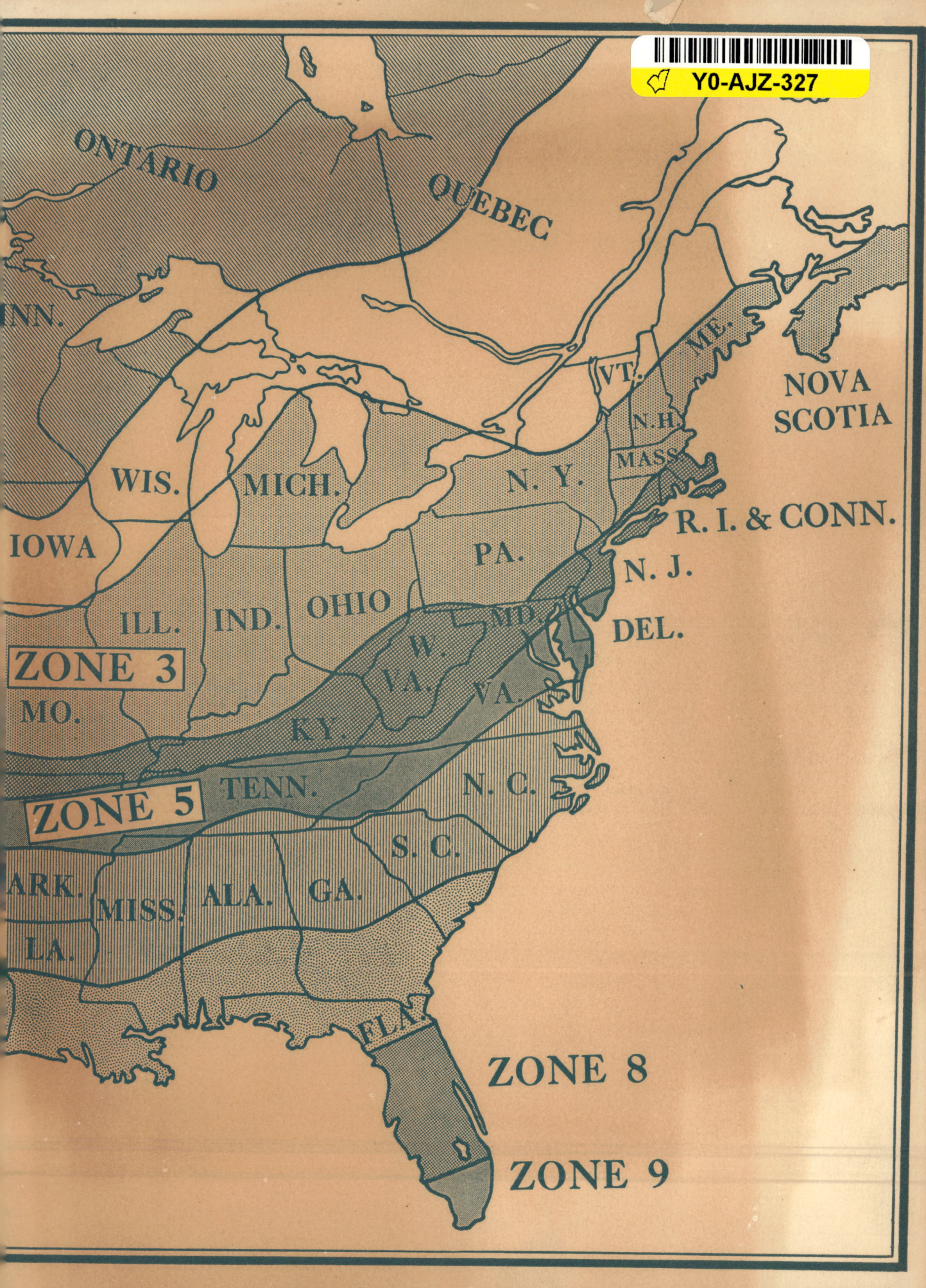

LARKSPURS NEAR THE SEA

THE GARDEN DICTIONARY

# THE PRACTICAL ENCYCLOPEDIA OF GARDENING

HORTICULTURE AND LANDSCAPE DESIGN

IN DICTIONARY FORM

EDITED BY

NORMAN TAYLOR

*De Luxe Edition*

GARDEN CITY PUBLISHING COMPANY, INC.

Garden City, New York

1941-42
GARDEN CITY PUBLISHING CO., INC.

COPYRIGHT, 1936 AND 1938, BY HOUGHTON MIFFLIN COMPANY
ALL RIGHTS RESERVED INCLUDING THE RIGHT TO REPRODUCE
THIS BOOK OR PARTS THEREOF IN ANY FORM

The Riverside Press
CAMBRIDGE · MASSACHUSETTS
PRINTED IN THE U.S.A.

# PREFACE

The effort to produce a comprehensive dictionary of gardening seems a hazardous venture; for the sponsors of it inevitably face two conflicting alternatives. There is the tendency on the one hand to write it only for the gifted few, who scarcely need it; or, on the other, to "write it down" for the many who may need it very much.

A reasonable solution of this dilemma is perhaps the one adopted in this book, and is embodied in the suggestion sent to all contributors: "Your article must not be written for the experts, but it must be apparent that it has been written by one." That has been the guiding principle throughout the preparation of THE GARDEN DICTIONARY — expert knowledge and advice translated into the simplest possible terms.

The completion of the book represents years of work and the hearty co-operation of many individuals and institutions. The garden public, even more than the publishers, are under a lasting obligation to these individuals and institutions. Without them the book never would fit the niche for which it was created — to be an indispensable reference work for all gardeners. Whether it comes measurably near to that ideal will ultimately be decided by those for whom it was written.

The Editor scarcely knows how to thank the sixty-eight devoted and ever-patient specialists who have contributed of their knowledge and experience to help make THE GARDEN DICTIONARY what it is. That such a distinguished body of men and women should always agree with each other or with the Editor is neither possible nor desirable. While inconsistencies as to advice or procedure have been reconciled in most cases, it has seemed best to let a few really conflicting statements stand as each contributor wrote them.

Special thanks are due Messrs. B. Y. Morrison, of the United States Department of Agriculture, W. H. Judd, of the Arnold Arboretum, and C. A. Weatherby, of the Gray Herbarium, all of whom have read the proofs; the first two for horticultural and botanical details, and the latter for the phonetic pronunciation of Latin names.

In addition, the Editor is most grateful for help and encouragement from Dr. N. L. Britton,† long director of the New York Botanical Garden; Dr. E. D. Merrill, of Harvard University; Mr. E. I. Farrington, of the Massachusetts Horticultural Society; Dr. J. H. Barnhart, of the New York Botanical Garden; Mr. Lee A. Strong, Chief of the United States Bureau of Entomology; Dr. H. H. Whetzel, of Cornell University; Mr. James H. Scarr, Meteorologist of the United States Weather Bureau at New York; Dr. C. C. Adams, director of the New York State Museum; Mr. Paul C. Standley, of the Field Museum, Chicago; Dr. George T. Moore, director of the Missouri Botanical Garden; Dr. Willis L. Jepson, of the University of California; Dr. Le Roy Abrams, of Stanford University; Mrs. Robert H. Fife, President of the Garden Club of America; and the Horticultural Society of New York.

The publishers are also under great obligation to the Agricultural Experiment Stations of the States of the Union and the Canadian Provinces for the material outlined below.

## STATES AND PROVINCES

Under the name of each State and Province appears an account of the garden possibilities, soils, and climate, together with an outline map showing where the zones of hardiness (*see* ZONE) cross the area, the significant frost data, the length of the growing season, and the rainfall when this is low enough to be a critical factor. All these articles, except one, were contributed by the technical staff of the station.

Few features of the book are more valuable, not only to the people who live in each State, but to those who garden both in the North and the South. Moreover, for those contemplating a permanent move —

† Died June 25, 1934.

from Des Moines to Los Angeles, for instance — the articles on Iowa and California are both indispensable. For, in the articles on the several States will be found just the information needed about climatic aids or obstacles, and especially about the different crops suited to each State — flowers, fruits, vegetables, and trees.

While THE DICTIONARY does not generally cater to the commercial production of crops, the articles on the different States and Provinces lay chief emphasis upon growing plants for profit. This has been done deliberately, because what professionals do for gain is apt to be a fair guide to what the amateur gardener may do for pleasure or for food.

## PLANTS

The selection of the plants found in this book was the work of years. THE GARDEN DICTIONARY does not contain all the plants cultivated in America, but it does include most of those likely to be of interest to the average intelligent or even inquisitive amateur. Rare or little known species by necessity have been excluded, particularly in groups dear to the hearts of certain specialists, but known to few others.

The judgment of no one person would be competent to settle what to include or exclude from such a book. The Editor, after months of work, finally sent lists of doubtful plants to many experts in different fields and regions, asking which of these items were, in their opinion, entitled to a place in a book like this. Their replies resulted in adding some fifty genera to the basic list compiled by the Editor. The completed book thus includes practically all the plants in general cultivation, and certainly all those of most garden value.

## NOMENCLATURE

While there is no mystery about the universal method of designating plants by their Latin names, few aspects of the garden world are so confusing to the beginner. The principles upon which such a scheme are based will not be repeated here, for they are discussed (in the body of the book) at PLANT NAMES.

For those familiar with the devious course of nomenclature in America, a few facts should here be recorded. In the first place, the International Botanical Congress held at Cambridge, England, in 1930 adopted an International Code of Botanical Nomenclature to which all responsible botanists agreed. That code has been followed here except for a few plants, the names of which apparently have never yet been made to conform to it. Upon the ground that a popular dictionary of gardening is no place to publish new combinations (in the technical sense of that term), the Editor has rejected all such in this book. The Latin names of plants are therefore the standard ones (*i.e.* in accordance with the International Code) or they are the next valid names available. Of the latter category there are, in any case, only a few, mostly among the cacti and a few other special groups.

The Editor has followed the practice long in use by zoologists and geneticists, and adopted in part by the second edition of Webster's New International Dictionary, in two departures from conventional rules — both of them pointing toward simplicity and uniformity. One is the dropping of the final *i* from all second declension genitives which usually or sometimes end in *ii*, and often most erratically so as used by various writers. Hence *grayi*, not *grayii*, *thunbergi*, not *thunbergii*.

The other departure has been the elimination of all capital letters from specific names, whether based upon geographical adjectives, proper nouns, or generic names. Hence *Berberis thunbergi*, not *Thunbergi*; *Amelanchier canadensis*, not *Canadensis*; and *Inula helenium*, not *Helenium*.

Because these Latin names are unfamiliar to many and their pronunciation and meaning still more so, much time and effort have been expended upon them. Every Latin name in the book is defined and phonetically pronounced at its proper alphabetic entry and, in addition, the etymology of all generic names is explained. There are thousands of such entries in THE DICTIONARY, the only ones omitted being names like *grayi* and *wilsoni*, which are obviously named for persons, and hence easily understood.

## TRADEMARKED PRODUCTS

There are countless commercial products of use to the gardener, often in a much more convenient form than any home-made equivalent. Because of the need for a permanent record of articles of merit, THE GARDEN DICTIONARY began the accumulation of the names of trademarked horticultural products; and through the courtesy of the *Florists Exchange* a notice to manufacturers was inserted of our intention to define worth-while products in the vocabulary, under their trade names. Upon their replies, and from the suggestions of many technical analysts in the Experiment Stations, brief definitions of acceptable products have been inserted.

The failure to find some trademarked product does not mean that it is not a worth-while one. Nor does the inclusion of any product mean that THE DICTIONARY recommends it. Sometimes the failure to include was because the manufacturer took no notice of the original invitation in the *Florists Exchange*. We, therefore, assume no responsibility for the inclusion or exclusion of any product. The definitions are simply like any others — put there for the convenience of readers and in the attempt to make the book as complete a reference work as possible.

## ILLUSTRATIONS

Thanks are due for the right to reproduce certain of the twenty colored plates in the book, especially to: The Right Reverend James E. Freeman for the Bishop's Garden at the Washington Cathedral (*see* LANDSCAPE ARCHITECTURE); Miss Katherine Bashford, Los Angeles, for the FORMAL GARDEN in San Marino, California; Mrs. C. I. DeBevoise, Greens Farms, Connecticut, for the ROCK GARDEN; Miss Laura Hills for a pastel at CALENDULA; Worcester Art Museum for the John Singer Sargent painting at TERRACE; Beacon Hill Garden Club, Boston, for the illustration at EXHIBITIONS AND SHOWS.

All the 502 line cuts were drawn especially for the book, most of them by Natalie Davis. Others were drawn by Laurence Blair, Armistead Fitzhugh, Robert L. Fowler, Jr., Dorothy Handsaker, Cecile Matschat, Jean Martin, Charles M. Stotz, and Georges Wilmet.

N. T.

NEW YORK
*January 2, 1936*

# CONTRIBUTORS

The contributors, and the initials used to designate their articles, are as follows:

| | |
|---|---|
| A. B. S. | A. B. Stout, Ph.D., Director of the Laboratories, New York Botanical Garden, New York, N.Y. Author of *Daylilies*. |
| A. D. H. | Arthur D. Houghton, M.D., Ph.D., Horticulturist, San Fernando, Calif. Author of *The Cactus Book*, etc. |
| A. D. S. | Arthur D. Slavin, U.S. Department of Agriculture, Soil Erosion Service, Elsberry, Mo. |
| A. F. | Armistead Fitzhugh, Landscape Architect, New York, N.Y. Member of the American Society of Landscape Architects; Secretary of the Fine Arts Federation of New York. |
| A. H. | Arthur Herrington, Garden Consultant and Lecturer; Secretary-Manager of the International Flower Show. New York, N.Y. |
| A. H. N. | Arno H. Nehrling, Secretary of the Chrysanthemum Society of America, Boston, Mass. |
| A. J. L. | Alfred J. Loveless, Horticulturist, Pittsfield, Mass. Contributor to *Standard Cyclopedia of Horticulture*, etc. |
| A. J. W. | Albert J. Winkler, Ph.D., Associate Professor of Viticulture, University of California, Davis, Calif. |
| A. P. S. | A. P. Saunders, Ph.D., Professor of Chemistry, Hamilton College, Clinton, N.Y. Producer of various strains of species hybrids in *Paeonia* and author of many articles on the genus. |
| B. J. L. | Bryan J. Lynch, Landscape Architect, New York, N.Y. |
| B. Y. M. | B. Y. Morrison, Division of Plant Exploration and Introduction, Bureau of Plant Industry, U.S. Department of Agriculture, Washington, D.C. Editor, *National Horticultural Magazine*. |
| C. A. W. | C. A. Weatherby, Assistant Curator, Gray Herbarium, Harvard University, Cambridge, Mass. |
| C. C. | Charles Chupp, Ph.D., Extension Professor of Plant Pathology, New York State College of Agriculture, Cornell University, Ithaca, N.Y. |
| C. E. F. G. | Carl E. F. Guterman, Ph.D., Assistant Professor of Plant Pathology, New York State College of Agriculture, Cornell University, Ithaca, N.Y. |
| C. H. M. | Cecile Hulse Matschat, Author of *Mexican Plants for American Gardens*. Croton Falls, N.Y. |
| D. L. | David Lumsden, Horticulturist, U.S. Department of Agriculture, Washington, D.C. |
| D. S. W. | Donald S. Welch, Ph.D., Assistant Professor of Plant Pathology, Cornell University, Ithaca, N.Y. |
| E. P. E. | Edward P. Eickhof, Landscape Architect, Chicago, Ill. |
| F. M. W. | F. M. Wadley, Ph.D., Associate Entomologist, Cereal and Forage Insect Investigations, Bureau of Entomology and Plant Quarantine, U.S. Department of Agriculture, Washington, D.C. |
| F. S. | Fletcher Steele, Fellow, American Society of Landscape Architects. Boston, Mass. |
| F. W. A. | Frank W. Allen, Associate Pomologist, California Agricultural Experiment Station, Davis, Calif. |
| G. H. P. | George H. Pring, Superintendent of the Missouri Botanical Garden; President of the St. Louis Horticultural Society, St. Louis, Mo. |
| G. L. P. | Guy L. Philp, Associate in Pomology, University of California, Davis, Calif. |
| G. W. S. | Gilbert W. Scott, Research Assistant in Truck Crops, University of California, Davis, Calif. |
| H. A. C. | Harold A. Caparn, Fellow, American Society of Landscape Architects. New York, N.Y. |
| H. B. T. | H. B. Tukey, Ph.D., Chief in Research, New York Agricultural Experiment Station, Geneva, N.Y.; and Professor of Pomology, Cornell University, Ithaca, N.Y. |
| H. C. T. | H. C. Thompson, Ph.D., Professor of Vegetable Crops and Head of Department of Vegetable Crops, Cornell University, Ithaca, N.Y. |
| H. E. D. | Henry E. Downer, Horticulturist and Superintendent of Grounds, Vassar College, Poughkeepsie, N.Y. |
| H. M. | Harold Mowry, Assistant Director, Florida Agricultural Experiment Station, Gainesville, Fla. |
| H. M. C. | Mrs. Jay Clark, Jr., Garden Editor of *House Beautiful*. Worcester, Mass. |
| H. M. F. | Helen Morgenthau Fox, Author of *Garden Cinderellas, Gardening With Herbs, Patio Gardens*. Peekskill, N.Y. |
| H. R. M. | Herbert R. Medlock, Garden Superintendent, estate of John S. Phipps, Esq., Westbury, L.I. Late Lecturer in Botany, University of London, Eng. |
| H. T. | Henry Teuscher, Horticulturist and Dendrologist, New York Botanical Garden, New York, N.Y. |
| I. N. G. | Ira N. Gabrielson, Chief, Bureau of Biological Survey, U.S. Department of Agriculture, Washington, D.C. |
| J. C. W. | John C. Wister, Landscape Architect, Philadelphia, Pa. President, American Iris Society, 1920–1934; Director, Arthur Hoyt Scott Horticultural Foundation, Swarthmore College, Swarthmore, Pa.; author of *The Iris, Lilac Culture, Bulbs for American Gardens*. |
| J. E. S. | J. E. Spingarn, Author, publicist, and horticulturist, Amenia, N.Y. |
| J. G. E. | James G. Esson, Head Gardener, estate of Mrs. Roswell Eldridge, Great Neck, L.I. |
| J. H. McF. | J. Horace McFarland, L.H.D., Author of *The Rose in America*, etc.; Editor, *The American Rose Annual*. Harrisburg, Pa. |
| L. B. | Leonard Barron, Horticultural Editor, *Country Life* and *The American Home*, Garden City, N.Y. |
| L. B. W. | Louise Beebe Wilder, Author of *The Fragrant Path, Colour in My Garden, What Happens in My Garden*, etc. Bronxville, N.Y. |
| L. D. D. | Luther D. Davis, Ph.D., Assistant Professor of Pomology, University of California, Davis, Calif. |
| L. R. | Lester Rowntree, Garden Consultant on California wild flowers; writer on horticultural subjects. Carmel, Calif. |
| L. Y. K. | Mrs. Francis King, Author of *The Well Considered Garden, Chronicles of the Garden, From a New Garden*, etc. South Hartford, N.Y. |
| M. A. | Mary Averill, Curator of Japanese Garden, Brooklyn Botanic Garden; Author of *Japanese Flower Arrangement, The Flower Art of Japan*. New York, N.Y. |

| | |
|---|---|
| M. A. H. | **Marshall A. Howe, Ph.D., Sc.D.,** Director, New York Botanical Garden, New York, N.Y. |
| M. C. | **Mary Chess,** President of Mary Chess Inc., New York, N.Y. |
| M. D. L. | **Mary Deputy Lamson,** Landscape Architect, New York, N.Y. |
| M. F. | **Montague Free,** Horticulturist, Brooklyn Botanic Garden, Brooklyn, N.Y. President, American Rock Garden Society. |
| O. E. W. | **Orland E. White, Sc.D.,** Professor of Agricultural Biology and Director of The Blandy Experimental Farm, University of Virginia, Charlottesville, Va. |
| P. Y. | **Perry Young,** Editor, *Garden*, New Orleans, La. |
| R. A. H. | **Roscoe Angus Huff,** Secretary, American Gladiolus Society, Goshen, Ind. |
| R. A. M. | **Ruth Averell Meigs,** Director of Garden Furnishing Department, Arden Studios, New York, N.Y. |
| R. E. G. | **Ralph E. Griswold,** Landscape Architect, Pittsburgh, Pa. |
| R. F. W. | **Ruth Frances Waters,** Author of *Growing Prize-Winning Chrysanthemums, The Poinsettia, Southern Seed-Sowing*, etc. Houston, Tex. |
| R. L. F., Jr. | **Robert Ludlow Fowler, Jr.,** Landscape Architect, New York, N.Y. Fellow of the American Society of Landscape Architects, and President of the New York Chapter of the American Society of Landscape Architects. |
| R. M. C. | **R. M. Crocket,** Nurseryman, seedsman, and florist, Cranford, N.J. |
| R. S. L. | **Robert S. Lemmon,** Managing Editor, *House and Garden*, New York, N.Y. |
| R. W. | **Richardson Wright,** Editor, *House and Garden*; author of *The Practical Book of Outdoor Flowers, The Gardener's Bedbook, The Story of Gardening*, etc. New York, N.Y. |
| R. W. H. | **Robert W. Hodgson,** Professor of Sub-tropical Horticulture, University of California, Los Angeles, Calif. |
| T. A. W. | **T. A. Weston,** Associate Editor, *Florists Exchange;* Fellow, Royal Horticultural Society; author of *Commercial Carnation Culture, Bulbs that Bloom in the Spring, Flowering Bulbs*. New York, N.Y. |
| T. R. A. | **Thomas R. Ashlee,** Department of Horticulture, University of Idaho, Moscow, Idaho. |
| U. P. H. | **U. P. Hedrick,** Director, New York State Agricultural Experiment Station, Geneva, N.Y. |
| V. E. K. | **Van Evrie Kilpatrick,** Director of Nature Education, New York City Public Schools; President and Founder of the School Garden Association of America. New York, N.Y. |
| W. H. C. | **William Henry Chandler, Ph.D.,** Professor of Pomology, University of California, Berkeley, Calif. |
| W. H. J. | **William Henry Judd,** Propagator, Arnold Arboretum, Harvard University, Jamaica Plain, Mass. |
| W. J. I. | **William J. Ing,** Horticultural Advisor, R. H. Macy & Co., New York, N.Y. |
| W. P. T. | **Warren P. Tufts, Ph.D.,** Pomologist, College of Agriculture, University of California, Davis, Calif. |
| W. T. I. | **William T. Innes,** Author of *Exotic Aquarium Fishes*; editor, *The Aquarium*. Philadelphia, Pa. |

# WHY A DICTIONARY?

BECAUSE plants and what we do with them never follow such an orderly sequence as the alphabet, for instance, one often hears the query: "Why follow the progression of the alphabet rather than the seasons?" Why, in other words, a garden dictionary at all?

The real answer to such a question is the reason this book was written. THE GARDEN DICTIONARY was planned to be an index to itself, so simply arranged that it is easy to find the things you want with a minimum of groping among momentarily useless features. Thousands of cross-reference items have been inserted to lead one directly to the needed information, and over 4400 common or vernacular names are similarly cross-referenced to the article where their culture is discussed.

There is, in the dictionary arrangement, another helpful feature, of which much has been made in this book: No words of special import (*i.e.* the jargon of gardeners, nurserymen, botanists, and such) have been used unless the word is defined at its proper vocabulary entry. In other words, you do not have to go to any other reference work to understand the terms used here. (*See*, below, HOW TO USE THE GARDEN DICTIONARY.) All such words are, in any case, marked with an asterisk (*), the significance of which will be found as the footnote to all pages.

The unquestioned advantage of the alphabetic arrangement of so much material has, however, one drawback — it gives us no *simultaneous* view either of the whole field of gardening, or of the contents of this book. To meet such a need the titles of the main articles in THE GARDEN DICTIONARY have been rearranged here according to the main divisions of gardening. Such a schematic plan, if followed as a reading guide, removes the only cogent reason for asking "Why a Dictionary?"

Such an outline may well be divided under ten main heads. It should be understood that it includes only the longer articles in the book, and the culture of all plants of secondary importance should be sought at the proper vocabulary entries, as well as thousands of briefer notes and definitions.

# MAIN ARTICLES IN THE GARDEN DICTIONARY

## 1. GREENHOUSES, CONSERVATORIES, COLD FRAMES, AND HOTBEDS

Greenhouse  Conservatory
Cold Frames (including hotbeds)

## 2. CLIMATE AND HARDINESS

Climate
Wind
Rainfall
Temperature
Snow

Frost and Frost Control
Hardiness
Zones (of hardiness in U.S. and Canada)
Protecting Plants
Windbreaks

## 3. SOILS AND SOIL OPERATIONS

Soils (general)
Acid and Alkali Soils
Humus
Lime
Manure
Fertilizers
Soil Operations (general)
Draining

Irrigation
Green Manuring (soil improvement)
Compost
Cultivation, Plowing, Harrowing
Raking, Digging, Hoeing, Trenching
Mulch and Mulching
Cover Crops

## 4. SPECIALIZED GARDENS

SEASONAL
Spring Garden
Summer Garden
Autumn Garden
Winter Garden

COLOR GARDENS
Red Garden
Blue Garden
Yellow Garden
Pink Garden
White Garden
Gray and Lavender Garden

SPECIALIZED GARDENS (ornamental)
Bog Garden
Border
Bulbs
Cacti
Ferns and Fern Gardening
Japanese Garden
Rock Garden
Rose Garden
Sand Garden
Seaside Garden
Shady Garden
Sub-tropical Garden
Succulents
Water Garden
Wild Garden

MISCELLANEOUS SPECIALIZED GARDENS
Cellar Gardening
Herb Gardening
Kitchen Garden
Window Gardening
Medicinal Plants
Muckland Gardening
School Gardening
Tub Gardening
Lawn

## 5. GARDEN PLANNING AND DESIGN

LANDSCAPE ARCHITECTURE (general)

GENERAL PLANNING

Backyard Garden       Home Grounds (suburban place)       Country Estate

SPECIAL LANDSCAPE FEATURES

Accent Plants
Arbors and Arches
Banks
Bridges
Drives
Gates and Gateways
Foundation Planting

Formal Garden
Informal Garden
Lighting (night illumination)
Modern Garden Design (modernistic)
Ornament and Furniture
Paths and Paving
Patio Gardens

Penthouse Gardens
Steps
Structures
Vista
Walls and Wall Gardening
Water

## 6. PROPAGATION

Propagation (general)
Seeds and Seedage
Budding

Cuttings
Division

Grafting
Layering

## 7. PLANT BREEDING

Crossing    Hybridizing    New Varieties    Mutation    And 26 shorter articles

## 8. PESTS

PLANT DISEASES (and their control)

Fungicides       Wood Rot       Damping-off

Also hundreds of brief notes on control at the crops needing it.

INSECT PESTS (and their control)
Insect Friends                    Fumigation
Insecticides                      Spraying and Dusting
Also hundreds of brief notes on control at the crops needing it.
ANIMAL INJURY (control of rodents, bird nuisances, etc.)

## 9. MISCELLANEOUS HORTICULTURAL OPERATIONS, SPECIAL TYPES OF GARDENING, AND MISCELLANEOUS ARTICLES

PLANTS
  Annuals
  Biennials
  Perennials
  Flowering Shrubs
  Fragrance
  Aquarium
  House Plants
  Grasses
  Bamboo
  Flower Arranging
  Everlastings
  Vines
  Mushroom
  Hanging Baskets
  Perfume Plants

OPERATIONS (except Soil Operations, for which see 3, and Propagating, for which see 6)
  Planting
  Potting
  Pruning
  Storage
  Training Plants
  Tree Surgery
  Tools and Implements
  Watering
  Weeds and Weeding
  Dwarfing
  Forcing
  Retarding

EDUCATIONAL AND REFERENCE
  Arboretum
  Botanic Garden
  Birds
  Exhibitions and Shows
  Garden Books
  Garden Calendar
  Garden Clubs
  Garden Magazines
  Garden History
  Garden Questions
  Garden Schools
  Garden Tables (statistics)
  Weights and Measures
  Poisonous Plants
  Bees and Bee Plants
  Labels
  Quarantine

## 10. SPECIAL CULTURAL ARTICLES ON THE BEST VARIETIES AND HOW TO GROW THEM

A. FLOWERS
  Special articles on:
    Anemone          Cineraria        Fuchsia            Michaelmas daisy    Primula
    Aster            Clematis         Gladiolus          Narcissus           Rose
    Begonia          Cosmos           Gloxinia           Nasturtium          Snapdragon
    Calceolaria      Crinum           Hollyhock          Orchids             Stocks
    Calla Lily       Crocus           Hyacinth           Pansy               Sweet Pea
    Camellia         Cyclamen         Iris               Pelargonium         Tulip
    Canna            Dahlia           Lilium             Peony               Violet
    Carnation        Daylily          Lily-of-the-valley Poinsettia          Water Lily
    Chrysanthemum    Delphinium       Marigold           Poppy

B. VEGETABLES. One long general article on Kitchen Garden
  Special articles on:
    Artichoke            Carrot                  Kale              Parsnip     Sea-kale
    Asparagus            Cauliflower             Kohlrabi          Pea         Spinach
    Bean                 Celery (and Celeriac)   Lettuce           Potato      Squash
    Beet (and Chard)     Chinese Cabbage         New Zealand       Pumpkin     Sweet Potato
    Broccoli             Corn                      Spinach         Radish      Tomato
    Brussels Sprouts     Cucumber                Okra              Rhubarb     Turnip
    Cabbage              Eggplant                Onion             Rutabaga    Watercress
    Cardoon              Endive                  Parsley

C. MISCELLANEOUS ECONOMIC AND ORNAMENTAL PLANTS
    Ginseng      Rice         Sugar Cane     Smilax           Horse-radish
    Hop          Sorghum      Tobacco        Vetch            Tarragon
    Peanut       Soybean      Nepenthes      Foliage Plants

D. NUTS AND TREES. Trees (general). Nut Culture (general)
  Special articles on:
    Almond       Eucalyptus   Magnolia       Pecan            Tung-oil tree
    Beech        Fir          Maple          Pine             Walnut
    Chestnut     Hazel        Oak            Poplar           Evergreens
    Coconut      Hickory      Palm           Spruce
    Elm          Litchi

E. ORNAMENTAL SHRUBS
    Azalea       Cotoneaster  Privet         Lilac            Hedges
    Box          Erica        Rhododendron   Flowering Shrubs Broad-leaved Evergreens

F. FRUIT CULTURE. General article, including eastern and western fruit culture
  Special articles on:
    Apple        Currant      Guava          Mulberry         Plum
    Apricot      Date         Lemon          Olive            Pomegranate
    Avocado      Dewberry     Lime           Orange           Prune
    Banana       Fig          Loganberry     Peach            Quince
    Blackberry   Gooseberry   Loquat         Pear             Raspberry
    Blueberry    Grape        Mango          Persimmon        Strawberry
    Cherry       Grapefruit   Melon          Pineapple        Watermelon
    Cranberry

# HOW TO USE THE GARDEN DICTIONARY

As in any other Dictionary, the items are entered in strict alphabetical sequence. Look for **red** oak, **New England** aster, **white** spruce, **black** oak, **pink** lady's-slipper, etc., under the boldface word, not under oak or spruce or lady's-slipper or aster. They will, of course, be found under oak or spruce or lady's-slipper or aster, but much more quickly and directly (*i.e.*, referred to the exact species) by going to the first word of names that contain two. For all other items the strictly alphabetical entry needs no explanation.

For those who are not familiar with the usual method of arranging plants under their Latin names, a sample of the first genus in the book is given below. *See also* PLANT NAMES.

|  |  |
|---|---|
| The genus or generic name of these plants, covering all species in the genus *Abelia*. Used exactly as Jones, Smith, or your own surname. If you are still uncertain what a genus is, *see* GENUS. | — |
| The preferred pronunciation indicated phonetically. | — |
| The family to which each genus belongs is always cited. *See* that family if you are interested in finding related plants. | — |

**ABELIA** (a-bee′li-a) A group of mostly Asiatic shrubs of the honeysuckle family grown for the small but showy flowers and often half-evergreen foliage. Leaves opposite,* nearly stalkless. Flowers mostly in leafy terminal clusters. Corolla bell-shaped or funnel-shaped. Fruit small, leathery, dry, and one-seeded. (Named for Dr. Clarke Abel, 1780–1826, a physician in China.)

- *Simple, non-technical description of the genus.*
- *All words or phrases so marked are the subject of special entries. They have a special significance or they would not be so marked.*
- *Origin or etymology of the generic name.*

Of the 25 species only the following are common in American gardens. They prefer well-drained soils, mixed with leaf mold, and full sunlight. Increased by cuttings of green wood (rooted under glass) in summer, or by mature wood in autumn, or by layers in spring. Can be grown in a cool greenhouse, using potting mixture* 3.

- *How grown and propagated.*
- *The proper soil mixture for plants grown in pots, window boxes, etc., is mentioned by number. See* POTTING MIXTURES.

**chinensis.** A spreading shrub 3–5 ft. high, with deciduous* oval leaves about 1 in. long and finely toothed. Flowers in dense terminal clusters, the corolla funnel-shaped, about ½ in. long, white. (China.) Summer and later. Hardy from zone* 5 southward.

**grandiflora.** Half-evergreen shrub 3–5 ft. high, with lustrous leaves and generally much like chinensis, but with loose flower clusters and the corolla flushed pink. The commonest cult. species, and of hybrid origin. (June–Oct.) Hardy from zone* 4 southward.

- *These are the species names of the plants belonging to* Abelia. *Species names correspond almost exactly to John or Mary. See* SPECIES *if you do not know its correct meaning. Because such species names are used many times, their pronunciation and meaning are not repeated wherever they occur, but are at* chinensis, grandiflora, *etc.*
- *The country of origin of all plants, hybrids excepted, is always stated if known.*
- *Period when in bloom. See* GARDEN CALENDAR *for further notes.*
- *Tells whether or not it is hardy in your vicinity. See the colored map at* ZONE.

If, in spite of thousands of cross-references inserted for the easy finding of what is wanted, the entry still proves elusive, *see* WHY A DICTIONARY, on page v. There will be found what amounts to a table of contents of all the leading articles, arranged according to subjects instead of alphabetically.

## ABBREVIATIONS
### USED IN WRITING THE GARDEN DICTIONARY

(NOTE: Common horticultural abbreviations are defined at their proper vocabulary entries: *i.e.*, B. & B., P.G., etc.) States of the Union and months of the year: Usual abbreviations.

Hort. = { Horticultural / Horticulture } according to context.    Cult. = { Cultivated / Culture / Cultivation } according to context.

| | | | |
|---|---|---|---|
| Af. = Africa | Eng. = England | L.I. = Long Island, N.Y. | S.A. = South America |
| As. = Asia | Eu. = Europe | N.Z. = New Zealand | U.S. = United States |
| Aust. = Australia | Jap. = Japan | N.A. = North America | W.I. = West Indies |
| E.I. = East Indies | | | |

in. = inches    ft. = feet

# THE PRACTICAL ENCYCLOPEDIA OF GARDENING

# THE GARDEN DICTIONARY

# A

**AARON'S-ROD** = *Thermopsis caroliniana*.

**ABACA** = *Musa textilis*.

**ABAMA** = *Narthecium*.

**ABELIA** (a-bee′li-a). A group of mostly Asiatic shrubs of the honeysuckle family grown for the small but showy flowers and often half-evergreen foliage. Leaves opposite,* nearly stalkless. Flowers mostly in leafy terminal clusters. Corolla bell-shaped or funnel-shaped. Fruit small, leathery, dry, and one-seeded. (Named for Dr. Clarke Abel, 1780–1826, a physician in China.)

Of the 25 species only the following are common in American gardens. They prefer well-drained soils, mixed with leaf mold, and full sunlight. Increased by cuttings of green wood (rooted under glass) in summer or by mature wood in autumn, or by layers in spring. Can be grown in a cool greenhouse, using potting mixture* 3.

    **chinensis.** A spreading shrub 3–5 ft. high with deciduous* oval leaves about 1 in. long and finely toothed. Flowers in dense terminal clusters, the corolla funnel-shaped, about ½ in. long, white. China. Summer and later. Hardy from zone* 5 southward.

    **grandiflora.** Half-evergreen shrub 3–5 ft. high with lustrous leaves and generally much like chinensis, but with loose flower clusters and the corolla flushed pink. The commonest cult. species, and of hybrid origin. June–Oct. Hardy from zone* 4 southward.

**ABELMOSCHUS** (a-bel-mos′kus) = Musky-seeded. See HIBISCUS ABELMOSCHUS.

**ABELMOSK** = *Hibiscus abelmoschus*.

**ABERIA** = *Dovyalis*.

**ABIES.** See FIR.

**ABOBRA** (a-bo′bra). A tropical, herbaceous vine of the cucumber family with a tuberous root, grown mostly for its small, showy fruits. Leaves alternate,* cut into linear divisions. Male and female flowers on separate plants, green and fragrant. Female flower solitary, the male usually in clusters. Fruit egg-shaped and berry-like. Stems tendril*-bearing, the tendrils usually forked. (*Abobra* is the Brazilian vernacular name.)

Easily grown from seed but only outdoors in zones* 8 and 9; northward in a warm greenhouse in potting mixture* 3.

    **tenuifolia.** Cranberry gourd. Stems quickly climbing to 20 or 30 ft. Leaves broadly oval in general outline, 2–4 in. long, white-dotted, their much cut segments almost thread-like. Fruit about ½ in. long, bright scarlet. Tropical S.A.

**ABORTIVE.** Imperfectly developed; especially failing to produce seeds.

**ABRONIA** (a-bro′ni-a). Sand verbena; also called wild lantana. A large genus of herbs, family Nyctaginaceae, mostly from western N.A. and one of them grown for its fragrant flowers that suggest a verbena. Leaves opposite,* stalked, somewhat inequilateral, usually sticky-hairy and with no marginal teeth. Flowers tubular, crowded in a loose head below which are 5 or more colored bracts.* Petals none, but the calyx is petal-like. Fruit leathery, 1-seeded. (Named from *abros*, Greek for delicate, in allusion to the bracts beneath the flower cluster.)

Among the 45 species only the following is of any hort. importance. While a perennial it is treated as an annual. Seeds which are slow to germinate may be started indoors or in the frame, or sown in place after danger of frost. The plant is useful for the border, rockery or for hanging baskets. See ANNUALS.

    **umbellata.** A prostrate, vine-like herb, often rooting at the joints, with long-stalked nearly oval leaves. Flowers about ½ in. long, pink, with usually 10–15 in an umbel*-like cluster that may be 2 in. across. Pacific Coast. June. The variety grandiflora has somewhat larger flowers.

**ABROTANIFOLIA, -us, -um** (a-bro-tay-ni-fō′li-a). Having leaves like the southernwood (*Artemisia abrotanum*).

**ABROTANUM.** An ancient name for some fragrant or beautiful plant. See ARTEMISIA.

**ABRUS** (ab′rus). Woody, tropical vines of the pea family chiefly grown for their scarlet, black-spotted seeds, commonly used in beadwork. Leaves compound,* with 10–15 pairs of small leaflets that fold up in cloudy weather. Flowers small, pea-like, in a stalked, lax cluster that arises in the leaf axil.* Fruit a somewhat woody pod. (Named from *abros*, Greek for delicate, in allusion to the leaflets.)

The only hort. species, the rosary pea, can be grown outdoors in zone* 9, elsewhere in a warm greenhouse in potting mixture* 3. Propagate by seeds, or by cuttings in moist sand. See VINES.

    **precatorius.** Rosary pea. Trailing on the ground for 8–10 ft. or on lattice in the greenhouse. Leaflets about ½ in. long, the whole leaf 2–3 in. long. Flowers small, pink, red, or purple, very rarely white. Pod about 1½ in. long. Seeds poisonous but showy, used for a variety of purposes in the tropics. Called also Indian licorice and (the seeds) Jequirity bean.

**ABSINTHIUM.** Classical name of the wormwood. See ARTEMISIA.

**ABUTILON** (a-bū′ti-lon). Flowering maple, also called Chinese bellflower. Over 100 species of tropical shrubs (rarely herbs) of the mallow family, only a few of which are grown in greenhouses, or as bedding plants in frost-free areas. Leaves alternate,* often veined and looking like a maple leaf, in some of the hort. varieties beautifully variegated. Flowers showy, solitary, and borne in the leaf-axils,* usually drooping and often trumpet-shaped. Fruit a circle of beaked, dry fruits that split off individually when ripe. (*Abutilon* is from the Arabic for some mallow.)

Grow in cool greenhouse in potting mixture* 4, or outdoors in zone* 8 or 9. Easily propagated by cuttings of young wood in spring or autumn. Very popular pot plants both for flowers and handsome foliage. Occasionally *Malvaviscus arboreus* is incorrectly sold for an abutilon.

    **hybridum.** Of hybrid and uncertain origin but the commonest of all in cultivation. Leaves variable, lobed like a maple leaf or unlobed, green and variously speckled or blotched. Flowers red, pinkish-purple, yellow or white, more or less bell- or trumpet-shaped. Many showy named forms belong here: Boule de Neige (white), Golden Fleece (yellow), Savitzi (grown for white-edged foliage).

    **pictum.** Leaves 3-lobed, the central lobe shorter than the others, the margins toothed. Flowers about 1½ in. long, yellow or orange veined with red. Southern S.A.

    **vitifolium.** Sturdy shrub with white-hairy foliage and twigs. Leaves prominently lobed, but roundish or heart-shaped in outline and 4–5 in. wide. Flowers lavender, often 2½ in. across, very showy. Chile.

**ABYSSINIAN BANANA** = *Musa ensete*.

**ABYSSINICA, -us, -um** (a-bis-sin′ee-ca). From Abyssinia.

**ACACIA** (a-kā′si-a, also a-kā′sha). An enormous genus of quick-growing shrubs and trees of the pea family found all over the tropical world, and a few in sub-tropical regions. About a hundred species are known to be cult. in America, of which the following are the most common — all of them

---

\* Special articles on the subjects indicated by an asterisk (\*) will be found at the words so marked.

# ACACIA

Australian. Some are thorny. Leaves normally twice compound,* the leaflets very numerous and small. In all species marked † there is a simple blade resembling a leaf (actually a modified leaf stalk and called a phyllodium) and no leaflets, a common feature in many species of *Acacia*. Flowers very small but crowded into dense finger-shaped or globular clusters, all yellow in the species below. The clusters may be solitary, but more often arranged in variously branched sprays, and consequently very handsome. Fruit like a pea pod, but often somewhat woody in maturity and sometimes twisted. (Named from the Greek for a point or thorn, in allusion to the many thorny species.) The Australian species are often called wattle.

Acacias are attractive, free-flowering shrubs and trees, easily grown outdoors in most of zone* 7 and all of zones* 8 and 9, elsewhere in a cool greenhouse in potting mixture* 3. They are not long-lived trees and this should be taken into account in planning a sub-tropical garden. Propagation by seed, which should be soaked in hot (not boiling) water for a few moments and then allowed to soak in cold water for a day or two. This softens the hard seed-coat. Plant while the seeds are still wet, but even with this treatment some species take four or five weeks to germinate. Propagated also by cuttings of half-ripened wood, with little or no bottom-heat.* From the cuttings or seedlings a taproot* develops which is sensitive to disturbance. Subsequent transplanting must therefore be done with great care. Water freely at first, but as the plants become established they should need little water for most species are drought-resistant.

Some acacias are common show plants in florists' windows, being much grown for their free bloom which is greatest in March and April. *See especially* A. ARMATA and A. PUBESCENS.

In Calif. a nice succession of acacia bloom is secured by planting *A. podalyriaefolia* (Dec. bloom), *A. baileyana* (Jan.), *A. cultriformis* and *A. decurrens dealbata* (Feb.), *A. pravissima* (March), and typical *A. decurrens* in April.

The species marked with a † bear phyllodia (*see* above).

**†armata.** Kangaroo thorn. A spiny shrub 6-8 ft. high, much grown in greenhouses as a decorative pot plant. Phyllodia about an inch long, usually pressed against the stem, prickle-tipped. Flower heads globular, solitary, about as big as a pea, but very numerous, bright yellow.

**baileyana.** Showy shrub or small tree, without spines, and beautiful, feathery, bluish-gray foliage. Leaves doubly compound,* the ultimate leaflets scarcely ¼ in. long, numerous enough to nearly hide the stem. Flower heads globular, only ⅛ in. across, but very numerous in large clusters that exceed the leaf in length. Commonly planted outdoors, and very popular in Calif.

**†cultriformis.** Stout shrub, with its oblique, blue-gray, knife-shaped, phyllodia numerous enough to nearly sheathe the stem and slightly prickle-tipped. Flower heads about ⅛ in. thick, globular, yellow, and very numerous in a terminal, much-branched cluster.

**decurrens.** Green wattle. Widely planted tree in Calif., often 50-60 ft. high. Leaves twice-compound,* the ultimate leaflets very numerous, about ⅓ in. long, always dark green. Flower heads about ¼ in. across, globular, cream-yellow, and arranged in a raceme.* Pods about 4 in. long. In addition to the typical form there are two widely grown varieties: var. **dealbata.** Silver wattle, has silvery-gray foliage; var. **mollis.** Black wattle, has white-hairy foliage and attractive purplish pods. All much planted in Calif.

**farnesiana.** Huisache; called, also, popinac, sponge tree and cassie. Probably Australian, but planted all over the tropical and sub-tropical world, the huisache is an attractive, very thorny shrub, much-branched and covered with twice-compound* leaves. Ultimate leaflets scarcely ⅛ in. long but very numerous. Flower heads globular, nearly ½ in. thick, deep yellow and fragrant, in rather dense clusters.

**†longifolia.** Golden wattle. Sydney golden wattle. A shrub or small tree, without prickles, the phyllodia nearly 6 in. long and more or less oblong. Flowers in finger-shaped clusters which are about 2½ in. long, and lemon yellow. Pod about 4½ in. long.

**†melanoxylon.** Lightwood. Black acacia. Tall, unarmed tree. Phyllodia more or less inverted lance-shaped, about 4½ in. long and an inch wide. Sometimes there are also doubly compound* leaves on young twigs. Flowers in dense, globular heads which are about ¼ in. across, cream-yellow, not particularly showy. Pod about 4 in. long, twisted. This tree yields the famous blackwood of Australia, which is very light. Much planted as a street tree in Calif.

**†podalyriaefolia.** Mount Morgan wattle. A bluish-gray, or even silvery, hairy shrub, much planted in Calif. Phyllodia oval or oblong, about 1½ in. long. Flowers golden-yellow, in ball-like heads that are clustered in long racemes.* Pod about 3 in. long.

**†pravissima.** Much-branched and twiggy tree usually not over 20 ft. high, the branches drooping. Phyllodia green, ovalish, about 1 in. long, somewhat resembling a helmet in silhouette. Flower heads yellow, scarcely ⅛ in. in diameter, in short clusters scarcely longer than the phyllodia. Pod about 3 in. long, distinctly twisted.

**pubescens.** Hairy wattle. Handsome shrub with pendulous branches and much grown in greenhouses for its showy bloom. Leaves twice-compound,* the ultimate leaflets usually in 16 pairs, scarcely ⅛ in. long. Flower heads yellow, about ⅓ in. in diameter in lax racemes* longer than the leaves. Pod flat. Common in florist-shop windows and a favorite because of its feathery foliage and free bloom in March or April.

**†saligna.** Golden wreath. A shrub or small tree with willow-like phyllodia often 8 in. long. Flower heads nearly ½ in. in diameter, in racemes.* Pod about 5 in. long and constricted between the seeds.

**†verticillata.** A small tree or shrub with very numerous phyllodia, which are needle-shaped, about ¾ in. long and whorled.* Flowers yellow in finger-shaped spikes which are about 1 in. long and usually solitary, but very numerous as there may be one at each whorl of phyllodia. Pod about 3 in. long.

**ACACIA FAMILY.** *See* LEGUMINOSAE.

**ACAENA** (a-seen'a). A small group of perennial herbs of the rose family, nearly or quite evergreen. Of the 40 or more, nearly all from the southern hemisphere, only the following are of much hort. importance. They are used mostly as ground-covers or in the rock garden, in mild climates. Leaves compound,* the pinnate* leaflets toothed. Flowers very small, but crowded in spikes or heads, prickly. Fruit dry. Most of the species are trailing or prostrate. (*Acaena*, Greek for thorn.)

Prefer open sunlight and a sandy soil. Propagation is easy, by cuttings in autumn or spring, or by seeds in early spring over gentle heat.

**buchanani.** Dwarf trailing perennial grown mostly for its beautiful bluish-gray leaves. Flowers insignificant, in tiny, stalkless heads, its spines yellowish. N.Z.

**microphylla.** New Zealand bur. Growing in large patches, but scarcely 3 in. high. Leaves, greenish, bronzy or slightly silky, but not bluish-gray. Flowers crimson in prickly heads, the spines red. N.Z.

**ACALYPHA** (a-ka-lee'fa, also a-ka-ly'fa). A very large genus of mostly tropical shrubs of the spurge family; a few weedy herbs in temperate regions. The hort. species are greenhouse plants or used for bedding or even hedges in zone* 9 and, sometimes, precariously, in zone 8. Leaves alternate, usually long-stalked. Flowers imperfect,* very minute, but crowded in a dense finger-thick, often bracted* cluster, hence often very showy. Fruit a 2-valved capsule.* (*Acalypha* was applied by Hippocrates to a nettle, but adopted by Linnaeus for these plants.)

As greenhouse plants grow in a warm house in potting mixture* 4. Outdoors (in zone* 8) they should be protected from occasional frosts. Propagated by cuttings in the autumn taken from bedded plants or from those in the greenhouse, over mild bottom-heat. Pots of any of the species may be plunged outdoors in the north for summer show, but all are tender and must be in the greenhouse before frost. *A. hispida* is a popular decorative plant for the conservatory, its long tassels of reddish-purple flowers being very striking.

**godseffiana.** Dense bushy shrub, grown mostly for its cream-margined, rather short-stalked leaves which are ovalish, but heart-shaped at the base and coarsely toothed. Flower spike greenish, half hidden by the leaves. New Guinea. By some considered only as a variety of *A. wilkesiana*.

**hispida.** Chenille plant. The leading hort. species, much cultivated for its long, drooping, reddish-purple spikes. These are three times as long as the leaves, which are green, broadly oval, about 6 in. long, and hairy-veined. East Indies. There is a variety with branched spikes, and another, more rare, with white spikes.

**wilkesiana.** Copper-leaf. Grown for its bronzy-green, usually red-mottled foliage. Leaves elliptic or oval, about 6 in. long, in some varieties handsomely mottled with green, white, yellow, brown or orange. Flower spike thinner than in *hispida*, reddish, and scarcely 8 in. long. Pacific Islands. Much planted in the far South for its extremely showy foliage.

**ACANTHACEAE** (a-kan-thā'see-e). The acanthus family comprises some 190 genera and nearly 2000 species, all but a handful tropical. Most of them are herbs, but there are some shrubs and vines. Leaves opposite,* simple, without stipules.* Flowers nearly always irregular, either 1-lipped or 2-lipped and generally crowded in a leafy cluster of some sort, often a spike. In some genera (*Pseuderanthemum, Odontonema, Barleria, Crossandra* and *Mackaya*) the flowers are nearly regular. Fruit a 2-celled capsule, often splitting elastically.

There are about a score of hort. genera, some of wide use in the garden or greenhouse because of showy flowers or bracts or colored foliage. Besides those mentioned above *see also*: ACANTHUS, APHELANDRA, BELOPERONE, FITTONIA,

---

* Special articles on the subjects indicated by an asterisk (*) will be found at the words so marked.

Graptophyllum, Hemigraphis, Peristrophe, Ruellia, Schaueria, and Strobilanthes, most of which are herbs or low shrubs, nearly all greenhouse plants in the north. *Thunbergia* comprises mostly twining vines, while among the showiest of the family are *Eranthemum, Jacobinia, Justicia, Pachystachys,* and *Sanchezia*.

Technical flower characters: Stamens 2, or 4, in the latter case in two pairs. Ovary superior,* its long, very slender style usually persistent, even after the corolla has fallen.

**ACANTHIUM.** Pre-Linnaean* name for the Scotch thistle (*Onopordon acanthium*).

**ACANTHOCEREUS** (a-kan-tho-see'ree-us). Little known trailing or climbing cacti with 3-angled stems, no leaves, and many spines borne at woolly cushion-like depressions. Flowers night-blooming, large, and funnel-shaped. Fruit a berry, which is sometimes spiny. (Named from the Greek for thorn and the genus *Cereus*.)

Grown outdoors in Fla. and Tex. As a greenhouse plant use potting mixture* 6, and a cool house. *See* Cacti.

pentagonus. Stems sometimes 20 ft. long and rooting at the tips, often half erect without support. Spines about 1½ in. long, usually 4–6 in a cluster. Flowers about 7 in. long, greenish-white and not so attractive as several other night-blooming species of cacti. Berry red. Fla. and Tex. and perhaps to the Argentine.

*ACANTHOCOMA, -us, -um* (a-kan-tho-kō'ma). With spiny hairs.

**ACANTHOLIMON** (a-kan-tho-ly'mon). Prickly thrift. Low evergreen perennial herbs, family Plumbaginaceae, with prickly or sharp-pointed, densely crowded and rigid leaves. Flowers small, crowded in one-sided racemes* or in a spike, pink or purple (in those below), the tiny flowers usually partly hidden by the many bracts. (Name from the Greek for spine, and limon, the sea lavender.)

Of the 80 species, all from the eastern Mediterranean region, only a handful are in cultivation and only those below are at all common in America. They are chiefly rock garden plants needing open sun, light and sandy soil and are slow growing. Propagation in late summer by cuttings wintered in a frost-protected cold frame, or by layering.* For related and more widely cultivated plants *see* Statice and Limonium.

glumaceum. Not over 6 in. high, its tufts of slender leaves making a considerable cushion. From this arises the stalk of the flower cluster, which is a one-sided raceme of rose-colored flowers. Summer. Can be grown, also, in the open border.

venustum. About 5 in. high. Leaves rather spiny, bluish-green, and in open rosettes. Flowers rose-pink, in relatively long-stalked dense spikes. Summer. A rock garden species doing best in sandy or gritty soil with perfect drainage.

**ACANTHOPANAX** (a-kan-tho-pay'nax). A genus of Asiatic shrubs or trees of the ginseng family, having 20 species of which only the following are of hort. significance in America. Leaves simple* in the first, but compound* in the second species. Flowers small, imperfect,* greenish-white, in small umbels,* but these sometimes grouped in a large, much-branched cluster. Fruit a black berry. (Named from the Greek for spine and the genus *Panax*.)

*Acanthopanax* is chiefly grown for the very handsome foliage. They make striking accents in a shrub border and fine specimen or lawn plants. They have no special soil requirements and are relatively free of pests. Propagation by seeds which should be stratified, or by root cuttings over bottom-heat.

pentaphyllum. A common name in the trade, but the plant is *A. sieboldianum*.

ricinifolium. A medium-sized tree with stout, prickly branches. Leaves nearly round in general outline, often a foot or more wide, and with 5–7 lobes, its stalk nearly 2 ft. long. Flowers whitish in small umbels,* but these grouped in a compound terminal cluster that is 15–18 in. wide. Berries about ⅓ in. in diameter. Jap. Summer. Doubtfully hardy in zone* 3, surely hardy from zone* 4 southward.

sieboldianum. A shrub usually not over 9 ft. high, usually without prickles. Leaves compound,* the 5–7 leaflets nearly stalkless, and generally wedge-shaped, and arranged fan-fashion. The general leaf-stalk is about 4 in. long. Flowers greenish-white in solitary, long-stalked umbels.* Berries about ½ in. in diameter. Jap. Summer. Zone* 4 southward. A good plant for smoky places.

**ACANTHUS** (a-kan'thus). A genus of perennial herbs, family Acanthaceae, comprising possibly 20 species, only the following of much hort. importance here. Leaves large, much cut, the segments or large teeth almost prickly, somewhat thistle-like. Flowers irregular,* one-lipped, in longish, erect spikes. Fruit a 4-seeded capsule. (*Acanthus* is Greek for thorn.)

*Acanthus* needs open sunshine, rich soil, and will not stand much water, especially in autumn and winter. It should be mulched from zone* 3 northward, in winter. Propagation by division* in spring.

mollis. Bear's-breech. A striking plant for the border, upright, its mostly basal leaves about 2 ft. long and half as wide, distinctly hairy on the upper surface. Flower spike about 1½–2 ft. long, the white, lilac, or rose-colored flowers with spiny bracts beneath. Southern Eu. Aug. There is a broader-leaved variety (**latifolius**), taller, and hardier.

**ACANTHUS FAMILY** = Acanthaceae.

**ACAULESCENT.** Apparently stemless, actually with the stem below ground. *See* Caulescent.

*ACAULIS, -e* (a-call'is). Acaulescent.

**ACCENT PLANT.** An accent plant is a type of plant with a well-defined decorative form. It is used to accentuate a particular feature in a design and should be used only where such emphasis is necessary. To use accents indiscriminately defeats their purpose.

Natural untrimmed forms of accent plants are vertical or emphatic; horizontal or prostrate; rounded or globose, and semi-formal (*see* illustrations). Other types of plants which do not assume these forms by their natural growth habit may be sheared into similar shapes. It is preferable to select plants for accent which assume a natural decorative form without shearing because they fulfill their intended purpose even when left to grow naturally. Except where special architectural forms are desired for a stylized effect sheared plants should be avoided.

Vertical forms are extremely emphatic and should be used only to arrest attention or to form a frame for some other feature. This type will create a very restless effect when repeated too often. Typical examples are the pyramid form of arborvitae, of the Chinese juniper, of the Irish yew (*Taxus baccata fastigata*), and *Populus alba pyramidalis*. Horizontal forms are more restful and are preferable where an emphatic accent is unnecessary. Steps and path intersections are better marked by this form. Typical examples are *Juniperus chinensis pfitzeriana, Juniperus horizontalis douglasi, Taxus cuspidata,* Swiss mountain pine, *Cotoneaster horizontalis*.

Vertical evergreens used as accent plants

A low and naturally informal accent plant

* Special articles on the subjects indicated by an asterisk (*) will be found at the words so marked.

# ACCLIMATION — ACHILLEA

Rounded or globose forms create a more decorative effect than horizontal forms but produce spottiness unless carefully placed. These forms may be used in the center of a design with less danger of restlessness than vertical forms. Typical examples are boxwood, *Azalea obtusa amoena*, Japanese holly, *Thuja occidentalis globosa*, *Chamaecyparis pisifera*, *Viburnum opulus nanum*, Japanese barberry. Semi-formal types are useful to frame other features when a more compact form is too definite. Typical examples are *Spiraea vanhouttei*, Rose-of-Sharon, mock-orange, *Azalea obtusa kaempferi*, hybrid lilacs, and *Pieris japonica*.

Globe-shaped evergreen as a low accent plant

A flowering shrub used as an informal accent plant

The successful choice of accent plants must take into account the ultimate size to which the specimens will grow, texture and color of foliage as well as the form of the plants. Variegated foliage plants and golden-hued evergreens are extremely difficult to harmonize with other plants and should be used only by the most skillful designers. Dark rich greens of fine foliage texture are best suited for accent plants. — R. E. G.

**ACCLIMATION.** The natural process by which plants come to tolerate a definite climate. It differs from acclimatization (which see at HARDINESS) because the latter involves the activities of man.

**ACCLIMATIZATION.** See HARDINESS.

**ACCOUNTS.** Garden bookkeeping is like any other. Most gardeners for fun don't want to keep a set of books. What they get out of a garden in pleasure, health, and the satisfaction of producing beautiful or useful plants far outweighs whatever expenditure they put into it.

However, there are times when it is necessary to know what it costs to have a garden, and, in many cases, whether it shows a real profit or not. Most agricultural economists admit that if corporation bookkeeping were applied to farms, scarcely any, except a few specialized ones, would show a profit. And in the field of gardening it is only the specialized fruit, vegetable and flower grower who knows exactly what production costs really are.

In garden bookkeeping the profit, outside of the satisfactions and intangibles, is real only if the following have been properly computed in the cost of production. Because they are so often forgotten, it seems well to list them:

Proportionate interest on investment in land occupied by the garden.

Depreciation at the rate of about 8 per cent a year on all garden tools, structures (greenhouses, frames, etc.) and equipment.

A sum to compensate for net loss of fertility to the land (necessary only if overcropped, without adequate replenishment of plant food).

Proportionate taxes (or rent) on garden land and insurance on garden equipment and structures.

All other costs of production are self-evident. But to labor, soil, manure, spraying materials, fertilizers, plants, seeds and bulbs, each gardener must add some reasonable allocation of the items in the list. Only so can he keep accurate garden accounts.

**ACEAE** (ā'see-e). A suffix found at the end of the name of most plant families signifying *belonging to*. Thus to the genus *Rosa* is added *aceae*, which then becomes Rosaceae, or the rose family. *Aceae* is the almost universal termination for plant family names, but there are exceptions like Umbelliferae, Labiatae, Gramineae, Leguminosae, and Compositae.

**ACER.** See MAPLE.

**ACERACEAE** (a-sir-ā'see-e). The maple family. The only genus here is the maple. *See* that entry for the characters of the Aceraceae.

***ACERIFOLIA, -us, -um*** (a-sir-ee-fō'lee-a). Having maple-like leaves.

**ACETOSA.** Pre-Linnaean* name for the common sorrel (*Rumex acetosa*).

**ACETOSELLA.** Pre-Linnaean* name for several plants with acid foliage, especially the sorrel and wood sorrel.

**ACHENE** (a-keen'). A dry, one-seeded fruit that does not split; typical examples being the fruit of the buttercup and the "seeds" on the surface of a strawberry (which see).

**ACHILLEA** (a-kil-lee'a). Yarrow. A large genus of perennial herbs, family Compositae, mostly from the north temperate zone and a few grown for their white, pink, or yellow flowers. Leaves toothed or parted or divided, and in some species finely dissected, often aromatic when crushed. Flower heads small, but usually numerous, in often flat-topped clusters. Of the 80 species only the following are of any hort. importance. (Named for Achilles who is supposed to have used some species to heal his wounds.)

Yarrow is easy to grow in ordinary garden soil and the taller species are attractive in the border. Low ones, like *A. argentea, ageratifolia, nana,* and *tomentosa* are chiefly rock garden* plants. Propagation, which is simple, is by root division in spring or autumn. Many species are rank growers and will crowd out more delicate plants. One (see *A.* PTARMICA below) is perhaps the most widely grown garden plant.

**ageratifolia.** Silvery-leaved, tufted, rock garden plant, scarcely 6 in. tall. Leaves cut feather-fashion, the margins crimped. Flowers white. Greece. The variety **aizoon** (often sold as *Anthemis aizoon*) has nearly uncut leaves. Summer.

**ageratum.** A border plant that reaches 1–2 ft. high. Leaves merely toothed, crowded in small clusters. Flowers yellow, the clusters slightly dome-shaped. Eu. Summer.

**argentea.** Not over 6 in. high. Leaves in dense clusters, mostly basal, silvery, cut nearly to the middle. Flowers white. A rock garden species from southern Eu. July–Sept.

**filipendulina.** A stout border plant frequently reaching 4 ft. high, the stems hairy and slightly furrowed. Leaves 6–7 in. long, densely clothing the stem, finely dissected. Flowers yellow, showy. Eurasian. Summer.

**millefolium.** Common yarrow, called also milfoil. Stem leafy, scarcely 2 ft. high. Leaves finely dissected. Flowers white. Rarely cult. and in fact a weed (see list at WEEDS). The *var.* **roseum**, the rosy milfoil, is grown, however, for its red or pink, attractive flower clusters. Eurasian. July.

**nana.** A European rock garden plant, scarcely 5 in. high. Leaves white-woolly, cut feather-fashion, distinctly aromatic. Flowers white. June.

**ptarmica.** Sneezewort. This, the parent form of widely planted garden varieties, is not very commonly grown. It is a stout herb 1–2 ft. high. Leaves lance-shaped, toothed. Flower heads white, not double, in loose open clusters. North temperate zone. Summer. Its double flowered varieties, especially The Pearl and Boule de Neige, are very old favorites, free bloomers during most of the summer, and are useful both in the border and for cutting, particularly the former.

**tomentosa.** A rock garden plant from the north temperate zone with green but woolly, cut leaves and yellow flowers. It needs a sandy soil and will bloom from June to Sept.

---
* Special articles on the subjects indicated by an asterisk (*) will be found at the words so marked.

**ACHIMENES** (a-kim'e-neez). Tropical American herbs, family Gesneriaceae, grown either in pots or hanging baskets for their showy gloxinia-like flowers. Of the 40 known species only two are commonly cult. and they have been so much hybridized that those below are more likely to represent the sorts in cultivation than the species themselves. Roots or rootstocks more or less tuberous. Leaves opposite* or in a whorl,* tinted on the lower side, always more or less toothed. Flowers in the leaf axils,* tubular, the tube curved, and with a spreading, somewhat irregular limb.* Fruit a 2-valved capsule. (From the Greek implying that the plants suffer from cold, which they do.)

*Achimenes* should be grown in the cool greenhouse in potting mixture* 4. When through flowering the tuberous root or rootstock should be taken from the pot, stored in clean sand, without watering, and in a temperature about 45°. In March or April re-pot, put in a greenhouse with a temperature of about 60°. Do not plant them deeply as they are shallow rooted. Give plenty of drainage. Easily propagated by division of the rhizome, or by cuttings in summer in a moist greenhouse. Rhizomes can also be purchased from seedsmen. Summer-flowering.

**grandiflora.** Stem erect, more or less covered with stiff hairs. Leaves ovalish, a little inequilateral at the base, reddish on the under side, about 1½ in. long. Flowers numerous, often more than 1 in an axil,* large and showy, bright red-purple. Mexico. Summer.

**longiflora.** Stems 1-2 ft. long. Leaves oval or oval-oblong, often in whorls* of 3 or 4, usually tinted on the lower side. Flower usually one in each axil, salver-shaped, with a long curving tube, violet-blue (or white in a variety). Guatemala.

Among the named hort. forms of *Achimenes*, not certainly referable to any particular species, are: Dainty Queen (white and pink-eyed), Galatea (deep lavender), Purple King (purple) and Supreme (lavender with whitish center).

**ACHIOTE** = *Bixa orellana*.

**ACHRAS** (ak'ras). A small genus of tropical American trees, family Sapotaceae, of no interest except for the marmalade plum which can only be grown outdoors in zone* 9. It is grown in the tropics for its fruit, rarely under glass in a warm greenhouse northward. (*Achras* is from Greek for the pear, in allusion to the fruit of the marmalade plum.) The tree is sometimes known as *Calocarpum* and the name *Achras* has also been applied to the sapodilla (see SAPOTA).

**zapota.** Marmalade plum, called also sapote. A tree up to 60 ft. Leaves without teeth, up to 15 in. long by 4 in. wide, usually clustered at the ends of the twigs. Flowers small, white, nearly stalkless, appearing on the old wood in the axils* of the fallen leaves. Fruit russet about 5 in. long, somewhat pear-shaped, with thick skin and firm, spicy, reddish flesh. Central America. The tree is also, incorrectly, known as *Lucuma mammosa*. It is sometimes called mamey sapote, but *see*, in this connection, MAMMEA.

**ACHYRANTHES.** See IRESINE

**ACHYRODES** = *Lamarckia*.

*ACIDA, -us, -um* (as'i-da). Tart or acid.

**ACID AND ALKALI SOILS.** Acidity and alkalinity of soils comes from two sources. The first, and probably most important, is the chemical nature of the rock from which the mineral soil is derived. In many specialized habitats, however, such as a bog, or humus* on the forest-floor, the chief source of acidity is the partial or complete decomposition of vegetation. Alkalinity, from the hort. standpoint, is confined to the comparatively limited areas of natural limestone, the salt marshes, and the alkali deserts of the West.

Much has been written, within the last ten years, on the acidity of soils and the "preference" of certain plants for soils of a definite degree of acidity. Technically, there may be no such preference. Much more accurately we can say that plants are acid-tolerant or alkali-tolerant, which implies that they grow in such places not because they prefer them but because they must.

From the practical gardening standpoint all we need to do is to provide acid-tolerant plants with the degree of acidity in which they mostly grow. This acidity is pretty well known for most of the plants where it is at all significant. But the bog-gardener, or wild-gardener, and often the rock-gardener does need a method of testing his soil to determine with reasonable accuracy whether his site meets these conditions.

### SOIL ACIDITY AND ALKALINITY

Of the many and often elaborate methods of determining the degree of soil acidity and alkalinity only one will be described here — the simplest and most convenient. What lies behind the reactions described hereafter belongs to the realm of chemistry — technical and perhaps quite unnecessary information for the gardener. The terms, however, and the nearly universal scale used in measuring acidity have been derived from the soil chemists and it will be necessary to define a few of them and explain what their significance may be.

Water, the common solvent of all soils, is $H_2O$. That is as near truth as most of us desire, but it is not exact truth, for, while the molecules of hydrogen and oxygen in water are mostly associated or combined with each other, they are not completely so. A small proportion are completely dissociated into positive, hydrogen ions and negative, hydroxyl ions. The latter is characteristic of alkalies, and the hydrogen ions of acids. If the number of hydrogen ions and hydroxyl ions were the same, water, or soil solutions, would be neither acid nor alkaline but neutral — as in distilled water.

If the water, or soil solution, or whatever you are testing, were acid, the hydrogen ions would be more numerous, while the hydroxyl ions would, contrariwise, be in the ascendant in alkali solutions. The amount of the divergence from neutral (neither acid nor alkaline) is thus commonly called the hydrogen ion concentration and the universal symbol for it, used here, is pH.

Chemists have devised a scale for measuring the acidity and alkalinity of soils based upon their hydrogen ion concentration or pH value as it is called. It utilizes (in the method below) the known color reaction of certain pH values for certain chemical indicators. Using this method does not need any greater knowledge of what lies behind such tests, than most of us know exactly what is behind the figures on a radio dial or a barometer. In other words, we now have a simple scale for measuring acidity and alkalinity, which any gardener can use.

### PRACTICAL APPLICATION

This scale is numbered from 4 to 9 which includes the whole range of soil in which plants can grow — 4 being the acid extremity of the scale and 9 the alkaline limits. It is divided into the following intervals:

| pH value | 4.0 | 5.0 | 6.0 | 7.0 | 8.0 | 9.0 |
|---|---|---|---|---|---|---|
| | Very acid | Acid | Slightly acid | Neutral (neither acid nor alkaline) | Alkaline | Strongly alkaline |

These intervals may be split into minute subdivisions, and usually are in many industrial applications, but for the gardener these are all we need, and of them 9.0 is confined only to such unhappy hort. sites as the alkali deserts.

Before making a test to determine what the degree of acidity may be, it will be worth while, perhaps even imperative, to see what ordinary soils contain, as to their acidity. For convenience of reference, they are listed (see page 6) together with a few special terms not elsewhere used in this DICTIONARY, as being unnecessary for the gardener, but frequently appearing in some publications.

For all practical purposes 6 and 7 do not concern the gardener because they comprise between them practically all normal garden soils. And most garden plants are very tolerant as to variations within the range of pH 6 and 7. In other words, one scarcely needs to consider by far the most widely occurring of pH values, nor the plants that grow in such places, insofar as their acidity or alkalinity requirements are concerned.

It is otherwise with pH 4.0 and 5.0. These degrees of acidity appear to be of such significance that a list of the commonly cultivated plants characteristic of each is re-

---

* Special articles on the subjects indicated by an asterisk (*) will be found at the words so marked.

## ACID AND ALKALI SOILS

### ACID AND ALKALI SOIL TYPES

**pH 4** Very acid. Found only in peat bogs covered with sphagnum moss and in the duff under coniferous trees. No lime is found in such places. Called, also, Superacid.

**pH 5** Acid. Peaty upland soils, rotted wood, some pine-barren sands, and fields or gardens heavily fertilized and scarcely ever limed. Called, also, Mediacid.

**pH 6** Slightly acid. Ordinary garden soils in a non-limestone region, including those without much manure and scarcely ever limed. Called Minimacid.

**pH 7** Neutral. Includes ordinary garden soils, especially where they have been limed occasionally, and even some more acid types that have been limed; also most compost, rotted manure, black leaf mold, etc.

**pH 8** Alkaline. Salt marshes, limestone soils or heavily limed soils. Called, also, Minimalkaline.

To the last three categories the general term of circumneutral has also been applied.

corded below. It will be noted that some are in both lists, which means, of course, that they tolerate either, or perhaps some (here unexpressed) degree of acidity between these figures.

### SOME ACID SOIL PLANTS
(Comprises only those entered in the DICTIONARY)

**pH 4** Very Acid
*Andromeda polifolia*
*Arethusa bulbosa*
*Arnica montana*
*Calla palustris*
*Calopogon pulchellus*
*Chamaecyparis thyoides*
*Coptis trifolia*
*Corema conradi*
*Cornus canadensis*
*Cypripedium acaule*
*Darlingtonia californica*
*Dionaea muscipula*
*Drosera* (all species)
*Epigaea* (see TRAILING ARBUTUS)
*Habenaria blephariglottis*
*Habenaria cristata*
*Helonias bullata*
*Ilex aquifolium* (see HOLLY)
*Kalmia polifolia*
*Ledum* (all species)
*Leiophyllum buxifolium*
*Linnaea* (both species)
*Loiseleuria procumbens*
*Lygodium palmatum*
*Magnolia virginiana*
*Menziesia pilosa*
*Paronychia argyrocoma*
*Pogonia ophioglossoides*
*Sarracenia* (see PITCHER-PLANT)
*Stenanthium robustum*
*Vaccinium* (see cultural notes at BLUEBERRY)
*Woodwardia areolata*
*Xerophyllum asphodeloides*
*Zantedeschia aethiopica* (see CALLA LILY)

**pH 5** Acid
*Abies* (see FIR)
*Acer pennsylvanicum* (see MAPLE)
*Aletris farinosa*
*Arenaria groenlandica*
*Arethusa bulbosa*
*Arnica montana*
*Azalea* (most species)
*Coptis trifolia*
*Corema conradi*
*Cornus canadensis*
*Cypripedium acaule*
*Cypripedium arietinum*
*Epigaea* (see TRAILING ARBUTUS)
*Habenaria blephariglottis*
*Habenaria fimbriata*
*Habenaria psycodes*
*Ilex aquifolium* (see HOLLY)
*Ilex opaca* (see HOLLY)
*Kalmia polifolia*
*Ledum* (all species)
*Linnaea* (both species)
*Loiseleuria procumbens*
*Lygodium palmatum*
*Magnolia virginiana*
*Menziesia pilosa*
*Polypodium aureum*
*Potentilla tridentata*
*Rhexia* (both species)
*Rhododendron* (see cultural notes at RHODODENDRON)
*Sorbus americana* (see MOUNTAIN-ASH)
*Streptopus* (both species)
*Trillium* (most species)
*Woodwardia areolata*
*Xerophyllum asphodeloides*
*Xolisma mariana*
*Xolisma ligustrina*
*Zantedeschia aethiopica* (see CALLA LILY)

*Note:* For plants requiring alkaline (mostly limestone) conditions, see LIMESTONE PLANTS.

Most of the above are wild garden or bog plants. Very few vegetables or ordinary garden flowers are so particular about the acidity of their soils, so long as it comes within the range of pH 6, 7 or 8. A few crops, however, seem to need special conditions or at least do better when provided with them. The most important and their apparent pH tolerance are the following:

|  | pH |  |
|---|---|---|
| *Aleurites fordi* (see TUNG-OIL TREE) | 5–6 | |
| *Ananas sativus* (see PINEAPPLE) | 5–6 | |
| *Citrullus vulgaris* (see WATERMELON) | 5–6 | (Neither above nor below these; intolerant outside this limited range of acidity.) |
| *Nicotiana tabacum* (tobacco) | 5–6 | |
| *Solanum tuberosum* (potato) | 5–6 | |
| *Spinacia oleracea* (spinach) | 6–8 | (Does not do well if pH is below 6.) |

### TESTING SOILS FOR ACIDITY

As mentioned above certain chemical indicators give definite color reactions when mixed with soils of a certain degree of acidity. Upon this principle a simple porcelain plate has been devised with a small well at one end, a shallow trough through the center and a much smaller well at the opposite end. On each side of the central trough is a series of colored bands, standardized at exactly the intervals of the pH values from 4 to 9 (see above).

All that is done to make a test is to put a pinch of soil (with a spoon, *not* the fingers) in the larger well, and drop enough of the liquid indicator (a few spots) to puddle the pinch of soil. Allow the puddle to stand for 2 or 3 minutes and then gently incline the plate so that the indicator will trickle through the central trough to the smaller well. Its color can then be exactly compared with the colored band that nearest matches it, and from that matching you can read the pH value, for the figures for these are put alongside of each of the color bands.

The above device, known as the Hellige Soil Tester, while the simplest and most direct, is by no means the only one. Others have several different indicators, some require distilled water in which the soil sample must be soaked, and there are a few (much more accurate) electrical devices for determining soil acidity. But, for the practical gardener, the simplicity and directness of the Hellige method will be all he needs.

### HOW TO INCREASE OR MAINTAIN SOIL ACIDITY OR ALKALINITY

Having made the test by this method and knowing the acid or alkali requirement of your plants, there remains still one more problem. Is it practicable to make a site more acid or more alkaline? In other words, can we change the soil environment to suit the plants we wish to grow, or should we limit our plantings to existing conditions?

On anything like a large scale there is no doubt that the latter alternative is the correct one, and that it is foolish attempting to make over a large tract. The only exception is the common one of increasing the alkalinity of fields, lawns or garden soil by the periodical addition of lime. This is both practical and effective. (For details, see LIME.)

To increase the acidity of a small bed or plantation is comparatively easy, however, and just as effective as liming on a much larger scale. Commercial aluminum sulphate applied according to the formula below will regulate soil acidity with sufficient accuracy for most plants if one keeps in mind two or three simple facts. Changing soil acidity requires different amounts of aluminum sulphate to increase acidity, depending upon the fineness of the soil particles. It needs less aluminum sulphate for sandy soils, more for loam and most for clay soils. (See SOILS for exact definition of sand, loam and clay.) With this caution, aluminum sulphate may be applied to bring acidity to the approximate level desired.

If your present soil is slightly acid (pH 6) and you wish to make it acid (pH 5) or very acid (pH 4); the aluminum sulphate should be spread on the soil at the following rates (assuming your soil now tests pH 6):

To make it Acid (pH 5) add aluminum sulphate at the rate of:

On sandy soils: 1 ton to the acre or nearly ½ lb. to the square yard.

On loam: 3 tons to the acre or a fraction over 1 lb. to the square yard.

On clay soils: 7 tons to the acre or 3½ lbs. to the square yard.

*Note:* To make the initial sample into a very acid one (pH 4), double the amounts of aluminum sulphate in the above table.

**ACIDANTHERA** (as-i-dan'the-ra). Bulbous African herbs of the iris family. Of the 18 species only the following is much grown here. Its summer-blooming, long-tubed flowers are handsome, somewhat resembling gladiolus.

* Special articles on the subjects indicated by an asterisk (*) will be found at the words so marked.

Leaves sword-shaped. Flowers in a long, loose, rather leafy spike, the corolla-tube slightly dilated toward the top. Fruit an oblong capsule. (Named from the Greek for a cusp and anther, in allusion to the cusp-like anthers of some species.)

*Acidanthera* (which is tender) should be treated exactly like gladiolus. Propagation by use of the many cormels* that start about the old corm.*

**bicolor.** The brownish corm* is about an inch in diameter. Stem unbranched, about 18 in. long. Leaves few, usually only one or two. Spike few-flowered, its leafy sheaths about 3 in. long. Flowers cream-white outside, splashed chocolate-brown inside, the slender tube about 4 in. long. Tropical Af. Summer.

**ACID FOR CUTTINGS.** See the aid of chemicals at Cuttings.

**ACID HUMUS.** See Humus.

**ACID LEMON.** See Lemon.

**ACID LIME.** See Lime.

*ACIDOSA, -us, -um* (as-i-do'sa). Acid or bitter.

**ACID PEAT.** See Peat.

**ACID PHOSPHATE.** See Phosphoric Acid at Fertilizers.

**ACID SOIL PLANTS.** See the list of them at Acid and Alkali Soils.

*ACINACIFOLIA, -us, -um* (as-i-nas-i-fō'li-a). With scimitar-shaped leaves.

**ACOELORRAPHE** (a-see-low-raff'e). A fan palm of southern Fla., the Bahamas and possibly from Cuba, useful only in zone* 9. Trunks slender, usually in clusters of 6–8, without prickles. Leaves long-stalked, the stalks spiny. Flowers small, 2 or 3 together, or often only 1. Fruit a black drupe. (Name of uncertain origin, possibly from Greek for not hollow, and *Raphe*, but that has little meaning here.)

**wrighti.** Everglade palm, called also, saw cabbage-palm. Handsome palm often 40 ft. high when full grown. Leaves green both sides, the blade 2½ ft. wide and cut nearly half way down into many divisions which are themselves split. Leafstalk 5 ft. long, its prickles upward curving. Fruit about ¼ in. in diameter. This palm, also known as *Serenoa arborescens* and *Paurotis wrighti*, is little known outside of Fla.

**ACOKANTHERA** (ak-o-kan'the-ra). A genus of African, very poisonous (not by contact), shrubs and trees, family Apocynaceae, one of which is a greenhouse plant with fragrant, whitish-pink flowers. Leaves opposite,* thick, leathery and without teeth. Flowers in small stalkless cymes,* tubular, the limb* slightly twisted to the left. Fruit a berry. (Name from Greek for pointed anthers.) Related, but not hort. species, furnish deadly arrow poisons.

Should be grown in warm greenhouse in potting mixture* 4. Propagation by cuttings in spring over bottom-heat. The plant is a rich feeder.

**spectabilis.** Shrub to 10 ft. but often kept as a much smaller pot plant. Leaves oblongish, about 4 in. long, narrowed at the base into a thick leafstalk. Flowers about 1 in. long. Berry ellipsoid about 1 in. long, blackish-purple. Tropical Af. Spring.

**ACONITE.** A plant of the genus *Aconitum*, or the sedative derived from them. See Monkshood.

*ACONITIFOLIA, -us, -um* (a-ko-ny-tee-fō'li-a). With leaves like a monkshood (*Aconitum*).

**ACONITUM.** See Monkshood.

**ACORUS** (ak'or-us). Marsh herbs of the arum family, hardy all over the United States and useful only in similar sites. Leaves long, parallel-sided, thickish, but otherwise grass-like, from a thick stout rootstock. Flowers greenish, minute, crowded on a stalkless spadix* that arises from a leaf-like sheath near the end of the stalk. Fruit berry-like, stalkless on the leaf-like stem. (*Acorus* is the classical name of the sweet flag.)

Suitable for bogs, water-sides or marshes, and of the easiest culture. Propagated by division of the creeping rootstock almost at any season. For uses see Herb Gardening.

**calamus.** Sweet flag. Stout perennial herb, its aromatic rootstock yielding calamus-root. Leaves usually about 2 ft. high, but sometimes twice this in rich soil. Spadix* about 2 in. long, finger-like. Throughout the north temperate zone. A yellow-striped form (*var.* variegatus) is more common in cultivation than the typical plant, but unknown wild.

**ACRE.** The common square measure for land. For its exact dimensions see Weights and Measures I. For the number of plants to an acre see Garden Tables I.

*ACRIS, -e* (ak'ris). Sharp.

**ACROCLINIUM.** See Helipterum.

**ACROCOMIA** (a-kro-kō'mi-a). Very spiny-trunked feather palms, all tropical American, and suitable for outdoor cultivation only in zone* 9 and sheltered parts of zone* 8. Trunk often swollen about half way up. Leaves pinnate,* the leaflets numerous, often drooping. Flower clusters appearing from amongst the dense crown of leaves, shiny sheathed, branched and drooping. Fruit round, thick-skinned. (From Greek for sharp and hair.)

Prefers moist sandy soil. The species below is a handsome palm suitable for lawn specimens but too spiny for street planting.

**totai.** This is also the native name for it in Paraguay and the Argentine where it frequently reaches a height of 40 ft. Trunk swollen, its long blackish spines borne in continuous bands around the trunk. Leaves green both sides, the leaflets narrow and rather sharp-pointed. Leafstalk felty and somewhat prickly. Fruit about ¾ in. in diameter.

*ACROSTICHOIDES* (a-kros-ti-koy'deez; but see Oïdes). Resembling a fern of the genus *Acrostichum*, which is scarcely in cultivation; but see, also, Elaphoglossum crinitum.

**ACROSTICHUM.** See Elaphoglossum crinitum.

**ACTAEA** (ak-tee'a). The baneberries are perennial herbs of the buttercup family, somewhat sparsely scattered over the north temperate zone. Leaves twice- or thrice-compound,* the ultimate leaflets sharply cleft and toothed. Flowers numerous, white, in thick terminal clusters. Fruit a red or white berry. (*Actaea* is the classical name of the elder, but adopted by Linnaeus for the baneberries.)

Useful and attractive herbs for the wild garden, these plants need a woods soil, but not a strongly acid one, and grow best in partial shade. Easily increased by root division in the early spring. The genus has received much attention from systematic botanists, and the names for the red and white baneberry below, while well known to gardeners, are possibly interpreted otherwise by some.

**alba.** White baneberry, also called white cohosh. Flowers white, in June. Fruit a white glistening berry on thick stalklets. Common in rich woods throughout eastern N.A.

**rubra.** Red baneberry, also called red cohosh. Similar to the above but the leaflets thinner, and the flower cluster not quite so elongate. Fruit a cherry-red, poisonous berry on very slender stalklets. Flowers about a week earlier than *A. alba*, and is rarer in the wild state. More common northward.

**ACTINIDIA** (ak-ti-nid'i-a). A group of 25 species of Asiatic woody vines, family Dilleniaceae, grown for their handsome foliage and ability to cover completely arbors and trellises. They have alternate simple leaves, the stalk of which covers the succeeding winter bud. Leaf-margins toothed. Flowers inconspicuous, cup-shaped, the male and the female often on different plants, or sometimes polygamous (see Hermaphrodite). Petals 5. Fruit a many-seeded berry. (From Greek for ray, in allusion to the radiating styles.)

They may be grown in ordinary garden soil, and climb rather quickly, either in full sun or part shade. Propagation is easily provided for by spring-sown seeds, cuttings of partly ripened wood in summer and matured wood under glass in winter. Layering* is also effective. See, also, stem climbers at Vines.

**arguta.** Tara vine. A high-climbing, densely leafy, woody vine, its broadly oval leaves about 5 in. long, lustrously green, the stalks about 2 in. long, reddish. Flower cluster shorter than the leafstalk, usually of three brownish-white flowers that are about ¾ in. across. Fruit ellipsoid, about 1 in. long, yellowish, sweet, and edible. Jap. and eastern As. July. Hardy from zone* 4 (and possibly from 3) southward.

**chinensis.** Yangtao. Often 30 ft. long, its branches and twigs covered with shaggy hairs that are red in youth. Leaves nearly round, about 6 in. diameter, heart-shaped at the base, green above, paler and felty beneath, the veins with red hairs. Flowers whitish, but ultimately yellowish, about 2 in. wide. Fruit nearly globular, about 2 in. in diameter, hairy, acid, but edible, not unlike a gooseberry in flavor. China. June.

---

* Special articles on the subjects indicated by an asterisk (*) will be found at the words so marked.

Perhaps the handsomest of the four but certainly hardy only from zone* 6 southward, and possibly in protected places in zone* 5.

**kolomikta.** Kolomikta vine. Not so high climbing, rarely over 10 ft., usually about 6 ft. high. Leaves (especially on the male plant) often white or pink-blotched, generally oblongish, about 5 in. long. Flowers white, about ¾ in. across. Fruit oblong or ovoid, about an inch long, greenish-yellow, sweet and edible. Eastern As. May. Hardy usually from zone* 3 southward, certainly so from zone* 4.

**polygama.** Silver vine. Sometimes climbing to 15 ft., the silver vine is attractive to cats. Leaves (especially on the male plant) often splashed with silvery white or yellowish blotches, generally oval-oblong, about 6 in. long. Flowers white, about ¾ in. across and fragrant. Fruit ovoid, beaked, yellow and edible. Eastern As. July. Hardy from zone* 3 southward. Male plants, which bear no fruit, have very attractive foliage.

**ACTINOLEPIS CORONARIA** = *Baeria aristata*.

**ACTINOPHLOEUS** (ak-tin-o-flee′us). A small genus of Australasian feather palms grown outdoors only in zones* 8 and 9, and elsewhere as tubbed specimens in the greenhouse. Leaves pinnate,* the leaflets more or less fringed, or jagged, or cut off obliquely at the tip. Flowers greenish, small, in a branched cluster that appears just below the crown of leaves. Fruit more or less cylindric, blunt-nosed, scarcely ¾ in. long. (From Greek for ray and bark, perhaps because of the ringed stems.)

Both the species below are slender graceful palms, usually suckering and sending up a number of thin prominently ringed stems. The first is usually a bushy plant, the second more graceful and, in its young state, a common pot plant. In the greenhouse grow both sorts in potting mixture* 4, feed well and provide plenty of water. *A. macarthuri* does well outdoors in southern Fla.

**macarthuri.** Cluster palm. Trunks greenish, scarcely more than 10 ft. high. Leaves about 2½ ft. long, paler beneath than above, the leaflets numerous (often over 36), about 8 in. long, always obliquely cut or jagged at the top. Fruit furrowed or wrinkled in drying. Aust. Identity still in doubt in many collections, as the plant is often offered as *Ptychosperma macarthuri* and *Kentia macarthuri*.

**sanderiana.** Resembling *A. macarthuri*, but more slender, especially its leaflets, some of which are long and narrow. Aust. Chiefly grown as a pot plant for its graceful foliage, often under the name of *Kentia sanderiana*.

*ACULEATA, -us, -um* (a-kew-le-ā′ta). Prickly.

*ACUMINATA, -us, -um* (a-kew-mi-nā′ta). See ACUMINATE.

**ACUMINATE.** Ending in a sharp, but distinctly tapering point. See ACUTE.

*ACUMINATIFOLIA, -us, -um* (a-kew-mi-na-ti-fō′li-a). With acuminate leaves.

*ACUTA, -us, -um* (a-kew′ta). See ACUTE.

*ACUTANGULA, -us, -um* (a-kew-tang′u-la). Sharply angled.

**ACUTE.** Ending in a sharp, but not a tapering, point. See ACUMINATE.

*ACUTIFOLIA, -us, -um* (a-kew-ti-fō′li-a). Sharp-leaved.

*ACUTILOBA, -us, -um* (a-kew-ti-lō′ba). With sharp-pointed lobes.

**ADAM-AND-EVE.** See APLECTRUM HYEMALE (an orchid), and ERYTHRONIUM GRANDIFLORUM (a western dogtooth violet).

**ADAM'S-APPLE** = *Tabernaemontana coronaria*.

**ADAM'S-NEEDLE** = *Yucca filamentosa*.

**ADANSONIA** (a-dan-sown′i-a). Huge tropical African trees, family Bombacaceae, grown as a curiosity only in zone* 9, rarely in the warm greenhouse. Frequently a shade tree in the tropics. Leaves compound,* palmate.* Flowers solitary, hanging on extraordinarily long stalks, from which, later, the huge fruit (known as monkey's-bread) also hangs. (Named for Michel Adanson, 1727–1806, French botanist.)

**digitata.** Baobab. A huge tree, the trunk sometimes 30 ft. in diameter in the wild state, much smaller in southern Fla. where it is sometimes grown. Leaflets usually 5, and about 5 in. long. Flowers white, nearly 6 in. across, the purple stamens very showy, soon withering. Fruit hard-shelled, white, about a foot long, the pulp mealy and acid. Tropical Af. July. The tree is leafless in the late spring and early summer.

**ADCO.** A trademarked chemical preparation for converting vegetable refuse into synthetic manure; useful in the compost pile. See Synthetic Manure at MANURE.

**ADDER'S-MOUTH** = *Pogonia ophioglossoides*.

**ADDER'S-TONGUE.** See ERYTHRONIUM.

**ADDER'S-TONGUE FAMILY** = OPHIOGLOSSACEAE.

**ADDER'S-TONGUE FERN** = *Ophioglossum*.

**ADDER'S VIOLET** = *Epipactis pubescens*.

**ADELIA** = *Forestiera*.

**ADENANTHERA** (a-den-ăn′the-ra). A small genus of acacia-like trees of the pea family, all from the Old World tropics. The only hort. species is grown outdoors in zone* 9 or in greenhouses northward, for its feathery foliage and yellowish and white flowers. Leaves many times compound,* the leaflets very numerous and small. Flowers in spike-like clusters, some white, others yellowish, in the same cluster. Fruit a linear pod that coils up when ripe. Seeds (often called Circassian seeds) red, showy, and lens-shaped. (From *adeno*, glandular or sticky, and *anther*, in allusion to the glandular anthers.)

The only cultivated species is easily grown in ordinary garden soil in zone* 9. In the greenhouse use potting mixture* 4. Propagation by seeds that have been soaked in warm water.

**pavonina.** Barbados pride, called also red sandalwood and flower fence. A tall tree in the tropics but in cultivated specimens scarcely over 20 ft. Foliage very fine and feathery. Flower clusters in the axils.* Pod about 8 in. long, its seeds used for beadwork. Tropical Af. and As.

**ADENOCARPUS** (a-den-o-kar′pus). A horticulturally unimportant genus of low trees or shrubs of the pea family cultivated in southern Calif., mostly native in the Orient and the Canaries. Leaves compound,* with only 3 small leaflets. Flowers pea-like, yellow, in terminal clusters. Fruit a sticky, linear pod. (From *adeno*, glandular or sticky, and *carpus*, fruit, in allusion to the sticky pod.)

The species below is grown in open sunlight and sandy soil in southern Calif., rarely in greenhouses where it should have potting mixture* 3. Propagated by cuttings of green wood in the spring or by seeds, or layering.*

**viscosus.** A sticky-stemmed shrub scarcely over 3 ft. high. Leaflets nearly oblong, often folded. Flower cluster crowded, somewhat sticky. Teneriffe. Hardy outdoors only in zones* 8 and 9.

**ADENOPHORA** (a-den-off′o-ra). About a dozen species of perennial herbs mostly from eastern Asia, closely related to the bellflowers (see CAMPANULA), two species grown for their handsome blue flowers. It differs from *Campanula* only in technical characters, and its cultivation is also like that genus. (Named for the gland-bearing nectary.)

**liliifolia.** A Eurasian leafy herb 2–3 ft. high. Lower leaves roundish and stalked, the stem leaves longer and stalkless, toothed. Flowers pale blue, fragrant, about an inch long, rather broadly bell-shaped and in pyramid-shaped, terminal clusters. Summer.

**potanini.** Hairy-stemmed Chinese herb with oval-lance-shaped leaves that are either coarsely and remotely toothed or without any teeth. Flowers blue, about ¾ in. long, in racemes.* Summer.

*ADENOPHYLLA, -us, -um* (a-den-off′il-la). Having sticky leaves.

**ADENOSTOMA** (a-de-nos′to-ma). A small group of chaparral shrubs of the rose family, common in southern Calif. and not much grown elsewhere. They have very small, evergreen, needle-shaped or heath-like leaves and small white flowers in a terminal truss. Petals 5. Fruit dry, partly enclosed by the calyx.* (From *adeno*, a gland, and *stoma-*mouth, in allusion to the glands on the calyx.)

While the species below will stand some frost it does not thrive in the comparatively humid east. Suitable mostly for southern Calif. and regions like it. Prefers sandy soil and open sunlight. Propagation by cuttings of green wood in the spring or by seeds.

**fasciculatum.** Chamiso. As a native, up to 15 ft., in cultivation considerably less. Leaves scarcely ¼ in. long, densely crowded. Flowers very small, nearly stalkless in a dense terminal cluster that is about 3 in. long. Calif.

**ADIANTUM** (a-dee-an′tum). A very large genus of mostly tropical ferns, the maidenhairs, family Polypodiaceae. A few species reach the temperate zone, notably our common maidenhair (*A. pedatum*). Of the nearly 200 known species, nearly 40 are supposed to be in cultivation in America, but

---

* Special articles on the subjects indicated by an asterisk (*) will be found at the words so marked.

of these only the following are generally grown — some on a great scale as greenhouse favorites.

Stems nearly always polished black or purplish. In all those below the fronds are twice- or thrice-compound* (simple-leaved species are known). The ultimate segments are characteristically fan-shaped or wedge-shaped in the wild species but often much altered in the horticultural forms. The outer margin is always slightly rolled and, in fertile forms, conceals the spore cases. The latter contains the spores which are the source of new plants (see the details at Spores and Reproduction in the article FERNS AND FERN GARDENING), unless the plants can be divided. (*Adiantum* is from the Greek not, and to wet, alluding to the water-shedding character of the leaflets.)

For the culture of the maidenhairs see FERNS AND FERN GARDENING, both for the greenhouse (tropical) species and our common maidenhair (*A. pedatum*) which can be easily grown in woods soil under shade. One of the greenhouse species (*A. cuneatum*) is grown by the million for house decoration or for ornamental grouping, its feathery, relatively resistant fronds being very beautiful. So are some of the horticultural varieties of maidenhair noted below. Some are common as florist's decorations.

**capillus-veneris.** Venus's-hair. In Europe this is the true or black maidenhair. It is a slender, somewhat spreading plant, its black unforked leafstalk arising from the slender, somewhat chaffy rootstock. Leaf twice- or thrice-compound,* its ultimate leaflets bright green, stalked, more or less wedge-shaped, about ½ in. wide. Old and New World tropics and rarely in the warmer parts of Eu. and N.A. Largely a greenhouse species, but hardy along the moister parts of the Pacific Coast and in the east from zone* 4 southward. There is a hort. form with fewer, almost crested leaflets.

**cuneatum.** The common maidenhair of the florists, and a native of Brazil. Stems brownish-black. Leaves twice- or thrice-compound,* the ultimate leaflets very numerous, stalked, dull green, broadly wedge-shaped and about ¼ or ⅓ in. wide. Of its many horticultural varieties the best known are forms with white-striped leaflets (*var.* **variegatum**); with crested ones (*var.* **grandiceps**); with very much smaller ones (*var.* **gracillimum**); and the *var.* **croweanum**, a florist's favorite because its sturdy fronds keep so well.

**pedatum.** The common hardy maidenhair of our rocky woods, somewhat resembling *A. capillus-veneris*, but its black-purple leafstalk always forked at the top. Leaves nearly round in general outline, the leaflets oblongish but wedge-shaped at the base, about ¾ in. long. N.A. A good wild garden plant and easy to grow in the shade.

**tenerum.** A tropical American, almost climbing maidenhair, scarcely known in ordinary greenhouse collections except for its *var.* **farleyense**. The latter is perhaps the showiest of all the greenhouse maidenhairs. It originated, as a supposed hybrid, at the Farley Hill garden, Barbados, produces no spores (in the typical form), so must be increased by division. Leaves 2–3 ft. long and nearly as wide, curving or falling in a spray-like mass. The ultimate leaflets about 2 in. wide, overlapping each other, light green or sometimes tinted pink, the generally wedge-shaped segments cut or fringed at the top.

**ADICEA** = *Pilea*.

**ADLAY.** See COIX.

**ADLUMIA** (ad-loom′i-a). A leaf-climbing, very delicate, biennial,* herb-like vine, family Fumariaceae, of rich woods in eastern N.A., sometimes grown in the wild garden for its spurred flowers. Leaves alternate, thrice compound,* its ultimate leaflets fragile and cut-lobed. Flowers white or purple, irregular, spurred, drooping in a loose cluster. Fruit a several-seeded pod. (Named for J. Adlum, 1759–1836, an amateur American botanist and grape breeder.)

Easily grown in nearly windless corners of the wild garden, in shade, and rich but not acid humus. Propagated by self-sown seeds. It often escapes.*

**fungosa.** Climbing fumitory. Often climbing many feet by its slender leafstalks. Flowers about ¾ in. long. Also called Allegheny vine and Mountain fringe. Summer.

**ADOBE LILY** = *Fritillaria plurifolia*.

**ADONIS** (a-don′is). Annual or perennial Eurasian herbs of the buttercup family, some of them old favorites in the flower garden. Of the 20 known species only three are common in cultivation. They have alternate, dissected leaves and a solitary flower with 5–16 petals. Fruit dry (an achene*) crowded into a roundish head. (Named for Adonis, from whose blood it is fabled to have sprung.)

The plants are of easy cult. in any ordinary garden soil (except *A. amurensis*) and are grown for their flowers, especially the annual species. Sow seeds in the spring for the pheasant's-eye; in spring or fall for the perennials, which may also be increased by spring division.

**amurensis.** A perennial, rock garden plant about 1 ft. high. Leaves crowded, almost fern-like, finely dissected. Flowers golden yellow, about 2 in. across. Eastern As. March. Needs rich loam. A double-flowered form is known.

**annua.** Pheasant's-eye. Often offered as *A. autumnalis*. Annual, about 18 in. high. Flowers red, about ¾ in. wide, with a prominent dark center. Eurasian. June and often later. The common species in cultivation and useful for the border or for cutting. See ANNUALS.

**vernalis.** Perennial, but grown as an annual, about 9 in. high, usually, though not necessarily, grown in the rock garden. Flowers 3 in. wide, yellow. Eu. May. Both white and double-flowered varieties are also grown. See ANNUALS.

**ADONIS GARDEN.** See the Greeks at GARDEN HISTORY.

**ADOPOGON** = *Krigia*.

**ADPRESSA, -us, -um** (ad-press′a). Pressed against; see also APPRESSED.

**ADSURGENS** (ad-sir′jens). Ascending.

**ADVENA, -us, -um** (ad-ven′a). Adventive; newly arrived.

**ADVENTITIOUS.** Arising at an unusual place, as adventitious buds which sometimes arise from severe pruning, or adventitious roots which may arise from a cut leaf, as in some begonias.

**ADVENTIVE.** A wild, usually weedy plant that becomes accidentally established, usually only for a brief period. Many foreign weeds are adventives, until they become naturalized. See also ESCAPE.

**ADZUKI BEAN** = *Phaseolus angularis*.

**AECHMEA** (eek′mee-a). A very large group of stemless South American air plants (see EPIPHYTES), family Bromeliaceae, grown only as greenhouse plants for their colored or scurfy foliage and rather handsome flowers in bracted* clusters. Leaves in a basal rosette,* the margins more or less spiny-toothed. Flowers yellow or red, often tipped with blue, in a branched cluster, on a long, often colored and bracted, stalk. Fruit many-seeded, berry-like. (Greek for a point, in allusion to the pointed sepals.)

Of the 100 known species only a handful are of hort. interest, and of these only the one below is at all commonly cult. For care, potting mixture, propagation, etc., see VRIESIA.

**fulgens.** A handsome Brazilian foliage plant with a dense rosette of basal leaves that form a nest-like cavity from which the flowering stalk arises. Leaves about 14 in. long and 2½ in. wide, with a few scattered, marginal and spiny teeth. Flower cluster longer than the leaves, branched. Flowers about ½ in. long, red, but blue-tipped, or some segments all bluish-violet. More common in cultivation is *var.* **discolor** with the under side of the leaves red or violet-red, often faintly striped.

**AEGOPODIUM** (ee-go-po′di-um). A small group of Eurasian perennial herbs of the carrot family one of which, the goutweed, is planted (mostly in its variegated form) as an edging or ground cover. Leaves twice-compound,* the ultimate leaflets toothed. Flowers small, white, in a compound umbel (see UMBEL). Fruit dry, seed-like, aromatic. (From the Greek for goat and a small foot, possibly from the outline of its leaflets.)

Easily grown in ordinary garden soil, but prefers partial shade. Increased by dividing its slender rootstocks in spring or fall.

**podagraria.** Goutweed, called also bishop's-weed. Stout coarse herb about a foot high. Leafstalks, especially the lower ones, winged and clasping. Flowers scarcely ⅛ in. wide, usually 12–15 in each umbel. June. Most popular in *var.* **variegatum** which has white-margined leaflets and is a useful foliage plant.

**AEONIUM.** See HOUSELEEK.

**AEQUINOCTIALIS, -e** (ee-kwi-nox-i-ale′is). Relating to the equinox.

**AEQUITRILOBA, -us, -um** (ee-kwi-try-lō′ba). Equally three-lobed.

**AERATION.** The exposing of soil to the air. This necessary operation is usually accomplished by plowing, cultivating or hoeing.

**AERIAL ROOT.** A root borne in the air, as in many epiphytic (air) plants, and on the stems of some vines like the ivy. See also VELAMEN.

---

* Special articles on the subjects indicated by an asterisk (*) will be found at the words so marked.

**AERIDES** (a-err′i-deez). Thirty tropical orchids from the East Indies region, all air plants (see EPIPHYTES), one of which is grown in greenhouses for its profusion of fragrant, purple- or carmine-spotted, white flowers. There is no pseudobulb.* Leaves two-ranked (see DISTICHOUS), rather fleshy, more or less clothing the stem. Flowers very irregular, the lip spurred, the profusely flowering pendent cluster appearing from the leaf bases. (*Aerides* is Greek for air in allusion to the epiphytic habit.) For culture see ORCHIDS (greenhouse species).

**odoratum.** Leaves strap-shaped, about 7 in. long. Flower cluster longer than the leaves. Flowers generally white, but some segments carmine-spotted; others, purple-spotted, or even lined and hence very showy. August.

**AERO CYANAMID.** A trademarked fertilizer containing 22 per cent nitrogen and 70 per cent hydrated lime; useful for preplanting applications to vegetable gardens and in preparing seed beds for lawns.

**AESCHYNANTHUS** = *Trichosporum*.

**AESCULACEAE** = HIPPOCASTANACEAE.

**AESCULUS.** See HORSE-CHESTNUT.

*AESTIVA, -us, -um* (ess-ty′-va). Summer.

*AESTIVALIS, -e* (ess-ti-vail′is). Pertaining to summer.

**AETHIONEMA** (e-thi-o-nee′ma). The stone cresses are dwarfish perennial herbs of the mustard family, mostly from the Mediterranean region. Of the 50 species those below are mostly rock garden plants related to candytuft. They have small, rather narrow leaves and variously colored, but rarely white flowers in terminal racemes.* Petals 4. Fruit a roundish, dry pod, usually winged (see WING). (From Greek to scorch and a filament, in apparent allusion to the brownish stamens of some species.)

The stone cresses are attractive, slightly woody, rock garden plants, all blooming in May or June. For the details of their culture see ROCK GARDEN.

**coridifolium.** About 6 in. high, somewhat bushy, the one-inch, narrow leaves bluish-gray and crowded. Flowers rose or lilac-pink in short compact clusters. Mt. Lebanon. Sometimes sold as *Iberis jucunda*.

**grandiflorum.** About 14 in. high, the stem not much branched. Leaves bluish-gray, 1½ in. long. Flowers about ¼ in. wide, rosy pink. Persia.

**pulchellum.** Resembling *A. coridifolium* but not so bushy and inclined to trail. Flowers in almost head-like clusters, rosy pink. Persia.

**schistosum.** Dwarf herb, the stems scarcely 2 in. high, but erect. Leaves very small and narrow. Flowers rose-pink, comparatively large for such a small plant. Asia Minor.

*AETHIOPICA, -us, -um* (ee-thi-ō′pi-ca). From Ethiopia, Africa.

*AFFINIS, -e* (af-fy′nis). Related or allied to another species.

*AFRA.* African.

*AFRICANA, -us, -um* (af-ri-cay′na). From Africa.

**AFRICAN CHERRY-ORANGE** = *Citropsis schweinfurthi*.

**AFRICAN DAISY** = *Arctotis stoechadifolia*. The name is also applied to plants in the genera *Dimorphotheca*, *Gazania* and *Gerbera*.

**AFRICAN HAIR.** See CHAMAEROPS HUMILIS.

**AFRICAN LILY** = *Agapanthus africanus*.

**AFRICAN MARIGOLD** = *Tagetes erecta*. See MARIGOLD.

**AFRICAN MILK-BUSH** = *Synadenium granti*.

**AFRICAN MILLET.** The name is applied to three unrelated grasses. See PENNISETUM GLAUCUM, ELEUSINE CORACANA, and HOLCUS SORGHUM CAFFRORUM.

**AFRICAN OIL PALM** = *Elaeis guineensis*.

**AFRICAN VALERIAN** = *Fedia cornucopiae*.

**AFRICAN VIOLET** = *Saintpaulia ionantha*.

**AGAPANTHUS** (ag-a-pan′thus). A tuberous rooted herb of the lily family much grown in tubs or pots for its showy flowers. Leaves all basal, numerous, long and narrow. Flowers numerous, in a terminal cluster (umbel*) which arises from between 2 sheath-like bracts.* Corolla funnel-shaped, its oblong segments about as long as the tube. Fruit a 3-celled pod. (From Greek for love flower.)

Grown in the greenhouse in potting mixture* 4, in large pots or tubs. Flowers in the summer, after which the plant should be rested over the winter (with little water and in a frost-free place). Very vigorous grower and needs a large pot or tub. If kept in the same one it should be fed liberally with liquid manure. The only species is

**africanus.** African lily, called also lily-of-the-Nile, but a native of South Africa. Leaves about 20 in. long, rather thick. Flower stalk longer than leaves, the cluster consisting of about 20 striking blue flowers. It may be grown outdoors in zones* 8 and 9, and flowered outdoors northward as a summer pot specimen. There are many hort. varieties, some larger than the type, some very much smaller, others with variegated leaves and still others with flowers paler blue, or violet, or white.

**AGARICUS.** See MUSHROOM.

**AGARITA** = *Mahonia trifoliolata*.

**AGATHAEA** = FELICIA.

**AGATHIS** (ag′a-thiss). Dammar pine. Evergreen Australasian and Malayan trees of the pine family useful outdoors only as indicated below. They have flat, broad (not needle-like) leaves, usually decidedly leathery, without marginal teeth. Male and female flowers on separate trees, the female in broad roundish cones composed of broad overlapping scales, between which are the solitary, winged seeds. (From Greek for ball or globe, alluding to the cones of the female tree.)

Rarely grown as greenhouse specimens.

**alba.** Up to 100 ft. high, but lower in cultivation. Leaves opposite,* about 3 in. long, more or less striated and dull green. Cone nearly globe-shaped, but slightly egg-shaped, about 3 in. long. Malaya. Zone* 8 in Calif. This plant is often sold as *Agathis orientalis*.

**australis.** Kauri pine. Sometimes 130 ft. high, the bark bluish-gray and flaky. Leaves opposite,* stalkless, more or less oblong and about 1 in. long on young trees, twice the size on old trees. Cone nearly globe-shaped, about 2½ in. in diameter, its scales faintly prickle-tipped. N.Z. Zone* 8 in Calif.

**robusta.** Tall tree, reaching 150 ft., its branches in whorls.* Leaves oval to oblong, about 3 in. long, faintly striated, usually alternate.* Cones from globe- to egg-shaped about 3½ in. long. Aust. Zone* 8 in Calif.

**AGATI** (a-gay′tee). Comprising only the following species, a medium-sized tree from tropical As. belonging to the pea family, cult. outdoors only in zone* 9 or in greenhouses for its showy flowers and fruit. Leaves compound,* the leaflets numerous, usually in about 25 pairs. Flowers pea-like. Fruit a long pod. (*Agati* is a Latinized derivative of the Hindu vernacular for this plant.)

When grown in greenhouses, use potting mixture* 4.

**grandiflora.** Pea tree. A short-lived but handsome tree, up to 25 ft. Leaves about 9 in. long, the many leaflets scarcely 2 in. long. Flowers very showy, in short clusters in the leaf axils,* red or white, about 2 in. long. Pod almost woody, flat and narrow, up to 2 ft. long and very striking. The tree is also called *Sesbania grandiflora*.

**AGAVE** (a-gah′vee). An immense genus of succulent, fleshy-leaved, semi-desert, tropical American plants, family Amaryllidaceae, of importance both in hort. and in industry. Of the 300 species much the best known is the commonly cult. century plant (*A. americana*), which, like many other species, blooms once and then dies. Other species flower periodically. Leaves in a basal rosette,* usually spiny-margined and often with a strong terminal prickle; persisting for many years. Flowers in a long terminal cluster, at the end of a very long stalk (40 ft. in some species). The flowers are greenish-yellow, funnel-shaped, with 6 segments. Fruit a capsule* with 3 valves. (From the Greek for noble or illustrious.)

Except the century plant, agaves are not so widely grown as they should be, for they are handsome succulents useful in dry, frost-free regions outdoors, and as cool-greenhouse or house plants where there is plenty of sun. All the species below, in the north, are improved by plunging outdoors during warm weather. Best grown in large pots or tubs in potting mixture* 6, although in their young stages they can be started in small pots.

Propagation is easiest by pulling off the usually many suckers* that arise from the base of old plants, especially

---

* Special articles on the subjects indicated by an asterisk (*) will be found at the words so marked.

just before they bloom. Bulbils* are sometimes produced in certain species and these can also be used for propagating. Root the bulbils in potting mixture* 1, but the suckers are already provided with roots and should be potted in the same mixture as mature plants. Seeds are rarely used, for most cult. species set no seeds unless the flowers have been hand pollinated. For general culture see SUCCULENTS.

**americana.** Century plant, also, but incorrectly, called American aloe. Stemless, the large leaves in a basal rosette* of huge size in mature plants. Leaves up to 5 or 6 ft. long, and 6–8 in. wide, decidedly grayish, their tips usually recurved, marginal spines stout and recurved. Stalk of flower cluster (rarely produced in cult. but likely any time after 10 or 15 years) from 25–40 ft. high, rather slender. Flowers about 2½ in. long, very numerous. Probably Mexico, but cult. so long and scarcely known in the wild state, that original habitat is uncertain. Of the hort. varieties one has yellow-margined leaves, another yellow- or white-striped leaves, and a third has a central yellowish band. A widely cult. plant, often growing to immense size in large tubs.

**atrovirens.** Pulque agave. A huge Mexican species widely cult. there as the source of pulque. Leaves up to 9 ft. long and a foot wide, their marginal spines gray, but the leaf generally green. Stalk of the flower cluster (rare in cult.) about 20 ft. high. Flowers about 3½ in. long.

**coerulescens.** This, in cult. specimens, is *A. lophantha coerulescens.*

**fourcroydes.** Henequen. Native, and an important plant, in Yucatan, where thousands of acres are devoted to its culture for a fiber resembling sisal. Produces a trunk 8–10 ft. high with a crown of narrow, green, nearly spineless leaves that are about 7 ft. long and 3 in. wide. Stalk of the flower cluster 20 ft., the flowers greenish, fetid, and about 3 in. long.

**lecheguilla.** Lechuguilla. A Mexican species somewhat grown as a pot plant for its handsome leaves which are bluish-green, pale banded along the midrib, but striped underneath, usually not over 18 in. long, prickly-margined. Stalk of flower cluster 4–8 ft., the flowers about 1½ in. long. Resembling the next and by some considered a variety of it.

**lophantha.** Bearing a short trunk and a crown of leaves that are about 3 ft. long and 3 in. wide, shiny-green above, striped beneath. Marginal spines not large but variously hooked. Stalk of the flower cluster about 12 ft. high, the flowers 1½ in. long. Mex. In cult. perhaps better known in the *var.* **coerulescens** which has bluish-gray leaves and no stripes beneath.

**sisalina.** Sisal. This, the commercial source of sisal hemp (mostly in S. Af.) is probably native in the Bahamas. It very much resembles *A. fourcroydes,* but usually produces no trunk, and has shorter leaves. Stalk of the flower cluster about 18 ft. high, the flowers green, fetid and about 2½ in. long.

**stricta.** Stemless and small enough to be easily grown as a pot plant. Leaves about a foot long and scarcely ⅓ in. wide, without prickles except for the terminal spine, somewhat triangular in cross-section, forming a dense, rather handsome cluster. Stalk of the flower cluster about 7 ft. high, the flowers about 1 in. long. Mexico. Widely cult., especially in some of its hort. forms with bluish-gray or purplish leaves, or in a dwarfish form with a distinct bloom* on the leaves.

**tequilana.** Tequila mescal. A Mexican stemless plant, one of the sources of mescal, and thus widely cult. Leaves about 2½ ft. long, 3 in. wide and bluish-gray. Stalk of the flower cluster up to 15 ft., the flowers about 2½ in. long.

**AGAVOIDES** (a-gah-voy′deez; but see OÏDES). Resembling a plant of the genus *Agave.*

**AGE OF TREES.** See GARDEN TABLES III.

**AGERATIFOLIA, -us, -um** (a-jur-a-ti-fo′li-a). With leaves like an ageratum.

**AGERATUM** (a-jur-ā′tum). A group of nearly 30 species of chiefly tropical American annual herbs, family Compositae, one of which is perhaps the most popular of all bedding and edging plants. Leaves opposite,* generally oval, the margins with rounded teeth. Flowers blue, rarely pink or white except in some hort. forms, in compact, clustered heads, without rays.* Fruit minute, dry. (*Ageratum* is from the Greek for not growing old, of uncertain application to these plants.)

*Ageratum* is as easily grown as it is deservedly popular. It is a tender annual. See ANNUALS. They can be used to give sheets of misty blue bloom in the border, but their greatest use is for bedding, for a carpet in which other plants are set, and for low edgings. They flower over most of the summer, and late fall or winter flowering can be had from potted plants, the seed for which is sown in early Sept. Keep these in a cool greenhouse.

**houstonianum.** Common garden ageratum. Leaves somewhat heart-shaped at the base, the typical form a plant about 14 in. high. Flower heads just over ¼ in. in diameter, blue, the outside somewhat sticky. There are many named hort. varieties of this old favorite, some white or pink, but the most useful are the dwarf sorts which are compact enough to be very valuable for edging.

For a related plant, sometimes called hardy ageratum, see EUPATORIUM COELESTINUM, better called mist-flower.

**AGGREGATE FRUIT.** See FRUIT.

**AGLAONEMA** (ag-la-o-nee′ma). Tropical Asian and Malaysian herbs of the arum family, one of the 40 species having recently become a very popular house plant. Stems lax, with a tendency to climb. Leaves without marginal teeth, always stalked, usually with a thick midrib, often splashed with white. Flowers minute (rare in cult. specimens), crowded on a short spadix,* beneath which is a soon-withering, green, or whitish spathe.* Fruit berry-like. (Greek for bright thread, of uncertain application here.)

The second species below is one of the most widely cult. house plants of recent introduction. It grows perfectly in water, even in comparatively dark, dry rooms. Like any other tropical aroid, however, it will grow much better in a warm, moist greenhouse in potting mixture* 4, to which charcoal has been added. Easily propagated by division of the rootstock, or by cuttings in moist sand.

**costatum.** A Malayan short-stemmed plant often branching at the base. Leaves handsome, about 8 in. long, and half as wide, tapering at both ends, the midrib white, and prominently marked with scattered white patches. A very satisfactory foliage plant, because its rather numerous leaves are crowded to make a compact specimen.

**modestum.** Chinese evergreen; called, also, Chinese water-plant and Japanese leaf. Erect or laxly spreading stem 3 ft. or more long, in cult. specimens commonly less. Leaves more or less loosely disposed towards the end of the stem, oblongish, nearly 10 in. long, green. Recently introduced but in practically every florist shop in America. The plant was formerly called *A. simplex.* See HOUSE PLANTS.

**AGNUS-CASTUS.** Classical name of the chaste tree (*Vitex agnus-castus*).

**AGONIS** (a-gō′nis). A genus of Australian shrubs and trees of the myrtle family, one grown outdoors in Calif. for ornament. Leaves alternate,* willow-like (in the species below). Flowers small, crowded in dense, globe-shaped, stalkless clusters. Fruit a leathery or nearly woody many-seeded capsule. (Greek, for gathering, perhaps alluding to its plentiful seed.)

**flexuosa.** Willow myrtle. A tree to 40 ft. high in the wild, less in cult. Leaves about 6 in. long. Flowers white, the dense globelike clusters about ½ in. thick, the numerous stamens* prominent. Cult. in southern Calif., scarcely known elsewhere. Sometimes called *Leptospermum flexuosum.*

**AGRICULTURAL LIME.** See LIME.

**AGRICULTURE.** Farming, as distinguished from horticulture.*

**AGRIFOLIA, -us, -um** (ag-ri-fō′li-a). Scabby- or rough-leaved.

**AGRI-PAX.** A trademarked pyrethrum insecticide, combined with a spreader, used only for chewing and sucking insects.

**AGROPYRON REPENS.** See Quack Grass in the list at WEEDS.

**AGROSTEMMA.** See LYCHNIS CORONARIA and L. COELI-ROSA.

**AGROSTIS** (a-gros′tis). Bent Grass. A large genus of widely distributed grasses, a few of which are much used in hay and lawn seed, although many wild species are weedy. They are annual or perennial grasses, some of the latter valuable because of their creeping stolons.* Leaves narrow. Flowers in small spikelets that are borne in open, loose panicles.* (*Agrostis* is Greek for field and Latin for some grass.)

Most of the species below form part of many pasture or lawn mixtures and are little grown otherwise. See the heading Lawn Mixtures at LAWN for the important ones and their value.

**canina.** Brown bent; also called dog bent and velvet bent. A perennial* grass up to 18 in. high. Leaves 2 in. long, scarcely 1/12 in. wide. N.A. Common in some lawn mixtures. See LAWN.

**capillaris.** Rhode Island bent. A common perennial* pasture grass, resembling redtop (*A. palustris*) but smaller and having shorter, more distinctly red flower clusters. Leaves about 6 in. long and ⅛ in. wide. Eu. but commonly naturalized in N.A.

**maritima.** Creeping bent. A roughish but very slender perennial* grass with plentiful creeping stolons which are harvested, cut into small pieces and sold for fine lawns where quick results are necessary. Leaves about 3 in. long and 1/12 in. wide. N.A. and Eu. Widely used for lawns, and sometimes sold as *A. stolonifera.*

**nebulosa.** Cloud grass. Annual* Spanish grass with very short and narrow leaves. Grown only for its wide cluster of tiny spikelets which

---

* Special articles on the subjects indicated by an asterisk (*) will be found at the words so marked.

are on very slender stalks and persistent enough to be used for dry bouquets.

**palustris.** Redtop, called also fiorin. A perennial* European pasture grass, naturalized in N.A. and much planted for hay and an ingredient of lawn mixtures. It reaches a height of about 3 ft. Leaves about 7 in. long and ¼ in. wide. Flower cluster greenish-red.

**AHUEHUETE** = *Taxodium mucronatum.*

**AILANTHUS** (ā-lăn′thus). A small genus of chiefly Asiatic trees, family Simaroubaceae, one widely grown in cities for its smoke-resistant, insect-free but ill-scented foliage. Leaves compound, with 6-12 pairs of leaflets, and an odd one at the end. (See CEDRELA SINENSIS.) Flowers small, yellowish-green, in large terminal clusters, the male and female mostly on different trees. Fruit winged, the seed surrounded by the wing, and rather showy when ripe. (Latinized form of the vernacular name for the tree in the Moluccas.)

**altissima.** Tree-of-Heaven. Stinkweed; also called *A. glandulosa.* A quick-growing, smooth-barked, medium-sized tree, easily propagated by fresh seed, or by root cuttings. Leaflets about 5 in. long, prominently toothed towards the base. China. Only female or fertile-flowered trees should be cult. as the odor of the male flower is noxious to many. Varieties with red fruit, with large drooping leaves and with purple leafstalks are often preferred to the ordinary ailanthus. No other tree will stand smoke and city conditions so well.

**AIRA:** *A. coerulea* = *Molina. A. capillaris* = *Aspris.*

**AIR LAYERING.** See LAYERING.

**AIR PLANT.** See BRYOPHYLLUM.

**AIR PLANTS.** See EPIPHYTES.

**AIR POTATO** = *Dioscorea bulbifera.*

**AIZOACEAE** (a-eye-zo-a′see-e). The carpetweed family, comprising 20 genera and perhaps 500 species of widely distributed herbs, is of no garden significance except for the genus *Mesembryanthemum* and for the New Zealand spinach (which see). Leaves often succulent or at least thickish, opposite* or alternate* or in whorls,* in some ice-plants (*Mesembryanthemum*) covered with glittering dots. Flowers regular, lacking petals in New Zealand spinach but with so many in *Mesembryanthemum* as to suggest a daisy-head. Fruit a capsule or nut-like, many-seeded.

Technical flower characters: Calyx 4-5 cleft or 4 parted. Stamens perigynous.* Ovary 3-5-celled, the ovules numerous in each cell.

**AIZOIDES** (a-eye-zoy′deez, but *see* OÏDES). Resembling a plant of the genus *Aizoon*, which is a relative of the ice-plants but scarcely cult.

**AIZOON.** See AIZOIDES.

**AJACIS** (a′ja-kiss). Old Greek name, said to relate to the marks on the petal of the rocket larkspur (*Delphinium ajacis*).

**AJANENSIS, -e** (a-jan-en′sis). From Ajan on the coast of Siberia.

**AJUGA** (ăj′oo-ga). Bugleweed. Annual or perennial herbs of the mint family, sometimes weedy, but a few cult. in borders and rock gardens for their profusion of white, blue, or sometimes reddish bloom. Flowers irregular* and 2-lipped, in close clusters or spikes. (*Ajuga* is Latin for not yoked, alluding to the calyx.)

The bugleweeds, all European, are of easy cult. in ordinary garden soil. Prop. by spring-sown seeds, by division, and by its freely rooting stems in *A. reptans*.

**brockbanki.** A long-current dealers' name for a blue-flowered bugle, of unknown origin and parentage.

**genevensis.** Flowers blue, in spiked but interrupted* close clusters. Leaves many-toothed, less than 3 in. long. Called, also, *A. alpina*, and a creeping or prostrate plant.

**reptans.** The common blue bugleweed, widely escaped from cult. in eastern N. Am. It is 4-10 in. high, but the stems are usually half-prostrate and often rooting. Lower leaves narrowed to a short stalk, the upper stalkless. In the typical form the flowers are blue or purplish, but the following are the preferred garden sorts: var. **alba**, with white flowers; var. **atropurpurea**, with bronze foliage and blue flowers; var. **metallica crispa**, with metallic, crisped leaves and blue flowers in uninterrupted spikes. Forms with deep purple (var. **rubra**) and white-blotched (var. **variegata**) foliage are also known.

**AKEAKE** = *Dodonaea viscosa.*

**AKEBIA** (a-kee′bi-a). Four species of Asiatic woody vines, family Lardizabalaceae, only the following cult. for shade and for covering walls or arbors. Leaves almost evergreen, compound,* the leaflets 3 or 5. Male and female flowers separate, spring-blooming, purplish-brown and in loose clusters. Fruit a black-seeded berry. (*Akebia* is the Japanese vernacular name for these plants.)

Propagation by seeds, by root-division and by cuttings over bottom-heat. *See, also,* VINES.

**quinata.** Leaflets 5 and without teeth. Flowers fragrant but small and inconspicuous. Fruit (often wanting in cult.) a purple berry, used as food in Japan. A stout, useful climber from zone* 4 southward, reaching a height of 20 ft. It blooms at night. Often planted in cool greenhouses.

**trifoliata.** Leaflets 3 and usually deeply toothed. Less grown than *A. quinata* and less worth it.

**AKEE** = *Blighia sapida.*

**ALABAMA.** The state lies wholly in zones* 5, 6, and 7. It has a mild climate, a long growing season, and a relatively high rainfall. A varied list of vegetables, fruits, and ornamentals is adapted to the soils and climate of the state.

SOILS. The soils of the state are divided into five major provinces, based largely on their geological origin. These provinces are: Limestone Valley, Appalachian Mountain, Piedmont Plateau, Coastal Plain, and Black Belt. The Tennessee Valley Province is located in the northern part of Alabama in the counties along the Tennessee River; the Decatur is the most important soil series. The Appalachian Province lies in northeast Alabama; the principal soil series is the Hartselle. The Piedmont Plateau, located in East Central Alabama, constitutes the oldest soil of the state geologically; the Cecil is the most important soil series. The Coastal Plain occupies the southern half of the state; the Norfolk is the principal soil series. The Black Belt occupies a strip beginning in Macon County and extending in a northwest direction across the state; soils range from those containing free limestone, as in the Sumpter, to very acid soils such as Oktibbeha, Lufkin, and Eutah. These soils are extremely plastic.

GARDEN CENTERS. Among the places in which unusual interest is shown in flowers, ornamentals, and beautification programs, should be mentioned: for South Alabama, Mobile; for Central Alabama, Selma, Montgomery, Opelika, and Auburn; for North Central Alabama, Birmingham, Gadsden, Talladega; and for North Alabama, Huntsville, Florence, and Decatur. Huntsville has for years been the center of large wholesale nurseries. The Azalea trail of Mobile is well known throughout the South for its beauty. Local markets for fruits and vegetables are especially good around Mobile, Montgomery, Selma, Birmingham, and Tuscaloosa. Curb markets are found in Montgomery, Mobile, Tuscaloosa, Gadsden, Birmingham, Anniston, Florence, Tuscumbia, Athens, Opelika, Dothan, Troy, Auburn, Selma, Jasper, Tuskegee, Eufaula, Clayton, and Talladega.

FRUITS. The variations in climatic conditions, soils, and elevation supply conditions favorable for a long list of fruits ranging from apples to satsuma oranges. Apples grow well in the upper one-half of the state, being especially well adapted to the area of higher elevation in North Alabama. Pears grow in all sections of the state, although in the southern counties only the Chinese type escapes fire-blight. Cherries are not adapted to this state except in a limited way on the mountains of northern Alabama. Dewberries and blackberries, both native and cultivated, grow throughout the state. Raspberries are not adapted generally to the state, although some raspberries are grown in the upper part of the state. Strawberries are produced very satisfactorily in all sections of the state, commercial quantities being grown in Cullman, Escambia, Conecuh, and Chilton counties. Satsuma oranges have for many years been grown quite generally in Mobile and Baldwin counties where many commercial orchards are found. Paper-shell varieties of pecans, both for commercial and home use, are grown extensively over the southern half of the state.

VEGETABLES. Almost the entire list of vegetables grown in this country are adapted to the state. Only rhubarb and celery, of a long list of commonly grown vegetables, seem not to be adapted to Alabama conditions. Winters are mild

---

* Special articles on the subjects indicated by an asterisk (*) will be found at the words so marked.

enough in central and southern portions for gardens to carry in them many vegetables throughout the winter.

FLOWERS. In the extreme southern portion of the state Indian azaleas, camellias, and oleanders are especially known for their beauty. The state has a varied display of native flowering and fruiting plants, including southern magnolia, sweet bay, yaupon, and Carolina jasmine in the southern half of the state, and mountain laurel, rhododendron and red buckeye in the more mountainous sections. Native azaleas, dogwood, redbud, American holly, and naturalized Cherokee rose are found throughout the state. The mild winters permit the planting and growth in the fall of many early spring grown annuals such as the larkspur, pansy, sweet pea, cornflower, calendula, stock, poppy and phlox. The long list of perennials grown successfully in the North is greatly abbreviated under southern conditions. A number of the perennials, however, are successfully grown as biennials. Among the bulbous plants, *Narcissus* varieties bloom from early February until May. The bulbs of these may remain in the same area indefinitely, while those of tulips and hyacinths must be replaced every third year. Many of the more tender bulbous plants as gladiolus, amaryllis, nerine, lycoris, crinum, and dahlia are grown outside without any winter protection for the roots.

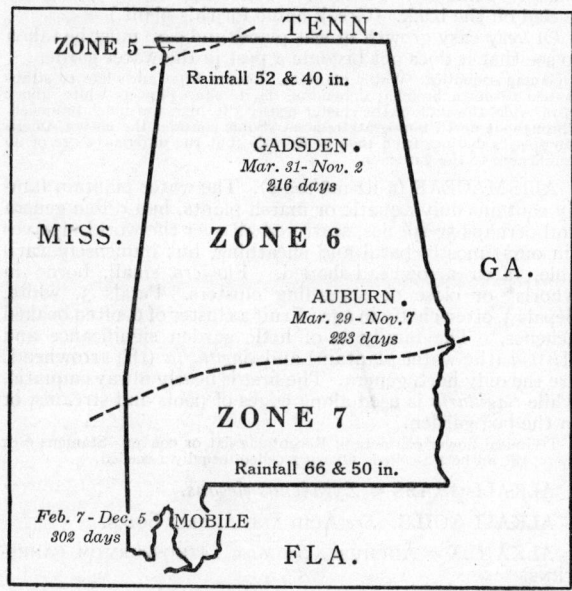

ALABAMA

The zones* of hardiness crossing Ala. are those shown on the colored map at ZONE, which should be consulted for details. The dates are the average latest killing frost in spring and the first one in the fall. The figures below the dates show the average length of the growing season. Rainfall figures are for total annual rainfall and for that falling in the growing season.

CLIMATE. The mean temperature of the state is 63.7°; for North Alabama it is 61°; for Central Alabama, 64°; and for South Alabama, 66°. Difference in temperature from north to south in mid-winter is 12°; in mid-summer it is only 3°. The mean daily minimum temperature in January ranges from 29° in Colbert County to 43.4° in Mobile. The mean daily maximum temperature for July ranges from 88° in Jackson County to 79° in Escambia County. The growing season ranges from 290 days in the Gulf counties to 200 days in northern counties.

|  | Average date of last killing frost in Spring | Latest known killing frost | Average date of earliest killing frost in the Fall | Earliest known killing frost |
|---|---|---|---|---|
| Mobile | Feb. 7 | April 6 | Dec. 5 | Oct. 31 |
| Auburn | Mar. 29 | April 25 | Nov. 7 | Oct. 16 |
| Gadsden | Mar. 31 | April 25 | Nov. 2 | Sept. 27 |

The average annual rainfall for the state is 52.4 inches. The range is from 52.4 inches in North Alabama to 66 inches along the Gulf. The average rainfall for the winter periods is 15.2 inches; for the spring period, 14 inches; for the summer period, 14.25 inches; and for the autumn period, 8.97 inches.

The address of the Agricultural Experiment Station, which has kindly supplied this information about the state, is Auburn, Alabama. The station is always ready to answer gardening questions.

Garden Club activities in the state include clubs of the Garden Club of America, the home office of which is 598 Madison Avenue, New York. There are also over 38 chapters of the Alabama Federation of Garden Clubs, information about which can be had by writing to Garden Editor, Houghton Mifflin Company, Boston, Mass.

**ALABAMENSIS, -e.** From Alabama.

**ALASKA CEDAR** = *Chamaecyparis nootkatensis.*

**ALATA, -us, -um** (a-lay′ta). Winged.

**ALATAMAHA.** Named for the Alatamaha River, Ga.

**ALATO-CAERULEA, -us, -um** (a-lay-toe-se-roo′lee-a). Blue-winged.

**ALBA, -us, -um** (al′ba). White.

**ALBERTA.** The Province lies wholly in zones* 1 and 2. Its soil and climatic conditions, and consequently its gardening possibilities, are so similar to the northern part of Idaho that it is needless to repeat them here. *See* IDAHO. *See also* BRITISH COLUMBIA.

**ALBIDA, -us, -um** (al′bi-da). White.

**ALBIFLORA, -us, -um** (al-bi-flow′ra). White-flowered.

**ALBI-PLENA, -us, -um** (al-bi-plee′na). With double, white flowers.

**ALBIZZIA** (al-bizz′ee-a). A large genus of tropical trees and shrubs of the pea family, three of which are grown for ornament. Their outdoor culture is mostly confined to zones* 8 and 9, except the first species, and scarcely known in greenhouses. Leaves alternate,* twice-compound,* the ultimate leaflets small, numerous, and more or less oblique. Flowers very small, congested ing lobe-shaped heads or in finger-shaped clusters. Fruit a large pod. (Named for Albizzi, an Italian naturalist.)

*Albizzia* closely resembles and is related to acacia. For greenhouse culture *see* ACACIA. The first and third species have very handsome foliage.

julibrissin. Silk tree. Medium-sized tree not over 30 ft. high, but with a broad spreading crown. Leaves with 12-20 or even 25 major divisions, each of which bears from 40-60 very oblique leaflets that are scarcely ¼ in. long. Flowers light pink, in slender-stalked, compact heads. Pod flat, about 5 in. long and 1 in. wide. Persia to Central China. Hardy from zone* 6 southward. There is a deeper pink form, the *var.* rosea, smaller than the type and hardy from zone* 4 southward.

lebbek. Siris; called also lebbek and East Indian walnut. Tall tree up to 80 ft. in the wild, less in cultivation. Leaves with 5-7 major divisions, each of which bears 12-18 stalkless, oblique leaflets that are about 1 in. long. Flowers greenish-yellow, in dense, small, short-stalked heads that are borne in the axils.* Pod 9-12 in. long, flat, just over an inch wide. Tropical As. and Aust. Hardy only in zone* 9, rarely in zone* 8. Sometimes called woman's-tongue tree.

lophantha. Usually a shrub, but sometimes a tree up to 20 ft. high. Leaves with 16-22 major divisions, each of which bears from 40-60, only slightly oblique, leaflets that are about ⅓ in. long. Aust. Hardy in zones* 8 and 9.

**ALBO-MACULATA, -us, -um** (al-bo-mac-u-lay′ta). White-spotted.

**ALBO-MARGINATA, -us, -um** (al-bo-mar-ji-nay′ta). White-margined.

**ALBO-PLENO** (al-bo-plee′no). White and double-flowered.

**ALBO-VARIEGATA, -us, -um** (al-bo-vare-i-gay′ta). With white markings.

**ALBULA, -us, -um** (al′bew-la). Whitish.

**ALCEA.** Pre-Linnaean* name for a mallow, probably *Malva alcea.*

---

* Special articles on the subjects indicated by an asterisk (*) will be found at the words so marked.

**ALCHEMILLA** (al-ke-mill'ya). Of thirty species of this genus of annual* and perennial* herbs of the rose family only the following two are of any garden importance. They are somewhat weedy plants with lobed or compound* leaves and small greenish-yellow flowers without petals. Fruit small, dry (an achene*), partly enclosed by the withered calyx.* (Latinized form of the Arabic vernacular name for these plants.)

They are of the easiest culture in any ordinary garden soil, and may be increased by division. Grown only for their silvery or grayish leaves. See ROCK GARDEN.

**alpina.** A European rock garden species with silvery, small leaflets, which are toothed towards the tip. It spreads to form a dense mat or carpet. Flowers inconspicuous. July.

**vulgaris.** Lady's-mantle. Rootstock stout and horizontal, producing a clump of erect long-stalked, grayish leaves, 4–5 in. wide, that have shallow rounded lobes, toothed throughout. Stalk of the flower cluster about 15 in. high, and bearing many, minute, greenish-yellow flowers. Eu. Summer.

**ALCICORNIUM** = *Platycerium*.

**ALCOCK SPRUCE** = *Picea bicolor*. See SPRUCE.

*ALDENHAMENSIS* (all-den-ham-en'sis). From Aldenham House, England.

**ALDER.** A large group of shrubs and trees belonging to the genus **Alnus** (al'nus) of the birch family grown as specimens or in the shrub border, especially in places too moist for other woody plants. They have rather handsome, often somewhat burnished or sticky, alternate,* leaves. Flowers in catkins, the male and female on the same plant, the latter becoming small, scaly, woody cones. (*Alnus* is the old Latin name of the alder.)

Of the 30 known species only the following are of much hort. importance, and these are useful only in cool moist parts of America. All bloom before the leaves unfold in spring. Easily grown in wet or moist places, and propagated by cuttings, or suckers, or by spring-sown seeds collected the autumn before. The species of *Alnus* here admitted are:

**A. glutinosa.** Black alder. A tree up to 70 ft., its twigs sticky. Leaves nearly round or ovalish, about 4 in. long, coarsely toothed, the teeth themselves also toothed. Eurasia. Commonly planted and often an escape* in eastern N.A. There are several hort. varieties, such as a golden-leaved form, one with much-cut leaves, another with oak-like leaves and one with red leaf veins and stalks. An important timber tree in its wild range and often called *Alnus vulgaris*.

**A. incana.** Speckled alder. Usually a shrub, rarely a medium-sized tree, the twigs hairy but not sticky. Leaves broadly elliptic, sharp at the tip, about 3½ in. long, dull green above, paler beneath. Found wild in many parts of the north temperate zone, especially Eu. and N.A. There are several hort. and wild varieties having yellow leaves or reddish twigs, or cut leaves, etc.

**A. rugosa.** Smooth alder. A branching, somewhat coarse shrub, very rarely a small tree. Leaves nearly elliptic but more or less wedge-shaped at the base, not over 4 in. long, finely toothed all round, green both sides. Common in swamps throughout eastern U.S. and often planted in such sites.

**A. viridis.** Green alder. Low shrub, not over 4–5 ft. high in cultivation. Leaves ovalish, about 2½ in. long, broader towards the base, green both sides, but paler beneath. Eu., especially in the mountains. Not much grown in U.S. and closely related to an American species, common in the mountains from Labrador to N. Car.

**ALDER BUCKTHORN** = *Rhamnus frangula*.

**ALDER FAMILY** = BETULACEAE.

**ALEPPO PINE** = *Pinus halepensis*. See PINE.

**ALERCE** = *Fitzroya cupressoides*; also *Libocedrus chilensis*, see INCENSE CEDAR.

**ALETRIS** (al'e-tris). A small genus of perennial herbs of the lily family, one grown for its stiff stalk of white tubular flowers. Leaves in a basal rosette* from which arises the flower stalk. Flowers tubular, in a spike, more or less as though mealy, white (in the species below). Fruit a tiny, beaked capsule, enclosed by the withered flower. (Greek for a female slave who grinds meal, in allusion to the mealy flowers.)

*Aletris* is easily grown in an acid (pH* 5) soil in full sunlight. Its erect stiff spikes are attractive enough to make it worth growing in the wild garden, but not to be attempted in ordinary garden soil.

**farinosa.** Colicroot; called also star-grass. Leaves broadly grass-like, bitter, flat on the ground, about 3 in. long. Flowers tubular, white, about ⅓ in. long, closely clustered in a slender spike at the end of the stiff stalk. Eastern U.S. July.

**ALEURITES.** See TUNG-OIL TREE.

*ALEXANDRINA*, *-us*, *-um* (a-licks-an-dry'na). From Alexandria.

**ALFALFA** = *Medicago sativa*.

**ALFILARIA** = *Erodium cicutarium*.

**ALGA** (plural algae). A flowerless plant of extremely simple structure, usually green, but, in the seaweeds, often beautifully colored. The algae range in size from the microscopic organisms which cover ponds with green scum (see SCUM) to the giant kelp, a seaweed over 100 ft. long. See LICHEN.

**ALGAROBA** = *Prosopis juliflora*. See MESQUITE.

**ALGERITA** = *Mahonia trifoliolata*.

**ALISMA** (a-liz'ma). Aquatic or marsh herbs, family Alismaceae, one grown along pond edges or in the water for its small white flowers. Leaves very variable, often narrow and grass-like if floating, but in mud forms with a distinct longish-oval blade and stalk. Flowers in a branched cluster (panicle*). Fruit dry, small (an achene*) slightly keeled on the back. (Greek name for this plant.)

Of very easy growth in wet places and care must be taken to see that it does not become a pest in the water garden.

**plantago-aquatica.** Water plantain. Leaves from grass-like to strap-shaped to much broader, depending on its site. Flowers white, about ½ in. wide, the stalk of the cluster nearly 3 ft. high and much-branched. Throughout north temperate regions. Some consider the native American species distinct from that of Eurasia, but the differences are of no significance to the gardener.

**ALISMACEAE** (a-liz-mā'see-e). The water plantain family contains only aquatic or marsh plants, in a dozen genera and perhaps 50 species, scattered all over the world. Leaves (in ours) mostly basal and sheathing, but immensely variable, often arrowhead-shaped. Flowers small, borne in whorls* or close or spreading clusters. Petals 3, white. Sepals 3, often chaffy in age. Fruit a cluster of 6, often beaked achenes.* The family is of little garden significance and *Alisma* (the water plantain) and *Sagittaria* (the arrowhead) are the only hort. genera. The first is nearly always aquatic, while *Sagittaria* is used along edges of pools and streams, or in the bog garden.

Technical flower characters: Receptacle flat or convex. Stamens 6 or more, the anthers 2-celled. Ovary 1-celled, usually 1-seeded.

**ALKALI-GRASS** = *Zygadenus elegans*.

**ALKALI SOILS.** See ACID AND ALKALI SOILS.

**ALKANET** = ANCHUSA. See also LITHOSPERMUM CANESCENS.

**ALKEKENGI.** Modern version of the Arab vernacular for *Physalis alkekengi*.

**ALLAMANDA** (al-la-man'da). A genus of handsome-flowered South American woody vines, family Apocynaceae, widely grown for ornament. Leaves opposite* or in whorls,* without marginal teeth. Flower funnel-shaped or nearly bell-shaped, its five lobes slightly, but distinctly, twisted. Stamens 5, alternating with the lobes of the corolla. Fruit a two-valved, prickly capsule.* (Named for J. N. S. Allamand, a European scientist.)

Allamandas are popular greenhouse vines, and are also much grown outdoors in zones* 8 and 9. They are profuse bloomers and quickly cover buildings and fences, but they will not cling to walls without being tied. In the greenhouse use potting mixture* 4, water freely and use liquid manure every few weeks throughout the growing season. Reduce watering to almost nothing from late autumn until early spring, when the vines can be cut back and re-potted, or left in place if planted in the ground. Easily propagated by cuttings. See VINES.

**cathartica.** Climbing up to 40 ft. Leaves often in groups of four, elliptic-oval, about 6 in. long, very glossy-green. Flowers about 3 in. wide, yellow, or golden-yellow and streaked with white. Brazil. Summer. There are many hort. varieties, of which the best is *var. hendersoni*. This

---

* Special articles on the subjects indicated by an asterisk (*) will be found at the words so marked.

is commonly called the golden trumpet and has more flowers than the type and they are often 5 in. across. This variety is the chief hort. favorite.

neriifolia. Yellow bell. Much shorter than *A. cathartica*, and often merely a sprawling shrub 3-5 ft. high. Leaves oblong or elliptic, about 4 in. long. Flowers golden-yellow, striped brownish-red inside, about 3 in. long and distinctly swollen and greenish at the base. Brazil. Summer.

**ALLÉE.** An allée is a glorified garden walk or promenade. There is no English term which exactly expresses the function of an allée. Although it was a common feature of Italian Renaissance gardens, the fashionable French of the sixteenth century put it to greatest use in garden design.

To meet their requirements for impressive garden settings these garden walks developed magnificent proportions and elaborate detail. As a result, the French term allée has been adopted by gardeners to indicate a type of walk or vista which performs a purely ornamental function. Although the English have developed the allée into a garden feature of exquisite dignity quite distinctive in its style, the term allée has nevertheless persisted. *See* PLEACH.

The characteristics of an allée are sumptuous proportions and ornamental or architectural planting with a purely decorative function. Compared with a garden walk which usually has a destination, an allée need not necessarily lead anywhere. It may have a purely visual destination with some ornamental feature to complete its effect. There can be no arbitrary rule for the design of an allée; it may be a single broad paved or gravel walk, bordered by generous turf strips and enclosed by high planting; it may be a double walk divided by a broad panel of turf with double rows of trees and enclosing hedges. Occasionally a long narrow pool extends down the center. In all cases the width between the bordering enclosure must be carefully proportioned to its height and length. To design successfully an allée it should be studied in perspective. If it is to be built on a slope or divided by steps the effect must be visualized in relation to the actual conditions where it is to be built.

An informal allée

There is no more dignified or impressive garden feature than a beautifully proportioned allée. It is also a most useful feature in uniting other elements of a garden, a very satisfactory means of focalizing the view from a terrace or window.

Although flowers are not ordinarily essential to the beauty of an allée they may be used if they are kept secondary in importance to the general effect. The most beautiful allées are compositions in green foliage with interesting plant or architectural forms arranged to create rhythmic and harmonious avenues. Obviously an allée requires skillful designing to be successful. The smaller the space available the more skillfully the design must be contrived to fit the site. This is not a desirable feature to be attempted in gardening unless space can be devoted to purely ornamental effect. — R. E. G.

**ALLEGHENY BARBERRY** = *Berberis canadensis*.

**ALLEGHENY SPURGE** = *Pachysandra procumbens*.

**ALLEGHENY VINE** = *Adlumia fungosa*.

**ALLEY.** An allée (which see).

**ALLIACEA, -us, -um** (al-lee-ace′ee-a). Onion-like.

**ALLIARIAEFOLIA, -us, um** (al-lee-air-ee-eye-fō′li-a). With leaves like the genus *Alliaria*, which is of little or no garden interest.

**ALLIGATOR PEAR.** *See* PERSEA AMERICANA.

**ALLIGATOR WAMPEE** = *Pontederia cordata*.

**ALLIONIACEAE** = NYCTAGINACEAE.

**ALLIUM** (al′li-um). A large genus of mostly onion-scented herbs which includes both the common onion, the leek, garlic, chives and shallot, as well as another group of perennial herbs grown for their ornamental flowers. All bear bulbs, often of considerable size in the common onion. Leaves mostly basal, typically hollow, but sometimes flat. Flowers few to a great many, always in a cluster (umbel)* the stalklets of which arise at one point and produce a usually ball-like flower cluster, variously colored. Fruit a small capsule. (*Allium* is the classical name of the garlic.)

The ornamental alliums are suitable border plants of easy culture in any ordinary garden soil. Most of the onion tribe produce bulbils* which provide easy method of propagation. Plant the bulbs in autumn or spring or sow seeds in spring. Some yield an onion-scented honey, especially in Calif.

**acuminatum.** An ornamental species from the Rocky Mts. usually less than 1 ft. high. Leaves about ½ in. wide. Flowers numerous, the umbels profuse, rose-purple. July.

**ascalonicum.** Shallot, sometimes called eschallot. About 1 ft. high and resembling the common onion but with small awl-like leaves, and small, more or less angular bulbs that break up into bublets.* Flowers not always present in the commonly cultivated form, when present violet or white. Possibly native of As., but may be a cultigen.* For culture *see* SHALLOT.

**azureum** = *Allium caeruleum*.

**caeruleum.** A stout herb 2-3 ft. high, cult. for ornament. Leaves 3-sided. Flower clusters (umbels)* dense, about 2 in. thick, deep blue. Turkestan and Siberia.

**cepa.** Onion. Bulb large. Leaves very various, usually bluish-gray and hollow. Flowering stalk about 18 in. high, the umbels profuse, white or lilac. Western Asia. For culture and garden varieties *see* ONION. There are in addition two well-marked hort. varieties: *var.* **solaninum,** the potato or multiplier onion which has separable bulbs used for propagation and a sparse flower cluster; and *var.* **viviparum,** the top onion, commonly propagated by its numerous bulbils,* which has small or undeveloped underground bulbs.

**fistulosum.** Welsh onion; called also spring onion. Bulb not much more swollen than the base of the flower stalk. Leaves and flower stalk thick, hollow, about 15 in. high, used for seasoning. Flowers whitish, the umbels very dense. As.

**moly.** Lily leek. A decorative species for use in the border or rock garden, usually not over 14 in. high, the leaves flat. Flowers showy, yellow, in a small, compact umbel. Southern Eu. July.

**neapolitanum.** Daffodil garlic. A decorative plant for borders in zone* 5 and southward, elsewhere safer to grow in pots with protection in the cold frame. Leaves flat, a little shorter than the stalk of the flower cluster. Flowers white, the cluster very profuse. Eu. June.

**porrum.** Leek. A stout herb, often 2½ ft. high. Leaves flat or slightly keeled, not hollow, 2½ ft. long and just less than 2 in. wide. Flowers white, in dense umbels. Probably a cultigen* of Eurasian origin. For culture and uses *see* LEEK.

**sativum.** Garlic. Smaller than *A. porrum*, its bulb with several, separable parts all enclosed in a white, membranous skin. Flowers pinkish. Eu. For culture and uses *see* HERB GARDENING.

**schoenoprasum.** Chive. Often forming tufts or sods with roots and few or no bulbs. Leaves flat, grass-like, but hollow. Flowers rose-purple in a close, head-like cluster. Eurasia. For culture and uses *see* CHIVES. *See, also,* HERB GARDENING.

**stellatum.** A native American decorative plant from the plains of Kan., Minn., Ill. and westward, usually about 2 ft. high. Leaves almost flat. Flowers pinkish-rose in stalked umbels. Summer and later. Easily grown in the border.

**validum.** A western U.S. wild plant grown for its showy umbels of rose or white flowers. Leaves nearly 2½ ft. long, flat, not hollow. Flower stalk erect, the cluster not nodding. Summer. It needs a moist soil.

**ALLOPLECTUS** (al-low-plek′tus). A group of 35 species of tropical plants, family Gesneriaceae, sometimes grown in greenhouses for the colored foliage and rather showy tubular flowers. Leaves opposite,* one of each pair not quite so large as the other. Flower clusters in the leaf-axils,* the clusters often bracted.* Flowers not quite regular,* somewhat sac-like at the base. Fruit a leathery, 2-valved pod. (*Alloplectus* is from the Greek meaning plaited diversely, in reference to the calyx.)

For culture *see* GLOXINIA.

**schlimi.** A woody herb or sub-shrub. Leaves ovalish, 3-4 in. long, somewhat heart-shaped at the base, purplish-violet below, green above. Flowers red, the calyx tube yellow below and red towards the tip. Brazil.

**ALLSPICE** = *Pimenta officinalis*.

---

* Special articles on the subjects indicated by an asterisk (*) will be found at the words so marked.

**ALLSPICE FAMILY** = MYRTACEAE.

**ALMOND** (*Amydalus communis*). Almonds are limited in production to areas less subject to cold and late spring frosts than the peach. Their production is confined mainly to Calif., though some are grown in other states west of the Rocky Mountains, where the winters are not too cold and late spring frosts do not occur.

The production of the almond is more limited than that of the peach because of its blossoming habit. The tree is as hardy as the peach, but it blossoms nearly a month earlier. In the almond-growing centers, orchard heating is a common practice in protecting the blossoms from frost. (For details, *see* FROST.)

Almonds are propagated by budding named varieties onto either peach or almond seedlings. The seed is stratified in sand and planted in the nursery row, generally in Feb. When almond seedlings are used, generally the wild bitter almond is used. Any variety of sweet almond will do, but it is more expensive than the bitter seed. In Aug. or Sept. the seedling is budded to the desired variety, using the common "T" or shield bud. The following spring the stock is cut back to the bud, which is allowed to grow for a season. At the end of the growing season, the one-year nursery tree is dug and ready to plant in the orchard.

The almond on almond root requires a sandy, well-drained soil. If the soil is a heavy loam, especially if wet during the growing season, the trees will die. The almond root is commonly used in orchards which are not irrigated, while the peach root is better adapted to irrigated orchards.

In preparation for planting, if one intends to irrigate, the land should be leveled. The field is laid out and tree positions located. Most people prefer the square system of planting — spacing the trees 20 to 30 feet apart. In planting the trees, injured roots should be cut back and the tree set in the orchard at the same depth at which it grew in the nursery. Great care must be taken to firm the soil around the roots. Almond trees can be planted any time from late Dec. to early March, the particular time being determined mainly by the moisture condition of the soil. One should wait until winter rains have moistened the soil, but it should not be so wet that it is sticky.

After planting, the tree should be cut back to 24-30 inches. If the side branches are strong and vigorous they may be headed moderately and saved for framework branches. Generally, however, they are not properly spaced and all are cut off. It is advisable to leave stubs about ¼ inch long when cutting off these side branches. After one season's growth in the orchard the trees should be pruned. Select three branches, preferably 6-8 inches apart and spaced equally around the trunk, for the primary framework. These should be headed lightly, generally to laterals. Care should be taken to see that the topmost primary is not subdued too much or the other two primaries will make more growth and tend to choke it out.

The second winter's pruning, if the trees have made normal, vigorous growth, should consist mainly of a thinning out. One should not try to save more than two secondary branches from each primary, otherwise the framework branches will crowd in later years. Subsequent pruning should consist of a moderate thinning out. Trees pruned as above outlined should begin to bear the third or fourth year.

Almonds, like any other fruit tree, require some type of cultivation. The amount of cultivation will depend a great deal on whether the orchard is irrigated or not. In non-irrigated orchards the cover crop or natural weed growth should be turned under either by disking or plowing fairly early in the spring. Subsequent weed growth should be controlled by sufficiently frequent cultivations for moisture conservation. If the orchard is irrigated, it is not necessary to cultivate as often, as the water used by weeds can be replaced by irrigation. In either irrigated or unirrigated orchards the ground should be cultivated just previous to harvest to facilitate the harvesting operations.

No general fertilizer program is practiced with almonds. If the orchard is planted on a good fertile soil, trees will probably show little or no response to fertilizers. Many growers occasionally apply barnyard manures to their almond trees, but no regular fertilizer program is followed.

As with other fruits, there are many individual varieties of almonds; however, there are only about six important ones. In their order of ripening, they are: Nonpareil, Ne Plus Ultra, I.X.L., Peerless, Drake, and Texas. The Nonpareil is the best of them. In planting almonds, it must be remembered that all varieties are self-sterile and will not set fruit when planted alone or in solid blocks. Also, Nonpareil and I.X.L. are inter-sterile and require that some other variety which blossoms at the same time be planted with them.

In the early fall the outer hull of the almond splits open. When most of the hulls in the centers of the trees have started to split, the trees should be harvested. The nuts are knocked off the tree by striking the smaller branches with long poles, or more recently by jarring the nuts off by striking the larger limbs with rubber hammers. To simplify gathering the nuts, large canvas sheets are spread under the trees before the almonds are knocked off.

After harvesting, the almonds must be hulled. This can easily be done by hand if the almonds have been grown under favorable conditions. However, it is cheaper and faster to use specially designed machines to hull the nuts. The hulled almonds are spread out, preferably in partial shade, to dry. When the kernels have dried so that they will be crisp, they may be sacked and kept a number of months in a cool, dry place, provided they are kept away from insects. Almonds which are sold commercially in the shell are generally bleached by moistening the shell and exposing them to sulphur fumes for a few minutes. However, care must be taken not to expose them too long or the sulphur fumes will penetrate the kernel and spoil its quality. — G. L. P.

INSECT PESTS: Insects of the peach may be expected to attack almond. On the Pacific Coast several scale insects, including the San Jose scale (*see* APPLE), as well as the peach-tree borer and the peach-twig borer, are likely to be important.

**ALMOND FAMILY.** *See* ROSACEAE.

*ALNIFOLIA, -us, -um* (al-ni-fō'li-a). With alder-like leaves.

**ALNUS.** *See* ALDER.

**ALOCASIA** (a-low-kay'zi-a). A large genus of tropical Asiatic and Malayan slightly woody herbs of the arum family, a few of which are grown in greenhouses for their handsome, often colored foliage. Leaves large, with long, sheathing stalks that usually end in or near the middle of the leaf blade (peltate*), which is often arrow-shaped with a heart-shaped base. Sheath of the flower cluster (spathe) boat-shaped, the spadix* shorter than it. Fruit a reddish berry. (*Alocasia* is an unexplained variant of *Colocasia*.)

Alocasias have a thick rootstock* and, in old plants, a tendency to be woody at the base. They need rich feeding and should be grown in potting mixture* 4 and watered freely. Do not let the greenhouse temperature fall below 60° in winter, and night temperatures of 70° are preferable. All of them need partial shade. Easily propagated by suckers, which are freely produced from the base, grown in sand over bottom-heat. More rarely grown from seed and sown in pots, with a temperature of 75°.

indica. In the typical (seldom grown) form the leaves are green. In *var.* metallica the leaves have a reddish-purplish sheen, while in *var.* variegata they are white-mottled. These are the commonly grown forms. Stem stout, and when full grown up to 6 ft. high. Leaves 2-4 ft. long, triangular-arrow-shaped, the basal lobes acutely pointed. Sheath of the flower cluster yellowish, often red inside. Malaya.

macrorhiza. Stem often 10 ft. tall, the plant handsome and striking. Leaves broadly triangular-oval, 3 ft. long, the basal lobes much shorter than the main part of the blade, green, but in many varieties with a white midrib,* or white-blotched. Sheath of the flower cluster grayish-green or greenish-yellow. India and Malaya.

sanderiana. Much smaller than the other two. Leaves peltate,* about a foot long, the blades triangular or narrower, the basal lobes blunter than the tip of the leaf, dark metallic green with white veins and white margins above, purplish beneath. Sheath of the flower cluster green. Philippine Islands.

**ALOE** (commonly ă'low; preferably a-low'ee). A genus of 100 species of mostly African, succulent plants of the lily

---
* Special articles on the subjects indicated by an asterisk (*) will be found at the words so marked.

family, a few grown in pots or tubs, often as specimen plants, for their striking usually spiny-toothed leaves, and red or yellow* flowers. Most species are stemless, with a rosette of basal leaves, but some have woody stems. Leaves with a sharp point and spiny or at least bony-toothed on the margin. Flowers (in those below) in a finger-shaped rather dense cluster, tubular or cylindric, often slightly curved, the tip separated into more or less spreading segments. Fruit a 3-angled pod (capsule*). (*Aloe* is the Latin version of alloch, its original Arabian name.)

Aloes are often confused with *Agave* or century plants which they superficially resemble, but the latter are all American. They will not stand much frost and are grown in the cool greenhouse in potting mixture* 6. See SUCCULENTS for general account of handling these plants, of which many species besides those below are to be had from fanciers and specialists in succulents. Propagated by suckers, or, in those producing stems, by cuttings.

**ciliaris.** Stems weak and sprawling, usually under 1 ft. Leaves many, thin, about 5 in. long, narrowed from a broader base, the margin white-toothed. Flowers red but green-tipped, about 1 in. long, the cluster long-stalked. South Africa.

**variegata.** A succulent resembling *Haworthia* in youth, mostly with basal leaves, but ultimately with a leafy stem. Leaves triangular or V-shaped, in three oblique ranks. Flowers red, about 1¼ in. long, the segments green-striped. South Africa.

**vera.** True aloe, sometimes called Barbados aloe, but not native there. Stemless, the rosette of basal leaves grayish-green. Leaves 1–2 ft. long, erect, juicy, spiny-margined, and, with other (not hort.) species, the source of bitter aloes. Flowers 1 in. long, yellow, the nodding cluster on a stalk somewhat longer than the leaves. Northern Africa, but widely naturalized throughout the tropical world and widely grown as a greenhouse pot plant.

**ALOE FAMILY.** See LILIACEAE.

*ALOIDES* (a-loy′deez; but *see* OÏDES). Aloe-like.

*ALOIFOLIA, -us, -um* (a-low-i-fō′li-a). With leaves like an aloe.

**ALONSOA** (a-lon-zō′a). A small group of tropical American herbs of the figwort family, grown as annuals outdoors, or as greenhouse plants for their attractive red, winter-blooming flowers. Leaves opposite* or in threes. Flowers in terminal finger-shaped clusters, the corolla very irregular, two-lipped,* and turned upside down by twisting of its individual stalklets, its tube nearly lacking. Fruit an oblongish pod (capsule*) with many small seeds. (Named for Alonzo Zanoni, a Bogotá official.) The plants are sometimes known as mask-flower.

Easily grown as summer annuals in any ordinary warm garden soil. For winter bloom sow the seed in potting mixture* 3 and put in cool greenhouse in November.

**acutifolia.** Bushy herb up to 3 ft. Leaves ovalish, deeply toothed on the margin. Flowers vermilion-red, the cluster leafy and elongated, the upper lip very large. Peru. There is a white-flowered hort. variety.

**warscewiczi.** Resembling the last but larger, the leaves with double-toothed margins and pale on the under side. Flowers scarlet-red, the cluster looser and not so leafy. Peru. The commonly cultivated plant, and offered with various names such as *A. grandiflora, A. compacta* and, perhaps, as *A. mutissi*.

*ALOPECUROIDES* (a-low-pee-cure-oy′deez; but *see* OÏDES). Like the meadow foxtail (*Alopecurus*).

**ALOPECURUS** (a-low-pee-cure′us). A genus of 30 species of meadow grasses mostly from the cooler parts of the north temperate zone, one widely used in grass mixtures for meadows. The only hort. species somewhat resembles timothy but is lower and has shorter spikes. (*Alopecurus* is Greek for foxtail.)

**pratensis.** Meadow foxtail. Perennial, the stem unbranched and erect from a creeping base, about 18 in. high. Leaves scarcely 6 in. long, slightly roughish. Spike dense, 1–3 in. long, usually standing above the leaves. Eu., but widely naturalized in N.A. A good meadow or pasture grass but too coarse for lawns.

**ALOYSIA** = LIPPIA.

*ALPESTRIS, -e* (al-pes′tris). Almost alpine.

*ALPINA, -us, -um* (al-py′na). Growing above timber line.

**ALPINE.** As a term it is strictly applicable to plants found only above timber line on mountains. By extension it has come to be used for any mountainous plant of high altitude, whether from above timber line or not. As part of a common name it may mean either and has been widely so used. Among the garden plants so called the following occur in THE GARDEN DICTIONARY:

Alpine azalea = *Lioseleuria procumbens;* Alpine catchfly = *Silene alpestris;* Alpine poppy = *Papaver alpinum.* See POPPY; Alpine savory = *Satureia alpina.* See SAVORY; Alpine wallflower = *Erysimum linifolium.*

**ALPINE GARDEN.** See ROCK GARDEN.

**ALPINIA** (al-pin′i-a). There are nearly 150 species of these ginger-like herbs from tropical Asia and the Pacific Islands, at least two of which are cultivated for ornament. They belong to the family Zingiberaceae and are leafy-stemmed herbs, some with colored foliage, and showy irregular* flowers in bracted* spikes. Leaves without marginal teeth, parallel-veined, the stalk or leaf-base more or less sheathing. Flowers very irregular,* orchid-like, in a terminal, ultimately nodding cluster. Fruit a slowly splitting capsule. (Named for Prosper Alpinus, Italian botanist.)

Can be grown outdoors only in zone* 9, or protected parts of zone* 8 in rich, moist sites. In the greenhouse use potting mixture* 4, give plenty of water and do not let the temperature fall below 60°. Easily propagated by division, which helps to reduce the otherwise large clumps that ultimately develop.

**sanderae.** A common greenhouse plant of uncertain identity. Leaves about 8 in. long and 1 in. wide, much like those of some cultivated dracaenas, but striped with white, not white-margined. Rarely flowering and the flowers sterile. Origin unknown. Common as a handsome foliage plant under glass.

**speciosa.** Shell-flower. A leafy-stemmed herb up to 10 ft. Leaves 1–2 ft. long, oblongish, bright green, not over 5 in. wide. Flowers very showy, orchid-like, the lip* yellow with brownish-red markings, the corolla white and tinged with purple. Eastern As. Often sold as *A. nutans* or as *Renealmia nutans.*

**ALSIKE CLOVER** = *Trifolium hybridum.* See CLOVER.

**ALSINACEAE.** See CARYOPHYLLACEAE.

**ALSINE.** Some cultivated plants so named belong to *Arenaria* (which see); for others, mostly weeds, *see* STELLARIA.

**ALSOPHILA** (al-soff′i-la). Tree ferns of wide distribution in the tropics and belonging to the family Cytheaceae. Of the 100 known species only a handful are of hort. significance and of these the one below is the best known. They have tall trunks covered with the remains of the frond stalks. Fronds (leaves) very large, in a handsome crown at the end of the trunk, the stalks often chaffy, the blade twice- or thrice-compound,* its ultimate segments of considerable size. (From Greek for grove-loving, in allusion to their shade tolerance.)

Alsophilas are very handsome tree ferns which can only be grown outdoors in the moister parts of zone* 9. Rather commonly grown in greenhouses for their graceful feathery foliage. For culture *see* Greenhouse Ferns in FERNS AND FERN GARDENING.

**australis.** Trunk up to 20 ft. Leaves usually 8 or 10 in the crown, from 5–10 ft. long, green above, bluish-green beneath, the primary segments about 18 in. long, the ultimate segments about 4–5 in. long and an inch wide. Foliage thus very showy and almost feathery. Aust.

**ALSTROEMERIA** (al-stre-meer′i-a). The Peruvian lilies comprise perhaps 50 species of South American herbs, family Amaryllidaceae, a few of which are grown in the greenhouse or outdoors (*see below*) for their showy, lily-like flowers. Roots fibrous or tuberous, the stem slender. Leaves often twisted at the base, narrow. Flowers slightly irregular* in a terminal cluster (umbel*) which is sometimes compound. Petals not united into a tube. Fruit (capsule*) 3-valved and with many seeds. (Named for Claus Alstroemer, a friend of Linnaeus.)

Peruvian lilies require special conditions to do well. *A. aurantiaca* can be planted outdoors in the spring, allowed to bloom through the summer, and lifted for storing in a cool, frost-free and dryish place over the winter. It needs some shade, a rich garden soil, and not too dry a site. Hardy everywhere, in summer, but will not survive the winter from about zone* 5 northwards. It is, in any case, better to lift it.

---

* Special articles on the subjects indicated by an asterisk (*) will be found at the words so marked.

Both *A. aurantiaca* and *A. chilensis*, which is not hardy, can be grown in a cool greenhouse in potting mixture* 4. Pot them up very carefully, for the roots are tender, in the autumn, and give occasional feeding with liquid manure. After blooming, store them as noted above.

Alstroemerias greatly increase their roots during a single season and need plenty of pot space. Divide them when lifting for the resting period and replant in pots or outdoors as needed. Propagated, also, but rarely, by spring-sown seeds. Do not disturb the seedlings the first year.

**aurantiaca.** Flowering stem erect, 2–4 ft. high. Leaves numerous (up to 50), lance-shaped, about 3½ in. long, whorled* under the flower cluster, scattered elsewhere. Umbel* compound, the flowers yellow, green-tipped and brown-spotted. Chile. Mulching will sometimes save it outdoors, but it is better lifted.

**chilensis.** Flowering stems about 3 ft. high, the few leaves scattered, bluish-green and fringed. Flowers rose-red or whitish, larger than in *A. aurantiaca*, but not so many in the umbel. Chile. Mostly a pot plant.

**ALTACIDE.** A trademarked weed killer useful for paths and roads.

**ALTERNANTHERA** = TELANTHERA.

**ALTERNARIA LEAFSPOT.** See Diseases at CABBAGE.

**ALTERNATE.** Having the point of attachment, as of leaves, twigs or branches, not exactly opposite each other. See LEAF.

*ALTERNIFOLIA, -us, -um* (all-ter-ni-fō′li-a). Having alternate leaves.

**ALTHAEA.** See HOLLYHOCK.

**ALTHEA.** An incorrect but very common spelling for *Althaea*, for which see HOLLYHOCK. *Althea*, in some catalogs, is also applied to shrubby species of *Hibiscus*, especially the rose-of-sharon. See HIBISCUS.

**ALTINGIACEAE** = HAMAMELIDACEAE.

*ALTISSIMA, -us, -um* (all-tiss′i-ma). Tallest.

**ALUMINUM SULPHATE.** This is used for increasing or maintaining the acidity of soils. For details see ACID AND ALKALI SOILS.

**ALUMROOT.** See HEUCHERA; see also GERANIUM MACULATUM and TELLIMA.

**ALYSSUM** (a-liss′some). The madworts comprise a large genus of Eurasian perennial herbs of the mustard family, widely grown for their deservedly popular and profuse bloom of yellow or white flowers. (For an annual sort, see SWEET ALYSSUM.) Leaves alternate.* Flowers in dense terminal clusters. (Greek for allaying rage, perhaps in allusion to its fabled quality of so doing; hence, madwort.)

Although most madworts are of easy culture in any ordinary garden soil, their profuse bloom and often prostrate habit have made them favorites in the rock garden, for pavement planting, and in dry walls. Widely used also in the flower border, for edging, and for cutting. Easily propagated by seed, or by fall or spring division of the roots.

**alpestre.** A European herb, not over 4 in. high, its grayish-white foliage tufted. Flowers yellow, in short clusters. Primarily a rock garden species which makes flat grayish-white masses. July. Often listed as *A. serpyllifolium*.

**argenteum.** Yellow tuft. Up to 15 in. high, dense and compact, the base a little woody. Leaves silvery-white underneath. Flowers in close, head-like clusters, deep yellow, blooming all summer. Eu. Often listed as *A. rostratum*. Mostly for the rock garden.

**maritimum** = *Lobularia maritima*. See SWEET ALYSSUM.

**montanum.** Compact or low and spreading, not over 9 in. high. Leaves ashy-gray, nearly linear. Flowers sweet-scented, yellow, mostly in June. A rock garden species from southern Eu. forming a carpet.

**rostratum** = *Alyssum argenteum*.

**saxatile.** Gold-dust; called also golden tuft and basket-of-gold. The most popular and widely grown of the madworts and easily grown almost anywhere in open sunlight. Leaves grayish, numerous, the plant forming dense mats or clumps. Flowers golden-yellow, in numerous clusters. Eu. May. Known in many named forms, such as Silver Queen and *var.* **compactum**, a particularly fine strain for pavement planting because of its dwarf habit. The var. **citrinum**, with lemon-yellow flowers, is also one of the best.

**serpyllifolium** = *Alyssum alpestre*.

**spinosum.** Densely bushy and spiny herb, about 12 in. high, the foliage silvery. Flowers white. July. Southern Eu. and northern Af. A rock garden species requiring sandy or gritty soil and full sun.

*AMABALIS, -e* (a-mab′a-lis). Lovable or pleasing.

**AMANO-GAWA.** See Japanese flowering cherries at PRUNUS.

*AMARA, -us, -um* (a-ma′ra). Bitter.

**AMARANTH.** See AMARANTHUS. For the globe amaranth see GOMPHRENA GLOBOSA.

**AMARANTHACEAE** (am-a-ran-thā′see-ee). The amaranth family contains about 40 genera and perhaps 500 species, comprising rather weedy herbs and a few woody plants of wide distribution, particularly in the tropics. The only hort. genera include important everlastings, the cockscomb, prince's-feather, love-lies-bleeding and several plants used in carpet bedding for their foliage.

Leaves alternate* in *Amaranthus*, *Deeringia* and *Celosia*, but opposite* in the other genera here mentioned. Flowers small, inconspicuous and without petals, often chaffy. The close-packed clusters in which they occur, however, are often brightly colored and very showy, especially in the cockscomb and prince's-feather. Fruit dry in all our genera except *Deeringia*, where it is berry-like. Besides those already mentioned, see GOMPHRENA, IRESINE and TELANTHERA. While the prince's-feather and love-lies-bleeding both belong to the genus *Amaranthus* it contains also some pernicious weeds. (See Prostrate Pigweed in the list at WEEDS.)

Technical flower characters: Calyx herbaceous or membranous, 2–5 parted. Stamens 1–5, mostly opposite the calyx segments. Ovary 1-celled.

**AMARANTH FAMILY** = AMARANTHACEAE.

**AMARANTH-FEATHERS** = *Humea elegans*.

*AMARANTHOIDES* (am-a-ran-thoy′deez; but see OÏDES). Resembling an amaranth.

**AMARANTHUS** (am-a-ran′thus). The amaranths are coarse, often weedy, mostly annual herbs, family Amaranthaceae, widely distributed and, except the following, of no garden importance. Leaves alternate,* often colored in the hort. forms, without marginal teeth. Flowers very small, without petals, but often conspicuous because congested in a chaffy, often brightly colored cluster. Fruit small, dry, 1-seeded. (From Greek meaning not fading, from the everlasting-like character of some species.)

The amaranths will grow nearly anywhere. If the soil is too rich the leaves will be larger, but the plant tends to lose its color. Dwarf varieties with variegated foliage are useful bedding plants. All need full sunshine. Sow seed in the border for tall sorts, and in frames for the bedding varieties, which may be transplanted any time after danger of frost is over.

**blitoides.** Prostrate pigweed. See list at WEEDS.

**caudatus.** Love-lies-bleeding; called also tassel-flower. Erect but spreading, up to 3 ft. high. Leaves ovalish or oblong, pointed both ends, green and stalked. Flower-spikes long and slender, often in branched clusters, drooping, the terminal one like a rat's tail, all deep red. Tropical. A very popular annual with varieties having blood-red foliage, green or yellow spikes, and one with close, head-like, red flower clusters. Called, by seedsmen, a variety of other names, such as *A. dussi*, *A. elegantissima*, *A. margaritae*, *A. superbus*, etc. See ANNUALS.

**hybridus.** A weedy herb not worth cult., except for its var. **hypochondriacus**, the prince's-feather. The latter is a showy plant 3–4 ft. high, the foliage reddish. Flower clusters dense, much-branched and chaffy, red or brownish-red. Tropical.

**salicifolius** = *Amaranthus tricolor*.

**tricolor.** Joseph's-coat, called also fountain plant. A very variable garden annual 1–4 ft. high, except in the dwarf forms. Flowers in stalkless, head-like clusters in the leaf-axils,* or sometimes spike-like and interrupted. Leaves sometimes blotched and colored, especially in the forms known as "Combustion," "Molten Fire," etc. Tropical. There are several hort. varieties, one with narrow drooping leaves, another with red foliage. See ANNUALS.

**AMARCRINUM** (am-ar-cry′num). A little-known and not much cult. hybrid between *Amaryllis* and *Crinum*, produced in Calif. where it can be grown outdoors in summer. As a pot plant it should be treated the same as amaryllis. (*Amarcrinum* is a contraction of *Amaryllis* and *Crinum*.) The only species.

**howardi.** Resembling an amaryllis. Flowers funnel-shaped, the segments recurving, the cluster dense, on stalks often 4 ft. long, fragrant, shell-pink. Garden hybrid.

*AMARICAULIS, -e* (am-air-i-call′iss). With a bitter stem.

* Special articles on the subjects indicated by an asterisk (*) will be found at the words so marked.

**AMARYLLIDACEAE** (am-a-rill-i-day'see-ee). The amaryllis family contains over 70 genera and nearly 900 species of mostly tropical plants. Lily-like in aspect, and differing from the lily family only in the technical character of the superior ovary. Many of the hort. genera of Amaryllidaceae are commonly called lilies. They have alternate* or basal leaves, without marginal teeth, but often prickly in *Agave* (century plant). Flowers typically of 6 segments, the three inner obviously petals, the outer ones sepals or often petal-like. Fruit a capsule* in all our genera except *Clivia, Curculigo* and *Haemanthus* which have berry-like or fleshy fruit.

The family contains many garden favorites (see SNOWFLAKE, SNOWDROP, TUBEROSE, *Lycoris* and *Narcissus*), as well as a group of bulbous greenhouse plants with showy, lily-like flowers (see AMARCRINUM, AMARYLLIS, AMMOCHARIS, BRUNSVIGIA, CRINUM, EUCHARIS, HIPPEASTRUM, HYMENOCALLIS, NERINE, PANCRATIUM, SPREKELIA and VALLOTA). Some of these are tropical, many from South Africa, and there are a few native American genera in cultivation, among them *Cooperia, Hypoxis* and *Zephyranthes*.

*Manfreda* and *Furcraea* are allied to *Agave* (the century plants); *Alstroemeria* comprises summer-blooming, fibrous-rooted South American herbs; *Anigozanthus* and *Doryanthes* are Australian genera grown mostly in Calif.; while *Sternbergia*, native in the Mediterranean region, resembles *Zepyranthes*.

Technical flower characters: Flowers arising from sheath-like bracts.* Stamens mostly 6, attached to the throat of the corolla or to the base of its segments. Ovary inferior, 3-celled.

**AMARYLLIS** (am-a-rill'is). Technically a genus of one species, a South African bulbous herb, family Amaryllidaceae. But, by extensive and not unnatural garden usage, plants belonging to the genera *Crinum, Hippeastrum, Brunsvigia, Sprekelia, Lycoris* and *Vallota*, are also called amaryllis, some, in hort. literature, always so.

The genus *Amaryllis* has large, showy, lily-like flowers on a tall solid stalk (hollow in *Sprekelia* and *Hippeastrum*), which bloom before the strap-shaped leaves appear. Flowers funnel-shaped, the tube short, its six segments erect and ascending. Fruit a globe-shaped pod (capsule*), its irregular bursting revealing the few pellet-like seeds. (*Amaryllis* is the classical name of this or a related plant.)

**belladonna.** Belladonna lily. Leaves strap-shaped, appearing usually after the plant blooms. Flowers typically rose-red (purple or white in some of the many named forms), sweet-scented, about 3½ in. long, in dense clusters (umbels*) at the end of a stout, naked stalk that is often 18 in. long. South Af. Blooms outdoors in summer, but before or after depending on when it is planted.

**formosissima** = *Sprekelia formosissima*.

The garden amaryllises may be considered as a cultural group, comprising all the genera mentioned above, except *Crinum* (which see). All are typically greenhouse subjects, but many of them can be grown permanently outdoors in zones* 8 and 9, and *Lycoris* (which see) is grown both indoors and under glass. A few, especially *Hippeastrum*, are used as pot plants for the window garden, or in the open border during summer.

These popular plants all agree in needing a prolonged resting period during the winter. Take up the bulbs and store in a cool, frost-free, dryish place. In the early spring, or even as early as January, re-pot (some large ones need tubs) in potting mixture* 3 and put in a greenhouse with a night temperature of 65° or more. Water once a fortnight with liquid manure, especially toward blooming time.

Those that are to go outdoors, or whose bloom is to be retarded, should be kept dormant longer. All have tender roots and must be handled carefully. After the plants bloom it is important to remember that they must be watered and fed so that the leaves will develop properly and that the bulbs will ripen sufficiently to permit of safe storage. This can be in the old pot (gradually dried out) or they may be plunged in clean dryish sand. Do not, however, allow them to shrivel.

The recently organized American Amaryllis Society is devoted to the culture of *Amaryllis* and related genera. It may be reached by addressing the Garden Editor, Houghton Mifflin Company, Boston, Mass.

**AMARYLLIS FAMILY.** See AMARYLLIDACEAE.

**AMATEUR GARDENER.** The garden amateur scarcely needs to be defined, except in terms of admiration. He never would be if it were not for the necessity of determining his status in a flower, fruit or vegetable show.

Where prizes are offered to both professional and amateur growers, an amateur is one who does it for pleasure, home consumption or charity; but not for profit. A fairly safe, but not absolute, criterion is whether or not a catalog is issued of plant material for sale. If it is, the person is, strictly, no longer an amateur. This allows an amateur to keep his status even if he occasionally sells surplus stock to the neighbors.

Both here and in England, some have tried to exclude from the amateur class those who hire professional gardeners. This is obviously unfair to the owner who is still amateur, so long as he sells nothing.

**AMATUNGULA** = *Carissa grandiflora*.

**AMAZONICA, -us, -um** (a-ma-zon'i-ka). From the Amazon.

**AMAZON LILY** = *Eucharis grandiflora*.

**AMBARELLA** = *Spondias cytherea*.

**AMBIGUA, -us, -um** (am-big'you-a). Ambiguous or uncertain.

**AMBLYODON.** An obsolete name for plants now included in *Gaillardia*.

**AMBROSIA ELATIOR** = ragweed. See list at WEEDS.

**AMBROSIOIDES** (am-bro-zee-oy'deez; but see OÏDES). Resembling the genus *Ambrosia* which contains the ragweed. See the list at WEEDS.

**AMELANCHIER** (am-e-lank'i-er). These plants are variously called shadbush, serviceberry and June-berry, while the profusion of white bloom is commonly called shadblow. They are shrubs or trees of the rose family, found throughout the north temperate zone, a few grown for ornament. Leaves alternate,* toothed, the buds prominently pointed. Flowers white, in terminal, rather profuse, clusters (racemes*), usually with 5 strap-shaped petals. Fruit like a miniature apple, but bony inside, sometimes used for jellies. (*Amelanchier*, as a name, is of unknown origin.)

The species below, all American except *A. ovalis*, are of easy culture in any ordinary garden soil. They are very attractive in early spring with their white flowers, later from their profusion of small often brightly colored fruit. Easily propagated by sowing ripe seeds, or sometimes by suckers. All are hardy from zone* 3 southward.

**canadensis.** A tree to 45 ft., but often shrubby. Leaves pointed prominently, white-hairy when young, green in age, about 2-3 in. long. Flower cluster about 2 in. long, blooming before or with the opening of the leaves. Fruit red-purple, nearly tasteless. April and May. Eastern U.S.

**laevis.** A tree to 30 ft., rarely shrubby. Leaves purplish-green when young, about 3½ in. long, rounded or slightly heart-shaped at the base, ultimately bright green. Flower clusters drooping, appearing with or after the unfolding of the leaves, making a striking contrast with the early foliage. Fruit purplish-black, sweet. May. Eastern N.A.

**ovalis.** A European shrub scarcely exceeding 6 ft., the leaves ovalish, whitish beneath when young, green in age. Flower cluster white-hairy, not drooping, blooming about the time the leaves unfold. Fruit bluish-black, with a bloom. May.

**stolonifera.** Dwarf June-berry. A low, more or less sprawling shrub, about 3 ft. high, often forming patches because of its underground stolons.* Leaves oblongish, or rounder, white-hairy on the under side when young, ultimately greenish throughout. Flower cluster upright. Fruit sweet, black-purple, with a slight bloom. Northeastern N.A. May, but blooming a few days later than *A. ovalis* where they are grown together. Sometimes cultivated for its jelly-making fruit under the name Success. Easily propagated by its stolons.*

There are many wild species of *Amelanchier* in America, any of which may be locally naturalized. Their technical differences are slight and very puzzling to the gardener.

**AMELLOIDES** (a-mell-oy'deez; but see OÏDES). Like a plant of the genus *Amellus* (which see).

**AMELLUS.** A genus name applied to plants of little hort. value. Derived from it is the specific name *amellus* (see ASTER AMELLUS). Both were named from the River Mella, in Italy, where *Aster amellus* was first found.

---

* Special articles on the subjects indicated by an asterisk (*) will be found at the words so marked.

**AMENT.** A catkin.*

**AMERICA.** A plant disseminated by Burbank, which turned out to be *Oenothera acaulis*. See EVENING PRIMROSE.

*AMERICANA, -us, -um* (a-me-ri-cay′na). From North or South America.

**AMERICAN.** As an adjective, widely applied to thousands of North or South American plants, usually to distinguish them from similar or related Old World species. The following apply only to the hort. species found in THE GARDEN DICTIONARY, although some of them are also used for other wild species not admitted to this book:

American abscess-root = *Polemonium reptans*; American aloe = *Agave americana*; American arborvitae = *Thuja occidentalis*; American beech = *Fagus grandifolia* (see BEECH); American Beauty. See Group 4 at ROSE; American centaury, see SABBATIA; American chestnut = *Castanea dentata* (see CHESTNUT); American colombo, see FRASERA; American cowslip, see DODECATHEON; American crab = *Malus coronaria*; American elder = *Sambucus canadensis* (see ELDER); American elm = *Ulmus americana* (see ELM); American globeflower = *Trollius laxus*; American hazel = *Corylus americana* (see HAZEL); American holly = *Ilex opaca* (see HOLLY); American hop-hornbeam = *Ostrya virginiana*; American hornbeam = *Carpinus caroliniana* (see HORNBEAM); American ipecac = *Gillenia stipulata*; American ivy = *Parthenocissus quinquefolia*; American larch = *Larix laricina* (see LARCH); American linden = *Tilia glabra* (see LINDEN); American lotus = *Nelumbium luteum*; American lungwort = *Mertensia virginica*; American mountain-ash = *Sorbus americana* (see MOUNTAIN-ASH); American mulberry = *Morus rubra* (see MULBERRY); American red elder = *Sambucus pubens* (see ELDER); American persimmon = *Diospyros virginiana* (see PERSIMMON); American redbud = *Cercis canadensis* (see REDBUD); American sanicle = *Heuchera americana*; American senna = *Cassia marylandica*; American smoke-tree = *Cotinus americanus*; American spikenard = *Aralia racemosa*; American Turk's-cap lily = *Lilium superbum*; American twinflower = *Linnaea americana*; American wayfaring-tree = *Viburnum alnifolium*; American white hellebore = *Veratrum viride*; American white water lily = *Nymphaea odorata*; American witch-alder, see FOTHERGILLA.

*AMETHYSTINA, -us, -um* (a-me-thiss′ti-na). Violet-colored.

**AMIANTHIUM** = *Zygadenus*.

**AMIESITE.** See DRIVES.

**AMMIACEAE.** See UMBELLIFERAE.

**AMMOBIUM** (am-moe′bi-um). A small genus of Australian herbs, family Compositae, the one below usually grown as an annual everlasting. Leaves white, felty, alternate* or basal. Flowers yellow, in chaffy heads which are solitary at the ends of the small branches and surrounded by silvery-white bracts.* Ray* flowers none. (Greek for growing in sand.)

Easily grown as a summer annual in ordinary garden soil. Sow the seeds where the plants are to stand. Before the flowers are mature cut and hang in a shady, cool place, when, upon drying, they will hold their color almost indefinitely.

alatum. Winged everlasting. Bushy herb up to 3 ft., the branches prominently winged.* Basal leaves shaped like a javelin; the stem leaves smaller and fewer. Heads about 1½ in. thick, the bracts* petal-like and silvery-white. The var. **grandiflorum**, with larger heads, is the best sort to grow. See ANNUALS.

**AMMOCHARIS** (am-mock′ar-is). A small genus of South African bulbous herbs, family Amaryllidaceae, the one below somewhat grown for ornament, mostly in the greenhouse. Bulb large (6–8 in. in diameter). Leaves strap-shaped, produced before the plant blooms. Flowers red, fragrant, perfectly regular,* about 30 in a terminal ball-shaped cluster (umbel*), on a solid stalk. Fruit a capsule.* (Greek, meaning sand beauty.)

Culture is the same as for the plants discussed at amaryllis.

falcata. Leaves 1–2 ft. long. Flowers with a cylindrical and straight tube, the segments clawed* and slightly recurved at the tip. Blooms in summer if grown outdoors, earlier if in the greenhouse.

**AMMONIA.** See PLANT FOODS.

**AMMONIUM SULPHATE.** See Synthetic Manure at MANURE.

**AMMOPHILA** (am-moff′i-la). A very small genus of sand-binding grasses of nearly world-wide distribution on sandy beaches and dunes. Of no hort. importance except to the seaside gardeners who have shifting dunes to capture, for which the species below is the best-known remedy. It will grow nowhere else, and will stand any amount of salt spray.

Rootstock creeping and deep below the surface. Leaves tough, wiry, with a minutely saw-toothed margin, pale green below, shining and leathery above. Flowering spike (rarely produced) about 1 ft. long. (Greek for sand-loving.)

Rootstocks, which may be dug or purchased, should be divided and planted about 6 in. apart, each way, and about 3 in. deep. Within a year or two the plant will completely stabilize a shifting dune.

arenaria. Beach grass; called also marram. Tough wiry grass growing naturally in isolated tufts or clumps. Leaves about 2 ft. long, the stalk of the flower spike (when produced) overtopping the leaves. By some this plant is considered as of world-wide distribution on sand dunes, but others consider the native American plant different and call it *A. breviligulata*. Horticulturally it matters little, for both are sand-binders par excellence.

*AMOENA, -us, -um* (a-mee′na). Pleasing.

**AMOLE** = *Chlorogalum pomeridianum*.

**AMOMUM** (a-mo′mum). A genus of 100 species of tropical Asian herbs, family Zingiberaceae, only the following sometimes grown for ornament or for its fragrant foliage. It differs only in technical characters from the ginger (*Zingiber*). Stem leafy, the leaves without marginal teeth. Flowers in dense spike-like clusters, the stalks arising directly from the creeping rootstock. (*Amomum* is from the Greek signifying a poison antidote, which some species may provide. *Amomum* is also used as a specific name for a *Cornus*.)

The species below is cultivated as is the ginger (which see).

cardamon. In spite of the specific name this is not the true source of cardamon (which see), but furnishes a cheap substitute for it. Herbaceous, fleshy, about 6 ft. tall. Leaves narrowly lance-shaped, 8–12 in. long. Flowering stalk much shorter than the stem of the plant. Flowers about 1 in. long, brownish-yellow, tubular, but with a distinct lip. Fruit a capsule. East Indies. The whole plant is spicy or aromatic.

**AMORPHA** (a-more′fa). False indigo. The group comprises a genus of 15 species of N.A. shrubs of the pea family, identified by rather technical characters. Leaves compound,* the numerous leaflets arranged feather-fashion, in pairs, but with a single terminal one. Flowers small, pea-like, in a dense, terminal, usually branched cluster. Fruit a small pod which does not split and is faintly sticky. (Greek for deformed, alluding to the imperfectly developed and small flowers.)

The species below are easily grown in ordinary garden soil throughout the climatic zones assigned to them. The plants are not particularly showy, but are sometimes used in the shrub border or as specimen plants, especially in cool regions. Easily propagated by seeds, cuttings, layers or suckers.

canescens. Lead plant. A white-hoary shrub up to 4 ft. Leaves with 15–45 leaflets that are oblongish, and usually less than an inch long. Flowers blue, the cluster about 4½ in. long. Central N.A. Hardy from zone* 2 southward. Summer.

fruticosa. Bastard indigo. A bushy shrub up to 15 or 20 ft., not grayish. Leaflets 11–25, more or less oval, about 1½ in. long. Flowers dull purplish or bluish, in clusters 6 in. long. Conn. to Fla., west to the central U.S. Hardy from zone* 3 southward. June. There are pale blue, white, and crisped-foliaged hort. varieties.

microphylla. Scarcely 3 ft. high, the foliage green. Leaflets 13–14, more or less oblong, about ½ in. long. Flowers purple, usually in an unbranched cluster that is nearly 6 in. long. Central N.A. Hardy from zone* 2 southward. June. This is often offered as *A. nana*.

**AMORPHOPHALLUS** (a-more-foe-fal′lus). For a plant often listed as *Amorphophallus rivieri*, see HYDROSME. True species of *Amorphophallus* are little known to gardeners, but the name has long been incorrectly applied to a species of *Hydrosme*.

**AMOUNT OF SEED REQUIRED.** For vegetables see the table at KITCHEN GARDEN.

**AMPELOPSIS** (am-pe-lop′sis). A genus of woody, tendril*-bearing vines, family Vitaceae, a few much grown for covering walls. All the species are North American or Asiatic and differ from the closely related grape vines mostly by their inedible fruit and by not having the shredding bark of the grape. Leaves simple* or compound,* the tendrils forking and without the sucking-disks* of the Virginia creeper (see PARTHENOCISSUS) and its relatives. Flowers small, greenish or yellowish. Fruit a 1–4-seeded berry. (Greek for vine-like.)

* Special articles on the subjects indicated by an asterisk (*) will be found at the words so marked.

These vines, which have no very strong soil preferences, will grow well on walls, but should be tied at first as they lack sucking-disks.* Propagated exactly as in the grape. See also VINES.

There is much confusion in the garden names of these vines. Besides the four species below, the following have been listed by some as belonging to the genus *Ampelopsis*. *A. henryana, quinquefolia, tricuspidata* and *A. vitacea*, all properly belonging to *Parthenocissus* (which see).

**acontifolia.** Tall growing but slender vine. Leaves compound,* 5 leaflets long-stalked, about 3 in. long, often divided and with toothed lobes. Fruit orange-yellow when ripe, bluish at first, about ¼ in. in diameter. China. Hardy from zone* 4 southward, possibly from zone* 3.

**arborea.** Pepper-vine. A slender vine with leaves twice-compound,* the ultimate leaflets broadly oval, about 2 in. long. The terminal leaflet is much longer-stalked than the others. Fruit nearly ½ in. in diameter, purple. Va. to Mex. Hardy from zone* 5 southward.

**brevipedunculata.** A stout, vigorous vine. Leaves simple,* more or less three-lobed, about 5 in. wide, the lobes coarsely toothed. Fruit pale blue at first, dark blue when ripe, about ¼ in. in diameter. China. Hardy from zone* 3 southward. Sometimes known as *A. heterophylla*.

**japonica.** A tuberous-rooted, graceful vine with shining foliage. Leaves compound, with 3-5 leaflets which may be cut nearly to the middle, the terminal leaflet much larger than the others. Fruit blue, about ¼ in. in diameter, faintly dotted. Northeastern As. Hardy from zone* 4 southward. See Wall-top Tumblers at VINES.

*AMPLEXICAULIS, -e* (am-plecks-i-call'is). Stem-clasping.

*AMPLEXIFOLIA, -us, -um* (am-plecks-i-foe'li-a). Leaf-clasping.

**AMSONIA** (am-sown'i-a). A few herbs, the ones below American, the rest Asiatic, belonging to the Apocynaceae, and sometimes grown for ornament. Leaves alternate,* without marginal teeth. Flowers small, funnel-shaped, the lobes long and slender, usually pale blue and in terminal branched clusters. Pods (follicles*) 2, long, slender, and with many seeds. (Named for Dr. Amson, an 18th-century Virginian physician.)

Amsonias are of easy culture in any ordinary garden soil. They are perennials, easily divided in spring or fall.

**tabernaemontana.** A bushy perennial up to 2 ft. Leaves taper-pointed, narrow, about 4 in. long. Flowers hairy on the outside, in a dense cluster, but each one scarcely ¼ in. long. N.J. to Tex. Grow in a cool, moist place. Often sold as *A. salicifolia*.

**texana.** Not over 2 ft. high, the leaves ovalish, about 2½ in. long. Flowers about ½ in. long, smooth on the outside. Tex. and Okla. Will stand drier and more open sites than *A. tabernaemontana*.

**AMUR CORK-TREE** = *Phellodendron amurense*.

*AMURENSIS, -e* (a-moor-en'sis). From Amur, Soviet Russia.

**AMUR PRIVET** = *Ligustrum amurense*. See PRIVET.

**AMYGDALACEAE.** See ROSACEAE.

*AMYGDALINA, -us, -um* (a-mig-da-ly'na). Almond-like.

**AMYGDALUS** (a-mig'da-lus). A very important genus of trees (rarely shrubs) of the rose family. It is of the greatest interest to all gardeners because it contains both the peach and the almond which, by some are considered to belong to the closely related genus *Prunus* (which see). Leaves alternate,* always toothed. Flowers of 5 petals (except in double-flowered hort. varieties), stalkless or nearly so, and blooming before the leaves unfold. Fruit fleshy, practically always fuzzy as in the peach, the stone pitted or smooth. (*Amygdalus* is the classical name of the almond.)

See ALMOND and PEACH for the hort. varieties and culture of these crops. *A. davidiana* is an ornamental tree with inedible fruit. It has no special soil requirements.

**communis.** Almond (which see for cult.). A medium-sized tree scarcely ever exceeding 25 ft., the bark gray. Leaves oval-lance-shaped, about 4 in. long, finely toothed. Flowers (in the fruiting trees) about 1½ in. wide, pink. Fruit oblong, 1½ in. long, its stone yielding the edible kernels (almonds). Asia. Because of its showy flowers the tree has many hort. varieties, some white and some double-flowered. The latter bear inedible fruit and are often called flowering almond, a name, however, also applied to *Prunus glandulosa* and *P. triloba*.

**davidiana.** An ornamental tree, closely related to the peach, and differing only in technical characters. Leaves finely toothed, the stalks sticky. Flowers pink, about ¾ in. across, usually solitary, blooming in March or April. Fruit round, inedible, yellow. China. Hardy from zone* 4 southward.

**nana.** See PRUNUS NANA.

**persica.** Peach. Not over 25 ft. high and a short-lived tree. Leaves lance-oblong, narrowly tapering at the tip, about 5 in. long, finely toothed. Flowers pink, usually solitary, very short-stalked or stalkless, blooming well before the leaves unfold. The fruit is the familiar peach (which see for hort. varieties and culture). China, but long cult. in Persia and once thought to have originated there.

There are many ornamental hort. varieties of the peach, grown only for their superb bloom. Some have purple foliage, others double flowers, and white or red forms are also known. Even striped flowers are offered, and as to habit, trees occasionally have weeping branches or a pyramidal outline. Some of them are called flowering peach.

**ANACARDIACEAE** (a-na-kar-di-a'see-ee). The sumac or mango family comprises nearly all tropical shrubs, trees, or vines. A few of the 60 genera and about 400 species, however, reach the temperate zone, especially *Rhus* (sumac and poison ivy) and *Cotinus* (smoke-tree). Leaves alternate,* simple* and often evergreen, or compound* and with many leaflets. Flowers often imperfect,* and in the pistachio (see PISTACIA) lacking even petals. Fruit a drupe* but differing widely, relatively large and fleshy in the mango and the genera *Spondias* and *Pleiogynium*, usually somewhat dry and much smaller in *Rhus*, *Schinus* and *Lithraea*. A peculiar fruit is the kidney-shaped one of *Anacardicum* (the cashew). Nearly all the plants have resinous bark.

All the hort. genera are tropical except *Rhus*, *Cotinus*, and possibly *Schinus* (the pepper-tree of Calif.). The mango is much the most important genus.

Technical flower characters: Calyx 3-7 cleft. Stamens as many as the petals or twice as many (5 in *Pistacia*). Ovary mostly 1-celled, rarely 3-5-celled, a single ovule in each cell.

*ANACARDIOIDES* (a-na-kar-di-oy'deez; but see OïDES). Resembling the cashew (*Anacardium*).

**ANACARDIUM** (a-na-kar'di-um). A tropical American genus of shrubs and trees of the sumac family, of garden interest only because it contains the cashew. It is an evergreen tree with simple* rather leathery leaves and many small flowers in terminal clusters. Fruit fleshy, red or yellow, technically part of the receptacle* and commonly called cashew-apple in the tropics. It is about 2½ in. long. The kidney-shaped nut (the true fruit) contains the edible kernel, which, when roasted, is the cashew-nut of commerce. (From Greek, heart-like, in allusion to the shape of the cashew-apple.)

Can be cult. outdoors only in zone* 9, but easily grown there as it appears to need no special soil conditions. It is propagated by seed or by budding. An irritating or poisonous oil in the shell of the nut makes harvesting the nuts a dreadful task. Even the smoke from the burning shells is irritating.

**occidentale.** Cashew. Not over 40 ft. high. Leaves 4-9 in. long, 2-3½ in. wide. Flowers fragrant, yellowish-pink. "Fruit" (the cashew-apple) more or less heart-shaped, neither edible nor safe when raw. The true fruit, the cashew-nut, must also be roasted before it is edible.

**ANACHARIS.** See ELODEA.

**ANAGALLIS** (a-na-gal'lis). The pimpernels are rather weedy, mostly prostrate herbs, family Primulaceae, comprising perhaps 25 widely distributed species, only two of which are of garden interest. Leaves opposite* or in whorls,* without marginal teeth. Flowers small, mostly solitary in the leaf-axils,* short-stalked, the corolla bell-shaped, its 5 lobes somewhat spreading. Fruit dry (a capsule*), splitting in a circle. (From Greek for delightful.)

There is no difficulty in growing pimpernels, but some difficulty in keeping the first species from becoming a pest. The second is a perennial* or biennial* and a worthy garden plant, propagated by spring-sown seeds or by division.*

**arvensis.** Scarlet pimpernel; called also poor-man's-weatherglass. A prostrate annual. See the list at WEEDS. Otherwise scarcely of garden interest.

**linifolia.** Erect, up to 18 in. high. Leaves narrowly lance-shaped, 1 in. long. Flowers blue, but reddish toward the base, especially on the outside, about ¾ in. wide. Southern Eu. June. There is a hort. variety with oval leaves and another with rose-purple flowers (*var.* **collina**). *A. linifolia* is sometimes sold as *A. grandiflora*.

*ANAGYROIDES* (a-na-ji-roy'deez; but see OïDES). Like a plant of the genus *Anagyrus*, which is scarcely of hort. interest.

**ANANAS.** See PINEAPPLE.

* Special articles on the subjects indicated by an asterisk (*) will be found at the words so marked.

**ANAPHALIS** (a-naff'a-lis). A large genus of wild everlastings, family Compositae, one of which is common as a weedy herb in America and is sometimes grown for its white, lasting flowers and gray, felty foliage. Leaves stalkless, alternate,* white-woolly throughout at first, ultimately dull green above. Flowers crowded in small heads, the bracts* of which are pearly-white, very numerous and fairly long-keeping. (*Anaphalis* is the Greek name for some everlasting, but lacks precise application to this genus.)

Easily grown in any sandy soil, and as easily transferred from the wild.

**margaritacea.** Pearly everlasting. Perennial erect herb to 20 in. high. Leaves narrow, pointed, about 5 in. long, without marginal teeth. Flower heads in a terminal cluster, the flowers all tubular, the heads about ¼ in. in diameter. For everlastings they are picked before maturity, dried, and by some, dyed various colors. Throughout the north temperate zone. June–July.

**ANASTATICA** (a-nas-tă'ti-ca). One extraordinary little desert plant of the mustard family grown for its remarkable ability to respond to alternate moisture and dryness. When moist it unfolds, revealing small, toothed leaves and minute white flowers. When dry or mature, its small branches curve inward, forming a tight ball which, in the deserts of Asia Minor, is driven by the wind. In this resting state it is often sold as a resurrection plant. (*Anastatica* is from the Greek signifying to make to stand [dryness].)

The only species is of easy culture in a warm, sunny place, preferably in a sandy soil. Sow seeds in spring.

**hierochuntica.** Rose-of-Jericho; called also, resurrection plant. When expanded, a fern-like herb perhaps a foot across, when dry, a tight ball the size of a small orange. In its dry state, it may be kept many years on a shelf but will expand and sometimes continue growth if put in water. Asia Minor. For other plants sometimes called resurrection plants, see POLYPODIUM POLYPODIOIDES and SELAGINELLA LEPIDOPHYLLA.

**ANATHERUM** = *Vetiveria*.

**ANATTO** = *Annatto*. See BIXA.

**ANCEPS** (an'seps). Two-headed or two-edged.

**ANCHISTEA.** See WOODWARDIA VIRGINICA.

**ANCHOR PLANT** = *Colletia cruciata*.

**ANCHUSA** (an-koo'sa). Alkanet; also called bugloss. A genus of perhaps 40 species of Old World herbs, family Boraginaceae, a few of which are grown for their showy flowers. The plants are all more or less hairy, and have alternate* leaves and leafy, usually one-sided, flower clusters not unlike (in some species) those of forget-me-not. Flowers small, trumpet-shaped, but somewhat closed at the throat. Fruit consists of 4 tiny nutlets. (From Greek for a paint for the skin, *i.e.* rouge.)

Anchusas are of easy cult. in any ordinary garden soil. Some of the hort. varieties of *A. azurea*, a perennial species, are popular plants for the border or for bedding. Easily propagated by spring-sown seeds or by division in spring or fall.

**angustifolia** = *Anchusa officinalis angustifolia*.

**azurea.** A stout perennial usually 3½ ft. high or more. Leaves oblongish or lance-shaped, 2–5 in. long, the base clasping or winged.* Flowers bright blue, about ½ in. wide, the cluster graceful and one-sided. Southern Eu. A widely cultivated plant grown for its splendid flowers. Among the best named forms are Dropmore (a lovely bright blue); Opal (sky blue); and Perry's (dark blue), all of which bloom in June and sometimes again in Sept. All are often sold as *Anchusa italica*.

**barrelieri.** A perennial, 1½–2 ft. high. Leaves ovalish or narrower. Flowers blue, the tube white, but with a yellow throat. Eu. and Asia Minor. Spring.

**capensis.** Cape forget-me-not. A biennial, usually less than 18 in. high. Leaves narrowly lance-shaped, about 2½ in. long. Flower buds red, the expanded flower blue, about ¼ in. wide. S. Africa. Used mostly as a pot plant. Not hardy in cold regions. There is a white-flowered variety.

**italica** = *Anchusa azurea*.

**myosotidiflora.** See BRUNNERA MACROPHYLLA.

**officinalis.** A biennial or sometimes a perennial, usually about 2 ft. high. Leaves lance-shaped, stalkless, about 4 in. long. Flowers blue, or purple or flesh-colored, in one-sided clusters and opening in pairs. Eu. June, and sometimes again in Sept. There is a narrow-leaved variety (*var.* angustifolia).

**ANDICOLA, -us, -um** (an-dick'o-la). From the Andes.

**ANDINA, -us, -um** (an-dy'na). From the Andes.

**ANDIRA** (an-dy'ra). Mostly tropical American trees of the pea family, the one below occasionally grown outdoors, only in zone* 9, rarely in greenhouses. Leaves alternate,* compound,* the leaflets arranged feather-fashion. Flowers pea-like, fragrant, rather showy, in terminal, branched clusters. Fruit a somewhat short, rather fleshy pod. (*Andira* is a Latinized form of a Brazilian name for these trees.)

If grown in the greenhouse use potting mixture* 4, giving plenty of heat and lots of water. The species below is chiefly of interest as the source of angelin. Propagated by cuttings over bottom-heat.

**inermis.** Angelin; called also cabbage tree. Not over 35 ft., usually less in cult. specimens. Leaflets in pairs, with an odd one at the tip, oval, or oval-lance-shaped. Flowers purple, the branched clusters rather short-stalked. Tropical America. Little grown outside of extreme southern Fla.

**ANDROMEDA** (an-drom'i-da). As here, and usually, restricted, a genus comprising only two species of the heath family. One of them, the bog rosemary or moorwort, is a bog shrub with evergreen leaves the margins of which are rolled. Flowers very small, pink, urn- or bell-shaped, in small drooping clusters. Fruit a capsule.* (Named for the mythological character of that name.)

Can be grown throughout the cooler parts of N.A. but only in very acid soils (*see* ACID AND ALKALI SOILS), preferably in the bog garden or in specially prepared soil in the rock garden. Extremely hardy northward. Easily propagated by division or by layering.

**polifolia.** Scarcely over 1 ft. high, with creeping roots and many small branches. Leaves oblong or narrower, about 1½ in. long. Flowers scarcely ¼ in. long, the clusters (umbels*) nodding. Throughout the north temperate zone. May–June. The only other species, a close relative, is confined to N.A. and scarcely in cult.

*Andromeda*, as a word, has suffered much from the attention of the name jugglers. The resulting confusion to gardeners is well illustrated by the following: All, and many others, were once included in *Andromeda*:

*Andromeda calyculata*. See CHAMAEDAPHNE CALYCULATA.
*Andromeda floribunda*. See PIERIS FLORIBUNDA.
*Andromeda japonica*. See PIERIS JAPONICA.
*Andromeda ligustrina*. See XOLISMA LIGUSTRINA.

**ANDROPOGON** (an-dro-pō'gon). Several wild species of grass, commonly called beard-grass, are properly included in the genus *Andropogon*, but they are of more agricultural than hort. interest. The name *Andropogon*, however, has been used for many other grasses of great interest to the gardener, and now included in *Holcus* (which see).

**ANDROSACE** (an-dros'a-see). The rock jasmines comprise a large genus of annual or perennial herbs, family Primulaceae, a few grown in rock gardens and not of particularly easy culture. They are low, often tufted plants, mostly from Eurasian mountains, nearly all with small basal leaves, often in rosettes.* Flowers resembling a miniature primrose, but the corolla constricted at the throat. (Greek name of uncertain application here.)

For the culture and uses of the species below *see* ROCK GARDEN.

**carnea.** Scarcely over 3 in. high; perennial. Leaves in rosettes,* very narrow, about ¾ in. long. Flowers about ⅓ in. wide, in clusters of 3–7, rose-pink or whitish, with a yellow eye. Mountains of Eu. May. A popular variety is *var.* brigantiaca, with white flowers.

**lactiflora.** An annual plant, erect, and usually up to 1 ft. Leaves lance-linear, about 2 in. long, mostly in rosettes.* Flowers white, about ½ in. wide, in rather large clusters. Siberia. June–July.

**lanuginosa.** Prostrate, white-silky, perennial herb. Some leaves basal, others on the short stem, about ¾ in. long. Flowers in a dense cluster, rose-pink, each flower not over ⅓ in. in diameter. Himalayas. June and July.

**sarmentosa.** A low perennial bearing runners that creep and may be 5 in. long. Leaves in rosettes,* silvery-white when young, about an inch long. Flowers rose-colored, about ¼ in. across in a profuse cluster that stands about 6 in. high. Himalayas. May.

**villosa.** A densely white-woolly perennial, scarcely 3 in. high. Leaves very small, in rosettes.* Flowers in umbels,* fragrant, rose-colored or white, the throat yellowish-red. Eurasia. June–July.

**vitaliana** = *Douglasia vitaliana*.

**ANDROSAEMIFOLIA, -us, -um** (an-dro-se-mi-fō'li-a). With leaves like the rock jasmine (*Androsace*).

**ANDROSTEPHIUM** (an-dro-stee'fi-um). A prairie genus of American bulbous plants of the lily family, one grown for its spring-blooming pretty blue flowers. Leaves all basal, linear or even grass-like. Flowers in a cluster (umbel*) at the end of a naked stalk. Corolla funnel-shaped,

---

* Special articles on the subjects indicated by an asterisk (*) will be found at the words so marked.

6-parted, with a crown at the throat. Fruit a capsule.* (Greek, referring to the crown in the flower.)

The only hort. species is of easy culture in a sandy soil. Plant the bulbs about 5 in. deep, and protect with a winter mulch of straw or manure. It is not hardy north of zone* 5, and not always so there, and may be increased by division of the bulbs.

**violaceum.** Slender perennial, scarcely up to 8 in. Leaves very narrow. Flowers blue, about 1 in. long, each of them stout-stalked, the naked stalk of the cluster about 6-8 in. high. Central U.S. May. Also known as *A. coeruleum*.

**ANEMONE** (correctly, a-nee-moe'nee; usually, a-nem'o-nee). Windflower or anemone. These most popular garden plants comprise a large genus of perennial herbs of the buttercup family, mostly confined to the north temperate zone. Leaves compound,* or if simple,* divided or dissected, mostly basal. Flowers usually showy, blooming in spring, summer and autumn, without petals, but with petal-like sepals.* The sepals are 5 in most species, but often (in hort. forms) much more numerous. Fruit a cluster of short-beaked achenes,* not so showy as in the closely related *Pulsatilla* (which see). (*Anemone* is the classical Greek name for these plants.)

For culture and uses *see* below.

**apennina.** A tuberous-rooted herb not over 9 in. high. Flowers solitary, about 1½ in. wide, azure-blue. Italy. March-April.

**blanda.** Tuberous-rooted and usually less than 6 in. high; otherwise resembling the last but with larger and darker blue flowers. Greece and Asia Minor.

**canadensis.** A native American species for the open border or wild garden and moderately showy. Perennial; hairy; not over 2 ft. high, its long-stalked 5-7-parted leaves basal, and above them a long flower stalk. Flowers few, about 1½ in. wide. Eastern N.A. June. Its creeping rootstocks make it an invasive plant; good for planting under shrubbery.

**coronaria.** Poppy anemone. This and *A. fulgens* and *A. hortensis* are the leading tuberous-rooted sorts for pot culture and much grown by florists. Roots irregularly swollen or tuberous, the plant essentially stemless. Leaves compound,* or twice-compound, the ultimate segments narrowly wedge-shaped. Flowers on a smooth stalk 10-18 in. high, solitary, poppy-like, red, blue, or white, or of many shades in hort. varieties, the best known of which are St. Brigid, The Bride and DeCaen. The outdoor cultivation of all of them is confined to Calif. or the South. Southern Eu. Some varieties are double-flowered.

**cylindrica.** Native American species resembling *A. canadensis*, but the flower greenish-white. Useful only for the wild garden. June. Its fruiting head is conspicuous, and more showy than the flowers.

**fulgens.** A French perennial, tuberous-rooted species, related to *A. coronaria* and differing from it chiefly in its brilliant scarlet or vermilion flowers which have conspicuous black stamens. Culture the same as for *A. coronaria*.

**globosa.** Western American species to 20 in. Flowers red or white or yellowish, always single, and about 1 in. wide. Suitable for the wild garden. May-Sept.

**hortensis.** The garden anemone, with other species. Related to *A. coronaria* and grown like it, differing only in having brownish stamens,* and in the leaves being only once-compound,* or even merely divided. Its flowers are rose-purple or red, and usually single. Southern Eu.

**hupehensis.** Related to *A. japonica*, but shorter and blooming about a month earlier. China. August to frost. See ROCK GARDEN.

**japonica.** Japanese anemone. One of the most popular garden perennials, and widely grown in the open border. It is a stout, branching plant, about 2½ ft. high, the leaves compound* but with only 3 leaflets. Flower stalks several, the flowers about 2½ in. wide, and, in some of the hort. varieties, of nearly every color except yellow and blue. Eastern As. There are scores of named hort. forms, many of which are double. All flower from Sept. to frost.

**multifida** = *Anemone globosa*.

**nemorosa.** European wood anemone. Resembles the common wood anemone of eastern N.A. (*A. quinquefolia*), but it has stouter flower stalks, and, in some forms, purplish flowers. See *A. quinquefolia*. May.

**patens** = *Pulsatilla patens*.

**pulsatilla** = *Pulsatilla vulgaris*.

**quinquefolia.** The common wood anemone of N.A. It is a delicate plant, useful only in the wild garden, and needs protection from too much sun and wind. Leaves compound,* the three leaflets wedge-shaped and deeply cut. Flowers solitary, white, about ¾ in. wide on very slender and weak stalks. May.

**sylvestris.** Snowdrop windflower. A beautiful Eurasian perennial suitable for the shaded border or wild garden. Basal leaves thrice cleft or divided, hairy below, the stem leaves long-stalked. Flowers one or two, pure white, about 2 in. wide, sometimes nodding, fragrant. May. See ROCK GARDEN.

**vernalis** = *Pulsatilla vernalis*.

### ANEMONE CULTURE

*Anemone japonica* and its hybrids are garden flowers making a grand display just before frost in Sept. and Oct. and will grow in almost any soil. They are easily propagated from root cuttings. Dig up a plant, chop off all roots, cut these into pieces 2 in. long, spread them on a flat or in a frame, cover with an inch of soil, and as they send up growths, pot singly, winter in cold frame and plant out in spring.

*Anemone coronaria*, *A. fulgens* and *A. hortensis*, the poppy anemones, are most popular and from these most of our present-day hybrids have originated, St. Brigid being the best known. The tubers can be bought at reasonable prices and should be planted in benches or flats in a rich loamy soil in the fall and allowed to grow along in a temperature of 40° to 45°. They come in the most gorgeous colors, the blue shades being particularly beautiful. They are easily raised from seed, and a wonderful assortment of colors in all the pastel shades is one of the desirable advantages in propagating by this means. Save seed from the largest flowers and the best colors, and when mature sow at once in good rich soil.

As the seed is very light a little care will be necessary to sow it evenly. Sow thinly and when the seedlings are large enough prick off into flats 2 in. apart each way, from which they can be transferred to permanent beds in a shady part of the greenhouse. Plant 4 in. apart and allow them to grow undisturbed until they flower. Do not try to hurry flowering by increasing the temperature as they are very impatient of heat and the temperature may be allowed to drop to 35° without any injury, in fact they enjoy it and will respond with better and larger flowers.

The outdoor species enjoy a rich loamy mixture of soil well drained, but partial shade at midday is helpful in keeping the young plants growing vigorously, and upon this will depend final results. Seedlings will start flowering early and keep up a continuous succession of bloom for many weeks if slightly shaded as the weather becomes warm.

If desired, the tuberous kinds can be taken up, well dried, and kept in dry sand for replanting in Sept. Or they may be left in the bench, and after a period of rest, by keeping absolutely dry, may be started again in Sept. for winter flowering. — A. J. L.

INSECT PESTS. Anemone is sometimes injured by a leaf tier (see CHRYSANTHEMUM) and by leaf miners.

**ANEMONE DAHLIA.** See DAHLIA.

*ANEMONEFLORA*, *-us*, *-um* (a-nem-o-ne-flow'ra). With flowers like an anemone.

**ANEMONELLA** (a-nem-o-nell'a), often called *Syndesmon*. A genus of N.A. woodland herbs closely related to *Anemone* and separated only by technical characters. The only species is **A. thalictroides**, the rue anemone, which can be grown best in a wind-sheltered, shady corner of the wild garden in rich woods soil. It is a delicate perennial with thrice-compound* leaves, the ultimate segments of which resemble those of the meadow rue (*Thalictrum*). Flowers several in a cluster (umbel*), white, about ¾ in. wide, fragile and on weak stalks. (*Anemonella* is a diminutive of *Anemone*.)

**ANEMONOPSIS** (a-nem-o-nop'sis). A Japanese genus of perennial herbs of the buttercup family, related to *Anemone* but differing in having both petals and petal-like sepals.* The only species, **A. macrophylla**, is a stout plant to 2½ ft. with thrice-compound* leaves, the segments of which are cut. Flowers in a loose cluster (raceme*), drooping, pale purple and about 1 in. wide. Suitable for the shady border or wild garden, in rich soil. Propagated by spring or autumn division of its roots. (*Anemonopsis* means *Anemone*-like.)

**ANEMONY** = *Anemone*.

**ANEMOPHILOUS** = Wind-pollinated.

**ANETHOIDES** (a-nee-thoy'deez, but *see* OÏDES). Like the dill (*Anethum*).

**ANETHUM.** See DILL.

**ANGELICA** (an-jell'i-ka). A very large genus of perennial, usually aromatic herbs of the carrot family, only the two following of much hort. interest. Leaves thrice-compound.* Flowers small, white or greenish, in a simple or

---

* Special articles on the subjects indicated by an asterisk (*) will be found at the words so marked.

compound, terminal umbel.* Fruit small, dry, usually aromatic. (Named for their supposed angelic virtue as medicinal plants.)

The first species is practically confined to herb gardens. For its uses and culture see HERB GARDENING. The second is a woodland plant of eastern U.S., useful only in the wild garden. Neither is showy.

**archangelica.** See HERB GARDENING. A stout plant, often 5 ft. high. Leaves twice-compound,* the ultimate segments 3-parted. Flowers greenish, in immense umbels.* Eurasia. July.

**curtisi.** Woods perennial up to 3½ ft. Leaves twice-compound,* the ultimate segments sharply and irregularly toothed. Umbels* 6 in. wide, the flowers white. Eastern U.S. Aug. This and one or two other wild species are occasionally grown in wild gardens.

**ANGELICA TREE.** See ARALIA; see also ZANTHOXYLUM AMERICANUM.

**ANGELIN** = *Andira inermis*.

**ANGELONIA** (an-jell-ō'ni-a). Over 20 species of herbs or low shrubs of the figwort family, only the following of garden interest, all tropical American and grown usually only in the greenhouse. Leaves prevailingly opposite.* Flowers blue or purplish in loose racemes.* Corolla prominently 2-lipped,* its tube almost none. Fruit a nearly round pod (capsule*) splitting by its two valves. (*Angelonia* is a Latinized version of a S.A. vernacular for another species.)

Grow in warm (65° or above) greenhouse in potting mixture* 4. Increased by seeds sown in early spring over bottom-heat, or by division of the roots. Outdoor cult. possible only in protected parts of zone* 9.

**grandiflora.** A sticky, perennial herb about 18 in. high. Leaves nearly without marginal teeth, lance-linear, about 3 in. long. Flowers blue or purplish-white, about ¾ in. wide, the cluster terminal and leafy. Brazil. May.

**ANGEL'S-TRUMPET.** See DATURA.

*ANGLICA, -us, -um* (ang'li-ka). English, or from England.

**ANGOPHORA** (an-goff'o-ra). An Australian genus of shrubs and trees of the myrtle family, the one below planted in southern Calif. and Fla. for ornament. The trees are closely related to *Eucalyptus* but have opposite* instead of alternate* leaves. Flowers white in terminal clusters. Fruit a woody pod (capsule*). (*Angophora* is Greek for bearing a vessel, in allusion to the fruit.)

Culture the same as *Eucalyptus*.

**lanceolata.** Gum-myrtle; also called orange gum and rusty gum. A medium-sized tree with smooth bark. Leaves broadly lance-shaped, about 5 in. long. Flowers white, rather showy. Little cultivated outside of Calif.

**ANGRAECUM** (an-gree'kum). An extraordinary group of tree-perching orchids from the Old World tropics, the one below sometimes cult. in greenhouses for its ivory-white flower which has a spur about 1 ft. long. The extreme length of this spur led Darwin to postulate some insect, then unknown, with a sucking apparatus long enough to reach the nectar at the base of the spur. Years after, such an insect was found. (*Angraecum* is the Latinized version of the Malayan vernacular angerek.)

For culture see the account of epiphytic orchid culture at ORCHIDS.

**sesquipedale.** Stem about 3 ft. long, clothed with two-ranked (distichous*) leaves 1 ft. long and about 2 in. wide. Flower about 5 in. wide, its petals and sepals nearly alike, the spur long and slender. There are usually 2-4 flowers in a cluster about the length of the leaves. Madagascar. Winter-blooming in the greenhouse.

*ANGUINA* (an-gwy'na). A species name derived from *anguis*, a serpent.

*ANGULARIS, -e* (an-gew-lar'is). Angled.

**ANGULAR LEAFSPOT.** See Diseases at CUCUMBER.

*ANGULATA, -us, -um* (an-gew-lay'ta). Angled.

*ANGURIA* (an-gew'ri-a). A specific name derived from a Greek word for a watermelon-like plant.

*ANGUSTA, -us, -um* (an-gus'ta). Narrow.

*ANGUSTIFOLIA, -us, -um* (an-gus-tee-fō'li-a). Narrow-leaved.

**ANIGOZANTHUS** (a-nig-o-zan'thus). A small genus of greenhouse herbs from Australia, family Amaryllidaceae, one grown for its greenish-red flowers. Rootstock fleshy but not bulbous. Leaves narrow and sword-shaped, mostly basal. Flowers in 1-sided, woolly clusters (racemes*), hairy inside, the tube long and flaring, slightly irregular. Fruit a capsule.* (Greek, an expanded flower, in allusion to the flaring corolla.)

Grow in cool greenhouse in potting mixture* 4. Propagated by division of its fleshy rootstocks, in spring. It needs less water during the winter season, but an ample supply during spring.

**manglesi.** Not over 3 ft. high, the stem red-woolly. Flowers about 3 in. long, the tube narrow, green at the base, red above, woolly. Usually flowers in May or June in the greenhouse. Little grown.

**ANIMAL INJURY.** Many small animals are injurious in the garden. Moles and pocket gophers destroy the roots and bulbs of plants; rabbits eat the tops; while rats and mice may do both. Slugs and snails eat the foliage and flowers.

MOLES. Moles are found on the Pacific Coast, and from the Atlantic west to about the one hundredth meridian, being absent from the intervening territory. They dig endless tunnels just beneath the surface, doing mechanical damage to the plant roots and drying out the fine feeding roots, in addition to feeding on the bulbs in a limited way.

Mole trap

Moles can best be trapped with choker, scissor-jaw, or harpoon traps. They travel their runways more or less regularly in search of food. If the runway is blocked, the animal will rebuild it exactly in its previous location, if not damaged beyond repair. The runway is opened and the trap set in a loose earth fill, the trigger being in such a position as to cause the animal to spring the trap during reconstruction operations. Some gardeners plant bulbs in wire baskets to prevent the ravages of moles.

MICE. Mice may construct small burrows or travel in those built by moles or pocket gophers. They eat succulent roots, cut and eat foliage and often completely girdle and kill large trees. Whenever serious damage occurs, the mice are usually so abundant that trapping is too slow, and poison must be used. There are ready-mixed poisons on the market, but a freshly mixed bait of rolled oats will usually give better results. The rolled oats should be slightly dampened with water or water and karo, and sprinkled with powdered strychnine alkaloid at the rate of one-eighth ounce of strychnine to two and one-half pounds of rolled oats. The bait should be stirred constantly while the strychnine is added. This should be dropped in mouse holes and scattered along their runways. It is best used in clear weather in fall and early winter.

Two quarts of sweet potatoes cut into one-half-inch cubes and sprinkled with a mixture of one-eighth ounce of powdered strychnine and one-eighth ounce of baking soda, makes a good summer bait. The strychnine and soda mixture should be sprinkled over the cut baits with a pepper shaker or similar instrument, stirring constantly to insure an even distribution. Use while fresh, dropping pieces in the small burrows.

---

* Special articles on the subjects indicated by an asterisk (*) will be found at the words so marked.

RATS. Rats are difficult animals to combat and constant warfare is necessary. All old piles of boards and other rubbish should be cleaned up. Following this, traps and poisons should be used alternately or together until the rats are under control.

The inexpensive wooden-base guillotine traps are as good as any. Baits should be changed frequently and the traps moved to new locations every few nights. There are many excellent rat poisons on the market which will give good results for a time, if used according to the directions on the package. It is advisable to avoid those containing phosphorus, particularly about buildings, because of the fire hazard. The safest of all is red squill, which is poisonous to rats and mice, but comparatively harmless to other forms of life. Better results will generally be obtained by buying the powdered squill, taking care to get one that has been standardized to a definite toxic strength. In this form it can be used on different baits such as hamburger, white-meated fish, peanut-butter, vegetables, and fruits. It is often advisable to feed the rats for several days on untreated bait to accustom them to finding that food at a certain place. When a number of them begin to feed freely, poisoned bait may be placed and a kill obtained quickly. Squill should not be used regularly, an interval of a week or more between exposures giving better results. If necessary to poison more frequently, alternate with some other material such as arsenic on a different bait.

RABBITS. Rabbits sometimes cause serious loss by eating the tops of valuable plants. Usually only a few animals are involved, and a No. 0 steel trap, set at the point where the animals are feeding, will generally catch the culprits. Box traps, baited with a bit of carrot or lettuce, may be substituted. Where the rabbits are too numerous to be dealt with in this fashion, split carrots sprinkled with powdered strychnine at the rate of one-eighth ounce to two pounds of carrots may be placed in the garden where the damage is occurring, or along the trails leading into it. These trails will inevitably appear if there are numbers of rabbits.

POCKET GOPHERS. Pocket gophers, like moles, make extensive underground tunnels which cause mechanical injury to roots and bulbs. In addition the gophers eat the roots of a wide variety of bulbs, herbaceous plants, shrubs, and trees. These animals are found throughout the territory west of the Mississippi and in the Gulf states to and including Florida. They are easily caught by setting a trap in the laterals to the surface mounds, or a pair of them in the main runway. After the traps are set and inserted, the runway may be left open or only partially closed, the trap being designed to catch the animal as it brings earth to plug the opening.

Practical trap for pocket gophers or for moles

The workings of gophers superficially resemble those of moles, but the tunnels are usually deeper, and the mounds decidedly fan-shaped and obviously built from one side, in contrast to the conical mounds of the mole, which are built from the center.

SLUGS AND SNAILS. These persistent garden pests require constant effort if control is obtained. Cleaning up rubbish, rotting vegetation, and weeds, will help in keeping down infestation.

A poison bait consisting of one ounce of calcium arsenate to sixteen ounces of bran, thoroughly mixed together dry and then moistened with barely enough water to cause the bran to stick together, has been found effective. This should be scattered evenly over the surface of the ground in the infested areas.

SQUIRRELS, including the red, gray and fox squirrels of the East and the silver-gray squirrel of the West, occasionally damage ornamental trees by gnawing the bark from the newer growth. Conifers are most frequently attacked and the damage usually occurs in late winter or early spring when other food becomes scarce. At such times the bark from the leader and topmost branches is stripped off and the cambium layer eaten off, the discarded outer bark being allowed to fall to the ground.

Shooting or trapping the offending individuals is the only sure remedy, though providing food supplies of corn, wheat, nuts, etc., will sometimes reduce the damage. For injurious birds, see BIRDS. — I. N. G.

**ANIMAL MATTER.** *See* MANURE.

**ANIMATED OAT** = *Avena sterilis.*

*ANISATA, -us, -um* (a-ni-say'ta). Anise-scented.

**ANISE.** The only garden species of the genus **Pimpinella** (pim-pi-nell'a), which comprises many perennial or annual herbs of the carrot family, from the north temperate zone, is the one below, yielding anise. They have twice- or thrice-compound* leaves, the ultimate segments mostly toothed. Flowers small, in a compound umbel.* (*Pimpinella* is possibly a confusion for bi-pinnata; uncertainly applied here.)

P. **anisum.** The common anise. Annual, not over 2 ft. high, with long-stalked basal leaves, and shorter-stalked stem leaves. Flowers yellowish-white, the cluster loose. Southern Eu. and Egypt. For culture and uses see HERB GARDENING. For the star anise see ILLICIUM.

**ANISUM.** An old word for anise; also, apparently, for dill.

**ANNATTO** = *Bixa orellana.*

**ANNATTO FAMILY.** The Bixaceae. *See* BIXA.

**ANNONA** (a-nō'na). A large genus of tropical trees, family Annonaceae. The species below yield fruits of secondary importance, all of them from tropical America, and little known in northern markets, because they cannot be shipped when fresh. Leaves alternate,* without marginal teeth. Flowers usually solitary or in clusters, the calyx tubular, the 6 separate petals in two series of three. Fruit large, fleshy, technically a syncarp.* (*Annona* is a Latinized version of some vernacular name for these trees.)

Of the species below, the cherimoya (*A. cherimola*) is by far the most important. Originally Peruvian, it is grown to a limited extent in southern Fla., and from Santa Barbara southward in Calif. It matures in late summer, and is quite variable in size and texture. The most favored form has the fruit beset with numerous tubercles, the pulp is white, aromatic and custard-like in texture. It must be eaten fresh.

The cherimoya can be grown in southern Fla., but requires greater elevations than are found there. It can survive light frosts, but bears poorly over most of the Cherimoya region in Fla. which extends from about Dade Co. southward. Plants raised from seedlings rarely come true, and the best plan is to cleft-graft or shield-bud desirable varieties upon the hardier stock of *Annona squamosa*, *glabra* or *reticulata*, all of which are also grown in Fla.

Trees should be spaced 25 × 25 ft. apart and yield some fruit after the fourth or fifth year. In Fla. they never bear as well as in tropical uplands.

**cherimola.** Cherimoya. Medium-sized tree, up to 25 ft., usually spreading, deciduous for part of the year. Leaves ovalish, 3-6 in. long, hairy below, dull green above. Flowers yellowish, fragrant, about 1 in. long. Fruit egg- or heart-shaped, varying from 4 ounces to over a pound, smooth in some, but tuberculate in the best varieties. Andes of Peru.

**glabra.** Pond-apple. Evergreen tree to 40 ft. Leaves more or less oblong, about 7 in. long. Flowers yellowish-red, about 1 in. long. Fruit ovoid, smooth, about 4 in. long. Tropical America. Fruit of little value, and the tree is useful chiefly as a stock for the cherimoya.

**muricata.** Soursop, also called guanabana. A tropical American evergreen tree scarcely exceeding 20 ft. in height. Leaves elliptic, about 5 in. long. Flowers yellow. Fruit ovoid, nearly 8 in. long, green and spiny on the outside. The flesh is white, juicy and tart, and used mostly for ices

---

* Special articles on the subjects indicated by an asterisk (*) will be found at the words so marked.

or beverages. The tree is also used as grafting stock for the cherimoya. Hardy only in zone* 9.

**reticulata.** Custard-apple, called also bullock's-heart. A deciduous or partly evergreen tree up to 30 ft. Leaves oblongish, about 8 in. long. Flowers yellowish. Fruit heart-shaped, up to 8 in. long, smooth, but marked with depressed lines. Its flesh is far inferior to cherimoya. Hardy only in zone* 9.

**squamosa.** Sweetsop, called also sugar-apple. A deciduous tree with bluish-gray, thin leaves 3–6 in. long. Flowers greenish-yellow. Fruit cone- or heart-shaped, yellowish-green, about 3 in. long, much broken up by its separable divisions (carpels). The flesh is sweet, custard-like, and much liked, but it is very perishable. Hardy only in zone* 9 and protected places in zone* 8.

**ANNONACEAE** (a-no-nay'see-ee). The custard-apple family contains about 45 genera and possibly 800 species of mostly tropical shrubs, vines and trees (one of ours hardy and native), widely cultivated for their often edible fruit in tropical and warm regions. They have alternate* leaves, without marginal teeth, rather inconspicuous flowers with mostly 6 petals. Fruit fleshy and consisting of an aggregation of carpels, or a berry, or even dry and inedible.

The custard-apple family is of little hort. importance in the U.S., and the only genera in this book are *Annona* (custard-apple), *Artabotrys*, *Asimina* (the papaw of eastern N.A.), and *Cananga* (ylang-ylang).

Technical flower characters: Sepals 3, or the calyx with 3 lobes; petals 6, their edges meeting but not overlapping; stamens numerous; carpels usually many, mostly distinct and separate.

*ANNUA, -us, -um* (an'new-a). Annual (which see).

**ANNUAL.** A plant which germinates, grows, flowers, fruits and dies within a single year. For the many garden plants treated as ANNUALS, see that term. See, also, BIENNIAL and PERENNIAL.

**ANNUAL BABY'S-BREATH** = *Gypsophila elegans*.

**ANNUAL CANDYTUFT** = *Iberis amara* and *I. umbellata*. See CANDYTUFT.

**ANNUAL MARJORAM** = sweet marjoram.

**ANNUAL PHLOX** = *Phlox drummondi*.

**ANNUALS.** No flower garden is complete without annuals. Their convenience, ease of handling and variety of color make them of the greatest use for bedding, for mixing in the perennial border, for following spring bulbs, and often they provide the best supply of cut flowers for the house. If they are chiefly to be used for the latter purpose, and a large supply is needed, it is often better to sow seed in rows as one does vegetables. Such a cutting garden will relieve the flower border which constant picking would otherwise sadly deplete of color.

Annuals are not in fact always annual* plants. Some biennials,* and a number of perennials,* will bloom from seed the first year, just as true annuals must, of course, always do. A few of the plants mentioned below are either biennials* or perennials* that bloom the first year from seed. For practical garden purposes, they are classed as annuals.

While annuals are a boon to both amateur and professional gardeners, they require some study as to their colors, their adaptability to the place you wish to plant them, and above all their suitability to your climate.

The last requirement is, of course, the most important. If you live in zone* 4 or north of it some annuals will be unable to bloom in the period after it is safe to sow them outdoors. Such are often called tender annuals, a common example being the petunia. Others, somewhat more hardy, but often started in the hotbed or greenhouse, are classed as half-hardy annuals. Tender and half-hardy annuals are scarcely very definite categories, but together they are properly set apart from ordinary annuals, the seed of which is sown in the place they are to grow.

These two groups are so definite and important that in all the lists below those needing to be started before outdoor planting (*i.e.* tender and half-hardy annuals) will be marked with a T. All others should be sown where they are to grow.

**TENDER ANNUALS.** Starting tender (and half-hardy) annuals in the greenhouse, hotbed, or in the kitchen window is almost exactly the same as raising tomato plants from seed (*see* TOMATO). In their need for warmth, in getting stocky plants, in planning their sowing so as to provide outdoor planting material at the proper time, the early culture of these annuals must approximate that of the tomato.

If you read the tomato article carefully, there is no need to repeat its directions here. The only variations from that procedure are that annual flower seeds should only just be covered with soil (instead of ¼ in. deep). You should pot up more seedlings than you think you need at first in order to replace failures. And, most important of all, do not try to beat the weather by setting out tender annuals until soil and air temperatures are definitely those of summer. Most tomato growers will gamble on this, but no grower of tender annuals needs to. Wait for settled warm weather.

When this has arrived, the plants may be knocked out of their pots or boxes and planted where desired. If you can choose a dull instead of a sunny day, do so, and a quiet rather than windy one. If neither can be done, see that each plant gets a cupful of water. In any case, disturb the roots as little as possible. A simple way to avoid this is to thoroughly water the pots the night before they are planted. The moist soil of such plants will hold the shape of the pot, and can be plunged in the ground with little or no root disturbance.

**HARDY ANNUALS.** These should always be sown directly where they are to grow. If they come up too thick, the plants can easily be thinned out to the required spacing, which depends, of course, upon the size of each plant. If you are unfamiliar with any of those in the lists, look them up elsewhere in this book. All are entered under the names used in the lists.

If, for some special purpose, you wish the color effect of a hardy annual before its normal blooming season, you can easily get it by treating it as a tender annual (*see* above). Some gardeners do this regularly in order to extend the normal blooming period of some favorite. In which case some are sown outdoors, while others, weeks before, have been raised in pots and planted outdoors at the time (or before or after) seed is sown.

The seeds of some annuals are so small that it is difficult to plant them properly. These may easily be handled by mixing the seed with about five times its bulk of fine sand. Stir the mixture thoroughly, then seed-and-sand may easily be planted together and the seeds properly spaced.

Even with this precaution the plants will be too thick at first. Begin thinning, except as noted below, as soon as the seedlings are three or four inches high, transplanting the thinned seedlings to other sites. The plants should be so spaced finally that they have a chance for proper development.

A few annuals, however, seem to prefer a bit of crowding and are best not thinned. In the list below they are Nos. 14, 15, 16, 20, 21, 24, 30, 33, 35, 36, 56, 62, 64 and 71.

### THE SEVENTY-FIVE BEST ANNUALS

In the body of THE GARDEN DICTIONARY there are described probably four hundred plants that are grown as annuals. Not all of them are of equal hort. merit, and many of them are grown only for special purposes. From them the list below has been selected with three things in mind: their value for color or foliage; their relative ease of growing; and their availability. All of them will be found in any good seed catalog.

They are here listed under the names used in the body of the DICTIONARY and should always be referred to there for additional information. A few seedsmen's names that differ from the ones here used are inserted at their proper vocabulary entry in the body of the book and cross-referenced to the correct name.

---

* Special articles on the subjects indicated by an asterisk (*) will be found at the words so marked.

AN ANNUAL GARDEN IN MASSACHUSETTS

# ANNUALS

Throughout this and subsequent lists the following symbols are used:
† = Useful for cutting.
T = Tender or half-hardy annuals (*see* above for cultural notes). All others, which are hardy annuals, should be sown where they are to grow.

| | | Height in Inches | Prevailing Color |
|---|---|---|---|
| 1. | †Ageratum T | 4–9 | Blue |
| 2. | Amaranthus caudatus (Love-lies-bleeding) | 36–50 | Red (foliage) |
| 3. | Amaranthus tricolor (Joseph's-coat) | 12–36 | Red (foliage) |
| 4. | Ammobium alatum grandiflorum (Winged everlasting) | 20–36 | White |
| 5. | †Arctotis breviscapa T | low | Orange |
| 6. | †Arctotis stoechadifolia T (African daisy) | 30–48 | Blue and yellow |
| 7. | Argemone grandiflora | 24–36 | Yellow |
| 8. | Brachycome iberidifolia T (Swan River daisy) | 8–18 | Various |
| 9. | Browallia speciosa major | 8–12 | Blue |
| 10. | †Calendula officinalis T (Pot marigold) | 8–20 | Yellow and orange |
| 11. | †Callistephus chinensis T (China aster) | 8–18 | Various (no yellow) |
| 12. | †Candytuft (Iberis, annual species) | 6 | Various |
| 13. | Castor-oil plant T (Ricinus communis) | 48–150 | Foliage plant |
| 14. | †Centaurea cyanus (Cornflower) | 12–24 | Blue |
| 15. | Centaurea moschata (Sweet sultan) | 18–24 | Various |
| 16. | †Clarkia elegans | 18–36 | Various |
| 17. | Cleome spinosa (Spiderflower) | 48–60 | Rose-purple |
| 18. | †Coreopsis atkinsoniana | 24–48 | Brown-purple |
| 19. | †Coreopsis drummondi T (Golden-wave) | 12–24 | Yellow |
| 20. | †Coreopsis stillmani T | 12–18 | Golden |
| 21. | †Coreopsis tinctoria T (Golden coreopsis) | 12–36 | Yellow |
| 22. | †Cosmos T | 60–100 | Various |
| 23. | Cynoglossum amabile (Chinese forget-me-not) | 18–24 | Blue |
| 24. | †Delphinium ajacis (Rocket larkspur) | 12–24 | Various |
| 25. | †Delphinium consolida (Field larkspur) | 12–18 | Blue |
| 26. | †Dianthus chinensis (China pink) | 12–18 | Various |
| 27. | Dimorphotheca annua T (Cape marigold) | 8–14 | Various |
| 28. | †Eschscholtzia californica (California poppy) | 12–20 | Yellow |
| 29. | Euphorbia marginata (Snow-on-the-mountain) | 8–12 | White |
| 30. | Forget-me-not (Myosotis, annual species) | 6–9 | Blue |
| 31. | †Gaillardia pulchella (Blanket-flower) | 12–20 | Red and yellow |
| 32. | Gilia capitata | 18–24 | Blue and white |
| 33. | †Godetia amoena T (Farewell-to-spring) | 12–30 | Various |
| 34. | †Gomphrena globosa T (Globe amaranth) | 8–12 | Various |
| 35. | †Gypsophila elegans grandiflora (Annual baby's-breath) | 10–18 | Various |
| 36. | †Gypsophila muralis | 6–8 | Pink |
| 37. | †Helichrysum bracteatum T (Strawflower) | 24–36 | Red and orange |
| 38. | Hollyhock T (Althaea rosea) | 48–60 | White and pink |
| 39. | †Hunnemannia fumariaefolia (Mexican tulip-poppy) | 12–20 | Golden |
| 40. | Impatiens balsamina T (Garden balsam) | 18–30 | Various |
| 41. | Kochia scoparia T (Summer cypress) | 20–36 | Yellow and red |
| 42. | Lathyrus odoratus T (Sweet pea) | 24–60 | All |
| 43. | Lavatera trimestris splendens | 24–40 | Pink |
| 44. | †Linum grandiflorum (Flowering flax) | 12–24 | Red |
| 45. | Lobelia erinus T (Edging lobelia) | low | Blue |
| 46. | Lychnis coeli-rosa (Rose-of-heaven) | 12–15 | Pink |
| 47. | †Marigold T (Tagetes) | 15–24 | Yellow and red |
| 48. | †Mathiola bicornis (Evening stock) | low | Purple-black |
| 49. | †Mathiola incana annua (Ten-weeks stock) | 12–20 | Various |
| 50. | †Mignonette (Reseda) | low | Yellow-green |
| 51. | Mirabilis jalapa T (Four-o'clock) | 14–30 | Various |
| 52. | †Nasturtium (Tropaeolum) | 7–15 | Yellow-red |
| 53. | †Nemesia strumosa suttoni T | 8–18 | Various |
| 54. | Nemophila insignis (Baby blue-eyes) | 6 | Blue and white |
| 55. | †Nicotiana alata grandiflora (Jasmine tobacco) | 24–40 | White |
| 56. | †Nigella damascena (Love-in-a-mist) | 12–15 | Blue and white |
| 57. | Petunia hybrida T | 7–12 | Various |
| 58. | †Phlox drummondi T | 9–18 | Various |
| 59. | Poppy (Papaver, annual species) | 12–20 | All but blue |
| 60. | Portulaca grandiflora (Rose moss) | low | Red and yellow |
| 61. | †Rudbeckia bicolor superba (Erfurt coneflower) | 12–20 | Yellow |
| 62. | Salpiglossis sinuata T | 18–30 | Various |
| 63. | Salvia splendens T (Scarlet sage) | 18–30 | Scarlet |
| 64. | †Scabiosa atropurpurea T (Sweet scabious) | 18–24 | Various |
| 65. | †Schizanthus retusus T | 18–24 | Rose-pink |
| 66. | †Schizanthus wisetonensis T | 36–50 | Various |
| 67. | Silene pendula | 6–10 | Various |
| 68. | †Snapdragon T (Antirrhinum) | 6–36 | All |
| 69. | Sunflower (Helianthus) | 48–120 | Yellow |
| 70. | Sweet alyssum (Lobularia maritima) | 6–12 | White |
| 71. | †Trachymene coerulea T (Blue lace-flower) | 18–30 | Blue |
| 72. | Venidium fastuosum T | 18–30 | Orange |
| 73. | Verbena hortensis T (Garden verbena) | low | All |
| 74. | Vinca rosea T (Madagascar periwinkle) | 12–18 | White and rose |
| 75. | †Zinnia elegans T (Youth-and-old-age) | 18–30 | All but blue |

Thoughtful gardeners will note the absence in this list of such plants as canna, chrysanthemum, pansy, dahlia, gladiolus and coleus, all of which are often treated as annuals, and some of them have annual species. For their culture and uses *see* the body of THE GARDEN DICTIONARY. For several annual vines, omitted from the list, *see* VINES.

How one uses the annuals in the above list is almost wholly a matter of personal taste in flower form and color. Conveniently enough, most of them are of average height, ranging from 9 to 24 in. A few much taller ones must be placed at the back of the bed or border. Numbers 13, 17, 22, 38, and 69 are the tallest of the lot, varying from 48–150 in. high.

Slightly less tall (30–50 in.) are numbers 2, 6, 42, and 66.

The annuals so low or even prostrate that they may conveniently be used for ground cover or for edging are numbers 45, 50, 60, 73, and forms of 30. Somewhat higher plants (4–12 in.) are numbers: 1, 5, 9, 12, 36, 48, and 54.

## TIME OF BLOOMING

Annuals are primarily plants that bloom in July and August over most of the country. Almost any of them will bloom in the south or in the warm sections of Calif. in other months, depending upon the time of planting them.

For the northern gardener who needs to extend his show of annual color, it is often necessary to plant varieties that bloom earlier and later than the average run of annual flowers. Here are the lists:

### Early-Blooming Annuals

(In the north usually in May or early June, often continuing later. For the numbers see the list.)

Cornflower (14). Sweet sultan (15). Forget-me-not (30). Sweet pea (42). *Nemesia strumosa suttoni* (53). Love-in-a-mist (56).

### Late-Blooming Annuals

(Flowering in summer but continuing to bloom until overtaken by frost.)

Numbers 5, 6, 10, 11, 12, 16, 21, 22, 23, 28, 29, 33, 39, 49, 58, 63, 69.

Most of the other annuals in the general list are midsummer bloomers not to be expected much before July first nor after September 15, although the season and locality may vary both dates.

---

\* Special articles on the subjects indicated by an asterisk (\*) will be found at the words so marked.

### Color

The variety of color among annuals is infinite. Many species, due to the skill of horticulturists, are now found in many other colors than their original one. Such are marked "various" or "all" in the list above.

A few annuals, however, come usually only in one definite color and, for convenience, they may be grouped thus:

WHITE: 4, 29, 70.
BLUE: 9, 71.
RED OR PINK: 2, 3, 36, 43, 44, 46, 63, 65.
YELLOW OR ORANGE: 5, 19, 20, 21, 28, 39, 69.

A few of the outstanding annuals that come in a wide range of colors will be found in numbers: 11, 12, 14, 15, 24, 42, 49, 53, 57, 58, 59, 60, 62, 64, 67, 68, 73, and 75.

### Some Secondary Annuals

Besides the seventy-five leading annuals listed above there are many others of nearly equal worth. Some of these, all of which are in the trade and can be had from some of the larger dealers, are here listed. Further information about them will be found in the body of the DICTIONARY under the names given below:

T = tender or half-hardy annual. For treatment *see* above.
All others are hardy and should be sown where needed.

IN VARIOUS COLORS: *Browallia americana, Datura metel* T, *Downingia pulchella, Gilia tricolor, Godetia grandiflora* T, *Linanthus parviflorus, Lupinus hartwegi, Saponaria vaccaria, Senecio elegans* T, *Silene armeria,* and *Zaluzianskya capensis* T.

ROSE-PINK OR RED: *Abronia umbellata grandiflora* T, *Adonis, Helipterum roseum* T, *Linaria maroccana* T, *Malope trifida rosea, Nicotiana sanderae* T, *Polygonum orientale.*

YELLOW AND ORANGE: *Arnebia cornuta, Coreopsis coronata* T, *Emilia sagittata lutea, Gamolepis tagetes* T, *Helipterum angustifolium* T, *H. manglesi, Layia elegans, Mentzelia lindleyi, Sanvitalia procumbens, Thelesperma burridgeanum, Ursinia anethoides* T, and *Venidium decurrens* T.

ORANGE-RED: *Collomia biflora.*

WHITE OR GREENISH-WHITE: *Artemisia sacrorum viride, Limnanthes douglasi.*

BLUE, VIOLET OR LILAC: *Campanula drabifolia, C. ramosissima, Collinsia bicolor, Dracocephalum moldavica, Felicia bergeriana, Heliophila leptophylla* T, *Ionopsidium acaule* T, *Lupinus texensis, Nicandra physalodes* T, *Nolana atriplicifolia* T, *Phacelia campanularia, P. tanacetifolia, P. viscida, P. whitlavia, Sedum caeruleum, Torenia fournieri* T.

Even this supplementary list by no means exhausts the roll of worthwhile annuals. For others, in genera not heretofore mentioned, *see*: ASPERULA, BAERIA, CALANDRINIA, DIASCIA, ECHIUM, ERYSIMUM, EUCHARIDIUM, GAZANIA, HEBENSTRETIA, HELIOTROPIUM, HIBISCUS, LASTHENIA, MALCOMIA, OXALIS, PODOLEPIS, SCHIZOPETALON, SPECULARIA, and TOLPIS.

**ANNUAL VINES.** *See* VINES.

**ANNUNCIATION LILY** = *Lilium candidum.*

**ANOMALA, -us, -um** (a-nom'a-la). Unusual or out of the ordinary. Also, of a species, of uncertain affinity or identity.

**ANTARCTICA, -us, -um** (ant-ark'ti-ka). From or near the Antarctic.

**ANTELOPE-BRUSH** = *Purshia tridentata.*

**ANTELOPE-HORNS** = *Asclepiadora decumbens.*

**ANTENNARIA** (an-ten-ar'i-a). A large genus of hort. unimportant, white-woolly herbs of the Compositae, very common as wild plants, and known as everlasting, cat's-foot and pussytoes. They have mostly basal leaves and small heads in loose clusters. Flowers all tubular, very minute, dirty-white, sometimes dried and kept for everlastings. (*Antennaria* is derived from antennae, in allusion to the resemblance of the pappus to the antennae of some insects.)

The species are all perennial, mostly somewhat weedy, and of the easiest culture in open, dry, sandy places. Others, besides *A. rhodantha,* are sometimes gathered from the wild, where they are common over much of the country. They spread so rapidly that they may become a nuisance.

rhodantha. Scarcely six in. high. Leaves spatula-shaped, about ¾ in. long. Flower heads about ½ in. long, the minute bracts* tipped with red. Wash. and Ore. Summer.

**ANTHEMIS** (an'them-is). A very large genus of Eurasian herbs, family Compositae, some cult. for ornament, some like the camomile for fragrant herbage, and a few are weeds. Leaves alternate,* often mostly basal, dissected or cut (in those below), generally strong-smelling. Flower heads with yellow or white rays and yellow disk flowers, not particularly showy except in *A. tinctoria.* (*Anthemis* is Greek for camomile.)

Easily grown in the open border from seeds or by division of the roots in spring or fall. Two plants often offered as *Anthemis* belong elsewhere. They are *A. aizoon* = *Achillea ageratifolia aizoon; A. arabica* = *Cladanthus arabicus.*

cotula. Mayweed. *See* list at WEEDS.
kelwayi. *See* ANTHEMIS TINCTORIA KELWAYI.
montana. A silky-hairy perennial herb, not over 15 in. high. Leaves much dissected. Ray flowers white. Summer. Eu.
nobilis. Camomile. Strong-smelling perennial herb up to 1 ft. Leaves dissected into fine, nearly thread-like segments. Ray flowers white. There is a double-flowered form and another (*var.* grandiflora) with larger, sometimes yellow flowers. For culture and uses *see* HERB GARDENING. For its use as an unusual grass substitute, *see* Lawn Mixtures at LAWN.
tinctoria. Golden marguerite; called also yellow camomile and oxeye camomile. The best garden plant of the genus. Perennial up to 3 ft. Leaves twice-cut, the segments oblongish, not dissected. Flower heads nearly 2 in. wide, golden-yellow. Summer. Eurasia. The *var.* kelwayi has dissected leaf segments and darker yellow flowers.

**ANTHEMOIDES** (an-them-oy'deez; but *see* OÏDES). Like a camomile (*Anthemis*).

**ANTHER.** The pollen-bearing part of a stamen. *See* FLOWER.

**ANTHERICUM** (an-ther'i-kum). A large genus of mostly African herbs of the lily family, only the following grown for its loose clusters of white flowers. Leaves narrow, strap-shaped, basal. Flowers small, white, in a long, loose, leafless cluster (raceme*), each flower nearly stalkless. Stamens* 6. Fruit a 3-celled pod. (*Anthericum* is Greek for flower hedge.)

The St. Bernard's-lily, the only commonly cult. species, is grown as a border plant in the South, elsewhere in the cool greenhouse. Use potting mixture* 4. Easily propagated by division of its rootstock.

liliago. St. Bernard's-lily. A European, unbranched, perennial herb, up to 3 ft. Leaves rather numerous in a basal cluster, about 10 in. long and an inch wide. Flowers ½-¾ in. wide, flattish, each with small bracts beneath.

For other plants often sold as *Anthericum, see* CHLOROPHYTUM.

**ANTHESIS.** The time of flowering.

**ANTHOLYZA** (an-tho-ly'za). African gladiolus-like herbs of the iris family sometimes grown for their showy, tubular, but slightly irregular,* flowers in tall spikes. Of the 20 known species only the following are known to most gardeners. They differ from *Gladiolus* mostly in the tube of the flower being long and slender, rather than shorter and broader. (*Antholyza* is from Greek for flower and rage, in allusion to the opening of the corolla resembling the mouth of an enraged animal.)

They are grown exactly as *Gladiolus* (which see).

aethiopica. Corm* bearing, branching herb up to 4 ft. Leaves about 18 in. long, and 1 in. wide. Spike 6-9 in. long, dense. Flowers reddish-yellow nearly 2 in. long. South Africa.
paniculata. Corm* large. Stem 3-4 ft. high, branched. Leaves 18-24 in. long, about 3 in. wide. Spike dense, about 1 ft. long, its stalk wavy. Flowers reddish-yellow, scarcely over 1½ in. long, the tube decidedly curved. Natal.

**ANTHORA** (an-thō'ra). A pre-Linnaean* name for some monkshood (which see).

**ANTHOXANTHUM** (an-thocks-an'thum). A small genus of Old World, mostly aromatic grasses, two of which are often ingredients of meadows or are common escapes* in N.A. They have flat, very narrow leaves, and narrow spike-like flower clusters. (*Anthoxanthum* is from Greek for yellow flower, probably in allusion to the pollen.)

---

* Special articles on the subjects indicated by an asterisk (*) will be found at the words so marked.

Neither is grown for ornament, but the second species sometimes for its fragrant foliage.

**aristatum.** European annual grass, scarcely 1 ft. high. Leaves 4 in. long and 1/8 in. wide. Flower cluster (a panicle*) about 1½ in. long, whitish-green, long-bristled. Common as an escape* in eastern N.A.

**odoratum.** Sweet vernal grass. A Eurasian perennial grass, usually 18–24 in. high. Leaves 6 in. long, rough above, nearly ¼ in. wide. Flower cluster (a panicle*) about 3 in. long, brownish-green. Nearly throughout N.A., mostly in meadows or as an escape.*

**ANTHRACNOSE.** A troublesome plant disease. For symptoms and control see the diseases at ORCHIDS, SWEET PEA, BEAN, CUCUMBER, GRAPE and RASPBERRY.

**ANTHRISCUS** (an-thris′kus). A small genus of Eurasian herbs of the carrot family, one considerably grown for its foliage, which is used like parsley. Leaves twice-compound,* the ultimate segments very fine. Flowers small, white in compound umbels.* (*Anthriscus* is Greek for flower fence.)

**cerefolium.** Salad chervil, but sometimes called merely chervil (which see). A hairy-leaved, Eurasian annual herb, with branching stem not over 18 in. high. Leaves much dissected, parsley-like. Flowers very small, white, in a stiff, compound umbel.* Fruits black and minutely beaked. For culture and uses see HERB GARDENING.

**ANTHURIUM** (an-thoor′i-um). An immense genus of tropical American perennial herbs of the arum family, some of which are widely grown greenhouse plants cult. for their fine foliage and often striking flowers. Leaves and habit very variable. Some are climbing aroids* with arrow-shaped or heart-shaped, often beautifully colored or variegated leaves. Flowers crowded in a dense spike (spadix*), beneath which or surrounding it is an often brightly colored spathe.* (For flower structure see ARACEAE.) Fruit berry-like. (*Anthurium* is Greek for tail-flower, in allusion to the tail-like spadix* of most species.)

Anthuriums are widely grown florists' plants, the first and third species for the showy flower cluster, the second and fourth for the very handsome foliage. They require a moist, warm greenhouse, not much below 60° at night and higher in the day. Give them plenty of water and keep the atmosphere as humid as possible. Use potting mixture* 4, to which should be added chopped-up fern roots or sphagnum moss or both to increase the humus. See that the roots are well covered (they tend to heave). As the plants get older they need re-potting only very occasionally.

**andraeanum.** A South American aroid* grown for its showy flower cluster. Leaves heart-shaped, green, deeply split at the base, about 12 in. long and 6 in. wide, the stalk as long as the blade. Flower spadix,* yellowish-white, its spathe* heart-shaped, leathery, 4–6 in. long, brilliant orange-red.

**crystallinum.** A showy foliage plant from Colombia. Leaves about 14 in. long and 10 in. wide, more or less heart-shaped, green and white-striped above, pale rose-pink beneath. Flower spathe* narrow, green.

**scherzerianum.** Flamingo-flower. One of the most widely grown florists' decorative plants, a native of Central America. Leaves oblongish, about 8 in. long and 2 in. wide, leathery, green and with a narrow tip. Flower spadix,* coiled, yellow, the spathe* red, yellow, rose, or white (depending upon which of many hort. varieties are grown). Some varieties, also, have scarlet or even white-spotted spathes,* all of which are more or less oval and about 3 in. long.

**veitchi.** The best-known foliage plant of the group, and a native of Colombia. Leaves oblong, nearly 3 ft. long and 10 in. wide, heart-shaped at the base, metallic-green, and hanging. It has prominent even showy veins on the under side. Flower spathe* scarcely 3 in. long, greenish-white, becoming recurved.

*ANTHYLLIDIFOLIA, -us, -um* (an-thil-lid-i-fō′li-a). With foliage like the kidney vetch (*Anthyllis*).

**ANTHYLLIS** (an-thil′lis). Old World perennial herbs of the pea family, comprising perhaps 20 species, two of which are of secondary hort. importance. They have compound,* silky leaves, the leaflets arranged feather-fashion, with an odd one at the end. Flowers pea-like, in rather showy spikes or heads. Pod mostly somewhat egg-shaped. (*Anthyllis* is Greek for downy flowers.)

The plants are of easy culture in open places, even if the soil is poor. Propagated by seeds or division of the roots. The first species is somewhat grown in rock gardens, the second scarcely known here but a common forage plant in Eu.

**montana.** A silky-hairy perennial herb from the Alps, mostly less than 12 in. high and with many leaflets. Flowers purple, in dense heads, below which is a leafy cluster of bracts.* A red-flowered variety (*var. rubra*) is somewhat grown in rock gardens. June.

**vulneraria.** Kidney vetch or woundwort; called, also, sand clover. A European perennial herb, about 12 in. high. Leaflets 5, rarely more. Flowers yellow or reddish, small. A clover-like plant, useful for forage in Eu., but occasionally grown for ornament here.

**ANTIGONON** (an-tig′o-non). A small group of showy, tropical American, tendril*-climbing vines, family Polygonaceae, one widely grown for ornament in warm regions where it approaches *Bougainvillaea* in its profuse bloom. Leaves alternate,* without marginal teeth. Flowers small but numerous, in drooping racemes* that come from the leaf-axils,* and end in a tendril.* (*Antigonon* means against or opposite an angle.)

Throughout zones* 8 and 9, the species below is common over porches, fences, and walls. Elsewhere, but rarely, it is a greenhouse plant. It is of the easiest culture in poor soils. See VINES. Propagated by seeds or easily rooted cuttings.

**leptopus.** Coral vine or corallita; called, also, pink vine or Confederate vine. Climbing to 30 ft. or more. Leaves arrow-shaped or heart-shaped, 1–3 in. long, but the lower leaves larger. Flowers pink, about 3/8 in. long. Fruit dry, bony, about 3/8 in. long, surrounded by the veiny remains of the withered flower. Mex. In the southern states it is sometimes called rosa montana.

*ANTILLANA, -us, -um* (an-til-lay′na). From the West Indian Antilles.

*ANTIQUORUM* (an-ti-quor′um). Of or belonging to the ancients.

*ANTIRRHINOIDES* (an-ti-ri-noy-deez; but see OÏDES). Like the snapdragon (*Antirrhinum*).

**ANTIRRHINUM.** See SNAPDRAGON.

**ANTS.** Many ants are harmless, although they may be very annoying in houses and on flowers. Some species attack plants or seeds, or bore in trees. Many ants care for aphids and mealybugs, and thus greatly increase their power of injuring plants. An ant colony in the soil has an organization something like a bee colony, with a queen, drones, and numerous workers. The workers are the ones usually seen, and it does little good to kill a few of them while there are many more in the nest and the queen continues laying eggs. If the colony can be located, it may be destroyed by making several holes leading into the nest, pouring an ounce or two of carbon disulphide down each of them, and covering the holes with soil. A simpler method is to put a weak poison syrup in tin salve boxes or paraffined pill boxes, having holes in the sides to admit the ants, but with the covers on. If these boxes are put where the ants work, they will carry this syrup to the nest, thus poisoning the queen and young ants, and in a few weeks causing the death of the entire colony.

The following poison syrup has proved to be effective in the control of certain species of ants:

Sugar . . . . . . . . . . . . . . 4 ounces
Water . . . . . . . . . . . . . 1 quart
Tartar emetic . . . . . . . . ½ ounce

The sugar is first dissolved in hot water, and then the tartar emetic is added.

The notorious Argentine ant of the South and California has been effectively controlled by the persistent use, during the period when natural food is not available, of bait made according to the following formula:

Granulated sugar . . . . . . . . . . . 9 pounds
Crystallized tartaric acid . . . . . 6 grams (93 grains)
Benzoate of soda . . . . . . . . . . . 8.4 grams (130 grains)
Water . . . . . . . . . . . . . . . . . . . . 9½ pints
Sodium arsenite . . . . . . . . . . . . 15 grams (230 grains)
Strained honey . . . . . . . . . . . . . 1¼ pounds

The sugar, tartaric acid, and benzoate of soda should be added to 9 pints of water, boiled slowly for 30 minutes (with replacement of evaporation loss), then cooled. The sodium arsenite should be dissolved in one half pint of hot water and allowed to cool. The poison should then be added to the syrup and stirred well. Finally, the strained honey should be added and the material again thoroughly mixed.

Both these baits are poisonous and should be handled with caution and kept out of reach of pets and children. A number of proprietary materials are made substantially according to these formulas.— F. M. W.

---

* Special articles on the subjects indicated by an asterisk (*) will be found at the words so marked.

**ANTWERP HOLLYHOCK** = *Althaea ficifolia.* See HOLLYHOCK.

*APENNINA, -us, -um* (ă-pĕ-ny′na). From the Apennine Mountains, Italy.

*APETALA, -us, -um* (a-pet′a-la). Without petals.

**APETALOUS.** Without petals, as the flowers of oak, beech, ash, and many other plants. *See* NAKED FLOWER.

**APHELANDRA** (a-fell-an′dra). A genus of 60 species of showy, tropical American shrubs or woody herbs, family Acanthaceae, the two below much grown in greenhouses for their attractive foliage and handsome, bracted* flowers. Leaves (in those below) opposite, sometimes in opposite pairs, often conspicuously veined or parti-colored. Flowers irregular,* somewhat 2-lipped,* crowded in dense bracted* spikes. Fruit a 4-angled pod. (*Aphelandra* is Greek for simple male, the anthers being 1-celled.)

Grown only in greenhouses where their culture is the same as for poinsettia (which see). Easily propagated by cuttings of partly ripened wood, or by seed, in *A. aurantiaca.*

**aurantiaca.** Low, perennial herb. Leaves oval or elliptic, 4-6 in. long, more or less wavy-margined, prominently veined, dark green above, paler green beneath. Flowers orange, rarely scarlet-tipped, the bracts* toothed. Mex. A popular greenhouse decorative plant.

**tetragona.** A shrub 3-4 ft. high, with the lower stems woody, the upper herbaceous and greenish-red. Leaves in opposite pairs, more or less elliptic, 8-12 in. long and about 4 in. wide, green. Flowers in erect, terminal spikes which are branched and profuse in bloom, scarlet, the bracts* merely hairy-margined. Brazil. The showiest species in cult.

**APHID.** *See* True Bugs at INSECT PESTS. They are common on many plants. *See* the insect pests mentioned at POTATO, APPLE, GRAPE, ROSE, CALLISTEPHUS, and CHRYSANTHEMUM.

**APHINE.** A trademarked liquid insecticide, combining nicotine, oils and soap; useful for the control of sucking insects and soft scale.

**APHRODITE.** The Greek goddess; often used as a varietal name for strikingly beautiful plants.

*APHYLLA, -us, -um* (a-fill′a). Leafless, or apparently so.

**APIACEAE.** See UMBELLIFERAE.

*APICULATA, -us, -um* (a-pick-you-lay′ta). Tipped with a short, often sharp, point.

*APIIFOLIA, -us, -um* (a-pi-i-fō′li-a). With celery-like leaves.

**APIO** = *Arracacia xanthorrhiza.*

**APIOS** (ā′pi-os). A small genus of tuberous-rooted vines of the pea family, the one below somewhat grown for its brownish flowers. Its roots were an important source of food to the Indians. Leaves compound.* Flowers pea-like, in short clusters, followed by long, flat, thickish, many-seeded pods. (*Apios* is Greek for pair, from the arrangement of the tubers.)

A moderately attractive vine of chief interest because its small tubers were long mistaken for the potato in the early history of that vegetable. Easily grown in any open sandy soil and propagated by seeds or planting the tubers.

**tuberosa.** Groundnut; called, also, potato bean and wild bean. A vine to 8 ft. long, its tuberous roots in strings like small potatoes. Leaflets 5-7. Flowers brown, with the fragrance of violets. Summer. Eastern N.A.

**APIUM.** *See* CELERY.

**APLECTRUM** (a-pleck′trum). One North American woods orchid, sometimes transferred from the forest to the wild garden, but not of easy cult. *See* Hardy Orchids at ORCHID. (*Aplectrum* is Greek for spurless.) The only species is **A. hyemale**, the puttyroot or Adam-and-Eve. It bears late in the summer a single, plaited, oval, many-veined, and winter-persisting leaf, followed early the next summer by the naked stalk of the loose flower cluster. Flowers brown or yellowish-brown, with strap-shaped sepals and a 3-lobed lip. June.

**APOCYNACEAE** (a-poss-i-nay′see-ee). The dogbane family comprises about 135 genera and over 1100 species of herbs, shrubs, vines or trees, scattered nearly throughout the world, but largely tropical. They have a milky juice and leaves without marginal teeth. Flowers regular, in clusters (cymes* or panicles*) or solitary. Fruit berry-like or fleshy in *Thevetia, Acokanthera* and *Carissa*, but mostly a dry pod (follicle*) in the other hort. genera.

The family includes several old garden favorites like the periwinkle (*see* VINCA) and the oleander. Also several showy woody vines like *Trachelospermum, Allamanda, Beaumontia, Dipladenia, Mandevilla,* and *Vallaris*, all tropical or sub-tropical. Among herbs are *Apocynum, Amsonia,* and *Tabernaemontana,* all of which are hardy over most of America, but their flowers are not so showy as those of the woody vines. Besides the oleander, there is another hort. genus of shrubs or trees, the frangipani (*see* PLUMERIA), widely planted in warm regions for ornament. Some genera have violently poisonous juice, notably *Acokanthera*, used by the natives for arrow poisons. A few genera, especially *Carissa*, bear edible fruits.

Technical flower characters: Calyx 5-parted. Corolla usually bell-shaped or funnel-shaped, its 5 lobes often distinctly twisted. Stamens 5, inserted on the tube of the corolla. Ovaries mostly 2, the seeds in the genera with pods, usually with a tuft of hairs (*see* APOCYNUM).

**APOCYNUM** (a-poss′i-num). The dogbanes are milky-juiced, tough-stemmed, perennial herbs, family Apocynaceae, somewhat grown for ornament, and for medicine. All are from the north temperate zone, those below, American. Leaves opposite,* without marginal teeth. Flowers small, bell-shaped, borne in loose clusters (cymes*). Fruit a long slender pod (follicle*), the seeds with a tuft of hairs. (*Apocynum* is the classical name of the dogbane.)

They are of very easy culture, preferring open, sandy soil. Both those below will stand considerable drought. Propagated by division of the roots in spring or fall.

**androsaemifolium.** Spreading dogbane; called, also, honey-bloom and wild ipecac. A stout, branching perennial 3-4 ft. high. Leaves 2-3 in. long, about half as wide, pale beneath. Flowers pinkish, about ⅓ in. wide. N.A.

**cannabinum.** Indian hemp; called also Choctaw-root. Nearly twice as tall as the above, the stem almost stringy-barked, and once cult. for its fiber. Leaves nearly 5 in. long, about half as wide. Flowers greenish-white, about ¼ in. wide. Eastern U.S. The root furnishes an emetic and cathartic.

**APOGON.** The group comprising the beardless irises. *See* IRIS.

**APONOGETON** (a-pon-o-jee′ton). The only genus of the family **Aponogetonaceae** (a-pon-o-jee-to-nay′see-ee), which are aquatic plants of the Old World tropics. Both those below are African and are widely cult. in greenhouse pools or in aquaria. They have tuberous rootstocks and submerged, permanently skeletonized leaves in the second species, but floating leaves in the Cape pondweed. Flowers very simple, in spikes, the flower parts (petals and sepals) usually only 2. Stamens 6. Ovary of three 1-celled carpels. (*Aponogeton* is of uncertain origin, possibly Celtic for water neighbor.)

These popular aquatics can be grown in any water that is kept at or above ordinary room temperatures. Plant the rootstocks, or offsets* in pots of rich loam and submerge at least 8 in. below the water surface, in full sunlight if possible. It is essential that the lace-leaf be grown in clear water to get the full effect of its extraordinary skeletonized leaves. Both species are sometimes sold as *Ouvirandra.*

**distachyus.** Cape pondweed or water hawthorn. Leaves floating, not skeletonized, long-stalked, narrow, about 4 in. long. Flowers minute, in a branched, emersed spike, white, fragrant, with one or two bracts beneath each flower. Cape of Good Hope.

**fenestralis.** Lace-leaf or lattice-leaf. One of the most extraordinary submerged aquatic plants in the world. Leaves broadish-oblong, notched at the tip, usually about 9 in. long and floating just beneath the water surface. The leaf consists only of several main parallel veins and a multitude of small lateral, connecting veins, the leaf thus permanently skeletonized. Flowers minute, white, the spikes borne on a stalk about 12 in. long. Madagascar.

**APOROCACTUS** (a-pore-o-kak′tus). A small group of tropical American cacti, the one below grown for its peculiar habit and crimson flowers. They are vine-like or clambering

---

* Special articles on the subjects indicated by an asterisk (*) will be found at the words so marked.

or prostrate succulents with thin, rat-tail-like stems which have 10-12 shallow ribs, brown spines and reddish, bristly fruit. Flowers day-blooming, funnel-shaped, the stamens protruding, gathered in a single, one-sided cluster. (The name is Greek for impenetrable cactus.)

The species below, a popular window plant, is one of the easiest cacti to grow. Plant joints in sandy loam and keep the pots near or in full sunlight. *See also* SUCCULENTS.

flagelliformis. Rat-tail cactus. Stems cylindric, about ¾ in. in diameter, erect, prostrate, climbing, or hanging, depending upon age and vigor. Flowers crimson, about 3 in. long, lasting 3 or 4 days. Fruit ½ in. in diameter. Probably Mexico. Often grafted on other cacti and its weak stems trained into grotesque designs.

**APPALACHIAN TEA** = *Viburnum cassinoides*.

*APPENDICULATA, -us, -um* (ap-pen-dick-you-lay'ta). Appendaged; *i.e.* with a crown, crest, hairs, etc.

**APPLE** (*Malus pumila*). Wherever general agriculture is practiced in the United States and Canada, the apple is the fruit of fruits. Temperature is the commonest limiting factor in its culture in North America. The apple cannot be counted upon to hold its own in regions where the temperature goes down with frequency to 20° below. Long, hot summers are as trying to the apple as cold winters. Dry weather is another limiting factor. The apple cannot be grown with much success in large areas between the Mississippi and the Rocky Mountains where irrigation is not possible but where a low rainfall does permit "dry farming." The rainfall might suffice, but the combination of a dry atmosphere and continuous winds takes too much moisture from apple trees to permit healthy growth.

The local climate as affected by site must be considered to secure freedom from unseasonable frosts, strong winds, and too great heat. It is well understood that large bodies of water give protection against both frosts and heat, while hills, mountains, and the lay of the land may be selected to modify the sweep of winds. Slopes which give air drainage, irrespective of direction, are better than level lands. These generalities are chiefly directed to orchard enterprises; a good gardener can grow a few apples under very adverse circumstances of climate and location.

SOILS. The apple grows in almost every agricultural soil in North America, faring worst on light sands and black mucks. Perhaps the soil most often recommended is a loam with an admixture of clay. A broad generalization is that apples thrive in any soils upon which the common cereals and the potato grow well. A soil ideal for corn is seldom suitable for the apple.

Generally, too little is said about the subsoil for apples. If the topsoil is shallow, the roots of trees may be down in the subsoil and must obtain from it both food and moisture. Moreover, the fruit-grower can seldom improve the subsoil by cultural methods. There are two extremes that must be avoided in subsoils for all fruit trees: One is hard, impervious strata, usually clays, into which the roots of trees can hardly penetrate and which do not permit drainage. The other is gravels and sands through which the water passes quickly out of the reach of roots.

PROPAGATION. No apple grower should attempt to grow his own trees, but the planter is often called upon to make a choice between trees propagated in different ways and to do this intelligently must know how the apple is propagated. The foundation of an apple tree is a seedling grown from seed taken from cider pomace. Apple varieties are grafted or budded on these seedling stocks.

If grafted, cions of varieties may be worked on "piece-roots" or "whole-roots." Experimenters find that one is as good as the other. In either case, the grafting is done in the winter, by the whip-graft method, after which the grafts are stored in sand in a cellar until spring when they are lined out in nursery rows.

In propagating the apple by budding,* the buds of varieties are inserted in July or August in yearling apple seedlings which have been lined out in nursery rows in the spring. The buds are set in the stocks about 2 in. above the surface of the ground by the shield-bud method. There is little if any difference between grafted and budded trees, but if the author has a preference it is for the budded.

PLANTING. Apple orchards are set in various parts of North America in squares, equilateral triangles, and quincunxes. Setting in squares is the simplest and commonest method. The objection urged against this method is that the trees are not equidistant from each other. But plowing, cultivating, spraying, and harvesting are carried on most conveniently in orchards laid out in squares; and in time roots and branches utilize all the space in a square. *See* illustration at FRUIT CULTURE.

The practice of planting temporary trees between rows of permanent ones in an apple orchard has much to recommend it in both home and commercial orchards. These filler trees can be used to advantage only when the permanent ones are set in squares. Then a filler may be put in the center of each square, giving nearly double the number of trees per acre. Or fillers may be set both ways between the permanents, giving three times as many fillers as permanents. Quick-bearing varieties only should be used as fillers. Some fruit growers plant cherries, peaches, or pears as fillers, but any of these in an apple orchard complicate orchard operations.

Trees are oftener set too close than too far apart. The notion that apples should be set only far enough apart so that branches will not overlap is wrong, as the roots of a mature tree spread farther than the branches, and should not compete for food and moisture. Cultivation, harvesting, and spraying can be well done only when trees are not crowded. In commercial orchards, 40 to 45 ft. apart each way is none too much. The gardener can reduce these distances somewhat. Dwarf apple trees, their size reduced by growing on Doucin or Paradise stocks, can be set much closer, 18 ft. for those on Doucin stock and 15 ft. for the smaller Paradise trees. Dwarf apples, however, are almost never grown in North America; for the reason that they are shallow-rooted and succumb to summer drouths and are blown over by heavy winds.

Two-year-old apple trees are chosen by most growers, but in some parts of the country, the South chiefly, one-year-olds are liked better. Trees that have stood three or more years in nurseries are occasionally used by gardeners. Some even succeed in transplanting bearing trees.

Early spring is the time for transplanting in cold or trying latitudes, but in the South and middle latitudes late fall, or even winter, in places where the ground can be worked, is better than spring. Fall planting, where possible, gets the work out of the way, and the tree starts more quickly in the spring. In transplanting it is necessary to cut away part of the branches to enable the injured root system to supply the top with sufficient food and water. The less the roots are injured and the better the condition of the tree, the less the top need be cut away. The roots should be exposed as little as possible to sun and wind. In planting, keep the trees in the field covered with earth or a wet sack until they are put in the ground. The chief care in setting should be to place moist soil in close contact with the roots of the plant. The trees should be set a little deeper than they stood in the nursery. Mulching after planting prevents evaporation and maintains an equable temperature favorable to root growth. Mulching is best done by frequent, shallow cultivation. Water thoroughly or not at all. For greenhouse culture, *see* Greenhouse Fruit at GREENHOUSE.

CULTURE. There are locations in which sod culture is a desirable special practice, but tillage should be the rule in most orchards. The orchard should be plowed in the autumn (or winter in the South), or as soon as the land can be worked in spring. The harrow ought to be put to work in early spring and kept at work until June in the South, July in the North. At the last time over with the cultivating tool a cover crop of one of the clovers, or peas, beans, vetch, oats, rye, millet, or buckwheat, as the orchard may demand, should be sown. The gardener can substitute manure or a mulch for the cover crop. In sod culture care should be taken to secure a good grass cover. For a permanent grass sod, bluegrass is best. Covers of alfalfa and clovers are also used and have the advantage of providing nitrogen for the

---

* Special articles on the subjects indicated by an asterisk (*) will be found at the words so marked.

trees. These legumes may attract destructive leaf hoppers. If either the legume or grass sod runs out or becomes thin and poor, it should be plowed up, the orchard cultivated for a season, and reseeded.

FERTILIZER. When an orchard is cultivated and cover crops follow, fertilizers are not necessary on average apple soils. In neglected orchards and those under sod culture nitrogenous fertilizers usually pay. A safe rule as to amount of fertilizer is ¼ pound of nitrate of soda, or its equivalent of some other nitrogen carrier (*see* FERTILIZERS), for each year of the tree's age.

PRUNING. In pruning a one-year-old tree, remove the branches and cut back the remaining whip to the height desired. If the tree is two years old, as is usually the case, or when the one-year-old plants have been set a year, shaping of the tree may be begun. This early pruning is more or less provisional, although an idea for the future tree must be plainly in the mind at the time. The frame-work should be established during the first two seasons. Usually the choice should be for a low-headed tree. A low-headed tree is more easily sprayed and pruned, the fruit is more readily thinned and harvested, crop and tree are less subject to injury by wind, the trunk is less liable to injury by sunscald* or winter-killing,* and the low-headed tree comes into bearing earlier. By "low-headed" is meant a distance from earth to the first limb of 1½ to 3 feet.

Apple growers usually prune trees too much. If trees are originally well selected, all that is needed is to remove an occasional branch which starts out in the wrong place and to take out dead, injured, or crossing limbs. Weak, sickly trees, or ones making long, willowy growth, may require somewhat more severe pruning. When a tree bears many small fruits, when the top contains dead branches, and when the seasonal growth is short and scant, the tree lacks vigor. Such trees may be reinvigorated by cutting back some branches and wholly removing others. In pruning trees with a spreading, drooping, or slender habit of growth, prune to buds that point upward; if the habit be upright and dense, cut to lower or outer buds. The "off-year" habit of bearing may be intensified by spasmodic and severe pruning; therefore prune biennial bearers lightly and yearly. The cut should be made close to the trunk so as not to leave a stub. The best covering for a wound is liquid grafting wax. Trees should be pruned between the fall of leaves and the coming of new ones. For cordon and other specially trained trees, *see* Fruit Trees at TRAINING PLANTS.

The productiveness of nearly all apples is increased by cross-pollination brought about by mixed plantings. Varieties that have poor pollen are of little value as pollinators. Not over 4 solid rows of apples should be set if the variety needs cross-pollination, and 2 or 3 are better.

RENOVATING OLD TREES. It is often difficult to tell whether it is worth while trying to save old, unproductive trees. If trunks or branches are badly rotted or if a quarter or a fifth of the top is dead through disease or winter injury, it is hardly worth trying to renovate. If it is decided that the trees are to be retained, the following treatment, somewhat in order of importance, should be given: —

Spray the trees, if necessary, to destroy San Jose scale or oyster-shell bark lice; cut out old wood and prune heavily to strong, new wood; remove all suckers that are not needed to replace the top; prune out interlacing branches and branchlets to open the trees to light and the circulation of air; if the trees are in sod, turn under or break up the turf or mulch heavily with lawn clippings, hay or manure; apply a dressing of some nitrogenous fertilizer at the rate of 12 to 18 pounds per tree. The work of renovation should be extended through several seasons.

VARIETIES. Out of several hundred varieties, perhaps 25 are representative of the region east of the Rocky Mountains. Human preferences dictate the choice of varieties rather more than the environment of plant zones. Varieties are named in order of ripening:

Yellow Transparent. — Fruit bright yellow, large, conical, subacid, very early. Tree very hardy, rather small and short-lived. All cold regions.
Red Astrachan. — Fruit bright crimson, round, medium size, subacid. Tree large, very productive, hardy, short-lived. All cold climates.
Early McIntosh. — Very like its parent, McIntosh, but two months earlier. Tree very productive, needs thinning. Best early red.
Duchess of Oldenburg. — Fruit above medium, thinly striped with red, round-oval, good for cooking. Tree medium size, very hardy, not very healthy. All cold regions.
Gravenstein. — Fruit medium in size, striped with crimson, round-oblate, splendid for table and cooking. Tree hardy, healthy, and productive. Northern regions.
Wealthy. — Fruit red, medium to large, round-ovate, good. Tree bears early, very hardy, good filler. All cold climates.
Twenty-Ounce. — Fruit large, striped, round-conical, excellent for cooking. Tree medium in size, health and hardiness. New York and neighboring states.
Fameuse (Snow). — Fruit bright red, small, round-oblate, high quality. Tree hardy, healthy, productive. New England and New York.
McIntosh. — Fruit bright red, striped, beautiful, round-oblate; flesh white, tender, juicy, aromatic, standard in quality. Tree satisfactory in all respects. New England and New York.
Sweet McIntosh. — Nearly identical with McIntosh, but sweet. Best of all sweet apples.
Cortland. — Fruit and tree of McIntosh type, fruit hangs better and ripens later than that of McIntosh. New York and New England.
Macoun. — Fruit dark red, medium to large, white, richly flavored flesh. Of McIntosh type, but ripens later. A good pollinator.
Delicious. — Fruit striped with red, medium in size, round-conic, high quality. Tree satisfactory, except a shy bearer, a good pollinator. Not adapted to northern apple regions.
Rhode Island Greening. — Fruit large, greenish-yellow, roundish, subacid, good in quality. Tree nearly perfect. New York and New England.
Baldwin. — Fruit large, red, round-oblate, subacid, good quality. Tree nearly perfect. Standard in New York and New England.
Rome Beauty. — Fruit large, red, striped, medium quality. Tree rather small, short-lived, very productive, and a good filler. South of New England and westward.
Grimes Golden. — Fruit golden-yellow, large, round-ovate, excellent quality. Tree medium in size, hardiness, productiveness and health. Virginia, westward to Missouri.
Jonathan. — Fruit bright red, below medium, round-conic, subacid, excellent quality. Tree late in bearing, long-lived, hardy, productive. Virginia and Maryland, west to Missouri.
Northern Spy. — Fruit striped with red, large, round-ovate, subacid, best quality. Tree hardy, healthy, long-lived, late in bearing. New York and New England.
Golden Delicious. — Fruit golden-yellow, medium in size, round-conic, splendid quality. Tree a little lacking in hardiness and productiveness. Maryland and Virginia, west to Missouri.
Yellow Newtown. — Fruit yellow, medium size, tender, crisp, excellent quality. Tree a shy bearer; excellent otherwise. Home orchards in all apple regions; commercial orchards, Virginia.
Winesap. — Fruit red, large, round-oblate, good, late keeper. Tree satisfactory. Virginia, west to Missouri.
Ben Davis. — Fruit striped red, large, round-conic, poor quality. Tree characters excellent. New York, south and west.
York Imperial. — Fruit large, red, round-oblique, fair quality. Tree tender to cold; otherwise satisfactory. Virginia and Maryland, west to Missouri. — U. P. H.

## APPLES IN IRRIGATED DISTRICTS

Practically all apple-growing districts west of the Rockies either rely upon or would be benefited by irrigation. Western-grown apples are therefore usually thought of as irrigated apples, even though some are produced under only natural rainfall.

According to the 1930 U.S. census, Washington, the leading apple-producing state of the United States, produces as many apples as all other western states combined. Two large, highly developed areas: the Wenatchee and Yakima valleys, produced, in 1926–1930, 95 per cent of the state's crop. The former area, centering at Wenatchee in north-central Washington, extends westward to the Cascade Mountains and north toward the Canadian boundary. General climatic conditions are arid, with summer temperatures relatively high. Annual rainfall during the winter and spring is 8 to 15 inches. The district is planted almost solidly to apples. Winesap, Delicious, Jonathan, and Rome Beauty varieties comprise 80 per cent of the trees. The first two sorts are of about equal importance and are grown in much the larger quantity.

The Yakima Valley, 50 miles south of Wenatchee, possesses similar climatic conditions to those in the Wenatchee Valley, although the district is somewhat more diversified in character. The principal varieties are the same as those produced in the Wenatchee Valley.

Smaller districts are those adjacent to Spokane, Walla Walla, and White Salmon. In addition to the above-mentioned varieties, Wagener is important in the Spokane area and the Yellow Newtown in the White Salmon district.

California is of second importance in apple production on

---

* Special articles on the subjects indicated by an asterisk (*) will be found at the words so marked.

the Pacific Coast, and about 25 per cent of its crop is usually dried. The Pajaro Valley, or Watsonville district, south of San Francisco, produces slightly over half the crop of the state. With frequent fogs and an annual rainfall of 20 inches or more during the winter and spring months, few orchards are irrigated. Yellow Newtown and Yellow Bellflower in the ratio of 2 to 1 are the principal varieties. The Sebastapol district in Sonoma County, another non-irrigated region, uses mostly the Gravenstein, a variety which ripens in July and August.

In southern California a third apple district is located on the mesa lands at Yucaipa in San Bernardino County. Other scattered plantings are to be found in the north coast counties and in districts in the Sierra Nevada foothills.

The Hood River Valley is the leading district of Oregon and was the first to establish a reputation for fruit of high quality. Yellow Newtown is the leading variety. Esopus Spitzenburg has also been of importance, but difficulties of production have caused its decline.

Idaho, in the irrigated districts adjacent to Boise, Twin Falls, and Lewiston, uses the same varieties as those grown in Washington.

Of the mountain states, Colorado is of first importance, with the principal districts on the western slope centering about Grand Junction, Delta, and Montrose. In addition to Jonathan, grown in largest quantities, Rome Beauty, Winesap, Gano, and Delicious are important. New Mexico, Utah, and Montana also have one or more centers of production.

CULTIVATION. This has been much more intensive in the far west than practiced in the central states, although in the Northwest this intensive cultivation now has been largely superseded by permanent cover crops, mainly alfalfa.

In the larger irrigated sections, water is diverted from streams at considerable altitude and brought to the district in large canals. From these it is taken and applied to individual orchards by means of 6 to 8 furrows run between each two rows of trees. Irrigations, usually 2 to 5 in number, continue for from 1 to 3 days, depending largely upon the topography, type of soil, and amount of water available.— F. W. A.

INSECT PESTS. The common apple worm, larva of the small, grayish-brown codling moth, is the worst pest of the fruit. Sprays of lead arsenate are applied to poison the newly hatched larva before it eats its way into the fruit. Poison residue should later be removed from the fruit by washing. Corrugated-paper bands on tree trunks will trap many larvae leaving trees in the summer.
Cankerworms, tent caterpillars, webworms, and other leaf-feeding caterpillars can be killed with arsenicals. Winter eggs of the fruit tree leaf roller are killed by strong dormant oil sprays.
The plum curculio, a small snout beetle, attacks young apples east of the Rocky Mountains, causing dropping or blemishing; arsenicals check it.
The flat-headed and round-headed borers, beetle larvae, can be killed with a wire after their burrows have been cut open in the autumn. Bark beetles, or shot-hole borers, affect sickly trees. By keeping trees healthy and cleaning up prunings the borers can be checked.
The grayish San Jose scale, which looks like ashes on the bark, often kills trees in the warmer sections of the country. The whitish scurfy scale and the larger oyster-shell scale (named for its shape) are less injurious. All are controlled with dormant sprays of lime-sulphur or oil.
Aphids, affecting leaves and fruit in the spring, yield to nicotine, as do redbugs, sometimes present in the East. Trees whose roots are affected by woolly aphids are helped by measures to promote vigorous growth.
The apple maggot, a fly larva, tunnels fruit late in the season in the Northeast. A midsummer spray of lead arsenate will kill adults. Poison residue must be removed from the fruit by washing.
Several kinds of small mites affect apple foliage, sometimes seriously. Dormant sprays kill the eggs of some species, and lime-sulphur in summer checks active forms.
A typical spray schedule for apples is given below:

| Time | Material | Against |
| --- | --- | --- |
| 1. Early spring | Lime-sulphur or oil | Scale insects and aphids |
| 2. Before blossoming | Lead arsenate and nicotine (with fungicides) | Cankerworms, aphids, etc. |
| 3. At blossom fall | Lead arsenate, fungicide | Codling moth, diseases |
| 4. One to several later sprays 10 days to several weeks apart | do. | Codling moth, curculio, diseases |

Since schedules vary in different sections of the country, state entomologists should be consulted. Apples sprayed when large should be washed in dilute hydrochloric acid or other solvent before marketing to remove excessive residues.

DISEASES. Scab is one of the outstanding troubles. It causes black blotches on the leaves and fruit, and defoliation. The fungus winters in the old leaves on the ground. The life history of this fungus is so complicated and so closely related to weather conditions and varietal development of the apple that important fruit areas usually have a spray service in which specialists advise regarding the materials to apply and the time of application. Lime-sulphur, 1-40, is commonly applied when the leaves of the bud clusters are beginning to open, when the blossoms are pink, at petal fall, and two or three times later in the summer. In hot weather the lime-sulphur may cause too much leaf burning, so that sulphur dust or various spray compounds are substituted when the temperatures are high.
Fly-speck, sooty-blotch, and fruit spot are controlled also by the same spray program. Blotch and bitter-rot may cause severe injury to the fruit in some of the warmer districts. Where these diseases are present the lime-sulphur spray in some of the applications is replaced by a weak bordeaux mixture which if used too lavishly causes severe russeting of the fruit. In all cases of doubt regarding the spray program, the grower should consult the state pathologist or other authorized expert on the subject. The same sprays suggested for scab also control various minor leaf spots, mildew, and fruit rots, and aid in reducing the amount of trunk and limb canker. Where cankers are present the spraying should be supplemented by the removal of the diseased portions, and covering large exposed areas of tissue with some recommended wound dressing. Fire-blight may cause serious damage on very susceptible varieties. The more resistant varieties should be planted if that is possible.
In localities where the red cedar grows in close proximity to apple orchards, cedar rust is likely to affect the leaves and fruit. For this reason, the cedar trees should be eradicated in all intensive apple districts.

**APPLE FAMILY.** See ROSACEAE.

**APPLE GERANIUM** = *Pelargonium odoratissimum*.

**APPLE MINT** = *Mentha rotundifolia*. See MINT.

**APPLE-OF-PERU** = *Nicandra physalodes*.

**APPRESSED.** Pressing against, as some leaves are appressed against the stem, or the scales against a cone. The botanical term is usually adpressed.

**APRICOT** (*Prunus armeniaca*). Besides the U.S., only Australia, the Union of South Africa, Syria, and Persia produce apricots in any considerable quantity, and production in the U.S. is practically confined to Calif., which has about 93 per cent of the total tonnage and 89 per cent of the trees, Wash. ranking next.

The other western states producing apricots do not seriously compete with the Calif. crop, which is sold dried (70 per cent), canned (25 per cent), and fresh (5 per cent). The earliest season is that of Calif. (May 15 to July 15). The apricot is also grown in British Columbia, and, locally, in Va.

VARIETIES. The ideal apricot variety is suitable for drying, canning, and marketing fresh. It should ripen both halves evenly, be free of the pit, and be well colored when canned or dried. In order of ripening, the four varieties constituting most of the tonnage are Royal, Blenheim, Tilton, and Moorpark.

The old French Royal variety and the English Blenheim were early introduced into Calif., where they are the foundation of the industry. At present no one can surely distinguish between them. In the interior valleys only Royal was planted; in the coastal counties, Blenheim. Royal now stands for a firm, well-colored, freestone apricot, highly flavored and medium to large, suitable for drying, canning, or shipping east. Blenheim, later in season, supposed to have less color and firmness, but better size, serves the same purposes. Trees of both are regularly productive. For the past 20 years, leading Calif. nurseries have increased the confusion by making no clear distinction between the two.

Tilton, a rather large, flat Calif. variety, tends to bear alternately unless carefully grown. It is prolific, having yielded 20 tons of good-sized cannery fruit per acre. In quality it ranks below Royal and Blenheim. It is lighter in color and blooms and ripens somewhat later. Its popularity is waning, no doubt through lack of annual crops of high quality. Although shipped and canned in a limited way, it is mostly dried.

Moorpark, an old English variety, has very large fruit, late and of the highest quality, used for local markets or drying. It is irregular and shy in bearing. This is the variety most widely grown in all western states except Calif.

For early shipment, Newcastle, Wiggan, Stewart, Derby, and others are occasionally planted. Newcastle and Wiggan, relatively soft, need more careful handling than the latter

* Special articles on the subjects indicated by an asterisk (*) will be found at the words so marked.

two, which closely resemble Royal and are commonly shipped as such.

Russian varieties such as Alexander and Budd are grown where winter temperatures are especially severe, but they are small and inferior.

All varieties are self-fertile and can be planted in solid blocks.

LOCATION. After the almond, the apricot is first to bloom. It is, however, apparently more susceptible to frost injury in both the flower and the young fruit, so that it must be planted in areas relatively free from frost. Many orchards in Calif. are artificially heated. (*See* FROST.) In order to break the "rest," winter temperatures should not be too mild; otherwise, fruit buds are shed instead of opening, and crops are reduced. With adequate irrigation, the apricot tree thrives in locations ranging from cool coastal to desert. It is more particular in its soil moisture requirements than some other fruits, such as the peach, so far as production is concerned; but the tree itself withstands drought better than the peach. During the growing season, the fruit responds directly to temperatures; it ripens when sufficient heat units have accumulated, whether in 100 or in 130 days, a fact explaining the earliness of certain districts. In most sections, however, temperatures of 103° F. and upward during the ripening season cause "pit burn" — a darkening of the flesh at the pit — which spoils the fruit for selling fresh or canning and lowers its value for drying.

CULTURE. The apricot can be grown successfully on many soils, but apparently prefers a deep, well-drained clay loam. Apricot, peach, and the myrobalan plum are satisfactory rootstocks, although with the myrobalan plum considerable breakage at the graft union occurs unless a congenial strain is secured. Peach root is used on light, well-drained soils; apricot on moderately heavy, well-drained soils; and myrobalan plum on wetter and heavier types. To plant apricots on soils so heavy that the apricot root will not thrive is economically questionable. According to some growers, peach root gives apricots of larger size and earlier maturity. Apricot root is more susceptible to gopher injury. On soils best adapted to apricots, there is probably little to choose between the peach and apricot stocks. Since adequate soil moisture is necessary for regular yields, most apricot orchards are irrigated from 2 to 8 times a season, depending upon age, type of soil, and climate. A permanent cover crop such as alfalfa may be grown, provided adequate irrigation water is available.

Apricot trees are planted from 20 to 30 ft. apart; on good soils 25 ft. should be the minimum. Usually a one-year-old tree is planted and immediately headed to about 30 in. During the next several years, light thinnings encourage an upright, natural habit of growth and first crops that will insure proper spread. Fruits are borne on spurs and new wood. The bearing tree should be pruned for a proper balance between renewal wood and crop — climatic conditions, soil, irrigation, and other factors being considered. Pruning for size of fruit is usually profitably supplemented by thinning of the fruit. Fruits are generally spaced about 4 in. apart.

HARVESTING. Apricots should be hand-picked. Proper maturity is largely determined by color. For distant shipment, for the cannery, and for drying, fruits are picked at successive degrees of firmness and color, being most mature for drying. For this last purpose, they should be fully ripe and yet firm enough to handle. The more nearly complete the ripening on the tree, the higher the sugar content and the consequent quality. After picking, there is no increase in sugar.

DRYING. Apricots should be halved, the pits removed, and placed on trays with cup up, and exposed to the fumes of burning sulphur from 2 to 6 hours and then dried in the sun. After 1 to 3 days, the trays are stacked; and the drying is completed in a week to ten days. A few apricots are artificially dehydrated; about 5 pounds fresh makes 1 pound dry. — W. P. T. *See also* PLUMCOT.

INSECT PESTS. The pests are similar to those of peach or plum. The plum curculio, a serious pest of the fruit, can be controlled with arsenical sprays at blossom fall and a little later. The peach-twig borer attacks twigs early in the season and the fruit later. It is controlled with a spray of either dormant-strength lime-sulphur or lead arsenate, applied just as the buds open. The peach borer sometimes attacks apricot (*see* PEACH). The San Jose scale is also a pest (*see* APPLE).

APRIL. *See* GARDEN CALENDAR.

APTENIA. *See* MESEMBRYANTHEMUM.

AQUARIUM. It is interesting to note the important part aquatic vegetation plays in successful aquarium management. There are five distinct ways in which plants benefit the aquarium, and an additional one which may be turned to the advantage of the aquarist. These values and their relationship to aquarium management may be listed thus:

FIRST. The ability of plants, under the influence of light, to develop free oxygen and to absorb carbon dioxide. Fishes, like other animals, must breathe oxygen. While pure water is composed of two parts of hydrogen and one of oxygen, it is not the oxygen of the water itself which supports fish life. Water absorbs or dissolves air into itself. It is this dissolved air which is absorbed by the gills of the fish and furnishes the oxygen necessary to life. As this oxygen in most aquariums is used by the fish more rapidly than it can be renewed by absorption at the water's surface, plants are most important. In a growing condition and under the stimulation of light, they give off much pure oxygen, most of which is absorbed directly into the water. When the plants are unusually active in this respect they furnish more oxygen than the water can take up, and we see tiny streams of bubbles rising from the leaves. This is to be observed when the light is strong. Excessive light, however, is not to be encouraged. The heat which usually goes with it raises the temperature of the water. This has the effect of *reducing* the oxygen content, for the warmer it gets, the *less* oxygen it can hold. Too much light also tends to turn the water green, and to produce that green mossy growth on the glass and plants — one of the aquarist's chief troubles. In justice to this green scum it should be said that it supplies oxygen and is a food for certain fishes.

The ideal situation for an aquarium is one in which it receives a strong diffused light, such as it would get at a large north window. If facing another direction, one or two hours' direct sunlight is not objectionable.

Before finishing point number one, it should be stated that fishes (again like other animals) exhale carbon dioxide. This is food for the plants, so that a beneficial exchange is thus set up. The term balanced aquarium has come into use to express that relationship between plant and fish life.

POINT NUMBER TWO. This also has to do with the chemistry of the aquarium. Fish in order to live must not only breathe; they must eat, and the certain result of eating is the discharge of contaminating substances into the water. These substances are fertilizers to the plants. They greedily absorb them through roots and leaves.

THE THIRD USE for aquarium plants is in helping to keep the water clear. This is accomplished in two ways — by shading and by food competition. Green water is produced by the presence of suspended microscopic vegetal organisms. To exist they must have food and light. Growing plants shade them and successfully compete for the food present in the water. The most effective plants for clearing the water are those which float, forming a green mantle. *Salvinia*, Duckweed and *Azolla* are the best plants for this purpose. The ideal arrangement is a growth of taller, grass-like plants, rooted in the sand, together with a floating mantle of plants. The disadvantage of small floating plants is that they get into the net when fish must be caught. They do *not* interfere with the absorption of oxygen by the water. On the contrary, they *furnish* it.

POINT NUMBER FOUR has to do with the very important part plants play in the breeding of fishes. Goldfishes and many of their cousins among the exotic aquarium fishes deposit their eggs on the finely divided leaves of plants like *Myriophyllum*. A number of the smaller fishes prefer depositing their eggs among loose masses of floating plants, such as *Riccia* or *Utricularia*. Plants of this character are of

---

* Special articles on the subjects indicated by an asterisk (*) will be found at the words so marked.

great value in the breeding of those popular fishes which have their young born alive. In most of those species the parents are cannibalistic and try to eat their new-born young. The babies, however, anticipate this, and quickly seek refuge among plants. *Riccia* is particularly good for the purpose. In a few weeks the babies are sufficiently grown to be out of danger of being eaten. *Azolla* is also used for this.

THE FIFTH POINT is by many considered to be the first. That is decorative value. As the aquarium is usually regarded in the light of a miniature bit of aquatic life, recreated in the home in as much completeness as possible, it is self-evident that the beauty of plant life is one of the first considerations. Plants not only give the most natural setting for fishes, but their mellow green furnishes the best possible background for the sparkling colors of the fishes.

The added personal advantage for the aquarist of plants is that there is always a ready market for aquarium-grown specimens. It is a recognized fact that they function better and live longer than do plants of similar species taken from the wild.

As to the most popular aquarium plants, there is no doubt that *Cabomba, Myriophyllum* and *Anacharis* (see ELODEA), are the commercial leaders. Each or all of them can be had wherever aquarium fishes are sold. Plants have different capacities in the production of oxygen. These three are fair in that respect. Most expert aquarists are more inclined to favor the two grass-like plants, *Vallisneria* (see EEL-GRASS) and *Sagittaria*, but they are not so well suited to aquaria of less than five-gallon capacity. Aquarium plants should be rooted in coarse sand in preference to pebbles.

Goldfish do best at temperatures between 60° and 70°, and ought to be fed once a day as much food as they can consume in five minutes. Besides prepared fish-foods they enjoy bits of boiled fish, shrimp, etc.

Exotic fishes (tropicals) should be kept within a range of 70° to 80°, and an average of 73° is satisfactory. At that temperature, or higher, they ought to be fed twice daily. They also should have variety.

No fish should be moved into water of a different temperature. All new water ought to be drawn a day before use, and stored in enamel or glass containers. Freshly drawn water, especially in winter, is also injurious to plants.

Many other plants, often suggested for aquaria, are quite unsuited to the maintenance of a properly balanced one. Such showy aquatics as the water hyacinth, water lily, water snowflake and many others are better suited to the water garden (which see) than to aquaria. — W. T. I.

**AQUATICA**, *-us, -um* (a-kwa'ti-ka). Growing in or near water.

**AQUATICS.** Water plants may be submerged, floating, or merely grow along the edge of a pool. Technically, the term should be restricted to plants that float upon the water (as do most water lilies) or are submerged in it (as is the eel-grass). But hort. usage has stretched the word to include not only true aquatics, but plants of marshes, meadows, swamps and bogs. For the chief garden aquatics see WATER GARDEN.

**AQUIFOLIACEAE** (a-kwi-fo-li-ā'see-ee). The holly family, sometimes called Ilicaceae, comprises only 3 genera, but nearly 300 species of trees and shrubs, of which *Ilex* (the holly) and *Nemopanthus* are the only cult. genera. They have alternate,* often evergreen, leaves, spiny-margined in some of the hollies, and small, inconspicuous, generally greenish-yellow flowers. Fruit berry-like (technically a small drupe*), often showy in some hollies. The family is of hort. importance only because of the fine evergreen foliage of the English and American holly trees and for their bright red fruit.

Technical flower characters: Calyx 3–6 parted, often persistent. Petals 4 or 5, distinct and separate, but slightly overlapping, often somewhat united only at the base. Stamens 4 or 5. Ovary superior,* 3- or many-celled.

**AQUIFOLIUM** (a-kwi-fō'li-um). The Latin name for the holly; literally *aqui*, a point, and *folium*, a leaf, in allusion to the spiny-margined leaves of some species.

**AQUILEGIA.** *See* COLUMBINE.

*AQUILEGIFOLIA*, *-us, -um* (a-kwi-lee-je-fō'li-a). With foliage like the columbine.

*AQUILINA*, *-us, -um* (a-kwi-ly'na). Aquiline; *i.e.* eagle-like.

**ARABIAN COFFEE** = *Coffea arabica*.

**ARABIAN JASMINE** = *Jasminum sambac*.

**ARABIAN PRIMROSE** = *Arnebia cornuta*.

*ARABICA*, *-us, -um* (a-rab'i-ka). From Arabia.

**ARABIS** (ar'ra-bis). The rock cresses comprise a large genus of herbs of the mustard family, much grown for ornament, especially in the wall garden, the rock garden, and in the open border. Of the hundred species, mostly from the north temperate zone, only the handful below are of garden interest. They have basal or stem leaves, usually hairy, and small, white or purple flowers, often in ample clusters (spikes* or racemes*). Fruit a long, narrow, usually flattened pod. (The name is a Latinized form of Arabia, from which some (not hort.) species came.)

The rock cresses are of very easy culture. The perennial sorts are easily propagated by spring or fall division of their roots. All prefer open sunlight and a warm, rather sandy soil, although they will often thrive in poor soils.

**albida.** Wall cress. A tufted, white-foliaged, hairy perennial from the Caucasus, usually less than 12 in. high. Leaves 1–3 in. long, coarsely toothed towards the relatively broad apex. Flowers white, fragrant, about ⅓ in. long, in loose clusters. May. There are double-flowered and variegated-leaved forms. A good plant for dry walls or the rock garden.*

**alpina.** A mountain plant from Eu., lower than the above and less hairy. Leaves more or less oblong, toothed throughout, 1–3 in. long. Flowers about ⅓ in. long, white. Primarily a rock garden species and often confused with *A. albida*. May. There is a double-flowered form; much finer than the typical one.

**aubrietioides.** A low, densely tufted perennial from Asia Minor, suited only to the rock garden. Leaves felty white or greenish, very small, blunt, and numerous, those on the stem appressed.* Flowers pink. May. Requires a gritty, sandy soil. *See* ROCK GARDEN.

**kellereri.** *See* list of plants at ROCK GARDEN.

**mollis.** A perennial, border plant from the Caucasus, usually 18–20 in. high. Leaves oval or roundish, heart-shaped at the base, often stem-clasping. Flowers white, about ½ in. long, in terminal clusters.

**ARACEAE** (a-ray'see-ee). The arum family (usually called simply aroids) comprises a huge aggregation of more than 100 genera and about 1500 species of herbs, the stems of some, especially in the tropical sorts, becoming woody and even tree-like. The family is often called the arum or *Calla* family. It contains not only these but such well-known plants as the calla lily, the Jack-in-the-pulpit (see ARISAEMA), the skunk-cabbage, the sweet flag (see ACORUS), and *Dracunculus*. All these, except the calla lily, are hardy, but most of the Araceae are tropical plants. All contain a bitter, often poisonous juice, sometimes milky.

Leaves various, wholly without marginal teeth, but often deeply lobed, very showy in some of the hort. genera, notably *Aglaonema, Alocasia, Anthurium, Caladium, Colocasia* (elephant's-ear), *Dieffenbachia, Schismatoglottis, Scindapsus,* and *Spathiphyllum*. All of these are handsome, tropical foliage plants of greenhouse culture, a few as summer bedding plants in the north.

There are, besides those above, two or three hardy native plants in *Orontium, Peltandra* and *Lysichitum*. There is one tropical aquatic (see PISTIA), and besides the taro (see COLOCASIA), another genus furnishes edible rootstocks (see XANTHOSOMA). For other hort. genera, all tropical, see HYDROSME, PHILODENDRON and MONSTERA, a curious plant with leaves full of holes, and edible fruit.

The flowers of the aroids are difficult for the gardener to fathom. What he calls a "flower," say the "Jack" in Jack-in-the-pulpit, is a collection of almost microscopic ones crowded on a column-like organ (the "Jack") technically known as a spadix. The spadix (which is the "flower" of most gardeners) may be a foot or more long in many tropical species, brightly colored and very showy, especially in *Anthurium*. *See* FLOWER.

Below the spadix there is a bract,* leaf-like but often colored in some genera, or funnel-shaped and completely

---

* Special articles on the subjects indicated by an asterisk (*) will be found at the words so marked.

surrounding the spadix as in the "pulpit" of the Jack-in-the-pulpit. This leaf-like or funnel-shaped organ is the spathe,* common (but soon withering in many tropical genera) throughout the Araceae. Fruit fleshy in all genera.

Technical flower characters: Sepals and petals none, or replaced by 4–8 scale-like substitutes. Stamens 1 or many, sometimes united. Ovary 1, with one to many carpels, each with one or more ovules. The individual flowers are extremely minute, and exact identification of the genera consequently difficult.

**ARACHIS.** See PEANUT.

*ARACHNOIDEA, -us, -um* (a-rak-noy'dee-a). Arachnoid; *i.e.* like a spider's web.

**ARALIA** (a-ray'li-a). A genus of 20 species of mostly spiny shrubs and trees, or unarmed perennial herbs, belonging to the ginseng family, and grown for ornament. All but a few are native in N.A. or eastern As. Leaves alternate,* compound,* or twice- or thrice-compound,* often very large and showy. Flowers greenish or whitish, in umbels, the latter often grouped in a large terminal cluster (panicle*). Fruit berry-like, with 2–5 flattened stones. (*Aralia* is of unknown origin.)

The shrubby and tree aralias, such as the angelica trees and the Hercules'-club, are striking plants for the shrub border or for specimens on the lawn. They need a rich soil and a reasonable amount of moisture. The perennial herbs are largely woods plants suited to the wild garden, where they should have partial shade and a rich humus. Propagation of the woody species by seeds sown in frames in the spring or by root cuttings over bottom-heat. The perennials are easily divided in the spring.

For some greenhouse decorative plants wrongly but commonly called *Aralia,* see POLYSCIAS and DIZYGOTHECA.

**californica.** Elk clover. A stout herbaceous perennial 6–10 ft. high. Leaves twice-compound,* the ultimate segments usually doubly toothed, nearly 12 in. long. Umbels* in a spreading panicle* nearly 18 in. long. British Columbia to Calif.

**chinensis.** Chinese angelica tree. A prickly shrub or small tree, not over 20 ft. high. Leaves very large, composed of 40–80, more or less oval leaflets that are about 7 in. long and closely toothed. Flower cluster very large, usually solitary, often 18 in. wide. Fruit black. China. Hardy from zone* 4 southward. The plant offered as *A. chinensis mandshurica* is often the next species.

**elata.** Japanese angelica tree. A stout prickly shrub or small tree, sometimes 25 ft. high. Leaves sometimes 3 ft. long, doubly compound,* the numerous leaflets narrowly elliptic, about 9 in. long, remotely toothed. They are dark green above, but paler beneath. Flower cluster large, hairy, the flowers whitish. Fruit black. Jap. and on the mainland. A very handsome tree with striking, bold foliage. Has hardier than *A. chinensis,* possibly only from the southern edge of zone* 4. There are white- and golden-variegated forms.

**japonica** = *Aralia elata.*

**nudicaulis.** Wild sarsaparilla. A low herb with a single, long-stalked, compound leaf and a ball-like cluster of greenish-yellow flowers. Eastern N.A. Will grow in a variety of places, and in pure sand. See SAND GARDENS.

**papyrifera** = *Tetrapanax papyriferum.*

**racemosa.** American spikenard; called also spikenard. A branching perennial herb 3–5 ft. high. Leaves twice-compound, the ultimate leaflets few, more or less heart-shaped, about 6 in. long, double-toothed. Flowers greenish, the umbels* arranged in a large cluster (raceme*). Fruit brownish-purple. Eastern N.A. The plant has spicy, aromatic roots.

**spinosa.** Hercules'-club, called, also, devil's-walking-stick. A North American spiny-trunked tree sometimes 40 ft. high. Leaves twice-compound,* long-stalked, the leaflets prickly, ovalish, about 4 in. long, pale on the under side. Flowers whitish in large, hairy clusters (panicles*). Fruit black. It forms an impenetrable, prickly barrier. See SMOKE.

**ARALIACEAE** (a-ray-li-a'see-ee). The ginseng family includes only a dozen or so hort. subjects among more than 50 genera of herbs, shrubs, vines or trees widely distributed over the world. They often have prickly stems among the shrubs and trees, but *Panax* (the ginseng) are unarmed herbs. Leaves simple* in *Hedera* (the English ivy), *Gilibertia, Echinopanax, Tetrapanax,* and *Fatsia,* but the blade may be variously cut or lobed even in these. All the other hort. genera have compound* or even twice- or thrice-compound* leaves, often of great size and consequently very showy.

Of the hardy woody genera (with compound* leaves), *Aralia* and *Acanthopanax* are the best known. Tropical or sub-tropical genera, mostly of greenhouse culture, include *Dizygotheca, Polyscias, Tupidanthus,* and *Nothopanax.*

The flowers of the ginseng family, never showy, are small, usually greenish or greenish-white, borne in umbels, but the latter often congested into a head-like cluster and borne in large, branched, umbel-like clusters (a compound umbel*) or in racemes* or panicles.* Fruit fleshy (a berry or a drupe*).

Technical flower characters: Calyx small, attached to the ovary. Petals 5, their margins touching or overlapping, or even slightly united. Stamens 5, epigynous.* Ovary inferior,* 1- to many-celled.

*ARAUCANA, -us, -um* (or-ro-kay'na). From Araucana, an old name for the southern part of Chile.

**ARAUCARIA** (or-ro-cay'ri-a). Stately evergreen trees of the pine family, one, the Norfolk Island pine, a widely grown decorative florist's plant in its young state; another, the famous monkey-puzzle. All are natives of the southern hemisphere. Branches in regular tiers. Leaves evergreen, prickly and scale-like or expanded into flat, thick, leathery blades, always stiff. The flowers and seeds are borne between the scales of an egg-shaped or globe-like cone which falls apart in age. (*Araucaria* is from *Araucana, see* above.)

The Norfolk Island pine (*A. excelsa*) is much grown in its young state as a pot plant. It needs a cool greenhouse, partial shade, and is best grown in potting mixture* 3. Propagation is by seed or cuttings of the terminal leader or its successors. Cuttings from lateral growth make unsymmetrical, lopsided plants. Planted in sand, the cuttings will root if kept at about 60°.

The other species are lofty trees, seldom grown in greenhouses, and outdoors only as indicated below, except the monkey-puzzle. This curious evergreen is hardy outdoors from zone* 5 southward, and, with protection (*see* PROTECTING PLANTS), in sheltered places north of this.

**araucana.** Monkey-puzzle, so-called from its habit of inextricable branching. The main branches are in tiers, but the ramifications twist and turn to form an impenetrable and very prickly growth. Leaves persisting for years, prickle-pointed, ovalish, flat, leathery, very stiff, and about 2 in. long when mature, bright green. Cone 6–8 in. in diameter. Hardy outdoors from zone* 5, and often planted for its grotesque habit. Chile. Long sold as *A. imbricata.*

**bidwilli.** Bunya-bunya. An Australian tree up to 150 ft., less in cult. and hardy only in zones* 8 and 9. Leaves glossy-green in distinct rows, sharp-pointed, stiff, oblong-oval, about 1½ in. long. Grown outdoors mostly in Calif. and Fla.

**cunninghami.** Moreton Bay pine, called, also, hoop pine. An Australian evergreen tree up to 150 ft., much less in cult., less symmetrical than the next, but often grown for ornament. Leaves stiff, sharp-pointed, needle-like, about 1½ in. long. There is also a variety with bluish-green foliage. Hardy outdoors only in zones* 8 and 9.

**excelsa.** Norfolk Island pine. As usually grown, a pot plant 2–10 ft. high; at home often 200 ft. high, and an important timber tree. Branches 5–7 in a tier, thickly beset with sharp-pointed leaves that are about ¼ in. long and curved at the tip. It practically never flowers or fruits in cult. An extremely popular florist's plant, grown by the million, and an excellent house plant. Norfolk Island (in the Pacific Ocean).

**imbricata** = *Araucaria araucana.*

**ARAUJIA** (a-raw'je-a). A small genus of mostly Brazilian, woody vines of the milkweed family, the one below sometimes grown as a greenhouse climber. Leaves opposite.* Flowers in sparse clusters in the axils* of the leaves, not very showy, the corolla bell-shaped. Fruit a leathery pod (follicle*). (Named for Araujo de Azevedo, Portuguese statesman.)

A greenhouse plant best grown in potting mixture* 5, in the cool house, and outdoors in zones* 8 and 9. Propagated by cuttings over bottom-heat, or by seeds sown outdoors in tropical and sub-tropical regions.

**sericofera.** A tall-growing, woody vine. Leaves oblongish, 2–4 in. long, with a tapering point, mealy on the under side. Flowers pale pink or white, about ¾ in. wide. Southern Brazil.

**ARBOR DAY.** A day set aside for the planting of trees, usually as a community enterprise, and largely by school children. The plan originated in Neb. in 1872 and is now general, although the day varies in the different states. Arbor Day in most states is in April or early May.

*ARBOREA, -us, -um* (ar-bore'ee-a). Tree-like; but often, as a specific name, indicating mere woodiness.

*ARBORESCENS* (ar-bore-ress'ens). Almost tree-like.

**ARBORETUM.** Strictly, a collection of trees grown for study, research or ornament; now, quite generally, any collection of woody plants so grown. By far the most important

---

* Special articles on the subjects indicated by an asterisk (*) will be found at the words so marked.

arboretum in this country is the Arnold Arboretum of Harvard University at Jamaica Plain, Mass. It occupies several hundred acres, has perhaps the greatest collection of trees, shrubs and woody vines in the world, and a large library and herbarium.*

There are many other arboreta in the country, some on private estates, in public parks, and various experimental collections of the U.S. Forest Service. Among the notable private collections are: Myron Stratton, Colorado Springs; Brett Palm Collection and the Montgomery Palm Collection, both at Coconut Grove, Fla.; Hunnewell Arboretum, Wellesley, Mass.; Childs Frick Arboretum, Roslyn, L.I.; and the John Evans Arboretum, Radnor, Pa.

Several botanic gardens* maintain very large collections of trees, shrubs and vines as part of their outdoor exhibits, especially the New York Botanical Garden, Missouri Botanical Garden and the Nichols Arboretum of the University of Mich. at Ann Arbor.

Many state and county park systems maintain collections of trees and in addition there are several public arboreta of more than local or civic importance. The leading public collections beyond those already mentioned are:

Boyce Thompson Southwestern Arboretum, Superior, Ariz.
Rock Creek Park Arboretum, Washington, D.C.
Los Angeles County Arboretum, Sierra Madre, Calif.
Letchworth Park Arboretum, Portageville, N.Y.
Portland Civic Arboretum, Portland, Ore.
Morris Arboretum, University of Pennsylvania, Philadelphia, Pa.
Lehigh University Arboretum, Bethlehem, Pa.
Public Park System, Rochester, N.Y.
Golden Gate Park, San Francisco, Calif.
Morton Arboretum, Lisle, Ill.

In addition the U.S. Forest Service maintains many tree collections in different parts of the country, mostly for study of silvicultural problems, involving the growing of trees in considerable stands. Such experiments are worth study to those with small pieces of forest on their estates, but lie outside the scope of the usual arboretum. *See also* BOTANIC GARDEN and Mount Vernon at TREES.

**ARBORICULTURE.** The culture of trees (which see).

**ARBORS AND ARCHES.** Arbors and arches are of two general types, one acts merely as a support for vines where the structure is subordinate to the planting; in the other the architectural structure is the important decorative feature, while the planting is secondary.

In construction it is important not to confuse the two types. If the plant effect is to dominate, the design of the structure should be simple and durable. In this case elaborate architectural detail is superfluous, since it is shrouded with vines. The structure, however, should be substantial, because repair work will be difficult after the vines have matured. The main supports of an arbor should be close enough together longitudinally to prevent sagging under weight of the vines. Distance between supports should not exceed eight feet. This same precaution applies to the width of the arbor and its cross-members. When the cross-span is too wide the supporting members must become disproportionately heavy to prevent sagging. For light-weight structures the longitudinal spacing between supports should be approximately equal to the cross-span. To secure a very light, airy effect the spacing between supports should be lengthened by using light, intermediate side supports

A formal architectural arbor

and arched cross-spans in place of horizontal members. Since the arch type of arbor combines greater strength with lighter structure, it is more graceful in its effect.

An arbor is merely a repetition of the same unit, depending upon the rhythm of this repetition for its effect. Hence, the cross-members should be reduced to the minimum lest they interrupt the view monotonously and destroy the effect of length. Whenever the longitudinal members of an arbor predominate there is a pleasing sense of continuity.

Details of arbor design are infinite in their variety. It is the purpose here to state general principles of construction, leaving individual ingenuity to develop details.

For the purely vine-supporting structure wood or non-rusting metal are the best materials. From the ornamental viewpoint wood is the most satisfactory. Cypress has proven to be the most durable wood for outdoor arbor construction; next in durability is redwood or fir. If the wood is given two coats of good lead and oil paint before erection, with two more coats after erection, a durable job is assured. To prevent further deterioration use copper nails and galvanized iron bolts. Wherever possible wood members should be fitted into each other to be self-supporting without nails. Durability of construction is important because nothing can be more exasperating than the collapse of an arbor when the vines have matured to their full beauty.

Although metal construction combined with wire vine supports can be very attractive it is less ornamental than wood and often burns the vines in very hot climates.

Wherever the architectural structure is the dominating feature masonry should be used for the main supports. Since the scale of this type of arbor is usually larger than the vine-covered type, both the longitudinal and cross-spans can be increased in length. The design of masonry arches is a real architectural problem requiring skill in the use of materials and construction. Unless the builder is endowed with creative ability it is wise to refresh his imagination from the many examples of architectural arbor design characteristic of Old World gardens. To insure permanency all supports must be carried below the frost line which averages three feet in the northern states. Unless the structure is securely built many types of vines in maturity will dislodge their supports to suit their growing convenience and the structural design will be destroyed.

An arbor made chiefly for vines

Arches are just short arbors and may be treated in much the same way. In its true sense an arch is merely an ornamental opening through a barrier. Therefore, when an arch is used as a gateway it should be flanked by planting so that it is the only opening through which one may pass. It is always inconsistent to see an arch floating in the open where it is just as convenient to go around it as to walk through. — R. E. G.

**ARBOR-TRISTIS, -e** (ar-bor-tris'tis). Sad, or grayish, tree.

**ARBORVITAE.** Properly, the evergreens of the genus *Thuja;* also, not quite so appropriately, evergreens of the genus *Thujopsis*. See both genera.

**ARBUTIFOLIA, -us, -um** (ar-bew-ti-fō'li-a). With leaves like the strawberry tree (*Arbutus*).

**ARBUTUS** (ar-bew'tus). A small genus of broad-leaved evergreen trees of the heath family, two of which are grown

---

* Special articles on the subjects indicated by an asterisk (*) will be found at the words so marked.

in warm regions for ornament. Leaves alternate* and stalked. Flowers white or pinkish, urn-shaped, in loose terminal clusters (panicles*). Fruit fleshy, red or orange. (*Arbutus* is the classical Latin name of a European species.)

These plants have nothing to do with trailing arbutus (which see).

Both the species below prefer well-drained, wind-sheltered sites, and the first is an important source of honey to Calif. bee keepers. Propagated by cuttings of partially ripened wood, taken in the fall and under glass, also by layers.

**menziesi.** Madroña; called also laurelwood and Oregon laurel. A tall tree found wild from British Columbia to Calif. Leaves oblongish, about 4 in. long, grayish-green beneath, and without marginal teeth. Flower cluster about 6 in. long, the flowers white, about ⅓ in. long. Fruit orange-red. June. Hardy outdoors only from zone* 6 southward, and seldom planted in greenhouses.

**unedo.** Strawberry tree. Less than half the height of the madroña, and a native of southern Eu. Branches sticky-hairy. Leaves elliptic or oblong, about 3½ in. long, toothed. Flower cluster drooping, about 2 in. long, the white or pink flowers about ¼ in. long. Fruit strawberry-like, about ¾ in. in diameter, orange-red. Hardy from zone* 6 southward, somewhat north of this with protection. Oct.

**ARBUTUS FAMILY.** The Ericaceae.

**ARCHANGELICA.** A disused generic name for plants now included in *Angelica*.

**ARCHES.** *See* ARBORS AND ARCHES.

**ARCHING LAYERS.** *See* LAYERING.

**ARCHITECTURAL STYLE.** Traditional styles of gardening correspond to the few major period changes in architectural styles. Because of the long time necessary for gardens to mature they did not follow temporary influence which caused many transitional styles in architecture.

Even though gardening has become a distinct art in modern times the influence of architecture on garden style is still inevitable when related to buildings. The distinct architectural styles in gardening are Italian, French, Spanish, English, Japanese and American Colonial. Although other countries and other influences added their own interpretation to these styles they were merely variations of the same basic style and purely local in their influence. For instance, the Mission garden of southern California is basically the same as the Spanish Patio garden, and the Dutch garden is similar in design to French and English gardens, with minor variations of architectural detail and planting. Likewise, everything that was worth retaining from the earlier styles of gardening in Egypt, Syria, Babylonia, Greece and Classic Rome has been incorporated in the Italian Renaissance style.

The Italian Renaissance gardens are intimately related to villas, casinos or palaces and, therefore, are architectural in character. Contrary to the popular conception that Italian gardens are highly artificial and pretentious, they are in reality in close harmony with natural conditions and the social life of the people for whom they were designed. In using the Italian precedent natural conditions must be given quite as logical consideration as any other style, and the design may be as unpretentious as a peasant garden or as grandiose as the social habits of the owner demand.

The characteristics of the Italian gardens are lavish use of water in cascades, fountains and pools; an extremely restrained use of plant materials, primarily box or yew hedges, cypress, stone pine and ilex trees; very little grass; large gravel areas, and almost no perennial flowers. Color is obtained by roses climbing on the walls, ornamental pots of annuals, and occasional parterre patterns of bedding plants. Walls, stairways, garden buildings and statuary are fanciful in their detail and large in scale.

Most Italian gardens were located on hillsides commanding magnificent views, and were designed at different levels to take advantage not only of the views but a natural gravity source of water. In adapting this style to modern use expensive materials are unnecessary; soft tufa rock and travertine were more often used than white marble. American sandstone, limestone and Wisconsin travertine are suitable substitutes for this type of garden architecture.

Stock sculptural ornaments and trivial wrought iron and ornamental pottery were unknown to the Italians who designed every detail for its special function. To attain the same result all ornaments must be equally genuine and not superficial embellishment.

The French gardens are an adaptation of Italian Renaissance design to less rugged topography and a more sophisticated social life. The basic design is the same but the architectural and planting details give it a character distinctly French. Parterre patterns, instead of being simple geometric designs, are more elaborate scroll patterns. Sculptural and architectural ornament is even more fanciful and romantic and smaller in scale; lead and bronze figures are more frequently used, turf and flowers take the place of gravel, water is more difficult to obtain and, therefore, more sparingly used. Treillage, wall decorations and garden pavilions are a distinct contribution of the French style.

Formal English gardens are also basically the same in design as Italian Renaissance gardens. The same general lines were followed, but balustrades, walls, steps, garden buildings and other architectural details followed the Elizabethan, Georgian or Jacobean architectural style. Brick trimmed with limestone or plain limestone was used in place of marble, travertine and stucco. Because of different climatic conditions turf and a wider variety of flowers are used in place of gravel, water and architectural ornaments. English gardens are primarily green with massive clipped evergreen hedges, broad expanses of lawn and luxurious growing trees.

The perennial border with a wide variety and profusion of flowers is distinctly English. The naturalistic English style of garden broke away entirely from the architectural influence and achieved nothing worthy of the name of art.

The American Colonial architectural style, coming as it did from England, was merely a simplification of the English Georgian style. Instead of emulating the pretentious Georgian architecture of England the colonists applied the same ideas to their modest means and materials. Wood was plentiful and replaced brick and stone. In using wood a new and distinctive style was created. A simple wooden paling or picket fence took the place of walls and balustrades. Graceful, unpretentious garden pavilions and the wooden pump replaced elaborate masonry summer houses and fountains; a profusion of flowers and a few simple wooden benches created interest sufficient for the busy colonists. *See also* MODERN GARDEN DESIGN. — R. E. G.

**ARCHONTOPHOENIX** (ar-kon-toe-fee′nix). An Australian genus of feather palms, one much planted for ornament in Calif. and Fla., rarely in greenhouses. They have tall trunks, crowned by a large collection of compound* leaves with numerous, sometimes split, leaflets. Flowers with the male and female flowers in separate clusters that are borne considerably below the crown of leaves. Fruit small, nearly round. (*Archontophoenix* is Greek for majestic palm.)

When planted outdoors (only possible in zone* 9 and especially favorable localities in zone* 8) these palms, which are very handsome, require rich soil and plenty of moisture. If the soil is too sandy or dry, dig it out and fill in with rich compost and loam.

**alexandrae.** A tall palm with a smooth trunk (often 60 ft. high), usually somewhat swollen at the base. Leaves 8–12 ft. long, the leaflets numerous, about 18 in. long and 1½ in. wide, green above but ashy-green beneath. Flower cluster about 12 in. long, the flowers greenish-yellow or whitish. Fruit not quite egg-shaped. A handsome palm sometimes known as *Ptychosperma alexandrae*.

**cunninghamiana.** This is the palm known to many growers as *Seaforthia elegans* and also as *Loroma*. It resembles *A. alexandrae*, but has no swelling at the base, and the leaves are green both sides, and with wider leaflets. Much more widely grown than the above, and not uncommon as a pot plant in greenhouses. It needs a cool greenhouse and should be planted in potting mixture* 4.

*ARCTICA, -us, -um* (ark′ti-ka). Arctic.

**ARCTIUM LAPPA** = Burdock. *See* list at WEEDS.

**ARCTOSTAPHYLOS** (ark-to-staff′i-los). A very large genus of woody plants, mostly North American, belonging to the heath family and containing such handsome garden plants as the bearberry and manzanita. They are shrubs or

---

* Special articles on the subjects indicated by an asterisk (*) will be found at the words so marked.

small trees (one a prostrate ground cover), with handsome evergreen leaves without marginal teeth. Flowers small, urn- or bell-shaped, often nodding. Fruit red or dull, fleshy. (*Arctostaphylos* is Greek for bear's grape.)

The tall shrubs or trees below (both natives of the Pacific Coast) have the same cultural and climatic requirements as the genus *Arbutus* (which see). They are useful bee plants in Calif. The bearberry (*A. uva-ursi*) is a handsome, vine-like, evergreen ground-cover found throughout sandy and rocky places in the north temperate zone. It is difficult to transplant unless one digs frozen clumps and plunges them in a prepared bed of 6 parts clean sand and 4 parts acid humus (*see* ACID AND ALKALI SOILS for details). In the spring the thawing clumps will become established. Potted plants offered by dealers should be put in the same mixture, preferably in early spring or from Aug. 15 to Sept. 15 in the North.

**glauca.** A tree or shrub, usually less than 20 ft. high. Leaves ovalish, 1–1½ in. long. Flowers white. Southern and Lower Calif.

**tomentosa.** Woolly manzanita. A tree or shrub rarely exceeding 20 ft. Leaves broadly oval, 1½–2 in., covered with white felt beneath. Flowers pink or white. British Columbia to Calif. Hardier than *A. glauca.* There are many other Californian species which may be in occasional cult.

**uva-ursi.** Bearberry; called, also, kinnikinnick. Prostrate, the stems often 5–6 ft. long and rooting at the joints to form large patches of handsome evergreen foliage that turns bronzy in winter. Leaves slightly broader upwards, about 1 in. long and ⅓ in. wide, the margins rolled and minutely fringed with hairs. Flowers white or pink. Throughout the north temperate zone and hardy throughout N.A. For culture *see* above.

**ARCTOTIS** (ark-toe'tis). A genus of South African, white-woolly, tender annual herbs, family Compositae, the two below widely grown as garden flowers. They have alternate* leaves, usually toothed or deeply cut, and handsome, long-stalked, blue, yellow or orange heads with both ray and disk flowers. (*Arctotis* is Greek for bear's ear, in allusion to the pappus scales.)

Both those below are grown as tender annuals. For culture *see* ANNUALS.

**breviscapa.** Low, stemless herb with oblongish leaves, 4–5½ in. long, cut feather-fashion. Heads 2 in. wide, the rays orange, the center darker. Flowers from the end of June to frost.

**stoechadifolia.** African daisy. A stout herb 30–48 in. high. Leaves ovalish, or broader towards the tip, about 3 in. long and toothed on the margin. Heads about 3 in. wide, blue and yellow, occasionally white or violet, flowering from end of June to frost. Often sold as *A. grandis.*

***ARCTURUS*** (ark-tew'rus). The specific name of a few plants named after the star Arcturus.

**ARDISIA** (ar-diz'i-a). The only hort. genus of the family **Myrsinaceae** (mur-sin-ā'see-ee), and including one widely grown pot plant (*A. crispa*) cult. for its bright red berries. They have alternate,* leathery, often shining green leaves, and small white or reddish flowers in clusters (cymes* or panicles*). Corolla united, 4–5-lobed, with 5 stamens opposite the lobes. Fruit a drupe.* The genus contains over 200 species of trees and shrubs, all tropical, and often called spearflower. (*Ardisia* is Greek for a point.)

The first species below is a very popular florist's pot plant, where it is a compact, bushy shrub. It should be grown in potting mixture* 5, in a cool greenhouse, and is propagated by spring-sown seeds or by cuttings of half-ripened wood over bottom-heat. Both species can be grown outdoors in zones* 8 and 9.

**crenulata** = *Ardisia crispa.*

**crispa.** A bushy shrub, but as usually grown, a compact, greenhouse pot plant. Leaves oblongish, about 2½ in. long, wavy-margined. Flowers red. Berries scarlet. Tropical As. A fine shrub, when in fruit, for Christmas decoration.

**paniculata.** Marlberry. A tropical American shrub or small tree, wild in southern Fla., but not very common in cult. Leaves more or less oblong, 5–7 in. long. Flowers white. Fruit shiny black.

**ARECA** (a-ree'ka). A small genus of tropical Old World feather palms, the only species of even secondary hort. interest being the famous betel palm, yielding the betelnut, which is somewhat grown for ornament in southern Fla. Leaves feather-parted, the leaflets numerous. Flower cluster branched, borne below the crown of leaves, the female flowers toward the base and the male flowers toward the tip of the cluster, fragrant. Fruit egg-shaped or nearly so, orange or red. (*Areca* is thought to be a Latinized version of a Malayan name.)

The species below is not the common areca palm of the florists which is usually *Chrysalidocarpus lutescens.* Other genera also sometimes called *Areca* are: *Dictyosperma, Hyophorbe,* and several others, the name *Areca* having once been widely applied.

For culture *see* CHRYSALIDOCARPUS.

**catechu** (spelled, also, **cathecu**). Betel palm. A graceful, unarmed, ring-stemmed, slender palm, sometimes 80 ft. high. Leaves 3–5 ft. long, the numerous leaflets soft, rather wide, irregularly cleft or notched towards the tip, sometimes with the upper leaflets more or less joined. Fruit about 1½ in. long, containing the betelnut, which is so widely used in the Far East that millions of trees are cult. for this purpose. Malaya or tropical As. The seed is sliced, rolled in a leaf of *Piper betel,* with a sprinkling of lime, and chewed. It stains saliva red and the teeth black, but is thought to aid digestion.

**ARECACEAE** = PALMACEAE.

**ARECASTRUM** (a-ree-kas'trum). A genus of South American feather palms, the only species of which is widely grown for ornament, both in greenhouses and outdoors in zones* 8 and 9. They have ringed trunks, compound* leaves with the leaflets arranged feather-fashion, unisexual* flowers borne in a cluster from the leaf-crown and nearly round fruits about 1 in. in diameter. (*Arecastrum* signifies *Areca*-like.)

Widely cult. by florists for its feathery ornamental foliage, often under the names of *Cocos plumosa* and *C. romanzoffiana.* It needs potting mixture* 4, a warm, moist-atmosphered greenhouse and plenty of water. Its outdoor cult. in Fla. and southern Calif. is very popular as it frequently reaches 40 ft. in height, is a fine avenue or street tree, and relatively hardy up to the limits of zone* 8.

**romanzoffianum.** Queen palm; called, also, plumy coconut. Trunk ringed, often clothed with a few dead, but persistent, leaves in old specimens. Leaves in mature plants 7–12 ft. long, much smaller in pot or tub specimens, the leaflets very numerous, never more than 1 in. wide. Flower cluster from between a spathe* 2–3 ft. long, the female flowers below the male and towards the tip. Fruits numerous, not over 1 in. in diameter, in large, hanging clusters.

Some regard the plant most common in cult. as a variety (*var.* **australe**) of the above, but this is not certain.

**ARENARIA** (a-re-nay'ri-a). The sandworts comprise a large genus of mostly low herbs of the pink family, a few grown in the border and rock garden for their profuse bloom. Of over 100 species, confined to the north temperate zone, only those below, all perennials, are of hort. interest. They have small leaves and mostly small white flowers, with 5 petals, in variously branched clusters, or solitary. Fruit a tiny dry pod. (*Arenaria* means growing in sandy places.)

The cult. sandworts are usually tufted plants of the open sunshine and require a sandy or gritty soil. They tend to make mats or low tufts and are especially suited to the wall garden or to the rock garden. They are easily propagated by division of the roots. Some of them are occasionally offered as *Alsine.*

**balearica.** Corsican sandwort. Scarcely 3 in. high and prostrate. Leaves ovalish, glossy, rather thick, very small and numerous. Flowers white, solitary. A moss-like plant, preferring moist sites in the rock garden.* July. Balearic Islands. Needs protection north of zone* 4.

**caespitosa** = *Arenaria verna caespitosa.*

**grandiflora.** A semi-prostrate herb from Europe, with creeping, wiry stems. Leaves awl-shaped, silvery-gray. Flowers white, solitary or in twos or threes. June.

**groenlandica.** Mountain sandwort; called also mountain starwort. A native, tufted plant suited to the rock garden in cool regions. It makes patches a foot wide and about 5 in. high. Leaves small, very numerous, about ½ in. long and 1/16 in. wide. Flowers in groups of 1–5. Greenland to mountains of N. Car. June. Use gritty soil with pH 5. (*See* ACID AND ALKALI SOILS.)

**juniperina.** A low, tufted plant with wiry stems, not over 6 in. high. Leaves resembling a juniper, greenish-gray. Flowers white, in small clusters. June. Southern Eu. and Asia Minor. A rock garden species needing protection north of zone* 4.

**montana.** A European rock garden species scarcely over 4 in. high. Leaves small and narrow. Flowers solitary, white. *See* ROCK GARDEN.

**saxifraga.** A mountain plant from southern Eu. and Asia Minor, used in the rock garden, but needing protection north of zone* 4. Leaves in rosettes, covered with sticky hairs, about ½ in. long. Flowers 2–7 in a cluster. July.

**verna.** A tufted plant from the European and Rocky Mountains, suited to the rock garden. Leaves flat, very narrow. Flowers solitary on very slender, thread-like stalks. June. The *var.* caespitosa is still lower, compact, and forms dense, moss-like clumps. It is also suited for a rocky wall.

**ARENGA** (a-ren'ga). A small group of Asiatic and Ma-

* Special articles on the subjects indicated by an asterisk (*) will be found at the words so marked.

layan feather palms, the one below somewhat cultivated outdoors in zone* 9, rarely in greenhouses. Leaves compound,* very large, the leaflets arranged feather-fashion, and having many, strong veins, gray beneath and often notched or cut off at the tip. Flower cluster much-branched, the male and female flowers usually in separate clusters on the same tree. Fruit more or less fleshy. (*Arenga* is of unknown origin.)

The species below rarely flowers and fruits in cult., whether outdoors or in greenhouses, which is fortunate, as the plants die once they have flowered and fruited. The greenhouse cult. is the same as for *Chrysalidocarpus*.

**saccharifera.** The gomuti, jaggery or sugar palm of Malaya, and widely cult. in the tropics for the sugar made from its sap. Trunk up to 40 ft., generally spineless. Leaves 15-20 ft. long (much less in cult.), with 100 or more leaflets on either side of the leafstalk. Leaflets arranged singly or in small bunches, nearly always toothed towards the tip. Fruit oblongish, nearly 2 in. long, flattened at the top.

*AREOLATA, -us, -um* (ar-ee-o-lay′ta). Pitted.

**ARETHUSA** (a-re-thoo′za). A small group of tuberous-rooted bog orchids, the one below cultivated for its beautiful fringed flowers, but suited only to the more acid sites of the bog garden. It prefers pH 4 or 5 (*see* ACID AND ALKALI SOILS). Besides two Asiatic (not cult.) species, the only other one is the dragon's mouth or wild pink, **Arethusa bulbosa**, of eastern N.A. It is about 8 in. high, bears a solitary leaf that appears after the plant blooms from the sheaths of the otherwise naked flower stalk. Flower solitary, hooded, rose-purple, fringed with yellow. May. *See* Hardy Orchids at ORCHIDS. (*Arethusa* was named for the nymph.)

**ARGANIA** (are-gain′i-a). A genus of Moroccan trees comprising only one species, the argan tree, of the family Sapotaceae. It is somewhat cult. in Calif. and Fla. for ornament, but widely grown for argan oil in northern Af. Leaves evergreen. Flowers greenish-yellow. Fruit a berry. (*Argania* is a Latinized version of arjan, a native name for the tree.)

**sideroxylon.** Argan tree. A tree seldom over 20 ft., up which goats scramble in Morocco for the fruits. Leaves dark green. Flowers in small cymes* in the leaf-axils.* Berry oblong. Little is known as to best method of cult. for this tree. In its native home it grows in the lowlands.

**ARGAN TREE** = *Argania sideroxylon*.

**ARGEMONE** (are-jem′o-nee). The prickly poppies are tropical American herbs of perhaps 10 species, belonging to the poppy family, one very widely grown as an annual. They are stout herbs with yellow juice, the cut leaves more or less toothed and spiny-margined. Flowers large, with 2 or 3 sepals and 4–6 rather showy petals. Fruit a prickly pod (capsule*), opening by terminal valves. (*Argemone* is a classical plant name of uncertain application here.)

*Argemone grandiflora* is a very popular hardy annual. For cult. *see* ANNUALS. The second species, also grown as an annual, should be similarly treated. It is not so well liked as the first species.

**grandiflora.** A stout, Mexican herb, 24-36 in. high, less spiny than the next. Leaves with white veins. Flowers summer-blooming, about 3 in. wide, yellow or white. Fruit about 1 in. long, not very spiny. A very showy, popular annual.

**platyceras.** Crested poppy. A tropical American herb 24-48 in. high, the stem, leaves and fruit densely clothed with weak or stiffish white spines. Leaves bluish-gray. Flowers about 2½ in. wide or less, mostly white (purple in a hort. form). The hedgehog poppy (*var.* **hispida**) has distinctly yellowish spines and is bristly as well. There is also a red-flowered variety.

*ARGENTATA, -us, -um* (are-jen-tay′ta). Silvery.

*ARGENTEA, -us, -um* (are-jen′tee-a). Silvery.

*ARGENTEO-MARGINATA, -us, -um* (are-jen-tee-o-mar-ji-nay′ta). Silvery-margined.

*ARGENTEO-VARIEGATA, -us, -um* (are-jen-tee-o-vare-i-e-gay′ta). With silvery patches.

*ARGILLACEA, -us, -um* (are-gil-lay′see-a). Pertaining to clay.

*ARGUTA, -us, -um* (are-gew′ta). Sharply toothed.

*ARGYRAEA, -us, -um* (are-jy-ree′a). Silvery.

**ARGYREIA** (are-jy-ree′a). A genus of 40 species of mostly Asiatic tropical vines of the morning-glory family, the one below grown for ornament outdoors in frost-free regions, more rarely in greenhouses. They have alternate, simple, usually large leaves, often hairy beneath. Flowers showy, rose-colored in the one below, in a few-flowered cluster, funnel-shaped. (*Argyreia* denotes the often silvery foliage.)

Easily grown outdoors in frost-free parts of Calif. and Fla. In greenhouses the plant may become a rampant nuisance. It is easily grown from seeds, or may be propagated by cuttings over bottom-heat.

**splendens.** Silver morning-glory. A handsome, tender, tall-climbing vine. Leaves nearly 7 in. long and about half as wide, with an angled base and silvery-hairy beneath. Flowers 1½ in. long, solitary, the stalk 1½-3 in. long. India.

*ARGYROCOMA, -us, -um* (are-jy-ro-ko′ma). Silvery-haired.

*ARGYRONEURA, -us, -um* (are-jy-ro-new′ra). With silvery veins.

*ARGYROPHYLLA, -us, -um* (are-jy-ro-fill′a). Silver-leaved.

*ARIA* (air′i-a). Ancient Greek name for the whitebeam (*Sorbus aria*).

*ARIETINA, -us, -um* (a-ri-e-ty′na). Resembling a ram's head.

**ARIL.** An extra, often colored, coat or appendage to a seed. It is the aril that provides the brilliant color to the bittersweet (*Celastrus scandens*). *See also* TAXACEAE.

**ARIOCARPUS** (air-i-o-kar′pus). A small genus of top-shaped cacti, mostly Mexican, and often called living-rock. They are small, half-buried succulents, grown as much for their curious habit as for their rose-colored or whitish flowers. Plant spineless, but much-tubercled, the sections sharp-pointed. Flowers arise from the center of the plant. Fruit fleshy, small, with black seeds. (*Ariocarpus* signifies having fruit like the whitebeam.) For culture *see* CACTI.

**retusus.** Seven-sisters; also called chaute. A low, flat-topped cactus, the plant body 3-7 in. wide and much cut up into tubercles, which are sharp when young but blunt in age, and often with a tuft of white hairs near the tip. Flowers rose-colored, or whitish-pink. Mex.

**ARISAEMA** (a-ri-see′ma). A genus of over 50 species of perennial herbs of the arum family, the ones below suited only to shady, moist places in the wild garden. They have tuberous, acrid roots, divided or compound* leaves and tiny flowers crowded on a spadix,* which is surrounded by, or has beneath it, a spathe.* (*See* ARACEAE for details of flower structure.) Fruit showy, fleshy. (*Arisaema* is Latin and Greek for blood arum, in allusion to the leaf color of some tropical species.)

The only commonly cult. species are plants of rich, moist woods, and they need a good humus soil, shade, and a moist site. With these conditions, their culture is easy. Propagated by division of their roots.

**dracontium.** Dragonroot; also called green dragon. A stout, fleshy herb 12-18 in. high, with a single, much, but irregularly, divided leaf, the 7-11 segments oblongish and pointed at the tip. Spathe* not pulpit-like (as in the next), green, tapering, and shorter than the long, slender spadix.* Eastern N.A. June.

**triphyllum.** Jack-in-the-pulpit; called, also, Indian turnip. Root very acrid, but used as food, when heated, by the Indians. Leaves usually 2, compound, the three leaflets more or less oval, pointed, about 2 in. long. The erect spadix* ("Jack") is surrounded by the spathe* ("pulpit") which also arches over the spadix. Eastern N.A. April–May.

*ARISTATA, -us, -um* (a-ris-tay′ta). Bearded; or with an awn.*

**ARISTEA** (a-ris′tee-a). A group of 30 species of largely South African herbs of the iris family, two of which, while not particularly showy, are grown in Calif. for ornament, rarely in greenhouses. They have alternate or two-ranked, narrow, grass-like leaves and small, blue, rather fleeting flowers, that twist after blooming, and suggest the blue-eyed grass (*Sisyrinchium*). Fruit a 3-valved pod (capsule*). (*Aristea* is derived from aristata.)

Their outdoor culture is confined mostly to Calif., where

---

* Special articles on the subjects indicated by an asterisk (*) will be found at the words so marked.

they should be planted in open, sandy loams. Propagated by division of the roots in spring.

**capitata.** A stout plant 2½–3½ ft. high, the leaves as long, but scarcely ½ in. wide and rather rigid. Flowers about ½ in. long, in narrow clusters. July.

**eckloni.** Not over 18 in. high, the leaves not rigid and dark green. Flowers about ⅓ in. long, in a small, flat-stemmed, rather profuse cluster. June.

**ARISTOLOCHIA** (a-ris-toe-loe′ki-a). A genus of 180 species of mostly tropical, woody vines, family Aristolochiaceae, and a few temperate species of vines and perennial herbs. They are widely grown for ornament, and for their extraordinary and usually evil-scented flowers. (See ARISTOLOCHIACEAE for details.) They have alternate,* often evergreen, and sometimes very handsome leaves. Fruit a capsule.* The species are often called birthworts, in allusion (as in *Aristolochia*) to their supposed value in child-birth.

The greenhouse species are handsome tropical vines with large leaves and, in one of them, remarkable flowers nearly 18 in. in diameter, with a tail still longer. They are easily grown in a warm, moist greenhouse and should be planted out in a place where their rampant growth will not shade other plants. Any rich soil will do. Propagated by seeds (for *A. elegans*), or by cuttings.

The hardy vines are grown for their fine rich foliage and their ability to cover unsightly objects with considerable speed. See Stem Climbers at VINES. The Virginia snakeroot, the only cult. herb, is a woods plant and needs rich humus and a shady, wind-free corner of the wild garden. The hardy vines and the last species below should be propagated only by seed.

**durior.** Dutchman's-pipe; called, also, pipevine. A tall, high-climbing vine of eastern N.A., widely cult. for its fine foliage. Leaves roundish or kidney-shaped, 6–14 in. wide, the stalks about ⅓ of this. Flowers about 1½ in. long, bent like a U, yellowish-brown. Long known as *A. macrophylla* and *A. sipho* and still offered under either name. See VINES.

**elegans.** Calico-flower. A slender, tropical vine for greenhouses kept about 60°. Leaves kidney-shaped or heart-shaped, rather long-stalked, but only about 2½ in. wide. Flower solitary, long-stalked, not badly scented, its tube yellowish-green and about 1½ in. long, the expanded limb heart-shaped, 3 in. wide, purple, and white-spotted. Brazil. A popular greenhouse vine and also grown outdoors in frost-free regions. See VINES.

**grandiflora.** Pelican-flower. A West Indian, greenhouse vine with heart-shaped leaves and extraordinary, solitary flowers. The flower-tube is inflated and yellowish-green, and at its end the broadened limb (6–8 in. wide) is wavy-margined, purple-spotted and purple-veined. At the apex of the limb is a long, slender, rather hairy, and colored tail. In the var. **sturtevanti**, which is the usual form in cult., the flower is often 18–24 in. wide and the tail nearly 3 ft. long.

**serpentaria.** Virginia snakeroot. A woodland plant of eastern U.S., useful only in the wild garden and cult. more for its medicinal root than for ornament. Not over 18 in. high, the stem rather wiry. Leaves more or less oval or oblong, the tip tapering, the base heart-shaped. Flower small, S-shaped, greenish, borne at or near the ground level. See MEDICINAL PLANTS.

**ARISTOLOCHIACEAE** (a-ris-toe-loe-ki-a′see-ee). The birthwort or wild ginger family is of little hort. importance, its only cult. genera being *Aristolochia* (mostly vines) and *Asarum* (herbs). Leaves alternate,* stalked, often heart-shaped. Flowers nearly always evil-smelling, the calyx petal-like and curiously tubular or bent (in *Aristolochia* often very large). Petals none. Fruit a capsule.*

Technical flower characters: Sepals united into a tubular, bent, trumpet-shaped or otherwise very irregular calyx, which often has a door-like flap that (at times) covers the opening, and may be tailed. Petals (in the hort. genera) none. Stamens 6–36, inserted on the ovary or joined to the style. Ovary superior,* 4–6-celled.

**ARISTOTELIA** (a-ris-tot-tee′li-a). The only cult. genus of the family Elaeocarpaceae (ee-lee-o-kar-pay′see-ee), which comprises about 7 genera and over 100 species of mostly tropical shrubs and trees, not distantly related to the lindens. The cult. genus has opposite,* evergreen leaves and polygamous* flowers with 4–5 sepals, 4–5 petals, many stamens, a superior* ovary, and fleshy, edible fruit. (Named for Aristotle.)

The species below are cult. for ornament in southern Calif. They grow well in the open, prefer sandy loam, and are propagated by layers or cuttings rooted under glass.

**macqui.** A Chilean shrub 3–6 ft. high. Leaves oblongish, 1½–3 in. long, toothed. Flowers greenish-white, in small clusters. Fruit dark purple, about ¼ in. in diameter, used for wine in Chile. April. A variegated-leaved form is also cult.

**racemosa.** New Zealand wineberry. A New Zealand shrub or small tree 8–25 ft. high. Leaves oval or nearly so, about 5 in. long. Flowers rose-colored, small, but in profuse clusters. Fruit purplish-black, about ¼ in. in diameter.

**ARITHMETIC AND GARDENING.** For sizes, volumes, measures, etc., see WEIGHTS AND MEASURES. For plants per acre, yields, amount of seed, height of trees, and other garden statistics, see GARDEN TABLES.

**ARIZONA.** The state lies in zones* 4, 5, 6, and 7, while zone* 8 crosses the small triangle near the mouth of the Gila River.

SOILS. Generalizations cannot be made on the soils of Arizona, as they vary from heavy clays to coarse sands, although the fine sands, sandy loams, and silt loams predominate.

Detailed Federal soil survey reports and maps are available for the following areas: Buckeye–Beardsley, Salt River Valley, Middle Gila Valley, Solomonville, Benson, San Simon, Winslow, Paradise Verde, and Gila Bend. Other areas, which have been surveyed but on which reports have not yet been published, are Nogales, Tucson, Santa Rita Range Reserve, St. Johns, and Yuma.

Arizona soils are on the whole quite fertile, provided they can be made to "take water" readily and are kept reasonably well aerated by the introduction of organic matter and by proper drainage. They contain very little organic matter and nitrogen; hence manure (both animal and green) is the most common fertilizer and is used extensively.

White and black alkali salts exist in widely scattered areas over southern Arizona. The reclamation of such areas depends largely upon the subsoil, as good drainage is the first essential for leaching operations. If underlain with sand or permeable substrata the removal of such alkali can be effected without excessive costs.

CHIEF GARDENING CENTERS. The central and southern parts of Arizona, containing the major irrigation projects, comprise the chief gardening centers. These, in order of their importance, are the Salt River Valley, Yuma Valley and Yuma Mesa, the Casa Grande, Safford, Duncan, Verde, Santa Cruz, San Pedro, and the Sulphur Springs Valleys. Even in these areas, gardening is limited to land with a reliable source of irrigation water. Garden centers of smaller area in northern Arizona are distributed along the Little Colorado River and its tributaries supplying irrigation water and to the Flagstaff district where rainfall is relied upon for soil moisture.

FRUIT AND GARDEN AREAS AND CROPS. Orchard fruits and vegetable crops are grown for home use in practically all parts of the state where farming operations are at all practicable. At the lower elevations the hardy group of vegetables are grown during the fall, winter, and spring months and many sub-tropical fruits may be planted in the home orchard. At higher elevations, vegetable production is limited to the spring, summer, and fall months and the temperate zone fruits must be grown.

The major truck crops produced in the state are cantaloupes and winter head lettuce. Several thousand cars of each are shipped annually, chiefly from the Salt River and Yuma valleys.

Other truck crops produced commercially to some extent in the irrigated valleys are asparagus, peas, white potatoes, sweet potatoes, carrots, and watermelons.

Of the small fruits, strawberries and blackberries are grown in limited quantity for markets within the state.

Apples, pears, and peaches of excellent quality are grown for Arizona market and home use in many of the higher mountain valleys of northern, eastern, and southeastern Arizona. Apricots, Japanese plums, and peaches succeed well in the lower irrigated valleys.

The European grape is grown extensively in home vineyards in the lower valleys of the state. In the Salt River Valley, a number of vineyards of considerable acreage are producing early table grapes of excellent quality for carlot shipment to eastern markets. American varieties of grapes are being grown successfully in home vineyards at elevations of more than 4000 feet.

---

*Special articles on the subjects indicated by an asterisk (*) will be found at the words so marked.*

Oranges and grapefruit of excellent quality and early maturity are produced in the Salt River Valley and on the Yuma Mesa. Some 20,000 acres have thus far been planted to these fruits. Dates are being planted more extensively each year. The choicest of Persian Gulf and North African varieties have been introduced, and offshoots of many of these are available for commercial plantings. While the cost of establishing a date garden is greater than for most any other orchard fruit, returns are correspondingly greater. See DATE.

Some 4000 acres of the lower irrigated valley lands have been planted to improved varieties of pecans. A high-quality, large-sized nut is being grown, and production of the groves now in bearing appears to be significantly greater than in the older-established pecan districts of the southeastern states.

At the lower elevations of the state, the winters are sufficiently mild so that the hardy flowers are planted in the fall for winter and spring bloom. Among these are stocks, African daisies, snapdragon, pansies, sweet peas, larkspur, petunias, and many others, including bulbs. These are spring planted for summer bloom at the higher elevations.

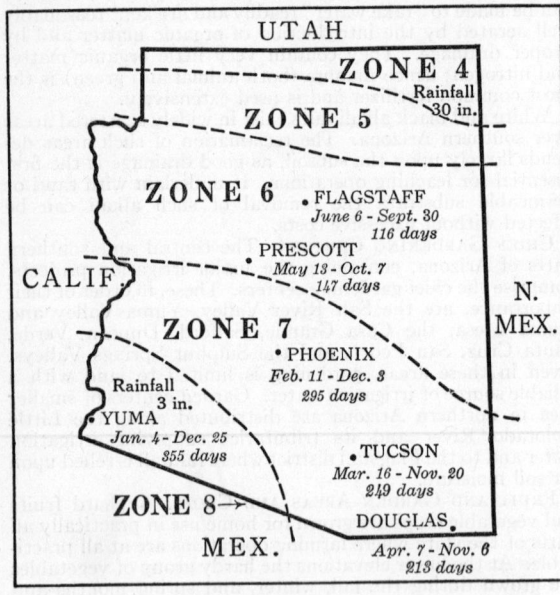

ARIZONA

The zones of hardiness crossing Arizona are those shown on the colored map at ZONE, which should be consulted for details. The dates are the average latest killing frost in spring and the first one in the fall. The figures below the dates show the average length of the growing season. Annual rainfall is not over 3 in. in the southwestern part of the state, but nearly 30 in. in the mountainous northern part.

Many ornamental trees from China, Japan, Australia, and the Mediterranean region are excellently adapted to the sub-tropical portions of southern Arizona. These include several species of eucalyptus and citrus, several palms, the carob, loquat, Chinese elm, Deodar cedar, olive, tamarisk, and the Aleppo pine. Native poplars, ash, sycamore, elderberry, mesquite, and cypress are widely used for ornamental planting.

Ornamental shrubs which succeed well are species of the following genera: *Pittosporum, Euonymus, Jasminum, Ligustrum, Rosa, Photinia, Punica, Feijoa, Myrtus, Plumbago, Cotoneaster, Pyracantha, Nandina*, and many others. At the higher elevations, trees and shrubs grown in the temperate regions of the Middle West and eastern United States are well adapted and commonly grown. The more common of these include the eastern elm, maple, ash, poplar, the sycamore (*Platanus*), both native and introduced, locust, Kentucky coffee-tree, China-tree, walnut; also a number of pines, junipers, and oaks. Shrubs include species of *Thuja, Berberis, Euonymus, Ligustrum, Viburnum, Philadelphus, Spiraea, Cercis, Rhus, Syringa, Tamarix, Lonicera*, and *Rosa*.

CLIMATE. The climate of Arizona is extremely varied, temperature conditions changing directly with changes in elevation and to a much less extent with latitude. At Yuma, and more particularly on the Yuma Mesa, more than 2 to 5 degrees of frost is rarely experienced in winter, while the summers are long, with the daily maxima ranging from 100° to as much as 118° for a 3 to 4 months' period. Near the other extreme is the Flagstaff district with considerable snow in winter and some sub-zero temperatures, while daily maximum temperatures in summer seldom reach 90°.

Killing frost and growing season data for a few points in Arizona are presented in the Table.

KILLING FROSTS AND LENGTH OF GROWING SEASON

| Station | Elevation | Average date of last killing frost in spring | Average date of first killing frost in autumn | Latest date of killing frost in spring | Earliest date of killing frost in autumn | Average length of growing season days |
|---|---|---|---|---|---|---|
| Alpine | 8500 | June 15 | Sept. 14 | June 27 | July 27 | 91 |
| Flagstaff | 6907 | June 6 | Sept. 30 | July 5 | Sept. 9 | 116 |
| Prescott | 5320 | May 13 | Oct. 7 | June 16 | Sept. 23 | 147 |
| Douglas | 3930 | Apr. 7 | Nov. 6 | May 1 | Oct. 19 | 213 |
| Tucson | 2423 | Mar. 16 | Nov. 20 | Apr. 18 | Oct. 19 | 249 |
| Phoenix | 1108 | Feb. 11 | Dec. 3 | Mar. 31 | Nov. 5 | 295 |
| Yuma | 141 | Jan. 4 | Dec. 25 | Feb. 18 | Nov. 30 | 355 |

PRECIPITATION. The mean annual rainfall in Arizona varies from about 3 to 30 inches. A topographic map of the state may be used with few changes as a rainfall map. Arizona, with an elevation of less than 150 feet at Yuma in the southwestern corner, rises more or less like a flight of steps in a northeasterly direction to an elevation at Greer, the highest weather-observing station in the state, of 8500 feet. The heavier precipitation on the mountains is often of great economic significance, inasmuch as much of it can be stored in reservoirs and used to irrigate the arid lowlands. A rainfall distribution curve for Arizona shows two distinct rainy seasons, the most important being in July, August, and September when approximately 43% of the entire year's rainfall occurs. The second period (December to March) is one of longer duration, but furnishes less water, as only 35% of the year's rainfall occurs during these 4 months. Summer rains are of a spontaneous nature, short-lived, and are often accompanied by wind, thunder, and lightning. Winter rains, as a rule, are gentle and may be of several days' duration.

IRRIGATION. With the exception of several relatively small areas in the northern part of the state which lie at high altitudes and are farmed without irrigation, all the cropped lands in Arizona require irrigation. The 1930 Federal Census shows a total of 575,590 acres, in 8523 farms, irrigated in 1929 and that the irrigation enterprises of the state are capable now of irrigating an additional area of 248,562 acres. The irrigated area is 0.8% of the land area of the state. It is possible that this may be increased in the future to about 2% of the total area as new enterprises are developed. Eighty-seven per cent of the present irrigated area is in the drainage basin of the Gila River and its tributaries, and 10% is irrigated directly from the Colorado River.

Water supplies for irrigation are obtained from flowing streams, or by pumping from wells, or from minor sources such as springs and artesian wells. Ephemeral flood flows are utilized in some localities. Eighteen per cent of the irrigated area is irrigated from pumped wells and 51% additional derives a part of its supply from wells. Ground-water supplies and pump irrigation are therefore of relatively high importance in Arizona.

The methods of applying water vary with the crop and, to a lesser extent, with topography and soil. Garden and truck crops are irrigated in furrows between the rows. Orchards

* Special articles on the subjects indicated by an asterisk (*) will be found at the words so marked.

are sometimes basined, 1 to 4 trees in a basin, sometimes irrigated by several furrows on each side of the tree row, and sometimes flooded in lands 330 or 660 feet long, the choice depending on the soil and other conditions.

The frequency of irrigation depends on the crop, the soil, and the season. Vegetables and young orchards may require weekly irrigations during midsummer.

CLIMATE AND AGRICULTURE. The mean annual rainfall of but 13.61 inches precludes the possibility of any great amount of dry-farming in Arizona.

Under arid or semi-arid conditions large amounts of water are lost to the soil by plant transpiration, the water requirement of crops being practically double that in humid regions. The Hopi and Navajo Indians practice dry-farming in a small way in northern Arizona, but Arizona farmers on the whole have not been entirely successful in attempts to "dry-farm." The Arizona Agricultural Experiment Station abandoned its dry farm at Cochise because the ordinary farm crops could not be satisfactorily grown by dry-farming methods. The Prescott Dry Farm has also proved a failure as a dry farm. Dry-farming, however, has possibilities in the higher and moister altitudes. Results of irrigating the valley lands have been highly successful, as most of the once desert land has proved to be fertile.

The address of the Agricultural Experiment Station which has kindly supplied this information about the state is the University of Arizona, Tucson, Arizona. The Station is always ready to answer gardening questions.

**ARIZONA CYPRESS** = *Cupressus arizonica.*

**ARIZONA FIR** = *Abies arizonica. See* FIR.

*ARIZONICA, -us, -um* (a-ri-zon′i-ka). From Arizona.

**ARJAN.** *See* ARGANIA.

**ARKANSAS.** The state lies wholly in zones* 4, 5 and 6. The soils of Arkansas are extremely variable, and very few sections can be said to be composed mainly of any one type. The types range from quite heavy clays to fine, sandy soil, and heavy and light soils may be found in close proximity in almost all parts of the state.

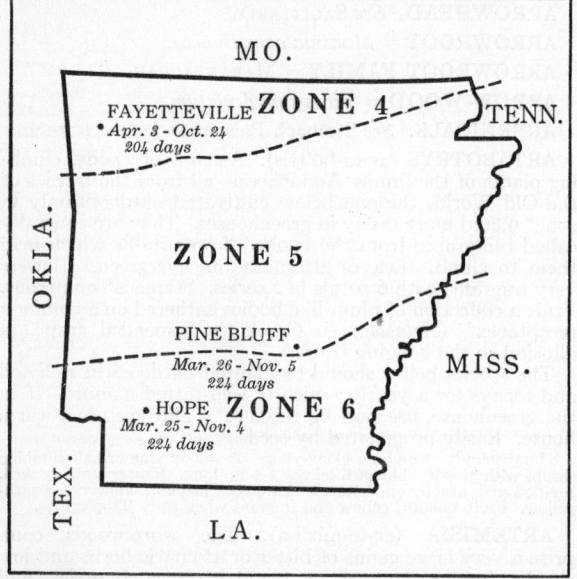

ARKANSAS

The zones of hardiness crossing Arkansas are those shown on the colored map at ZONE, which should be consulted for details. The dates are the average latest killing frost in spring and the first one in the fall. The figures below the dates show the average length of the growing season. Rainfall of about 40 in. per year is adequate, but there is sometimes a summer deficiency.

With reference to fruit, the state may be divided into two main areas as far as climatic and soil conditions are concerned, although several local areas of production have been developed. In the higher altitudes of northwest Arkansas commercial apple production has been established for many years. This region also produces Concord grapes and strawberries in large quantities. Peach-growing has never been developed in this region to any extent because of the frost hazard. The centers of peach production are in southwest Arkansas and along a narrow, high portion of ground known as Crowley's Ridge which runs north and south through eastern Arkansas. Peaches can be produced all over the southern and eastern part of Arkansas where the land is high enough to afford good drainage. There is a large commercial center of strawberry production in White County. Blackberries are grown for canning in northwest Arkansas. There are commercial plantings of raspberries in the Crowley's Ridge sections and in northwest Arkansas. Aside from these commercial centers, fruit is produced for home consumption and local markets all over the state.

The southern part of the state is rapidly developing in the growing of high-grade pecans. A considerable planting of short-season pecans is taking place in the hill sections of the state.

American grapes other than Concord are grown all over the state for home consumption. The Concord grape is not grown in the lowlands because of a tendency to uneven ripening of the fruit. Muscadine grapes thrive in the southern part of the state.

With reference to vegetables it may be said in general that there are no centers of non-commercial production except in suburban areas where there are centers of population with land available for gardening. All parts of the state can and do produce vegetables (for home consumption) at some season of the year.

Commercial vegetable production is a fairly important part of the agriculture of the state. Sweet potatoes and white potatoes are grown extensively in almost all parts of the state, the latter primarily for early summer harvest. Cantaloupes and, to a lesser extent, cucumbers, are shipped from the southern and eastern regions. Watermelons are shipped from the southwestern part and are grown for local sale on suitable soils in all parts of the state. Tomatoes are grown for shipment especially in the southern region, and to some extent in other areas. They are grown extensively for canning in the northern part.

Minor commercial vegetable crops include spinach, sweet corn, asparagus, and onions, as well as a wide variety of crops grown for local sale. Vegetables which may be and are grown for home consumption include practically all the common ones grown in temperate climates.

FROST DATES IN NORTHERN, SOUTHERN, AND EASTERN ARKANSAS

| Name of town | Average date of last killing frost in spring | Average date of first killing frost in fall |
|---|---|---|
| Fayetteville | April 3 | October 24 |
| Hope | March 25 | November 4 |
| Pine Bluff | March 26 | November 5 |

The state may be roughly divided into two main areas with respect to climate: the northwestern hill section, and the southern and eastern lowlands. In the first-mentioned region the winters are moderate, with occasional periods of freezing and sometimes sub-zero weather, usually interspersed with periods of mild weather in which slow growth of plants sometimes occurs. In other parts of the state the winters are usually quite mild. In many years no heavy freezes are reported in these areas, although cold waves do sometimes sweep far enough south to do serious damage. In most years, however, hardy plants such as cabbage may be overwintered in the open without any danger. Light freezes and cool weather, of course, prevent the winter culture of tender plants.

Rainfall in the state is usually well above forty inches, and has varied since 1891 between thirty-five and sixty-two

---

* Special articles on the subjects indicated by an asterisk (*) will be found at the words so marked.

inches per year. The precipitation, however, is usually during the fall, winter, and spring months, and in many years there is a shortage of water for optimum plant growth during the mid-summer months. For this reason many garden crops succeed best when produced in seasons other than mid-summer. Abundant sunshine throughout the year is a climatic character of advantage to many garden plants.

The address of the Agricultural Experiment Station which has kindly supplied this information about the state is the Arkansas Agricultural Experiment Station, Fayetteville, Arkansas. The station is always ready to answer gardening questions.

The Garden Club activities in the state include over 60 chapters, and 48 junior chapters of the Arkansas Federation of Garden Clubs, information about which can be had by writing to Garden Editor, Houghton Mifflin Company, Boston, Mass.

**ARM.** Loosely, any branch of a tree. Technically, in grape culture, a branch of a vine that is more than one year old.

*ARMATA, -us, -um* (are-may'ta). Armed; that is, provided with thorns, prickles, or spines, assumed to be, but not necessarily for, defense.

*ARMENIACA* (ar-men-i-ā'ka). An old generic name for the apricot, so called because it was once thought to be native in Armenia.

**ARMERIA** = Statice.

*ARMILLARIS, -e* (ar-mil-lar'is). Ringed, as with a collar or bracelet.

**ARMORACIA.** See Horse-radish.

**ARNATTO** = Annatto. See Bixa.

**ARNEBIA** (ar-nee'bi-a). A genus of perhaps a dozen species of Asiatic and African herbs, family Boraginaceae, the two below grown in the flower garden for their attractive bloom. They have alternate leaves and small flowers in more or less 1-sided clusters. Corolla nearly regular, its 5 lobes blunt. Fruit of 4 nutlets, hidden by the withered flowers. (*Arnebia* is a Latinized version of an Arabic vernacular.)

The species below are of the easiest culture. Sow seed of the first where it is to stay as it is a hardy annual (*see* Annuals). The second species is a perennial, easily propagated by division of its roots, but it requires partial shade.

 cornuta. Arabian primrose. A hardy annual from the Orient, rather bushy, and 18–24 in. high. Leaves lance-shaped or narrower. Flowers about ¾ in. wide, orange and black-spotted, fading to red and finally to yellow. Summer.
 echioides. Prophet-flower. A perennial herb 4–10 in. high. Leaves oblong or slightly wider upward. Flowers in a 1-sided cluster, yellow and purple-spotted, fading to yellow. Southeastern Eu. and Armenia. June. Good for shaded part of a rockery.

**ARNICA** (ar'ni-ka). A large genus of perennial herbs, family Compositae, many from N.A., but the one below European. They are little grown except *A. montana*, which yields tincture of arnica. Leaves opposite. Flowers yellow, the long-stalked heads with conspicuous rays. (*Arnica* is the classical name for these plants.)

Can be grown in the open border, but prefers a distinctly acid soil (pH 4, *see* Acid and Alkali Soils). Best propagated by division of its roots. Best suited to drier parts of the country.

 montana. A European herb whose roots yield tincture of arnica; 12–20 in. high. Leaves without teeth, oblongish, smooth. Flowers on branching stalks, the head showy, nearly 3 in. wide. See also Medicinal Plants.

**ARNOLD ARBORETUM.** See Arboretum.

**AROID.** Any plant of the arum family. See Araceae.

*AROMATICA, -us, -um* (a-roe-mat'tick-a). Fragrant or aromatic.

**ARONIA** (a-rone'i-a). A small genus of North American shrubs of the rose family, often grown in informal shrubberies for their attractive white flowers and persistent, colored, but bitter fruits; hence the name chokeberry. Leaves alternate,* always toothed. Flowers in terminal clusters, blooming early in May, the white petals and black anthers making an interesting contrast. Fruit fleshy, a small berry-like pome.* (*Aronia* is derived from *Aria*, which see.)

The shrubs are of the easiest culture in a variety of soils, and are readily propagated by seeds, cuttings or by layering. They are not particularly showy, but useful because of their early bloom. They are sometimes offered as *Pyrus* from which they are separated only by technical characters.

 arbutifolia. Red chokeberry. Not over 8 ft., usually half that. Leaves gray beneath, oblongish, about 2 in. long. Fruit brilliant red, winter-persisting. Mass. to Fla. Fine red foliage in the fall. Zone* 4 and southward.
 atropurpurea. Purple chokeberry. Somewhat taller than the first. Leaves merely hairy beneath. Fruit purple-black. Newfoundland to Fla. Zone* 3 and southward.
 melanocarpa. Black chokeberry. Lower than either of the others, rarely exceeding 4 ft. Leaves without hairs, or only a few, shining. Fruit shining black, but shriveling and soon dropping. Nova Scotia to Fla. Zone* 3 and southward. Called, also, *Aronia nigra*.

**ARRACACIA** (ar-ra-kay'si-a). A large genus of mostly South American herbs of the carrot family, the only cult. species being a parsnip-like plant much grown in the tropics for its edible root. This plant, called apio in Porto Rico, is *A. xanthorrhiza*, a native of the Andes. It has twice-compound* leaves, small, white flowers in compound* umbels, and a thick, branched, yellowish, starchy root. Little known in the U.S. and suited only to zone* 9. (*Arracacia* is the Spanish name of some of the species.) Sometimes known as *A. esculenta*.

**ARRHENATHERUM** (ar-re-nath'er-rum). A genus of tall, oat-like, perennial grasses of European origin, of no garden interest except as it occurs in meadows. Stems tall, up to 3½ ft. high, the coarse leaves rough on the edges. Flower cluster a narrow panicle, the male spikelets long-awned.* (The name implies a masculine awn, alluding to the male spikelets.)

 elatius. Tall oat grass; also called tall meadow oat. Leaves about 12 in. long, ¼ in. wide, and distinctly rough. Flowering panicle 12 in. long, its numerous branches erect, purplish-green. Common as a naturalized grass in the N.A. There is a tuberous-rooted variety (*var.* tuberosum) which is sometimes known as *A. bulbosum*.

**ARROW-ARUM.** See Peltandra.

**ARROWHEAD.** See Sagittaria.

**ARROWROOT** = *Maranta arundinacea*.

**ARROWROOT FAMILY** = Marantaceae.

**ARROW-WOOD** = *Viburnum dentatum*.

**ARSENICALS.** See Stomach Poisons at Insecticides.

**ARTABOTRYS** (ar-ta-bō'tris). A genus of woody, climbing plants of the family Annonaceae, all from the tropics of the Old World, the one below cultivated outdoors only in zone* 9, and more rarely in greenhouses. They are generally called tail-grapes from the hooked flower stalks which help them to climb. Leaves alternate and evergreen. Flowers very fragrant, with 6 petals in 2 series. Stamens* numerous. Fruit a collection of plum-like bodies gathered on a common receptacle.* (*Artabotrys* is Greek for suspended grape, in allusion to the hanging fruits.)

The species below should be planted outdoors in rich soil and repays for a yearly mulch of well-rotted manure. If in the greenhouse, use potting mixture* 5 and keep in a warm house. Easily propagated by seeds.

 odoratissimus. Climbing ylang-ylang. A woody vine or half-climbing shrub, with glossy, oblongish leaves 3–6 in. long. Flower stalk hooked, 1–2-flowered, usually opposite a leaf, woody when old. Flowers greenish-yellow. Fruit smooth, yellow and fragrant when ripe. Tropical As.

**ARTEMISIA** (ar-te-miz'i-a). The wormwoods comprise a very large genus of bitter or aromatic herbs and low shrubs, family Compositae, found in most countries, and cult. since ancient times for their aromatic qualities, for ornament, or as seasoning (*see* Tarragon). They have alternate,* mostly divided or dissected leaves. Flowers in small heads, wholly made up of disk flowers (*see* Compositae), not showy except in a few species, prevailingly greenish-yellow. (*Artemisia* is the Latin name of the mugwort.)

---

* Special articles on the subjects indicated by an asterisk (*) will be found at the words so marked.

Many of the species have silvery coating to the leaves and like similarly clothed plants they do not tolerate much winter moisture. Otherwise, except as noted below, they are of easy culture, generally growing better in poor and sandy soils than in rich ones. The perennials are easily increased by division of the roots, the others by seeds. All bloom in the summer, and prefer open sunshine.

**abrotanum.** Southernwood; called, also, old man. A green-foliaged, woody, perennial herb, 2½-4 ft. high. Leaves divided into thread-like sections. Flower heads ⅛ in. in diameter, yellowish-white. Southern Eu. For uses and culture see HERB GARDENING.

**absinthium.** The classical wormwood, and an ingredient of absinthe. A white-hairy, woody, perennial herb, 2½-4 ft. high. Leaves divided in 2 or 3 oblongish segments. Flower heads ⅛ in. wide, greenish, very numerous. Eu.

**albula.** Sometimes grown as Silver King artemisia. Not over 4 ft. high. Leaves ovalish, 3-5-lobed, white-felty, the upper ones narrower and unlobed. Flowers inconspicuous. Southwestern U.S.

**canadensis.** Sea or wild wormwood. An American perennial herb, seldom over 2 ft. high, usually grayish, but without hairs. Leaves with 2 main divisions, but these much cut into fine segments. Flower heads about ⅛ in. across, greenish and very plentiful in long, narrow clusters. Eastern N.A. and westward.

**canescens** = *Artemisia vulgaris*.

**dracunculus.** Tarragon; called, also, estragon. A perennial, green, completely smooth herb, the aromatic foliage of which is used for seasoning. Leaves basal and on the stem, the latter narrow and undivided, the basal ones 3 parted toward the tip. Flower heads ⅛ in. wide, whitish-green. Eurasia. For culture see TARRAGON.

**frigida.** Mountain sage; called, also, wormwood sage and wild sage. A perennial herb, 9-15 in. high, with silvery-white foliage. Leaves twice divided, the ultimate segments very narrow. Flower heads yellow, about ¼ in. wide, nodding, in racemes.* Western U.S. and As.

**glacialis.** An alpine perennial for the rock garden, scarcely over 4 in. high, with much-divided leaves and small, golden-yellow flower heads. European Alps. Plant in gritty or sandy soil.

**lactiflora** = *Artemisia vulgaris lactiflora*.

**pontica.** Roman wormwood. A shrubby, perennial herb, 2-4 ft. high. Leaves much dissected into linear segments that are ashy-gray beneath. Flower heads ⅛ in. wide, whitish-yellow, but often failing to develop, when the plant is a patch of feathery shoots. Eu.

**sacrorum.** Russian wormwood. A tall, stiff herb, often 5 ft. high, with whitish, cut, but not dissected leaves and greenish-white, nodding heads in slender racemes. Siberia. The form most worth growing is *var.* **viride**, the summer fir. This is tree-like in habit, grown mostly as a bold foliage plant, and treated as an annual. See ANNUALS.

**stelleriana.** One of the plants called dusty miller; called, also, beach wormwood and old woman. A densely white-woolly, perennial herb seldom over 24 in. high. Leaves cut, but not dissected, the segments oblong, toothed or sometimes without teeth. Flower heads ¼ in. wide, yellow, crowded in dense racemes.* A splendid beach plant. Coasts of northeastern U.S. and As. For culture see HERB GARDENING. See also SAND GARDENS.

**vulgaris.** Mugwort. A much-branched, often purplish-stemmed perennial herb 2-3½ ft. high. Leaves fragrant, white-hairy beneath, cut into oblong, mostly toothed segments. Flower heads yellow, ⅛ in. wide in clustered spikes. Eurasia and naturalized in N.A. An especially fine form, with white heads, is called *var.* **lactiflora**.

*ARTEMISIOIDES* (ar-te-miz-i-oy′deez; but see OÏDES). Resembling the wormwood (*Artemisia*).

**ARTICHOKE** (*Cynara scolymus*). A vegetable, the edible portion of which consists of the unripe flower head and its attendant parts — the scales and receptacle.* It is often known as bur-artichoke or globe-artichoke, and should not be confused with Jerusalem artichoke, which neither comes from Jerusalem nor is an artichoke (see HELIANTHUS TUBEROSUS). For the Chinese artichoke, see STACHYS SIEBOLDI.

Globe-artichoke is a perennial, does not ordinarily come true from seed, and must therefore be propagated by planting the numerous suckers that arise from the base of old plants. In starting a plantation of them, put these suckers at least 6 ft. apart in rows 8 ft. apart, for mature plants are large and spreading. The suckers should be well cut back and planted 6 or 8 in. deep. While the artichoke may live for many years, it is advisable to renew a plantation every three or four years to ensure not only the largest yield but the tenderest and most juicy heads. They must not be moved once they are planted, so pick a site for them that they will monopolize for the next three or four years.

Frequent cultivation is necessary, and if the plants have been set at exactly the intervals given above, cultivation may well be in both directions. In cultivating, care must be taken not to injure the plants as they become full grown and ready for the harvesting of the heads. Artichoke is a rich feeder. At least 10 tons of stable manure per acre is plowed in after the final crop of heads is harvested and the plants are cut down to the ground. Some growers also use 400 pounds to the acre of nitrate of soda, applied just before the first heads are ready for harvesting.

Artichokes are harvested throughout the latter part of the growing season of the plant. Never allow one of the large buds to become old enough so that its scales get hard or woody, for it is the succulence of these that one seeks in a good globe-artichoke. Cut off all old stems that have borne harvested heads, either plowing them in between the rows or feeding them to cattle.

The plant came originally from the southern Mediterranean region, and its climatic requirements have resulted in certain parts of California being the chief places where it is grown, notably in Monterey, San Mateo and Santa Cruz counties. It is primarily a winter vegetable, and, in Calif., the suckers are started so as to ensure winter production of heads. This means an essentially frost-free area in winter, but cool and foggy in summer. Without these peculiar climatic conditions the production of artichokes is not advisable, although the plant, as a perennial herb, may be grown in many frosty regions under the conditions mentioned below.

Throughout the Calif. region of production the plants must be irrigated, but they will not tolerate standing water any more than the heads will stand frost.

Outside of Calif. and a few places along the Gulf Coast, artichoke, as a perennial herb, can be grown if cut down to the ground at the approach of frost. Cover the crown with a box and mulch the box and surrounding soil heavily with manure. Plants not covered with a box or inverted flower pot will gather too much moisture around the crown and probably die. Artichoke protected as described will produce heads, but not very good ones, in the late summer. Few people, outside Calif., take the trouble to grow them.

INSECT PESTS. Plant lice, controlled with nicotine, and the caterpillar of the painted lady butterfly, which succumbs to lead arsenate, are occasionally injurious. Some general feeders attack artichoke.

DISEASES. A leaf-spot and mildew affect the leaves. Spraying with bordeaux is suggested. The root rots in storage are avoided if the temperature is kept near 32° F.

*ARTICULATA, -us, -um* (ar-tick-you-lay′ta). Articulated; that is, jointed at obviously, or apparently, separable nodes or joints, as the stems of some bamboos, the joints of a cactus, or the point at which a fruit falls from a stem.

**ARTIFICIAL FERTILIZERS.** Chemical fertilizers. See FERTILIZERS.

**ARTIFICIAL MANURE.** See Synthetic Manure at MANURE.

**ARTIFICIAL STONE.** See CONCRETE.

**ARTILLERY-PLANT** = *Pilea microphylla*.

**ARTOCARPACEAE.** See MORACEAE.

**ARTOCARPUS** (ar-toe-kar′pus). A large genus of tropical, mostly Asiatic, milky-juiced trees, family Moraceae, the two below grown for their fruit. Leaves alternate,* lobed or unlobed (in ours). Male and female flowers in different clusters on the same plant, the male in spikes, the female in heads, both small. There is no distinction between petals and sepals, which are united to form a small tube. Fruit a syncarp,* edible in the breadfruit, and enormous in the jackfruit. (*Artocarpus* is Greek for breadfruit.)

Outdoor culture possible only in zone* 9; rarely cult. in greenhouses for the handsome stiff leaves and curious flowers and fruit. Propagated by seeds or cuttings, and they should not be moved once they are planted as they do not stand transplanting very well. Both are typically tropical plants of moist lowlands and their culture is thus restricted to extreme southern Fla., and risky even there.

**communis.** Breadfruit. A tree up to 50 ft., its profuse foliage dense and striking. Leaves 18-24 in. long, thick and leathery, ovalish, but deeply lobed with sharp segments. Male spikes 6 in. long, yellowish, drooping or curving downward. Female cluster nearly globe-shaped. Fruit 4-8 in. in diameter, yellow, the outside weakly spiny, the flesh delicious; seedless in the true breadfruit, but with seeds in a variety known as breadnut. The latter is grown for these seeds which are cooked. Polynesia. The plant is also offered as *A. incisa*.

---

* Special articles on the subjects indicated by an asterisk (*) will be found at the words so marked.

**integrifolia.** Jackfruit; called, also, jak. Frequently up to 70 ft. and much cult. in the tropics for its fruit, one of the largest known. Leaves stiff, glossy-green, without lobes, 6-8 in. long. Male spikes 3-4 in. long. Female spike arising only from the bark of the trunk or larger branches. Fruit 1-2 ft. long, often weighing 40 pounds or more, knobby, the flesh edible but insipid. Seeds numerous, edible when cooked, and prized by some tropical natives. Offered, also, as *A. integra.*

**ARUM** (air'um). Eurasian relatives of the Jack-in-the-pulpit, and requiring the same culture (see ARISAEMA), except for the black calla (see below). The genus comprises a dozen species of tuberous-rooted perennial herbs with mostly arrow-shaped leaves. The flowers are borne on a naked spadix* which is partly surrounded by the much more showy spathe.* (See ARACEAE for minute structure.) Fruit a fleshy berry. (*Arum* is the classical name for these plants.)

**maculatum.** Lords-and-ladies; called, also, cuckoopint. A fleshy herb about 12 in. high. Leaves more or less arrow-shaped, usually black-spotted, withering in summer, long-stalked. Spathe* 6-10 in. long, pinched at the middle, purple-spotted or purple-margined or both, much exceeding the spadix.* Southern Eu. There are whitish-spathed and all-purple-spathed varieties. Called wakerobin in England. See POISONOUS PLANTS.

**palaestinum.** Black calla; called also Solomon's lily. A tender, greenhouse plant grown for its handsome foliage and flowers like the calla lily, but blackish-purple inside the spathe.* Leaves 6 in. wide, arrow-shaped and with a heart-shaped base. Spathe green outside, blackish-purple within, the tip often drooping. Palestine. Its soil and culture requirements are the same as for *Caladium* (which see).

**ARUM FAMILY.** The aroids, as they are often called, comprise an immense family of mostly tropical herbs, but some native plants like the Jack-in-the-pulpit and skunk-cabbage. Most of the hort. genera are chiefly greenhouse plants like the anthuriums, the elephant's-ear and the edible-fruited ceriman. For the peculiar flowers of this family and the hort. genera see ARACEAE.

**ARUNCUS** (a-run'kus). A genus of spirea-like herbs of the rose family, differing from the closely related *Spiraea* in having compound* leaves, which are twice- or thrice-compound. Flowers small, white, crowded into showy panicles, the male and female on different plants. Petals 5. Stamens many. Pistils 3 (5 in *Spiraea*). Fruit a collection of follicles.* (*Aruncus* is the classical name of these plants.)

The goatsbeard is an attractive hardy perennial with feathery foliage and masses of small white flowers. It is a fine plant for the border, does best in partial shade, and will grow in any good garden soil. Propagated by division.

**sylvester.** Goatsbeard. A strong-growing plant 4-6 ft. high. Leaves much dissected, the ultimate leaflets ovalish, sharply and doubly toothed, about 1½ in. long. Flowers about ⅛ in. wide, nearly stalkless on the branches of a wide-spreading, open cluster 6-10 in. high. N.A. and As. Much confused with *Spiraea* and *Astilbe* and offered under both names.

*ARUNDINACEA, -us, -um* (a-run-di-nay'see-a). Reed-like.

**ARUNDINARIA** (a-run-di-nay'ri-a). Tall, bamboo-like, but nearly hardy grasses, much grown for their fine foliage and somewhat showy, plume-like flower clusters. They differ from the mostly tropical bamboos (*Bambusa*) only in technical characters, although usually, in temperate climates, *Arundinaria* does not have a woody stem as in the bamboos. Leaves flat, short-stalked, from persistent sheaths. Flowers grass-like, in flattish spikes which are gathered in large, often plumy clusters. (*Arundinaria* is derived from *Arundo*.)

For the culture and garden uses of these handsome plants see GRASSES. Some of the species below are credited by some to *Sasa*, a genus not here maintained. Most of them are not hardy above the southern edges of zone* 5. See also BAMBOO.

**falcata.** Stems very slender, 10-15 ft. high, bluish and waxy when young, yellow-green in age. Leaves 3-6 in. long, about ½ in. wide, striped, the margins roughened with minute teeth. Flower cluster a raceme,* which is slightly arched. Himalayas. The stems die down to the ground each year, except in the south.

**fastuosa.** Stems stout, 20-30 ft. high, usually with purple-brown markings. Leaves 5-7 in. long and about 1 in. wide, green above, bluish-gray beneath. Jap. Stems persisting all year, somewhat woody.

**japonica.** The hardiest of the group and safely planted from zone* 4 southward. Stems 5-8 ft., bluish-waxy. Leaves 4-12 in. long, about 1½ in. wide, green and shining above, whitish and minutely hairy beneath. Jap. Stems dying down each winter in the north.

**macrosperma.** Southern cane; called also cane reed. The chief plant of the canebrakes from Va. southward. Stems persistent, 10-25 ft. high.

Leaves nearly 12 in. long, about 1½ in. wide, very rough and cutting on the margin. Less showy than the Asiatic species.

**simoni.** The handsomest of the group, the stems 10-20 ft. high and usually persisting southward. Leaves 8-12 in. long and about 1 in. wide, often white-striped. There is also a shorter plant with smaller, yellow-mottled leaves. China and Jap.

**veitchi.** Not over 3 ft. high and hardy, with protection, as far north as the central part of zone* 4. Leaves 5-8 in. long, about 2 in. wide, green above, bluish-gray beneath, the margins often yellowish. Jap.

**ARUNDO** (a-run'doe). A genus of very ornamental grasses from the Old World, the one below widely planted for ornament. It is not hardy north of zone* 5, rarely in zone* 4 with protection. Stems tall and woody. Leaves long, stiff and more or less two-ranked on the stems. Flowers grass-like, crowded into a large, silky, plume-like and striking cluster (panicle*), seldom produced except southward. (*Arundo* is the classical name for the reed.)

For culture and uses in the garden see GRASSES.

**donax.** Giant reed; called also Italian reed. A stout plant 10-15 ft. high, the stems somewhat woody. Leaves 1-2 ft. long, about 2½ in. wide. Flower cluster spire-like, often 2 ft. long. Southern Eu. There is a variety with yellow- or white-striped leaves.

*ARVENSIS, -e* (ar-ven'sis). From cultivated fields.

**ASAHI-BOTAN.** See Japanese Flowering Cherries at PRUNUS.

*ASARINA.* An old, now obsolete name for a plant with heart-shaped leaves. See *Antirrhinum asarina* at SNAPDRAGON.

**ASARUM** (ass'a-rum). Woodland, perennial plants with aromatic rootstocks and usually kidney-shaped leaves, useful only in shady places in the wild garden. They are usually called wild ginger from their strong scent and flavor. Of 30 known species, belonging to the Aristolochiaceae, only a handful are of secondary garden interest. Leaves stalked, heart-shaped or kidney-shaped. Flowers brownish-purple, borne at or near the ground and hidden by the relatively dense foliage (for structure see ARISTOLOCHIACEAE). Fruit a rather fleshy capsule.* (The name *Asarum* is of unknown significance here.)

The wild gingers need shade, a humus soil, and plenty of moisture. Given these, they spread readily and will cover considerable areas in a few years. Easily increased by division of their creeping rootstocks. All those below are North American.

**canadense.** Leaves 3-6 in. wide, kidney-shaped, the stalk about 6-8 in. long. Flowers 1 in. wide. Eastern N.A. See MEDICINAL PLANTS.

**caudatum.** Leaves 2-5 in. wide, more or less heart-shaped, the stalk 5-7 in. long. Flowers with the lobes prolonged into 2-in. tails. Pacific Coast.

**virginicum.** Resembling the first, but with smaller, usually somewhat mottled leaves, and much smaller flowers. Mountain woods from Va. to Tenn.

*ASCALONICA, -us, -um* (as-ka-lon'i-ka). Named for Ascalon, a village in Palestine.

**ASCENDING.** Rising upwards, but not stiffly or erectly so.

**ASCLEPIADACEAE** (as-kleep-i-a-day'see-ee). The milkweed family, as its name implies, nearly always has a milky juice. Of its 220 widely distributed genera and over 2000 species only a handful are of any garden significance. Among the most curious are *Stapelia, Huernia,* and *Huerniopsis,* which are succulent, almost cactus-like genera from South Africa. The rest of the hort. genera are herbs, shrubs or vines, the leaves of which scarcely ever have marginal teeth. Flowers regular,* rarely solitary, mostly in terminal clusters, sometimes in the axils.* Fruit a dry pod (follicle*), the seeds with a tuft of hairs.

A few are hardy genera (see MILKWEED, ASCLEPIODORA, CYNANCHUM, and PERIPLOCA), but most of the family are tropical. Among the latter are woody vines in *Araujia, Cryptostegia, Hoya,* and *Stephanotis,* while *Ceropegia* is a prostrate, fleshy-stemmed vine from South Africa.

Technical flower characters: Sepals 5, separate or nearly so. Petals joined to form a united corolla, the 5 lobes of which are usually bent backward. Stamens 5, the filaments usually united into a column.* Between the stamens and petals is usually a crown-like organ (corona*). Ovaries 2, each of them 1-celled but many-seeded, superior.*

*ASCLEPIADEA, -us, -um* (as-kleep-i-ā'dee-a). Milkweed-like.

---

* Special articles on the subjects indicated by an asterisk (*) will be found at the words so marked.

**ASCLEPIAS.** See MILKWEED.

**ASCLEPIODORA** (as-kleep-ee-o-dō′ra). A small genus of North American, milkweed-like, perennial herbs, differing from *Asclepias* (see MILKWEED) chiefly in technical characters, and in having alternate* leaves. The only species in cult. is **A. decumbens,** called antelope-horns (in N. Mex.) and snakeroot (Tex.). It is a stout herb 18–24 in. high, with short-stalked, oblongish leaves 3–5 in. long, and greenish-purple flowers in a loose cluster (umbel*). Fruit a follicle.* Suitable only for dry, open places. (The name is derived from *Asclepias*.)

**ASCYRUM** (a-sy′rum). A small genus of mostly North American, shrubby, perennial herbs, family Hypericaceae, only the St. Andrew's-cross of much garden interest. Leaves opposite,* without marginal teeth. Flowers bright yellow, in terminal clusters (cymes*), with numerous stamens and 4 petals. Fruit a small, dry, valved pod (capsule*). (*Ascyrum* is Greek for not hard or rough, and of uncertain application here.)

The St. Andrew's-cross is a pretty little bushy plant useful in the border and effective when planted in masses. It prefers open sunshine and a decidedly sandy soil. Easily propagated by division or by seeds. They need an annual shearing to keep them tidy.

hypericoides. St. Andrew's-cross. A bushy plant 18–24 in. high. Leaves numerous, oblongish, about 1 in. long. Flowers usually 3 to a cluster, the petals narrowly oblong. Native from Mass. to tropical America, but needs winter covering from zone* 4 northward. Not very long-lived. It is sometimes sold as *A. crux-andrae.*

*ASELLIFORMIS, -e* (a-sell-i-for′mis). Shaped like a wood-louse.

**ASEXUAL.** Sexless. As applied to flowers asexual implies that they have no stamens or pollen and no pistil or ovules and are consequently quite sterile. As applied to propagation, asexual reproduction indicates any method of increasing plants except by seeds. See PROPAGATION.

**ASH.** The group of ash trees, all belonging to the genus **Fraxinus** (frax′i-nus) of the olive family, are more important as timber than as ornamentals. Of the 65 known species, mostly from the north temperate zone, only six are of hort.

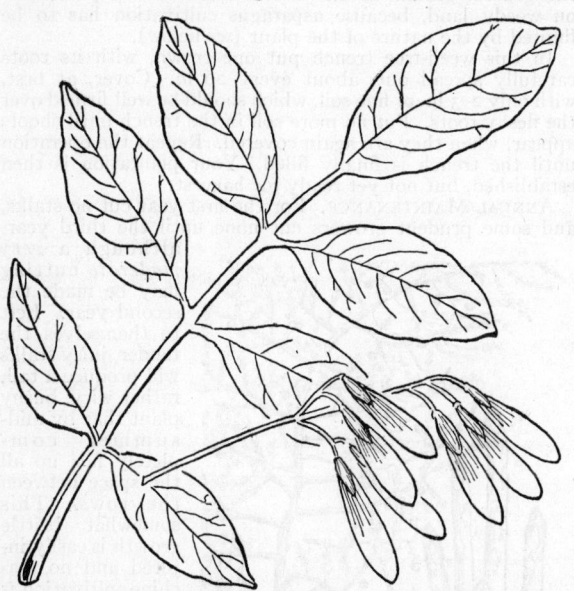

Leaf and fruits of white ash (*Fraxinus americana*)

interest. These are handsome trees with compound,* opposite* leaves, and (in ours) 5 or more leaflets. Flowers small, greenish or whitish, perfect or unisexual (polygamous*), without petals in all except the flowering ash (*F. ornus*). Fruit a small nutlet, partly surrounded by an elongated wing (a samara*). (*Fraxinus* is classical Latin for the ash.)

The flowering ash is the only really showy tree of the group. It has large clusters of whitish flowers blooming about the time the leaves appear. The others flower before the leaves unfold and lack petals. All will grow in most ordinary garden soils, but they are not trees for dry sites, especially the black ash, which prefers moist places. Easily propagated from seeds which should be stratified (see SEEDS AND SEEDAGE), and may not sprout until the second year. All are subject to borers, which must be kept down (see Beetles at INSECT PESTS; see also Insect Pests at APPLE and MAPLE).

**F. americana.** White ash. A tree 60–120 ft. high, the young twigs lustrous-green. Leaflets mostly 7 (rarely 5 or 9), stalked, more or less oval, 3–5 in. long. Fruit oblong, about 1½ in. long. Eastern N.A. Hardy from zone* 2 southward, and not particular as to site.

**F. excelsior.** European ash. Taller than the last, the twigs smooth but not lustrous. Leaflets mostly 9 (rarely 7 or 11), stalkless, oblongish, 3–5 in. long, dark green above, paler beneath. Fruit very narrow, the wing often notched at the tip, about 1½ in. long. Eu. and Asia Minor. Hardy from zone* 3 southward.

**F. nigra.** Black ash; called also hoop ash. Not over 75 ft. high, the twigs smooth. Leaflets 7–11, usually 9, stalkless, rather broad-oblong, green both sides, 4–6 in. long, and with rusty tufts of hair along the mid-rib beneath. Fruit narrow-oblong, 1–1½ in. long, the wing surrounding the nutlet. Eastern N.A. Hardy from zone* 2 southward. Prefers moist sites.

**F. ornus.** Flowering ash; called also manna ash. A Eurasian round-headed tree, not over 50 ft., usually much less. Leaflets usually 7, stalked, oblong or oval, the terminal one larger than the others, which are 2½–3½ in. long. Flowers whitish, fragrant, in dense terminal clusters, opening usually after the leaves unfold. Fruit about 1 in. long, cut-off or notched at the tip. Hardy from zone* 4 southward. The commonest species in cult. and much the showiest. A sweetish manna is collected from it in Asia Minor.

**F. pennsylvanica.** Red or river ash. Much resembles the first but with usually 9 leaflets, and with fruit wing more completely surrounding the nutlet. A variety (**F. pennsylvanica lanceolata**) known as green or swamp ash has irregularly toothed leaflets. Both are found wild over much of eastern N.A., and are hardy from zone* 2 southward. The variety is suited to wind-swept regions in the prairie states.

**F. quadrangulata.** Blue ash. A tree not usually over 70 ft. high, the twigs 4-angled and mostly slightly winged. Leaflets mostly 9 (rarely 7 or 11), short-stalked, yellow-green, more or less narrowly oval, 3–5 in. long. Fruit notched at the tip, winged to the base, 1½–2 in. long. Central U.S. Hardy from zone* 3 southward. Its foliage turns pale yellow in the fall.

For other plants sometimes called ash see MOUNTAIN-ASH and ZANTHOXYLUM.

**ASH AND ASHES.** To the gardener ash is the unburnable residue left from the combustion of plant tissue. It contains various chemicals, all of which are part of the food of plants (see PLANT FOODS). Practically, however, ash means wood ashes or coal ashes.

To dispose of the latter first, coal ashes have no place in the soil of the garden. Chemically they are useless and physically they are far better replaced by sand. Some people put coal ashes in heavy clay soils to lighten them. This is to be avoided. Use sand instead.

Coal ashes have some value as material in which to plunge* potted plants for the summer, because they are more or less antiseptic and discourage worms.

Wood ashes, and the burned vegetable refuse of the garden, both yield an appreciable amount of available potash and are therefore valuable. Wood ashes may be used at the rate of a pound to a cubic yard of soil, in heaps, or scattered on the surface at the rate of about 4 ounces per square yard. Those from the fireplace are the best, and refuse burnings are best mixed with the compost pile, after screening out the rubbish. They furnish a quick-acting, very soluble form of potash, containing from 4–6% of it.

**ASH FAMILY** = Oleaceae.

*ASIATICA, -us, -um* (a-she-at′i-ka). From Asia.

**ASIATIC GLOBEFLOWER** = *Trollius asiaticus.*

**ASIATIC REDBUD** = *Cercis chinensis.* See REDBUD.

**ASIMINA** (as-sim′i-na). A small genus of North American shrubs and trees, family Annonaceae, the one below, the only tree of the group, cult. for its fine foliage, handsome flowers and (to some) desirable fruit. Leaves alternate,* large, without teeth. Flowers in the leaf-axils,* green at

---

* Special articles on the subjects indicated by an asterisk (*) will be found at the words so marked.

first, changing to purple, red and yellow. Sepals 3. Petals 6. Stamens numerous. Fruit fleshy, oblong, suggesting an old potato in color and shape. (*Asimina* is a Latinized version of a French and Indian vernacular name for the species below.)

The tree grows in rich woods, and prefers good rich soil and not too much sun. It transplants with considerable difficulty and is best raised from seeds sown in the fall, or stratified (*see* Seeds and Seedage) and sown the following spring.

**triloba.** Papaw; called also custard-apple in the Central States. A medium-sized tree, usually not over 25 ft. high. Leaves more or less oval-oblong, wedge-shaped at the base, 8–12 in. long. Flowers blooming when the leaves expand, about 2 in. wide. Fruit 2–6 in. long, dark brown when ripe, the flesh yellow, aromatic, but banana-flavored, and surrounding the flattish seeds. Eastern and Central U.S. Hardy from zone* 4 southward. For another plant called papaw *see* Carica.

*ASPARAGINA, -us, -um* (as-pa-ra-geen′a). Asparagus-like.

*ASPARAGOIDES* (as-pa-ra-goy′deez; but *see* Oïdes). Asparagus-like.

**ASPARAGUS** (as-pa′ra-gus). An Old World, but chiefly African, genus of 150 species of largely desert herbs and vines, of the lily family. It comprises such unlike plants as the "smilax" of the florist, the common garden asparagus, and the so-called asparagus fern used for trimming countless bouquets. All have tuberous or fleshy roots and no true leaves, which are reduced to scales or wholly lacking, or, in some, like the florist's "smilax," are replaced by flat, leaf-like branches. Flowers very small and greenish. Fruit a berry. (*Asparagus* is the Greek name for the vegetable.)

For the culture of the common garden asparagus, *see* below. For the culture of *A. asparagoides* (the florist's "smilax") *see* Smilax. The other species below, especially the asparagus fern, are widely grown commercially for their feathery foliage, rivaling in delicacy the finest ferns, but, being leafless, are far more resistant to the heat and dryness of an ordinary room. They are thus the most popular material for trimming bouquets and funeral wreaths in America. Their culture is easy in a cool greenhouse, in potting mixture* 4, and they can be propagated from seed which is plentifully produced on old plants.

**asparagoides.** The "smilax" of the florists. A South African, branching, leafless vine, the leaf-like branches oval, about 1 in. long, bright and lustrous-green. Flowers greenish-white, sparse. Berry dark purple, pea size. For culture and uses *see* Smilax (2). Often sold as *Myrsiphyllum asparagoides*.

**falcatus.** Sickle thorn. A tall-climbing, leafless, spiny vine, the leaf-like branches sickle-shaped, leathery, 2–3 in. long, dark green. Flowers white, fragrant. Berry brown. South Africa. Cult. in Fla. as an ornamental vine that reaches 40 ft. in height.

**officinalis.** Garden asparagus. A Eurasian seacoast plant originally very different from the modern vegetable, and perhaps not now in cult. For culture *see* below.

**plumosus.** Asparagus fern, called also, with as little reason, fern asparagus (it is no fern). A feathery, fern-like, climbing vine from South Africa, the leaves reduced to needle-like bodies about ¼ in. long, and the green stems and twigs functioning as leaves, but wiry. Flowers very small, whitish. Berry purple-black, pea size. In some of its many forms, very widely grown for the florist trade.

**sprengeri.** A South African low-growing vine, cult. for ornament in greenhouses. Leaf-like branches narrow, linear, about ¾ in. long, freely dropping. Flowers pinkish, in racemes. Berry bright red. An attractive plant for the hanging basket.

**verticillatus.** A medium-sized, somewhat woody vine sometimes reaching a height of 15 ft. Leaves reduced to thread-like bodies nearly 2 in. long. Flowers whitish-green. Berry red, pea size. Persia and Central As. Hardy outdoors from zone* 6 southward.

### Asparagus Culture
(*Asparagus officinalis*)

The young tender shoots of asparagus ("grass" to the illiterate) have been used as a vegetable for over two thousand years. It can be grown, and is, in practically every part of the United States, except in areas of extreme heat.

Varieties. Several score are known. Of these only a handful have survived the test of public taste and the ravages of various pests. The outstanding sorts, often generally called Washington asparagus, are the two varieties named Martha Washington and Mary Washington and the latter is easily the leading variety in cult., both on the score of public taste and its resistance to rust. Next to Mary Washington, varieties like Palmetto, Argenteuil, Barr Mammoth, Columbian Mammoth White, and Reading Giant have found favor in special regions.

California (44 per cent) and New Jersey (23 per cent) lead all other states in total asparagus production of U.S., the combined production of South Carolina, Illinois and Maryland scarcely equaling that of New Jersey. Asparagus production, outside these five states, totals only about 11 per cent of the country's consumption and is grown mostly for local market or home use. It should be noted that most of these regions have winters where the ground freezes at least a few inches and the crop appears to benefit by such conditions.

Culture. Asparagus is the most permanent of all vegetable crops. Once established, it used to be assumed, and still is in England, that it will last a lifetime. The best practice now is to renew plantings every 15 years. Because of this it is obvious that the home gardener should plan to put asparagus in areas that do not have to be plowed every year. (For suggestions as to site *see* Kitchen Garden.)

No soil is too rich for asparagus. It will grow in any ordinary good garden soil, but it will not produce tender stalks without liberal supplies of stable manure and plenty of moisture. One of the most successful growers in America grows it on fairly sandy soil, but the permanent water-table is only three feet below the surface and capillarity assures a steady supply to the roots.

For the home gardener it is usually too troublesome to start asparagus from seed. For a moderate price he can purchase dormant one-year-old crowns or roots, thus hastening ultimate production by several years. It takes from 60 to 70 roots for 100 ft. of row. While the old-fashioned idea was to make an "asparagus bed," it is much better planted in rows which should be at least 4–5 ft. apart.

Having selected a rich, well-drained soil, start operations as early in spring as the ground is workable by plowing a deep furrow. This must be deep enough so that when the bottom is smoothed it will still be at least 10 in. below the general ground level. Never start such a plantation on weedy land, because asparagus cultivation has to be limited by the nature of the plant (*see* below).

In this weed-free trench put one crown, with its roots carefully spread out, about every 20 in. Cover, at first, with only 2–3 in. of fine soil, which should be well firmed over the fleshy roots. Put no more soil in the trench until shoots appear, when they are again covered. Repeat the operation until the trench is finally filled. Your plantation is then established, but not yet ready for harvest.

Annual Maintenance. For the first year cut no stalks, and some prudent growers cut none until the third year, although a *very moderate* cutting may be made the second year. Left to themselves the tender, juicy stalks will produce a tall, rather wiry, bushy plant that by midsummer completely fills up all the space between the rows. This somewhat brittle growth is easily injured and no machine cultivation is possible once this growth is well developed. Before it starts, and while the shoots are soft, cultivate frequently and keep the plantation as weed-free as possible up to the end of June.

Asparagus ready for harvesting (at the left) and the summer condition of the plant

---

* Special articles on the subjects indicated by an asterisk (*) will be found at the words so marked.

In the fall cut the bushy growth down to the ground, but never cut it away in midsummer, for it is this summer growth that nourishes the roots for next year's production of shoots. Many growers, besides the initial stable manure, plow in extra supplies in the fall or early spring, or top-dress with a liberal application of commercial fertilizer. If manure is plowed in, care must be taken not to injure the roots which, however, are not injured by any amount of surface cultivation.

HARVEST AND YIELDS. A very moderate cutting may be made the second year, and beginning with the third year all stalks should be cut as soon as they are the usual length, but not for more than three weeks. From the fourth year all stalks should be cut throughout the season. Cut just below the ground level with an asparagus knife, or an ordinary knife will do. Care must be taken to cut so that no young, and still buried, shoots are injured. *See* Section 1, TOOLS AND IMPLEMENTS.

Cutting can begin as soon as the season will permit, but all cutting must stop by June 20, or latest by July 1, when summer growth should be allowed to start. This feathery summer state of the plant is quite unlike the tender spring stalks, but essential to the continued vigor of the plantation.

For those who prefer white stalks some growers heap earth around the emerging shoot. This cuts off the light, and the normally green shoot becomes white, except at the tip. The variety Columbian Mammoth White is normally white.

One hundred feet of row should furnish an ample supply of asparagus for a family of 5, assuming that it is served twice a week and that the plant has been well grown. Good commercial growers expect 2000 bunches per acre, but yields of 3500 bunches are not unknown.

INSECT PESTS. The common asparagus beetle is blue and red and about ¼ in. long. Both adults and the dark, grublike larvae feed on the shoots and leaves. Shoots should be kept well cut during the harvest season. Afterwards the plants should be sprayed or dusted with lead arsenate; the spray should be strong, 3 pounds to 50 gallons, and include a soap spreader. Young plants should be especially protected. The somewhat similar, 12-spotted asparagus beetle injures in the same way except that its larvae feed in the berries. The asparagus miner, a fly larva, may be reduced in numbers by cleaning up old stems and spraying in summer with nicotine sulphate.

DISEASES. Rust is the most serious disease. It causes red or black pustules on the stems which later may die. The Washington strains of asparagus, which are resistant to the disease, are recommended. Other diseases are stem and root cankers, which are controlled by setting healthy plants into a new bed.

**ASPARAGUS BEAN** = *Vigna sesquipedalis*.

**ASPARAGUS BROCCOLI** = *Brassica oleracea italica*. For culture *see* BROCCOLI.

**ASPARAGUS FERN** = *Asparagus plumosus*.

**ASPARAGUS LETTUCE** = *Lactuca sativa asparagina*.

**ASPARAGUS PEA** = *Psophocarpus tetragonolobus*.

**ASPECT.** *See* SITE.

**ASPEN.** *See* POPULUS.

**ASPERA, -us, -um** (as'per-a). Rough.

**ASPERRIMA, -us, -um** (as-per'ri-ma). Very rough.

**ASPERULA** (as-per'u-la). A large genus of Old World annual or perennial herbs of the madder family, with square stems, the few below long cult. for ornament, one a pretty popular annual. Leaves in whorls* of 6 or more. Flowers small, more or less funnel-shaped, and very numerous in forking clusters (cymes*). Fruit leathery but somewhat fleshy, minute. (*Asperula* is diminutive of *aspera*, in allusion to the roughish stems of some species.)

The plants are often called woodruff, and *A. odorata* and *A. tinctoria*, the perennial species, are old favorites in the garden, especially suited to partially shady places. *A. orientalis* is an annual, not so well known as it should be. The perennial species are easily divided in the spring, or raised from seed.

azurea setosa = *Asperula orientalis*.
odorata. Sweet woodruff. A Eurasian, low-spreading, perennial herb, the dried foliage fragrant. Leaves in whorls* of 8, narrow. Flowers white. Prefers a moist site.
orientalis. A Eurasian, hardy annual, easily grown from seed sown in the place they are to grow, not over 12 in. high. Leaves in whorls* of 8, narrow. Flowers blue. A pretty garden flower for open sunlight. *See* ANNUALS.
tinctoria. Dyer's woodruff. A red-rooted, European perennial herb 18-24 in. long, but straggling. Leaves in whorls* of 4 or 6. Flowers red or pinkish-white. Prefers somewhat moist sites.

**ASPHODEL.** The asphodel of poetry is often a narcissus. The asphodel of the ancients is *Asphodeline lutea*. For another plant, also called asphodel, *see* ASPHODELUS. For the bog asphodel *see* NARTHECIUM AMERICANUM.

**ASPHODELINE** (as-fo-de-line'e). A genus of 14 species of perennial herbs of the lily family found in the Mediterranean region and of chief interest because it contains the traditional asphodel. This is a yellow-flowered herb differing from the genus *Asphodelus* only in having a leafy flower stalk. (*Asphodeline* means one of the asphodels.) Sometimes called Jacob's-rod.

The culture of the asphodel is easy in any ordinary garden soil, either in partial shade or the open. Propagated by spring or fall division of the roots.

lutea. The traditional asphodel is a thick-rooted herb 2-3½ ft. high. Leaves 4-10 in. long, rough-margined, mostly basal but also found along the stalk of the flower cluster. Flowers yellow, numerous, in finger-shaped clusters (racemes*) 7-15 in. long and toward the top of the stalk, each about ⅔ in. thick, which have membranes and persistent bracts.* Southern Eu. and Arabia. June.

*ASPHODELOIDES* (as-fo-del-oy'deez; but *see* OÏDES). Asphodel-like.

**ASPHODELUS** (as-fo-del'us). A genus of herbs of the lily family from the Mediterranean region, the one below cultivated for ornament under the name of asphodel (but *see* ASPHODELINE). They are stemless herbs with basal, narrow leaves and lily-like, white flowers in finger-shaped, sometimes branched, clusters (racemes*). Corolla funnel-shaped, of 6 segments, each segment distinctly veined on the back. Stamens 6. Fruit a capsule.* (*Asphodelus* is the classical Greek name of the true asphodel, now included in the genus *Asphodeline*.)

Culture the same as for *Asphodeline*.

ramosus. Often called asphodel. A perennial herb 3-5 ft. high. Leaves all basal, narrow, not so long as the naked stalk of the flower cluster. Flowers white, about ¾ in. long, in a dense, usually branching raceme* which bears also buff-colored bracts. Southern Eu. May.

**ASPIDISTRA** (as-pi-dis'tra). A small but important genus of foliage plants of the lily family, the one below from southern China, and a most resistant house plant. They have basal, numerous, tough evergreen leaves that arise from a mat of shallow rootstocks (often exposed). Flowers (rare in household plants) solitary, borne at the ground level, thus usually hidden by the foliage, dull brown or purplish-brown, bell-shaped. Stamens 8. Fruit a berry. (*Aspidistra* is Greek for small, round shield, in allusion to the stigma.)

The only cult. species is widely grown for house ornament, for window boxes, and wherever conditions are unfavorable for other foliage plants. It will stand so much abuse that it is often called cast-iron-plant, and is so common in saloons that it is frequently called lager-beer-plant. Florists grow it extensively for decorations that must stand dust, smoke, heat and cold. They are best grown in pots in a cool greenhouse, where they grow rapidly and are easily increased by division of their numerous rootstocks. Use potting mixture* 4.

elatior. Cast-iron-plant. Leaves plentiful, 15-20 in. long, stiff and leathery, deep green, sharp-pointed but more or less oblong and with a stout, channeled stalk about a third the length of the blade. Flowers about 1 in. long. Southern China. Can be grown outdoors in zones* 8 and 9. Often sold as *A. lurida*. There is a variegated (white-striped) variety which loses its stripes if planted in too rich a soil.

**ASPIDIUM.** A much-confused name for ferns usually, and here, assigned to other genera, especially to *Dryopteris*, *Polystichum* and *Cyrtomium*.

*ASPLENIFOLIA, -us, -um* (as-plee-ni-fō'li-a). With leaves like a spleenwort (*Asplenium*).

**ASPLENIUM** (as-plee'ni-um). The spleenworts comprise a genus of 200 species of widely distributed ferns, family Polypodiaceae, both temperate and tropical, and of great diversity of habit. All those below, except *A. nidus*, have fronds that are once- or twice-compound,* their ultimate

---

* Special articles on the subjects indicated by an asterisk (*) will be found at the words so marked.

segments small and the foliage thus fine and feathery. *Asplenium nidus*, the bird's-nest fern, has undivided fronds. The fronds have free (not reticulated) veins along which are the elongated spore cases; see FERNS AND FERN GARDENING. (*Asplenium* is Greek for not the spleen, in allusion to their supposed medicinal properties.)

*Asplenium bulbiferum* and *A. nidus* are tropical species to be grown in the greenhouse. The other two are hardy ferns for the outdoor fernery or wild garden. See FERNS AND FERN GARDENING for culture of both groups. *See also* ATHYRIUM.

**bulbiferum.** Mother spleenwort. A curious fern with much-divided fronds 12–18 in. long, the ultimate segments tapering to a point. The fronds often bear bulbils which sprout into new plants while still attached. Tropical Af. and Australasia. Grown by florists for decoration and its proliferating* fronds.

**nidus.** Bird's-nest fern. A handsome tropical fern with undivided fronds without marginal teeth, all of which arise at the ground level and diverge to form a bird's-nest-like clump. Fronds 1–3 ft. long, short-stalked, about 3 in. wide, bright green. A very striking greenhouse fern frequently grown. It is found wild from southern Fla. to Brazil, and in the Old World tropics.

**platyneuron.** Ebony spleenwort. A hardy American fern with fronds 8–15 in. long. Leaflets 30–35 pairs, each of which has an enlarged, ear-like lobe at the base. A woods fern for the shady nook.

**trichomanes.** Maidenhair spleenwort. A hardy, evergreen fern found in rich woods throughout the north temperate zone. Fronds thickly clustered, only once-compound,* about 5 in. long and less than 1 in. wide. Leaflets about ½ in. long, very numerous and crowded, slightly toothed on the upper side. A delicate fern for the shaded part of the wild garden.

**ASPRIS** (as'pris). A small genus of very delicate annual grasses from the Mediterranean region, one grown for dry bouquets. They have hair-like or thread-like leaves and spreading clusters (panicles*) of tiny, persistent spikelets. (*Aspris* is the Greek name of the one below.) It is of the easiest culture. Sow seed in any open, reasonably good, preferably sandy, loam.

**capillaris.** Hair grass. Not over 15 in. high. Leaves extremely fine, less than 1/16 in. thick. Flower clusters (panicles) with many-spreading, hair-like branches. Southern Eu. Grown for dry bouquets and of little use otherwise; often offered as *Aira capillaris*.

**ASSONIA** = DOMBEYA.

**ASSURGENT** = ASCENDING.

**ASSURGENTIFLORA, -us, -um** (as-sir-gent-i-flow'ra). With an ascending flower cluster.

**ASTER.** As a name aster is confusing. To many gardeners it implies the garden or China aster, a popular annual of world-wide cult. This plant, however, does not belong to the genus *Aster* but to *Callistephus*, which see for the garden aster.

*Aster* as a genus is an immense group of mostly perennial herbs, family Compositae, very common throughout N.A., much less so in Eu. and As. They are common features of our autumnal landscapes, with a variety of color in their ray flowers (nearly all but yellow). Most of them are stout plants of the woods or fields, easily grown and often too weedy for the border or bed, but useful for bold effects in half-wild sites. Leaves alternate.* Flower heads usually clustered, made up of ray flowers and often yellow disk flowers (see COMPOSITAE for details). They differ only in technical characters from *Erigeron*. (*Aster* is Latin for star, hence the little-used name of starwort.)

Of more than 200 species, those below are most likely to be found in cult., although many native species are occasionally dug from the wild. All those below flower in late summer and fall, except those specified otherwise. For the blue garden the hort. forms Blue Gem, Climax and Feltham Blue are useful. These and many more have been derived from a few, chiefly native American species, from which the English, mostly, have developed a fine strain of hybrid asters called Michaelmas daisies. These are finer garden plants than any of those below, especially as grown in England. See MICHAELMAS DAISY.

**acris.** A rough-hairy perennial from southern Eu., 2–3 ft. high. Leaves very narrow, without teeth, about 1½ in. long. Ray flowers blue, the heads about 1 in. wide, clustered. Autumn.

**alpinus.** Rock aster. Mostly a rock garden species, usually less than 10 in. high. Leaves spatula-shaped or lance-shaped, 1½–2 in. long. Ray flowers blue or violet, the heads solitary, about 1½ in. wide. Mountains of Eurasia and in the Rockies. May. The *var*. **himalaicus** has lilac ray flowers, and is a lower plant. The *var*. **ruber** has rose-pink flowers. For the *var*. **speciosus** see ROCK GARDEN.

**amellus.** Italian aster. A rough-hairy Eurasian herb 1–2 ft. high, with oblongish leaves with marginal teeth. Ray flowers purple, the heads clustered and about 1½ in. across. The *var*. **bessarabicus** has deeper purple ray flowers. There are several named forms such as Arethusa, Mrs. Perry, etc. August.

**cordifolius.** Blue wood aster. A much-branched North American herb 3–5 ft. Basal leaves very large, heart-shaped and stalked, the stem leaves narrow-oblong, about 5 in. long. Ray flowers violet or blue, the heads about ¾ in. wide and very numerous. Prefers partial shade.

**diplostephioides.** A Himalayan herb 2–3 ft. high and hairy. Leaves lance-shaped, 2–3 in. long and without marginal teeth. Ray flowers blue or pale purple, the solitary heads nearly 3 in. wide.

**divaricatus.** White wood aster. Somewhat similar to *A. cordifolius* but the ray flowers white. A stout North American species common in dry woods.

**ericoides.** Heath aster. A wiry, branching herb 2–3 ft. high. Leaves very small and heath-like, seldom over 1½ in. long, but very numerous. Ray flowers white, the heads very small but numerous, and in profuse clusters. Eastern U.S.

**grandiflorus.** A hairy, much-branched herb 2–3 ft. high, its leaves oblongish, about 1½ in. long and hairy. Ray flowers deep purple or violet, the heads solitary and nearly 2 in. wide. Va. to Fla.

**novae-angliae.** New England aster. A tall branching herb, 3–5 ft. high. Leaves very numerous, lance-shaped, 3–4 in. long. Ray flowers deep purple, the heads crowded and nearly 1½ in. wide. Eastern N.A. One of the finest wild species. See MICHAELMAS DAISY for its many named forms.

**novi-belgi.** New York aster. A perfectly smooth herb 2–3 ft. high, its leaves narrow, pointed, 4–6 in. long. Ray flowers bluish-violet, the heads about 1 in. wide and very numerous in large, branched clusters. Eastern N.A.

**porteri.** A Rocky Mountain herb seldom over 12 in. high, and suited to the rock garden. Leaves smooth, narrow, 2–3½ in. long. Ray flowers white, the heads small but numerous. July.

**ptarmicoides.** White upland aster. A North American herb 18–24 in. high. Leaves very narrow, 4–6 in. long, nearly without marginal teeth. Ray flowers white, the heads about 1 in. wide and in profuse, branching clusters. New England to Colo.

**spectabilis.** A low, early-blooming native aster with oval or oblongish leaves 3–5 in. long. Ray flowers bright purple-violet, the heads 1½–2 in. wide and rather sparse. Mass. to Del. Prefers moist sites and open places. July.

**subcoeruleus.** A rock garden aster seldom over 1 ft. high, the foliage hairy. Leaves oblongish, 1–2 in. long. Ray flowers blue or pale blue, the heads nearly 2 in. wide, showy, but solitary. July. Himalayas.

**tataricus.** Tartarian aster. The largest of the hort. asters, often 6–8 ft. high and wide-spreading. Lower leaves ovalish or lance-shaped, nearly 2 ft. long, the upper leaves much smaller. Ray flowers blue or violet-purple, the heads 1 in. wide but in numerous and profuse clusters. Siberia. A handsome and striking plant needing plenty of space.

Various plants are offered from time to time as yellow asters. No true *Aster* is ever yellow so far as known. See CHRYSOPSIS for the golden aster, which is sometimes called yellow aster.

**ASTERACEAE.** See COMPOSITAE.

**ASTER DAISY** = *Chrysanthemum arcticum*.

**ASTER FAMILY.** See COMPOSITAE.

**ASTEROIDES** (as-ter-roy'deez; but *see* OÏDES). Like an aster.

**ASTILBE** (as-til'be). A genus of spirea-like herbs, of the family Saxifragaceae, widely grown as handsome border perennials and much forced by florists who commonly, but incorrectly, sell them as spirea. They superficially resemble the genus *Aruncus*, but the latter have many stamens, while *Astilbe* has 8–10. Leaves simple,* or twice- or thrice-compound,* the ultimate leaflets cut or toothed. Flowers mostly unisexual.* Petals 4–5, sometimes lacking, white, pink, or reddish. Pistils* 2 or 3. Fruit a group of follicles.* (*Astilbe* is Greek for not shining, in allusion to the leaflets.)

The astilbes are fine garden plants of easy culture in any ordinarily good soil. Their flowers, while small, are borne in profuse, spire-like clusters, blooming mostly in June, but often continuing to August. For forcing in the greenhouse the roots should be potted up in the fall and held in a pit or cold frame. When brought into a moderately warm greenhouse, give plenty of water and allow about 12 weeks until blooming time.

**arendsi.** See ASTILBE DAVIDI.

**astilboides.** A Japanese herb 2–3 ft. high. Leaves twice- or thrice-compound,* the ultimate leaflets ovalish, sharply toothed, 1½–2½ in. long. Flowers white in dense, spike-like clusters, which are grouped into a panicle.* Often sold as *Aruncus astilboides* and *Spiraea astilboides*.

**davidi.** A very showy Chinese herb 4–6 ft. high. Leaves compound,*

---

* Special articles on the subjects indicated by an asterisk (*) will be found at the words so marked.

the leaflets resembling an elm leaf, coarsely toothed, about 2 in. long. Flowers rose-pink (but the anthers* blue), clustered in long, narrow panicles 12-20 in. long. Under the name of *A. arendsi*, hybrids of this and other species comprise very fine plants, with flowers ranging from purple to white. Some of the best named forms are Meta Immink, America, Gloria, Gruno, Queen Alexandra and Rose Pearl. See PINK GARDEN.
    **japonica.** A Japanese herb 1-3 ft. high. Leaves twice- or thrice-compound,* the ultimate leaflets lance-oval, wedge-shaped at the base, sharply toothed. Flowers white, in terminal, spire-like clusters, or a few clusters in the leaf-axils.* A good house plant.
    **simplicifolia.** A low Japanese herb, seldom over 12 in. high. Leaves simple, more or less oval, deeply cut, 2-3 in. long. Flowers white, in slender, narrow clusters. Less showy than the others.

**ASTILBOIDES** (as-til-boy'deez; but *see* OÏDES). Like a plant of the genus *Astilbe*.

**ASTRAGALUS** (as-trag'a-lus). An enormous genus of vetch-like herbs of the pea family scattered over most of the world. Of the 1500 known species, which include some of the cattle-poisoning locoweeds of the West, only a handful are of secondary garden interest. They have alternate,* compound* leaves and small, pea-like flowers in clusters. Fruit a legume,* smaller than the garden pea. The plants are often called milk vetch. (*Astragalus* is an óld Greek name for some shrub, and of uncertain application here.)
    The species below are occasionally seen in the border or rock garden. They do not stand transplanting very well and are best raised from seed, but these germinate slowly and poorly. The roots may also be divided, but with care, and see that some of the old soil is transplanted with the divided clump to the new site.
    **austrinus.** A half prostrate or straggling annual or biennial herb 8-12 in. high. Leaflets about ¼ in. long. Flowers purple, in close, head-like clusters (racemes*). Southwestern U.S. and Mex. July.
    **drummondi.** A perennial herb 15-24 in. high, the foliage hairy. Leaflets about ½ in. long. Flowers cream-yellow, in clusters (racemes*) 2-4 in. long. Rocky Mountains. July.
    **hypoglottis.** A low, somewhat prostrate herb scarcely exceeding 6 in. in height. Leaflets numerous (19 or more), oblongish, about ⅓ in. long. Flowers bluish-purple, in small, spike-like clusters that are rarely over 1 in. long. Eu. July. The best known of the cult. species and sometimes grown in pots for its attractive bloom.
    **mexicanus.** Not Mexican but a prairie plant found wild from Ill. to Tex. Perennial, more or less straggling, its leaflets ¼-½ in. long. Flowers cream-white, but blue at the tip. July.

**ASTRANTIA** (as-tran'she-a). A small group of Eurasian, perennial herbs of the carrot family, one commonly cult. as a garden plant for its attractive flower clusters. They have aromatic roots and compound* leaves, with the leaflets arranged finger-fashion, or the upper leaves may be nearly simple.* In both there is a wide-margined or winged* leafstalk. Flowers small (for details *see* UMBELLIFERAE), in tiny umbels,* beneath which are bracts* that often exceed the umbel in length and are attractively colored. (*Astrantia* is derived from *Aster*, in allusion to the star-like bracts.)
    The plant below is of the easiest cult. in any ordinary garden soil. It is attractive in June, with its numerous umbels* of small flowers set in the center of the star-like bracts.* Best propagated by division of its roots.
    **major.** Masterwort. A stout plant 2-3 ft. high. Leaves chiefly basal, the 3-5 leaf segments (leaflets) deeply lobed or toothed. Flower clusters (umbels*) pinkish-rose or white, the bracts* beneath usually purplish. Eu.

**ASTROPHYTUM** (as-trow-fy'tum). A small genus of Mexican cacti, cult. in succulent gardens for their curious, globose or flattened, rarely cylindric, habit. The plant body is ribbed or winged, often giving the plants a star-like appearance, hence their general name of star cactus. They have a few weak spines, or none. The large, quickly fading flowers are borne at the top of the plant; in ours yellow or orange. Fruit fleshy. (*Astrophytum* means star-like plant.) For culture and uses *see* CACTI.
    **capricorne.** Biznaga. Plant nearly globe-shaped, rarely cylindric, about 8 in. high, usually with 7 or 8 deep ribs. Spines nearly 2 in. long, weak or sometimes wanting. Flower lemon-yellow, about 2½ in. long, its numerous petals spreading orange at the base.
    **myriostigma.** Mitra. Not over 2 in. high, the globose plant body suggesting a bishop's hood. Ribs mostly 5, lacking spines. Flowers orange-yellow, about 2 in. long, the petals brown-tipped.
    **ornatum.** The most ornamental of the hort. species. Plant body nearly globe-shaped, 10-15 in. high, covered with whitish tufts of hair. Ribs usually 8, armed with spines about 1 in. long. Flowers lemon-yellow, about 3½ in. long and showy.

**ATAMASCO.** North American Indian name for *Zephyranthes atamasco*.

**ATAMASCO LILY** = *Zephyranthes atamasco*.

**ATAMOSCO.** An untenable generic name (derived from atamasco) for *Zephyranthes*.

**ATHEL TREE** = *Tamarix articulata*.

**ATHYRIUM** (a-thir'i-um). A very large genus of ferns, separated only by technical characters from *Asplenium*, and found almost throughout the world, chiefly in warm regions. Fronds (in ours) once- or twice-compound,* the ultimate leaflets numerous. (*Athyrium* is from the Greek for oblong shield, in allusion to the spore cases.)
    The only fern of much garden interest is *A. filix-femina*, the lady fern, widely grown for ornament in many hort. forms. For culture and uses *see* FERNS AND FERN GARDENING.
    **acrostichoides.** Silvery spleenwort. A hardy fern, the fronds 20-30 in. long, twice-compound, on long, yellowish-green stalks. Ultimate leaflets very numerous, toothed. In rich woods, eastern N.A. Sometimes known as *A. thelypteroides*.
    **angustifolium.** Swamp spleenwort. A hardy fern with fronds 18-24 in. long, only once-compound,* the ultimate leaflets nearly 4 in. long, narrow, and nearly without teeth, short-stalked. In rich woods, eastern N.A. Often called *A. pycnocarpon*.
    **filix-femina.** Lady fern. A delicate, feathery, very popular fern with bright green fronds 24-30 in. long and twice-compound.* Ultimate leaflets very numerous, generally deeply cut or toothed, but of infinite variety in the many hort. named forms, some crested and crisped. Nearly throughout N.A.; also (perhaps a different form), in Eu. and As. Very variable and much cult.
    **pycnocarpon** = *Athyrium angustifolium*.
    **thelypteroides** = *Athyrium acrostichoides*.

**ATLANTICA, -us, -um** (at-lan'tick-a). From or near the Atlantic; also from Mt. Atlas.

**ATLAS CEDAR** = *Cedrus atlantica*.

**ATOMIZER.** *See* SPRAYING AND DUSTING.

**ATRAGENE.** *See* CLEMATIS.

**ATRIPLEX** (at'ri-plex). A large genus of herbs and salt-tolerant shrubs, of the goosefoot family, of wide distribution. One is a secondary garden vegetable, several are troublesome weeds, and *A. breweri* is a Californian shrub. Leaves mostly alternate,* or rarely opposite,* often mealy or whitish. Flowers inconspicuous, mostly unisexual,* in simple or branched clusters (for flower structure *see* CHENOPODIACEAE). Fruit dry, partly or wholly hidden by the persistent, tiny bracts.* (*Atriplex* is Greek for orach.) The wild (not hort.) shrubs of the West are commonly called greasewood or saltbush. Some of the wild species are useful in the re-vegetation of arid regions. *See also* SAND GARDENS.
    The garden orach, whose herbage is used like spinach, is an annual whose seeds should be sown in spring in drills 8 in. apart, and thinned, when about 2 in. high, to 6 in. apart in the row. The leaves should be used while young, as they become stringy and tough when old. *Atriplex breweri* is useful for seaside planting along the coast of southern Calif., and for hedges in dry regions of the Southwest.
    **breweri.** Quail-brush. A shrub 3-5 ft. high. Leaves oval or oblongish, silvery-gray, 1-2½ in. long. Southern Calif.
    **hortensis.** Garden orach. A stout, annual herb 1-3 ft. or more. Leaves somewhat triangular or arrow-shaped, or heart-shaped, short-stalked, 4-5 in. long, varying from yellow-green to pale red. As. Sometimes called sea purslane.
    **patula.** See Orach in the list at WEEDS.

**ATRIPLICIFOLIA, -us, -um** (at-ri-pli-si-fō'li-a). With leaves like a saltbush (*Atriplex*).

**ATROCARPA, -us, -um** (at-ro-kar'pa). With blackish fruit.

**ATROCAULIS, -e** (at-ro-call'is). With blackish (or dark) stems.

**ATROPA** (at'ro-pa). A genus of only two species of Eurasian herbs of the potato family, the one below a dangerous garden plant, for its berries are poisonous and its sap yields the drugs atropine and belladonna. Leaves large, alternate,* without marginal teeth. Flowers bell-shaped, the calyx* enlarging in fruit, the corolla with 5 rather

---

\* Special articles on the subjects indicated by an asterisk (\*) will be found at the words so marked.

pointed, short, recurved lobes. Fruit a berry. (Named for Atropus who cut the thread of life.)

Belladonna can be grown in any ordinary garden soil and propagated by division of its roots. The percentage of the alkaloid in its sap, however, under American conditions, does not warrant its culture for atropine. It appears to prefer limestone soils, and north of zone* 4 is apt to be winter-killed. See MEDICINAL PLANTS.

**belladonna.** Belladonna. A perennial herb 2–3 ft. high. Leaves more or less oval, 3½–5 in. long. Flowers nodding, singly or in pairs, purplish-red, about 1 in. long. Berry black, about ½ in. in diameter, poisonous. Eurasia.

*ATROPUNICEA, -us, -um* (at-ro-pew-niss′i-a). Dark red or dark reddish-purple.

*ATROPURPUREA, -us, -um* (at-ro-pur-pure′ee-a). Dark purple.

*ATROSANGUINEA, -us, -um* (at-ro-san-gwin′ee-a). Deep blood-red.

*ATROVIRENS* (at-ro-vy′rens). Dark green.

**ATTALEA** (at-tay′lee-a). A large genus of tropical American feather palms, only one of which is likely to be cult., and this only in frost-free parts of Fla. Leaves compound,* long, graceful, and curving outward at the tip. Leaflets often standing edgewise on the main leafstalk. Flower cluster from among the crown of leaves, issuing from an erect, boat-shaped spathe,* the latter recurved. Flowers unisexual,* mostly yellow. Fruit (in ours) a short-beaked, fibrous-coated drupe,* its nut very hard. (*Attalea* is from the Latin for magnificent.)

The cohune palm can only be grown outdoors in zone* 9, where it prefers low, rich soils. It is too big for pot or tub culture.

**cohune.** Cohune palm. An erect palm 50–60 ft. high, with a ringed trunk. Leaves in a tremendous terminal crown, each leaf often 20 ft. long. Leaflets 30–50 pairs, each leaflet about 18 in. long, the leafstalk flat above and rounded beneath. Flower cluster 4–5 ft. long. Fruit about 3 in. long. Honduras.

**ATTAR OF ROSES.** See ROSA ALBA SUAVEOLENS and R. DAMASCENA.

*ATTENUATA, -us, -um* (at-ten-u-ā′ta). Narrowed to a point.

*ATTICA, -us, -um* (at′tick-a). From Athens, Greece.

**AUBERGINE.** See EGGPLANT.

**AUBRIETIA** (au-bree′shee-a). A small genus of Old World perennial herbs of the mustard family, the only hort. species very popular as a mat-forming plant for edgings, the rock garden or the open border. They have more or less crowded leaves and relatively large 4-petaled flowers in short terminal clusters (see CRUCIFERAE for details). Fruit an oblong pod. (Named for Claude Aubriet, French natural history painter.) The name is sometimes spelled *Aubrieta* and *Aubretia*.

For culture and uses see ROCK GARDEN.

**deltoides.** Purple rock cress. Usually 3–6 in. high. Leaves more or less triangular, hairy, with one or two teeth, scarcely 1 in. long. Flowers typically purple or violet, the petals with a stalk-like base. Fruit about ½ in. long. Italy and Greece. June. There are many varieties and named forms, some dwarf, others with larger flowers or bigger leaves, and some with pink flowers.

*AUBRIETIOIDES* (au-bree-shee-oy′deez; but see OÏDES). Like the purple rock cress (*Aubrietia*).

**AUCUBA** (aw-kew′ba). A small genus of Asiatic, evergreen shrubs, family Cornaceae, very popular as foliage plants, especially for city window boxes in the North, and in the cool greenhouse. Leaves opposite,* without marginal teeth or distantly toothed. Male and female flowers on different plants, small and greenish. Fruit a usually orange or scarlet berry. (*Aucuba* is a Latinized form of the Japanese vernacular name for these plants.)

The species below is widely grown by florists for decoration, in the cool greenhouse and in potting mixture* 4. Grown mostly as a pot plant, and propagated by cuttings of half-ripened wood, taken when convenient, and rooted in a cutting bench under glass. The plant is perfectly hardy outdoors from zone* 5 southward, and often in sheltered parts of zone* 4 where it often merely winter-kills without protection. It prefers half-shade and plenty of moisture. Greenhouse plants should be plunged in a frost-free, but unheated, pit over the winter.

**japonica.** Shrub 4–15 ft. high southward; usually much smaller as cult. Leaves glossy, dark green, more or less oval, 4–8 in. long, rather distantly toothed. Berry mostly scarlet, and not produced without male plants. Eastern As. The *var.* **variegata**, often called the gold-dust tree, has yellow-spotted leaves. There are other varieties with narrower leaves and with coarse teeth.

*AUCUPARIA* (aw-kew-pay′ri-a). A specific name implying bird-catching, from the use of the fruits for this purpose. See MOUNTAIN-ASH.

**AUDIBERTIA** (o-di-ber′shee-a). A genus of mostly Californian perennial herbs or under-shrubs of the mint family and closely related to salvia. They have roughish, opposite, often woolly or hairy leaves, and irregular, 2-lipped flowers in mostly terminal but not profuse clusters. Calyx deeply cleft, almost spathe*-like. (Named for Urbain Audibert, French botanist.) The species are sometimes called *Ramona*.

The plants, commonly called sage in Calif., are cult. more there than in the East, for ornament and *A. stachyoides* as an important bee plant. They are of easy cult. and may be propagated by division.

**grandiflora.** Crimson sage, called also bee sage. A sticky-hairy perennial 1–3 ft. high. Leaves woolly or felty on the under side, more or less arrow-head-shaped, 3–7 in. long. Flower 1–1½ in. long, crimson-purple or red, the bracts* crowded and showy. Calif.

**polystachya.** White sage, called also greasewood (but not the true greasewood). A shrubby herb 4–8 ft. high, its foliage densely white-hairy. Flowers ½–¾ in. long, white. Calif.

**stachyoides.** Black sage. A stiff, perennial herb 2–3 ft. high and one of the important Calif. bee plants. Leaves green above, grayish beneath, oblongish and short-stalked, 2–3 in. long. Flowers about ⅓ in. long, white or lilac. Calif.

**AUGUST.** See GARDEN CALENDAR.

*AURANTIACA, -us, -um* (aw-ran-ty′a-ka). Orange-colored.

*AURANTIFOLIA, -us, -um* (aw-ran-ti-fō′li-a). With leaves like the orange.

*AURANTIUM.* An old generic and specific name for the Seville or sour orange.

*AURATA, -us, -um* (aw-ray′ta). Golden.

*AUREA, -us, -um* (aw′ree-a). Golden.

*AUREO-MACULATA, -us, -um* (aw-ree-o-mac-kew-lay′ta). Golden-spotted.

*AUREO-MARGINATA, -us, -um* (aw-ree-o-mar-ji-nay′-ta). Golden-margined.

*AUREO-REGINA, -us, -um* (aw-ree-o-re-jine′a). Golden queen.

*AUREO-RETICULATA, -us, -um* (aw-ree-o-re-tick-ew-lay′ta). With golden veins.

*AUREO-VARIEGATA, -us, -um* (aw-ree-o-vair-ee-i-gay′ta). With golden markings.

**AURICLE.** An ear-shaped organ, often surrounding a leafstalk, or partly sheathing a flower cluster; or an ear-shaped appendage to a petal.

*AURICULA.* A pre-Linnaean* name for plants now included in *Primula*. See PRIMULA AURICULA.

*AURICULATA, -us, -um* (aw-rick-kew-lay′ta). Eared; *i.e.* auricled.

*AURITA, -us, -um* (aw-ry′ta). Eared; *i.e.* auricled.

*AUSTRALASICA, -us, -um* (os-tray-lay′zi-ka). From Australasia.

**AUSTRALIAN.** Many plants from Australia and neighboring islands, wholly unrelated to European plants which they recalled, were, by early settlers, named Australian beech, etc. Of the hundreds so called the following are found here:

**Australian beech** = *Eucalyptus polyanthemos*; **Australian bluebell creeper** = *Sollya heterophylla*; **Australian brush-cherry** = *Eugenia pani-*

---

* Special articles on the subjects indicated by an asterisk (*) will be found at the words so marked.

*culata australis;* **Australian fan palm** = *Livistona australis;* **Australian honeysuckle** (see BANKSIA); **Australian laurel** (see PITTOSPORUM); **Australian lilac** = *Hardenbergia monophylla;* **Australian oak family** = PROTEACEAE; **Australian pea** = *Dolichos lignosus;* **Australian pine** (see CASUARINA); **Australian rye grass** = *Lolium multiflorum;* and **Australian teatree** = *Leptospermum laevigatum.*

**AUSTRALIS,** *-e* (os-tray′lis). Southern.

**AUSTRIACA,** *-us, -um* (os-try′a-ka). From Austria.

**AUSTRIAN BRIER** = *Rosa foetida.*

**AUSTRIAN COPPER BRIER** = *Rosa foetida bicolor.*

**AUSTRIAN PINE** = *Pinus nigra.* See PINE.

**AUSTRINA,** *-us, -um* (os-try′na). Southern.

**AUTOMATIC GREENHOUSE CONTROL.** See GREENHOUSE.

**AUTUMNALIS,** *-e* (aw-tum-nay′lis). Autumnal.

**AUTUMN CROCUS.** See COLCHICUM.

**AUTUMN FOLIAGE.** The fall color of foliage is most gorgeous in the plants of eastern North America and eastern Asia, and it is from these two regions that the gardener must get his best autumnal foliage plants.

Mixing autumn foliage in the border or in vistas requires just as much care as mixing flower color. Taste and individual preference will dictate what one plants. It is well to remember, however, that it is possible to overdo the brilliant scarlet of Japanese barberry, and that a judicious mixture of evergreens, both conifers and broad-leaved evergreens, will help any group planted for autumn color effects.

Some plants not in the tabulation below are planted for their gay twigs, especially Tatarian dogwood of eastern Asia and the native American red dogwood, but these are not primarily fall foliage plants.

From the segregation of colors below the skillful gardener may get almost any effect within the range from bright scarlet to brown. Scores more could be cited, but the following are the easiest grown and provide all that one needs for autumn foliage effects.

RED OR SCARLET. Sassafras, red maple, sumac, Japanese barberry, red oak, scarlet oak, pin oak, flowering dogwood, sweet gum, sour gum, and a few native blueberries.

BRONZE. Many broad-leaved evergreens, such as *Mahonia,* some rhododendrons, *Leucothoë, Pieris, Arctostaphylos,* and *Galax.* Some of these will stay green in protected or warm places but become bronzy in exposed or cold sites.

YELLOW OR ORANGE. Sugar maple, Norway maple, *Ginkgo,* larch, witch-hazel, persimmon, moosewood (see MAPLE), yellow-wood, cucumber tree, wild red cherry, tulip-tree and some wild hickories.

Less showy are the brownish or neutral shades of many oaks, the elms, and hosts of common trees. For other autumn effects in the garden, see AUTUMN GARDEN, and the section headed Food Supply in the article BIRDS.

**AUTUMN GARDENS.** The autumn garden may be marked by opulence of bloom and richness of color if planting is done with this end in view. There are fewer flowering plants and shrubs to call upon than are available in the earlier seasons, but those blossoming at the later date are in the main characterized by luxuriance of habit and warmth of hue. Many annuals and perennials linger over from the late summer and add a valuable quota to the autumn assemblage, but the majority of the annuals will be cut off by the early frosts, and reliance should be placed chiefly upon such hardy plants as sunflowers, ironweed, Michaelmas daisies, heleniums, aconites, Japanese chrysanthemums and Japanese anemones, aconites and rudbeckias whose brightness outlasts many frosts and some of which continue to bloom well on towards December. To increase the splendor of the autumn garden free use should be made of such trees and shrubs as bear decorative fruits or whose foliage colors handsomely. See AUTUMN FOLIAGE.

The autumn-flowering bulbs should also be more widely employed than is commonly the custom. These include *Colchicum, Crocus* and *Sternbergia.* For the best results they should be planted as early in August as they may be procured.

AUTUMN-FLOWERING PLANTS AND BULBS. *Aconitum autumnale,* 4–5 ft. dark blue, *A. fischeri,* 4 ft. bright blue; *Allium stellatum,* 2 ft. rose; *Anemone hupenensis,* 18 in. rose, *A. japonica* vars., 2–5 ft. pink, rosewhite; *Artemisia vulgaris,* 4 ft. cream; *Aster acris* vars. lavender, *A. amellus,* in varieties of mauve, rose, violet, *A. cordifolius,* 3–5 ft. small flowers, white, lilac, pale rose, *A. ericoides,* 2–3 ft. small flowers, pale blue, white, *A. novae-angliae,* 3–5 ft. purple, deep rose, pink, *A. novi-belgi,* 2–3 ft. all tones of rose, pink, lavender, mauve, purple and white, *A. tataricus,* 6 ft. lavender; *Ceratostigma plumbaginoides,* 18 in. pure blue; *Chrysanthemum arcticum,* 18 in. white, *C. nipponicum,* 2 ft. white, C. Japanese vars. white, yellow, orange, bronze, russet, rose, pink; *Cimicifuga simplex,* 3 ft. white; *Colchicum* species and vars., *autumnale, bornmulleri, speciosum,* white, rose, purplish; *Cosmos,* 4–6 ft. pink, rose, white; *Crocus* species, *longiflorus, nudiflorus, pulchellus, sativus, speciosus, zonatus,* white, mauve, lavender, violet; Dahlias, many vars. all colors, sizes and heights; *Eupatorium urticaefolium,* 4 ft. white; *Gentiana andrewsi,* 18 in. blue, *G. crinita,* 18 in. blue; *Helenium autumnale rubrum,* 5 ft. russet; *Helianthus* (see SUNFLOWER) Miss Mellish, 6 ft. yellow, *H. maximiliani,* 8 ft. orange-yellow (the latest to flower), *H. orgyalis,* 6–8 ft. orange-yellow; *Helleborus niger,* 12–18 in. white; *Hosta japonica tardiflora,* 18 in. lavender-blue; *Kniphofia uvaria grandiflora* and other species and vars. orange, scarlet, yellow; *Liriope muscari variegata,* 1 ft. blue; *Lobelia cardinalis,* 2 ft. scarlet; *Oxalis bowieana,* 1 ft. pink; *Phlox* Jeanne d'Arc, 4–5 ft. white; *Rudbeckia laciniata hortensia,* 6 ft. yellow; *Sedum sieboldi,* pink, *S. spectabile,* 18 in. pink; *Solidago* species and vars. yellow; *Sternbergia lutea,* 6–8 in. yellow; *Tricyrtis hirta,* 2–3 ft. purplish; *Tritonias,* scarlet, orange, yellow; *Vernonia altissima,* 8 ft. purple.

SHRUBS. *Abelia chinensis,* 4–6 ft. pinkish; *Caryopteris incana,* 3–4 ft. lavender or white; *Clerodendron trichotomum,* 10 ft. white; *Elsholtzia stauntoni,* 5 ft. lilac-purple; *Hamamelis virginiana,* 15 ft. yellow; *Lespedeza formosa,* 4–5 ft. rose-purple; *Vitex agnus-castus,* 10 ft. blue.—L. B. W.

**AUTUMN PLANTING.** Because the season is waning, and dormancy instead of a mass of growth is to follow, fall or autumn is an ideal time to do much planting that the spring rush has left undone.

This applies to most woody plants, except plane trees (*Platanus*), and to the division of many perennial herbs. Of course such work should be completed before hard freezing weather is to be expected, and for the dates of this see the article on your own state.

Within the category of fall planting comes the late summer or early fall planting of coniferous evergreens and such broad-leaved evergreens as *Rhododendron, Kalmia, Pieris, Leucothoë,* and many others. These can be moved with success between August 20 and September 20 nearly throughout zones* 3, 4, and 5. That gives them time to become established before hard frost is to be expected.

Most deciduous* woody plants should not be moved until their foliage is well colored or better yet, dropping. For a general time-table of fall work, as distinguished from autumn planting *per se,* see the fall months at GARDEN CALENDAR.

**AUTUMN SQUASH** = Winter Squash. See SQUASH.

**AUTUMN WORK.** See GARDEN CALENDAR.

**AVAILABLE NITROGEN.** See FERTILIZERS.

**AVELLANA,** *-us, -um* (a-vel-lan′a). From Avellino, in Campania, Italy.

**AVENA** (a-vee′na). The oats are chiefly agricultural grasses of little interest to the gardener. They are mostly Old World annual plants with flat, grass-like leaves and bristly, long-awned,* usually hanging spikelets which are grouped in loose clusters (panicles*). Fruit the familiar oat, or a modification of it. (*Avena* is Latin for oat.)

The common oat is often a weed in gardens, but easy to control because of its annual habit. Winter oats are hardy strains for autumn planting, maturing the following spring. All others are spring-planted annuals.

**fatua.** Wild oat. A Eurasian, oat-like grass, 3–4 ft. high. Leaves 6–9 in. long, ¼–½ in. wide. Spikelets drooping, rather broad, grouped in stout panicles* 8–12 in. long. Naturalized on the Pacific Coast.

**sativa.** The common oat. Foliage resembling *A. fatua,* but the leaves more or less rough. Flower cluster (panicle*) terminal, its flattish, long-awned spikelets spreading on all sides, except in the variety known as side oats, where the spikelets are arranged in one-sided clusters. A cultigen,* perhaps derived from *A. fatua.*

**sterilis.** Animated oat. A shorter grass from the Mediterranean region, grown chiefly for its curious spikelets, which twist or move when exposed to sudden moisture, due to the hygroscopic action of its awns.* It has a twisted stem.

---

* Special articles on the subjects indicated by an asterisk (*) will be found at the words so marked.

**AVENS.** See GEUM.

**AVENUE PLANTING.** See STREET TREES.

**AVERAGE BEARING AGE.** See GARDEN TABLES I.

**AVERRHOA** (a-ver-rō′a). A small genus of Asiatic trees, family Oxalidaceae, the one below somewhat planted in Fla. (zone* 9 only) for its pleasant, quince-scented fruit. Leaves alternate,* compound,* the leaflets arranged feather-fashion. Flowers small, fragrant. Petals 5. Stamens 10, five shorter than the other five. Fruit fleshy, drooping. (Named for Averroes, Arabian philosopher.)

The tree needs rich soil and plenty of rainfall. It is propagated by shield-budding or by seeds.

**carambola.** Carambola. A symmetrical tree 20–30 ft. high. Leaflets 5–9, increasing in size towards the tip of the leaf, 1–2 in. long, closing when touched or at night. Flowers in the leaf-axils,* not over ¼ in. long, white, but purple-marked. Fruit yellowish-brown, smooth-skinned, about 4 in. long, nearly egg-shaped, 3–5-angled or ribbed, thus star-shaped in cross-section. Pulp watery, somewhat acid-sweet, used fresh or for jellies. Malayan region. Like the jackfruit, the fruit is apt to be borne on old wood. See CAULIFLORY.

*AVICULARIS, -e* (a-vick-kew-lă′ris). Relating to birds.

*AVIUM* (ā′vee-um). Of the birds; a not inappropriate specific name for the cherry.

**AVOCADO** (*Persea americana*). This fruit holds high rank among the tropical food fruits and is now extensively cult. in both Fla. and Calif. *Persea* is native to tropical America and, according to place of origin, is divided into the Mexican (var. *drymifolia*), Guatemalan and West Indian groups or races. The trees require a warm climate, but the races differ somewhat in cold resistance, their hardiness being in the order named. In their native habitats, the trees are not grown in orchards but as scattered seedlings, and it was not until their comparatively recent introduction into the U.S. that orchard plantings were made and propagation of varieties initiated.

The avocado's popularity, especially as a salad fruit, is steadily increasing, and it is now classed as a staple article of diet rather than a novelty. Containing from 7 to 23 per cent fat, 1.5 per cent protein and above 1.5 per cent mineral matter, it is of high nutritional value. The fat percentage varies with variety; highest in the Mexican and lowest in the West Indian races.

In Fla., the West Indian and Guatemalan varieties are chiefly grown, and in Calif. mainly those of the Mexican and Guatemalan races. Fruits of the 3 races are distinct in general appearance, shape, size, fat content and season of maturity. Wide variation in season gives a succession of ripening fruit extending from early summer until late spring. It has been found that non-setting of fruit is due mainly to an unusual sex-reversal of the flowers that prevents pollination. The difficulty is overcome by interplanting compatible varieties to insure cross-pollination. Varieties have been classified as either "a" or "b" (as below), and selections from the two classes should be interplanted. Of the numerous varieties, the following are among the most popular:

WEST INDIAN (season July into Oct.) — Pollock (b), Waldin (a), Trapp (b); GUATEMALAN (Dec. into March) — Taylor (a), Schmidt (b), Eagle Rock (b); MEXICAN (June into Oct.) — Gottfried (a), Puebla (a), San Sebastian (b); HYBRIDS (Nov. to Feb.) — Collinson (a), Lula (a), Fuerte (b).

The trees are adapted to a wide range of soils, but must have an ample supply of soil moisture coupled with good underdrainage. Fertilizers are required. Heavy mulching with organic litter has been especially beneficial, and growing leguminous cover crops is practiced. Planting distances vary with variety, but about 20 × 20 ft. with 30 ft. rows for roadways at intervals is now recommended. Propagation is by seeds and shield-budding or cleft- and side-grafting, the latter method now superseding the former. Nursery stock is propagated for the most part in plant boxes instead of the nursery row to overcome loss in transplanting. — H. M.

INSECT PESTS. A scale insect and a whitefly, often injurious, can be controlled with a spray of lubricating-oil emulsion, 1 part of stock to 70 of water, applied late in the fall and again in the spring. A small beetle that eats the blossoms and a leaf-folding caterpillar are controlled with lead arsenate. A blossom thrips is checked with nicotine. Red spiders, lace bugs, and thrips, often injurious in winter, also yield to nicotine spray. Lime-sulphur, 1–60, is excellent for mites if the fruit is off.

DISEASES. Among the troubles found are scab, which attacks the young foliage, shoots and fruits; black spot and blotch on the fruit; and rusty blight on the foliage and young branches. All of these diseases are in part controlled by spraying with bordeaux mixture, 3-3-50 or 4-4-50. The first application is made before any new growth is put out; the second, before the blossoms open; third, at petal-fall; fourth, three weeks later; and fifth, six weeks later.

**AWINC.** A trademarked pyrethrum insecticide, sold with directions for use as a contact spray.

**AWL-SHAPED.** Gradually tapering from a thickened base to a slender, often prickly, tip, like an awls.

**AWN.** A bristle-like appendage, sometimes hair-like or stiff, found in the spikelets of certain grasses (oat, etc.), on the fruits of other plants, or even on anthers.

**AWNLESS BROME GRASS** = *Bromus inermis*.

**AXIL.** Classically an armpit; in modern botany and hort. the point at which a stalk or branch diverges from the stem or axis to which it is attached. Many flower clusters are borne in leaf-axils.

*AXILLARIS, -e* (ax-il-lar′is). Axillary, *i.e.* borne in an axil.*

**AXIS.** The main stem of a plant or a flower cluster. The trunk is the axis of a pine tree.

**AXONOPUS** (ax-o-nō′pus). A small genus of mostly tropical grasses of no hort. interest except for *A. compressus*, the carpet grass, which is widely used in the South for places where better lawn grasses will not grow. It is a perennial grass which spreads by stolons,* has narrow, grass-like, flat leaves about 4 in. long and ¼ in. wide, and 1-sided clusters of spikelets. It is native from Va. to La. and tropical America. For its use see Lawn Mixtures at LAWN. (*Axonopus* is from the Greek for axis and foot, in allusion to the creeping stolons.*)

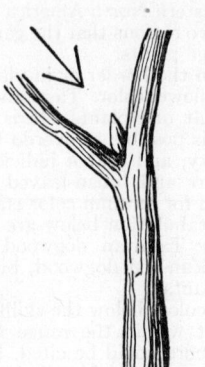

The arrow points to the axil

**AXSEED** = *Coronilla varia*.

**AYRESHIRE ROSE** = *Rosa arvensis ayreshirea*.

**AZALEA** (a-zay′lee-a). A group of well-known garden shrubs and trees of the heath family, perhaps not technically different from *Rhododendron* (which see), but kept distinct from that genus by most gardeners, and here. There are many species and named forms, comprising some of the handsomest flowering shrubs in the world. All are natives of the north temperate zone, chiefly N.A. and eastern As. Leaves alternate* and stalked. Flowers more or less irregular,* usually in terminal, umbel*-like clusters, the stamens often far-protruding. Fruit a dry pod (capsule*), splitting lengthwise, the seeds very numerous and small. (*Azalea* is Greek for dry, in allusion to the old, and false, idea that the plants require dry sites.)

For culture see below.

**amoena** = *Azalea obtusa amoena*.

**arborescens.** Tree azalea. A native, deciduous* shrub 8–20 ft. high. Leaves more or less oblong, hairy on the margins, 1½–2½ in. long. Flowers funnel-shaped, about 2 in. long, fragrant, white or pinkish, and hairy on the outside. Mountain woods Pa. to Ga. Hardy from zone* 4 southward. June.

**calendulacea.** Flame azalea. A native, deciduous* shrub 6–12 ft. high. Leaves broadly elliptic, 2–3 in. long. Flowers 5–7 together, blooming after the leaves unfold, yellow, orange or scarlet, not fragrant, sticky-hairy on the outside, the stamens* much protruding. Mountains, Pa. to Ga. May–June. One of the most magnificent native shrubs and known in many hort. forms. Often sold as *A. lutea*. Zone* 4 and southward.

---

* Special articles on the subjects indicated by an asterisk (*) will be found at the words so marked.

**californica** = *Azalea occidentalis*.

**canescens.** Mountain azalea. Native American, deciduous* shrub 6-12 ft. high. Leaves oblong or broader above, 2½-4 in. long, grayish-hairy beneath. Flowers nearly odorless, blooming with or before the leaves unfold, pink or white, funnel-shaped, about 1½ in. long. N.C. to Fla. and eastern Texas. May. Hardy from zone* 5 southward.

**gandavensis.** Ghent azaleas. A group of hort. important azaleas derived by hybridizing native American species and some from the Old World. There are hundreds of named forms, many of them of unknown parentage, although *A. japonica* is often involved. *See below.*

**hinodegiri** = *A. obtusa* var. *hinodegiri*. One of the Kurume azaleas with scarlet flowers.

**indica.** A race usually called Indica azaleas and derived from a mixture of Japanese and Chinese species. *See below at* AZALEA CULTURE.

**japonica.** A Japanese deciduous* shrub 2-5 ft. high. Leaves 2-4 in. long, hairy on the margin. Flowers narrowly bell-shaped, only slightly irregular, orange to scarlet, about 1½ in. long, but numerous, the stamens within the corolla. Hardy from zone* 4 southward. May.

**kaempferi** = *Azalea obtusa kaempferi*.

**ledifolia** = *Azalea mucronata*.

**macrantha.** Leaves glossy-green above, pale beneath, 2-3 in. long. Flowers usually 1 or 2 together, broadly funnel-shaped, nearly 3 in. across, white or pink. June. Hardy from protected places in zone* 4 southward.

**mollis.** A beautiful Chinese deciduous* shrub, 2-4 ft. high, with golden-yellow flowers, the young branches hairy. Leaves oblongish, 4-6 in. long, gray and hairy on the under side. Flowers broadly funnel-shaped, about 2 in. wide. Hardy from sheltered places in zone* 4 southward. May.

**mucronata.** An evergreen, Chinese shrub, 4-6 ft. high, with brilliantly white, fragrant flowers. Leaves more or less elliptic, 1½-2½ in. long, matted with dense, gray or brownish hairs. Flowers 1-3 in a cluster, nearly 2 in. wide. Hardy from sheltered places in zone* 4 southward. May. A very popular azalea with double, and often variously colored flowers in some hort. varieties. It is often sold as *A. ledifolia*.

**nudiflora.** Pinkster flower. A native American shrub, 2-5 ft. high, deciduous,* and growing naturally in rich woods. Leaves green both sides, elliptic or oblongish, 2-4 in. long. Flowers 6-10 in a cluster, appearing before the leaves, pink or whitish-pink, about 1½ in. wide, the stamens* far-protruding. Eastern U.S. Hardy from zone* 4 southward. May. There are white and rose-colored hort. varieties.

**obtusa.** In its wild state (seldom cult.) a half-evergreen Japanese shrub 12-30 in. high, and much-branched. Leaves shining dark green above, hairy on the midrib beneath, more or less elliptic, ¾-1 in. long. Flowers 2-3 in a cluster, orange-red or red, about 1½ in. wide. Hardy from zone* 5 southward. April-May.

From this plant many hort. important varieties have been derived by selection and hybridization, largely in Japan. From near Kurume, Japan, have come a beautiful series known as Kurume azaleas. (See below.) Other well-known varieties are: *var.* **hinodegiri**, brilliant scarlet; *var.* **amoena**, with magenta, often double flowers, and hardier than the typical species; *var.* **kaempferi**, often called Kaempfer's azalea, with larger and reddish-pink flowers. The number of named, mostly Japanese, forms is legion.

**occidentalis.** A native American, deciduous* shrub 5-9 ft. high. Leaves oblongish, but with a small, prickle-like point, 2-4 in. long. Flowers white or pinkish, yellow-blotched, about 2 in. wide. Ore. and Calif. Hardy from zone* 5 southward. June-July. Foliage yellow or scarlet in autumn.

**poukhanensis** = *Azalea yedoensis poukhanensis*.

**rosea** = A form of *Azalea viscosa* with rose-colored flowers.

**schlippenbachi.** A deciduous* shrub 9-15 ft. high. Leaves clustered at the ends of the twigs, green above, pale beneath, ovalish but broader towards the short-pointed tip, 3-5 in. long. Flowers pink, brown-spotted, 3-6 in a cluster, about 2½ in. wide. Eastern As. Hardy from zone* 4 southward. May.

**vaseyi.** One of the finest native shrubs, 6-12 ft. high, with deciduous* foliage. Leaves oblong or elliptic, 3-5½ in. long, hairy-margined. Flowers distinctly 2-lipped, light rose color, but spotted with orange or brownish-orange, about 1½ in. long. N. Car. Hardy from zone* 4 southward. April-May.

**viscosa.** White swamp azalea, commonly called swamp honeysuckle. A deciduous* shrub 6-10 ft. high. Leaves ovalish, 1½-2½ in. long, green both sides. Flowers 4-9 in a cluster, glandular-hairy, white or faintly pinkish, very fragrant, nearly 2 in. long, the stamens far-protruding. Swamps and bogs, Me. to S. Car. June. Hardy from zone* 3 southward. There is a variety with rose-colored flowers, and another with bluish-gray foliage.

**yedoensis.** Korean azalea. A deciduous* or half-evergreen shrub 2-3 ft. high. Leaves narrowly elliptic, 2-3 in. long, pointed both ends, dark green above, paler beneath, evergreen southward. Flowers 1-3 in a cluster, double, rosy-lilac and purple-spotted, about 1½ in. long. Eastern As. Hardy from zone* 5 southward. Often sold as *A. yodogava*. A fine, taller variety, with larger, single, fragrant flowers and more hardy than the type, is *var.* **poukhanensis**. There are also many named forms.

**yodogava** = *Azalea yedoensis*.

Most of the above azaleas are unsuited to regions where the rainfall is below 25 in. per year. See the name of your state for rainfall figures in your locality.

## AZALEA CULTURE

From the gardener's viewpoint azaleas fall into two sections, deciduous and evergreen, although some of the latter become deciduous, at least in part, if they are grown at the northern limit of their hardiness. In the first group are our own native species, several Oriental species and one European species, as well as the garden races resulting from their interbreeding; the second section is essentially Oriental. All are acid-soil plants, the deciduous species usually more strictly so than the evergreen sorts. They range in size from small, almost prostrate shrubs to tall, slender, almost tree-like forms.

Because of their masses of relatively shallow, fibrous roots, they are impatient of dry soil conditions, although many of the deciduous forms can adapt themselves to positions if the conditions are uniform throughout the year. All form their flower buds during the late summer, and this factor limits their use in the North, where the plants may be hardy, but the flower buds tender, as is the case with peaches. Our American species have tubular flowers with five expanded lobes and conspicuously protruding stamens and pistils that add to the beauty of the flowers that are produced in rounded heads. Most of them flower just before the leaves or just as the leaves appear, although there are several species that bloom in summer with their leaves. In color they fall into two series, one white through pink to deep rose-pink, the other white through yellow and orange to deep brick-red. In many cases there is a blotch of contrasting color, usually yellow, on the upper lobe.

The Oriental species have wider, more bowl-shaped flowers with the typical five lobes, and range in color from pale yellow through orange-reds. The conspicuous exception is *A. schlippenbachi*, with exquisite pink flowers, that resembles our pale rose-pink American *A. vaseyi*. There are several Oriental forms with rosy-purple flowers, notably the plant usually offered as *Rhododendron dilitatum*.

From the crossing of our American species with *A. mollis* and *A. japonica* has come the race usually referred to as Ghent azaleas, which resemble our own species in form, but offer some variations in color and pattern. From crossing *A. mollis* and *A. japonica* has resulted the hybrid *mollis* forms that vary little from their parent types, except that all are more vigorous than *mollis*, which is somewhat tender to cold.

For the garden, the most useful evergreen azaleas are the forms of *A. obtusa*, long known as *Azalea amoena* in the trade and more recently by the many Kurume azaleas, with flowers so lavishly produced as to hide the plant, and varying in color from pure white through every hue of pink to deep crimson with variations toward cerise and salmon, but not to orange. In this section are many flaked and blotched varieties and many of the hose-in-hose type in which the sepals have become petal-like, giving a semi-double appearance. All these make very dense, wide-spreading bushes that eventually reach four or five feet, entirely evergreen in the South and semi-evergreen in the North.

Related to them, and considered by some as a sub-variety, is Kaempfer's azalea which is more nearly deciduous, more hardy in the North, and eventually much taller. Its flowers are usually salmon-red, but there are variations toward pink and toward deeper red. For best results this should have some light shade at flowering time to prevent the fading of the petal color in the sunlight.

The large-flowered Oriental azaleas of the evergreen section are *A. mucronata*, *A. macrantha*, *A. yedoensis*, and the somewhat mongrel race known as the Indica azaleas. The first is most commonly known in its white form, although there are blush-tinted, crimson-blotched and pinkish-lilac forms. *A. yedoensis*, the Korean azalea, is pinkish-lilac and most useful in its single form, *poukhanensis*. The last are variable from white, through pinks to deep crimson-purples and crimson-reds. In some there is a variable striping and flaking of color on white or light ground, and in many a darker blotch on the upper lobe. Among them are many difficult magenta varieties. For the most part they are tender to cold both in their flower buds and as a result of the splitting of the thin bark. Their use is restricted to the South and as pot plants in the North.

All azaleas can be raised from seed, from layers, both branch and mound, and in the evergreen section from cut-

---

* Special articles on the subjects indicated by an asterisk (*) will be found at the words so marked.

tings of half-ripe wood in sand or sand and peat mixture. A gentle bottom-heat hastens rooting, which occurs all along the stem and not at the joint or node. Selected forms of deciduous azaleas can be increased by grafting, in winter, either on seedling stocks or piece roots.

Although all require considerable moisture, especially after flowering, when new shoots are forming, it is best to limit watering outdoor plants as summer advances, to check new growth, and insure ripening of the wood, which will help to prevent bark-splitting during winter.

While nearly all will flourish in full sun, a light, passing shade helps to preserve the flower color. None will flower freely in dense shade.

All may be grown in pots, and brought into bloom in the winter, if they are forced gradually and at relatively low temperatures, which will prevent the dropping of foliage and assure an even and simultaneous development of the flowers. *See* RETARDING.

All respond freely to pruning if this is necessary to check irregular growth. It should be done just after flowering, to assure ripening of the wood and proper formation of flower buds for the next season. If fertilizer is given, it should be either old, well-rotted manure or cottonseed meal with an occasional dose of aluminum sulphate if the soil tends to lose its acidity. A mulch of humus should be maintained always, and the soil should be well supplied with both humus and sand, to provide a mixture that retains moisture without becoming over-saturated. — B. Y. M.

INSECT PESTS. Azalea is attacked by a small and pretty lace bug, the adults and nymphs of which suck juices from the leaves; a nicotine spray will control them. A tiny whitefly can be controlled with oil sprays at a summer dilution. A borer, caterpillar of a clear-winged moth, also attacks this plant (*see* RHODODENDRON).

DISEASES. Leaf galls or blisters on azalea are caused by a fungus, which causes a similar disease on *Rhododendron* and *Vaccinium*. The galls are at first green, turning to reddish or purple, and later covered with the spore stage of the fungus, which appears like a whitish film over the surface of the gall. Control it by removing and destroying the galls in the early stages before they produce spores. For other diseases of azalea *see* RHODODENDRON, where there is a discussion of several diseases common to both plants.

AZALEA POT. *See* FLOWER POTS.

AZARA (a-zah'ra). A small genus of mostly Chilean evergreen shrubs or vines, family Flacourtiaceae, the two below grown for ornament in Calif., rarely under glass. Leaves leathery, alternate,* short-stalked, one of the stipules* enlarged and leaf-like. Flowers small, fragrant, greenish-yellow, without petals, but with 4-5 persistent sepals. Fruit a berry. (Named for J. N. Azara, Spanish patron of botany.)

The second species is often trained as a vine in Calif., and is handsome in fruit. They need open sunlight and are propagated by seeds or cuttings of ripe wood.

gilliesi. A shrub 8-12 ft. high. Leaves broadly oval, 2½-3 in. long, with coarse, spiny teeth. Flowers in nodding heads. Chile. Blooms in Feb.-March in Calif.

microphylla. A sprawling, but erect, shrub 6-12 ft. high, often trained to cover walls. Leaves ½-¾ in. long, somewhat toothed, shining. Clusters few-flowered. Fruit orange. Chile. Flowers in Feb. and March in Calif. Hardy, in the East, from sheltered places in zone* 5 southward.

*AZEDARACH.* A pre-Linnaean* name for the China-tree (*see* MELIA).

AZOLLA (a-zol'la). A small genus of minute, floating aquatic, flowerless plants, family Salviniaceae, the one below of little garden interest except to make attractive floating patches on the surface of pools or aquaria. They grow so rapidly and so close together that *Azolla* may also become a scum-like nuisance if not kept in check. The plants have minute stems, fleshy, 2-lobed leaves, upon which the microscopic spores* are borne. (*Azolla* is Greek for destroying by drying.)

caroliniana. Appearing like a reddish, moss-like patch. Plant body scarcely ½ in. long, the leaves much smaller. Its spore characters are technical and microscopic. In quiet water nearly throughout U.S.

*AZORICA, -us, -um* (a-zaw'ri-ka). From the Azores.

AZTEC MARIGOLD = *Tagetes erecta*. *See* MARIGOLD.

*AZUREA, -us, -um* (a-zoor'ee-a). Sky-blue.

# B

B & B = Ball and burlap method of handling nursery stock. *See* PLANTING.

BABIANA (bā-bi-ā'na). A genus of chiefly South African herbs of the iris family, comprising over 30 species, of which one is sometimes grown in greenhouses, or outdoors in frost-free regions, for its showy flowers. Leaves mostly basal and sword-shaped, hairy in the one below. Flowers nearly regular, in lax clusters, the slender corolla tube broadening into 6 segments. Stamens 3. Fruit a dry pod (capsule*), splitting into 3 segments. (*Babiana* is from the Dutch for baboon, who are credited with eating the corms.) The plants are sometimes called baboon-root.

The culture is the same as for *Freesia*.

stricta. A corm*-bearing herb 8-12 in. high, the corm covered with fibers. Leaves shorter than the stem, hairy. Flowering stem slightly twisted, bearing 1-3, spike-like but few-flowered clusters. Flowers red (lilac, blue or yellow in some of the named forms), about ¾ in. long. South Africa. Spring-blooming.

BABOON-ROOT. *See* BABIANA.

BABY BLUE-EYES = *Nemophila insignis*.

*BABYLONICA, -us, -um* (bab-i-lon'i-ka). From ancient Babylon, now near Bagdad.

BABY PRIMROSE = *Primula forbesi*.

BABY RAMBLER = *Rosa chinensis minima*.

BABY'S-BREATH. Usually applied to *Gypsophila paniculata* and related species; also to *Galium mollugo* and *Muscari*.

BABY'S-SLIPPERS = *Lotus corniculatus*.

BABY-TEARS = *Helxine soleiroli*.

*BACCATA, -us, -um* (bak-kay'ta). Baccate; *i.e.* a berry, or berry-like.

BACCHARIS (bak'kar-is). A very large genus of American shrubs, family Compositae, chiefly inhabitants of salt marshes or alkali deserts and of little garden interest except for similar sites. Leaves thick and more or less fleshy. Flowers very small, yellowish or dirty-white, all tubular and crowded in small heads, the fruiting of which is a white and rather showy collection of pappus* bristles (*see* COMPOSITAE for details). (The plants commemorate Bacchus, but without much signification.)

The first species is a salt-marsh shrub useful for seaside planting, less so in ordinary garden soil, although it will grow there if given open sunshine. The last two are Californian species somewhat grown there for ornament, and unsuited to most of the country. All are easily propagated by cuttings and may be dug from the wild.

halimifolia. Groundsel bush or groundsel tree. A much-branched shrub 6-10 ft. high. Leaves oblongish, short-stalked, 1-3 in. long, wedge-shaped at the base and coarsely toothed, more or less resinous. Flower heads about ¼ in. long, crowded in dense clusters, the fruiting head snowy-white. Brackish marshes. N. Eng. to Tex.

pilularis. Kidneywort; called also coyote-brush, chaparral broom and squaw waterweed. An evergreen shrub 2-3 ft. high. Leaves nearly stalkless, broadest towards the tip, scarcely 1 in. long, toothed. On dry hills and dunes, Ore. to Calif.

viminea. Mule-fat; called also guatemote. A leafy, branching shrub, 4-8 ft. high. Leaves willow-like, oblongish, 1-3 in. long (more on sterile shoots). Flowering cluster leafy, the heads in close clusters, which are grouped in a branching inflorescence. In river-beds, Calif.

BACHELOR'S BUTTON = *Centaurea cyanus*; also *Bellis perennis*, and *Gomphrena globosa*.

---

* Special articles on the subjects indicated by an asterisk (*) will be found at the words so marked.

**BACK-BULB.** One of the old pseudobulbs of an orchid. See Dividing Greenhouse Orchids at ORCHID.

**BACKCROSS.** Result of a hybrid crossed on one of its parents.

**BACKGROUND PLANTING.** See BORDER.

**BACKYARD GARDEN.** Backyard gardening is the art of creating the rural charm of an outdoor living-room in the rear of a city house. Its success depends chiefly upon the condition of the soil. Sunlight and water are the other essentials.

The majority of city soils are sour and filled with poisonous vapors. A soil test will determine the degree of sourness, thus indicating the amount of lime required to sweeten it. (See ACID AND ALKALI SOILS.) If the ground is filled with débris, excavate to a depth of approximately two feet in places where you desire plantings; fill in with fresh soil. An excellent mixture is one-third loam, one-third well-rotted manure, and one-third leaf mold. (If unable to obtain manure use a commercial substitute.) If the ground is clayey, supply drainage at the bottom of the excavation by means of broken pots, bricks, or stones. After the beds have settled, top-dress with lime. Lime, applied every other spring, will counteract the acid effects of the year's accumulation of soot and gases, and kill also wire worms and slugs.

Should the ground be merely hard-packed, sooty, and uncultivated, use trenching. In digging, keep the top-soil on one side and the sub-soil on the other side of the trench. Loosen up the packed earth at the bottom, then refill with alternate layers of manure and sub-soil. Then mix your top-soil with a little lime and finish filling in. Do not plant until the beds are well settled.

Watering should always be done after sundown, and a thorough soaking given. Sponging off the leaves of broad-leaved evergreens with water and castile soap to remove soot and grime will often prolong their life. Use a fine overhead spray in order thoroughly to cleanse all the foliage. Pests and diseases may cause trouble. (See INSECT PESTS; PLANT DISEASES.) Plants mentioned in this article are selected because of their suitability for city conditions, especially for their smoke-resistant qualities.

WALLS. The most common enclosure of a city garden is a high board fence. Paint this white to create an effect of sunlight, or some neutral shade, and break the bare expanse with vines. Desirable ones are *Akebia*, trumpet-creeper, *Clematis paniculata*, English ivy, wistaria, and grape. A focal point of interest can be created by an arbor and trellises at the extreme end of the garden, a seat against the wall, or a small statue surrounded by an arch of ivy. Brick, stucco, and slabs make desirable backgrounds, but they are expensive. A shrub hedge or a high fence serves also as a wind-break in winter. Broad-leaved evergreens, such as *Ilex crenata*, *Mahonia aquifolia*, and *Pyracantha coccinea*, provide excellent winter effects. The ailanthus is the tree most commonly seen. Smaller trees and shrubs, as hawthorn, magnolia, Cornelian-cherry, Ibota privet, mock-orange, common lilac, and snowberry, may be used.

A brick or paved terrace, raised slightly above the garden level, creates an atmosphere of space at the same time that it ties together house and garden. This may be covered with an awning and used as an outdoor dining-room. Paths may be of brick, stepping-stones, or earth. Too many break up a small space and make it appear choppy. See PATHS AND PAVING.

A garden with little or no direct sunlight will sustain only a limited variety of plants. A grass plot is almost an impossibility. Ground covers, such as English ivy, *Pachysandra terminalis*, and *Vinca minor*, may be substituted. Tuberous-rooted begonias, fuchsias, English daisies, annual ageratum, foxgloves, and garden pinks will grow in partial shade.

In a garden with a certain amount of full sunlight numerous aquatics may be grown in a lily pool. Annuals may be bought in flats ready to set out or grown direct from seed. Potted plants and evergreens may always be used for fillers, but they are usually costly, unless bought in special group collections at reduced prices.

If the garden is very small, leave the central plot open. Plant it with grass or ground cover or pave with old flags. Small succulents and tufts of turf may be planted between. Encourage moss to grow on the paving, as it will absorb the strong sunlight. Plant perennial borders on three sides with iris, peonies, and phlox, to obtain a long succession of bloom and attractive foliage. *Phlox subulata*, pansies, and violets may be used as edgings and ground covers. Small shrubs should be planted at irregular intervals in the background. The following are attractive both winter and summer: *Acanthopanax sieboldianum*, Japanese barberry, *Cornus alba sibirica*, Japanese flowering quince, gumi, forsythia, bush honeysuckle, and the mountain currant. For a list of specially smoke-resistant woody plants, see SMOKE.

Garden furniture and decorations must conform to the general type of garden created, as an unwise selection creates discord. See ORNAMENT AND FURNITURE. — C. H. M.

The Department of Horticulture of Cornell University has issued valuable lists of plants suited to the unfavorable conditions of the average city backyard in the northeastern states. With some modifications they are listed below. All are treated in more detail at the different articles on the genera mentioned.

SHADE-ENDURING* WOODY PLANTS FOR USE IN CITY GARDENS

*Acer negundo*  
*Aesculus parviflora*  
*Ampelopsis*  
*Aronia arbutifolia*  
*Benzoin aestivale*  
*Celastrus orbiculatus*  
*Clematis paniculata*  
*Cornus*  
*Euonymus japonicus*  
*Euonymus radicans*  
*Forsythia*  
*Hamamelis virginiana*  
*Hedera helix*  
*Ilex crenata*  
*Lonicera japonica halliana*  
*Lycium halimifolium*  
*Mahonia aquifolia*  
*Pachysandra terminalis*  
*Polygonum auberti* (not woody)  
*Rhamnus cathartica*  
*Ribes alpinum*  
*Symphoricarpos orbiculatus*  
*Viburnum acerifolium*  
*Viburnum dentatum*  
*Vinca minor*

DRY-SOIL-ENDURING WOODY PLANTS FOR USE IN CITY GARDENS

*Actinidia arguta*  
*Ailanthus altissima*  
*Amorpha fruticosa*  
*Ampelopsis*  
*Berberis thunbergi*  
*Campsis radicans*  
*Caragana arborescens*  
*Catalpa bignonioides nana*  
*Celastrus orbiculatus*  
*Cornus mas*  
*Cornus racemosa*  
*Elaeagnus angustifolia*  
*Forsythia*  
*Hamamelis virginiana*  
*Hibiscus syriacus*  
*Ligustrum*  
*Lonicera*  
*Lycium halimifolium*  
*Mahonia aquifolia*  
*Philadelphus* (see MOCK-ORANGE)  
*Phlox subulata*  
*Polygonum auberti* (not woody)  
*Pyracantha coccinea*  
*Rhamnus cathartica*  
*Rhodotypos tetrapetala*  
*Rhus*  
*Ribes*  
*Sophora japonica*  
*Spiraea bumalda*  
*Symphoricarpos orbiculatus*  
*Syringa vulgaris*  
*Ulmus pumila*  
*Wistaria sinensis*

BEST VINES FOR USE IN CITY GARDENS

*Actinidia arguta*  
*Akebia quinata*  
*Ampelopsis*  
*Campsis radicans*  
*Clematis paniculata*  
*Euonymus radicans*  
*Hedera helix*  
*Lonicera henryi*  
*Lonicera japonica halliana*  
*Polygonum auberti*  
*Wistaria sinensis*

EIGHT GOOD GROUND-COVER PLANTS FOR USE IN CITY GARDENS

*Cotoneaster horizontalis*  
*Euonymus radicans minimus*  
*Hedera helix*  
*Iberis sempervirens*  
*Pachysandra terminalis*  
*Phlox subulata*  
*Rosa wichuraiana*  
*Vinca minor*

---

* Special articles on the subjects indicated by an asterisk (*) will be found at the words so marked.

**BACTERIA.** Microscopic, one-celled organisms, the cause of most diseases in man, animals, and plants, and popularly called microbes. While many of them are baleful, not a few are of the utmost use to the gardener, because some of them inhabit soils and greatly aid, with fungi, in the decomposition of vegetable matter into humus. Perhaps their most important garden use is the ability of some kinds to aid plants of the pea family in gathering nitrogen from the air (for which see LEGUME INOCULATION). For those causing disease, see Bacteria at PLANT DISEASES.

**BACTERIAL BLIGHT.** See Diseases at DELPHINIUM and BEAN.

**BACTERIAL SPOT.** See Diseases at PEACH.

**BADIAN.** See ILLICIUM VERUM.

**BADMINTON.** A lawn game, the court of which is 44 × 17 ft., or 20 ft. for doubles.

**BAERIA** (bay′ri-a). Californian yellow-flowered herbs, commonly called goldfields, the two below grown as annuals for their profuse bloom. There are over 20 species, family Compositae, and all have opposite leaves and flower heads with both ray and disk flowers. (Named for K. E. von Baer, Russian naturalist.)
Both species are hardy annuals, the seed of which should be sown where the plants are needed. See ANNUALS. The plants are sometimes offered as *Hymenoxis*.

aristata. A low, weak annual, scarcely exceeding 8 in. in height and used for edging. Leaves compound,* the leaflets arranged feather-fashion, the ultimate segments narrow. Flower heads about ½ in. wide, yellow. Calif. Sometimes known as *Actinolepis coronaria*.

macrantha. Erect, often unbranched annual, 12–18 in. high. Leaves simple,* very narrow, 3–4½ in. long, toothed and hairy on the margin. Flower heads about 1 in. wide, yellow. Calif.

**BAG-FLOWER** = *Clerodendron thomsonae*.

**BAGWORM.** See Moths at INSECT PESTS. See also the insect notes at SPRUCE and MULBERRY.

**BAHAMA GRASS** = *Cynodon dactylon*.

*BAICALENSIS, -e* (by-kal-en′sis). From Lake Baikal, Siberia.

**BAIT.** Poisoned bait is used to control both insects and small animal pests. For kinds and uses see Stomach Poisons at INSECTICIDES; see also ANIMAL INJURY.

**BALAKA** (ba-lah′ka). A genus of Fiji Island feather palms of two species, the one below cult. for ornament outdoors only in zone* 9 or in greenhouses. It is a medium-sized palm, not prickly, with a ringed trunk, and leaves about 4 ft. long. Leaflets very broad, often somewhat rhomboid, or oblique, their tips deeply cut or toothed. Flower cluster from below the crown of leaves, branched. Fruit more or less egg-shaped. (*Balaka* is the Fijian vernacular for one of the species.)
The only cult. species is a useful pot palm for room decoration and is grown by florists for that purpose, but not widely. It is somewhat grown, outdoors, in extreme southern Fla. For culture see PALM.

seemanni. A slender palm, usually not over 10 ft. high, the trunks ringed and about 1 in. in diameter. Leaves 3–4 ft. long, the segments or leaflets broad and toothed and more or less cut at the tip, oblique. The palm is often called *Ptychosperma seemanni*.

**BALCONY GARDEN.** See PENTHOUSE GARDEN.

**BALD CYPRESS** = *Taxodium distichum*.

*BALDENSIS, -e* (ball-den′sis). From Mt. Baldo, Italy.

*BALDSCHUANICA, -us, -um* (bald-shoo-ăn′i-ka). From Baldschuan, Bokhara.

**BALDWIN.** See APPLE.

*BALEARICA, -us, -um* (bal-ee-ă′ri-ka). From the Balearic Islands, near the Mediterranean coast of Spain.

**BALISIER** = *Heliconia bihai*.

**BALL AND BURLAP.** See PLANTING.

**BALL DAHLIA.** See DAHLIA.

**BALL FERN** = *Davallia bullata*.

**BALLOON-BERRY** = *Rubus illecebrosus*.

**BALLOON-FLOWER** = *Platycodon grandiflorum*.

**BALLOON-VINE** = *Cardiospermum halicacabum*.

**BALLOTA** (bal-low′ta). A genus of 30 species of Eurasian perennial herbs, of the mint family, of little garden interest except for the black horehound, a moderately decorative plant. It has opposite, toothed leaves, a square stem and small, 2-lipped, irregular* flowers in dense whorls clustered in the leaf-axils,* or rarely terminal. (*Ballota* is Greek for a plant, but not certainly this one.)
The black horehound is of the easiest culture in almost any garden soil, and is naturalized* or an escape* in the eastern U.S.

nigra. Black horehound; called also fetid horehound. A strong-smelling, erect and hairy herb 15–20 in. high. Leaves ovalish, 2–3 in. long. Flowers reddish-purple or paler, about ½ in. long. Eu. June.

**BALM.** See MELISSA. See also for plants sometimes called balm, MONARDA, NEPETA, COLLINSONIA, and MOLUCELLA.

**BALM-OF-GILEAD** = *Populus candicans*.

**BALM-OF-HEAVEN** = *Umbellularia californica*.

**BALSAM.** See FIR (*Abies balsamea*) for the tree so called. For the garden balsam see IMPATIENS.

**BALSAM APPLE** = *Momordica balsamina*.

*BALSAMEA* (ball-same′ee-a). A specific name derived from the genus *Balsamea*, which is of no hort. interest.

**BALSAM FAMILY** = Balsaminaceae.

**BALSAM FIR** = *Abies balsamea*. See FIR.

*BALSAMIFERA, -us, -um* (ball-sam-if′fe-ra). Balsam-bearing.

*BALSAMINA, -us, -um* (ball-sam-eye′na). Balsam or balsam-like.

**BALSAMINACEAE** (ball-sam-i-nay′see-e). The jewel-weed or balsam family contains only two genera, one of which, *Impatiens*, comprises nearly 500 species, among which are our common jewelweeds (or touch-me-not) and a handful of garden balsams. All are rather weak, soft, almost succulent herbs with stalked leaves. Flowers very irregular,* one of the usually 3 sepals petal-like and produced into a long spur. Fruit (in *Impatiens*) an elastically explosive pod (capsule*) that discharges its seeds if touched when ripe.

Technical flower characters: Sepals 3, two of them small and green the third petal-like and spurred. Petals 5, but often appearing as if three by the union of two pairs. Ovary 5-celled, many-ovuled, the style short and produced into 5 stigmas.

*BALSAMITA.* A pre-Linnaean* name for certain plants with the odor of balsam.

**BALSAM PEAR** = *Momordica charantia*.

**BALSAM POPLAR.** See POPULUS.

**BALSAM TREE FAMILY** = Guttiferae.

*BALTICA, -us, -um* (ball′tick-a). From the region of the Baltic Sea.

**BALTIMORE BELLE.** See ROSA SETIGERA.

**BAMBOO.** True bamboos are tall, woody, hollow-stemmed grasses of imposing aspect and multifarious uses in regions where they thrive. They belong to the genus *Bambusa* (which see), are nearly all tropical, and grow to such size and with such speed (a foot a day in favorable places) that they are difficult to manage in all but the loftiest greenhouses. Their outdoor culture in U.S. is mostly confined to zone* 9 and to especially sheltered places in zone* 8, although some of the cult. species can be grown up to the limits of zone* 5.
The name bamboo is also, somewhat loosely, applied to many other tall-growing, woody grasses, closely related to *Bambusa*, and popularly mistaken for that genus. Some of these are much more hardy than the tropical bamboos, and are widely planted for ornament in many parts of the

---
* Special articles on the subjects indicated by an asterisk (*) will be found at the words so marked.

U.S. For these, and other bamboo-like grasses, see ARUNDINARIA, DENDROCALAMUS (mostly tropical), and PHYLLOSTACHYS.

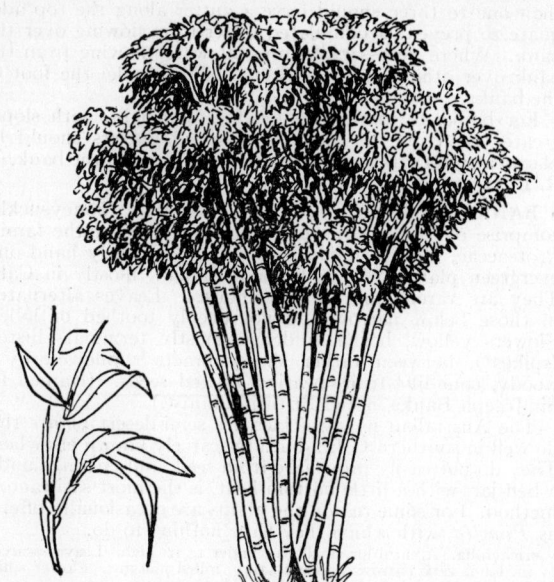

A clump of bamboos and a spray of their foliage

Bamboos, in the broad sense, supply planting material which is duplicated by no other plants. Their tall stems, feathery and handsome foliage, and their slender, arching, often grouped trunks make garden pictures of great beauty. In the tropics, where they frequently reach a height of 100 ft., they make majestic clumps impossible to reproduce in the U.S. But on a reduced scale the same effects may be gained by selecting species from the genera named above.

For the culture of both the tropical and half-hardy sorts see GRASSES.

**BAMBOO FERN** = *Coniogramme japonica*.

**BAMBOO RAKE.** See Section 1, TOOLS AND IMPLEMENTS.

**BAMBUSA** (bam-boo′sa). The true bamboos comprise a large genus of often gigantic, woody, hollow-stemmed, Old World, and chiefly tropical grasses, grown for ornament and for innumerable construction uses in the tropics. The usually polished, hollow stems are interrupted by a partition at the joints which conspicuously ring the trunk. Some species have a few spines on the stem. Leaves short-stalked, parallel-veined or, in some species, netted-veined. Flowers (rarely produced in cult. specimens) in few or many-flowered spikes, which are bunched on the branches of the cluster (panicle*). Stamens 6. Fruit dry, thin-walled (a caryopsis*). (*Bambusa* is a Latinized version of the Malayan vernacular for these plants.)

For culture and uses, see GRASSES. The technical names of the bamboos are confusing. Some authorities consider that certain species belong to the genus *Sasa*, not here maintained. For other grasses, also called bamboo, see ARUNDINARIA, DENDROCALAMUS and PHYLLOSTACHYS.

**disticha.** A dwarf species rarely over 3 ft. high. Stems slender, often zigzag, green or tinged with purple. Leaves 2–2½ in. long and about ⅓ in. wide, minutely toothed on the edges, netted-veined, and borne in paralleled, 2-ranked rows. Japan. Hardy from zone* 5 southward.

**nana.** A yellow-stemmed bamboo 8–15 ft. high. Leaves bluish-gray, rough on the edges, 2–3 in. long, scarcely ⅓ in. wide. A very handsome plant with hort. varieties having also variegated (yellow and silvery) leaves. China. Hardy from zone* 5 southward.

**palmata.** A purple-stemmed grass 3–8 ft. high. Leaves green above, pale bluish-green beneath, about 8 in. long and 2½ in. wide. Japan. Hardy from zone* 5 southward.

**vulgaris.** The commonest bamboo of the tropics and often reaching (there) a height of 100 ft. It has yellowish stems, often banded lengthwise. Leaves green both sides, 8–10 in. long, about 1 in. wide, and smooth-margined. Probably a native of Java, and will stand no frost.

**BAMBUSOIDES** (bam-boo-zoy′deez; but see OÏDES). Resembling a bamboo.

**BANANA** (*Musa sapientum*). Bananas are native to southeastern As. and are now cult. throughout the tropics. They are among the best known of tropical fruits, and have become a staple food fruit of temperate climates, their popularity being due to their high food value and agreeable flavor, coupled with the year-round season of ripening and availability at all times through refrigerated transportation facilities. Banana culture within the continental U.S. is limited to peninsular Fla., with an occasional plant grown as an ornamental in protected situations in southern Calif. and the coastal area of the Gulf states. Fruit is rarely produced outside of Fla., and there only in local commercial quantity, since severe damage accompanies temperatures below freezing.

The banana plant is large, herbaceous and tree-like. It suckers freely, but usually only 2 to 4 stalks are allowed to grow in a clump. Each stalk fruits but once, after which it is cut to the ground. New stalks, arising as suckers, give a succession of ripening fruit. In adapted situations growth is rapid and the first fruit matures from 12 to 14 months after planting.

Of the several tall-growing varieties, the Lady Finger (Hart's Choice) is the most popular, with the Apple, Orinoco (horse-banana) and Red Jamaica grown in limited number. Gros Michel, principal commercial variety of the western tropics, is seldom planted. The Cavendish or Chinese banana (*M. cavendishi*), often called dwarf banana, is considered the most resistant to cold and wind and is widely planted; it is but 5 to 7 feet tall, stout-stemmed, and produces good quality but easily bruised fruit.

Fertile, porous soils with a goodly content of organic matter are best suited. The plants require much moisture, but must have adequate drainage, and thrive best in full sun with protection from wind. Heavy mulching and fertilizers are beneficial. Planting distances vary from 8 to 14 or more feet, according to variety and soils. Propagation is by suckers or by sections of the stem "bulb." — H. M.

INSECT PESTS. A black snout beetle, the grublike larva of which bores in the corms, is found in some places in the U.S. Adults may be collected by baits of banana stem. Insect-free planting stock should be used, and the old, dried, outside leaves removed from the plants.

DISEASES. Probably the most serious disease of banana is wilt, which may kill large plantings of this crop. The soil should be kept in an excellent condition culturally, including an application of lime where the soil is very acid. Certain varieties are resistant to wilt and should be grown where they meet market requirements. Other diseases are the root and stem rot, Moko disease, nematodes, black spot, bonnygate disease, and black head. Aside from the suggestions made for wilt control, few preventive measures can be suggested. Spraying with bordeaux mixture has been advised in the case of black spot.

**BANANA FAMILY** = Musaceae.

**BANANA-SHRUB** = *Michelia fuscata*.

**BANEBERRY.** See ACTAEA.

**BANGALAY** = *Eucalyptus botryoides*.

**BANKING.** The heaping-up of soil to preserve moisture or coolness in cultivating some crops like potatoes. Or the similar heaping of earth around celery (which see) to aid blanching.* A specialized use of the term banking applies to considerable mounds of earth, with a brush top for ventilation, used, but certainly not recommended, for storing sweet potatoes (which see).

**BANKS.** Banks or abrupt slopes are sometimes essential to take care of differences in grade, and other times deliberately created for effect.

When limited space requires that a bank occupy the minimum area it may be as steep as one foot perpendicular to one and one-half feet horizontal. This rate of slope is very difficult to maintain and should be avoided whenever possible. If it must be used it should be planted with a rank, close-growing ground cover such as *Lonicera japonica halliana*. Since the rainfall which accumulates on the bank itself will wash out the planting, no bank of this steepness should exceed eight feet in height without rip-rap protection.

Rip-rap protection is flat field stone almost buried at

---

* Special articles on the subjects indicated by an asterisk (*) will be found at the words so marked.

right angles to the slope of the bank and paralleling the longitudinal direction. Another form of cheap, effective rip-rap is to half bury six-inch logs, paralleling the longitudinal direction of the bank, holding the logs in place by stakes driven down to the top of the logs on the lower side. If the bank is too stony to permit driving wooden stakes, use three-quarter-inch iron pins. Vines planted above these logs will soon cover them, giving the effect of a completely green bank. Locust logs are the most durable, but any wood which will last long enough for the plants to become well established will serve the purpose.

The most commonly used slope for banks where economy of space is necessary is one foot vertical to two feet horizontal. Any extension of slopes beyond these dimensions is unnecessary except for special purposes or appearance. If a bank is to be walked over without steps the minimum slope should be one foot vertical to three feet horizontal.

All banks should avoid a sharply defined edge at the top and bottom. These sharp edges are extremely difficult to maintain and are rarely justified for design effect. Moisture does not reach the grass or plants at the extreme sharp edges of a bank and natural wear and tear breaks down such edges. The ideal bank has a rolled top and bottom, forming a broad letter "S" by the junction of the top and bottom curves with the normal slope of the bank. Do not exaggerate the top curve so that it overhangs the normal slope. Both top and bottom curves should merge easily with the main slope.

For slopes steeper than one foot vertical to three feet horizontal ground-cover vines or compact cover plants are preferable to turf which is difficult to mow and water satisfactorily. Types of plants for banks should be of compact growing habit with no tendency to get leggy as they mature. If rank, tall-growing plants are used and kept cut back they ultimately become stubby and unattractive. Groundcovers such as myrtle (*Vinca minor*), *Lonicera japonica halliana*, and prostrate roses are most suitable for steep slopes.

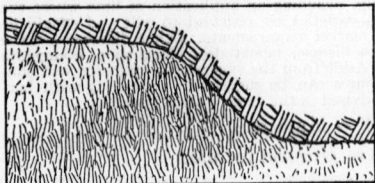

Above — an incorrect bank with sharp edges
Below — a correct one with rolled or rounded edges

On more gradual slopes such plants as matrimony vine (*Lycium halimifolium*), weeping golden bell, Japanese barberry, Regel's privet and fragrant sumac (*Rhus canadensis*) are satisfactory. So is *Jasminum nudiflorum*, if it is hardy in your region. See JASMINUM.

Pocket planting, which consists of preparing a separate hole of proper size for each plant, is the most satisfactory method of bank planting. Pot-grown myrtle is the best for banks and should be planted in trowel-depth holes at least two to the square foot of surface. The intervening space should be covered with a minimum of four inches of good growing soil. For vines like honeysuckle or roses a spacing of five feet on center is a maximum distance, and for quick covering two and one-half feet is preferable. Plants like barberry or privet should have holes prepared not less than 18 in. deep and 18 in in diameter. The more generous the prepared growing space the more satisfactory will be the growth. In backfilling the holes around the plants leave a depression on the upper side in order that rain will collect and not run off without soaking in. For the first season it is advisable to mulch deciduous plants with a strawy manure to hold moisture and prevent erosion.

In purchasing stock, two-year vines, 18 in. barberry, 2 ft. privet and 3 ft. forsythia, are the best sizes for ordinary purposes.

All banks over eight feet in height with a slope greater than one to three should have a gutter along the top adequate to prevent accumulated water from flowing over the bank. Where necessary to prevent water flowing from the bank over other areas a gutter should parallel the foot of the bank.

For banks of more than ten feet in height, with slopes greater than one to three, intervening gutters should be placed at intervals of every ten feet of height on the bank. — R. E. G.

**BANKSIA** (banks'i-a). The Australian honeysuckles comprise over 40 species of shrubs and trees of the family Proteaceae, all Australian. One is a sufficiently handsome evergreen plant to be cult. for ornament, mostly in Calif. They are rarely cult. in greenhouses. Leaves alternate,* in those below narrow and not deeply toothed or lobed. Flowers yellow, borne in dense, mostly terminal clusters (spikes*), between rather showy bracts,* followed by a woody, cone-like fruit, bearing winged seeds. (Named for Sir Joseph Banks, noted British botanist.)

The Australian honeysuckles are semi-desert plants that do well in southern Calif., but are scarcely known elsewhere. They do not easily propagate from seed, and cuttings under a bell-jar, with a little bottom-heat, is the most satisfactory method. For some reason the plants are occasionally offered as *Pimelea*, with which they have nothing to do.

ericaefolia. A shrub or small tree under 14 ft. high. Leaves scarcely ½ in. long, very narrow, and with tiny, rolled margins. Flower spikes 6-10 in. long, usually solitary in the axil* of a twig.

integrifolia. A tree 20-30 ft. high. Leaves oblongish, 6-8 in. long, about 1 in. wide, green above, white-hairy or felty beneath. Flower spikes 4-6 in. long, mostly terminal.

**BANKS ROSE** = *Rosa banksiae*.

**BANNER.** See STANDARD 2.

**BANYAN** = *Ficus benghalensis*.

**BAOBAB** = *Adansonia digitata*.

**BAOBAB FAMILY** = Bombacaceae.

**BAPTISIA** (bap-tiz'i-a). The false indigo or wild indigo is a general term for nearly 25 species of perennial herbs of the pea family, all from N.A., a few grown in the flower border for ornament. They are stout plants with compound* leaves, the three leaflets arranged finger-fashion. Flowers pea-like, in showy clusters (racemes*), followed by more or less inflated, short pods. (Named from the Greek to dye, from the indigo-like dye yielded by some species.)

The two below are useful plants in drier parts of the border or wild garden. They need full sun, an open, porous, somewhat sandy soil, and can be increased by division.

australis. Blue false indigo; called, also, rattle-bush. From 3-5 ft. high. Leaflets 1½-2½ in. long, more or less wedge-shaped. Flower blue, the cluster 2-3 in. long. Pa. to Ga. and westward. June.

tinctoria. Clover broom; called, also, shoofly. A dome-shaped herb 18-30 in. high. Leaflets about ¾ in. long. Flowers yellow, the clusters sparsely flowered but very numerous. Me. to Fla. July. Turns black in drying.

*BARBADENSIS, -e* (bar-ba-den'sis). From Barbados, W.I.

**BARBADOS.** As an adjective applied to many plants native to or grown in Barbados. The ones of hort. interest and found in THE GARDEN DICTIONARY are:

Barbados aloes = *Aloe vera*; Barbados cherry = *Malpighia glabra*; Barbados flower-fence = *Poinciana pulcherrima*; Barbados gooseberry = *Pereskia aculeata*; Barbados nut = *Jatropha curcas*; Barbados pride = *Poinciana pulcherrima* and *Adenanthera pavonina*; Barbados royal palm = *Roystonea oleracea*.

*BARBARA, -us, -um* (bar'ba-ra). Foreign.

**BARBARA'S-BUTTONS.** See MARSHALLIA.

**BARBAREA** (bar-ba-ree'a). The winter or upland cresses are rather weedy herbs of the mustard family, of secondary use as substitutes for watercress, and of little ornamental value. They have divided or compound leaves, small yellow flowers in terminal clusters (racemes*) and narrow pods (siliques*). (The name is from St. Barbara, one of

---

* Special articles on the subjects indicated by an asterisk (*) will be found at the words so marked.

the species being anciently known as herb of St. Barbara.)
The plants are of such easy culture as to suggest weeds, which they much resemble.

**verna.** Early cress; called, also, Belle Isle cress and scurvy-grass. A biennial or perennial herb 12–18 in. high. Leaves irregularly cut, with 5–8 lobes. Flowers scarcely ⅛ in. wide. Pod 1–2 in. long. Eu. One of the earliest blooming weedy plants, sometimes cult. for winter salad, as its foliage is pleasantly acid.

**vulgaris.** The common winter cress; also called bitter winter cress. Similar to *B. verna*, but with 1–4 lobes or leaflets. Pod 1 in. or less long. Eu. Blooms later than *B. verna* and is widely naturalized nearly throughout N.A. as a weed.

**BARBATA, -us, -um** (bar-bay′ta). Barbed or bearded.

**BARBERRY.** See BERBERIS.

**BARBERRY FAMILY** = Berberidaceae.

**BARBERTON DAISY** = *Gerbera jamesoni*.

**BARBINERVIS, -e** (bar-bi-ner′vis). With barbed nerves or veins.

**BARBINODIS, -e** (bar-bi-nō′dis). Bearded at the joints.

**BARBULATA, -us, -um** (bar-bew-lay′ta). Shortly, or somewhat, bearded.

**BARCINONENSIS, -e** (bar-sin-o-nen′sis). From Barcelona, Spain.

**BARK.** The outer, usually more or less woody or corky layer of the stems of most woody plants, best exemplified on tree trunks. It appears to have no other function than protection of the tissue within, consequently being of little importance from the standpoint of garden operations.

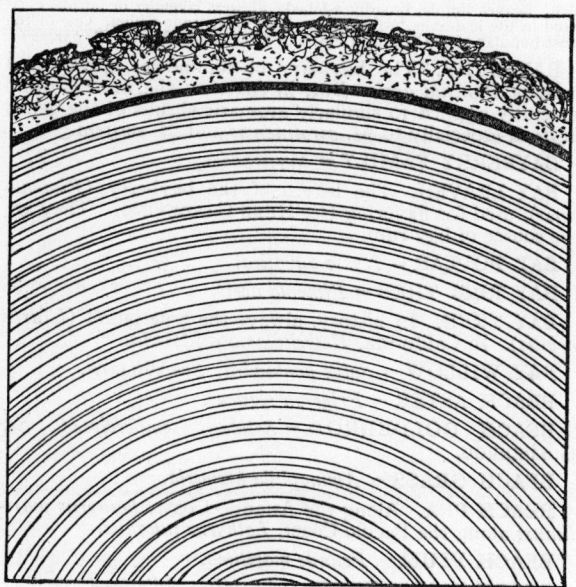

A much enlarged cross-section of a woody stem. Beneath the outer, dead, corky bark is the living, green cambium shown by a dark line. See text for the role of cambium in hort. operations.

It is quite otherwise with the green inner bark, known as cambium. Unlike the outer bark, which is dead, this cambium layer is alive and functionally very important to most woody plants. For it is this layer that carries the foods manufactured in the leaves to the roots. Cutting a complete ring of cambium from a tree trunk will, in most cases, ultimately kill it, a fact well known to the Indians. From this cambium layer also springs all the protective covering which trees throw out over wounds. See also GRAFTING.

**BARK BEETLE.** See the Insect Pests at APPLE, CHERRY and PEACH.

**BARK GRAFTING.** See GRAFTING.

**BARLERIA** (bar-leer′i-a). Greenhouse herbs or small shrubs, of the family Acanthaceae, and comprising over 150 species, nearly all natives of the Old World tropics. The two below are grown for their very showy, bracted* flowers. Leaves opposite,* without marginal teeth. Flowers somewhat irregular,* crowded in the leaf-axils* or in spikes, and from between showy, often spiny, bracts.* Corolla tube slender below, its five lobes flaring and somewhat unequal above. Fruit a normally 4-seeded pod (capsule*). (Named for Jacques Barrelier, French botanist.)

These plants need a warm, moist greenhouse and potting mixture* 4. Occasionally they are used as bedding plants in extreme southern Fla. Propagated by cuttings of young wood over bottom-heat.

**coerulea.** A shrubby herb 3–4 ft. high. Leaves ovalish, 6–8 in. long. Flowers blue, 1–1½ in. long, in bracted spikes, the bracts* showy, prominently veined, but not spiny. India.

**cristata.** An herb or low shrub 2–3 ft. high. Leaves ovalish, 1½–3 in. long. Flowers resembling the *B. coerulea*, but with spiny bracts.* India.

**BARLEY** = *Hordeum vulgare*.

**BARN OR BARNYARD GRASS** = *Echinochloa crus-galli*.

**BARN SWALLOW.** See BIRDS.

**BAROMETZ.** A Tartar word meaning lamb. For centuries the "vegetable lamb of Tartary" was supposed to be a fern (see CIBOTIUM). Actually it was cotton.

**BARREL GARDENING.** See TUB GARDENING.

**BARREN STRAWBERRY** = *Waldsteinia fragarioides*; also *Duchesnea indica*.

**BARRENWORT.** See EPIMEDIUM.

**BARRINGTONIA** (bar-ring-tō′ni-a). A genus of 30 species of very showy trees, family Lecythidaceae, only one of any garden interest and confined to southern Calif. and extreme south Fla. Leaves evergreen, mostly crowded at the ends of the twigs, and large. Flowers in loose clusters, very handsome from their numerous and protruding stamens. Fruit a 4-sided, box-like, woody pod. (Named for Daines Barrington, English naturalist.)

Little is known of the culture or propagation of *B. speciosa*, beyond the need for heat and moisture. It grows naturally in coastal regions of India.

**speciosa.** A spreading tree 30–50 ft. high. Leaves without marginal teeth, stalkless, shining, 12–15 in. long and broadest towards the tip. Flowers few in the cluster, the petals white, the stamens purple and showy. Fruit nearly 3 in. wide.

**BARROW.** See TOOLS AND IMPLEMENTS, Section 1.

**BARTLETT.** A pear variety. See PEAR.

**BARTONIA AUREA** = *Mentzelia lindleyi*.

**BARTRAM'S GARDEN.** The garden of John Bartram, at Philadelphia, is one of the oldest in America. He was a correspondent of Linnaeus* who called him "the greatest natural botanist in the world." There still grows at this famous garden many of the plants which Bartram collected in America or which were sent to him from all over the world. He died in 1777, but the garden is still in existence at 54th Street and Lindley Avenue, and is open to the public.

**BARYXYLUM** = PELTOPHORUM.

**BASAL ROT.** See Diseases at NARCISSUS.

**BASELLA** (ba-sell′a). The Malabar nightshades comprise only one or two species of tropical, annual (or rarely biennial) vines, family Basellaceae, the foliage used for greens in the tropics, but the vines cult. for ornament in the north. Leaves succulent, without marginal teeth. Flowers white or red. (See BASELLACEAE for details.) (*Basella* is a native Malabar name.)

Mostly grown in the greenhouse, but may be started as a tender annual (see ANNUALS) and planted outdoors after danger of frost is past. Propagated by seed.

**alba.** Perhaps not distinct from the following, but it has leaves longer than broad and white flowers. Tropical As.

**rubra.** A moderately tall but rampant climbing vine, the stems greenish-purple. Leaves 2–6 in. broad, about as long, nearly round, and somewhat heart-shaped at the base. Flowers in short clusters (spikes*), reddish. Tropical As.

---

* Special articles on the subjects indicated by an asterisk (*) will be found at the words so marked.

**BASELLACEAE** (ba-sell-ā'see-e). The Madeira-vine family comprises a small group of tropical, herbaceous vines with only two of its six genera of any hort. significance. They have tuberous rootstocks and rather fleshy, alternate leaves without marginal teeth. Flowers regular,* in finger-shaped clusters (racemes*), each with 2 bracts,* the clusters sometimes branched. Fruit small, not splitting, usually enclosed within the withered flower. The only two hort. genera are *Basella* and the much better known *Boussingaultia* (the Madeira-vine), both containing rampant-growing vines grown for their rather ornamental red or white flower clusters.

Technical flower characters: Sepals 2. Petals 5, separate or partly united, scarcely opening. Stamens 5 and opposite the petals. Ovary 1-celled, superior,* with a single ovule, usually with 3 styles.

*BASELLOIDES* (ba-sell-loy'deez; but *see* OÏDES). Like a plant of the genus *Basella*.

**BASIC SLAG.** *See* Phosphoric Acid at FERTILIZERS.

**BASIL** = *Ocimum basilicum*.

**BASILICUM** (ba-sill'i-kum). Ancient name for the basil (*Ocimum basilicum*) in allusion to its reputed healing qualities.

**BASIN.** The depression in an apple, pear, quince, and related fruits at the apex of them; *i.e.* at the end opposite their stalks.

**BASIN IRRIGATION.** *See* IRRIGATION.

**BASKET FERN** = *Nephrolepis pectinata*.

**BASKET-FLOWER.** Commonly, *Centaurea americana*, but also *Hymenocallis calathina* (*see* SPIDER-LILY).

**BASKET GRASS** = *Oplismenus compositus*.

**BASKET-OF-GOLD** = *Alyssum saxatile*.

**BASKET PLANTS.** *See* HANGING BASKET.

**BASSWOOD** = *Tilia*. *See* LINDEN.

**BASTARD INDIGO** = *Amorpha fruticosa*.

**BASTARD MAHOGANY** = *Eucalyptus botryoides*.

**BASTARD SANDALWOOD** = *Myoporum sandwicense*.

**BASTARD SPEEDWELL** = *Veronica spuria*.

**BASTARD TRENCHING.** *See* TRENCHING.

**BATATAS.** A very interesting vernacular to all gardeners. It was the aboriginal Haitian word for the sweet potato, and possibly spelled *batata*. From a corruption of the latter came the English word potato. As the specific, Latinized name of plants it has been applied to *Ipomoea* and *Dioscorea*.

**BATOKO PLUM** = *Flacourtia indica*.

**BAUERA** (bow-ear'ra). In Australia, where the only three species are known, they call these pretty little shrubs native rose. They are not roses, but small shrubs of the family Saxifragaceae, with evergreen, 3-parted, opposite* leaves and white or pink, slender-stalked, 5-petaled flowers, which may be solitary or in small, terminal clusters. Stamens few or many, borne on a ring-like disk. Fruit a 2-valved pod (capsule*). (Named for a German, Bauer, variously credited as a botanist, jurist, botanical draftsman, and professor.)

The only hort. species has long been a favorite cool-greenhouse plant (winter temperature 45°–50°). Plant in potting mixture* 3 and do not allow them to become pot-bound until they reach the size you want, which (for indoor plants) should be 1–2 ft. high. Keep well watered, as the plants naturally grow in wet places. They will bloom most of the winter and early spring under glass, but the pots are best plunged in ashes, in partial shade, during our summer (their winter). Propagated by cuttings of half-ripened wood, in April, preferably under a bell-jar.

rubioides. At home a shrub 4–6 ft., in cult. much less. Leaf segments more or less oblong, ¼–½ in. long, toothed. Flowers pink or white, the petals blunt. Australia.

**BAUHINIA** (baw-hin'i-a). An immense genus of tropical shrubs, trees and woody vines of the pea family, a few planted outdoors in zones* 8 or 9 (see below) for their showy flowers and their fine, very interesting foliage. Leaves compound,* with two oblique leaflets, or merely simple* and with 2 oblique lobes, much resembling the redbud, to which it is related. Flowers showy, not pea-like, with 5 rather unequal petals, each narrowed into a claw.* Fruit a long, flat pod. (Named for the brothers John and Caspar Bauhin, noted herbalists, the twin leaflets suggesting the two brothers.)

Bauhinias are slow-growing and relatively unsuccessful plants for greenhouse culture. In southern Calif. and Fla. they are handsome but not large trees, their showy flowers being indicated by such names as orchid tree and butterfly-flower. They bloom in the winter and very early spring, after which most species drop their leaves. They need well-drained soils, are easily raised from seed and no pests are as yet serious. The U.S. Department of Agriculture is introducing many other species than those listed below, but they are not yet generally available.

acuminata. A shrub 5–6 ft. high. Leaves compound,* the 2 leaflets folding at night. Flowers white, 2–3 in. wide. Pod about 5 in. long. Indo-Malaya. Blooms when only a few months old in Fla.

grandiflora = *Bauhinia variegata*.

monandra. Butterfly-flower; called, also, Jerusalem date. Shrub or small tree, not over 25 ft. Leaves simple,* the 2 lobes broad. Flowers pink, streaked with purple, in showy terminal clusters (racemes*). Pod about 8 in. long. Probably French Guiana.

purpurea. Tree, not over 30 ft., usually less. Leaves simple,* cleft about ⅓ their length into 2 rounded lobes, leathery. Flowers reddish-purple, 2–3 in. wide, in lax clusters, fragrant. Pod about 12 in. long. Indo-China. There is a white variety, and another, called Simpson's Pink, with pink flowers. Both the latter may be varieties of *B. variegata*.

tomentosa. St. Thomas tree. A shrub or small tree, not over 15 ft. high. Leaves simple,* with 2 broad lobes. Flowers yellow, but with one of the petals chocolate-blotched. Pod about 4 in. long. Tropical Africa and Asia.

triandra = *Bauhinia purpurea*.

variegata. Orchid tree; called also mountain ebony. Tree 10–25 ft. high. Leaves simple, broadly 2-lobed. Flowers lavender or purple, clustered in the leaf-axils.* Pod about 9 in. long. Indo-China. One of the most popular of the group in Fla. and often confused with *B. purpurea*.

**BAYBERRY.** The bayberry of commerce, history and hort. is *Pimenta acris*. But, in America, the word is quite generally applied to similarly aromatic shrubs of the genus *Myrica*, especially to *M. carolinensis* and *M. cerifera*.

**BAYBERRY FAMILY** = Myricaceae.

**BAY LEAVES.** The leaves of the bayberry (*Pimenta acris*), used for flavoring (*see* HERB GARDENING). They are the source of bay rum.

**BAY POPLAR** = *Nyssa aquatica*.

**BAY RUM TREE** = *Pimenta acris*.

**BAY TREE.** In history, always the true laurel (*Laurus nobilis*). In California, *Umbellularia californica*.

**BAY WILLOW** = *Salix pentandra*. *See* WILLOW.

**BEACH ASTER** = *Erigeron glaucus*.

**BEACH GOLDENROD** = *Solidago sempervirens*. *See* GOLDENROD.

**BEACH GRASS** = *Ammophila arenaria*.

**BEACH PEA.** Along the Atlantic Coast, *Lathyrus maritimus*; along the Pacific Coast, *Lathyrus littoralis*.

**BEACH PLUM** = *Prunus maritima*.

**BEACH WORMWOOD** = *Artemisia stelleriana*.

**BEAD-PLANT** = *Nertera depressa*.

**BEAD-RUBY** = *Maianthemum canadense*.

**BEAKED HAZEL** = *Corylus cornuta*. *See* HAZEL.

**BEAN.** To the average gardener the word bean implies only two main types — the string bean (often called snap, kidney, or stringless bean) and the lima bean, both of which are derived from the genus *Phaseolus* (which see). Neither was known before the discovery of the New World, as both types are natives of tropical America.

Beans, however, mean much more than this. The traditional bean of the Old World is *Vicia faba*, often called the broad bean, and little grown here, except in Canada, mostly as a forage or for the ground meal from its seeds. It is a bushy annual which does not like hot, dry summers. Other plants called beans, grown for ornament, soil improvement

---

* Special articles on the subjects indicated by an asterisk (*) will be found at the words so marked.

or for forage will be found in the genera *Dolichos*, *Vigna*, *Glycine* (soybean) and among other species of *Phaseolus*.

### CULTURE OF STRING BEAN (*Phaseolus vulgaris*)
(Commonly called, also, snap, kidney, or stringless bean; or haricot)

The string bean (stringless or nearly so in the best varieties) is cult. more generally than any other plant of the bean tribe, both for its delicious, edible green pods and, later, for the very nutritious seeds. The wax or butter bean is a yellow-podded variety preferred by some, but nothing like as much grown as the common string bean. Both are grown as field crops for commercial production and for canning.

The string bean comes in two main types, a low or bush bean (*Phaseolus vulgaris humilis*) and the pole bean (*P. vulgaris*). Most home growers prefer the bush variety because it avoids the trouble and expense of poles.

VARIETIES. Of the hundreds that are known the consensus of expert opinion indicates the following as most generally successful:

Low or bushy varieties (often called dwarf beans).
   Green podded: Burpee Stringless. Bountiful. Black Valentine (for the South). Red Valentine. Refugee. If grown especially for shell beans use Goddard or Dwarf Horticultural. *See also* PINTO BEAN.
   Golden or wax podded: Improved Golden Wax. Burpee Kidney.
Pole or high-climbing varieties.
   Green podded: Lazy Wife (practically stringless). Creaseback. Kentucky Wonder.
   Golden or wax podded: Kentucky Wonder Wax. Golden Cluster. White Creaseback. Golden Carmine.

SOILS AND FERTILIZER. Beans will grow in almost any soils except heavy muck ones, but will do best in well-drained, warm, garden soils that are sandy rather than heavy, or that have too much clay. The soil should have a moderate amount of humus and plenty of plant food.

The latter is best assured by the application, at planting time, of a 4-8-10 commercial fertilizer (*see* FERTILIZERS) at the rate of 500–600 pounds per acre (2½ pounds per 100-foot row). It may be broadcast or sprinkled in the drills, but in the latter case care must be used to mix it thoroughly with the soil, as the naked fertilizer may injure the seeds. Because all beans gather nitrogen from the air, the nitrogen content of the fertilizer can be lower than for many other crops.

If available, stable manure, plowed in two weeks before planting time at the rate of a ton to the acre, will be a satisfactory substitute for commercial fertilizer. Some growers also make small applications of commercial fertilizer between the rows after the plants have started.

PLANTING. String beans will not stand frost, and should not be planted until two weeks after the last killing frost in your neighborhood (see the name of your state for dates). It takes about ¾ pound of seed for a row 100 feet long, 1½ pounds for a garden 50 × 100 feet, and 8 pounds for an acre garden.

For a succession, plant every ten days or two weeks until about the middle of August. Seed sown after this will probably be caught by early frosts. In the South or other regions of long frost-free periods the bean season may be much longer. Bush beans mature in from 45 to 70 days, depending on heat; pole beans take from 75 to 80 days. Both these periods should be kept in mind in making final plantings. Because early beans are so desirable few gardeners will not gamble a little on the first planting of beans. If you win (*i.e.* escape the last frost), you may considerably extend the bean season.

For the bush varieties make the drills about 1½ inches deep and 2 feet apart and put the seeds about 2 inches apart in the row. For the tall sorts put the poles (at least 6 feet high) in rows at least 3 feet apart and the poles about 4 feet apart in the row. At each pole plant 5 or 6 seeds (ultimately thinned to 3 or 4 plants). In planting both sorts see that the soil is slightly tamped over the seeds.

CULTIVATION AND YIELDS. Cultivate frequently with a wheel hoe or hand weeder, or with a scuffle hoe. Never do this in the early morning or just after a rain. All evidence points to the foliage of the bean as dangerously likely to spread disease if implements or clothing brush past it while it is wet. Keep this in mind also when picking the crop. (*See* DISEASES, below.)

Beans must be hand picked, preferably before the pods show much of the outline of the still immature seed, unless it is the latter (shell beans) that are desired, when picking should be delayed. All the varieties are better (*i.e.* more completely stringless) when picked young.

Bush beans enough for a family of 5 can usually be harvested from 100 feet of row, but more will be needed if there are frequent pickings and several plantings.

### CULTURE OF LIMA BEAN (*Phaseolus limensis*)

Even more than the string bean the lima bean is sensitive to frost. Not only should there be no danger of frost, but the ground must have warmed up enough to ensure the proper development of this essentially tropical crop. Safe planting dates for it are generally as follows (but see climatic data at the name of your state):

|  | Earliest in Spring | Last Planting |
|---|---|---|
| Zone* 3 | About June 1 | June 20 |
| Zone* 4 | About May 20 | July 1 |
| Zone* 5 | About May 1 | July 15 |

In zones* 6, 7, and 8 the season is considerably longer, but in zones* 1 and 2 the culture of the lima bean is generally impossible or extremely risky because of the short growing season and lack of heat.

Many growers, impatient of these climatic restrictions, start the plants in the cold frame or even the greenhouse. Seeds sown in paper pots or old strawberry baskets are started three or four weeks before outdoor planting is safe. When settled warm weather makes planting advisable, the boxes or pots are plunged in the ground at intervals of 6 inches apart, in rows that are 3 feet apart (for the bush limas). The pole kinds are set out 2 feet apart, in rows 3½ feet apart.

OUTDOOR PLANTING AND SOILS. Soil requirements are the same as for string beans, and so are the fertilizers. Some growers prefer a slightly acid soil (*see* ACID AND ALKALI SOILS), but this does not appear to be a country-wide factor.

Drills should be 3 feet apart and about 1½ inches deep. Put the seeds about 3½ inches apart in the row, cover, and tamp down slightly. Because the seeds are large it takes about ¾ pound for 100 feet of row (¾ peck to the acre).

CULTIVATION. Same as for string bean (see above).

HARVESTING AND YIELDS. Lima beans take much longer to mature than string beans. It takes from 75–90 days from outdoor planting to harvest, so that over much of the country only one crop can be grown.

They must be hand picked, and as it is the seeds that are used, it is useless to pick until the pod shows indication of some seed formation. Young lima beans, however, are so delicious that many gardeners pick them earlier than the commercial grower would find profitable. If left too long on the plants, lima beans become tough and then are best suited for drying and winter storage.

PREFERRED VARIETIES OF LIMA BEAN.
   Low or bush sorts. Fordhook Bush. Henderson Bush. Burpee Bush. Wonder.
   Tall or pole sorts. Leviathan. Hopi and Lewis (Calif.). Sieva (South). King of the Garden.

Many growers, especially commercial ones, prefer to grow the tall varieties on wire trellises and in drills, instead of on poles set at intervals. A continuous, fence-like wire trellis 6 ft. high is then constructed, with the wires stretched diagonally up and down, instead of laterally as in a fence. Few home growers will bother with such equipment, or with the poles, and bush limas are consequently most pre-

---

* Special articles on the subjects indicated by an asterisk (*) will be found at the words so marked.

ferred. If poles are used they should be rough, preferably with their bark on. (*See also* KITCHEN GARDEN.)

INSECT PESTS. The Mexican bean beetle, a brownish-spotted ladybird beetle, is a serious pest in the East and in the Rocky Mountain region. The larva is a bright yellow grub. Both adults and larvae feed on snap and lima beans throughout the season. Snap beans are easily injured by sprays, and most arsenicals cannot be used on them. A spray of magnesium arsenate, 2 pounds to 50 gallons, or a dust of calcium arsenate and lime will give control if *put on the underside* of the leaves, and will cause little injury to the beans. Poisons should not be put on after the pods form. Vines should be removed and destroyed after the crop has been picked. The bean leaf beetle, the larvae of which feed on the roots of beans, and the spotted cucumber beetle are sometimes injurious early in the season; the same arsenicals will check them. Black plant lice, sometimes found on beans, can be controlled with nicotine. Bean weevils on seed beans may be controlled by fumigation with carbon disulphide.

DISEASES. The most serious diseases of field or snap beans are anthracnose, bacterial blight, mosaic, and dry root rot. Anthracnose and bacterial blights may cause dying of the young plants, spotting of the pods, and injury to the leaves. Rotation of crops, plowing under deeply diseased refuse, and planting resistant or healthy seed include the most common control measures. Snap bean seed from Idaho and Red Kidney seed from some parts of California are free from these diseases and may safely be planted. A number of dry bean seeds, as Robust pea and Perry Marrow, have been bred for disease resistance. Mosaic causes mottling and corrugation of the leaves, and dwarfing of the plant. The virus causing it is carried in the seed, so that stock from a healthy field, or resistant strains should be planted. The dry root rot is caused by a fungus which may live years in the soil. It also is disseminated with manure containing affected bean straw. Rotations of six years or longer, and not placing bean straw on the soil are the recommended control measures. In some states, especially where Kentucky Wonder pole beans are grown, rust causes large black pustules. Resistant varieties now are available for planting.

Lima beans are affected by pod blight and downy mildew. Both may kill the pods and turn them black. The mildew first produces a downy white growth over the affected parts. Spraying with bordeaux mixture or dusting with copper-lime dust, holds these two diseases in check, especially when accompanied by the use of healthy seed, and rotation of crops.

**BEAN FAMILY.** See LEGUMINOSAE.

**BEANPOLE FENCING.** See FENCES.

**BEAN-TREE.** Usually applied to *Catalpa bignonioides;* also to *Laburnum anagyroides.*

**BEARBERRY.** Commonly applied to *Arctostaphylos uva-ursi;* in California, to *Rhamnus purshiana.*

**BEAR-BUSH** = *Ilex glabra.* See HOLLY.

**BEARD.** A bristle-like awn,* especially a tuft of such. Also, any fringe-like growth on a petal, as in many irises and some orchids.

**BEARDED DARNEL** = *Lolium temulentum.*

**BEARDED IRIS.** See IRIS.

**BEARD-GRASS.** See ANDROPOGON.

**BEARDLESS IRIS.** See IRIS.

**BEARDTONGUE.** See PENTSTEMON.

**BEAR GRASS.** This is applied to several plants with grass-like or sword-shaped leaves, all members of the lily family. See NOLINA, DASYLIRION TEXANUM, YUCCA FILAMENTOSA, Y. GLAUCA, and CAMASSIA QUAMASH.

**BEARING AGE.** For the normal time when trees may be expected to bear fruit, etc., see GARDEN TABLES I.

**BEAR'S-BREECH** = *Acanthus mollis.*

**BEAR'S-GRAPE.** See UVA-URSI.

**BEAR-TONGUE.** See CLINTONIA.

**BEAUMONTIA** (bo-mon'ti-a). A small genus of trees or woody vines, family Apocynaceae, the one below from India, the rest Javanese. Leaves opposite,* without marginal teeth. Flowers large, fragrant, white, and funnel- or trumpet-shaped, the corolla with 5 broad lobes. Fruit long, cylindric, splitting into two follicles.* (Named for Lady Beaumont of Bretton Hall, England.)

The herald's-trumpet would be a splendid greenhouse vine if it could be kept within bounds. It cannot be confined to a pot or tub and should be planted in the soil of a greenhouse large enough to contain it. It needs a warm house (65° or more), and plenty of moisture. Some growers regularly thin out its large leaves which might otherwise make a greenhouse into a dusky nook. Can be grown outdoors only in zone* 9.

grandiflora. Herald's-trumpet. A tall-growing, woody vine. Leaves ovalish, 6–9 in. long. Flowers 5 in. long and nearly as wide, spring-blooming in the greenhouse. India, where the floss from its seeds is used as a vegetable silk.

**BEAUTY-BERRY.** See CALLICARPA.

**BEAUTY-BUSH** = *Kolkwitzia amabilis.*

**BEAVER-POISON** = *Cicuta maculata.*

**BEDDING.** When plants are grouped together for mass effect they form a planting bed and the term Bedding is applied to this type of arrangement.

One of these types is called Carpet Bedding, which is an arrangement of low, compact, mostly foliage plants in conventional patterns resembling carpet design.

The outline shape of the beds varies from a simple circle to elaborate scroll patterns, and in some cases the bedding plants are used to lay out flags, shields or other insignia.

Since this kind of bedding remains exactly the same throughout the summer it is too monotonous and also too expensive for private garden use and has, therefore, been confined to public gardens which are seen only occasionally by different people. In public gardens there are skilled gardeners specially trained for this very difficult type of bedding design. It is beyond the scope of this article to attempt to go into the intricacies of carpet-bedding design.

Another type of bedding, known as Parterre work, is well adapted to ornamental planting in private gardens. The term Parterre means a geometric arrangement of ornamental shaped beds separated by a pattern of walks or turf areas. Variations in parterre design are unlimited, the simplest form being four beds arranged symmetrically around a central ornamental feature. The shapes of these beds are related one to the other so that they form a complete pattern from which no one bed can be eliminated without having the pattern incomplete.

To lay out a parterre design within any given area, determine first what the major feature in the garden is to be and where it is to be placed. If it is to be a pool, a sundial or flower bed in the center of the garden, lay out a symmetrical path system leading up to this feature. The resulting shape of the areas in between the paths forms the pattern of the parterre. This pattern should be outlined by formal, trimmed hedges within which the surface may be planted with grass or flowers, according to personal preference.

Sometimes an additional pattern of low hedges, separating beds of different colored flowers, is laid out within the larger areas. Such patterns are often very elaborate scroll designs resembling embroidery, which was characteristic of the French style of embroidery gardening.

If the major feature is to be at one end of the garden the same process of laying out the pattern will apply, but all paths will lead up to this terminal feature.

Annuals are the most suitable plants for parterre bedding because of their continuous profusion of bloom. Any type of plant which has a short season of bloom leaves a blank in the pattern at some one season or another. Typical annuals for parterre bedding are heliotrope, ageratum, single petunias, snapdragons, dwarf annual phlox, geraniums, dwarf marigolds and lantanas. Colored foliage plants such as *Coleus* and *Telanthera* are excellent for very formal parterre planting, but less satisfactory among annuals or more informal plants.

The beauty of the parterre is its pattern design and the flowers are only the color spots which create this pattern. Each division of the pattern should, therefore, be a solid color of a single variety. To see properly the beauty of the pattern it must be viewed from a height sufficient to comprehend the whole pattern. For this reason the parterre is most effective when seen from a terrace or slightly elevated, surrounding walk. If such elevation is not possible, then the pattern should be created with very low-growing plants. Originally these patterns were laid out with boxwood edgings, but *Taxus cuspidata nana* or dwarf forms of *Thuja* are satisfactory evergreen substitutes. *Teucrium chamaedrys,*

---

* Special articles on the subjects indicated by an asterisk (*) will be found at the words so marked.

*Nepeta mussini, Euonymus radicans carrieri*, or *Berberis thunbergi minor* are deciduous alternatives.

Spring Bedding is similar in design to other types of bedding, but the color is created by spring-flowering bulbs instead of annuals. See BULBS.

A Ribbon Bed is a long, narrow-shaped bed with special pattern conforming to its length. Such beds parallel paths or drives, and the pattern is a rhythmic repetition of the same design. The materials used are similar to other types of bedding.

The parterre at the Medici Gardens—the finest type of bedding

The term Flower Bed means any shape of bed within which there may be a great many varieties of flowers, and the bed is not a part of a general pattern. In this case the interest is created by a variety of plants arranged for succession of bloom, color and foliage composition. There is no limitation of height, type of plant, or arrangement for a flower bed. Perennials and annuals may be intermixed, and since the outline of the bed is secondary in importance to the plants within it there is no necessity for a surrounding hedge. The scattering of unrelated and different-shaped flower beds on a lawn is one of the worst vagaries of amateur design. The parterre is far more artistic. *See also* BORDER.

Low-growing flowers are used around the outside of the bed and built up to higher plants in the center, or if it is a border bed the front is kept low and built up to a high background. In place of a surrounding hedge a border plant should be used to unify the composition.

The only limitation to the size and shape of flower beds is the practical consideration of being able to get into the bed to cultivate the plants. A skillful gardener can easily cultivate a bed twelve feet wide, but a practical width for the ordinary border bed which does not require skillful maintenance is eight feet.

To determine the number of plants required for any kind or size of bed the number of square feet within the bed should be figured. For rank-growing perennials such as larkspur, phlox and chrysanthemums allow two square feet for the ultimate requirements of each plant; for peonies four square feet; for tea roses three square feet; for hybrid, perpetual roses four square feet; for annuals such as ageratum or petunias one square foot. See GARDEN TABLES IV.

In figuring dwarf hedges count one plant for each six inches in length; for perennial or annual border plants eight to ten inches. The tendency is to overcrowd perennials for immediate effect on new plantings, which results in ultimate stunted growth. It is better to allow adequate room for ultimate growth and interplant with bulbs such as tulips, lilies or gladiolus for temporary filler. — R. E. G.

**BEDDING PANSY.** *See* VIOLA CORNUTA.

**BEDDING ROSES.** *See* Group 5 at ROSE.

**BEDSTRAW.** *See* GALIUM.

**BEE.** *See* BEES AND BEE PLANTS.

**BEE BALM** = *Monarda didyma;* also *Melissa officinalis.*

**BEECH.** These ornamental trees, all belonging to the genus **Fagus** (fay'gus), of the family Fagaceae, comprise only 9 species, all of which are confined to temperate regions of the northern hemisphere. The two below are the only species, so far, of any interest to the gardener, but they are among the most decorative and hardy of all cult. trees (*see* Culture below). Leaves alternate, toothed (in those below). Male and female flowers in separate clusters on the same tree. Male flowers in slender-stalked heads, without petals, but with 4–7-lobed calyx, and 8–16 stamens.* Female flowers usually 2, surrounded by many united bracts. Fruit a triangular or egg-shaped nut in a woody, 4-valved, prickly covering. (*Fagus* is classical Latin for the beech.)

**F. grandifolia.** American beech; called, also, red or white beech. A tree 90–100 ft. high, with light gray bark. Leaves oblong-oval, broadly wedge-shaped at the base, coarsely toothed, 4–7 in. long, bluish-green above, light green beneath, beautifully silky when unfolding. Eastern N.A.

**F. sylvatica.** European beech. Somewhat taller than the American beech. Leaves dark, lustrous-green, finely and somewhat remotely toothed, more or less elliptic-ovate, 3½–5 in. long. Eu. For the many beautiful hort. forms of this *see* below.

## CULTURE OF THE BEECH

The beech is among the most beautiful of the larger ornamental trees. Although seven species are hardy in the U.S., only the native and European representatives are well known. The species from China, Japan, and Northern Asia have been in cultivation but a short time, when the natural life span of this group is considered, and are not commonly cultivated.

The beech is quite soil tolerant, although it prefers a well-drained, light soil. Care in transplanting is the only rigid requirement for successful cultivation. A long tap root is present and should be preserved. For this reason, the moving of large specimens is a dangerous operation unless the tree is first prepared by a gradual process of root pruning. Nurserymen make a practice of transplanting this group regularly to develop a vigorous root system without long tap roots.

Propagation is by seed which is planted in the fall in beds which have been screened to keep out rodents. The varieties are grafted on seedlings of the European species. This work is done in the greenhouse during late winter. A cleft graft is sometimes used, although veneer or tongue grafting is more common.

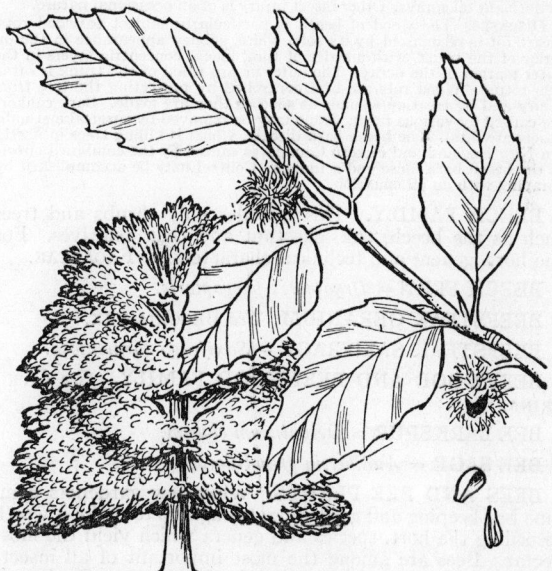

The habit, foliage and fruit of the American beech (*Fagus grandifolia*)

The European beech (*Fagus sylvatica*) is perhaps the most beautiful of the group. Hardy throughout this country, it often reaches a height of more than one hundred feet. When grown as a specimen tree, it forms a huge, broad top with horizontal and ascending branches extending from a generally low, bulky trunk which sometimes measures six feet in

---

* Special articles on the subjects indicated by an asterisk (*) will be found at the words so marked.

diameter. In wooded areas the habit is less broad and the trunk often clean for a height of forty feet. Its smooth, light gray bark and lustrous, dark green foliage combine to furnish a delightful color contrast.

The many varieties of the European beech may be considered as among the most coveted of the ornamental trees. The purple beech, *Fagus sylvatica atropunicea*, is identical with the type, except for its purple leaves, and is one of the finest trees with colored foliage. *Fagus sylvatica cuprea*, the copper beech, although less widely distributed, is identified by its bright copper or rosy-colored leaves. It is slower-growing than the variety *atropunicea*. The pendulous form, *Fagus sylvatica pendula*, has pendulous branches which often completely hide the trunk. A combination of the pendulous branches and purple-leaved forms is known as *Fagus sylvatica purpurea-pendula*. It combines the characters of both forms, but is rather slow growing and seldom exceeds forty feet in height. The fern-leaved beech, *Fagus sylvatica laciniata*, has sharply cut, fern-like leaves which cover the tree with a beautiful, dense, shimmering mantle of green throughout the summer. A lesser known form is the *var. fastigiata*, the upright beech. This tree raises its branches in an almost vertical fashion, forming a narrow, spire-like tree. Many other forms are grown in Europe. Chief among these are a number of varieties with intermediate shades of purple-colored foliage or cut leaves. The European beech holds its green color later in the fall than the American tree, and is thus valuable where late greenery is an advantage.

The American beech (*Fagus grandifolia*) is quite similar in general appearance to the European representative. The bark is a lighter gray and the leaves are larger and duller in color. It is more beautiful in autumn, as its foliage turns a bright yellow, whereas that of the European species turns red. Although most commonly employed as a specimen tree, it is sometimes used for large hedges and is becoming popular for allée work. — A. D. S.

INSECT PESTS. Woolly-white aphids infest beech, one species on the leaves and another in masses on the limbs. The one on the leaves will succumb to nicotine and soap sprays if applied thoroughly. For the second species nicotine in oil emulsion, applied early in the spring, is advised. In New England a scale insect occurs on this tree; it succumbs to dormant oil sprays. Other insect injury is of an occasional nature.

DISEASES. The wood of beech is particularly subject to wood rots. Heart rot is recognized by its soft, white, spongy appearance in the interior of the trunk, with a series of thin, black, concentric layers in the outer margin of the decay. The outer or sap wood of the trunk is often also rotted. Wood rots are best controlled by protecting the tree from injury and by treating wounds as soon as they are made. Bark cankers are caused by various fungi. Some may be removed by surgical methods, others are fatal. The beech bark disease, which is killing trees in northern New England and eastern Canada, is caused by the combined effects of the beech bark louse and a fungus. Control may be accomplished by spraying with an oil emulsion.

**BEECH FAMILY.** This includes only shrubs and trees such as the beech, oak, chestnut and their relatives. For the hort. genera and technical characters see FAGACEAE.

**BEECH FERN** = *Dryopteris phegopteris*.

**BEEFSTEAK GERANIUM.** See BEGONIA REX.

**BEEFSTEAK SAXIFRAGE** = *Saxifraga sarmentosa*.

**BEEFWOOD AND BEEFWOOD FAMILY.** See CASUARINA.

**BEE LARKSPUR** = *Delphinium elatum*.

**BEE SAGE** = *Audibertia grandiflora*.

**BEES AND BEE PLANTS.** While few gardeners combine bee-keeping and gardening, enough do to make it worth recording the hort. species and genera which yield the most nectar. Bees are among the most important of all insects in carrying pollen, especially in the fruit trees. See POLLINATION.

Besides such favorites as buckwheat and the lindens, there are a few other genera that yield enough honey so that they are planted in quantity for the purpose, especially in Calif. Among the most important bee plants are:

All clovers (*Trifolium*)
Lindens (*Tilia*)
Nearly all the sages (*Salvia*)
Bluecurls (*Trichostema lanceolatum*)
Mesquite (*Prosopis juliflora*)
Nearly all milkweeds
Orange (in Calif. and Fla.)
All sweet clovers (*Melilotus*)
Buckwheat (*Fagopyrum*)
Button-bush (*Cephalanthus*)
Nearly all fruit trees, especially apple
Eucalyptus (in Calif.)
Alfalfa (*Medicago sativa*)
*Borago officinalis*
*Cleome serrulata*
Tulip-tree (*Liriodendron*)
Nearly all wisterias
Lima bean
Toyon (*Heteromeles arbutifolia*) in Calif.
*Vitex*

Miscellaneous garden flowers, while useful, and regularly visited by bees, are not so attractive to them as the above, some of which should be planted in quantity by those who want to combine gardening and bee-keeping.

**BEET.** The beet and Swiss chard belong to **Beta** (bee'ta), (family Chenopodiaceae), which is a genus of Old World herbs having leaves quite without hairs. Flowers greenish, in spikes or panicles,* without petals, and extremely simple. Usually there are minute bracts* beneath the 5-cleft calyx.* Fruit an aggregate of 2 or more flowers joined together at the base, and forming a dry, corky body (utricle*) which, while not a true seed, is commonly the best "seed" of the markets. (*Beta* is the Latin name of the beet.) The only cult. species is:

**B. vulgaris.** Beet, commonly called beetroot in England. A biennial grown for its much-thickened red (white in the sugar beet) root. Stem produced from the root the second year, rarely seen in cult. specimens, 2–4 ft. high. Leaves oblongish, often red-stalked. Perhaps a cultigen,* but derived from a wild species on the coasts of Eu. The *var. cicla*, the leaf beet and Swiss chard, produces no fleshy root and its foliage, often brightly colored or with white veins or leafstalks, is grown both for ornament and for greens. (See Swiss Chard below.) An agricultural variety of the beet, with much-enlarged roots used for stock food, is known as the mangel, or mangel-wurzel.

BEET CULTURE (*Beta vulgaris*)

Beets are one of the easiest of vegetables to grow, doing well in almost every type of garden soil, except those too rocky to allow proper root development. A rich, sandy loam, easily worked, is ideal.

While somewhat tolerant of soils, the beet will not grow well in the warm sections of the country, and is primarily a crop for zone* 4 and northward. The commercial production in the South for northern winter markets is based upon the use of the brief cool periods that come before the heat of summer. (See CALIFORNIA.)

VARIETIES. Of the many on the market the best varieties of beet for the ordinary garden are, in order of preference: Crosby's Egyptian, Detroit Dark Red, Early Wonder. For winter storage, or for canning, use Long Season, which, unlike the turnip-shaped varieties cited above, is a half-long, more carrot-shaped sort. Early Wonder is one of the quickest from seeding to harvest, averaging, in good soil and favorable climate, about 42 days. The others take from 45–50 days.

PLANTING. If you are to cultivate with a hoe or wheel hoe, the rows should be 12 in. apart. If horse or power cultivation is to be used, the rows should be twice that or even a little more. Make the drills deep enough to allow the seed to be covered with an inch of soil.

In planting the seed it is well to remember that the "seed" of the beet is really a fruit containing several seeds. This fruit (hereafter called a seed) is thus likely to sprout with several small plants at each interval. This matters little because the best method is always to sow beet seed thicker than the final stand is to be, and then thin out the plants enough to allow proper root development.

Plant about 10 seeds to a foot of row (at this rate it takes about 2 ounces for 100 ft. of row). Because the seed germinates a little slower than some vegetables, it is a good plan to sprinkle a few radish seeds in the row before covering the beet seed. The radishes sprout quickly, so marking the row plainly for a possible cultivation before the beets are up.

CULTIVATION AND THINNING. Cultivate frequently and deeply at first, being careful not to disturb the young seedlings, however. When the plants get to be 4 in. high you must decide whether you finally want a great many, fairly small, roots or fewer and larger ones, or a combination of both. Thin to 2 in. apart if you want small roots, and to 5½ in. apart for big ones. Many home growers prefer to let thinning be dictated by how thickly the seed has sprouted, the different development of the individual plants, and whether or not they wish to use the plants they pull out as beet

---

* Special articles on the subjects indicated by an asterisk (*) will be found at the words so marked.

greens. These are a good substitute for spinach. If the larger roots are ultimately desired, it is often possible first to harvest a crop of small roots, and then one or two lots of beet tops, the result being that you have by such harvesting left the final roots spaced so they can develop properly.

Still another use of thinned beets is to transplant them at once. While some growers, with a moist soil or a watering system, can do this successfully, the plants stand moving rather poorly.

In the later stages great care must be used in cultivating to avoid injuring the fleshy roots, which are prone to bleed and become useless if nicked by hoe or cultivator.

Beets are rich feeders, and the soil should be correspondingly rich, especially if quick growth is to be secured, and it should be. Slow growth means tough roots, while quick growth means juicy and tender ones. Do not plow in green or fresh stable manure before planting — use only well-rotted cow or stable manure. If neither is available, broadcast a good commercial fertilizer (1500 pounds to the acre, or 3½ pounds to 100 ft. of row). In addition, many find it profitable to broadcast and cultivate in (between the rows), when the plants are 6 in. high, about 200 pounds of nitrate of soda to the acre (about 8 ounces to 100 ft. of row).

### Swiss Chard Culture (*Beta vulgaris cicla*)

Chard (sometimes called the silver beet) is simply a variety of the common beet that develops no turnip-shaped or carrot-shaped root, but whose leaves (due to breeding and selection) are much larger and more succulent than the ordinary beet. A few varieties, often called leaf beet, are variously colored and grown sometimes for ornament. But the chief use is for greens that make a splendid substitute for spinach. This is the ordinary chard of the kitchen garden, sometimes called spinach-beet.

As now developed, some varieties of this have a much-enlarged, white leafstalk which is the only part that many growers use. Others cook the whole leaf (often white-veined), leafstalk and all.

VARIETIES. The best general variety is Lucullus, but if you care only for the stalks, it is better to plant Large-ribbed White.

CULTURE. Chard is planted and cultivated exactly as the beet (see above), but because the plants are very leafy, it is well to thin them to 6 in. apart in the row (using thinned plants for greens). Harvesting can begin whenever the leaves are 6 in. or more long. If the soil is rich, moisture adequate, and the season not too hot, you can keep on cutting until frost. But if the plants show a tendency to become exhausted (*i.e.* produce fewer and smaller leaves), it is a good plan to start another crop. This can be done anytime up to 40 days before you expect the first killing frost of autumn (*see* the name of your state for frost data in your vicinity).

Unlike spinach, chard wilts quickly and cannot be shipped to any great distance. It is thus a home-grown delicacy which is pretty infrequent in the markets. (*See also* KITCHEN GARDEN.)

INSECT PESTS. The spinach flea beetle often attacks young beets (*see* SPINACH); arsenicals will check it. Both garden beets and sugar beets are attacked by webworms, the larvae of moths; arsenical sprays will control them. In the West sugar beets are attacked by a root aphid, which is controlled by frequent irrigation; and by a leafhopper, which carries a serious disease and is hard to control. Beet leaf beetles can be controlled with arsenicals. Grasshoppers often seriously damage sugar beets; poisoned-bran bait, sowed thinly in fields and borders early in the morning, is effective against them.

DISEASES. Curly top has almost driven western sugar beet growers out of the industry. Resistant or tolerant varieties are now being developed. The beet leaf spot, light-colored in the center and with a purplish border, is much more common on sugar beet and mangel than on garden beets. Spraying with bordeaux mixture or dusting with copper-lime has been suggested where the leaf spot has caused much injury. The common potato scab may cause unsightly roughening on the root if beets are grown in infested soil that is inclined to be alkaline. Long rotations and the reduction of soil alkalinity will reduce scab, but not completely control it. Damping-off is very prevalent on seedling beets. Treating the seed with red copper oxide, or the soil with dilute formaldehyde, protects the young plants. Beets are heirs to many other less serious or slightly known diseases.

**BEET FAMILY** = Chenopodiaceae.

**BEETLES**. See Beetles at INSECT PESTS. *See also* the insect pests at GRAPE and ROSE.

**BEETLEWEED** = *Galax aphylla*.

**BEGGAR-LICE** = *Desmodium canadense*.

**BEGGAR-TICKS** = *Desmodium canadense*; also *Bidens frondosa* (see the list at WEEDS).

**BEGGARWEED** = *Desmodium purpureum*.

**BEGONIA** (bee-gō'ni-a). An immense genus of tropical foliage and flowering herbs, with soft or succulent stems, and the only hort. genus of the family **Begoniaceae** (bee-gō-ni-ā'see-ee). Leaves alternate, often brightly colored or with colored veins, nearly always oblique in general outline. Flowers red, pink, yellow or white, slightly irregular, the male and female always separate. Male flowers with 2-5 or more parts scarcely distinguishable as petals and sepals. Ovary inferior,* 2-celled, the fruit a many-seeded capsule.* (Named for Michel Begon, French antiquary and patron of botany.)

As *Begonia* is a genus of over 400 species, has been widely diversified by breeders, and is now found in a multitude of hort. forms, the names are still in much confusion. Many of the hort. forms have been given Latin names exactly as though they were true wild species, which has simply made the confusion worse.

From the gardening standpoint, those in cult. are best divided into two groups: (a) Tuberous-rooted begonias, and (b) Fibrous-rooted sorts.

(a) Tuberous-rooted begonias (all marked *a* in the list below). Here belong *B. socotrana*, *B. lloydi*, the tuberous begonia hybrids, and *B. evansiana*, the latter the hardiest of all begonias and even standing zero weather. All others are tender plants killed by frost.

(b) Fibrous-rooted begonias (all marked *b* in the list below). Here belong *B. bunchi*, *B. feasti*, *B. fuchsioides*, *B. heracleifolia*, *B. incana*, *B. manicata*, President Carnot, *B. rex*, *B. sanguinea*, and *B. semperflorens*. The latter includes most of the common bedding begonias.

For culture and uses *see* Culture (below).

**bunchi** (b). A hybrid plant with nearly round, thick leaves, green above, and red beneath, the margins growing out like crests.

**evansiana** (a). A smooth, branching plant 1-2 ft. high. Leaves more or less oval, but lobed and the lobes toothed, red on the underside. Flowers large, flesh-pink. China and Jap. It is the hardiest of all cult. forms, and stands temperatures of zero at Washington, D.C.

**feasti** (b). Leaves red beneath, nearly round, thick and fleshy, from a creeping mass of stems. Leaf-margins distinctly hairy. Flowers light pink, long-stalked. Of hybrid origin.

**fuchsioides** (b). A popular greenhouse begonia with slender stem, 2-3 ft. high, the branches shaggy. Leaves lopsided, ovalish, 1-1½ in. long. Flowers suggesting a fuchsia, scarlet, ½-¾ in. wide. Mex.

**heracleifolia** (b). A hairy, creeping-stemmed plant with large leaves on long stalks. Leaves nearly round, nearly a foot wide, deeply cut into 5-9 narrow lobes. Flowers scarcely 1 in. wide, white or pink, on stalks that are 15-20 in. long. Mex.

**incana** (b). An upright plant, 1-2 ft. high, the stems, leafstalks and leaves covered with brownish-red hairs. Leaves with the stalk arising near the center of the blade, nearly round, 4-9 in. wide. Flowers white, long-stalked clusters. Brazil.

**lloydi** (a). A hybrid (or series of them), with more or less drooping habit and thus suited to hanging baskets. Leaves narrow, the stalk arising at the base of the blade. Flowers small, single or double, in all colors but blue in some of the many named forms. The so-called Zeppelin types, with brilliant flowers, are beautiful and graceful for temporary house decoration.

**manicata** (b). A plant with creeping rootstocks, without hairs, except on the margins and veins of the leaves, which are green above, reddish beneath, ovalish, 4-8 in. long and with wavy, toothed margins. Flowers pink, about ½ in. long, the stalk longer than the leaves. Mex. There are crisp-margined forms and others with thin, yellow-mottled leaves.

**President Carnot** (b). A tall plant (or group of hybrids), the stems often 6 ft. high. Leaves large. Flowers deep coral-pink. Exact origin unknown.

**rex** (b). The common rex begonia of many homes and greenhouses. Rootstocks creeping. Leaves large and long-stalked, the stalk shaggy-hairy. Blade marbled, blotched or banded with metallic markings above, reddish beneath, nearly 9 in. long. Flowers rose-pink, about 1½ in. wide. Occurs in many hort. forms, all derived from a plant from Assam, and is sometimes called beefsteak geranium. For preferred varieties *see* Culture (below).

**sanguinea** (b). A smooth and shining plant, its several stems red, scarcely over 20 in. high. Leaves green above, red beneath, more or less heart-shaped or oval, about 5 in. long, without marginal teeth. Flowers white, about ¾ in. wide, the cluster usually above the foliage. Brazil.

**semperflorens** (b). As usually cult., not over 1 ft. high, mostly less than 8 in., the whole plant nearly without hairs and rather fleshy. Leaves

---

* Special articles on the subjects indicated by an asterisk (*) will be found at the words so marked.

ovalish, glossy-green, 2-4 in. long, very finely toothed, and the margins fringed with minute hairs. Flowers white, pink or red (in some of the many forms), about 1 in. wide, blooming rather continuously when planted out for summer decoration. Brazil. Of the many varieties of this species, the leading bedding begonia, the best are: Gracilia, Fire King, Zulu King, Triomphe de Lorraine and Gigantea rosea.

socotrana (a). A low begonia from the island of Socotra, interesting for itself, but widely used by hybridizers in the production of hort. forms often credited to other species. Stems not over 1 ft. high, usually branched. Leaves nearly round, 6-7 in. wide, the stalk arising in the middle of the blade. Flowers rose-pink, about 1½ in. wide, in a long-stalked, forking cluster. Among its many named forms the best are: Mrs. Peterson, Melior, and Gloire de Lorraine. Some are called Christmas begonias because they are widely sold then by florists.

tuberhybrida (a). A group name for many hybrid, tuberous-rooted begonias. They have not more than 2-3 stems. Leaves large, the stalk arising at the base of the blade. Flowers large, in all colors except blue, single or double, some of the forms camellia-like, others narcissus-like.

### CULTURE AND USES OF BEGONIA

Most of the species above are derived from plants of moist, hot forests. Naturally they thrive best in a greenhouse that approximates these conditions, and, to make their best growth and produce their finest foliage, demand them. Many of them, however, will tolerate a reasonably warm, preferably moist, living-room, especially forms of the rex begonia, and those derived from *B. socotrana*, and most of the fibrous-rooted kinds.

All begonias when in active growth are gross feeders and require plenty of liquid manure, but when growth stops they require a short resting period, during which water is reduced and feeding entirely stopped. After new growth begins they may be re-potted in potting mixture* 4.

For those who have no greenhouse, plants wintered over in the living-room (a kitchen window, without a gas stove is better) may be brought outdoors after all danger of frost is passed, well watered, and kept in partial shade.

A begonia leaf held down on the sand by stones and forming new plants at the places where the veins were cut

Begonias are not good as cut flowers, as they are too delicate. However, nothing is more beautiful than a table piece of tuberous begonias with fern or smilax, while a cascade of flowers of Berthe de Chateaurocher or President Carnot is a sight to be remembered.

The rex begonia now comprises hundreds of named garden forms, all hybrids or crosses of other ornamental species and varieties. They are favorites because of their beautiful leaves, variously marked with spots, colored bands, and metallic shadings. The best of the named forms are: Louise Closson, with purple-bronze veins and a metallic luster with the effect of a blotch of blood on a black leaf; Jules Chrétien, dark green, sprinkled with rose-pink points and a central pink band passing to white; Countess Louise Erdody, with leaves whorled in a spiral of 4 turns, silvery above, reddish and hairy beneath; Bettina Rothschild, whole plant covered with long red hairs with appearance of chenille.

PROPAGATION. Begonias are grown from stem cuttings, leaf cuttings, division of the tubers, seeds, and in *semperflorens* varieties by root division. These can best be taken as directed below.

STEM CUTTING. Cut below a joint with a sharp knife, insert in moist sand, at room temperature. LEAF CUTTING. Rex begonia leaf cuttings 1½ in. long with main vein running through them, inserted in sand with bottom-heat, will root and form new plants; whole leaves of these varieties placed under benches and kept moist will develop plants on the surface of the leaves. Christmas begonias, hybrids of *B. socotrana*, are propagated by inserting the stalk of the leaf in sand or even in soil, or water. Still another method, especially for *B. evansiana*, is to use the bulbils* which sprout at the apex of the leafstalk where it joins the blade. A quick method is to spread the bulbils over the surface of potting mixture* 1, press down and cover with glass. The bulbils* will soon produce young plants. DIVISION OF TUBERS. Cut tubers as in potatoes, leaving an eye on each cut, dust with charcoal, cover lightly with peat. When sprouted, plant in potting mixture* 4. SEEDS. These are as fine as dust, and are sown in potting mixture* 1 by placing in a groove of a bent card, which is tapped lightly to give an even distribution. Do not cover with soil, but place a sheet of glass and paper over the pot or pan. Water from below by dipping pot. ROOT DIVISION. The *semperflorens* varieties form clumps with many shoots; these are readily separated into pieces consisting of root and shoot, which may be immediately planted in potting mixture* 4. — A. D. H.

INSECT PESTS. Mealybugs are sometimes injurious (*see* COLEUS). Whiteflies can be checked by several fumigations with calcium cyanide, ¼ ounce to 1000 cubic ft., or by sprays for mealybugs.

DISEASES. Root knot, leaf nematode and gray mold are the three common diseases of begonias. For root knot see Root Knot, PLANT DISEASES. The leaf nematode disease is characterized by rusty or dark brown dead areas on the leaves. Control can be obtained by keeping the foliage dry, removing infected leaves and isolating diseased plants. Gray mold causes a rot or blight of leaves and flowers. Sanitation and increased ventilation will give control.

**BELAMCANDA** (bel-am-kan'da). A single Chino-Japanese, perennial herb of the iris family, usually called the blackberry lily, grown for ornament in the open border throughout the country. It has long, sword-shaped, 2-ranked leaves and red-spotted, orange flowers. Flower segments 6, scarcely distinguishable as petals and sepals, the three inner ones shorter than the rest. Fruit a 3-valved capsule,* splitting in the autumn and revealing the blackberry-like seeds. (*Belamcanda* is a Latinized form of an Asiatic vernacular.)

chinensis. Blackberry lily. From 2-4 ft. high. Leaves 10 in. long, 1 in. wide, iris-like. Flowers 1½-2 in. wide, soon withering. Fruit about 1 in. long. Easily grown in any ordinary garden soil and as easily propagated by spring division of its stout rootstock. June.

**BELGIAN ELM** = *Ulmus hollandica belgica*. See ELM.

*BELGICA, -us, -um* (bel'ji-ka). From Belgium.

*BELLA, -us, -um.* Handsome or pretty.

*BELLADONNA* (bel-la-don'na). From Italian for beautiful woman. One plant so named contains a red sap used as a cosmetic. See ATROPA and AMARYLLIS.

**BELLADONNA LILY** = *Amaryllis belladonna*.

**BELLE ISLE CRESS** = *Barbarea verna*.

**BELLFLOWER.** See CAMPANULA, and OSTROWSKIA.

**BELLFLOWER FAMILY** = Campanulaceae.

*BELLIDIOIDES* (bel-lid-i-oy'deez; but *see* OÏDES). Resembling a plant of the genus *Bellium* (which see).

**BELLIS** (bel'lis). A small genus of European herbs, family Compositae, one of them cult. for centuries as the true daisy, and a very popular bedding plant. Leaves mostly basal, forming a tuft in the one below. Flower heads solitary, on a naked stalk, its ray flowers, in the typical form, white or

* Special articles on the subjects indicated by an asterisk (*) will be found at the words so marked.

pink, the center of the head (disk* flowers) yellow. (The name is from the Latin *bella*, pretty.)

Plants for bedding should be raised from seed sown the previous year. It is a perennial, but often treated as a biennial (see BIENNIALS), and often escapes into lawns or borders, or even to roadsides. Its cheerful, early bloom has made it a favorite bedding plant for mass effects and it is also widely used for window boxes. Most of the finer double-flowered varieties, or those with quilled rays, do not come true from seed and should be propagated by division.

**perennis.** The true daisy of history and literature, but here commonly called English daisy or bachelor's-button. Not over 6 in. high. Leaves broadest towards the tip, in basal tufts. Flower heads nearly 2 in. wide, on stiff, erect stalks. Eu. Among the more desirable named forms, some widely used in city parks, are: Double Quilled, Longfellow (white), The Bride, and *var.* **ranunculiflora**, which is double and comes in white, pink, and red.

**BELLIUM** (bel′li-um). A small genus of annual herbs of the Mediterranean region, family Compositae, sometimes grown in rock gardens for their small, solitary, daisy-like heads of white flowers. Leaves in a basal rosette. Ray flowers white, the disk* flowers yellow. The genus differs from *Bellis* only in technical flower characters, and in being annuals. (*Bellium* means resembling a little *Bellis*.)

For culture and uses *see* ROCK GARDEN.

**bellidioides.** Not over 4 in. high with creeping stolons.* Leaves spatula-shaped. Flower heads about ½ in. wide. June.

**minutum.** Shorter, and with narrower leaves. Flower heads about ⅓ in. wide. July.

**BELL-JAR.** A glass, bell-shaped jar with a knob at the top, often used to give the plant over which it is set uniform atmospheric conditions, and to protect it from draughts or other disturbing factors. A modification of the bell-jar is the cloche, in which a small glass tent is made of separate pieces of glass clipped together at the edges. *See* CUTTINGS.

**BELL PEPPER** = *Capsicum frutescens grossum*.

**BELLWORT.** *See* UVULARIA.

**BELOPERONE** (bel-o-per-own′e). A tropical American genus of 30 species of herbs or low shrubs, family Acanthaceae, only one of secondary interest to gardeners. The genus is separated only by technical characters from *Jacobinia*. Leaves opposite,* without marginal teeth. Flowers tubular but irregular* and 2-lipped, crowded in dense spikes and from between relatively showy, overlapping bracts.* Fruit a capsule.* (*Beloperone* is Greek, in allusion to the arrow-shaped anthers.)

The only cult. species is used as a border plant in zones* 8 and 9, elsewhere, but rarely, as an attractive greenhouse plant. It requires plenty of moisture and liquid manure, and should be planted in potting mixture* 4.

**guttata.** Stems several, 12–18 in. high. Leaves ovalish, 1½–2½ in. long, and tapering to a slender stalk. Flowers in nearly cone-like clusters (spikes*), which are about 3 in. long and beset with numerous, reddish-brown bracts,* from between which the flowers are borne. Flowers about 1½ in. long, white, but spotted with purple. Mex.

**BELVEDERE** = *Kochia scoparia*.

**BENCH.** A raised platform in a greenhouse,* in or upon which plants are grown. *Bench* is often used as a verb meaning that plants or seedlings are transferred from propagating beds, from outdoors, or brought from a resting period and planted in, or their pots put on, the bench.

**BEN DAVIS.** *See* APPLE.

**BENDY TREE** = *Thespesia populnea*.

**BENE** = benne; *see* SESAMUM ORIENTALE.

**BENEDICTUS.** Blessed; *see* CNICUS.

**BENEFICIAL INSECTS.** *See* INSECT FRIENDS.

**BENGAL ROSE** = *Rosa chinensis*. *See* Group 5 at ROSE.

**BENGHALENSIS, -e** (ben-gall-en′sis). From Bengal, India.

**BENINCASA** (ben-in-kay′sa). A tender, annual, pumpkin-like and tendril*-bearing, Asiatic vine, belonging to the cucumber family. It is little known here, except as an ornamental, but in China is the source of the Chinese preserving melon (variously called zit-kwa, tunka and Chinese watermelon). The vine is fleshy, creeping, and has forked tendrils.* Leaves alternate,* large and angled. Flowers solitary, yellow, large, the stamens and pistils never in the same flower. Fruit large, melon-like, but without a hard rind. (Named for Giuseppe Benincasa, who founded the botanic garden at Pisa.)

The vine is grown mostly in warm countries, but can be grown here if treated as we do cucumbers or melons.

**hispida.** Wax gourd or white gourd (*see* above for other names). A long-trailing vine, the stem brown-hairy. Leaves broadly oval, heart-shaped at the base, 6–9 in. wide and angled on the margins. Flowers 3–4 in. wide. Fruit round-oblong, hairy, 8–15 in. long. Tropical As.

**BENJAMIN-BUSH** = *Benzoin aestivale*.

**BENNE** (and **Benny**) = *Sesamum orientale*.

**BEN OIL.** *See* MORINGA OLEIFERA.

**BENT GRASS.** *See* AGROSTIS.

**BENZOIN** (ben′zoin). A group of 60 species of aromatic shrubs and trees of the laurel family, most of them tropical, but the one below the well-known spicebush of our swamps and woods. Leaves (in ours) without marginal teeth, alternate.* Flowers small, yellow, blooming long before the leaves unfold, unisexual.* Sepals 6, colored. Petals none. Male flowers with 9 stamens.* Fruit fleshy, nearly round. (*Benzoin* is probably Arabic, and means gum or perfume.)

The spicebush is of the easiest culture in most garden soil. If it has any preference it is for partial shade and a moist site. The bush is particularly attractive very early in the spring for its mass of yellow bloom. Sometimes offered as *Lindera*.

**aestivale.** Spicebush; called also spicewood and Benjamin-bush. A shrub 8–15 ft. high. Leaves more or less oblong, but wedge-shaped at the base, 3–5 in. long. Flowers small, crowded in small, nearly stalkless clusters that are about ⅓ in. long. Me. to Fla. and westward. March–April. Hardy from zone* 3 southward. Fall foliage yellow.

**BERBERIDACEAE** (ber-berry-day′see-e). The barberry family comprises perhaps a dozen genera of herbs or shrubs widely scattered over the north temperate zone, rare elsewhere. Much the most important genus is *Berberis*, comprising the barberries. The only other woody plants of garden interest are found in *Mahonia* and *Nandina*, both of which have compound* leaves, while the barberry has simple* leaves and often spiny branches.

All the rest of the hort. genera are herbs. Some have compound* leaves with many leaflets, like *Caulophyllum*, *Epimedium*, and *Vancouveria*. The rest have simple* leaves that often appear compound because some are lobed, finger-fashion, to or beyond the middle of the blade. (*See* MAYAPPLE, JEFFERSONIA, DIPHYLLEIA.)

Flowers rather large and solitary in the mayapple and *Jeffersonia*, smaller and in variously arranged clusters in all other hort. genera, mostly in racemes.* Fruit a berry or a capsule.*

Technical flower characters: Sepals and petals with their margins overlapping. Petals often replaced by nectaries. Ovary superior, 1-celled, its style short or none.

**BERBERIDOPSIS** (ber-berry-dop′sis). A single Chilean shrub, half vine-like, belonging to the family Flacourtiaceae, and grown outdoors in southern Calif. for its evergreen foliage and red flowers. Leaves alternate,* stalked and toothed. Flowers long-stalked, in clusters (racemes*), the cluster with many bracts. Petals, sepals and bracts scarcely distinguishable from one another, totaling 9–15 segments. Stamens 7–10. Fruit a berry. (*Berberidopsis* is Greek for like *Berberis*.)

The plant will grow in a variety of soils, but if grown in the greenhouse use potting mixture* 4, and keep in a cool house. Propagated by spring-sown seeds, by green wood cuttings or by layering in the fall.

**corallina.** A low shrub inclined to sprawl or climb. Leaves oblongish, with a heart-shaped base, 2–3 in. long, spiny-toothed. Flowers nearly round, about ½ in. in diameter, the bracted* raceme about 4 in. long.

**BERBERIS** (ber′ber-iss). The barberries (family Berberidaceae) are of first-rate hort. importance. The genus in-

---

* Special articles on the subjects indicated by an asterisk (*) will be found at the words so marked.

cludes upwards of 175 species of evergreen or deciduous shrubs, all more or less spiny, and scattered throughout the north temperate zone (mostly in As.), with a few in North Af. and S.A. They have yellow wood and inner bark (cambium), and usually 3-branched spines in most of the axils.* Leaves simple,* appearing in small clusters at the ends of short spurs. Flowers yellow, in longish clusters (racemes*) or in closer clusters, all spring-blooming. Petals and stamens 6, the latter irritable and explosively discharging the pollen when touched. Fruit a berry. (*Berberis* is the Latinized form of an Arabic vernacular for the fruit.)

The barberry is used for its foliage, which turns to scarlets, orange or yellow in the fall, its flowers, and for its handsome fruit, which in *B. sieboldi* and *B. thunbergi*, lasts through the winter. In the others the fruits shrivel or lose their color late in the fall.

A number are evergreens and not quite hardy in extreme winters (*see* Hardiness, notes below). Others, like the Japanese barberry, are widely planted for hedges or as specimen plants for the gorgeous autumnal foliage and persistent red berries. The box-barberry is a favorite plant for edging, where a low and much cheaper, but deciduous, substitute for real box is desirable.

There is a wide variety of color, stature and habit to be found in the species below, which are the leading ones of over 50 known to be cult. in America. They are horticulturally so desirable that it is a pity that some must be rigorously excluded from wheat-growing regions. The European and some other barberries are an alternate host* for a serious wheat rust, and have been much exterminated because of this, especially *B. vulgaris*. Those that serve as hosts for rust are so marked below. The others may be considered free of the wheat rust at least.

Most of the species grow readily in ordinary garden soil, and are easily raised from seed. June-made cuttings, also, may be rooted in moist sand, preferably in a shaded hotbed.

For the plants with compound* leaves and no spines, sometimes credited to *Berberis*, *see* MAHONIA. These are also called barberry. All the species below drop their leaves in the fall unless noted as evergreen.

**amurensis.** From 3–8 ft. high, and related to the common barberry of Eu. (*B. vulgaris*), but with the leaves brighter green and with a more upright habit. Eastern As. Hardy from zone* 2 southward. Sometimes rust-infected.

**atrocarpa.** An evergreen shrub 2–5 ft. high, the young twigs reddish. Leaves elliptic or oblong, dark green above, paler beneath, spiny-margined, 1½–4 in. long. Flowers about ½ in. wide. Fruit bluish-black. China. Hardy from zone* 5 southward, possibly in sheltered parts of zone* 4.

**buxifolia.** Magellan barberry. Upright, not over 8 ft., and usually less in cult. Leaves evergreen, wedge-shaped at the base, prickle-tipped, ½–1¼ in. long. Flowers only one or two in a cluster, orange-yellow. Fruit dark purple. Southern Chile. Hardy from zone* 4 southward. One of the best of the evergreen sorts and known, also, in a compact dwarf form and also in another where the spines are longer than the leaves.

**canadensis.** Allegheny or Canada barberry. A native shrub much resembling the common barberry of Eu. (*B. vulgaris*), but with the leaves grayish beneath. In the woods, Va. to Ga. and Mo. Hardy from zone* 4 southward. Sometimes rust-infected.

**darwini.** Handsome evergreen shrub 5–8 ft. high. Leaves oblongish, or broader towards the tip, ½–1½ in., rather remotely, but spiny-toothed, and with a 3-pronged spine at the tip. Flowers golden-yellow in drooping clusters (racemes*). Fruit dark purple. Chile. Hardy from zone* 6 southward. A related, somewhat more hardy species, is *B. ilicifolia*. It has orange-yellow flowers in shorter clusters, and is perhaps hardy in zone* 5. Both are offered by many nurserymen, but the plant sold as *B. ilicifolia* is usually *Mahoberberis neuberti*.

**gagnepaini.** An evergreen shrub 4–6 ft. high, the branches spreading. Leaves narrow, lance-shaped, 1–3 in. long, with a wavy, but spiny-toothed margin. Flowers in clusters of 3–10, about ½ in. wide. Fruit bluish-black, with a bloom. Western China. Hardy from zone* 5 southward. Sometimes rust-infected.

**ilicifolia.** *See* BERBERIS DARWINI.

**julianae.** Wintergreen barberry. An upright evergreen shrub 4–6 ft. high. Leaves narrowly elliptic, 1½–3 in. long, the margins toothed and spiny, dark green above, pale beneath. Flowers in close clusters. Fruit bluish-black, with a bloom. Central China. Hardy from zone* 4 southward, the hardiest of the evergreen species, and one of the most popular of all the newer Chinese species.

**sargentiana.** Evergreen, the branches somewhat spreading, not usually over 5 ft. high. Leaves elliptic or oblong, 2–4½ in. long, closely toothed and the teeth spiny, dark green above. Flowers in close clusters, each about ½ in. wide. Fruit bluish-black, with a bloom. Central China. Hardy from zone* 6 southward.

**sieboldi.** A low shrub, rarely over 4 ft. high. Leaves oblong or broader towards the tip, 1½–3 in. long, not spiny-margined, but densely fringed along the leaf-edge with hairs. Flowers 3–6 in a cluster. Fruit shining red, winter-persisting. Japan. Hardy from zone* 4 southward. Fall foliage red. Sometimes rust-infected.

**stenophylla.** Evergreen and from 6–8 ft. high. Leaves narrowly lance-shaped, ¾–1½ in. long, spiny-tipped, but with a rolled margin, dark green above, whitish beneath. Flowers about ½ in. wide, in clusters of 2–6, golden-yellow. Of hybrid origin. Hardy from zone* 5, and in sheltered parts of zone* 4 southward.

**thunbergi.** The Japanese barberry, more widely cult. than almost any other shrub, and usually 4–6 ft. high when mature. Branches ultimately purple-brown. Leaves variable, usually broader towards the tip, ½–1½ in. long, without teeth. Flowers yellow, but red-tinged outside, about ⅓ in. wide, solitary or in close clusters of 2–5. Fruit bright red, winter-persisting. Japan. Hardy from the southern part of zone* 3 southward. Autumn foliage brilliant scarlet. There are several hort. varieties, some with variegated leaves. The best-known one, *var.* **minor**, commonly called box-barberry, is a dwarf, dense form with smaller leaves and rarely exceeds 15 in. in height if trimmed, otherwise it may reach 3 ft.

**triacanthophora.** Low, evergreen shrub, rarely more than 3½ ft. high. Leaves narrow, 1–2½ in. long, less than ½ in. wide, finely and bristly toothed, green above, bluish-gray beneath. Flowers whitish-yellow, tinged with red. Fruit blue-black, with a slight bloom. Central China. Hardy from zone* 4 southward.

**verruculosa.** Evergreen and not over 3 ft. high, the branches warty. Leaves ovalish or elliptic, ¾–1½ in. long, glossy-green, remotely spiny-toothed, and pale beneath. Flowers larger than in most barberries, golden-yellow, about ¾ in. wide. Fruit bluish-black, with a bloom. Western China. Hardy from zone* 4 southward.

**vulgaris.** The common or European barberry. A somewhat arching shrub 5–9 ft. high. Leaves elliptic or oblongish, 1–2 in. long, green but not shining green. Flowers in short-stalked clusters (racemes*). Fruit bright red or purple. Eu. Hardy from zone* 2 throughout the country and frequently naturalized. Much less valuable as a garden plant than most of the others. It resembles *B. amurensis* and *B. canadensis*, and like them is pretty apt to be rust-infected.

**wilsonae.** A prostrate or erect, half-evergreen, and very spiny shrub, sometimes 6 ft. high. Leaves ⅓–¾ in. long, without teeth, but tipped with a short prickle, pale green. Flowers golden-yellow, about ⅓ in. wide, in various sorts of small clusters. Fruit coral-red or salmon-colored. Western China. Hardy from zone* 5 southward. Sometimes rust-infected. The variety sold as Tom Thumb, with slightly toothed leaves and prolific red fruit, apparently belongs to this species.

**BERCHEMIA** (ber-kee'mi-a). A small genus of woody vines, family Rhamnaceae, grown for the ornamental foliage. Leaves alternate,* without marginal teeth but with conspicuous parallel veins. Flowers greenish or greenish-white, in branched clusters (panicles*), but small and inconspicuous (for detailed structure *see* RHAMNACEAE). Fruit fleshy. (*Berchemia* is of unknown origin.)

The species below are moderately decorative, but not high-climbing vines, as cult., and without special soil preferences. They may be propagated by spring-sown seeds or root cuttings or by cuttings of ripened wood in autumn.

**racemosa.** A woody vine 10–15 ft. long. Leaves ovalish, somewhat heart-shaped at the base, 1½–2½ in. long, green above but paler beneath. Flowers greenish, the clusters about 4 in. long. Fruit red at first, ultimately black. Japan and Formosa. Hardy from zone* 5 southward.

**scandens.** Supplejack. Climbing to 15–20 ft. in cult., but to the tree-tops in the wild. Leaves elliptic or oblong-oval, not over 2 in. long. Flowers greenish-white, the clusters scarcely 2 in. long. Fruit bluish-black. In woods Va. to Fla. and Tex. Hardy from zone* 5 southward.

**BERGAMOT.** *See* MONARDA and CITRUS BERGAMIA.

**BERGAMOT LIME** = *Triphasia trifolia*.

**BERGAMOT MINT** = *Mentha citrata*. *See* MINT.

**BERGENIA** (ber-gen'i-a). Half a dozen Asiatic, perennial herbs, family Saxifragaceae, three of which are grown in the border for their ornamental foliage and very early-blooming pink or white flowers. They have thickened root-stocks and from them the plants grow in pretty dense clumps or colonies. Leaves mostly basal, thick and fleshy, pitted, half evergreen, the stalks with a sheathing base. Flowers large, in nodding clusters (panicles* or racemes*), the stalk thick and fleshy. (Named for K. A. von Bergen, a German botanist.)

Closely related to *Saxifraga*, grown like them, and all the species below are often offered as *Saxifraga*. The first two are hardy over most of the country, but are better protected with a light straw mulch in the North. *B. ligulata* is not certainly hardy north of zone* 5. The genus is sometimes known as *Megasea*.

**cordifolia.** A stout, fleshy herb 12–18 in. high. Leaves thick, shining, nearly round, wavy-margined, somewhat heart-shaped at the base. Flowers rose-pink, the clusters among the leaves. Siberia. There are also white and purple-flowered hort. forms.

**crassifolia.** Siberian tea. Similar to the above, but the leaves longer

* Special articles on the subjects indicated by an asterisk (*) will be found at the words so marked.

and with the blade extending down the leafstalk. Flowers rose-pink or lilac, the clusters standing above the foliage. Eastern As.

ligulata. A very showy plant with large leaves nearly round but tapering towards the base, the margins somewhat scalloped and fringed with hairs. Flowers white, or rose-purple, in nodding clusters (racemes*). Himalayas. Not certainly hardy north of zone* 5, but sometimes so with protection. There are several named hort. varieties and forms, a very striking one being var. leichtlini, with crimson leaves and rose-colored flowers.

**BERGEROCACTUS** (ber'jer-o-kak-tus). A single species of cactus found in southern and Lower Calif. and cult. for its habit of making large colonies or patches and for its day-blooming, yellow flowers. The only species, **B. emoryi**, is an erect-growing plant, 1–2 ft. high, with many closely ribbed, cylindric branches covered with sharp, yellow spines, the stems not over 2 in. thick. Flowers about ¾ in. wide. Useful for decorative plantings in desert gardens and scarcely cult. otherwise. (Named for Alwin Berger, a horticulturist and botanist long interested in succulents.)

**BERMUDA BUTTERCUP** = *Oxalis cernua*.

**BERMUDA GRASS** = *Cynodon dactylon*.

**BERMUDA LILY.** The Easter lily. *See* LILIUM.

**BERMUDA PALMETTO** = *Sabal blackburniana*.

*BERMUDIANA, -us, -um* (ber-mew-di-ā'na). From Bermuda.

*BEROLINENSIS, -e* (ber-o-lin-en'sis). From Berlin.

**BERRY.** A confusing term. Commonly, almost any fleshy fruit such as strawberry, blackberry, raspberry, cranberry, currant or blueberry, but technically the first three are not berries at all. In the strict botanical sense a berry is a fleshy or pulpy fruit that does not usually split open, has few or many seeds, but no stone. It always develops from a single enlarged ovary. Typical examples of true berries are currant, blueberry, cranberry, grape, tomato, and eggplant. *See* STRAWBERRY. *See also* PEPO.

**BERSEEM** = *Trifolium alexandrinum*. *See* CLOVER.

**BERTHOLLETIA** (ber-thoe-lesh'i-a). A genus of South American trees, family Lechythidaceae, of no garden interest except to those living in the warmest parts of zone* 9. Of the two known species, one, **B. excelsa**, is the Brazil-nut or Pará-nut, the seeds of which (often called nigger-toes) are the Brazil-nuts of commerce. It is a tall tree, needing heat, moisture and a rich soil for proper development. Leaves leathery, oblong, nearly 2 ft. long. Flowers cream-white, in spike-like clusters (racemes*), with no petals, but colored sepals. Fruit a hard, woody, brown structure about 4 in. in diameter, containing 18–24 of the familiar nuts. (Named for C. L. Berthollet, French chemist.)

**BERTOLONIA** (ber-toe-low'ni-a). A small, Brazilian genus of showy-foliaged herbs, family Melastomaceae, grown in greenhouses for their attractive, opposite,* 3–9-veined and sometimes banded leaves. Flowers rose-colored or purple, in one-sided clusters (racemes*). Petals 5. Stamens 10. Fruit a 3-valved pod (capsule*), enclosed by the persistent calyx. (Named for Antonio Bertoloni, Italian botanist.)

The species below are attractive foliage plants that need a warm (70°) greenhouse, plenty of moisture and a partially shaded section of the house. Use potting mixture* 4. Easily propagated by cuttings in moist sand over bottom-heat.

maculata. Stems low or creeping, densely covered with rusty hairs. Leaves with magenta or purple bands along the veins, hairy, generally green, but sometimes spotted with color. Flowers rose-pink.

marmorata. Similar but not so hairy-stemmed and with whitish bands along the leaf-veins. Flowers purple.

*BESSARABICA, -us, -um* (bess-a-rab'i-ka). From Bessarabia, in eastern Rumania.

**BESSERA ELEGANS** = *Milla biflora*.

**BETA.** *See* BEET.

*BETACEA, -us, -um* (bee-tay'see-a). Beet-like.

**BETCHEL'S CRAB.** *See* MALUS IOENSIS.

**BETELNUT, BETEL PALM.** *See* ARECA CATECHU.

**BETHLEHEM SAGE** = *Pulmonaria saccharata*.

**BETHROOT** = *Trillium erectum*.

*BETONICIFOLIA, -us, -um* (bee-ton-i-ki-fō'li-a). With leaves like a plant of the genus *Betonica*, weedy herbs of no garden interest.

**BETONY.** *See* STACHYS.

**BETULA.** *See* BIRCH.

**BETULACEAE** (bet-you-lay'see-e). The birch family, often called alder or hazel family, contains only trees and shrubs of the northern hemisphere. Five of its six known genera are cultivated for ornament, or for the nuts, in the hazel. All have alternate* leaves with relatively straight (not curved or arching) veins. Male and female flowers in separate catkins on the same plant. Male catkins, long, in small groups and hanging. Female catkins shorter, almost headlike. Fruit a small nut with membranous wings in the birch (*Betula*) but large and edible, and without the wing, in the hazel (*Corylus*).

The other hort. genera include the hornbeam (*Carpinus*), Ostrya (the hop hornbeam), and the alder (*Alnus*).

Technical flower characters: Petals none. Female catkins with or without a minute calyx; ovary 2-celled, each cavity of it with a single ovule. Male catkins with a 2–4-parted calyx in the birches and alders, but without a calyx in the hornbeam and hazel.

*BETULAEFOLIA, -us, -um* (bet-you-lee-fō'li-a). With leaves like a birch.

*BETULINA, -us, -um* (bet-you-ly'na). Birch-like.

*BETULOIDES* (bet-you-loy'deez; but *see* OÏDES). Resembling a birch.

*BETULUS.* An old name for a birch-like tree, or perhaps for the birch itself. *See* CARPINUS.

**BICHLORIDE OF MERCURY.** *See* Mercury at FUNGICIDES.

*BICOLOR* (by'color, also bick'o-lor). Two-colored.

*BICORNIS, -e* (by-cor'nis). Two-horned.

**BIDENS** (by'dens). A large genus of somewhat weedy herbs, family Compositae, generally called bur-marigold, stick-tight or tickseed. The only species of garden interest is **B. ferulaefolia**, a Mexican annual with yellow flowers. They have usually divided or dissected leaves with toothed segments. Flowers yellow, with bright rays in the one below (often rayless in some native weeds). Fruit a small, flat, 2-pronged and barbed achene,* which, in our weeds, is a familiar fall pest to woolen clothed walkers. (*Bidens* is Latin for 2-toothed, in reference to the fruit.)

*Bidens ferulaefolia* is an easily cult. annual. Sow the seeds in any ordinary garden soil, after danger of frost is past. For **B. frondosa** (often called beggar-ticks, boot-jack, or Spanish needles), which is a troublesome weed, *see* Beggar-ticks in the list at WEEDS.

ferulaefolia. Smooth and branching annual herb. Leaves dissected into narrow segments. Flower heads about ¾ in. wide, in close or open clusters (corymbs*), bright yellow. Mex. Mid-summer.

**BIENNIAL.** Requiring two growing seasons for the completion of its life. True biennials die after they have set seed. (*See* ANNUAL and PERENNIAL.) For the garden uses and culture of biennial plants *see* BIENNIALS.

**BIENNIALS.** Plants listed as biennials, as a class, are not difficult of culture. The chief objection to them is their brief period of life. Of the ornamental kinds the majority bloom the second year from seed sown the previous mid-summer. A few of the hardier sorts are treated as perennials, seed being sown directly into the ground where they are to remain during their lifetime. This is satisfactory only in localities where winter-killing or rotting of the crowns need not be feared. Foxgloves and Canterbury bells (*see* CAMPANULA MEDIUM) are examples of biennials that nearly always rot when the seed is sown in the aforesaid manner. Short-lived perennials are in many instances, for convenience, classified as biennials and cult. as such. Examples of flowering plants that are commonly grown as biennials are Canter-

---

* Special articles on the subjects indicated by an asterisk (*) will be found at the words so marked.

bury bells, hollyhocks, foxgloves, English daisies, some forget-me-nots, honesty, *Lychnis* (some species), horn poppy, verbascums, the improved sweet-Williams, pansies, and Siberian wallflowers.

The best and safest way to treat biennials is to plant the seed in June or July in flats. Later prick out and transplant the seedlings to 3-in. pots and put in the cold frame. Do not transplant them to the garden from the flats. Plunge the pots up to the rim in soil, allowing 8 in. between them. Keep a uniform temperature throughout the winter. Cover with boards or regulation hotbed cover. A light mulch of dry leaves, marsh hay or strawy litter should be placed around the crowns to keep them dry, and among the foliage in such a way that the centers are not smothered. Transfer to beds or borders when the weather permits in the spring. Should you have failed to start your biennials the previous midsummer, try planting them in flats in Feb. Prick them out as soon as the tiny second leaves appear and again transplant, once or twice more, to insure continuous growth. Feb. planting is not, however, so satisfactory a method. If your flats or young plants are grown under the ordinary conditions of home and not in a greenhouse, newspapers may be used as night coverings.

Where biennials are to be included in the mixed border, they must be treated as annual plants. The young seedlings should be placed in the desired position where they are to bloom, and renewed by other plants the following year. Even those biennials which are hardy and self-sowing, such as the hollyhocks, are not to be depended upon. Second-year plants in many cases have a tendency to be weak and straggling, with much smaller blooms. The larger plants should be massed at the back, with the low-growing sorts in the front of the border, to facilitate handling. By so doing the ground may be prepared for their occupancy with the least amount of disturbance of the perennials and hardy shrubs.

Canterbury bells and the "cup and saucer" form are indispensable garden flowers which like a good rich soil and last much longer in bloom if planted in a half-shady place. Sow the seed in flats in separate rows as to color, and water thoroughly, transplanting later to the cold frame. The "cup and saucer" type make excellent pot and conservatory plants for table decoration.

The improved sweet-William (*Dianthus barbatus*) is really a perennial but does much better when treated as a biennial. As a matter of fact, all the perennial species of *Dianthus* should be renewed every two or three years, preferably by seeds when named varieties are not included. The rich color of the flowers produces a splendid effect in beds and borders.

The common foxgloves are usually treated as biennials, seed sown early in the spring producing flowering plants the following year. *Digitalis purpurea* and its horticultural varieties are great favorites for general plantings, making excellent accent plants for the border. Hollyhocks are best used either in massed plantings or as background for low-growing plants.

Forget-me-nots may be planted out-of-doors, in moderately moist soil, if given winter protection. The annual sorts bloom the first year from seed; the biennials bloom early the second year. Pansies give their best bloom on young plants. Grown as perennials, with care they may survive for many years, but new stock should be kept coming on every year if the large choice blooms are to be had. Seed sown in mid-August gives blooming plants in early spring; seed sown in January makes blooming plants by early summer. Siberian wallflowers are sometimes handled as annuals, as they will bloom during the summer from seed sown early in the spring. Their dwarf height makes them good rock garden subjects.

*BIENNIS, -e* (by-en'nis). Biennial (which see).

*BIFLORA, -us, -um* (by-flow'ra). Two-flowered.

*BIFOLIA, -us, -um* (by-fō'li-a). Two-leaved.

*BIFURCATA, -us, -um* (by-fur-kay'ta). Twice-forked.

**BIGARREAU CHERRY** = *Prunus avium duracina.*

**BIG-CONE PINE** = *Pinus coulteri.* See PINE.

**BIGENERIC HYBRID.** The result of a cross between plants belonging to different genera. They are known between *Crinum* and *Amaryllis* (see AMARCRINUM), the radish and cabbage, *Selenicereus* and *Heliocereus*, between *Cytisus* and *Laburnum*, *Sorbus* and *Aronia*, *Sorbus* and *Pyrus*, and between several orchid genera. See BRASSOCATTLEYA, LAELIOCATTLEYA and BRASSOLAELIA.

**BIG LAUREL** = *Magnolia grandiflora.*

**BIG MARIGOLD** = *Tagetes erecta.* See MARIGOLD.

**BIGNONIA** (big-known'i-a). A beautiful woody vine, usually called the cross-vine, is the only species now included in the genus *Bignonia*, once considered as including many other plants (see below). The cross-vine, or **Bignonia capreolata,** or trumpet-flower as it is sometimes called, is an evergreen, high-climbing, woody vine. It has compound* leaves with 2 stalked leaflets which are without marginal teeth, and a terminal tendril.* Leaflets 4–6 in. long. Flowers funnel-shaped, but slightly irregular, about 2 in. long, reddish-orange but pale within, grouped in clusters (cymes*) in the leaf-axils.* Fruit a long, narrow, slightly flattened pod, 5–8 in. long. (Named for the Abbé Jean Paul Bignon, court librarian to Louis XIV.)

The cross-vine is a handsome creeper (see VINES) found wild from Va. and southern Ill. to Fla. and La. It is hardy from zone* 4 southward, and is sometimes merely winter-killed north of this.

Other plants of the family Bignoniaceae, once, and sometimes still, credited to the genus *Bignonia*, are:

*Bignonia buccinatoria* = *Phaedranthus buccinatorius.*
  "   *grandiflora* = *Campsis chinensis.* See TRUMPET-CREEPER.
  "   *radicans* = *Campsis radicans.* See TRUMPET-CREEPER.
  "   *speciosa* = *Clytostoma calystegioides.*
  "   *stans* = *Stenolobium stans.*
  "   *tweediana* = *Doxantha unguis-cati.*
  "   *unguis-cati* = "           "
  "   *venusta* = *Pyrostegia ignea.*

**BIGNONIACEAE** (big-known-i-ā'see-ee). The trumpet-creeper family, often called catalpa or cross-vine family, comprises nearly 100 genera and over 600 species of widely distributed trees, shrubs and woody vines, many of which are handsome garden plants. The only herbaceous hort. genus is *Incarvillea*.

While most are tropical, a few well-known ones are temperate zone plants, notably the trumpet-creeper (*Campsis*), the catalpa, and *Bignonia* or cross-vine.

Leaves opposite, simple* or of many leaflets. The only hort. genera with simple leaves are *Chilopsis*, *Catalpa* and the calabash (*Crescentia*), all the others having compound leaves and many of the vines having the terminal leaflet replaced by tendrils.* Flowers perfect,* nearly always in showy clusters, more or less tubular or funnel-shaped and always slightly irregular* or two-lipped.* Fruit usually a longish pod, splitting lengthwise, its seeds usually winged.

Upright trees and shrubs of garden interest are found in *Spathodea*, *Stenolobium*, *Tabebuia*, *Jacaranda*, *Kigelia*, *Oroxylon*, and *Parmentiera*. But woody vines are among the most handsome of the plants in this family: see CLYTOSTOMA, CYDISTA, ECCREMOCARPUS, PANDOREA, PHAEDRANTHUS, PITHECOCTENIUM, PYROSTEGIA, TECOMARIA, and DISTICTIS. See also TECOMA.

Technical flower characters: Ovary superior,* the style slender, with a 2-lobed stigma. Calyx tubular, its lobes blunt or 5-toothed. Corolla slightly irregular, its five lobes unequal. Stamens usually 4, rarely 5 or 6, and if so, one or more sterile.

*BIGNONIOIDES* (big-known-i-oy'deez; but see OÏDES). Resembling the cross-vine (*Bignonia*).

**BIG SHAGBARK** = *Carya laciniosa.*

**BIG-TREE** = *Sequoia gigantea.*

*BIHAI.* A tropical American vernacular name for the wild plantain (*Heliconia bihai*).

*BIJUGA, -us, -um* (by-jew'ga). Yoked; two in a pair.

**BILLBERGIA** (bill-ber'ji-a). A genus of 40 or more species of tropical American air plants (see EPIPHYTES) be-

---

* Special articles on the subjects indicated by an asterisk (*) will be found at the words so marked.

longing to the family Bromeliaceae, a few of which are cult. by fanciers for their foliage and showy, bracted* flower clusters. Only the one below is at all common in greenhouse collections and is also offered by florists. They have spiny, pineapple-like leaves in a basal rosette from which arises a long, branching flower cluster. Flowers with a 3-parted calyx,* 3 petals, and 6 long-protruding stamens.* Beneath the flowers and at many of the joints of the cluster are showy bracts,* scarlet and narrow in the one below. Fruit fleshy. (Named for J. G. Billberg, Swedish botanist.)

Billbergias need a warm, moist greenhouse (70°–80°) and plenty of moisture at the roots while they are actively growing and blooming (spring and summer). In the winter they need less watering, and when actually in flower, it is better to reduce the amount of water. They should be planted in wooden or latticed boxes, in hanging baskets, or in pans. If pans or pots are used, be sure that there is at least 2 in. of broken flower pots in the bottom. Use one half of potting mixture* 3 and one half fern roots or coconut fiber to which should be added a little charcoal. It is better to hang the boxes or pans about 2 ft. from the greenhouse roof than to grow billbergias on the bench.

**nutans.** A stemless air plant with long, linear leaves (1–2 ft.) remotely and finely toothed on the margin and finely striped on the back. Flowers 4–8 in a drooping cluster, the flowers green but blue-edged. Brazil.

**BINDWEED.** See CONVOLVULUS.

**BING.** A cherry variety. See CHERRY.

**BIOTA.** See THUJA ORIENTALIS.

**BIPINNATA, -us, -um** (by-pin-nay′ta). Twice pinnate* or twice pinnately cut; that is, the segments or leaflets arranged feather-fashion.

**BIRCH.** Medium or tall trees (rarely shrubs) of more economic importance for timber or aromatic properties than for ornament. All belong to the genus **Betula** (bet′you-la), of the family Betulaceae, which comprises over 40 species, mostly North American or Asiatic. Leaves alternate,* always toothed and with relatively straight veins. Flowers without petals, in early-blooming catkins or spikes, or (in the female flowers) in small, cone-like but leafy-bracted clusters (strobiles*), the bracts 3-pointed and dropping at maturity with the minute nut. (*Betula* is the classical name of the birch.)

Most of the birches are not particular as to soil, and few of them are of much value as lawn specimens except the beautiful white-barked sorts from N.A. and the Old World. Unfortunately, all are rather short-lived. Grouped with evergreens the white or paper birch makes beautiful winter pictures. Some of the weeping and cut-leaved hort. forms are also widely planted for ornament. Aromatic, as used below, means the familiar birch-bark odor which is found, however, only in some species. The trees are easily propagated by seeds (fresh sown or stratified); they are also easily grafted. All the birches are wind-pollinated.

**B. alba.** A common name in nursery catalogs. It applies to the white-barked canoe birch (*B. papyrifera*) of N.A. and the European white birch (*B. pendula*).

**B. fontinalis.** Red birch, also called black birch. More or less shrubby tree, usually in clumps and (in cult.) not over 25 ft. high, the bark aromatic. Leaves broadly oval, double-toothed, 1–2 in. long, glandular*-dotted on the under side. Female flower cluster (strobile*) nearly as large as the leaves. Alaska to Ore. and Colo. Hardy from zone* 4 northward.

**B. lenta.** Sweet birch; called also black birch and cherry birch. An aromatic tree up to 75 ft. high, the bark dark, reddish-brown. Leaves oblong-oval, 3–5 in. long, tapering at the tip and heart-shaped at the base, double-toothed. Female flower cluster (strobile*) ⅓ as long as the leaf. Me. to Ala. Hardy from zone* 3 southward.

**B. lutea.** Yellow birch. A most important timber tree but less so horticulturally, often 80–90 ft. high, the bark yellowish and characteristically unrolling like shavings, aromatic. Leaves ovalish or oval-oblong, 4–7 in. long, with pale hairs on the veins beneath. Female flower cluster (strobile*) about ⅓ as long as the leaves. Newfoundland to Ga. and Tenn., mostly in the mountains. Hardy from zone* 3 southward, but does not like the heat of the coastal plain.

**B. nigra.** River birch; called also red birch. A tree 60–80 ft. high, its reddish-brown, ragged bark not aromatic. Leaves somewhat rhombic or ovalish, 1½–3½ in. long, doubly toothed, whitish below when young. Female flower cluster (strobile*) about half as long as the leaves. Mass. to Fla. and westward, and hardy throughout the country, but it needs a moist or even wet site.

**B. papyracea** = *Betula papyrifera*.

**B. papyrifera.** Canoe or paper birch; it is the white birch of eastern N.A. A tree up to 90 ft. or more, its brilliantly white bark not aromatic. Leaves more or less oval, but narrowed or wedge-shaped at the base, 3–5 in. long, double-toothed. Female flower cluster (strobile*) about ⅓ the leaf length. Almost throughout the cooler parts of N.A. and preferring zone* 4 and northward in cult.

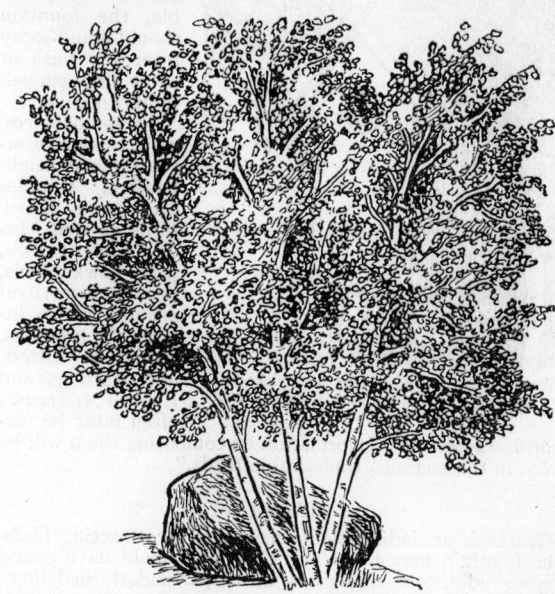

The white bark of these birches makes a very striking winter contrast against dark evergreens.

**B. pendula.** European white birch. A tree resembling our canoe or paper birch, but not so tall, and in old trees with more or less drooping branches, and with resinous twigs. Leaves rhombic or ovalish, mostly wedge-shaped at the base, doubly toothed, 3–5 in. long. Female flower cluster (strobile*) 1–1½ in. long. Eu. and As. Minor. Hardy from zone* 2 southward, but not long-lived. This is the commonest white birch of cult. It is found in many attractive forms, especially one with finely divided leaves, another with still more drooping branches (nearly a weeping form) and one with a compact, bushy crown having no drooping branches.

**B. populifolia.** Gray birch. A weedy and horticulturally useless tree included here because its similarity to *B. papyrifera* often leads to unscrupulous substitution. The gray birch is (in maturity) much smaller, has dirty black bark (brilliant white in youth) and its more or less triangular leaves are broadest at the base. Nova Scotia to Del. Useful only where other trees will not thrive. It will grow in very poor, stony soil, or even on sandy or cindery wastes, but is short-lived.

**BIRCH FAMILY.** A small family of shrubs and trees comprising, in the hort. genera, the birch, alder, hazel, hornbeam and the hop-hornbeam. For the characters of the family see BETULACEAE.

**BIRD BATH.** See BIRDS.

**BIRD BILLS.** See DODECATHEON.

**BIRD BOXES.** See BIRDS.

**BIRD CHERRY** = *Prunus padus*.

**BIRD-OF-PARADISE BUSH** = *Poinciana gilliesi*.

**BIRD-OF-PARADISE FLOWER** = *Strelitzia reginae*.

**BIRD PEPPER** = *Capsicum frutescens*.

**BIRDS.** Birds are an attractive and very useful garden feature which can be increased by attention to a few fundamentals. Protection, food, water, and nesting sites must be provided.

### PROTECTION

About gardens cats are the worst enemies of small birds. They are natural predators, no matter how well fed. Stray cats may be trapped in box traps and turned over to the Humane Societies, or killed humanely.

Nest boxes and feeding trays placed in trees or on poles may be made secure against feline depredations by metal

---

* Special articles on the subjects indicated by an asterisk (*) will be found at the words so marked.

bands a foot in width and six feet from the ground. Bird baths and fountains should be of metal, concrete, or stone, and afford the best protection if two or more feet above the ground. Where this is not possible, the fountain should stand away from any bush or plant large enough to afford cover.

Wren's bird house. If used for chickadees or nuthatches make the hole larger as shown by the dotted lines.

Cat-proof fences, while expensive, often prevent neighborhood troubles and save many birds as well. Individual crows, jays, hawks, owls, or other natural enemies which invade the premises, should be killed, and starlings and English sparrows often must be vigorously persecuted. Information on combating them will be given in the section "Undesirable Birds."

### WATER

Water is an indispensable necessity in attracting birds. The fountain may be of any size, but should have gently sloping sides, otherwise many birds, particularly fledglings, will be drowned.

### NESTING SITES

Most birds naturally nest in trees or bushes, and the normal plantings provide their requirements. Ground-nesting birds, likewise, need no special provision. Bluebirds, wrens, swallows, martins, woodpeckers, chickadees, and nuthatches, will take advantage of artificial nest boxes. For wrens, boxes should be four inches square and eight inches deep, with an entrance-opening one inch in diameter. Chickadees and nuthatches need the same size box with one-fourth inch larger entrance. Bluebirds and swallows should have boxes five inches square, eight inches in depth, with a one-and-one-half-inch doorway, while martins require dimensions a trifle larger, with a two-and-one-half-inch opening.

Bluebirds need a larger house than wrens. See text for dimensions.

Swallows and martins will use houses containing several apartments, and prefer them located in the open on a tall pole. All others prefer individual houses which are not too close to those already occupied. These boxes should face away from the prevailing wind and rain, with the entrance-opening well toward the top, leaving the cavity available for the nest. Designs may suit personal taste, although frequently birds prefer structures of natural wood or stained lumber to painted ones. Robins, phoebes, and barn swallows will often build their nests on shelves placed about buildings, or in trees. These can be any type, though those built with a roof and open sides afford the most protection.

### FOOD SUPPLY

Even when water, shelter, and protection are available, an adequate food supply must be provided to increase the bird population. This can be accomplished by selecting trees and shrubs that furnish edible berries or fruits.

Among those groups which will grow over most of this country and which will furnish a food supply for summer and early fall, are raspberries, blackberries, mulberries, wild cherries, wild grapes, bush honeysuckles, dogwoods, sour gum, elderberries, Juneberries, and Virginia creeper. Buckwheat, when in seed, is also an excellent food.

Valuable ornamentals which carry their fruits far into the winter and provide emergency cold-weather rations for birds, are barberries, cotoneasters, hawthorns, mountain-ash, roses, sumac, viburnum, snowberries, and holly. In each group are some forms which will grow in almost any part of this country. Any local nurseryman will recommend those best suited to your garden.

Food trays and boxes placed on posts, hung in trees, or made as window shelves, will attract juncos, towhees, woodpeckers, chickadees, nuthatches, and many others. These feeding stations should be supplied with suet for insect-eating birds, and wheat, wheat screenings, hemp, sunflower seed, or millet for the seed-eating birds. Sliced apple, dried raisins, and lettuce leaves, are also often appreciated by the feathered folk, and water should be provided when not available naturally.

A several-chambered house on a pole or in a tree is preferred by martins and swallows.

By providing these four essentials one may expect to attract woodpeckers, swallows, thrushes, sparrows, orioles, chickadees, nuthatches, wrens, and thrashers, as nesting birds; while in winter quail, jays, blackbirds, sparrows, thrushes, waxwings, grosbeaks, chickadees, nuthatches and many others, are possibilities. The number and variety attracted will vary according to geographic and climatic conditions.

### BIRD NUISANCES

Comparatively few birds are undesirable. Crows, blackbirds, starlings, brown thrashers, catbirds, cardinal birds and horned larks, are sometimes destructive to seedling corn, peas, and other vegetables. Robins, catbirds, thrushes, starlings, waxwings, bluebirds, and some kinds of woodpeckers, attack ripening fruit, especially cherries and strawberries. Purple finches, linnets, and pine siskins, eat fruit buds of cherries, apricots, and peaches, sometimes destroying the entire crop. Ring-necked pheasants are frequently bold enough to invade gardens where they do as much damage as domestic chickens in scratching out seedling vegetables and flowers. In such cases wire netting can be placed over the flower beds until the plants have developed to withstand attack. Sometimes it is necessary to shoot or trap the offending individual. For a method of protecting corn seed from crows, see CORN.

Starlings and English sparrows frequently drive out more desirable birds in addition to becoming nuisances themselves. If the openings to nest boxes are made in sizes specified above it will protect wrens, chickadees, and nuthatches from the raids of sparrows and will prevent the starlings from destroying the nests of birds up to the size of bluebirds. Both species may be discouraged by constantly breaking up their nests and where no local ordinances prevent, by shoot-

* Special articles on the subjects indicated by an asterisk (*) will be found at the words so marked.

ing the invading individuals as fast as they appear. A twenty-two rifle shooting dust shot, is an effective weapon for this purpose. Many sparrows can also be taken by traps.

Seedlings can be partially protected by streamers of paper or cloth on stakes stuck into the ground at frequent intervals. In small gardens netting may be fastened a few inches above the seed beds until the plants have become several inches tall.

Damage to ripening fruit is more difficult to prevent. Scarecrows in trees do little good, the birds quickly becoming accustomed to them. Single trees may be protected by a netting cover, though this is expensive. Planting of mulberries which ripen with the cherries, is frequently successful in diverting the attention of the birds from the fruit, though it will not entirely prevent damage. Shooting has little effect unless one wishes to continue until the nesting bird population is eliminated. For other animal pests, see ANIMAL INJURY. — I. N. G.

**BIRD'S-EYE PRIMROSE** = *Primula farinosa*.

**BIRD'S-EYES** = *Gilia tricolor*.

**BIRD'S-FOOT TREFOIL** = *Lotus corniculatus*.

**BIRD'S-FOOT VIOLET** = *Viola pedata*.

**BIRD'S-NEST FERN** = *Asplenium nidus*.

**BIRTHROOT** = *Trillium erectum*.

**BIRTHWORT.** See ARISTOLOCHIA; for birthwort family see ARISTOLOCHIACEAE.

**BISCHOFIA** (bi-show'fi-a). A single tropical Asiatic tree of the spurge family, known in outdoor cult. only in zone* 9 or in most sheltered parts of zone* 8, where, in Fla., it makes vigorous growth. The only species is the toog, **Bischofia javanica** (sometimes called *B. trifoliata*). It is a quick-growing tree up to 65 ft., with attractive, bronzy foliage. Leaves compound,* the 3 leaflets ovalish, tapering and finely toothed, 3–5 in. long. Flowers small, greenish, without petals, the male and female flowers on different trees and in branched clusters. Fruit a pea-sized, blackish berry. (Named for G. W. Bischoff, a German professor.)

*BISERRATA, -us, -um* (by-ser-ray'ta). Twice or doubly toothed.

**BISHOP'S-CAP** = *Mitella diphylla*.

**BISHOP'S-WEED** = *Aegopodium podagraria*.

**BISNAGA** = *Biznaga*.

*BITERNATA, -us, -um* (by-ter-nay'ta). Twice-ternate. See TERNATE.

**BITING INSECTS.** See INSECT PESTS; see also Stomach Poisons at INSECTICIDES.

**BITTER ALOES.** See ALOE VERA.

**BITTER-BUTTONS** = *Tanacetum vulgare*.

**BITTER CRESS.** See CARDAMINE; see also BARBAREA VULGARIS.

**BITTER HERBS.** See HERB GARDENING.

**BITTER ORANGE.** The sour or Seville orange. See CITRUS AURANTIUM.

**BITTER-ROOT** = *Lewisia rediviva*.

**BITTER-STEM PALM** = *Hyophorbe amaricaulis*.

**BITTERSWEET.** Generally, in America, *Celastrus scandens*, but also, and certainly first applied to, *Solanum dulcamara*. The attempt to call *Celastrus scandens* false bittersweet does not make much headway.

**BITTERSWEET FAMILY** = Celastraceae.

**BITTER VETCH** = *Vicia ervilia*.

**BITTER WINTER CRESS** = *Barbarea vulgaris*.

**BITTERWORT** = *Gentiana lutea*.

**BIXA** (bick'sa). A single tropical American tree and the only hort. genus of the family **Bixaceae** (bick-say'see-ee), often called annatto family. They have alternate,* simple* leaves without marginal teeth and rather showy and (in ours) red or pink regular* flowers. Sepals 5. Petals 5, overlapping and twisted in the bud. Stamens many. Ovary superior,* 1-celled. Fruit a reddish, 2-valved, nearly egg-shaped pod (capsule*) which is covered with soft, reddish, weak prickles. (*Bixa* is a South American vernacular for the tree.)

The annatto can be grown outdoors only in zone* 9, where it is purely an ornamental tree, although in the tropics it is raised as the source of annatto or achiote dye, used for coloring butter and cheese. Easily propagated by seeds or by cuttings.

orellana. Annatto (also, incorrectly, spelled anatto and arnatto); called also achiote. As cult. in Fla., not over 25 ft. high, and a handsome tree when in flower or fruit. Leaves ovalish, 5–7 in. long. Flower about 2 in. wide. Fruit about 2 in. long, the pulp around the seeds yielding the orange-red dye. Tropical America. It drops its leaves in midwinter in Fla.

**BIZARRE TULIP.** See Garden Tulips at TULIPA.

**BIZNAGA.** A name for several cacti in the southwestern U.S. and adjacent Mex., most of which have a globular or cylindric, ribbed plant body, plentifully beset with spines. The two hort. species are *Astrophytum capricorne* and *Ferocactus wislizeni* (which see).

**BLACK ACACIA** = *Acacia melanoxylon*.

**BLACK ALDER** = *Ilex verticillata* (see HOLLY); also *Alnus glutinosa* (see ALDER).

**BLACK ARROW.** A trademarked pyrethrum insecticide, sold with directions for use as a contact dust.

**BLACK ASH** = *Fraxinus nigra*. See ASH.

**BLACK BEAD** = *Pithecolobium unguis-cati*.

**BLACK BEAN** = *Castanospermum australe*.

**BLACKBERRY** (derived from various species of *Rubus*). Wild species of blackberries, of which there are many, are widespread in the north temperate zone in both the Old and the New World, but have been domesticated only in North America. Here they have been under cultivation about one hundred years, but in this brief time at least seven wild types of this fruit have been brought under subjugation. With these facts in mind one may generalize and say that some blackberry may be found for about every agricultural region in North America; and further say that no fruit has proved itself better fitted to fill a place in orchards and gardens, and none varies more rapidly and offers greater opportunities to develop new types.

The blackberry is at home in any climate in which the tree fruits, the hardiest excepted, are grown. Perhaps it is a little more tender to cold than the apple. It is cosmopolitan as to soils, but reaches greatest perfection in strong loams which contain more clay than sand. It is generally agreed that a good soil for this bramble must be retentive of moisture and yet be well drained. A soil too moist or too rich in humus supports a plant so rank in growth that it falls short in fruitfulness; while, on the other hand, light loams and sands will not carry the blackberry through the droughts that accompany every American summer. A cool northern exposure suits this fruit well. Cover crops supply all the humus and fertility that need to be added to a good blackberry soil.

Blackberries are usually propagated from root-cuttings, although suckers naturally spring up and supply new plants for a few varieties. In propagating from cuttings, roots the size of a lead pencil, a little larger if they can be had, are dug in the fall, cut into 4-in. lengths, stratified in sand during the winter, and planted 3 or 4 in. apart in nursery rows in the spring. The following spring these nursery plants are ready for the field. Suckers may well be used for gardens, but are usually too few and cost too much in care for large plantations.

Blackberries are set either in hills or hedgerows; perhaps hills suit gardeners best, hedgerows, growers for markets. The plants want plenty of roots, sun and air, and 6 × 7 ft. are

---

* Special articles on the subjects indicated by an asterisk (*) will be found at the words so marked.

not too great distances for hills, and 8 ft. between rows and 4 ft. between plants are usual distances in hedgerows.

The soil in a blackberry plantation must be stirred early in the spring and frequently thereafter until the berries are ripe. Perhaps greater care is needed in cultivating blackberries than any other small fruit. The plantation persists for several years and weeds and suckers must be kept down; yet if the cultivator runs a shade too deep the roots are injured and sucker growth is stimulated. The gardener can always use a hoe to advantage, and the owner of a large plantation must hand-hoe it once or twice a year to keep down weeds and suckers.

After the picking season is over, a cover crop must be sown to furnish humus and to check succulent growths which would be winter-killed. Barley, oats, buckwheat, and millet are good cover crops, since none live over winter to plague the cultivator in the spring. Whatever the crop, it should be plowed under in the fall at which time a heavy furrow should be thrown up to the canes as winter protection. A cover crop, or a mulch in gardens, is all-important to the blackberry, since the limiting factors in fruit production are humus and moisture in the soil. Experiments with fertilizers for this fruit have given only negative results. Nitrate of soda and its equivalents increase cane growth but not the quantity of fruit.

Pruning the blackberry is not difficult but very necessary, and, because of the thorns, is a very disagreeable task. The work of pruning begins by putting on heavy gloves and arming oneself with a brush-hook and long-handled pruning-shears. As soon as they have borne a crop, the canes, which are biennials, should be cut out. Promptness in removing and burning old canes helps to keep down insect and fungous pests and permits fuller development of young canes. The blackberry, permitted to have its own way, is a sprawling, unmanageable plant, to avoid which the young canes should be clipped in June with a sickle or pruning-shears to a height of 2 ft. This clipping is very important also because it induces early branching, a stocky growth, and stout laterals which will hold a heavy crop of fruit. In the spring pruning, the fruiting canes are cut back somewhat and laterals reduced to 2 ft. or a little less. Not more than 4 or 5 canes are left in a hill. Gardeners, and some commercial growers, support tall-growing varieties on a trellis of one or two wires.

In cold climates, some winter protection is demanded by the blackberry. A mulch helps, but sometimes the plants must be bent over and the tips covered with earth, a method feasible only for gardeners. The blackberry suffers from drouth in winter as well as cold. In the states of the plains, persistent winds dry the canes out unless protection is given and the soil well soaked before winter comes on.

The fruit of the blackberry should be left on the bush until dead ripe; it is not ready to pick when it first turns black. Premature picking has given this fruit an undeserved reputation for sourness. From first to last the berries should be kept cool and dry. The crop is marketed in quart baskets packed in 32-quart crates. The blackberry outyields all other bramble fruits. "Plentiful as blackberries" comes to us from Shakespeare.

Some variety of blackberry can be found for every zone* excepting zones* 1 and 8 and 9, extremes of cold and heat. The following varieties are all successfully grown:

BRITON (Ancient Briton). Berries large, not very firm, very good in quality. Season medium to late. Bush vigorous, very hardy, very productive. Zones* 1 and 2, especially Wisconsin and Minnesota.

EARLY HARVEST. Berries medium in size, firm, good in quality. Season very early. Bush vigorous and does not sucker. Not hardy in the North, and subject to rust in the South; recommended for California.

ELDORADO. Berries medium to large, firm, sweet, very good. Season early to medium and very long. The best variety for zones* 2, 3, and 4 east of the Rocky Mountains.

KITTATINNY. Berries large to very large, firm, sweet, very good. Season medium early. Bush vigorous, half-hardy, productive. Susceptible to rust in the South. Zones* 2, 3, and 4.

LAWTON. Berries large, soft, sweet, very good. Season medium. Bush vigorous, half-hardy, productive. Susceptible to rust. Zones* 2, 3, 4, and California.

MERSEREAU. Berries large, firm, sweet, very good. Season medium, short. Bush medium in vigor, hardiness, and productiveness. Zones* 2, 3, and 4 east of the Rocky Mountains.

SNYDER. Berries of medium size, firm, seedy, poor in quality. Season medium and short. Bush vigorous, very hardy, productive. Parts of all zones where hardiness is requisite.

TAYLOR. Berries medium, soft, very good. Season late. Bush vigorous, hardy, productive, free from rust. Grown for a late berry east of the Rocky Mountains in zones* 1, 2, 3, and 4.

Besides the foregoing blackberries, all of which have biennial canes, there are two with perennial canes much grown in the Pacific states and somewhat grown in the eastern states, where, however, they are seldom hardy, except south of Pennsylvania. These are: EVERGREEN, with perhaps a half dozen synonyms; and HIMALAYA. Both have large, sweet berries, ripen very late. Canes long and trailing for which reason they are grown on 3 or 4 wire trellises. See also LOGANBERRY and DEWBERRY. — U. P. H.

INSECT PESTS. Insect injury to blackberry is seldom serious. The pale green tree crickets sometimes puncture the canes and lay eggs in them. The application of arsenical sprays early in the summer and the destruction of old canes will check them. A green, spiny sawfly larva sometimes eats the leaves late in the spring; it is easily killed by arsenicals. The rose scale, a conspicuous white scale insect, infests the canes occasionally; a good dormant spray early in the spring will control it. Several insects bore in the canes at times; one, a beetle larva ½ in. long, makes an indefinite swelling; another is a small wasp, the larva of which produces a definite gall. Both these gall makers may be controlled by removing the affected cane in the spring. Larvae of a beetle and a fly sometimes bore in young canes; affected canes should be removed during the summer. A leaf miner occurs, but is not a serious pest. Small mites cause trouble at times, especially to fruit; they should yield to a sulphur spray or dust.

**BLACKBERRY LILY** = *Belamcanda chinensis*.

**BLACK BINDWEED** = *Polygonum convolvulus*. See list at WEEDS.

**BLACK BIRCH.** In the East, *Betula lenta*; in the West, *B. fontinalis*. For both see BIRCH.

**BLACK CALLA** = *Arum palaestinum*.

**BLACKCAP RASPBERRY** = *Rubus occidentalis*. For cult. see RASPBERRY.

**BLACK CHOKEBERRY** = *Aronia melanocarpa*.

**BLACK COHOSH** = *Cimicifuga racemosa*.

**BLACK COSMOS** = *Cosmos diversifolius*.

**BLACK CURRANT** = *Ribes nigrum*.

**BLACK-EYED SUSAN.** Usually some species of *Rudbeckia*, especially *R. hirta*, the yellow daisy; also *Thunbergia alata*.

**BLACK GRAM** = *Phaseolus mungo*.

**BLACK GUM** = *Nyssa sylvatica*.

**BLACK HAW** = *Viburnum prunifolium*.

**BLACK-HEART.** See Environmental Influences at PLANT DISEASES.

**BLACK HILLS SPRUCE** = *Picea glauca albertiana*. See SPRUCE.

**BLACK HOREHOUND** = *Ballota nigra*.

**BLACK HUCKLEBERRY** = *Gaylussacia baccata*. See HUCKLEBERRY.

**BLACK-KNOT.** See Diseases at CHERRY.

**BLACK-LEAF-40.** A trademarked liquid insecticide, containing 40 per cent nicotine sulphate, and sold with directions for use as a contact spray.

**BLACK-LEG.** See Diseases at CABBAGE.

**BLACK LOCUST** = *Robinia pseudo-acacia*; see LOCUST; also *Gleditsia triacanthos*; see HONEY LOCUST.

**BLACK MAPAU** = *Pittosporum tenuifolium*.

**BLACK MEDIC** = *Medicago lupulina*.

**BLACK MUSTARD** = *Brassica nigra*.

**BLACK NIGHTSHADE** = *Solanum nigrum*.

**BLACK OAK** = *Quercus velutina*; see OAK.

**BLACK POPLAR** = *Populus nigra*.

**BLACKROOT** = *Veronica virginica*.

**BLACK-ROOT.** See DAMPING-OFF.

---

* Special articles on the subjects indicated by an asterisk (*) will be found at the words so marked.

**BLACK-ROT.** *See* Diseases at Cabbage, Cucumber and Grape.

**BLACK SAGE** = *Audibertia stachyoides*.

**BLACK SALSIFY** = *Scorzonera hispanica*.

**BLACK SAMPSON** = *Echinacea purpurea*.

**BLACK SCALE.** *See* the insect pests at Orange and Olive.

**BLACK SNAKEROOT** = *Cimicifuga racemosa*.

**BLACK SPOT.** *See* Diseases at Rose.

**BLACK SPRUCE** = *Picea mariana; see* Spruce.

**BLACK TARTARIAN.** A cherry variety. *See* Cherry.

**BLACKTHORN.** In America, *Crataegus tomentosa* (better spelled black thorn), and a very different plant from the blackthorn of the Irish, which is *Prunus spinosa*, the sloe.

**BLACK WALNUT** = *Juglans nigra* and *J. Hindsi; see* Walnut.

**BLACK WART.** *See* Diseases at Potato.

**BLACK WATTLE** = *Acacia decurrens mollis*.

**BLACK WILLOW** = *Salix nigra; see* Willow.

**BLACKWOOD** = *Acacia melanoxylon*.

**BLADDER-FERN.** *See* Cystopteris.

**BLADDER-NUT.** *See* Staphylea.

**BLADDER-POD** = *Vesicaria utriculata; see also* Lesquerella.

**BLADDER SENNA** = *Colutea arborescens*.

**BLADDERWORT.** *See* Utricularia.

**BLADDERWORT FAMILY** = Lentibulariaceae.

**BLADDERY.** Inflated and usually with papery or thin walls, as in some fruits.

**BLADE.** The usually flat, expanded part of a leaf, as distinguished from its stalk; less commonly, the similar expansion of a petal which is better called the limb.*

**BLADEAPPLE** = *Pereskia aculeata*.

**BLAKSLEY BOTANIC GARDEN.** *See* Botanic Garden.

**BLANCHING.** A not unusual garden operation having for its object the reduction or practical disappearance of the green coloring matter of certain plants. This substance (chlorophyll) needs light for proper development, and blanching involves cutting off direct light. It is done by banking up earth, by boards, or by paper or cardboard individual plant covers. The chief crops in which blanching is a factor are celery, sea-kale and endive. See these for details.

*BLANDA, -us, -um* (blan'da). Mild or bland, not bitter or strong.

**BLANKET-FLOWER.** *See* Gaillardia, especially *G. aristata*.

**BLAST.** *See* Diseases at Rice.

*BLATTARIA*. A pre-Linnaean* name for certain mulleins now included in the genus *Verbascum*.

**BLAZING STAR** = *Liatris squarrosa*, *Mentzelia laevicaulis*, and *Chamaelirium luteum*. *See also* Tritonia.

**BLEACHING.** A process designed to maintain the color of apples when cut for drying. In ordinary air, discoloration of apple flesh is rapid, but when exposed to the fumes of burning sulphur, the fruit keeps its fresh whitish color. The sliced apples must be put in an air-tight chamber through which the sulphur fumes slowly pass from an entrance pipe at the bottom to a vent at the top. The amount of sulphur to be burned and the time of exposure to the fumes both vary according to the variety of apple and the condition (water content) of the fruit. A fair average is 45 minutes' exposure, and for 100 pounds of apples, the fumes resulting from the burning of about six ounces of sulphur. It is, however, safer to experiment with a small lot and thus arrive at some exact figures. The exposure to the fumes should be no longer than is necessary to preserve the color of the fruit.

**BLECHNUM** (bleck'num). A very large genus of mostly tropical ferns, family Polypodiaceae, a few of which reach temperate regions. They are rather coarse, stiff-fronded ferns grown for ornament and comparatively immune to the unfavorable conditions of a living-room. Fronds with many leaflets or divisions arranged feather-fashion. Along the midrib, on the under side of the leaflets or segments, are the more or less continuous, brown spore-cases, containing the spores.* (*Blechnum* is Greek for some fern, but perhaps not these.)

Blechnums are useful ferns for florists and for house decoration largely because they will stand abuse. This means they can stand a dry atmosphere, but they need water at the roots. Do not sprinkle or syringe the foliage. For soil and greenhouse conditions *see* Ferns. Some species are offered under the name *Lomaria*.

brasiliense. A greenhouse fern with a short trunk (2–3 ft.) and a bushy crown of leaves. Fronds 2–3 ft. long and about 12 in. wide, its segments set at an acute angle. Brazil and Peru. Can be grown outdoors only in zone* 9.

serrulatum. Saw fern. A greenhouse fern without a trunk, the fronds stalked and arising at the ground level. Fronds 12–20 in. long, and about 10 in. wide, their segments many, narrow, stiffish, with nearly parallel edges which are minutely toothed. Fla. to Brazil, mostly in wet places.

spicant. Deer fern; called also hard fern. A hardy fern suitable for the outdoor fern garden. Fronds evergreen, 2½–3½ ft. long, in a dense cluster. The frond is divided into many small segments which are without marginal teeth or sometimes faintly toothed. In Eurasia and in N.A. from Alaska to Calif.

**BLEEDING-HEART** = *Dicentra spectabilis;* also, in Calif., *D. formosa*.

**BLEEDING-HEART FAMILY** = Fumariaceae.

**BLENDING.** *See* Dominant.

**BLENHEIM.** *See* Apricot.

*BLEO.* Brazilian vernacular name for *Pereskia bleo*.

**BLEPHARIGLOTTIS.** A once-current name for orchids here included in *Habenaria*.

**BLESSED THISTLE** = *Cnicus benedictus*.

**BLETIA HYACINTHINA** = *Bletilla striata*.

**BLETILLA** (ble-till'a). A small group of Asiatic orchids, one suitable to shady parts of the wild garden. Unlike most temperate region orchids, they have a pseudobulb* and a leafy stem. Leaves plaited like a fan. Flowers very irregular, in a terminal cluster (raceme*). Sepals and petals very similar, but the lip* 3-lobed, and the middle lobe toothed. (*Bletilla* is diminutive of *Bletia*, a (non-hort.) genus named for Louis Blet, a Spanish botanist.)

The species below is not well known, but is a desirable plant for the wild garden. It prefers half-shady places, and will form good-sized clumps. Propagated by spring division of the clumps.

striata. Pseudobulbs tuber-like and from them the stems rise 8–15 in., along which are 3–6 plaited leaves. Flowers amethyst-purple, and showy. China and Jap. Sometimes offered as *Bletia hyacinthina*.

**BLIGHIA** (bly'gi-a). Three tropical African trees, family Sapindaceae, one of which is cult. in southern Fla. for its edible fruit (the akee). Leaves compound,* the leaflets arranged feather-fashion. Flowers in racemes,* very fragrant, greenish-white. (For details *see* Sapindaceae.) Fruit a 3-celled capsule,* in each cell a single black seed to which is attached the edible white aril.* (Named for William Bligh, commander of the "Bounty.")

The akee can only be grown outdoors in zone* 9 as it is susceptible to frost. When the pods split open the furrowed aril* is gathered. From its brain-like appearance it is often called vegetable brain or sesal vegetal. Only ripe arils should be used, preferably fried in butter. Over- or under-ripe arils are apt to be poisonous. The tree is propagated by seeds or by shield-budding.

sapida. Akee. A tree up to 25 ft. or a little more. Leaflets 3, 4 or 5 pairs, more or less oblong and without teeth. Flowers hairy, white, fragrant, the oblong, greenish-white petals somewhat showy. Capsule

---

* Special articles on the subjects indicated by an asterisk (*) will be found at the words so marked.

3–4 in. long, yellowish-red. Aril* generally white, but with a pinkish portion (apt to be poisonous) between its white lobes. Tropical Africa.

**BLIGHT.** An indefinite and loose term for various discolorations on or for the sudden death of plants. Most blights are caused by one or more plant diseases (which see). See also Diseases at PEONY, SNAPDRAGON, GINSENG and PEACH.

**BLIND.** Failure to produce flowers or fruit, usually from disease, improper nourishment, or too deep or too early planting.

**BLIND FURROW.** See PLOWING.

**BLIND WOOD.** See Softwood Cuttings at CUTTINGS.

**BLISTER BEETLE.** See Beetles at INSECT PESTS; see also the insect pests at POTATO.

**BLISTER-CRESS.** See ERYSIMUM.

**BLISTER-FLOWER** = *Ranunculus acris.* See BUTTERCUP.

*BLITOIDES* (bly-toy′deez; but *see* OÏDES). Resembling *Blitum*, an old name for the strawberry-blite, which *see* in the list at WEEDS.

**BLITUM CAPITATUM** = *Chenopodium capitatum.* See Strawberry-blite in the list at WEEDS.

**BLOOD.** See Nitrogen at FERTILIZERS.

**BLOODBERRY** = *Rivina humilis.*

**BLOOD-FLOWER** = *Asclepias curassavica.* See MILKWEED.

**BLOOD-LEAF.** See IRESINE.

**BLOOD-LILY.** See HAEMANTHUS.

**BLOODROOT.** The bloodroot is an ideal wild garden plant where it thrives in rich woods soil (not especially acid) and in partial shade. It is the only known species of the genus **Sanguinaria** (san-gwi-nair′ree-a), belongs to the poppy family, and is confined to the forests of eastern N.A. The only species, **S. canadensis**, has a red, perennial root, red sap, and sends up in early spring a single, lobed leaf which is often 4–6 in. wide. Flower solitary, on a stalk 6–8 in. high. Sepals 2. Petals 8–12, white or pinkish, waxy and about 1 in. long. Stamens many. Fruit a pod about 1 in. long. A very handsome wild flower blooming early in May, but completely dying down by midsummer. It is also called redroot, tetterwort, or Indian plant. (*Sanguinaria* refers to the blood-like juice.) For culture *see* WILD GARDEN.

**BLOODROOT FAMILY** = Papaveraceae.

**BLOODWOOD TREE** = *Haematoxylon campechianum.*

**BLOODWORT FAMILY** = Haemodoraceae. See LACHNANTHES.

**BLOODY BUTCHERS** = *Trillium sessile.*

**BLOOM.** The delicate powdery coating on some fruits, and occasionally on other parts of plants, of unknown origin and of no known use. Technically bloomy plants or fruits are said to be *pruinose. Bloom*, of course, is also synonymous with blossom.

**BLOOMERIA** (blue-meer′i-a). A genus of only two Californian bulbous plants of the lily family, one of which is cult. for its summer-blooming flowers that suggest the ornamental species of *Brodiaea*. Leaves all grass-like and basal. Flower cluster an umbel* on a long, naked stalk. Flowers wheel-shaped, orange-yellow, the segments of the corolla parted nearly to the base, about ¾ in. across. (Named for Dr. H. G. Bloomer, an American botanist.)

The only hort. species prefers a well-drained, sandy soil and open sunlight. While it will stand considerable frost, it is safer to cover with straw or light mulch in regions of severe winters. Pot culture is often better than planting in the open ground, especially in cool regions, and it is better, in any case, to dig up the corms after they have ripened (about a month after blooming time), store in a dry place and replant in the fall.

*crocea.* Golden stars. A perennial with a crocus-like corm.* Leaf solitary, ¼–⅓ in. wide. Stalk of the flower cluster 6–15 in. high, roughish. Flowers many, golden-orange, the stamens* nearly as long as the petals. Southern Calif. Often offered as *B. aurea.*

**BLOOM-FELL** = *Lotus corniculatus.*

**BLOOM-FOOD.** A trademarked chemical preparation sold in tablet form, with directions for use in aiding cut flowers to be kept fresh.

**BLOSSOM.** Any flower, but especially the collection of them when fruit trees are in bloom.

**BLOSSOM BLIGHT.** See Diseases at TULIP.

**BLOSSOM-END-ROT.** See environmental influences at PLANT DISEASES; *see also* Diseases at TOMATO.

**BLUE ANEMONE** = *Hepatica americana.*

**BLUE ASH** = *Fraxinus quadrangulata.* See ASH.

**BLUEBEARD.** See CARYOPTERIS.

**BLUE BEECH** = *Carpinus caroliniana.* See HORNBEAM.

**BLUEBELL.** Many plants are called bluebell, the most common hort. species being *Campanula rotundifolia, Polemonium reptans, Eustoma russellianum,* and *Clematis crispa.* In England, and sometimes here, bluebells is also applied to *Scilla nonscripta.*

**BLUEBELL-OF-SCOTLAND** = *Campanula rotundifolia.*

**BLUEBELLS** = *Muscari botryoides; see also* MERTENSIA and SCILLA NONSCRIPTA.

**BLUEBERRY.** Blueberries, all derived from species of *Vaccinium*, are often mistaken for huckleberries, which come from shrubs of the genus *Gaylussacia*. The latter has 10 seed-like nuts in the fleshy fruit, while the blueberry is a real berry with many small seeds.

Until a few years ago blueberries were known only as a wild fruit, some derived from low plants but the finest from the high-bush blueberry. The latter includes several species known to botanists, notably *Vaccinium corymbosum* in the North and *V. virgatum* in the South. These are shrubs 6–10 ft. high and (in the wild) with fruit about ⅓ in. in diameter. From these and other species have been developed hort. forms having fruit up to ¾ in. in diameter, and which can be cultivated in the garden with proper care. Most wild species of *Vaccinium* are not garden plants, and are difficult to grow.

The cult. blueberry of today is best purchased as a rooted shrub from a reliable dealer who is necessarily a specialist in propagating these plants, which is a somewhat technical and difficult process. These plants are therefore expensive.

Blueberries cannot be grown in ordinary garden soil nor in one that contains lime. Like most plants of the heath family, they rely for their food upon microscopic organisms attached to their roots, which appear to function only when certain soil conditions are approximated. These are soil acidity and proper aeration.

If your soil is sandy and has a pH of 5 (*see* ACID AND ALKALI SOILS for details), you are safe in starting a blueberry plantation. If it is neither, you must make a prepared bed for the plants, preferably a month or six weeks before the plants are set out, or better, six months before.

Dig or scrape out about 2 ft. of your ordinary garden soil and fill in with the following mixture:

4 parts of chopped-up peat, half-rotted oak leaves, or one of the commercial acid peats. From whatever source, this material must test to pH 5 or better (*i.e.* pH 4.5 or pH 4). See ACID AND ALKALI SOILS for details of the tests.

1 part pure sand. (Do not use sand from the seashore nor any other with an alkali reaction.)

Mix these thoroughly and put them in the excavated bed or trench. If the latter is underlaid by clay, break it up or dig out still more soil and fill in with sand or fine gravelly sand. In any case, see that there is 2 ft. of the peat and sand mixture, even after it has settled.

---

* Special articles on the subjects indicated by an asterisk (*) will be found at the words so marked.

BLUEBIRD 79 BLUE GARDEN

The young plants, usually sold 8-15 in. high, will come with a ball of roots, and should be set in the soil mixture very early in the spring or late in the fall. (In midwinter in Fla.) Put them 5 ft. apart each way, or the rows can be 7 ft. apart in the North, but at least 15 × 15 ft. in Fla. Do not allow the roots to become exposed to the sun or wind. Water them for the first week or so, but once established they need no more water than their wild ancestors. Do not use any manure, and if you wish to mulch the plants, use only oak leaves or those from the mountain laurel (*Kalmia*).

Each year, or every other year, apply the following fertilizer to each acre of blueberry plants:
- 100 pounds of nitrate of soda
- 260 pounds of rock phosphate
- 40 pounds of sulphate of potash.

From planting time, it will be 3 or 4 years until the bushes are big enough to begin bearing. The plantation will last a lifetime, but the plants should not be disturbed, although weeds must be kept down. A mature bush (10 or 15 years old) should yield about 14 quarts of berries, and much more than this in later years, especially in some of the Fla. varieties.

VARIETIES. From zone* 5 northward the best varieties are: Ruvel, Pioneer, Katherine and Jersey. In Fla. and the South there are several varieties, mostly derived from *Vaccinium virgatum*.

The commercial production of blueberries is best developed in N.J., Minn., Mich., and Fla.

INSECT PESTS. A maggot closely allied to the apple maggot is the worst pest of blueberries. It works in the berries late in the summer. Calcium-arsenate dust applied twice in July, when adults are present, has been effective. The chain-dotted measuring worm, larva of a moth, feeds on the plant in summer; it should yield to arsenicals, as should other leaf-feeding caterpillars. Spittle insects (much like leafhoppers) are usually checked by the burning practiced in some sections. Thrips have been controlled in Me. by burning, which is aided by the scattering of hay or straw, in June. A small flea beetle and a larger leaf beetle, with their larvae, can be controlled with arsenicals applied in June. Cutworms can often be controlled with poisoned bran bait.

DISEASES. The most important disease of blueberry is the mummy berry, which causes the fruit to rot, turn brown, or gray, and fall to the ground. It is known wherever blueberries are grown in the East. It is best controlled by destroying the old mummies either by sweeping them up or by burying them when cultivating. Witches'-broom caused by a rust is common throughout the northern states. It produces abnormal proliferation of the branches, which may be killed. In severe cases the whole plant may die. The recommended control measure is cutting out and burning the young brooms as soon as they can be observed.

**BLUEBIRD.** See BIRDS.

**BLUE BLAZING STAR** = *Liatris scariosa*.

**BLUE BLOSSOM** = *Ceanothus thyrsiflorus*.

**BLUE BONNETS** = *Centaurea cyanus*. See also LUPINUS TEXENSIS.

**BLUEBOTTLE** = *Centaurea cyanus*.

**BLUE COHOSH** = *Caulophyllum thalictroides*.

**BLUECURLS.** Low herbs in the East, but much taller and somewhat woody in Calif., where some species are widely cult. as bee plants. All belong to the genus Trichostema (try-kos'ti-ma), of the mint family, and are natives of N.A. Leaves opposite.* Flowers blue or purple, irregular and 2-lipped, the long-protuding stamens arched, whence the name bluecurls. Usually the flowers are solitary at the ends of slender stalks or in small clusters in the leaf-axils.* (*Trichostema* is Greek for hair and stamen.)

Both those below are little grown outside Calif. They prefer the open sun and will stand much summer heat. Neither is hardy in the East, where they are replaced by several wild species that are scarcely garden plants.

T. lanatum. Ramero. A shrubby herb to 4 ft. high. Leaves narrow, slender, scarcely 2 in. long, very hairy on the lower surface. Flowers clothed with a blue or purplish wool, about ½ in. long. Calif.

T. lanceolatum. Vinegarweed; called also camphorweed. Flowers mostly in the leaf-axils,* blue, and blooming from August to frost in Calif. In dry, sandy places Calif. to Oregon. A very important bee plant.

**BLUE DAISY** = *Felicia amelloides*.

**BLUE DANDELION** = *Cichorium intybus*.

**BLUE DAWN-FLOWER** = *Ipomoea leari*.

**BLUE DICKS** = *Brodiaea capitata*.

**BLUE DOGWOOD** = *Cornus alternifolia*.

**BLUE-EYED MARY** = *Collinsia verna*.

**BLUE FALSE INDIGO** = *Baptisia australis*.

**BLUE FESCUE** = *Festuca ovina glauca*.

**BLUE FLAG** = *Iris versicolor*.

**BLUE GARDEN.** In planting a blue garden or border the pure blues such as those of gentian and *Anchusa* and the purple-blues as seen in many campanulas should not be placed side by side. They may be separated by breadths of green or gray foliage or by the intervention of white or some bright-hued flower. A few yellow-flowered plants add immensely to the effectiveness of a collection of blue flowers, and even a touch of orange or scarlet may be introduced with advantage. Woodwork and accessories may be light green, white or yellow. In the following lists the purple-blues are indicated by a dagger (†). All the plants mentioned will be found under their names in the body of THE GARDEN DICTIONARY.

SHRUBS

*Amorpha canescens* 3-4 ft., Aug.-Sept.; *Caryopteris incana*† 5 ft., autumn; *Hibiscus syriacus coelestis*† 10-12 ft., July-Aug.

TALL PLANTS FOR USE IN BACKGROUND

SUMMER-FLOWERING. *Aconitum fischeri* 4 ft., *A. napellus*† 4-5 ft., *A.* Spark's Variety† 4-6 ft. (see MONKSHOOD); *Anchusa azurea* and vars. 4 ft.; *Campanula pyramidalis*† 4-6 ft.; *Delphinium* hybrids, many vars. 4-6 ft.; *Echinops exaltatus* 4 ft., *E. sphaerocephalus*† 5-8 ft.; *Phlox* Blue Hill† 3-4 ft.; *Salvia azurea* 4-5 ft.

AUTUMN-FLOWERING. *Aconitum autumnale*† 4-5 ft.; *Aster* Blue Gem 4-5 ft., *A.* Climax† 5 ft.; *Verbena hastata* 4-6 ft.

PLANTS OF MEDIUM HEIGHT

SPRING-FLOWERING. *Aquilegia caerulea* (see COLUMBINE) 1½ ft.; *Camassia leichtlini*† 2 ft.; *Linum narbonense* 2 ft., *L. perenne* 2 ft.; *Mertensia virginica* 2 ft.; *Polemonium caeruleum* 2-3 ft.; *Pulmonaria angustifolia* 1 ft.; *Tradescantia virginiana*† (see SPIDERWORT) 2-3 ft.

SUMMER-FLOWERING. *Adenophora potanini* 18 in.; *Amsonia tabernaemontana*† 2½ ft.; *Anagallis linifolia* (biennial) 1½ ft.; *Anchusa capensis* (annual) 1½ ft.; *Baptisia australis* 3-4 ft.; *Borago officinalis* 2 ft.; *Browallia americana*† (annual) 2 ft.; *Campanula persicifolia*† 2-3 ft.; *Catanache caerulea* 2 ft.; *Centaurea cyanus* (annual) 2-3 ft., *C. montana* 2 ft.; *Clematis davidiana* 4 ft.; *C. integrifolia* 3 ft.; *Commelina coelestis* 2 ft. (tender); *Cynoglossum amabile* (biennial) 2 ft.; *Delphinium ajacis* (rocket larkspur) 2-3 ft., *D. grandiflorum* vars. 1-2 ft.; *Echinops ritro*† 3 ft.; *Eryngium alpinum*† 2 ft., *E. amethystinum*† 2 ft., *E. bourgati*† 1½ ft., *E. olivierianum*† 3 ft., *E. planum* 3 ft.; *Geranium platypetalum*† 2 ft.; *Lupinus polyphyllus* vars. 2-4 ft.; *Pentstemon unilateralis* 2-2½ ft.; *Platycodon grandiflorum* 2½ ft., var. *mariesi* 1½ ft.; *Salvia farinacea*† 3 ft., *S. patens* (half-hardy) 2 ft., *S. pratensis*† 2 ft.; *Veronica austriaca* 2 ft., *V. maritima* var. *subsessilis* 2 ft., *V. spicata* 2 ft., *V. spuria* 2 ft.

AUTUMN-FLOWERING. *Aster* Feltham Blue† 2 ft.; *Eupatorium coelestinum* 2 ft.; *Gentiana andrewsi* 2 ft.; *Lobelia syphilitica* 2-3 ft.

LOW-GROWING PLANTS FOR FOREGROUND

SPRING-FLOWERING. *Ajuga genevensis*, *A. reptans* (creepers); *Brunnera macrophylla* 1-1½ ft.; *Campanula garganica* vars. 3-4 in.; *Chionodoxa luciliae* 3 in., *C. sardensis* 3 in. (bulbs); *Gentiana acaulis* 3 in.; *Globularia cordifolia* 4 in., *G. trichosantha* 6 in.; *Hyacinthus azureus* 3 in., *H. amethystinus* 4-5 in., *H. orientalis* vars. 8-10 in. (bulbs); *Linum alpinum* 6 in.; *Muscari botryoides* 4 in., *M.* Heavenly Blue 5 in. (bulbs); *Myosotidium hortensia* 12-18 in.; *Myosotis* vars. 4-10 in.; *Phyteuma scheuchzeri* 1 ft.; *Polemonium humile* 1 ft., *P. reptans* 6 in.; *Primula vulgaris caerulea* 6 in.; *Scilla hispanica* 1 ft., *S. nonscripta* 1 ft., *S. sibirica* 4 in. (bulb); *Sisyrinchium angustifolium* 8 in.; *Veronica gentianoides* 1 ft.; *Vinca minor* (creeping).

* Special articles on the subjects indicated by an asterisk (*) will be found at the words so marked.

SUMMER-FLOWERING. *Asperula orientalis* (annual) 1 ft.; *Convolvulus mauritanicus* (prostrate), *C. tricolor* (annual); *Gentiana cruciata* 6 in., *G. septemfida*; *Jasione perennis* 6–9 in.; *Lobelia* (annual vars.); *Nemesia* Blue Gem (annual) 8 in.; *Nemophila insignis* (annual); *Nigella damascena* Miss Jekyll 1 ft.; *Pentstemon angustifolius* 1 ft.; *Petunia* Heavenly Blue (annual); *Phacelia campanularia* (annual) 6–8 in.; *Prunella grandiflora*† 9 in.; *Veronica incana* 8 in.

AUTUMN-FLOWERING. *Ceratostigma plumbaginoides* (semi-prostrate). — L. B. W.

See also GRAY AND LAVENDER GARDEN.

**BLUEGRASS.** See POA PRATENSIS.

**BLUE GUM** = *Eucalyptus globulus*.

**BLUE HUCKLEBERRY** = *Gaylussacia frondosa*. See HUCKLEBERRY.

**BLUE JASMINE** = *Clematis crispa*.

**BLUE LACE-FLOWER.** See TRACHYMENE.

**BLUE LILY-TURF** = *Liriope muscari*.

**BLUE-LIPS** = *Collinsia grandiflora*.

**BLUE LOBELIA** = *Lobelia syphilitica*.

**BLUE LOTUS** = *Nymphaea caerulea*.

**BLUE MARGUERITE** = *Felicia amelloides*.

**BLUE MELILOT** = *Trigonella caerulea*.

**BLUE MOLD.** See Diseases at HOP.

**BLUE MYRTLE** = *Ceanothus thyrsiflorus*.

**BLUE OXALIS** = *Parochetus communis*.

**BLUE PHLOX** = *Phlox divaricata*.

**BLUE SPIREA** = *Caryopteris incana*.

**BLUE SPRUCE** = *Picea pungens*. See SPRUCE.

**BLUESTEM** = *Sabal minor*.

**BLUE STONE.** See Copper at FUNGICIDES.

**BLUE SUCCORY** = *Catananche caerulea*.

**BLUE THISTLE** = *Echium vulgare*.

**BLUETS** = *Houstonia coerulea*.

**BLUE VERVAIN** = *Verbena hastata*.

**BLUE VIOLET** = *Viola cucullata*.

**BLUE VITRIOL.** See Copper at FUNGICIDES.

**BLUEWEED** = *Cichorium intybus*; also *Echium vulgare*.

**BLUE WING FLOWER** = *Torenia fournieri compacta*.

**BLUE WOOD ASTER** = *Aster cordifolius*.

**BLUMENBACHIA** (blew-men-back'i-a). A small genus of annual South American herbs of the family Loasaceae, mostly covered with stinging hairs. Leaves opposite* and lobed. Flowers solitary in the leaf-axils,* bracted.* (For details see LOASACEAE.) (Named for J. F. Blumenbach, German professor.)

The only cult. species is not much grown, on account of its stinging hairs. It has odd-shaped flowers and is to be treated as a tender annual. (For details see ANNUALS.)

insignis. A twining plant not over 2 ft. high. Leaves deeply 5-cleft or lobed, the divisions arranged finger-fashion. Flowers white, the petals more or less hooded and with a claw-like base that is spotted with red and yellow. Summer.

**BLUSHWORT.** See TRICHOSPORUM.

**BOARIA.** Probably derived from the aboriginal name in Chile for the mayten (*Maytenus boaria*).

**BOCCONIA.** A name somewhat common in the catalogs, but it is doubtful if any true *Bocconia* is of much interest to gardeners. For the plants usually listed as *Bocconia*, see MACLEAYA.

**BOEHMERIA** (bo-meer'i-a). A large genus of trees, shrubs or herbs, family Urticaceae, and widely scattered. A few are weedy herbs in N.A., but the one below is widely grown in China, and to some extent in the southern U.S., for the fine fiber taken from its inner bark. Leaves opposite.* Flowers green, without petals, unisexual,* crowded in small heads which are grouped in a spike-like cluster. Fruit an achene.* (Named for G. R. Boehmer, German professor.)

In Fla. and La. the ramie is a shrubby plant, its tall, annual shoots being harvested for the fiber. If grown in the greenhouse the plant becomes tree-like and very handsome. Easily propagated by division. It requires a rich, moist soil, and is not hardy north of zone* 6.

nivea. As cult. for fiber a bushy plant 4–6 ft. high, its stems hairy. Leaves broadly oval, 4–7 in. long, coarsely toothed, rough above, felty-white beneath. As. The common form yields rhea, or China-silk, but a tropical variety yields the true ramie. Ramie, however, as a name, is also applied to the fiber of the typical *B. nivea*, the only form known to be cult. in the U.S.

***BOERHAAVIAEFOLIA, -us, -um*** (boor-hah-vi-eye-fō'li-a). With leaves like a *Boerhaavia*, which is scarcely of hort. interest.

**BOG.** See BOG GARDENING.

**BOG ASPHODEL** = *Narthecium americanum*.

**BOGBEAN** = *Menyanthes trifoliata*.

**BOG GARDENING.** This is somewhat of an English institution which has of late years gained much favor in the United States. This was to be expected, for it is in North America that the major portion of the most useful cultivated bog plants are to be found.

The bog garden is a sanctuary for the wildings that by nature live in wet, acid places, on the sides of lakes, ponds, and streams or in peaty hollows. The plants are particularly easy of culture. Woody plants, herbaceous perennials, and some species of bulbs furnish the major portion of the plant material used in the development of such a garden. In making a bog garden we must remember that the plants which inhabit the bog will not thrive in any harsh, bare, and dry position. Bog plants are at home only when planted in moist situations, cradled in sphagnum, or other mosses of wet, spongy ground, or in a moist peat soil which is acid in character.

### SOIL

A good rich and acid soil is the keynote to success in bog gardening, and correct soil conditions are of more importance to the plants than moisture.

In selecting a soil, preference should be given to one such as is furnished by natural boggy soil. In texture this soil contains a good quantity of decayed humus and is full of fiber, the pH value of the substrata running between 4.5 and 5. (See ACID AND ALKALI SOILS.) Bog plants require an acid soil, and acidity must not be overlooked when the soil is selected. The turf should be cut and laid on a pile and to each two layers of this, add one layer of decayed cow manure. The fall is the best time to prepare the compost. After the pile has laid for a few weeks the turf should be chopped down with a spade in order to cut the fiber mass and thoroughly incorporate the manure. Aluminum sulphate added and well mixed with the compost, using it at the rate of fifty pounds to the ton of soil, will be of great benefit to the plants. The compost, after having been turned a few times, will be ready for use in building the mounds which will be placed here and there throughout the garden.

Nature, in order to retain soil acidity, provides means by utilizing the decaying leaves from the hardwood growths and the needles from the pine growths as soil acidifiers. Dressings of peat moss, decaying leaves, and vegetation, also sawdust from hardwood trees, when used as a top dressing or mulch, adds acidity and food to the soil.

### SITE

The bog garden should be so developed that it will be natural and picturesque in appearance, and it should be so shaped as to fit into the surrounding landscape in a naturalistic manner. A well-designed bog garden is an interesting feature on any estate, and it is a continuous source of pleasure to the owner. On many estates we find tracts of boggy ground

---

* Special articles on the subjects indicated by an asterisk (*) will be found at the words so marked.

which would be worthless for average garden purposes. These could be converted into ideal bog gardens.

Assuming that we have at our disposal a low section of ground inundated part of the year, unfit for garden crops or for the culture of garden flowers, such a spot can be made a thing of beauty at a comparatively low cost and the maintenance afterwards is almost nil. Nature unrestrictedly has clothed her bog gardens with numerous species of moisture-loving plants. Our first duty, then, in developing the garden would be to root out one and all of the undesirable plants, leaving the ones which are ornamental and those which will fit into the composition.

During the process of cleaning the ground it may be necessary to construct temporary trenches to allow the water to drain off, as the removal of brush, roots, and debris is much facilitated if the ground is in a dry and workable condition. After the ground has been cleaned, attention should be given to the soil. In most cases it will not be necessary to add anything to the natural bottom, but it would be best to plough, dig, or cultivate the surface so that the soil will be in good condition for planting. The proper method of working is to draw a plan to scale of the plot, having previously taken the dimensions of the ground and considered its topography, the source of water supply, its inlet and outlet. After deciding upon the plan, stakes are set showing the margin and the depths for excavation.

A well-designed bog garden is usually constructed so that the depression is from 10 inches to one foot below the average surrounding soil. Excavate for the paths running through the garden, utilizing the soil, if good, for the mounds, 12–18 inches high, which will be placed here and there throughout. Place drainage consisting of stones, cinders, brick bats, or other such material below the paths to keep them dry, finishing the surface with three inches of soil in which imbed stepping stones. These will insure a dry walk, giving facilities for the free inspection of the plants at any time without suffering the inconvenience of wet feet. Mounds of various sizes should be made to accommodate the diversified plants which will inhabit them.

## Treatment of Margins

The margin of the bog is every bit as important as the bog itself and it should receive the same care and consideration in planting. Remember, the bog is the picture and the margin the frame; therefore, in design, try to avoid making one part incongruous to the other. The sloping banks at the edge of the garden will furnish ideal positions to naturalize species of the dwarfer bamboos, alders, willows, birches and *Ilex verticillata* (see Holly). Other good shrubs for such places are: *Myrica gale*, *Chamaedaphne calyculata*, *Andromeda polifolia*, and *Kalmia polifolia*. *Ilex verticillata* is quite conspicuous in the fall and early winter with its display of red berries. Plants of the willow herb (*Epilobium*), purple loosestrife (*Lythrum salicaria*), *Iris sibirica*, Japanese iris (*Iris laevigata* or *I. kaempferi*), not forgetting *Iris pseudacorus*, the eulalia (*Miscanthus sinensis*), and the goatsbeard (*Aruncus sylvester*.) The plume poppy (*Macleaya cordata*) is an excellent subject if massed here and there on the slightly higher ground. Other interesting plants most useful for marginal plantings are the marsh marigold (*Caltha palustris*), horsetail (*Equisetum hyemale* and *E. praealtum*), and the knotweed (*Polygonum cuspidatum*). The Asiatic primrose (*Primula bulleyana* and *P. beesiana*), planted on the mounds, makes a charming picture when massed.

## Bog Plants

In the depressions, and at a lower level, excellent results may be obtained by introducing plants of the royal fern (*Osmunda regalis*), the ostrich fern (*Pteretis struthiopteris*), maidenhair fern (*Adiantum pedatum*), the chain fern (*Woodwardia virginica*) and other species of ferns which by nature are dwellers in wet or boggy soils. Next come the lilies. These should be planted in the prepared mounds in the bog. *Lilium pardalinum*, *L. canadense*, and *L. superbum*, these three lilies are children of the bog. As companions to the lilies we may place the trilliums, such species as *Trillium grandiflorum*, *T. erectum*, *T. stylosum*, and *T. undulatum*. All are pleasingly beautiful when in flower and grow vigorously in a wet-damp situation. Also the foliage of these plants furnishes a mantle to the young growths of the *Lilium*, protecting them from the late spring frosts.

Sections of the mounds could be used to naturalize species of the beautiful native orchids: *Cypripedium parviflorum* and *C. parviflorum pubescens*, although the latter is better suited to the wild garden (which see). The showy orchis (*Orchis spectabilis*) and *O. rotundifolia* are also suited to the mounds.

In the depressions: *Cypripedium arietinum*, *Habenaria ciliaris* and *H. psycodes*, will be at home, as will the rose pogonia. All these plants are moisture lovers and are at their best in an acid soil.

The cardinal flower (*Lobelia cardinalis*) should be given a prominent place in the bog garden and it is seen to advantage when given the companionship of *Primula sikkimensis*. The bleeding-heart (*Dicentra spectabilis*) is a worth-while subject for the bog garden and is at home when growing in peaty soil. All the varieties of *Astilbe japonica* do best in moist situations and are adaptable to any color combination from warm white to deep pink. The arrowheads (*Sagittaria*) are attractive plants and revel in a position near the margin of the water. The bogbean or buckbean (*Menyanthes trifoliata*) is one of the attractive subjects of the moist bog, its flowers are white, pink or purplish, bearded inside with white hairs.

One of the showy native plants is the pickerelweed (*Pontederia cordata*). Its upright habit of growth and its thick, parallel-veined leaves make it a very worthy subject for any wet position in the bog. In the cool and damp edges surrounding the bog garden the beautiful gentians will thrive; such species as *Gentiana asclepiadea*, *G. andrewsi*, and the fringed gentian (*G. crinita*). The forget-me-nots (*Myosotis*) are happy dwellers in moist situations, are readily naturalized and become a beautiful feature of the bog.

Unless the bog is in the immediate vicinity of the flower garden, showy flowering plants massed for effect look at their best when they are detached from each other as they appear in nature. It is much better when planting the bog garden to bear in mind that the naturalistic is to be followed rather than the formal. Nature has no use for the formal in her wild garden arrangement. If the bog adjoins the garden proper, then a more free use can be made of garden plants, but even in this case the emphasis should be placed on natural plantings rather than on the well-groomed appearance of the flower garden. See Informal Garden.

Mass plantings of cat-tails are appropriate when placed in moist soil near the edge of the bog. Excellent summer effects are produced by a planting of *Cyperus papyrus*. This plant is not hardy and will require the protection of a cool greenhouse during winter. *Zizania aquatica*, a wild rice, is one of the most interesting of our native hardy plants. It is an annual and will spread rapidly, therefore the young plants should be removed in the early spring where they encroach on other plants.

## The Small Bog Garden

Where space will not admit the making of a bog garden on the scale of the one discussed, a miniature garden may be constructed by the use of cement pools and barrels cut in half and sunk in the ground. These are best placed in the lowest part of the garden, if low ground is available; if not, they may be kept moist by artificial means. The space where the tubs and bog plants are to be placed should be excavated to a depth of a foot or more. Prepared soil as outlined above should then be filled in. When filling in, the ground should be sunk four or five inches below the level of the surrounding land. This will tend to keep the soil in a fairly moist condition.

Plants recommended for the smaller bog garden are: *Anagallis linifolia*, *Caltha palustris*, *Cypripedium pubescens* and its variety *parviflorum*, *Drosera longifolia* and *D. rotundifolia*, *Gentiana andrewsi*, *Helonias bullata*, *Menyanthes trifoliata*, *Myosotis palustris*, *Parnassia caroliniana*, *Pinguicula vulgaris*, *Rhexia virginica*, and *Sarracenia purpurea* (see Pitcher-plant). The latter is one of a group of insectivo-

---

* Special articles on the subjects indicated by an asterisk (*) will be found at the words so marked.

**BOG MYRTLE** = *Myrica gale.*

**BOG ROSEMARY.** See ANDROMEDA.

**BOG RUSH** = *Juncus effusus.*

**BOG VIOLET** = *Pinguicula vulgaris.*

**BOIS D'ARC** = *Maclura pomifera.*

**BOKHARA CLOVER** = *Melilotus alba.*

**BOLDO** = *Peumus boldus.*

**BOLDUS.** Latinized form of the Chilean vernacular boldo (*Peumus boldus*).

**BOLIVIENSIS, -e** (bo-liv-i-en′sis). From Bolivia.

**BOLTING TREES.** See TREE SURGERY.

**BOLTONIA** (bole-tone′i-a). A small genus of aster-like perennial herbs of the family Compositae, the two below native in the U.S. and planted in the border for ornament. They are erect, leafy plants with alternate* leaves that usually stand vertical by a slight twisting of the essentially stalkless base. Flowers in short-stalked heads, the many rays rather showy, white or violet or purplish. (Named for James Bolton, English botanist.)

These tall, stout, native plants, often called false camomile, false starwort or thousand-flowered aster, are of the easiest culture. They should be planted in the open sunlight and towards the rear of a bed or border. Their profuse bloom in late summer and early fall makes them attractive garden plants. Easily propagated by spring or fall division.

asteroides. From 5–8 ft. high and bushy. Leaves lance-shaped, 3–5 in. long, nearly without marginal teeth, pale green. Flower heads about ¾ in. wide, very numerous, generally white, but sometimes violet or even purple. Conn. to Fla., mostly near the coast, and westward to Neb. Sometimes sold as *B. laevigata.*

latisquama. Similar, but with larger heads (about 1 in.) that are violet-blue. Mo. to Okla. The commonest species in cult., especially its *var.* nana, which is only 2–3 ft. high and has pink flower heads.

**BOMBACACEAE** (bom-ba-kay′see-ee). The silk-cotton tree family (often called the baobab family) comprises only about 20 genera and possibly 150 species of tropical, often huge, trees. All the hort. genera have compound* leaves, the leaflets arranged finger-fashion. Flowers solitary or in clusters (panicles*), appearing before the leaves unfold in *Adansonia, Bombax* and *Ceiba*. The only other cult. genera, *Pachira*, has solitary flowers about a foot long, while *Chorisia* has solitary yellow flowers about 3 in. wide.

Few of these genera are much cultivated outdoors in U.S. except as curiosities or for shade in zone* 9. The fruit of the baobab (*see* ADANSONIA) and kapok (*see* CEIBA) are both of interest, and the flowers of *Pachira* are extremely showy.

Technical flower characters: Calyx 5-toothed. Petals 5. Stamens* 5 or many, often showy. Ovary superior,* the style one, the stigmas 2–5.

**BOMBAX** (bom′backs). Very large, soft-wooded, tropical trees, family Bombacaceae, its 60 species of little hort. interest outside of the tropics, although the cotton tree is planted outdoors in the southern part of Fla. It is too big for greenhouse culture. They have compound* leaves, the 3–7 leaflets arranged finger-fashion. Flowers large, red, appearing when the tree is leafless, hence very showy. (For flower structure *see* BOMBACACEAE.) Fruit a capsule,* its seeds embedded in a fluffy mass of cotton-like hairs. (*Bombax* is Latin for cotton or cotton wadding.)

malabaricum. Cotton tree. A spiny tree up to 80 ft. Leaflets 5–7 in. long, but the tree leafless from Dec. to April. Flowers nearly 4 in. long, clustered towards the ends of the branches, blooming in Jan. Fruit 4–6 in. long. Indo-Malaya.

**BONA-NOX** (bone-a-nocks′). Good night.

**BONAVIST** = *Dolichos lablab.*

**BONE AND BONE MEAL.** See FERTILIZERS.

**BONESET.** See EUPATORIUM.

**BONUS-HENRICUS** (bone-us-hen′ri-kus). Good (King) Henry. See CHENOPODIUM.

**BOOKS ON GARDENING.** See GARDEN BOOKS.

**BOOT-JACK** = BEGGAR-TICKS. See list at WEEDS.

**BORAGE.** See BORAGO.

**BORAGE FAMILY** = Boraginaceae.

**BORAGINACEAE** (bore-aj-i-nay′see-ee). The borage family (often called the heliotrope or comfrey family) contains many well-known garden plants among its 85 genera and over 1500 species. Most of them are herbs of the temperate zone, but *Cordia* and *Ehretia* are tropical shrubs and trees.

Leaves mostly alternate,* the foliage generally rough-hairy. Flowers usually small, but in attractive, 1-sided clusters in most genera, especially in forget-me-not (*Myosotis*), *Anchusa, Brunnera, Echium, Mertensia,* and *Heliotropium.* In some other garden genera the flower cluster is not at all one-sided.

The characters that distinguish the genera of the borage family are mostly technical and based on the tiny, nut-like fruit. From the garden standpoint, the remaining genera are perhaps best grouped thus: *Lindelofia* and *Omphalodes* somewhat resemble forget-me-not; *Lithospermum, Lithodora,* and *Moltkia* are closely related to each other; *Pulmonaria* is allied to *Mertensia; Arnebia* has spotted, yellow flowers; *Cerinthe* has yellow, but purple-tipped flowers; *Borago* and *Cynoglossum* are usually blue or purple-flowered; and the remaining garden genera, *Myosotidium, Onosma,* and *Symphytum* are variously colored.

Technical flower characters: Calyx and corolla 5-cleft, the calyx often persistent. Corolla often with an appendage.

**BORAGO** (bore-ray′go). A small genus of European herbs, family Boraginaceae, the one below grown in the blue garden for its flowers, which are much liked by bees; also in the herb garden (*see* HERB GARDENING). It is an annual with stiff-hairy foliage. Leaves alternate.* Flowers blue, more or less wheel-shaped, in a loose, leafy cluster. (*Borago* is derived from the Latin *burra*, rough-hairy.)

The borage is a hardy annual, the seeds of which should be sown where the plants are to bloom.

officinalis. Borage. Not over 2 ft. high. Leaves oblongish, 3½–5 in. long, generally narrowed to a winged stalk or base. Flowers about ¾ in. wide, the stamens protruding as much as ¼ in. Southern Eu. and northern Af. Blooming all summer.

**BORBONIA** (bor-bō′ni-a). An old and now untenable generic name for certain plants included in *Persea* (which see).

**BORBONICA, -us, -um** (bore-bon′i-ka). From Réunion (once called Bourbon) Island, in the Indian Ocean. Also applied to some species named for the Bourbon kings of France.

**BORDEAUX MIXTURE.** For directions on how to prepare it *see* under Copper at FUNGICIDES. For its use in insect control *see* Repellents at INSECTICIDES.

**BORDER.** As generally understood this term refers to any more or less long and narrow strip of land in the garden, and is not necessarily confined to plantings along the property margins. Borders may be made close to the house, parallel with walks and drives, and designed to form inclosures or garden compartments. They should be laid out with due regard to proportion with the rest of the place, and as a rule be of rather simple outline. Borders are generally planted with a variety of plants arranged chiefly for mass effect. The planting may consist entirely of shrubs; of herbaceous or annual flowers both hardy and tender; or a mixture of both shrubs and herbs. A border may be entirely in the open, exposed to full sunlight, or be subject to shade in varying degree. In any case a selection of plants can be made that will thrive and give good results, providing the planter has exercised good judgment in making the choice.

Flowers appear to best advantage against some kind of background. Shrubs are good if far enough back so as not to smother and rob of food all but the more robust kinds of flowers. A clipped hedge is good if there is a walk or strip of turf between it and the border. Sometimes a wall is ideal, especially one laid up with native stone of a pleasing character, in not too mechanical a manner. When partly clothed with

---

* Special articles on the subjects indicated by an asterisk (*) will be found at the words so marked.

climbing plants it becomes an attraction as well as a protection. In other surroundings a picket fence, or one made of more rustic material, will seem to be just the thing for a suitable background and to support such plants as roses and clematis.

### Preparing the Border

Whatever the designation of the border may be, it is of the utmost importance that the work of preparing the soil for planting should be of the most thorough nature, especially when the occupants are to be of a somewhat permanent character. The general run of cultivated plants do not thrive in a water-logged soil, so if the site is one not naturally well drained, the surplus water must be taken care of by tile drains or other means. The ideal soil is a spade-depth or more of good free working loam, but too often soil far from ideal has to be dealt with. The addition of sand or coal-ashes works wonders in improving the texture of a heavy soil, and only if the sub-soil is exceptionally hard and unkind are excavation and replacement necessary. Light soils are naturally improved by the addition of heavier loam or powdered clay, while a plentiful supply of leaf-mold or good humus will greatly increase its moisture-retaining capacity.

Deep cultivation by double digging pays sure dividends on the extra effort required, in the form of better and happier-looking plants. By this excellent form of exercise the soil is stirred up to a depth of two feet, which creates a deeper root run and storage place for plant food. The method is to open a trench two feet wide and a foot deep at one end by removing that much soil and putting it on one side for the finish. The bottom twelve inches is then forked over, and to make a good job some rotted manure or leaf-mold should be dug in. In the case of a retentive sub-soil this is the time to work in something of a gritty nature to render it more porous and so improve drainage. The next spit of top-soil is then turned on top of this, and so the work proceeds to the end of the strip, with two layers of soil well cultivated and enriched, still in their former positions. Sub-soil should not be brought to the surface until improved by such treatment.

### Hardy Flower Border

Some flower borders are designed to give a very definite display for a short period of the year only, but for most people the best kind of border is one composed chiefly of hardy, herbaceous perennials selected to keep up a succession of bloom over the longest possible season. Hardy bulbs open the display, although sometimes the minor ones at least are thought to be a nuisance in the flower border. But to most people clumps of snowdrops, crocuses, scillas and the like, mean far more than the tallest sunflower, and if there is no other place for these cheery harbingers of spring they can be kept along the front edge in amongst the "mat" plants such as dwarf phlox, rock-cress, pinks and other good front-line plants. The various types of narcissus, followed by the glowing, May-flowering tulips appear to fine advantage amongst the young growth of hardy perennials, and do not need annual replacement. *See* Bulbs.

Varieties of columbines, irises and pyrethrums strike a dominant note as the tulips fade out of the picture, and from this time on there should be a succession of bloom until the season ends. Good backbone plants for the hardy border are to be found amongst peonies, anchusas, lupins, hemerocallis, delphiniums, campanulas, anthemis, coreopsis, gaillardias, heleniums, phlox, veronicas, asters, boltonias, anemones and chrysanthemums. All of these may be represented by good garden varieties, and there are many lesser lights to add to the general interest and display if need be. Many of the true lilies are good-natured enough to get along in the average border and should not be overlooked.

### Planting

In most parts the planting of this kind of border can be done to good advantage in the fall. The soil is then in good working condition, new roots are quickly formed, and the spring rush of work is eased. The chief gain is for the plants, as they are all set to grow from the first in spring. If planting has to be done then the work should be pushed forward as soon as the soil is dry enough to work freely if ordinary clump divisions are used. Pot plants of most kinds are available for unavoidable late planting. There is no hard and fast rule concerning arrangement. Much depends on personal taste, but it is well to give some thought to the succession of bloom, so as to have flowers fairly well distributed throughout the border all during the season. Plant in groups of three or more of a kind rather than in lines, while a free-and-easy effect is generally more pleasing than a too-well-graded outline.

Elaborate color schemes do not always come out according to plan, and here again the personal taste enters, but color harmony is doubtless more appealing to the majority of people than vivid contrasts. White and pale yellow have a pacifying effect between groups of clashing colors, and in general strong colors should be kept in the background, with pastel shades to the fore. It is well to avoid a too regular grouping and even spacing of the color masses, or a feeling of spottiness rather than a blending of colors will prevail. (*See* Color Gardens.)

### Maintenance

The suggestion has often been put forward as an argument in their favor, that hardy perennials will take good care of themselves and give a good display year after year with little or no attention. It is true that such ones as peonies, dictamnus and gypsophila can remain happy for a long time without disturbance at the root, but the majority need to be dug up and divided every so often if they are to keep going in vigorous condition. Certain groups, such as phlox, helenium and aster, are the better for being divided every second or third year, but for most this can be deferred for another year or two. A little observation will show when and how division of the clumps should be performed. Double digging and enrichment of the soil is in order whenever this dividing takes place, and for the old settlers remaining undisturbed some fresh food should be placed within reach at such times. In most instances the work of renovation can be done in the fall, and of course this is always the time to make any replacements of spring-flowering bulbs. Narcissus clumps need to be divided about every fourth year, and this can be safely done at this time also, even though new roots will have been made. They suffer no apparent harm so long as not allowed to get dry, and may be kept out of place for days during a renovating job, if kept covered with moist material. A cultural detail worth doing in the late fall is to fork lightly over the border just before putting on the winter covering. When the cover comes off in spring a light scratching of the surface will give that well-groomed effect, with little danger of injuring pushing shoots of bulbs and other plants.

Winter protection is provided in the form of a not too heavy covering of some material that will not pack into a sodden mass. A shake of partly rotted manure is good, affording nourishment as well as protection. Salt hay is much used and corn stalks have a value in this connection. Pine needles make good clean covering, and where pine and hemlock trees abound it is possible to get evergreen boughs, than which there is nothing better for covering those plants with persistent foliage. The important thing is not to cover before winter has really taken possession, and to proceed with caution about removing the material in spring. The real purpose of covering is not to keep the plants warm, but rather to maintain even conditions about the plants during the periods of freezing and thawing, and to guard against the ill effects which follow extreme weather changes. For further details *see* Mulch and Mulching.

A sprinkling of bone meal scratched in early in spring is safe and good for the average flower border and helps to maintain a healthy but not soft growth throughout the season. Wood ashes are also excellent to apply at this time. If in early summer it appears an extra feeding is required, sheep manure or some other quick-acting fertilizer lightly scattered during a rainy time, or watered in, will keep growth moving. Watering is a vexatious problem

---

\* Special articles on the subjects indicated by an asterisk (\*) will be found at the words so marked.

in a dry time. It is often started before really needed and for lack of a proper understanding of its function little or no good follows. Sprinklings are of no use, the job must be done thoroughly if at all. Surface cultivation before a crust forms after rain or waterings helps conserve soil moisture, as does the application of a fine mulch. The matter of staking calls for attention early in the season, before the growth is far enough advanced to be injured or broken in storms. The art of staking is to provide support without it being too obvious or detracting from the natural appearance of the plants. Bamboo canes are good for the heavier ones, while twiggy brush worked in amongst the lighter plants gives ample support without tying. (See STAKES AND STAKING.) The prompt removal of faded flowers ensures a trim appearance, and in many cases lengthens the flowering period.

### ANNUALS

The use of annuals in the hardy border has come to be accepted as a matter of course, and they add greatly to the floral display. They are really necessary to cover the gaps left by the passing of the spring bulbs and other early flowers. While it is possible to sow seeds of the more robust kinds in place, it is generally better to have plants coming along in pots, or ready to transplant from a seed-bed, for this style of work. To fill gaps along the front of the border, such kinds as ageratum, verbena, petunia, phlox, pinks and candy-tuft offer colorful and good varieties. The intermediate forms of antirrhinum make good fillers behind the front row. Other desirable kinds for this section are to be found amongst arctotis, browallias, calendulas, cynoglossum, gaillardias, and nigella. Of larger growth for the back of the border, cosmos, scabious, larkspur, helichrysum, nicotianas, and helianthus are all first-class. *Salvia farinacea* is one of several plants that are perennial in a mild climate, but that can be grown and flowered as annuals. This should find a place in any border. Its long spikes of lavender-blue flowers blend well and are good for a long time.

A well-planned border of annuals alone can be a source of much beauty and satisfaction. Perhaps because they are easy to grow and not expensive, they do not always receive the good treatment they deserve. They appreciate well-prepared soil and should be given ample room to develop their individual habit of growth. (*See* ANNUALS.)

### THE SHRUB BORDER

A border of shrubs gives a feeling of greater permanency than a flower border, so perhaps for that reason it is likely to receive less care. It is quite a common occurrence to plant shrubs too close for the sake of immediate effect. This does very well if thinning out and re-arrangement are attended to when crowding begins. Too often, however, this is entirely neglected and the result is a tangled mass of growth of no great decorative value. In the selection of kinds for a particular place some thought should be given to their ultimate size. In most cases, of course, when planted in a border they are not expected to attain the same size as when grown as single specimens. One bad feature of a random selection is likely to be the excessive use of pruning shears, thereby sacrificing flowers and beauty of form.

There is a wealth of good material to select from. Desirable new introductions follow a collector's trip from time to time, while some old families have produced improved forms through the skill of the hybridist, so there is really no excuse for the planting of a commonplace and uninteresting shrub border. The list should be scanned with an eye to values in leaf and berry effect as well as just for flower, so beauty and interest will remain throughout the season. To secure a harmonious composition in the arrangement of various shrubs in a large border requires careful study. This is difficult to achieve if too great an assortment of kinds is used, although related species or varieties generally go together very well. Shrubs with variegated leaves should be used with restraint and not spotted all over the place. Those with colored stems, so effective in providing a touch of color in winter, are likewise best when grouped together.

The acid-soil lovers can be used to give interesting and valuable combinations in lime-free sections. The choice of broad-leaved evergreens for northern gardens is strictly limited by climatic conditions. For such as rhododendron, kalmia, pieris, and leucothoë, it is well worth a little effort to try to accommodate these with a sheltered place whenever possible. The showy flowers of azaleas show to best advantage against coniferous evergreens, and are more lasting in partial shade. The earliest kinds begin to flower before spring frosts are over, and when spring has really arrived a representative collection of azaleas will give a gorgeous outburst of color when happily placed. (*See* AZALEA.) *Enkianthus* belongs in this group, and while its flowers are not so showy, it has a lot of character, and is outstanding in the fall with a brilliant display of red leaf coloring. Good low evergreens to associate with this group are the various forms of calluna (heather), kept in good condition by a spring shearing. Where the climate will permit, certain of the closely related ericas (heath) will add their quota of interest. *Leiophyllum buxifolium* (sand myrtle) and *Pachistima canbyi* are also worthy of planting in the best of borders.

All the plants mentioned in this group do well in sandy loam and should have a perpetual mulch of leaves, pine-needles or peat-moss. This is one border that should not be forked over or tidied up by removing the mulch. Yearly additions keep up the essential soil acidity and help to maintain that desirable condition of coolness and moisture at the roots.

Shrubs which flower before winter has quite passed are more than welcome. A native witch-hazel (*Hamamelis vernalis*) is one of these, and often its curious and fragrant flowers are opened in abundance before the year is very old. Another early bloomer, and the showiest member of the family, is the Chinese species, *Hamamelis mollis*, which is likely soon to be more widely known. Where space is not limited the Cornelian cherry (*Cornus mas*) and the aromatic spicebush are worth a place for their early clusters of tiny yellow flowers. They come in just ahead of the more showy forsythias, which lead the main show. *Lonicera fragrantissima* is another of the early indispensables, the first to bloom of a genus containing many good flowering and fruiting kinds. *Viburnum carlesi* must be included in any border for its charming and fragrant clusters. Several others of this genus also have strong claims for inclusion, particularly for fine berry effects late in the season. Some of the old stand-bys can be represented by newer and even more desirable forms. The Japanese flowering quince is available in a colorful assortment, while the many species and varieties of lilacs often put a strain on available space. Spireas and deutzias, weigelas and mock-orange each offers good varieties to carry on the wealth of flower into early summer. *Rhodotypos* is excellent in flower and form, and especially good for its green leaf effect late in the fall, when most other deciduous shrubs are bare. The old-fashioned kerria is fine to tie a planting to the ground, and its bright green stems have good winter value. Another good "facer" is the hybrid *Symphoricarpos chenaulti*, with lacy foliage held late. For bold foliage *Hydrangea quercifolia* is good. Its large panicles of mixed perfect and sterile flowers have summer value, and in fall the fine leaves take on a deep ruddy tint. Varieties of Rose-of-Sharon must have a place for their colorful display in late summer and fall. Only passing mention can be made of berried shrubs, but genera like *Aronia, Berberis, Cotoneaster*, and *Euonymus* contain many of outstanding value.

The maintenance of a shrub border is not very exacting if the preparatory work was well done. Pruning is usually the bugbear, and before the shears are brought into play the natural habit and the manner of flowering should be understood. With most it is a matter of thinning out the older parts rather than a cutting back of everything. (*See* PRUNING.) Feeding is too often neglected. Organic manures are best, and a mulch of rotted manure or leaves put on in the fall is advantageous.

---

\* Special articles on the subjects indicated by an asterisk (\*) will be found at the words so marked.

## The Mixed Border

The planting of shrubs and herbaceous perennials together may sometimes be worked out in an interesting manner, especially where there is room to do it on an ample scale. In a small garden only the smaller kinds should be considered, but there are enough of these to make an interesting grouping. Some of the dwarf forms of coniferous evergreens, such as yew and juniper, give a pleasing year-round effect, while equally valuable shrubs are to be found amongst the euonymus, barberries and cotoneasters. Often a good arrangement of the shrubs is in a series of bays, bringing to the fore such plants as perennial candytuft, sun-rose, pachysandra and *Daphne cneorum*. *Daphne mezereum* should find a place in such a planting, both for its early fragrant flowers, neat habit, and scarlet berries in summer. Only the choicest kinds of shrubs should be chosen and not very closely planted, so as to allow room for good individual development. *Rosa hugonis* and other roses of this habit make good background plants, while the improved forms of shrubby cinquefoil make neat groups for the foreground. In some sections certain shrubs may be more or less killed back by severe weather, and in fact respond well if treated like an herbaceous plant, except that the cutting down should be left until spring. Certain shrubby members of the verbena family, such as callicarpa, clerodendron, caryopteris, and vitex, have this tendency. They are valuable for late flower or fruit display and fit in well with a mixed group. Some buddleias and lespedezas also respond to this treatment and flower freely. Some yuccas might be introduced here and there for a stately effect, while the eremurus might find just the protection it needs for the proper development of its towering spikes, known as desert candles. Several of the lilies could be so grouped as to get protection from the shrubs when they first push up their tender shoots, and add much to the summer display. (*See* Lilium.) All kinds of narcissus are invaluable for spring display, while irises and peonies just seem to belong in this kind of border. Such robust growers as thermopsis, baptisia, plume poppy, eryngium, echinops, aster, boltonia, helenium, helianthus, and verbascum associate with shrubs to good advantage. The Japanese anemone does well in partial shade and for a moist place the giant mallows are well suited. The list can easily be extended to suit any particular place.

## The Shady Border

The satisfactory planting of shady borders is often a real problem, especially when flowers are desired. Sometimes shade alone is not the only factor to deal with. The cause of the shade may be the root of the trouble, the presence of large trees which have their full nine-tenths of possession. Just cutting back the roots gives a very temporary relief where this condition prevails. In extreme cases about the only thing possible is to use evergreen ground-covers such as English ivy, the creeping forms of euonymus, and pachysandra, depending on the early spring bulbs for floral effect. The soil will need to be loosened and perhaps added to, working in a good dressing of humus to stimulate the new plants into action. Moisture will be their chief need for a time. With shade and a fair degree of moisture, a good "woodsy" combination of flowering herbs, ferns and shrubs may be worked out in a most attractive manner. Amongst the general run of garden flowers certain kinds are tolerant of shade if other handicaps are not too great. Bulbs, forget-me-nots, primroses and violets lead the way. *Mertensia*, Solomon's-seal, lily-of-the-valley, and the bleeding-heart are always reliable. So, too, is the good-natured plantain-lily. *Epimedium* attracts with its curious flowers and good leaf value. Valerian, garden heliotrope, bellflowers, monkshoods and foxgloves all do well, and a very happy combination for late summer is red turtlehead and mist-flower. (*See* Eupatorium.) Four-o'clocks and nicotianas give both color and delightful fragrance, while the common spiderwort gives a long succession of its fleeting flowers. Broad-leaved evergreens are valuable shady-place plants if given liberal treatment in food and moisture. Amongst deciduous shrubs dogwoods, privets, barberries and some viburnums are reliable. The old-fashioned sweet-shrub is happy in shade, and the mock-orange is also quite tolerant. Forsythias with their golden showers, and single and double kerrias will brighten up a shady corner, and when all flowers are past the extremely tolerant snowberry makes a good contrast with the red fruits of the winterberry. *See also* Shady Garden.

## Rock Border

In this case not the conventional rock garden border is considered, but rather a border or slope where boulders occur naturally or otherwise. The dwarf form of the common juniper and the numerous trailing garden varieties of other junipers are well adapted for this style of planting in open situations. In the shade, if not too dry, the ground hemlock will thrive, and in really damp places the ostrich and royal ferns will grow to perfection and adorn the boulders. The prostrate kinds of cotoneaster and the varied forms of *Euonymus radicans* never appear better than when nestling up to a shapely boulder. Where plants of larger growth would be appropriate the fragrant sumach and scotch broom (*see* Broom) are useful, the latter especially so in sandy or gravelly soil. *Lonicera syringantha* and *Forsythia suspensa* are still larger, and their pendulous habit makes them effective on slopes. Where hardy, *Jasminum nudiflorum* is valued for its early bloom and sprawling habit. Matrimony vine, trumpet-creeper, Japanese honeysuckle, bittersweet, virgin's-bower, and various kinds of ampelopsis are more robust sprawlers that seem to love to clamber over rocks.

## Tender Border Plants

Where frost is only a casual visitor many plants familiar in northern greenhouses are seen to advantage outdoors. Tender relatives of generally hardy families may be associated with the very exotic-looking shrubs from S.A., Aust., and N.Z., and a greater wealth of evergreens is available. Only samples can be mentioned here, but amongst evergreen shrubs with attractive flowers or fruit *Berberis darwini* and others take high rank, as does the related and handsome *Nandina*. *Viburnum* is well represented by the notable laurustinus. The amazing variety in *Veronica* is proved by the shrubby natives of N.Z., while the elegance of *Abelia* is developed to the full. With modest flowers but delightful fragrance, *Daphne odora*; *Diosma ericoides*, known as breath-of-heaven; the compact pittosporums, clipped or natural; the neat *Azara microphylla*. Rosemary and lemon verbena both deserve a special place. *Ceanothus* hybrids with their clouds of pale-blue flowers go well with the glossy and fragrant *Choisya ternata*. Acacias with feathery flowers and foliage; the showy *Chorizema*; *Coronilla glauca*; *Cytisus* in variety, including the genista of the florist, are worthy representatives of the Pea family.

English Holly, box-huckleberry, the glossy escallonias, and the classic myrtle are choice plants for hedges as well as informal growth. Vines of distinction are jasmine, passion-flower, coral vine and *Solanum jasminoides*. See the body of this Dictionary for notes on the hardiness of all these tender border plants. — H. E. D.

**BOREALIS, -e** (bor-ree-ā'lis). Northern.

**BORECOLE** = *Brassica oleracea acephala*. For culture see Kale.

**BORERS.** See the section under Bees and under Beetles at Insect Pests. For the best methods of control of the different sorts of borers, see the Insect Pests at Apple, Azalea, Blackberry, Corn, and Sunflower.

**BORINQUENA, -us, -um** (bor-rin-kwen'a). Derived from an old Spanish name for the island of Porto Rico.

**BOROL.** A paradichlorobenzene preparation sold with directions for use against borers.

**BORONIA** (bor-ro'nee-a). A large genus of Australian, fragrant and evergreen shrubs of the rue family, two of which are grown for ornament, mostly in the greenhouse or outdoors in frost-free regions. Leaves opposite, compound* (in the two below), with a few lateral leaflets. Flowers

---

* Special articles on the subjects indicated by an asterisk (*) will be found at the words so marked.

solitary or in twos, borne mostly along the stem, often so thickly as partially to hide it. Stamens 8, 4 small, yellow and pollen-bearing, the other four large, purple, but sterile. Fruit capsule*-like. (Named for Francesco Borone, an Italian friend of Sir Joseph E. Smith, British botanist.)

Boronias are very aromatic greenhouse shrubs cult. for their pleasing odor and profusion of flowers. They need a cool greenhouse, not much or certainly not excessive watering, and potting mixture* 5. They should be cut back to the ground after blooming and renewed completely every second or third year. Propagated by cuttings, preferably under a bell-jar.

elatior. A leafy shrub up to 4 ft. high. Leaves stalked, the leaflets 2-6 pairs, with an odd terminal one, very narrow. Flowers rose-purple or red, about ¼ in. wide, very numerous, and often of different colors on the same plant.

megastigma. A sparsely leafy shrub, but twiggy and 12-20 in. high. Leaves stalkless, the leaflets 1 or 2 pairs, with an odd terminal one, about ¾ in. long. Flowers yellow inside, purple outside, nearly ½ in. wide.

**BOSTON FERN** = *Nephrolepis exaltata bostoniensis*.

**BOSTON IVY** = *Parthenocissus tricuspidata*.

**BOSTON MARROW.** A smooth-skinned winter squash. See SQUASH.

**BOTANIC GARDEN.** Primarily an institution for research in the field of botany, by extension, an institution which may include horticulture, or any of several applications of the science of plant life to practical affairs. The modern, well-balanced botanical garden is apt to have, besides research laboratories, a library and herbarium, large collections of growing plants both outdoors and in the greenhouse. All of the more important ones in America also maintain a department of horticulture and often elaborate gardens to illustrate it.

There are two botanic gardens in the country which from age, endowments, staff and research are easily the leading institutions of the sort and well worth any gardener's visit. The oldest (established 1860) is the Missouri Botanical Garden at St. Louis, Mo. The largest and most important is the New York Botanical Garden, Bronx Park, New York City, established in 1898.

The Missouri Botanical Garden, besides its systematic collections, has the following features of special interest to gardeners: one of the finest collections of greenhouse orchids in the world; a tropical fruit greenhouse; the best collection of hardy and tender water lilies in the U.S.; a fine formal garden; a special garden of hardy perennials; a large collection of hardy and tropical ferns; and over 11,000 species of plants under cultivation. The garden comprises about 75 acres at St. Louis and fifteen hundred more at its arboretum at Gray Summit, Mo.

The New York Botanical Garden (area over 500 acres), besides its great prestige as a research institution, maintains the following collections of outstanding interest to the gardener: the greatest collection of hardy and tender cacti in the U.S.; large collections of such garden favorites as dahlias, irises, bulbs, daylilies, and roses; very large shrub and tree collections and another of evergreens; and a small model garden. It has nearly 12,000 species of plants in cultivation, both outdoors and under glass.

The Brooklyn Botanic Garden (established 1911, area 50 acres) has the following features of interest to gardeners: one of the best rock gardens in the U.S.; Japanese garden; rose garden; a fine collection of Japanese iris.

Two other botanic gardens, both more recent, demand attention. One is the United States Botanic Garden, established 1934. It should be the culmination of many years of devoted effort to create a real national botanic garden, and may be found at Maryland Avenue and 1st Street, S.W., Washington, D.C. The other is the Blaksley Botanic Garden, Santa Barbara, Calif., which maintains a fine collection of succulents and sub-tropical ornamentals. A new, recently opened botanic garden is at Ft. Worth, Tex.

A unique botanic garden is the Rancho Santa Ana, at Santa Ana Cañon, Orange County, Calif. It is devoted to the native plants of Calif., many hundreds of which are already in cult. there in an extremely attractive setting. The garden also maintains an herbarium of Calif. plants, a reference library, and co-operates with schools and colleges in an educational program.

Most universities maintain a botanic garden, usually as an adjunct of their work in the classroom. Most of them are an acre or so and, while growing many plants of great interest or merit, their horticultural significance is slight. The leading gardens of this type are at Johns Hopkins, Harvard, University of Pennsylvania, Yale, University of Michigan, Ohio State University, Smith College, and Bryn Mawr.

See also ARBORETUM, BARTRAM'S GARDEN, BOYCE THOMPSON INSTITUTE, HOSACKIA and DESERT LABORATORY.

**BOTANY.** The science of plant life. One of its applications is to horticulture and gardening, the main purpose of this book. Botany, as such, is not. Some features of botany, however, should be known to all gardeners. (See LEAF, FLOWER, FRUIT, ROOT, etc.; see also the various entries under PLANT.)

**BO-TREE** = *Ficus religiosa*.

**BOTRYCHIUM** (bo-trick'i-um). The grape ferns or moonworts, family Ophioglossaceae, are little grown except in the wild garden. Of the 40 known species only two are likely to be cult. They have underground stems from which arises at intervals a single compound* leaf (frond), the leaflets arranged feather-fashion. On an apparently separate stalk, usually exceeding the frond, is a branched, grapelike (but small) cluster of spore cases. This is the fertile frond. (*Botrychium* is Greek for grape-like.)

The species below are both hardy over most of the country. They need the shade of trees or buildings, a good rich woods soil (not acid or only mildly so) and plenty of moisture.

dissectum. An evergreen fern 6-15 in. high, the fronds in 3 main, stalked segments but these dissected, the ultimate segments scarcely 1/16 in. wide. Fertile frond taller than the leaf-like one. Eastern U.S. There is a var. *obliquum*, with much wider ultimate segments. It is sometimes known as *Botrychium ternatum*.

virginianum. Rattlesnake fern. From 6-20 in. high, the fronds with 3 main, stalked segments, the ultimate divisions oblongish and toothed towards the tip. Fertile frond scarcely exceeding the leaf-like one. North temperate zone. The most satisfactory species of the two, but neither is of much garden interest except to fern fanciers.

**BOTRYOIDES** (bo-tree-oy'deez; but see OÏDES). Grapelike or with grape-like clusters.

**BOTRYS.** An old classical name for the feather-geranium (*Chenopodium botrys*).

**BOTRYTIS, -e** (bo-try'tis). With a grape-like cluster.

**BOTRYTIS BLIGHT.** See Diseases at LILIUM and TULIPA.

**BOTTLE-BRUSH.** See CALLISTEMON and MELALEUCA.

**BOTTLE FERN** = *Cystopteris fragilis*.

**BOTTLE GARDEN.** See TERRARIUM.

**BOTTLE GENTIAN** = *Gentiana andrewsi*.

**BOTTLE GRAFTING.** See GRAFTING.

**BOTTLE PALM** = *Hyophorbe amaricaulis*.

**BOTTLE-TREE.** See BRACHYCHITON.

**BOTTOM-HEAT.** Heat applied underneath a greenhouse bench in which propagating material is growing. Application of bottom-heat is a common and useful aid in getting cuttings to root, and in the germination of some seeds. It is most widely used in making cuttings of tender plants which root more easily if the soil temperature (due to bottom-heat) is several degrees warmer than the air temperature of the greenhouse. A bench with bottom-heat needs close watching to keep it from drying out.

**BOTTOM ROT.** See Diseases at LETTUCE.

**BOUGAINVILLAEA** (boo-gen-vill-ee'a). Perhaps the handsomest, and certainly the most widely planted ornamental vines of the tropics, and a great favorite in the southern U.S. and in Calif. Of the 10 known species, all South American and belonging to the family Nyctaginaceae,

---

* Special articles on the subjects indicated by an asterisk (*) will be found at the words so marked.

the three below are the best known. They are tall-growing, woody vines with alternate,* stalked leaves. Flowers small and not at all showy, all the color coming from the large, showy bracts,* three of which surround each flower. (For flower characters see NYCTAGINACEAE.) Fruit a 5-ribbed achene.* (Named for de Bougainville, a French navigator.) There are several variations in spelling to be found in the catalogs. Two of the best known are *Buginvillaea* and *Bouginvillea*.

These vines, for arbors, porches, or for covering the corner of a house, are among the finest creepers known. They will grow in any ordinary garden soil and will stand considerable periods of drought. Outdoors their culture is limited to the most sheltered parts of zone* 7, but they are thoroughly at home in zones* 8 and 9, and, of course, throughout the tropics. Occasionally grown in northern greenhouses, but usually too rampant to be confined. Some florists keep them as trimmed pot plants. They need a cool greenhouse and potting mixture* 4. Propagated by cuttings.

**glabra.** A vine with a stout, woody and spiny but not hairy, stem, often 60–100 ft. long (in the tropics), much less in the U.S. Leaves oblongish, narrowed both ends. Flowers scattered on wand-like, lateral, usually drooping branchlets, the bracts magenta or purple and about 1 in. long, very showy. Brazil. There is a form with variegated leaves and another, *var.* **sanderiana**, with even more flowers than the typical form. It blooms most of the year.

**spectabilis.** Similar to *B. glabra*, but the stems densely hairy and with larger and more showy bracts. The bloom does not, however, last as long as in the other species, and the plant is a more rampant climber than *B. glabra*. Bracts reddish in the typical form, but in the variety Crimson Lake, crimson-red. This is the most popular variety in Fla. and Calif. Brazil.

**BOULDER BANK.** See Rock Border at BORDER.
**BOULDER RASPBERRY** = *Rubus deliciosus*.
**BOULE de NEIGE.** See DEUTZIA LEMOINEI.
**BOUNCING BET** = *Saponaria officinalis*.
**BOUNDARIES.** See SCREEN PLANTING. See also FENCES.
**BOUQUET.** See FLOWER ARRANGING.
**BOUQUET LARKSPUR** = *Delphinium grandiflorum*.
**BOURBON ROSE** = *Rosa borbonia*. See Group 5 at ROSE.

**BOUSSINGAULTIA** (boo-sin-galt'i-a). A small genus of tropical American herbaceous vines, family Bassellaceae, one grown for ornament in warm regions and an escape* in Fla. and Tex. They have a tuberous rootstock and alternate* leaves without marginal teeth. Flowers in spike-like clusters (racemes*). Sepals 2; petals 5, and the flower with 2 bracts beneath it. Fruit fleshy, enclosed by the persistent, withered flower. (Named for J. B. Boussingault, French chemist.)

The Madeira-vine is grown outdoors in the South, and its root, with some winter covering, will survive up to zone* 6. North of this the roots should be dug and stored for the winter in a cool, frost-free place.

**baselloides.** Madeira-vine; called also mignonette-vine, from the fragrance of its flowers. A tall creeper with ovalish or heart-shaped, taper-pointed leaves 2–3 in. long. Flowers white (black in age), small, but the slender, drooping racemes* often 12 in. long and showy. Tropical America. It produces tubercles in the axils* of the leaves which, if planted in moist sand, will produce new plants. Also called manetti-vine.

**BOUVARDIA** (boo-var'di-a). A genus of 30 species of attractive greenhouse shrubs of the madder family, most of them tropical American, and grown for their showy flowers. Leaves opposite* or in whorls.* Flowers tubular, in showy, terminal, flattish clusters (cymes*). Corolla-tube terminated by 4 spreading lobes. Stamens 4. Stigmas 2. Fruit a capsule.* (Named for Charles Bouvard, French physician.)

Bouvardias are handsome, but not much cult. shrubs, the hort. species evergreen and possibly not the original wild species as outlined below, as they were once much hybridized. They need a warm-temperate greenhouse (50°–55°), plenty of water, and should be grown in potting mixture* 5.

**humboldti.** A shrub 2–4 ft. high with opposite, ovalish leaves with a tapering tip. Flowers white, very fragrant, the tube nearly 2½ in. long, the limb about 1½ in. wide. Of uncertain origin, but probably a hort. form.

**ternifolia.** A shrub 4–6 ft. high, the leaves in whorls* of 3 or 4, more or less lance-oval. Flowers red, hairy on the outside, ¾–1¼ in. long. Tex. to Mex. Called also *B. triphylla*.

**BOWER PLANT** = *Pandorea jasminoides*.
**BOWIEA** = *Schizobasopsis*.
**BOWLING GREEN.** A bowling green is a level, compact turf area 120 ft. square, comparable to a putting green. Since the bowling concentrates wear at the two ends of the rink the play should be alternated from East–West to North–South weekly, to allow the end sod to recuperate while the other is being used.

Surrounding the rink is a gutter six inches below the level of the green with a creosoted wooden curb 2 × 8 inches supporting the edge of the gutter next to the green. The curb is held in place by stakes 2 × 4 × 18 inches driven into the ground on 5-ft. centers and nailed to the curb on the inside edge with the top of the stake ½ in. below the level of the green. The width of the gutter may vary from one to two feet, with either a wooden backboard or a turf bank to keep the bowls from roll-

Bowling Green

ing beyond. The floor of the gutter should be gravel 18 in. deep, underdrained by a 4-in. agricultural tile.

For bowling, the turf should be absolutely perfect because any undulation counteracts the skill of the bowler. The seed bed should be prepared exactly the same as for a putting green, with perfect underdrainage and at least six inches of good growing topsoil. A mixture of five parts good topsoil to one part peat moss or humus and one part well-rotted manure, with one pound of bone meal to each cubic foot of soil should be put into a concrete mixer and thoroughly mixed, then laid down in an even, six-inch layer over the subgrade. This should be rolled to a perfect level, seeded with Washington creeping bent (see LAWN) which should be raked lightly into the surface, and kept watered daily until satisfactory turf is developed. Just before the first cutting this turf should be rolled, and immediately after the cutting should be top-dressed with a mixture of sifted topsoil and humus, which should be repeated again twice during the first growing season.

Any ornamental planting or shelter around the bowling green depends upon its location and proposed use. For public use a building is necessary for rest rooms, changing of shoes and storage of equipment. — R. E. G.

**BOWMAN'S-ROOT** = *Gillenia trifoliata*.
**BOWSTRING HEMP.** See SANSEVIERIA.

**BOX.** The box, or as many call it, boxwood, is perhaps our most valuable broad-leaved evergreen. Of the thirty known species, all belonging to the genus **Buxus** (bucks'us), family Buxaceae, only two are in common cult. But from these, and their numerous hort. varieties, many historic gardens, especially in Md. and Va., have taken on an atmosphere of grace, charm and solidity that no other shrubs could give them. And since the days of the Romans it has been the best of all plants for hedges and topiary work.

Leaves opposite,* evergreen, without marginal teeth. Flowers small and inconspicuous, without petals, the male and female on the same plant, but not together, and usually the female flowers above the male ones. Female flowers with 6 sepals, the male flowers with 4. Fruit a 3-horned capsule.* (*Buxus* is classical Latin for the box.) For the Victorian box see PITTOSPORUM UNDULATUM.

---

* Special articles on the subjects indicated by an asterisk (*) will be found at the words so marked.

For Culture *see* below.

**B. harlandi.** An evergreen shrub, related to the next species, but not hardy northward. Its great merit is that it provides a box suitable for places where the summers are too hot and dry for the common box. China.

**B. microphylla.** A Japanese evergreen shrub, rarely over 3 ft. high, and resembling ordinary box, but with its leaves smaller and broadest above the middle, and with its branchlets prominently 4-angled or winged. This is more hardy than common box, often living up to zone* 4, especially in the *var.* **japonica**, which is also a little taller. The *var.* **koreana** (from Korea) is shorter than the typical form, rarely exceeding 18-20 in., and, like the *var.* **japonica**, more hardy.

**B. sempervirens.** The common box which (in some of its forms) ranges from a dwarf, globular shrub up to a tree 25 ft. high, the latter only in the most favorable sites. Leaves broadest at or below the middle, ¾-1½ in. long, lustrous-green both sides, but darker above. A native of southern Eu., northern Af. and western As., consequently not certainly hardy above zone* 4, but often grown there in locally favorable places or with winter protection. Of its many hort. forms there are weeping, pyramidal, globe-shaped and tree-like varieties, some with variegated foliage. One of the best is *var.* **suffruticosa**, the edging box, a permanent dwarf and used for centuries to edge beds and in formal gardens.

### CULTURE OF BOXWOOD

The box is a slow-growing plant, its hard, uniform wood having furnished Albrecht Dürer with material for his wood-blocks, and it still does for most artists. Because of its slow growth and evergreen habit it stands moving rather poorly. Its roots must not be exposed to the sun and wind, and it is safest moved with a large ball of earth tightly wrapped in stout canvas, not in porous bagging.

Box is not particular as to soils, and most ordinary garden soils will suit it. If large plants are to be transferred, dig a hole at least a foot deeper and wider than the ball of soil surrounding it. And the bottom of the hole should be of well-tamped, fine garden soil, not sandy or rocky. No matter what the size, the plants should be set a little deeper than their old ground level, and the new soil thoroughly packed around the root ball. Water copiously the first few weeks after planting, which, in the North, should be early in the spring or from Aug. 15 to Sept. 15. Recently transplanted large specimens should be shaded from the sun, winter or summer, until thoroughly established.

In clipping box it should be remembered that well-sheared forms, and, of course, all topiary work, are only secured by regular attention. However, along the northern edge of its hardiness range (*see* notes at SPECIES), clipping is best done in August or later, as earlier clipping may provoke young growth that will winter-kill if it does not have time to ripen its wood.

Like any other shrub they respond to mulching with well-rotted manure, and all old plants should be so treated every year. The beauty and popularity of box are so great that gardeners are always tempted to grow it beyond its natural range of hardiness. Such venturesome growers should read the articles on zones and on protecting plants.

Box is propagated by cuttings of mature wood taken early in the autumn. If in zone* 5 or 4, they should be kept in a cool greenhouse, in moist sand, without bottom-heat. Farther south the cuttings may be put in a shady place outdoors. It is also sometimes propagated by layers, and, in the edging box, by division. Growing box from seed is interminable.

INSECT PESTS. A tiny fly larva mines in the leaves of box. Nicotine spray, to which is added 1 part of molasses to 6 parts of water, applied about twice a week the first half of May, when adults are active, has been effective. Fumigating plants with hydrocyanic acid under covers in the dormant season and dipping small plants into warm water (120° F.) for 10 minutes are also good control measures. Mites can be controlled with sulphur sprays. The oyster-shell scale is sometimes troublesome and hard to check.

DISEASES. Canker of stems accompanied by yellow or straw-colored leaves and brittle twigs is caused by a fungus. Scorch or winter injury frequently produces similar symptoms. Twigs dead from whatever cause should be removed at once by careful cutting below the killed part. All dead twigs and leaves should be shaken from the plant, removed from the ground and burned. Where its appearance is not objectionable, bordeaux mixture may be used.

**BOX-BARBERRY** = *Berberis thunbergi minor*.

**BOX-ELDER** = *Acer negundo*. *See* MAPLE.

**BOX FAMILY** = Buxaceae.

**BOX-HUCKLEBERRY** = *Gaylussacia brachycera*. *See* HUCKLEBERRY.

**BOX-THORN.** *See* LYCIUM.

**BOXWOOD.** *See* Box. The name is also applied to *Cornus florida*.

**BOYCE THOMPSON INSTITUTE.** The Boyce Thompson Institute for Plant Research, at Yonkers, N.Y., is perhaps the leading botanical research institution in the U.S. Most of the experimental work done there is of the first interest to all intelligent gardeners, especially the work on different sorts of light rays, on gases, and on many problems affecting the growth of plants. It also maintains the Boyce Thompson Southwestern Arboretum at Superior, Ariz.

*BRACHYBOTRYS* (brack-ee-bō'triss). Short-clustered, like a bunch of grapes.

*BRACHYCERA*, *-us*, *-um* (bra-kiss'e-ra). Short-horned; sometimes short-tipped.

**BRACHYCHITON** (brack-ee-ky'ton). The bottle-trees, so named for the bottle-like swellings of the trunk, comprise a small genus of Australian trees, family Sterculiaceae, the two below planted for ornament in Fla. and Calif., rarely in greenhouses northward. They have alternate, and (in ours) simple* but deeply lobed leaves. Flowers unisexual* or polygamous,* very showy because of the clusters (mostly panicles*) of scarlet or yellowish bloom. Petals none, but the calyx bell-shaped and corolla-like. Stamens 10-15, in a column surrounding the pistil.* Fruit woody, tardily splitting. (*Brachychiton* is Greek for overlapping hairs or scales.)

These showy trees are hardy outdoors only in zones* 8 and 9, where, especially in Calif., the first species is much prized. It blooms in midsummer, after which the foliage falls quickly. Neither is particular as to soil, but apparently partial to the shade of larger trees for at least some of the day. Propagated by seeds or by ripe-wood cuttings.

**acerifolium.** Flame-tree. Frequently 40-55 ft. high. Leaves usually 8-10 in. wide, long-stalked and deeply lobed with 5-7 rounded divisions, or sometimes there are fewer lobes or none. Flowers brilliant scarlet, about ¾ in. long, smooth. Fruit smooth, black, about 4 in. long. Often called *Sterculia acerifolia*.

**populneum.** Kurrajong. A taller tree, the leaves very variable, scarcely more than 3 in. long, lobed, or unlobed and ovalish. Flowers yellowish-white, but reddish inside, and sometimes dark-spotted on the outside, hairy when young. Fruit 1-2½ in. long. Often called *Sterculia diversifolia*.

**BRACHYCOME** (bra-kick'o-me). A large genus of mostly Australian herbs of the family Compositae, one, the Swan River daisy, a very popular, tender annual. It has alternate,* rather small leaves, divided, feather-fashion, into narrow segments. Flower heads solitary on the ends of long stalks, the rays white, blue, or rose (in a hort. form). (The name is Greek for short hair, in allusion to the short bristles of the pappus.)

For culture *see* Tender Annuals at ANNUALS.

**iberidifolia.** Swan River daisy. A branching herb 8-18 in. high Leaves with few, but very narrow, segments. Flower heads about 1 in. wide, the rays blue or white, or rose color in some of the hort. forms. It is an excellent edging plant, and for making an attractive, low covering of bare places in the border.

*BRACHYPETALA*, *-us*, *-um* (brack-i-pet'a-la). With short petals.

**BRACKEN** = *Pteridium aquilinum*. *See* BRAKE.

**BRACT.** A small, leaf-like or membranous or even brightly colored organ usually confined to the stalks of a flower cluster or just beneath the flower itself. In many plants they look like miniature leaves and are commonly mistaken for them. Sometimes there are many small bracts surrounding a head, as in the Compositae (there called involucral bracts). But in other plants the bracts are the showiest part of a flower cluster, although a bract is not technically part of the flower. It is the highly colored bracts that make poinsettia, the flowering dogwood, and many plants in the Bromeliaceae, the showy things they are. Bracts are very common throughout the mallow and carrot families, and not unusual in many other garden plants.

*BRACTEATA*, *-us*, *-um* (brack-tee-ā'ta). Having bracts.

*BRACTEOSA*, *-us*, *-um* (brack-tee-ō'sa). Bearing bracts.

---

* Special articles on the subjects indicated by an asterisk (*) will be found at the words so marked.

**BRACTESCENS** (brack-tess'enz). Having bracts.

**BRACTLET.** A small bract.

**BRADBURYA** = CENTROSEMA.

**BRAHEA** (bra-he'a). A small genus of mostly Mexican, medium-sized fan palms, the palma dulce cult. outdoors in southern Calif. for ornament. The stout trunks, toward the top, are usually covered with the persistent but dead and drooping leaves, the lower part ringed and spineless. Leaves divided to the middle or deeper with many slender divisions. Flowers perfect,* the cluster appearing in the crown of leaves, branched and woolly. Sepals and petals 3 each. Stamens 6. (Named for Tycho Brahe, Danish astronomer.)

Outdoors the palma dulce does not need any special soil. If grown in the greenhouse, use potting mixture* 4, give plenty of water and keep in the cool greenhouse. The plant resembles the California fan palm in holding its dead leaves for years.

dulcis. Palma dulce. Usually in groups of several trunks, each 12-20 ft. high and 6-9 in. in diameter. Leaves 4-5 ft. long, its leaflets or segments 36-50, slender and tapering. Flower cluster (spadix*) 6-8 ft. long, hanging. Fruit oblongish, ½ in. long, yellow and edible.

**BRAKE.** The bracken or brake is a fern of nearly worldwide distribution, but of slight garden interest. It is the only species of the genus **Pteridium** (ter-rid'ee-um), family Polypodiaceae. Fronds on black, polished, and in age, very tough stems, the frond immense and twice- or thrice-compound,* its ultimate divisions innumerable and somewhat tough. The only species, *P. aquilinum*, is about 2-4 ft. high in N.A., thrice that or more in the tropics. Fronds 3-4 ft. wide, the ultimate segments oblongish, sometimes toothed. (*Pteridium* means *Pteris*-like.) Other plants sometimes called brake are also found in the genus *Pteris*. The true brake will grow almost anywhere and is too coarse a fern except for the most informal plantings.

**BRAMBLE.** Loosely, any prickly shrub. As used in hort., any plant of the genus *Rubus*, especially the blackberry and raspberry, which are thus often called bramble fruits.

**BRAMPTON STOCK** = *Mathiola incana*.

**BRAN BAIT.** See Stomach Poisons at INSECTICIDES. See also ANIMAL INJURY.

**BRANCH.** Any shoot, stalk, or stem that springs from a main one, as a branch does from a tree trunk, or a secondary axis from the main one in a flower cluster.

**BRANCHING BROCCOLI** = *Brassica oleracea italica*. For culture see BROCCOLI.

**BRANCH ROT.** See Diseases at CARNATION.

**BRANDY MINT** = *Mentha piperita*. See MINT.

**BRASENIA** (bra-si'ni-a). A single, nearly world-wide aquatic plant, family Nymphaeaceae, common in still water over most of the U.S. and sometimes cult. for its purple flower. It roots in the mud and sends up long, jelly-coated stalks which are attached to the middle of the blade of a floating leaf that is oval and 3-4 in. long. Flowers about ½ in. in diameter, purple, with 3 or 4 narrow petals. Fruit small, club-shaped, not splitting. The only species, **B. schreberi** (sometimes called *B. peltata*) is the water shield. (*Brasenia* is of unknown origin.)

*BRASILIENSIS, -e* (bra-zill-i-en'sis). From Brazil.

**BRASSAVOLA** (bras-a-vō'la). A genus of 20 species of tropical American, tree-perching orchids, the one below, and perhaps others, grown in the greenhouse for their showy flowers. They have small pseudobulbs* (see ORCHIDACEAE) and one or two thick, leathery leaves. Flowers large, solitary in the one below, the sepals and petals spreading, small, and greenish, the lip* white. (Named for A. M. Brassavola, Venetian botanist.)

For culture see Epiphytes in the article on culture of greenhouse ORCHIDS.

digbyana. Pseudobulb 3-6 in. long and bearing a single (rarely 2) leaf 5-8 in. long. Flower fragrant, 4-5 in. wide, greenish-white, the lip deeply fringed or bearded. Mex. and Honduras. Blooms in the summer in the greenhouse. Sometimes offered as *Laelia digbyana*.

**BRASSIA** (brass'i-a). Thirty tropical American, tree-perching orchids, commonly called spider orchids, and cult. for their beautiful and odd flowers. These have narrow, often long-tailed and spreading sepals and petals, a single flower thus suggesting the legs of a spider. The lip* is nearly stalkless, without teeth or a fringe, and much shorter than the sepals. (Named for William Brass, a botanist friend of Robert Brown.)

The brassias are scarcely showy enough to be grown by florists, but their generally yellowish, spider-like bloom makes them attractive to orchid lovers. They have a pseudobulb* with one or two leaves and the flowers in weak, more or less drooping, open clusters. For culture see greenhouse ORCHIDS. The plants are epiphytes.* Of six known hort. species the following are best known.

lawrenceana. The pseudobulb 4-5 in. long, its two lance-shaped leaves 8-10 in. long. Stalk of the flower cluster 12-20 in. long, and bearing 10-15 flowers. Sepals and petals yellow, brown-spotted, the sepals about 3 in. long. Brazil. In the greenhouse blooms in May or June.

longissima. Pseudobulb 1-3 in. long, its one or two leaves 8-10 in. long and about 2 in. wide. Stalk of the flower cluster 18-24 in. long, bearing 10-15 flowers. Sepals and petals golden-yellow, brown-spotted at the base, the sepals often 9 in. long. Lip white, but spotted with red-brown. Costa Rica. Blooms in June in the greenhouse.

**BRASSICA** (brass'i-ka). A botanically confusing but horticulturally important genus of temperate Old World annual or biennial herbs of the family Cruciferae, containing not only the mustard, but all the vegetables of the cabbage tribe, as well as rape, turnip, and others (see below). Some, also, are pernicious weeds (see Wild Mustard at WEEDS). They have mostly smooth, often bluish-green, water-shedding leaves which may be cut, lobed or toothed. Flowers (lacking in most of the vegetables as harvested) yellow or white, with 4 petals, and in terminal clusters (racemes*). Fruit a long pod (silique*), usually stalked. (*Brassica* is the classical name for cabbage.) The exact home of most of the species is lost in antiquity. Many of the vegetables have been cult. over 2000 years.

alba. White mustard. A stout, branching annual, 2-4 ft. high, the foliage sometimes slightly hairy. Leaves ovalish, but divided to or near the midrib, and with a large terminal lobe. Flowers yellow, ⅓-½ in. wide. Pods ¾-1½ in. long, constricted between the seeds. Eurasia; also a weed in U.S. Not the chief source of mustard (see *B. nigra*). See HERB GARDENING.

arvensis. Charlock. A weedy plant resembling, in some stages, other plants of this genus. It is an annual, 2-3 ft. high, has green, somewhat stiff-hairy foliage, and small yellow flowers. The pod is about ¾ in. long and tipped by a beak at least ½ in. long. Eurasia, but common as a weed in U.S.

caulorapa. Kohlrabi. A biennial, not over 18 in. high, with bluish-green leaves 7-9 in. long borne on a stout stem, the swollen part near the ground level being edible. Flowers cream-yellow. For culture see KOHLRABI.

chinensis. Pak-choi. A Chinese annual or biennial herb, grown there, and a little here, as a pot herb. It has a tight basal cluster (not as tight as cabbage) of leaves which are broadest towards the tip, and have white, margined stalks. The stem leaves are clasping. Flowers cream-yellow. Pods 1½-2½ in. long.

juncea. Leaf mustard. An annual, 2-4 ft. high. Lower leaves lobed or divided, the edges scalloped; stem leaves narrower, but not clasping. Flowers yellow. Pod 1-1½ in. long. A well-known form, called Southern Curled, has the leaf-margins crisped, and is grown for greens.

napobrassica. Rutabaga, called also Swede and Swedish turnip. A biennial with an underground, yellow or white-fleshed, tuberlike swelling (the rutabaga). Leaves very thick, bluish-green, perfectly smooth, rather long and large and with lyre-like divisions. Flowers whitish-yellow. Pods widely spreading, the stalks stout.

napus. Rape or colza. An annual resembling the rutabaga, but with a thin taproot, and with ascending pods on more slender stalks. It is cult. in Eu. as the source of rape seed, but in the U.S. mostly as a farm cover crop.

nigra. Black mustard. The chief source of commercial mustard and a tall annual, 4-6 ft. high, with stiff-hairy, mostly green foliage. Leaves lobed or cut, the terminal lobe larger than the lateral ones. Flowers yellow, in many, short clusters. Pods about 1 in. long, hugging the stem. Cult. for mustard but also a widely dispersed weed.

oleracea. A thick-leaved, bluish-gray herb, probably native along the coasts of northwestern Eu. but not now cult. in its original form, which appears to have been a biennial or perennial. From it have been derived the following important vegetables: Var. **acephala**. Kale, also collards, borecole and cow cabbage. A form with many leaves but not in dense, cabbage-like heads or rosettes. For culture see KALE. Var. **botrytis**. Cauliflower. A stemless form in which there is a whitish, much-thickened head consisting of a much-modified flower cluster. For culture see CAULIFLOWER. Var. **capitata**. Cabbage. A stemless form having a single dense head of consolidated leaves. For culture see CABBAGE. Var. **gemmifera**. Brussels Sprouts, called also sprouts and Thousand-headed-cabbage. With a stout stem, a terminal or nearly terminal crown of leaves, and button-like heads like miniature cabbages along the stem. For culture

---

* Special articles on the subjects indicated by an asterisk (*) will be found at the words so marked.

*see* BRUSSELS SPROUTS. *Var. italica.* Broccoli, called also sprouting, branching, Italian and asparagus broccoli; also calabrese. A form in which the thickened flower branches are in a loose, not compact, head. For culture *see* BROCCOLI.

**pekinensis.** Chinese cabbage, but commonly called celery cabbage in the markets, or, more rarely, pe-tsai. A plant of Chinese origin in which there is a cylindrical, tender, almost lettuce-like head of whitish, crisp leaves. For culture *see* CHINESE CABBAGE.

**rapa.** Turnip. A biennial with green leaves and a yellow or white-fleshed, tuberous, edible, underground portion. It has long, soft but stiff-hairy leaves, divided lyre-fashion. Flowers yellow. Pods 1½–2½ in. long. There are two varieties. One is *var.* **lorifolia,** the strap-leaved turnip, with nearly unlobed leaves. The other is *var.* **septiceps,** the seven-top turnip or Italian kale, which has no tuberous thickening, but its edible shoots are harvested.

**BRASSICACEAE** = Cruciferae.

**BRASSOCATTLAELIA** (brass-o-cat-lay′li-a). An interesting orchid resulting from hybridizing the genera *Brassavola, Cattleya* and *Laelia* — one of the few-known trigeneric hybrids. They are not much cult., except by orchid specialists.

**BRASSOCATTLEYA** (brass-o-cat′lee-a). A bigeneric* hybrid between the orchid genera *Brassavola* and *Cattleya.* More than a dozen such crosses are known, but they are mostly confined to the collections of fanciers.

**BRASSOLAELIA** (brass-o-lay′li-a). A bigeneric* hybrid between the orchid genera *Brassavola* and *Laelia.* Three or four known crosses have been recorded, but the plants are little known outside the collections of orchid specialists.

**BRAUNERIA** = Echinacea.

**BRAZILIAN GUAVA** = *Psidium guineense.* See GUAVA.

**BRAZILIAN MORNING-GLORY** = *Ipomoea setosa.*

**BRAZILIAN PEPPER-TREE** = *Schinus terebinthifolius.*

**BRAZIL-NUT** = *Bertholletia excelsa.*

**BREADFRUIT; BREADNUT** = *Artocarpus communis.*

**BREAK.** See MUTATION.

**BREAKING.** Premature leafing or flowering; as a cion may *break* before it should, or a lily may *break* (flower) before it is expected.

**BREATH-OF-HEAVEN** = *Diosma ericoides.*

**BRECK, J.** See America at GARDEN BOOKS.

**BREEDER TULIPS.** See Garden Tulips at TULIPA.

**BREEDING.** See PLANT BREEDING.

**BRETT PALM COLLECTION.** See ARBORETUM.

*BREVIFOLIA, -us, -um* (brev-ee-fō′lee-a). Short-leaved.

*BREVIPEDUNCULATA, -us, -um* (brev-i-pe-dunk-you-lay′ta). With a short flower stalk.

*BREVIPES* (brev-ĭ-peez′). Short-stalked.

*BREVISCAPA, -us, -um* (brev-i-skape′a). With a short scape or flower stalk.

**BREVOORTIA** (bre-voor′ti-a). A single, California bulbous plant of the lily family, separated from *Brodiaea* only by technical characters. Its only species, *B. ida-maia,* the floral fire-cracker, is a perennial with basal, narrow leaves, a stalk 2–3 ft. high, upon which is a cluster (umbel*) of tubular, scarlet flowers, tipped with green. (Named for J. C. Brevoort, American naturalist, and for Ida-May, the daughter of a Calif. stagecoach driver who first brought the plant to the notice of Alphonso Wood.)

The floral fire-cracker has the same cultural requirements as *Brodiaea.*

**BREYNIA** (bry′nee-a). A small genus of shrubs or trees of the spurge family, the one below from the South Sea Islands and cult. for hedges or ornament in zones* 8 and 9, rarely in greenhouses. Leaves alternate,* without marginal teeth. Flowers without petals, the male and female separate, the female solitary in the leaf-axils,* the male in small clusters, and with a turban-shaped calyx* and 3 stamens.* Fruit a berry. (Named for J. P. Breyn, a German botanist.)

The snow bush is somewhat grown in Calif. and Fla., where it appears to have no special soil requirements. If grown in the greenhouse, use potting mixture* 4 and keep in a cool house.

**nivosa.** Snow bush. A loosely branched shrub 3–4 ft. high, the stems somewhat zigzag. Leaves 1½–2 in. long, white-speckled or white-mottled. Flowers greenish, small, inconspicuous. Fruit red. There is a variety with dark purple leaves (*var.* **atropurpurea**) and another with the leaves mottled with pink and red (*var.* **roseo-picta**). The plant is offered also as *Phyllanthus nivosus.*

**BRICK.** See MUSHROOM GROWING. See also PATHS AND PAVING.

**BRICK WALLS.** See WALLS AND WALL GARDENING.

**BRIDAL ROSE.** See MATRICARIA INODORA PLENISSIMA.

**BRIDAL WREATH** = *Spiraea prunifolia* and *S. vanhouttei,* and possibly *S. trichocarpa.* See also FRANCOA RAMOSA.

**BRIDE.** See ANEMONE CORONARIA.

**BRIDEWORT** = *Spiraea salicifolia.*

**BRIDGE GRAFTING.** See GRAFTING.

**BRIDGES.** For private roads, bridle trails or even pedestrian walks the arched stone bridge is the handsomest and most permanent type of bridge. Where appearance and permanence are to be considered stone should always be used in preference to concrete, which is very little cheaper and is much less attractive than stone.

The simplest form of stone bridge for streams with a normal flow less than three feet wide and six inches deep is a culvert type built with large tile. Lay concrete drain tile four or five feet in diameter in the stream bed with the inside of the tile level with the normal bottom of the stream. Use enough lengths of tile to make a bridge at least two feet wider on each side than the path or road crossing the bridge.

Construct a stone wall at right angles to the pipe at both ends, using the pipe as a form for the top of an arch in the stone wall. The wall should rest on a foundation extending three feet below finished grade. This foundation should also carry across the stream bed under the end of the tile to prevent the stream forcing its way under the tile. To conceal the ends of the tile the stone should overhang at least six inches.

For permanence and beauty the stone arched bridge is unrivaled.

The side walls should extend from bank to bank with the bottom of the wall following the natural shape of the ground and the top of the wall following the grade of the path or road. Carry the walls a foot or a foot and a half above the level of the path to act as a guard rail.

After the masonry shell is built fill it in with broken stone, slag or compact soil to the required level of the path, and lay the path surface in the same way as on the ground.

When the width of the stream is too great for pipe use a regular masonry arch. To construct an arch of eight or ten feet diameter a form of clay can be built over a temporary drain to take care of the stream flow during construction.

Model the arch opening in clay held in place at the ends by wooden forms. Lay the stone on this clay form just as you would on a wooden form, building from the foundation up to the center of the arch. The stone should be laid with just enough cement mortar to hold it in place and after the arch is completed the whole top of the arch slushed in with very wet mortar. After the mortar is set the clay form and

---

* Special articles on the subjects indicated by an asterisk (*) will be found at the words so marked.

temporary drain should be moved out from under the arch and the joints underneath filled with mortar.

The wing walls connecting the arch with the banks should be constructed over the arch after it is well set.

For bridges with a span of over ten feet a wooden form must be constructed to support the arch during construction. The design and construction of a masonry bridge of this size is a problem requiring the services of a competent designer.

The capacity load of a stone arch bridge when properly constructed is almost unlimited and will stand any ordinary use.

WOODEN BRIDGES. The simple wooden bridge with a span not exceeding fifteen feet may be constructed by laying beams lengthwise from buttress to buttress and nailing the flooring directly onto the cross-beams. The guard rail may be of some ornamental design, or a simple, protective rail spiked directly onto the outer beams.

For a fifteen-foot span use 8 × 12-in. chestnut or oak beams two feet on center, cross-braced at the center and ends. The flooring should be two-inch oak or chestnut planking laid with a quarter-inch opening between planks and securely spiked to the beams. Such a bridge will carry a maximum load of five tons. To increase the strength of this type of bridge a second plank flooring may be laid lengthwise on top of the first floor.

A timbered bridge for foot passage over a small stream

For lighter loads and shorter spans the size of the beams may be decreased proportionately. Common sense will determine the size beams for this small type of bridge quite as adequately as an engineer's calculations. A generous factor of safety is not an extravagance on small structures.

It should be remembered that the entire support of the bridge depends on the ends of the beams. These should be protected by waterproof paint and kept dry.

This type of bridge is not very ornamental. An attractive guard rail will give it added interest, but the flat span is neither graceful nor imaginative.

A more attractive type of construction for simple wooden bridges is some form of truss. The usual form is the inverted "V" truss which is a simple piece of carpentry. More difficult trusses to build are the arched or bowed truss and the more complicated trusses seen in our old-fashioned covered bridges.

There is a prevalent notion that bridges to be picturesque should be rustic. As a matter of fact nothing could be more illogical than a bridge whose real structural form is disguised by gnarled and twisted tree limbs.

The most beautiful wooden bridge is one which is structurally logical, with its members properly proportioned and gracefully fitted into a structural pattern. Rough-hewn timbers of oak or chestnut creosoted or filled with boiled linseed oil far surpass the contortions of so-called rustic work in beauty and picturesqueness. — R. E. G.

**BRIGANTIACA**, *-us, -um* (bri-gan-ty'a-ka). From Briançon (formerly Brigantium), a town in the French Alps.

**BRINJAL.** *See* EGGPLANT.

**BRISBANE BOX** = *Tristania conferta.*

**BRITISH COLUMBIA.** The province lies wholly within zones* 2, 3, 4, 5, and 6, which from the proximity of the mountains and the effect of the sea run approximately north and south instead of east and west as over most of North America. The area is so influenced by diverse factors, however, that any statement of a general nature may well be challenged. In a given district soils, rainfall and temperature are so unlike other districts a few miles distant, that one area may be producing abundant crops while the other is quite barren.

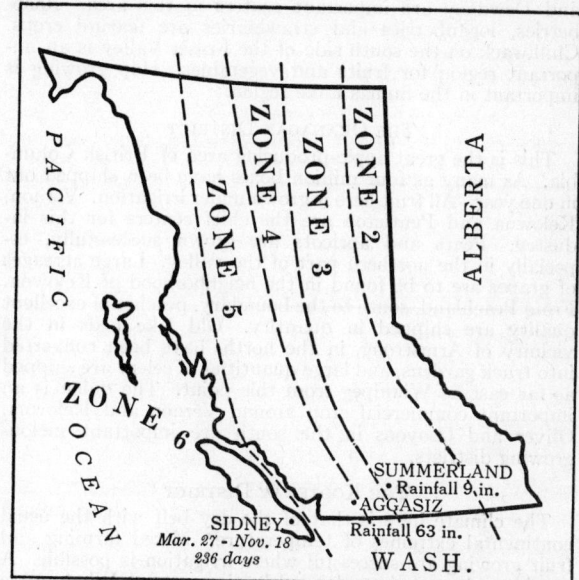

BRITISH COLUMBIA

The zones of hardiness are those described in detail at ZONE (which see), but their exact limits are uncertain owing to lack of data for the northern part of the province. The number of days is the length of the growing season at and near Vancouver. Rainfall figures are for total annual rainfall (and snow) at the places shown.

SOILS. On Vancouver Island every type of soil may be found, sometimes in close proximity to each other and without apparent cause. Large areas of one type of soil are rarely found. Maywood clays, sandy soils, peat and silt are well distributed over the southern half of the island. Some of the best soils are found in the Fraser Valley, especially the rich alluvial bottom lands. The soils in the Okanagan region, for the most part a volcanic ash, are exceedingly fertile and capable of producing abundant crops if water is available. Much land on the benches around the lake is irrigated. If water should be withheld the crop would perish.

GARDENING CENTERS. Owing to the great parallel mountain chains which traverse British Columbia from north to south, the areas of fertile lands suitable for cultivation are found in the river and lake valleys that lie between the mountain ranges. Settlement in the province is, therefore, confined to well-defined districts and those areas of horticultural importance are dealt with here.

VANCOUVER AND ADJACENT ISLANDS

Adjoining the city of Victoria lie the fertile lands of the Saanich Peninsula. Two of the best-known strawberry-growing districts of the coast, Gordon Head and Keating, are located here. These districts export annually to the prairie provinces large quantities of delicious berries. The loganberry is grown extensively as well. Sidney is one of the near-by fruit centers.

This fertile area also provides a never-failing supply of fresh vegetables and fruit for the city of Victoria. Pears do exceptionally well in this area, while cherries, plums and apples are grown chiefly for local markets. The Cowichan River Valley is adapted to mixed farming, with dairy farming predominating. Other fertile areas include the Comox Valley, of which the town of Courtenay is the center, and Salt Spring and Pender Islands.

---

* Special articles on the subjects indicated by an asterisk (*) will be found at the words so marked.

### The Lower Fraser Valley

The lands of this valley area may be divided into two classes, the rich heavy bottom lands along the river, and the lighter bench lands rising to the mountains. On the north bank of the Fraser from Pitt Meadows to Yale the bench lands produce both small and tree fruits in abundance, as well as quantities of early vegetables. Mission, Hatzic and Dewdney are important centers in this area. Raspberries, loganberries and strawberries are feature crops. Chilliwack on the south side of the Fraser Valley is an important region for fruits and vegetables. Hop growing is important in the Sumas Lake region.

### The Okanagan District

This is the great apple-producing area of British Columbia. As many as four million boxes have been shipped out in one year. All fruit here is grown under irrigation. Vernon, Kelowna and Penticton are the chief centers for this industry. Pears and apricots are grown successfully, especially in the northern part of the valley. Large acreages of grapes are to be found in the neighborhood of Kelowna. From Peachland, south to the boundary, peaches of excellent quality are shipped in quantity. Old lake beds in the vicinity of Armstrong, in the north, have been converted into truck gardens, and large quantities of celery are shipped as far east as Winnipeg from this point. The onion is an important commercial crop around Vernon and Kelowna. Oliver and Osoyoos in the south are important melon-growing districts.

### The Kootenay District

The climate here is that of the dry belt with the usual continental extremes of temperature. Mixed farming and fruit growing are successful where irrigation is possible. A considerable area is under cultivation around Windermere Lake. Along the Kootenay Lake from Erickson and Creston to Sirdar the benches along the east bank have been developed, and a well-known fruit are aestablished. Apples, plums, pears, cherries, as well as strawberries, are grown here in increasing quantities.

### The Arrow Lakes

Here, too, on the fertile bench lands, fruit culture and mixed farming are carried on. Tree fruits do well. Some of the chief centers here are Nakusp, Edgewood, Robson, Burton City and West Demars.

CLIMATE. In common with many other things in British Columbia, the variation in climate from year to year is marked. At Sidney, the site of the Experimental Station, official records of climate are kept, but averages are not available for purposes of comparison with other places.

SIDNEY, B.C.

Average date of last killing frost in spring.....March 27th.
Latest known killing frost...................May 9th.
Average date of earliest killing frost in fall....Nov. 18th.
Earliest known killing frost..................Oct. 30th.

AGASSIZ, B.C., FOR 1933

Highest Temperature..................96.0
Lowest Temperature ..................7.0
Rainfall ..............................75.64 in.
Snowfall.............................62.9 in.
Average Snow for 10 years.............29.7 in.
Average Precipitation for 10 years......63.47 in.
Average Sunshine for 10 years..........1,414 hrs.

SUMMERLAND, B.C., FOR 1933

Highest Temperature..................96.0
Lowest Temperature ..................7.0
Rainfall ............................. 8.28 in.
Snowfall.............................53.4 in.
Average Snow for 10 years.............31.1 in.
Average Precipitation for 10 years....... 9.76 in.
Average Sunshine for 10 years..........2,018 hrs.

### Rainfall

Rainfall for Agassiz and Summerland has been referred to. The average rainfall at Sidney, B.C., for 20 years is 29.11 inches. Though this amount is fair, if obtained at the right time, it is nevertheless true that during the growing season the crops suffer much during certain years, while irrigation water is not available. At Agassiz, being representative of the Fraser Valley, rainfall is abundant and sufficient to meet all needs. At Summerland, as pointed out, the rainfall is not sufficient, but lakes, streams and melting snows furnish the irrigation water in quantity for all purposes.

The address of the Experimental Station, which has supplied the information about British Columbia, is Saanichton, R.R. 1, B.C. The Station is always ready to answer gardening questions.

**BRITISH OAK** = *Quercus robur*. See OAK.

**BRITTLE FERN** = *Cystopteris fragilis*.

**BRITTLE THATCH** = *Thrinax microcarpa*.

**BRIZA** (bry′za). A group of slender grasses, the spikelets of which are often on hair-thin stalks, hence usually called quaking grass. They are small, annual or perennial grasses, the spikelets suggesting small, flattened hops, often nodding on their thread-like stalks. (*Briza* is Greek for some grain.)

The quaking grasses are sometimes grown in the garden for their attractive panicles* of spikelets. Sow the annuals where they are to stay. The perennial one is easily propagated by division. The dried panicles are used for winter decoration.

**maxima.** An annual 1–2 ft. high. Leaves 4–6 in. long and ⅓–¾ in. wide. Spikelets ½ in. long, pale or metallic in age, nodding. Southern Eu. Perhaps the handsomest of the quaking grasses.

**media.** A perennial 10–18 in. high, with very narrow, slender leaves. Panicle 5–10 in. long, branched, the spikelets broadly oval, purplish, not over ¼ in. long, the stalks stiffish. Eurasia, and naturalized in U.S.

**minor.** An annual 6–15 in. high. Leaves 3–5 in. long, about ⅓ in. wide. Panicle* compound, broad, about 5 in. long, the spikelets about ⅛ in. long and green. Eu. and naturalized in U.S.

**BRIZAEFORMIS, -e** (bry-ze-for′mis). Like a grass of the genus *Briza*.

**BRIZOIDES** (bry-zoy′deez; but see OÏDES). *Briza*-like.

**BROAD BEAN** = *Vicia faba*.

**BROAD-LEAVED EVERGREENS.** A common designation among gardeners for outdoor plants with relatively broad, evergreen leaves, that do not belong to the cone-bearing plants such as the spruces, firs, pines, yew, etc. (the conifers).

The broad-leaved evergreens are extremely valuable plants to all gardeners. Box, rhododendron, the Japanese holly, *Pachysandra*, the holly, *Leucothoë*, *Pieris*, the mountain laurel, *Cotoneaster*, *Daphne*, some species of *Euonymus*, and the evergreen species of *Berberis* provide the choicest plants of this sort for most northern gardeners. See each of these for notes on culture and their hardiness in different sections of the country.

Most of them do poorly or cannot be grown at all in regions where the annual rainfall is below 20 in. (See the name of your state for rainfall figures.) They grow best in regions of relatively mild winters near the sea. Nearly all of them should have a permanent mulch of leaves.

Farther south there are scores, perhaps hundreds, of plants, not conifers, to which the term could equally well be applied, for they have evergreen or nearly evergreen leaves. But most of them are of tropical affinities, and broad-leaved evergreen, as a term, is not usually applied to them.

**BROCCOLI** (*Brassica oleracea italica*). Broccoli is a word that has been in some confusion in recent years because two plants are comprised under the one term. In England, and by the technically minded here, the word and vegetable are practically synonymous with the cauliflower (*Brassica oleracea botrytis*). See CAULIFLOWER. In America, broccoli, largely of Italian culture and interest until lately, means a cauliflower-like plant in which the malformed flower head (the edible part of cauliflower) instead of being white, close and ball-like, is more open, branchy and green. To this now very common vegetable, various names have been applied, such as sprouting broccoli, branching broccoli, asparagus broccoli, Italian broccoli and calabrese (the original Italian word for it). All these are now quite generally shortened simply to broccoli. The notes below apply only

---

* Special articles on the subjects indicated by an asterisk (*) will be found at the words so marked.

# BROCCOLI

to this sprouting or branching broccoli. For the original and perhaps true broccoli (really a winter cauliflower) see CAULIFLOWER. *See also* OREGON.

Broccoli (as above restricted) is a branching herb about 2 ft. high. Some or all of the lateral branches, and the terminal one, end in a malformed, green, more or less open flower head. This, which should be cut before it actually flowers, and cooked like cauliflower, is a delicious, succulent vegetable, rich in the vitamins of the cabbage tribe to which it belongs. In cooking, however, it lacks most of the tenement house odor of cabbage.

CULTURE. The plant prefers coolness and moisture rather than heat and dryness. Unless you are in a particularly favorable place (*i.e.* along the sea coast or close to the shores of the Great Lakes), broccoli is best treated as a two-season crop. The first is started in the hotbed or greenhouse in February or March (depending on locality) and planted out after the last frost (*see* the name of your state for frost data). The second crop is sown in the seed bed in June or July and transplanted to the garden a month or six weeks later. The latter crop can be harvested through the cool autumn months.

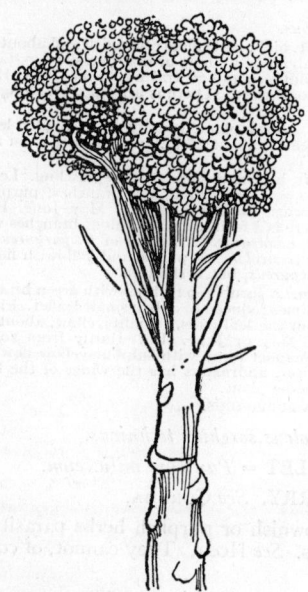

Broccoli ready for harvesting

It is absolutely essential to get pure seed of a first-class seedsman if you intend raising your own plants. Considerable instability still exists in the various strains of broccoli (even some weedy, mustard-like plants occasionally appearing). Avoid such accidents by getting the best seed obtainable of the following two varieties: Calabrese or Italian Green Sprouting.

Because of this uncertainty many home gardeners prefer to buy young plants from a dealer. But even in this case it is well to insist that they be of one of the two varieties mentioned.

PLANTING. Seeds sown in the greenhouse, hotbed or seed bed, should be planted in flats or boxes where their management is exactly the same as for cabbage (which see).

When the seedlings are ready to be put out in the garden, they should be set 2 ft. apart in the rows which are themselves 2 ft. apart. A single row of fifty plants (100 ft.) is ample for a family of 5, and unless the family has a particularly strong liking for it, the 100 ft. may well be split between the early and late crops (as outlined above).

The plants do well in any ordinary garden soil, but it should be reasonably moist. They are moderately rich feeders and manure or commercial fertilizers should be applied before the plants are set out. (See CABBAGE for details.) Some also top-dress with nitrate of soda three weeks after the plants have been set out, at the rate of 200 pounds per acre (1 pound per 100-ft. row), and repeat the process just as the plants begin to head.

If the plants have been set out exactly on the two-foot intervals they can, in the early stages at least, be cultivated both ways. In any case, they must be kept free of weeds, and, to conserve moisture, the ground should be kept pulverized, especially after every rain.

HARVESTING. As the plants come to maturity the somewhat abortive and grotesque heads of flowers begin to develop. Some mature quicker than others, but they must be cut well before the true whitish-yellow flowers "break" from the cluster. If the immature heads, which should vary from 4 to 7 in. in diameter, are constantly cut, the plant will force out other heads. This considerably prolongs the harvesting period. The whole flower head and its thick, succulent branches should be green, not white or yellow, when the head is harvested.

PESTS. Broccoli is subject to the same insects and diseases as cabbage. For their control *see* CABBAGE.

**BRODIAEA** (bro-di-ee'a). An attractive group of 30 species of chiefly Californian herbs of the lily family, with crocus-like corms,* and narrow, grass-like leaves. They are mostly grown in Calif., but can be grown in the South and elsewhere as directed below. Leaves few, narrow. Flowers mostly funnel-shaped, solitary or in loose clusters (umbels*) that arise from spathe*-like, membranous bracts.* Petals or colored sepals 6. Stamens 6, 3 often sterile. Fruit a pod (capsule*), splitting by valves. (Named for James Brodie, Scotch botanist.) Sometimes the species are offered under the name *Triteleia*.

The triplet lilies, as they are often called, are easily grown in Calif., and do well in most soils, except wet or shaded ones, but prefer gritty or sandy sites. In the East they are not hardy outdoors north of Va. without protection, and it is safer to plant them in pans or boxes in the frame. Plant at the same time as for fall bulbs. In the spring they may be taken out of the frame and planted outdoors. After flowering, the corms (in the East) should be dug and stored over the summer, for they will not stand summer humidity nor too much rain. Some, as noted below, are forced in the cool greenhouse.

**californica.** Not over 1 ft. high. Flowers about 1½ in. long, violet-purple. Southern Calif.
**capitata.** Blue dicks. Not over 2 ft. high. Flowers about ⅔ in. long, blue, in head-like clusters (umbels*). Ore. to Calif.
**coccinea** = *Brevoortia ida-maia*.
**coronaria.** From 12–18 in. high. Flowers violet-purple, 1–1½ in. long. This is often offered as *Hookera* (or even *Hookeria*) *coronaria*, and as *Brodiaea grandiflora*. It is found wild from British Columbia to Calif.
**crocea.** From 8–12 in. high. Flowers yellow, ½–¾ in. long.
**grandiflora** = *Brodiaea coronaria*.
**ixioides.** Pretty-face. One of the showiest, and from 10–18 in. high. Flowers salmon or salmon-yellow, streaked with dark purple, ½–¾ in. long. Ore. to southern Calif. Best grown in the cool greenhouse.
**lactea.** Wild hyacinth. From 10–18 in. high. Flowers lilac or white, ⅓–½ in. long. British Columbia to Calif.
**laxa.** Triplet lily. Not over 2 ft. high. Flowers about 1½ in. long, purple or white. Calif.
**uniflora.** Spring starflower. The best-known and most widely cult. species, usually not over 8 in. high, and somewhat onion-scented. Flowers solitary, white but tinged with blue, about 1 in. long. Argentina. Must be grown in the cool greenhouse in the North. It is also known as *Milla uniflora* and *Leucocoryne uniflora*.
**volubilis.** Snake lily. Unlike all the others in having a twining stem 3–8 ft. high. Flowers rose-red or pink, ½–¾ in. long. It is sometimes offered as *Stropholirion californicum* and is best grown in the frame or cool greenhouse.

**BROKEN TULIP.** *See* Garden Tulips at TULIPA.

**BROME GRASS** = BROMUS.

**BROMELIA** (bro-mee'li-a). A genus of perhaps 25 species of tropical American, pineapple-like herbs, family Bromeliaceae, with spiny-margined leaves. The only cult. species is the pinguin, **Bromelia pinguin**, too coarse to grow in greenhouses, but a valuable hedge plant in extreme southern Fla. It has a rosette of long, sword-shaped leaves 4–6 ft. high, very spiny on the margins. Flowers red, in a dense cluster (panicle*) on a mealy, or whitish, stout stalk. Fruit plum-like, acid. (Named for Olaf Bromel, Swedish botanist.) It will grow in pure sand or on bare coral rock in the tropics. Native of the W.I.

**BROMELIACEAE** (bro-mee-li-ā'see-ee). The pineapple family is exclusively tropical American, with a few stretching into sub-tropical Florida. All are herbs, many of them air plants (*see* EPIPHYTES), and of the 40 genera and perhaps 1000 species, a good number are cult. in greenhouses either for their showy flowers or as extremely handsome, often brightly colored, foliage plants. Not one is a true parasite,

---

*Special articles on the subjects indicated by an asterisk (*) will be found at the words so marked.

although often thought to be from their usually tree-perching habit.

For the only important fruit plant *see* the PINEAPPLE (*Ananas*). All the rest of the garden genera are cult. for ornament, although some genera yield fine fibers. The plants are usually scurfy, have stiffish, sometimes spiny-margined, leaves that are mostly in rosettes. In some genera the rosette and leaf-bases hold such considerable amounts of water as to be mosquito breeders in the tropics.

Flowers regular, often very showy, usually in long-stalked, handsome spikes that have colored bracts*; sometimes stalkless. Fruit a dry pod (capsule*) in *Guzmania*, *Puya*, *Tillandsia* and *Vriesia*, but fleshy in all the other garden genera. The flower cluster is prominently stalked in *Aechmea* and *Billbergia*, but close to the rosette of leaves in *Cryptanthus*, *Nidularium*, *Greigia*, and *Canistrum*. *Dyckia* and *Hechtia* are mostly small desert plants with spiny leaves, while *Bromelia* is the pinguin. One of the most characteristic plants in the pineapple family is the Spanish or long moss that drapes live oak and cypress trees in the southern states (*see* TILLANDSIA).

Technical flower characters: Ovary superior* in the genera that bear capsules; inferior* in the rest. Flowers regular,* of 6 segments, the 3 inner, or the 3 outer, or sometimes both, united into a tube. Stamens 6. Ovary 3-celled.

**BROMUS** (brō′mus). Brome grass is a general term applied to this large genus of grasses, most of which live in the north temperate zone. Only one is of secondary garden interest, although others are valuable forage grasses. The cult. species are annuals or perennials with rather coarse, flat leaves. They have large, open, terminal clusters (panicles*) consisting of often drooping spikelets. (*Bromus* is Greek for food, in allusion to a weedy grass long thought to "grow into wheat.")

**brizaeformis.** Quake grass. A useful plant for dry bouquets. It is an annual with leaves up to 8 in. long and about ¼ in. wide. Cluster (panicle*) 6–8 in. long, the branches nodding and with many flattened spikelets that are oblong, about 1 in. long and have no awn.* Eurasia, and naturalized in U.S.

**inermis.** Hungarian brome grass; called, also, awnless brome grass. A perennial 2–4 ft. high. Leaves nearly 1 ft. long and about ¼ in. wide. Clusters (panicles*) 8–10 in. long, the branches ascending. Spikelets not awned, oblong, about 1 in. long. Eu. Not much grown except in pastures.

**unioloides.** Rescue grass. An annual 18–30 in. high. Leaves 8–12 in. long and about ⅓ in. wide. Clusters (panicles*) 6–9 in. long, the spikelets much flattened, the branches of the cluster ascending. Tropical America and northward to our southern states where it is used in pastures.

**BROOK.** *See* WATER.

**BROOKLYN BOTANIC GARDEN.** *See* BOTANIC GARDEN.

**BROOM.** A somewhat confusing term because it has been applied to plants in several different genera. As here used it comprises shrubs of the genus *Cytisus* (sit′i-sus) of the pea family. But this genus contains not only the "genista" of the florists (not the genus *Genista*) but the Scotch broom and several related plants. (For the butcher's-broom *see* RUSCUS, and for the Spanish broom *see* SPARTIUM.)

*Cytisus* includes perhaps 50 species of generally spineless shrubs, mostly from the Mediterranean region and western As., grown for their profuse bloom of pea-like flowers. They have compound* leaves with 3 leaflets. Flowers yellow, purple, or white, solitary or in small clusters (usually racemes*). Calyx irregular* and 2-lipped. Flowers typically pea-like. Fruit a flat pod (legume*). (*Cytisus* is Greek for some clover-like plant, in allusion to the 3 leaflets.)

All except *C. canariensis* (the genista of the florists) are deciduous shrubs for the open border, but they will not stand much frost and should be planted outdoors only as shown below. They are not particular as to soil, but transplant poorly when mature, so that they should be set out while young in the place they are to stay.

The genista of the florists (*C. canariensis*) should be grown in the cool greenhouse in potting mixture* 4. Keep in a semi-dormant condition during the late fall and early winter by reducing its water. In February or March (earlier if needed) begin more active watering and increase the temperature by a few degrees. The plant will then flower profusely and should afterwards be cut back and re-potted. Put the pots outdoors, partly in the shade, until frost threatens, when they should be brought into the cool greenhouse. This species is widely forced by florists for spring bloom.

**C. albus.** A low shrub, usually not over 18 in. high. Leaflets broadest above the middle, about ¾ in. long. Flowers yellowish-white, nearly 1 in. long in a terminal, close, head-like cluster. Southeastern Eu. June. Hardy outdoors from zone* 4 southward. Sometimes offered as *C. leucanthus.*

**C. canariensis.** The genista of the florists. An evergreen shrub 4–6 ft. high. Leaflets wedge-shaped, about ⅓ in. long. Flowers slightly fragrant, yellow, about ¾ in. long, in dense terminal clusters (racemes*). Canary Islands. Blooms normally in spring and summer, except when forced. A greenhouse plant (*see* above).

**C. kewensis.** A low plant, nearly prostrate and suited to rock gardens, never over 1 ft. high. Leaflets very narrow, softly hairy, sometimes reduced to only 1. Flowers yellowish-white, about ½ in. long or less, mostly on slender, lateral branches. Of hybrid origin, and not certainly hardy north of zone* 4.

**C. leucanthus** = *Cytisus albus.*

**C. nigricans.** A shrub 4–6 ft. high, its leaflets oblongish and about 1 in. long. Flowers bright yellow, about ¾ in. long or less, in a slender-stalked, terminal cluster (raceme*). Southern and central Eu. June–July. Hardy outdoors only from zone* 4 southward. There is a form (*var*. **elongatus**) that blooms again in the fall.

**C. praecox.** A handsome, hybrid plant, usually with simple* leaves. Flowers yellowish-white or yellow, about ½ in. long. Hardy from zone* 5 southward.

**C. purpureus.** Not over 2 ft. high and more or less sprawling. Leaflets not over 1 in. long. Flowers scattered along the branches, purple, or white, or pink in some hort. forms. Southern Austria. May–June. Hardy from zone* 4 southward. There is a form with pendulous branches which is sometimes grafted high on *Laburnum*. A hybrid of *C. purpureus* and another species, known as *C. versicolor*, has purple and yellowish flowers. It otherwise resembles *C. purpureus*, but is showier.

**C. scoparius.** Scotch broom. A shrub 4–9 ft. high with green branches. Leaflets ⅓–½ in. long, sometimes reduced to only a single leaflet. Flowers usually one or two together in the leaf-axils,* bright yellow, about 1 in. long, blooming profusely in May or June. Eu. Hardy from zone* 3 southward. A lower, more compact form, with sulphur-yellow flowers, is the Moonlight Broom. The *var*. **andreanus** has the wings of the flower crimson, and is a very handsome plant.

**C. versicolor.** *See* CYTISUS PURPUREUS.

**BROOMCORN** = *Holcus sorghum technicus.*

**BROOMCORN MILLET** = *Panicum miliaceum.*

**BROOM CROWBERRY.** *See* COREMA.

**BROOMRAPE.** Brownish or purplish herbs parasitic on the roots of other plants. *See* HOST. They cannot, of course, be cult.

**BROUSSONETIA** (broo-so-nesh′ee-a). The paper mulberry is the only cult. tree of the three known species of this Asiatic genus belonging to the family Moraceae. It has alternate,* often lobed leaves and the male and female flowers are borne on different trees. Male flowers in hanging catkins. Female flowers in small, compact heads. Neither has any petals. Fruit an aggregate of many carpels (a syncarp*). (Named for T. U. V. Broussonet, French naturalist.)

The paper mulberry (its bark yields a sort of paper) is hardy from zone* 4 southward and will stand considerable abuse as to site. It is occasionally a good street tree in New York. Easily propagated by seeds, suckers, or by layering.

**papyrifera.** Paper mulberry. A tree 25–40 ft. Leaves generally oval, 6–8 in. long, usually deeply and roundly lobed in young leaves, very rough above. Fruit cluster (syncarp*) densely hairy, about ¾ in. in diameter. China and Jap., sparingly naturalized from N.Y. to Fla. There are cut-leaved, white-fruited, and variegated forms.

**BROWALLIA** (brow-wall′i-a). A genus of mostly tropical American herbs, belonging to the potato family, several widely grown as very popular, mostly blue-flowered, annuals. Leaves simple,* mostly alternate.* Flowers solitary or in somewhat 1-sided clusters (racemes*). Calyx tubular, usually with 5 teeth. Corolla tubular, the 5-lobed limb* more or less irregular.* Fruit a capsule,* included within the persistent calyx. (Named for Bishop John Browall, a Swedish botanist.)

The browallias, especially *B. speciosa major* and *B. americana*, are widely grown hardy annuals. (*See* ANNUALS for culture.) *B. americana*, with bluish-purple flowers, is useful for those who want that color in the blue garden (which see). Seeds sown in pots in midsummer will provide winter bloom if kept in the cool greenhouse, especially *B. speciosa major*.

**americana.** A branching annual herb 12–20 in. high, its foliage hairy. Leaves round-oval, stalked, 1–2 in. long. Flowers bluish-purple, solitary

---

* Special articles on the subjects indicated by an asterisk (*) will be found at the words so marked.

in the leaf-axils,* or in loose clusters, the tube about ½ in. long, the expanded limb a little larger and notched. S.A. There are hort. forms with pure blue, and with white flowers. Often called *B. demissa* and *B. elata*.
   **jamesoni** = *Streptosolen jamesoni*.
   **speciosa**. A smooth-branching annual 8–12 or rarely 15 in. high. Leaves alternate* or opposite,* ovalish, but pointed at the tip. Flowers with the tube about 1 in. long, the expanded limb larger and not notched, purplish. S.A. The *var.* **major**, the form most grown; has steely-blue flowers. There are also hort. forms with violet or with white flowers. See ANNUALS.

**BROWN BENT** = *Agrostis canina*.

**BROWN CANKER.** See Diseases at ROSE.

**BROWN-EYED SUSAN** = *Rudbeckia triloba*.

**BROWNPATCH.** See Diseases at GRASSES.

**BROWN-ROT.** See Diseases at CHERRY and PEACH.

**BROWN-TAIL MOTH.** See Insect Pests at OAK.

**BROWN TIP.** See Diseases at LILIUM.

**BRUCKENTHALIA** (brook-en-thay′li-a). A single species of evergreen shrubs of the heath family, native in southeastern Eu. and Asia Minor, grown for ornament, and sometimes planted in rock gardens. It has narrow, very short leaves, crowded and densely clothing the twigs. Flowers bell-shaped but deeply 4-lobed, in short, dense spikes. Fruit a capsule enclosed by the persistent calyx. (Named for S. von Bruckenthal, an Austrian nobleman.)
   A pretty little heath-like shrub needing a gritty soil in the border or rock garden, open sunshine, and a winter mulch of dried leaves in severe places. It can be propagated by seeds or by cuttings.
   **spiculifolia**. Spike heath. Not over 8–10 in. high. Leaves not over ⅓ in. long. Flowers pink, about ¼ in. long, the whole spike scarcely ¾ in. long. Hardy from zone* 4 southward.

**BRUNFELSIA** (brun-felz′i-a). A genus of 20 species of tropical American shrubs or trees of the potato family, the one below grown in greenhouses for its yellowish-white, extremely fragrant flowers. Leaves alternate* and without marginal teeth. Flowers (in the one below) solitary, the calyx bell-shaped, the corolla funnel-shaped, and with a long tube. Stamens 4. Fruit (in ours) fleshy. (Named for Otto Brunfels, one of the earliest German botanists.)
   Of the half-dozen species known to be in cult. in America, the lady-of-the-night is the best known. It needs a warm greenhouse (not below 55° at night) and should be grown in potting mixture* 5. The bloom is better if the plants are kept slightly pot-bound. Easily propagated from cuttings of new wood in spring.
   **americana**. Lady-of-the-night; called also Franciscan nightshade. A shrub 6–8 ft. high. Leaves 3–4 in. long, ovalish. Flowers white, fading to yellow, the tube 3–4 in. long, the expanded part nearly 2 in. wide, especially fragrant at night. Fruit berry-like, yellow, about ¾ in. wide. W.I. Can be grown outdoors in zone* 9 and in sheltered parts of zone* 8.

**BRUNNERA** (brun′er-ra). An anchusa-like herb of the Caucasus and Siberia, family Boraginaceae, rather commonly cult. as *Anchusa myosotidiflora*. It has large, heart-shaped, basal leaves, erect, somewhat hairy stems, and flowers in a naked cluster. The only cult. species, **Brunnera macrophylla**, is a perennial and should be grown like an *Anchusa*. It is 12–18 in. high and has stem leaves narrower and more tapering towards the top of the plant. Flowers blue, spring-blooming, not over ¼ in. wide, but the clusters showy and handsome. See BLUE GARDEN. (Named for Samuel Brunner, German botanist.)

**BRUNSVIGIA** (bruns-vig′i-a). South African, greenhouse herbs of perhaps 12 species, belonging to the family Amaryllidaceae, the one below popular for its showy, lily-like flowers. They differ only in technical characters from *Amaryllis* (which see), and are grown in the same way. (Named for the House of Brunswick.)
   **josephinae**. Josephine's-lily. A perennial with a very large bulb. Leaves sword-shaped, 24–30 in. long, about 1¾ in. wide, ribbed and fleshy. Stalk of the flower cluster naked, stout, solid, about 18 in. high and at least an inch thick. Flowers about 3 in. long, red, in an open umbel,* the tubular part of the flower scarcely more than ½ in. long.

**BRUSH.** Twiggy branches used to support peas and other plants. Often used as a verb implying the putting out of such brush. See PEA.

**BRUSH DEAL** = *Cupania anacardioides*.

**BRUSSELS SPROUTS** (*Brassica oleracea gemmifera*.) This vegetable, called simply sprouts by some and thousand-headed-cabbage by others, is a peculiar member of the cabbage tribe. It is an erect, usually single-stalked herb with some leaves on its stout, thick stalk, but most of them at the summit. At the base of the lower leafstalks the "buttons," or small, ball-like sprouts, appear. They are quite stalkless, and in properly grown plants very numerous. Depending on the variety and the success of its culture, the sprouts (which are simply immature but very large buds) should be from 1–1½ or even 2 inches in diameter, close packed and with no loose leaves.
   Brussels sprouts are primarily a fall and winter vegetable. The plant will not mature properly in intense heat and dryness. That is why plants set out about August 1st on the cool south shore of eastern Long Island do so well. Plants set out the same day in the interior of the country would be apt to fail.
   Some growers (in the East) insist on starting Brussels sprouts at the same time as early cabbage, but even if they mature properly before hot weather (which is not always certain), the harvest comes at the time when most people have given up Brussels sprouts until the following autumn. August-set plants, however, begin bearing about October 1st. Because the plant is pretty resistant to cold, the harvest may continue until well after Christmas, at which period it is a most seasonable vegetable.

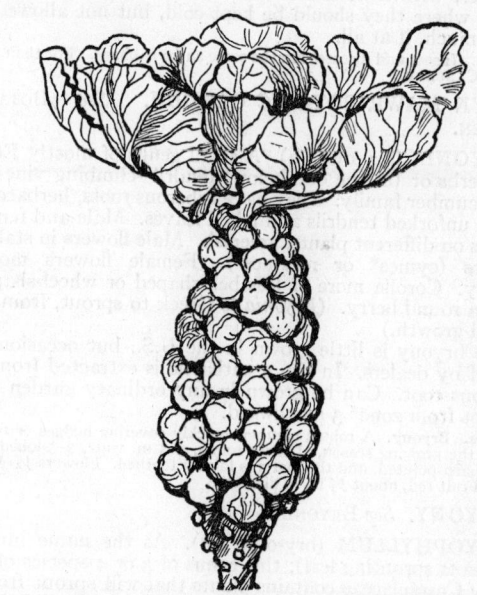

A good Brussels Sprouts plant ready for harvesting

PLANTING. Upon the theory that most gardeners will prefer to harvest their crop from October to Christmas or beyond (depending upon locality), the following directions are for plants set out at a time to accomplish this.
   The plant is closely related to the cabbage, and Brussels sprouts (for fall use) are, in their early stages, treated exactly like a crop of late cabbage. See CABBAGE. Seed sown in the seed bed outdoors in late May should be ready for transplanting to their permanent place in the garden by the latter part of July or early August. They should then be somewhat leggy plants 5–7 inches high.
   Pinch off a few of the leaves, and set out the plants about 18 in. apart, in rows that are two ft. apart. They should have a rich soil, but most ordinary kitchen garden soils will grow good sprouts if the plants are top-dressed, about 2 weeks after setting out, with nitrate of soda at the rate of 250 pounds to the acre (1 pound per 100 ft. of row).

---

* Special articles on the subjects indicated by an asterisk (*) will be found at the words so marked.

CULTIVATION AND MANAGEMENT. Cultivate frequently, especially after rains. The dust mulch so secured is invaluable for conserving soil moisture, and these plants need moisture, especially if, in spite of late planting, there should be much hot weather. Of course cultivate enough to keep down all weeds.

The sprouts begin forming at the leaf bases of the lower leaves first. To stimulate their production it is a good plan to break off (leaving a stump an inch or two long) most of the lower leaves of the plant, beginning about October 1st or when the buds develop. Be sure to leave the terminal crown of leaves intact. This also forces more food into the forming sprouts, the lowest of which should be picked first. Later sprouts are better flavored than the earliest ones to be picked, as the product is much improved by a few sharp frosts.

Between 50 and 66 plants are usually enough for a family of 5, depending, of course, upon their fondness for them. Each plant should yield a quart of sprouts.

VARIETIES. Long Island is one of the chief commercial centers of production, and the variety called Long Island Improved is by far the best one. Other good varieties are Burpee Danish Prize and Dreer Select Matchless. As in all the cabbage tribe, pure seed is essential, whether you start your own plants or buy them ready for transplanting.

WINTER STORAGE. Some gardeners, faced by the destruction of unharvested sprouts when zero weather overtakes them, prefer to store their plants with the sprouts attached. This may be done by pulling up the plants and packing them together, with a little soil at their roots, in a pit or cold frame, where they should be kept cold, but not allowed to freeze much, if at all.

PESTS. Insect and diseases are the same as for cabbage. For their control see CABBAGE.

**BRYN MAWR BOTANIC GARDEN.** See BOTANIC GARDEN.

**BRYONIA** (bry-own'i-a). A small genus of mostly Eurasian herbs or (in the one below) tendril*-climbing vines, of the cucumber family. They have tuberous roots, herbaceous stems, unforked tendrils and lobed leaves. Male and female flowers on different plants, greenish. Male flowers in stalked clusters (cymes* or racemes*). Female flowers mostly solitary. Corolla more or less bell-shaped or wheel-shaped. Fruit a round berry. (*Bryonia* is Greek to sprout, from the annual growth.)

The bryony is little grown in the U.S., but occasionally offered by dealers. In Eu. a cathartic is extracted from its tuberous root. Can be grown in any ordinary garden soil, but not from zone* 3 northward.

dioica. Bryony. A robust climber, quickly covering hedges or fences during the growing season. Leaves rough, 3–5 in. wide, 3–5-lobed, the lobes sharp-pointed, and the margins faintly toothed. Flowers ½–¾ in. wide. Fruit red, about ⅓ in. in diameter.

**BRYONY.** See BRYONIA.

**BRYOPHYLLUM** (bry-o-fill'um). As the name implies (it means sprouting leaf), this genus of 3 or 4 species of the family Crassulaceae contains plants that will sprout from a leaf. In the one below new plants, starting as bulbils,* will sprout from the notches of a leaf if pegged down on moist sand or on blotting paper. They are perennial herbs with opposite,* and in the one below, compound* leaves with 3–5 thick, fleshy leaflets. Flowers in a stalked, drooping cluster, the 4-lobed corolla partly covered by the inflated calyx. Stamens 8. Fruit a follicle.*

These easily grown and most interesting plants need a cool greenhouse over the winter, or they will do fairly well in a moderately heated living-room. They will not stand frost, but may be left outdoors all summer. Propagation is almost laughably easy due to the great tendency to proliferation at the leaf notches. Sometimes new plants will start while the leaf is still attached to its old stalk, especially in the second species.

pinnatum. Air plant; also called life plant and floppers. An herb 2–5 ft. high, its stems round and hollow. Leaflets almost stalkless, ovalish-oblong, 2–5 in. long, notched or wavy on the margins and a new plant likely to spring from each notch. Flowers 1–1½ in. long, the calyx greenish-white and papery, the corolla red. Origin in the tropics but not certainly known where. The best of all plants to illustrate propagation by leaves. Sometimes known as *B. calycinum*.

tubiflorum. A succulent plant, 12–18 in. high. Leaves cylindric, in whorls* of 3, the whorls about 1 in. apart, the leaves 4–5 in. long, about ⅛ in. thick, and grooved on the upper side, the tip 5–7-toothed. Young plants sprout from the tips of the leaves and remain attached until roots form, when they drop off. Madagascar.

**BUBBLE BOUQUET.** See SUBMERGED FLOWER ARRANGEMENT.

**BUCARE** = *Erythrina poeppigiana*.

**BUCCANEER PALM** = *Pseudophoenix vinifera*.

**BUCCINATORIA, -us, -um** (bew-sin-a-tor'i-a). Like a crooked horn or trumpet.

**BUCKBEAN.** See MENYANTHES.

**BUCKBEAN FAMILY.** See GENTIANACEAE.

**BUCKBRUSH** = *Symphoricarpos occidentalis;* see also CEANOTHUS.

**BUCKEYE.** See HORSE-CHESTNUT.

**BUCKEYE FAMILY** = Hippocastanaceae.

**BUCKEYE-ROT.** See Diseases at TOMATO.

**BUCKTHORN.** See RHAMNUS.

**BUCKTHORN FAMILY** = Rhamnaceae.

**BUCKWEED.** See EPILOBIUM ANGUSTIFOLIUM.

**BUCKWHEAT.** Farm plants of little interest to the gardener unless he keeps bees, which greatly favor the plant. The common buckwheat, also, is one of the best plants for soil improvement or for smothering weeds. Sow as often as possible during the growing season, allowing plants to get about 8 in. high and then plow under, after which a new planting can be made.

Buckwheat belongs to the genus **Fagopyrum** (fag-o-py'rum), family Polygonaceae, and comprises about 6, mostly annual, quick-growing herbs with alternate,* usually angled leaves. Flowers small, white, in racemes in those below. Fruit a pointed, triangular achene* which furnishes the buckwheat of commerce.

F. esculentum. The common buckwheat. A weak, fleshy herb, inclined to sprawl in age. Leaves more or less triangular-oval, the stalk stouter than in the next species. Flowers fragrant, white, beloved of bees. Sides of its triangular fruit not grooved. Central Asia.

F. tataricum. India wheat; called also Kangra buckwheat and duck-wheat. Similar to common buckwheat but more slender and smaller. Leaves broadly halberd-shaped, the basal lobes wide-spreading. Flowers in a loose cluster and the sides of the fruit with a distinct groove. India. More hardy than the common buckwheat. Sometimes called Tartarian or Iceland buckwheat.

**BUCKWHEAT FAMILY** = Polygonaceae.

**BUD.** See BUDS.

**BUD CUTTING.** See CUTTINGS.

**BUDDING.** Budding is a form of grafting in which a bud rather than a cion is inserted upon the stock. Since only a single bud is used, it is more economical of wood. It is used to propagate nursery plants and to top-work young trees. Some plants are better adapted to budding than cion grafting, as stone fruits, for the reason that cherry, peach, or plum wood does not split well for grafting, while the bark slips readily for budding.

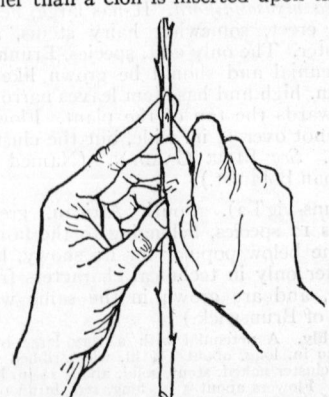

The right way to make the cut in budding, with a slanting, shallow cut

As in any form of grafting, budding depends upon bringing together the growing regions of the "bud" and of the

---

* Special articles on the subjects indicated by an asterisk (*) will be found at the words so marked.

stock under such conditions that they will unite and grow as one (see GRAFTING). This growing region, or cambium zone, is at the point where the bark separates from the wood and all operations should be carried on with this thought in mind. Sharp tools, clean cuts, careful matching of cambium regions, snug fitting and tying, and careful protection from drying of tissues both before and after the budding operation, are conducive to success. Although there are various forms of budding, they are essentially the same in general principle, the differences lying in adaptability to some particular material or object in view. Accordingly, June budding refers to the time of the year in which the operation is performed; shield, plate, and patch budding refer to the shape of the bud portion used. T-budding, commonly known as shield budding, and H-budding, refer to the type cut made in the stock; while up-budding and down-budding refer to the manner of insertion of the bud in the stock. Budding may be done at any time that the bark of the stock will slip and yet mature buds are available. In general practice this limits the operation to summer after buds of the current season have matured and before the bark of the stock has tightened. Below are given the approximate dates for budding fruit trees and rose stocks in the nursery region of western New York. The dates may be earlier in a dry season or on light soils and in southern regions.

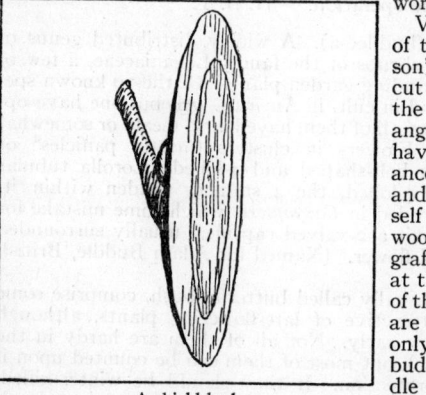
Do not cut a bud with a deep, horizontal stroke of the knife

Rose .....................July 1 to July 15
Pear .....................July 10 to July 20
Apple ....................July 15 to Aug. 10
Plum (St. Julien stock)...July 1 to Aug. 1
Plum (Myrobalan stock)....Aug. 15 to Sept. 1
Cherry (Mazzard stock)....July 20 to Aug. 1
Cherry (Mahaleb stock)....Aug. 15 to Sept. 1
Quince ...................July 25 to Aug. 15
Peach ....................Aug. 20 to Sept. 10

SHIELD OR T-BUDDING

Shield or T-budding is the most common form of budding, used both for propagating fruit trees and ornamentals in the nursery and for top-working older trees. Vigorous shoots of the current season's growth are cut for bud wood, the buds in the angles of the leaves having an appearance of maturity and the stick itself having a firm, woody feel. As in grafting, the buds at the tip and base of the year's growth are discarded and only plump, hard buds near the middle are used. The leaves on the bud-sticks are trimmed away, leaving about ¼ in. of the stem as a handle to the bud. After trimming, the sticks are wrapped in a damp burlap, for once they become dried they are worthless.

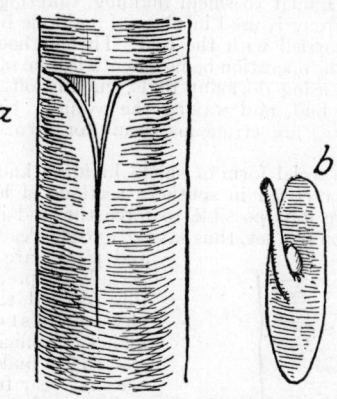
A shield bud

A shield bud (b), and the T-shaped incision in the bark (a), prepared to receive it

At the point where the bud is to be inserted a T-shaped incision is made, the transverse cut being made by a rocking motion of the knife and the vertical one by drawing the knife upward lightly from a point about an inch below the first cut. Before removing the knife a slight twist of the blade will loosen the edges. Here the advantage of the straight-pointed knife over the curved form is apparent, for the latter could not be twisted to open the bark without boring into and injuring the tender tissue beneath.

The bud is cut from below upward, with a drawing motion of the knife. The entire thickness of the bark is cut at the point of the bud, so that it will not crumple when inserted into the stock.

No wood is cut away with the bud unless just under the "eye"; but, on the other hand, the bud must not be cut so thin that the soft, growing tissue between the bark and wood is injured. With fruit plants, one may leave a thin strip of wood, while with roses it is customary to remove all the wood by making the first upward cut very deep and severing the bark by a cross-cut above the bud. Grasping the shield firmly between the thumb and forefinger, it is carefully lifted from the wood, without tearing the bud. With the leaf stem as a handle, the bud is inserted into the T-shaped incision and pushed down until its "heel" is flush with the transverse cut. When the T-incision is inverted the bud must be pushed upwards and the operation is called up-budding or reverse T-budding as contrasted with down-budding. Sometimes with plants with large buds, as some pear varieties, a vertical cross is better than a T-incision.

No waxing is necessary, but the bud must be tied. For this purpose raffia and rubber budding strips are used. Raffia is cut into lengths of 18 or 20 inches and moistened to make it flat and pliable. Rubber strips are sold already cut into 2-in. lengths, ⅜ in. in width. The strand is first brought firmly across the upper end of the bud to keep it from working out. Beginning then at the bottom of the slit, the material is wound smoothly upward, covering everything but the eye, and fastened. It is essential that this winding be tight, for it must hold the bud immovably in place and must be air-tight. In from 2 to 4 weeks, depending on the growth of the stock, the tie should be cut to prevent girdling. The bud will not put forth growth, but will lie dormant until the following spring, when the stock is cut away just above the bud. Any new growth from the stock must be removed as soon as it appears.

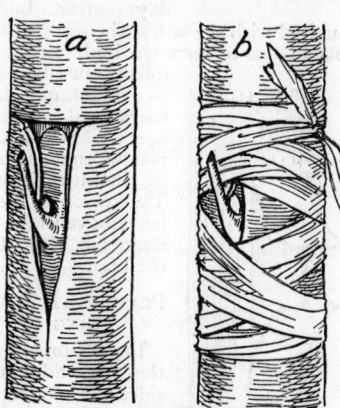
A bud inserted (a), bound with raffia (b), and ready for growth

* Special articles on the subjects indicated by an asterisk (*) will be found at the words so marked.

In the case of nursery trees the bud is inserted on the stock 2 inches above the ground-line. The following spring the stock is cut off above the bud. The work may be done in two operations, the first cut being made 2 or 3 in. above the bud so as to leave a stub to which the new shoot may be loosely tied for support. Several weeks later when the new shoot has hardened somewhat, the old stub may be cut off smooth, close to the bud, when the new growth will rapidly heal the wound.

Young trees up to 5 years old are well adapted to topworking by budding, and since budding is economical of wood, it is suited to new varieties, the bud wood of which may be scarce. Branches of trees larger than ½ in. in diameter, or with thick bark, are not overly successful. Older trees may be budded by severely cutting back so as to induce vigorous new growth of small diameter which may in turn be budded.

PRONG BUDDING is similar to shield budding, differing in that a short spur or prong is used in place of a simple bud. No wood should be carried with the bud. The method is adapted to nut trees, the operation being essentially the same as dormant grafting, using dormant buds, cutting off the stock just above the bud, and waxing the wound. *Cion, sprig,* and *twig budding* are erroneous terms for forms of grafting (see GRAFTING).

JUNE BUDDING. A special form of shield budding known as June budding is practiced in southern sections of long growing season, where it is possible to force the bud into growth the same season it is set, thus saving a year. Peaches and plums are especially adapted to this method since the rootstock makes sufficient size to be budded the first year from seed, yet other material may also be used to advantage. The difficulty of securing buds sufficiently mature from the current season's growth may be met by holding dormant wood in storage from the previous season until needed. Five or ten days after budding, when the bud has united with the stock, the top should be bent or partially broken so as to force the bud. Enough foliage must be left to maintain the stock until the foliage of the new shoot is sufficient to nourish the entire plant. The stock may then be removed with a clean cut close to the bud.

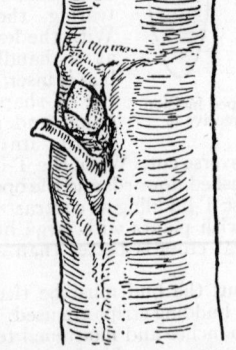

A bud with the raffia removed and thoroughly established in its new home

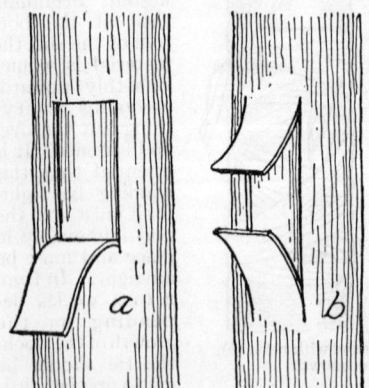

The stock prepared for plate budding (a), and H-budding (b)

PLATE AND H-BUDDING

In plate budding, the top and both sides of a rectangle are cut through the bark of the stock, and the resulting flap of bark turned down, exposing a rectangular area. The bud to be united is cut with a similar rectangle of bark attached so as just to fit the exposed area on the stock. No wood is taken with the bud. After the bud is set in place on the stock, the flap of bark is brought up over the bud and securely tied. This method is useful with the olive. Treatment following budding is the same as for shield budding.

Sometimes a double rectangular cut is made in the bark of the stock to form the letter H, hence the name H-BUDDING. Both flaps of bark are turned back, a bud with rectangular shield is placed to match the exposed area, and both flaps turned back over the bud and tied. Where the bark is thick, the H-bud makes a less bunglesome job than would simple plate budding.

PATCH BUDDING

Patch budding differs from plate budding in that no hanging strip of bark is left on the stock, otherwise it is essentially the same. A rectangular piece of bark is cut out from the stock and a bud with bark of corresponding size and shape is fitted into the exposed area and tied. Since this method is at present so widely used owing to popular interest in pecans, nut trees in general, mango, and other heavy-bark plants, a special knife is to be had which cuts a rectangle on the stock of identical size as the bud to be inserted. It is patterned after a machinist's die, consisting of a sharp-edged metal box, which when pressed against the stock and the cion, cuts out identical areas. The work is usually done in late spring with dormant buds of the last season's growth, but may be done in summer with buds of the current season's growth.

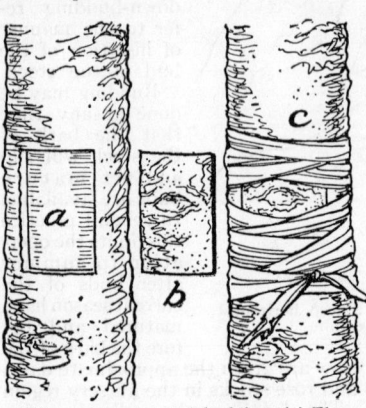

Three stages in patch budding: (a) The stock prepared for the bud; (b) The bud; (c) The bud inserted and bound with raffia

There are several other modifications of the three main types of budding as described above. Some of them are used by professional fruit growers or nurserymen, but the average home grower will find that all his ordinary budding needs will be met by shield or T-budding, by plate or H-budding, or by patch budding. To list and describe other minor sorts of budding is merely to confuse a comparatively simple operation. — H. B. T.

**BUDDLEIA** (bud'lee-a). A widely distributed genus of mostly tropical shrubs of the family Loganiaceae, a few of which are outstanding garden plants. Of the 70 known species six are found in cult. in America. All but one have opposite* leaves and all of them have hairy, mealy or somewhat scurfy foliage. Flowers in clusters (mostly panicles* or spikes*). Calyx bell-shaped and 4-lobed. Corolla tubular or bell-shaped, 4-lobed, the 4 stamens hidden within it. (They are protruded in *Caryopteris* which some mistake for this genus.) Fruit a 2-valved capsule,* usually surrounded by the withered flower. (Named for Adam Buddle, British botanist.)

The shrubs, usually called butterfly-bush, comprise some of the most attractive of late-flowering plants, although some bloom very early. Not all of them are hardy in the North (*see* below), but most of them can be counted upon if given winter protection. If they should be winter-killed, they can be cut back to the ground as the roots nearly always survive. Some growers prefer to cut back most of the cult. species and mulch the crowns with light, strawy manure. They need a rich but not heavy soil and it should be well drained. Easily propagated by cuttings of half-ripe wood

---

* Special articles on the subjects indicated by an asterisk (*) will be found at the words so marked.

and rooted in the fall in the greenhouse. For winter bloom most of them can be grown in the cool greenhouse. See GREENHOUSE.

**alternifolia.** The only cult. species with opposite leaves and a shrub up to 10 ft., thus too big for cutting back. Leaves lance-shaped, 1–4 in. long, green above, grayish and scurfy beneath. Flowers lilac-purple, about ½ in. long, in short, dense, leafy clusters on last year's branches. China. A beautiful plant with arching or pendulous branches and hardy only from zone* 5 southward. June–July.

**asiatica.** A shrub 2–6 ft. high, the leaves narrow, 5–8 in. long, green above, rusty-hairy or felt-like beneath. Flowers white, fragrant, in slender, drooping clusters that are often 5 in. long. Southern China and India. Not hardy above zone* 5. April–May.

**davidi.** Orange-eye butterfly-bush. The best known of the cult. species and the hardiest. A shrub 4–10 ft. high, but often much less in those cut back for the winter. Leaves oval-lance-shaped, 6–9 in. long, finely toothed, green above, white-felty beneath. Flowers lilac, fragrant, orange at the throat, in usually nodding spikes 5–12 in. long. China. Blooms from late July to frost. The var. **magnifica** has rose-purple and larger flowers. Var. **veitchiana** has mauve flowers with an orange eye. There are several other varieties, all of them and the typical form often called summer lilac.

**farquhari.** A beautiful hybrid shrub 3–7 ft. high. Leaves rusty-yellow and felt-like beneath, narrow, about 7 in. long. Flowers pale pink, in elongated, slender spikes that are grouped in clusters. Not certainly hardy north of zone* 5.

**lindleyana.** Not over 5 ft. high, the branchlets somewhat 4-angled or winged. Leaves oval to oblong, 2½–4 in. long, green both sides, but paler beneath. Flowers purplish-violet in erect, dense spikes. Eastern China. Hardy from zone* 6 southward. Aug.–Sept.

**officinalis.** A shrub 2–6 ft. high, the branchlets round and gray-scurfy. Leaves lance-oblong, or narrower, 4–7 in. long, grayish above, white or rusty-hairy beneath. Flowers in dense, stalked cymes,* fragrant, lilac with an orange eye. China. April–May. Not hardy north of zone* 6.

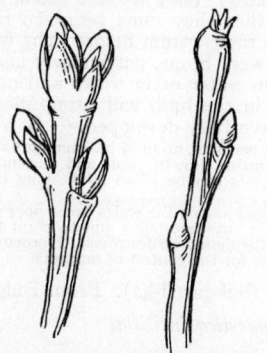

Winter buds, often sticky or varnished, are Nature's best protection for the shoots to follow in spring.

At the left a fruit bud and at the right a leaf bud. In pruning it is often necessary to distinguish between them.

**BUD DROP.** See Diseases at SWEET PEA.

**BUD GRAFTING** = BUDDING.

**BUD MUTATION.** See MUTATION.

**BUD ROT.** See Diseases at CANNA and CARNATION.

**BUDS.** Nature's protection to undeveloped flowers or leaves. They vary from the eyes on a potato to the delicately tinted rose bud. From the gardening standpoint, the most important are the winter buds, which ensure next year's supply of fresh green leaves or flowers. They are often elaborately protected by coatings of hair, scales, felt-like coverings, gums, and some are apparently varnished.

It is upon the knowledge of this function of buds that all grafting, budding, and the making of cuttings is based. For all these operations merely rely upon the bud to develop into a shoot or new plant.

Leaf buds and flower buds are usually formed many months before either will open, and in most temperate climates a winter usually intervenes. It is often a practical matter, therefore, both in pruning and grafting, to know which are flower buds and which will produce only foliage. The accompanying figures tell this better than words.

The underground buds on rootstocks are also important to the gardener. Each of them will send up a new shoot the following spring, and if the rootstock is cut or divided, a bud must be included in order to ensure a new plant. See also ADVENTITIOUS.

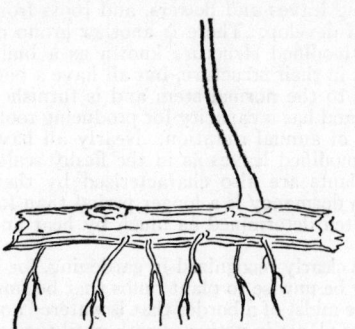

Underground buds on a rootstock. The bud scar at the left shows where a shoot once grew.

**BUD-SPORT.** An unusual, and sometimes valuable, variation from the type, originating from the bud of an otherwise normal plant — cause unknown. One of the most famous bud-sports is the navel orange.

**BUD STICK.** A shoot from which buds are removed for propagation; often called merely a *stick*.

**BUD-VARIETY.** A bud-sport.

**BUFFALOBERRY.** See SHEPHERDIA.

**BUFFALO CURRANT** = *Ribes odoratum.*

**BUGBANE.** See CIMICIFUGA.

**BUGINVILLAEA** = BOUGAINVILLAEA.

**BUGLE.** See AJUGA.

**BUGLE-LILY.** See WATSONIA.

**BUGLOSS** = ANCHUSA.

**BUGS.** See True Bugs at INSECT PESTS. See also the Insect Pests at CURRANT and GOOSEBERRY.

**BULB.** A much swollen, usually underground stem, of which the onion is a typical example, and from the bottom of which roots always arise. The scale-like coverings are actually much modified, food-storing leaves which completely surround, protect and feed the bud. True bulbs like onion and tulip always have these scale-like coverings, and sometimes the outermost layer is parchment or skin-like. Such bulbs were once, and are sometimes still, called tunicated bulbs to distinguish them from corms (which see). For the many valuable bulb-bearing garden plants and their uses see BULBS.

*BULBIFERA, -us, -um* (bul-biff'e-ra). Bulb-bearing.

**BULBIL.** A small bulb, differing from a bulblet in being borne above ground, usually among the flowers, as in some onions, but sometimes in the axil* of a leaf.

**BULBLET.** A small bulb, borne about a larger one, as in many bulbous plants (see MOTHER BULB). The term bulblet is often, but somewhat loosely, applied to a bulbil (which see). See also SET.

**BULB NEMATODE.** See Diseases at ONION.

**BULBOCODIUM** (bul-bo-cō'dee-um). A single, crocus-like, European herb of the lily family, grown for its very early spring bloom. They bear corms* which should be planted in the same way and at the same time as crocuses. The only species, **B. vernum,** the spring meadow saffron, bears 1–3 purple, funnel-shaped flowers close to the ground, followed by a cluster of narrow, basal leaves. (*Bulbocodium* is Greek for woolly bulb.)

*BULBOSA, -us, -um* (bul-bō'sa). Bearing bulbs; also applied to other swollen underground stems or even to swollen roots.

---

* Special articles on the subjects indicated by an asterisk (*) will be found at the words so marked.

**BULBO-TUBER.** A corm.*

**BULBOUS CHERVIL** = *Chaerophyllum bulbosum*.

**BULB PAN.** *See* FLOWER POTS.

**BULBS.** Most perennial plants at the time of their dormancy have stems furnished with buds from which will develop shoots, bearing leaves and flowers, and roots from which other roots will develop. There is another group of plants which have a modified structure known as a bulb. These vary somewhat in their structure, but all have a portion that corresponds to the normal stem and is furnished with buds for growth and has a capacity for producing roots which often are only of annual duration. Nearly all have parts that represent modified leaves as in the fleshy scales of the lily. These plants are also characterized by their growth cycle in which dormancy is a longer period than for most plants and is often determined as much by heat and dryness as by cold.

This factor must be clearly recognized in gardening, for it is obvious that it may be unwise to plant bulbs that become dormant in June in the midst of a border that is watered and fed to keep herbaceous plants in active growth until the approach of cold weather.

It should be understood that some bulbs renew themselves almost entirely each year, forming a bulb of flowering size annually, and that others are relatively permanent, dividing slowly within their mass until each branch becomes a unit of sufficient size to separate or be separated from the oldest portion of the plant. Tulips and Spanish iris are good examples of the first type and narcissus of the second. This means that the tulip bulb, when planted, must be given suitable conditions and enough food so that, in addition to flowering, it can immediately form also a new bulb strong enough to flower the next season. Narcissus on the other hand continues to grow from the original base and produces leaves even if there is not food enough to produce flowers. This explains sometimes why tulips that are poorly planted may not flower a second year after planting. It also suggests why tulips are so often treated as annuals and planted for one season's show only, and why narcissus is so often found in deserted homesteads still vigorous but unflowering.

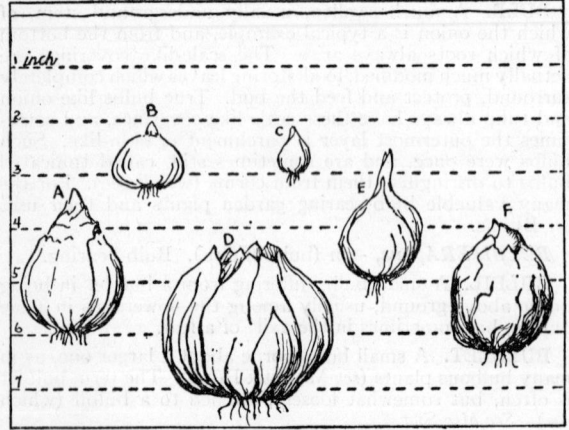

The correct depths for planting common bulbs: (*a*) Narcissus; (*b*) Crocus; (*c*) Snowdrop; (*d*) Lily; (*e*) Tulip; (*f*) Hyacinth

Bulbs, therefore, must be used where they can find food for their continued growth and in sufficient quantity and of proper character to assure annual flowering. This is particularly true of the bulbs of cold climates, for many that come from warm regions, notably members of the Amaryllis family, do not make strictly annual root growth, but have more or less permanent roots that are added to each season.

GARDEN BULBS. In the garden, bulbs are prized because of the prodigality of their blooming and the brilliance of their flowers. Since their flower buds are formed inside the bulb at the time of purchase, the gardener is practically assured of flower the next season unless he commits some signal cultural error.

We commonly group bulbs according to their season of bloom, a purely arbitrary and artificial classification. From the moment snow leaves, they commence with scilla, chionodoxa, snowdrop, crocus, grape hyacinth (*see* MUSCARI), wild tulip, and narcissus until the great army of garden and horticultural forms of hyacinth, tulip and narcissus bring about the spring climax. This yields in turn to the lilies, amaryllis, lycoris, and nerine of summer and early autumn, with zephyranthes, sternbergia, colchicum, or autumn crocus for late autumn and early winter for northern gardens, to name only the most common of the garden bulbs, a galaxy that can be greatly increased in warmer regions by many of the amaryllis relatives.

All of these plants are discussed at their proper entries, but it is possibly wise to mention both hyacinth and tulip here. The first is essentially a garden plant, the result of years of selection and cultivation. It comes to the garden ready for its best flowering, and then the bulb splits up enough to give only smaller stalks of bloom that each year grow stronger, until they again reach a maximum and the cycle repeats itself. Obviously this points to care in feeding, for the richer the soil the more rapidly the dividing young bulbs will reach their new peak of growth. Being a hungry plant, it enjoys the richly manured soil that would mean ruin to some other bulbs. The tulip, on the other hand, while needing rich food and a warm soil so that it may have a full summer rest, should grow enough to flower well each year. That is why tulips are so often bedded or treated as a crop plant, being lifted and followed by annuals.

In general terms, planting should always recognize these points — food located below the bulb to be reached by the roots annually renewed; drainage to prevent danger of decay of bulb during dormancy; proper location to insure a period of summer dormancy during which growth goes on below ground and within the bulb to insure next year's flowering; and a proper depth to insure full root growth and prevent undue division of the bulb at the expense of all else. The general rule that the bulb should be two and one-half times its depth below the surface is safe except for a few bulbs that must be shallow and are noted elsewhere. In some mole-infested gardens bulbs are occasionally planted in wire baskets to prevent the bulbs from being eaten.

Bulbs that renew themselves annually are best treated as annuals in garden beds, those that are permanent can be combined with any reasonable amount of herbaceous growth, provided they get their summer rest. Beside use in garden beds, bulbs are successful in lawns, meadows and near shrubbery where their masses of bloom make spectacular sheets of color and where their maturing foliage, that must not be cut off, can die away normally. They are also useful in pots for forcing, remembering that they must be given time in the dark to develop a fine root system before light is given to bring about leaf and flower. Some, particularly narcissus and hyacinth, are grown in water or in water and pebbles, where the stored-up food in the bulb will bring about the flowering once the roots have fully developed. — B. Y. M.

INSECT PESTS. Two species of maggots, up to ¾ in. long, bore and feed in bulbs, causing decay and stunting growth. Soft and unsound bulbs should be destroyed. The maggots can be killed by keeping bulbs in water at 110° F. for 2 to 3 hours.

Tiny mites working on bulbs and among the scales cause poor growth. Efforts should be made to obtain mite-free bulbs and to plant them in uninfested soil, and unsound bulbs should be destroyed. Dormant bulbs can be treated with hot water as for the control of maggots.

*BULGARICA*, *-us*, *-um* (bul-gare'i-ka). From Bulgaria.

**BULLACE** = *Prunus domestica insititia*.

**BULLACE GRAPE** = *Vitis rotundifolia*.

*BULLATA*, *-us*, *-um* (bul-lay'ta). Bullate; *i.e.* blistered or puckered.

**BULL BAY** = *Magnolia grandiflora*; also *Persea borbonia*.

**BULLOCK'S-HEART** = *Annona reticulata*.

---

* Special articles on the subjects indicated by an asterisk (*) will be found at the words so marked.

**BULL PINE** = *Pinus ponderosa.* See PINE.

**BULRUSH.** See SCIRPUS.

*BUMALDA* (bew-mal′da). An old generic name of uncertain application as a specific name for *Spiraea bumalda.*

**BUMELIA** (bew-mee′lee-a). A genus of not very ornamental shrubs and trees, comprising 25, chiefly tropical American, species, belonging to the family Sapotaceae. The only species of much cult. interest extends northward to Va. It is a shrub or small tree with hard wood and usually spiny branches. Leaves alternate,* without marginal teeth, persistent and green, but not evergreen. Flowers minute, white, in small, many-flowered clusters. Fruit berry-like. The cult. species is **B. lanuginosa,** variously called gum elastic, chittamwood (also shittimwood), and false buckthorn. Its leaves are 1½–4 in. long, shining green above and rusty beneath. Flowers scarcely ⅛ in. long. Fruit black, ellipsoid, about ½ in. long. It is little grown except as transferred from the wild, where it grows in woods from Va. to Fla. and Tex. (*Bumelia* is Greek for some ash tree, of uncertain application here.)

**BUNCHBERRY** = *Cornus canadensis.*

**BUNCHBERRY FAMILY** = Cornaceae.

**BUNCHFLOWER** = *Melanthium virginicum.*

**BUNCHFLOWER FAMILY.** See LILIACEAE.

**BUNCH PEANUT.** See PEANUT.

**BUNCH PINK** = *Dianthus barbatus.*

**BUNYA-BUNYA** = *Araucaria bidwilli.*

**BUPHTHALMUM** (bewf-thal′mum). A small genus of Eurasian herbs, family Compositae, usually called oxeye, from their yellow, dark-centered flower heads. They are grown somewhat in the perennial border for their rather large flowers. Leaves alternate.* Ray flowers, long and strap-shaped. (*Buphthalmum* is Greek for oxeye.)

Both the species below are of easy culture in any ordinary garden soil and may be increased by division.

**salicifolium.** A perennial herb 1–2 ft. high. Leaves willow-like, toothed and white-hairy, about 3 in. long. Flower heads solitary, about 2 in. wide, the disk darker than the bright yellow rays. Southeastern Eu. Late summer.

**speciosum.** Taller than the last, the leaves more or less heart-shaped, coarsely toothed, and very large in the lower ones, smaller and ovalish toward the top of the plant. Heads in clusters of 2–5, or solitary. Southern Eu.

**BUR.** Any prickly or spiny covering or fruit husk, as in the chestnut; also applied to many plants bearing prickly flowers or fruits.

**BUR-ARTICHOKE.** See ARTICHOKE.

**BURBANK.** A cherry variety. See CHERRY. See also the account of the origin of western fruit varieties at FRUIT CULTURE.

**BUR CLOVER** = *Medicago hispida.*

**BURDEKIN PLUM** = *Pleiogynium solandri.*

**BURDOCK** = *Arctium lappa.* See list at WEEDS.

**BUR GHERKIN** = *Cucumis anguria.*

**BURGUNDY.** See *vinifera* varieties at GRAPE.

**BURGUNDY TREFOIL** = *Medicago sativa.*

**BURL.** An overgrown excrescence or knot found on the trunks of some trees, and sometimes called a knaur. The burls of the redwood (*Sequoia sempervirens*), and of some other trees, will sprout into cutting-like growth if given heat and moisture. Standing the burl in a dish of water will produce the growth in a few days, and such freely sprouting burls make interesting centerpieces.

**BUR-MARIGOLD** = *Bidens.*

**BURN.** See WATER BLISTER.

**BURNET.** See SANGUISORBA.

**BURNET ROSE** = *Rosa spinosissima.*

**BURNING-BUSH** = *Euonymus americanus;* also *Dictamnus albus.*

**BURNING RUBBISH.** See RUBBISH.

**BUR OAK** = *Quercus macrocarpa.* See OAK.

**BURRAWANG** = *Macrozamia spiralis.*

*BURSA-PASTORIS* (bur-sa-pass-tor′is). An old generic name for the shepherd's-purse, which *see* in the list at WEEDS.

**BURSARIA** (bur-sar′i-a). A genus of only two species of Australian shrubs, family Pittosporaceae, the one below grown in Calif. for ornament, rarely cult. in greenhouses. Branches spiny. Leaves alternate.* Flowers small, white, in clusters, soon failing. Petals, sepals, and stamens each 5. Fruit dry (a capsule*), resembling the shepherd's-purse. (Named for *Bursa*, a pouch, in allusion to the pod.)

**spinosa.** Shrub or small tree, the branches pendulous. Leaves oblong-wedge-shaped, ½–1 in. long. Flowers in pyramidal clusters, which are showy, although each flower is very small. Grown outdoors only in Calif., mostly in the southern part of the state.

**BURSTWORT.** See HERNIARIA.

**BURYING VEGETABLES.** See STORAGE.

**BUSH.** See SHRUB. The word is also applied to a certain type of trained fruit tree, for which see TRAINING PLANTS.

**BUSH BASIL** = *Ocimum minimum.*

**BUSH BEAN** = *Phaseolus vulgaris humilis.* For culture see BEAN.

**BUSH BROOM** = *Hypericum prolificum.* See ST. JOHN'S-WORT.

**BUSH CLOVER.** See LESPEDEZA.

**BUSHEL.** See WEIGHTS AND MEASURES 3.

**BUSH FRUITS.** A collective term for various small fruits borne on a shrub, notably blackberry, raspberry, gooseberry, and currant. The loganberry and a few others, usually called bramble* fruits, make up the largest part of the bush fruits. For their culture *see* the different entries under the above names.

**BUSH HONEYSUCKLE** = *Lonicera tatarica, L. xylosteum,* and any other shrubby *Lonicera*, as distinguished from the vines. See also DIERVILLA.

**BUSH HUCKLEBERRY** = *Gaylussacia dumosa.* See HUCKLEBERRY.

**BUSH LIMA BEAN** = *Phaseolus limensis limeanus.* For culture see BEAN.

**BUSH PEA** = *Thermopsis mollis.*

**BUSH POPPY** = *Dendromecon rigidum.*

**BUSH PUMPKIN; BUSH SQUASH** = *Cucurbita pepo melopepo.*

**BUSH TREFOIL** = *Desmodium canadense.*

**BUTCHER'S-BROOM** = *Ruscus aculeatus.*

**BUTIA** (bew′ti-a). A small group of tropical South American feather palms, closely related to the coconut palm. The one below is widely grown by florists as *Cocos australis*, and is also planted outdoors in zones* 8 and 9. Trunk stocky, solitary, not spiny, clothed in nature with the withered leaves or their scars. Leaves rather stiff, drooping beyond the middle, the leaflets curving. Flower cluster arising from between the lower leaves, the male flowers with 6 stamens. Fruit globe-like or somewhat egg-shaped. (Named for the Earl of Bute.)

**capitata.** The pindo palm. Trunk stout, 12–18 ft. high, nearly 18 in. in diameter. Leaves long and arching, the leaflets many, about 2 ft. long, and grayish beneath, often in bunches of 3 or 4. Fruit nearly egg-shaped, about 1 in. long. Brazil. Common in Fla. and Calif.

---

* Special articles on the subjects indicated by an asterisk (*) will be found at the words so marked.

**BUTNERIA** = *Calycanthus*.

**BUTOMACEAE** (bew-to-may'see-ee). The flowering rush family, of secondary garden importance, comprises only 4 genera and perhaps 10 species of aquatic or marsh plants — *Butomus*, *Hydrocleis*, and *Limnocharis* being the cult. genera. All are closely related to the Alismaceae (which see).

One of the genera is a plant of the pond-edge with iris-like leaves, milky juice, and rose-colored flowers (*see* BUTOMUS), while *Limnocharis* and *Hydrocleis* have yellow flowers and grow in the water. Fruit small, dry (an achene*).

Technical characters: Differs from Alismaceae chiefly in having numerous ovules.

**BUTOMUS** (bew-tō'mus). A single Eurasian, aquatic or pond-edge herb, family Butomaceae, grown for its rose-colored flowers. It has long, narrow leaves 18–30 in. long and a many-flowered umbel* on a naked, rush-like stalk, 2–3½ ft. high. Flowers rose or pinkish, with three petals and 3 sepals, the individual flowers very small, but the cluster attractive. The only species, **B. umbellatus**, the flowering rush, is easy to grow in pools or along their edges. It is hardy in all except the coldest regions. (*Butomus* is from the Greek for ox and to cut, in allusion to the leaves being too sharp for fodder.)

**BUTTER-AND-EGGS** = *Linaria vulgaris*.

**BUTTER BEAN.** A form of *Phaseolus vulgaris*. See BEAN.

**BUTTERBUR.** See PETASITES.

**BUTTER-BUSH** = *Pittosporum phillyraeoides*.

**BUTTERCUP.** The crowfoots or buttercups comprise a large group of mostly north temperate herbs, all belonging to the genus **Ranunculus** (ra-nun'kew-lus), of the family Ranunculaceae. They include, besides the field buttercups, the common florists' ranunculus, which is much grown for winter bloom (*see* below). They have tuberous or fibrous roots, and simple* or compound* leaves, often much cut, lobed or divided. Flowers prevailingly yellow, but white or even red in some hort. varieties. Petals and sepals 5 each. Stamens* numerous. Fruit a tiny cluster of dry achenes.* (*Ranunculus* is Latin for a little frog, in allusion to the meadow habit of many wild species.)

All those below, except the florists' ranunculus, are easily grown outdoors in any ordinary garden soil, and as easily propagated by division in the spring or fall. Some are more weedy than decorative, and one is a weed in one form but a garden plant in another (*see* R. REPENS).

R. aconitifolius. Related to *R. asiaticus*, but taller and with usually branching stems. Flowers about 1 in. wide, often double in the hort. forms, usually white, but yellow in some of the hort. varieties. Eu. Its culture is the same as for the florists' ranunculus (*see* below).

R. acris. The common field buttercup; called also blister-flower and butter-rose. Weedy in the wild state but often double-flowered and handsome in the garden forms. Root fibrous, the stem branched and hairy, 2–2½ ft. high. Leaves divided into three segments, these stalkless and again thrice-divided or cut. Flowers about ½ in. wide, yellow. Eu., but widely naturalized throughout the U.S.

R. asiaticus. The florists' ranunculus, better called the turban or Persian buttercup. Root bulbous, from which springs a simple (rarely branched) stem 6–15 in. high. Leaves compound,* the three leaflets toothed and somewhat blunt. Flowers 1–4 on a stem, long-stalked, about 1½ in. wide, yellow and mostly double, with broad, blunt petals. Eurasia. For culture and varieties see below.

R. bulbosus. The bulbous buttercup, which *see* in the list at WEEDS.

R. repens. Creeping crowfoot or buttercup; called also sitfast. A creeping, weedy plant with long runners, often a nuisance as a weed (*see* the list at WEEDS). It roots at the joints and sends up erect, flowering stems 12–20 in. high. Lower leaves long-stalked and nearly round, the margins wavy. Flowers single, yellow. Eu., but a common weed in U.S. Its *var.* pleniflorus, a double-flowered form, is a widely grown garden plant. It has much-doubled, very profuse flowers about ¾ in. wide. It is also called *R. repens flore-pleno* and *R. speciosus*.

R. speciosus = *Ranunculus repens pleniflorus*.

### CULTURE OF THE FLORISTS' RANUNCULUS
(*Ranunculus asiaticus*)

This is valuable as a cut flower and for the gay display it may make in the garden. It is recorded by early garden writers, and although it may have lost popularity at one time, today gardeners are returning to an appreciation of its good qualities. In many respects it resembles the poppy-flowered anemone from the Mediterranean region, except that the predominating shades in this anemone are blue, while those of *Ranunculus asiaticus* are orange and yellow. Improved types are offered with larger and more colorful flowers that are very double.

Although the tubers may be planted out of doors after danger of frost has gone, it is in the greenhouse as a winter bloomer that it is most useful. The tubers may be planted in pots or benches in potting mixture* 4 and succeed best under a temperature dropping to 50° at night. They can also be raised from seed sown in May for early spring flowering. As soon as the seedlings are large enough to handle with ease, plant singly in thumb pots in potting mixture* 2, from which they may be transferred when ready, putting three in a 6-inch pot. When the roots become pot-bound in this, apply weak liquid fertilizer once a week. — J. G. E.

**BUTTERCUP FAMILY.** A very large family of plants, nearly all herbs, and containing among its many genera such garden favorites as the larkspur, monkshood, peony, columbine, clematis, and anemone. For the other genera and the characters of the family *see* RANUNCULACEAE.

**BUTTERFLIES.** See Moths at INSECT PESTS.

**BUTTERFLY-BUSH.** See BUDDLEIA.

**BUTTERFLY-FLOWER.** See SCHIZANTHUS; *see* also BAUHINIA MONANDRA.

**BUTTERFLY-LILY.** See HEDYCHIUM.

**BUTTERFLY-ORCHID** = *Oncidium papilio*.

**BUTTERFLY-PEA** = *Clitoria mariana*; also *Centrosema virginianum*.

**BUTTERFLY-VINE** = *Stigmaphyllon ciliatum*.

**BUTTERFLY-WEED** = *Asclepias tuberosa*. See MILKWEED.

**BUTTERNUT** = *Juglans cinerea*. See WALNUT.

**BUTTER-ROSE** = *Ranunculus acris*. See BUTTERCUP.

**BUTTERWORT.** See PINGUICULA.

**BUTTONBALL TREE.** See PLATANUS.

**BUTTON-BUSH.** The common button-bush (called button willow in Calif.) of N.A. is the only American species and the only one worth the gardener's attention in the genus **Cephalanthus** (sef-a-lan'thus) of the madder family. While growing naturally in swamps, it is perfectly at home in most ordinary garden soils and is hardy over most of U.S. **C. occidentalis**, the cult. species, is a shrub 5–12 ft. high with opposite or whorled* leaves without marginal teeth. From Aug. to late Sept. it has ball-like, fragrant clusters of small, white, tubular flowers. (For technical characters *see* RUBIACEAE.) Easily propagated by seeds or cuttings. (*Cephalanthus* is Greek for flower-head.)

**BUTTON SNAKEROOT.** See LIATRIS; *see* also ERYNGIUM AQUATICUM.

**BUTTON WILLOW** = *Cephalanthus occidentalis*. See BUTTON-BUSH.

**BUTTONWOOD** = *Platanus occidentalis*.

**BUXACEAE** (bucks-ā'see-ee). The box family is small but horticulturally important because it yields not only box (*Buxus*) but *Pachysandra*. Of its six known genera and about 40 species, the only other one of garden interest is *Sarcococca*. They are widely distributed, but mostly tropical or subtropical.

Leaves alternate* (or opposite in the box) and in hort. genera, evergreen, the plants all shrubs or trees (herb-like in *Pachysandra*). Flowers small, greenish or inconspicuous, without petals. Fruit a pod (capsule*) or fleshy. Much the most important genus is the box (*Buxus*).

Technical flower characters: Flowers monoecious,* without petals. Calyx 4–12-parted, or sometimes none. Ovary superior,* 3-celled. Ovules 2.

---

* Special articles on the subjects indicated by an asterisk (*) will be found at the words so marked.

***BUXIFOLIA, -us, -um*** (bucks-i-fō'li-a). With leaves like the box (*Buxus*).

**BUXUS.** *See* Box.

**BYBLOEM TULIP.** *See* Garden Tulips at TULIPA.

**BYRNESIA** (burnz'ee-a). A single Mexican succulent plant, family Crassulaceae, grown in the greenhouse for its handsome bluish leaves and white flowers. Leaves mostly in a basal rosette,* thick, fleshy, about 2 in. long, pale bluish-gray, and bluntly keeled on the underside. Flowers small, in spreading clusters (cymes*) at the end of the stem, which rarely exceeds 6 in. (For flower characters *see* CRASSULACEAE.) The only species, *B. weinbergi*, needs a cool greenhouse, in the North and potting mixture* 6, but it is grown outdoors in southern Calif. Often called *Echeveria weinbergi*, and an attractive succulent. For related plants *see* ECHEVERIA, COTYLEDON, and HOUSELEEK. (Named for E. M. Byrnes, an expert grower of *Echeveria*, a related genus.)

***BYZANTINA, -us, -um*** (bi-zan-ty'na). From Byzantium, ancient name for Stamboul (Constantinople).

# C

**CABBAGE** (*Brassica oleracea capitata*). The cabbage is a cultigen* that originated many centuries ago from *Brassica oleracea*, a mustard-like, mostly sea-coast weed of the Old World. Today there are hundreds of varieties found in every country with a temperate climate, and this climatic exclusiveness should not be forgotten in our own culture of the plant. It will not stand extreme heat or dryness, and will grow well only where there is some moisture and coolness. To ensure the latter, cabbage is rightly divided into two groups — early and late. Midsummer crops are not sought at all, or are secondary with this crop.

Pointed and flat-headed types of cabbage

The seasonal nature of the crop and its wide uses have largely dictated the varieties that are grown here. Some are used for boiling, some only for coleslaw, others only for sauerkraut, some are green, others red, and there is the Savoy Cabbage with blistered, puckery leaves.

VARIETIES. Depending on their use and season, the best varieties are:
Early. Jersey Wakefield (conical head). Charleston Wakefield (larger than Jersey Wakefield). Early Copenhagen. Golden Acre.
Midseason. Glory.
Late. Danish Ballhead. Flat Dutch. Wisconsin All Season (for sauerkraut). Drumhead Savoy (a Savoy Cabbage).

There are many other varieties, some suited to the special requirements of the market gardener. But the home gardener, from the above list, can select those that best fit his needs. For those who want a red cabbage, Red Drumhead or Mammoth Rock Red should be chosen. The Danish Ballhead is one of the best varieties if you wish to store the heads for winter cabbage.

SOILS AND FERTILIZER. Most good garden soil will produce satisfactory cabbage if it is properly enriched. Commercially it is grown on soils ranging from sandy loam to fairly heavy clays or even muck. Perhaps more important than texture is the supply of soil moisture. This must be adequate and conserved by constant cultivation (*see* CULTIVATION). Adequate soil moisture may well compensate for long heat spells which cabbage does not like. It will not develop properly if these are too frequent or too long continued.

Most important of all is fertility. No crop repays so richly the expenditure for manure or fertilizer. A good grade of commercial fertilizer with a 4–8–10 ratio (*see* FERTILIZERS) should be applied, before planting, at the rate of one ton to the acre (11 pounds per 100 ft. of row). If well-rotted stable manure is available, spread it 3 in. thick and plow in at least two weeks before the plants are set out.

Some commercial growers, where intensive returns are necessary (8000 heads of cabbage per acre), use both manure and fertilizers.

Home growers will find it will pay also to top-dress, about three weeks after the plants are set out, with nitrate of soda at the rate of 250 pounds to the acre (1¼ pounds per 100-ft. row). The nitrate of soda application is necessary only for the early season varieties (*see above*).

SEED SOWING. There are several different methods of which the most practical is the following (for early cabbage): Sow the seeds in fine soil in flats in the hotbed or greenhouse in February or March. Do not make the soil too rich, as it is likely to make the seedlings grow too fast and become leggy. Make small drills about ½ in. deep and 2–3 in. apart, and put 8–10 seeds in each inch of drill. Water and keep in a reasonably cool temperature (50°–60°).

When the seedlings are large enough (3–4 in. high), prick out and replant farther apart in flats or boxes. This ensures stocky instead of spindling plants. The seed-sowing should be timed a month or six weeks earlier than the plants are to be set out.

The method of raising seedlings of the late varieties is exactly the same, except that the flats or boxes are kept outdoors instead of under glass. It will take from four to six weeks to get plants large enough for their permanent location.

Long Island, and the northeastern seaboard generally, the shores of the Great Lakes, and along the Pacific Coast are the preferred cabbage localities, but it is raised very well in many other states. Some quite warm states can grow good crops by picking the coolest season.

SETTING THE PLANTS. Cabbage is set at different intervals, depending on the variety. A useful guide is the following:

Early varieties.      14 in. apart.   Rows 28 in. apart.
Midseason varieties.  16 in. apart.   Rows 30 in. apart.
Late season.          24 in. apart.   Rows 36 in. apart.

To plant much closer may mean crowding and result in smaller heads. If the plants are sold by the head (not by the pound), closer planting may pay, although it makes cultivation more difficult at first and impossible later.

---

* Special articles on the subjects indicated by an asterisk (*) will be found at the words so marked.

Early varieties can be set out as soon as there is no danger of hard frost (for the dates see the name of your state). Late varieties should, over most of the northern states, be in place by August first.

Depending on the variety, it will take from 67 (early) to 40 plants (for late varieties) for a row 100 ft. long, which is ample, or perhaps too much, for a family of five.

CULTIVATION. To keep down weeds and conserve moisture, frequent cultivation is essential. If only a hoe is used, there need be little trouble about this. But if a wheel hoe or horse or motor machine is used, great care must be taken not to break the rather brittle leaves of the plants.

One way to minimize this is to cultivate only between 10 in the morning and 4 in the afternoon, when the leaves are more pliable or even partly wilted, than earlier or later, and less likely to injury. Keep up the cultivation as long as possible because, even with the spacing outlined above, the plants will ultimately prevent all but hand weeding. But if cultivation has been clean, the plants properly spaced, and they have grown well, their foliage should keep down the last crop of weeds.

HEADING. If the varieties listed above have been well grown, they should form the well-known, compact head without any extraneous aid. No commercial grower could afford *not* to have normally heading plants. But if the climate or soil or culture is not up to requirements and the plants are only heading poorly, tie up the outer leaves.

For the preferred position and sequence of cabbage in your garden *see* KITCHEN GARDEN.

INSECT PESTS. Several greenish leaf-feeding caterpillars attack cabbage and related plants. They include the cabbage worm, larva of a white butterfly, the cabbage looper, some webworms, and others. Spraying or dusting with Paris green is recommended in the early stages of the development of the crop, but the poison should not be applied when the crop is bearing the leaves that will be marketed or consumed. Derris or pyrethrum sprays and dusts may then be used.

The grayish cabbage aphid occurs in thick masses on the leaves, stunting and distorting plants; it yields to nicotine, especially when applied as a dust.

The red and black harlequin bug occurs south of the 40-degree latitude line; adults and nymphs suck the sap. It is hard to kill. A small patch of mustard planted early will attract adults, and may then be destroyed; hand picking is of some value. Cabbage, radish, etc., should be cleaned up after their season to avoid harboring these bugs.

A root maggot injures small plants in the spring in the North. Corrosive sublimate solution, 1 ounce to 10 gallons, sprinkled on the soil around the plant, will check the pest.

Cutworms often destroy young transplants (*see* TOMATO). Flea beetles also attack them sometimes (*see* TURNIP).

DISEASES. Black-rot, caused by a bacterium that lives over winter on the seed, produces a black ring in the stem, and soon kills the plant. Black-leg, caused by a fungus that penetrates the seed and which also remains alive in the soil for three years, destroys the plant with equal facility. The *Alternaria* leafspot fungus is not so deadly in its action, but injures the seedlings, affects the leaves, and on cauliflower, may blacken the blanched curd. These three diseases are controlled by treating the seed with hot water (cabbage 25 minutes, other crucifers 18 minutes, at 122° F.), and by long rotations with non-related crops.

Club root caused by a slime-mold lives for years in the soil but is not carried with the seed. Treating the seedlings in the bed by pouring corrosive sublimate solution (1 part in 1280 parts of water) along the row, long rotations, and treating the soil in affected fields with hydrated lime are profitable if the disease has been present. This corrosive sublimate solution also controls damping-off and wire-stem which so often injure the seedlings.

Wilt causes symptoms almost identical with those of black-rot. The only effective control measure is the procuring of wilt-resistant seed. Suitable strains of all the more common varieties are now available. Cabbage and especially cauliflower are very susceptible to injury from acid soils, hot, dry weather, and lack of potash. The cauliflower leaves under such conditions may become narrow and thick (known as whiptail) and the curd becomes brown and bitter. The cabbage leaves are tip-burned, especially if the ratio of potash to the superphosphate is not great enough. Time of planting, humus content of the soil, and proper liming must be taken into consideration in correcting these environmental deficiencies. Other diseases are soft rot, mildew, and peppery leaf spot.

**CABBAGE FAMILY** = Cruciferae.

**CABBAGE PALM** = *Roystonea oleracea*.

**CABBAGE PALMETTO** = *Sabal palmetto*.

**CABBAGE ROSE** = *Rosa centifolia*.

**CABBAGE TREE** = *Andira inermis*; also *Cordyline australis*.

**CABBAGE WORM.** See Insect Pests at CABBAGE.

**CABOMBA** (ka-bom′ba). A genus of six species of aquatics, family Nymphaeaceae, one widely used in aquaria for its finely divided, submerged leaves, which are good for supplying oxygen to the water. Floating leaves oblong, often lacking. Submerged leaves very finely divided, hair-like, and numerous on the weak stems. Flowers white, with 3 sepals and 3 petals, blooming on the water surface. (*Cabomba* is derived from an aboriginal name for the plant.)

The species are generally called fanwort or water shield and have little use outside of aquaria. Without some soil in the tank the plant will live only a few weeks. It is easily propagated by division, but should be propagated under water.

**caroliniana.** Washington plant; called also fish-grass and Carolina water shield. Submerged leaves hair-like, about ¾ in. long. Flowers about ⅓ in. wide, white, but with yellow spots at the center. Native from Ill. to Tex. and Fla., often a pest in outdoor pools because of its rampant growth, especially in the South.

**CABOMBACEAE.** See NYMPHAEACEAE.

**CABUYA** = *Furcraea gigantea*.

**CACALIA.** See EMILIA SAGITTATA LUTEA.

**CACANAPA** = *Opuntia lindheimeri*.

*CACAO*. Aztec name for the chocolate tree, and still the name for the tree and for chocolate in most tropical countries. See THEOBROMA.

**CACTACEAE** (kak-tay′see-ee). The cactus family is an immense group of succulent, mostly spiny, desert plants, all but a handful confined to dry or desert regions of the New World. There are perhaps 100 genera and over 1300 species, many of which are cultivated for their grotesque form, their often showy flowers, their sometimes edible fruit, and often because they make good, if odd-looking, house plants.

True leaves with expanded blades are lacking in mature specimens of most cacti, except in *Pereskia* and *Pereskiopsis*. All the rest have tiny or ephemeral leaves, and the green stem, often separated into leaf-like but swollen joints, functions as do leaves. The stem of some genera is immense, notably in the giant cactus (*see* CARNEGIEA), and in other genera where it stores great quantities of water in barrel-like enlargements. Practically all the genera are spiny, some horribly so, but *Rhipsalis* and *Hatiora* are spineless, and so are the very different plants known as crab cactus or Christmas cactus. (*See* EPIPHYLLUM and ZYGOCACTUS.)

In habit the cacti are often fantastic, sometimes erect and tree-like, sometimes climbing vines, others small and globular growths in the ground. Some, as in *Opuntia*, bear edible fruit; others yield beautiful night-blooming flowers (*see* HYLOCEREUS, SELENICEREUS, and NYCTOCEREUS). Except for the forage value of a few species of *Opuntia*, the cacti have little economic importance, the notable exception being *Nopalea*, which was commercially cult. for the cochineal insect in Mex.

From the garden standpoint, the remaining hort. genera may be divided into three groups:

1. *Cereus* and its allies.
2. Globular or low-growing plants without elongated stems.
3. *Echinocactus* and its allies.

The technical differences between these groups are difficult. But so far as the cult. genera are concerned, the three sections may be separated thus:

1. *Cereus* and its allies: Here belong the cacti with obvious stems, sometimes thick, branched and tree-like, or again vine-like, or some prostrate vines. All bear spines, sometimes on the ridges of the stem. For the hort. genera in this group see:

| MORE OR LESS ERECT, SOMETIMES TREE-LIKE | CLIMBING VINES | PROSTRATE OR LOW |
|---|---|---|
| *Bergerocactus* | *Acanthocereus* | *Echinocereus* |
| *Cereus* | *Aporocactus* | *Machaerocereus* |
| *Cephalocereus* | *Deamia* | *Wilcoxia* |
| *Escontria* | *Harrisia* | |
| *Heliocereus* | | |
| *Lemaireocereus* | | |
| *Myrtillocactus* | | |
| *Pachycereus* | | |
| *Peniocereus* | | |

---

* Special articles on the subjects indicated by an asterisk (*) will be found at the words so marked.

It is mostly from this group that the grotesque desert forms come, and some genera furnish close, spiny, hedge plants in many parts of the Southwest and in tropical America.

2. Globular or low-growing plants without elongated stems: Here belong the small, button-like genera, used for centerpieces, and also some other genera with a larger plant body but no very obvious elongated stem. The hort. genera of this group may be separated thus:

| Low, button-like or ball-like cacti, often half-hidden in the ground; sometimes cylindric | Often a foot high or more, but ball-like or barrel-shaped |
|---|---|
| *Ariocarpus* | *Escobaria* |
| *Astrophytum* | *Melocactus* |
| *Coryphantha* | *Pediocactus* |
| *Epithelantha* | |
| *Neomammillaria* | |
| *Pelecyphora* | |

3. *Echinocactus* and its allies: In this group belong cacti with a single, usually unbranched plant body that is stout, cylindric or barrel-shaped, usually too large for pot culture, but the plants are often grown in effective groups outdoors in frost-free areas. The plant body is usually prominently ribbed or grooved and very spiny. The hort. genera in this group are the following: *Echinocactus, Echinomastus, Ferocactus, Gymnocalycium, Hamatocactus, Homalocephala, Sclerocactus, Strombocactus,* and *Thelocactus.*

All the cacti are inclined to have very showy flowers, but the petals and sepals are often indistinguishable, as they merge insensibly one into the other. In some genera the flower is tubular; in others, of separate segments. The fruits are nearly always berry-like, and edible in some prickly pears (*see* Opuntia).

Besides the spines, some genera bear small tufts of often barbed bristles, and in some the spine arises in a small pit which also is the seat of the tuft of bristles (*see* Glochid). For cactus culture and uses *see* Cacti.

**CACTI.** Most of the cacti native in our southwestern states and in adjacent Mexico are adapted to outdoor culture in regions where the conditions approximate their own — a low annual rainfall and extremely warm summer temperature. While there are a few hardy sorts, most cacti will not stand much frost, which perhaps explains why only a single wild prickly pear (*Opuntia*) is native in the northeastern states, and it does not grow much above Cape Cod along the coast. And in all the area east of the 100th meridian and north of Va., there are less than 15 wild species of cacti, all the rest of the U.S. species growing in desert and semi-desert regions, most of which have an annual rainfall of 12 in. or less, sometimes much less, and little of which falls in the winter.

The outdoor culture of most cacti must therefore be confined to these regions of deficient rainfall and summer heat, areas where slush, sleet, fog, and other evidence of winter moisture are lacking. Some hardy collections are kept outdoors by providing a wooden roof to keep off snow and rain, even as far north as Mich.

### Outdoor Cactus Garden

Assuming you live within the climatic restrictions as outlined above (*see* the name of your state for rainfall and frost data), it is not difficult to have an outdoor cactus garden. In it one can grow scores of species from small, button-like plants to the huge, barrel-like or cylindric ones, or even the giant cactus (*Carnegiea*) if you have the space.

For most of the small kinds it is better to grow them in pots, using potting mixture* 6, and plunge* the pots in the prepared bed. The larger ones had better be planted directly in the bed in a soil mixture approximating potting mixture* 6.

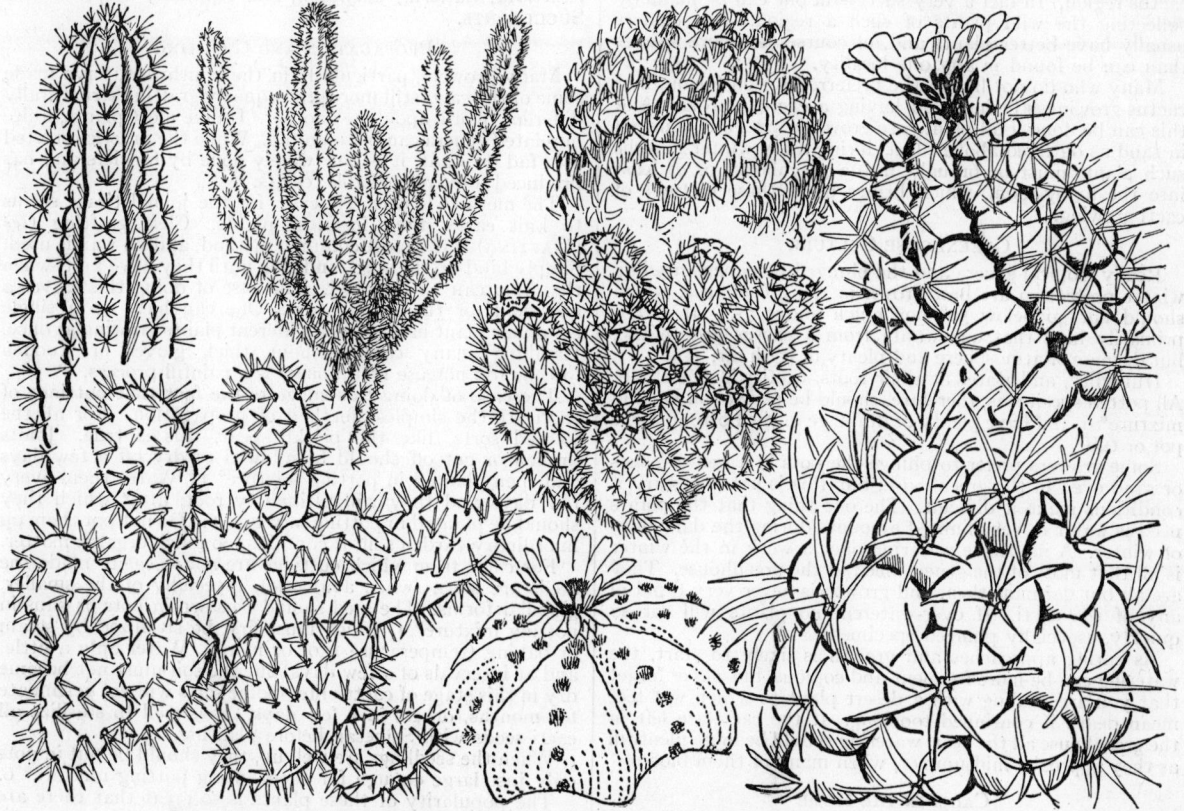

Decorative types of Cacti. Top row (*left to right*): *Pachycereus, Cephalocereus, Neomammillaria, Thelocactus*
Bottom row (*left to right*): *Opuntia, Astrophytum, Echinocactus*
The plant in the middle is *Echinocereus.*

---

* Special articles on the subjects indicated by an asterisk (*) will be found at the words so marked.

Whether the pots are plunged or the cacti planted in the bed, it is essential that proper drainage be provided. If the local soil is rocky or gravelly, there will be no trouble about this. But if it tends to hold water, dig out to a depth of at least 2½ ft. Fill in about 6 in. of broken stone, cinders or gravel. When this is settled, the rest of the bed should be filled up to the top with the soil that approximates potting mixture* 6, especially if cacti are to be planted directly in it.

Many growers limit their collections to plants that are best grown in pots. Most of the small cacti are easier handled in pots, and these may be plunged so that no pots show. If your cactus collection is only of these potted specimens, the bed for plunging may be filled with sand instead of potting mixture* 6, but the under-drainage is necessary in any case.

What you grow will depend a little upon the region in which you live. If winter rains or spring humidity are even moderate, you should not attempt many genera, especially tropical sorts.

Over much of the outdoor cactus country, however, you can grow at least some species in the genera *Opuntia, Cereus, Cephalocereus, Echinocactus, Echinocereus, Selenicereus, Coryphantha, Melocactus, Astrophytum, Ariocarpus,* and others. See CACTACEAE for the different genera of this family.

With such a beginning one can get the most grotesque and fantastic effects. Some creep, others climb, some look like burnt buttons, others like a Turk's-head, and there is often a bewildering array of colors in their flowers.

With some genera, notably in the taller forms of *Cereus* and its allies, desert landscapes can be made, with a mixture of ocotillo and *Agave*, neither of which is cacti but are often mistaken for them.

Such an outdoor cactus garden, and some of them in southern Calif., Ariz., and N. Mex. are very extensive and elaborate, needs no water except rainfall if it is in a natural cactus region. In fact a very successful one can be made by collecting the wild plants of such a region. But dealers usually have better plants and, of course, far more species than can be found in any one locality.

Many who do not live in the preferred region for outdoor cactus-growing still insist on having a cactus garden. And this can be done if all plants are grown in pots and plunged in sand as outlined above. But during rainy winter months such plants must be brought into a greenhouse or at least into the living-room, which brings us to these features of cacti-growing.

### GREENHOUSE CULTURE

Really tropical genera and the plunged specimens needing winter protection are best grown in the greenhouse, which should not go below 50° nor much above 75°. It is not primarily heat that one wants from a cactus greenhouse, but dryness of atmosphere and plenty of fresh air.

Humidity, and water at their roots, cacti will not stand. All potted specimens, therefore, should be planted in potting mixture* 6, and have plenty of drainage in the bottom of the pot or tub.

Some growers prefer to plunge the pots in a bed of ashes or sand even in the greenhouse, but this is not necessary if conditions make it difficult. The one thing that the plants need is water in very limited amounts during the dark days of winter. A moderate watering once a week in the winter is all that most of the genera need in the greenhouse. They are all but dormant then, and growth is never very rapid in any of the cacti. If over-watered, no plants will rot so quickly, especially plunged specimens.

As spring approaches and growth is likely to start, the watering can be more frequent and copious, but never forget that you are dealing with a desert plant to which wet feet mean death if continued too long. If the cacti are left in the greenhouse all the year, watering should be more plentiful as they approach midsummer, when many of them bloom.

### CACTI IN THE HOME

Without a greenhouse many enthusiasts are still able to have quite extensive cactus collections — all of course in pots, pans, or the fancy containers sold by the dealers. They should be potted exactly as are the usually larger greenhouse plants (*see* above). Plunge them in a bed of sand or ashes during the frost-free period, but in the fall bring them indoors.

No plants are so light-demanding as cacti, so that it is an affront to put them too far from a window. They are peculiarly sensitive to illuminating gas and should not be in the kitchen if there is a gas stove. A good, light, preferably well-ventilated living-room is the best, and emphatically not on a shelf over the radiator. Ordinary room temperatures will do.

Nearly all the trouble with house cacti comes from over-watering during their normal dormant period, which is winter. The plants, whatever their size, need to be kept between the points where they shrivel from too much dryness, or rot from too much water. If the room is very hot and dry (*i.e.* without evaporating pans on the radiator), the cacti will stand more water than in a relatively cool or moister room. No absolute guide can be given. But if planted in the proper mixture and with adequate drainage, they should not need watering more than every six or eight days. And some kinds will last three weeks or more without water.

This does not apply to the genera *Epiphyllum* and *Zygocactus*, long favorite house plants under the name of Christmas or crab cactus. These plants need more water and should be planted in potting mixture* 5. These, too, should be plunged outdoors in summer.

Most of the successful cacti for house culture, especially those suitable for the attractive, miniature desert gardens and for centerpieces, are found in the genera *Ariocarpus, Astrophytum, Coryphantha, Epithelantha,* and *Neomammillaria,* or in the juvenile states of otherwise much larger plants in the genera *Echinocactus, Melocactus, Ferocactus,* and many others. With these, especially in the prepared dishes of the florists, there are often other plants (not cacti) of the genera *Echeveria, Gasteria, Cotyledon,* and especially *Stapelia.* See SUCCULENTS.

### PROPAGATION AND GRAFTING

Many growers, particularly in the Southwest, have made some of the cacti still more grotesque by grafting structurally different plants upon one another. Unlike most plants, quite unrelated genera can be so united. While the practice started as a fad or stunt, it is now widely done by fanciers and has produced some remarkable results.

The method is perfectly easy, for the joined tissue seems to knit easier than in most plants. Cleft grafting (*see* GRAFTING) is the most common method, and no wax is used. Simply bind up the stock and cion until they have knit, when the raffia can be removed. The ease of doing this leaves a free field for the imagination. One can have on a single columnar plant half a dozen different plants growing at once. Handling many cacti without thick gloves or wooden forceps (do not use metal ones) is a painful process.

The ease of doing this suggests the fact that cuttings of cacti are the simplest method of propagation. For all the jointed sorts, like the prickly pear, this is true. Joints broken or cut off should be allowed to dry off a few days and then planted in potting mixture* 1. Water them every few days and they will ultimately root, after which they should be planted in potting mixture* 6. Do not pot them up in ordinary garden soil; it contains too much organic matter.

For cacti from which cuttings are not so easily made the seeds are sown (when available), especially of the smaller, globular forms. The seed should be sown in pots or pans in potting mixture* 1, which must first be sterilized by steam or baking (temperature 150° or more). Water only a little, and at intervals of a few days, but the soil must not become dry in this stage of cactus life. Some sorts will not germinate for months, others in a few days. It is well to sterilize all cacti seeds with Semesan before planting.

When the seedlings are well up, they should be put in pots only just large enough for them, using potting mixture* 6.

The popularity of these plants is so great that there are now many cactus societies whose members exchange specimens and cultural notes. For the address of your nearest

---

\* Special articles on the subjects indicated by an asterisk (*) will be found at the words so marked.

cactus club write the Garden Editor, Houghton Mifflin Company, Boston, Mass.

INSECT PESTS. Ornamental cacti are attacked by several species of scale insects and mealybugs, especially in greenhouses. Light oil emulsions or soap and nicotine sprays are suggested for their control. In Aust. cactus insects have been introduced to keep down the plague of cactus in fields.

**CACTUS DAHLIA.** See DAHLIA.

**CACTUS FAMILY** = Cactaceae.

*CAERULEA.* Same as *Coerulea.*

**CAESALPINIA** (see-zal-pin′i-a). A genus of important tropical shrubs and trees of the pea family, not one of which is of much garden interest. One of them is the source of brazilwood. The name *Caesalpinia,* however, is often incorrectly applied to the following cult. trees and shrubs. See their correct names for a description of them:

Caesalpinia gillesi = Poinciana gillesi.
Caesalpinia pulcherrima = Poinciana pulcherrima.
Caesalpinia regia = Delonix regia.

**CAESALPINIACEAE.** See LEGUMINOSAE.

*CAESIA, -us, -um* (see′si-a). Bluish-green (glaucous).

*CAESPITOSA, -us, -um* (sess-pi-tō′sa). Cespitose; *i.e.* tufted and forming dense, turf-like clumps or mats.

*CAFFRA.* Native South African name for the kei-apple (*Dovyalis caffra*).

*CAFFRORUM* (caff-ror′um). Pertaining or relating to the Kafirs of South Africa.

*CAHIOTA* = *Sechium edule.*

*CAINOTO.* West Indian vernacular for the star-apple (*Chrysophyllum cainito*).

**CAIOPHORA** (ky-off′o-ra). A large genus of often climbing, South American herbs, family Loasaceae, only one of secondary garden interest, and beset with stinging hairs. Leaves opposite.* Flowers regular,* but the petals hooded, very showy. Alternating with the petals are 5 scale-like, sterile stamens*; the fertile stamens numerous. Fruit a spirally twisted pod which splits along its valves but is closed at the top. (*Caiophora* is Greek for burn-bearing; from the stinging hairs.)

The plant below should be treated as a tender annual. See ANNUALS.

lateritia. An annual, climbing vine 10-15 ft. long. Leaves long-stalked, deeply cut, the segments toothed or lobed, 1-3 in. long. Flowers about 1½ in. long, the petals orange-red, the scale-like, sterile stamens greenish-yellow, the flower long-stalked. Fruit 2-3 in. long.

*CAJAN.* A specific name adapted from a Sudanese vernacular for the pigeon pea (*Cajanus cajan*).

**CAJANUS** (kay-jay′nus). A single tropical shrub of the pea family widely cultivated throughout the tropics for its edible seeds. It has compound leaves,* with 3 leaflets that are resinous-dotted beneath. Flowers typically pea-like, in clusters (racemes*) borne in the leaf-axils.* Fruit a compressed pod (legume*) with diagonal depressions, the seeds nearly round. (*See* CAJAN for origin of name.)

The pigeon pea is somewhat grown outdoors in extreme southern Fla. It is also occasionally grown as an annual in the greenhouse for its showy flowers.

cajan. Pigeon pea. A much-branched, hairy shrub 5-8 ft. high. Leaflets narrowly lance-shaped, about 3 in. long, hairy on both sides. Flowers orange-yellow, brownish on the back or otherwise irregularly colored. Pod about 2½ in. long, its seeds brown with a white "eye," about ¼ in. in diameter. Probably Old World tropics.

**CAJEPUT.** See CAJUPUT-TREE.

**CAJUPUT-TREE** = *Melaleuca leucadendron.*

*CALABA.* South American native name for *Calophyllum antillanum.*

**CALABASH.** The name calabash is applied to two or more unrelated plants. One is the gourd *Lagenaria leucantha* (which see), from which calabash pipes are made. The other is a tropical tree of the genus **Crescentia** (kres-sen′-tee-a), family Bignoniaceae, which bears the huge fruits so widely used for dippers and utensils, and is somewhat grown in Fla. Of the 5 known species, all tropical American, the only cult. one is the calabash tree, **Crescentia cujete,** which grows from 25-50 ft. high. It has broad leaves 4-6 in. long, mostly borne in clusters. Flowers solitary, hanging, yellowish but red or purple-striped, tubular. Fruit a hard-rinded berry, more or less oval, or round in some trees, from 6 in. in diameter to 20 in. long. The dried rind is water-tight and the split shell has many uses. Hardy outdoors only in zone* 9. (Named for Pietro Crescenzi, an Italian. See Herbals at GARDEN BOOKS.)

**CALABASH GOURD** = *Lagenaria leucantha.*

**CALABAZILLA** = *Cucurbita foetidissima.*

**CALABRESE** = *Brassica oleracea italica.* For culture see BROCCOLI.

*CALABRICA, -us, -um* (ka-lab′ri-ka). From Calabria, Italy.

*CALACINUM* = MUEHLENBECKIA.

**CALADIUM** (ka-lay′di-um). An important genus of greenhouse foliage plants widely cult. for their beautifully colored leaves, usually under the gardener's name of fancy-leaved caladiums. Of the 12 or 14 species, all tropical American and belonging to the family Araceae, two are widely known greenhouse subjects. They have thin leaves, the stalk of which (in ours) is joined to, or near, the middle of the blade, not to the base. Leaves variously colored, not usually green, more or less arrowhead-shaped. The flowers (for characters *see* ARACEAE), and white, berry-like fruit are seldom produced in the greenhouse except by breeders. (*Caladium* is from a Malay word for a related plant that is not now included in the genus *Caladium.*)

Caladiums, properly grown, are among our most gorgeously colored foliage plants. They are tuberous-rooted herbs, at home in tropical rain-forests. They, therefore, need heat, moisture and plenty of rich soil. For summer bedding, for which they are very popular, start the tubers in flats, in chopped moss, covering them about one inch. Keep the moss moist and maintain a greenhouse temperature between 75° and 85°. When the tubers have rooted in the moss, remove and pot up each (depending on its size) in a pot only just large enough. Use potting mixture* 2. When they have started good growth, they should be shifted to larger pots, but kept relatively pot-bound; use potting mixture* 3. Keep the temperature 75° or more, and the plants should be as near the glass of the greenhouse as possible. Shade the glass (*see* SHADING) or the leaves will burn. The air should be moist at all times, and frequent wetting-down of floors and the benches is advisable. The plants should also be fed with liquid manure every two weeks.

There are perhaps dozens of named hort. forms of caladiums, but the names and identities are in such confusion that there can be no attempt to list them here. Most of them seem to be derived from the following two species, although they are sometimes listed as *Colocasia.*

bicolor. The commonest sort in greenhouses. Leaves ovalish, colored above in various patterns, but bluish-green or metallic beneath, the leaf-stalk at least 4 times longer than the blade. Tropical America.

esculentum = *Colocasia esculenta.*

picturatum. Leaves more or less lance-shaped, variously colored above but paler beneath. Leafstalks shorter than in *C. bicolor* and variegated. Peru and Brazil.

**CALAMONDIN ORANGE** = *Citrus mitis.*

**CALAMUS** (kal′a-mus). A specific name derived from the genus *Calamus* or rattan palms, which are little known to gardeners. Originally the word was from the Latin for reed. See ACORUS.

**CALAMUS-ROOT.** See ACORUS CALAMUS.

**CALANDRINIA** (kal-an-drin′i-a). A rather large genus of somewhat fleshy herbs, family Portulacaceae, found in western N.A. and S.A. and of secondary garden interest, although two are grown as annuals. They are commonly called rock purslane in Calif. Leaves alternate* or basal. Flowers somewhat ephemeral, in bracted clusters (racemes*).

---

* Special articles on the subjects indicated by an asterisk (*) will be found at the words so marked.

Petals 3-7, rose-pink or red. Sepals 2 and persistent. Fruit a globe-shaped pod (capsule*) with numerous seeds. (Named for J. L. Calandrini, Geneva botanist.)

The plants are of easy culture if treated as hardy annuals. See ANNUALS.

**caulescens menziesi.** Red Maids. More or less sprawling and 1-2 ft. high. Leaves narrow, not over 2 in. long. Flowers about ½ in. long, rose or crimson. Western U.S. The plant is also called *C. menziesi* and *C. speciosa*. It is not much grown.

**grandiflora.** A perennial, but grown as an annual and the best-known one in cult. More or less erect and 12-18 in. high. Leaves ovalish, 5-7 in. long. Flowers rose-pink or purplish. Chile.

**menziesi** = *Calandrinia caulescens menziesi.*
**speciosa** = *Calandrinia caulescens menziesi.*

**umbellata.** A perennial, but treated as an annual and not over 6 in. high. Leaves all basal and very narrow. Flowers red or crimson-magenta. Peru.

**CALANTHE** (ka-lan'the). A large genus of tropical orchids, one of which is a favorite greenhouse plant in which the large plaited leaves appear after the showy flowers have passed. In the one below there are pseudobulbs* that are grayish and angled, from which spring a few stalked, plaited leaves. The flowers are borne on a long, hairy and bracted* stalk. Flowers very showy, yellowish-white in the one below, the petals and sepals similar, but the lip clawed,* flat and lobed. (*Calanthe* is Greek for beautiful flower.)

For culture see Greenhouse Orchids at ORCHID.

**vestita.** Leaves 18-24 in. long, broadly lance-shaped, the pseudobulbs* 3-5 in. long. Flowering stalk 18-30 in. long, its bracts* conspicuous. Flowers 2-3 in. wide, borne in 6-10-flowered racemes. Petals and sepals cream-white, the lip yellow-orange. Malaya. ¡ Blooms in midwinter in the greenhouse.

**CALATHEA** (kal-a-thee'a). A genus of over 100 species of handsome foliage plants, family Marantaceae, mostly tropical American, but a few in tropical Africa. The cult. species below are favorite greenhouse plants which suggest, in their finely marked and colored foliage, the fancy-leaved *Caladium*, which, however, belong to a different family. They differ from *Caladium* in having thicker leaves in which the stalk joins the base of the blade instead of the middle of it, as in *Caladium*. In those below the leaves are mostly basal and relatively long-stalked, barred, mottled, or striped in various colors, often with a metallic sheen. Flowers (seldom produced in cult. foliage specimens) in cone-like, bracted* clusters among the leaves, not showy. (*Calathea* is Greek for basket, in allusion to the basket-like flower cluster.)

The greenhouse cultural requirements are the same as for *Caladium* (which see). In some parts of zone* 8 and in all of zone* 9 *Calathea* can be grown outdoors in rich, moist soil. They should be cut back to the ground and heavily mulched with well-rotted manure. They are gross feeders, and without it their finest coloring cannot be produced. The plants are sometimes offered as *Maranta*, a close relative.

**bicolor** = *Maranta bicolor.*

**illustris.** A low, showy, compact plant, not over 9 in. high. Leaves ovalish and sharp-pointed, 4-6 in. long, dark olive-green, with a metallic sheen, and with white along the midrib and along the margin on the upper side, but dull red on the lower side. Ecuador.

**insignis.** From 15-30 in. high. Leaves long-stalked, oblongish but tapering both ends, about 1 ft. long, generally yellowish-green, but olive-green along the margins and along some of the main veins above, dull red beneath. Brazil.

**makoyana.** A handsome plant 2-3½ ft. high. Leaves broadly oblong, more or less blunt and generally olive-green, but blotched or ribbed with darker green. The under side is red, but patterned, as is the upper surface. Brazil.

**ornata.** One of the best-known cult. species, often offered as *Calathea sanderiana*. Stout, compact plant 18-36 in. high. Leaves generally elliptic, but heart-shaped at the base, 12-24 in. long, in maturity plain green above, purple-red beneath. In young or juvenile states (often sold) the leaves are handsomely striped between the veins with pink or white. Northern S.A., but offered in many hort. forms and under a variety of names.

**roseo-picta.** Small plant not over 8 in. high. Leaves nearly round, about 6 in. long, dark green, but red-ribbed and red-blotched near the margin above, purplish beneath. Brazil. Sometimes mistaken for and offered as *Maranta bicolor.*

**sanderiana** = Mostly forms of *Calathea ornata.*

**vittata.** Dwarf or rarely up to 3 ft. Leaves lance-elliptic, 8-10 in. long, pointed, light green, but with cross-bands of white on the upper side, green and tinted yellowish-green beneath. Colombia (?).

**zebrina.** The zebra-plant and the commonest species in cult. Not over 3 ft., usually less, and of compact habit. Leaves bluntish, more or less elliptic, 12-20 in. long, about half as wide. The upper side is generally velvety green, but from the midrib the side veins are alternately barred with pale yellow-green and much darker green. The lower leaf surface, purplish-red. Brazil.

**CALATHINA, -us, -um** (kal-a-thy'na). Like a basket.

**CALCARATA, -us, -um** (kal-ka-ray'ta). Having a spur.

**CALCAREA, -us, -um** (kal-care'ee-a). Pertaining to lime.

**CALCEOLARIA** (kal-see-o-lay'ri-a). A very large genus of tropical American herbs or shrubby plants of the figwort family and collectively called slipperworts from the slipper-shaped, showy flowers. *Calceolaria crenatiflora* is a very popular florists' flower, and the other two cult. species are occasionally grown. Leaves opposite* or in whorls.* Flowers in irregular, often 1-sided clusters, generally yellow, but often spotted with orange-brown. Corolla very irregular* and 2-lipped, the upper lip small, the lower one large, inflated and slipper-like. Stamens 2. Fruit a capsule,* splitting at the top. (Name from *calceolus*, Latin for slipper.)

For Culture see below.

**crenatiflora.** The usual slipperwort of the florists. An herb 1-2 ft. high, bushy and softly hairy throughout. Leaves simple,* broadly oval, the lower ones 4-7 in. long, the upper ones smaller and stalkless. Flowers about ¾ in. long, yellow, but spotted orange-brown, the large lower lip wavy or fluted. Chile. There are several hort. forms, variously colored. Sometimes called *C. hybrida*.

**hybrida** = *Calceolaria crenatiflora.*

**integrifolia.** Shrubby or actually woody and 2-5 ft. high, usually sticky. Leaves simple,* oblong-oval, 1-3 in. long, rough, the margins with wavy teeth. Flowers about ½ in. long, yellowish to red-brown, but not spotted. Chile. Rather common in cult. and sometimes used as a summer bedding plant. There are several named forms, some of them hybrids.

**scabiosaefolia.** An annual herb 1-2 ft. high, the leaves deeply cut or even compound, 5-8 in. long, the base of the leafstalks practically surrounding the stem. Flowers numerous, not over ½ in. long, pale yellow. Chile to Ecuador. Less grown than the other two.

### CALCEOLARIA CULTURE

Calceolarias are a very popular florists' flower. Grown from seed, they require careful attention from the time the seed is sown until ready to flower. Seed should be sown in May, and being very small, care must be taken not to bury it in the soil. Potting mixture No. 1 finely sifted may be used. Fill the pot or pan two-thirds full of roughage from the sifted soil in which you sow the seed, and this will give perfect drainage; press it down firmly, fill the pot level with the finely sifted soil, press this gently, particularly around the edge, finishing as level as possible 1 in. below the rim. Should the soil be dry water with a fine spray and defer sowing until the next day.

Open the seed packet carefully and pour contents on a sheet of white paper, then sow evenly over the surface; no covering of soil will be necessary. Place seed pan up near the light and cover with a sheet of glass. When germination takes place give a little air and encourage the seedlings to grow as sturdy as possible, and as they develop remove glass, always allowing a free circulation of air; avoid direct sunlight at all times. When the plants are large enough to handle prick off in other pots, pans or flats, using a pointed stick for this purpose. Pot singly when the plants touch each other, using small pots and after the first shift use potting mixture No. 4 and pot more firmly.

Do not allow the plants to become pot-bound, but as soon as the roots form a network around the pot shift into a larger size; good plants can be grown in 6-in. pots, but if extra-large specimens are desired an 8-in. may be used for the final potting, which should be completed by Nov. A temperature of 45°-50° should be maintained, and good plants may be grown in cold frames, if kept properly shaded from direct sunlight, a northern aspect being preferable, and given plenty of air, but cold draughts should be avoided. During winter keep on the dry side, but never allow the plants to suffer for want of water, and use as little artificial heat as possible; never allow water to touch the flowers, as they spot very easily.

When the flower spikes appear, liquid fertilizer is advisable to feed the mass of fine roots with which the pot should now be filled and to increase the size of the flowers. Neat stakes may be needed to support the flowers, but use as few as possible.

---

* Special articles on the subjects indicated by an asterisk (*) will be found at the words so marked.

*From a pastel by Laura Coombs Hills*

POPPIES, CALENDULAS, AND EUPHORBIA

When the plants are mature and ready to flower, plenty of room should be allowed for them to develop into shapely specimens.

The shrubby varieties are not popular, but the Kelway hybrids make very satisfactory pot plants, and the same treatment applies to all varieties. Give plenty of air, keep clean and water carefully. — A. J. L.

INSECT PESTS. Red spiders can be controlled with derris spray. Leaf tiers attack the plant. See CHRYSANTHEMUM.

DISEASES. Leafblight, presumably caused by a bacterium, is characterized by brown spots on the lower leaves. Infected leaves should be removed. Gray mold causes a rot or blight of the leaves and flowers. The removal of infected leaves, adequate ventilation, and maintenance of the foliage in a dry condition are measures for control.

**CALCIUM.** See LIME.

**CALCIUM ARSENATE.** See Stomach Poisons at INSECTICIDES.

**CALCIUM CASEINATE.** See Contact Sprays at INSECTICIDES.

**CALCIUM CYANIDE.** See FUMIGATION.

**CALCIUM NITRATE.** See Nitrogen at FERTILIZERS.

**CALCIUM OXIDE.** See LIME.

**CALENDAR OF GARDEN WORK.** See GARDEN CALENDAR.

**CALENDULA** (ka-len'dew-la). A genus of 15 species of herbs of the family Compositae, chiefly from the Mediterranean region. Only one is of much garden interest, the pot marigold, but it has been cult. for centuries as a popular annual. Unlike other plants known as marigold (which see), the pot marigold has undivided and not strong-smelling leaves, which are alternate,* simple and faintly toothed. Flower heads large, the rays yellow or orange in the typical forms. (From Latin *calends*, throughout the months, alluding to the long blooming period.)

The pot marigold is one of the most popular of tender annuals (which *see* at ANNUALS for culture). Through breeding and long culture there are many varieties with innumerable shades from whitish-yellow to deep orange. The plant can also be grown for winter bloom in the greenhouse. Sow the seeds in pans in August and pot up the seedlings before frost. Grow in a cool greenhouse and by dis-budding the remaining flower heads may be 4 in. wide. See Pinching at TRAINING PLANTS.

officinalis. Pot marigold. A tender annual 12–20 in. high. Leaves oblongish, 2–3 in. long, more or less stem-clasping. Flower heads solitary, stalked, 1½–2 in. wide, the day-blooming and night-closing rays usually flattish and orange-yellow. Southern Eu. June to frost. Comes in many hort. named forms. Very good for cutting, as the flower heads are lasting.

*CALENDULACEA, -us, -um* (ka-len-dew-lay'see-a). Like a marigold (*Calendula*) in its brilliant color. See AZALEA.

**CALICO-BUSH** = *Kalmia latifolia*.

**CALICO-FLOWER** = *Aristolochia elegans*.

**CALIFORNIA.** As an adjective California is used to designate many plants that grow in that and neighboring states. The ones of garden interest in THE GARDEN DICTIONARY are:

California barberry = *Mahonia pinnata*; California bleeding-heart = *Dicentra formosa*; California bluebell = *Phacelia campanularia* and *P. whitlavia*; California dandelion = *Hypochaeris radicata* (see Cat's-Ear at list of WEEDS); California fan palm = *Washingtonia robusta*; California fuchsia = *Zauschneria californica*; California gold fern = *Pityrogramma triangularis*; California holly (see TOYON); California laurel = *Umbellularia californica*; California lilac = *Ceanothus thyrsiflorus*; California live oak = *Quercus agrifolia* (see OAK); California nutmeg = *Torreya californica*; California pepper tree = *Schinus molle*; California phlox (see LINANTHUS GRANDIFLORUS); California pitcher-plant = *Darlingtonia californica*; California poppy = *Eschscholtzia californica*; California privet = *Ligustrum ovalifolium* (see PRIVET); California redwood = *Sequoia sempervirens*; California rose = *Convolvulus japonicus*; California scrub oak = *Quercus dumosa* (see OAK); California tree poppy = *Romneya coulteri*; California walnut = *Juglans californica* (see WALNUT); California white oak = *Quercus lobata* (see OAK).

**CALIFORNIA.** The state lies wholly in zones* 4, 5, 6, 7 and 8, which instead of running east and west as in most parts of America, run approximately north and south, due to the proximity of high mountains and the warm Japanese current which flows along the California coast.

SOILS. The soils of California are exceedingly variable in all characteristics, and soils of markedly different value may occur in any given tract of land. Textures range from the heaviest clays to the lightest sands. Some soils vary from high quality pervious soils to dense claypans and hardpans. A few soils are acid. Many more soils contain sufficient alkali to injure plants, while the great bulk of soils are intermediate or neutral in their reaction and may be expected to give satisfactory results for many crops when properly managed. Every piece of California farm land requires individual examination to determine the actual character and condition of the soils. General statements cannot be made that will apply to any extensive area.

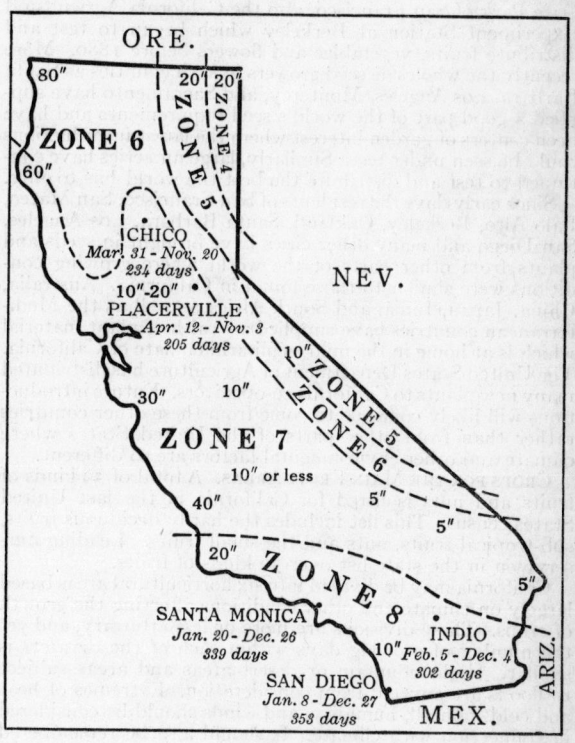

CALIFORNIA

The zones of hardiness crossing California are those shown on the colored map at ZONE, which should be consulted for details. The dates are the average latest killing frost in spring and the first one in the fall. The figures below the dates show the average length of the growing season. The figures scattered over the map show the total annual average rainfall in inches in the different regions of the state.

CHIEF GARDEN CENTERS. The oldest garden centers in California are to be found in fertile valleys along the coast from San Diego County northward. Mission San Diego was founded in 1769, and in time 21 Spanish missions were established, extending as far north as Sonoma County. The mission grounds served as demonstration plots where the first American settlers observed the apple, apricot, fig, grape, peach, pear, olive, almond, walnut and orange, also such vegetables as peas and beans. Horticulture still flourishes near old missions at San Diego, San Gabriel, Los Angeles, Ventura, Santa Barbara, Santa Ynez, Lompoc, San Luis Obispo, Monterey, Mission San José, Santa Clara and Sonoma.

As transportation and irrigation facilities improved, such cities as Pomona, Riverside, Redlands, San Bernardino, Indio, El Centro, Bakersfield, Fresno, Porterville, Merced, Modesto, Stockton, Sacramento, Napa, Santa Rosa, Eureka, Woodland, Marysville, Chico, Red Bluff and Redding became the centers of thriving horticultural communities. Special im-

---

* Special articles on the subjects indicated by an asterisk (*) will be found at the words so marked.

petus was also given to fruit growing by the early distribution of grafted trees from such counties as Alameda, Contra Costa, Sacramento, Napa and San Francisco. At the same time early settlers in many districts were growing and testing seedling trees which in time gave rise to many standard varieties of the present day.

While the first Spanish missionaries brought in flower seeds to plant around the missions, the more important ornamentals have been distributed more recently from such cities as San Francisco, Santa Barbara, Santa Monica, Los Angeles, Pasadena, and San Diego where even the tenderest plants could be carefully tested. Nurserymen living outside of the larger cities have also assisted in distributing ornamentals as well as many excellent fruit varieties. Other centers of distribution include some of the city parks, such as Golden Gate Park of San Francisco, also the California Agricultural Experiment Station at Berkeley which began to test and distribute fruits, vegetables and flowers before 1880. More recently the wholesale seed growers in such counties as Santa Barbara, Los Angeles, Monterey, and Sacramento have supplied a good part of the world's seed requirements and have been centers of garden interest where the latest introductions could be seen under test. Similarly, large nurseries have continued to test and distribute the best the world has to offer.

Since early days the residents of San Francisco, San Mateo, Palo Alto, Berkeley, Oakland, Santa Barbara, Los Angeles, San Diego and many other cities have brought in seeds and plants from other parts of the world where growing conditions were similar to those found in California. Australia, China, Japan, India, and South Africa as well as the Mediterranean countries have supplied a wealth of plant material which is at home in the mild, semi-arid climate of California. The United States Department of Agriculture has distributed many new plants to California co-operators. Future introductions will likely continue to come from these other countries rather than from other parts of the United States where climate and other environmental factors are so different.

CROPS FOR THE MAIN FRUIT AREAS. A total of 39 kinds of fruits and nuts is listed for California in the last United States census. This list includes the hardy deciduous fruits, sub-tropical fruits, nuts and the small fruits. Leading nurserymen in the state list over 50 kinds of fruits.

California may be divided into six horticultural areas based largely on climate and other conditions affecting the growth of crops. These divisions are more or less arbitrary, and yet the number of growing days within each of the districts is similar. High mountain or desert areas and areas subject to floods are omitted from consideration. Extremes of heat and cold, rainfall, humidity, and winds should be considered in connection with climate. It should also be remembered that climate is only one of several factors which control plant growth. The nature of the soil, soil moisture, and topography may be involved within a particular area. A site involving an excessive expenditure might not be suitable, regardless of what crops it would grow. The following lists will give some idea of what crops are important in the six areas here defined. (1) *North Coast*, extending from Marin County on the south, northward to the state line and including Napa and Lake counties; (2) *Sacramento Valley*, bounded on the south by the Solano County, the state line on the north, and the mountains on the east; (3) the *Central Valley*, bordered by the counties of Stanislaus, Tuolumne, Amador, and San Joaquin; (4) *Central Coast*, extending from San Mateo County south to San Luis Obispo County and inland through the counties of Alameda, Santa Clara, and San Benito; (5) *San Joaquin Valley*, extending from Merced County on the north to and including Kern County on the south; (6) *Southern California*, which includes the eight counties below the districts described above.

*Fruits for the Leading Horticultural Districts.* (The more important kinds listed first — county name mentioned for limited area.)
*North Coast.* Apples, cherries, grapes, pears, prunes, walnuts, plums, and small fruits such as blackberries, loganberries, strawberries and gooseberries.
*Sacramento Valley.* Peaches, plums, almonds, cherries, olives, pears, apricots, figs, grapes, citrus fruits (Butte, Glenn, and Sacramento counties), prunes, walnuts, jujubes, persimmons, and strawberries.
*Central Valley.* Cherries, grapes, peaches, almonds, apples, apricots, plums, figs, olives, pears, prunes, walnuts, bush fruits and strawberries.
*Central Coast.* Almonds, apples, apricots, prunes, cherries, pears, walnuts, grapes, plums, figs, peaches, prickly pears (Santa Clara County), bush fruits, and strawberries.
*San Joaquin Valley.* Figs, grapes, olives, peaches, citrus fruits (Tulare and Fresno County districts), apricots, plums, apples (mountain valleys), pears, prunes, persimmons, pomegranates, walnuts, bush fruits and strawberries.
*Southern California.* Avocados, lemons, oranges, pomelos (grapefruit), walnuts, grapes, peaches, cherries (Riverside and San Bernardino counties), olives, almonds, apricots, pears, figs, plums, prunes, pecans, bush fruits, strawberries, and miscellaneous sub-tropical fruits such as prickly pear and passion fruit (San Diego County), guavas, loquats, persimmons, pomegranates, and dates (Coachella and Imperial valleys).

CROPS FOR THE MAIN VEGETABLE AREAS. About 50 kinds of vegetables are listed in the ordinary seed catalogues, but the United States census enumerates only 32 kinds of California vegetables as being important commercially. Most of these vegetables can be grown at some season of the year in practically all California gardens, although extremes of temperature and moisture may limit the choice or season of certain vegetables such as lettuce, globe artichokes, beans, peas, and squashes. Vegetables grown extensively in the different districts are mentioned below.

*Vegetables for Leading Horticultural Districts.*
*North Coast.* Artichokes (Marin County), green beans, sweet corn, green peas, tomatoes, carrots, parsnips, potatoes, squashes, turnips.
*Sacramento Valley.* Asparagus (delta region), onions, cabbage, cucumbers, spinach, tomatoes, green beans, sweet corn, lettuce, lima beans, carrots, green peas, sweet potatoes, beets.
*Central Valley.* Celery (delta region), sweet potatoes, cantaloupes, onions, spinach, tomatoes, watermelons, green beans, cabbage, carrots, parsnips, sweet corn, garlic, lettuce, potatoes, green peas, squashes, beets.
*Central Coast.* Artichokes, lettuce, cabbage, garlic, spinach, carrots, cauliflower, broccoli, Brussels sprouts, sweet corn, cucumbers, green peas, peppers, tomatoes, green beans, rhubarb, lima beans, beets, cantaloupes, celery, potatoes, onions, squashes.
*San Joaquin Valley.* Sweet potatoes, onions, potatoes, watermelons, green beans, lima beans, cantaloupes, cucumbers, garlic, asparagus, carrots, parsnips, cauliflower, sweet corn, beets, lettuce, green peas, peppers, tomatoes, squashes.
*Southern California.* Green beans, lima beans, cantaloupes, carrots, parsnips, cauliflower, broccoli, Brussels sprouts, cabbage, celery, sweet corn, cucumbers, lettuce, peppers, watermelons, onions, green peas, rhubarb, spinach, white potatoes, sweet potatoes, tomatoes, squashes, asparagus, garlic, chayote, eggplant.

ORNAMENTAL FLOWERS, SHRUBS AND TREES. There is probably no place in the world where more kinds of ornamentals can be grown than in California. This may be accounted for by the great extremes of rainfall, snow, temperature, humidity, wind, soil, and elevation within the borders of the state. It is, therefore, not surprising that California has from 800 to 900 species of native woody plants and has more native lilies than any other state. Many exotics find a congenial home some place in the state. Seed catalogues normally mention from 200 to 225 or more genera of flowering plants. Bulb catalogues have listed more than 80 genera. A single nursery catalogue may list 20 genera of conifers, over 100 genera of evergreen trees and shrubs, more than 40 deciduous trees and shrubs and about 20 vines and trailers. It would be a very easy task to list 1000 genera of ornamental plants grown in California and still leave out many natives and the less common exotics.

The evergreen trees and shrubs include both hardy and tender species. Most of the broad-leaved evergreen trees thrive best in districts where there are no killing frosts, as in parts of southern California, in the various coastal areas, and to a limited extent in the warmer parts of the interior valleys. Such conifers as the firs, cedars, junipers, Monterey cypress, pines, redwoods, arborvitae and spruces are generally hardy against cold but may not thrive with high summer temperatures found in the interior. This is also true of some deciduous trees like the maple, beech, birch, and mountain-ash. The flowering peach and cherry may not break their rest period properly with mild winters. A few conifers like *Araucaria* should not be exposed to freezing winter temperatures. Palms and bananas are best suited to frostless districts.

Some evergreen shrubs like *Bouvardia, Hibiscus, Gardenia, Grevillea, Iochroma, Lantana, Lavatera, Michelia, Poinsettia, Sesbania, Streptosolen, Tibouchina,* and *Wigandia* are decidedly sub-tropical in their climatic requirements and should not be planted in frosty situations. Other shrubs

---

* Special articles on the subjects indicated by an asterisk (*) will be found at the words so marked.

like *Abelia, Azalea, Buxus, Cistus, Cotoneaster, Cytisus, Erica, Escallonia, Euonymus, Fremontia, Melaleuca, Nerium, Pyracantha, Rhododendron,* and *Viburnum tinus* may be expected to stand at least a few degrees of frost. A little frost with short duration in the dormant season may do no serious harm, but prolonged freezing temperatures will cause frost injury to all of the more tender evergreen shrubs.

Deciduous shrubs are for the most part hardy in California. *Lagerstroemia* (crape myrtle) does best in the warm interior. The lilac needs cold winters to break the rest period. This is also true of several other cold-climate trees and shrubs.

Evergreen vines and trailers include both hardy and tender species. *Bougainvillaea, Chorizema, Distictis, Hoya, Passiflora, Solandra* and *Thunbergia* are popular tender plants, while the bignonias, jasmines, and English ivy are reasonably hardy. Deciduous vines may be considered hardy in California, except when frost occurs during the early growing season.

Several kinds of plants with bulbs or rootstocks live over winter in California and therefore require mild winter temperatures to thrive. The calla lily, *Dierama,* and *Strelitzia* are good examples. The great majority of bulbs will grow in any locality except where the sun is very hot in summer. Such diseases as basal rot of the narcissus may be serious where high summer temperatures prevail.

True annuals which complete their life cycle in one year will be listed in all seed catalogues and can be grown in all parts of California. Some flowering plants often listed as annuals in other states are biennials or perennials in growth in the milder parts of the state. These include such plants as *Antirrhinum* (snapdragon), *Calendula, Calonyction* (moonflower), *Chrysanthemum coccineum* (pyrethrum), *Cobaea scandens, Diascia, Dolichos lignosus* (Australian pea), *Eschscholtzia* (California poppy), *Maurandia,* pansy, petunia, *Quamoclit lobata, Scabiosa atropurpurea* and *Thunbergia gibsoni.* Most people prefer to treat pansies, snapdragons and petunias as annuals, even though they may live for more than one year in California gardens.

California has a long list of native wild flowers. Some of the very popular annuals include the following genera: *Clarkia, Collinsia, Eschscholtzia, Gilia, Godetia, Layia, Lupinus, Mentzelia, Nemophila* and *Phacelia.* In addition to these annual wild flowers might be mentioned a large number of native bulbs such as *Bloomeria, Brodiaea, Calochortus, Erythronium, Iris* and *Lilium.*

CLIMATE. California possesses all of the climatic variations in other states and has a few more besides. The state has been credited with having the hottest and coldest weather, the wettest and driest, and the sunniest and foggiest. Typical variations in frost conditions are shown below.

| Place | Average date of last killing frost in spring | Latest known killing frost | Average date of earliest killing frost in spring | Earliest known killing frost |
|---|---|---|---|---|
| San Diego | none | Jan. 20 | none | Dec. 26 |
| Santa Monica | Jan. 8 | March 11 | Dec. 27 | Nov. 28 |
| Indio | Feb. 5 | March 16 | Dec. 4 | Nov. 12 |
| Chico | March 31 | April 30 | Nov. 20 | Oct. 21 |
| Placerville | April 12 | June 15 | Nov. 3 | Sept. 15 |

Rainfall in the state varies from none in some years in desert areas to more than 100 inches in exceptional years along the extreme north coast. The summers are typically dry, while during the months of December, January, February, and March about 60 to 75 per cent of the annual precipitation is expected. Humidity also varies widely over the state, being lowest in the hotter inland valleys and highest along the coast. At Fresno the daily range is 39 to 73%, Los Angeles 51 to 77%, Sacramento 50 to 82%, San Francisco 64 to 85%, and Eureka 79 to 91%. The low humidity in warm districts tends to make the heat less oppressive but at the same time greatly affects plant selection. Daily moisture stresses may lead to sunburn on such trees as the birch, beech, mountain-ash, juniper, Monterey cypress, Douglas fir, and several others; consequently these plants may not thrive in the hot, dry, inland valleys away from the moist coastal influences, although these hardy plants will tolerate any reasonable amount of cold. Plants which grow naturally with great moisture variations in the soil are considered drouth-resistant. Such drouth-resistant plants have been imported from Australia and other countries to supplement similar native plants for such extreme conditions.

The number of days above freezing varies from 365 days along the coast at San Diego, Santa Monica, Santa Barbara, and San Francisco to less than 100 growing days in the high mountain areas. Those areas with 200 or more growing days, as listed on weather maps, will include the primary horticultural districts of the state, but within this large area there is a vast difference in growing conditions. The higher mountains and hills and the desert areas may be excluded from consideration. Even a short distance from a weather-recording station weather conditions may differ. For example, there may be no frost in ordinary years at the higher elevations in parts of Santa Barbara, which is credited with 325 growing days. In most years the calla lily and other tender plants may grow throughout the winter in mild districts where air drainage is good, as far north as San Francisco Bay.

The so-called frostless belts are scattered throughout southern California and extend along the coast as far north as Marin County. But the more northern districts are much cooler in spite of being frostless in some places. This accounts for differences in the growth of sub-tropical plants. For example, the mean average annual temperature at Santa Monica and Santa Barbara is 60 degrees, while frost-free areas near San Francisco Bay average 56 degrees. Lack of heat rather than excessively low winter temperatures in such cases accounts for the difference in plant growth. In other cases inland districts average a much higher annual temperature, the average being 61° F. at Chico, 63° at Los Angeles, Fresno, and Riverside, and over 73° at Indio. A date palm may fail to mature fruit with an average of 63 degrees, but 10 more degrees average annual temperature at Indio has overcome the deficiency. In a similar way such plants as the jujube, olive, oleander, crape myrtle and zinnia require considerable heat during the growing season to reach perfection. Such variations in temperatures and temperature requirements help account for the great variety of plants grown over the state.

Fogs, winds, and occasionally snow affect growing conditions. Warm days and cool nights are typical for many parts of the state. Fogs are prevalent at certain seasons of the year in some districts, while only a few miles away fogs may rarely occur. From 80 to 90% of the days are sunny in the drier southern districts, about 75% in the larger interior valleys, 64% at San Francisco and 45% at Eureka. A few localities exposed to the continuous sweep of strong winds are unsuitable for horticultural purposes. Occasional strong winds, such as the "northers" and "Santa Anas," may require the planting of windbreaks to check the wind velocity. The cool "coast breeze" or sea breeze from offshore in southern California is normally pleasant. Snow is largely limited to the higher elevations. The principal horticultural districts of the main valleys do not have snow except at rare intervals. But such cities as Alturas, Colfax, and Nevada City average a foot or more of snow in winter. The snowfall in the higher mountains is an important source of irrigation water for many irrigated areas in California. The type of horticulture developed in each district is generally related to the climatic factors just mentioned.

The address of the Agricultural Experiment Station, which has kindly supplied this information about the state, is the Agricultural Experiment Station of the University of California, Berkeley, California. The Station is always ready to answer gardening questions.

Garden Club activities in Calif. are extensive. There are chapters of the Garden Club of America, the home office of which is 598 Madison Avenue, New York. There are also over 70 chapters of the California Garden Club Federation, information about which can be had by writing to the Garden Editor, Houghton Mifflin Company, Boston, Mass. There

* Special articles on the subjects indicated by an asterisk (\*) will be found at the words so marked.

are also several garden papers published in the state. *See* Garden Magazines. *See also* Horticultural Societies.

**CALIFORNIA SCHOOL OF GARDENING.** *See* Garden Schools.

*CALIFORNICA, -us, -um* (kal-i-for'ni-ca). From California.

**CALIMERIS** (ka-lim'er-is). A genus of 10 Asiatic perennial herbs, family Compositae, closely related to the genus *Aster*. The only cult. species is grown for ornament in the perennial border. Leaves alternate.* Flower heads with yellow disk* flowers and purple or white ray flowers, the heads solitary at the ends of small branchlets. (*Calimeris* is from the Greek for beautiful arrangement.)

The species below, which is not much grown, is an aster-like herb needing the same culture as the perennials of the genus *Aster* (which see). Easily propagated by fall or spring division.

**incisa.** A leafy-stemmed, hairy herb 12-20 in. high, branching at the top. Leaves oblongish, more or less irregularly cut or deeply toothed, smaller towards the top and without teeth. Flower heads solitary, about 1 in. wide, the rays usually purple, shading to white. Siberia. There is also a pink-flowered variety.

**CALLA** (kal'la). A single species of mud or aquatic herbs of the family Araceae, confined to the north temperate zone and very different from the plant known as calla lily (which see). The genus *Calla* has long-stalked, oval or heart-shaped leaves, springing from a slender, bitter rootstock. The spathe* is green on the outside but white within. Spadix* cylindric, crowded with the minute green flowers (see Araceae for structure). Fruit a head of red berries. (Calla is the classical name of the only species.)

The water arum is easily grown along the edges of ponds, in the mud or in shallow water, but not in dry soils. It prefers the acid edges of bogs where the muck has a pH of 4-5 (*see* Acid and Alkali Soils).

**palustris.** Water arum, also called wild calla. Leaf-stalks 4-8 in. long, fleshy. Leaves coarse, thick, without marginal teeth, 2-4½ in. long, not covering the spadix which is about 1 in. long. May. Berries ripe in July.

**CALLA FAMILY** = Araceae.

**CALLA LILY.** A group of tropical herbs of the genus *Zantedeschia* (zan-te-desh'i-a) of the arum family (Araceae), quite different from the genus *Calla* (which see). The calla lilies are popular florists' flowers, widely used for decoration. They have thick rootstocks and basal, long-stalked leaves that are chiefly arrowhead-shaped or more or less oval-heart-shaped. They are chiefly grown for the showy, solitary spathes* which are beautifully colored, and suggest a large corolla. (*See* Araceae for flower structure.) Fruit berry-like. (Named for Francesco Zantedeschia, an Italian botanist.)

For Culture *see* below.

**Z. aethiopica.** The common calla lily of the florists. A stout herb 18-30 in. high. Leaves smooth, usually arrowhead-shaped, nearly 15 in. long and ⅔ as wide. Spathe* 6-9 in. long, brilliantly white, the upper part tapering to a sharp point. S. Af. Fragrant.

**Z. albo-maculata.** Spotted calla lily. Resembling the first but smaller and the leaves white-spotted. Spathe* somewhat cream-white or yellowish, tinged purple in the throat, not over 5 in. long. Cape of Good Hope.

**Z. elliottiana.** Golden or yellow calla lily. Leaves long-stalked, more or less oval-heart-shaped, 7-10 in. long, sporadically white-spotted. Spathe* about 5 in. long, trumpet- or funnel-shaped, golden-yellow, not purple-tinged. S. Af.

**Z. rehmanni.** Red or pink calla lily. Differing from the others in having narrow, tapering leaves which are often white-spotted. Spathe* 3-4 in. long, trumpet-shaped, the limb narrowed to a point, rose-red, rarely white. Natal, S. Af.

### Calla Lily Culture

The chief essentials for growing the common calla lily under glass are plenty of food, light and water. The dormant, fleshy roots or tubers are usually obtainable by midsummer and should be potted up, one tuber to a 6-in. pot, or three tubers to a 9-in. pot, using a rich soil made up of 2 parts old cow manure, 1 part sharp sand, 2 parts loam, 2 parts leaf mold and a 7-in. pot of bone meal to each bushel of the mixture. Keep the pots at first under the benches or in a cool, semi-dark spot and do not over-water. In two or three weeks the roots will be well started and the plants are then given a light open place in the greenhouse with plenty of water. In sections of the country where the sunlight is very strong the glass should be whitewashed or some other semi-shade provided. Apply liquid fertilizer as soon as the pots are filled with roots and increase applications after the flower-stalks appear. Winter temperature under glass should not fall below 55° F. nor rise much above 65° F. After all fear of frost is over the pots may be sunk out of doors and taken in before the weather turns cold. If callas are grown for bloom only, the tubers can be planted directly in the greenhouse bench in very rich soil.

The pink and yellow varieties of calla lily, both of which are readily obtainable, will thrive in a higher temperature than the above and should be kept at about 60° F. during the growing period. These must remain under glass the year round, are more difficult of culture and less robust than the white *Z. aethiopica* and never so prolific, but respond well to careful cultivation.

After the blooming period is over the tubers must be rested and dried before re-potting for next season's bloom. If plants are to be raised from seed this should be sown in light soil in November. They can also be propagated from suckers which are potted up in the same manner as the tubers.

Tubers of calla lilies are grown out of doors in great quantities for commerce in the frostless, foggy coastal region of central California. There they cover large areas of lowland, often escaping and naturalizing themselves in moist places. — L. R.

**Diseases.** Root rot and soft rot are the common diseases of the calla lily. Plants infected with root rot exhibit yellowing along the leaf margins followed by gradual wilting. Infected roots have a water-soaked, rotted appearance. With soft rot, the leafstalks or upper part of the corm are attacked near the soil line, resulting in a malodorous, mushy rot. The control measures for both diseases are similar. When dormant, the corms should be sorted and then soaked for ½ to 1 hour in corrosive sublimate 1-1000 or 2% formaldehyde solution. Pot culture, soil sterilization, and the use of a well-drained, acid soil are also suggested. Manure contaminated with vegetable debris and fertilizers high in nitrate should be avoided.

**CALLIANDRA** (kal'li-an-dra). A large genus of tropical shrubs and trees, family Leguminosae, separated from *Acacia* only by technical characters and of very similar culture. Unlike many acacias, this genus is not usually thorny. Leaves twice-compound,* the ultimate leaflets numerous and small. Flowers small, crowded in dense, globular heads which are covered by the silky, protruding stamens.* Fruit a flattened and sometimes curled legume.* (*Calliandra* is from the Greek for beautiful stamens.)

For culture *see* Acacia.

**californica.** A much-branched, hairy shrub 3-4 ft. high. Leaves with 7-8 divisions each of which is composed of many, small, oblong leaflets. Flower heads about 1½ in. in diameter, the stamens purple. Lower Calif. and not hardy northward.

**portoricensis.** Pich. A West Indian shrub or small tree with very numerous leaflets that fold up at evening. Flower heads white, in clusters of 3 and blooming at night. Pod straight and narrow. Can be grown outdoors only in zone* 9.

**tweedi.** A small, Brazilian shrub for the greenhouse or outdoors in zone* 9. Leaflets very numerous, narrow but blunt and shining. Flower heads on slender stalks from the leaf-axils,* the showy stamens* purple.

**CALLICARPA** (kal'li-kar-pa). A genus of 30 species of shrubs, family Verbenaceae, the three below grown for ornament, although the fruits are more showy than the flowers. Leaves opposite,* toothed, the teeth often bluntish. Flowers small, tubular, 4-lobed at the top, the four stamens protruding. Fruit nearly globe-shaped, berry-like. (*Callicarpa* is Greek for beauty fruit.)

The bushes are often called beauty-berry, but *C. americana* is commonly called French mulberry, although it is neither French nor a mulberry. They can be grown outdoors as indicated below, preferably in full sun and in a rich soil. If they should winter-kill, they will usually come from the base as in *Buddleia*. They can also be grown in the cool greenhouse. Easily propagated by seeds or by cuttings of mature wood.

**americana.** French mulberry. A shrub 4-5 ft. high. Leaves 4-6 in. long, bluntly toothed, green above, rusty beneath. Flowers about ⅛ in. long in a compact, short-stalked cluster (cyme*), bluish. Va. to Tex. and in

---

* Special articles on the subjects indicated by an asterisk (*) will be found at the words so marked.

the W.I. May. The fruit is violet, but a white-fruited form is offered and is conspicuous in winter. Not generally hardy north of zone* 6.

**dichotoma.** A shrub 2-4 ft. high. Leaves 1-3 in. long, bluntly toothed towards the base, without teeth towards the tip. Flowers pink, about ⅛ in. long, the cluster usually few-flowered. Eastern As. Aug. The fruit is violet or lilac. Hardy to zone* 4. Often sold as *C. purpurea.*

**japonica.** Not over 4 ft. high. Leaves 3-5 in. long, finely toothed. Flowers white or pink, about ¼ in. long, the clusters stalked and profuse. Fruit violet. Jap. Aug. A white-fruited variety is also offered. Hardy, with protection, to zone* 5.

**purpurea** = *Callicarpa dichotoma.*

## CALLIOPSIS. See COREOPSIS.

## CALLIRHOË (kal-lir'o-ee).
The poppy mallows comprise a small genus of North American herbs of the family Malvaceae, well liked for their showy flowers. They have alternate* usually cleft or dissected leaves. Flowers mostly in the leaf-axils,* reddish-purple or pinkish, the petals irregularly cut but not notched at the ends. (Named for the goddess.)

Both the cult. species are easy to grow in ordinary garden soil, and are propagated by spring or fall division of their clumps. They are natives of the prairie region of the central U.S. and prefer dry sites.

**digitata.** A perennial not over 18 in. high. Leaves usually deeply cut into narrow segments, but not compound.* Flowers 1-2 in. wide, handsome, the petals more or less wedge-shaped, red-purple or violet. Flowers from May to July.

**involucrata.** Perennial from a deep rootstock, not over 24 in. high and inclined to sprawl. Leaves 3-5-parted, finger-fashion, the segments mostly wedge-shaped. Flowers 1½-2½ in. wide, the calyx leafy, the petals oblongish and pale red-purple. May-Aug.

## CALLISTEMMA = CALLISTEPHUS.

## CALLISTEMON (kal-lis-tee'mon).
A showy genus of Australian shrubs and trees of the family Myrtaceae, often cult. outdoors in Calif. and in northern greenhouses for their handsome flowers. They have many scattered or crowded, small, but stoutish leaves that are narrow or pointed. Flowers in dense spikes, each flower minute, but the spike very showy from the handsome, protruding and numerous stamens,* hence their common name of bottle-brush. Fruit a somewhat woody capsule.* (*Callistemon* is Greek for beautiful stamens.)

The outdoor cult. of bottle-brushes is popular in Calif., less so in Fla., where they can be safely planted in zones* 8 and 9. They are not particular as to soil. Propagated by cuttings of ripened wood or by spring-sown seeds harvested the previous fall. Indoor cult. demands potting mixture* 4 and a cool greenhouse.

**coccineus.** A shrub or rarely a tree 15-25 ft. high. Leaves sharp-pointed, about 1½ in. long Spikes 3-5 in. long, not dense, the stamens* red but tipped with a yellow anther.*

**lanceolatus.** A shrub (rarely a tree in cult.) 10-30 ft. Leaves lance-shaped, about 2½ in. long. Spikes 2-4 in. long, not dense, the bright red stamens about 1 in. long, the spike thus very showy.

**rigidus.** Mostly a shrub 6-10 ft. high, rarely a tree. Leaves very narrow, sharp-pointed and rigid, 2½-5 in. long. Spikes very dense, 2-4 in. long, the stamens red.

**speciosus.** A shrub or tree 10-30 ft. high. Leaves lance-shaped, 3-4 in. long and about ¼ in. wide. Spikes very dense, 3-5 in. long, the showy red stamens* tipped with a yellow anther.* Perhaps the handsomest of the four.

## CALLISTEPHUS (kal-lis'tee-fuss).
A single, extraordinarily variable, Asiatic, annual herb, family Compositae, known throughout the world as the China or garden aster. It is not very closely related to the true genus *Aster*, but to most gardeners aster means only *Callistephus*. (For other plants called aster see MICHAELMAS DAISY and ASTER.)

As a garden plant the only species, **C. chinensis,** a native of China and Jap., is a hairy plant from 9-24 in. high, with broadly ovalish, deeply but irregularly toothed leaves. Flower heads solitary at the ends of the relatively long stalks, the rays showy and flat (but see below) in the simple types, of nearly every color but yellow, predominately blue or violet. (*Callistephus* is Greek for beautiful crown.) The plant is also sold as *Callistemma*.

### CULTURE OF GARDEN OR CHINA ASTER

The plant is a true annual, and for the earliest bloom should always be treated as a tender annual (which see at ANNUALS). For the late or main crop, many prefer to sow the seed directly where the plants are to go. This may be done after danger of frost is well over. (For frost data see the name of your state.)

They need a rich, well-drained soil and open sunlight. No plants so well repay clean cultivation and frequent watering if the season is dry, especially in late summer, and early fall, when most of the varieties are at their best. But the garden aster is so popular and comes in such a multitude of varieties that it is possible to have aster bloom from early July until frost. Scarcely any other annual is so useful for cutting, and as outlined below they come in many forms, with flower heads ranging from about 2 in. wide (smaller in the dwarfs) to 5 in.

TYPES AND VARIETIES. The original or simple type of the garden aster seems to have been one with flat rays in only one or two rows or circles. It is from this that what we call single asters are derived. They are less showy than some of the strains listed below, but preferred by many, especially for mid-season bloom.

Another class, known as incurved, have many more rays than the single asters, and the rays are curved towards the center of the head. Still another group, known as reflexed, have about the same number of rays, but their tips curve outwards. A fourth, and very popular strain, called quilled asters, have the rays all tubular. The latter are divided into two groups: (1) German quilled, in which the quills are very short at the center but longer at the periphery. These are also called Sunshine asters. (2) The other group of quilled has the tubular flowers of approximately even length.

From these four main types have sprung hundreds of named varieties and forms. No attempt can be made here to list them, but the enthusiast should understand that most of them come in early, mid-season, and late-flowering strains, and that they are also to be had in dwarf, branching, and tall-branching strains. And, of course, they come in all colors except yellow. A few of the leading varieties or forms are:

Giant Branching (also called American Branching); 2½ ft., late, the rays loosely incurved.

Beauty; 2-3 ft., late, long-stalked heads with incurved rays.

Crego; about 2 ft., mid-season, the rays twisted and reflexed and twisted.

Royal; early-branching, nearly single type.

King; 2 ft., mid-season, quilled and incurved.

Comet; 2 ft., mid-season, nearly double-flowered.

Astermum; 2 ft., resembling a small chrysanthemum head.

Peony-flowered; 2-3 ft., huge, double flowers, some nearly 4½ in. wide.

While these are widely advertised and grown, the exact names and identities of each are very uncertain because of the multitudinous varieties and named forms that are constantly offered. From them every garden aster need can be easily filled.

INSECT PESTS. Stem borers can be checked by carefully cutting them out and by keeping down weeds of the Compositae family. Blister beetles (see POTATO) can be kept off plants by the use of arsenicals, or by a cover of netting. Root aphids are controlled by planting in soil free from them, working tobacco dust into soil, and keeping down ants. Leafhoppers which carry disease can be kept away by a cover of netting, which also improves plant growth.

DISEASES. Asters are subject to three serious diseases known as rust, wilt and yellows. For rust see Rusts at PLANT DISEASES. When infected with wilt, asters turn yellow, wilt and suddenly die. Black discoloration of the lower stem and roots will be observed. Plants are susceptible at any stage of growth. The use of wilt-resistant asters is the only effective means of control. These strains, highly resistant to the disease, can be obtained in several varieties and types of colors. Yellows is a virus disease characterized by stunted plants, spindly yellow shoots and green, distorted flowers. Many ornamentals, food plants and weeds are susceptible to this disease. An insect known as the six-spotted leafhopper serves to carry the virus from diseased to healthy plants. Control is dependent upon the removal and destruction of all infected plants. The use of insect-proof cloth tents for growing asters is also effective.

## CALLITRIS (kal-ly'tris).
A small group of Australian evergreen trees of the pine family suitable for outdoor culture only in zones* 8 and 9, and usually too large for greenhouse culture. They are commonly called cypress-pines, and have cypress-like leaves that are reduced to scales that cover the angled and jointed branchlets. The male flowers, consisting only of stamens,* are in catkin-like clusters, but the female flowers are borne between the woody scales of a cone. (*Callitris* is from the Greek for beautiful.)

---

* Special articles on the subjects indicated by an asterisk (*) will be found at the words so marked.

The cypress-pines are rapid-growing trees, considerably planted for their fine foliage in Fla. and Calif. They have many erect branches, so that the trees make a compact growth not unlike a cedar. They are tolerant of a variety of soils.

**cupressiformis.** A tall tree, up to 50 ft., its foliage resembling the true cypress. Its cones are scarcely more than ½ in. wide, nearly globular and often borne in clusters. Not so much grown as *C. robusta*.

**rhomboidea** = *Callitris cupressiformis*.

**robusta.** A pyramidal tree 70–100 ft. high, its branches beginning nearly at the ground level, its foliage light green. Cones nearly globular. ¾–1 in. wide.

***CALLOSA*, *-us*, *-um*** (kal-low'sa). Callused (*see* CALLUS).

**CALLUNA.** *See* HEATHER.

**CALLUS.** The protective or healing tissue that forms over a wound, notably over the cut surface of a cutting or slip. Callus also signifies the hard, knob-like protuberance on some tree trunks. It is from the callused surface that the roots of cuttings arise.

**CALOCARPUM** = *Achras*.

**CALOCHORTUS** (kal-o-kor'tus). A charming group of 40 species of chiefly Californian, bulbous herbs of the lily family, grown there for ornament and hardy with protection, as indicated below, in other parts of the country. They bear corms,* erect stems and narrow, grass-like, but somewhat fleshy leaves. Flowers terminal, solitary or in small clusters, usually very showy and almost tulip-like, hence their name of globe tulip (also called Mariposa lily). The flower has 3 inner and showy segments and 3 outer and sepal-like ones. Stamens 6. Fruit a 3-angled capsule.* (*Calochortus* is Greek for beautiful grass.)

The culture of Mariposa lilies is simple in their native region of western U.S., and in Calif. they do well in a light, sandy, porous soil, preferably slightly acid, but not too rich. Manure is not advised. In the East, while they can stand considerable cold, they do not tolerate alternate freezing and thawing, the mucky conditions of the latter being particularly trying. They are thus best grown in pots in potting mixture* 2, to which should be added a little spent tanbark and charcoal. Plant the corms* in late fall and plunge the pots in a cold frame for the winter. After spring growth and blooming, lift the corms and keep them in a dry place until planting time. In Calif. they can stay in the ground continuously, and *C. albus* will often live over winter without lifting as far north as Washington in the East. Two of the most satisfactory in the East are *C. gunnisoni* and *C. macrocarpus*.

**albus.** White Globe lily. About 2 ft. high. Flowers nodding, more or less globe-shaped, white, the petals purplish at the base, about 1½ in. long. Calif.

**catalinae.** From 18–30 in. high. Flowers nearly 2 in. long, white or lilac-purple, the petals maroon-red at the base. Southern Calif. and Catalina Island.

**clavatus.** Nearly 3 ft. high. Flowers 2–3 in. long, deep rich yellow, the petals lined with brown. Calif.

**gunnisoni.** About 18 in. high, the flowers nearly 1¾ in. long, white but purple-streaked. Central U.S.

**luteus.** From 15–30 in. high, the stem sometimes branching. Flowers 1½–2 in. long, the petals yellow or orange but brown-spotted at the base, and brown-striped. Calif. There is a variety with lemon-yellow flowers, and another with pure white. Both are brown-spotted.

**macrocarpus.** Nearly 2 ft. high, the flowers about 2 in. long, purple, but with a green stripe down the center of each segment. Pacific Coast.

**splendens.** From 15–24 in. high. Flowers numerous (sometimes 30), pale lavender or lilac and unspotted, about 2 in. long. Calif. There is also a reddish-lilac variety.

**venustus.** White Mariposa lily. Not much over 1 ft. high, usually less. Flowers about 2 in. long, very pale lilac, the petals with a reddish-brown spot at the base. Calif. An improved sort is *var.* **superbus,** and *var.* **roseus** has a rose-colored spot near the tip of the petals.

**CALOMEL.** *See* Mercury at FUNGICIDES.

**CALONYCTION** (kal-o-nik'tee-on). The moonflowers are perennial vines closely related to the morning-glories, family Convolvulaceae, but bloom at night instead of in sunshine. Of the 3 or 4 species, the two below are of garden interest only in zones* 8 and 9; otherwise, rather rarely cult. greenhouse vines. They have alternate,* broad leaves and fragrant white or purple, large, salver-shaped flowers. Sepals 5. Corolla with a long, but not dilated tube from which the stamens protrude. (*Calonyction* is Greek for night beauty.)

While the plants are perennial they are mostly grown from seed and will bloom the first year. They will not stand much frost.

**aculeatum.** A milky-juiced vine with somewhat prickly stems. Leaves broadly oval, 6–8 in. long, sometimes 3-lobed. Flowers white but sometimes green-banded, the tube 5–6 in. long, the expanded part 5–6 in. wide. Tropical America and in southern Fla. Sometimes offered as *Ipomoea bona-nox*.

**muricatum.** Similar but smaller and with purplish flowers about half the size of *C. aculeatum*. Tropical America.

**CALOPHYLLUM** (kal-lo-fill'um). A genus of 25 species of resinous, aromatic, chiefly Asiatic and tropical trees of the family Guttiferae, the one below somewhat grown in zone* 9 or the most sheltered parts of zone* 8 in Fla. Leaves opposite,* evergreen, without marginal teeth. Flowers polygamous,* white, fragrant, in small clusters (racemes*), not showy. Petals, if present, 1–4, often replaced by the colored sepals. Fruit fleshy. (*Calophyllum* is from the Greek for beautiful leaf, from the handsome foliage.)

A very beautiful shade tree in the tropics, but useful only in warm, frost-free regions.

**antillanum.** Calaba, also called Maria and Santa Maria tree. A tall-branching tree up to 100 ft., casting a very dense shade. Leaves oval-oblong, blunt, 5–6 in. long, bright shiny-green and leathery. Flowers scarcely ½ in. long. Fruit about 1 in. in diameter. W.I. Long known as *Calophyllum calaba*.

**CALOPOGON** (kal-lo-pō'gon). A small genus of mostly native American bog orchids, the only one of garden interest being the grass pink, which is also called the swamp pink. This cult. species, **C. pulchellus,** is a tuberous-rooted herb with a single narrow leaf 8–12 in. long. Flowers in a sparse cluster at the end of a naked stalk 6–15 in. long. Sepals and petals similar, rose or purple-pink, the lip beautifully fringed and mostly yellowish-orange. The plant can only be grown in an acid bog, preferably with a pH of 4–5 (*see* ACID AND ALKALI SOILS). (*Calopogon* is Greek for beautiful beard, from the fringed lip.) June. The plant is also known as *Limodorum tuberosum*.

**CALOTHAMNUS** (kal-lo-tham'nus). Australian shrubs of perhaps 25 species, family Myrtaceae, the one below grown outdoors in Calif., rarely in greenhouses elsewhere. They have scattered, rigid, heath-like leaves. Flowers in clusters which, like *Callistemon*, are showy because of the numerous, protruding, colored stamens,* but the spikes do not resemble a bottle-brush as in *Callistemon*. Fruit a woody capsule.* (*Calothamnus* is from the Greek for beautiful bush.)

The culture is the same as for *Callistemon*.

**quadrifidus.** A shrub 6–8 ft. high. Leaves round in sections, ½–1 in. long, very numerous. Flowers in small, stalkless clusters, the stamens* red, about 1 in. long, and in bundles or clusters.

**CALTHA.** *See* MARSH MARIGOLD.

**CALYCANTHACEAE** (kal-ee-kan-thay'see-ee). The sweet-shrub or strawberry-shrub family contains only two genera of shrubs, both of which, *Meratia* and *Calycanthus*, are cultivated for ornament. They have opposite* leaves without marginal teeth, and solitary flowers on leafy, side branchlets. The fruit consists of many, dry, mostly 1-seeded achenes,* all enclosed in a small, pear-shaped or egg-shaped receptacle.

*Meratia* is Asiatic and has yellow flowers, while *Calycanthus*, with heavily aromatic, brownish-purple flowers, is the sweet-shrub of N.A.

Technical flower characters: Sepals and petals alike, overlapping in many series. Stamens numerous. Ovaries numerous, each 1-celled, and developing into an achene.

**CALYCANTHUS** (kal-ee-kan'thus). Aromatic North American shrubs, so fragrant that they are variously called sweet-scented shrub, sweet-shrub, strawberry-shrub, and sometimes merely shrub. Of the four known species three are cult. for their fragrant flowers, which have the sepals and petals similarly colored and either brown or brownish-purple. (*See* CALYCANTHACEAE for details.) (*Calycanthus* is from the Greek for calyx and flower, in allusion to the colored calyx.)

While they have no special soil preferences, these shrubs do best in rich soils with plenty of moisture but also well-

* Special articles on the subjects indicated by an asterisk (*) will be found at the words so marked.

drained. Easily propagated by layers, suckers, division, or seeds. All of them are occasionally called *Butneria*.

**fertilis.** A smooth shrub 4-8 ft. high. Leaves oval or oblong, 4-6 in. long, bluish-green beneath. Flowers brownish-purple, 1½-2 in. wide. Pa. to Ga. and Ala., mostly in the mountains. Hardy from zone* 4 southward.

**floridus.** Carolina allspice. A densely hairy shrub 4-8 ft. high. Leaves oval or elliptic, 3-5 in. long, pale on the under side. Flowers dark purple-brown, about 2 in. wide. Va. to Fla., mostly near the coast. Hardy from zone* 4 southward.

**occidentalis.** Called spicebush in Calif., and a shrub 7-12 ft. high. Leaves oblongish, 6-8 in. long, green both sides. Flowers light brown, 2-3 in. wide. Calif. Hardy only from zone* 5 southward.

**CALYCINA, -us, -um** (kal-ee-sy'na). Like a calyx.

**CALYCULATA, -us, -um** (ka-lik-kew-lay'ta). Calyculate; *i.e.* bearing a calyx,* or within one, as are some fruits.

**CALYPSO** (ka-lip'so). A single bog orchid of the north temperate zone, of little hort. importance except as grown in the bog garden by enthusiasts in native orchids. The only species, *C. bulbosa* (also called *C. borealis*), is a bulbous herb with a single, stalked, round-oval leaf 1-1½ in. wide. Flower solitary at the end of a naked stalk 3-6 in. high. Sepals and petals alike, variegated purple, pink, and yellow. Lip large and pouch-like, twice-divided below, and with patch of yellow hairs. (Named for the goddess.)

**CALYPTRATA, -us, -um** (ka-lip-tray'ta). Calyptrate (having a calyptra); *i.e.* furnished with a cap-like hood or covering.

**CALYSTEGIOIDES** (kal-is-tee-ji-oy'deez; but *see* OÏDES). Resembling a plant of *Calystegia*, an obsolete name for some morning-glory.

**CALYX.** A collective term for all the sepals* of a flower, whether separate or united. While the calyx is usually green and very different from the corolla in color and texture, some flowers have no corolla. Then the calyx is often colored like a corolla and replaces it, as in the common hepatica and in anemone. Some plants are grown for the edible calyx, as in roselle. *See* FLOWER.

**CAMARA.** South American vernacular for *Lantana camara*.

**CAMAS** = *Camassia quamash*.

**CAMASSIA** (ka-mas'si-a). A small genus of North American bulbous herbs of the lily family, the two below somewhat grown for their showy flowers. They have narrow or grass-like leaves, mostly basal, and a bracted* stalk to the flower cluster (raceme*), which usually over-tops the leaves. Flower not tubular, of six separate segments each with a stamen* inserted at the base. Fruit a 3-valved capsule,* the seeds black. (Latinized form of the Indian *camas* or *quamash*.) The plants are occasionally called *Quamasia*. The bulbs should be planted like tulips in the fall and not disturbed. Put them 3-5 in. apart in a loamy soil in which there is some sand. The plants, particularly the first species, are prized in the open border.

**leichtlini.** Up to 18-24 in. Leaves narrow, but tough, ¾ in. wide and 3 ft. long. Flowers usually purplish-blue, sometimes whitish, the withered remains tightly clasping the pods. British Columbia to Calif.

**quamash.** Camas or bear grass. Usually 2-3 ft. tall, the leaves basal, long and strap-shaped. Flowers blue or white in a long, terminal raceme,* the whole cluster often 1 ft. long, the individual flowers about 1 in. long. British Columbia to Calif. The bulbs of this species were once eaten by the Indians.

**CAMBRICA, -us, -um** (kam'bri-ka). From Cambria; *i.e.* Wales.

**CAMBIUM.** *See* BARK.

**CAMEL GRASS; CAMEL HAY** = *Cympopogon schoenanthus*.

**CAMELLIA** (ka-mee'li-a). Asiatic, evergreen shrubs or small trees of the family Theaceae, one widely grown for its wax-like, very showy and lasting bloom. They have alternate, toothed leaves, and usually solitary, nearly stalkless flowers, red in the typical plant, but of other colors or even double in the many hort. forms (*see* below). Petals mostly five. Sepals 5-7, often falling away. Fruit a woody capsule.* (Named for George J. Camellus, a Jesuit traveler in Asia.) For Culture *see* below.

**japonica.** The common camellia. A shrub or rarely a tree up to 25-30 ft. Leaves ovalish, 3-4 in. long, shining dark green. Flowers 3-5 in. wide, waxy, the petals roundish. China and Jap. The plant is sometimes offered as *Thea japonica*, and is often called merely japonica.

### CAMELLIA CULTURE

Camellias grow outdoors in varied soils and under varied conditions. They are found in red clay, pure sand, rich delta soil, and black mud. Soil that will grow ordinary plants will grow camellias. Unlike azaleas, camellias do not prefer acid soil, though they do grow in the same climates. Camellias prefer good, friable, natural soil to which well-rotted barnyard manure has been added. And although they often are found with their roots growing in water, they do best with good drainage. The plants should be raised 1 to 1½ in. above the surrounding soil.

White camellias prefer partial shade; they will grow in dense shade if it does not come down too low.

Camellias are generally set out in the early fall, but with reasonable care may be set out at any time. It is best to select a plant without buds, and if the plant is in good condition it is not necessary to prune it. Don't undo the burlap, but set the plant down in a hole 4 or 5 times as large as the ball of earth the shrub is packed in. Fill in the soil around the plant 2 or 3 in., then remove the burlap or else loosen it well so that it will not bind the plant. Water well to exclude all air, and do not let it become dry until well established. Peat moss is not required, but in the spring a mulch with strawy, barnyard manure or pine straw helps keep the plant cool. The mulch may extend up to 3 or 4 in.

Fertilizer should be added to the soil in the amount of 1 in. of fertilizer to every ft. depth of soil. Chicken manure is excellent but must be used carefully. Save the manure in an old barrel and cover over with ⅓ wood ashes. Chop up thoroughly. This releases the ammonia and prevents burning.

If the plant is vigorous, two buds side by side on each shoot may be left, otherwise leave only one. Save the growth around the bud, for it is the new growth for next year. The wood should not be picked. For the good of the plant flowers really should be picked off and wired as they are in Europe.

Drought often causes the buds to drop off, especially the second buds — after a late frost has killed the first growth. The second-growth buds are not as satisfactory as the first. When camellia buds won't open, usually it is because the variety is not suitable for out-of-door growing.

Camellias come in single, semi-double, double, peony, and pompon varieties, and the most popular shades are white, pink, violet, and dark red with white streaking. Because of the fact that camellias often have different-looking flowers on one plant the names of camellia varieties are not definitely fixed. Sometimes one variety has as many as five different trade names. The upper range of outdoor culture is zone* 6. Above this they must be grown in the cool greenhouse in potting mixture* 5. — R. F. W. For another plant sometimes called camellia, *see* STEWARTIA.

INSECT PESTS. Camellia is attacked by several kinds of scale insects. Rather dilute miscible-oil sprays are suggested for control. A beetle which occasionally attacks the plant can be killed with pyrethrum dust. The black vine weevil, a snout beetle, can be checked by the use of bran bait.

**CAMMARUM** (kam-mar'um). A pre-Linnaean* name for some monkshood.

**CAMOMILE** = *Anthemis nobilis*. But *Matricaria chamomilla* is also, not very properly, called camomile. It is better called false or German camomile.

**CAMOMILE LAWN.** *See* Lawn Mixtures at LAWN.

**CAMPANULA** (kam-pan'you-la). The bellflowers comprise an important group of garden plants of the family Campanulaceae, over two dozen of its 250 known species being in common cult. for their handsome bloom. While some are perennials for the open border or for the rock

---

* Special articles on the subjects indicated by an asterisk (*) will be found at the words so marked.

garden, a few make handsome pot plants and at least two are annuals.

Root leaves often unlike the stem leaves, sometimes markedly so, the latter alternate.* Flowers typically bell-shaped, often very showy, mostly blue or white, the calyx* persistent on the egg-shaped pod (capsule*) which opens by a terminal pore in some, by valves in others. (*Campanula* is Latin for little bell.)

The perennial species below (including the related genus *Adenophora*) are of simple culture in any ordinary garden soil, unless they are rock garden species, in which case their culture is treated at ROCK GARDEN. Most of the rest can be grown in the open border and divided in the spring or fall. Or seeds may be started in pans with a glass cover in the greenhouse in February and the seedlings put outdoors after danger of frost.

Some of the biennials are best sown as seeds in summer, transplanted to the garden in early fall and given a mulch of dried leaves for the winter. They will bloom the next season. The annuals should be treated as hardy annuals. See ANNUALS.

No garden plants offer such a variety of blue color as the bellflowers. While many of the hort. forms, some of which make fine pot plants for the porch or terrace because of their long-continued bloom, are in other colors than blue, it is the latter which predominates throughout the genus.

One of the best for pot culture is *C. pyramidalis*. Among the rock garden species are *C. bellardi*, *C. garganica*, *C. carpatica*, and *C. excisa*, while several of the others are splendid in planning for the blue garden (which see). Most of them bloom in May or June, but a few bloom for several weeks after this. Most of them appear to tolerate some lime in the soil. See LIMESTONE PLANTS.

**alliariaefolia.** A perennial 1-2 ft. high. Leaves oval to heart-shaped, 1-3 in. long, felty beneath, the basal ones long-stalked. Flowers white, ¾-1¼ in. long, nodding. As. Minor and the Caucasus.
**attica** = *Campanula drabifolia*.
**barbata.** A rock garden perennial 6-9 in. high. Leaves basal, long-lance-shaped, 4-6 in. long and hairy. Flowers pale blue, 1 in. long, nodding in loose racemes.* Alps.
**bellardi.** A European perennial plant 4-6 in. high. Flowers blue, solitary, nodding, about ½ in. long. For culture see ROCK GARDEN. It is often sold as *C. pusilla*.
**carpatica.** Perennial, 9-15 in. high. Leaves ovalish, toothed, about 1 in. long. Flowers solitary, erect, blue, nearly 2 in. wide and very handsome. Eastern Eu. See ROCK GARDEN for culture. There are white and sky-blue varieties.
**drabifolia.** An annual 4-6 in. high, useful for the border or rock garden, the foliage hairy. Flowers blue, sometimes with a white tube, solitary and about ½ in. long. Greece and Asia Minor. See ANNUALS. Sometimes sold as *C. attica*.
**excisa.** An alpine perennial scarcely 5 in. high, with narrow leaves about 1 in. long. Flowers solitary, nodding, about ½ in. long, pale blue. Alps. For culture see ROCK GARDEN.
**garganica.** Somewhat sprawling and about 10 in. long. Leaves ovalish, toothed. Flowers more wheel-shaped than bell-shaped, solitary, blue, about ½ in. wide. Dalmatia. For culture see ROCK GARDEN.
**glomerata.** A hardy, border perennial 12-20 in. high, with large, long-stalked, ovalish leaves 3-5 in. wide. Flowers blue or white, about ¾ in. long, in dense clusters. Eurasia. There is a double-flowered form and a variety with deep violet flowers in large clusters.
**isophylla.** A trailing plant useful for hanging baskets, with small, oval, or heart-shaped leaves 1-1½ in. wide. Flowers usually numerous, but not in clusters, shallowly bell-shaped, pale blue and about 1 in. wide. Italy. Not hardy northward.
**lactiflora.** A stout, border perennial 2-4 ft. high. Leaves oval or oblong, 1-3 in. long. Flowers white or pale blue (in a variety), about 1 in. long, in long, terminal, showy clusters (panicles*). Caucasus.
**latifolia.** A showy Eurasian border perennial, 2-4 ft. high, with broad, toothed, hairy leaves 4-6 in. wide. Flowers purplish-blue, solitary, about 1½ in. long. The *var.* **macrantha** has flowers nearly twice as large.
**loreyi** = *Campanula ramosissima*.
**medium.** Canterbury bells. A much-planted biennial herb from southern Eu., 2-4 ft. high. Leaves hairy, long-oblong, 6-9 in. long, toothed and wavy. Flowers violet-blue, solitary or in loose racemes,* about 1 in. wide. See BIENNIALS. It has some interesting forms. In one the calyx and corolla are similarly colored and produce a hose-in-hose* type. Another, known as cup-and-saucer, has a colored calyx, like a saucer, below the cup-shaped corolla.
**muralis** = *Campanula portenschlagiana*.
**persicifolia.** Peach bells. A perennial herb 2-3 ft. high and attractive for the border. Leaves narrow, finely toothed, 6-8 in. long. Flowers blue or white, about 1½ in. long, in showy terminal clusters (racemes*). Eu. There are several varieties with larger, white, or double flowers, and many handsome named forms.
**portenschlagiana.** A Dalmatian perennial, useful for the rock garden and not over 6-8 in. high. Leaves nearly round or kidney-shaped, long-stalked, about 1 in. wide. Flowers few, bluish-purple, about ¾ in. long. For culture see ROCK GARDEN.
**punctata.** A hairy-stemmed perennial 1-2 ft. high, with broad, coarsely toothed leaves 3-5 in. wide, the lower long-stalked. Flowers white, lilac-spotted inside, about 2 in. long, solitary and nodding. Asia. In the popular form, known as Marian Gehring, the corolla is pure lilac and unspotted.
**pusilla** = *Campanula bellardi*.
**pyramidalis.** Chimney bellflower. A smooth, bushy perennial 3-5 ft. high, useful for the border and for pot plants. Leaves ovalish, about 2 in. long, the lower heart-shaped and long-stalked. Flowers in free-blooming, narrow clusters, pale blue, flat, bell-shaped, about 1 in. long. Southern Eu. There is also a white-flowered variety.
**raddeana.** A perennial herb 8-12 in. high, with ovalish, toothed leaves, the lower long-stalked. Flowers about ¾ in. long, solitary in the leaf-axils,* dark purple. Caucasus.
**ramosissima.** An annual, not over 12 in. high, with oblongish leaves 1-2 in. long. Flowers solitary, erect, somewhat saucer-shaped, about 1½ in. wide, violet, but whitish at the base. Southeastern Eu. There is also a white-flowered variety. See ANNUALS. The plant is sometimes sold as *C. loreyi*.
**rapunculoides.** A Eurasian perennial, 2-3 ft. high, often an escape* in eastern U.S. Leaves oval or longer, 2-4 in. long, toothed, the lower ones heart-shaped and long-stalked. Flowers blue, 1 in. long, in a loose, terminal, 1-sided cluster. Apt to run wild.
**rotundifolia.** Bluebell or harebell, but better known as the blue-bells-of-Scotland. A slender, weak perennial with basal, round leaves and narrow stem leaves, the former often withering. Flowers bright blue, about ¾ in. long, in a lax, few-flowered cluster. Throughout the north temperate zone. There is a white variety and another with apparently double flowers with shredded petals.
**speculum** = *Specularia speculum-veneris*.
**trachelium.** Coventry bells. A rough-hairy, Eurasian, border perennial, 2-3 ft. high. Leaves narrowly oval, 2-3 in. long, coarsely toothed. Flowers nodding, in a loose cluster (raceme*), the corolla bluish-purple and about 1 in. long. There is also a white variety. A vigorous plant and apt to run wild.

**CAMPANULACEAE** (kam-pan-you-lay'see-ee). The bellflower family is of considerable garden interest because it contains *Campanula* and *Platycodon*, both widely cult. for their showy flowers. Of the 40 known genera in the family, about a dozen are cultivated in gardens, all of them herbs with alternate* leaves. Some tropical genera of no garden interest are shrubs or even trees.

Flowers regular,* solitary or in clusters, quite often blue or white, and usually more or less bell-shaped. The fruit is a dry pod (capsule*), the splitting of which provides the only, if somewhat technical, difference between the garden genera. Besides those mentioned above, these comprise the following: *Adenophora*, *Symphyandra* and *Trachelium* which resemble the bellflowers (*Campanula*); *Wahlenbergia* and *Edraianthus*, both herbs of the Old World with blue flowers; *Jasione* and *Phyteuma* which have their flowers in dense heads or spikes; *Michauxia* of Asia Minor, a tall herb with flowers 2 in. long; and *Specularia* which has wheel-shaped flowers. See also OSTROWSKIA.

Technical flower characters: Flowers hermaphrodite,* the calyx tube united to the usually inferior* ovary. Corolla prevailingly bell-shaped, its lobes 5. Stamens 5. Ovary 2-5-celled. Style 1.

**CAMPANULARIA, -us, -um** (kam-pan-you-lay'ri-a). Bellflower-like.

**CAMPANULATA, -us, -um** (kam-pan-you-lay'ta). Campanulate; *i.e.* bell-shaped.

**CAMPANULOIDES** (kam-pan-you-loy'deez; but see OÏDES). Like a bellflower (*Campanula*).

**CAMPECHIANA, -us, -um** (kam-pee-chi-ā'na). From Campeche on the peninsula of Yucatan.

**CAMPERDOWN ELM** = *Ulmus glabra camperdowni*. See ELM.

**CAMPERNELLE JONQUIL** = *Narcissus odorus*.

**CAMPESTRIS, -e** (kam-pes'tris). Growing in a field or in flat country.

**CAMPHORA** (kam-for'a). An old and obsolete generic name for the camphor tree.

**CAMPHOR TREE** = *Cinnamomum camphora*.

**CAMPHORWEED** = *Trichostema lanceolatum*. See BLUE-CURLS.

**CAMPION.** See LYCHNIS; see also SILENE.

**CAMPSIS.** See TRUMPET-CREEPER.

* Special articles on the subjects indicated by an asterisk (*) will be found at the words so marked.

**CAMPTOSORUS** (kamp-toe-sore′rus). A genus of two species of hardy ferns, family Polypodiaceae, the one below North American and grown only in the wild garden or in ferneries; the other Asiatic and scarcely in cult. Fronds evergreen, undivided, rooting at the tip. Spore* cases narrow, line-like, scattered along the veins of the fronds. (*Camptosorus* is Greek for a curved sorus.*)

The walking fern naturally inhabits limestone ledges or limey woods and should only be attempted if one has access to crushed limestone which should be mixed with well-decayed (non-acid) humus. The plants prefer at least partial shade.

**rhizophyllus.** Walking fern or walking leaf. Fronds basal, evergreen, 7–8 in. long, and narrow, heart-shaped at the base, but tapering at the apex to a long, thread-like tip which roots (hence walking fern). Quebec to Ala. and westward.

*CAMTSCHATENSIS, -e* (kam-chat-ten′sis). From Kamchatka, Siberia.

*CAMTSCHATICA, -us, -um* (kam-chat′i-ka). From Kamchatka, Siberia.

**CANADA.** As an adjective Canada is part of the common name of many plants. Originally most of them were supposed to be confined to Canada, but are now known from many other parts of N.A. The hort. species that appear in THE GARDEN DICTIONARY, and their proper equivalents, are:

Canada barberry = *Berberis canadensis;* Canada bluegrass = *Poa compressa;* Canada crookneck squash (see CUCURBITA MOSCHATA); Canada moonseed = *Menispermum canadense;* Canada pest = *Eustoma russellianum;* Canada plum = *Prunus nigra;* Canada potato = *Helianthus tuberosus* (see SUNFLOWER); Canada thistle = *Cirsium arvense* (see list at WEEDS); Canada violet = *Viola canadensis.*

*CANADENSIS, -e* (kan-a-den′sis). From Canada or described as from there (see CANADA).

**CANAFISTULA** = *Cassia fistula.*

**CANAIGRE** = *Rumex hymenosepalus.*

**CANANGA** (ka-nan′ga). Also spelled *Canangium*. A small Malayan genus of aromatic trees, family Annonaceae, one of which, the ylang-ylang, is occasionally grown for ornament in zone* 9. It is hardy nowhere else in U.S. Leaves evergreen, alternate,* without marginal teeth. Flowers hanging, greenish-yellow, very fragrant and the source of perfume in the Pacific Islands. Petals 6. Sepals 3. Fruit a collection of stalked, fleshy, and many-seeded carpels. (*Cananga* is a Latinized version of a native Malayan name.)

**odorata.** Ylang-ylang. A tree 60–80 ft., much less in extreme southern Fla., the branches drooping. Leaves oblongish, 6–8 in. long, bright green above, a little hairy beneath. Flowers about 2 in. long, the petals narrow. Fruit about 1 in. long, greenish. Indo-Malayan region.

*CANARIENSIS, -e* (ka-nay-ri-en′sis). From the Canary Islands.

**CANARY-BIRD FLOWER** = *Tropaeolum peregrinum.* See NASTURTIUM.

**CANARY GRASS** = *Phalaris canariensis.*

**CANAVALIA** (kan-a-vale′ee-a). A genus of herbs or vines of the pea family, widely distributed in the tropics. Of the 25 known species the only two of much garden interest are grown from zone* 7 southward, somewhat for ornament but usually for stock food, or the beans occasionally for human food. They have compound* leaves, usually with 3 leaflets. Flowers rather large, showy, typically pea-like, and with a 2-lipped* calyx. Fruit a large, flat, somewhat woody pod (legume*), the seeds white or reddish-brown. (*Canavalia* is the Latinized version of an aboriginal name.)

The seeds should be planted in rows 3 ft. apart and put 8–15 in. apart in the rows. The plants need a long growing season to mature.

**ensiformis.** Jack bean. An annual, erect herb 2–4 ft. high. Leaflets oblong or elliptic, 3–5 in. long, the tip pointed. Flowers purple, about 1 in. long, in showy, drooping clusters 10–12 in. long. Pod 8–12 in. long, slightly curved, the white seeds nearly ¾ in. long. W.I.

**gladiata.** Sword or saber bean. Resembling *C. ensiformis,* but a twining vine with shorter, much-curved pods and the seeds reddish-brown. Old World tropics.

**CANDEBOBE** = *Lemaireocereus weberi.*

*CANDICANS* (kan′di-kanz). White-hairy or white-woolly.

*CANDIDA, -us, -um* (kan′di-da). White and shining.

*CANDIDISSIMA, -us, -um* (kan-di-dis′see-ma). Very hoary or white-hairy.

**CANDLE LARKSPUR** = *Delphinium elatum.*

**CANDLEMAS BELLS.** See SNOWDROP.

**CANDLE TREE** = *Parmentiera cerifera.*

**CANDLEWICK** = *Verbascum thapsus.*

**CANDLEWOOD.** See FOUQUIERIA.

**CANDYTUFT.** These valuable garden plants, belonging to the genus **Iberis** (eye-beer′is), of the mustard family, comprise perhaps 25 species of annual or perennial herbs, mostly from the Mediterranean region. The cult. species are about equally divided between those which are annuals or treated as such and the perennials. Leaves divided or undivided, alternate.* Flowers in flat-topped or finger-shaped clusters, the 4 petals separate. Sometimes the outer flowers of a cluster are sterile.* Fruit a nearly round or ovalish pod, flattish and often notched at the tip. (Named from *Iberia,* the ancient name for Spain, where some species are native.)

The annual candytufts can be treated as hardy annuals and the seed sown where needed. They bloom in about 6 weeks from sowing and keep on blooming until frost. The plants should be thinned to about 6 in. apart. The perennials are easily propagated by division, and are useful plants for edging or for the rock garden. Both sorts tend to run to seed (*i.e.* stop flowering) if kept too dry, so they are best watered during droughts if bloom is to be maintained, and they are helped by picking.

**I. amara.** Rocket candytuft. One of the annual species, more or less erect and about 12 in. high. Leaves broadest towards the tip, 3–4 in. long. Flowers fragrant, white, the finger-shaped cluster ultimately getting long. Eu. Much grown both in the garden and by florists, for cutting, and known in many forms, some dwarf.

**I. gibraltarica.** A perennial species, not so much grown, and sometimes called the Gibraltar candytuft. Leaves 1–2 in. long. Flowers light purple or lilac, in flat-topped clusters. Spain.

**I. jucunda.** See AETHIONEMA CORIDIFOLIUM.

**I. sempervirens.** Edging or perennial candytuft. The best perennial species, the foliage evergreen in most regions. Leaves narrow, oblongish, ¾–1¼ in. long. Flowers in longish, finger-shaped clusters, white. Eurasia. A fine hort. form is QUEEN OF ITALY.

**I. umbellata.** Globe or annual candytuft. The leading annual garden species, more or less erect, 8–15 in. high. Leaves narrow, thin, 2–3½ in. long. Flowers in close clusters, pink, red, lilac, or violet, not fragrant. Eu. Here belong the colored candytufts that are annuals.

**CANE.** The stem of a bush fruit like the raspberry.

**CANE BLIGHT.** See Diseases at RASPBERRY.

**CANE BORER.** See Insect Pests at BLACKBERRY and RASPBERRY.

**CANE PALM** = *Chrysalidocarpus lutescens.*

**CANE REED** = *Arundinaria macrosperma.*

*CANESCENS* (kan-ness′senz). Canescent; *i.e.* covered with ashy-gray, more or less matted hairs.

*CANINA, -us, -um* (kan-eye′na). Pertaining to a dog, as in *Rosa canina,* the dog rose.

**CANISTEL** = *Lucuma nervosa.*

**CANISTRUM** (ka-niss′trum). A genus of ten species of scurfy-leaved herbs, family Bromeliaceae, the two below sometimes grown in greenhouses for their rather showy flower clusters. Leaves finely spiny on the margins, borne in a dense, basal, water-holding rosette, but narrow or sword-shaped toward the tip. Flower stalks with a showy, colored whorl* of bracts* beneath the cluster. Flowers yellow-orange or greenish-white. (For structure see BROMELIACEAE.) Fruit a many-seeded berry. (*Canistrum* is from Greek for basket, in allusion to the cup-like whorl of bracts.)

These are showy greenhouse plants, needing a temperature of 60°–75° and plenty of water during spring and summer, but much less in winter, when growth is nearly stopped.

---

* Special articles on the subjects indicated by an asterisk (*) will be found at the words so marked.

Plant in pots or wooden cribs in a soil made up of ⅓ potting mixture* 3 and ⅔ chopped fern roots or other coarse fiber.

**amazonicum.** Leaves many, the blades 12–18 in. long, about 2½ in. wide, brownish but not spotted. Flowering stalk short, terminated by a dense head of narrow bracts, the flowers greenish-white. Sometimes sold as *Nidularium amazonicum*.

**aurantiacum.** Leaves 10–12 in. long, green but spotted or banded with darker green. Flowering stalk crowned by a head of green and red bracts, the flowers orange-yellow and about 1½ in. long.

**CANKER.** *See* Bacteria at PLANT DISEASES.

**CANKER LETTUCE** = *Pyrola americana*.

**CANKER-ROOT** = *Coptis trifolia*.

**CANKERWORMS.** *See* Insect Pests at APPLE, ELM, and MAPLE.

**CANNA** (kan'na). A very useful and handsome genus of tropical herbs, constituting the family **Cannaceae** (kan-nay'see-ee) which was once included in the Scitamineae. They have mostly tuberous rootstocks and stately, broad, often colored leaves, without marginal teeth, but prominently veined, the leafstalk sheathing. In the garden canna (there are 40 others, mostly non-hort. species) the flowers are very showy, sometimes gorgeous, in a terminal cluster and very irregular.* Sepals 3 and greenish. Petals 3, resembling the sepals. Nearly all the color comes from the much-enlarged, colored, and petal-like, sterile stamens (staminodes). Fruit a 3-angled, roughish pod (capsule*), surrounded by the withered calyx. (*Canna* is an old name for some reed-like plant.)

The lack of species names below is frankly an evasion of the problem of the true parentage and specific identity of the hundreds of named forms of these most popular bedding plants. They have been so much hybridized that it is doubtful if any modern canna can now be assigned definitely to any of its wild ancestors, and even the parentage of many of them is wholly unknown.

### CANNA CULTURE AND VARIETIES

Over most sections of the country cannas must be grown as summer bedding plants, as they are tropical plants that will not tolerate frost. In parts of Calif. and the Far South, however, they may be left in the ground and treated like any other perennial herb.

Until a few years ago cannas were mostly grown for their handsome foliage, particularly the old-fashioned Indian Shot (*Canna indica*), with green leaves and often growing 5–7 ft. high. Today we chiefly grow them for the gorgeous flowers that have been developed by the plant breeders, mostly French. These plants are shorter than the Indian Shot, often have bronze-colored leaves and a wide range of color in their very showy flower clusters.

Their culture is easy if one will prepare a bed 18–24 in. deep. They like a good rich soil and if the proposed canna bed is poor or stony dig it out and fill in with any good garden loam to which has been added about ¼ its bulk in well-rotted manure. In making such a bed it is well to leave the center 4–6 in. higher than the edges.

In order to lengthen the canna season it is best to use potted plants instead of planting the rootstocks. The former are cheap and in the markets at the proper time in your locality which is long after all danger of frost is over. The idea is not merely to dodge a sporadic late frost but to put the plants in soil warm enough to be congenial for a tropical plant — in other words, they need summer heat.

Space the rootstocks or potted plants 18 in. apart each way, and, of course, see that tall varieties are at the center of the bed. The foliage and flower color of cannas are so strikingly different from most other garden plants that a canna bed needs careful placing with relation to the rest of your garden. By itself, with a background of shrubbery and trees, or in the center of a formal courtyard, a canna bed may be very stunning. But a scattered clump peppering up the front lawn or a patch of canna in a perennial border looks, and is, incongruous.

Summer care is very simple. If the bed is kept thoroughly watered over drought periods, and free of weeds, the canna will do well over most of the country, provided there is plenty of heat. When autumn frosts threaten they should be dug up and stored just as one stores dahlias. Their culture is very similar to that of dahlias, except that they require more heat. In the early spring, if you intend raising your own plants, divide the rootstock so that there will be at least one, but not more than two, buds to a piece of rootstock. Pot up the pieces in early April and put in a warm greenhouse. If you have only a hotbed, it is better to wait until May to start the cannas. And if you have neither, the rootstocks may be planted directly in the bed, but not before the soil temperature at 6 in. deep is at least 65°; in other words, tomato-planting time or later. The latter procedure, of course, delays matters so much that most home gardeners prefer to buy pot plants ready for outdoor planting.

VARIETIES. If you merely want a handsome, green-foliaged bedding plant, the old-fashioned Indian Shot is one of the best. It has, also, red flowers, but these are nothing like so striking as in the varieties listed below. The plant is about 4 ft. high, has leaves about 18 in. long, and, in the warmer sections of the country, it frequently escapes.*

The modern cannas are all of hybrid origin and the list of named forms is confusing. Often the different dealers will offer the same plant under different names. It is, therefore, of the greatest importance to buy plants or rootstocks from a reputable dealer, whose named forms come true. From hundreds that are offered the following promise the best chances of success, and provide as wide a choice of color and stature as most growers desire. Novelties, at much increased prices, are constantly being offered. Your curiosity and pocketbook are the only limits to trying such.

The relatively standard varieties are:

The Ambassador; 5 ft.; cherry-red flowers; bronze leaves; free bloomer.
City of Portland; 3½ to 4 ft.; clear rose-pink; green foliage; free bloomer.
King Humbert; O. 5 ft.; large, orange-scarlet flowers; bronzy foliage; popular.
Mrs. Alfred F. Conard; 4 ft.; salmon-pink; large-size blooms; bright green foliage.
Mrs. Pierre S. duPont; 4 ft.; watermelon-pink; large flowers; massive trusses.
Nokomis; 4½ ft.; deep crimson flowers; bronze-green foliage; perhaps best in its color.
The President; 4 ft.; crimson flowers; vigorous; free-flowering; green foliage.
Wintzer's Colossal; O. 6 ft.; immense trusses of bright scarlet flowers.
Wyoming; O. 6 ft.; immense spikes of orange flowers; bronze-purple foliage.
Yellow King Humbert; O. 4½ ft.; yellow flowers dotted orange; sport from King Humbert.

Those marked O are the so-called orchid-flowered cannas, in which the petals become re-curved. They are very handsome plants. Other canna varieties, and by some preferred to the ten above, are:

Hungaria; 3½ ft.; pink; bluish-green foliage.
Eureka; 4½ ft.; white; green foliage.
Copper Giant; 4 ft.; red and old rose; green foliage.

For the number of plants needed for a round bed *see* GARDEN TABLES IV.

INSECT PESTS. Two species of leaf-rolling caterpillars attack canna, especially in the South. Hand-picking or sprays or dusts of lead arsenate will give control.

DISEASES. Cannas are susceptible to a bacterial disease called bud rot, which results in a black decay of the young tissues. The injury may extend into the stem and flower buds. Sterilization of dormant rootstocks for 2 hours in a 1–1000 corrosive sublimate solution, selection of rootstocks from healthy plants and the avoidance of overwatering are measures for control.

**CANNABINA, -us, -um** (kan-na-by'na). Hemp-like.

**CANNABINACEAE** (kan-na-bi-nay'see-ee). There are only two genera in the hemp family — *Cannabis* and the hop (*Humulus*) — both of which are widely cultivated for fiber, narcotics, for the making of beer, or sometimes for ornament. *See* VINES.

They have alternate* leaves and small, greenish and inconspicuous flowers. The fruit is a dry achene* in *Cannabis* (the hemp), but a catkin-like or cone-like cluster in the hop. In both genera the male and female flowers are on different plants. From the closely related fig family (Moraceae), with which they are sometimes included, the hemp family is easily distinguished by not having a milky juice.

**CANNABIS** (kan'na-bis). A single species of annual herb,

---

* Special articles on the subjects indicated by an asterisk (*) will be found at the words so marked.

family Cannabinaceae, a native of temperate As., and of little garden, but great economic, importance because it yields both hemp and hashish. The only species, **C. sativa**, the hemp, is a strong-smelling herb, with a rough, almost woody stem from which the hemp (not Manila hemp) fiber is derived. It has compound* leaves, the 3–7 long, slender leaflets arranged finger-fashion. Flowers green, small, inconspicuous, the male and female on different plants. Widely grown for hemp, then only as an agricultural crop in warm regions. It has little or no garden value and the cult. of female plants is forbidden in many countries because from their dried flowers is derived the narcotic hashish, usually here called marihuana. (*Cannabis* is the classical name of the hemp.)

**CANNACEAE** (kan-nay′see-ee). The canna family. See CANNA.

**CANOE BIRCH** = *Betula papyrifera*. See BIRCH.

**CAÑON LIVE OAK** = *Quercus chrysolepis*. See OAK.

*CANTABRICA*, *-us*, *-um* (kan-tab′ri-ka). From Cantabria, an old name for northern Spain.

**CANTALOUPE.** See MELON.

*CANTERBURYANA*, *-us*, *-um* (kan-ter-berry-ā′na). From Canterbury, New Zealand; rarely from Canterbury, England.

**CANTERBURY BELLS** = *Campanula medium*.

*CANTONIENSIS*, *-e* (kan-ton-i-en′sis). From Canton, China.

**CANTUA** (kan′chew-a). A small genus of South American shrubs or small trees, family Polemoniaceae, the one below grown outdoors in Calif. and elsewhere in zones* 8 and 9, rarely in the greenhouse. Leaves opposite,* without marginal teeth (in ours). Flowers in hanging, terminal clusters, the corolla with a long tube and 5 short, spreading lobes. Fruit a 3-valved capsule,* with many seeds. (Name is a Latinized form of a Peruvian vernacular.)

In Calif., where it is sometimes called magic tree, from its quick response to rainfall after a drought, the species below is a handsome, showy garden shrub. For indoor cult. it needs a cool greenhouse and potting mixture* 4. Easily propagated by cuttings.

buxifolia. Shrub 5–8 ft. high. Leaves about 1 in. long, rather crowded. Flowers 2–3 in. long, numerous, the tube pinkish-red but yellow-striped. Andes.

**CAPE AND CAPE BULBS.** Early hort. literature is full of references to "The Cape" and to Cape bulbs — all referable to bulbous or tuberous plants from the Cape of Good Hope, South Africa. As exploration uncovered the garden treasures of this extraordinary country, the list of Cape Bulbs grew. Among them are *Babiana*, *Ixia*, *Freesia*, *Sparaxis*, *Lachenalia*, *Tritonia*, *Gladiolus*, and many others.

**CAPE COD WEEDER.** See Section 1, TOOLS AND IMPLEMENTS.

**CAPE COWSLIP.** See LACHENALIA.

**CAPE FORGET-ME-NOT** = *Anchusa capensis*.

**CAPE FUCHSIA** = *Phygelius capensis*.

**CAPE GOOSEBERRY** = *Physalis peruviana*.

**CAPE HONEYSUCKLE** = *Tecomaria capensis*.

**CAPE JASMINE** = *Gardenia jasminoides*.

**CAPE MARIGOLD.** See DIMORPHOTHECA.

*CAPENSIS*, *-e* (ka-pen′sis). From the Cape (which see).

**CAPE PONDWEED** = *Aponogeton distachyus*.

**CAPE PRIMROSE.** See STREPTOCARPUS.

**CAPER** = *Capparis spinosa*.

**CAPER FAMILY** = Capparidaceae.

**CAPE STOCK.** See HELIOPHILA.

*CAPILLARIS*, *-e* (ka-pil-lay′ris). Capillary; *i.e.* hair-like.

*CAPILLATA*, *-us*, *-um* (ka-pil-lay′ta). With capillaries or fine hairs.

*CAPILLUS-VENERIS* (ka-pil-lus-ven′er-is). Venus's hair. See ADIANTUM.

*CAPITATA*, *-us*, *-um* (ka-pi-tay′ta). Capitate; *i.e.* having flowers or fruits in a dense head (capitulum).

*CAPITULATA*, *-us*, *-um* (ka-pit-you-lay′ta). Having small heads, as in some flower clusters.

*CAPPADOCICA*, *-us*, *-um* (kap-pa-dō′si-ka). From Cappadocia in eastern Asia Minor.

**CAPPARIDACEAE** (kap-par-i-day′see-ee). The caper family consists of over 30 genera and 450 species of mostly tropical or warm region shrubs or herbs, only two of which, *Capparis* and *Cleome*, are of any garden interest. They have usually alternate* leaves, without marginal teeth and a watery sap. Flowers more or less irregular, the four petals often with a claw.*

The fruit is a berry in *Capparis* (the flower buds of which furnish the familiar caper), while it is a dry pod (capsule*), often stalked, in *Cleome*, which is cult. for its handsome flowers.

Technical flower characters: In the garden genera, sepals and petals 4. Stamens numerous in *Capparis*; 6 in *Cleome*, and often long and showy. Ovary 1-celled, with many ovules.

**CAPPARIS** (kap′par-ris). A large genus of shrubs and trees, family Capparidaceae, widely distributed but mostly tropical, only one of which, the caper, is of any garden interest, and this chiefly in southern Europe where it is cult. for capers. (For flower and fruit characters see CAPPARIDACEAE.) The cult. species, **C. spinosa**, the source of capers, is a spiny, somewhat straggling shrub 3–6 ft. high, with simple,* roundish or oval leaves 1–2 in. long. Flowers (the unopened buds are the capers) white, solitary, borne in the leaf-axils* on stout stalks, the petals about 1 in. long. Mediterranean region. Not hardy above zone* 6, but it is sometimes grown northward as a tender annual. (*Capparis* is the classical name of the caper.)

*CAPREA* (kap′ree-a). A specific name pertaining to a goat, applied to a willow (*Salix caprea*); of uncertain application there.

*CAPREOLATA*, *-us*, *-um* (kap-ree-o-lay′ta). Twining or winding.

*CAPRICORNIS*, *-e* (kap-ri-cor′nis). Like a goat's horn; sometimes, also, applied to plants from or below the Tropic of Capricorn.

**CAPRIFIG; CAPRIFICATION.** See FIG.

**CAPRIFOLIACEAE** (kap-ri-foe-li-ā′see-ee). The honeysuckle family, often called the elder or twinflower family, is a large aggregation of herbs, shrubs, woody vines or trees, most of its 350 species growing within the north temperate zone. All of its 12 genera are of garden interest, some, as *Weigela*, *Lonicera* (the honeysuckles), *Symphoricarpos*, and *Viburnum* being among the most popular shrubs and vines in cult. Leaves opposite*; compound* in the elder (*Sambucus*), but simple in all the other genera. Flowers regular,* and more or less tubular in *Abelia*, *Kolkwitzia*, *Leycesteria*, *Linnaea* (the twinflower), *Triosteum*, *Weigela*, and *Viburnum*, but more or less irregular* in *Diervilla* and *Dipelta*, and noticeably so in the honeysuckles.

All the genera are shrubs, trees, or woody vines, except *Linnaea* and *Triosteum*, both of which are herbaceous. The fruit is a berry or fleshy in some genera (especially the elder), but dry in others.

Technical flower characters: Ovary inferior.* Calyx 4-5-toothed or lobed, its tube joined to the ovary. Corolla 4-5-lobed, the stamens alternating with its lobes. Ovary 1-5-celled.

*CAPRIFOLIUM* (kap-ri-fō′lee-um). Pre-Linnaean* name for a honeysuckle.

**CAPRIOLA** = CYNODON.

---

* Special articles on the subjects indicated by an asterisk (*) will be found at the words so marked.

**CAPSELLA BURSA-PASTORIS** = Shepherd's purse. *See* list at WEEDS.

***CAPSICASTRUM*** (kap-si-kas'trum). Like a pepper of the genus *Capsicum*.

**CAPSICUM** (kap'si-kum). A confused but hort. important genus of tropical, woody plants of the potato family, yielding red (but not black) pepper, tabasco, and cayenne pepper, as well as the milder peppers commonly grown for seasoning and as vegetables. Most of the species (or there may be only one with many varieties, as here treated) are from tropical America, but in the North they are grown as tender annuals. Leaves alternate,* simple,* without marginal teeth. Flowers white or greenish-white, usually stalked and solitary or in 2-3-flowered clusters, generally wheel-shaped and 5-lobed. Fruit typically a pod-like berry, with a thickish rind, but much diversified as to shape and color, and easily divided, as to taste, between the mild and very pungent sorts. (*Capsicum* is Latin for a box or chest, apparently in reference to the fruit.)

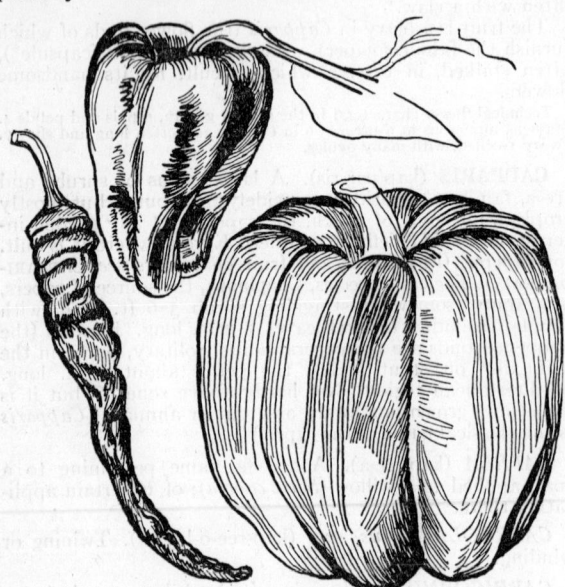

Three common types of garden peppers

For Culture *see* below.

As here, and usually, treated, all the garden peppers are derived from a single species, *C. frutescens* (also called by others *C. annum* and *C. baccatum*) and probably native in tropical America, although it may have been wild also in the Old World tropics. Its progeny, in scores of forms, are now found all over the tropical world. It is a woody shrub 6-8 ft. tall, with variously shaped leaves, flowers about ½ in. in diameter, and the fruits represented by the bird pepper (also called chili and spur pepper), which is red but scarcely 1 in. long. This plant is rare or altogether lacking among the numerous modern cult. varieties, being chiefly tropical. The varieties derived from it, while of tropical origin, are cult. here as annuals. The chief cult. peppers are:

**frutescens cerasiforme.** Cherry pepper. Leaves 2-3 in. long. Fruit roundish or heart-shaped, about ¾ in. in diameter, red, yellow, or purplish and very pungent, erect or re-curved.

**frutescens conoides.** Cone pepper. Like the cherry pepper, but the fruit cone-shaped or cylindrical, 1-2 in. long, and erect.

**frutescens fasciculatum.** Red cluster pepper. Leaves narrow and clustered. Fruit in small bunches, narrow, slender, 3 in. long and pencil-thick, red, very pungent and erect.

**frutescens grossum.** Bell or sweet pepper. Leaves larger than in the others, oblongish, 4-5 in. long. Flowers nearly 1 in. in diameter. Fruit large, generally bell-shaped or oblongish, more or less puffy, the sides ridged or furrowed, variously colored, but of mild flavor.

**frutescens longum.** Long pepper. Fruit hanging, 4-10 in. long and tapering to a point, but the base often 2 in. wide, red or yellow. Here belongs the variety yielding cayenne pepper, and other very pungent sorts.

PEPPER CULTURE

From zone* 6 northward peppers are treated as summer annuals, very much like tomatoes. They need more heat than tomatoes and a longer growing season, so that above zone* 4 their culture, while safe enough for household needs, is too risky for commercial production.

If you do not wish to grow your own plants, they can always be purchased at the proper time, which is outdoor tomato-planting time in your locality (*see* TOMATO). If you raise your own plants, the procedure is the same as for tomato.

Whichever method you follow, it is essential to know exactly what sort of peppers you wish to raise and pick them from the following named varieties:

Hot peppers for flavoring, sauces, etc.
  Small Chili.
  Long Red. Long, pointed, very pungent.
  Long Red Cayenne. Long, pointed, and fiery hot.
  Red Squash. Best for northern sections.
  Tabasco. For Calif.

Mild-flavored peppers for stuffing, pickling, or even slicing and eating like tomatoes.
  Chinese Giant.
  Bull Nose.
  Harris Early Giant.
  Ruby King. *See* next paragraph.

There is still a third category of garden peppers, the pimiento. They are raised chiefly in Calif. or south of zone* 6, and the most satisfactory varieties are Perfection (for Calif.) and Panama. If the variety Ruby King is grown with either of these pimiento peppers, it will hybridize with them so that seed is no longer pure for successive crops. They should be kept apart.

As one approaches the tropics, peppers, instead of being summer annuals, tend to revert to the perennial or woody ancestral form. In some parts of Fla. they are so grown.

The diseases of the pepper, while caused by different organisms, are very like those on the tomato and so are the controls. *See* Diseases at TOMATO.

INSECT PESTS. The black flea beetles of potato occasionally attack pepper. In parts of Tex., Mex., and Calif. a black snout beetle, or weevil, ⅛ in. long, punctures buds and fruits and lays eggs in them. The larvae feed within, causing the buds to die and the fruits to fall. Rotation, destruction of infested fruits and crop remnants, and keeping down nightshade, on which the pest breeds, are advised.

***CAPSULARIS***, -e (kap-soo-lay'ris). Capsular; *i.e.* bearing a capsule.*

**CAPSULE.** A dry fruit of more than one, often several, compartments or cells. It always splits open by one or more seams or valves, or rarely by terminal or basal pores. In splitting, it usually does so lengthwise. In a few capsules, it splits around the circumference, hence when split it is in two cup-like sections. Typical capsules are found in iris, all the poppy family, many of the lily family, the trumpet-creeper, the rhododendron, and hundreds of other plants.

***CARACALLA.*** An obsolete name for plants now included in *Phaseolus*.

***CARACASANA***, -us, -um (ka-ra-ka-say'na). From Caracas, Venezuela.

**CARAGANA** (ka-ra-gay'na). Decorative shrubs and trees of the pea family comprising nearly 50 species which are mostly native in central Asia. The one below is a spiny shrub or small tree with compound* leaves, the numerous leaflets arranged feather-fashion, without an odd one at the end. Flowers typically pea-like, yellow in the one below. Legumes* narrow and nearly round. (*Caragana* is a Latinized form of the Mongolian *caragan*, a native name for one of the species.)

The pea tree or pea shrub is a hardy plant easily grown in any garden soil, preferably in full sunlight. As hedge plants for windbreaks and snow traps few plants are superior in regions of intense cold. Propagated by seeds (first soaked in hot water) or by cuttings.

**arborescens.** Pea tree or pea shrub. Not over 20 ft., usually less, the spines often lacking. Leaves 1-3 in. long, composed of 4-6 pairs of tiny leaflets about ⅓ in. long each. Flowers nearly ¾ in. long, yellow, borne singly, but several close together, hence showy when in bloom. Pod

---

* Special articles on the subjects indicated by an asterisk (*) will be found at the words so marked.

(legume*) 1½–2 in. long, stalked. Siberia. Hardy from zone* 1 southward. There are dwarf forms suitable for hedges, and valuable in regions where privet is not hardy.

**CARAMBOLA.** Vernacular name in the Orient for *Averrhoa carambola*.

**CARANDAS.** Native name for the karanda (*Carissa carandas*).

**CARAWAY.** This fragrant condiment is derived from one of about 20 species of the genus **Carum** (kair'um), of the carrot family, all of which are herbs of the temperate zone. Leaves mostly basal, much compounded into tiny segments. Flowers minute, white, in small umbels* which are grouped in larger umbels. Fruit the familiar and aromatic caraway seed. (*Carum* is probably from Caria, Asia Minor, where some species are wild.) See CARICA.
For culture and uses see HERB GARDENING.

C. carvi. The common caraway. An annual or biennial 1–2 ft. high. Leaves so finely divided that the ultimate segments are thread-like. Flowers scarcely 1/10 in. wide, the umbel often with some sterile flowers. Fruit strongly ribbed. Eurasia. Summer.

**CARBONATE OF POTASH.** See Potash at FERTILIZERS.

**CARBON DIOXIDE.** See PLANT FOODS.

**CARBON DISULPHIDE.** See FUMIGATION.

**CARDAMINE** (kar-dam'i-nee). The bitter cresses comprise a large genus of annual or perennial herbs of the mustard family, only one of which is of secondary garden interest. They have leaves cut feather-fashion, sometimes lyre-shaped, the principal segments in 3–7 pairs. Flowers usually in lax clusters, white or purplish, the 4 petals rather large and conspicuous for such a slender plant. Fruit a long and slender, somewhat flattened silique.* (*Cardamine* is a classical name for some cress.)

The only cult. species is easily grown in sites that approximate its wild home, which is always in moist or even wet, preferably shaded, places. It will stand open sunlight if kept moist.

pratensis. Lady's-smock; also called cuckoo-flower and milkmaids. An erect, but not stiff, perennial 8–15 in. high. Leaves with the segments scarcely ½ in. long. Flowers in a terminal cluster, rarely double, about ½ in. wide. Cooler parts of the north temperate zone. June.

**CARDAMON.** The true cardamon is derived from the plant below, which is the only species of the genus **Elettaria** (el-et-tay'ri-a), of the family Zingiberaceae. It is a stout herb, closely related to *Amomum*, and native in tropical As. The only species, **Elettaria cardamomum**, rarely cult. outdoors in zone* 9, or in a warm greenhouse, is about 5–9 ft. high, with large leaves that are hairy on the under side. Flowering stalk arising from the thick rootstock, and naked, the flowers in loose spikes or racemes, very irregular.* Fruit a capsule,* the seeds being cardamons, except that inferior cardamons are often substituted from the related plant *Amomum cardamon* (which see also for the culture of *Elettaria*, which is a Latinized version of a native Malabar name).

**CARDIACA** (kar-dy'a-ka). Pre-Linnaean* name for the motherwort (*Leonurus*).

**CARDINAL-FLOWER** = *Lobelia cardinalis*.

**CARDINAL CLIMBER** = *Quamoclit sloteri*.

**CARDINALIS, -e** (kar-din-nay'lis). Cardinal-red.

**CARDIOSPERMUM** (kar-dee-o-sper'mum). A genus of perhaps 15 species of chiefly tropical, herbaceous vines of the family Sapindaceae, one cultivated, mostly in warm regions, for ornament. See VINES. Leaves alternate,* twice-compound,* the ultimate leaflets coarsely toothed. Flowers small but numerous, unisexual,* in clusters that bear tendrils. Sepals and petals each 4, the latter slightly irregular* or unequal. Fruit a papery, inflated and veiny capsule,* 3-valved, and with black seeds with a white, heart-shaped spot, hence the common name of heart-seed for these vines. (*Cardiospermum* is from the Greek for heart and seed.)

The balloon-vine is a quick-growing plant useful for trellises and low buildings. While native in the tropics, it can be treated as an annual in the North.

halicacabum. Balloon-vine. Not usually over 10–12 ft. high. Leaflets ovalish, pointed. Flowers white, the clusters scarcely longer than the leaves. Pod 3-angled, about 1 in. long, the seeds pea-size. Tropical regions, and naturalized in the southeastern U.S.

**CARDON** = *Lemaireocereus weberi*.

**CARDOON** (*Cynara cardunculus*). This thistle-like, spiny-leaved perennial herb is a close relative of the true artichoke, but its edible portion is the thickened (and blanched) leafstalk, which is boiled and used like spinach, or sometimes eaten fresh. Because the leafstalks are somewhat bitter, the cardoon is decidedly one of our secondary vegetables.

Its culture is much like the artichoke (which see) and it has somewhat the same climatic requirements. Being a tender vegetable, it will not ordinarily stand the rigors of a northern winter. Plants must be raised in the hotbed, very much as tomato plants are, and planted outdoors after settled warm weather arrives. Put them about 3 ft. apart each way. In the South or in Calif. the seed may be sown directly outdoors.

In the autumn, draw the leaves together and wrap the stalks in heavy paper, or slip a cardboard cylinder over them. Or any other method of blanching may be used except heaping soil which may rot them. If you want cardoon for winter use, dig up the plants and replant in a frost-free, dark cellar or pit, where blanching will naturally occur.

The plant needs a rich soil and plenty of moisture, but not mucky sites or poorly drained ones.

**CARDUACEAE.** See COMPOSITAE.

**CARDUNCULUS** (kar-dun'kew-lus). A small thistle. See CYNARA.

**CARDUUS** (kard'you-us). An immense genus of thistles, mostly weedy, and belonging to the family Compositae. They are sometimes called plumeless thistles, and the one below is occasionally cult. in the border for ornament. (For other thistles see CNICUS and CIRSIUM.) The only cult. species of much garden interest is **Carduus kerneri**, a biennial or perennial herb 2–3 ft. high, with a winged and spiny stem. It has deeply lobed, spiny-toothed leaves and solitary heads of rose-purple flowers, the head surrounded by a series of spiny-toothed bracts.* There are no ray flowers in the head. The plant is probably native in the Balkans and is easily grown in ordinary garden soil. (*Carduus* is the classical name for a thistle.)

**CARE OF HOUSE PLANTS.** See HOUSE PLANTS.

**CARE OF TOOLS.** See Section 8, TOOLS AND IMPLEMENTS.

**CAREX** (cay'rex). The sedges are an enormous genus of grass-like plants of the family Cyperaceae, but of over 900 species scarcely a handful are of any garden interest, and the two below are only seldom cult. for their greenish spikes. From grasses, for which many take them, they are distinguished by having solid (not hollow), 3-angled stems. The two below are tufted perennials with grass-like leaves. The flowers are minute, green, and crowded in flattish, spike-like clusters (for flower structure see CYPERACEAE), which are grouped at the top of the slender, grass-like stalks. (*Carex* is the classical name for the sedges.)

The first species is native in N.A., and can be grown in the open border. The second, a native of Japan, is sometimes grown as a pot plant in cool greenhouses or for edging greenhouse walks. It is not certainly hardy outdoors north of zone* 5. Propagation, which is simple, is by division of the grass-like clumps.

fraseri. A tufted perennial with flat, grass-like, evergreen leaves, about 18 in. high, and nearly 1½ in. wide. Stalk of the flower cluster about as long. In woods, Va. to N. Car.

morrowi. Leaves flat, grass-like, about 12 in. long, evergreen, and sometimes white-striped in cult. forms. Flower spikes flattish, clustered at the ends of stalks about as long as the leaves. Jap.

**CARIBAEA, -us, -um** (kar-i-bee'a). From some island of the Caribbean Sea.

---

* Special articles on the subjects indicated by an asterisk (*) will be found at the words so marked.

**CARICA** (ka'rick-a). The papaya is an important tropical American fruit tree and the only cult. genus of the family **Caricaceae** (ka-ri-kay'see-ee). It is sometimes called papaw (or pawpaw), but this name also applies to another tree (see ASIMINA). *Carica* has a straight, palm-like trunk, with a milky juice, topped by a cluster of immense leaves that are deeply lobed, finger-fashion, and very long-stalked. Male and female flowers usually on different trees, only the female producing fruit. Male flowers in slender, long-stalked, hanging clusters (racemes*), yellow, funnel-shaped, and about 1 in. long. Female flowers nearly stalkless, yellow, the 5 petals distinct. Fruit suggesting a yellow or orange melon, in some varieties oblong, in others globe-shaped, the flesh aromatic and delicious. Seeds black. (*Carica* is Latin for Caria, from which the specific name of the edible fig was derived. Caria is a division of southwestern Asia Minor, but neither the fig nor papaya is native there.)
For Culture see below.

**papaya.** The papaya. Not usually over 25 ft. high, bearing trees often being half this. Branches usually none. Leaves nearly 2 ft. across, round, deeply 7-lobed, the lobes again lobed, distinctly pale beneath, the leafstalks hollow and 2 ft. long. Fruit 4–20 in. long. Tropical America, but now naturalized throughout the tropical world, and widely planted there in improved varieties.

### PAPAYA CULTURE

The tree is safely grown only in zone* 9 and most favored locations in zone* 8. One good frost will kill it, and too much near-frost will prevent its fruiting. It will grow in a variety of soils, but prefers rich ones and a good amount of moisture.

There are thousands of naturalized and relatively worthless papaya trees, the pollen of which infects good cult. varieties in Fla. Care must therefore be taken to root out these strays before planting to good varieties. Plant the trees on 8-foot intervals, using 8 female trees to 1 male tree to ensure pollination by a desirable variety.

The fruit, borne singly on short stems just below the terminal crown of leaves, ripens from mid-winter to June in Fla. It is delicious, somewhat mucilaginous, and quickly perishes when ripe. Its milky juice and black seeds are rich in papain, and the juice is often used in tropical countries to soften tough meat.

The trees will respond to a dressing of good commercial fertilizers, but many trees in the tropics that get none are prolific bearers. Each tree should bear from 12–30 fruits a year, and do this for perhaps four years, but not much longer. Some growers only allow the trees to fruit one or two years. Propagation is by seeds, and the tree will bear about 12 months after being transferred from the seed bed to the open ground.

**CARICATURE PLANT** = *Graptophyllum pictum*.

**CARINATA, -us, -um** (ka-ri-nay'ta). Carinate; *i.e.* keeled.

**CARINTHIACA, -us, -um** (ka-rin-thy'a-ka). From Carinthia, Austria.

**CARISSA** (ka-ris'sa). A genus of 30 species of spiny shrubs of the family Apocynaceae, chiefly South African, two somewhat grown for ornament or hedges, more rarely for their fruit. Leaves opposite,* without marginal teeth. Flowers in stalked clusters (cymes*), the corolla salver-shaped, white or pink. Stamens 5, inserted in the corolla tube. Fruit a fleshy berry. (*Carissa* is of unknown origin.)

Both species can be grown outdoors throughout zones* 8 and 9, where they are used for hedge plants and are boy-proof from the plentiful spines. Fruits of the second species, the Natal plum, have a reddish pulp suggestive of the raspberry, but are little known outside of Fla., Calif., and the tropics.

**carandas.** Karanda. Shrub or small tree, the spines not forked. Leaves oblong-oval, 2–3 in. long. Flowers white or pink, the tube about ¾ in. long. Berry reddish-black, about ¾ in. long, more or less elliptic. India.
**grandiflora.** Natal plum or amatungula. Very bushy shrub up to 15 ft. high, the spines forked. Leaves ovalish, 1–2½ in. long. Flowers white, nearly 2 in. wide. Berry egg-shaped, red, 1–2 in. long. South Africa.

**CARLUDOVICA** (kar-loo-dō'vi-ka). A genus of perhaps 35 species of palm-like, but apparently stemless, tropical American plants, and the only cult. genus of the family **Cyclanthaceae** (sy-clan-thay'see-ee). They have palm-like leaves which are long-stalked and fan-like. Flowers resembling those of the palms (see PALMACEAE) and differing from them only in technical characters. Fruit a syncarp.* (Named for Carlos IV and Ludovia, king and queen of Spain.)

The species below is not infrequent in greenhouse palm collections, but is of far more hort. interest from the fact that, in Ecuador, it is the plant from which Panama hats are made. The plant is not native at Panama. For greenhouse cult. see PALM.

**palmata.** Jipi-japa; the Panama-hat plant. An essentially stemless, palm-like plant, the leafstalks channeled, arising from the ground, and 4–6 ft. long. Leaves fan-like, the blade split into four main divisions, each of which is again split, and the segments drooping at the tip. Peru and Ecuador.

**CARMICHAELIA** (kar-my-kay'li-a). Perhaps 20 species of New Zealand shrubs of the pea family, the green, flattened or cylindrical branches often functioning as leaves while the latter fall. Leaves compound* (in ours), the few leaflets arranged feather-fashion, soon falling and leaving the plants with bare green twigs. Flowers pea-like, small, in lateral clusters (racemes*). Pod (legume*) small, leathery, nearly round. (Named for Dugald Carmichael, Scotch botanist.)

The two below are somewhat grown for their odd habit and pretty flowers in Calif. They appear to be without much soil preference, but will not stand much frost.

**grandiflora.** A shrub 4–6 ft. high, very twiggy. Leaflets 3–5, dropping after the plant blooms. Flowers purplish, but with violet veins, about ¼ in. long, 8–12 in a cluster. Pod about ½ in. long.
**odorata.** Larger than *C. grandiflora*, the branches hanging. Leaves not over ¾ in. long, with 3–7 leaflets or 3–7-parted. Flowers about ⅙ in. long, 10–20 in a cluster, white or lilac. Pod about ¼ in. long.

**CARMINE CRABAPPLE** = *Malus atrosanguinea*.

**CARNATION** (*Dianthus caryophyllus*). To most people the word carnation means a flower which the florists display in their windows from October to May. But this is only part of the truth. *Dianthus caryophyllus* is just as much a pink as many other species of *Dianthus*, and in some parts of the country can be treated as a hardy perennial. While this is a common method in England, few American gardeners treat the plant in this way. And it can be grown so only in regions of comparatively mild winters. They are grown outdoors successfully in Calif., where the preferred varieties for this purpose are:

| San Remo. Yellow | Beauty of Nice. Rose-pink |
| Villa Franca. White | Mentone. Scarlet |
| Cannes. Pink | Monaco. Crimson |

While these bedding or border carnations will bloom from seed in 6 or 8 months, they are often treated as perennials, raised from seed or cuttings and planted out in the early spring. None is really hardy in regions of severe winters. It is among these plants that the fragrant or aromatic clove pink of England is found. They are not so showy as the ordinary carnation of the florists, but have a charm, and particularly a fragrance, that the commercially produced flower ordinarily lacks. Here also belongs the picotee carnation in which each petal is edged with some color that differs from the general color of the petal. Usually the edging is pink.

GREENHOUSE CARNATIONS. Anyone with a greenhouse that can be kept during the winter between 50° (night) and 60° during the day can grow the ordinary florist's carnation if the following directions are adhered to. The year-round procedure is this:

(1) In November and December cuttings are made from plants growing in the greenhouse bench (see below). They should be taken from prolific-flowering stems, cut about half way between the swollen joints and rooted in potting mixture* 1, which should take from 4–5 weeks. When thoroughly rooted, the plants should be potted up in potting mixture* 2 and grown along until the next step of the process.

(2) After all danger of frost is past, the potted cuttings should be planted outdoors in rows 16–24 in. apart and the plants set 8–10 in. apart in the row. The plants are then

---
* Special articles on the subjects indicated by an asterisk (*) will be found at the words so marked.

grown all summer very much like any other perennial, that is, the weeds must be kept down and the rows cultivated. Few or no blooms will appear, and if any do, the buds should be pinched off. Some time before frosts are expected the plants should be carefully dug, ready for the final step in their life cycle. Many professional growers omit the outdoor program and plant the cuttings in the greenhouse bench.

(3) The dug plants should be planted out directly in the greenhouse bench. The bench should have been filled several days or a week or two before with rich garden loam or with potting mixture* 3. Never allow the old soil of the previous year to be used the following one. Space the plants 6 in. apart in the rows and have the rows about 12 in. apart. If you want all the flowers you can get from each plant, they can be grown without further attention except plentiful watering and an occasional dose of liquid manure.

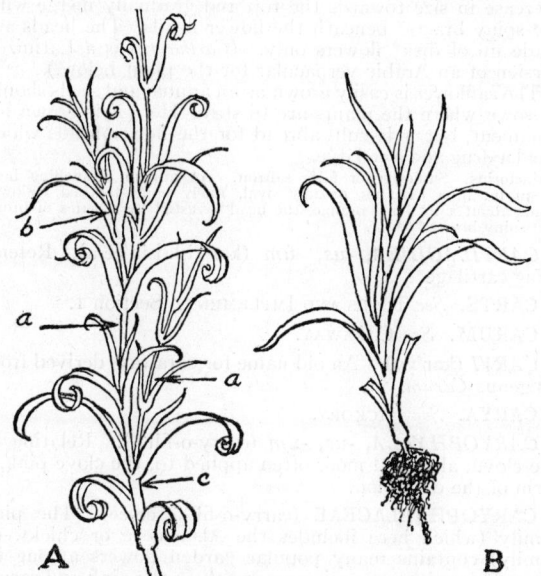

Carnation Cuttings
A. A shoot of carnation showing (*a*) the proper sort of cutting; (*b*) cutting made too high; and (*c*) cutting made too low.
B. A sturdy, well-rooted carnation cutting.

Keep the temperature between 50° and 60° — more heat will be most detrimental. If it is necessary to ventilate, however, see that no cold, winter air currents blow on the plants. Assuming that you want the finest blooms rather than quantity, it is necessary to follow the commercial procedure. The plants should be grown to a single stem which is accomplished by pinching off all side shoots. If this is done, the plants should begin blooming about 7 weeks after planting in the bench, and, with successive pickings, keep on blooming until the following May or June. If you have given them the right conditions, each plant should produce 12–18 good flowers. But the number of these and the length of the stem (an important commercial feature) will depend upon the care in growing. The greenhouse glass must be shaded from early in January until the plants are ready to go outdoors. The plants are, also, extraordinarily sensitive to one of the constituents of illuminating gas — ethylene. If there is the least danger of escaping gas in the greenhouse, test the air with potted tomato plants (see TOMATO). Carnation flowers protrude their usually hidden and useless stamens if ethylene is present in the greenhouse in the proportion of 1 part of ethylene to 2 million parts of air — a concentration indetectable chemically. But the flowers are ruined by it.

VARIETIES. The varieties of florists' carnations are legion and change rapidly with the public taste. Not many of the named forms last very long, but the following will provide a standard assortment for any grower:

| VARIETY | AVERAGE NUMBER OF BLOOMS PER SEASON |
|---|---|
| Bettie Lou. Cerise pink. | 13 |
| Enchantress Supreme. Light pink. | 15 |
| Hilda. Pink (with red splashes). | 14 |
| Maine Sunshine. Yellow. | 16 |
| Morning Glow. Pink. | 16 |
| Mrs. C. W. Ward. Dark Pink. | 13 |
| White Eldora. White. | 18 |
| Harvester. White. | 17 |
| Spectrum. Red. | 17 |
| Sophelia. Dark Pink. | 18 |

INSECT PESTS. Red spider mites (*see* ORANGE) are the most important pests; they are controlled with sprays of dilute lime-sulphur followed by water spray a couple of days later. Thrips can be checked by nicotine dust. The cabbage looper, the greenhouse leaf tier (same as celery leaf tier), the corn ear worm, and other leaf feeders can be controlled with arsenical spray applied before blossoming.

DISEASES. The important diseases of carnations are rust, leafspot, branch rot, stem rot and bud rot. For rust, *see* Rusts at PLANT DISEASES. Leafspot is caused by various fungi and in one case a bacterium. For control, use healthy cuttings, spray with Bordeaux mixture, keep the foliage dry, and ventilate to reduce humidity. Branch rot is characterized by white spots on the foliage and a dry rot of the branches. With stem rot, the plant is attacked just below the soil level. A wet decay of the stem and wilting are the chief symptoms. The control for branch and stem rot is the same. Use healthy cuttings, spray with Bordeaux mixture plus a spreader, practice rotation in the field, use light, well-drained soils and avoid wounds as much as possible. Bud rot is a disease which results in decay of the unopened blossoms. Mites are responsible for spread of the disease to healthy buds. The disease can be checked by avoiding high humidities, by spraying or fumigating for mite control, and by picking and destroying infected buds.

*CARNEA, -us, -um* (kar'nee-a). Flesh-colored.

**CARNEGIEA** (kar-nay'gee-a). A single, gigantic cactus, the largest in the world, and localized in extreme southeastern Calif., southern Ariz., and the neighboring Mexican state of Sonora. It may be grown in that region and attempted in greenhouses, but it does not take kindly to cultivation. (Named for Andrew Carnegie, in recognition of his aid in establishing the Desert Laboratory at Tucson.)

gigantea. The giant cactus, locally called suwarro, sahuaro, and saguaro. A huge, post-like, erect plant body 20–60 ft. high and often 2 ft. thick, with many ribs and stout, strong spines. Old specimens have 3–4, candelabra-like, huge branches that curve upward. Flowers white, produced only at the tips of the stem or branches, 4 in. long, and half as wide. Fruit edible, egg-shaped and as big, red, widely used for sweetmeats. A full-grown plant may weigh 6 tons and be 250 years old.

**CARNEGIE INSTITUTION.** *See* DESERT LABORATORY.

*CARNEROSANA, -us, -um* (kar-ner-o-san'a). From the Carnerosa Pass, Mexico.

**CARNIVOROUS PLANTS.** *See* INSECTIVOROUS PLANTS.

*CARNOSA, -us, -um* (kar-nō'sa). Fleshy.

**CAROB.** This evergreen tree from the eastern Mediterranean region is the only species of the genus **Ceratonia** (see-ra-tone'ee-a) of the pea family, the pods of which are familiar as St. John's-bread (the "wild locusts" of John the Baptist). The only species, **C. siliqua**, is a tree 20–40 ft. high. Leaves compound,* with 2–3 pairs of broad, leathery leaflets that are 2–4 in. long. Flowers red, unisexual,* not pealike, without petals. Pods 4–12 in. long, slightly flattened, not splitting, the seeds surrounded by a sweetish, nutritious pulp. Both male and female trees must be planted to ensure fruit. Probably hardy only from zone* 7, certainly from zone* 8, southward. (*Ceratonia* is from the Greek for horn in allusion to the fruit.)

*CAROLINA, -us, -um* (ka-ro-ly'na). From North or South Carolina.

**CAROLINA ALLSPICE** = *Calycanthus floridus*.

**CAROLINA HEMLOCK** = *Tsuga caroliniana*. *See* HEMLOCK.

**CAROLINA JASMINE** = *Gelsemium sempervirens*.

**CAROLINA MOONSEED** = *Cocculus carolinus*.

**CAROLINA POPLAR** = *Populus canadensis*.

**CAROLINA VANILLA** = *Trilisa odoratissima*.

**CAROLINA WATER SHIELD** = *Cabomba caroliniana*.

---

* Special articles on the subjects indicated by an asterisk (*) will be found at the words so marked.

**CAROLINENSIS, -e** (ka-ro-ly-nen'sis). From North or South Carolina.

**CAROLINIANA, -us, -um** (ka-ro-lin-i-ā'na). From North or South Carolina.

**CAROSELLA** = *Foeniculum vulgare piperitum*. See FENNEL.

*CAROTA* (ka-rō'ta). Latin for carrot.

**CARPANTHEA.** See MESEMBRYANTHEMUM.

*CARPATICA, -us, -um* (kar-pat'ti-ka). From the region of the Carpathian Mountains.

**CARPEL.** See PISTIL.

**CARPENTERIA** (kar-pen-teer'i-a). A single shrub of the family Saxifragaceae, native in the southern part of the Sierra Nevada Mountains in Calif. and grown in that region for its handsome white flowers. It differs from *Philadelphus* (mock-oranges) only in technical characters, and in being evergreen. (Named for Wm. M. Carpenter, American physician.)

This shrub, while perhaps able to stand the cold of northeastern U.S., will not stand wet winters. In its own region it is easily propagated by layers or by seeds, and prefers a light, well-drained soil.

*californica.* Shrub 6–8 ft. high. Leaves opposite,* evergreen, oblongish, 3–4 in. long. Flowers fragrant, showy, white, 2–3 in. wide, and borne singly or in clusters of 2 or 3. June.

**CARPET BEDDING.** See BEDDING.

**CARPET GRASS.** See AXONOPUS COMPRESSUS; see also LIPPIA.

**CARPETWEED FAMILY** = Aizoaceae.

*CARPINIFOLIA, -us, -um* (kar-py-ni-fō'li-a). With leaves like the hornbeam (*Carpinus*).

**CARPINUS.** See HORNBEAM.

**CARPOBROTUS.** See MESEMBRYANTHEMUM.

**CARRION-FLOWER.** See STAPELIA; see also SMILAX HERBACEA.

**CARROT.** An important root vegetable derived from an annual or perhaps biennial herb belonging to the genus *Daucus* (daw'kus) of the family Umbelliferae. Of the sixty species of *Daucus* only one is involved in the cultivated carrot, **Daucus carota**, the common, weedy Queen Anne's-lace of our roadsides. This is a Eurasian herb, often called the wild carrot, and is without the large root development of the ordinary garden carrot which is known as **Daucus carota sativa**. The genus *Daucus* has rather bristly, much-divided or compound* leaves, the ultimate segments fern-like. Flowers very small, in a flat-topped cluster (really a compound umbel*), below which is a whorl* of leaf-like bracts.* (*Daucus* is the classical Greek name for this plant.)

Carrot culture is very simple. The ordinary procedure is to sow the seeds rather thickly (germination is slow and poor) in drills about ½–¾ in. deep, the rows being far enough apart for working between them (12–24 in., depending on hand or machine cultivation). Thin the plants to 3–4 in. apart in the row. If the soil is rich and friable there will be no trouble about root development, but remember that young, tender, quick-growing carrots are better flavored than old or slow-growing ones, which are fit only for stock feed. If the soil is not rich, apply a good commercial fertilizer at the rate of 6 pounds per 100 ft. of row. It takes about 1 oz. of seed for a row this length. See also MUCKLAND GARDENING.

In order to hasten matters, some growers start the plants in the cold frame and transplant later to the garden. This is a troublesome procedure, scarcely warranted unless especially early crops are needed. A succession of ordinary carrots may be sown every two weeks up to the middle of July. Later sowings may not mature before frost.

INSECT PESTS. Insects are usually not very injurious to carrots. A root maggot, a beetle resembling a June bug, a grayish aphid, and the grub-like larva of a snout beetle attack the roots occasionally. Their control has not been well worked out. The celery caterpillar (see CELERY) sometimes eats the leaves. The vegetable weevil is serious in the South (see TURNIP.)

DISEASES. Leafblight and leafspot may cause serious damage on bunching carrots by disfiguring the foliage. Three to five applications of copper lime dust at weekly intervals protect the plants satisfactorily. There are several serious root rots, which may cause damage in storage. Low temperatures and layers of carrots alternated with layers of straw to absorb excess moisture hinder decay.

**CARROT FAMILY.** A huge family of plants, mostly herbs, and containing such diverse garden favorites as carrot, celery, parsley, parsnip, dill, caraway, and anise, as well as the popular blue lace-flower from Australia. For the many kinds and their chief characteristics see UMBELLIFERAE.

*CARTHAGINENSIS, -e* (kar-ta-jin-en'sis). From Cartagena, Spain or Colombia.

**CARTHAMUS** (kar'tha-mus). A genus of 20 species of Old World herbs of the family Compositae, only one of much garden interest. They have spiny, alternate* leaves which decrease in size towards the top and gradually merge with the spiny bracts* beneath the flower heads. The heads are made up of disk* flowers only. (*Carthamus* is a Latinized version of an Arabic vernacular for the plant below.)

The safflower is easily grown as an annual and seeds should be sown where the plants are to stay. Here it is grown for ornament, but it is cult. abroad for the flower heads which yield a drug and a red dye.

*tinctorius.* Safflower or false saffron. An annual, branching herb 12–30 in. high. Leaves broadly oval, finely spiny-toothed. Flower heads about 1 in. long, orange, the head invested by a series of broad and spiny bracts.* Asia.

*CARTILAGINEA, -us, -um* (kar-ti-laj-in'ee-a). Resembling cartilage.

**CARTS.** See TOOLS AND IMPLEMENTS, Section 1.

**CARUM.** See CARAWAY.

*CARVI* (kar'vy). An old name for caraway, derived from its genus *Carum*.

**CARYA.** See HICKORY.

*CARYOPHYLLA, -us, -um* (carry-o-fill'a). Relating to the clove; also, and more often applied to, the clove pink, a form of the carnation.

**CARYOPHYLLACEAE** (carry-o-fill-ā'see-ee). The pink family (which here includes the Alsinaceae or chickweed family) contains many popular garden flowers among its 70 genera and 1200 species, among them the pink and carnation. All are widely distributed herbs having opposite* leaves without marginal teeth, and swollen joints. All, except the carnation, are of outdoor cult., many of them extremely popular annuals or perennial garden plants.

The flowers are regular,* with 4 or 5 petals (fringed in some), often very showy, but wanting in *Herniaria*, and small in *Arenaria, Cerastium, Gypsophila, Sagina, Stellaria,* and *Tunica*. But in several of these, notably *Gypsophila* (baby's-breath), the flowers are so numerous as to make the plants showy. Much larger and handsomer flowers are found in *Dianthus* (the pink and carnation), *Lychnis, Saponaria, Silene,* and *Petrocoptis*. The fruit is a dry pod (capsule*) in all the garden genera.

Technical flower characters: Ovary superior,* usually 1-celled. Sepals and petals 4 or 5, the latter often with a claw,* and in some genera notched or fringed. Stamens 8–10.

**CARYOPSIS.** A small, 1-seeded fruit that does not split and is so closely invested with its outer husk that the seed inside and the fruit are inseparable. It is characteristic of the grasses, and what is ordinarily called grass seed (*i.e.* a grain of wheat) is actually a caryopsis.

**CARYOPTERIS** (carry-op'ter-is). Attractive, Asiatic shrubs of the family Verbenaceae, grown for their showy bloom. Of the six species the one below is the best known, usually as bluebeard or blue spirea. Leaves opposite,* short-stalked, and toothed. Flowers in profuse clusters (cymes*), the corolla irregular,* one of its 5 lobes larger than the others and fringed. Stamens 4 protruding (see BUDDLEIA). Fruit dry, separating into 4, slightly winged nutlets. (*Caryopteris* is Greek for nut and wing.)

---

\* Special articles on the subjects indicated by an asterisk (\*) will be found at the words so marked.

This is a popular greenhouse pot plant and needs a cool house and potting mixture* 3. Outdoors it is hardy from zone* 5 southward, and north of this is frequently planted, but winter-kills. If the shrub is cut back to the ground, as are some buddleias, and well mulched with manure, the new shoots will bloom the next autumn, unless the winter has been very severe.

**incana.** Blue spirea. A grayish-hairy shrub 1–5 ft. high. Leaves ovalish, coarsely but bluntly toothed, 2–3 in. long. Flower clusters showy, mostly in the leaf-axils,* bluish-purple or blue. Sept. Eastern As. Often known as *C. mastacanthus*.

**CARYOTA** (carry-ō'ta). The fish-tail palms comprise a genus of perhaps 12 species of tall feather palms, chiefly from the Indo-Malayan region, some of which sucker from the base and hence have several stems. Leaves twice-compound,* the ultimate segments broad towards the tip and jagged or cut fish-tail-fashion. Male and female flowers in different clusters on the same plant, appearing among the lower leaves of the terminal crown and fruiting successively down the trunk. When the flowering and fruiting is completed, the palm dies, but it may take several years to do so. Fruit small, oblongish or globe-shaped, not over ¾ in. in diameter. (*Caryota* is Greek for the date palm and of uncertain application here.)

The toddy palm is well suited for outdoor cult. in zones* 8 and 9, but is likely to be caught by occasional frosts in zone* 8. In Fla. it grows vigorously in almost any good soil and makes very decorative specimens. *Caryota mitis*, a smaller palm, is less known. *C. urens* is widely cult. in India for the delicious wine made from it (12 quarts a day from tapped trunks). The plants are usually too big for all but the largest greenhouses.

**mitis.** Usually with several smooth stems, the trunk larger than the suckers, not over 25 ft. high. Leaves 4–8 ft. long, the ultimate segments light green, faintly ribbed, the tips irregularly lobed, but generally triangular. Fruit ½ in. in diameter, bluish-black. Indo-Malaya.

**urens.** Toddy palm or wine palm; called also jaggery palm and kittul. A tall, single-stemmed palm 30–70 ft. high or more (in India). Leaves 12–20 ft. long, the ultimate segments stiff, strongly ribbed, fish-tail-shaped, or some, jagged or irregularly cut, the tips mostly drooping. Fruit about ¾ in. in diameter, red. Indo-Malaya.

*CARYOTAEFOLIA, -us, -um* (carry-o-ti-fō'li-a). With leaves like the fish-tail palms (*Caryota*).

**CASABA MELON.** See MELON.

**CASCADE.** See WATER.

**CASCARA SAGRADA** = *Rhamnus purshiana*.

**CASHEW** = *Anacardium occidentale*.

**CASHEW FAMILY** = Anacardiaceae.

*CASHMERIANA, -us, -um* (cash-meer-i-ā'na). From Kashmir, India.

**CASIMIROA** (ka-see-mi-rō'a). Of the four species of this tropical American genus of trees of the rue family, only one, the white sapote, is of much garden value. It can be grown outdoors in zones* 8 and 9, and in Fla. is moderately valued for its fruit. Leaves alternate,* compound,* the leaflets arranged finger-fashion. Flowers greenish and inconspicuous. (For structure see RUTACEAE.) Fruit fleshy (a drupe*), its pulp agreeably sweet and yellow. (Named for Casimiro Gomez de Ortega, Spanish botanist.)

The white sapote appears to have no soil preferences in Fla. It will stand occasional mild frosts, and its fruit begins ripening in May.

**edulis.** White sapote; also called Mexican apple. A tree (in cult.) rarely over 30 ft. high. Leaflets 3–7, mostly 5, each short-stalked, pointed both ends, 3–5 in. long. Fruit tomato-like in size and shape, gray or yellowish-green on the outside, yellow-fleshed and soft inside, with usually 3, hard, oblong seeds. Mex. and Central America.

**CASSABANANA** = *Sicana odorifera*.

**CASSAVA** = *Manihot esculenta*.

**CASSENA** = *Ilex vomitoria*. See HOLLY.

**CASSIA** (cash'i-a). Under the general term senna are grouped an immense genus (perhaps 500 species) of herbs, shrubs and trees of the pea family, the trees mostly tropical, but a few herbs in the temperate zone. They have compound* leaves, the leaflets arranged feather-fashion, and without an odd one at the end. Flowers not pea-like, very nearly regular,* but one of the clawed* petals often a little larger than the other 4. (See LEGUMINOSAE.) Fruit a flattened or roundish pod (legume*), usually 4-angled or winged. (*Cassia* is the old Greek name for these plants.)

All those below, except *C. marylandica*, are shrubs or trees that are hardy outdoors only in zones* 8 or 9, where they are grown for their usually showy flowers or for interest. Some of them, especially *C. corymbosa*, are occasionally grown in the cool greenhouse and should be planted in potting mixture* 4. *Cassia marylandica* is native in the U.S. and a bold, handsome border perennial of easy culture.

**artemisioides.** A compact shrub with silky-gray foliage. Leaflets 6–8, needle-like, about 1 in. long. Flowers yellow, in racemes* that arise in the leaf-axils.* Australia.

**corymbosa.** A smooth shrub 4–8 ft. high. Leaflets 6, oblongish. Flowers yellow, in mostly flat-topped clusters from the leaf-axils. Argentina. A free-flowering, handsome shrub more grown in the greenhouse than the other tropical species.

**fistula.** Pudding-pipe tree or canafistula; called, also, golden shower and drumstick tree. A tree 20–30 ft. Leaflets 8–16, ovalish, about 2 in. long. Flower cluster 1 ft. long, the flowers yellow and blooming before the leaves appear in early spring. Pod cylindric, nearly 2 ft. long. India.

**marylandica.** Wild or American senna. A stout, perennial herb 3–7 ft. high. Leaflets 10–20, oblongish, about 1½ in. long. Flowers yellow, in racemes, some in the leaf-axils, some terminal. Pod narrow, flat, about 3½ in. long. Eastern U.S. Hardy in the perennial border and a striking plant, blooming in June.

**tomentosa.** Shrub 10–12 ft. high, the twigs felty-hairy. Leaflets 12–18, oblongish, but with a minute, soft prickle at the tip, gray-hairy beneath. Flowers nearly 1 in. wide, deep yellow. Pod hairy, flat, nearly 5 in. long. Mex.

**CASSIA-BARK TREE** = *Cinnamomum cassia*.

**CASSIE** = *Acacia farnesiana*.

**CASSINE.** North American Indian name for the dahoon (*Ilex cassine*).

**CASSINOIDES** (cas-si-noy'deez; but see OÏDES). Like the cassine.

**CASSYTHA.** A generic name for dodder-like (non-hort.), tropical plants, and applied to *Rhipsalis cassytha*, which somewhat resembles them.

**CASTALIA** = NYMPHAEA.

**CASTANEA.** See CHESTNUT.

**CASTANOPSIS** (cas-ta-nop'sis). A genus of chiefly Asiatic evergreen trees of the beech family, the only cult. species being a native of the Pacific Coast and hardy in the East only south of zone* 5. It is closely related to the chestnut. The cult. species, **C. chrysophylla**, called giant or golden chinquapin, is a tree up to 100 ft. Leaves without teeth, oblongish, 4–6 in. long, green above, golden beneath. Flowers in catkins. Fruit in a spiny bur, the nut (not edible) usually solitary. Ore. to Calif. and Nev. Little grown in the East. A shrubby, but little known, form is hardier than the type. (*Castanopsis* is Greek for resembling chestnuts.)

**CASTANOSPERMUM** (cas-tan-o-spur'mum). Two tall trees of the pea family, the only cult. species being the Moreton Bay chestnut from Australia, which is grown outdoors only in Calif. and Fla. Leaves compound,* the leaflets arranged feather-fashion with an odd one at the end. Flowers not truly pea-like, in loose clusters. Petals 4, the stamens long-protruding. Pod 8–9 in. long, the seeds as big as Italian chestnuts. (*Castanospermum* is from the Greek for chestnut and seed, in allusion to the large seed.)

In Fla. and Calif. (only in zones* 8 and 9) the tree is a handsome ornamental, grown as such rather than for the seeds which are edible only if roasted.

**australe.** Moreton Bay chestnut; also called black bean. A tree 40–60 ft. high. Leaves 18 in. long, the 11–15 leaflets broad, and thickish. In early spring the tree is covered with its striking yellow-orange flowers in loose racemes. Australia.

**CASTILLA** (cas-till'ya). A small genus of Central American, milky-juiced trees of the mulberry family, the one below an important source of rubber when the latter is fairly high-priced. It yielded the rubber balls found by Columbus. It can be grown outdoors only in zone* 9 and

---

* Special articles on the subjects indicated by an asterisk (*) will be found at the words so marked.

is occasionally cult. there for interest (not for rubber production, which needs more heat). This cult. species is **C. elastica**, the ule or Mexican rubber-tree. It has alternate* leaves without marginal teeth, and small, unisexual* flowers, without petals. (Named for Juan Castillo y Lopez, Spanish botanist.)

**CASTILLEJA** (cas-til-lee'ya). Most gardeners will try to grow the painted-cups, a genus of 35 species of gorgeously colored herbs of the figwort family, but they will practically always fail. The plants are partially or wholly parasitic on the roots of other plants, hence nearly impossible of cultivation. They are perennial herbs with alternate* leaves. Flowers small, the corolla tubular, the top very irregular and 2-lipped. The color comes chiefly from the showy bracts,* from between which the flowers are borne in a strikingly beautiful spike. (Named for D. Castillejo, Spanish botanist.) The species most likely to be attempted are:

**californica.** Indian paint-brush. Erect, 12–18 in. high. Leaves narrow, about 1½ in. long. Flowers red, about 1 in. long, the bracts* red or red-tipped. Calif.

**latifolia.** Seaside painted-cup. A sticky-hairy herb 12–15 in. high. Leaves thickish, more or less oval, about ¾ in. long. Flowers about ¾ in. long, the bracts* leafy, yellow or red. Calif.

**parviflora.** Indian paint-brush. A hairy perennial 12–20 in. high. Leaves much cut into narrow segments, or the upper ones uncut. Flowers about 1 in. long, the bracts* red, yellow or white. Western U.S.

The scarlet painted-cup of the eastern U.S. has so far resisted cultivation.

**CAST-IRON PLANT** = *Aspidistra elatior.*

**CASTLE GARDENS.** See GARDEN HISTORY.

**CASTOR-BEAN.** The fruit of the castor-oil plant.

**CASTOR-OIL PLANT.** A single gigantic herb (tree-like in the tropics), and the only species of the genus **Ricinus** (ris'i-nus) of the spurge family. It is grown as a striking annual foliage plant or for summer bedding, also, far south, for its seeds, which yield castor-oil. The only species is **Ricinus communis,** a native of tropical Africa, often called palma christi in Spanish countries. See MEDICINAL PLANTS, and POISONOUS PLANTS.

As grown in the North, the castor-oil plant is a tender annual (*see* ANNUALS) 48–150 in. high. Leaves alternate,* often 3 ft. wide, the stalk attached to the middle of the blade, which is divided nearly to the middle by several lobes. Flowers in a dense, terminal cluster often 1–2 ft. high, the individual flowers small, without petals, the sexes separate. Fruit a spiny pod (capsule*) containing the beautifully marked, poisonous seeds. (*Ricinus* is the classical Latin name of this plant.)

The common castor-oil plant is usually grown in the form with green foliage, but there are several other varieties. One has much larger, green leaves. Another has red stems and bluish-gray leaves, and there are several with red and one with variegated leaves. One with white-veined leaves is offered as "mosquito-plant."

**CASUARINA** (cas-you-a-ry'na). The names beefwood, she-oak, or Australian pine are all applied to this curious group of chiefly Australian trees, the only genus of the family **Casuarinaceae** (cas-you-a-ry-nay'see-ee). They have apparently leafless twigs, covered with minute, scale-like leaves, the foliage thus suggesting the horsetail. The illusion is further carried out by the twigs being jointed and often ridged, as in some horsetails. True foliage leaves lacking. Flowers extremely simple, lacking true petals or sepals, the flower-parts scale-like, becoming a dry, cone-like or ball-like body. Fruit a winged nutlet, surrounded by 2 bractlets. (*Casuarina* is supposed to refer to the feathery branches being like the feathers of a cassowary.)

The two species below make excellent seaside trees along the coasts of frost-free regions such as southern Fla. and Calif. They cannot be grown anywhere else outdoors and are not usually greenhouse subjects.

**equisetifolia.** Horsetail tree; also called beefwood. A tall tree, the drooping branches and leafless twigs swaying wildly in a wind. Branchlets wire-like, jointed, much like the stems of the horsetails (*Equisetum*). Cones stalked, about ½ in. in diameter. Aust., but naturalized in Fla. and much planted there.

**stricta.** Smaller, or shrub-like, the branches drooping. Branchlets with the joints about ½–¾ in. apart (¼ in. in the other species). Cones about 1 in. in diameter.

*CATALINAE* (kat-a-ly'ne). From Santa Catalina Island, Calif.

**CATALINA IRONWOOD** = *Lyonothamnus floribundus.*

**CATALOGUES.** Seedmen's and nurserymen's catalogues, issued by hundreds of U.S. firms, are often of the greatest value to the gardener. Most reputable firms strike a happy medium between attractively advertising their products and sound information on how to grow them. Some specialists' catalogues in such things as rock gardens, cacti, aquatic plants, or fruit trees, contain more varieties than many technical books.

Extravagant claims of merit and a deficiency of specific information about the advertised product are, of course, open to suspicion in hort. as in any other field. Most good catalogues avoid this, but some do not. While current catalogues are pretty accurate reflections of the progress of hort., old ones are often valuable as history. If you find a catalogue in the attic dated any time before 1850, it may be valuable.

While all the plants in THE GARDEN DICTIONARY are in the trade you cannot find all of them in any one, and probably not in any dozen catalogues. If you are unable to find a dealer for any plant mentioned here, write to the Garden Editor, Houghton Mifflin Company, Boston, Mass.

**CATALONIAN JASMINE** = *Jasminum grandiflorum.*

**CATALPA** (ka-tal'pa). A genus of attractively flowering trees of the family Bignoniaceae, nearly all North American, but some Asiatic, much planted for ornament. They have long-stalked, opposite,* and usually large leaves. Flowers showy, the corolla irregular* and 2-lipped,* the flowers grouped in handsome, branched clusters (panicles*). Fertile stamens only 2. Fruit a long, cylindric, very narrow pod (capsule*), the many seeds with a tuft of white hairs at each end. (*Catalpa* is the North American Indian name for these trees.)

The catalpas are valuable lawn or street trees because of their profuse flowering. It should be remembered, however, that they are quick-growing, soft-wooded trees that reach maturity and then soon begin to fail. Consequently, they should be used with other, more permanent trees in any mass planting. They are easily grown in any ordinary garden soil, and young trees make an astonishing growth in a single season. Easily propagated by seeds, cuttings, root cuttings, or layering.

**bignonioides.** The common catalpa or Indian bean; also called bean-tree, cigar-tree, and smoking bean tree (from its long pods). A round-headed tree 30–40 ft. high, often less in cult. Leaves broadly oval, 6–8 in. long, bad-smelling when crushed. Flower cluster 6–9 in. long, pyramidal, the flowers about 1¼ in. long, white, but yellow-striped inside, and spotted with purple-brown. Pod 9–14 in. long. June–July. Native from Ga. to Fla. and Miss., but naturalized in the northeastern U.S. Hardy from zone* 3 southward. The *var.* **nana**, the umbrella or standard catalpa, is a popular, dwarf, globe-shaped tree (often sold as *Catalpa bungei*). It is a high-grafted plant forming a standard, and most useful for accents,* along drives, or in formal plantings.

**bungei** = *Catalpa bignonioides nana.*

**kaempferi** = *Catalpa ovata.*

**ovata.** A tree usually less than 30 ft. Leaves broadly oval, 5–7 in. long, often shallowly lobed. Flower cluster as in *C. bignonioides*, but the flowers yellowish-white and orange-striped inside and with violet spots. Pod 10–15 in. long. Eastern Asia. May–June. Hardy from zone* 4 southward.

**speciosa.** Hardy catalpa. Often up to 60 ft., the bark dark reddish-brown. Leaves oval or oval-oblong, 8–12 in. long, densely hairy on the under side, not malodorous when crushed. Flower cluster rather sparse and open, about 7 in. long, the flowers white, but yellow-striped inside, and inconspicuously spotted purple-brown. Pod 12–20 in. long. Native in the central U.S. Hardy from zone* 3 southward. June.

**CATALPA FAMILY** = Bignoniaceae.

**CATANANCHE** (kat-a-nan'ke). Of the five known species of this genus (family Compositae) only the blue succory is of garden interest. It is a flower garden perennial grown for its showy blue heads. Leaves mostly basal and narrow. Flowers in handsome, long-stalked heads, the rays flat and slightly toothed. It has dandelion-like heads of fruit. (*Catananche* is of confused or uncertain origin.)

---

\* Special articles on the subjects indicated by an asterisk (\*) will be found at the words so marked.

The blue succory is of easy cult. as a hardy perennial and will grow in any ordinary garden soil. Propagated by division or by seeds.

**caerulea.** Blue succory; also called Cupid's-dart. Not over 2 ft. high. Leaves very hairy, oblongish, with a few scattered teeth. Flower heads nearly 2 in. wide, the rays blue (white or white-margined in a hort. variety). Summer. Southern Eu.

**CATAPPA.** East Indian name for the Indian almond (*Terminalia catappa*).

**CATARIA** (ka-tay'ri-a). Latin for cat. See NEPETA.

**CATAWBIENSIS, -e** (ka-taw-bi-en'sis). From or near the Catawba River in the Blue Ridge Mountains of N. Car.

**CATBRIER.** See SMILAX (1).

**CATCH CROP.** See Intercropping at KITCHEN GARDEN.

**CATCHFLY.** See LYCHNIS and SILENE.

**CATECHU.** Asiatic vernacular for several plants yielding tanning extracts; also for the palm yielding the betelnut. See ARECA.

**CATERPILLARS.** The elongated, worm-like larvae of any moth or butterfly, often very destructive to plants in this stage of their life-history. See Moth at INSECT PESTS, and Stomach Poisons at INSECTICIDES.

**CATGUT** = *Tephrosia virginiana*.

**CATHARTICA, -us, -um** (ka-thar'ti-ka). Yielding a purge.

**CATHAYENSIS, -e** (kă-thay-en'sis). From China.

**CATJANG.** Oriental name of *Vigna catjang*.

**CATKIN.** A flower cluster typified by the pussy-willow and the poplar. It is often called an ament and consists of a scaly spike, the flowers in which have no petals. It is found also in birches and some trees of the beech family.

Catkins; poplar at the left, oak at the right

**CAT-MINT** = *Nepeta cataria*.

**CATNIP** = *Nepeta cataria*.

**CATS.** Garden enemies or household pets? They are both. For those who wish to attract them, catnip (*Nepeta cataria*) is an old favorite. Less known, but most interesting, is the liking shown by cats for the vine *Actinidia polygama* (which see). For those who need to preserve the birds and know that prowling cats are their worst enemies, see BIRDS.

**CAT'S-CLAW** = *Pithecolobium unguis-cati*; also *Doxantha unguis-cati*.

**CAT'S-EAR** = *Hypochaeris radicata*. See list at WEEDS.

**CAT'S-FOOT.** See ANTENNARIA.

**CAT'S-TAIL SPEEDWELL** = *Veronica spicata*.

**CAT-TAIL.** The cat-tails are marsh rather than garden plants and belong to the genus **Typha** (ty'fa), the only genus of the family **Typhaceae** (ty-fā'see-ee). They are reed-like plants with long, narrow, stiffish leaves and thick rootstocks. The flowers are extremely minute, hundreds being crowded in the dense, terminal, brownish spike. They have neither petals nor sepals, which are represented merely by a ring of bristles or hairs. (*Typha* is the Greek name for the cat-tail.)

The plants are easily grown in wet, open places and are suited for no other sites. Care must be taken to keep them from spreading too far or too fast. They are rampant growers.

**T. angustifolia.** Perhaps not very different from the following, but with generally narrow leaves and an interrupted spike. Nearly throughout the world.
**T. latifolia.** The common cat-tail, often called flag or reed mace. Growing in dense stands, the leaves 5–9 ft. long, scarcely ¾ in. wide. Flowering spike cylindric, brownish, about 6–8 in. long, continuous at the tip of a stalk as long as the leaves. Throughout the world.

**CATTLEYA** (kat'lee-a). To most city folk this is *the* orchid. It is the most widely grown of the florists' orchids and is one of a genus of perhaps 40 species of tropical American plants, most of which grow in the trees (true epiphytes*). They have club-shaped, thickened stems very like a pseudobulb,* from which arise 1–3, thick, fleshy leaves. Flowers sometimes solitary, often 2 or 3 together or more, large and very showy, the petals and sepals alike, or the petals broader than the sepals. There is a striking, apparently tubular lip,* the summit of which is 3-lobed, with the middle lobe spreading and larger than the side ones. (Named for William Cattley, English plant lover.)

For the culture of cattleyas *see* the section on Greenhouse Orchids at ORCHID. Of the 40 or more known species only a few have contributed to the modern florists' cattleya. But these have been so much hybridized that over 300 named forms are known, many of them of obscure parentage. Of these, 75 are fairly common in the collections of orchid fanciers, but lie outside the scope of this book. The species and varieties that appear to be the most common are listed below. Most of them are considered by many orchid specialists as only varieties of *Cattleya labiata*. The flowering months are those under greenhouse culture.

**bowringiana.** Stems club-shaped, about 12 in. long. Leaves 2, oblongish, 6–8 in. long. Flowers usually 5–9, not over 3 in. wide, the sepals and petals rose-purple. Lip rose-lilac, with a large, white, but maroon-bordered spot in the throat. British Honduras. Sept.–Dec.
**citrina.** Tulip orchid. Leaves narrow, 8–10 in. long. Flower solitary, on a stalk 8–10 in. long, drooping. Petals and sepals almost tulip-like, yellow, the lip white-edged and wavy. Mex. Oct.–April.
**labiata.** The commonest cult. orchid in America. Stem club-shaped, topped by a single, flattish, thickish leaf 5–7 in. long. The stem is green-sheathed when young, furrowed when old. Flowers 2–5, usually about 6 in. wide, the sepals and petals rose-lilac, the petals wider than the sepals. Lip magenta-purple, the throat yellow but orange-spotted, the central lobe of the lip crisped on the margin. Brazil. Oct.–June. This and perhaps 200 named forms and varieties are the chief sources of the cattleya found in the florists' windows. The genus has entered into many hybrids with other genera. See BRASSOCATTLAELIA and BRASSOCATTLEYA.
**mendeli.** Resembling *C. labiata*, but with larger, white or rosy flowers, the limb of the purple lip wavy, the throat yellow. Colombia. June–Nov.
**mossiae.** Resembling *C. labiata* and perhaps only a variety of it, but the flowers decidedly larger and rose-colored, the wavy lip with a purplish limb variegated with violet and white-margined. Venezuela. April–July. There is also a variety with violet-blue flowers.
**percivaliana.** Resembling *C. mossiae*, but the flowers smaller, darker-colored and blooming from Jan. to March. It is probably only a variety of *C. labiata*. Venezuela.
**skinneri.** San Sebastian. Leaves 4–6 in. long, more or less cylindric. Flowers 4–6, not over 4 in. wide, rose-purple, the lip with a yellow throat. Guatemala. March–June. There is also a white-flowered variety.
**trianae.** Next to *C. labiata*, of which it may be only a variety, the most widely cult. of the cattleyas. Leaves oblong, 6–8 in. long. Flowers 2 or 3, not over 7 in. wide, rose or rose-purple, the lip purple, its limb wavy and its throat yellow. Colombia. Dec.–Feb. There are several varieties, one with fragrant pink flowers, another with white or lilac-tinged flowers.

**CAUCASIAN LILY** = *Lilium monadelphum*.

**CAUCASICA, -us, -um** (kau-kay'si-ka). From the Caucasus Mountains.

**CAUDATA, -us, -um** (kau-day'ta). Tailed.

**CAULESCENS** (kau-les'senz). See CAULESCENT.

**CAULESCENT.** Having an obvious stem, usually above ground; not stemless. See ACAULESCENT.

**CAULIFLORA, -us, -um** (kau-lee-flow'ra). See CAULIFLORY.

**CAULIFLORY.** The bearing of flowers and fruit on the trunk or larger branches. It is mostly found on tropical trees, notably in the chocolate tree, the carambola, and the jackfruit.

**CAULIFLOWER** (*Brassica oleracea botrytis*). This, one of the most delicious of the cabbage tribe, is a cultigen,* originating from the European weed *Brassica oleracea*. See

---

* Special articles on the subjects indicated by an asterisk (*) will be found at the words so marked.

# CAULIFLOWER

CABBAGE. Like the others it does not like heat and dryness.

The plant comes in two main types. One is the ordinary cauliflower of the markets. The other is known as winter cauliflower here, and as broccoli in England and also by some here. (See BROCCOLI.) Its culture is largely confined to the extreme northwest coastal states. In both sorts we eat the whitened, much enlarged and crowded flower head of the plant, the curd. Ordinary cauliflower will develop in a single season, while winter cauliflower (sometimes called heading broccoli) needs parts of two growing seasons (see below). See OREGON.

Cauliflower is more difficult to grow than any other plant of the cabbage tribe. Like most of them it will not stand heat and drought, which limits its culture in this country to areas free of these conditions. Proximity to the sea, and cool uplands of plentiful moisture are ideal. It will not, however, stand as much frost as cabbage or Brussels sprouts, and if there is protracted warm weather, it will not head. Commercial culture is chiefly on Long Island, Colorado, California, Florida, and about the Great Lakes. It must be grown only in the cool seasons of the South, and northward its cultivation, for the same reason, is divided into an early and late crop, just as in cabbage.

VARIETIES. For ordinary cauliflower the best varieties are: Snowball, Erfurt, and Snowstorm for the early sorts. For the late crop Seafoam, Dry Weather, and Autumn Giant are preferred.

SOILS AND FERTILIZER. Soil and fertilizer conditions are the same as for cabbage (which see). All growers agree, however, that assured of the proper degree of coolness and moisture, any good soil will grow cauliflower, sometimes called rich-man's cabbage from the difficulty and expense of growing it.

RAISING YOUNG PLANTS. For both early and late varieties the method of raising young plants and their subsequent management is the same as for cabbage (which see). A possible variation is the much greater expense of cauliflower seed and the consequent need to carefully preserve all thinned seedlings for pricking out. Most home gardeners will prefer to buy rooted plants, but be sure they are true to name and come from a reliable dealer. No crop is more likely to go wrong than cauliflower.

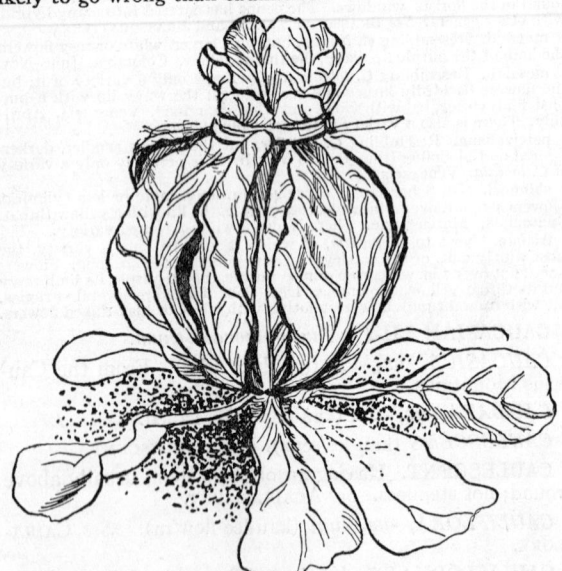

A cauliflower head tied up

PLANTING OUT. For both early and late varieties set the plants 2 ft. apart in the row and make the rows 3 ft. apart. This will allow 50 heads of cauliflower to a 100-ft. row, which should be more than ample for a family of five.

CULTIVATION AND HEADING. Cultivate frequently and cleanly, being careful not to injure the brittle foliage if machines are used. As in cabbage, if cultivation is confined to mid-day, there is less chance of injury than earlier or later (see Cultivation at CABBAGE).

Cauliflower will not head of itself. Frequently, if poor seed has been used, or it gets too dry or too hot, the button-like center of the plant will "break," send up a flower stalk, and ruin the plant as a marketable cauliflower. The only way to force the plant to produce a solid white head (the curd) is to start the day the first button-like swelling appears. The safest and most certain method of doing this is to gather the outer leaves and tie them over the center of the plant. Don't pull the cord or tape or raffia tight enough to injure the outer leaves, which must still keep on growing.

These leaves are simply bent over the developing head, shield it from the heat of the sun, and gradually (from lack of light) turn it white. Some growers prefer to bend the leaves over the center and pin them with a toothpick, but this method is not so satisfactory as to tie them up.

HARVESTING. Cauliflower heads will stand no frost, and when they are ready to be picked (i.e. plump, firm and white), they cannot be left on the plant as a cabbage head may be — perhaps for a fortnight. Harvest at once by cutting well below the head those that are ready to harvest. If freezing weather is likely, all remaining heads should be harvested. The heads are easily damaged and must be handled with great care.

WINTER CAULIFLOWER (sometimes called heading broccoli). This is similar to cauliflower, but it needs the late fall and the following very early spring to develop. That limits its culture to parts of the South or the coastal regions of the Northwest. Its chief value is a commercial one — to deliver to the great markets cauliflower that is far out of the normal season of ordinary cauliflower. Winter cauliflower, impossible of growth in regions of cold winters, is therefore of little interest to the average home gardener. For pests see CABBAGE.

**CAULINE.** Having a stem.

**CAULOPHYLLUM** (kau-lo-fill'um). A genus of only two species of perennial herbs of the family Berberidaceae, one Asiatic, the other North American and grown in the wild garden. They have thickened rootstocks and large, thrice-compound* leaves. Flowers greenish-purple, with 6 petals and 6 sepals, and borne in a terminal cluster (panicle*). Fruit berry-like, blue. (*Caulophyllum* is from the Greek for stem and leaf.)

The only cult. species needs a rich woods soil, not particularly acid, and the shade of trees. It is unsuited to open, sunny places. Easily propagated in early spring by division of the rootstocks.

**thalictroides.** Blue cohosh; also called papoose-root and squaw-root. A perennial herb 1-3 ft. high. Leaves usually 2, one near the flower cluster, the other below it. Leaflets resembling the meadow rue, 3-5 lobed at the tip. Flowers about $\frac{1}{3}$ in. long. Fruit nearly round, about $\frac{1}{3}$ in. in diameter, on short, stout stalks. Eastern N.A. May.

**CAULORAPA, -us, -um** (kau-lo-ray'pa). With a turnip-like stem as in kohlrabi.

**CAVENDISH BANANA** = *Musa cavendishi*. For culture see BANANA.

**CAVITIES IN TREES.** See TREE SURGERY.

**CEANOTHUS** (see-a-nō'thus). A large genus of very handsome North American shrubs of the family Rhamnaceae, only a few cult., and of these the hardiness is restricted as indicated below. Leaves evergreen in some species, nearly always 3-nerved or veined at the base. Flowers small, blue or white, but showy from the dense, branched clusters in which they are borne. Sepals incurved and often colored. Petals hooded and with a narrow shank. Fruit dry, 3-lobed, and separating into 3 segments when ripe. (*Ceanothus* is from the Greek for a kind of thistle and of uncertain application here.)

These American plants have been more prized in Eu. than here, especially in France where there are many hybrid, named forms. Few of these are hardy here, except in Calif.

---

* Special articles on the subjects indicated by an asterisk (*) will be found at the words so marked.

Those species not quite hardy can often be grown by digging them out before cold weather sets in, and storing them in frost-free pits, either in pots or heeled in. They all prefer open sunlight and a light, porous soil. Propagated by seeds or by cuttings, layering or by grafting the hybrid sorts. In Calif. they are generally called wild lilac or buckbrush.

**americanus.** New Jersey tea, Indian tea, Walpole tea, and redroot. A shrub not over 3 ft. high. Leaves ovalish, 2-4 in. long, finely but irregularly toothed. Flowers white, in flat-topped, small clusters. Canada to S. Car. and westward. Hardy from zone* 3 southward, but the least showy of the cult. species.

**arboreus.** Tree or island myrtle. An evergreen shrub or tree-like, not over 25 ft. Leaves ovalish, densely white-felty beneath. Flowers pale blue and fragrant. Calif. coast and Islands. Hardy only from zone* 7 southward.

**coeruleus.** A shrub 10-15 ft. Leaves oblong-oval, 2-4 in. long, white-felty beneath. Flowers deep blue in large-branching clusters. Mex. Scarcely hardy except in zones* 8 and 9, but the origin of many fine hybrids that are somewhat hardier.

**prostratus.** Mahala mat. A beautiful prostrate shrub with wedge-shaped, evergreen leaves having spiny teeth on the margins. Flowers blue. Pacific Coast. Hardy only from zone* 6 southward.

**spinosus.** Red-heart. A shrub 8-10 ft. high or tree-like and somewhat higher. Leaves oblong, about 1½ in. long, nearly without marginal teeth. Flowers white or pale blue. Calif. Hardy from zone* 7 southward.

**thyrsiflorus.** Blue blossom or blue myrtle; called also Calif. lilac. The finest and most popular of the cult. species. Evergreen and often up to 25 ft. high. Leaves oblong, 1-2½ in. long, lustrous. Flowers blue, numerous in lateral clusters (panicles*). Ore. to Calif. Hardy from zone* 5 southward.

**verrucosus.** A low shrub, the small leaves somewhat larger toward the tip, pale on the under side. Flowers white. Lower Calif. and southern Calif. Hardy only from zone* 8 southward.

**CECROPIA** (see-crow'pi-a). A genus of peculiar, mostly hollow-trunked, tropical American trees of the mulberry family, one sometimes planted in southern Fla. and Calif. The only cult. species, C. palmata, the snakewood, has a milky juice and large leaves, with 7-11 lobes, and the leaf-stalk attached to the center of the blade, which is conspicuously white beneath. Flowers greenish, in dense catkins, the male and female on different trees. (Named for King Cecrops of Attica.)

**CEDAR.** A widely used term in botany and hort. For the traditional cedar see CEDRUS (which includes the cedar-of-Lebanon). Also commonly called cedars are trees and shrubs of *Juniperus* (which includes the common red cedar). For other plants sometimes called cedar see CEDRELA, LIBOCEDRUS, TORREYA, and CHAMAECYPARIS.

**CEDAR MOSS** = *Ceratophyllum demersum.*

**CEDAR-OF-LEBANON** = *Cedrus libanotica.*

**CEDAR RUST.** See Diseases at APPLE.

**CEDRELA** (see-drell'a, also sed-ree'la). A widely distributed genus of trees of the family Meliaceae, one or two of the temperate zone, but most of them tropical. They have alternate,* compound* leaves, the usually large leaflets arranged feather-fashion. Flowers not showy, but small and usually in branched clusters (panicles*). Petals 4-5, keeled inside. Ovary on a short stalk, followed by a capsule* containing many winged seeds. (*Cedrela* is derived from *Cedrus*, in allusion to the wood resembling some cedars.) Some of the species are also called *Toona*.

The only hardy species is C. sinensis, which grows well up to zone* 4, or possibly in protected places in zone* 3. It has no special soil preferences. The other two can be grown outdoors only in zones* 8 and 9, and are frequently planted in southern Calif. and Fla.

**odorata.** Spanish cedar or West Indian cedar. A tree to 100 ft. high, its wood used for cigar boxes. Leaflets 12-20, 4-6 in. long, without marginal teeth, and without an odd leaflet at the end. Flowers yellowish-green, the cluster shorter than the leaves. Tropical America.

**sinensis.** A hardy tree (see above), usually not over 50 ft. high. Leaflets 10-22, without an odd one at the end, 4-7 in. long and remotely toothed. Flowers greenish-white, the cluster a little shorter than the leaves. China. June. The tree somewhat resembles the ailanthus, but the latter has an odd leaflet at the end.

**toona.** Toon. Almost evergreen tree 50-70 ft. high. Leaflets 10-20, without an odd one at the end, oval or lance-shaped, 3-6 in. long. Flowers greenish-white, honey-scented, the clusters shorter than the leaves. Himalayas. Often called *Toona ciliata*.

**CEDRUS** (see'drus). A genus of four species of handsome, evergreen trees of the pine family, three of which are widely cult. for ornament. They are the traditional cedars, the most famous being the cedar-of-Lebanon and the deodar. Leaves stiff, needle-like, 4-angled, scattered or arranged in small, dense clusters. Flowers unisexual,* the male and female on the same tree, wholly without petals or sepals. Cones erect, its scales closely appressed,* the seeds between them triangular and broadly winged. (*Cedrus* is from the old Greek name for a resinous tree.)

The cedars can be grown in the zones indicated for each species. They need open places and ordinary good soil, preferably not too moist. They make handsome specimen evergreens for lawns or parks, and somewhat resemble larches in the arrangement of their leaves, but unlike larches are true evergreens.

**atlantica.** Atlas cedar. An upright tree 40-100 ft. high (much less as usually cult.), having a main leader or trunk. Leaves bluish-green, just under an inch long, rigid. Cones 1-3 in. long, light brown. Northern Af. Hardy from zone* 5, or in protected sites from zone* 4, southward. There are fine hort. forms or varieties with silvery-white leaves and with drooping branches.

**deodora.** The deodor. A tree up to 150 ft., but less as usually cult. Leaves dark bluish-green, nearly 2 in. long, not very rigid. Cones 3-5 in. long, reddish-brown. Himalayas. Hardy from zone* 6 southward and a handsome evergreen. Varieties are offered with silvery leaves, with stiff and shorter leaves, and some forms have pendulous branches. The *var.* **crassifolia** is a much shorter, almost stunted tree with shorter and thicker leaves.

**libani** = *Cedrus libanotica.*

**libanotica.** Cedar-of-Lebanon. A tree up to 100 ft. (usually less in cult.), with a single trunk or more often splitting into trunk-like branches. Leaves dark green, about 1 in. long. Cones 2-4 in. long, brown. Asia Minor and Syria. Hardy from zone* 4 southward. There is a dwarf, compact form (often called Comte de Dijon), and another with silvery or bluish leaves.

**CEIBA** (say-ee'ba). Gigantic tropical trees, often with widely flaring buttresses, belonging to the family Bombacaceae, one planted in southern Fla. for interest. Leaves compound,* the 7 leaflets arranged finger-fashion. Flowers large and showy, the 5 petals hairy on the outside. Stamens numerous, in one group. Fruit a leathery capsule,* the seeds surrounded by a cotton-like fiber (the kapok of commerce). (*Ceiba* is the native name for them in tropical America.)

**pentandra.** Silk-cotton tree. A tree 100-150 ft. high, its branches huge and wide-spreading, the twigs often spiny. At the base the trunk flares out into immense, flank-like buttresses which may extend 30 ft. from the trunk. Leaflets oblongish but tapering, 4-6 in. long. Flowers white or pinkish, in clusters that are 6-8 in. long. Fruit 3-6 in. long. Tropical America. A very striking tree, cult. in Fla. for shade (it is deciduous in mid-winter), and in Java as the source of kapok.

**CELANDINE** = *Chelidonium majus.*

**CELANDINE POPPY** = *Stylophorum diphyllum.*

**CELASTRACEAE** (see-lass-tray'see-ee). The staff-tree or bittersweet family comprises about 45 genera and over 400 species of widely distributed shrubs, trees, and woody vines, a few of which furnish valuable garden plants, some of them evergreen. The leaves are alternate* in *Celastrus* (the bittersweet), *Maytenus*, and *Tripterygium*, but opposite* in most of the other garden genera. The flowers are never conspicuous in this family, usually small and greenish or whitish. The fruit is dry or fleshy and in some genera, notably in *Euonymus* and *Celastrus*, very showy from the often brightly colored aril.* Beautiful evergreen vines are found in *Euonymus* (as well as shrubs), while *Pachistima* is a dwarf evergreen shrub with opposite* leaves. All the garden genera are of outdoor cult. over most of America, but *Elaeodendron* is tropical and can be grown outdoors only in zones* 8 and 9, or in the greenhouse.

Technical flower characters: Calyx 4-5-parted or lobed, usually persistent. Petals 4 or 5, their margins overlapping, inserted on a conspicuous disk. Ovary superior* or half inferior.* Style 1, the stigma 3-5-lobed.

**CELASTRUS** (see-las'trus). While most of this genus are woody vines, they are sometimes called staff-tree, instead of by the better known name of bittersweet. There are more than 30 species (family Celastraceae), mostly Asiatic, American, or Australian, and two of them are cult. as ornamental vines. (See VINES.) They have alternate,* stalked leaves, and small, greenish, unisexual flowers. (For details see CELASTRACEAE.) Fruit a usually yellow capsule,* which,

---

* Special articles on the subjects indicated by an asterisk (*) will be found at the words so marked.

upon splitting, discloses the fleshy crimson aril* of the seeds. (*Celastrus* is from the Greek for some evergreen tree.)

These vines are useful for walls, trellises or arbors, not only for the handsome foliage but for the brilliant autumn fruit. They root easily and may be propagated by cuttings or by suckers. Also raised from seed.

**articulatus.** Often reaching 30 ft. and a handsome vine. Leaves nearly round or oblongish, 3–5 in. long. Flowering and fruiting clusters mostly in the leaf-axils,* thus often partly hidden. Fruit orange-yellow. Western China. Hardy in protected parts of zone* 4 and southward. Often sold as *C. orbiculatus*.

**orbiculatus** = *Celastrus articulatus*.

**scandens.** Bittersweet, shrubby bittersweet, waxwork, and fever-twig. A rampant but not tall-growing, woody vine very suitable for covering low wall-tops. Leaves oblong-oval, 2½–5 in. long, tapering at the tip. Flower and fruit clusters mostly terminal, hence not much hidden by the foliage. Fruit yellow, the aril* a brilliant crimson. N.A. Hardy from zone* 2 southward. The attempt of the bookish to call this false bittersweet does not make much headway. For another plant called bittersweet *see* SOLANUM DULCAMARA.

**CELERY.** This vegetable and the closely related celeriac both belong to the genus **Apium** (ā′pi-um) of the carrot family, which comprises about 20 species of herbs, mostly from the north temperate zone. They have compound* or twice-compound* leaves, often with sheathing leafstalks (as in celery). Flowers small, white, many in a compound umbel.* Fruit a prominently 2-angled, small carpel. (*Apium* is Latin for parsley, a related plant.)

**A. graveolens.** Not in cult., and interesting as a Eurasian, biennial herb, from which the varieties below have been derived. *Var.* **dulce.** Celery. A strong-smelling herb without much enlargement of the root. Leaves with many leaflets, the stalks (celery) channeled and sheathing. For culture *see* below. *Var.* **rapaceum.** Celeriac. Very similar, but cult. for the edible, thickened, turnip-like root. Leafstalks not as in common celery. For culture *see* below.

## CELERY CULTURE

The ordinary celery of the markets was derived from *Apium graveolens*, a white-flowered herb from Europe and Asia. Celeriac, often called turnip-rooted celery (*Apium graveolens rapaceum*), is also derived from the same wild plant, but instead of having edible leafstalks, has practically none, but an edible root for which it is cult. *See* CELERIAC, below.

Successful celery culture is based on the right climate and the right soils. As to the first, the plant requires coolness. In the commercially important areas, as along the Great Lakes, it gets this for most of the growing season. Elsewhere there are two distinct celery crops, one utilizing the cool spring months for growth; the later and much more important crop matures in the late fall, and, by protection, is extended well through the winter. The very important commercial production of celery in the winter months, as practiced in the South and California, is based upon the use of their brief period of coolness.

SOILS AND FERTILIZER. No garden crop grown is such a rich feeder as celery. The soil must have depth and mellowness and an abundant supply of moisture. If rainfall and moisture retentiveness do not supply this, an overhead watering system or irrigation is essential. It is absolutely impossible to make it grow in hard, dry or sun-baked land. So important is this depth, mellowness and soil moisture that the most successful commercial growers in the country have utilized drained muck lands for celery farms. In the region about the Great Lakes there are thousands of acres so utilized, and elsewhere muck lands are also highly favored. *See* MUCKLAND GARDENING.

The average home gardener has no muck, but to grow good celery he must approximate the conditions of such places as nearly as possible. This means adding humus for moisture-holding and mellowness and plant food for enrichment.

An excellent method is to plow in 15–20 tons of well-rotted stable manure to the acre (4–5 wheelbarrow loads to a 100-ft. row). This adds humus and plant food, but besides this it is advisable to add 1500 pounds per acre (about 6 pounds per 100-ft. row) of commercial fertilizer with a 4-8-12 ratio (*see* FERTILIZERS). These should be thoroughly and deeply plowed under at least three weeks before the plants are set in the garden. It is almost impossible to get the soil too rich or to plow too deeply for successful celery culture.

VARIETIES. The best early season celery varieties are: Golden Self-Blanching, Wonderful, or Golden Plume. For the late and more important, because more seasonable, varieties use Easy Blanching, Green Top, Giant Pascal, and Salt Lake. Some of these are the so-called self-blanching types, others frankly need blanching. For the details of this *see* below.

RAISING CELERY FROM SEED. For the average home gardener this is apt to be sufficiently difficult and tedious to suggest the desirability of buying plants ready to be set in his specially prepared soil. Good plants are offered by dealers of both the late and early sorts.

If plants are raised from seed they must be handled very carefully. Celery seed is small, germinates slowly and a considerable number fail to germinate at all. Germination is hastened by soaking the seeds (in a cotton bag) in water for 24 hours. Then mix the seeds with an equal quantity of fine sand, which greatly facilitates their planting.

Sow the seeds and sand in a fine drill (not over ¼ in. deep), or sow them broadcast if you prefer, covering with about ¼ in. of finely sifted soil. Keep the flats or boxes moist in which they have been planted, or even rather wet. This can be done by covering them for some time, before germination, with wet burlap.

For the early varieties this seed should be sown in the cool greenhouse or hotbed, approximately 8 or 9 weeks before the plants are ready to go to their permanent position. For the late varieties the procedure and timing are the same, except that the seed is sown in flats or boxes outdoors. In either case it will take perhaps 3 weeks before the first plants show above ground.

These young seedlings are very delicate and spindling at first. They are greatly improved by two or three subsequent transplantings, at each move spacing them farther apart. This is an expensive and tedious process, and the loss from wilting and damping-off is considerable. But the survivors are much more stocky and better able to stand conditions in the open garden. If the plants are from seed sown in the greenhouse, it is important that the temperature for the young seedlings be kept around 50° or a little above. Do not let it get down to 40° or 45°.

PLANTING CELERY. The plants should be about 4–5 in. high when set out in the garden, stocky, and with plenty of roots. See that these requirements are met, whether you have raised them yourself or bought them from a dealer.

Set out the plants only when the ground is wet or you can make it so. Setting celery plants in dry soil will certainly kill them. If you have only 100 ft. of celery, the young plants should be watered every day for the first three days — more if you happen to be caught by a dry spell. They should be planted in a trench 3–4 in. deep, which is gradually filled in as the plants grow.

Early varieties should be planted after danger of frost is over (see the name of your state for the dates). Late varieties are best planted from mid-July to August 1st.

The plants should be put about 5 in. apart in the row and the rows cannot be nearer than 2½ ft. apart, and 4 ft. is better, as will appear presently, especially for the late crop. The plants must be cultivated frequently and kept absolutely free of weeds. A weedy celery row will greatly increase the difficulty of blanching.

Some growers, in spite of the liberal applications of manure and fertilizer already mentioned, use nitrate of soda in addition. They put on 250 pounds to the acre (1½ pounds to a 100-ft. row) two or three times at intervals of 15 days, starting a week or two after the plants have been put out.

BLANCHING AND HARVESTING. Most of the early varieties are of the sort described as self-blanching, which means that they are supposed to be white and tender without having the light excluded from them. Most of the late (and most desirable) varieties are naturally green and useless without blanching.

---

* Special articles on the subjects indicated by an asterisk (*) will be found at the words so marked.

For the late varieties the most satisfactory method of blanching is gradually to heap soil about the plants so that only the tops finally show above the raised mounds. This operation must be done carefully and not much before September 15 in most northern localities. No soil must be allowed to fall into the heart of the plant, which, if too spreading, should be tied up before starting to heap up the soil. It will take considerable, and preferably weed-free soil, to do a thorough blanching job, which is the chief reason for the wide spacing and thorough cultivation.

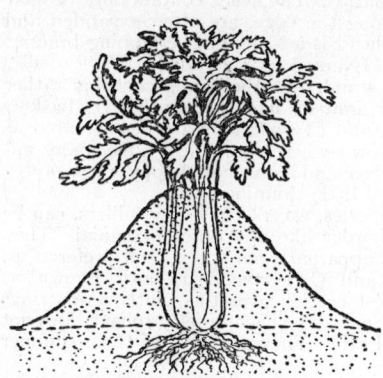
Blanching celery with earth

All the late varieties are better for this soil blanching, and if the tops are protected with a deep dressing of salt hay or straw, the celery may be kept for a good part of the winter and dug as wanted.

The early varieties cannot be soil-blanched, as soil about the stems will almost certainly cause rot. Some prefer paper cylinders slipped over each plant. Others use long boards (a foot wide) each side of the row and pinched nearly together over the plants with wire hooks. Even the self-blanching types are improved by this treatment, and some growers of late celery prefer boards to soil for blanching.

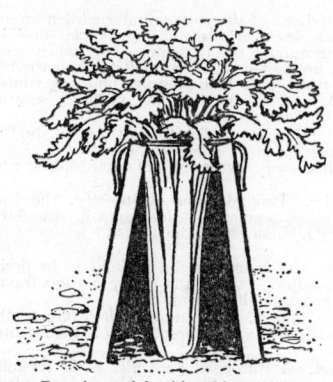
Boards used for blanching celery

Both early and late varieties are harvested by digging out a few plants at a time. A 100-ft. row should yield about 200 plants, or a little more if they are put exactly 5 in. apart.

CELERIAC CULTURE (*Apium graveolens rapaceum*)

The turnip-rooted celery or celeriac is grown in exactly the same way as celery. But because there is no development of leafstalk, and the delicious root is the final harvest, the plants need no blanching and the rows can be put 20 in. apart. It is less subject to diseases than celery and, needing no blanching, is easier to grow. It is sometimes known as knob celery.

INSECT PESTS. The celery leaf tier, a webbing caterpillar, injures celery. It cannot be controlled with arsenicals, because of the danger of poison on the celery; a dust of equal parts pyrethrum and lime or tobacco dust, blown well down between the stalks, is effective. The green and black celery caterpillar, larva of the black swallowtail butterfly, occasionally feeds on celery. It may be hand-picked. A celery looper, similar to the cabbage looper, sometimes occurs. In the North a small, ill-smelling black plant bug has occasionally damaged celery; it may be killed with a spray of nicotine sulphate, 1 to 500.

DISEASES. The organisms which cause early and late blights, and the bacterial leafspot are carried with the seed and in old diseased celery refuse. If seed treated with formaldehyde is planted in clean soil, and the plants sprayed with bordeaux or dusted with copper-lime dust at weekly intervals both in the seed bed and in the field, healthy plants can be grown. Wilt or yellows is the result of a soil-borne fungus, which can be controlled only by planting resistant strains. Root rot which causes a greenish decay at the base of the plant is partly combated by long rotations with other crops, and care in selecting the seed bed. Storage rots are avoided if the temperatures are kept slightly below 32° F.

**CELERY CABBAGE.** = *Brassica pekinensis*. For culture see CHINESE CABBAGE.

**CELERY FAMILY** = Umbelliferae.

**CELLAR GARDENING.** More than a dozen crops will furnish food throughout the winter when grown in a cellar. The only real drawback is the danger of coal or illuminating-gas fumes. Gas in such minute quantities as to be apparently odorless will kill and stunt the growth of many plants. A temperature of 50 to 60 degrees is best for vegetables. For the growing of those which require darkness, a corner of the cellar may be curtained off, or a box, with a few holes bored for ventilation, turned over the one containing the forced roots.

Rhubarb is the easiest vegetable to force. The clumps must be old and well established, as winter growth is due to the nourishment stored in the roots. Allow the clumps to freeze hard before taking indoors. Store in a cool place. Start a few in Dec. in boxes of earth with a little fresh manure under the roots. Better stalks are obtained by forcing in a dark, moist spot. They will be ready for use in about six weeks.

Dig asparagus roots in the fall and transplant them into boxes of earth. Keep in a light, heated spot; water well. Edible-size stalks will soon appear. If an extra supply of roots is dug, kept in a cool place, and forced at intervals, asparagus may be enjoyed until the new crop arrives.

French endive, sold in expensive restaurants and hotels, is really Witloof chicory. Sow seed in the garden in June. In the late fall dig and store the roots in a cool cellar. Start forcing at intervals of two or three weeks. Pack close. Cover the crowns with about 4 in. of sand; water and keep warm. The new tops which push up will be creamy-white, tender, and ready for use in three to four weeks. Do not cut too close to the roots, as second and third cuttings may be made. This plant is commonly, but mistakenly, called simply endive in the shops. See the illustrations at ENDIVE.

Mushrooms, seakale, chard, parsley, dandelions for salad, and chives for seasoning also may be grown.

In cellars where the heating apparatus is partitioned off, or where fuel other than coal or gas is used, many plants suitable for the cool greenhouse may be grown. Benches may be placed beneath the windows or artificial lighting may be used. This is an ideal place in which to start bulbs and other plants for house decoration. Bench planting can be practiced as in ordinary greenhouse culture. Rock garden seedlings and many half-hardy annuals, such as verbenas, can be started and carried through the winter. Small seedlings for next year's plants also do well here through the hot summer. *See also* STORAGE.

**CEL-O-GLASS.** See Sash at COLD FRAME.

**CELOSIA** (sell-ō'si-a). A large genus of tropical herbs or shrubs of the family Amaranthaceae, the chief cult. sorts grown as tender annuals (*see* ANNUALS) for their often fantastic or grotesque, chaffy flower clusters (the cockscombs). Leaves alternate.* Flowers minute and chaffy, crowded into dense spikes which are much enlarged, flattened, crested, or otherwise modified and often brilliantly colored. The minute flower characters are technical. (*Celosia* is from the Greek for burned, in allusion to the brilliant scarlet inflorescence.)

These showy garden plants are of easy culture if treated as tender annuals. They are extremely useful and widely grown to give lasting color in shades of red, yellow, green, purple or white, and come in many different forms.

**argentea.** A tropical Asiatic weed, scarcely in cult., with a silvery-white, more or less oblong spike. It is the parent of the *var*. **cristata**, the cockscomb. This is lower than the type, usually 1–2 ft. Flower clusters very diverse. One common type has a crested or rolled cluster very like a cockscomb and from 3 to 6 in. wide; or congested and monstrous. Some are very broad and fan-like, others spire-like, some open and feathery, all chaffy and in a variety of colors, to which all sorts of names have been applied such as Plumed Knight, etc.

**floribunda.** A shrubby plant 8–10 ft. high. Leaves triangular or oval, often 7 in. long. Flowers very numerous in tight clusters (panicles*). Lower Calif. and not hardy in the East. Some plants called by seedsmen *C. floribunda* are actually forms of the cockscomb and do not belong here.

---

* Special articles on the subjects indicated by an asterisk (*) will be found at the words so marked.

**CELSIA** (sell'zi-a). Thirty species of mullein-like herbs of the figwort family, the two below somewhat grown for ornament, but not hardy over much of the country. They are separated only by technical characters from the mulleins, and have a terminal flower cluster (spike or raceme*) of yellow, usually bracted* flowers. (Named for Olaus Celsius, teacher of Linnaeus.)

The plants are best treated as biennials. Start the seeds in the greenhouse or hotbed and set them out only after settled warm weather has come. While perennials, they often die in our cold, wet winters.

**arcturus.** Cretan bear's-tail. An erect herb with a single, hairy stem 10–18 in. high. Leaves ovalish and toothed or the lower cut lyre-fashion. Flowers yellow, distinctly stalked, in a loose raceme, the anthers* purple. Crete and Asia Minor.

**cretica.** Cretan mullein. Hairy and 3–5 ft. high. Leaves ovalish, more or less clasping, the lower ones cut lyre-fashion. Flowers yellow, almost stalkless in the spike, and marked with purple. Mediterranean region.

**CELTIS.** See HACKBERRY.

*CEMBRA* (sem'bra). Modern form of the ancient *zember*, the name of the Swiss stone pine.

*CEMBROIDES* (sem-broy'deez; but *see* OÏDES). Resembling the Swiss stone pine. (*See* CEMBRA.)

**CEMENT FLAGGING.** See PATHS AND PAVING. For mixing *see* CONCRETE.

**CEMETERY.** There are two general types of cemetery; the traditional type with monuments and vaults, and the modern type in which the graves are marked only by bronze plaques laid level with the grass. The special problems of cemetery design require the services of a skilled designer and are beyond the scope of this article.

The fact that all are alike in death should characterize the cemetery landscape. If there is a harmonious arrangement of trees, masses of planting and flowers, the entire cemetery will have the appearance of quiet beauty in keeping with its memorial purpose.

Trees along the drives should be uniform in character, spaced fifty feet apart to allow mature growth without crowding one another or the edge of the road. High-branched trees such as *Ulmus americana* create an appearance of dignity and still permit a satisfactory turf underneath.

Within the blocks of private lots trees should be placed on public easements where they need not be disturbed by future graves. Use permanent hardwood trees with deep root systems and clean foliage habits such as the oaks, Norway maple, European linden. Avoid quick-growing, softwood trees such as willows and poplars, and shallow-rooted trees like buckeye or sugar maple.

Cemeteries are not botanical gardens and should be planted for a quiet, dignified effect rather than botanical display. For evergreen trees use *Tsuga canadensis, Pinus strobus, Pinus sylvestris, Pinus nigra.* For lower evergreens use *Taxus cuspidata, Ilex crenata microphylla, Buxus sempervirens, Rhododendron* in variety, *Kalmia latifolia, Juniperus chinensis pfitzeriana.* Among the suitable deciduous small trees and shrubs are *Crataegus oxyacantha, Malus floribunda, Magnolia virginiana, Cornus florida, Syringa vulgaris, Philadelphus coronarius, Pyracantha, Spiraea vanhouttei,* and *Azalea nudiflora.* Flowers should be used only for general decorative effect and not scattered in small beds on individual lots. A fine display of iris, phlox or hardy chrysanthemums, arranged in masses at the entrance and in various locations throughout the cemetery, will be effective throughout the growing season and eliminate the necessity of a great many scattered plantings. For a selection useful in warmer regions *see* SUB-TROPICAL GARDEN and CALIFORNIA. — R. E. G.

**CENCHRUS TRIBULOIDES.** See Sandbur in the list at WEEDS.

*CENISIA, -us, -um* (se-nee'zi-a). From Mt. Cenis in the Alps.

**CENTAUREA** (sen-tor'ree-a). A genus of chiefly Eurasian herbs of the family Compositae, comprising over 500 species, a few of which are among our most popular garden flowers. They are annuals or perennials of diverse leaf-form but with their flowers in heads. The heads contain only tubular flowers, but some, along the edge, are often expanded and ray-like. Below the head is a series of overlapping bracts,* often cut or fringed. (Named for Centaur.)

From the garden standpoint the genus contains rather diverse plants. The annuals like the cornflower, basket-flower, sweet sultan, and *C. imperialis* are best treated as hardy annuals and sown where wanted. Unlike many annuals, they flower better and seem most happy when pretty crowded, so they need little thinning.

All the perennial species, except the dusty millers, can be grown in the open border like any other perennial. They are thrifty plants of apparently no special soil preferences. *Centaurea cineraria* and *C. gymnocarpa*, both known as dusty millers, are best carried over the winter as cuttings rooted the previous Sept. Their white-felty foliage does not like winter slush and rain. They are most of them summer bloomers.

**americana.** Basket-flower. Annual, and 4–6 ft. high, the leaves oblongish and mostly without marginal teeth. Heads 4–5 in. wide, the marginal flowers ray-like, hence the head set as though in a rose- or flesh-colored, shallow basket. The bracts below the head have fringed tufts. Central U.S. to Mex. A handsome garden favorite.

**cineraria.** Dusty miller. A perennial, 12–18 in. high, its foliage prominently white-felty. Leaves parted into blunt but narrow lobes. Heads large, yellow or purple. Southern Italy. For the garden cineraria *see* that entry.

**cyanus.** The cornflower and one of the most popular garden annuals, cult. under such names as bachelor's-button, bluebottle, and blue bonnets. A rather sprawling annual 1–2 ft. high, woolly when young, green later. Leaves narrow, nearly 5 in. long, without teeth or the lower sometimes cut. Heads typically pale blue (purple, pink, or white in hort. forms), the marginal flowers expanded and ray-like. Southern Eu. There is also a double-flowered form.

**dealbata.** A perennial of the dusty miller type, 18–24 in. high, its white-felty leaves cut into coarsely toothed lobes, the lower leaves sometimes a foot long. Heads with inner flowers red, the outer pink or white. Persia and Asia Minor.

**gymnocarpa.** Dusty miller. Perennial and white-felty, the leaves twice-cut into narrow, toothless segments. Heads small, rose-purple, grouped in clusters (panicles*), but mostly hidden by the leaves. Capri. A handsome foliage plant.

**imperialis.** An annual plant of hybrid origin, thought to be derived from a variety of the sweet sultan. It is 2–4 ft. high, and has fragrant heads in varied colors (white, purple, lilac or pink).

**macrocephala.** A perennial, 2–3 ft. high, the ovalish leaves toothed. Flower heads nearly 4 in. wide, yellow, the bracts* below them fringed. Armenia.

**montana.** Mountain bluet. A European perennial herb, its foliage white-hairy only when young. Leaves oblongish. Heads blue, often 3 in. wide, the marginal flowers much enlarged and ray-like. The bracts beneath the head are black-fringed.

**moschata.** Sweet sultan. Next to the cornflower the most popular of the annual centaureas. It is smooth, 1–2 ft. high, the leaves toothed or cut feather-fashion. Heads solitary, usually fragrant, yellow, red, purple, pink or white in some of the hort. forms and very handsome. The marginal flowers are much enlarged, ray-like or even fringed. Orient.

**nigra.** Knapweed; also called hardheads and Spanish buttons. A rough-hairy, rather weedy or coarse perennial, frequent as an escape all over the temperate world. Leaves oblongish, toothed or not, 4–6 in. long. Heads solitary, ball-like, rose-purple, usually less than 1 in. across. Eu.

**ruthenica.** A perennial, 2–3 ft. high, the leaves cut into fine, toothed segments. Flower heads pale yellow, the marginal ones larger than the center flowers, the bracts* beneath the head not toothed or fringed. Eurasia.

**CENTAURIUM** (sen-tor'ee-um). A comparatively unimportant genus of chiefly annual or biennial herbs of the family Gentianaceae, of little garden interest. They have opposite* leaves without marginal teeth, and without leafstalks. Flowers small, usually numerous in spikes or branched clusters (panicles*). Corolla salver-shaped, its lobes slightly twisted. Fruit a 2-celled capsule. (*Centaurium* is Latin for 100 gold pieces, in allusion to the supposed medicinal value.) The genus is often called *Erythraea*.

The only cult. species among the 25 known is suited only to sandy soils where it can be protected from too much sun. Treated as a hardy annual or biennial.

**confertum.** Centaury. An annual or biennial, not over 4 in. high, the stems usually several. Leaves fleshy, the lower ones mostly in a basal rosette, the upper ones narrow but blunt. Flowers small, rose-pink. Southwestern Eu. and England. Sometimes called *C. chloodes*.

**CENTAURY.** See CENTAURIUM CONFERTUM.

**CENTERPIECE.** See TERRARIUM.

---

* Special articles on the subjects indicated by an asterisk (*) will be found at the words so marked.

**CENTIFOLIA,** *-us, -um* (sen-ti-fō′li-a). A hundred-leaved.

**CENTIPEDE-GRASS** = *Eremochloa ophiuroides.*

**CENTIPEDE-PLANT** = *Muehlenbeckia platyclados.*

**CENTIPEDES.** See Insect Pests at SWEET PEA.

**CENTRADENIA** (sen-tra-dee′ni-a). Attractive greenhouse foliage plants of the family Melastomaceae, comprising perhaps half a dozen tropical American species, one not uncommon in cult. Branches 4-winged. Leaves opposite, one in each pair smaller than the other. Flowers rose-pink in a dense cluster (cyme*) that is shorter than the leaves. Calyx tubular, 4-lobed. Petals 4. Stamens 8. Fruit a 4-valved pod (capsule*). (*Centradenia* is from the Greek for spur and gland, referring to a feature of the anthers.*)

The plant below needs potting mixture* 2 and a warm-temperate greenhouse. If grown near the glass (shaded) it will respond with good color in its leaves. Easily propagated by cuttings.

    **grandifolia.** A showy, Mexican under-shrub, not over 2 ft. high. Leaves oval-lance-shaped, but unequal, 4-6 in. long and with generally 5 leading veins, bright red on the under side. Flowers rose-pink, in many-flowered clusters.

**CENTRANTHIFOLIA,** *-us, -um* (sen-tran-thi-fō′li-a). With foliage like the red valerian (*Centranthus*).

**CENTRANTHUS** (sen-tran′thus). A small group of mostly perennial herbs of the family Valerianaceae, from the Mediterranean region, the one below an attractive flower garden plant. Leaves opposite,* faintly or not at all toothed. Flowers small, red (in ours), in a dense terminal cluster, the corolla with a slender tube, but spurred at the base, 5-parted at the top. Stamen only 1. Fruit crowned by a bristly crest. (*Centranthus* is Greek for spurred flower.)

    **ruber.** Red valerian or Jupiter's-beard; also called scarlet lightning. A perennial, bushy herb 1-3 ft. high. Leaves oval or narrower, 3-4 in. long, stalkless and broad at the base. Flowers many, fragrant, about ½ in. long, the spur slender, red in the typical form but often crimson or white in some varieties. Eu. and southwestern As. An easily grown and favorite perennial garden plant. Sometimes offered as *Valeriana rubra.*

**CENTROPOGON** (sen-tro-pō′gon). Of over 100 species of tropical American under-shrubs of the family Lobeliaceae, only the following is of much garden interest. It is a favorite plant for hanging baskets, but needs a warm, moist greenhouse for proper growth. Leaves alternate,* stalked and finely toothed (in ours). Flowers scarlet or carmine (in the one below), solitary, on long stalks in the leaf-axils,* or in clusters. Corolla tubular, slightly irregular* from being somewhat split. Fruit a berry. (*Centropogon* is Greek for spur and beard, in allusion to the fringed stigma.)

    **lucyanus.** A little woody and 12-20 in. high. Leaves oblongish or oval. Flowers mostly in terminal clusters, rather showy, the corolla about 1½ in. long. Stamens* protruding, the anther* white-bristly.

**CENTROSEMA** (sen-tro-see′ma). Of over 30 species of these chiefly tropical American vines of the pea family only the butterfly-pea is cult. for ornament. The others, sometimes grown as cover crops in the tropics, are little known here. Leaves compound,* with 3 leaflets, the central one longer-stalked than the other two. Flowers typically pea-like, solitary or few in a long-stalked cluster. Pod long and narrow, tipped by a slender, weak point. (*Centrosema* is from the Greek for spur and a sign or standard.) The plants are sometimes called *Bradburya*.

The butterfly-pea is a pretty, summer-blooming stem climber, not much grown in the tropics and found wild from N.J. to tropical America. (*See* VINES.)

    **virginianum.** Butterfly-pea. A weak vine, not very tall-growing, often prostrate in the wild state. Leaflets ovalish, pointed at the tip, without teeth, 1-2 in. long. Flowers purple and white, about 1 in. long. Pod 4-5 in. long.

**CENTURY PLANT** = *Agave americana;* also, generally, any species of *Agave.*

**CEPA** (see′pa). Latin name for the onion.

**CEPHALANTHUS.** See BUTTON-BUSH.

**CEPHALARIA** (seff-a-lay′ri-a). Coarse, scabious-like herbs of the family Dipsacaceae, comprising over 30 species, mostly from the Mediterranean region, of which two are somewhat cult. in the flower garden. They are tall herbs with coarse, deeply cut leaves and roundish flower-heads at the ends of long stalks, the heads surrounded by a series of small bracts.* Flowers very small, densely packed in the head, yellow or white, the corolla 4-parted. Fruit a ribbed achene,* the minute calyx often crowning it. (*Cephalaria* is from the Greek for head, in allusion to the flower heads.)

Both the plants below are suited to the back of the more informal border. They are easily propagated by division, as both are stout perennials.

    **alpina.** Erect, 4-6 ft. high. Leaves much cut, feather-fashion. Flower heads about 1½ in. across, sulphur-yellow. Southern Eu.
    **tatarica.** Stiff, and 5-6 ft. high. Leaves cut feather-fashion into many, toothed segments. Flower heads nearly 2 in. across, white. Western As.

**CEPHALOCEREUS** (sef-fal-lo-seer′e-us). A striking group of perhaps 50 species of column-like cacti, chiefly Mexican and South American, a few cult. for their odd habit and the interesting, long, white, hair-like "wool" found on the old-man cactus (and some others) near the top of the plant. The plant body has many longitudinal ribs and sharp spines. Flowers chiefly night-blooming, small for the cacti, some of the flower often clinging to the fleshy fruit. (*Cephalocereus* is from the Greek for head and *Cereus*.) They are sometimes known as *Pilocereus*.

For culture *see* CACTI.

    **euphorbioides.** Usually a single column up to 15 ft. high, and a foot thick, prominently 8-ribbed, the spine-bases cottony. Flowers day-blooming, not over 2 in. long, brownish outside, rose-red in the inner petals. South American (?). Not much known outside the collections of specialists.
    **polylophus.** Tall, columnar, usually unbranched and occasionally 40 ft. high in Mex., much less in cult. Ribs 15-18, the spine-bases felted but not white-woolly. Flowers red, about 2 in. long.
    **senilis.** Old-man cactus. A popular and widely grown Mexican species, the plant body columnar, 30-40 ft. tall in the wild, usually much less in cult. Ribs 20-30. The top of the plant is crowned with a thatch-like collection of long white hairs. Flowers red, about 2 in. long.

**CEPHALONICA,** *-us, -um* (sef-fal-lon′i-ka). From Cephalonia, an Ionian Island.

**CEPHALOSTACHYUM** (sef-fal-lo-stake′i-um). A small group of East Indian bamboo-like grasses grown outdoors only in zone* 9. They have large leaves and many scattered spikelets in heads, these grouped in a large-branched cluster (panicle*). (*Cephalostachyum* is from Greek for head and spike.)

The only cult. species, little known in America, needs the same culture as the most tender of the bamboos.

    **pergracile.** Often 40 ft. high, its slender, ringed stems bluish-green. Leaves 9-12 in. long, 1½ in. wide, rough, and with a minutely saw-toothed leaf margin. The heads of flower spikelets about 2 in. apart. East Indies.

**CEPHALOTAXUS** (sef-fal-lo-tax′us). The plum-yews are Asiatic evergreen trees of the yew family (Taxaceae), often cult. for their fine foliage, and remarkable for the stalked, plum-like fruit. Leaves needle-like, very numerous and scattered, green above but with 2 bluish-gray bands beneath. For flowers *see* TAXACEAE. Fruit stalked, not cone-like, but fleshy, more or less egg-shaped and maturing the second season. (*Cephalotaxus* is from Greek for head and *Taxus*, in reference to the shape of the male flower.)

While both the cult. species are trees, they are usually shrubby as grown here. They are handsome evergreens, unsuited to regions of summer heat or dryness, but perfectly at home near the sea coast in the zones indicated below. They much resemble the closely related true yews, but the latter do not have the leaves 2-banded beneath.

    **drupacea.** A tree up to 30 ft., usually shrubby in cult. Leaves 1-2 in. long, pointed. Plum-like fruit green, about 1 in. long. Japan. Hardy from zone* 4 southward. The two best known of the many horticultural varieties are: var. **pedunculata,** with longer leaves and longer-stalked fruit (sometimes sold as *C. harringtoniana*); and var. **fastigiata,** with upright, columnar habit.
    **fortunei.** A tree up to 30 ft., usually with several stems, or in cult. shrubby. Leaves spreading nearly horizontally, 2-4 in. long. Fruit purple, about 1 in. long. Central China. Hardy from zone* 5 southward. When perfectly grown it should be a broad-headed tree with the tips of its branches pendulous.

**CEPHALOTES** (sef-fal-lō′tees). Like a small head.

---

\* Special articles on the subjects indicated by an asterisk (\*) will be found at the words so marked.

*CERASIFERA, -us, -um* (see-ra-sif′fer-ra). Bearing cherries or cherry-like fruit.

*CERASIFORMIS, -e* (see-ras-i-for′mis). Cherry-shaped.

**CERASTIOIDES** (see-ras-tee-oy′deez; but *see* OÏDES). Resembling a chickweed (*Cerastium*).

**CERASTIUM** (see-ras′tee-um). The 100 or so species of chickweed or mouse-ear chickweed, which belong to the pink family, are mostly weedy herbs (sometimes pests), but three of them are attractive garden plants. They have opposite* leaves, without marginal teeth, and slightly swollen joints, the foliage often hairy. Flowers small, white, but relatively showy from being in profuse, forked clusters in the cult. species. Sepals mostly 5. Petals 5, often 2-notched at the tip. Fruit a small capsule.* (*Cerastium* is from Greek for horn, alluding to the shape of the pod.)

The three cult. species are all perennials of the easiest culture, increased by division. Snow-in-summer is an extremely popular prostrate herb, very useful in the rock garden or border for its ground-covering habit, its mats of white foliage and white flowers.

**arvense.** Starry grassweed or field chickweed. A densely tufted perennial, 6–10 in. high. Leaves very narrow, about 1 in. long. Flowers many, white, about ⅓ in. wide. North temperate zone. April–May. Frequently a mere weed, but one of the earliest of white-flowered plants.

**biebersteini.** A creeping perennial, not over 6 in. high, the leaves about 1½ in. long and ⅙ in. wide, grayish-woolly. Flowers white, in May and June. Asia Minor.

**tomentosum.** Snow-in-summer. A popular, prostrate, garden plant, not over 6 in. high and forming large patches. Leaves numerous, about ½ in. long and ⅛ in. wide, conspicuously white-woolly. Flowers white, nearly ½ in. wide. June. Eu. It will grow in pure sand. *See* SAND GARDENS.

**vulgatum.** *See* Mouse-ear Chickweed in the list at WEEDS.

*CERASUS* (ser′a-sus). Classical name for the cherry.

**CERATONIA.** *See* CAROB.

**CERATOPHYLLUM** (ser-rat-o-fill′um). A single, submerged, aquatic plant and the only genus of the family **Ceratophyllaceae** (ser-rat-o-fil-lay′see-ee). They have finely dissected leaves, with thread-like segments at intervals along a fine, thread-like stem. Flowers extremely minute, without a true calyx or corolla. The only species, **C. demersum,** called hornwort, fish-blankets or cedar moss, is a delicate, submerged, water plant very useful in aquaria, to which it is easily transferred from the wild, where it grows in ponds or slow streams. (*Ceratophyllum* is from Greek for horn and leaf, in allusion to the stiffish, though very slender, leaves.)

**CERATOPTERIS** (ser-ra-top′ter-is). The floating or water ferns are the only cult. genus of the family **Parkeriaceae** (par-keer-ee-ā′see-ee). They are the only really aquatic ferns and have two sorts of fronds. While rooted in the mud, the sterile fronds are usually floating, but the fertile (spore*-bearing) fronds are erect, and twice or even more compound.* Both sorts are borne in rosettes. (*Ceratopteris* is from the Greek for horned fern.)

These more interesting than decorative plants can be best grown by planting in pots which are just below the surface of the water. They are useful for aquaria or greenhouse pools, but are not hardy where it freezes. The plants must be renewed each year, which may be done by detaching the buds from the leaves. These buds will produce new plants if kept just submerged and planted in good soil.

**pteridoides.** Sterile fronds floating, short-stalked, broadly triangular, the margins lobed. Fertile fronds divided into whip-like segments. Fla. to Brazil.

**thalictroides.** Segments of the sterile fronds more or less triangular, the frond long-stalked, floating, but some partly erect. Fertile frond similar, but the segments much finer. Tropics of the Old World.

**CERATOSTIGMA** (ser-rat-o-stig′ma). A small genus of herbs or low shrubs of the family Plumbaginaceae, from China and Africa, one grown as a border plant for its blue flowers. They have alternate leaves, hairy on the margins, and flowers in loose, head-like clusters which are surrounded by a series of stiff bracts. Corolla tubular, its limb* salver-shaped, the stamens* inserted in the tube. Fruit a 5-valved capsule, inclosed in the persistent, tubular calyx.* (*Ceratostigma* is from the Greek for horn and stigma.)

The only cult. species is an attractive, fall-blooming border plant with no special soil preferences. It is propagated by division.

**plumbaginoides.** A low or semi-prostrate, shrubby herb or woody, not over 1 ft. high. Leaves 2–3 in. long, broadest above the middle and tapering to the base. Flowers deep blue, not over ½ in. wide. China. Hardy from zone* 4 southward and an attractive plant for the blue garden. Aug.–Sept. Sometimes offered as *Plumbago larpentae.* A related Chinese shrub, *C. willmottianum,* with blue, but pink-tubed flowers, is also grown in Calif.

**CERCIDIPHYLLUM** (sir-sid-i-fil′lum). A single, Asiatic tree, commonly called the katsura tree, belonging to the family Trochodendraceae, and frequently cultivated for ornament. Leaves opposite* or nearly so, mostly borne on short spurs, the veins arranged finger-fashion. Male and female flowers on different trees. They are small, have no petals and are borne on the spurs as the leaves unfold. Fruit a splitting pod, with many seeds. (*Cercidiphyllum* is from *Cercis* and the Greek for leaf.)

**japonicum.** Katsura tree. A tree 30–50 ft., usually less in cult., and often divided into several trunks or stems. Leaves nearly round, heart-shaped at the base, 2–4½ in. long, shallowly and bluntly toothed, pale beneath. Jap. Hardy from zone* 3 southward. The *var.* **sinense,** with usually a single trunk and longer-stalked leaves, is hardy from zone* 4 southward. These are handsome foliage trees, the leaves purplish when unfolding, changing in the autumn from green to yellow and scarlet.

**CERCIDIUM** (sir-sid′i-um). A small genus of chiefly tropical American shrubs or trees of the pea family, one of which is wild in the southwestern U.S. and adjacent Mex. and is somewhat cult. in its native region. This cult. species, **C. torreyanum,** is the palo-verde or green-barked acacia, a desert shrub, that is green-barked, spiny and leafless for much of the year. Leaves (when present) alternate,* twice-compound,* falling at the end of spring. Flowers showy, yellow, not pea-like, but nearly regular,* about ¾ in. wide. Pods (legumes*) about 3 in. long. (*Cercidium* means like *Cercis*.)

**CERCIS.** *See* REDBUD.

**CERCOCARPUS** (sir-ko-kar′pus). In the western U.S., especially in Calif., is a group of evergreen shrubs or small trees of the rose family, commonly called the mountain mahogany, but not related to the true mahogany. Of the 20 known species only two are usually found in gardens and these are not hardy everywhere (*see below*). They have alternate* leaves, and small, greenish-white flowers without petals, usually in small clusters in the leaf-axils.* Stamens many, borne on the cup-shaped calyx.* Fruit small, dry, crowned by a long, silky plume. (*Cercocarpus* is from the Greek for tailed fruit.)

The chief attraction of these plants is their feathery, tailed fruits, the early bloom not being showy. The shrubs need open sunlight, a well-drained site, and are propagated by seeds or cuttings.

**betulaefolius** = *Cercocarpus betuloides.*

**betuloides.** A shrub, rarely a small tree, with scaly bark. Leaves oblongish, but broadest towards the tip, 1–2 in. long, bluntly toothed. Plume of the fruit 2½–4 in. long. Calif. Hardy from zone* 6 southward.

**montanus.** A shrub not over 5 ft. high, the bark fissured. Leaves rounded at the tip, 1–2½ in. long, finely hairy and pale beneath, coarsely toothed. Plume of the fruit 3–5 in. long. Western U.S. Hardy from zone* 5 southward.

*CEREALIS, -e* (seer-ee-ā′lis). Cereal-like, and named for Ceres, the goddess of agriculture.

*CEREFOLIA, -us, -um* (seer-ee-fō′li-a). A specific name of uncertain meaning; perhaps implying that leaves are like those of the genus *Chaerophyllum,* or named from the goddess Ceres.

**CERESAN.** A trademarked mercury fungicide, containing ethyl mercury phosphate, sold with directions for use.

**CEREUS** (seer′ee-us). As once understood, an immense genus of cacti, of very diverse habit, and popularly including the beautiful night-bloom cereus, now known to belong to other genera. As now restricted, *Cereus* has about 20 species, mostly South American and West Indian, three of which are cult. in the warmest parts of U.S. or in green-

---

* Special articles on the subjects indicated by an asterisk (*) will be found at the words so marked.

houses. They are mostly tall, even tree-like, plants with a columnar plant body that is deeply angled or ribbed, spiny, but without the long tufts of white hair found in the old-man cactus. Flowers funnel-shaped, night-blooming, white. Fruit fleshy and naked. (*Cereus* is Latin for a wax candle, perhaps in allusion to the shape of some former species.)

For culture *see* CACTI.

For the plants usually known as night-blooming Cereus *see* SELENICEREUS, NYCTOCEREUS, and HYLOCEREUS.

For other plants hitherto, and by some still called Cereus, *see* CORYPHANTHA, HELIOCEREUS, CEPHALOCEREUS, HOMALOCEPHALA, TRICHOCEREUS, ESCONTRIA, PACHYCEREUS, LEMAIREOCEREUS, BERGEROCACTUS, HARRISIA, MACHAEROCEREUS, APOROCACTUS, MYRTILLOCACTUS, CARNEGIEA, PENIOCEREUS, ECHINOCEREUS, WILCOXIA, and DEAMIA.

**jamacaru.** Mandacaru. Much-branched, often 20 ft. high and with a woody trunk at base. Ribs 4–6, with many sharp spines. Flowers nearly 12 in. long, white, but green on the outside. Brazil.

**peruvianus.** Tree-like, much-branched and sometimes 40 ft. high, the branches green or bluish-green, and with 4–9 ribs. Spines long, slender, needle-like. Flowers about 6 in. long, white, but reddish on the outside. Southeastern S.A.

**validus.** Not over 6 ft. high, more or less shrubby, bluish-green when young. Ribs 4–8, and blunt, the spines 5 in a cluster, short and stout. Flowers white, but reddish on the outside. Argentina.

***CERIFERA, -us, -um*** (see-rif'fer-ra). Wax-bearing.

**CERIMAN** = *Monstera deliciosa.*

**CERINTHE** (sir-rin'the). A small group of Eurasian herbs of the family Boraginaceae, one of them an annual flower garden plant cult. for its showy bloom. Leaves alternate,* often red or white-spotted. Flowers in 1-sided clusters, yellow, borne among numerous purple bracts.* Corolla nearly regular,* tubular. Fruit a group of 2 erect nutlets, very small. (*Cerinthe* is from the Greek for wax flower, the ancients assuming that bees harvested wax from them.)

The only commonly cult. species is a hardy annual easily grown from seed sown where wanted.

**retorta.** Honeywort. Not over 18–20 in. tall, the leaves generally bluish-green, the upper nearly stem-clasping by the eared base, gradually passing into the colored bracts* of the flower cluster. Flowers yellow, tipped with purple, protruding beyond the bracts.* Greece.

***CERNUA, -us, -um*** (sir'new-a). Cernuous; *i.e.* nodding.

**CEROPEGIA** (seer-ro-pee'ji-a). Tropical vines, or shrubby plants, comprising over 160 species of the milkweed family, all from the Old World, one of which is a greenhouse vine with wax-like flowers. Leaves opposite* (sometimes none), fleshy. Flowers in pairs (in ours), their long stalks in the leaf-axils.* Corolla tubular, a little curved and swollen at the base. Fruit a slender follicle.* (*Ceropegia* is from the Greek for wax fountain, in allusion to the waxy flowers.)

The only cult. species needs a warm, moist greenhouse and potting mixture* 3. Easily propagated by cuttings over bottom-heat.*

**woodi.** Prostrate or trailing and needing support for growing on walls. Leaves ovalish or roundish, about ½ in. long, heart-shaped at the base. Flowers pinkish-purple, waxy, about ½ in. long. Fruit smooth, 2–3 in. long. Natal.

**CEROXYLON** (see-rox'i-lon). Immensely tall feather palms from the northern Andean region, comprising 4 or 5 species, one of which, in the young state, is cult. outdoors in southern Calif. and in greenhouses. The trunk is ringed and spineless, crowned by huge leaves. The leaflets are long, rigid, and sword-shaped. Flowers unisexual,* rather large for a palm. Stamens 9–15. Fruit purplish, berry-like. (*Ceroxylon* is Greek for wax and wood, *see* below.)

In southern Calif. the wax palm is somewhat cult., but it does not approach its wild stature. (For greenhouse cult. *see* PALM.)

**andicolum.** Wax palm. Nearly 200 ft. high in the wild, far less in cult., the trunk slightly swollen about the middle, covered (at home) with a whitish, commercially important, wax. Leaves 15–25 ft. long, the under side of the leaflets white-scurfy. Fruit purple-red, just less than an inch in diameter. Andes of Colombia and Ecuador.

***CERRIS*** (ser'ris). A specific name of uncertain application to the turkey oak; perhaps from the Latin for fringe. (*See* OAK.)

**CERTINENSIS POPLAR** = *Populus berolinensis.*

**CESPITOSE.** *See* CAESPITOSA.

**CESTRUM** (ses'trum). A fragrant group of shrubs (some vine-like) or low trees, comprising over 150 species of the potato family, all tropical American and a few widely grown for their beautiful bloom. Leaves alternate,* without marginal teeth. Flowers numerous, in clusters at the ends, or the clusters in the leaf-axils.* Corolla tubular, the expanded part salver-shaped, the tube sometimes enlarged or contracted near the top. Fruit small, berry-like. (*Cestrum* is an old Greek name for some plant, of uncertain application here.)

These are handsome greenhouse plants, but also popular outdoors in zones* 8 and 9. They need a cool greenhouse and potting mixture* 4. Some are night-blooming and exceptionally fragrant, and a few are vine-like, especially *C. elegans.*

**aurantiacum.** More or less sprawling or half-climbing. Leaves ovalish, 2½–4 in. long. Flower clusters terminal, the flowers orange-yellow, about 1 in. long, the tips recurved. Guatemala.

**diurnum.** Day jasmine. A shrub 8–12 ft. high. Leaves oblongish or oval, 2–3½ in. long. Flower clusters on long stems from the axils,* the flowers white, about ½ in. long, very fragrant by day. W.I. Commonly planted in Fla.

**elegans.** Coral jasmine; also called purple cestrum. A shrub up to 10 ft. high, often vine-like, its branches softly hairy. Leaves 2–4 in. long, about 1½ in. wide. Flowers in terminal, nodding clusters, the corolla about ¾ in. long, red-purple, and constricted at the throat. Fruit red. Mex. The most popular of the cult. species, with forms also offered with rose-colored flowers and variegated leaves.

**nocturnum.** Night jasmine. A shrub 6–9 ft. high. Leaves oblongish or oval, 6–9 in. long. Flower clusters in the axils,* the flowers about ¾ in. long, greenish-white to cream-colored, very fragrant by night. W.I.

**parqui.** Willow-leaved jasmine. A shrub 3–6 ft. high, the leaves willow-like, 4–6 in. long. Flower clusters terminal and in the axils,* the flowers whitish or yellowish, about 1 in. long, very fragrant at night. Chile.

**CEYLON GOOSEBERRY** = *Dovyalis hebecarpa.*

**CHABLIS.** *See vinifera* varieties at GRAPE.

**CHAENOMELES** (kee-nom'e-lees). All the known species of the flowering quince, which belong to the rose family and come from eastern Asia, are popular garden shrubs, among the earliest to bloom. While closely related to the quince (*see* CYDONIA) and bearing many-seeded, quince-like fruits; these are, if not quite worthless, used only occasionally for preserves. Leaves alternate.* Flowers solitary or in small, close clusters, blooming before or with the unfolding of the leaves. Petals 5, showy. Stamens* many. Fruit a pome,* with brown seeds. (*Chaenomeles* is from the Greek meaning to split and apple, applied to these plants under the erroneous notion that they have splitting fruits.)

The flowering quinces are popular as specimen plants and they also are widely used for hedges. While they will not stand so much clipping as privet, their beautiful spring bloom offsets their usual lack of architectural symmetry. They are not particular as to soil and may be propagated by cuttings, layers, or by root cuttings.

**japonica.** Dwarf Japanese quince. Scarcely more than 3 ft. high, the branches often spiny. Leaves broadly oval, 1½–2 in. long, coarsely toothed. Flowers brick-red, about 1 in. wide. Fruit yellow, about 1½ in. long. Japan. March–April. Hardy from zone* 3 southward. Often sold as *Cydonia japonica,* and sometimes called merely japonica. It stands smoke.*

**lagenaria.** Japanese quince, or Japanese flowering quince. A shrub 4–6 ft. high, the branches somewhat spiny. Leaves oval-oblong, 2–3 in. long, finely toothed. Flowers scarlet-red (in the typical form), 1–1¾ in. wide. Fruit yellowish-green, nearly 2 in. long. China. March–April. Hardy from zone* 3 southward. There are varieties with pink or white flowers. The best of the flowering quinces for hedges.

**sinensis.** Chinese quince. A large shrub or small tree 8–20 ft. high and without spines. Leaves elliptic-oval, 2–3 in. long, sharply but finely toothed. Flowers light pink, usually solitary, about 1 in. wide. May. China. Hardy from zone* 4 southward.

**CHAEROPHYLLUM** (kee-ro-fil'lum). Of 30 or more species of this genus (family Umbelliferae), only the turnip-rooted chervil, or, as some call it, the bulbous chervil, is of any garden interest. Known as **C. bulbosum,** it is a European biennial which is somewhat cult. for its fleshy, edible root. Leaves compound,* the leaflets arranged feather-fashion. Flowers small, white, in a compound umbel.* The edible, spindle-shaped, tuberous root is blackish, but the flesh is yellowish. It is little grown here. (*Chaerophyllum* is from the Greek for scented foliage.)

* Special articles on the subjects indicated by an asterisk (*) will be found at the words so marked.

**CHAETOCHLOA** = Setaria.

**CHAFER.** For the control of rose chafer, see Insect Pests at Rose.

**CHAFEWEED** = *Gnaphalium sylvaticum*.

**CHAFF, CHAFFY.** The bracts* of many flowers, or sometimes the flower parts themselves, are chaffy or made up of chaff. This is thin, membranous, usually dry, and often brittle. Typical examples are found in the flowers of everlastings and in many grasses. Sometimes it is colored, as in the cockscomb.

**CHAIN FERN.** See Woodwardia.

**CHAINING TREES.** See Tree Surgery.

**CHAIRS AND AWNINGS.** See Ornament and Furniture.

**CHALCAS** = *Murraya*.

*CHALCEDONICA, -us, -um* (chal-see-don'i-ka). From Chalcedon (now Kaidiköi), near Istanbul.

**CHALICE VINE** = *Solandra guttata*.

**CHALK.** A poor substitute for lime in soil treatment, but common in the literature of gardening that originates in England, where chalk is also common. It has perhaps twice the bulk and half the value of lime (which see).

**CHALTA** = *Dillenia indica*.

*CHAMAECISTUS* (ka-mee-sis'tus). A specific name for a dwarf rockrose. See Cistus.

**CHAMAECYPARIS** (kam-ee-sip'ar-is). Very valuable timber trees and equally valuable as ornamental evergreen shrubs or trees of the pine family. In their young or juvenile (often permanent) form they are widely planted as retinispora (or retinospora) — perhaps the commonest evergreens in cult. and coming in many named forms. Leaves in mature plants scale-like, minute, closely pressed against the flattened, often fan-like branchlets. In the juvenile (often permanent) state the leaves are needle-like, but softish and stand out from the twigs. In some cult. specimens both sorts of leaves will be found, but in most retinisporas the needle-like leaves predominate. Flowers minute and of no hort. value. Fruit round, maturing the first season, the scales of the small cone, pointed or keeled in the middle, the cones not showy as in pines or firs. (*Chamaecyparis* is from the Greek for ground cypress.)

These extremely popular evergreens, often called false cypress, are grown throughout the U.S. unless it be the dry, hot plains and deserts. They do best in regions reasonably near the sea, and better in acid soils than in neutral or alkaline ones. (See Acid and Alkali Soils.) Where used in group plantings it is better to mulch the ground between them with straw or leaves, as the roots of some of the cult. forms are shallow.

For mass evergreen plantings, these and the arborvitaes and cedars are perhaps the finest of our conifers. Because many garden retinisporas die every year is no reason to stop planting them. But we must remember that they need moisture, do not like hot, dry winds, and, in some sections, should be protected during the winter (see Protecting Plants). Otherwise their culture is no more difficult than any other evergreen, but they repay for feeding, and some of them must be pruned to keep them shapely.

**lawsoniana.** Port Orford cedar, also called (in the West) Oregon or white cedar. In the forest a timber tree often 150 ft.; in cult. much less and forming a pyramidal tree with branches down to the ground, the bark reddish-brown. Foliage green or bluish-green, the leaves all scale-like, each often minutely white-streaked. Cones about ⅔ in. thick, reddish-brown, often with a bloom. Ore. to northern Calif. Hardy from zone* 4 southward if the rainfall is 30 in. per year or more. Will not stand long summer heat or drought. A magnificent evergreen known, especially in Eu., in over 80 garden forms. Three of the best are *var.* **glauca**, with steel-blue foliage; *var.* **argentea**, with foliage silvery; and *var.* **lutea**, where the young growth is yellow.

**nootkatensis.** Alaska cedar; also called Nootka, Sitka, or yellow cypress. In the forest taller than the last, but much less in cult., where it is uncommon, and the branches usually droop at the tip. Branchlets or twigs in fan-like growths, particularly toward the upper part of the tree. Leaves flat and scale-like, green both sides, rarely needle-like. Cones about ½ in. thick or less. Alaska to Ore. Hardy from zone* 4 southward, if the summers are reasonably moist. It will not stand high winds and dryness, especially in Feb. and March.

**obtusa.** Hinoki cypress. This and the next comprise most of the plants offered by nurserymen as retinisporas. It is a tree up to 120 ft. in Japan, much less in cult., where it has a multitude of forms. Leaves scale-like, pressed flat against the twigs in mature specimens, needle-like in the ordinary juvenile cult. forms, green above, faintly white-streaked beneath. Cones about ¾ in. thick, orange-brown, the scales with a sharp, but not prickly, tip. Hardy from zone* 3 southward, but it will not stand drought or hot drying winds.

Of its many hort. forms the following are most worth attention:
Color forms: *var.* **albo-spicata**, young foliage white-tipped
   *var.* **aurea**, foliage golden-yellow
Habit forms: *var.* **erecta**, columnar form
   *var.* **gracilis**, compact and pyramidal
   *var.* **compacta**, a low, broadly conical form and one of the most widely grown
   *var.* **pygmaea**, a very dwarf form with almost creeping branchlets

**pisifera.** Sawara cypress. A Japanese tree up to 150 ft., much lower in cult., where it makes a pyramidal tree of rather loose habit. The branchlets are flattened and fan-like, the closely appressed, scale-like leaves green above, white-streaked beneath. Cones about ⅓ in. in diameter, dark brown. Hardy from zone* 3 southward, but only in moist regions free from great summer heat and drying winds. It has many color forms, as those with silvery, golden, or variegated foliage. Habit varieties include *var.* **plumosa**, having dense, conical habit, and frond-like, feathery foliage; *var.* **filifera**, a pyramidal form with slender, drooping branches; and *var.* **squarrosa**, a dense bush or small tree, feathery, but the branchlets not flattened or frond-like.

**thyoides.** White cedar, also called southern white cedar. A bog or swamp tree usually not over 75 ft. high, mostly less, its bark reddish-brown. Foliage dark green, the leaves scale-like, keeled on the back and glandular.* Cones bluish-purple, about ⅓ in. in diameter. Me. to Fla. and Miss., especially common southward. Not much grown, but the hardiest of all the cult. species; far less attractive than the Asiatic species.

*CHAMAECYPARISSUS* (kam-ee-sip-a-ris'sus). Greek for a dwarf cypress.

**CHAMAEDAPHNE** (kam-ee-daf'ne). A single, evergreen bog shrub of the heath family, suitable to the bog garden but of little hort. value otherwise. The only species, **C. calyculata**, the leatherleaf, is found throughout the north temperate zone. It has alternate,* leathery, scurfy leaves, 1½–2 in. long, and small, white, nearly bell-shaped flowers in a terminal, leafy cluster (raceme*). Stamens 10. Fruit a small, dry pod. (*Chamaedaphne* is from Greek for ground or dwarf laurel.) The plant was once called *Andromeda calyculata*.

**CHAMAEDOREA** (kam-ee-dor'ree-a). A large genus of tropical American feather palms, of which many are cult. in Mexico, but only the following much known in greenhouse collections, although it is planted outdoors in southern Calif. and Fla. **Chamaedorea elegans** has a green, reed-like, ringed, spineless stem, usually several in a cluster, and not over 6–8 ft. high. Leaves having several narrow, long-pointed leaflets that are green both sides, not stiff or ridged. Male and female flowers on different plants, often not produced in cult. specimens. The plant is much used as a tubbed specimen for outdoor use, particularly in Fla. and Calif. patios. (*Chamaedorea* is from the Greek for a dwarf gift.) For cult. see Palm.

*CHAMAEDRYS* (kam-ee'dris). Pre-Linnaean* name for some germander. See Teucrium.

*CHAMAEIRIS* (kam-ee-eye'ris). A specific name meaning low iris. See Iris chamaeiris.

**CHAMAELIRIUM** (kam-ee-leer'i-um). A single, white-flowered herb of the lily family, found in the eastern U.S. and sometimes cult. in the wild garden. The only species is **C. luteum**, the devil's-bit (also called blazing star and fairy wand), a perennial with a bitter rootstock, mostly basal leaves that are broadest above the middle and 2–8 in. long. Male and female flowers on different plants, the spikes borne at the end of a wand-like stalk that reaches up 2–3½ ft. Stamens* (in the male flower) 6. Fruit a 3-lobed and 3-valved pod. (*Chamaelirium* is from the Greek for low lily.) Not much cult., as its tall spike is not particularly showy and each flower is scarcely ⅓ in. long. It needs a moist, partly shady place, and flowers in June.

**CHAMAEPEUCE** = *Cirsium diacantha*.

**CHAMAEROPS** (kam'ee-rops). A genus of only two, low, fan palms of the Mediterranean region, one of them widely

---

* Special articles on the subjects indicated by an asterisk (*) will be found at the words so marked.

cult. for ornament and perhaps the hardiest of all known palms. They commonly have several trunks or stems, not over 3 ft. high in cult., higher in the wild. Leaves fan-like, but deeply cut into many segments, the leafstalk slender and usually spiny. Male and female flowers on different plants or sometimes merely unisexual* on the same plant, borne in short, dense clusters among the leaves. Stamens 6–9. Fruit yellowish or reddish, small. (*Chamaerops* is from the Greek for low or dwarf bush.)

The species below is commonly planted outdoors throughout the warm parts of the U.S. almost up to the area of fairly severe frosts. It is also widely cult. in the cool greenhouse, where it is a very serviceable, bushy, foliage plant, well suited for decoration. Also useful for porches or for summer bedding, where it should be plunged. In Eu. and northern Africa it is grown as the source of African hair, a fiber extracted from the leaves.

humilis. Dwarf fan palm; also called European fan palm. As cult. mostly with several or many stems. Leaves bluish-green, the segments stiff, not drooping at the ends which are often deeply cleft. An easy palm to grow. For plants sometimes called *C. excelsa* and *C. fortunei*, see TRACHYCARPUS.

**CHAMISE LILY** = *Erythronium grandiflorum*.

**CHAMISO** = *Adenostoma fasciculatum*.

**CHAMOMILE** = Camomile.

*CHAMOMILLA* (kam-o-mill′ya). An old name for the wild camomile.

**CHAMPNEY ROSE** = *Rosa noisettiana*.

**CHA-NIWA.** A tea garden. See JAPANESE GARDEN.

**CHAPARRAL BROOM** = *Baccharis pilularis*.

**CHAPARRAL LILY** = *Lilium rubescens*.

**CHAPARRAL SNAPDRAGON** = *Antirrhinum coulterianum*. See SNAPDRAGON.

**CHAPMAN.** A cherry variety. See CHERRY.

**CHARACTER.** In ordinary hort. and botanical usage a character is any distinctive characteristic of a plant or its organs, common examples being height, color, texture, and many other *characters*. As a term in genetics character is used as an expression of a gene* or genes in a given environment and is used to designate any form, function, color, or other feature of an organism.

**CHARACTER PINE.** See Trees at JAPANESE GARDEN.

*CHARANTIA* (ka-ran′shee-a). Pre-Linnaean* name for the plant *Momordica charantia*.

**CHARCOAL.** This common form of carbonized wood has some garden uses, especially in sweetening soil mixtures for succulents, sometimes in the cutting bench, and in the rooting of plants like begonia. Ordinary fuel charcoal broken up in small pieces or powdered is all that is necessary. In the soil of the cutting bench it is of use to prevent or check damping-off.*

**CHARD.** The Swiss chard; for culture *see* BEET.

**CHARIEIS** (kar-ree′is). A single, South African herb of the family Compositae, sometimes grown as a hardy annual in the flower garden. It is of the easiest culture, seeds being sown where wanted. Lower leaves opposite,* without marginal teeth, the upper alternate.* Flower heads solitary, on long stalks, the disk* flowers yellow, the rays usually blue. (*Charieis* is from the Greek for elegant.)

heterophylla. An annual, more or less sprawling herb 6–12 in. high. Leaves oblongish, 1–2½ in. long. Flower heads about ¾ in. wide, the rays blue (occasionally violet or reddish-violet in varieties). Summer. South Africa.

**CHARITY** = *Polemonium caeruleum*.

**CHARLOCK** = *Brassica arvensis*.

**CHASTE TREE** = *Vitex agnus-castus*.

**CHAUTE** = *Ariocarpus retusus*.

**CHAYOTE** = *Sechium edule*.

**CHECKERBERRY** = *Gaultheria procumbens*.

**CHECKERBLOOM** = *Sidalcea malvaeflora*.

**CHECKERED LILY** = *Fritillaria meleagris;* and, in Calif., *F. lanceolata*.

**CHECK IRRIGATION.** See IRRIGATION.

**CHEDDAR PINK** = *Dianthus caesius*.

**CHEESES** = *Malva rotundifolia*. See Mallow in the list at WEEDS.

**CHEESEWOOD** = *Pittosporum undulatum*.

**CHEILANTHES** (ky-lan′theez). A large genus of mostly rock-loving ferns of the family Polypodiaceae, a few grown in the greenhouse or in the outdoor fern garden. They are widely distributed both in the tropics and in temperate regions. They have no obvious stem, the fronds all arising from the rootstock. Fronds twice- or thrice-compound,* the ultimate segments arranged feather-fashion, often hairy or scaly. The spore* cases are terminal on the veins. (*Cheilanthes* is from the Greek for lip and flower.) Most of them are called lip-ferns.

If grown in the greenhouse, care should be used to keep the house cool and well ventilated, and do not let the foliage stay wet. *See* FERNS AND FERN GARDENING.

densa. A tough, stout fern, the fronds not over 13 in. long (including the stalk) and thrice-compound,* the ultimate segments with a rolled margin. Western N.A.

gracillima. Lace-fern. A tufted, small fern with fronds scarcely more than 4 in. long, the stalk dark brown. Fronds twice-compound,* the ultimate divisions or segments about 9 to each primary division. Western U.S.

lanosa. Fronds 4–9 in. long, the stalk wiry and chestnut-brown, and covered with rusty hairs. The ultimate segments of the frond are more or less triangular or ovalish, regularly toothed, hairy. Conn. to Ga. and westward.

tomentosa. Fronds 4–8 in. long, the stalks densely covered with brown hairs. The ultimate segments of the frond very small, rather distant, the frond thus more open than in the other cult. species. Va. to Ga. Tex. and Mex.

*CHEILANTHIFOLIA*, -us, -um (ky-lan-thi-fō′li-a). Having leaves like a lip-fern (*Cheilanthes*).

**CHEIRANTHUS** (ky-ran′thus). Perhaps a dozen perennial herbs of the mustard family, scattered from Madeira to the Himalayas, one the widely cult. wallflower, *C. cheiri*. It is a hardy plant 12–13 in. high, covered with minute, forked hairs. Leaves narrow, with few or no marginal teeth, 1–3 in. long and often clustered beneath the flowers, which are in terminal clusters (spikes* or racemes*). Flowers with 4 clawed* petals, yellow or orange-brown, fragrant. Fruit a pod 2–2½ in. long, thickish, angled and with a short, protruding tip. (Origin of the name obscure.)

The wallflower has been a garden favorite from remote antiquity. Originally a native of southern Eu., it has been much improved, so that it now comes also in reddish or reddish-black shades and some forms have double flowers. Some of the special color varieties do not come true from seed and should be increased by division or even by cuttings. The plant does not like wet or slushy winters and in such places is better wintered in the cold frame. The wallflower blooms early in the spring, and, as its name implies, it is useful in the rock wall. But it is also much grown for the border and a bedding plant. In the latter case, seeds sown the previous August are potted up and carried over the winter in the cold frame. For the plant sometimes called *Cheiranthus allioni* see ERYSIMUM ASPERUM; for *C. linifolius* see ERYSIMUM LINIFOLIUM.

*CHEIRI* (ky′ree). An Arabic name for some plant, but of uncertain application to the wallflower. See CHEIRANTHUS.

**CHELIDONIUM** (kelly-dō′ni-um). A single, perennial, somewhat weedy, Eurasian herb of the poppy family, commonly called celandine, killwort, or sightwort. This plant, *C. majus*, is of secondary hort. importance, but frequently escapes* from old gardens. It is 12–30 in. high, and has deeply divided or cleft leaves, distinctly pale bluish-green beneath. Flowers yellow, in small, stalked clusters (umbels*). Sepals 2. Petals 4, the flower not over ⅔ in. long. Fruit a slender pod, splitting from the base upward. (*Chelidonium* is Greek for swallow, in allusion to the plant blooming when

---

* Special articles on the subjects indicated by an asterisk (*) will be found at the words so marked.

swallows arrive.) There is also a *var.* **laciniatum** with more finely divided leaves.

**CHELONE** (kel-lō'nee). A small group of North American perennial herbs of the family Scrophulariaceae, two of which are garden subjects, and one, the red turtlehead, a showy plant. Leaves opposite,* toothed. Flowers irregular* and 2-lipped, the upper lip arching and notched. The flowers are stalkless in a compact, terminal spike, only one or two flowering at a time. Stamens 5, one sterile and shorter than the other 4. Fruit a capsule.* (*Chelone* is Greek for turtle's head.)

The plants need partial shade and a reasonably moist site, especially the first species, which inhabits swampy woods or moist thickets. They are easily propagated by division.

**glabra.** Turtlehead; called also snake-head and shell-flower. Not usually over 24 in. high, often half that. Leaves oblong-lance-shaped, 3–6 in. long, short-stalked. Flowers white (rarely pinkish), about 1 in. long. Newfoundland to Ga. and westward. Summer.

**lyoni.** Red turtlehead. The most desirable for the garden. Leaves ovalish, 4–7 in. long and longer-stalked. Flowers rose-purple, about 1 in. long. Mountains of the Carolinas and Tenn., but hardy much farther north. Summer.

**CHENILLE PLANT** = *Acalypha hispida*.

**CHENOPODIACEAE** (ken-o-po-di-ā'see-ee). The goosefoot family, often called the beet or spinach family, is of the greatest interest to gardeners because it contains among its 75 genera and perhaps 600 widely distributed species, not only the beet and spinach (which see), but a few garden ornamentals of wide cultivation, as well as many pernicious weeds (the goosefoots).

The family contains mostly annual or perennial herbs, and a few shrubby plants, most of them with scurfy foliage and alternate* leaves. Flowers always inconspicuous, prevailingly greenish or whitish, without petals, often unisexual,* and sometimes with male and female flowers on different plants. Fruit dry (an achene* or a utricle*) or berry-like in the strawberry-blite and *Rhagodia*.

Besides the spinach and beet (which includes chard), the garden genera are *Atriplex* (the orach), *Chenopodium* (mostly weedy, but including Good-King-Henry); and *Kochia* (summer cypress). *Rhagodia* and *Salsola* are salt-tolerant plants of little garden interest, but sometimes planted in saline situations.

Technical flower characters: Plants monoecious* or dioecious,* or at least unisexual.* Calyx 2–5-parted, or merely of 1 sepal, or none. Petals none. Ovary superior,* 1-celled, 1-ovuled, its styles 1–3.

**CHENOPODIUM** (ken-o-pō'di-um). The goosefoots or pigweeds comprise a genus of 60 species of herbs of the family Chenopodiaceae, many of them pernicious weeds. The two below are of moderate hort. interest. Leaves alternate,* often angled and toothed, usually mealy. Flowers small and inconspicuous. (For details see CHENOPODIACEAE.) Fruit small, dry, often enclosed by the persistent calyx. (*Chenopodium* is Greek for goosefoot, in allusion to the shape of the leaves of some species.)

The ones below are of very easy culture and any of them may soon become weedy if not kept under control.

**album.** See Pigweed in the list at WEEDS.

**ambrosioides.** See Mexican Tea in the list at WEEDS.

**bonus-henricus.** Good-King-Henry; also called mercury. A rank perennial with a deep rootstock from which arise several stems 12–30 in. high. Leaves spinach-like and sometimes grown for greens, more or less triangular, the margins slightly wavy. Eu.

**botrys.** Feather geranium or Jerusalem oak. A rank-smelling annual, much-branched and 12–24 in. high. Leaves more or less wavy-margined or somewhat toothed or cut. Flower clusters profuse, not showy, but much aggregated into sprays or collections of small, head-like clusters. Eurasia and Af., also widely naturalized in N.A.

**capitatum.** See Strawberry Blite in the list at WEEDS. This is also called *Blitum capitatum*.

**CHERIMOLA.** An adaptation of the vernacular *cherimoya*.

**CHERIMOYA** = *Annona cherimola*.

**CHEROKEE ROSE** = *Rosa laevigata*.

**CHERRY.** Three representatives of the great genus *Prunus* to which cultivated cherries belong are commonly cultivated in North America: sweet cherries, sour cherries, and the dukes, hybrids between sweet and sour sorts. All three groups are profoundly influenced by the natural environment in which they are grown — sweet cherries rather more so than any other fruit, either soil or climate dictating whether they may or may not be grown. Still some cherry may be grown in almost every agricultural region of the continent. The cherry industry, east of the Rocky Mountains, is of importance only in the states touching on or near the Great Lakes.

Cherries are propagated by budding on seedlings of two wild stocks, known by nurserymen as Mazzard and Mahaleb. Experience the country over and experiments at several experiment stations have demonstrated that the Mazzard is so much the better stock that no cherry grower should ever plant a tree on Mahaleb stock; yet, because the latter is the cheaper stock to grow, most of the sour cherries offered by nurserymen are on the worthless Mahaleb.

The sour cherry is the hardiest to cold of any of the tree fruits and the vagaries of weather in the growing season seldom affect it. The sweet cherry, on the other hand, must be coddled at every turn in climatic requirements since it is tender to cold, subject to spring frosts, and heat and rain cause the ripening cherries to crack. The dukes fall in between the sweets and sours in adaptability to climates — some following the sours, others the sweets.

SOILS. Sweet and sour cherries grow with proper vigor in quite different soils. Growers of sweet cherries conceive an ideal soil for this fruit to be a dry, warm, friable, gravelly or sandy loam. The sour cherry excels on strong, fertile loams or clays, well-drained, yet retentive of moisture. Soils with wet, cold, clammy subsoils furnish a combination for any cherry which defies the best of care and culture. Either sweet or sour cherries can be grown on soils other than that set down as ideal, but for a large, finely finished product only the soils described are suitable.

Often the uncertainty in the setting of the cherry crop is not due to either climate or soil but to self-sterility of varieties. In selecting varieties, ascertain whether or not they need cross-pollination, and if so plant to make sure of its taking place.

PLANTING. All of the refinements of soil preparation and good planting are needed in setting cherry trees, for no other tree fruit suffers greater loss between nursery and orchard. Moist, mellow soil, good root-run, roots carefully spread, soil firmed — these are the most important items in planting. It is patent to the eye of every passer-by that cherries are often set too close. Sour cherries should be set 20 × 20 ft. and the sweets 24 × 24 ft., these distances to be varied in accordance with soil and variety. Spring is the best time to set sweet cherries and perhaps most sours are put out in this season, although fall would probably suit sour cherries as well. Most fruits are cut back at setting time, but cherries grow better when the branches are not headed back.

Two forms of top are in vogue, the spire-shape and the vase-shape. Sour cherries are almost always grown to spires with a close center, but a good many sweets are vase-form with an open center, though more and more all cherry trees are trained to center trunks with many subsidiary branches. Cherry trees are pruned but little after the first two or three years, by which time the saplings are shaped. As with every fruit tree, dead, injured, crowded and crossed branches must be taken out. Perhaps the cherry needs less pruning than any other inhabitant of the orchard. For fan or espalier trees and the method of producing them, *see* Fruit Trees at TRAINING PLANTS.

CULTIVATION. The general tuning up in the cultivation of the orchard during the last quarter-century has had its influence on cherry culture. Perhaps in this time purposeful cultivation has doubled the cherry output throughout the country. When drouth comes, as so often happens when cherries are ripening, the crop on sod-bound trees is ruined. A cherry orchard should be plowed in late fall, and in the spring cultivators should be kept steadily at work over the ground once in two weeks until cherry-picking, after which a

---

* Special articles on the subjects indicated by an asterisk (*) will be found at the words so marked.

cover crop should be sown. Cherries seldom respond to commercial fertilizers, the exceptions being on light soils where nitrate of soda at the rate of 200 pounds to the acre more than pays for its cost.

Cherries are picked for the markets a few days before full ripeness, but should be dead ripe for home use. Sweet cherries go to market in small baskets, of which 4-pound and 8-pound sizes are commonest; larger sizes for the sours are generally used. In fancy grades all of the fruits are layered stems down.

Varieties of the three groups are described in order of ripening.

### SWEET CHERRIES

Seneca. Fruit purple-black, round-cordate, soft, richly flavored. Tree tall, very vigorous, productive. Zones* 3 and 4 except in the plains states.

Governor Wood. Fruit yellow, small, soft-fleshed, sweet, very good. Tree hardy, not always productive, fairly vigorous. Zones* 3 and 4 east of Mississippi.

Black Tartarian. Fruit purplish-black, medium-sized, soft, juicy, delicious flesh. Tree very vigorous, productive, hardy. Suitable for all localities east of the Rocky Mountains.

Napoleon. Fruit yellow, with a red blush, large, firm-fleshed, splendid quality, sometimes crack at ripening. Tree large but fastidious as to soil and not very hardy. Favored parts of zones* 2 and 3 east of the Great Lakes.

Schmidt. Fruit black, round-cordate, large, firm, sweet. Tree healthy, hardy, productive. All cherry regions in zones* 2, 3 and 4.

Bing. Fruit dark red, large, broad-cordate, flesh firm, sweet, very good. Tree large, vigorous, fastidious as to soils and not very hardy. Favored spots in zones* 2, 3, and 4 east of the Great Lakes.

Giant. Fruit purplish-black, large, round-cordate, firm, sweet, rich, very good. Tree vigorous, productive, fairly hardy. Cherry regions in zones* 2, 3, and 4.

Windsor. Fruit purple, large, firm, crisp, sweet, very good. Tree very vigorous, hardiest of the sweets, productive. Zones* 2, 3, and 4 wherever cherries can be grown.

### DUKES

Reine Hortense. Fruits light red, firm, large, handsome, delicious in quality. Tree hardy and vigorous but sometimes unproductive. Zones* 2, 3, and 4 in all cherry regions.

Royal Duke. Fruits dark red, very large, handsome, sprightly and refreshing. Tree large, vigorous, very productive. Cherry regions in zones* 2, 3, and 4.

### SOUR CHERRIES

Early Richmond. Fruits small, early, culinary purposes. Tree large and very vigorous, hardy, and productive. Zones* 2 and 3 where sour cherries can be grown.

Montmorency. Fruit bright red, large, tart, firm flesh. Tree large, very hardy, vigorous and productive. The standard sour cherry for zones* 2, 3, and 4.

English Morello. Fruit reddish-black, medium size, firm, very late, excellent for cooking. Tree small, vigorous, hardy. Zones* 2 and 3 where sour cherries are grown. — U. P. H.

### WESTERN CHERRY GROWING

Cherry growing in the Far West is confined mainly to Calif., Oreg., Wash., Idaho and Utah. According to the 1930 census there are 2,974,236 sweet cherry trees in the above 5 states. Of this total, it is estimated that they are distributed as follows: Calif. 47%, Oreg. 25%, Wash. 17%, Utah 6%, and Ida. 5%. About 90% of all the sweet cherries produced in the U.S. are grown in these states, and 10% or less of the sour cherries, none of which are produced commercially in California.

VARIETIES. While a great number of varieties are grown, the important ones are: Napoleon (Royal Ann), Bing, Lambert, Black Tartarian, and Republican. The Chapman and Burbank are grown extensively in the early sections of Calif.

The sweet cherry presents a serious pollination problem in the West, in that all varieties are self-sterile, and the three most important varieties — Napoleon, Lambert, and Bing — are intersterile. Black Tartarian and Republican are quite satisfactory pollinizers for Napoleon and Bing, but most years the Lambert blossoms too late to be pollinized by them. Several other varieties are also used as pollinizers.

CULTURE. Most growers practice clean culture during the summer. They may plant cover crops in the fall, or depend upon weed growth, which is turned under in the spring. Quite frequent summer cultivations are given, and in many cases excessive cultivation is practiced. Where irrigation water is plentiful, many growers use a permanent cover crop — generally alfalfa. The alfalfa may be cut and removed, left in the orchard to rot, or allowed to grow undisturbed. There seems to be some evidence to indicate that permanent cover cropping is a desirable practice where it can be followed.

The fertilizer practice is quite variable, and there is practically no experimental basis for the practices used. A common practice is to apply a nitrate fertilizer, 2 to 4 pounds per tree, just previous to bloom. In some older orchards as much as 15 to 20 pounds are applied.

The sweet cherry crop of the West is either sold fresh as dessert fruit or processed (canned, frozen pack, or barreled). The Napoleon, a white variety, is the only one used extensively for processing. All the other important varieties grown are black sorts and are disposed of fresh.

The disposition of the crop determines the care in harvesting. Cherries for eastern shipment must be picked and handled with the utmost care. The cherries are sometimes taken to the packing house in the picking receptacles, but generally are dumped into various types of field boxes. Fruit for processing is generally delivered in 50-pound boxes.

All fruit for distant markets is packed in boxes. Many sizes and styles of packages are used from the standard 10-pound box of Calif. to boxes containing 25 to 30 pounds. Most of the smaller packages are faced by placing the individual fruits in rows and then the box is filled with uniform fruit. — G. L. P. For the flowering cherry see PRUNUS.

INSECT PESTS. The plum curculio (see APPLE) affects cherry; the larvae feed in the fruit, causing wormy cherries. Lead arsenate sprays before and after blossoming, with perhaps one or two applications later about 2 weeks apart, give control. Excessive arsenical residue may be removed by washing in a strong stream of water. Two species of maggot, similar to the apple maggot, injure fruit in the North. The sprays for curculio will kill adults. The pear slug, dark olive-green larva of a sawfly, feeds greedily on cherry leaves. Early injury may be controlled with the lead arsenate sprays applied as for the plum curculio; injury later in the season is easily stopped by spraying with arsenicals after the fruit is off. Fungicides are often included in these sprays.

Scale insects are not abundant or hard to control on sour cherry, but San Jose scale is very serious on sweet cherry; it yields to dormant sprays of oil or lime-sulphur. Black cherry aphids can be controlled with nicotine, applied before blossoming. Mites and bark beetles sometimes affect cherry, as they do other orchard fruits.

DISEASES. The three outstanding diseases on cherries are brown-rot, yellow leaf or shot-hole, and black-knot. Each name is descriptive of the symptoms. The brown-rot attacks the fruit after it has begun to ripen, and is especially destructive during shipment. The fruit decays and is covered with an ashen-gray mold. Later the host tissue shrivels into a dried mummy, and may remain hanging on the tree. When the affected fruit drops to the ground and is protected from total decomposition by being covered with old leaves or straw, the fungus causing the disease remains alive until spring, when it produces cup-like fruiting bodies which bear an immense number of spores. These float upward and finally affect the new crop. The blossoms may be blighted, the fruit rotted and the leaves affected. The fungus spreads rapidly in wet weather during the summer.

The yellow leaf of cherry causes defoliation, after the leaves have become spotted and discolored. This defoliation not only weakens the trees so that they succumb to low temperatures during the winter, but it also reduces the number of fruit buds for the following year, and delays ripening of the current crop so that maggots have more opportunity of causing damage. The fungus lives in the old leaves on the ground from which the spores are splashed to the new foliage in the spring. It then spreads rapidly until the whole tree from a distance may appear yellow.

Black-knot occurs also on wild cherries and plums, and is most injurious in orchards that have been neglected for some time. The disease affects only the woody parts. The knots begin by an enlargement and cracking of the wood which finally develops into olive-green knots of varying shape and size. Later the knots turn black and become hard and brittle. The fungus does not spread rapidly, but when the knots are not removed they may finally destroy the value of the tree.

The control measures are the removal of a dead or injured wood, cankers and knots as soon as these occur, and having a careful spray or dust program. On sour cherries, lime sulphur, 1–40, should be applied just before blossoms open, at petal-fall, when shucks have fallen, just before the fruit turns red and when yellow leaf is serious, after the fruit is picked. On sweet cherries a dilution of 1–50 is recommended since they are susceptible to spray injury.

**CHERRY BIRCH** = *Betula lenta*. See BIRCH.

**CHERRY FAMILY.** See ROSACEAE.

**CHERRY LAUREL.** See LAUROCERASUS.

**CHERRY PEPPER** = *Capsicum frutescens cerasiforme*.

**CHERRY PIE** = *Valeriana officinalis* and *Heliotropium arborescens*.

**CHERRY PLUM** = *Prunus cerasifera*.

---

* Special articles on the subjects indicated by an asterisk (*) will be found at the words so marked.

**CHERRY TOMATO** = *Lycopersicum esculentum cerasiforme.* See TOMATO.

**CHERVIL.** For the salad chervil see ANTHRISCUS CEREFOLIUM. For the bulbous or turnip-rooted chervil see CHAEROPHYLLUM BULBOSUM. Both are often called merely chervil.

**CHESTNUT.** A small group of important nut and timber trees constituting the genus **Castanea** (kas-tay'nee-a) which belongs to the family Fagaceae. They are mostly tall trees with furrowed bark and alternate, toothed leaves that have several parallel veins arising at the midrib. Male flowers in small, erect catkins,* its calyx 6-parted; petals none. The female flower on the lower part of the male catkin. Fruit the familiar chestnut, usually 3 in a prickly bur. Of the eight known species four are in cult. and one or two of them are important. (*Castanea* is the classical Latin name for the chestnut.) In Eu. chestnut usually refers to the horse-chestnut (which see).

For Culture see below.

C. crenata. Japanese chestnut. Usually not over 30 ft., often considerably less, and shrub-like. Leaves oblong or elliptic, 4–7 in. long, with rounded, not sharp, teeth. Bur about 2 in. in diameter, the nuts 2 or 3. Japan. Hardy from zone* 4 southward. More useful for breeding possibly blight-free hybrids than for its own fruit. Often sold as *Castanea japonica.*

C. dentata. American chestnut. A tree up to nearly 100 ft. high, now nearly exterminated in the northeastern U.S., but freely suckering from the bottom. Leaves oblongish, 5–9 in. long, coarsely toothed. Bur 2–3½ in. in diameter, the nuts usually 3. Me. to Mich. and Ala. Hardy from zone* 3 southward, but not now planted within the area of the blight (see below).

C. japonica = *Castanea crenata.*

C. pumila. Chinquapin. A shrubby, American tree usually not over 20 ft. Leaves oblongish, 3–7 in. long, coarsely toothed or the teeth merely bristles, white and felty beneath. Bur about 1½ in. in diameter, the nut mostly solitary. Pa. to Fla. and Tex. Hardy from zone* 4 southward.

C. sativa. Spanish chestnut. A tree up to 90 ft., usually round-headed in age. Leaves oblongish, 7–12 in. long, coarsely toothed, hairy or even felty beneath. Bur 2–4 in. in diameter, the nuts 1–3, nearly twice the size of the native American chestnut. Mediterranean region. Hardy from zone* 5, or in protected places in zone* 4, southward. The finest of all the chestnuts for size of the nut and productiveness. There are several hort. varieties. See below.

### CHESTNUT CULTURE

Growing chestnut trees for their fruit is dependent upon freedom from the blight which has destroyed nearly all the native American chestnut trees from central Maine, N.H. and Vt. to most of Mich., and southwestward to include the Alleghenies. In other words, any attempt to grow chestnuts is extremely dangerous or impossible in the following states: Me., N.H., Vt., Mass., R.I., Conn., N.Y., Pa., N.J., Del., Md., Va., West Va., Ohio, Southern Mich., Ind., and in some of the mountainous parts of Ky., Tenn., S. Car., N. Car., Ga., and Ala.

And the blight is constantly spreading so that only last-minute information on your area would be of any value, and should be secured from your local experiment station before attempting a plantation.

In blight-free areas, preferably many miles from the nearest infestation, good crops of the native American species and of the much larger-fruited Spanish chestnut can be raised. The trees are not particular as to soil, except that low wet sites are to be avoided. Rocky, well-drained hillsides are ideal, and they thrive in sandy loams.

Occasional trees of both the European and American chestnuts appear to be immune to blight. These are now being worked over by plant-breeding experts to determine whether they can be successfully propagated, and used for crossing with Japanese and Chinese varieties which are either immune or nearly immune to the disease. The chinquapin also is of use, as this has so far escaped the blight.

While many varieties of both the European and American chestnut have been developed in the past, and commercial production of the nuts was important, the blight has thrown chestnut cultivation into such a chaotic condition that it is impossible as yet to specify blight-free varieties. Some years of breeding the European, American, Japanese and Chinese kinds are still necessary before chestnut production in the area now occupied by blight will be safe. There are a few successful chestnut orchards left in the Middle West. The most promising feature of an admittedly difficult problem is the research of the U.S. Department of Agriculture in breeding new and disease-resistant varieties.

INSECT PESTS. Snout beetles or weevils, ¼ to ½ in. long, deposit eggs in chestnuts on trees late in the summer. The larvae feed within the chestnuts, causing them to become wormy. Destruction of infested nuts will reduce future numbers of weevils; it has been suggested that arsenical sprays late in the summer may destroy adults. The weevils in the nuts may be killed by fumigation with carbon disulphide. The larva of the two-lined chestnut borer works between the bark and the wood. By keeping the trees healthy borer injury can be avoided.

DISEASES. The most important disease of chestnut is the blight or *Endothia* canker for which there is no known cure. Introduced about 1900, this disease has destroyed practically every chestnut tree in the eastern U.S. See above. The fungus spores enter through wounds and infect the inner bark. Branches are girdled and the leaves shrivel and appear blighted. Leaves thus killed cling to the tree for months and are useful in recognizing the disease. The fungus does not penetrate below the ground level, hence the tree roots remain alive for a long time. Numerous sprouts arise from these roots and these often give the impression that the tree is recovering. Sooner or later, however, these are killed and their places taken by new shoots. Such sprouts are not likely to develop immunity to the disease, since they are but a part of the old tree which was originally attacked, and the sprouts are in no way different from the parent tree.

Asiatic species of chestnut are resistant to the disease, but hybrids of these with the American chestnut have been of uncertain value. Chestnut heartwood is very resistant to decay, but the sapwood succumbs easily to the attacks of wood-rotting fungi. The most common leaf disease of chestnut is powdery mildew. Where this disease threatens, control it by the use of sulphur fungicides.

**CHESTNUT FAMILY** = Fagaceae.

**CHESTNUT OAK.** In the East, *Quercus montana* (see OAK); on the Pacific Coast, *Lithocarpus densiflora.*

**CHEWING INSECTS.** See INSECT PESTS.

**CHIANTI.** See *vinifera* varieties at GRAPE.

**CHICKADEE.** See BIRDS.

**CHICKASAW PLUM** = *Prunus angustifolia.*

**CHICKEN-CORN** = *Holcus sorghum drummondi.*

**CHICKEN GRAPE** = *Vitis cordifolia.*

**CHICKEN MANURE.** See MANURE.

**CHICK-PEA.** See CICER.

**CHICKWEED.** See CERASTIUM and STELLARIA; see also Chickweed in the list at WEEDS.

**CHICKWEED FAMILY** = Caryophyllaceae.

**CHICKWEED WINTERGREEN** = *Trientalis borealis.*

**CHICLE TREE** = *Sapota achras.*

**CHICORY** = *Cichorium intybus.*

**CHICORY FAMILY.** See COMPOSITAE.

**CHILDREN'S GARDEN.** See SCHOOL GARDENING.

**CHILDS FRICK ARBORETUM.** See ARBORETUM.

**CHILEAN ARBORVITAE** = *Libocedrus chilensis.* See INCENSE CEDAR.

**CHILEAN BELLFLOWER** = *Lapageria rosea* and *Nolana atriplicifolia.*

**CHILEAN GUAVA** = *Myrtus ugni.*

**CHILEAN JASMINE** = *Mandevilla suaveolens.*

**CHILEAN TARWEED** = *Madia sativa.*

*CHILENSIS, -e* (chill-en'sis). From Chile.

**CHILI PEPPER** = *Capsicum frutescens.*

*CHILOENSIS, -e* (chill-o-en'sis). From Chile.

**CHILOPSIS** (ky-lop'sis). A single, rather showy, small tree or shrub of the family Bignoniaceae, found in the southwestern U.S. and adjacent Mex. The only species, **C. linearis**, the desert or flowering willow, is cult. there for ornament, and also in other warm parts of the country. It seldom exceeds 15 ft. Leaves narrow, willow-like, 3–5 in. long. Flowers in a short terminal cluster (raceme*). Corolla crimped, lilac, with a pair of yellow stripes inside, about 1½ in. long. Fruit a cylindric, many-seeded pod, nearly

---

* Special articles on the subjects indicated by an asterisk (*) will be found at the words so marked.

12 in. long. While the plant grows in dry regions it favors moist sites in them. (*Chilopsis* is from the Greek for lip-like.) It is sometimes called mimbre in N. Mex. and Mex.

**CHILOTES.** See EPITHELANTHA MICROMERIS.

**CHIMAERA** (ky-meer'ra). A specific name of uncertain application, possibly a mythological reference to a flame.

**CHIMAPHILA** (ky-maf'fil-a). A small genus of low, evergreen herbs of the heath family, the two below natives in N.A., and attractive wild flowers. They are suited only to the wild garden. They are perennials, with slightly woody stems and clustered, leathery leaves. Flowers nodding or spreading, in a sparse terminal cluster. Petals 5, concave, somewhat waxy. Stamens 10. Fruit a dry, 5-valved capsule. (*Chimaphila* is for winter-loving, in reference to the evergreen leaves.)

These plants are not of easy culture. They must be grown in rich woods soil, preferably leaf mold that is well decomposed and not too acid. They may also rely on fungus or bacterial organisms at their roots for part of their food supply. Consequently, they must be dug from the wild with plenty of their native soil and even then often fail. See WILD GARDEN.

*maculata.* Spotted wintergreen, also called rheumatism-root and dragon's-tongue. Stem more or less prostrate, partly underground, sending up occasional flowering and leafing shoots. Leaves lance-shaped, pointed, 1-3 in. long, with distant teeth and mottled white along some of the veins. Flowers white, rarely pinkish, nodding. Me. to Minn. and southward. Summer.

*umbellata.* Pipsissewa; also called prince's-pine and wintergreen. Similar to the other species but taller and the leaves blunter and not white-mottled, and the flowers spreading rather than nodding. Nearly throughout N.A., also in Eurasia. Summer.

**CHIMERA.** Sometimes, apples occur on a tree representing in one fruit, but in different areas, both cion and stock characters. In other words, the upper half of such apples may be red and slightly acid, indicating their origin from the cion tissue, while the lower half may be sweet and yellow, representing the stock tissue. Such apples are called chimeras. Trees bearing chimeras are grafted trees, and usually certain limbs bear these apples, while other limbs may bear red sour, and other yellow sweet apples. Chimeras, in such cases, arise through adventitious* buds at the graft union and consist of both cion and stock tissue. Other types have cion skin and a stock core. Chimeric plants often arise naturally through bud sporting, and their occurrence is widespread. Variegated foliage plants of some types are of this nature, *e.g.* variegated euonymous. — O. E. W. See POMATO.

**CHIMNEY BELLFLOWER** = *Campanula pyramidalis.*

**CHIMONANTHUS FRAGRANS** = *Meratia praecox.*

**CHINABERRY** = *Melia azedarach.*

**CHINA FIR.** See CUNNINGHAMIA.

**CHINA PINK** = *Dianthus chinensis.*

**CHINA ROSE** = *Hibiscus rosa-sinensis.* See also Group 5 at ROSE.

**CHINA-TREE** = *Melia azedarach;* also *Koelreuteria paniculata.*

**CHINA WOOD-OIL TREE.** See TUNG-OIL TREE.

**CHINCH BUG.** See True Bugs at INSECT PESTS, and Repellents at INSECTICIDES.

*CHINENSIS, -e* (chi-nen'sis). From China.

**CHINESE.** As an adjective Chinese has been applied to many plants and other things from China or the region near it. Those occurring in THE GARDEN DICTIONARY and their equivalents are:

Chinese angelica tree = *Aralia chinensis;* Chinese anise = *Illicium verum;* Chinese artichoke = *Stachys sieboldi;* Chinese banana = *Musa cavendishi* (for culture see BANANA); Chinese bellflower (see ABUTILON); Chinese cabbage (see next main entry below); Chinese elm = *Ulmus parvifolia* (see ELM); Chinese evergreen = *Aglaonema modestum;* Chinese fan palm = *Livistona chinensis;* Chinese fleece-vine = *Polygonum auberti;* Chinese forget-me-not = *Cynoglossum amabile;* Chinese hat-plant = *Holmskioldia sanguinea;* Chinese houses = *Collinsia bicolor;* Chinese jujube = *Zizyphus jujuba;* Chinese juniper = *Juniperus chinensis;* Chinese lantern-plant = *Physalis alkekengi;* Chinese layering = air layering (see LAYERING); Chinese loquat (see LOQUAT); Chinese monthly rose = *Rosa chinensis semperflorens;* Chinese parasol tree = *Firmiana simplex;* Chinese pistachio = *Pistacia chinensis;* Chinese potato = *Dioscorea batatas;* Chinese preserving melon = *Benincasa hispida;* Chinese primrose = *Primula sinensis;* Chinese quince = *Chaenomeles sinensis;* Chinese radish = *Raphanus sativus longipinnatus* (see RADISH); Chinese sacred lily = *Narcissus tazetta orientalis;* Chinese scholar tree = *Sophora japonica;* Chinese silk plant = *Boehmeria nivea;* Chinese tallow-tree = *Sapium sebiferum;* Chinese trumpet-creeper = *Campsis chinensis* (see TRUMPET-CREEPER); Chinese watermelon = *Benincasa hispida;* Chinese water plant = *Aglaonema modestum;* Chinese wisteria = *Wistaria sinensis;* Chinese yam = *Dioscorea batatas.*

**CHINESE CABBAGE** (*Brassica pekinensis*). This most popular salad vegetable, called in China pe-tsai, and in our markets the celery cabbage, has come into American gardens within the last few years. It is now raised commercially in Mich., and for fall and winter use in Calif.

The celery cabbage has little of the cabbage flavor, and when well grown its tender, central core of leaves is crisp, almost lettuce-like, and similarly used. The outer, coarser leaves are used as cooked greens. It is a leaf vegetable, the closely packed cylindric head being 12-18 in. long and 4-5 in. in diameter.

For early harvest the plants should be raised as for early cabbage and set out in the field as soon as the ground can be worked. It does well on reclaimed muck soils, but will grow in ordinary garden soils if they are deep and rich, and there is plenty of moisture. This early crop is not so likely to be tender as one maturing in late autumn. For this crop, sow the seeds as for late cabbage and set the plants in the field about the last week of July. They should be spaced about 8 in. apart and the rows wide enough to allow frequent cultivation. See MUCKLAND GARDENING.

The finest celery cabbage in the country is now raised in Calif., where magnificent white heads are harvested from Oct. through the winter. The plant is a rich feeder and the soil must be well fertilized. It will not thrive in areas of great summer heat or drought. For its insect pests and diseases see CABBAGE.

**CHINKAPIN** = CHINQUAPIN.

**CHINQUAPIN.** In the East, *Castanea pumila,* see CHESTNUT; in Calif. = *Castanopsis chrysophylla.*

**CHIOGENES** (ky-oj'je-nees). A genus of only two evergreen, creeping, herb-like shrubs of the heath family, one of them *C. hispidula,* usually called the creeping snowberry, moxieberry or running-birch. It has a creeping, slender stem, and small, alternate leaves that are ovalish and scarcely ¼ in. long. Flowers white, bell-shaped, not over ⅕ in. long, solitary and nodding in the leaf-axils.* Fruit aromatic (birch flavor), white, berry-like, and scarcely ⅕ in. in diameter. It grows in cold bogs and wet, often evergreen, woods in the northern part of N.A., and is suited only to similar places in the wild garden. (*Chiogenes* is from Greek for snow-born, in allusion to the white fruit.)

**CHIONANTHUS** (ki-o-nan'thus). Two handsome shrubs or small trees of the olive family, one widely and the other somewhat cult. for their showy white flowers. Leaves opposite,* without marginal teeth. Flowers in loose, often hanging clusters. Petals 4, strap-shaped, slightly united at the base. Fruit fleshy, 1-seeded, blue. (*Chionanthus* is from the Greek for snow and flower. It occurs as a specific name in the genus *Eomecon.*)

These are desirable shrubs (rarely trees), but care must be used in selecting individuals because sometimes male and female flowers are on separate plants. While the male flowers are larger, they produce no fruit. They are easily grown in open, light soils and require no special attention. Propagated by layers or cuttings of plants forced for the purpose. Occasionally grafted on the closely related ash tree.

*retusa.* Often 10-18 ft. high, usually a shrub, the leaves elliptic or oblongish, 2-4 in. long. Flower cluster about 4 in. long, at the ends of leafy shoots. Petals ¾-1½ in. long. Fruit nearly egg-shaped, about ¾ in. long, dark blue. China. June-July. Hardy from zone* 4 southward.

*virginica.* Fringe-tree or old-man's-beard. A shrub or tree up to 25 ft. high. Leaves narrowly elliptic or oblongish, 6-8 in. long. Flower cluster about 7 in. long. Petals 1-2 in. long. Fruit egg-shaped, ¾-1¼ in. long. Pa. to Fla. and Tex. May-June. Hardy from zone* 3 southward.

---

* Special articles on the subjects indicated by an asterisk (*) will be found at the words so marked.

**CHIONODOXA** (ki-on-o-dock'sa). Bulbous herbs of the lily family, mostly from Crete and Asia Minor, widely planted in the blue garden or rock garden for their attractive bloom. They are commonly called glory-of-the-snow, from their early flowering. There is a very short stalk from the bulb, narrow, toothless leaves, and small blue flowers in tiny racemes* at the end of the stalk. Corolla bell-shaped, the tube very short, its 6 stamens attached to the throat. Fruit a 3-angled capsule.* (*Chionodoxa* is Greek for glory of the snow.)

For Culture *see* below.

**luciliae.** About 3 in. high, while in flower, longer in fruit. Leaves nearly grass-like, shorter than the stalk of the flower cluster, in fruit longer. Flowers about 5 in a cluster, the lower nodding, blue with a white center. Asia Minor. There is also a pink and a white-flowered variety.

**sardensis.** Similar, but the blue flowers without the white eye. Asia Minor.

### CHIONODOXA CULTURE

Chionodoxas are among the earliest and most beautiful of spring-flowering bulbs. They are perfectly hardy and flourish and increase freely in good soil of a gritty nature, and they like plenty of light and some moisture. Planted in low, sunny sections of the rock garden, or massed closely about such contemporaneous shrubs as *Magnolia stellata*, forsythias and flowering almond, their blue color shows to perfection. Their best display comes in the years following their first blossoming, so that on no account should they be disturbed, but may be allowed to seed and increase from year to year until a carpet of color is attained. An occasional mulch of old manure in autumn keeps the soil in good condition. *C. luciliae* and *C. sardensis* are the best for general use. The bulbs should be planted in September or October 3 in. deep and 3 in. apart. — L. B. W.

**CHIOTILLA.** Mexican name of the cactus *Escontria chiotilla*.

**CHITTAMWOOD** = *Bumelia lanuginosa*; also *Cotinus americanus*.

**CHIVES** (*Allium schoenoprasum*). An onion-scented, perennial herb that does not produce the bulbs of the typical onion and is grown for its hollow, cylindrical leaves, which are cut and used for seasoning. (*See* HERB GARDENING.) While it is chiefly grown for these leaves, the plant produces attractive, rose-purple flowers, unless cut too much. It needs no special attention and can be grown either in the ordinary soil of the vegetable garden or in the flower border. Every two or three years it should be dug up, divided and replanted, especially if cutting is frequent. The insect pests are those of the onion.

**CHLOODES** (klo-ō'deez). Grass-green.

**CHLORIS** (clow'ris). A genus of perhaps 40 species of grasses, mostly from warm regions, and commonly called finger-grass. While most of them are of no garden interest, the Rhode's-grass, **C. gayana**, is somewhat planted in the South for ornament or forage. It is an erect, perennial grass, but spreads by running branches that root at the joints. Stems 3–4 ft. high, leafy, the joints brownish. Leaves numerous. Flower cluster well above the leaves, umbel*-like, and composed of 6–15 spikes that are 3–5 in. long. S. Af. (*Chloris* is from the Greek for green.)

**CHLOROGALUM** (clow-rog'a-lum). A genus of 3 species of California, bulbous plants of the lily family, closely related to *Camassia*, and grown like them. The only cult. species is **C. pomeridianum**, the soap plant or amole, which is an important bee plant in Calif. It has an onion-like bulb and a tall, many-branched stem 3–5 ft. high. Leaves long, narrow and wavy-margined at the base of the stem, diminishing in size and frequency towards the top of the plant. Flowers white, purple-veined, the cluster a terminal panicle.* Petals 6. Stamens 6. The Indians used the bulb to make soap. (*Chlorogalum* is from the Greek for green milk.)

**CHLOROPHYLL.** The basic green coloring matter of nearly all plants. For its all-important function *see* PLANT FOODS.

**CHLOROPHYTUM** (clow-ro-fy'tum). A group of 60 species of perennial, tropical herbs of the lily family, one very commonly grown in the green house for its numerous, bright green leaves and for its long-stalked, branched flower cluster. They differ from *Anthericum* only in technical characters, but the species below has wider leaves than *Anthericum liliago* (which see). (*Chlorophytum* is from the Greek for green plant.)

It is odd that this very common greenhouse plant has no common name, although it is locally sometimes called spider plant. It is of easy, almost rampant growth in the cool greenhouse in potting mixture* 3, and is easily propagated by division of its rootstocks, and by its runners.

**elatum.** Leaves long, flat, often 1 in. wide, green in the typical form, but white-margined, variegated, or yellow-banded in some of the hort. forms. Flowering stem 2–3 ft. long, lax and inclined to sprawl. Flowers white, about ½ in. long. S. Af. The plant or some of its forms is also, but incorrectly, called *Anthericum vittatum, A. mandaianum, A. picturatum*, and *A. variegatum*.

**CHLOROSIS.** A plant disease of obscure or unknown origin, usually followed by a loss of green color. *See* Diseases at PEANUT.

**CHOCOLATE.** *See* THEOBROMA CACAO.

**CHOCOLATE FAMILY** = Sterculiaceae.

**CHOCOLATE-FLOWER** = *Geranium maculatum*.

**CHOCTAW-ROOT** = *Apocynum cannabinum*.

**CHOISYA** (shaw'si-a). A single, aromatic, evergreen shrub of the family Rutaceae, grown for its fine foliage and for fragrant, white flowers in early spring. Leaves opposite,* compound,* the three leaflets nearly stalkless and without marginal teeth. Flowers in 3–6-flowered, slender-stalked clusters (cymes*). Petals 5. Stamens 10. Fruit of 5 two-lobed carpels. (Named for J. D. Choisy, Swiss botanist.)

The Mexican orange is a handsome shrub for the tender border, much grown in Fla. and Calif. and occasionally hardy up to zone* 6 or even 5 in sheltered places. It has no special soil preferences and is propagated by cuttings of old wood in the frame.

**ternata.** Mexican orange. A shrub 6–8 ft. high. Leaflets 2–3 in. long. Flowers 1–1½ in. wide. Mex.

**CHOKEBERRY** = *Aronia*.

**CHOKE CHERRY.** Properly, *Prunus virginiana*, but *P. serotina*, the wild black cherry, is often called choke cherry.

**CHOLLA.** *See* OPUNTIA.

**CHORISIA** (ko-ris'i-a). A genus of South American trees of the family Bombacaceae, one planted for ornament but hardy only in zones* 8 and 9. It is related to the silk-cotton tree (*Ceiba*) and differs chiefly in the lack of the huge buttresses of the latter. It has alternate,* compound* leaves, the leaflets arranged finger-fashion. Flowers large (for details *see* BOMBACACEAE). Fruit a capsule,* the seeds with a silky floss. (Named for Ludwig Choris, botanical artist.)

**speciosa.** Floss-silk tree. A spiny tree up to 50 ft., occasionally planted for ornament in southern Fla. Leaflets usually 5, stalked, more or less lance-shaped and toothed. Flowers solitary in the axils,* nearly 3 in. wide, pink, appearing in early winter when the tree is without leaves. Brazil.

**CHORIZEMA** (core-riz'ee-ma). Of 15 Australian evergreen shrubs of this genus (family Leguminosae) only one is in general cult. in the U.S. It is pretty widely planted outdoors in Calif. and Fla. for its handsome foliage and showy flowers. Unlike nearly all plants of the pea family, it has simple* leaves, which, in the one below, are spiny-margined. Flowers typically pea-like, in terminal racemes.* Fruit a short pod (legume*). (*Chorizema* is a fanciful Greek name of unknown application here.)

If grown in the greenhouse, they need a cool house, and potting mixture* 4, to which should be added a little acid peat. They need plenty of water. Outdoors they need open sunshine and a well-drained soil. Easily propagated by cuttings of young wood in the greenhouse.

**cordatum.** A weak-stemmed shrub 3–8 ft. high, often better grown over a small trellis in the greenhouse, as it tends to sprawl. Leaves roundish or ovalish, heart-shaped at the base, about 1 in. long, the mar-

---

* Special articles on the subjects indicated by an asterisk (*) will be found at the words so marked.

gins with small teeth or prickles. Flowers about ¾ in. long, the upright standard* scarlet, the rest of the flower purplish. Very showy, as the flowers are numerous in early spring. Greenhouse plants should be plunged outdoors in summer, in partial shade. The plant is sometimes offered as *C. ilicifolium.*

**CHOROGI** = *Stachys sieboldi.*

**CHRISTMAS BEGONIA.** See BEGONIA SOCOTRANA.

**CHRISTMAS-BERRY** = *Heteromeles arbutifolia* (see TOYON); also = *Schinus terebinthifolius,* which is called Christmas-berry tree in Calif.

**CHRISTMAS CACTUS** = *Zygocactus truncatus.*

**CHRISTMAS FERN** = *Polystichum acrostichoides.*

**CHRISTMAS GREENS.** The custom of decking the house with Christmas greens is older than Christmas and survives all attempts of the conservationists to stop it. A better plan is to utilize the foliage of the common native fir of northeastern America, which is worthless from the forestry standpoint. It is also much the best for a Christmas tree. Avoid all spruces and hemlocks, which not only drop their needles very soon in the heat of a room, but are too valuable as trees to warrant trimming or destruction for transitory decoration. Some plantations of Norway spruce are grown for Christmas trees in Mich., however, but the fir is more satisfactory.

There is no justification for wreaths made of ground pine or other native evergreens in danger of extermination and any garden club should exert local pressure upon dealers to stop this. Good wreaths can be made of mountain laurel and other broad-leaved evergreens grown for the purpose and harvested annually.

**CHRISTMAS ROSE** = *Helleborus niger.*

**CHRISTOPHINE** = *Sechium edule.*

**CHRIST'S-THORN** = *Paliurus spina-christi.*

**CHRYSALIDOCARPUS** (kris-sal'i-do-kar-pus). Madagascan feather palms of perhaps 10 species, one of which is the palm perhaps most widely grown by florists, who generally call it areca. They have clustered, smooth, ringed stems, never very high in cult. Leaves compound,* the leaflets numerous, arranged feather-fashion, very graceful and handsome, and drooping at the tip, the plant thus plumelike. Flowers in a short cluster near the leaves, the sepals, petals, and stamens 6 each. Fruit turban-shaped, dark violet or black. (*Chrysalidocarpus* is from the Greek for golden fruit, in allusion to the yellow fruit of another species.)

The florists' areca, better known as cane palm (from its slender, bamboo-like stems), is a favorite tub and pot palm in greenhouses and for house decoration. Not so tough and houseworthy as the kentias (see HOWEA), it is a far more graceful palm. It is widely grown for decoration outdoors in southern Fla. and all over the world in the tropics. In greenhouses it needs the same general culture as *Arenga* and the genus *Areca.* That means a house kept at about 60° at night and 70°–75° during the day. Use potting mixture* 4 and keep the plants, whatever their size, slightly pot-bound. While they need plenty of water, loosely filled pots with meager root development invite stagnant, water-soaked soil and poor growth.

**lutescens.** The areca of the florists; better called cane palm. Stem clustered, usually not over 10 ft. high, often much less as a pot plant. Leaves olive-green, their stalks yellow, not all at the top of the stem as in most palms. Leaflets 40–60 pairs, about ¾ in. wide or less, with a strong midrib. Fruit about ¾ in. long. Madagascar. Often offered as *Areca lutescens.*

**CHRYSAMPHORA** = DARLINGTONIA.

*CHRYSANTHA, -us, -um* (kris-san'tha). Golden-flowered.

**CHRYSANTHEMUM** (kris-san'thee-mum). An important genus of garden plants, comprising over 150 species of the family Compositae, nearly all from the temperate or sub-tropical regions of the Old World. Some have been in cultivation for over 3000 years in China and Japan, and today the genus includes such unlike plants as the florist's chrysanthemum, the garden pyrethrums, the costmary, and the common white daisy of our fields, as well as the well-known Shasta daisy and Marguerite. They are usually erect herbs (but *C. frutescens* is a little woody), often with strong-smelling foliage, and generally much-branched. Leaves alternate,* often more or less divided. Flowers in heads, of all colors except blue and purple, the rays* much modified by long selection and cultivation, the heads usually showy and of immense size in the florist's chrysanthemum, but small and button-like in others. (*Chrysanthemum* is from the Greek for golden flower.) "Mum" is florist's slang for Chrysanthemum.

**arcticum.** Aster daisy. A hardy, border perennial, 12–15 in. high, useful in the autumn garden. Stems more or less prostrate at first, the tips ascending. Flowers white or lilac, the heads aster-like, nearly 2 in. wide. Arctic regions.

**balsamita.** Costmary; called also mint geranium, and the leaves are sometimes called "lavender." A hardy perennial 2–3 ft. high. Leaves toothed. Flower heads numerous, scarcely ⅓ in. wide, the white rays very short, sometimes none. Asia. Grown for its aromatic foliage. See HERB GARDENING.

**carinatum.** A half-hardy annual, smooth and 2–3 ft. high, not much branched. Leaves cut into narrow segments. Flower heads about 2½ in. wide, white, red, or yellow, with a differently colored ring at the base of the rays.* Morocco. For culture see Tender Annuals at ANNUALS.

**coccineum.** Pyrethrum. A very popular, summer-blooming, perennial herb, 1–2 ft. high, and little, if at all, branched. Leaves much-divided and fern-like. Flower heads large, very showy, often 2½ in. wide, red, pink, lilac, or white, and sometimes double. Caucasus and Persia. There are scores of named forms, some of them very fine plants for the border, although they are not hardy in severe climates. They are also grown as pot plants by florists. Sometimes known as painted lady.

**coreanum.** A common name in the literature of chrysanthemum, but of uncertain application. Among gardeners it always means a hardy, white, single-flowered plant, but the origin and nativity of it are unknown. From it have originated the Korean hybrids. [See Culture below.

**coronarium.** Crown daisy. A hardy annual, stout, branched, and 3–4 ft. high. Leaves deeply divided, the segments also cut or toothed. Flower heads numerous, about 1½ in. wide, sometimes double, yellowish-white. Southern Eu. A variety is grown in Jap. and China for the edible young shoots.

**frutescens.** Marguerite or Paris daisy. A tender, very beautiful, much-branched herb, 2–3 ft. high, the base usually woody. Leaves rather coarsely divided, a little fleshy. Flower heads daisy-like, 1½–2½ in. wide, white or pale yellow. Canary Islands. Can only be grown in the greenhouse and should be treated the same as the florist's chrysanthemum. See below. For a method of increasing the number of flowers, and changing the shape of the plant, see Pinching at TRAINING PLANTS.

**hortorum.** A doubtful name for the group of plants comprising the florist's chrysanthemum, and here listed as *C. morifolium.*

**indicum.** A hardy border perennial, 2–3 ft. high. Leaves divided, white-woolly on the under side. Flower heads yellow, numerous, about ¾ in. wide, showy only en masse. China. Considered as having contributed, in part, to the modern florist's chrysanthemum.

**leucanthemum.** Common, white, or oxeye daisy, and often weedy in the fields. Not over 2 ft. high, the stems normally unbranched. Leaves cut or divided. Flower heads long-stalked, usually solitary, about 1½ in. wide, the rays* white, the disk* yellow. Eurasia. Not much grown as a garden plant and sometimes a pest.

**maximum.** Chiefly grown in large-flowered form known as the Shasta daisy, although originally from the Pyrenees. It is a fine perennial border plant, but soon dies out and is best treated as a biennial. (See BIENNIALS.) Stems not much branched, 1–2 ft. high. Leaves long, narrow, toothed, but not deeply cut. Flower heads 2–4 in. wide, white and daisy-like. It is widely cult. and there are a variety of named forms.

**morifolium.** Florist's chrysanthemum. Probably a Chinese perennial herb, originally 2–4 ft. high and much-branched, but often, as grown today, much larger and of various habit (dome-shaped, etc.), due to pinching and disbudding. Leaves broad, strong-scented, lobed, and more or less grayish-hairy. Flower heads of many forms (see below) and colors, often immense. For Culture see below. Sometimes called *C. hortorum.*

**nipponicum.** A hardy, perennial, border plant, 1½–2 ft. high, a little woody at the base, branched above. Leaves thickish, blunt, only slightly toothed towards the end. Flower heads solitary at the ends of the branches, white, 2–3 in. wide. Jap.

**parthenium.** Feverfew. A bushy, hardy perennial for the border, the stems leafy, 2–3½ ft. high. Leaves more or less cut, and, in varieties, yellowish or crisped. Flower heads many, scarcely ¾ in. wide, the rays white, short or lacking altogether. Eurasia. Sometimes offered as *Matricaria capensis* and as *M. parthenioides.*

**segetum.** Corn marigold. A much-branched annual herb, to be sown where wanted. Stems 1–2 ft. high. Leaves notched, or somewhat cut, but not deeply so. Flower heads 1½–2½ in. wide, white or yellowish, solitary at the ends of the branches and daisy-like. Eurasia. There are many named forms of this popular annual.

**uliginosum.** Giant daisy. A hardy, perennial border plant, 4–7 ft. high and much-branched. Leaves narrow and sharply toothed, but not deeply cut. Flower heads solitary at the ends of the branches, daisy-like, about 2½ in. wide. Eu.

CHRYSANTHEMUM CULTURE

The species from which the present-day florist's varieties mostly originated appear to be *Chrysanthemum indicum* and *Chrysanthemum morifolium.*

---

* Special articles on the subjects indicated by an asterisk (*) will be found at the words so marked.

Since the hybridizer began his work in the United States, about 3000 varieties have been grown and listed. The majority of these are not hardy and must be grown under glass. Every year new varieties are disseminated, while others are discarded, and not over 75 or 80 varieties are now actually in cultivation.

PROPAGATION. Except for the new varieties (which are grown from seed), chrysanthemums are propagated by means of cuttings and division. These cuttings are taken in March or April, grown on in pots, and by July they should all be transferred to the greenhouse benches or beds where they are allowed to flower. The early ones come into bloom by September first, the so-called midseason sorts from October 15 to November 15, and the late varieties for the Thanksgiving market. However, the hybridizer is constantly striving to increase the length of the blooming period and there are now in existence a number of varieties that will flower as late as January. Shading with black cloth will hasten the blooming period.

When grown under glass the plants require a good compost soil to which about one-quarter well-rotted cow manure should be added. In the course of the growing season they will require additional fertility, which may be supplied in the form of a cow-manure mulch, manure water or in the form of some chemical fertilizer such as nitrate of soda or ammonium sulphate. Potash and phosphorus must also be supplied if the basic soil happens to be low in these essential elements. The greenhouse should be kept between 50° and 60°.

All the other details in culture, such as ventilation, watering, staking, disbudding, cultivating, fumigating, spraying, etc., must be given careful attention. For the production of the immense, so-called cascade chrysanthemum plants, sometimes seen at flower shows, *see* Pinching at TRAINING PLANTS.

Because of the variation in the flowers of the chrysanthemum the following classification has been quite generally adopted: Incurved, Reflexed, Japanese, Hairy, Anemone, Pompon, Single, Spidery, Plumed and Feathery. These types in a number of cases have again been subdivided according to size.

OUTDOOR CULTURE. As a garden flower the culture of the chrysanthemum dates back to the early colonial gardens. Until recent years the majority of the so-called hardy forms belonged to the *C. morifolium* group. Some varieties proved hardy in certain localities, while others stood only the winters in the South and West. The term hardiness, especially after the severe winter of 1933–34, has lost its meaning to a certain extent, and this is especially true of chrysanthemums.

In addition to the *C. morifolium* types two annual species, *C. coronarium* (crown daisy) and *C. segetum* (corn marigold), make excellent garden flowers. The seeds of these annual forms should be sown in April under glass or in the home.

Of the perennial forms, *C. maximum*, which includes the Shasta daisy, makes an excellent garden flower. This species may be grown from seed, but a more satisfactory method is by division of the clumps. Another perennial form is *C. arcticum*, the aster daisy, excellent for rock gardens, or low garden borders. It flowers in September and October and may also be grown from seed or by division. *C. parthenium* (feverfew) is another species often found in perennial borders.

No perennial border is complete unless it contains a good collection of hardy chrysanthemums. If sufficient room is available they may be planted by themselves, and with the variety, types and colors now available, beautiful effects may be created.

A good many of the varieties of the florist's chrysanthemum are perfectly hardy, although it is difficult to state in the case of any given variety just where it will live through the winter. Soil and moisture conditions are important factors when the matter of hardiness is taken into consideration.

In addition to the *morifolium* varieties there are now available varieties of *C. coreanum* which have proven thoroughly hardy in the severest climates. *C. coreanum* and its varieties Ceres, Daphne and Mercury lived through the winter of 1933–34 without any protection in Massachusetts and many other parts of the country.

While these Korean hybrids are so far all singles, other types, such as semidoubles, decoratives, and pompons, are soon likely to be available. The hybridizer is now giving much of his time and attention to the hardy types and is working with *C. coreanum*, *C. articum*, *C. maximum*, *C. parthenium* and other hardy species. This work is really in its infancy and the results anticipated are most promising.

PREPARATION OF THE SOIL. The soil for hardy chrysanthemums should be light, rich and above all, well drained. In the preparation of the new border an abundant supply of manure should be spaded into the soil. When new plants are being added to the border, it is a good method to work a shovelful of manure into the place where the plants are to be set. The value of sufficient fertilizer cannot be overemphasized in the growth of the chrysanthemum, for it is a plant which must not be checked in its development by lack of food or moisture.

PLANTING. Hardy chrysanthemums may be planted either in the fall or the spring, although spring is the more suitable time, enabling the plants to become thoroughly established before the cold weather sets in. Fall planting must of necessity be late, since the blooming period is rarely over before freezing weather sets in. The distance between plants will vary with the type, but ordinarily 18 to 24 inches will give sufficient space. The depth of the plants should be such as to have the soil come to the top of the crown of the roots. It is wise to give the plants a good watering after planting.

For outdoor culture the plants may be propagated by cuttings of the stem and by division of the crown. New varieties are, of course, grown from seed. Stem cuttings should be taken early in the season when the new growths have attained the height of four or five inches. The actual method does not differ from that of taking a cutting of any other type of plant as, for example, a geranium. When greenhouse space is not available, the cuttings may be rooted in a small hotbed, or in the home small quantities may be rooted in an ordinary wooden box filled with sand. This should have a cover of glass. After the insertion of cuttings into the rooting medium to a depth of two inches, the cover should be put on and a sheet of newspaper or cloth placed over the glass. This should be kept on until the plants are well rooted. Every day more and more air should be admitted, until by the time the cuttings are rooted the cover should be left off entirely. As soon as rooted, the plants may be potted and placed in another frame where they should be protected from cold and sun.

In three or four days the protection may be gradually removed and in two or three weeks the new plants may be set out in their permanent quarters or into a nursery row from which they may be transplanted later in the season.

Propagating plants by means of division may also be done in the spring, although fall division is also practiced. It is accomplished by lifting the old plants and separating them into two, four or more sections with a knife or spade. Immediate replanting is desirable.

DISBUDDING AND PINCHING. In the course of the growing season frequent pinching of the terminal shoots is necessary if stocky, bushy plants are desired. For the best results, however, the plants should not be pinched after August first, as in the case of the early varieties they begin to set their buds about that time. Pinching is not necessary when a plant develops numerous branches from the base. Disbudding* must be practiced if large flowers are desired.

CULTIVATION. The soil in which the plants are growing should be cultivated from time to time and the weeds should be removed when necessary. These operations can be entirely eliminated by placing an inch mulch of peat around the plants early in the spring or after the first cultivation. An occasional heavy watering during especially dry periods of midsummer is beneficial, but it is decidedly harmful unless it is done properly. Frequent light watering discourages deep rooting of the plants and leaves them at the greater mercy of the scorching sun.

---

* Special articles on the subjects indicated by an asterisk (*) will be found at the words so marked.

### GARDEN CHRYSANTHEMUMS

**1** Early Bronze

2  Korean — Daphne  
3  Jean Cumming  
4  Barbara Cumming  

5  Korean — Mercury  
6  Jean Treadway  

**7** Granny Scoville

The plants may need additional fertility during the growing season. This may be applied in the form of liquid manure, solutions of nitrate of soda or sulphate of ammonia. After the buds have set and if the growth is strong no further feeding is necessary. As a means of protection it is a good plan to put a light mulch around the plants after the ground is frozen. This is done not so much to keep the plants from freezing but rather to prevent heaving through alternate freezing and thawing. Strawy manure or leaves may be used for this purpose.

VARIETIES. No two people will select the same list of varieties. Some people prefer the button types while others are fond of the simplicity found in the single types. There is considerable difference of opinion in selecting, for example, the twelve best varieties from the standpoint of beauty and hardiness.

Following are twelve varieties quite universally grown and appreciated at the present time:

Barbara Cumming. One of the first to bloom and still the best large yellow pompon.
Early Bronze. An early-blooming, attractive bronze pompon.
Mercury. The earliest of the Korean hybrids.
Apollo. A superbly colored terra cotta and salmon Korean.
Amelia. A dwarf pink variety ideal for rock garden.
Jean Treadway. Perhaps the most appealing of all medium pompons.
Daphne. A daphne pink Korean, the last to bloom, but whose flowers remain unharmed by heaviest frost.
Ruth Cumming. A pompon with reddish-bronze flowers. Strong grower.
Mrs. J. Willis Martin. A crushed-strawberry pompon.
Jean Cumming. A fine handsome white decorative pompon.
Granny Scoville. Immense, shaggy, reddish-orange, large pompon.
Louise Schling. Shaggy, deep rose single with double layer of petals. — A. H. N.

INSECT PESTS. Aphids, especially a black species, are injurious both outdoors and in greenhouses. Nicotine spray or dust, or nicotine fumigation indoors, will control them, as well as leaf miners and thrips. In greenhouses larvae of the chrysanthemum gall midge form small, lumpy leaf galls, checking and warping growth. Planting stock should be free of them, and infested leaves should be removed when they first appear. Heavily infested plants may be treated by nightly fumigation with calcium cyanide for a week or two. The greenhouse leaf tier (same as celery leaf tier) can be checked by spray or dust of lead arsenate before blossoming, as can occasional leaf feeders.

DISEASES. Rust, mildew, wilt, leafspot, flower blight and yellows are the important chrysanthemum diseases. For rust and mildew see Rusts and Mildews at PLANT DISEASES. Yellow leaves, wilting and black discoloration of the stem are symptoms of wilt. Select healthy stock for cuttings and plant in new or sterilized soil. With leafspot, dark brown to black dead areas of varying size will be noted on the foliage. The disease appears first on the lower leaves. For control, remove infected leaves, spray with bordeaux mixture and keep the foliage dry. Remove the early infections, increase ventilation, avoid crowding, and water from below, thus keeping the foliage and flowers dry. Chrysanthemums are susceptible to the aster yellows disease, for which see Diseases at CALLISTEPHUS.

Amateur growers are welcome as members of The Chrysanthemum Society of America, which fosters interest and research in their favorite flower. Its officers change from time to time, but its current headquarters can always be reached by writing Garden Editor, Houghton Mifflin Company, Boston, Mass.

**CHRYSOBALANUS** (kris-o-bal'a-nus). A small group of tropical trees of the rose family, one sometimes planted in southern Fla., very rarely in greenhouses. The only cult. species is **C. icaco**, the coco-plum or gopher-plum, which is also wild from southern Fla. to Brazil. It is usually a shrub in Fla. (a tall tree in the tropics) with alternate,* leathery, evergreen leaves, 2-3 in. across and nearly round. Flowers white, in small clusters (cymes*) in the leaf-axils.* Petals 5, with a claw.* Stamens many. Fruit dryish, but a fleshy, yellow drupe,* edible but somewhat insipid, about 1 in. long, its stone pointed and ridged. (*Chrysobalanus* is from the Greek for golden acorn, in allusion to the fruit.) It is useful for seaside planting in zone* 9.

**CHRYSOLEPIS, -e** (kris-ol'ep-is). Golden-scaled.

**CHRYSOLEUCA, -us, -um** (kris-o-loo'ka). Yellow and pale or whitish.

**CHRYSOPHYLLA, -us, -um** (kris-o-fil'la). Yellow- or golden-leaved.

**CHRYSOPHYLLUM.** See STAR-APPLE.

**CHRYSOPSIS** (kris-sop'sis). The golden asters (not true asters, which are never yellow) comprise a group of North American perennial herbs of the family Compositae, almost weedy in the wild state, but occasionally transferred to the garden for their yellow flower heads and their ability to grow in dry, sandy soils. They are low herbs with woolly or hairy leaves and rather large heads of yellow ray and disk* flowers, usually in small clusters at the ends of the branches. (*Chrysopsis* is from the Greek for golden aspect.)

The golden asters are of the easiest culture in any garden soil and may be increased by division in the spring. All bloom in midsummer.

falcata. Ground gold-flower. Not over 1 ft. high, the leaves narrow, crowded, rigid, and hairy, 2-4 in. long. Flower heads about ⅓ in. wide. In sandy soil, Mass. to N.J.
mariana. Golden star. From 12-20 in. high, the leaves oblongish, 2-4 in. long. Flower heads about 1 in. wide, numerous. In dry sand L.I. to Fla.
villosa. Rosinweed. From 10-18 in. high, the leaves oblongish, 1-2 in. long. Flower heads about 1 in. wide, rather sparse. In plains and prairies, Minn. to British Columbia and N. Mex.

**CHUCHU** = *Sechium edule*.

**CHUFA** = *Cyperus esculentus*.

**CHYSIS** (ky'sis). A small genus of tropical American tree-perching orchids, not much grown in greenhouses, but very handsome. Without true pseudobulbs,* the stems are somewhat thickened and spindle-shaped, leafy. Leaves less fleshy than in many orchids, soon falling, when the stems thicken still more. Flowers showy, in short clusters (racemes*) produced from the leaf-axils,* and usually shorter than the leaves. One of the sepals and the petals are alike in shape, the other sepals forming a foot with the base of the column.* Lip with the lateral lobes erect, and surrounding the column. (*Chysis* is from the Greek for melting, in reference to a technical character of the pollen.)

These plants need to be grown in a basket or wooden crib, or in well-drained pans in a tropical atmosphere. For details see Culture of Epiphytic Orchids at ORCHID.

aurea. Flowers 5-8 in a cluster, about 2 in. wide. Sepals and petals oblongish, yellow. Lip with the lateral lobes yellow, the middle lobe downy, white, but red- and yellow-spotted. Brazil.
bractescens. A leafy orchid with drooping stems. Flowers 3-5 in a cluster, about 3 in. wide. Sepals and petals white. Lateral lobes of the lip white outside, yellow within, red-striped. Middle lobe of the lip yellow, but red-streaked. Mex.
chelsoni. Flowers 5-7 in a cluster, about 2½ in. wide, sepals, petals and lip generally yellow, all spotted or blotched with red. Of hybrid origin, *C. bractescens* being one of the parents.

**CIBOL.** The Welsh onion; also the shallot.

**CIBOTIUM** (sy-bō'ti-um). A small group of sturdy tree ferns of the family Cyatheaceae, found in tropical America and in the tropics of the Far East. Two are rather common greenhouse ferns which (under cult.) do not produce the usually shaggy trunk of wild trees. They are coarser-foliaged than other tree ferns but easier to grow and hence (especially *C. schiedei*) popular florists' ferns. Fronds twice-compound,* the ultimate segments narrow. Spore cases at the ends of the veinlets. (*Cibotium* is from the Greek for a little seed-vessel.)

For the culture of these greenhouse ferns see FERNS AND FERN GARDENING.

barometz. Scythian lamb. As cult., a trunkless fern with the large, feathery leaves arising from the ground level, the stalks shaggy and brownish. Ultimate segments of the frond narrowly oblong, 4-6 in. long, pale bluish-green beneath. Indo-Malaya. This was one of the plants to which ancient legend ascribed the production of vegetable wool, hence its name of Scythian lamb. (See BAROMETZ.)
schiedei. In the wild, 15 ft. high or more, but often much less and nearly trunkless in cult. Fronds 3-5 ft. long, drooping and graceful, the stalks brown-hairy. Ultimate segments of the frond 5-8 in. long, much cut, bluish-green beneath. Mex. The best known and most popular as a cult. fern, being well suited to decorations because of its sturdy growth.

**CIBOUL** = CIBOL.

**CICER** (sy'sir). Perhaps a dozen Asiatic herbs of the pea family of no garden interest except for the chick-pea or garbanzo, a plant long cult. (little in U.S.) for its edible seeds. Leaves compound,* the leaflets arranged feather-fashion with (in the one below) an odd leaflet at the end. Flowers small, but pea-like, solitary and long-stalked. Pod (legume*)

---

* Special articles on the subjects indicated by an asterisk (*) will be found at the words so marked.

short and swollen, with only 1 or 2 seeds. (*Cicer* is the classical name for the chick-pea.)

The chick-pea is an annual long cult. in southern Eu. for food. Unlike the garden pea, it will stand considerable summer heat. Sow the seeds 6–8 in. apart in drills about 2 in. deep, and space the rows at least 2 ft. apart. The plant is of easy culture.

**arietinum.** Chick-pea or garbanzo. A sticky-hairy annual, 1–2 ft. high and branched. Leaflets 9–15, ovalish, about ½ in. long, finely toothed. Flowers white or pinkish, scarcely ⅜ in. long. Pod nearly 1 in. long and half as wide, the seed wrinkled, about ⅓ in. in diameter, one end pointed as though a ram's horn, white, red or black. Western Asia.

**CICHORIACEAE.** See COMPOSITAE.

**CICHORIUM** (sick-kor′i-um). A remarkably versatile group of herbs of the family Compositae, containing such unlike garden plants as the chicory, endive, and the witloof or French endive. Leaves alternate (much modified in the endive), usually towards the base of the stem. Flowers in heads, composed only of ray* flowers, the heads sometimes solitary and stalkless, or a few terminal and short-stalked. (*Cichorium* is a Latinized version of an Arabic name for one of the species.)

**intybus.** Chicory; called also succory, blueweed, blue dandelion, and coffeeweed, the latter from the use of its ground-up root as an adulterant of coffee. A stout perennial 3–6 ft. high, nearly leafless toward the top. Leaves variable, generally oblongish, clasping, the lower ones sometimes dandelion-like. Heads usually blue, sometimes white or pink, about 1½ in. wide. Eu. Summer. For culture and for the witloof see below.

**endivia.** Endive. Annual or biennial, the stem leafy, 2–3 ft. high. Leaves most numerous at the base, oblong, brittle, lobed or cut in the wild form. Flower heads purple, below them a series of leafy bracts that exceed the head. India (?). For culture see ENDIVE.

### CHICORY AND WITLOOF CULTURE

The common chicory is abundant as a weed along roadsides throughout N.A. It is cult. as a farm crop in some sections, where its roots are harvested and are the source of commercial chicory. Such culture is easy, the plants being handled like any other perennial. Young roots are planted in spring in rows 3 ft. apart or seed is sown instead, the ground is kept cultivated, and the plants kept spaced about 18 in. apart in the rows.

Less known in U.S., but common in France, is the French endive or witloof. It is a form or variety of chicory in which the blanched leaves are eaten. They may be forced in a cellar (see CELLAR GARDENING) after the roots have been dug from the ground in the fall and stored as other root crops. Seed of witloof should be sown in drills in the spring, spaced about 6 in. apart. In the fall cut the tops off and dig the roots. When ready to force, follow the directions given at CELLAR GARDENING.

**CICUTA** (sy-kew′ta). The water hemlock is scarcely of garden importance except to warn children against its dangerously poisonous roots. It is one of a small genus of perennial herbs of the carrot family found in the north temperate zone, and sometimes **C. maculata** is transferred to pond edges or bogs, where it thrives. Commonly called water hemlock (not the poison hemlock that killed Socrates); it is also known as spotted cowbane, musquash-root, and beaver-poison. It has compound,* rather graceful or feathery leaves, and tiny white flowers in terminal, compound umbels.* Its roots contain a deadly alkaloid. (*Cicuta* is the classical Latin name of these plants.)

*CICUTARIA, -us, -um* (sick-kew-tay′ri-a). Like the water hemlock (*Cicuta*).

**CIDER.** In choosing apples for cider it is obvious that the varieties with most juice will give the greatest yield. But early varieties do not make as good cider as late apples. Consequently, choose one of those towards the end of the list of desirable apple varieties in the article on the apple. Also apples with yellow fruit do not make a cider with as good a color as red-fruited varieties. Winesap, McIntosh, Jonathan, Baldwin, and Wealthy are all good cider apples, as well as having many other fine qualities. See APPLE.

**CIGAR-FLOWER** = *Cuphea platycentra*.

**CIGAR-TREE** = *Catalpa bignonioides*.

*CILIARIS, -e* (silly-ā′ris). See CILIATA.

*CILIATA, -us, -um* (silly-ā′ta). Ciliate; *i.e.* with marginal hairs as those on the edges of many leaves or petals.

**CILICIAN FIR** = *Abies cilicica*. See FIR.

*CILICICA, -us, -um* (sil-lis′i-ka). From Cilicica, Asia Minor.

*CILIOSA, -us, -um* (silly-ō′sa). Slightly fringed or ciliate. See CILIATA.

**CIMICIFUGA** (sim-mi-siff′you-ga). The bugbanes are tall, rather showy, summer-blooming perennial herbs of the buttercup family, well suited to the wild garden or the shadiest part of the border. They have large, thrice-compound* leaves. Flowers small, white, with few or no petals, but crowded in a dense, terminal, finger-shaped cluster at the end of a tall stalk, hence striking, and standing well above the foliage. Stamens many and giving the chief color to the flower. Fruit a collection of small, dry pods (follicles*), differing from the closely related and somewhat similar *Actaea*, which has fleshy fruit. (*Cimicifuga* is Latin for bugbane.)

The two American species are best suited to the wild garden, while *C. simplex* is quite at home in a partly shady border of ordinary garden soil. The American plants grow in the woods and should have similar soil (not especially acid). A good mixture for them is black leaf mold and rotted sods mixed half and half.

**americana.** Snakeroot. Not over 4 ft. high, usually about 3 ft. Ultimate leaflets oval or oblong, 1–3 in. long, thin, deeply cut or toothed. Flower cluster 1–2 ft. long, usually branched. Fruits about ¼ in. long. N.Y. and Pa. to Tenn. and Ga. Aug.–Sept.

**racemosa.** Black snakeroot; also called black cohosh and rattlesnakeweed. Taller than the others, and sometimes 6 ft. high. Ultimate leaflets thin and tapering at both ends, 2–4 in. long, toothed or deeply cut or both. Flower cluster branched, its main spike 9–24 in. long and showy. Eastern N.A. July–Aug.

**simplex.** Not over 3 ft. high, usually less. Ultimate leaflets thickish, tapering towards a broad base, about 2 in. long, toothed. Flower cluster usually unbranched. Kamtchatka. Aug.–Oct.

**CINCHONA** (sin-kō′na). A genus of perhaps 60 species of mostly Andean trees of the family Rubiaceae, of little garden interest, but important as the source of quinine. The quinine tree is not cult. in the U.S. or in S.A., its commercial production centering in Java. A related tree, the one below, is somewhat planted in extreme southern Fla. and is hardy nowhere else. They have opposite,* stalked leaves and small flowers in terminal clusters (panicles*). Corolla tubular, its 5 lobes spreading. (For details see RUBIACEAE.) Fruit a capsule,* splitting from the base upward. (Named for Doña Francisca Henriquez de Rivera, wife of the Count of Chinchon, and the first prominent European to be cured of malaria by quinine, in Lima, in 1630.)

**officinalis.** A tree long thought to be the best source of quinine, now replaced by Javanese hybrids. Commonly called quina or Peruvian bark. Leaves oval, or longer, 3–5 in. long. Flowers rose-pink, ½ in. long, the clusters 5–6 in. long. Peru and Bolivia. Somewhat planted from Palm Beach southward, but of little decorative value, and of no importance as a source of quinine.

**CINERARIA.** As a name cineraria is a little confusing. To the florist it means very showy greenhouse plants with usually bright blue flowers. And some of the hort. varieties are of many other colors, except yellow. These are all derived from a single, woolly-leaved, perennial herb from the Canary Islands properly called *Senecio cruentus* (which see for botanical characters).

But cineraria also applies to some plants known as dusty miller, and for these see *Senecio cineraria*. And cineraria, as a specific name, has also been used for a species of *Centaurea*.

From the hort. standpoint we can dismiss all but the florists' cineraria (*Senecio cruentus*). This is a very widely grown greenhouse plant forced into profuse bloom, especially in the fall. Their culture should not be attempted without a greenhouse, and this must be kept cool (50° at night, not over 60° in the day).

---

* Special articles on the subjects indicated by an asterisk (*) will be found at the words so marked.

Part of the attraction of a finely flowered cineraria plant is the large truss of flowers well above the handsome foliage. To secure this the following directions should be noted. For fall and winter bloom all the single varieties are started from seed sown in May, preferably in flats in the cold frame or in a cool greenhouse. As the seedlings develop pot them up in successively larger pots, but always keep them on the edge of being pot-bound. By fall most plants should be only in 5- or 6-in. pots, only the largest in 8-in. pots. Use potting mixture* 3.

During growth up to the 6-in. pot stage many of the plants will have a tendency to bloom. This must be checked by pinching out all buds. Also, to keep the plants bushy so that the final truss of flowers will stand well above the foliage, pinch off any branches that will make the plant leggy.

In the case of the double-flowered varieties they are best increased by cuttings that may be made of the vigorous shoots that start after the flowering top is cut off. After rooting in sand, these are potted up and handled exactly as are the seedlings from single varieties.

Cinerarias make fine window garden plants, but only if the room is a cool one. Any temperature above 65° will quickly spoil them.

INSECT PESTS. Aphids, thrips, and leaf tiers (see CHRYSANTHEMUM), whiteflies (see BEGONIA), and red spider mites (see CARNATION) are important pests. Sowbugs and thousand-legs (millipedes) in greenhouses can be killed with bran bait, mixed extra sweet.

DISEASES. Cinerarias are susceptible to two diseases, rust and downy mildew. For rust, see Rusts at PLANT DISEASES. Downy mildew is characterized by the appearance of dark brown dead areas on the foliage. As the disease progresses, the leaves may die and drop from the plants. In general, this trouble is not particularly prevalent. Remove and burn all infected leaves, lower the humidity and avoid wetting the foliage when watering.

**CINEREA, -us, -um** (sy-neer′ee-a). Cinereous; *i.e.* ashy or ash-colored.

**CINNABARINA, -us, -um** (sin-na-ba-ry′na). Vermilion-red.

**CINNAMOMEA, -us, -um** (sin-a-mō′mee-a). Cinnamon-like, or of cinnamon color.

**CINNAMOMUM** (sin-na-mō′mum). A genus of commercially important, aromatic, evergreen trees of the family Lauraceae, mostly from tropical Asia, two of them widely grown as the source of camphor and cinnamon. Leaves often distinctly 3-veined from the base. Flowers small, not showy, without petals, the calyx 6-lobed. Stamens* 9 or fewer, in three series together with a fourth series of sterile stamens. Fruit a berry, set in a cup-like receptacle.* (*Cinnamomum* is the old Greek name for cinnamon.)

The two below are occasionally planted in zone* 9, or the most favorable sites in zone* 8, not so much for ornament as for the interest of their products. Neither is of commercial importance in the U.S., and true cinnamon (*C. zeylanicum*) is rarely cult. here but is an important industry in Ceylon. Outdoors the trees do well in a sandy loam or on a variety of other soils in southern Fla. In the greenhouse they need a warm house (60°-75°) and potting mixture* 5.

camphora. Camphor tree. Not over 40–50 ft. high. Leaves alternate,* more or less elliptic, but tapering at the tip, 4–5 in. long, pale underneath. Flowers yellow, the clusters shorter than the leaves. China and Japan. Bruised foliage is camphor-scented, and the wood (in Formosa) is the commercial source of camphor. Occasionally planted as a street tree in southern Calif. and Fla.

cassia. Cassia-bark tree. A tree 30–45 ft. high with opposite* leaves that are oblongish and 4–6 in. long. Flowers yellowish-white, the densely hairy clusters as long as the leaves. China. Largely grown in the Far East as a fraudulent adulterant of true cinnamon. Little grown here, but occasionally seen in southern Fla. and Calif.

**CINNAMON FAMILY** = Lauraceae.

**CINNAMON FERN** = *Osmunda cinnamomea*.

**CINNAMON ROSE** = *Rosa cinnamomea*.

**CINNAMON VINE** = *Dioscorea batatas*.

**CINQUEFOIL.** See POTENTILLA.

**CION** (sy′on). Often spelled scion. A detached shoot of a woody plant, containing two or more buds to be used in grafting.* The purpose of a cion (as distinguished from a cutting which will be rooted) is to insert it in a stock. When cion and stock have completely united the buds of the cion will continue to produce growth similar to the plant from which it was cut, not that of the stock into which it was grafted. Upon this fact has been built the whole reason and technique of grafting.* See also BUDDING.

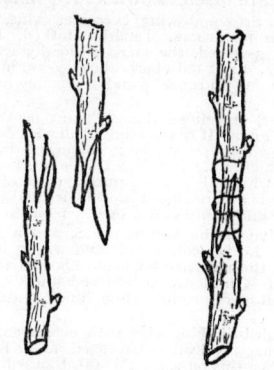

Cion and stock. At the left the cion, above, and the stock below cut ready for grafting. At the right cion and stock waxed and bound ready for uniting.

**CION BUDDING.** An erroneous term for a form of grafting (which see).

**CIRCASSIN SEEDS.** See ADENANTHERA.

*CIRCINALIS, -e* (sir-si-nay′lis). Coiled.

*CIRCINATA, -us, -um* (sir-si-nay′ta). Coiled.

**CIRCULAR BEDS.** For the number of plants needed for circular or round flower beds, see GARDEN TABLES IV.

**CIRCULAR TANKS.** For contents see WEIGHTS AND MEASURES 5.

**CIRCUMNEUTRAL.** A term for most ordinary garden soils whose range of soil acidity is indicated by the pH value 6.00–8.00. Most garden plants appear to be relatively indifferent to a soil acidity or alkalinity within this range. For details see ACID AND ALKALI SOILS.

**CIRCUMPOSITION** = Air layering. See LAYERING.

**CIRSIUM** (sir′si-um). Thistles are more often weeds than garden plants. Of 200 known species (family Compositae) scattered over the north temperate zone, only a very few are of any garden interest, and some are most pernicious weeds. They are prickly herbs with alternate* or basal leaves that are nearly always cut or lobed, and horribly spiny-margined. Flowers tiny, tubular (all disk* flowers), crowded in a dense, usually spiny-bracted,* head, and often very handsome. (*Cirsium* is from the Greek for a kind of thistle.)

The two garden plants are biennials of easy culture in any garden soil. See BIENNIALS.

arvense. Canada thistle. One of the worst weeds in N.A. See Canada thistle in the list at WEEDS.

diacantha. Fishbone thistle. Not over 3 ft. high. Leaves narrowly lance-shaped, not deeply cut, about 4 in. long, smooth above but densely white-hairy beneath. Flower heads purple. Syria. Summer.

occidentale. A beautiful, white-woolly herb 2–3 ft. high. Leaves oblongish, 6–9 in. long, toothed or somewhat deeply cut, prickly. Flower heads about 2 in. across, rose-purple and showy. Calif. and southern Ore. The *var.* coulteri differs in having long branches with a single head; the *var.* venustum has heads more webby than white-woolly.

**CIRUELA.** See SPONDIAS.

**CISSUS** (sis′sus). A very large genus of chiefly tropical, grape-like vines (a few non-hort. herbs) of the family Vitaceae, differing from the closely related grape in having an inedible berry, and in technical characters. The cult. species are thick-leaved, handsome-foliaged vines, much grown outdoors in southern Calif. and Fla. (hardy elsewhere only as indicated below) and in greenhouses. Leaves sometimes evergreen, alternate,* simple* and lobed, or compound.* All climb by tendrils.* Flowers small, inconspicu-

---

* Special articles on the subjects indicated by an asterisk (*) will be found at the words so marked.

ous, with 4 expanding petals. (*Cissus* is from the Greek for ivy.) The cult. species are often known as treebine.

**capensis.** Evergreen grape. Strong-growing evergreen vine, much used in nearly frost-free regions for arbors. Tendrils* forked. Leaves simple,* 4-8 in. wide, strongly 3-veined, the margin broadly wavy or toothed, the young growth rusty. Fruit red-black, about ½ in. in diameter. S. Africa. Hardy outdoors only in zones* 8 and 9, possibly in zone* 7 in protected places.

**discolor.** A beautiful, slender, greenhouse foliage plant persistently cursed with the name trailing begonia. It has nothing to do with *Begonia*. Leaves simple,* oblongish or ovalish, 4-6 in. long, somewhat tapering at the tip, finely toothed and highly colored. The leaves are generally green above, but blotched with white, pink or red-purple, or all of them; and purple beneath. Java. Needs a warm, moist greenhouse and potting mixture* 4. Not high-climbing, and easily grown over a bamboo trellis.

**incisa.** Marine ivy. A native of the southern U.S. and a strong-growing vine up to 30 ft. long. Leaves compound* and with 3 leaflets, or simple* and deeply 3-lobed, the ultimate segments about 1 in. long and toothed. Fruit black, about ¾ in. long, on recurved stalks. Mo. to Ariz., Tex. and Fla. Hardy outdoors possibly from zone* 5, certainly from zone* 6, southward.

**striata.** A low, shrubby, tendril-climbing vine with evergreen, hairy foliage. Leaves compound,* the 3-5 leaflets arranged finger-fashion, usually not over 1 in. long (thrice this on some shoots), toothed. Fruit small, 2-4-seeded. S.A. Hardy outdoors in zones* 8 and 9, elsewhere to be grown in the cool greenhouse in potting mixture* 4.

**CISTACEAE** (siss-tay'see-ee). The rockrose family is a small one, and of its 8 genera and over 150 species, only *Cistus* and *Helianthemum* are of any garden interest. They are low shrubs or woody herbs, mostly from the north temperate zone, usually with quickly wilting or ephemeral, but often showy, flowers.

Leaves usually opposite,* but the upper ones alternate* in *Helianthemum*. Flowers regular,* usually with 5 petals, solitary or in small clusters. In *Cistus* the flowers are showy, and there are many garden hybrids with white, lilac, or rose-pink bloom. In *Helianthemum* the flowers are usually smaller and of various colors. The fruit in both genera is a dry pod (capsule*) splitting into 3, 5, or rarely 10 valves.*

Technical flower characters: Sepals 5, the three inner often persistent, the two outer ones bract*-like, smaller, and sometimes lacking. Petals mostly 5. Stamens numerous. Ovary superior,* 1-celled, or rarely incompletely 5- or 10-celled, with 2 to many ovules. Style with a 3-lobed or single stigma.

**CISTERNS.** To estimate contents *see* WEIGHTS AND MEASURES 5.

**CISTUS** (sis'tus). Mediterranean shrubs of low stature and usually called rockrose (family Cistaceae). Long known in Old World gardens, they are less known here, perhaps because they do not stand northern winters. Leaves opposite,* simple,* without marginal teeth,* evergreen or nearly so, generally softly hairy. Flowers large, somewhat suggesting a single rose, with 5 separate petals, but many stamens.* Fruit a capsule splitting by 5 or 10 valves. (*Cistus* is the classical Greek name for these plants.)

The rockroses are handsome garden plants, but need particular attention to soil and climatic restrictions. Most of them are partial to well-drained, open soils, not acid, and preferably somewhat derived from limestone. They must have open sunlight, and will not tolerate slushy, bitter winters. In Calif. and the South they are easily grown, elsewhere only as indicated below. The plants are difficult to move, except when young, consequently seedlings are best kept in pots until ready to be planted out, and then the plants should be let alone. They may also be increased by layering. But an easier method is to make cuttings of non-flowering side shoots, rooted in a sand-filled box covered with glass, preferably from Aug. to Oct. The lower-growing species are excellent rock garden plants.

**albidus.** From 4-6 ft. high, the foliage white-hairy. Leaves stalkless, oblongish or elliptic, 1-2½ in. long. Flowers about 2 in. wide, rose-lilac, blotched yellow at the center. June. Hardy from zone* 6 southward.

**creticus** = *Cistus villosus creticus.*

**crispus.** Not over 2 ft. high, and a compact shrub. Leaves stalkless, softly white-hairy, more or less elliptic, about 1 in. long and wrinkled. Flowers deep purple-red, about 2 in. across, in a close terminal cluster. June-July. Hardy possibly from zone* 5, surely from zone* 6, southward.

**ladaniferus.** A sticky-branched shrub scarcely over 4 ft. high. Leaves slightly stalked, green and sticky above, densely white-hairy beneath, lance-shaped, 3-4 in. long. Flowers solitary, white, but purple-blotched at the center, nearly 3½ in. wide. July-Aug. Hardy from zone* 6 southward. The *var.* **maculatus** has a brownish-red center to the flower, and *var.* **albiflorus** has white but yellow-centered flowers.

**laurifolius.** A shrub 5-8 ft. high. Leaves stalked, ovalish, 1¾-2½ in. long, green above and sticky, densely white or brown-hairy beneath. Flowers nearly 2½ in. wide, in clusters (cymes*), white, with a yellow center. July to Sept. Hardy from zone* 6 southward.

**villosus.** A compact shrub not over 3 ft. high. Leaves stalked, elliptic or ovalish, 1-2½ in. long, rough and hairy, especially beneath. Flowers about 2½ in. wide, rose or rose-purple, but with a yellow center, borne in a cyme.* June-July. Hardy from zone* 5, and possibly from zone* 4, southward. The *var.* **creticus** has smaller leaves and purple flowers. The *var.* **tauricus** is a lower shrub and has some leaves roundish. It is more hardy than the typical form or than the *var.* **creticus**.

Besides these species there are many hybrids. Of these the following are worth attention, especially in Calif.: *Cistus corbariensis* (white) and *C. purpureus* (pink and red-centered).

**CITHAREXYLUM** (sith-a-rex'i-lum). Tropical American trees or shrubs of the family Verbenaceae, of secondary garden interest except for their occasional planting in southern Fla. for ornament. Commonly called fiddlewood. Leaves opposite,* rather leathery. Flowers white (in those below), in small, finger-shaped clusters (racemes*), terminal or in the leaf-axils.* Corolla slightly irregular,* its 5-lobed limb oblique. Fruit fleshy, set in the persistent calyx. (*Citharexylum* is from the Greek for zither and wood.)

**ilicifolium.** Shrubby, the branches 4-angled. Leaves elliptic or oblong, 1-2 in. long, the margin rolled. Flowers about ⅓ in. long, the clusters terminal. Fruit pea-sized. Ecuador.

**spinosum.** A handsome tree up to 50 ft., its branchlets 4-angled. Leaves oblongish, 5-8 in. long, its stalk nearly an inch long. Flowers nearly ⅓ in. long, fragrant, the cluster nearly 12 in. long and sometimes branched. Fruit about ½ in. long. W.I.

**CITRANGE.** A hybrid citrus fruit derived from crossing the sweet orange with *Poncirus trifoliata*. It has little or no value for fresh fruit, but is used somewhat in cooking or for making citrangeade. The plant is hardier than the sweet orange, and can be grown as far north as zone* 7. The fruits, as yet of little importance, are about 2-3 in. in diameter, and are more acid and have a more distinctive odor than the orange. The citrange is chiefly of use as material for professional citrus breeders.

**CITRANGEQUAT.** An interesting plant to citrus breeders, derived from crossing the citrange and the kumquat. It has yellow, orange, or reddish fruits 1½-2 in. in diameter, of no commercial importance, but used in cooking and for beverages.

*CITRATA, -us, -um* (sit-tray'ta). Citrus-like as to color, flavor or odor.

*CITRIFOLIA, -us, -um* (sit-tri-fō'li-a). With leaves like *Citrus*.

*CITRINA, -us, -um* (sit-try'na). Like, or colored like, citron.

*CITRIODORA, -us, -um* (sit-tri-o-door'ra). With the fragrance of the lemon.

*CITROIDES* (sit-troy'deez; but *see* OÏDES). Citron-like.

**CITRON.** The preserved rind of *Citrus medica*, or the tree itself. Citron also applies to a form of the watermelon better known as the citron melon or preserving melon. *See* WATERMELON.

**CITRONELLA.** *See* COLLINSONIA CANADENSIS, but this is not the source of citronella, for which *see* CYMBOPOGON.

**CITRONELLA GRASS** = *Cymbopogon nardus*, the source of citronella.

**CITRON MELON** = *Citrullus vulgaris citroides*. *See* WATERMELON.

**CITROPSIS** (sit-trop'sis). Spiny African trees of the family Rutaceae, one of them of interest to citrus breeders and somewhat as an ornamental in southern Calif. and Fla. Spines usually in pairs. Leaves compound,* the 3-5 leaflets arranged feather-fashion. Flowers much as in the orange, but the petals strap-shaped. Fruit like a lime in appearance but sweet. (*Citropsis* is from Greek for *Citrus*-like.)

**schweinfurthi.** African cherry-orange. A shrub or small tree. Leaflets broadly lance-shaped, 2-5 in. long. Flowers in clusters of 4-10, not over

---

* Special articles on the subjects indicated by an asterisk (*) will be found at the words so marked.

1 in. wide. Fruit about 1½ in. in diameter. S. Africa to the Congo. Little known in U.S. as yet.

**CITROSMA, -us, -um** (sit-tros′ma). Lemon-scented.

**CITRULLUS.** See WATERMELON.

**CITRUS** (sit′rus). Here belong the incomparably important citrus fruits, all derived from this genus of only a dozen species of the family Rutaceae. All of them came originally from tropical or sub-tropical Asia or Indo-Malaya, but are now spread all over the world as cult. fruits of the greatest importance, or as innumerable escapes,* many of which are worthless. They are (or were before cult. modified them) often spiny, rather small, highly aromatic trees which have a compound* leaf on which only a single leaflet is found (therefore appearing as if with simple leaves). In most of them there is a distinctly winged leafstalk. Flowers solitary or in few-flowered clusters, often very fragrant (orange, especially). Petals 5, white, often waxy. Fruit a special form of berry known as a hesperidium. This is globose or lemon-shaped, often has several compartments separated by the rag,* much pulpy juice, and a spongy rind beset with aromatic oil glands. (*Citrus* is a classical name applied to some other tree, but adopted by Linnaeus for the citrus fruits.)

Besides the common citrus fruits there are several other plants in the genus *Citrus* grown for ornament. They are also described below. For the culture and best varieties of the important ones see the special articles at ORANGE, LIME, LEMON, and GRAPEFRUIT. In addition to those below there are the interesting hybrids known as citrange, citrangequat, limequat, and tangelo (see these terms). See also FORTUNELLA (for the kumquat).

**aurantifolia.** Lime. A small spiny tree. Leaves elliptic or oblongish, 2-3 in. long, the stalk narrowly winged. Flowers scarcely ½ in. long. Fruit generally round-oval, 1½-2½ in. in diameter, very acid. Asia. For culture and varieties see LIME. The sweet lime (*C. limetta*) is a variety or perhaps a separate species. See LIME.

**aurantium.** Seville or sour orange. A small tree with long but not especially sharp spines. Leaves oval or oblong, 3-4 in. long, stalk broadly winged. Flowers very fragrant, about ¾ in. long. Fruit acid, the rag* also bitter, flattened-globe-shaped, about 3½ in. in diameter. Cochin-China. Little cult. in the U.S., but in Spain, the finest orange for marmalade. It is more hardy than the common orange. See ORANGE.

**bergamia.** Bergamot. A spiny tree with oblong-oval leaves, the stalks winged. Fruit sour, pear-shaped, about 3½ in. in diameter. It yields an essential oil, as cult. in Eu., but is little known here.

**grandis** = *Citrus maxima*.

**japonica** = *Fortunella japonica*.

**limonia.** Lemon. A small tree, its spines or thorns short and stiff. Leaves oblong or elliptic, 2-3½ in. long, finely but bluntly toothed, the stalk very narrowly winged or merely margined. Flowers ⅓-⅔ in. long, white, but pinkish outside. Fruit egg-shaped, but with a nipple-like projection at the end (umbonate), very sour. Asia. For culture and varieties see LEMON.

**maxima.** Shaddock, also pummelo and pompelmous. Tropical tree 15-25 ft. high, not usually spiny. Leaves 4-8 in. long, hairy beneath, the stalk widely winged. Fruit pear-shaped, very large, the flesh coarse and inferior to the grapefruit. East Indies, from which a Capt. Shaddock brought it to Barbados in 1696. Little known here except in southern Fla.

**medica.** Citron. A shrub or small tree with stiff, short spines. Leaves 4-6 in. long, toothed, the stalk without wings. Flowers about 1½ in. long, white, but purplish outside. Fruit 7-10 in. long, more or less oval or oblong, lemon-yellow, its rough, thick skin highly aromatic and adapted to make commercial citron. Asia. Much grown in southern Eu., only occasionally in Fla. and Calif.

**mitis.** Calamondin orange; called, also, Panama orange, although a native of the Philippines. A nearly spineless small tree with oblongish leaves having narrowly winged stalks. Flowers about ⅓ in. long. Fruit globe-shaped or slightly flattened at the ends, about 1 in. in diameter, the skin loose, the pulp acid. Hardier than the orange, but little grown.

**nobilis.** King orange. A nearly spineless tree with broadly oval leaves that are only narrowly winged on the leafstalk. Flowers about ⅓ in. long. Fruit orange or reddish, flattened at each end, with a loose, thin skin, and sweet or slightly acid pulp. Cochin-China. Little grown but of interest as the source of two varieties: *var.* **deliciosa**, tangerine, also the mandarin orange. Leaves oval-lance-shaped, 1½-2½ in. long, the stalks scarcely margined. Fruit 2-3 in. in diameter, smooth, reddish-orange, the segments so easily separating that the fruit is sometimes called kid-glove orange, *i.e.* it need not moisten the hands; *var.* **unshiu**, Satsuma orange. Leaves 3-4 in. long and broader than in the tangerine. Fruit depressed-globose, about 2½ in. in diameter, the pulp orange-color, sweet. A very hardy variety.

**paradisi.** Grapefruit; called, also, pomelo. A tree much like *C. maxima* but larger, and with the leaves not hairy beneath. Fruit 4-8 in. in diameter, usually borne in clusters, the pulp fine-grained, moderately acid. Origin unknown. For culture and varieties see GRAPEFRUIT.

**sinensis.** The common or sweet orange. A medium-sized tree (15-25 ft. as cult.) with a few bluntish spines or none. Leaves oblong-oval, 3-5 in. long, the stalk narrowly winged. Flowers white, fragrant, but not so fragrant as those of the sour orange. Fruit a depressed sphere, 3-5 in. in diameter, the pulp sweet. China. For culture and varieties see ORANGE.

**taitensis.** Otaheite or Tahiti orange. A pretty little miniature orange tree much grown by florists, of unknown origin but not from Tahiti (Fiji) in spite of its widely used common name. Usually not over 2-3 ft. high. Leaves oblongish, 2-3½ in. long, the stalk narrowly winged. Flowers white, but pinkish outside. Fruit bright orange, but lemon-shaped, about 1½ in. long, ornamental because they are numerous, but of insipid taste. A decorative plant well suited for the window garden, but best grown in a cool greenhouse in potting mixture* 4.

**trifoliata** = *Poncirus trifoliata*.

**CITRUS CANKER.** See Diseases at ORANGE.

**CITRUS FAMILY** = Rutaceae.

**CITRUS FRUITS.** The chief ones, each the subject of a special article, are orange, lemon, grapefruit, and lime. For other citrus fruits see CITRUS.

**CITY GARDEN.** See BACKYARD GARDEN.

**CLADANTHUS** (kla-dan′thus). A single herb of the family Compositae, a native of southern Spain and Morocco and grown as a hardy annual in the flower garden. The only species, *C. arabicus*, is a branching herb 2-3½ ft. high, with strongly scented foliage. Leaves alternate,* parted feather-fashion, the segments narrow and 3-toothed or divided at the end. Flowers yellow, the heads composed of both ray and disk* flowers, the head solitary and the plant often forking beneath it. It is sometimes listed as *Anthemis arabica* and is of easy culture if the seed is sown where the plant is wanted. See ANNUALS. (*Cladanthus* is from the Greek for branch and flower, in allusion to its peculiar branching habit.)

**CLADOCALYX** (klad-o-cay′licks). With a club-shaped calyx.*

**CLADODE.** A cladophyll.

**CLADOPHYLL.** An expanded, leaf-like branch, a common example of which is found in the butcher's-broom. See RUSCUS.

**CLADRASTIS** (kla-dras′tis). A small genus of North American and eastern Asiatic decorative trees of the pea family, the native yellow-wood, often planted for ornament. They have alternate,* compound* leaves, the leaflets arranged feather-fashion, with an odd one at the end. Flowers fragrant, white (in ours), pea-like, in showy clusters (panicles*). Pod (legume*) oblongish, flattened. (*Cladrastis* is from the Greek for fragile and branch, in allusion to the usually brittle twigs.)

The yellow-wood is deservedly popular for its showy bloom, and will thrive in a variety of soils. Easily propagated by spring-sown seeds.

**lutea.** Kentucky yellow-wood; also called gopherwood. A smooth-barked tree, 30-50 ft. high, its wood yellow. Leaflets 7-9, ovalish and about 3-4 in. long. Flowers about 1 in. long, the cluster 10-20 in. long and drooping. Pod 4-5 in. long. N. Car. to Ky. and Tenn. Hardy from zone* 3 southward. The tree was for long known as *C. tinctoria*.

**CLAMMY LOCUST** = *Robinia viscosa*. See LOCUST.

**CLARET.** See *vinifera* varieties at GRAPE.

**CLARIN** = *Phaedranthus buccinatorius*.

**CLARKIA** (clark′i-a). Very showy annual herbs of the family Onagraceae, mostly from the western U.S., one of them popular in the flower garden, and the other also much grown. They have alternate,* narrow leaves, without marginal teeth or very small ones, and handsome flowers which are solitary or in few-flowered clusters. Petals 4, clawed,* the upper part widely spreading and sometimes 3-toothed. Fruit a somewhat 4-angled, narrow capsule.* (Named for Captain Wm. Clark of Lewis and Clark fame.)

The two below are of the easiest culture if treated as hardy annuals (see ANNUALS). Unlike many others, these should not be thinned out too much, as they appear to bloom better when somewhat crowded. They flower from July 1 or soon after, until Oct.

**elegans.** Stems erect, reddish, 18-36 in. high. Leaves ovalish, remotely toothed. Flowers purple or rose-colored, but whitish in some hort. forms, nearly 2½ in. wide. Claw* of the petal not toothed. Pod about 1 in. long. Calif. A good named form is Salmon King, and a red variety is called Vesuvius.

---

* Special articles on the subjects indicated by an asterisk (*) will be found at the words so marked.

pulchella. Lower and with narrower leaves. Flowers lilac (white in some hort. forms), the claw* of the petal with 2 recurved teeth. British Columbia to Calif.

There are many hybrids between these two species, some of them double-flowered, and all of them superior to the wild species. They make fine flowers for cutting.

**CLARK, J. T. C.** See America at GARDEN BOOKS.

**CLARY** = *Salvia sclarea.*

**CLASPING.** Surrounding the stem, as the leaves of some honeysuckles.

***CLAVA-HERCULIS, -e*** (kla-va-her'kew-lis). Club of Hercules. See ZANTHOXYLUM.

***CLAVATA, -us, -um*** (kla-vay'ta). Clavate; *i.e.* club-shaped.

**CLAW.** The long, usually narrow, basal part of a petal, common in some flowers of iris, rose, lily, pink, *Clarkia*, and many others. Such petals are said to be *clawed*.

**CLAW-FERN.** See ONYCHIUM.

**CLAY.** See SOILS.

**CLAYPAN.** See HARDPAN.

**CLAYTON FERN** = *Osmunda claytoniana.*

**CLAYTONIA** (clay-tō'ni-a). The spring beauty of our meadows is one of perhaps two dozen species of slender, perennial herbs of the family Portulacaceae, sometimes transferred to the wild garden. Both those below need partial shade and a moist site. They have tuberous roots (corm*), and slender, weak, narrow leaves without marginal teeth. Flowers blooming very early in spring, pink or white, often streaked, borne in few-flowered, lax clusters. Petals 5. Stamens 5. Fruit a small pod with 3 valves. (Named for John Clayton, early American botanist of Virginia.)

Both the plants below will completely disappear by mid-summer. They bloom just before the forest canopy comes into leafage, but soon die down. Their culture is easy in moist places under partial shade, impossible on dry sites.

caroliniana. Resembling the next, but with broader leaves and smaller flowers. A mountain plant chiefly in wet woods, eastern N.A. April.

virginica. The common spring beauty, commonly called Mayflower, grass-flower, and good-morning-spring. A slender herb 4–6 in. high. Leaves narrowly lance-shaped, 2–5 in. long. Flowers white, but often tinged with pink or streaked with it, about ⅝ in. wide, very fleeting, and wilting at once if picked. In moist thickets or woods throughout eastern N.A.

**CLAYWEED** = *Tussilago farfara.*

**CLEANING FLOWER POTS.** See FLOWER POTS.

**CLEAR-EYE** = *Salvia sclarea.*

**CLEAVERS.** See GALIUM.

**CLEFT GRAFTING.** See GRAFTING.

**CLEISTOGAMOUS FLOWERS.** Small, often partly underground flowers that never open and are self-pollinated. Some plants, as the violets, have both ordinary and cleistogamous flowers.

**CLEMATIS** (klem'a-tis). A genus of perhaps 300 species of herbs, or shrubby or woody vines of the buttercup family, widely distributed, but most numerous in eastern As., the Himalayas, and N.A. Leaves mostly compound,* sometimes simple,* but usually with 3–5, or more, leaflets, the leafstalk often curling and acting as a tendril.* Flowers frequently very showy, without petals, but with 4 petal-like sepals, sometimes 5–8. Stamens* numerous, some of them occasionally sterile or even petal-like. Fruit a collection of 1-seeded achenes,* each (in some species) with a plumed, feathery, and often showy, tail-like appendage. (*Clematis* is from the Greek for a slender vine.) Many of the species are called virgin's-bower.

For culture and many beautiful hybrids *see* below.

alpina. A woody vine, 4–7 ft. high. Leaflets nearly stalkless, ovalish, 1–3 in. long, coarsely toothed. Flowers violet-blue, bell-shaped, about 1½ in. long. Fruits plumed. Eurasia. April–May. Hardy to zone* 2.

apiifolia. A woody vine 5–9 ft. high. Leaflets oval-lance-shaped, 2–4 in. long, coarsely toothed or even lobed. Flowers dull white, ½–1 in. wide, in loose clusters (panicles*) in the leaf-axils.* Fruits shortly plumed. Jap. Sept.–Oct. Hardy from zone* 1 southward.

armandi. An evergreen, woody vine 10–15 ft. high. Leaflets 3, on twisted stalks, generally oblongish, 3½–5½ in. long. Flowers white, 1½–2½ in. wide, in leafless clusters. Fruits long-plumed. China. May. Hardy from zone* 6 or 7 southward.

coccinea = *Clematis texensis.*

columbiana. Climbing or trailing vine, 4–10 ft. long. Leaflets 3, stalked, generally oblong-oval, 1½–4 in. long, mostly without teeth. Flowers blue or purple, the sepals narrow. Fruits long-plumed. May–June. Western U.S. Hardy from zone* 3 southward. Perhaps a western form of *C. verticillaris.*

crispa. Blue jasmine, called also bluebell, and curly clematis. A shrubby vine, 6–9 ft. high. Leaflets ovalish, 1¾–3½ in. long, sometimes lobed. Flowers nodding, solitary, bell-shaped, blue or bluish-purple to pale pink, ¾–1½ in. long. Fruits with silky, not plumed, appendages. June–Sept. Va. to Fla. and Tex. Hardy from zone* 3 southward.

davidiana. Upright, usually not over 4 ft. tall. Leaflets 3, more or less wedge-shaped, coarsely toothed, 2½–5 in. long. Male and female flowers on different plants, bright blue, ¾–2 in. long. China. Aug.–Sept. Hardy from zone* 3 southward. See BLUE GARDEN.

douglasi. Sugar-loaf. An erect herb, 12–20 in. high. Leaves twice- or thrice-compound,* the leaflets narrow. Flowers solitary, about 1 in. long, tubular, purple inside but paler outside. Colo. to Wash. May–July. Hardy up to zone* 2.

durandi. A hybrid. See Clematis Culture (below).

eriophora. An erect herb 9–18 in. high, its foliage white-hairy. Leaves twice-compound,* the leaflets narrow. Flowers solitary, nodding, a little less than 1 in. long, bell-shaped and purple. Wyo. to N. Mex. May–June. Hardy from zones* 2 or 3 southward.

flammula. A woody vine 10–15 ft. high. Leaves twice- or thrice-compound,* the leaflets broadly oval or narrower, ¾–2 in. long. Flowers fragrant, white, nearly 1½ in. wide, in many-flowered clusters (panicles*). Mediterranean region to Persia. Aug.–Oct. Hardy, possibly, from zone* 5 southward.

fremonti. An erect herb 10–18 in. high. Leaves simple,* leathery and stalkless. Flower solitary, nodding, bell-shaped, purple, about 1 in. long. Mo. to Neb. May–Aug. Hardy everywhere.

graveolens = *Clematis orientalis.*

integrifolia. An herb or undershrub, usually not over 2½ ft. Leaves simple, stalkless, oval-oblong, and without teeth. Flowers solitary and terminal, violet-blue (rarely white), 1½–2 in. long, the stamens yellow. Fruit plumed. Eurasia. June–Aug. Hardy everywhere. See BLUE GARDEN.

jackmani. A showy, woody climber, perhaps the most widely cult. of all clematis, and of hybrid origin. Leaves compound,* or the upper ones simple, large and ovalish. Flowers usually in threes, sometimes 6 in. and usually more than 4 in. wide, violet-purple. July–Oct. Hardy from zone* 2 southward. For its numerous varieties or named forms *see* below.

jouiniana. A hybrid. See Clematis Culture (below).

ligusticifolia. Hill clematis. A woody climber 10–15 ft. high. Leaves compound,* the 5–7 leaflets ovalish or narrower, 1½–3½ in. long. Male and female flowers on different plants, about 1 in. wide, white, in cymes.* Western N.A. July–Oct. Hardy everywhere.

missouriensis. Closely related to *C. virginiana* and differing mostly in the leaflets being hairy beneath. Neb. to Mo. Hardy from zone* 3 southward.

montana. A woody vine up to 20 ft. Leaflets 3, oblong or ovalish, short-stalked, 1¼–4½ in. long, deeply toothed (rarely without any). Flowers 1–5, slender-stalked, white, 1½–3½ in. wide. Fruit plumed. China and Himalayas. May. Hardy without protection from zone* 4, with it from zone* 3, southward. The *var. rubens* has purplish young foliage and pink flowers. The *var. wilsoni* has larger white flowers than the typical form and blooms 1–2 months later. The first variety is somewhat more hardy than the typical *C. montana*, but the second variety a little less so.

orientalis. A woody vine 10–15 ft. high. Leaves compound* or twice-compound,* the leaflets ovalish or oblong, ¾–2 in. long. Flowers yellow, 1½–3 in. wide, solitary or in few-flowered clusters. Fruit long-plumed. Aug.–Oct. Persia to Himalayas. Hardy from zone* 2 or 3 southward. Sometimes called *C. graveolens.*

paniculata. Japanese clematis. A woody climber 20–30 ft. high. Leaflets 3–5, ovalish, 1½–4 in. long, without teeth, but sometimes lobed. Flowers white, fragrant, about 1½ in. wide, in a many-flowered cluster. Fruit plumed. Jap. Sept.–Oct. Hardy from zone* 2 southward.

pitcheri. A woody, high-climbing vine. Leaflets usually 3–6, ovalish, 1½–3½ in. long, with a fine, short tip at the end. Flowers urn-shaped, solitary, long-stalked, about 1½ in. long, purplish. Fruit not plumed. Central U.S. June–Sept. Hardy from zone* 3 southward. Sometimes called *C. simsi.*

recta. An erect herb 2–5 ft. high. Leaflets 5–9, usually without teeth. Flowers white, fragrant, about 1 in. wide, in many-flowered clusters, mostly terminal. Southern Eu. June–Aug. Hardy everywhere, as are several varieties, one with double flowers.

scotti. An erect herb 10–18 in. high. Leaves twice-compound,* the leaflets ¾–1½ in. long, the stalks often twisted. Flower solitary, urn-shaped, about 1 in. long, purple-brown. Wyo. and S. Dak. to N. Mex. and Mex. May–July. Hardy from zone* 3 southward.

serratifolia. A woody vine 6–9 ft. high. Leaves twice-compound,* the leaflets ovalish or narrower, 1½–3 in. long, toothed and sometimes 2–3-lobed. Flowers 1–3 together, yellow, 1–1½ in. long. Fruits plumed. Korea. Aug.–Oct. Hardy everywhere.

simsi = *Clematis pitcheri.*

tangutica. Golden clematis. A woody vine 6–9 ft. high. Leaves compound, the leaflets oblongish, 1½–2½ in. long. Fruits plumed. Northeastern As. June, and often again in the fall. Hardy everywhere.

texensis. Scarlet clematis. A slightly woody vine, 4–6 ft. high. Leaflets 4–8, the uppermost often replaced by a tendril,* broadly oval, 1¾–3½ in. long, bluish-green. Flowers solitary, stalked, urn-shaped, scarlet

---

* Special articles on the subjects indicated by an asterisk (*) will be found at the words so marked.

to rose-pink, about 1½ in. long, constricted near the top. Fruits plumed. Tex. July–Sept. Hardy from zone* 3 southward. Sometimes called *C. coccinea.*

**troutbeckiana.** A climbing vine, 6–10 ft. high, the stems reddish-brown and striped. Lower leaves simple,* the upper compound,* the leaflets elliptic, ¾–2½ in. long, without marginal teeth. Flowers urn-shaped, lavender or pinkish-purple, but yellowish-green inside. Fruits plumed. July–Aug. Of unknown, but possibly of hybrid origin. Hardy from zone* 2 southward.

**veitchiana.** A slender, woody vine, the leaves twice-compound.* Ultimate leaflets ovalish or narrower, 1½–2½ in. long, coarsely toothed or 3-lobed, silky underneath. Flowers bell-shaped, nodding, fragrant, yellowish-white, about ¾ in. long, in bracted* clusters. Western China. Sept.–Oct. Hardy from zone* 4 or 5 southward.

**versicolor.** A vine 9–12 ft. high. Leaves compound, the leaflets bluish-green beneath, very veiny, ¾–3 in. long. Flowers urn-shaped, solitary, nodding, purplish. Mo. and Ark. July. Hardy from zone* 3 southward.

**verticillaris.** Climbing up to 10 ft. or weak and sprawling without support. Leaflets 3, stalked, ovalish-oblong, 1½–3½ in. long, coarsely toothed or without teeth. Flowers solitary, nearly 3 in. wide, purple or bluish-purple. Fruits long-plumed. Eastern N.A. May–June. Hardy everywhere.

**viorna.** Slender, woody vine, 6–9 ft. high. Leaflets 5–7, ovalish or oblong, 1½–3½ in. long, more or less wedge-shaped at the base, sometimes lobed. Flowers solitary, nodding, urn-shaped, dull reddish-purple, about 1 in. long. Fruits with brownish plumes. Pa. and Ala. westward. May–Aug. Hardy everywhere.

**virginiana.** Woodbine; also called love-vine and old-man's-beard. Climbing, often up to 18 ft. or often sprawling as a wild plant. Leaflets ovalish, 2½ to 4 in. long, coarsely toothed. Male and female flowers on separate plants, white, ¾–1½ in. wide in clusters (panicles*) in the leaf-axils. Fruits plumed, the cluster of them nearly 2½ in. in diameter. Eastern N.A. Aug.–Oct. Hardy everywhere.

**vitalba.** Traveler's-joy; called, also, old-man's-beard and withywind. A high-climbing, woody vine, sometimes up to 25 ft. Leaflets usually 5, oval-lance-shaped, 1½–4 in. long, coarsely toothed or sometimes 3-lobed. Flowers white, slightly fragrant, about 1 in. wide, in terminal clusters (panicles*) or these sometimes in the leaf-axils.* Fruits long-plumed. Eu. and northern Africa. July–Oct. Hardy from zone* 3 southward.

**viticella.** Vine bower. Slender, woody vine, not over 12 ft. high. Leaflets ovalish or narrower, ¾–2 in. long, blunt, without marginal teeth, but sometimes 3-lobed. Flowers 1–3, rose-purple or violet, about 1¾ in. wide, the stamens* yellow. Fruit scarcely or not at all plumed. Eurasia. June–Aug. Hardy from zone* 2, perhaps from zone* 1, southward. There is also a white-flowered *var.* **alba**.

Various students of *Clematis* have, at times, split that genus into several others, notably *Atragene, Viticella, Flammula,* and *Viorna,* but there does not seem sufficient evidence to maintain them here.

The selection of the species treated above and the specifications of their hardiness in the different zones* are based upon the work of J. E. Spingarn, Esq., of Troutbeck, Amenia, N.Y., who has also contributed the notes on *Clematis* culture below. The hardiness notes are based upon his collection at Amenia and upon others at Roslyn, L.I.; Bar Harbor, Me.; Montreal; Dropmore, Manitoba; and scattered reports from the South and West.

## Clematis Culture

"Many years' experience among my plants," writes Wm. Robinson in the fifteenth edition of his *English Flower Garden,* "makes me more than ever convinced that the clematis is the most beautiful of our northern climbing plants." The genus is distinguished as much by variety as by beauty. It includes nearly three hundred species and an even larger number of beautiful hybrids. The colors include white, yellow, pink, red, lavender, mauve, violet, purple, and a host of intermediate shades. The shapes are almost as diverse, but fall more or less into three general forms, a type with small white flowers in panicles* or loose and irregular spreading clusters (*C. paniculata*), one with bell-shaped or urn-shaped flowers (*C. texensis*), and one with more or less flat or open flowers (*C. montana, C. jackmani*).

Clematis can be made to serve a great variety of purposes. They can be grown on trellises, fences, pergolas, walls, over mounds and tree-stumps, or to cover the side of a house. Most of the wild species are found under shrubs or small trees, over which they scramble into the sunlight; and this practice should be more generally followed by gardeners, for nearly all species and varieties love a cool root-run with their heads in the sun.

SMALL- AND MEDIUM-FLOWERED SPECIES. *Clematis* species are scattered all over the world, but are especially numerous in Eastern Asia, the Himalayas, and North America. They are for the most part climbers, growing from five to fifty feet high. Of these every garden should contain at least such slender climbers as *C. tangutica* (yellow), *C. texensis* (scarlet to rose-pink), *C. crispa* (pale purplish-pink), and *C. viticella* or *C. viticella alba* (white), as well as the more rampant climbers like *C. montana* (white), *C. montana rubens* (pink), *C. paniculata* (white), and the pale lavender hybrid, *C. jouiniana*. Besides these there are some interesting non-climbers which are admirable for the herbaceous border or the front of the shrubbery, such as *C. davidiana* (blue), *C. recta* (white), *C. integrifolia* (blue with a mass of yellow stamens*), and the attractive blue hybrid *C. durandii.* The gardener need not be dependent on nurseries for the rarer species, for most of them can easily be grown from seed, which can be obtained from American specialists in rare seeds or from European seedsmen; among the delightful sorts that can be grown this way are *C. alpina, C. orientalis, C. serratifolia,* and *C. viticella*. It is a pity that American gardeners do not take more interest in our native species; two have already been mentioned, *C. texensis* and *C. crispa,* but other sorts, such as *C. versicolor, C. troutbeckiana, C. scotti, C. virginiana* or its western kinsman *C. ligusticifolia,* are also interesting.

LARGE-FLOWERED HYBRIDS. The large-flowered hybrids are the showiest members of the clematis clan, and are worthy of a place in the proudest garden. The first was produced in 1855, but it was not until *jackmani* was exhibited in 1863 that they captured the imagination of Europe. Since then about 500 varieties have been created, of which about 175 are still listed by European nurserymen; one English nursery alone offered 92 varieties in 1934. They were produced by crossing four species, three large-flowered ones from China and Japan (the creamy-white *C. florida,* the white to violet-blue *C. patens,* and the very large pale lavender *C. lanuginosa*) and one medium-flowered species from southern Europe (the rosy-purple *C. viticella*). The hybrids are grouped into five general types according to the dominant strain in each, four of them receiving their names from the above-mentioned species and the fifth from *jackmani*, which has all the characteristics of a species or established form. The *florida* type and *patens* type bloom on old wood, while the *lanuginosa* type, *jackmani* type, and *viticella* type bloom on the growing summer shoots. This determines the treatment to be given the plants, the first two requiring little or no pruning, and the last three enduring or in fact requiring more severe pruning.

The hybrids can be propagated by grafting, layering, or from cuttings; but plants on their own roots (that is, from cuttings or layering) should always be preferred when obtainable, and nurserymen should be discouraged from selling grafted plants. Nodal or internodal cuttings of young shoots taken in the greenhouse in January or February usually root in sand more readily than internodal cuttings taken, according to the older method, from half-ripe wood in late summer.

Only a few varieties are obtainable in this country at present, but this was certainly not always the case (one American nursery listed 73 in its 1890 catalogue), and it is not likely to remain the case for long, as the interest in *Clematis* is growing by leaps and bounds. Eight varieties, most of them hardy as far north as Montreal, are widely accessible, and have proved their adaptability to our climate over a considerable period of years: *jackmani* (violet-purple), Gipsy Queen (dark velvety purple, an improvement on *jackmani*), *henryi* (white, very large), Ramona (blue), Ville de Lyon (purplish-red), Madame Edouard André (rich purplish-carmine), Madame Baron-Veillard (rose-lilac), and the double-flowered Duchess of Edinburgh (white); all except the last bloom on growing summer shoots. The novice should perhaps begin with these varieties before experimenting with other sorts which are now, or are soon to become, available in this country, such as *lanuginosa* (pale lavender), *lanuginosa candida* (white), Nelly Moser (pale mauve with red bar down the center of each sepal), Prince Hendrick (blue), Fairy Queen (pale flesh), Lady Northcliffe (deep lavender), *ascotiensis* (azure blue), Belle of Woking (double, silver-gray), and Lady Betty Balfour (deep velvety purple).

Besides the five types already mentioned, there is a sixth,

---

* Special articles on the subjects indicated by an asterisk (*) will be found at the words so marked.

the *texensis* type, with trumpet-shaped instead of open or flat flowers. This is the result of crossing our native *C. texensis* with some of the large-flowered hybrids; and of the charming varieties of this type Duchess of York, Countess of Onslow, and Duchess of Albany are likely to be available here in the not distant future.

CULTURE. Clematis likes a cool, rich, moist, well-drained soil, preferably with lime in it. Most of the wild species, including those from which the large-flowered hybrids have been derived, are natives of limestone regions, but whether lime or the texture of the soil is of primary importance remains to be determined. Many species and varieties will thrive in a well-drained, lime-free soil, and in some cases grow even under pine trees, but all are apparently benefited by the use of lime. The addition of lime, leaf mold, and sand when planting is therefore recommended; and the plants should never be allowed to become too dry. They should be given a stable support as soon as they are set out, for the stems are brittle and easily broken by the swaying of the wind; and shade of some sort should be provided for their root-runs if possible. An annual mulch of well-rotted manure is advisable, especially in the case of the large-flowered hybrids. Directions in regard to pruning have already been given, and it is merely necessary to add that *C. montana* and its varieties, as well as the hybrids of the *florida* and *patens* types, should receive no pruning except the cutting out of dead wood, while other species and hybrids will endure a considerable amount of pruning. But too much pruning is usually more dangerous than too little, and in any event lessens the picturesque effect. — J. E. S.

INSECT PESTS. A root- and crown-boring caterpillar may be carefully cut out.

DISEASES. Rust, root knot, leafspot and stem rot are the common diseases. For rust and root knot *see* Rusts, Root Knot at PLANT DISEASES. Leafspot is characterized by small, tan, angular spots with red margins. Control can be obtained by sanitation and the use of sulphur dust or spray. A sudden wilting and death of single shoots is the chief symptom of stem rot. Infection occurs on the stems near the soil line. Remove infected stubs, select healthy cuttings and use clean soil. Spraying around the point of infection with a weak solution of Semesan is also beneficial.

**CLEOME** (klee-ō'me). Of the 75 known species of *Cleome*, which belongs to the family Capparidaceae, only one is of much garden importance, while another is an important bee plant in the western U.S. They are usually strong-smelling herbs, chiefly tropical, and (in ours) with compound* leaves with 3–7 leaflets arranged finger-fashion. Flowers solitary or in clusters, appearing irregular from the 4 long-clawed* petals, the long stamens and the stalked ovary.* Fruit a narrow pod (capsule*) on a long stalk. (*Cleome* is of unknown origin.)

The two below, both annuals, are of the easiest culture if the seeds are sown where the plants are wanted. The spiderflower needs plenty of space, which must be allowed for in thinning out the seedlings.

serrulata. Rocky Mountain bee-plant, also called stinking clover. An annual 2–3 ft. high. Leaflets 3. Flowers pink or white, 2–3 in. long and wide, the petals short-clawed.* Western U.S. and an important bee-plant, especially in Calif., where it is planted for the purpose.

spinosa. Annual herb 4–5 ft. high and bushy. Leaflets 5–7, oblongish, long-stalked. Towards the top of the stem the leaves may be simple* and smaller. Flowers 2–3 in. long and wide, rose-purple or white, the petals long-clawed, and the stamens 2–3 in. long. Stalk of the fruit 3–6 in. long. Tropical America. Summer. A very popular garden annual sometimes sold as *C. pungens*, and often called spiderflower.

**CLERODENDRON** (kler-ro-den'dron). A genus of perhaps 100 species of chiefly tropical shrubs, vines or trees of the family Verbenaceae, the cult. species often called glory-tree or glory-bower. They have opposite (or whorled*) leaves, often lobed but not compound.* Flowers showy, in clusters (often panicles* or racemes*). Calyx often colored, more or less bell-shaped, and sometimes handsomer than the tubular corolla. Stamens 4, long-protruding and curved. Fruit fleshy, enclosed by the withered calyx. (*Clerodendron* is from Greek for chance and tree, and of no known application here.)

All except *C. trichotomum* are adapted to outdoor cult. only in zones* 8 and 9. Otherwise they must be grown in the cool greenhouse, in potting mixture* 4. They may be propagated by cuttings of half-ripened wood over bottom-heat, in a greenhouse kept at about 70°.

fragrans. A showy shrub 5–7 ft. high. Leaves broadly oval, 6–9 in. long, coarsely toothed. Flowers fragrant, in hydrangea-like clusters, white or pink, each flower about 1 in. long and with protruding stamens.* China and Jap. Seldom seen in cult. except in the *var.* **pleniflorum**, a form with showy trusses of double flowers.

thomsonae. Bag-flower. A handsome, woody vine, much grown in greenhouses and outdoors in Fla. and Calif. *See* VINES. Leaves ovalish, 3–5 in. long, without teeth. Flowers very showy, in branching clusters, the calyx ivory-white, the corolla crimson. West Africa. There are varieties with rose-magenta flowers and with variegated leaves.

trichotomum. A shrub or small tree 7–20 ft. high. Leaves ovalish or elliptic, 3–7 in. long, tapering at the tip. Flowers fragrant, in long-stalked clusters, the corolla white, the calyx conspicuously reddish-brown. Fruit blue, set in the showy, reddish calyx. China and Jap. Aug.–Sept., the fruit lasting into late Oct. Hardy from zone* 5 southward.

**CLETHRA** (kleth'ra). White-flowered, usually very fragrant shrubs and trees of the heath family, comprising perhaps 30 species, most common in N.A. and eastern Asia, a few tropical. Leaves alternate,* toothed, short-stalked. Flowers in terminal, spire-like clusters (racemes*) with 5 sepals and 5 petals, neither tubular. Stamens 10. Fruit a 3-valved, many-seeded capsule.* (*Clethra* is the classical Greek for alder, which some species suggest.) Commonly called white alder.

The three below, especially *C. alnifolia*, are of the easiest culture in lime-free soils. All are native and may often be dug from the wild. Division of young growth is the easiest method of propagation.

acuminata. Shrub or small tree 10–18 ft. high. Leaves oval-oblong, 5–8 in. long. Flower cluster 4–10 in. long, the flowers nodding in the cluster, not fragrant. Va. and W. Va. to Ga. and Ala. Aug.–Sept. Hardy from zone* 5 southward.

alnifolia. Sweet pepperbush; also called spiked alder and summer-sweet. A shrub 3–9 ft. high. Leaves oblongish, pointed, 2½–5 in. long. Flowers very fragrant, the clusters numerous, erect, and about 5 in. long. Me. to Fla. Aug.–Oct. Hardy from zone* 2 southward. There is also a pink-flowered variety.

barbinervis. A Japanese shrub or small tree 10–25 ft. high. Leaves oblongish, 3–6 in. long, tapering at the tip, wedge-shaped at the base. Flowers fragrant, in branched, hairy clusters. Aug.–Oct. Hardy from zone* 4 southward.

**CLETHRACEAE.** *See* ERICACEAE.

**CLETHROIDES** (kleth-roy'deez; but *see* OÏDES). Like a white alder (*Clethra*).

**CLEYERA** = EURYA.

**CLIANTHUS** (kly-an'thus). Showy, Australian, vine-like plants of the pea family often grown on trellises in greenhouses or outdoors in zones* 8 and 9. *See* VINES. Leaves compound,* the many leaflets arranged feather-fashion, with an odd one at the end. Flowers red, typically pea-like, in profuse or sparse clusters, usually from the leaf-axils,* and drooping. Pod (legume*) cylindric and leathery. (*Clianthus* is Greek for glory-flower.)

Greenhouse culture demands a cool house and potting mixture* 3. The plants will sprawl if not tied to a trellis. They are extremely showy plants. Propagation of the parrot's-bill by seeds or cuttings, of the glory-pea by grafts on a stock of *Colutea arborescens*. In the greenhouse they usually bloom in April or May.

dampieri. Glory-pea. Not over 4 ft. high and grayish-green, the stem white-hairy. Leaflets numerous, stalkless. Flower cluster with 4–6 blooms. Flowers nearly 3 in. long, scarlet, but with a black splotch on the lower part of the standard.* Pod silky-hairy. Aust.

puniceus. Parrot's-bill; also called parrot-beak and red kowahi. Taller, and practically without hairs on the stem. Leaflets short-stalked. Flower cluster with about 8 blooms. Flowers 3–4 in. long, crimson but soon fading, somewhat white-streaked at the base of the standard.* Pod smooth. N. Zeal. There is a white-flowered variety.

**CLIFF BRAKE.** *See* PELLAEA.

**CLIMATE.** The accumulation of all the weathers, and the greatest single factor in the growth of plants. For purposes of analysis the Weather Bureau must separate climate into its significant parts, and for the gardener these are temperature, rainfall, and wind (*see* these terms). Of these, temperature and rainfall are much the most important. Both affect the suitability of plants for a particular section of the country and the last frost of spring and the first one in autumn dictate the time of many garden operations.

---

* Special articles on the subjects indicated by an asterisk (*) will be found at the words so marked.

To discuss adequately the climate of the U.S. would take a volume bigger than this one. But the significant details of temperature and rainfall are so necessary to all intelligent gardeners that they have been prepared for each state of the Union and for the Canadian provinces. See the name of your state or province for these details.

How plants respond to the totality of these things — the climate — is quite another thing. It affects their hardiness (which see), and it is responsible for the separation of all the woody plants in this book into definite zones of hardiness. For a complete account of this see ZONE and the map there.

**CLIMBING FERN.** See LYGODIUM.

**CLIMBING FIG** = *Ficus pumila*.

**CLIMBING FUMITORY** = *Adlumia fungosa*.

**CLIMBING HYDRANGEA** = *Hydrangea petiolaris*.

**CLIMBING NIGHTSHADE** = *Solanum dulcamara*.

**CLIMBING PLANTS.** See VINES.

**CLIMBING ROSES.** See Group 6 at ROSE.

**CLIMBING SAILOR** = *Cymbalaria muralis*.

**CLIMBING YLANG-YLANG** = *Artabotrys odoratissimus*.

**CLINGSTONE.** See FREESTONE.

**CLINTONIA** (klin-tone′i-a). A small genus of woodland, perennial herbs of the lily family found in N.A. and eastern Asia, not infrequently grown in the wild garden. They have long, underground rootstocks and basal, broad leaves without marginal teeth. Flowers at the end of a short stalk, usually in loose, lax umbels.* Petals and sepals scarcely distinguishable as such, totaling 6, and lily-like. Fruit a fleshy berry. (Named for DeWitt Clinton, Governor of N.Y.) The plants are sometimes called bear-tongue.

They need rich woods soil, a reasonably moist site, and at least partial shade. Not as difficult to grow as some wild flowers and easily propagated by division of the rootstock. Not suited to open borders or beds.

borealis. Cow-tongue. Leaves broadly oval, but broadest toward the end, 4–7 in. long. Flowers ¾ in. long, greenish-yellow, nodding, the umbel* with 3–6 blooms. Berry blue. Eastern N.A. May.

umbellata. Dog-plum, also called wild corn. Resembling the last, but with smaller, white flowers (more numerous in the cluster) and black fruit. Mountain woods, N.Y. and N.J. to Ga. June.

For a totally unrelated plant, often mistakenly named *Clintonia pulchella*, see DOWNINGIA.

**CLINTON'S FERN** = *Dryopteris clintoniana*.

**CLIPPING.** See PRUNING.

**CLITORIA** (kly-tow′ri-a). A large genus of chiefly tropical, perennial, but not woody vines of the pea family, the ones below natives of the U.S. and As. and sometimes grown for ornament. Leaves compound,* the leaflets arranged feather-fashion. Flowers pea-like, showy, the standard* much larger than the rest of the flower. Pod (legume*) stalked, narrow and flattened. (The origin of *Clitoria* is unprintable.)

*Clitoria mariana* is almost a weedy vine scrambling over bushes in the wild. It is easily grown in open, sandy soils. *C. ternatea*, a far more showy plant, is tropical and can be grown outdoors only in zones* 8 and 9, where it is an attractive vine.

mariana. Butterfly-pea. A smooth-stemmed vine, not over 4–5 ft. long. Leaflets 3, very veiny, oblongish or narrower. Flowers pale blue, nearly 2 in. long, appearing as if upside down. Pod about 2 in. long. N.J. to Fla. May–June.

ternatea. Taller, the slender stem hairy. Leaflets 5–7, ovalish, 1–2 in. long. Flowers dark blue, sometimes streaked with lighter blue, about 2 in. long. Pod about 4 in. long. Probably tropical Asia, but now naturalized all over the tropical world. June. Flowers sometimes double.

**CLIVIA** (kly′vi-a). Three South African species of perennial herbs of the family Amaryllidaceae, one a widely popular greenhouse plant and well suited for house decoration when in bloom. They have fleshy roots and a bulb-like swelling of the lower part of the stem formed by the expanded leaf-bases. Leaves strap-shaped, evergreen. Flowers in a terminal umbel, the corolla funnel-shaped, the three inner segments wider than the outer ones. Fruit a red berry. (Named for a Duchess of Northumberland, one of the Clive family.)

The species below is a very stout herb needing plenty of space in the pot or tub. Its culture is the same as for *Amaryllis*.

miniata. Leaves thick, two-ranked, more or less strap-shaped and 1–2 in. wide. Flowers 10–18 in the cluster, lily-like, scarlet but yellowish inside, the corolla 2–3 in. long. Berry about 1 in. long. Blooms in early spring, as a greenhouse plant.

*CLIVORUM* (kly-vor′rum). Of the hills.

**CLOCHE.** See BELL-JAR.

**CLOISTER GARDEN.** See GARDEN HISTORY.

**CLONE** (also spelled **Clon**). A group of plants, often many thousands, all of which originated from one seedling plant, from which they have subsequently increased only by asexual reproduction, often by cuttings, by division, or by any method other than by seeds. Many garden plants are considered as units of a clone, notably the Baldwin apple, the Concord grape, and the iris known as Ambassadeur. Because gardeners and botanists have not always recognized the concept of a clone, many clones have been given varietal and specific names. At present there is no nomenclatorial machinery for differentiating clones from species or true varieties grown from seeds, but such distinctions would be a desirable addition to the nomenclature of horticulture and botany. See DAYLILY and POPULUS CANDICANS.

**CLOSED GENTIAN** = *Gentiana andrewsi*.

**CLOSE-FERTILIZATION.** See SELF-FERTILIZATION.

**CLOTH.** Commercial growers of summer cut flowers, grown outdoors, have found it profitable, at times, to protect their plants with a covering of cloth. Snapdragon, the garden aster, dahlia, chrysanthemum, gladiolus, *Clarkia*, marigold, and zinnia are among many garden flowers that were benefited.

The advantages are longer stems, larger and better blooms, protection from insect and fungus pests and from heavy rains or violent winds. While commercial growers construct elaborate cloth shelters, with insect-proof doors, most home gardeners will not need such an outlay. A tent-like cheese-cloth box, stretched over one's plants, will accomplish the same purpose. If there are high winds or the structure is to be used for long periods, the cloth should be that supplied by dealers in florists' supplies. It should be 6–8 ft. high and sealed at all corners and at the ground level. The most extensive use of cloth is for the growing of tobacco for cigar wrappers. The shade helps to reduce the thickness of the leaf.

**CLOTHES YARD.** See SERVICE YARD.

**CLOTH-OF-GOLD** = *Crocus susianus*.

**CLOUD GRASS** = *Agrostis nebulosa*.

**CLOVE.** As a hort. term, one of the small divisions of a separable bulb, as in garlic and shallot. The tree producing cloves (the spice) is not much, or perhaps not at all, cult. in the U.S.

**CLOVE-PINK** = *Dianthus caryophyllus*. See CARNATION.

**CLOVER.** Extremely useful agricultural, forage plants of secondary interest to the gardener, except as some of them are constituents of lawn mixtures, and the value of the coarser ones as green manure. The genus **Trifolium** (try-fō′li-um), to which belong all those below, comprises over 300 species of the pea family, nearly all from temperate regions. Leaves compound,* in all of ours with 3, usually toothed, leaflets, most of them stalkless. Flowers small, scarcely pea-like, or at least so proved only by careful dissection, crowded in dense heads. Fruit small, dry, 1–2-seeded, usually covered by the withered calyx. (*Trifolium* is Latin for 3 leaves.) All are splendid bee plants.

Few or none of those below are garden plants grown for ornament. Their value lies in the fact of their ability to absorb free nitrogen from the atmosphere and add it to the soil. For two thousand years before this was definitely es-

---

* Special articles on the subjects indicated by an asterisk (*) will be found at the words so marked.

tablished, clovers were cult. for soil improvement, a practice just as sound today. *See* LEGUME INOCULATION.

    **T. alexandrinum.** Berseem or Egyptian clover. A branching annual 1-2 ft. high. Leaflets oblongish, blunt, ¾-1 in. long, faintly toothed. Flower heads globe-shaped, white or yellowish-white. Egypt and Syria. Grown for soil improvement in alkali and dry regions of Calif. and the Southwest. Not suited to the North and East.

    **T. hybridum.** Alsike clover, called also Swedish clover. Resembling the common white clover (*T. repens*) when prostrate, but in youth an erect perennial, 1-2 ft. high, ultimately sprawling or prostrate. Leaflets ovalish, not notched at the tip. Flower heads globe-shaped, pink. Eu. Much used for soil improvement.

    **T. incarnatum.** Crimson clover, called also Italian clover. An annual 20-30 in. high and branched. Leaflets ¾-1½ in. long, faintly toothed, more or less wedge-shaped at the base. Flower heads oblong, 1½-2½ in. long, crimson. Eu. Perhaps the most widely used for soil improvement and for forage.

    **T. medium.** Zigzag clover, called also cow clover. A perennial 8-15 in. high, its rootstock creeping, the stems zigzag. Leaflets elliptic or oblong, nearly without teeth, not blotched as in the next. Flower heads globe-shaped, stalked, deep purple. Eu. Less cult. than the others and sometimes confused with mammoth clover.

    **T. pratense.** Red clover, also called honeysuckle clover. A perennial, 1-2 ft. high, but not long persisting. Leaflets ovalish or oblong, 1½-2½ in. long, often notched at the tip and usually white-blotched. Flower heads globe-shaped, rose-purple. Eu. The common clover of our meadows. The *var. serotinum*, the mammoth clover, is a stouter plant that blooms later and it does not need such frequent renewal.

    **T. repens.** White or Dutch clover. A low, creeping perennial. Leaves long-stalked, the leaflets notched, minutely toothed. Flower heads solitary, on long stalks arising from the ground, globe-shaped and white. Eu. A low plant forming flat mats. It is the chief clover in grass mixtures and makes a valuable constituent of lawns. On March 17 it annually appears in flats or pans, forced for the purpose as the "shamrock" (which see).

Several of these clovers, from wholly unknown causes, occasionally produce leaves with 4, or even 5 or 6 leaflets. For other plants sometimes called clover *see* MELILOTUS, MEDICAGO, and LESPEDEZA.

**CLOVER BROOM** = *Baptisia tinctoria.*

**CLUB GOURD** = *Trichosanthes anguina.*

**CLUB MOSS AND CLUB MOSS FAMILY.** *See* LYCOPODIUM.

**CLUBROOT.** *See* Slime-molds at PLANT DISEASES; *see* also the diseases at CABBAGE.

**CLUMP.** A cluster or group of shrubs; more usually, in the hort. sense, a mass of roots or rootstocks, such as one divides or moves — as a *clump* of iris.

**CLUSIACEAE** = Guttiferae.

**CLUSTER.** As applied to flowers a cluster is an indefinite but convenient designation for inflorescence.* As applied to the stems of shrubs or the trunks of trees it is still more indefinite, suggesting merely a group.

**CLUSTER PALM** = *Actinophloeus macarthuri.*

**CLYTOSTOMA** (kly-tos'to-ma). Evergreen woody vines, of the family Bignoniaceae, all the 8 species South American, one of which is popular for outdoor cult. in zones* 8 and 9 (possibly in zone* 7) because of its showy bloom. Leaves compound,* of 2 leaflets, the end of the main leafstalk prolonged into a slender, unbranched tendril.* Flowers in clusters of 2, the calyx* bell-shaped, the corolla funnel-shaped, its lobes wavy. Fruit a prickly capsule.* (*Clytostoma* is from the Greek for splendid and mouth, in reference to the showy corolla.)

The only cult. species is not particular as to soils and makes an attractive, medium-sized vine for Fla., Calif. and other regions of mild climate. It is slow-growing until thoroughly established. Propagated by cuttings of last season's wood.

    **callistegioides.** A frequent error for the next.

    **calystegioides.** Leaflets only 2, evergreen, glossy, oblongish, 2½-3 in. long. Flowers in terminal pairs, about 3 in. long, light purple or lavender, streaked darker purple inside. April-May. Argentina and southern Brazil. Sometimes known as *Bignonia speciosa.*

**CNEORUM** (nee-ō'rum). Pre-Linnaean* name for some plants of the genus *Daphne;* also a modern genus name for plants little known in cult. and not here included.

**CNICUS** (ny'kus). A single, thistle-like annual herb, **C. benedictus,** of the family Compositae, and commonly called blessed thistle, Our Lady's thistle, or sometimes, sweet sultan. It is a native of the Mediterranean region, easily grown from seed, and not especially showy or desirable. Stems 1-2 ft. high, branching. Leaves oblong, deeply lobed or toothed, the lobes spiny-margined. Flowers yellow in dense, thistle-like heads about 1 in. in diameter, which terminate the branches and are set in a collection of spiny bracts.* (*Cnicus* is Latin for some thistle-like plant.) The plant is sometimes offered under the names *Carduus* and *Centaurea.*

**COACH-WHIP** = *Fouquieria splendens.*

**COAL ASHES.** *See* ASH AND ASHES.

*COARCTATA, -us, -um* (ko-ark-tay'ta). Crowded.

**COAST LIVE OAK** = *Quercus agrifolia. See* OAK.

**COAST REDWOOD** = *Sequoia sempervirens.*

**COAST TRILLIUM** = *Trillium ovatum.*

**COBAEA** (ko-bee'a). Tendril*-climbing, tropical American woody vines of the family Polemoniaceae, one widely grown for its quick growth and showy bloom when treated as a tender annual. Leaves alternate,* compound,* the leaflets arranged feather-fashion, the terminal one replaced by a branched tendril.* Flowers solitary, on long stalks from the leaf-axils.* Corolla bell-shaped, or cylindric, its limb 5-lobed, the stamens protruding. Fruit a leathery, 3-valved capsule.* (Named for Father Cobo, a Spanish Jesuit naturalist.)

    **scandens.** Cup-and-saucer vine; Mexican ivy. Growing from 10-25 ft. high in a single season when sown as an annual in the greenhouse, window box, or outdoors in the South. Leaflets 4-6, oval-oblong, the lowest with an ear-like base and nearly stalkless. Flowers violet or greenish-purple, about 2 in. long, the calyx inflated and leaf-like, the protruding stamens curved. Mex. Seeds are often sold by street hawkers under a variety of catch-penny names. *See* VINES. There is a white-flowered form.

**COBNUT** = *Corylus avellana grandis. See* HAZEL.

**COBWEB HOUSELEEK** = *Sempervivum arachnoideum. See* HOUSELEEK.

**COCA.** Native South American name for the plant yielding cocaine. *See* ERYTHROXYLON.

**COCA FAMILY** = Erythroxylaceae. *See* ERYTHROXYLON.

**COCAINE PLANT** = *Erythroxylon coca.*

*COCCIGERA, -us, -um* (kok-kidj'er-ra). Berry-bearing.

*COCCINEA, -us, -um* (kok-sin'ee-a). Scarlet.

**COCCINIA** (kok-sin'i-a). Tendril*-climbing, tropical Asiatic, or African, perennial vines of the cucumber family, with tuberous roots. One of them, the ivy gourd, **C. cordifolia,** is rarely grown in greenhouses, but somewhat cult. outdoors in frostless regions for ornament. It has slender, high-climbing, furrowed but hairless stems, and angled or lobed leaves 2-3 in. wide and heart-shaped at the base. Male and female flowers on different plants, white, bell-shaped, about 1½ in. long, the lobes flaring. Fruit berry-like, scarlet, 1-2 in. long. Southeastern Asia. (*Coccinia* is derived from *coccinea*, scarlet.)

**COCCOLOBIS** (kok-o-low'bis). Sometimes spelled *Coccoloba.* A genus of 125 species of tropical American shrubs and trees of the buckwheat family, often growing along the sandy beaches, remarkable for their large, leathery leaves which are alternate* and without marginal teeth. Little known as cult. plants outside of Fla., where the sea grape or seaside plum, **C. uvifera,** is both wild and cult. It is a shrub or tree up to 25 ft. high. Leaves nearly round, 6-8 in. wide, heart-shaped at the base. Flowers small, greenish-white, not showy, but in clusters 6-9 in. long (for details *see* POLYGONACEAE). Fruit resembling a bunch of grapes, purple, about ½ in. in diameter and sometimes used for jelly. (*Coccolobis* is from the Greek for a colored seed or fruit.)

**COCCOTHRINAX** (kok-o-thry'nacks). Tropical American fan palms, often cult. outdoors in zones* 8 and 9 for ornament, rarely in greenhouses outside of botanic gardens. The chief cult. species is **C. argentea,** the thatch-palm or

---

* Special articles on the subjects indicated by an asterisk (*) will be found at the words so marked.

silvertop palmetto (often known as *Thrinax argentea*). It may grow up to 30 ft. high, but as usually cult. it has a short trunk or is practically stemless. Leaves fan-like, nearly round, 2–3 ft. wide, pale green above, silvery beneath, the smooth leafstalk about 3 ft. long. Flowers perfect,* the cluster just at the crown of leaves. Stamens 9–12. Fruit berry-like, black, round and about ⅜ in. in diameter. Native from southern Fla. to the Bahamas and larger W.I. (*Coccothrinax* is Greek for berry and *Thrinax*.)

**COCCULUS** (kok'kew-lus). A small genus of very widely distributed woody vines or shrubs of the family Menispermaceae, often called moonseed or snailseed. Of the 11 known species two are cult. for ornament, and present no difficulty in any good garden soil, preferably in somewhat moist sites. Leaves alternate,* the veins arranged finger-fashion. Male and female flowers on different plants, small and inconspicuous (for details see MENISPERMACEAE). Fruit fleshy (a true drupe*), the stone flattened and ribbed crosswise. (*Cocculus* is a Greek diminutive meaning small berry.)

**carolinus.** Carolina moonseed. A twining, woody vine 6–12 ft. high. Leaves roundish or triangular-oval, 3–4 in. long, without teeth but often shallowly lobed, pale beneath. Flowers greenish, the clusters 3–5 in. long. Fruit red, about ⅔ in. long. June–July. Va. to Fla., Ill. and Tex. Hardy from zone* 4 southward.

**laurifolius.** Evergreen shrub and not over 15 ft. high. Leaves leathery, glossy, oblongish, 3–6 in. long. Flower clusters only 2 in. long. Fruit black. Himalayas. Hardy from zone* 7 southward.

*COCHENILLIFERA, -us, -um* (ko-chen-il-lif'e-ra). Bearing cochineal.

**COCHINEAL PLANT** = *Nopalea cochenillifera*.

**COCHLEARIA** (kok-lee-ā'ri-a). Of the 20 species of this genus of herbs of the mustard family, only **C. officinalis**, the scurvy-grass, is of any garden interest. It is sometimes cult. as a salad plant, but its rather tarry flavor suggests its medicinal qualities, which are as a cure for scurvy. It is a biennial or perennial herb, usually not over 4–5 in. high, but planted as an annual. Leaves long-stalked, kidney-shaped or heart-shaped, practically all basal. Flowers scarcely ¼ in. wide, white (for details see CRUCIFERAE), in a close cluster that elongates as the somewhat inflated pods develop. The plant is wild in the cooler parts of the temperate zone and far northward. (*Cochlearia* is from Greek for spoon, in reference to the shape of the leaves.)

*COCHLEARIS, -e* (kok-lee-ā'ris). Spoon-shaped.

**COCKSCOMB** = *Celosia argentea cristata*.

**COCK'S EGGS.** See SALPICHROA RHOMBOIDEA.

**COCK'S-FOOT** = *Dactylis glomerata*.

**COCKSPUR GRASS** = *Echinochloa crus-galli*.

**COCKSPUR THORN** = *Crataegus crus-galli*.

**COCONUT** (*Cocos nucifera*). The coconut as a cult. plant has a wide distribution in tropical and some sub-tropical regions of both hemispheres. The trees, strongly wind-resistant and with slender, leaning trunks, reach heights exceeding 80 ft. and are among the most beautiful of the large palms. Probably unexcelled in importance among the world's tree fruits, the coconut yields food, drink and fiber, and is planted to the extent of millions of acres. Most of the cult. acreage is in Asia and the East Indies; only approximately 2 per cent of the total is in tropical America. A frost-free and humid climate is required and planting in the U.S. is limited to the warmest portions of Fla., where the tree thrives but is grown only as an ornamental.

The oily meat of the nut — termed copra when dried — is the source of desiccated coconut and of the coconut oil used extensively in cooking oils, blended fats and soaps; the freshly husked nuts are sold widely; the coir fiber of the husks is utilized for cordage, coarse matting and brushes and as fiber for planting material; the shells are made into household utensils and high quality charcoal; and even the leaves are utilized for thatching, mats and other local uses. Toddy, the sap obtained by tapping the unopened inflorescence, is a sweet and pleasant drink and a source of sugar, alcohol and vinegar. Fresh coconut meat contains about 30 per cent oil, copra more than twice that amount, and the "milk" about 4 per cent sugar.

There are numerous varieties, several having been introduced into Fla. Propagation is by seeds which are planted in a nursery or in the place where the tree is wanted. The mature, unhusked nuts are placed on their sides and only partially covered. Most will germinate within 4 to 5 months in moist soil and be ready for transplanting when the sprout is 6 to 12 inches high. Planting distances vary widely, but 70 to 80 trees to the acre is most generally recommended for highest nut production. Fruiting begins within 5 to 7 years and full bearing is reached at about 20 years. Annual tree yields are from 20 to 200 nuts, with the average near the lower figure. The nuts mature over a year-round season. Greatest vigor of growth is obtained by planting in large, well-prepared holes and following with annual applications of complete fertilizers. Additions of organic materials and growing of leguminous cover crops have proved beneficial. The tree thrives on many soil types and even though it grows well on brackish soils close to the sea neither salt nor close proximity to the ocean is essential to its growth. — H. M.

INSECT PESTS. Scale insects on coconut trees are usually controlled by their natural enemies if these enemies are not protected by ants. If scales become injurious, controlling the ants by poisoned syrups will help to reduce scale populations. Injuries to the trunk, which attract borers, should be avoided. Large beetles boring in the trunk can be dug out when their work is first evident.

DISEASES. Bacterial bud rot is a disease of the buds and other tender parts caused by a bacterial organism. Control is accomplished by cutting and burning affected trees. Red ring disease is caused by a nematode worm. The stem and leaves are invaded, the latter turning yellow, orange or brown, while a red ring appears in the stem. Sanitation by the complete removal and destruction of diseased trees, including roots, is the best method of control. Bud rot is a similar disease to the bacterial bud rot, but caused in this case by a fungus. Early recognition and eradication have been effective. Stem rot or stem bleeding is a disease of unknown cause. It responds to careful surgical methods if followed by thorough applications of crude oil or distillate. The treatment should be applied early and trees frequently re-examined.

**COCONUT-OIL SOAP.** See Contact Sprays at INSECTICIDES.

**COCO-PLUM** = *Chrysobalanus icaco*.

**COCOS** (ko'kos). As originally understood a very large genus of feather palms, but now considered as including only the coconut palm, **C. nucifera**, a native of the tropical Old World, and introduced into tropical America by the Portuguese and Spanish, and now of world-wide occurrence in tropical regions. It is perhaps the most important of all cult. palms. For a description of the tree and notes on its culture see COCONUT. The fruit of the coconut is technically a drupe,* what is generally called the nut being merely the seed of this drupe, which is fleshy and green when young, but very tough when the nut is ripe.

For the commonly cult. palms formerly included in *Cocos*, see ARECASTRUM, BUTIA, and SYAGRUS.

**CODIAEUM** (ko-di-ee'um). Gorgeously colored, tropical foliage plants of the family Euphorbiaceae, universally called crotons. Of the six known species, only the one below is of garden interest, but in its many forms it is cult. throughout the tropical world and extensively in northern greenhouses. Leaves alternate,* without marginal teeth, but sometimes lobed, probably green in its original state, but in the only cult. forms, variously marked, streaked, blotched, or banded with green, white, the reds, and yellow, often spectacularly so when properly grown. Flowers small and inconspicuous (for details see EUPHORBIACEAE). Fruit a roundish capsule,* splitting into 2 berry-like segments. (*Codiaeum* is from Greek for head, in allusion to the leaves being used for wreaths.)

In Fla. and southern Calif. where crotons can be grown outdoors they require no special soil or culture beyond that given to any other shrub. They do better in good soils and with a reasonable amount of moisture, but they need heat most of all. They are widely used in parks and as specimen plants on the lawn and often, as tubbed plants, are showy features of porches or patios.

The greenhouse culture of crotons demands a house kept at 70°–75° at night, more in the day, and the atmosphere

---

* Special articles on the subjects indicated by an asterisk (*) will be found at the words so marked.

must be kept moist by wetting down the paths (not the plants) and the space under the greenhouse bench every three or four hours during the day. Large plants can be grown in tubs, but frequently these become leggy, when cuttings should be made of all bushy shoots, and these grown along in pots until they are fit for exhibition or for summer bedding. They make excellent foliage plants for the latter purpose, coming in so many color combinations that any desired effect can be produced. Do not put outdoors until settled warm weather has arrived.

Use potting mixture* 4 and give plenty of water while the plants are in active growth, but less as growth slackens. To get the finest color, the glass of the greenhouse should be ground-glass or have a thin wash of white paint. Clear glass will burn the leaves and most roller or lath shades make the greenhouse too dark. If possible, the best time to make the cuttings is during the winter months. They need bottom-heat and a house temperature of 80°. Most young plants in the florists' shops are grown annually in this way.

**variegatum pictum.** The common croton of the florists. A shrub or small tree with smooth, ovalish or oblong (very narrow in some varieties) leaves, which are variously colored (*see* above). Flower cluster sometimes 7–9 in. long. Fruit white. Java, Aust. and South Pacific Islands. Over a hundred named forms are pretty common in cult. Besides the color variations, some forms have the leaves finely cut, some curled, others crisp-margined, some spirally twisted.

**CODLING MOTH.** See Moth at INSECT PESTS; see also the Insect Pests at APPLE, LOQUAT, and WALNUT.

**COELESTINA, -us, -um** (see-les-ty'na). Sky-blue.

**COELESTIS, -e** (see-les'tis). Sky-blue.

**COELI-ROSA** (see-li-rō'sa). A species name meaning rose of the sky (heaven). See LYCHNIS.

**COELOGYNE** (see-lŏ'jen-ee). A very large group of chiefly Indo-Malayan, tree-perching (epiphytic*) orchids, one a very popular greenhouse flower and another somewhat grown by orchid fanciers. They have clustered pseudobulbs,* each of which usually bears 2 leaves. Flowers few or many in racemes,* the petals and sepals somewhat similar. Lip* stalkless at the base of the column* and 3-lobed, the side lobes erect, the central one spreading or curved backward. (*Coelogyne* is from the Greek suggesting a depressed or hollow stigma.)

*Coelogyne cristata* is a widely grown greenhouse orchid. *C. dayana*, while less known, is a handsome orchid with a drooping flower cluster nearly 3 ft. long. For culture *see* Greenhouse Orchids at ORCHID.

**cristata.** The common species in cult. and a fine plant with several drooping clusters of showy flowers. Leaves 9–12 in. long and about 1 in. wide. Flowers white, the sepals and petals oblong or narrower, sharp-pointed. Throat orange-yellow. The middle lobe of the lip is slightly toothed. Tropical Himalayas. Jan.–April, as a greenhouse plant.

**dayana.** Necklace orchid. Leaves 15–20 in. long, 3–4 in. wide. Flowers nearly 2½ in. wide, the cluster almost 3 ft. long, white, the lip reddish-brown. Malaya. April–June.

**COERULEA, -us, -um** (see-roo'lee-a). Dark blue.

**COERULESCENS** (see-roo-les'senz). Almost dark blue.

**COFFEA** (kof'fee-a). The shrubs or trees yielding coffee, of the family Rubiaceae, are of no commercial importance in the U.S., but the two below are often grown for interest in extreme southern Fla. and occasionally in greenhouses. Leaves usually opposite,* evergreen. Flowers white or cream, the corolla salver-shaped, the stamens* in or below the throat. Fruit a fleshy berry, its seeds the source of coffee and usually (but incorrectly) called coffee berries. (*Coffea* is a Latinized version of the Arabian name for coffee.)

Can be grown (as an ornamental) outdoors only in zone* 9. For commercial production it needs more heat, and preferably a tropical tableland between 2000 and 3000 ft., conditions not found in the U.S. For greenhouse cult. use potting mixture* 4 and keep in a moist, warm (75°) house.

**arabica.** Common or Arabian coffee. A usually many-stemmed shrub 10–15 ft. high. Leaves oblongish, 3–6 in. long, prolonged into a tip about ½ in. long. Flowers white, faintly fragrant, star-shaped, about ¾ in. long. Fruit red. Tropical Africa; from thence introduced into Arabia and long thought to be native there.

**liberica.** Liberian coffee. A somewhat similar shrub, but the leaves 9–12 in. long, the flowers about 1 in. long, and with black fruit.

**COFFEE.** See COFFEA.
**COFFEEBERRY** = *Rhamnus californica*.
**COFFEE FAMILY** = Rubiaceae.
**COFFEE-TREE** = *Gymnocladus dioica*.
**COFFEEWEED** = *Cichorium intybus*.

**COGGYGRIA** (kog-ji'gri-a). Old Greek name for the smoke-tree.

**COHOSH.** Several plants are so called. See ACTAEA, CAULOPHYLLUM, and CIMICIFUGA RACEMOSA.

**COHUNE.** Vernacular tropical American name for the cohune palm. See ATTALEA.

**COIR.** See COCONUT.

**COIX** (kō'icks). A small genus of leafy-stemmed grasses of the Indo-Malayan region, one grown in the East for centuries for its edible grain and here for ornament or as a curiosity. Stem obviously jointed. Flower cluster terminal, the male clusters at the end, the female below. From the latter develops the peculiar, white or dirty-white, bead-like structure, inside which is the kernel, the source of the cereal food, adlay, in the Philippines. (*Coix* is the Greek name for this grass.)

**lacryma-jobi.** Job's tears. An annual grass 3–6 ft. high. Leaves 1–2 ft. long, ¾–1¼ in. wide, sword-shaped and with a prominent midrib. Beads about 1½ in. wide, very striking, hard and shiny. Tropical Asia. There is also a variety with yellow-striped leaves. Can be grown as an annual from zone* 7 southwards, but north of this it may not fruit.

**COLA** (kō'la). Tropical African trees comprising over 100 species of the family Sterculiaceae, only one of which is of hort. interest, and this only in extreme southern Fla. This is the tree, **C. acuminata,** that yields the kolanut or Goora-nut, widely used as a stimulant in soft drinks. It is a tree up to 40 ft. high, with alternate,* simple leaves, 6–8 in. long, and without marginal teeth. Flowers without petals, the calyx bell-shaped, yellowish-green, about ½ in. wide. Fruit a collection of 4–5 woody or leathery pods (follicles*), 5–6 in. long, each containing many seeds (kolanuts). Little grown in the U.S., but an important tree in the tropics. (*Cola* is the African vernacular for these trees.)

**COLBIT.** A weatherproof, bituminous emulsion, used in the construction of garden walks, driveways and tennis courts.

**COLCHICA, -us, -um** (kol'chi-ka). From Colchis, an ancient country now included in Georgia, Transcaucasia.

**COLCHICUM** (kol'chi-cum). A genus of 30 species of mostly autumn-blooming, crocus-like, bulbous herbs of the lily family, very popular in the autumn garden and in the rock garden. Leaves sometimes none at flowering time, but sometimes appearing with the flowers, both arising from the ground, the plant thus apparently stemless. Flowers tubular, the segments 6, and the 6 stamens inserted within the tube. Fruit a 3-valved capsule.* (*Colchicum* is derived from *colchica*, which see.) They are commonly called autumn crocus or meadow saffron, although there are several autumn-blooming plants of the genus *Crocus* (which see).

For Culture and color notes *see* below.

**autumnale.** Leaves in spring, 8–10 in. long and about 1½ in. wide, the plant leafless in summer. Flowers 3–4 in. wide. Fruit usually maturing with the leaves in spring. Eu. and northern Africa.

**bornmuelleri.** Flowers larger, often nearly 5 in. wide, blooming in autumn. Asia Minor. Leaves in spring, about 8 in. long and 2 in. wide.

**speciosum.** Flowers nearly 6 in. wide. Leaves the following spring, nearly a foot long and 3–4 in. wide. Caucasus. Autumn-blooming. There is also a variety with pure white flowers, var. **album.**

### COLCHICUM CULTURE

This beautiful genus of flowering bulbs has suffered undeserved neglect from American gardeners.

The blooms come, in northern latitudes, from the beginning of September until November, thus giving a succession of flowers for the decoration of house or garden at a time when most of the summer flowers are past. Their general color is a light pink inclining to mauve; but there are varieties in deeper shades, and all the colors are pleasant, many

* Special articles on the subjects indicated by an asterisk (*) will be found at the words so marked.

of them lovely. Sometimes the petals are tessellated in white and pink, or light and dark pink.

The only species at all commonly found in cultivation is *C. autumnale*; this bears rather small flowers and is not comparable in beauty with the larger-flowered types. Especially to be recommended is *C. bornmuelleri*, one of the earliest to bloom, and one of the best. The large, mauve, cup-shaped flowers stand from six to eight inches above the ground. The flower stem goes down to the base of the bulb and if the flowers are pulled up instead of being broken off, most of them will come up with stems about a foot long.

The different forms of *C. speciosum* come later and are equally lovely; particularly good is the rather capricious *C. speciosum album*.

The best forms of *C. autumnale* include the wild pink form so common in southern Europe; also a white single variety, and a double pink and a double white.

Bulbs should be purchased in July or August, when they are dormant. At no other time can they be safely shipped; but for moving about in one's own garden, or for dividing, the clumps may be lifted when in bloom; they should, however, be immediately replanted, as root growth is then active.

The bulbs should be set so that their tops are at least three or four inches below the surface of the soil. They produce their rather coarse leaf growth in spring, hence they should not be put in a position where their lush foliage will mar the appearance of the garden. The best plan is to give them a corner by themselves.

The seeds of the previous year's flowers mature in July when the leaves turn brown. The bed may then be lightly hoed, leaving the ground clear for the flowers which shoot up without any leaves in the autumn. Seeds may be sown when ripe. They often lie dormant until the second or third year; but in time they do germinate, and after three or four years' growth the bulbs reach the blooming stage.

In recent years some extremely good hybrid forms have been put on the market by the firm of van Tubergen in Holland. These are grand additions to the group, and need only to be known to come into wide popularity. Among the best of these new sorts are: Autumn Queen, Lilac Wonder, The Giant, and Water lily. — A. P. S.

**COLD.** *See* TEMPERATURE.

**COLD FRAME.** DEFINITION OF TERMS. A frame or garden frame is, ordinarily, a bottomless, box-like structure with a removable top glazed with glass or covered with some transparent material. Frames are used for protecting, propagating or growing plants. A cold frame is any unheated frame; a heated frame is any frame that has a device for heating the air in the frame; a hotbed is a frame that has a device for heating the soil bed of the frame. A heated frame approximates a glasshouse more nearly than the others. A hotbed in a heated frame is of the greatest garden value.

A single frame consists of a frame that will accommodate a single sash.

The sash, or light, is the top of the frame, and the most convenient dimensions are approximately 3 ft. × 6 ft. The most useful non-commercial sizes for frames are of four or six sash.

CONSTRUCTION OF FRAME. If the frame is to be movable, a very convenient feature, it is perhaps best constructed of 2-in. planks; the planks may either be rough or dressed. In the case of dressed planks there is a loss of ⅝ in. on all sides, but a much better job can be made of painting. The minimum practicable height for a frame is about 16 in. back, 10 in. front and 6 in. slope. The back and front may be of any convenient height, the slope, however, never need exceed 10 in.

The wood should be the most durable that cost will permit, white cedar, western cedar, redwood and cypress are excellent, but one often has to make use of pine or other woods, or even of box boarding.

For a frame 6 ft. wide, outside measure, the front may consist of 2 × 10 in. planking, the back of two such planks and the sides of one 2 × 10 in. plank for the lower piece, the top piece of a like plank cut diagonally to provide the slope.

Frames may be double and of any width up to 12 ft., the ridge is constructed of 2 × 4 in. material on edge supported every 6 ft. by 4 × 4 in. posts. The sash is hinged on the ridge and a 1 × 6 in. board nailed flat on the top of the ridge to form a coping. A double frame 12 ft. wide is too cumbersome for most uses, but if high on the sides and if the hinges have readily removable pins, work such as sowing, pricking-off, digging and harvesting is greatly facilitated. The inconveniences with any frame over 8 ft. wide are greatly increased for watering or harvesting individual plants.

SASH-SUPPORTS. These are best made of 2 × 4 in. lumber and free from large knots. They must be spaced to allow free sliding of the sash, a leeway of about ⅝ in. is usually sufficient. The supports are most effectively fixed by being checked in the planks, but they may be nailed on a rest of 2 × 2 in. material. It is an advantage to nail a 1 × 1 in. strip down the center of the sash support to act as a sash guide. The length of the sash supports for a 6-ft. frame with a 10-in. slope will be 6 ft. 3 in. Mistakes in the exact position of the sash supports may be avoided by placing the sash in a trial position before fastening. If the frames are not portable and cost is very important, the lumber used may be of ship-lap or any kind of 1-in. boarding. In this case the boards are nailed to 4 × 4 in. uprights, if the uprights are on the outside of the frame there will be found to be considerable saving in space, particularly when flats or boxes are used as containers. In districts where the winters are long and severe, take-down frames offer advantages in the matter of convenient storage. A simple method of construction is to make the units of two or three sash sizes. The ends, backs and fronts are fastened securely by means of cleats; at the end of both back and front a groove of two 2 × 4 in. material is nailed to receive the ends, the back and front may be held firmly in place by means of stakes; bolts are, however, more workmanlike. The sash supports are made four inches longer (6 ft. 7 in. for 10-in. slope) and a piece of 2 × 2 in. material nailed at both ends to act as lugs. Frames may also be constructed of brick and concrete. Concrete walls must be raised from about a foot below the ground level and may taper from 4 in. to 2½ in. from bottom to top. It is necessary to stabilize the wall by providing concrete piers at 6-ft. intervals below the wall to the depth of 2 ft. The piers are usually 8 × 8 in. × 2 ft. The grout is 4 parts gravel, 2 parts sand and 1 of cement; this is thoroughly mixed and wetted, then poured into the form.

SASH. The 3 × 6 ft. one-man sash glazed with 10 × 12 in. glass is the most desirable. The single-weight strength is sufficient and lightest, double-weight glass is stronger, but unless the district is subject to heavy hail-storms adds unnecessary weight.

Standard sash material is generally purchasable in populous districts, but the following specifications may help. The sides and upper ends of 3 × 1½ in. material are grooved to receive glass, the lower end of 1 × 5 in. material and the two center strips of 1 × 1½ in. material. Paint the sash twice before glazing and once afterwards. The glass may be butted or lapped, but if lapped the slope needs to be of about 12 in. to shed the water

A notched stick is the simplest device for ventilating cold frames or hotbeds.

quickly enough. Either putty or a good putty substitute may be used. If difficulty is encountered in obtaining standard or approximately standard lumber, sash may be

---

* Special articles on the subjects indicated by an asterisk (*) will be found at the words so marked.

constructed of dressed 2 × 4 in. material, in this case all but the lower end is ripped. This makes a very neat and rigid sash, and by cutting ⅜-in. grooves for the glass, the sash will be about 35 in. wide.

Of late years substitutes for glass have been offered in several forms. Cloth dressed with paraffin and other waterproofing waxes is obtainable. The cellulose products mentioned below allow as much or more ultra-violet rays to penetrate as ordinary glass, but cut off the longer rays to a greater extent, thus giving a different but not necessarily inferior plant light value. They have a low melting point, so cannot be used in positions of direct sunlight during late spring or summer. They are, however, suitable for north frames throughout the growing season, or south frames in early spring. Waterproofed cloth has the advantage of being light and cheap, but has a relatively short life. Excellent plants are raised under such sash.

Cellulose products under various proprietary names are offered, *i.e.* Cel-o-glass, Vimlite, etc. These materials are principally galvanized wire netting coated with a suitable form of cellulose. Sash of these materials are practically unbreakable, but unbreakability, in these cases, is not synonymous with useful life. New Cel-o-glass and like materials allow up to approximately 50% of the ultra-violet rays to pass; this condition is not lasting and changes progressively until stability is reached at about 20%. This is scarcely a good glass substitute, and, when rust sets in, although the covering may be waterproof, it will also be practically light-proof because the iron oxide absorbs the ultra-violet rays, and whether new or old, much less of the longer rays pass than does in the case of glass. On the other hand, cellulose glass substitutes, until they become coated with a film of iron rust, are superior to common glass as sash under which to grow alpine plants. Alpine plants under these conditions, in spite of the apparently less intense light, retain their normal dwarf stature even after being under such protection for many months. Spring bedding plants, tomatoes, cabbage, etc., show no measurable difference when compared with the same kind of plants grown under glass. Modern greenhouse glass is much superior to the glass of twenty years ago in that much more ultra-violet rays are able to pass; thus the problem of leggy plants, the bane of the grower in the old days, arises only in cases of dull weather sustained over a long period.

MATS AND SHUTTERS. Shutters are wooden covers of the same size as the sash used as protection from the cold. They are either used alone or to cover mats. Shutters are satisfactorily made of dressed ship-lap. Shutters should always be painted. Mats may be of burlap or cheap canvas, plain or quilted. Quilted mats may be stuffed with straw, excelsior or bracken, or an old bed quilt may be used.

SITE AND SLOPE. For most garden purposes a slope to the south is desirable, but a slope to the north has many uses. If protection is afforded by a building it is generally sufficient; if the frame is away from a building, a hedge or board fence is imperative. A hedge on three sides is a splendid protection and also ornamental.

HOTBEDS. The best known hotbed material is stable manure. If this is mixed with leaves of oak, beech, birch, elm or any such tree to the extent of one-third of the bulk, the length of the heating period will be greatly extended and a less range in temperature result. With the plain stable manure, plus bedding straw, the period of heat is completed within two months. As a rule, by the addition of leaves, in the case of a bed 2½ ft. deep, the heating period is extended to 10 or 12 weeks. On obtaining the stable manure and leaves they must be well mixed and placed in a pile about 4 ft. wide and about 4 ft. high and extended to any length as occasion demands. In piling the material it must be wetted thoroughly but not saturated with water. Within a week active fermentation takes place, as is clearly indicated by the steaming. After steaming has been pronounced for about 2 days, the pile is changed by remixing the material, taking care to change the material from the outside to the center. Heating takes place much more rapidly after the second time of piling, so that in 10 or 11 days from the commencement it is ready for the hotbed. The amount of material used in any given case depends entirely on the season of the year and crop to be grown.

A hotbed of a minimum depth of 18 in. of firmly packed material will suffice for most crops. If the frame is shallow, that is, with a 10-in. front or less, it is generally better to excavate below to the depth of about 2 ft. to provide room for subsequent crops to develop; or the frame may be placed on the top of the pile of fermenting material. In this case, the hotbed must extend beyond the dimensions of the frame on all sides for 18 in. and be banked up the sides of the frame to the top. The material must be spread evenly in the frame and firmly packed after heating takes place. After packing the soil must then be added. The kind of soil depends on the crop to be raised. The depth is 5 or 6 in. except when the plants are being raised in flats or pots, then only about three inches are needed. Seeds may be sown when the temperature of the bed is falling from 90° Fahrenheit.

FIRE OR HOT-AIR HEATED HOTBED. This is the frontier hotbed and in practicability depends on a plentiful supply of firewood and readily available rough logs or split trees. In this case a trench is dug, gradually becoming shallower, from the fire box to the end of the frame. A rise of about one foot is usually sufficient for a frame 25 ft. long. The sides of the trench and top may be simply of stones, but it is better to use 6-in. sewer pipe if available. A chimney 6 or 10 ft. high is necessary at the upper end. The fire box may be simply of stones or bricks and of sufficient size to take cord wood or less. If a sewer pipe is used, a cheap laundry stove or some other type of heater answers admirably. It is desirable when heating a frame in this manner to construct a bench of split cedar, or some other readily available wood, about 1 ft. above the top of the flue, for the whole width and length of the frame; this provides even bottom-heat for the bed. Such frames in frontier districts cost little more than the labor involved and are remarkably efficient. A sash covered with whitewashed burlap used with one of these frames enables one to raise early plants in a satisfactory manner. Glass is, however, always best.

HOTBEDS IN HEATED FRAMES. Heated frames are generally heated by means of hot water or steam, and this is usually done by extending the heating system of glass-houses or dwelling to the frames. In the case of hot-water heating a 2½-in. pipe on either side of the frame is sufficient, because it is practically impossible to use a frame during very cold weather. With steam 1¼-in. pipe is sufficient, but the pipe must be higher in the frame owing to the greater heat injuring plants near them. If a hotbed is to be made of piping either for steam or hot water, it is advisable to have an air-space at 6 or 8 in. below the bed to ensure even heating. Pipes in the soil are unsatisfactory, as they give uneven bed temperature and, in case of steam, unless very deeply buried, will kill the plants. Pipes spaced 18 in. apart are sufficient for any hotbed, and such a hotbed should be valved in such a way as to have the bed under control. Hotbeds in heated frames are as near to perfection for growing plants as any can be other than a glass-house. The cost, however, of erecting higher sides and thus making a forcing-house, is not appreciably greater than a hotbed-heated frame. A hotbed of manure in a heated frame is very satisfactory, and the covering at night and during inclement weather is not so imperative, though covering by night is a safeguard and during very cold weather is necessary.

ELECTRICALLY HEATED HOTBEDS. The thermostatically controlled electrically heated hotbed is the most up-to-date method of hotbed heating. This idea was first carried out in Sweden, followed by Germany, and has been used and investigated in the United States since 1928. The greater initial cost of installation is very largely offset by the permanent nature of the equipment and trifling labor of making changes from time to time. What appears to be the most desirable heating device is a special resistance wire insulated from a lead sheath which forms a waterproof protection for the wire and insulation. This cable or wire is very flexible and can be bent or turned in any way desired. It may be buried in the soil of the bed at any depth desired, but ob-

---

* Special articles on the subjects indicated by an asterisk (*) will be found at the words so marked.

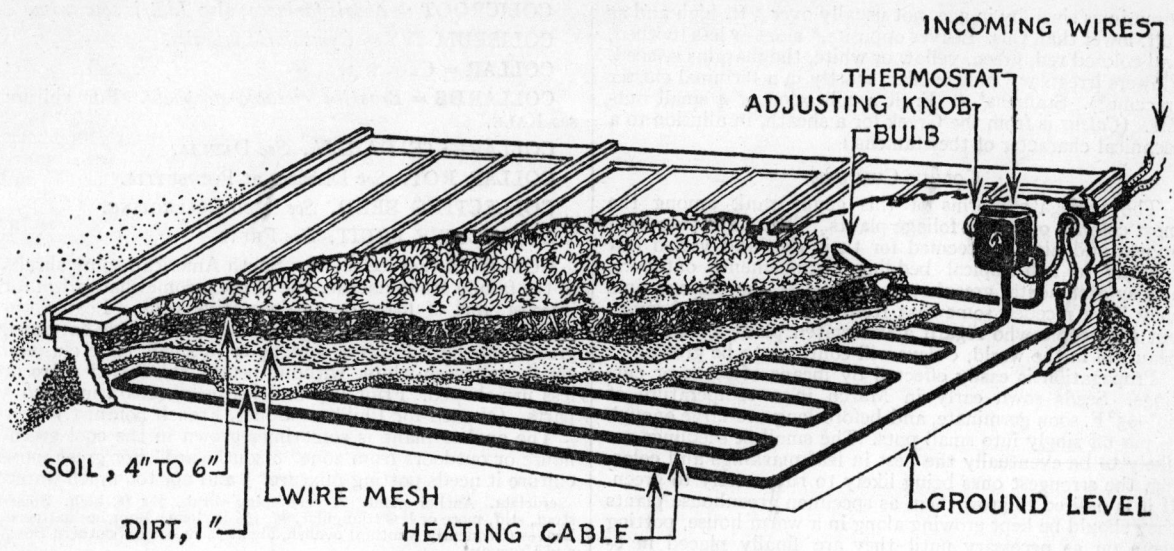
Cross-section of an electrically heated hotbed. For details see text.

viously 6 or 7 in. would suffice in most cases of growing plants; 2 or 3 in. are sufficient if pots or flats are to be used for the plants, seeds or cuttings. The thermostatic control allows the operator to fix any desired heat for the bed. If the plants are in containers of any kind and soil not desirable, ashes, sand or sawdust may be used to imbed the cable, or flats may be laid directly on the cable — but the soil, apparently by reason of its greater moisture capacity, is more economical and injures the cable much less than ashes. The cost of the cable is about seven cents a foot, thermostats cost from $6.00 up and power consumption may average about 1.64 kilowatt hours per 6 × 3 ft. sash per day. The cable is laid to and fro about 12 in. apart, but the cable is better about 6 in. apart in case of two outside lines, unless the sides of the frame are well banked.

The other type of electrical heating device used consists of three industrial-type strip heaters under a metal shield; this device is so much less convenient than the hotbed wire that it merely calls for note. It, however, would serve anyone who desires only a single frame of permanent construction.

MANAGEMENT OF FRAMES. Probably the most neglected feature of any frame management is that of ventilation. The means of ventilating are of two kinds, the most popular with professional gardeners is by sliding the sash up and down for the distance required; the earlier ventilation of the season is usually only 2 or 3 in. at the top, later, alternately top and bottom of varying distances up to about 15 in. The other means is by a notched piece of 2 × 4 in. material to act as a prop. At any time before the average frost-free date it is distinctly advantageous, if not imperative, to close the frame before the sun loses its afternoon power. After the frame has had time to get warm, if not already warm enough, the sash should be covered with mats or shutters to prevent the escape of heat. It is obvious, of course, that if the frame is being used only for the protection of hardy plants, early closing may unnecessarily force the plants.

Watering is usually better done in the morning of a bright day; this is not always possible, but it will be found surprising how few times in dull weather water is imperative, if advantage is taken of bright weather to water sufficiently. Watering late in the day is to be avoided, especially in the case of small seedlings, because excess moisture on the plants and surface of the bed encourages damping-off.* Weeding, and cultivating by stirring the surface of the soil, should always be attended to.

USES OF COLD FRAMES. Cold frames have many uses, the most popular being that of starting plants of either flowers or vegetables in advance of safe sowing weather conditions. Radishes may be matured before the end of the average frost-free date, because a cold frame may be sown four to six weeks before that date. A wide range of annuals can be had large enough to plant out at the time it would otherwise be only time to sow them. The same is true of lettuce, cabbage, cauliflower and other cool-season vegetables. After the first crop of plants is out the cold frame may be used to raise cucumbers, melons or tomatoes to maturity in districts where the growing of these subjects is uncertain. Other uses of cold frames are for the growing of violets for winter or early spring, for the protection of biennials that are unable to withstand severe northern winters. Cold frames that face north form excellent propagating frames for conifers and other evergreens, and are the most desirable structures for protecting and growing ferns or plants that have been collected during the growing season.

Portable cold frames are useful to afford autumnal protection for the late fruit of everbearing strawberries or late-sown china asters or hardy chrysanthemums, also parsley is get-at-able during winter when covered by a frame.

USES OF HOTBEDS. Hotbeds are of greater use than cold frames in that tender plants may be started as soon or sooner than cool-season plants may be started in a cold frame. After the bed is cold, or bottom-heat no longer required, the hotbed still has all the uses of a cold frame. Early crops of radish, carrots, turnips, lettuce, cucumbers, melons, tomatoes, eggplants, etc., can be assured by using a hotbed.

Warm-season subjects like the cucumber and tomatoes may be matured in the frame or planted out as advanced plants. In the case of a manure-heated hotbed, mushroom spawn may be planted with the cucumbers that are to mature in the frame and often succeed well. Forcing beans are another very useful crop. Cannas, dahlias, or tuberous begonias may be started, and dahlias may readily be propagated by cuttings with bottom-heat. — T. R. A. *See also* the tools and appliances at Section 6, TOOLS AND IMPLEMENTS.

COLD STORAGE. *See* STORAGE.

COLE. An indefinite term for plants of the cabbage tribe, including kohlrabi and rutabaga.

COLEUS (kō'lee-us). Foliage plants of the Old World tropics comprising over 90 species of the mint family, commonly called *Coleus*, but all through the Middle West called simply "The Foliage Plant." The only cult. species is C. blumei from Java, and its *var.* verschaffelti, which is the usual garden plant. It is a somewhat weak or soft herb,

* Special articles on the subjects indicated by an asterisk (*) will be found at the words so marked.

sometimes shrubby in age, not usually over 3 ft. high and as cult. lower than this. Leaves opposite,* more or less toothed, and colored red, green, yellow or white, the margins crisped. Flowers irregular,* blue or lilac, mostly in a terminal cluster (raceme*). Stamens* 4. Fruit a collection of 4 small nutlets. (*Coleus* is from the Greek for a sheath, in allusion to a technical character of the stamens.)

### COLEUS CULTURE

The variegated forms of this genus rank among the most colorful of tender foliage plants. They have long been known and highly esteemed for their rich and varied leaf coloring in sub-tropical bedding arrangements outdoors, and as ornamental greenhouse plants. At the present time they have receded somewhat from their position of favor, but for people who regard a variegated plant as the most beautiful in the world, *Coleus* will continue to be grown.

Propagation is easily effected by means of seeds or cuttings. Seeds sown early in March in a temperature of 60°–65° F. soon germinate, and before long are large enough to pot off singly into small pots. The smallest seedlings are likely to be eventually the best in leaf markings and coloring, the strongest ones being likely to run mostly to green. If it is desired to grow them as specimen greenhouse plants they should be kept growing along in a warm house, potting them on as necessary until they are finally placed in 8- or 10-in. pots, using potting mixture* 3. Pot rather firmly to ensure the desired short-jointed growth. Pinching out the growing points of some of the shoots will also be necessary to secure well-furnished plants of bushy habit. Flower buds should always be pinched out on sight, as the decorative value of these plants depends entirely on the leaves.

In the days of more formality than at present, large specimens trained on wire frames were considered the acme of a grower's skill and sure to be regarded with great admiration. Specimens when established in their final pots appreciate a watering with diluted liquid manure now and again. Large plants do not carry over the winter in good condition as a rule. Cuttings rooted in Sept. can be carried along safely in a moderately warm greenhouse, keeping them rather on the dry side at the roots. These are stock plants, and with the advent of good growing conditions in Feb. and March numerous cuttings will be obtainable. These root readily in clean, sharp sand in a temperature of 60°–65° F. Later on their tips afford good cuttings if needed. Being so tender *Coleus* cannot be used for bedding until all likelihood of frost has passed, which makes their season of effectiveness rather short in many sections. For this reason it is well to have nicely established plants in 4-in. pots all ready to plant when the weather is right.

Many named varieties of former years have disappeared from present-day lists, though *verschaffelti*, one of the first and best for bedding and conservatory decoration, is still offered. With leaves of rich crimson and green-frilled edges, this has been one of the most outstanding varieties ever introduced. Golden Bedder still ranks as the best yellow and among the leaders. Her Majesty, with bronze-red leaves margined with orange, is one of the best to grow as a specimen pot plant. Brilliancy, in the same color class, gives a still more rich effect. Salvador, with green-edged rose and maroon leaves; and Sun Ray, with leaves combining reddish-purple, yellow and bronze, are among the most highly colored varieties of today. — H. E. D.

INSECT PESTS. Sluggish white mealybugs are important pests of this and other greenhouse plants. Washing strong plants with a hose will check them; nicotine sulphate spray 1-500 (with soap) and calcium cyanide fumigation also give some control. Mealybugs should be prevented from getting a start, if possible. Whiteflies are also injurious (see BEGONIA).

DISEASES. This plant is fairly free from diseases, although cutting rot and gray mold may be troublesome. Cutting rot, a disease affecting young cuttings, is caused by at least two soil-inhabiting fungi. A dark-colored rot on the lower part of the stem is characteristic of the disease. For control, select cuttings from healthy plants, use clean sand or soil for the rooting medium, and avoid excess water. Sterilization of the sand or soil with steam or formaldehyde is also beneficial. Plants affected with gray mold exhibit light brown dead areas on the leaves. Remove all infected leaves, lower the humidity and keep the foliage dry.

**COLEWORT** = Cole.

**COLICROOT** = *Aletris farinosa*; also *Liatris squarrosa*.
**COLISEUM IVY** = *Cymbalaria muralis*.
**COLLAR** = CROWN 1.
**COLLARDS** = *Brassica oleracea acephala*. For culture see KALE.
**COLLARETTE DAHLIA.** See DAHLIA.
**COLLAR ROT.** See Diseases at POINSETTIA.
**COLLECTING SEED.** See SEED COLLECTING.
**COLLECTIVE FRUIT.** See FRUIT.

**COLLETIA** (kol-lee'shi-a). South American spiny shrubs of the family Rhamnaceae, one of them somewhat grown for interest, but of little or no decorative value. Leaves opposite,* small, often lacking and the plant with flattened, green branches. Flowers solitary or in small, close clusters, small, yellowish-white, without petals, the calyx* more or less urn-shaped. Fruit dry and leathery, separating into 3 parts. (Named for Philibert Collet, French botanist.)

The anchor plant is sometimes grown in the cool greenhouse or outdoors from zone* 8 southward. For greenhouse culture it needs potting mixture* 3 and not too much water.

**cruciata.** Anchor plant. A very spiny shrub, 3-4 ft. high. Spines stout, stiff, more or less triangular, ¾-1½ in. long. Branches flattened. Leaves (frequently wanting) ovalish, about ¼ in. long. Southern Brazil and Uruguay.

**COLLINSIA** (kol-lin'si-a). A genus of 20 species of attractive annual herbs of the family Scrophulariaceae, three often grown in the flower garden. Most of them are natives of western N.A. Leaves opposite* or in threes. Flowers solitary or in small clusters in the leaf-axils,* the corolla irregular* and 2-lipped, the calyx bell-shaped. The lower lip is 3-lobed and spreading. Fruit a capsule.* (Named for Zaccheus Collins, Philadelphia botanist.)

The species below may be easily grown if treated as hardy annuals, the seed being sown in spring, after warm weather has arrived, in the place where wanted.

**bicolor.** Chinese houses. Not over 2 ft. high, the leaves oblongish, 1-2 in. long, toothed. Flowers 1 in. long, nearly stalkless, the upper lip* white, the lower rose-purple or violet. Calif. Summer. The var. **candidissima** has pure white flowers.

**grandiflora.** Blue-lips. From 8-15 in. high, the leaves narrow, ¾-1½ in. long, toothed. Flowers about ¾ in. long, the stalks about the same length, the upper lip* purple or white, the lower blue or violet. British Columbia to Calif.

**verna.** Blue-eyed Mary. From 1-2 ft. high, the leaves ovalish, 1-2 in. long. Flowers long-stalked, about ⅓ in. long, the upper lip white or purple, the lower blue. N.Y. to Ky. and Wisc.

**COLLINSONIA** (kol-lin-sō'ni-a). Three woodland species of herbs of the mint family, of eastern N.A., one of them grown in the wild garden but not of much decorative value. The cult. species, **C. canadensis**, variously called horse balm, stoneroot, rickweed, and citronella, is a strong-smelling perennial 2-4 ft. high. Leaves opposite,* broadly oval, 4-8 in. long. Flowers yellow, lemon-scented, irregular,* about ½ in. long, in a long, terminal, often branched cluster (raceme*). Its culture in the wild garden is easy if kept in woods soil and given shade. (Named for Peter Collinson, British botanist.) It is not the source of citronella. See CYMBOPOGON.

**COLLOMIA** (kol-lo'mi-a). Attractive annual herbs of the family Polemoniaceae, found in western N.A. and in S.A., three of them useful plants in the flower garden. They have usually alternate* leaves and flowers suggesting those of *Gilia* from which they are separated only by technical characters. Corolla mostly funnel-shaped, the stamens usually protruding. (*Collomia* is from the Greek for glue, in allusion to the seeds, which are mucilaginous when wet.)

*Collomia biflora* is a showy-flowered annual well worth a place in the flower garden. This and the other species should be grown as hardy annuals. See ANNUALS. They bloom very freely with a minimum of attention.

**biflora.** Usually not over 9 in., rarely up to 15 in. high. Leaves narrow, 1-2 in. long, toothed or cut. Flowers in leafy clusters, the corolla about 1 in. long, orange-red or scarlet. Bolivia to Chile and Argentina. Sometimes offered as *C. coccinea*.

**coccinea** = *Collomia biflora*.

---

* Special articles on the subjects indicated by an asterisk (*) will be found at the words so marked.

# FLOWER COLORS

The colors on the plate facing this page are the usual ones found in a great range of garden flowers. Unfortunately, the names of colors vary widely; the gardeners, artists, silk manufacturers, chemists, and other groups each having a system of their own. And, as will be seen from the chart, Nature often provides tints and shades found nowhere else. Because of this confusion of names, the colors in the list below, so far as possible, have been designated in accordance with the standard color nomenclature of Webster's New International Dictionary, Second Edition. Black and white are omitted from the chart.

It must also be understood that color names like mulberry, plum, peach, geranium, lilac, etc., are not necessarily the color of the flowers or fruits from which the name of the color was derived.

### Key to Flower Colors

| | | |
|---|---|---|
| 1. Jonquil Yellow. | 22. Geranium. | 43. Mauvette. |
| 2. Greenish-yellow. | 23. Coral. | 44. Lavender. |
| 3. Lemon Yellow. | 24. Vermilion. | 45. Pansy Violet. |
| 4. Chrome Yellow. | 25. Scarlet. | 46. Royal Purple. |
| 5. Golden-yellow. | 26. Carmine. | 47. Plum. |
| 6. Indian Yellow. | 27. Cherry. | 48. Mulberry. |
| 7. Yellow Ochre. | 28. Raisin. | 49. Eggplant. |
| 8. Straw Yellow. | 29. Pink. | 50. Hyacinth Blue. |
| 9. Peach. | 30. Mallow Pink. | 51. Gentian Blue. |
| 10. Chrome Orange. | 31. Cardinal. | 52. Wistaria Blue. |
| 11. Marigold Yellow. | 32. Crimson. | 53. Violet. |
| 12. Yellow-orange. | 33. Claret. | 54. Amethyst. |
| 13. Orange. | 34. Ruby. | 55. Mauve. |
| 14. Henna. | 35. Chocolate. | 56. Purple-violet. |
| 15. Salmon Pink. | 36. Lilac. | 57. Gray. |
| 16. Tile Red. | 37. Orchid. | 58. Blue-gray. |
| 17. Spectrum Red. | 38. Mallow Purple. | 59. Sky Blue. |
| 18. Terra-cotta. | 39. Magenta. | 60. Italian Blue. |
| 19. Scarlet Vermilion. | 40. Burgundy. | 61. Cobalt Blue. |
| 20. Burnt Sienna. | 41. Maroon. | 62. Royal Blue. |
| 21. Sepia. | 42. Heliotrope. | 63. Antwerp Blue. |

## FLOWER COLORS

The colors on the plate facing this page are the usual ones found in a great range of garden flowers. Unfortunately, the names of colors vary widely, the gardeners, artists, silk manufacturers, chemists, and other groups each having a system of their own. And, as will be seen from the chart, Nature often provides tints and shades found nowhere else. Because of this confusion of names, the colors in the list below, so far as possible, have been designated in accordance with the standard color nomenclature of Webster's New International Dictionary, Second Edition. Black and white are omitted from the chart.

It must also be understood that color names like mulberry, plum, peach, geranium, lilac, etc., are not necessarily the color of the flowers or fruits from which the name of the color was derived.

*Key to Flower Colors*

| | | |
|---|---|---|
| 1. Jonquil Yellow. | 22. Geranium. | 43. Mauvette. |
| 2. Greenish-yellow. | 23. Coral. | 44. Lavender. |
| 3. Lemon Yellow. | 24. Vermilion. | 45. Pansy Violet. |
| 4. Chrome Yellow. | 25. Scarlet. | 46. Royal Purple. |
| 5. Golden-yellow. | 26. Carmine. | 47. Plum. |
| 6. Indian Yellow. | 27. Cherry. | 48. Mulberry. |
| 7. Yellow Ochre. | 28. Raisin. | 49. Eggplant. |
| 8. Straw Yellow. | 29. Pink. | 50. Hyacinth Blue. |
| 9. Peach. | 30. Mallow Pink. | 51. Gentian Blue. |
| 10. Chrome Orange. | 31. Cardinal. | 52. Wisteria Blue. |
| 11. Marigold Yellow. | 32. Crimson. | 53. Violet. |
| 12. Yellow-orange. | 33. Claret. | 54. Amethyst. |
| 13. Orange. | 34. Ruby. | 55. Mauve. |
| 14. Henna. | 35. Chocolate. | 56. Purple-violet. |
| 15. Salmon Pink. | 36. Lilac. | 57. Gray. |
| 16. Tile Red. | 37. Orchid. | 58. Blue-gray. |
| 17. Spectrum Red. | 38. Mallow Purple. | 59. Sky Blue. |
| 18. Terra-cotta. | 39. Magenta. | 60. Italian Blue. |
| 19. Scarlet Vermilion. | 40. Burgundy. | 61. Cobalt Blue. |
| 20. Burnt Sienna. | 41. Maroon. | 62. Royal Blue. |
| 21. Sepia. | 42. Heliotrope. | 63. Antwerp Blue. |

grandiflora. Similar to *C. biflora*, but the leaves without teeth and the flowers salmon or buff. Western U.S.

linearis. Not over 15 in. high, the leaves narrow and without teeth. Flowers reddish-purple or pinkish. Western N.A.

**COLOCASIA** (ko-lo-kay′zee-a). Large, tuberous-rooted, tropical Asiatic herbs of the arum family, commonly known as elephant-ear, and widely grown for their ornamental foliage, and, in the tropics, for the edible tubers of the taro. They have a short, or no, stem and very large leaves with long, fleshy, sheathing leafstalks. The blade of the leaf is usually arrowhead-shaped, or halberd-shaped, deeply cut at the base and the leafstalk attached to or near the middle of the blade (peltate*). Flowers minute (for details see ARACEAE), crowded on a spadix,* the boat-shaped spathe* longer than the spadix.* Fruit fleshy. (*Colocasia* is from the Greek for an Egyptian plant resembling the water lily; of uncertain application here.)

As a garden plant the elephant-ear is a striking summer bedding herb, its fine foliage being unlike any plant similarly used. Well-grown specimens should be covered with the large leaves, which should hang nearly to the ground. Plants should not be put outdoors until settled warm weather, and they need plenty of space and the soil cannot be too rich. Keep the bed thoroughly watered, and if it is in shade for part of the day, so much the better. The young plants, ready for summer bedding, can be purchased from dealers, but to raise your own, dig up the tubers from the old plants and store in a frost-free, but cool place all winter. In April plant them in potting mixture* 4, water well and put in a moist, warm greenhouse (75°–80°). They will be ready for bedding out by June.

antiquorum. The common bedding elephant-ear. A stout herb, when properly grown, 6–9 ft. high and as wide, usually less as cult. Leaves green, thick and fleshy, about 2 ft. long, the stalks 4–5 ft. long. East Indies. While this common green form is the most widely grown, there are several varieties, as *var. illustris*, with purple leafstalks and larger leaves which are dark-spotted between the veins, and others with violet leaf margins and veins.

esculenta. Taro, eddo, dasheen. A plant very similar to *C. antiquorum*, but its tubers yield an edible, starchy vegetable, a staple food in the Pacific Islands. Little grown in the U.S. except in the South where the form known as dasheen is cult. for food. Small tubers are planted in regions with at least 7 months of warm weather (generally from zone* 7 southward). Put them 2 ft. apart in the row, and the rows about 4 ft. apart. They may be grown, harvested, and stored like sweet potatoes, except that the tubers need no curing. They are cooked and eaten like potatoes. Often known as *Caladium esculentum*.

**COLOMBO AGENT** = *Scindapsus aureus*.

**COLONIAL GARDEN.** See ARCHITECTURAL STYLE.

**COLOR.** For the usual colors found in garden flowers see the colored plate. See also COLOR GARDENING.

**COLORADO.** The state lies wholly in zones* 3 and 4. Although these zones are based upon average minimum temperatures, the problem of plant hardiness is complicated in this state by large differences in snowfall and the ameliorating influence in certain localities of steep-sided mountains and rock palisades.

Colorado soils are extremely variable in depth, structure, and the parent material from which they are derived. This is particularly true in the mountains that divide the state into "eastern Colorado and the western slope."

The principal rivers in eastern Colorado are the Platte and the Arkansas; on the western slope, the Gunnison and the Colorado. These rivers and their flood plains include much of the state's agricultural land.

Some fine soils are isolated geographically and economically by mountains. North Park, Middle Park, South Park and the San Luis Valley form an extensive area nearly continuous throughout the length of the state in which only a small part of the arable land is tilled.

Colorado soils, in general, are slightly alkaline, but alkalinity is seldom the limiting factor where other conditions are suitable to plant growing. For plants which require distinctly acid soils, especially if they are at all deep-rooted, it is often difficult to maintain the acidity necessary even with the approved methods of using chemicals or peats. The drainage essential to normal growth of most plants carries off acidulated solutions, making the task of acidifying a continuous one rather than simply a single item in original preparation.

The chief gardening centers of eastern Colorado are along the foothills and mostly in the vicinity of Denver, Pueblo, and Canon City. On the western slope Grand Junction, Delta and Montrose are the chief centers.

Horticulture is practically confined to the 2,000,000 irrigated acres. Fruit is grown on about 30,000 of these acres. The other important horticultural crops and their approximate acreages in recent years are:

| | |
|---|---:|
| Potatoes | 90,000 |
| Cantaloupes | 10,000 |
| Lettuce | 8,000 |
| Green peas (table) | 7,000 |
| Onions | 4,000 |
| Green peas (manufacture) | 3,000 |
| Cabbage | 3,000 |
| Cauliflower | 3,000 |
| Cucumbers (seed) | 3,000 |
| Cucumbers (pickles) | 2,500 |
| Snap beans | 2,000 |
| Tomatoes (manufacture) | 2,000 |
| Tomatoes (table) | 1,000 |
| Celery | 900 |
| | 139,400 acres |

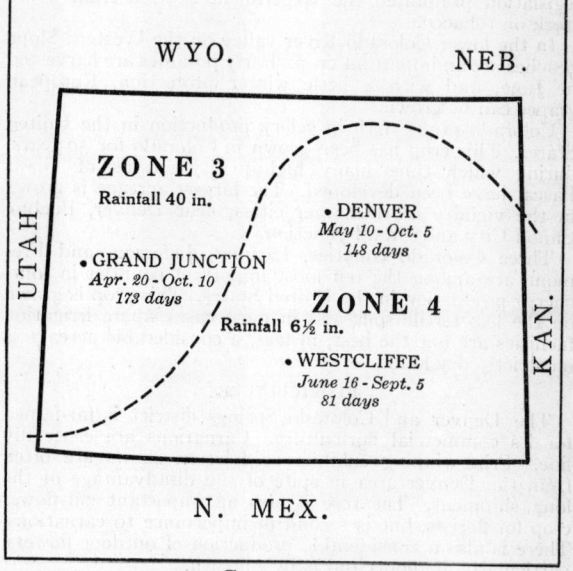

COLORADO

The zones of hardiness crossing Colorado are those shown on the colored map at ZONE, which should be consulted for details. The dates are the average latest killing frost in spring and the first one in the fall. The figures below the dates show the average length of the growing season. The rainfall figures show the total annual rainfall, in inches, for two significant localities.

CHIEF GARDENING CENTERS

The Arkansas Valley is the most important section in the United States in the production of melon seeds, besides being an important source of the melons themselves. Zinnia seed is produced commercially in this section also. Colorado leads in the United States in fall shipments of cauliflower, which is grown in the San Luis Valley, Pueblo, Denver, and Brighton districts as well as on many scattered mountain farms.

High altitude head lettuce, growing in mountain valleys from 7000 to 9000 feet elevation in the early '20's, encouraged buyers and established packing sheds at rail points, particularly in the San Luis Valley, the Eagle Valley, and Middle and South Parks. The growth of the lettuce-growing industry was too rapid to be a healthy one. This boom was its undoing in many places, but cauliflower and peas have replaced some of the surplus lettuce acreage. These cool-season crops grow to perfection in the mountains. Growing seasons are short, but plant growth is correspondingly rapid, which makes for quality.

---

* Special articles on the subjects indicated by an asterisk (*) will be found at the words so marked.

Exceptionally fine potatoes and tremendous yields are produced on these high-altitude farms. L. G. Schutte of Monte Vista holds the United States record for high yield of potatoes. He produced 1145 bushels of Brown Beauties on a measured acre. The Greeley area in Weld County formerly was the important potato-growing section of the state, but in the past few years it has dropped from first place, which is now held by the San Luis Valley. This valley is at 7500 feet elevation, the Greeley district, 5000. Colorado is famous for its Peachblow potatoes, especially the dark red strain.

As may be noticed from the weather statistics to follow, one of these mountain farming districts (Westcliffe) has only a 2-day growing season, considering its latest and earliest recorded frost dates. The average, however, is 81 days. The other extreme in Colorado climate is reached in the gardening sections of the lower Arkansas and Colorado River valleys. In the Arkansas Valley in eastern Colorado, besides an important melon crop, Valencia onions are matured from seed, sweet potatoes are grown to a limited extent, and though it is not a commercial crop, tobacco can be grown. It is interesting to note that early state legislation prohibited the Experiment Station from doing work on tobacco.

In the lower Colorado River valley on the Western Slope peaches are an important crop. Early potatoes are harvested in June, and with a little winter protection, European grapes can be grown.

Colorado ranks sixth in celery production in the United States. This crop has been grown in Colorado for 50 years, during which time many high-quality strains of Giant Pascal have been developed. The largest acreage is grown in the vicinity of the larger cities; near Denver, Pueblo, Canon City and Grand Junction.

Three Colorado counties, Larimer, Jefferson, and Fremont, are among the ten most important counties in sour-cherry production in the United States. This crop is grown on the less fertile soils and in most cases where irrigation facilities are not the best, in fact, a considerable acreage is on strictly dry land.

### Floriculture

The Denver and Colorado Springs district is far-famed for its commercial floriculture. Carnations are especially fine. Prize-winning exhibits at Eastern shows are often from the Denver area in spite of the disadvantage of the long shipment. The rose is also an important cut-flower crop for florists, but is second in importance to carnations. There is also a considerable production of outdoor flowers, particularly gladiolus and baby's-breath.

### Ornamentals

Colorado Blue Spruce is the crowning glory of Colorado's outdoor ornamentals. The pines, firs, and junipers native to the state are also used extensively. Of the broad-leaf trees, American elm is the best all-around shade and street tree. Other much-used trees are Chinese elm (*Ulmus parvifolia*), American linden, European weeping birch, and the Carolina and Lombardy poplars, as well as *Populus alba pyramidalis*.

The most satisfactory of the medium-high shrubs is Vanhoutte spirea. Other commonly used shrubs are the mock-orange, sumacs, lilacs, several species of *Viburnum*, dogwoods, *Caragana*, and Russian olive.

For windbreaks and shelter belts the kinds used are poplar, cottonwood, ash, box-elder, Chinese elm, honey locust, willow, *Caragana* and Russian olive. It is recommended that such evergreens as Ponderosa pine, Rocky Mountain red cedar, Douglas fir, and Colorado blue spruce also be included for permanency.

### Rainfall

Although Colorado is an arid state, the mountains are a great storehouse of water for irrigation. Average snowfall at a number of points is over 20 feet annually. This snow is barely melted each year when new snow falls. Snow in summer is common and Colorado's glaciers are famous. This large reserve of water, plus the fact that about three-fourths of the annual precipitation occurs as small showers through the growing season, makes gardening profitable in extensive areas which appear quite arid in the climatological data.

The average annual precipitation for the state is 17½ inches. The lowest average is 6½ inches in the San Luis Valley, and the highest above 40 inches in the San Juan Mountains and some other restricted areas. In spite of the low average rainfall of the San Luis Valley, its agricultural areas are literally afloat at times during the growing season by reason of the enormous quantities of water used in the sub-irrigation universally practiced in crop production there.

### Frost Data

A general statement conveys little meaning on account of the wide range of elevations in Colorado. The mean annual temperature for the entire state is 44.3 degrees F., though it varies from about 31 degrees in some mountain districts to 54 degrees in parts of the Arkansas Valley.

|  | Average date of last killing frost in Spring | Latest known killing frost | Average date of earliest killing frost in Fall | Earliest known killing frost |
|---|---|---|---|---|
| Grand Junction | April 20 | May 14 | Oct. 10 | Sept. 14 |
| Denver | May 10 | June 6 | Oct. 5 | Sept. 12 |
| Westcliffe | June 16 | July 29 | Sept. 5 | Aug. 1 |

The address of the Agricultural Experiment Station, which has kindly supplied this information about the state, is at Fort Collins, Colorado. The station is always ready to answer gardening questions.

Colorado's garden club activities include chapters of the Garden Club of America, the home office of which is 598 Madison Avenue, New York. There are also several chapters of the Colorado Federation of Garden Clubs, information about which may be had by writing to Garden Editor, Houghton Mifflin Company, Boston, Mass.

**COLORADO BLUE SPRUCE** = *Picea pungens.* See Spruce.

**COLORADO FIR** = *Abies concolor.* See Fir.

**COLORADO GRASS** = *Panicum texanum.*

**COLORADO POTATO BEETLE.** See Beetle at Insect Pests and the Insect Pests at Potato.

**COLORADO RED CEDAR** = *Juniperus scopulorum.*

*COLORATA, -us, -um* (kol-or-ray′ta). Colored.

**COLOR GARDENING.** Taste or preference may at times dictate the carrying out of a garden wholly or in part with plants having flowers in tones of a special color. In this case, while the preferred color will predominate, a more pleasing effect is brought about if a few flowers or foliage plants of harmonizing or contrasting hues are introduced as foils or accents. In such a planting the colors of near-by buildings or walls should be taken into consideration so that they will not bring about a lack of harmony; and all garden accessories such as trellis-work, fences, gates, seats or arbors should be painted or otherwise treated with the general color scheme in view, while care should be taken that jars, pots, umbrellas and such minor accessories do not introduce a discordant note. The success of a special color garden depends upon keeping all its component parts in pleasant harmony.

If the color garden is a subdivision of a larger garden its effectiveness is greatly enhanced if it is walled or fenced or hedged about so that other portions of the garden do not intervene to detract from the impression it is intended to create. If merely a border it should be placed or screened so that it does not come within the same vision-scope as parts of the garden that would not accord with it. In planting such a garden or border use should be made of flowering shrubs, climbers, bulbs, perennial and annual plants of all types and heights and seasons of blossoming.

---

\* Special articles on the subjects indicated by an asterisk (\*) will be found at the words so marked.

See Blue Garden, Red Garden, White Garden, Pink Garden, Yellow Garden and Gray and Lavender Garden. — L. B. W.

**COLPROVIA.** See Drives.

**COLQUHOUNIA** (ko-hoon'i-a). A small and horticulturally unimportant genus of Asiatic plants of the mint family, C. vestita somewhat cult. outdoors, from zone* 7 southward, for ornament. It is an erect, white-woolly plant 3-4 ft. high. Leaves opposite,* large below but smaller and bract*-like above. Flowers irregular,* orange-scarlet, winter-blooming, the corolla about ¾ in. long. The flowers are in whorls in the upper leaf-axils.* (Named for Sir Robert Colquhoun, British worthy.)

**COLTSFOOT** = *Tussilago farfara.*

*COLUBRINA, -us, -um* (kol-you-bry'na). Pertaining to or shaped like a snake.

*COLUMBIANA, -us, -um* (ko-lum-bi-ā'na). From British Columbia, or from Colombia, S.A.

**COLUMBINE.** Many attractive garden herbs, all perennials, belonging to the genus **Aquilegia** (a-kwee-lee'ji-a) of the buttercup family. Of the 40 known species, all from the north temperate zone, about a dozen are very popular plants for the border or rock garden. Leaves twice- or thrice-compound.* Flowers showy, usually at the ends of the branches. Sepals and petals colored alike, the 5 petals with long, hollow spurs,* some of which are knobbed, others hooked at the end. Sepals shorter than the spurs. In many of the garden hybrids double-flowered forms are common. These are possibly derived from *A. coerulea, A. chrysantha,* or others, but the parentage of some of the finest is uncertain. Fruit a collection of dry, erect pods (follicles*) which split off separately. (*Aquilegia* is of uncertain origin.)

The columbines are well divided into those whose original habitat makes the rock garden their best cult. home, and those, more tolerant, that can be grown in the open border. The latter group includes the long-spurred hybrids as well as several of the Old World species. They do best in open, sandy loam in the perennial border. The others, as indicated below, are rock garden species and their culture should be sought there. All the columbines are best increased by division of the clumps in the spring.

A. alpina. Not over 1 ft. high. Flowers nearly 2 in. wide, blue, the spurs long and incurved. The Alps. July-Aug. For cult. see Rock Garden.

A. canadensis. The common columbine of eastern N.A. A beautiful herb 15-24 in. high. Flowers about 1½ in. wide, the sepals yellow, the spurs red, almost straight, knobbed at the end. Eastern N.A. May. A fine plant for the shady nook in the wild garden, preferably in woods soil. Also grown in the rock garden. See Wild Garden.

A. chrysantha. A very showy border columbine, 2-4 ft. high, and branched. Flowers nearly 3 in. wide, yellow, the spurs straight, nearly 2½ in. long. Rocky Mountains to Tex. May-Aug.

A. coerulea. A native American columbine, 2-3 ft. high. Flowers up to 2 in. wide, bluish-purple, the spurs straightish and knobbed at the ends. May-June. Rocky Mountains. A fine border plant, but also grown in the rock garden (which see).

A. flabellata. Not over 18 in. high, the flowers lilac, nodding, and about 2 in. wide. Spurs rather short, the ends incurved. Jap. July-Aug. There is a much smaller, almost dwarf var. nana with pure white flowers. For its culture see Rock Garden.

A. formosa. A striking columbine for the open border, 2-3 ft. high. Flowers about 1½ in. wide, nodding, red and yellow, the spurs red, straight, and not knobbed. Western N.A. and Siberia. May-Aug. There are several hort. varieties or forms, some of them of hybrid origin, including dwarfs, a double-flowered form and one with nearly white flowers.

A. glandulosa. A Siberian columbine for the border, usually not over 18 in. high. Flowers nodding, up to 3 in. wide, lilac-blue, the shortish spurs much incurved. June-Aug. The var. jucunda has whitish, somewhat double flowers.

A. jucunda = *Aquilegia glandulosa jucunda.*

A. longissima. A showy perennial 2-3 ft. high, the foliage silky-hairy. Flowers golden-yellow, nodding, the spurs about 5 in. long. Southwestern Tex. and northern Mex. July-Oct.

A. pyrenaica. A low columbine, usually not over 12 in. high. Flowers about 2 in. wide, dark blue, the spurs short but distinctly incurved. Pyrenees. Summer.

A. skinneri. A handsome columbine from the mountains of Mex. and Guatemala, often 2½-3 ft. high. Flowers about 1½ in. wide, nodding, the sepals greenish-yellow, the spurs red, nearly 2 in. long and straight. July-Sept. There is also a double-flowered form.

A. vulgaris. Perhaps the best known of the columbines for the open border, and often up to 2 ft. high. Flowers 1½-2 in. wide, nodding, usually blue, but sometimes purple or white, the spurs decidedly incurved and knobbed at the ends. Eurasia. Summer. There are many color forms and hybrids, some dwarf, white and double-flowered, some lilac, and one with yellow-lined leaves.

**COLUMBO.** See Frasera.

*COLUMELLARIS, -e* (kol-you-mel-lay'ris). Relating to a small collar or to a pillar.

**COLUMN.** The structure formed by the union of stamens* and pistils in orchid flowers, or of the stamens* in the flowers of the mallow family (Malvaceae).

*COLUMNARIS, -e* (kol-um-nay'ris). Columnar.

*COLURNA* (ko-lur'na). Classical name of the hazel.

**COLUTEA** (ko-lew'tee-a). Eurasian shrubs of the pea family, the one below often grown for ornament, and as a stock for grafting cions of the glory-pea (*Clianthus dampieri*). Of the 10 known species only C. arborescens, the bladder-senna, is much cult. It is about 4 ft. high and has compound* leaves, the leaflets arranged feather-fashion, with an odd one at the end. Leaflets without teeth, usually 9-13, and about 2 in. long. Flowers pea-like, bright yellow, about 1 in. long, in long-stalked clusters (racemes*) from the leaf-axils.* Pod (not a legume) papery, inflated and not splitting, about 2½ in. long. Southern Eu. May-July. Hardy from zone* 4 southward, and of easy culture in ordinary garden soils. (*Colutea* is from the Greek for some pea-like tree.)

**COLZA** = *Brassica napus.*

**COMBRETACEAE** (kom-bret-tay'see-ee). A family of tropical shrubs, trees and woody vines of little garden interest except for the Indian almond (see Terminalia) and the Rangoon creeper (see Quisqualis), both of which can be grown outdoors only in frost-free regions.

Leaves mostly alternate* in *Terminalia*, but opposite in *Quisqualis*, a rank-growing, woody vine with rusty young foliage and white flowers. *Terminalia* is a tall tree with large, glossy leaves and a dry fruit with an edible seed.

Technical flower characters: Flowers in spikes,* panicles,* or heads,* the cluster bracted* at the base. Sepals 4 or 5. Petals (in ours) 4 or 5. Stamens inserted on the calyx, usually 10, in 2 series. Ovary inferior,* 1-celled, with a single style.*

**COMFREY.** See Symphytum.

**COMFREY FAMILY** = Boraginaceae.

**COMMELINA** (kom-mel-ly'na). The day-flowers are weak, watery-juiced, quickly wilting herbs of the family Commelinaceae, with jointed stems and alternate leaves without marginal teeth. Of the 100 known species, of wide distribution, only 3 are of any garden interest. They have quickly fading flowers, blue in those below, solitary or in small clusters, below which is a boat-shaped bract* or spathe.* Flowers irregular,* the 3 sepals often colored and joined. Petals 3, two of them long-clawed.* Stamens 6, 3 of them infertile. Fruit a 3-celled capsule.* (Named for Caspar and Johann Commelin, Dutch botanists.)

*Commelina angustifolia* and *C. nudiflora* are hardy, with protection, over most of the country. Both of them tend to sprawl and prefer moist, shady places. *C. coelestis* is more often almost a weed under greenhouse benches, but can be grown outdoors in the blue garden if south of zone* 6. All are easily propagated by rooting bits of their jointed stems in moist sand.

angustifolia. More or less prostrate, the stems up to 2 ft. long. Leaves very narrow, 3-5 in. long. Flowers blue, the bract* below it purplish. Southern U.S.

coelestis. A perennial up to 2 ft. high, but usually half sprawling. Flowers dark blue, nearly 1 in. long. Common in greenhouses and hardy outdoors south of zone* 6. Mex.

nudiflora. More or less creeping perennial, easily rooting at the joints. Flowers blue, scarcely ½ in. wide. A somewhat weedy perennial hardy up to zone* 4. Widely distributed from N.J. to S.A., Africa, and Asia.

**COMMELINACEAE** (kom-mel-ly-nay'see-ee). The spiderwort or day-flower family is familiar to all gardeners from containing the wandering Jew and the spiderwort (which see). All of its 26 genera and over 300 species are fleshy herbs,

---

* Special articles on the subjects indicated by an asterisk (*) will be found at the words so marked.

mostly of warm regions, but *Commelina* and the spiderwort (*Tradescantia*) are also found in the temperate region. Most of the garden genera have fleshy, watery-juiced stems that quickly wilt when picked. Leaves alternate,* without marginal teeth. Flowers regular* or irregular, the 3 petals soon withering, but often rather showy. Fruit a dry pod (capsule*).

Besides those mentioned above, the garden genera include *Dichorisandra*, *Spironema* and *Rhoeo*, all tropical plants of greenhouse cult., and *Zebrina*, which contains one of the plants called wandering Jew (for the other *see* SPIDERWORT).

Technical flower characters: Ovary superior,* 2–3-celled, its ovules few or many. Sepals 3, free, or sometimes united into a sheath-like organ, green. Petals 3, free, or rarely united into a short tube (in *Zebrina*), usually brightly colored.

**COMMUNIS, -e** (kom-mew'nis). Common or general.

**COMMUNITY GARDENS.** The term Community Garden in relation to landscape architecture is a public garden designed to be of common interest to a particular community. In a sense this is a special type of public park devoted to horticultural or garden interest rather than active recreation.

The plan of such a garden will depend on its natural location, but there are general principles which apply to all such projects. Paths should be a minimum of six feet wide, and paved with a durable surface such as bituminous-bound macadam, brick, flagstone, or well-drained gravel. Since the paths are often crowded to capacity the beds should be protected by brick or stone curbs elevated two to four inches above the level of the walk. Surface drainage on the walks should be picked up at intervals by drain inlets set level with the walk frequently enough to prevent the accumulation of water at any point.

There should be a major center of interest, which may be a garden building, a fountain or a pool. The location of this major feature should dominate the entire garden and the paths leading directly from it should be proportionately larger than the minimum-width paths.

Any building should be of masonry construction, intimate in character, and avoid any public-institution appearance. A pool should be designed not over two feet deep to avoid any risk of public liability and be a minimum of twenty feet in diameter to grow a display of water lilies.

In order to segregate the garden from its surroundings the property lines should be planted with trees high enough to shut out any view of adjacent buildings and massed with low planting for proper background. If the property lines are on street frontage a masonry wall, at least seven feet high, should shut off the garden from the street, leaving entrance gateways for adequate access for the community. This type of garden is intended for leisure-time interest and need not be opened up for the benefit of the hurried passer-by.

There are many classes of plants which may be included, according to the amount and type of space available. Collections of flowering trees, flowering shrubs, perennials, rock plants and annuals — each has its particular interest, but it is necessary to select the groups which fit the location and not attempt to crowd in all of them. It is better to concentrate on a representative collection of one or two classes of plant materials than to sacrifice the garden effect for too much variety. — R. E. G.

**COMMUTATA, -us, -um** (kom-mew-tay'ta). Changing or changeable.

**COMOSA, -us, -um** (ko-mō'sa). Long-haired.

**COMPACTA, -us, -um** (kom-pack'ta). Compact or dense.

**COMPANION CROPPING.** See KITCHEN GARDEN.

**COMPASS-PLANT** = *Silphium laciniatum*.

**COMPETITION.** While garden plants are often assumed to be free of the bitter struggle which wild plants wage for food, water, and a place in the sun, this is only a half-truth. By cultivating, fertilizing, and watering, we remove some of the most difficult of the hazards that wild plants must meet or die. But we should not forget that garden plants are themselves engaged in the age-old warfare of survival. And this competition should not be ignored by the gardener. Space, light, food, and water must be provided, and the greatest use of these is best accomplished by judicious thinning — in other words, destroy the weaklings for the sake of the survivors.

**COMPLANATA, -us, -um** (kom-plan-nay'ta). Flattened.

**COMPLETE.** A flower is said to be complete when it bears sepals, petals, stamens, and a pistil. See PERFECT; see also ESSENTIAL ORGANS. For a complete fertilizer see FERTILIZER.

**COMPLEXA, -us, -um** (kom-plecks'sa). Encircled or embraced.

**COMPOSITA, -us, -um** (kom-poz'i-ta). Compound.

**COMPOSITAE** (kom-poz'i-tee). The largest family of plants in the world, comprising shrubs, trees, vines and thousands of herbs, many of which are among the finest garden flowers, such as dahlia, chrysanthemum, coreopsis, marigold, aster, cosmos, and others to be mentioned presently.

It is variously called the thistle, aster, daisy, cosmos, or goldenrod family, but its technical difficulty, because of the tremendous number of other genera involved, is very great. Many specialists consider it is best divided into three families — Carduaceae, Cichoriaceae (often, thence, called the chicory, lettuce, dandelion, or hawkweed family), and the Ambrosiaceae (mostly weeds of little garden interest).

Cross-section of a flower head of the Compositae, showing ray flowers (around the margin) and disk flowers in the center

Here considered as one big family, the Compositae comprise perhaps 800 genera and over 12,000 species of world-wide distribution. While the leaves are very various — opposite,* alternate* or whorled* — the flowers of the Compositae are all alike in being borne in heads,* the individual florets of which are small, often minute, and may consist of *ray* flowers (often supposed to be the "petals" of a daisy) or *disk* flowers (the small, tubular flowers in the center of a head of black-eyed Susan) or of both.

One section of the family (the old Cichoriaceae) has only ray flowers (ligules*). Such flowers are said to be radiate. Most of these plants have a milky juice. Here belong chicory (see CICHORIUM), lettuce, *Crepis*, dandelion, *Hieracium*, *Hypochaeris*, *Krigia*, *Catananche*, *Malacothrix*, *Scolymus*, *Scorzonera*, *Tolpis*,

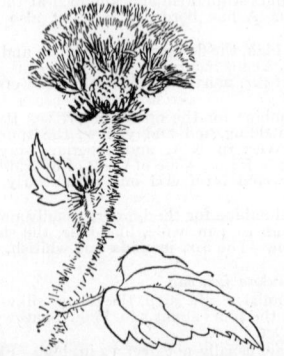

Ageratum, a type of Compositae flower head (like many others) that has disk flowers but no ray flowers

---

* Special articles on the subjects indicated by an asterisk (*) will be found at the words so marked.

and *Tragopogon*. Among these garden genera, some are weedy, but *Scorzonera*, *Tragopogon* and *Scolymus* furnish vegetables such as black salsify, the Spanish oyster plant and salsify.

All the remaining plants in the Compositae bear disk flowers, or disk flowers and ray flowers, but not ray flowers alone. The disk may be flat or cone-shaped (as it is in the cone-flower and many sunflowers). Below the head and usually tightly surrounding it, all plants of the Compositae have a series of small, overlapping and minute, leaf-like, or chaffy scales (involucral bracts).

Among the disk flowers there is usually a collection of minute bristles (the pappus), and upon this, and upon the shape of the involucral bracts and upon still other technical characters, the different garden genera are separated.

Such characters lie outside the scope of this book and if included would exhaust the patience of the most enthusi-

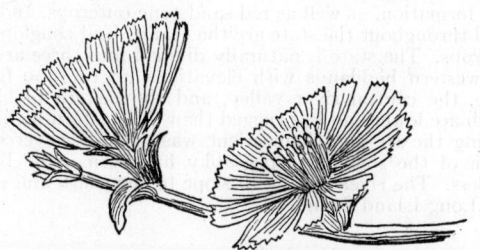

Chicory, a type of Compositae flower head (like many others) that has ray flowers but no disk flowers

astic gardener. From the hort. standpoint, the following genera are those of importance and you should turn to those that most nearly meet your garden interest in this complex and huge plant family.

The chief garden genera, including only herbs of usually outdoor cultivation, are: *Achillea, Ageratum, Artemisia, Aster, Bellis, Bidens, Boltonia, Brachycome, Calendula, Callistephus, Centaurea, Chrysanthemum, Coreopsis, Cosmos, Dahlia, Gaillardia, Helenium, Helianthus* (see SUNFLOWER), *Matricaria, Parthenium, Rudbeckia, Senecio* (including cineraria), *Stokesia, Tagetes* (see MARIGOLD), and *Zinnia*.

Secondary, mostly outdoor, garden genera, nearly all herbs, include the following: *Ammobium, Anaphalis, Antennaria, Anthemis, Arctotis, Arnica, Baeria, Bellium, Buphthalmum, Calimeris, Carthamus, Charieis, Chrysopsis, Cladanthus, Cotula, Dimorphotheca, Doronicum, Echinacea, Echinops, Emilia, Encelia, Erigeron, Eriophyllum, Eupatorium, Gazania, Gnaphalium, Grindelia, Helianthella, Helichrysum, Heliopsis, Helipterum, Inula, Lasthenia, Layia, Leontopodium* (see EDELWEISS), *Lepachys, Liatris, Ligularia, Linosyris, Madia, Marshallia, Perezia, Petasites, Podolepis, Polypteris, Santolina, Sanvitalia, Silphium, Solidago* (see GOLDENROD), *Spilanthes, Tanacetum, Thelesperma, Townsendia, Trilisa, Tussilago, Ursinia, Venidium, Verbesina, Vernonia, Vittadinia, Wyethia, Xanthisma,* and *Xeranthemum*.

A few genera are grown chiefly in the greenhouse, or outdoors in the warmer parts of the country: *Erlangea, Felicia, Gamolepis, Gerbera, Gynura, Humea, Montanoa, Mutisia, Olearia, Othonna, Piqueria,* and *Tithonia*. Some of these are used as summer bedding plants or even as summer annuals, as well as being grown under glass, and some are tropical shrubs and trees.

Thistle-like or frankly weedy genera include: *Arctium* (see Burdock in the list at WEEDS), *Carduus, Cirsium, Cnicus, Onopordon,* and *Silybum*.

There remain still a few cult. genera in this huge family of plants. *Cynara* (artichoke), *Lactuca* (lettuce), and *Cichorium* (the endive) are the only genera yielding important vegetables, while *Baccharis* is the only hardy shrubby genus of the garden genera. *Olearia* and *Montanoa* include greenhouse plants from the tropics; both are woody.

**COMPOST PILE.** Compost is a kind of manure, made up of a variety of fermented or decomposed materials, or refuse matter, adaptable to use as a fertilizer. It may be composed of some or all of the following ingredients: manure, mushroom soil, straw, leaves, lawn clippings, vegetable refuse, peat moss, sod, rubbish, etc., and topsoil, muck, or sand. It is an excellent source of humus, and the best "filler" or base to use in the distribution of commercial fertilizers.

The object in making or keeping a compost pile is to make use of all refuse, vegetable matter, manures, etc., and to have on hand a source of top-dressing highly valuable as an organic fertilizer, used to improve the mechanical condition of the soil.

It may be used to fertilize flower beds, trees, shrubs, etc., and is invaluable as a top-dressing for lawns; especially for turf which is thin and poor or coarse, and which covers soil which is (1) excessively light, (2) excessively heavy, or (3) which contains an excess of decayed vegetable matter. Grass does not like an overabundance of any one ingredient in the soil, and by means of top-dressings it is possible eventually to correct such a condition as far as the uppermost layer of soil is concerned.

A comparatively heavy dressing of compost should be given before winter, a medium heavy dressing in spring, and a very light dressing several times during the summer, to maintain a healthy, heavy, weed-free turf, or beautiful lawn.

The value of compost depends greatly upon its composition and upon the soil on which it is to be used. For light soils the mixture should contain a large percentage of good topsoil, to aid in the retention of moisture, and, eventually, to give weight to the soil, thereby preventing excessive leaching.

For heavy or clayey soils, a preponderance of sand is best, for this will gradually work down into the soil, making it more porous and absorbent of moisture.

The physical condition of the soil should be the determining factor regarding the correct proportioning of the materials to be used.

Never use materials infected with fungous diseases or infested by insect pests. Burn these immediately when noticed.

The process of decomposition is aided, and leaching to some extent prevented by the addition of topsoil, muck, or sand. Excessive leaching may be prevented by providing a roof of some sort, or by covering the heap with several inches of topsoil.

The pile of earth and manurial matter should preferably be in pyramid section, in order to shed rain. In constructing the storage pile the manure, vegetable matter, or rubbish should be spread in a layer 4 in. thick; the topsoil, muck, or sand 3 in. thick over it; continuing to spread alternate layers in this proportion until the pile reaches a height of 5 or 6 ft. A small amount of a complete commercial fertilizer may be spread over each layer of soil.

If there is danger of foul odor from the compost heap, a small amount of acid phosphate sprinkled over it will correct this condition, and preserve the gases valuable for plant food, though this is unnecessary where the mixed fertilizer has been added in the process of mixing.

Where a large amount of compost is to be made it is advisable to make the pile long and narrow. This facilitates mixing or stirring the compost, a necessary procedure, which aids decomposition and mellows the mixture. The pile should be turned or spaded over occasionally, mixing it thoroughly and completely, yet must be kept compact and sufficiently moist to exclude oxygen and prevent the loss of nitrogen. It should not be allowed to become dry, or fermentation and proper decomposition will cease.

The addition of 150 pounds of Adco to each ton of material will aid and hasten decomposition. Screen compost through a half-inch screen before applying. — E. P. E. See also Artificial Manure at MANURE.

**COMPOUND.** As applied to a leaf, compound means having more than one blade to a single leafstalk. A compound leaf is thus composed of from two to any number of

---

\* Special articles on the subjects indicated by an asterisk (\*) will be found at the words so marked.

leaflets,* as in the rose, locust, ash, and many other plants. Some leaflets are arranged feather-fashion (*see* PINNATE) as in the locust, others finger-fashion (*see* PALMATE) as in the horse-chestnut.

Compound is also applied to a flower cluster. *See* INFLORESCENCE.

**COMPOUND PISTIL.** *See* PISTIL.

**COMPOUND RACEME.** *See* RACEME.

*COMPRESSA, -us, -um* (kom-pres′sa). Compressed or flattened.

**COMPTONIA** (komp-tō′ni-a). A single, highly aromatic shrub of the family Myricaceae, found in sandy or rocky soils throughout eastern N.A. The only species, **C. asplenifolia**, the sweet-fern or shrubby fern (actually no fern) is also called sweet-bush. It is a hairy shrub up to 5 ft., but often much less. Leaves alternate,* stalked, fragrant when crushed, rather narrow and about 4–5 in. long, the margins obliquely cut into rounded lobes. Flowers small and inconspicuous, green, in catkins* (for details *see* MYRICACEAE). Fruit a small nutlet, beneath which are narrow bracts,* the fruit thus bur-like. The shrub, suited to open, dry places, is of secondary garden importance, and should be given a sandy or peaty-sandy soil. (Named for Henry Compton, Bishop of Oxford.)

*CONCHIFLORA, -us, -um* (konk-i-flow′ra). With shell-shaped flowers.

*CONCINNA, -us, -um* (kon-sin′na). Neat, natty, or even elegant.

*CONCOLOR* (kon′kul-or). Colored the same throughout.

**CONCRETE.** The best general-purpose mixture for concrete is:
1 part Portland cement
2 parts sharp sand
3 parts crushed stone or gravel, ½–¾-in. sizes

Mix the ingredients thoroughly and add enough pure water to allow the mixture to be poured easily. Such a mixture is useful for pools (but *see* WATER GARDEN for a caution regarding first use of concrete pools) or for any structures for which forms are made into which concrete is poured. For the uses of concrete in path making *see* PATHS AND PAVING.

**CONDIMENT PLANTS.** *See* HERB GARDENING.

**CONE.** Typically the flower and fruit cluster of the pine and its relatives. *See* PINACEAE. Most cones consist of a central stem or axis, around which are arranged a series of overlapping, often woody, scales (the cone scales) between which the naked ovule* is borne, and from which the ripe seed is shed. Cone is also, somewhat loosely, applied to many cone-shaped organs, such as the fruits of magnolia and the strobiles* of a hop.

**CONEFLOWER.** *See* ECHINACEA, RUDBECKIA, and LEPACHYS.

**CONE PEPPER** = *Capsicum frutescens conoides.*

**CONFEDERATE JASMINE** = *Trachelospermum jasminoides.*

**CONFEDERATE ROSE** = *Hibiscus mutabilis.*

**CONFEDERATE VINE** = *Antigonon leptopus.*

*CONFERTA, -us, -um* (kon-fer′ta). Crowded.

*CONGLOMERATA, -us, -um* (kon-glom-er-ray′ta). Crowded.

*CONICA, -us, -um* (kon′i-ka). Conical or cone-shaped.

**CONIFERS.** The cone-bearing trees and shrubs, especially the pines, spruces, firs, cedars. *See* PINACEAE. Their overwhelmingly evergreen habit makes the conifers of the greatest garden importance. For this feature of them *see* EVERGREENS.

**CONIOGRAMME** (kon-i-o-gram′me). A small genus of useful greenhouse ferns of the family Polypodiaceae, **C. japonica**, the bamboo fern, being grown for ornament. It is found in Jap. and the Pacific Islands, and is excellent for house decoration as it stands ordinary room conditions better than most ferns. Fronds usually compound,* 18–24 in. long, the ultimate segments 6–12 in. long and about 1 in. wide, veiny. Spore* cases extending along the main veins. Grown best in a cool greenhouse in potting mixture* 3 to which about ⅓ its bulk of chopped peat has been added. It is a strong-growing, useful fern. (*Coniogramme* is from the Greek for dust line, in reference to the spore cases along the veins.)

**CONIUM.** *See* POISON HEMLOCK.

**CONNECTICUT.** The state lies wholly in zones* 3 and 4, but its southern shore is bounded by the waters of Long Island Sound, which softens the climate of the shore lands.

SOILS. There are many types of soils found in Connecticut, and the geological formation has had much to do with this condition. In the western part of the state are outcrops of limestone ledges, in the central part are large areas of trap rock formation, as well as red sandstone outcrops, and scattered throughout the state are the granite and conglomerate outcrops. The state is naturally divided into three areas — the western highlands with elevations up to 1300 feet or more, the central river valley, and the eastern highlands, which are lower and less rugged than the western highlands. During the ice age Connecticut was entirely covered and much of the soil and topography has been made by the glaciers. The river valleys all slope to the south and empty into Long Island Sound.

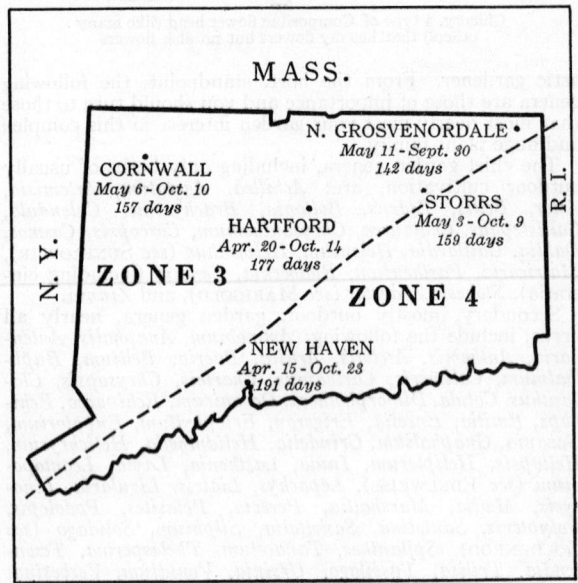

CONNECTICUT

The zones of hardiness crossing Connecticut are those shown on the colored map at ZONE, which should be consulted for details. The dates are the average latest killing frost in spring and the first one in the fall. The figures below the dates show the average length of the growing season. Rainfall is adequate.

The outstanding horticultural soils are Charlton loam, Wethersfield loam, Gloucester fine sandy loam, Merrimac and Hartford sandy loam and the Podunk soils. The eastern and western highlands are covered by Charlton loam soils that are brown at the surface, yellowish-brown or yellowish-olive below, and rest on tight, compact substrata with so much clay that drainage may be retarded in many instances. In the central river valley is found the Wethersfield loam; this soil and subsoil are reddish in color from the iron oxides derived from the parent sandstone and shale rocks. Gloucester fine sandy loam soils are brown soils with yellow-brown subsoils and open, porous substrata; they are characteristic

* Special articles on the subjects indicated by an asterisk (*) will be found at the words so marked.

soils of the higher hills in both the western and eastern parts of the state. These are all till soils resulting from glacial action. The Merrimac sandy loam and the Hartford sandy loam are water-laid soils. The first is a brown soil with yellow subsoil resting on a sand and gravel substratum. The Hartford sandy loam is similar, except for a reddish color in both the soil and subsoil. Then there is the river flood plain Podunk light soils which are annually flooded during the spring thaws.

The soils, however, do not determine the horticulture of the state. There are commercial apple orchards in at least 130 of the 164 towns of the state. The other branches of horticulture are as extensively scattered.

FRUIT GROWING. Many apple orchards are growing on either Charlton or Wethersfield loams or Gloucester sandy loam soils. The apple-tree population in Connecticut, according to the 1930 census, is

Non-bearing 266,976
Bearing 540,117
807,093

Peach growing is not as extensive as it was, because of the fact that the peach trees have been removed from the apple orchards which were planted with peach fillers. Peaches are not grown extensively in northern Litchfield and Windham counties.

Pear growing is increasing slightly as a commercial enterprise, several growers have orchards of from three to ten acres. The quince industry has gradually declined, due to lessened demand for canning, and also because of the damage done to the fruit by the Oriental fruit moth. The growing of grapes was stimulated a few years ago, and there are many vineyards of from five to fifteen acres.

The most commonly grown varieties of the several tree fruits are:

APPLES — McIntosh, Baldwin, Delicious, R.I. Greening, Cortland.

PEARS — Clapp's Favorite, Bartlett, Beurre Bosc.

PEACHES — Elberta, J. H. Hale.

GRAPES — Concord, Worden.

The small fruits are almost exclusively the strawberry and red raspberry. Most of the strawberries are grown by vegetable gardeners; they seem to work in with vegetables better than with the orchard fruits. The Howard 17 is the most commonly grown strawberry, and Latham is the raspberry with the greatest acreage. Few growers care to make extensive plantings of currants because of the white pine blister rust and the limited demand. Climatic conditions are not favorable for the commercial production of sweet cherries, but there are many farms with a few sweet cherry trees which are productive. Sour cherries produce good crops annually.

VEGETABLE GROWING. Thirty of the leading vegetables, including potatoes, are grown throughout Connecticut. Their culture is not confined to any one soil type, for there are large truck garden areas near all of the cities and towns.

COMMERCIAL FLORISTS AND NURSERIES. There are greenhouse establishments near all the cities and most of the small towns. One of the largest floral establishments in the United States is located near Middletown, where numerous houses are devoted to the growing of orchids, to gardenias, to ferns, and, of course, to roses and carnations. A large dairy herd of over 100 cows is maintained to supply some of the manure needed for the roses. There are also 362 nursery firms, devoted to the growing of nursery stock. While the seed industry is of small importance the breeding of special strains of vegetables is being carried on by the Connecticut Agricultural Experiment Station at its farm at Mt. Carmel and the sub-station at Windsor.

CLIMATE. There is considerable variation in temperature within such a small state as Connecticut, and fruit trees bloom from 10-14 days later in Litchfield County than in the southern part of the state.

| Station and Elevation | Average date of last killing frost in spring | Latest known killing frost | Average date of earliest killing frost in fall | Earliest known killing frost in fall |
|---|---|---|---|---|
| Storrs, 640 ft. | May 3 | May 29 | Oct. 9 | Sept. 22 |
| New Haven, 68 ft. | April 15 | May 6 | Oct. 23 | Oct. 2 |
| Cornwall, 1300 ft. | May 6 | May 29 | Oct. 10 | Sept. 11 |
| Hartford, 159 ft. | April 20 | May 22 | Oct. 14 | Sept. 11 |
| No. Grosvenordale, 355 ft. | May 11 | June 21 | Sept. 30 | Sept. 10 |

Total average annual rainfall at Storrs = 43.67"
The 45-year average rainfall at Storrs for months of:

April . . . . . . . . . 3.47"
May . . . . . . . . . 3.43"
June . . . . . . . . . 3.01"
July . . . . . . . . . 4.30"
August . . . . . . . . 4.06"
Sept. . . . . . . . . . 3.70"

There are two Experiment Stations in Connecticut. The Connecticut Agricultural Experiment Station at New Haven, and the Storrs Agricultural Experiment Station at Storrs, which has supplied this information about Connecticut. Both stations are ready to answer gardening questions.

Data about climate, crops, and soils are the basic factors upon which all gardening is based — in Conn. as elsewhere. Such information does not tell one what a wealthy and long-settled people have done, nor that in this small state are some of the finest developments of the art of gardening to be found in America. Outstanding examples are to be found near Greenwich, New Canaan, New Haven, Hartford (a municipal rose garden), Litchfield, New London, and in dozens of quite perfect little villages. In some of the latter there have been fine gardens since before the Revolution — not large nor expensive, but reflecting long traditions of garden lore.

The Garden Club of America has several chapters in Conn. Its home office is 598 Madison Avenue, New York. There are also over 60 chapters of the Federated Garden Clubs of Connecticut, information about which may be had by writing to the Garden Editor, Houghton Mifflin Co.

CONOIDES (kŏ-noy'deez; but *see* OÏDES). Cone-shaped or cone-like.

CONSERVATION. The preservation of forests and other natural areas is primarily a function of governmental agencies, such as the Forest Service and the U.S. Biological Survey. But garden clubs can often, and should, help in such activities by influencing legislation or public opinion. *See* GARDEN CLUBS and ROADSIDE IMPROVEMENT.

CONSERVATORY. The difference between a conservatory and a greenhouse is not clearly defined. Both are glazed structures erected for the accommodation of plants, yet certain differences relating chiefly to growing conditions are readily apparent. Any greenhouse adjoining a dwelling may be commonly called a conservatory.

The technical difference may be stated thus: In a conservatory plants are arranged for display, while in a greenhouse plants are propagated and grown along until they reach the display stage. The old-time conservatory, especially when constructed on a grand scale to conform to an ornate mansion, required a good deal of greenhouse space to keep it furnished with a continuous display of plants in good condition. Where space permitted, and a minimum temperature of around 60° F. could be maintained, palms and other tropical plants were planted in beds of well-drained, friable soil. Climbing plants would drape pillars, clothe walls, and hang from the rafters; while staghorn ferns and other plants which display their charms best in hanging baskets, all added to the tropical jungle effect. Side tables were usually erected, and these kept bright with a variety of flowering and foliage plants, renewed as required from other houses. Walks were often made of ornamental tile and wide enough to admit of promenading. To ensure subdued light all the time, the roof was of ground or frosted glass. During the brightest weather, lath shades of roller type would be used, often on the sides

---

* Special articles on the subjects indicated by an asterisk (*) will be found at the words so marked.

as well as the roof, to intensify the shade and keep the temperature down to a pleasant level.

There are many reasons why this type of conservatory belongs definitely to the past. It is being replaced by less pretentious structures, equally attractive and correct in architectural detail, and likely to be of more practical use. The most modern type permits of social affairs in comfort, even to the extent of including a bathing pool. By the use of a special kind of glass, which admits the ultra-violet rays from the sun, it may become even more of a health room for all members of the family.

In many cases there will be no other glass-house on the place, and it is quite likely to be a single compartment in which all the work is performed by members of the household. Many and varied are the plants which may be grown with satisfaction in such a house, providing, of course, that not only personal taste but conditions also are taken into account. Where flowers are the first consideration a situation capturing a good deal of sunlight is necessary. On the other hand a north-side house can be most attractive, filled with ferns and other foliage plants. If orchids are preferred above all else it is possible to make a selection from this fascinating family which the enthusiastic amateur can handle with good results (see ORCHID). Interesting and good companions for orchids can be chosen from the several genera of the pineapple family. The begonia family is another which contains so many interesting species, hybrids and varieties that an entire house could easily be filled with only a selection. If fancy turns to nature's oddities it may be well satisfied with a selection from the great assortment of cacti and other succulents which offer such interesting forms and variation in leaf, stem and flower.

For most people, however, a variety of flowering and foliage plants in pots, with perhaps a little bench space given over for the supply of cut flowers, will give the most satisfaction. A high temperature is not necessary in order to have a gay conservatory, although if tropical plants are desired a night temperature of not less than 60° F. with plenty of atmospheric moisture is desirable. Around 50° F. at night is warm enough for the welfare of a great many attractive plants. Many of these need not be permanent occupants either, as a considerable number can be grown from seed sown in late summer and early fall. This permits of variation from year to year at very little expense, and with a little planning a succession of bloom will come along until early summer. If desirable to have the house unoccupied during the hot weather, any permanent plants in pots can be plunged* outside.

The improved strains of such annuals as calendula, nemesia, stock, clarkia, larkspur, sweet sultan, cornflower, schizanthus, salpiglossis, and phlox will give plenty of flowers for cutting and display in winter and spring, either grown in pots or in the bench. For hanging baskets *Browallia speciosa major* blooms almost the year through, and the new nasturtiums are fine in baskets also. Calceolarias, cinerarias, primulas, impatiens, and the colored nicotianas are all good pot plants, easily grown and flowered in a few months from seed.

Bulbs, of course, are indispensable. A few pots of freesias will give color and fragrance early in the year, while ixias and iris add an interesting touch along with the more familiar bulbs of spring. Among the more or less permanent plants a few of the various scented-leaved geraniums, and just one plant of *Osmanthus fragrans* will make their presence known in a delightful way. As transient plants cease blooming, space becomes available in which to root cuttings and raise seedlings for the outdoor garden. The best fun of all will be in experimenting.

Hot water heat is best, and is sometimes supplied from the dwelling house system. However, it is more satisfactory if a separate heater with modern controlled appliances can be installed, as the time of required heat in each is different. For general principles of conservatory management *see* GREENHOUSE. — H. E. D.

**CONSOLIDA, -us, -um** (kon-sol'i-da). Solid or stable.

**CONSPICUA, -us, -um** (kon-spic'kew-a). Conspicuous or showy.

**CONSUMPTION-WEED** = *Pyrola americana*.

**CONTACT SPRAYS.** *See* INSECTICIDES.

**CONTINUOUS LAYERING.** *See* LAYERING.

**CONTROL OF PESTS.** *See* INSECT PESTS, PLANT DISEASES, ANIMAL INJURY.

**CONVALLARIA.** *See* LILY-OF-THE-VALLEY.

**CONVALLARIACEAE.** *See* LILIACEAE.

**CONVENT GARDEN.** *See* GARDEN HISTORY.

**CONVOLVULACEAE** (kon-voll-view-lay'see-ee). The garden genera of the morning-glory family are all vines, but shrubs and trees are found among its 45 other genera which contain about 1000 species of world-wide, but especially tropical, range. Leaves alternate.* Flowers mostly funnel-shaped or long-tubular, expanded into a broad limb, nearly always twisted in the bud. Fruit mostly a pod (capsule*), but sometimes fleshy.

Of the 7 garden genera, *Ipomoea* (the morning-glory and sweet potato) is the most important, the closely related *Calonyction* (which are night-bloomers) and *Convolvulus* coming next. *Argyreia, Jacquemontia, Porana,* and *Quamoclit* are chiefly tropical. While grown occasionally outdoors (in the summer) northwards they are chiefly greenhouse plants, or some can be grown outdoors only in frost-free regions. *See* VINES.

Technical flower characters: Flowers regular* and complete.* Calyx with 5 lobes often persistent. Corolla gamopetalous,* its flaring limb usually 5-angled or 5-lobed. Stamens 5, inserted deep in the corolla. Ovary superior,* mostly 2-celled, and with 2 ovules in each cell.

**CONVOLVULUS** (kon-voll'view-lus). The bindweeds include a few garden plants and some very pernicious weeds, among the 175 widely distributed species of the family Convolvulaceae. They are trailing or twining plants with alternate* leaves usually without marginal teeth or lobes. Flowers chiefly day bloomers but sometimes closing by noon, solitary or a few in the leaf-axils,* often long-stalked. Corolla bell-shaped or funnel-shaped, usually showy, but not as handsome as the closely related morning-glories (*see* IPOMOEA), from which they differ in having 2 stigmas.* Fruit a 4-valved, irregularly bursting capsule.* (*Convolvulus* is Latin to entwine.)

All those below are perennials except *C. tricolor,* which is an annual, useful in the blue garden. *C. arvensis* and *C. sepium* are two very troublesome weeds. The other species are of the easiest culture, but even these should be watched to prevent their rampant growth from becoming a nuisance.

**arvensis.** See Field Bindweed in the list at WEEDS.

**japonicus.** California rose. A perennial climber up to 20 ft., twining by its coiled stems. Leaves narrowly arrow-shaped. Flowers about 2 in. wide, pink. Eastern Asia. Summer. Throughout the eastern states there is a double-flowered, sterile form of this which is often a troublesome weed, and is usually prostrate.

**mauritanicus.** Perennial and prostrate. Leaves roundish or oval, about 1½ in. wide. Flowers blue, or violet-purple, about 2 in. wide. Africa. Useful for hanging baskets or in the blue garden.

**sepium.** See Hedge Bindweed in the list at WEEDS.

**tricolor.** Dwarf morning-glory. An annual with stems more or less erect or semi-prostrate, not over 1 ft. long, usually branched. Leaves narrowly oblong. Flowers about 1½ in. wide, blue, but with the throat yellow, and white-margined. Southern Eu. A good annual for the blue garden, the seeds of which may be sown where wanted.

**COOKING WITH HERBS.** *See* that section of HERB GARDENING.

**COOL GREENHOUSE.** *See* GREENHOUSE.

**COOLWORT** = *Tiarella cordifolia*.

**COONTIE** = *Zamia floridana*.

**COOPERIA** (koo-peer'i-a). There are only three species of the rain lily or prairie lily, two of which are sometimes cult. in the flower garden. They are bulbous herbs of the family Amaryllidaceae, found in the southwestern U.S. and adjacent Mex., with grass-like, basal leaves and night-blooming flowers. Leaves often twisted. Flower fragrant, solitary at the end of the stalk, and beneath it is a bract*-

---

* Special articles on the subjects indicated by an asterisk (*) will be found at the words so marked.

like spathe,* tubular or funnel-shaped. (Named for Joseph Cooper, English gardener.)

Of easy culture in their native region. Elsewhere, especially in regions of slushy winters, the bulbs should be dug in the fall, stored in a frost-free but cool place and planted in the spring. Both species bloom in summer, and bloom repeatedly after rains.

**drummondi.** Evening star. Bulb about 1 in. in diameter, its leaves erect and about 12 in. long. Flower stalk hollow, weak, 7–12 in. long, the tube of flower 3–5 in. long, its expanded limb about ¾ in. wide, white, but reddish-tinged outside. Tex. and N. Mex. to Mex.

**pedunculata.** Stouter and larger than the last, but the tube of the flower shorter, the limb about 1½ in. wide, reddish outside. Tex.

*COPALLINA*, -us, -um (ko-pal-ly′na). Gummy or resinous.

**COPPER.** See Copper at FUNGICIDES.

**COPPER ACETO-ARSENITE.** See Stomach Poisons at INSECTICIDES.

**COPPER BEECH** = *Fagus sylvatica cuprea*. See BEECH.

**COPPER CARBONATE.** See Copper at FUNGICIDES.

**COPPER-LEAF** = *Acalypha wilkesiana*.

**COPPER-SULPHATE.** See Copper at FUNGICIDES.

**COPRA.** See COCONUT.

**COPROSMA** (kō-prŏs′ma). A large genus of chiefly New Zealand shrubs or small trees of the family Rubiaceae, one of them very generally grown outdoors from zone* 7 southward, and sometimes in greenhouses northward. Leaves opposite,* persistent or half-evergreen, thick and shining in the one below. Male and female flowers on different plants, small, greenish-white, in short, dense heads. Fruit fleshy. (*Coprosma* is from the Greek for dung, in allusion to the vile odor of some species.)

The plant below is a favorite specimen and hedge plant in southern Calif., less so elsewhere in the South. It stands clipping very well, and without it makes a handsome bush 10–25 ft. high. In greenhouses it needs a cool house and potting mixture* 4.

**baueri.** Leaves nearly evergreen, oval or oblongish, 2–3 in. long, usually notched or blunt at the tip. Fruit, on female plants only, orange-yellow, about ⅓ in. long. N. Zeal. The var. **variegata** has yellow-blotched leaves.

**COPTIS** (kop′tis). Weak, low, perennial herbs of the buttercup family, one somewhat grown for interest, and, by some, for its medicinal root. Of the eight known species, all from the cooler parts of the north temperate zone, the only cult. plant is **C. trifolia**, the goldthread, yellowroot, or canker-root, found in northern N.A., Eu., and As. (By some the American plant is called *C. groenlandica*.) It has creeping, golden-yellow, thread-like roots and basal, compound,* long-stalked leaves, with 3 wedge-shaped, toothed leaflets. Flowers small, white, the 5–7 sepals colored like the petals. Fruit a small, dry, pointed pod. The goldthread needs shade, moisture, and a peaty or sandy soil with a pH of 4–5 (see ACID AND ALKALI SOILS). It is suited only to the wild garden. (*Coptis* is from the Greek for cut, in allusion to the leaflets.)

**COQUITO PALM** = *Jubaea spectabilis*.

*CORACANA* (kor-ra-kā′na). A Latinized version of a name in India for the African millet. See ELEUSINE.

**CORAL BELLS** = *Heuchera sanguinea*.

**CORALBERRY** = *Symphoricarpos orbiculatus*.

**CORALBUSH** = *Templetonia retusa*.

**CORAL HONEYSUCKLE** = *Lonicera sempervirens*.

**CORAL JASMINE** = *Cestrum elegans*.

**CORAL LILY** = *Lilium tenuifolium*.

*CORALLINA*, -us, -um (kor-ral-ly′na). Coral-like; also coral-red.

**CORALLITA** = *Antigonon leptopus*.

*CORALLODENDRON* (kor-ral-lo-den′dron). The specific name for the coral tree. See ERYTHRINA.

**CORAL PLANT** = *Russelia equisetiformis*.

**CORAL TREE.** See ERYTHRINA.

**CORAL VINE** = *Antigonon leptopus*.

**CORCHORUS** (kor′ko-rus). Annual, tropical herbs, belonging to the family Tiliaceae, of no garden but much commercial interest, and sometimes cult. here. They are quick-growing herbs with alternate,* toothed leaves, and stems, in *C. capsularis*, yielding jute. Flowers not showy, small, yellow, usually with 5 petals and 5 sepals. Fruit a 2–6-valved capsule.* (*Corchorus* is from the Greek for an eye remedy which one of the 35 species was supposed to yield.)

Jute is nowhere grown commercially in the U.S., and the plant is of scarcely any other interest. *Corchorus*, as a name, has also been applied by gardeners to two widely cultivated shrubs. See KERRIA and RHODOTYPOS.

**capsularis.** Jute. A usually single-stemmed annual up to 15 ft. high. Leaves oblongish, 2–4 in. long, toothed, the two lower teeth long and sharp-pointed. Capsule globe-shaped, 5-valved. India, but widely escaped in tropical countries.

**olitorius.** Jew's mallow. Similar, but with the cylindric capsules having 3–6 valves. India.

*CORDATA*, -us, -um (kor-day′ta). Cordate; *i.e.* heart-shaped or with a heart-shaped base.

**CORDATE.** See CORDATA.

**CORDIA** (kor′di-a). A very large genus of tropical trees of the family Boraginaceae, many of them important timber trees, and the one below cult. outdoors in zone* 9 for its showy bloom. **C. sebestena**, the geiger tree or sebesten, is native from southern Fla. to tropical America, and is an evergreen tree not usually over 35 ft. high. Leaves alternate,* rough-hairy, ovalish, 6–8 in. long, the margins wavy but not toothed. Flowers in showy clusters blooming most of the year. Corolla tubular or somewhat bell-shaped, 1½–2 in. long, scarlet or orange-red. Fruit fleshy, surrounded by the persistent calyx. Occasionally cult. in the warm greenhouse, where it should have potting mixture* 4 and plenty of room. (Named for Valerius Cordus, German botanist.)

*CORDIFOLIA*, -us, -um (kor-di-fō′li-a). With heart-shaped leaves.

**CORDON FRUIT TREES.** A method of training fruit trees to grow a single main stem and laterals from it that are usually trained along parallel wires, or in other ways. Cordon trees are very popular in England, but not so well known here. For cordons, and other special methods of training and pruning fruit trees, *see* TRAINING PLANTS.

**CORDULA.** See CYPRIPEDIUM.

**CORDYLINE** (kor-di-ly′ne). Here belong some, but not all, of the handsome foliage plants which the florists call dracaena; others belong to the genus *Dracaena* (which see). *Cordyline* is a genus of perhaps a dozen species of tropical foliage plants, three of which are very popular greenhouse subjects and widely used for summer bedding, ornamental vases, window boxes, and for house plants. In nature they have a single stem or trunk and a terminal crown of leaves suggesting a palm, but usually in the North cult. plants are much shorter. Leaves long and sword-shaped, or broader, wholly without teeth or prickles, in some species the tips gracefully arching. Flowers greenish or whitish, not showy, mostly in small, but sometimes in larger, branched clusters. Corolla tubular or funnel-shaped, its 6 segments scarcely separable into petals and sepals. Fruit a berry. (*Cordyline* is from the Greek for club, in allusion to the thick roots.)

*Cordyline* and *Dracaena* are separated only by technical characters. Because of this and the fact that both genera contain popular foliage plants, the names have been loosely applied to both genera and are in much confusion. So far as the cult. plants are concerned, the identity of them is best understood by reading the descriptions below and at *Dracaena*.

The culture of both genera is essentially the same. They are grown outdoors in Fla. and southern Calif. and make valuable additions to any sub-tropical garden, because only

---

\* Special articles on the subjects indicated by an asterisk (\*) will be found at the words so marked.

there is the proper trunk-like habit developed. For house plants, window boxes, porch specimens, and for their wide use as summer bedding plants in the North, a greenhouse is necessary for propagation and best growth.

They should be grown in a warm, moist greenhouse in potting mixture* 3. Their finest color, and the variegated leaves are their chief attraction, is best developed, however, by gradually reducing the heat and watering just before they are to be planted out or used by florist or householder as potted specimens. This is particularly true of *Dracaena fragrans* and *Cordyline terminalis*. Such treatment adds greatly to the ability of these plants to withstand household conditions. Both genera may be propagated by seeds, but the more usual way is to strip off the leaves and cut up the woody stem into pieces about 3 in. long. These are half buried in sand in the propagating bench, bottom-heat* of about 80° applied, and they should be well watered. New plants will soon start from the "eyes" (buds), which can then be separated and potted up for growing.

The cult. species of *Cordyline* are:

**australis.** Ti tree; called, also, tuft tree and cabbage tree. This is the plant commonly sold by florists as *Cordyline indivisa* and sometimes as *Dracaena australis*. Trunk (outdoors) up to 40 ft. Leaves in a rosette-like, terminal crown, the blades 18–30 in. long, about 1⅓ in. wide, green, without a stalk, but with an abruptly contracted base. N. Zeal. The *var.* **veitchi,** much cult., has the midribs and leaf bases bright crimson.

**indivisa** = Mostly *Cordyline australis*, the true *C. indivisa* of N. Zeal. being rare or unknown as a cult. plant here.

**stricta.** From 6–12 ft., the leaves less crowded than in the next. Leaves without a stalk, 12–20 in. long, scarcely 1 in. wide, and narrowed at the base to half this. Aust. There are also colored forms, one bronzy-purple.

**terminalis.** Not over 10 ft. high. Leaves crowded at the end of the stem, the blades with a distinct, narrowed, channeled stalk, the blade oval-lance-shaped, 12–24 in. long, 2–5 in. broad, tapering to a point both ends. Eastern Asia. The typical form has green leaves, but dozens of hort. forms or varieties have red, pink, white, metallic, purple, and variegated or striped leaves. The names of these are indefinite and in much confusion.

***COREANA, -us, -um*** (kor-ee-ā'na). From Korea.

**COREMA** (ko-ree'ma). Two species of heath-like, bushy but low shrubs of the family Empetraceae, **C. conradi,** the broom crowberry, sometimes cult. in the wild garden or rock garden. It is scarcely 18 in. high and native from N.J. to Newfoundland, and can be grown in this or similar regions but only in sandy or rocky soils with a pH of 4–5 (*see* Acid and Alkali Soils). It has crowded, very narrow leaves about ⅕ in. long. Flowers small and inconspicuous (for details *see* Empetraceae). Fruit very small, fleshy (a drupe*), but dryish. (*Corema* is from the Greek for a broom.)

**COREOPSIS** (ko-ree-op'sis). Handsome garden flowers commonly called tickseed, comprising a genus of about 70 species of the family Compositae, perhaps a dozen of which are widely cult. for their showy bloom. They are annual or perennial herbs, the annuals being the most popular. Leaves generally opposite,* often lobed or dissected but entire* in some. Flower heads solitary or in branched clusters, composed of central, usually yellow disk* flowers, and showy ray* flowers which are prevailingly yellow, but white, pink, or sometimes variegated in certain hort. varieties. There are usually about 8 rays in the single sorts, more in the double varieties. Fruits flattish, but becoming curved, small, dry, crowded in the head. (*Coreopsis* is from the Greek for bug, in allusion to the shape of the fruit.)

Coreopsis is almost weed-like in its ease of culture. Many of those below are tender annuals and should be treated as such. *See* Annuals. The perennials are readily divided in spring or fall. All grow in any ordinary garden soil. Most of them are among the most lasting of cut flowers. All are summer bloomers, and many of them are occasionally offered under the name *Calliopsis*.

**atkinsoniana.** A perennial, but often treated as a hardy annual (*see* Annuals), not usually over 36 in. high. Leaves twice- or thrice-compound,* the ultimate segments narrow. Flower heads long-stalked, the rays yellow, but brownish-purple at the base. Western N.A.

**atrosanguinea** = *Thelesperma burridgeanum*.

**coronata.** A tender annual 12–20 in. high. Leaves oblongish, 2–3 in. long, sometimes the lower 3-parted, but generally unlobed. Flower heads yellow, the rays* dark-lined, about ½ in. long. Texas.

**delphinifolia.** A perennial 3–5 ft. high. Leaves suggesting a larkspur, usually 3-parted finger-fashion, about 2½ in. long, each segment divided into narrow, almost thread-like divisions. Heads nearly 2½ in. wide, the disk flowers brownish, the rays yellow. Va. to Ga. and Ala.

**drummondi.** Golden-wave. A tender annual 12–24 in. high. Leaves divided into narrow lobes. Flower heads nearly 2 in. wide, long-stalked, the rays notched, yellow at the ends, brownish-purple at the base, the head thus with a dark center. Texas.

**grandiflora.** A perennial up to 2 ft. high. Leaves narrow, usually 3–5-parted. Flower heads long-stalked, about 2½ in. wide, the ray* and disk* flowers yellow, the rays often notched or lobed. Southern U.S.

**lanceolata.** A perennial up to 2 ft. high, often an escape* in eastern N.A. Leaves lance-shaped, mostly basal, undivided. Flower heads very long-stalked, the disk and ray flowers yellow, the ray flowers notched. Eastern N.A. There is a double-flowered variety.

**maritima.** Sea dahlia. A perennial up to 3 ft. high, with leafy, hollow stems. Leaves much-divided, the segments narrow. Flower heads long-stalked, nearly 3 in. wide, yellow, solitary. Coast of southern Calif. and Mex. Not hardy in regions of slushy winters. Sometimes offered as *Leptosyne maritima*.

**rosea.** Swamp tickseed. A weak, slender-stemmed perennial up to 2 ft. high. Leaves very narrow, or 3-parted and the segments narrow. Flower heads short-stalked, about 1 in. wide, the rays rose-pink, the center yellow. Eastern U.S. A beautiful wild flower preferring open, sunny, and moist places, but it grows well in the border.

**stillmani.** A beautiful tender annual, 12–18 in. high, with somewhat fleshy stems. Leaves divided, the segments long and narrow. Flower heads nearly 2 in. wide, golden-yellow. Calif. An annual that blooms best when somewhat crowded. Sometimes offered as *Leptosyne stillmani*.

**tinctoria.** Golden coreopsis. The best known and most popular of the tender annual species. Erect and from 20–36 in. high. Leaves divided into narrow segments. Flower heads long-stalked, red-brown in the center, the ends of the rays notched and pure yellow. Central U.S. Blooming from July 1st to Oct. Do not thin out, as the plant blooms best when crowded. There are forms with all-crimson rays, and with double flowers.

**verticillata.** A perennial with ascending stems up to 3 ft. Leaves finely divided, the segments thread-like. Flower heads nearly 2 in. wide, dark yellow, the rays not notched. Eastern and Central U.S.

***CORIACEA, -us, -um*** (kor-ee-ā'see-a). Coriaceous; *i.e.* thick and leathery.

**CORIANDER.** Aromatic plants, one of which is grown for the seeds used in seasoning. There are only two species of the genus **Coriandrum** (kor-ee-ăn'drum), which belongs to the carrot family. One of them, **C. sativum,** is the common coriander, a native of southern Eu. It is an annual herb with twice- or thrice-compound leaves, the lower less divided than the upper which are dissected into very narrow segments. Flowers small, white, in compound umbels,* the outer flowers in each umbel sometimes enlarged and ray-like. Fruit ribbed, the coriander "seed" of the markets. For culture and uses *see* Herb Gardening. (*Coriandrum* is from the Greek for this plant.)

**CORIANDRUM.** *See* Coriander.

**CORIARIA** (ko-ri-ā'ri-a). A small group of herbs or shrubs, the only genus of the family **Coriariaceae** (kor-ree-air-ree-ā'see-ee), one of them a Japanese shrub, **C. japonica,** cultivated for ornament. It grows usually to 3, rarely to 7–8 ft. in height and has nearly stalkless, opposite,* ovalish leaves 2–4 in. long and 3-veined. Flowers regular,* greenish, small. Sepals 5. Petals 5, ultimately becoming fleshy and enclosing the fruit. Stamens 10. Fruit fleshy, bright red at first, ultimately black, pea-sized. The plant, not much grown as yet, is hardy from zone* 4 southward. (*Coriaria* is derived from *coriacea*, leathery, in reference to one species used for tanning.)

***CORIDIFOLIA, -us, -um*** (kor-rid-i-fō'li-a). With leaves like a plant of the genus *Coris*.

***CORIS.*** A specific name for a St. John's-wort, based upon its similarity to the genus *Coris*, which includes an irregular-flowered plant of the primrose family, scarcely of garden interest.

**CORK.** Practically the same as bark.* In some plants, notably the cork oak, this bark is much developed and yields the cork of commerce.

**CORK ELM** = *Ulmus racemosa*. *See* Elm.

**CORK FIR** = *Abies arizonica*. *See* Fir.

**CORK OAK** = *Quercus suber*. *See* Oak.

**CORKSCREW-FLOWER** = *Phaseolus caracalla*.

**CORK-TREE.** Properly, the cork oak, but cork-tree is more generally applied to *Phellodendron* and to *Entelea arborescens*.

* Special articles on the subjects indicated by an asterisk (*) will be found at the words so marked.

**CORKWOOD** = *Entelea arborescens*.

**CORM.** A solid, bulb-like, underground stem, resembling a bulb but without its scales. Typical examples are the corms of crocus and gladiolus. Corms are often called solid bulbs or bulbo-tubers. They bear roots at the base and nourish the young plant, just as in bulbs, and from the base of them arise young *cormels*, which are commonly detached and grown along as propagating material, ultimately forming mature corms.

**CORMEL.** See CORM.

**CORN.** The most valuable food plant contributed by the New World to the Old. Doubt exists as to its true botanical origin, but as now considered, all corns belong to the genus **Zea** (zee'a) of which there is only one species, Z. mays. What the prototype of this may have been is lost in Pre-Incan, Pre-Mayan, and Pre-Aztec antiquity. Modern corn is a tall, annual grass with a jointed, solid stem (most grass stems are hollow), and bearing numerous, relatively broad, sword-shaped leaves, which in many varieties have a cutting edge. Male flowers in a terminal cluster (spike) which produces plentiful supplies of pollen. Female flowers in small clusters, borne below the males and only one or two in the upper leaf-axils.* It is the long, thread-like styles* of these female flowers that constitute corn silk. From these the familiar, heavily sheathed ear of corn develops, the kernels of which are the seeds. (*Zea* is a Greek name for some cereal.)

Common Indian corn or maize is not a garden plant. It is the field corn of agriculture and of enormous economic importance. But several varieties of it are grown in gardens for interest, and the sweet corn is one of the most delicious of American vegetables. (It is almost unknown in Eu.) See Culture of Sweet Corn below.

The species and varieties of corn are:

**mays.** Common field corn, often called Indian corn or maize. Useless as a garden plant, this is taller (up to 12 ft.), coarser, and more vigorous than any of its varieties. Its kernels contain too much starch and too little sugar to be of any value as sweet corn.

*var.* **curagua.** The curagua of Chile, where it yields a kind of popcorn. It is little grown here as an ornamental, being a robust, leafy, green-leaved form.

*var.* **everta.** Popcorn. Resembling sweet corn, but has small ears which have very hard, pointed seeds that explode when heated. Its culture is the same as sweet corn (*see* below).

*var.* **indentata.** Dent corn. A tall (8–10 ft.) variety, the seeds of which are yellow or white and indented at the top. Scarcely a garden plant, but occasionally grown.

*var.* **indurata.** Flint corn; Yankee corn. A medium-sized corn, little grown as a garden plant, with dark yellow, hard, smooth seeds.

*var.* **japonica.** As an ornamental the most valuable of all the corn varieties. Its leaves are striped up and down with yellow, white, or pink; — a handsome grass.

*var.* **rugosa** = *Zea mays saccharata*.

*var.* **saccharata.** Sweet corn, and, from the garden standpoint, the most important of all the varieties of corn. Generally lower than field corn, its kernels are soft and sweet in the young state, wrinkled when old. For culture and best strains *see* below. Also called sugar corn.

*var.* **variegata.** A variegated form of *Zea mays japonica* and a good ornamental grass.

In Mexico, and sometimes in the southern U.S., there are many other varieties or forms of corn to be found, but they are of little interest to the gardener. Some of them appear to be related to the teosinte (see EUCHLAENA MEXICANA).

CULTURE OF SWEET CORN (*Zea mays saccharata*)

Of all the varieties of corn mentioned above sweet corn is the only one of real interest to the home gardener. Field corn takes too much space in the garden, is useless for the table, and if dried corn is needed for chickens it can be bought cheaper than you can raise it.

Sweet corn, or corn as it is quite generally but not very accurately called, can be raised in every state of the Union having a growing season of 70–80 days and plenty of summer heat. This means that corn can be grown throughout the country at some season, but the best corn is raised in the summer months.

Someone has said that anyone can grow corn, that the Indians and Aztecs (it is purely an American plant) grew it under very primitive conditions, and hence no directions are necessary. Anyone *can* grow it, but to get the best varieties to mature in the shortest time possible requires a bit of planning and considerable attention to cultivation.

SOILS. Any good garden soil (and many poor ones) will grow corn. But it will mature quicker and be more tender if a ton of a 3–5–7 commercial fertilizer (*see* FERTILIZERS) is used per acre. For a row of 100 ft. use 11 pounds of such a fertilizer. Some growers prefer 8 tons of stable manure to the acre (about 5 wheelbarrow loads to a 100-ft. row), plowed in two weeks before planting time. A few seacoast gardeners still follow the old Indian method of burying a dead fish or two at each hill.

VARIETIES. Getting the first corn in their locality is almost a fetish with home gardeners. To accomplish this, and to maintain a steady supply until frost, means that early, midseason and late varieties must each be planted in sufficient amount and at the proper intervals of time. The best varieties and their normal periods from seeding to harvest are:

Early sorts (white kernels). Early Market. Whipple Early. 60–65 days.

Early sorts (yellow kernels). Extra Early Bantam. Golden Bantam, Canada Gold, Black Mexican (mixed yellow, black and white kernels). 60–65 days.

Midseason sorts. Whipple Yellow. Surprise (white). Sunshine (yellow). 70–75 days.

Late sorts (mostly taller-growing varieties). Stowell Evergreen. Country Gentleman. Bantam Evergreen. 75–80 days.

Most of the early sorts are fairly short plants (3–4 ft. high), while the later kinds frequently run from 5–7 feet, or even more on rich soils. Because of this it is often a question, in small gardens, whether one should not plant only a succession of the early sorts because of the space saved. Of all the early sorts Golden Bantam has the best-filled ears, but Canada Gold is a few days earlier, as is Black Mexican, which is often all black.

PLANTING. Generally speaking, it is better to plant the early varieties in drills and the late sorts in hills so spaced that cultivating may be done both ways. If, in spite of all directions, your garden is weedy, it is better to plant all varieties in hills, because it is thus possible to control weeds easier than if the plants are in long rows.

For early varieties make the drills 2–2½ ft. apart and 1½ in. deep. (If in hills make them 2½ ft. apart each way.) For growing in rows, put a seed every 3 in. in the drill, with the expectation of thinning to 6-in. intervals, as soon as possible. The thinned plants cannot be transplanted, without such a serious check that your next succession will easily overtake them.

If you plant in hills (as you should for the late varieties or on weedy land), put the hills 3 ft. apart each way and plant 6 seeds to a hill. These should soon be thinned to 3 or at the most 4 plants to a hill. Do not make the hill before planting. Simply put the seed about 1½ in. below the general ground level and leave the making of the hill until later.

If you want variety in your corn diet, it will pay to plant the different sorts at 12-day intervals, beginning only after settled warm weather has arrived. A good indicator of this in your locality is to plant the first corn just after the common lilac has definitely passed out of bloom.

The last planting of the late varieties must allow about 75–80 days from seeding to the expectation of the first frost in your locality, and it is safer to allow 80–85 days because of waning heat. (For frost dates see the name of your state.) This requires such perfect timing that many growers prefer to run no risks. They keep on planting early varieties because they mature faster and are less likely to be caught by the first frost.

Crows may scratch out the seed. If they are numerous the seed should be treated with creosote. This should be used at the rate of about a tablespoonful to a half bushel of seed, which has been previously heated with warm water, and then drained. A continued stirring of the grain will eventually permit an even coating of creosote. The seed must then be spread on a dry surface, or drying may be facilitated by the application of some absorbent medium, such as ashes, land plaster, or powdered earth. When thoroughly dried the grain may be used in a planter.

CULTIVATION AND CARE. Clean cultivation is essential,

---

* Special articles on the subjects indicated by an asterisk (*) will be found at the words so marked.

# CORN

whether your corn is in rows or hills. If in the latter, you can run the wheel cultivator in both directions. In any case see that no weeds are stealing the food your corn should have.

Corn plants, especially the tall, late sorts, nearly always develop a ring of secondary roots just above the level of the ground. These are the well-known prop roots that tend to stiffen the plant in a strong breeze. It much helps the formation and usefulness of these prop roots to draw up on each side of the plants enough soil to cover them. In doing so you make all the "hill" the corn plant needs — usually not over 8 in. high.

Corn showing how the hill of soil provides food and anchorage for the prop roots

In the early varieties (most of which are in rows) the same object is accomplished by a shallow plowing along each side of the row. This, except in very stony land, will usually bury the prop roots about 5–6 in., which is all these shorter varieties need. Some growers do not bother to cover the prop roots of the early varieties at all, upon the theory that the plants need the support less and that the roots will penetrate the soil without aid. Both are true, but covering them helps, especially in a violent wind. It can, of course, be done with a hoe, if a wheel cultivator is lacking.

All corn plants tend to send up suckers from the base. Much has been written upon the desirability of pulling or not pulling these suckers. Except in California, most growers are now convinced that suckering is not necessary.

For the preferred position and sequence of sweet corn in your garden see KITCHEN GARDEN.

HARVESTING AND YIELDS. No instructions are necessary except the old one that the ears should not be picked before the water for them is boiling. Flavor and succulence are soon lost after picking, which is why those used to home-grown corn are never satisfied with the store kind. The ears are ready to be picked when the kernels are plump. If you are uncertain, pry open a few of the outer husks and see when it is prime. Most corn plants should average two ears to a plant, occasionally 3, and if poorly grown, one or even none. From this you can easily estimate the amount you should grow.

INSECT PESTS. Many insects attack garden corn, but usually not severely enough to destroy the crop. Control is not well developed; the methods worked out for cornfield insects are often not adapted to gardens. The corn ear worm, a smooth caterpillar, gnaws the tips of roasting ears, especially in the South and on late sweet corn. It is hard to control; a dust of lead arsenate on fresh silks is only partially successful. The European corn borer tunnels in stalks and cobs in the Northeast; it is controlled by community-wide winter clean-up of stalks. Chinch bugs are sometimes injurious in the Middle West (see SORGHUM). Thorough cultivation, clean-up of woody borders, crop rotation, and bran baits (for cutworms) all have value against corn insects.

DISEASES. The terms root rots, stalk rots, ear rots, and seedling diseases, describe briefly a rather long list of diseases which affect corn and the control measures of which are somewhat similar. These include long rotations with crops other than cereals, the use of fertilizer containing potash; soil humus, seed selection and seed treatment. Seed ears are chosen from plants standing firmly upright, the ripened husks cover the kernels, the shank breaks off without shredding, and all parts of the ear are free from mold. Each ear should be tested in a germinator. The grains from the ears which prove healthy are then treated with some recommended organic mercury compound and planted in warm, moist soil.

The smut that causes the unsightly black boils on the ears and stalks, and the less evident type of smut are difficult to control. Removal of affected parts and burying have been suggested. Bacterial wilt kills the early varieties, especially of sweet corn and popcorn. Planting late varieties or early varieties late and the use of resistant strains in so far as they are available, are recommended.

**CORNACEAE** (kor-nay'see-ee). The dogwood or bunch-berry family, so far as its garden genera are concerned, comprises only woody plants (but *see* the bunchberry (*Cornus canadensis*). Most of them are shrubs and trees, some with handsome flowers and showy fruits. Leaves simple,* alternate* or opposite,* often, but not exclusively, without marginal teeth. Flowers in terminal clusters, the cluster sometimes surrounded by showy white bracts* commonly mistaken for flowers. (See CORNUS.) Fruit a 1- or 2-seeded drupe,* or a berry.

Two of the cultivated genera, *Nyssa* (which includes the tupelo and sour gum) and *Davidia* (an Asiatic tree), are, with other genera, sometimes considered as a separate family, Nyssaceae, not here recognized as such. The other cult. genera of the Cornaceae are *Aucuba*, *Cornus*, and *Griselinia*, of which *Cornus* is by far the most important, because it contains all the cornels, the flowering dogwood, and the bunchberry. Many of its species much resemble *Viburnum*.

Technical flower characters: Flowers sometimes unisexual* or dioecious. Calyx 4–5-toothed, sometimes wanting. Petals 4 or 5, or none. Stamens 4–5. Ovary inferior.* Style 1.

**CORN EAR WORM.** See Moths at INSECT PESTS. See also Insect Pests at CORN, CARNATION, PEANUT and TOBACCO.

**CORNEL.** See CORNUS.

**CORNEL FAMILY** = Cornaceae.

**CORNELIAN CHERRY** = *Cornus mas*.

**CORNFLOWER** = *Centaurea cyanus*; less frequently applied to *Uvularia grandiflora*.

*CORNICULATA, -us, -um* (kor-ni-kew-lay'ta). Horned.

**CORNISH HEATH** = *Erica vagans*.

**CORN LILY.** See GLADIOLUS.

**CORN MARIGOLD** = *Chrysanthemum segetum*.

**CORN MAYWEED** = *Matricaria inodora*.

**CORN MINT** = *Mentha arvensis*. See MINT.

**CORN POPPY** = *Papaver rhoeas*. See POPPY.

**CORN SALAD** = *Valerianella locusta olitoria*.

*CORNUCOPIAE* (kor-new-kō'pĭ-ee). Like a cornucopia.

**CORNUS** (kor'nus). The dogwoods or cornels comprise an important genus of garden shrubs and trees (one an herb) of the family Cornaceae, much grown for their handsome flowers, often brighly colored fruits, and in some species for the winter effect of their colored twigs. All the 40 known species are native in the north temperate zone. Leaves generally opposite,* without marginal teeth. Flowers small, with 4 small petals and 4 stamens. In many species these flowers are white and grouped in flat-topped or rounded clusters (cymes*); such resemble viburnums, but the latter have 5 stamens and a united corolla.* In a few species the flowers are inconspicuous, greenish, and set in the midst of several colored bracts* (often mistakenly called petals), as in the flowering dogwood and the bunchberry. One has yellow flowers. Fruit fleshy. (*Cornus* is the old Latin name of the Cornelian cherry.)

* Special articles on the subjects indicated by as asterisk (*) will be found at the words so marked.

Fortunately, most of the cornels are of easy culture in any good garden soil, the exceptions being noted at each species. Propagation by cuttings of old wood or by layering. Some choice varieties are occasionally grafted on commoner sorts.

**alba.** Tartarian dogwood. A showy shrub, 6-10 ft. high, its twigs bright red. Leaves ovalish, 3-5 in. long, bluish-green beneath. Flowers white, the clusters numerous and about 2 in. wide. Fruit whitish-blue. Eastern Asia. May-June. Hardy everywhere and widely cult., also in the var. **argenteo-marginata,** with white-margined leaves; the var. **sibirica,** with coral-red twigs; and the var. **spaethi,** with yellow-edged leaves.

**alternifolia.** Blue dogwood; also called pigeonberry. A shrub or small tree 8-15 ft., the only cult. species with alternate* leaves, which are elliptic or ovalish, 2-4 in. long. Flowers white, the clusters about 2½ in. wide. Fruit bluish, with a bloom. Eastern N.A. and hardy everywhere. May-June.

**amomum.** Silky cornel. A shrub 6-8 ft. high, its branches purplish. Leaves ovalish or longer, 2-4 in. long, generally silky beneath. Flowers white, the clusters about 2½ in. wide. Fruit pale blue. Eastern N.A. and hardy everywhere. June.

**baileyi.** An American representative of *C. alba* and very much like it; useful for seashore planting. See SEASIDE GARDENS.

**canadensis.** Bunchberry, also called crackerberry. Scarcely over 6 in. high, and a woody herb. Leaves in a usually basal whorl,* ovalish, 1-2½ in. long. Flowers greenish, inconspicuous, set among 4-6 large white and petal-like bracts.* Fruit scarlet. Northern N.A. and Asia, and on mountain tops southward. May. A plant for the wild garden. It needs coolness and moisture and often grows wild in sphagnum moss. See WILD GARDEN.

**florida.** Flowering dogwood, also called boxwood. A showy tree up to 30 ft. Leaves oval, 3-5 in. long. Flowers small, greenish, set in the midst of 4 large, showy, white, notched and petal-like bracts.* Fruit scarlet. Eastern U.S. May-June. In its natural state the flowering dogwood is a tree of the under-canopy of the forest. While it can be grown in the open it prefers partially shady sites. There is a very popular red- or pink- bracted var., **rubra,** commonly called the red dogwood, and cult. here since 1731. There is also a form with weeping branches. All have bright scarlet autumnal foliage. Not quite hardy north of zone* 3.

**kousa.** An Asiatic representative of our flowering dogwood, there called kousa. It is a lower tree, has smaller leaves, very similar flowers and bracts, but its pinkish fruits are in a head-like cluster. Japan and Korea. June. Hardy from zone* 4 southward. The var. **chinensis** has longer and more showy bracts.*

**mas.** Cornelian cherry. A shrub or small tree, the naked twigs of which are crowded with short-stalked, small, head-like clusters of minute yellow flowers in March or April. Leaves oval or elliptic, 3-4 in. long. Fruit edible, but acid, scarlet, ripening in Aug. Eurasia. Hardy from zone* 3 southward. It stands smoky atmosphere better than most shrubs.

**nuttalli.** Pacific dogwood. A western representative of the flowering dogwood (*C. florida*), but a much taller tree, and it usually has 6 petal-like white or pinkish bracts,* instead of 4. Fruit red or orange. May. British Columbia to southern Calif. and easily cult. there but, in the East, doubtfully hardy above zone* 6.

**paniculata** = *Cornus racemosa.*

**racemosa.** Gray dogwood. A shrub, 6-10 ft. high with gray twigs. Leaves elliptic or narrowly oval, 2-4 in. long, tapering at the tip, but wedge-shaped at the base. Flowers white, the cluster branched, not flat-topped. Fruit white. Eastern U.S. Hardy from zone* 2 southward. June-July.

**rugosa.** Green osier. A shrub 3-8 ft. high, the twigs green, faintly purple-spotted. Leaves nearly round, about 3 in. long. Flowers small, the flat-topped cluster nearly 2½ in. wide. Fruit blue. May-June. Eastern N.A. Hardy from zone* 2 southward.

**sanguinea.** Red dogwood. For hort. purposes very similar to *C. alba,* and differing chiefly in having black fruit. Eurasia. May-June. Hardy from zone* 3 southward. See SMOKE.

**stolonifera.** Red osier. A shrub, rarely above 6 ft. high, its red branches erect, but spreading by underground, prostrate stems, thus making large clumps. Leaves ovalish or narrower, 3-5 in. long. Flowers white, small, in flat-topped clusters that are often 2½ in. wide. Fruit bluish-white. N.A. May-June. Hardy everywhere. The var. **flaviramea** has yellow twigs.

*CORNUTA, -us, -um* (kor-new'ta). Horned.

**COROLLA.** The petals, collectively, of a flower. They are often separate, as in a rose, but many plants have a united corolla, as in a bellflower or morning-glory. See FLOWER.

*COROLLATA, -us, -um* (kor-ro-lay'ta). Corolla-like.

**CORONA.** Any crown or crown-like appendage in a flower, usually between the petals and the stamens, but often applied also to a crown-like appendage on the corolla.

*CORONARIA, -us, -um* (kor-ro-nay'ri-a). Pertaining to a corona,* also to any garland or crown.

*CORONATA, -us, -um* (kor-ro-nay'ta). Crowned.

**CORONILLA** (kor-ro-nil'la). A genus of perhaps 20 species of herbs or shrubs of the pea family, scattered from the Canary Islands to western Asia, a few of secondary hort. interest. They have compound* leaves, the leaflets arranged feather-fashion, with an odd one at the end. Flowers pea-like, in long-stalked clusters (umbels*) from the leaf-axils.* Fruit a slender pod (legume*) constricted between the seeds. (*Coronilla* is Latin for a little crown, alluding to the umbels.*)

The three below present no difficulties, but their hardiness should be noted. They are occasionally grown in the cool greenhouse in potting mixture* 3. Propagated by seeds, or by cuttings for *C. emerus* and *C. glauca.*

**emerus.** Scorpion senna. A shrub, usually 3-7 ft. high, its twigs green-striped. Leaflets 7-9, usually broadest towards the tip, not over 1½ in. long. Flowers yellow, about ¾ in. long. Pod about 2 in. long. Southern Eu. May-Sept. Hardy from zone* 4 southward.

**glauca.** A low shrub 2-4 ft. high. Leaflets 5-7, blunt, bluish-green. Flowers yellow, usually 7-9 in a cluster, heavy-scented. Southern Eu. May-Sept. An attractive border plant, not certainly hardy north of zone* 7, and a favorite in Calif. There is also a variety with variegated foliage.

**varia.** Crown vetch or axseed. A perennial, usually sprawling, vine-like herb, not over 18 in. high. Leaflets 11-25, oblongish and blunt (but fine-tipped), about ⅝ in. long. Flowers about ½ in. long, pink, in dense clusters. Eu. June-Oct. A useful creeper or sprawling plant for the perennial border.

*CORONOPIFOLIA, -us, -um* (kor-ro-no-pi-fō'li-a). With leaves like a weed of the genus *Coronopus,* which is scarcely in cult.

**CORREA** (kor'ree-a). Australian shrubs or small trees of the family Rutaceae, two of the 6 known species cult. outdoors in zones* 8 or 9 for their showy flowers, rarely in greenhouses. Leaves opposite,* dotted with resinous glands, and rather thick. Flowers solitary, or 2 or 3 together, hanging, apparently tubular, but actually of 4 separate, hairy petals. Stamens 8. Fruit composed of 4 nearly distinct segments (carpels). (Named for Jose Francesco Correa de Serra, Portuguese botanist.)

*Correa speciosa* is a valuable shrub for dry, sandy places in Calif. It is little grown elsewhere, and *C. alba* is even less known outside Calif.

**alba.** A much-branched, bushy shrub 3-4 ft. high, the twigs rusty-hairy. Leaves generally roundish, blunt, ½-1 in. long. Flowers white or pink, about ½ in. long, the petals ultimately spreading, so that the flower no longer appears as if tubular.

**speciosa.** Compact shrub, 2-3 ft. high, its twigs rusty-hairy. Leaves varying from roundish to oblong, about 1 in. long, wrinkled, whitish beneath. Flowers about 1 in. long, scarlet, remaining as though tubular, and the tips of the petals often greenish-yellow.

**CORROSIVE SUBLIMATE.** A poison ingredient of various spraying mixtures and for destroying earthworms (which see). See also Contact Sprays at INSECTICIDES and Mercury at FUNGICIDES.

*CORSICA, -us, -um* (kor'si-ka). From Corsica.

**CORSICAN HEATH** = *Erica stricta.*

**CORSICAN NETTLE** = *Helxine soleiroli.*

**CORSICAN PINE** = *Pinus nigra calabrica.* See PINE.

**CORSICAN SANDWORT** = *Arenaria balearica.*

**CORTADERIA** (kor-ta-deer'i-a). Pampas grass is confined to southern S.A. and the genus contains only six species of tall, reed-like grasses. One of them, **C. selloana** (sometimes called *C. argentea*), is cult. for its showy plumes, but is not hardy outdoors north of zone* 7. It grows in clumps, the stems 8-20 ft. high. Leaves numerous, rough-margined, long and narrow, usually not over ¼ in. wide. Male and female flowers on different plants, only the female producing the showy, terminal cluster of feathery, plumed spikes. These are silvery, 1-3 ft. long and, as one traveler has expressed it, pampas grass *en masse* looks like "a rolling sea of silver." (*Cortaderia* is the Latinized version of the Argentine vernacular for this grass.)

*CORTUSOIDES* (kor-tu-zoy'deez; but see OÏDES). Like a plant of the genus *Cortusa,* which are primrose-like herbs scarcely in cult.

**CORYDALIS** (kor-rid'a-lis). A large genus of usually weak-stemmed, often prostrate herbs of the family Fumariaceae, most of them from the north temperate zone. Of the 90 known species only those below are of much garden

---

* Special articles on the subjects indicated by an asterisk (*) will be found at the words so marked.

interest, mostly for the open border, but *C. sempervirens* primarily for shady parts of the wild garden. They have lobed or finely dissected leaves, often bluish-green. Flowers in dense or lax clusters (racemes*), the 4 petals spurred as in the bleeding-heart. Stamens 6. Fruit a slender pod. (*Corydalis* is from the Greek for lark, the spur of the flower suggesting a lark's spur.)

The plants below are not so much grown as they should be. Their handsome, spurred flowers, mostly spring and early summer-blooming, are fine for the border, but not lasting enough for picking. Most of them, except *C. sempervirens*, can be grown in the open border, but preferably in a partly shady section of it.

**cheilanthifolia.** A low perennial from a thickened rootstock, the leaves finely dissected and fern-like, nearly 8 in. long. Flowers about ½ in. long, yellow. China.

**glauca** = *Corydalis sempervirens*.

**lutea.** Annual or sometimes perennial herb, erect or spreading, not over 8 in. high. Leaves bluish-green, much-divided, the segments generally wedge-shaped. Flowers pale yellow, about ½ in. long. Southern Eu.

**nobilis.** An erect perennial 6–9 in. high. Leaves deeply cut, the few segments wedge-shaped and toothed. Flowers white, but tipped yellow and purple-spotted, the spur about 1 in. long, the clusters terminal and dense. Siberia.

**sempervirens.** Pink or pale corydalis. An annual with weak, pale, bluish-green foliage, the stems straggling. Leaves lobed, the segments spoon-shaped or knife-shaped. Flowers about ½ in. long, in a loose, branched cluster, pink, but tipped with yellow. N.A. Prefers shady site and woods soil in the wild garden, preferably among rocks or boulders. Sometimes known as *C. glauca*.

**thalictrifolia.** A perennial, scarcely over 1 ft. high, the rootstock woody. Leaves suggesting the meadow rue, but more finely dissected. Flowers yellow, about 1 in. long, the clusters large and spreading, mostly opposite the leaves. China.

**CORYLOPSIS** (kor-ril-lop'sis). A small group of Asiatic shrubs of the family Hamamelidaceae, related to the witchhazel, but flowering in early spring before the leaves unfold, hence sometimes called winter hazel. They have alternate,* stalked, prominently veined and toothed leaves. Flowers yellow, in nearly stalkless, nodding clusters (racemes*). Petals 5, clawed.* Stamens* 5. Fruit a 2-beaked pod (capsule*) with 2 black seeds. (*Corylopsis* is from the Greek for like hazel.)

The two below prefer a somewhat peaty, sandy soil, but can be grown in any ordinary garden soil that is not too heavy. Propagated by seeds or by cuttings of green wood under glass.

**pauciflora.** Shrub up to 6 ft. Leaves ovalish, obliquely heart-shaped at the base, 2–3 in. long. Flowers about ¾ in. long, the cluster sparse. Jap. Feb.–March. Hardy from zone* 4 southward.

**spicata.** Similar to *C. pauciflora* in height, but with leaves nearly twice the size. Flowers in clusters of 7–10, yellow, fragrant about ¾ in. long. Jap. Feb.–March. Hardy from zone* 4 southward.

**CORYLUS.** See HAZEL.

**CORYMB.** A flower cluster in which the individual flower stalks elongate, so that the cluster is nearly or quite flat-topped. It blooms from the edge towards the center of the cluster. Common examples are some of the spireas, the ninebark (*Physocarpus*) and the fire thorn (*Pyracantha*).

**CORYMBOSA, -us, -um** (kor-rim-bō'sa). Bearing corymbs.

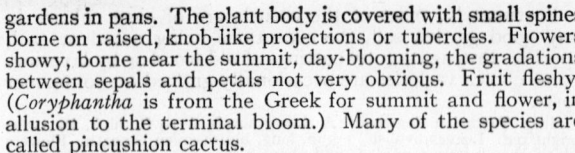
Corymb

**CORYPHANTHA** (kor-ri-fan'tha). A group of small, ball-like or button-shaped (rarely cylindric) cacti, mostly from the southwestern U.S. and adjacent Mex., a few of them popular for pot culture, especially for miniature desert gardens in pans. The plant body is covered with small spines borne on raised, knob-like projections or tubercles. Flowers showy, borne near the summit, day-blooming, the gradations between sepals and petals not very obvious. Fruit fleshy. (*Coryphantha* is from the Greek for summit and flower, in allusion to the terminal bloom.) Many of the species are called pincushion cactus.

For culture see CACTI.

**elephantidens.** Plant body nearly globe-shaped, never more than 5 in. Spines 8 to each group, all interlocking, there being no central erect one. Flowers nearly 4 in. wide, rose-pink. Mex.

**macromeris.** Plant body somewhat cylindrical, 6–8 in. long, densely spiny, the spines interlocking except the central black one of each group. Flowers nearly 3 in. wide. Western Tex. and Mex.

**recurvata.** Plant body a flattened globe, 3–7 in. in diameter, often in masses. Spines many, about 22 to a group, 20 of them interlocking and curved, the two central ones erect. Flowers about 1 in. long, yellow inside, brownish outside. Ariz. and Mex.

**robustispina.** Devil's-pincushion; called also pineapple cactus. Plant body nearly globe-shaped, 2–4 in. in diameter, practically concealed by the numerous spines. At each spine group are 12–15 interlocking spines, 3 lower and stouter ones, and a central solitary one. Flowers salmon-pink, about 2 in. long. N. Mex., Ariz., and Mex.

**CORYTHOLOMA** (kor-rith-o-lō'ma). A large genus of tropical American, tuberous-rooted herbs of the family Gesneriaceae, only one, *C. cardinalis*, cult. in greenhouses for its showy red flowers. Leaves opposite* or in 3's. Flowers irregular,* the tube often long and curved, its limb 2-lipped,* the upper lip helmet-shaped and projecting, the lower almost lacking. Stamens mostly 4, borne on the corolla. (*Corytholoma* is from the Greek for helmet and throat, in reference to the shape of the flower.)

*Corytholoma* and *Alloplectus* (which see) both require the same culture as gloxinia to which they are related. See GLOXINIA.

**cardinalis.** Not over 1 ft. high, the stem hairy. Leaves ovalish or heart-shaped, 4–6 in. long, wavy-toothed. Flowers in the leaf-axils* or crowded at the summit, the corolla* hairy, red, about 2¾ in. long. Somewhere in tropical America. The plant is sometimes offered as a *Gesneria*.

**COS LETTUCE** = *Lactuca sativa longifolia*. For culture see LETTUCE.

**COSMIDIUM.** See THELESPERMA BURRIDGEANUM.

**COSMOS** (kos'mus). Tropical American garden plants, of the family Compositae, the annual species of the greatest popularity and the easiest culture. Of the 20 known species, mostly Mexican, only three are of garden interest, and all the popular annual varieties have been derived from *C. bipinnatus*. Leaves opposite,* in those below much cut into fine segments. Flowers in heads, the latter solitary and long-stalked or in loose, open clusters. Ray* flowers showy, of many colors, the rays often notched, the disk flowers (center of the head) yellow or red. (*Cosmos* is from a Greek word implying orderliness; *i.e.* beauty.)

For Culture and varieties see below.

**bipinnatus.** The common garden cosmos. An annual 7–10 ft. high, the stems green, not very stout. Leaves cut into fine, almost thread-like segments. Flower heads 1–2 in. wide (wider in some hort. forms), the rays white, pink, or red, the disk* flowers yellow. Mex. See below.

**diversifolius.** Black cosmos. A perennial up to 15 ft. high, but often grown as an annual, with dahlia-like, but smaller tubers. Leaves parted into 5–7 segments, the terminal one much the largest. Flower heads solitary, the rays velvety, dark red or purplish, the disk* flowers red. Mex. Sometimes offered as *Cosmos dahlioides*.

**sulphureus.** A much-branched, hairy annual, 4–7 ft. high. Leaves up to 12 in. long, twice- or thrice- cut into narrow lobes that are hairy on the margins. Flower heads solitary, long-stalked, both ray* and disk* flowers orange-yellow. Mex.

## COSMOS CULTURE

The common annual cosmos, derived from *Cosmos bipinnatus*, is a tall-growing, erect, but weak-stemmed plant from the tableland of Mexico. While it can be planted as a hardy annual (seeds sown where wanted), it is better treated as a tender annual (see ANNUALS).

Unlike most garden plants, cosmos does not need a rich, heavily manured soil. If given such conditions, it will grow to great size but produce few flowers. Given relatively indifferent and preferably sandy soils, it blooms profusely from July to frost, and sometimes even a few straggling heads may be gathered in late November if the season hasn't

---

* Special articles on the subjects indicated by an asterisk (*) will be found at the words so marked.

been too severe. Of course no one plant will bloom so long, but by a selection of varieties cosmos flowers may be had from July 1 to the end of the season.

Such a popular garden annual has been much hybridized and selected, so that today there are numerous named forms and strains. Perhaps the most desirable are the old-fashioned single sorts, in which the rays are neither quilled nor doubled. They come in early and late varieties and in red, pink, crimson, and white.

Another race comprises the double or crested cosmos. In these the ray* flowers are unchanged, but the disk flowers are modified into many petal-like enlargements. The outer part of the head is thus single, but the center is double. These are sometimes called anemone cosmos, and come in the same colors and in both early and late strains. Some of the early varieties will bloom in 50 days from seed planting. Such plants, and several of the hort. strains, are apt to be lower than the old-fashioned single cosmos — often not over 3 ft. high. All yellow-flowered varieties are derivatives of *Cosmos sulphureus*, and are to be treated the same as the common kinds. Insect troubles are few. Stem borers are sometimes injurious (see CALLISTEPHUS). Aphids can be controlled with nicotine.

**COSMOS FAMILY.** See COMPOSITAE.

**COSTA RICA NIGHTSHADE** = *Solanum wendlandi*.

*COSTATA, -us, -um* (kos-tay'ta). Ribbed.

**COSTMARY** = *Chrysanthemum balsamita*.

*COTINOIDES* (ko-ty-noy'deez; but see OÏDES). Resembling the smoke-tree (*Cotinus*).

**COTINUS** (ko-ty'nus). Two species of shrubs or small trees of the sumac family, both cult. for ornament, and having a strong-smelling juice. Leaves alternate,* short-stalked, without marginal teeth. Flowers yellowish, not very showy, small, polygamous,* in large-branching, terminal clusters. Petals 5, longer than the sepals.* Fruit fleshy (a drupe*), but somewhat dry, slightly lopsided. The fruiting cluster consists mostly of the lengthened stalks of the numerous sterile flowers, which are plumed, silky, and form, in the mass, the most attractive feature of these plants, which are generally known as smoke-tree. (*Cotinus* is an old Greek name for the wild olive, and of uncertain application here.)

Both species are of easy culture in any ordinary garden soil, preferably not too rich or moist. They make handsome lawn specimens, the plumy fruiting cluster suggesting greenish-buff smoke from a distance, especially in the second species. Easily raised from seed, but not easy to get started, hence needing water and attention after planting out. Later they grow easily.

**americanus.** American smoke-tree, also called chittamwood. A small tree 15–20 ft. high. Its foliage resembles the next, but the leaves are generally wedge-shaped at the base, and the fruiting cluster not so showy. Ala. to Tex. Flowers in July, fruiting cluster in Aug.–Sept. Hardy from zone* 5 southward, perhaps in zone* 4 with protection. Sometimes known as *Rhus cotinoides*.

**coggygria.** A Eurasian shrub, 10–15 ft. high. Leaves ovalish, 2–3 in. long, abruptly narrowed at the base. Fruiting cluster (mostly sterile) much-branched, 7–10 in. long, covered with long, spreading, purplish-green hairs, the actual fruits few, kidney-shaped, scarcely ¼ in. wide. Flowers in July, fruiting cluster in Aug.–Sept. Hardy from zone* 4 southward. Often known as *Rhus cotinus*.

**COTONEASTER** (ko-tō'nee-as-ter). An important group of garden shrubs or small trees of the rose family, comprising perhaps 40 species, many of which are widely planted for ornament. Leaves alternate,* stalked, without marginal teeth, in some species (specified below) evergreen. Flowers small, white or pinkish, usually in small clusters (corymbs*). Petals 5, upright or spreading. Stamens about 20. Fruit small, fleshy, apple-like, crowned by the persistent calyx,* and with 2–5 stones. (*Cotoneaster* is from the Greek meaning like quince, in reference to the quince-like leaves of some species.)

For Culture *see* below. All those below drop their leaves in the autumn unless noted as evergreen. All are spring-blooming.

**adpressa.** A low, prostrate shrub suited to the rock garden. Leaves ½ in. long, wavy-margined. Flowers pinkish, the petals upright. Fruit red. Western China. Hardy from zone* 4 southward.

**dammeri.** An evergreen, prostrate shrub, its trailing branches often rooting at the joints, and thus a valuable plant for the rock garden. Leaves about 1 in. long, pale beneath. Flowers white, solitary, the petals spreading. Fruit red. Central China. Hardy from zone* 5, or with protection from zone* 4, southward.

**dielsiana.** An erectish shrub 2–7 ft. high, the branches arching. Leaves 1 in. long, densely hairy beneath. Flowers pinkish, the petals upright. Fruit red, very showy in autumn. China. Hardy from zone* 5 southward.

**divaricata.** Upright shrub, 3–7 ft. high, its branches wide-spreading. Leaves ¾ in. long, pale beneath. Flowers pinkish, the petals erect. Fruit bright red, profusely borne and showy, ultimately becoming plum-red. China. Hardy from zone* 4 southward.

**foveolata.** An upright shrub 4–8 ft. high, the branches spreading. Leaves 2½–4 in. long, hairy. Flowers pinkish, the petals upright. Fruit black. Central China. Hardy from zone* 4 southward.

**francheti.** A partly evergreen, upright shrub, 4–8 ft. high, the branches spreading. Leaves 1–1½ in. long, densely hairy beneath. Flowers pinkish, the petals erect. Fruit orange-red. Western China. Hardy from zone* 5 southward.

**horizontalis.** A low shrub, its branches forked and almost trailing. Leaves half-evergreen or dropping in the northern edge of its hardiness range, nearly round, ½ in. long. Flowers pinkish, the petals upright. Fruit red. Western China. Hardy from zone* 4 southward. The *var. perpusilla* has smaller but more numerous fruit, and it has many more small branches. Its foliage turns orange-red in autumn.

**lucida.** An upright shrub, 4–10 ft. high, the branches ascending or erect. Leaves 1–2 in. long, shining above, pale beneath. Flowers pinkish, the petals upright. Fruit black. Northern Asia. Hardy from zone* 3 southward.

**microphylla.** Rock spray. A low, evergreen shrub, its branches somewhat upright, but the plant forming dense masses. Leaves about ¼ in. long, shining above, pale or grayish-hairy beneath. Flowers white, the petals spreading. Fruit scarlet, profuse. Himalayas. Hardy from zone* 4 southward. The *var. thymifolia* has narrower leaves and smaller flowers and fruit.

**pannosa.** Evergreen or half-evergreen shrub, 3–6 ft. high, the branches arching. Leaves 1 in. long, dull green above, white-woolly beneath. Flowers white, in profuse clusters, the petals spreading. Fruit dull red. Southwestern China. Hardy from zone* 6 southward and much planted in Calif.

**prostrata.** Evergreen shrub, 6–10 ft. high, branches arching, and plant forming dense masses. Leaves about ¾ in. long. Flowers white, the petals spreading. Fruit red. Himalayas. Hardy from zone* 5 southward.

**pyracantha** = *Pyracantha coccinea*.

**racemiflora.** A shrub 3–6 ft. high, the branches ascending or erect. Leaves nearly round, ¾–1¼ in. wide, whitish-hairy beneath. Flowers white, the petals spreading. Fruit red. Eurasia and northern Africa. Hardy from zone* 4 southward. The *var. songarica* from western China has leaves less hairy beneath. There are several other varieties of this most variable species.

**rotundifolia.** An upright, half-evergreen shrub, 5–8 ft. high, but making dense patches. Leaves ½–¾ in. long, dark green above. Flowers pinkish-white, the petals erect. Fruit scarlet. Southwestern China. Hardy from zone* 4 southward.

**salicifolia.** An upright shrub 7–12 ft. high. Leaves evergreen southward, half-evergreen northward, 1½–3 in. long, the veins and stalk sometimes reddish. Flowers white, the petals spreading, the clusters densely woolly. Fruit red. Western China. Hardy from zone* 5 southward. The *var. floccosa* has the under side of young leaves densely hairy.

**simonsi.** Upright shrub, 7–12 ft. high, often partly evergreen. Leaves ¾–1¼ in. long, hairy beneath. Flowers white, the petals upright. Fruit scarlet. Himalayas. Hardy from zone* 5 southward.

### COTONEASTER CULTURE

Cotoneasters form a useful group of shrubs or rarely small trees with deciduous or persistent to evergreen leaves. They are valued more for their showy black or red fruits than for their small white to pinkish flowers. They prefer sunny locations in well-drained soils with an alkaline rather than acid reaction. In limited quarters one might choose only the species with red fruits as they are more striking than those with black fruits. In growth habit they vary from almost vine-like, prostrate shrubs, such as *C. dammeri*, through low, wide-spreading forms like *C. horizontalis*, wide-spreading bushes such as *C. divaricata* and *C. salicifolia* to erect, almost tree-like forms. Nearly all of the deciduous forms are hardy in the North, while the evergreen sorts are best in the South, as, for example, the handsome *C. pannosa*. The several varieties of *C. salicifolia* are the best evergreen sorts for the North. Nearly all cotoneasters are impatient of moving when once established and should be planted where needed, with preference for spring planting. Propagation is by seed, which is often slow to germinate, or by cuttings of green wood with heat, or half-ripe wood with enough bottom-heat to stimulate root action. — B. Y. M.

INSECT PESTS. *Cotoneaster* is attacked by several scale insects, including the San Jose scale and oyster-shell scale. A dormant spray of miscible oil is used, but the oyster-shell scale is rather difficult to control on *Cotoneaster*.

DISEASES. Cotoneasters are subject to the diseases of pears, which *see* for control.

---

* Special articles on the subjects indicated by an asterisk (*) will be found at the words so marked.

**COTTAGE TULIPS.** See Garden Tulips at TULIPA.

**COTTON.** See GOSSYPIUM.

**COTTON GRASS.** See ERIOPHORUM.

**COTTON GUM** = *Nyssa aquatica.*

**COTTON ROSE** = *Hibiscus mutabilis.*

**COTTONSEED MEAL.** A by-product of the oil mills and valuable as a fertilizer on lawns and acid-tolerant plants, particularly kalmias, etc., at the rate of 3–5 lbs. per 100 sq. ft. The formula is about 6–3–2. (See FERTILIZER; also MANURE.)

**COTTON THISTLE** = *Onopordon acanthium.*

**COTTON TREE** = *Bombax malabaricum.* For the silk-cotton tree see CEIBA.

**COTTONWOOD.** See POPULUS.

**COTTONY JUJUBE** = *Zizyphus mauritiana.*

**COTULA** (kot′you-la). An unimportant genus of herbs of the daisy family from the southern hemisphere, one, **C. squalida**, occasionally planted in the rock garden for its fern-like foliage. It is a low perennial, scarcely 2 in. high, but the stems creeping and often 1 ft. long. Leaves alternate,* about 2 in. long, deeply cut into fern-like segments. Flower heads scarcely ¼ in. in diameter, stalked, without rays, the head wholly of minute disk flowers. N. Zeal. The genus is sometimes called *Leptinella.* (*Cotula* is from the Greek for cup, perhaps in reference to the cup-shaped flower heads.)

**COTYLEDON.** The first or seed-leaf, folded within the seed. It is obvious upon germination of the common bean, but remains hidden within the seed in many other plants. See DICOTYLEDON, MONOCOTYLEDON, and POLYCOTYLEDON.

**COTYLEDON** (kot-ee-lee′don). A large group of succulent plants of the family Crassulaceae, all from the Old World and many from desert regions of South Africa. Leaves mostly in rosettes,* the latter basal or borne on the stem, thick and fleshy. Flowers in terminal clusters (cymes* or racemes*), the calyx 5-parted, the corolla tubular or urn-shaped. Stamens 10. Fruit a collection of pods (follicles*), each with several seeds. (*Cotyledon* is from the Greek for a cavity, in reference to the cup-like leaves of some species.)

For culture see SUCCULENTS. The species below is sometimes offered under the name *Umbilicus.*

**elegans** = *Oliveranthus elegans.*

**umbilicus.** Navelwort; called, also, pennywort. Not over 12 in. high, the leaves round, the stalk attached to the middle of the blade, the margins coarsely toothed. Flowers yellowish-green, about ⅓ in. long, drooping, and borne in a raceme. Eurasia. Can be grown in the rock garden southward.

**COUGHWORT** = *Tussilago farfara.*

**COULTER PINE** = *Pinus coulteri.* See PINE.

**COUNTRY ESTATE.** A country estate is a complete residential unit with considerable acreage, detached from the immediate influence of city or suburb. The residence should be located as far as possible from the main highway and approached by a private drive. Among the facilities included in the plan of a country estate are garage, stables, cottages for gardener and chauffeur, pleasure garden, cutting and vegetable gardens, tennis court, swimming pool, and sometimes facilities for cattle, sheep and chickens.

An independent water and drainage system is necessary where municipal facilities are not available. Often the location of the residence is controlled by available water supply and drainage outlets, the former being an important factor in fire protection.

There are so many elements which may ultimately be required in the plan of a country estate that it is wise to make preliminary provision for all of these elements, even though they may not all be developed. A tennis court or a swimming pool may not seem necessary at the outset, but possible locations for them should be taken into account in order that they may be built without disrupting other features when and if they are desired. It is well, therefore, to set up a preliminary budget for all possible requirements. For an average country estate of forty acres the budget would be approximately:

| | |
|---|---:|
| 1. Topographical survey and preliminary plans | $ 1,000.00 |
| 2. Entrance road 15 ft. wide, 1500 ft. long, including grading, sub-drainage and surface drainage | 15,000.00 |
| 3. Residence, average masonry construction, ten rooms (exclusive of furnishings or special decorations), including water system, drainage and sewage disposal | 83,000.00 |
| 4. Lawns, gardens, planting, orchard | 32,500.00 |
| 5. Greenhouse 18 × 50 ft. with potting shed | 7,000.00 |
| 6. Automatic underground sprinkling system for gardens and terrace | 5,000.00 |
| 7. Boundary fence | 10,000.00 |
| 8. Tennis court complete with fence | 2,500.00 |
| 9. Swimming pool 25 × 75 ft., complete with dressing rooms, filtration plant and chlorinating system | 15,000.00 |
| 10. Garage, gardener's cottage and stables | 25,000.00 |
| | $196,000.00 |
| 11. Architect's and Landscape Architect's fees, 10% | 19,600.00 |
| | $215,600.00 |

To maintain adequately grounds of this size, based on the above investment, will require an annual operating budget approximately as follows:

| | |
|---|---:|
| Head gardener | $2,400.00 |
| Labor assistance | 2,000.00 |
| Supplies, including fertilizer, spray materials, grass seed, annual plants, maintenance and replacement of equipment | 500.00 |
| | $4,900.00 |

If the original investment is made according to a far-sighted plan the operating cost can be minimized. Adequate hose connections around the residence and in the garden should be located to reach any part of these areas with a fifty-foot length of hose. Planting beds prepared with at least 18 in. of good growing soil, and lawn seed beds prepared with at least 6 in. of good topsoil, produce vigorous growth and reduce maintenance labor.

All masonry construction should extend at least 3 ft. 6 in. below finished grade. Paved walks or terraces should be on a 6-in. bed of cinders or gravel with tile underdrainage. Bituminous bound or paved entrance drives eliminate dust and ruts which require expensive upkeep.

The entrance road should be a minimum of 15 ft. wide to permit the easy passing of two cars in opposite directions. Sharp curves should be avoided, and wherever possible the minimum inside radius should be 90 ft. Grades in excess of 10% increase the driving hazard in winter and should be avoided. In the open country a generous entrance turn-around with a minimum outside turning radius of 40 ft. and immediate access to the entrance door is important.

The service court or garage court should be convenient to the house without crowding, yet should be located so that the garage doors and service court are not visible from the entrance area. Where a chauffeur is retained it is advisable to detach the garage entirely from the residence, using the second story for the chauffeur's living quarters.

A gardener's cottage and greenhouse should be convenient to the cut-flower and vegetable gardens. Often these gardens are quite as attractive as the pleasure garden and a circulating walk should make them conveniently accessible.

In connection with the gardens there must be a root cellar for storing roots and bulbs under proper temperature during the winter, and also storage space for potted plants or furnishings which must be protected during the winter.

Gardens should be located not to conflict with any distant view. There is sufficient interest in the garden to be an attraction in itself and if this attraction is interposed on an interesting vista one will detract from the other.

Stables, or buildings for other live stock, must be located in relation to the prevailing winds to prevent objectionable odors and flies being carried to the residence. It is also essential that the residence should be oriented to take advantage of prevailing winds for cross-ventilation.

Plant permanent hardwood shade trees which are not subject to local infectious diseases or pests. The average hardwood shade trees should be allowed a minimum diameter of 80 ft. and small flowering trees such as crabapples or cherries a minimum of 30 ft. Deciduous shrubs should be

---

* Special articles on the subjects indicated by an asterisk (*) will be found at the words so marked.

An attractive, but somewhat expensive, type of courtyard garden. For simpler and less expensive treatments see BACKYARD GARDENS.

spaced not less than 8 ft. apart to allow for mature development, or 6 ft. apart for massed planting.

For boundary planting and natural landscape composition plants native to the same environment are preferable to gardenesque or exotic varieties. Native hawthorns, dogwood or any equivalent thicket plants are most desirable for mass effect. — R. E. G. For the general principles of laying out such a place see LANDSCAPE ARCHITECTURE.

**COURBARIL** (koor-bar′il). South American native name for *Hymenaea courbaril*.

**COURTYARD GARDENS.** Courtyard gardens are an integral part of the house and are enclosed on at least two sides by important rooms. Ordinarily the living room and dining room open directly into the court, although there are special cases where the house completely surrounds such a garden. This type of garden, enclosed by the major rooms of the house, is an additional outdoor room and should be treated as such. It is protected and sheltered from the winds and permits of an entirely different type of planting than an open garden somewhat removed from the house.

By reason of its intimate connection with the interior rooms of the house it requires refined plant materials and architectural detail consistent with the rooms to which it relates.

Only the rambling type of house justifies a courtyard garden. For example, the patio garden characteristic of the Spanish style; the court characteristic of the Italian villa, and the French and English intimate small gardens found both in the rambling provincial country houses and the formal city residences. See PATIO GARDENS.

The courtyard garden is invariably small in area, and all available space must be used to the greatest advantage. Materials should be choice evergreens such as *Buxus sempervirens*, *Taxus cuspidata*, or *Ilex crenata*, which can be controlled in their growth and should take the place of the more rampant-growing deciduous shrubs. The walls surrounding the court are as important a part of the garden as the horizontal area and should be treated as part of the ornamental scheme. Espaliered fruit trees, *Hedera helix*, *Euonymus radicans*, or pillar roses and wisteria are more suitable than rank-growing vines.

Courts are invariably shaded on one side or the other part of the day, which is part of their charm, and the plant materials must be selected to thrive in this shade. At best the plant materials are merely a background in a courtyard and should not be crowded. Large paved areas are necessary to provide space for furniture, and the remaining ground space should be covered with hardy ground covers such as *Hedera helix*, *Pachysandra terminalis* or *Vinca minor*. This ground cover may be made more interesting by interplanting *Narcissus* and *Scilla*, which will poke up through the ground cover in the spring. During the summer lilies thrive under these same conditions, and a mass effect of *Lilium testaceum*, followed by *Lilium regale* and then *Lilium speciosum* will give continued interest.

Where the courtyard is sufficiently open to allow ample sunlight for perennials they may take the place of the ground cover and those plants which thrive only under shaded conditions. If the garden is to be used only in summer use annuals; for yellow, dwarf marigolds; for white, small, single bedding petunias; for blue, *Ageratum* or *Lobelia*; for purple, blue petunias or heliotrope; for pink or red either petunias or geraniums.

If windows open on to the courtyard color may be added by window boxes filled with fuchsias, lantanas or petunias. Where space does not permit of bedding plants use ornamental pots of geraniums, *Hibiscus* or Shasta daisy. In cases where most of the court is taken up by paving set standard heliotrope, geraniums, lantanas or fuchsias, also *Agapanthus* or tuberous-rooted begonias, around in informal groups to break up the severity of the paving.

Nothing is more ornamental or pleasant in a courtyard garden than a small pool or fountain surrounded by a few potted plants. The water has a cooling effect and adds life and interest to the court. Such fountains must be proportionate in size to the court, but have infinite possibilities for variation in design. If the pool is raised 15 in. from the

* Special articles on the subjects indicated by an asterisk (*) will be found at the words so marked.

surrounding walk level, with the coping 12 to 15 inches wide, it is just the right height to serve as a seat.

Large, picturesque trees like apple or hawthorn should be included incidentally in the plan of the court to offset the severity of its architectural surroundings. The courtyard should be much more imaginative and picturesque than the rooms which it adjoins. Such an effect can be obtained by mature rhododendrons, tubbed oleanders, *Pieris japonica*, *Azalea yedoensis poukhanensis*, *Azalea mucronata*, *Magnolia virginiana*, or mature *Taxus cuspidata*. There is already sufficient architectural interest in the surrounding walls without repeating similar architectural forms in the planting. Compact, formal-shaped evergreens like *Juniperus communis hibernica*, *Juniperus chinensis globosa*, or *Juniperus chinensis pyramidalis* may accentuate entrances to the courtyard, but this type of compact emphatic form, either in upright spiky effects or low, clipped, globular forms like *Thuja occidentalis globosa*, should be used sparingly. Plants which require large space for maturity, like the pines and spruces, have no place in the courtyard. *Pyracantha*, *Taxus*, *Buxus*, or *Ilex* which can be controlled are preferable in this sort of work.

If the center of the garden is sunken, with two or three steps leading down into it, the appearance of size and interest is greatly increased. The apparent space is also enhanced by keeping the center of the garden simple, either in plain turf or paving, with the planting arranged around the edges next to the walls. Such an area should be regarded as a room and treated as such. — R. E. G.

**COVENTRY BELLS** = *Campanula trachelium*.

**COVER CROP.** A temporary crop to cover the ground, sometimes for protecting the land from erosion, to smother weeds, or for soil improvement. Sown broadcast and fairly thickly, any of the following will accomplish this: rye, oats, millet, and many legumes such as clovers, vetch, and peas. One of the best, for summer use, is buckwheat. Most cover crops are plowed under in the spring, but some, like buckwheat, are plowed under as soon as there is danger of their flowering. The legumes are the most valuable because of the nitrogen they gather and add to the soil.

**COWAGE** = *Stizolobium pruritum*.

**COWBANE.** See CICUTA.

**COWBERRY** = *Vaccinium vitis-idaea*.

**COW CABBAGE** = *Brassica oleracea acephala*. For culture see KALE.

**COW CLOVER** = *Trifolium medium*. See CLOVER.

**COWHERB** = *Saponaria vaccaria*.

**COWITCH** = *Stizolobium pruritum*.

**COW LILY** = *Nymphozanthus advenus*.

**COW MANURE.** See MANURE.

**COW PARSNIP.** See HERACLEUM.

**COWPEA** = *Vigna sinensis*.

**COWSLIP.** As a garden plant, *Primula veris*; as a wild flower, *Caltha palustris* (see MARSH MARIGOLD). See also DODECATHEON and LACHENALIA.

**COW-TONGUE** = *Clintonia borealis*.

**COW VETCH** = *Vicia cracca*.

**COXE, W.** See America at GARDEN BOOKS.

**COYOTE-BUSH** = *Baccharis pilularis*.

**COYOTE MINT** = *Monardella villosa*.

**C.P.O.** Trademarked soaps, both solid and liquid, especially prepared for contact spraying.

**CRAB, CRABAPPLE.** See MALUS.

**CRAB CACTUS** = *Zygocactus truncatus*.

**CRAB GRASS** = *Syntherisma sanguinale*. See Crab Grass in the list at WEEDS.

**CRAB-TREE.** See MALUS.

*CRACCA* (krak'ka). An obsolete generic name applied to several vetch-like plants. See VICIA and TEPHROSIA.

**CRACKERBERRY** = *Cornus canadensis*.

**CRAMBE** (kram'be). Perhaps 20 species of fleshy-leaved, mostly bluish-foliaged herbs of the mustard family, scattered from the Canary Islands to western Asia, **C. maritima**, the sea-kale, being the only one of garden interest. It is a perennial with cabbage-like leaves nearly 2 ft. long, oblongish, lobed and notched. Flowers white, about ½ in. wide, in a large terminal cluster often 3 ft. high. (For details see CRUCIFERAE.) Fruit a hard, pea-like body with a single seed in each pod. The original plant is native along the sea coasts of western Eu. For culture see SEA-KALE. (*Crambe* is the Greek name for this plant.)

**CRANBERRY** (*Vaccinium macrocarpon*). The culture of the common cranberry (purely an American species, although the name is also applied to *V. oxycoccus*) is not to be attempted unless one has or can make the specialized conditions it needs for growth. As to climatic requirements, the location of the commercial growers in Mass., N.J. and Wisc. should be a guide to anyone.

While climatic conditions are important, the soil is still more so: It cannot be grown on upland soils, so that its culture is confined to a place having a low, relatively flat topography with a sluggish stream in it, or where ditches can be dug. And in addition, it must have an acid muck or peaty soil with a pH of 4.5-5 (see ACID AND ALKALI SOILS). A natural site with such a soil will be dominated by wild bog shrubs or herbs such as *Chamaedaphne calyculata*, the cranberry itself, much sphagnum moss, the pitcher-plant (*Sarracenia purpurea*), the sundews, or other acid-tolerant plants. In some places there may even be taller shrubs or trees like the white cedar (*Chamaecyparis thyoides*), or, in the North, tamarack or spruce.

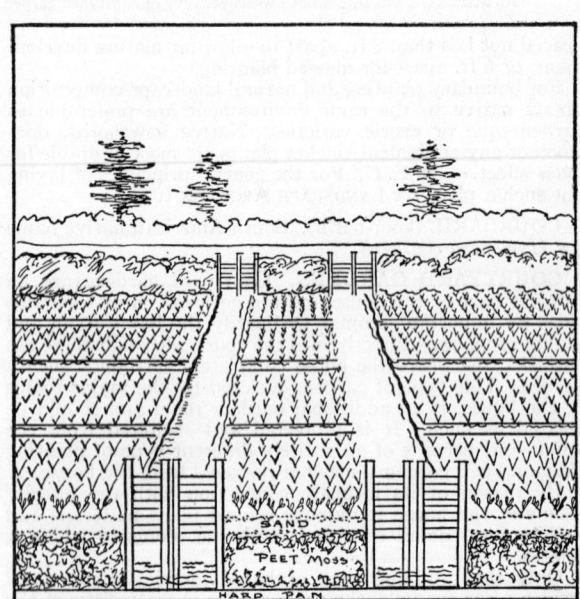

Cross-section of a prepared cranberry bog, showing stratification of plants, soils, and water. The water gates in the foreground are used to control the periodic flooding of the bog.

Underlying the soil in which such plants are rooted is generally a layer of hard-pan, often, and in the most favorable conditions, about 5 ft. below the surface. This maintains a steady supply of relatively acid water in the upper layer of muck.

To start operations, all live vegetation must be removed by burning or by a complete flooding and submergence for two years. Flooding is such an essential feature of subse-

---

* Special articles on the subjects indicated by an asterisk (*) will be found at the words so marked.

quent culture that it is better to build a dam, with gates, at the start, so constructed that it is possible to cover the whole bog, plants and all, as needed.

Having completely cleaned the site, the cuttings of the vine are planted in a layer of clean, moist sand about 2 in. thick. Put the rows 12–20 in. apart, and usually 2 cuttings are put at each 8-in. interval in the row. It will take them considerable time to cover completely all the ground and in the meantime weeds must be kept down. When once established, little weeding is necessary. Ordinarily it will be 2 or 3 years before such a plantation begins to bear in any quantity. Yields run from 3000–14,000 pounds per acre, depending on the variety and season.

FLOODING. Cranberry is sensitive to frost and the bogs are usually flooded soon after the final picking, which should be over by November 20 or earlier in some regions. They must be flooded (i.e. the plants submerged) from Dec. 15 to May 8 in N.J. and elsewhere to correspond with the worst of the cold weather and late spring frosts.

There are other temporary floodings for pest controls as outlined below. The necessity for these floodings is so imperative that no plantation should be contemplated unless adequate water supplies (i.e. of acid water) are available for storage, and arrangements made for conducting it quickly. Growers will temporarily flood a bog if late afternoon temperatures get down to 28° or 29°. While the berries are able to stand 28° without injury, 24° or 22° will quite likely ruin them.

FERTILIZER. Of course the native growth of wild cranberries gets no special feeding. But commercial growers have found, after a long series of experiments, that their crop is greatly increased by an application of a special fertilizer. Due to the acid soil condition of the site, this fertilizer must be made according to the following formula:

| Sodium nitrate | 75 pounds |
| Dried blood | 75 pounds |
| Rock phosphate | 300 pounds |
| Sulphate of potash | 50 pounds |

A single application of such a mixture at a rate of 500–800 pounds per acre is beneficial, but it should not be done more than once in three or four years. On some cranberry soils even this single application may stimulate vine growth at the expense of fruit production. It is safer, therefore, to experiment on a small part of the bog to determine if your soil type responds favorably to fertilizer.

VARIETIES. The leading horticultural varieties of cranberry are:
Howes. Oval, dark red berries. Ripens in October.
Early Black. Bell-shaped, very dark red berries. Ripens in September, but a good keeper.
Centennial. Nearly round, medium red berries, larger than any other variety. Ripens about October first. Much subject to disease.
McFarlin. Size and color of berries variable, hence an inferior variety, but much grown because of its disease resistance.

INSECT PESTS. Several species of small caterpillars, called fireworms, eat and kill cranberry leaves. Nicotine sprays have been used with success against them. Winter flooding held until some time in May also checks them, and has also been effective against another caterpillar, the fruitworm, and against the blunt-nosed leafhopper, which carries disease. The rootworm is the larva of a leaf beetle; adults may be killed by arsenical sprays in midsummer. Such sprays also control occasional injury by leaf-feeding caterpillars or flea beetles. The girdler, a caterpillar girdling the runners, can be checked by flooding for a week about the first of Oct.

DISEASES. Of the several diseases some are kept under control by the flooding outlined under insect pests above. Others such as scald and blast and a rot are best controlled by five applications of a 4-4-50 bordeaux mixture to which one-half pound of a fish-oil soap is added to each 50 gallons. The 5 applications should be sprayed on about (1) June 1, (2) just before bloom, (3) just after blooming ends, (4) two weeks later and (5) two weeks later. For false blossom, a virus disease, there is no known cure.

**CRANBERRY BUSH** = *Viburnum trilobum*.
**CRANBERRY GOURD** = *Abobra tenuifolia*.
**CRANBERRY TREE** = *Viburnum opulus*.
**CRANESBILL.** See GERANIUM.
**CRANESBILL FAMILY** = Geraniaceae.
**CRAPE JASMINE** = *Tabernaemontana coronaria*.
**CRAPE MYRTLE** = *Lagerstroemia indica*.

*CRASSIFOLIA, -us, -um* (kras-si-fō′li-a). Thick-leaved.
*CRASSIPES* (kras′si-peez). Thick-stalked.
**CRASSULA** (krass′you-la). A very large genus of succulent herbs or shrubs of the family Crassulaceae, all from the Old World, and most from South Africa. One of those below is very widely grown as a pot plant and in miniature desert gardens, where it rarely blooms, but in Calif. it grows outdoors and blooms annually. Leaves opposite,* very thick and fleshy, without teeth (in ours). Flowers (rarely produced in house plants) white or pink, in compact clusters (often cymes*), the petals, sepals and stamens 5, the petals sometimes joined at the base. Fruit dry. (*Crassula* is Latin diminutive of *crassus*, thick.)

For general notes on culture *see* SUCCULENTS. *Crassula portulacea* is one of the commonest succulent plants in the U.S., every florist offering specimens that range from only a few leaves to compact, well-grown, bushy plants containing scores of leaves. As a house plant it will stand more abuse than almost any other, but it will not stand overwatering. While it will stand house conditions, it is best grown in the cool greenhouse.

coccinea = *Rochea coccinea*.
multicava. A low, greenhouse herb, but grown outdoors in Calif. Leaves ovalish, 2–3 in. long, the bases of the leaves joining so that they surround the stem. Flowers white. South Africa.
portulacea. The common species in cult., but without an appropriate common name, the florists' names of Japanese laurel and Japanese rubber-plant being misleading. As grown in Calif., a thick-stemmed, branching shrub 6–10 ft. high, as a pot plant much smaller and often unbranched. Leaves very thick and shining, oval to roundish, about 1½ in. long, the broad base appearing as though merged with the stem. Flowers, which may not bloom for years (or ever in house plants), rosy red. South Africa.
quadrifida = *Crassula multicava*.

There are many other species to be found in the collections of specialists in succulents.

**CRASSULACEAE** (krass-you-lay′see-ee). The orpine or stonecrop family is easily recognized if only its garden representatives are considered. They are characteristically fleshy-leaved plants with often handsome, prevailingly red or yellow, rarely white, flowers. They are chiefly grown as pot plants, especially *Rochea, Crassula, Cotyledon, Bryophyllum, Kalanchoe, Pachyphytum, Urbinia,* and *Echeveria,* but many are grown in the open border and some, especially in *Sedum,* are popular rock garden plants.

Leaves (in our genera) thick and fleshy (scale-like in some sedums). Flowers perfect,* nearly always in clusters, often in cymes,* the individual flower small, but the cluster often very showy, especially in *Sempervivum* (*see* HOUSELEEK), *Gormania, Graptopetalum,* and *Oliveranthus.* The only other garden genera are *Monanthes,* from Morocco and the Canaries, and *Byrnesia,* which is Mexican. The family contains over 900 species, in perhaps 20 genera, the identification of which is puzzling. For the culture of the garden genera *see* SUCCULENTS.

Technical flower characters: Sepals or lobes of the calyx 4 or 5. Petals 4 or 5, sometimes united into a tube (*Cotyledon, Echeveria, Bryophyllum, Kalanchoe,* etc.). Stamens 4 or 5, or double these numbers. Fruit dry, 1-celled, a follicle.*

**CRATAEGUS** (kra-tee′gus). Under the name hawthorn, thorn, or thornapple is grouped an enormous genus (over 1000 species) of thorny shrubs and trees of the rose family, found in the north temperate zone but most common in eastern N.A. Less than a dozen are really garden plants, although any of the wild species may be transferred to informal plantings. Leaves alternate,* always toothed or lobed, none truly evergreen. Flowers white (red or pink in some hort. forms), nearly always in small clusters (corymbs*). Sepals and petals 5, the stamens 5–25, sometimes the anthers* pink or purple. Fruit resembling a miniature apple, nearly always brightly colored, and a most attractive autumn feature of the group. (*Crataegus* is the old Greek name for these plants, implying strength, from their hard wood.)

The native hawthorns are extremely attractive in flower (May–June) and in fruit (Sept.–Oct.). While most of those below will grow in ordinary garden soil, they prefer limestone regions and an open, sandy loam. Because of their

---
* Special articles on the subjects indicated by an asterisk (*) will be found at the words so marked.

thorns, impenetrable barriers can be made of them, although they do not stand being clipped for hedges. Of the Old World species much the best known is the English hawthorn or May. Propagation is by seeds and a slow process. Allow the pulp of the fruit to decay or soak it off in water, after which the seeds must be stratified (*see* SEEDS AND SEEDAGE). Ordinarily they take two years to sprout. Another and quicker method is by root cuttings (*see* CUTTINGS). All those below can be purchased as rooted plants from nurserymen. Some of them are known as haw.

The flowers are white unless otherwise noted, and the hardiness of the American species is indicated by their wide range.

**arnoldiana.** A tree up to 20 ft. or even more, the thorns thin, straight, about 3 in. long. Leaves 2–3 in. long, doubly toothed and shallowly lobed. Flowers nearly ¾ in. wide. Fruit pear-shaped, red, about ¾ in. long. Mass. to N.Y.

**carrieri** = *Crataegus lavallei.*

**coccinea** = *Crataegus intricata.*

**cordata** = *Crataegus phaenopyrum.*

**crus-galli.** Cockspur thorn. A large shrub or small tree up to 30 ft., the thorns numerous, slender, 3–4 in. long. Leaves oblongish, wedge-shaped at the base, 2–3 in. long, toothed in the upper part. Flowers about ½ in. wide. Fruit nearly round, about ½ in. in diameter. Quebec to Mich. and N. Car.

**intricata.** A shrub 5–8 ft. high, the thorns few, curved and 3–4 in. long. Leaves elliptic to ovalish, 2–3 in. long, doubly toothed and also with 3–4 pairs of sharp lobes. Flowers nearly 1 in. wide. Fruit nearly round, reddish-brown. Mass. to N.Y. and N. Car. Sometimes known as *C. coccinea.*

**lavallei.** A hybrid tree up to 20 ft., the thorns stout and about 2 in. long. Leaves elliptic or oblongish, 3–4 in. long, unequally toothed. Flowers white, with a red disk, about ¾ in. wide. Fruit persisting through the winter, brick-red, about ½ in. long. Hardy from zone* 4 southward.

**mollis.** Red haw. Tree up to 30 ft., the thorns stout and 2 in. long or less. Leaves broadly oval, 3–4 in. long, doubly toothed. Flowers white, with a red disk, about 1 in. wide. Fruit nearly 1 in. in diameter, scarlet. Ohio to S. Dak. and Kan.

**monogyna.** English hawthorn, but the name applies also to the next. A shrub or small tree, not over 15 ft. high, the thorns about 1 in. long. Leaves broadly oval, cut into 3–5 lobes that are shallowly toothed. Flowers white, about ½ in. wide. Fruit scarlet. Eurasia. Hardy from zone* 3 southward. There are many varieties, some with pink, red, or double flowers, and one with upright branches and columnar habit.

**oxyacantha.** English hawthorn, but *see* C. MONOGYNA. Similar, but a tree up to 30 ft., and with the leaves more deeply lobed and the lobes toothed only in the upper part. Eurasia and northern Africa. Hardy from zone* 3 southward. Often confused with the last. Of the many varieties offered the most noteworthy are those with drooping branches, another with bloom extending into mid-August, and one with fern-like foliage.

**phaenopyrum.** Washington thorn. A dense, round-headed tree, 20–30 ft. high, the thorns slender, up to 3 in. long. Leaves broadly triangular, 3–7-lobed, the lobes doubly toothed. Flowers ½ in. wide. Fruit bright red, about ¼ in. in diameter. Va. to Ala. Hardy from zone* 4 southward.

**tomentosa.** Pear haw; also called black thorn. A shrub or small tree up to 15 ft. high, the thorns short or none. Leaves elliptic or oblongish, 3–5 in. long, toothed and sometimes slightly lobed. Flowers about ½ in. wide. Fruit somewhat pear-shaped, orange-red, about ½ in. long. Ontario to Ga. westward to Minn. and Kan.

**CREAM BUSH** = *Holodiscus discolor.*

**CREAM-CUPS.** A single, rather attractive, annual Californian herb belonging to the genus **Platystemon** (plat-i-stee'-mon) of the family Papaveraceae. The only species, **P. californicus,** covers great areas there and is often grown as an annual in the flower garden elsewhere. It is an erect plant 6–12 in. high, the leaves narrow, clasping the stem and about 2 in. long. Flowers solitary, long-stalked, with 3 sepals and 6 petals, the latter cream-colored or light yellow. Stamens* numerous, some of them flattened and petal-like. Fruit a head of small pods. (*Platystemon* is from the Greek for broad and stamen.) Seeds should be sown where the plant is wanted, but only after warm weather has arrived.

**CREEPERS.** *See* VINES.

**CREEPING.** As a descriptive word for plants of prostrate or trailing habit, creeping is part of the common name of many plants. Those found in this DICTIONARY are:

**Creeping barberry** = *Mahonia repens;* **Creeping bent** = *Agrostis maritima;* **Creeping buttercup** = *Ranunculus repens* (*see* BUTTERCUP. *See also* Creeping buttercup in the list at WEEDS); **Creeping Charlie** = *Lysimachia nummularia;* **Creeping crowfoot** = *Ranunculus repens* (*see* BUTTERCUP. *See also* the creeping buttercup in the list at WEEDS); **Creeping fig** = *Ficus pumila;* **Creeping forget-me-not** = *Omphalodes verna;* **Creeping Jennie** = *Lysimachia nummularia;* **Creeping Juniper** = *Juniperus horizontalis;* **Creeping lily-turf** = *Liriope spicata;* **Creeping myrtle** = *Vinca minor;* **Creeping snowberry** = *Chiogenes hispidula;* **Creeping thyme** = *Thymus serpyllum* (*see* THYME).

***CRENATA, -us, -um*** (kree-nay'ta). Crenate; *i.e.* scalloped or with an irregularly waved margin; mostly applied to leaf margins.

***CRENATIFLORA, -us, -um*** (kree-nay-ti-flow'ra). Having flowers with scalloped edges.

***CRENULATA, -us, -um*** (kren-you-lay'ta). Somewhat crenate or scalloped.

**CREOLE EASTER LILY.** *See* Flowers at LOUISIANA.

**CREOSOTE.** *See* Repellents at INSECTICIDES.

**CREOSOTE BUSH** = *Larrea tridentata.*

**CREPIS** (creep'is). Rather weedy herbs, some actual pests, but one an annual flower garden plant. The hawksbeards, which comprise the genus *Crepis,* include well over 200 species, but only **C. rubra** is of any garden interest. It is a branching annual 8–18 in. high, with a leafy stem and milky juice. Leaves largely basal, dandelion-like, the lower ones with a winged stalk. Flowers in small, solitary, long-stalked heads, red or flesh-colored. Italy. Summer. A showy annual to be sown where wanted. *See* ANNUALS. For the plant known as *Crepis barbata see* TOLPIS. (*Crepis* is Greek for sandal and of uncertain application here.)

***CREPITANS*** (krep'i-tanz). Crackling or rustling.

**CRESCENTIA.** *See* CALABASH.

**CRESCENZI, P.** *See* Herbals at GARDEN BOOKS.

**CRESS.** Many plants of the mustard family are known as cress, the most important being watercress (which see). For other cresses *see* LEPIDIUM, BARBAREA, CARDAMINE, and ARABIS.

**CRESS FAMILY** = Cruciferae.

**CRESTED.** Bearing a crest. In plants the crest is often a ridge or appendage, sometimes toothed or elevated and irregular. The crest may be on the petals, as in some iris, or it may modify the whole flower cluster as in the cockscomb.

**CRESTED DOG'S-TAIL** = *Cynosurus cristatus.*

**CRESTED IRIS.** *See* IRIS.

**CRESTED POPPY** = *Argemone platyceras.*

**CRESTED SHIELD FERN** = *Dryopteris cristata.*

**CRETAN BEAR'S-TAIL** = *Celsia arcturus.*

**CRETAN MULLEIN** = *Celsia cretica.*

**CRETAN SPIKENARD** = *Valeriana phu.*

***CRETICA, -us, -um*** (kree'ti-ka). From Crete.

**CRICKETS.** *See* Grasshoppers at INSECT PESTS.

**CRIMSON CLOVER** = *Trifolium incarnatum. See* CLOVER.

**CRIMSON FLAG** = *Schizostylis coccinea.*

**CRIMSON GARDEN.** *See* RED GARDEN.

**CRIMSON GLORY VINE** = *Vitis kaempferi glabrescens.*

**CRIMSON RAMBLER.** *See* ROSA CATHAYENSIS PLATYPHYLLA.

**CRIMSON SAGE** = *Audibertia grandiflora.*

***CRINITA, -us, -um*** (kry-ny'ta). Long-haired.

**CRINKLEROOT** = *Dentaria diphylla.*

**CRINUM** (kry'num). A genus of perhaps 100 species of thick- or bulbous-rooted, lily-like herbs of the family Amaryllidaceae, mostly tropical, a few cult. for their very showy flowers. Leaves persistent or evergreen, thick or almost fleshy, strap-shaped or sword-shaped, stalkless. Flowers in an umbel* at the end of a tall, solid stalk, beneath the umbel 2 spathe*-like bracts. Corolla funnel-shaped, but with a long, slender tube, the summit ending in narrow segments. Fruit an irregularly bursting capsule.* (*Crinum* is the Greek name for a lily.)

These handsome plants, sometimes called crinum lilies,

* Special articles on the subjects indicated by an asterisk (*) will be found at the words so marked.

are grown **outdoors** chiefly in the South, although some of them can be wintered over up to zone* 5 with a good mulch of strawy manure. They are naturally rich feeders and do best in good soils and with plenty of water. In the South they should be left where planted, as they dislike moving and may not flower for two or three seasons after being lifted. If let alone they are apt to make striking, large clumps.

Greenhouse culture is rare because the plants get too big for easy handling. If grown in the greenhouse the roots of most of them should be stored over the winter in a cool but frost-free place, potted up in early March and put in a warm, moist greenhouse, using potting mixture* 4. Greenhouse culture of the evergreen sorts demands that they be potted up continuously but rested by reduction of heat and partial drying-out during the winter. For insect pests see BULBS.

Most of the species produce small offsets* from the base of the bulb-like root. These can be detached and provide the easiest method of propagation as they root easily. If the plants set fruit, which is seldom, propagation by seeds is possible, but it will take at least 2 or 3 years before the seedlings will bloom.

**americanum.** Swamp lily (not a true lily, however). Leaves few, long and narrow. Flowers white, the segments long and narrow. Stalk of the flower cluster 18-24 in. long, usually arising before the leaves appear. Fla. to Tex.

**asiaticum.** A large, strong plant, its bulb-like root often 1 ft. long. From this spring large clumps of closely placed leaves, that are 3 ft. long, 3-4 in. wide, and with a tapering tip. Flowers fragrant, white, at least 20 in the cluster, which is borne on a 2-edged stalk that slightly overtops the leaves. Tropical Asia. Blooming all summer and beyond.

**capense** = Crinum longifolium.

**fimbriatulum.** Leaves narrow, 2-3 ft. long, the margins fringed with short hairs. Flowers funnel-shaped, greenish-white, the tube 4-5 in. long, the segments red-striped, the whole cluster sparsely flowered. Tropical Africa.

**kirki.** Leaves narrow, strap-shaped, 3-4 ft. long. Flowers about 12 in a cluster, greenish, the tube about 4 in. long and curved, the segments with a bright red keel. Zanzibar.

**longifolium.** The commonest crinum in cult. and hardy, with protection, up to zone* 5. Leaves long and narrow, the margins roughish. Flowers white or pink, about 12 in the cluster, 3-4 in. wide, the tube 3-4 in. long and curved. Segments about 1 in. wide. South Africa.

**moorei.** A larger plant than the last, the leaves at least 3 in. wide and smooth on the edges. Flowers nearly 4 in. wide, red. South Africa. Tender in the North and only for greenhouse culture there.

**scabrum.** Leaves scarcely 2 in. wide, the margins rough. Flowers white, the back of the segments crimson, the tube greenish, curved and 3-5 in. long, the segments half that length. Tropical Africa. Not hardy north.

**CRISPA, -us, -um** (kriss'pa). Crisped or curled.

**CRISTA-GALLI.** A specific name meaning a cock's comb or like one, but not applied to the plant cockscomb.

**CRISTATA, -us, -um** (kriss-tay'ta). Crested.*

**CROCATA, -us, -um** (kro-cay'ta). Yellow.

**CROCEA, -us, -um** (krō'see-a). Crocus-yellow.

**CROCOSMAEFLORA, -us, -um** (kro-kos-mi-flow'ra). With flowers like the genus *Crocosmia* (which see).

**CROCOSMIA** (kro-kos'mee-a). A single, South African herb of the iris family, having gladiolus-like corms,* and to be grown, in the North, in the same way. The only species, **C. aurea**, is a branching herb up to 3½ ft. high, with only a few small, scattered leaves, the lower shorter than the upper, sword-shaped. Flowers nearly regular,* bright orange-yellow, the tube about 1 in. long, the segments longer and spreading. The flowers are in spikes and these are sometimes branched. Not much grown in the North. Related to *Gladiolus*, but differing in having the valves of the spathe* not notched. (*Crocosmia* is from the Greek for saffron smell, which is evident when the dried flowers are soaked in water.) It is one of the parents of the common garden montbretia. See TRITONIA CROCOSMAEFLORA.

**CROCUS** (krō'kus). A genus of perhaps 75 species of very popular garden plants of the iris family, ranging from the Mediterranean region to southwestern Asia. They are apparently stemless plants arising from a corm* (the crocus "bulb" of the shops). Leaves narrow or grass-like, appearing before, or with, or after the flowers. Flowers blooming very early in spring or in autumn, but the plant commonly called autumn crocus belongs to the genus *Colchicum*. Crocus flowers are produced at the ground level, are stemless or very short-stalked, and have 6 segments and 3 stamens.* Fruit a capsule,* ripening at or below ground level. (*Crocus* is the Greek name of the saffron, *Crocus sativus*.)

For Culture and uses, see below. The common garden crocus is *C. vernus*.

**aureus.** A spring-blooming sort sometimes called Dutch crocus or simply Dutch yellow. Flowers bright yellow, the segments about 1½ in. long. Southeastern Eu. and Asia Minor.

**biflorus.** Scotch crocus (but a native of southeastern Eu. and Asia Minor); a useful, spring-blooming plant for the rock garden. Flowers purple-tinged, the outer segments purple-striped, the throat yellow. There are several named forms or varieties, most of them color variants.

**imperati.** Spring-blooming, the flowers lilac or white, the outer segments purple-striped and about 1¾ in. long. One of the first to bloom. Italy.

**longiflorus.** Autumn-blooming, the flowers lilac, the segments about 1 in. long, the throat slightly bearded and yellow. Southern Eu.

**nudiflorus.** Autumn-blooming, the flowers lilac, the segments nearly 2 in. long. Southern Eu. This and *C. longiflorus* are good plants for the autumn garden (which see).

**pulchellus.** Autumn-blooming, the flowers lilac, but faintly striped. Segments about 1½ in. long, the throat yellow. Greece to Asia Minor.

**sativus.** Saffron crocus; called also vegetable gold. Autumn-blooming, the flowers white or lilac, the segments nearly 2 in. long, the throat bearded, the stigmas* orange. Asia Minor. A common form has a yellow throat. See below for cult. See also HERB GARDENING.

**speciosus.** A good rock garden, autumn-blooming crocus with lilac or purple-tinged flowers, the segments 2 in. long. Eurasia.

**susianus.** Cloth of Gold. Spring-blooming, the flowers orange-yellow, but brownish outside, the segments about 1¼ in. long. Crimea. See ROCK GARDEN.

**tomassinianus.** Spring-blooming, the flowers pale reddish-blue, the segments about 1½ in. long, often dark-spotted at the tip. Dalmatia and Serbia.

**vernus.** Common crocus, spring-blooming and in a variety of colors (see Culture below), the segments about 1½ in. long, bearded. Eu. Very like the last except for the beard.

**zonatus.** A rock-garden, autumn-blooming crocus, the rose-lilac flowers streaked with purple, and orange-spotted inside. Segments about 2 in. long, the throat yellow and bearded. Asia Minor. See ROCK GARDEN.

## CROCUS CULTURE

Possibly none of the smaller spring bulbs will make a braver show than crocus if one remembers to plant them in a warm, well-drained soil where the first spring sun will make them open wide their brilliant flowers accented by the showy yellow stamens* and pistils.* From the corms, that resemble small gladiolus, they push up the sharp noses from which rise grassy leaves with silver middle stripes and masses of bloom, white, white with purple and violet stripes, lavenders, lilacs, gray-blues, rosy purples and deep, warm purples darkening in the throat — King of the Whites and Kathleen Parlow for white; Albion, white with purple stripes; Pallas, violet-striped purple; Maximilian, soft lavender; Gladstone, reddish-purple; and *purpureus grandiflorus*, very deep purple, should surely be represented. All these are forms of *Crocus vernus*.

For pure yellow, one must turn to the species *Crocus aureus*, which is usually listed with the Dutch crocus as Dutch Yellow, or *C. susianus*, which sometimes is called Cloth of Gold. The first is pure yellow, the second is striped with dark brown on the outside of the petals. Like many of the other species crocus, these do not flower with the garden forms and so one cannot depend on a garish combination of purple and gold, although sometimes their seasons overlap.

Crocus should always be planted where they may self-sow, for the little seedlings that look much like grass come up all about the parent bulbs and soon yield flowering bulbs and sometimes color varieties that are valuable. They should also be planted deeply enough so that the bulbs do not multiply too rapidly and go to foliage. Drainage and a warm summer sun also help to keep them in health, conditions that do not always obtain when crocus are planted in lawns that must be mown and watered during summer.

Finally, after having enjoyed the robust beauty of the garden varieties, the gardener might well turn to the more slender crocus species that flower in both spring and fall, choosing for spring certainly *C. biflorus* in its many forms, *C. imperati* and *C. tomassinianus*; and for autumn many of the forms of *C. speciosus* and *C. zonatus*, but not the saffron crocus, *C. sativus*, unless a specially warm spot can be given, for otherwise it will yield leaves but no flowers with their lax orange stigmas. — B. Y. M.

**CROCUS FAMILY** = Iridaceae.

**CROOKNECK SQUASH.** See SQUASH.

**CROQUET.** A lawn game, the standard area for which is 36 × 72 ft.

**CROSSANDRA** (kros-san'dra). Showy greenhouse plants, comprising perhaps 20 species of herbs or shrubs of the family Acanthaceae, all from the Old World tropics. The only one of hort. interest is C. infundibuliformis, a shrub 1-3 ft. high from India. Leaves generally opposite,* narrowly oval, 3-5 in. long, more or less wavy-margined. Flowers orange-scarlet, in a large, dense, hairy, 4-sided spike. Corolla tubular, its limb 1-sided, about 1 in. long, each flower from within the leafy bracts,* which are persistent and about as long as the capsules.* The plant needs a warm, moist greenhouse and potting mixture* 3. (*Crossandra* is from the Greek for fringed anthers.)

**CROSS-BREED.** The result of a cross between plants of varieties of one species. Synonyms are *half-breed, mongrel, variety hybrid*. — O. E. W.

**CROSS-FERTILIZATION: CROSS-POLLINATION.** A sexually produced seed may result from either cross- or self-pollination and subsequent fertilization. In the former case two plants are involved; in the latter only one. The pollen and egg parent plants may be simply two individuals of the same variety, or plants more distantly related, *i.e.* representing two varieties, two species or even two genera. Natural cross-pollination is probably more common than self-pollination. — O. E. W.

**CROSSING.** This involves the artificial transfer of pollen from one flower to another for the purpose of producing a hybrid* and in crossing or hybridizing plants, at least six essentials must be kept in mind: (1) The prevention of self-pollination*; (2) The protection of the pistil and its receptive surface from injury during the removal of the stamens (emasculation); (3) Guarding the pistil from pollen other than that with which it is to be crossed; (4) Using pollen that is both viable and otherwise effective in producing a seed; (5) Using such protective devices on the crossed flower that will not facilitate wilting, mold, or cause it to fall; and (6) Proper labeling.

Many plants self-pollinate themselves in the bud, so that it is necessary to remove or otherwise destroy the effectiveness of the pollen in such cases, before the pollen is shed. This is sometimes done with water and a syringe, but usually the bud is carefully slit with a sharp scalpel and the immature anthers are picked off with a pair of straight tweezers or with a spear-headed dissecting needle. Extreme care is used not to mutilate the flower more than is necessary, since some plants have flowers that are very prone to fall due to their sensitiveness to injury. One soon discovers which these are.

(1) Plants commonly self-pollinated* are wheat, barley, oats, tomatoes, sweet peas, beans, garden peas, commercial tobacco, peanuts and four o'clocks.

(2) Various devices are used to guard the pistil, crossed or uncrossed, from undesired pollination. Among these are square-bottomed manila paper bags of various sizes fastened over the flowers with either string or paper clips; celluloid cylinders with cotton plugs where maximum light is needed to keep flowers from falling; cellophane or glassine bags, or tooth-brush or cigar holders; muslin or cheesecloth cages covering the whole plant. In some cases the flower envelope itself can be closed with paper clips. Which device is used depends on the plant involved.

(3) In the case of many self-pollinating species, it is probably most practical, where this can be done, to cross-pollinate them at once, and provide no protection, since the chance of contamination would be rare under these conditions, in such plants as sweet peas and peanuts. Obviously wind-pollinated plants require greater flower protection to prevent undesirable crossing than most insect-pollinated forms, since this type of pollen is more easily and more profusely distributed.

(4) Pollen of different species varies much in its length of life or viability, even under the most optimum conditions. Pansy pollen is said to be "good" for 26 days, that of the peony and some grape species for 60 days, while date palm pollen is saved from year to year by the Arabs as a precaution against a poor supply or a bad season. Tomato growers save tomato pollen from the summer flowers to use several months later on greenhouse plants. Carnation pollen will live for several weeks, sweet cherry pollen is viable for 28 days, nasturtium pollen for 88 days, while the pollen of some grasses dies in a day or two. The drier pollen is kept (within certain limitations), the longer it lives. Nasturtium pollen wetted for 2 minutes and then dried, remained alive for 2 days, as against 88 days for the unwetted sample, while sweet cherry pollen in 60 per cent humidity was viable for 25 days as against 126 days in moisture-free air. Shallow, sterilized dishes with covers are often used as pollen containers. Molds are great enemies of stored pollen. Storage is unnecessary where the plants to be crossed are both in bloom.

Pollen may be viable and it may even germinate on the "strange" pistil, but never produce a seed. In general the more closely related plants are, the more likely they are to successfully cross. Thus varieties within a species usually hybridize, but successful crosses between species of a genus are less certain; though in certain genera common (*Rosa, Salix, Gladiolus, Viola*); in others rare (*Lathyrus*). All our varieties of petunia are said to have come from crossing the two species, *Petunia violacea* and *Petunia axillaris*. Crosses between genera within a given family are still more problematical, although there are a sufficient number recorded to show there is a chance of securing them. Crosses between orchid genera are comparatively common, and many have a commercial value. Startling results were obtained from crossing a cabbage (*Brassica*) and a radish (*Raphanus*). As a rule, most profitable and practical results can be expected from crosses between species of a genus or between varieties of a species. See BIGENERIC HYBRID.

(5) In using the various devices against undesirable pollination, experiment is necessary, since what works with one may be quite unsuccessful in the case of another species. Paper and cellophane bags may involve too high a temperature, or in the case of paper bags, shut out too much light, thereby causing the flowers to wilt, dry up, or fall. Bags once used should not be used again.

(6) Labeling is usually done with marking tags — only cardboard types should be used — as the others peel when wetted. Besides the date, the tag should indicate the parents involved in the cross, the mother first — Baldwin × Jonathan — either names or numbers being used.

### CROSSING TECHNIQUE

The actual mechanics of crossing are simple, once one knows his material. It consists of transferring viable pollen from the flowers of the plant used as father to the receptive stigmatic surface of the flower to be used as the mother. There are many ways of doing this. In the sweet pea and the garden pea, the pistil somewhat reminds one of a miniature tooth brush — the brush end being the stigmatic surface. In crossing such plants, it is most convenient to collect on the stigma of the same flower pollen from the pollen sacs, and transfer it by rubbing the pollen-loaded, brush-like stigma on that of the flower to be crossed. In morning-glories and the four o'clocks the pollen grains are large enough to be handled singly with a small camel's hair brush or with tweezers. Camel's hair brushes are often used, but after each type of cross, if accurate knowledge of parentage is important, the brush should be cleansed in alcohol.

In hybridizing such plants as maize and conifers, pollen is collected in paper bags and these are placed over the female flowers, made tight, and shaken, raising within the bag a pollen dust storm. For day-blooming plants, the morning is, in general, the best time to pollinate. For night bloomers, early evening is the most practical. At these

---

* Special articles on the subjects indicated by an asterisk (*) will be found at the words so marked.

times, the stigmas are more likely to be receptive. Likewise the pollen is more plentiful and less spoiled, since the anthers or pollen sacs have just opened. Pollen should be taken only from protected flowers (bagged), since insects are great mixers of pollen. Some plants, such as avocados, are very definitely timed as to anther bursting and stigma receptiveness. — O. E. W. See PLANT BREEDING.

**CROSS-LEAVED HEATH** = *Erica tetralix*.

**CROSS-POLLINATION.** The act of transferring pollen from one flower to another on a different plant.

**CROSS-STERILITY.** When, under the most favorable environmental conditions, two normal plants of the same species cannot be crossed, they are said to be cross-sterile. They may belong to different varieties of this species, or they may be members of a segregating hybrid population, involving closely related species. Cross-sterility is widespread among cultivated plants, especially fruits. In Oregon, Napoleon, Lambert and Bing varieties of sweet cherries are all cross-sterile with each other. Theoretically, it is assumed that both cross- and self-sterility are due to the inability of the pollen to reach the ovary before the pistil dies. — O. E. W.

**CROSS-VINE** = *Bignonia capreolata*.

**CROSS-VINE FAMILY** = Bignoniaceae.

**CROSSWORT.** See CRUCIANELLA.

**CROTALARIA** (kro-ta-lay′ri-a). A genus of probably 250 species of herbs or shrubs of the pea family, largely tropical, but scattered also in the temperate zone, only two of any garden interest and these only in zones* 8 and 9. Leaves alternate,* consisting of only a single leaflet (thus appearing simple-leaved) in the two below. Flowers pea-like, yellow, showy, usually in handsome clusters (racemes*). Fruit a roundish pod, not pea-like, the seeds loose in it, hence the name rattlebox for most of the species. (*Crotalaria* is from the Greek for a rattle.)

The plants below are scarcely grown outside the warmer parts of Fla. and Calif., where they are sometimes offered as "yellow-flowering pea." The seeds germinate more easily if soaked in warm water for a few hours. They are valuable plants for green manuring in the South.

candicans. A medium-sized shrub, its many branches covered with brownish, silky hairs. Leaves oblongish or ovalish, 2–4 in. long, pointed at the tip. Flowers nearly 1 in. wide, the standard nearly round and silky. Pod 1½ in. long, swollen and a little hairy. India. In Fla. it is winter-blooming.

retusa. An annual herb 1–3 ft. high. Leaves 2–3 in. long, blunt, and broadest towards the tip, grayish-hairy. Flowers ¾–1 in. long, the standard yellow but variegated. Pod 1–1½ in. long, beaked. Indo-Malaya. Grown as an annual cover crop in Fla. and often escaping.

**CROTON.** There is a genus *Croton* of the spurge family, but it contains no garden plants. To all gardeners and to many others the word croton means handsome tropical foliage plants. They all belong to the genus *Codiaeum* (which see).

**CROWBERRY.** See EMPETRUM; for broom crowberry see COREMA.

**CROWBERRY FAMILY** = Empetraceae.

**CROWDED PLANTS.** Most garden plants suffer if too closely crowded — suffer from lack of light, air, water and plant food. The need for thinning is thus obvious. But a few annuals appear to bloom better and more profusely if left a bit crowded. For a list of such see ANNUALS.

**CROWFOOT.** See BUTTERCUP.

**CROWFOOT FAMILY** = Ranunculaceae.

**CROWN.** 1. That part of a plant between the root and the stem, usually at or near the ground level; often called the *collar* of a plant.

2. The whole upper foliage of a tree; its *canopy* in the forestry sense.

3. = Corona.*

**CROWN DAISY** = *Chrysanthemum coronarium*.

**CROWN-GALL.** See Bacteria at PLANT DISEASES; see also the diseases at ROSE, GRAPE, and RASPBERRY.

**CROWN GRAFTING.** See Bark Grafting at GRAFTING.

**CROWN IMPERIAL** = *Fritillaria imperialis*.

**CROWN-OF-THORNS** = *Euphorbia splendens*.

**CROWN ROT.** See Diseases at DELPHINIUM and IRIS.

**CROWN TUBER.** See PIP.

**CROWN VETCH** = *Coronilla varia*.

**CROWS.** See Bird Nuisances at BIRDS.

**CROW'S-TOES** = *Dentaria laciniata*.

**CRUCIANELLA** (kroo-si-a-nell′a). The crossworts are annual or perennial herbs of the family Rubiaceae, all Old World, only **C. stylosa** of secondary garden interest, and mostly confined to shady places in the rock garden. It is a prostrate annual, 6–9 in. high, the leaves in whorls of 8–9, generally lance-shaped and stiff-hairy. Flowers small, dark pink or rose-red, crowded in a dense, globe-shaped head about ½ in. in diameter, the corolla funnel-shaped. Fruit dry. (*Crucianella* is Latin for a little cross, in allusion to the arrangement of the leaves.)

*CRUCIATA, -us, -um* (kroo-si-ā′ta). Cross-like or cross-shaped.

**CRUCIFER.** Any plant of the mustard family. See CRUCIFERAE.

**CRUCIFERAE** (kroo-siff′er-ee), often called Brassicaceae, is a family of over 200 genera and perhaps 2000 species, nearly all herbs of wide distribution. It is commonly called the mustard, cabbage, cress, or radish family, but besides these and other important vegetables it contains many popular garden plants like candytuft, sweet alyssum, honesty, *Aethionema*, and the stocks.

Leaves prevailingly alternate,* often bitter but never poisonous, simple* or compound.* Flowers always (except in double-flowered forms) with 4 petals arranged cross-fashion (hence Cruciferae = cross-bearing), usually with a claw.* Fruit a dry pod, when long called a silique*; when as broad as long (as in honesty) called a silicle.*

The garden genera of the Cruciferae furnish many important vegetables and condiments. See HORSE-RADISH, CABBAGE, CAULIFLOWER, BROCCOLI, MUSTARD, BRUSSELS SPROUTS, TURNIP, KOHLRABI, RADISH, the genera BRASSICA and RORIPA (watercress).

Among the chief ornamental genera are: *Aethionema*, *Alyssum*, *Aubrietia*, *Cheiranthus*, *Hesperis*, *Iberis* (candytuft), *Lobularia* (see SWEET ALYSSUM), and *Mathiola*, some of which have been garden favorites for centuries. Lesser known and less ornamental genera include: *Arabis*, *Barbarea* (largely weedy), *Cardamine*, *Cochlearia*, *Dentaria*, *Draba*, *Erysimum*, *Heliophila*, *Hutchinsia*, *Ionopsidium*, *Isatis*, *Lepidium* (largely weedy), *Lesquerella*, *Malcomia*, *Peltaria*, *Ricotia*, *Schizopetalon*, *Stanleya*, and *Vesicaria*.

Of the three remaining garden genera two furnish minor vegetables or salad plants — *Crambe* (sea-kale) and *Eruca* (rocket salad). *Anastatica* (which see) includes an extraordinary little desert plant often called Rose-of-Jericho or resurrection plant.

Technical flower characters: Flowers small, usually very numerous in mostly unbranched clusters (racemes*). Sepals 4, soon withering. Petals 4. Stamens typically 6, four long and two short. Ovary superior,* developing into dry pods (siliques* or silicles*).

*CRUENTA, -us, -um* (kroo-en′ta). Blood-colored or bloody.

*CRUS-GALLI* (kruss-gal′li). A specific name implying that a plant or its organs are like a cock's spur.

*CRUX-ANDRAE* (krux-an′dree). A specific name implying that the plant is named for St. Andrew's-Cross.

**CRYOLITE.** See Stomach Poisons at INSECTICIDES.

**CRYOPHYTUM.** See MESEMBRYANTHEMUM.

**CRYPTANTHUS** (krip-tan′thus). Perhaps a dozen tree-perching, South American foliage plants of the family

---

* Special articles on the subjects indicated by an asterisk (*) will be found at the words so marked.

Bromeliaceae, two of which are very common greenhouse subjects. They have practically no stems and a basal rosette of stiff, spiny-margined leaves, in the center of which is nested the stalkless, dense head of white flowers. The outer segments of the flower are united into a tube, the inner ones free and usually narrowed at the base or with a claw.* Fruit dry but berry-like. (*Cryptanthus* is from the Greek for hidden flower.)

Both species, especially *C. zonatus*, are very common foliage plants, much grown by florists. They are best grown in the greenhouse in pots, baskets, or wooden cribs, allowing plenty of drainage. Use potting mixture* 3, to which one half its bulk of chopped fern fibers or coir should be added. During winter the plants need much less water than in spring and summer. The house should be kept between 55° and 65° in winter, but 10° above this when more active growth starts in March. They usually flower in summer under glass.

 **acaulis.** Leaves 6-12 in a basal rosette, 3-5 in. long, about 1 in. wide, the margins prominently wavy and finely toothed. Upper surface green, lower surface whitish and scurfy. Brazil. Sometimes sold as *C. undulatus*.

 **undulatus** = *Cryptanthus acaulis*.

 **zonatus.** Very similar to *C. acaulis*, but the leaves longer (5-9 in.), and with prominent white or brownish bands across the blades. Brazil. The most popular species in cult. because of its handsome variegation. Occasional plants of both species, when well grown, will show a pinkish tinge to the foliage.

**CRYPTOGAM, CRYPTOGAMOUS.** Literally meaning a hidden marriage, but as applied to plants meaning any that do not produce flowers or seeds in the ordinary garden sense of those terms. Cryptogams reproduce by spores (see FERNS AND FERN GARDENING). Common examples of cryptogamous plants are the ferns, club mosses, horsetails, and mushrooms. Nearly all plant diseases are caused by microscopic cryptogams. See PHANEROGAMS.

**CRYPTOGRAMMA** (krip-to-gram'ma). Mostly northern or alpine ferns of the family Polypodiaceae, comprising four species generally known as rock brakes. One, *C. acrostichoides*, the parsley-fern, is a native of northern N.A. and is sometimes grown in the fern garden or in the rock garden. It has a short, stout, chaffy rootstock, and two sorts of fronds — fertile and sterile. The latter are leaf-like, twice-divided or compound,* the ultimate segments rounded, more or less toothed. Fertile fronds longer than the leaf-like ones, similarly divided, but the ultimate segments very narrow, the spore* cases at or near the margin, which is rolled over and hides them before maturity. (*Cryptogramma* is from the Greek and implies hidden spore* cases.)

**CRYPTOMERIA** (krip-to-meer'ri-a). A single species of Japanese evergreen tree of the pine family, **C. japonica**, known as the Japan cedar or sugi. It is a magnificent, pyramidal tree up to 125 ft. in its native home and much used there for the planting of temple gardens and ceremonial avenues. Here it is much lower, hardy only up to zone* 4, and often failing there, and nearly always turning a bronzy color in winter, but becoming green the following season. Farther south it does much better. Bark reddish-brown and shreddy. Leaves small, awl-shaped, the tips always curved inward, more or less completely clothing the twigs, spirally arranged, and keeled. Cones nearly globe-shaped, about 1 in. in diameter, the scales wedge-shaped but pointed at the tip. (*Cryptomeria* is from the Greek for hidden and part; of uncertain application here.)

The tree is less particular as to soil than to climatic conditions. Near the sea-coasts and south of zone* 5 it grows well. It cannot be grown in regions of great summer heat and deficient rainfall, nor anywhere that has bitter winds and zero temperatures. In its proper climatic range a very stately evergreen. There are several important hort. varieties of *C. japonica*:

 var. **compacta.** A compact conical form with bluish-green leaves. About as hardy as the typical form.

 var. **dacrydioides.** A form having closely set, brownish leaves. Hardiness not certainly known.

 var. **elegans.** Densely branched, somewhat bushy form, not very long-lived, but useful for quick effects.

 var. **lobbi.** The commonest form in cult. in the U.S., not differing materially from the type, but apparently a little more hardy. Useful for the northern limits of *Cryptomeria* culture.

**CRYPTOSTEGIA** (krip-tō-stee'ji-a). Handsome woody vines of the milkweed family from tropical Africa and Madagascar, two of them grown for ornament in greenhouses or in the open in zones* 8 and 9, where they are very showy. They have opposite* leaves and a milky juice, and large, funnel-shaped flowers in 3-branched clusters (cymes*). Corolla with a short tube and a corona* of 5 scales attached to it, the stamens* forming a tube around the stigma.* Fruit an angled or winged pod (follicle*). (*Cryptostegia* is from the Greek for conceal and cover, in allusion to the corona.*)

Both species should be grown in the warm greenhouse, preferably planted out in rich, loamy soils rather than in pots. In southern Fla. they grow profusely in most ordinary garden soils. Propagated by cuttings, preferably in spring, over bottom-heat.* In Africa some species yield rubber, and those below do so in Fla., but not in commercial quantities.

 **grandiflora.** A sturdy, woody vine, not very high-climbing. Leaves oblongish, 3-4 in. long, thick, glossy, and without teeth. Flowers purplish, about 2 in. wide, the lobes of the corolla not divided. Tropical Africa.

 **madagascariensis.** Somewhat like the last, but the leaves are red-veined, the flowers pink or white, and the corolla lobes are divided. Madagascar.

*CRYSTALLINA, -us, -um* (kriss-tal-ly'na). Resembling crystals, or crystalline; *i.e.* transparent.

**CRYSTAL TEA** = *Ledum palustre*.

**CUBAN LILY** = *Scilla peruviana*.

**CUBAN ROYAL PALM** = *Roystonea regia*.

**CUBEB** = *Piper cubeba*.

**CUBEBA.** An obsolete generic name for plants now included in *Piper*.

**CUBIC MEASURE.** See WEIGHTS AND MEASURES, 2.

**CUCKOO-FLOWER** = *Cardamine pratensis*; also *Lychnis flos-cuculi*.

**CUCKOOPINT** = *Arum maculatum*.

**CUCULLARIA** (kew-kew-lay'ri-a). An obsolete generic name for a genus of plants scarcely in cult., signifying a hood, and used as a specific name for a *Dicentra*.

*CUCULLATA, -us, -um* (kew-kew-lay'ta). Hooded.

**CUCUMBER** (*Cucumis sativus*). Gardeners with limited space cannot afford to grow cucumbers which, for outdoor culture, must be planted in hills at intervals of at least 4½ ft. each way. (See below.) The plant is a sprawling, tendril-bearing vine. It requires considerable heat, a lot of moisture and a rich soil. Cucumbers are much more sensitive to frost than most vegetable crops. They can only be grown in regions that not only have plenty of heat but a frost-free period of 75-90 days. (See the name of your state for frost data.)

In some regions with insufficient heat cucumbers can be grown in hotbeds which have already been used for raising tomato or other tender plants. Put two vines under each sash and at first, on cool days and every night, put on the glass and, at night, a mat. When settled warm weather arrives, the sash is left off and the plants matured in the frame. This is often an ideal arrangement, for it utilizes the spent manure of the hotbed.

SOILS. Warm, sandy loam, especially if it has a gentle slope southward, is the best soil for outdoor cucumbers. No other method of fertilizing is so satisfactory as putting 2 forks of thoroughly rotted manure (horse or cow) under each hill, and a scant wheelbarrow load is better. Broadcasting manure or fertilizer, for plants spaced so far apart, is merely wasteful.

PLANTING. See that the manure is covered sufficiently so that no seed touches it. This is easily accomplished by forming a circular hill about a foot wide and 4 in. deep over each lot of buried manure, the site of which had better be marked with a stick, if some days intervene between burying it and planting time.

---

* Special articles on the subjects indicated by an asterisk (*) will be found at the words so marked.

Planting cannot be done until warm or hot weather is assured, a fair criterion for most regions being that catalpa blossoms are budding, or that Japanese iris are beginning to bloom.

Plant 6 seeds at each hill, expecting to reduce them to three as soon as germination is complete and it is possible to select the three best plants. The seeds should be planted about 1½ in. deep.

Commercial growers often take elaborate precautions to protect the young plants from cold or frost, which they feel forced to ignore in the race to produce the first cucumbers for the market. Most home growers need not bother with such methods, but if they do, any of the small, glass-covered, individual frames or boxes may be put over the young plants on cold days and every night until the vines become too long.

CULTIVATION. As the vines become large they will fill all the space between the hills which should never be less than 4 ft. apart each way, and many put them 5 ft. apart or even more.

This means that while the plants are young, cultivation must be very thorough or you will have a very weedy cucumber patch when it is no longer possible to get between the plants with implements. In the later stages this cannot be done at all, as the vines are very fleshy and easily injured. Hand weeding is the only sequel to early neglect of thorough, clean cultivation. Some, to avoid this trouble, grow the so-called bush cucumbers, but they are not so prolific as the ordinary sort.

VARIETIES. Cucumbers are grown mainly for two purposes: to slice and eat fresh or cooked, and for pickling. For slicing the larger-fruited varieties are used, of which the best are White Spine, Kirby, Early Fortune, and Davis Perfect. These should be from 5 to 9 in. long when harvested.

For pickling the small-fruited varieties like Chicago Pickling, Snow Pickling and National Pickling are the most favored. These are usually harvested when the fruits are from 1½–3 in. long. Some cucumber enthusiasts also pickle the large-fruited sorts cut into longitudinal sections.

Most families will be amply provided for by a dozen hills of ordinary cucumbers. The fruit is indigestible to some and almost a poison to others. It is a not very distant relative of a plant yielding an arrow poison in the Amazon. Growing pickling cucumbers is largely a commercial business.

For the preferred position and sequence of cucumbers in your garden see KITCHEN GARDEN.

INSECT PESTS. The striped cucumber beetle, black and yellow and about ⅓ in. long, feeds on and sometimes kills seedlings. The adults also bring disease to the plants, and lay eggs from which root-feeding larvae hatch; these larvae are seldom seen, but they do some damage. The beetles should be kept off with an arsenical dust or spray, applied several times while the plants are small. The spotted cucumber beetle, larvae of which feed on corn roots, attacks similarly, and may be controlled in the same way.

The melon aphid, a plant louse of varying shades of green, clusters in colonies under the leaves in summer, twisting and sapping them. The aphids may be killed with a spray of dust of nicotine, but it is hard to hit them all on tangled vines. It is better to spray or dust under the leaves before the vines begin to run, and later to watch for the first appearance of plant lice and destroy them before they spread to all the vines.

The melon worm and the related pickle worm attack cucumbers in the South and East (see MELON). Cucumbers are occasionally attacked by the squash bug, the squash ladybird, and the squash vine borer (see SQUASH).

DISEASES. The disease pathogenes* carried with the seed cause scab, anthracnose, leafblight, angular leafspot, and others. The seed treatment recommended is dipping the seeds in a corrosive sublimate solution (1 tablet for each pint of water) for five minutes, rinsing and drying. These same diseases, as well as downy and powdery mildews, stem canker, various leafspots, timber rot, and others occur in the field and may in part be controlled by spraying or dusting at weekly intervals. Care must be taken to get the fungicide on every leaf. Since the bacterium causing bacterial wilt lives over winter in the cucumber beetle, an insecticide must be added to the spray or dust. Cucurbits are very susceptible to spray or dust injury in hot weather. The mosaic or white pickle virus lives over winter in the seeds of wild or bur cucumbers and in the living roots of catnip, milkweed, and ground cherry. These weeds should be eradicated.

**CUCUMBER FAMILY.** All the squashes, melons, watermelon, pumpkin, gourds, and several ornamental vines belong to the cucumber family. All the cult. genera have creeping or climbing, herbaceous stems, bear tendrils, and have sometimes showy but rather ephemeral flowers. The fruit is always a modified berry known as a pepo.* For the cult. genera see CUCURBITACEAE.

**CUCUMBER MOSAIC.** See Diseases at SPINACH.

**CUCUMBER TREE** = *Magnolia acuminata*.

*CUCUMERIFOLIA*, *-us*, *-um* (kew-kew-mĕ-ri-fō′li-a). With cucumber-like leaves.

**CUCUMIS** (kew-kew′mis). A genus of probably 30 species of trailing or climbing vines of the cucumber family, mostly tropical African or Asian, two of them of outstanding garden interest as yielding the cucumber and all the melons (but not the watermelon). The cult. species are frost-tender, annual, tendril*-bearing vines with generally hairy stems and alternate,* usually large leaves. Male and female flowers on the same plant but in separate flowers, which are solitary, but not large as in the closely related pumpkins. Corolla more or less bell-shaped, yellow. Fruit fleshy, smooth or netted or ribbed in the melons, but with weak, fleshy prickles or tubercles in the cucumber. (*Cucumis* is Latin for some plant with a cucumber-like odor.) The tendrils* are not forked in these plants, but branched in the closely related watermelon (which see).

anguria. Bur Gherkin, also called West India Gherkin. A trailing vine with angled, rough-hairy stems. Leaves 1½–3 in. long, rough, 3-lobed, each lobe again lobed, the margins wavy and toothed. Flowers less than ½ in. wide. Fruit oval or oblongish, about 2 in. long, its stalks crooked, the skin furrowed and prickly. Southern U.S. to Brazil. While the fruit is called gherkin, the "gherkins" of most pickle mixtures are young cucumbers little known outside of the deep South.

melo. Melon. Here belong all the cultivated melons except the watermelon (which see). The vines are soft-hairy trailers, seldom climbing, the tendrils* not forked. Leaves roundish-oval, 3–5 in. wide, more or less angled on the margin but scarcely lobed, rough. Flowers about 1 in. wide, usually 1 in a leaf-axil.* Fruit the melon. Probably Central Asia. For an account of all the cult. varieties of the melon and how to grow them see MELON.

sativus. Cucumber. A trailing, rarely climbing, rough-hairy, annual vine. Leaves triangular-oval, 3–6 in. long, more or less angled or 3-lobed, the middle lobe pointed. Flowers 1–1½ in. wide, the male flowers often several to a leaf-axil,* very short-stalked. Fruit the familiar cucumber, which varies from nearly globe-shaped (rare) to the long-cylindric type forced in England. Here the fruit is, when mature, 3–9 in. long (3 ft. in England), always with minute, soft prickles. For culture and varieties see CUCUMBER.

**CUCURBITA** (kew-kur′bi-ta). Mostly tender, annual, trailing or climbing vines of the family Cucurbitaceae, comprising perhaps 10 species, the original home of some uncertain, but chiefly tropical. The genus includes the squash, pumpkin, and many ornamental gourds grown for interest (but *see also* GOURDS). They are mostly rough-hairy vines with forked tendrils,* and large leaves, often lobed. Flowers yellow, large, usually more or less bell-shaped, but lobed half way down the tube. Fruit a large berry of the sort known as a pepo,* smooth-skinned in some, deeply furrowed in others, and, in the various cult. varieties, of great variety as to form (see below). (*Cucurbita* is Latin for gourd.) The species are little understood.

For the culture of the ornamental gourds *see* GOURD. For culture of the squash and pumpkin, *see* those entries.

ficifolia. Malabar gourd. A running or climbing vine grown for ornament, its fruit inedible. Leaves nearly round or kidney-shaped, 7–10 in. wide, the margins wavy or lobed, more or less weakly prickle-toothed. Flower with spreading, large lobes, the tube funnel-shaped. Fruit roundish or oblong, 6–12 in. long, smooth, green, but white-striped, the seeds black. Eastern Asia.

foetidissima. Calabazilla; called also Missouri gourd and wild pumpkin. A perennial, native American, prostrate and long-running vine, with inedible fruit. Leaves triangular-heart-shaped, whitish beneath, finely toothed, long-stalked. Flowers 2½–4 in. long. Fruit smooth, orange-shaped, green and yellow-splashed. Mo. and Kan. to Calif. and Mex. A gourd for the South, but it often fails to ripen fruit in the North. Will stand much heat and a sandy soil.

maxima. Squash. Here belong the autumn and winter squashes, the well-known Hubbard squash, and, sometimes, very large squashes that pass for pumpkins. An annual vine, the stems prostrate, and not very rough or prickly. Leaves roundish or heart-shaped, blunt, but usually not lobed. Flowers yellow, the lobes recurved, or drooping, and soft, the tube bulging towards the base. Fruit very variable, spherical or oblong, sometimes immense, the top of its stalk not swollen. Seeds white. Origin unknown. For culture see SQUASH. The turban squash, sometimes called a "squash-within-a-squash," has turban-shaped fruit. It is the *var.* turbaniformis.

moschata. Canada crookneck squash; winter crookneck squash; cushaw. A soft-hairy annual vine, the leaves more or less limp, somewhat velvety, more or less broadly oval or roundish, usually not lobed, often

---

* Special articles on the subjects indicated by an asterisk (*) will be found at the words so marked.

white-blotched. Flowers large, the corolla lobes wide-spreading and crinkly. Fruit very variable, often crook-necked, the stalk distinctly bulged at the point of attachment. The fruits, often called pumpkins, are harvested for autumn and winter use. Origin unknown.

**pepo.** The common field pumpkin belongs here, but so does the vegetable marrow. A confusing species of harsh, annual, prostrate vines, with prickly stems and leafstalks. Leaves triangular-oval, usually prominently lobed, 6-12 in. long, and pointed at the tip. Flower large, the corolla lobes pointed, erect or spreading, not recurved. Fruit large, furrowed, usually orange, not keeping as in the winter squashes, the stalk enlarged at the point of attachment. Origin unknown. The *var. melopepo* includes the bush pumpkins or squashes, which are more or less compact plants without tendrils. The fruits are summer-maturing and include such well-known types as the Pattypan, scallop, and summer crookneck squash. The *var. ovifera* includes running vines producing hard-shelled, ornamental yellow gourds which are inedible but showy. For culture of the pumpkin, see PUMPKIN. For the squashes, see SQUASH.

**CUCURBITACEAE** (kew-kur-bi-tay'see-ee). The cucumber family is often called (with equal reason) the gourd, melon, or squash family. It comprises about 90 genera and perhaps 700 species of mostly tropical, generally fleshy-stemmed vines, all of which usually bear tendrils, except *Ecballium*.

Leaves alternate,* usually broad and simple,* but sometimes cut, or divided or even compound.* Flowers regular, often large and showy, but in some genera small, greenish and inconspicuous, funnel-shaped or with 5 separate petals. The fruit is large, fleshy and usually with a rind in *Citrullus* (see WATERMELON), *Cucumis, Benincasa, Cucurbita* (which contains the squash and pumpkin), *Luffa, Sechium, Lagenaria,* and *Sicana.* These genera contain all the important garden plants in the family, because they include the cucumber, gourds, melons, squash, pumpkin, and chayote.

Less well known, and with much smaller fruit, usually fleshy, are *Abobra, Bryonia, Coccinia, Cyclanthera, Ecballium* (the squirting cucumber), *Echinocystis, Melothria, Momordica,* and *Trichosanthes.* Most of these are cult. only for ornament. See VINES.

Technical flower characters: Plants with male and female organs mostly in separate flowers on the same plant. Corolla united and more or less funnel-shaped, or of 5 separate petals. Calyx joined to the 5-lobed ovary. Stamens 5, but with 2 pairs united, thus with apparently only 3 stamens.

**CUDWEED.** See GNAPHALIUM.

**CUJETE** (kew-yee'te). Brazilian vernacular name for the calabash (*Crescentia cujete*).

**CULINARY HERBS.** See HERB GARDENING.

**CULTIGEN.** A plant assumed to have originated in cultivation, and unknown as a wild plant. Cabbage and cauliflower are cultigens, as well as many other garden plants.

**CULTIVATION.** Like many other garden terms cultivation has a double meaning — the cultivation of a crop and the cultivation of the soil. This book is packed with notes on the cultivation of various crops, consequently this phase of cultivation will be ignored here.

Soil cultivation, however, is one of the most important of gardening operations. It is to be distinguished from those soil operations which usually precede planting, such as plowing, rolling, raking, harrowing, etc. Cultivation, as here treated, and as ordinarily understood by gardeners, means the cultivation or tillage of the soil while occupied by a crop and for its benefit.

BENEFITS. There are two main reasons for soil cultivation — to conserve moisture and keep down weeds. Both are important enough to warrant separate treatment.

The conservation of soil moisture makes certain dry areas of America possible as garden sites, and there is no garden that is not improved by cultivation with this as the chief object. Wherever practiced, it is based upon a purely physical characteristic of soils and soil water which every gardener should understand.

Soil water, or what soil scientists call the water table, usually lies a long way below the roots of most garden plants. Here lies the permanent water reservoir of the soil which only appears at the surface in pools, lakes, marshes, or bogs. In all other garden soils the water table is far below the surface and reaches the roots of plants only by capillarity. Water rises in soils just as it will rise if put at the base of a lump of sugar. On its way up to the surface this soil moisture is absorbed by the roots of whatever plants grow there, and the rest reaches the surface to be lost by evaporation.

Upon the continuity of this capillary water all plants, except aquatics, depend for their moisture supply. And upon the breaking of this capillarity depends the prevention of water loss by excessive evaporation at the surface. Cultivation does this more effectively than anything else, in the following manner:

DUST MULCH. Thoroughly pulverized surface soil is dried almost at once by the sun and wind. Even roughly cultivated soil dries out pretty rapidly. And in the process of drying it creates a dust mulch, which, depending on the type of soil and on how well you have done the job, will vary from one inch to several inches thick. Through this dusty upper layer, capillary water finds it very difficult to penetrate and escape into the air as water vapor. In other words, the dust mulch, if it does not completely stop the ascent of capillary water, stops so much of it that roots growing under a dust mulch have far more available water than without it. Upon this fact rests the whole theory and practice of cultivation. In other words, successful cultivation means the creation of an effective dust mulch. Weeds play no part in such a program, but in properly carrying it out, most weeds are necessarily destroyed. (See WEEDS AND WEEDING.)

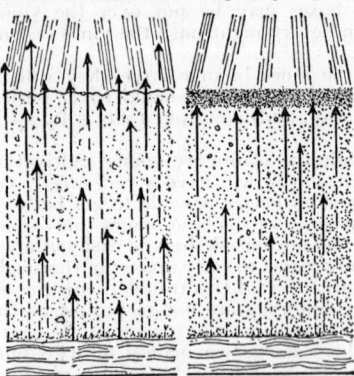

How the dust mulch (the black layer) prevents evaporation of soil moisture (*at the right*) and the water lost by evaporation without the dust mulch (*left*).

MAKING THE DUST MULCH. Various methods of cultivation (the creation of the dust mulch) are in vogue, depending upon the size of the soil particles, presence of stones, the weather, and the size of the area to be cultivated. For very small gardens with reasonably stone-free soil, any of a number of small hand cultivators are available at any seedsman's. The principle upon which all of them work is the same. Teeth, or spikes, or knives are so arranged that they scratch or scuffle up the surface soil, leaving it pulverized instead of in the normal packed or caked condition of untouched surface soil. A simple precaution is to so plan your work that cultivated soil is ahead (*i.e.* finished) and uncultivated soil is behind you. In other words, don't walk over freshly cultivated soil (*see below*).

The time to cultivate, because its object is the conservation of soil moisture, is after every good soaking rain. In heavy soils with much clay or silt this cannot be done at once or your implements will become mud-caked, and you can also do more harm than good by packing the soil into cement-like hardness. A good guide of when to start is to take a handful of soil and press it into as hard a cake as you can with one hand. Let the cake fall and if it breaks apart it is usually safe to begin. If the cake sticks together, it is better to wait a few hours or days.

Between rains there is less reason for cultivating, except to keep down any weeds that may not have been killed by the last cultivation. Some gardeners keep up cultivating, however, according to a schedule, regardless of when the last rain happened to come. They know that dew and wind may have slightly packed the old dust mulch, and to maintain its effectiveness they cultivate even an apparently dry soil. The theory is absolutely sound, and most good commercial growers follow it, but it means, of course, more time and labor. In periods of long drought, or in regions where

---

* Special articles on the subjects indicated by an asterisk (*) will be found at the words so marked.

rainfall is always deficient, these between-rain cultivations are imperative. There is, paradoxically enough, no better moisture conserver than dry surface soil. For other methods of conserving soil moisture see MULCH AND MULCHING.

DEPTH TO CULTIVATE. For most ordinary garden soils a dust mulch of one inch is sufficient. For some deep-rooted crops and with machine cultivators in operation, the upper layer of dusty soil will be thicker — up to 3 or 4 inches. The depth is far less important than the thoroughness of pulverization — dusty, not lumpy, soil is what is needed.

EQUIPMENT. The illustrations at TOOLS show the best and simplest types of hand cultivators. For all small gardens, tubs, cold frames, and hotbeds, they are the most convenient and effective. Next in simplicity and for larger-scale operations are the different types of long-handled hoes. The ordinary draw hoe you can use only by drawing it toward you, a disadvantage in cultivating overcome by the scuffle hoe which you use by pushing it away from the operator.

For vegetables or anything else planted in rows, the most effective tool is a single-wheel cultivator to which are fitted various blades that scuffle up the soil and cut weeds at the same time. Its easiest method of operation is to push it ahead of you and this has the disadvantage that you are constantly walking over the soil just cultivated. Some operators, to avoid this, work backwards. They cultivate by a few thrusts of the knives forward and backward, and then walk backwards, repeating the operation. This is more tedious, but at the end of the row you have walked on no cultivated soil. If this seems a needless precaution, it is well to remember that your footprints destroy the dust mulch by partially restoring capillarity, and that you may firm down an uprooted weed just enough to let it get a fresh start.

In using any type of wheel cultivator, whether man- or power-driven, it is necessary to be very careful about fleshy-rooted crops, which are easily injured by tools. The rows must be straight and spaced for whichever type of cultivator you use. In large gardens with motor-driven tractor cultivators such as one sees on farms, the rows must have been spaced for them. To most home gardeners the loss of planting space, in order to accommodate such cultivators, precludes their use. See Section 1, TOOLS AND IMPLEMENTS.

*CULTRIFORMIS, -e* (kul-tree-for'mis). Knife-shaped.

**CULVER'S-ROOT** = *Veronica virginica.*

**CUMIN** = *Cuminum cyminum.*

**CUMINUM** (kew-my'num). A single species of annual herb of the carrot family, **C. cyminum,** the cumin, a native of the Mediterranean region, long cult. for its aromatic fruit. (See HERB GARDENING.) It is a delicate little herb, scarcely 6 in. high, the leaves dissected into thread-like segments. Flowers very small (for details see UMBELLIFERAE), in compound umbels,* usually white, rarely pinkish. Fruits dry, bristly, scarcely ¼ in. long, aromatic. June. (*Cuminum* is the old Greek word for this plant.)

**CUMMIN** = Cumin.

*CUNEATA, -us, -um* (kew-nee-ā'ta). Cuneate; *i.e.* wedge-shaped, usually with the narrow end downward.

*CUNEIFOLIA, -us, -um* (kew-nee-i-fō'li-a). With wedge-shaped leaves.

**CUNILA** (kew-ny'la). An unimportant genus of 16 species of aromatic, American herbs of the mint family, one cult. for ornament in the border or wild garden, but of secondary garden interest. The only cult. species is **C. origanoides,** the stone mint or Maryland dittany. It is a perennial herb about 12 in. high and branching. Leaves opposite,* nearly stalkless, ovalish, toothed, about 1 in. long, and dotted with aromatic oil-glands. Flowers small, irregular* and 2-lipped* (for details see LABIATAE), purplish-pink, crowded in small whorls* which are variously scattered in clusters. Aug. Coastal N.Y. to Ohio and Fla. (*Cunila* is Greek for some mint.)

**CUNNINGHAMIA** (kun-ning-ham'i-a). Two Asiatic evergreen trees of the pine family, the one below cult. for ornament from zone* 6 southward, possibly also in protected places in zone* 5. The only cult. species is **C. lanceolata,** the China fir, which is sometimes offered as *C. sinensis.* It is a noble evergreen up to 75 ft. high, with brownish outer, and reddish inner bark, the branches spreading and inclined to droop at the ends. Leaves crowded, narrow, about 2 in. long, broad at the base, but sharply pointed at the tip, green above, and with 2 white bands beneath. Cones nearly round, about 2 in. long, persisting after the shedding of the seeds, 3 of which are at each scale. The tree resembles *Araucaria* in habit. (Named for J. Cunningham, British explorer in Asia.)

**CUP-AND-SAUCER.** See CAMPANULA MEDIUM.

**CUP-AND-SAUCER VINE** = *Cobaea scandens.*

**CUPANIA** (kew-pay'nee-a). A genus of 30 species of tropical trees and shrubs, family Sapindaceae, one occasionally planted for ornament in zones* 8 and 9, and of secondary garden interest. The only cult. species is an Australian tree, which they call brush deal, otherwise **C. anacardioides.** It is about 40 ft. high and has compound* leaves, the 6–10 leaflets arranged feather-fashion, without an odd one at the end, broadly oval, 3–4 in. long and without marginal teeth. Flowers small, white (for details see SAPINDACEAE), arranged in loose clusters (panicles*). Fruit a leathery capsule,* nearly ⅔ in. wide, almost stalkless and somewhat 3-lobed. (Named for Francis Cupani, Italian botanist and monk.)

**CUPFLOWER.** See NIEREMBERGIA.

**CUPHEA** (kew'fee-a). An immense group of chiefly tropical American herbs or shrubs of the family Lythraceae. Of over 200 species only 3 are of any garden interest, and they are mostly greenhouse plants grown for their attractive flowers. They are also, but rarely, grown outdoors in zones* 8 and 9. Leaves opposite* or crowded. Flowers irregular,* the calyx* tubular and corolla*-like, often exceeding the 6 unequal petals, sometimes swollen and pouch-like, or curved at the base. In one species there are no petals. Stamens generally 11. Fruit a capsule,* enclosed by the persistent calyx.* (*Cuphea* is from the Greek for curved, in reference to the curved calyx* of some species.)

The cigar-flower is a popular greenhouse plant considerably cult. by florists. It and the others need a cool or warm-temperate greenhouse and potting mixture* 3. They are of easy cult. and best propagated by cuttings, or by seeds, from which blooming plants may be had in one season.

**hyssopifolia.** A much-branched, hairy, small shrub. Leaves crowded, very narrow, usually less than ½ in. long, stalkless. Flowers numerous, stalked in the leaf-axils,* scarcely ¼ in. long, violet-white, the calyx* tube straight. Mex. and Guatemala.

**ignea** = *Cuphea platycentra.*

**micropetala.** An erect, little-branched shrub 1–2 ft. high. Leaves stalked, oblongish, 2–5 in. long. Flowers in a long, leafy, terminal cluster (raceme*). Calyx* tubular, about 1 in. long, yellowish, but scarlet at the base, longer than the petals, but shorter than the protruding red stamens.* Mex.

**platycentra.** Cigar-flower. A popular pot plant, often used for summer bedding. It is a shrub (but may be grown as a tender annual) 8–15 in. high. Leaves lance-shaped, 1–2½ in. long. Flowers solitary, slender-stalked and chiefly in the leaf-axils.* Calyx tube about ¾ in. long, spurred at the base, red but with a darker ring near the tip and an ash-white mouth; petals none. Mex. Often sold as *C. ignea.*

**CUPID'S-DART** = *Catananche caerulea.*

**CUP-PLANT** = *Silphium perfoliatum.*

*CUPREA, -us, -um* (kew'pree-a). Coppery.

*CUPREATA, -us, -um* (kew-pree-ā'ta). Copper-colored.

*CUPRESSIFOLIA, -us, -um* (kew-pres-si-fō'li-a). With cypress-like leaves.

*CUPRESSIFORMIS, -e* (kew-pres-si-for'mis). Resembling the cypress (*Cupressus*).

*CUPRESSINA, -us, -um* (kew-pres-sy'na). Cypress-like.

*CUPRESSOIDES* (kew-pres-soy'deez; but see OÏDES). Resembling the cypress (*Cupressus*).

---

* Special articles on the subjects indicated by an asterisk (*) will be found at the words so marked.

**CUPRESSUS** (kew-pres'sus). Magnificent evergreen trees of the pine family (the true cypress), mostly from the warmer parts of the Old World, a few from western N.A., most unfortunately not hardy over great stretches of the U.S. Of the 12 known species, half are in common cult. over most of the warmer sections of the world. They have aromatic foliage and the branchlets are densely clothed with small, usually 4-angled leaves that are pressed against the twigs. The very small leaves are opposite,* scale-like. Sometimes, on young plants or shoots, the leaves are longer and spreading, otherwise they hug the twigs. Cones nearly globe-shaped, composed of 6-12 woody scales, often nearly prickly at the scale-tip, at each scale many narrowly winged, flattish seeds. (*Cupressus* is the classical name of the Italian cypress.)

Outdoor culture of those below is only possible in the indicated zone* or south of it. The trees are closely related to *Chamaecyparis*. See EVERGREENS.

**arizonica.** Arizona cypress. An evergreen tree up to 40 ft., its foliage pale bluish-green. Leaves thick, keeled, pointed and resinous. Cones about 1 in. in diameter, bluish-green. Ariz. Hardy from zone* 6 southward, and particularly good for exposed places and for windbreaks.*

**funebris.** Mourning cypress and much planted in cemeteries along the Mediterranean. A beautiful tree up to 60 ft. high, its main branches drooping. Twigs flattened, the leaves sharp-pointed, light green. Cones about ½ in. in diameter. China. Hardy from zone* 7 southward.

**lusitanica.** Portuguese cypress. Both the Latin and common names of this Mexican tree are misleading, but it was long thought to be native in Portugal. Tall tree (40-60 ft.), its main branches drooping. Leaves sharp-pointed, bluish-green. Cones about ½ in. in diameter, with a bloom. Hardy from zone* 7 southward.

**macnabiana.** Macnab cypress, also called white cedar and Shasta cypress. A bushy tree up to 35 ft., usually less, often with several stems, its branches very slender. Leaves dark green, blunt, resinous. Cone about 1 in. in diameter. Ore. and Calif. Hardy from sheltered places in zone* 4 southward. The hardiest of all the cypresses. There is a variety with yellow twigs.

**macrocarpa.** Monterey cypress. A tree up to 75 ft. high, broad and spreading in age, pyramidal in youth. Leaves blunt or 4-sided (rhomboid*), dark green. Cones nearly 1½ in. in diameter. Calif., south of Monterey. Hardy from zone* 6 southward. There are several hort. varieties, one with the young foliage yellow.

**sempervirens.** Italian cypress, and the cypress of history. A tree up to 75 ft., its branches erect or horizontal. Branchlets or twigs flattened, the leaves dark green, blunt, 4-sided (rhomboid*). Cones nearly 1½ in. in diameter. Southern Eu. and southwestern As. Hardy from zone* 6 southward. The var. **horizontalis** has branches that spread out in a flat plane. The var. **stricta**, a common form in cult., has a columnar habit.

**CUPRO-JABONITE.** A trademarked fungicidal dust, containing 18-20% metallic copper, sold with directions for use.

*CURAGUA* (kew-rah'gwa). Chilean name for a kind of popcorn. See CORN.

*CURASSAVICA, -us, -um* (cure-ras-săv'i-ka). From Curaçao, West Indies.

*CURCAS* (kur'kaz). Pre-Linnaean* name for the purging-nut (*Jatropha curcas*).

**CURCULIGO** (kur-kew-ly'go). Perhaps a dozen species of greenhouse herbs of the family Amaryllidaceae, one a well-known foliage plant needing a warm, moist greenhouse, never much below 75° and potting mixture* 4. The only cult. species, C. **capitulata** (formerly known as *C. recurvata*), a native of tropical Asia and Aust., is a stemless herb which makes a cluster of handsome foliage. Leaves all basal, 1-3 ft. long, the blade plaited like a fan, recurved, 1-3 ft. long, 2-6 in. wide, the stalk channeled. Flowers yellow, nearly ¾ in. wide, borne on short, recurved stalks, the cluster near the ground level and half hidden by the foliage. (For details see AMARYLLIDACEAE.) Fruit somewhat fleshy. (*Curculigo* is from Latin for a weevil, in allusion to the beaked ovary.)

**CURCULIO.** See Insect Pests at ROSE.

**CURCUMA** (kur-kew'ma). A genus of about 50 species of aromatic, perennial herbs of the family Zingiberaceae, all from the tropics of the Old World, two sometimes cult. for interest here, but the turmeric widely grown in India. They are ginger-like herbs with thick rootstocks, and stout leafy stems, the leaves generally large, lance-shaped, and sheathing at the base. In many cult. plants there is no stem, the leaves arising at the ground level. Flowers in a dense, bracted* spike, two irregular* flowers at each bract,* the top of the spike with a cluster of large, colored bracts. Corolla funnel-shaped, its summit 2-lipped.* Some of the stamens* are sterile and petal-like. Fruit a spherical, 3-valved capsule. (*Curcuma* is a Latinized version of an Arabic name for the turmeric.)

These plants need a warm (70°-80°) greenhouse and moist air as well as plenty of moisture at their roots. Use potting mixture* 4. Little grown outdoors and only possible in zone* 9. In the Far East turmeric is widely grown as an ingredient of curry powder.

**longa.** Turmeric. Rootstock stout and the source of turmeric. Leaves oblongish to lance-shaped, 12-18 in. long, 4-8 in. wide, the sheathing stalk about as long. Flower spike 4-7 in. long, nearly 2 in. thick, the stalk from within the leaf-sheaths. Flowers pale yellow. India.

**petiolata.** Smaller in all its parts than *C. longa*, the leaves rounded at the base. Flowers yellowish-white, the tuft of bracts* at the end of the spike purple. Eastern Asia.

**CURD.** The edible and often whitish flower head of plants like cauliflower and broccoli. It is, of course, a much modified and monstrous form of flower cluster.

**CURDWORT** = *Galium verum*.

**CURING.** Few vegetables need curing in the sense that sweet potatoes must be cured to be kept. The process involves the introduction of heat, the forcing out of excess moisture and provision for the elimination of the latter as water vapor rather than its accumulation on the walls of the curing room. For the details of curing see SWEET POTATO.

**CURLED DOCK** = *Rumex crispus*. See the list at WEEDS.

**CURLED MALLOW** = *Malva crispa* and *M. verticillata*.

**CURLY CLEMATIS** = *Clematis crispa*.

**CURLY-GRASS** = *Schizaea pusilla*.

**CURLY PALM** = *Howea belmoreana*.

**CURLY TOP.** See Diseases at BEET.

**CURRANT** (*Ribes*). The red currant is a modern fruit, its domestication having taken place within the last three or four hundred years in several widely separated regions and from at least three species. All red currants are natives of cool, moist climates and their culture is restricted to northern latitudes and regions where summer rainfall is fairly copious. Currants do not thrive in the gulf states and grow but poorly under the dry, hot summers of the plains states.

Any gardener can propagate currant plants easily, but nurserymen grow them so cheaply that home propagation is seldom worth while. In home propagation hard-wood cuttings are taken in the autumn after leaves have dropped. Customarily they are 8 or 10 in. long and are planted at once 6 in. apart in nursery rows. Or they may be tied in bundles and stored, butts up, in moist sand and held until early spring. The cuttings are grown in nursery rows two seasons.

Currants are very hardy and may be grown north of fruit-tree latitudes without fear of injury. A cool, moist, well-drained loam or clay, even a stiff clay, are the most suitable soils for currants. Light soils and southern exposures are unsuitable. In the South and the prairie states the shade of buildings or trees sometimes makes currant-growing possible.

The plants are best when set in the fall, as plants often open their buds in the spring before the ground can be made ready for planting. In the North, at least, a furrow should be plowed up to the newly set rows to prevent heaving. Distances apart vary with the soil and the variety. Strong-growing varieties need a distance of 6 × 6 ft.; for weaker-growing sorts, 5 × 5 ft. suffice. A plantation lasts for many years.

Cultivation should be shallow since currant roots are surface feeders. In home gardens and small plantations, mulching with grass or straw may take the place of cultivation. Stable manure will furnish both a mulch and a fertilizer. Currants need organic matter and cover crops of barley, buckwheat, or oats, crops which do not live through the

---

* Special articles on the subjects indicated by an asterisk (*) will be found at the words so marked.

winter, should be turned under in the fall. Several experiments seem to show that currants do not make a satisfactory response to chemical fertilizers.

Pruning is simple but very necessary. The aim in pruning should be to maintain an abundant supply of young wood, since the currant bears fruit on the base of one-year canes and on spurs of older wood. All canes over three years old should be cut out as well as very weak ones and those that sprawl on the ground. Usually there should be 6 or 8 strong canes, according to the vigor of the bush. Heading back is a poor practice, since it makes the bark too dense. Pruning is best done in early winter.

Currants are most used for jelly and for this purpose must be picked before fully ripe. The berries should be dry when picked and should not be stripped from the cluster stem. Ripe currants hang on the bushes for several weeks, to be picked in a moment for the table. Currants are sold in quart baskets packed in 32-quart crates, or in 12-quart Climax baskets.

The culture of black currants does not differ from that of red currants except that the plants require more room. The cultivation of black currants is forbidden in some states because the bush is a host plant to the pine blister rust.

Five red currants may be recommended. Cherry is an early sort with very large, dark red berries. Diploma is one of the handsomest and best in quality. Fay is a standard midseason variety. Perfection is an early midseason currant liked best of all for table use. Wilder is the best commercial variety because of its vigorous, productive, long-lived bush. White Imperial and White Grape are the best white currants. Naples is the best black. One thrives as well as another in plant zones* 1, 2, 3, 4, and 5 and 6 in the Pacific states. — U. P. H. Dried "currants" are usually the dried fruits of the Black Corinth grape. See *vinifera* varieties at GRAPE.

INSECT PESTS. San Jose scale is a severe pest of currant, and is occasionally found on gooseberry. Dormant-strength oil or lime-sulphur sprays applied early in the spring will check it. The spotted green larvae of the currant sawfly eat leaves rapidly. They are easily controlled with arsenicals or, if the fruit is on, with hellebore spray. The currant aphid and sometimes other plant lice are often injurious; they can be killed by nicotine, but it should be applied early, before the leaves are twisted. The currant borer, the larva of a clear-winged moth, bores in canes; it may be controlled by removing and burning sickly canes in the spring. Both adults and nymphs of the four-lined plant bug (adults about ⅓ in. long), injure leaves by sucking. A strong nicotine spray or dust will reduce their numbers.

DISEASES. Leafspots, anthracnose, cane blight, European rust, American powdery mildew, root-rot and silver-leaf, are some of the more important diseases on currants and gooseberries. Most of these diseases may not only defoliate the plants and cause a reduction in yield, but may so weaken the bushes that root-rots and winter-injury later can kill them. The plants should be inspected at regular intervals and all diseased or dead wood removed and burned; the rows should be far enough apart and clean enough from weeds to permit good aeration. Spraying at two-week intervals with lime-sulphur, 1-50, or spray with bordeaux mixture, 3-3-50, or dusting with sulphur is recommended. Some English varieties are susceptible to spray injury, so that a wettable form of sulphur is preferable to other sprays. (For pine blister rust, see PINE.)

**CURRANT TOMATO** = *Lycopersicum pimpinellifolium*. See TOMATO.

**CURUBA** = *Sicana odorifera*.

**CURVIFOLIA**, *-us, -um* (kur-vi-fō'li-a). With curved leaves.

**CUSHAW** = *Cucurbita moschata*.

**CUSH-CUSH** = *Dioscorea trifida*.

**CUSHION PINK** = *Silene acaulis*.

**CUSHION PLANT.** See TUFTED.

**CUSHION SPURGE** = *Euphorbia epithymoides*.

**CUSPIDATA**, *-us, -um* (kus-pi-day'ta). Having a sharp, stiff point (cusp).

**CUSTARD-APPLE.** In the Central States, *Asimina triloba*; in Fla. and the tropics, *Annona reticulata*.

**CUSTARD-APPLE FAMILY** = Annonaceae.

**CUT-AND-COME-AGAIN.** See *Helianthus annuus* at SUNFLOWER.

**CUT FLOWERS.** No one needs to have a list of the common florist's offering of cut flowers. They are shown with the greatest profusion during the changing seasons and one never need be without flowers from this source.

For the home gardener, however, nothing quite replaces the things he can raise himself, and if properly planned, the flower garden will yield a supply for all months including winter. Not all garden flowers, however, keep well when cut. Some wilt too soon, and others never should be picked at all for they seem more at home on the plant than you can ever make them in the house.

Annuals are always the best source of cut flowers, for they can be raised like vegetables, in rows, if large quantities are needed. Those best suited to picking, their colors, and the times to expect their bloom, are all designated in the list at ANNUALS.

Among perennial garden flowers the following have proved the most satisfactory for cutting. Notes on the culture and best varieties of each are scattered throughout the DICTIONARY and should be consulted for these details. The names in the list are the same as those under which they are entered in the DICTIONARY:

| | | |
|---|---|---|
| Achillea | Foxglove | Milkweed |
| Anchusa | Galega | Mignonette |
| Anemone | Gypsophila | Monkshood |
| Boltonia | Helenium | Peony |
| Campanula | Hemerocallis | Phlox |
| Candytuft | Heuchera | Platycodon |
| Chrysanthemum | Iris | Poppy (some sorts) |
| Columbine | Kniphofia | Rudbeckia |
| Coreopsis | Limonium | Scabiosa |
| Dahlia | Lilium | Snapdragon |
| Delphinium | Lupinus | Sweet Alyssum |
| Dianthus | Marigold | Sweet Pea |
| Forget-me-not | | |

There are some annuals in certain of the plants listed above, but many more good ones will be found in the list at ANNUALS.

To annuals and perennials should be added the bulbous plants like tulip, hyacinth, and, for summer, the gladiolus. Less well known bulbous plants, many of them suited for cutting, will be found at BULBS.

Cut flowers should be cut, not torn off the plant. Make a clean cut with a good, stout pair of shears, never leaving the stems out of water for more than a few minutes and it is far better to plunge them at once in a pail of water. More flowers wilt in consequence of the first few minutes of neglect than one would ordinarily expect. Cutting, after all, is a shock, and it should be done early in the morning or late in the afternoon, never at midday nor in a wind. And carry your treasures into the shade of a tree or indoors as soon as possible.

While most cut-flower stalks are best plunged immediately into cold water, it is better to put dahlias, heliotrope, poinsettias, and oriental poppies in water of about 170° at once, after which they may be put in water of room temperature. Also do not submerge any more leaves than is necessary, for they soon decay and induce wilting. Aspirin, salt, sugar, and various other chemicals are useless in spite of newspaper notices to the contrary. A commercial preparation known as Bloom-Food has some adherents. Each day the ends of flower stalks should be cut, under water, as the old end tends to heal and cut off water entrance.

What you do with cut flowers is a reflection of your taste in color, form, and arrangement. No one can dictate that to you, but the main principles of it are well known. See FLOWER ARRANGING. See also CLOTH.

**CUTLEAF BEECH** = *Fagus sylvatica laciniata*. See BEECH.

**CUTLEAF BLACKBERRY** = *Rubus laciniatus*.

**CUTTAGE.** The making and care of cuttings (which see).

**CUTTING BENCH.** A bench in a greenhouse for rooting cuttings. It is ordinarily sand-filled, is often covered with a frame and sash, and sometimes provided with bottom-heat.*

**CUTTING GARDEN.** For a list of the 1000 plants which will provide, from outdoor material, flowers for every month in the year, see GARDEN CALENDAR.

---

* Special articles on the subjects indicated by an asterisk (*) will be found at the words so marked.

**CUTTING-GRAFTAGE.** *See* GRAFTING.

**CUTTING ROT.** *See* Diseases at COLEUS and PELARGONIUM.

**CUTTINGS.** A cutting is a piece of a plant without roots but used to produce roots after it has been severed from the parent plant. Layers, suckers, etc., already have roots when they are cut off. The term *slip* applies to softwood cuttings because the side-shoots of which they frequently consist are sometimes pulled or slipped off the main stem without the use of a knife.

### ADVANTAGES OF PROPAGATING BY CUTTINGS

Propagation by cuttings is a cheap and convenient way to increase a stock of plants. Sizeable plants are usually much more quickly obtained in this manner than from seeds. Besides, many garden varieties and hybrids vary greatly if raised from seeds, while from cuttings one is sure to obtain a very uniform set of plants which resemble the parent plant in every way. Certain plants, also, do not readily produce seeds in cultivation or, as is the case for instance with willows and poplars, are rather difficult to propagate from seeds.

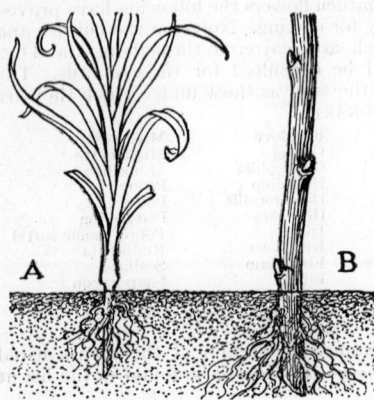

A softwood cutting (A) and a hardwood cutting (B)

Skilled propagators claim that there is no plant which cannot be propagated from cuttings. This, unquestionably, is true, but certain plants, notably most of our fruit trees, grow so much better and are so easy to propagate from buds or grafts that with them these latter methods are to be preferred.

### TYPES OF CUTTINGS

We can distinguish between the following types of cuttings:

a. Stem cuttings, consisting of parts of the stem, to be divided into:
  1. Softwood or green cuttings, taken from the plant while it is in leaf and growth, thus providing half-ripened wood.
  2. Hardwood cuttings, taken from the leafless, dormant plant, after it has finished and ripened its yearly growth.
  3. Single eye cuttings, consisting of only one bud or eye with not more than a part of the stem attached.
b. Leaf cuttings, consisting only of a leaf, with or without its stalk.
c. Root or rootstock cuttings.

### SOFTWOOD CUTTINGS

Easiest and most frequently used is the softwood cutting. For best results, cuttings of this type should be taken when the plant is at a certain intermediate stage of growth — that is, when the cuttings are neither too soft and succulent nor too mature. If the young shoots, when bent, neither snap off like glass nor crush without breaking, they are in the right condition to use. For only a few plants does this rule not hold true. Lilacs and azaleas, for example, have been found to root most readily when the cuttings are very soft, while others, like varieties of *Weigela* and *Hydrangea*, give better results if the cuttings are almost mature. June to August are the months in which outdoor plants may be propagated in this manner. Softwood cuttings of greenhouse or bedding plants are usually taken in the early spring.

The shoot chosen for a cutting must be healthy and in good condition and must show the characteristics which are typical for the variety we wish to propagate. The most vigorous shoots, however, never make the best cuttings. The best results are usually obtained with side-shoots of intermediate strength, and if these are cut directly at their base, they will root most readily. The frequently recommended "heel," a small slice of the main stem left on the base of the side-shoot cutting, is with many plants more a hindrance than a help. Only with certain hollow-stemmed alpines has the heel been found to be of definite advantage.

With certain plants not all side-shoots make equally desirable cuttings. On carnations, for instance, only the side-shoots from the center of the stem make flowering plants of good habit.

With roses, cuttings of side-shoots — so-called flowering wood — give earlier and more free-flowering plants than do tip cuttings, so-called blind wood.

If small side-shoots are not available, we have to use the tips of longer shoots, and with them we find that usually the cuttings root best if the basal cut is made from ¼ to ½ inch below a leaf or a pair of leaves, as the case may be, since it is from the part of the stem below the node* that roots are most likely to arise. The old and long-accepted rule that all cuttings should be cut at a node,* that is, directly below a leaf, has been disproved by recent extensive experiments. Only a few of our hardy shrubs, such as box, *Caragana*, *Clethra*, *Cotoneaster*, *Kolkwitzia*, *Laburnum*, *Photinia* and *Pyracantha*, give decidedly better results if the cut is made at a node. The weigelas and some of the privets root most readily if the cut is made slightly above a node,* leaving a long internode beneath the first pair of leaves.

An important point with softwood cuttings is that they must be put into the cutting bench as soon as they are cut and before they have had a chance to wilt. To put cuttings in a pail of water in order to keep them fresh, however, is a mistake, since the water has an undesirable effect on the cut surface, preventing the formation of a protective fatty layer for which the oxygen of the air is necessary, and rendering the cutting susceptible to rot. Cuttings which are collected outdoors may be wrapped in a moist cloth and in this manner be kept fresh for an hour or two.

Also, in the future treatment of the cuttings it is absolutely essential that they never be allowed to wilt. Frequent sprinkling — on hot days several times during the day — is necessary. On the cutting bench in the greenhouse the cuttings may be covered with cheesecloth over which the sprinkling may take place until callus has been formed. The cutting bench must have bottom-heat* and should have a temperature of 60°–65° F. The electrically heated frame, now obtainable in the trade at a reasonable price, will be found a great help by the amateur who does not have a greenhouse. (*See* COLD FRAME.)

The *best medium* in which to root cuttings is a mixture of sand and peat in equal parts, surfaced with about a quarter-inch of pure sand. There are only a few plants which root better in pure sand, like *Euonymus* and *Magnolia*, while pure peat is a rather unsatisfactory medium, since it provides poor aeration. The surface of the rooting medium is smoothed and is gently but not too firmly pressed down. Then the cuttings are inserted in rows, so far apart that their leaves barely touch. Their lowermost leaves may be cut off, if they interfere. It is advisable not to use a dibble in putting in the cuttings, since this may easily leave an air space beneath the cutting, which is a serious disadvantage.

Taking the cutting between three fingers of one hand, a slight downward pressure will be sufficient for inserting it in the rooting medium deeply enough to make it stand upright, though never more than half its length. After all cuttings are in place, the rooting medium is settled firmly around them by a thorough soaking with water. This is better than to firm it down with the fingers or with a piece of wood.

### A SIMPLE AID IN PROPAGATION

The amateur without a greenhouse will find the following simple arrangement effective for small amounts of cuttings:

In a seedpan (6–7 in. diam.) a smaller pot (2½–3 in. diam.) with closed drainage hole is inserted. The drainage hole of the seedpan must be kept open. The space between the two pots holds the rooting medium (peat and sand).

---

* Special articles on the subjects indicated by an asterisk (*) will be found at the words so marked.

The cuttings are inserted close to the rim of the inner pot, which is kept filled with water. Since the moisture seeps slowly through the pores of the pot, no direct watering of the cuttings is necessary. A large bell-jar* covering the seedpan will prevent wilting of the cuttings. It must be shaded if set in a sunny window.

After the cuttings have formed callus* it is advisable on warm days to put a small block of wood under one side of the bell-jar to permit a change of air. The root development of the cuttings can easily be watched by taking out the center pot from time to time with a twisting movement which prevents disturbance of the soil.

### HARDWOOD CUTTINGS

One advantage of hardwood over greenwood cuttings is that they are much easier to handle, being less perishable, and may even be shipped safely over great distances. Many hardy deciduous shrubs can be propagated in this manner, and, though various ways of handling are advocated, the following is probably the simplest and most effective.

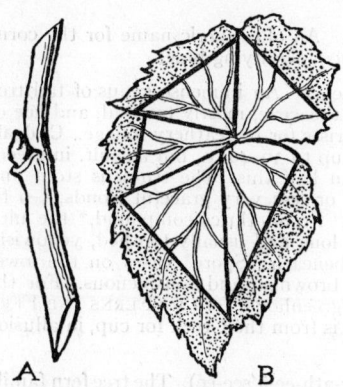

A single-eye woody cutting (A) and a leaf cutting of begonia (B). The dark lines on the inset enlargement of the veins show where they should be cut to induce new plants to sprout. See BEGONIA.

The mature shoots of last season's growth are collected as soon as the leaves have fallen, usually in October or November, and are cut up into sticks 6–10 in. long. The cut on the lower end should be just below a node. Tied in small bundles, they are set upright in trenches about 1 foot deep, preferably in a cold frame.* The trenches then are filled with sand to not more than 1 inch above the tips of the cuttings. There they are left to form callus. In the spring they may either be rooted in the cutting bench in the greenhouse or lined out in beds outside, where they must be buried to the uppermost pair of buds and planted 4–6 in. apart. *Deutzia*, *Forsythia*, privet, *Lonicera*, mock-orange, *Populus*, *Ribes*, willow, spireas, and other shrubs may be propagated in this manner.

CONIFER CUTTINGS are also taken from the mature wood, November being the best time for them. Short side-shoots, cut at the very base, or with a small heel,* are usually most successful. They may be rooted in the cutting bench or in small quantities in the double-pot arrangement mentioned under softwood cuttings. The rooting medium and general treatment are also the same as mentioned there. *Cephalotaxus*, *Chamaecyparis*, *Juniperus*, *Taxus* and *Thuya* are readily rooted in this manner, though some of them, in particular *Juniperus* and some of the *Chamaecyparis*, may take a whole year before they produce roots. Excessive callus formation to which they are inclined hinders the production of roots. If this is observed, it is advisable to pare off the callus with a sharp knife. Spruces and pines are difficult to root from cuttings mainly because of the resin which is exuded at the cut surface and which hinders callus and root formation. This may be overcome by dipping the lower ends of the cuttings for a few minutes in fairly hot water (130°–150° F.) before they are inserted in the cutting bed.

Broad-leaved evergreens, like *Aucuba*, box, *Daphne*, *Euonymus*, *Osmanthus*, *Phillyrea*, *Stranvaesia*, *Vinca*, heathers, holly, ivy, etc., are readily rooted in the same manner. Their cuttings, however, should be taken just at the end of the growing season, and before they are fully mature. Towards the end of August they are usually in the most favorable condition.

### BUD CUTTINGS

Bud cuttings, consisting of only one single bud with a part of the stem, are employed particularly with grapes.

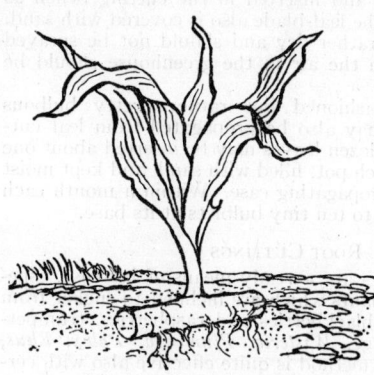

A stem cutting of dracaena

In November the budsticks are collected and cut up into single eye pieces, about ½ in. above and ½ in. below the eye. The stem is then split lengthwise through the center and the halved stems with the eye up and the cut surface downward are placed in boxes filled with peat and sand.

The cuttings are pressed only lightly into the rooting medium and covered thinly with pure sand until only the eyes show. Sphagnum moss is then spread over the sand to the thickness of 1 inch and the box, covered with a pane of glass, is stored for at least 6–8 weeks in a cool greenhouse or cellar to form callus. After that the box is removed to a warmer place to induce root formation.

LEAFBUD CUTTINGS may be used for quick increase of dahlias, but this is done in the spring from shoots which have been forced from the tubers in the greenhouse in February. In this case the leafstalk and at least half of the leaf-blade form part of the cutting besides the bud, and usually only a small slice of the stem is left at the base. Cotyledons are also propagated in this manner, and pelargoniums and various other plants may be so propagated in an emergency.

### LEAF CUTTINGS

Propagation by leaf cuttings is widely practiced, especially with *Begonia rex*. Large, well-matured leaves are selected, and are cut off with or without a small part of the stalk. The principal veins are cut on the underside in a few places and the leaf is placed flat on the sand bed in a warm propagating house, and weighted down with sand or small pebbles. If carefully shaded, young plants will develop from each incision.

Other begonias are usually propagated from leaf cuttings in November or December. Healthy, well-matured leaves are cut off with their stalks and the stalks are inserted in the sand bed to about half their length. With these begonias the leaf-blade must not rest on the bed and the individual leaves must be

Cuttings growing in a flower pot in which another pot is sunk and kept filled with water. This is the easiest way of rooting cuttings in the house, as it keeps the cuttings moist but not wet.

spaced in such a manner that they do not touch each other, or they will start to rot. The danger of damping-off* may be further reduced by sprinkling charcoal dust over the sand of the cutting bed. A temperature of 70 degrees is required for best results.

---

* Special articles on the subjects indicated by an asterisk (*) will be found at the words so marked.

Gloxinias and saintpaulias and other members of the same family (Gesneriaceae) are frequently propagated from leaf cuttings, but gloxinias only if one particularly fine form is to be perpetuated. In their case the leaf is cut with about one inch of its stalk and inserted in the cutting bench so that a small part of the leaf-blade also is covered with sand. They must be kept rather dry and should not be sprayed with water, although the air in the greenhouse should be always moist.

Lachenalias, old-fashioned but rather pretty bulbous greenhouse plants, may also be propagated from leaf cuttings. About half a dozen leaves may be inserted about one inch deep in a five-inch pot, filled with sand, and kept moist and shaded in the propagating case. Within a month each one will produce five to ten tiny bublets at its base.

### ROOT CUTTINGS

Pieces of true roots are a ready means of increase, especially for all those plants which are inclined to sucker from their roots, such as blackberries and raspberries, trumpet-creeper, Osage orange, *Wisteria*, *Plumbago*, *Phlox*, *Rhus*, *Ailanthus*, etc. This method is quite effective also with certain other trees and shrubs from which stem cuttings do not root readily, for example: *Acanthopanax*, *Crataegus*, *Gymnocladus*, locust, *Sophora*, *Xanthoceras*, etc.

The roots are dug up in the autumn, as soon as the leaves have fallen, cut into 1–3-inch pieces and stored in boxes in moist sand either in the cold frame or in a cold but frost-proof cellar. The root cuttings of those varieties which are slow to respond to this treatment have to be brought into the greenhouse in February, where with gentle bottom-heat they may be induced to form buds. All others may be lined out in beds in the spring, the distance depending on the variety, but far enough apart to allow the young plants to develop. Plant them horizontally about 2 in. deep.

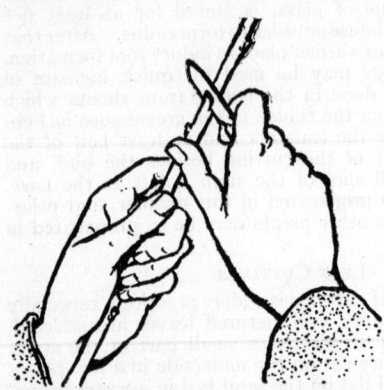
A clean, slanting cut with a sharp knife is best for making slips or cuttings.

The creeping rootstocks of many perennials may also be used for propagation. During the resting period of the plant, which with the spring-flowering plants usually is in midsummer, the rootstocks are dug up and cut into small pieces (¼ inch long will do in most cases), and are stored in sand in a cool place. Their further treatment is like that of root cuttings.

### THE AID OF CHEMICALS

Treatment with potassium permanganate has been found to be very helpful with certain slow-rooting cuttings, by inhibiting excessive callus* growth, preventing damping-off, and hastening the formation of roots. With softwood cuttings it is most effective, if the rooting medium is soaked 24 hours prior to the insertion of the cuttings with a solution of 1 ounce of potassium permanganate to 5 gallons of water at the rate of 2 quarts per square foot of surface. Evergreen cuttings or mature wood cuttings may be immersed with their lower ends to a depth of about 1½ in. in a slightly stronger solution of potassium permanganate and left to soak for about 24 hours. They are then placed in the cutting bench without rinsing.

To increase the acidity of the rooting medium by adding three teaspoonfuls of ordinary white vinegar to each gallon of water with which the cutting bed is watered, is sometimes recommended, but is apparently of small if any consequence.

The use of ordinary cane-sugar water to wet down the rooting medium, while it has some adherents, does little good, and often induces decay rather than rooting. — H. T.

**CUTWORM.** See Moths at INSECT PESTS. For control see Stomach Poisons at INSECTICIDES; also the Insect Pests at TOMATO, BLUEBERRY, and FLAX.

**CYANEGG.** A trademarked sodium cyanide preparation, sold with directions, for fumigating.

**CYANOCLADA, -us, -um** (sy-an-ok′la-da). Blue-twigged.

**CYANOGAS.** A trademarked insecticidal powder containing not less than 40% calcium cyanide, and useful for fumigating against ants, rats, moles, and other burrowing pests.

**CYANUS** (sy-an′us). An old generic name for the cornflower (*Centaurea cyanus*), signifying blue.

**CYATHEA** (sy-ăth′ee-a). An immense genus of tall tree ferns of the family Cyatheaceae, mostly tropical, and one of them much cult. by florists for its feathery foliage. C. dealbata grows in N. Zeal. up to 30–40 ft., but as cult. in greenhouses usually less than half this. The trunk is stout and crowned with a dozen or less very graceful fronds, 5–9 ft. long and 2–4 ft. wide. Frond thrice-compound,* the ultimate segments 2–4 in. long and usually toothed, yellowish-green above, whitish beneath. Spore* cases on the lower surface of the fronds, brownish and conspicuous. For the cult. of this handsome greenhouse fern see FERNS AND FERN GARDENING. (*Cyathea* is from the Greek for cup, in allusion to the spore* cases.)

**CYATHEACEAE** (sy-ath-ee-ā′see-ee). The tree fern family includes, among garden plants, only 4 genera of arborescent ferns of great beauty, cult. only in greenhouses or in the most sheltered parts of zone* 9. All of its 7 genera and over 300 species are plants of moist, warm, or hot tropical forests. For their culture see FERNS AND FERN GARDENING.

The leaves (fronds) are often of great size, being twice- or thrice-compound,* and the ultimate segments often deeply cut or lobed, the foliage thus being of great beauty and of feathery texture. The leafstalk is often smooth or polished, but in some genera prickly. The minute technicalities that separate *Alsophila*, *Cibotium*, *Cyathea*, and *Dicksonia*, the only hort. genera, and Cyatheaceae from the Polypodiaceae are quite outside usual garden practice and may be left to the experts. Some of the tree ferns which, in cult. specimens, do not have much of a trunk (but often 60 ft. high in the tropics), are widely grown by florists.

**CYCAD.** Any plant of the family Cycadaceae.

**CYCADACEAE** (sy-ka-day′see-ee). The cycas or sago palm family, geologically very ancient, has only 9 existing genera and perhaps 75 species of woody, fern-like or palm-like plants that once nearly covered the earth. They are, however, quite unlike ferns in bearing cones and seeds. The only cult. genera are *Cycas* (which contains the common, and funereal, sago palm), *Macrozamia*, which is confined to Australia, and *Zamia* which is American and includes the coontie. All are of greenhouse cult. or planted outdoors only in zones* 8 and 9.

They are ornamental, evergreen plants with a trunk or trunk-like base, compound,* usually leathery leaves that, in opening, uncoil like a fern frond. The leaves are usually borne in a crown or rosette* at the top of the trunk, and are often very handsome (notably in the sago palm, *Cycas revoluta*).

Technical characters: Plants gymnospermous,* the male and female flowers usually borne naked between the scales of a cone-like structure that mostly arises in the center of the rosette of leaves. Fruit fleshy.

**CYCAS** (sy′kas). A group of fern-like or palm-like plants of the family Cycadaceae, comprising only 16 species, chiefly from Asia and Australasia. Two of them are widely cult. greenhouse plants and grown outdoors in Fla. and Calif.

---
* Special articles on the subjects indicated by an asterisk (*) will be found at the words so marked.

They have a stout, unbranched, but not very tall, trunk-like stem and a large crown of frond-like leaves, for which they are mostly cult. Leaves long and stiffish, divided feather-fashion into innumerable rigid, often pointed segments which have no veins but the midrib. Male and female flowers on different plants, neither with any petals, but crowded in cone-like structures between the scales of which are borne the naked male and female organs of reproduction. (*Cycas* is from the Greek for some palm tree, which these are not.)

The second species is more widely grown for funeral wreaths than any plant in America, its crossed fronds tied with a ribbon being nearly universal. Both need a warm, moist greenhouse (65°–75°) and plenty of water. Use potting mixture* 3. Young plants do not have a trunk, but old ones have trunks of considerable height, mostly concealed beneath the persistent bases of the old leaves. Propagated by suckers which should be detached when dormant, that is between the periods when the plant is forcing out a new crop of leaves, all of which appear at once, often in May–June when planted outdoors, but forced at will by the florists.

**circinalis.** Palm-like, the trunk 10–12 ft. Leaves in a terminal crown, 5–8 ft. long, the stalk spiny at the base. Ultimate leaf segments alternate,* 10–12 in. long, the margins flat. Male cone nearly 2 ft. long and 5 in. in diameter (rarely produced in cult.). Tropical Africa to the islands of the Pacific.

**revoluta.** This, the commonest cycad in cult., is universally called sago palm in spite of the fact that it does not produce commercial sago nor is it a palm. It is palm-like, with a trunk 6–10 ft. high. Leaves in a terminal crown, 2–7 ft. long, somewhat arching at the tip, glossy-green, the ultimate segments numerous, crowded, stiff, spine-tipped, 3–5 in. long and with rolled margins. Male cone 18–20 in. long. Java or Japan. Common as a specimen plant in sub-tropical gardens and hardier than *C. circinalis*. See above for its use for funeral wreaths.

**CYCAS FAMILY** = Cycadaceae.

**CYCLAMEN** (sy'kla-men, also sick'la-men). About 20 species of tuberous, stemless, perennial herbs of the family Primulaceae, mostly from central and southern Eu., one a very popular florists' pot plant, grown for its handsome flowers. Leaves all basal, long-stalked, the blade roundish or kidney-shaped. Flowers solitary on each stalk, which is less than 12 in. high. Calyx with 5 divisions. Corolla with a very short tube, the 5 lobes much longer, contorted, and with strongly recurved tips. Fruit a 5-valved capsule* splitting from the top downward. (*Cyclamen* is the classical name for these plants.)

For culture *see* below.

**coum.** A perennial herb resembling *C. indicum*, but hardy. Leaves nearly round, or kidney-shaped. Flowers smaller than in *C. indicum*, purple-spotted and odorless. Southeastern Eu. Spring.

**hederaefolium** = *Cyclamen indicum*.

**indicum.** The common cyclamen of the shops. A stemless herb, the leaves roundish-heart-shaped, 2½–3 in. wide, the margins with rounded teeth. Flower stalk 6–8 in. high, the flower about 2 in. wide, white or rose, dark purple at the mouth (much variation exists in some of the hort. varieties). Greece to Syria. Blooming in early spring where grown outdoors, but winter-flowering as grown under glass by florists. There are many forms in cult. One has flowers nearly twice the normal size. Others have double flowers and some have the petals crested or shredded.

**neapolitanum.** A late summer-blooming perennial herb with large, black-skinned tubers. Leaves roundish or eared, wavy-margined. Flowers pink or rarely white, the petals twisted. Southern and eastern Eu.

**persicum** = *Cyclamen indicum*.

## Cyclamen Culture

*Cyclamen indicum*, the common cyclamen of the florists, needs a greenhouse for best results. The other species can be grown as hardy perennials, being suited especially to the rock garden or shaded borders. They are generally hardy up to zone* 3, and need good garden loam and moisture.

*Cyclamen coum* is a spring-bloomer, while *C. neapolitanum* blooms in the late summer or early fall.

The common cyclamen of the florists needs rather special attention. For good bloom the plants should be started from seed, allowing 18 months from that time until they are ready to flower. Seeds should be sown in flats in July or August, in potting mixture* 2, and the young seedlings transferred to other flats with potting mixture* 3 when large enough to move. Only on the last move should the plants be transferred to pots. They need plenty of water, but will rot if the drainage is not good. Keep the greenhouse about 55° during the period of active growth, and do not allow the plants to be shaded in winter either by trees outside, or by a wash on the greenhouse glass. During the summer the glass should be shaded.

Just before the blooming period the temperature should be reduced to 45°–50°, to prevent too short a flowering period, which is likely to happen if the temperature is too high. Cyclamens are occasionally raised from seed in cold frames and brought to maturity as house plants.

INSECT PESTS. Greenhouse cyclamen is injured by little mites which cause weak, twisted growth. Uninfested stock should be obtained, and empty greenhouses should be well fumigated before planting. Immersing infested plants in water at 110° F. for 15 minutes will give control. Black vine weevils (*see* CAMELLIA) and thrips (*see* CARNATION) are also occasional pests.

**CYCLAMEN POT.** *See* FLOWER POTS.

**CYCLANTHACEAE.** *See* CARLUDOVICA.

**CYCLANTHERA** (sy-klan'theer-ra). A group of over 30 species of chiefly tropical American vines of the cucumber family, *C. pedata* being the only one of much garden interest. It is an herbaceous vine grown as an annual and reaches up to 10 ft. or beyond. Leaves alternate,* compound* or nearly so, the 5–7 segments or leaflets arranged feather-fashion, lobed or toothed. Flowers small and inconspicuous, the male and female separate, but on the same plant, greenish-white. (For details *see* CUCURBITACEAE.) Fruit oblongish, about 2 in. long, short-stalked, its yellowish-white husk covered with soft prickles. The vine grows quickly and soon covers fences or a lattice screen. (*Cyclanthera* is from Greek for circle and anther, in allusion to a stamen character.)

**CYCLOPHORUS** (sy-klof'for-us). Mostly tropical Indo-Malayan ferns of the family Polypodiaceae, of the 75 known species **C. lingua**, the tongue-fern or Japanese fern, commonly grown in greenhouses. It has slender, shaggy rootstocks from which arise many undivided fronds that are lance-shaped, 5–6 in. long, half of which is stalk. The under side of the frond is rusty-colored, and often almost completely covered with the conspicuous, circular spore* cases. There is a form with the tip of the frond crested,* and another with variegated fronds. For culture *see* FERNS AND FERN GARDENING. (*Cyclophorus* is from Greek for circle-bearing, in reference to the shape of the spore cases.) It is sometimes known as felt-fern.

**CYDISTA** (sy-dis'ta). A single species of tropical American, woody vine of the family Bignoniaceae, related to the trumpet-creeper, and grown in the far South for its showy flowers. The only species, **C. aequinoctialis**, is a tendril-bearing vine with opposite,* compound* leaves composed of only 2 leaflets and a terminal tendril.* Leaflets leathery, wavy-margined, 4–6 in. long. Flowers in racemes,* the corolla funnel- or trumpet-shaped, nearly 3 in. long, white or purplish. Fruit a slender pod 9–12 in. long. It is a popular vine in Fla. but little known and not hardy much north of it. (*Cydista* is from the Greek for most glorious, in reference to the beautiful flowers.)

**CYDONIA.** *See* QUINCE. For the flowering quince *see* CHAENOMELES.

**CYLINDRICA, -us, -um** (sil-lin'dri-ka). Cylindrical.

**CYMBALARIA** (sim-ba-lay'ri-a). A genus of 10 species of generally prostrate, Old World herbs of the family Scrophulariaceae, one very common as a greenhouse vine or in hanging baskets, the other two less grown. They have herbaceous stems and alternate* or opposite* leaves, sometimes lobed and veined finger-fashion. Flowers solitary in the leaf-axils,* irregular* and spurred, usually small, the throat nearly closed. Stamens 4. Fruit a small capsule, shedding its seeds through small pores. (*Cymbalaria* is from the Greek for cymbal, in allusion to the leaf-shape of some species.)

All those below are often listed as of the genus *Linaria*.

The Kenilworth ivy is a popular, widely grown plant for hanging baskets and for small trellises in the living room, conditions it withstands very well. It is almost weedy under many greenhouse benches. While a perennial, it often persists as a self-sown escape outdoors. The other two are

---

* Special articles on the subjects indicated by an asterisk (*) will be found at the words so marked.

chiefly plants for the cool greenhouse, or outdoors in the South, or in the rock garden.

**aequitriloba.** Creeping perennial herb, the leaves opposite,* 3–5-lobed or unlobed. Flowers small, pale mauve, the top of the corolla reddish-purple. Southern Eu. *See* ROCK GARDEN.

**hepaticaefolia.** Prostrate, the leaves usually opposite,* slightly 3–5-lobed or unlobed. Flowers nearly ½ in. long, lilac-blue, the upper part of the corolla yellowish inside. Corsica.

**muralis.** Kenilworth ivy; called also Coliseum ivy and climbing sailor. A creeping vine easily rooting at the joints. Leaves generally alternate,* roundish or kidney-shaped, more or less shallowly 3–7-angled or lobed. Flowers about ⅓ in. long, lilac-blue, the upper part of the corolla yellowish inside. Eu. Sometimes persisting or naturalized outdoors in eastern N.A. There are white and pink-flowered varieties and one with larger flowers. A useful vine for hanging baskets or window boxes, never growing more than 3 ft. or so.

**CYMBIDIUM** (sim-bid'i-um). Nearly 50 species of handsome, tree-perching (epiphytic*) orchids of the Old World tropics, many grown by orchid fanciers, and one rather generally in greenhouses. The commonly cult. species, **C. lowianum,** has a compressed, oblongish pseudobulb,* from which arise narrow, sharp, curved leaves 2–3 ft. long, which are usually persistent. Flowers very showy in an arching cluster (raceme*) that may have 20 blooms. Flowers 3–4 in. wide, the sepals and petals alike, greenish-yellow with brown or reddish streaks. Lip* yellowish-tan on the side lobes, the front lobe maroon with a yellow margin. Burma. For culture *see* Epiphytes at the culture of greenhouse ORCHIDS. (*Cymbidium* is from the Greek for boat, in allusion to the shape of the lip.*)

***CYMBIFORMIS, -e*** (sim-bi-for'mis). Boat-shaped.

**CYMBOPOGON** (sim-bo-pō'gon). Tropical Old World, mostly perennial grasses, often aromatic, of the 40 known species the three below grown for their fragrant oil, or rarely for ornament. Here they are little known, but they are the source in India of perfumes and drugs. They have grass-like leaves and flowers in twin spikelets, the spikelets grouped in a branched, often hairy, cluster (panicle*). Sometimes the spikelets are awned.* (*Cymbopogon* is Greek for boat and beard, in reference to the spikelets.)

The three below can be grown outdoors only in the warmest parts of the U.S. They are scarcely cult. otherwise.

**citratus.** Lemon grass. Differs from *C. nardus* chiefly in technical characters of the spikelets and in the lemon-scented foliage. Origin unknown, but cult. in India for centuries.

**nardus.** Citronella grass, its roots and herbage the source of citronella oil. A perennial grass 4–6 ft. high. Leaves 2–3 ft. long, about ¾ in. wide, bluish-green. Flower cluster 1½–2½ ft. long, usually branched. Tropical As., but naturalized in tropical America.

**schoenanthus.** Camel hay or camel grass. Resembling *C. nardus*, but rarely over 2 ft. high. Foliage very fragrant. Joints of the flowering cluster hairy. Southern As. and northern Af.

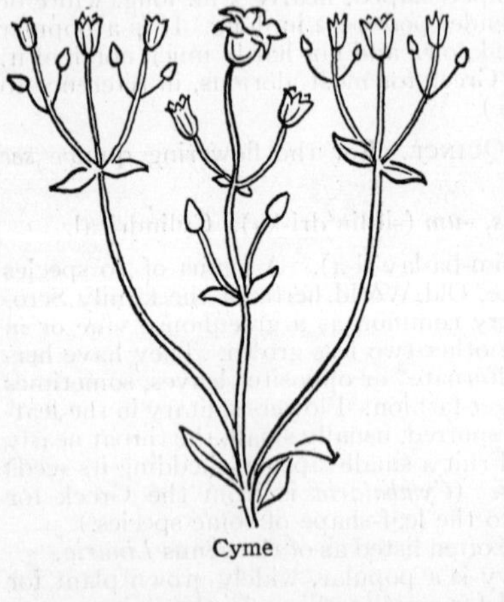
Cyme

**CYME** (syme). A broad, often flat-topped, branching flower cluster that blooms from the center towards the edges, and in which the main stalk or axis is always terminated by a flower. Typical examples are many plants of the pink and gentian families. Such clusters are said to be cymose.

***CYMINUM*** (sym-my'num). A variant spelling of *Cuminum*, the cumin.

***CYMOSA, -us, -um*** (sy-mō'sa). Cymose; *see* CYME.

***CYNANCHOIDES*** (sy-nan-choy'deez; but *see* OÏDES). Resembling the mosquito-trap (*Cynanchum*).

**CYNANCHUM** (sy-nan'chum). A genus of Old World perennial herbs of the milkweed family, one of them, **C. acuminatifolium,** known as the mosquito-trap or mosquito-plant, and of easy cult. in any ordinary garden soil. It is a Japanese herb, often somewhat vine-like at the tip. Leaves opposite,* arrow-shaped, grayish and hairy on the under side. Flowers whitish, sometimes entrapping small insects. (*See* ASCLEPIADACEAE.) Fruits resembling the common milkweeds. The plant is sometimes known as *Vincetoxicum acuminatum*, and is of only secondary garden interest. (*Cynanchum* is from the Greek for dog-strangling, of remote application here.)

**CYNARA** (sin'a-ra). Perhaps a dozen coarse, thistle-like herbs of the family Compositae, mostly from the Mediterranean region, two of them yielding garden vegetables. Leaves large, more or less lobed or cut or both, sometimes spiny, in one of them with thickened, edible leafstalks. Flowers in large, dense heads, one of which terminates most of the larger branches. Flowers all tubular and disk* flowers, there being no rays. Below and surrounding each head is a cluster of bracts* in many series (much modified in the artichoke), spiny-tipped in the cardoon. (*Cynara* is from the Greek, implying that the spiny bracts are like a dog's tooth.)

**cardunculus.** Cardoon. Stout perennial up to 6 ft. high. Root and thickened leafstalks edible. Leaves large, very deeply cut, grayish-green above, but white-felty beneath, densely spiny. Flower heads with spiny-tipped bracts,* the flowers purple. Southern Eu. For culture *see* CARDOON.

**scolymus.** Artichoke (for Jerusalem artichoke *see* SUNFLOWER). Shorter than the last, the leaves not so, or not at all, spiny. Flower heads with the bracts* much modified, broad-based and compactly crowded upon the much swollen receptacle,* which, together, yield the vegetable. Supposed to be derived from the cardoon. For culture *see* ARTICHOKE.

**CYNODON** (sin'o-don). A small genus of perennial grasses of the Old World, of no garden significance except in the far South where **C. dactylon,** the Bermuda grass (called also scutch grass and Bahama grass), will make a lawn where many other grasses cannot live. It has a creeping rootstock which spreads rapidly in dry and sandy soils. Leaves short and flat, mostly near the base of the stems, which rise 3–16 in. high. There are also many leaves arising directly from the rootstocks. Flower cluster of flattened spikelets, without an awn,* arranged somewhat finger-fashion. A useful, but sometimes a weedy grass in warm regions, much planted in Fla. (*Cynodon* is from Greek for dog-tooth, perhaps in allusion to the teeth-like sheaths on the runners.)

**CYNOGLOSSUM** (sin-o-gloss'um). A genus of 75 species of widely scattered herbs of the family Boraginaceae, most of them pretty weedy, but the two below often grown in the flower garden for their blue, purple, or pink flowers. They have alternate,* undivided, often roughish leaves, and small flowers in often arching, always one-sided clusters (racemes*). Corolla funnel-shaped, its limb with 5 rounded lobes. Fruit a collection of small, minutely prickly nutlets. The wild plants are commonly called hound's-tongue, and some of the species are occasionally credited to the genus *Omphalodes*. (*Cynoglossum* is from the Greek for hound and tongue, in allusion to the roughish leaves.)

*Cynoglossum grande* is a perennial of easy culture in any ordinary garden soil, and is propagated by division in spring or fall. The first species is the more desirable garden plant, and, while a biennial, will bloom from seed the first year and is usually grown as a hardy annual. *See* ANNUALS.

**amabile.** Chinese forget-me-not. Biennial, but grown as an annual, 18–24 in. high. Leaves oblongish or narrower, 2–3 in. long, rough. Flowers about ⅓ in. long, in a relatively showy cluster, usually blue, but a pink form is known. Eastern As. Blooms from July 1 to Oct.

**grande.** Perennial, 2–3 ft. high, the leaves mostly basal and ovalish. Flowers nearly ½ in. long, blue or purple, but the center white. Pacific Coast of U.S. Not much grown in the East.

**CYPERACEAE** (sy-per-ray'see-ee; also sip'er-ray-see-ee). The sedge family comprises 85 genera and over 2500 species of grass-like plants, differing from true grasses in technical characters, and, usually, in the more easily recognized triangular, solid stem, instead of a hollow round one. They are found throughout the world, usually in moist places.

The only cult. genera are *Carex*, *Cyperus*, and *Scirpus*,

* Special articles on the subjects indicated by an asterisk (*) will be found at the words so marked.

all of minor garden importance, although *Cyperus papyrus*, often grown in aquaria, is the paper-making papyrus of the Egyptians. Sometimes *Eriophorum* is grown in the bog garden.

The flowers are small, green, inconspicuous, and crowded in usually tightly bracted* spikes. Like the grasses they are wind-pollinated. Fruit a tiny, dry, usually 3-sided achene.*

**CYPERUS** (sy-peer'us). An enormous genus, with perhaps 600 species of grass-like herbs, of the family Cyperaceae, only three of any garden interest. The cult. species are of very different origin and aspect. *C. alternifolius* and *C. papyrus* are tall-stemmed, practically aquatic sedges suited to greenhouse pools or pots, while *C. esculentus* is a dry-land, hardy perennial that bears edible tubers. Flowers inconspicuous, borne in crowded spikelets, these often arranged in large, branching clusters. (*Cyperus* is the old Greek word for these sedges.) The species, especially the chufa, are often called galingale.

**alternifolius.** Umbrella plant. A common pot plant, but requiring much moisture at its roots. It usually has several stems from a mass of roots. Stems slender, 2-4 ft. high, essentially leafless but having brownish sheaths. At the top of each stem is an umbrella-shaped cluster of leaves, from which the flower spikelets arise. Africa. Widely grown in greenhouses and easily propagated by detaching the leaf-crown, which, in moist sand, will send up a new plant from most of the axils.* The var. **gracilis** has shorter terminal leaves (2-3 in. long), and the var. **variegatus** has white-margined foliage.

**esculentus.** Chufa; called also earthnut and earth almond. A common sedge of sandy places over most of the north temperate zone. It is a perennial 2-3 ft. high, rising from an edible rootstock, pieces of which are planted in spring for harvesting in the fall. Leaves mostly at the ends of the stem and in a crown-like cluster just below the nearly stalkless spikelets. More cult. in Eu. than here.

**papyrus.** The papyrus of the Egyptians from which they made paper. An aquatic sedge, the stems 6-8 ft. high, essentially leafless but clothed with sheaths. Terminal cluster of flower spikelets umbel*-like, with 50-100 drooping rays that are thread-like, 12-18 in. long, and longer than the leaves beneath them. Southern Eu. and Northern Af. A striking plant for greenhouse pools, supposed to be the "bulrush" of Moses.

**CYPHOMANDRA** (sy-fo-man'dra). Perhaps 30 species of South American herbs, shrubs, or trees of the potato family, only **C. betacea**, the tree tomato, of hort. interest. It is a tree-like shrub, 8-10 ft. high, with alternate,* heart-shaped or ovalish, soft-hairy leaves 8-12 in. long. Flowers pinkish, fragrant, about ½ in. wide, mostly in small clusters (cymes*). Corolla bell-shaped, its lobes long and narrow and spreading. (For details see SOLANACEAE.) Fruit a smooth, dull-red, egg-shaped berry about 3 in. long, the flesh somewhat tomato-like in flavor, but acid. Somewhat cult. for its fruit in zones* 8 and 9, but of secondary interest. (*Cyphomandra* is from the Greek for hump and man, in reference to an anther character.)

**CYPRESS.** The traditional cypress belongs to the genus *Cupressus*. Many other evergreen trees are so called, or cypress makes part of their name. See TAXODIUM and CHAMAECYPARIS.

**CYPRESS GARDENS.** See SOUTH CAROLINA.

**CYPRESS-PINE.** See CALLITRIS.

**CYPRESS-VINE** = *Quamoclit pennata*.

**CYPRIPEDIUM** (sip-pri-pee'di-um). Very beautiful orchids, nearly always growing in the ground, and cult. both in the greenhouse and outdoors for their showy flowers. As here understood, the lady's-slippers, as they are generally called, comprise a genus of several hundred species, scattered in temperate regions and in the tropics. Certain of the tropical species have been separated into the genera *Cordula*, *Paphiopedilum*, *Phragmopedilum*, and *Selenipedium*, all of which are orchids of greenhouse culture, reserving for the hardy plants the name *Cypripedium*. As here inclusively considered, *Cypripedium* comprises all these genera, which are stemless or stemmed orchids with fleshy, usually brittle root systems, sometimes fibrous-rooted. Leaves usually plaited like a fan, many-nerved, generally with a sheathing base. Flowers solitary or few. Sepals 3, two of them often united, erect and showy. Petals mostly spreading, oblong or narrower. Lip very striking, much enlarged, sac-like or pouch-like (hence the name lady's-slipper), often beautifully colored. Fruit a 3-valved capsule.* (*Cypripedium* is a corruption of the Greek for Venus and shoe.)

†All the species below marked with a dagger are greenhouse orchids. See the culture of greenhouse orchids at ORCHID. The others are hardy plants for the bog garden, wild garden, or other special sites or soils as indicated.

**acaule.** Moccasin flower; pink lady's-slipper. A stemless perennial herb with two basal, ovalish leaves, 6-8 in. long. Flower solitary at the end of a scurfy-hairy stalk 6-10 in. long, nearly 4 in. wide, the lip pink (rarely white), the petals yellowish-green. In dry woods, N.A. May-June. Needs a dry soil with a pH of 4-5 (see ACID AND ALKALI SOILS). Difficult to grow and maintain. See WILD GARDEN.

**arietinum.** Ram's-head lady's-slipper. A slender-stemmed orchid bearing 3 or 4 lance-shaped leaves, which are nearly smooth. Flower about 1½ in. wide, the 3 sepals separate, narrow and purple, the lip whitish but crimson-streaked. In bogs or moist woods, northeastern N.A. and China. May-June. Needs a moist soil with a pH of 4-5 (see ACID AND ALKALI SOILS). See also BOG GARDENING.

†**barbatum.** Stemless, the leaves marked like a checkerboard, usually less than 6 in. long. Flower solitary, about 2 at the end of a hairy stalk, about 3 in. wide. Sepals white or purplish, greenish at the base. Petals narrow, purple at the tip, black-dotted on the upper margin. Lip helmet-shaped, brownish-purple, the lobes spotted. Malaya. Feb.-June. The parent of many hybrid greenhouse plants, one of them being the next.

†**harrisonianum.** Commonly grown by florists, resembling the last, but with the upper sepal nearly black-purple, and white-margined. Lip pale purple, but darker-veined. Hybrid origin. Jan.-March.

†**insigne.** Stemless, the leaves not marked like a checkerboard, about 12 in. long and ¾ in. wide, longer than the densely hairy flower stalk. Flowers mostly solitary, sometimes 2, about 4 in. wide, glossy. Sepals white and green, brown-spotted. Petals narrow, spreading, wavy, yellow-green but purple-veined, the margins hairy. Lip yellowish-green, shaded with brown. India. The parent of many hybrid species and very variable. Nov.-Jan.

**japonicum.** A stemmed orchid, the leaves 2 to a stem, and 3-5 in. long. Flower solitary, about 2½ in. wide, the greenish sepals spotted red at the base. Petals white, spotted with red-brown at the base. Lip generally white and red-spotted, sometimes pinkish. Eastern As. May-June. For culture see BOG GARDEN.

†**lawrenceanum.** Stemless, the leaves marked like a checkerboard, 8-10 in. long, about 2 in. wide, the hairy flower stalk a little longer. Flower solitary, rarely 2, about 4 in. wide. Sepals white, purple-veined, roundish. Petals narrow, hairy on the margin, green but purple-tipped, warty on the margin. Lip dull purple, green underneath but brownish above. Borneo.

†**leeanum.** Stemless and resembling *C. insigne*, but with purple spots on the upper sepal, the lower one green, and with the lip yellowish-brown. Of hybrid origin. Jan.-May.

**macranthum.** A Siberian orchid, the stems with 3-4 leaves. Flowers solitary, large, the sepals and petals purple, the lip dark red and contracted at the mouth. May-June. For culture see BOG GARDENING.

**parviflorum.** Smaller yellow lady's-slipper. A showy native orchid with a leafy stem 10-25 in. high, the leaves ovalish, 4-8 in. long, about half as wide. Flowers about 2 in. wide, the sepals and petals greenish, flushed purple, the lip yellow, ¾-1¼ in. long. Eastern N.A. May-July. The var. **pubescens**, usually called the larger yellow lady's-slipper, has a golden yellow lip nearly twice as large. The species is chiefly a bog plant (see BOG GARDENING), but the variety is mostly a plant of rich woods and one of the easiest to grow of the native orchids. See WILD GARDEN.

**reginae.** Showy lady's-slipper. Stemmed and up to 2 ft. high. Leaves several, 5-7 in. long, ovalish. Flowers nearly 3 in. wide, the sepals and petals white. Lip much inflated, white, but crimson-magenta in front. Eastern N.A. May-June. Prefers moist, mossy places in the shade. Difficult to grow. See WILD GARDEN.

†**spicerianum.** Stemless, the leaves not checkerboard-marked, 8-12 in. long, about 2 in. wide, nearly equaling the smooth flower stalk. Flower solitary, nearly 3 in. wide. Sepals white, crimson-banded, a green-spotted blotch at the base. Petals greenish-brown. Lip violet. India.

**CYRTOMIUM** (sir-tō'mi-um). A small genus of ferns from the Old World tropics, of the family Polypodiaceae, the one below a very popular greenhouse plant well suited to the living room. The genus differs only in technical characters from *Polystichum*. They have rather stiff, firm fronds which are divided feather-fashion, and the large, brown spore cases are scattered over the leaf segments.

(*Cyrtomium* is from Greek for arching and merging, in allusion to the behavior of the veins.)

The holly fern is easily grown in any reasonably moist greenhouse, and is commonly cult. by the florists because of its lasting qualities under unfavorable room conditions. For culture see FERNS AND FERN GARDENING.

**falcatum.** Holly fern. A stiff, erect fern, 1-2 ft. high, the leafstalks very shaggy. Fronds with alternate, deep green and glossy segments that are short-stalked, 2-4 in. long, somewhat suggesting a holly leaf. Widely dispersed in warm regions of the Old World. There is also a var. **compactum** which is shorter and denser in habit. The plant is often offered as *Polystichum falcatum*.

**CYSTOPTERIS** (sis-top'ter-is). The bladder-ferns comprise a small genus of plants of the family Polypodiaceae, of little garden significance except in the outdoor fern garden

---

* Special articles on the subjects indicated by an asterisk (*) will be found at the words so marked.

(which see for culture). They are delicate ferns with twice- or thrice-compound* leaves, the ultimate segments cut-toothed. Spore cases on the veins, on the back of the segments. (*Cystopteris* is from the Greek for bladder and fern.)

**bulbifera.** Common bladder-fern. Fronds 18–24 in. long, the many segments tapering, toothed or cut on the margin, bearing on the upper surface small bulbils* from which new plants can be germinated. Eastern N.A., mostly on limestone rocks in the woods.

**fragilis.** Brittle fern, called also bottle fern. Fronds shorter and grayish-green, the stalk very brittle. Segments ovalish, or narrower, irregularly cut or toothed, the stalklet usually margined or winged. Rocky woods nearly throughout N.A.

**CYTHEREA** (sith-eer'ee-a). A specific name derived from that of the goddess.

**CYTISUS.** See BROOM.

# D

**DABOECIA** (dab-ee'shi-a). A single species of heath-like, low shrub, of the family Ericaceae. The only species, **C. cantabrica,** the Irish heath, and a native of Western Eu., is cult. for its evergreen foliage and nodding purple flowers. It is suited to the rock garden or other sites where a sandy, peaty, moderately acid soil can be mixed for it, and the plant is seldom hardy north of zone* 4 without protection. It is an upright shrub about 18 in. high, the leaves alternate* but numerous, elliptic and about ½ in. long. Flowers in a terminal cluster (raceme*), from June–Oct., the corolla bell-shaped or urn-shaped, about ½ in. long. Fruit a small, 4-valved pod. There are variously colored forms, one a beautiful white, and one a dwarf variety with smaller leaves. (Named for St. Daboec and sometimes called St. Dabeoc's-heath.) Sometimes sold as *Menziesia polifolia.*

**DACRYDIOIDES** (day-krid-i-oy'deez; but *see* OÏDES). Like a plant of the genus *Dacrydium.*

**DACRYDIUM** (day-krid'i-um). A genus of chiefly Australian evergreen, tender trees of the family Taxaceae, little known outside of Calif., where they are sometimes grown for ornament. The leaves are scale-like, suggesting a juniper, on old twigs, but often needle-like on the young growth. Male and female flowers on different trees (for details *see* TAXACEAE). Cones much modified in some, but with cone scales and more typically cone-like in others. Seeds nut-like, surrounded by an aril.* (*Dacrydium* is from a Greek diminutive for a tear, with allusion to the tear-like gum.) The trees are commonly called mountain pine in N. Zeal. and Aust. They have the general aspect of *Podocarpus.*

**cupressinum.** Rimu. A tall tree, up to 100 ft., its branches drooping when young. Leaves scale-like on old twigs, about ¼ in. long, smaller and needle-like on young growth. Nutlet nearly ⅛ in. long, in an aril.* N. Zeal.

**franklini.** Huon pine. A tall tree up to 100 ft., the branches horizontal, but the branchlets drooping. Leaves all scale-like and scarcely 1/20 of an in. long, closely pressed against the twigs. Cones very small, composed of 4–8 tiny scales. Tasmania.

**DACTYLIFERA, -us, -um** (dak-til-lif'fer-a). Finger-bearing or finger-like.

**DACTYLIS** (dak'til-is). A single species of Old World, perennial grass, **D. glomerata,** the orchard grass or cock's-foot, widely naturalized in N.A. and an ingredient of many pasture grass mixtures. It is of no garden interest except rarely for a silvery-margined variety sometimes cult. for ornament. It is a stout perennial, 2–3 ft. tall and usually forming dense, tussock-like clumps. Leaves flat, about ⅓ in. wide, rough. Grass-like flowers in a large, terminal, branching cluster (panicle*) often 6 in. long. (*Dactylis* is from the Greek for finger, and of uncertain application here.)

**DACTYLON** (dak'till-on). Finger-like.

**DAFFODIL.** See NARCISSUS.

**DAFFODIL GARLIC** = *Allium neapolitanum.*

**DAGGER FERN** = *Polystichum acrostichoides.*

**DAHLIA** (dahl'ya, also day'li-ya). A small but very important genus of tuberous-rooted herbs of the family Compositae, the source of all the garden dahlias. Of the dozen or so species, the ones below have contributed to the making of the modern dahlia, and all are from the uplands of Mexico. A few other species are Central American or from northern S.A. Ours are perennials with tuberous roots and opposite* leaves which are often compound* or twice-compound,* the leaflets or segments toothed or cut. Flowers very various, due to breeding, but the wild types always with both ray* and disk* flowers. For details *see* below. (Named for Andreas Dahl, Swedish pupil of Linnaeus.)

The exact identity of the species below is open to much question. The description of them, being based on cultivated plants, is more apt to reflect the hort. development of them than it does their actual wild prototypes.

For the different classes of modern dahlias and their culture *see* below.

**imperialis.** A tall herb, woody at the base, from 6–18 ft. high and one of the plants known as tree dahlia. Leaves large, thrice-compound,* the ultimate segments ovalish, 1–2 in. long, stalkless, sharp-pointed and with incurved teeth. Flower heads long-stalked, nodding, 4–7 in. wide, white, but red-tinged, the rays* about 8, narrow and not notched at the tip. Mex.

**juarezi.** Cactus dahlia. Resembling the common dahlia (*D. pinnata*), but the rays* with recurved margins, of unequal length, and overlapping. Perhaps of hybrid origin, but supposed to be based upon a wild plant from Mexico.

**maxoni.** Resembling *D. imperialis,* and one of the tree dahlias, 6–18 ft. high. It differs from *D. imperialis* in the much narrower ultimate leaf segments, which are sharply toothed. Rays lavender-pink or lilac, ovalish, scarcely more than 2 in. long. Mex. and adjacent Guatemala. It flowers freely in southern Calif.

**mercki.** A low, slender, smooth herb 2–3 ft. high. Ultimate leaf segments 1–2 in. long and about as broad, toothed. Flower heads erect (not nodding), the rays* short, blunt, lilac, not over 2 in. long, usually less. Mex.

**pinnata.** Common garden dahlia, usually 4–8 ft. high. Leaves usually grayish underneath, the ultimate segments ovalish, more or less blunt-toothed, and the axis of the leaf usually winged.* Flower heads more or less nodding, at least 4 in. wide, but much wider in some of the classes (*see* below), and less than this in the smallest form, originally with 8 rays, and rose or lilac, but much modified as now cult. Mex.

### DAHLIA CULTURE

Dahlias, as they occur in the wild state in the mountains of Mexico, Central America, and northern S.A., are nearly always "single-flowered" plants, using the word "flower" in the popular sense. As a result of cultivation and of crossings of perhaps two or three natural species and of their numerous hort. varieties, a great number — at least 14,000 (1934) of named garden varieties — most of them double-flowered, have been introduced to the trade. The flowers of any seedling very rarely match accurately the flowers of the seed-parent (the pollen-parent, in actual practice, is commonly unknown), so it has been customary to give hort. names to any seedlings that are considered worthy of introduction. Exhibitors and commercial growers require classifications, which differ to some extent in different countries. No classification is wholly satisfactory or ever can be. The latest (1931) classification sponsored by the American Dahlia Society recognizes fourteen groups, as follows, with definitions here slightly abbreviated and modified:

1. *Single.* Open-centered flowers, with only one row of ray florets* ("petals").
2. *Mignon.* Flowers as in *Single,* but the plants not exceeding 18 inches in height.
3. *Anemone.* Open-centered flowers, with only one row of ray florets and with tubular disk florets* elongated, forming a pin-cushion effect.
4. *Collarette.* As in *Single,* but with the addition of one or more rows of petaloids, usually of a different color, forming a collar around the disk.
5. *Duplex.* Open-centered flowers, with only two rows of ray florets.*

---

* Special articles on the subjects indicated by an asterisk (*) will be found at the words so marked.

## GARDEN DAHLIAS

Satan  
Yellow Beauty

Fort Monmouth

Jersey's Beauty  
Jane Cowl

6. *Peony.* Open-centered flowers, with not more than four rows of ray florets, with the addition of smaller curled or twisted floral rays around the disk.
7. *Incurved Cactus.* Fully double flowers, with the margins of the majority of the floral rays turned back for half or more of their length, the rays tending to curve toward the center of the flower.
8. *Recurved and Straight Cactus.* As in 7, but the floral rays recurved or straight.
9. *Semi-cactus.* As in 7 or 8, but with the margins of the majority of the floral rays turned back for less than half their length.
10. *Formal Decorative.* Fully double flowers, with margins of the floral rays slightly or not at all turned back, the rays generally broad, the outer tending to recurve and the central tending to be cupped, all in a somewhat regular arrangement.
11. *Informal Decorative.* As in 10, but the floral rays generally long, twisted or pointed, and usually irregular in arrangement.
12. *Ball.* Fully double flowers, ball-shaped or slightly flattened, floral rays in spiral arrangement, blunt or rounded at tips and quilled or with markedly turned-in margins, the flowers more than three inches in diameter.
13. *Miniature.* All which normally produce flowers not exceeding four inches in diameter, *Pompons* excluded, to be classified according to the foregoing definitions.
14. *Pompon.* As in *Ball*, but, for show purposes, not more than two inches in diameter.

The tendency during the last two decades, in the U.S., has been towards the development of large-flowered exhibition varieties of the Decorative classes, but a distinct trend towards the popularization of the Miniatures and Pompons and of low-growing, bedding sorts is now recognizable. These are more amenable to inclusion in a general flower-border planted for succession and are also considered more suitable for household bouquets than are the giant-flowered kinds.

Dahlias thrive best on a well-drained loam. They like plenty of water after they begin to bloom, but, like roses and peonies, they seem to resent "wet feet." As a rule, they do better on a slope than on level ground. Sunny positions are preferred, though dahlias often perform very well when they have only five or six hours of direct sunlight a day. A heavy clay soil that bakes hard in the summer is distinctly unfavorable, but such may be improved by spreading on sand to a depth of four or five inches and mixing it well with the soil.

FERTILIZERS. Bone meal is commonly recommended as a safe and effective fertilizer. It is valuable for its phosphorus compounds; these, however, are more immediately available from commercial superphosphate (acid phosphate), which is more directly soluble. Most soils are said to be well supplied with potash, yet, in many cases, a healthier, more vigorous growth is obtained by applications of muriate of potash or of unleached wood-ashes, which contain the same substance. One pound of the muriate (or 10 lbs. of wood-ashes) and 5 lbs. of raw bone meal (or 2 lbs. of superphosphate) for each 100 square ft. may be raked deeply into the surface after spading or plowing in the spring. Or, instead, a balanced mixed fertilizer may be broadcast to the amount of about 10 lbs. to 100 sq. ft. and raked in as directed above. If cow or horse manure is used, it is better to apply and turn it under in the autumn. Manuring "in the hill" at the time of planting is not to be recommended, for close contact of the tuberous root and animal or chemical fertilizers is often injurious.

Dahlias seem to thrive best when fed from the surface, after they have made a good start. It is a good plan to use a top-dressing about Aug. 15. For every 10 hills, one may apply 2 lbs. raw bone meal, and ½ lb. of muriate of potash, keeping it away about six inches from the base of the plant and raking into the surface. For producing large exhibition flowers, one may repeat this treatment two weeks later, or may use dilute liquid manure in a shallow trench a foot from the plant. If sodium nitrate is ever used, it must be done with caution and restraint. In some cases, a small handful to a plant, raked into the surface, some distance from its base, is beneficial. However, such a forcing of rapid growth commonly results in large, sappy roots which do not winter well and often produce inferior plants the next season. The healthiest stock comes from field-grown plants that have had no special feeding. Dahlias are tolerant of a mildly acid soil, but results are often improved, especially in newly turned land and in ground rich in humus, if lime is added at the rate of 1 lb. for 20 or 30 sq. ft. In a moderately acid soil at the Conn. Agr. Exp. Sta., it was found that both flowers and root crop reached best development when lime was added to a complete balanced fertilizer.

PLANTING AND CULTIVATION. Where the growing season is short, dahlias should be put out as soon as safe from freezing and, in some cases, should be previously started in the house or in cold frames. Where a longer season is assured, as along the mid-Atlantic seaboard, the last of May and the first week of June are the preferred planting dates. On the Pacific Coast of the U.S., planting is done considerably earlier than in the East. In ordinary field culture, the rows are commonly 3 or 4 ft. apart, with the plants 2 to 3 ft. apart in the row, but for the development of large exhibition flowers, the plants should stand at least 4 ft. apart in all directions.

It is desirable to stake all except the dwarf varieties and it is well to drive the stakes before the actual planting is done. The root should be laid down horizontally, eye upward and towards the stake, in a hole about six inches deep. Cover two or three inches at first, drawing the soil in later, as the shoot grows, leaving the general surface level, or, in most soils, a little concave to facilitate watering. Let only one, or at most two, shoots develop. Stir the soil freely — once a week — up to the middle of August. At this time, or by Sept. 1, the fine feeding roots are close to the surface and hoeing may do more harm than good. A mulch of stable manure, compost, or granulated peat at about this time helps to hold the moisture and supply food. If desirable to do artificial watering, as is usually the case in the blooming period, it is better to apply the water copiously, once a week, perhaps — so that it will soak down a foot — than to water lightly every evening. However, after a hot day, a good sprinkling of the leaves seems to have a cooling and healthful effect.

DIVISION OF ROOT CLUMPS. The enlarged underground parts of a dahlia are sometimes called "bulbs" or "tubers," but, properly speaking, they are always *tuberous roots*. This distinction has become of practical importance since the passage of a U.S. law authorizing the patenting of new varieties of plants propagated by roots and denying that right to those propagated by tubers.

Beginners often make the mistake of planting a whole clump of roots, which, in most cases, is not only a waste but the results are usually not so good as when the clump is properly divided. All of the eyes are in the "crown" or upper end, which is essentially a part of the base of last year's stem. Sometimes there are more roots than there are eyes and sometimes more eyes than roots. Amateurs with a few root clumps divide them in May or late in April. If the roots are still dormant, and really alive, one may hasten the visibility of the eyes by keeping them moist and moderately warm, or, if danger of freezing is past, may heel them in out of doors, before dividing. Or one may take chances in dividing and treat the divisions in a similar way to find out which have good eyes. Long cellar sprouts should be carefully cut back to a length of about a quarter-inch. Roots of medium size are the best. Large ones should have the lower half or two-thirds removed.

PROPAGATION. Growers who have glass houses commonly develop so-called "green plants" from slips. It is a widespread belief that plants thus started are healthier and produce better flowers than those grown from the tuberous roots. However, to get good results, such plants should be well rooted and properly hardened off before being set out. The root clumps should be brought to the greenhouse benches about March 1. Whether divided or not, they may be more conveniently handled if kept in boxes, flats, or large pots. Light soil may be placed around the roots, leaving the crown free, and, at first, they should be sparingly watered. High temperatures should be avoided, about 60° F. being the most favorable.

When the shoots have developed three or four pairs of leaves, they should be cut off carefully, leaving on the stump a pair of scales or leaf rudiments. From the axils* of these, two new sprouts will soon appear. The cuttings are then

---

* Special articles on the subjects indicated by an asterisk (*) will be found at the words so marked.

rooted in moist sand, being kept shaded by cheesecloth or newspapers during the day. Bottom-heat* for the propagating bed may range from 65° to 70° F. Some varieties root easily, others with difficulty. In from 10 to 21 days roots should appear, soon after which the little plants may be placed in light or medium loam in 2½ or 3-inch pots. They should never be overwatered or allowed to dry out. A plant that has become hardened is useless. When well established, the potted plants may be removed to a cold frame. Green plants are commonly put out later than the tuberous roots, often about June 15 on the Atlantic seaboard.

SEEDS AND SEEDLINGS. It is from the planting of seeds that the new varieties originate. It is a common belief, not yet fully substantiated, that the double, large-flowered dahlias do not set seed to their own pollen. Many of the originators of new varieties raise only a few of the better kinds and allow the bees to do the cross-pollinating. Others, more particular and wishing to know the pollen-parent, carefully remove all the stamens in the 100 to 300 florets in a head before any pollen is set free, cover the "flower" with a paper bag to keep away pollen-carrying insects, bring pollen-dust from the desired male parent, sift it on the stigmas when mature and receptive, and then restore the covering for a few days. If, under these circumstances, viable seeds are obtained, one may feel fairly certain that the desired cross has been made. Seeds, if planted in a greenhouse in March, commonly make plants that flower the same season and develop plenty of tuberous roots for carrying the variety over the next winter. The more critical of the growers of seedlings often consider only four or five out of a thousand to be worthy of naming and preservation. The American Dahlia Society maintains test gardens at Storrs, Conn., and East Lansing, Mich., where new varieties are judged and those scoring 85 points are granted certificates of merit.

PRUNING AND DISBUDDING. Certain varieties (and others when not thriving properly) have a dense, shrubby growth, and in such cases a freer blooming may often be induced by removing one-half or two-thirds of the branches, allowing better lighting and better circulation of air. The bud terminating the main stem commonly produces the best flower, and its size and beauty are enhanced and better stems for cutting are developed if the lateral buds and branches for two, three, or four pairs of leaves directly underneath are soon snipped out. Growers of exhibition flowers often develop "standards," or only one flower to a plant, all laterals being removed. Many growers, especially of large fields, "crown out" or "top" their plants when they have formed three pairs of good leaves. Removal of the terminal bud then allows six lateral branches to develop and take the place of the single main stem. If these six are disbudded, one gets six large, long-stemmed flowers to a plant. Crowned-out plants do not grow so tall as normally and they require less staking. The operation sets back the opening of the first flower about two weeks, and it should rarely be attempted in the more northern regions.

SELECTION OF VARIETIES. Of the 14,000 dahlia varieties that have been introduced, perhaps 2000 are on the market at the present time. Few of these date back more than 15 years, so that any selected list of the "best varieties" is soon outmoded. However, an old variety that is still in cultivation must have its virtues, two of which would be disease-resistance and good wintering qualities. Without including some of the promising newest, not yet sufficiently tested, twenty-two of the most popular varieties of the large-flowered groups are the following: Jane Cowl (buff, gold, and rose), Jersey's Beauty (pink), Lord of Autumn (canary-yellow), Satan (scarlet), Kathleen Norris (rose), Monmouth Champion (scarlet-orange), Jersey's Beacon (scarlet and buff), Fort Monmouth (dark claret), Murphy's Masterpiece (red), Amelia Earhart (salmon-apricot), Adirondack Sunset (scarlet, with old-gold edges and backs), Frau O. Bracht (light primrose-yellow), Paul Pfitzer (primrose and shell-pink), Ambassador (yellow and salmon-pink), Eagle Rock Fantasy (violet-rose), Jersey's Dainty (white), Arelda Lloyd (yellow, flushed pink), Grace Curling (lilac), Golden Eclipse (gold and salmon), Betty Colter (salmon-red), Thomas A. Edison (dark violet-purple), and Lady Moyra Ponsonby (yellow).

The Pompons find a place with other kinds of flowers in a general border or in front of the taller, larger-flowered dahlias or may make attractive beds by themselves. They average of considerably lower growth than the ordinary dahlias. As cut flowers they are widely useful and charming. The Pompons, in keeping with their smaller size, are commonly more profuse in blooming than are the giant-flowered forms. They should not be disbudded. Of the many good varieties in cultivation, fifteen of the better are: Little Edith (primrose-yellow, tipped carmine), Little David (russet-orange), Sunny Daybreak (lemon-yellow, tipped cardinal), Bronze Beauty (golden apricot), Johnny (maroon), Honey (primrose-yellow, suffused red), Atom (fiery red), Dee Dee (pale lilac), Yellow Gem (canary-yellow), Brunette (crimson and white, variegated), Joe Fette (white), Betty Moore (rosy buff), Douglas Tucker (gold and crimson), Belle of Springfield (red) and Tom Thumb (garnet-red).

The Miniatures, mostly of low growth like the Pompons, and with small and numerous flowers, may be used as described above for the Pompons. The flowers, apart from their size, commonly fall in the Decorative, Cactus, Peony groups; they are often known in the British Isles as Charm Dahlias! Some of the better Miniatures are: Baby Royal (salmon-pink), Little Jewel (peach-blossom pink), Pink Pearl (rose), Garden Love (salmon-rose), Picture (rosy orange), Corona (white), Mrs. Kathleen Carwithen (crimson-scarlet), Lillian Courtney Page (scarlet-orange), Bishop of Llandaff (brilliant red), and Little Jenny (single, bronze, yellow, and red).

Of the dwarf Singles, now known as Mignons, the most popular is Coltness Gem (red). Of the taller singles, favorites are Newport Wonder (crushed raspberry), Crawley Beauty (velvety maroon), Scarlet Century (bright scarlet), Purity (white), and James Weller (yellow, tinged red).

STORAGE. Soon after the first killing frost, the roots should be lifted carefully, with as little breaking of necks as possible. Cut off stump a second time, down to about one inch in height, dry off three or four hours in sunshine, cover stump copiously with sulphur, filling hollow, if any, and pack away. The largest clumps keep better if stump is split. In a furnace-heated cellar, dahlia roots need some kind of covering to prevent excessive shrinkage and possible death. Sand, granulated peat, ashes, newspapers, gunny sacks, etc., are commonly used. Strike a happy medium, learned by experience between too much covering and too little. A storage temperature of 35°–50° F. is the most favorable.

The American Dahlia Society publishes a quarterly *Bulletin* containing much practical information and notes of new varieties. The society welcomes as members any interested in dahlias. Its officers change from time to time, but its present address can always be had by writing to Garden Editor, Houghton Mifflin Company, Boston, Mass. — M. A. H.

INSECT PESTS. Occasional leaf feeders can be controlled with arsenicals. The tarnished plant bug, yellowish brown and ¼ in. long, attacks this and other flowers. Its feeding depletes sap and causes distortion. The bugs are reduced in number by keeping down weeds. Nymphs yield to contact sprays, but the adults are too active to be easily hit. Stem borers are sometimes injurious (*see* ASTER).

DISEASES. Dahlias are subject to four common diseases, namely, mildew, leafspot, wilt and stunt. For mildew *see* Mildew at PLANT DISEASES. Leafspot, in general, is not serious and a careful cleanup of all plant debris in the fall will prevent infection another season. Wilt is characterized by yellowing and wilting of infected plants, soft rot within the stems and tuber rot in storage. Propagate only from healthy plants, practice rotation and remove diseased plants together with some of the surrounding soil. The symptoms of stunt, a virus disease, are dwarfed, mottled and distorted leaves, stunted plants, and malformed flowers. Aphids are responsible for spread of the disease. Methods of control involve spraying for insects, selection of healthy plants for propagation, and the destruction of all affected individuals. Certain varieties such as Jersey's Beauty and Jane Cowl are tolerant of the disease and can be grown successfully even when infected.

**DAHOON** = *Ilex cassine*. See HOLLY.

**DAHURIAN LARCH** = *Larix gmelini*. See LARCH.

---

* Special articles on the subjects indicated by an asterisk (*) will be found at the words so marked.

*DAHURICA, -us, -um* (da-hoor′i-ka). From Dahuria, Siberia.

**DAIKON** = *Raphanus sativus longipinnatus*. See RADISH.

**DAISY.** The traditional daisy is *Bellis perennis*, commonly called English daisy here. For the many other plants to which the name daisy is also applied see CHRYSANTHEMUM, TOWNSENDIA, ARCTOTIS, ASTER and RUDBECKIA. *See also* COMPOSITAE.

**DAISY FAMILY.** *See* COMPOSITAE.

**DAISY TREE.** *See* OLEARIA.

**DALBERGIA** (dal-ber′ji-a). A large genus of tropical vines or valuable timber trees of the pea family, only one, **D. sissoo**, the sissoo, of any garden interest and this only in zones* 8 and 9. It is a tree up to 80 ft. high. Leaves compound* and comprising 5 nearly round leaflets, narrowed at the tip, 3–4 in. long. Flowers small, pea-like, yellowish-white, in short clusters (panicles*) which arise at the leaf-axils. Fruit a flattened pod (legume*) about 3 in. long. India, but planted for ornament in Fla. (Named for Nils Dalberg, Swedish botanist.)

**DALIBARDA** (dal-i-bar′da). A single species of perennial herbs of the rose family, found in rich woods in eastern N.A., and of garden interest only for shaded places in the wild garden. The only species, **D. repens**, the false violet or dewdrop, is a tufted,* half-prostrate herb with long-stalked, scalloped leaves that are heart-shaped at the base, roundish, and about 1½ in. in diameter. Flowers white, long-stalked, about ½ in. in diameter, with 5 rounded petals and many stamens. Near the base there are also one or two cleistogamous* flowers. Fruit a collection of 5 dryish, drupe*-like bodies, enclosed by the persistent calyx. (Named for T. F. Dalibard, French botanist.)

*DALMATICA, -us, -um* (dal-mat′i-ka). From Dalmatia, Yugoslavia.

*DAMASCENA, -us, -um* (da-ma-see′na). From Damascus, Syria.

**DAMASK ROSE** = *Rosa damascena*.

**DAME'S-ROCKET** and **DAME'S-VIOLET** = *Hesperis matronalis*.

**DAMEWORT.** *See* HESPERIS.

**DAMMAR PINE** = *Agathis*.

**DAMPING-OFF.** Damping-off, black-root, or wire-stem in the seedbed is caused by a half-dozen or more fungous parasites. They usually grow very near the surface, and enter the plant at the point where the seedling emerges from the ground. All of them require for quick growth a high moisture content of the soil and the air.

If the air and the surface of the soil are kept as dry as is consistent with good growth of the plant, damping-off can fairly well be held in check. In addition, the seed should be sown thinly enough in the bed so that later the plants will not be crowded. The beds in cold frames should be protected from fog or excessive rain. If the soil in the bed is heavy and slow-drying, it can be improved by mixing with it a small amount of sand or by sprinkling sand over the surface. The watering should be done in the morning and preferably on bright days. Heavy applications of water at long intervals are more desirable than are frequent light sprinkling. Stirring the surface soil after an application of water helps it to dry and thereby reduces the chances of damping-off.

Correct conditions cannot always be maintained, particularly in hotbeds or in low greenhouses. Tight wooden rooms or metal boilers can be built, or bought, into which flats filled with dirt can be piled, and steam forced in until the soil is sterilized. If nematodes are not present, the soil may be drenched with formaldehyde, 1–50. Where steam or formaldehyde sterilization cannot be practiced, the application of another fungicide is desirable. Copper carbonate, which does not dissolve in water, is one of the safest compounds to use so far as freedom from plant injury is concerned. One pound is mixed with 25 gallons of water, and poured over the newly seeded soil at the rate of 1 pint for each square foot of surface, or it is poured along the row as the plants are coming through the ground. It may be applied later at the rate of 1 pint for each 5 feet of row. The applications are repeated as often as found necessary.

Corrosive sublimate, one ounce in 15 gallons of water, may be used in the same manner as suggested for the copper carbonate. It is a better fungicide, but there is more danger of seed injury with its use. A test should be made before large areas are treated to make sure that the conditions and the nature of the crop will permit the use of this mercury compound. Cabbage, cauliflower, and brussels-sprouts seedbeds are benefited especially by this treatment.

Various organic-mercury compounds have been used successfully by some growers. These compounds should always be applied according to the directions on the containers.

Red cuprous oxide; one pound shaken up with thirty pounds of seed, has proved especially successful for tomato, spinach, beet, peas, peppers, and eggplant, and has been satisfactory on a number of other vegetable and flower seeds. — C. C. *See also* PLANT DISEASES and FUNGICIDES.

**DAMSON** = *Prunus domestica insititia*.

**DANDELION.** The common dandelion, one of the six known species of the genus **Taraxacum** (ta-racks′a-kum), is chiefly noted as a weed, but others have spoken of it as the "tramp with a golden crown." It belongs to the section of the family Compositae which have milky juice and only ray flowers in the head. Perennial herbs with a deep taproot (in ours), the leaves in a basal rosette, the blades cut into more or less triangular sections, the tips of which are curved or bent downwards (runcinate). Flower head solitary at the end of a hollow stalk. Below the head is a series of calyx-like bracts,* some bent downward, the inner ones erect. Rays numerous, golden-yellow. Fruit a collection of minute, plumed achenes,* the mass forming a globe-shaped cluster. (*Taraxacum* is from the Greek for disquiet or disorder, in allusion to the medicinal qualities of the herbage.)

T. officinale. The common dandelion. For its eradication *see* Dandelion in the list at WEEDS. It is of European origin, but naturalized everywhere in U.S. A larger-leaved form is sometimes cult. for its bitter-juiced foliage used as greens.

**DANDELION FAMILY.** *See* COMPOSITAE.

**DANGLEBERRY** = *Gaylussacia frondosa*. *See* HUCKLEBERRY.

**DAPHNACEAE.** *See* THYMELAEACEAE.

**DAPHNE** (daf′nee). Sometimes evergreen, very desirable Eurasian shrubs of the family Thymelaeaceae, a few widely grown for their pretty flowers, some of which bloom before the leaves unfold. Leaves generally alternate,* without marginal teeth, evergreen in those so specified below. Flowers in small clusters (racemes or umbel*-like heads), without petals, but the usually bell-shaped calyx* corolla-like. Stamens 8 or 10, in two rows, not protruding. Fruit leathery or fleshy, a 1-seeded drupe.* (*Daphne* is the Greek name for the true laurel and of misleading application to these plants.)

*Daphne* comprises beautiful shrubs for low borders or for the rock garden, but some of the best of them are not hardy over much of the country. They prefer a loose loam with a fair amount of sand, although most of them will grow in ordinary garden soil. If grown in the greenhouse, use potting mixture* 3 to which ⅓ its bulk of chopped-up peat has been added. They may be propagated by layers or by hardwood cuttings, or seed may be used, but it should either be sown at once or stratified. (*See* SEEDS AND SEEDAGE.)

cneorum. Low-creeping, evergreen shrub forming large mats, useful as a ground cover or in the rock garden. Leaves crowded, more or less oblong, about 1 in. long, blunt at the tip and with a minute point. Flowers fragrant, pink, about ⅓ in. wide, in terminal clusters. Fruit yellow-brown. Mountains of Eu. April–May. Hardy from zone* 4, and, with protection, from zone* 3, southward. Sometimes called garland-flower.

laureola. Spurge laurel. An erect, bushy shrub, 18–30 in., the foliage evergreen. Leaves oblongish, 2–3 in. long, gradually narrowed at the base. Flowers yellowish-green, in nearly stalkless clusters (racemes*). Fruit bluish-black. Pyrenees. March–April. Hardy from zone* 5, and, with protection, from zone* 4, southward.

mezereum. Mezereon. An upright shrub 18–36 in. high, the foliage

---

* Special articles on the subjects indicated by an asterisk (*) will be found at the words so marked.

not evergreen. Leaves oblongish, 2–3 in. long, wedge-shaped at the base. Flowers in stalkless clusters of 3, blooming before the leaves unfold, lilac-purple or rosy-purple, and very fragrant. Fruit scarlet. Eurasia, sometimes an escape* in eastern N.A. March–April. Hardy from zone* 3 southward.

**odora.** An evergreen shrub 3–5 ft. high. Leaves oblongish or elliptic, 2–3 in. long, narrowed at both ends but bluntly-pointed. Flowers rosy-purple, fragrant, in dense head-like, terminal clusters. Japan and China. March–April. Hardy from zone* 6 southward. There is a *var.* **marginata** with yellow-bordered leaves.

**DAPHNIPHYLLUM** (daf-ni-fill'um). Twenty-five species of evergreen, Asiatic shrubs or trees of the spurge family, only **D. macropodum** much known here. It is a shrub or small tree, rarely up to 30 ft., with alternate,* stalked leaves and red twigs. Leaves oblong, 4–7 in. long, dark green above, paler or bluish beneath, the stalk and midrib often red. Flowers pale green and inconspicuous (for details *see* EUPHORBIACEAE). Fruit fleshy, oblong, 1-seeded, about ½ in. long. Cult. chiefly for its handsome foliage. Hardy from zone* 6, possibly from zone* 5 (with protection), southward, but most at home in Calif. and the South. Eastern As. (*Daphniphyllum* is from Greek for laurel and leaf.)

*DAPHNOIDES* (daf-noy'deez; but *see* OÏDES). Like a plant of the genus *Daphne*.

**DARLING PEA.** *See* SWAINSONA.

**DARLINGTONIA** (dar-ling-tō'ni-a). A single species of insect-catching herbs of the family Sarraceniaceae, sometimes sold as *Chrysamphora*. **C. californica**, the California pitcher-plant, the only species, is sometimes cult. for its interesting habit. It is a bog plant needing acid moss of pH 4–5 (*see* ACID AND ALKALI SOILS) and plenty of water. It can be grown outdoors north of zone* 5, in the East, only with protection; otherwise, in the cool greenhouse. Native from Ore. to Calif. The plant has a basal rosette of tubular, water-holding leaves, 12–30 in. long, capped by an arched, white-spotted, hooded flap, and a forked appendage. Flowers solitary, yellowish-purple, about 1¼ in. long. (For details *see* SARRACENIACEAE.) *See also* INSECTIVOROUS PLANTS. (Named for William Darlington, American botanist.)

**DARNEL** = *Lolium temulentum*.

**DARWIN TULIPS.** *See* Garden Tulips at TULIPA.

**DASHEEN** = *Colocasia esculenta*.

*DASYCARPA, -us, -um* (das-i-kar'pa). Thick-fruited.

**DASYLIRION** (das-i-lir'i-on). Attractive desert plants of the lily family, from the southwestern U.S. and adjacent Mex., cult. there and in greenhouses northward for their foliage and tall-stalked, flowering clusters. They have a superficial resemblance to agave when young but as the trunk develops they have a terminal crown of leaves more like a dracaena. Generally called sotol in the Southwest. Leaves very narrow, prickly margined in those below, often shreddy at the tip or margin. Male and female flowers on different plants, always in large, branched clusters at the end of a very tall (12–18 ft.) stalk. Flowers lily-like, the male flowers with 6 protruding stamens. Fruit dry and not splitting. (*Dasylirion* is from Greek for tufted lily.)

Both the plants below will stand a little frost, but not slushy, wet winters. Outdoors they must have sandy or rocky soils, brilliant sun, and much summer heat. For greenhouse culture *see* SUCCULENTS.

**glaucophyllum.** Trunk not tall, the leaves 3–4 ft. long and about ½ in. wide, bluish-green, the prickles yellowish-white. Flowering stalk 12–18 ft. high, the flowers small, white. Fruit about ⅜ in. long. Mex.

**texanum.** Bear grass. Trunk short, partly underground. Leaves glossy-green, 2–3 ft. long, about ½ in. wide, the prickles yellowish-brown. Flowering stalk 9–15 ft. high. Fruit about ¼ in. long. Tex.

*DASYPHYLLA, -us, -um* (das-i-fil'la). Thick-leaved.

**DASYSTEMON** (da-sis'te-mon). With thick stamens.

**DATE** (*Phoenix dactylifera*). The date palm can be cultivated in any warm, frost-free part of the U.S. or in a conservatory, but such trees will not bear fruit unless they can get the requisite amount of heat during the fruiting period. Its demands for heat exceed almost any other cult. plant, so much so that the U.S. Department of Agriculture made careful studies of the summer climatic needs of the date in Egypt.

These show that the date will not ripen nor produce good fruit here unless the mean temperature is somewhere near that of at least a dozen famous date plantations in Egypt. The figures are critical. It also needs dryness during the ripening period.

MEAN TEMPERATURES (= MAXIMUM + MINIMUM ÷ BY 2) FOR EGYPTIAN DATE PLANTATIONS AND FOR THE ONLY POSSIBLE DATE REGIONS IN THE U.S.

|       | Egypt | South Ariz. | Near Mecca, Calif. |
|-------|-------|-------------|--------------------|
| April | 76–84 | 66          | 70                 |
| May   | 78–92 | 73          | 77                 |
| June  | 88–92 | 82          | 85                 |
| July  | 82–90 | 88          | 90                 |
| Aug.  | 82–90 | 86          | 90                 |
| Sept. | 76–86 | 81          | 83                 |

The kernel of these temperature figures lies in the fact that just when the date needs a good deal of heat, in April and May, the U.S. localities are deficient in it by 10 degrees on the average. And another unfavorable U.S. climatic feature in our only possible date regions is the prevalence of night dews and, in irrigated regions, too high a water-table. The date is a palm of desert regions of extreme heat, so that its cult. in U.S. is always something of a problem.

There are date plantations in Ariz., Calif., and in parts of Texas in spite of the climatic handicaps. The trees are set on 30-ft. intervals, usually started from suckers, and should begin bearing within 5 or 6 years, but full bearing will not be reached for 15 years and may then yield 100–200 pounds of dates for many years. The suckers are produced freely by old plants and should be gradually removed whether needed for new plants or not. If they are to make new plants, they should be gathered when 3–4 years old, well headed back, and planted directly in the field. Only a few suckers from each old tree should be taken at a time — to take all at once may prevent the old plant from setting fruit for a couple of years. Most suckers are produced from the base of fairly young trees, but suckering may occur well up on the trunks of old trees. The latter should not be used for propagating.

The male and female flowers of the date are on different trees (the suckers are the same sex as the parent tree). Consequently, pollination is a problem. Naturally they are wind-pollinated, but this is too precarious for commercial production. The best practice is to plant one male tree for every 300 females and hand-pollinate the latter. This is done by tying a piece of pollen-producing inflorescence (a few inches long) to the female flower cluster. It is safer to repeat the process in a few days. More expert pollination is practiced in Arabia where bottled pollen of especially fine varieties brings high prices and is used sparingly on only the finest female clusters.

The fruits ripen on the trees if the season is favorable, but most commercial growers prefer to ripen them off the trees in heated rooms. Some criterion of the ability of our climate to ripen dates is shown by the fact that dates usually fail to ripen at Fresno, Calif., and Tucson, Ariz., but complete that process, usually, at Phoenix and Tempe, Ariz., and at Mecca, Calif. The leading varieties for the U.S. are the Saidy and Deglet Noor. *See also* Fruits at LOUISIANA.

While the plant needs an intensely dry, hot atmosphere, it also needs some moisture at its roots, but not too much. This is accomplished in the oases of Egypt and in our Southwest by irrigation.

INSECT PESTS. Several species of scale insects attack date palm under the fiber around the trunk. They can be controlled by clearing away this protection and singeing the trunk. The Parlatoria date scale has been a serious pest in Ariz. and Calif., but its eradication has been undertaken by public authorities and appears to be nearly completed. The red date scale is less injurious. Mites sometimes injure developing fruit; they should yield to sulphur spray or dust.

DISEASES. There are several diseases on dates, as decline, black scorch, brown-spot, black-nose, various leaf diseases and stem-rots. The only general control is to use healthy date palms, destroy diseased material, and use great care to ensure uniform watering. In the case of the decline disease, copper sulphate in solution may be applied to the soil about the tree. For the others see the local plant pathologist. — C. C.

**DATE PLUM** = *Diospyros lotus*. *See* PERSIMMON.

---

* Special articles on the subjects indicated by an asterisk (*) will be found at the words so marked.

**DATURA** (dah-toor'ra). A genus of only 12 or 15 species of the potato family, ranging from annual weeds to tropical trees. Some are poisonous, especially the jimsonweed. Leaves alternate,* often coarsely but remotely toothed. Flowers usually trumpet-shaped, solitary, usually from the leaf-axils.* Calyx* with a long tube, splitting lengthwise or across. Corolla with a spreading limb.* Fruit a large capsule,* often prickly or spiny; rarely the fruit is fleshy. (*Datura* is a Latin version of an East Indian vernacular for some species.)

Only *Datura metel* is of much garden interest. It is to be grown as a tender annual (*see* ANNUALS). The jimsonweed merely needs eradication and a warning about its poisonous juice. *D. arborea* and *D. suaveolens* are tropical shrubs or trees and can be grown outdoors only in zones* 8 and 9. Sometimes grown in the warm-temperate greenhouse where they should have potting mixture* 4.

**arborea.** Angel's-trumpet. A showy, medium-sized Peruvian tree. Leaves of various shapes, but of two sizes, one a third shorter than the other. Flowers 6–9 in. long, white but green-striped, the corolla lobes long-pointed. Fruit about 2½ in. long, without prickles.

**metel.** Tender annual herb, 3–5 ft. high. Leaves ovalish, oblique at the base, 7–9 in. long, or some considerably smaller. Flowers about 7 in. long, the calyx* purple and tubular, the corolla white, violet or yellow. Fruit about 1½ in. long, prickly. India. Resembling the jimsonweed, but with larger flowers. There are double-flowered varieties, and some have variously colored flowers.

**stramonium.** Jimsonweed, also called thornapple. A tropical, annual herb, 3–5 ft. high, naturalized as a weed over most of the country, its juice poisonous, deadly so when the plant is wilted. Leaves more or less lobed, 5–8 in. long. Flower erect, about 4 in. long, white or violet. Fruit very spiny, about 2 in. long. A dangerous weed against which children should be warned. Sometimes called Jamestownweed.

**suaveolens.** Angel's-trumpet, also called floripondio. Closely related to *D. arborea*, but leaves up to 1 ft. long. A shrub 10–15 ft. high, the solitary, nodding, white flower sometimes 12 in. long. Fruit spindle-shaped, 2½–5 in. long. Brazil.

**DAUBENTONIA** (do-ben-tō'ni-a). A genus of tropical shrubs and trees of the pea family, only **D. punicea** of any hort. interest. It is a South American shrub 5–9 ft. high, which is grown for ornament, and has escaped along the Gulf Coast from Fla. to Miss. Leaves compound,* the 12–14 leaflets about 1 in. long, without an odd one at the end. Flowers pea-like, rose-purple, scarcely over ¼ in. long, but the clusters (racemes*) showy, about 4 in. long, from the leaf-axils.* Fruit a 4-winged pod nearly 4 in. long. The plant is sometimes known as *Sesbania punicea*. (Named for L. J. M. Daubenton, French naturalist.)

**DAUCUS.** *See* CARROT.

**DAURICA, -us, -um** (dau'ri-ka). Same as *dahurica*.

**DAVALLIA** (da-val'li-a). A genus of perhaps 70 species of tropical Old World ferns of the family Polypodiaceae, three rather popular as greenhouse ferns. Most of them have thin, pliant rootstocks that tend to creep along the surface or even over the edge of whatever they grow in, thus being ideal for hanging baskets, and commonly used to make fern balls. Fronds very much divided and feathery, more delicate than most cult. ferns, the spore cases on or near the margins of the leaf segments. (Named for Edmund Davall, Swiss botanist.) Some of them are called hare's-foot ferns.

All are greenhouse ferns. For culture *see* FERNS AND FERN GARDENING.

**bullata.** Ball fern, also called squirrel's-foot fern. The commonest species in cult. and often used in fern balls. A slender fern, its fronds 6–12 in. long and about half as wide, at least 4 times compound,* the ultimate segments sharply toothed, not narrow as in *D. fejeensis*. Indo-Malaya and Jap. Its fronds usually droop and fall off in age.

**dissecta.** A stouter plant than *D. bullata*, its rootstocks strongly creeping. Leaves (fronds) 12–18 in. long, 4 times compound,* the ultimate segments somewhat wider than in *D. bullata*. Java. Less grown than the last, but offered sometimes as *D. elegans* and a very beautiful, finely dissected fern.

**fejeensis.** An evergreen fern, its fronds drooping but persistent. Fronds 4 times compound, its numerous ultimate segments very narrow, the leaf more delicate and feathery than the other cult. species. Fiji Islands. The most beautiful of the davallias, and cult. in several forms, one, var. **plumosa**, having especially feathery and gracefully drooping fronds.

**DAVIDIA** (day-vid'i-a). A single species of Chinese tree of the family Cornaceae, grown for ornament. **D. involucrata**, the only species, is an upright tree, up to 50 ft., branching like a linden, with alternate,* short-stalked, toothed leaves that are broadly oval, 4–6 in. long, and silky-hairy underneath. Flowers small and inconspicuous, without petals, in dense heads, beneath which are 2 showy, cream-white bracts,* which make the tree very attractive in bloom. One of the bracts* is nearly 6 in. long, the other about half this, both drooping. Fruit fleshy, green but with a bloom, pear-shaped, about 1½ in. long. May–June. Hardy from zone* 5, or in protected parts of zone* 4, southward. (Named for Armand David, French missionary and botanist in China.)

**DAY-FLOWER.** *See* COMMELINA. For day-flower family *see* COMMELINACEAE.

**DAY JASMINE** = *Cestrum diurnum*.

**DAYLILY.** The term is applied to the plantain-lily (which see), and to the plants below, all of which belong to the genus **Hemerocallis** (hem-mer-o-kal'lis), which comprises about half a dozen wild species of lily-like herbs, found from Central Eu. to Jap., and several hybrid forms recently developed. Roots somewhat fleshy, the leaves nearly all basal, narrow, sword-shaped and keeled. The stem or stalk of the flower cluster is often branched and usually exceeds the leaves. Flowers funnel-form or bell-shaped, widely expanding above. Stamens 6, inserted on the throat of the corolla. Fruit (which is rare) a capsule. (*Hemerocallis* is from the Greek for beautiful for a day.)

For varieties and culture *see* below.

**H. aurantiaca.** Leaves up to 3 ft. long and 1 in. wide. Flowers burnt-orange or salmon-orange, not fragrant. Jap. Spring and summer.

**H. citrina.** Up to 4 ft. high, the leaves about 3 ft. long and 1 in. wide. Flowers light lemon-yellow, nearly 5 in. long, fragrant. China. Summer.

**H. dumortieri.** Scarcely over 1½ ft. high, the leaves 1 ft. long, about ½ in. wide. Flowers pale orange, about 2½ in. long, the tube short. Jap. Spring.

**H. flava.** Lemon daylily. Flowering stalk 2–3 ft. high, the leaves less and about ¾ in. wide. Flowers yellow, 3–4 in. long, the stalks weak and arching. Eastern As. Rarely an escape* in eastern U.S. Spring and summer.

**H. fulva.** Up to 5 ft. high, the leaves 2 ft. long and 1⅛ in. wide. Flowers not fragrant, 3–5 in. long, rusty-orange-red, often with dark lines. Eurasia. Summer. Quite common as a roadside escape* in the eastern U.S.

**H. middendorffi.** Scarcely over 1½ ft. high, but the leaves about 1 in. wide. Flowers pale orange, about 2½ in. long, the segments curving backward in age. Siberia. Spring.

**H. minor.** About 20 in. high, but the leaves scarcely ¼ in. wide. Flowers yellow, about 4 in. long, fragrant. Eastern As. Spring and summer.

**H. thunbergi.** About 3 ft. high, the leaves 2 ft. long and about ¾ in. wide. Flower stalk stiff, somewhat 3-angled. Flowers lemon-yellow, 2–3 in. long, a little fragrant. Jap. Summer. One of the commonest species in cult., mostly night-blooming.

### DAYLILY CULTURE

Daylilies rank among the valuable herbaceous perennials, for their hardiness, ease of culture, and freedom from disease. Their grass-like foliage is attractive and substantial and their colorful flowers open in succession for a rather extended period. The recent addition of new species and the production of horticultural types by selection breeding and hybridization have greatly diversified the group and now give promise of further developments. With this diversity, daylilies are rapidly gaining in popular interest and acclaim.

SELECTION OF DAYLILIES. Several of the named species of daylilies are to be ranked highly as garden plants. *Hemerocallis flava* (lemon daylily) is early-flowering and semi-robust and the flowers are lemon-yellow and odorous. The true *H. minor* blooms with the lemon daylily but is lower in stature and has grass-like foliage. *H. thunbergi* is another yellow-flowered daylily; but it blooms in early July. *H. fulva*, with tawny-red coloring in the flowers, is widely distributed and extremely variable in the Orient, and the cultivated clones* of it include the well-known single-flowered types known as Kwanso, Flore-Pleno, and Variegata. There are low-growing and dwarf types of *H. dumortieri* and *H. minor* that are of value for the rock garden. But with few exceptions the various species of *Hemerocallis* are surpassed as garden plants by the hybrid seedlings that are being propagated for garden culture.

Nearly 200 seedlings of *Hemerocallis*, mostly of hybrid origin, have now been named as horticultural clones* or clonal varieties. Also numerous seedlings of recent hybridi-

* Special articles on the subjects indicated by an asterisk (*) will be found at the words so marked.

zation are being propagated for distribution in the near future. These will provide gardeners with a wide diversity in types in respect to habits of growth, season of bloom, and range in the color and the size of the flowers. At the present time at least twenty-five different daylilies must be selected if one wishes a collection which includes the best of the various classes. Naturally the choice of daylilies deemed most desirable will depend somewhat upon individual taste. But a list of good or excellent horticultural clones* which will meet the approval of most gardeners would, it seems certain, include many of the following daylilies. Flowering in the region about New York City in May and June: Gold Dust, Estmere, Apricot, and Tangerine. These are low-growing, either yellow or orange in flower color, and they bloom with the somewhat taller lemon daylily (*H. flava*). Flowering mostly during June: Winsome, Modesty, Aureole, Queen of May, and Ajax. Flowering in late June into July: Wau-Bun, Mikado, Vesta, Luteola, Sirius, Cinnabar, and Parthenope. Flowering in July: Soudan, Golden Dream, Radiant, Royal, Bijou, Princess, Majestic, Taruga, Vulcan, Theron, and Jubilee. For late July into August: Ophir, Anna Betscher, Hyperion, and Margaret Perry, and of the recent introductions, Star of Gold and Gay Day have been highly recommended for August. Critical comparisons of the new daylilies recently offered in catalogues for 1934 and 1935 will no doubt add others to the list of choice daylilies. In making selections of the new daylilies, the gardener is advised to see plants in flower whenever this is possible and to make his own comparisons between the different clones.* This is especially advisable for the class of fulvous and red-colored daylilies now being introduced in considerable number.

CULTURE OF DAYLILIES. Daylilies thrive without special care or attention in the soil of any ordinary garden. Many of them are easily established in naturalistic plantings in almost any location ranging from dry, rocky slopes to the moist banks of lakes or streams. Daylilies have no serious fungous diseases or insect pests. Throughout north temperate regions most daylilies are either fully hardy or are not seriously affected by winter injury. *H. aurantiaca* clone* *major* requires in winter some protection such as a cover of coarse hay or straw. In tropical and semi-tropical regions the "evergreen" type thrive somewhat better than do those with "deciduous" foliage (as *H. minor, H. dumortieri, H. middendorffi*). In northern regions daylilies thrive best in sunny locations or in only partial shade, except for those that are more or less night-blooming or whose flowers fade badly in full sunlight (as *H. thunbergi, H. citrina*, and the clones* Calypso, Lady Hesketh, Ochroleuca, Modesty, and Hyperion). In tropical lands daylilies usually make the best appearance when planted in somewhat shaded localities.

PROPAGATION OF DAYLILIES is by division. A plant may be separated into sections of convenient size, except that the smallest should include at least one bud of the crown with some roots attached to it. In garden culture, plants of daylilies may be left undisturbed for several years. When the branches in the crown become crowded and the central part somewhat elevated, it is time to break up the plant, to remove the accumulation of dead roots, and then to replant. With reasonable care daylilies may be transplanted at any time, but the most seasonable time for dividing, resetting, and planting is in early spring before growth starts. This work may, however, be done in late summer as soon as the plants cease flowering. — A. B. S.

**DEAD-ARM.** *See* Diseases at GRAPE.

**DEADLY NIGHTSHADE** = *Solanum nigrum.*

**DEAD NETTLE.** *See* LAMIUM.

*DEALBATA, -us, -um* (dee-al-bay'ta). Nearly white.

**DEAMIA** (deem'i-a). A single species of climbing cactus found from southern Mex. to Colombia, once called *Cereus* but now called **Deamia testudo**, and cult. for interest and for its huge, day-blooming flowers. It climbs naturally over rocks and trees, its stems or joints about 4 in. wide, with 3 (rarely 5–8) high ribs or wings. Spines 10 or more to a cluster, brown and spreading. Flower yellowish-white, nearly a foot long, the long, slender, hairy tube expanding into many narrow corolla segments and with many stamens* (for details *see* CACTACEAE). Fruit fleshy. A very handsome cactus needing greenhouse culture (*see* CACTI). (Named for Charles C. Deam, American botanist.)

*DEBILIS, -e* (deb'il-is). Weak or frail.

**DE CAEN.** *See* ANEMONE CORONARIA.

*DECANDRA, -us, -um* (de-kan'dra). With ten stamens.*

*DECAPETALA, -us, -um* (dek-a-pet'a-la). With ten petals.

**DECAYED WOOD.** *See* WOOD ROT.

**DECEMBER.** *See* GARDEN CALENDAR.

*DECIDUA, -us, -um* (de-sid'you-a). *See* DECIDUOUS.

**DECIDUOUS.** Dropping its leaves, petals, fruits, etc. Most broad-leaved trees are deciduous, as distinguished from plants whose leaves are persistent or evergreen, but even these are ultimately deciduous.

*DECIPIENS* (dee-sip'ee-enz). Deceptive or at least not obvious.

**DECODON** (dek'ko-don). A single species of woody herb of the family Lythraceae, found in bogs and swamps of the eastern U.S. and of little garden interest except for similar sites. Commonly called swamp loosestrife, water willow, or wild oleander, **D. verticillatus** makes large clumps of gracefully arching stems 3–8 ft. high, rooting at the tip. Leaves opposite* or in opposite pairs, narrow, willow-like, 2–5 in. long. Flowers pink-purple, in a dense, nearly stalkless cluster at the leaf-axils,* half the 10 stamens prominently protruding, the others hidden. Fruit a 3–5-chambered capsule. Of easy culture in wet places and rooting freely from its arching tips, hence soon covering large areas. (*Decodon* is from the Greek for ten-toothed, in allusion to the toothed calyx.*)

*DECORA, -us, -um* (de-cō'ra). Becoming; comely.

**DECORATIVE DAHLIA.** *See* DAHLIA.

**DECUMARIA** (de-koo-mare'ee-a). A small genus of woody vines of the family Saxifragaceae, related to *Hydrangea*, but without the sterile flowers. Of the two known species one is Chinese, the other, **D. barbara**, is a stem-climbing vine (*see* VINES) hardy from zone* 5 southward, and native from Va. to Fla. and La. It has peeling, shreddy bark, its stem often climbing up to 30 ft. Leaves opposite,* ovalish, 2–4 in. long, nearly or quite without marginal teeth, often half-evergreen. Flowers small, white, in terminal clusters (corymbs*). Calyx turban-shaped, its 7–10 sepals small. Petals 7–10. Stamens* 20–30. Fruit a small, ribbed capsule, splitting between the ribs. It prefers moist, low situations. (*Decumaria* is derived from the Latin for 10, in allusion to the flower parts.)

*DECUMBENS* (dee-kum'benz). Decumbent; *i.e.* trailing, but the tips upright.

*DECURRENS* (dee-kur'renz). Decurrent; *i.e.* a leaf-base or other organ that merges with or runs into the stem or stalk below it.

*DECUSSATA, -us, -um* (dee-kus-say'ta). Decussate; *i.e.* arranged in pairs, but each pair diverging at right angles to the pair above and below it.

**DEER FERN** = *Blechnum spicant.*

**DEER GRASS** = *Rhexia virginica.*

**DEERHORN CACTUS** = *Peniocereus greggi.*

**DEERINGIA** (deer-in'ji-a). A small genus of herbs or shrubby vines of the family Amaranthaceae, the only cult. species being **D. amaranthoides** of Aust., sometimes sold as *D. baccata*. It is a woody vine 10–15 ft. high, grown in Calif. and suited only to similar climates. Leaves alternate,* ovalish or narrower, without marginal teeth. Flowers small and inconspicuous, in branched clusters (for details *see* AMARANTHACEAE). Fruit an inedible, but decorative bright red

---

* Special articles on the subjects indicated by an asterisk (*) will be found at the words so marked.

berry about ¼ in. in diameter, for which the vine is chiefly grown. There is also a form with variegated foliage. (Named for George C. Deering, British botanist.)

**DEER'S-TONGUE** = *Frasera speciosa*.

**DEER VINE** = *Linnaea americana*.

**DEHISCENCE.** The splitting or other mode of opening of a seed pod for the release of seeds; or the opening of an anther to discharge pollen. Fruits or anthers that never split are called indehiscent.

**DELAWARE.** The state lies wholly in zones* 4 and 5. Except in the northern part of the state the topography is level or very gently rolling, and is characteristic of the Atlantic Coastal plain. The northern part of the state is hilly, with occasional outcrops of rock, and belongs to the Piedmont.

SOILS. In general the soils are of a loamy, or sandy loam, or loamy sand type and are usually deficient in lime, phosphoric acid and available potash. Crops on these types of soils respond very quickly to commercial fertilizers. In the Piedmont section, the soils are of granitic formation, and are basically more fertile than the Coastal plain series. The most productive soils are Chester loams, and soils of the Sassafras series. Along the western side of the state the soils are, in general, not well drained. The eastern side of the state has a fringe of tidal, swampy land not adapted to crop production.

GARDENING. Except near the City of Wilmington, Delaware has no great area of market gardening. But truck farming on a large scale is fairly well distributed over the state. Fruit farming is quite localized in the central part of the state, especially the Dover-Wyoming area in Kent County, and the Bridgeville area in Sussex County. The principal fruits are apples, both summer and winter varieties; peaches; grapes; and strawberries. There are also some pears and blackberries produced on a commercial scale.

The vegetable crops are chiefly sweet potatoes, cantaloupes, cucumbers, tomatoes, sweet corn, string beans, and lima beans. Some cabbage, spinach, broccoli, peppers and a few other vegetables are produced. Flowers grown for market, on a small scale, include dahlias, cockscomb, strawflowers, snapdragons, roses, asters, *Scabiosa*, golden glow, zinnias, marigolds, and others. There is also a substantial greenhouse business in the northern part of the state, mostly the production of roses, sweet peas, snapdragons, and carnations. There is also an extensive mushroom industry in the vicinity of Hockessin.

The outstanding hort. development of Delaware centers around the magnificent estates near Wilmington, mostly the result of a century-old fondness for gardening of one family. Upon one of them is the largest private greenhouse in America, housing world-famous collections of exotics. Landscape design is also carried to an extent almost unknown elsewhere in the U.S.

*Climate.* The climate of the state is fairly uniform. The winters are mild and the summers quite warm. The greatest drawback to the Delaware climate is its high humidity, along the coast, especially during the summer months.

Weather records have been kept for many years in various parts of the state. The following table gives the frost dates.

| Place | Average date of last killing frost | Latest known killing frost | Average date of earliest killing frost | Earliest known killing frost |
|---|---|---|---|---|
| Milford | April 16 | May 12 | October 24 | October 2 |
| Dover | April 17 | May 12 | October 23 | October 7 |
| Newark | April 20 | May 12 | October 17 | October 2 |

The average monthly temperatures are:

| | | | | | |
|---|---|---|---|---|---|
| January | 34.0 F. | May | 63.3 F. | September | 68.8 F. |
| February | 34.1 | June | 70.4 | October | 57.6 |
| March | 43.2 | July | 76.4 | November | 46.1 |
| April | 52.8 | August | 74.5 | December | 36.4 |

The average rainfall for the year is 42.77 inches, and is distributed quite evenly as is shown by the following table:

| | | | | | |
|---|---|---|---|---|---|
| January | 3.29 in. | May | 3.53 in. | September | 3.37 in. |
| February | 3.30 in. | June | 3.73 in. | October | 3.03 in. |
| March | 3.63 in. | July | 4.64 in. | November | 2.71 in. |
| April | 3.51 in. | August | 4.50 in. | December | 3.53 in. |

The proximity of the Delaware River, Delaware Bay and the Atlantic Ocean on the East and the Chesapeake Bay on the West, has an important effect not only upon rainfall but also in the prevention of extremes of temperature.

The address of the Agricultural Experiment Station, which has kindly supplied this information about Delaware, is Newark, Delaware. The Station is always ready to answer gardening questions.

The Garden Club of America, whose home office is 598 Madison Avenue, New York, has a club at Wilmington.

**DELICIOSA, -us, -um** (del-ish-i-ō'sa). Delicious.

**DELICIOUS.** An apple variety. *See* APPLE.

**DELONIX** (dee-lon'icks). The royal poinciana, peacock-flower, or flamboyant is admittedly the most showy tree cult. in the warmer parts of Fla. and Calif. Sometimes known as *Caesalpinia regia* or *Poinciana regia*, this Madagascan tree of the pea family is better known as **Delonix regia**. It is a broad-headed tree and not over 40 ft. high. Leaves twice-compound,* 1-2 ft. long, composed of scores of small, oblong leaflets, of which there is no odd one at the end of each series. Flowers not pea-like, 3-4 in. wide, the 5 long-clawed* petals brilliant scarlet, or one of them yellow-striped. The flowers are in clusters (racemes*) and these are so numerous that the flame-like color may be seen far off. Fruit a flat, woody pod (legume*) about 2 in. wide and 8-20 in. long. This most gorgeous of cult. trees will stand a variety of soils, but can be grown outdoors only in zones* 8 and 9. It blooms in summer and is usually leafless in spring. (*Delonix* is from the Greek for long claw, in reference to the petals.)

**DELPHINIFOLIA, -us, -um** (del-fin-i-fō'li-a). With leaves like a larkspur.

**DELPHINIUM** (dell-fin'i-um). The larkspurs comprise a genus of over 250 species of annual or perennial herbs of the buttercup family, all from the north temperate zone, and they include some of the finest of hardy garden flowers. Leaves always lobed or divided finger-fashion and alternate.* Flowers very showy, generally in a long, terminal cluster (raceme* or spike*), these sometimes on stalks several feet high, but lower in some of the annual sorts. The flowers are

DELAWARE

The zones of hardiness crossing Delaware are those shown on the colored map at ZONE, which should be consulted for details. The dates are the average latest killing frost in spring and the first one in the fall. The figures below the dates show the average length of the growing season.

---

* Special articles on the subjects indicated by an asterisk (*) will be found at the words so marked.

prevailingly blue, but of other colors in some cult. forms, and very irregular.* Sepals 5, petal-like, one of them produced into a long spur.* Two of the petals are also short-spurred, the other petals (sometimes wanting) are short, small, and usually clawed.* Stamens numerous. Fruit a collection of small, splitting follicles.* (*Delphinium* is from the Latin for dolphin, in allusion to the shape of the flowers.) All of them have a poisonous juice. *See* POISONOUS PLANTS.

For the culture of the common, perennial, garden larkspur *see* the article below. The identity and parentage of this garden favorite are in so much confusion that it is still impossible to assign definite Latin names that mean very much. The other perennial species are also in some doubt as to their identity, and the names here given are likely to be changed, as the group is better understood.

The annual larkspurs, *D. ajacis* and *D. consolida*, may be treated as hardy annuals (*see* ANNUALS), or if earlier bloom is desired, they may be started earlier and treated as tender annuals.

**ajacis.** Rocket larkspur. An annual, 12-24 in. high, erect and branching. Leaves usually bunched at the joints and rather finely divided. Flowers violet, rose, pink, blue or white (in some of the many garden strains). Southern Eu. June-Aug.

**cardinale.** Scarlet larkspur. An erect or arching perennial herb, 2-3 ft. high. Leaves thickish, divided into many, narrow, almost line-like segments. Flowers scarlet, but the petals yellowish, the spurs* long, the flowers borne in long, open or lax-flowered racemes.* Calif. Summer.

**cashmerianum.** A leafy-stemmed perennial, 1-2 ft. high. Leaves nearly round in outline, but cut into broad, toothed lobes. Flowers blue, hairy, in a broad cluster (corymb*), the spurs short and somewhat curved. Fruits hairy. Himalayas. Summer.

**consolida.** Field larkspur, also called knight's-spur. A forking annual herb 12-18 in. high. Leaves scattered, cut into long, narrow segments. Flowers in sparse clusters at the ends of the branches, nearly 1 in. wide, blue or violet. Fruit smooth. Eu. Often confused with *D. ajacis.*

**elatum.** Candle larkspur; also called bee larkspur. A perennial herb up to 6 ft. high, the branches upright. Leaves cut into broad segments that are sharply cut or toothed at the tip. Flowers in a long, terminal, spike-like raceme,* each flower scarcely over 1 in. wide, blue, smooth, the spurs not very long, slender, and somewhat curved. Petals small and closing over the throat. Fruits only slightly hairy. Eurasia. Summer. Perhaps not cult. in its true wild form, but it may be one of the parents of the tall garden larkspurs.

**garden larkspur.** Of uncertain origin, but almost certainly comprising a group of hybrids. Many Latin names have been applied to the presumed parents and to the finished product, which is the perennial garden larkspur of today. None of these names can be used with certainty and they are therefore omitted here. *See* below.

**grandiflorum.** Siberian larkspur; also called bouquet larkspur. A branched perennial, 2-4 ft. high, often blooming from seed the first year. Leaves much divided into very narrow, nearly feathery segments. Flower clusters lax, open, and more or less scattered. Flowers blue or whitish, 1-1½ in. wide, the spur longish. Fruits hairy. Eastern As., and widely grown.

**nudicaule.** Red larkspur. A slender, perennial herb 12-24 in. high, resembling *D. cardinale*, but the leaf segments broad and blunt. Flowers red, the spurs long, the much smaller petals yellow. Fruit hairy at first, smooth later. Ore. and Calif.

**sinense** = *Delphinium grandiflorum.*

## LARKSPUR CULTURE

The perennial garden *Delphinium* is a confused hybrid of uncertain origin and probably several European and Siberian species are the foundation of this popular garden flower. This garden hybrid is quite easy to grow in the North and isn't exacting as to soil, provided it is deep enough for the roots to penetrate freely to their full length.

Of recent years the garden *Delphinium* has had an enormous vogue in America and is spoken of as being temperamental and difficult, but the basic fact is that it is a northern-region, cold-country plant that does not take kindly to warm climates and hot soils.

*Delphinium* is raised easily from seed best sown as soon as ripe in the late summer or early fall. Much complaint about the poor viability of *Delphinium* seed is due to improper storage conditions through the winter. It keeps best in totally sealed packets and preferably at a temperature around 50°.

Though in Europe named varieties are well established and commonly grown, and such can also be had in Canada, in the other parts of the American continent it is most satisfactory to raise plants constantly from seed. Such named varieties as are offered are usually field selections from mixed sowings from selected strains.

Propagation of particular varieties is possible and not really difficult by division of the clumps in the spring or fall or even by cuttings of the young shoots in the spring. It is so much easier to raise seedlings, however, that vegetative propagation is rarely resorted to. Under average conditions seeds sown in fall will give plants that flower sparsely the following summer when selections of the desired types can be made and the following year the plant gives its best bloom.

If the flower stalk is cut down as soon as the blooms fade a second flowering in fall will be quite satisfactory although not as good as the early bloom. The ordinary practice is to discard the plants after this second bloom, but this is purely a cultural convenience, because of the difficulty of getting them permanently established and carrying them through for later years. Strenuous effort is being made to introduce some native American species into the garden strains, but progress along this line is only just beginning.

The plant is valued in the garden for its height and stature, and there has thus been a tendency towards selection of tall-growing individuals which, however, often need staking to prevent damage from wind. Some specialists, therefore, prefer a lower stature and more heavy type of stem that will withstand the storms.

PLANTING. For permanent planting, open up the earth 2 ft. deep and allow 2 ft. of space for each plant, putting a liberal quantity of old manure with the soil in the lower part of the hole. After setting, tamp well. In heavy soils make holes deeper and put an undertrench in the extra space of coarse gravel or stony rubble. Have plenty of humic matter in the soil that is filled in. Incorporate sand with clay soils to prevent caking. Set the crowns 2 in. below the surface. Plant in an open, airy place not heavily overshaded by trees or buildings or where there are roots of trees.

When growth starts in spring stir the soil around each plant, uncovering the ground shallowly, and add at this time a mixture of commercial plant food, but keep it away from the crowns. Water regularly, preferably by flooding the ground rather than showering overhead. As the flower stalks develop tie lightly to stakes and after blooming cut spikes away to prevent seeding. If seed is desired select only one or two of the early good flowers on a given spike and prevent all others from ripening.

The type of flower cluster varies from a strict cylindrical column to pyramidal with lateral branching, which includes the Wrexham strain. An ideal type is one in which the flowering stalk is about two-thirds of the whole height with foliage well up to the lowest flowers. The type of individual flower varies from single, semi-double (most popular) and fully double or ranunculus-flowered in which the bloom is a rather tight rosette. The semi-double type in which the conspicuously colored sepals form a nearly solid circle is preferred, and the base of the petals may be white, brown, yellowish or black.

The leading strains offered today are selections of English growers which again have formed the basis of strains offered by American specialists, but it can hardly be said as yet that an American type has been developed in *Delphinium*. Particularly on the Pacific Coast, the breeding of American strains of larkspur seems to hold most promise. The object of this is to give to the American garden a plant that will withstand the average conditions of all America — a wiry stem to endure winds, combined with a constitution to resist the onslaught of insidious diseases. We are well on the way to that difficult goal. Rather than a plant that grows to a height of eight or nine feet, our ideal would seem to be a plant of lesser stature but greater stability. Mere height can hardly be an ideal of accomplishment.

In the transition stage, such as we are going through at the present time with the delphinium, strains and types will vary with local conditions as well as with the ideals of the individual grower. If the gardener wants a simple pyramidal spike for garden accent,* he can have it in the Pudor strain. Or, again, if his desire be for one that will show a strong development of lateral branchlets that will give abundance of short-stemmed flowers for cutting, he can find that in the Barber varieties and seedlings. Plants of lesser stature, with

---

* Special articles on the subjects indicated by an asterisk (*) will be found at the words so marked.

more wiry stems, are possessed by the Vanderbilt hybrids. All these are from the Pacific Coast.

The individual strains are fairly well determined, and there are three recognized classes of flower forms:

1. *Single:* one row of sepals and at least five petals forming the eye.
2. *Semi-Double:* two rows of sepals; eyes present or absent.
3. *Double:* more than two rows of sepals; eyes present or absent.

The Wrexham delphinium, an especially fine English or Welsh strain, is very popular here, and is best raised from imported seed. The spike is more spire-like than columnar and very handsome. While named *Wrexham* from a village in Wales, this strain originated in Somerset, England, about 1908. They are often called hollyhock delphiniums. — L. B.

INSECT PESTS. A leaf-eating caterpillar, controlled with arsenicals, and occasional stem borers (*see* CALLISTEPHUS) are among pests of larkspur. In the greenhouse and field the cyclamen mite (*see* CYCLAMEN) and the red spider (*see* CARNATION) are important. A leaf miner, not very important, should succumb to nicotine spray.

DISEASES. Mildew, crown rot and bacterial blight are the important diseases. For mildew *see* Mildew at PLANT DISEASES. Crown rot is characterized by yellowing of the lower leaves, wilting of the plants and a black rot of the crowns and roots. Small, tan, seed-like resting bodies of the fungus are frequently found around the rotted crowns. Control is difficult once the disease becomes established. Use healthy plants, sterilize or change the soil, avoid crowding and remove diseased individuals. Drench the remaining soil with 1-2000 corrosive sublimate solution. In cases of recent or partial infection, the plants may be cut back and the crowns drenched with the corrosive sublimate solution. The symptoms of bacterial blight are irregular, black spots on the upper surfaces of the leaves. Rake up and burn all plant debris in the fall. Drench the crowns with 1-2000 corrosive sublimate solution before growth starts in the spring.

The American Delphinium Society is active in furthering interest in the larkspur and its culture, and welcomes members in sympathy with its aims. Its officers change from time to time, but can always be reached by writing to the Garden Editor, Houghton Mifflin Company, Boston, Mass.

**DELTOID.** Triangular, usually with a broader base than sides; delta-shaped.

**DELTOIDEA, -us, -um** (del-toy'dee-a). Deltoid.

**DELTOIDES** (del-toy'deez; but *see* OÏDES). Deltoid.

**DEMAZERIA** (de-ma-zeer'i-a). A small, unimportant genus of grasses of South Africa and the Mediterranean region, only **D. sicula**, the spike grass of moderate hort. interest. It is an annual grass sometimes used for edgings, scarcely over 12 in. high. Leaves flat, grass-like, about 6 in. long and ⅛ in. wide. Flower spikes green, strongly flattened, the cluster unbranched, terminal, and 2-3 in. long. The compressed spikelets are about ½ in. long, and there are 12-15 of them in the cluster. (Named for M. Desmazières, French naturalist, the genus hence spelled *Desmazeria* by some.)

**DEMERSA, -us, -um** (de-mer'sa). Submerged.

**DEMISSA, -us, -um** (de-mis'sa). Weak or low.

**DENDROBIUM** (den-drō'bi-um). Next to *Cattleya* the most popular greenhouse orchids in cultivation, although they lack a common name. Of over 600 species, chiefly from the steaming forests of the Indo-Malayan region, few are in cult., but from them have been developed scores of hort. important hybrids and named forms much prized by orchid fanciers and by florists. All are tree-perching (epiphytes*), without true pseudobulbs,* but with often thickened stems that are usually jointed and often leafless at flowering time. Leaves various, but neither strap-shaped nor folded like a fan. Flowers extremely showy, in all those below in few or many-flowered clusters (racemes*) which are terminal, or from along the sides of the stem. Sepals nearly equal in length, the two side ones joined to the foot of the column,* and forming a spur-like sac. Petals resembling the odd sepal. Lip* joined to the base of the column.* (*Dendrobium* is from the Greek for tree and life, in allusion to their epiphytic habit.)

For the culture of these greenhouse orchids *see* ORCHIDS.

densiflorum. Stems 4-angled, club-shaped, 12-18 in. long and leafy. Leaves 3-5, leathery, about 6 in. long. Flowers golden-yellow, or whitish and with an orange-yellow lip, about 2 in. wide, the many-flowered, showy, hanging cluster 7-10 in. long. Himalayas. March-April.

formosum. Stems round, about ⅓ in. thick, 12-18 in. long, in youth bearing a few blackish hairs on the sheath. Leaves oval-oblong, about 5 in. long, more or less stem-clasping. Flowers 2-3 in. wide, white, but with a yellow-marked lip,* usually only 3-5 blooms in the cluster, which is near the end of the stem. Himalayas. Feb.-May. A *var.* giganteum has flowers 4-5 in. wide.

nobile. Much the commonest dendrobium in cult., and frequently offered by florists. Stems round, 1-2 ft. long. Leaves lasting 2 years, ovalish or narrower, 3-4 in. long. Flowers about 2½ in. wide, usually only 2 or 3 in a cluster, white or rosy-purple, the lip edged white, with a rose-purple tip and dark purple throat. Himalayas. March-June. There are innumerable varieties, the colors and markings of which are too variable to make it worth cataloguing them here.

phalaenopsis. Stems finger-thick, 12-20 in. long, leafy, especially at the end. Flower cluster nearly 2 ft. long, terminal, containing 8-15 flowers that are about 3 in. wide, and white, rose, and purple, the lip maroon-purple. A very showy plant. East Indies and Aust.

pulchellum. Stems 2-3 ft. long, finger-thick. Flowers 6-9, or more, in a hanging cluster, yellowish-brown, with a purple spot in the throat. Sepals much narrower than the petals. India. April-June.

wardianum. Stems 2-3 ft., pencil-thick, the leaves about 3 in. long. Flowers only 2-3 in the cluster, white but rose-tipped, with a yellow throat and two deep purple spots. The flowers are nearly 4 in. wide and when blooming the stems are leafless. Burma. March-June.

**DENDROCALAMUS** (den-dro-kal'a-mus). Indo-Malayan, tree-like grasses usually called giant bamboos (*see* BAMBOO), and of outdoor cult. only in zones* 8 and 9. Of the 12 known species, the two below are somewhat cult. in southern Fla. and Calif., and one of them is an imposing plant. They have jointed, greenish, or yellowish, usually hollow stems, and leaves wider than in most grasses. Flowers in globe-shaped clusters, which are grouped in long, branching clusters (panicles*). Stamens 6. Fruit small and hard (a caryopsis*). (*Dendrocalamus* is from the Greek for tree reed.)

For culture *see* GRASSES. *See also* BAMBOO.

latiflorus. A very straight-stemmed bamboo 60-70 ft. high. Leaves 7-10 in. long, 1-2 in. wide, tapering at the tip, very short-stalked, with a prominent midrib* and about 9 veins on either side of it. India to Cochin-China. A popular bamboo in southern Calif.

strictus. Male bamboo. Stems often solid or partly so, 40-50 ft. high, bluish-green in youth, ultimately greenish-yellow. Leaves 4-9 in. long, about 1 in. wide, softly hairy when young, with 3-6 veins on either side of the midrib,* and with the tip of the leaf slightly twisted. India, Burma, and Java.

**DENDROIDEA, -us, -um** (den-droy'dee-a). Woody or tree-like.

**DENDROL.** A trademarked miscible oil, sold with directions for use as a dormant spray for scale insects.

**DENDROMECON** (den-dro-mee'kon). A single species of Californian shrub of the poppy family, **D. rigidum**, the tree or bush poppy, often cult. there for its handsome yellow flowers. Its culture in the East is infrequent and difficult, probably because its usually evergreen habit and fondness for dry, sandy sites suffer from the wet, slushy winters and alternate thawing and freezing. Even in Calif. it occasionally loses most of its leaves and should then be cut back to the ground. A stiff, rigid shrub 2-8 ft. high, and very leafy. Leaves lance-shaped, stiff, leathery, veiny, generally persistent or evergreen, and pale green. Flowers solitary, 1-3 in. wide, golden-yellow, with 2 sepals,* 4 petals, and many stamens.* Fruit a narrow, curved, and grooved pod, 2-4 in. long, splitting by 2 valves. Some authorities have split the tree poppy into 20 species. (*Dendromecon* is from the Greek for tree and poppy.)

**DENDROPANAX** = *Gilibertia.*

**DENNSTAEDTIA** (den-stet'i-a). A large genus of chiefly tropical ferns of the family Polypodiaceae, **D. punctilobula**, the hay-scented fern common in eastern N.A. and sometimes transferred to the hardy fern garden (*see* FERNS AND FERN GARDENING for culture). It is a fern with minutely hairy fronds and grows in moist, shady places. Fronds thrice-compound,* nearly 3 ft. long and 9 in. wide, the ultimate segments thin, cut-toothed, sweet-scented (especially when dry). Spore* cases round, brownish, each at the end of a vein and borne near the margin of the leaf segments. A very handsome wild fern. (Named for August Wilhelm Dennstaedt, German botanist.)

**DENSA, -us, -um** (den'sa). Dense or compact.

**DENSIFLORA, -us, -um** (den-si-flow'ra). With dense flowers or a densely compacted flower cluster.

---

* Special articles on the subjects indicated by an asterisk (*) will be found at the words so marked.

**DENTARIA** (den-tay'ri-a). Perhaps 20 species of chiefly woodland, perennial herbs of the mustard family from the north temperate zone, the two below natives and sometimes grown in the wild garden. They have toothed or scaly rootstocks (hence the name toothwort) and few leaves that (in ours) are deeply divided, but not compound.* Leaf lobes usually 3, bluntly and irregularly toothed. Flowers in a loose, open, few-flowered, terminal cluster, the petals 4. Stamens 6. Fruit a very narrow, flat pod (silique*) splitting from the bottom upwards. (*Dentaria* is derived from Latin *dens*, a tooth, in allusion to the toothed rootstocks.)

The toothworts are of easy culture in woods soil, in partly or wholly shady places, in the wild garden, but useless in the open border. Easily propagated by division of their rootstocks in fall or very early in spring. They flower both early in May and late in April.

**diphylla.** Crinkleroot, also called pepper-root. Rootstock strongly toothed, the plant 6–12 in. high. There are 2 stem leaves, 3-lobed and toothed, as well as the similar but basal leaves. Flowers white inside, flushed pinkish outside, about ½ in. wide. Eastern N.A.

**laciniata.** Pepper-root, also called crow's-toes. Rootstock thicker, deeper in the ground, tuber-like. Stem leaves 3, the lobes deeply cleft and toothed. Basal leaves (sometimes wanting) similar. Flower purplish or white, about ¾ in. wide. Eastern N.A.

***DENTATA, -us, -um*** (den-tay'ta). Dentate; *i.e.* toothed.

**DENT CORN** = *Zea mays indentata. See* CORN.

***DENTICULATA, -us, -um*** (den-tick-you-lay'ta). Slightly toothed.

***DENUDATA, -us, -um*** (dee-noo-day'ta). Naked.

**DEODAR** = *Cedrus deodara.*

***DEODARA*** (dee-o-dar'ra). Native name in India for the deodar.

***DEPRESSA, -us, -um*** (de-pres'sa). Depressed or flattened.

**DERRIS.** *See* Contact Sprays at INSECTICIDES.

**DERRIS** (der'ris). A genus of tropical woody vines or shrubs of the pea family, of secondary garden interest except for the one below, and for another, non-hort. species, *D. elliptica*, the source of the insecticide derris. The only cult. species is **D. scandens,** the Malay jewel-vine, a native of the Malayan region and cult. for ornament in Fla. It is a woody climber with compound* leaves, the leaflets stalked, about ½ in. long, and usually 5–13 to a leaf. Flowers small, white, pea-like, showy because they are borne in large clusters, sometimes exceeding the leaves in length. Pods (legumes*) about 3 in. long. A handsome vine, but only suitable for zone* 9. (*Derris* is from the Greek for a leather covering, perhaps in allusion to the pod.)

**DERRISOL.** A trademarked insecticide containing derris and pyrethrum, sold with directions for a contact spray.

**DESERT CANDLE.** *See* EREMURUS.

**DESERT GARDEN.** For the plants suited to the desert garden and for some of the conditions that make for success in such sites, see the articles on cacti and succulents. For additional plants suited to the desert *see also* AGAVE, FOUQUIERIA, HAWORTHIA, YUCCA, STAPELIA, MESQUITE, MESEMBRYANTHEMUM, EUPHORBIA; also the families Amaryllidaceae and Crassulaceae.

Technically there is no true desert (*i.e.* absolutely rainless) in the U.S. What we call the desert has a rainfall of from 3–10 in. a year. See the name of your state for rainfall figures in your vicinity, and if the annual precipitation is much over 15 in., it is better not to try growing many desert species. They will stand extremes of heat and, in some kinds, considerable cold, but few will tolerate much winter moisture.

**DESERT GUM** = *Eucalyptus rudis.*

**DESERT LABORATORY.** Short for The Desert Laboratory of the Carnegie Institution, Tucson, Ariz., a center for research upon problems of desert plant life. It maintains collections of cacti, and conducts experiments upon transpiration and water needs of desert plants, the results and publication of which are of the first importance to gardeners in the Southwest. It also maintains a station at Carmel, Calif.

**DESERT WILLOW** = *Chilopsis linearis.*

**DESIGN.** *See* LANDSCAPE ARCHITECTURE.

**DESMAZERIA** = *Demazeria.*

**DESMODIUM** (des-mō'di-um). A very large but horticulturally secondary genus of herbs of the pea family, mostly tropical, but a few reaching temperate N.A., where they are weedy plants of indifferent garden interest. Leaves compound,* the leaflets usually 3, the central one often longer-stalked than the lateral pair. Flowers small, pea-like, usually in branched, sometimes sparse clusters. Fruit a prominently jointed legume (loment*), the segments of which may become detached separately and, in the native species, often stick to the clothing, hence their names of tick trefoil and tick clover. (*Desmodium* is from the Greek for a chain, in reference to the jointed pods.)

*See* cultural notes at each species.

**canadense.** Bush trefoil; called, also, beggar-lice and beggar-ticks. A perennial herb 3–5, rarely up to 8 ft. high. Leaflets oblongish, about 1½ in. long. Flowers about ¾ in. long, purple, the cluster rather showy. Pods about 1 in. long, with 3–5 joints. Eastern N.A. A plant of open, sandy woods and of the easiest culture in loose, warm soils. Easily propagated by division. *See* SAND GARDEN.

**gyrans.** Telegraph plant. A tropical Asiatic perennial herb (often grown as an annual in the warm greenhouse) of interest for the movements of its leaflets. It grows 2–4 ft. high, the terminal leaflet larger than the lateral pair which constantly (but slowly) move in all directions. Flowers purple or violet, about ¼ in. long. Pods about 1½ in. long, 6–10 jointed. A greenhouse curiosity long studied by Darwin for the telegraph-like regularity of the movement of its leaflets. Best raised from seed.

**purpureum.** Beggarweed. A West Indian perennial herb, grown as an annual cover crop in the far South and practically unknown elsewhere. It is 5–7 ft. high, and its leaflets are ovalish or oblong, 3–4 in. long and have a minute, soft prickle at the tip. Flowers blue or purple, scarcely ⅓ in. long. Pods about 1 in. long, the joints 2–6. Grown from seed as a forage or cover crop, preferably in moist soil, but of the easiest cult. and freely seeding itself.

**DETERMINER.** *See* GENE.

**DEUTZIA** (doot'zi-a). A group of garden shrubs of the first importance, comprising perhaps 50 species, 2 from Mex., all the rest Asiatic, and belonging to the family Saxifragaceae. They have usually hollow twigs and mostly shreddy bark. Leaves opposite,* short-stalked and toothed. Flowers mostly in terminal clusters (cymes* or panicles*), generally white. Calyx* with 5 teeth. Petals 5 (more in some double-flowered hort. forms). Stamens 10. Fruit a 3–5-valved capsule,* its seeds minute. (Named for Johan van der Deutz, Dutch patron of botany.)

These well-known shrubs, which have no common name, are of the easiest culture in any ordinary garden soil. They provide a fine display of bloom in bushes from 12 in. to several feet in height, mostly in the spring. Besides the species below there are many named garden forms, some of hybrid and uncertain parentage. Greenwood or hardwood cuttings, which root easily, are the best method of propagation. They can be forced to bloom in the greenhouse if kept at about 50°, but the process is not likely to succeed more than once.

**campanulata** = *Deutzia rosea campanulata.*

**candida.** A shrub 6 ft. high and of hybrid origin, the shreddy bark brownish. Leaves ovalish, or oval-oblong, 1½–2½ in. long, finely toothed and slightly rough. Flowers white, nearly 1 in. wide, in rather loose clusters 1½–3 in. wide. Hardy from zone* 4 southward.

**crenata** = *Deutzia scabra.*

**gracilis.** Much the best known of all the deutzias and a shrub not over 5 ft., usually lower and bushy, its bark not very shreddy and yellowish-gray. Leaves oblong or narrower, 1½–2½ in. long. Flowers very numerous, white, about ¾ in. wide, the clusters loose. Jap. One of the best known shrubs in cult. and often forced for late winter bloom. For the pink-flowered form sometimes called *D. gracilis rosea see* DEUTZIA ROSEA. Hardy from zone* 3 southward.

**kalmiaeflora.** A hybrid shrub up to 6 ft. high. Leaves oval-oblong, 1–2 in. long, a little hairy beneath. Flowers cup-shaped, nearly 1 in. wide, white, but flushed carmine outside, in rather loose 5–12-flowered clusters. Hardy from zone* 4 southward.

**lemoinei.** The best known of the taller deutzias and a hybrid shrub up to 7 ft. high. Leaves elliptic or narrower, 3–4 in. long, sharply toothed. Flowers pure white, about ¾ in. wide, very numerous in pyramidal or flattish clusters 2–4 in. wide. Petals broadest towards the tip. Hardy from zone* 3 southward. Here belong many named garden forms, among them the old favorite "Boule de Neige."

* Special articles on the subjects indicated by an asterisk (*) will be found at the words so marked.

**parviflora.** Shrub 4–6 ft. high. Leaves ovalish, 3–4 in. long, somewhat wedge-shaped at the base, unequally but finely toothed. Flowers pure white, about ¾ in. wide, the clusters 2–3½ in. wide. A handsome, free-flowering shrub from China and hardy from zone* 3 southward.

**purpurascens.** A shrub 4–6 ft. high, the shreddy bark brownish. Leaves oblong or ovalish, 1½–2½ in. long, rounded at the base and roughish above. Flowers nearly 1 in. wide, star-shaped, white, but distinctly purplish on the outside. Western China. Hardy from zone* 5 southward.

**rosea.** A shrub much resembling *D. gracilis*, but the flowers pinkish and decidedly bell-shaped. Of hybrid origin and hardy from zone* 4 southward. The var. **campanulata** (often sold as *D. campanulata*) has bell-shaped, but white flowers that are nearly 1½ in. wide.

**scabra.** A widely cult. shrub, especially in a double-flowered variety known as "Pride-of-Rochester." It is a branching, more or less arching shrub 5–8 ft. high, the shreddy bark reddish-brown. Leaves ovalish, 2–3 in. long, hairy both sides. Flowers white, or pinkish outside, nearly 1¼ in. wide, the clusters spire-like and 3–5 in. long. Eastern Asia. June–July. Hardy from zone* 4 southward. There are many hort. forms, especially dwarf ones and others with white-dotted or white-marbled leaves. It is a good shrub for a smoky atmosphere.

**DEVIL-IN-THE-BUSH** = *Nigella damascena*.

**DEVIL'S-BIT** = *Liatris spicata*; also *Chamaelirium luteum*.

**DEVIL'S-CLUB** = *Echinopanax horridum*.

**DEVIL'S-PAINTBRUSH** = Orange hawkweed. *See* list at Weeds.

**DEVIL'S-PINCUSHION** = *Coryphantha robustispina*.

**DEVIL'S-TONGUE** = *Hydrosme rivieri*.

**DEVIL'S WALKING-STICK** = *Aralia spinosa*.

**DEVILWOOD** = *Osmanthus americanus*.

**DEWBERRY.** The dewberry is simply a prostrate form of the blackberry, the trailing stems of which root at the joints or at the tip and make, consequently, rather unmanageable patches, if not kept under control. The only real difference between blackberry and dewberry from the hort. standpoint is that the fruits of dewberry are generally ripe from one to two weeks earlier than the ordinary tall blackberries.

While botanists are not agreed upon the specific identity of most dewberries — purely an American fruit — they are, generally speaking, prostrate forms of the genus *Rubus*, possibly derived from *R. flagellaris* and *R. trivialis*. They have blackberry-like fruits and are more at home in the southeastern and southern states, as a garden crop, than the upright blackberries. Texas and some of the states to the eastward are thus the chief dewberry-producing areas.

The culture of dewberry is the same as for blackberry (which see), except that the prostrate canes must either be trained on wires or kept in control if allowed to sprawl. Training on wires strung between posts is expensive, but makes cultivation easier. The alternative is to confine the vines, by cutting off the tips, into flat patches, between which one may walk for cultivating or harvesting. The chief commercial varieties, mostly of hybrid origin, are Lucretia and Manatee, while Aughinbaugh and Skagit are better suited to Calif. Most of the cult. dewberries do indifferently as far north as Ohio, although several wild species are found in the North. Its diseases are the same as the raspberry (which see), and its insect pests are not usually important.

**DEWDROP** = *Dalibarda repens*.

**DEW PLANT** = *Drosera rotundifolia*.

**D-HOE.** A Dutch hoe. *See* Tools and Implements, Section 1.

*DIACANTHA*, **-us, -um** (dy-a-kan'tha). Two-spined.

**DIAMOND-LEAF LAUREL** = *Pittosporum rhombifolium*.

*DIANTHIFLORA*, **-us, -um** (dy-an-thee-flow'ra). With flowers like a pink (*Dianthus*).

**DIANTHUS** (dy-an'thus). Nearly 200 species of annual or perennial herbs of the family Caryophyllaceae, mostly Eurasian, some, as the pink, Sweet William, and carnation being important garden plants. They have opposite,* usually narrow leaves and swollen joints. Flowers terminal, solitary in the carnation and some others, but usually grouped in small, often dense, clusters (cymes* or panicles*). Calyx veiny, and with 5 teeth, often with 2 or more bracts beneath it. Petals 5 (much doubled in some hort. forms), fringed or toothed in some species, always with a longish basal shank (claw*). Stamens 10. Fruit a 4-valved capsule.* (*Dianthus* is from the Greek for flower of Jove.)

There are many valuable garden plants in *Dianthus*, of which several types demand comment. For *D. caryophyllus* and its culture *see* Carnation. All the others are hardy, and all except those designated otherwise are perennials. These are of the following types: (1) the grass pinks (*D. plumarius*) which are low, tufted herbs, usually with fragrant foliage; (2) the maiden pinks (*D. deltoides*) which make turf-like mats and have small flowers; (3) the Sweet William (*D. barbatus*) and its allies which have dense, nearly globular flower clusters; (4) species of pinks grown less frequently than any of the above groups.

The culture of the perennials is usually easy in any ordinary garden soil, but they are inclined to die out if left alone for two or three years. To avoid this, keep a fresh stock coming along by division, layering or by cuttings, all of which are easily managed, as the plant roots freely. In the mat-forming sorts it is better to cut off all flowering stalks in the fall, nearly to the base of the plant. Of the 80 or so species of *Dianthus* known to be cult. in the U.S. the following are the best known. Most of them are spring-blooming.

**alpestris.** A European alpine plant chiefly suited to the rock garden. Leaves narrow, shorter than the stalk of the flower cluster, which has 1 or 2 deep pink or rose-colored flowers about 1 in. wide, the petals notched and without fragrance.

**alpinus.** A tufted plant scarcely 4 in. high, useful only in the rock garden (which see for culture). Leaves short, broad and blunt. Flowers usually solitary, rose or purplish and crimson-eyed, nearly 1½ in. wide, not fragrant. Mountains of Eurasia.

**arenarius.** A tufted plant with many slender stems 6–15 in. high. Flowers white, not very fragrant, long-stalked, the petals finely cut or almost fringed. Central Eu.

**barbatus.** Sweet William; also called bunch pink. A popular garden plant with many named forms, such as the Newport Pink. While a perennial, it is better grown as a biennial, especially for the improved sorts (*see* Biennials). The seedsmen also have strains that bloom from seed the first year and such can be treated as hardy annuals (*see* Annuals). The typical form is a smooth herb 12–24 in. high, with green, flat, and broader leaves than in most pinks. Flowers not fragrant, in dense, close heads, red, rose-purple, white or sometimes varicolored, and in a few forms double-flowered. Eurasia and sometimes an escape* in eastern U.S.

**caesius.** Cheddar pink. A low, mat-forming plant, its bluish-green, numerous stems usually unbranched and 3–9 in. high. Flowers usually solitary, fragrant, rose-colored, very handsome and with fringed petals. Eu. For culture *see* Rock Garden.

**caryophyllus.** Carnation; also the clove pink. A smooth-tufted* herb 1–3 ft. high, the foliage grayish, the stems stiffish. Flowers usually solitary, very fragrant, about 2 in. wide (more in nearly all the much-doubled forms of the carnation), the petals cut or slightly fringed. Eurasia. For the culture of the carnation and hardy derivatives of it, *see* Carnation.

**chinensis.** China pink, also called Indian pink. A green-foliaged, tufted* plant 12–18 in. high, its stems erect and stiffish. Flowers faintly fragrant, red, white, or lilac, solitary or in sparse clusters, about 1 in. wide. Eurasia. Sometimes sold as *D. sinensis*, and as *D. seguieri*, by some considered the European form of *D. chinensis*. For cult. *see* Annuals, although the plant is a biennial or perennial.

**cruentus.** A tufted,* grayish-foliaged herb, its stems forked and 8–15 in. high. Flowers deep red, in small, dense, head-like clusters, the petals toothed. Eastern Eu.

**deltoides.** Maiden pink; called also meadow pink and spink. A turf-forming plant forming mats of green foliage, the leaves scarcely 1 in. long and very narrow. Flowering stalks forked, 4–12 in. high, the flowers scarcely ¾ in. wide, red, or pink (white with a crimson eye in some hort. forms). Western Eu. to eastern As. The var. **glaucus** has bluish-gray foliage. For culture *see* Rock Garden, but it may also be grown in the open border.

**glacialis.** A rock garden tufted herb 3–4 in. high, the stems unbranched and with 1–2 flowers that are about ½ in. wide, not fragrant, reddish-purple, the petals toothed and yellowish underneath. Mountains of southern Eu. Sometimes offered as *D. neglectus*, which is a closely related plant.

**graniticus.** A rock garden plant with 4-angled stems 4–7 in. high. Leaves chiefly basal, very narrow. Flowers solitary (rarely 2 or 3), about ¾ in. wide, the petals purplish and toothed but paler beneath. Pyrenees.

**knappi.** A rough-stemmed border plant 8–16 in. high, unbranched, the foliage bluish-gray. Flowers yellow, not fragrant, about ¾ in. wide, in a dense, solitary head at the end of each stem. Southern Eu.

**latifolius.** Probably a hybrid between the Sweet William and the China pink. An erect, branching herb, 9–18 in. high, the foliage green and roughish, the leaves 2–3 in. long and about ½ in. wide. Flowers in a few-flowered head, rose-pink, shading to dark red (double in some varieties).

**neglectus.** A plant closely related to *D. glacialis*, and sometimes sold for it, but *neglectus* always has a solitary flower, the bracts* below the calyx 4. Southern Eu. For culture *see* Rock Garden.

**petraeus.** Tufted, usually mat-forming herb with smooth, slender, sometimes forked stems 6–15 in. high, the leaves green and 3-veined. Flowers about ¾ in. wide, fragrant, the petals fringed. Eastern Eu.

* Special articles on the subjects indicated by an asterisk (*) will be found at the words so marked.

**plumarius.** Grass pink and including many common garden pinks; sometimes called Scotch pink. Mat-forming herb with smooth, bluish-gray foliage, the stems erect, sometimes forked, 9-18 in. high. Flowers 2-3, fragrant, rose-pink to purplish or white or with variegated colors, the petals fringed. Eurasia. An old garden favorite, known in many named forms and varieties, some double-flowered. The *var.* **semperflorens**, with long-continuing bloom, includes many of the common garden pinks.

**seguieri.** See DIANTHUS CHINENSIS.

**sinensis** = *Dianthus chinensis*.

**superbus.** A border pink 1-2 ft. high, its stems branched and smooth. Leaves flat, narrow, 3-5-veined. Flowers fragrant, nearly 1½ in. wide, lilac or pale rose, the petals deeply fringed and bearded. Eurasia.

Some of the most desirable of the many named forms of the common garden pink are Her Majesty, Homer, Jean, Mrs. Sinkins, Napoleon Third, Robert, Rose de Mai, and White Reserve. The parentage of these is uncertain.

**DIAPENSIACEAE** (dy-a-pen-si-ā'see-ee). The galax or pyxie family consists of only 6 genera of evergreen, low shrubs or herbs, all from the north temperate zone, four of which are of garden interest. *Galax* is found in every florist shop in America, its glossy, evergreen leaves being much used in funeral wreaths.

Leaves simple,* very small and crowded in *Pyxidanthera*, long-stalked and much larger in *Galax* and in *Schizocodon*, a Japanese relative of the American *Shortia*. Most of these garden genera are of rock garden culture. Flowers solitary in all the cult. genera, white or pink. Fruit a dry pod (capsule*), with many minute seeds.

Technical flower characters: Flowers regular,* the calyx and corolla more or less bell-shaped, 5-lobed. Stamens 5, borne on the corolla. Ovary superior,* 3-celled.

**DIASCIA** (dy-ass'si-a). A large genus of South African herbs of the family Scrophulariaceae, only **D. barberae** of secondary garden interest. It is a tender annual (see ANNUALS for cult.), 8-15 in. high, with opposite,* toothed, ovalish leaves 1-1½ in. long. Flowers irregular* and 2-lipped,* rose-pink but yellow-throated, about ½ in. long, the lower lip with 2 spurs. The plant is showy because of the terminal flower cluster (raceme*) which is often 6 in. long. Fruit a roundish pod. (*Diascia* is probably from a Greek word meaning to adorn.)

**DIBBER, DIBBLE.** See TOOLS AND IMPLEMENTS, Section 1.

**DICENTRA** (dy-sen'tra). A small genus of slender, rather weak, somewhat watery-juiced herbs of the family Fumariaceae, some Asiatic, the rest from N.A. They have fleshy rootstocks, and feathery, much dissected, often basal leaves which are sometimes compound.* Flowers in terminal racemes,* very irregular,* the petals joined into a heart-shaped or long-spurred corolla. Fruit a slender, 2-valved pod, the seeds minutely crested.* (*Dicentra* is from the Greek for two-spurred, in allusion to the spurred corolla.)

The first and third species should only be grown in the deep shade of the wild garden, preferably in a wind-free place. After their early bloom, the leaves die down and the plant is not seen until the following season. The others may be grown in open borders or in the rock garden, and present no special difficulty. All are increased by division in early spring.

**canadensis.** Squirrel-corn or turkey-corn. Very similar to *D. cucullaria*, but with the flower spurs not diverging. In rich woods, eastern N.A.

**chrysantha.** Golden eardrops. A stout, leafy-stemmed herb 3-5 ft. high, the foliage bluish-green. Flowers yellow, the spurs very short, the flower cluster large and often branched. Calif. Not much cult. and difficult to grow in the East.

**cucullaria.** Dutchman's-breeches; called also white eardrops. A delicate, stemless herb, the feathery leaves all basal. Flowering stalk 5-8 in. high, the cluster sparse. Flowers white but tipped with yellow, about ¾ in. long, the two spurs diverging, the flowers appearing forked. Rich woods, eastern N.A.

**eximia.** Wild bleeding-heart. A native herb suited to the rock garden (which see for cult.). Leaves all basal. Flowers nodding, in a branched cluster, rose-colored or pink, the spurs short and rounded. In woods, N.Y. to Ga. A related species, *D. formosa*, commonly called California bleeding-heart, may not be distinct, but it has rose-purple (rarely white) flowers.

**formosa.** See DICENTRA EXIMIA.

**spectabilis.** The common garden bleeding-heart, and a leafy-stemmed herb 12-24 in. high. Flowers in an unbranched, 1-sided cluster, rose-colored or red, the spurs short and rounded. Jap. An old garden favorite of the easiest cult. in the open border. Sometimes sold as *Dielytra spectabilis*.

**DICHORISANDRA** (dy-kor-i-san'dra). About 30 species of tropical American perennial herbs of the family Commelinaceae, the two below infrequently grown in greenhouses for their fine foliage and blue flowers. They have erect or somewhat sprawling, usually unbranched stems which bear the few leaves at or near the top. Leaves without teeth, nearly stalkless, and with a sheathing base. Flowers blue, borne in a dense cluster (panicle*). Sepals and petals each 3. Stamens usually 6. Fruit a 3-angled pod, with few seeds. (*Dichorisandra* is from the Greek and refers to a technical stamen character.)

Should be grown in the warm greenhouse in potting mixture* 4. During the growing season give plenty of water, but after blooming the plant dies down to the ground until it puts forth a new shoot (usually only 1) the following spring. It may not do this unless kept a bit pot-bound.* During dormancy reduce its watering materially. Easily propagated by division, preferably during winter dormancy or when re-potting.

**mosaica.** Stem lower than in the next, and spotted. Leaves broadly elliptic, about 6 in. long, 3-4 in. wide, white-lined above, rich purple beneath. Flower cluster short and dense, but often wanting in cult. Peru. A very handsome foliage plant, which in the *var.* **gigantea** has blue flowers more sure than in the typical form.

**thyrsiflora.** Stems stout, 3-6 ft. high. Leaves green both sides, 6-10 in. long, about 2 in. wide. Flower cluster showy, usually branched, sepals and petals blue, or the sepals sometimes greenish. Brazil. More showy in bloom, but a less desirable foliage plant.

*DICHOTOMOUS* (dy-kot'o-mus). Forked in pairs.

**DICKSONIA** (dik-sō'ni-a). A small genus of comparatively hardy tree ferns of the family Cyatheaceae, **D. antarctica** frequently grown in the warm-temperate or cool greenhouse for ornament. It is an Australian fern with a trunk 30-40 ft. high in the wild, much less as usually cult., the stem plentifully studded with leaf-bases. Leaves (fronds) thrice-compound,* not over 6 ft. long, the ultimate segments lance-shaped, toothed, and about 2 in. long. Spore* cases near the margin and at the tips of the veins. One of the most useful of the tree ferns for decoration. Not so feathery as some, it is much more able to stand unfavorable conditions. For culture see FERNS AND FERN GARDENING. (Named for James Dickson, English botanist.)

**DICOTYLEDON.** A plant having two cotyledons* or seed leaves. Dicotyledonous plants usually have netted-veined leaves, and the parts of their flowers (petals, stamens, etc.) in fours or fives or multiples of these. Most garden plants except the palms, aroids,* lilies, grasses, iris, amaryllis, and their allies are dicotyledons. See MONOCOTYLEDON and POLYCOTYLEDON.

**DICTAMNUS** (dik-tam'nus). A single species of hardy, Eurasian, perennial herb of the family Rutaceae, long cult. for ornament in the open border where it may persist for generations. The only species is **D. albus**, variously called gas-plant, dittany, fraxinella, and burning-bush. It is so called because the strong odor of its foliage and flowers will faintly ignite if a lighted match is put to it on a windless summer evening. It is a somewhat woody herb, 2-3 ft. high, its leaves compound,* the 9-11 leaflets ovalish and leathery. Flowers in a terminal cluster (raceme*), white, about 1 in. long. Petals 5. Stamens 10. Fruit a 5-divided, hard, almost woody capsule.* Of the easiest culture, but not tolerating change, so it is better planted where wanted permanently, and avoid dividing if possible. Seeds sown in the fall, outdoors, will sprout the next spring and provide the easiest method of propagation. *Var.* **purpureus** has purple, and *var.* **rubrus**, red flowers. (*Dictamnus* is the classical Greek name of the plant.)

**DICTYOSPERMA** (dik-ti-o-sper'ma). A single species of feather palm (some say 2 others are known) from the Mascarene Islands, much grown for ornament in greenhouses or outdoors in the warmer parts of Fla. and Calif. It is a spineless palm with large, feathery, gracefully arching leaves. Flowers in a short-stalked cluster, the branches of which are rope-like and upon which the flowers are in scattered bunches

---

* Special articles on the subjects indicated by an asterisk (*) will be found at the words so marked.

of 3, of which the central one is female, the two others male. Stamens 6. Fruit fleshy, somewhat olive-shaped. (*Dictyosperma* is from the Greek for netted seed.) The genus is also called *Linoma*, and some of the forms are often sold as arecas.

The young state of the species below is a fairly common pot palm with the florists. For its greenhouse cult. see PALMS. In Fla. and Calif. it grows fairly rapidly in a variety of soils, but should not be planted outdoors except in zone* 9 and the more favorable sites in zone* 8.

album. In Fla. about 30 ft. high, much less under glass, and twice that in its own home, bulging at the base. There is a striking terminal crown of 10–15 gracefully drooping leaves about 10 ft. long, the long, drooping segments arranged feather-fashion, 2–3 in. wide, light green. The var. rubrum has reddish veins and leafstalks in youth, and the var. aureum is similarly yellow-tinged. All of them are very attractive palms whether as juvenile pot plants or in maturity.

**DIDISCUS.** See TRACHYMENE.

***DIDYMA, -us, -um*** (did'i-ma). In pairs.

**DIEFFENBACHIA** (dee-fen-bak'i-a). Handsome tropical American foliage plants of the family Araceae, much grown in greenhouse for their attractive leaves. They are erect, shrubby plants (apparently stemless in youth), bearing near the summit a few oblong, large leaves without marginal teeth and with sheathing leafstalks. Flowers minute, unisexual,* crowded on an erect spadix,* about as long as the oblong spathe* (for details see ARACEAE). Fruit fleshy. (Named for J. F. Dieffenbach, German botanist.)

These popular aroids* need a warm greenhouse (70°–80°) during the growing season, plenty of water, and should be planted in potting mixture* 4. They prefer a partially shaded greenhouse and moist atmosphere. Easily propagated from cut sections of the partially dormant stems, which should be half buried, lengthwise, in moist sand over bottom-heat. The rooted stem cuttings can then be potted up. The plants are rich feeders and respond well to occasional doses of liquid manure. All have an acrid, some a poisonous, juice.

magnifica = *Dieffenbachia picta magnifica*.
picta. Not over 4 ft. high. Leaves oblong or elliptic, at least 3 times as long as broad, the sheathing leafstalks nearly as long as the blade, which is green, but with many irregular, oblongish or narrower, lighter-colored, usually yellowish markings between the veins. S.A. There are at least 2 dozen named forms of this popular foliage plant, perhaps the best being var. magnifica, with white markings. The others are variously banded, feathered, or blotched with white or yellow.
seguine. Dumb cane, so called because chewing it causes temporary speechlessness. A taller, stouter plant than *D. picta* and less well known in cult. Leaves about twice as long as broad, slightly heart-shaped at the base, green, irregularly spotted with unequal sized and shaped yellowish blotches or dots or both. W.I. There are few cult. varieties, but one has a yellow stripe along the midrib.*

**DIELYTRA SPECTABILIS** = *Dicentra spectabilis*.

**DIERAMA** (dy-ray'ma). A genus of only two species of South African herbs of the iris family, both of which are cult. outdoors in southern Calif., rarely in greenhouses northward. They have gladiolus-like corms,* but culturally they must be grown the same as *Ixia* (which see), outside of Calif. and neighboring regions. Leaves chiefly basal, long and rigid. Flowers large, showy, usually in branched spikes, the corolla funnel-shaped but expanded at the throat. Stamens* 3. Fruit a 3-valved capsule.* (*Dierama* is from the Greek for funnel, in allusion to the shape of the flowers.)

pendula. Nearly 4 ft. high, the chiefly basal leaves 12–20 in. long, about ¼ in. wide. Flowers about 1 in. long, grouped in slender, drooping clusters (spikes*), white to lavender.
pulcherrima. Nearly 4 ft. high, the leaves stiff, 12–20 in. long, about ¼ in. wide. Flowers about 1½ in. long, in drooping clusters (spikes*), reddish-purple. Sometimes sold as *Sparaxis pulcherrima*.

**DIERVILLA** (dy-er-vil'la). A small genus of low shrubs of the honeysuckle family, all North American, two of them of secondary garden interest. They are useful under shade or in the wild garden, where they make rather extensive patches from the spreading of their underground stems. Leaves opposite,* short-stalked and toothed. Flowers yellow, funnel-shaped, mostly in small, leafless clusters, from the leaf-axils.* Corolla irregular,* slightly 2-lipped. Stamens 5. Fruit a 2-valved capsule* crowned with the narrow lobes of the calyx. (Named for Dierville, French surgeon in Canada.) The plants are usually called bush honeysuckle. For related plants, much more important as decorative shrubs, see WEIGELA.

The species below are of the easiest culture, preferring shade, but doing pretty well in open sunshine. They grow freely from suckers or may be increased by division.

lonicera. Gravelweed. Never over 3 ft. high, usually about 2 ft. Leaves ovalish or oblong, 2–4 in. long, taper-pointed. Flowers usually 3 to a cluster, the corolla about ¾ in. long. June. Nearly throughout N.A. and hardy everywhere.
sessilifolia. Somewhat taller and with longer, narrower leaves. Flowers usually 3–7 to a cluster, the corolla shorter than in *D. lonicera*. In mountain woods N.C. to Tenn., Ga., and Ala. June. Hardy from zone* 3 southward.
trifida = *Diervilla lonicera*.

***DIFFUSA, -us, -um*** (dif-few'sa). Diffuse; i.e. spreading.

**DIGGING.** The simplest, best, but most laborious method of turning the soil in anticipation of planting. All machine or horse-implement substitutes have the disadvantage of the operator of the machine walking over the turned-up earth, which never happens in spading or forking because one necessarily walks backward as digging progresses. Forking is simply digging with a spading fork, which one does if the roots of plants are apt to be cut with the broad blade of a spade. It is also easier to fork in manure than to spade it in.

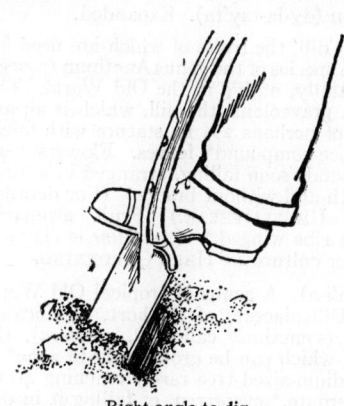

Right angle to dig

Whether the operation is digging or forking, it would scarcely seem necessary to give any directions for a process as old as gardening. It would not be, except that there is a right and a wrong way to dig, both for the operator and for the soil.

The main objects of digging are to loosen up the soil, allow it to aerate, and in the process to cover up all weeds, vegetable trash, or spent manure. This cannot be done properly by shallow (i.e. slantwise) digging, but is usually completely successful if the spade or fork is driven almost vertically into the ground and nearly or quite the depth of its blade. While the illustrations show the right and wrong ways to dig, they cannot convey the fact that the wrong method is much the most laborious.

Wrong angle to dig

There is also the obvious caution about the time to dig. Late fall is good if the turned-up soil is left in the rough over the winter. Frost and snow are good for it. Many fall-dug soils will be ready for raking and planting in spring, especially if they are light, loamy, or sandy loam soils, which will not pack over the winter. If there is much clay or silt,

---

* Special articles on the subjects indicated by an asterisk (*) will be found at the words so marked.

digging is best left to the spring and even then must be approached with caution.

Heavy clay or silt soils pack badly when wet and may be unworkable by midsummer if you begin digging them too soon. Wait until a clod of earth breaks or crumbles when dropped off the spade. If it packs or sticks together, it is too early to dig. If you insist, the penalty may be unmanageable chunks of cement-like hardness by the time your soil should be in its most friable condition for root development and for cultivation.

**DIGITALIS.** See FOXGLOVE.

**DIGITARIA SANGUINALIS** = Crab Grass. See the list at WEEDS.

*DIGITATA, -us, -um* (dij-i-tay'ta). Digitate; *i.e.* with the leaflets,* or with the lobes of a simple leaf, all arising from one point, as in the horse-chestnut. See PINNATE.

*DILATATA, -us, -um* (dy-la-tay'ta). Expanded.

**DILL.** The common dill, the fruits of which are used for seasoning, is one of two species of the genus *Anethum* (a-nee'-thum) of the carrot family, native in the Old World. The only cult. species is *A. graveolens*, the dill, which is an annual or biennial herb of perhaps 2½ ft. stature with finely dissected, usually thrice-compound* leaves. Flowers very small, yellowish, the petals soon falling, arranged in a large umbel* which is smooth and without bracts.* (For detailed flower structure see UMBELLIFERAE.) Fruit aromatic, flattened, some of the ribs winged.* (*Anethum* is classical Greek for the dill.) For culture see HERB GARDENING.

**DILLENIA** (dil-leen'i-a). A genus of tropical Old World trees of the family Dilleniaceae, of no hort. significance except for **D. indica** (sometimes called *D. speciosa*), the chalta of tropical As., which can be grown only in zone* 9. It is a handsome, medium-sized tree rarely reaching 40 ft. in height. Leaves alternate,* evergreen, or failing it in dry seasons, oblongish, coarsely toothed, and 7–11 in. long. Flowers large, pure white, nearly 6 in. wide, the stamens* yellow and conspicuous. Petals 5, separate. Fruit hard, about 3½ in. wide, greenish, the fleshy part mostly the enlarged calyx, edible if you like fruits as sour as rhubarb. (Named for Johann J. Dillenius, one of the fathers of modern botany and a professor at Oxford.)

**DILLENIACEAE** (dil-leen-i-ā'see-ee). The silver vine family has only three genera of garden interest among its 11 genera and 300 species of mostly trees, shrubs, or woody vines, all of which are tropical except *Actinidia*. This genus of woody vines, often grown for ornament, is sometimes included in Actinidiaceae, a family not here maintained.

Leaves mostly alternate.* Flowers unisexual* in *Actinidia*, perfect* in the other cult. genera, mostly rather showy. The fruit is fleshy and sometimes edible in *Actinidia* and *Dillenia*. The only other cult. genus is *Hibbertia*.

Technical flower characters: Petals 5, their margins overlapping, as do the 5 sepals which are persistent and sometimes enlarged in fruit. Stamens numerous. Ovary superior,* the styles spreading.

**DIMORPHOTHECA** (dy-more-fo-thee'ka). The Cape marigolds comprise perhaps 20 species of annual or perennial, South African herbs of the family Compositae, one a popular, tender annual. They have alternate* or basal, few-toothed leaves and showy, solitary, long-stalked flower heads. Rays* long and strap-shaped, chiefly yellow, orange, or white, the disk flowers yellow or orange. (*Dimorphotheca* is from the Greek for two-formed achenes, in allusion to a technical fruit character.)

While *D. aurantiaca* is a perennial, it will bloom from seed the first year, and, like *D. annua*, is best treated as a tender annual. See ANNUALS. The exact botanical identity of the plants below is in grave doubt, as there has been much crossing of these popular flowers. Sometimes grown in the greenhouse and bedded out in summer. They are sometimes called African daisy.

annua. A rough-hairy herb 8–14 in. high, the leaves oblongish, practically stalkless. Flower heads showy, the rays white, yellow, or orange, but somewhat purplish below, and in some hort. forms double. As the flowers wane, the head is nodding. Summer. Of this, or possibly of the next, there are many fine, showy, garden forms, but their identity or parentage is very doubtful.

aurantiaca. A perennial, in age somewhat woody at the base. Leaves narrowly oblong, a little rough but not, or only a little, hairy. Flowers generally orange-yellow (white, bluish, or red in some hort. forms). Easily flowered from seed in a single season if treated as a tender annual, but it requires a long season and plenty of heat.

**DIOECIOUS** (dy-ee'shus). Having male and female flowers on separate plants, as in the willow, in *Aucuba*, and many other plants. See MONOECIOUS.

*DIOICA, -us, -um* (dy-ō'i-ka). Dioecious.

**DIONAEA** (dy-o-nee'a). A single, remarkable, insectivorous plant of the family Droseraceae, found only in North and South Carolina, and cult. for its interesting method of catching and digesting insects. The only species, **D. muscipula**, the Venus's-flytrap, can be grown outdoors in its native region, but is easier managed in the frame or cool greenhouse. It grows perfectly in wet sphagnum moss with a pH about 4.0 or 4.5 (see ACID AND ALKALI SOILS) or in a similarly acid mixture of sand and peat, both kept saturated. The plant is a perennial with a basal rosette of flat-stalked leaves, the blade of which consists of two hinged lobes which are fringed with bristles. The lobes close together when irritated with a pencil or by an insect, completely trapping the latter, which is subsequently digested. Flowers white, small, in a terminal cluster (umbel*), the stalk of which is 8–12 in. long. (For structure of flowers see DROSERACEAE.) Fruit a capsule.* (*Dionaea* is a Greek name for Venus.) See also INSECTIVOROUS PLANTS.

**DIOSCOREA** (dy-os-kor-ree'a). A very large genus of chiefly herbaceous, twining vines of the family Dioscoreaceae, most of them tropical and a few cult. for food (the yam) or ornament. They have usually large underground tubers (the air potato has them in the foliage) and rather various, but prevailingly alternate* leaves. Flowers small, white or greenish, usually in spikes* or racemes.* (For details see DIOSCOREACEAE.) Fruit a strongly 3-angled or 3-winged, sometimes inflated, seldom a fleshy, pod. (Named for Dioscorides, one of the Greek fathers of botany.)

The yams grown for food must be confined to zone* 7 or southward, as they need a long season and considerable heat. Those grown for ornament are hardy up to zone* 4 or possibly to zone* 3, as their tops die down, but the roots persist. All are of the easiest culture, preferably in sandy, warm soils. The tubers may be planted almost at any time of the year in the South, preferably in spring in the North.

batatas. Chinese yam or potato; usually called cinnamon vine in the North where it is cult. for ornament. Tubers 2–3 ft. long, deep in the ground. Stem angled, sometimes twisted, tall-climbing. Leaves opposite,* often with small tubers in the axils,* ovalish, but broad or angled at the base. Flowers cinnamon-scented, in small clusters from the leaf-axils.* China.

bulbifera. Air potato. An Indo-Malayan vine, tender in the North, and without the large underground tuber of most yams. Stems round, often bearing in the leaf-axils* large tubers 8–12 in. long and weighing several pounds. Leaves alternate,* heart-shaped or roundish, the stalk longer than the blade. Flowers in many drooping, slender spikes. Chiefly grown for the aerial tubers.

trifida. Yampee, also called cush-cush. Underground tubers, not large, but prized for their flavor. Stem more or less winged or angled, without tubers. Leaves 3–5-lobed, the lobes extending nearly to the middle. Flowers in racemes* (male flowers) or the female ones in spikes. S.A. Can only be grown far south.

villosa. Wild yam. A native vine with a woody but not large rootstock. Leaves ovalish, heart-shaped at the base, with 9–11 main veins. Flowers in drooping clusters. Almost a weedy vine, native from R.I. to Fla. and Tex. Little cult. and hardy to zone* 3.

**DIOSCOREACEAE** (dy-os-kor-ree-ā'see-ee). The yam family would be of no garden interest if it were not for the food value of the yam (*Dioscorea*) and for the only other cult. genus, *Rajania*, also yam-like. Like the other 8 genera and upwards of 200 species, these are herbaceous vines often with tremendous underground (rarely in the air) tubers which furnish the yams of commerce.

Leaves alternate* or opposite.* Flowers small, greenish or whitish, usually in clusters (spikes* or racemes*), nearly always unisexual.* Fruit a decidedly 3-angled or winged

---

* Special articles on the subjects indicated by an asterisk (*) will be found at the words so marked.

capsule.* Both genera are cult. mostly for their edible tubers, but some vines in *Dioscorea* are decorative.

Technical flower characters: Flowers regular,* the 6 segments not easily separable as sepals and petals. Stamens 6 or 3. Ovary 3-celled, its styles 3 and distinct.

**DIOSCORIDES.** *See* GARDEN BOOKS.

**DIOSMA** (dy-ōs'ma). Aromatic, small, heath-like, South African shrubs of the family Rutaceae, only **D. ericoides,** the breath-of-heaven, of much garden interest. It is a tender border shrub in Calif. and Fla., more often grown as a greenhouse plant needing potting mixture* 4 and a cool house. It is a much-branched, bushy shrub, 1–2 ft. high. Leaves alternate,* scarcely ½ in. long, needle-shaped and much crowded. Flowers about ⅕ in. wide, in clusters of 1–3, but the clusters very numerous. Petals 5, reddish. Calyx deeply 5-parted. Fruit a collection of 5 carpels, ultimately separable as 5 distinct capsules,* each 1-seeded. An attractive and floriferous little bush. (*Diosma* is from the Greek for divine fragrance, from the aromatic foliage.)

**DIOSPYROS.** *See* PERSIMMON.

**DIPELTA** (dy-pel'ta). A small genus of Chinese shrubs of the honeysuckle family, only **D. floribunda** of interest to the shrubbery enthusiast. It is 8–15 ft. high and has shreddy bark. Leaves opposite,* short-stalked, ovalish or narrower, 2–4 in. long, mostly without marginal teeth. Flowers fragrant, in slender, nodding clusters of 2–6 blooms. Corolla pale rose, but orange in the throat, tubular but a little 2-lipped,* about 1½ in. long. Beneath the flower is a series of bracts* of unequal size. Stamens* 4. Fruit a capsule,* partly enclosed by the persistent bracts. An ornamental shrub, resembling beauty-bush, blooming in May, hardy from zone* 4 southward, and tolerant of most ordinary garden soils. (*Dipelta* is from the Greek for twice and shield, in allusion to the unequal bracts.*)

***DIPETALA, -us, -um*** (dy-pet'a-la). With two petals.

***DIPHYLLA, -us, -um*** (dy-fil'la). Two-leaved.

**DIPHYLLEIA** (dy-fil-lee'ya). A genus of two species of the family Berberidaceae, one Asiatic, the other **D. cymosa,** the umbrella leaf, a woodland perennial herb of the southeastern U.S., cult. in the wild garden. It is an erect, stout herb with a single, basal, long-stalked leaf 12–20 in. in diameter, and 2 stem leaves, shorter-stalked. Both sorts are deeply 2-lobed, the lobes more or less cut or lobed also, and the leafstalks arise from or near the middle of the blade (peltate*). Flowers white, in a small, terminal cluster (cyme*), the 6 petals and 6 sepals similar. Stamens 6. Fruit a blue berry about ½ in. in diameter. The plant needs shade and woods soil and prefers mountain forests to sandy lowlands. (*Diphylleia* is from the Greek for double-leaf, in allusion to the two stem leaves.)

**DIPLACUS.** *See* MIMULUS.

**DIPLADENIA** (dip-la-dee'ni-a). Forty species of tropical American woody vines of the family Apocynaceae, two sometimes cult. in the greenhouse or outdoors only in zone* 9. Leaves opposite,* without marginal teeth, their juice milky. Flowers large, showy, in few-flowered clusters (racemes*). Corolla funnel-shaped, slightly twisted, the 5 stamens* inserted in its throat. Fruit a pair of divergent, narrow pods (follicles*). (*Dipladenia* is from the Greek meaning double gland, in reference to a technical character of the disk.*)

These are very handsome woody vines which in youth are somewhat shrubby and only climb later. They need a warm-temperate greenhouse and potting mixture* 3 to which is added about ⅛ its bulk in charcoal. Propagated by cuttings over bottom-heat. In extreme southern Fla. they appear to thrive on a variety of soils.

**boliviensis.** Leaves 2–3½ in. long, narrowed at the base, and stalked. Flowers about 1½ in. long, white, the throat yellow, the stalk of the cluster shorter than the leaves. Bolivia.

**splendens.** Leaves elliptic, 4–8 in. long, the heart-shaped base nearly stalkless. Flowers nearly 4 in. long, white or rose-flushed, the throat purple, the stalk of the cluster longer than the leaves. Brazil. The most popular in cult. and often sold under a variety of names. It is also likely to be the origin of some hybrid forms.

***DIPLOSTEPHIOIDES*** (dip-low-stee-fi-oy'deez; but *see* OÏDES). Like a plant of the genus *Diplostephium,* which is of little garden interest.

**DIPPER GOURD** = *Lagenaria leucantha.*

**DIPSACACEAE** (dip-sa-kay'see-ee). The teasel family, closely related to the Compositae, contains mostly weedy herbs in perhaps 7 Old World genera and about 140 species. The only cult. genera are *Cephalaria, Morina, Scabiosa,* and *Dipsacus,* the latter yielding fuller's teasel from its spiny-tipped fruiting head.

Leaves usually opposite* or whorled.* Flowers small, in bracted* heads, except in *Morina* where they are in interrupted spikes. Unlike the Compositae, there are no ray flowers, all being tubular in the Dipsacaceae. Fruit dry, small (an achene*).

The only important hort. genus is *Scabiosa,* one species of which is the parent of popular flower garden annuals.

Technical characters: Flowers mostly in heads, the heads bracted. Ovary inferior,* 1-celled, the calyx-tube joined to it. Ovules 1.

**DIPSACEAE** = Dipsacaceae.

**DIPSACUS** (dip'sa-kus). Coarse, thistle-like, Old World herbs of the family Dipsacaceae, none of any real garden interest, but one of them cult. for the peculiar fruiting head, known as teasel and used to raise the nap on woolen cloth. It is **D. fullonum,** the fuller's teasel, a biennial European herb 4–6 ft. high, coarse and hairy. Leaves opposite,* nearly 1 ft. long, the bases connected and cup-like. Flowers pale lilac, all tubular and minute, crowded in a dense, cylindric head, somewhat resembling those in the Compositae. The head is provided with a number of hooked bracts,* which are spine-tipped (the teasel). Grown commercially for these teasels near woolen factories. (*Dipsacus* is Greek for thirst, in allusion to the water-holding leaf-bases.)

***DIPTERA, -us, -um*** (dip'ter-ra). Two-winged.

***DIPTEROCARPA, -us, -um*** (dip-ter-ro-kar'pa). Having two-winged fruit.

**DIRCA** (der'ka). Two species of North American shrubs of the family Thymelaeaceae, the alternate* leaves having no marginal teeth. The only cult. species is **D. palustris,** commonly called leatherwood, leather bush, wicopy, or rope bark. It is a tough-wooded, but pliable shrub, 3–5 ft. high, the leaves elliptic, 2–3 in. long, short-stalked. Flowers blooming before the leaves unfold (March–April), yellow, without petals but the calyx* petal-like, grouped in small, nearly stalkless clusters in the axils* of old wood. Fruit fleshy, egg-shaped, reddish or green. The shrub is wild in eastern N.A., mostly in moist places, but it can be grown in any ordinary garden soil and is hardy from zone* 3 southward. (*Dirca* is Greek for a mythological fountain, perhaps in allusion to their moist sites.)

**DIRT GARDENER.** Really to understand the fundamentals of gardening everyone should be a dirt gardener. In no other way can one get the feel and texture of soil. How you treat it will decide whether you should be a gardener at all. Its needs and handling are the foundation of all successful gardening. *See* the series of articles on SOILS and SOIL OPERATIONS.

**DISBUDDING.** The pinching of certain buds for the benefit of those left to grow. It has in reality two phases. The first is the pinching-off of leaf buds that would otherwise form perhaps unwanted shoots. It is easy to control the shape and branching of woody plants by this process. But as its objects are the same as pruning, this feature of disbudding will be found at the article PRUNING. It is also possible to change very greatly the form or growth of herbaceous plants by pinching out certain buds. *See* Pinching at TRAINING PLANTS.

The pinching of flower buds is in a somewhat different category. While the object is to increase the chances of the

* Special articles on the subjects indicated by an asterisk (*) will be found at the words so marked.

# DISC 212 DIVISION

remaining flowers, it does not ordinarily change the habit or permanent shape of the plant as pinching off leaf buds always does.

Disbudding for better bloom is so common among professional gardeners that it is extraordinary how many amateurs all but ignore it. At the blooming stage plants are at the peak of their activity and Nature is usually perfectly reckless about the number of blossoms produced, perhaps upon the sound theory that the more blooms the greater the chances of survival from a large crop of seeds. Disbudding is the interruption of this process.

A plant needing disbudding

No absolute rules can be given for disbudding because conditions vary so much in different plants and in different seasons. A little practice will inform any observant gardener whether he wants 6 fair blooms or 2 splendid ones. Scattered throughout the cultural articles in the DICTIONARY there are notes on the need for reducing the number of blooms for the sake of the remainder. The only general, necessary direction is that if you are to disbud, do it early. Then a minimum of the plant's strength will have passed into flower buds that are to be pinched out.

Same plant disbudded for the sake of the remaining bloom

**DISC.** The disk in the flower heads of plants of the family Compositae (which see). See also SUCKING DISC.

**DISCIFORMIS, -e** (dis-kee-for′mis). Disk-shaped.

**DISCOLOR** (dis′color). Of different, and usually of two distinct colors.

**DISEASES.** See PLANT DISEASES.

**DISHCLOTH GOURD.** See LUFFA.

**DISINFECTION.** See Disinfection at PLANT DISEASES.

**DISK** (also spelled **Disc**). The structure which bears the central flowers in the head of plants of the family Compositae (which see). See also RECEPTACLE.

**DISK FLOWER.** See COMPOSITAE.

**DISK HARROW.** See Section 1, TOOLS AND IMPLEMENTS.

**DISKING.** See HARROWING.

**DISPORUM** (dy-spore′um). A genus of perennial herbs of the lily family, some Asiatic, the two cult. species North American. They are sometimes called fairy bells and are woodland herbs with creeping rootstocks, suited to shady places in the wild garden, preferably in rich (not very acid) humus. Leaves somewhat downy, nearly stalkless, alternate* on the stem. Flowers bell-shaped, the six segments scarcely identifiable as petals or sepals. Stamens* 6, thread-like. Fruit a fleshy red berry. (*Disporum* is from the Greek for double seed, in allusion to a technical ovary character.)

These are scarcely of much garden interest, as their flowers are too ephemeral, but they are sometimes cult. by wild-flower enthusiasts. Both bloom in the spring.

**lanuginosum.** Liverberry. Not over 30 in. high, usually less. Leaves taper-pointed, roundish at the base, 3–4½ in. long, about 2 in. wide. Flowers greenish-yellow, about ½ in. long, solitary or in small umbels.* Eastern N.A.

**oreganum.** Not quite so tall as the last, the leaves smaller and heart-shaped at the base. Flowers white, about ½ in. long, solitary or in small umbels.* Western U.S.

**DISSECTA, -us, -um** (dis-sek′ta). Dissected, *i.e.* divided into numerous fine, sometimes almost thread-like, segments.

**DISSITIFLORA, -us, -um** (dis-si-ti-flow′ra). Loosely flowered; not compact.

**DISTACHYA, -us, -um** (dy-stack′ee-a). Two-spiked.

**DISTICHA, -us, -um** (dis′ti-ka). Distichous.

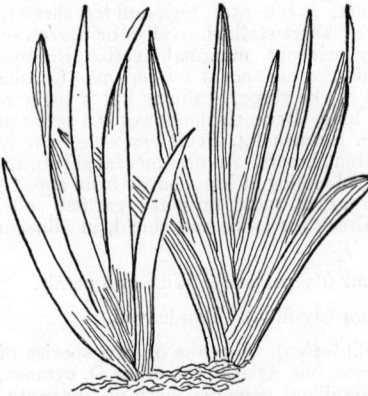

A two-ranked (distichous) arrangement of leaves

**DISTICHOUS.** Arranged in two vertical rows or ranks on opposite sides of a stem; often called two-ranked. The leaves of some iris and of the traveler's-tree are distichous. It results in a flat, fan-like arrangement.

**DISTICTIS** (dis-tick′tis). A small genus of tropical American, woody vines of the family Bignoniaceae, **D. lactiflora** somewhat cult. in Calif. for its showy clusters of purple flowers. It is a high-climbing, tendril*-bearing vine with twice- or thrice-compound* leaves. Leaflets 2 or 3, without teeth, ovalish and 1–2 in. long. Flower purple, the corolla funnel- or bell-shaped, 2–3½ in. long. The flower cluster is branched (panicle*) and very handsome, usually at the ends of the twigs. Fruit a smooth pod 2½–3½ in. long. The plant is not hardy above zone* 8, and is sometimes sold as *D. cinerea*. (*Distictis* is from Greek for twice-dotted and of uncertain application here.)

**DITCH-MOSS** = *Elodea canadensis.*

**DITTANY.** See CUNILA; see also DICTAMNUS ALBUS.

**DIURNA, -us, -um** (dy-er′na). Day-flowering.

**DIVARICATA, -us, -um** (dy-var-i-kay′ta). Divergent; spreading widely.

**DIVERSIFOLIA, -us, -um** (dy-ver-si-fō′li-a). With variable leaves or with different ones.

**DIVERSILOBA, -us, -um** (dy-ver-si-lō′ba). Variously lobed.

**DIVIDED.** Parted or cut to the base or center, as the segments of some leaves. However deeply divided, such leaves are not compound,* and bear no leaflets.

**DIVISION.** Division is an important method of propagation used for all kinds of plants that increase in size by suckers, rhizomes or underground growths. The majority of herbaceous plants spread by the development of eyes or growth buds, each of which, though attached to the parent root, makes independent growth the following season. Most bulbs also increase by division, but in a different way,

---

* Special articles on the subjects indicated by an asterisk (*) will be found at the words so marked.

# DIVISION

the parent bulb splitting up into several. Some shrubs likewise spread by underground sucker-like shoots or root eyes which develop into independent plants though attached to the parent.

Divide asters and similarly rooted plants as shown above.

While practically all such plants can be and usually are propagated commercially from cuttings because of the greater numbers possible, division is the simplest and quickest method of propagation for the amateur. Almost all the hardy perennials lend themselves to division, including the fleshy-rooted subjects like the peony. Lift an old peony root and it will be seen that it is composed of a number of crowns, each having several eyes or growth buds. These crowns may be pulled apart or severed with a knife, so that several independent pieces, each with roots, are secured. Of a

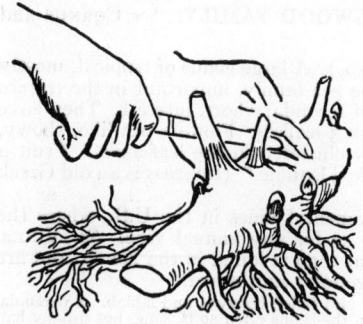
Peony rootstocks should be cut so as to provide several eyes and roots.

different character is the dahlia, which has fleshy, tuber-like roots with the eyes or growth buds on the stems to which are attached the fleshy roots. The latter, unlike true tubers, have no eyes and will not grow if severed from the stem. A large dahlia root with several stems may be pulled apart, but the division of a one-stemmed root necessitates the use of a knife, so that each fleshy root has a portion of the woody stem attached.

The herbaceous perennials vary in their root formation. The *Delphinium* root with several stems must

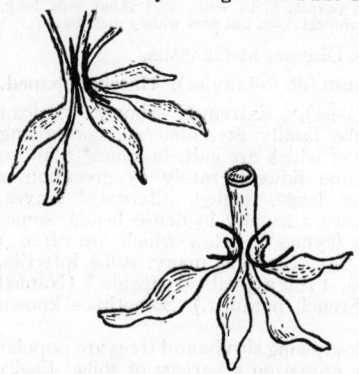
In dividing dahlia roots it is essential to see that part of the bud-bearing stem (*i.e.* with "eyes") is secured. The upper figure shows a clump which may or may not have eyes; the lower figure has eyes and should be divided where indicated.

be divided by a knife, each stem at the base having several eyes. *Helleborus niger*, like the peony, develops crowns, but in larger numbers, and these may readily be pulled or cut apart. Some irises, too, can easily be divided. The tall phlox develops numerous stems with eyes at the base, and they likewise can be pulled or cut apart so that each division possesses some roots. The perennial asters spread by the development of eyes or suckers underground, and every shoot is capable of becoming a separate plant. Low-growing subjects, like the various dwarf or creeping phloxes or violas, when cut back a little in the early fall, may shortly after be pulled into many divisions, which, if planted right away, will make strong plants the following season.

The best time to divide most herbaceous perennials is in the early fall after they are through blooming or early in the spring. Cut them to the ground and lift, and if large and woody, tear them apart by the aid of two digging forks; tearing or pulling apart is better than chopping with a spade or axe. Evergreen low-growers can be pulled apart with

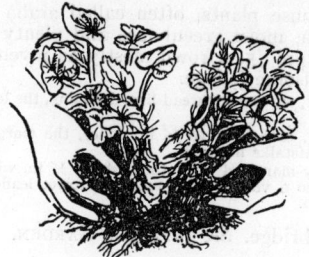
Violet clumps are easily divided by pulling apart.

the fingers. For some subjects that have woody or fleshy roots and few crowns, a spade if carefully used is the best tool.

Tallish-growing herbaceous perennials — plants that die down in the fall — that may be divided are: *Anemone japonica*, *Artemisia*, asters, *Astilbe*, *Boltonia*, *Campanula persicifolia*, *Cimicifuga*, *Coreopsis*, *Delphinium*, *Dicentra*, *Doronicum*, *Erigeron*, all kinds of ferns, gaillardias,

Phlox and similar clumps are best divided by cutting with a spade.

*Helenium*, *Lobelia cardinalis*, phloxes, rudbeckias, thalictrums, *Trollius*, and *Veronica maritima subsessilis* and *V. spicata*. A few low-growing, more or less evergreen subjects easily divided are: *Androsace*, *Arabis*, *Aubrietia*, *Campanula garganica* and kindred types, geums, heucheras, *Phlox subulata* and kindred sorts, primulas, pyrethrums, saxifrages, sedums, sempervivums and violas.

Some perennials have tuber-like roots which are readily separated, among the most common being aconitums, *Liatris* and montbretias. Corm-rooted subjects like *Gladiolus* may be divided or cut into several pieces, but it is not prac-

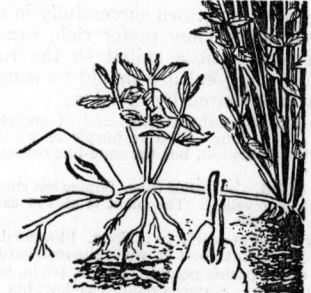
Shrubs that bear suckers or creeping roots should be divided by cutting as indicated.

ticed except when rare forms have to be increased more rapidly than the natural increase by bulblets allows. Shrubs that spread by underground shoots are *Symphoricarpos albus*, *Kerria japonica*, *Clethra alnifolia*, etc. Cut off at the point of union, these shoots quickly make plants. — T. A. W. See also PROPAGATION.

**DIZYGOTHECA** (di-zee-go-thee′ka). Tender, greenhouse foliage plants of the family Araliaceae, probably from the Pacific Islands, but of uncertain identity, as they rarely flower in cult. They are shrubby plants with no spines and compound* leaves, the leaflets arranged finger-fashion and very variable. Sometimes the leaflets are broad and leathery, others, on the same plant or at a different age, being graceful, thread-like and drooping. Whether any of the plants below really belong here is still uncertain. (*Dizygotheca* is from the

---

* Special articles on the subjects indicated by an asterisk (*) will be found at the words so marked.

Greek for having double the usual number of anther* cells.)

These popular greenhouse plants, often called aralia or false aralia, need a warm, moist greenhouse and plenty of water. Use potting mixture* 5. Grown mostly as juvenile pot plants for their handsome foliage.

**elegantissima.** Leaflets 7–11, narrow or thread-like, drooping, the leafstalk mottled white.

**kerchoveana.** Leaflets 7–11, broad (up to ½ in. wide), the margins conspicuously notched, the leafstalks mottled.

**veitchi.** Leaflets 9–11, wavy-margined or toothed, about ¼ in. wide, reddish beneath. There is also a variety with much narrower leaflets, white-striped along the midrib.

**DO-BASHI.** Earthen bridge. See JAPANESE GARDEN.

**DOCK.** See RUMEX.

**DOCKMACKIE** = *Viburnum acerifolium.*

**DOCTOR WALTER VAN FLEET** = Dr. Walter Van Fleet. See Group 6 at ROSE.

**DODDER.** Sprawling, yellow, thread-like plants, parasitic on the foliage of other plants, often completely smothering them. See HOST. As a garden pest dodder is to be controlled only by pulling it out.

**DODECANDRA, -us, -um** (do-deck-an'dra). Having 12 stamens.

**DODECATHEON** (do-deck-kath'ee-on). Beautiful North American wild flowers comprising perhaps 30 species, family Primulaceae, a few of which are cult. in the wild garden or in the rock garden. They are perennial, essentially stemless herbs with basal leaves and cyclamen-like, nodding flowers. Leaves wavy-margined, without teeth, usually narrowed at the base into a winged stalk. Flowers in a small terminal cluster (umbel*) at the end of a stalk arising from the ground. Sepals* 5, turned backwards. Corolla with a very short tube, the 5 lobes turned backwards. Stamens* 5, the anthers* united into a characteristic cone-shaped structure. Fruit a 5-valved capsule. In various sections of the country these plants are called shooting star, American cowslip, and bird bills. (*Dodecatheon* is from the Greek for 12 gods and of no significance here.)

The woodland species cannot be grown successfully in the open border nor in heavy soils. They prefer rich, sandy, woods soil and partial shade. Those suited to the rock garden are so indicated and their culture should be sought at ROCK GARDEN. Easily propagated by division.

**clevelandi.** A perennial herb from southern Calif. and of uncertain culture elsewhere. Leaves 2–2½ in. long. Flowers purple or whitish, the base yellow. The stamens* are purplish, but the cone-like collection of anthers* is yellow.

**hendersoni.** Mosquito bills; called, also, sailor caps. Somewhat similar to the last, but the anthers* deeper yellow. The plant is also of easier cult., as it is native from Calif. to Wash.

**jeffreyi.** Sierra shooting star. Leaves nearly 12 in. long. Flowers deep reddish-purple throughout. Western N.A., best grown in the rock garden.

**meadia.** Shooting star; also called prairie pointer. Leaves 4–6 in. long. Flowers rose-pink, whitish at the base. Stamens reddish-yellow, but the cone-like collection of anthers* purple. A wild garden plant native from Pa. to Tex.

**radicatum.** A rock garden herb, the leaves 4–5 in. long. Flowers rose-pink or reddish, the cone-like collections of anthers purple. Central and southwestern U.S.

**DODONAEA** (do-do-nee'a). A genus of 50 species of tropical and chiefly Australian shrubs and trees of the family Sapindaceae, two grown for ornament in zones* 8 and 9, but of secondary hort. significance. They have alternate* leaves, not compound in those below, without marginal teeth. Flowers small, often of one sex only, without petals, the 3–7 sepals inconspicuous. Stamens 8. Fruit an angled capsule.* (Named for Rembert Dodoens, Dutch physician.)

These bushes, which usually have sticky foliage, are not uncommon in sub-tropical gardens, especially in Fla. and Calif. They are of easy cult. and not particularly attractive. In Aust., and sometimes here, they are called hop-bush.

**cuneata.** A much-branched shrub, the leaves oblongish, ½–1 in. long, wedge-shaped at the base. Flowers mostly in terminal, sometimes branched clusters (racemes*), not showy. Aust.

**viscosa.** Akeake. A shrub, 8–12 ft. high. Leaves oblongish, 3–4 in. long, about an inch wide. Flowers in generally terminal clusters (racemes*), not showy. Of uncertain nativity, perhaps tropical American, but certainly wild in New Zealand from whence comes the vernacular akeake.

**DODONAEACEAE.** See SAPINDACEAE.

**DOES THE GARDEN PAY?** See ACCOUNTS.

**DOGBANE; DOGBANE FAMILY.** See APOCYNUM and APOCYNACEAE.

**DOG BENT.** See AGROSTIS CANINA.

**DOGBERRY** = *Ilex verticillata.* See HOLLY.

**DOG FENNEL** = mayweed. See the list at WEEDS.

**DOG-HOBBLE** = *Leucothoë catesbaei.*

**DOG-PLUM** = *Clintonia umbellata.*

**DOG ROSE** = *Rosa canina.*

**DOGTOOTH VIOLET.** See ERYTHRONIUM.

**DOGWOOD; DOGWOOD FAMILY.** See CORNUS and CORNACEAE.

**DOLICHOS** (dŏ'li-kos). A large genus of tropical, mostly herbaceous vines of the pea family, important in the tropics as forage plants, but of secondary hort. interest. They have compound* leaves with 3 leaflets. Flowers pea-like, showy, often solitary or a few clustered in the leaf-axils.* Fruit a curved, flat, often beaked legume.* (*Dolichos* is an old Greek name for a bean.)

Grown only as ornamental vines in the U.S., where the seeds should be sown as for any annual vine. See VINES. They require more heat than is found in the North, and are most successful from zone* 7 southward.

**lablab.** Hyacinth bean; also called bonavist and lablab. A perennial (grown as an annual) vine, the stems often 30 ft. long, but usually half this. Leaflets broadly oval, the side ones lopsided, and 3–6 in. long. Flowers purple or white, ¾–1 in. long. Pod flat, 1–2½ in. long, papery and beaked, the seeds black or white. Old World tropics and of considerable economic importance there; *i.e.* food, forage, acids, etc.; here only an ornamental.

**lignosus.** Australian pea. Less common in cult., and an evergreen, somewhat woody vine. Leaflets more or less triangular-oval, 1–1½ in. long. Flowers white or rose-purple, ⅓ in. long. Pod about 1 in. long, the seeds black. Probably tropical Asia, but now widely distributed.

**DOLLARSPOT.** See Diseases at GRASSES.

**DOLOBRATA, -us, -um** (do-lo-bray'ta). Hatchet-shaped.

**DOMBEYA** (dom'bee-a). Extremely showy, African shrubs and trees of the family Sterculiaceae, comprising over 100 species, three of which are cult. in zones* 8 and 9 for their very handsome flowers, rarely in greenhouses northward. They have large, angled, alternate* leaves, often long-stalked. Flowers usually in dense heads, sometimes in loose clusters (cymes*), below which are often 3 bracts.* Petals 5 and flat. Stamens many, some infertile, others joined into a tube. Fruit a 5-valved capsule.* (Named for Joseph Dombey, French botanist.) Sometimes known as *Assonia*.

These valuable, quick-growing shrubs and trees are popular in Fla., where they are grown on a variety of soils. Easily propagated by seeds, or by cuttings over bottom-heat.* They bloom in winter in Fla.

**punctata.** A shrub 6–10 ft. high. Leaves angled or toothed on the margin, densely hairy beneath. Flowers pink, fragrant, in umbel-like but not profuse clusters. Mauritius.

**spectabilis.** A shrub 10–15 ft. high, but sometimes taller and tree-like. Leaves very large, long-stalked, angled but not toothed on the margin, white- or rusty-hairy beneath. Flowers white, about ½ in. wide, in dense, branched, many-flowered clusters. Madagascar and tropical Africa.

**wallichi.** A tree up to 30 ft. and the most popular in cult. Leaves somewhat 3-lobed, roundish, nearly 12 in. wide, long-stalked. Flowers pink, about 2 in. wide, in dense, umbel*-like, hanging clusters. Madagascar and tropical Africa.

**DOMESTICA, -us, -um** (do-mes'ti-ka). Domesticated; not wild.

**DOMINANT.** The exclusion or partial exclusion of any effect from the other member of a cross; the opposite from *recessive*. A character is often referred to as dominant or recessive as tall (dominant) and dwarf (recessive) garden peas or as the *dominance* of tall over dwarf. Dominance is seldom complete, most hybrids showing imperfect domi-

---

* Special articles on the subjects indicated by an asterisk (*) will be found at the words so marked.

nance or, as it is often called, blending. In such cases, the height is intermediate between the parents, or the color of the flower may be diluted. Thus yellow × white in certain four-o'clock crosses is light yellow. Dominant variations are far less common than recessive variations, and most of the valuable characteristics that distinguish wild from cultivated plants are recessive variations. — O. E. W.

**DONAX** (dō′nacks). Classical name for the reed, which may have been the cat-tail; now applied to another plant. See ARUNDO.

**DOODIA** (doo′di-a). A genus of chiefly Australasian, dwarf, dense-growing ferns of the family Polypodiaceae, **D. aspera**, the hacksaw fern, popular as a window box and house plant. It is not usually over 12 in. high, often half this, and has rigid, stiffish fronds that are deeply cut into fine segments, but not compound.* Segments 1½–3 in. long, very rough. Spore cases in one or two rows between the midrib and the margins of the segments. Aust. Of easy culture in the cool greenhouse, but it does not like water standing at its roots and the glass should be shaded. See FERNS AND FERN GARDENING. (Named for Samuel Doody, London apothecary.)

**DORMANCY.** See HARDINESS.

**DORMANT GRAFTING.** See GRAFTING.

**DORONICUM** (do-ron′i-kum). Eurasian perennial herbs of the family Compositae, comprising 20–30 species, of which a few are widely grown garden plants under the name leopard's-bane. They are stout, often unbranched herbs with basal, and with alternate* stem leaves, the latter often clasping. Flower heads yellow, long-stalked, with a single row of ray* flowers. (*Doronicum* is a Latinized version of the Arabic name for these plants; it is also a specific name for a *Senecio*.)

The leopard's-banes are of very simple cult. in the border or flower bed, and are considerably grown, especially in the well-filled perennial border. Easily propagated by division. They are mostly spring-blooming.

**caucasicum.** A single-stemmed herb 1–2 ft. high, the leaves coarsely toothed and hairy, the basal ones heart-shaped and long-stalked. Flower head usually one, about 2 in. wide, long-stalked at the end of the main stem. Caucasus and elsewhere in southern Eu.

**clusi.** Nearly 2 ft. high, the stem leaves clasping or partly so, remotely or not at all toothed. Flower heads solitary. Southern Eu.

**plantagineum.** The most popular of the cult. leopard's-banes, and often somewhat branching, 18–30 in. high. Stem leaves stalkless, but not clasping, the basal leaves ovalish or oblong, the base narrowed into a winged stalk. Flower heads more numerous, terminating most branches, 1½–4 in. wide. Eu. There are several named forms, some with many more than a single row of rays, and more handsome garden plants than the typical species; possibly not belonging here at all.

**DOROTHEANTHUS.** See MESEMBRYANTHEMUM.

**DOROTHY PERKINS.** See ROSA WICHURAIANA.

**DORSAL.** The back, or outside, or under side of an organ; as the dorsal side of a leaf is the under side of it. See VENTRAL.

**DORYALIS** = *Dovyalis*.

**DORYANTHES** (dor-i-an′theez). A genus of Australian desert plants of the family Amaryllidaceae, little known in the U.S. outside of Calif. or Fla., where they are cult. for ornament. They much resemble the century plant (*Agave*) in having a basal rosette of thick, fleshy, but not prickly-margined, leaves. There is an immense central stalk topped by a large cluster of showy, red flowers. Petals and sepals distinct. Fruit a capsule.* (*Doryanthes* is from the Greek for spear and flower.) They are commonly called spear lily.

For culture see AGAVE, to which they are related.

**excelsa.** Torch lily. Leaves sword-shaped, 2–4 ft. long, numerous. Flowering stalk 12–18 ft. high, the flowers 4 in. long, in dense heads nearly 1 ft. wide, its bracts* green.

**palmeri.** Leaves very narrow, up to 6 ft. long, the outer arching, the inner erect and hugging the flowering stem which may be 25 ft. high. Flower cluster branched (a panicle*), nearly 3 ft. long, the flowers about 2½ in. long, scarlet. An extremely handsome plant in bloom.

**DOUBLE FLOWERS.** Producing more, and usually much more, than the usual number of petals. The ordinary single flower has, usually, a definite number of petals (or rays in a head), which are pretty apt to be uniform. There are, for instance, 5 petals in an ordinary wild rose. But for some cause, mostly quite unknown, a plant will occasionally produce a flower with more than the usual number of petals. Such plants are a boon to the breeder, whether they happen to be garden possibilities at the moment or not. For they have the capacity to vary in the direction of producing more petals. Most of the double-flowered garden plants have been derived from such variants. The production of petals goes so far that some flowers have lost stamens or pistils, or even both. Double flowers are very common in the rose, peony, garden aster, dahlia, and hundreds of others. Double flowers are extremely rare among wild plants.

**DOUBLE GRAFTING.** See GRAFTING.

**DOUBLE ORANGE DAISY** = *Erigeron aurantiacus*.

**DOUBLE WALL.** See WALLS AND WALL GARDENING.

**DOUBLE WORKING** = Double Grafting. See GRAFTING.

**DOUCIN.** A dwarf variety of apple used for the stock of dwarf apple trees. See APPLE.

**DOUGLAS FIR.** See PSEUDOTSUGA.

**DOUGLASIA** (dug-las′si-a). A small genus of European alpine plants of the family Primulaceae, suited to the rock garden. The only species much grown here is **D. vitaliana** (sometimes known as *Androsace vitaliana*) of the Alps and Pyrenees. It is a tufted,* more or less prostrate perennial herb with a basal rosette of small, narrow, hairy leaves. Flowers 1 or 2, at the end of a short stalk 2 in. high, arising from the rosette. Corolla yellow, the tube long. Fruit a small capsule. The plant resembles *Androsace* and needs the same culture. See ROCK GARDEN. (Named for David Douglas, Scotch botanist who explored the Northwest.)

**DOVE FLOWER; DOVE ORCHID** = *Peristeria elata*.

**DOVYALIS** (do-vi-ā′lis). A genus of 12 species of Old World tropical shrubs or small trees of the family Flacourtiaceae, two of them cult. in Fla. and Calif. as the source of minor fruits. They have alternate,* short-stalked leaves and inconspicuous, small flowers, the male and female on different plants. (For details see FLACOURTIACEAE.) Fruit an edible, but acid, berry. (*Dovyalis* is of unknown origin.) Often called *Aberia* and sometimes spelled *Doryalis*.

Both of those below must have male plants interspersed with female ones to ensure the latter setting fruit. They are not particular as to soils, doing very well on the sandy soils of Fla. The kitambilla can be grown up to the northern edge of zone* 8, but the kei-apple is not so hardy. Propagated by seeds or by shield budding.

**caffra.** Kei-apple; also called umkokolo. A thorny shrub or small tree 10–20 ft. high, the thorns long and stiff. Leaves often clustered at the base of the thorn, 1½–2 in. long. Flowers greenish. Fruit nearly round, about 1 in. in diameter, yellow, the juicy pulp also yellow, cranberry-flavored and good only when cooked. South Africa.

**hebecarpa.** Kitambilla; also called Ceylon gooseberry. About the same size as *D. caffra*, but more branched. Leaves 3–4 in. long. Fruit about 1 in. in diameter, velvety, maroon-purple, less acid than the kei-apple. India and Ceylon.

**DOWN-BUDDING.** See BUDDING.

**DOWNING, A. J.** See America at GARDEN BOOKS.

**DOWNINGIA** (down-in′ji-a). Rather showy, low-growing, annual herbs of the family Lobeliaceae, the two cult. species from the Pacific Coast, others in S.A. Leaves alternate,* without teeth, diminishing upward into small bracts.* Flowers stalkless in the axils* of the upper bracts. Corolla irregular* and 2-lipped, but tubular below. Upper lip much narrower than the 3-lobed lower lip. Stamens 5. Fruit a capsule splitting lengthwise, tipped by the leafy, persistent lobes of the calyx.* (Named for Andrew Jackson Downing, American horticulturist.)

These attractive little summer-blooming plants are hardy annuals. For their culture see ANNUALS.

**elegans.** Not over 7 in. high. Leaves oblongish, ½–¾ in. long. Flowers light blue, but white-throated, and the throat streaked green or yellow, the stamens* long-protruding. Wash. to Calif.

---

* Special articles on the subjects indicated by an asterisk (*) will be found at the words so marked.

pulchella. From 4–6 in. high. Leaves oblongish or ovalish, about ½ in. long. Flowers deep blue, the center of the lower lip white, splotched yellow and purple, the stamens scarcely protruding. Ore. to Calif. Often offered as *Clintonia pulchella.*

**DOWNY.** Softly and weakly hairy.

**DOWNY MILDEW.** *See* Diseases at CINERARIA, GINSENG, HOP, and GRAPE.

**DOWNY MYRTLE** = *Rhodomyrtus tomentosa.*

**DOXANTHA** (docks-an′tha). Two species of tropical American woody vines of the family Bignoniaceae, one of them, **D. unguis-cati**, the cat's-claw, grown in the South and in greenhouses northward. It is a handsome vine with compound,* evergreen leaves composed of 2 leaflets and a terminal, 3-parted, claw-like tendril* by which it clings to supports. Flowers showy, solitary or in small clusters (racemes*), the corolla trumpet-shaped, about 2 in. long, yellow, but the throat orange-streaked. Fruit a narrow pod nearly 12 in. long. Argentina. It is hardy up to the edge of zone* 7, and north of this should be in the cool greenhouse in potting mixture* 4. An extremely handsome vine sometimes offered as *Bignonia unguis-cati* or *B. tweediana*. (*Doxantha* is from the Greek for glory flower.)

**DRABA** (dray′ba). Whitlow grass is a general name for perhaps 175 species of small, usually tufted,* herbs of the mustard family, a few of which are cult. in the rock garden, rarely in borders. They are mostly spring-blooming annuals or perennials from the north temperate zone, with the small leaves chiefly in basal rosettes, and nearly always hairy. Flowers small, but usually numerous and grouped in racemes*; white, yellow, or pinkish-purple. Petals 4. Fruit a small pod. (*Draba* is an old Greek name for some cress.)

All of the drabas below are suited only to the rock garden (which see for their culture).

aizoides. A tufted perennial, not over 4 in. high. Leaves narrow, pointed, without teeth, about ½ in. long. Flowers yellow. Mountains of southern Eu.
cuspidata. A tufted perennial, not over 4 in. high. Leaves narrow, blunt, about ½ in. long. Flowers purplish-pink. Mountains of southern Eu.
fladnizensis. A tufted perennial, making flattish cushions not over 3 in. high. Leaves oblongish, blunt, scarcely ½ in. long. Flowers greenish-white. Mountain tops of Eu. and N.A. and in the Arctic.
hirta. A perennial 5–10 in. high. Leaves narrow, sometimes toothed at the tip, ½–¾ in. long. Flowers white. Northern Eurasia.
olympica. A cushion-like, tufted perennial, 2–4 in. high. Leaves scarcely ¼ in. long, hairy on the margins. Flowers orange. Southern Eu.
repens = *Draba sibirica.*
sibirica. Stems more or less prostrate and often 12 in. long. Leaves not in rosettes, oblongish, hairy, pointed and without teeth. Flowers yellow on slender, upright stems. Siberia and in the Caucasus.

*DRABIFOLIA, -us, -um* (dra-bi-fō′li-a). Having leaves like the genus *Draba*.

**DRACAENA** (dra-see′na). Handsome foliage plants of the lily family, chiefly from the Old World tropics, comprising perhaps 50 species, of which a few are popular greenhouse subjects. They are tree-like, with a crown of leaves suggesting a palm, or more often shrubby and grown in pots for their handsome foliage. Leaves narrow and sword-shaped or wider and with a distinct stalk. Flowers small, greenish or yellowish, rarely produced in greenhouse specimens. They differ only in technical characters from *Cordyline*, with which the cult. species are often confused. Petals and sepals 6 in all, not easily separable as such. Stamens 6. Fruit a 1–3-seeded berry. (*Dracaena* is from the Greek for female dragon, in reference to the first species.)

The dracaenas, especially popular for house decoration and for summer bedding, are only to be grown in the greenhouse in the north, but do well outdoors in southern Fla. and Calif. For their culture and propagation *see* CORDYLINE.

draco. Dragon tree. Rare in cult., but interesting as being the famous dragon tree of the Canary Islands, known to the Greeks before the Christian era. It is a gigantic tree, now over 60 ft. high, but the trunk nearly 20 ft. in diameter. Leaves bluish-green, about 2 ft. long and 1½ in. wide. Flowers greenish. Fruit orange. Canary Islands. Planted outdoors in Calif., but rare in greenhouses and very slow-growing. It was long thought to be the source of commercial dragon's blood.
fragrans. A very common greenhouse plant, usually small and unbranched, but in maturity tree-like, up to 20 ft., and branched. Leaves handsome, in a terminal, rosette-like cluster, about 3 ft. long and 4 in. wide, green, or, in several hort. varieties, variously white-striped or yellow-margined, but not banded crosswise. Flowers (rare in greenhouse plants) yellowish, fragrant. Central Af.
godseffiana. Somewhat similar, but the leaves not over 10 in. long, about 2½ in. wide, narrowed into a channeled stalk, green and irregularly splotched or banded crosswise with white. Flowers, when produced, greenish-yellow. Central Af. A popular foliage plant.
goldieana. Leaves long-stalked, ovalish, 4–8 in. long, about 4 in. wide, short-pointed, green, but banded crosswise with gray-green. Flowers (rare in the greenhouse) white. Central Af.

*DRACAENOIDES* (dra-see-noy′deez; but *see* OÏDES). *Dracaena*-like.

**DRACO** (dray′ko). A specific name meaning dragon and applied to the dragon tree. *See* DRACAENA.

**DRACOCEPHALUM** (dra-ko-seff′a-lum). The dragonheads, so called from the shape of their flowers, comprise about 40 species of herbs of the mint family, a few grown in the flower garden, but of secondary importance. The cult. species are summer-blooming, moderate-sized herbs with opposite* leaves and square stems. Flowers irregular,* 2-lipped,* crowded in dense heads in the leaf-axils* or in terminal spikes (for details *see* LABIATAE). The upper lip is arched and notched, the lower 3-divided. (*Dracocephalum* is Greek for a dragon's head.)

All those below, except *D. moldavica*, are perennials of easy culture in the open border, but prefer partial shade and a fairly moist site. They can be divided in spring or fall.

grandiflorum. A handsome Siberian herb 6–12 in. high. Leaves oblongish, toothed, diminishing upward. Flowers nearly 2 in. long, blue, hairy, in terminal spikes.*
moldavica. A hardy annual, 12–18 in. high. Leaves lance-shaped, toothed, 1–1½ in. long. Flowers bluish-violet, or white, usually less than 1 in. long, in a long, leafy cluster (raceme*). For culture *see* ANNUALS. Eurasia.
nutans. A perennial 8–12 in. high. Leaves ovalish or oblong, 1–2 in. long, toothed. Flowers about ½ in. long, blue, in short, terminal spikes. Siberia. There is also a white-flowered variety which is shaded with blue.
virginianum = *Physostegia virginiana.*

**DRACONTIUM** (dra-kon′she-um). A specific name derived from the genus *Dracontium*, which is of little garden interest. *See* ARISAEMA.

**DRACUNCULUS** (dra-kun′kew-lus). A small group of putrid-smelling aroids* from the Mediterranean region, **D. vulgaris**, the green dragon sometimes cult. in the greenhouse or outdoors south of zone* 7. It has a tuberous rootstock and a few, basal, long-stalked leaves that are deeply cleft into 11–15 segments, the whole leaf often 12 in. wide. Flowers crowded upon a spadix* (for details *see* ARACEAE), which is surrounded by a spathe* that is tubular, green and purple-striped at the base, but purple at the apex and nearly 12 in. long. When in bloom, the odor is offensive. Fruit fleshy. More a curiosity than a garden asset. (*Dracunculus* is Latin for a dragon; also a specific name at *Artemisia*.)

**DRAGGING.** *See* HARROWING.

**DRAGON FLY.** *See* INSECT FRIENDS.

**DRAGONHEAD.** *See* DRACOCEPHALUM.

**DRAGONROOT** = *Arisaema dracontium.*

**DRAGON'S-MOUTH** = *Arethusa bulbosa.*

**DRAGON'S-TONGUE** = *Chimaphila maculata.*

**DRAGON TREE** = *Dracaena draco.*

**DRAINING.** The underdraining of land is usually too expensive to be worth undertaking. But there are tracts where the water-table is so near the surface that it must be carried off or lowered to prevent ordinary garden plants from being killed by water suffocation. And, of course, water must be kept from beneath roads and drives. *See* DRIVES.

While the regulation of excess water under the surface demands an engineer or surveyor if it is to be done on any large scale, the home gardener can often do for himself all that is necessary. First of all, determine, after a dry spell, how much of the site is really water-soaked. This can easily be seen, as capillarity will keep the surface soil moist or even muddy in such places, long after the rest of your garden is already showing a dry or dryish surface.

---

* Special articles on the subjects indicated by an asterisk (*) will be found at the words so marked.

# DRAINING       217       DRIED FLOWERS

Having determined the area of water-soaked soil, the next step is to see if, upon your own land, there is an outlet low enough to be well below the lowest part of your proposed drainage system. If these two factors are favorable, it will be possible to make an effective system. And even if there is no natural outlet such as a stream or pond, it is sometimes possible, especially in suburban areas, to empty your drainage system into a town main.

Assuming that the area is known and a drainage outlet is provided for, there then comes the question of grade and depth and spacing of the tile drains and their diameter. These tiles are made for the purpose, without collars or sleeves, and baked enough so that practically no water enters through their pores as it does through the side of a flower pot.

If the wet area is a small one (25 × 25 ft.), a single line of tile drains will often be enough. But if the area is larger, especially if of irregular shape, a more elaborate system of laterals will be necessary.

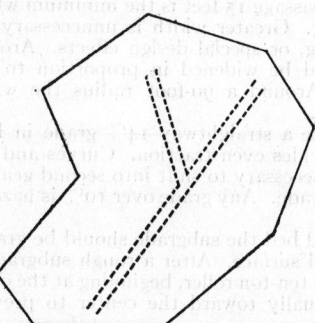

A simple plan for draining a small area. Usually only a few lateral branches are needed.

Some gardeners prefer to solve the draining difficulty by merely digging a ditch. Others improve upon this by filling up the ditch with loose stones. Such makeshifts are inadvisable, on the score both of looks and efficiency. Tile drains properly laid are buried out of sight and will last almost indefinitely.

DEPTH AND PITCH. Drains should not be nearer than 2 ft. below the surface, nor, except in special cases, more than 3 ft. deep. It is better not to use drains of less than 4 in. diameter, and if there is to be only a single line, it is better to use 6-in. pipe.

The pitch at which the system is laid is naturally of the greatest importance. Sometimes the general grade of the land will determine this, but usually the area to be drained is level enough to hold too much standing water and the pitch of the system can be arranged as desired.

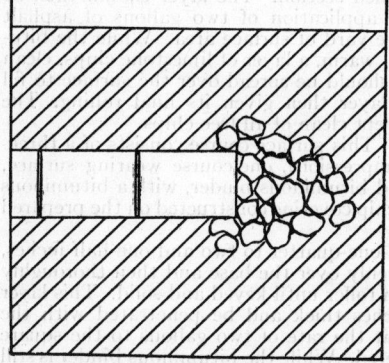

See that the upper end of the tile drain is set in a collection of stones or loose gravel to allow water but not soil to get in.

A good general rule is that the system shall fall at least 3 in. in each 100 ft. That allows a free flow through the tile and a current sufficiently active to carry off any fine soil particles that may seep into the system. It requires considerable ingenuity to determine accurately the proper levels, but it can be done with a spirit level and a string stretched tightly over the trench. Of course an engineer will do it better, but any intelligent gardener can plan his own system with a little care.

Assuming that only one line of tile is to be laid, dig a trench of the proper depth and pitch to carry off the excess water. If in a nice garden, separate topsoil and subsoil as you dig, so that refilling will not leave the subsoil on the top. Then place the drains end to end as closely as possible. They are not made to "nest" like sewer pipe, but they must be so tightly placed end to end that only water and not soil will seep in at the joints.

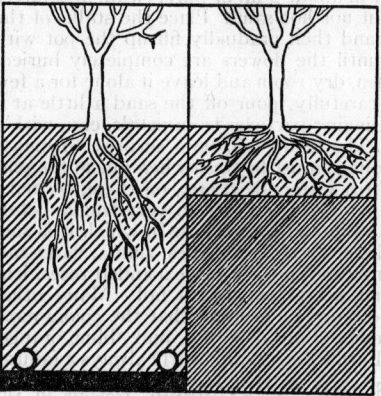

At the right a root system prevented from developing by a water table too high. At the left the same area drained so the roots can develop.

Having laid the tile, it is wiser, before rough filling of the trench, to cover every joint carefully with a little coarse soil or cinders or tar paper. And any irregularity in the bottom of the trench must be taken up as each tile is laid. Either scoop out enough, or if too deep, put the tile on a stone or brick to bring it exactly at the desired depth below your taut string. All this needs care and patience. But properly done, it will transform boggy, useless land into a garden site.

There then remains only the final filling of the trench which may be cinders below but earth above. See also that the outlet is kept free of leaves and debris. The system will then be in operation. It will work no wonders at first. But as the years go on the underdrainage will gradually be carried by your system instead of seeping through the ground generally.

**DRAM.** See WEIGHTS AND MEASURES 4.

**DRAW; DRAWING.** A term of somewhat limited application in the propagation of the sweet potato (which see). A draw is a slip in the propagating bed and drawing is the pulling of such slips, with their roots, for planting in the field.

**DRAWN.** See LEGGY.

**DRESSING.** The trimming and preparation of nursery stock for grafting, budding, or for making cuttings. See these articles for the details.

**DRICONURE.** A trademarked preparation of humus consisting of sphagnum moss, treated to make it neutral, rendered weed-free, and impregnated with cow manure. It is useful for garden soils or for top-dressing lawns.

**DRIED BLOOD.** See Nitrogen at FERTILIZERS.

**DRIED FLOWERS.** Most of the everlastings (which see) and a few of the finer grasses that hold their panicles (see AGROSTIS NEBULOSA, ASPRIS CAPILLARIS, BRIZA, ERAGROSTIS, CHLORIS GAYANA and PANICUM) make good subjects for dried flowers. Their use is dependent upon their holding their color or form or both when perfectly dry. The best method is to dry them slowly, in the shade, and not over artificial heat. Hang them with heads down in an ordinary living room (not over a radiator) until they are brittle, after which they must be handled carefully. The only real objection to them is the dust they gather. See also HONESTY and SYNGONANTHUS.

The fad for dyeing dried flowers has little to recommend it, but is widely practiced. Various aniline dyes can be used, a common one being the green used for carnations on St. Patrick's Day. And the foliage of the butcher's-broom (*Ruscus aculeatus*) is generally colored red for Christmas decorations. The dyes should be sprayed on the dried flowers if they are fragile, but many can simply be dipped in a bath of the desired dye.

An interesting method of drying flowers is offered to careful operators by the sand method. This is suited to certain

---

\* Special articles on the subjects indicated by an asterisk (\*) will be found at the words so marked.

types of flowers that cannot ordinarily be saved at all. Take an ordinary flower pot, deep enough to allow your specimens to be completely submerged. Cover the hole in the bottom with paper and pour in about 2 in. of pure, clean, absolutely dry (oven-baked) but not hot sand. Place the stalks of the flowers in the sand and then gradually fill up the pot with similarly dry sand until the flowers are completely buried. Put the pot in a warm, dry room and leave it alone for a few weeks. Then, very carefully, pour off the sand a little at a time, brushing the clinging particles from petals, etc., with a camel's-hair brush. The result will be a surprise to many.

The flowers and foliage must be fresh when put in the pot, with not a drop of free water, dew, etc., on them, to make the sand method a success. And certain very fragile petals will be ruined by sand immersion. Those in which it is successful are: gaillardia, cosmos, water lilies, zinnia, narcissus, marigolds, and young rose buds. Fully expanded roses, iris, poppy, daylilies, and portulaca always fail. Many other flowers may be tried, keeping in mind that the colors most likely to be best preserved are deep red, pink, blue, orange, yellow, and white. Purple flowers are nearly always a failure.

**DRIED FRUITS AND VEGETABLES.** Except in the desert regions, it is usually impossible to dry fruits and vegetables outdoors in the U.S. Artificial heat is therefore necessary, but this must not be too violent, as drying, not cooking, is the object. For the home gardener the best drying apparatus is the kitchen range if it burns coal or cheap electricity. Put the fruit in slat racks, which will allow plenty of air circulation, as the process involves driving off much moisture.

The racks can be put in the oven, leaving the door open and keeping the temperature between 160° and 190°. A slower method is to suspend the racks over the stove where of course there is merely a warm-air current passing through them. When thoroughly dry, the material must be stored in some place where there will be no re-absorption of moisture. Among the best for drying are apple rings, halved pears, apricots (in Calif.), currants, beans, shredded carrots, and peas. The process is troublesome but worth the effort to preserve an excess harvest.

**DRILL.** A trench in which seeds are planted. Short and shallow ones can be made with a hoe or sharp stick. But much better drills can be made with a proper attachment to a wheel cultivator. Do not, generally speaking, make your drills until ready to plant them, otherwise they become sun-baked and dry.

**DRILL SEEDER.** *See* Section 1, TOOLS AND IMPLEMENTS.

**DRIP.** Rain water dripping off certain trees has a bad effect upon some garden plants and often on the lawn. Tests of the run-off from oaks, pines, firs, beeches, spruces, and the walnut, show clearly that the acid dissolved from bark, twigs, or leaves is so highly concentrated that it injures some garden plants. This is especially true of the first run-off following a prolonged drought. Nothing, of course, can be done about this, but in planting the tree it is well to keep its run-off in mind. The acidity of the run-off may be tested in the same way as soil (*see* ACID AND ALKALI SOILS). The often poisonous drip from city smoke-infested trees, is more serious. For a list of plants that will stand this worst form of drip *see* SHADY GARDEN.

**DRIVES.** There are five essential factors in the design of drives — alignment, width, grade, road-bed construction and drainage.

To determine the alignment of a drive the points of entrance from the highway and arrival at the house must first be fixed. Between these two known points the drive should follow the easiest grade along the most direct and attractive route without unnecessary winding. Curves should be used only when they appear logical, to follow the natural shape of the ground or to avoid permanently fixed obstacles.

The connection with the main highway should be at right angles wherever possible and where this is not possible the angle should favor the direction from which the property is most often approached. Widen the drive at the highway connection by flaring the drive edges on a 30-foot radius. This radius should meet the drive and highway edges at their points of tangency.

Set stakes along the proposed center line of the road at 25-foot intervals. Line the stakes by eye into a pleasing alignment free from abrupt changes in direction, and, after a satisfactory center line is established, set side line stakes opposite each center stake. Avoid curves less than 90-foot inside radius and grades exceeding 10%.

For drives involving considerable grading an engineer will have to be called in.

Around curves the inside curve should be at least 1 foot lower than the outside. If the curve is on a steep grade it should be banked even more. For a 90-foot radius on a 10% grade make the inside curve 18 inches lower than the outside.

For a single-way drive 10 feet is ample width for practical driving. For two-way passage 15 feet is the minimum width for comfortable passing. Greater width is unnecessary except for curves, parking, or special design effects. Around curves the drive should be widened in proportion to the radius of the curve. Around a 90-foot radius the width should be at least 18 ft.

Modern cars can take a straightway 14% grade in high gear if the surface provides even traction. Curves and uneven surfaces make it necessary to shift into second gear on anything over a 10% grade. Any grade over 10% is hazardous for winter driving.

To construct the road bed the subgrade should be graded exactly like the finished surface. After a rough subgrade is established roll it with a ten-ton roller, beginning at the outer edges and rolling gradually toward the center to prevent squeezing out the edges.

On the subgrade lay the base course of the material of which the drive is to be constructed. The best private drive material is some form of bituminous-bound crushed slag or stone. Concrete is not a desirable surface for private drives except on short city property drives and even in this case paving block or brick is more suitable.

The essentials for a bituminous-bound macadam drive for ordinary passenger car and delivery truck wear are: The base should be an eight-inch slag base laid down in two layers or courses on the approved subgrade. The bottom course should be a layer of two-and-one-half to five-inch hard heavy slag which, when thoroughly rolled with a ten-ton roller, must be four inches thick, and have the same crown or bank as the finished section.

The second or upper course of the base must be a layer of the same slag, which, when thoroughly rolled with a ten-ton roller, should be four inches thick and have the same crown or bank as the finished section. The layer should then be penetrated with an application of two gallons of asphalt or tar to each square yard of surface area. While the bituminous binder is still warm, a layer of limestone chips, clean and free from dust, should be spread over the surface to fill the voids and the layer then given its final rolling. The surface should be swept clean of all free chips.

DRIVE SURFACE. This surface course consists of a three-inch (after final compression), one-course wearing surface, composed of slag and bituminous binder, with a bituminous seal coat and stone-chip covering constructed on the prepared base course.

The slag, one and one-quarter to two and one-half inches, should be spread evenly over the base and then thoroughly rolled with a ten-ton roller until keyed and solid. This layer should be three inches thick and be penetrated with the bituminous binder at the rate of two gallons to the square yard of surface covered. While the bituminous binder is still warm, enough limestone chips should be spread over the surface to fill all the voids and the drive thoroughly rolled again. All excess chips should be brushed off and then the entire surface given a seal coat of bituminous binder at the rate of one-half a gallon to each square yard of surface covered. Before this is cold the surface should be covered with a thin layer of limestone chips and rolled lightly. The entire surface must be thoroughly rolled after this application and additional chips applied as required to take up all excess

---

\* Special articles on the subjects indicated by an asterisk (\*) will be found at the words so marked.

bituminous material and leave the finished surface uniform and conforming to grades.

Variations in surface treatment may be substituted for the above specifications to meet special requirements. For a smoother, more perfect surface a pre-mix material such as Amiesite or Colprovia may be used in place of a penetration surface. To disguise the macadam texture granite chips of various colors, or silica gravel, may be rolled into the surface.

The life and durability of a drive depend on its drainage. To keep water off the surface, crown the drive two to three inches higher in the middle than at the edges, and provide gutters adequate to collect all surface drainage from the drive and any slopes pitching toward the drive.

Water must be kept out from under the drive base. A wet base means a soft road bed and frost will soon destroy the most perfect construction under such conditions. See DRAINAGE. — R. E. G.

A drive or path with provision for draining off excess water

**DROPMORE.** See ANCHUSA AZUREA.

**DROPPER.** See TULIP DROPPER.

**DROPWORT** = *Filipendula hexapetala*.

**DROSERA** (dros'sir-ra). Interesting insectivorous plants, commonly called sundew from their glistening foliage. The genus comprises over 90 species, widely distributed, but most abundant in Aust. All those below are found in N.A., where they grow in sphagnum bogs or on the sandy shores of them. All require similar conditions to thrive under cult., although a good substitute is a sphagnum-filled pot in the cool greenhouse. Whether indoors or out, the mixture in which they grow must be about pH 4 (see ACID AND ALKALI SOILS for details). They are small, perennial herbs with a basal rosette of much-modified leaves covered with glistening, sticky hairs. Flowers in a sparse cluster at the end of a short stalk arising from the rosette of leaves (for details see DROSERACEAE). Fruit a capsule.* (*Drosera* is from the Greek for dewy, in allusion to the glistening leaf hairs.)

For their methods of digesting insects see INSECTIVOROUS PLANTS.

**filiformis.** Leaves long and thread-like, 6–9 in. long, green, but the hairs purplish. Flower cluster about as high as the leaves, or a little more, the flowers pinkish-purple, about ¼ in. wide. Mass. to Fla.
**longifolia.** Leaves broadest towards the tip, narrowed to a very slender base, usually about 1½ in. long, green or reddish, the hairs reddish-purple. Flowers white, the cluster 6–8 in. high. North temperate zone.
**rotundifolia.** Common sundew; called also dew plant and rosa solis. Leaves close to the ground and having a round, flat blade, about ¾ in. in diameter, narrowed to a flat stalk, the whole red or green, the hairs always reddish-purple. Flowers white or pinkish, the stalk 4–10 in. high. North temperate zone.

**DROSERACEAE** (dros-sir-ray'see-ee). The sundew family is one of the few plant families having the ability to digest animal matter directly (*see also* NEPENTHACEAE and SARRACENIACEAE). Of its four known genera, two are often cult. for their interesting habit of catching and digesting insects. *Drosera*, the sundew, does this by the sticky-glistening hairs on its foliage, while *Dionaea*, the Venus's-flytrap, has hinged, hairy, valve-like leaves that close on its prey. Both are bog plants; *Drosera* being cosmopolitan, but *Dionaea* localized in N. Car. and S. Car.

Leaves unlike ordinary foliage leaves (*see* DROSERA and DIONAEA). Flowers usually in small clusters, white or pinkish (in ours), followed by a small pod (capsule*).

Technical flower characters: Flowers regular. Sepals and petals 5, the stamens 5 or more. Ovary superior,* 1-celled, the single style rather long, the ovules 3 to many.

**DROUGHT-RESISTANT PLANTS.** Regions with deficient or seasonal rainfall present difficult problems to the gardener. There is no need here to repeat information on the plants suited to such localities. See the articles on CACTI, SUCCULENTS, SAND GARDENS, DESERT GARDENS, and the rainfall data at the name of your state or province. *See also* RAINFALL and the discussion of cultivation at EVERGREENS.

**DRUMMOND PHLOX** = *Phlox drummondi*.

**DRUMSTICK TREE** = *Cassia fistula*.

**DRUPACEA, -us, -um** (droo-pay'see-a). Bearing drupes.

**DRUPACEAE.** See ROSACEAE.

**DRUPE.** A fleshy, 1-seeded fruit that does not split. The seed is enclosed in a bony stone, hence such fruits are often called stone fruits, common examples being peach, plum, cherry, and olive.

**DRUPELET.** A little drupe, often one of many, as in the raspberry.

**DR. WALTER VAN FLEET.** See Group 6 at ROSE.

**DRYANDRA** (dry-ăn'dra). A large genus of Australian shrubs and trees of the family Proteaceae, little known here except for the two shrubs below which are cult. in Calif. They have alternate* leaves, and yellow flowers without petals, but showy because crowded in dense heads beneath which are bracts* and foliage leaves. (For detailed flower structure *see* PROTEACEAE.) The flowers are decidedly woolly, as are also the pods. (Named for Jonas Dryander, Swedish naturalist.)

These shrubs are not certainly hardy north of zone* 8, but do not appear to have any very definite soil preferences. They are propagated by cuttings of side shoots taken in summer and rooted in sand under shade and with mild bottom-heat.

**floribunda.** Shrub 6–8 ft. high. Leaves practically stalkless, more or less wedge-shaped, prickly, 1–2 in. long. Flower heads small, terminal, the bracts* beneath it about ½ in. long. Flowers almost 1 in. long.
**formosa.** Shrub 10–15 ft. high. Leaves divided nearly to the midrib, 6–8 in. long. Flower head larger, terminal, the bracts beneath it about 1½ in. long. Flowers about 1½ in. long.

**DRYAS** (dry'as). Rock garden herbs of the cooler parts of the north temperate zone, family Rosaceae, two of the half dozen known species sometimes grown in the rock garden. They are somewhat woody, perennial herbs with alternate,* usually evergreen leaves, and rather showy, solitary flowers borne at the end of slender stalks. Sepals 8–10, more or less persistent. Petals 8–10, yellowish or white. Stamens* many. Fruit a collection of feathered or plumed achenes,* suggesting *Geum*. (*Dryas* is from Greek for wood nymph.) The plants are sometimes called mountain avens.

For culture see ROCK GARDEN.

**octopetala.** Densely tufted, prostrate plant, the leaves oblongish, about 1 in. long, and white-felty beneath. Flowers about 1½ in. wide, white, upright. Fruiting plumes about 1 in. long. Mountain and northern parts of Eu., As. and N.A.
**suendermanni.** Somewhat similar, but the flowers yellow in the early stage, ultimately white, nodding. Of hybrid origin.

**DRYING FLOWERS.** See DRIED FLOWERS.

**DRYING FRUITS AND VEGETABLES.** See DRIED FRUITS.

**DRY MEASURES.** See WEIGHTS AND MEASURES, 3.

**DRYMIFOLIA, -us, -um** (dry-mi-fō'li-a). With leaves like the genus *Drimys*, which is here of little garden interest.

**DRYMOCALLIS GLANDULOSA** = *Potentilla glandulosa*.

**DRYOPTERIS** (dry-op'ter-is). The shield ferns, of nearly world-wide distribution, and containing perhaps hundreds of species of the family Polypodiaceae, are, so far as the cult. plants are concerned, chiefly hardy ferns for the outdoor

* Special articles on the subjects indicated by an asterisk (*) will be found at the words so marked.

fern garden. For other plants sometimes included here see POLYSTICHUM. Some of the shield ferns are also still called *Aspidium* and *Thelypteris* by dealers. They have usually erect, handsome fronds that may be twice- or thrice-compound,* the ultimate segments somewhat or very much toothed. Spore* cases near the center or along the edges of the segments that bear them. (*Dryopteris* is from Greek for oak fern.)

For culture of these chiefly hardy ferns see FERNS AND FERN GARDENING.

**acrostichoides** = *Polystichum acrostichoides*.
**clintoniana.** Clinton's fern. Much resembling the next and perhaps only a variety of it, but the ultimate frond segments are 4-6 in. long. N.A. and northern Eu.
**cristata.** Crested shield fern. Fronds 18-30 in. long, erect and striking, twice-compound,* the ultimate segments 2-3 in. long, finely toothed, the foliage thus beautifully feathery. North temperate zone.
**filix-mas.** Male fern. Leaves (fronds) in dense crowns, nearly evergreen, 2-3½ ft. long, and almost 1 ft. wide, twice-compound,* the ultimate segments deeply toothed or cut. N.A. and Eu. A popular fern garden plant, offered also in a crested and in a dwarf form.
**goldieana.** Goldie's fern. Fronds in a dense crown, each leaf 2½-4 ft. high, nearly 18 in. wide and twice-compound.* Ultimate segments dark green, broadest at the middle, toothed. Eastern N.A. and one of the finest of our native ferns.
**hexagonoptera.** A lower and more open fern, the fronds more or less triangular in outline, about 15 in. long and 12 in. wide, and only once-compound, often somewhat sticky beneath. Ultimate segments oblongish and a little toothed, but the lowermost pair much longer than the others and deeply lobed or toothed. Eastern N.A.
**linnaeana.** Oak fern. Fronds more or less triangular, about 11 in. long and as wide, twice-compound,* the ultimate segments narrow and wavy-toothed or nearly without teeth. North temperate zone.
**marginalis.** Evergreen wood fern. Fronds growing in a dense crown, nearly evergreen, 8-24 in. high, twice- or thrice-compound.* Ultimate segments lobed or without lobes, the spore cases conspicuously dotted along the margins. Eastern N.A. Very common in woods and much gathered for florists' decorations. Of easy cult. in the shade. See FERNS AND FERN GARDENING.
**phegopteris.** Beech fern. Fronds more or less triangular, about 9 in. long and 8 in. wide, once-compound.* Ultimate segments mostly without teeth, but the lowermost pair recurved and standing forward. Spore cases near the margin. North temperate zone.
**spinulosa.** Fronds about 18 in. long and half as wide, persistent or nearly evergreen, twice-compound,* the ultimate segments deeply cut. North temperate zone.
**thelypteris.** Marsh fern. Rootstock creeping, the erect fronds very graceful, nearly 30 in. long, and about 6 in. wide, once-compound,* the ultimate segments deeply cut, the margin slightly rolled. North temperate zone, especially in open, wet places. It needs less shade and more moisture than the others.

**DRY ROT.** See Diseases at GLADIOLUS.

**DRY STRAWBERRY** = *Waldsteinia fragarioides*.

**DRY WALL.** See WALLS AND WALL GARDENING.

**DRY WINES.** See *vinifera* varieties at GRAPE.

**DUCHESNEA** (doo-shay'nee-a). Two Asiatic species of perennial herbs of the rose family, D. indica of secondary garden interest. It is commonly called the mock strawberry or Indian or barren strawberry from its *Fragaria*-like aspect. It is a trailing herb with runners, the compound* leaves with 3 leaflets, which are ovalish and coarsely toothed. Flowers yellow, solitary, about ¾ in. wide, the petals 5. Fruit red, surrounded by the persistent calyx, suggesting a strawberry, but inedible. It is established as a weedy plant in various parts of the U.S. and is of the easiest cult. Of some use as a ground cover. (Named for Antoine Nicolas Duchesne, French student of the true strawberry.)

**DUCK MANURE.** See MANURE.

**DUCKWEED.** See LEMNA.

**DUCKWHEAT** = *Fagopyrum tataricum.* See BUCKWHEAT.

**DUC VAN THOL TULIP.** See Garden Tulips at TULIPA.

**DUDAIM MELON** = pomegranate melon. See MELON.

**DUFOUR, J. J.** See America at GARDEN BOOKS.

**DUKE CHERRY** = *Prunus avium regalis*.

**DULCAMARA** (dul-ka-mā′ra). Latin for bittersweet. See SOLANUM.

**DULCIS, -e** (dul'sis). Sweet.

**DUMB CANE** = *Dieffenbachia seguine*.

**DUMOSA, -us, -um** (doo-mō′sa). Shrubby.

**DUNG.** See MANURE.

**DUPLEX DAHLIA.** See DAHLIA.

**DURACINA, -us, -um** (du-ra-sy′na). With hard fruit or berries.

**DURANTA** (du-ran′ta). Perhaps a dozen species of tropical American shrubs and trees of the family Verbenaceae, D. repens (sometimes called *D. plumieri*) cult. outdoors in Fla. and Calif. for ornament. It is commonly called tropical lilac, pigeonberry or sky-flower, and is a shrub or small tree 12-20 ft. high, its 4-angled branches often drooping or even trailing. Leaves generally opposite* (sometimes whorled*), ovalish, about 3½ in. long, toothed or without teeth. Flowers in a terminal cluster (raceme*), showy, but the corolla* only about ½ in. wide, lilac, slightly tubular, its five lobes slightly oblique, minutely hairy on the edges. Fruit fleshy, yellow, 8-seeded, about ½ in. in diameter. Fla. to Brazil. Rarely cult. in northern greenhouses, where it needs a warm-temperate house and potting mixture* 4. (Named for Castor Durantes, Roman botanist.)

*DURIUS, -or* (dur′ee-us). Harder or tougher.

*DURIUSCULA, -us, -um* (dur-ee-us′kew-la). Rather hard or tough.

*DURRA.* Native name in Egypt for *Holcus sorghum durra*.

**DUSTER.** See SPRAYING AND DUSTING.

**DUSTY CLOVER** = *Lespedeza capitata*.

**DUSTY MILLER.** An old plant name of rather wide and somewhat confusing application. Perhaps it should be confined to *Senecio cineraria* or *Artemisia stelleriana*, but it is also used for *Centaurea cineraria, C. gymnocarpa, Lychnis coronaria*, and many other wild plants.

**DUTCH BULBS.** A loose designation for bulbs raised in Holland, notably tulip, hyacinth, crocus, etc.

**DUTCH CASE-KNIFE BEAN** = *Phaseolus coccineus albus*.

**DUTCH CLOVER** = *Trifolium repens*. See CLOVER.

**DUTCH CROCUS.** See CROCUS AUREUS.

**DUTCH ELM** = *Ulmus hollandica*. See ELM.

**DUTCH ELM DISEASE.** See ELM.

**DUTCH GARDEN.** See ARCHITECTURAL STYLE.

**DUTCH HOE.** See TOOLS AND IMPLEMENTS, Section 1.

**DUTCH HOLLY.** See *Ilex aquifolium* at HOLLY.

**DUTCH IRIS.** See IRIS.

**DUTCHMAN'S-BREECHES** = *Dicentra cucullaria*.

**DUTCHMAN'S-PIPE** = *Aristolochia durior*.

**DUTCH RUSH** = *Equisetum hyemale*.

**DUTCH YELLOW.** See CROCUS AUREUS.

**DUTOX.** A trademarked insecticide containing barium fluosilicate, sold with directions for use as a stomach poison.

**DWARF.** As an adjective *dwarf* is part of the name of many garden plants, usually signifying low stature or small parts. Those found in THE GARDEN DICTIONARY, with their proper equivalents, are:

Dwarf alder = *Fothergilla gardeni;* dwarf banana = *Musa cavendishi* (for culture see BANANA); dwarf dandelion = *Krigia virginica;* dwarf elm = *Ulmus pumila* (see ELM); dwarf fan palm = *Chamaerops humilis;* dwarf ginseng = *Panax trifolium;* dwarf goldenrod = *Solidago nemoralis* (see

* Special articles on the subjects indicated by an asterisk (*) will be found at the words so marked.

GOLDENROD); **dwarfing** (see next main entry); **dwarf Japanese quince** = *Chaenomeles japonica*; **dwarf June-berry** = *Amelanchier stolonifera*; **dwarf laurel** = *Kalmia angustifolia*; **dwarf lima bean** = *Phaseolus limensis limeanus* (for culture see BEAN); **dwarf morning-glory** = *Convolvulus tricolor*; **dwarf nasturtium** = *Tropaeolum minus* (see NASTURTIUM); **dwarf palmetto** = *Sabal minor*; **dwarf pea** (see PEA); **dwarf poinciana** = *Poinciana pulcherrima*; **dwarf Russian almond** = *Prunus nana*; **dwarf sumac** = *Rhus copallina*.

**DWARFING.** Many naturally dwarf forms of tall plants exist, these being sports or mutations that retain their dwarf character. Thus we have extremely dwarf varieties of antirrhinums, petunias and other annuals that come true from seed, the dwarf habit being fixed by prolonged selection. There are also many dwarf varieties of coniferous evergreens which, while retaining the general characteristics of the parent species, persist in remaining dwarf, their short-jointedness and slow growth resulting in a stature that is only a fraction of the normal type of the same age.

An old pine dwarfed by years of effort

The dwarf evergreens for which Japanese gardeners are famous are, however, artificially produced. Some of these specimens growing in shallow dishes or earthenware urns may be anywhere between 10 and 80 years old, possessing all the gnarled, aged appearance of full-grown specimens of the same age, though they be no more than two feet tall. Infinite patience is required to obtain such specimens, and some examples, imported from Japan before the Quarantine Law forbade the entry of plants growing in soil, represented the work of three or four generations of gardeners. Such specimens now existing in the United States are few and are in the hands of skilled gardeners who can give them the necessary attention.

Few occidental gardeners are inclined to devote years to growing artificially dwarf trees of this character, but the process is more a matter of patience than anything else. Seedlings or rooted cuttings, healthy but not the most vigorous, should be chosen, and they should be kept in the smallest pots possible. Before potting into 2-in. pots, cut off part of the tap root, and pot very firmly, using a heavy soil and a bit of moss at the bottom to prevent clogging of the drainage hole. Cut away any roots that push through the bottom of the pot, and keep the latter in a larger pot packed with moist moss to prevent drying out. Allow to stand outdoors sheltered from hot sunshine during the summer and keep in a frost-free house during the winter. Give no more water at any time than is essential and only fertilize in minute doses. Some Japanese growers, however, water constantly, apparently on the theory that over-watering impoverishes the soil, by leaching. Constant pinching of the growths is necessary, and to encourage an aged appearance the various branches should be tied down or twisted as fancy dictates. Re-potting should be done in the spring, each shift being into a pot only slightly larger than the previous one, which means that root pruning must be vigorous. Pines, firs, taxodiums, junipers, cryptomerias, etc., may be dwarfed in this way, as may some of the hard-wooded, flowering shrubs, such as azaleas, *Pieris, Pyracantha*, Japanese cherries and Japanese quinces, as well as foliage shrubs such as cut-leaf maples, hollies, *Osmanthus* and *Rhus typhina laciniata*.— T. A. W.

**DYCKIA** (dike′i-a). Over 60 species of desert, succulent, South American plants of the pineapple family, two of which are sometimes cult. outdoors in Fla. and Calif., more rarely in northern greenhouses. They resemble miniature century plants in having a basal rosette of spiny-margined leaves. Flowers (in those below) yellow or orange in a bracted cluster which arises from the leaf rosette (for details of flower structure see BROMELIACEAE). Fruit a capsule.* (Named for Prince Salm-Dyck, German botanist.)

For culture see SUCCULENTS.

**rariflora.** Leaves 4–6 in. long, about ⅛ in. wide, the spines sharp and upward-pointing. Flowers nearly stalkless in the cluster, orange, about ½ in. long, the cluster nearly 18 in. long. Brazil.

**sulphurea.** Leaves 5–8 in. long, about ⅓ in. wide, the spines smaller. Flowers yellow, about ⅓ in. long, distinctly stalked in the cluster, which may be up to 12 in. long. Brazil.

**DYEING FLOWERS.** See DRIED FLOWERS.

**DYER'S GREENWEED** = *Genista tinctoria*.

**DYER'S WOAD** = *Isatis tinctoria*.

**DYER'S WOODRUFF** = *Asperula tinctoria*.

**DYNAMITE.** An unusual, but very useful, garden adjunct, to be employed only by an experienced, usually professional, operator. There is no substitute for it in destroying layers of hardpan or other compacted material. Such a subsoil often makes tree-growing impossible, but a stick of dynamite exploded where each tree is to be planted will shatter the most refractory material.

It is also commonly employed for making tree holes in stony or rocky land, especially where layers of impervious rock underlie an orchard or garden site. Needless to add is the caution to remove to a safe place all topsoil while the charge is exploded.

---

* Special articles on the subjects indicated by an asterisk (*) will be found at the words so marked.

# E

**EARDROPS.** See DICENTRA.

**EARLY.** A common hort. designation for crops that mature quickly, regardless of when they are planted. Early corn, for instance, may take 45 days from seeding to harvest, while late corn requires from 55–65 days. The term *early* thus has two distinct meanings in the garden world: the usual one of being early in the season and this somewhat special one which relates to speed of maturity.

**EARLY BLIGHT.** See Diseases at POTATO.

**EARLY CRESS** = *Barbarea verna*.

**EARLY DWARF PEA** = *Pisum sativum humile*. See PEA.

**EARLY McINTOSH.** See APPLE.

**EARLY MEADOW RUE** = *Thalictrum dioicum*.

**EARLY PERENNIAL PHLOX** = *Phlox suffruticosa*.

**EARLY RICHMOND.** A sour cherry. See CHERRY.

**EARLY SAXIFRAGE** = *Saxifraga virginiensis*.

**EARLY TULIPS.** See Garden Tulips at TULIPA.

**EAR ROT.** See Diseases at CORN.

**EARTH ALMOND** = *Cyperus esculentus*.

**EARTHNUT** = *Cyperus esculentus*.

**EARTH WALL.** See WALLS AND WALL GARDENING.

**EARTHWORMS.** True earthworms do not belong to the same branch of the animal kingdom as insects, crabs and spiders. They inhabit moist, fertile soils in most of the humid regions. Because their habits of mixing the soil by burrowing, and of bringing bits of decaying vegetable matter into the soil, tend to increase soil fertility, they are listed among beneficial organisms. Their usefulness as fish bait is well known. Occasionally, however, they cause complaint by making little heaps of soil on the surface of the ground, marring the appearance of lawns and interfering with the playing qualities of golf greens, and this sometimes leads to requests for control methods.

Several substances applied to the soil have been found to kill earthworms. Most effective and convenient is a solution of corrosive sublimate, 2 or 3 ounces to 50 gallons of water. It should be sprinkled over the lawn at the rate of 50 gallons to 1000 square feet, and the treatment should be followed by watering. As the corrosive sublimate is very poisonous, caution should be used in handling it, and metal containers used for it should be washed promptly to prevent corrosion. — F. M. W.

**EASTER-BELL** = *Stellaria holostea*.

**EASTER DAISY** = *Townsendia exscapa*.

**EASTER LILY** = *Lilium longiflorum eximium*.

**EASTERN BLUE STEM.** See Diseases at RASPBERRY.

**EAST INDIAN LOTUS** = *Nelumbium nelumbo*.

**EAST INDIAN ROSE BAY** = *Tabernaemontana coronaria*.

**EAST INDIAN WALNUT** = *Albizzia lebbek*.

**EBENACEAE** (ee-be-nay'see-ee, also ebb-e-nay'see-ee). The ebony or persimmon family, largely tropical, contains only 6 genera of unusually hard-wooded trees or shrubs. One of its few genera found in the temperate zone is *Diospyros* (see PERSIMMON), widely cult. for its edible fruit.

Leaves alternate,* without marginal teeth, mostly rather leathery. Male and female flowers often on separate trees, but always separate even if on the same tree, solitary or in small clusters in the leaf-axils.* Fruit (in the cult. genera) fleshy.

The persimmon and a close relative, *Maba*, which is tropical, are the only cult. genera.

Technical flower characters: Calyx 3–7-lobed, sometimes persistent and much enlarged in fruit. Corolla more or less bell-shaped or tubular, 3–7-lobed. Stamens inserted on the base of the corolla, the same number as the corolla-lobes or twice as many, some (or all in the female flowers) sterile. Ovary superior,* 2–16-celled. Styles 2–8.

**EBONY FAMILY** = Ebenaceae.

**EBONY SPLEENWORT** = *Asplenium platyneuron*.

**ECBALLIUM** (ek-băl'lee-um). The squirting cucumber, **E. elaterium**, is the only species in this curious genus of vines of the family Cucurbitaceae. It is grown more for its remarkable fruits than for ornament (but *see* VINES). It is a hairy, perennial, herbaceous vine from the Mediterranean region, with alternate,* triangular-ovalish leaves, 3–4 in. long and grayish-felty beneath. Male and female flowers separate on the same plant, both yellow. Female flower solitary, the male flowers in racemes,* sometimes both in the same leaf-axil.* Fruit an oblongish berry, 1½–2 in. long, rough-hairy, which at the moment of detachment from its stalk squirts out its brownish seeds with explosive force. (*Ecballium* is from the Greek to eject.)

**ECCREMOCARPUS** (ek-krem'o-kar-pus). A small genus of Andean vines of the family Bignoniaceae, **E. scaber** grown for its very handsome flowers. It is a stem-climbing, tendril*-bearing vine with opposite, twice-compound* leaves. Leaflets ovalish, about 1 in. long. Flowers orange-red, in a showy, summer-blooming, terminal raceme.* Corolla about 1 in. long, tubular, but the limb 2-lipped, hence slightly irregular.* Fruit a slender pod (capsule*) about 1½ in. long. Chile. Hardy as a perennial vine from zone* 7 southward, but in the North it blooms from seed if treated as a tender annual (*see* ANNUALS). (*Eccremocarpus* is from the Greek for pendulous fruit.)

**ECHEVERIA** (ech-e-veer'i-a). A large genus of tropical American, chiefly Mexican, succulent plants of the family Crassulaceae, a few grown as summer bedding plants and in the greenhouse. They have thick, often grayish leaves, chiefly in a basal rosette, resembling the houseleeks. Flowers in a cluster at the end of a stalk that arises at the leaf rosette. Calyx tubular and 5-parted, nearly as long as the 5 petals, which are rarely or only slightly united into a tube. Stamens* 10. Fruit dry. (Named for Atanasio Echeverra, botanical artist in Mexico.)

All the plants below can be grown in the cool greenhouse (*see* SUCCULENTS). They are often used for summer carpet bedding. While they grow perfectly outdoors in Calif. and the Southwest, they cannot stand the wet, slushy winters of much of the North. *Echeveria secunda* and *E. glauca* are nearly hardy as far north as Washington, D.C.

*agavoides* = *Urbinia agavoides*.

**gibbiflora.** A branching plant 1–2 ft. high. Leaves somewhat wedge-shaped or oblongish, 5–7 in. long, grayish-blue or becoming pinkish, mostly in a basal rosette, but a few clustered towards the ends of the branches. Flowers red, about ½ in. long, in a 1-sided cluster. Mex.

**glauca.** Leaves all basal, nearly round, about ¾ in. wide, pale bluish-green, the terminal point purplish. Flowers about ½ in. long, pink outside, yellowish inside, the stalks reddish, the cluster 1-sided. Mex. Sometimes offered as *E. secunda glauca*.

**secunda.** Similar to *E. glauca*, but the leaves reddish along the margins, and with red flowers. Mex.

*weinbergi* = *Byrnesia weinbergi*.

**ECHINACEA** (ek-in-ā'see-a). Almost weedy, North American perennial herbs of the family Compositae, commonly called coneflower or purple coneflower and sometimes offered under the name *Brauneria*. They are coarse herbs with black, pungent roots, stout, hairy stems, and alternate* leaves, the basal ones long-stalked. Flower heads solitary on long stalks at the end of the stems, the center of the head distinctly conical. Ray flowers not numerous,

---

* Special articles on the subjects indicated by an asterisk (*) will be found at the words so marked.

rose or rose-purple, withering but persistent. Below the head is a close-set series of small bracts,* the tips of which are finally recurved. (*Echinacea* is from the Greek for hedgehog, in allusion to the sharp bracts.*)

The two below are of the easiest culture in the open border. Both are native in the U.S. and grow wild in a variety of sites. They will stand sun and wind, are easiest propagated by division, and are summer bloomers.

**angustifolia.** Purple daisy. Usually not much-branched, 1-2 ft. high. Leaves broadly lance-shaped or narrower, about 8 in. long, narrowed at the base into a long stalk, without marginal teeth. Ray flowers 1-2 in. long, 2-toothed at the tip. Central cone of the head nearly 1 in. high. Central and western N.A.

**purpurea.** Hedgehog coneflower; called also Black Sampson. Usually branched, 2-3 ft. high. Leaves broader, ovalish, toothed, the long stalk winged* or not. Flower heads similar to *E. angustifolia*, but more numerous. Central U.S.

**ECHINOCACTUS** (ee-ky'no-kak-tus). A small but badly confused genus of generally globular, or columnar, ribbed cacti, ranging from the southwestern U.S. to Mex. Botanists have attributed nearly a thousand different species to the genus, all but 9 of which are now considered as of other genera (*Ferocactus, Astrophytum, Echinomastus, Thelocactus*, etc.). While some of the species of *Echinocactus* are cult. by fanciers, the one of chief interest is **E. grusoni**. It is a large plant, orange-shaped, 16-30 in. in diameter, with many ribs and numerous golden-yellow spines. Flowers at the summit of the plant, red and yellow, day-blooming, 1½-2½ in. long, partly hidden by the dense wool that clothes the top of the plant. Fruit oblongish, ½-¾ in. long, white-woolly, its seeds black and shining. Mex. For culture see CACTI. (*Echinocactus* is Greek for spine and cactus.)

**ECHINOCEREUS** (ee-ky-no-seer'ee-us). A genus of nearly 60 species of generally low, prostrate or hanging cacti, all from the southwestern U.S. and Mex., two grown for ornament or interest in desert regions or in the greenhouse. They usually form large clumps, the stems cylindrical or nearly globular, strongly ribbed, sometimes jointed. The ribs are plentifully beset with spines. Flowers solitary, borne on the sides but toward the top of the branches, day-blooming, more or less funnel-shaped or bell-shaped, the tube spiny. Fruit fleshy, thin-skinned, edible in some species. (*Echinocereus* is Greek for spine and *Cereus*.)

More than 30 species are known to be cult., most of them confined to the collections of experts or fanciers. For the cult. of the two below, which are the commonest in the trade, see CACTI.

**pectinatus.** Stems usually unbranched, cylindric, 4-6 in. long, about 1½ in. in diameter. Ribs about 20, covered with many interlocking spines, which are in groups with about 30 laterals and a few erect at each center. Flowers 2-3 in. long, purple. Mex.

**polyacanthus.** One of the cacti with edible fruit called pitahaya. It is a low plant forming dense clumps of 20-50 pale, reddish-tinged stems. Ribs about 10, not very prominent. Spines yellow or grayish, becoming purplish in age. Flowers crimson, about 2 in. long, the tube spiny and woolly. New Mexico, Ariz. and Mex.

**ECHINOCHLOA** (ee-ky-nock'lō-a). Rather weedy grasses of little or no garden interest, but often cult. for forage, and sometimes persisting in the garden as weeds, especially in the South. Of the dozen species only **E. crus-galli** of Eu. is likely to be met. It is commonly called barn, or barnyard, or cockspur grass and is an annual, stout, coarse grass 3-6 ft. high, very leafy, and usually branched. Leaves 18-24 in. long, about 1 in. wide. Flowering cluster terminal, the spikelets awned. There is a *var.* **edulis**, the Japanese barnyard millet, which has denser clusters and purplish spikelets without awns.* (*Echinochloa* is from the Greek for hedgehog grass.)

**ECHINOCYSTIS** (ee-ky-no-sis'tis). Herbaceous, usually quick-growing vines, comprising about 25 species of the cucumber family, all from N.A. or S.A., only one of secondary garden interest. It is **E. lobata**, the wild balsam apple, often called wild or mock cucumber. It is an annual, North American, tendril*-bearing vine, often reaching 20 ft. and useful for quick covering. Stems slender, angled. Leaves alternate,* more or less ovalish-heart-shaped, 3-5 in. long, 3-7-lobed, the lobes with a minute soft prickle. Flowers small, whitish, in branched racemes* (for structure see CUCURBITACEAE). Fruit a puffy, rather papery, weak-spined pod about 2 in. long. (*Echinocystis* is from the Greek for hedgehog and bladder, in allusion to the spiny pod.) Sometimes offered as *Micrampelis*. See GOURDS.

**ECHINOMASTUS** (ee-ky-no-mas'tus). A small genus of chiefly Mexican cacti, two of them sometimes grown in desert gardens or in northern greenhouses. They are small, nearly globular or short-cylindric cacti, with many, rather low ribs which are divided into tubercles. Spines several at each cluster, but often without a central spine or with few. Flowers central, usually purple. Fruit small, scaly, becoming dry. (*Echinomastus* is from the Greek denoting spiny breast, in allusion to the spiny tubercles.)

For culture see CACTI.

**intertextus.** Nearly globular and about 4 in. in diameter. Ribs 13. Spines 16-25 at each cluster, with 4 erect, central ones. Flowers purple, about 1 in. long. Tex., Ariz. and Mex.

**macdowelli.** Nearly globular, but about 3 in. high and a little more in diameter. Ribs 20-25. Spines 15-20 at a cluster with 3 or 4 erect, darker-colored, central spines. Flowers rose-purple, nearly 1½ in. long. Northern Mex.

**ECHINOPANAX** (ee-ky-no-pay'nacks). Three species of horribly prickly but ornamental shrubs of the family Araliaceae, some native in eastern As., but **E. horridum**, the devil's-club, from Alaska to Calif. It is a bushy shrub 6-10 ft. high, spiny throughout, with large, alternate,* long-stalked, deeply 5-7-lobed leaves that are roundish in general outline, nearly 10 in. wide and prickly both sides. Flowers small, greenish-white (for details see ARALIACEAE), crowded in small umbels,* which are grouped in a large, terminal, branched cluster (panicle*). Fruit fleshy, scarlet, about ⅓ in. long. A handsome shrub with fine foliage and showy fruit; hardy from zone* 4 southward and of easy culture, although it prefers moist sites in proximity to the sea. (*Echinopanax* is from the Greek for hedgehog and *Panax*, which see.) The plant is sometimes sold as *Fatsia horrida*.

**ECHINOPS** (ek'i-nops). Decidedly handsome, thistle-like, Old World herbs of the family Compositae, commonly called globe thistle and popular plants in the hardy border. Of the 60 known species the ones below, especially *E. ritro* and *E. exaltatus*, are useful both for their handsome, white-woolly foliage and blue flowers. See BLUE GARDEN. Leaves alternate,* more or less prickly toothed or lobed, the under surface white. Flower heads densely beset with spiny bracts,* and each flower in the head so furnished, the bracts usually metallic blue. (*Echinops* is Greek for like a hedgehog, in allusion to the spiny heads.)

These bold, showy plants are of easy culture in any ordinary garden soil, and may be increased by division or raised from seed like any other perennial or biennial. They need plenty of space.

**exaltatus.** A biennial,* 3-4 ft. high, scarcely branched, the stem cobwebby. Leaves unevenly cut, the spines small. Flower head large, blue, some of its bracts hairy on the margin. Russia. Late summer.

**humilis.** A perennial, 3-4 ft. high, usually unbranched and with a single spiny flower head. Leaves cobwebby above, white-felty beneath, lobed or cut, but wavy-margined and not very spiny. Siberia. Summer.

**ritro.** A perennial 1-3 ft. high and the most widely cult. of the four. Stems branched and white-felty. Leaves nearly smooth above, white-felty beneath, cut into narrow segments. Flower heads blue. Eurasia. July-Sept.

**sphaerocephalus.** A stout perennial, 5-8 ft. high, and branched. Leaves roughish and green above, hairy beneath, cut into triangular, spiny lobes. Flower head nearly 2 in. wide, blue. Eurasia and northern Af. Aug.-Oct. Sometimes confused with *E. ritro*.

**ECHIOIDES** (ek-ee-oy'deez, but see OÏDES). Resembling *Echium*.

**ECHIUM** (ek'i-um). A genus of over 30 species of Eurasian herbs or shrubby plants of the family Boraginaceae, a few grown for ornament, and *E. vulgare*, a common roadside, naturalized weed in eastern N.A. They have rough foliage, with alternate,* simple leaves. Flowers rather showy, prevailingly blue, in forked or unforked, one-sided spikes.* Corolla funnel-shaped or trumpet-shaped, its limb somewhat oblique, the flower hence a little irregular.* Stamens 5, nearly always protruding. Fruit a collection of 4, erect, wrinkled nutlets. (*Echium* is from the Greek for viper, some of the species being called viper's-bugloss.)

---

*Special articles on the subjects indicated by an asterisk (*) will be found at the words so marked.

The first species is a shrub suited to outdoor cult. only in Calif. and similar regions. The others are of easy culture anywhere and may be raised from seed. Flowering in summer.

**fastuosum.** Shrub 4–6 ft. high, the foliage gray-hairy. Leaves lance-shaped. Flowers purplish or dark blue, the stamens* red. Canary Islands.

**plantagineum.** An annual or biennial 15–20 in. high, but usually grown as a hardy annual. See ANNUALS. Leaves ovalish or oblong, diminishing upward into bracts.* Flowers blue, rarely light purple. Southern Eu.

**vulgare.** Blueweed, called also blue thistle. A somewhat weedy biennial 18–30 in. high. Leaves oblongish, 2–6 in. long. Flowers at first pink, in maturity brilliant blue, about ⅞ in. long and very handsome. Eurasia, but common as a weed and little grown as a garden plant.

**wildpreti.** A beautiful, white-hairy, biennial herb, 2–3 ft. high, with narrow, stalkless leaves. Flowers rose-colored, in showy, terminal clusters (cymes*), the stamens much-protruding. Canary Islands. Suited to Calif. and similar climates.

**EDDO** = *Colocasia esculenta*.

**EDELWEISS.** A much publicized but not particularly beautiful alpine herb comprising the genus **Leontopodium** (lee-on-to-pō′di-um), native in the mountains of Eurasia and S.A. The only cult. species is **L. alpinum**, the edelweiss of the Alps, which is sometimes sold as *Gnaphalium leontopodium*. It is a white-woolly perennial herb with erect or ascending stems usually about 6 in. high. Leaves lance-shaped but broader towards the tip, ultimately shedding the white wool from the upper surface. Flower heads solitary at the ends of the branches, wholly of yellow disk* flowers, not showy, but beneath which is a series of dry, silvery bracts,* much longer than the width of the head. For culture see ROCK GARDEN. (*Leontopodium* is Greek for lion's-foot.)

**EDGEWORTHIA** (edj-wor′thi-a). A small genus of Asiatic shrubs of the family Thymelaeaceae, one of secondary garden interest. It is the paper tree or paper bush, **E. papyrifera**, which is also called by some *E. gardneri* and *E. chrysantha*, and is a Chinese and Japanese shrub. Leaves alternate,* mostly crowded at the ends of the twigs, oblongish, 4–5 in. long, unfolding after the yellow flowers appear. Flowers in dense, head-like clusters, fragrant, rather small (for details see THYMELAEACEAE). Fruit fleshy but somewhat dry. The bark yields a paper-making fiber in China and Japan. Not hardy north of zone* 6, nor does it like the extreme summer heat of much of the Middle West. (Named for M. P. Edgeworth, English botanist.)

**EDGING.** A border of flowers, wood, metal or stones used to define the edge of a lawn, drive, path or a flower bed.

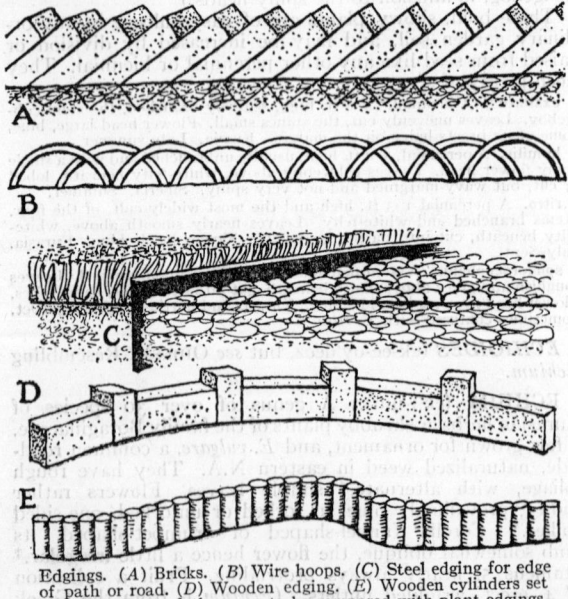

Edgings. (*A*) Bricks. (*B*) Wire hoops. (*C*) Steel edging for edge of path or road. (*D*) Wooden edging. (*E*) Wooden cylinders set on end. None of these are to be compared with plant edgings, but (*C*) is often necessary on drives.

Whether composed of plants or other materials, edgings are the features that first strike the eye. Metal edgings, of rolled steel and zinc, as well as iron, are obtainable in various sizes to fit all spaces. A standard size of one-quarter inch by five inches is preferred in most cases. These are used to retain the soil in raised beds, to obtain clean-cut lines on walks and drives, and to confine gravel or loose-stone paths and roadways within their proper limits. Cement, stone, or brick curbs may be used if preferred. Turf is often used as a border edging, although constant care is required to keep it from acquiring a ragged appearance. There are also attractive wooden edgings, but they are not permanent.

Upon the width and type of the border depend to a large extent the plants used as edging material. Low, compact-growing plants must be used with small or formal borders, while taller, less formal, massed plantings may have as an edging the plants that often make up the small border proper. Long borders, either straight or winding, are usually edged with a variety of plants varying in form and color, but sometimes a ribbon of one variety runs the entire length.

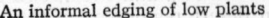

An informal edging of low plants

The edging strip is an excellent place for low-growing annuals which provide a brilliancy not found in many perennials. Very early-blooming bulbs, such as *Muscari*, snowdrops, crocuses, and tulips may be used to prolong the season of bloom, by filling in the space later with petunias, dwarf snapdragons, ageratum, *Lobelia erinus*, and pansies, to cover the dying foliage. Of the quickly maturing annuals, sown where they are to bloom, the most popular is the sweet alyssum. Other good annuals for edgings are abronia, the annual candytufts, dwarf coreopsis, dianthus, godetia, nemophila, nigella, phlox, and portulaca.

Perennial edgings, such as the violas and dwarf campanulas, cannot be changed each year. Variety may be obtained by replacing old or winter-killed plants with new seedlings or substituting taller-growing specimens for mat-like species. Good perennials for both sun and shade are *Dianthus caesius*, *Veronica incana*, and *Iberis sempervirens* (see CANDYTUFT).

*Romanzoffia* is a garden plant which does well in shady or half-shady situations. It succeeds very well when used in conjunction with brick or

A formal clipped edging of low shrubs such as box or box barberry

stone edgings. Box* is one of the most popular of all edgings, and the most desirable for formal plantings, especially in the dwarf edging form (see BOX). A good substitute, and much cheaper, is the box barberry (see BERBERIS THUNBERGI MINOR).

* Special articles on the subjects indicated by an asterisk (*) will be found at the words so marked.

**EDGING BOX** = *Buxus sempervirens suffruticosa*. See BOX.

**EDGING CANDYTUFT** = *Iberis sempervirens*. See CANDYTUFT.

**EDGING KNIFE.** See Section 3, TOOLS AND IMPLEMENTS.

**EDGING LOBELIA** = *Lobelia erinus*.

**EDIBLE-PODDED PEA** = *Pisum sativum macrocarpon*. See PEA.

**EDRAIANTHUS** (ed-dry-an'thus). A small genus of herbs of the family Campanulaceae, mostly from the Mediterranean region, E. tenuifolius sometimes cult. in the rock garden (which see). It is sometimes known as *E. dalmaticus* or as *Wahlenbergia dalmatica*. It is a perennial, tufted* herb, scarcely 6 in. high, with alternate,* very narrow leaves, and blue flowers in dense, terminal, and bracted clusters. Corolla bell-shaped, the upper part 5-lobed. Fruit a 2-5-valved capsule.* (*Edraianthus* is from the Greek for [essentially] stalkless flower.)

**EDUCATION FOR GARDENING.** See GARDEN SCHOOLS.

*EDULIS, -e* (ed'you-lis). Edible.

**EEL-GRASS.** Common submerged, aquatic herbs of the genus Vallisneria (val-lis-neer'i-a) of the family Hydrocharitaceae, of no garden interest except for aquaria, but of absorbing fruiting habits. The only cult. species is **V. spiralis,** often called tape-grass or wild celery, a favorite feed of wild ducks. It has long, very narrow, tape-like leaves and minute flowers, the male and female on different stalks. (See HYDROCHARITACEAE.) Male flowers white, at first submerged and on short stalks near the bottom, ultimately released and reaching the surface detached. Here they fertilize the female flowers which are on long, coiling stalks that ultimately contract. Fruit a minute achene,* which ripens far beneath the surface. The American representative of this nearly world-wide aquatic is sometimes designated as *V. americana*. (Named for Antonio Vallisneri, Italian naturalist.) Many of the wild plants are in danger from a disease which does not yield to control measures.

**EELWORM.** See Root Knot at PLANT DISEASES.

**EFFECTIVE TEMPERATURE.** See TEMPERATURE.

*EFFUSA, -us, -um* (eff-you'sa). Loosely spreading.

**EGGFRUIT** = *Lucuma nervosa*.

**EGGPLANT** (*Solanum melongena esculentum*). The eggplant, sometimes, in one of its varieties, called snake eggplant, is essentially a tropical crop needing heat for its proper development. While it can be grown as far north as zone* 4, its best development is in the warmer parts of the country. Other names for it are aubergine, brinjal, Jew's-apple and mad-apple.

Because it will not stand the cold, it is better to plant seed in the hotbed or in the greenhouse, allowing 6-8 weeks from seeding until the plants are ready to be put outdoors, which should not be before settled warm weather has arrived. Its early handling is very much the same as for the garden peppers or for tomatoes, but the plant is even more sensitive to cold than either of them.

SOILS. While eggplant will grow on a variety of soils, it prefers rich, reasonably moist, sandy loams. It will not thrive if there is enough clay to hold too much moisture at its roots. If the soil is too sandy or deficient in plant food, a good all-around commercial fertilizer may be applied, after the plants are set out, a little being worked in around each plant.

While the eggplant needs humus, it is better not to use stable manure, unless it is old and thoroughly composted. Some commercial growers prefer to get humus through plowing in a leguminous crop the season before.

PLANTING. Having raised your seedlings to the stage of being about 6 in. high, preferably each in its own pot, you are ready for outdoor planting, assuming the seedlings have been gradually hardened-off as with tomato plants (which see). Put the plants 3-4 ft. apart each way, and if it is a dry period, give each a little water. If, however, you are using potted plants, these may be given a thorough soaking the night before planting and then should show little effects from the shift to outdoor culture.

YIELDS AND VARIETIES. For the South, use Black Beauty and Florida Highbush. For the North, and especially for the home gardener, the preferred varieties are New York Improved, Black Pekin, and also Black Beauty. A good plant, with the right soil and plenty of heat, will bear 3-8 fruits, often less, but sometimes more under favorable conditions. The fruit is so heavy it should be cut, not torn, from the plant.

INSECT PESTS. A tortoise beetle, the larvæ of which carries a load of trash, sometimes feeds on eggplant; arsenicals will kill it. A pretty little sucking insect, the lace bug, may be killed with contact sprays if abundant. The Colorado potato beetle, flea beetles, and the potato stalk borer are occasional pests; the first two yield to arsenicals.

DISEASES. Wilt, in which the leaves turn yellow and later the whole plant dies, is caused by a soil organism which affects many crops. Planting the crop on new soil is the only satisfactory control measure. Fruit rots and various leafspots are common, and in part combated by procuring seed from healthy fruit or by treating the seed with corrosive sublimate and spraying or dusting the plants, both in the seed bed and the field. The damping-off of the young plants may be controlled by treating the seed with red copper oxide, or the soil with formaldehyde dust.

**EGLANTERIA** (egg-lan-teer'i-a). A Latinized version of an old French name for the sweetbrier.

**EGLANTINE** = *Rosa eglanteria*. For another plant sometimes called eglantine see LONICERA PERICLYMENUM.

**EGYPTIAN CLOVER** = *Trifolium alexandrinum*. See CLOVER.

**EGYPTIAN GARDENS.** See GARDEN HISTORY.

**EGYPTIAN LILY** = Calla lily (*Zantedeschia aethiopica*).

**EGYPTIAN LOTUS.** See NELUMBIUM NELUMBO. Also the white lotus (*Nymphaea lotus*) and the blue lotus (*N. caerulea*) are both called Egyptian lotus.

**EHRETIA** (er-ree'shi-a). A genus of nearly 50 species of chiefly tropical shrubs and trees of the family Boraginaceae, two somewhat grown for ornament. They have alternate* and (in ours) toothed leaves and small, white flowers in terminal clusters. Corolla shortly funnel-shaped, its 5 spreading lobes blunt. Stamens 5, inserted on the tube of the corolla. Fruit fleshy, with 4 nutlets. (Named for G. D. Ehret, German botanical artist.)

While *E. thyrsiflora* will survive in the North as indicated below, it is most at home in central and northern Fla., where it flowers and fruits much more freely than in the North. It is partial to a variety of soils.

acuminata = *Ehretia thyrsiflora*.

microphylla. A shrub 8-12 ft. high. Leaves clustered, toothed, broadest above the middle, 1½-2½ in. long. Flowers solitary or in clusters of 2-4. Indo-Malaya. Not hardy north of zone* 9, and little grown.

thyrsiflora. A tree 20-45 ft. high. Leaves oblongish or broadest above

Eggplant

---

* Special articles on the subjects indicated by an asterisk (*) will be found at the words so marked.

the middle, 4–7 in. long, toothed. Flowers about 1/3 in. wide, the clusters (panicles*) 5–7 in. long and showy. Fruit orange, ultimately brownish-black. Eastern Asia. Hardy from zone* 4 southward. June–July. Popular in Fla.

**EICHHORNIA.** *See* WATER HYACINTH.

**ELAEAGNACEAE** (ell-ee-ag-nay'see-ee). All of the three known genera of the oleaster family contain plants of garden interest. They are shrubs or trees mostly of the warmer parts of the north temperate zone, but some species of *Elaeagnus* extend far northward. Most of the plants have scurfy or golden-brown foliage.

Leaves alternate* in *Elaeagnus* and *Hippophaë*, but opposite* in *Shepherdia*, without marginal teeth in all genera. Flowers not very showy, in small clusters in the leaf-axils,* or solitary, or in racemes.* Fruit actually a dry nut or achene,* but appearing fleshy because the fleshy receptacle* encloses the true fruits. This fleshy receptacle is often incorrectly called a berry (*see* GUMI at *Elaeagnus multiflora*). The shrubs of this family are widely planted for their ornamental, often silvery foliage, and for their brightly colored, often edible "fruits" (*i.e.* receptacles*).

Technical flower characters: Flowers hermaphrodite* in *Elaeagnus*, but mostly dioecious* in the other two genera, without petals. Calyx tubular, 2–4-lobed, petal-like. Stamens 2–4, or twice as many. Ovary 1-celled, with long style and a single ovule.

**ELAEAGNUS** (eel-ee-ag'nus). A handsome genus of shrubs or trees of the family Elaeagnaceae, comprising perhaps 40 species of the north temperate zone, several cult. for their ornamental foliage and for their decorative or edible fruits. Leaves alternate,* short-stalked, more or less dotted with silvery or scurfy scales. Flowers not showy, without petals, the calyx* tubular or bell-shaped, 4-lobed. Stamens 4. Fruit berry-like but not a true berry (actually the modified receptacle*). (*Elaeagnus* is from the Greek for olive and the chaste tree.)

These are hardy, wind-resistant shrubs or small trees, useful as windbreaks in the prairie states, and they will grow easily in a variety of dry sites. They are easily propagated by root cuttings, layers or by grafting. Stratified seeds sown the second season will also yield new plants.

**angustifolia.** Oleaster; called also Russian olive and Trebizond date. A Eurasian, sometimes spiny tree 10–20 ft. high. Leaves silvery beneath, oblongish, 2–3½ in. long. Flowers greenish, 1–3 together. Fruit egg-shaped, about ½ in. long, yellow but silvery-scaled, the flesh sweet but mealy. June. Hardy from zone* 2 southward. There are varieties with spiny branches and with larger, greenish leaves.

**argentea.** Silverberry, also called wolfberry. An erect shrub 8–12 ft. high, spreading by stolons.* Leaves short-stalked, ovalish to oblong, 1–4½ in. long, silvery. Flowers fragrant, silvery-yellow, about 1 in. long, in clusters of 1–3. Fruit silvery, short-stalked. May–July. N.A. Hardy everywhere.

**longipes** = *Elaeagnus multiflora.*

**multiflora.** Gumi. A spreading shrub 4–9 ft. high. Leaves more or less elliptic, 1–3 in. long, silvery beneath. Flowers yellowish-white, silvery and brown-scaly on the outside. Fruit red, scaly, of a pleasant acid flavor. April–May. Eastern As. Hardy from zone* 4 southward. There are several varieties with minor foliage differences. The plant is also offered as *E. longipes.* It is smoke-resistant.

**pungens.** A usually spiny, spreading shrub 10–15 ft. high, the foliage evergreen. Leaves wavy-margined, silvery beneath, oblongish, 2½–5 in. long, stalked. Flowers 1–3, hanging, silvery-white. Fruit brown at first, then red. Japan. Oct.–Nov. Hardy from zone* 6 southward and commonly cult. in the South. The *var.* **aurea** has yellow-margined leaves; *var.* **maculata** has yellow-blotched leaves; *var.* **variegata** has white or yellowish-white-margined leaves; the *var.* **reflexa** has wavy-margined leaves, brown-scaly beneath; the *var.* **simoni** has somewhat larger leaves, scarcely scaly beneath.

**umbellata.** A branching shrub 10–18 ft. high, the branches brown-scaly. Leaves elliptic to oval-oblong, 1½–3½ in. long, silvery beneath, the margins often crisped. Flowers fragrant, yellowish-white, scaly on the outside, about ¾ in. long. Fruit brown, then red. May–June. Eastern As. Hardy from zone* 3 southward.

**ELAEIS** (ee-lee'is). A small group of feather palms from tropical Af. and America, one, **E. guineensis**, the African oil palm, cult. outdoors only in zone* 9. Economically important in the African oil trade, it is of little hort. importance in the U.S., although it is a handsome palm, up to 70 ft. (less in cult. here), in the young state resembling a *Phoenix.* Leaves 10–15 ft. long, often long-persistent even when dead. Leaflets very numerous, ridged, stiffish. Flowering cluster among the crown of leaves, branched, short and head-like, sometimes spiny. Fruit egg-shaped or conical, about 1 in. long, red or orange-yellow. Af. (*Elaeis* is Greek for olive, in allusion to the fruit.)

**ELAEOCARPACEAE.** *See* ARISTOTELIA.

**ELAEODENDRON** (ee-lee-o-den'dron). A genus of 45 species of warm-country shrubs or trees of the family Celastraceae, one grown for ornament in Calif. and other nearly frost-free places, and in the greenhouse. They have leathery leaves and small, whitish or greenish flowers in small clusters in the leaf-axils.* Of several species in cult., **E. orientale**, the false olive, is most likely to be of interest. It is a handsome shrub, the juvenile and mature leaves being very different. Mature leaves oblongish, scalloped, 2–3 in. long, the young ones narrower and very graceful, the shrub chiefly grown for them. Fruit olive-like, but inedible. Use potting mixture* 5 and grow in a warm greenhouse. (*Elaeodendron* is from the Greek for olive tree.)

**ELAPHOGLOSSUM** (e-laff-o-gloss'um). Nearly 300 species of tropical ferns of the family Polypodiaceae, with undivided fronds and creeping rootstocks. Only one, **E. crinitum**, the elephant-ear fern of tropical America, is of any garden interest, and is widely grown in the greenhouse for its hardy, resistant foliage. Fronds stout, thick, 12–20 in. long, the stalk conspicuously shaggy, the blade without teeth, paddle-shaped and nearly 7 in. wide, often hairy on the margins. Spore cases completely covering the under side of some of the narrower fronds, felt-like and brownish. The plant needs greenhouse culture, with plenty of water but perfect drainage. *See* FERNS AND FERN GARDENING. (*Elaphoglossum* is from the Greek for deer tongue, in allusion to the fronds.)

***ELASTICA, -us, -um*** (ee-las'ti-ka). Elastic or rubber-producing.

***ELATA, -us, -um*** (ee-lay'ta). Tall.

***ELATERIUM*** (ell-a-teer'i-um). Old Greek word implying to drive. *See* ECBALLIUM.

***ELATIUS, -or*** (ee-lay'ti-us). Taller.

**ELDER.** Attractive shrubs comprising the genus **Sambucus** (sam-bew'kus) of the honeysuckle family. There are perhaps 20 species, of which those below are in common cult. for their flowers and some for their fruit used for making both wine and jelly. They have pithy branches and opposite,* compound* leaves, the leaflets arranged feather-fashion with an odd one at the end, all toothed. Flowers small, white, in terminal, much-branched, often flat-topped clusters (corymb* or panicle*). Corolla small, wheel-shaped, the calyx very small or nearly abortive. Fruit berry-like, with 3–5 one-seeded nutlets. (*Sambucus* is the classical Latin name of the elder.)

The elders, or, as they are often called, the elderberries, are rather showy shrubs but inclined to be sprawling and more suited to informal shrubberies than for specimen plants. Some of the cut-leaved varieties of *S. racemosa* are, however, valued for their foliage. And the fruits of *S. canadensis* were once very widely gathered for wine-making. All are of the easiest culture, although most of them do better in moist sites than in dry ones. They are easily increased by cuttings or by suckers,* which are very common in most of them.

**S. canadensis.** American elder or elderberry. A very common North American shrub 6–10 ft. high, its branches brittle. Leaflets mostly 7, short-stalked, 2½–6 in. long, tapering at the tip. Flowers small (about 1/10 in. wide), the cluster slightly convex but essentially flat-topped, nearly 4 in. across. Fruit purple-black, about ⅙ in. in diameter. June–July. Hardy from zone* 2 southward. There are golden-leaved varieties, and the *var.* **acutiloba** has dissected leaflets. All forms stand smoke better than most shrubs.

**S. nigra.** European elder. A shrub up to 25 ft. high, sometimes tree-like. Leaflets mostly 5, elliptic to ovalish, short-stalked, 2–5½ in. long. Flowers yellowish-white, heavy-scented, the essentially flat-topped cluster about 3 in. wide. Fruit black, about ¼ in. in diameter. Eurasia and northern Af. Hardy from zone* 3 southward. The *var.* **aureo-variegata** and the *var.* **albo-variegata** have golden-yellow and white-blotched foliage, respectively.

**S. pubens.** American red elder. A spreading shrub 8–12 ft. high. Leaflets 5–7, generally ovalish or oblongish, 2½–4 in. long. Flower cluster pyramid-shaped. Fruit scarlet, inedible. Eastern N.A. but west to Colo.

* Special articles on the subjects indicated by an asterisk (*) will be found at the words so marked.

May. Hardy from zone* 3 southward and possibly in protected parts of zone* 2. Not much grown, but common in moist, mountain woods.

**S. racemosa.** Red-berried elder. A commonly cult. Eurasian shrub, perhaps the best of the four, scarcely over 10 ft. high. Leaflets 5–7, practically stalkless, ovalish or elliptic, 2–3½ in. long, tapering at the tip. Flowers yellowish-white, the cluster not flat-topped. Fruit scarlet. April–May. Of its many varieties two are: *var.* **laciniata,** with the young foliage green and the leaflets dissected; and *var.* **plumosa,** with the young foliage purplish and the leaflets cut to nearly the middle.

For other plants sometimes called elder *see Acer negundo* at MAPLE, and STENOLOBIUM STANS.

**ELDERBERRY** = elder, especially *Sambucus canadensis. See* ELDER.

**ELDER FAMILY** = Caprifoliaceae.

**ELECAMPANE** = *Inula helenium.*

**ELECTRIMMER.** A patented, motor-driven hedge-clipper.

**ELECTRO-HORTICULTURE.** Twenty years of experiment in the use of electricity for plants has resulted in little of practical importance. Most of the experimental work has been with light rays of different color, intensity, or duration. Astonishing response to such stimuli, especially long-continued night illumination, has demonstrated that the speed of growth can, in certain plants, be tremendously accelerated, usually to the plant's disadvantage. While increasing the length of winter days, by the judicious use of electric illumination, appears to be practical, its cost, so far, outweighs its advantages.

Much more practical is the substitution of electric coils for heating hotbeds instead of using stable manure. For details *see* COLD FRAME. *See also* LIGHTING.

***ELEGANS*** (el'lee-ganz). Beautiful or elegant.

***ELEGANTISSIMA*** (el-lee-gan-tiss'i-ma). Most beautiful or elegant.

**ELEPHANT-EAR.** *See* COLOCASIA.

**ELEPHANT-EAR FERN** = *Elaphoglossum crinitum.*

***ELEPHANTIDENS*** (el-ee-fan'ti-denz). Large-toothed.

**ELETTARIA.** *See* CARDAMON.

**ELEUSINE** (el-you-sy'ne). Perhaps half a dozen species of Old World grasses, one yielding a minor grain, one a weed, and none particularly ornamental. Ours are annuals, or treated as such, with tufted* stems and narrow, grass-like leaves. Flowers minute (for details *see* GRAMINEAE), usually arranged in 1-sided spikes which are grouped in a terminal, umbel*-like cluster. (*Eleusine* is Greek for the town where Ceres, the goddess of agriculture, was worshiped.)

*Eleusine coracana* is somewhat grown here for ornament, but in the Old World its grain is a secondary cereal. Like the others it is easily raised as an annual.

**barcinonensis** = *Eleusine tristachya.*

**coracana.** African millet. From 1–4 ft. high. Leaves 8–12 in. long, about ¼ in. wide. Flowering spikes erect, about 1½ in. long and ¼ in. wide. Fruit (a caryopsis*) nearly round, with a loose husk. As. and Af., probably.

**indica.** Wire grass. A weedy, sometimes troublesome Old World grass naturalized* in N.A., not over 2 ft. high. Leaves 8–12 in. long, about ¼ in. wide. Flowering spikes spreading, 2–4 in. long.

**tristachya.** Usually less than 12 in. high. Leaves 3–7 in. long, about 1/16 in. wide. Flowering spikes about 1 in. long and ⅛ in. wide. India.

**ELGIN BOTANIC GARDEN.** *See* HOSACKIA.

**ELK CLOVER** = *Aralia californica.*

**ELK-GRASS** = *Xerophyllum tenax.*

***ELLIPTICA, -us, -um*** (el-lip'ti-ka). Elliptic; *i.e.* oval, but narrowed towards the rounded ends.

**ELM.** No trees could replace elms in the American landscape. They all belong to the genus **Ulmus** (ul'mus) of the family Ulmaceae, and of the 18 known species, all from the north temperate zone, nearly half are in pretty common cultivation for their beautiful habit and fine foliage. They are mostly tall trees with alternate,* short-stalked leaves that are usually somewhat oblique and doubly toothed. Flowers without petals, the calyx* bell-shaped and inconspicuous. Fruit a compressed nut surrounded by a flat, often hairy wing (a samara). (*Ulmus* is the classical Latin name of the elm.)

For Culture *see* below.

**U. americana.** American elm, also called white elm and water elm. A magnificent tree, vase-like in outline when mature, up to 120 ft. in height and with light gray, scaly, but deeply fissured bark. Leaves oval-oblong, 3–7 in. long, unequal at the base, smooth or roughish above, sometimes hairy beneath. Flowers small, on stalks ½–¾ in. long, 3 or 4 together. Fruit about ⅜ in. long, notched at the tip, hairy on the margin. N.A., east of the Rocky Mountains. Flowering before the leaves unfold. Hardy everywhere. The *var.* **pendula,** often called the weeping American elm, has the ends of the main branches drooping. Both are widely planted as street trees.

**U. campestris.** English elm. A tall tree, more round-headed than the American elm, often 100–150 ft. high. Leaves oval or elliptic, 2½–4 in. long, very oblique at the base, rough above, softly hairy beneath. Flowers short-stalked, appearing before the leaves unfold. Fruit nearly round, about ¾ in. in diameter, not hairy. Eu. Somewhat planted here, but surely hardy only up to zone* 3. Sometimes known as *U. procera.* There are many varieties of this handsome tree, some with variegated foliage, some purple-tinged, and some with more erect branches than the typical plant.

**U. chinensis** = *Ulmus parviflora.*

**U. foliacea.** Smooth-leaved elm. A tree rarely over 75 ft. high. Leaves very oblique, smooth both sides, glossy-green, 2–4 in. long. Flowers in dense clusters. Fruit elliptic, but wedge-shaped at the base, the seed close to the closed notch. Eurasia and northern Af. Hardy from zone* 3 southward. There are several varieties in cult., the best known being *var.* **umbraculifera,** with a globe-shaped crown, and *var.* **wheatleyi,** the Jersey elm, which has stiffer, more erect branches.

**U. fulva.** Slippery elm. Rarely over 60 ft. high. Leaves very oblique at the base, rough above, hairy beneath, 5–9 in. long. Flowers short-stalked, but in dense clusters. Fruit nearly round, almost 1 in. long, hairy in the center. Eastern N.A. Hardy from zone* 2 southward, but not much planted. Its bruised twigs have a characteristic odor.

**U. glabra.** Wych elm. A smooth-barked tree up to 120 ft. Leaves short-stalked, oblongish or elliptic, 3½–7 in. long, rough above, but usually hairy beneath. Flowers in dense clusters. Fruit broadly elliptic, over 1 in. long, smooth. Eurasia. A widely planted tree for lawns or parks, hardy from zone* 3 southward. Of its many cult. varieties the following are best liked: *var.* **atropurpurea,** with dark purple young foliage; *var.* **camperdowni,** the Camperdown elm, which has drooping branches; *var.* **crispa,** with twisted and incurved leaf teeth; and *var.* **fastigiata,** with upright branches forming a columnar tree.

**U. hollandica.** Dutch or Holland elm. A hybrid elm, intermediate in characters between the wych elm and the smooth-leaved elm. It is best known in two varieties long cult. for ornament: *var.* **belgica,** the Belgian elm, a tall tree with upright branches and a broad crown, its leaves more or less elliptic, 3½–5½ in. long, somewhat rough above, and very oblique at the base. The *var.* **vegeta,** usually known as the Huntingdon elm, is a tall tree, usually with a forking trunk, the leaves very oblique at the base, smooth above, 4–7½ in. long, generally elliptic. Both the Dutch elm and its two varieties are hardy up to zone* 3.

**U. parvifolia.** Chinese elm. A small, smooth-barked tree usually not over 40 ft. high, and inclined to forking. Leaves more or less elliptic, 1–2½ in. long, shining above, hairy beneath at first, at length smooth. Flowers in small clusters, blooming in Aug.–Sept. Fruit about ½ in. long, notched at the tip. Eastern As. A small, quick-growing tree, hardy from zone* 3 southward, the fall foliage red or purple in the North, but persistent and green southward. Sometimes known as *U. chinensis.*

**U. procera** = *Ulmus campestris.*

**U. pumila.** Dwarf elm. Somewhat resembling *U. parvifolia,* but much taller, the bark rough, the flowers appearing before the leaves unfold, and the branches still more inclined to fork. Leaves 1½–3½ in. long, smooth both sides. Fruit nearly 1 in. long. Northeastern As. Hardy from zone* 3 southward. Unfortunately the name dwarf elm became attached to this species, although it reaches a height of 80 ft. in its native home. It is called by many the Chinese elm.

**U. racemosa.** Rock elm, also called cork elm. A tree up to 90 ft. high, its twigs corky-winged. Leaves roughish above, oblongish, 2½–5 in. long, unequal at the base. Flowers in small, hanging clusters (racemes*). Fruit elliptic, ¾–1½ in. long, slightly notched at the tip, hairy. Eastern N.A. Not much planted, but handsome in the fall when its foliage turns yellow. Hardy from zone* 2 southward.

### ELM CULTURE

The Elm is without doubt the most commonly planted ornamental tree in the northeastern states. About fifteen species and many varieties are hardy. This group is easily transplanted and is not particular as to soil requirements. Neither does it mind severe pruning. Its greatest drawback is its susceptibility to insect attack and disease. At the present time, plantings in this country are in great danger due to an infection known as the Dutch Elm Disease (*see* below). This has become so serious, especially in the north-eastern states, that thoughtful owners are already on the lookout for elm substitutes. There is, of course, no real substitute for the incomparable branching of the American elm.

* Special articles on the subjects indicated by an asterisk (*) will be found at the words so marked.

Good shade trees, however, can be found among the lindens. *See also* TREES.

The American Elm is the most common of the group. At the present time several upright forms are being propagated in large numbers for situations that require a narrow tree and for street work.

*Ulmus fulva*, the Slippery Elm; *Ulmus glabra*, the Wych Elm; and *Ulmus campestris*, the English Elm, are all hardy and fast-growing. The hybrid, *Ulmus hollandica*, is commonly used for street ornamentation in Europe and to some extent in this country. It cannot compete, however, with the American Elm in size or rate of growth in the northeastern states.

The Camperdown Elm, *Ulmus glabra camperdowni*, a rounded or flat-headed form with pendulous branches, is generally grafted head high and is an excellent small tree for the garden.

Several of the Asiatic species such as *Ulmus pumila* and *parviflora* are now commonly planted. The former is especially noted for its fast growth. However, because of its brittle wood, it is not a clean tree, and cannot be recommended for avenue ornamentation. An upright form is now being propagated for this purpose, but it will never make a really satisfactory street tree. It is excellent in the garden where fast growth is desired.

The Elm is most commonly propagated by seed which is sown immediately after it ripens in June. Germination takes place soon after it is sown and the following year the seedlings will be six inches to more than a foot high. They are then lined out in nursery rows. The varieties and hybrids are generally budded on the American Elm. Some propagators prefer grafting, but it can hardly be recommended as it is more expensive and does not produce as good a tree as budded stock. In rare instances, layering and softwood cuttings are used, but the results are seldom satisfactory when carried out on a large scale. In recent years it has become the custom with many nurserymen to bud the American Elm in order to obtain standardized trees, a practice to be particularly recommended where the material is to be used for street plantings. — A. D. S.

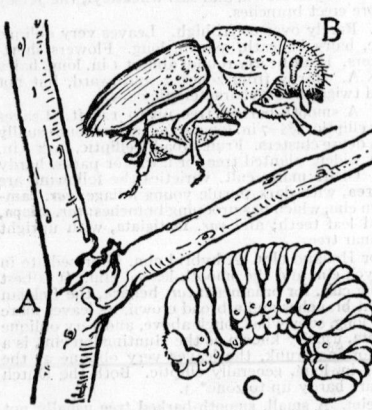

Dutch Elm Disease. (*A*) The incision made by the European bark beetle; (*B*) The beetle. The grub of this beetle; (*C*) The grub. (Both much enlarged.) The beetle is the carrier of the disease.

INSECT PESTS. The oyster-shell and scurfy scales (*see* APPLE), and the European elm scale, oval and 1/10 in. long, yield to dormant spray of miscible oil. Woolly and green aphids are controlled with contact sprays, although sometimes with difficulty. The aphid causing cockscomb gall may be controlled with dormant oil spray. Cankerworms feed on leaves in the spring; the adult female moths are wingless, and cannot climb trees to lay eggs if sticky tree-banding material is on the trunks from late fall to spring. Tussock-moth females are also wingless, but they frequently lay eggs on the trees where they fed as caterpillars; they may be checked by destroying the cocoons and white egg masses on bark in winter, or by the use of arsenicals to kill the large tufted larvae in summer. The elm leaf beetle, greenish black and 1/4 in. long, feeds late in the spring, and its spotted larvae feed in the summer; arsenicals applied late in the spring will control it and other leaf feeders. The elm borer, resembling the round-headed apple tree borer, is controlled by keeping trees healthy. The smaller elm bark beetle is not very injurious, but is suspected of carrying disease. The leopard moth is another borer in elm (*see* MAPLE).

DISEASES. The Dutch Elm Disease is the most serious disease of elm. It has been known in this country since 1930 and in its severe form it is at present limited to an area within about fifty miles of New York City (1935). The disease is spreading in all directions and unless checked, will cause widespread destruction. The disease is associated with a bark beetle which appears to be the chief carrier and inoculating agent. The insect breeds in dead or dying trees and branches of elm and the removal of these will tend to reduce the number of insects. No spray is known to be effective. Prompt eradication and destruction of affected trees is the only known method of control.

The black leaf spot of elm may be controlled by eradication of fallen leaves and application of bordeaux mixture spray. A canker disease of young elms in nurseries is caused by a fungus affecting the bark in small, localized lesions. Affected trees should be removed and destroyed at once. Older elms frequently suffer from chronic leaking or slime flux, satisfactory treatment of which requires the services of an experienced and skillful tree surgeon.

Die-back and a wilt are two diseases frequently confused with the Dutch Elm Disease. Affected parts should be cut out and burned. In city streets elms frequently die from gas poisoning of the roots caused by illuminating gas leaking from mains into the soil. Symptoms are a general dying back at the top without any apparent cause, and a loosening of the bark around the lower trunk. Recently killed roots show a bluish color when the inner bark is cut. Positive diagnosis depends upon the discovery of gas in the soil, which may be detected by crow-bar holes or by digging a pit. Severely injured trees will not recover.

Discolored elm twigs attacked by the Dutch Elm Disease

**ELM FAMILY** = Ulmaceae.

**ELODEA** (ee-low'dee-a). A small genus of American submerged, aquatic, perennial herbs of the family Hydrocharitaceae, useful in aquaria or in pools, but apt to choke both if not kept under control. They have soft leafy stems, the leaves small, opposite* or whorled,* pellucid. Flowers minute, mostly unisexual,* without true petals, the segments sometimes petal-like, less than 1/12 in. wide. Fruit a minute nutlet that ripens under water. (*Elodea* is from the Greek for marshy.)

The plants are of no garden interest except for aquaria, where they are widely popular. Easily grown if rooted in the mud, and very graceful and feathery, under-water plants. Sometimes known as *Anacharis*.

canadensis. Water-weed; called also ditch-moss. Leaves about 1/4 in. long, scarcely 1/12 in. wide, densely crowded. N.A., but introduced into Eu. and sometimes a pest there. For the plant sometimes called *Elodea canadensis gigantea* see the next.

densa. Resembling the last, but the leaves less crowded, nearly 1 in. long and 1/8 in. wide. Argentina. A better plant for aquaria than the native species.

*ELONGATA*, *-us*, *-um* (ee-lon-gay'ta). Elongate; *i.e.* lengthened or stretched out, as in many leaves.

**ELSHOLTZIA** (el-sholt'zi-a). A genus of 20 species of chiefly Asiatic, aromatic under-shrubs of the mint family, E. stauntoni somewhat grown for its late-blooming flowers. It is a low shrub or shrubby herb, 2–4 ft. high, its opposite* leaves short-stalked, toothed, oval-oblong, 3–5 in. long, and sticky beneath. Flowers lavender, in a dense, 1-sided spike, 6–12 in. long. Corolla only slightly 2-lipped,* its stamens long-protruding. The plant is easily grown in the open border south of zone* 4 and blooms in Sept.–Oct. Choose a sunny place and propagate by greenwood cuttings, or by seed. (Named for Johann Sigismund Elsholtz, Prussian physician and botanist.)

**ELYMUS** (el'i-mus). Grasses usually known as wild rye or lyme grass, and comprising over 40 species, all from temperate regions. They are perennial grasses of secondary garden interest, although *E. arenarius* is a good sand-binder. They have flat, grass-like leaves and a dense terminal spike, usually unbranched. (*Elymus* is from the Greek to roll up, in reference to a technical flower character.)

*Elymus arenarius*, a Eurasian species, is well adapted for binding shifting dune sand. The other species is occasionally grown for ornament.

arenarius. Sea lyme grass. A stout perennial grass 5–8 ft. high. Leaves about 12 in. long and 3/8 in. wide, rough on the upper surface, the margin rolled in age. Flowering spikes about 8 in. long, not awned.*

* Special articles on the subjects indicated by an asterisk (*) will be found at the words so marked.

glaucus. An ornamental grass 3-5 ft. high. Leaves about 12 in. long, nearly ⅓ in. wide, bluish-green. Flowering spike 5-7 in. long, with rather stiff, long awns.* Turkestan.

*EMARGINATA, -us, -um* (ee-mar-ji-nay′ta). Emarginate; *i.e.* shallowly notched at the tip, as in some leaves and fruits.

**EMASCULATION.** *See* CROSSING.

**EMBROIDERY GARDENING.** *See* BEDDING.

**EMBRYO.** The minute plantlet within the seed, and sometimes called the seed-germ, a term to be frowned upon.

**EMERUS.** Pre-Linnaean* name of uncertain application. *See* CORONILLA.

**EMILIA** (e-mil′i-a). Perhaps a dozen species of chiefly tropical herbs of the family Compositae, one a rather widely grown flower-garden annual sometimes offered as *Cacalia*. The only cult. species, **E. sagittata**, the tassel-flower or Flora's paintbrush, is sometimes offered as *E. flammea*. It is a showy, erect annual, 1-2 ft. high, with alternate,* more or less elliptic leaves that are narrowed to a winged stalk. Flower heads loosely clustered, about ½ in. in diameter, without rays, red or scarlet. Tropical America. More popular is the *var.* **lutea**, with yellow or golden flowers. Both are of the easiest culture if treated as hardy annuals. *See* ANNUALS. (*Emilia* is probably named for someone, but for whom is unknown.)

**EMMENANTHE** (em-me-nan′thee). A single Californian annual herb of the family Hydrophyllaceae, grown in the flower garden for its loosely branched clusters of cream-yellow flowers. The only species is **E. penduliflora**, the yellow bells, golden bells, or whispering bells, a rather sticky-foliaged, branching herb 12-18 in. high. Leaves cut into fine segments, but not compound.* Flowers bell-shaped, persistent, about ½ in. long, hanging on longish stalks, the whole cluster loose but much-branched. Fruit a 2-valved capsule. Should be grown as a hardy annual, or as a tender annual, if early bloom is desired. *See* ANNUALS. (*Emmenanthe* is from Greek for abide and flower, from the lasting corolla.)

**EMPETRACEAE** (em-pe-tray′see-ee). The crowberry family contains only 3 genera of low, evergreen, heath-like shrubs, two of which, *Empetrum* and *Corema*, are sometimes grown under the specialized conditions necessary for both genera.

Leaves very small, crowded, deeply grooved or furrowed on the under side. Flowers very small, without petals, regular.* The flower is solitary and the fruit fleshy in *Empetrum*, but in *Corema* the flowers are in tiny heads and the fruit is dry. Of little hort. but of considerable botanical interest, *Empetrum* extends to the Arctic Circle. *Corema* (one species) is localized from Newfoundland to N.J.

Technical flower characters: Flowers polygamous* or dioecious* without petals. Sepals 2 or 3 (or sometimes wanting), a little petal-like. Stamens 2 or 3, often colored. Ovary superior,* 2-9-celled, the 2-9 stigmas parted or fringed; all very minute.

*EMPETRIFORMIS, -e* (em-pee-tree-for′mis). With the form or aspect of the crowberry (*Empetrum*).

**EMPETRUM** (em-pee′trum). Evergreen, prostrate, or mat-forming shrubs, comprising only 5 species of the family Empetraceae, only **E. nigrum**, the crowberry, likely to be in cult. It is an alpine plant of the northern hemisphere, adapted only to the rock garden and frequently makes patches 2-3 ft. across. Leaves very numerous, heath-like, narrow, about ½ in. long. Flowers solitary in the leaf-axils,* mostly unisexual* (for details *see* EMPETRACEAE), purplish, not over ¼ in. long. Fruit black, berry-like, about ¼ in. in diameter. There is also a variety with purple fruit. May. It needs a strongly acid, rather gritty soil, preferably cool moisture at its roots, and it will not stand continued summer heat. (*Empetrum* is Old Greek for on rocks.) *See* ROCK GARDEN.

**ENCELIA** (en-see′li-a). A group of herbs or undershrubs of the family Compositae, ranging from western N.A. to Chile, two sometimes grown in Calif. and the Southwest for their showy heads of yellow flowers. Leaves alternate* or opposite,* sometimes silvery, and usually strong-scented. Flower heads with conspicuous yellow rays,* the disk* flowers sometimes purple, the heads on naked stalks. (Named for Christopher Encel, who wrote on oak galls in 1577.)

**californica.** A strong-smelling, woody, perennial herb 3-4 ft. high. Leaves ovalish or a little narrower, 2-2½ in. long. Flower heads solitary, nearly 2½ in. wide, the disk* flowers purple, the rays golden-yellow. Calif., and little grown outside that state.

**farinosa.** Incienso. A showy, desert, shrubby plant, 3-5 ft. high, the clumps very handsome when in bloom. Leaves ovalish, 1¾-2½ in. long, generally silvery. Flower heads yellow throughout, about 1 in. in diameter, in branched clusters (cymes*). Calif., Ariz. and Mex.

*ENCELIOIDES* (en-see-li-oy′deez, but *see* OÏDES). Like a plant of the genus *Encelia*.

**ENCINA** = *Quercus agrifolia*. *See* OAK.

**ENDIVE** (*Cichorium endivia*). This delicious salad plant is troublesome to bring to perfection. It is grown for the rosette of leaves, which when tied up and blanched constitutes practically the whole plant. While endive is chiefly fancied in the cool autumn or early winter months, it may also be had in midsummer by sowing the seeds in April or May. The frilled sort is sometimes known as escarole, a name not applied, however, to the French endive, a very different plant.

Common and true endive; a frilled variety is often called escarole.

Generally, seed may be sown 2 weeks apart from June 10 to August 20, which will provide a succession from early fall well into cold weather. They may be sown in shallow drills directly in the garden or raised as seedlings much like young lettuce and transplanted to the row, preferably about 9 in. apart in the row, and the rows 18-24 in. apart.

During the early stages endive needs no more attention

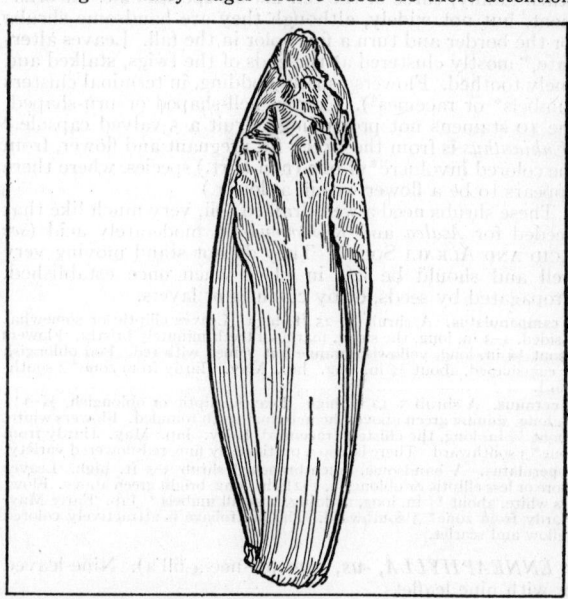

French endive (Witloof chicory). This plant is commonly called endive in vegetable shops.

---

* Special articles on the subjects indicated by an asterisk (*) will be found at the words so marked.

than any hardy vegetable beyond rather constant cultivation and, of course, freedom from weeds. But as the plants approach maturity, the necessity for blanching arrives and this is both troublesome and hazardous. The leaves will not turn white nor become crisp without excluding the light. Many good growers prefer to tie up each plant by hand. Others put boards each side the row, pinch them together over the endive and thus cut off all light. The real difficulty in either method is that if drops of water are left, or subsequently get into the heart of the plant, it will probably rot before it blanches. Great care is needed in this operation, and some professional growers even open up the heart of the plant after each rain to allow drops of water to dry off before letting the blanching process go on.

Also, if the late crops are likely to be overtaken by frost, which they cannot stand, they must be carefully lifted and brought into a cold frame and covered with mats every night. By doing this, blanching may often be carried on until the weather gets too severe for further endive culture.

For the culture of the plant known as French endive, which is really Witloof chicory, *see* CELLAR GARDENING.

***ENDIVIA.*** An East Indian word adapted into Latin, and, with *intybus*, applied to chicory and endive; the application to both being quite uncertain.

**ENDOTHIA CANKER.** *See* Diseases at CHESTNUT.

**ENGELMANN'S SPRUCE** = *Picea engelmanni*. *See* SPRUCE.

**ENGLISH.** As an adjective English has naturally been applied to many plants, things, gardens, etc., which originated in, or have long been associated with, England. Those that occur in THE GARDEN DICTIONARY, and their proper equivalents, are:

**English daisy** = *Bellis perennis;* **English elm** = *Ulmus campestris* (*see* ELM); **English garden** (*see* ARCHITECTURAL STYLE); **English gooseberry** = *Ribes grossularia;* **English hawthorn** = *Crataegus monogyna* and *C. oxyacantha;* **English holly** = *Ilex aquifolium* (*see* HOLLY); **English iris** (*see* IRIS); **English ivy** = *Hedera helix;* **English laurel** = *Laurocerasus officinalis;* **English meadow grass** = *Lolium perenne;* **English Morello**, a sour cherry (*see* CHERRY); **English oak** = *Quercus robur* (*see* OAK); **English primrose** = *Primula vulgaris;* **English scuffle hoe.** *See* Section 1, TOOLS AND IMPLEMENTS. **English sparrow** (*see* Bird Nuisances at BIRDS); **English walnut** = *Juglans regia* (*see* WALNUT); **English yew** = *Taxus baccata.*

**ENKIANTHUS** (en-ki-an'thus). Asiatic shrubs of the heath family, three of the ten known species cult. for ornament, but not widely, although they are handsome shrubs for the border and turn a fine color in the fall. Leaves alternate,* mostly clustered at the ends of the twigs, stalked and finely toothed. Flowers usually nodding, in terminal clusters (umbels* or racemes*). Corolla bell-shaped or urn-shaped, the 10 stamens not protruding. Fruit a 5-valved capsule.* (*Enkianthus* is from the Greek for pregnant and flower, from the colored involucre* of one (non-hort.) species, where there appears to be a flower within a flower.)

These shrubs need a well-drained soil, very much like that needed for *Azalea* and *Rhododendron*, moderately acid (*see* ACID AND ALKALI SOILS). They do not stand moving very well and should be left in place when once established. Propagated by seeds, or by cuttings or layers.

**campanulatus.** A shrub 15–25 ft. high. Leaves elliptic or somewhat 4-sided, 1–3 in. long, the small, marginal teeth minutely bristly. Flowers about 5/8 in. long, yellowish-orange but veined with red. Pod oblongish or egg-shaped, about 1/4 in. long. Jap. May. Hardy from zone* 3 southward.

**cernuus.** A shrub 5–12 ft. high. Leaves elliptic or oblongish, 3/4–1 1/2 in. long, shining green above, the marginal teeth rounded. Flowers white, about 1/3 in. long, the clusters (racemes*) hairy. Jap. May. Hardy from zone* 3 southward. There is also a particularly fine, red-flowered variety.

**perulatus.** A handsome, much-branched shrub 3–5 ft. high. Leaves more or less elliptic or oblongish, 1–2 1/2 in. long, bright green above. Flowers white, about 1/3 in. long, nodding, in small umbels.* Jap. Early May. Hardy from zone* 3 southward. The fall foliage is attractively colored yellow and scarlet.

***ENNEAPHYLLA, -us, -um*** (en-nee-a-fill'a). Nine-leaved or with nine leaflets.

***ENSETE.*** Abyssinian vernacular for *Musa ensete.*

***ENSIFOLIA, -us, -um*** (en-see-fō'lee-a). With sword-shaped leaves.

***ENSIFORMIS, -e*** (en-si-for'mis). Sword-shaped.

**ENTELEA** (en-tee'lee-a). A single, New Zealand tree, **E. arborescens,** usually called cork-tree or corkwood, somewhat grown in southern Calif. for ornament, but little known elsewhere. It belongs to the family Tiliaceae and scarcely exceeds 20 ft. in height. Leaves alternate,* ovalish or heart-shaped, 9–12 in. long, sometimes 3-lobed, and usually toothed. Flowers white, about 1 in. wide, the stamens numerous. Fruit a capsule,* covered with weak bristles or stiffish hairs. (*Entelea* is from the Greek for complete, in allusion to the fertility of all the stamens.)

**ENTIRE.** Whole; as wholly without teeth, as are many leaf margins.

**ENTRANCE GATES.** *See* GATES AND GATEWAYS.

**ENVIRONMENT.** The total influences arising outside a given plant, such as soil, temperature, light, disease, moisture, fertilizer, wind, sunshine, insects, and other plants. Certain types of characters are much more influenced by environment than others. Examples are height and size. Flower and fruit colors and shapes are much less likely to be affected, depending on the nature of the soil ingredients. Thus, certain varieties of hydrangeas in some soils or with certain chemicals applied are either pink or blue. The relation of heredity and environment is best illustrated by the farmer and his three cornfields planted with Boone County White. He planted one with poor seed, but cultivated it well and fertilized it well. The yield was 30 bushels per acre. (Poor heredity, good environment.) Field 2 he planted with the best seed to be had, but it was neither cultivated nor fertilized. The yield was 30 bushels per acre. (Good heredity, poor environment.) The third field was given the best of seed and the best of care and the yield was 60 bushels. (Good heredity, good environment.) — O. E. W.

**EOMECON** (ee-o-mee'kon). A single, Chinese herb of the poppy family, **E. chionantha,** rather commonly and easily cult. under the name snow poppy. It is a showy perennial with a stout, creeping rootstock and basal, long-stalked leaves that are heart-shaped, wavy-margined, and 4–6 in. wide. Flowers white, poppy-like, nearly 2 in. wide, blooming in spring. Petals 4. Stamens numerous. Fruit a capsule. (*Eomecon* is Greek for eastern poppy, in reference to its Chinese nativity.)

**EPAULETTE-TREE** = *Pterostyrax hispida.*

**EPHEDRA** (ef-fee'dra). Remarkable little plants and the only cult. genus of the family **Gnetaceae** (ne-tay'see-ee), cult. for thousands of years in China, where one of them yields ma-huang, a source of ephedrine. They are chiefly low or climbing, essentially leafless, desert shrubs, the green twigs resembling the horsetail (*Equisetum*). The plants are not of much garden importance, for the minute flowers are very primitive and the red, berry-like fruit is rarely produced in cult. specimens. Male and female flowers on separate plants, consisting of only 2–4 very small, scarcely petal-like organs, 2–8 stamens (in the male flower), and the female flower consisting of a single upright ovule.* (*Ephedra* is an old Greek name, probably of a horsetail.)

Of the 30 known species, commonly known as joint-fir, only 2 are likely to be found in cult. The Bureau of Plant Industry is experimenting on a large scale with ephedras to be planted as ground cover in the arid regions of Calif. and Ariz., and in the hope of developing a U.S. source of ephedrine. The plants are easily propagated by division of the clumps.

**altissima.** A sprawling or climbing shrub from northern Af., suited only to the desert regions of the Southwest. Unlike most of the other species, it has definite leaves that are nearly 1 in. long, and scattered along the bluish-green, jointed stems.

**distachya.** A low, nearly prostrate, shrubby plant, the dark green, jointed stems scarcely 1/12 in. thick, and less than 2 ft. long. Leaves reduced to opposite* scales, which sheathe the stems. Eurasia. Hardy from zone* 4 southward.

**EPHEMERAL.** Lasting only one day, as some flowers. *See* FUGACIOUS.

* Special articles on the subjects indicated by an asterisk (*) will be found at the words so marked.

**EPIDENDRUM** (ep-i-den′drum). An enormous genus (500 species) of tropical American, tree-perching (epiphytic) orchids, the one below sometimes cult. in the ordinary greenhouse, but many others appearing in the collections of orchid specialists and fanciers. The only one in reasonably common cult. is **E. vitellinum** from Mex. and Guatemala. It has pseudobulbs* nearly 2 in. long and somewhat stiffish, bluish-green, rather narrow leaves, 6–9 in. long. Flowers 10–15 in a terminal, lax, branching cluster, each flower about 1½ in. wide, generally cinnabar-red, the petals and sepals nearly similar. The lip* and column* are orange-yellow. There is a *var.* **majus** with shorter pseudobulbs and more brightly colored flowers. For their culture *see* Greenhouse Orchids at ORCHIDS. (*Epidendrum* is from the Greek for on trees, in allusion to their epiphytic habit.)

**EPIGAEA.** *See* TRAILING ARBUTUS.

**EPILOBIUM** (ep-i-lō′bi-um). The willow-herbs are usually herbaceous, but some a little woody, and comprise perhaps 200 species of the family Onagraceae, widely distributed in temperate regions, some almost weedy. Those below are grown for ornament and by bee-keepers, and one of them in the rock garden. Leaves usually willow-like, often, but not always, toothed. Flowers in showy terminal clusters or sometimes only a few in the leaf-axils.* Petals 4, broadest toward the end. Stamens 8, of unequal length. Fruit a long, 4-sided pod (capsule*), its seeds with a tuft of silky hairs. (*Epilobium* is from the Greek for upon the pod, in allusion to a technical flower character.)

The first species is the famous fireweed that follows so many forest fires, but the plant is also cult. in Calif. as an important bee plant. *E. hectori*, a New Zealand species, is not hardy outside of Calif. and similar regions. The last species is a rock garden plant, for which *see* ROCK GARDEN.

**angustifolium.** An erect herb 3–4 ft. high, wand-like in the wild, but often branched in cult. Leaves alternate,* narrow, 2–6 in. long. Flowers rose-purple, in a showy, terminal cluster, the petals widely spreading. Pod 3–4 in. long. Summer. Throughout the north temperate zone, especially after forest fires, and of the easiest culture. The plant has a variety of names, as fireweed, giant willow-herb, French willow, rose bay, and in Calif., buckweed.

**hectori.** A nearly prostrate herb rooting at the tips, but some stems erect and 6 in. high. Leaves chiefly opposite,* scarcely ½ in. long, oblongish. Flowers rose-purple, about ¼ in. wide, in the upper leaf-axils.* N. Zeal.

**nummularifolium.** A creeping and tufted herb, the stems 6–9 in. long. Leaves opposite,* nearly round, about ½ in. wide. Flowers about ⅓ in. wide, pink or white, solitary or few in the leaf-axils. N. Zeal. For culture *see* ROCK GARDEN.

**EPIMEDIUM** (ep-i-mee′di-um). Rather woody, perennial herbs of the family Berberidaceae; of the 10 known species, all from the north temperate zone, three widely cult. for their fine flowers. They have compound* leaves, the leaflets finely toothed and arranged feather-fashion. Flowers in simple or branched clusters, either terminal or opposite the leaves. Sepals 8 and petal-like. Petals 4, mostly in the form of spurs* that are sometimes longer than the sepals. Stamens 4. Fruit a few-seeded capsule.* (*Epimedium* is from the Greek for like Medion, a plant thought to grow in Media.) The plants are called barrenwort.

Chiefly of use in the rock garden (which see), and valuable as ground cover. They prefer partial shade and, with a little protection, their foliage may keep green over the winter. Propagated by division, but the first two species are slow to increase.

**alpinum.** A European herb, usually less than 1 ft. high, not much cult. except in the *var.* **rubrum**, which has red-margined leaflets and red flowers with short spurs. May–June.

**macranthum.** An erect herb 6–9 in. high. Leaves thrice-compound.* Flowers with outer segments red, the inner violet, the spurs white, and nearly 1 in. long. Jap. May–June. The *var.* **niveum** has pure white flowers; the *var.* **violaceum** has the spurs violet.

**pinnatum.** Leaves only twice-compound.* Flowers brilliant yellow, the short spurs red. Persia and the Caucasus. The *var.* **colchicum** has yellow flowers throughout, and is offered by some as *sulphureum.* It spreads rapidly by its stem-like rootstocks.

**sulphureum** = *Epimedium pinnatum colchicum.*

**EPIPACTIS** (ep-i-pak′tis). Woodland orchids suitable only for specialized sites in the wild garden. Of the 25 known species, mostly from temperate regions, only the three below are likely to be grown. They have a basal rosette of often variegated leaves and an erect, often bracted or sheathed flower stalk terminated by a small, often 1-sided spike or very irregular* flowers, which have 2 free sepals and one united with the petals into a small, hood-like structure. (*Epipactis* is from the Greek for coagulating milk and of uncertain application here.)

For culture *see* Hardy Orchids at ORCHIDS. Some of those below are occasionally offered as *Goodyera* or *Peramium.*

**pubescens.** Rattlesnake plantain; also called adder's violet. Leaves 1–2 in. long, margined towards the winged base, prominently and regularly white-mottled. Flowering stalk 7–18 in. high, densely sticky-hairy, the flowers greenish-white, about ¼ in. long. Eastern N.A., mostly in dry woods. July–Aug.

**repens.** Squirrel's-ear. Leaves ½–1 in. long, rather irregularly white-blotched, the base a sheathing leafstalk. There are also a few leaves on the lower part of the stem. Flowering stalk 5–9 in. high, densely sticky-hairy, the spike decidedly 1-sided. Flowers scarcely ⅛ in. long, greenish-white.

**tessellata.** Leaves oblongish or oval, 1–1½ in. long, tapering to a winged base, green but conspicuously white-blotched. Flowering stalk 6–9 in. high, the flowers white, about ⅓ in. long. Eastern N.A., mostly in evergreen woods. Aug.–Sept.

**EPIPHYLLUM** (ep-i-fill′um). Tree-perching (epiphytic), usually spineless cacti, ranging from Mex. to Brazil, very popular for greenhouses, window gardens, or as potted plants on porches. They are leafless in age, but the jointed, flattened branches are green and leaf-like, and are sometimes winged. Flowers showy, but often not blooming as house plants, the many stamens long and handsome. For details of flower structure *see* CACTACEAE. (*Epiphyllum* is from the Greek for on a leaf, in allusion to the leaf-like branches which bear the flowers.)

While these are true cacti, they are not desert plants, but inhabitants of much moister climates. They need a richer soil and more water than most cacti (which see). Some of the plants below are occasionally offered under the names *Phyllocactus* and *Zygocactus.* The latter includes the Christmas or crab cactus, often mistaken for some of the plants below.

**ackermanni.** Stems many, up to 3 ft. long, inclined to droop at the tips. Branches usually less than 12 in. long, the midrib and side ribs obvious. Flowers day-blooming, 4–6 in. wide, scarlet outside, carmine inside, the throat greenish-yellow. Of unknown origin, probably Mexican.

**crenatum.** Stems nearly 3 ft. high, erect, the margins strongly scalloped, the midrib thick. Flowers about 8 in. long and 4 in. wide, day-blooming, fragrant, white but yellow in age. Mex. and Central America.

**truncatum** = *Zygocactus truncatus.*

**EPIPHYTES.** Plants that grow on other plants is the exact meaning of this term, but by extension it has come to include all the air plants or tree-perchers. The epiphytic habit is so common in the tropics and so rare in the temperate zone that a few words regarding it may be useful to all who grow plants from both regions.

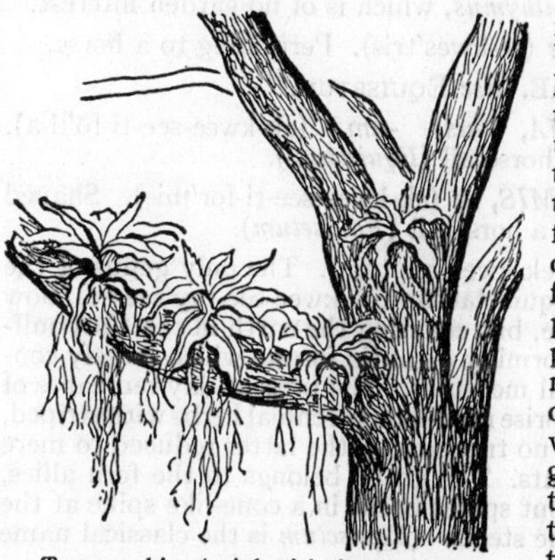

Tree-perching (epiphytic) plants at home in the tropics

A true epiphyte is a plant driven by demands for light or moisture to seek a perch upon a tree rather than succumb upon the dark forest floor. Thousands of orchids, aroids,* ferns, and other plants are epiphytes, and their need for that sort of an environment we translate into greenhouse practice every day. *See* the articles on culture of epiphytic ORCHIDS. *See also* BROMELIACEAE.

Epiphytes are often rooted in moss or debris in the fork of a branch, very rarely are they actually rooted upon the green surface of another plant. But no myth of the vegetable

* Special articles on the subjects indicated by an asterisk (*) will be found at the words so marked.

world is harder to kill than the assumption that epiphytes are parasites.* They never are, for they steal not food (as would be a true parasite), but merely a place to perch in the light. Hence they are here often called tree-perching to avoid the technical term of epiphyte. So little do they rely upon the nature of the support that, in the tropics, many epiphytes cling to telegraph wires or the eaves of buildings.

Many of them have special mechanisms for absorbing atmospheric moisture, which most plants never do. See VELAMEN.

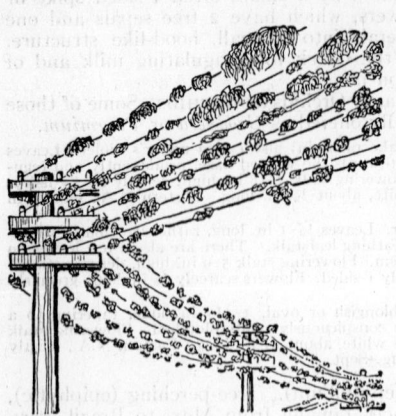
Epiphytic tillandsias on telegraph wires are sufficient proof that air plants do not get food from their perch.

**EPISCIA** (ep-piss'i-a). Thirty species of tropical American herbs of the family Gesneriaceae, **E. cupreata** widely grown in hanging baskets, but it needs a warm, moist greenhouse. Stems slender, branching, rooting at the joints, the tips drooping. Leaves opposite,* unequal, rough-hairy above, reddish beneath, nearly round or ovalish, the margin scalloped. Flower solitary in the leaf-axils,* scarlet, about ¾ in. wide, the corolla somewhat irregular* and sac-like. A very handsome plant for the greenhouse needing support or a chance to droop. Nicaragua. (*Episcia* is from Greek for shady, in allusion to their habitat preference.)

**EPITHELANTHA** (ep-i-thel-an'tha). A single, small, globe-shaped, cactus, **E. micromeris** of western Tex. and Mex. often cult. for interest, especially in small desert gardens or as a center-piece decoration. It has a tubercular plant body usually less than 2½ in. in diameter, almost globe-shaped, but flattened somewhat at the ends and a little depressed at the top. Spines numerous, white. Flowers from near the center of the plant, surrounded by spines and wool, scarcely ¼ in. wide, white or light pink. Fruit edible, but slightly acid, known to the natives as chilotes. For culture see CACTI. (*Epithelantha* is from the Greek meaning upon an anther.)

*EPITHYMOIDES* (ep-i-thy-moy'deez, but *see* OÏDES). Like the genus *Epithymus*, which is of no garden interest.

*EQUESTRIS, -e* (ee-kwes'tris). Pertaining to a horse.

*EQUISETACEAE.* See EQUISETUM.

*EQUISETIFOLIA, -us, -um* (ek-kwee-see-ti-fō'li-a). With leaves like a horsetail (*Equisetum*).

*EQUISETIFORMIS, -e* (ek-kwee-see-ti-for'mis). Shaped like, or resembling a horsetail (*Equisetum*).

**EQUISETUM** (ek-kwee-see'tum). The only genus of the horsetail family, **Equisetaceae** (ek-kwee-see-tay'see-ee), now of little importance, but covering the earth in the Carboniferous period and forming gigantic forests which largely contributed to the coal measures. The present-day remnants of the horsetails comprise rush-like, perennial herbs with striped, hollow stems, and no true leaves, the latter reduced to mere sheaths at the joints. The group belongs to the fern allies, bears no flowers, but spores borne in a cone-like spike at the ends of some of the stems. (*Equisetum* is the classical name of the horsetails.)

These plants are of much more historical than garden interest, for they link modern plants with an incredibly ancient type of vegetation. The first two are of easy culture in any ordinary garden soil, preferably a moist one. E. arvense, common along railway embankments, is often a nuisance. Only a single (non-hort.) Brazilian species is tree-like.

**arvense.** Common horsetail. *See* list at WEEDS.
**hyemale.** Scouring rush; called also Dutch rush, and many other names, all implying that its tough, wiry, rough stems are used for scouring. Stems furrowed, evergreen, 3–4 ft. high. Scale-like leaves pointed, clustered at the joints. The cone-like spikes that bear the spores are pointed. Throughout the north temperate zone, mostly in moist places.
**praealtum.** An evergreen, rush-like plant, the tough, wiry stems 3–10 ft. high, nearly 1 in. in diameter. Scale-like leaves pointed, the base of the sheath of which they are part black-girdled. Western N.A.; also in As. Sometimes known as *E. robustum*.
**robustum** = *Equisetum praealtum*.

**ERAGROSTIS** (e-ra-gros'tis). A genus of over 100 species of annual or perennial grasses of minor economic importance, but a few somewhat grown for their delicate, spray-like flower spikes. All those below are annuals and should be sown where wanted. The small flower spikes are borne in open, lax, branching clusters (panicles*), the spikes not awned. (*Eragrostis* is from the Greek for love grass and of uncertain application here.)

**abyssinica.** Teff. A North African, fragrant grass, there yielding a cereal grain (teff), but grown here only for ornament, and 1–3 ft. high. Leaves grass-like, 4–6 in. long, about 1/10 in. wide. Flowering cluster nearly 1 ft. long, its hair-like branches more or less erect. In Abyssinia teff is an important cereal grain.
**elegans** = *Eragrostis japonica*.
**japonica.** Usually 1–2 ft. high, rarely 3 ft. Flower cluster nearly half the height of the plant, narrow, rather interrupted, its spikelets very numerous but small. Jap. Sometimes known as *E. elegans*.
**suaveolens.** A delicate grass sometimes grown for dry bouquets. It resembles *E. abyssinica*, but it is not fragrant and its cluster of flowering spikes is less spreading, and the spikelets more compact. Western As.

**ERANTHEMUM** (ee-ran'thee-mum). Tropical Asian shrubs or woody herbs of the family Acanthaceae, **E. nervosum** of India a popular ornamental greenhouse shrub 2–4 ft. high, which can also be grown outdoors in zones* 8 and 9. It has thickish, prominently-veined, ovalish leaves, 4–8 in. long, faintly toothed and long-stalked. Flowers blue, in closely bracted* spikes, either terminal or in the leaf-axils.* Corolla nearly regular,* about 1 in. long, its tube long and somewhat curved. Stamens (fertile ones) 2. The bracts* of the spike are prominently veined. Fruit an oblongish capsule. Indoor culture demands potting mixture* 3, a warm-temperate greenhouse, and plenty of water. The plant is sometimes offered as *E. pulchellum*. (*Eranthemum* is from the Greek for lovely flower.) For the plant occasionally known as *E. reticulatum, see* PSEUDERANTHEMUM RETICULATUM.

**ERANTHIS** (e-ran'thiss). Tuberous, Eurasian herbs of the buttercup family. Of the six known species **E. hyemalis**, the winter aconite, is a deservedly popular plant for the rock garden or border because its yellow flowers bloom very early in spring or even in late winter if the season has not been too severe. It is an erect, usually unbranched perennial, 3–8 in. high, the leaves all basal, roundish, long-stalked, and much cut into fine segments. Flower solitary, the petals none or much reduced. Sepals 5–8, yellow and petal-like, about ⅝ in. long. Fruit a collection of small pods (follicles*), somewhat resembling a miniature bean pod. For culture *see* below. (*Eranthis* is Greek for flower of spring.) It is sometimes called New Year's Gift.

### WINTER ACONITE CULTURE

Winter aconite thrives in any good, well-drained garden soil. One of its recommendations is that it will flourish in shade, and a woodland bank suits it well. Being a free seeder in such a position, it increases rapidly, and may be left undisturbed year after year. It may also be planted thickly beneath early-flowering shrubs, where the bright color showing during the first months of the year is very welcome. If mingled with such bulbs as snowdrops, *Scilla sibirica*, chionodoxas, *Crocus imperati* and *Hyacinthus azureus*, a brave show is made for many weeks. After seed is formed the plants die down and the tuber rests during the summer months, growth beginning early in the autumn. It is thus important to get the tubers into the ground as early as possible. Plant them in August or early September,

---
\* Special articles on the subjects indicated by an asterisk (\*) will be found at the words so marked.

3 inches deep and for the best effect not more than 3 in. apart. — L. B. W.

***ERECTA, -us, -um*** (ee-rek'ta). Upright.

**EREMOCHLOA** (e-ree-mock'lō-a). Asiatic or Australian perennial grasses of little garden interest, except for **E. ophiuroides** of China, commonly called centipede-grass, and useful for lawns in places too warm for ordinary lawn mixtures. It creeps by runners, from the ends and joints of which arise the bluish-green leaves that are about 3 in. long and ¼ in. wide. Flowering spikes terminal, rather narrow, somewhat arching, composed of many 1-sided, small spikelets. (*Eremochloa* is from the Greek for lovely grass.)

**EREMURUS** (e-ree-mure'us). Magnificent Asiatic, perennial herbs of the lily family, with thick, cord-like or fibrous roots. They need careful culture, but few border herbs are so striking or showy. They are generally known as foxtail lily or desert candle, perhaps from the very tall, flowering stalk. Leaves all basal, rather narrow, without teeth, and forming tufts or rosettes. Flowering stalks from 4–10 ft. high, the spire-like cluster (raceme*) usually 1–3 ft. long. Flowers very numerous, bell-shaped, but the petals only slightly connected at the base, usually with 1 prominent vein. Stamens 6, sometimes protruding. Fruit a capsule.* (*Eremurus* is from the Greek for lonely tail, probably in reference to the solitary flower cluster.)

The foxtail lilies are among the most striking garden plants, the tall, flowering cluster often containing several hundred flowers. Because they have peculiarly brittle roots they must be planted very carefully, and the cord-like branches of the root must be spread out very gently, looking when planted not unlike a star-fish. Plant at least 6–9 in. deep in a rich, well-drained soil. They are voracious feeders and the soil can scarcely be too rich. Fall planting is best, after which top-dress the soil with strawy manure, and this is best repeated each year, for the plants are not quite hardy north of zone* 4, and a good mulching is always safer. Of the species below the best known are *E. himalaicus* and *E. robustus*, and they are the easiest to grow. But some of the others, and particularly some of the newer hybrids, are even better worth growing. All are most attractive when planted against a background of shrubbery.

**bungei.** Leaves narrow, about 1 ft. long. Flowering stalk 4 ft. high, the cluster about 5 in. long. Flowers yellow or orange. Persia. July.

**elwesi.** Leaves ovalish-oblong or narrower, bluish-green. Flowering stalk 10–12 ft., the cluster nearly 2½ ft. long. Flowers pink. Of unknown, but probably of hybrid origin. The *var.* **albus** has white flowers.

**himalaicus.** Leaves narrow, about 18 in. long. Flowering stalk 6–8 ft. high, the cluster 18–30 in. long. Flowers white. Himalayas. June. The best known in cult.

**robustus.** Leaves strap-shaped, up to 2 ft. long. Flowering stalk 8–10 ft. high, the cluster 2–3 ft. long and nearly 5 in. thick. Flowers bright pink. Central As.

**tubergeni.** A hybrid between *E. himalaicus* and *E. bungei.*

**ERFURT CONEFLOWER** = *Rudbeckia bicolor superba.*

**ERIANTHUS** (e-ri-an'thus). Perhaps 20 species of chiefly tropical grasses, usually called plume grass, most of them perennials and **E. ravennae,** the Ravenna grass, commonly grown for ornament. It is a stout, strong-growing grass, 8–12 ft. high, the stems smooth and stiff. Leaves nearly 3 ft. long, about ½ in. wide, the veins roughish, the sheath at the base hairy and very rough. Flowering plume much-branched, very silky and showy, much resembling pampas grass (*see* CORTADERIA). Southern Eu. to India. Scarcely hardy above zone* 4, but easily grown in any ordinary garden soil. (*Erianthus* is from the Greek for wool-flower, in allusion to the silky plume of inflorescence.)

**ERICA** (ĕ'ri-ka). The true heaths comprise a genus of over 500 species of the family Ericaceae, largely from South Africa and the Mediterranean region, a few scattered elsewhere. They are sometimes tree-like, more often low shrubs and some are nearly prostrate. Leaves characteristically heath-like, *i.e.* small, narrow, and needle-like, usually in clusters of 3–6, but so numerous as to be often densely crowded, prevailingly evergreen. Flowers sometimes solitary, more often in small clusters (umbels* or spikes*), often nodding. Corolla urn-shaped or bell-shaped, never large, with 4 small lobes. Stamens 8. Fruit a many-seeded capsule. (*Erica* is from the Latin for heath.)

For Culture *see* below.

**arborea.** Tree heath. A shrub or small tree 10–20 ft. high, the twigs hairy. Leaves in 3's. Flowers white, about ⅕ in. long, fragrant, in large, branching clusters. Not hardy north of zone* 6. Southern Eu.

**carnea.** Spring or winter heath. Not over 12 in. high, mostly prostrate. Leaves in 4's. Flowers red, about ¼ in. long, in 1-sided clusters. March–May, or earlier with protection. *See* WINTER GARDEN. Southern Eu. Hardy up to zone* 3. The *var.* **alba** has white, and the *var.* **rosea,** rose-colored, flowers. All are often grown in the rock garden (which see).

**ciliaris.** Fringed heath. Not over 12 in. high, mostly prostrate. Leaves in 3's, hairy on the edges. Flowers rosy-red, about ⅓ in. long, the terminal clusters (racemes*) about 5 in. long. Eng. to Spain. Spring. Hardy up to zone* 6, possibly to zone* 5 with protection.

**cinerea.** Twisted heath; also called Scotch heath (for the heather *see* CALLUNA). A dense, much-branched shrub 12–18 in. high. Leaves in 3's. Flowers rosy-purple, about ¼ in. long, the clusters about 3 in. long. Western Eu. June–Sept. Hardy up to zone* 3, and naturalized at Nantucket.

**mediterranea.** A shrub 6–10 ft. high. Leaves in 4's or 5's. Flowers deep red, about ¼ in. long, the stamens* protruding. Spring. Western Eu. Hardy from zone* 5, and, with protection, from zone* 4, southward. The *var.* **alba** has white flowers.

**melanthera.** A South African heath, rarely over 2 ft. high. Leaves in 3's. Flowers winter-blooming, rose-red, very profuse at the ends of the twigs, the corolla scarcely ⅕ in. long. For culture and hardiness *see* below.

**persoluta** = *Erica subdivaricata.*

**stricta.** Corsican heath. A shrub 6–9 ft. high, the leaves usually in 4's. Flowers rosy-purple, about ¼ in. long, summer-blooming. Southern Eu. Hardy only up to zone* 6.

**subdivaricata.** Garland heath. A South African heath never over 2 ft. high. Flowers rose-red (or white in a variety), about ⅙ in. long, borne in terminal racemes* in spring. For culture and hardiness *see* below. Sometimes offered as *E. persoluta.*

**tetralix.** Cross-leaved heath. Not over 2 ft. high, the branches mostly prostrate. Leaves in 4's, hairy on the edges. Flowers rose-red, about ¼ in. long, in dense terminal clusters. Eu. June–Oct. Hardy up to zone* 3 and naturalized in Mass.

**vagans.** Cornish heath. A spreading, but not prostrate, shrub, 8–12 in. high. Leaves in 4's or 5's. Flowers pinkish-purple, about ⅕ in. long, in leafy clusters that may be 6 in. long. Western Eu. Aug.–Oct. Hardy from zone* 4 southward.

**ventricosa.** A South African heath 4–6 ft. high. Leaves in 4's, hairy on the edges. Flowers red, pink, or white, up to ⅔ in. long, in dense clusters (umbels*). For culture *see* below.

**verticillata.** A South African heath 3–5 ft. high. Leaves usually in 4's or 6's, not hairy on the edges. Flowers more tubular than bell-shaped, nearly ¾ in. long, in dense racemes.* For culture *see* below.

### ERICA CULTURE

The heaths are represented by two groups, those of Europe, particularly southern Europe, and those from South Africa that were once more used than now as pot plants for winter bloom. The hardy heaths vary from white through pink to deep rose and the tender heaths add yellow and orange to the range.

All require firm mixtures of peat and sand. The hardy forms, such as *Erica carnea, ciliaris, cinerea, stricta, tetralix* and *vagans*, are best used in masses with callunas and other related plants, either in the open or with passing shade. The taller Mediterranean forms are most useful in California, as are some of the South African species. The latter, however, particularly *melanthera* for winter and *verticillata, ventricosa* and *subdivaricata* for late winter and early spring, are best suited to pot culture, using mixture No. 5, growing them in a house with a temperature of about 45° F., with ample ventilation and no excess of moisture.

All are easily propagated by cuttings of half-ripe wood in sand or sand and peat with mild bottom-heat. — B. Y. M.

**ERICACEAE** (e-ri-kay'see-ee). The heath family, often called the arbutus, heather or wintergreen family, is of outstanding garden importance because it includes both azalea and rhododendron, as well as the showy South African and European heaths, and many valuable hort. genera, including splendid, broad-leaved evergreens.

As here understood it is a very large family of herbs, shrubs or rarely small trees, largely evergreens, comprising over 70 genera and 1500 species, most of which are plants of somewhat, or decidedly, acid soils and are confined mostly to the north temperate zone.

By many authorities this large family is split into four:

**Clethraceae,** or white alder family, which includes only *Clethra.*

**Pyrolaceae** or shinleaf family, which (in the garden genera) includes only *Chimaphila, Pyrola* and *Moneses.*

* Special articles on the subjects indicated by an asterisk (*) will be found at the words so marked.

Vacciniaceae, or huckleberry family, which includes only (in the garden genera) the huckleberry and *Vaccinium* (the blueberry).

Ericaceae, or heath family, here considered as including not only the plants sometimes restricted to it but all those often included in the three above.

The Ericaceae (as a whole) have alternate,* very rarely opposite* but sometimes much-crowded leaves. Flowers often very showy (as in azalea and rhododendron and many cult. genera), regular,* or highly irregular* in *Azalea*, solitary or in various sorts of clusters, quite often bell-shaped or urn-shaped, but sometimes of separate petals. The fruit is a dry pod (capsule*) in the Ericaceae proper, but fleshy in the huckleberry, blueberry (*Vaccinium*) and its relatives.

The garden favorites in the heath family, all of outdoor culture over most of the U.S., are *Azalea*, *Calluna* (see HEATHER), *Kalmia* (the mountain laurel), *Leucothoë*, *Pieris*, *Rhododendron*, and the beautiful *Rhodora*, and *Xolisma*.

Among the lesser known garden genera, some of which require specialized culture, dealt with at each genus, are: *Andromeda*, *Arctostaphylos*, *Bruckenthalia*, *Chamaedaphne*, *Chiogenes*, *Daboecia*, *Epigaea* (see TRAILING ARBUTUS), *Gaultheria*, *Ledum*, *Leiophyllum*, *Loiseleuria*, *Menziesia*, *Pernettya* and *Phyllodoce*.

There are in addition a few shrubs and tree genera, which instead of being evergreen, drop their leaves in the fall, among them being: *Enkianthus*, *Oxydendrum* (a tree) and *Zenobia*.

The only genera of greenhouse culture are Erica (in part) and *Arbutus*, both of which are also mostly hardy from zone* 6 southward outdoors.

Technical flower characters: Ovary superior* in most genera, except the blueberry and its relatives, where it is inferior.* Corolla bell-shaped or urn-shaped or more or less tubular in nearly all genera, but of separate petals in *Ledum*, *Leiophyllum*, some azaleas, *Clethra* and partly so in *Chimaphila* and *Moneses*. Calyx 4-5-parted. Stamens as many as the petals or corolla lobes or twice as many, the anthers opening mostly by terminal pores. Ovary 2-5-celled, in the genera with dry fruit (see above), many-seeded.

*ERICAEFOLIA, -us, -um* (e-ri-see-fō′li-a). With heath-like leaves.

*ERICOIDES* (e-ri-koy′deez, but *see* OÏDES). Like a heath (*Erica*).

ERIGENIA (e-ri-jee′ni-a). A single bulbous herb, E. bulbosa, the harbinger-of-spring, of the carrot family, an inhabitant of rich woods of eastern N.A., and suited only to the wild garden. It is a smooth, delicate perennial, scarcely 8 in. high, the leaves thrice-compound, and its leaflets narrow or oblongish and rather blunt. Flowers very small, white, in a terminal, leafy umbel* (for details *see* UMBELLIFERAE). Fruit a collection of kidney-shaped, 5-ribbed carpels. The plant blooms in April or early May, and is not widely grown. (*Erigenia* is from the Greek for born in spring.)

ERIGERON (e-rij′er-on). The fleabanes comprise perhaps 150 species of annual or perennial herbs of the family Compositae, of wide distribution, but mostly of temperate regions. A few are fine garden plants, much resembling wild asters, from which they differ only in technical characters, and some are merely weedy. Plants sometimes nearly stemless and with basal leaves, but the taller sorts have alternate* leaves. Flower heads solitary or in branched clusters, the disk* flowers yellow, but the rays* numerous, mostly violet-purple, yellow, or rose-red, but white in a few weedy species. (*Erigeron* is from the Greek for old man in spring, in allusion to the hoary leaves of some species.)

The ordinary border fleabanes are of very simple culture in any usual garden soil, and may be propagated by division in spring or fall. A few, such as E. alpinus, E. aurantiacus, etc., are, as indicated below, best suited to the rock garden (which see). All bloom in summer.

alpinus. A rock garden plant from the mountains of Eurasia and the Rocky Mountains, over 1 ft. high. Leaves narrow, without marginal teeth. Flower heads mostly solitary, about ¾ in. wide, mostly purple, sometimes whitish.

aurantiacus. Double orange daisy. A rock garden perennial from Turkestan, and not over 10 in. high. Leaves narrow, broadest towards the tip. Flower heads solitary or 2, about 1 in. wide, orange-yellow.

coulteri. A stout perennial 12-20 in. high and useful in the open border. Leaves lance-shaped, or broader towards the tip, somewhat toothed.

Flower heads solitary, about 1½ in. wide, whitish or purplish-white. Western U.S. There are one or two named forms in the trade.

glaucus. Beach aster or seaside daisy. A seaside plant of the Pacific Coast, not much grown elsewhere and not hardy in the East. Leaves chiefly basal, oblongish, without marginal teeth. Flower heads solitary, about 1½ in. wide, violet or lilac.

karvinskianus. A rock garden or border perennial, not over 18 in. high, the stems mostly creeping or trailing. Leaves about 1 in. long, toothed or lobed, especially towards the tip. Flower heads several, but solitary on each stalk, about ¾ in. wide, pinkish-white. Tropical America. Not hardy northward and sometimes used as a summer bedding plant, as it blooms from seed the first year. Offered as E. mucronatus, but more often as *Vittadinia australis*.

mucronatus = *Erigeron karvinskianus*.

multiradiatus. Himalayan fleabane. A rock garden perennial, 6-18 in. high. Leaves oblongish or narrower, without marginal teeth. Flower heads solitary, very showy, purple, nearly 3 in. wide. Himalayas.

pulchellus. Poor Robin's-plantain or Robin's-plantain. A border herb, almost weedy, bur rather showy, 12-20 in. high, producing offsets.* Leaves chiefly basal and tufted, more or less oblong. Flower heads 1-6, in a loose, terminal cluster, violet or violet-purple, about 1½ in. wide. Eastern U.S.

speciosus. A showy border perennial from western N.A. and the best known of all the cult. species. It grows from 15-30 in. high, and has narrow leaves without teeth. Flower heads dark violet, about 1¼ in. wide, numerous in showy corymbs.* There are many named forms, especially with larger, double, or rose-colored heads.

*ERINOIDES* (e-ri-noy′deez, but *see* OÏDES). Resembling the genus *Erinus*.

ERINUS (e-ry′nus). A single, tufted, spring-blooming, perennial herb of the figwort family, found in the mountains of Europe and suited chiefly for the rock garden, where the cult. of E. alpinus is noted. The plant is scarcely 3½ in. high, and has basal, coarsely toothed leaves about ½ in. long. Flowers purple, about ½ in. wide, the cluster (raceme*) about 2 in. long. Corolla slightly irregular. Stamens 4. There are white- and red-flowered varieties. (*Erinus* is from the Greek indicating early bloom.)

ERIOBOTRYA (e-ri-o-bō′tri-a). A small genus of Asiatic, evergreen trees and shrubs of the rose family, E. japonica, the loquat, widely cult. for its fruit, and as an ornamental. It is a tree up to 20 ft. high, the leaves nearly stalkless, thick, stiff, nearly 1 ft. long, and rusty-hairy beneath. Flowers fragrant, white, about ½ in. wide, in hairy clusters (panicles*) nearly 6 in. long. Petals 5, clawed.* Stamens* about 20. Fruit fleshy (a pome*), plum-shaped, 1-2-seeded, its yellow flesh agreeably acid. Some of the improved cult. varieties have fruits nearly 3 in. long. There is also a variegated leaved form grown chiefly for ornament. For culture *see* LOQUAT. The tree is hardy, with protection, up to zone* 6, and is commonly grown far southward, rarely in the cool greenhouse. (*Eriobotrya* is from the Greek for woolly cluster, in allusion to the hairy flower cluster.)

ERIOGONUM (e-ri-ŏg′o-num). A very large genus of western American, mostly woolly herbs of the buckwheat family, decidedly of secondary garden interest except for their culture in Calif. as bee plants. They have chiefly basal leaves without teeth, the stem leaves, when present, alternate* or whorled.* Flowers small, inconspicuous, in various sorts of close clusters. (For detailed flower structure *see* POLYGONACEAE.) Fruit a 3-angled achene.* (*Eriogonum* is from the Greek for woolly joint, in allusion to the hairy stems.)

These are not easy to grow in eastern gardens because of the cold, wet winters. While the plants can stand intense, dry cold, their woolly foliage is unsuited to slush and winter rains. In the West they thrive in dry, open soils, thoroughly drained. The second species does well, however, in the East, as far north as Washington, D.C.

fasciculatum. Wild buckwheat; called also flat-tops in Calif., in which state and Nev. is native. Stems woody at the base, 2-3 ft. high. Leaves oblongish or narrower, about ¾ in. long, densely white-woolly on the under side. Flowers white, the cluster a simple or compound umbel.*

umbellatum. Sulphur-flower. Not over 1 ft. high, the leaves chiefly basal, ovalish, about 2 in. long, white-woolly on the under side. Flowers golden-yellow, the umbels* simple. Pacific Coast and Wyo.

*ERIOPHORA, -us, -um* (e-ri-off′o-ra). Woolly. The genus *Eriophorum*, the cotton grasses, are sometimes planted in the bog garden. They are grass-like plants belonging to

* Special articles on the subjects indicated by an asterisk (*) will be found at the words so marked.

the sedge family, with cottony, terminal heads; mostly native in cool-region bogs.

**ERIOPHYLLUM** (e-ri-o-fill'um). Western North American herbs of the family Compositae, often called woolly sunflower, from their often white-woolly foliage and sunflower-like heads. They have alternate,* and, in ours, deeply lobed leaves. Flower heads small, resembling a miniature sunflower, the disk* and ray* flowers yellow. (*Eriophyllum* is from the Greek for woolly leaf.)

The woolly sunflowers are not happy in our eastern, usually slushy or wet, winters. In the Far West they are occasionally transferred to open, sandy borders where they do well.

**caespitosum.** A perennial, 9–18 in. high. Leaves deeply 3–5-parted or lobed, green above, white-woolly beneath. Flower heads mostly solitary, light yellow, about 1 in. wide. Calif. Summer.
**lanatum.** A perennial 9–18 in. high. Leaves deeply 5–7-parted or lobed, the segments oblongish or narrower. Flower heads chiefly solitary, about 1 in. wide, golden-yellow. Idaho and British Columbia to Calif. Summer.

**ERLANGEA** (er-lan'jee-a). A genus of chiefly tropical African herbs or shrubby plants of the family Compositae, only E. tomentosa occasionally cult. in the greenhouse for its long-blooming, flat-topped cluster of lilac or mauve flower heads. It is a densely hairy shrub, 3–5 ft. high, with generally opposite* leaves that are scented, toothed, oblongish but blunt, and 3–5 in. long. Flower heads wholly of disk* flowers, of which there may be 40, the heads about ⅔ in. wide and clustered in a generally flat-topped panicle.* Grow in a warm greenhouse and use potting mixture* 4. (Named for the University of Erlangen in Bavaria.)

**ERODIUM** (ee-rō'di-um). Nearly 60 species of widely distributed herbs of the family Geraniaceae, a few grown for ornament, some weedy, a few planted for forage in dry regions, and one or two fairly important as bee plants in Calif. They are closely related to the genus *Geranium* (not the garden geranium), from which they differ in having the outer stamens* bearing no anthers,* while all the 10 stamens of *Geranium* are anther-bearing. Leaves generally divided or compound,* feather-fashion. Petals 5. Fruit a collection of spindle-shaped carpels, all attached to the styles which coil up in age. The plants are commonly called stork's-bill or heron's-bill. (*Erodium* is from the Greek for heron's-bill.)

Erodiums are of very easy culture in open, sandy or loamy soils. Outside of their use as forage, they are of secondary garden interest, and are readily raised from spring-sown seed or increased by division.

**cheilanthifolium.** A perennial not over 4 in. high. Leaves basal, twice-compound,* gray-felty. Flowers about ¾ in. wide, white, veined with rose. Southern Spain and Morocco. Useful in the rock garden.
**chrysanthum.** A silvery-leaved, tufted perennial best suited to the rock garden, and not over 4 in. high. Leaves twice-compound,* chiefly basal. Flowers ½ in. wide, yellow. Greece.
**cicutarium.** Alfilaria; called also filaree and pin-clover. The best known of the heron's-bills and widely cult. for forage, and in Calif. for bees. It is an annual, erect or sprawling, 6–15 in. high, and with chiefly basal, much-divided leaves. Flowers ¼ in. wide, purplish-pink. Southern Eu., but naturalized in the U.S.
**macradenum.** A perennial 8–12 in. high, the leaves all basal and only once-compound.* Flowers nearly ½ in. wide, light purple but dark-spotted. Pyrenees. Rock garden plant.
**manescavi.** Resembling the last, but the flowers rosy-purple, about twice as large, and without the spots. Pyrenees. Rock garden plant.

*EROSA, -us, -um* (ee-rō'sa). Jagged or gnawed.

**EROSION.** In regions of little or no forest cover, steep slopes, and sandy soil, the washing of soil in rainy weather is a serious menace. To overcome such, on any considerable scale, the attention of trained foresters and engineers is needed. Local erosion in a garden is best stopped by sodding, or, if that is impossible, see the methods and plants mentioned at BANKS.

*ERUBESCENS* (er-roo-bes'senz). Blushing.

**ERUCA** (ee-roo'ka). A small genus of Eurasian annual or biennial herbs of the mustard family, E. sativa rather rarely grown here as a salad plant under the name of rocket salad, roquette, or simply rocket. It is a mustard-like, half-hardy annual, branching, 18–30 in. high, and does not like summer heat. Leaves large, deeply toothed or cut. Flowers yellowish-white, about ¾ in. long, the 4 petals with purple veins, the flower cluster erect, terminal, and a raceme.* Fruit an erect, flattish, beaked pod (silique*). Sow seeds as for early and late cabbage; *i.e.* avoid midsummer heat. The leaves should be ready for harvesting in about 65 days from sowing the seed. Quick growth and a cool season help to reduce the peculiar odor that makes many dislike the plant. (*Eruca* is the classical name of some mustard-like plant, but perhaps not this one.)

**ERVIL** = *Vicia ervilia.*

*ERVILIA.* Ancient classical name, used by Pliny for some legume, but now a specific name for a vetch. See VICIA.

**ERYNGIUM** (er-rin'ji-um). Very striking and handsome, chiefly perennial, spiny-leaved herbs of the carrot family, widely cult. for the border or rock garden, and commonly called eryngo or sea holly. Of over 200 species the following seven are very popular as tall, bold plants, especially for the blue garden (which see). Unlike most plants of the carrot family, eryngo has simple* leaves, generally cut or lobed, and the margins usually spiny. Flowers prevailingly blue in the cult. sorts, but sometimes white or green, crowded in dense, bracted,* head-like clusters. Calyx showy, spiny-toothed, the petals less conspicuous, erect and stiffish. Fruit egg-shaped, without ribs, several in a cluster. (*Eryngium* is Greek for a thistle, which some of the plants suggest.)

The sea hollies thrive in any ordinarily good garden soil, preferably a reasonably moist one. They may be increased by division or by sowing fresh seed. Extremely handsome plants for the border, but they need plenty of space. Most of them are summer-blooming.

**alpinum.** About 2 ft. high, the plant bushy. Leaves triangular-heart-shaped, bluish, the upper ones often 3-lobed. Flower heads bluish-purple, rarely white, about 1½ in. wide, below a series of finely divided bracts.* Eu.
**amethystinum.** A perennial, not over 2 ft. high. Leaves deeply lobed or sometimes quite compound.* Flower heads about ½ in. long, bluish-purple, the bracts* below them lance-shaped. Eu. Sometimes confused with E. planum.
**aquaticum.** Button snakeroot; also called rattlesnake master. A stout, bushy herb 4–6 ft. high. Leaves stiff, rigid, very narrow, bristly margined. Flower heads pale blue or whitish. Eastern U.S.
**bourgati.** Scarcely over 18 in. high. Leaves nearly round, stiff, spiny-toothed, and divided finger-fashion into 3–5 segments. Flower heads ½ in. long, bluish-purple, the bracts* beneath long and spine-tipped. Southern Eu.
**giganteum.** Five to seven feet high and much-branched. Leaves heart-shaped or triangular, the upper ones 3-lobed. Flower heads nearly 4 in. wide, blue or pale green, the bracts beneath long, stiff and much cut. Caucasus. A very handsome plant.
**oliverianum.** A perennial 2–3 ft. high. Leaves various, the lower undivided, the upper 4–5-parted or lobed, finger-fashion. Flower heads about 1½ in. wide, blue or bluish-purple, the bracts* below rigid, very narrow and stiff. Of hybrid origin.
**planum.** Not over 3 ft. high, the lower leaves undivided, the upper 3–5-parted. Flower heads blue, about ½ in. wide, the bracts* beneath rigid, narrow and stiff. Eurasia.

**ERYNGO.** See ERYNGIUM.

**ERYSIMUM** (e-riss'i-mum). A large genus of Old World herbs of the mustard family, closely related to the common wallflower (see CHEIRANTHUS) and differing only in technical characters from it. *Erysimum*, usually called blister-cress, contains a few flower garden plants, somewhat resembling stocks, with yellow, lilac, or blue flowers, usually in terminal clusters (racemes*) that lengthen considerably as the long, 4-sided pods (silique*) ripen. The pods are usually beaked. (*Erysimum* is from the Greek to draw blisters.)

The blister-cresses are of very easy culture in any garden soil. The plants are almost weedy in their ability to withstand unfavorable conditions. Under usual garden culture they flower profusely. Sow the annuals where wanted, while the perennials and biennial species should be sown the season before they are to be planted out. The Latin names below are still in much confusion.

**asperum.** Siberian wallflower. A supposedly North American, but possibly Asiatic, perennial herb, best treated as a biennial (see BIENNIALS). It is erect, 1–3 ft. high, the foliage rough-hairy. Leaves rather narrow, 2–4 in. long, the lower ones remotely toothed. Flowers orange-yellow. Pods slender, 2–4 in. long. Often sold as *Cheiranthus allioni.*
**linifolium.** Alpine wallflower. A grayish, perennial herb, 6–12 in.

---

* Special articles on the subjects indicated by an asterisk (*) will be found at the words so marked.

high, but the branches somewhat prostrate. Leaves narrow, nearly linelike. Flowers lilac or mauve. Spain. Often sold as *Cheiranthus linifolius*.
**murale.** An old, flower garden, hardy annual (*see* ANNUALS), grown or offered under a variety of names, one of the most widely used being *E. perofskianum* (a name properly applied to another non-hort. species). It is a showy herb 12–18 in. high, leafy, and with the leaves little, if at all, toothed. Flowers golden-yellow, in compact clusters. Pods not much over 1 in. long, rather thick. Eu. A much-confused species as to name, but long in cult.
**perofskianum.** *See* ERYSIMUM MURALE.
**pulchellum.** A tufted, perennial herb 12–24 in. high, the stem erect. Leaves oblongish, toothed or with lyre-shaped lobes, the upper ones narrower and deeply toothed. Flowers dark orange. Pod slender and erect. Asia Minor and Greece. Sometimes the plant offered as this is *E. murale*.

**ERYTHEA** (e-ri-thee'a). Mexican fan palms, three of the five known species grown for ornament outdoors in zones* 8 and 9, especially in Fla. and Calif. They are not very tall, the trunk without spines but sometimes very shaggy, as in the not distantly related California fan palm. Leaves fan-like, the stalk sometimes prickly, the blade split into many (20–80) segments, the tips of which often droop. Flowers perfect,* the cluster from among the leaf crown, the spadix* provided with a spathe.* Stamens 6. Fruits about ¾ in. long or a little less. (Named for one of the Hesperides, The Daughter of Evening.)

For culture *see* PALM.

**armata.** Mexican blue palm. Not over 40 ft. high, the trunk covered by the remains of the withered leaf bases and their attendant shag. Leaves bluish-green, waxy, cut deeply into nearly 50 segments, the leafstalk spiny. Flowering cluster long, protruding beyond the crown of leaves. Fruit nearly round, fleshy. Baja Calif. The tree is also offered as *Glaucotheca*.
**brandegeei.** Taller than the last, and the trunk usually not shaggy. Leaves green above, pale beneath, cut to the middle or beyond into many segments that are about 1 in. wide and droop at the tip, where each segment is also cut. Leafstalk 3–5 ft. long, spiny-toothed. Fruit about ½ in. in diameter.
**edulis.** Guadalupe palm. A stout, ringed palm, usually less than 30 ft. high, the trunk not shaggy. Leaves green both sides, but paler beneath, cut about ⅓ to the middle into 70–80 segments that are about 1 in. wide, and deeply cleft at the tip. Leafstalk usually without spines. Fruit globe-shaped, black, about ⅞ in. thick, in a long cluster. Guadalupe Island and Baja Calif. Commonly planted in Calif. and Fla.

**ERYTHRAEA** = *Centaurium*.

**ERYTHRINA** (e-ri-thry'na). A very large genus of handsome tropical shrubs or trees (rarely herbs) of the pea family, of many uses in the tropics, but planted only for ornament in zones* 8 and 9, where their usually showy flowers are mostly borne before or after, not with, the leaves. Commonly called coral trees because of their striking flowers. Leaves compound,* the leaflets usually only 3 and broad. Flowers almost pea-like, very handsome, borne in large clusters (racemes*). Pod (legume*) long, somewhat woody, usually constricted between the seeds, which are usually brightly colored. (*Erythrina* is from the Greek for red, in allusion to the flower color.)

The three below, all tropical American, are somewhat grown in zone* 9 or protected parts of zone* 8 in Fla., where they are highly prized. They appear to have no special soil preferences. Propagated by seeds or cuttings. Most of them are thorny and winter-blooming.

**corallodendron.** Not over 20 ft. high, usually prickly. Leaflets more or less rhomboid.* Flowers scarlet, the cluster loose, but very handsome. Pod about 4 in. long, the seeds black-spotted, but scarlet. Tropical America.
**crista-galli.** A shrub or small tree, not over 15 ft. high. Leaflets often spiny on the midrib and sometimes on the stalk. Flowers crimson, the cluster loose. Brazil.
**poeppigiana.** Bucare. This, a very common coral tree, universally used to shade young coffee and chocolate plantations, is nearly 50 ft. high and very prickly. Leaflets oval. Flowers cinnabar-red, the clusters short and close, but very numerous. Probably Peruvian, but now widely dispersed over the tropical world.

*ERYTHROCARPA, -us, -um* (e-ri-throw-kar'pa). Red-fruited.

**ERYTHRONIUM** (e-ri-throw'ni-um). A dozen species of generally woodland, bulbous, spring-blooming herbs of the lily family, all but one North American. They have 2, often mottled, basal leaves and rather handsome flowers that are nodding, usually in small clusters or solitary. Petals and sepals not easily distinguishable as such, but the segments separate. Stamens* 6. Fruit an oblongish, somewhat 3-angled pod. The plants are generally called dogtooth violet, adder's-tongue, or trout flower. (*Erythronium* is from the Greek for red flower.)

Except for the rock garden species, noted as such below, all the dogtooth violets are best suited to the wild garden, where they do well in partial shade, and in moist woods soil, not especially acid. They are best propagated by offsets, although they may be raised from seed if one is willing to wait for 3–4 years for the first flowers. Some of them are among the most attractive of American wild flowers, the western ones best treated as bulbous plants that need a long rest after blooming.

**albidum.** Spring or fawn lily. Not over 12 in. high. Leaves green or brown-mottled. Flowers white or pinkish-purple, about 1½ in. long, the segments curved backward. Eastern N.A.
**americanum.** The common dogtooth violet or yellow adder's-tongue. Leaves 4–6 in. long, the blade mottled with brown. Flowers yellow, about 1½ in. long, the segments curved backward. Eastern N.A., especially in rich, moist woods. Often grown in the rock garden (which see), but also suited to the wild garden.
**californicum.** Fawn lily. About 1 ft. high, the leaves strongly mottled with brownish or whitish spots. Flowers 1¼ in. long, cream-white. Native in Calif. and not much suited to other parts of the country.
**grandiflorum.** Adam-and-Eve; called, also, in Calif., the chamise lily, and little grown outside that state. It grows nearly 24 in. high and has unmottled leaves and bright yellow flowers nearly 2 in. long, the flower segments strongly bent backwards. Western N.A.
**hendersoni.** Not over 12 in. high, the leaves mottled. Flowers about 1½ in. long, purple, the segments strongly bent backwards. Southern Ore.
**johnsoni.** By some considered only a variety of *E. revolutum*, but the leaf mottling is darker brown and the leaves look as though varnished. Flowers dark rose color, the center orange. Calif. For culture *see* ROCK GARDEN.
**revolutum.** A fine, rock garden, bulbous herb, up to 12 in. Leaves mottled. Flowers lavender-white, ultimately turning purple. British Columbia to Calif. For culture *see* ROCK GARDEN.

**ERYTHROXYLON** (e-ri-throx'i-lon). The only cult. genus of the coca family, Erythroxylaceae (e-ri-throx-i-lay'-see-ee), and comprising over 90 species of South American shrubs or small trees. The only cult. species is **E. coca,** the coca plant, which is the only source of cocaine. It can be grown only in zone* 9 or the most favorable places in zone* 8, and nowhere in the U.S. does it produce leaves worth cocaine extraction. It is a shrub 8–12 ft. high, with alternate* leaves about 2 in. long, which the Peruvians chew to relieve fatigue. Flowers small, regular, yellowish, scarcely ¼ in. wide. Fruit a reddish drupe* about ⅓ in. long, the stone furrowed. Best propagated by cuttings over bottom-heat. (*Erythroxylon* is from the Greek for red wood, true of some non-hort. species.)

**ESCALLONIA** (es-ka-low'ni-a). Handsome, chiefly evergreen shrubs and trees of the family Saxifragaceae, unfortunately not hardy in the North, but widely grown southward. Of the 60 known species, mostly from the Andes, those below are popular in Calif., but can be grown northward only as indicated below. Leaves alternate,* toothed. Flowers white, red, or pink, in terminal clusters (racemes* or panicles*) or these occasionally in the leaf-axils.* Sepals 5, the tube turban-shaped. Petals with a long claw.* Stamens 5. Fruit a 2–3-valved capsule.* (Named for Escallon, Spanish traveler.)

These useful and handsome shrubs are very popular in Calif., where their late autumn or winter bloom is most welcome. They do not need any specialized soil conditions, but do better in rich soils than in poor ones. Some of them are trained on walls or trellises. Best propagated by autumn cuttings rooted in a cold frame and planted out the following spring, a procedure possible only in mild climates. They have not done well in the sub-tropical, moister climate of Fla.

**alba** = *Escallonia montevidensis*.
**macrantha.** A densely leafy, compact shrub 7–10 ft. high. Leaves thickish, broadly oval, 2–3 in. long. Flowers crimson, about ½ in. long, in short, leafy clusters. Chile. One of the best-known of the cult. species and offered under a variety of names, such as *rosea*, *alba*, etc. Hardy only up to zone* 7.
**montevidensis.** A shrub or small tree, the leaves oblongish, 2–4 in. long, slightly notched at the tip. Flowers white, about ½ in. long, the cluster rounded. Uruguay and southern Brazil. Hardy only up to zone* 7.
**organensis.** Not over 6 ft. high, the branches resinous or sticky. Leaves narrowly oblongish, sometimes red-margined, 2–3 in. long. Flowers about ½ in. long, rose-red, in short, dense clusters. Brazil, in the Organ Mountains. Hardy only up to zone* 7.

---

* Special articles on the subjects indicated by an asterisk (*) will be found at the words so marked.

**pulverulenta.** A densely sticky shrub 9–12 ft. high. Leaves oblongish, tapering towards the base, 2–4 in. long, finely toothed, shining on the upper surface. Flowers white, small, crowded in a tail-like cluster nearly 9 in. long. Chile. Hardy, with protection, up to zone* 6, and a very handsome shrub.

**punctata.** A sticky shrub 7–9 ft. high. Leaves 1–2 in. long, tapering both ends, and toothed chiefly towards the tip. Flowers crimson, solitary in the leaf-axils,* or more generally in sticky, terminal clusters. Chile. Hardy, with protection, up to zone* 6.

**ESCALLONIACEAE.** *See* SAXIFRAGACEAE.

**ESCAPE.** A cultivated plant that has run wild and maintains itself without further cultivation. Common examples of garden escapes are found in phlox, lily-of-the-valley, some pinks, many bulbous plants and fruit trees. *See* ADVENTIVE.

**ESCAROLE.** *See* ENDIVE.

**ESCHALLOT** = Shallot.

**ESCHSCHOLTZIA** (esh-sholt′zi-a). Very popular flower garden annuals (or treated as such) of the poppy family, all from western N.A., **E. californica,** the California poppy, being the finest, and a widely grown favorite. It is 12–20 in. high, perennial, but grown as an annual (*see* ANNUALS), and has finely dissected, long-stalked, bluish-green leaves. Flower long-stalked, solitary, very showy, 3–4 in. wide, orange-yellow, opening in sunshine, the 4 petals each with a deep orange spot at the base. Fruit a strongly ribbed pod (capsule*) 3–4 in. long. A splendid garden annual blooming from July 1 to Oct. (Named for J. F. Eschscholtz, who sailed with Otto von Kotzebue to the Pacific Coast in 1816.) A fine hort. form with reddish flowers is known as Geisha.

**ESCOBARIA** (es-ko-bay′ri-a). A small genus of cylindric or somewhat globe-shaped cacti from Mex. and the Southwest, **E. tuberculosa** cult. for ornament and interest in the cactus garden (*see* CACTI). It grows in clumps, the plant body more or less cylindric, 8–10 in. high, crowded with spirally arranged tubercles. Central spines brownish or blackish, few; the lateral spines white and numerous at each spine cluster, never hooked. Flowers about 1 in. wide, pink, appearing at the top of the plant. Fruit oblong, red, about ¾ in. long. (Named for Escobar y Mendoza, Spanish Jesuit.)

*ESCOBITA* = *Orthocarpus purpurascens.*

**ESCONTRIA** (es-kon′tri-a). A striking Mexican cactus called there the jiotilla or chiotilla, comprising only the species **E. chiotilla.** It is tree-like, much-branched, and up to 20 ft. high, the few-ribbed branches bright green, rather weak and easily broken. Ribs 7–8, rather sharp-edged. Spines of 2 sorts at each cluster, a central group with one longer than the others, and 7–10 lateral, shorter, and slightly hooked spines. Flowers yellow, about 1 in. long, borne near the ends of the branches (for details *see* CACTACEAE). Fruit about ¼ in. in diameter, edible, and sold in Mexican markets. Little cult. and suited only to the warmest cactus regions. *See* CACTI. (Named for Señor Don Blas Escontria of Mexico.)

*ESCULENTA, -us, -um* (es-kew-len′ta). Edible.

**ESPALIER.** A method of training fruit and other trees. *See* TRAINING PLANTS.

**ESSENTIAL ORGANS.** In flowers, those upon which the perpetuation of the species depends. Flowers can get along without petals or sepals, and some have neither (*see* NAKED FLOWER), but most plants cannot produce seed unless their flowers contain the essential organs of stamen* and pistil.* *See* COMPLETE, PERFECT.

**ESTIMATING TREE HEIGHT.** *See* GARDEN TABLES III.

**ESTRAGON** = *Artemisia dracunculus.*

**ETHERIZATION.** The subjecting of dormant plants, both perennial herbs and shrubs and trees, to the effects of ether vapor in order to hasten their starting into growth. Much experimental work has been done on this, and the period of normal dormancy can be shortened by the use of ether, especially on woody plants like maple, horse-chestnut, birch, barberry, redbud, deutzia, spirea, etc. Ordinary procedure calls for exposure to ether fumes for about 48 hours, split into 2 equal periods and separated by a day of ether-free atmosphere. Concentrations of one part of ether to 400–500 parts of air seem to be the best, and even this concentration becomes less effective as the plant approaches the natural end of its dormancy. Etherization is useful, if at all, early in January.

**EUCALYPTUS** (you-ka-lip′tus). An enormous genus of chiefly Australian, sometimes gigantic, very aromatic, evergreen trees of the myrtle family, widely planted in zones* 8 and 9, and even in sheltered parts of zone* 7, for their striking flowers and foliage, but not hardy elsewhere. They are especially popular in Calif., where many of the over 365 known species have been introduced from Aust., and are prized for their freedom from pests, and some for their use as bee trees. Leaves prevailingly alternate* (opposite* in the closely related cult. genus *Angophora*), without marginal teeth, often very variable on the same plant. Flowers usually in the leaf-axils,* often in small umbels,* but sometimes in branched clusters, white, yellow, or red. Calyx bell-shaped or turban-shaped, the calyx-lobes and petals forming a lid at flowering time, and separating from the calyx-tube. Fruit a capsule* opening at the top by 3–6 valves. The fruits are often colored and sent East as winter decorations. (*Eucalyptus* is from the Greek for well and to cover, in allusion to the lid-like arrangement of the flowers.)

The trees are generally called gum tree or stringy-bark, and of over 70 species known to be in cult. here (mostly in Calif.), the following are perhaps the best selection for the average grower. No attempt is made here to include many valuable timber trees, although some are cult. on a great scale for this purpose as they grow quickly and some to an incredible height (300 ft. or more). For Culture *see* below.

**amygdalina.** Peppermint gum. A fibrous-barked tree up to 300 ft., the foliage peppermint-scented. Leaves lance-shaped. Flowers small, in profuse umbels.* Fruit about ¼ in. wide.

**botryoides.** Bastard mahogany; also called bangalay. Not over 150 ft. high, the bark persistent and furrowed. Leaves lance-shaped. Flowers nearly stalkless, large. Fruit about ⅓ in. wide.

**citriodora** = *Eucalyptus maculata citriodora.*

**cladocalyx.** Sugar gum. A tree 80–120 ft. high, the bark smooth but deciduous.* Leaves ovalish or lance-shaped. Flowers nearly ½ in. wide in umbels* of 7–12 blooms. Fruit about ¼ in. wide.

**cornuta.** Yate-tree. A tree up to 80–120 ft. high. Leaves oblongish or broadly lance-shaped. Flowers greenish-yellow, in dense, head-like umbels.* Fruit about ⅓ in. wide.

**ficifolia.** Scarlet-flowered gum; also called scarlet bloom. Not much over 30 ft., the bark dark and furrowed. Leaves ovalish or narrower. Flowers white, pink or scarlet, nearly 1½ in. long. Fruit nearly 1½ in. wide.

**gigantea** = *Eucalyptus obliqua.*

**globulus.** Blue gum, and one of the most widely cult. It may reach 300 ft. in height, the trunk smooth and bluish-white. Leaves broad and very bluish on young growth, later narrower. Flowers about 1½ in. wide, solitary or a few together. Fruit nearly 1 in. wide.

**maculata.** Not over 150 ft. high, the bark peeling off in patches. Leaves lance-shaped. Flowers about ½ in. long, in a many-flowered, branched cluster. Fruit about ½ in. wide. The var. **citriodora,** the lemon-scented gum, has lemon-scented foliage and is often offered by dealers as *E. citriodora.*

**obliqua.** Tasmania stringy-bark. A tree up to 300 ft., the bark persistent but fibrous. Leaves ovalish, very oblique. Flowers small, in umbels.* Fruit about ⅓ in. wide. Sometimes offered as *E. gigantea.*

**polyanthemos.** Red box; also called Australian beech. A tree up to 150 ft. high, the bark persistent. Leaves ovalish or even roundish, gray-green. Flowers small, in a profuse, branched cluster. Fruit about ¼ in. wide.

**resinifera.** Red mahogany. A tree scarcely over 100 ft., the bark rough and persistent. Leaves lance-shaped, thickish. Flowers small, in umbels.* Fruit about ⅓ in. wide.

**robusta.** Swamp mahogany; also called mahogany gum. A widely planted tree, not over 100 ft. high, with rough, persistent bark. Leaves ovalish or lance-shaped. Flowers about ¾ in. wide, in umbels.* Fruit about ½ in. wide.

**rostrata.** Red gum. A popular tree in Calif., 150–200 ft. high, the smooth gray bark deciduous.* Leaves narrowly lance-shaped. Flowers nearly ½ in. wide, in umbels.* Fruit about ¼ in. wide.

**rudis.** Desert gum. Not over 100 ft. high, the rough, gray bark persistent. Leaves lance-shaped. Flowers about ½ in. wide, in umbels.* Fruit about ½ in. wide.

**sideroxylon.** Red ironbark. Not over 100 ft. high, the dark red or blackish, rough bark persistent. Leaves narrowly lance-shaped, the young growth even narrower. Flowers yellowish-white, in umbels.* Fruit about ½ in. in diameter. There are also red or rose-colored forms and one with silvery foliage.

**tereticornis.** Gray or slaty gum. Up to 150 ft. high, the smooth, **gray**

---

* Special articles on the subjects indicated by an asterisk (*) will be found at the words so marked.

bark deciduous.* Leaves broadly lance-shaped or even ovalish. Flowers nearly ¾ in. wide, in umbels.* Fruit about ¼ in. wide.

**viminalis.** Manna gum. A beautiful tree, up to 300 ft. high, the branches hanging. Leaves lance-shaped. Flowers about ½ in. wide, in umbels.* Fruit about ¼ in. wide.

### EUCALYPTUS CULTURE

The culture of eucalyptus in Calif. is simple, as they do well in a variety of soils. The easiest method of propagation is by seeds. Take the unopened fruits from the trees and put them in a dry place until the small seeds are loosened. Then sow in flats in potting mixture* 2, preferably in July or Aug. Press the seeds in gently and sprinkle a little charcoal dust over them, cover the flat with a sheet of glass and put in the shade. They should germinate, if the seed is reasonably fresh, in about 5 days. This is much better than trying to propagate by cuttings, budding, or grafting.

The southern Calif. skyline is dominated by gum trees, especially *E. amygdalina, globulus, rudis, robusta,* and the lemon-scented gum. The latter is also grown in the cool greenhouse for its fragrant foliage. Of lesser height, at least as grown in Calif., are *Eucalyptus ficifolia, cladocalyx, cornuta,* and *resinifera.* — A. D. H.

**EUCHARIDIUM** (you-ka-rid′i-um). Californian annual herbs of the family Onagraceae, two of the three known species rather popular flower garden annuals, closely related to *Clarkia.* Leaves alternate.* Flowers showy, in terminal clusters (mostly spike-like racemes*). Petals 4, with a long claw,* the broadly expanded limb 3-lobed. Stamens 4. Fruit a 4-angled, 4-valved, many-seeded capsule.* (*Eucharidium* is from the Greek for charming.)

Both those below should be grown as hardy annuals. See ANNUALS.

**breweri.** Fairy fans. Not over 9 in. high, the leaves lance-shaped. Flowers deep pink, the petals fan-shaped, one of the lobes longer than the other two.

**concinnum.** Red ribbons. Twice as tall as the above, the leaves ovalish or oblong. Flowers rose-purple, the petals with the three lobes nearly equal. A very handsome plant sometimes offered as *E. grandiflorum.*

**grandiflorum** = *Eucharidium concinnum.*

**EUCHARIS** (you′kar-is). South American bulbous herbs of the family Amaryllidaceae, **E. grandiflora,** the Amazon lily, a popular greenhouse and pot plant, or occasionally grown outdoors in southern Fla. and Calif. It has a stout bulb, nearly 2 in. in diameter, from which spring the leaves and stalk of the flower cluster which is 1–2 ft. high. Leaves 8–12 in. long, about half as wide, the slender leafstalk 8–12 in. long. Flowers pure white, fragrant, in a terminal umbel,* the stalk round. Corolla cylindric and tubular below, the lobes spreading, in all about 2½ in. wide and very showy. Stamens 6, inserted in the throat of the corolla and shorter than its segments. Fruit a 3-lobed capsule.* Colombia. Its culture is the same as for *Amaryllis* (which see). (*Eucharis* is from the Greek for very graceful.) Often sold as *E. amazonica.*

**EUCHLAENA** (you-klee′na). A genus of corn-like Mexican or Central American grasses of secondary garden significance, except for **E. mexicana,** the teosinte, which may have been a remote ancestor of modern corn. The teosinte today is chiefly grown for forage in the South, and is an annual grass 6–10 ft. high, with a very leafy stem. Leaves 3–5 ft. long, about 1½ in. wide, the midrib prominent. Male and female flowers in separate clusters, the male in terminal spikelets, the female in clusters in the upper leaf-axils, as in corn, from the husks of which the silk-like styles* protrude. The grain (seed) is about ¼ in. long and shining, not borne in "ears" like corn, but on a jointed spike enclosed by the husk. (*Euchlaena* is from the Greek for well-covered, from the husk-enclosed fruit.)

*EUCHLORA* (you-clow′ra). Well, *i.e.* thoroughly green.

**EUCOMIS** (you-kō′mis). A small genus of South African bulbous herbs of the lily family; only **E. punctata,** the pineapple-flower, of garden interest. It is a greenhouse plant related to *Scilla,* and 1–2 ft. high. Leaves brown-spotted beneath, nearly 2 ft. long and 3 in. wide, in a basal rosette. Flowers greenish-white, borne in a leafy-topped, terminal raceme,* the flower about ½ in. long, its segments separate. Stamens 6. Fruit a 3-valved capsule. South of zone* 6 the bulbs may be allowed to stay in the ground over the winter, but in the North they should be handled as pot subjects in the cool greenhouse. (*Eucomis* is from the Greek for beautiful topknot, from the leafy tuft at the end of the flower cluster.)

**EUCOMMIA** (you-kom′mi-a). A single Chinese tree, the only genus of the family Eucommiaceae (you-kom-mee-ā′-see-ee) and of more interest as the only hardy woody plant producing rubber than as an ornamental. (The rubber is of no commercial importance as yet.) The only species, **E. ulmoides,** is an elm-like tree up to 50 ft. high. Leaves alternate,* stalked and toothed, elliptic or oblongish, 2–3 in. long. Flowers unisexual,* blooming in April before the leaves unfold, without petals or sepals. The male flowers with red anthers,* the female consisting only of a 1-celled ovary. Fruit a stalked, 1-seeded, and winged nutlet. Hardy from zone* 4 southward, and of easy culture. (*Eucommia* is from the Greek for well and gum, in allusion to the rubber it contains.)

**EUGENE POPLAR** = *Populus canadensis eugenei.*

**EUGENIA** (you-jee′ni-a). Perhaps a thousand species of chiefly tropical, generally aromatic, shrubs and trees of the myrtle family, of great economic and garden interest, both for the often edible fruits and for the fine ornamental plants used throughout the tropical and sub-tropical world, especially in Calif. and Fla. Leaves opposite,* evergreen. Flowers solitary in the leaf-axils* or in few-flowered clusters (cymes*). Calyx* turban-shaped, the sepals 5. Petals 4–5. Stamens numerous, in several series, usually longer than the petals. Fruit a berry. (Named for Prince Eugene of Savoy, plant patron.)

South of zone* 7 these plants are of easy culture in any usual soil and are propagated by seeds or by cuttings over bottom-heat or in the frame outdoors. They are not usually cult. in the greenhouse.

**apiculata.** A shrub 4–5 ft. high. Leaves ovalish, ¾–1 in. long. Flowers white, in 3's, nearly ½ in. wide. Fruit black. Chile.

**cauliflora.** Jaboticaba. A large shrub or small tree, usually less than 35 ft. high. Leaves lance-shaped or broader, 3–4 in. long, tapering at the tip. Flowers white, small, borne in clusters along the older wood. Fruit edible, nearly round, about 1 in. in diameter, purple. Brazil, and a popular fruit there, but little known in the U.S.

**hookeriana** = *Eugenia paniculata.*

**jambos.** Rose-apple; also called jambu. A branching, broad-headed tree, usually not over 30 ft. Leaves narrowly lance-shaped, tapering both ends, 6–8 in. long. Flowers 2–3 in. wide, greenish-white, the numerous stamens* showy. Fruit edible (as preserves), greenish-yellow, about 2 in. in diameter. Tropical Asia.

**myrtifolia** = *Eugenia paniculata australis.*

**paniculata.** A widely popular ornamental tree, especially in Calif. Leaves oblongish, 2–3 in. long, tapering both ends. Flowers about ½ in. wide, white, the stamens numerous and showy. Fruit edible (for jelly), purple, about ½ in. in diameter. Aust. Often sold as *E. hookeriana.* Even more popular is var. **australis,** the Australian brush cherry (often sold as *E. myrtifolia*), which is a bushier form, popular in Calif. for topiary work, but its flowers and fruits are less desirable than in the typical form.

**uniflora.** Pitanga; called also Surinam cherry. A shrub or tree not over 25 ft. high. Leaves ovalish or narrower, 1–2 in. long. Flowers fragrant, white, about ½ in. wide. Fruit edible, crimson, ribbed. Brazil.

*EUGENIOIDES* (you-jee-nee-oy′deez, but *see* OÏDES). Resembling the genus *Eugenia* (which see).

**EULALIA** = *Miscanthus sinensis.*

**EUONYMUS** (you-on′i-mus). Also spelled *Evonymus.* Shrubs, vines, or trees of the greatest garden importance and belonging to the family Celastraceae. Of the 120 known species, generally called spindle-tree, over a dozen are very popular garden plants, although their flowers are inconspicuous. They are grown either for their showy fruits or often evergreen foliage, or both, and some are extremely valuable vines (which see). Leaves opposite,* stalked, nearly always smooth. Flowers greenish, white, or yellowish, small, in small clusters (cymes*) in the leaf-axils.* Sepals and petals 4–5. Fruit a capsule,* often lobed, the splitting of which discloses the seeds which are enclosed or partly surrounded with a showy, fleshy, orange aril.* (*Euonymus* is the old Greek name for the spindle-tree.)

---

* Special articles on the subjects indicated by an asterisk (*) will be found at the words so marked.

These valuable plants are not particular as to soil, nor exposure, but all are not hardy, as indicated below. They may be propagated by stratified seeds, or by cuttings taken of the old wood, which in evergreen sorts should be rooted under glass. All are spring-flowering (May–June), and set their attractive fruits from July to frost. All are deciduous,* unless mentioned as evergreen.

**alatus.** Winged spindle-tree. A stiff, spreading shrub 6–9 ft. high, the twigs corky-winged. Leaves elliptic to ovalish, 1½–3 in. long. Flowers yellowish. Fruit purplish, about ½ in. long. Eastern As. Hardy from zone* 3 southward.

**americanus.** Burning-bush; called also strawberry-bush and skewer-wood. A sparsely branched shrub 5–8 ft. high. Leaves oval or oblongish, 1½–4 in. long, wavy-toothed. Flowers greenish. Fruit pinkish, warty, about ½ in. thick. N.Y. to Fla. and Tex. Hardy from zone* 4 southward.

**atropurpureus.** Wahoo or burning-bush. A shrub or small tree 8–20 ft. high. Leaves elliptic or ovalish, 2–5 in. long, finely toothed, and hairy beneath. Flowers greenish-purple. Fruit scarlet, 4-lobed, the aril* crimson. N.Y. to Fla. and Tex. Hardy from zone* 3 southward. There is also a variegated-leaved form.

**bungeanus.** A shrub or small tree, not over 18 ft. high. Leaves elliptic or ovalish, 2½–5 in. long, wedge-shaped at the base. Flowers yellowish. Fruit when open disclosing the showy, orange aril* of the seeds. China. Hardy from zone* 4 southward.

**europaeus.** Spindle-tree; also called prick-timber. A shrub or small tree 9–20 ft. high. Leaves oblongish, 1½–4 in. long, wavy-toothed, wedge-shaped at the base. Flowers yellowish-green, larger and more showy than in the others. Fruit 4-lobed, red or pink, nearly ¾ in. wide, the aril* orange. Eurasia, sometimes an escape in the U.S. Hardy from zone* 3 southward.

**japonicus.** An evergreen shrub up to 15 ft. or more, the twigs a little angled. Leaves narrowly elliptic or broadest towards the tip, 1–3 in. long, bluntly toothed. Flowers greenish-white. Fruit nearly round, pinkish, the aril* orange. Southern Jap. Hardy from zone* 5 southward. An extremely popular plant also offered in var. **albo-marginatus**, with white-margined leaves; var. **aureo-marginatus**, with yellow-margined leaves; and var. **microphyllus** (often offered as E. pulchellus), with smaller leaves.

**latifolius.** A Eurasian shrub or small tree 9–20 ft. high. Leaves oblongish, 3–5½ in. long, broadly wedge-shaped at the base, the teeth rounded. Flowers greenish. Fruit bright red, nearly 1 in. wide, 4-winged, the aril* orange. Hardy from zone* 4 southward.

**obovatus.** Running strawberry-bush. A prostrate or procumbent shrub, never over 18 in. high. Leaves elliptic or broadest towards the tip, 1½–3 in. long, blunt-toothed. Flowers greenish-purple. Fruit crimson, 3-lobed, warty, the aril* scarlet. Eastern N.A. Hardy from zone* 2 southward.

**patens.** Evergreen or half-evergreen shrub, 4–8 ft. high, the lower branches sometimes prostrate and rooting. Leaves oblongish, 2½–4 in. long, bluntly fine-toothed. Flowers greenish-white. Fruit nearly round, about ⅝ in. wide, pinkish, the aril* orange-red. China. Hardy from zone* 5, or, with protection, from zone* 4 southward.

**pulchellus** = Euonymus japonicus microphyllus.

**radicans.** A trailing or climbing evergreen vine and the finest of all the cult. species, especially in some of its varieties. Leaves ovalish or broadly elliptic, ¾–2½ in. long. Flowers greenish-white. Fruit nearly round, pale-pink. Eastern As. Hardy from zone* 4, and, with protection, from zone* 3 southward, and occasionally hardy farther north. Of the many varieties the best are: var. **argenteo-marginatus**, with silvery-margined leaves; var. **acutus**, with smaller leaves, and an especially good climber; var. **carrieri**, a low, shrubby form, with showy fruit, useful for bedding; var. **minimus**, a very small-leaved form, the veins whitish, useful in the rock garden (which see, sometimes sold as var. **kewensis**); and var. **vegetus**, the best and the hardiest of all the evergreen vines.

**yedoensis.** A large Asiatic shrub 4–10 ft. high, the leaves oblongish or broadest towards the tip, 3–5½ in. long, bluntly fine-toothed. Flowers yellowish. Fruit deeply 4-lobed, pinkish, the aril* orange. Hardy from zone* 4 southward. Fall foliage brilliant scarlet.

**EUPATORIUM** (you-pa-toe′ri-um). The bonesets or thoroughworts comprise a genus of over 600 species of chiefly tropical American herbs of the family Compositae, a few reaching temperate regions and prized for the flower garden, and the only sorts here treated. Some of the tropical species are occasionally grown in the greenhouse, but are little known to the average greenhouse owner. The hardy species are perennial herbs with opposite* or whorled* leaves. Flowers showy in numerous small heads crowded in various sorts of clusters, some of them arching and lax, others close and dense. Ray flowers none, as the head is composed of many small, tubular flowers suggesting the garden ageratum, to which Eupatorium is closely related. The minute branches of the styles* usually protrude beyond the general level of the head, which thus appears roughish and accounts for the name mist-flower for some species. (Named for an ancient King of Pontus who is supposed to have used some species for healing.)

All the bonesets are of easy culture in ordinary garden soils. They are prized for their profuse, usually late summer or autumn bloom. Propagated by division in spring.

**aromaticum.** Wild hoarhound; also called poolroot. A stout herb much resembling E. urticaefolium, but the leaves thicker, blunter, and usually hairy. Flowers white. Mass. to Fla. along the coast, and especially suited to sandy soils. Not aromatic.

**coelestinum.** Mist-flower, blue boneset, and often called the hardy ageratum. It is a perennial up to 2 ft. Leaves stalked, more or less triangular-ovalish, thin and coarsely toothed. Flower heads numerous, small, but very attractive; light blue or violet blue, and late-blooming. N.J. to Mich. and southward. See BLUE GARDEN.

**hyssopifolium.** A low herb with whorled,* narrow leaves and a terminal, flat-topped cluster of small, white flower heads. It is of no garden interest except for the fact that it will grow in pure sand (see SAND GARDEN). Eastern U.S.

**perfoliatum.** Boneset; called, also, Indian sage and feverwort. A coarse, stout herb, 3–6 ft. high, somewhat rank-smelling. Leaves pointed at the tip, but broadening towards the base and united with the leaf opposite it. Flower heads white, in a dense, flat-topped cluster. Nearly throughout N.A. and preferring low grounds. Long cult. as a domestic medicine.

**purpureum.** Joe-pye-weed; also called purple boneset. A rank-growing herb 7–9 ft. high, less in dry ground. Leaves in whorls* of 5 or 6, oblongish or ovalish, coarsely toothed and taper-pointed. Flower heads purple, in a roundish, much-branched and showy terminal cluster. Nearly throughout N.A., in some of its forms, mostly in moist places.

**urticaefolium.** White snakeroot; called also Indian sanicle and richweed. A branching herb 2–4 ft. high, the leaves smooth or nearly so and thin, long-stalked, ovalish, but broad towards the base, sharply toothed. Flower heads in a loosely branched cluster, white. Eastern N.A. and blooming from midsummer to frost. See AUTUMN GARDEN.

**EUPHORBIA** (you-for′bi-a). Probably over 1000 species of wide distribution and great diversity of habit, belonging to the family Euphorbiaceae, some tropical, cactus-like succulents, others weeds, and one the popular flower garden annual snow-on-the-mountain. The cactus-like plants from Africa and the East Indies, such as E. lactea, are widely planted for hedges in warm regions, and are usually as leafless as most cacti. E. splendens is a prickly, creeping plant from Madagascar, but bears a few leaves, and is a greenhouse favorite. E. marginata, E. corollata, and E. epithymoides are herbs. The flowers in all of them have no petals or sepals and would not be showy if it were not for the often highly colored bracts.* (For structure see EUPHORBIACEAE.) Fruit a capsule,* which often opens explosively. All the plants have a milky juice and in some the juice is poisonous. (Euphorbia is from a Greek word of uncertain significance as applied to these plants.)

The plants are of such diverse habit and origin that cultural notes are appended for each. Some of them are called spurge, especially the herbs.

**corollata.** Flowering spurge; also called milk purslane. A hardy, perennial herb best grown for cutting, or as a bedding plant. It is 18–30 in. high, sparsely branched. Leaves ovalish-oblong, 1–2 in. long, diminishing upward and opposite near the flower cluster. Flower cluster with showy white appendages, for which the plant is grown. Eastern U.S., especially in sandy soil. See SAND GARDENS.

**epithymoides.** Cushion spurge. A European, hardy, perennial herb, the 12-in. stems usually forming a cushion-shaped or roundish clump. Leaves oblongish, green, becoming yellow near the flower cluster when the latter blooms. A good accent plant for the border, its bracts and foliage very attractive.

**fulgens.** Scarlet plume. A Mexican shrub to be grown in the greenhouse as one does poinsettia (which see for culture). It is a small bush with slender, usually drooping branches. Leaves long-stalked, green, generally lance-shaped. Bracts* of the flower cluster bright scarlet and very showy.

**heterophylla** = Poinsettia heterophylla.

**lactea.** A tall, branching, candelabra-like and cactus-like plant, frequently 20 ft. high, but less as clipped for hedges in the warm sections of Fla. and throughout the tropics. Joints broadly but bluntly winged, plentifully beset with light-colored spines, 1–2 in. long. Through the middle of each joint there is generally a white-marbled area. Leaves very small, soon falling and for months the plant is leafless. It requires the same treatment as tree-like cacti (which see). East Indies.

**maculata.** See the Spotted Spurge in the list at WEEDS.

**marginata.** Snow-on-the-mountain. A prairie plant widely grown as one of the most popular of flower garden annuals. For culture see ANNUALS. It is a bushy herb 8–15 in. high, much-branched. Leaves oblongish, 1–3 in. long, the lower green, the upper white-margined. The bracts* of the flower cluster, for which the plant is grown, are also white and very showy. South Dakota to Tex. July 15–Oct. An old garden favorite, and sometimes sold as E. variegata.

**myrsinites.** A European, hardy, perennial herb, the many stems almost prostrate. Leaves numerous, fleshy, bluish-green, oblongish, pointed and a little concave. Bracts* of the flower clusters yellow. Useful for dry walls or in the rock garden.

**pulcherrima** = Poinsettia pulcherrima.

**splendens.** Crown-of-thorns. A creeping, spiny, greenhouse plant, best trained over a small trellis, its stems not over 3 ft. long, usually dull purple-brown, but the young growth often green. Spines about 1 in. long, thick and stout. Leaves oblongish, thin, 1–2 in. long, rather sparse and the plant often leafless. Flower clusters long-stalked, the bracts*

* Special articles on the subjects indicated by an asterisk (*) will be found at the words so marked.

brilliant red. Madagascar. It blooms most of the year, but most freely in the winter. Treat as a greenhouse succulent (which see).
variegata = *Euphorbia marginata*.

**EUPHORBIACEAE** (you-for-bi-ā'see-ee). The spurge or poinsettia family, while of huge size and diverse habit, furnishes only a few genera of garden significance. Of its 250 genera and over 4000 species, world-wide in their distribution, only 19 are of hort. interest, and of these *Poinsettia*, *Codiaeum* (the garden crotons), *Ricinus* (see CASTOR-OIL PLANT), *Aleurites* (see TUNG-OIL TREE) *Euphorbia* and *Acalypha* are much cult.

The family comprises herbs, shrubs or trees (some cactus-like, nearly leafless succulents), many of which have a milky (often poisonous) juice and alternate* leaves. The true flowers (see below) are usually small and inconspicuous, but the bracts around or beneath them are extremely showy in some genera, notably in the scarlet-bracted *Poinsettia*, in some euphorbias, and in *Pedilanthus*. The fruit in nearly all genera is a dry, 3-lobed capsule,* but fleshy in *Bischofia*, *Breynia* and *Daphniphyllum*, none of which, though in cultivation, are of much garden importance.

A few tropical genera are of outstanding importance. They include *Hevea* (rubber), *Hura* (sandbox tree) and *Manihot* (cassava). The other cult. genera are *Jatropha*, *Mercurialis*, *Phyllanthus*, *Sapium*, *Synadenium* and *Xylophylla*.

Technical flower characters: Flowers monoecious* or dioecious.* The naked female flower is often surrounded by several male flowers. This whole cluster is, in some genera, surrounded by a series of brightly colored bracts* (often mistaken for flowers in poinsettias and snow-on-the-mountain). Calyx and corolla both sometimes wanting, when present of separate petals or sepals. Stamens many or 1. Ovary superior,* 3-celled.

**EUPHORBIOIDES** (you-for-bee-oy'deez, but see OÏDES). Like a plant of the genus *Euphorbia*.

**EUPHORIA** (you-foe'ri-a). Half a dozen Asiatic tropical trees of the family Sapindaceae, E. longana, yielding the longan or lungan, which are fruits of secondary interest for outdoor culture only in zones* 8 and 9. It is a tree 30-40 ft. high, the leaves compound* and composed of 2-5 pairs of blunt, oblongish or narrower leaflets. Flowers small, yellowish-white, in small terminal clusters, or these in the leaf-axils.* (For details see SAPINDACEAE.) Fruit nearly round, about 1 in. in diameter, yellowish-brown, the outer husk thin and shell-like, the white, juicy pulp edible. India. As grown in Fla. and Calif. the trees are indifferent to soils, and will even stand slight frosts, but they do better in the shade of larger trees than in full sunlight. Propagated by seeds or by grafting. (*Euphoria* is from the Greek for carries well, in allusion to the fruits.)

**EUPTELEA** (you-tee'lee-a). Three Asiatic species of shrubs or small trees of the family Trochodendraceae, two of them grown for ornament. Leaves alternate,* toothed, appearing after the flowers bloom. Flowers not showy, without petals or sepals, small, crowded in small, head-like clusters or racemes.* Stamens many. Fruit a small, winged nut (samara*) or a splitting pod (follicle*). (*Euptelea* is from the Greek for well or handsome and elm, in allusion to the fruit.)

Both those below are chiefly grown for the young foliage, which is reddish, changing to green and, in the fall, a bright yellow or red. They do well in well-drained, moist soils, and may be increased by seeds or root grafts.

francheti. Resembling the next, but the leaves rather regularly toothed and the fruit a samara.* China. Hardy from zone* 3 southward.
polyandra. A large shrub or small tree not over 40 ft. high. Leaves roundish-oval, 3-5 in. wide, with a point at the tip, coarsely and irregularly toothed. Fruit a slender, stalked pod (follicle*), about ¾ in. long. Jap. Hardy from zone* 3 southward.

*EUROPAEA, -us, -um* (you-ro-pee'a). From Europe.

**EUROPEAN.** As an adjective *European* has been part of the name of many European plants or insects, especially since the discovery of America, where most of the names below are in pretty common use. All will be found at the proper entry in THE GARDEN DICTIONARY:

European ash = *Fraxinus excelsior* (see ASH); **European aspen** = *Populus tremula*; European barberry = *Berberis vulgaris*; **European beech** = *Fagus sylvatica* (see BEECH); European birch = *Betula pendula* (see BIRCH); **European bird cherry** = *Prunus padus*; European black currant = *Ribes nigrum*; European cantaloupe (see MELON); European chestnut = *Castanea sativa* (see CHESTNUT); European corn borer (see Moth at INSECT PESTS; see also Insects at CORN); European elder = *Sambucus nigra* (see ELDER); European fan palm = *Chamaerops humilis*; European fly-honeysuckle = *Lonicera xylosteum*; European globeflower = *Trollius europaeus*; European hazel = *Corylus avellana* (see HAZEL); European hornbeam = *Carpinus betulus* (see HORNBEAM); European larch = *Larix decidua* (see LARCH); European linden = *Tilia vulgaris* (see LINDEN); European mallow = *Malva alcea*; European mountain-ash = *Sorbus aucuparia* (see MOUNTAIN-ASH); European raspberry = *Rubus idaeus*; European sweet cicely = *Myrrhis odorata*; European twinflower = *Linnaea borealis*; European white birch = *Betula pendula* (see BIRCH); European white hellebore = *Veratrum album*; European white water lily = *Nymphaea alba*; European wood anemone = *Anemone nemorosa*.

**EURYA** (your'i-a). A genus of over 35 species of evergreen shrubs and trees of the family Theaceae, found in the warmer parts of Asia and America and grown for ornament in the greenhouse or outdoors in the South. Leaves alternate,* rather leathery. Male and female flowers chiefly on different plants, solitary or in clusters in the leaf-axils,* small and not showy. Petals and sepals 5 each. Stamens* usually many. Fruit a berry. (*Eurya* is Greek for broad or large and of little or no significance as applied to these plants.)

The indoor and outdoor culture of the two below is the same as for camellia (which see), to which they are related. But they lack the showy flowers of camellia; *Eurya* is valued chiefly for its foliage. Both are sometimes offered under the name *Cleyera*.

japonica. A smooth, smallish shrub. Leaves short-stalked, more or less elliptic and irregularly toothed. Flowers greenish-white, in small clusters. Eastern As. A variegated form has white-blotched leaves.
ochnacea. Somewhat similar to *E. japonica*, but the leaves without marginal teeth and with cream-white, fragrant, but small flowers. Berry red. Himalayas to Jap. There is also a variegated-leaved variety.

**EUSTOMA** (you-stō'ma). A small genus of North American prairie herbs of the gentian family, E. russellianum sometimes grown in the flower garden, although in its native home (Neb. to Tex.) it is called Canada pest. It is an attractive hardy annual (see ANNUALS) 2-3 ft. high, with bluish-gray foliage and opposite* leaves that are ovalish and 2-3 in. long. Flowers pale purple, but with dark purple blotches at the base, usually in a branched cluster (panicle*), the corolla nearly bell-shaped, but flaring, and about 2 in. long and wide. Fruit a many-seeded capsule.* It may also be treated as a biennial, as well-established seedlings may be carried over winter in the cold frame. (*Eustoma* is from the Greek for good mouth, in allusion to the flaring corolla.) In Tex. it is sometimes called bluebell.

**EUTOCA.** See PHACELIA VISCIDA.

**EVANS ARBORETUM.** See ARBORETUM.

**EVAPORATED FRUIT.** See DRIED FRUIT.

**EVAPORATION.** See TRANSPIRATION.

**EVENING BLOOM.** See NOCTURNAL FLOWERS.

**EVENING CAMPION** = *Lychnis alba*.

**EVENING PRIMROSE.** The evening primroses and their day-blooming relatives, the sundrops, both belong to the genus *Oenothera* (ee-no-thee'ra, also ee-nŏth'er-ra), which comprises nearly 100 species of herbs of the family Onagraceae, all American. They have been credited to various other genera at times, especially to *Hartmannia*, but all are here treated as of the genus *Oenothera*. Leaves alternate.* Flowers very showy, day- or night-blooming, prevailingly yellow, but also white or rose-color in some species, generally one or 2 in the leaf-axils.* Calyx* tubular, usually 4-sided, its 4 lobes often bent backward and usually soon falling. Petals 4, mostly very broad. Fruit a 4-lobed or 4-angled capsule, splitting by 4 valves. (*Oenothera* is from the Greek for wine-scenting and of uncertain application here.)

The evening primroses are of easy culture if given an open, sandy or loamy site. All the perennial kinds can easily be increased by division. Some are biennials, but seed so freely that they are easily maintained. The sundrops are day-bloomers, and so are some others, as indicated below. The others bloom at night or on dark days. All bloom in the summer.

---

* Special articles on the subjects indicated by an asterisk (*) will be found at the words so marked.

**O. acaulis.** A biennial sundrops, apparently stemless, but ultimately producing prostrate stems. Leaves much cut, the terminal segment larger than the others. Flowers nearly 4 in. wide, white or pink, the tube long. Chile. It is the plant put out by Burbank as "America."

**O. biennis.** Evening primrose. A weedy, biennial herb 3–5 ft. high, of less garden interest than for its wide use by plant breeders to illustrate principles of that science. Flowers yellow, 1–2 in. wide. Nearly throughout N.A. and widely naturalized in Eu. The *var.* **grandiflora**, chiefly from the southern states, has larger flowers and is a better garden plant, but its botanical identity is uncertain.

**O. fruticosa.** Sundrops. A perennial herb, 1–3 ft. high, usually woody at the base, the stems reddish. Leaves lance-oblong, usually short-stalked, 1–2 in. long. Flowers yellow, nearly 2 in. wide. In dry soil nearly throughout eastern N.A. The *var.* **major** has more profuse bloom and is bushier. *Var.* **youngi** is a strong, stocky form, and a profuse bloomer with larger leaves.

**O. glauca.** A sundrops related to *O. fruticosa*, but the foliage usually bluish-green, and the leaves essentially stalkless. Va. to Ky. and southward. The *var.* **fraseri** has nearly ovalish leaves that are slightly stalked.

**O. lamarckiana.** An evening primrose closely related to *O. biennis*, but with larger flowers, broader and crinkled leaves, and a stem that is red-dotted. Unknown as a wild plant, but long cult. in old gardens.

**O. missouriensis.** Missouri primrose. A perennial, day-blooming herb, not over 12 in. high, the base a little woody. Leaves hairy, narrowly oval, 3–5 in. long. Flowers yellow, showy, nearly 4 in. wide. Fruit 2–3 in. long and nearly that wide. Central U.S. A garden favorite, but less known eastward than in the prairie states.

**O. perennis.** A common perennial sundrops throughout the eastern U.S., often known as *O. pumila* or *O. pusilla*, the latter name indicating its habit of often blooming when scarcely 3 in. high. Normally the plant is 12–24 in. high, and has lance-oblong leaves without marginal teeth. Flowers yellow, about 1 in. wide.

**O. rosea.** A half-prostrate biennial (blooming from seed the first year), with hairy stem and ovalish or narrower leaves. Flowers rose-purple, about ½ in. wide, night-blooming, and also blooming the next day. Central U.S. to S.A.

**O. speciosa.** Showy primrose. A fine, day-blooming, garden perennial, the stems erect or nearly so, and finely hairy. Leaves lance-shaped or narrower. Flowers nearly 3 in. wide, white, but changing to pink. Central U.S. Sometimes offered as a *Hartmannia*.

**O. trichocalyx.** A day-blooming biennial or perennial, 6–12 in. high, the stem silky-hairy. Leaves narrowly lance-shaped, wavy-toothed, 1–2 in. long. Flowers white, about 2 in. wide. Colo., Wyo., and Utah.

**EVENING PRIMROSE FAMILY** = Onagraceae.

**EVENING STAR** = *Cooperia drummondi*.

**EVENING STOCK** = *Mathiola bicornis*.

**EVERBLOOMING ROSES.** See Group 3 at Rose.

**EVERGLADE PALM** = *Acoelorraphe wrighti*.

**EVER GREEN.** A patented, liquid, non-poisonous insecticide containing pyrethrum, oil, and a spreader; sold with directions for controlling chewing and sucking insects.

**EVERGREEN.** Holding its foliage over the winter, or, in the tropics, over the dry season. For the garden uses of such plants, *see* Evergreens.

**EVERGREEN CHERRY** = *Prunus ilicifolia*.

**EVERGREEN GRAPE** = *Cissus capensis*.

**EVERGREEN IVY** = *Hedera helix*.

**EVERGREEN MAGNOLIA** = *Magnolia grandiflora*.

**EVERGREEN WHITE OAK** = *Quercus engelmanni*. See Oak.

**EVERGREEN WOOD FERN** = *Dryopteris marginalis*.

**EVERGREENS.** No woody plants can replace the evergreens. No matter what the size or extent of the garden, its winter attractiveness is tremendously enhanced by the judicious use of these plants.

As a term, evergreens is somewhat confusing, for in ordinary hort. speech it means two things, and maybe three. The first comprises the non-cone-bearing, broad-leaved evergreens, which form an important group of garden plants. But all belong to other families than the evergreens as here treated, and for their culture and kinds, *see* Broad-leaved Evergreens.

The second, and to the northern gardener, the least important group, comprises those tropical plants that hold most of their foliage continuously. Such plants are truly evergreen, but the term is seldom applied to them.

By far the most important group of evergreens comprise the subject of this article. All of them are gymnosperms,* so that we do not cultivate them for their flowers, because they have none in the garden sense of flower. Nearly all of them bear cones, the commonest example of which is the familiar pine cone. But some, especially the yews, junipers, and some others, have fleshy fruits not in the least cone-like. So many of the evergreens are cone-bearing, however, that the group is commonly called conifers and no one is confused by the term *coniferous* tree for a pine, hemlock, spruce, or fir.

From the garden standpoint, it is their winter-persisting foliage that makes the evergreens so important. But, as in so many things botanical, there are exceptions. The larch and the bald cypress (see Taxodium) both drop their leaves, but are universally included among evergreens because of their cones.

Evergreens do well in most ordinary garden soils. They do not bear transplanting as well as plants that drop their leaves. Consequently, most careful nurserymen will deliver them with a ball of earth tightly wrapped in bagging. They cannot stand drying of the roots, and climatically there are restrictions to their culture in a country so large as ours.

Many of the firs and spruces range far northward in Eurasia and N.A. and will stand much cold. But they cannot stand a deficiency of summer moisture. It is chiefly for this reason that evergreens are really unsuited for great sections of the country. Generally speaking, they are precariously happy, or impossible, in regions that have 25 in. of rain a year or less. See the name of your state or province for the rainfall in your locality. It is also important that the moisture be distributed throughout the year.

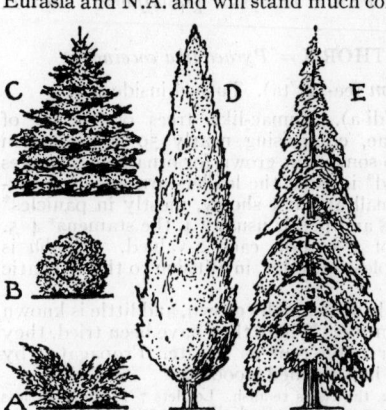
Forms of evergreens. (*A*) *Juniperus chinensis pfitzeriana*. (*B*) Low-growing arborvitae. (*C*) Colorado blue spruce. (*D*) Italian cypress. (*E*) Incense cedar.

There are special cultural articles on the pine, spruce, hemlock, and fir. *See* these entries for the details, as these comprise the most important group of evergreens. All the other evergreens in The Garden Dictionary will be found listed at the entries Pinaceae, Taxaceae, Ginkgoaceae, and a related, but not hardy family, the Cycadaceae. Among other especially important genera are *Chamaecyparis*, *Juniperus*, *Thuja*, and *Taxus*, some of which are widely used for foundation planting.

Propagation of evergreens, especially the trees, is usually by seeds which germinate readily if kept stratified, or sometimes they are planted fresh. Sow them in rows about 6 in. apart in flats or boxes, in which the soil should be fine, mellow, and preferably a little sandy. Cover the flats with pine needles or a light, strawy mulch, and keep them moist. All this is best done in the cold frame. When the seedlings are a few inches high, they should be spaced to allow for proper development, but they must be grown for the first year under a lath screen or under some other shade. Keep them constantly moist, but not wet. As they get older, they will stand more exposure, but it must not be forgotten that evergreens do best along the Atlantic Coast and in regions like Oregon and Washington, where there is abundant moisture, much fog, and a consequent reduction of direct sunshine.

Some of the ornamental sorts, especially the forms of peculiar habit or with variegated or colored foliage, will not come true from seed. Such are propagated by cuttings. For the details of this process *see* Cuttings.

While most of the evergreens do well in ordinary garden soil, the larches, bald cypress, and some species of *Chamaecyparis* are especially suited to lower and moister

---

*Special articles on the subjects indicated by an asterisk (*) will be found at the words so marked.

sites, as is the arborvitae (*see* THUJA). Pines and spruces do better on drier sites. All of them should be kept clear of weeds in their young state, and a mulch of leaves or strawy manure often helps to conserve moisture. The insect and fungus pests of evergreens are treated at the description of the different sorts.

**EVERLASTING.** Valuable garden plants for winter decoration because their chaffy or papery flower parts hold their color when thoroughly dry. For the details of drying *see* DRIED FLOWERS.

The best everlastings will be found in the genera *Ammobium, Anaphalis, Antennaria, Gomphrena, Helichrysum, Helipterum, Statice,* and *Xeranthemum*. All are the subject of special articles. To them are often added the plumes of certain of the grasses like the pampas grass, and the fine panicles of grasses like *Briza* and *Panicum*. Also the fine colored fruits of some species of *Physalis* are a welcome addition, as well as the pods of honesty.* For a recent and interesting addition to everlastings *see* SYNGONANTHUS.

**EVERLASTING PEA** = *Lathyrus grandiflorus* and *L. latifolius*.

**EVERLASTING THORN** = *Pyracantha coccinea*.

*EVERTA, -us, -um* (ee-ver′ta). Turned inside out.

**EVODIA** (ee-vō′di-a). Sumac-like trees or shrubs of the family Rutaceae, comprising nearly 50 species from Asia and Aust., two somewhat grown for ornament. Leaves opposite,* compound* in ours, the leaflets arranged featherfashion. Flowers small and not showy, mostly in panicles* or corymbs.* Sepals and petals usually 4, the stamens* 4–5. Fruit a collection of 4–5 pods, each 2-valved. (*Evodia* is from the Greek for pleasant odor, in allusion to the aromatic foliage.)

These trees are only occasionally grown, and little is known of their soil requirements. Where they have been tried, they appear to be rather indifferent as to site. Propagated by seeds or cuttings of half-ripened wood.

**danielli.** A small tree, the twigs reddish. Leaflets 7–11, more or less ovalish, 2–4½ in. long, very finely toothed. Flowers scarcely ⅛ in. long, whitish, the clusters hairy and nearly 8 in. long. Pods with a hooked beak. Eastern As. June. Hardy from zone* 3 southward. Much liked by bees.

**hupehensis.** A tree up to 25 ft. Leaflets 5–9, oblong or ovalish, 3–4½ in. long, oblique at the base. Flowers pinkish, nearly ¼ in. long, the cluster pyramidal and nearly 6 in. thick. China. June. Hardy from zone* 3 southward.

**EVOLUTION OF FLOWERS.** Flowers are comparatively recent in the history of the world. There were none during the Carboniferous, when only the ancestors of our modern ferns and pines covered the earth. When the first recognizable flower evolved no one exactly knows, but it appears to have been some ancestor of *Magnolia* or a relative of it, and was a flower with *separate* petals. This first appears in the fossil record millions of years after the remains of the flowerless plants of the Carboniferous were already making coal.

From plants with separate petals, like magnolias, buttercups, and roses, those with a *united* corolla, like bellflowers, morning-glories, and many others, are assumed to have been derived, and those with irregular* flowers, like snapdragon and the lobelias, are still more recent. Last of all, as the evolutionists picture the story, came the huge family of the Compositae* (the daisy, aster, and relatives), which are certainly our most recent flowering plants.

Whether the development of grasses, lilies, palms, and their allies (the monocotyledons*) came before or after the rest of our flowering plants is still a disputed point. But all agree that the final and most recent development of this chapter of floral history is the perfection of floral structure, complexity, and beauty found in the orchids. *See* ORCHIDACEAE.

Far older, in fact many millions of years older, are plants which rely upon spores for reproduction. Among these are the algae,* fungi,* mosses,* and ferns,* none of which bear flowers and are considered as very ancient ancestors of flowering plants.

**EVONYMUS** = *Euonymus*.

**EXACUM** (ecks′a-kum). A genus of 30 species of herbs or undershrubs of the gentian family, all from the Old World tropics, the two below grown for ornament in the greenhouse or outdoors in zones* 8 and 9. Leaves opposite,* mostly stalkless or very short-stalked, without marginal teeth. Flowers in forked clusters (cymes*), the calyx* 4–5-parted. Corolla more or less twisted, its lobes usually 5 and blunt or pointed. Stamens 4–5, attached to the throat of the corolla. Fruit a roundish, 2-valved capsule.* (*Exacum* is of wholly uncertain application here.)

These are best treated as warm-greenhouse plants in potting mixture* 3. Sow seeds in pots in March for *E. affine*, and they should bloom in August. Or they may be treated as greenhouse perennials and plunged outdoors in the summer and in the shade.

**affine.** A much-branched herb 1–2 ft. high. Leaves elliptic or ovalish, not over 1½ in. long, faintly 3–5-veined. Flowers bluish, about ¾ in. wide, the corolla lobes pointed. Socotra.

**macranthum.** Only slightly branched and less than 2 ft. high. Leaves oblongish, strongly 3-veined. Flowers purplish-blue, nearly 2 in. wide, the corolla lobes blunt. Ceylon.

*EXALTATA, -us, -um* (ecks-all-tay′ta). Very tall.

*EXCELSA, -us, -um* (ecks-sell′sa). Tall.

*EXCELSIOR.* Taller.

**EXHIBITIONS AND SHOWS.** A competitive, almost a sporting event, having for its object the appraisal of the hort. skill of the exhibitors, whether they grow flowers, fruits or vegetables.

In arranging and staging a flower show there are certain things which must be done. Any society or garden club should select a committee and empower it to proceed, having first decided the plan and scope, and the extent of its financial allowance in prizes, if cash awards are to be made. This committee should meet, elect a chairman and secretary, and then proceed to arrange for conducting the Show.

SCHEDULE. The important thing to do is to make up a schedule of desirable classes for competition. To each class must be apportioned prizes adequate to the extent or importance of the class, and care should be exercised to keep the total amount of prizes within the limits of the amount apportioned. Don't preface each class with "the best" this, that, or the other. It is the province of the judges to determine the best exhibit and reward it accordingly.

Make every class designation most explicit as to number of specimens and manner in which they are to be shown; if in one or more containers, and with or without accessories such as added foliage. (*See* the sample schedule, Section 1, below.) This of course applies only to classes in which the exhibits are of subjects to be judged for individual perfection of growth and flowers. In classes where arrangement is to govern the making of the award detailed information should be given to prevent an exhibit having to be passed by the judges because it is not in accord with specified conditions. These seemingly little things may suddenly become of great importance if an exhibit is later found to have been given an award and does not fully comply with class conditions.

In many small shows no cash prizes are offered. Ribbons are given, blue for first prize, red for second prize and white for third. A special prize of any desired kind is then awarded to the exhibitor winning the greatest number of points on the following point system.

    First    .... 5 points
    Second .... 3 points
    Third   .... 1 point

The following is a sample schedule for a show to be held in August. It can be changed to cover any season from June to October.

### SECTION I

#### SPECIMEN CLASSES

Exhibits in these classes must be grown by the exhibitor.

**Dahlia.**
  Class 1. "Single." 3 blooms, one variety, on long stem.
  Class 2. "Decorative." 3 blooms, one variety, on long stem.
  Class 3. Single specimen in any class.

---

* Special articles on the subjects indicated by an asterisk (*) will be found at the words so marked.

### CITY YARD GARDEN

Exhibited by the Beacon Hill Garden Club at the Centennial Exhibition of the Massachusetts Horticultural Society and awarded the Mrs. Gardner M. Lane Bowl.

**Delphinium.**
  Class 4. Single spike.
  Class 5. Collection. 5 spikes or less.
**Gladiolus.**
  Class 6. 3 spikes, yellow, any variety.
  Class 7. 3 spikes, white, any variety.
  Class 8. 3 spikes, pink or salmon, any variety.
  Class 9. 3 spikes, blue or purple, any variety.
**Herb.**
  Class 10. 2 specimens, each of 3 varieties. (It is requested that these be tagged with both botanical and common name.)
**Larkspur.**
  Class 11. Collection, tones of blue, 6 spikes.
  Class 12. Collection, tones of pink, 6 spikes.
**Lilium.**
  Class 13. Specimen stalk of *Lilium speciosum rubrum*.
  Class 14. One vase, 1 stalk each of 3 species.
**Perennial Phlox.**
  Class 15. Collection, 10 clusters, not less than 4 varieties.
**Scabiosa.**
  Class 16. Collection, dark tones of red and purple, not less than 12 or more than 18 blooms.
**Giant Zinnia.**
  Class 17. Collection, pastel colors, 10 blooms.
  Class 18. Collection, other colors, 10 blooms.

## SECTION II
### ARRANGEMENT CLASSES

Exhibits in these classes need not be grown by exhibitor. Arrangements should be in proportion to space occupied.

**Silhouettes.** (Space approximately 19 × 25 in.)
  Class 19. Open class, no restrictions.
**Still Life.** (Staging space 2 ft. square, 3 ft. high)
  Class 20. Flower arrangement, any container, mirror background. Colored bulbs for lighting and material under exhibit permitted. Nothing supplied to exhibitor by committee but staging space. No accessories.
**Lunch Tables.**
  Class 21. Flower arrangement, in tones of blue, any container. Accessories to contain color contrast. Card tables supplied by exhibitor, to be set with service for one, all accessories including a course.
**Submerged Flower Arrangement** (which see).
  Class 22. Open class, no restrictions.
**Miniature Models.**
  Class 23. Roadside planting, either an imaginary or an actual problem. Scale, ¼ in. to 1 ft.
**Miniature Arrangement.** (Space approx. 1 cu. ft.)
  Class 24. Airy flower arrangement in glass container. No accessories except optional teakwood stand.

When sending out the schedule to prospective exhibitors there should be a blank entry form and return envelope enclosed with instructions printed on the entry blank as to filling it out by enumerating the classes the exhibitor proposes to compete in.

### ENTRY FORM

To be filled in by the exhibitor and returned at once to the secretary.

| Class No. | Description of Class |
|---|---|
| ......... | ................................... |
| ......... | ................................... |
| ......... | ................................... |
| ......... | ................................... |
| ......... | ................................... |
| ......... | ................................... |
| ......... | ................................... |
| ......... | ................................... |

Date entry was received..................................

Each exhibitor agrees to conform to all rules governing this exhibition.
Exhibitor..........................................
Superintendent..................................
Gardener.........................................
  Address.......................................

### READ THE RULES CAREFULLY, THEY WILL BE STRICTLY ENFORCED

**RULES AND REGULATIONS.** There must be certain rules and regulations for any show if it is to be staged and managed without friction or confusion.

If an entry fee is to be charged, the fact should be plainly stated, giving the amount, also if it is general, covering every entry, or if the charge applies to each class.

In larger shows a distinction should be made between professional and amateur growers, with separate sections and classes for each group. If there are classes open to all regardless of any condition, this fact should be clearly stated. (*See* AMATEUR GARDENER.)

In conducting any show there can be no efficiency unless there is a closing date at which entries must be in the hands of the secretary. In no case should this be less than 24 hours in advance of the opening day of the show, and for larger ones from two to three days is essential. Whoever has the responsibility of staging needs to know just what may be expected in order to allot each class sufficient staging space.

In recording the entries and tabulating them under their proper classes methods vary, and some in common practice are distinctly bad. There is a standard method which has stood the test of many years, and those who follow it continue to do so, for it is simple, practical and completely informative. This is called the **Class Book.** In a small show any blank book with ruled pages will suffice. Each page should be devoted to one class only with the class number at the top. At the left side of the page rule off a column about one inch wide the length of the sheet. Then you take the entry blank sent in by an intending exhibitor, and enter his or her name and address under each class in which the exhibitor proposes to compete, with a number in the column at the left.

The exhibitor whose entry is first recorded will of course be number one, but only in the classes in which an entry has been made. In other classes another exhibitor will be number one, but no confusion arises from this as the record for each class is a complete statement of the exhibits which may be staged in that class. After writing out the exhibitors' cards they should each be placed in an envelope and on the face of the envelope there is written Class —— with exhibitor's number, as recorded in the class book.

From the class book the secretary prepares the **Judges' Book,** writing in the class numbers and the number of entries in each class.

The judges merely mark the envelope and record the award made against the corresponding number in their book. The judges should sign their book upon completion of their duty, return it to the secretary, who should forthwith make corresponding entries in the class book which then becomes a complete record of the winners.

The judges should not be residents of the community or live in the immediate vicinity. There should be three in each set or group to offset any differences of opinion.

The judges should not enter the show until everything is ready for judging, and no one but the official attendants should be permitted to remain in or enter the show until the judging is concluded. In any show, even the small ones, there should be great care in the selection of those who are to be entrusted with making the awards, and they must be allowed ample time to make their decision.

**JUDGING.** In competitive shows where awards are to be made the most important function is judging. There may be some shortcomings or errors in other details of management, but usually they can be reasonably excused. There can be no apology for or satisfactory explanation of incompetence in awarding the prizes. As a helpful basis for arriving at a satisfactory conclusion scales of points have been adopted and are now in general use. They are, however, only a means to an end, and to experienced judges the end is often achieved without reference to them. Occasionally there may be two exhibits each so near the accepted standard of perfection that recourse may be had to the scale of points to ascertain in what particular specification one exhibit may have a slight but none the less a deciding advantage over the other.

The following **Scales of Points** are helpful and informative

---
* Special articles on the subjects indicated by an asterisk (*) will be found at the words so marked.

to the extent that they show the relative qualities and proportionate values which competent judgment considers essential. Two or more competing exhibits may at first examination appear equal. The scale applying to those exhibits is a means of finding out why a decision gave one of them the first award.

## SCALES OF POINTS FOR JUDGING

### No. 1 — Groups of Foliage Plants

| | |
|---|---|
| Staging or Arrangement | 35 |
| Cultural Perfection | 30 |
| Distinctiveness | 20 |
| Rarity | 10 |
| Correct and Suitable Labeling | 5 |
| | 100 |

### No. 2 — Groups of Flowering Plants

| | |
|---|---|
| Staging or Arrangement | 45 |
| Cultural Perfection | 35 |
| Quality and Suitability of Accessories | 15 |
| Correct and Suitable Labeling | 5 |
| | 100 |

### No. 3 — Groups of Miscellaneous Plants

| | |
|---|---|
| Staging or Arrangement | 40 |
| Cultural Perfection | 30 |
| Variety | 20 |
| Rarity | 5 |
| Correct and Suitable Labeling | 5 |
| | 100 |

### No. 4 — Groups of Orchid Plants

| | |
|---|---|
| Staging or Arrangement | 20 |
| Cultural Perfection | 20 |
| Condition of Flowers | 20 |
| Variety | 15 |
| Rarity | 10 |
| Quality and Suitability of Accessories | 10 |
| Correct and Suitable Labeling | 5 |
| | 100 |

### No. 5 — Orchid Plants — Single Specimen

| | |
|---|---|
| Size of Plant | 25 |
| Cultural Perfection | 25 |
| Condition of Flowers | 20 |
| Color | 15 |
| Floriferousness | 15 |
| | 100 |

### No. 6 — Specimen Foliage Plants

| | |
|---|---|
| Cultural Perfection | 40 |
| Size of Plant | 25 |
| Distinctiveness | 15 |
| Rarity | 10 |
| Form | 10 |
| | 100 |

### No. 7 — Specimen Flowering Plants

| | |
|---|---|
| Cultural Perfection | 40 |
| Size of Plant | 20 |
| Floriferousness | 15 |
| Color | 15 |
| Foliage | 10 |
| | 100 |

### No. 8 — Garden Exhibits

| | |
|---|---|
| Design | 20 |
| Quality of Plant Material | 20 |
| Proportion to Scale | 20 |
| Appropriateness and Seasonability | 15 |
| Quality and Suitability of Accessories | 10 |
| Condition of Plant Material | 10 |
| Correct and Suitable Labeling | 5 |
| | 100 |

### No. 9 — Naturalistic Planting or Garden

| | |
|---|---|
| Naturalistic Reproduction | 45 |
| Condition of Plants | 15 |
| Suitability of Plants | 15 |
| Natural Arrangement of Planting Material | 10 |
| Seasonability | 10 |
| Labeling | 5 |
| | 100 |

### No. 10 — Garden Accessories with Suitable Planting

| | |
|---|---|
| Design of Accessories | 25 |
| Suitability of Plant Material | 25 |
| Proportion to Scale | 20 |
| General Design of the Exhibit | 15 |
| Condition of Plant Material | 10 |
| Correct and Suitable Labeling | 5 |
| | 100 |

### No. 11 — Rock Garden Exhibits

| | |
|---|---|
| Suitability and Arrangement of the Rocks | 25 |
| Placing and Planting of the Plants | 25 |
| Quality of Plant Material | 15 |
| Suitability of Plant Material | 10 |
| Rarity of Plant Material | 10 |
| Seasonability | 10 |
| Correct and Suitable Labeling | 5 |
| | 100 |

### No. 12 — Bird Feeding Stations

| | |
|---|---|
| General Design | 30 |
| Suitability and Arrangement of Plant Material | 25 |
| Suitability and Arrangement of Accessories | 20 |
| Proportion to Scale | 20 |
| Correct and Suitable Labeling | 5 |
| | 100 |

### No. 13 — Displays of Cut Flowers

| | |
|---|---|
| Arrangement and Effect | 45 |
| Cultural Perfection | 30 |
| Quality and Suitability of Accessories | 20 |
| Correct and Suitable Labeling | 5 |
| | 100 |

### No. 14 — Cut Roses
Adopted by the American Rose Society

| | |
|---|---|
| Color | 20 |
| Stem | 20 |
| Foliage | 15 |
| Form | 15 |
| Size | 15 |
| Substance | 15 |
| | 100 |

### No. 15 — Rose Novelties for Certificates
Adopted by the American Rose Society

| | |
|---|---|
| Color | 20 |
| Stem | 15 |
| Foliage | 15 |
| Form | 15 |
| Size | 10 |
| Substance | 10 |
| Distinctiveness | 10 |
| Fragrance | 5 |
| | 100 |

### No. 16 — Cut Carnations
Adopted by the American Carnation Society

| | |
|---|---|
| Color | 25 |
| Size | 20 |
| Stem | 20 |
| Substance | 15 |
| Form | 10 |
| Calyx | 5 |
| Fragrance | 5 |
| | 100 |

### No. 17 — Cut Peonies
Adopted by the American Peony Society

| | |
|---|---|
| Color | 25 |
| Form | 15 |
| Size | 15 |
| Distinctiveness | 15 |
| Substance | 10 |
| Stem | 10 |
| Odor | 10 |
| | 100 |

### No. 18 — Cut Sweet Peas
Adopted by the American Sweet Pea Society

| | |
|---|---|
| Size | 25 |
| Length of Stem | 25 |
| Color | 20 |
| Number of Flowers on Stem | 15 |
| Substance | 15 |
| | 100 |

### No. 19 — Cut Irises
Adopted by the American Iris Society

| | |
|---|---|
| Flower: | |
|   Quality | 15 |
|   Color | 15 |
|   Form | 10 |
|   Substance and Texture | 10 |
|   Size, according to variety | 10 |
|   Condition | 10 |
|   Fragrance | 5 |
| Stalk: | |
|   Poise and Grade, according to section | 10 |
|   Number of Blooms in Bud, according to variety | 5 |
|   Height, according to section | 5 |
|   Branching, according to section | 5 |
| | 100 |

---

\* Special articles on the subjects indicated by an asterisk (\*) will be found at the words so marked.

## No. 20 — Cut Chrysanthemums
*Adopted by the Chrysanthemum Society of America*

| | |
|---|---|
| Size | 30 |
| Color | 15 |
| Fullness | 15 |
| Form | 15 |
| Depth | 15 |
| Stem | 5 |
| Foliage | 5 |
| | 100 |

## No. 21 — Cut Chrysanthemums — Pompon and Single Varieties

| | |
|---|---|
| Color | 40 |
| Form | 20 |
| Substance | 20 |
| Stem | 10 |
| Foliage | 10 |
| | 100 |

## No. 22 — Cut Gladioli
*Adopted by the American Gladiolus Society*

Flower:
| | |
|---|---|
| Color | 20 |
| Substance | 10 |
| Size | 12 |
| Form | 5 |
| Condition | 5 |

Spike:
| | |
|---|---|
| Florescence | 15 |
| Harmony | 15 |
| Arrangement of Blooms | 10 |
| Length of Stem | 5 |
| Foliage | 3 |
| | 100 |

## No. 23 — Cut Gladioli — Primulinus Hybrids

| | |
|---|---|
| Color | 20 |
| Arrangement of Blooms | 15 |
| Harmony | 15 |
| Size | 12 |
| Substance | 10 |
| Florescence | 10 |
| Form | 5 |
| Length of Stem | 5 |
| Condition | 5 |
| Foliage | 3 |
| | 100 |

## No. 24 — Cut Dahlias
*Adopted by the American Dahlia Society*

| | |
|---|---|
| Size | 40 |
| Form | 40 |
| Color | 20 |
| | 100 |

## No. 25 — Cut Dahlias — Pompons

| | |
|---|---|
| Form | 40 |
| Diminutiveness | 35 |
| Color | 15 |
| Foliage and Arrangement | 10 |
| | 100 |

## No. 26 — Hybrid Delphiniums
*Adopted by the American Delphinium Society*

| | |
|---|---|
| Color | 25 |
| Length of Flower Spike | 10 |
| Symmetry of Flower Spike | 10 |
| Size of Florets | 10 |
| Form of Florets | 10 |
| Placement of Florets | 10 |
| Substance of Florets | 5 |
| Foliage | 10 |
| Special Features, such as fragrance, new types of petals or spikes, new colors, etc. | 10 |
| | 100 |

**Note** — Since foliage cannot be satisfactorily considered in indoor judging, the ten points allotted to the foliage may be used by the judge at his discretion.

## No. 27 — Cut Tulips

| | |
|---|---|
| Color | 25 |
| Substance and Texture | 20 |
| Culture | 20 |
| Form | 15 |
| Stem | 10 |
| Condition | 10 |
| | 100 |

## No. 28 — Cut Daffodils (Narcissi)

| | |
|---|---|
| Substance of Perianth | 25 |
| Culture | 25 |
| Color | 20 |
| Size Suitable to the Variety | 15 |
| Balance between Crown and Spread of Perianth | 15 |
| | 100 |

## No. 29 — Table Arrangements

| | |
|---|---|
| Harmony of Arrangement with Accessories | 25 |
| Distinctiveness | 20 |
| Condition | 20 |
| Proportion | 15 |
| Originality | 10 |
| Suitability to the Occasion | 10 |
| | 100 |

## No. 30 — Arrangements of Cut Flowers in Baskets or Other Decorative Containers

| | |
|---|---|
| Color Combination of Flowers | 25 |
| Container | 25 |
| Proportion and Balance | 20 |
| Originality | 15 |
| Condition | 15 |
| | 100 |

## No. 31 — Shadow Boxes (which see)

| | |
|---|---|
| Originality of Composition | 20 |
| Color Harmony | 20 |
| Perfection of Detail | 20 |
| Suitability of Accessories | 15 |
| Proportion and Arrangement | 15 |
| Condition of Material | 10 |
| | 100 |

## No. 32 — Porch or Window Boxes

| | |
|---|---|
| Color Harmony | 30 |
| Arrangement and Adaptability of Material | 25 |
| Proportion of Planting Material to Container | 25 |
| Cultural Perfection | 20 |
| | 100 |

## No. 33 — Arrangement of Flowers, Fruits and/or Vegetables Adapted to a Definite Purpose such as a Mantel, Wall, Porch, Table or the like

| | |
|---|---|
| Suitability to Purpose | 30 |
| Color Harmony | 25 |
| Distinctiveness | 25 |
| Relation of Material to Receptacle | 20 |
| | 100 |

## No. 34 — Contest Posters

| | |
|---|---|
| Design | 30 |
| Advertising Appeal | 30 |
| Originality | 20 |
| Decorative Quality | 20 |
| | 100 |

## No. 35 — Terrariums

| | |
|---|---|
| Design and Arrangement of Planting | 35 |
| Suitability of Material | 35 |
| Condition | 25 |
| Correct and Suitable Labeling | 5 |
| | 100 |

## No. 36 — Aquariums

| | |
|---|---|
| Arrangement of Plants and Accessories | 20 |
| Variety and Rarity of Fish | 20 |
| Variety of Plant Material | 15 |
| General Artistic Effect | 15 |
| Design of Aquarium | 10 |
| Quality of Plant Material | 10 |
| Other Aquatic Fauna | 10 |
| | 100 |

## No. 37 — Miniature Gardens

| | |
|---|---|
| Landscape Design | 25 |
| Originality of Design | 20 |
| Scale and Proportion | 20 |
| Quality and Type of Material | 15 |
| Color Harmony | 10 |
| Perfection of Detail | 10 |
| | 100 |

## No. 38 — Grapes

| | |
|---|---|
| Freedom from Blemishes | 20 |
| Form of Bunch | 20 |
| Size of Bunch | 15 |
| Flavor | 15 |
| Size of Berry | 10 |
| Color | 10 |
| Firmness | 5 |
| Bloom | 5 |
| | 100 |

\* Special articles on the subjects indicated by an asterisk (\*) will be found at the words so marked.

### No. 39 — Apples, Pears and Quinces

| | |
|---|---|
| Freedom from Blemishes | 25 |
| Color | 20 |
| Uniformity | 20 |
| Quality | 15 |
| Form | 10 |
| Size | 10 |
| | 100 |

### No. 40 — Plums

| | |
|---|---|
| Uniformity | 20 |
| Quality | 20 |
| Freedom from Blemishes | 20 |
| Size | 15 |
| Color | 15 |
| Form | 10 |
| | 100 |

### No. 41 — Peaches and Cherries

| | |
|---|---|
| Uniformity | 20 |
| Quality | 20 |
| Freedom from Blemishes | 20 |
| Form | 15 |
| Color | 15 |
| Size | 10 |
| | 100 |

### No. 42 — Display of Fruits

| | |
|---|---|
| Staging or Arrangement | 40 |
| Quality | 35 |
| Variety | 20 |
| Correct and Suitable Labeling | 5 |
| | 100 |

### No. 43 — Display of Vegetables

| | |
|---|---|
| Staging or Arrangement | 35 |
| Quality and Color | 30 |
| Variety | 20 |
| Trueness to Type | 10 |
| Correct and Suitable Labeling | 5 |
| | 100 |

In judging collections or displays of vegetables, many prefer a different scale from that of Table 43. Upon this theory, the varieties shown have varying degrees of merit according to the actual cultural skill required to produce them. For example, 6 perfect beets should be accorded more points than 6 perfect turnips.

For judging such exhibits the following scale has been found entirely satisfactory:

### SCALE OF POINTS FOR JUDGING VEGETABLES
#### Lenox Horticultural Society

| | No. to form a dish or to be exhibited in collections | Points |
|---|---|---|
| Artichoke, globe | 6 | 100 |
| Artichoke, Jerusalem | 12 | 50 |
| Asparagus | 25 | 100 |
| Beans, string, green | 40 pods | 100 |
| Beans, string, yellow | 40 pods | 80 |
| Beans, Lima | 24 pods | 100 |
| Beans, runner | 24 pods | 75 |
| Beans, broad | 21 pods | 75 |
| Beet, long | 6 | 90 |
| Beet, round | 6 | 90 |
| Cauliflower | 6 | 100 |
| Cardoon | 3 | 35 |
| Cabbage | 3 | 50 |
| Cabbage, Savoy | 3 | 50 |
| Cabbage, red | 3 | 50 |
| Carrot, long | 6 | 90 |
| Carrot, short | 6 | 65 |
| Celery | 6 | 100 |
| Celeriac | 6 | 55 |
| Cucumber, frame | 2 | 100 |
| Cucumber, outdoor | 6 | 50 |
| Chicory | 6 | 35 |
| Corn, sweet | 6 | 100 |
| Eggplant | 3 | 90 |
| Endive | 6 | 80 |
| Horseradish | 6 | 35 |
| Kohlrabi | 6 | 50 |
| Leek | 6 | 90 |
| Lettuce | 6 | 90 |
| Mushrooms | 18 | 100 |
| Onion | 6 | 100 |
| Okra | 12 | 70 |
| Parsnip | 6 | 75 |
| Peas | 40 pods | 100 |
| Peppers, red, green or red and green | 9 | 65 |
| Potatoes | 9 | 100 |
| Pumpkin | 2 | 25 |
| Rhubarb | 6 | 50 |
| Radishes | 12 | 35 |
| Salsify | 12 | 45 |
| Scorzonera | 12 | 45 |
| Spinach | 10 | 35 |
| Sprouts, Brussels | 40 | 75 |
| Squash | 2 | 25 |
| Shallots | 24 | 25 |
| Tomatoes | 10 | 100 |
| Turnip | 6 | 40 |
| Vegetable Marrow | 2 | 25 |
| Arrangement | | 100 |

Staging the Show. When staging a show one must also consider the facilities available. Our British friends make some remarkable displays in summer and early fall in tents. The use of tents in this country, however, is of doubtful expediency. If the weather is fine a tent usually becomes too hot, or a sudden summer storm may arise and in a few moments wreck everything.

Buildings or places of permanent construction are really essential, such as large halls or spacious rooms with a floor area to accommodate the contemplated exhibit. The disposition and arrangement of the exhibits is the next important matter to consider. This calls for some careful advance planning. The exhibits when finally assembled should be displayed attractively, so as to create a pleasing spectacle to those who have less interest in the actual prize winners, but a keen appreciation for artistic disposition and colorful effectiveness. The building should be cool, there must be plenty of water available, and it is of advantage that the floor can be hosed down, both to remove dirt and keep the atmosphere moist.

Plant exhibits, either as specimens or in groups, usually look best when staged upon the ground. It is better to look down upon them than up at them, if they are three feet or more in height. The same applies to tall cut flowers such as delphiniums, hollyhocks, foxgloves, lilies, *Gladioli*, and others which meet the eye more effectively staged on the ground.

In making space allotments for exhibits on the ground or on tables the requirements are governed by size of plants or of containers in the case of cut flowers. If the competing items in any class are in single containers allot to each one sufficient space to display its individuality, yet the entire class should be held together to facilitate judging. In groups or display classes the allotted space is usually stated in the schedule, and a space approximately two feet should be left open between exhibits to show and accentuate the group effect desired. All these things must be thought out and prepared for in advance of the arrival of the exhibitors with their entries.

Tables are usually most desirable for staging such exhibits as generally make up the smaller shows. These may be of the simplest kind, ordinary three-legged trestles with board tops, and not to exceed four or five feet in width if the exhibits placed thereon are to be viewed from one front. Where space permits tables may be set up eight feet in width, so that one can walk around them. The exhibits, in their respective classes, are then staged, so that one set faces one side, and the other faces the opposite side.

The use of suitable drapery of appropriate color and character helps to improve the effect of table exhibits, especially in front of a wall, but it should be for all or none. It should be put up by the management, not left to the option of the exhibitor, or some bizarre things may be done, quite out of harmony with and even detrimental to the general effect. A wide table with exhibits facing both ways may advantageously have a central division line of dark green burlap tacked to a light framework extended to a height of about four feet above the table. Here again leave nothing to the discretion of the exhibitor, but treat the whole table uniformly.

The table-tops should be covered with a waterproof paper or burlap, and the sides may be draped with burlap in a neutral tint so that one cannot see beneath the tables.

It may happen at certain seasons that many of the exhibits will lack sufficient height to permit of effective staging.

* Special articles on the subjects indicated by an asterisk (*) will be found at the words so marked.

For example, at a June show when roses and other short-stemmed flowers predominate, these will have a poor effect upon a flat table. A step table is the solution of such a problem. A three-step, shelf-like arrangement, simple and easy to put up on the table itself, can be made. It should set back one foot from the front of the table, with a three-step rise, each six inches in height, carrying a ten-inch-wide shelf. This will permit the effective display of four rows at equal heights and show all the exhibits to much better advantage.

Another important detail is to have proper class designations. A numbered class card eight inches long and five inches wide should be set up on a little stand where it can be easily seen. It fixes the space allotted for that class both for the exhibitor and the public; a seemingly small matter, yet one which can cause considerable grief to a penalized exhibitor. The judges have an unpleasant duty to perform when they have to disqualify an exhibit which might be a prize winner because there may be eleven or thirteen blooms in the vase in a class which calls for twelve. Such errors are usually unintentional. They often result from the exhibitor wisely bringing one or two extra flowers in case of accident and in the haste of arranging the exhibit forgetting to count. A deficiency may also result from some breakage on the way to the show, with no extra flowers at hand.

It is the exhibitors' responsibility to stage in exact accordance with the requirements of the schedule, and neglect or inadvertence to do so must be penalized in justice to those exhibits which fully conform to specified conditions.

For some reason plants, flowers and ferns seem more popular in the garden club world than fruits and vegetables. But when classes are provided for the latter and worth-while exhibits staged they are greatly admired. The show value of a few plates of apples or pears may not be especially appealing, but a display of edible fruits and berry-bearing trees and shrubs in combination can be made most attractive. In vegetables the largest cabbage or pumpkin is merely of incidental interest, but when such collections of vegetables are staged as at the November shows of the Horticultural Society of New York, the visitors accord them unbounded admiration. In anything that grows, if you can only invoke a competitive spirit, it becomes a stimulus to expert cultivation.

The old adage that "trifles make perfection, but perfection is no trifle" is most apparent on the show table. In the last analysis it is the intangible something not measurable by points which influences the rendering of the actual judgment.

A few terms used in a special sense by judges need definition:

## MEANING OF TERMS COMMONLY USED BY JUDGES

**Accessories.** Material used in an exhibit but not necessarily called for in the schedule. Cut foliage and foliage plants, stands and containers, as well as sundials, bird baths, garden furniture, textile backgrounds, draperies, throws, etc., are classed as accessories.

**Arranged for effect.** This term is used to emphasize the necessity of staging a group or display to create an attractive and aesthetic impression. The proper selection and use of accessories usually is important in such exhibits.

**Collection.** As understood in schedules, this means several varieties of plants, flowers, fruits or vegetables in one exhibit. It differs from a group in that the number of different varieties is an important factor. Artistic arrangement is desirable but not required unless so stated in the schedule.

**Color.** This is understood to mean the natural color and not any variation produced by rubbing or polishing. In the case of apples an exception is made, polishing being permitted.

**Condition.** This refers to the quality or nearness to perfection at the time of judging — not what the material probably looked like the previous day or may look like the following day.

**Display.** Unless otherwise specified in the schedule, a display calls for an exhibit of cut flowers, vegetables or fruits, artistically arranged to create a striking effect. Any accessories, including cut foliage and foliage plants, are permitted.

**Distinctiveness.** Difficult to define but having that quality of elegance and finish which makes an exhibit stand out as above the ordinary exhibit.

**Form.** This refers to the normal type or shape of the variety.

**Novelty.** A variety of recent introduction or still undisseminated and not previously shown at an exhibition of this Society.

**Originality.** This is understood to mean unusual plant material or common plant material set up in an unusual way. This does not mean bizarre or freakish.

**Size.** Exhibition flowers and fruits and vegetables may be somewhat above the average size of the particular variety, but the selection of abnormally large-sized specimens should be avoided, especially when size tends to impair quality.

**Specimen.** A single fruit, vegetable, plant, bloom, spike or stalk.

**Spike.** A thick, upright stem carrying several flowers. The gladiolus, foxglove and delphinium are examples.

**Stalk.** A stiff stem carrying one or more flowers and buds. It may be branched. The bearded iris is an example.

**Substance.** This is understood to mean firmness as characteristic of the flower at its best.

**Undisseminated.** A variety is considered undisseminated when it cannot be exhibited by any person other than the originator or his agent.

**Uniformity.** This means that all specimens on a plate, or flowers in a vase, etc., should be as nearly as possible alike in size, form and color. — A. H.

*EXIMIA, -us, -um* (ecks-im'i-a). Out of the common run; distinguished.

*EXCISA, -us, -um* (ecks-sy'za). Excised; *i.e.* cut away.

**EXOCHORDA** (ecks-o-kor'da). A small but important genus of Asiatic shrubs of the rose family, E. racemosa, the pearl bush, being a very popular garden plant, and useful for forcing (which see). It is a spreading shrub, 5–10 ft. high, the leaves alternate,* more or less elliptic-oblong, 1–3 in. long, generally without marginal teeth. Flowers white, nearly 2 in. wide, in a showy, terminal, but not very profuse, cluster (raceme*). Sepals 5. Petals 5, broad but with a short claw.* Stamens 15. Fruit a 5-angled capsule.* China. April–May. Hardy from zone* 3 southward and often sold as E. grandiflora. This handsome shrub is of the easiest culture in any ordinary garden soil. Propagated by seeds, layers, or by softwood cuttings. (*Exochorda* is from the Greek for an external chord, in allusion to a technical ovary character.)

*EXONIENSIS, -e* (ecks-o-ni-en'sis). From Exmouth, England.

*EXOTICA, -us, -um* (ecks-ot'i-ka). Exotic; *i.e.* not native; from another region.

*EXPANSA, -us, -um* (ecks-span'sa). Expanded.

**EXPERIMENT STATIONS.** The state experiment stations and the U.S. Department of Agriculture do more for the gardener than any other agencies dealing with the growth of plants. While some of them, especially the National Government, carry on much original research, their chief function is the preparation of first-hand, practical directions on how to grow plants and how to combat the pests that attack them.

You will find the name and address of your own experiment station under the name of your state or province in THE GARDEN DICTIONARY, where you will also find an account of the garden possibilities of your state contributed by the experiment station. Few other features of the DICTIONARY are so useful.

**EXPOSURE.** Within the general hardiness range of whatever plant you wish to grow, there are places where it will do better or worse, depending on many contributing factors. One of the most important of these secondary contributors to success or failure is exposure. Whether your plant will be exposed to too much sun or wind, or have to stand cooler nights, depends in great measure upon the place you finally select for it. No hard-and-fast rules can be given, but it is well to study the wild range and cultivated hardiness of your proposed plant, and to read the articles on SITE, HARDINESS, and ZONES, before you choose what the exposure will be.

*EXSCAPA, -us, -um* (ecks-skay'pa). Without a stalk (scape).

**EXSERTED.** Protruding. Exserted is the usual technical term for stamens* that protrude beyond the corolla.

**EXTRAVASATED SAP** = bleeding.

**EYE.** A bud on a cutting, or a bud on a tuber, as the eyes on a potato. *Eye* is also very commonly applied to the differently colored center of a flower, very conspicuous in some pinks, forget-me-nots, and in *Hibiscus oculiroseus*, which has a white flower with a conspicuous red eye (center). Many garden flowers have them.

**EYEBRIGHT** = *Mimulus ringens*.

---

* Special articles on the subjects indicated by an asterisk (*) will be found at the words so marked.

# F

**F₁, F₂, F₃.** Symbols used to indicate first, second, and third hybrid generations from a given mating or cross, F meaning filial. The original parents are often designated P₁ and P₂.

*FABA* (fay'ba). Classical name of the bean.

*FABACEA, -us, -um* (fay-bay'see-a). Bean-like.

**FABACEAE.** See LEGUMINOSAE.

**FABIANA** (fay-bi-ā'na). Low, heath-like, South American shrubs of the potato family, comprising perhaps 20 species, of which **F. imbricata**, the false heath, is often grown for ornament in greenhouses or outdoors in Calif. and Fla. It is an erect, branching shrub 4–7 ft. high, the branches numerous and softly hairy. Leaves small, crowded, heath-like or scale-like. Flowers nearly stalkless, white, solitary, but many of them at the ends of short spurs. Corolla tubular, not over ½ in. long, the 5-lobed limb scarcely evident. Stamens* 5, of unequal length. Fruit an oblong, 2-valved capsule.* Peru. Of easy culture in the cool greenhouse in potting mixture* 3, and outdoors in any frost-free area. Propagated by cuttings taken in Aug. (Named for Francisco Fabiano, Spanish botanist and Archbishop.)

**FACTOR.** See GENE.

**FAGACEAE** (fay-gay'see-ee). The beech family is, with equal reason, called also the oak or chestnut family. See these three trees for the chief genera. The only other genera are *Castanopsis* and *Lithocarpus*, but of the 450 species known in the whole family, less than 50 are of much garden importance, although many furnish valuable timbers, and the nuts of the chestnut are widely harvested for food.

Leaves alternate* (evergreen in some trees). Flowers without petals, all the male flowers in catkins,* the female solitary or in small clusters, both on the same tree, and always wind-pollinated. Fruit a 1-seeded nut, partly enclosed in a cup (in oaks), or completely surrounded by a bur (in the chestnut), and by bracts* in some other genera.

Technical flower characters: Petals none. Calyx extremely simple, 4–8-lobed. Stamens 4–20. In the female flower the calyx is joined to the 3–7-celled ovary. Styles 3–7.

**FAGOPYRUM.** See BUCKWHEAT.

**FAGUS.** See BEECH.

**FAILURE TO BLOOM.** Many are the disappointments caused by the failure of favorite flowers to bloom, or the failure of fruit trees to flower as freely as they should. In the latter case, it is often a case of improper pruning, and in the apple article this trouble is discussed. *See* APPLE. *See also* STERILITY OF FRUIT TREES.

Failure to bloom should be separated into woody and herbaceous examples of it, for the underlying causes are often different.

In the case of herbs, few annuals, unless diseased, ever fail to produce flowers at the normal time. But not a few perennials, especially the peony, bloom poorly or not at all the first season after planting. There is no remedy for this, except to leave the plants alone. After the second or third season there is usually no trouble about this. The same is true of many slow-growing, long-lived perennials. Time is the only cure. But sometimes they have too much nitrate of soda or other nitrogenous fertilizer, which tends to produce leafage at the expense of flowers. Phosphorus and potash will usually correct this. *See* FERTILIZERS. Too deep planting of perennials also retards bloom.

In the case of all woody plants, there are occasional or periodic "off years" when there is little or no bloom. The cause and the remedy are as yet unknown. Many early-flowering shrubs and trees fail to bloom because a late frost may have caught their flower buds — notably the peach and apricot. But the chief cause in woody plants is improper pruning. This is discussed in detail in the article on pruning.

Disease and poor culture will, of course, tend to reduce bloom, and improper site, such as too much or too little sunlight. The notes on habitat and country of origin should be studied with this in mind for any plant that habitually fails to bloom. Often it is simply too weak to do so.

**FAIRWAY FOOD.** A trademarked fertilizer with a 6-6-4 ratio (*see* FERTILIZERS), mixed with tobacco stems, sold for use on lawns or golf courses.

**FAIRY BELLS.** See DISPORUM.

**FAIRY CUP** = *Mitella diphylla*.

**FAIRY FANS** = *Eucharidium breweri*.

**FAIRY GLOVE** = *Digitalis purpurea*. See FOXGLOVE.

**FAIRY PRIMROSE** = *Primula malacoides*.

**FAIRY ROSE** = *Rosa chinensis minima*.

**FAIRY WAND** = *Chamaelirium luteum*.

*FALCATA, -us, -um* (fal-kay'ta). Falcate; *i.e.* sickle-shaped.

**FALL COLOR.** See AUTUMN FOLIAGE and AUTUMN GARDEN.

**FALL FOLIAGE.** See AUTUMN FOLIAGE.

**FALL GARDEN.** See AUTUMN GARDEN.

**FALLOW LAND.** From very ancient days it has been known that allowing land to rest, without any crop on it, did for it what no amount of cultivation will accomplish. Part of the benefits are undoubtedly due to the uninterrupted play of sun, wind, rain, and especially frost upon the soil. While it is not often possible to let land occupied by ornamentals lie fallow, it can often be managed in the vegetable garden. And, of course, all intelligent farmers follow a pretty steady rotation of fallowing. It is really a part of soil management and is discussed there in more detail.

**FALL PLANTING.** See AUTUMN PLANTING.

**FALLS.** See IRIS.

**FALL WEBWORM.** See Moths at INSECT PESTS.

**FALL WORK.** See the autumn months at GARDEN CALENDAR.

**FALSE.** As an adjective *false* is linked with the names of many plants, usually indicating that they are like, or may be mistaken for, some other plant. Those that occur in THE GARDEN DICTIONARY, and their proper equivalents, are:

False acacia = *Robinia pseudo-acacia* (see LOCUST); False aloe = *Manfreda virginica*; False alumroot = *Tellima grandiflora*; False anemone = *Isopyrum biternatum*; False aralia (see DIZYGOTHECA); False arborvitae = *Thujopsis dolobrata*; False bittersweet (see BITTERSWEET); False bugbane = *Trautvetteria carolinensis*; False camomile (see MATRICARIA and BOLTONIA); False cypress (see CHAMAECYPARIS); False dragonhead = *Physostegia virginiana*; False heath = *Fabiana imbricata*; False hellebore (see VERATRUM); False indigo (see BAPTISIA and AMORPHA); False ipecac = *Gillenia trifoliata*; False Jerusalem cherry = *Solanum capsicastrum*; False loosestrife (see LUDWIGIA); False mallow (see SIDALCEA and MALVASTRUM); False mermaid family = Limnanthaceae; False mitrewort (see TIARELLA); False olive = *Elaeodendron orientale*; False saffron = *Carthamus tinctorius*; False Solomon's-seal (see SMILACINA); False spirea (see SORBARIA); False starwort (see BOLTONIA); False sunflower = *Helenium autumnale* and *Heliopsis helianthoides*; False syringa = *Philadelphus coronarius* (see MOCK-ORANGE); False violet = *Dalibarda repens*.

**FAMEUSE.** See APPLE.

**FAMILY.** See PLANT FAMILY.

**FANCY GERANIUM** = *Pelargonium domesticum*.

**FANCY-LEAVED CALADIUM.** See CALADIUM.

**FAN PALM.** A palm with fan-like leaves. See the illustration at PALMACEAE.

**FAN TRAINING.** See Fruit Trees at TRAINING PLANTS.

---

* Special articles on the subjects indicated by an asterisk (*) will be found at the words so marked.

**FANWORT.** See Cabomba.

**FANWORT FAMILY.** See Nymphaeaceae.

**FAREWELL-TO-SPRING** = *Godetia amoena*.

*FARFARA* (far'fa-ra). Pre-Linnaean* name for the coltsfoot (*Tussilago farfara*).

**FARFUGIUM KAEMPFERI** = *Ligularia kaempferi*.

*FARINACEA, -us, -um* (far-ri-nay'see-a). Farinaceous; *i.e.* starch-yielding.

*FARINOSA, -us, -um* (fa-ri-nō'sa). Mealy.

*FARLEYENSIS, -e* (far-lee-en'sis). From Farley Hill Gardens, Barbados.

**FARMYARD MANURE.** See Manure.

*FARNESIANA, -us, -um* (far-nee-zi-ā'na). Named for the Farnesian Garden, Rome.

**FASCIATED; FASCIATION.** An abnormal widening and flattening of the stem, often of a flower stalk. While generally of unknown origin, it is sometimes due to disease (see Diseases at Sweet Pea). Fasciation is not at all uncommon among garden plants, particularly in the genus *Nicotiana*, and in *Celosia* and *Lilium*.

*FASCICULATA, -us, -um* (fa-sick-kew-lay'ta). Fascicled; *i.e.* in a close, dense cluster.

*FASTIGIATA, -us, -um* (fas-tij-ji-ā'ta). Fastigiate; *i.e.* having the branches erect and close together, as in the Lombardy poplar.

*FASTUOSA, -us, -um* (fast-you-o'sa). Proud.

**FATHER HUGO'S ROSE** = *Rosa hugonis*.

**FATSIA** (fat'si-a). A single, evergreen, Japanese shrub or small tree of the family Araliaceae, much planted south of zone* 7 for its tropical-looking foliage. The only species, F. japonica, is an unarmed, bushy shrub or small tree 10-20 ft. high. Leaves alternate,* its stalks 8-12 in. long, the blade nearly round in outline, 9-15 in. wide, cut into 5-9 ovalish, broad, toothed lobes, shiny and stiff. Flowers small, whitish, in small umbels,* many of which are grouped in a large, rather showy, branched cluster. (For details see Araliaceae.) Fruit black, berry-like, about ¼ in. in diameter. The plant grows well in nearly every type of soil, but prefers rich, sandy ones. Propagated by seeds, or by cuttings in spring. There is also a form with variegated leaves. For a related plant sometimes offered as *F. papyrifera*, see Tetrapanax papyriferum. And for the plant sometimes offered as *F. horrida*, see Echinopanax horridum. (*Fatsia* is derived from a Japanese vernacular for the plant.)

*FATUA, -us, -um* (fat'you-a). Simple; or, in horticultural usage, simply insipid.

**FAWN LILY** = *Erythronium albidum* and *E. californicum*.

**FEATHER-BALL** = *Neomammillaria plumosa*.

**FEATHER-FASHION.** With the leaflets of a compound leaf arranged as are the segments of a bird's feather, *i.e.* arising from opposite sides of a common axis.* The technical term is pinnate (which see).

**FEATHER-GERANIUM** = *Chenopodium botrys*.

**FEATHER-GRASS.** See Stipa.

**FEATHER-HYACINTH** = *Muscari comosum monstrosum*.

**FEATHER PALM.** A palm in which the segments of the leaf are arranged feather-fashion; not like a fan. See the illustration at Palmaceae.

**FEBRUARY.** See Garden Calendar.

**FEDERATED GARDEN CLUBS.** See Garden Clubs.

**FEDIA** (fee'di-a). A single, annual herb of the family Valerianaceae, native in the Mediterranean region, and grown chiefly for ornament, and rarely as a salad plant. The only species, F. cornucopiae, the African valerian, is a stout, purplish-stemmed, leafy herb, 10-15 in. high. Leaves opposite,* ovalish or spatula-shaped, 2-4 in. long, shiny and green. Flowers red, small, in dense terminal clusters (cymes*), the corolla tubular but slightly 2-lipped.* Stamens 2. Fruit like a grain of wheat. To be grown as a hardy annual (see Annuals). (*Fedia* is of unknown origin.)

**FEEDING PLANTS.** See Fertilizers. See also Manure. For Feeding Trees see Tree Surgery.

**FEIJOA** (fa-jo'a). A small genus of South American shrubs or small trees of the myrtle family, F. sellowiana, the pineapple guava, grown in Fla. and Calif. for its delicious, white-fleshed fruit. It is hardy surely only south of zone* 7, although it stands an occasional drop to 14°. Leaves opposite,* oval-oblong, 2-3 in. long, white-felty beneath. Flowers solitary, ¾-1½ in. long, white-felty outside, purplish inside, long-stalked, blooming in April. Petals 4. Stamens* many, red, protruding and showy. Fruit (ripe in Aug.-Sept.) a greenish-red berry, 2-3 in. long. The pineapple guava is grown both in the dry Calif. climate and in the moister one of Fla. They do well in sandy, rich loam, and should be planted 15-20 ft. apart each way. Seeds germinate 2-3 weeks after sowing. Cuttings and layers are both very slow. To ensure a good set of fruit it is well to stagger varieties in the row, some of the best being Andre, Coolidge, Choice, and Superba. Otherwise, pollination may fail. (Named for J. da Silva Feijo, a Spanish naturalist.)

*FEJEENSIS, -e* (fee-jee-en'sis). From the Fiji Islands.

**FELICIA** (fe-liss'i-a). A large genus of chiefly South African under-shrubs (rarely annuals) of the family Compositae, F. amelloides, the blue daisy or blue Marguerite, a popular greenhouse plant grown for ornament, sometimes under the name *Agathea*. It is a bushy shrub 1-3 ft. high, the leaves opposite,* more or less elliptic, mostly without teeth, and tapering at the base to a winged stalk. Flower heads solitary, daisy-like, about 1 in. wide, the numerous rays* blue, the small disk* flowers yellow. It is a handsome, winter-blooming plant to be grown in potting mixture* 3 and in the cool greenhouse. A recently advertised species, F. bergeriana, is said to be a hardy annual with blue, aster-like flowers. Nothing is known of its origin. (Named for Herr Felix, a German official.)

**FELT-FERN.** See Cyclophorus.

**FEMALE.** Male and female are common terms among gardeners, indicating flowers with stamens* and pistils,* respectively. The preferable, but botanical, terms, staminate (for male) and pistillate (for female), appear unlikely to replace male and female as the usual garden terms for the reproductive functions of plants. See Fertilization.

**FENCES.** Fences should harmonize with their surroundings, combining decorative design with practical usage. A fence, to act as a screen, and not just a barrier, must have no openings. French hand-riven chestnut palings, pointed at the top and closely woven together, are best for this purpose, but they rot if buried in the soil. This fence is durable, economical, cannot be seen through, and fits into the landscape. With formal houses of brick, stone, or stucco, house and garden may be tied together by using this type in panels between piers, plain or ornamental, built of the same material as the house walls. In small gardens where every inch of space is precious but privacy is desired, solid board or thin masonry fences may be used. There are many variations of the latter, the most

Good type of woven-paling fence

---
* Special articles on the subjects indicated by an asterisk (*) will be found at the words so marked.

common being of metal lath fastened to tee irons set into concrete at intervals of six to eight feet. The entire structure is then stuccoed and a stucco base and top molding added. Stone or brick may be used for a heavy fence.

Lattice, with large or small openings, or a combination of both, intricate designs, and ornamental finials and moldings, serve a variety of purposes. The wood hurdle fence and the heavy post and rail fence are ideal for country boundaries. The old-fashioned picket fence is well adapted to the Colonial style of architecture. Pickets may vary in width, shape, and spacing; they may be flat and wide with pointed tops, square, or round. Chestnut, white or red cedar, and locust make excellent durable posts. Give a priming coat of lead and oil to all parts before erecting.

Common types of wooden fences and railings. The split-rail type of fence at the bottom encloses some of the finest gardens in America at East Hampton, L.I., usually covered (only partly) with honeysuckle, clematis or climbing roses.

For protection, especially on country estates, heavy metal chain link or woven wire fences are best. They do not provide privacy, but climbers or dense hedges of privet or shrubs may be grown inside them.

**FENESTRALIS, -e** (fen-es-tray'lis). Having window-like openings.

**FENNEL.** The common garden fennel is one of 4 species of European herbs of the genus **Foeniculum** (fe-nick'you-lum) of the carrot family, and is grown for its aromatic fruits and foliage. It has twice-compound* leaves, the leaflets arranged feather-fashion, and small, yellow flowers in compound umbels* (for details see UMBELLIFERAE). (*Foeniculum* is a Latin diminutive for hay, in allusion to the odor of its foliage.)

Of the four known species, the only one of garden interest is the common fennel and its varieties. For culture and uses see HERB GARDENING.

F. officinale = *Foeniculum vulgare*.

F. vulgare. Common fennel. A perennial, but grown usually as an annual or biennial. Stems 3-5 ft. high, bluish-green. Ultimate leaflets very numerous, thread-like. Flower-cluster (umbel*) large, the number of flowers in each umbel 15-25. Summer. The *var.* dulce, the Florence or sweet fennel, which is also called finnochio, has the leaf-base enlarged, and, when blanched, is used as food, and is considerably grown in Calif. The *var.* piperitum, the carosella, is grown for its tender young stems which are eaten, and sometimes made into a glacé confection.

**FENNEL-FLOWER** = *Nigella sativa*.

**FEN ORCHIS** = *Liparis loeseli*.

**FENUGREEK** = *Trigonella foenum-graecum*.

**FERN ALLIES.** The fern allies are not true ferns but like them in being reproduced by spores. Not many fern allies are of much garden significance. For those in THE GARDEN DICTIONARY, see EQUISETUM, LYCOPODIUM, MARSILEA, and SALVINIACEAE.

**FERN ASPARAGUS** = *Asparagus plumosus*.

**FERN BALL.** A compact, pudding-shaped mass of the rhizomes* of certain ferns, notably *Davallia bullata*, mostly made in Japan and imported in a dry, dormant condition. The mass is tightly tied together, and when soaked in water and hung in a warm, moist, partly shaded greenhouse will soon be covered with the beautiful, feathery foliage of *Davallia*. Subsequent care is the same as for any greenhouse fern. (See FERNS AND FERN GARDENING.) Fern balls may well replace hanging baskets on a summer porch, but it must not be a windy or dry one. Watering is most easily done by dipping the whole fern ball, foliage and all, in a bucket of water. They must be kept moist.

**FERNLEAF BEECH** = *Fagus sylvatica laciniata*. See BEECH.

**FERNS AND FERN GARDENING.** Ferns are perennial, flowerless plants of more than 6000 species, divided into several families, which are widely distributed throughout the temperate and tropical regions of the world. Long before the Age of Man, gigantic ancestors of our ferns formed mighty forests which were in their turn submerged, and slowly became vast beds of coal, while higher plant life gradually evolved above them. Today the extinct species of ferns far outnumber the living.

Two groups are recognized by gardeners. The hardy kinds are chiefly terrestial species from temperate regions, which may be planted in gardens if given conditions approximately like those of their natural habitat. The greenhouse kinds, of tropical regions, include the epiphytic* varieties, which require special growing facilities approximating their environmental conditions.

### SPORES AND REPRODUCTION

For many years the development of ferns, their methods of fertilization and reproduction, were wholly unknown. In the middle of the nineteenth century it was shown that these plants pass through two complete stages in their life cycles. The first consists of a tiny, green, flattened body, often heart-shaped, connected with the soil by hair-like roots, and bearing on its lower surface both of the reproductive organs. This is termed a *prothallus*. The union of these reproductive organs does not, as in flowering plants, form seed. Instead of this seed-formation, the germ-cell in the fern develops into the second stage, or fern-plant proper. The first fronds are very small and simple,* quite unlike the later ones. For a time the little plant is nourished by the prothallus, but as soon as it is sufficiently vigorous to shift for itself, the prothallus dies away, and the fern maintains an independent existence. This fern-plant, in turn, develops the spores which produce the prothallus, thus completing its life cycle.

### PROPAGATION

Ferns are propagated by division, by the buds or offsets* that form on the fronds of certain varieties, and by means of spores. These spores are collected in spore cases clustered in dots or lines, usually on the back of a frond or leaf, or along its margin. Spores differ from seeds in that they are not the immediate result of the interaction of reproductive organs; they resemble seeds in that they are expelled from the spore cases upon attaining maturity, and germinate on contact with moisture. Ripened spores may be shaken from the parent plant, and put in sacks of paper to dry. Sow in one or two weeks in flats or pots on light, moist, well-sifted soil. Equal parts of garden loam and leaf mold, with sand for drainage, make a good mixture. Do not cover the spores with earth or water on top; the flat or pot should be kept in a frame or house at a temperature of about 60 degrees. After the tiny prothalli appear, a little more air may be given. When large enough to be handled easily, prick out little

---

* Special articles on the subjects indicated by an asterisk (*) will be found at the words so marked.

sporelings and transplant them, later re-transplanting them individually into separate pots. From ten months to a year are required to produce good ferns by this method.

### Hardy Ferns

To many people ferns have an aesthetic value in the landscape not surpassed by any class of flowering plants. Their immense variety and geographical distribution make it possible to select species adapted to almost any location. Almost all may be introduced into our gardens if their preferences are consulted, and reasonable attention given to their simple cultural requirements. The majority are terrestrial in habit; a few climb; some prefer dry, sunny places, and others are at home in humid, moisture-laden swamps. Being so varied in their characteristics, they are adapted to a wide variety of purposes — exposed northern spots where flowers will not grow, massed plantings, walk edgings, rock gardens, bog gardens, sunny walls and banks. Many of the plants will thrive under ordinary conditions, but a little leaf mold added to common soil, will in general prolong the life of all ferns. Early spring or late fall is to be preferred for planting, as the roots are then least apt to be disturbed. Autumn planting, with a mulch of leaves during the cold months to give protection and to retain moisture in the soil until new rootlets have started to grow, is probably the best.

The spots in our garden that cause us the most worry and trouble are those where flowers do not thrive — the north side of the house, wall and foundation plantings, bare spots under trees, or any place where light is not abundant.

Some types of hardy ferns. Above, *Dryopteris marginalis* (*left*) and *Woodsia*; below, the Christmas fern (*left*) and the cinnamon fern.

The evergreen wood fern, *Dryopteris marginalis*, as its name signifies, flourishes throughout the winter, and comes nearer being a "tree" fern than any other of our northern species. It requires deep shade and has a liking for rocks or stones. It grows equally well in neutral or acid soil. An excellent companion for massing under shrubs, to form an evergreen ground cover, is *D. spinulosa*, which requires more moisture than *D. marginalis*. The crowns should be placed just at the surface, about a foot apart. The Christmas-fern, *Polystichum acrostichoides*, is easily grown in dry, shady places and is indifferent to soil. *Polystichum brauni* will succeed in any rich, neutral soil. It prefers shaded locations. These last two plants require moderate watering. Set the crowns to show above the surface. Other useful ferns with a decided preference for shaded situations are Goldie's fern, and the maidenhair-spleenwort. All this group are propagated by spores or division.

Some ferns will grow in either sun or shade. Regardless of soil, exposure or moisture, the lady fern is one of our most graceful and valuable hardy plants. For the best results a little shade is desirable. It makes good undercover, a background for smaller ferns, and transplants readily. Sometimes variable in form. The hay-scented fern is a favorite wild garden subject. It has no preference as regards soil or moisture. Both are propagated by spores. One of the easiest to cult., the ostrich fern is propagated by means of underground runners, and soon forms dense growths of almost tropical luxuriance. These ferns thrive best in a mixture of swamp muck and fine loam; a portion of the crown should be left above the surface. A light mulch of leaves will give protection until they are well established.

In moist, shady places in open woods, deep ravines and river banks, grow some of our loveliest native ferns. Even though we may not have the identical landscape facilities, nearly all gardens have certain spots where we can use some of them.

The foliage of certain wildflowers much resembles that of our northeastern maidenhair, which is the most popular of all ferns. Easily cult., it prefers a rich, moist soil and well-drained location. If planted in masses, place them 8 in. apart; cover the roots lightly with leaf mold. The spleenworts are indifferent as to soil, if the roots are not covered too deeply; place them 1 ft. apart. *Dryopteris cristata* is splendid for edging walks in damp woodlands; its larger relative, *D. clintonianum*, is desirable for the fern bed. Set so the crowns are above the surface; both are indifferent to soil. All of this group may be propagated by spores or division.

For wet ground, such as lake borders, bogs and meadowland, the royal fern is the most beautiful. Like others of the *Osmunda* family, it prefers full sunlight. They will flourish in still water of 2 or 3 in., provided the crowns are above the high-water line. *Osmunda claytoniana* requires the same cult. Propagation by spores.

Dry, rocky ledges and rock gardens are always glad to welcome low-growing, hardy plants which may be used as backgrounds. The common polypody forms dense mats when set 4 in. apart. *Woodsia ilvensis* and *W. obtusa* are good covers for bare spots, easy of cult. and need little moisture. Cover the crowns partially in planting. For a dry limestone wall *Pellaea atropurpurea* is an attractive and unique plant. Propagation by the creeping rootstocks or spores.

Although southern Fla. and the tropics are blessed with a number of climbing species of the fern family, we of the North must be content with one only, *Lygodium palmatum*. Potted plants bought from dealers and set out in an acid soil of pH 4-4.5 (*see* Acid and Alkali Soils), preferably among mountain laurel and blueberry bushes, will grow and flourish. Each season give a heavy mulch of oak leaves; the bushes will protect it from a too-hot sun. *Polystichum munitum*, an evergreen species known as giant holly fern, is hardy in the Northeast.

### Greenhouse Ferns

The most commonly grown ferns in conservatory and greenhouse are found in the genera *Adiantum, Alsophila, Blechnum, Cibotium, Cyathea, Cyrtomium, Davallia, Dicksonia, Lygodium, Nephrolepis, Platycerium, Polystichum* and *Pteris*.

In general the night temperature should be a minimum of 55 degrees, with a rise of 10 to 15 degrees during the day. Extremes of heat and cold should be avoided. Standing water must never be left in the pots. Never use stable manure or fresh commercial fertilizer. Watch closely for signs of pot-binding; re-pot often. Do not use clay soil. Propagation chiefly by spores. If by division, break the crowns in small pieces and place in a pan of live sphagnum moss. Cover with glass. Keep at a temperature of 65 to 70 degrees. When the eyes develop and one or two fronds appear, pot and place in shaded house. Ventilate, but keep

---

\* Special articles on the subjects indicated by an asterisk (\*) will be found at the words so marked.

atmosphere moist and even. In a few cases where propagation is by bulbils,* as in the hardy *Cystopteris bulbifera*, separate and put directly into small pots.

Many ferns grown in the North as house and greenhouse plants are hardy in central and southern Fla. and Calif. With the slight protection of a lath-house, practically all will do well there. Tree ferns are unable to withstand more than slight frost and dislike extreme heat and drought. Whether in pots or gardens, they must have perfect drainage and sweet soil. Use potting mixture* 5; add a little charcoal. *Alsophila australis* is commonly grown under glass; *Cyathea dealbata* does well in sheltered gardens; *Cibotium schiedei* is beautiful but so slow-growing it may be used as a house plant. Wrap the trunks with moss to provide moisture. Damp down the house often; a humid atmosphere is essential.

The maidenhair ferns of this class do best under shelter. A liberal supply of water must be given during the growing season. Use potting mixture* 4 with broken pots for drainage, and add charcoal. Keep a fairly moist atmosphere of about 65 degrees and protect from full sun. *Adiantum cuneatum* and its varieties are the best known and most important of the genus and make good house plants.

The leathery texture of the foliage of the spleenworts and their ease of cult. make these species popular. Under glass they must not be exposed to strong sunlight. If kept too wet they lose color in the dormant season. Use potting mixture* 4. *Asplenium bulbiferum* is propagated by bulbils.* *A. nidus*, the bird's-nest fern, is as well suited for house cult. as for the greenhouse. Do not re-pot this species very often. After pot is well filled with roots, give occasionally a little very weak liquid manure.

A few species of blechnums are cultivated chiefly as backgrounds for orchids. They are good specimen plants. Average temperature 60 degrees. Dry atmosphere, with plenty of moisture at the roots. They are practically free from pests. While they will grow in any soil, it is better to use potting mixture* 5. Excellent for outdoor cult. in Fla.

Greenhouse ferns: Above, *Pteris cretica* (*left*) and *Cyrtomium falcatum*; below, the bird's-nest fern (*left*) and the Boston fern.

The sword-ferns are greenhouse, house and porch subjects, sometimes grown in baskets. The epiphytic species do well in conservatories. *Nephrolepis cordifolia* grows on palms; *N. exaltata*, of which the Boston fern is a variety, grows luxuriantly on the trunks of palmettos, live oaks and other moss-covered trees in Fla. All varieties of the Boston type make excellent living-room plants. Propagation by means of rooting runners.

*Platycerium* does not appear to be a fern at all. They are striking-looking plants when old and well grown. Propagation may be by suckers as well as spores. The common staghorn, *P. bifurcatum*, is an excellent conservatory plant. It may be grown on a piece of tree-fern trunk if given a little peat and moss for a foothold. Add a little bonemeal now and then and occasionally some charcoal. These plants will, in the open, endure a temperature of 30 degrees.

The claw-ferns remain fresh longer and are as attractive, when used with cut flowers, as maidenhair ferns. *Onychium japonicum* is excellent for a conservatory, and its small size makes it suitable for a centerpiece. Use potting mixture* 4.

Polypodiums are both terrestrial and epiphytic, many being hardy in Fla. and Calif. They will do well in either potting mixture* 4 or 5, as they are not particular as regards soil. Propagate by division of clumps or spores. The golden polypody is a good, hardy, house plant. This particular species grows on palms, where it self-sows by means of spores. The rootstocks adhere tightly to the trunk. It grows well in pots in patios in the Southwest. *Polypodium polypodioides*, the resurrection fern, is the most abundant of all the epiphytic ferns in Fla. Many of these are sold by the trade, as the dry, shriveled fronds expand when put in water and become as beautiful as ever. The tongue-fern (*Cyclophorus*), often called felt-fern, is much like the polypody and is often listed as such. This plant does not stand dry weather well, if grown in the open. It requires plenty of moisture in the greenhouse and does not always do well even there. However, it is worth growing because of its beautiful, variegated foliage. Otherwise cult. the same as polypody.

The cyrtomiums are half-hardy or glasshouse ferns of easy culture, thriving admirably in places where light is not abundant. For this reason forms of *Cyrtomium falcatum*, are, next to the Boston fern, the best for apartment use. A dwarf variety, *compactum*, makes a good centerpiece. Same cult. as the spleenworts.

*Pteris* is among the best of all fern types for northern greenhouse cult. They thrive in lath-houses in deep, rich soil in Fla. and Calif. Potting mixture* 4 will suit the majority, although they are not fastidious as regards soil. Some few burn easily when placed in full sunlight at midday. The crested forms are in great demand for pan and fern dishes and for table decorations, particularly *Pteris cretica* and *P. serrulata* and their varieties. *P. serrulata* grows wild in Fla. on limestone ledges and old walls in full sun. It dislikes shade and heavy rains. These ferns do well in terrariums* and in window gardens, under ordinary conditions.

The davallias are popular for hanging-basket and fern-ball use. *Davallia bullata* is hardy in Fla. and Calif. These plants are deciduous, shedding their dry leaves in winter. If grown in a basket, the rootstocks should be bound over sphagnum moss by the use of copper wire. If the fern-ball type is preferred, a good plan is to soak thoroughly before hanging, as the plants will be received in a dormant condition. Propagation is by division of the old plants and spores; keep at a temperature of 65 degrees.

The asparagus fern, commonly grown in conservatories and apartments, is not a fern. It is *Asparagus plumosus* and belongs to the lily family.

All the genera of ferns in THE GARDEN DICTIONARY will be found listed at the entries POLYPODIACEAE, CYATHEACEAE, OPHIOGLOSSACEAE, OSMUNDACEAE, and SCHIZAEACEAE. *See also* CERATOPTERIS and FERN ALLIES.

Fern lovers are welcome as members of the American Fern Society, a national organization devoted to ferns. It publishes a journal, but its officers change from time to time. It can always be reached by writing the Garden Editor, Houghton Mifflin Company, Boston, Mass. — C. H. M.

**FEROCACTUS** (fer'o-kak-tus). Horribly spiny cacti from Mexico and the southwestern U.S., comprising perhaps 30 species, of which two, and sometimes more, are cult. in the desert garden, less commonly in the greenhouse. They have a cylindric or globe-shaped, often large plant body,

---

* Special articles on the subjects indicated by an asterisk (*) will be found at the words so marked.

prominently ribbed and plentifully beset with stout or needle-like spines. Flowers not usually large, funnel-shaped, mostly borne just above a spine-cluster (for details see CACTACEAE). Fruit thick-walled and dry, the seeds black and pitted. (*Ferocactus* is from fierce and cactus, in allusion to the spines.)

For culture see CACTI.

**glaucescens.** Plant body nearly globe-shaped, 9-15 in. in diameter, bluish-green and with 11-15 prominent ribs. Spines in clusters of 7, one solitary and erect, the others spreading, all straight. Flowers nearly 1 in. long, yellow. Mex.

**wislizeni.** Biznaga. Roundish in youth, cylindric and nearly 6 ft. high in age, the prominent ribs at least 25. Spines in large clusters, several erect but most of them spreading, all long and needle-like. Flowers 2-3 in. long, yellow. Western Tex., Ariz., and Mex.

**FERRUGINEA, -us, -um** (fer-rew-ji-nee'a). Rusty.

**FERTILE.** As to flowers, bearing both stamens* and pistils* and thus able to produce seed. As to soil, see FERTILITY.

**FERTILIS, -e** (fer'till-iss). Fertile; *i.e.* having both stamens* and pistils.*

**FERTILITY.** Soil fertility is a combination of many things. Chief among them are the proper ingredients for plant growth, the right soil texture, the acidity or alkalinity of it, and the proper conditions of soil moisture.

There is no simple chemical test for fertility, because the ability to produce a satisfactory crop is a combination of all the four factors outlined above, and a fifth, the presence of soil organisms like the microscopic fungi. The best test for fertility is to grow plants, preferably under carefully controlled conditions. These should consist of corn sown in pots, thinning the seedlings to 4 in a pot. After 3 weeks measure the growth and compare with a sample pot in which potting mixture* 3 has been used. If the crop is poor, study the articles on soils, and also the following: CULTIVATION, ACID AND ALKALI SOILS. To increase the amount of plant food in the soil some sort of fertilizer or manure is indicated. See FERTILIZERS, MANURE, PLANT FOODS.

There are various chemical tests for the amount of nitrogen, phosphoric acid, and potash in soils, but they are somewhat complicated and are better left to the soil chemists at the Experiment Stations, especially those in Mass., N.J., N.Y., Mich., Ill., and Calif., all of whom have well-equipped laboratories for such tests. For the average home grower the pot culture of plants under uniform conditions provides the best ready measure of fertility.

**FERTILIZATION.** The process, in flowering plants, after pollination,* which results in the impregnation of the ovule by the sperm (male) cell. Immediately after it is placed upon a stigma,* the pollen begins a (microscopic) process of downward elongation, forming the pollen tube which carries the sperm cell. The growth of the pollen tube inside the tissue of the style,* is culminated by the impregnation of the ovule by the sperm cell. Only when this is completed is fertilization accomplished and a future seed assured. Sometimes, but loosely, this final union of male and female elements is called pollination, but the latter process is merely a preliminary to fertilization. See POLLINATION and the account of the fertilization of ferns at FERNS AND FERN GARDENING.

**FERTILIZERS.** As here, and usually understood, fertilizers include the so-called artificial, or chemically prepared, commercial fertilizers, but not manure (which see), the latter being mostly of animal origin.

A complete fertilizer should theoretically contain all the plant food that could be derived from a perfect soil. But plants use so many different chemical elements and their compounds, and so many of them are present in more than adequate amounts in all soils, that a complete fertilizer is now understood to contain the three most essential elements only — nitrogen, phosphoric acid, and potash. It is upon these three, especially nitrogen, that the fertility of most soils depends, and all commercial fertilizers contain these substances in varying ratios, depending upon the crop and the soil to which the fertilizer will be added. For the complete list of substances that make up the food of plants, see PLANT FOODS. Here we shall deal only with the three that are often deficient, and which, in varying amounts, are found in all fertilizer mixtures.

No one today needs to buy fertilizers blindly. They are forced to contain a specified amount of available nitrogen, phosphoric acid, and potash, and their claims are checked by the chemists of the Agricultural Experiment Stations. Most of the stations publish annually a list of fertilizers which shows what they claim and what was actually found in them. All seedsmen and supply houses carry standard brands with a guaranteed formula on the bag. To buy any others is to invite deception and in the old days deception was rife in the fertilizer business — some of the samples being inert or actually detrimental substances, such as borax, for instance. All high-priced, small-packaged brands, without a formula, should be purchased with caution. Even when they are of value, their cost is generally far too high.

FERTILIZER MIXTURES. The uninitiated, however, can still be misled, or can buy fertilizers wastefully, by not understanding exactly what the figures on a fertilizer bag mean. It is, for instance, a common thing to see a bag labeled 4-8-4, or 2-5-7, or 3-5-9, or almost any other combination of three numbers separated by hyphens. Throughout the U.S. such figures always mean that the first figure is the percentage of nitrogen, the second figure the percentage of phosphoric acid, and the third figure the percentage of potash, in the mixture. Represented diagrammatically, such a simple formula as 4-8-4 would thus mean:

| 4 | — | 8 | — | 4 |
|---|---|---|---|---|
| = 4% of Nitrogen | | = 8% of Phosphoric acid | | = 4% of Potash |

Throughout THE GARDEN DICTIONARY, and in horticultural literature generally, especially in Experiment Station bulletins, these symbols of fertilizer constituents are used, the significance of which is important to all gardeners. For the right kind of fertilizer often means success, while the wrong kind, if it does not spell failure, at least means a useless waste of money.

Many intelligent gardeners often ask why use commercial fertilizers at all, considering that it is only since the rise of industrial chemistry that they have been available. This is true, and if manure in sufficient quantities could be found, chemical fertilizers would not be needed. But the motor age and the passing of the horse have made animal manure available only near large cities or on stock farms, and its cost far exceeds what one pays for even the finest commercial fertilizers. But manure is still the best for the soil and is an extremely valuable plant food. See MANURE.

Before coming to specific fertilizer suggestions for different crops, it will make them more intelligible to understand the role of the chief constituents.

NITROGEN. The most valuable, most expensive, and soonest exhausted of all fertilizer constituents. Outside of the nitrogen gathered from the air by plants of the pea family, there is no other method of replacing the nitrogen which the current crop has used, except by fertilizers or manure. Of course some sort of a crop can be grown without applying nitrogen, just as wild vegetation must rely upon the nitrogen naturally in the soil. But to get the best crops, there must be a renewal of nitrogen, for this is the substance that stimulates vegetative growth (as distinguished from flowering and fruiting). Hence crops like cabbage, Brussels sprouts, kale and kohlrabi, celery, endive, Swiss chard, and asparagus thrive on a fertilizer with a high nitrogen content.

The quickest-acting and most effective source of nitrogen is nitrate of soda. It is available almost as soon as applied to the ground as it dissolves at the first rain and is immediately available thereafter. Its disadvantage is that, once applied, it is soon lost (*i.e.* absorbed by the crop) and consequently builds up little or no residue of nitrogen for later crops. But other sources of nitrogen will supply this deficiency.

One of them is bone meal. This ground-up bone dust dissolves much more slowly than nitrate of soda and is consequently of value in small gardens, as top-dressing for pots, frames, or for feeding house plants. And because of its slow

---

* Special articles on the subjects indicated by an asterisk (*) will be found at the words so marked.

action, it is safer to use than nitrate of soda, an overdose of which can easily injure or even kill a crop. *See* the Formulas below. Bone meal also contains much phosphoric acid.

Other valuable sources of nitrogen are tankage and dried blood, both prepared by-products of the slaughter houses, and, like bone meal, more useful for permanent enrichment than for quick effects. Calcium nitrate, sulphate of ammonia, and urea are also valuable sources of nitrogen.

PHOSPHORIC ACID. This, mostly supplied by rock phosphates and superphosphates, is, next to nitrogen, the most valuable of fertilizer constituents. Its especial function is the stimulation of cereal crops, but it is also absolutely necessary for most vegetable and flower crops. Many soils are deficient in phosphorus and the lack of it often slows up final crop production. Various basic slags and ground-up acid phosphates, carrying from 12-20% of phosphoric acid, are available, and still another source of it is bone meal.

POTASH. The chief use of potash is the stimulation of root crops like beets, carrots, turnips, radishes, and parsnips. But as part of the balanced ration for perfect growth, potash must be a constituent of all fertilizer mixtures. It is used chiefly in the form of muriate of potash (mostly for vegetables), sulphate of potash for potatoes, kainit for asparagus and a few other succulent vegetables, and as carbonate of potash. Wood ashes contain from 4-6% of potash.

While different plants need different amounts of these three substances, only nitrate of soda is usually applied alone, and this for the quick stimulation of leafage as outlined above. Most fertilizers contain judicious mixtures of the three, hence the common advertising of so-called "complete fertilizers." There never can be a really complete one, but long experience has shown that the following come as near being complete as one can expect.

THE COMPLETE FERTILIZER. There is available today the greatest range of fertilizer ratios. From them every fertilizer need can be met and a few of the most important mixtures and their uses are outlined below. The application of any of them would be a simple matter if *all* of their constituents were to be used by the end of the season. But there is always a residue, and what is left has an effect upon the soil that cannot be ignored by any intelligent gardener. Sulphate of ammonia (a common source of nitrogen), muriate of potash, sulphate of potash, and acid phosphate all tend to leave a soil more acid; in other words, they are acid-residue fertilizers. But nitrate of soda, carbonate of potash, and some of the commercial phosphates are inclined to leave the soil more alkaline. Repeated applications of these, in the same ratios, would have a bad effect upon the soil, even though they might have benefited successive crops. For the acid-residue fertilizers, and to some extent all fertilizers, have a tendency to exhaust the humus content of the soil. This may do more harm than no fertilizer at all. And overdoses of fertilizers may also have the same effect. The remedy, of course, is rotation of crops, an occasional season of fallow* land, and the use of different mixtures in successive years.

With these cautions the following fertilizer mixtures have been found helpful. (For the meaning of the figures *see* FERTILIZER MIXTURES, above.)

5-8-7. A widely used mixture for potatoes, for root crops, and for general purposes. Use at the rate of 2000-3000 lbs. per acre.
4-8-4. An all-round mixture, especially valuable for sweet corn and the vegetable garden. Use at the rate of 1500-2500 lbs. per acre.
4-12-4. A good general purpose mixture for lawns, flower gardens, and the kitchen garden. Use at the rate of 1500-2500 lbs. per acre.
6-6-6. A special mixture found valuable for celery. Used at the rate of 2500-3500 lbs. per acre, the results were profitable. When used at the rate of 10,000 lbs. per acre, the higher yield was more than offset by the greater cost of the fertilizer.
8-4-4. A special celery mixture applied at the rate of 8000 lbs. per acre, and found profitable.
4-2-10. A special lettuce mixture applied at the rate of 6000 lbs. per acre, and found very profitable on a sandy loam.
4-6-6. A special tomato mixture applied at the rate of 3000 lbs. per acre, a fertilized section yielding 9 times the crop of an unfertilized part of the same field.

NOTE: TO REDUCE ALL THESE ESTIMATES TO SMALLER UNITS, FIGURE THAT A PLOT 33 x 66 FT. IS EXACTLY 1/20 OF AN ACRE.

Some of the mixtures above would scarcely interest the ordinary home gardener, for they were made by specialists who had to make every fertilizer penny yield a profitable return. Two of the best all-round mixtures are ratios of 5-8-7 and 4-8-4 applied at the rate of 1500-3000 lbs. per acre, the higher figure, of course, to be used for the poorer soils.

Another important feature of fertilizers is the proper distribution of them. All commercial fertilizers contain a legally determined amount of "filler" (inert matter, usually sand), which is thoroughly mixed with the salts and helps to ensure their even distribution. But even with this filler, raw fertilizer should never be put directly at the roots, nor against germinating seed. It is better to rake or harrow in the fertilizer a day or two before planting, or else top-dress between the rows after the plants are up. For regular and even distribution the use of a fertilizer spreader is by far the best. *See* Section 1, TOOLS AND IMPLEMENTS.

In quick-acting fertilizers like nitrate of soda, the only method should be top-dressing after the crop is up. Specific directions for the use of nitrate of soda will be found at the cultural notes on each crop. Generally speaking, it should not be applied at a rate of more than 400 lbs. per acre, and half of this is usually enough. *See also* COTTONSEED MEAL.

The use of fertilizers does not offset good tillage nor will it produce crops if ordinary care is not used. Study the group of articles at SOIL, CULTIVATION, LIME, and ACID and ALKALI SOILS.

**FERULA** (fer′you-la). A genus of 60 species of Eurasian and northern African herbs of the carrot family, only **F. communis**, the giant fennel, of any garden interest. It is a stout perennial plant 8-12 ft. high, grown occasionally for its handsome foliage and large clusters of small, yellow flowers. Leaves twice- or thrice-compound,* the basal sheaths very large, the ultimate leaflets fine and thread-like. Flowers small (for details *see* UMBELLIFERAE), in umbels* which are grouped in a large, compound umbel,* the central umbel nearly stalkless, all the other umbels* in the cluster long-stalked, the latter mostly male flowers. Fruit flattened, about ½ in. long. Southern Eu. and northeastern Af. A striking plant of simple culture easily propagated by division. It flowers in the spring. (*Ferula* is perhaps from the Latin for ferule, a stick, in allusion to the tall stems.)

*FERULAEFOLIA, -us, -um* (fer-you-lee-fō′lee-a). With leaves like the giant fennel (*Ferula*).

**FESCUE GRASS.** *See* FESTUCA.

*FESTIVA, -us, -um* (fess-ty′va). Festive or gay.

**FESTUCA** (fess-too′ka). The fescue grasses comprise a genus of nearly 100, annual or perennial, usually tufted,* grasses mostly from the temperate regions, some of them found in pasture or lawn mixtures, and a few of moderate interest as ornamentals. They are generally small grasses, the leaves flat and typically grass-like, but in some with rolled or coiled leaves that thus appear very fine and thread-like. Flowering cluster usually a narrow panicle,* the spikelets generally not awned.* Stamens* 1-3. (*Festuca* is an old Latin name for some grass.)

For meadows and pastures the leading fescue grasses are the tall fescue (*F. elatior*), the sheep′s-fescue (*F. ovina*), and the red fescue (*F. rubra*).

duriuscula = *Festuca ovina duriuscula*.
elatior. Tall or meadow fescue. An upright perennial grass, the stems smooth and 2-4 ft. high. Leaves flat, grass-like, nearly 12 in. long, about ⅛ in. wide, a little rough. Flowering cluster (panicle*) 3-8 in. long, not much-branched. Eu., but commonly naturalized nearly throughout N.A., and sometimes called *F. pratensis*. Common in meadow and pasture mixtures.
glauca = *Festuca ovina glauca*.
ovina. Sheep′s-fescue. A low grass, its many stems very fine and slender, tufted,* 8-20 in. high, producing no stolons.* Leaves rolled, thread-like, not over 6 in. long. Flowering cluster (panicle*) 2-6 in. long, often 1-sided. North temperate zone, and useful in dry places. Often entering poor lawns. The var. duriuscula, the hard fescue, has stiffish leaves; var. glauca, the blue fescue, has silvery-blue foliage; var. capillata has awned* spikelets and still narrower leaves. It is a good variety for shady places. *See* LAWNS.
pratensis = *Festuca elatior*.
rubra. Red fescue. A perennial grass creeping by stolons,* the stems 8-30 in. high and reddish at the base. Leaves rolled, very narrow, somewhat finely hairy, shorter than the stems. Flowering cluster (panicle*) 2-5 in. long, green, reddish, or bluish-green. North temperate zone, and found mostly in meadows.
tenuifolia = *Festuca ovina capillata*.

**FETERITA** = *Holcus sorghum caudatus*.

**FETID.** Evil-smelling, as are some flowers of the arum family and a few other plants.

---

* Special articles on the subjects indicated by an asterisk (*) will be found at the words so marked.

**FETID HOREHOUND** = *Ballota nigra*.

**FETTER-BUSH** = *Leucothoë catesbaei* and *Xolisma lucida*.

**FEVERFEW** = *Chrysanthemum parthenium*.

**FEVER-TWIG** = *Celastrus scandens*.

**FEVERWORT.** See TRIOSTEUM and EUPATORIUM PERFOLIATUM.

*FICIFOLIA, -us, -um* (fy-si-fō′li-a). With fig-like leaves.

**FICUS** (fy′kus). A huge genus (700–800 species) of chiefly tropical trees, shrubs, or vines of the family Moraceae, one of which is the common fig, but including also many ornamentals like the banyan and the much-domesticated rubber-plant. Some of them are epiphytes* at first, some are strangling trees in the tropics, and many, like the banyan, produce numerous aerial roots, whip-like at first, but ultimately reaching the ground and becoming trunk-like in age. Nearly all have a milky juice. Leaves alternate.* Flowers and fruits (achenes*) minute, borne on the inside face of a closed, fleshy receptacle (syncarp), which is edible in the common fig, but in few others. See FIG. (*Ficus* is classical Latin for the fig.)

The ornamental figs are hardy only in zones* 8 and 9, but are popular in Calif. and Fla., where they grow in a variety of soils. Two species are widely grown as greenhouse plants, *F. pandurata* and *F. elastica*, and the latter, the household rubber-plant, is one of the most widely known tender plants grown in the U.S. While it will do best in a warm, moist greenhouse, it will stand a surprising amount of abuse. Do not over-water it during the winter, and preferably plunge* it outdoors, in the shade, during warm weather. It is easily propagated by air layering (see LAYERING). Household plants that become leggy may be shortened, and a new crop of young plants obtained by air layering the ends of the shoots. "Fruits," as used below, means the whole syncarp (see FIG).

**altissima.** A spreading tree, the aerial roots few. Leaves thick, ovalish, 4–6 in. long. Fruit about ¾ in. long. India.

**aurea.** A banyan-like tree, well suited to seashore planting in subtropical regions (zones* 8 and 9). While at first an epiphyte,* it ultimately becomes a tree up to 50 ft. high. Leaves oblongish, narrowed both ends. Fruit nearly stalkless, yellow, about ⅓ in. in diameter. Southern Fla.

**benghalensis.** Banyan. A widely spreading tree with many aerial roots that ultimately become additional trunks (one such tree in India covers nearly an acre). Leaves broadly oval, 4–8 in. long. Fruit red, about ½ in. long, borne in pairs. India.

**carica.** The common fig. An irregularly branching tree, usually not over 25 ft. high. Leaves deeply 3–5-lobed, rough above, hairy beneath. Fruit the edible fig. Mediterranean region. For cult. see FIG.

**elastica.** The common household rubber-plant, naturally a large tree, but as usually grown a pot plant. Leaves oblong-elliptic, 6–11 in. long, green and glossy. Fruit yellowish, ½ in. long. Malaya. The *var.* **variegata** has white-blotched leaves. It was once an important source of rubber. For the true rubber-tree see HEVEA.

**lyrata** = *Ficus pandurata*.

**macrophylla.** Moreton Bay fig. A large, Australian tree, very popular in Calif. It has gray bark, bulging roots and broadly oblong leaves, nearly 10 in. long and brownish underneath. Fruit stalked, purplish but white-spotted, about 1 in. in diameter.

**nitida** = *Ficus retusa*.

**pandurata.** A medium-sized tree in the wild, but usually a pot plant as cult., and much grown by florists for its large, fiddle-shaped, lasting leaves which are often 15 in. long. Fruit nearly 2 in. in diameter. White-dotted. Sometimes sold as *F. lyrata*.

**pumila.** Climbing or creeping fig. A popular greenhouse vine that grows flat against walls, except for the fruiting branches. Leaves very numerous, oval-heart-shaped, about ¾ in. long, except on the fruiting branches where 2–4 in. long. Fruit pear-shaped, yellowish, about 2 in. long. Tropical As. and Aust. A widely grown plant both in the greenhouse and outdoors in the South (see VINES). Long, but incorrectly, known as *F. repens*.

**religiosa.** Peepul; also called bo-tree. A fig sacred to many millions in India, and sometimes planted in Fla. and Calif. Leaves roundish or ovalish, 4–6 in. long, the tailed tip 2–3 in. long. Fruit purplish, about ½ in. long. India.

**repens** = *Ficus pumila*.

**retusa.** A popular Indo-Malayan tree, much planted in the warmer parts of Fla. Leaves broadly ovalish, 2–4 in. long. Fruit yellowish-red, about ¼ in. long. Sometimes offered as *F. nitida*.

*FICUS-INDICA, -us, -um* (fy-kus-in′di-ka). The Indian fig. See OPUNTIA.

**FIDDLENECK** = *Phacelia tanacetifolia*.

**FIDDLEWOOD.** See CITHAREXYLUM.

**FIELD BALM** = *Nepeta hederacea*. See also Ground Ivy in the list at WEEDS.

**FIELD BINDWEED** = *Convolvulus arvensis*. See list at WEEDS.

**FIELD CHICKWEED** = *Cerastium arvense*.

**FIELD LARKSPUR** = *Delphinium consolida*.

**FIELD MINT** = *Mentha arvensis*. See MINT.

**FIELD PEA** = *Pisum sativum arvense*. See PEA.

**FIELD SALAD** = *Valerianella locusta olitoria*.

**FIELD SCORPION GRASS** = *Myosotis arvensis*. See FORGET-ME-NOT.

**FIESTA-FLOWER** = *Nemophila aurita*.

**FIG** (*Ficus carica*). What we call the "fruit" of an ordinary fig is a syncarp (a fleshy receptacle), and without an understanding of its structure and function, fig culture is next to impossible. Upon the inside of the "fruit," which in most varieties never opens, are scores of minute male and female flowers which thus bloom and mature wholly in the dark interior. There is, however, in most varieties a tiny terminal pore or opening, which is sometimes a clear passageway and in other varieties a passageway well blocked, or apparently so blocked, by a series of minute, overlapping scales. The female flowers ultimately develop into the "seeds" so familiar in the commercial fig, but these "seeds" are actually small fruits (achenes*) which in some varieties can only develop after pollination.* This looks like an impossible process, and would be quite so were not a pollen-coated insect able to force its way through the terminal pore of the "fruit" and accomplish this. Such insects are bred for the purpose in Calif. and carry into the immature fruit a load of pollen from another kind of fig. This fertilizes the desired kind and mature fruits result from the process. This is known as caprification from the fact that the insects come pollen-laden from the caprifig, a variety otherwise useless, but grown for the fact that it produces much pollen and is a suitable temporary home for the insects that carry it.

In the notes below the varieties that will set "fruit" only by aid of caprification are marked with a dagger (†), and it is useless to grow such without providing a supply of caprifigs.

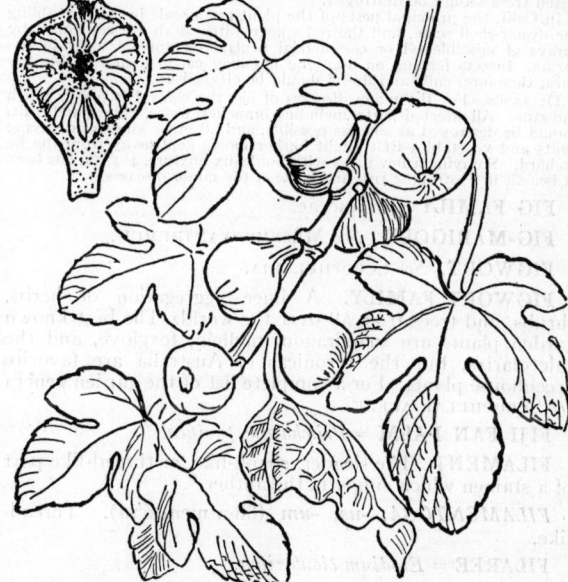

A branch of the common fig with foliage and "fruit." In the upper left-hand corner a cross-section of the receptacle ("fruit") showing the true fruits inside. See text for explanation of fruit structure and caprification.

---

* Special articles on the subjects indicated by an asterisk (*) will be found at the words so marked.

The others produce edible, but of course sterile, fruits without caprification.

The tree will stand occasional cold weather, and by pruning, the branches may be kept low enough to be bent down and covered with earth during the winter, up to the limits of zone* 7 or even farther north. But the preferred climatic localities for fig culture are southern Calif. and the Gulf Coast of Tex. where all the commercial production is centered. Soils vary from open, sandy ones in Calif. to the much heavier and blacker soils of the Tex. fig region. Summer heat and freedom from long-continued winter cold are more important than soil conditions.

VARIETIES. In Calif. the figs of the Smyrna type are represented by †Calimyrna, †Kassaba, and †Bardajie, mostly used for drying figs. Other valuable sorts are †Adriatic and †Kadota. The †Mission, sometimes called †Black Mission, is a black fig, popular only for drying. †Turkey is grown chiefly for fresh figs. One of the most popular varieties is Magnolia, the only sort grown in Tex. and usually successful without caprification. For the home orchard, Osborn's Prolific, Ronde Noire, and White Genoa are preferred, at least in Calif. The leading varieties of caprifigs, grown only as a source of pollen and a breeding place for the pollen-carrying insect, are Roeding No. 1, Milco, Roeding No. 3, and Stanford. The caprifigs are not interplanted with the regular sorts but are kept separate, and the fruits picked and carried to the vicinity of the trees to be pollinated. Usually the insects will complete their work within 24 hours. But care must be taken to see that the caprifigs are plentifully supplied with pollen before the regular kinds are exposed to the insect visitors. Sterility will otherwise be the only result of all the trouble.

Figs of a sort can, of course, be grown without the above somewhat elaborate precautions. They often are, and occasional fig trees may be found as far north as New York or Mich. They are interesting curiosities more than anything else, because successful fig production is chiefly based upon summer heat and caprification. The best method of propagation is by cuttings which root easily.

For greenhouse cult. of the fig, see Greenhouse Fruit at GREENHOUSE.

INSECT PESTS. In the Gulf states wood-boring larvae of the three-lined fig borer, a beetle nearly 1 in. long, are sometimes injurious. Broken branches should be promptly removed, and the stubs trimmed and painted with a mixture of 5 parts of coal tar to 1 of creosote; badly infested trees should be destroyed.

In Calif. the principal pests of the plant are a scale insect resembling the oyster-shell scale, and the red spider mite. Both are controlled by sprays of miscible oil or commercial neutral oil applied early in the spring. Insects feeding on decaying figs may carry disease to healthy ones; therefore, culls and drops should be cleaned up.

DISEASES. For the many diseases of figs the control is pretty much the same. All affected parts, including branches, twigs, foliage and fruit, should be destroyed as soon as possible, and all other kinds of decaying fruits and vegetables that might harbor molds kept away from the fig orchard. Spraying a few times with bordeaux mixture, 4-4-50, has been of benefit in controlling rust and some of the minor diseases.

**FIG FAMILY** = Moraceae.

**FIG-MARIGOLD.** See MESEMBRYANTHEMUM.

**FIGWORT.** See SCROPHULARIA.

**FIGWORT FAMILY.** A huge aggregation of herbs, shrubs, and trees from all over the world. The best known garden plants are snapdragon, mullein, foxglove, and the calceolarias, but the veronicas of Australia are favorite greenhouse plants. For a complete list of the garden genera see SCROPHULARIACEAE.

**FIJI FAN PALM** = Pritchardia pacifica.

**FILAMENT.** The slender, shank-like, or thread-like part of a stamen which supports the anther.*

*FILAMENTOSA, -us, -um* (fill-a-men-tō'sa). Thread-like.

**FILAREE** = Erodium cicutarium.

**FILBERT** = Corylus maxima. See HAZEL.

*FILICAULIS, -e* (fill-i-caw'lis). With thread-like stems.

*FILICIFOLIA, -us, -um* (fil-iss-i-fō'li-a). Fern-leaved.

*FILIFERA, -us, -um* (fy-liff'e-ra). Bearing threads.

*FILIFORMIS, -e* (fill-i-for'mis). Filiform; i.e. thread-like.

**FILIPENDULA** (fill-i-pen'dew-la). A genus of free-flowering herbs of the rose family, all from the north temperate zone, half of the ten species grown for ornament in the border and sometimes sold as spirea. They have alternate,* compound* leaves, the leaflets alternate, arranged feather-fashion with an odd one at the end which is sometimes lobed. Flowers numerous in large terminal clusters (panicles* or corymbs*), the individual flowers small and usually with 5 petals. Stamens* numerous. Fruit a collection of small, capsule*-like but non-splitting bodies. (*Filipendula* is from the Latin for hanging thread, in allusion to the root-tubers of some species hanging together by threads.)

All the species below are of easy culture in any ordinary garden soil and may be propagated by division of the clumps in early spring.

**camtschatica.** A stout herb 5-8 ft. high. Terminal leaflet oval or heart-shaped, more or less 3-5-lobed, the other leaflets often lacking. Flowers white. Northeastern As. Sometimes sold as *Spiraea camtschatica*.

**hexapetala.** Dropwort. A perennial herb 2-3 ft. high, the rootstocks tuberous. Leaves finely dissected and fern-like, the leaflets numerous and much cut. Flowers white. Eurasia. Sometimes offered as *Spiraea filipendula*. The var. **flore-pleno** has double flowers.

**palmata** = *Filipendula purpurea*.

**purpurea.** A perennial herb 2-4 ft. high. Terminal leaflet* large, 5-7-lobed, the other leaflets much smaller and unlobed or wanting. Flowers pinkish-purple. Jap. The var. **alba** has white flowers and the var. **elegans** has white flowers with red stamens.*

**rubra.** Queen-of-the-prairie. A stout but graceful perennial herb 4-7 ft. high. Terminal leaflet* large, 7-9-lobed, and the other leaflets also lobed. Flowers magenta-pink. Eastern U.S. The var. **venusta** has deep pink flowers.

**ulmaria.** Queen-of-the-meadow. A feathery, beautiful herb 3-5 ft. high. Terminal leaflet* 3-5-lobed, the other leaflets smaller, toothed, and white-felty beneath. Flowers white, north temperate zone, mostly in moist places. Sometimes offered as *Spiraea ulmaria*. The var. **flore-pleno** has double flowers.

*FILIPENDULINA, -us, -um* (fill-i-pen-dew-ly'na). Like the genus *Filipendula* (which see).

*FILIX-FEMINA* (fy-licks-fem'i-na). The lady fern. See ATHYRIUM.

*FILIX-MAS* (fy-licks-mas'). The male fern. See DRYOPTERIS.

**FILLER.** Inert matter (often sand) used in fertilizers to ensure an even distribution of their constituents. See FERTILIZERS.

*FIMBRIATA, -us, -um* (fim-bri-ā'ta). Fimbriate; i.e. fringed.

*FIMBRIATULA, -us, -um* (fim-bri-at'you-la). Somewhat fringed.

**FINES HERBES.** See Cooking with Herbs at HERB GARDENING.

**FINGER-FASHION.** Arranged as are the fingers on the hand; i.e. all arising from approximately the same point. The technical term is palmate (which see). See also FEATHER-FASHION and PINNATE.

**FINGER-FLOWER** = *Digitalis purpurea*. See FOXGLOVE.

**FINGER-GRASS.** See CHLORIS. See also Crab Grass in the list at WEEDS.

**FINGER-LIME** = *Microcitrus australasica*.

**FINNOCHIO** = *Foeniculum vulgare dulce*. See FENNEL.

**FIORIN** = *Agrostis palustris*.

**FIR.** Magnificent evergreen trees comprising perhaps 35 species of the genus **Abies** (ah'bee-āz) of the family Pinaceae, all from the north temperate zone, and many of them among our finest cultivated evergreens. They are generally of pyramidal habit, with whorls* of graceful branches. Leaves narrow, line-like, wholly without marginal teeth, stalkless and persistent when dry (the spruces shed their leaves when dry), flattened, but usually grooved beneath and with 2 pale whitish bands. They are often arranged as though 2-ranked, the spray of foliage hence flattened. Cones erect

---

* Special articles on the subjects indicated by an asterisk (*) will be found at the words so marked.

(hanging in the spruces), the cone-scales never prickle-tipped. (*Abies* is the classical Latin name of the fir.)

For Culture *see* below; *see also* EVERGREENS.

**A. alba.** Silver fir. A tree up to 150 ft., the bark grayish. Leaves just over 1 in. long, slightly notched at the tip. Cones reddish-brown, 3–5 in. long. Eu. Hardy from zone* 4 southward, but *see* notes below. Sometimes offered as *A. pectinata*.

**A. amabilis.** A tree up to 200 ft., with silvery-white bark. Leaves nearly 1 in. long, notched at the tip. Cones purplish, nearly 6 in. long. British Columbia to Ore. See notes below for hardiness.

**A. arizonica.** Arizona or cork fir. A tree resembling *A. lasiocarpa* and thought by some to be only a variety of it; differing in having silvery bark and leaves whiter on the under side. Ariz. and N. Mex.

**A. balsamea.** Balsam fir; the only species native in the northeastern states. It is most unsatisfactory as a cult. tree, being difficult and sometimes impossible to establish. Not over 70 ft. high, usually less. Leaves about ¾ in. long. Cones 2–2½ in. long, violet-purple. Labrador to the mountains of W. Va. west to Iowa. Our chief and best Christmas tree.

**A. cephalonica.** Greek fir. A tree up to 90 ft., the bark grayish-brown. Leaves about 1 in. long, sharp-pointed. Cones brownish, nearly 7 in. long. Greece. Hardy from zone* 4 southward.

**A. cilicica.** Cilician fir. A handsome tree up to 90 ft., the bark ashy-gray. Leaves about 1 in. long, slightly notched at the tip. Cones reddish-brown, 7–9 in. long. Asia Minor and Syria. Hardy from zone* 3 southward. One of the largest and oldest specimens in the U.S. is at Watermill, L.I.

**A. concolor.** White or Colorado fir. One of the most satisfactory of the cult. firs and widely planted (*see* below). It is a grayish-barked tree up to 125 ft. Leaves nearly 2 in. long, not notched. Cones 3–5 in. long, greenish-purple. Colo. to N. Mex. and northern Mex. There are several hort. varieties with variously colored young foliage.

**A. fraseri.** A southern representative of the common balsam fir (*A. balsamea*), and a much more satisfactory cult. tree. It differs only in technical characters from *A. balsamea*. Mountains of W. Va. to Tenn. Hardy up to zone* 3.

**A. grandis.** Giant fir. A magnificent tree up to 300 ft. high, much less as cult. Leaves nearly 2½ in. long, rounded and notched at the tip. Cones greenish, 3–4 in. long. Vancouver to northern Calif., east to Mont. Not hardy in the East (*see* below).

**A. homolepis.** Nikko fir. An extremely valuable Japanese tree, widely and deservedly planted, rarely over 75 ft. high. Leaves about 1 in. long. Cones 2–4 in. long, purplish. Hardy from zone* 3 southward. *See* below.

**A. lasiocarpa.** Rocky Mountain fir. A fine fir, up to 90 ft. high, but not suited to the eastern states. Leaves nearly 1⅓ in. long, not notched. Cones purplish, 3–4 in. long. Alaska to the Rocky Mountains. For hardiness *see* below. *See also* A. ARIZONICA.

**A. nobilis.** A magnificent fir of the forests of Wash., Ore., and northern Calif. unsuited to the East in its typical form which may reach 250 ft. The var. **glauca**, usually a semi-dwarf form, with beautiful bluish-green leaves 1–1½ in. long, is hardy in the East up to zone* 3 and is a valuable hort. fir. Cones (rarely produced in the East) 6–9 in. long, [purplish-brown.

**A. nordmanniana.** Nordmann fir. A popular and very widely planted evergreen, rarely over 125 ft. high. Leaves 1–1½ in. long, rounded and notched at the tip. Cones reddish-brown, 4–6 in. long. Asia Minor, Caucasus and Greece. Hardy from zone* 3 southward.

**A. pectinata** = *Abies alba*.

**A. veitchi.** A valuable fir, and one of the most easily cult., rarely over 70 ft., but handsome, especially when young. Leaves about 1 in. long, notched at the tip. Cones bluish-purple, 1½–2½ in. long. Jap. Hardy from zone* 2 southward.

### FIR CULTURE

The fir is one of our most valuable economic trees and, for ornamental work, leaves little to be desired. Unfortunately, it does not enjoy a wide distribution, as its dislike for smoke or dust and hot, dry climates limits its successful cultivation mostly to the Pacific Coast and Atlantic Seaboard where, even in these localities, it must be kept away from industrial centers if a healthy specimen is desired. To many the fir is looked upon as a sort of spruce and is, in fact, sometimes known by that name. Differentiation between the two is quite simple (*see* above).

The firs are without doubt the most particular of all of the conifers as regards proper conditions for good growth. Practically all members of the group are inhabitants of high altitudes and, in some instances, will not succeed on low land. *Abies lasiocarpa*, from the Rocky Mountains, is rarely a success in the East. Their great need of good air and light is clearly evidenced by the fact that most of the species in cultivation lose their lower branches and become scrawny after they reach the twoscore mark. To a large extent this condition is impossible of cure with many of the species, but it can be held off for a considerable time if the tree is given full advantage of sun and light. This does not mean undue exposure to dry winds or scorching sun, for no conifer is more sensitive to drought than the fir.

Probably the best combination for the successful cultivation of this group is a planting on a north slope with surrounding specimens of other conifers set sufficiently close to break the wind without hindering a free circulation of air or light. In like manner does the fir demand exactness in the condition of the soil. Fertility is not paramount and, while many species will grow on poor land, good drainage without dryness is an absolute necessity. Fertility will, of course, aid greatly and may be accomplished by the application of well-rotted manure spaded in about the base of the tree every few years.

For general planting in the temperate parts of this country, several species recommend themselves highly. *Abies concolor*, from the Rocky Mountains, will thrive in locations too difficult for any other species. *Abies homolepis* and *A. veitchi* from Japan are among the finest of our exotic trees and appear hardy in practically all parts of the country. *Abies nordmanniana* and *cilicica*, from the Caucasus and Asia Minor, are excellent trees for the Middle Atlantic states. The Pacific Coast species, *Abies amabilis* and *grandis*, do not thrive in the East. Unlike most of the conifers, the fir is not represented by a great number of varieties or forms, although one of our western species is best known by a semi-dwarf, bluish-leaved form which is indeed beautiful. Known as *Abies nobilis glauca*, it is the one representative of the species which thrives in the East.

Transplanting of the fir follows the usual method of most conifers. The roots must not be permitted to dry out and, hence, are moved with a ball of earth. This operation is greatly facilitated by systematic root pruning for one or two seasons previous to moving for the purpose of developing a large number of fibrous roots within a small area. Pruning the fir is seldom necessary except for the removal of dying branches near the base and the removal of secondary leaders. In some cases medium-sized specimens grow too fast and do not develop their lateral branches properly. This condition, which creates a bare, open appearance, may be easily corrected by pinching out the terminal buds on the longer branches, thus forcing lateral growth. Do not remove the buds on the main leader.

As most of the firs are represented by species, propagation from seed is most common. The seed is sown in late spring and carefully shaded during the first two years. Seedling firs are very sensitive to strong sun and must be well protected. Forms of the species are veneer-grafted in the greenhouse during Jan. and the plants set out in propagating frames in late spring. — A. D. S.

INSECT PESTS. Aphids attack and sometimes disfigure firs; a nicotine and soap spray will control them. Sawfly larvae may be killed by arsenicals. The spruce budworm, a caterpillar that gnaws the buds in the spring, may be killed by an arsenical spray applied early in the season; it is more injurious in forests than on ornamental trees.

DISEASES. Most of the difficulties encountered in growing balsam fir under artificial conditions are due to the lack of one or more of the requirements of this tree. Rust fungi cause leaf diseases and witches'-brooms on fir. Removal of the alternate hosts is the only effective control. Avoidance of wounds and prompt attention to unavoidable injuries that involve the heartwood are the most efficient methods of control of heart rot.

**FIRE-BLIGHT.** See Bacteria at PLANT DISEASES. See also Diseases at PEAR.

**FIRE-LILY** = *Xerophyllum tenax*.

**FIRE-PINK** = *Silene virginica*.

**FIRE-PLANT.** See POINSETTIA.

**FIRE-THORN.** See PYRACANTHA.

**FIREWEED** = *Epilobium angustifolium*.

**FIREWORM.** See Insect Pests at CRANBERRY.

**FIR FAMILY** = Pinaceae.

**FIRMIANA** (fir-mi-ā′na). Ornamental, Asiatic trees, comprising about 10 species of the family Sterculiaceae, **F. simplex**, the Chinese parasol tree or Phoenix-tree, being the only cult. species. It is planted for ornament from zone* 7 southward and is a round-headed tree up to 40 ft. Leaves alternate,* nearly round or heart-shaped, almost 12 in. wide, and split into 3–5 sharp-pointed lobes. Flowers small, greenish-white, usually in branched clusters (for

* Special articles on the subjects indicated by an asterisk (*) will be found at the words so marked.

structure see STERCULIACEAE). Fruit a collection of follicles,* each of which splits into a leaf-like expansion to which cling the still unripened seeds. A handsome, green-barked tree, popular in Fla. and Calif. because of its showy foliage and peculiar fruits. It is not particular as to soil. (Named for Karl Joseph von Firmian, governor of Lombardy.)

**FISH.** See MANURE.

**FISH-BLANKETS** = *Ceratophyllum demersum*.

**FISHBONE THISTLE** = *Cirsium diacantha*.

**FISH GERANIUM** = *Pelargonium hortorum*.

**FISH-GRASS** = *Cabomba caroliniana*.

**FISH-OIL SOAP.** See Contact Sprays at INSECTICIDES.

**FISH-TAIL PALM.** See CARYOTA.

**FISTULA.** See FISTULOSA.

*FISTULOSA, -us, -um* (fist-you-lō'sa). Fistulose; *i.e.* cylindrical and hollow, as is a reed or pipe (fistula).

**FITTONIA** (fit-toe'ni-a). Tropical American foliage plants of the family Acanthaceae, **F. verschaffelti**, which is probably the only species, widely grown in the greenhouse for its handsome leaves. It is a low herb with creeping, shaggy or hairy stems. Leaves opposite,* without marginal teeth, ovalish, 3–4 in. long, more or less heart-shaped at the base, dark green above, but red-veined beneath. Flowers small, yellow, not showy, in scaly spikes* (for details see ACANTHACEAE). Fruit a long-stalked capsule.* The var. **argyroneura** has white-veined leaves. These plants are of the easiest culture in a warm (60°–75°), moist greenhouse. They need plenty of water and root so easily from cuttings that the plants often become established from broken bits that root under the greenhouse bench. Use potting mixture* 3. (Named for Elizabeth and Sarah Fitton who wrote "Conversations on Botany.")

**FITZROYA** (fitz-roy'ya). A single, Chilean, evergreen tree, or as cult., usually shrubby, belonging to the pine family, and grown outdoors only from zone* 7 southward. The only species, **F. cupressoides**, the alerce, is sometimes called *F. patagonica* and is related to the arborvitae and the genus *Chamaecyparis*. It has deeply furrowed, reddish bark and small, usually overlapping leaves about ⅛ in. long, dark green above, keeled, and with 2 white lines beneath. Cones (see PINACEAE) nearly globe-shaped, about ⅓ in. in diameter, the cone-scales with a prominent but blunt projection (umbonate). Occasional specimens are found north of zone* 7, but as cult. the plant is slow-growing and inclined to be straggly. (Named for Captain R. Fitzroy of the British navy.)

**FIVE-SPOT** = *Nemophila maculata*.

*FLABELLATA, -us, -um* (fla-bel-lay'ta). Flabellate; *i.e.* having fan-like parts.

*FLABELLIFER* (fla-bell'i-fer). Fan-shaped.

*FLABELLIFORMIS, -e* (fla-bel-li-for'mis). Fan-shaped.

**FLACOURTIA** (fla-koor'ti-a). Old World tropical, often spiny shrubs or trees of the family Flacourtiaceae, comprising perhaps 15 species, only **F. indica**, a secondary fruit tree, of any garden interest. It is grown in Fla. and Calif. (zones* 8 and 9) as the ramontchi, governor's-plum, or Batoko plum, and is sometimes called *F. ramontchi*. Not over 25 ft. high and often shrubby. Leaves alternate,* ovalish or elliptic, 2–3 in. long, the teeth rounded. Flowers unisexual,* small, yellowish, without petals, and mostly in small clusters (see FLACOURTIACEAE). Fruit fleshy, nearly globe-shaped, about ¾ in. in diameter, dark red, somewhat resembling a plum. Commonly grown in Fla., but care must be taken to grow several plants together as the plant is dioecious* and solitary specimens will not fruit. Easily propagated by seeds. Native of Madagascar and southern As. (Named for Etienne de Flacourt, once a governor of Madagascar.)

**FLACOURTIACEAE** (fla-koor-ti-ā'see-ee). The Indian plum family is wholly composed of tropical shrubs and trees in about 70 genera and perhaps 500 species. Of these only *Azara, Dovyalis, Flacourtia* and *Berberidopsis* are of garden interest, chiefly because the edible kei-apple and Indian plum are derived from two of them.

Leaves (in ours) alternate.* Flowers regular,* without petals in all the garden genera, but the sepals colored like petals, or greenish in *Azara*, not showy in any of the cult. genera. Fruit fleshy and edible in *Flacourtia* and *Dovyalis*, a showy but inedible berry in *Azara*. *Azara* and *Berberidopsis* are cult. for ornament, outdoors in relatively frost-free regions. *Flacourtia* and *Dovyalis* can be grown outdoors only in zones* 8 and 9.

Technical flower characters: Flowers dioecious* in *Dovyalis*, mostly hermaphrodite* in the other genera. Sepals 4 or more, their edges overlapping. Petals none in cult. genera. Stamens many, some often sterile. Ovary superior* or essentially so, 1-celled.

*FLADNIZENSIS, -e* (flad-ni-zen'sis). From Fladungen in northwestern Bavaria.

**FLAG.** Many plants are called flag, or with various combinations, blue flag, yellow flag, etc. For those in THE GARDEN DICTIONARY see CAT-TAIL, IRIS, SCHIZOSTYLIS, ACORUS.

*FLAGELLARIS, -e* (fla-jell-ar'is). Whip-like.

*FLAGELLIFORMIS, -e* (fla-jell-i-for'mis). Whip-shaped.

**FLAGGING.** See PATHS AND PAVING. See also WILTING.

**FLAMBOYANT** = *Delonix regia*.

**FLAME AZALEA** = *Azalea calendulacea*.

**FLAME FLOWER.** See KNIPHOFIA.

**FLAME-OF-THE-WOODS** = *Ixora coccinea*.

**FLAME-TREE** = *Brachychiton acerifolium*.

**FLAME-VINE** = *Pyrostegia ignea*.

**FLAMINGO-FLOWER** = *Anthurium scherzerianum*.

*FLAMMEA, -us, -um* (flăm'ee-a). Flame-colored or flame-like.

*FLAMMULA* (flăm'you-la). A Pre-Linnaean* name for *Clematis flammula*, and some related species, and signifying a little flame. See CLEMATIS.

**FLANNEL-BUSH** = *Fremontia californica*.

**FLANNEL-LEAF** = *Verbascum thapsus*.

**FLAT.** See Section 6, TOOLS AND IMPLEMENTS.

**FLAT PALM** = *Howea forsteriana*.

**FLAT-TOPS** = *Eriogonum fasciculatum*.

*FLAVA, -us, -um* (flay'va). Yellow.

*FLAVESCENS* (flay-ves'zens). Yellowish.

*FLAVICOMA, -us, -um* (flay-vick'o-ma). Yellow-haired.

*FLAVIRAMEA, -us, -um* (flay-vi-ray'me-a). Yellow-branched.

**FLAVOR.** The distinctive flavor of most fruits is instantly identified but impossible to define. It is the result of concentration of what the botanists call cell-sap. No definite rules can be given for increasing that concentration, except the obvious one that, as fruit is maturing, the plant's water supply is best reduced. Much fruit naturally ripens towards the end of summer, and Nature takes care of this reduction of water supply by a usually diminished rainfall. It is this that makes non-irrigated fruits, picked when ripe, of such fine flavor.

In irrigated trees the reduction of water as the fruit is ripening is imperative. Again, no rule can be given because varieties and soils and sunshine vary so much. But overwatering during this ripening period may well result in mealy or watery fruit, while a reduction of water would nearly always allow the proper concentration of cell-sap and a fine flavor.

---

* Special articles on the subjects indicated by an asterisk (*) will be found at the words so marked.

**FLAVOVIRENS** (flay-vo-vy'renz). Yellowish-green.

**FLAX.** Commercially grown, common flax (*Linum usitatissimum*) is raised as a farm crop in this country chiefly for the oil expressed from the seeds (linseed or flaxseed oil). The fiber of the stem, from which linen is made, does not attain the perfection here that it does abroad; consequently, flax-growing for linen production does not amount to much in the U.S. For several other sorts of flax, grown only for ornament, *see* LINUM. For New Zealand flax, *see* PHORMIUM TENAX.

**FLAX FAMILY** = Linaceae.

**FLAX LILY** = *Phormium tenax*.

**FLEABANE.** *See* ERIGERON.

**FLEA BEETLE.** *See* Beetle at INSECT PESTS. For control *see* the Insect Pests at POTATO, SPINACH, TURNIP, PEPPER, MINT, and BLUEBERRY.

**FLEA HOPPER.** *See* Insect Pests at SMILAX.

**FLEECE-VINE** = *Polygonum auberti*.

**FLEUR DE LYS** = *Iris pseudacorus*.

*FLEXILIS, -e* (flecks'il-is). Pliant or flexible.

**FLEX-NEK.** A patented nozzle holder which converts an ordinary hose nozzle into a practical lawn sprinkler.

*FLEXUOSA, -us, -um* (flecks-you-ō'sa). Flexuose; *i.e.* more or less tortuous or zigzag; usually applied to stems.

**FLINT CORN** = *Zea mays indurata*. *See* CORN.

**FLOATING ARUM** = *Orontium aquaticum*.

**FLOATING FERN.** *See* CERATOPTERIS.

**FLOATING HEART** = *Nymphoides lacunosum*.

*FLOCCOSA, -us, -um* (flock-kō'sa). Woolly.

**FLOPPERS** = *Bryophyllum pinnatum*.

**FLORAL EMBLEMS.** *See* STATE FLOWERS; also NATIONAL FLOWERS.

**FLORAL FIRE-CRACKER** = *Brevoortia ida-maia*.

**FLORAL HISTORY.** *See* EVOLUTION OF FLOWERS.

**FLORA'S-PAINTBRUSH** = *Emilia sagittata*.

**FLORENCE FENNEL** = *Foeniculum vulgare dulce*. *See* FENNEL.

*FLORE-PLENO* (floor-re-plee'no). Double-flowered; often abbreviated Fl. Pl.

**FLORET.** One of the individual, and usually small flowers, that comprise the flower head* in plants of the Compositae (which see). Also, but less correctly, any small flower in a dense cluster of them.

*FLORIBUNDA, -us, -um* (floor-i-bun'da). Blooming freely; floriferous.

**FLORICULTURE.** Strictly speaking, the raising of flowers, as distinguished from general horticulture (which see). By extension, and now quite generally, *floriculture* has come to mean any branch of horticulture that has to do with plants grown chiefly for ornament, whether trees, shrubs, or herbs. In this broad sense floriculture is synonymous with ornamental horticulture.

*FLORIDA, -us, -um* (flŏ'ri-da). Freely flowering.

**FLORIDA.** The state lies wholly in zones,* 7, 8, and 9.
SOILS. Surface soils are mostly sandy, having been derived from unconsolidated marine sands. Some small areas are of limestone origin, while others have developed as organic soils in lakes and marshes. The Norfolk soils, comprising the most extensive uplands, and closely related series, together with the various hammock lands, are adapted to a wide range of truck, fruit and farm crops. Most of the grassy flatwoods and marl areas, when drained, are good truck and farm lands. The organic soils, of which the Everglades of approximately 5,000,000 acres is the largest uniform body, consist of peat and muck and usually are quite fertile when drained. Swamps, savannahs and river flood plains are rarely cropped.

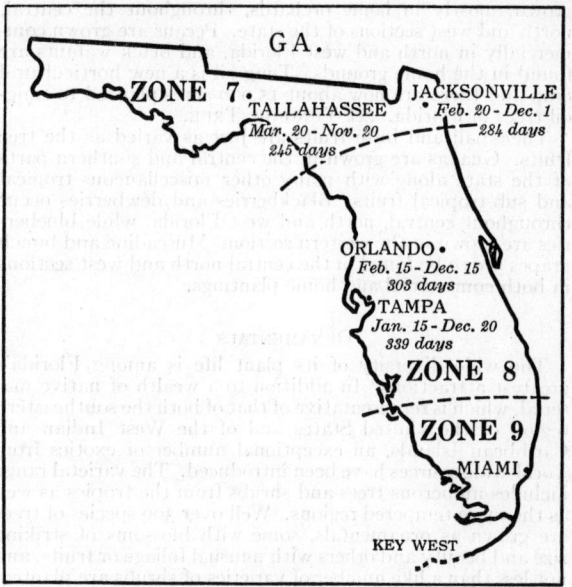

FLORIDA
The zones of hardiness crossing Florida are those shown on the colored map at ZONE, which should be consulted for details. The dates are the average latest killing frost in spring and the first one in the fall. The figures below the dates show the average length of the growing season. From the northern edge of zone 9 southward killing frosts are rare (but liable in half the years), except at and near Key West where a killing frost has never been recorded.

The production centers for vegetables are localized in such places as are particularly adapted for the production of particular crops. Thus, Hastings is the center of an area in which potatoes are produced; Sanford of a region in which celery is the principal crop, although lettuce, endive and peppers are also shipped in considerable quantities; Sarasota, on the west coast, is another important celery-production center. Manatee County, also on the west coast, produces a number of vegetable crops, the most important being tomatoes, lettuce, peppers and celery. Alachua County is the center of an area shipping watermelons, spring cucumbers, beans, cabbage and potatoes. Marion County, located directly south of Alachua, each year ships approximately 3000 carloads of watermelons, tomatoes, green beans, lettuce and cabbage. Plant City, in Hillsborough County, is the strawberry center of Florida, the Starke–Lawtey area producing in lesser quantity. Approximately 1000 carloads are shipped yearly from Plant City and adjoining stations. Tomatoes, peppers and green beans are also raised in this area. Leesburg, in Lake County, is the center of the earliest watermelon-producing area within the United States.

In the southernmost part of the state there are three important regions. The coastal areas of Palm Beach, Broward, and other adjoining counties produce large quantities of tomatoes, peppers, green beans and eggplants. The production region known as the Everglades is situated on the southeastern shores of Lake Okeechobee. Green beans have been the most important crop in this area. Large quantities of green peas, tomatoes, potatoes and cabbage also are grown. In coastal glades of Dade County potatoes and tomatoes are the principal crops, with an increasing amount of miscel-

---
* Special articles on the subjects indicated by an asterisk (*) will be found at the words so marked.

laneous crops, as rhubarb, Chinese cabbage, broccoli and cauliflower, being produced.

The tree crops of Florida are varied and include tropical, sub-tropical and temperate-zone types. Citrus predominates, with an annual production of 16,000,000 boxes of oranges and tangerines and 12,000,000 boxes of grapefruit. In the extreme south and other well-protected areas, limes, avocados, mangos and many other tropical fruits occur, while persimmons, figs, peaches and blight-resistant pears are grown, mostly in home orchards, throughout the central, north and west sections of the state. Pecans are grown commercially in north and west Florida, and black walnuts are found in the home grounds. Tung-oil is a new horticultural crop and there are now about 15,000 acres planted to tung-oil trees in Florida. See TUNG-OIL TREE.

The small and bush fruits are just as varied as the tree fruits. Guavas are grown in the central and southern parts of the state along with many other miscellaneous tropical and sub-tropical fruits. Blackberries and dewberries occur throughout central, north and west Florida, while blueberries are grown in the western section. Muscadine and bunch grapes are to be found in the central north and west sections in both commercial and home plantings.

ORNAMENTALS

The wide diversity of its plant life is among Florida's greatest attractions. In addition to a wealth of native material, which is representative of that of both the southeastern region of the United States and of the West Indian and Caribbean Islands, an exceptional number of exotics from world-wide sources have been introduced. The varietal range includes numerous trees and shrubs from the tropics as well as the more tempered regions. Well over 300 species of trees are grown as ornamentals, some with blossoms of striking size and beauty and others with unusual foliage or fruits, and not less than a like number of varieties of shrubs are planted. Of these, comparatively few are deciduous, and conifers are sparingly used. Most of the common herbaceous garden annuals and perennials are grown, many of the former flowering during the winter and spring months.

The palms, of which there are 12 native and many introduced species, with bamboos and numerous other tropical trees and plants, many of the last with varicolored foliage or an abundance of gorgeous bloom, combine to give Florida gardens, and especially in the southern areas, a true atmosphere of the tropics. See PALM, BAMBOO. See also SUB-TROPICAL GARDEN for a list of the plants most suited to the state.

CLIMATE. The geographical location of Florida favors long summers and moderate winters. The Gulf of Mexico and the Atlantic Ocean have a tempering effect on the summer as well as winter temperatures. The many lakes within the state tend to modify the local temperature and frequently prevent the occurrence of frost or freeze damage. Average seasonal temperatures for the state are: Summer, 80.8; Autumn, 72.5; Winter, 59.8; and Spring, 70.4.

The normal annual rainfall for the state is 52.35 inches, seasonally divided as follows: Spring, 3.12 inches; Summer, 6.94 inches; Autumn, 4.39 inches; Winter, 3.00 inches a month. One-half of the rainfall occurs from June to September. While Florida is so situated as to justify the expectation of sufficient rainfall the state is not immune from drought. Many of the horticultural crops are produced during the dry period of the year. Thus the artesian water supply available in the state south of Tampa and Orlando and the east coast south of Jacksonville is often used for irrigation purposes. Many lakes in the state are also used as a source for irrigation waters. See IRRIGATION.

The principal horticultural crops are produced during the fall, winter and spring months. Therefore, the occurrence of frost and freezes is of vital importance. The southern half of the state is normally free from serious freezes, although the mainland areas of the state have been subjected to occasional freezing temperatures. The significant frost dates for various localities are:

| Town | Average date of last killing frost | Latest known killing frost | Average date of earliest killing frost in fall | Earliest known killing frost |
|---|---|---|---|---|
| Tallahassee | Mar. 20 | April 10 | Nov. 20 | Nov. 10 |
| Jacksonville | Feb. 20 | April.10 | Dec. 1 | Nov. 17 |
| Orlando | Feb. 15 | March 23 | Dec. 15 | Nov. 10 |
| Tampa | Jan. 15 | Feb. 6 | Dec. 20 | Nov. 21 |
| Miami† | † | Mar. 9 | † | Nov. 21 |

† Frost occurs infrequently at this locality, the greater part of the year being entirely free from frost.

The address of the Agricultural Experiment Station, which has kindly supplied this information about the state, is Gainesville, Florida. The station is always ready to answer gardening questions.

Garden Club activities include clubs of the Garden Club of America, the home office of which is 598 Madison Avenue, New York. There are also over 40 clubs affiliated with the Florida Federation of Garden Clubs. For the one nearest your locality write the Garden Editor, Houghton Mifflin Company, Boston, Mass.

**FLORIDA CAT'S-CLAW** = *Pithecolobium unguis-cati.*

*FLORIDANA, -us, -um* (flo-ri-day'na). From Florida.

**FLORIDA VELVET BEAN** = *Stizolobium deeringianum.*

**FLORIFEROUS.** Bearing many, or a few large, flowers.

**FLORIPONDIO** = *Datura suaveolens.*

**FLORIST.** One who sells, and sometimes grows, cut flowers and potted plants. While the florist business aggregates many millions of dollars annually, such a purely commercial aspect of floriculture lies outside the scope of this book. The chief flowers offered by florists can, however, be raised by anyone willing to take the trouble. The cultural articles at camellia, carnation, sweet pea, rose, chrysanthemum, *Lilium*, *Viola*, buttercup, orchid, and ferns and fern gardening will be found useful. See also FREESIA, FUCHSIA, GARDENIA, and SNAPDRAGON. Some plants that florists offer are sold under names that are often confusing. See the next few entries.

**FLORISTS' CHRYSANTHEMUM** = *Chrysanthemum morifolium.*

**FLORISTS' GENISTA** = *Cytisus canariensis.* See BROOM.

**FLORISTS' GERANIUM** = *Pelargonium.*

**FLORISTS' SMILAX** = *Asparagus asparagoides.* See SMILAX (2), for cult.

**FLORISTS' SPIREA.** See ASTILBE, FILIPENDULA, ARUNCUS.

**FLORISTS' VIOLET** = *Viola odorata.*

*FLOS-CUCULI* (floss-kew'kew-li). Cuckoo flower. See LYCHNIS.

*FLOS-JOVIS* (floss-joe'vis). Flower of Jove. See LYCHNIS.

*FLOS-REGINAE* (floss-re-jy'nee). The queen's flower.

**FLOSS-SILK TREE** = *Chorisia speciosa.*

**FLOURINE.** See Stomach Poisons at INSECTICIDES.

**FLOWER.** An absolutely essential organ in all seed plants, usually brightly colored, often very beautiful. While it caters to man's conceit to assume that flowers were created for his enjoyment, their true function is far more important. Without them most vegetation would perish in a generation or two, for flowers contain within them the mechanism of perpetuation. No one who raises them for pleasure should, and absolutely no plant breeder can, ignore the fact that flowers are the seat of sexual activity in all flowering plants. See PLANT BREEDING. And this necessary reproductive

* Special articles on the subjects indicated by an asterisk (*) will be found at the words so marked.

# Flower

function is usually enclosed within one, or generally two, series of outer coverings, the calyx and corolla.

In a complete* flower the outermost, usually greenish, series of organs are the sepals (collectively called the calyx) and it is these that often cover the unopened flower bud. Inside them is the second series of floral envelopes, the petals (collectively called the corolla). It is these that usually give color to a flower, and sometimes the petals are separate, as in a rose or buttercup, or they are united and tubular or bell-shaped or even 2-lipped and irregular.* Many flowers have no petals, as in some ash trees, and in some the lack of petals is made up by the sepals being colored and petal-like, as in the common hepatica. See APETALOUS.

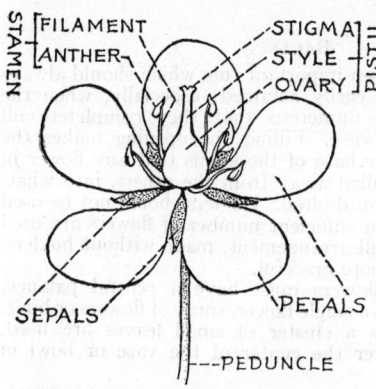

Diagram of a perfect and complete flower

But within the calyx and corolla are the really essential organs (which see) of a flower. These consist of the male and female organs of reproduction. The female is usually in the center and consists in the typical case of a swollen base, the ovary,* within which are the ovules,* a shank-like style,* and a club-shaped, forked or swollen tip, the stigma.* Around the style and stigma, and hence next to, or often inserted on the petals, are the male organs of reproduction — the stamens.* A typical stamen consists of a threadlike or club-shaped shank, the filament,* and a terminal organ of various shapes, the anther,* within which the male fertilizing element, the pollen,* is produced. It is the union of this, usually yellow, dust-like pollen and the ovule that ensures the production of seed. See POLLINATION, FERTILIZATION. Some flowers bear only stamens or only pistils (see PERFECT, UNISEXUAL, MONOECIOUS) and in a few plants the sexes are on different individuals (see DIOECIOUS).

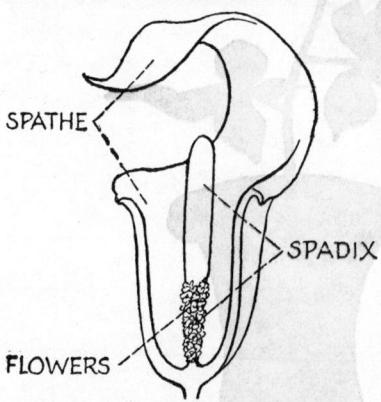

The flowering apparatus in the Jack-in-the-pulpit, a type of flower cluster found in the arum family. For details see ARACEAE.

It is obviously impossible to mention even part of the common garden flowers in this brief account of the true function and structure of them. Those wishing such lists should turn to the articles on annuals, biennials, perennials, border, bedding, and cut flowers, and the various entries cross-referenced from them.

For those plants that bear no flowers or seeds, in the garden sense of these terms, see FERNS AND FERN GARDENING, and FERN ALLIES.

**FLOWER ARRANGING.** Short is the bridge connecting gardening and flower arranging. With the increasing interest in gardens and flower shows comes a natural desire for definite aid in arranging the blossoms so long and patiently waited for. In spite of good taste in color combinations and choice of flower containers, the majority of real flower lovers feel keenly that the beauty of arranging cut flowers has yet to be attained. The fortunate, who can choose from a wealth of material from their own gardens, those who pick sparingly from tiny gardens, and we who deny ourselves in order to buy a few flowers, feel alike the lack of beauty in

Spring arrangement of white and lavender lilacs, daffodils, Poet's narcissus, and purple tulips in a gray porcelain vase

most flower arrangements. In few instances is the beauty of the flower enhanced by the manner in which it is placed in the vase. A truly good grouping of flowers should convey something of the personality of the arranger as well as enhancing the natural charm of the flowers.

With adherence to a few practical rules, accompanied by a knowledge of the nature of the growth of flowers, and a desire to make them appear natural, we should be able to work out endless variety in flower arranging. Flower arranging in one's own home gives greater freedom than an exhibit in a flower show. But even in the home, the result is better when some thought is given to the arrangement. In the home it is necessary to consider in which room you wish flowers, and where they are to be placed. Next select a vase, and then go to the garden and get the best possible flowers for that especial place and vase. This method will be found more satisfactory than first running to the garden and gathering whatever pleases your fancy, without any thought of the receptacle to be used or where the arranged flowers are to be placed when completed. This applies equally well to flowers bought from a florist.

BOUQUET. It is impossible to write of flower arrangement without mention of the quaint little bouquet (*bosquet, boschetto*), a small bunch of flowers or leaves — a nosegay with its dainty lace paper frill holding the rather stiff bunch in place, and covering the stems to protect "my lady's" hands. All nations have been charmed by this delightful grouping of small flowers of various varieties together. The plan is always the same, a central flower considerably larger than the others in the group, and surrounded by circle after circle of flowers of different varieties. Italy and France have woven

---

* Special articles on the subjects indicated by an asterisk (*) will be found at the words so marked.

# Flower Arranging

many interesting customs about it. "Mettre le bouquet" is still used figuratively at having finished a task or any rather difficult work. An old English word for a nosegay is tussie-mussie. In Colonial days, the ladies were given to wearing these gay little bouquets on their corsage, the carefully wrapped stems protecting their delicate gowns. Oliver Wendell Holmes once said, "I'm a florist in verse, and what would people say, if I went to a banquet without a bouquet!"

Typical bouquet arrangement

RULES. A few rules would be found useful to many. Why, then, should we hesitate in going to the only source where definite rules have been found and used successfully for centuries — Japan? Japan offers these rules not to be followed with precision, but to create in each person who has thoroughly acquired them a flexibility and individuality blended with creative charm — not a repeating of some pleasing arrangement done by another person. So the following few rules are given.

The value of foliage without flowers; — the leaves of narcissus or other bulbous plants

## NATURE

Nature will be found the finest of all guides. He who follows nature closest will be most liberally rewarded. For variety of line and beauty of form will be apparent in the result of all who reflect nature's perfect plan in their flower arranging. Look for the outline of a growing plant, for the form of a group to be made indoors, as well as the forms of flowers and lines of the stems. If this has not been your habit, you will be surprised and rewarded by the variety of new forms nature will suggest for your indoor flower groups. Nature brings first the foliage; therefore, in making an arrangement try always to have more leaves than flowers and put the leaves first into the vase. Next place the blossoms among the leaves in as natural a way as possible. The result will be that your group of flowers will look like a growing plant. It will give to you and all who see it keener pleasure, for it expresses a living group. Look at the lines of your flower stems, and, where you find a curve of stem or an unusual form of flower which takes your fancy, place it so that the foliage or a space left about it leaves it clean-cut and striking. The following of nature's suggestions adds strength and character as well as beauty to any arrangement of flowers.

## BALANCE

Balance, although an important rule which should always be kept in mind, is easily attained; especially, when the flowers used are so numerous that they completely fill the opening in the vase. Filling the opening makes the flowers so firm at the base of the stems that any flower in the group can be pulled away from the others, into whatever height or position desired. Holders should not be used in high vases where a sufficient number of flowers are used to fill the vase. A full arrangement, made without holders, is much softer and more graceful.

Every group of flowers must have a central balance. By this we mean that a single flower, spray of flowers or buds, or in some instances a cluster of small leaves are used, must be directly over the center of the vase or bowl in

A single rose flower in perfect balance

which the flowers are placed. This is essential to all arrangements of flowers. The position of the other flowers in the group is not vital to a good composition. The placing of all the other flowers in the arrangement may be left to the taste of the individual, guided by the form or peculiar growth of the flowers which will suggest to the arranger where each flower should be placed in the group. It is,

---

* Special articles on the subjects indicated by an asterisk (*) will be found at the words so marked.

however, impossible to make an attractive arrangement of flowers without a central balance.

It is not wise in arranging many flowers to start by putting the central flower, which is to be the pivot or balance of the arrangement, first in the vase. Place the flowers in the vase, one at a time, allowing each flower to fall, as it naturally will, towards the rim of the vase. The next flowers placed in the vase will bring the flowers first placed into a more nearly upright position. Working from the outside edge of the group towards the center, there will be left finally a small opening in the center for your balance flower. You can then bring it into any position you desire; for now, supported by all the other flowers, it will stand upright and not fall out of balance as it would have done had it been placed first in an empty vase without the support of the rest of the flowers. A few flowers loosened at the sides and a pulling out of a few towards the front and your composition is complete, balanced, and yet graceful. This method will bring about a better result than by using flower holders in tall vases. It will also do away with a too uniform balance of the whole group. An equal balance of the sides of the arrangement should always be avoided.

### Color

We need to be more daring in color combinations. The value of contrasts is the color of flowers used in the same arrangement, as well as a contrast between the vase and the flowers placed in it. Such color contrasts are more difficult and must be placed with utmost care. We can never go wrong with a harmony of flowers and vase. But there are places in every interior where a more striking arrangement will bring out a dark corner to advantage. For instance, a group of delphinium in the various shades of blue, arranged in a vase of soft gray or brown colored pottery, would be harmonious and exquisite, properly placed. But it fails in bringing the brightness of sunshine given by a different variety of flowers and color introduced. Place the same delphinium in a black vase and a few sprays of flame-colored gladiolus, here and there; it will key up such an arrangement like a high note in music. Never be afraid of combining a number of different varieties of flowers together. Adding another variety of flowers has the same effect in bringing out the beauty of the flowers already in the vase as the adding of foliage to any group of flowers.

### Form

The form or outline of any arrangement of flowers has a great influence on the result of all grouped flowers. A form which is too regular or symmetrical is not pleasing, as it falls at once into merely a decoration of color and mass, and the natural grace of the flowers is wasted. With the variety of an irregular form is given an opportunity of showing the natural lines of the flowers used. It is always best to avoid an overcrowding of too many flowers in one vase, which ruins the form of any group of flowers and produces only a hard mass of color without character or grace.

The natural lines of stems and forms of flowers are very beautiful, and always give suggestions of form more lovely than anything which the arranger's own mind could create. The thickest mass of flowers or foliage should always occupy the center of the arrangement, which should taper off toward the top and the bottom of the group, with a fuller effect at the base than at the summit. This results in bringing all arrangements into a triangle. If one flower insists upon falling out a trifle more on one side than the other, it will add to the appearance of the arrangement and should not be disturbed, provided the central balance is kept.

### Height

The height of the longest or central stem should be at least once and one half the height of the vase. This length is taken from the surface of the water in the vase to the tip of the flower, exclusive of the stem in the vase beneath the water. The height of the other flowers is left to the taste of the arranger, guided, as much as possible, by the natural growth of stems and forms of flowers. The buds of flowers should always have a higher position in the group than the partially open or full-blown flowers, only changing this rule when nature sees fit to place a bud on a short stem.

The highest spray in all arrangements should be formed by a bud, collection of buds, or a cluster of very small leaves. This gives a tapering and more graceful appearance than a full-blown flower at the extreme top of the group. From this, the central height of the arrangement, the flowers should come down to the surface of the water in the vase, by irregular heights of stems, but not in even steps. After having shortened a number of stems, begin to lengthen also some others. In shortening or lengthening of stems in an arrangement, shorten or make longer several flowers at a time, making each flower of these small groups a different height. Thus, by uneven lengthening and shortening, is brought about a less stiff and better arrangement.

A suggestion for a table arrangement with a fern and rock

### Holders

Holders are so numerous that it is a problem to select which of the many varieties is most useful. Flower holders are so generally used that every individual flower arranger has found, by now, those best for their particular needs. Therefore, it may prove of greater assistance to suggest when not to use holders. Any of the lead, glass, or bronze holders about two inches in height should never be placed in a tall flower container. If a support is necessary to hold flowers upright in a tall vase, a very fine-woven wire holder, fitting over the mouth of the vase, is excellent for that use.

Flower arrangements made in the low bowls with wide openings must have a holder in order to bring the flowers of any height into an upright position. The low, wide flower containers, with the surface of the water exposed and not hidden entirely by the flowers placed in them, make very attractive arrangements to be used for table decoration. A few iris or narcissus leaves, when no blossoms are to be had, will give a charming effect. Try, also, a group of ferns arranged about a stone of good form and color.

### Flower Combinations

The following combinations will make attractive arrangements, and are available to all gardeners.

WHITE AND LAVENDER LILACS, daffodils, narcissus, pink and purple tulips make a happy combination of spring flowers.

FRUIT BLOSSOMS. Nothing makes a more lovely arrangement, getting them in tight buds, so that the pleasure of watching the blossoms come to full bloom may be enjoyed indoors.

---

* Special articles on the subjects indicated by an asterisk (*) will be found at the words so marked.

*A Japanese arrangement of a pine representing an anchored boat*

PANSIES of brown, yellow, white, deep purple, and lavender, with a few white cyclamens for height and balance. This makes a beautiful low arrangement in pewter or glass.

WILD FLOWERS make exquisite groups — common cat-tail for height and balance, black-eyed susans and Queen Anne's lace combined in a tall vase, preferably of copper, will prove most pleasing.

BEGONIA which may be had all winter, with its strong, well-formed foliage, makes not only an arrangement of charm but lasts longer than most cut flowers. This appears at its best in any kind of metal vase.

PELARGONIUMS or pink Martha Washington geraniums arranged with the buds and flowers of pale shades of yellow scabiosas with a few sprays of tall heliotrope. The arrangement should have an abundance of geranium foliage at the base. The scabiosas are the highest of the group, which will be very charming in a soft gray or brown porcelain vase.

In summing up the essential points of a flower arrangement of merit, the arranger need not be overburdened by rules. With a knowledge of the natural form of the flowers or branches used, a perfect central balance is always kept. The colors of the flowers well thought out, in accord with the vase, will aid in an harmonious arrangement. If an arrangement of contrasts, they must not be too strikingly different for one flower to overshadow another. The form of an arrangement must always make irregular, lovely lines. The heights of the stems must show a pleasing variety. The arrangement when completed should suggest life, and therefore bring refreshment wherever placed. This requires more than a beautiful vase and exquisite flowers. We have all suffered from the ruin of good material by poor arranging. Yet, what might seem undesirable material, properly arranged, can be made most attractive. For the details of keeping flowers fresh, *see* CUT FLOWERS. — M. A.

**FLOWER BED.** *See* BEDDING. For the number of plants needed for beds of different shapes, *see* GARDEN TABLES IV.

**FLOWER BORDER.** *See* BORDER.

**FLOWER BOX.** *See* WINDOW GARDENING.

**FLOWER BUD.** *See* BUDS.

**FLOWER COLOR.** *See* COLOR.

**FLOWER EVOLUTION.** *See* EVOLUTION OF FLOWERS.

**FLOWER FENCE** = *Adenanthera pavonina*.

**FLOWER GARDEN.** To the average American this term connotes a collection of perennials or annuals, or both, arranged in beds. For several reasons, practical and esthetic, these beds tend to be of formal pattern. The plants are easier to care for if assembled into clearly defined beds. If assembled, their collective effect becomes greater and may be made continuous, from early spring until late fall. And if the shape of the beds is good, it may be emphasized by a border of box or other plants, so that it remains a decorative feature throughout the year, excepting when covered with snow.

The most common and useful layout of a flower garden is rectangular, which continues or repeats the lines of the house. Patterns of beds should be simple. It might seem that flower gardens of few and simple beds would soon get monotonous by repetition of similar or near-similar patterns, but this is not the case. There is no more reason for monotony in two rectangular gardens than in two rectangular rooms. There may be a central or terminal feature, a fountain or figure. The garden may be enclosed by a hedge, wall or fence with vines with or without a border planting of shrubs or flowers.

Border and accent* plants may be evergreen or deciduous or both. Size, proportions of beds and intervening spaces, character of setting, by which is meant the building and planting along the boundaries, construction of paths, garden furniture and the planting in the beds themselves, may and do vary endlessly. The way to get something different and individual in a garden layout is not to use eccentric shapes, but to make something growing, as it were, out of the surroundings.

It is far better to concentrate the flowers (perennials and annuals) into one place than to scatter a few here and a few there. Isolated beds in the lawn generally look as if they had been dropped casually to be left till called for, and if put in the borders of the shrubbery, leave bare spaces before and after they develop.

---

* Special articles on the subjects indicated by an asterisk (*) will be found at the words so marked.

This does not mean that annuals and perennials cannot be used informally, or that there cannot be a good informal flower garden. When successful, informal flower gardens are usually made on rolling or irregularly shaped sites, and there are many situations where it would be better to make an informal flower garden than to level off the surface for the reception of a formal pattern. For a formal pattern should be laid down on a flat surface or it loses its formal character and becomes neither formal nor informal, but merely shapeless.

In an informal flower garden the flowers are usually better for a background of foliage, and a mass planting of shrubs and trees should, generally speaking, follow, rather than cross, the contours of the ground, *i.e.* lines of shrubs on a convex surface should convex, on a concave surface concave. Flowers suited to the situation may be set effectively in the recesses of such plantations. The successful design and maintenance of an informal flower garden requires especial judgment and knowledge of plant material, one reason being that lines are less definite than in a formal garden and more dependent on the plant material itself.

A common error in flower planting is to scatter them around and about the shrubbery with long bandages of tulips, narcissus, and annuals along the edges. This kind of thing soon cheapens the flowers and makes them tiresome by repetition. It also greatly increases the upkeep. But flowers concentrated in a relatively small area gain by contrast with the other, less vivid, parts of the grounds.

A tantalizing characteristic of a perennial garden is the short duration of bloom of most of the plants: but this is also part of its charm, for before one kind of flower has had time to become stale it disappears only to be followed by others. If the garden is well planned, there is something new almost every day. In midsummer there is apt to be a period of scarcity of flowering perennials, and the empty spaces may be filled with bedding plants such as ageratum, cockscomb, heliotrope, geraniums, salvia. The use of these is highly debatable, and each must decide whether their use in the flower garden is to be tolerated or not.

Some of the colors are hard to reconcile with other colors: but, if care be taken to keep reds, orange and pinks apart, there are likely to be few clashes of hues in the beds that the sunlight and a little distance will not harmonize. In considering the effect of a flower garden one should not concentrate on local color combinations, but on the impression produced by the whole. Better, for the most part, are annuals, the most popular of which seem to be zinnias, marigolds and salpiglossis, although these are the least easy to reconcile with their perennial neighbors. *Phlox drummondi*, petunias, hunnemannia, snapdragons, centaurea, alyssum, annual larkspurs, shirley poppies, stocks and asters are much more sympathetic.

It is not possible to give precise directions as to the arrangement of plants in a flower garden. The large masses of one kind, advocated by many, are striking in themselves and may be used in informal plantings with shrub backgrounds effectively, but in formal beds they tend to cut the beds into visual sections and thus concentrate on themselves the attention that should be given to the garden. When their flowering season is over, they leave large, unsightly, blank spaces.

Groups of plants should vary with the size and shape of the beds. Thus, in a long border, the groups would tend to be long and narrow: in a square or round bed they would not differ much in length and width. When using a large number of plants of one kind in a formal bed it is better to distribute them up and down the bed in groups of different sizes so that the eye may be carried from one to the other. Taller plants may be brought near the edge of the beds at irregular intervals forming bays containing lower plants. Varieties should be distributed through a bed so that, as far as may be, there is something in bloom in different parts of the bed throughout the season. For the details of what to plant, *see* COLOR GARDENING, ANNUALS, BIENNIALS, PERENNIALS, and BULBS. — H. A. C.

**FLOWER GATHERING.** *See* CUT FLOWERS.

**FLOWERING ALMOND.** *See* PRUNUS GLANDULOSA, P. NANA and P. TRILOBA. *See also* AMYGDALUS COMMUNIS.

**FLOWERING ASH** = *Fraxinus ornus*. *See* ASH.

**FLOWERING BEAN** = *Phaseolus coccineus*.

**FLOWERING CHERRY** = *Prunus lannesiana*, *P. serrulata*, and *P. yedoensis*.

**FLOWERING CURRANT** = *Ribes aureum* and *R. sanguineum*.

**FLOWERING DOGWOOD** = *Cornus florida*.

**FLOWERING FLAX** = *Linum grandiflorum*.

**FLOWERING MAPLE.** *See* ABUTILON.

**FLOWERING MOSS** = *Phlox subulata*, *Sedum pulchellum*, and *Pyxidanthera barbulata*.

**FLOWERING PEACH.** *See* AMYGDALUS PERSICA.

**FLOWERING QUINCE.** *See* CHAENOMELES.

**FLOWERING RASPBERRY** = *Rubus odoratus* and *R. deliciosus*.

**FLOWERING RUSH** = *Butomus umbellatus*.

**FLOWERING RUSH FAMILY** = Butomaceae.

**FLOWERING SHRUBS.** All shrubs must, of course, bear flowers of some sort, but many of them have small or inconspicuous ones and are hence grown mostly for foliage or fruits. But some genera are noteworthy for the beauty of their flowers. Among the best flowering shrubs, all of which are the subjects of special articles, are (the predominantly tender ones, in the East, are marked with a dagger [†]):

| | | |
|---|---|---|
| †Abelia | Daphne | Lilac |
| †Acacia | Deutzia | Lonicera |
| Azalea | Diervilla | Magnolia |
| †Bauhinia | Elder | Malus |
| †Broom | †Erica | Mock-orange |
| Buddleia | Exochorda | †Osmanthus |
| †Callistemon | Forsythia | †Pittosporum |
| Calycanthus | †Fuchsia | Prunus |
| †Camellia | Gardenia | Rhododendron |
| Caryopteris | †Grevillea | Ribes |
| Cassia | Heather | Rosa |
| †Ceanothus | Hydrangea | †Solanum |
| Cercis | Itea | Spiraea |
| †Cestrum | Ixora | Symphoricarpos |
| Chaenomeles | Jasminum | †Veronica |
| †Clerodendron | Kalmia | Viburnum |
| Cornus | †Lagerstroemia | Vitex |
| Crataegus | †Lantana | Weigela |

**FLOWERING SPURGE** = *Euphorbia corollata*.

**FLOWERING TIME.** *See* PHENOLOGY for the factors that control it. For the progression of bloom in the garden, *see* GARDEN CALENDAR.

**FLOWERING WILLOW** = *Chilopsis linearis*.

**FLOWERING WINTERGREEN** = *Polygala paucifolia*.

**FLOWERING WOOD.** *See* Softwood Cuttings at CUTTINGS.

**FLOWER-OF-AN-HOUR** = *Hibiscus trionum*.

**FLOWER-OF-JOVE** = *Lychnis flos-jovis*.

**FLOWER POTS.** The best permanent container for most potted plants is the common clay flower pot, porous, unglazed, and with a hole in the bottom to allow the escape of excess water. They come in sizes from 1¾ in. to 14 in. diameters, the standard sizes for which are as follows:

### STANDARD FLOWER POTS

| Inside diameter (inches) | Inside diameter (inches) | Inside diameter (inches) |
|---|---|---|
| 1¾ | 3¾ | 6½ |
| 2 Thimble pot | 4 | 7 |
| 2¼ | 4½ | 8 |
| 2½ Thumb pot | 5 | 9 |
| 3 | 5½ Lily pot | 10 |
| 3½ | 6 | 12 |
| | | 14 |

---

\* Special articles on the subjects indicated by an asterisk (\*) will be found at the words so marked.

From such a series one can take care of nearly every potting need from the pricking out of seedlings to a potted plant needing the largest of the standard sizes — 14 in. Above this diameter the cost and breakage of clay pots become so great that tubs are more economical. See TUBS.

There are some growers, especially bulb growers, who prefer shallower pots than those of the standard sizes. For such, the following are to be had in the sizes specified below:

THREE-QUARTER OR AZALEA POTS. These are clay pots much like the ordinary ones but only three-quarters the regulation depth. They come in all sizes from 6-in. to 12-in. diameters.

CYCLAMEN POTS. The same as three-quarter pots, but with 5 holes in the bottom. They come only in 5-6-7-in. diameters.

PANS (often called Bulb or Seed Pans). These are clay pots of about half the depth of standard flower pots, and have many uses for shallow-rooted plants, for bulbs, or for pricking out seedlings. They are to be had in all diameters from 5 in. to 12 in.

Some rose growers, and those specializing in raising evergreen seedlings or in small budded or grafted stock, use a specially deep sort of pot known as a ROSE POT. Because they are needed only in the young state of the plant, they come only in the following sizes:

ROSE POTS

| Inside diameter (inches) | depth (inches) |
|---|---|
| 2 | 2½ |
| 2¼ | 2¾ |
| 2¼ | 3¼ |
| 2½ | 3¼ |

SAUCERS. In rooms, and sometimes in the greenhouse, flower pots must stand in some sort of a saucer which collects excess water or sometimes holds water that is applied at the base of the pot. Clay saucers are made in all sizes from 3- to 14-in. diameters. Because of the downward flare of all flower pots, a 6-in. saucer will fit a 6-in. pot.

Only fancy and one's pocketbook need dictate the use of many glazed, glass, colored, enamel, or metal containers for the growing of plants. But they are expensive and not so practical as the common clay flower pot.

To keep pots clean, especially to free them from the green scum or moss so common in moist greenhouses, they should be soaked in a solution of 2½ ounces of carbonate of copper, and 1½ pints of ammonia in about 20 gallons of water, given a good scrubbing, and then rinsed in clear water.

PAPER POTS. For all temporary purposes paper pots are most useful. They come in all the smaller sizes, are far cheaper than clay pots, and for the few weeks they are needed answer every purpose. They will not stand much wear, but for young vegetable plants or tender annuals waiting for outdoor planting, paper pots are very satisfactory. Even cheaper substitutes are the discarded paper drinking cups, especially the corrugated sort with a rim. Empty tin cans are sturdy, but ugly, and do not allow aeration, for which only clay pots properly provide.

**FLOWERS FOR INDOOR DECORATION.** See CUT FLOWERS and FLOWER ARRANGING.

**FLOWER SHOW.** See EXHIBITIONS AND SHOWS.

**FL. PL.** Short for *flore-pleno;* i.e. double-flowered.

**FLUES.** An old-fashioned method of heating greenhouses, now abandoned for steam or hot water. Flues are still used for somewhat primitive hotbeds. See COLD FRAME.

*FLUITANS* (flew'i-tanz). Floating.

**FLUME.** See IRRIGATION.

*FLUMINENSIS, -e* (flew-mi-nen'sis). Named for the flumen (river) at Rio de Janeiro, when it was supposed that the harbor of that city was part of a river. See TRADESCANTIA.

**FLY-HONEYSUCKLE.** See LONICERA.

**FLY-SPECK.** See Diseases at APPLE and ORANGE.

**FOAM FLOWER** = *Tiarella cordifolia.*

**FOENICULUM.** See FENNEL.

*FOENUM-GRAECUM* (fee-num-gree'kum). Literally, Greek hay. See TRIGONELLA.

*FOETIDA, -us, -um* (fe'ti-da). Evil-smelling.

*FOETIDISSIMA, -us, -um* (fe-ti-diss'i-ma). Most evil-smelling.

**FOG FRUIT.** See LIPPIA.

*FOLIACEA, -us, -um* (foe-li-ā'see-a). Foliaceous; i.e. leafy or leaf-like. Many bracts* are foliaceous, others are colored.

**FOLIAGE PLANTS.** As generally used, foliage plants refers to greenhouse subjects grown primarily for their handsome leaves, some of which are variegated or otherwise colored. Among the best greenhouse ones are plants in the genera *Begonia, Calathea, Aglaonema, Ficus, Grevillea, Pandanus, Dracaena, Cordyline, Araucaria, Peperomia, Caladium,* and *Polyscias;* all of which are described at their generic names. See also FERNS AND FERN GARDENING and PALMS, some of which are among our finest foliage plants.

Among hardy plants or summer bedding ones, those grown chiefly for their foliage are less numerous than the tropical genera. But the castor-oil plant, *Coleus, Colocasia,* and a variety of *Ligularia* are mostly so grown. So are some of the bamboo-like grasses. See BAMBOO. Other hardy plants, some species of which have especially fine foliage, are the maples, some of the vines (*see* VINES), *Acanthopanax, Echinopanax,* and box. See also EVERGREENS; BROAD-LEAVED EVERGREENS.

*FOLIOSA, -us, -um* (fo-lee-o'sa). Leafy.

**FOLLICLE.** A dry, one-chambered fruit, which, unlike a legume (pea), splits only along one seam. The fruits of peony, monkshood, and the milkweed are follicles.

**FONTANESIA** (fon-ta-nee'zi-a). Asiatic shrubs of the olive family, both the two known species cult. for ornament, although their flowers are not particularly showy. Leaves opposite,* without, or nearly without, marginal teeth, and short-stalked. Flowers small, in leafy clusters (panicles*), the calyx* very small and 4-parted, the 4 petals also small and narrow. Stamens* 2, a little longer than the petals. Fruit a small, flat, winged nutlet. (Named for René Louiche Desfontaines, French botanist.)

Both the shrubs below are of easy culture in any ordinary garden soil. They may be increased by seeds, or by layering.

californica = *Fontanesia fortunei.*

fortunei. A slender, smooth, upright-branching shrub, 6-12 ft. high. Leaves lance-shaped, or ovalish, shining green, 2-4 in. long. Flowers greenish-white. Fruit oval, nearly ¾ in. long. China. May-June. Hardy from zone* 4 southward.

phillyreoides. Closely related to *F. fortunei,* but lower, and with smaller and more oblongish leaves, which are minutely toothed on the margin, and gray-green. Fruit nearly round, ½-¾ in. in diameter. Hardy from zone* 5 southward.

*FONTINALIS, -e* (fon-ti-nay'lis). Pertaining to a spring.

**FOOD PLANTS.** Outside the cereals, which are agricultural rather than garden crops, many food plants come within the scope of THE GARDEN DICTIONARY. See the several articles on fruit culture, kitchen gardening, herbs, and herb gardening. See also the name of your state or province, for the chief food plants suitable to your region.

**FOOD TRAYS.** See BIRDS.

**FOOT.** See WEIGHTS AND MEASURES 2.

**FOOT-ROT.** See Diseases at RHUBARB and ORANGE.

**FORCING.** The forcing of flowers, fruits, and vegetables out of season is not a new innovation, it having been in practice in European countries for many years.

In America the forcing of vegetables, potted plants and cut flowers has developed into an enormous industry and many acres of land are covered with greenhouses and frames

---

* Special articles on the subjects indicated by an asterisk (*) will be found at the words so marked.

in order to produce various specialized crops out of season for the markets.

Probably no horticultural industry requires more skill than that of forcing plants in order to harvest the crops when in most demand. In the case of an amateur grower having a small greenhouse at his disposal, success can be achieved in the forcing of plants if the following simple general instructions are followed:

*a.* See that the plants are well rooted and in a good healthy condition.

*b.* Commence with a minimum temperature, increasing a few degrees weekly until the maximum is reached. *See* RETARDING.

*c.* Maintain a buoyant atmosphere in the forcing house by the liberal use of water sprayed under the benches and walks and on the foliage of the plants.

*d.* Administer air during all seasonable weather, avoiding drafts, closing the ventilators in the early afternoon.

*e.* Do not allow the plants to become dry from the time forcing has commenced.

*f.* Fumigate or vaporize regularly to keep down insect pests. *See* FUMIGATION.

BULBS. Hyacinths, tulips, narcissus, and lilies. Use potting mixture* No. 3. Place the bulbs as soon as received in pots or pans 4–8 inches in diameter, allowing one to ten bulbs in each. As soon as potted, water thoroughly and place where they can be kept cool in order to give the roots an opportunity to develop. If a frame is convenient they may be placed in that or they may be placed in a block outside where they will be shaded from the sun. Cover with three or four inches of sand or coal ashes. This will keep the pots from drying out. As soon as the bulbs develop a good root system they may be taken out and placed in the greenhouse in a temperature of 50° F., later increasing the temperature to 60°–65°.

AZALEA, RHODODENDRON. Use potting mixture* No. 5. These plants should be kept in a cool house until wanted for forcing, 40°–45° at night, with plenty of air through the day. When the buds have developed forcing may begin. Place in a temperature of 55° to start, increasing to 60°–65°. Frequent watering and syringing will be necessary. Do not at any time allow the plants to get dry at the roots. Best results are obtained in a well-ventilated and lightly shaded greenhouse. It is important to keep the buds of the rhododendrons moist to encourage evenness in breaking. Spray the foliage with the hose at least twice on all bright days.

HYDRANGEA. Use potting mixture* No. 3. As a house plant *Hydrangea* is very popular. Flowering at Easter, it has become one of the most useful florists' plants, as it lends itself readily to forcing. The young plants are bedded out during the summer and in late September or October are taken up, potted, and placed in a block outside on the dry ground. This is done to check the vigorous growth and to encourage its ripening. Force as recommended for azaleas.

Hydrangeas are great water lovers, therefore they should not be allowed to become dry. They are also gross feeders and an occasional watering with liquid manure is very beneficial to them. Force in a temperature 50° F., increasing to a maximum of 60° F.

HARDY PLANTS. Use potting mixture* No. 3. Hardy plants have been forced for many years in Europe; it is, however, a new industry in this country. The flowers of many of these plants are most useful for cutting, and many lend themselves admirably for decoration in the home when grown as pot plants. A number of the species of the hardy shrubs are well adapted for forcing, the best results being obtained from those flowering early in the season.

Well grown and shapely plants should be selected that have been prepared for the purpose. They require a resting period of from two to three months before they are brought into the forcing house. Among the most useful for forcing are: *Zenobia pulverulenta, Pieris floribunda, Azalea mollis, Kalmia latifolia, Exochorda racemosa, Spiraea vanhouttei, Viburnum tomentosum sterile, Viburnum opulus sterile, Deutzia gracilis, Deutzia lemoinei, Deutzia scabra, Lagerstroemia indica, Clethra alnifolia, Daphne cneorum, Syringa vulgaris* (see LILAC), *Buddleia alternifolia, Kolkwitzia amabilis, Viburnum carlesi, Forsythia intermedia spectabilis, Philadelphus virginalis* (see MOCK-ORANGE) and *Hamamelis vernalis.*

Young stock should be planted in the nursery or garden rows and grown for two or three seasons, transplanting each year to ensure a mass of fibrous roots that will adapt them for their growth in pots. Pruning should be attended to in order to shape the plants. When strong and vigorous enough for forcing they may be dug as the leaves fall. Place in pots of a suitable size. Water thoroughly and plunge* in a frame or in a sheltered spot outside. Water occasionally as their needs require. Early in January the first plants may be started, bringing in other plants at intervals of two weeks for succession.

Place at first in a cool greenhouse, 45° F., increasing the temperature gradually until a maximum of 60°–65° F. is reached. Spray frequently on all sunny days to encourage a free and even breaking of the growths.

Fruiting plants in pots such as the pear, apple, fig, etc., may be forced under these same cultural conditions.

FORCING PLANTS IN FRAMES. The frame method of forcing has been in use for many generations, decaying manure or electricity being the medium from which the heat is furnished, supplemented with the rays of the sun. For the details of hotbed and cold frames *see* COLD FRAMES.

Many excellent crops can be grown in frames if careful with regard to watering, protection and ventilation. Crops such as lettuce, radish, carrots, and cucumbers may be grown in the hotbed. As a medium on which to start early plants from seed, it is also most useful. — D. L.

**FORCING HOUSE.** Any greenhouse in which plants are forced into harvest out of season. *See* FORCING.

**FORESTIERA** (fo-res-ti-ee'ra). A genus of 20 species of New World shrubs of the olive family, only two of rather secondary ornamental value. Often sold as *Adelia,* they have opposite,* short-stalked leaves, and small, unisexual,* greenish flowers, without petals, which bloom before the leaves unfold in *F. acuminata.* Sepals 4–6, unequal, often soon falling, thus apparently wanting. Stamens* 2–4. Fruit small, black, fleshy (a drupe*), mostly 1-seeded. (Named for Charles Le-Forestier, French naturalist and physician.)

The swamp privet, as its name indicates, will thrive best in moist places, while *F. ligustrina* is more tolerant of drier sites. Both the cult. species are native in the southeastern U.S. and are hardy only as indicated below. Easily propagated by seeds or by layering.

**acuminata.** Swamp privet. Usually a shrub up to 9 ft., rarely tree-like and up to 25 ft. Leaves ovalish-oblong, 2–4 in. long, tapering at the tip. Flowers very small, the male in bracted* clusters, the female in panicles.* Fruit oblongish, about ½ in. long. Southern Ill. to Ga. and Tex. April–May. Hardy from zone* 4 with protection, and from zone* 5 without it, southward.

**ligustrina.** A shrub, never over 9 ft. high. Leaves oblong or elliptic, blunt at the tip, 1–1½ in. long. Flowers almost stalkless. Fruit egg-shaped, about ⅝ in. long. Tenn., Ga. and Fla. Aug. Hardy from zone* 6, or with protection from zone* 5, southward.

**FORESTRY.** While commercial forestry lies outside the scope of this book, the management of small woodlands on country estates demands some knowledge of forestry principles. The successful management of such depends upon the willingness of the owner to manage the woods in such a manner as to come within one of three categories. It is true that a woodland may to some extent serve all purposes, but one purpose must be dominant.

SUPPLY WOODLANDS. The object of supply woodlands is to provide a succession of timber supplies: cordwood, fenceposts, railroad ties, or replacements for farm implements.

Succession is brought about by planting a stand composed of several species of trees that are mutually tolerant and maturing, or become usable, at varying ages. The composition of such woodlands is easily determined if the land is not derelict. The trees native to the original forests of the region will provide the range to select from. Should the land be derelict, the owner is confronted with a problem in regeneration, owing to the changes that have taken place in the soil since the original forest was removed. In this case

---

* Special articles on the subjects indicated by an asterisk (*) will be found at the words so marked.

the most reliable procedure is to note carefully all trees that are succeeding, or show promise of succeeding, under similar conditions in the locality. It will frequently be found that non-native trees offer the greater promise, so use them. In cutting out trees it is imperative that the wood be not opened up to the play of the prevailing wind. Cut or thin in alternate strips at right angles to the prevailing wind and leave the exposed boundary till the strip under its lee is established.

PROTECTION WOODS. The primary object of such woods is to prevent rapid soil erosion and consequent floods or to afford privacy or protection from wind. These woods may also have esthetic features and likewise serve as game preserves. Protection woods should not be so densely planted with trees as supply woods, because shrubs are essential to impede erosion, the trees providing shade to slow up the melting of snow, in addition to wind protection.

The problem of management, apart from the removal of diseased and insect-infested trees, is to see that the outer tree stand is composed of wind-resisting trees planted sufficiently thick so as to act as an efficient windbreak, and that shrubbery is sufficiently dense, at intervals, and at approximately right angles to the run-off. See WINDBREAKS.

ESTHETIC WOODS. Esthetic woodlands may serve protective purposes, but wind and erosion problems greatly limit these possibilities. In order to have a diversity of trees an adequate depth of soil must be present to allow the inclusion of deeply rooting species. This type of wood may, in the center, be of the nature of an arboretum by allowing the trees to be sufficiently widely spaced as to allow full development as specimens. In addition glades may be formed for the establishment of bulbous and other perennial herbaceous plants; also adequate space can be allowed for shrubbery masses. A diversity of species lessens the probability of mass trouble with insects and fungi.

Whichever type of woodland one maintains, it is well to remember that one is keeping a small piece of forest and that the forest floor should not be kept "picked up" or cleaned. Humus, the one great asset in any forest, can only be accumulated by letting fallen leaves, twigs, or even branches decay as they would naturally. Such an accumulation increases the fire hazard, but this can be guarded against by plowing a few furrows (leaving the plowed earth untouched) completely around the piece of forest. Few small or grass fires will jump such a dirt barrier. — T. R. A.

**FORGET-ME-NOT.** Mainly blue-flowered, but sometimes pink or white-flowered, annual or perennial herbs of the genus **Myosotis** (my-o-so′tis) of the family Boraginaceae, most of the 40 species European, but a few throughout the north temperate zone. They are usually branching, often weak or prostrate, generally hairy, plants of very easy culture. Leaves alternate,* without marginal teeth. Flowers small, in branched or unbranched, sometimes 1-sided, clusters. Calyx short, tubular, 5-toothed at the top. Corolla salver-shaped, 5-lobed, the throat crested and often of a different color (with an eye*). Fruit a collection of 4 small, smooth nutlets. (*Myosotis* is from the Greek for mouse-ear, in allusion to the leaves.)

Most garden forget-me-nots, especially *M. arvensis* and *M. sylvatica*, are best treated as hardy annuals or biennials. See ANNUALS; BIENNIALS. Some, like *M. scorpioides*, are true perennials and should be so grown, and may easily be divided in early spring. The beautiful color and low growth make the forget-me-nots very attractive bedding plants, especially as a carpet under tulips or other bulbs. All of them do better when a bit crowded, the annuals especially, and most of them prefer partial shade and plenty of moisture. Can also be grown in the greenhouse for winter bloom.

**M. alpestris.** A common name in the catalogues, but the plant, and its white and pink-flowered forms, are usually *M. sylvatica*. The true *M. alpestris* is scarcely known in gardens.

**M. arvensis.** Field scorpion grass. An annual or biennial, somewhat sprawling, but occasionally up to 18 in. high. Leaves oblongish, ¾–1 in. long. Flowers blue or white, about ⅕ in. wide. North temperate zone.

**M. dissitiflora** = *Myosotis sylvatica*, so far as cult. plants are concerned.

**M. palustris** = *Myosotis scorpioides*.

**M. scorpioides.** Common perennial forget-me-not of the gardens, the stems more or less prostrate and up to 12 in. long. Leaves oblongish or narrower, about 1 in. long. Flowers blue, but with a yellow, pink, or white eye.* Eurasia. Spring. The *var.* semperflorens is a lower form which blooms through the summer.

**M. sylvatica.** A Eurasian annual or biennial, not over 9 in. high, usually less. Leaves oblongish or narrower, about ¾ in. long. Flower blue, but sometimes pink or white, the eye differently colored, often yellow. May–Aug.

**FORK.** See TOOLS AND IMPLEMENTS.

**FORKING.** See DIGGING.

**FORMALDEHYDE.** See Formaldehyde at FUNGICIDES.

**FORMAL GARDEN.** A garden, geometric in shape, enclosed and laid out with regularity according to established methods of classic design, is called a formal garden. In it one feels the presence of a studied scheme, a conscious effort for a dignified effect. It serves a valuable purpose by affording a natural transition between the house and the informal landscape, which satisfies the eye and is logically correct.

Being symmetrical, such a garden may well continue an important axis of the house, becoming thus a part of the house itself extended and open to the sky, where nature meets man and each agrees to understand the other.

Not only does the large house need a frame of some formality, but the small estate dominated by one or more houses might best be designed formally, as an informal or naturalistic setting would generally look absurd — more pathetic than pleasant.

In laying out a formal garden the designer must guard against the confusion which arises from trying to include too many features. He should first study the size, shape, and levels of the proposed garden, making it as large and as interesting as conditions of space and upkeep will permit. He should secure, if possible, one or at most two notes of dominating interest, such as a good distant view, an attractive garden pavilion, a fountain, an urn, a few steps, a gate, or even a bird bath. The less important features can be made to lead the interest up to these points.

A formal garden

There may be an object of dominating interest at either end of the garden or at the center. In the first case, the center axis will be left open as a wide path or a grass panel. In the second case, a central dominating object will best be surrounded by an open space. The first develops the stronger axis as the second produces a feeling of radiation towards a center. The first might best be used for the long garden and

---

* Special articles on the subjects indicated by an asterisk (*) will be found at the words so marked.

A FORMAL GARDEN IN SAN MARINO, CALIFORNIA

(Courtesy of Katherine Bashford)

the second for the garden which more nearly approaches a circle or a square.

Having settled on the size, shape, and dominating features of the garden, the designer must consider the proper relationship of the various parts and the minor features, such as flower beds, paths, seats, or the color scheme. It must be remembered that a minor feature in one garden may be used as a major feature in another, as there is infinite scope for the clever designer. He may venture on a fountain at the center or a wall fountain at the end of a path, for the sight and sound of water are always pleasant. He may radiate his paths from the center or run them parallel to or vertical to the axis. He may include definitely shaped flower beds. A change of level dispels monotony, so he may lower the center of the garden not less than five inches so that he can get one or more steps, for steps lie as a terminal object and introduce a pleasant suggestion of human use. Seats in the formal garden should be well designed and not too rustic; in fact, furniture should be as important to the garden as to the living room. In more pretentious gardens the designer may use robust statuary, lead, stone, or bronze urns and variously colored flower pots.

When the construction of the formal garden is finished, it may look too stiff and uncompromising. This can always be corrected by the clever use of plants of informal or romantic aspect — an old apple tree, a lilac, or a dogwood. Thus the informal softens the formal and each lends charm to the other.

It must be remembered that all areas and features of the formal garden must be definite in outline and as simple as is consistent with sufficient interest. The formal garden, in the right place, need not be defended and it will have that backbone and that measure of fitness which are the foundations of all good art. — R. L. F., Jr.

**FORM-O-FUME.** A copyrighted fungicide, containing formaldehyde and sold with directions for the control of damping-off.

*FORMOSA, -us, -um* (for-moe'sa). Handsome.

*FORMOSANA, -us, -um* (for-moe-say'na). From the island of Formosa.

*FORMOSISSIMA, -us, -um* (for-moe-sis'i-ma). Most showy or handsome.

**FORSYTHIA** (for-sĭth'i-a; *also* for-sy'thi-a). Very handsome, spring-blooming, Old World shrubs of the olive family, widely planted for their profuse, usually yellow, flowers that bloom before or with the unfolding of the leaves. Commonly called golden bell, the shrubs are inclined to be arching or spreading, and some varieties root at the ends of the pendulous branches. Leaves opposite,* stalked. Flowers in clusters of 1–6 in the leaf-axils,* practically stalkless, and so numerous as nearly to cover the stems in some varieties. Calyx 4-lobed and persistent. Corolla bell-shaped below, but split into 4 strap-shaped lobes which look casually like 4 separate petals. Stamens 2. Fruit a 2-celled capsule.* (Named for William Forsyth, British horticulturist.)

Fortunately, the golden bells are of the easiest culture in any garden soil. They root as easily as privet, and cuttings of the stems, or uprooting the usually plentiful supply of suckers, will always provide new plants. They are extremely effective when planted in large masses, especially against an evergreen background. All are hardy up to zone* 2, but sometimes slightly winter-killed,* especially the flower buds, which are more sensitive than the leaf buds. Most of them stand smoke better than such decorative shrubs usually do.

**intermedia.** A hybrid between the other two cult. species and by far the best of the golden bells. It is a shrub up to 9 ft. high, with arching or spreading, pithy branches. Leaves oblong or ovalish, 3–5 in. long, sometimes 3-parted, but usually merely toothed. Flowers yellow, usually several at each cluster, about 1½ in. long, the clusters very numerous. The *var.* **primulina** has pale yellow flowers, which are more numerous towards the ends of the branches. The *var.* **spectabilis** has more flowers at each cluster and each corolla may be up to 1½ in. long. This variety is probably the finest *Forsythia* in cult. It is useful for forcing (which see).

**ovata.** A Korean shrub, not over 5 ft. high, the branches arching.

Leaves broadly oval, 2–3 in. long. Flowers solitary,* but very numerous, amber-yellow. April–May, usually blooming before any of the others. Hardy from zone* 3 southward, possibly in zone* 2.

**suspensa.** Weeping golden bell. An upright shrub up to 12 ft. high, the tips of the long, arching, hollow branches often pendulous and, in age, rooting at the tip. Leaves oval-oblong, toothed, 3–5 in. long. Flowers golden-yellow, about 1 in. long, mostly 1–3 at each cluster. China. If left unpruned this may sometimes act like a vine over a wall. See VINES. The *var.* **atrocaulis** has dark purple, young branches; *var.* **fortunei** is chiefly erect and has few or no pendulous branches; *var.* **sieboldi** has slender, almost trailing branches.

**viridissima.** A nearly erect shrub up to 10 ft., the branches pithy. Leaves 4–6 in. long, toothed only towards the tip. Flowers greenish-yellow, about 1 in. long, usually only 1–3 at each cluster. China. Less grown than the other two, but a variety from Korea is welcomed by some. It has bright yellow flowers.

**FORTUNELLA** (for-tew-nel'la). Evergreen, Chinese trees or shrubs, commonly called kumquat, belonging to the family Rutaceae and closely related to the orange. Leaves alternate,* compound,* but reduced to a single leaflet with a margined or winged stalk and prominently dotted with glands on the under side. Flowers resembling an orange blossom (see CITRUS). Fruit orange-like, but small, its cells 3–7 (8–15 in the orange), aromatic and chiefly used for preserves. (Named for Robert Fortune, English traveler who introduced the kumquat into Eu.)

The kumquats should be grown in the same way as oranges, but they will stand more cold than the common sweet orange. See ORANGE. They are sometimes grown on the stock of *Poncirus trifoliata*, when they are still more frost-resistant. They have been crossed with other citrus fruits and the citrangequat* and limequat* both have kumquat blood in them.

**crassifolia.** Meiwa kumquat. A shrub or small tree 8–15 ft. high, sometimes spiny. Leaves thick, the stalks narrowly winged. Fruit nearly egg-shaped, about 1½ in. in diameter, its cells 6 or 7.

**japonica.** Round kumquat; also called Marumi kumquat. A shrub or small tree 7–10 ft. high, usually much-branched. Leaves bluntish, broad, about 2½ in. long. Fruit globe-shaped, about 1¼ in. in diameter, its cells 5 or 6. Sometimes offered as *Citrus japonica*.

**margarita.** Oval or Nagami kumquat. A spineless shrub or small tree, the leaves narrow-oblong, 3–4 in. long, pointed at the tip. Fruit ovalish-oblong, about 1 in. thick, the cells 4 or 5.

**FOTHERGILLA** (foth-er-gil'la). A small genus of North American shrubs of the family Hamamelidaceae, commonly called witch-alder or American witch-alder, related to the witch-hazel, but lacking petals. Leaves coarse, toothed, alternate,* resembling those of the witch-hazel. Flowers small, white, in small terminal heads or spikes, without petals, the only showy feature being the numerous white stamens.* Fruit a beaked capsule. (Named for John Fothergill, English physician.)

The witch-alders are rather ornamental shrubs blooming in April or May, and prefer rather low, moist places. Propagated by seeds or by root cuttings, or suckers.

**carolina** = *Fothergilla gardeni*.

**gardeni.** Dwarf alder. A low shrub, usually under 3 ft. high, the broadly wedge-shaped leaves 1–2 in. long, bluish-white and hairy on the under side. Flowers white, the spikes oblongish and about 1 in. long, blooming before the leaves unfold. Va. to Ga. Hardy from zone* 4 southward. Sometimes offered as *F. carolina*.

**major.** A shrub 7–10 ft. high, the nearly round or ovalish leaves 2–5 in. long, pale and a little hairy on the under side. Flowers white, the clusters 1½–4 in. long, blooming with the unfolding of the leaves. Ga. Hardy from zone* 4 southward.

**FOUNDATION PLANTING.** Few buildings, whether private or public, fail to be enhanced in their appeal to the eye when the line from the base to the ground is softened by well-balanced groups of living plants. The primary function of such plantings is to tie together house, gardens, shrubbery, and walks as an harmonious whole, rather than to conceal faulty lines or remedy other defects in building design. Plantings serve to anchor the building to the ground.

Shrubs, carefully chosen, are one of the most practical solutions. The north side, which is shaded at least half the day, should be planted only with such material as is, to a certain extent, shade-enduring. Choice is somewhat restricted, although some of those available have brilliantly tinted autumn and winter foliage, but small, inconspicuous flowers. The best is Japanese barberry, which is extremely hardy in the East, requires no special attention as to soil, is practically

* Special articles on the subjects indicated by an asterisk (*) will be found at the words so marked.

A house with and without foundation planting

drought-resistant, and impervious to cold. *Berberis thunbergi atropurpurea*, although the more brilliantly tinted of the Japanese barberries, should not be used for a northern planting, as it requires full exposure to the sun to develop its gorgeous coloring. To relieve the monotony occasioned by a foundation planting of only one type of shrub, shade-loving plants such as the tuberous-rooted begonias may be placed in front of the shrubbery, or a hardy border used for accent.

An attractive treatment of a corner with foundation planting

The west side of the house allows of more leeway. A mixed planting of such shrubs as rhododendron, deutzia, forsythia, and privet makes a good combination, and is sometimes successfully used on the north side also, although it usually requires special winter protection; many of the shrubs may blossom but seldom. Where the house faces east or south, the difficulties are much less. Here shrubs can be chosen which will give a succession of bloom; by setting out those which flower at different seasons of the year, some may be had in flower nearly every month. While waiting for the shrubs to attain blooming size, the spaces between them may be filled with petunias, centaureas, and other quick-growing, showy annuals. Regardless of the location, however, choose only shrubs suited to the type of house and garden and remember that foundation plantings require plenty of moisture, due to their proximity to the house walls.

Evergreens, when well chosen and carefully placed, are among the most desirable of material. The arborvitae gives a wide range from pyramid to globe forms, broad-leaved evergreen shrubs include many dwarf species, while *Taxus* provides many very hardy as well as beautiful subjects. Among the junipers are dwarf forms of *Juniperus chinensis*, and *J. sabina*, and the prostrate *J. sabina tamariscifolia* for use beside rocky steps.

Flowers may be used as foundation plantings, but their period of bloom is not continuous, and unless an exceptionally heavy type of plant is used, they often appear thin and out of place at the base of a massive building.

**FOUNTAIN-GRASS** = *Pennisetum ruppeli*.

**FOUNTAIN-PALM** = *Livistona chinensis*.

**FOUNTAIN-PLANT** = *Russelia equisetiformis* and *Amaranthus tricolor*.

**FOUNTAINS.** See WATER.

**FOUQUIERIA** (foo-kwee-ee'ri-a). The only cult. genus of the family **Fouquieriaceae** (foo-kwee-air-ee-ā'see-ee), the torch tree family, which comprises cactus-like, fantastic, desert plants from Mex. and the adjacent U.S. The only cult. species is **F. splendens**, which is usually called ocotillo, coach-whip, vine cactus, candlewood, or Jacob's staff. It is cactus-like and consists of several very prickly, rigid stems 8–20 ft. high, which are apparently leafless, although there are clusters of small leaves in the axils* of the spines in early spring. Flowers scarlet, tubular, about 1 in. long, with 5 sepals and a 5-lobed corolla, beyond which the 10–17 stamens* protrude. Flower clusters very showy, often branched and 6–10 in. long. Fruit a capsule about ¾ in. long. A showy, desert, hedge plant, fine for the desert garden or in a greenhouse suitable for cacti (*see* CACTI). It is not hardy northward. (Named for Pierre E. Fouquier, French professor of medicine.)

*FOURCROYDES* (foor-croy'deez; but *see* OÏDES). A name derived from, and meaning like, the genus *Furcraea*.

**FOUR-O'CLOCK** = *Mirabilis jalapa*.

**FOUR-O'CLOCK FAMILY** = Nyctaginaceae.

*FOVEOLATA, -us, -um* (foe-vee-o-lay'ta). Slightly pitted.

**FOX GERANIUM** = *Geranium robertianum*.

**FOXGLOVE.** Handsome, sometimes poisonous or medicinal herbs comprising the genus **Digitalis** (di-ji-tay'lis) of the figwort family, some of them deservedly popular garden flowers. Of the 25 known species, all Eurasian, only a few are in cult. and of these the common garden foxglove (*D. purpurea*) is by far the most important. They are erect, biennial or perennial herbs, with alternate* leaves or the lower ones sometimes crowded. Flowers in long, terminal, often 1-sided clusters (racemes*), often very showy, usually purple, yellow, or white. Corolla more or less bell-shaped at the base, the tube a little inflated, the top slightly 2-lipped. Stamens 4. Fruit a capsule.* (*Digitalis* is Latin for the finger of a glove, in allusion to the shape of the corolla.)

All the foxgloves below are either perennials or biennials, but most of them, especially the common garden sort, tend to die out and are best treated as biennials. *See* BIENNIALS. If they are treated as perennials they may be divided in spring. All are of simple culture in ordinary garden soil, but the common *D. purpurea* does much better in relatively cool, moist climates, especially along the sea coast of New England and in Wash. and Ore. It is one of the handsomest of garden plants.

**D. ambigua.** Yellow foxglove. A hairy herb 2–3 ft. high. Leaves stalkless, toothed, oval-lance-shaped. Flowers nearly 2 in. long, yellowish but brown-marked. Eurasia. Sometimes sold as *D. grandiflora*.

**D. grandiflora** = *Digitalis ambigua*.

**D. laevigata.** A perennial herb up to 3 ft. high. Flowers yellow but purple-marked. Southern Eu. A handsome species but not much grown.

**D. lanata.** A biennial or perennial, rarely over 3 ft. high. Flowers white, but with fine veins. Southern Eu. Little known in cult.

**D. lutea.** A perennial 12–20 in. high. Flowers yellowish-white, scarcely more than ¾ in. long, in 1-sided clusters. Eu.

**D. purpurea.** Common foxglove of the gardens and called by many other names such as purple foxglove, fairy glove, and finger-flower. It is generally a biennial, 2–4 ft. high, but much higher in favorable places. Leaves roughish, the lower long-stalked, the upper shorter-stalked and smaller. Flowers 2–3 in. long, hanging, purple but spotted, borne in a 1-sided raceme 12–24 in. long. Western Eu. The finest of the foxgloves and planted in several forms, especially the *var.* **alba**, with white flowers; *var.* **gloxiniaeflora**, with longer flower clusters; and *var.* **maculata superba**, the leopard foxglove, which is a showy, spotted form.

---

*Special articles on the subjects indicated by an asterisk (*) will be found at the words so marked.

**FOXGLOVE BEARDTONGUE** = *Pentstemon digitalis*.

**FOXGLOVE FAMILY** = Scrophulariaceae.

**FOX GRAPE** = *Vitis labrusca*.

**FOXTAIL.** See ALOPECURUS.

**FOXTAIL LILY.** See EREMURUS.

**FOXTAIL MILLET** = *Setaria italica*.

**FRAGARIA.** See STRAWBERRY.

*FRAGARIOIDES* (fra-gay-ri-oy′deez, but *see* OÏDES). Strawberry-like.

*FRAGILIS, -e* (fră′ji-lis). Easily broken or, often, easily wilted.

**FRAGRANCE.** Fragrance adds so much to the pleasure derived from a garden that special effort should be made to insure a succession of sweet-scented flowers throughout the growing season, both for cutting and for garden decoration. It is quite possible to fill a garden with fragrant flowers alone and for those who like to specialize, a small enclosed "nose-garden" or border devoted to them is both practicable and pleasant. But it is commonly more satisfactory to distribute the fragrant flowers generously among the others in order that the choice of material shall not be limited, but the whole garden impregnated by agreeable odors. In any collection of plants those with aromatic leaves should be prominently featured. They are especially useful in bouquets and nosegays of unscented blooms. Climbers with sweet-scented flowers may be trained about the windows of the dwelling and over porches and arbors, and if there is a favorite walk its verges may be planted with shrubs and herbs giving forth pleasant aromas.

Many flowers are fragrant only at night, like the evening stock, and the sweetness of many others is greatly increased with the coming of dusk. This is true of the tuberose, garden pink (*Dianthus plumarius*) and honeysuckles. If the night-scenting plants are massed in the vicinity of the dwelling their fragrance is carried into the rooms on the night breezes. Some flowers give off their sweetness freely to the air, others release it most readily under a hot sun, or after rain, or in a warm room. The garden is most full of scents when the air is mild and somewhat damp. Certain leaves that must ordinarily be pressed to loose their aromas give it forth readily after a rain. This is true of the sweetbrier and the box. Heliotrope and many sweet herbs are intensely fragrant after a light frost.

Flower scents are of many types and not all are pleasing to all persons, but few will be found to be unpleasant in the open air or to clash with each other. Each week of the growing year has its special scents and with a little forethought these may be given pre-eminence.

Early scents come from snowdrops, daffodils, jonquils, poet's narcissus, *Crocus imperati*, hyacinths, grape hyacinths, many tulips, especially of the early and Cottage varieties; from *Viola odorata*, wallflowers, primroses, cowslips, *Arabis*, lily-of-the-valley, and from such shrubs as *Daphne mezereum*, *Lonicera fragrantissima*, *L. standishi*, *L. syringantha*, *Viburnum carlesi*, flowering currant, *Magnolia stellata*, *M. denudata*, *Mahonia aquifolium*, azaleas, *Corylopsis*, English hawthorn, Carolina allspice and many flowering fruit trees, both domesticated and exotic. Later-flowering shrubs are mock-oranges, lilacs and the fringe-tree. Sweet-scented climbers include *Akebia quinata*, *Wistaria* and *Clematis montana* and its variety *rubens*.

With the coming of summer arrives a wealth of roses, irises, peonies, garden heliotrope, fraxinella, pinks, hardy carnations, *Lilium candidum*, and *Clematis recta*. Later come *Clematis ligusticifolia*, tall phlox, *Lilium regale*, *L. speciosum* and *L. auratum*, white plantain-lily, *Campanula lactiflora*, *C. pyramidalis*, *Malva moschata*, meadowsweet and many annuals. Among the annuals are heliotrope, sweet alyssum, sweet peas, sweet sultan, sweet scabious, mignonette, four-o'clocks, stocks, snapdragons, verbenas, petunias, *Abronia*, candytuft, lupines and daturas. At this season also we have the pungent odors of marigold, tansy, *Calendula* and chrysanthemums. Summer-flowering shrubs and trees are *Clethra alnifolia*, *Magnolia virginiana* and *Elaeagnus angustifolia*. Climbers include *Apios tuberosa*, honeysuckles, moonflower, and *Clematis paniculata*.

Some sweet-scented, late-flowering bulbs are *Lycoris squamigera*, *Crocus longiflorus*, *Colchicum speciosum* and *C. bornmuelleri*.

Important among night-scenting flowers are bouncing Bet, evening stock, *Nicotiana*, *Hesperis matronalis*, *Lychnis alba*, *Akebia quinata*, *Lonicera heckrotti*, *Zaluzianskya villosa*, *Schizopetalon walkeri* (annual), *Gladiolus tristis*.

Plants and shrubs with fragrant leaves are the following: sweet geraniums (tender), lemon verbena (tender), bergamot, mints, thymes, southernwood and other artemisias, lavender, rosemary (tender), sweet marjoram, sweet basil, tansies, winter and summer savory, costmary, balm, *Teucrium marum*, *Nepeta mussini*, camomile, feverfew, yarrow, *Micromeria*, hyssop, rue, bayberry, *Sassafras* and sweetbriers.

Southern gardens may enjoy a variety of jasmines, pittosporums, *Osmanthus*, *Gardenia*, myrtles, tender daphnes and magnolias, as well as *Gelsemium*, *Azara microphylla* and *Choisya ternata*, also *Acacia*, *Boronia megastigma*, *Camellia*, *Cestrum nocturnum*, *Murraya exotica*, camphora tree, clerodendrons, *Diosma ericoides*, *Eriobotrya japonica*, *Escallonia*, *Cytisus fragrans* (see BROOM), sweet bay, oleander and the laurustinus. — L. B. W.

*FRAGRANS* (fray′granz). Fragrant.

*FRAGRANTISSIMA, -us, -um* (fray-gran-tiss′i-ma). Most fragrant.

**FRAGRANT SUMAC** = *Rhus canadensis*.

**FRAME.** See COLD FRAME.

**FRANCISCAN NIGHTSHADE** = *Brunfelsia americana*.

**FRANCOA** (fran-ko′a). Chilean perennial herbs of the family Saxifragaceae, two grown outdoors in Calif. and in similar climates, or rarely in the greenhouse, for their white or pink flowers, in long-stalked spikes or racemes.* Leaves mostly basal, lyre-like, and coarsely toothed. Flowers about 1 in. wide, the cluster very floriferous, the 4 petals broad, but with a claw.* Stamens 4. Fruit a 4-angled capsule.* (Named for a Doctor Franco, a Spanish patron of plants.)

While chiefly suited to warm or mild regions, the francoas can be wintered in the cold frame in the East, and are sometimes grown in the cool greenhouse in potting mixture* 3. Propagate by division of the thick rootstocks.

**appendiculata.** A perennial herb 18–30 in. high, the leaves long-stalked, the lowest lobes of the leaf far from the base of the stalk. Flowers pink or paler, the petals sometimes spotted.

**ramosa.** Maiden's-wreath, sometimes called bridal wreath. A showy, perennial herb 20–36 in. high, often grown in pots for Calif. patios. Flower spikes showy, white, often 2 ft. long and nearly an inch thick. Leaves prominently crinkled.

**FRANGIPANI.** See PLUMERIA.

*FRANGULA* (fran′gew-la). An old name for the alder buckthorn (*Rhamnus frangula*).

**FRANKLINIA** = *Gordonia alatamaha*.

**FRASERA** (fray′zer-ra). Stout North American herbs of the family Gentianaceae, commonly called columbo or American columbo, and suited only to shady parts of the wild garden. They are sometimes known as *Swertia*, and are large, perennial herbs with chiefly basal leaves without marginal teeth, if on the stem then opposite,* or whorled.* Of the 15 known species the two cult. sorts are from the Far West. They are fine plants for the open border in Calif. and the Pacific Coast, but not much grown elsewhere. They have rather large flowers in terminal clusters (panicle* or thyrsus*), the calyx 4-parted and the corolla wheel-shaped, the 4 corolla lobes each with a fringed gland. Fruit a somewhat leathery,

---

* Special articles on the subjects indicated by an asterisk (*) will be found at the words so marked.

2-valved, flattened capsule.* (Named for John Fraser, a noted botanical collector in America.)

The plants are of easy culture in the region west of the Rockies, but they are not partial to the cold, wet winters in the East. Propagated by division.

**parryi.** Not over 36 in. high, the chiefly basal leaves nearly 8 in. long and white-margined. Flowers greenish-white, the corolla lobes black-spotted, the clusters nearly 1 ft. long. Southern Calif.

**radiata** = *Frasera speciosa*.

**speciosa.** Deer's-tongue. A stout herb 3-5 ft. high, the chiefly basal leaves green and sometimes 12 in. long. Flowers greenish-white, the corolla lobes purple-spotted, the clusters (panicles*) narrow and nearly 2 ft. long. Mont. to Ore. and Calif. A very handsome plant often sold as *Frasera* (or *Swertia*) *radiata*.

**FRAXINELLA** = *Dictamnus albus*.

**FRAXINUS.** See ASH.

**FRAZERIA.** A somewhat common error for *Frasera*.

**FREESIA** (free′zi-a). Very fragrant and beautiful, South African, bulbous herbs of the iris family, deservedly popular for their winter-blooming flowers. They are of greenhouse culture and bear bulb-like corms,* and mostly narrow, basal, sword-shaped leaves. Flowers typically white or yellow, in terminal, not very floriferous clusters (spike-like racemes*), which are mostly at right angles to the stem. Corolla funnel-shaped, or tubular, the limb* slightly irregular.* Stamens 3. Fruit a small capsule.* (Named for someone, but for whom is not known.)

Freesias are extremely popular florists' flowers, but may be grown by anyone with a cool greenhouse, and the culture of the related *Babiana* and that of *Lachenalia*, which belongs to the lily family, are the same. The corms* should be planted in potting mixture* 3 about the middle of Aug. Keep in a cool greenhouse, and even during the winter the night temperature should not be above 45°-50°. Keep them reasonably moist, and in about 3½ months the first flowers of the earliest varieties should appear, when they should be watered freely. If a succession of bloom is desired, delay the planting of some for 2-3 weeks. As the flowering spike elongates, the plants had better be staked, for they are weak-stemmed. If the bulbs are held in a cool, moist place, they may be started in February for window-box blooming in spring. Whenever they have finished blooming, reduce the water, and when the leaves are dying, shake out the corms* and store in a cool, moist, dark place until the following Aug.

While freesias are typically white or yellow, they have been much hybridized, and some of the newer hort. forms are pink but lack the wonderful fragrance of the older sorts. The first two below are considered, by some, as mere variants of *F. refracta*, and there are over 40 named forms, mostly produced by English or Dutch hybridizers, but some American forms were sponsored by the late Walter van Fleet.

**armstrongi.** Resembling *F. refracta*, but with the white corolla orange at the base, and with the segments rose-purple on the margins.

**hybrida.** Here are grouped many hort. hybrids, probably all derived from *F. refracta*, and having much variation in flower color, notably tinted or veined with pink, purple, blue, orange, and even brown. Not generally as fragrant as the next.

**refracta.** A corm*-bearing herb up to 18-20 in. high, the leaves long, narrow, sword-shaped or even grass-like. Flowers about 2 in. long, yellow or greenish-yellow (white in *var. alba*, in which the tube is gradually narrowed). There are several other varieties, all yellow, but differing in the corolla tube being abruptly narrowed.

**FREESTONE.** Peaches and nectarines are divided by the fact that in some varieties the flesh clings to the stone (clingstone), while in others the flesh slips easily from the stone (freestone). These differences have existed ever since the peach was first grown by the Chinese, perhaps 2500 B.C.

**FREMONTIA** (free-mon′ti-a). A small genus of chiefly Californian, evergreen shrubs of the family Sterculiaceae, suited only to climatically similar regions, but hardy in the East only up to zone* 6. The only cult. species is **F. californica,** variously called flannel-bush, leatherwood, mountain leatherwood, and, in Calif., the slippery elm (no elm, however). It is a shrub 6-10 ft. high, with alternate,* lobed leaves about 1 in. long and felty-hairy beneath. Flowers yellow, showy, nearly 2 in. wide, solitary in the leaf-axils* (for details see STERCULIACEAE). Fruit a capsule.* It is best propagated by seeds or by cuttings of green wood over bottom-heat. (Named for John C. Fremont, an explorer, who discovered the plant.)

**FRENCH ENDIVE.** For botanical identity see CICHORIUM. For culture see CELLAR GARDENING.

**FRENCH GARDEN.** See ARCHITECTURAL STYLE.

**FRENCH HONEYSUCKLE** = *Hedysarum coronarium*.

**FRENCH LAVENDER.** See LAVANDULA STOECHAS and L. SPICA.

**FRENCH MARIGOLD** = *Tagetes patula*. See MARIGOLD.

**FRENCH MULBERRY** = *Callicarpa americana*.

**FRENCH NETTLE** = *Lamium purpureum*.

**FRENCH ROSE** = *Rosa gallica*.

**FRENCH TAMARISK** = *Tamarix gallica*.

**FRENCH WILLOW** = *Epilobium angustifolium*.

**FRIABLE.** Easily crumbled or pulverized. A soil is friable when it can be easily cultivated or dug, which cannot be done to wet clay or silt soils which become friable with difficulty after a downpour. See TILTH.

**FRICK ARBORETUM.** See ARBORETUM.

*FRIGIDA, -us, -um* (fri′ji-da). Growing in cold regions.

**FRINGE-CUPS** = *Tellima grandiflora*.

**FRINGED GALAX** = *Schizocodon soldanelloides*.

**FRINGED GENTIAN** = *Gentiana crinita*.

**FRINGED HEATH** = *Erica ciliaris*.

**FRINGED LOOSESTRIFE** = *Steironema ciliatum*.

**FRINGED ORCHIS.** See HABENARIA.

**FRINGED POLYGALA** = *Polygala paucifolia*.

**FRINGE-FLOWER.** See SCHIZANTHUS.

**FRINGE-TREE** = *Chionanthus virginica*.

**FRITILLARIA** (fri-til-lay′ri-a). Fine, old-fashioned garden flowers of the lily family, all from the north temperate zone and usually called fritillary, although *F. imperialis* is the well-known crown imperial. Of the 70 known species only the following are much cult. They are bulbous, mostly unbranched herbs with alternate* or whorled* leaves, sometimes in a terminal cluster above the flowers, which are mostly early-blooming. Flowers lily-like, pendent, the 6 segments alike (there is no apparent calyx*). Stamens 6. Fruit a many-seeded, 3-valved capsule.* (*Fritillaria* is from the Latin for dicebox, in reference to the flower markings of some species.)

The Old World fritillaries, especially the crown imperial, are old garden favorites which persist for years and are of simple culture in most ordinary garden soils. *F. meleagris* is best grown in the rock garden.* All of them pay for dividing and re-setting every second or third season, and are best propagated by offsets. Most of the western species are not very partial to the cold, wet winters of the eastern U.S.

**imperialis.** Crown imperial. A stout, strong-smelling herb, 2-4 ft. high, the stem purple-spotted. Leaves many, some in a terminal whorl* above the flowers, usually lance-shaped. Flowers nearly 2 in. long, purplish, or yellow-red, or terra-cotta-colored, the segments veined. Persia.

**lanceolata.** Checkered lily. Not over 2 ft. high, the leaves ovalish or lance-oval. Flowers about 1½ in. long, in few-flowered clusters (racemes*), the segments dark purple but mottled greenish-yellow. British Columbia to Calif. Not happy in eastern gardens.

**meleagris.** Toad or checkered lily; called also snake's-head or guinea-hen flower. An erect herb 12-18 in. high. Leaves few, oblongish or narrower. Flowers usually solitary, bell-shaped, 2-3 in. wide, the segments checkered and veined purplish or maroon. Eurasia. There are also white- and yellow-flowered forms. For culture see ROCK GARDEN.

**pluriflora.** Adobe lily or pink fritillary. Not over 12 in. high, the leaves oblongish or lance-shaped. Flowers about 1½ in. long, in a 6-12-flowered raceme,* the segments pinkish-purple. Calif. and not much suited to the East.

**pudica.** Yellow fritillary. Not over 9 in. high, the leaves narrow, but broader towards the tip. Flowers about ¾ in. long, only 1-3 in a cluster, the segments orange-yellow, but purple-tinged. British Columbia to Calif. and N. Mex.

**recurva.** Scarlet fritillary. A stoutish herb 15-30 in. high, the leaves narrowly lance-shaped. Flowers about 1½ in. long, in a cluster of 3-6,

---

* Special articles on the subjects indicated by an asterisk (*) will be found at the words so marked.

the segments brilliant scarlet, but yellow-checkered. Southern Ore. to Calif. A showy plant, but not suited to most eastern gardens.

**FRITILLARY.** See FRITILLARIA.

**FROG'S-BIT** = *Hydrocharis morsus-ranae*.

**FROG'S-BIT FAMILY** = Hydrocharitaceae.

**FROND.** Properly, a fern leaf, but the term is also applied to the leaves of some palms.

*FRONDOSA, -us, -um* (fron-do'sa). Leafy.

**FROST AND FROST CONTROL.** Destructive or killing frosts should not be confused with white or hoar frosts, which may do little or no damage, except to the tenderest plants. And the killing frosts of autumn usually do little damage, as most plants are in any case approaching dormancy.

It is quite otherwise with the late or unseasonable frosts of spring, which may ruin the flowers of early-blooming fruit trees, especially the apricot, almond, peach, and some citrus fruits. For these and a few other plants the frost hazard is so great that somewhat elaborate and effective measures are taken to reduce it. Successful control can be based only upon rather accurate knowledge of what frost is and how it works.

Upon still, calm nights, especially in dry climates, there begins about sundown a rapid, and sometimes violent radiation of heat from the air just above the ground level. This process goes on for an hour or two until the loss of heat, which, of course, rises, begins to affect the air at considerable elevations (500-1000 ft.) above the surface. When this is well under way there starts an inversion which results in the much colder, upper air finally reaching the ground, a process usually known as cold-air drainage. It is this, if the general temperature is near 32°, which may cause a killing frost to occur sometime in the early morning.

Effective fighting of such a condition requires careful reading of accurate thermometers put all over the orchard and especially on the edges of it. Some thermometers, also, should be put at elevations (if possible) of 30, 60, and 100 ft. above the surface. If the temperatures between sundown and 10 P.M. indicate that cold air-drainage may be serious within a few hours, frost control must be started at once.

FROST CONTROL. For many years it was supposed that smoky fires or smudges were the best means of preventing cold-air drainage, but scientific fruit growers have found it cheaper and more effective to use heat. Nor does this involve the apparent absurdity of heating all outdoors. It is based solely upon the fact that to stop radiation of heat will prevent cold-air drainage or so reduce it that little or no damage will result. When the hourly readings of the thermometers show that radiation from the surface is very rapid, the grower must start his fires. Because the control is expensive, the fires should not be burned an hour longer than necessary, which usually means that they are not started until the rate of falling temperature indicates that a killing frost is an hour or two away. They must, of course, be started if the temperature is anywhere near 32°, although some fruits will stand temperatures as low as 27°.

Various types of small, portable, oil-burning furnaces are the best for general use. Orchard-heating-oil, sold for the purpose, is available wherever frost control is feasible. And the furnaces, which should hold enough fuel to burn all night, are also available in frost-control regions.

It will need about 400-600 gallons of oil per acre for citrus fruits and about half this for deciduous fruits, in a single night of serious frost hazard. The number of heaters or furnaces varies from 20 to 100 per acre, depending upon topography (*i.e.* danger of cold-air drainage), the temperature, and the crop to be protected. See the different cultural articles for frost susceptibility of the different fruit crops.

If there is a general hard freeze, or a wind, no frost control by heating can be effective, but it saves much fruit in Calif., where the operation is well managed on a large scale. In the East it seldom pays, where moisture conditions of the atmosphere or wind make frost control very often impossible. It is, for instance, generally ineffective in the citrus region of the lower Rio Grande valley in Tex., largely because of the wind. See PROTECTING PLANTS.

**FROST GRAPE** = *Vitis cordifolia* and *V. vulpina*.

**FROST HEAVING.** See HEAVING.

**FROSTWEED.** See HELIANTHEMUM.

*FRUCTESCENS* (fruk-tess'zens). Fruitful.

**FRUIT.** The term fruit has two somewhat specialized meanings. In the ordinary garden sense a fruit is any edible development from a flower, such as a peach, apple, pear, or plum. For fruits in this sense *see* FRUIT CULTURE.

Fruit, as a botanical term, is of much wider significance. It is technically important in all schemes of plant classification because the seed-bearing organs of plants vary much less than the foliage. Upon this relative stability of the form and structure of fruits and the flowers that produce them depends the classification of plants into families and genera, and sometimes even species in the same genus have decidedly different fruits.

A fruit in this restricted, wholly botanical sense is the ripened ovary and the seeds within or upon it, together with other parts of the flower, which often change materially in the process of ripening. In the apple, for instance, the only development of the ovary is the papery core and its seeds, all the rest of the fruit being the much-enlarged and juicy development of the receptacle* and part of the calyx.*

Fruits in this sense may be edible or not, usually they are worthless in the hort. sense. But it makes much of the descriptive matter in THE GARDEN DICTIONARY more useful to understand the classification of the more important fruits in the botanical sense as given below. All with an asterisk are defined at their proper entries.

Dry Fruits which split: Legume* (pea), Capsule* (Iris), Follicle* (peony), Silique* (mustard). (All these are the product of a single ovary.)
Dry Fruits which do not split: Achene* (buttercup), Utricle* (Chenopodium), Caryopsis* (wheat), Samara* (maple), Schizocarp* (mallow), Nut* (acorn). (All these are the product of a single ovary.)
Fleshy Fruits: Berry* (grape), Drupe* (plum), Pome* (apple). (All these are the product of a single ovary.)
Aggregate Fruits: Strawberry, Raspberry, Magnolia. (All these are the products of the several ovaries of a single flower.)
Collective Fruits: Mulberry, Fig, Pineapple. (All these are the products of the fused ovaries of several flowers.)

This comparatively simple table does not comprise all the fruits recognized by the systematic botanist, but it does include most of those of any interest to the gardener. For other specialized fruit structures *see* CITRUS (for a hesperidium), LOMENT, SILIQUE (for a silicle), PEPO.

Another important botanical feature of the fruits that split is the way they do so. Some, like the iris, split lengthwise along their seams or valves. Others split around the capsule, as in the common weedy plantain. Still others discharge their seeds through pores, as in the poppy.

**FRUIT BUDS.** See BUDS.

**FRUIT CULTURE.** Rather roughly we may describe a fruit in the sense in which it is used in this discussion as a product which has its origin in the flower of a tree, bush, or vine, to which the strawberry, an herbaceous perennial, is an exception. Fruits are commonly grouped as tree, vine, bush, and bramble fruits, but this classification also leaves out the strawberry. Hardy tree fruits are divided into pomes (apples and pears) and drupes (peaches, cherries, plums, and apricots). Almost synonymous with fruit culture is *pomology*, which differs in that it includes the classification and description of fruits.

Fruits are used almost universally in cookery and to eat out of hand. They supply the human system with comparatively little real food, if calories be called the chief attribute of a food, but do furnish indispensable tonics, appetizers, regulators, liquids, medicines and vitamins. (*See* below.) Thus, fruits form an almost indispensable part of the food regimen of every person. Fruits supply a great part of the product for the canning industry of the country, are preserved as well in large quantities by evaporation, and there is now a rapidly growing demand for frozen fruits. Millions

---

* Special articles on the subjects indicated by an asterisk (*) will be found at the words so marked.

# Fruit Culture

of homes in America are supplied either by the housewife or through commerce with preserves, pastries, ices, and confections made from fruits.

Hardy tree fruits and some bush and bramble fruits have been grown in American gardens since the first European settlers brought them here. Commercial fruit growing, however, is a comparatively recent development in North America. There could not be much trade in the products of orchards until transportation facilities permitted shipments from the country to cities and towns, and these did not come until toward the middle of the nineteenth century.

An inventory of the hardy fruits now grown in America is longer than the layman would think in both native and exotic types. The native American fruits are: red and black raspberries and the hybrid purple; several species of blackberries and nearly as many of the closely related dewberries, with hybrids within and between the two groups; five or six species of plum between which there are many hybrids; several species of grapes and many hybrids; and at least one species each of the strawberry, cranberry, blueberry, elderberry, gooseberry, mulberry, crabapple and persimmon. (*See* these terms.)

Fruits from foreign countries are fewer in number, but are of much greater importance. They are: apple, pear, quince, peach, plum (European and Asiatic types), cherry (sweet, sour, and the Dukes, hybrids between the sweets and sours), apricot and nectarine; currant, gooseberry (English type), persimmon (Oriental), grape (*vinifera* type) and two or three species of mulberry.

The value and importance of such of these fruits as appear in the census of 1930 are expressed in millions of dollars as follows: apples, 250; peaches, 100; grapes, 100; plums (including prunes), 48; strawberries, 45; pears, 42; cherries, 38; apricots, 35; raspberries, 35; blackberries and dewberries, 35; cranberries, 3; currants, 2; and gooseberries, 1.

CULTIVATION. The cultivation of hardy fruits east of the Rocky Mountains is localized in several great regions, the most perfect of which is the vast area extending from Nova Scotia on the northeast west to Lake Michigan, south to Virginia, and west to Illinois. In parts of this great area, all the hardy fruits grow with vigor, are long-lived, healthy, and produce fruits in abundance of high quality and of great beauty. High lands in the states south of Virginia, in southern Illinois, in the Ozarks of Missouri and Arkansas, and in the mountains and foothills of the plains region provide some splendid lands for hardy fruits. The strawberry is at home not only in the regions named but in the lowlands of the Gulf and South Atlantic states.

Fruits, even more than vegetables, and greatly more than farm crops, are grown by small land owners, and give vastly greater pleasure to collectors and gardeners than other food products of the soil. Indeed, those who grow fruits as a business but poorly supply the necessaries of a wholesome and a palatable fruit diet. The human palate seeks a greater variety of flavors and aromas and the human eye delights in more shapes and colors in fruits than commercial growers provide. Through the many varieties found in collections more purposes can be served, the season for these products can be lengthened, and new habitats can be found. For these reasons fruit growing is the chief agricultural hobby, "an elegant branch of agriculture" as one old writer puts it.

There is great similarity in planting plans, cultivation, pruning, and general care of home and commercial orchards in America, and the treatment of pests is identical. The differences between professional and amateur fruit growing are chiefly in the selection of varieties and in the harvesting and keeping of the products. Only the several chief operations in fruit growing can receive consideration; the details are left to the discussion of each of the fruits.

PLANTING. In home plantations one must plant the ground he has. A man, however, who grows fruit for the market must select his soil with the greatest care, since he must grow fruit at the lowest cost to meet competition. In a small way, if the earth's crust is not all arable soil, it can be made so by him who would grow fruits for his own use. Impediments can be removed and land enriched. Usually any lands on which the cereals or the potato thrive, are good fruit soils. If there is choice as to sites, choose one above surrounding country which is rolling, near a body of water, with an exposure toward the water, with good atmospheric drainage, and one not swept by strong winds.

A wood is a maze, but an orchard must have a plan if the owner is to get the most out of his land. Getting the most out of the land may not be getting the most on the land. Thus, though one may plant an orchard in squares, quincunxes or hexagons, getting more trees on the land by the last two than the first plan, he is likely to get more out of his land by planting in squares. Trees planted in squares are much more easily cared for and a plant searching for sun, food, and moisture sends its branches and roots quickly into the waste areas of sunlight and soil, if such there be in a square. The quincunx is an arrangement whereby five trees are used in a figure, one in each corner and one in the center of the square. The hexagon permits the planting of all trees at exactly the same distance apart in every direction, thus giving 15 per cent more trees than when planted in squares. Most of the orchards in North America are planted in squares.

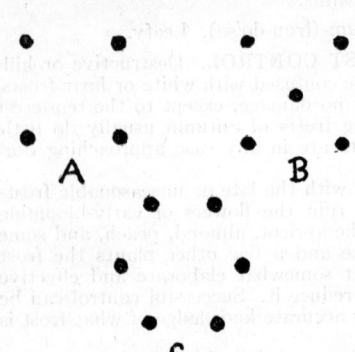

Types of orchard planting. (*A*) In squares. (*B*) Quincunx. (*C*) Hexagon planting.

Growers who want to get more out of the land than they can by planting in squares usually set temporary plants among the permanent plants. These temporary plants are called fillers. Usually fillers should be early-bearing varieties of the same fruit or of a shorter-lived species. Early-bearing apples should be set in the center of a square in the apple orchards, or peaches, cherries, quinces, or small fruits may be set in the apple orchard. Again, small fruits may be set in peach or cherry orchards. The trouble with this filler plan is that when permanents and fillers interlock their boughs, the axe must lay the fillers low and most owners are loath to do this thinning.

Orchards occupy the land longer than any other crop. Preparing the land for fruits, therefore, needs to be done with greater care than for other crops. Underdrainage must be provided if the soil is wet. *See* DRAINING. A soil without organic matter is but a skeleton — dead, inert, and lifeless — and fruits will not grow in the framework of a soil. Green crops or manure must be turned under to put flesh on the soil's skeleton. Always before planting the soil must be made fine and mellow by plowing or spading and then by harrowing and smoothing. The better the preparation, the greater the yield of fruit. If the land is properly prepared, planting is easily, quickly, and safely done. On such land, there need be no such pottering over-niceties as laying out the roots to preserve the fibers and inserting the plant in a gingerly fashion to make sure that it stands in its new abode exactly as it stood in the old. In land well prepared the hole is really as large as the orchard, and all that needs to be done in planting is to throw the surface soil to one side and put in the plant.

In the actual work of setting, the plants should be put in the ground about as deep as they stood in the nursery, though in light, hungry, or thirsty soils, the roots should go a little deeper and in heavy soils not quite so deep. The soil must be packed firmly about newly set plants, which is best done by tramping. Watering at planting time is necessary only when the land is unduly dry. When necessary, water should be used liberally, always leaving the sur-

---

* Special articles on the subjects indicated by an asterisk (*) will be found at the words so marked.

face soil loose and dry. Newly set plants do not need outside nourishment. To put rank manure or strong fertilizers about the roots of young trees is inviting plant infanticide.

Small fruits should always be cultivated and most plantations of tree fruits do better under cultivation. Generally speaking, orchards should be plowed in late autumn. Tillage should begin in early spring and continue until July or August in the North and June or July in the South, after which a cover crop should be sown to keep up the organic matter in the soil.

COVER CROPS. In some soils commercial orchards are best kept in grass which is cut two or three times and left on the ground as a mulch. This method of managing orchard soils is called sod culture or sod mulch. It can be used only on deep, rich, moist lands. In most home plantations sod culture suffices.

Clover, vetch, oats, rape, rye, barley, or buckwheat are the common cover crops in the North, to which may be added soybeans and cowpeas for the South. Usually a cover crop is sown after the last cultivation, provided that at this time a moist seedbed can be had.

In the average orchard, big or little, if the land is well drained, well tilled, and well supplied with organic matter from cover crops, commercial fertilizers are little needed. The exceptions are found in sandy and gravelly soils; in those subject to drouth; or on soils of such shallowness or such mechanical texture as to limit the root-range of the plants; or in soils so wet or so dry as to prevent bacteriological activities in the soil. All the fruits thrive in either alkaline or acid soils, and lime is never needed to neutralize acidity. Potash and phosphorus are seldom needed. Nitrogen is usually the limiting factor, a liberal amount of which is 200 pounds to the acre of nitrate of soda or its equivalent in some other nitrogen carrier. If phosphorus is needed, 300 pounds of acid phosphate to the acre should suffice. If potash is indicated, 200 pounds of muriate to the acre might be tried. *See* FERTILIZERS. Commercial fertilizers are best applied in the spring, as soon as the ground can be worked, spreading the chemicals over an area considerably greater than that covered by the branches of the plant.

Pruning is a different operation for every fruit, the details of which are given for each in the discussion of the several fruits. Perhaps it ought to be emphasized here that usually fruits are pruned more than need be and without knowledge specific enough as to what each of the different kinds and varieties need. A good orchardist will not put a knife in a branch without knowing exactly why he does so. *See* NEGLECTED ORCHARDS.

STORAGE. The commercial fruit grower needs little instruction in the art of conservation, since his crop usually goes in cold storage, where it is looked after by professional storage men. The home gardener must usually depend upon common storage and here a few items of advice may be helpful. Fruits must be kept in a cool place, neither too wet nor too dry, and where they will not absorb odors from vegetables or other products. The ideal temperature is just above the freezing point, but most tree fruits may be kept well where the temperature occasionally goes up to 40° or 45° F. Windows that can be opened and closed as occasion requires are great helps in controlling the temperature. The moisture can be kept at the right degree by having a dirt floor or by occasionally sprinkling a cement floor. It is always helpful, in these small storage rooms, to wrap each apple or pear or bunch of grapes in a paper to conserve moisture. Cellophane is ideal for this purpose. Wrappers keep out odors and prevent the spread of decay. In a very dry room, fruit containers should be lined with paper and kept tightly covered. Pears are best stored in shallow trays. It is useless to store bruised, decayed, diseased, or over-ripe fruit. — U. P. H.

For the culture of greenhouse fruit, *see* GREENHOUSE.

## FRUIT WEST OF THE ROCKY MOUNTAINS

Considerably more than half the commercial fruit crop of the country is grown in the eleven Pacific Slope and Mountain states: more than half the apples, more than three-fourths the pears, grapes, plums, avocados, figs, and persimmons, all the prunes, nearly half the peaches, practically all the apricots, almonds, walnuts, lemons, olives, dates, more than two-thirds of the oranges, some of the grapefruit, and much of the small fruit crop. In parts of the West average annual yields are much larger than in the East, due, in part, to the specialized climatic conditions that obtain in the West. The most important are noted below. The details of culture and best varieties for the West will be found at the special articles on each fruit.

FROST. In this region all the climatic zones of the United States are represented, except the very warmest: the southern part of Florida. Sections for commercial fruit growing must be chosen cautiously; but in much of the region all the temperate-zone fruits and nuts may be grown, at least in a small way, for home use. In two states, California and Arizona, all the sub-tropical fruits can be grown, and in the warmest parts, tropical fruits, such as the mango, have occasionally ripened well.

In the Mountain states a large percentage of the total area is frosty. In Pacific Coast states, except at high elevation, crops are less frequently lost from spring or autumn frosts than in most other sections. Because of this and other influences, the fruit crop of the Pacific Coast states tends to be more uniform than that of other sections.

In the northern Pacific Coast fruit-growing districts, winter temperatures tend to be well above the danger point to winter wood, but there have been cold nights in a few years that caused much damage. In California and Arizona, except at high elevations, there are no winter temperatures that kill the wood of common temperate-zone fruits, but there have been frosts in which much damage was done to citrus and other sub-tropical fruit trees. Because they blossom and grow in winter or very early spring, these fruits must be protected by heating during cold nights. *See* FROST AND FROST CONTROL.

DRY SUMMERS AND DEEP SOILS. The tendency to bear large crops annually seems to be due in part to absence of high water tables, in late spring and summer, which kills the deeper roots or makes the soil unfavorable for the development of strong root systems in the deeper layers. Naturally, the more soil a tree has filled completely with roots, the larger will be the leaf surface it can supply with water and, therefore, the larger the amount of fruit it can bear.

Of course, even in the best districts, not all soil is suitable for good root growth to such depths.

ABUNDANT SUNSHINE AND HIGH SUMMER TEMPERATURE. In most of the fruit-growing districts of these states, there is little cloudiness in summer: more hours of sunshine than at the same latitudes in the East. And the sunlight tends to be more intense. The average daily amount of plant activity should therefore be greater.

Sunny weather at blossoming time, characteristic of much of the West, is certainly favorable to insect pollination and therefore to the setting of fruit, whenever there are blossoms not killed by frost.

There is a tendency for both fruit and wood to be firmer in the Pacific slope states, except at high elevations. Whether this is due to abundant sunshine and the resulting abundant food supply to form thick cell walls, or to high temperature, or to something else, we cannot be certain. This greater firmness is sometimes associated with a milder flavor: more pleasant flavor in varieties that tend to be too tart, more insipid flavor in varieties that are naturally mild.

High summer temperatures do not prevail in all western districts. Near the Pacific Ocean the summers tend to be cool. In some coastal districts where sub-tropical fruits are grown, the summers are moderately cool and the fruit may ripen several months later than fruit of the same varieties ripens a few miles farther from the coast. Farther north in some coastal districts, such as that near Watsonville, California, owing partly to fog, the summer temperature is lower than in any fruit-growing districts in the mountains or in the East. Many kinds of temperate-zone fruits will not develop normal flavor, and even apples grown there tend to develop troubles in storage that do not often develop on fruit grown in sections with warmer summers.

---

\* Special articles on the subjects indicated by an asterisk (\*) will be found at the words so marked.

In many mountain districts where the summer temperature tends to be moderate, western mountain fruit tends to resemble eastern fruit of the same varieties.

HIGH WINTER TEMPERATURE. For most of the sub-tropical fruits grown in southern California and Arizona, mean temperatures above 50° F. may be beneficial, but for some of the temperate-zone fruits and nuts, if the mean temperature for December, January, and February is appreciably above 50° F., blossoming and beginning of growth in spring are delayed and straggling. It requires two or three months of mean temperature below about 50° F. to break the rest of the buds of many kinds of temperate-zone plants. Fruit buds of some kinds, such as the apricot and the peach, may fall without opening. Flowers or young fruits of other kinds, such as the apple, the pear, and, sometimes, the walnut, may fall, perhaps in part because the young fruit set so late that the weather is hot and dry. The delay in starting of growth may be several months, and then only a small percentage of the buds may grow. This straggling growth cannot form as many fruit buds as would be formed on a normal tree. The crop in the second year after a warm winter will, therefore, be rather small, even if that winter is cold enough to break the rest period. The average annual crop may, therefore, be considerably reduced, even in sections where the winters are harmfully warm only once in two or three years. There are several kinds of deciduous fruits, such as the Japanese persimmon, the fig, the almond, most varieties of *vinifera* grapes, blackberries from western species and apparently from eastern species also, that will start normally after such winters, and others, like Oriental plums, some chestnut varieties, and some grape varieties, that may be delayed somewhat in starting after such winters, but seldom, if ever, enough to prevent the trees from making a full season's growth and bearing a good crop. The starting of leaf buds of the apricot is never delayed enough to prevent the trees from making a normal season's growth, though the flower buds fall badly.

This bad effect of warm winters is seen only rarely north of latitude 35°, except mildly with apples and Bartlett pears and a few varieties of peaches in warm valleys near the coast. Even in southern California it is not usually serious at elevations above 3000 feet. At such elevations, and in sections like the San Joaquin and Sacramento valleys of California, where the mean winter temperature is usually kept somewhat below 50° F. by the heavy fogs that prevent air and trees from warming up much during the day, the rest period may not be completely broken when the weather becomes warm enough for growth, but it causes only a beneficial delay: enough to reduce considerably the danger of frost to the blossoms or young fruits.

ORIGIN OF VARIETIES. (For lists of most suitable varieties for the West see articles concerning each kind of fruit.) Most of the varieties grown in the West have originated as chance seedlings in the East or the West or have been introduced from the Old World. For example, apple varieties are mostly those from chance seedlings in the East, though the pear, apricot, plum, and sweet cherry varieties are mostly from Europe. Shipping peach varieties are eastern seedlings, the principal ones being the same in East and West. *Vinifera* grape and fig varieties are from Asia. Almond varieties and peach varieties for canning and drying are seedlings from California orchards. Walnut varieties are from France and from California seedlings of strains introduced by Felix Gillet and Joseph Sexton.

A few varieties of plums, as well as one slightly important variety of quince, two of cherries, and two of blackberries, were introduced by Luther Burbank. Many people seem to attribute much of western success in fruit growing to the work of Burbank in introducing "scientifically" developed varieties; yet, except for Oriental plums, his varieties have been of very little value. His Sugar prune is better than other varieties in some poor soils and the Standard prune is good in some places for the fresh fruit market, but probably as many people have suffered loss as have profited by having planted one of these varieties instead of the French prune, which is a much better variety for most situations. Even the Oriental plums were not the result of skillful or scientific plant breeding. They came from twelve trees sent to him from Japan by Isaac Bunting. Two of his varieties, Burbank and Satsuma, were from two of these trees direct, and the others, it seems, were seedlings descended from some of them. They were all of strains developed in Japan.— W. H. C.

**FRUIT FLIES.** *See* Two-Winged Flies at INSECT PESTS. *See also* Insect Pests at MANGO.

**FRUIT ROOM.** *See* Storage at FRUIT CULTURE.

**FRUIT SHOW.** *See* EXHIBITIONS AND SHOWS.

**FRUIT-TREE SPRAYING.** *See* SPRAYING AND DUSTING.

**FRUITWORM.** *See* Insect Pests at CRANBERRY.

*FRUTESCENS* (froo-tess'zens). Shrubby.

*FRUTICOSA*, *-us*, *-um* (froo-ti-ko'sa). Fruticose; *i.e.* shrubby.

*FRUTICULOSA*, *-us*, *-um* (froo-tick-you-lō'sa). Somewhat shrubby.

**FUCHSIA** (few'sha, but properly fuke'zi-a). A genus of perhaps 80 species of showy shrubs of the family Onagraceae, all but a handful tropical American, the rest from New Zealand. They are very popular as greenhouse plants, for summer bedding, and for window boxes, but may be grown outdoors all year in zones* 8 and 9, where they are very handsome, especially in Calif. Leaves simple,* opposite* or alternate.* Flowers usually very showy, often hanging, and mostly in small clusters, or solitary in the leaf-axils,* red, purple, blue, or white, or sometimes all four. Calyx* tubular or bell-shaped, the limb with 4 spreading tips. Petals usually 4 (wanting in *F. procumbens*). Stamens 8, usually unequal and nearly always long-protruding and showy, as is the style.* Fruit a 4-celled, pulpy berry. (Named for Leonard Fuchs, a German botanist.) The plants are sometimes called lady's-eardrops.

As commonly grown by florists or by amateurs with a cool greenhouse, fuchsias are usually propagated each year from softwood cuttings rooted in pots or in the propagating bench. They need potting mixture* 3 and a greenhouse temperature of 50°–60°. They are usually trained to a central stem or into a bushy crown, largely by pinching. Outdoors, or if kept over the blooming season, they become much larger. If this is done, they bloom more freely if the branches are cut back after the current blooming season. The height dimensions below are for plants as grown permanently outdoors, the usual greenhouse specimens being much smaller. Fuchsias make good house plants, and during the summer they may be plunged outdoors, preferably in the shade. They are pretty free of diseases, the only one of importance being a rust (which see at PLANT DISEASES). The American Fuchsia Society welcomes those interested in this flower. Its officers change from time to time, but may be reached by writing to the Garden Editor, Houghton Mifflin Company, Boston, Mass.

For the California fuchsia *see* ZAUSCHNERIA.

**hybrida.** A hybrid plant and including most of the common fuchsias in cult., probably derived from *F. magellanica* and a Mexican species. It differs from the former species in having sturdier twigs, broader leaves, and larger flowers. As a greenhouse plant always shrubby. Calyx crimson, but the petals white, rose, or purple, and shorter than the calyx*-lobes. Some hort. varieties have flowers 3 in. long. See Pinching at TRAINING PLANTS.

**magellanica.** As grown on walls or trained on a trellis, often 20 ft. high in Calif., where it is very popular, much lower in the greenhouse. Leaves opposite* or in 3's, oval or oval-lance-shaped, 1½–2 in. long, wavy and toothed on the margin. Flowers 1–2 in. long, the calyx* red and the petals blue, the stamens long-protruding. Peru to southern S.A. The *var. conica* has a scarlet calyx* and purple petals; *var. globosa* has small, reddish-purple flowers, the buds of which are globe-shaped; and the *var. gracilis* is a lower, more slender shrub with a scarlet calyx and purple petals.

**procumbens.** Trailing fuchsia. A prostrate or trailing plant useful for hanging baskets. Leaves alternate,* roundish-oval, long-stalked, about 1 in. long. Male and female flowers on different plants, solitary in the leaf-axils,* erect, nor over ¾ in. long, the calyx orange-purple, the petals none. N. Zeal.

INSECT PESTS: The following general greenhouse pests attack fuchsia: mealybugs (*see* COLEUS), whiteflies (*see* BEGONIA), aphids and thrips (*see* CHRYSANTHEMUM), and the cyclamen mite (*see* CYCLAMEN).

**FUCHSIA FAMILY** = Onagraceae.

*FUCHSIOIDES* (fuke-zi-oy'deez, but *see* OÏDES). Fuchsia-like.

**FUGACIOUS.** Soon withering or falling off, but not truly ephemeral (which see).

*FUJISAN-SAKURA.* See Japanese flowering cherries at PRUNUS.

*FULGENS* (ful'jenz). Glistening or shining.

*FULGIDA*, *-us*, *-um* (ful'ji-da). Shining.

**FULLER, A. S.** *See* America at GARDEN BOOKS.

---

* Special articles on the subjects indicated by an asterisk (*) will be found at the words so marked.

**FULLER'S TEASEL** = *Dipsacus fullonum*.

**FULLONUM** (full-lō'num). Of or pertaining to the fullers (of cloth), the Latin for whom was *fullo*.

**FULVA, -us, -um** (full'va). Of a tawny or smoky orange-yellow.

**FUMARIA.** See FUMITORY.

**FUMARIACEAE** (few-mare-i-ā'see-ee). The fumitory or bleeding-heart family comprises only 5 genera and about 170 species, four of which contain garden plants, and one, *Dicentra*, the ever-popular bleeding-heart and Dutchman's-breeches. The other cult. genera are *Adlumia, Corydalis*, and *Fumaria* (see FUMITORY).

All are relatively weak herbs with more or less glistening foliage and highly irregular* flowers with a conspicuous spur, sometimes very showy.

Leaves simple* and much cut, or compound,* and sometimes thrice-compound. All the plants have a watery juice (unlike the often milky juice of the closely related poppy family). Fruit a dry pod (capsule*) which splits by valves in all the genera except *Fumaria*, which bears a small, nut-like fruit.

Technical flower characters: Sepals 2, small and scale-like. Petals 4 in two series. One or both of the outer series prolonged into a spur or merely swollen. Stamens 6. Ovary superior.*

**FUMARIAEFOLIA, -us, -um** (few-mare-i-ee-fō'li-a). With fumitory-like leaves.

**FUMARIOIDES** (few-mare-i-oy'deez, but *see* OÏDES). Like the fumitory.

**FUMIGATION.** The types of fumigation of most interest to the horticulturist are the use of nicotine fumes in greenhouses; the use of hydrocyanic acid gas in greenhouses and rooms, and under tents; the use of carbon disulphide in seeds and soil; and the use of paradichlorobenzene in soil, against the peach borer. The use of heat may also be considered here, although it is not strictly fumigation. Formaldehyde is useful against disease organisms, but is *not* effective as an insecticide.

The space to be fumigated should be made as nearly airtight as possible (except in soil fumigation), and its volume in cubic feet should be calculated. The cubic contents of a rectangular room are easily computed, and the tents used in tree fumigation are standardized for contents. The cubic contents of a greenhouse are a little more difficult to calculate. The best method is to get the area in square feet of the end of each house and multiply it by the length in feet. The area can be obtained by making a diagram of the end to scale, dividing it into one or more triangles and rectangles, computing the area of each, and adding the different areas.

### NICOTINE PREPARATIONS

Nicotine fumes are deadly to plant lice and other greenhouse insects, but will not injure plants, unless used at high temperatures and in bright sunshine. The concentrated preparations are poisonous to man, but the fumes are not dangerous unless inhaled in large quantities. Coarse tobacco or stems may be burned to produce smoke, but commercial preparations, extracts of nicotine sulphate or free nicotine, used according to directions, are more reliable in their action and give better results. The extract may be vaporized by heating or placing on steam pipes. Free nicotine is more often used than the sulphate. Other preparations are sold, usually in the form of nicotine papers or powders, to be burned slowly. Fumigation of greenhouses with nicotine is most successful at temperatures between 50° and 70° F. and is usually done in the evening or at night, after which the fumes are allowed to leak away gradually and the house is aired in the morning. For persistent pests repeated fumigations may be necessary.

### HYDROCYANIC ACID

Hydrocyanic acid is a light gas at ordinary temperatures and pressures. It is a deadly poison and must not be breathed, but if carefully and properly handled it is a very effective and satisfactory fumigant. This gas may be produced by the action of atmospheric moisture on calcium cyanide, by the action of dilute sulphuric acid on sodium cyanide or potassium cyanide, or by exposing to the air diatomaceous earth or other inert materials impregnated with liquid hydrocyanic acid. These cyanides are themselves deadly poisonous, and should be handled with care. Hydrocyanic acid can also be obtained in steel cylinders, as a liquid under pressure.

Hydrocyanic acid gas has a tendency to burn leaves, varying with different plants and air conditions. It works best between 60° and 70° F., with the plants dry and the air still, and in the absence of the sun. Night is usually chosen for fumigation. Every precaution should be taken to make the building tight, to get out before the gas begins to diffuse, to keep others from entering (a warning notice on the door is best), and to ventilate the building thoroughly before entering after the fumigation. It is not safe to fumigate an ordinary room with this gas if adjoining rooms are occupied.

Fumigation with calcium cyanide is the safest method for general use. The calcium cyanide is spread out on paper in a thin layer, in different parts of the room to be fumigated. Since the gas is given off less rapidly than when evolved from sodium cyanide or potassium cyanide and sulphuric acid, the operator has more time to get away. It is used at the rate of 12 to 16 ounces per 1000 cubic feet in empty buildings or greenhouses, and at nearly this strength on dormant nursery stock, but on living plants in greenhouses the concentration should be much weaker. The grower is often advised to try ⅛ ounce per 1000 cubic feet, and, if this does not prove strong enough, to increase the strength. If the plants show injury, the strength must be decreased. This material is usually allowed to remain overnight.

By the "pot" method of fumigation, in which sodium cyanide or potassium cyanide is treated with sulphuric acid, the gas is given off much more rapidly than when calcium cyanide is used, and this method is therefore more dangerous to use. The acid is an additional danger. A common dosage for an empty room or dormant plants is 10 ounces of sodium cyanide, 15 ounces of sulphuric acid (concentrated), and 30 fluid ounces of water per 1000 cubic feet of space. For greenhouse plants a very much weaker dosage is used; from ⅛ to ¼ ounce of the cyanide, depending on the tightness of the greenhouse, per 1000 cubic feet, with water and acid correspondingly reduced. The exposure should be for 1 hour only. Stoneware crocks should be used to hold the materials, several if the space is large. The water should always be put in the crock first and then the acid; and the liquid should not come within several inches of the top. The proper quantity of cyanide for each crock should be weighed out and placed in a paper bag. The bags should be dropped quickly in the crocks, and then, while the acid is eating through the paper, the operator should leave the room and shut the door. The room should be aired by opening it from the outside, and the residue in the crocks should be buried.

Pests of citrus trees in Calif. are usually controlled by fumigation, for since these trees do not shed their leaves they are liable to be injured by a strong dormant spray. The fumigation is usually conducted under tents. Most frequently liquid hydrocyanic acid in cylinders is released by means of special apparatus in the tents, where it turns to a gas, although sometimes calcium cyanide dust is blown into the tents, and formerly the pot method was used. This sort of fumigation is usually done commercially by skilled operators.

### CARBON DISULPHIDE

Carbon disulphide is a heavy liquid which quickly evaporates when exposed, forming a gas heavier than air. It is deadly to insects, too injurious to use on living plants, but not so deadly to man as hydrocyanic acid. It is more explosive than gasoline, and should be kept away from fire or heat.

When used for fumigation in empty rooms, the carbon disulphide is exposed in small dishes placed near the ceiling. It should be used at the rate of 1 or 2 pounds per 100 cubic feet, when the temperature is between 70° and 100° F., and

* Special articles on the subjects indicated by an asterisk (*) will be found at the words so marked.

allowed to remain overnight or longer. For treating seeds in a box or bin, it may be put on rags placed at the top of the bin. As in the case of other fumigants, the room or bin should be tight. For soil fumigation this material should be used in beds. A small hole several inches deep is made in each square foot, a tablespoonful of the liquid poured into it, and then covered with soil. The fumigant will diffuse and finally evaporate without further treatment.

A carbon disulphide emulsion may be used to kill Japanese beetle larvae and other soil insects in lawns and golf greens. It is prepared from 10 parts by volume of carbon disulphide, 3 parts of water, and 1 part of rosin-fish oil soap; mixed as in the preparation of kerosene emulsion (*see* SPRAYING). The stock mixture is diluted with water, 1 to 400, and sprinkled on the soil, 3 pints of diluted emulsion per square foot.

PARADICHLOROBENZENE

This is a strong-smelling white crystalline substance. It is used to combat clothes moths and also in soil fumigation, particularly soil around peach trees to kill young peach borers (*see* PEACH).

HEAT

Insects succumb readily to exposure to moderate heat; few can withstand temperatures of 120° to 130° F. for very long. It is difficult to apply heat to living plants without injuring them; however, it is practicable in some cases, as in the control of cyclamen mites on various plants. Bulbs can be freed of some pests by immersion in warm water (110° F.) for 3 hours. Soil that is to be used for the growing of plants can be sterilized by steaming or otherwise heating, and greenhouse pipes or tiles can easily be arranged to steam soil in beds before planting. — F. M. W. (*See also* SPRAYING, INSECT PESTS, *and* INSECTICIDES.)

**FUMITORY.** An old garden plant, the only cult. species of 40 herbs of the genus **Fumaria** (few-may'ri-a) of the family Fumariaceae, all from the Old World temperate regions. The only one of even secondary garden interest is **F. officinalis**, which is also called hedge fumitory, wax dolls, and a dozen other names. It is an annual or biennial herb with finely dissected, almost fern-like leaves and a weak stem. Flowers small, in racemes,* the 4 petals purplish but crimson at the tip, one of them spurred. Stamens 6. Fruit small, stalked, not splitting, the lower ones usually ripe before the upper flowers of the cluster have finished blooming. The plant is of the easiest culture in any garden soil. It was once widely grown as a remedy for scurvy. (*Fumaria* is from the Latin for smoke, in allusion to the smoky odor of some species.) *See also* ADLUMIA FUNGOSA.

**FUMITORY FAMILY** = Fumariaceae.

**FUNEBRIS, -e** (few-nee'bris). Funereal.

**FUNGI** (fun'jy). Plural of fungus (which see). For the edible fungi *see* MUSHROOM. For the harmful fungi *see* PLANT DISEASES.

**FUNGICIDES.** At present relatively few chemicals are used as fungicides, but there is no doubt that many more will be discovered and used in practical control measures. Among those now employed are various forms of sulphur, copper, mercury, formaldehyde, and a few minor substances. In addition, heat is commonly used to destroy various parasites.

SULPHUR. When sulphur and lime are boiled together, the resulting dark red liquid is known as lime-sulphur. The commercial product usually has a standard concentration known as 32° Baumé, and is diluted with water before being applied as a spray to plants. The liquid is heavy and unpleasant to handle, therefore a number of dry lime-sulphur brands in the form of dust are now on the market. These materials are mixed with water, and also applied as sprays.

Some plants, such as peach trees, are injured by lime-sulphur, therefore a mild form of sulphur-lime has been devised. Finely ground sulphur is mixed with hydrated lime and some spreader, such as dried milk, and the mixture stirred into water for spraying.

Sulphur, in minute enough particles to be fluffy, is used to dust all kinds of plants. When the particles are large a sufficient dust fog is not formed to envelop the plant. Some of the sulphur dust is stained green to be more nearly invisible on green foliage of ornamental plants.

COPPER. Blue stone or blue vitriol, as copper-sulphate is known to most growers, is used as a fungicide in various ways. It is the fungicidal ingredient of bordeaux mixture. Two to five pounds, depending upon the concentration desired, are dissolved in twenty-five gallons of water. At the same time the same number of pounds of hydrated lime are mixed in twenty-five gallons of water in another barrel. The contents of the two barrels are then slowly poured together and stirred vigorously. The resulting spray is a sky blue suspension that deteriorates rapidly after mixture, therefore should be applied as soon as prepared. The concentrations of both the copper and lime as well as the method of mixing may be varied to fit the needs of the plant and the convenience of the grower. Throughout this book bordeaux mixture with strengths of 2-2-50, 4-4-50, 4-2-50, 5-5-50, etc., are recommended for different plants. The first number represents the number of pounds of copper sulphate; the second, the pounds of lime; and the third, the number of gallons of water. When a small, three-gallon sprayer only is to be filled, about three ounces of copper sulphate and the same amount of hydrated lime is required. Insect poisons may be added to the spray if necessary. *See* LIME for exact meaning of hydrated lime.

In making a copper dust, the factory heats the blue stone crystals until most of the water is removed, then grinds them exceedingly fine. This is known as monohydrated copper sulphate, and is mixed with hydrated lime, and applied as a dust to plants when dew or other moisture is present. When twenty pounds of the monohydrated copper dust is mixed with eighty pounds of lime the concentration is a 20-80 dust. Other concentrations may be recommended. Arsenate of lead may be added for insect control.

One pound of copper sulphate may be dissolved in five gallons of water and used for scrubbing walls and floors which require treatment with a fungicide. Seeds, such as tomatoes and spinach, may be dipped in the same solution for disinfection.

Other copper compounds commonly employed are copper carbonate and red cuprous oxide. The carbonate is mixed with wheat seed (about 3 ounces for each bushel) in controlling stinking smut. The red oxide is mixed with various vegetable and flower seeds for the control of damping-off.

MERCURY. One of the most effective fungicides known is mercury in its various forms. Mercuric chloride, also known as corrosive sublimate or bichloride of mercury, may be bought in powder form or as a tablet, and is widely employed as a tuber and seed disinfectant. The concentration most generally recommended is 1-1000, or one tablet dissolved in each pint of water. If the powder form is used, one ounce is dissolved in a little hot water, then enough cold water is added to make seven and one-half gallons. The solution may be employed cold or hot. If it is much cooler than 60° F. the poison does not react, and if much hotter than 126° F. the seeds or tubers may be killed. A more dilute solution, 1-1500 or 1-2000 is poured along the rows of crucifer seedlings to control damping-off.

Mercurous chloride or calomel is mixed with water to treat tubers or seeds, and also is sprayed or dusted over lawns to control brown patch. It has the one disadvantage of being so heavy that it sinks to the bottom almost immediately when placed in water. Constant agitation is required to keep it in suspension.

Mercuric oxide or yellow oxide of mercury, 1 pound in 20 gallons of water, has proved effective in treating potato seed.

There are now on sale a very large number of organic mercury compounds, some of which have proved excellent fungicides. They should always be applied according to the directions on the container.

FORMALDEHYDE is a gas forced into water to the saturation point, or about 37%. This liquid is diluted to various strengths for use in disinfecting soil, boards, flats, walks, and

---

* Special articles on the subjects indicated by an asterisk (*) will be found at the words so marked.

walls. It also is used widely for controlling oat and onion smuts. It is an effective fungicide, but the fumes are so disagreeable that it has in many cases been replaced by some other chemical. In order to overcome some of this disagreeableness, formaldehyde has been mixed with absorbent dusts, and may now be applied in dust form.

Among other chemicals that are sometimes employed as fungicides are aluminum sulphate, zinc oxide, acetic acid, potassium permanganate, zinc sulphate, and a rather long list of other materials. — C. C.

**FUNGINE.** A trademarked liquid fungicide, sold with directions for use against mildew and rust.

**FUNGO.** A trademarked liquid fungicide, containing sulphur, and sold with directions for use against mildew.

*FUNGOSA, -us, -um* (fun-go'sa). Related to or resembling a fungus; also, spongy.

**FUNGOUS DISEASES.** See PLANT DISEASES.

**FUNGUS** (fun'gus). Plural fungi.* One of a huge group of flowerless plants, of little interest to the gardener except for the mushroom (which see) and for the many plant diseases* caused by the microscopic forms. Unlike nearly all flowering plants, the fungi contain no green coloring matter and are therefore wholly parasitic or else live on the dead remains of other plants (*see* SAPROPHYTE). They bear no flowers, but are reproduced by microscopic spores, a common example being the cloud of such given off by a puffball. While the great majority of the fungi can only be seen under the microscope, *en masse* even these are very noticeable, as in the mold on bread or jam, or the blights on leaves. Others, however, are large, as in the mushroom and toadstools, or the often very large bracket fungi on tree trunks. See WOOD ROT.

**FUNKIA.** See PLANTAIN-LILY.

**FURCRAEA** (fur-kree'ya). Tropical American plants of the family Amaryllidaceae, resembling the century plants in habit, and grown like them. *See* AGAVE. They have fleshy, long, sword-shaped leaves in a basal rosette from which springs a tall flowering stalk with a terminal cluster (panicle*) of greenish-white flowers, after the blooming of which the plant dies. Corolla* more or less wheel-shaped, the 6 segments spreading but united at the base. Stamens 6. Fruit an oblong, 3-sided capsule.* (Named for Antoine François de Fourcroy, French chemist.)

**gigantea.** Giant lily; called also cabuya, and sometimes Mauritius hemp for which it is grown commercially. Leaves nearly 8 ft. long and 6-7 in. wide, very fleshy and with only a few, distant, marginal teeth. Flowering stalk about 20 ft. high, the flowers about 1½ in. long. Brazil. There is a hort. variety with variegated, wholly spineless leaves. Both are very striking plants for the desert garden. They seldom or never produce a trunk, the leaves all being basal.

**selloa.** Leaves about 4 ft. long and 3 in. wide, the rosette basal or at the end of a short, stout trunk. Marginal leaf-prickles curved. Flowering stalk 15-20 ft. high, the flowers about 1½ in. long. Colombia. The *var. marginata* has yellow- or white-margined leaves.

**FURNACE ASHES.** See ASH AND ASHES.
**FURNITURE.** See ORNAMENT AND FURNITURE.
**FURROW.** See PLOWING.

**FURZE.** Very showy, spiny, yellow-flowered, mostly Eurasian shrubs comprising the genus **Ulex** (you'lex) of the pea family, and often called gorse or whin. Of the 20 known species only the two below are much cult. They are low shrubs, mostly leafless, or the leaves represented only by a thorny leafstalk. Flowers pea-like, mostly in the axils* of thorns, but inclined to be crowded at the ends of the twigs. Fruit a small, egg-shaped legume.* (*Ulex* is the classical Latin name for this plant or one like it.)

Furze is not easy to transplant and should be let alone once it is established. Some growers prefer to sow seeds directly where the plants are wanted. They prefer a sandy, slightly acid soil, and when once established they are fine plants for sandy banks or open wastes. They are not hardy everywhere (see below).

**U. europaeus.** A much-branched, twiggy and spiny shrub 2-3 ft. high, the leaves scale-like, none, or reduced to spines. Flowers about ¾ in. long, bright yellow. Pod about ½ in. long, brown and hairy. Eu. April-July (all the year in Calif.). Hardy from zone* 4 southward.

**U. nanus.** A dwarf, spiny shrub, 12-20 in. high, sometimes half prostrate, very twiggy. Flowers golden-yellow. Pod about ½ in. long, enclosed by the persistent calyx. Aug.-Sept. Eu. Hardy from zone* 5 southward.

**FUSARIUM ROT.** See Diseases at GLADIOLUS.

*FUSCA, -us, -um* (fuss'ka). Brown.

*FUSCATA, -us, -um* (fuss-kay'ta). Brownish.

*FUSCO-RUBRA, -us, -um* (fuss-ko-roo'bra). Brownish-red.

**FUSIFORM.** Spindle-shaped; *i.e.* narrowed both ends from a swollen middle.

**FUTURISTIC GARDEN.** See MODERN GARDEN DESIGN.

# G

**GACHIPAES** = *Guilielma gasipaes*.

**GADGETS.** See Section 7, TOOLS AND IMPLEMENTS.

**GAILLARDIA** (gay-lar'di-a). Showy North American herbs of the family Compositae, the three below very popular flower garden plants from the western U.S. They are leafy, erect, branching herbs with alternate* or basal leaves which are more or less dotted. Flower heads extremely handsome, the rays 3-toothed or almost fringed, yellow, orange, or orange-red (white in a hort. form), the head appearing fringed. Disk* flowers purple. (Named for Gaillard de Marentonneau, French botanist.)

The annual blanket-flower (*G. pulchella*) and *G. amblyodon* are both hardy annuals and should be grown as such. *See* ANNUALS. The blanket-flower is a widely grown garden favorite, especially fine for cutting. The other species is a perennial and, like the annuals, is partial to light, open soils and full sunlight. It is propagated by division, spring or fall. They are chiefly summer-bloomers.

**amblyodon.** A leafy-stemmed, hairy annual, 12-24 in. high, the foliage rough-hairy. Leaves oblongish, stalkless, more or less eared at the base. Flower heads about 2 in. wide, the rays brownish-red. Tex.

**aristata.** Blanket-flower. A popular flower garden hardy perennial, 2-3 ft. high, more or less rough-hairy. Leaves nearly 5 in. long, more or less lance-shaped, sometimes deeply cut. Flower heads 3-4 in. wide, the rays yellow. Western N.A.

**drummondi** = *Gaillardia pulchella*.

**pulchella.** Annual blanket-flower; Indian blanket. A very showy, popular flower garden annual, 12-20 in. high, the foliage softly hairy. Leaves oblongish, 3-4 in. long. Flower heads 2-3 in. wide, the rays yellow at the tip, rose-purple at the base, the head thus with a dark eye.* Central U.S. A popular form is *var. picta*, with the rays in various shades of red, yellow, or white. Burgundy is a good red variety.

*GALACIFOLIA, -us, -um* (gay-las-i-fō'li-a). With the leaves of *Galax* (which see).

**GALANTHUS.** See SNOWDROP.

**GALAX** (gay'lacks). A single, perennial, evergreen herb of the family Diapensiaceae, the only species being **G. aphylla,** the beetleweed, a native in mountain woods from Va. to Ga. It is a stemless, tufted herb, the leaves nearly round, 3-4½ in. wide, green, but bronze in age, and widely used for funeral decorations. Flowers white, in a spike-like cluster (raceme*), the slender stalk of which may be 25 in. high. Petals 5. Stamens 10, five of them sterile and petal-like. Fruit a 3-valved capsule.* The plant is suited only to the moister and shadier parts of the rock garden or wild garden, and prefers a rich, woods soil, not too acid. (*Galax* is from the Greek for milk, perhaps in allusion to the white flowers.) For the fringed galax see SCHIZOCODON.

**GALAX FAMILY** = Diapensiaceae.

---
* Special articles on the subjects indicated by an asterisk (*) will be found at the words so marked.

*GALE.* Ancient European name, of uncertain origin, applied to the sweet gale (*Myrica gale*).

**GALEGA** (ga-li'ga). A small genus of Eurasian perennial herbs of the pea family, G. officinalis, the goat's-rue, a good garden plant and of easy culture in any ordinary soil. It is an erect herb 2–3 ft. high, with compound* leaves, the leaflets arranged feather-fashion and with an odd one at the end. Leaflets oblongish, 1½–2 in. long. Flowers pealike, purplish-blue, about ½ in. long, arranged in terminal clusters (racemes*) or these in the leaf-axils.* Summer. The *var.* carnea, with rose-pink, double flowers is fine for cut flowers. There are also white-flowered and variegated-leaved forms. All are readily propagated by division. (*Galega* is from the Greek for milk, as some species were supposed to increase its flow.)

*GALEGIFLORA, -us, -um* (ga-lee-gi-flow'ra). With flowers like the goat's-rue (*Galega*).

**GALEN,** Claudius. *See* Early Greek and Roman writers at GARDEN BOOKS.

**GALINGALE.** *See* CYPERUS.

**GALIUM** (gay'li-um). Weak, almost weedy, perennial herbs, commonly known as bedstraw or cleavers, and comprising a widely distributed genus of perhaps 200 species of the family Rubiaceae. They are suited only to informal plantings in the border or rock garden, are of the easiest culture, and are of only secondary hort. interest. Stems often prostrate or arching, 4-sided, often finely barbed. Leaves stalkless, usually 4–10 in a whorl.* Flowers very numerous, but small, white or yellow, the corolla wheel-shaped or deeply 4-parted. Stamens 4. Fruit small, dry, not splitting, 2-lobed, sometimes minutely prickly. (*Galium* is from the Greek for a plant supposed to curdle milk.)

boreale. Northern bedstraw. Forming mats or patches, the stems smooth, 1–3 ft. long. Leaves 4 at a joint, narrow, ¾–1 in. long, sometimes with smaller leaves in the axils.* Flowers scarcely 1/10 in. wide, white. N.A. Summer.

mollugo. White bedstraw; called, also, wild madder and baby's-breath. A smooth-stemmed herb, erect or arching, 1–3 ft. high. Leaves 8 or rarely 6 at a joint, not over 1 in. long. Flowers about 1/10 in. wide, white, in practically leafless clusters. Eu., but naturalized in eastern N.A. Summer.

verum. Yellow bedstraw; also called curdwort or (Our) Lady's-bedstraw. A perennial herb with narrow leaves about 1 in. long that are bristle-tipped and minutely barbed on the margins. Leaves 8 or 6 at a joint. Flowers about ⅛ in. wide, yellow. Eu., but naturalized in eastern N.A. June–Oct.

*GALLICA, -us, -um* (gal'li-ka). From France.

**GALL INSECTS.** *See* Two-winged Flies at INSECT PESTS. *See also* the insect pests at BLACKBERRY, CHRYSANTHEMUM, and SPRUCE.

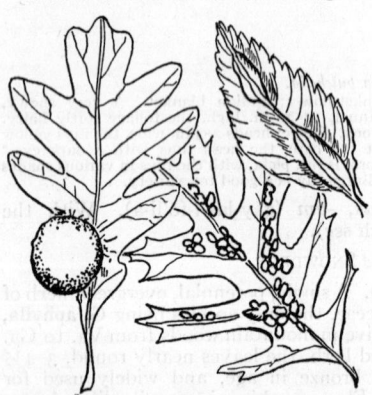

Some common types of insect galls. Oak gall (*left*), wart gall on oaks (*center*), and a midrib gall on a leaflet of the ash. Galls are not usually serious garden pests.

**GALLON.** *See* WEIGHTS AND MEASURES, 3.

**GALTONIA** (gall-tō'ni-a). A small genus of South African bulbous herbs of the lily family, G. candicans, the summer hyacinth or giant summer hyacinth, a garden plant with showy white flowers. It has strap-shaped, basal leaves 2–3 ft. long and 1–2 in. wide, and an erect, flowering stalk 2–3 ft. high, terminated by a long, rather sparsely flowered raceme.* Flowers short-tubed, fragrant, about 1 in. long, narrowly bell-shaped, the segments longer than the tube. Stamens 6. Fruit a somewhat 3-sided capsule.* The plant is not really hardy north of zone* 5 unless well mulched. Increased by offsets. (Named for Sir Francis Galton, British anthropologist.)

**GAMES.** For the minimum space requirements of lawn games *see* BADMINTON, BOWLING GREEN, CROQUET, and TENNIS.

**GAMOLEPIS** (gam-ol'e-pis). South African herbs or shrubs of the family Compositae, the only cult. species being G. tagetes, a tender annual grown for its yellow or orange-yellow flowers. It is a wiry, much-branched herb 4–6 in. high, and has alternate,* usually cut leaves, the segments toothed. Flower head solitary, about ¾ in. wide, the bracts beneath it forming an urn-shaped involucre.* It is best treated as a tender annual (*see* ANNUALS), and is often used for low edging. (*Gamolepis* is from the Greek meaning united scales, in allusion to the urn-shaped involucre.)

**GAMOPETALOUS.** Having the petals united to form a one-piece, or nearly one-piece corolla,* as in the bellflower and many other plants. The opposite term, *polypetalous*, indicates that the petals are separate, as in the rose and hundreds of garden flowers. Whether flowers are gamopetalous or polypetalous is of greater botanical than hort. importance, for upon the character of separate or united petals the botanists have classified whole sections of the plant world.

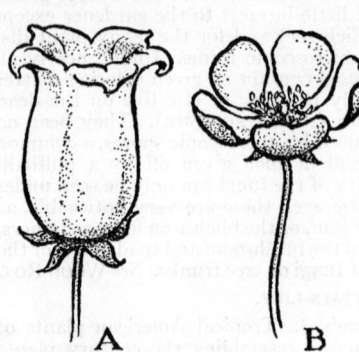

(*A*) A united (gamopetalous) corolla. (*B*) A flower with separate petals (polypetalous).

*GANDAVENSIS, -e* (gan-da-ven'sis). From Ghent, Belgium.

**GARAGE.** *See* SERVICE YARD.

**GARAMBULLO** = *Myrtillocactus geometrizans.*

**GARBANZO** = *Cicer arietinum.*

**GARCINIA** (gar-sin'i-a). A large genus of Old World tropical trees of the family Guttiferae, only one, G. mangostana, the mangosteen, suitable for outdoor cult. in the U.S., and this only in the warmest sections of zone* 9. It is a handsome tree up to 30 ft., with opposite,* thick, leathery, shining green leaves, 6–9 in. long, that have several prominent cross-veins. Flowers rose-pink, nearly 2 in. wide, usually polygamous.* Petals and sepals 4. Stamens* many. Fruit reddish-purple, about 2½ in. in diameter, its outer rind thick, but the 5–7 orange-like, white segments of flesh, juicy, of superb flavor, and highly prized in the Indo-Malayan region where the tree is native. Grown here only occasionally in extreme southern Fla., where it needs a moist, well-drained soil. It may be propagated by seeds, budding, or by inarching (*see* GRAFTING). (Named for Laurence Garcin, French botanist.)

**GARDEN.** Traditionally, a more or less enclosed place in which to grow plants, nearly always in conjunction with a house. This restricted, old meaning of the term is now stretched to include almost any outdoor collection of plants, and easily merges with one's concept of a small farm, such, for instance, as a commercial market garden. In spite of this stretching of its meaning, *garden* still implies a home garden to most of us, whether a backyard or a country estate. For the development of the garden from ancient times to the present, *see* GARDEN HISTORY. *See also* LANDSCAPE ARCHITECTURE and ARCHITECTURAL STYLES.

What we do *with* a garden is a reflection of our taste, knowledge, and pocketbook. No rule can be stated that

---

* Special articles on the subjects indicated by an asterisk (*) will be found at the words so marked.

would apply for everyone. In THE GARDEN DICTIONARY are many articles designed to guide the seeker. Perhaps the surest way towards one's garden hopes and aspirations is to scan the list of subjects below, all of which have special articles about them:

| Soils | Herb Gardening | Backyard Garden |
| Kitchen Garden | Rock Garden | Home Garden |
| Annuals | Wild Garden | Country Estate |
| Biennials | Trees | Water Garden |
| Perennials | Shrubs | Ferns and Fern Gardening |
| Fruit Culture | Vines | Garden Calendar |

For what we do *in* a garden, and the daily routine of garden management, *see* the various subjects treated at GARDEN OPERATIONS.

**GARDEN ACCOUNTS.** *See* ACCOUNTS.

**GARDEN ALTERATIONS.** *See* the winter months at GARDEN CALENDAR.

**GARDEN AMATEUR.** *See* AMATEUR.

**GARDEN ANEMONE** = *Anemone hortensis.*

**GARDEN APPLIANCES.** *See* TOOLS AND IMPLEMENTS.

**GARDEN ASPARAGUS.** *See* ASPARAGUS.

**GARDEN BALSAM** = *Impatiens balsamina.*

**GARDEN BOOKS.** Books about gardening are almost as old as the art itself, and they are legion. At the beginning there are, of course, only the rudest inscriptions to tell us of the first rescue of wild plants by our still wilder ancestors. Some of that story you can read at another entry. *See* GARDEN HISTORY.

But long before the Christian Era, cultivated Greeks not only developed beautiful gardens but wrote books about them. One of the greatest was Theophrastus of Eresus, born 370 B.C., and a favorite pupil of Aristotle. He is thought to have written over 200 books, but only two of them survive, the *History of Plants* and the *Causes of Plants*, and these only in part. But the remarkable thing about them and their author, who also developed the first known botanical garden, is that, almost alone, they carried Greek learning about plants and gardens to the Renaissance. No greater glory in the history of hort. literature can exceed this — to have impressed one's knowledge and standards upon the world for close to 16 centuries. And many of the observations of Theophrastus are current right down to our own time.

He had many elaborators, copyists, and some pupils. Today their writings give us much light on gardening and the plants grown for pleasure and use over two thousand years ago, but none of them left such an impress upon garden literature as the genius of Theophrastus. Chief among the Greeks who followed their master was Dioscorides, whose *Materia Medica* has been issued in countless editions. Another was Crenatus who illustrated the first Herbal. Then came Claudius Galen, born 130 B.C., a talented Greek physician who wrote an Herbal, *De Simplicium*, of which only 83 out of 400 parts have been preserved. But that fragment influenced all subsequent writing about medicinal plants down to almost modern times.

EARLY ROMAN. Of the many Roman books about gardens and flowers only a few need notice here. While the art of gardening and the development of country estates made far greater progress in Rome than in Greece, the writers about it were mostly elaborating upon the writings of Theophrastus. Two Romans stand out especially. They were Pliny, who wrote a *Natural History*, and Marcus Terentius Varro, whose *De Re Rustica* is a remarkable garden book full of sound advice on topiary work, olive trees, pools, fountains, and the kitchen garden. Also at Rome was published the first garden calendar by Palladius Rutilius in the fifth century.

HERBALS. From the Greeks and Romans to the Renaissance there stretches what are popularly called the Dark Ages. So far as the printed or written word is concerned perhaps they were. But it should not be forgotten that the art of gardening was carried through these dark centuries almost wholly by the Church. In many a Cathedral and Cloister garden, not only the plants and methods, but the very books themselves of the talented Greeks and proud Romans were preserved for the flowering of the Renaissance, which was soon to astonish a sluggard world.

One of the first evidences of a revival of garden learning was the publication in 1471 of *Opus Ruralium Commodorum* by Pietro Crescenzi, an Italian lawyer, who became enamored of country life after the Roman plan of centuries earlier. Published in Latin, the book was quickly translated into Italian, French, and German. While it borrowed heavily from the Greeks and Romans, especially from Varro's *De Re Rustica*, its great merit was that it showed to a relatively gardenless world the pleasures of having a garden and how to go about making one. While not an Herbal in the usual sense of that term, Crescenzi's book was followed by many that were. And in fact garden books within the next century or two became as popular as they are today.

Among the Herbals, which are systematic accounts of the plants known at the time, especially their "virtues" as medicine and condiment, the following English examples should be consulted by all students of the development of garden literature:

William Turner's *Herbal;* 1568.
John Gerard's *Herball or Generall Historie of Plantes;* 1597.
John Parkinson's *Herbal*, but called by him *Paradisi in Sole Paradisus Terrestris;* 1629.

There were, in addition, many other Herbals, mostly by the German fathers of botany, and hundreds of books on gardening were published in England between 1500 and 1700. But, with the settlement of America and the beginnings of gardening here, came the first truly American hort. literature.

AMERICA. While most of us think that American gardening began in Mass. or Va. soon after 1600, the Spanish and Portuguese had long before brought the incomparable art of the Moors to Mexico, Central America, Peru, and Brazil. Upon an elaborate system of Aztec and Inca horticulture they reared a garden structure of which too little is known. To the New World cultivation of corn, tobacco, chocolate, potato, and many other plants, they brought wheat, rye, sugar cane, banana, the olive, fig, the citrus fruits, and many Old World flowers. The literature, both Aztec and Spanish, of this tremendously interesting period of American gardening is much too extensive to cite here. Some of it is well summarized in Cecile Hulse Matschat's *Mexican Plants for American Gardens*.

Who wrote the first real garden book in the U.S. will always be in dispute. So much was written by botanists, travelers, and horticulturists, and so many of the books were a mixture of all three subjects, that it is impossible to pick out one as the first. George Washington's diaries, for instance, are full of valuable horticultural notes. Some writers give the distinction to William Yong, Jr., of Philadelphia, who published in Paris in 1783 his *Catalogue d'Arbres Arbustes et Plantes Herbacées d'Amérique*. It is chiefly a catalogue of plants he grew in his garden with notes on their culture. But others credit a Mrs. Martha Logan of Charleston, S.C., with the first real garden book, *The Gardener's Kalendar*. It may have been only a pamphlet, but of its existence there is no doubt. She died in 1779 and her book was published soon after, so that it may well antedate the catalogue of William Yong, Jr.

If both these early claimants are excluded, the earliest hort. book, written by an American and published here, is Robert Squibb's *Gardener's Kalender*, Charleston, 1787. In Boston, in 1799, was published an American edition of *Introduction to the Knowledge and Practice of Gardening*, an English book by the Rev. Charles Marshall. The second really American garden book was printed at Washington, D.C., in 1804. It was entitled *The American Gardener* and was written by John Gardiner and David Hepburn.

With the opening of the nineteenth century, American gardening and books about it grew as rapidly as the country. There is no space here to catalogue that literature, which includes hundreds of titles. Some of the landmarks, however, are worth notice, and a few of them are listed below in the order of their publication. They have been selected

---

\* Special articles on the subjects indicated by an asterisk (\*) will be found at the words so marked.

not only for their importance, but for diversified subject matter.

1806. Bernard M'Mahon. *American Gardener's Calendar.* Philadelphia. Ran through eleven editions, the last in 1857. His name is also spelled McMahon.
1817. William Coxe. *A View of the Cultivation of Fruit Trees, and the Management of Orchards and Cider.* Philadelphia. Perhaps the first American book devoted wholly to fruits.
1826. John James Dufour. *The American Vine Dresser's Guide.* Cincinnati. Not the first, but one of the most important books on early grape culture.
1828. Ronald Green. *Treatise on the Cultivation of Flowers.* Boston. The first American book devoted only to garden flowers.
1838. Robert Manning. *Book of Fruits.* Salem, Mass. Chiefly responsible for the introduction into America of pears raised by Van Mons of Belgium.
1839. Edward Sayers. *A Treatise on the Culture of the Dahlia and Cactus.* Boston. Apparently the first book on the special culture of both groups.
1841. Andrew Jackson Downing. *A Treatise on the Theory and Practice of Landscape Gardening.* New York. Probably the most important book ever published in America on landscape architecture. Subsequently revised and enlarged in nine later editions.
1844. Andrew Jackson Downing. *Cottage Residences: or a Series of Designs for Rural Cottages and Cottage Villas.* New York. This, for the small place, did what his earlier book accomplished for more pretentious ones.
1845. Andrew Jackson Downing. *The Fruits and Fruit Trees of America.* New York. Considered the most influential fruit book of its time, and perhaps greater than all others since.
1846. Samuel B. Parsons. *The Rose: Its History, Poetry, Culture and Classification.* New York. Not the first, but perhaps the first important, rose book.
1849. John J. Thomas. *The American Fruit Culturist.* Auburn, N.Y. Subsequently issued in 13 separate editions.
1851. Joseph Breck. *The Flower-Garden; or Breck's Book of Flowers.* Boston. This, and enlargements or revisions of it, was issued several times, the last edition in 1866.
1853. Thomas Meehan. *The American Handbook of Ornamental Trees.* Philadelphia.
1856. John T. C. Clark. *The Amateur's Guide and Flower-Garden Directory.* Washington, D.C.
1858. Edward Kemp. *How to Lay Out a Garden.* New York.
1866. Edward Sprague Rand. *Bulbs: A Treatise on Hardy and Tender Bulbs and Tubers.* Boston. One of the first books on bulb culture.
1867. Peter Henderson. *Gardening for Profit.* New York.
1871. Edward Sprague Rand. *The Rhododendron and American Plants.* Boston. Perhaps the first American book on the special culture of plants of the heath family.
1872. Henry T. Williams. *Window Gardening.* New York. The 14th edition was issued in 1884.
1877. James Hogg. *The Vegetable Garden.* New York.
1880. Peter Henderson. *Gardening for Pleasure.* New York.
1887. Andrew S. Fuller. *The Propagation of Plants.* New York.
1889. Edward J. Wickson. *The California Fruits and How to Grow Them.* San Francisco. An excellent résumé of earlier books on California gardening, which had appeared as early as 1859, some, Mexican and Spanish, much earlier.
1891. Samuel Parsons, Jr. *Landscape Gardening.* New York.
1893. Mrs. Schuyler Van Rensselaer. *Art Out-of-Doors: Hints on Good Taste in Gardening.* New York. One of the first women to write with taste and discrimination on landscape design.
1894. L. R. Taft. *Greenhouse Construction.* New York. For years a standard reference work on the building of greenhouses, frames, pits, etc.
1896. P. H. Rolfs. *Vegetable Growing in the South.* Richmond, Va.
1897. William Tricker. *The Water Garden.* New York.
1899. Samuel T. Maynard. *Landscape Gardening as Applied to Home Decoration.* New York.

It is, of course, idle to claim that these were the only important garden books written in the U.S. from 1800 to 1900, but they have the distinction among hundreds of others of setting a standard for their day. No browser among American hort. literature should ignore them, and many of their facts are as true today as when they were written.

But some are not, and science keeps driving the gardener to new methods, while exploration and plant breeding have given us many plants not found in these classics of American horticulture. Among the writers since 1900, who have helped to bring hort. literature down to date, perhaps the outstanding will be found in the list of contributors to THE GARDEN DICTIONARY. But there are many others, especially upon the staffs of the Experiment Stations and at the universities that have Horticultural Departments. *See also* GARDEN MAGAZINES.

**GARDEN CALENDAR.** All calculations for outdoor work in a normal growing season are based on work and plant materials suitable for the "White" Belt on the accompanying map.

This map shows by Belts the average dates on which the last killing frost in spring may be expected to occur. The earliest date from which it is possible to show the *average* time of the last killing frost is March 1st and the last date is June 1st. Either before or after these dates the times of killing frosts are too irregular to base any accurate figures upon. In high elevations in the West large areas, which are used for sheep and cattle grazing, are subject to frosts after June 1.

Variations in frost dates are smaller near the Atlantic Coast and in the strip of country lying east of the Rocky Mountains. There will be, of course, in all areas a variation of a few days each year from the given average. The greatest variations are in sections west of the Rocky Mountains and in regions where frost is less common, such as parts of Florida and the Gulf Coast. The only absolutely frost-free area in the United States is near Key West, Florida.

Plantings must be made late enough to be safe from too great a risk of spring frost and early enough for the crops to mature before being in danger from autumn frosts. In general, the frost-free period is, depending entirely upon the location, between 15 and 50 days longer than the average number of days fit for ordinary garden operations.

It is an impossibility to devise any planting schedule which will be absolutely accurate and applicable to all parts of the country at the same time. For this work, therefore, a section of the country has been selected which, so far as possible, has pretty much the same planting conditions and the average length of growing season. Differences in soil, rainfall, length of the days, the amount of sunshine, etc., all tend to influence the kind of crops grown, as well as their planting dates. As always elevation plays an important part; the higher the altitude the later the season.

Common sense applied to all gardening problems will be the greatest guide in the use of this Calendar. Mountains, deserts, valleys, etc., will cause a variation of a few days in either direction from the average dates given. For example, in the "White" Belt there is a difference of 30 days, *i.e.* April 1 to April 30, between dates when a planting may be made in sheltered valleys and the same crop planted in unsheltered regions or mountain tops. A legend on the map shows the approximate dates of the last killing frosts. *See also* the name of your state or province for definite frost data in your locality.

---

* Special articles on the subjects indicated by an asterisk (*) will be found at the words so marked.

# GARDEN CALENDAR

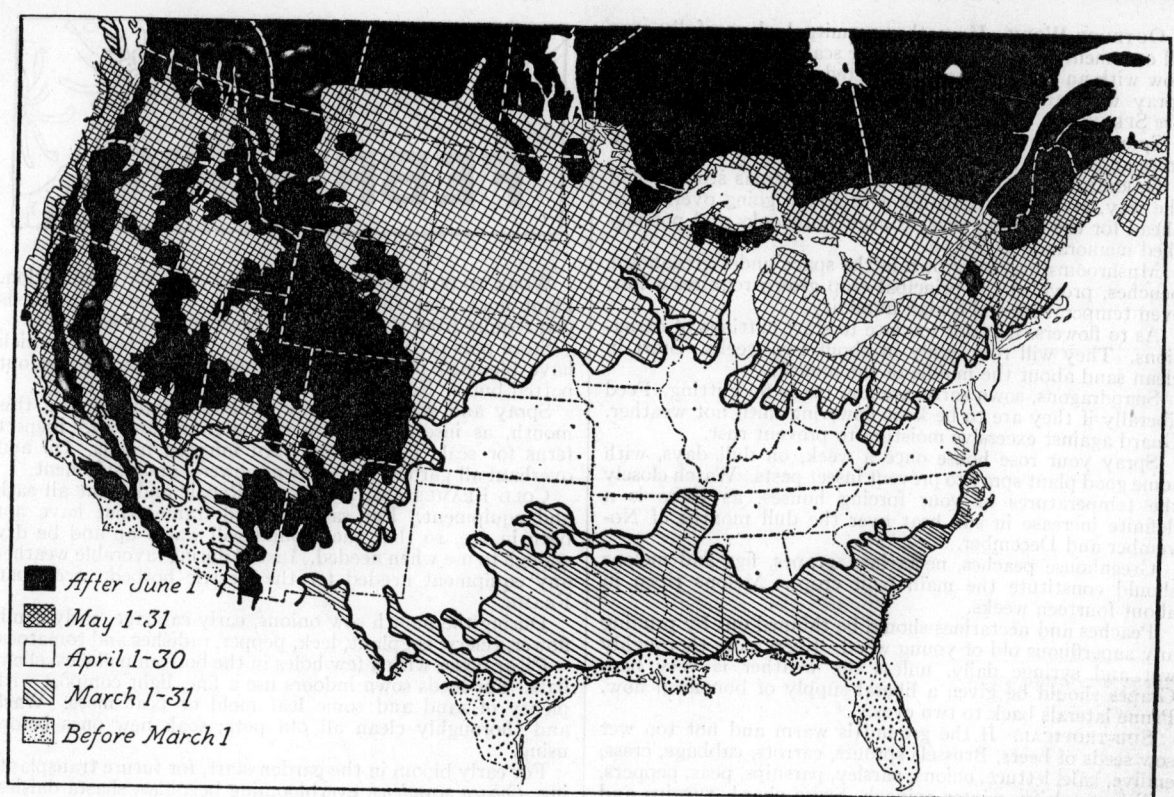

### THE ONSET OF SPRING

The map shows the average dates of the last killing spring frosts, which coincide with the beginning of many garden operations, as outlined in the introduction to the Garden Calendar. The Weather Bureau data for the Canadian Provinces is not so complete as for the United States, so Canadian gardeners should be guided by local observations.

For the regions where the last killing frost is safely passed by March 1st, or where there is none, as in Key West, long growing seasons make special directions necessary. At the end of each month you will find these under the heading *Sub-tropical.*

It should also be mentioned that the *Calendar* suggests many simple, or sometimes more difficult, hort. operations, without defining them here. All are treated elsewhere in THE GARDEN DICTIONARY and should be looked for there.

FLORAL TIME-TABLE. At the end of the work to be done in each month there is included a list of the plants one expects to find in bloom that month. All species or varieties mentioned in these lists will be found in THE GARDEN DICTIONARY at their proper entries, where all notes on their culture should be sought. It was found impractical to include all the plants in THE DICTIONARY, but one thousand of the most desirable ornamentals have been arranged under their usual flowering months, including selections from shrubs, trees, herbs, and not omitting some native plants grown mostly in the wild garden.

Such a time-table must be based upon records kept in one or two standard regions, and the one adopted here is the White Belt on the accompanying map. For regions north or south of it, or for especially high elevations, the dates will, of course, be somewhat hastened or retarded. A year or two's observation will soon determine how much your local conditions make it necessary to subtract from or add to the dates. But this amount of variation will not greatly change the schedules, because all records south of zone* 5, including, of course, sub-tropical plants, have had to be excluded, as the flowering periods are so different from those of cooler regions.

It should also be noted that some plants given as winter-blooming do so only when provided with the protection of a wall. Those expecting to get winter bloom would do well to read the article WINTER GARDEN, before planting one. *See also* SEASONAL GARDENS.

WORK TO DO INDOORS. Look over all stored tubers and bulbs. Discard all diseased roots.

Send for new seed and nursery catalogues; make plans for next year's gardening activities. Sow in flats pansies, forget-me-not, phlox and hardy poppies.

Inspect house plants for mealybugs, which appear as white, cottony masses, and destroy them immediately.

Repair and paint or make garden furniture, trellises, archways, etc.

Force as house plants lilies-of-the-valley, paper-white narcissus, tulips, hyacinths and Chinese Sacred Lily.

Heather, cyclamen, and Jerusalem cherry plants need to be kept well watered. Underwater Christmas cactus as soon as the buds begin to form. Poinsettias do best in an even temperature, with thorough watering every day. The end of this month store them for the balance of the season.

Start tuberous-rooted begonias from seed now.

---

*Special articles on the subjects indicated by an asterisk (\*) will be found at the words so marked.

OUTDOOR WORK. If weather permits, look carefully over all ornamental trees and shrubs for scale infestation. Spray now with an oil emulsion. If infected with euonymus scale, spray with an oil spray mixed with a nicotine solution. *See* SPRAYING.

Sprays of pussywillow, forsythias and other flowering trees and shrubs may be cut for indoor forcing.

GARDENING UNDER GLASS. With Christmas stock out of the way, give the greenhouse a thorough going over. Plan ahead for the coming year; consult notebooks and potting-shed memoranda at length.

Mushrooms may be grown in the space under greenhouse benches, provided the principal crop grown requires a low, even temperature and a high humidity.

As to flowers, it is not too late to start cuttings of carnations. They will root easily in about two weeks. Start in clean sand about the middle of the month.

Snapdragons, sown early, are now ready for cutting. Feed liberally if they are to be kept flowering until hot weather. Guard against excessive moisture to prevent rust.

Spray your rose house once a week, on dull days, with some good plant spray to prevent insect pests. Watch closely the temperatures of your forcing houses, as there is a definite increase in sun heat over the dull months of November and December.

Greenhouse peaches, nectarines, grapes, figs and melons should constitute the main fruit crops. Melons ripen in about fourteen weeks.

Peaches and nectarines should be thinned out by pruning any superfluous old or young wood. Keep roots thoroughly wet and syringe daily, unless the weather is very bad. Grapes should be given a liberal supply of bonemeal now. Prune laterals back to two eyes.

SUB-TROPICAL. If the ground is warm and not too wet sow seeds of beets, Brussels sprouts, carrots, cabbage, cress, endive, kale, lettuce, onions, parsley, parsnips, peas, peppers, radishes, salsify, winter spinach, Swiss chard, turnips and watermelons.

Set out onion sets, Chinese cabbage, eggplant, kohlrabi, squash and tomatoes. Plant potatoes. Start an asparagus bed.

Set out fruit trees such as loquats, guavas, pomegranates, etc.; also berries and muscadine grape vines. While the older plantings of fruit trees are dormant, spray, paying especial attention to the peaches.

In the flower garden sow in the open ground seeds of *Helipterum*, alyssum, *Mentzelia*, calendula, candytuft, centaurea, clarkia, godetia, lupine, nigella, poppies (including *Eschscholtzia*), schizanthus, California wild flower seeds, sweet peas and lawn grasses.

Plant bulbs of amaryllis, gladioli, Japanese lilies, narcissus, Mexican tuberoses and tuberous begonias. Columbines, delphiniums, phlox and snapdragons should be sown in seed flats. Take chrysanthemums (rooted cuttings) from the edge of the old clumps and heel-in* until needed. Transplant into the open border from flats seedlings of foxgloves, Shasta daisies, etc. Plant young cinerarias in shaded or semi-shaded situations.

Trim wisteria vines, and dig around established trees and shrubs and fertilize and prune wherever necessary. Set out deciduous trees and shrubs and broad-leaved evergreens.

Place tropical foliage plants such as acalyphas, crotons and dracaenas where they get their full quota of sun. Inspect any such as aralias, marantas, and dieffenbachias for pests.

### PLANTS IN BLOOM — JANUARY

HERBACEOUS PLANTS: 1. *Crocus aureus*; 2. *Galanthus byzantinus*; 3. *Galanthus nivalis*; 4. *Galanthus* (double-flowered form).

SHRUBS AND TREES: 5. *Hamamelis japonica arborea*; 6. *Hamamelis vernalis*; 7. *Jasminum nudiflorum*; 8. *Lonicera fragrantissima*; 9. *Parrotia persica*.

Also numbers 999 and 1000 (*see* DECEMBER).

WORK TO DO INDOORS. Test all old seeds for germination. Plant none that show poor viability. Decide what seeds you require from the new catalogues and order early.

Store pots used for narcissi, tulips, hyacinths, etc., which have bloomed in the house during the winter. Bring out potted bulbs. Set in a light window for spring forcing.

Spray and watch carefully all house plants during this month, as insect pests are active from now on. Inspect ferns for scale insects and burn infected fronds. Oil and overhaul all garden tools, lawn-mowers, and equipment.

COLD FRAMES AND HOTBEDS. Repair and paint all sash and equipment. Put sash on cold frames that have not been in use, so that the ground will warm up and be dry enough to use when needed. Install during favorable weather any equipment needed for the electric hotbed. *See* COLD FRAME.

During the month sow onions, early cabbage, early cauliflower, celery, eggplant, leek, pepper, radishes and tomatoes.

Cigar boxes with a few holes in the bottom make excellent flats. For seeds sown indoors use a fine, light compost with plenty of sand and some leaf mold or peat moss. Wash and thoroughly clean all old pots; soak new ones before using.

For early bloom in the garden start, for future transplanting, *Cobaea scandens*, everblooming begonias, shasta daisies, candytuft, stocks, annual canterbury bells, delphiniums, snapdragons, pentstemons and gaillardias.

Asters sown now will flower in June; all annuals may be sown for spring planting to be followed by another sowing later in the season, if desired.

PRUNING AND OUTSIDE WORK. Prune at this time only late-flowering spring shrubs. Never prune the early varieties before flowering. If too thick, cut at the ground level a few of the oldest canes. Apple and pear trees may be pruned in moderate weather. Remove all broken limbs with a sharp saw. Remove weak, straggly growths from wisteria vines. This is a good month to prune grape vines throughout the country, wherever the weather is not freezing.

Look over irises and herbaceous plants for aphids. Inspect all your rose canes, including the climbing sorts, for signs of canker disease, which will start wherever the bark is broken. Move large deciduous trees now. Paint egg clusters of the gypsy moth with creosote to eliminate caterpillars next summer. Rake and dispose of all actual refuse.

This is a bad month for boxwood, in the northern states, where there is much freezing and thawing. Protect as much as possible. (*See* PROTECTING PLANTS.) Southern states will find this a good month to trim and shape boxwood.

GARDENING UNDER GLASS. Make as much room as possible for young stock. Cinerarias, nemesias and clarkias need plenty of room to spread. Amaryllis seeds may be sown now.

For Easter bloom of lilies temperatures will need to be adjusted, in order that the plants may flower on time. *Lilium longiflorum* and *L. longiflorum harrisi* do well at 55°–60°. Pink roses are the most popular at this time. Water and feed freely. Push the temperature up two to four degrees as growth advances. Watch out for red spiders. Shrubs require a forcing temperature of 50°–55°. All forcing bulbs require more water at this time.

About the middle of the month start cuttings of chrysanthemums and evergreens in sand. Water liberally and shade from direct sun. Take cuttings now of all old plants saved

* Special articles on the subjects indicated by an asterisk (*) will be found at the words so marked.

for that purpose. Sow seeds of begonias, *Streptocarpus*, asparagus, smilax, saintpaulias and Jerusalem cherries.

Re-pot foliage plants and ferns. Top-dress dracaenas and cinerarias, or re-pot if pot-bound.

Look over all your orchids carefully, before new growth starts. If necessary, separate and re-pot firmly, giving especial attention to drainage. Shade from full sun. *See Culture at* ORCHIDS.

SUB-TROPICAL. Sow any seeds mentioned last month as well as those of beans, canteloupes, cabbage, collard, eggplant, kohlrabi, leek, mustard, sweet corn, New Zealand spinach, squash and tomatoes. Transplant from frames cucumbers, lettuce, tomatoes, etc. Sow in flats seeds of plants for late crops.

Among the fruits put out stock plants of strawberries for runners. Fertilize well. Set out peaches, pears, plums, persimmons, mulberry and fig trees. Place pecan trees wherever shade is desired.

Sow in the open ground flower seeds mentioned last month and those of African daisies, calliopsis, early cosmos, dahlias, gypsophilas, *Linum*, nasturtium, nemophila, scabiosa. Do not sow poppies later than the end of the month.

Plant bulbs listed in January; also cannas, caladiums and ranunculus (*see* BUTTERCUP).

Sow in flats ageratum, asters, begonias, fuchsias, hollyhocks, lobelias, nemesias, pentstemons, petunias, and stocks. Transplant December seedlings.

Set out Japanese iris and rose bushes. Prune old bushes for spring and summer bloom. Inspect all potted plants in the patio; stir up the soil and give plant food or re-pot.

### PLANTS IN BLOOM — FEBRUARY

HERBACEOUS PLANTS: 10. *Crocus imperati*; 11. *Symplocarpus foetidus*; 12. *Crocus susianus*; 13. *Crocus tomassinianus*; 14. *Crocus vernus*; 15. *Eranthis hyemalis*.
SHRUBS AND TREES: 16. *Corylopsis pauciflora*; 17. *Cornus mas*; 18. *Daphne mezereum*; 19. *Erica carnea*; 20. *Hamamelis mollis*.

Also numbers 1, 2, 3, 4, 5, 6, 8, and 9 (*see* JANUARY); and numbers 999 and 1000 (*see* DECEMBER).

OUTDOOR WORK. Clean around shrubbery and garden corners; burn actual refuse to eliminate pests. Near the end of the month you will be able gradually to remove windbreaks and coverings from tender shrubs, evergreens, roses, bulbs and many perennials.

Transplanting of small trees and ornamentals may be done to advantage now in the South. Plant dormant roses in these states and prune back sharply.

Give lawn a top-dressing of some good plant food. As soon as the frost is out of the ground sow your grass seed.

Plant fruit trees. Finish all pruning and dormant spraying left over from last month. Cut cions of fruit trees now and store in sand; graft next month.

Late this month, below New York, or in sheltered places, seeds may be sown of certain annuals such as border stocks, Shirley poppies, gypsophila, larkspur, lupines, lavatera, *Phlox drummondi*, coreopsis, *Mentzelia*, calendulas and chrysanthemums. The last day of the month sow sweet peas.

Dig and store all oyster plants, parsnips, etc., that have wintered in the ground, in a cold cellar. Force clumps of rhubarb ahead of season by covering with a temporary frame or sash. Toward the end of the month put out cabbage plants that have wintered in the cold frame, if weather is warm.

Apply lime now to sour soil. Uncover the asparagus beds and check weeds; apply nitrate of soda in small quantities to beds.

When soil does not stick to the tools, sow thickly but very shallow, peas, radishes, carrots, beets and parsnips.

Raspberries and blackberries may be thinned now of old canes, and tied up. Top back any canes that are too tall. Gooseberries bear on old wood, so prune carefully, only cutting out extra shoots.

COLD FRAMES AND HOTBEDS. Transplant all plants started last month. Sow kohlrabi, lettuce and early beets in the hotbed, and Brussels sprouts in the cold frame.

Air frames that have been in use during the winter and protect the plants on cold nights.

Transplant to the hotbed small plants from seeds sown in January, such as pansies, etc. Plants sown indoors in small paper pots will transplant easily later, in the open. Sow seeds of such plants as China asters, dahlias, monkey-flower, salpiglossis, *Salvia patens*, verbena and *Vinca rosea* in frames, or indoors.

GREENHOUSE. Watch closely the temperatures of your houses this month; sun heat is more intense; and give more ventilation to them than usual.

Peaches and nectarines should be in flower; admit air and sunshine to encourage pollination. Give figs plenty of moisture at the roots; feed heavily.

Continue propagation of chrysanthemums, carnations, evergreens, coleus, *Plumbago indica*, roses and any other plants desired for use now or for fall and winter flowers, as rooting from now on will be difficult. Re-pot any that have large roots. Inspect for thrips; spray and fumigate.

Watch young rose plants for black spot. Allow *Rosa wichuraiana* and hybrid roses in pots, recently brought in from the outdoors, at least three months before forcing into bloom. Best start them now. Re-pot any that seem pot-bound; top-dress.

Look over hydrangeas, oleanders and such to see if they need new top-dressing and cleaning. Inspect white lilies at this time of year for aphids. Water *Astilbe japonica* heavily before flowering time.

Bring dahlias to daylight; shade and water thoroughly. Start cannas, caladiums and bouvardias.

Begonia tubers should be laid now on the bench, singly, over bottom-heat, and potted as soon as well started.

Shrubs, such as the flowering dogwood, may now be forced easily.

Seeds sown in January and February must be carefully tended now. Re-pot into larger sizes as quickly as they show advanced root growth.

SUB-TROPICAL. Sow seeds of pole lima, bush and field beans; cabbage, carrots, chufas; sweet and pop corn; crotalaria, cucumbers, kale, leek, lettuce, mustard, okra, onions, parsnips, parsley, peppers; garden peas; peanuts, pumpkins, radishes, rhubarb, rice, early roselle, tomatoes, turnips, sage, salsify, sorghum, soy-beans, squash, sunflowers and watermelons. Celery requires summer protection from the sun if planted in the open.

Transplant seedlings from flats. Set out stock strawberry plants.

Sow in the open any flower seeds listed in February and in addition *Amaranthus*, balsam, *Brachycome*, celosia, four-o'clocks, gomphrena, helichrysum, kochia, larkspur, salpiglossis and annual vines.

Plant in seed flats *Bellis*, coleus, *Trachymene*, matricaria, castor-oil plant, *Statice*, stocks, *Tithonia*, and verbena.

Set out bulbs such as cannas, dahlias, hemerocallis, *Zephyranthes*, and *Tigridia*. Plant in the border, to recuperate, bulbs used for forcing in the house.

Transplant pinks, stocks, verbena, etc., for early bloom. Transplant broad-leaved evergreens such as camphor, holly and yaupon. Divide if necessary such perennials as heucheras, salvias, etc. Plant in shady places azaleas, erythrinums, hydrangeas, oxalis, etc. Cut away dead leaves and stalks of bananas, *Plumbago*, *Hibiscus*, roses and other like shrubs and plants.

Move or prune any summer- and fall-blooming shrubs, if

---

* Special articles on the subjects indicated by an asterisk (*) will be found at the words so marked.

necessary, if they are not yet in bud. Set out eucalyptus, acacias, *Hibiscus, Duranta*, jasmine, oleander, crape myrtle and pepper trees. Take cuttings of *Brunfelsia* from new growth; grow in half-shade. Take cuttings of crotons, pot and give full sun when well rooted.

### PLANTS IN BLOOM — MARCH

HERBACEOUS PLANTS: 21. *Scilla verna;* 22. *Chionodoxa luciliae;* 23. *Chionodoxa sardensis;* 24. *Crocus biflorus;* 25. *Iris reticulata;* 26. *Rosmarinus officinalis;* 27. *Scilla amoena;* 28. *Scilla peruviana;* 29. *Scilla sibirica;* 30. *Tussilago farfara.*

SHRUBS AND TREES: 31. *Magnolia stellata;* 32. *Chaenomeles japonica;* 33. *Chaenomeles lagenaria;* 34. *Forsythia ovata;* 35. *Meratia praecox;* 36. *Pieris floribunda;* 37. *Pieris japonica;* 38. *Amygdalus davidiana;* 39. *Rhododendron arboreum;* 40. *Rhodora canadensis;* 41. *Lonicera standishi.*

Also numbers 1, 2, 3, 4, 5, and 8 (*see* JANUARY); numbers 10, 11, 12, 13, 14, 15, 16, 17, 18, 19, and 20 (*see* FEBRUARY); and numbers 999 and 1000 (*see* DECEMBER).

FLOWER GARDEN. Remove winter coverings; dry burlap and store. Keep newly transplanted material well watered. If bare spots show in the lawn, rake and sow grass seed.

Prepare all vacant beds. Uncover your bulb beds and perennial borders. Dig up and divide summer- and fall-flowering perennials; enrich the soil and re-plant. Cut back to the ground any shrubs that have apparently winter-killed, they may send out new shoots.

Cut back roots of trees or hedges that are robbing the soil. Remove all dead foliage from around foxgloves, larkspurs, hollyhocks, monkshood, and phloxes. Fertilize well between herbaceous plants. Shear back, mulch with humus and fertilize English ivy, *Pachysandra* and *Vinca minor*.

Plant deciduous nursery stock as soon as received. Treat gladiolus corms for thrips and plant the last of the month at successive intervals of two weeks until July, for a succession of flowers.

In the East, if warm, plant garden roses. Spray rose beds if buds have not started as yet. Prune tops of hybrid teas and hybrid perpetuals and cut out weak wood. Fertilize with well-rotted stable manure.

Transplant native ferns and flowering plants.

FRUITS. Uncover the strawberry bed and fertilize between the rows. Set out new plants of strawberries, raspberries and blackberries at once.

Plant new fruit trees and graft, before growth starts, the cions cut and stored in sand last month. Examine peach trees for borers. Begin to prune and train dwarf varieties. *See* TRAINING PLANTS.

VEGETABLE GARDEN. Prepare your ground carefully and plant, if the weather is moderate, beets, early cabbage, carrots, early cauliflower, cress, kohlrabi, lettuce, mustard, onions, parsley, parsnips, radishes, peas, spinach, Swiss chard, salsify and turnips, to be followed by successive sowings of peas, if desired. Later transplant from the frames the hardiest of the plants which have been hardened-off.* Treat potatoes for scab before planting.

Many seeds, such as cabbage, cauliflower, tomato, pepper, eggplant, beets and spinach should be treated for disease before planting. Thyme, sage, dill and other herbs may be sown in small beds.

NUT TREES. Plow under cover crop in new walnut orchards. One-year grafted trees should be cut back to 5 or 6 feet. Hickories require little pruning.

Pecan seedlings should be cultivated in spring the same as corn crops. Do not bud or graft until the second season. Watch bearing trees, especially western varieties, for pecan scab. Spray thoroughly. Spray also for pecan casebearer.

COLD FRAMES AND HOTBEDS. It is not too late to sow the vegetable seeds mentioned in February and March; in addition sow asparagus, cucumbers, eggplant and melons. Harden-off* all plants still in the frames.

Set out in the garden all plants which were moved into the hotbeds last month, such as pansies, forget-me-nots, and columbines.

Move into the hotbed, from benches in the greenhouse, bedding plants such as geraniums. Harden out in a mild hotbed excess stock grown in the greenhouse, give them plenty of ventilation and water; cover during cold nights.

GREENHOUSE. With increased sun power and longer days place your plants with regard to their physical requirements. Give sweet peas and carnations light and ventilation; cyclamen a northern exposure during the summer; sun for euphorbias; half-shade for calanthes and gloxinia; all ferns and orchids some shade to prevent burning; all require more water and air.

Sow cinerarias, greenhouse primulas and *Streptocarpus* for winter flowering. Calanthe bulbs should be started early this month. Pot as soon as they start growth; water sparingly and shade young foliage.

Chrysanthemums can still be rooted. Start violets for next winter's flowering from cuttings; discard the old stems.

Prune at the end of the month and pot all roses to be carried over another year. Feed and water freely. Watch for red spider.

Pot up from the bench any plants started last month which have good root growth; later continue re-potting into larger sizes.

Memorial Day flowers, such as hydrangeas, cinerarias, lilies and early-flowering shrubs which are being forced, must be inspected for pests. Feed heavily. When in full flower move into the cool house.

Peaches and nectarines must be gone over carefully. Give plenty of water to those which have set fruit.

SUB-TROPICAL. Sow seeds from list mentioned last month. Set out plants of cauliflower, tomatoes, etc., from frames.

Sow in open ground *Abronia, Arctotis grandis*, African marigold, *Nigella*, portulaca, *Phlox drummondi, Helipterum*, valerian, zinnias, etc., and any seeds from March list suitable to your locality.

Asters, carnations, primulas, etc., may be grown in seed flats for earlier flowering. Plant summer-flowering bulbs. Set out chrysanthemums and tender seedlings from frames. Bring out house plants, fertilize and set in the border or re-pot.

Shrubs such as *Abelia, Allamanda*, camellias, gardenias, and lantanas may be planted until the middle of the month.

### PLANTS IN BLOOM — APRIL

HERBACEOUS PLANTS: 42. *Adonis vernalis;* 43. *Myosotis arvensis;* 44. *Dicentra chrysantha;* 45. *Allium neapolitanum;* 46. *Allium moly;* 47. *Alyssum saxatile compactum;* 48. *Geranium maculatum;* 49. *Alyssum saxatile;* 50. *Brunnera macrophylla;* 51. *Cerastium arvense;* 52. *Uvularia grandiflora;* 53. *Anemone canadensis;* 54. *Corydalis sempervirens;* 55. *Aquilegia canadensis;* 56. *Aquilegia formosa;* 57. *Aquilegia vulgaris;* 58. *Arabis albida;* 59. *Arabis alpina;* 60. *Arabis mollis;* 61. *Draba hirta;* 62. *Draba aizoides;* 63. *Bellis perennis;* 64. *Bloomeria crocea;* 65. *Bulbocodium vernum;* 66. *Caltha palustris;* 67. *Iberis sempervirens;* 68. *Claytonia caroliniana;* 69. *Claytonia virginica;* 70. *Arisaema triphyllum;* 71. *Draba alpina;* 72. *Dicentra canadensis;* 73. *Dicentra cucullaria;* 74. *Dicentra formosa;* 75. *Dentaria diphylla;* 76. *Epimedium alpinum;* 77. *Erythronium americanum;* 78. *Erythronium albidum;* 79. *Erythronium hendersoni;* 80. *Erythronium grandiflorum;* 81. *Erysimum linifolium;* 82. *Euphorbia epithymoides;* 83. *Euphorbia myrsinites;* 84. *Fritillaria imperialis;* 85. *Fritillaria lanceolata;* 86. *Fritillaria*

---

* Special articles on the subjects indicated by an asterisk (*) will be found at the words so marked.

recurva; 87. *Fritillaria meleagris*; 88. *Fritillaria pudica*; 89. *Viola pedata*; 90. *Omphalodes cappadocica*; 91. *Helonias bullata*; 92. *Hepatica acutiloba*; 93. *Hepatica americana*; 94. *Hyacinthus orientalis*; 95. *Hydrastis canadensis*; 96. *Omphalodes linifolia*; 97. *Leucojum aestivum*; 98. *Leucojum vernum*; 99. *Leucocrinum montanum*; 100. *Lychnis alba*; 101. *Lychnis alpina*; 102. *Mertensia virginica*; 103. *Muscari botryoides*; 104. *Muscari conicum*; 105. *Muscari comosum*; 106. *Muscari moschatum*; 107. *Narcissus cyclamineus*; 108. *Narcissus bulbocodium*; 109. *Narcissus incomparabilis*; 110. *Narcissus jonquilla*; 111. *Narcissus pseudo-narcissus*; 112. *Omphalodes verna*; 113. *Ornithogalum nutans*; 114. *Papaver nudicaule*; 115. *Phlox drummondi stellaris*; 116. *Phlox subulata*; 117. *Primula vulgaris*; 118. *Primula vulgaris caerulea*; 119. *Pulmonaria saccharata*; 120. *Pulsatilla patens*; 121. *Pulsatilla vulgaris*; 122. *Puschkinia scilloides*; 123. *Pyxidanthera barbulata*; 124. *Sanguinaria canadensis*; 125. *Bergenia cordifolia*; 126. *Bergenia crassifolia*; 127. *Saxifraga oppositifolia*; 128. *Saxifraga virginiensis*; 129. *Iris cristata*; 130. *Statice caespitosa*; 131. *Trillium cernuum*; 132. *Trillium erectum*; 133. *Trillium grandiflorum*; 134. *Trillium stylosum*; 135. *Trillium undulatum*; 136. *Viola* Mauve Queen; 137. *Viola odorata*; 138. *Viola pubescens*; 139. *Viola tricolor hortensis*; 140. *Trollius asiaticus*; 141. *Townsendia grandiflora*; 142. *Tulipa* Duc van Thol; 143. *Tulipa* (Mayflowering); 144. *Veronica gentianoides*; 145. *Viola blanda*; 146. *Viola canadensis*; 147. *Viola cucullata*; 148. *Viola cornuta*.

SHRUBS AND TREES: 149. *Azalea mollis*; 150. *Azalea nudiflora*; 151. *Salix babylonica*; 152. *Salix nigra*; 153. *Cercis canadensis*; 154. *Clematis montana*; 155. *Cornus alba*; 156. *Cornus florida*; 157. *Salix discolor*; 158. *Amelanchier canadensis*; 159. *Daphne cneorum*; 160. *Forsythia suspensa*; 161. *Forsythia viridissima*; 162. *Forsythia intermedia*; 163. Japanese flowering cherries; 164. *Magnolia soulangeana*; 165. *Prunus triloba*; 166. *Amygdalus persica*; 167. *Prunus avium*; 168. Kurume azaleas; 169. *Exochorda racemosa*; 170. Plum blossom; 171. *Acer platanoides*; 172. *Spiraea prunifolia*; 173. *Spiraea thunbergi*; 174. *Syringa vulgaris*; 175. *Viburnum carlesi*; 176. *Vinca minor*; 177. *Cercis chinensis*; 178. *Benzoin aestivale*.

Also numbers 3 and 4 (see JANUARY); numbers 15, 18, and 19 (see FEBRUARY); numbers 21, 22, 23, 24, 26, 27, 28, 29, 30, 32, 33, 34, 36, 37, 38, 39, 40, and 41 (see MARCH); and numbers 999 and 1000 (see DECEMBER).

FLOWERS AND SHRUBS IN THE GARDEN. Prepare beds and sow seeds of hardy annuals early in the month; tender sorts later. Biennials and perennials may be sown for next year's flowers.

Empty places in the border may be filled with sowings of larkspur, candytuft, poppies, marigolds and nasturtiums. For quick results sow Virginia stocks.

Make up your bulb beds for lilies, the new daylilies, dahlias, tuberous begonias (for shaded places), tigridias and tuberoses.

Clean and prepare your lily pool. Water lilies are only a small part of the many aquatics to order and plant in or around your pool. See WATER GARDEN.

Plant out toward the end of the month all the stock moved last month from the greenhouse into the frames to harden. About the same time set out pot-grown roses in full leaf. Do not cut back the tops. Set out early asters. Have in readiness annuals, to fill in tulip beds and borders where the plants have finished blooming.

Inspect tulips and iris for aphids. Spray. Destroy tent caterpillar nests. Watch rose foliage for insects and disease. Destroy iris borers as they start to hatch. Control cutworms with bait. Spray Madonna lilies and clear away all dead or diseased foliage. Eliminate ants from the lawn. Look out for boxwood leaf-miner and canker.

After flowering *Arabis* and *Aubrietia* must be cut back hard; cut *Achillea* to the ground to secure a second flowering later. Pinch back garden chrysanthemums to keep them dwarf, if you are south of zone* 4.

Mulch broad-leaved evergreens with rotted oak leaves, straw, grass clippings, etc. Pinch back all annuals that have any tendency to become leggy.

Give lilacs and peonies a good top-dressing. Prune lilacs when removing dead flower sprays. Prune all early-flowering shrubs immediately after flowering.

AROUND THE HOUSE. Repair and fill window and porch boxes. If annuals are used, do not crowd the young seedlings. Cut back trailing sorts to make bushy plants. Tuberous begonias are excellent for shaded locations. Hanging baskets may be brought out the latter part of the month. Plunge* many house plants in the borders or other garden spots to recuperate.

FRUITS AND BERRIES. Fertilize the strawberry bed; hoe and cultivate to eliminate weeds and to aerate the soil. Watch gooseberries and currants for mildew and worms respectively. Spray fruit trees for scale, codling moth and aphids. Properly tie and train grape vines. See GRAPE.

COLD FRAMES AND HOTBEDS. As soon as annuals and tender plants are cleared, the sash may be dispensed with. If desired, melons, cucumbers or the like may be grown in this space.

VEGETABLE GARDEN. Prepare and fertilize the soil and sow any of the following: artichokes, asparagus, bush beans, beets, carrots, early cauliflower, celery, sweet corn, kohlrabi, leek, lettuce, onions, parsley, peas, radishes, salsify, spinach, Swiss chard, herbs, pumpkins, late cabbage, late cauliflower, endive, rutabaga and kale. Thin out the young seedlings as soon as they are well established. Set out the balance of any tender plants still in the cold frames and hotbeds. Plant successive sowings of lettuce, endive, string beans, etc., for steady supply until frost.

Watch for cutworms; root maggots; Colorado potato, asparagus and cucumber beetles; lace bugs or any insects which attack early, tender vegetable plants. See INSECT PESTS.

Stake and prune tomato vines. Brush tall-growing varieties of peas. Cut only a small amount of asparagus from the new bed. In cutting, gather both the large and small stalks. Do not cut after the last of June.

Sow or plant mint in beds; okra may be sown in rows the end of the month. Try planting different vegetables such as Jerusalem artichokes, Witloof chicory, black salsify, and cardoon.

GREENHOUSE. Transfer all remaining bedding stock to cold frames and sheltered places in the open, prior to their final placement in the garden. As fast as the houses are cleared, paint any woodwork, limewash any wall space, repair benches where necessary, and look after all drainage and pipe equipment.

Train and tie new growth of climbers in any class where necessary. Pot all subjects propagated in March and April. Root in moist sand *Plumbago indica*. Shade slightly Memorial Day flowers now coming into bloom. Ventilate and water well.

Pot and gradually bring to the light any bulbs started in the hothouse which have made new growth. Shade slightly. Feed heavily all plants in flower in the houses. Woody plants may be placed outdoors. Begonias, etc., may be put in cold frames to harden.

Ferns that had rest periods during the winter should now begin new growth; re-pot if necessary, feed with weak liquid manure and shade until well established. Bench carnations from pots; spray frequently for a few days.

Now that the greenhouse is less congested, with many of the benches cleared, run a crop of melons, especially in northern sections where early ones cannot be depended

---

* Special articles on the subjects indicated by an asterisk (*) will be found at the words so marked.

upon. Use any small house. Little or no fire is needed as it becomes warmer. Cover seeded pots with glass to protect against mice. Train the young plants on wires as soon as they are benched. Inspect the base of the plant for canker. Hand pollinate. Support the fruits in nets. One of the best to grow is Sutton's *Superlative*.

Plant early gardenias, or whatever similar flowers are to be the main crop for next winter.

November's show chrysanthemums must be kept growing without check. Do not over-water; watch for aphids; give bonemeal in moderation; tie and stake up wherever necessary.

Sow seeds of stocks, snapdragons and other winter-flowering plants in flats.

Look after *Calanthe* bulbs started last month. Do not water too freely. Give odontoglossums full sun; raise the temperature of the house and water heavily. Give cattleyas plenty of light, but not full sun. Water those grown on blocks at the roots every day during the summer.

SUB-TROPICAL. Sow seeds of beets; pole, lima and field beans; cabbage, carrots, cauliflower, celery, sweet and pop corn; cucumbers, kale, okra, onions, parsley, parsnips, peanuts, peppers, pumpkins, radishes, rice and salsify. Sow in flats sorts required for second plantings. Plant chayote seeds where they are to grow.

Sow in the open seeds mentioned last month; also helichrysum, *Piqueria*, tropical vines such as *Passiflora*, *Antignon leptopus*, etc.

Transplant to beds and borders seedlings from flats from last month's and previous sowings, if thoroughly hardened. Sow in flats asters, carnations, pinks, gaillardia, matricaria, *Nicotiana*, salvias, and *Schizanthus*.

## PLANTS IN BLOOM — MAY

HERBACEOUS PLANTS: 179. *Achillea ptarmica*; 180. *Actaea alba*; 181. *Actaea rubra*; 182. *Aethionema coridifolium*; 183. *Ajuga reptans alba*; 184. *Anemonella thalictroides*; 185. *Anemone cylindrica*; 186. *Anemone fulgens*; 187. *Anemone nemorosa*; 188. *Anemone sylvestris*; 189. *Aquilegia coerulea*; 190. *Aquilegia chrysantha*; 191. *Arenaria verna*; 192. *Arenaria verna caespitosa*; 193. *Asarum canadense*; 194. *Asperula odorata*; 195. *Aubrietia deltoides*; 196. *Begonia semperflorens*; 197. *Bergenia ligulata*; 198. *Tulipa* (Darwin tulips); 199. *Centaurea moschata*; 200. *Cerastium biebersteini*; 201. *Convallaria majalis*; 202. *Cypripedium acaule*; 203. *Cypripedium macranthum*; 204. *Dianthus plumarius*; 205. *Dicentra spectabilis*; 206. *Diphylleia cymosa*; 207. *Doronicum plantagineum*; 208. *Lupinus texensis*; 209. *Dentaria laciniata*; 210. *Iberis amara*; 211. *Dryas suendermanni*; 212. *Epimedium macranthum*; 213. *Erigeron glaucus*; 214. *Erodium cicutarium*; 215. *Gentiana acaulis*; 216. *Geum montanum*; 217. *Geum chiloense*; 218. *Hemerocallis*; 219. *Schizocodon soldanelloides*; 220. *Primula denticulata*; 221. *Heuchera lithophila*; 222. *Heuchera sanguinea*; 223. *Hutchinsia alpina*; 224. *Hyacinthus azureus*; 225. *Iberis umbellata*; 226. *Iberis gibraltarica*; 227. *Polemonium caeruleum*; 228. *Iris pumila*; 229. *Iris sibirica*; 230. *Iris* (tall-bearded varieties); 231. *Polygala paucifolia*; 232. *Tiarella cordifolia*; 233. *Anemone quinquefolia*; 234. *Jeffersonia diphylla*; 235. *Lamium maculatum*; 236. *Lewisia columbiana*; 237. *Lilium sargentiae*; 238. *Linum perenne*; 239. *Lithodora diffusa*; 240. *Lupinus polyphyllus roseus*; 241. *Lychnis haageana*; 242. *Mazus japonicus*; 243. *Mitella diphylla*; 244. *Corydalis lutea*; 245. *Myosotis sylvatica*; 246. *Myosotis scorpioides*; 247. *Podophyllum peltatum*; 248. *Pedicularis canadensis*; 249. *Narcissus poeticus*; 250. *Nymphaea alba*; 251. *Oenothera acaulis*; 252. *Oenothera trichocalyx*; 253. *Ornithogalum umbellatum*; 254. *Papaver alpinum*; 255. *Papaver orientale*; 256. Peonies (early white varieties); 257. Peonies (early pink varieties); 258. *Pelargonium* (garden geranium); 259. *Phlox amoena*; 260. *Phlox arendsi*; 261. *Phlox divaricata*; 262. *Phlox* Miss Lingard; 263. *Phlox ovata*; 264. *Phlox adsurgens*; 265. *Polemonium reptans*; 266. *Primula auricula*; 267. *Primula polyantha*; 268. *Primula sikkimensis*; 269. *Primula veris*; 270. *Pentstemon menziesi*; 271. *Ranunculus repens pleniflorus*; 272. *Salvia nemorosa*; 273. *Polygonatum biflorum*; 274. *Saponaria ocymoides*; 275. *Saxifraga aizoon baldensis*;

276. *Saxifraga decipiens*; 277. *Senecio doronicum*; 278. *Scilla hispanica*; 279. *Scilla nonscripta*; 280. *Sedum acre*; 281. *Trillium sessile*; 282. *Trollius europaeus*; 283. *Viola* Apricot Gem; 284. *Viola lutea splendens*; 285. Wallflowers.

SHRUBS AND TREES: 286. *Akebia quinata*; 287. *Aesculus hippocastanum*; 288. *Amelanchier stolonifera*; 289. *Aristolochia durior*; 290. *Calycanthus floridus*; 291. *Cornus canadensis*; 292. *Aronia arbutifolia*; 293. *Aronia melanocarpa*; 294. *Epigaea repens*; 295. *Euonymus alatus*; 296. *Halesia carolina*; 297. *Azalea calendulacea*; 298. *Cornus alternifolia*; 299. *Crataegus crus-galli*; 300. *Malus atrosanguinea*; 301. *Malus halliana parkmani*; 302. *Malus ionensis* (Bechtel's double crab); 303. *Pachysandra procumbens*; 304. *Pachysandra terminalis*; 305. English hawthorn; 306. *Crataegus phaenopyrum*; 307. *Philadelphus virginalis*; 308. *Pyracantha coccinea lalandi*; 309. *Deutzia purpurascens*; 310. *Enkianthus campanulatus*; 311. *Halesia diptera*; 312. *Rhododendron carolinianum*; 313. *Rhododendron catawbiense*; 314. *Rhododendron californicum*; 315. *Rhododendron ponticum*; 316. *Azalea mucronata*; 317. *Laburnum anagyroides*; 318. *Lonicera maacki*; 319. *Lonicera tatarica*; 320. *Rhodotypos tetrapetala*; 321. *Rosa hugonis*; 322. *Sambucus pubens*; 323. *Symplocos tinctoria*; 324. *Vaccinium corymbosum*; 325. *Gaylussacia baccata*; 326. *Spiraea crenata*; 327. *Spiraea trilobata*; 328. *Spiraea vanhouttei*; 329. *Viburnum acerifolium*; 330. *Syringa* Mme. Marie Lemoine; 331. *Syringa persica*; 332. *Magnolia acuminata*; 333. *Magnolia grandiflora*; 334. *Tamarix africana*; 335. *Viburnum alnifolium*; 336. *Viburnum opulus sterile*; 337. *Viburnum dentatum*; 338. *Weigela florida*; 339. *Weigela* Madame Lemoine; 340. *Wistaria floribunda*; 341. *Wistaria sinensis*; 342. *Wistaria floribunda macrobotrys*.

Also numbers 21, 22, 23, 27, 28, 30, 36, 37, 39, and 41 (see MARCH); and numbers 42, 43, 44, 45, 46, 47, 48, 49, 50, 51, 52, 53, 54, 55, 56, 57, 59, 60, 61, 62, 63, 64, 66, 67, 68, 69, 70, 71, 72, 73, 74, 75, 76, 77, 78, 79, 80, 81, 83, 84, 85, 86, 87, 88, 89, 90, 91, 92, 93, 94, 95, 96, 97, 98, 100, 101, 102, 103, 104, 105, 106, 107, 108, 109, 110, 111, 112, 113, 114, 115, 116, 117, 119, 120, 121, 122, 123, 124, 125, 126, 127, 128, 129, 130, 131, 132, 133, 134, 135, 136, 137, 138, 139, 140, 141, 142, 143, 144, 145, 146, 147, 148, 149, 150, 154, 155, 156, 159, 163, 164, 168, 169, 172, 173, 174, 175, and 176 (see APRIL).

FLOWERS. A longer blooming period for annuals may be had by keeping the flowers cut and pinching back terminal growth. Feed and water well all plants during blooming season. Keep coreopsis cut close and sweet peas picked. Pick off all dead leaves or flowers. Cut lupines to the ground after flowering. Keep seed pods off snapdragons, sweet peas, violas and nasturtiums.

Early spring-flowering perennials may be propagated by division and transplanted. Iris, polyanthus, alyssum, etc., should be so treated. If left in the border, clean off old leaves and flowering matter, top-dress with rotted manure and a little soil. Water delphiniums well while buds are setting.

Tulips, not hardy, may be lifted and stored. Darwin tulips must be so handled in the Middle West. Dry off slowly. Burn all diseased tops. When cutting peony blooms, leave two or more leaves on the stalk. Continue to set out gladiolus bulbs and toward the end of the month dahlia roots.

Water lilies and aquatics may go into the pool; also the fish.

THE ROSE GARDEN. Where rose bugs are numerous and spraying has proved ineffective, try shallow cultivation in light soil; in heavier soils mulch without cultivation. Fertilize now so as to get the roses well established before hot weather. Spray often for control of black spot and mildew. Gather and burn leaves as soon as they fall. Tie up young

---

\* Special articles on the subjects indicated by an asterisk (\*) will be found at the words so marked.

growth which is to take the place of the old wood. Potted roses may still be planted.

SEED SOWING AND GENERAL WORK. A seedbed in the open ground, sheltered, will take care of many perennials which will be large enough to be transplanted by fall to permanent quarters. Use new seeds preferably of delphiniums, primroses and polyanthus.

Biennials such as wallflowers, sweet Williams, Canterbury bells, hollyhocks, columbines, forget-me-nots, daisies and verbascums may be sown now. Annuals, to be sown for late summer bloom, are calendulas, asters, zinnias, alyssum, candytuft, marigolds, cornflowers, larkspur, snapdragons, clarkia, lupine, poppy, mignonette, stock, verbena, and annual sunflowers. Sow deeper as the weather becomes warmer.

Set palms, house plants and tub plants outdoors in a shady place. Begin to collect and save seeds from choice plants.

Spray boxwood foliage with water every day during the summer, when shaded. Clip and trim all hedges. Prune back straggling branches on small evergreens. Do not shear newly planted ones until they are established. Do not mow the lawn closely during hot, dry weather. Clip edges of borders and grass plots. Prune early-flowering shrubs as soon as they have finished blooming. Do not prune heavily those which are depended upon for fall fruiting effects.

Stake large herbaceous plants or any of weak or straggly growth.

FRUITS AND BERRIES. If everbearing strawberry plants were set out late in the spring, keep the blossoms picked off until the end of July. Mulch around strawberries, currants, etc., to keep moisture around the roots. Prune young fruit trees (new growth only) and feed heavily to secure large fruits.

VEGETABLE GARDEN. Those who raise vegetables for their own use should plant late-maturing varieties for storing purposes, as carrots, pumpkins, onions, parsnips, turnips, squash, winter radishes, cabbage, beets and tomatoes. Cared for correctly, they may be kept long after frost.

Plant outdoors for summer and fall use, bush and lima beans, Brussels sprouts, late cabbage, beets, carrots, late cauliflower, sweet corn, cucumbers, endive, kale, lettuce, melons, okra, peas, pumpkins, salsify, Swiss chard, radishes, squash and herbs. Set out plants of celery, peppers, tomatoes, broccoli and eggplants which were grown late in the cold frames. Plan definitely for a steady succession of crops.

Asparagus should not be cut after the end of the month. Grow eggplant and peppers together, as they give a heavier yield. Prune a little of the pepper herbage to obtain a larger pepper.

Spray potatoes, cabbages, melons, and squash. Watch closely for all pests mentioned last month.

GREENHOUSE. The next four months are vital ones to gardeners growing next winter's flowers. Young growth is tender; shade is essential. Use roller shades rather than permanent shading. Spray often as a preventive.

Pot up chrysanthemums. Spray the foliage for a day or so before watering heavily. Move those not for exhibition onto the bench where they are to flower. Pot for winter flowering such plants as poinsettias, cyclamen and Jerusalem cherry. Do not bench field-grown carnations until July. Bench now any still in small pots. Do not over-water outdoor stock; do not bring in weak, spindly plants. Young seedlings of stocks, snapdragons, etc., sown last month should be large enough to prick off now.

Inspect the gardenias planted last month. Spray often and damp down to promote moist atmosphere. They are liable to attack by mealybugs.

Sow seeds of stock, cinerarias, *Primula malacoides* and varieties, for winter flowers.

Train up any new or two-year trees of dwarf fruits. Cut and tie. Look for red spiders. Water and feed moderately. Shade slightly. Keep houses well ventilated.

Give terrestrial species of *Calanthe* and other orchids considerable heat and watering during their growing period.

Destroy brown and white scale. Syringe between pots of *Cattleya* during the growing season on fine days. Do not keep odontoglossums too warm.

SUB-TROPICAL. Sow seeds of beets; velvet, soy and garden beans; broccoli, cabbage, carrots, cauliflower, celery; corn; cucumbers, melons, okra, mustard, parsley, peanuts, peppers, pumpkins, radishes, rice, New Zealand spinach, Swiss chard and tomatoes. Transplant seedlings from flats.

Make permanent strawberry beds. Fertilize. Set out plants from runners from early stock settings. Look over fruit orchards for spraying needs. Sow cover crop in young orchards.

Sow outdoors calendulas, candytuft, late cosmos, African marigolds, nasturtiums, phlox, portulacas, zinnias, and annual vines. Bermuda grass should be planted from now until November for good lawn effects.

Cinerarias should be sown in frames. Plant gladioli and dahlias. Perennial plants in gallon cans may be set out at any time.

## PLANTS IN BLOOM — JUNE

HERBACEOUS PLANTS: 343. *Anchusa azurea;* 344. *Achillea filipendulina;* 345. *Achillea millefolium roseum;* 346. *Aconitum uncinatum;* 347. *Adenophora potanini;* 348. *Aethionema pulchellum;* 349. *Aethionema grandiflorum;* 350. *Ageratum houstonianum;* 351. *Allium azureum;* 352. *Alyssum argenteum;* 353. *Anagallis linifolia;* 354. *Anemone coronaria;* 355. *Anthemis tinctoria;* 356. *Dianthus caesius;* 357. Snapdragons; 358. *Aquilegia flagellata;* 359. *Aquilegia skinneri;* 360. *Arenaria montana;* 361. *Aster alpinus;* 362. *Aster subcoeruleus;* 363. *Astilbe davidi;* 364. *Astilbe japonica;* 365. *Baptisia australis;* 366. *Coreopsis rosea;* 367. *Borago officinalis;* 368. *Brachycome iberidifolia;* 369. *Satureia alpina;* 370. *Satureia hortensis;* 371. *Calendula officinalis;* 372. *Callirhoë involucrata;* 373. *Cooperia pedunculata;* 374. *Campanula carpatica;* 375. *Campanula garganica;* 376. *Campanula glomerata;* 377. *Campanula latifolia;* 378. *Campanula latifolia macrantha;* 379. *Campanula medium;* 380. *Campanula persicifolia;* 381. *Campanula portenschlagiana;* 382. *Campanula punctata;* 383. *Campanula rotundifolia;* 384. *Campanula trachelium;* 385. *Catananche caerulea;* 386. *Centaurea americana;* 387. *Centaurea montana;* 388. *Centaurium confertum;* 389. *Centranthus ruber;* 390. *Cephalaria alpina;* 391. *Cerastium tomentosum;* 392. *Chrysanthemum coccineum;* 393. *Coreopsis grandiflora;* 394. *Coreopsis lanceolata;* 395. *Coreopsis verticillata;* 396. *Coreopsis tinctoria;* 397. *Crucianella stylosa;* 398. *Cymbalaria muralis;* 399. *Mazus pumilio;* 400. *Delphinium cashmerianum;* 401. *Delphinium consolida;* 402. *Delphinium* (garden larkspur); 403. *Delphinium elatum;* 404. *Digitalis lutea;* 405. *Delphinium grandiflorum;* 406. *Dianthus arenarius;* 407. *Dianthus alpinus;* 408. *Dianthus barbatus;* 409. *Astilbe* (Gruno); 410. *Dianthus chinensis;* 411. *Dianthus cruentus;* 412. *Dianthus glacialis;* 413. *Dianthus* (Hybrid sweet William); 414. *Dianthus latifolius;* 415. *Dianthus petraeus;* 416. *Echinacea angustifolia;* 417. *Dianthus superbus;* 418. *Dicentra eximia;* 419. *Dictamnus albus;* 420. *Digitalis ambigua;* 421. *Digitalis lanata;* 422. *Digitalis purpurea;* 423. *Draba olympica;* 424. *Dracocephalum grandiflorum;* 425. *Duchesnea indica;* 426. *Emilia sagittata;* 427. *Eremurus bungei;* 428. *Eremurus himalaicus;* 429. *Eremurus robustus;* 430. *Erigeron coulteri;* 431. *Erigeron pulchellus;* 432. *Erigeron speciosus;* 433. *Epilobium angustifolium;* 434. *Eriophyllum caespitosum;* 435. *Erodium macradenum;* 436. *Erodium chrysanthemum;* 437. *Eryngium amethystinum;* 438. *Euphorbia corollata;* 439. *Filipendula purpurea;* 440. *Filipendula rubra;* 441. *Hosta coerulea;* 442. *Hosta sieboldiana;* 443. *Gaillardia aristata;* 444. *Galega officinalis;* 445. *Galium verum;* 446. *Geranium ibericum;* 447. *Geranium pratense;* 448. *Geranium sanguineum;* 449. *Geranium sanguineum album;* 450. *Geranium wallichianum;* 451. *Geum ciliatum;* 452. *Gladiolus* (early varieties); 453. *Globularia trichosantha;* 454. *Grindelia robusta;* 455. *Gypsophila elegans;* 456. *Gypsophila repens;* 457. *Hedysarum coronarium;* 458. *Hedysarum pabulare;* 459. *Helianthemum nummularium;* 460. Heliotrope; 461. *Oxalis acetosella;* 462. *Nicotiana sylvestris;* 463. *Hemerocallis;* 464. *Senecio jacobaea;* 465. *Nigella damascena;* 466. *Hesperis matronalis;* 467. *Horminum pyre-*

---

* Special articles on the subjects indicated by an asterisk (*) will be found at the words so marked.

naicum; 468. *Hyssopus officinalis;* 469. *Incarvillea delavayi;* 470. *Inula glandulosa;* 471. *Polygonum amplexicaule;* 472. *Belamcanda chinensis;* 473. *Iris laevigata;* 474. *Nicotiana sanderae;* 475. *Iris xiphium;* 476. *Kniphofia tuckii;* 477. *Lathyrus latifolius;* 478. *Lathyrus grandiflorus;* 479. *Leontopodium alpinum;* 480. *Lewisia rediviva;* 481. *Lepachys pinnata;* 482. *Lilium canadense;* 483. *Lilium candidum;* 484. *Lilium chalcedonicum;* 485. *Lilium columbianum;* 486. *Lilium concolor;* 487. *Lilium elegans;* 488. *Lilium hansoni;* 489. *Lilium japonicum;* 490. *Lilium martagon;* 491. *Lilium monadelphum;* 492. *Lilium parryi;* 493. *Trientalis borealis;* 494. *Lilium regale;* 495. *Lilium tenuifolium;* 496. *Lilium testaceum;* 497. *Lilium washingtonianum;* 498. *Linaria dalmatica;* 499. *Linaria maroccana;* 500. *Linum grandiflorum;* 501. *Linum flavum;* 502. *Linnaea americana;* 503. *Lotus corniculatus;* 504. *Lupinus perennis;* 505. *Lupinus polyphyllus;* 506. *Lychnis chalcedonica;* 507. *Lychnis coronaria;* 508. *Campanula raddeana;* 509. *Lychnis flos-cuculi;* 510. *Lychnis flos-jovis;* 511. *Lychnis viscaria;* 512. *Lysimachia nummularia;* 513. *Lysimachia punctata;* 514. *Lysimachia japonica;* 515. *Lysimachia vulgaris;* 516. *Lythrum virgatum;* 517. *Malva alcea;* 518. *Malva moschata;* 519. *Matricaria chamomilla;* 520. *Meconopsis cambrica;* 521. *Mimulus cardinalis;* 522. *Monarda punctata;* 523. *Monarda didyma;* 524. *Morina longifolia;* 525. *Nepeta;* 526. *Nierembergia rivularis;* 527. *Oenothera lamarckiana;* 528. *Oenothera biennis grandiflora;* 529. *Oenothera fruticosa;* 530. *Oenothera glauca fraseri;* 531. *Oenothera missouriensis;* 532. *Oenothera speciosa;* 533. *Onobrychis viciaefolia;* 534. *Opuntia compressa;* 535. *Origanum vulgare;* 536. *Papaver orientale* (Goliath); 537. *Pentstemon acuminatus;* 538. *Pentstemon barbatus;* 539. *Pentstemon diffusus;* 540. *Pentstemon digitalis;* 541. *Pentstemon hartwegi;* 542. *Pentstemon glaber;* 543. *Pentstemon hirsutus;* 544. *Pentstemon unilateralis;* 545. *Pentstemon spectabilis;* 546. Peonies (Madame Jules, Dessert, La Perle, Emile Galle, Solange); 547. Peonies (Eugenie Verdier, Therese, Walter Faxon, Venus, Mabel Franklin); 548. Peonies (La Rosière, Le Cygne, Primevère, Alice Harding, Kelway's Glorious); 549. Peonies (Adolphe Rousseau, M. Martin, Cahuzac, Cherry Hill); 550. Peonies (Japanese-Isani-gidui, Aureolin, Tamatbaku, Ama-no-sode); 551. *Petalostemon purpureum;* 552. *Petasites japonica;* 553. *Petunias;* 554. *Phlomis fruticosa;* 555. *Phlomis tuberosa;* 556. *Phlox stolonifera;* 557. *Phlox maculata;* 558. *Phlox suffruticosa;* 559. *Phyteuma hemisphaericum;* 560. *Platycodon grandiflorum;* 561. *Polemonium humile;* 562. *Portulaca grandiflora;* 563. *Potentilla grandiflora;* 564. *Potentilla atrosanguinea;* 565. *Potentilla hybrida;* 556. *Potentilla russelliana;* 567. *Calopogon pulchellus;* 568. *Primula japonica;* 569. *Prunella vulgaris;* 570. *Reseda odorata;* 571. *Sabbatia dodecandra;* 572. *Salvia argentea;* 573. *Salvia officinalis;* 574. *Maianthemum canadense;* 575. *Aruncus sylvester;* 576. *Saxifraga umbrosa;* 577. *Scabiosa atropurpurea;* 578. *Chamaelirium luteum;* 579. *Scabiosa caucasica;* 580. *Scabiosa japonica;* 581. *Chiogenes hispidula;* 582. *Polygala senega;* 583. *Cypripedium parviflorum pubescens;* 584. *Sedum aizoon;* 585. *Sedum reflexum;* 586. *Sedum lydium;* 587. *Sedum middendorfianum;* 588. *Sedum pulchellum;* 589. *Sedum rupestre;* 590. *Sedum sexangulare;* 591. *Clintonia umbellata;* 592. *Sempervivum arenarium;* 593. *Sempervivum calcareum;* 594. *Sempervivum glaucum;* 595. *Sempervivum montanum;* 596. *Sempervivum tectorum;* 597. Shasta daisy; 598. *Sidalcea candida;* 599. *Sidalcea malvaeflora;* 600. *Silene acaulis;* 601. *Silene compacta;* 602. *Silene schafta;* 603. *Silene virginica;* 604. *Sprekelia formosissima;* 605. *Stachys corsica;* 606. *Stachys grandiflora;* 607. *Stachys lanata;* 608. *Stokesia laevis;* 609. *Thalictrum glaucum;* 610. *Thalictrum minus;* 611. *Thermopsis caroliniana;* 612. *Thymus serpyllum;* 613. *Thymus vulgaris;* 614. *Tigridia pavonia;* 615. *Tradescantia virginiana;* 616. *Xerophyllum asphodeloides;* 617. *Tropaeolum majus;* 618. *Tunica saxifraga;* 619. *Valeriana officinalis;* 620. *Verbascum chaixi;* 621. *Verbascum olympicum;* 622. *Verbascum phoeniceum;* 623. *Veronica incana;* 624. *Veronica maritima subsessilis;* 625. *Veronica spicata;* 626. *Veronica spuria;* 627. *Veronica teucrium;* 628. *Yucca filamentosa;* 629. *Zephyranthes.*

SHRUBS AND TREES. 630. *Actinidia chinensis;* 631. *Cladrastis lutea;* 632. *Lycium halimifolium;* 633. *Catalpa bignonioides;* 634. *Campsis radicans;* 635. *Cotoneasters;* 636. *Kalmia latifolia;* 637. *Celastrus scandens;* 638. *Chionanthus virginica;* 639. *Clematis integrifolia;* 640. *Clematis recta;* 641. *Liriodendron tulipifera;* 642. *Philadelphus coronarius;* 643. *Philadelphus lewisi;* 644. *Deutzia gracilis;* 645. *Deutzia lemoinei;* 646. *Duetzia scabra;* 647. *Sambucus canadensis;* 648. *Sorbus aucuparia;* 649. *Echinocactus simpsoni;* 650. *Genista tinctoria;* 651. *Hydrangea arborescens;* 652. *Hypericum moserianum;* 653. *Styrax japonica;* 654. *Syringa reflexa;* 655. *Viburnum rhytidophyllum;* 656. *Jasminum officinale;* 657. *Kerria japonica;* 658. *Kolkwitzia amabilis;* 659. *Lonicera henryi;* 660. *Lonicera japonica halliana;* 661. *Lonicera sempervirens;* 662. *Potentilla fruticosa;* 663. *Viburnum lantana;* 664. *Viburnum pubescens;* 665. *Spiraea cantoniensis;* 666. *Laburnum;* 667. *Robinia hispida;* 668. *Spiraea latifolia;* 669. *Aesculus pavia;* 670. *Rosa* (The New Dawn); 671. *Rosa* (climbing and ramblers); 672. *Rosa laevigata;* 673. *Rosa multiflora;* 674. *Rosa rugosa;* 675. *Rosa xanthina;* 676. *Rosa centifolia;* 677. *Rosa odorata;* 678. *Rosa setigera;* 679. *Photinia villosa;* 680. *Physocarpus opulifolius;* 681. Late hawthorns; 682. *Phyllodoce coerulea;* 683. *Spiraea japonica;* 684. *Symphoricarpos albus;* 685. *Syringa josikaea;* 686. *Syringa japonica.*

Also numbers 47, 55, 56, 57, 63, 67, 74, 84, 85, 88, 96, 114, 115, 128, 130, 131, 132, 139, 146, and 148 (see APRIL); and numbers 179, 180, 181, 183, 186, 187, 189, 190, 193, 194, 195, 196, 199, 200, 201, 204, 205, 207, 211, 213, 214, 215, 216, 217, 222, 223, 225, 226, 229, 235, 236, 237, 238, 239, 240, 241, 242, 244, 245, 250, 251, 252, 253, 254, 255, 256, 258, 260, 262, 263, 265, 271, 272, 274, 276, 277, 280, 282, 283, 284, 285, 289, 291, 303, 304, 307, 312, 313, 315, 322, 327, 328, 335, 338, and 339 (see MAY).

THINGS TO DO IN THE GARDEN. Keep soil loose around newly planted shrubs and bedding plants. Water thoroughly. Syringe foliage often to remove dust or soot.

Gladiolus may be planted up to the fifteenth. For late iris use varieties of Siberian and tall-bearded groups, or Japanese iris. When transplanting discard diseased or real old rhizomes. Stake all tall, slender plants. Bedding plants in pots will take care of last-minute vacancies. Use begonias and fuchsias for shaded spots; for sunny places buy young annuals or geraniums, lantanas, lobelias, heliotrope, etc.

Provide for the July slump by following larkspur cutting with phlox Miss Lingard; early phlox varieties; *Achillea;* *Hemerocallis;* climbing roses; hardy pinks; French marigolds and lavender.

Destroy weeds in the gravel walks; never use weed-killer near edging plants, etc. Trim back and remove seed pods of rock plants. Eradicate Canada thistles, burdock, etc.

Keep sweet peas and cornflowers well watered. Picking the flowers as fast as they bloom will prolong the flowering season. Transplant Oriental poppies.

THE ROSE GARDEN. Prune climbing roses after blooming. Prune standard rose bushes. Cut off withered flowers and leaves from the polyanthas daily. Mulch newly planted roses. Never feed newly planted roses during mid-summer. Cut back small flowered sorts to the ground. From large-flowered climbers thin but do not remove all the old canes. Root cuttings of climbers in moist, sandy soil.

INSECTS AND DISEASES. Look the lawn over carefully for signs of the lawn webworm.

Give lime to bearded irises that have rusty spots on the leaves. Transplant them from now on. Trim off any rusty-looking foliage.

Look for the Mexican bean beetle on bean leaves and spray. For late crops spray again in a couple of weeks. Spray evergreens, laurel and rhododendrons for red spider for the first and lace-wing fly for the two latter. Remember Japanese beetles are still active.

* Special articles on the subjects indicated by an asterisk (*) will be found at the words so marked.

FALL BLOOM AND ODD JOBS. Early this month sow zinnias, candytufts, larkspurs, early cosmos, scabious, coreopsis, gypsophilas, etc. Keep seed pods off hollyhocks and phlox and they will bloom again in the fall.

Order and plant Madonna-lily bulbs. Water window-box plants regularly. Pinch back shoots on geraniums that you will use as house plants later.

FRUIT AND VEGETABLES. Go over the peach and apple orchards and thin out fruit on all heavily laden trees. Clean up all fruits dropped in June.

Bag grapes with paper bags from the grocery. Cut small holes in the bottom for drainage. Thin out berry canes.

Bleach cauliflower by tying the outside leaves together as soon as the center hearts are formed.

Sow for late-season crops beans, beets, carrots, sweet corn, cress, cucumbers, corn salad, string beans, okra, early peas, rutabaga, squash, turnips, Chinese cabbage, kale and kohlrabi. Set out plants of late cabbage, late cauliflower, celery, kale, endive, and Brussels sprouts.

Feed tomatoes liberally if you wish large quantities of well-ripened fruits. Place a general fertilizer three or four inches away from the stems, after it has been mixed with some soil so that the vines will not be over-stimulated.

GREENHOUSE. Root poinsettias for Christmas flowering. Avoid any drying or airy conditions in the house. Shade the glass and keep a continuously moist atmosphere. Insert cuttings firmly and water well. Cheesecloth placed above plants will often give just the extra amount of protection necessary. Propagation may also be carried on in a frame on the north side of a building or hedge.

Pot freesias for Christmas flowers. Put about fifteen corms in a pot and stand them in an open frame. Water sparingly until roots are well established.

Continue all routine work with carnations, chrysanthemums, etc. For early flowers of salpiglossis sow seed about the fifteenth. Give it all the light possible.

Many orchids rest during the summer months. A few cattleyas will be in flower and all must be inspected and guarded against the *Cattleya* fly. Many summer-blooming coelogynes should be grown in the same temperatures as the cattleyas. Grow them in pots or baskets. Do not allow the cypripediums to get too dry at the roots, as they require little rest.

SUB-TROPICAL. Sow beets, beans, broccoli, cabbage, carrots, celery, collard, mustard, okra, peanuts, peppers, rice, soybeans, sunflowers, turnips and rutabagas. Eggplants for fall crops may be planted from June through August. If set in the open during the summer protect from full sun.

Continue the setting out of strawberry plants from stock runners. After harvesting early berry crops clean out old canes, etc.

Sow in open seeds of all flowers mentioned last month. Transplant strong plants of cinerarias, etc., and sow delphiniums in especially prepared flats. Fill in bare spots in the perennial border with zinnias and asters. Start strelitzias before the fall; shelter from cold winds.

## PLANTS IN BLOOM — JULY

HERBACEOUS PLANTS: 687. *Gladiolus* (mid-season varieties); 688. *Aconitum anthora;* 689. *Aconitum lycoctonum;* 690. *Aconitum napellus;* 691. *Steironema ciliatum;* 692. *Adenophora liliifolia;* 693. *Adlumia fungosa;* 694. *Hypericum calycinum;* 695. *Chimaphila maculata;* 696. *Cimicifuga americana;* 697. *Althaea* (hollyhocks); 698. *Apocynum cannabinum;* 699. *Convolvulus tricolor;* 700. *Arctotis grandis;* 701. *Arenaria grandiflora;* 702. *Argemone grandiflora;* 703. *Arnica montana;* 704. *Asclepias tuberosa;* 705. *Asphodeline lutea;* 706. *Aster ptarmicoides;* 707. *Macleaya cordata;* 708. *Boltonia asteroides;* 709. *Boltonia latisquama;* 710. *Pyrola elliptica;* 711. *Dalibarda repens;* 712. *Parnassia caroliniana;* 713. *Browallia americana;* 714. *Clarkia pulchella;* 715. *Callistephus* (China aster); 716. *Campanula alliariaefolia;* 717. *Campanula drabifolia;* 718. *Campanula ramosissima;* 719. *Cannas;* 720. *Cardiospermum halicacabum;* 721. *Lathyrus maritimus;* 722. *Potentilla tridentata;* 723. *Aletris farinosa;* 724. *Veronica virginica;* 725. *Cassia marylandica;* 726. *Centaurea dealbata;* 727. *Centaurea cyanus;* 728. *Centaurea cineraria;* 729. *Cephalaria tatarica;* 730. *Ceratostigma plumbaginoides;* 731. *Chelone glabra;* 732. *Chelone lyoni;* 733. *Chrysanthemum uliginosum;* 734. *Lilium philadelphicum;* 735. *Hypoxis hirsuta;* 736. *Impatiens holsti;* 737. *Cimicifuga racemosa;* 738. *Clarkia elegans;* 739. *Cleome spinosa;* 740. *Convolvulus japonicus;* 741. *Cosmos;* 742. *Cynanchum acuminatifolium;* 743. *Cynoglossum amabile;* 744. *Impatiens sultani;* 745. *Clematis ligusticifolia;* 746. *Smilacina racemosa;* 747. *Baptisia tinctoria;* 748. *Trachymene coeruleus;* 749. *Dimorphotheca aurantiaca;* 750. *Echinacea purpurea;* 751. *Echinops humilis;* 752. *Eomecon chionantha;* 753. *Epipactis pubescens;* 754. *Eryngium planum;* 755. *Eryngium alpinum;* 756. *Eupatorium coelestinum;* 757. *Eupatorium aromaticum;* 758. *Filipendula ulmaria;* 759. *Filipendula camtschatica;* 760. *Clematis texensis;* 761. *Hosta plantaginea;* 762. *Galax aphylla;* 763. *Galtonia candicans;* 764. *Gloriosa rothschildiana;* 765. *Gypsophila acutifolia;* 766. *Gypsophila cerastioides;* 767. *Gypsophila paniculata;* 768. *Helianthus decapetalus;* 769. *Heliopsis helianthoides;* 770. *Nicotiana alata;* 771. *Hemerocallis;* 772. *Herniaria glabra;* 773. *Hibiscus moscheutos;* 774. *Hosta undulata;* 775. *Quamoclit sloteri;* 776. *Iris kaempferi* (Japanese iris); 777. *Kniphofia uvaria;* 778. *Lavandula spica;* 779. *Liatris pycnostachya;* 780. *Liatris scariosa;* 781. *Lilium auratum;* 782. *Lilium giganteum;* 783. *Lilium longiflorum;* 784. *Lilium tigrinum;* 785. *Hypericum polyphyllum;* 786. *Lobelia cardinalis;* 787. *Hydrophyllum virginianum;* 788. *Pycnanthemum virginianum;* 789. *Gillenia stipulata;* 790. *Lysimachia clethroides;* 791. *Lythrum salicaria;* 792. *Marigold;* 793. *Michauxia campanuloides;* 794. *Monarda fistulosa;* 795. *Ophiopogon jaburan;* 796. *Alisma plantago-aquatica;* 797. *Pontederia cordata;* 798. *Sagittaria latifolia;* 799. *Nepeta mussini;* 800. *Ononis rotundifolia;* 801. *Rudbeckia maxima;* 802. *Cooperia drummondi;* 803. *Spiranthes cernuua;* 804. *Euphorbia marginata;* 805. *Physalis alkekengi;* 806. *Physostegia virginiana;* 807. *Platycodon grandiflorum mariesi;* 808. *Asclepias incarnata;* 809. *Gilia rubra;* 810. *Quamoclit pennata;* 811. *Romneya coulteri;* 812. *Eryngium giganteum;* 813. *Achillea ageratifolia;* 814. *Rudbeckia speciosa;* 815. *Salvia pratensis;* 816. *Salvia splendens;* 817. *Sedum album;* 818. *Sedum hispanicum;* 819. *Sedum sarmentosum;* 820. *Sedum stoloniferum;* 821. *Senecio pulcher;* 822. *Solidago latifolia;* 823. *Limonium vulgare;* 824. *Symphyandra hofmanni;* 825. *Teucrium chamaedrys;* 826. *Tropaeolum peregrinum;* 827. Tuberoses; 828. *Ursinia anethoides;* 829. *Verbena canadensis;* 830. *Verbena hortensis;* 831. *Veronica maritima;* 832. Zinnias.

SHRUBS AND TREES: 833. *Abelia grandiflora;* 834. *Buddleia davidi;* 835. *Sorbaria aitchisoni;* 836. *Sorbaria arborea;* 837. *Clematis orientalis;* 838. *Clematis jackmani;* 839. *Sophora japonica;* 840. *Hypericum prolificum;* 841. *Clethra alnifolia;* 842. *Cephalanthus occidentalis;* 843. *Koelreuteria paniculata;* 844. *Gaultheria procumbens;* 845. *Spiraea billiardi;* 846. *Spiraea alba;* 847. *Hypericum patulum henryi;* 848. *Hibiscus syriacus;* 849. *Spiraea* (Anthony Waterer); 850. *Spiraea tomentosa;* 851. *Cotinus coggygria;* 852. *Stewartia pentagyna;* 853. *Vitex agnus-castus.*

Also numbers 74, 114, 115, 130, 139, and 148 (see APRIL); numbers 180, 186, 190, 196, 207, 214, 216, 217, 222, 235, 236, 238, 239, 250, 251, 258, 262, 274, 283, 284, and 289 (see MAY); and numbers 344, 345, 346, 347, 350, 351, 352, 355, 357, 359, 364, 366, 367, 368, 370, 371, 372, 373, 374, 376, 377, 378, 380, 381, 382, 383, 384, 385, 386, 387, 389, 390, 392, 393, 394, 395, 396, 397, 398, 399, 400, 401, 402, 403, 404, 405, 406, 407, 408, 411, 413, 414, 415, 416, 418, 419, 420, 421, 422, 424, 426, 427, 429, 431, 432, 433, 434, 435, 436, 437, 438, 439, 440, 441, 442, 443, 444, 445, 446, 447, 448, 449, 450, 454, 455, 456, 457, 458, 459, 460, 461, 462, 464, 465, 466, 467, 468, 469, 471, 473, 474, 476, 477, 478, 479, 480, 481, 482, 483, 485, 486, 487, 488, 489, 491, 492, 494, 495, 496, 498, 499, 500, 501, 502, 503, 504, 505, 506, 507, 509, 510, 512, 513, 514, 515, 516, 517, 519, 520, 521, 523, 524, 525, 526, 527, 528, 529, 530, 531, 532, 533, 534, 535, 536, 537, 538, 539, 540, 541, 542, 543, 544, 545, 551, 552, 553, 554, 555, 556, 557, 558, 559, 560, 561, 562, 563, 564, 565, 566, 568, 569, 570, 571, 572, 573, 575, 576, 577, 578, 579, 580, 584, 587, 588, 590, 591, 592, 596, 597, 598, 599, 600, 602, 603, 604, 605, 606, 607, 608, 609, 610, 611, 612, 613, 614, 615, 616, 617, 618, 619, 620, 621, 622, 623, 624, 625, 626, 627, 628, 629, 630, 632, 633, 634, 639, 640, 649, 650, 651, 652, 657, 659, 661, 662, 666, 668, 670, 671, 673, 674, 676, 681, 683, and 684 (see JUNE).

---

\* Special articles on the subjects indicated by an asterisk (\*) will be found at the words so marked.

ROCK GARDEN. Weed and remove all dead flower heads and water according to general soil requirements. Remove all excess parts of plants instead of systematic shearing back, to initiate natural growth. Top-dress stem-rooting sorts. Give gentians and primulas some very old, screened cow manure with sand and leaf mold added, after heavy rainstorms. The very last of the month sow seeds for next spring's planting. Winter them over in the cold frame.

FLOWER GARDEN. Evergreens may be transplanted now. (See AUTUMN PLANTING.) Separate large clumps of naturalized bulbs and replant. Set out Madonna lilies, Oriental poppies, hardy amaryllis; divide *Chrysanthemum coccineum*, trollius, and hepaticas, if absolutely necessary to disturb the latter.

Water lawns after the sun is down. Weeds can be removed by application of weed-killer, but boards or some such protection should be laid against boxwood, etc., to protect it if the weeds are in its vicinity. Sow new lawns where needed.

Candytuft, if cut back after flowering, may be propagated by cuttings. Take cuttings also of hardy phlox, carnations, snapdragons, etc.

If cool weather, sow in frames to flower in early spring *Linaria*, California poppies, larkspur, candytuft, forget-me-nots, English daisies, pansies, and hollyhocks. If the weather is very warm, sow in September. Sow delphinium seeds as soon as they ripen.

Spray phlox for mildew; nasturtiums for lice. Cut and burn webworm nests.

Prune and trim into shape wisteria vines. Cut back all suckers on grafted flowering shrubs and trees.

VEGETABLES, FRUITS AND BERRIES. Thin late beets; pick cucumbers for pickling; water heavily in dry weather the foliage of parsnips, turnips, and other leafy sorts.

Sow bush beans, corn salad, endive, lettuce, dwarf peas for a late crop, also cress, spinach and radishes. It is not too late to set out kale, endive and rutabaga.

In picking August apples, be careful not to bruise in picking or packing, as they rot quickly. Mulch around blackberry and raspberry bushes; mulch with grass clippings beneath gooseberry and currant bushes; cut back strawberries and mulch between the plant rows.

The cut-off runners of strawberries make the best propagative material for next year's bed. Cut the runners so as to provide only one bud (see Illustration at STRAWBERRY), and plant directly on the site of next year's bed — about three feet apart in the row and the rows two feet apart.

Begin, also, to cut out old and useless canes of raspberry, blackberry, and other bramble fruits.

Currant bushes should be cut back to induce young growth for next year's bearing.

GREENHOUSE. Carry on all routine work in the houses, such as show chrysanthemums, carnations, snapdragons, etc. Do not pinch chrysanthemums after the fifteenth.

Stand the hardiest of the greenhouse plants out of doors now. Give them regular attention, as though they were still in the houses. Water with hose-pipe or watering can. Spray azaleas overhead often and keep in an airy, shaded location.

Pot primulas and annuals for winter flowering. Sow for early spring flowers annual lupines. *Lupinus mutabilis* is one of the best for this purpose. For Christmas sweet peas sow a few in pots. Give plenty of sunshine, keep fairly cool and ventilate thoroughly.

Cyclamen for show or marketing do best sown this month. Do not hurry to prick out the seedlings or to pot.

Pot lilies as soon as they are received. *Lilium longiflorum eximium* should be potted with Easter flower requirements in mind. Water during the winter months with lukewarm water and feed heavily. Do not crowd the plants. Start *Lilium speciosum* and *L. tigrinum* from cold storage. Keep a succession of these planted until about the end of September, for successive bloom periods.

Move gloxinias, caladiums and achimenes which have finished their growth to a cool house. Tie climbers to their supports, but take care not to fasten too tightly. *Pentas* may be put away for a rest period until the early part of the winter.

SUB-TROPICAL. Plant early varieties of beets and beans, broccoli, Brussels sprouts, cabbage, cauliflower, carrots, celery, collards, cucumbers, endive, kale, kohlrabi, leek, lettuce, mustard, onions, parsley, peppers, fall potatoes, radishes, spinach, squash, turnips and rutabagas.

Sow in the open calendulas, early cosmos, winter-flowering sweet peas, French marigolds, nasturtiums, phlox and salpiglossis.

Sow in frames carnations, canterbury bells, columbines, delphiniums, foxglove, forget-me-not, hollyhocks, pansies, perennial poppies, snapdragons, stocks, verbena and violas. Set out bulbs such as callas, freesias, German iris, ornithogalums and oxalis.

Buy alpinias and plant this autumn for spring and summer bloom. They make excellent foundation plantings. The amomums and sanchezias do best in the lath house.

## PLANTS IN BLOOM — AUGUST

HERBACEOUS PLANTS: 854. *Eupatorium perfoliatum;* 855. *Amaryllis belladonna;* 856. *Gladiolus* (main late varieties); 857. *Ammobium alatum grandiflorum;* 858. *Echinocystis lobata;* 859. *Anemone japonica;* 860. *Artemisia vulgaris lactiflora;* 861. *Artemisia stelleriana;* 862. *Ipomoea pandurata;* 863. Michaelmas daisies; 864. *Ipomoea purpurea;* 865. *Boussingaultia baselloides;* 866. *Clematis virginiana;* 867. *Celosia argentea;* 868. *Dianthus deltoides;* 869. *Cobaea scandens;* 870. *Gentiana pneumonanthe;* 871. *Saponaria officinalis;* 872. Dahlias (Jane Cowl, Jersey's Beauty, Satan, Kathleen Norris, etc.); 873. Dahlias (dwarf singles); 874. Dahlias (pompons); 875. Dahlias (miniatures); 876. *Sanguisorba canadensis;* 877. *Eupatorium hyssopifolium;* 878. *Eupatorium urticaefolium;* 879. *Gentiana asclepiadea;* 880. Golden Glow; 881. *Sanguisorba minor;* 882. *Helianthus angustifolius;* 883. *Helianthus mollis;* 884. *Helenium autumnale;* 885. *Helipterum roseum;* 886. *Hemerocallis;* 887. *Hymenocallis calathina;* 888. *Chrysopsis mariana;* 889. *Polygala lutea;* 890. *Impatiens balsamina;* 891. *Ipomoea* (Heavenly Blue); 892. *Physalis peruviana;* 893. *Kniphofia uvaria pfitzeri;* 894. *Lilium philippinense;* 895. *Lilium speciosum;* 896. *Lilium superbum;* 897. *Lycoris squamigera;* 898. *Moneses uniflora;* 899. *Solidago sempervirens;* 900. *Rudbeckia triloba;* 901. *Salvia azurea;* 902. *Salvia pitcheri;* 903. *Sedum spectabile;* 904. *Tagetes erecta;* 905. *Tagetes tenuifolia pumila;* 906. *Tritonia* (hybrids); 907. Nasturtium (Golden Gleam); 908. *Abutilon* (as bedding plant).

SHRUBS AND TREES: 909. *Vitex negundo;* 910. *Clethra acuminata;* 911. *Callicarpa dichotoma;* 912. *Calluna vulgaris;* 913. *Clematis davidiana;* 914. *Clematis paniculata;* 915. *Clerodendron trichotomum;* 916. *Tamarix pentandra;* 917. *Aralia spinosa;* 918. *Hydrangea paniculata grandiflora;* 919. *Pueraria thunbergiana;* 920. *Aralia chinensis.*

Also numbers 74, 115, 130, 139, and 148 (see APRIL); numbers 186, 190, 196, 207, 214, 216, 236, 239, 250, 258, 262, 283, 284, and 289 (see MAY); numbers 347, 350, 355, 357, 359, 367, 368, 371, 372, 374, 377, 381, 383, 385, 386, 387, 393, 394, 396, 398, 402, 403, 413, 426, 433, 435, 437, 443, 444, 445, 446, 447, 450, 454, 460, 468, 474, 476, 481, 498, 500, 502, 503, 519, 523, 525, 526, 528, 530, 531, 534, 538, 540, 543, 551, 553, 560, 564, 577, 578, 580, 584, 597, 603, 608, 612, 614, 615, 617, 629, 634, 643, 652, 657, 659, 661, 662, 668, 670, 673, 674, and 684 (see JUNE); and numbers 688, 689, 690, 691, 692, 693, 696, 697, 699, 700, 702, 703, 704, 706, 707, 708, 709, 713, 715, 717, 719, 720, 725, 727, 729, 730, 731, 732, 733, 737, 738, 740, 741, 743, 745, 748, 749, 750, 752, 753, 754, 755, 756, 757, 758, 760, 761, 763, 764, 765, 767, 768, 769, 772, 773, 775, 777, 778, 779, 780, 781, 782, 783, 784, 786, 790, 791, 792, 795, 799, 800, 801, 807, 810, 811, 814, 816, 821, 822, 823, 825, 826, 827, 828, 829, 830, 831, 832, 833, 834, 837, 838, 841, 842, 843, 844, 845, 846, 847, 848, 849, 850, 852, and 853 (see JULY).

---

\* Special articles on the subjects indicated by as asterisk (\*) will be found at the words so marked.

Concerning Plants in General. Plant peonies. Select only strong divisions. Firm down and water thoroughly. Old clumps may be divided and moved. Make late plantings of, lift, divide or transplant Siberian and Japanese irises.

Order and plant all sorts of bulbs, such as chionodoxas, narcissi, crocus, etc. Order choice bulbs early, for next month's planting. Remove ripe bulblets from lilies and plant in a cold frame.

Divide lilies-of-the-valley. Divide and reset perennials that require attention, but not the autumn-flowering sorts. Plant or transplant daylilies.

Plant oxalis bulbs in hanging baskets for winter flowering. Plant bulbous irises. Set out *Eremurus* roots. Rock garden plants may be set out in old, established gardens. Allow new soil to fallow over winter. *See* Fallow Land.

Trim vines of *Akebia*. Prune drastically if too heavy. Late this month prune lilac roots, if they are not blooming well. Cut off dead wood and top-dress.

Around the Grounds. Make all necessary rose beds in time to allow the ground to settle. Remove from tender shrubs, vines or rose bushes any wires attached to labels; tie the canes and branches with soft strings instead.

Remove tender aquatics from the pool and put tropical fish in the aquarium. Plant bog plants, etc.

Take indoors before frost any tender tubbed plants. Lemon verbena should be potted and used as a house plant in the North. Cut trailing nasturtiums three to four feet long to blossom indoors in water. Protect newly potted or young ferns from full sunlight.

At the end of the month transplant trees and shrubs. Rake and burn any leaves or herbage which might be pest-infected.

Cut grass on lawns and repair or remake if necessary. New lawns should have soil left for some weeks, weeds hoed under, then grass seed sown this month. Dig in bonemeal and humus.

Stake heavily growing plants such as dahlias; give plenty of freedom to bushy ones such as hollyhocks. Stake chrysanthemums; water and fertilize well.

Herbaceous plants may be purchased and planted in the reserve garden for transplanting next year.

Insects and Sprays. Inspect dahlia stems for the borer. Fork about in the soil a good soil fumigant. Watch tulip bulbs, etc., for green flies. Store the bulbs in a cool, airy place. Spray to destroy poison ivy, if it cannot be dug now. Spray spruce gall aphids, and the underside and tips of all spruce branches, especially the new growth.

Fruits. Plant cover crops under trees. Pick all ripe fruit without bruising. Clean and remove dropped leaves, twigs, fruit, etc., from beneath the trees.

Cold Frames. Sow seeds of *Lilium philippinense*. Transplant later into the greenhouse. Plant St. Brigid anemones for very early bloom next spring. Store fuchsias and withhold water; bring into heat and light in a couple of months.

Greenhouse. Propagate geraniums for use as house plants from cuttings. Pot small plants of zinnias, pansies, and begonias and bring to blooming point before moving to house.

Feed roses for October flowering with weak liquid cow manure. Guard against any sudden drop in temperatures. Watch for black spot and red spider. Give chrysanthemums plenty of light and air.

This is also the time to see that all greenhouse equipment is in perfect order for winter use. Note carefully the condition of the boiler and the piping and see that all valves and shut-offs are in shape for use.

Potting mixtures* should be prepared and put in the bins. All benches that are to have soil in them should be thoroughly cleaned of old soil, hosed down, and allowed to dry out before fresh soil is put into them. Sterilize soil for plants needing it (*see* Soil Sterilization). See that all ventilators are in order and oil all connections. Examine for loose lights of glass and putty-up those needing it.

Forcing Bulbs and Autumn-flowering Plants. Pot irises. Water thoroughly and place under bench in carnation house. Do not give narcissi bottom-heat. Tie and disbud bush chrysanthemums. Spray regularly against mealybugs.

Raise gloxinias from seed for second blooming period. Fall-blooming plants are *Achimenes* and *Naegelia*, and all of which may be raised from spring-sown seeds. Feed all well just before the flowering period.

Sub-tropical. Sow in open ground seeds of beets, bush beans, broccoli, cabbage, carrots, cauliflower, collards, endive, kale, kohlrabi, leek, lettuce, mustard, okra, onion seed and sets, parsnips, peas, potatoes, radishes, spinach, squash, Swiss chard and turnips.

Before the fig season is over next month go over the orchard and decide which trees to eliminate; destroy all fruit trees not in good condition. Set out strawberry plants from runners of June and July stock. Train loganberry runners on wire trellises.

Flower seeds may be sown outdoors of *Mentzelia*, *Centaurea*, *Dimorphotheca*, *Gypsophila*, *Linum*, *Nemesia*, all poppies and wildflower mixtures. Unlike eastern sorts California wild flowers do not require so much moisture.

Sow in flats seeds of columbines, carnations, coreopsis, cineraria, foxglove, hollyhocks, phlox, and wallflowers. Plant for spring blossoms bulbs or rootstocks of *Allium*, anemones, calla-lily, Dutch and tall-bearded iris, freesias, lilies, ornithogalums, oxalis and watsonias.

Old rose bushes may be pruned to increase size and number of winter-blooming roses. All pot-grown plants may be bought and set out.

## PLANTS IN BLOOM — SEPTEMBER

Herbaceous Plants: 921. *Aconitum fischeri*; 922. *Gaura coccinea*; 923. *Gladiolus* (late varieties); 924. *Aster divaricatus*; 925. *Aster cordifolius*; 926. *Aster amellus*; 927. *Vernonia altissima*; 928. *Aster noviae-angliae*; 929. *Aster novi-belgi*; 930. *Gentiana linearis*; 931. *Aster tataricus*; 932. *Liatris spicata*; 933. *Anemone hupehensis*; 934. Dwarf garden asters (*Callistephus*); 935. *Aster ericoides*; 936. *Begonia evansiana*; 937. *Gentiana crinita*; 938. *Vernonia noveboracensis*; 939. *Gentiana andrewsi*; 940. *Chrysanthemum* (Korean hybrids); 941. *Chrysanthemum morifolium*; 942. Chrysanthemums (*see* main article for hort. varieties); 943. *Chrysanthemum nipponicum*; 944. *Cimicifuga simplex*; 945. *Colchicum autumnale*; 946. *Colchicum bornmuelleri*; 947. *Gentiana septemfida*; 948. *Crocus sativus*; 949. *Gaura lindheimeri*; 950. *Scutellaria alpina*; 951. *Gentiana cruciata*; 952. *Rudbeckia fulgida*; 953. *Helianthus giganteus*; 954. *Helianthus maximiliani*; 955. *Helianthus orgyalis*; 956. *Helianthus tuberosus*; 957. *Colchicum speciosum*; 958. *Helichrysum bracteatum*; 959. *Heliotropium arborescens*; 960. *Chrysanthemum* (Daphne); 961. *Iris unguicularis*; 962. *Cunila mariana*; 963. *Kniphofia foliosa*; 964. *Pycnanthemum incanum*; 965. *Kniphofia rufa*; 966. *Lespedeza striata*; 967. *Leucojum autumnale*; 968. *Lythrum alatum*; 969. *Lespedeza bicolor*; 970. *Nemesia strumosa*; 971. *Polygonum cuspidatum*.

Shrubs and Trees: 972. *Baccharis halimifolia*; 973. *Polygonum auberti* (herbaceous vine); 974. *Hamamelis virginiana* (earliest bloom); 975. *Abelia chinensis*; 976. *Erica vagans*; 977. *Caryopteris incana*; 978. *Clematis apiifolia*; 979. *Clematis missouriensis*; 980. *Elsholtzia stauntoni*.

Also numbers 74, 130, 139, and 148 (*see* April); numbers 196, 214, 216, 236, 239, 250, 258, 262, 283, 284, and 289 (*see* May); numbers 350, 355, 357, 367, 371, 374, 381, 393, 394, 396, 402, 413, 437, 443, 445, 454, 460, 476, 481, 503, 523, 525, 528, 530, 534, 538, 551, 553, 560, 564, 580, 597, 608, 615, 617, 634, 657, 661, 662, 673, and 684 (*see* June); numbers 696, 700, 702, 708, 709, 719, 730, 732, 741, 743, 745, 748, 749, 750, 755, 763, 764, 768, 775, 781, 786, 792, 807, 810, 811, 814, 816, 821, 828, 829, 830, 832, 833, 834, 837, 838, 847, and 848 (*see* July); and numbers 855, 857, 859, 860, 865, 866, 867, 870, 872, 878, 879, 880, 882, 883, 884, 885, 887, 890, 891, 893, 894, 895, 900, 901, 902, 903, 904, 905, 906, 907, 908, 912, 913, 914, 916, and 918 (*see* August).

* Special articles on the subjects indicated by an asterisk (*) will be found at the words so marked.

GENERAL OUTDOOR WORK. Many vines, such as wisterias, are best planted at this time in localities near the Pacific Coast and south of New York City. Plant crocus and snowdrops in bare places underneath trees.

Sow hardy annuals such as cosmos, calendulas, cornflowers, snapdragons, petunias, marigolds, larkspurs, Shirley poppies, etc. Cover the seed beds with a light mulch before heavy frost, to prevent frost heaving. Label all plantings, such as late bulb flowering and perennials. Write labels in indelible inks.

Mow and edge lawns, grass walks, etc., as long as the grass continues to grow. Destroy all possible weeds to prevent germination of seeds.

Prepare beds for new garden roses. Order plants for November delivery. Clear away leaves and dead stems from under old bushes.

Move evergreens, or plant replacements, during warm weather. Water heavily if ground is dry. Water shrubs thoroughly until freezing weather. *See* HARDINESS. Cut peony plants back to the ground. Destroy the tops.

Cut off dahlia tops, dig, dry the roots and store them, not later than the end of this month. Cut back gladiolus and burn the tops. Dry corms well in the sunshine; then store. Dig tuberous begonias and dry thoroughly. After the tops fall off clean the tubers; pack in sand. Take up root clumps of cannas with plenty of sand around them and pack close together in a box. In all sections where *Tritoma* is not hardy dig and store the roots.

Pot sturdy clumps of hardy annuals, such as zinnias, for winter-flowering house plants. Tender chrysanthemums may be lifted in clumps, potted and transferred to the greenhouse.

Plant amaryllis, tulips, hyacinths, etc., and store in a cold frame or cool, dark place until time for forcing.

VEGETABLES. Cover all plants possible when hard frosts threaten. Leave beets, carrots, salsify, and turnips in the ground until just before severe freezing. Allow parsnips to be stored to freeze slightly before digging, to improve flavor. Pull tomato plants and remove to warm place so that green tomatoes may ripen gradually indoors. Bleach celery by banking; dig and store in prepared trenches. Before frost harvest pumpkins. Store in a warm place.

FRUIT TREES. Attach wire guards, or something similar, around the base of fruit trees to protect from mice. Pick fruit at varying intervals, as it ripens.

THE NUT HARVEST. Early this month cover crops may be sown. Prune all weak or superfluous wood. Nuts may be shaken down by the use of poles with hooks. Wash and dry thoroughly before packing.

If your filbert crop has not already been gathered, do so at once. Dry the nuts thoroughly before storing in an unheated room. In pruning, thin moderately and head back if necessary, to stimulate a moderate amount of new growth. Set out any new trees on north slopes that are protected from prevailing winds. *See* HAZEL.

GREENHOUSE. Chrysanthemums are the most important flowers grown this month. Show flowers now in bud need a drier atmosphere. Guard against overcrowding. Mildew must be watched for. Feed heavily until the flowers show color.

Give dracaenas and other warmhouse plants some shade during the hottest part of the day. After the fifteenth begin to harden up and mature them for their rest period.

Gloire de Lorraine types of begonia, as well as hybrid sorts, should be given plenty of ventilation. Cease syringing overhead. Dampen freely between the plants and on all bare spots. Stake with wire or bamboo stakes.

Thin out established climbers. Water carefully, giving just enough to keep the wood filled out. There is still time to propagate fuchsias. Ventilate freely.

Early spring-flowering bulbs must all be in pots or flats by the fifteenth. Watch temperatures and avoid drafts. Bulbs for Christmas flowering must be given plenty of light. Plants such as the Amazon lily will benefit from a feeding of weak liquid cow manure. Water if the leaves show the least sign of wilting. Place nerines in the cool house. Water thoroughly at the roots and overhead. Feed regularly with liquid cow manure. *Nerine curvifolia fothergilli* makes the best greenhouse plant for forcing.

Ease off watering gradually any bulbs or plants which are ready for a rest period.

SUB-TROPICAL. Sow in the garden beets, broccoli, Brussels sprouts, cabbage, cress, kale, lettuce, parsley, garden peas, radishes, spinach, and turnips. Any plants desired for early vegetables should be started in frames.

Sow in open beds *Helipterum*, *Mentzelia*, calendula, clarkia, godetia, larkspur, *Linum*, lupine, mignonette, Nemophila, *Schizanthus*, winter-flowering sweet peas.

Sow in seed flats flowers listed last month and canterbury bells, double daisies, delphiniums, forget-me-nots, pentstemon, petunias, snapdragons, stocks and Sweet Williams.

Plant bulbs of those mentioned last month and in addition amaryllis, crocus, hyacinths, ixias, native California bulbs (for California and like climates), *Sparaxis*, tulips, and Easter lilies. Work fertilizer in between sprouted bulbs.

Order for winter planting deciduous trees and shrubs. Re-pot where necessary tub plants in house or patio. Late this month pot up perennial seedlings and set out from flats calendulas, stocks and violas. Start a perennial border with plants which do not drop their leaves in winter.

## PLANTS IN BLOOM — OCTOBER

HERBACEOUS PLANTS: 986. *Allium stellatum;* 987. *Aster acris;* 988. *Crocus speciosus;* 989. *Solidago altissima;* 990. *Sternbergia lutea;* 991. *Tithonia rotundifolia;* 992. *Tricyrtis hirta;* 993. *Venidium fastuosum.*

SHRUBS AND TREES: 981. *Hamamelis virginiana;* 982. *Clematis veitchiana;* 983. *Lespedeza formosa;* 984. *Prunus subhirtella autumnalis;* 985. *Arbutus unedo;* 994. *Lycium halimifolium* (second flowering).

Also number 130 (*see* APRIL); numbers 196, 236, 258, 262, and 289 (*see* MAY); numbers 350, 357, 371, 374, 381, 396, 443, 460, 503, 551, 553, 580, 657, and 661 (*see* JUNE); numbers 700, 702, 719, 743, 745, 748, 750, 792, 810, 816, 832, 834, 837, and 838 (*see* JULY); numbers 866, 867, 872, 882, 893, and 914 (*see* AUGUST); and numbers 921, 922, 927, 928, 930, 931, 932, 933, 936, 940, 942, 943, 944, 945, 946, 948, 951, 953, 954, 955, 958, 960, 961, 963, 965, 966, 968, 970, 973, 977, 978, and 980 (*see* SEPTEMBER).

THE GARDEN CLEAN-UP. Collect leaves in piles ready to add to the compost heap. Cover undecayed leaves for mulching so they will not freeze. Rake and burn all diseased foliage.

Remove some of the water from the pool to allow for expansion. Leave it deep enough to care for hardy goldfish.

Plant the garden roses you ordered last month. Plant English hawthorn, oaks, California privet, etc. Continue to plant tulips and lilies, or any bulbs not planted last month. Prepare beds for the foreign sorts not yet available and mulch to prevent the ground being frozen when they arrive. Plant deciduous trees and shrubs where necessary.

Mulch around the crowns of perennials with large rosettes, such as hollyhocks, foxgloves, etc. Do not cover the tops. Mulch the lily-of-the-valley bed with a light covering of

---

\* Special articles on the subjects indicated by an asterisk (\*) will be found at the words so marked.

leaf mold or well-rotted manure. Just before freezing mulch all newly planted shrubs and trees with clean leaves, straw or salt hay. Mulch newly planted roses. Cover old-established rose beds. Tender roses such as Emily Gray do best when the canes are laid on the ground and protected with mulch. Be careful not to mulch too early.

POTTED BULBS AND PLANTS. Force cowslips in a cool window, where they receive a fair amount of sun. Pot up chrysanthemums for indoor flowering.

Pot up bulbs for winter bloom. Plunge the pots in a cold frame or store in a cool, dark, frost-free cellar. Keep moist until roots appear; then bring to the light. Paper-white narcissus started by the fifteenth will bloom at Christmas. Choose only heavy bulbs.

Re-pot foliage plants, Boston ferns, and any others in which the roots show through the hole in the bottom of the pot.

VEGETABLE GARDEN. Clean up the vegetable plot as carefully as you do the garden. Plow up and leave the vegetable garden rough-surfaced over the winter. If the soil is sour, sprinkle lightly with lime. Otherwise cover with a thin layer of manure, which will be spaded under in the spring. Never use both lime and manure. Plow under the corn stubble if any trouble has been had with the corn borer.

A cover of well-rotted manure should be spread around rhubarb.

Among the vegetables which may be stored for winter use are celery, carrots, cabbage, beets, onions, leeks, parsnips, potatoes, winter radishes, pumpkins, salsify, winter squash and turnips. Others, such as eggplant, cauliflower, peppers and tomatoes may be kept for a long time. Hard freezing injures nearly all vegetables, inasmuch as their saving qualities are concerned; take in before freezing.

If you have not previously done so, make provisions to grow as many vegetables as possible in the cellar. See CELLAR GARDENING.

FRUIT AND BERRIES. The strawberry bed must not be mulched until after a hard freeze. Use no mulch that contains weed seeds. Prop up any weak limbs on the fruit trees which might be damaged by heavy wind or ice storms. Clean up under the trees. Before freezing weather spray for scale. Prune out and burn any black spots on cherry or plum trees. Never leave rotted plums on the ground; they might spread brown rot.

GREENHOUSE. Dispense with all shading; water and damp down with care; ventilation and temperatures must be closely watched.

Christmas plants, such as poinsettias, require forcing, with all available light and considerable heat. Do not overwater or feed. *Coleus*, after flowering, must be cut back and rested. Take cuttings for next year's plants in the spring, when new growth starts.

Begonias do best propagated at this time from leaf cuttings, particularly the low growers. Give them a warm, moist house.

Pick off all leaves which show any signs of decay or leaf-spot on the blooming chrysanthemums. Keep the atmosphere fairly dry. On extra cold or damp nights have the house slightly heated to cause a circulation of drier air.

Nasturtiums, mignonette, calendula, nemophila and early-flowering sweet peas may be planted in flats to insure early spring flowers.

SUB-TROPICAL. Sow vegetable seeds mentioned last month and also endive, kohlrabi, leek, mustard, onions, onion sets, parsnips, salsify and Swiss chard.

Flower seeds sown in the open this month are slower in germinating, but many hardy annuals such as *Browallia*, *Clarkia*, godetia, phlox, poppies, larkspur, *Linaria*, *Nemophila*, *Nigella*, Virginia stocks and the like do well. Many of these may be planted among early-blooming bulbs which will have finished blooming before the annuals are ready to flower.

For winter flowers set out between well-sprouted bulbs small plants from seed flats or nurseries of candytuft, verbena, dwarf ageratum, forget-me-nots and primulas. Snapdragons set out now will bloom in late March or April.

Replace zinnias and asters in the combination annual and perennial border with stocks and wallflowers. Sow in flats seeds of all flowers listed in October. Set out bulbs mentioned last month.

## PLANTS IN BLOOM — NOVEMBER

HERBACEOUS PLANTS: 995. *Chrysanthemum articum;* 996. *Crocus pulchellus;* 997. *Crocus nudiflorus.*

SHRUBS AND TREES: 998. *Jasminum gracillimum.*

Also numbers 371, 381, and 443 (see JUNE); number 702 (see JULY); numbers 940, 945, 961 and 976 (see SEPTEMBER); and number 984 (see OCTOBER).

INDOOR WORK. Store garden seats and other furniture. All statuary must be taken in unless covered with waterproof shelter. Bird baths, etc., of artificial stone, are liable to frost-crack; take in and store. Oil all tools to prevent rust before putting them away.

Get out all old catalogues and study them carefully. Get the new books on horticulture. Then lay out your garden on paper, figure any proposed changes and new effects for next year.

Look over all stored bulbs and cut out any diseased spots.

HOUSE PLANTS. Attach a humidifier to the radiator; this will benefit house plants as well as humans.

Newspapers placed against the window will protect plants from cold drafts at night. Spray insecticides on house plants with an atomizer. While flowering, feed liquid fertilizer to house plants every two or three weeks.

Poinsettias must be watered daily; hold any cut sprays over a flame or in hot water until the ends of the stems are sealed.

Keep azaleas cool, but water freely. Set the entire pot in a basin of water to saturate all the soil.

Cyclamen, as well as primroses, do best in cool temperatures, but must be given three or four hours of sunlight a day.

Stand potted heaths or ericas in water. Give orange trees some sunlight and feed moderately. Flowering begonias (large varieties) need some sun and much water, but chilling is fatal.

Coal or illuminating gas will cause plants like Christmas peppers and Jerusalem cherries to drop their leaves.

FORCING BULBS. When well rooted, bring in early single tulips, freesias, Roman hyacinths, scillas, crocuses, oxalis and daffodils for forcing. Avoid strong light or excess heat for the first few days. Lily-of-the-valley pips must be kept in a dark, moist place until well started. Then bring to the light.

Tie up tall, slender or weak bulbous plants, like freesias, with thin stakes and soft strings. All forced bulbs must be watered abundantly.

OUTDOOR WORK. Look over the garden carefully and decide what improvements or additions you should make. Cut down any undesirable trees, shrubs, etc. Protect with mulch any tender plants. Mulch rose beds as soon as the ground freezes.

After heavy wind or ice storms inspect the grounds; see that all mulches are in place; take care of any broken limbs or tops; sprinkle sand over plant beds to help melt the ice.

Make regular feeding stations for the birds. Hang their food, such as suet, etc., out of the reach of stray cats.

Plant the bulbs of *Lilium auratum* and *L. speciosum* as soon as they are available. Keep ground used for these lilies from freezing by use of heavy mulch.

---

\* Special articles on the subjects indicated by an asterisk (\*) will be found at the words so marked.

In moderate weather dig any poison ivy and burn the plants when dry, but keep away from the smoke.

GREENHOUSE. Guard against too high temperatures in the warmhouse. Give less water during the rest period of the plants. Damp walks, etc., down frequently where hot-water pipes cause quick evaporation. Rose house must have fairly dry atmosphere; spray on bright mornings. Give carnations plenty of light and air. Pick off any leaves affected with rust; spray with bordeaux.

Bring in shrubs, such as lilacs, etc., for late winter flowers. Do not push your temperature above 55 degrees, so the leaves will develop freely.

Narcissus, tulips, hyacinths, ornithogalums in variety, etc., should be forced. Also sow calendulas, schizanthus and other annuals. Give ventilation to all crops scheduled for February and March flowering. Fumigate to eliminate pests; avoid overcrowding of plants.

SUB-TROPICAL. Sow seeds of beets, Brussels sprouts, cabbage, carrots, cauliflower, celery, collards, cress, endive, leek, lettuce, parsnips, potatoes, garden peas, radishes, winter spinach, Swiss chard, turnips and rutabagas.

Sow in the open *Helipterum, Alyssum*, calendulas, candytuft, annual chrysanthemums, dianthus, lupines, standard sweet peas, *Schizanthus* and lawn grasses.

Complete rose pruning, cultivate, water and surface-fertilize. Set out new bushes. Plant late-flowering lilies such as *Lilium auratum* and *L. speciosum*. Gladioli, calla-lily, amaryllis, hyacinths, narcissus, ranunculus and tulips may be planted for late spring flowering. Prepare and set out evergreen ferns. Do not bury the crowns deeply if at all. Sow in flats columbine, larkspur, pansies, phlox and snapdragons.

**PLANTS IN BLOOM — DECEMBER**

HERBACEOUS PLANTS: 999. *Galanthus elwesi*; 1000. *Helleborus niger*.

Also number 996 (see NOVEMBER). See also the plants in bloom in January, some of which may flower before Christmas in favorable sites. — C. H. M.

**GARDEN CHEMICALS.** Many chemical substances enter into modern garden practice or into the life history of the plant itself. There is no need to list them here for all are noted where they belong. See FERTILIZERS, INSECTICIDES, FUNGICIDES, Weed Killers (at WEEDS AND WEEDING), and PLANT FOODS.

**GARDEN CLUB OF AMERICA.** See GARDEN CLUBS.

**GARDEN CLUBS.** Second only to the Experiment Stations, the garden clubs are the greatest single agency for the advancement of gardening in America. Their lectures, test gardens, and influence for better standards of the art of horticulture are of incalculable value. Some of their lecture courses are as complete as a first-class school of horticulture. Overwhelmingly they are managed by women who thus exert an immense influence for civic betterment, school gardens, flower shows, conservation, and for the general raising of the standards of garden art.

Unfortunately, there is no one national organization or amalgamation of the garden clubs of the country. United they could do more, especially with legislation, than is possible under present conditions.

All the clubs mentioned below are women's activities, but there are a few clubs for men only, notably in N.J. and Ill. The leading women's garden club amalgamations, in the order of their establishment, are:

GARDEN CLUB OF AMERICA. A national association of garden clubs, formed in 1913 and scattered over most of the country. It wields potent influence for good, issues a journal eight times a year, devoted to gardening, and has affiliated clubs in most of the states of the Union. Its national headquarters and permanent office are at 598 Madison Avenue, New York.

FEDERATED GARDEN CLUBS. A national association or amalgamation which includes nearly all the local garden clubs not affiliated with the Garden Club of America. There are 1927 clubs scattered practically throughout the country, and the total membership is well over 100,000.

Some, but not all, of these clubs are affiliated with The National Council. It is obviously impossible to list here all the clubs in this large federation of widely scattered clubs. See the name of your state for the garden club possibilities in your region. Or, for the name of your nearest local club, which usually has no permanent home and changes officers yearly, write to the Garden Editor, Houghton Mifflin Company, Boston, Mass.

INTERNATIONAL GARDEN CLUB. A small but powerful organization of generally wealthy men and women, who maintain beautiful gardens and a hort. library and clubhouse in the borough of the Bronx, New York City. Unlike both the above organizations, they have maintained for years a fine garden designed by a noted landscape architect and kept with skill and taste. The club's membership is largely made up of New York women and its address is International Garden Club, Pelham Bay Park, New York City.

There are, in a few states, garden clubs affiliated with none of those mentioned above. But every passing year sees a drift from sectional isolation towards amalgamation with one of the associations of national scope. This is a natural development, for there are times, especially in state or national legislatures, where a united stand has to be made for the good of the cause. This is especially true on large-scale plans for parks, parkways, or the conservation of wild flowers.

**GARDEN COLOR.** See COLOR.

**GARDEN CRESS** = *Lepidium sativum*. See also WATERCRESS.

**GARDEN CURRANT** = *Ribes sativum*.

**GARDEN DESIGN.** See LANDSCAPE ARCHITECTURE.

**GARDEN DIARY.** Keeping a garden diary is an intelligent pastime for any gardener. The trouble with such an undertaking is that when most is happening, there is the least time to write about it. The rush of spring planting and summer harvest often make daily entries difficult. And the long winter evenings give us plenty of time, but little to write about. However, there is no better way to keep a record of failures and successes of varieties, times of blooming, etc., than in a garden diary which comes ready printed for use. Another fine feature of its use is to jot down far before the fateful day arrives things which must be done on or about a certain date. In this connection see GARDEN CALENDAR.

**GARDEN EDGINGS.** See EDGING.

**GARDEN ENEMIES.** The only serious ones are all the subject of special articles. See INSECT PESTS, PLANT DISEASES, ANIMAL INJURY, and Bird Nuisances at BIRDS.

**GARDENER'S-GARTERS** = *Phalaris arundinacea picta*.

**GARDEN ESCAPE.** See ESCAPE.

**GARDEN EXPERIMENTS.** No inquisitive gardener can help making some yearly experiments, for knowledge of the art of gardening has come chiefly by this route. Depending upon your bent, they may take various forms.

If they have to do with the suitability of plants for certain soils, it will help to read the general article on soils and all the cross-references there suggested.

If, however, it is climate and hardiness which chiefly interest you, see the articles under HARDINESS, ZONE, and the cross-references there suggested. See also PROTECTING PLANTS.

For the most aggravated form of the urge to experiment there is no remedy, unless it be to look up all possible references to the plant in hand. For this kind of garden experiment involves the age-old quest for new or desirable substitutes for old favorites. For such seekers only patience and study can bring a reward. Sometimes it will pay to find out what family the plant belongs to and turn to the description of that family. All are described in THE GARDEN DICTIONARY, and all related genera will be found at one place under each family.

---

\* Special articles on the subjects indicated by an asterisk (\*) will be found at the words so marked.

**GARDEN FENCES.** See FENCES.

**GARDEN FLY-HONEYSUCKLE** = *Lonicera tatarica*.

**GARDEN FRAME.** See COLD FRAME.

**GARDEN FURNITURE.** See ORNAMENT AND FURNITURE.

**GARDEN GADGETS.** See Section 7, TOOLS AND IMPLEMENTS.

**GARDEN GATES.** See GATES AND GATEWAYS.

**GARDEN GERANIUM.** See PELARGONIUM.

**GARDEN GLOVES.** See Section 2, TOOLS AND IMPLEMENTS.

**GARDEN GOOSEBERRY** = *Ribes grossularia*. For culture see GOOSEBERRY.

**GARDEN HEDGES.** See HEDGES.

**GARDEN HELIOTROPE** = *Valeriana officinalis*.

**GARDEN HISTORY.** Gardens first appeared when primitive man, no longer depending on the chase or migratory stock-raising for his sustenance, settled down in one chosen spot. Here, alongside his hut, his womenfolk scarred the ground with a crotched stick or a hoe made by lashing a shell or animal shoulder-blade to a length of branch. To this patch they brought wild edible grains and roots collected from the meadows, and soon found that better crops resulted from intensive cultivation. A fence of woven branches or thorns or a cactus hedge kept out straying cattle. As water was necessary, the garden was usually located either by a brook or around a water hole. From this source, runnels carried water to the plants.

In these primitive attempts we see the beginnings of the fenced or hedged garden, irrigation and horticulture. These first gardens were made for no aesthetic reasons, however. They were gardens of necessity. Not until man "built finely," as Bacon put it, did he begin to garden for the delight of his eye. His crops were food crops and such herbs as were necessary for family doctoring.

Climate, the nature of the soil, and religious beliefs were further factors in the evolution of the garden from those primitive conditions to the various garden forms we know today. Thus in Persia and India, where intense heat required much water to cool the air and fill bathing tanks, water was much in evidence. This style, carried to Spain, was developed in Saracenic gardens, which were the progenitors of Spanish gardens as we know them today in Florida and California.

Religious taboos and predilections also gave rise to garden forms and garden adjuncts. From the totem and Tree of Life set up in gardens by primitive man for purposes of worship, we can trace the lineage of garden statuary and fountains. The effect of Buddhism, as it spread over through the East by way of the Straits Settlement and China to Japan, brought about a taste for gardens that copied the features of Nature, and from these, in turn, we have inherited the informal style of garden design.

The nature of the soil, together with climate, decided what plants grew in gardens. For a long time the plants used in decorative gardens were such as grew naturally in the locality together with some few brought in by conquests or commerce. Commerce was responsible for the distribution of plants almost up to the threshold of our own times, when plant explorers and traveling botanists made a special business of plant importation.

EGYPTIAN GARDENS were produced by a peculiar local condition. The Nile, the main source of water, was dammed, and the flood gates opened at certain required seasons. Consequently, Egyptians made their gardens for ease of irrigation, *i.e.* formal in patterns and divided by irrigation ditches. The grapevine was an early favorite plant of Egyptians, and its proper cultivation required the vines being raised on wooden supports. From these supports grew the pergola that the Romans later developed into a decorative feature and which is a commonplace adjunct of gardens today.

Both Egyptian and Sumerian temples were situated on either natural or artificial hills called Ziggurats, and the surrounding area given over to the cultivation of trees and herbs especially adapted. As most of these early temples were also the meeting place of the priest-physicians, they served as the ancestors of those later monastic enclosures in which the herb garden, for the cure of the ailing, was a necessary feature. From the Ziggurats can be traced the garden mount which appeared in Roman gardens and many centuries later was made a feature in gardens of mediaeval Europe and Tudor England. Used first as a lookout or a spot from which to enjoy a panorama of the garden and the surrounding country, it was later topped by a pavilion for entertainment. See Gazebo at STRUCTURES.

Throughout the Near East the plane and the palm were the trees most grown. The latter was especially valued since so many necessary products were derived from it. Though the Persians allowed their trees to grow naturally, the Egyptians clipped them into columnar forms, thus affording the first instance of topiary work.

GREEK GARDENS, in the beginning, were not extensive, nor can the early Greeks be said to have advanced garden practices. The usual home garden was in the rear of the house, enclosed by two projecting wings. On these three sides was built a covered terrace or peristyle. Sometimes the peristyle ran around all four sides. When it was not built on the fourth, the ground was banked up and lined with trees. In this enclosure was laid out a formal garden. In the center was a water basin, into which roof water drained and which served as a source for watering the garden. Around it were beds of fragrant flowers, since it was believed that fragrant plants had prophylactic properties, keeping the air pure and warding off disease. Between the columns of the peristyle were set deep flower boxes and on the walls behind were trained vines. However, if vines would not grow in this shade the walls were painted with garden scenes. This use of garden perspectives cropped up again in seventeenth-century France.

Two other garden features, of which gardens of subsequent civilizations were the heirs, first appeared in Greece — grottos and the Adonis garden. Originally believed to be the abode of nymphs, grottos were made to serve as cool retreats in hot weather. Built of rock and decorated with shells and often watered by a spring, they were comfortable adjuncts to the garden. As they copied Nature, they also were almost the only naturalistic effects in these classical Greek gardens.

The Adonis garden consisted of small pots of quickly growing seeds set around a statue of Adonis either in the garden or on the housetop. Adonis was the god of the growing world; in autumn when winter brought death to plants, he was believed to disappear into the bowels of the earth; in spring he reappeared again. To celebrate his reappearance these gardens were made. From them can be traced the Mediterranean custom of clustering potted plants around the foot of a statue or the basin of a fountain. Roof gardens may also find some semblance of a heritage in this custom, since the Adonis garden, made for a short display at a particular season, gave rise to rooftop gardens, made for all the seasons. However, the crowding of cities and the restricted areas of cultivatable space also were factors in the evolution of the roof garden.

After the conquests of Alexander, the Greeks began to enjoy some of the luxuries of Persian living; they began developing country villas, and when they planted their colonies in Sicily and along the Mediterranean, these settlements soon became famous for the luxury of their gardens.

ROMAN GARDENS carried on the heritage of Greece and developed it further. Whereas the Greeks preferred city life, country living came naturally to the Romans, and the art of horticulture was part of their national tradition. The early writers on land improvement — Cato and Varro and Columella — were among the farm heroes. Rome was early a garden city. Nobles developed much of the lands within the city limits into elaborate estates. These were laid out formally. Two features appeared in them — the

---

* Special articles on the subjects indicated by an asterisk (*) will be found at the words so marked.

*gestatio* or area for taking a "constitutional," and the *hippodromo* or horse-pacing ring. Even the poor citizen had his window-box garden — which can still be seen in the poor quarters of Italian cities. Where tillable space was scarce, Romans planted their housetops into roof gardens or *sylvae in tectus*.

The crowded condition of Rome caused the city to spill over into the Campagna and the near-by hills. This countryward movement was quickened by the publication of Virgil's Georgics. A man of ordinary means had a *suburban inn* or little country place where he kept a *villicus* or farm manager and his wife. Those with more means might possess either a *villa rustica*, a farm on which special crops were grown and where the owner went at harvest times; or he might have a *villa urbana*. The latter was an elaborate country place with building designed in the manner of city dwellings, and where little or no farming was pursued. Such pleasure gardens the Younger Pliny maintained on the seashore at Laurentium and on his larger place in the Tuscan Hills. His letters describing them afford us the most authentic records of country living and garden design of the times.

In these Roman country gardens were found two features that handed on their lineage — water-tricks and topiary work. Neatly calculated garden benches, when one sat on them, sprayed water on the sitter or caused it to flow in a fantastic design. Even more popular was shrub-sculpture or topiary clipping of trees and shrubs into amusing and decorative effects. A large estate would keep a special gardener or *topiarius* to care for these; at the same time actual statuary was not neglected, and indeed the Roman garden was well populated with figures of the gods and national heroes.

Eventually both in Rome itself and in the surrounding countryside garden luxury grew to such proportions that agriculture was neglected. When Alaric descended on Rome he found some 1700 villas with gardens. At the arrival of invaders owners of these estates fled to the cities and their country places fell into ruin. Southern Europe entered on the Dark Ages, during which the only garden light that burned was found in monastic gardens.

MONASTERY GARDENS in Europe first followed the form of Roman gardens, since many of them were located in *villa urbana* and *villa rustica*. Before this, the cenobites of Egypt had their vegetable patches. When the monastic ideal was adapted for western Europe by St. Benedict, gardening was made one of the required labors. Benedict's rule set the pattern for subsequent regulations of both monasteries and convents.

The convent gardens, tended by women, could scarcely be expected to grow field crops that entailed heavy manual labor; consequently, within their enclosures they grew flowers and herbs with which to deck their chapels and from which they decocted specifics and cosmetics. These arts they taught to women.

The garden of a well-equipped monastery, such as St. Gall on Lake Constance, of which we have plans, contained four parts — a physic garden, a cloister garth, a vegetable garden and a combined orchard-vineyard and burial ground. Altar flowers were grown in the cloister garden or else the sacristan had his own patch devoted to this purpose. Many of the flowers which we grow for decorative purposes today, in those times were used for making medicine. Among the many services the monastery rendered gardens in the Dark Ages was the preservation of strains of fruit and vegetables that, without their care, would have disappeared. In later times the monastery also afforded new varieties of fruit, some of which are still grown today.

CASTLE GARDENS. In this same era the domestic garden of the castle and the burgher home alike was restricted in size, being laid out in the narrow limits between castle and town walls. Returning Crusaders and other travelers from the East brought home new concepts of gardens and new plants to grow in them. As safety in country living became more assured, gardens crept beyond the walls, increased in size and were equipped with structures and amenities that both gave them a marked architectural pattern and suited them for outdoor living. This mediaeval pattern was formal — a series of geometric beds around a central fountain, and the garden was square, oblong or circular, a wall or fence marking its limits.

RENAISSANCE GARDENS were produced by two main influences — humanistic thought, which aroused interest in old Roman traditions, and an awakening appreciation of the beauties of Nature. These, together with the increasing safety of the countryside, revived country living and brought the country villa into prominence once more. By gradual steps the garden passed from the old house terrace of the Romans to those elaborate patterned gardens dominated by architectural effects that well-nigh submerged horticultural effort. At the same time the revived interest in tradition brought into the garden old Roman statues or copies of them and all manner of classical embellishments and water effects.

Though architecture was its main feature, nevertheless an interest in new plants began to appear in Renaissance gardens. This was the dawn of the age of exploration, and from distant corners of the world came roots, seeds and plants that the botanically minded tried to grow in their gardens. This age also saw the rise of the botanical garden, a service to science and the public which continues down to our own day.

From Italy the Renaissance garden spread to France, Germany, Spain, Holland and England, each country making its own interpretations and adaptations of the style, according to its environment. Thus the grand proportions of Renaissance gardens could not be copied in Holland, nor did the public interest tend in that direction. Holland early became the nursery of Europe and produced many new plants. The French clung to their mediaeval moated castle gardens for a long time, then eventually, with the assistance of Italian garden designers and water engineers, began to evolve an elaborate Renaissance style, the parterre being an especial subject for development into complicated designs. England, on the other hand, was evolving its own style of garden.

THE ENGLISH MEDIAEVAL contained the same features found in mediaeval French gardens — the pleached bower, the turf seats, the flower-spangled lawns, the sanded walks, the herbary and the orchard — but not until the late Renaissance did the pleasance appear as a separate entity. Up to that time it had been combined with the orchard or the physic garden. The gardens described by Chaucer are mediaeval and early Renaissance; those found in Shakespeare show later influence. One of the most pronounced influences was the diversity of flowers that were planted in gardens. England began to awaken to the natural beauties of her own countryside and at the same time to those foreign plants that were trickling in. Not for several centuries, however, did new plants affect the form of gardens.

LE NOTRE, with the gardens in the grand manner he created at Vaux de Vicomte and Versailles and other magnificent places, displayed the ultimate flowering of the Renaissance. His style was formal and required extensive space.

The main features of his style were the planting of bosquets or groups of trees to make decorative arbors in which were placed architectural or water effects; the goose-foot style of allées, *i.e.* several allées radiating from a central point; the elongated water canal; the complicated and decorative use of water in cascades and fountains; the abundance of statuary to which the greatest artists of the time contributed; the development of treillage or architectural lattice work for backgrounds and garden structures; and the relegation of flowers to especial spots for immediate effect. At the same time he did not neglect the more utilitarian parts of the garden, for the vegetables and fruits at Versailles, entrusted to the care of Jean de la Quintinie, set the style for an interest in these matters that was reflected not alone in other French estates but in other countries as well. Both as a horticulturist and as a garden author, de la Quintinie was one of the greatest figures of all time, as Le Notre was in the world of garden designing.

---

* Special articles on the subjects indicated by an asterisk (*) will be found at the words so marked.

This influence of Le Notre soon spread over the continent, although in England it did not appear to have been generally accepted. There the taste ran more to the small formal garden or the garden in the Dutch manner, in which the living plant was the object of more solicitude than the setting given it. Moreover, since England was reaching out to empire limits by its explorations and colonizations, it became the home of plants found in those far-flung countries, as countless books on the subject attest. From the multitude of authors and gardeners who contributed to the advancement and appreciation of gardening and plants in this era, three stand out supreme — John Gerard, John Parkinson and the Tradescants.

ORIENTAL GARDENS of China and Japan began to make their influence felt at this stage and acted as a counter-influence to the formality of Le Notre. Returning missionaries and travelers brought news of the naturalistic gardens found in the East. As we saw previously, the followers of Buddha were worshipers in natural groves and their temples were set in naturalistic gardens. This lost its influence to the types of domestic and palace gardens that were made for many centuries in China and Japan. A favorite glimpse of a mountain or a stream was scaled down to the limited proportions of a home garden. Soon each of its elements was given a name and a symbolic significance, a custom developed into a highly complicated ritual of garden design by the Zen Buddhist priests in Japan. Meantime a deep love for the beauty of particular flowers was growing. The peony, the peach blossoms, the chrysanthemum were all subject to hybridization, tender care and poetic adulation. See JAPANESE GARDEN.

This Oriental influence came to Europe at exactly the right time. Formalism reached its apex and was going into a decline; the naturalism of the Orient was seized on enthusiastically.

To this Oriental influence can be traced the later stages of the naturalistic garden movement in England and the rococo taste in France.

THE NATURALISTIC GARDEN of England first appeared as a revolt against the trifles and formality of the Dutch Garden, together with an enthusiasm for the painting of Salvator Rosa, who depicted Nature in all her grandeur, and an awakening to the beauties of Nature as found in the writings of Rousseau. Gardens were supposed to copy that grandeur. Great formal gardens were destroyed that they might give place to the rustic visions of "Capability" Brown and Humphrey Repton that made gardens appear a part of the surrounding countryside. In its later phase this movement adopted all sorts of picturesque effects — ruins, Gothic chapels and hermitages. It also gave rise to the fancy farm. The taste was quickly copied in France. The hameau at Versailles, made to please the fancies of Marie Antoinette, still stands as a reminder of this taste.

At the same time in both England and France there appeared the pronounced Chinese taste in the design of garden structures. This gave rise to the Oriental rococo that, for more than fifty years, maintained its influence. At the same time interest in Chinese plants increased as the English and Dutch imported them into their gardens.

Since much of the early exploration went to tropical countries, the first plants brought from distant lands could be raised only in warm climates. However, in England the desire to grow them soon gave rise to the development of the greenhouse in which oranges and other warm-climate fruits and flowers were eventually grown to perfection.

The threshold of our own time finds the garden inheriting several traditions — classical formalism and its opposite, informal naturalism. Advances in horticultural technique and the study of plants preceded a wider appreciation of the material grown in gardens. Nevertheless garden styles were still marked by pronounced nationalistic influences. The gardens Spanish conquistadors and their descendants made in Spanish colonies showed marked influences from the homeland. The same was true of gardens in Dutch colonies and in those settled by the English. The gardens of Early America, indeed gardens made here until almost the present time, are directly traceable to English influence. The early settlers brought their own seeds from the Old Country and grew many of the plants they had known at home. In the Georgian era, the estate gardens laid out along the Atlantic seaboard were patterned after gardens of that time in England. When the naturalistic English school began spreading its influence, the same sort of gardens appeared in the United States.

The later years of the nineteenth century saw England combining many types of garden in one place — there would be an Italian garden, a bit of Spain, something from Holland and a reminiscence of France. This taste also is found today in the United States. However, another factor brought about specialized gardens.

SPECIAL PLANT GARDENS were produced by the better understanding of the requirements of plants. The contemporary rose garden, water garden, rock garden, naturalistic planting of daffodils, bog garden and garden of wild flowers, all represent an effort to produce on the home grounds the environments in which special groups of plants naturally thrive. Interest in these plants has caused the founding of special societies and an extensive body of literature. Today gardeners are apt to be specialists, choosing one group of plants and making them dominate the garden.

In more recent years we have witnessed a revolt against the informalism of the naturalistic type of garden and a gradual creeping in of traditional garden shapes and architecture. Gardens have lost their pronounced nationalistic atmosphere and become eclectic. Our gardens today combine features from all the gardens of the past, and in them are grown flowers from all countries of the world.

ROOF GARDENS, however, can be called America's latest contribution to garden practice. Here again we have only revived an ancient art. The stepping back of architecture in high buildings, necessitated by the demand for sunlight in the lower floors and on the street, caused a series of flat terraces suitable for roof-top gardens. Most of the plants are grown in pots or deep boxes of soil, and in this respect they repeat the experience and technique of the Babylonians when they made their hanging gardens and the custom of the Greeks when their women set potted gardens around the statue of Adonis, to celebrate the return of spring. See PENTHOUSE GARDEN. — R. W.

**GARDEN HOSE.** See Section 1, TOOLS AND IMPLEMENTS.

**GARDEN HUCKLEBERRY.** See SOLANUM NIGRUM. See also HUCKLEBERRY.

**GARDENIA** (gar-dee′ni-a; also gar-din′i-a). A genus of over 50 species of tropical Old World shrubs and trees of the family Rubiaceae, one a very popular, fragrant, florists' flower. They have opposite* evergreen leaves, some of which are occasionally found in 3's at a single joint. Flowers large, white (in ours), usually solitary in the leaf-axils* (always so when disbudded by the grower). Calyx tubular. Corolla salver-shaped or short-tubular, its limb with 5–11 spreading, more or less twisted, waxy, petal-like lobes. Stamens 5–9. Fruit stalkless, leathery, or fleshy. (Named for Doctor Alexander Garden, Charleston physician and friend of Linnaeus.)

The Cape jasmine, which is the florists' gardenia, is grown exactly as in *Camellia* (which see). The only difference is that in *Gardenia* the size and fragrance of the flowers is enhanced by pinching off all but a few blossoms, especially when more than one occurs at a leaf-axil.* Such disbudding is always practiced by commercial growers.

florida = *Gardenia jasminoides*.
fortunei = *Gardenia jasminoides fortuniana*.
jasminoides. Cape jasmine and the common gardenia of the florists. A shrub 2–5 ft. high. Leaves generally lance-shaped or broader towards the tip, 3–4 in. long, thick, leathery, and occasionally variegated. Flowers 2–3½ in. wide, very fragrant. China, but long supposed to come from the Cape of Good Hope, hence its common name. The *var.* **fortuniana** is a larger-flowered form and is sometimes called *G. veitchi*.
radicans = *Gardenia jasminoides*.
veitchi = *Gardenia jasminoides fortuniana*.

**GARDEN JOURNALS.** See GARDEN MAGAZINES.

* Special articles on the subjects indicated by an asterisk (*) will be found at the words so marked.

**GARDEN LABELS.** See LABELS.

**GARDEN LINE.** See Section 1, TOOLS AND IMPLEMENTS.

**GARDEN LITERATURE.** See GARDEN BOOKS.

**GARDEN MAGAZINES.** The number of garden periodicals in America is very great. Many of them are of special interest or local significance only, and no attempt will be made here to list them. Nor can space be found, usually, for the transactions or reports of horticultural societies,* garden clubs, botanic gardens, nor for the periodical literature of the Experiment Stations. In the list below are included only those garden journals of wide circulation, and a few others, often devoted to outdoor subjects, which carry a regular garden department. Those marked with a dagger (†) are devoted wholly to some branch of hort. The place of publication, year of establishment, and annual subscription price (1936) are also included:

  American Home (including Garden Magazine). Garden City, N.Y. Monthly. 1905. $1.00.
  Better Homes and Gardens. Des Moines, Iowa. Monthly. 1922. $1.00.
  †Cactus and Succulent Journal. Los Angeles, Calif. Monthly. 1929. $3.00.
  †California Garden. San Diego, Calif. Monthly. 1919. $1.00.
  †Canadian Horticulture and Home Magazine. Peterborough, Ontario, Canada. Monthly. 1877. $1.00.
  The Country Home (formerly Farm and Fireside). New York, N.Y. Monthly. 1877. $.25.
  Country Life. Garden City, New York. Monthly. 1907. $5.00.
  †Desert Plant Life. Pasadena, Calif. Monthly. 1928. $1.50.
  Farm and Fireside. See THE COUNTRY HOME.
  †The Flower Grower (includes former Modern Gladiolus Grower). Calcium, N.Y. Monthly. 1914. $2.00.
  †Garden. New Orleans, La. Quarterly. 1935. $1.00.
  †Garden Digest (formerly Home Acres). Pleasantville, N.Y. (Reviews and condensations of articles published elsewhere.) Monthly. 1928. $1.00.
  †The Gardeners' Chronicle of America. New York, N.Y. Monthly. 1905. $2.00.
  †Garden Gossip. Richmond, Va. Monthly. 1925. $1.00.
  Garden Magazine. See AMERICAN HOME.
  †The Garden Quarterly. San Francisco, Calif. Quarterly. 1933. $1.50.
  Home Acres. See GARDEN DIGEST.
  Home and Field. See HOUSE BEAUTIFUL.
  †Horticulture. Boston, Mass. Fortnightly. 1904. $1.00.
  House and Garden. New York, N.Y. Monthly. 1901. $3.00.
  House Beautiful (including Home and Field). New York, N.Y. Monthly. 1900. $3.00.
  Landscape Architecture. Cambridge, Mass. Quarterly. 1910. $3.00.
  †Minnesota Horticulturist. St. Paul, Minn. Monthly (except July, Oct., and Dec.). 1894. $.50.
  Modern Gladiolus Grower. See THE FLOWER GROWER.
  †Bulletin of the National Council of State Garden Clubs. New York, N.Y. Monthly (except July and Aug.). 1930. $.50.
  †National Horticultural Magazine. Washington, D.C. Quarterly. 1922. $3.00.
  New Jersey Farm and Garden. Sea Isle City, N.J. Monthly. 1929. $.80.
  Southern Home and Garden. Fort Worth, Tex. Monthly. 1934. $1.00.
  Sunset Magazine. San Francisco, Calif. Monthly. 1898. $.50.
  Town and Country. New York, N.Y. Fortnightly. 1846. $7.50.

**GARDEN MEASURES.** For sizes, volumes, weights and measures, see WEIGHTS AND MEASURES. For plants, yields, amount of seed, plants per acre, etc., see GARDEN TABLES.

**GARDEN MINT** = *Mentha spicata*. See MINT.

**GARDEN NASTURTIUM** = *Tropaeolum majus*. See NASTURTIUM.

**GARDEN OPERATIONS.** What has to be done in a garden comprises the different skills one learns from the seeding to harvesting of the final crop. Naturally these different garden operations divide themselves into things that are done to the soil or to the plants themselves. And there is no need to repeat in detail here all the things that are treated extensively in other parts of THE GARDEN DICTIONARY.

But suggestions of where to find these special articles are helpful enough to summarize here.

SOIL. For all details having to do with the soil, see SOILS (and the cross-references there mentioned). See also CULTIVATION, DRAINING, DIGGING, FERTILIZERS, WATERING.

PLANTS. In the treatment of your plants, whether herbs or trees, there are certain things you must know about their care, protection from pests, or perpetuation. See, especially, the articles on PLANTING, PROPAGATION, WATERING, FORCING, INSECT PESTS, PLANT DISEASES, ANIMAL INJURY. There are also many cultural notes on special crops which should be looked for under their common names (*i.e.* apple, cabbage, carnation, fig, etc.).

GREENHOUSE OR COLD FRAME. For the things to do in daily management of a greenhouse or conservatory, see both these words. For the management of a hotbed or a cold frame, see COLD FRAME.

HOUSE PLANTS. See that entry.

**GARDEN ORACH** = *Atriplex hortensis*.

**GARDEN ORNAMENT.** See ORNAMENT AND FURNITURE.

**GARDEN PATHS.** See PATHS AND PAVING.

**GARDEN PHLOX** = *Phlox paniculata*.

**GARDEN PLANNING.** See LANDSCAPE ARCHITECTURE.

**GARDEN POETRY.** Garden poetry appears to be older than other garden books, for no purely hort. work goes back to 1300 B.C. But from that day to this there have been poems on the garden, and the poets range from Vergil to Edna St. Vincent Millay. No attempt can be made here to quote even the finest of them, and the reader is referred to the best modern compilation, Sylvia Spencer's *Up from the Earth: A Collection of Garden Poems 1300 B.C.–1935*.

**GARDEN PORTULACA** = *Portulaca grandiflora*.

**GARDEN QUESTIONS.** No lecture ever ends without inevitable questions by members of the garden club. Several thousands have accumulated in the past, most of which have ultimately reached the editorial office of THE GARDEN DICTIONARY, either in the form of printed lists or in direct queries. Sifting them out gives one a cross-section of the doubts and perplexities of the average gardener.

To list them here is impossible. To sort them into categories and steer the seeker to the proper reference in this book seems not only possible but perhaps the most helpful way of answering them. Most garden questions have to do with (1) specific plants; (2) the soil in which they grow; (3) their pests; (4) their suitability for the place in which you wish to grow them. Still another set of questions (5) are grouped around the more difficult subject of design, or questions of taste in home surroundings; and (6) the question of "How to do things." To take the questions in order, let us see where, in THE GARDEN DICTIONARY, you are most likely to find the answers.

(1) SPECIFIC PLANTS. All the plants in this book are listed under their generic names and under as many vernacular names as are in common use. If you know the Latin or common name of the plant in question, turn to that entry and you will soon learn its culture and the varieties most worth growing, its diseases or insect pests, and much other useful information on propagation. There are also special articles on the culture of all the important fruits, vegetables, flowers, and trees.

(2) SOILS. Read the article on SOILS and the cross-refer-

---

* Special articles on the subjects indicated by an asterisk (*) will be found at the words so marked.

ences there suggested. *See also* FERTILIZERS, PLANT FOOD, ACID AND ALKALI SOILS, SOIL OPERATIONS.

(3) PESTS. Read first the general articles on INSECT PESTS, PLANT DISEASES, and ANIMAL INJURY. If your query is a specific pest on some plant, turn to that plant, where you will find an account of the control of all insect or fungous pests thought worth including by the Contributing Editors in charge of this section of THE GARDEN DICTIONARY.

(4) SUITABILITY. The whole question of a plant for your locality is tied up with your local climate and the hardiness of the plant involved. *See* HARDINESS, ZONE, PROTECTING PLANTS, and, especially, the climatic data on temperature and rainfall at the name of your state or province.

(5) GARDEN DESIGN. *See* the article headed LANDSCAPE ARCHITECTURE and the cross-references there suggested. For specific problems *see* such special articles as BRIDGES, DRIVES, FENCES, PATHS, and many others.

(6) HOW TO DO THINGS. Perhaps the most difficult of all the different sorts of garden questions. The best way to start is to read the article on GARDEN OPERATIONS, and the cross-references there suggested.

If, in spite of these possible question answerers, there are still problems that puzzle you, *see* the Classified List of Main Articles in the Introduction, or write to the garden editor, Houghton Mifflin Company, Boston, Mass.

**GARDEN ROCKET** = *Hesperis matronalis*.

Garden room which encloses a lily pool and a tea house

**GARDEN ROOM.** This should serve as a center for outdoor living. A garden room should be an intimate area containing plant material and sufficiently defined in extent and purpose to be a recognized entity.

Garden rooms extend from a simple open area beneath the canopy of great spreading tree branches to a highly organized architectural unit forming an integral part of a garden scheme.

The purpose of a garden room is to provide a place accessible, yet apart, and amid natural growing things where one may be quiet and free to sit and think or to meditate on the heart's desires.

Its intimate use gives the place a certain distinction. Interesting variations in ground level and frank recognition of existing dominant features adjacent to the site, such as a building or large tree, add an air of permanence and suggest a sympathetic relationship between landscape elements. To be convincing, such a unit area should obviously suggest its function. The treatment of its various features should all contribute toward successfully carrying out the general purposes of the garden room, which is detachment and privacy outdoors.

A simpler outdoor living room

The choice of materials employed to create the setting of such an area is governed by individual requirements and is usually dependent upon local conditions.

Floor areas are generally paved with flagstone or brick, and a carpet of turf is also used where dampness and mosquitoes are not deterrent factors.

The enclosure strikes the dominant note in the composition of the room. For formal effect, a wall or hedge usually serves as a boundary, and occasionally an arbor or covered seat is used, or a combination of such elements. For informal effects, the limits are not so severely defined. A dry stone wall or flanking mass of shrubs may be used, or a group of trees or possibly one large low-branched tree.

Supplementing necessary furniture, such as seats and tables, the judicious use of potted or tubbed plants, sculptural ornament, and the use of water, all definitely contribute to the character and atmosphere of the place, providing they are in keeping with the spirit of the room.

Where feasible and desirable, electric outlets can be provided for a portable electric stove or a percolator. Also for evening occasions, electric illumination of the garden room has proved an interesting feature and the effects are quite adaptable to the mood desired. *See* LIGHTING. — A. F.

**GARDEN SAGE** = *Salvia officinalis*.

**GARDEN SCHOOLS.** Nearly every State University has a well-equipped department of Horticulture, the most notable being at Cornell, Iowa, Wisconsin, Illinois, Pennsylvania State College, Purdue, and Ohio State University. *See also* SCHOOL GARDENING, for children's instruction.

Special courses in various garden subjects are offered from time to time by the botanic gardens (which see), especially the New York Botanical Garden, Brooklyn Botanic Garden, and the Missouri Botanical Garden. There are, in addition, a few special schools of horticulture or courses offered in gardening, of which the most noteworthy are:

California School of Gardening for Women. Hayward, Calif.
Horticultural Society of New York. New York, N.Y. (Courses for amateur and professional gardeners.)
Lowthorpe School of Landscape Architecture for Women. Groton, Mass.
School of Horticulture for Women. Ambler, Pa.
State Institute of Applied Agriculture. Farmingdale, Long Island, N.Y. (Courses in horticulture.)

**GARDEN STATISTICS.** *See* GARDEN TABLES.

**GARDEN STATUARY.** *See* ORNAMENT AND FURNITURE.

**GARDEN SUMMER HOUSE.** *See* STRUCTURES.

**GARDEN TABLES.** There is apt to, but need not be, confusion between this entry and WEIGHTS AND MEASURES. At the latter entry look for all statistics having to do with the standard dimensions or contents of things, like a mile, foot, yard, bushel, acre, pint, or the contents of a cistern, etc.

But here are grouped many tables that most gardeners need to consult from time to time. For ready reference they may be separated into various sections:

---

* Special articles on the subjects indicated by an asterisk (*) will be found at the words so marked.

I. Yields, Plants per Acre, Average Bearing Age, Seeds Needed for 100 Feet of Row and for an Acre.
II. Weight of Seeds, Viability of Seeds, Percentage of Seed Germinating.
III. Tree Height, Age or Longevity of Trees, Rate of Growth, How to Estimate Tree Height.
IV. Number of Plants for Oval, Round, or Square Flower Beds.

# I

## AVERAGE YIELDS

The average yields per acre of various garden crops are given below. They vary, of course, with locality, cultural methods, and the variety grown.

| | |
|---|---|
| Artichoke | 200 to 300 bushels |
| Beans, String | 75 to 120 bushels |
| Beans, Lima | 75 to 100 bushels of dry beans |
| Beets | 400 to 700 bushels |
| Carrots | 400 to 700 bushels |
| Corn | 50 to 75 bushels, shelled |
| Cranberry | 100 to 300 bushels |
| Cucumber | About 150,000 fruits per acre |
| Currant | 100 bushels |
| Eggplant | 1 or 2 large fruits to the plant for the large sorts, and from 3 to 8 fruits for the smaller varieties |
| Gooseberry | 100 bushels |
| Grape | 3 to 5 tons |
| Horseradish | 3 to 5 tons |
| Kohlrabi | 500 to 1000 bushels |
| Onion, from seed | 300 to 800 bushels |
| Parsnips | 500 to 800 bushels |
| Pea, green in pod | 100 to 150 bushels |
| Peach | In full bearing, a peach tree should produce from 5 to 10 bushels |
| Pear | A tree 20 to 25 years old should give from 25 to 45 bushels |
| Pepper | 30,000 to 50,000 fruits |
| Plum | 5 to 8 bushels may be considered an average crop for an average tree |
| Potato | 100 to 300 bushels |
| Quince | 100 to 300 bushels |
| Raspberry and Blackberry | 50 to 100 bushels |
| Salsify | 200 to 300 bushels |
| Spinach | 200 barrels |
| Strawberry | 75 to 250 or even 300 bushels |
| Tomato | 8 to 16 tons |
| Turnip | 600 to 1000 bushels |

## PLANTS PER ACRE

*Plants Needed for an Acre of Land when Set the Indicated Number of Inches Apart*

NOTE: *To estimate for smaller areas figure that a plot 33 × 66 ft. is exactly 1/20 of an acre.*

| Inches | Plants | Inches | Plants |
|---|---|---|---|
| 1 × 1 | 6,272,640 | 3 × 8 | 261,360 |
| 1 × 2 | 3,136,320 | 3 × 10 | 209,088 |
| 1 × 3 | 2,090,880 | 3 × 12 | 174,240 |
| 1 × 6 | 1,045,440 | 4 × 4 | 392,040 |
| 1 × 9 | 696,960 | 4 × 6 | 261,360 |
| 1 × 12 | 522,720 | 4 × 8 | 196,020 |
| 2 × 2 | 1,568,160 | 4 × 10 | 156,816 |
| 2 × 3 | 1,045,440 | 4 × 12 | 130,680 |
| 2 × 4 | 784,080 | 5 × 5 | 250,905 |
| 2 × 6 | 522,720 | 5 × 7 | 179,218 |
| 2 × 8 | 392,040 | 5 × 9 | 139,392 |
| 2 × 10 | 313,632 | 5 × 12 | 104,544 |
| 2 × 12 | 261,360 | 6 × 6 | 174,240 |
| 3 × 3 | 696,960 | 6 × 8 | 130,680 |
| 3 × 4 | 522,720 | 6 × 10 | 104,544 |
| 3 × 6 | 348,480 | 6 × 12 | 87,120 |

## PLANTS PER ACRE, *continued*

| Inches | Plants | Inches | Plants |
|---|---|---|---|
| 7 × 7 | 128,013 | 10 × 48 or 4 ft. | 13,068 |
| 7 × 10 | 89,609 | 10 × 60 or 5 ft. | 10,454 |
| 7 × 12 | 74,674 | 15 × 15 | 27,878 |
| 8 × 8 | 98,010 | 15 × 20 | 20,908 |
| 8 × 10 | 78,408 | 15 × 36 or 3 ft. | 11,616 |
| 8 × 12 | 65,340 | 15 × 48 or 4 ft. | 8,712 |
| 9 × 9 | 77,440 | 15 × 60 or 5 ft. | 6,969 |
| 9 × 10 | 69,696 | 18 × 18 | 19,360 |
| 9 × 12 | 58,080 | 18 × 24 or 2 ft. | 14,520 |
| 10 × 10 | 62,726 | 18 × 36 or 3 ft. | 9,680 |
| 10 × 12 | 52,272 | 18 × 48 or 4 ft. | 7,260 |
| 10 × 15 | 41,817 | 20 × 20 | 15,681 |
| 10 × 18 | 34,848 | 20 × 24 or 2 ft. | 13,168 |
| 10 × 20 | 31,362 | 20 × 36 or 3 ft. | 8,712 |
| 10 × 24 or 2 ft. | 26,132 | 20 × 48 or 4 ft. | 6,534 |
| 10 × 30 | 20,908 | 20 × 60 or 5 ft. | 5,227 |
| 10 × 42 | 14,935 | | |

## PLANTS PER ACRE

*Plants Needed for an Acre of Land when Set the Indicated Number of Feet Apart*

NOTE: *To estimate for smaller areas figure that a plot 33 × 66 ft. is exactly 1/20 of an acre.*

| Feet | Plants | Feet | Plants |
|---|---|---|---|
| 1 × 1 | 43,560 | 9 × 12 | 403 |
| 1 × 2 | 21,780 | 9 × 14 | 345 |
| 1 × 3 | 14,520 | 9 × 15 | 322 |
| 1 × 4 | 10,890 | 9 × 18 | 268 |
| 1 × 5 | 8,712 | 9 × 20 | 242 |
| 1 × 6 | 7,260 | 10 × 10 | 435 |
| 1 × 8 | 5,445 | 10 × 12 | 363 |
| 1 × 10 | 4,356 | 10 × 15 | 290 |
| 1 × 12 | 3,630 | 10 × 18 | 242 |
| 2 × 2 | 10,890 | 10 × 20 | 217 |
| 2 × 4 | 5,445 | 10 × 24 | 181 |
| 2 × 6 | 3,630 | 10 × 30 | 145 |
| 2 × 8 | 2,722 | 10 × 36 | 121 |
| 2 × 10 | 2,178 | 10 × 42 | 103 |
| 2 × 12 | 1,815 | 10 × 45 | 96 |
| 3 × 3 | 4,840 | 10 × 48 | 90 |
| 3 × 6 | 2,420 | 10 × 54 | 80 |
| 3 × 8 | 1,815 | 10 × 60 | 72 |
| 3 × 10 | 1,452 | 12 × 12 | 302 |
| 3 × 12 | 1,210 | 12 × 15 | 242 |
| 4 × 4 | 2,722 | 12 × 18 | 201 |
| 4 × 6 | 1,185 | 12 × 20 | 181 |
| 4 × 8 | 1,361 | 12 × 24 | 151 |
| 4 × 10 | 1,089 | 12 × 30 | 121 |
| 4 × 12 | 907 | 12 × 36 | 100 |
| 5 × 5 | 1,742 | 12 × 42 | 86 |
| 5 × 7 | 1,244 | 12 × 48 | 75 |
| 5 × 9 | 968 | 12 × 54 | 67 |
| 5 × 11 | 792 | 12 × 60 | 60 |
| 5 × 12 | 726 | 15 × 15 | 193 |
| 6 × 6 | 1,210 | 15 × 18 | 161 |
| 6 × 8 | 907 | 15 × 20 | 145 |
| 6 × 10 | 726 | 15 × 24 | 121 |
| 6 × 12 | 605 | 15 × 30 | 96 |
| 7 × 7 | 888 | 15 × 36 | 80 |
| 7 × 8 | 777 | 15 × 42 | 69 |
| 7 × 9 | 691 | 15 × 48 | 60 |
| 7 × 10 | 622 | 15 × 54 | 53 |
| 7 × 11 | 565 | 15 × 60 | 48 |
| 7 × 12 | 518 | 18 × 18 | 134 |
| 8 × 8 | 680 | 18 × 20 | 121 |
| 8 × 9 | 605 | 18 × 24 | 100 |
| 8 × 10 | 544 | 18 × 30 | 80 |
| 8 × 11 | 495 | 18 × 36 | 67 |
| 8 × 12 | 453 | 18 × 42 | 57 |
| 9 × 9 | 537 | 18 × 48 | 50 |
| 9 × 10 | 484 | 18 × 54 | 44 |
| 9 × 11 | 440 | 18 × 60 | 40 |

* Special articles on the subjects indicated by an asterisk (*) will be found at the words so marked.

# Garden Tables

## Plants per Acre, continued

| Feet | Plants | Feet | Plants |
|---|---|---|---|
| 20 × 20 | 108 | 38 × 42 | 27 |
| 20 × 24 | 90 | 38 × 48 | 23 |
| 20 × 30 | 72 | 38 × 50 | 22 |
| 20 × 36 | 60 | 38 × 54 | 21 |
| 20 × 42 | 51 | 38 × 60 | 19 |
| 20 × 48 | 45 | 40 × 40 | 27 |
| 20 × 54 | 40 | 40 × 42 | 25 |
| 20 × 60 | 36 | 40 × 48 | 22 |
| 24 × 24 | 75 | 40 × 50 | 21 |
| 24 × 30 | 60 | 40 × 54 | 20 |
| 24 × 36 | 50 | 40 × 60 | 18 |
| 24 × 42 | 43 | 42 × 42 | 24 |
| 24 × 48 | 37 | 42 × 48 | 21 |
| 24 × 54 | 33 | 42 × 54 | 19 |
| 24 × 60 | 30 | 42 × 60 | 17 |
| 30 × 30 | 48 | 48 × 48 | 18 |
| 30 × 36 | 40 | 48 × 54 | 16 |
| 30 × 42 | 34 | 48 × 60 | 15 |
| 30 × 48 | 30 | 50 × 50 | 17 |
| 30 × 54 | 26 | 50 × 54 | 16 |
| 30 × 60 | 24 | 50 × 60 | 14 |
| 36 × 36 | 33 | 54 × 54 | 14 |
| 36 × 42 | 28 | 54 × 60 | 13 |
| 36 × 48 | 25 | 60 × 60 | 12 |
| 36 × 54 | 22 | 70 × 70 | 8 |
| 36 × 60 | 20 | 80 × 80 | 6 |
| 38 × 38 | 30 | 90 × 90 | 5 |
| 38 × 40 | 28 | 100 × 100 | 4 |

## Average Bearing Age of Fruit Plants from Time of Setting Out to First Full Crop

| | Years | | Years |
|---|---|---|---|
| Apple | 4–10 | Peach | 2 |
| Blackberry | 1 | Pear | 3 or 4 |
| Citrus fruits | 3–6 | | dwarfs in 5–7 |
| (oranges, lemons, etc.) | | Persimmon, or Kaki | 1–3 |
| | | Plum | 3–5 |
| Cranberry | 3 | Quince | 2–3 |
| Currant | 1–2 | Raspberry | 1–2 |
| Gooseberry | 1–2 | Strawberry | 1–2 |
| Grape | 4 | | |

## Seeds Needed per 100 Feet of Row, per Acre, and per Foot of Various Crops

| Crop | Seeds per 100-ft. row | Seeds per acre | No. of seeds per foot |
|---|---|---|---|
| Asparagus | 1–2 oz. | | 7–10 |
| Beans, String | 8 oz. | 1 bu. | 5–8 |
| Beans, dry shell | 4–8 oz. | ¾ bu.–1½ bu. | 5–8 |
| Beets | ½ oz. | 4 lb. | 10 |
| Brussels Sprouts | 1/20 oz. | ½ lb. | 5–8 |
| Cabbage | 1/20 oz. | ½ lb. | 5–8 |
| Carrot | 1/10 oz. | 2 lb. | 15–20 |
| Cauliflower | 1/20 oz. | ¼–½ lb. | 5–8 |
| Celery | 1/20 oz. | ¼–1 lb. | 10–20 |
| Cucumber | ¼ oz. | 1–2 lb. | 5–6 (per hill) |
| Eggplant | 1/20 oz. | ¼–½ lb. | 6–8 |
| Endive | 1/10 oz. | 4 lb. | 8–10 |
| Lettuce | 1/10 oz. | 3 lb. | 8–10 |
| Muskmelons | ¼ oz. | 2 lb. | 5–6 (per hill) |
| Onion | ½ oz. | 4–5 lb. | 10–15 |
| Onion sets | 1–2 lb. | 8–12 bu. | 5–6 |
| Onions, Winter | 1–2 lb. | 8–12 bu. | 5–6 |
| Parsley | 1/10 oz. | 3 lb. | 8–10 |
| Parsnips | ¼ oz. | 3–5 lb. | 8–10 |
| Peas | ½ lb. | 1½–4 bu. | 5–8 |
| Peppers | 1/20 oz. | ¾–1 lb. | 4–5 |
| Potatoes | 5–6 lb. | 12–15 bu. | |
| Radish | ½ oz. | 10–12 lb. | 8–10 |
| Rutabaga | 1/10 oz. | 2–3 lb. | 8–10 |
| Salsify | ½ oz. | 6–8 lb. | 5–8 |
| Spinach | ½ oz. | 12–20 lb. | 10–12 |

## Seeds Needed per 100 Feet of Row, continued

| Crop | Seeds per 100-ft. row | Seeds per acre | No. of seeds per foot |
|---|---|---|---|
| Squash, Winter | 1 oz. | 3–5 lb. | 5–6 (per hill) |
| Sweet Corn | ¼ lb. | 10–15 lb. | 3–4 |
| Tomatoes | 1/20 oz. | 2–4 oz. | 6–8 |
| Turnips | 1/10 oz. | 1–2 lb. | 5–8 |

For the amount of vegetable seed needed for gardens 100 × 50 ft. and 200 × 100 ft., see Kitchen Garden.

## II

### Average Weight of Some Common Garden and Tree Seeds

These weights are apt to vary with the variety and the thoroughness with which the seeds have been dried.

| Garden seeds | Weight of a quart of seed in ounces | Garden seeds | Weight of a quart of seed in ounces |
|---|---|---|---|
| Anise | 11.6 | Marjoram, Sweet | 21.3 |
| Balm | 21.3 | Muskmelon | 13.9 |
| Basil | 20.5 | Nasturtium, Tall | 13.2 |
| Bean | 24.2 to 33.0 | Nasturtium, Dwarf | 23.3 |
| Beet | 9.7 | Okra | 24.0 |
| Borage | 18.7 | Onion | 19.4 |
| Broccoli | 27.1 | Pea | 27.1 to 31.0 |
| Cabbage | 27.1 | | |
| Caper | 17.8 | Peanut | 15.5 |
| Caraway | 16.3 | Pepper | 17.4 |
| Cardoon | 24.4 | Pumpkin | 9.7 |
| Carrot with the spines | 9.3 | Radish | 27.1 |
| | | Rhubarb | 3.1 to 4.6 |
| Cauliflower | 27.1 | | |
| Celery | 18.6 | Rosemary | 15.5 |
| Chervil | 14.7 | Rue | 22.5 |
| Chicory | 15.5 | Sage | 21.3 |
| Coriander | 12.4 | Salsify | 8.9 |
| Corn | 24.8 | Savory, Summer | 19.4 |
| Cucumber | 19.4 | Savory, Winter | 16.6 |
| Dill | 11.6 | Spinach | 14.5 |
| Eggplant | 19.4 | Spinach, New Zealand | 8.6 |
| Endive | 13.2 | | |
| Fennel, Common or Wild | 17.4 | Squash | 16.6 |
| | | Strawberry | 23.3 |
| Fennel, Sweet | 9.1 | Sweet Cicely | 9.7 |
| Hop | 9.7 | Tansy | 11.6 |
| Horehound | 26.4 | Thyme | 26.4 |
| Hyssop | 22.3 | Tomato | 11.6 |
| Kohlrabi | 27.1 | Turnip | 26.0 |
| Leek | 21.3 | Watermelon | 17.8 |
| Lettuce | 16.6 | | |

### Approximate Number of Some Tree Seeds to a Pound

| Tree seeds | Approximate number of seeds to a pound | Tree seeds | Approximate number of seeds to a pound |
|---|---|---|---|
| Apple | 12,000 | Norway Maple | 7,231 |
| Cherry (pits) | 1,000 | Sugar Maple | 7,488 |
| Peach | 200 | Red Cedar | 8,321 |
| Pear | 15,000 | White Ash | 9,858 |
| Plum | 600 | Osage Orange | 10,656 |
| Quince | 15,000 | Box Elder | 14,784 |
| Mulberry | 200,000 | Catalpa | 19,776 |
| Butternut | 15 | Ailanthus | 20,161 |
| Black Walnut | 25 | White Pine | 20,540 |
| Hickory | 78 | Red Maple | 22,464 |
| Chestnut | 90 | Green Ash | 22,656 |
| Silver Maple | 2,421 | Black Locust | 28,992 |
| Honey Locust | 2,496 | Slippery Elm | 54,359 |
| Black Cherry | 4,311 | American Elm | 92,352 |
| Black Ash | 5,629 | Mountain-ash | 108,327 |
| Linden | 6,337 | | |

* Special articles on the subjects indicated by an asterisk (*) will be found at the words so marked.

## Viability of Seeds

While some seeds, under specialized conditions, will hold their germinating power for many years, the average period is rather short. All tales of seeds from Egyptian mummies still holding the power to germinate are false. The extreme viability of wheat is about 30 years, usually far less. The average and extreme longevity of some typical garden plants are as follows:

| | Average: in years | Extreme: in years |
|---|---|---|
| Angelica | 1 or 2 | 3 |
| Anise | 3 | 5 |
| Asparagus Bean | 3 | 8 |
| Balm | 4 | 7 |
| Basil | 8 | 10+ |
| Bean | 3 | 8 |
| Beet | 6 | 10+ |
| Borage | 8 | 10+ |
| Broccoli | 5 | 10 |
| Cabbage | 5 | 10 |
| Caraway | 3 | 4 |
| Cardoon | 7 | 9 |
| Carrot | 4 or 5 | 10+ |
| Cauliflower | 5 | 10 |
| Celery | 8 | 10 |
| Chervil | 2 or 3 | 6 |
| Chicory | 8 | 10+ |
| Coriander | 6 | 8 |
| Corn | 2 | 4 |
| Cucumber | 10 | 10+ |
| Dandelion | 2 | 5 |
| Dill | 3 | 5 |
| Eggplant | 6 | 10+ |
| Endive | 10 | 10+ |
| Fennel, Common or Wild | 4 | 7 |
| Fennel, Sweet | 4 | 7 |
| Gourds | 6 | 10+ |
| Hop | 2 | 4 |
| Horehound | 3 | 6 |
| Hyssop | 3 | 5 |
| Kohlrabi | 5 | 10 |
| Leek | 3 | 9 |
| Lettuce | 5 | 9 |
| Lovage | 3 | 4 |
| Marjoram, Sweet | 3 | 7 |
| Marjoram, Winter | 5 | 7 |
| Muskmelon | 5 | 10+ |
| Mustard | 4 | 9 |
| Nasturtium, Tall | 5 | 5 |
| Nasturtium, Dwarf | 5 | 8 |
| Okra | 5 | 10+ |
| Onion | 2 | 7 |
| Orach | 6 | 7 |
| Parsley | 3 | 9 |
| Parsnip | 2 | 4 |
| Pea | 3 | 8 |
| Pepper | 4 | 7 |
| Pumpkin | 4 or 5 | 9 |
| Purslane | 7 | 10 |
| Radish | 5 | 10+ |
| Rhubarb | 3 | 8 |
| Rosemary | 4 | (?) |
| Rue | 2 | 5 |
| Sage | 3 | 7 |
| Salsify | 2 | 8 |
| Savory, Summer | 3 | 7 |
| Savory, Winter | 3 | 6 |
| Spinach | 5 | 7 |
| Spinach, New Zealand | 5 | 8 |
| Squash | 6 | 10+ |
| Strawberry | 3 | 6 |
| Tansy | 2 | 4 |
| Thyme | 3 | 7 |
| Tomato | 4 | 9 |
| Turnip | 5 | 10+ |
| Watermelon | 6 | 10 |

## Average Percentage of Vegetable Seed Usually Germinating under Ordinary Garden Conditions

| Kind of seed | Per cent | Kind of seed | Per cent |
|---|---|---|---|
| Artichoke | 70 | Okra | 70 |
| Asparagus | 80 | Onion | 75 |
| Beans | 85 | Parsley | 60 |
| Beets | 70 | Parsnip | 65 |
| Cabbage | 80 | Peas | 85 |
| Carrot | 70 | Pepper | 60 |
| Cauliflower | 70 | Pumpkin | 75 |
| Celery | 60 | Radish | 85 |
| Chicory | 70 | Rutabaga | 80 |
| Cress | 70 | Salsify | 70 |
| Cucumber | 80 | Spinach | 65 |
| Eggplant | 65 | Squash | 80 |
| Endive | 75 | Sweet Corn | 80 |
| Kale | 70 | Swiss Chard | 75 |
| Kohlrabi | 75 | Tomato | 75 |
| Lettuce | 75 | Turnip | 80 |

### III

## Tree Statistics are Grouped under Three Heads
### Average Height of Some Mature Trees under Reasonably Good Culture

| | Height in feet |
|---|---|
| White pine (*Pinus strobus*) | 70 |
| Pitch pine (*Pinus rigida*) | 40 |
| Austrian pine (*Pinus nigra*) | 70 |
| Scotch pine (*Pinus sylvestris*) | 75 |
| Larch (*Larix laricina*) | 50 |
| White spruce (*Picea glauca*) | 60 |
| Blue spruce (*Picea pungens*) | 50 |
| Douglas fir (*Pseudotsuga taxifolia*) | 150 |
| Balsam (*Abies balsamea*) | 40 |
| Cilician fir (*Abies cilicica*) | 60 |
| Hemlock (*Tsuga canadensis*) | 60 |
| Arborvitae (*Thuja occidentalis*) | 40 |
| Red cedar (*Juniperus virginiana*) | 35 |
| Redwood (*Sequoia sempervirens*) | 250 |
| Big Tree (*Sequoia gigantea*) | 220 |
| Ginkgo (*Ginkgo biloba*) | 70 |
| White poplar (*Populus alba*) | 50 |
| Aspen (*Populus tremuloides*) | 35 |
| Balm of Gilead (*Populus candicans*) | 45 |
| Lombardy poplar (*Populus nigra italica*) | 70 |
| Butternut (*Juglans cinerea*) | 30 |
| Walnut (*Juglans nigra*) | 60 |
| English walnut (*Juglans regia*) | 70 |
| Hop-hornbeam (*Ostrya virginiana*) | 30 |
| Ironwood (*Carpinus caroliniana*) | 25 |
| Black birch (*Betula lenta*) | 60 |
| Yellow birch (*Betula lutea*) | 75 |
| Paper birch (*Betula papyrifera*) | 60 |
| American beech (*Fagus grandifolia*) | 65 |
| European beech (*Fagus sylvatica*) | 75 |
| White oak (*Quercus alba*) | 65 |
| Bur oak (*Quercus macrocarpa*) | 60 |
| Swamp white oak (*Quercus bicolor*) | 50 |
| Chestnut oak (*Quercus montana*) | 45 |
| Red oak (*Quercus rubra*) | 70 |
| Pin oak (*Quercus palustris*) | 45 |
| Scarlet oak (*Quercus coccinea*) | 45 |
| Black oak (*Quercus velutina*) | 60 |
| Slippery elm (*Ulmus fulva*) | 50 |
| English elm (*Ulmus campestris*) | 70 |
| American elm (*Ulmus americana*) | 85 |
| Hackberry (*Celtis occidentalis*) | 30 |
| Red mulberry (*Morus rubra*) | 30 |
| White mulberry (*Morus alba*) | 35 |
| Cucumber tree (*Magnolia acuminata*) | 45 |
| Umbrella tree (*Magnolia tripetala*) | 25 |
| Tulip-tree (*Liriodendron tulipifera*) | 65 |

*Special articles on the subjects indicated by an asterisk (*) will be found at the words so marked.

## Tree Statistics, continued

| | Height in feet |
|---|---|
| Sassafras (*Sassafras variifolium*) | 45 |
| Sweet gum (*Liquidambar styraciflua*) | 50 |
| Plane tree (*Platanus occidentalis*) | 75 |
| London plane (*Platanus acerifolia*) | 60 |
| Black cherry (*Prunus serotina*) | 40 |
| Common cherry (*Prunus avium*) | 50 |
| Sour cherry (*Prunus cerasus*) | 30 |
| Peach (*Amygalus persica*) | 15 |
| Honey locust (*Gleditsia triacanthos*) | 50 |
| Locust (*Robinia pseudo-acacia*) | 30 |
| Ailanthus (*Ailanthus glandulosa*) | 60 |
| Eucalyptus (various species) | 30–250 |
| Sugar maple (*Acer saccharum*) | 75 |
| Silver maple (*Acer saccharinum*) | 55 |
| Red maple (*Acer rubrum*) | 50 |
| Norway maple (*Acer platanoides*) | 50 |
| Sycamore maple (*Acer pseudo-platanus*) | 50 |
| Box elder (*Acer negundo*) | 45 |
| Horse-chestnut (*Aesculus hippocastanum*) | 65 |
| American linden (*Tilia glabra*) | 70 |
| European linden (*Tilia vulgaris*) | 75 |
| Flowering dogwood (*Cornus florida*) | 25 |
| Black gum (*Nyssa sylvatica*) | 45 |
| White ash (*Fraxinus americana*) | 60 |
| Black ash (*Fraxinus nigra*) | 70 |
| Catalpa (*Catalpa speciosa*) | 50 |
| Paulownia (*Paulownia tomentosa*) | 60 |

### Age or Average Longevity of Trees

The big trees of Calif., the ahuehuete, and the Dragon tree of the Canary Islands may well be among the oldest of living things, certainly 2000–3000 years old. But most ordinary trees are far younger when disease or old age overtakes them. Not many accurate records have been kept of cultivated trees, but a few are known, at least for fruit trees and a few ornamental species.

| | Years | | Years |
|---|---|---|---|
| Apple | 40–100 | Peach | 8–12 |
| Beech | 200–400 | Pear | 50–75 |
| Citrus | 50–60 | Persimmon | 25–40 |
| Cryptomeria | 300–700 | Plum | 20–25 |
| Olive | 300–600 (some known to be over 1500 years) | White oak | 300–700 |
| | | Yew | 200–800 |

### Rate of Growth of Some Commonly Planted Trees

The following, if given reasonably good care, and assuming that they were each planted as saplings of 3 in. in diameter, should, in 20 years, have the following diameters:

| | Inches | | Inches |
|---|---|---|---|
| White elm | 19 | Red maple | 16 |
| Plane tree | 18 | Silver maple | 21 |
| Tulip-tree | 18 | Sugar maple | 13 |
| Linden | 17 | Horse-chestnut | 13 |
| Catalpa | 16 | Red oak | 13 |
| Ailanthus | 16 | Pin oak | 13 |
| Cucumber tree | 15 | Scarlet oak | 13 |
| Chestnut | 14 | White oak | 12 |
| Common locust | 14 | White ash | 12 |
| Honey locust | 13 | Hackberry | 10 |

### How to Estimate the Height of Trees

While professional foresters use an instrument known as a hypsometer for measuring the exact height of a tree without putting a tape-measure on it, the gardener or landscape architect is often satisfied with a reasonably close approximation of the true height, which can be determined with no more equipment than a yardstick and the sun.

1. Measure the exact distance from the trunk to the extremity of the shadow of the tree (on level ground, if possible).
2. At the extremity of the shadow stand a yardstick (3 ft.) as nearly erect as possible.
3. Measure the exact length of the *shadow* of the yardstick, which, of course, projects beyond the shadow of the tip of the tree.
4. Divide the length of the tree shadow by the length of the yardstick shadow and multiply by 3, which gives the height of the tree.

*Example:* A tree throws a shadow 20 ft. long; the shadow of the yardstick is 4 ft. 20 divided by 4 = 5 ft. × 3 = 15 ft., which is the height of the tree.

## IV
### Number of Plants for Round, Oval, or Rectangular Flower Beds
#### Plants Needed for a Round or Circular Bed

| Diameter of bed | Plants 6 in. apart | Plants 12 in. apart | Plants 18 in. apart | Plants 24 in. apart | Plants 30 in. apart |
|---|---|---|---|---|---|
| 3 feet | 28 | 7 | .. | .. | .. |
| 4 feet | 48 | 12 | 6 | .. | .. |
| 5 feet | 80 | 20 | 8 | .. | .. |
| 6 feet | 112 | 28 | 13 | 7 | .. |
| 7 feet | 152 | 38 | 17 | 9 | .. |
| 8 feet | 200 | 50 | 23 | 12 | .. |
| 9 feet | 256 | 64 | 28 | 16 | .. |
| 10 feet | 320 | 80 | 36 | 20 | 13 |
| 11 feet | 380 | 95 | 42 | 24 | 16 |
| 12 feet | 452 | 113 | 50 | 28 | 18 |
| 13 feet | 528 | 132 | 59 | 33 | 22 |
| 14 feet | 612 | 153 | 68 | 39 | 25 |
| 15 feet | 704 | 176 | 78 | 44 | 28 |
| 16 feet | 804 | 201 | 89 | 50 | 32 |
| 17 feet | 904 | 226 | 100 | 57 | 36 |
| 18 feet | 1016 | 254 | 113 | 63 | 40 |
| 19 feet | 1132 | 283 | 126 | 71 | 46 |
| 20 feet | 1256 | 314 | 139 | 78 | 50 |

#### Plants Needed for an Oval Bed

Assuming that the bed is a perfect oval, *add* the breadth and length of the bed and *divide* by 2. The result is exactly the same as though the bed were round and the above table for round beds should then be used.

*Example:* An oval bed is 9 × 7 ft.
Add 9 + 7 = 16, which divided by 2 = 8.
Use the table for a round bed 8 ft. in diameter.

#### Plants Needed for a Rectangular Bed (Square or Oblong)

1. Determine the exact area of the bed.
2. Determine what fraction of an acre (*see* Weights and Measures) the bed may be.
3. Use the table at I (Plants per Acre) to see how many plants will be needed for your fraction of an acre.

A somewhat simpler, but not so accurate method is illustrated thus:

A rectangular bed is 12 × 10 ft. and plants are to be 6 in. apart and 6 in. from all edges.
Along the 12 ft. edge 23 plants will be needed.
Multiply this by the 19 needed along the 10 ft. edge
19 × 23 = 437 plants.

**GARDEN TOOLS.** *See* Tools and Implements.

**GARDEN VIOLET** = *Viola odorata*.

**GARDEN WALLS.** *See* Walls and Wall Gardening.

*GARGANICA, -us, -um* (gar-gan'i-ka). From or near Gargano, Italy.

**GARLAND CRABAPPLE** = *Malus coronaria*.

---

* Special articles on the subjects indicated by an asterisk (*) will be found at the words so marked.

**GARLAND-FLOWER** = *Hedychium coronarium* and *Daphne cneorum*.

**GARLAND HEATH** = *Erica subdivaricata*.

**GARLIC** (*Allium sativum*). The dried bulblets or cloves* of an onion-like plant, familiar enough as sold in (mostly Italian) vegetable shops, where they hang in dried braids. For culture see HERB GARDENING.

**GARNISHES.** See Cooking with Herbs at HERB GARDENING.

**GARRYA** (gă'ri-a). A small genus and the only one of the family **Garryaceae** (ga-ri-ā'see-ee), comprising perhaps 15 species of evergreen shrubs chiefly from the western part of N.A., and sometimes cult. for ornament. The only species of much garden interest is **G. elliptica**, the silk-tassel tree, which is also called tassel-tree or quinine bush (it does not yield quinine). It is a hairy-branched shrub up to 6 ft. high. Leaves opposite,* without marginal teeth, leathery, elliptic or oblong, 2–3 in. long and densely hairy beneath. Male and female flowers on different plants, without petals, and in catkin*-like, rather long clusters (racemes*). Sepals 4. Stamens 4. Fruit a nearly round, velvety berry. Jan.–March. Hardy only in the region from Ore. to Calif., and not particularly handsome. (Named for Nicholas Garry, secretary of the Hudson's Bay Company.)

**GARRYACEAE.** See GARRYA.

**GAS INJURY.** Common illuminating gas is death to most plants, if in concentrations sufficient to be detected by odor, and sometimes in concentrations so minute that no one can smell it. One of the constituents of illuminating gas is ethylene, which, strangely enough, may actually stimulate the growth of some plants. One part of ethylene in two million parts of air, a concentration too weak to be detected chemically, will force the stamens of carnations to protrude, thus making the blooms unfit for sale.

From a practical garden standpoint the chief danger from gas is from leaky pipes, especially where street trees are near them. Sometimes the first warning will be a sudden yellowing of leaves, much too rapid to be the result of a fungous pest. Prompt stopping of the leak is the only remedy. If it is allowed to go on, the plants will certainly be killed.

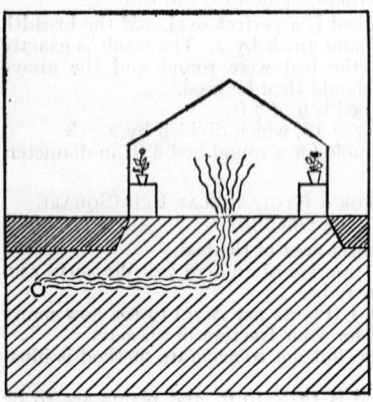

Escaping gas, held down by frozen surface soil, leaking through the warm soil of a near-by greenhouse. This and tree injury are the most serious effects of leaky gas mains.

Another example of the danger of leaking gas is that under frozen ground. It will often seep along below the frozen layer and come up through the unfrozen soil in a greenhouse. At the slightest hint of such trouble it is best to bring into the greenhouse a few potted tomato plants. They are more sensitive to gas poisoning than almost anything else. If enough tomato plants are scattered about the greenhouse, it is usually possible to localize the trouble, for the plants will show discoloration or droop within a few hours in a gas leakage so slight that no one can smell it. See the note at TOMATO.

*GASIPAES* (gă'si-peez). Latinized form of gachipaes, a tropical American native name for the palm *Guilielma gasipaes*.

**GAS-PLANT** = *Dictamnus albus*.

**GASTERIA** (gas-steer'ri-a). South African desert plants of the lily family, suitable for desert gardens outdoors in Calif. and the Southwest, the two below also grown for interest or ornament in the greenhouse. Of the 50 known species, several are grown by fanciers, the two below most commonly. They are essentially stemless plants with a dense, basal rosette of thick, 2-ranked, often dotted leaves. Flowers greenish, but the tips red or pink, in rather loose, lax clusters (racemes*). Corolla with a curved tube, swollen at the base. Fruit a capsule. (*Gasteria* is from the Greek for belly, in allusion to the swollen flower.)

The gasterias are aloe-like plants, but smaller, and need the same culture. See ALOE. See also SUCCULENTS.

*acinacifolia.* Leaves very fleshy, 8–12 in. long, about 2 in. wide, not much dotted, more or less 3-edged. Flower cluster nearly 4 ft. long, sometimes branched, the flowers about 2 in. long, not much inflated.

*verrucosa.* Leaves 4–6 in. long, about ¾ in. wide, the surface conspicuously white-dotted, more or less 3-sided. Flower cluster about 2 ft. long, usually unbranched, the flowers pink, about 1 in. long, swollen. The most popular species in cult. and a good house plant. There are several varieties, mostly differing in the shape or wartiness of the leaves.

**GATES AND GATEWAYS.** A gateway is an opening in a wall or enclosure, made for purposes of entrance and exit, and capable of being closed with a barrier. A gate is the barrier which closes a gateway. Generally, the term "gate" is used to indicate the opening, together with its barrier, as one unit.

A gate has two, double functions: one, to exclude and retain; the other, to permit access and egress. Where privacy is desired, the gate should clearly express its function of exclusion, by its narrowness, by its height, or by the strength and solidity of its construction. These same characteristics will also serve to hold one's attention within the enclosed area and prevent it from wandering to some less pleasing area beyond. Such a gateway is eminently suited to the walled city garden, adjacent to a street or service walk, or to any similar situation where it is desirable to avoid intrusion from without and to limit one's perceptions to the pleasant area within. Inherent in any gateway is a slight suggestion of discrimination, a hint that someone or something is to be excluded, but in many situations this feeling should be subdued until the dominant note is one of welcome — beckoning one onward. Such a character is suitable to the entrance gateway of a country home where hospitality is the keynote of daily life, or to the gateway between a quiet garden and a woodland walk, where the essential spirit of the two areas is very similar, and an interruption in transition from one to the other undesirable. A generous width of opening, a light and open gate structure, or even the use of piers without any actual barrier will give the gateway the character here desired. Between these two extremes of openness and guarded seclusion there are gradations of feeling which may be expressed in gate design.

A simple but effective garden gate of iron

It is desirable that the gate be in character with the wall, fence or hedge in which it forms a passage, the gate and enclosure combining in a harmonious unit. Both should express the character of the area enclosed. An entrance gateway should conform in feeling to the house to which it gives access. It should be simple and unpretentious if it leads to a small, unassuming house, but given a dignified architec-

* Special articles on the subjects indicated by an asterisk (*) will be found at the words so marked.

tural treatment if it leads to a large, imposing building. Often the same structural materials are used in the entrance gate as in the house itself, creating a harmony of relationship between the two. A garden gateway may be delicately graceful, severely architectural, rugged, or rustic, depending upon the character of the garden itself. Occasionally the gateway may be given something of the character of each of two areas between which it forms a connecting link, suggesting slightly some pleasing quality of each.

A high wall and a wooden gate, suitable for screening an entrance court or service yard from the garden

While it would be absurd to place a gate where it could not possibly have any real use, it may nevertheless be employed in situations where its decorative qualities far overshadow its actual usefulness as an exit or barrier. An enclosed garden with but a simple means of entrance and exit would create in the mind a disturbing sense of confinement. But a gateway at the far end, while it might seldom be used as an exit, would give a feeling of spaciousness and freedom, and at the same time could be made a dominant decorative feature. A gate can be successfully used as the terminus of a garden or as the terminus of a minor-, or cross-axis. It may close the end of an allée* or serve as the frame for a vista.* Sometimes its chief purpose is to relieve a blank expanse of wall, its open grille-work contrasting pleasantly with the wall's smooth, unbroken surface.

There is an almost limitless variety of forms which a gate may take, depending upon the function to be served and the materials used in its construction. The latter should be chosen with due regard to the former, but necessity for economy is sometimes an influential factor.

Gates may be high or low, single or double, depend-

An inviting wooden garden gate, effective because of the arch and planting

ing upon function and proportional relationship to walls, etc. The materials chiefly employed in their construction are wood and iron. Wooden gates may be of either solid or open construction. They may be plain or they may be decorated with pickets, panels, moldings, perforations, lattice-work, spindles, or applied iron work. Iron gates may be extremely simple or they may assume the infinitely varied and complicated forms peculiar to wrought-iron work. Gates may also have supporting posts or piers of wood, brick, stone, or iron work. These likewise may be plain, or may be decorated with such ornaments as caps, moldings, tiles, finials, or sculptured figures and escutcheons.

Careful thought and good taste can do much to achieve suitability and harmony of design in a gateway, but for best results the advice of a trained designer is indispensable. — A. F. and B. J. L.

**GAULTHERIA** (gaul-theer′ri-a). Beautiful evergreen shrubs (one herb-like) of the family Ericaceae, most of the 100 species from the Andes, a few from eastern As. and the two below North American. They are low or prostrate plants with usually alternate,* toothed leaves. Flowers solitary in the leaf-axils* in *G. procumbens*, but in small, terminal clusters in *G. shallon*. Calyx* ultimately becomes fleshy, colored and enclosing the fruit, which is really a capsule, although the fruit is apparently berry-like. Corolla urn-shaped. Stamens 10. (Named for a Doctor Gaultier, a physician in Quebec.)

Both the plants below need a decidedly acid soil and are best grown in sandy soils in the rock garden, preferably in partial shade. They do not transplant easily, and it is better to plant potted specimens than to attempt transferring them from the wild. They may be propagated by cuttings of half-ripened wood, or by seeds sown in peaty sand under a hand glass. But the seeds are extremely minute and hard to handle.

**procumbens.** The common wintergreen of our dry woods; called also checkerberry, teaberry, and spiceberry. A prostrate, herb-like, evergreen, woody plant, the stems half underground, the tips upright and about 4 in. high. Leaves ovalish, about 1¾ in. long, the marginal teeth often bristly. Flower solitary, nodding, white or pinkish, about ¼ in. long. Fruit scarlet, pea-size. N.A. May–July. Hardy everywhere. See also HERB GARDENING.

**shallon.** Salal. A Pacific Coast, evergreen shrub, more or less spreading and not over 18 in. high. Leaves round-oval, 3–5 in. long. Flower cluster terminal, 2–5 in. long, the corolla pink or white, about ½ in. long. Fruit purplish-black, nearly ½ in. in diameter. Alaska to Calif. May–June. Hardy from zone* 4 southward, but chiefly suited to the rock garden.

**GAURA** (gau′ra). Perhaps 25 species of rather coarse, chiefly perennial, North American herbs of the family Onagraceae, the two below somewhat grown for ornament in the more informal border. They are stout herbs with alternate* leaves and white or pink, summer-blooming flowers in terminal clusters (spikes or racemes*). Calyx* tubular below, but its 4 lobes separate and bent backward. Petals slightly unequal, separate, the base narrowed into a claw.* Fruit 4–5-ribbed, nut-like. (*Gaura* is from the Greek for superb.)

Both species are of the easiest culture in any ordinary garden soil, and are readily increased by spring or fall division. The first species is more hardy than *G. lindheimeri*, which needs a mulch north of zone* 5.

**coccinea.** Wild honeysuckle (not a true honeysuckle). A perennial herb 12–30 in. high. Leaves oblongish, about 1 in. long. Flowers about ½ in. long, pink, red, or white. S. Dak. to Mex.

**lindheimeri.** A perennial herb 2–4 ft. high and bushy. Leaves lance-shaped, 1½–3½ in. long, stalkless, and more or less hairy. Flowers about ¾ in. long, white. La. to Tex.

**GAY-FEATHER** = *Liatris scariosa* and *L. spicata*.

**GAYLUSSACIA.** See HUCKLEBERRY.

**GAY ORCHIS** = *Orchis spectabilis*.

**GAY-WINGS** = *Polygala paucifolia*.

**GAZANIA** (ga-zay′ni-a). Showy, South African flower garden herbs of the daisy family, comprising about two dozen species, a few long cult. for their handsome flower heads. Leaves alternate,* but the plants often nearly stemless and the leaves thus basal. Flower heads solitary, long-

---

* Special articles on the subjects indicated by an asterisk (*) will be found at the words so marked.

stalked, day-blooming, but closing at night or in cloudy weather. Rays yellow, golden, or white (in ours), often with a dark spot at the base, the head thus with a dark eye.* (Named for Theodore of Gaza, a translator of Theophrastus.)

*Gazania longiscapa* is a fine, summer-blooming plant, best treated as a tender annual. (See ANNUALS.) The other two are perennials, not quite hardy north of zone* 5 without mulching. In the South they may bloom nearly all year. Propagated by division, or by cuttings of basal shoots taken in Aug. and rooted in sand. They are sometimes called African daisy.

**longiscapa.** Practically stalkless. Leaves more or less deeply cut, feather-fashion, felty-white beneath. Flower heads golden-yellow, dark-eyed, the flower stalk smooth, 6–8 in. long.

**rigens.** A perennial herb, the stems leafy, short, and branched. Leaves spatula-shaped, felty-white beneath. Flower heads about 1½ in. wide, the stalk smooth, the rays* orange, but with a white-eyed black spot near the base.

**splendens.** Perhaps a hybrid plant and unknown in the wild. An erect perennial 9–18 in. high, the leaves silky, and very narrow. Flower heads large and showy, the rays orange, but with a black and white spot at the base.

**GAZEBO.** See STRUCTURES.

**GEIGER TREE** = *Cordia sebestena*.

**GELSEMIUM** (gel-see′mi-um). Two (or perhaps three) evergreen, woody vines of the family Loganiaceae, one Asiatic, the other, G. sempervirens, of the southeastern U.S., and famous as the Carolina or yellow jasmine, although it is not the true jasmine (see JASMINUM). It is a beautiful vine, climbing 10–20 ft. high, the leaves usually opposite,* oblongish, 2½–4 in. long and shining. Flowers bright yellow, very fragrant, in a dense cluster (cyme*) usually in the leaf-axil.* Corolla funnel-shaped, about 1 in. long. Stamens 5, alternating with the 5 short lobes of the corolla. Fruit a flattened, short-beaked pod (capsule*) about ¾ in. long, its seeds winged. This beautiful porch-climbing vine, very popular from Charleston southward, can be grown in any ordinary garden soil, and can be propagated by seeds or cuttings. It is not hardy north of zone* 6. (*Gelsemium* is a Latinized version of *gelsomino*, the Italian for jasmine.)

*GEMINIFLORA*, *-us*, *-um* (jem-i-ni-flow′ra). Twin- or several-flowered.

*GEMINISPINA*, *-us*, *-um* (jem-i-ni-spy′na). Twin- or several-spined.

*GEMMIFERA*, *-us*, *-um* (jem-mif′er-ra). Bearing buds.

**GENE.** The unit of inheritance, sometimes called a factor or determiner. It is the lowest amount that hereditary material is ordinarily divided into and corresponds somewhat to the chemical atom. Genes may differ in size, and they are contained in the chromosomes in linear arrangements.

**GENERA.** Plural of genus (which see).

**GENERAL WASHINGTON.** For the trees he planted, see Mount Vernon at TREES.

**GENETICS.** See HEREDITY.

*GENEVENSIS*, *-e* (je-nee-ven′sis). From Geneva, Switzerland.

**GENIP** = *Genipa americana* and *Melicocca bijuga*.

**GENIPA** (jen′i-pa). A small genus of chiefly West Indian shrubs or trees of the family Rubiaceae, one, **G. americana,** the genip or genipap, somewhat grown in extreme southern Fla. for its edible fruits. It is not hardy north of zone* 9. It is a tree 30–50 ft. high, with opposite,* short-stalked, leathery, oblongish leaves that are nearly 12 in. long. Flowers yellowish-white, in few-flowered cymes.* Corolla salver-shaped, about 1 in. wide, its 5–6 blunt lobes slightly twisted to the left. Fruit a russet-brown berry about 2½ in. in diameter with large, dark brown seeds. The tree, sometimes called marmalade box, is popular in the tropics, but not much known in the U.S. It needs heat and moisture for proper growth. The juicy fruit is largely used for preserves or in making beverages. (*Genipa* is the Brazilian vernacular for the tree.)

**GENIPAP** = *Genipa americana*.

**GENISTA** (je-niss′ta). Low, rather handsome, often evergreen or nearly leafless shrubs of the pea family, all from temperate or mild regions of the Old World, and comprising over 100 species. Of these only those below are much cult. in this country, and some are not hardy northward. While some of them are called broom, the common broom is a *Cytisus* (see BROOM), and the common genista of the florists is *Cytisus canariensis* (see BROOM). The genus name *Genista* is properly applied to the plants below. They are sometimes spiny, usually green-barked shrubs with compound* leaves, the leaflets often reduced to one (rarely 3), and without teeth. Flowers typically pea-like, yellow or white, usually borne in terminal clusters (racemes* or heads*), rarely in the leaf-axils.* Fruit a longish, flattened pod (legume*), usually several-seeded. (*Genista* is the classical Latin name of these plants.)

The shrubs do well in dry, open places, but they do not transplant easily and should not be moved when once established. They can be increased by seeds or by layering.*

**hispanica.** Spanish broom. A densely branched, spiny, often leafless shrub, not over 18 in. high, usually less. Leaflet one, ovalish, about ½ in. long, often soon deciduous.* Flowers golden-yellow, in a dense head of 2–10 blooms. Pod hairy. Southern Eu. May–June. Hardy from zone* 4 southward. The *var.* **nana** is about half as high.

**monosperma.** A nearly leafless shrub 3–8 ft. high. Flowers fragrant, white, in clusters in the leaf-axils. Spain and northern Africa. March–April. Hardy from zone* 6 southward. Little known in this country.

**pilosa.** Prostrate and warty, the leaflets one, oblongish, scarcely ½ in. long. Flowers yellow in sparse clusters in the leaf-axils. Pod nearly 1½ in. long, silky. Southern Eu. May–July. Hardy from zone* 4 southward.

**sagittalis.** Nearly prostrate shrub, chiefly suited to the rock garden, its branches 2-winged. Leaflets one, ovalish or narrower, nearly 1 in. long. Flowers yellow, in terminal clusters. Eurasia. June. Hardy from zone* 4 southward. For culture see ROCK GARDEN.

**tinctoria.** Woadwaxen (or woodwaxen); called also dyer's greenweed, and the best known species in cult. It is an upright shrub 24–36 in. high, with a single leaflet to each leaf. Leaflets oblongish, ½–1½ in. long, smooth, but fringed with hair on the margin. Flowers yellow, in profuse clusters. Pod narrow-oblong, often slightly hairy. Eurasia. June–Aug. Hardy from zone* 3 southward. There are several hort. forms, mostly varying in habit, some of them dwarf. The *var.* **plena** has double flowers.

**GENTIAN.** See GENTIANA.

**GENTIANA** (jen-she-ā′na). The gentians comprise a genus of perhaps 300 species of herbs, family Gentianaceae, some of them choice plants for the rock garden, border, or wild garden, and all of them needing somewhat specialized culture. While most of them are perennials, a few, like our fringed gentian, are biennials, and some are annuals. They are chiefly plants of cool, moist regions, especially mountain meadows and some on alpine summits. Leaves opposite,* rarely in 3's, stalkless in the main, and without marginal teeth. Flowers showy, often solitary or in few-flowered clusters, prevailingly blue, but occasionally purple, yellow, or white. Corolla 4–5-lobed, often with teeth between the lobes, which in some (the fringed gentian) are beautifully fringed. Stamens 5, inserted in the tube of the corolla. Fruit a capsule.* (Named for King Gentius of Illyria, who is credited with faith in the medicinal value of gentians.)

Cultural directions are difficult because the plants have such diverse habitat preferences. Those suited to the rock, wild, or bog garden are specified below and their culture should be sought at ROCK GARDEN or BOG GARDEN or WILD GARDEN. For the others there are special cultural notes. See also BLUE GARDEN.

**acaulis.** A perennial rock garden plant and the common blue gentian of European mountains. Not usually over 4 in. high, with elliptic or narrower leaves. Flower solitary, deep blue, about 2 in. long, sometimes spotted inside. Mountains of the Alps and Pyrenees. Summer. For its forms, or perhaps species, and their culture, see ROCK GARDEN.

**andrewsi.** Closed gentian, or bottle gentian. A North American perennial herb 12–20 in. high. Leaves ovalish or narrower, 1–2 in. long. Flowers about 1½ in. long, purplish-blue, more or less permanently closed; *i.e.* the corolla inarching and not open. Eastern N.A. Aug.–Oct. For culture see BOG GARDENING.

**asclepiadea.** A European perennial herb, 12–18 in. high and suited to the shadier parts of the herbaceous border. Leaves ovalish to lance-shaped. Flowers dark blue, about 1½ in. long, usually solitary in the leaf-axils,* or in small clusters resembling leafy racemes.* Southern Eu. Summer.

**crinita.** Fringed gentian. A beautiful biennial, North American meadow herb that is practically hopeless to dig from the wild. Leaves

---

* Special articles on the subjects indicated by an asterisk (*) will be found at the words so marked.

GENTIANACEAE 309 GEORGIA

lance-shaped or broadest towards the tip. Flowers bright blue, usually solitary and terminal, about 2 in. long and very showy, the lobes of the corolla beautifully fringed. Eastern N.A. Sept. and Oct. For culture see WILD GARDEN.

**cruciata.** A Eurasian perennial herb 4–10 in. long. Leaves ovalish or narrower. Flowers with a corolla about ¾ in. long, dark blue, usually in small clusters in the leaf-axils.* Suited to the hilly regions north of zone* 4. See BLUE GARDEN.

**farreri.** A more or less prostrate perennial herb, the ascending stems not over 4 in. high. Leaves very narrow or line-like, usually partly united at the base. Flowers deep blue, solitary, about 1½ in. long, the corolla lobes with a white or yellowish band. China. Aug.–Sept.

**linearis.** A slender bog perennial 12–20 in. high, with narrow leaves. Flowers in terminal clusters, blue or white, the corolla nearly 2 in. long. Eastern N.A. Should be grown in the bog garden (which see) or on wet, rocky ledges. Sept.

**lutea.** Yellow gentian or bitterwort. A perennial, often 3–4 ft. high, and cult. for centuries in Eu. for its bitter, tonic rootstock. Flowers yellow, about 1 in. long, the calyx resembling a small spathe.* Eu. and Asia Minor. Little grown in the U.S., but suited to the perennial border.

**pneumonanthe.** A Eurasian perennial herb 5–14 in. high, and suited to the open border. Leaves oblongish or narrower. Flowers dark blue, but green-striped on the outside, about 1½ in. long. Aug.–Sept.

**septemfida.** An Asiatic rock garden perennial, sometimes grown in the border (see BLUE GARDEN). It is erect, 9–15 in. high. Flowers dark blue, about 2 in. long, and grouped in a terminal cluster. Aug.–Sept. For culture see ROCK GARDEN.

**tibetica.** A Himalayan perennial 9–15 in. high, the leaves lance-shaped. Flowers about 1½ in. long, yellowish-white, but lilac-tinted, mostly crowded in the upper leaf-axils.* Aug. For culture see ROCK GARDEN.

**walujewi.** A rock garden perennial not over 8 in. high, the leaves elliptic or lance-shaped. Flowers whitish, but blue-dotted, usually crowded in a terminal cluster. Turkestan. Aug.–Sept. For culture see ROCK GARDEN.

**GENTIANACEAE** (jen-she-a-nay′see-ee). The gentian family, mostly herbaceous, contains 70 genera and over 700 widely distributed species of often showy plants, but few of the genera are much known in the garden. Two of them, *Menyanthes* and *Nymphoides*, are aquatic or bog plants, sometimes, but not here, considered as belonging to a separate family, the Menyanthaceae. Both have alternate* leaves.

Leaves otherwise opposite,* without marginal teeth. Flowers usually showy, often grouped in cymes,* the corolla more or less tubular or spreading, sometimes beautifully fringed (see GENTIANA). Fruit a 2-valved pod (capsule*).

Less than a dozen genera are of garden interest. *Centaurium* consists of mostly annual herbs. *Eustoma* is the Canada pest and attractive in spite of its name. *Exacum* contains Old World herbs not hardy in cold regions; *Frasera* contains the columbo; while *Sabbatia* is mostly confined to salt marshes. Of all the cult. genera *Gentiana* is by far the most important, many of the species being rare and interesting plants from mountain meadows and summits.

Technical flower characters: Corolla regular, 4–5-lobed (more in *Sabbatia*). Calyx 4–12-parted, often persistent. Stamens 4–12, inserted on the corolla. Ovary superior,* 1-celled or rarely 2-celled, with numerous ovules.

**GENTIAN FAMILY** = Gentianaceae.

*GENTIANOIDES* (jen-she-a-noy′deez, but see OÏDES). Gentian-like.

**GENUS** (plural, genera). The simplest grouping or category of plants, so classified because they are more like each other than like any other group. Common examples are *Rosa* (genus name for all the roses), *Quercus* (genus name for the oaks). No one needs to be confused by the use of such generic names for an easily recognized category of plants, but many gardeners and all beginners are apt to confuse genus and species.

A genus is a group of species (which see), linked together by usually obvious, but sometimes rather puzzling, botanical characters. To take a simple illustration: the genus name of the larkspur is *Delphinium*, a generic name properly printed in italics and with a capital *D*. This typography for genus names is followed throughout THE GARDEN DICTIONARY (unless the generic name is the usual bold-face entry word or a cross-reference). To this genus *Delphinium* belong all the larkspurs, each one of which is a separate species. In THE GARDEN DICTIONARY there are eight species of larkspur noted under *Delphinium*, but as in most reference works, the name *Delphinium* is not repeated at each of the eight, but it is understood to cover all of them. Also, as in practically all reference works, *Delphinium* is abbreviated to *D*. after the first use of the full name.

Some genera have only a single species. Common examples of such monotypic genera, as they are called, are *Sanguinaria*, which contains only the single species *canadensis*, the bloodroot. Another is *Chamaedaphne*, with only the species *calyculata*, or leatherleaf. But most genera have several or many species, and some are enormous (see CAREX, SOLANUM, EUPHORBIA, and CRATAEGUS).

In THE GARDEN DICTIONARY there are over 1700 genera of sufficient hort. interest to demand inclusion, but there are thousands of other genera of ferns and flowering plants known in the world.

Another feature of generic names that sometimes leads to confusion is the type in which they are printed when they have become so common that everyone uses them as the common name of the plant. Examples are *Rhododendron* (a generic name) and rhododendron (the common name for these plants). There are many other such generic names, of which a few are:

*Aster* and aster.
*Chrysanthemum* and chrysanthemum.
*Cosmos* and cosmos.
*Delphinium* and delphinium.

This difference in typography between generic names and common ones derived from the genus is maintained throughout THE GARDEN DICTIONARY. See also SPECIES, PLANT NAMES, PLANT FAMILY.

*GEOMETRIZANS* (jee-o-met′ri-zans). In a geometrical pattern.

**GEORGE PEABODY ARBORVITAE** = *Thuja occidentalis lutea*.

**GEORGE WASHINGTON.** For the trees he planted, see Mount Vernon at TREES.

**GEORGIA.** The state lies wholly in zones* 6 and 7.

SOILS. Georgia is roughly divided into the Limestone Valley of northwest Georgia, the mountainous or northern section, the Piedmont Plateau or north central portion, and the Coastal Plain or south central and southern section.

The soils of the mountainous section are typically mountain soils, with rich, loamy valleys and draws. There is a section in northwest Georgia known as the Limestone Valley section. The Piedmont is typified by the red Cecil clays and Cecil clay loams. The southern or Coastal Plain region is generally level and typified by sandy soils and Palmetto flats near the coast.

CHIEF GARDENING CENTERS. The chief gardening centers are Athens and Atlanta in the upper central section, Macon in central Georgia, and Savannah on the Atlantic Coast. The mountainous section of Georgia is the site of a thriving and productive apple industry, which fact is not generally known in other parts of the country. Displays of Georgia-grown apples usually rank surprisingly high or near the top when shown in competition at various apple shows.

The peach is the fruit that has rightfully made Georgia famous. There is quite an acreage of peaches in the upper Piedmont. However, the bulk of the production is from the lower Piedmont and south central sections located generally around the Macon, Fort Valley, Thomaston, and Griffin sections. Elberta is the leading variety, but there are large plantings of Early Rose, Hiley, Georgia Belle, J. H. Hale, and other varieties.

Georgia is one of the largest producing states of improved varieties of pecans. The largest producing areas are in the lower Piedmont and Coastal Plain region from Albany, Georgia, to points located a little north of Macon.

The mountainous section, owing to its high altitude and heavy rainfall, is admirably located and suited to late vegetable production, including Irish potatoes. There are extensive fruit and vegetable areas around the larger cities,

---

* Special articles on the subjects indicated by an asterisk (*) will be found at the words so marked.

and a large vegetable industry along the coast and throughout the Coastal Plain section.

Central Georgia has developed a large pimiento growing and canning industry.

South Georgia is famous for its fine watermelons, and ships thousands of cars to the northern markets annually.

The Piedmont and southern sections of Georgia are very well suited to the production of the Muscadine type of grape, of which the Scuppernong, Thomas and Hunt are the leading varieties. This type of grape is native to these sections of the state, is long-lived, very productive, and offers great commercial possibilities.

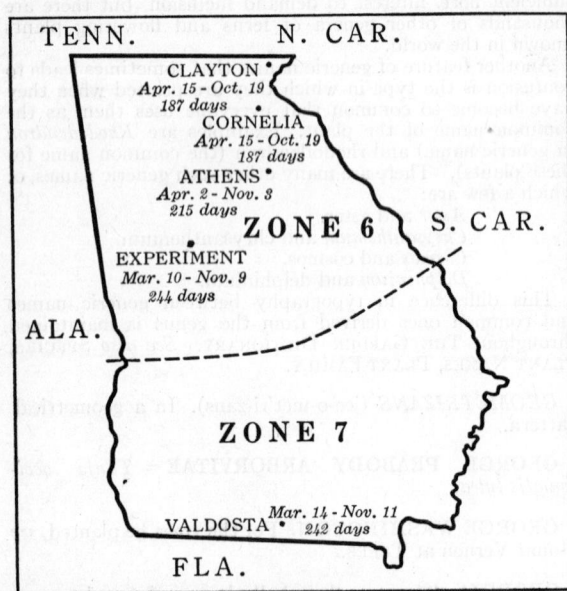

GEORGIA

The zones of hardiness crossing Georgia are those shown on the colored map at ZONE, which should be consulted for details. The dates are the average latest killing frost in spring and the first one in the fall. The figures below the dates show the average length of the growing season.

The growing of tung-oil trees for the production of tung oil for use in making high-grade paints and varnishes is a promising new industry in southern Georgia.

Georgia is admirably adapted to growing a host of blossoming flowers. Roses, dahlias, azaleas, iris, tulips, gladiolus, and numerous others, including commercial bulb production along the coast, flourish in this state. Dogwood, mountain laurel, rhododendron, azaleas, redbud, mimosa, maples, hickories, large, stately oaks, holly, pine, and cedars lend beauty to the landscape. Such shrubs and plants as *Abelia, Nandina, Weigela, Pyracantha, Forsythia, Buddleia,* arborvitae, box, *Euonymus, Photinia, Deutzia, Philadelphus* (see MOCK-ORANGE), crape myrtle, *Wistaria,* ivy, and many others thrive in lawn and park plantings over the state.

CLIMATE. Geographically, Georgia extends from the Gulf and South Atlantic regions on the south to the Southern Appalachian Mountain region on the north.

January is the coldest month, the monthly average of temperature being 40° F. in the northeast corner and approximately 52° F. on the southern border. July is the hottest month, and for this month the average temperatures are 75° F. in the northeast corner of the state and approximately 82° F. on the southern border. The other months are intermediate. The average daily change from the lowest to highest temperature is about 20 degrees in winter and summer and 22 to 23 degrees in fall and spring. The highest temperatures observed at stations in Georgia are about 30 degrees above the monthly average and the lowest about 30 degrees, except in winter when they are about 40 degrees below the average. Killing frosts are probable when the average monthly temperature is 57 degrees or lower.

FROST DATES

| Town | County | Average date of last killing frost in spring | Latest known killing frost | Average date of earliest killing frost in fall | Earliest known killing frost |
|---|---|---|---|---|---|
| Clayton | Rabun | April 15 | May 10 | Oct. 19 | Oct. 1 |
| Cornelia | Habersham | April 15 | May 10 | Oct. 19 | Oct. 1 |
| Athens | Clarke | April 2 | April 21 | Nov. 3 | Oct. 11 |
| Experiment | Spalding | March 10 | April 17 | Nov. 9 | (?) |
| Valdosta | Lowndes | March 14 | April 16 | Nov. 11 | Oct. 21 |

RAINFALL. The annual rainfall of Georgia is approximately 50 inches. It is slightly lower in the southeastern and eastern parts of the state and considerably higher in the mountainous northeastern section. In the northern section the winter and summer rainfalls are about equally divided. In the southern half of the state the summer rainfall is greater.

In central Georgia there are generally periods of low rainfall in late April and May, followed by greater rainfall in June, July, and August, and then followed by dry and hot weather during most of September and October.

The address of the Georgia Agricultural Experiment Station, which has kindly supplied this information about the state, is Experiment, Georgia. The Station is always ready to answer gardening questions.

Garden club activities include clubs of the Garden Club of America, the home office of which is at 598 Madison Avenue, New York, N.Y. There are also over 110 clubs affiliated with the Garden Club of Georgia. For the one nearest your locality write the Garden Editor, Houghton Mifflin Company, Boston, Mass.

**GERANIACEAE** (ger-ray-nee-ā′see-ee). The geranium or cranesbill family is of great hort. interest because it contains the common garden geranium (*Pelargonium*) and the cranesbill or wild geranium which belong to the genus *Geranium*. The only other cult. genus is *Erodium*, but the family comprises 11 genera and over 600 species widely distributed in temperate regions and in South Africa.

All are herbs, but some become woody. Leaves simple* (but often cut) in *Geranium* and *Pelargonium*, compound in *Erodium* and fragrant in many species. Flowers showy (spectacularly so in the garden forms of *Pelargonium*), typically of 5 separate petals, but often doubled and with a spur in the garden geranium (*Pelargonium*). Fruit a collection of dry, 1-seeded pods, each splitting separately from the base upward.

Technical flower characters: Sepals 5, distinct from one another. Petals (typically) 5, separate, but with the margins overlapping, sometimes much doubled and one or more produced into a spur. Stamens 5 or 10, rarely 15, usually joined at the base. Ovary superior,* 3–5-lobed.

**GERANIUM** (ger-ray′ni-um). Hardy perennial, biennial, or rarely annual herbs, commonly called cranesbill, and comprising over 250 species of the family Geraniaceae. The genus does not include the common garden geranium, as this belongs to *Pelargonium* (which see). The genus *Geranium* includes several plants of garden interest, mostly suited to the border or to the wild garden. They are generally low, often half-prostrate herbs, with forking stems and more or less dissected or lobed, roundish leaves divided finger-fashion. Flowers regular, not spurred as in *Pelargonium* (the garden or common geranium), the petals 5, the stamens 10. Fruit a collection of elastically splitting, beaked carpels which persist for some time. (*Geranium* is from the Greek for a crane, the beaked fruits resembling a crane's bill.)

The cranesbills are of easy culture, and the perennial species are readily increased by division of the clumps in spring or fall. The only annual, *G. robertianum*, should be raised from seed sown where wanted. Some of them, as noted below, are woodland plants, and such should be grown

* Special articles on the subjects indicated by an asterisk (*) will be found at the words so marked.

in partially shaded parts of the wild garden. Nearly all of them bloom in early spring.

**argenteum.** A biennial or perennial herb, scarcely over 6 in. high, the white-silvery leaves 5-7-parted. Flowers about 1 in. wide, pink, but darker-veined. Northern Italy. For culture *see* Moraine at Rock Garden.

**endressi.** A perennial 12-18 in. high. Leaves 5-parted or lobed nearly to the middle. Flowers about ½ in. wide, rose-pink. Pyrenees.

**grandiflorum.** A perennial herb 8-15 in. high. Leaves deeply 5-parted nearly to the middle. Flowers almost 1½ in. wide, lilac, but with purple veins. Northern As.

**ibericum.** A perennial 10-20 in. high. Leaves 7-lobed almost to the middle. Flowers nearly 1½ in. wide, purple. Southwestern As. There is also a white-flowered variety.

**incisum.** A perennial 12-24 in. high. Leaves 3-5-parted, the segments also cut or coarsely toothed. Flowers about ½ in. long, pinkish-purple. British Columbia to Calif.

**maculatum.** Wild geranium of eastern woodlands; also called alumroot and chocolate-flower. A perennial 12-20 in. high. Leaves 3-5-parted nearly to the middle. Flowers about 1 in. wide, rose-purple. April-May. N.A., especially rocky woods. Grow in the wild garden.

**platypetalum.** A Chinese perennial 12-24 in. high and well suited to the border. *See* Blue Garden. Leaves deeply 5-parted. Flowers about ¼ in. wide, purplish-blue.

**pratense.** A stout, Eurasian perennial 18-30 in. high and well suited to the open border. Leaves 7-parted. Flowers about ½ in. wide, purple.

**pylzowianum.** A Chinese perennial scarcely over 12 in. high. Leaves 5-parted, each segment 3-lobed. Flowers about 1 in. wide, purple.

**robertianum.** Herb Robert; called, also, red shanks and fox geranium. A nearly prostrate annual or biennial, the stems sometimes erect or sprawling and as much as 15 in. high. Leaves 3-parted, the segments deeply cut or toothed. Flowers numerous, about ¼ in. wide, reddish-purple. North temperate zone and northern Africa, mostly in woods or thickets. Grows best in the wild garden.

**sanguineum.** A commonly grown Eurasian perennial, 12-18 in. high, the foliage white-hairy. Leaves 5-7-parted. Flowers about ¾ in. wide, reddish-purple. The best of the cranesbills for the open border. There is a white-flowered variety and one with prostrate habit and lighter-colored flowers.

**wallichianum.** A prostrate, Himalayan perennial, best suited to the rock garden (which see). Leaves 3-5-parted, the segments deeply toothed. Flowers nearly 2 in. wide, purple.

For other plants sometimes called geranium, or where geranium is part of the name (*i.e.* strawberry geranium, etc.) *see* Saxifraga sarmentosa, Chenopodium botrys, Chrysanthemum balsamita, Pelargonium.

**GERANIUM FAMILY** = Geraniaceae.

**GERARD, J.** *See* Herbals at Garden Books.

**GERARDIA** (ger-rar′di-a). A badly mixed-up genus of which no species appear to be in cult. The name is also used by some for plants now included in *Agalinis* and *Aureolaria*, neither of which appears to be in cult.

**GERBERA** (ger′ber-ra); also spelled *Gerberia*. A genus of perhaps 40 species of South African or Asiatic, mostly stemless herbs, of the family Compositae, only **G. jamesoni**, the Transvaal or Barberton daisy, of any hort. interest. It is an erect, hairy herb, with leaves in a basal rosette. Leaf-blade about 8 in. long and considerably cut or parted feather-fashion, very woolly on the under side. Flower heads solitary at the ends of long, hairy stalks, the head nearly 4 in. wide, the rays a brilliant orange or orange-red in the typical form, but in the **var. hybrida**, white, pink, salmon, or violet. South Africa. Not hardy outdoors north of zone* 6, but often grown in the cool greenhouse in potting mixture* 3, for its very showy, usually winter-blooming flowers. (Named for Trang Gerber, German naturalist.) Often called by florists the African daisy.

**GERMAN CAMOMILE** = *Matricaria chamomilla*.

**GERMAN CATCHFLY** = *Lychnis viscaria*.

**GERMANDER.** *See* Teucrium.

**GERMANDER SPEEDWELL** = *Veronica teucrium*.

**GERMANICA, -us, -um** (ger-man′i-ka). From Germany.

**GERMAN IRIS.** *See* Iris germanica.

**GERMAN IVY** = *Senecio mikanioides*.

**GERMAN MILLET** = *Setaria italica stramineofructa*.

**GERMINATION.** For a general account of the things that help seeds to sprout or germinate *see* Seeds and Seedage. For the average percentage of germination of some garden seeds *see* Garden Tables II.

**GESNERIA.** There seem to be no cult. plants in the true genus *Gesneria*. For some cult. plants often incorrectly credited to Gesneria *see* Corytholoma and Naegelia.

**GESNERIACEAE** (jez-near-i-ā′see-ee). A large family of mostly tropical herbs (rarely woody plants), without any well-recognized common name, but yielding many fine greenhouse plants, among them the gloxinia (*Sinningia*). Of its over 80 genera and perhaps 500 species, about a dozen are in cultivation, all of them herbs of greenhouse culture except *Trichosporum* which contains Japanese woody vines with showy flowers, and *Alloplectus* which is shrubby. The leaves are simple* in all genera.

Some are popular plants for hanging baskets, especially *Episcia*. Two genera, *Haberlea* and *Ramondia*, are European and can be grown outdoors in some parts of the U.S. But most of the cult. genera contain showy-flowered greenhouse plants, the most important being *Achimenes*, *Corytholoma*, *Isoloma*, *Naegelia*, *Saintpaulia* (the African violet) and *Streptocarpus*. Fruit dry in all the garden genera, fleshy in some others.

Technical flower characters: Calyx tubular, 5-parted or 5-lobed. Corolla tubular (often with a considerable tube), the five lobes usually unequal, and often definitely 2-lipped and strikingly irregular.* Stamens mostly 4, two shorter than the others. Ovary superior* (in *Episcia*, *Alloplectus*, *Trichosporum*, *Streptocarpus* and *Saintpaulia*), more or less inferior in the other genera.

**GEUM** (jee′um). Perennial herbs of the rose family, most of the 50 known species from the cooler parts of the North Temperate Zone, and usually called avens. A few are grown in the border or rock garden for ornament, although only one, *G. chiloense*, is at all popular. They have chiefly basal leaves which are compound* or so deeply cut or lobed as to appear so, the terminal segment or leaflet much larger than the others. There are often a few smaller leaves on the stem. Flowers solitary or a few, in corymbs,* yellow, white, or red. Calyx usually bell-shaped, its 5 lobes alternating with 5 bractlets. Petals 5, rather broad. Stamens* numerous. Fruit a collection of silky-plumed achenes which are often as showy as the flowers. (*Geum* is of unknown significance here.)

The avens are of simple culture in most garden soils, and are readily increased by division. Some of the taller ones are striking plants for the border, but the best of the avens is *G. chiloense*, which is rarely over 2 ft. high. Mostly summer-blooming. An absurd, but phonetic, plural for *Geum* is "gums," which has some currency among the illiterate.

**atrosanguineum** = *Geum chiloense*.

**bulgaricum.** Not over 2 ft. high. Leaves with a large, heart-shaped end leaflet or segment, and many smaller side leaflets. Flowers bright orange or yellow, about 1 in. wide, nodding. Bulgaria.

**chiloense.** Not over 2 ft. high. Terminal leaflet or segment much larger than the numerous side ones, all hairy. Flowers nearly 1½ in. wide, bright scarlet. Chile. A popular border perennial known also in several forms, one double-flowered. Others, like Mrs. Bradshaw, have long been favorites.

**ciliatum.** Prairie smoke; also called Johnny smokers. A North American perennial 12-18 in. high, its leaves much cut into silky segments. Flowers about ½ in. wide, purplish, not so handsome as the fine head of silky-plumed fruit.

**coccineum.** The garden plants so called are mostly *Geum chiloense*, the true *G. coccineum* being not much cult.

**kolbianum.** A garden plant of unknown origin, said to be a hybrid, and to have orange-red flowers.

**montanum.** Not over 12 in. high, the terminal leaf segment or leaflet much larger than the many smaller side ones. Flowers nearly 1½ in. wide, golden-yellow. Southern Eu.

**sibiricum.** A plant listed in some catalogues. It may be a form of *G. chiloense*, although it is a lower plant and the flowers are coppery-red. There is no true *Geum sibiricum* known to be in cult.

**triflorum** = *Geum ciliatum*.

**GHENT AZALEA.** *See* Azalea gandavensis.

**GHERKIN.** Usually a gherkin is a young cucumber used for pickling; but *see also* Cucumis anguria.

**GIANT.** A cherry variety. *See* Cherry.

**GIANT.** As an adjective giant enters into the name of many plants. Those occurring in The Garden Dictionary and their proper equivalents are:

Giant arborvitae = *Thuja plicata*; Giant arrowhead = *Sagittaria montevidensis*; Giant bamboo, *see* Dendrocalamus; Giant cactus = *Carnegiea gigantea*; Giant chinquapin = *Castanopsis chrysophylla*; Giant daisy =

---

* Special articles on the subjects indicated by an asterisk (*) will be found at the words so marked.

*Chrysanthemum uliginosum;* **Giant fennel** = *Ferula communis;* **Giant fir** = *Abies grandis* (see FIR); **Giant granadilla** = *Passiflora quadrangularis;* **Giant holly fern** = *Polystichum munitum;* **Giant lily** = *Furcraea gigantea;* **Giant reed** = *Arundo donax;* **Giant sequoia** = *Sequoia gigantea;* **Giant snowdrop** = *Galanthus elwesi* (see SNOWDROP); **Giant summer hyacinth** = *Galtonia candicans;* **Giant sunflower** = *Helianthus giganteus* (see SUNFLOWER); **Giant willow-herb** = *Epilobium angustifolium.*

**GIBBIFLORA, -us, -um** (gib-bi-flo'ra). Having flowers with a pouch-like swelling on one side.

**GIBRALTAR CANDYTUFT** = *Iberis gibraltarica.* See CANDYTUFT.

**GIBRALTARICA, -us, -um** (gib-ral-tar'i-ka). From or near the Rock of Gibraltar.

**GIGANTEA, -us, -um** (ji-gan'tee-a). Large or immense.

**GILIA** (gil'li-a). A genus of nearly 100 species of herbs of the family Polemoniaceae, most of them from the western U.S., a few rather showy garden annuals, or occasionally biennial or perennial. They have alternate* or opposite* leaves, usually without marginal teeth, but some with lobed or divided leaves. Flowers rather various, mostly in clusters. Corolla more or less bell-shaped or funnel-shaped, the stamens* attached to the tube of the corolla. Fruit a 3-valved capsule. (Named for Philipp Salvador Gil, Spanish botanist, or, according to some, for Filippi Luigi Gillii, an Italian.)

Gilias are showy plants, most of which are best treated as hardy annuals. (*See* ANNUALS.) Even biennial or perennial plants like *G. rubra* will often flower from seed within a single season, although some prefer fall-sown seed, and wintering of the seedlings, as in a biennial. (*See* BIENNIALS.) All of them need open sunny places and a soil not too heavy or wet.

**abrotanifolia.** A Californian annual, 12–20 in. high. Leaves divided into very narrow, line-like segments. Flowers blue, in a dense terminal truss.

**californica.** Prickly phlox. A perennial, Californian herb or woody shrub 2–3 ft. high. Leaves divided, finger-fashion, into 5–9 rather rigid, stiff segments that are about ⅛ in. long. Flowers nearly 1½ in. wide, in few-flowered clusters. Corolla rose-pink or lilac. Not suited to the cold, slushy winters of the East, unless grown in a cold frame. Often sold under the name *Leptodactylon.*

**capitata.** An extremely popular flower-garden annual, 18–24 in. high. Leaves divided or dissected, feather-fashion, into very narrow segments. Flowers light blue or white, in stalked, head-like clusters that are about 1 in. wide. Wash. to Calif. Flowers fine for cutting.

**coronopiflora** = *Gilia rubra.*

**densiflora** = *Linanthus grandiflorus.*

**rubra.** A showy perennial or biennial, 3–5 ft. high, and known by a variety of names, of which tree cypress, standing cypress, Texas plume, and trailing fire are the best known. Leaves dissected, feather-fashion, into thread-like segments. Flowers in a narrow cluster (panicle*), very showy. Corolla scarlet outside, but yellow and red-dotted inside. S. Car. to Fla. and Tex. It is sometimes sold under the name *Ipomopsis.*

**tricolor.** Bird's-eyes. A Californian annual, 18–24 in. high, and next to *G. capitata* the most widely grown of the annual gilias. Leaves finely dissected into narrow segments. Flowers in loose clusters, the corolla lilac or violet above, the tube yellowish but purple-streaked. There is a variety with rose-pink flowers.

**GILIBERTIA** (gil-li-ber'ti-a). Asiatic, tender shrubs or trees of the family Araliaceae, only **G. japonica,** from Japan, of any hort. interest. It is a medium-sized shrub or small tree with alternate,* 3-lobed or entire,* ivy-like leaves about 3 in. wide. Flowers small, greenish (for details *see* ARALIACEAE), borne in umbels* that are scarcely 1 in. wide. Fruit berry-like. Rarely cult. and needing the same greenhouse conditions as *Polyscias.* (Named for J. E. Gilibert, French botanist and physician.) Sometimes offered as *Dendropanax.*

**GILLENIA** (gil-len'i-a). North American perennial herbs of the rose family, both the known species occasionally cult. in the wild garden and commonly called Indian physic. They are erect, branching plants having compound* leaves with 3 leaflets, or simple* ones which are deeply 3-parted. There are often, in addition, 2 leaf-like stipules,* the whole leaf thus appearing as with 5 leaflets or segments. Flowers white, in loose, terminal clusters (panicles*). Petals 5, narrow and spreading, a little unequal. Stamens 10–20, not protruding. Fruit a collection of 5 follicles,* each of which is 2–4-seeded. (Named for A. Gille, or Gillenius, a German botanist.)

Both the species are woodland plants suited to the wild garden, preferably in partial shade, and they should have rich woods soil, not too acid. In such places they are of easy cult. Propagated by division of the clumps in spring.

**stipulata.** American ipecac. A wand-like herb, 2–4 ft. high. Leaves usually 3-parted, sometimes compound, the two stipules* prominent and leaf-like. Flowers about ½ in. wide. N.Y. to Ga. and La. July.

**trifoliata.** Bowman's root; also called false ipecac and Indian hippo. Much resembling *G. stipulata,* but with compound* leaves and with the leaflets toothed. Stipules* small and very narrow, hence not so leaf-like as in the other species. Eastern N.A. June.

**GILLIFLOWER** = Gillyflower.

**GILL-OVER-THE-GROUND** = *Nepeta hederacea.* But *see also* Ground ivy in the list at WEEDS.

**GILLYFLOWER** = *Mathiola incana.*

**GINGER.** The common ginger is derived from an herb of the genus **Zingiber** (zin'gi-ber), of the family Zingiberaceae. Of the 50 or more species, all from moist tropical forests in southeastern Asia, only the ginger, **Z. officinale,** is likely to be cult. in the U.S., and its outdoor cult. must be confined to frost-free regions of Fla. where there is abundant moisture and a rich soil. It is chiefly grown as an ornamental, as commercial ginger production needs more heat than is found anywhere in the U.S. It has a stout cane-like stem 3–4 ft. high, rising from a thick rootstock (the source of ginger). Leaves sheathing at the base, oblongish or narrower, 8–12 in. long. Flower cluster a bracted spike, the bracts* usually persistent and with one flower at each. Flower irregular,* yellowish-green, about ¾ in. long, the irregular lip* purple, but yellow-spotted. Fruit a capsule.* While the plant is not much grown outdoors, it is frequent in greenhouse collections. Together with the closely related *Amomum,* it needs a warm (70°–80°) greenhouse, potting mixture* 3, and a large pot or tub to take care of its stout rootstock. During nine months of the year it needs plenty of water and will repay an occasional application of liquid manure. But during the winter the plant should be allowed to become half dormant by reducing the heat and keeping it as dry as possible. (*Zingiber* is a Latinized version of the Sanskrit name for ginger.)

**GINGER FAMILY** = Zingiberaceae.

**GINGER-LILY.** See HEDYCHIUM.

**GINKGO** (gink'o, jin'ko). A remarkable, deciduous,* Chinese tree, the only species and only genus of the family **Ginkgoaceae** (gink-ko-a'see-ee), once a widely distributed group stretching back to the Carboniferous, but now a

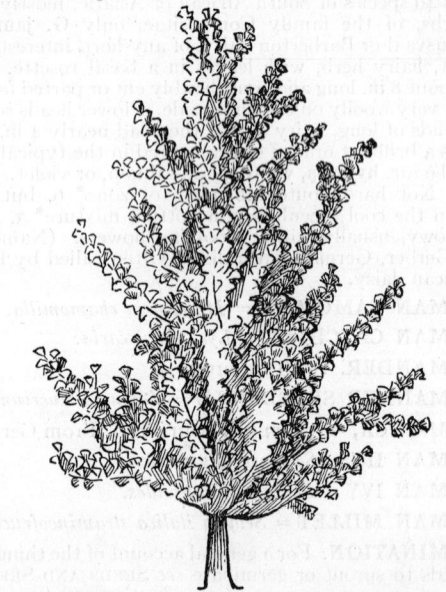

It will take nearly 20 years for this ginkgo to lose its gawky habit of branching and become a round-headed tree.

---

* Special articles on the subjects indicated by an asterisk (*) will be found at the words so marked.

dwindling family with only this survivor. Until recently, it was unknown as a wild tree, all the cult. specimens having been derived from trees preserved around Chinese temples. But wild trees have now been discovered. It is a resinous tree with deciduous, fan-shaped leaves. Male and female flowers on separate trees, both without sepals or petals. The male flowers consist of naked pairs of anthers* in catkin-like clusters. Female flowers consist only of a naked ovule, which, unlike all other trees, is fertilized by motile sperm-cells, as in the ferns. Fruit fleshy, drupe*-like, foul-smelling, but the kernel edible. (*Ginkgo* is the Chinese name for the tree.)

The ginkgo or maidenhair tree is one of the finest street and specimen trees in the temperate world. Only male trees should be planted, because of the foul odor of the fruit. For the first few years it is gawky, but in age it is a magnificent, round-headed, full-foliaged tree. Practically immune to all pests and standing street conditions very well.

**biloba.** Ginkgo or maidenhair tree. A smooth tree up to 120 ft. Leaves alternate,* fan-shaped, more or less cut at the broad tip, wedge-shaped at the base, 2½–3½ in. wide, and much resembling a segment of the frond of a maidenhair fern. The foliage turns a soft yellow in autumn. Fruit yellow. China. Hardy from zone* 3 southward. The var. **aurea** has yellow leaves, at least in youth; var. **fastigiata** has upward-pointing branches and is columnar in habit; var. **pendula** has hanging branches; var. **variegata** has yellow-blotched leaves.

*GINNALA* (gin-nay′la). Asiatic vernacular name for the maple, *Acer ginnala.* See MAPLE.

**GINSENG.** Two species of *Panax,* one, native to this country, *Panax quinquefolium,* the other, *Panax schinseng,* indigenous to eastern Asia, are the source of ginseng. The roots are much prized by the Orientals and are used for medicinal purposes. The native American species is chiefly grown and harvested in the United States and Canada for export.

SOIL. Ginseng grows naturally on the slopes of ravines and in other situations where the drainage is good and when the soil is slightly acid, which is formed from the decaying leaves of hardwood trees.

Ginseng growing under a lath shade

For cultivated ginseng, the soil should be well drained, fairly light; a soil suitable on which to grow early vegetables would be in right condition for its culture, substituting decayed leaves for manure. Sandy soil should not be used, as it is apt to produce plants whose roots are fibrous and hard and of inferior value.

The plant is grown from seeds which are slow in germination. When gathered, they should never be permitted to become dry. They may be stratified by mixing them with twice their bulk of moist sand, fine loam or old sawdust and stored in a cool, damp building until they are planted in early spring. As a rule the seeds do not germinate until a year from the summer following their ripening, and they do not reach a marketable size until about the sixth year from seed. Autumn and spring are the proper times for transplanting to permanent beds. Plants are usually placed at a distance of five inches apart each way.

FERTILIZERS. The best fertilizers to use are woods soil or well-decayed hardwood leaves, well spaded into the soil. Raw bonemeal is also beneficial to the plants, used at the rate of 1 lb. to each square yard of bed.

SHADE AND CULTIVATION. Ginseng grows naturally in rather dense shade, therefore it will be necessary to grow the plant under lath houses or frames covered with lath screens. It requires little cultivation, the mere pulling out of grass and weeds from the beds and a light cultivation to leave a dust mulch on the bed to keep it from caking being sufficient. A winter mulch is also advisable; this prevents the heaving by frost. Hardwood leaves applied to the depth of four inches when freezing weather sets in, prove the best protection to the plants.

MARKETING. Late September to mid-October is the most favorable time. The drying of the roots is best effected in a heated storage with a temperature of 60° to 90° F. Approximately a month is required to cure the larger roots. — D. L.

DISEASES. Blight, downy mildew, wilt, and various root rots tend to make ginseng a difficult crop to grow successfully. The blight and the mildew may not completely kill the plants but do reduce the yield. The removal and destruction of all diseased refuse are of great importance. In addition the soil should be well drained, and occasionally sterilized with steam or chemicals, and the plants should be sprayed carefully with bordeaux mixture to which arsenate of lead has been added.

**GINSENG FAMILY.** Besides the ginseng itself, this family comprises shrubs like the greenhouse aralias, trees like the Hercules'-club, and vines like the English ivy. See ARALIACEAE.

**GIRASOLE** = *Helianthus tuberosus* (the Jerusalem artichoke). See SUNFLOWER.

**GIRDLE.** To strip a ring of bark from a tree, a practice well known to the Indians. It cuts off the food supply and will ultimately kill most trees. See BARK.

**GIRDLER.** See the Insect Pests at CRANBERRY, PECAN, and PERSIMMON.

*GLABELLA, -us, -um* (glay-bell′la). Nearly smooth.

*GLABER* (glay′ber). Same as *glabra.*

*GLABRA, -us, -um* (glay′bra). Smooth.

*GLABRATA, -us, -um* (glay-bray′ta). Glabrate; *i.e.* somewhat smooth.

**GLABROUS.** Completely smooth; *i.e.* altogether lacking hairs, pustules, warts, or any sort of roughness; mostly applied to leaves and stems. The opposite of pubescent (which see).

*GLACIALIS, -e* (glay-see-ā′lis). Growing on or near a glacier.

**GLAD.** Florists' slang for gladiolus.

*GLADIATA, -us, -um* (glay-dee-ā′ta). Sword-like.

**GLADIOLUS** (gla-dy′o-lus, also glad-i-ō′lus). Very popular, summer-blooming plants of the iris family, many of them from South Africa, but a few from tropical Africa and elsewhere. More than 200 species are known, and from a few of them the breeders have developed several thousand named forms among which are very striking plants. The gladioli bear corms from which grows a usually erect, unbranched, leafy stem. Leaves commonly sword-shaped, long, and narrow, handsome. Flowers very showy, in a long, terminal, spike-like cluster composed of leafy bracts (spathe*) between every two of which there is a single, stalkless flower (for color variations see Culture below). They bloom

---

* Special articles on the subjects indicated by an asterisk (*) will be found at the words so marked.

# GLADIOLUS

from the bottom upward. The flowers are more or less funnel-shaped, but with the tube dilated, and usually curved upward. Flower segments 6, the upper three larger than the lower, hence the flower is slightly irregular.* Stamens 3. Fruit a large capsule,* its seeds usually flattened or winged. (*Gladiolus* is Latin for a small sword, in allusion to the shape of the leaves.) Old names for them are sword lily and corn lily.

It is almost impossible to assign the modern gladiolus of the garden to any of the botanical species below. The list is therefore more of a guide to the species that have been used in *breeding* the modern flower, than a list of species actually in cult. in gardens today. With thousands of named forms, and the parentage of many of the hybrids quite uncertain, any list of species of *Gladiolus* is frankly tentative. For a discussion of the leading classes and varieties and how to grow them *see* Culture below.

**blandus.** About 2 ft. high, the stems sometimes branched. Leaves usually 4, nearly 12 in. long and ½ in. wide. Flowers 4-8 in the spike, white, or red-tinged, or pink, the segments pointed, the upper one about ¾ in. wide. South Africa.

**cardinalis.** Usually unbranched and 3-4 ft. high. Leaves 2-3 ft. long, bluish-green. Flowers 5-10 in the spike, crimson or scarlet, the upper segment larger and hooded, the lower ones blotched with white. South Africa. Thought to be one of the parents of *G. gandavensis*.

**colvillei.** Usually not over 2 ft. high. Flower spikes short, early-blooming, the flowers scarlet and with oblong blotches. It is supposed to be a hybrid between a form of *G. tristis* and *G. cardinalis*.

**dracocephalus.** Not over 2 ft. high, the stem unbranched. Leaves about 18 in. long and nearly 1 in. wide. Flowers 3-5 in the spike, yellow-green, but purple-spotted, the tube much curved and nearly 2 in. long. South Africa.

**gandavensis.** A hybrid, very popular and long-cult. garden gladiolus, perhaps derived by crossing *G. psittacinus* and *G. cardinalis* or *G. oppositiflorus*. It is late-blooming, has broad leaves and a rather long, dense, flowering spike. Flowers prevailingly red or reddish-yellow, often streaked or penciled. It is certainly the origin of many named forms.

**oppositiflorus.** Occasionally branched, the stem 3-4 ft. high. Leaves usually 4, nearly 18 in. long and 1 in. wide. Flower spike 2-sided, the flowers numerous, nearly 3 in. long, white. South Africa.

**primulinus.** One of the most important parents of many garden forms, and a tender species from the moist regions of tropical Africa.

**psittacinus.** Probably one of the parents of *G. gandavensis*, and with a usually unbranched stem 3-4 ft. high. Flowers numerous in the spike, the tube nearly 3 in. long, the lower flower segments red and yellow and smaller than the larger upper one, which is crimson. South Africa.

**saundersi.** A South African gladiolus which has entered into several hybrid forms or strains. It is 2-3 ft. high, usually unbranched. Leaves, 4-6, nearly 2 ft. long and 1 in. wide, prominently ribbed. Flowers scarlet, 6-8 in the spike, the three lower segments white-blotched.

**tristis.** Not over 2 ft. high, unbranched. Leaves 3, round in section, about 18 in. long and ribbed. Flowers night-blooming, white or yellowish-white, but purple-streaked and very fragrant, the tube about 2 in. long. South Africa. There is a *var.* concolor with pure white flowers.

## GLADIOLUS CULTURE

It is probable that *Gladiolus blandus*, *G. cardinalis*, *G. dracocephalus*, *G. psittacinus*, *G. oppositiflorus* and *G. primulinus* have contributed most to the creation of the varieties now generally known. But *Gladiolus gandavensis* is considered the original of the large-flowered or exhibition type, while the introduction of *G. primulinus* blood has probably brought about the forms in which small size, charm and daintiness have created a classification called Small Decorative.

The origin and history of gladiolus reach far into the past. As late as A.D. 1000 gladioli were known as sword lilies and about A.D. 200 Dioscorides described several different *corn* lilies, which today we know were gladiolus species.

CULTURE. The corms, generally but incorrectly called bulbs, are planted 3-6 inches deep, but only the larger corms should be put as deep as 6 inches. They must not be put in the ground until settled warm weather has arrived. The plant is then cultivated and fertilized, and the new crop is harvested and handled very much like the potato, except that the new corms have the old ones attached at digging and must be separated before curing and storage.

After harvest, the corms require a rest or dormant period before replanting. Storage for the corms should be at a temperature of from 35° to 50° in a place neither too damp nor too dry and with ventilation facilities. For the amateur who has but few bulbs, a cellar or a place proper for the storage of fruits or root crops is suitable.

In the temperate zone, winter cold induces the rest period of the corms, but in warm regions artificial cold storage is necessary for a period of approximately three months to bring about the required dormancy. In the Far South, the corms may be planted at any time of the year, following the proper rest period, but in the north and south temperate zones, a general rule is to plant about the time the deciduous trees native to the vicinity begin to unfold their leaves in the spring.

The time between the planting of the corms and the actual blooming season varies in the different varieties, the range being from 50 to 140 days, though weather, moisture and climatic conditions may, to some extent, lessen or lengthen the blooming period of the different varieties. Maturity or digging time is indicated by the gradual browning of the plant foliage.

For an ornamental or garden planting, varieties are chosen with the date of bloom in mind. With properly chosen varieties, one may plant all corms at the same time and be assured of blooms for cutting continuously through several months. Similar results may be obtained by planting several different sizes of corms. But usually the smaller corms do not produce as large and beautiful blooms as No. 1 or large corms.

CLASSES. There are only three types into which all gladiolus varieties are classified for exhibition or commercial purposes: Exhibition, Large Decorative and Small Decorative. The Exhibition type embraces the huge varieties wherein size and the number of flowers are the most important features, and where the possibility of a sometimes rather stiff and mechanically precise arrangement of the flowers does not bring a penalty. The Large Decorative type embraces those with size ranging from 3 in. across the largest flower as a minimum, extending to varieties with flowers 6 and 7 in. across, but which are more informal and graceful. The Small Decorative type embraces varieties 3 in. across the largest flower as a maximum and ranging to the tiny miniatures, some of which are no more than ½ or ¾ in. across. Other than size, these are replicas of the larger-growing varieties.

The varieties of today range in color from pure white to clear scarlet, from lovely rose to bright yellow and true violet, with literally thousands of different color combinations and markings. There are many forms of the individual flowers, of which a number make up the spike.

There are many forms or shapes into which the three officially designated types may be subdivided. The petals may be plain, ruffled, fringed, recurved, needlepoint, rosebud, tulip, twilled, elongated or twisted, with certain varieties having a combination of two or more of these. In color there are monotones, duotones, etc., followed by such descriptions of petal markings as edged, feathered, plumed, flecked, stippled, blotched, striped and veined, these markings being in different colors.

VARIETIES. The American Gladiolus Society has, for many years, annually arranged a "Symposium of Favorites," and tabulated the results from the votes of its members. The last symposium resulted in the table which follows, in which are given the twenty-five highest of nearly a thousand varieties, arranged in the order of preference. The country of origin and the color of the flower are also indicated:

1. Picardy, (Can.), Salmon Pink
2. Minuet, (U.S.), Lavender
3. Marmora, (Aust.), Smoky
4. Betty Nuthall, (U.S.), Salmon Pink
5. Mr. W. H. Phipps, (U.S.), Salmon Pink
6. Commander Koehl, (Ger.), Red
7. Mother Machree, (U.S.), Smoky
8. Pfitzer's Triumph, (Ger.), Scarlet
9. Dr. F. E. Bennett, (U.S.), Scarlet
10. Mrs. Leon Douglas, (U.S.), Salmon Pink
11. Albatross, (Ger.), White
12. Golden Dream, (Can.), Yellow
13. Mammoth White, (Hol.), White
14. Aflame, (U.S.), Scarlet
15. Emile Auburn, (Aust.), Smoky
16. Red Glory, (Aust.), Red

---

* Special articles on the subjects indicated by an asterisk (*) will be found at the words so marked.

GARDEN GLADIOLUS

1 Mrs. Leon Douglas
2 Golden Dream
3 Coryphee
4 Mother Machree
5 Giant Nymph
6 Minuet
7 Pfitzer's Triumph
8 Red Glory

17. Maid of Orleans, (Ger.), White
18. Giant Nymph, (U.S.), Pink
19. Mrs. P. W. Sisson, (U.S.), Light Pink
20. Ave Maria, (Ger.), Light Violet
21. Bagdad, (Can.), Smoky Rose
22. Our Selection, (Aust.), Salmon
23. Pelegrina, (Ger.), Dark Violet
24. Coryphee, (Ger.), Light Pink
25. Johnkeer Van Tets, (Ger.), White

Forcing. Gladioli can be grown under glass for cut flowers if the corms are planted in potting mixture* 3, in Jan. or early Feb. They should then be in bloom by April or May. Earlier planting may occasionally produce earlier bloom, but there is apt to be a fairly large proportion of blind plants if the corms are planted earlier than Jan. Corms should be planted only 2 in. deep and 6 in. apart each way. Keep the night temperature about 52° and day temperatures of 58°-60°. Some of the best varieties for forcing are Chicago White, Halley, Mrs. Francis King, Mrs. Frank Pendleton, Flanders, Seafoam, and Virginal.

After blooming, the corms should be dug and stored as outlined above. There is some evidence that forced corms, even when properly stored, do not repay for subsequent forcing. For safety, therefore, it is better to use fresh, outdoor corms for each set of forced gladioli. — R. A. H.

The American Gladiolus Society welcomes members who are interested in the culture of these beautiful flowers. It has published a descriptive catalogue which names and briefly describes more than 5000 varieties. It also publishes revisions and additions to this list in *The Gladiolus Review*, the monthly publication. The address of the society may be had by writing to the Garden Editor, Houghton Mifflin Company, Boston, Mass.

Insect Pests. A species of tiny thrips has recently been very injurious to gladiolus. It lives in the stored corms and infests new plantings, destroying their beauty. Corms may be treated while dormant with naphthalene flakes or with warm water (see Bulbs).

Diseases. The more important diseases of gladiolus such as *scab, hard rot, Fusarium rot, dry rot,* and *Penicillium rot* are characterized by distinct lesions on the corms. With certain of these diseases, lesions also may occur on the stems. For control, maintain a four- or five-year rotation, plant in light, well-drained soil, avoid injuries when harvesting, dry thoroughly and store in a cool, well-ventilated room where the temperature is maintained at around 40° F. Chemical treatments can be made prior to planting. A two-hour soak in corrosive sublimate, one ounce to 7½ gallons of water, is suggested. When calomel is preferred, use at the rate of 1 ounce in 1 gallon of water and dip corms for 3 to 5 minutes.

**GLADIOLUS FAMILY** = Iridaceae.

**GLAND, GLANDULAR.** Minute, often sticky or glistening bodies common on the stems, leaves, petals, or flower stalks of many plants. The gland itself is often too small to see, but its secretions, especially those of the glandular hairs of some plants, make them very sticky. Typical examples are seen on the stems of tomato or the flowers of *Azalea viscosa.*

*GLANDULIFLORA, -us, -um* (glan-dew-li-flow'ra). With glandular flowers.

*GLANDULOSA, -us, -um* (glan-dew-lō'sa). Glandular.

**GLASS.** A general term for hotbeds, cold frames,* greenhouses,* or conservatories*; it usually occurs in the phrase *under glass,* implying that the plant is not grown in the open.

**GLASSHOUSE.** A greenhouse* or conservatory.*

**GLASS SUBSTITUTES.** See Sash at Cold Frame.

*GLAUCA, -us, -um* (glaw'ka). Glaucous (which see).

*GLAUCESCENS* (glaw-ses'senz). Glaucescent; *i.e.* almost, or becoming glaucous (which see).

**GLAUCIUM** (glaw'si-um). Stout, biennial or perennial herbs of the poppy family, usually with bluish-green or grayish foliage and yellow juice. Of the dozen known species, which are often called sea or horn poppy, all from the Mediterranean region, only G. flavum is of much garden interest. It is a branching biennial, 2-3 ft. high, often planted in the border. Lower leaves cut or lobed and stalked, the stem leaves clasping and wavy-toothed or lobed, all bluish-gray. Flowers solitary, long-stalked, orange-yellow, nearly 2 in. wide. Sepals 2. Petals 4. Stamens* numerous. Fruit a narrow capsule 8-12 in. long. For culture *see* Biennials. The plant is showy, but its flowers do not last long. It is naturalized, especially along sea beaches, in eastern N.A. (*Glaucium* is from the Greek for glaucous,* in allusion to the foliage.)

*GLAUCOPHYLLA, -us, -um* (glaw-ko-fill'a). With glaucous* leaves.

*GLAUCOTHEA* = *Erythea armata.*

**GLAUCOUS.** Covered with a minute whitish or grayish powder that will often rub off, as it will in the bloom on some fruits. Glaucous leaves are, due to the green beneath the powder, conspicuously blue-green or gray-green, as in the common blue spruce.

**GLECOMA** (glee-ko'ma). An obsolete generic name once applied to *Nepeta hederacea.*

**GLEDITSIA.** See Honey Locust.

**GLIRICIDIA** (gli-ri-sid'ee-a). Tropical American trees of the pea family, G. sepium, the madre de cacao, occasionally planted in extreme southern Fla. for ornament. It is hardy nowhere else in the U.S., but is commonly planted as a shade for coffee and chocolate plantations in the tropics. It is a tree 10-20 ft. high, with alternate* compound* leaves, the leaflets arranged feather-fashion, with an odd one at the end. Leaflets 5-15, without marginal teeth, oblongish, purple-blotched beneath. Flowers pea-like, pink, about ¾ in. long, in large clusters (racemes*) that bloom usually after the leaves drop in early spring. Fruit a narrow, shiny, flattened pod 4-6 in. long. (*Gliricidia* is from the Greek for rodent poison, in allusion to the poisonous properties of some species.)

**GLOBE AMARANTH** = *Gomphrena globosa.*

**GLOBE ARTICHOKE.** See Artichoke.

**GLOBE CANDYTUFT** = *Iberis umbellata.* See Candytuft.

**GLOBE DAISY** = *Globularia trichosantha.*

**GLOBEFLOWER.** See Trollius.

**GLOBE MALLOW.** See Sphaeralcea.

**GLOBE THISTLE.** See Echinops.

**GLOBE TULIP.** See Calochortus.

*GLOBIFERA, -us, -um* (glō-bif'fe-ra). Bearing globe-like or head-like clusters.

*GLOBOSA, -us, -um* (glo-bō'sa). Globe-shaped.

**GLOBULARIA** (glob-you-lay'ri-a). A small group of chiefly blue-flowered, Eurasian herbs, and the only cult. genus of the family **Globulariaceae** (glob-you-lair-ee-ā'see-ee). They are often cult. in the border or rock garden (*see* Blue Garden) for their early spring bloom. The ones below are all low or prostrate herbs, sometimes a little woody, with alternate* leaves. Flowers small, in dense, globular heads and crowded between small bracts.* Corolla 2-lipped,* the upper lip 2-lobed, the lower one 3-lobed. Stamens* 2-4. Fruit a tiny nutlet included within the persistent calyx. (The name is derived from the arrangement of the flowers in globular heads.)

All those below do better in partial shade, and are easily grown in the border or rock garden if provided with it and a reasonably well-drained soil. They are readily propagated from seeds or by division of the plants in early spring.

**cordifolia.** A prostrate, woody herb or under-shrub, not over 4 in. high. Leaves about 1 in. long, broader towards the end and notched at the tip. Flower heads about ½ in. wide, blue. May. Southern Eu.

**nana.** A prostrate, somewhat woody herb, with tiny, club-shaped leaves that are scarcely ¼ in. long. Flower heads about ¼ in. wide, pale blue. Southern Eu. April-May.

**nudicaulis.** More or less erect, and sometimes 8-10 in. high. Leaves nearly 3 in. long, without teeth or notches. Flower heads nearly ¾ in. wide, blue. Southern Eu. May.

**trichosantha.** Globe daisy. The best-known species in cult. and a nearly erect perennial up to 8 in. high. Leaves about 1 in. long, finely toothed. Flower heads about ½ in. wide, blue. Asia Minor. June.

* Special articles on the subjects indicated by an asterisk (*) will be found at the words so marked.

**GLOBULARIACEAE.** See **GLOBULARIA.**

**GLOBULUS** (glob'you-lus). A little globe.

**GLOCHID.** One of the barbed bristles found on the joints of some cacti, especially the prickly pears. Sometimes the spines arise at the glochids. See CACTACEAE.

**GLOMERATA, -us, -um** (glom-er-ray'ta). Glomerate; i.e. in dense, often globe-shaped and compact clusters.

**GLOMULIFERA, -us, -um** (glom-you-lif'fer-ra). Bearing small, globe-shaped heads or clusters.

**GLORIOSA** (glow-ri-ō'sa). Glory-lily. Weak-stemmed, tuberous-rooted, showy vines of the lily family, natives of tropical Af. and As., mostly grown in the greenhouse, but suited to outdoor culture in the Far South. (See VINES.) They have narrow leaves, the segments of which are prolonged into tendril*-like organs by which the plants climb. Flowers lily-like, solitary in the upper leaf-axils,* mostly red or yellow, the segments separate, rather narrow, sometimes crisped. Stamens* 6. Fruit a capsule.* (*Gloriosa* is from the Latin for glorious, in allusion to the showy flowers.)

Greenhouse culture demands a warm-temperate house (day temperature of 55°–65°), and potting mixture* 3. The tubers should be potted soon after Jan. and will then bloom in late summer and autumn, after which they need a rest (reduce their water). For outdoor cult. see VINES. It is sometimes, in the North, grown as a summer annual, the tubers of which, of course, must be stored over winter. Propagated by division of the tubers during dormancy.

**rothschildiana.** A tall-climbing vine, the leaves broadly lance-shaped. Flowers bent downward, 2–3 in. long, yellowish-white near the base, crimson towards the tip, the segments not crisped, but sometimes wavy. Tropical Af.

**superba.** Not so high-climbing as the last, usually not over 10 ft. Leaves narrowly lance-shaped. Flowers 2–3 in. long, yellow, but changing to red, the segments narrow, much-crisped and appearing as though twisted. Tropical Africa. A very handsome plant and the most widely grown of the genus.

**GLORY-BOWER.** See CLERODENDRON.

**GLORY-LILY** = *Gloriosa.*

**GLORY-OF-THE-SNOW** = *Chionodoxa.*

**GLORY-PEA** = *Clianthus dampieri.*

**GLORY-TREE.** See CLERODENDRON.

**GLOVES.** See Section 2, TOOLS AND IMPLEMENTS.

**GLOXINIA.** The florist's gloxinia is one of a small group of chiefly Brazilian herbs belonging to the genus **Sinningia** (sin-nin'ji-a) of the family Gesneriaceae. They are tuberous-rooted, nearly stemless herbs with opposite, long-stalked leaves. The only cult. species is S. *speciosa*, the common gloxinia of the greenhouses, long cult. for its very showy flowers. It has oblongish or oblong-oval, toothed leaves, 6–8 in. long. Flowers solitary or a few in a cluster, the corolla tubular or bell-shaped, somewhat swollen on one side, nearly 3 in. long, usually violet or purple, but sometimes reddish and white-spotted. Stamens 5, not protruding. Fruit a 2-valved capsule.* (Named for Wilhelm Sinning, German gardener.)

### GLOXINIA CULTURE

The culture of gloxinia, and of the related genera *Alloplectus, Isoloma* and *Corytholoma*, is essentially the same. They are plants of the warm, humid rain-forests and need, during their growing season, a warm greenhouse (70°–80°). Because they are plants primarily of the lower canopy of the forest or of the forest floor, they must have shade and this must be provided by painting the greenhouse glass or by the roller type of shades. Also, after blooming, which corresponds with the beginning of a dry season in their natural environment, they need a resting period. This means that after the blooming period, the corm-like tubers should be taken up and stored in a temperature of about 45°, in the dark, until Feb. or early March, when they may be started up again.

Then they should be potted up or put in pans in potting mixture* 3 and put into the warm greenhouse. Be careful to give them plenty of water, but see that none of it gets on the foliage. Liquid manure may be given every three weeks, especially as they approach the flowering period.

Gloxinias, and in fact most of the family Gesneriaceae to which they belong, are more easily propagated by leaf cuttings than by any other method. (See Leaf Cuttings at CUTTINGS.) They may also be increased by seeds, but either method needs a propagating bench, shade, moisture, and heat. Both methods should produce plants ready to flower within a year. Gloxinias make good house plants.

**GLOXINIAEFLORA, -us, -um** (glocks-in-i-ee-flow'ra). With flowers like a gloxinia.

**GLOXINIOIDES** (glocks-in-i-oy'deez, but see OÏDES). Like a gloxinia.

**GLUMACEA, -us, -um** (gloo-may'see-a). Bearing chaffy scales or glumes.*

**GLUME.** A chaffy bract* or scale, especially one of the two empty bracts* often found at the base of a grass spikelet.

**GLUTINOSA, -us, -um** (gloo-ti-nō'sa). Glutinous; i.e. sticky or gluey.

**GLYCINE.** See SOYBEAN.

**GLYCYRRHIZA.** See LICORICE.

**GNAPHALIUM** (na-fā'li-um). Cudweed. Few, or perhaps only one, of this genus of the family Compositae, are of much interest to the gardener. They are woolly-foliaged plants resembling an everlasting, and one of them, *G. sylvaticum*, is so grown occasionally in the hardy border. There are over 120 widely distributed species of usually perennial herbs in the genus, with alternate* leaves and rather dirty-white flower heads arranged in corymbs,* spikes, or other clusters. There are no ray* flowers, the heads being composed only of disk* flowers, and rather compact and button-like. (*Gnaphalium* is from the Greek for wool, in allusion to the woolly foliage of most species.)

The woodcud weed is easily grown in open, sandy soil, and can be increased by division of the clumps in early spring. As noted below, some plants credited to *Gnaphalium* belong elsewhere.

**lanatum** = *Helichrysum petiolatum.*
**leontopodium** = *Leontopodium alpinum.* See EDELWEISS.
**sylvaticum.** Wood cudweed; also called owl's-crown and chafeweed. A rather weedy, perennial herb 6–18 in. high, the stem mostly unbranched. Leaves narrow, sharp-pointed, about 1½ in. long. Flower heads numerous, about ¼ in. wide, in a more or less leafy spike. North temperate zone and common in northeastern N.A. July.

**GNETACEAE.** See EPHEDRA.

**GOA BEAN** = *Psophocarpus tetragonolobus.*

**GOATSBEARD.** See ARUNCUS and TRAGOPOGON.

**GOAT'S-RUE** = *Tephrosia virginiana* or *Galega officinalis.*

**GOAT WILLOW** = *Salix caprea.* See WILLOW.

**GOBO** = *Arctium lappa.* See list at WEEDS.

**GODETIA** (go-dee'she-a). A genus of perhaps 25 species of New World, prevailingly annual herbs of the family Onagraceae, some of them very popular as flower garden annuals. They have alternate,* stalkless or short-stalked leaves, and showy, day-blooming flowers in leafy clusters (racemes*) or in spikes. Calyx* tubular, often colored like the petals which are 4, usually pink, lilac-purple or white, and sometimes crimson- or purple-spotted. Stamens* 8, 4 shorter than the others. Fruit a 4-valved capsule, its seeds numerous. (Named for C. H. Godet, Swiss botanist.)

All those below are best grown as tender annuals. (See ANNUALS.) The first species is extremely popular and makes a fine plant for cutting. Like a few other annuals, it blooms more profusely if the plants are a bit crowded; in other words, do not thin them out too much.

**amoena.** Farewell-to-spring. A slender, branching herb 12–30 in. high. Leaves lance-shaped or narrower, ¾–2 in. long, often with smaller ones in the axils.* Flowers 1–2 in. wide, the petals satiny, lilac-crimson or reddish-pink. Fruit roundish in cross-section. Mid-July to Oct. British Columbia to Calif. There are many fine garden forms, some white, some double-flowered, and one crimson-blotched. A very showy and desirable annual sometimes known as satin-flower.

---

* Special articles on the subjects indicated by an asterisk (*) will be found at the words so marked.

**bottae.** Resembling *G. amoena*, but the buds nodding, and the petals light pink or light crimson, and the pods flattish. Southern Calif. Summer.

**grandiflora.** An unbranched annual 8–14 in. high, its leaves oblongish, tapering both ends. Flowers in a short spike, the corolla 3–5 in. wide, red but deeper red-blotched at the center. There are also pure white, crimson, and carmine forms. Pods 4-sided. Calif. Summer.

**GOLD-DUST** = *Alyssum saxatile* and *Sedum acre*.

**GOLD-DUST TREE** = *Aucuba japonica variegata*.

**GOLDEN.** As an adjective, *golden* is part of the name of many plants with yellow, orange, or golden-colored flowers or fruit. Those in THE GARDEN DICTIONARY and their proper equivalents are:

Golden aster (see CHRYSOPSIS); Golden bamboo = *Phyllostachys aurea*; Golden bell (see FORSYTHIA); Golden bells = *Emmenanthe penduliflora*; Golden calla lily = *Zantedeschia elliottiana* (see CALLA LILY); Goldenchain = *Laburnum anagyroides*; Golden chinquapin = *Castanopsis chrysophylla*; Golden clematis = *Clematis tangutica*; Golden club = *Orontium aquaticum*; Golden coreopsis = *Coreopsis tinctoria*; Golden crown-beard = *Verbesina encelioides*; Golden cup = *Hunnemannia fumariaefolia*; Golden currant = *Ribes aureum*; Golden eardrops = *Dicentra chrysantha*; Golden-eyed grass = *Sisyrinchium californicum*; Gold fern (see PITYROGRAMMA); Golden flax = *Linum flavum*; Golden garden (see YELLOW GARDEN); Goldenglow = *Rudbeckia laciniata hortensia*; Golden gram = *Phaseolus aureus*; Golden larch (see PSEUDOLARIX); Golden loosestrife = *Lysimachia vulgaris*; Golden marguerite = *Anthemis tinctoria*; Golden moss = SEDUM *acre*; Golden osier = *Salix vitellina* (see WILLOW); Golden polypody = *Polypodium aureum*; Golden queen = *Trollius ledebouri*; Golden ragwort = *Senecio aureus*; Goldenrod (see second main entry below); Goldenseal (see fourth main entry below); Golden shower = *Cassia fistula*; Golden star = *Chrysopsis mariana*; Golden stars = *Bloomeria crocea*; Golden thistle = *Scolymus hispanicus*; Golden-top = *Lamarckia aurea*; Golden trumpet = *Allamanda cathartica hendersoni*; Golden tuft = *Alyssum saxatile*; Golden wattle = *Acacia longifolia*; Golden-wave = *Coreopsis drummondi*; Golden wonder millet = *Setaria italica stramineofructa*; Golden wreath = *Acacia saligna*.

**GOLDEN GATE PARK.** See ARBORETUM.

**GOLDENROD.** Coarse, rather weedy herbs belonging to the genus **Solidago** (sol-i-day'go) of the family Compositae. All but a handful of the 140 known species are from the New World, with scattered species in Eu. and As. They are usually perennial herbs, often branched or arching, and have alternate,* usually toothed leaves. Flower heads mostly yellow (white in one hort. species), the small heads very numerous and crowded in sometimes one-sided clusters, or these branched and consisting of compound panicles* or racemes.* While the whole inflorescence is often showy, the plants are little used in the garden outside of the more informal borders. (*Solidago* is from the Latin implying to strengthen or draw together, in allusion to the supposed medicinal properties.)

The goldenrods are of very easy culture and make attractive groupings with native asters (see ASTER) and other fall-blooming wild flowers. While they improve with cultivation, the soil should not be too rich, or they may develop more foliage than flowers. They can easily be divided, and in fact some species spread so fast that they need to be watched.

**S. bicolor.** Silver-rod, or white goldenrod. Not usually over 3 ft., the stems wand-like, or sometimes branched. Leaves oblongish, 2–4 in. long, hairy and toothed. Flower heads white, in a narrow, spike-like cluster 5–7 in. long. Eastern N.A.

**S. caesia.** Wreath goldenrod. A smooth-stemmed, often bluish-green herb 1–3 ft. high. Leaves lance-shaped, 3–5 in. long, and toothed. Flower heads yellow, in clusters in the axils,* the whole flower cluster thus leafy. Eastern N.A. and west to Tex.

**S. canadensis.** Rock goldenrod; also called yellow-weed. A tall, striking, branching plant often 4–6 ft. high. Leaves narrowly lance-shaped, 3–5 in. long, prominently 3-veined, but without teeth. Flower heads yellow in very large, terminal, 1-sided clusters. Eastern N.A.

**S. latifolia.** A smooth-stemmed, somewhat zigzag perennial 18–36 in. high. Leaves broadly oval, pointed both ends, sharply toothed. Flower heads yellow, in short clusters in the upper leaf-axils,* long pointed at the ends of the branches. Eastern N.A.

**S. nemoralis.** Dwarf or gray goldenrod. A grayish-hairy, wand-like plant not over 2 ft. high. Leaves broadest towards the tip, 4–6 in. long, the margins wavy-toothed. Flower heads yellow, in congested, prominently 1-sided, terminal clusters. Eastern N.A. A fine plant for dry, sandy banks.

**S. rigida.** A coarse, stiff-hairy herb 3–5 ft. high, its leaves oblongish or oval, 1½–3 in. long, mostly without teeth. Flower heads yellow, mostly in terminal clusters (corymbs*) that are not conspicuously 1-sided. Mass. to Ga. and Tex.

**S. sempervirens.** Beach or seaside goldenrod. A completely smooth, stout, thick-stemmed herb 5–8 ft. high. Leaves thick or even fleshy, oblongish, 6–10 in. long, without teeth. Flower heads yellow, in large, branched, terminal and 1-sided clusters. On sea beaches or salt marshes, eastern N.A. and south to Mex. A fine plant for the seaside garden, although it will also grow in any good sandy loam.

**GOLDENROD FAMILY.** See COMPOSITAE.

**GOLDENSEAL.** Two species of perennial herbs of the genus **Hydrastis** (hy-dras'tis) of the buttercup family, one Asiatic, the other **H. canadensis** of the richer woods of the eastern U.S., and cult. in the wild garden under the name of yellow puccoon, yellowroot, and Indian dye. It has a thick, yellow, medicinal rootstock, for which it is often cult. commercially. Leaves chiefly basal, nearly 8 in. wide and deeply 5–9-lobed. Stem leaves usually 2, the upper one just beneath the flowers and stalkless. Flowers about ¼ in. wide, greenish-white, without petals, but with 3 petal-like sepals.* Stamens* numerous. April–May. Fruit a collection or head of red berries. Its culture for ornament should be in the shadier part of the wild garden. Its commercial culture is the same as for ginseng (which see). See also MEDICINAL PLANTS. (The origin of the name is unknown.)

**GOLD FERN.** See PITYROGRAMMA.

**GOLDFIELDS.** See BAERIA.

**GOLD-FLOWER** = *Hypericum moserianum*. See ST. JOHN'S-WORT.

**GOLDIE'S FERN** = *Dryopteris goldieana*.

**GOLDILOCKS** = *Linosyris vulgaris*.

**GOLDTHREAD.** See COPTIS.

**GOMESA** (go-mee'za). Brazilian tree-perching orchids, little known in cult. except **G. planifolia**, which is best grown in a moderately cool greenhouse. See Epiphytic Greenhouse Orchids at ORCHIDS. It bears pseudobulbs* that are about 2 in. long, and from which spring 2–3 narrow leaves. Flowers yellowish-green in hanging clusters (racemes*) that are profuse-flowered and about 8 in. long. One of the sepals* and the petals alike, partially united and wavy. Lip* shorter than the sepals, with 2 crests. In the greenhouse it blooms in June–July. (Named for Bernardinus A. Gomes, Portuguese surgeon interested in Brazilian botany.)

**GOMPHRENA** (gom-free'na). A genus of over 90 tropical, Old World herbs of the family Amaranthaceae, **G. globosa**, the globe amaranth, a deservedly popular flower garden annual, grown for its fine bloom which is so lasting when dried that the plant is one of the more useful everlastings. It is 8–20 in. high, and superficially resembles a clover. Leaves opposite,* oblongish or elliptic, 2–4 in. long, without teeth, but the margins minutely hairy. Flowers chaffy, in dense, long-stalked, clover-like heads of red, pink, white, or yellow flowers without petals. Fruit 1-seeded, dry (a utricle*). The globe amaranth, which is found in many hort. forms, is a fine plant for summer and later bloom, and for cutting. It should be treated as a tender annual. (See ANNUALS. See also DRIED FLOWERS, for the best method of preserving these everlastings. (*Gomphrena* is an old name for some amaranth, but possibly not for this one.) Occasionally called bachelor's button.

**GOMUTI** = *Arenga saccharifera*.

**GOOBER.** See PEANUT.

**GOODIA** (good'i-a). A small genus of Australian shrubs of the pea family, **G. lotifolia** grown outdoors in southern Calif., but scarcely known elsewhere. It is an ornamental, much-branched shrub with compound* leaves and 3 ovalish leaflets about ¾ in. long and without teeth. Flowers pea-like, yellow, but the standard* purple at the base, grouped in racemes* that are about 3–4 in. long. Fruit a flattish pod (legume*) about 1 in. long. (Named for Peter Good who found the plant.)

**GOOD-KING-HENRY** = *Chenopodium bonus-henricus*.

**GOOD-MORNING-SPRING** = *Claytonia virginica*.

**GOODYERA.** See EPIPACTIS.

**GOOLS** = *Caltha palustris*. See MARSH MARIGOLD.

**GOORA-NUT** = *Cola acuminata*.

**GOOSEBERRY** (*Ribes*). The gooseberry is a neglected fruit in America. Perhaps not more than a dozen varieties are grown in the United States and Canada, whereas in

---

* Special articles on the subjects indicated by an asterisk (*) will be found at the words so marked.

Great Britain not less than a thousand sorts have been listed for British gardeners, with whom it is a great favorite. Americans seem not to have acquired or cultivated a taste for the gooseberry.

Gooseberries do not "strike" readily from cuttings and so are usually propagated from mound layers. In this operation vigorous, healthy bushes, 5 or 6 years old, are cut back closely in the dormant season. About the middle of July friable earth is piled up around the bushes until only the tops of the shoots are uncovered. Shoots of American varieties are well rooted by the following fall, but English sorts are left a year longer. The rooted shoots are set in nursery rows for 1 or 2 years after being detached. Rich, moist, well-drained clay soils suit gooseberries best. This is a fruit that cannot be coaxed to thrive in sands or light loams. It is just as particular about climate. English gooseberries find the hot sun of any part of America trying and refuse to grow in any part of the country except the north Atlantic and north Pacific seaboards and close to the Great Lakes. If the soil is suitable, a gooseberry will stand more shade than any other cultivated fruit, and in trying climates cannot be grown without it.

Perhaps the gooseberry is best transplanted in autumn, and if in spring it must be early, since the buds open with the first burst of spring warmth. The plants are spaced variously, depending upon the soil and the vigor of the varieties. Five feet apart each way is a fair average. Some growers like to set them close in the row with greater distances between rows. Plants well cared for last many years, and ground should be in good tilth* before planting.

In commercial plantations, gooseberries should receive shallow cultivation, but in gardens they thrive under mulches of straw or grass. Barnyard manure supplies a good mulch and a fertilizer as well. Chemical fertilizers seldom pay for their cost. If the culture of gooseberries is attempted in the interior states it is a good practice to plant them in the shade of trees, fences, or grapevines. Under shade the plants should be grown with open heads to discourage mildews.

Pruning and training is very simple but quite necessary. The fruit is borne for most part on 2- and 3-year-old wood, and pruning is close with the view to keeping a vigorous supply of bearing wood. Cut out canes older than three years and feeble ones of lesser age. Gooseberries can be trained to single stems, but the bush form is better. A sprawling habit can be corrected by cutting back. Sometimes it is necessary to prune out the tops to lessen mildew and thin the crop.

Gooseberries, especially American varieties, are nearly always picked green, an unpleasant task, since the canes and shoots bristle with thorns. The berries are best picked by raising and steadying a cane with one hand and stripping the pendent berries off with the other — gloves on both hands. The berries are usually sent to market in quart baskets packed in 32-quart crates, or in 12-quart Climax baskets.

Gooseberries belong to two quite distinct species, which gardeners classify as American and European. Downing, ripening in midseason, is the most commonly grown American sort. Josselyn (Red Jacket of some) is a good early variety. Poorman is noteworthy for its large productive bushes and handsome fruits of high quality. Out of several hundred European varieties Chautauqua and Fredonia are best and these may be grown only in the eastern parts of zones* 2 and 3, and on the Pacific Coast in zone* 4. Gardeners trained in Europe, who know this fruit well, can, with a little care, grow a good many of the splendid English varieties. — U. P. H.

Its pests and their control are the same as for the currant (which see).

**GOOSEBERRY FAMILY.** See SAXIFRAGACEAE.

**GOOSEBERRY-TREE** = *Phyllanthus acidus*.

**GOOSEFOOT.** See CHENOPODIUM.

**GOOSEFOOT FAMILY.** Besides many weeds, this large family of plants includes a few shrubs, often of desert or alkali regions, and such well-known garden plants as the beet, spinach, summer cypress, and the orach. For the other genera and a description of the family see CHENOPODIACEAE.

**GOPHER-BERRY** = *Gaylussacia dumosa*. See HUCKLEBERRY.

**GOPHER-PLUM** = *Chrysobalanus icaco*.

**GOPHERS.** See ANIMAL INJURY.

**GOPHERWOOD** = *Cladrastis lutea*.

**GORDONIA** (gor-dō'ni-a). Rather rare, and botanically interesting, late-blooming shrubs or trees of the family Theaceae, all but two of the species Asiatic, but both the native ones grown for ornament. They have half-evergreen, or completely evergreen, alternate,* stalked leaves without marginal teeth, or remotely toothed. Flowers large, solitary, white, the 5 sepals unequal, the petals sometimes partly united. Stamens* many. Fruit a woody capsule, its seeds flat. (Named for James Gordon, English nurseryman.)

The first species has a remarkable history. It was introduced into cult. in 1770, but has never been seen again in the wild state, although it was recently reported (erroneously) as re-discovered. Both species need low, moist, peaty soils. They may be propagated by seeds, layers, or by cuttings.

**alatamaha.** A shrub or small tree, not over 25 ft. high, the branches erect. Leaves oblongish, 5–7 in. long, remotely toothed, long-persistent, but ultimately bright crimson in the late fall. Flowers cup-shaped, about 3½ in. wide. Fruit nearly globe-shaped, ½–¾ in. in diameter. Ga. Sept.–Oct. Hardy from zone* 5, or with protection, from zone* 4 southward. Sometimes known as *Franklinia*.

**lasianthus.** Loblolly bay; also called tan bay. An evergreen tree up to 60 ft. high. Leaves 5–6 in. long, oblongish, turning reddish before they fall, which is irregularly. Flowers fragrant, 2–3 in. wide, long-stalked. Fruit egg-shaped and slightly pointed. Va. to Fla. and Miss. July–Aug. Hardy from zone* 6 southward, and considerably planted in Fla. for ornament.

**GORMANIA** (gor-man'i-a). Succulent plants of western N.A., related to and resembling *Sedum*, and belonging to the family Crassulaceae. They have chiefly basal, roundish, blunt leaves, those on the stem fewer and smaller, but otherwise similar. Flowers in terminal clusters, red or yellowish, the 5 petals more or less united at the base. Stamens* 10. Fruit a collection of follicles.* (Named for M. W. Gorman, of Portland, Ore., a collector of plants from the Pacific Northwest.)

For culture, see SEDUM.

**obtusata.** Not over 6 in. high, the foliage sometimes bluish-green. Leaves about ¾ in. long, broadest towards the blunt tip. Flowers yellowish, the segments of it pointed, the cluster rather narrow. In the Sierras of Calif. Sometimes offered as *Sedum obtusatum*.

**oregana.** Not over 6 in. high, always green. Leaves less than ¾ in. long, more or less wedge-shaped at the base, broader towards the tip. Flowers yellow, fading to pink or reddish, the cluster nearly 3 in. wide and branched. Alaska to Northern Calif. Sometimes offered as *Sedum oreganum*.

**GORSE.** See FURZE.

**GOSMORE** = *Hypochaeris radicata*. See Cat's-ear in the list at WEEDS.

**GOSSYPIUM** (gos-sip'i-um). While cotton is in no sense a garden plant, its huge commercial culture for fiber, and the fact that the different species are occasionally grown for interest or ornament, make a brief note on them necessary here. The flowers are also favorites of the bees, although it is scarcely cult. for that purpose, except possibly in parts of Calif. The genus contains perhaps 30 species, belonging to the family Malvaceae, some of them woody herbs, but some tree-like. Practically all of them are grown as annuals in the U.S. All are of tropical origin and need a long season and much heat to produce seed. Consequently, their commercial culture is confined to the cotton belt, which roughly coincides with the region from zone* 7 southward, although the plant will flower much farther north. Leaves alternate,* more or less lobed or ribbed finger-fashion, often dotted. Flowers usually solitary in the leaf-axils,* large, showy, generally white, yellow, or pinkish-purple, but often changing color soon after opening. Below the flower is a collection of 3–7, often fringed or cut bracts.* Calyx* 5-lobed. Petals 5. Stamens numerous, joined together to form a tube around the style.* Fruit a capsule* (the cotton boll), containing the seeds, to which is attached the fiber (cotton). (*Gossypium* is a very old name for the cotton plant.) There are now many

---

* Special articles on the subjects indicated by an asterisk (*) will be found at the words so marked.

valuable named forms of the species below, and these are the ones chiefly grown commercially.

**arboreum.** Tree cotton; also called Indian tree cotton. An erect plant 8–10 ft. high, the branches glossy and purple. Leaves leathery, 3–7-lobed, sometimes deeply so. Flowers small, pale yellow or whitish-pink, sometimes blotched at the center (with an eye*). Fruit egg-shaped or ovalish, the lint of the seeds dull white or reddish. Old World tropics. Not one of the commercial cottons in the U.S.

**barbadense.** Sea-island cotton; sometimes called tree cotton, and widely grown commercially here and in Egypt. It is a shrubby plant 5–8 ft. high. Leaves as broad as long, 3–5-lobed, the lobes pointed, the base more or less heart-shaped. Flowers yellow, but purple-tinged. Fruit 3–4-valved, the lint of the seeds yielding fine long-staple cotton. Tropical America, but described first from Barbados, W.I.

**herbaceum.** Levant cotton. Stem not woody, annual. Leaves generally heart-shaped, 5–7-lobed, the lobes not deeper than half the distance to the center. Flowers yellow, the center purplish. Fruit 4–5-celled, the lint of the seeds grayish. Asia Minor or Arabia, probably. Not grown commercially, but assumed as one of the parents of certain short-staple U.S. cotton varieties.

**hirsutum.** Upland cotton and a commercially important source of both long- and short-staple varieties. Mostly an annual, much-branched, reddish-stemmed plant 2–5 ft. high. Leaves 3–6 in. wide, 3-lobed, the lobes broad below but pointed at the tip. Flowers yellowish-white, but soon turning purplish-pink. Fruit 1½–3½ in. long, 4-celled, the lint white. Tropical America.

**mexicanum.** Mexican cotton. A shrubby plant of no commercial importance in the U.S., 3–5-lobed leaves that are divided only about ⅓ the distance to the center. Flowers yellowish-white, tinged with pink. Lint or fuzz of the seeds grayish. Mex.

**punctatum.** Jamaica cotton. A shrubby, non-commercial cotton, the stems 4–5 ft. high. Leaves softly hairy, divided halfway to the middle, strongly dotted. Flowers yellow, the center brown. Lint or fuzz of the seeds grayish or rusty. Tropical America and Africa.

**GOURD FAMILY** = Cucurbitaceae.

**GOURDS.** As distinguished from the edible melons, pumpkins, squashes and cucumbers, the ornamental gourds are chiefly grown for show. All belong to the family Cucurbitaceae, and their need for heat, moisture, and rich soil is the same as for the melons (which *see* for cultural directions).

All the ornamental gourds in THE GARDEN DICTIONARY are described at the following genera: *Abobra, Cucumis, Cucurbita, Lagenaria, Luffa,* and *Trichosanthes*.

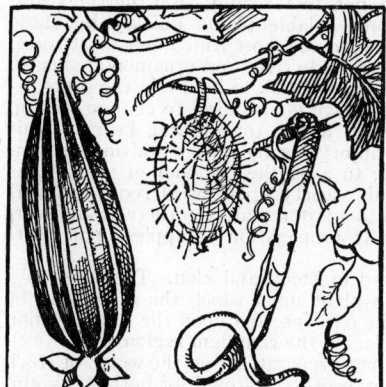

Gourds. At the left, the dishrag gourd; in the center the mock-cucumber, a hardy, native gourd; at the right the snake gourd.

Some of them have grotesque fruits, as shown in the illustrations, while others are extremely decorative and are grown to cover porches, screens, or fences, which they do in a very short time. (See VINES.) While they can be treated as tender annuals, they do not bear transplanting well, and are better sown where wanted, after settled warm weather has arrived. If grown in an open bed, some sort of a rough-barked, twiggy post or trellis must be provided for them. All are tendril-bearing vines,

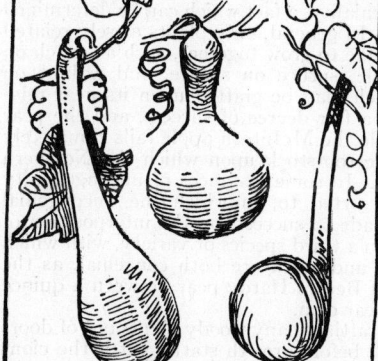

Various forms of the bottle gourd

which, without support, will sprawl like a pumpkin vine.

Some of their fruits make handsome table decorations. A hardy, native one is *Echinocystis lobata,* the mock-cucumber.

**GOUTWEED** = *Aegopodium podagraria.*

**GOVERNOR'S-PLUM** = *Flacourtia indica.*

**GRABOWSKIA** (gra-bou'ski-a). A small genus of New World, chiefly tropical shrubs of the potato family, one of them, **G. boerhaaviaefolia,** planted in Calif. and similar climates for ornament. It is a sprawling bush resembling the matrimony vine, with alternate,* grayish-green leaves that have in most of the axils* spines about ¼ in. long. Some of the twigs or spurs are also spine-like. Flowers blue or pale whitish, solitary, or in small clusters at the ends of the smaller branches. Corolla funnel-shaped, not very showy, its limb* 5-lobed and spreading. Stamens* 5, protruding. Fruit fleshy, berry-like, about ½ in. long. Scarcely known outside Calif. Native of Peru. (Named for H. E. Grabowsky, German botanist.)

*GRACILIPES* (gra-sill'i-peez). Slender-stalked; literally slender-footed.

*GRACILIS, -e* (grass'i-lis). Slender and graceful.

*GRACILLIMA, -us, -um* (gra-sill'i-ma). Very slender or graceful.

**GRADING FRUIT.** The grading of fruit is mostly a commercial business which involves the reasonable, and honest, segregation of different sizes and qualities. For the home grower, ordinary selection of the best fruit is all that is needed. But if large quantities of fruit are raised and some of it sold or stored, it is well to keep in mind the practice of those commercial growers who have found that honest grading is the best policy in a highly competitive field like the fruit business. This is especially true in the West, where various fruit exchanges and marketing organizations have worked out elaborate scales of perfection in fruit.

Grading can be of at least three sorts — for size, color, and blemishes. In large-scale operations it is possible to get any number of mechanical sorting machines that will segregate different sizes of the larger fruits, the skins of which are not injured by such equipment. But there is no machine which will pick out color or blemishes, both of which must be done before the fruit is graded for size.

For most small-scale operations a padded sorting table is the best. It can be of ordinary table height with a rim about three inches high around all edges, and the rim and table-top should be thinly padded to prevent bruising. Make the pad removable for washing, as fruit juices from blemished fruit will be sure to soak into it. Much grading can, of course, be avoided by careful picking, but if the fruit is the general run of the orchard, a grading table is a useful bit of equipment.

**GRADING LAND.** In reshaping land for use the term grading is used in engineering practice where utility is the primary purpose. Grading as applied to landscape design should be more than an engineering operation, it should be a process of modeling land primarily for appearance. Wherever it is necessary to change the natural shape of land for practical use the remodeling is quite as essential to landscape beauty as any other phase of composition. No amount of planting or architectural ornamentation will compensate for ugly grading.

Study grading in the preliminary stages of planning to take advantage of excesses or shortages of soil. Collaborative planning between architects, engineers, and landscape architects, or equivalent comprehensive planning by individuals, is essential to efficient and well-designed grading.

Use excavation from building foundations, roads or walls as subsoil to create terraces or improve the general grade. Gardens and terraces can usually be made to utilize excess excavation or, when necessary, to provide extra fill. When such adjustments are left to afterthought, opportunities for utilizing these differences to advantage are often lost. With modern engineering equipment it is possible to anticipate and utilize the exact amount of grading involved in any construction operation. Before starting any subgrading, con-

---

* Special articles on the subjects indicated by an asterisk (*) will be found at the words so marked.

Two methods of correcting an unfortunate natural grade (shown at top). In the middle a wall (or bank) rises from the street level. The lowest figure shows the most satisfactory but expensive solution, a gently sloping surface from sidewalk to the house.

serve all existing topsoil and pile in convenient piles out of the way of all construction. On large operations a power shovel can skim soil as thin as six inches. On smaller jobs plow to the depth of good soil and use a scoop to collect the soil in piles. A haul of over 100 yards is not efficiently done by scoops; for longer hauls load on 2-ton dump trucks. Where properties are less than an acre, and topsoil is not over six inches deep, move by hand labor and wheelbarrows.

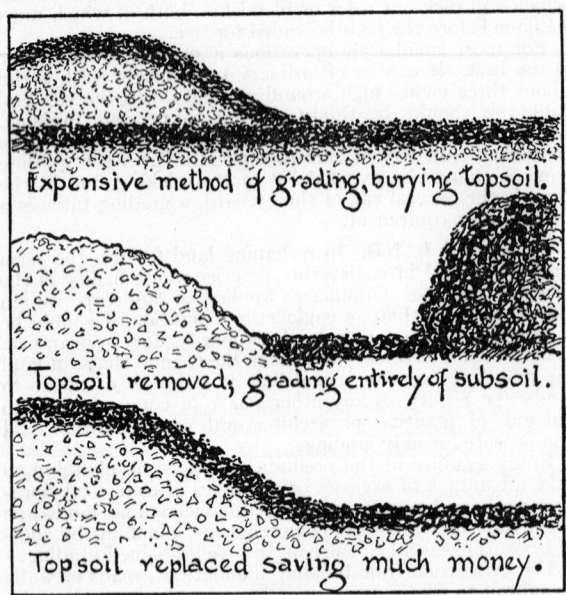

Much money is wasted in grading if expensive topsoil is buried. Study the two lower figures to see how this can be avoided.

The subgrade should be modeled to conform to the finished grade, allowing six inches for topsoil on lawn areas, and at least 24 inches for planting beds. Planting pockets should be dug in the subgrade according to the planting plan in order that all subsoil may be distributed before topsoil is replaced. If possible, mix manure with topsoil when it is piled and if weeds grow on the pile keep them cut to avoid weed seeds.

The solution of the drainage system is a part of the grading problem and they should be planned together. Unless they are equally well planned one or the other is bound to be unsatisfactory. One of the practical reasons for grading is to control drainage. Wherever possible open drainage gutters should be avoided in landscape grading. By providing frequent drain inlets water can be carried away in underground lines cheaper than constantly repairing surface gutters. Properly modeled land surfaces should be drained effectively without causing erosion or allowing water to accumulate where it can cause damage. Inadequate drainage will result in erosion, and unsatisfactory grading will result in drains being clogged or washed out. — R. E. G.

*GRAECA, -us, -um* (gree′ka). Grecian.

**GRAFT-HYBRID.** The assumed influence of a stock upon the cion into which it has been grafted. Much has been written upon this subject, but authentic instances of it are extremely rare. Specialists insist that the correct term for graft-hybrids is chimera (which see). *See also* POMATO.

**GRAFTING.** Graftage involves the bringing together of the growing regions of two different individuals under such conditions that they will unite and grow as one. It is used to propagate plants that do not reproduce true from seed, and which either do not root readily from cuttings and layers or do not make salable plants quickly by these processes. Such plants include most fruit trees, most roses, many evergreens, some shade trees and ornamental shrubs, and a few succulents. In addition to its use in the propagation of new plants, graftage is also used to change the top of an established plant, as by top-working bearing fruit trees; to correct an injury, as by bridge-grafting and in-arching girdled trees; to alter the behavior of the top, as by propagating a fruit variety upon dwarf roots to dwarf the entire plant; and to adapt a plant to otherwise unfavorable conditions, as the propagation of apples upon roots resistant to root rot.

A graft is composed of **stock** and **cion**. The stock is a plant or portion of a plant upon which the graft is to be made. The cion is the part inserted upon the stock. **Union** is accomplished by placing the **cambium region** (*see* BARK), the region where the bark separates from the wood, of stock and of cion against each other. Growth of both stock and cion in the cambium region results in so-called union, by an interlacing and dovetailing of tissues. Sharp tools, clean, straight cuts, careful matching of cambium regions, snug fitting and fastening, and careful protection from drying of tissues both before and after the grafting operation, are conducive to success.

The union of plants with one another by grafting is limited by their congeniality, a fact which can be determined solely by experience. In general, only plants closely related botanically can be made to grow together, such as peach on peach, apple on apple, spruce on spruce, and walnut on walnut. Yet the peach may be grafted upon its near relative, the plum, with a fair degree of success, and the pear upon the quince, while the McIntosh apple fails completely upon a selected apple rootstock upon which the Northern Spy variety succeeds. In some instances of uncongeniality **double-working** is resorted to, in which the uncongenial cion and stock are made to succeed by the interposition of a portion of stem from a third species or variety, with which the uncongenial cion and stock are both congenial, as the use of a stem-piece of Beurré Hardy pear between a quince root and a Bartlett pear cion.

The best time for grafting many woody plants out of doors is in early spring just before growth starts, yet if the cions are maintained dormant by storage under cool, moist conditions, grafting may be done even after the stock has begun new growth. With grafting of plants in full leaf and active growth, success is dependent largely upon maintaining the

---

* Special articles on the subjects indicated by an asterisk (*) will be found at the words so marked.

cion from drying out, as by enclosing the grafted plants in closed frames with high humidity.

Cion wood of deciduous woody plants should be dormant both when it is collected and when it is used. Wood should be taken from vigorous shoots of the past season's growth, 12 in. or more in length. It is possible, however, to use 2- and even 3-year-old wood. It should be collected in late fall or early winter, tied in bundles, packed in sawdust or peat moss, and stored in a cool, damp place, such as a cool cellar. A temperature of 40° is best. Two or 3 in. of the base and a portion of the tip of the shoot should be discarded, since the buds at the base of the shoots are frequently poorly developed, while the tip is frequently soft. If it becomes necessary to collect frozen wood, it should be carefully handled and should be thawed slowly, as in a cool room, but not in water.

Grafts are classified and named according to:
(1) Time, as summer grafting, winter grafting, or dormant grafting;
(2) Place, as root graft, crown graft, stem graft, and top graft;
(3) Part used, as root graft, twig graft, sprig graft;
(4) Description of method or type of cut, as cleft graft, bridge graft, bark graft, saddle graft, veneer graft, side graft, and tongue graft. Accordingly, a plant may be root grafted by tongue grafting, it may be top grafted by cleft grafting, and so on. **Budding,** in which a single bud is used in place of a cion, may quite properly be included as a method of grafting, but is treated separately. *See* BUDDING.

There are endless modifications of the principal forms of graftage, each named by its originator or user for convenience, or because it describes a method found successful with some particular material or in some particular locality. Most of them are merely variations of the forms described under the following general headings.

### CLEFT GRAFTING

The cleft graft is most often used on large trees. Trees of more than 8 years of age are better top-worked during more than one season because of the severe pruning incident to cleft grafting. Work the center and top of the tree the first season, otherwise the grafts may be shaded; and work the sides and lower portions the next and succeeding seasons.

The most favorable time for cleft grafting is just before growth starts, although it may be done both during the winter and also after growth has started. The cion wood, however, must be dormant. Choose branches ranging from 1 to 4 in. in diameter; those about 1½ to 2 in. across are the most convenient and satisfactory. For very large limbs the *bark graft*, described later, is preferred. The limb should be sawed off squarely and split with a grafting chisel and mallet.

In making the split care should be taken to see that it does not run into a knot, but extends straight down on either side of the limb. In cases where four or more cions are wanted, the extra clefts should be made parallel to the first and not across it. The two halves of the limb are spread apart by the wedge on the grafting chisel.

Cleft grafting, showing (*top center*) the two cions and (*bottom center*) the stock, both cut ready for grafting. At the right the cions inserted in the stock. At the left the finished graft with its coating of wax.

Cions should bear two or three buds, preferably three, although it is possible to use only one when economy of wood is essential. Beginning on either side of a bud, with two strokes of the knife cut the lower end of the cion in the form of a wedge, one side of which should be slightly narrower than the other. If the sides of the cion are not cut clean and straight so as to taper evenly, the point of contact may be only at the thickest portion of the cion rather than through its length. The wedge of the cion is then inserted into the cleft with its narrower side toward the center of the stock, thus allowing the outer and thicker edge of the cion to be firmly gripped when the parts of the stock spring together. Utmost care should be taken to match the growing layer, or inner bark, of the cion with that of the stock. They must come in contact. If the cion is set too far towards the center of the cleft, the cambium zones will not match.

The final step is waxing. The wax should be spread in a thin coat over all the cut surfaces, including the tip of the cion, and extending down the limb on both sides covering the cleft.

A variation of the cleft graft may be used to propagate varieties of grapes of both American and European species upon phylloxera*-resistant or more vigorous roots, and also to change a bearing vine to another variety. The work may be done after active growth has passed, or preferably, just before growth starts in early spring. Established vines, preferably not over 6 or 8 years old, are sawed off at the ground. With a thin-bladed saw a cleft is cut down through the center of the stock for about 2 in. Cions are cut with two buds, with the wedge starting at the lower bud. A single cion is then inserted in the cleft as already described for fruit trees. Two cions may be used if the stock is large. No wax is used, and it is usually not necessary to tie the graft except with young vines. Dry dirt is mounded over the graft, covering the top of the cion, so as to keep the graft uniformly moist and at a more even temperature. Two or three times during the summer the mound should be removed to cut away any sprouts which come from the stock and any roots which come from the cion.

WEDGE GRAFTING. This is the same in general principle as the cleft graft, differing in that a wedge is cut in the stock rather than merely splitting it. It generally involves herbaceous or softwooded plants, both stock and cion being of nearly the same size, and the cion being held in place by tying.

### WHIP GRAFTING

The whip graft, also called **tongue graft,** is used for small limbs, for grafting grapes, and for root grafting nursery stock. It is easily made, and because of the several uniting edges, forms a good union. In the case of trees, the stock should be cut off with a slanting cut 1½ in. long. Half an inch down from the cut end of the stock, cut, but do not split, a tongue downwards about half an inch. The objection to splitting the tongue is that it leaves a rough surface which will not fit the cion.

The base of the cion is prepared in the same way as the stock, and the two are then fitted to match the growing parts along one side. The union should be bound with common twine, grafting tape, or, if available, waxed string or waxed cloth strips, and then thoroughly waxed. After growth is well started, usually in June, the strings under the wax should be cut to prevent girdling. This is best done by drawing a sharp knife up the back side of the graft.

In grafting the grape, the procedure is similar, the best results being secured in March. For the stock, sections of 1-year canes should be used 8 to 10 in. in length and at least ¼ in. in diameter, the top cut being made 1½ in. above the top bud and all buds removed so as to lessen sucker growth. The cion is made with one bud, the lower cut being made 2½ in. below the bud and the upper cut 1½ in. above. The stock and cion are joined as described above, and tied with wax string. The resulting grafts are packed upright in a box in wet sawdust and stored at 70° to 75°. They are planted out in the nursery row before the buds have started.

---
* Special articles on the subjects indicated by an asterisk (*) will be found at the words so marked.

## Root Grafting

In the case of root grafting with nursery stock, seedling roots are cut into pieces 4 or 5 in. long and cions are prepared of the same length and of as nearly the same diameter as the roots as possible. The process is the same as in top-working, except that no wax is used, while grafting tape and waxed string are preferred for tying. The grafts are packed away in damp moss or sand in a cool cellar until spring when they are planted in nursery rows, leaving only the upper bud above ground. Careful matching of stock and cion will reduce loss from callus knot formation. Sometimes a whole root is used instead of short pieces, when the graft is known as a **whole-root graft**, as contrasted with **piece-root graft**. In cases where it is desired to secure a cion-rooted plant, a **nurse-root graft** may be used, in which the cion of a root graft is planted deep so as to encourage rooting of the cion, after which the nurse root is cut off. A copper wire may be placed just above the union so as gradually to constrict the nurse root and automatically cut it off without the necessity of digging the entire plant to remove it.

There are various modifications of the whip graft of which the **side whip graft** is one, in which the cion is placed on the side of a stock rather than on the end of it. The cut end of the cion may be left long or the tie allowed to hang down so as to rest in a container of water and supply water by absorption while the graft is uniting. This is sometimes called **bottle grafting**, more interesting than useful.

## Splice Grafting

Splice grafting, used for tender wood which does not split readily and for small shoots, is perhaps the simplest form of grafting. The cion and stock are cut with a diagonal cut as for whip grafting, the tongue being omitted, and tied together. Sometimes a pin is placed vertically in the stock, and the cion pressed down upon it, so as to make the graft more firm. With cions which have a terminal bud, and with some soft and herbaceous plants, as cacti, the stock is cut flat wedge-shaped and the cion, with a split or wedge-shaped cut in the lower end, placed upon it, whence the name **saddle graft**.

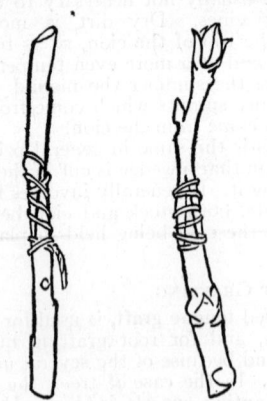

At the right a saddle graft; at the left a splice graft

## Side Grafting

The side graft is a form of grafting used with both dormant and full-growing plants, in which the cion is inserted in the side of the stock, the stock being cut off just above the point of insertion either immediately after grafting, at a later time, or not at all, as the case may demand. It is used in grafting woody ornamentals with slender stems, particularly potted junipers, arborvitae, and spruce; and because of the rapidity of the method it may be used in top-working fruit trees. In the case of evergreens, potted stocks are used whose diameter is 2/16 to 3/16 in. A cut is made in the side of the stock about 1½ in. long, running just inside the wood, the flap of bark and wood being left attached at the lower end. The cion is prepared wedge-shaped, with smooth cuts of similar length, and the two cut surfaces placed carefully against each other, the flap of bark and wood from the stock being brought up along the cion and the graft and securely tied. In 3 or 4 weeks part of the stock is cut off so as to force the cion into growth, and four weeks later the remainder is removed just above the union.

In its use in top-working fruit trees during the dormant season small branches not over ¾ in. in diameter are best. A downward-slanting cut is made nearly to the pith, and the cion is prepared wedge-shaped as already described. The stock is then bent so as to open the cut, the cion pushed down into it, the stock cut off just above the cut, and the entire graft waxed. No tying is necessary, since the spring of the wood holds the cion in place.

The side grafting of evergreens. At the left the stock cut to receive the cion (*in the center*).

There are several minor forms of grafting which are but variations of the side graft, suited to particular material. One of these is the **shield graft** or **sprig graft**, used advantageously in grafting the mulberry with dormant cions in early spring, and for the weeping and purple beech in fall with freshly cut cions. A T-shape incision is cut in the bark of the stock as for budding (*see* Budding). Into this incision, a wedge-shaped cion is inserted, tied in place, and waxed, the stock being headed back and eventually cut off just above the cion.

## Veneer Grafting

The veneer graft is a very useful form of side graft used largely with ornamentals, as evergreens, *Rhododendron*, and Japanese maples. In general principle it consists in exposing a portion of one side of both stock and cion, matching them, and tying and waxing. In practice, a thin, wedge-shaped section about 1 in. long is cut from the stock, the lower end of the cut extending into the stem a distance equal to about ⅓ the diameter. The cion is prepared by making a cut along one side and diagonally across the end so as to match the cut in the cion, at least along one side and at the lower end. If both sides can be matched, success is more likely. The union is tied and waxed, and subsequent care is as described under side graft.

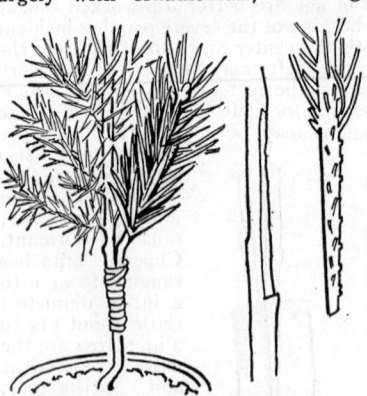

Veneer grafting, showing finished graft (*left*), the stock (*center*) and cion (*right*), both cut ready for grafting.

## Bark Grafting

Bark grafting is employed in place of cleft grafting with material the bark of which does not split well, as the cherry, and when the stock is much larger than the cion. The work is done in the spring when the bark will slip. The cion must be dormant. The stock is cut off, as for the cleft graft, and a slit made downward in the bark for about 1½ in. from the end of the stub in the positions where the

---

\* Special articles on the subjects indicated by an asterisk (\*) will be found at the words so marked.

cions are to be placed. The cions are cut flat and wedge-shaped on one side and pushed down between the slit bark, held in place with slender brads, and the entire graft covered with wax. The cions may be prepared quite thin by cutting a shoulder in them so that they will slip under the bark more easily. The bark graft is used in rehabilitating trees of large diameter cut off near the crown, whence it has been unfortunately called **crown graft**.

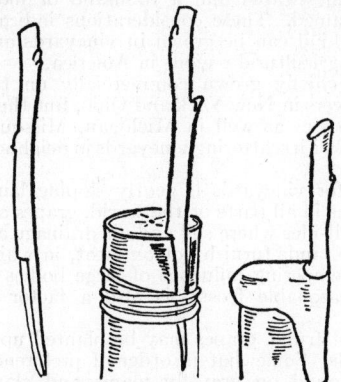

Bark grafting. Cion (*left*), stock (*center*) with cion inserted near the bark, and the finished, waxed job at the right.

### INLAYING

Inlaying refers to a refinement in various forms of grafting to adapt that method to particular material. It consists in carefully removing a definite area of the stock and preparing a similar area of the cion so that it will exactly fit into the stock. It is a useful refinement in the case of the bark graft and the bridge graft, where the stock has heavy bark, and will not split readily. In such cases a piece of bark is cut from the stock just the size of the cion to be received. Where the wood of the stock is curly or otherwise difficult to split for the cleft graft, a sloping, *V*-shaped groove is cut in the stock, and the cion prepared with a sloping triangular edge to match. A special tool may be procured for this work to insure accuracy. The cions must be strongly tied, since there is no such support from the stock as when the cleft graft is used. European gardeners prefer this form of grafting for top-working, but in America the cleft graft is more popular.

### INARCHING OR GRAFTING BY APPROACH

Inarching or **grafting by approach** is a method used for uniting plants still attached to their own roots, and is useful for plants which are otherwise difficult to unite, for rapid propagation of rare specimens, and for repairing and bracing injured or weak trees and crotches. Either the veneer or the tongue graft may be used, the principal feature being to expose the cambium regions of both plants, and fastening them together in such a position that they will unite. When union has been accomplished one plant may be severed from its own roots just below the union. Merely twisting together and tightly fastening young shoots from opposite forks of a crotch will produce a natural graft for strengthening the crotch, although best results are secured by exposing the cambium regions of both shoots by thinly slicing the bark from where the shoots are in contact. Grafting by approach has been used to secure early flowering of seedling roses in breeding work, in which the new plants, while only a few weeks old from seed, are grafted to a vigorous potted stock.

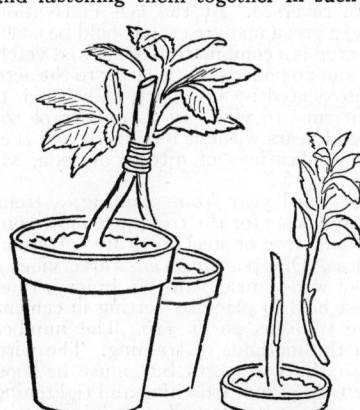

Inarching or grafting by approach. See text for explanation.

### CUTTING-GRAFTAGE

Cutting-graftage combines the rooting of cuttings with the operation of grafting, useful with plants which are difficult to root, are uncongenial, or are otherwise difficult to unite. Nurse-rooting grafting (*see* Whip Grafting) is a form of cutting-graftage. Still another mode is to permit the cion or "cutting" to project downward beyond the point of union with the stock and to stand in moist soil, a dish of water, or damp peat moss so as to keep the cion fresh until union has been accomplished. The lower projecting portion of the cion is later cut off.

### BRIDGE GRAFTING

This form of grafting is used to preserve trees injured or girdled by rodents or suffering from winter injury or disease. Ragged edges and loose bark should be cleanly cut away. In case the injury extends to the roots, the earth must be removed from the base of the tree and the larger roots until sound bark is uncovered. A longitudinal slit is made in the bark, both above and below the wound, and the edges of the slits loosened. With older trees with thick bark, make two parallel slits as far apart as the cion is wide so as to lift a tongue of bark. A cion should then be cut 2 or 3 in. longer than the space to be bridged, one side beveled off at both ends, and inserted in the slits, beveled face against the wood of the trunk. When the space to be covered is more than 12 in., the cion should be long enough to stand out an inch from the trunk when in place. In order to

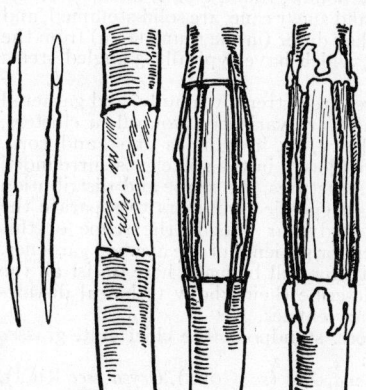

Bridge grafting. For details *see* text.

guard against any accidental displacement, it is well to drive a small brad through each end of the cion, which, however, must not be split in the operation.

Other cions in a like manner may be inserted at intervals of about 2 in. around the injured surface, taking care to ensure cions directly under the main branches. The ends of the cion should be covered with wax, but it is not necessary to cover all of the bridge portion of the trunk. If the tree is so small as to wave in the wind, it should be tied to a strong stake.

With old trees having very thick bark, and on old roots, the method of inlaying is used in which a piece of bark is removed 3 or 4 in. long and as wide as the end of the cion. The cion is cut flat on one side and fitted into the place in the stock prepared to receive it and is fastened with small brads driven through it.

In cases of extensive injury, young trees may be grafted by approach by planting around the injured tree and their tops either inserted or veneer grafted above the wound. — H. B. T.

**GRAFTING KNIFE.** See Section 5, TOOLS AND IMPLEMENTS.

**GRAFTING WAX.** An essential feature of this material is that it will "work" without becoming "tacky." One way to avoid both troubles is to keep the fingers greased while using the wax. But unless of the proper consistency, no grafting wax is likely to be very workable. A good formula for the average grafting wax:

    1 lb. of tallow
    2 lbs. of common beeswax
    4 lbs. of resin

---

\* Special articles on the subjects indicated by an asterisk (\*) will be found at the words so marked.

These should be melted together and thoroughly mixed, after which the mixture should be poured into a tub of cold water. Before it thoroughly hardens it should be "pulled" just as molasses candy is pulled, after which it can be stored almost indefinitely. It will, of course, harden somewhat after long storage, but, if properly made, will soften up enough through the heat of one's hand to be workable.

There are also several prepared, commercial substitutes for the above. If they exclude the air for the necessary time and do not harden too much, they save the trouble of making the above mixture.

**GRAM.** See Phaseolus aureus and P. mungo.

**GRAMINEAE** (gra-min'ee-ee). The grass family (often called Poaceae) is an immense aggregation of plants of world-wide distribution and of supreme importance because it yields the world's cereals, all its forage and lawn grasses, the bamboos and sugar cane, some drugs, and not a few decorative garden plants. Of its 400 known genera and over 4500 species many are in extremely common cultivation.

Typically they have hollow, round stems, but two of the most important, corn and sugar cane, are solid-stemmed, and so are a few others. They differ (in the round stem) from the closely related sedges, which have typically 3-angled stems (see Cyperaceae).

The flowers of grasses are extremely minute, and gathered in small spikelets, which are variously grouped in clusters, some of which are showy, as in pampas grass and corn. Each individual flower (floret) in the spikelet is surrounded by minute, scale-like structures, the shape and distribution of which are used as diagnostic characters to separate the different genera — a study far outside the scope of this book and the equipment or patience of the average gardener. For this reason no attempt will be made here to list all the cult. genera, nor to describe their wholly technical distinctions at their vocabulary entries.

From the purely hort. standpoint the chief cult. grasses may be grouped thus:
  CEREALS: *Euchlaena, Zea* (see CORN), *Oryza* (see RICE), *Secale* (see RYE), *Avena, Coix, Pennisetum, Triticum, Hordeum, Eleusine,* etc.
  PASTURE AND LAWN GRASSES: *Alopecurus, Agrostis, Arrhenatherum, Axonopus, Bromus, Dactylis, Festuca, Cynodon, Lolium, Phleum, Poa,* etc.
  BAMBOO AND ITS RELATIVES: Tall and woody. *Bambusa, Arundinaria, Phyllostachys, Dendrocalamus, Cephalostachyum,* etc.
  ORNAMENTAL GRASSES, without much economic value, and grown chiefly for show: *Miscanthus, Vetiveria, Anthoxanthum, Erianthus, Cortaderia, Phragmites, Lamarckia, Demazeria, Tricholaena, Uniola, Stipa, Lagurus,* etc.
  SUGAR-PRODUCING: *Saccharum* (sugar cane) and some sorghums (see HOLCUS).

Besides these there are many other cult. genera, and not a few grasses are pernicious weeds (see the list at WEEDS).

**GRAMINIFOLIA,** -us, -um (gra-mi-ni-fō'li-a). With grass-like leaves.

**GRANADILLA.** See PASSIFLORA.

**GRANATUM** (gra-nā'tum). Pre-Linnaean* name for the pomegranate.

**GRANDIFLORA,** -us, -um (gran-di-flaw'ra). Large- or showy-flowered.

**GRANDIFOLIA,** -us, -um (gran-di-fō'lee-a). Large-leaved.

**GRANDIS,** -e (gran'diss). Large or showy.

**GRAND RAPIDS DISEASE.** See Diseases at TOMATO.

**GRANITICA,** -us, -um (gra-nĭ'ti-ka). Growing on granite or in granite crevices.

**GRAPE.** There are 20 or 30 species of wild grapes on the continent, some one of which is found in nearly every American agricultural region. At least five of these wild species have been domesticated and a thousand or more varieties have been named. These considerations indicate that a grape of some kind can be grown in vineyards and gardens in almost all agricultural regions in America.

Native grapes are chiefly grown commercially on the borders of lakes and rivers in New York and Ohio, but there are minor grape industries as well in Michigan, Missouri, Georgia, and Alabama, with scattering vineyards in neighboring states.

The ideal location for vineyards is gently sloping land, although in America, as in all parts of the world, grapes are grown well on steep hillsides where soil and air drainage are nearly perfect and the lands furnish bottom-heat, in which grapes delight. The tempering influence of large bodies of water, to avoid unseasonable frosts, is also a factor of prime importance.

SOILS. As with most fruits, grapes may be planted upon a great variety of soils. Somewhat in order of preference, good vineyards are found on gravelly loams and clays. With the grape, however, it is not so much a matter of the kind of soil as it is of texture, which should be rather coarse; of drainage, which should be as nearly perfect as possible; and of a high degree of bottom-heat, to be secured by heat-retaining gravels and stony gravels. Whatever the soil, a considerable admixture of organic matter should be provided by the addition of stable manure or plowing under cover crops before the vines are planted.

For the propagation of the grape see Cleft Grafting and Whip Grafting at GRAFTING.

PLANTING. The plants in commercial vineyards are usually 8 ft. apart in rows 9 ft. apart. Sometimes these distances are less, seldom greater. In planting, furrows 9 ft. apart are opened up, 8 in. deep, and the plants are set in the bottom of these. The rows must be straight, not simply as a matter of professional pride but because posts must be set and wires strung — these to be tightened yearly — and wires on posts out of alignment bind in tightening. When the vineyard is more than 3 acres, driveways running both parallel and crosswise to the rows should be provided to facilitate handling the crop and hauling out prunings.

Grapes thrive only under thorough tillage, which begins in the spring with shallow plowing or, less desirable, the ground is broken up with a disc-harrow. Usually discing should follow plowing for a time or two, the disc, in turn, being followed by the spring-tooth harrow two or three times. In early summer the grape-horse-hoe is used to pull the soil away from the vines and in late summer the hoe and the operation are reversed. At the last cultivation, toward the end of July, a green manure crop should be sown. Perhaps the best such crop is a combination of rye and vetch, 1 bushel of the former and 20 pounds of the latter to the acre. The grape is easily intoxicated by too much plant food, to the end that the plant runs to vine. In a good grape soil the grape may go several years without fertilizers, and then is satisfied with light applications of nitrate of soda, say 200 pounds to the acre.

In the spring of the third year from planting, a trellis must be put up. Perhaps posts for the trellis are most commonly locust or red cedar. Iron or steel posts are better and in the long run cost less. One post to every three vines is sufficient. End posts of wood must be firmly braced; those of iron or steel are best held in place by setting in cement. The best wire for the trellis is #9 or #10. The number, 2 or 3, depends upon the methods of training. The wires are firmly attached to the end posts but must be loose enough on between posts to permit loosening and tightening.

TRAINING. There are many "systems" of training grapes. Perhaps the most generally used east of the Rocky Mountains is the Single-stem Four-cane Kniffin System. In this method of training a single trunk is carried to the top wire of the trellis. This can be done in most vineyards the second or third year after setting. The top wire is at an average height of five and a half feet above the ground,

---

*Special articles on the subjects indicated by an asterisk (*) will be found at the words so marked.

the lower wire two feet lower. Four canes are taken from side spurs on the trunk and laid to the right and left on each wire. The upper canes should be longer than the lower ones, as the vines are most vigorous at the extremity of the stem. The trunk is permanently tied to each wire. Pruning, then, consists of cutting out all but four of the canes that have developed from the spurs of the canes of previous years, selecting the most vigorous and those that are closest to the main trunk. Even if grapes are grown on an old-fashioned arbor, pruning should still be done with a view of keeping as much fresh young cane as possible.

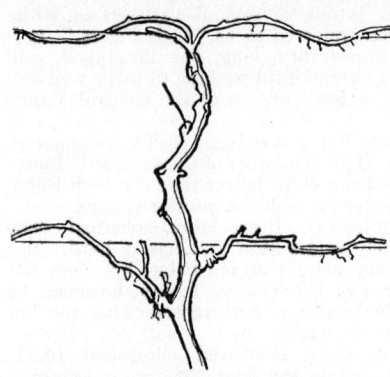

The Four-cane Kniffen System of pruning and training grapes, used for most varieties except *vinifera* grapes. *See below.*

**VARIETIES.** Out of several hundred varieties, the following are selected as best for table grapes and the various kinds of wines that can be made from the eastern grapes. The varieties are named in the order of ripening, and are adapted to all grape soils in zones* 2, 3, 4, and 5, and cool parts of 6:

FREDONIA. Fruit black with heavy bloom, cluster and berry large, very early, quality good. Plant vigorous, healthy, hardy, and productive.

ONTARIO. Fruit golden-yellow, bunch and berry medium, very early. Plant satisfactory in all respects.

WORDEN. Fruit black, bunch and berry large, skin tender, early, very good. Plant very vigorous, hardy, productive.

BRIGHTON. Fruit red, bunch long, straggling, early, very good. Plant satisfactory, but must be planted with other varieties for cross-pollination.

DELAWARE. Fruit red, cluster and berry small, sweet and delicious. Plant rather small but fairly productive. One of the best for all white wines.

NIAGARA. Fruit light golden, cluster and berry large, sweet, perfumed, good. Plant not very healthy nor regular in bearing.

CONCORD. Fruit black, bunch and berry large, sweet, good quality. Plant very vigorous, healthy, productive, and adapted to many soils. A table grape, not suited for wines.

ELVIRA. Fruit light golden, bunch and berry medium, skin thin, fair in quality. Plant vigorous, hardy, healthy, productive. Missouri and neighboring states; much used for white wines.

SHERIDAN. Fruit black, cluster and berry large, sweet, very good. Plant vigorous healthy, hardy, productive. Very good for all red wines.

IVES. Fruit black, berry and cluster above medium, sweet and good. Plant vigorous and productive, but erratic in fruit bearing. One of the best for all red wines.

BROCTON. Fruit light golden, bunch large, sweet, excellent quality. Plant satisfactory. One of the best for all white wines.

IONA. Berries light red, clusters large, sweet, delicious. Plant not very vigorous nor productive. About the best for all white wines.

GOLDEN MUSCAT. Fruit golden-yellow, cluster and berry very large, Muscat flavor, excellent. Plant not very vigorous.

CLINTON. Berry black, below medium in cluster and berry. Plant very vigorous, productive, healthy. Not a table grape, but one of the best for all red wines.

NORTON. Berry blue, medium in cluster and berry. Plant very vigorous, healthy, and productive. Not a table grape, but the best eastern grape for red wines.

CATAWBA. Berry red, bunch large, quality excellent, standard late variety. Plant vigorous, productive, healthy. A good table grape and one of the best for all white wines.— U. P. H.

While the above include most of the important grape varieties grown east of Calif., the latter state is the chief source of an entirely different set of grape varieties based upon a European plant, *Vitis vinifera*. This is the classical "vine" of history and poetry and the present-day source of nearly all worth-while wine grapes, raisins, and all the finer sorts of table grapes. They are commonly called *vinifera* grapes to distinguish them from the varieties mentioned above.

### VINIFERA GRAPE GROWING

The production of *vinifera* grapes in the United States is practically confined to the states of California, Arizona, and Oregon. During the period 1922 to 1932 California shipped an average of 59,000 carloads out of the state. Arizona shipped between 25 and 75 cars and Oregon less than ten cars yearly.

In California grapes are grown principally in the great central valley and in the coastal valleys below 1000 feet elevation. Variations in climate caused by various combinations of temperature, rainfall and atmospheric humidity make it possible to divide the grape-growing areas of the state into a number of regions as follows:

THE COAST REGION comprises the coastal valleys from Mendocino County to San Diego. The temperatures are moderate and have a relatively small range between day and night and between summer and winter. Fogs are frequent during the spring and early summer but diminish in duration from north to south and with distance from the ocean. The rainfall varies the same way, being ample towards the northern limit and somewhat deficient towards the southern. This region is commonly subdivided into the north coast and south coast. The former includes the counties around San Francisco Bay and the adjoining counties of Mendocino, San Benito and Monterey. This is the great "Dry-Wine Region" and is not well suited for the commercial production of either table or raisin grapes. The south coast includes the coast counties from Santa Barbara to San Diego and the western portion of Riverside and San Bernardino counties. It is also a dry-wine region, but a few table grapes and even raisins are successfully produced in the warmest locations.

THE GREAT INTERIOR VALLEY, extending from Shasta to Kern County, is characterized by hotter summers and cooler winters than the Coast Region and by greater difference between day and night temperatures. The rainfall, on the other hand, is less and varies from just about enough at the north to a negligible amount at the extreme south. Spring and summer fogs are rare. It embraces three sub-regions: (1) the *San Joaquin Valley region*, from Bakersfield to Modesto, (2) the *Central Valley region*, from Modesto to Sacramento, (3) the *Sacramento Valley region*, extending from Sacramento to Redding.

In the *San Joaquin Valley* the average temperature increases from north to south. It is favorable for varieties of grapes that need abundant heat. The annual rainfall decreases gradually from about 14 inches at Modesto to four or five inches at Bakersfield, hence irrigation is everywhere necessary. This is the great raisin-producing region but also produces many excellent table grapes.

The *Central Valley* is the coolest part of the interior valley and has a moderate rainfall of from 14 to 20 inches. It owes its relative coolness to the influence of the ocean breezes which pass through the gaps in the coast range north and south of the Golden Gate. It is the great Tokay region but also has limited areas of several other commercial table grapes and large areas of heavily producing wine grapes.

To the north of the Central Valley lies the *Sacramento Valley*. As we proceed north through this valley, the influence of the ocean breezes gradually diminishes and the average seasonal temperature increases so that Chico

---

* Special articles on the subjects indicated by an asterisk (*) will be found at the words so marked.

has nearly the same temperature as Fresno. The rainfall also increases from south to north; reaching about 24 inches at Chico and 36 inches at Redding. Irrigation, though favorable, is not in all cases necessary. Grape growing in this region has been less developed than in the San Joaquin Valley. There are, however, many scattered vineyards of wine grapes and some raisin vineyards in the central part of the valley. The climatic conditions of the area in Oregon where *vinifera* grapes are grown are similar to those of the upper Sacramento Valley.

The *Desert Region* of the Imperial and Coachella valleys is the hottest grape-growing area of California. The Thompson Seedless and Malaga are the principal varieties grown. Raisins are not made, because the table grapes ripening in June and early July are more profitable, and because the grapes produced under such severe condition of temperature are not suited to the production of raisins. The climatic conditions of the Salt River Valley, where the majority of Arizona's grapes are produced, are intermediate between those of the Hot Desert and the southern end of the San Joaquin Valley regions.

VARIETIES. In the vineyards and collections of California there are growing probably eight hundred or more varieties of *vinifera* grapes. Of this horde, a small number, not more than one hundred and fifty, are grown in commercial quantities.

*Vinifera* grapes can be divided into three large classes, (1) raisin grapes, (2) table grapes, and (3) wine grapes.

### RAISIN GRAPES

MUSCAT OF ALEXANDRIA. Berries large, white, egg-shaped, pulpy, with a strong, Muscat flavor; maturing in mid-season. It is the variety from which the Muscat raisins of California are made. It has no rival for quality as a "cluster" or dessert raisin. It is grown most extensively from Madera south to Kern County in the San Joaquin Valley and the interior of the South Coast region. It is also a very good table grape.

THOMPSON SEEDLESS. Berry medium to small, oval, yellow, seedless; early maturing. From this grape the Seedless raisins of California are made, as are the Sultana raisins of Smyrna and Australia. It is at present the most largely grown grape in California. It is grown throughout the grape areas of the San Joaquin, Sacramento and Hot Desert regions. It ranks second to Tokay in volume shipped as table grapes.

BLACK CORINTH. Berry very small, nearly spherical, black or dark purple, seedless; very early maturing. It is from this grape that the dried "currants" are made. It succeeds well in California when girdled and given the requisite special care, but has not generally been found profitable. It is adapted to the cooler areas of the raisin-producing region.

### TABLE GRAPES

TOKAY. Berry large, irregularly short ovoid; maturing in late mid-season. Its most valuable quality is its brilliant red color, which it attains, however, only in limited localities, of which the principal one is the Central Valley region. In the cooler regions its ripening is late and irregular and in the hotter regions it fails to color sufficiently even when ripe.

THOMPSON SEEDLESS. See Raisin Grapes.

EMPEROR. Berry large, long, oval, rose-purple or red; maturing very late. This variety, like the Tokay, has a limited range wherein it is successful. In both cases it is a matter of attaining a desired color. The Emperor has been most profitable in localities where it reaches only a light purplish-red color. The principal Emperor region is near the Sierra foothills, along the east side of the San Joaquin Valley, in Fresno and Tulare counties.

MALAGA. Berry large, short, oval, white; maturing in mid-season. This grape is widely grown, but does best in the east-central part of the San Joaquin Valley.

ALMERIA (Ohanez). Berry large, cylindrical, white; very late maturing. It is of fair quality when well grown and ripe, but its chief value lies in its keeping qualities. It has been grown for many years in California in the Emperor district on a small scale with indifferent success, both in quality and productiveness.

MUSCAT. See Raisin Grapes.

RISH BABA. This is one of several varieties of white grapes which are often referred to as "Ladyfingers." It is of very attractive appearance, long, spindle-shaped, and matures early. It requires skillful packing to carry well and is produced by only a few growers in the Central Valley region.

OLIVETTE BLANCHE. Berry very large, fusiform elongated, white; late maturing. This is another of the so-called "Ladyfingers." It bears well and ships better than the Rish Baba. It does well in the hotter parts of the interior valleys.

RED MALAGA (Molinera). Berry large, spherical, deep red; maturing in early mid-season and has a hard, crisp texture. It has a very attractive red color, but does not equal the brilliant red of the Tokay. It can, however, be grown successfully in localities that are somewhat too hot for the Tokay, and is earlier.

CORNICHON. Berry large, elongated, ellipsoidal, black, often somewhat flattened on one side; maturing in late mid-season. Its irregularity of bearing with ordinary methods of pruning and its inferior quality should restrict further plantings. It does best in the Central Valley.

RIBIER (Alphonse Lavallée). Berry very large, irregularly spherical, black; maturing early to early mid-season. It is the principal one of the two very large, black varieties grown. This is a hot-region grape, doing best in the San Joaquin Valley.

GROS COLMAN. Similar to the Ribier, except that the berries are more nearly spherical and the shoots and leaves are more woolly. It does not require quite so much heat as the Ribier.

### WINE GRAPES

The number of wine varieties is so large and the differences employed in identification are so small that it is beyond the scope of this treatise to attempt a separation of the varieties. The most important varieties will be grouped under the principal types of wines for which they are best adapted.

### DRY WHITE WINES

*Sauterne-type wines* are made usually of blends of Semillon and Colombar, with smaller portions of Sauvignon blanc, Muscadelle du Bordelais, etc.

*Chablis-type wines* are made of Pinot Chardonay, Pinot blanc, Gamai blanc, Golden Chasselas, Green Hungarian, etc.

*Riesling-type wines* are made of Johannisberg Riesling, Franken Riesling, Orleans Riesling, Traminer, etc.

### DRY RED WINES

*Claret-type wines* are made of Cabernet Sauvignon, Carignane, Petite Sirah, Alicante Bouschet, Mataro, Zinfandel, Malbec, St. Macaire, etc.

*Burgundy-type wines* are made of Petite Sirah, Pinot noir, Gamai noir, etc.

*Chianti and other Italian-type wines* are made of Nebbiolo, Barbera, Refosco, Fresa, Bonarda, Lagrain, Gros Manseuc, etc.

### SWEET WINES

*Port-type red wines* are usually made by blends of Zinfandel, Mission, Petite Sirah, Grenache, Tinta de Madeira, Tinta Amarella, Tinta Câo, etc.

*Sherry-type wines* are made of Palomino, Beba, Boal de Madeira, Malmsey, Verdelho, etc.

*Muscatel-type wines* are made principally from the raisin Muscat and to a less extent from the Malvasia Bianca, Aleatico, Moscatello fino, etc. — A. J. W.

### CULTURE OF VINIFERA GRAPES
(*Where it differs from that of the eastern varieties*)

*Vinifera* grapevines require somewhat more pruning than others to keep them from becoming devitalized by

---

* Special articles on the subjects indicated by an asterisk (*) will be found at the words so marked.

overbearing. Many *vinifera* varieties fruit satisfactorily from the two or three buds at the base of a cane and can therefore be pruned to the head system: — a vertical trunk branching at the top into several arms ascending to form a vase-like structure. One or more spurs, containing three or more buds, are left on each arm. The number of arms, spurs, and buds left depends on the variety, size, and vigor of a vine. If at pruning time a vine is seen to have grown rather short shoots in the preceding summer, fewer spurs and buds are left so the crop will be lighter and the vine permitted to grow more vigorously. Head-pruned vines require no trellises and can be cultivated in both directions. Labor of pruning is minimized also.

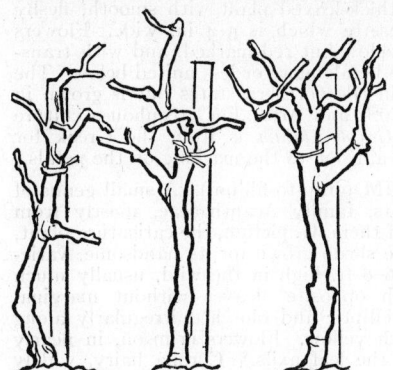

The head system of pruning and training *vinifera* grape varieties. The figure at the left is after the third winter pruning, the central one after the fourth winter pruning, and the right one after the fifth winter pruning.

Some varieties will not fruit well at the top of a short trunk, but will from canes on long trunks; which results in vertical, unilateral, or bilateral cordons. With unilateral or bilateral cordon pruning, as with cane pruning, cultivation can be in only one direction. Vines of some varieties will be weakened by cane pruning, unless some of the flower clusters are removed when they appear. By leaving more buds and cutting out some of the flower clusters, vines of many varieties will bear more and better fruit and still maintain their vigor.

The vine is cut back to one bud at planting and, usually, to two buds after the first year's growth. In the second summer a shoot is tied up to a stake and all other shoots kept removed close to the trunk. When the shoot left is a little higher than the point desired for the head, the end is pinched off to force branching. For cordon pruning, the vine may be cut back to two buds after the second summer so that the shoot to be tied up will be more vigorous and will give the longer trunk desired. In the second summer, or third with some cordon vines, all shoots from the lower part of the trunk are kept removed, as are also all shoots from buds on the lower side of the cordon, and from other buds where arms are not wanted. If suckers are kept removed closely during the first few years there will not be many to remove from the trunk when it is older.

Where *vinifera* grapes are grown in America there is little or no summer rainfall and irrigation is generally practiced. Vines seem to be injured more than fruit trees from having the soil muddy in summer for more than two days. If winter rainfall does not wet the soil to the deepest roots, irrigation in late winter, when long muddiness is not injurious, is advisable. In summer irrigations, the water can then be left in the furrows only long enough to wet the upper two or three feet of soil, where the roots are thickest. Frequency of irrigation depends upon the soil and the amount of leaf surface. Irrigation is not necessary until the soil is nearly dry enough for leaves to remain wilted during the night. — W. H. C. For indoor grape culture, see Greenhouse Fruit at GREENHOUSE.

INSECT PESTS. The larvae of the small grape-berry moth feed in or on the grapes and web them together. They are combated by clean culture, and by two thorough applications of calcium-arsenate spray, 1 pound to 50 gallons, one just before blossoming, and a second immediately after the blossoms fall. The grape-flea beetle and its little grub-like larva, which feed on the leaves, are controlled by applications of the spray before blossoming. These sprays usually include fungicides.

The grape-root worm may weaken the vines; the adult, a grayish leaf beetle, may be killed by the spray mentioned above, while feeding on leaves early in the summer. The rose chafer, a gray beetle about ½ in. long, sometimes destroys blossoms and young fruit; it is also checked with arsenicals. Various leaf-eating caterpillars may be controlled with calcium-arsenate sprays, also a small snout beetle, the larvae of which sometimes attack the fruit.

The handsome little yellow and red grape leafhopper often saps leaves; it is controlled with nicotine spray or dust. The phylloxera, an aphid, makes galls on leaves and sometimes roots; it does not injure American varieties, but is very destructive to European grapes (grown principally in Calif.). European varieties grafted on American roots, however, are not injured.

Several grape pests are reduced by clean culture around the vineyard.

DISEASES. Among the diseases affecting grape are black rot, downy mildew, powdery mildew, anthracnose, crown gall, dead-arm, white rot, and ripe rot. There also are a number of troubles the exact causes of which are not known, or are the result of unfavorable environmental conditions, as black measles, California disease, brunissure, and shelling. Black rot causes a rot of the berry, which finally becomes a hard and shriveled mummy. The fungous-fruiting bodies produce numerous minute black dots over the affected fruits and in the circular brown spots on the leaves.

Downy mildew causes a white cottony growth on the under side of the leaves, on the young stems, and on the fruit. The affected berries harden and finally shrivel. The parasite spreads rapidly when the atmosphere is moist and cool. Powdery mildew makes a talcum-like growth over the upper leaf surface and on the young stems and fruit. Anthracnose causes small, sunken cankers on the stems and bird's-eye spots on the fruit. Some varieties, like the Concord, are not often seriously affected with anthracnose, but the more susceptible varieties may be injured seriously. Crown gall rarely is a serious trouble. It produces large swellings, especially on the roots. Dead-arm is quite descriptive of the trouble, in which the foliage on the branch or whole vine remains dwarfed, finally becomes yellow and the plant dies.

In controlling all of the grape diseases, the first requisite is the establishment of the vineyard in a location favorable for grape growing. The rows should be far enough apart to permit the use of horse-drawn dusters or sprayers and weeds should be eradicated so that aëration is afforded. Healthy stock should be procured from inspected nurseries, and planted into disease-free soils. The plants should be sprayed carefully with bordeaux mixture, 4-4-50, according to the recommendations of local pathologists. The environment and the diseases present determine the number of applications and the time they should be applied. In the case of powdery mildew, sulphur dusting is suggested on some varieties. Most American varieties are very susceptible to sulphur injury, so that it should be applied only when specifically recommended.

**GRAPE FAMILY** = Vitaceae.

**GRAPE FERN** = *Botrychium*.

**GRAPEFRUIT.** Grown first in Florida and later extended to California, Arizona and Texas, the grapefruit or pomelo (*Citrus paradisi*) is now the second most important citrus fruit. It is believed to have originated in the West Indies and to have developed from the thick-skinned and worthless pummelo or pompelmous (*Citrus maxima*), which in this country is known as the shaddock. In any event the grapefruit as we know it is of modern origin and is known in the Eastern Hemisphere only as an introduced fruit.

Like the other citrus fruits, the grapefruit is a tender subtropical evergreen. In frost resistance it stands intermediate between the sweet orange and sour orange, though closer to the former than the latter (see ORANGE). For this reason a comparatively small part of the acreage is provided with frost protection. (For details see FROST.) The grapefruit requires a high total amount of heat for the production of good-quality fruit; it succeeds better than any other citrus fruit in the tropics and in the desert, in the latter, of course, only with irrigation.

In the best commercial orange and lemon districts the grapefruit is sour and bitter and ripens late; this may be a commercial advantage, however, in that it is ready for market after the better-quality fruit has been consumed. In California the best-quality fruit is produced in the desert sections where the amount of heat is sufficient to ripen the fruit 9 or 10 months after bloom; this fruit ripens at the same period as does that in Arizona, Texas and Florida. In the other citrus-growing regions of California more than one growing season is required to ripen the grapefruit. Advantage is taken of this fact, however, and by growing this fruit in four climatic zones, differing mainly in amount of heat, tree-ripened grapefruit is shipped every month in the year.

The grapefruit is less affected by heat and more resistant to wind than any other citrus fruit. It therefore has a wider range of climatic adaptation. Its culture in the United States is limited to central and south Florida, the lower Rio Grande Valley of Texas and areas of mild winters in Arizona and California. In the Gulf Coast states frost and

---

\* Special articles on the subjects indicated by an asterisk (\*) will be found at the words so marked.

cyclonic winds are the principal climatic hazards, in California, frost.

There is no pollination problem in grapefruit culture for, like other citrus fruits, it does not require seed formation for fruit setting, unpollinated fruits being seedless. The major variety, Marsh, is commercially seedless because it normally has few functional ovules; all other varieties are regularly seedy. Two commercial varieties, Foster and Thompson, and several others exhibit pink-colored flesh and juice, and the former has a pink blush on the rind.

PROPAGATION. Like other citrus fruits, the grapefruit is propagated by budding on seedling rootstocks and the nursery trees are usually planted as year-old budlings. In Florida the rootstock most used is the rough lemon (see LEMON), which seems not to cause the undesirable effects associated with the use of this rootstock for the orange (see ORANGE). In Texas, California and Arizona, and on the heavier soils in Florida, the sour orange is preferred because of its resistance to root and bark diseases. The sweet orange and grapefruit are also used to some extent in California but seem not to have any special advantages.

The planting of bare-rooted nursery trees is the regular practice in Florida but elsewhere the use of balled trees is preferred. Fall and early spring planting are practiced in Florida and Texas; in California and Arizona spring planting is preferable and protection against sunscald is advisable. Because of the large size ultimately attained, planting distances should not be less than 25 ft., and in Texas and Florida 30 ft. is considered the minimum safe distance.

SOILS. The grapefruit appears to have an even wider range of soil adaptation than do the other citrus fruits. It does not require deep soils, for its root distribution is comparatively shallow; it is sensitive to alkali and excessive moisture, however, and requires good drainage. It is essential that only irrigation water of good quality be used.

In general the orchard-management requirements of the grapefruit are similar to those of the orange and the same practices are employed (for more specific details see ORANGE). Because of the larger average size of the trees somewhat more water is required; the number of irrigations ranges from 4 to 15 or more per season, depending on climatic conditions.

For satisfactory yields and high-quality fruit regular and heavy fertilization is required. The usual program employed is similar to that used for the orange, though the application of chemical fertilizers in early spring to favor the setting of the fruit is not considered so important. A total application of 200 pounds of nitrogen per acre per year is considered adequate, not less than half of which is supplied from bulky organic substances. The usual practice consists in the application, in summer or fall, of manures, and, in the winter or spring, of chemical-nitrogen carriers.

In California winter cover crops are usually grown, and also summer cover crops where the water supply permits. Tillage operations are usually confined to the turning under of cover crops, weeds and fertilizers, and furrowing or basining for irrigation. Pruning is of less importance than with other citrus fruits. Insects and diseases are the same as for other citrus fruits. Melanose is by far the worst disease in Florida and Texas, and is controlled by spraying with bordeaux-oil mixtures.

VARIETIES. Marsh, seedless and late-ripening, is the most important variety and the only one grown in California and Arizona. Seedy varieties of importance in Florida, and to some extent in Texas, are Duncan, Walters, Triumph, Hall and McCarty. The pink-fleshed Foster and Thompson, the latter seedless, are grown to some extent. — R. W. H. See also CITRUS FRUITS.

INSECT PESTS. The pests of grapefruit are those of citrus fruits in general — scale insects, whiteflies, mealybugs, and others. The purple scale and whiteflies are most often mentioned, and the most important control measures are spraying with oils or with lime-sulphur, and fumigation with hydrocyanic acid. (See ORANGE for general treatment of citrus insects.)

**GRAPE-HYACINTH.** See MUSCARI.

**GRAPTOPETALUM** (grap-to-pet′a-lum). A genus of chiefly Mexican, succulent plants of the family Crassulaceae, only G. orpeti of Ariz. as yet much known among gardeners. It is a thick-leaved plant with smooth, fleshy leaves in a basal rosette which is 3–4 in. wide. Flowers about ½ in. wide, yellow but red-marked, and with transverse dots or bands. Petals more or less united below. The plant is not hardy in the northern states but is grown in desert gardens in Calif. and Ariz. For greenhouse culture see SUCCULENTS. (Graptopetalum is from the Greek for variegated petals, in allusion to the marking on the petals.)

**GRAPTOPHYLLUM** (grap-to-fill′um). A small genus of tender, foliage plants, family Acanthaceae, mostly from tropical India, one of them, G. pictum, the caricature plant, a popular greenhouse shrub grown for its handsome, variegated leaves. It is 6–8 ft. high in the wild, usually much lower as cult., with opposite* leaves without marginal teeth, more or less elliptic and blotched irregularly along the central vein with yellow. Flowers crimson, in nearly stalkless whorls* in the leaf axils.* Corolla hairy, widely gaping, the tube inflated, but the limb 2-lipped,* the lower lip 3-parted. Stamens* 2. Fruit an oblongish capsule. Nativity unknown. It should be grown as a pot plant in a warm, moist greenhouse, preferably in potting mixture* 3. While the leaves are usually yellow-marked as indicated, the plant is very variable as to this and some have leaves with marginal yellow markings. (Graptophyllum is from the Greek signifying variegated foliage.) Sometimes known as G. hortense.

**GRASSES.** The grass family supports the temperate and tropical world, for it contains wheat, corn, rice, rye, barley, oats, and also the sugar cane. Horticulturally, it is nothing like so imposing as the world crops found within it; most grasses, outside the bamboos, being of secondary decorative value. An exception to the latter statement are the beautiful silky plumes of the pampas grass and the genera Arundinaria, Arundo, and Phragmites, as well as some grown for their value in dry bouquets. See DRIED FLOWERS.

It is impossible to list here all the genera of grasses found in THE GARDEN DICTIONARY, for they have already been listed at the description of the family. (See GRAMINEAE.) But some of the horticulturally more important grasses are found in so many gardens that notes on their culture and uses are quite essential. Nor can we repeat here the merits of the many grasses that enter into lawn or meadow mixtures. For this feature of grasses see LAWNS.

GARDEN USES. For bold, tropical effects none of the grasses excel the bamboos and related genera. While many of them can only be grown in the warmer sections of the country, some bamboo-like grasses are hardy northward, and should be planted in large masses by those seeking such effects. See BAMBOO.

Lower, and not so striking, are many other grasses that are widely grown for special garden compositions — some for their decorative foliage, as in a variety of Coix, and in the variegated or colored-leaved form of sweet corn. (See CORN.) Others are, of themselves, of little value, but in masses or as edgings they are decorative enough. Among genera especially suited for such purposes are: Anthoxanthum, Axonopus, Demazeria, Elymus, Eragrostis, Lamarckia, Miscanthus, Pennisetum, Setaria, Tricholaena, and Uniola. Some of these are annuals of which the seed should be sown where needed.

The perennial grasses are best grown as are any perennial garden flowers. Seeds sown in flats in the cold frame in Aug. will be ready to set out permanently the following spring. After the second or third year they may then be easily divided in spring or fall, and often they should be, to prevent too rapid encroachment into other parts of the bed or border.

Grasses are so world-wide in their distribution that, as a family, they tolerate nearly every sort of soil. This freedom from soil preferences is reflected in the variety of garden soils in which they will grow. Most cult. grasses will grow in any ordinary garden soil, and, once established, need very little attention, except to keep them from spreading

---

* Special articles on the subjects indicated by an asterisk (*) will be found at the words so marked.

too fast. This is particularly true of the low-growing sorts that will form a sod if not checked.

Garden grasses are chiefly grown for their often feathery habit and foliage, rather than for the flowers which are minute, wind-pollinated, and conspicuous only because they are crowded in dense or branching clusters (usually panicles*). These, especially in the genera *Briza*, *Bromus*, *Chloris*, *Eragrostis*, and *Panicum*, are first dried and then dyed various colors. Some of these dyed grasses are common in florists' shops and, to some, have decorative value. But the form and branching of most grass clusters are their chief charm, to which little or nothing is added by dyeing. See DRIED FLOWERS.

As noted at the different genera (*see* GRAMINEAE), a few cult. grasses are essentially tropical. This tropical distribution may dictate hardiness if the grass is a perennial species, but many tropical annuals will, if sown outdoors in the north, usually produce fine plants during a single season.

Annual grasses, not necessarily all tropical, may be sought in the genera *Aspris*, *Avena*, *Bromus*, *Coix*, *Echinochloa*, *Euchlaena*, *Lagurus*, *Panicum*, *Phalaris*, and *Zea* (*see* CORN). These can all be sown where wanted, or if needed earlier, they may be sown in flats or pots in the hotbed or greenhouse and transplanted, just as are tender annuals. See ANNUALS.

A few grasses are grown more for interest than for ornament, two especially being mostly so grown. One is the curious animated oat (*see* AVENA) and the other is the well-known Job's-tears (*see* COIX), with its bead-like fruits.

DISEASES. Brown patch, dollarspot, spotblight and snow mold are the common diseases. Brown patch, both "large" and "small," causes irregularly shaped, brown areas of varying size. Avoid overwatering, excessive nitrogen and high soil acidities. Corrosive sublimate, calomel or a combination of the two may be applied to infected areas at the rate of three ounces per thousand square feet. The amount must be reduced during hot weather. Dollarspot has symptoms similar to small brown patch, except that the dead areas are lighter in color. Control is the same as for brown patch. Spotblight, caused by another fungus, results in small dead spots grouped together to form streaks. Excessive watering during periods of high temperatures should be avoided. Snow mold occurs during the winter or early spring. Its presence is indicated by a thick, cottony growth of the fungus in patches. For control, hasten drying of the turf in the spring. Fall applications of calomel or corrosive sublimate, 2 to 5 ounces per thousand square feet, have been effective.

**GRASS FAMILY.** See GRAMINEAE.

**GRASS-FLOWER** = *Claytonia virginica*.

**GRASS HOOK.** See Section 3, TOOLS AND IMPLEMENTS.

**GRASSHOPPERS.** See Grasshoppers at INSECT PESTS. For control *see* Stomach Poisons at INSECTICIDES.

**GRASS-OF-PARNASSUS.** See PARNASSIA.

**GRASS PINK** = *Dianthus deltoides*; also *Calopogon pulchellus*.

**GRASS SHEARS.** See Section 3, TOOLS AND IMPLEMENTS.

**GRASS STEPS.** See STEPS.

**GRASSWORT.** See CERASTIUM ARVENSE.

*GRATISSIMA*, *-us*, *-um* (gra-tiss′i-ma). Most pleasing or agreeable.

**GRAVEL.** See SOILS.

**GRAVEL WALKS.** See PATHS AND PAVING.

**GRAVELWEED** = *Diervilla lonicera*.

**GRAVENSTEIN.** See APPLE.

*GRAVEOLENS* (gra-vee′o-lenz). Strong-smelling.

**GRAVEYARD.** See CEMETERY.

**GRAY AND LAVENDER GARDEN.** Gardens planted in tones of lavender, violet and purple, with a few pale pink and pale yellow flowers and a plentiful admixture of gray foliage, are very lovely and restful in effect. Stone walls make a fine background for such gardens or borders, and the trellises, arbors and seats that are made of wood are best painted silver-gray, or, when near the sea, allowed to weather. Besides the plants given in the following lists, those marked with a dagger at BLUE GARDEN may be made use of.

SHRUBS

*Buddleia davidi*, 8–12 ft., summer; *Callicarpa purpurea*, 3 ft., purple berries in autumn; *Cercis canadensis*, small tree, spring; *Cytisus purpureus* (*see* BROOM), semi-prostrate, spring; *Daphne mezereum*, 3–4 ft., spring; *Hibiscus syriacus coelestis*, 8–10 ft., summer; *Lonicera syringantha*, 5–8 ft., spring, *L. thibetica*, 5 ft., spring; *Rhododendron* hybrids and many varieties; *Syringa* (Lilac) *persica*, *S. vulgaris*, many hybrid varieties, mauve, lilac, purple, etc.; *Vitex agnus-castus*, 6 ft., late summer.

TALL PLANTS FOR USE IN BACKGROUND

SUMMER-FLOWERING: *Aster*, various forms; *Boltonia latisquama*; *Campanula latifolia*; *Delphinium*, lavender varieties; *Iris*, Japanese varieties; *Ostrowskia magnifica*; *Thalictrum dipterocarpum*.

AUTUMN-FLOWERING: *Aster grandiflorus*, *A. novae-angliae*, *A. novi-belgi*, *A. tataricus*; *Vernonia crinita*.

PLANTS OF MEDIUM HEIGHT

SPRING-FLOWERING: *Aquilegia* long-spurred hybrids (*see* COLUMBINE); *Geranium grandiflorum*; *Nepeta mussini*.

SUMMER-FLOWERING: *Ageratum* (annual); *Aster acris*, *A. cordifolius*; China aster (annual); *Campanula medium* (Canterbury Bells); *Delphinium* annual varieties; *Trachymene coerulea*; *Erigeron speciosus*; *Geranium pratense*; *Galega officinalis*; *Gilia capitata* (annual); *Hesperis matronalis*; *Hosta fortunei*, *H. sieboldiana*; *Iris* tall-bearded varieties; *Limonium latifolium*; *Monarda fistulosa*; *Pentstemon diffusus*; *Phlox maculata*; *Salpiglossis* (annual); *Salvia nemorosa*, *S. sclarea*; *Scabiosa* (annual), *S. caucasica*, *S. japonica*; *Stokesia laevis*; *Thalictrum aquilegifolium purpureum*; *Verbascum phoeniceum*.

AUTUMN-FLOWERING: *Aster ericoides*, and other species (*see* ASTER); *Cheloni lyoni*.

DWARF PLANTS FOR FOREGROUND

SPRING-FLOWERING: *Pulsatilla vulgaris*; *Aquilegia vulgaris* (*see* COLUMBINE); *Aster alpinus*; *Aubrietia* (lavender); *Campanula portenschlagiana*; *Crocus imperati*, *C. tomassinianus*, *Crocus*, Dutch varieties; *Erysimum linifolium*; *Iris* (dwarf-bearded); Pansies; *Phlox arendsi* Louise, *P. divaricata*, *P. subulata*; *Primula denticulata*; *Viola cornuta*, *V. gracilis*.

SUMMER-FLOWERING: *Ageratum* (dwarf annual varieties); *Alyssum* (annual); *Aster acris*, *A. subcoeruleus*; *Iberis gibraltarica* (*see* CANDYTUFT); *Petunia*, Heavenly Blue, Violet Queen, and Balcony Blue; *Phlox drummondi*; *Primula capitata*; *Sedum caeruleum* (annual).

AUTUMN-FLOWERING: *Colchicum autumnale*, double and single, *C. speciosum* (bulbs); *Crocus longiflorus*, *C. nudiflorus*, *C. speciosus*, *C. zonatus* (bulbs).

CLIMBERS

*Akebia quinata* (spring); *Clematis crispa*, *C. jackmani* (summer); *Dolichos lablab*; Morning-glory (annual); Sweet Peas (annual); *Wistaria sinensis*, *W. floribunda macrobotrys*.

PLANTS WITH GRAY FOLIAGE

*Arabis alpina* (prostrate); *Artemisia abrotanum*, 2 ft., *A. vulgaris*, 3–4 ft., *A. stelleriana*, 2 ft.; *Cerastium tomentosum* (prostrate); *Dianthus plumarius*, 1 ft.; *Elymus arenarius*, 2 ft.; *Eryngium* and *Echinops*; *Festuca ovina glauca*, 6–8 in.; Lavender; *Ruta graveolens*, 2 ft.; *Salvia argentea*; *Santolina chamaecyparissus*; *Stachys lanata*, 8–10 in.; *Thalictrum glaucum*, 5 ft.; *Thymus serpyllum lanuginosus* (creeping); *Verbascum olympicum*, 8 ft. For the culture and hardiness of all these plants *see* the various genera cited above.— L. B. W.

**GRAY BIRCH** = *Betula populifolia*. See BIRCH.

**GRAY BULB ROT.** See Diseases at TULIPA.

**GRAY DOGWOOD** = *Cornus racemosa*.

**GRAY GOLDENROD** = *Solidago nemoralis*. See GOLDENROD.

---

* Special articles on the subjects indicated by an asterisk (*) will be found at the words so marked.

**GRAY GUM** = *Eucalyptus tereticornis*.

**GRAY MOLD.** See Diseases at Begonia, Calceolaria, Coleus, Orchid, and Lettuce.

**GRAY PINE** = *Pinus banksiana*. See Pine.

**GREASEWOOD.** In the west, *greasewood* is applied chiefly to *Larrea tridentata* and to species of *Atriplex*. But to most gardeners, greasewood is *Audibertia polystachya*.

**GREAT BURDOCK** = *Arctium lappa*. See the list at Weeds.

**GREATER STITCHWORT** = *Stellaria holostea*.

**GREAT LAUREL** = *Rhododendron maximum*.

**GREAT LOBELIA** = *Lobelia syphilitica*.

**GREAT NETTLE** = *Urtica dioica*. See Nettle.

**GREAT SOLOMON'S-SEAL** = *Polygonatum commutatum*. See Solomon's-seal.

**GREAT WHITE TRILLIUM** = *Trillium grandiflorum*.

**GREEK FIR** = *Abies cephalonica*. See Fir.

**GREEK GARDENS.** See Garden History.

**GREEK JUNIPER** = *Juniperus excelsa*.

**GREEK VALERIAN** = *Polemonium caeruleum*.

**GREEN ALDER** = *Alnus viridis*. See Alder.

**GREEN ARROW-ARUM** = *Peltandra virginica*.

**GREEN ASH** = *Fraxinus pennsylvanica lanceolata*. See Ash.

**GREEN-BARKED ACACIA** = *Cercidium torreyanum*.

**GREENBRIER.** See Smilax (1).

**GREEN CLOVER WORM.** See Insect Pests at Soybean.

**GREEN CUTTINGS.** See Cuttings.

**GREEN DRAGON** = *Dracunculus vulgaris* and *Arisaema dracontium*.

**GREEN GRAM** = *Phaseolus aureus*.

**GREENHOUSE.** The word greenhouse was first used for a house in which plants that never required a very high temperature were placed for winter protection. Today, it is generally applied to any form of glass structure that is erected for the growing of plants, with the exception of frames and pits. Terms denoting the particular use of a house, such as hot-house, forcing-house, and temperate-house, have become pretty well merged with *greenhouse* in common usage. The house in which plants are arranged for display, and usually attached to the dwelling, is known as a conservatory (which see).

The early-style greenhouses were not nearly so light, either in materials or growing conditions, as are those of the present time. Anyone who has seen a real old-timer can only marvel at the patience and skill of the gardener who succeeded in growing good plants under such poor conditions. In the modern house the heavy wood framework has been generally replaced with metal of much smaller dimensions. The small panes of roof-glass set in removable sash have given way to large panes of improved quality set in a fixed roof. Whether the heat is supplied by hot water or steam, it is in marked contrast to the early methods of heating by the use of fermenting material or the horizontal smoke-flue. By the use of modern automatic appliances, much of the drudgery of firing has been eliminated, and heat fluctuation brought under better control.

There is a wide variation in the size and use of greenhouses, from the small, cool house of simple design to the ornamental and spacious range divided into numerous compartments. Here, separated only by glass partitions, conditions can be maintained to suit a wide variety of plants from cool, temperate and tropical regions. Desert natives can dwell next door to tropical aquatics and epiphytes,* while choice fruits and vegetables may be produced out of season, as well as the usual flowering and foliage plants grown to delight the eye.

LOCATION. In the location of greenhouses a situation admitting plenty of light and air is to be preferred. There are several types of construction to choose from, and in sizes that are pretty well standardized, although a special can be designed to suit any particular place. The selection will depend upon the site, the plants to be grown, and the amount of money available.

The most economical in construction and heating costs is the lean-to, an old-style house that can be fitted into a smaller space than any other type. As the name implies it is built against a wall, usually of the dwelling or other building, and can be made to harmonize with the particular style of architecture to which it is attached. Where there is a choice of location, a south or southeast exposure is preferable, so as to get the benefit of the maximum amount of light possible in a house of this type. But anywhere it will be useful, especially in connection with other houses, where it is well adapted for propagating purposes and the growing of plants that prefer a partially shaded existence. Under certain conditions of attachment to a building it is necessary to protect the glass from sliding snow and ice.

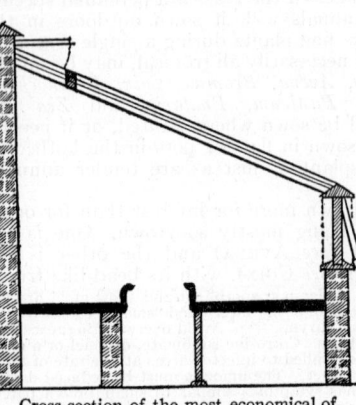

Cross-section of the most economical of greenhouses — the lean-to. In some the bench near the inner wall is arranged in steps so that the plants at the rear may be nearer the glass. Note the ventilators both at the top and side.

The three-quarter span, or hip-roof style, admits more light than the lean-to and can be built upon a lower back wall. It is usually only erected when some peculiar condition of grade or grouping with other houses has to be met.

The best type of greenhouse for general growing purposes is the span-roof house standing alone. This permits the maximum amount of light on all sides. The curvilinear roof has been used for a long time on private estates and in public parks, but its value seems to be solely for external artistic effect rather than the betterment of growing conditions. The even span with straight roof and curved eaves is now considered the best, for both light and appearance. It also frees itself of snow and ice better than any other.

The ridge-and-furrow type of span construction is often adopted by commercial growers. First costs are lessened because of fewer side walls to build, and for the same reason there is a reduction in heating costs. It works out very well when plants grown in the different houses require similar conditions. However, if need be, a partition can be put in to allow of running a single house at a different temperature. The plants are subject to rather more shade than when the houses stand singly, but with many this is not a vital factor. Improved methods of construction have largely overcome the disadvantages caused by the accumulation of snow in the furrows, and the drip-drip-drip that follows this and heavy rains.

As with any permanent building a good foundation is important, and has much to do with the durability of the structure. The depth in the ground depends somewhat on the nature of the soil and frost penetration. The sides will be mostly of glass, but it is well to build the side-

---

* Special articles on the subjects indicated by an asterisk (*) will be found at the words so marked.

walls up 2 or 3 ft. above grade. For this, brick, stone or concrete gives a more lasting job than wood. The total height from ground to eave is variable, but 5 ft. is a good average.

Very useful small greenhouses of moderate cost are obtainable in sections, all ready to erect on the foundation and complete from side walls to the heating system. With the newest method of hot-water heating the need of a boiler pit is eliminated, and very little space is lost by having the boiler inside the house. Care must be taken, however, to keep the actual greenhouse space free from combustion fumes.

### Greenhouse Interior

Adequate ventilation is one of the important things in greenhouse management. With the modern ventilating apparatus it is easier to get a change of air and temperature without drafts. In most cases top ventilators are hinged on both sides of the ridge, so that only one or both together may be opened as conditions warrant. Side ventilation is desirable in hot weather, so the side sash is usually hinged also. In some cases box ventilators are built into the foundation wall, through which air is admitted over the heating pipes under the bench.

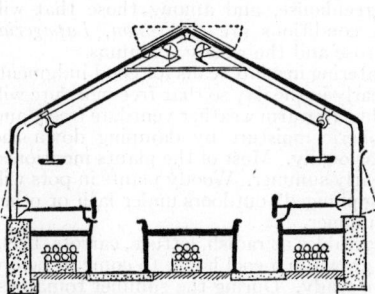

Cross-section of even-span greenhouse, showing preferred arrangement of ventilators, benches for plants, with heating pipes below them, the paths, and the best method of constructing the walls.

Internal arrangements of staging and growing space will vary to suit the kinds of plants to be grown and the method of culture to be followed. For cut flowers and vegetables, solid beds close to the walk level may serve the purpose. Sometimes beds are built up to a more convenient level for working, and kept in place with brick or concrete sides. Raised benches made of wood or concrete, with sides 6 in. deep, are much used for this purpose also. As plants are pulled out of the soil this may be removed and the space used for pot plants. A convenient height for benches is 30 in. and width 3 ft., but plenty of variations either way are to be found. As a rule it is easier to grow plants for cut flowers in beds or benches rather than in pots. Wooden stages, stepped up, are sometimes used in a display house for pot plants. They are satisfactory while kept in good repair, and especially useful in a lean-to house.

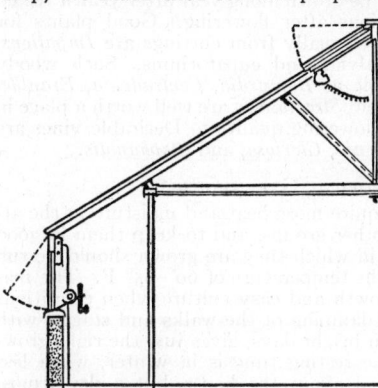

The mechanism for opening and closing the top and side ventilators of a greenhouse

The best table for pot plants is made up of an angle-iron frame supported on gas-pipe legs, with a bottom of slate or tile rather than wood. This is covered with a layer of crushed stone, gravel or screened cinders, the latter being the better moisture retainer, though not as clean.

An adjoining workroom is a practical necessity in most cases, and is often built over the boiler room. Space under the potting bench serves as a convenient place for the storage of loam and the other materials needed for the potting composts. Racks on which pots can be kept in their separate sizes are also part of the essential equipment; while a cupboard in which to keep seeds, tools and supplies should also be provided.

Cold frames, and pits either cold or sufficiently heated to keep out frost, are invaluable in which to shelter certain plants prior to their entry into the greenhouse; then in spring to relieve the inevitable pressure for space that is bound to be felt.

SHADING. Although a site allowing the maximum amount of sunlight is the most desirable, some shade is necessary for the majority of plants under glass during hot weather. This is not only to give protection from sunburn, but also to help maintain more uniform conditions of temperature and moisture. Where appearances count for much, lath blinds on rollers are most satisfactory in every respect. With these it is possible to give the plants the advantage of full light on dull days, while lowering them on cold and windy nights will check heat loss and so to an extent cut fuel costs. In early spring only certain things are likely to need the protection of temporary shading, and this can be given on the inside by the use of paper or scrim. The slap-dash method of spraying lime-wash all over the glass and framework is not recommended. A good temporary shading to apply on the glass is a thin mixture of whiting and gasoline. For a shading to last the summer substitute white lead for the whiting. If a green tint is desired add a little Brunswick green to the mixture. A powdered preparation known as Summer Cloud, obtainable in white or green, mixed according to directions, also makes a satisfactory shading. Whatever is applied to the glass, the best effect is obtained by stippling it on with a wide brush.

A type of roller shades for the outside of the greenhouse

### Greenhouse Management

The daily routine to be followed in greenhouse management varies with the seasons, and must even be modified from day to day with sudden weather changes. Success is based on attention to numerous small details given at the proper time, and is more easily achieved if experience is aided by a study of underlying principles.

Cleanliness is an important factor in the growing of healthy plants and should prevail at all times and in all places. Certain insect pests are bound to appear and select their favorite plants, while an ever-watchful eye must be kept to detect plant diseases from the beginning. In either case immediate steps should be taken to apply measures of control and to correct bad conditions if needed. For details of treatment see FUMIGATION, INSECT PESTS, and PLANT DISEASES.

The operation of the ventilators is a most important detail, especially when plants are in their most active state of growth. Drafts are harmful, and fluctuating temperatures should be avoided as much as possible. Watch the thermometer closely as it rises from the early-morning minimum, and on a rise of about 5° F. ventilate slightly. Thereafter it is increased or decreased as the temperature rises or falls,

---

* Special articles on the subjects indicated by an asterisk (*) will be found at the words so marked.

and the more gradually it happens the better. In hot weather of course the night temperature will be above the winter minimum, but this will be offset by night ventilation. Certain groups of plants have a rather definite temperature which they prefer. Too high a temperature for any particular group, especially at night, is conducive to soft growth and loss of texture in the flowers. On very cold nights a drop of a few degrees below normal is not harmful, and on dull days it is unwise to try and make up the loss of sun heat by driving the boilers. If the weather is damp and foggy in early fall it is often advisable, instead of closing the house entirely, to have a little heat in the system at night with the ventilators slightly open. This will prevent the accumulation of moisture on the foliage and so help to ward off mildew and other troubles.

Overcrowding is a common fault in many greenhouses. Each individual plant should be given ample room for proper development. If there is a good reason for retaining poor or sickly specimens, hospital quarters should be provided and short shift given any that do not respond to treatment. Many greenhouse plants are propagated by cuttings or other vegetative means, and only healthy specimens should be selected for this purpose.

For those who have no gardener to watch for changes of weather the commercial designers of greenhouses have perfected devices for the automatic control of heat, humidity, ventilation, and even shading, for which an "electric eye" provides the stimulus for raising or lowering the slat shades. Such devices are expensive and not much favored by commercial growers, but have their uses for those who cannot attend continuously to greenhouse management.

Greenhouse plants are roughly divided into two groups, hard-wooded and soft-wooded. Many of the former are seldom cultivated today outside of botanic gardens. One reason is because they call for more skill and attention in growing than do those of the soft-wooded group. Improved forms have been more readily produced in the latter class, and many kinds can be raised from seed and flowered within a year. Hard-wooded plants flower chiefly in spring and early summer. They have a very definite growing, resting and flowering period. Any necessary pruning and shaping are done after flowering, and re-potting as the new growth begins. To encourage good growth a somewhat close and moist atmosphere is desirable at this time. Later, more airy and drier conditions will ensure thorough ripening of the wood, which leads up to well-flowered specimens. Over-potting should be avoided in all cases. With woody plants the old ball of soil may often be sufficiently reduced to allow of enough new soil being added to carry the plant for another year in the same sized pot or tub. The potting on of soft-wooded plants tends to continue their growth and delay flowering, a fact which growers often use to extend the season of bloom in certain cases. For a full discussion of the best methods in potting, see POTTING.

### COOL GREENHOUSE

For the cool house, with a minimum night temperature of 45°–50°, choice can be made from a wide variety of plants. Improved forms of many garden annuals give a great display in winter and spring, and can be grown either in pots or benches with good results. Seeds sown in Aug. of such kinds as calendula, clarkia, nemesia, stock, and the new tall and long-stemmed pansies, give a wealth of flowers for cutting. *Nemesia* sown again early in the year, together with sweet sultan and salpiglossis, can be grown to advantage to replace those passing out of bloom, and carry on until outdoor flowers are available. Pot plants, easily raised from summer-sown seeds to give a bright display in winter and spring, are various primulas, cinerarias, calceolarias, schizanthus, and nicotianas. *Cyclamen* belongs with this group also, but requires more than a year to flower from seed.

Bulbous plants in variety are indispensable, and can be brought in from their cold quarters at intervals to keep up a succession of bloom for many weeks. Certain native plants and garden perennials that bloom in spring can be brought along to flower in advance with very little trouble. Selected plants, potted in the fall and kept in frames until the turn of the year, will respond readily to gentle heat. Later on they can be set out in the garden.

Examples of hardwooded flowering plants that can be kept growing from year to year under cool-house treatment are certain kinds of *Acacia*, *Azalea*, *Boronia*, *Camellia*, *Cytisus*, and *Erica*. Sizable plants of *Buddleia asiatica* can be grown from spring cuttings for winter bloom, and just one specimen will fill the house with fragrance. Fancy pelargoniums and fuchsias grow into good plants within a year from cuttings, and can be grown for several years if cut back annually when rested after flowering. Some of the scented-leaved pelargoniums are worth a place in a general collection. Chrysanthemums of course are indispensable, and may be grown in pots inside or planted out in the garden and carefully lifted and benched in Sept. Vines add to the attractive furnishing of any greenhouse, and among those that will flourish under cool conditions are *Antigonon*, *Lapageria*, *Manettia*, Cherokee rose and the woody solanums.

In a cool house, watering in winter calls for good judgment, and should be done early in the day so that free moisture will evaporate before night. In warm weather ventilate freely and increase the atmospheric moisture by damping down the walks and stages occasionally. Most of the plants mentioned will be discarded in early summer. Woody plants in pots will be benefited by being plunged* outdoors under lath or other light shade for the summer.

If desired, such vegetables as radish, lettuce, carrots, beets and spinach may be grown in a cool house to come in before the outdoor crops are ready. During the summer tomatoes, cucumbers, and melons may be grown to advantage, and be out of the way in time to prepare the house for new occupants in the fall.

### WARM-TEMPERATE GREENHOUSE

There is an interesting group of plants that prefer conditions between cool and tropical, and these thrive in what is known as a warm-temperate house, with a minimum night temperature of 50°–55°. Many of these are more or less permanent, but it is a good plan to keep up a stock of vigorous young plants from cuttings. A genial, moist atmosphere is required during their active season, and during the summer free ventilation with shading. A varied selection can be made from begonias to give an interesting group featuring attractive form, foliage and flowers. *Achimenes*, gloxinia, *Isoloma*, *Streptocarpus* and *Saintpaulia* are related plants with attractive flowers that can be grown along year after year if rested under cooler conditions after flowering. Good plants for winter bloom grown annually from cuttings are *Impatiens*, jacobinias, tender salvias and eupatoriums. Such woody plants of bushy habit as *Bouvardia*, *Centradenia*, *Eranthemum*, *Strobilanthes*, and *Streptosolen* are well worth a place in this house for their flowering qualities. Desirable vines are *Clerodendron*, *Dipladenia*, *Gloriosa*, and *Stephanotis*.

### TROPICAL GREENHOUSE

Tropical plants require more heat and moisture in the atmosphere than the other groups, and to keep them in good condition the house in which they are grown should be run with a minimum night temperature of 60°–65° F. The majority are of free growth and easy culture when conditions are right. Frequent damping of the walks and stages, with overhead spraying on bright days, gives just the right growing atmosphere. The resting time is in winter, when less moisture is distributed about the house, but a dry atmosphere must be avoided, especially near the heating pipes.

Most of the re-potting takes place toward spring, and care must be taken to avoid saturating the soil until new roots are active. The soft-wooded group prefers more shade than the hard-wooded section, and this can be managed to a certain extent by careful arrangement in the house. Early shading is necessary, and for this purpose lath roller blinds, run down and up as conditions require, are especially good. Ventilation must be closely watched and sparingly given until hot weather arrives.

Numerous fine foliage plants belong in this group. Such

---

* Special articles on the subjects indicated by an asterisk (*) will be found at the words so marked.

kinds as *Alocasia, Calathea, Dieffenbachia, Codiaeum* (the garden crotons), *Cordyline, Dracaena, Fittonia, Pandanus, Sanchezia*, and *Xanthosoma* provide a colorful display of varied leaf forms. Anthuriums, with their brightly colored spathes,* should also have a place. Tillandsias, and other plants of the family Bromeliaceae, show much of interest in leaf form and color as well as colorful bracts* and flowers.

Good woody flowering plants can be selected from *Acalypha, Ixora, Hibiscus, Medinilla, Pentas* and *Posoqueria*. A few plants of *Nepenthes*, the tropical pitcher-plants, suspended in baskets from the roof, will also add to the interest. If vines can be accommodated, such kinds as *Allamanda, Bougainvillaea, Passiflora*, and *Thunbergia* will give colorful displays.

### Greenhouse Fruit

The culture of fruit under glass can be made to yield results of much satisfaction. While generally planted out in a border and formally trained, it is possible to grow bush or pyramid trees in pots or tubs. They are started in a cool house early in the year (Jan.–Feb.), and at no time need hard forcing. Until growth is well started watering and spraying need to be carefully done. When the flowers are open a rather dry and buoyant atmosphere is required to ensure a good pollination. As the fruit swells atmospheric moisture is increased, watering carefully attended to and supplemented with liquid manure occasionally until ripening begins, when somewhat drier conditions with more air should prevail.

After the fruit is gathered the trees are plunged* outdoors in a sunny place to ensure thorough ripening of the wood.

Grapes in the greenhouse

Re-potting is done in Oct. and should be very firmly done, using a mixture of good fibrous loam and real old manure in the proportion of 3–1 and adding a little bone meal. Avoid overpotting by reducing the old ball of soil as much as possible. Water only enough to keep the soil just moist, mulch the pots if need be to protect from frost, and keep the trees in a cold place until the time comes to start them in the house again. Varieties of apples, pears, plums, peaches, nectarines, figs and grapes may be grown in this way. See also MELON.

While most people may prefer a general assortment of plants in a greenhouse, if one wishes to specialize, such groups as ferns, succulents and orchids offer a wide field of interest. — H. E. D.

**GREEN MANURING.** No soil-improvement scheme should be without at least one phase of green manuring, for the process supplies humus to the soil in the cheapest and most effective way. Particularly is this true where stable manure is impossible to get or too expensive to use on the necessary scale. See HUMUS.

OBJECTS. Green manuring has for its greatest object the increase in the water-holding capacity of the soil. Any ordinary subsoil, which is usually without humus, will hold only as much water as its particles will absorb, which, in the case of sandy or gravelly ones, is not much. Even fairly good garden soils will not hold as much water as they should. And the capacity of all, except muck soils, to hold adequate amounts of soil moisture is tremendously increased by the humus that green manuring adds to them.

The process, in short, involves the plowing under of green crops, usually grown for the purpose. It may well begin by plowing under the initial weed crop, preferably in late May or early June, before many of them have gone to seed. Try to cover the weeds with soil as completely as possible, so that decay may start at once and to prevent a few of them from sprouting again. This initial plowing should be as deep as possible with an ordinary plow. Or on a small scale, dig the weeds in as thoroughly as possible.

Diagrammatic outline of the green crop (*at right*), the furrow (*center*), and the buried green crop (*at the left*), the complete covering of which is essential in correct green manuring for soil improvement.

SUCCESSIVE STEPS. Assuming the worst — that the land you are to improve consists only of subsoil, or contractors' fill — in other words, a weedy lot — after the first plowing in of all possible weeds, allow the rough furrows to stand as they are for 10–15 days. Then disk-harrow or coarsely rake the area and sow very thickly a crop of ordinary buckwheat. Even on pretty poor land the buckwheat will make a fair stand and should be allowed to grow only about 8 in. high when it too is turned under. Wait another 10 days and sow another crop of buckwheat as before, which will germinate and grow considerably better than the first one.

This rotation of buckwheat can be repeated as often as possible until the final crop is plowed under, which should be, in the North, about Sept. 20. Then let the land lie fallow until about Oct. 15, when a heavy seeding of winter rye should be given. This will germinate before heavy frosts and go through the winter looking much like a coarse lawn. In the spring, plow under the rye when it is about 9 in. high. Then, if necessary, begin the buckwheat series again.

Not all green-manuring schemes will need to be so intensive as the one just outlined. Sometimes only a crop or two will suffice to add all the humus the particular soil will need. And there are some regions of heavy rainfall where decay may be too sluggish, in which case there should be a light application of lime only once in the season.

NITROGEN GATHERERS. While the rotation just outlined does a tremendous amount for the physical texture of a soil, it adds little real plant food to it. This is best accomplished by planting legumes like pea, clover, vetch, alfalfa, and, in the South, *Lespedeza striata*. There is little use in planting such crops at once if the initial soil is as poor as the one noted above, for most of the legumes would not grow in such a soil or grow so poorly as to make a trial too expensive or wasteful of time.

But if the soil has already been partially improved by green manuring, then one of the legumes may be planted. Their great advantage is that they absorb nitrogen from the air and add it to the soil. No other plants can do this, and consequently, no other plants are as valuable for green manuring as these nitrogen gatherers. The objection to them is getting them established on poor soils. Some, too, are perennials and not so easy to handle as rye and buckwheat.

**GREEN MINT** = *Mentha spicata.* See MINT.

**GREEN OSIER** = *Cornus rugosa.*

**GREEN, R.** See America at GARDEN BOOKS.

**GREEN ROSE** = *Rosa chinensis viridiflora.*

**GREENS.** See CHRISTMAS GREENS. See also SALAD PLANTS.

**GREEN WATTLE** = *Acacia decurrens.*

---

* Special articles on the subjects indicated by an asterisk (*) will be found at the words so marked.

**GREIGIA** (gry'gi-a). A small and horticulturally rather unimportant genus of herbs of the pineapple family found in rocky places in the Andes. The only cult. species, G. **sphacelata**, of Chile, resembles the pineapple in having stout, prickly margined leaves. Flowers rose-pink, in a dense, bracted* cluster from between the leaf bases, the bracts* sharp and spiny-margined. Little grown here, but a showy plant needing the same culture as *Cryptanthus* (which see) to which it is related. (Named for Major-General Greig, Russian horticulturist.)

**GREVILLEA** (gre-vil'lee-a). Australasian shrubs or trees of the family Proteaceae, comprising more than 200 species, but only the following of much garden interest. They are planted south of zone* 7 for street or avenue trees or specimen plants, but *G. robusta* is often used as a pot plant in northern greenhouses for its fine foliage. Leaves alternate,* sometimes small and heath-like, or much larger and divided or deeply parted, feather-fashion, into five segments. Flowers in close clusters (racemes* or heads), without petals, but the calyx* more or less tubular, the 4 lobes joined even after the flower has opened. Stamens 4. Fruit a woody follicle.* (Named for Charles F. Greville, British patron of botany.)

The chief feature of the grevilleas is the long, showy styles* which protrude much above the general level of the flower cluster. The plants are easily raised from seed sown as soon as ripe in warm, moist sand. In Calif., where they are widely grown, the species are at home in a variety of soils, and stand the summer drought very well. In greenhouses *Grevillea robusta* needs potting mixture* 3 and a temperature of 50°–60°.

**banksi.** A shrub or tree, not over 20 ft. high. Leaves about 4 in. long, split into 9–11 narrow segments, silky beneath. Flowers red, very showy, in 1-sided, terminal clusters that are 2–4 in. long. There is also a white-flowered variety. Both are planted for ornament in Fla.

**hilliana.** A tree 30–50 ft. high. Leaves nearly 12 in. long, silvery beneath, cut into 2–3 deep lobes at the end, or divided into 5–7 lobes. Flowers red, pink, or sometimes white, in dense, finger-shaped clusters (racemes*) that are 6–8 in. long and borne in the leaf-axils.* A very showy tree.

**robusta.** Silk-oak. In outdoor cult. a tree 100–150 ft. high, but as grown in the juvenile state in the greenhouse 2–3 ft. high. Leaves twice-divided into graceful, feathery, fern-like segments. Flowers orange, in 1-sided clusters (racemes*) that are up to 4 in. long, and borne on leafless branches. A popular street tree in southern Calif.

**thelemanniana.** A shrub not over 5 ft. high, the leaves about 2 in. long and divided into many narrow segments. Flowers pinkish, tipped with green, the clusters terminal, 1-sided, and not over 1½ in. long.

**GREYIA** (gray'ee-a). A genus of only 3 species of South African trees of the family Melianthaceae, **G. sutherlandi** grown for ornament in Calif. It is a small tree with alternate,* simple,* toothed leaves that are roundish or oval-oblong, 2–3 in. long and deeply heart-shaped at the base. Flowers bright scarlet, about 1½ in. long, very profuse in showy racemes* 8–10 in. long. Sepals and petals both 5, not united. Stamens* 10, both they and the style long-protruding. Fruit a 5-valved, membranous capsule.* It does well in Calif. on a variety of soils and blooms plentifully long before it is full grown. Propagated by cuttings of partially ripened wood, or by seeds. (Named for Sir George Grey, Governor of Cape Colony.)

**GRIDIRON TRAINING.** See Fruit Trees at TRAINING PLANTS.

**GRILL.** See TRELLISES.

**GRINDELIA** (grin-dee'lee-a). New World, resinous or gummy herbs, of the family Compositae, most of the 30 known species from the western U.S. and of little hort. interest, although some non-hort. species furnish medicines. Commonly called gum plant or tarweed, they are often woody at the base and have decidedly sticky foliage. The only cult. species of much garden interest is G. **robusta**, a perennial herb 1–2 ft. high, with alternate,* clasping, ovalish or lance-shaped leaves 1–2 in. long and toothed. Flower heads solitary, gummy, about 1½ in. wide, both the rays* and disk* yellow. Calif., and not much suited to regions with wet, cold winters. The var. **latifolia** (sometimes known as *G. latifolia*) has broader and more clasping leaves. (Named for H. Grindel, Riga professor.)

*GRISEA, -us, -um* (gri'see-a). Gray.

**GRISELINIA** (gri-se-lin'ee-a). Attractive evergreen shrubs and trees of the family Cornaceae, mostly from New Zealand and Chile, the two below somewhat grown for ornament south of zone* 6, especially in Calif. They are related to and suggest *Aucuba*. Leaves alternate,* rather leathery and shiny. Male and female flowers on different plants, small, greenish, inconspicuous and sometimes (in the female flowers) without petals. In both those below the flowers are borne in small, branched clusters (panicles*). Fruit a berry. (Named for Franc Griselini, Venetian botanist.)

Little is known as to the cult. of the two below, for they are seldom grown.

**littoralis.** Kapuka. A tree 20–40 ft. high, the twigs brown-hairy. Leaves oblongish or wedge-shaped, 2–4 in. long. Flowers in panicles* 1½–3 in. long, chiefly in the leaf-axils.* New Zealand. There is a variegated-leaved form.

**lucida.** Puka. A shrub or small tree, 5–20 ft. Leaves oblongish, 5–7 in. long, unequal at the base. Flower clusters (panicles*) nearly 6 in. long, the flowers without petals. New Zealand.

**GRIT CELLS.** See STONE CELLS.

*GROENLANDICA, -us, -um* (green-lan'di-ka). From Greenland.

**GROMWELL.** See LITHOSPERMUM.

**GROSBEAK.** See BIRDS.

*GROSSA, -us, -um* (grō'sa). Great or large.

**GROSSULARIA.** See RIBES.

**GROSSULARIACEAE.** See SAXIFRAGACEAE.

**GROUND CEDAR** = *Lycopodium complanatum*.

**GROUND CHERRY.** See PHYSALIS.

**GROUND COVERS.** On the best ordered property there are places that refuse to be pleasant ones to look upon. Under shady trees the absence of light and the heavy drip of every rain obliterates grass year after year. In another place the surface roots of forest trees have taken up all nourishment intended for the lawn grasses.

There may be steep banks facing the noonday sun, and these are constant sources of expense and trouble. New turf shrivels up and becomes a prey to crab grass; if it is seeded a rain often carries new seed and prepared soil into the gutters below. Or a wood clearing of brush requires a cover to restore the natural effects.

With these vexations to overcome it is a relief to know that there are good plant materials that will provide covers for every condition. Weeds and fickle grass can be replaced by plants that are both happy and attractive.

The shade and drip of trees are not an ideal condition for most plants, but some native herbs and shrubs can be made to grow. And often no more expense is involved than for the work of clearing and attempting the impossible. See SHADY GARDEN.

The materials listed are those suitable for shade and woods; for moist places; for full sun, and for sun and shade at choice. Whenever possible choose shrubs that have edible berries, many of these have a threefold feature in spring flower, summer foliage and autumn fruit. See the body of the DICTIONARY for cultural notes on the different species, and for their hardiness. Here only their names and flower color are given.

GROUND COVERS FOR SHADY PLACES:
Lily-of-the-valley. *Convallaria majalis*. White, spring.
St. John's-wort. *Hypericum calycinum*. Yellow, summer.
*Leiophyllum buxifolium*. White, May, evergreen.
*Leiophyllum lyoni*. White, April, evergreen.
*Sarcococca ruscifolia*. Evergreen, spring or late fall, fragrant white flowers.
Ground ivy. *Nepeta hederacea*. Blue, May to Sept., but weedy.
Navelwort. *Omphalodes verna*. Blue, March.
*Sedum spurium*. Dense evergreen carpet. For cult. see ROCK GARDEN.
Speedwell. *Veronica chamaedrys*. Blue, all summer.

---

* Special articles on the subjects indicated by an asterisk (*) will be found at the words so marked.

Periwinkle. *Vinca minor.* Blue, summer.
*Euonymus radicans minimus.* Small evergreen leaves.
Moneywort. *Lysimachia nummularia.* Yellow.

GROUND COVERS FOR PARTIALLY SHADY PLACES:
Allegheny spurge. *Pachysandra procumbens.* Deciduous.
Japanese spurge. *Pachysandra terminalis.* Evergreen.
Ground hemlock. *Taxus canadensis.* Evergreen.
Creeping thyme. *Thymus serpyllum.* Evergreen, May–June.
Bugleweed. *Ajuga reptans variegata.* Blue and white, summer. Deciduous.*
*Pachistima canbyi.* Leaves dark green, but purplish in winter. Evergreen.
*Hedera helix baltica.* Evergreen.
Wintergreen. *Gaultheria procumbens.* Evergreen.
Honeysuckle. *Lonicera japonica.* Evergreen in the South.
Creeping barberry. *Mahonia repens.* Yellow, all summer, evergreen.
*Mazus japonicus.* Blue, summer, evergreen.
*Nertera depressa.* Good for Calif.; not hardy eastward.

GROUND COVERS FOR SUNNY PLACES:
Snow-in-summer. *Cerastium tomentosum.* Silvery foliage, white flowers in spring.
*Dianthus arenarius.* White flowers in June.
Candytuft. *Iberis sempervirens.* White, spring, evergreen.
*Phlox amoena.* Purple, spring.
*Polemonium reptans.* Blue, spring.
*Silene maritima.* White, June.
*Veronica repens.* Blue, July.
*Veronica teucrium prostrata.* Blue, summer.
*Cytisus kewensis.* White, May. For culture see ROCK GARDEN.
*Galax aphylla.* White, June, leaves purple in winter.
*Berberis verruculosa.* Foliage bronzy in winter.
*Buxus microphylla koreana.*
*Dryas octopetala.* White, summer.
*Rosa wichuraiana.* Pink, red and white; and forms a dense mat of glossy foliage.

GROUND COVERS FOR MOIST PLACES:
*Phlox divaricata.* Blue, spring.
*Phlox stolonifera.* Purple, spring.
Swamp dewberry. *Rubus hispidus.* White, June.
*Bergenia crassifolia.* Pink, spring; large foliage.
*Epilobium nummularifolium.* Pink, July.
Star violet. *Houstonia serpyllifolia.* Blue, summer.
Partridge-berry. *Mitchella repens.* White, April; red berries all summer.
Forget-me-not. *Myosotis scorpioides.* Blue, all summer.
Woodland ferns. — W. J. I.

**GROUND GOLD-FLOWER** = *Chrysopsis falcata.*

**GROUND HEMLOCK** = *Taxus canadensis.*

**GROUND HONEYSUCKLE** = *Lotus corniculatus.*

**GROUND IVY** = *Nepeta hederacea.* See also the list at WEEDS.

**GROUND LAUREL** = *Epigaea repens.* See TRAILING ARBUTUS.

**GROUND LILY** = *Trillium cernuum.*

**GROUND LIMESTONE.** See LIME.

**GROUNDNUT** = peanut; also *Apios tuberosa.*

**GROUND PINE.** See LYCOPODIUM.

**GROUND PINK** = *Phlox subulata.*

**GROUND RATTAN** = *Rhapis excelsa.*

**GROUNDSEL.** See SENECIO.

**GROUNDSEL BUSH, OR TREE** = *Baccharis halimifolia.*

**GRUBS.** See LARVA. See also INSECT PESTS.

**GUABA** = *Inga vera.*

**GUADALUPE PALM** = *Erythea edulis.*

*GUAJAVA.* The name in Spanish-America for the guava.

**GUAMA** = *Inga laurina.*

**GUAMACHIL** = *Pithecolobium dulce.*

**GUANABANA** = *Annona muricata.*

**GUANO.** See MANURE.

**GUARDIAN STONE.** See JAPANESE GARDEN.

**GUARDS FOR TREES.** See STREET TREES.

*GUATEMALENSIS, -e* (gwa-te-ma-len'sis). From Guatemala.

**GUATEMOTE** = *Baccharis viminea.*

**GUAVA.** A group of perhaps 150 species of the genus Psidium (sid'i-um), family Myrtaceae, all tropical American shrubs and trees, the three below, especially *P. guajava,* widely cult. in warm regions for their fruit, which is the common guava and the source of such widely used products as guava jelly and guava paste (the guayabada of the Brazilians). They are medium-sized trees or tall shrubs with opposite* leaves. Flowers large and showy, usually 1–3 on stalks that are often in the leaf-axils* or on the sides of the branches, never terminal. Calyx,* or its base, bell-shaped or pear-shaped, its lobes 4–5. Petals 4–5. Stamens* numerous, in several series. Fruit a berry, the tip crowned with the persistent calyx lobes or sepals. (*Psidium* is the Greek name for the pomegranate which the fruit somewhat resembles.)

For Culture and varieties *see below.*

**P. cattleianum.** Strawberry guava. A shrub or small tree, not over 25 ft. high, the bark smooth and grayish-brown. Leaves elliptic or broadest towards the tip, leathery, 2–4 in. long, the veins not prominently depressed. Flowers about 1 in. wide, white, the stamens* about as long as the petals. Fruit roundish, 1–1½ in. long, purplish-red, the flesh white. Brazil.

**P. guajava.** Common guava. A shrub or tree not over 30 ft., the twigs 4-angled, the bark brownish-green and scaly. Leaves oblongish, 3–6 in. long, the veins prominently depressed above, ridged beneath. Flowers about 1 in. wide, white. Fruit egg-shaped or pear-shaped, 2–4 in. long, yellow, the flesh whitish-yellow or pinkish. Tropical America.

**P. guineense.** Brazilian guava, but once supposed to be African, hence the specific name of *guineense.* A shrub, usually not over 8–10 ft. high. Leaves oblongish, 3–5 in. long. Flowers in clusters of 2–3. Fruit about 1½ in. long, greenish-yellow, the flesh white. S.A.

### GUAVA CULTURE

Culture of the common guava, a native of tropical America, is restricted to a limited area of So. Calif. and to peninsular Fla. where it has become naturalized in many places. It is primarily a jelly and preserve fruit, the high pectin and acid content of sour varieties making possible a yield of 3½ lbs. of jelly from each pound of fruit. It is also eaten fresh, cooked and canned, and made into butters, paste, relishes, catsups and chutneys. High in both mineral value and vitamin C, the guava is important in the diet, but because of the characteristic odor the fruit is not at first relished in the fresh state by everyone.

The plants fruit at an early age and bear regularly and abundantly. Beginning in early summer, a succession of ripening fruit is produced over a season of several weeks. There are two distinct fruit types, the pyriform (pear guava) and globose (apple guava), but no named hort. varieties are grown. Many seedling forms are planted and are differentiated mainly according to shape, flesh color — white and yellow to deep pink, and degree of acidity — sour to sweet. Acid varieties are chosen for jellies and pastes, and those of large size with meaty fruit and sub-acid flavor are preferred for other uses.

Plants of the red-fruited strawberry guava (*Psidium cattleianum*) bear little or no resemblance to the common guava and are included in ornamental as well as fruit plantings. They are much hardier, the range extending to the protected areas of the Gulf Coast and southern Calif. Like the common guava, they are precocious and prolific but the fruits are small and used principally for jelly making.

Guavas thrive on nearly any except marsh soils. Good drainage is desirable, although ample soil moisture must be available throughout the season of growth and fruit development for maximum yield. Several planting distances, varying with soils and variety, from 10 × 15 ft. to 25 × 25 ft., are

---

* Special articles on the subjects indicated by an asterisk (*) will be found at the words so marked.

used, but the closer spacing ultimately results in crowding of mature trees. Either clean culture, with cultivation, or mulching* is practiced, and material benefits are derived from both manures and commercial fertilizers.

Propagation is mainly by seeds, and to a much lesser extent by root cuttings, budding and grafting. Sprout growth from desirable varieties may be forced by severing roots of large plants 2 or 3 ft. from the main trunk and allowing to grow in place until large enough for transplanting.

Guavas are remarkably free of insect pests and diseases. Whiteflies, and a few scale insects, occasionally attack the plants and are controlled by weak dilutions of a miscible oil spray. — H. M.

**GUAVA FAMILY** = Myrtaceae.

**GUAYABO** = *Rajania pleioneura*.

**GUAYULE.** See PARTHENIUM ARGENTATUM.

**GUELDER ROSE** = *Viburnum opulus sterile*.

**GUERNSEY LILY** = *Nerine sarniensis*.

**GUIANA CHESTNUT** = *Pachira aquatica*.

**GUILIELMA** (gwe-li-el'ma). Chiefly Brazilian, spiny, feather palms, comprising perhaps 3 species, only G. gasipaes, the pejibaye or gachipaes, known to be in cult., and confined to the warmest parts of peninsular Fla. It has one or several trunks, 30–50 ft. high, usually spiny. Leaves in a showy terminal crown, each leaf 8–12 ft. long, with many, strongly ribbed leaflets that are deeply 2-toothed at the tip, the ribs and margins with stiff bristles. Flower cluster from just beneath the crown of leaves, the stalk spiny, the male and female flowers separate in the same cluster. Stamens* 6. Fruit 1–2 in. long, yellowish-orange, more or less top-shaped, the flesh edible and much prized in tropical America, where there is also a seedless variety. The plant is sometimes known as G. utile. (Named for Frederick William III, King of Prussia.)

**GUINEA GRASS** = *Panicum maximum*.

**GUINEA-HEN FLOWER** = *Fritillaria meleagris*.

*GUINEENSIS, -e* (gi-ne-en'sis). From Guinea, West Africa.

**GUMBO** = *Hibiscus esculentus*. For culture, see OKRA.

**GUMBO LILY** = *Mentzelia decapetala*.

**GUM ELASTIC** = *Bumelia lanuginosa*.

**GUMFINGER.** A patented lawn and leaf rake with tough, durable rubber teeth that do not clog or dig in.

**GUMI** = *Elaeagnus multiflora*.

*GUMMOSA, -us, -um* (gum-mō'sa). Gummy.

**GUMMOSIS.** A gummy exudation, usually caused by disease, often found on the trunks of certain trees, especially on plum, cherry, and on citrus fruits. See Diseases at ORANGE.

**GUM-MYRTLE** = *Angophora*.

**GUM PLANT.** See GRINDELIA.

**GUMS.** An uncommon, illiterate, and phonetic attempt to construct a plural for *Geum* (which see).

**GUM TREE.** See EUCALYPTUS. Trees of the genus *Nyssa* are also so called, but are better known as sour, tupelo, or black gum. See also SWEET GUM.

**GUNDA** = *Rajania pleioneura*.

**GUNNERA** (gun'ner-ra). Very showy foliage plants little known in American gardens, but interesting as being large herbs in a family, the Haloragidaceae, otherwise aquatic. Of the 25 known species, all from the southern hemisphere, the following are occasionally grown for bold effects in the border or on a lawn. They are perennial herbs with stout, creeping rootstocks, the leaves all basal, stalked, usually very large and striking. Flowers unisexual* or polygamous* in often dense spikes or panicles, the cluster sometimes spadix-* like. Petals 2, or none. Stamens 1 or 2. Fruit a drupe.* (Named for J. Ernest Gunner, Swedish bishop and botanist.)

The gunneras are extremely handsome foliage plants that need much space, a moist, rich soil, and, north of zone* 6, a thick winter mulch of straw or strawy manure. It is useless to attempt growing them in poor or dry soil. Propagated by division of the rootstocks.

chilensis. A stout herb, the leafstalks green, 6 ft. long, and covered with stiff, bristly hairs. Leaf blade nearly 6 ft. in diameter, roundish or heart-shaped, divided finger-fashion into many large segments. Flower cluster a spike nearly 3 ft. long, the individual flowers small and without petals. Fruit red. Ecuador, Colombia, and Chile. Sometimes known as G. scabra.

manicata. Resembling the above but larger, the leaves considerably larger and with the reddish-spiny leafstalk attached to the middle of the leaf blade. Southern Brazil.

scabra = *Gunnera chilensis*.

*GUTTA.* East Indian vernacular for many plants yielding products like rubber or gutta-percha. See PALAQUIUM.

**GUTTA-PERCHA TREE** = *Palaquium gutta*.

*GUTTATA, -us, -um* (gut-tay'ta). Speckled.

**GUTTIFERAE** (gut-tiff'er-ree). The balsam tree or mamey family, sometimes called the Clusiaceae, includes only tropical shrubs and trees, few of which are cultivated. Of the many genera and perhaps 500 species only 3 are known to gardeners in the extreme South, *Calophyllum*, *Garcinia* and *Mammea*. The two latter are of interest only for the edible fruit (mangosteen and the mamey).

They are resinous or aromatic trees with opposite* leaves having no marginal teeth, rather showy, sometimes waxy flowers which are solitary or in clusters, and (in ours) fleshy, usually edible fruit. See also HYPERICACEAE.

Technical flower characters: Flowers mostly polygamous* or dioecious.* Sepals and petals separate and free, usually 4, but sometimes 2 or 6. Stamens usually very numerous, some sterile, and often joined into groups at the base. Ovary superior,* with 2 or more cells.

**GUYING TREES.** See PLANTING.

**GUZMANIA** (guz-man'i-a). A genus of 75 species of handsome tropical American plants of the family Bromeliaceae, one or two grown in greenhouses for their handsome foliage and the white or yellow flowers borne in nearly stalkless clusters among the foliage. Leaves stiffish, in a dense basal rosette in the practically stemless G. musaica, but the rosettes on the stout stems of G. lingulata. Flower clusters with showy bracts,* the flowers more or less tubular. (See BROMELIACEAE.) Fruit a capsule.* (Named for A. Guzmann, Spanish naturalist.)

For culture see TILLANDSIA.

lingulata. A tree-perching, stout-stemmed plant, the numerous leaves scurfy, sword-shaped, remotely toothed, 12–18 in. long and about 1 in. wide. Flowers yellowish below, the tip purplish, crowded in a dense, red-bracted* cluster. Tropical America.

musaica. Normally growing in the ground and stemless. Leaves 12–20 in. long and 2–3 in. wide, round-tipped, with wavy cross-bands that are dark green on the upper side and purple on the lower surface. Flowers yellowish, the cluster 2–3 in. long, its bracts* golden-yellow and pink-striped. Colombia.

*GYMNOCARPA, -us, -um* (jim-no-kar'pa). Naked-fruited.

**GYMNOCLADUS** (jim-nock'lay-dus). A genus of only two species of trees of the pea family, one of them Chinese; the other, G. dioica, the Kentucky coffee-tree (often called simply coffee-tree), which is scattered from N.Y. and Pa. to Minn., Okla., and Tenn., and sometimes cult. for ornament. It is a tree up to 90 ft. high (less in cult.), with twice-compound* leaves, the leaflets arranged feather-fashion, in 3–7 pairs, more or less ovalish, without teeth, 2–4 in. long. Male and female flowers (in ours) on separate trees, or the flowers polygamous,* in terminal clusters, not pea-like but more or less regular. Calyx* tubular, 5-lobed. Petals 5, oblongish, greenish-white. Fruit a thick, flat, pulpy legume,* 8–12 in. long, the seeds large and flattened. The plant is of easy cult. in most ordinary garden soils, but it is certainly hardy only from zone* 3 southward. It is best propagated from root cuttings, or by seed. (Gymnocladus is from the Greek for naked and branch, in reference to some of the branches which are without twigs.)

**GYMNOGRAMMA** = *Pityrogramma*.

---

* Special articles on the subjects indicated by an asterisk (*) will be found at the words so marked.

**GYMNOSPERM.** The exact meaning of the term is naked-seeded, but the botanical and hort. significance of gymnospermous plants is greater than the mere meaning of the term would imply. Nearly all flowering plants have ovules* in a closed ovary,* the development of which results in some sort of a fruit with the seeds (developed ovules) inside. Gymnosperms have no ovary, no petals, sepals, nor any "flower" in the ordinary hort. sense of that word. Instead they have naked ovules typically borne between the scales of a cone as in the common pine. Or the male flowers consist merely of naked, pollen-bearing organs in various sorts of clusters. Upon fertilization the naked ovules (the female flowers) develop into seeds which are common in pines, spruces, and other cone-bearing plants. For the genera in THE GARDEN DICTIONARY that are included in the gymnosperms see PINACEAE, TAXACEAE, CYCADACEAE, GINKGO, and EPHEDRA.

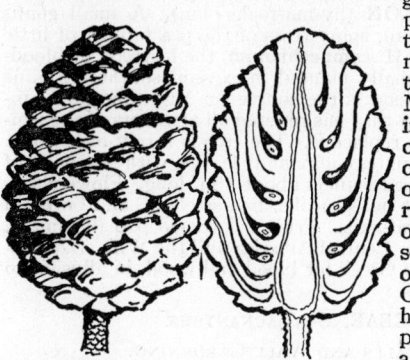

A pine cone (a gymnosperm), the cross-section showing the position of the naked ovules (the future seeds) between the cone scales.

**GYNURA** (jy-noor'ra). Handsome, greenhouse foliage plants of the family Compositae, most of the 25 species from tropical Asia or Africa. The only cult. species, G. aurantiaca, the velvet plant, is a native of Java, and is grown in the warm greenhouse for its handsome foliage. It is a shrubby, but somewhat fleshy herb, 2–3 ft. high, more or less velvety, with violet or purple hairs. Leaves alternate,* soft, ovalish, raggedly toothed, the blades narrowed at the base into winged stalks. Flower heads in loose clusters, not very showy, the flowers all in the disk and yellow or orange. The plants need a good light in order to bring out the color of the leaves, for which these plants are grown. (*Gynura* is from the Greek for tailed stigmas,* in allusion to a technical flower character.)

**GYNANDRIUM.** A structure found only in orchid flowers whereby the male and female organs are united into a column. See ORCHIDACEAE.

**GYPSOPHILA** (jip-sof'fill-a). Handsome, although small-flowered, annual or perennial herbs of the pink family, some of the sixty, chiefly Eurasian species very popular garden plants, known generally as baby's-breath from the profusion of mostly small, white or pink flowers. They are bluish-green herbs with opposite,* small leaves and slightly swollen joints. Flowers many, in usually profuse branched clusters (panicles*). Calyx* 5-toothed. Petals 5, sometimes toothed, usually with a minute claw.* Stamens* 10. Fruit a 4-valved capsule.* (*Gypsophila* is from the Greek for gypsum-loving, in reference to the preference of some species for limey soils.)

The annual and perennial species of *Gypsophila* are very popular garden plants because of their ease of culture and the profusion of bloom which makes snowy (or pink) patches in the border or bed, and are most useful as trimming for bouquets. While *G. cerastioides* and *G. repens* are most at home in the rock garden (which see), *G. elegans* and *G. muralis*, both annuals, are of the simplest cult. if the seeds are sown where wanted. Both will bloom more freely if not thinned out too much, as, like some annuals, they seem to prefer a bit of crowding. The perennial species are easily propagated by division. All of them need full sunlight and open, not too rich, soils.

**acutifolia.** Very like the common baby's-breath (*G. paniculata*), but the foliage less bluish-green, and the leaves only slightly 3-veined. Flowers white or pink. Caucasus.

**cerastioides.** A perennial with prostrate habit and creeping stems not over 4 in. high and downy. Lower leaves long-stalked, the upper nearly stalkless and broadest toward the tip. Flowers nearly ¾ in. wide, white, but pink-veined. Himalayas. For culture see ROCK GARDEN.

**elegans.** Annual baby's-breath. Upright, forking, and 10–18 in. high. Leaves sharp-pointed, lance-shaped, a little fleshy. Flowers small, long-stalked, white or pinkish, the petals slightly notched. Caucasus. Blooms from June 15 to Oct. The *var.* **grandiflora** has larger, white, pink, or rose-colored flowers and is the usual form in cult. The *var.* **carminea** has carmine flowers.

**muralis.** An annual pink-flowered herb, more or less sprawling and not over 8 in. high. Leaves narrowed at both ends. Flowers usually solitary in the leaf-axils,* the tiny petals more or less wavy-margined. Eu. and rarely escaped in the eastern U.S. June 15–Oct.

**paniculata.** Baby's-breath; called also gypsum pink and mist. The best known of the perennial species and often much-branched and 20–30 in. high. Leaves 2–4 in. long, much smaller on the flowering branches, 3-veined. Flowers very numerous, small, white, the clusters (panicles*) much-branched. Spring and summer. Eurasia. There are also double-flowered, named forms of the *var.* flore-pleno.

**repens.** A perennial scarcely 6 in. high, the foliage pale blue-green. Leaves very narrow, smooth. Flowers nearly ½ in. wide, white or pinkish, the clusters rather few-flowered. Mountains of Eu. For culture see ROCK GARDEN. The *var.* **rosea** has rose-pink flowers, and the *var.* **monstrosa** is merely a larger form.

**GYPSUM PINK** = *Gypsophila paniculata*.

**GYPSY MOTH.** See Moths at INSECT PESTS. See also Insect Pests at OAK.

**GYRANS** (jy'ranz). Gyrating or revolving.

**GYROTHECA** = *Lachnanthes*.

# H

**HABENARIA** (ha-be-nay'ri-a). A large and showy genus of orchids, mostly of the temperate regions, and commonly called fringed orchis from the beautifully fringed flowers of all the cult. species. All those below are wild flowers of N.A., needing rather special conditions for successful cult. They have (in ours) leafy stems and fleshy or tuberous roots, the leaves usually with a sheathing base. Flowers few or several in a terminal, bracted* spike, very irregular* and spurred. Sepals broad or spreading, the lip usually fringed or 3-parted, and toothed. Spur* longer than the lip. Fruit a capsule.* (*Habenaria* is from the Greek for rein, in allusion to the long, narrow spur of some species.)

It is useless to attempt growing the species of *Habenaria* without supplying the conditions they demand. All of them need a decidedly acid soil mostly from pH 4.0 to 5.0 (see ACID AND ALKALI SOILS). Where noted below, the bog is the best place for some species, but others are acid-soil plants of drier sites. There are many other wild species, some of them without the beautiful fringed flowers of the cult. sorts. While the average grower will prefer to buy roots from a dealer, it is possible to dig them from the wild. If the latter plan is adopted, it is better to mark wild plants when in flower and dig them out, with ample soil about their roots, at least 6 weeks after they are through blooming. But such digging should be done with discretion, as orchids are rare flowers worth preserving in their native habitat.

**blephariglottis.** White fringed orchis. A bog orchid differing from *B. ciliaris* in having longer spurs, but generally smaller and pure white flowers. Eastern N.A. Should only be grown in an acid bog. July–Aug.

**ciliaris.** Yellow fringed orchis; also called rattlesnake master. A slender orchid 12–28 in. high, the leaves lance-shaped, 4–8 in. long, the upper smaller and merging into the bracts.* Flowers showy, orange-yellow, the lip* much-fringed, the spur 1–1½ in. long. In meadows or bogs, eastern N.A. July–Aug. For culture see BOG GARDEN.

**cristata.** A bog orchid 8–20 in. high, the leaves narrow, 2–8 in. long. Flowers orange or yellow, the lip* deeply fringed, but not 3-parted, the spur scarcely ⅓ in. long. In pine-barren bogs, N.J. to Fla. and La.

**fimbriata.** Purple fringed orchis; also called meadow pink. A very

---

*Special articles on the subjects indicated by an asterisk (*) will be found at the words so marked.

beautiful native orchid 12–36 in. high. Leaves ovalish or lance-shaped, 5–10 in. long, the base more or less stem clasping. Flowers fragrant, purplish-lilac, the lip deeply 3-parted and each of the segments fringed, the spur 1–1½ in. long. In woods or moist places, eastern Canada to N. Car. June–July.

**psycodes.** Pink fringed orchis; also called soldier's-plume. Resembling the last, but the flowers pinkish or lilac, smaller, and less fringed. The spur is shorter than in *H. fimbriata* and has a knob at the end. In woods or bogs, eastern N.A. July–Aug.

**HABERLEA** (ha-ber-lee′a). A small genus of tufted, perennial herbs of the family Gesneriaceae, only the two below sometimes grown in the rock garden. They are low herbs with chiefly basal leaves and slightly irregular,* nodding flowers borne on a naked stalk, the corolla generally tubular and irregularly 5-lobed. Fruit a capsule.* (Named for Karl Konstantin Haberle, Austrian botanist.)

These are attractive little herbs suited to the rock garden. They are related to *Ramondia*, the cult. of which is discussed at ROCK GARDEN (which see, also for the cult. of *Haberlea*).

**ferdinandi-coburgi.** Resembling the next, but smaller and with the leaves smooth above and the flowers smaller and dark blue. Balkans.

**rhodopensis.** A perennial herb scarcely 6 in. high. Leaves somewhat broader towards the tip, hairy above, 2–3 in. long and coarsely toothed. Flowers pale lilac, about 1 in. long. Balkans.

**HABRANTHUS.** See HIPPEASTRUM.

**HACKBERRY.** Elm-like, but usually medium-sized, round-headed trees comprising the genus **Celtis** (sell′tis), of the family Ulmaceae, only a few of the 70 widely distributed species cult. for ornament. They are much less attractive than the closely related elms. Leaves alternate,* stalked, more or less oblique at the base and 3-veined. Flowers inconspicuous, unisexual* or polygamous,* without petals and with a 4–5-lobed calyx.* Stamens* 4–5. Fruit a greenish or blackish, bony, egg-shaped or roundish drupe,* the pulp scanty. (*Celtis* is the classical Greek name for a tree with a sweet fruit, but not certainly applicable to these trees.)

The hackberry is of the easiest culture in any ordinary garden soil, but they are hardy only as indicated below. Propagation is easiest from fall-sown seeds or from cuttings taken in the fall. The species much resemble one another and are hard to distinguish.

**C. australis.** A tree 40–70 ft. high. Leaves ovalish, 4–6 in. long, sharply toothed, more or less pale and hairy beneath. Fruit purplish-green. Eurasia and northern Af. Little grown outside of Calif. and similar climates, and not hardy north of zone* 5.

**C. laevigata.** Sugarberry. A tree 50–90 ft. high. Leaves almost without marginal teeth, oblongish, but long-tapering at the tip, 2½–4 in. long. Fruit at first orange-red, ultimately black-purple, almost ⅓ in. in diameter. Central U.S. to Fla. and Tex. Hardy from zone* 3 southward. Sometimes known as *C. mississippiensis*.

**C. mississippiensis** = *Celtis laevigata*.

**C. occidentalis.** The common hackberry of eastern N.A., and a tree up to 100 ft., usually much lower and round-headed. Leaves ovalish or oblongish, 3–5 in. long, tapering at the tip, but roundish at the base, usually toothed except towards the base. Fruit greenish-orange, but ultimately blackish-purple, nearly ⅓ in. long, somewhat pear-shaped. Eastern N.A. Hardy from zone* 2 southward. Called also nettle tree.

**HACKMATACK** = *Larix laricina*. See LARCH.

**HACKSAW FERN** = *Doodia aspera*.

**HAEMANTHUS** (hy-man′thus). Blood-lily. Showy, bulbous, African herbs of the family Amaryllidaceae, comprising over 60 species, the two below grown in greenhouses for their handsome flowers. They have chiefly basal, broad, blunt leaves and a somewhat flattened, solid flower stalk, crowned by a dense head of (in ours) red flowers beneath which is a whorl* of spathe*-like bracts. Flowers more or less tubular, the segments erect or spreading. Stamens* sometimes showy and protruding. Fruit berry-like, not splitting. (*Haemanthus* is Greek for blood flower, in allusion to the red flowers of many species.)

The blood-lilies should be grown in a cool greenhouse (not over 55° night temperature) in potting mixture* 3. Grown in such a house, they flower in late summer and early autumn, when the bulbs should be rested through the winter and started into growth in the spring. The bulbs may be dug and stored in a cool, dark, frost-free cellar, or the pots gradually dried off and similarly stored.

**coccineus.** Leaves thick and fleshy, nearly 20 in. long and 8 in. wide. Flowering stalk about 12 in. high. Flowers red, about 1 in. long, the cluster about 3 in. wide. South Africa.

**katherinae.** Leaves thin, 10–14 in. long and about 6 in. wide. Flowers bright red, nearly 2½ in. long, the cluster nearly 9 in. wide and very showy. South Africa.

**HAEMATOXYLON** (hy-ma-tocks′i-lon). A small genus of tropical American, spiny trees of the pea family, of little hort. interest, but **H. campechianum**, the logwood or bloodwood tree, occasionally planted in extreme southern Fla. as a curiosity. Its wood is the source (in Yucatan and Campeche) of a red dye that has resisted all attempts of the synthetic chemists to replace it. The tree is rarely over 40 ft. high and has alternate, compound* leaves, with 2–4 pairs of broad, wedge-shaped leaflets about 1 in. long. Flowers yellow, irregular* but not pea-like, bad-smelling, and borne in racemes* in the leaf-axils. Fruit a flattened pod (legume*), about 1½ in. long. Central America and the W.I. (*Haematoxylon* is from the Greek for blood and wood, in allusion to the red wood.)

**HAEMODORACEAE.** See LACNANTHES.

**HA-HA.** See WALLS AND WALL GARDENING.

**HAIR-BRUSH CACTUS** = *Pachycereus pecten-aboriginum*.

**HAIR GRASS.** See ASPRIS.

**HAIRY WATTLE** = *Acacia pubescens*.

**HAKEA** (hă′kee-a). A genus of over 100 species of evergreen Australian shrubs of the family Proteaceae, useful for outdoor cult. only from zone* 7 southward, a few of them popular plants in Calif. Leaves alternate,* in the cult. species either flat or needle-like. Flowers crowded, in pairs, in a dense, globe-shaped or finger-shaped cluster. Corolla tube slender, its 4 lobes joined even after the tube has opened. Fruit a hard, woody, 2-valved capsule.* (Named for Baron von Hake, German patron of botany.)

While popular in Calif., *Hakea* is little grown elsewhere, although it can stand an occasional frost. Mostly they are useful in semi-desert conditions and thrive there in a variety of soils, but prefer well-drained, light ones. Propagated by seeds, which are very slow to germinate, as they are extremely hard, and are best kept in a cool place for a year before being planted. Also the capsules will not discharge their seeds for some time unless kept in a warm, dry place.

**elliptica.** A shrub 5–8 ft. high, and of compact habit, the young twigs bronzy. Leaves ovalish or elliptic, nearly stalkless, 2–4 in. long, wavy-margined. Flowers white, in stalkless, nearly globe-shaped clusters. Fruit egg-shaped, 1–1¼ in. long, beaked.

**laurina.** Sea urchin; called, also, pincushion-flower. A tall shrub or small tree, sometimes up to 25 ft. high. Leaves elliptic or narrower, 5–6 in. long, about ¾ in. long, narrowed at the base into an obvious stalk, 5–7-veined. Flowers crimson in dense, stalkless, nearly globe-shaped clusters. Fruit egg-shaped, about 1 in. long, short-beaked.

**pugioniformis.** A spreading shrub 8–10 ft. high. Leaves needle-shaped, stiff, almost prickle-tipped, 1–3 in. long. Flowers white, the clusters stalkless, the corolla hairy. Fruit about 1 in. long, and ¼ in. wide, crested obliquely around the middle. Aust. and Tasmania.

**saligna.** A shrub 5–8 ft. high, the foliage grayish. Leaves oblongish, 4–6 in. long, short-stalked, the tip with a small, callused point. Flowers white, the clusters dense and stalkless. Fruit about 1 in. long, more or less warty.

**suaveolens.** A round-headed shrub, 6–10 ft. high. Leaves needle-like, spiny-tipped, often divided into several needle-like, spiny segments. Flowers fragrant, white, short-stalked clusters, the corolla smooth. Fruit about 1 in. long, corrugated, the small beak incurved.

*HALEPENSIS, -e* (ha-le-pen′sis). From Aleppo, Syria; or from the region anciently so called, which is supposed to be the "Eastern Mediterranean."

**HALESIA** (ha-lee′zi-a). Three or four species of rather showy, medium-sized trees of the family Styracaceae, one Chinese, all the others from the southeastern U.S. and cult. for ornament. They have alternate,* stalked, toothed leaves. Flowers in small, hanging clusters from the twigs of the previous season. Corolla bell-shaped, prevailingly white, 4-lobed. Stamens* 8–16. Fruit an oblongish, rather fleshless and dry drupe,* the stone with 1–3 seeds. (Named for Stephen Hale, an early botanical author.)

Some of these handsome trees are called silver-bell or snowdrop tree, from their profusion of white flowers in early spring. They are chiefly trees of the under-canopy of the forest and prefer sheltered to windy sites, and a rich, well-drained soil. If raised from seed, this should be stratified for

---

* Special articles on the subjects indicated by an asterisk (*) will be found at the words so marked.

one season, or they may be propagated from layers or by root cuttings. They are sometimes offered as *Mohrodendron*.

**carolina.** Silver-bell tree; also called snowdrop tree. Not over 40 ft., usually half this as cult. Leaves ovalish or oblong, 2-4 in. long, finely blunt-toothed. Flowers 2-5 in a cluster, the stalks about ¾ in. long. Corolla white, about ¾ in. long. Fruit oblongish. May. W. Va. to Fla. and Tex. Hardy from zone* 3 southward. Sometimes sold as *H. tetraptera*.

**diptera.** Snowdrop tree; also called silver-bell tree. A tree or large shrub, rarely over 20 ft. high. Leaves elliptic or wider towards the tip, 2½-5 in. long, remotely wavy-toothed. Flowers 3-6 in a cluster, or this with more flowers and raceme*-like. Corolla about 1 in. long, white, deeply lobed. Fruit nearly 2 in. long, 2-winged. May. S. Car. to Fla. and Tex. Hardy from zone* 5 southward; possibly in zone* 4 if in a sheltered place.

**monticola.** Tisswood. A larger tree than the others, 90 ft. in the wild, and about half this as usually cult. in the South. Leaves elliptic or oblongish, tapering at the tip, 5-9 in. long. Flowers 2-5 in a cluster, the corolla white, about 1 in. long, deeply lobed. Fruit nearly 2 in. long, 4-winged. May. N. Car. to Tenn. and Ga. Hardy from zone* 4 southward.

**tetraptera** = *Halesia carolina*.

**HALF-BREED.** See CROSS-BREED.

**HALF-HARDY.** See HARDINESS.

**HALF-HARDY ANNUAL.** See ANNUALS.

**HALF-HYBRID.** The result of a cross between a species and a variety of another species.

**HALF-MOON.** A hoe. See Section 1, TOOLS AND IMPLEMENTS.

*HALICACABUM* (ha-li-ka-kay′bum). Pre-Linnaean* name for the balloon-vine. See CARDIOSPERMUM.

*HALIMIFOLIA, -us, -um* (ha-li-mi-fō′li-um). With leaves like the genus *Halimium*, which is of no garden interest.

**HALIMODENDRON** (ha-li-mo-den′dron). A single species of salt-tolerant shrubs of the pea family, known as the salt tree, although it is a shrub scarcely 5 ft. high. The only species, **H. halodendron**, has compound* leaves, having 2-4 pairs of stalkless, rounded leaflets that are 1-2½ in. long, the main leafstalk often spiny. Flowers pea-like, pale purple, about 1 in. long, the clusters (racemes*) usually with only 2-3 flowers. Fruit a pod (legume*), 1-2 in. long, inflated and brownish-yellow. May-June. Vicinity of Turkestan. While an original inhabitant of alkali deserts, it is a fine ornamental shrub for ordinary gardens from zone* 4 southward, and may be propagated by seeds or by cuttings over bottom-heat,* rarely by grafting on *Laburnum* or *Caragana*. (*Halimodendron* is from the Greek for maritime and tree, in allusion to its saline habitat.)

**HALODENDRON** (ha-lo-den′dron). An obsolete generic name for *Halimodendron* (which see).

**HALORAGIDACEAE** (hal-or-ra-ji-day′see-ee). The water milfoil family is a puzzle to gardeners who cannot see the relationship of its only two cult. genera. One, *Myriophyllum*, is the beautiful submerged aquatic known as parrot′s-feather, while *Gunnera* comprises huge herbs with very large, expanded leaves. There are six other genera and over 100 species of wide distribution.

Leaves hair-like in *Myriophyllum*, nearly always submerged, but often six feet across and on stalks 6 ft. long in *Gunnera*, which is grown as a decorative foliage plant. Flowers very small, inconspicuous, but in *Gunnera* often crowded in dense clusters, nearly always unisexual.* Fruit dry and nut-like in *Myriophyllum*, fleshy in *Gunnera*.

Technical flower characters: Flowers unisexual* or polygamous.* Calyx joined to the ovary, or none. Petals 2-4, or none, if present very fleeting. Ovary inferior,* 1-4-celled.

**HAMAMELIDACEAE** (ha-ma-mell-i-day′see-ee). The witch-hazel family, except for the cult. genera, is chiefly tropical or sub-tropical. It comprises about 20 genera and possibly 50 species of trees or shrubs, none except the sweet gum (*Liquidambar*) and the winter- or fall-blooming witch-hazel being particularly handsome.

Leaves alternate* and simple, the veins arranged finger-fashion in *Liquidambar* (see sweet gum), but feather-fashion in all the rest of the cult. genera. Some writers consider that the sweet gum and a few other (non-hort.) genera should be included in a separate family, Altingiaceae, not here so considered.

There are no petals in *Parrotia* and *Fothergilla*, but all the other cult. genera have them. The only reasonably showy garden plants are *Hamamelis* (witch-hazel) with yellow flowers, *Loropetalum*, an evergreen Chinese shrub, with mostly white flowers, and *Corylopsis*, whose yellow flowers appear in spring before the leaves unfold. Fruit a woody capsule* which explosively discharges the seeds in the witch-hazel.

Technical flower characters: Sepals 4 or 5, sometimes 6 or 7. Petals 4-7, often strap-shaped, or lacking. Stamens 4 or 5, rarely none. Ovary inferior* or nearly so. Styles 2.

**HAMAMELIS** (ha-ma-mell′is). A small genus of rather coarse shrubs, family Hamamelidaceae, confined to N.A. and eastern As., usually called witch-hazel or winter-bloom, the latter in allusion to their blooming from Oct. to April, while the twigs are bare. Leaves alternate,* short-stalked, oblique at the base, more or less wavy-toothed. Flowers yellow, crumpled in the bud, the 4 petals strap-shaped. Stamens* 4. Fruit a 2-valved, explosively splitting capsule, which shoots its 2 black, shining seeds for a considerable distance. (*Hamamelis* is an old Greek name for a plant with a pear-shaped fruit, perhaps the medlar, and of little applicability to the witch-hazel.)

The witch-hazels are of the easiest cult., for they thrive in any ordinary garden soil, although preferring moist sites to dry ones. As the seeds take two years to germinate, the plants are most easily propagated by layers. They are good plants for the shrub border or for a border screen.

**japonica.** A shrub or small tree 10-25 ft. high. Leaves roundish or broadly oval, 3-4 in. long. Flowers about ¾ in. long, bright yellow. Jap. Jan.-March. Hardy from zone* 3 southward. The *var.* **arborea** is more tree-like in habit, and has golden-yellow flowers.

**mollis.** A shrub or small tree 10-25 ft. high. Leaves roundish or broadest towards the tip, 3½-7 in. long, finely toothed, and grayish-hairy beneath. Flowers golden-yellow, but reddish at the base, about ¾ in. long. China. Feb.-March. Hardy from zone* 3 southward.

**vernalis.** A shrub, often with many stems, usually less than 6 ft. high. Leaves oblongish, or broadest towards the tip, 3-5 in. long, coarsely toothed above the middle. Flowers about ½ in. long, light yellow, or reddish towards the base. Central U.S. Jan.-March. Hardy from zone* 4 southward. A useful shrub for forcing (which see).

**virginiana.** Common witch-hazel. A coarse shrub up to 15 ft. high. Leaves elliptic or broadest towards the tip, 4-6 in. long, coarsely toothed. Flowers bright yellow, about ¾ in. long. Eastern N.A. Sept.-Nov. Hardy from zone* 2 southward.

**HAMATOCACTUS** (ha-ma-toe-kak′tus). A single species of globe-shaped or oblongish cactus, **H. setispinus**, from southern Tex. and adjacent Mex. It is scarcely 6 in. high and has usually 13 rather thin ribs. Spines 12-16 in a cluster, with 1-3 central and larger spines in the center of each spine cluster. Flowers funnel-shaped, yellow, 2-3 in. long, its outer scales somewhat fringed. Fruit red, small, berry-like. The plant is cult. outdoors in the desert regions of the U.S. and in greenhouses. See CACTI for details of culture. (*Hamatocactus* is from the Greek for hook and *Cactus*, in reference to the hooked spines of some related cacti, although this plant has straight spines.)

**HAMBURG PARSLEY.** See PARSLEY.

**HAMELIA** (ha-me′li-a). Showy, evergreen, tropical American shrubs of the family Rubiaceae, favorite garden plants in the tropics, but cult. outdoors in the U.S. only in zones* 8 and 9, especially in Fla. They have generally opposite* leaves and handsome, tubular, red or yellowish flowers in terminal, branching clusters (cymes*). Corolla regular, 5-lobed. Stamens usually 5, not protruding. Fruit a berry. (Named for Henry L. Duhamel, French botanist.)

The hamelias are very fine garden shrubs in warm regions and respond to rich soils and plenty of moisture, although they will grow in a variety of less favorable sites. Propagated by cuttings of partially ripe wood rooted under glass, or by seeds.

**erecta.** Rat-poison plant. A stout, branching shrub 8-20 ft. high, more or less grayish-hairy on the twigs. Leaves ovalish, 4-6 in. long. Flowers about ¾ in. long, usually scarlet, but sometimes orange. Fruit about ¼ in. long, reddish-purple, more or less egg-shaped. Fla. to Brazil. Sometimes mistaken for *Ixora* (which see). Sometimes called scarlet-bush.

**patens** = *Hamelia erecta*.

**sphaerocarpa.** A hairy, branched shrub 6-10 ft. high. Leaves oblongish,

---

* Special articles on the subjects indicated by an asterisk (*) will be found at the words so marked.

2-4 in. long, more or less wavy-margined. Flowers about 1 in. long, orange-yellow. Fruit small, globe-shaped, purplish-black. Peru.

**HAND CULTIVATOR.** See Section 1, TOOLS AND IMPLEMENTS.

**HAND POLLINATION.** *See* Crossing Technique at CROSSING.

**HANDSOME HARRY** = *Rhexia virginica*.

**HANGING BASKET.** A basket-like contrivance of wood or wire, suspended from the roof, and filled with soil and suitable plants. Its chief value is decorative, and in the greenhouse or hanging from a porch roof, a series of well-filled hanging baskets may be very handsome.

While very showy, painted, wooden baskets are to be had from the dealers, the most lasting and practical are made of wire stout enough to hold the weight of soil and plants. Also wire baskets stand daily watering better than wooden ones. Another type is the so-called self-watering basket. It is made of iron with a double bottom, the space below the soil container being filled with water which is poured down a tube that projects up to the soil level. Such baskets are thus sub-irrigated and avoid the inevitable drip that follows ordinary watering as outlined below. They are more costly than wire baskets, and do not need watering until the reservoir is dry.

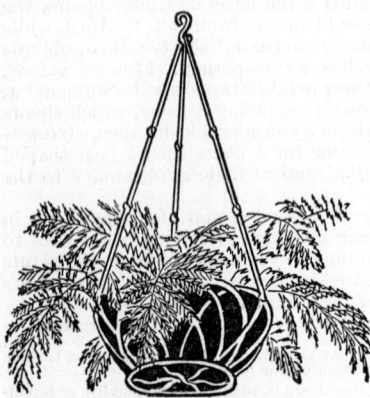

Old-fashioned, moss-lined hanging basket with fern

It adds to the attractiveness of wire baskets, and also holds the soil, to line them next the wire with fresh slabs of green moss. See that the moss completely covers the inner side of the basket, and it is better to fit the moss a bit at a time as the soil is put in. For most hanging baskets, potting mixture* 3 will be the best. Pack the soil reasonably well so that the moss is tightly pressed against the wire. Then dip the basket in a pail of water and allow the soil to settle for a day or so. Then fill in any holes that may have developed and you are ready for planting.

BASKET PLANTS. Very attractive hanging baskets can be made by using plants like dwarf nasturtiums, sweet alyssum, *Browallia*, *Vinca minor*, *Vinca major*, the English ivy, *Cobaea scandens*, *Thunbergia*, *Saxifraga sarmentosa*, wandering Jew, or the Kenilworth ivy. These, and more desirable plants to be mentioned presently, will form drooping sprays without which a hanging basket looks rather naked. These trailing or drooping plants should be planted near the edge or even plunged in the sides of the basket, which may be done with a dibble if the plants are young. In fact most hanging-basket plants are best started elsewhere and transplanted into the basket when still quite young.

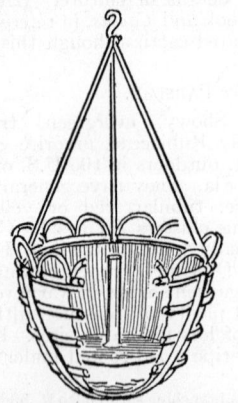

So-called self-watering hanging basket with a basal reservoir and pipe. For details *see* text.

Usually the center of the basket should have some erect plant, or several if they are small, around which are grouped the smaller or trailing species. Good plants for the center are: geraniums, petunia, *Cordyline*, *Dracaena*, begonia, coleus, *Cuphea*, platycentra, fuchsia, and ferns. Some very fine hanging baskets consist only of the Boston fern and its drooping variety.

While an all-fern basket is often very attractive, there are some very fine greenhouse plants with beautiful flowers that are suited to hanging baskets. They must be purchased from the florist or grown in one's own greenhouse. And the plants listed below will not stand too much wind or dry air. Hanging baskets containing them should therefore be put in quiet, wind-free porches or kept in the greenhouse. Some of these choicer basket plants are:

*Centropogon lucyanus*  *Convolvulus mauritanicus*
*Begonia lloydi*  *Episcia cupreata*
*Fuchsia procumbens*  *Solanum jasminoides*

WATERING. Because they are exposed to the air on all sides, hanging baskets dry out much more quickly than ordinary flower pots. If they are in a sunny or windy place, they will need a thorough watering at least every other day, and often every day. Much the most satisfactory method is to dip the basket, plants and all, in a tub of water, but begonia leaves should not be submerged. Watering from a ladder with a watering pot is apt to wash out the soil, especially in freshly planted baskets, where the roots of the plants have not yet bound the soil. If the plants in your basket show signs of yellowing, they may need fertilizer. The best plan, so as not to disturb the plants, is to work into the soil a little complete fertilizer (*see* FERTILIZERS), or water with liquid manure. See also FERN BALL.

**HANGING GARDEN.** No garden really hangs, but the term hanging gardens has been applied to roof gardens from the days when elaborate ones were made in Babylon to the modern penthouse garden.

**HARBINGER-OF-SPRING** = *Erigenia bulbosa*.

**HARBOURIA** (har-boor'i-a). A single species of Rocky Mountain, perennial herb of the carrot family, little grown except in open places in the rock garden. The only species, **H. trachypleura**, is a feathery herb 12–20 in. high, the leaves thrice-compound and having the finest thread-like segments or leaflets. Flowers yellow, in long-stalked, paired clusters (umbels*). Fruits flattened, ribbed. It has no special soil preferences, beyond needing good drainage. (Named for J. P. Harbour, a collector of Rocky Mountain plants.)

**HARDENBERGIA** (har-den-ber'ji-a). A small genus of Australian woody vines of the pea family, the two below much grown in Calif. and south of zone* 7 for their long clusters of small flowers. They have compound* leaves, the leaflets 3–5, or reduced to 1 in *H. monophylla*. Flowers pea-like, very small, but in long, showy racemes.* Fruit a swollen or flat pod (legume*). (Named for Franziska, Countess of Hardenberg.)

While popular as outdoor vines in Calif., both can be grown in the cool greenhouse. Use potting mixture* 3, to which about ⅓ its bulk should be added of peaty, slightly acid humus. They are best propagated by greenwood cuttings taken in spring and kept under glass.

**comptoniana.** Leaflets mostly 3, rarely 5, ovalish or narrower, 1½–3 in. long, blunt-tipped. Flowers blue or violet blue, scarcely ½ in. long. Pod flattish, 1½–2 in. long.

**monophylla.** Leaflet only 1, ovalish or oblong, 2–4 in. long, blunt at the tip. Flowers scarcely ½ in. long, violet or rose-color. Pod more or less swollen. The *var*. **alba** has white flowers and the *var*. **rosea** has pink ones.

**HARDENING OFF.** This is a gardener's term used to describe the process of making plants ready for outdoors. All plants raised in frames or greenhouses, whether from seeds, cuttings or otherwise, are necessarily tender at first, and if exposed to outdoor conditions without being hardened off, would suffer severely from sunscald* or chilly winds. Hardy annual or hardy perennial seedlings if raised in the open may be transplanted without much fear of damage, even from light frost.

---

* Special articles on the subjects indicated by an asterisk (*) will be found at the words so marked.

If raised in a greenhouse, or even a cold frame, the same plants would, if put outdoors right away, lose much of their foliage and perhaps be severely cut back by late frosts. Geraniums, petunias and similar tender subjects that are raised under glass would likewise suffer injury, even if not planted out until the end of May.

Hardening off, therefore, means making such plants hardy enough to withstand outdoor conditions. If raised indoors or in a greenhouse, the usual plan is to place the plants in a cold frame, keeping the sash closed for two or three days, then gradually allowing more and more air until eventually the sash is removed entirely. The hardening process takes about two weeks — that is, if the plants are to be set out at the end of May, they should spend two weeks in the frame, the sash being dispensed with the last few days.

If no frame is available the plants, whether in pots or boxes, should be stood outdoors in a partially shaded, sheltered place when weather permits, either covering with a temporary canvas arrangement or bringing them indoors at night, especially if frost threatens. By degrees the plants may be brought more into the open until they are thoroughly inured to sun and light.

The time for hardening off depends largely upon the class of plants and when they are to be planted out. Most half-hardy annuals such as petunias, verbenas, salpiglossis, etc., are sown in heat in March and are not safe outdoors until mid-May; therefore the hardening process should begin the latter part of April. Geraniums and similar plants wintered indoors are usually planted out after the end of May, and therefore should be given their hardening treatment from the middle of that month, special precautions against cold winds and night frosts being taken. If the nights are very cold, mats on the frame are advisable at night.

Vegetable and even flowering plants raised in a hotbed, if space is lacking for full hardening off in frames, may be planted outside and covered with paper cones known as Hotkaps. These paper cones ward off both wind and hot sunshine and serve as miniature greenhouses. The plants can gradually be ventilated until it is safe to remove the protector entirely. Hotkaps are largely used by vegetable growers, even for the raising of cucumbers, melons, etc., the seeds being sown under the covers, which are allowed to remain until the plants no longer can be protected by them. — T. A. W.

**HARD FERN** = *Blechnum spicant*.

**HARD FESCUE** = *Festuca ovina duriuscula*.

**HARD-FLESHED CHERRY** = *Prunus avium duracina*.

**HARDHACK** = *Spiraea tomentosa*; also *Potentilla fruticosa*.

**HARDHEADS** = *Centaurea nigra*.

**HARDINESS.** No terms are more common in hort. literature than hardy, tender, and half-hardy, and none more difficult to define. For we try to reduce to such terms many factors that determine the climatic fitness of a plant for outdoor culture. The difficulty is that in their own home all plants are hardy, while the average garden has dozens of plants that come from a variety of climates. Some are hardy, some merely root hardy (which means they may winter-kill*), while others are tender. And some are hardy for one season but not for others.

Hardiness, for most ordinary purposes, means trying to answer the question, "Will it live over the winter?" In other words, hardiness is a temperature response, and only this, to most gardeners. While this is true in a general way, so many other things besides winter cold contribute to hardiness, that they are worth noting.

DORMANCY. For all woody plants, except evergreens, there comes a period of winter dormancy, coinciding with leaf-fall and the onset of cold weather in the fall, and ending with the onset of spring. For all wild plants, in any locality, this periodic dormancy is automatic, or the plants, instead of being acclimated, would have long since perished.

This dormancy is a very definite physiological response to cold. The plant cells, the air spaces between them, and the concentration of cell-sap change materially during cold weather — mostly in the direction of lessened water content. The effectiveness of this dormancy also depends upon a rather delicate balance which can withstand sudden warm spells in mid-winter, when an untimely bursting into leaf would be fatal. But no native plant ever does this, nor do they change by more than a few days their yearly rhythm of dormancy. Resistance to cold is based upon these facts, although the physiology of what goes on in the dormant wood is more complicated than there is space to enlarge upon here.

When this is thoroughly understood, hardiness takes on a somewhat different meaning. If resistance to cold depends not only upon the intensity of winter temperature, but upon water content and concentration of the cell-sap, it is imperative to know more about these very important factors of hardiness.

Woody plants enter the winter with a water content dictated by the amount and distribution of summer rainfall. If there has been a gradual slackening of rainfall as mid-August or September approaches, then the season's growth will tend to ripen and the plant will enter the winter as well prepared to meet it as possible.

If, on the other hand, there is much late-summer rainfall, the season's growth will continue green, there will be little ripening of wood, and the plant will enter the winter in the worst possible state to meet its rigors. Such a plant will almost surely winter-kill, and it may be killed outright. In other words, it is not "hardy."

With many plants their hardiness is thus a matter of summer rainfall rather than winter cold. A study of their condition during the early fall will tell us much about their chances of winter survival. If their growth is too lush and if the wood has not ripened, then pruning or protection is advisable. See PROTECTING PLANTS.

INCREASING HARDINESS. While, as we shall see presently, it is impossible to make tender plants (*i.e.* climatically unsuited ones) hardy, there are many things that a resourceful gardener can do to increase the hardiness of plants that are on or near the edge of their hardiness range. All of them point in the same direction, the gradual slackening of the plant's activity as it enters the winter. The chief things to avoid are:

1. Do not cultivate the soil after late summer; it may induce a lot of new shoots that will enter the winter unprepared for it. For the same reason do not use nitrogen fertilizers (*see* FERTILIZERS) late in the season, and do not over-water after Aug. 15, especially on rich but poorly drained soils.

2. Do not, if possible, allow shrubs to suffer from midsummer drought, which usually checks growth, induces a premature ripening of wood, and may be followed by a lush fall growth that will be unfit to face the winter.

3. If you have allowed a smothering overgrowth or a crowded plantation to go through the summer without thinning, do not clean it up in the fall. This merely means that you expose tissue which was not given the proper chance to ripen. For the same reason vigorous summer pruning may induce a lot of fresh, and therefore vulnerable, growth.

4. If possible, use plants raised from cuttings made in your locality or a climatically similar one. Such are more likely to have become acclimatized than plants raised from seeds which often, or may, come from the South and are therefore more likely to produce tender plants. This is especially true of some evergreens. The reverse, of course, is true of seeds coming from more severe climates than yours.

5. Some plants known to be tender or only half-hardy may often be used if one studies the site or exposure. In regions where cold-air drainage naturally reaches the lowest part of your grounds with the greatest intensity, avoid such sites for your questionably hardy plant. (*See* FROST.)

6. The really important feature of hardiness in nearly all woody plants is to grow them in a well-drained soil, get their ordinary spring growth well ripened, and then trust to their going through the winter with a minimum of damage. They will do this if they are climatically suited for your region. In other words, do they come within certain climatic zones

---

* Special articles on the subjects indicated by an asterisk (*) will be found at the words so marked.

of hardiness, outside of which it is impossible to grow them?

ZONES OF HARDINESS. It is possible, and has been done for most woody plants in THE GARDEN DICTIONARY, to assign them to definite zones of hardiness, north of which it is unreasonable to expect them to grow. While, as we have seen, the hardiness of a plant in a particular site is a compound of many things besides temperature, it is still true that winter cold is the chief factor which dictates the climatic zonation of vegetation from the Arctic to the tropics. While many refinements of method have been used for plotting such zones, perhaps the most readily workable one is the plan evolved by Alfred Rehder of considering the lowest mean temperature of the coldest month. Concentrated in such periods are the extremes of unfavorable temperatures, the plant's survival of which will probably mean its continued growth.

For THE GARDEN DICTIONARY an extension of the Rehder system had to be made to cover the whole country, as his published map only includes, roughly, the region north of a line from N. Car., Ark., northern Tex. and westward. The plan here adopted separates the region north of Mex. into 9 zones.* For a complete description of them and a map see ZONE.

While such a scheme certainly operates over large areas, many local conditions of hardiness are affected by slope, site, exposure, and by some of the purely hort. operations of cultivation, pruning, watering, and fertilizing, such as are outlined above. For all herbs there is also the protection of a snow blanket, or of a mulch (which see). Both so change the cold hazard that it is impossible to assign most herbs to any of these countrywide zones of hardiness.

There are some plants, too, especially a group of Californian bulbs and certain cacti, which while able to stand pretty severe winter temperatures (10°–23°) in their own region, succumb at once in a higher temperature in the East when this is accompanied by winter slush or rain. Whether such a condition of winter dryness is properly considered as hardiness is a moot point. That is why there are notes at most such genera explaining their peculiar climatic requirements. While these may well be outside the scope of hardiness, the term also covers the ability of a plant to survive, no matter whether the hazard it must overcome is too much cold or heat or unfavorable factors such as drought.

The same is also true of the unfitness of certain conifers and many broad-leaved evergreens for large sections of the country due to insufficient rainfall. See EVERGREENS, BROAD-LEAVED EVERGREENS. The survival of such plants is due to a combination of moisture and temperature to which hardiness should perhaps be applied in a sense far from the usual one of being able to withstand winter cold.

**HARDPAN.** A layer of compact clay or silt below the usual penetration of the roots of most shallow-rooted plants. It often prevents the penetration of shrub or tree roots, and especially so for taproots. Hardpan may cause an accumulation of relatively stagnant water, which, in some dry regions, is a benefit. But to most gardeners, in a reasonably moist climate, hardpan is a nuisance to be destroyed by digging or dynamite.*

At the left a root system driven laterally by hardpan. At the right the root system developing normally after removal or breaking-up of hardpan.

**HARD ROT.** See Diseases at GLADIOLUS.

**HARDWOOD CUTTINGS.** See CUTTINGS.

**HARDY.** See HARDINESS.

**HARDY AGERATUM.** See EUPATORIUM COELESTINUM.
**HARDY ANNUAL.** See ANNUALS.
**HARDY BORDER.** See BORDER.
**HARDY CATALPA** = Catalpa speciosa.
**HARDY CLIMBING ROSES.** See Group 6 at ROSE.
**HARDY GLOXINIA.** See INCARVILLEA DELAVAYI.
**HARDY ORANGE** = Poncirus trifoliata.
**HAREBELL** = Campanula rotundifolia.
**HARE'S-FOOT FERN.** See DAVALLIA. See also POLYPODIUM AUREUM.
**HARE'S-TAIL GRASS** = Lagurus ovatus.
**HARICOT** = Phaseolus vulgaris. See BEAN.
**HARLEQUIN BUG.** See Insect Pests at CABBAGE and HORSE-RADISH.

**HARRISIA** (har-riss'i-a). Night-blooming, mostly climbing or vine-like cacti, most of the 20 known species from the W.I. and S.A., none from Mex. or the southwestern U.S. They have angled or fluted and 8–10-ribbed branches which bear at intervals a group of straight spines. Flowers solitary, funnel-shaped, the tube scaly but not spiny, the sepals* greenish-pink, the petals white. Fruit fleshy, spineless but tubercled or deeply warty. (Named for William Harris, Superintendent of the Public Gardens of Jamaica.)

The cult. species are tropical cacti to be grown in the greenhouse or outdoors only in extreme southern Fla. or Calif. See CACTI for details of soil and handling.

**bonplandi.** Climbing, often 8–10 ft. high. Branches 2–3 in. in diameter, 4-angled. Spines 6–8 at each cluster. Flowers 8–9 in. long, usually closing after sunrise. Southern S.A.

**eriophora.** Not much over 12 in. high, the branches about 1½ in. in diameter, 8–9-ribbed. Spines dark-tipped, 8–9 at a cluster. Flowers nearly 9 in. long, pinkish outside. Cuba.

**gracilis.** High-climbing (15–20 ft.) and much-branched, the branches with 9–10 ribs. Spines black-tipped, 10–16 at a cluster. Flowers about 8 in. long, the outer scales hairy in their axils.* Jamaica.

**tortuosa.** An erectish but arching, not high-climbing cactus, its branches about 1½ in. in diameter and 7-ribbed. Spines 6–10 at each cluster. Flowers 5–6 in. long. Argentina.

**HARROW.** See TOOLS AND IMPLEMENTS, Section 1.

**HARROWING.** What we do to the soil by hand raking, harrowing does with a machine. For the several sorts of harrows see TOOLS AND IMPLEMENTS.

Whether the machine is horse-drawn or motor-driven does not matter, but the operation can be done most effectively by recognizing a few simple facts. Harrowing practically always follows plowing, and it is best to harrow as soon after plowing as convenient. The soil is most workable then and we shall accomplish the greatest object of harrowing, which is thoroughly to pulverize the soil. Hand raking does this for small areas, but for anything over ¼ acre, harrowing is far easier and just as effective.

When the land is left in furrows by the plow, it is best to use first the disk harrow, the rotating knives of which break up the lumps and begin the process of smoothing out the ridges left by plowing.

Some operators run a disk harrow several times over a field and in different directions, but this is not usually necessary. And it saves time to begin harrowing with an ordinary toothed harrow immediately after one or two disk harrowings. The toothed or spring-toothed harrow has a series of spike-like teeth so arranged that as the implement is dragged over the land it acts much like a rake. Run it as long as necessary in order to make finely pulverized soil, for this is the only real object of raking or harrowing. In other words, both operations usually precede planting and have nothing to do with cultivation, which is a soil operation that follows planting.

Like any other soil operation, harrowing cannot be done successfully if the land is wet. See CULTIVATION for a discussion of the handling of soils after a rain.

**HARTFORD FERN** = Lygodium palmatum.

---

* Special articles on the subjects indicated by an asterisk (*) will be found at the words so marked.

**HARTMANNIA SPECIOSA** = *Oenothera speciosa.* See EVENING PRIMROSE.

**HART'S THORN** = *Rhamnus cathartica.*

**HARTSTONGUE FERN** = *Phyllitis scolopendrium.*

**HARVARD BOTANIC GARDEN.** See BOTANIC GARDEN.

**HASHISH.** See CANNABIS SATIVA.

*HASJOO.* Japanese name for the Yokohama bean.

*HASTATA, -us, -um* (has-tay'ta). Hastate; *i.e.* shaped like the head of a spear or arrow, but the basal lobes widely spreading.

**HATCHET-CACTUS** = *Pelecyphora aselliformis.*

**HATIORA** (ha-ti-or'ra). A small genus of tree-perching, spineless cacti, found in tropical American forests, and unlike most cacti, not true desert plants. They have round, usually pencil-thick branches, which are much-branched, and the small terete branchlets are more or less club-shaped and about 1 in. long in the only cult. species, **H. salicornioides**. Its main branches are frequently 6 ft. long and pendulous. Flowers day-blooming, about ⅓ in. long, more or less wheel-shaped, the petals erect and salmon-colored. Fruit mistletoe-like. Brazil. This is a cactus of greenhouse culture, where it blooms in late winter, and is closely related to *Rhipsalis*, where notes on how to grow both will be found. (*Hatiora* is an anagram of *Hariota*, an untenable name.)

**HAULM.** The stem; especially of peas, beans, **or grasses.** The term is more common in England than here.

**HAUTBOIS STRAWBERRY** = *Fragaria.* See STRAWBERRY.

**HAW.** See VIBURNUM and CRATAEGUS.

**HAWKS.** See BIRDS.

**HAWKSBEARD.** See CREPIS.

**HAWKWEED.** Very showy and handsome, but pestiferous, weeds belonging to the genus *Hieracium*. The two worst are the orange hawkweed and the mouse-ear hawkweed, both of which will be found in the list at WEEDS.

**HAWKWEED FAMILY.** See COMPOSITAE.

**HAWORTHIA** (ha-wor'thi-a). Generally stemless, South African succulent plants of the lily family, often grown in desert gardens and in miniature groups of cacti and other succulents for table decorations. They have mostly a basal rosette* of thick, fleshy leaves, which are often white-warty or tubercled, and in some species crowded on a short stem. Flowers greenish or whitish, usually in sparse clusters (panicles* or racemes*) at the end of a slender stalk that arises from the leaf rosette.* Corolla tubular, its limb slightly irregular.* Stamens* 6. Fruit a 3-valved capsule, its numerous seeds flat and somewhat angled. (Named for A. H. Haworth, English succulent fancier and botanist.)

For culture *see* SUCCULENTS.

**attenuata.** Leaves 30-40 in a rosette,* the thick blades white-warty on the back, 2-3 in. long and about ¾ in. wide. Flowers rose-red, the stalk of the cluster nearly 2 ft. long.

**coarctata.** Leaves in a rosette,* but at the end of a stem 5-7 in. long. Leaves about 2 in. long and ¾ in. wide, prominently white-warty. Flowers reddish, the cluster unbranched, its stalk not over 12 in. high.

**cymbiformis.** Leaves pale bluish-green, 1-1½ in. long and about ¾ in. wide, not warty, but very thick. Flowers pinkish-green, the cluster unbranched, its stalk about 12 in. high.

**margaritifera.** With 30-40 much-tubercled leaves in a dense basal rosette.* Leaves 2-3 in. long, about 1 in. wide. Flowers whitish, the cluster (raceme*) long-stalked and about 6 in. long.

**turgida.** Leaves 20-30 in a basal rosette,* the thick, keeled blades scarcely 1 in. long, ⅓ in. wide, the upper side lined with pale green toward the tip. Flowers very short-stalked in a spike-like raceme,* which is few-flowered.

**HAWTHORN.** See CRATAEGUS. For other plants sometimes called hawthorn *see* APONOGETON and RAPHIOLEPIS.

**HAY-SCENTED FERN** = *Dennstaedtia punctilobula.*

**HAZEL; HAZELNUT.** The hazel (hazelnut is best restricted to the fruits) is a general term comprising all the shrubs and trees of the genus **Corylus** (kor'i-lus) of the birch family, all the 15 species being found in the north temperate zone. Some of them yield hazelnuts and filberts, both of which are cult. commercially for the nutritious nuts. Leaves alternate,* doubly toothed, stalked, and generally hairy. Male and female flowers in separate clusters on the same plant, both without petals. Male flowers in scaly catkins,* the female in a partially enclosed, stalkless, head-like, dense cluster, only the red styles* protruding, both blooming before the leaves unfold. Stamens 4-8. Fruit an egg-shaped, roundish or oblong nut with a hard, smooth shell, partly or wholly surrounded by a leafy, sometimes tubular, structure (involucre*). (*Corylus* is the classical name for the hazel.)

For Culture *see* below.

**C. americana.** American hazel. A shrub 5-8 ft. high. Leaves broadly ovalish, 3-5 in. long, irregularly double-toothed. Fruits 2-6 in the cluster at the ends of the twigs, the leafy, lobed involucre* twice as long as the nut, which is nearly round and about ⅝ in. wide. N.A. Hardy from zone* 2 southward. Nuts of little value.

**C. avellana.** European hazel. A shrub 10-15 ft. high. Leaves roundish or broadest towards the tip, 3-4 in. long, heart-shaped at the base. Fruits 1-4, the leafy, deeply lobed involucre* as long as or shorter than the nut which is about ¾ in. long. Eu., and commonly grown there for the nuts, but here mostly for ornament. Hardy from zone* 2 southward. The *var.* **aurea** has yellowish leaves; *var.* **fuscorubra** has purplish or brownish-red leaves. The *var.* **grandis**, the cobnut, is usually grown for the nut which is larger than the typical form.

**C. colurna.** Turkish hazel. A tree up to 60 ft. and grown chiefly for ornament, its branches corky. Leaves broadly oval, heart-shaped at the base, 3-5 in. long. Fruits clustered, the leafy involucre* divided into narrow, sticky lobes, the nut about 1 in. wide. Western As. and southeastern Eu. Hardy from zone* 3 southward. Used, also, for grafting stock for the filbert.

**C. cornuta.** Beaked hazel. A shrub 3-8 ft. high. Leaves ovalish or broadest towards the tip, 2½-4½ in. long, densely double-toothed. Fruits 1-2 in a cluster completely hidden by the long, tubular, leafy involucre* which is nearly 3 times as long as the nut. The latter is thin-shelled, about ⅝ in. long, and more or less egg-shaped. Eastern N.A., but west to Saskatchewan. Hardy from zone* 3 southward. Formerly known as *C. rostrata.* The nuts are nearly worthless.

**C. maxima.** Filbert. A shrub 10-30 ft. high, sometimes tree-like (*see* below), the twigs and foliage sticky-hairy. Leaves roundish-oval, suddenly tapering at the tip, 3-5½ in. long. Fruits 1-3 in the cluster, the leafy, tubular, usually lobed involucre* about twice as long as the nut, which is oblongish, its kernel with a red or whitish skin. Western As. and southeastern Eu. Hardy from zone* 3 southward. The *var.* **purpurea,** chiefly grown for ornament, has dark purple leaves.

HAZEL CULTURE

Growing shrubs of *Corylus americana* and *C. cornuta* presents no difficulties, for both are common on a variety of soils in many parts of eastern N.A. But the nuts of both species are inferior to the filberts of the Old World which are imported into this country on a large scale.

Hazelnuts, which are chiefly the product of these two American and some Old World species, are generally roundish, and include also the cobnut, a variety of *Corylus avellana*. They are, from the commercial standpoint, not worth cultivating, but will always be collected from the wild.

Filberts, on the other hand, include various hort. varieties of *Corylus maxima*, widely grown in Europe for the nuts which are decidedly oblong and far better than our hazelnuts or the cobnut. Unfortunately, the plant does not grow so well in the eastern U.S. and its commercial production in the U.S. is chiefly limited to Washington and Oregon. There the plant is trimmed to a tree-like form and often reaches a height of 20-30 ft. It is planted upon 25-ft. intervals.

While it can be propagated by stratified seeds, most of the better varieties are budded or grafted upon stock of *Corylus colurna* or sometimes on *C. avellana*.

The culture of filberts in the East seems to be still in an experimental stage, although many new American and European hybrids are now being produced, and offer better chances of success with the hazel than formerly, especially in the East. The plant does much better in the moist coolness of Washington and Oregon than in New York, where experimental plantings are still to demonstrate their value. Small plantations show that some of the varieties are at least hardy, but they should not be planted on southern or warm sites because the warmth may force them into flower, only to have a late frost kill all chances of a later crop of nuts.

---

* Special articles on the subjects indicated by an asterisk (*) will be found at the words so marked.

VARIETIES. For Washington and Oregon the outstanding variety of filbert is Barcelona, there allowed to become treelike, but usually a shrub as grown in the East, where it is also the best variety for general purposes. It may be the same as the Barcelona variety of Spain, which produces large crops of Old World nuts. Other varieties of promise are Kentish Cob (a cobnut), Daviana, and Red Lambert, but all of them do better in the Pacific Northwest than in the East. Winter injury to or premature flowering of the male catkins is a trouble of nearly all varieties in the East, as well as disease.

INSECT PESTS. A tiny mite affects buds of hazel and filbert; lime-sulphur spray in May has been suggested for its control in Ore. Weevils, similar to those on chestnut, injure the nuts; infested nuts should be destroyed. An aphid is sometimes injurious in the West; it may be controlled with nicotine dust. Occasional leaf feeders yield to arsenicals.

**HAZEL FAMILY** = Betulaceae.

**H-BUDDING.** See BUDDING.

**HEAD.** Any tight or head-like flower cluster. Technically, *head* should perhaps be restricted to the flower clusters of the daisy, chrysanthemum, aster, and all the other plants of the huge family of Compositae (which see for details). But to most gardeners a head is any close cluster of flowers. For *head* in the sense of a head of lettuce *see* the next entry.

**HEADING.** A few plants, notably lettuce, endive, cabbage, cauliflower, and Chinese cabbage and some others, have, by selection and the work of the plant breeder, developed a more or less congested head of leaves, or of flowers, as in the cauliflower. All but the outside leaves of such heads are cut off from light and consequently produce no green coloring matter.

This fact means that the production of such an abnormal thing as a head puts a tremendous burden upon the functionally normal leaves. It is the latter that support the development of the head, for it is ordinary green leaves that produce plant food, while the head merely produces food for us.

It is for this reason that the cultural notes on cabbage, cauliflower, lettuce, etc., stress the fact that the only way to insure good heading is good, quick growth. Sluggish growth, weedy gardens, too much shade, and any other major disturbance of the plant's economy will make heading difficult and it may make it impossible. Do not forget that heading is something man has forced upon some plants, and to get the best results from such an unusual process, the best of care must be given.

In a few, like endive and cauliflower, no amount of good care will force the plants to head properly. Such have to be tied up, a laborious process described at both crops.

**HEADING BROCCOLI** = *Brassica oleracea botrytis.* See CAULIFLOWER.

**HEADING-IN.** See PRUNING.

**HEAD LETTUCE** = *Lactuca sativa capitata.* For culture *see* LETTUCE.

**HEAL-ALL** = *Prunella vulgaris.* See also the list at WEEDS.

**HEALING.** See TREE SURGERY.

**HEART CHERRY** = *Prunus avium juliana.*

**HEARTSEASE.** See VIOLA TRICOLOR HORTENSIS.

**HEART-SEED.** See CARDIOSPERMUM.

**HEAT.** See TEMPERATURE.

**HEATH.** See ERICA.

**HEATH ASTER** = *Aster ericoides.*

**HEATHER.** A single, remarkably variable, low shrub, comprising the genus **Calluna** (ka-loo′na) of the family Ericaceae, found all over Eu. and in Asia Minor, and widely cult. for its evergreen foliage and profusion of small, nodding, rosy-pink flowers (in the typical sort). The only species, **C. vulgaris**, the common heather, usually grows in dense masses,

and is mostly less than 18 in. high. Leaves small, opposite,* stalkless, keeled, mostly in 4 ranks and so numerous as to completely clothe the twigs. The leaves are scarcely 1/10 in. long. Flowers in dense, terminal spikes. Corolla bell-shaped, 4-parted above, ultimately becoming membranous and long-persisting. In the closely related genus *Erica* the corolla falls off after blooming. The corolla of the heather is exceeded also by a bell-shaped colored calyx.* Stamens* 8, included within the corolla. Fruit a small 4-valved capsule* which is hidden by the persistent corolla. (*Calluna* is from the Greek to sweep, in allusion to the ancient use of the twigs to make brooms.)

The heather makes a splendid plant for naturalizing on sandy banks or slopes, and has become naturalized in the northeastern U.S. in a few places having such conditions, notably at Nantucket. For details of its culture *see* ERICA, as it needs the same conditions as the hardy species there noted. The heather, which blooms from July to Oct., has been so long cult. and is so popular that many hort. varieties are to be had. The best of them include:

*C. vulgaris alba.* White-flowered.
*C. vulgaris alporti.* Crimson-flowered and taller than the typical form.
*C. vulgaris aurea.* Foliage golden-yellow.
*C. vulgaris carnea.* Flowers pink.
*C. vulgaris coccinea.* Flowers deep red. Sometimes known as *C. vulgaris rubra.*
*C. vulgaris cuprea.* Summer foliage golden; winter foliage bronzy.
*C. vulgaris hammondi.* Flowers white; taller than the typical form.
*C. vulgaris hirsuta.* Foliage gray-hairy.
*C. vulgaris humilis.* Lower than the typical form; flowers white.
*C. vulgaris nana.* Scarcely 6 in. high; flowers purple.
*C. vulgaris rubra* = *C. vulgaris coccinea.*
*C. vulgaris searlei.* Flowers white; taller and of looser growth than the typical form.

**HEATHER FAMILY** = Ericaceae.

**HEATH FAMILY.** Horticulturally an important family of woody plants, because it includes the heaths, heather, mountain laurel, rhododendron, azalea, trailing arbutus, wintergreen, rhodora, shinleaf, cranberry, blueberry, and huckleberry. Most of them have showy flowers and a few produce edible fruits, but some are poisonous. The family furnishes many broad-leaved evergreens of great garden value. For all the cult. genera and a description of the technical characters of the family, *see* ERICACEAE.

**HEAVING.** Many soils with a considerable amount of clay or silt in them, and any soils that are water-soaked, are likely to heave in the spring. It is caused by the alternate thawing and freezing of the upper layer of the soil. Such frost or soil heaving will likely throw out loosely rooted perennials, especially ones planted the fall before.

Heaved-out roots that have no chance to get anchored, because of shallow or indifferent planting

It is a minor nuisance in the garden because it exposes the roots of such plants to the cold or dryness and kills many of them. This is true not only of recently planted perennials but of some long-established ones if they happen to have shallow and fleshy, but few, fibrous roots.

---

* Special articles on the subjects indicated by an asterisk (*) will be found at the words so marked.

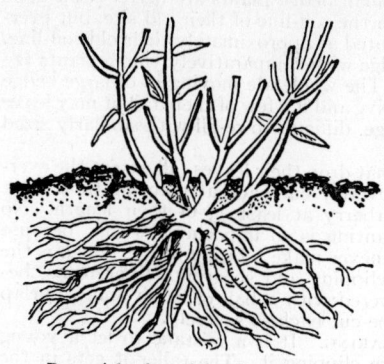
Perennials planted deeply and firmly enough do not heave.

One remedy is to practice spring transplanting in heavy or wet soils. If this is impossible, try to be especially careful to plant securely, and even a little too deep, those plants which may be heaved out in the spring. Another is to mulch* the plants with manure or straw which will prevent alternate thawing and freezing. But care has to be used in mulching very wet soils, as the mulch may cause rotting if not taken off in time.

**HEAVY SOIL.** See SOIL MOISTURE.

**HEBE.** See VERONICA.

*HEBECARPA, -us, -um* (he-be-kar'pa). Hairy-fruited.

**HEBENSTRETIA** (he-ben-stree'shi-a). A genus of 30, mostly South African, herbs or shrubs of the family Scrophulariaceae. **H. comosa** often grown as a flower garden annual. It is an annual herb (or treated as such), 2–3½ ft. high. Leaves alternate,* lance-shaped, ¾–2 in. long, distantly sharp-toothed. Flowers yellow or white, fragrant, in dense terminal clusters (spikes*) 3–6 in. long and resembling mignonette. Corolla irregular,* tubular, the limb deeply cut and with an orange-red blotch. Stamens 4. Fruit not splitting, otherwise capsule*-like. The plant can be grown as a half-hardy annual (see ANNUALS) or treated as a tender annual. (Named for John E. Hebenstreit, German professor of medicine.)

**HECHTIA** (heck'ti-a). A small genus of chiefly Mexican, semi-desert, spiny-toothed plants of the family Bromeliaceae, the two below sometimes cult. in the greenhouse for their foliage. They have dense rosettes* of leaves that are purple above, towards the tip, but silvery beneath. Male and female flowers on separate plants, white but not showy, scarcely ⅓ in. wide, borne in small, bracted,* interrupted clusters on a slender stalk about 2 ft. high. (Named for J. G. H. Hecht.)

*argentea.* Leaves about 12 in. long, silvery, stiff, and spiny. Flowers nearly stalkless, but numerous in each of the many small clusters. Mex. (?).

*glomerata.* Leaves 12–18 in. long and about an inch wide at the base, leathery and rigid, but gradually narrowed towards the sharp-pointed tip. Not such a good foliage plant as *H. argentea.* Mex.

**HEDEOMA** (he-de-ō'ma). Aromatic, pungent-scented herbs, comprising about 15 species of New World annuals or perennials of the mint family, only **H. drummondi** of secondary garden interest. It is a perennial herb, 12–20 in. high, with small, opposite* leaves about ⅓ in. long. Flowers pinkish-purple, about ¼ in. long, in small, nearly stalkless clusters in the leaf-axils.* Corolla irregular,* 2-lipped.* Fruit a collection of tiny nutlets, hidden within the hairy, sharply toothed, irregular* calyx.* Tex. April–Aug. An herb resembling the wild pennyroyal and not much grown, for its flowers are too small to be very decorative. (*Hedeoma* is from the Greek for sweet smell, in allusion to the aromatic foliage.)

**HEDERA** (hed'er-ra). This genus of evergreen, woody vines of the family Araliaceae comprises only 5 Eurasian and North African species, generally called ivy, but one of them (*H. helix*) cultivated throughout the temperate world as the English ivy, although it is native from England to the Caucasus. They have woody stems and climb by aerial rootlets which cling very easily to brick or masonry, but less so to wood. Leaves alternate,* evergreen, stalked, usually more or less lobed or coarsely toothed. Flowers greenish, not very conspicuous, and produced only on the oldest specimens of the English ivy, mostly in small umbels,* but these often in branched clusters on bushy branches. Petals 5, the sepals small or obsolete. Stamens* 5. Fruit a 3–5-seeded berry. (*Hedera* is the classical name of the ivy.)

The English ivy is one of the most valuable of evergreen vines, useful for walls, rocks, and any rough surface like the bark of a tree, and is often trained on decorative trellises. It is fine for hanging baskets or window boxes, but it should be remembered that it does not like open, sunny places and does best under shade, on the sides of buildings where the walls are in shade for part of the day, or it will make a splendid ground cover under trees where grass cannot be maintained.

The plant is perfectly hardy up to the limits of zone* 4, and even in many parts of zone* 3, if not planted in full sun and if the moisture conditions are right. The latter feature of its needs is well taken care of in places near the sea from Boston southward and along the Pacific Northwest. In many sections of the interior the summers are too hot and dry for it.

Ivy is easily propagated by cuttings, many of which are already provided with aerial roots. The cuttings may be started in sand in the greenhouse in winter, or almost any time during the growing season in frames or outdoors in sandy soil. Of the three species noted below only *H. helix*, the English ivy, and its varieties are much grown in the U.S., where millions of plants are propagated for landscape and cemetery planting, for house plants, or for window boxes. For the latter purposes it is better to buy potted plants, although its propagation is easy if one has a stock from which to make cuttings.

Rooting ivy cuttings in sand (or water) is one of the simplest of hort. operations.

*canariensis.* Perhaps only a form of *H. helix* found on Madeira and Canary Islands and in North Africa and hardy only from zone* 7 southward. It is a stout, high-climbing vine with roundish or heart-shaped, usually 5–7-lobed leaves that are 2–6 in. long. Fruit black, larger than in the English ivy (*H. helix*).

*colchica.* A high-climbing vine, the leaves broadly oval or elliptic or on some branches oblongish, 5–10 in. long and usually not lobed, dark green and leathery. Fruit black. Caucasus, Asia Minor, and Persia. Not hardy above zone* 6.

*helix.* The common English or evergreen ivy. Creeping, or if allowed to climb frequently reaching a height of 80–90 ft. and completely covering walls in favorable places. Ordinary leaves 3–5 lobed, 2–5 in. long, dark green above, yellowish-green beneath. On flowering branches (mostly produced only in very old plants) the leaves are larger and squarish but not lobed. Flowers green, inconspicuous, the umbels* globe-shaped. Fruit nearly round, almost ½ in. in diameter, black. For its hardiness and uses see above. There are many hort. varieties of this plant, some for special places and with different degrees of hardiness. The best-known ones are:

The juvenile form (*a*) and the fruiting or mature form (*b*) of the English ivy. Most ivy plants never get beyond the juvenile stage.

var. *arborescens.* An upright shrub with essentially unlobed leaves; perhaps originating from cutting of only flowering branches.

---
* Special articles on the subjects indicated by an asterisk (*) will be found at the words so marked.

*var.* **argenteo-variegata.** Vine-like, the leaves white-variegated or white-margined.
*var.* **aureo-variegata.** Leaves yellow or variegated with yellow.
*var.* **baltica.** A small-leaved form very useful for a ground cover (which see); also more hardy than the typical *H. helix* or than any other of its varieties.
*var.* **conglomerata.** A slow-growing, creeping form with small, crowded, unlobed or only 3-lobed leaves. For culture *see* ROCK GARDEN.
*var.* **gracilis.** A small-leaved form, the foliage turning bronzy in winter. One small-leaved form is commonly sold as Japanese ivy.
*var.* **minima.** A very popular form with small leaves having wavy margins.

There are at least two dozen other sorts.

**HEDERACEA,** *-us, -um* (hed-er-ray'see-a). Ivy-like.

**HEDERAEFOLIA,** *-us, -um* (hed-er-ry-fō'li-a). With ivy-like leaves.

**HEDGE BINDWEED** = *Convolvulus sepium*. *See* list at WEEDS.

**HEDGE-BOY.** A trademarked, electric hedge-shearing machine.

**HEDGE FUMITORY** = *Fumaria officinalis*. *See* FUMITORY.

**HEDGEHOG CONEFLOWER** = *Echinacea purpurea*.

**HEDGEHOG POPPY** = *Argemone platyceras hispida*.

**HEDGES.** A clipped or informal hedge is in many ways better than a wooden or wire fence. For the purely architectural features of hedges see the section devoted to this below. Here we are concerned only with hedge plants, their care, clipping, and advantages and disadvantages.

All the plants mentioned below are entered in other parts of THE GARDEN DICTIONARY and should be looked for at their regular entries for additional details about them, especially for the notes on their hardiness. It is needless to repeat these details here, but neglect of them may mean failure in the case of some of the rarer and finer hedge plants.

In making a hedge it is important to decide which type of plant will be used, whether they will be closely planted or whether they are large enough to make individual holes necessary. For privet and most small plants that will be planted a foot or less apart, the best plan is to dig a trench 2 ft. wide and 2 ft. deep and fill it in with good topsoil into which dig a 3-in. layer of well-rotted manure. Let the soil settle until after the first good rain and then fill up to the general ground level if there has been

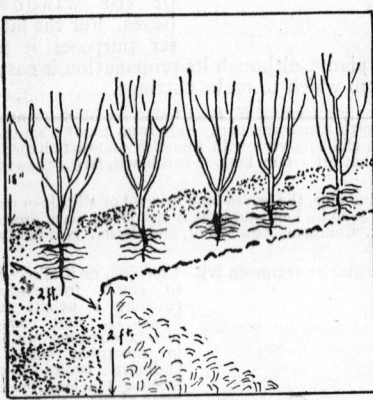

The trench method of planting privet. For details *see* text.

much sinking. Some prefer to make such a trench for evergreens or larger plants, but these can be planted in separate holes if expense is a factor.

PLANTING. For all hedge plants that drop their leaves, planting can be done in the usual spring or fall planting time in your locality. For evergreens the planting should be done either in early spring or between Aug. 15 and Sept. 15 over most of the country. In sub-tropical regions the planting of hedges will naturally follow the very different conditions in such places. *See* the section Sub-tropical under each month at GARDEN CALENDAR.

For most small plants it is better to stretch a line so as to ensure straight planting, and it may be well to use a line for larger ones, although if it gets in the way of handling them, drive stakes where the larger plants are to go and remove the line. Plant in single, not double, rows. For all but large plants and evergreens, a good average distance apart is 12 in., but many fine privet hedges were planted only 6 in. apart.

Privet and most small hedge plants are better set a little deeper (2–3 in.) than the soil-line of their old site, but evergreens should be planted at approximately their old soil-line. Always start the hedge with comparatively young plants (2–3 years for privet). The wholesale moving-in of large hedge plants is very expensive and if a few of them fail, it may leave bad holes in the hedge, difficult to re-fill with similarly sized plants.

All hedge plants that drop their leaves (all except the evergreens) should be severely cut back at planting time. Cut back privet and barberry at least $\frac{1}{3}$ of their length. No feature of hedge planting is so important as this, because "leggy" plants will never make a bushy hedge, which is the object of all early clipping and shearing. Evergreens, because they are delivered with a ball of earth and a burlap covering, need not be cut back so severely.

CLIPPING OR SHEARING. It is a mistake to let a young hedge get tall before clipping it. The taller it gets in the young state the less chance is there of making it fill out towards the base. During the first year after planting, cut it back two or three times in the growing season, the permanent height of the clipped hedge being increased only a few inches after each clipping. This will force out a lot of new growth towards the base of the hedge and permit the start of the most important feature of the properly shaped hedge.

Start the young hedge properly by forcing it to produce twigs from the base. Cut at first as shown at the right.

When there is an ample growth of twigs near the base and the hedge (in the case of privet) is still only 3–4 ft. high, begin trimming so that the base of the hedge will always be a little wider than the top. If the reverse is done (a common failing in amateur hedge-shearing), the top will be wider than the bottom, and enough light will be screened off the base of the hedge to kill or partially suppress the twigs near the base. This is why so many old hedges are naked at the bottom but fine enough at the top. No matter how high or wide the hedge may become, always plan its trimming so that the top is left slightly narrower than the bottom. Such a hedge also sheds snow more easily.

While for small hedges clipping is best done with an old-fashioned hedge shears (*see* TOOLS AND IMPLEMENTS), there are, for extensive hedges, several types of electrically driven hedge-clipping machines. They remove one of the chief objections to hedges. Three times in a growing season is enough for

As it matures see that the hedge is slightly narrower at the top, not broader at the top as shown in the lower figure. *See* text for details.

---

* Special articles on the subjects indicated by an asterisk (*) will be found at the words so marked.

# HEDGES

clipping most hedges, unless they are wanted in the most perfect symmetry, when they will need clipping more often. It all depends upon the season and the plant used.

## Hedge Plants

Well-sheared, perfect hedges can only be made from plants that will stand regular clipping. Very fine, but more informal, hedges can be made of plants that will stand a good deal of occasional pruning, but resent the more or less constant clipping necessary for plants like privet and boxwood. These informal hedge plants are far more numerous than the sorts which thrive upon regular clipping, but they cannot be moulded into architectural forms such as privet and the others. In the list below those that can be clipped regularly are marked with a †. All others can be pruned from time to time, a disadvantage, in a hedge plant, perhaps overcome by the fact that many of them flower profusely. Few clipped hedge plants do so.

† = Can be clipped as much as necessary. All others may be more or less shaped by occasional pruning.

*Note:* See the entries in THE GARDEN DICTIONARY under which the plants are listed below, for essential notes on hardiness.

†Privet (*Ligustrum*). The best all-round hedge plants in the U.S., especially *L. ovalifolium*, the California privet, which holds its leaves most of the winter. Other good privets are *Ligustrum obtusifolium* (the ibota privet) and *L. obtusifolium regelianum* (Regel's privet). The common privet (*L. vulgare*) is not so good as California privet as it drops its leaves long before *L. ovalifolium*. In the South *L. japonicum* makes beautiful evergreen hedges.

†Box (*Buxus*). The finest evergreen hedge plant, but slow-growing and expensive. Not hardy everywhere. *See* Box.

†Taxus. The yews make magnificent hedge plants, but are generally slow-growing. *See* TAXUS.

†*Thuja occidentalis* (arborvitae). One of the best of the coniferous evergreens for hedges, but useless near big cities.

Some rather common but not particularly desirable kinds of hedge shearing. Compare with the next illustration.

Old hedges are often 20 ft. high and 10 ft. thick. For low arborvitae hedges use some of the dwarf varieties. *See* THUJA.

Hemlock (*Tsuga canadensis*). A splendid evergreen, but useful only in regions where it thrives. *See* HEMLOCK. It will not thrive in or near big cities nor in regions of extreme summer heat. Will not stand severe clipping, especially when young, but it may be pruned and shaped fairly well. As a tall, hedge-like screen the hemlock is fine.

Spruce (*Picea glauca*). The white spruce is a beautiful evergreen, very similar to the hemlock in its growth requirements, and will do well in the North or along the seashore, but not in the South. Needs careful pruning to shape it. Will not stand steady shearing in youth.

*Berberis thunbergi.* The Japanese barberry makes a fine informal, round-headed hedge plant. Its fine foliage and red berries are especially attractive. Will not stand close shearing, but it needs little because of its close, twiggy growth. There is also a dwarf variety. *See* B. THUNBERGI. Another fine barberry is *B. julianae*.

*Berberis vulgaris.* The common barberry is less desirable than the Japanese one, but grows taller. A purple-leaved variety is especially fine. Will stand, and needs for hedge purposes, a good deal of pruning, but not close shearing.

*Chamaecyparis.* Several of the lower-growing species and varieties make fine informal, evergreen hedges, but they will not stand shearing. *See* CHAMAECYPARIS.

†*Acanthopanax pentaphyllum.* Will stand clipping when old, and severe pruning in youth.

*Poncirus trifoliata.* Hardy orange. A fine, prickly, defensive hedge plant, not hardy northward. *See* PONCIRUS.

†*Elaeagnus angustifolia.* Russian olive. Good for open, wind-swept places.

*Rosa rugosa.* A good hedge plant which will stand severe pruning but not shearing. Very attractive in flower and for its showy fruits.

†Hornbeam (*Carpinus betulus*). The European hornbeam is a tall-growing, stout hedge plant. It needs very careful clipping to make it well furnished with foliage at the base. Perhaps a better substitute is *Ulmus pumila*.

Besides these there are many other plants suitable for hedges. Some of them are lilac, mock-orange, beech, *Chaenomeles japonica* (flowering quince), *Deutzia gracilis* and *D. lemoinei*, *Maclura*, *Osmanthus ilicifolius*, *Crataegus*, several spireas (*see* SPIRAEA), *Viburnum cassinoides*, *V. tinus*, and *V. dentatum*, *Kerria japonica*, and *Caragana arborescens*. The latter is the best of all hedge plants for regions of long, severe winters, such as the northern prairie states and far into Canada, where privet is often killed outright or severely winter-killed. Most of them, except the flowering quince, need careful pruning in youth to make them satisfactory hedge subjects. In the South the crape myrtle is often used for hedges.

## Garden Uses

A hedge is a line of trees or shrubs formalized in semblance to a wall or fence, and usually serves to define the limits of a given area.

It is desirable that the height and form of a hedge be in character with the function, size and shape of the area it bounds, as well as with the nature of the general surroundings. The use to which an area is to be put plays an important part not only in dictating the general type of hedge to enclose it but also the texture and density of its foliage mass. Treated architecturally, for formal effects, a hedge may be regulated to definite lines and clean-cut surfaces. Used more informally, it may be allowed to grow freely as a thicket, within its natural limitations.

The beauty and dignity of a hedge rightly used

---

* Special articles on the subjects indicated by an asterisk (*) will be found at the words so marked.

As an element in landscape design, a hedge may be employed to act as a windbreak, barrier, screen, edging, background, or an enclosure for privacy. As a boundary barrier, it may serve as a protection and screen from neighboring grounds, or be used to provide a feeling of seclusion. A hedge may create a sense of unity by separating a given space from any unrelated features which otherwise would visually intrude and tend to distract the eye and mind from the essential purpose of the area as designed.

As a contributing element in relating structural features to the landscape, by seemingly tying a building to the ground, a hedge is often used as a dominant horizontal line. It accentuates the base lines and defines and recalls certain architectural space relationships in softer, more dynamic texture and in a natural vital color. To frame a formal vista, or to act as a definite yet unobtrusive foreground for a broader view, a controlled and regulated line of shrubs or trees is most useful.

A low, compact hedge may bound a flower bed, a lawn area, or a walk or terrace, clearly defining in the third dimension the pattern of the area enclosed. As a quiet background for perennials, a hedge presents an ideal surface of uniform texture and color to contrast with the delicate forms and shadings of the flowers.

The play of light and shade gives the hedge a distinct appeal by outlining ever-changing patterns, whose subtle variations in hue and color are a constant source of interest and delight. — A. F.

**HEDGE SHEARS.** *See* Section 4, TOOLS AND IMPLEMENTS.

**HEDRAIANTHUS** = *Edraianthus*.

**HEDYCHIUM** (he-dich'i-um). Tropical Asiatic (one Madagascan) herbs of the family Zingiberaceae, often called ginger-lily or butterfly lily, grown in the greenhouse, or from zone* 6 southward outdoors, for their ornamental foliage and very fragrant flowers. They have large, 2-ranked leaves, without marginal teeth, and sheathing at the base. Flowers showy, irregular,* borne from between bracts* in a terminal cluster (spike or panicle*). For details of flower structure *see* ZINGIBERACEAE. Fruit a capsule.* (*Hedychium* is from the Greek for sweet snow, in reference to the often white, fragrant flowers.)

The ginger-lilies, which differ only in technical characters from the true ginger, have stout underground rootstocks by which they are propagated and which should be divided every two or three years. They need a warm greenhouse, potting mixture* 3, and plenty of water. Some, like *H. coronarium*, can even be submerged up to the crown. They also require liberal applications of liquid manure, because they are gross feeders. After blooming, the plants should be gradually dried off, and when the foliage is browned, the pots had better be rested for two months or so, after which the growth should be renewed by liberal watering. They will stand no frost, although their rootstocks may be left in the ground all year below zone* 7, even if the tops are ruined by frost. They are popular bedding plants throughout the tropics, where 15 or more species may be grown. In the U.S. the four below are the most likely to be seen. Most of them bloom in the late fall.

**chrysoleucum.** A stout herb 3–5 ft. high. Leaves 12–20 in. long, about 4 in. wide. Flowers red, but the base of the lip* orange-yellow. India.

**coronarium.** Garland-flower, and by far the most widely grown species. Stems 4–7 ft. high, the leaves 15–30 in. long, about 5 in. wide. Flowers 2–3 in. long, white, very fragrant, the bracts of the cluster whitish-green, firm. The lower part of the lip* is sometimes yellow-tinged. Tropical As.

**flavum.** From 3–5 ft. high. Leaves 8–14 in. long, tapering to a slender point. Flowers nearly 2½ in. wide, yellow, with an orange spot on the base of the lip.* India.

**gardnerianum.** Not over 6 ft. high, the leaves 9–18 in. long, but nearly 6 in. wide. Flowers nearly 2 in. long, the corolla yellow, but the long-protruding stamen red. The flowering spike is nearly 18 in. long. India. A very showy plant.

**HEDYSARUM** (hed-i-sar'rum). A large genus of chiefly Old World herbs of the pea family, perhaps a dozen of its 60 species found in N.A. They are perennial herbs or undershrubs with compound* leaves, the leaflets arranged feather-fashion and with an odd one at the tip. Flowers small, pea-like, mostly in showy racemes. Fruit a jointed legume (a loment*), usually flattened. (*Hedysarum* is from the Greek for sweet smell, in allusion to the fragrance of some species.)

Both the species below are of easy culture in open, preferably sandy soils. One of them is an old garden plant, but not so much grown as formerly. Readily propagated by seeds or by division.

**coronarium.** French honeysuckle; called, also, sulla clover. A bushy, perennial herb 2–4 ft. high, and long cult. in old gardens. Leaflets in 3–7 pairs, elliptic or roundish, hairy. Flowers deep red, fragrant, densely crowded in spikes or racemes* from the leaf-axils.* Eu. Summer. A white-flowered variety is also offered.

**pabulare.** A prairie herb not over 30 in. high. Leaflets in 4–7 pairs, oblongish, about ¾ in. long. Flowers purplish, nearly ½ in. long. Mont. to N. Mex. Summer.

**HEDYSCEPE** (hed-i-see'pe). A single species of unarmed feather palm from Lord Howe's Island in the Pacific. The only species is **H. canterburyana**, often called umbrella palm, and sometimes offered as *Kentia canterburyana*. It is somewhat grown for ornament in Fla. and southern Calif., more often in the greenhouse for its fine foliage. Mature plants may be 30 ft. high (much lower in the greenhouse), the gracefully arching or drooping leaves in a dense crown at the top of the trunk. Leaf-segments numerous, narrow, but broader at the base than at the tapering and drooping tip. Flowers in a dense, branched cluster from among the leaf-crown, the male and female in different parts of the cluster. Fruit more or less egg-shaped, about 2 in. long. For its greenhouse culture *see* PALM. (*Hedyscepe* is from the Greek for sweet covering.)

**HEEL.** The basal end of a cutting, tuber, or other propagative material, especially if there is some of the old stock taken with it.

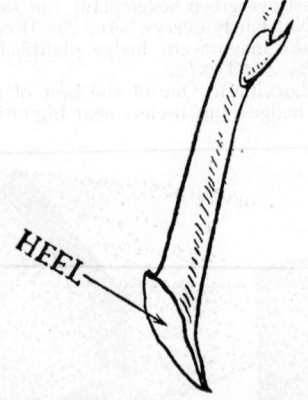

Heel of a cutting. Most practical gardeners do not attach much importance to the heel in propagating. *See* CUTTINGS.

**HEEL-IN.** To cover temporarily with soil the roots of plants awaiting permanent planting. It should always be done upon the arrival of nursery stock. An old term for it is *to sheugh*. *See* the illustration at PLANTING.

**HE-HUCKLEBERRY** = *Xolisma ligustrina*.

**HEIGHT OF TREES.** *See* GARDEN TABLES III.

**HELENIUM** (hell-lee'ni-um). The sneezeweeds are rather tall, coarse, New World herbs of the family Compositae, useful chiefly towards the rear of the informal herbaceous border, or in open places in the wild garden. All the cult. species are stout perennials with alternate* leaves and profuse heads of yellow or brownish flowers (red in a hort. variety), the heads containing both ray* and disk* flowers. Clusters usually flat-topped, the flowers mostly blooming in late summer and fall. They have a superficial resemblance to sunflowers. (Named for Helen of Troy; and *Helenium* is also used as a specific name at Inula.)

Almost any garden soil will suit sneezeweeds, which, in the case of *H. autumnale*, may need curtailing, as it tends to become weedy. Easiest propagated by spring division of the clumps.

**autumnale.** Yellow star; false sunflower. Stout, branching perennial 4–6 ft. high. Leaves lance-oval, 3–5 in. long, toothed, the base decurrent on the stem. Flower heads nearly 2 in. wide, the rays* lemon-yellow, the disk* flowers darker yellow. Eastern N.A. The *var.* **grandiflorum** has larger flowers; *var.* **pumilum** (sometimes offered as *H. pumilum*) is only about 2 ft. high; *var.* **rubrum** has deep red flowers and is a useful plant for the autumn garden (which see). There are also many desirable named hort. forms.

---

* Special articles on the subjects indicated by an asterisk (*) will be found at the words so marked.

**bigelovi.** A Californian perennial, not over 4 ft. high. Leaves lance-shaped, 6-9 in. long, narrowed into a decurrent* base. Flower heads about 2 in. wide, the rays* yellow, the disk* flowers brownish.

**hoopesi.** A perennial, not over 3 ft. high. Leaves lance-shaped or narrower, 4-6 in. long, without marginal teeth and not decurrent* at the base. Flower heads nearly 3 in. wide, solitary or a few in a cluster, yellow. Rocky Mountains westward to Ore. and Calif.

**HELIANTHELLA** (he-li-an-thell′la). Western American, sunflower-like, perennial herbs of the family Compositae, only one of the 13 known species at all likely to be cult. This is **H. quinquenervis**, a nearly smooth, essentially unbranched herb 2-4 ft. high, its leaves mostly opposite, 4-8 in. long, the upper ones stalkless. Flower heads showy, 3-5 in. wide, solitary or in few-flowered clusters, pale yellow. Rocky Mountains. Summer. The plant is of easy culture in most garden soils, and can be increased by division. (*Helianthella* is Latin for a small sunflower.)

**HELIANTHEMUM** (he-li-an′thee-mum). Usually prostrate or sprawling woody plants or herbs of the family Cistaceae, comprising perhaps 120 widely distributed species, of which only a few are cult. in the garden for their rose-like flowers. They are chiefly suited to the rock garden in the East, but are very popular in Calif., a climate that suits them well. They are usually called frostweed or sun-rose, and have evergreen or half-evergreen, usually opposite* (sometimes alternate*) leaves without marginal teeth. Flowers very fleeting, in few-flowered clusters or solitary, prevailingly yellow, and of two kinds. Some flower earlier than the others and are larger and with showy petals, while the later flowers are smaller and may have no petals. Large-flowered petals usually 5. Stamens* numerous. Fruit a 3-valved capsule.* (*Helianthemum* is from the Greek for sun and flower, in allusion to their day-blooming.)

For culture see ROCK GARDEN.

**chamaecistus** = *Helianthemum nummularium*.

**halimifolium.** Not over 2 ft. high. Leaves oblongish or narrower, conspicuously white-felty when young. Flowers yellow, about 1½ in. wide, the petals dark-spotted. Southern Eu. and northern Af. Summer.

**nummularium.** The commonest sun-rose in cult. and coming in many hort. varieties. The typical form is usually less than 12 in. high. Leaves ovalish or narrower, 1-2 in. long, gray-hairy on the under side. Flowers about 1 in. wide, yellow. Mediterranean region. Summer. Often offered as *H. chamaecistus* and *H. vulgare*. For the many hort. varieties of this popular plant and their culture see ROCK GARDEN.

**vulgare** = *Helianthemum nummularium*.

**HELIANTHOIDES** (he-li-an-thoy′deez, but see OÏDES). Sunflower-like.

**HELIANTHUS.** See SUNFLOWER.

**HELICHRYSUM** (hell-i-kry′zum). One of the better-known groups of everlastings, and comprising a genus of over 300 species belonging to the family Compositae, all from the Old World. They are herbs or shrubs with chiefly alternate* leaves without marginal teeth. Flower heads wholly of disk* flowers, the parts chaffy, mostly yellow (red, orange, or white in hort. varieties of the strawflower), and holding their color long after drying. The bracts* of the involucre* beneath the heads are also colored, almost petal-like. (*Helichrysum* is from the Greek for sun and gold, in allusion to the gay flower heads.)

The first species is the well-known strawflower from Australia and one of the most satisfactory plants for winter bouquets as its chaffy flower heads will hold their color for months. See DRIED FLOWERS. It is a tender annual and should be grown as such. See ANNUALS.

**bracteatum.** Strawflower. A tender annual from Australia, 24-36 in. high, usually branched. Leaves oblongish or narrower, 2-5 in. long, roughish. Flower heads 1-2 in. wide, the bracts of the involucre* petal-like, red, yellow, orange, or white (in some of its varieties), the true disk* flowers yellow. Widely grown for its bloom, which besides its use for dry bouquets is good for summer cutting.

**petiolatum.** A South African, shrubby, perennial herb, somewhat woody at the base, the stems woolly, its slender shoots vine-like. Leaves ovalish, woolly. Flower heads (often lacking in cult. specimens) in branching clusters (corymbs*), the disk* flowers yellow, the bracts of the involucre* cream-white. Must be grown in the cool greenhouse in potting mixture* 3, or may be plunged outdoors in the summer. Chiefly an interesting foliage plant. Sometimes known as *Gnaphalium lanatum*.

**HELICONIA** (hell-i-kō′ni-a). Large, tropical American, banana-like herbs of the family Musaceae, comprising over 40 species, the only cult. species being **H. bihai**, the wild plantain or balisier. It is a large herb, 10-15 ft. high, its leaves banana-like, transversely ribbed. The leafstalks are very long, all arising from the ground, the plant thus differing from the banana and without a true stem. Flowers borne on long stalks, showy, but still more striking are the scarlet, boat-shaped bracts often 5-10 in. long, from between which the flowers are borne. Corolla irregular,* its tube short. Fruit a bluish capsule* which ultimately separates into berry-like segments. There is a variety (or perhaps a separate species) with yellow striped or splashed leaves. The culture of the wild plantain, outdoors, is the same as for banana (which see). Also grown in the tropical greenhouse, where it needs plenty of moisture, a humid atmosphere, and rich soil. (Named for Mt. Helicon, seat of the Muses, and purely fanciful as applied to these plants.)

**HELIOCEREUS** (he-li-o-seer′ee-us). A small genus of chiefly Mexican and mostly climbing or sprawling cacti, only of secondary hort. interest. They are sometimes erect as cult. in the greenhouse, and have strongly angled or ribbed branches, and mostly needle-like spines that are all alike. Flowers day-blooming, showy, funnel-shaped, prevailingly scarlet. The plants differ only in technical characters from *Cereus*. (*Heliocereus* is from the Greek for sun and *Cereus*, in allusion to their desert habitat.)

For culture see CACTI. The plants are of less interest as ornamentals, especially *H. speciosus*, than as material for making interesting cactus crosses. Some breeders have used this species as one of the parents in a cross with *Selenicereus pteranthus*, which produces a bigeneric* hybrid.

**elegantissimus.** Branches or stems (as cult.) usually less than 1 ft. high, sometimes sprawling, nearly 2 in. thick and 3-4-angled. Flowers nearly 6 in. long, scarlet, the lobes of the stigma* white. Mex.

**speciosus.** Santa Marta. More or less branching, the stems seldom erect, 3-5-angled or with 3-5 ribs. Flowers 6-7 in. long, scarlet, the lobes of the stigma* red. Mex. and Central America.

**HELIOPHILA** (he-lee-o-fy′la). South African, annual or partly woody, perennial herbs of the mustard family, comprising over 80 species, of which three are occasionally grown in the flower garden, some of them of recent introduction. All the cult. species are tender annuals with leafy stems and a terminal, usually leafless cluster (raceme*) of white or blue flowers, or blue flowers with a yellow or white eye. Petals 4. Fruit a 2-celled pod (silique*), the seeds in a single row. (*Heliophila* is from the Greek for sun-loving.)

For culture see Tender Annuals at ANNUALS. The plants are sometimes called Cape stock.

**leptophylla.** A loosely branched herb, 10-30 in. high, the leaves narrow, about 3 in. long and sparse. Flowers blue, with a white eye. A useful border plant or may be grown in pots in the cool greenhouse for winter bloom. Sow seeds for the latter purpose in Oct.-Nov.

**linearifolia.** Not over 12 in. high, the leaves thickish and bluish-green. Flowers a brilliant blue.

**pilosa.** A variable, hairy-stemmed herb 6-20 in. high, the lower leaves opposite, the upper alternate,* hairy. Flowers sky-blue, but with a yellow eye.

**HELIOPSIS** (he-li-op′sis). Perennial, sunflower-like, North American herbs of the family Compositae, useful for the informal border or wild garden, but otherwise rather coarse, tall, yellow-flowered, summer-blooming plants. They have opposite,* rather coarsely toothed, 3-veined leaves, often very rough on one or both surfaces. Flower heads long-stalked, showy, the long rays* generally yellow, the disk* flowers darker. (*Heliopsis* is from the Greek for like the sun, in allusion to the yellow flower heads.)

There is no difficulty in growing either of the species, both of which are wild and almost weedy throughout most of the eastern U.S. Propagated by division. The plants are called oxeye by some, but the name is better applied to some daisies.

**helianthoides.** False sunflower. Three to five ft. high and with an essentially smooth stem. Leaves oblong or ovalish, 3-5 in. long, rough above, smooth beneath. Flower heads 1½-2½ in. wide, yellow, rays* about 1 in. long. The *var. pitcheriana* has deeper yellow flowers.

**scabra.** Orange sunflower. Similar to the last, but the leaves very rough on both sides and the flower heads fewer and orange-yellow. There are several hort. varieties, some with the flower heads double, and others with paler yellow flowers. One of the best is *var. zinniaeflora*, which is double-flowered.

---

* Special articles on the subjects indicated by an asterisk (*) will be found at the words so marked.

**HELIOTROPE.** See HELIOTROPIUM. For the garden heliotrope see VALERIANA OFFICINALIS, which is perhaps better known as the common valerian. For winter heliotrope see PETASITES FRAGRANS.

**HELIOTROPE FAMILY** = Boraginaceae.

**HELIOTROPIC.** Turning towards the sun, as do many leaves and flowers.

**HELIOTROPIUM** (he-li-o-trō′pi-um). A genus of over 200 species of mainly tropical or sub-tropical herbs (some woody) of the family Boraginaceae, one of them a widely cult. garden plant grown for its fragrant flowers. Leaves mostly alternate,* usually hairy. Flowers rather small, borne in forking, usually 1-sided clusters (sometimes cymes*). Calyx* tubular, as long as the corolla in some species. Corolla tubular, regular, the stamens not protruding from it. Fruit a collection of 4 small nutlets surrounded by the persistent calyx. (*Heliotropium* is from *heliotropic*, which see.)

The cult. heliotropes may be treated as greenhouse plants or as tender annuals (see ANNUALS). For fragrance it is better to grow them in the greenhouse, but still as annuals. They need plenty of heat and a rich soil. If grown as tender annuals outdoors, the stems may be pegged down, especially young shoots, which will root. They may also be propagated by cuttings.

**arborescens.** Common heliotrope. A perennial herb 2-4 ft. high, usually grown as a tender annual. Leaves ovalish or oblong. Flowers small, purple or violet (white in a hort. variety), scarcely ¼ in. long, strongly vanilla-scented. Peru. Sometimes offered as *H. peruvianum*, and is called by some cherry pie (but see also VALERIANA OFFICINALIS).

**corymbosum.** Not very different from *H. arborescens*, but with narrower leaves, and the flowers narcissus-scented. Peru (?). It may be only a form of *H. arborescens*.

**peruvianum** = *Heliotropium arborescens*.

**HELIPTERUM** (hell-lip′ter-rum). An important group of garden everlastings from South Africa and Aust., belonging to the family Compositae, and widely grown as tender annuals for dried bouquets (see EVERLASTINGS; also DRIED FLOWERS). They have alternate,* often white-felty leaves without marginal teeth. Flower heads wholly of disk* flowers, generally yellow, chaffy, and holding their color for long periods. Below the flower head are bracts of the involucre* that are green, or petal-like and white, yellow, or rose-pink. (*Helipterum* is from the Greek for sun and wing, in reference to a technical pappus character.) The plants are sometimes offered under the names of *Acroclinium* and *Rhodanthe*.

These are fine flower garden everlastings or immortelles, and are best grown as tender annuals (see ANNUALS), although the seed may be sown in place if planted after settled warm weather has come.

**anthemoides.** A green-leaved, perennial herb scarcely 12 in. high, with very narrow leaves. Flower heads nearly 1 in. wide, mostly solitary, the bracts of the involucre* white, but brownish-tinged. Aust.

**humboldtianum.** A white-felty herb 8-18 in. high, the leaves very narrow. Flower heads small, yellow, in branched clusters, the bracts of the involucre* yellowish-green. Aust. Sometimes offered as *H. sanfordi*.

**manglesi.** Swan River everlasting. A green-leaved herb 8-15 in. high, the leaves ovalish. Flower heads mostly solitary, 1½ in. wide, the bracts of the involucre* white or pink (spotted red in *var.* maculatum). Aust. The most popular of the cult. species, sometimes known as *Rhodanthe*.

**roseum.** A green-leaved herb 12-20 in. high, the leaves lance-shaped or narrower. Flower heads usually solitary, nearly 2 in. wide, the bracts of the involucre white or rose-colored. Aust. Often offered under the name *Acroclinium roseum*.

**sanfordi** = *Helipterum humboldtianum*.

*HELIX* (he′licks). Latin for ivy.

**HELLEBORE.** For the plant see HELLEBORUS. For the poison see Stomach Poisons at INSECTICIDES. For the plant yielding the poison, which is properly known as false hellebore, see VERATRUM.

**HELLEBORUS** (hell-e-bore′rus). A small genus of Eurasian, perennial herbs of the buttercup family, one of them the ever-popular Christmas rose, so called from its very late bloom. They are nearly stemless plants with thick but fibrous roots and chiefly basal, long-stalked, compound* or divided leaves, the leaflets or segments arranged finger-fashion. Flowers solitary or few, showy, and with 5 petal-like sepals.* Petals very small and mostly hidden by the numerous stamens. Fruit a collection of papery or leathery follicles.* (*Helleborus* is the classical name of the Christmas rose.) These are the true hellebores, yielding drugs, and the root of the first species is also a violent poison. See POISONOUS PLANTS.

The Christmas rose will grow in most garden soils, but it prefers moist ones and partial shade. It may be propagated by division of the roots in Aug.–Sept. Division must be done carefully, for the roots are brittle. The plant may also be forced in the greenhouse. See FORCING.

**niger.** Christmas rose; also called winter rose. Leaves evergreen, its 7 or more leaflets or segments oblong. There are also a few small leaves or bracts on the stem. Flower nearly 2½ in. wide, white or pinkish-green. Eu. Depending on locality the plant will bloom in late fall (see AUTUMN GARDEN), at Christmas, or in the early spring, sometimes under the snow. It is occasionally called the Lenten rose. For a related winter-blooming plant see ERANTHIS.

**orientalis.** Related to the last, but differing in having a cluster of 2-6 flowers on a branched, leafless stem. It has basal leaves similar to *H. niger*. Asia Minor. Not much grown here, but very popular in Eu., especially in Germany, where there are numerous fine hort. varieties.

**HELONIAS** (hell-lō′ni-as). A single, perennial, bog herb of the lily family, **H. bullata**, the swamp pink, found wild in bogs from N.J. to N. Car. It has basal leaves nearly 15 in. long and 2 in. wide, without marginal teeth. Flowers white or pinkish, scarcely ¼ in. long, borne in a dense cluster (raceme*) about 3 in. long, which terminates a 2-ft. hollow stalk. Fruit a 3-valved capsule.* Its outdoor culture is possible only in the bog garden (which see), where it needs a very acid soil (pH 4-5; see ACID AND ALKALI SOILS). Propagated by division. (*Helonias* is probably from the Greek for a swamp [bog], in allusion to its habitat.)

**HELXINE** (hell-zy′nee). A single, Sardinian and Corsican, prostrate, moss-like plant of the family Urticaceae, mostly grown in the cool greenhouse for its minute foliage. The only species, **H. solieroli**, the baby-tears or Corsican nettle, is an extremely delicate plant with very numerous, somewhat inequilateral, moss-like leaves of very unequal size, but none over ¼ in. long, and generally roundish. Flowers extremely minute, greenish, solitary and stalkless in the leaf-axils* (for details see URTICACEAE). In warm regions it can also be used to cover rock walls, but it needs plenty of moisture. (*Helxine* is Greek for the pellitory, a related plant.)

**HEMEROCALLIS.** See DAYLILY.

**HEMIGRAPHIS** (hem-i-graff′is). A genus of 30 species of chiefly tropical, Asian, perennial herbs of the family Acanthaceae, one of them, **H. colorata**, of secondary hort. importance. It is a prostrate or trailing plant with opposite,* simple* leaves, 2-3 in. long and purplish. Flowers tubular, more or less irregular,* white, about ¾ in. long, borne between large bracts in a dense terminal head. The plant is little grown outside of Fla., where it is sometimes used as a basket plant or as a ground cover. It will not stand frost. Java. (*Hemigraphis* is Greek for half-written, and of no application here.)

**HEMIONITIS** (hem-i-o-ni′tis). A small genus of tropical ferns of the family Polypodiaceae, the only cult. species the ivy fern or strawberry fern, **H. palmata**, of tropical America. It is sometimes grown in the warm greenhouse for its foliage, and has 5-parted, stiff fronds about 6 in. long, the divisions triangular and hairy. The fertile or spore-bearing fronds are longer-stalked, the spore cases being borne along the veins. For culture see Greenhouse Ferns at FERNS AND FERN GARDENING. (*Hemionitis* is Greek for mule, the plants having been thought to be sterile.)

*HEMISPHAERICA, -us, -um* (hem-i-spheer′i-ka). Shaped like half a sphere.

**HEMLOCK.** In the U.S. beautiful evergreen trees, as noted below, but generally in Eu. hemlock means the poison hemlock which killed Socrates. For this plant see CONIUM. For the water hemlock see CICUTA. For the ground hemlock see TAXUS CANADENSIS.

---

* Special articles on the subjects indicated by an asterisk (*) will be found at the words so marked.

# HEMLOCK

The evergreen trees called hemlock in America all belong to the genus **Tsuga** (soo′ga) of the pine family, which comprises only 10 species, chiefly from N.A. and eastern As., at least six of which are valuable trees in any garden landscape. Some are magnificent trees with more or less horizontal or pendulous branches and deeply furrowed bark. Leaves 2-ranked, very numerous, their arrangement resulting in the foliage being in flattish, fan-like sprays. The leaves (which drop off quickly when dry) are flattish, minutely grooved on the upper surface, and with 2 white lines on the lower side. Cones usually small, the scales somewhat woody, but not stiff. Seeds 2 under each scale. (*Tsuga* is the Japanese name for one of the Asiatic hemlocks.)

Habit, foliage and cones of the common hemlock (*Tsuga canadensis*)

While the common hemlock of eastern N.A. is a very hardy tree, like most of the others below it dislikes open, wind-swept places. They will thrive in many different soil types, but generally they are trees of moist, rich woods. In the great bulk of the central, wheat-growing section of N.A. the hemlocks will grow with difficulty or not at all, for they cannot stand great summer heat nor a deficiency of summer rainfall. East of the Alleghenies and along the northern coastal region of the Pacific states they do well, but there is little use trying them in or near big cities, as few evergreens are so sensitive to dust and smoke. With these restrictions in mind, they are magnificent lawn or estate trees, and *T. canadensis* can be made into a fine evergreen hedge. The acid drip after a rain, and the shade beneath hemlocks, make the cult. of most plants impossible beneath them.

**T. canadensis.** The common hemlock of the northeastern states, and often called hemlock spruce (it is not a spruce). It may reach 90 ft., but is usually shorter as cult., the branches gracefully drooping in age. Leaves lustrous dark green above, bluish beneath, about ⅝ in. long, sometimes slightly notched at the tip, never over 1/16 in. wide, almost microscopically saw-toothed on the margins. Cones short-stalked, slightly egg-shaped, about ¾ in. long. Eastern N.A. Hardy from zone* 2 southward, but often failing in cult. because of unfavorable moisture conditions. Useful for hedges (which see). The *var*. **compacta** is a dwarf, cone-shaped tree; *var*. **gracilis** is a slow-growing form with shorter leaves and the smaller branches drooping at the tip; *var*. **pendula** is a compact, bushy form, usually broader than high, with pendulous branches.

**T. caroliniana.** Carolina hemlock; sometimes called spruce pine, although it is no spruce or pine. Resembling the last, but generally lower, the leaves very similar, but without the minute marginal teeth. Cones oblongish, 1–1¾ in. long. Mountains of Va. to Ga. Hardy from zone* 3 southward, and often doing better in cult. than *T. canadensis*.

**T. diversifolia.** Japanese hemlock. A pyramidal-headed tree rarely over 80 ft. high, less in cult. specimens. Leaves less than ½ in. long, about 1/16 in. wide, notched at the tip, dark, glossy, and green above. Cones practically stalkless, more or less egg-shaped, about 1 in. long. Jap. Hardy from zone* 3 southward and a fine evergreen.

**T. heterophylla.** Western hemlock; also called hemlock spruce. A Pacific Coast evergreen tree of noble stature, but not well suited to the East. Trunk often 120 ft. high. Leaves dark green and glossy above, not notched, about ¾ in. long. Cones stalkless, about 1 in. long. Hardy in the East only from zone* 4 southward, and often failing because of insufficient summer moisture.

**T. mertensiana.** Mountain hemlock. A tree up to 90 ft. or even more, the branches drooping. Leaves bluish-green, not notched, ¼–¾ in. long. Cones stalkless, oblongish, 1½–3 in. long, generally purplish. Alaska to Mont., Idaho, and Calif. Resembling *T. heterophylla* in general aspect, sometimes confused with it, and with the same climatic requirements.

**T. sieboldi.** A tree up to 80 ft., the branches spreading horizontally. Leaves notched at the tip, ¼–¾ in. long, nearly ⅙ in. wide, dark and glossy-green above. Cones stalked, more or less egg-shaped, about 1 in. long. Jap. Hardy from zone* 4 southward.

**HEMLOCK SPRUCE.** In the East, *Tsuga canadensis*; in the West, *T. heterophylla*. Neither is a true spruce. See HEMLOCK.

**HEMP.** The true hemp is *Cannabis sativa* (which see). For other plants called hemp, or where hemp is part of their names, see SANSEVIERIA, APOCYNUM, MUSA TEXTILIS (the Manila hemp), and the next few entries.

**HEMP FAMILY** = Cannabinaceae.

**HEMP PALM** = *Trachycarpus fortunei*.

**HEMP TREE** = *Vitex agnus-castus*.

**HEN-AND-CHICKENS** = *Sempervivum tectorum*. See HOUSELEEK.

**HENBANE.** See HYOSCYAMUS.

**HENDERSON, PETER.** See America at GARDEN BOOKS.

**HENEQUEN** = *Agave fourcroydes*.

**HEN MANURE.** See MANURE.

**HENNA.** See LAWSONIA INERMIS.

**HEPATICA** (he-pat′i-ka). Low, perennial herbs of the buttercup family, comprising only a few species from the north temperate zone, generally called hepatica, liverleaf, or liverwort. They should only be grown in rich woods soil (not too acid) and in shadier parts of the wild garden. Leaves basal, long-stalked, 3-lobed, evergreen through the winter, but a new crop developing after the plant blooms. Flowers solitary, without petals, the sepals petal-like, and below them a calyx-like involucre* of 3 bracts. Fruit a collection of small achenes.* (*Hepatica* is from the Greek for liver, in allusion to the shape of the leaves.)

The hepaticas are charming little wild flowers, but not suited to open places (see above). They are easily propagated by division. They bloom early in the spring. For culture see WILD GARDEN.

**acutiloba.** Resembling the next species, if indeed distinct from it, the only difference being the sharper lobes of the leaf. Eastern U.S.

**americana.** The common hepatica of eastern N.A., often called Mayflower and blue anemone, and for long named *H. triloba*. It is a perennial herb, usually under 6 in. high, the stalk of the leaves and flowers silky-hairy. Leaves 3-lobed, the lobes rounded. Flowers about ¾ in. wide, lavender-blue, white, or even rose-pink. Eastern N.A., west to Manitoba.

**nobilis.** A European representative of the last, also once called *H. triloba*. It differs from *H. americana* in having less hairy stalks and in the larger flowers. Little grown in the U.S. There are double-flowered varieties in Eu.

**triloba.** Long the name of the common hepatica of N.A., now known as *H. americana*. Also *H. triloba* was once incorrectly applied to the European hepatica, now known as *H. nobilis*.

**HEPATICAEFOLIA,** *-us*, *-um* (he-pat-i-see-fō′li-a). With leaves like the hepatica.

**HEPATICA FAMILY** = Ranunculaceae.

**HERACLEAEFOLIA,** *-us*, *-um* (her-ra-klee-ee-fō′-li-a). With leaves like the genus *Heracleum* (which see). Sometimes spelled *heracleifolia*, as at *Begonia*.

**HERACLEUM** (her-ra-klee′um). The cow parsnips comprise a genus of tall, coarse herbs of the carrot family, chiefly from the north temperate zone, and of little hort. interest except for moist places in the wild garden or for very informal border plantations. They are perennials, with immense, thrice-compound* leaves, the stalks of which

---

*Special articles on the subjects indicated by an asterisk (*) will be found at the words so marked.

are often sheathed. Flowers small, usually white, crowded in huge, compound umbels* (for details see UMBELLIFERAE). Fruits flattened and grooved. (*Heracleum* was named for Hercules.)

There is no difficulty in growing the cow parsnips. All they need is open sunshine and a moist site. The first is weedy in wet places nearly throughout N.A. Propagated by division.

**lanatum.** Cow parsnip; also called masterwort. Nearly 8 ft. high and nearly as wide. Leaves at least 18 in. wide, the leaflets broadly oval, toothed and lobed, felty beneath. Flowers white, the compound clusters (umbels*) 12–20 in. wide. N.A. Summer.

**mantegazzianum.** Nearly 9 ft. high, the leaves 3 ft. long, the leaflets deeply cut. Flower cluster nearly 4 ft. wide (a compound umbel*), the flowers very small, white. Caucasus. Summer.

**HERALD'S-TRUMPET** = *Beaumontia grandiflora*.

**HERB.** A plant without a permanent woody stem. Most herbs have fleshy stems and die down to the ground over the winter. But some herbs are evergreen, and a few, like the banana, attain the size of trees, although they still have a fleshy stem. Some, like the castor-oil plant, are herbs as grown in the North, but immense, tree-like shrubs in the tropics.

Most herbs come up year after year, and are then called perennial (which see). Others live two years, while a few complete their growth and die within a single year. See ANNUAL; BIENNIAL.

As garden plants herbs furnish us with most of our color. For the uses of herbs in the garden see ANNUALS, BIENNIALS, PERENNIALS, BORDER, HERB GARDENING, and the cross-references suggested at each entry.

*HERBACEA, -us, -um* (her-bay'see-a). Herbaceous (which see).

**HERBACEOUS.** Having a stem that is fleshy and often green. Most herbs have herbaceous stems, which in some sorts are stiff, but usually not woody as in shrubs or trees. *Herbaceous* is also used, more rarely, to designate an organ that is green and leaf-like, instead of being membranous or scarious, as an *herbaceous* bract.*

**HERBACEOUS BORDER.** See BORDER.

**HERBAL AND HERBALIST.** Old, usually pre-Linnaean* books of the greatest possible interest to the gardener, although their authors (the herbalists) made many quaint mistakes about plants and what they called "their virtues." The great value of these books, most of them 16th-century English and German works, is that they contain a complete description of what was cult. at the time. Many of them were illustrated. Although the names they used for plants are confusing today, the pictures make identification of these garden plants of long ago fairly certain. The three best collections in America of these priceless old books are at the New York Botanical Garden, the Missouri Botanical Garden, and the library of the U.S. Department of Agriculture. See also Herbals at GARDEN BOOKS.

**HERBARIUM.** A collection of dried specimens of plants, usually, in America, mounted on stiffish paper or thin cardboard, 11½ × 16½ in. While all systematic studies of the wild flora of the different countries are based on herbarium specimens, there are few such for garden plants.

An herbarium specimen should consist of as much of the plant as possible, but to be of real use as a permanent record it must have leaves and flowers, or if not, of leaves and fruit. Each specimen should be ticketed with the names of the plant and its collector, the date, locality, the color of the flower, and any other helpful notes that may aid identification. The specimens must be pressed flat and thoroughly dried between blotters before mounting. Such collections are an invaluable record of plants which may long since have died.

**HERB GARDENING.** Herbs are plants the stems of which die down to the ground after flowering, as distinguished from woody plants with persistent stems. The plants here noted are a special class of herbs, most of them used as condiments, and selected for the aromatic properties of their roots, stems, leaves, seeds, flowers, or flower buds. As in all definitions there are many exceptions, and a few of the herbs such as the artemisias, thymes, sages, perennial savories and rue have woody stems which die back only a little in the cold winter months. Herbs differ from vegetables in that the herbs are used to flavor other dishes, while vegetables are eaten for themselves. But here too are exceptions, for example, the celery, carrots and onions, which, although considered vegetables, are also used to flavor other dishes, whereas such herbs as fennel, angelica and lovage can be eaten as vegetables. The basils, savories, or chervil are sweet herbs with pleasantly tasting leaves, seeds or roots, while bitter herbs taste either bitter or sharply. Wormwood is said to be the bitterest of all. When it comes to matters of taste and smell people react very differently, and although coriander has a pleasantly tasting seed, it is eaten at the Jewish Feast of Passover as one of the bitter herbs, while rue, generally considered decidedly bitter, is eaten with bread by the Italians and Spanish.

The herbs here included can be used today for flavor or fragrance by the amateur cook or distiller and can be grown by him in his garden. A few have been added to our list because of their sentimental associations. Herbs used only for medicine are not included, because almost every plant has been used medicinally at some time and the list would be far too long. A "simple" is a medicinal herb or the medicine made from it (see MEDICINAL PLANTS).

LIST OF HERBS †

Angelica, *Angelica archangelica*, persists until it sets seed. Stems are candied for decorating pastry; seeds and stems are used for flavoring. The blanched stalks were formerly eaten as a vegetable. Oil distilled from root flavors liqueurs.

Anise, *Pinpinella anisum*, annual. Leaves in salads or as a garnish, seed for flavoring. Oil from seeds in perfumes and also liqueurs.

Balm, *Melissa officinalis*, perennial. Leafy tips flavor drinks, dried leaves make tea. Oil distilled from whole plant in perfumes. Called, also, lemon balm.

Basil, *Ocimum basilicum*, annual. Same uses as balm.

Bee balm, *Monarda didyma*, perennial. Dried leaves for tea, but leaves of *M. fistulosa* and *M. citriodora* make better teas. Oil from *M. didyma* formerly used in perfumes.

Borage, *Borago officinalis*, annual. Flower sprays and leafy tops impart flavor of cucumber to cool drinks. Leaves when cooked can be eaten as spinach.

Burnet, *Sanguisorba minor*, perennial. Young leaves for salads, and to flavor cool tankards.

Camomile, *Anthemis nobilis*, perennial. Dried yellow disk flowers make tea for medicine and as a cosmetic.

Caraway, *Carum carvi*, biennial. Roots eaten as vegetable, leaves for garnish and in salads, seeds as a condiment. Oil distilled from seeds in liqueurs, sachets and perfumes.

Carnation, *Dianthus caryophyllus*, perennial. Flowers formerly conserved, and also flavored wine and vinegar.

Chervil, *Anthriscus cerefolium*, annual. Leaves flavor salads, soups and are an ingredient of *fines herbes*. (See below.)

Chives, *Allium schoenoprasum*, perennial. Leaves are condiments.

Clary, *Salvia sclarea*, biennial. Leaves formerly flavored many varieties of drinks; also put into omelettes. Flowers make tea. Oil distilled from plant used in perfumery. Leaves used in sachets.

Coriander, *Coriandrum sativum*, annual. Seeds when crushed a condiment, also an ingredient in curry powder, mixed spices and liqueurs. Oil distilled from seeds in toilet waters.

Costmary, *Chrysanthemum balsamita*, perennial. Leaves for flavorings, and for tea.

Cowslip, *Primula veris*, perennial. Flowers make a narcotic tea, formerly made into wine. Leaves can be eaten in salads. Flowers and leaves used as a pot herb in England.

Cumin, *Cuminum cyminum*, annual. Seeds flavor cheese,

---

* Special articles on the subjects indicated by an asterisk (*) will be found at the words so marked.

bread, sauerkraut. An ingredient of curry powder. Oil distilled from seeds flavors liqueurs.

Damask Rose, *Rosa damascena*, shrub. Petals make a jam and scent potpourris. When distilled they yield rose oil for perfume and condiment.

Dill, *Anethum graveolens*, annual. Leaves, flowering tops, and seeds are condiments. Oil from seeds perfumes soaps.

Fennel, *Foeniculum vulgare*, annual. Stems of flowering plant eaten, seeds and leaves a condiment.

Fennel-flower, *Nigella sativa*, annual. Seeds a condiment. Oil from seeds in perfumery.

Florence Fennel, *Foeniculum vulgare dulce*, annual. Thickened stem bases a vegetable, also used to aromatize wine. Seeds a condiment.

Fraxinella, *Dictamnus albus*, perennial. Leaves make a tea.

German Camomile, *Matricaria chamomilla*, annual. Oil distilled from plant used in perfumes and for coating glass and porcelain.

Horehound, *Marrubium vulgare*, perennial. Juice from boiled plants made into horehound candy, given for colds. In England beer is made from the plant.

Hyssop, *Hyssopus officinalis*, perennial. Leaves and flowering tops a condiment. Leaves make a tea. Oil extracted from green portions an ingredient of eau de cologne.

Lavender, *Lavandula spica*, perennial. Calyx of flowers yields oil for perfume. Dried flower buds highly fragrant.

Lemon verbena, *Lippia citriodora*, shrub in South, pot plant in North. Leaves for flavoring drinks, fruit cups and when dried for tea.

Lovage, *Levisticum officinale*, perennial. Young stems a condiment, leafstalks and stem bases when blanched eaten as a vegetable, seeds are condiments and roots used medicinally.

Pot Marjoram. *Origanum vulgare*, perennial. Leaves for flavoring, also in sachets and with tobacco.

Sweet Marjoram. *Majorana hortensis*, annual. Leaves for seasoning, as a garnish, cooked with spinach. Oil from plant highly fragrant and present in perfumes.

Mustard, black. *Brassica nigra*, annual. Leaves mixed with salads, bruised seed flavors sauces. Oil from seeds used for making soaps and in East for lighting.

Mustard, white. *Brassica alba*, annual. Same as above.

Nasturtium, *Tropaeolum minus* and *T. majus*, annuals. Flowers as garnish, stems and young leaves can be eaten in salads; seeds, chopped, used in sauces as a condiment.

Old Woman, *Artemisia stelleriana*, perennial. Used medicinally and as a charm by the Chinese.

Parsley, *Petroselinum hortense*, biennial. Leaves for condiment and garnish; seed and root for medicine.

Peppermint, *Mentha piperita*, perennial. Leaves and flowering tops flavor drinks; leaves make tea. Oil from plant flavors toilet articles and chewing gum.

Opium Poppy. *Papaver somniferum*, annual. Seeds for flavoring; opium gum comes from the juice of the unripe pod, but is not found in the seeds.

Pot Marigold, *Calendula officinalis*, annual. Rays flavor puddings and color butter; also, a substitute for saffron.

Provence Rose, *Rosa gallica*, shrub. Same use as damask rose.

Rose Geranium, *Pelargonium graveolens*, shrub in South, pot plant in North. Leaves flavor jellies and desserts. Oil distilled from leaves is used in perfumery.

Rosemary, *Rosmarinus officinalis*, perennial. Leaves flavor certain foods, notably soup. Oil extracted from leafy portions of plant and flowers used medicinally and in perfumery.

Rue, *Ruta graveolens*, perennial. Leaves for flavoring by some people, but are very strong. Oil distilled from leafy portions of plant in toilet preparations.

Saffron Crocus. *Crocus sativus*, perennial. Dried stigmas for perfume, flavor and formerly for coloring.

Sage, *Salvia officinalis*, perennial. Leaves a condiment, and make tea for sore throats and colds. Oil distilled from whole plant perfumes soaps.

Summer Savory. *Satureia hortensis*, annual. Leafy portions of plants and flowering branches flavor foods; also make medicinal teas.

Winter Savory. *Satureia montana*, perennial. Same as above, only less delicate as a flavoring.

Sesame, *Sesamum orientale*, annual. Seeds as a condiment and food. Oil extracted from seeds used in cooking in East, and medicinally everywhere.

Southernwood, *Artemisia abrotanum*, perennial. Dried stems and leaves said to keep moths and ants away. Also used medicinally.

Spearmint, *Mentha spicata*, perennial. Leaves flavor vinegars, cold drinks and certain vegetables. Oil extracted from plant used medicinally, as a condiment and for toilet preparations.

Sweet flag, *Acorus calamus*, perennial. Leaves flavor certain desserts. Pulverized roots made into sachet powders. Bark of root yields oil used in perfumery.

Tansy, *Tanacetum vulgare*, perennial. Leaves in puddings; said to destroy fleas; have long been used medicinally, but reputed poisonous.

Tarragon. See TARRAGON, in the body of the DICTIONARY.

Thyme, *Thymus vulgaris*, perennial. Leaves and flowering tops a condiment. Oil distilled from them used medicinally and for perfume.

Violet, *Viola odorata*, perennial. Flowers sometimes candied, used as a dye and for perfume.

Wintergreen, *Gaultheria procumbens*, perennial. Berries in brandy make a drink like bitters. Leaves used formerly for tea. Oil distilled from leaves used medicinally and for perfume.

Wormwood. *Artemisia absinthium*, perennial. Dried leaves an ingredient in absinthe. Fruit in beer. Was formerly used medicinally.

† All these plants are entered elsewhere in THE GARDEN DICTIONARY, under their Latin and English common names. See these entries for additional information about them.

## EARLY HISTORY

Herbs were used long before the days of written history, and man may have learned his first herb lore by watching the animals, who take certain of them, such as fennel, as purgatives and others as emetics. Herbs were so important in the lives of early man that in their wanderings the Indo-Europeans undoubtedly carried them from Europe to India and the Eastern tribes brought others to western Europe.

Magical properties were attributed to them because of their medicinal potency, and as time went on superstition gradually obscured much of the original herb lore. The Chinese use *Artemisia vulgaris* as a charm, while in France babies of the Middle Ages were rubbed with the juice of *Artemisia abrotanum* so they never would feel cold. The Brahmins regard the basils as holy and women pray to a basil plant every day. The Greeks and Romans thought one should curse when sowing the basil to insure its germination. In Italy a maiden stands a pot of basil in her window as a signal to her lover that he is expected. As with the basil, so most herbs have many superstitions and old customs associated with them.

The first men and women gathered the fragrant thymes, rosemary and lavender from the rocky ledges on the hillsides, sweet woodruff in the woods, fennel from the seacoast and others wherever they grew wild. But as people settled down into an agricultural and stationary life, they planted herbs in their gardens. Seeds of coriander were found in Egyptian tombs of the twenty-first dynasty, and of caraway among the debris of the Lake Dwellers of Switzerland.

Mint, lavender, rue, wormwood, anise and cumin are mentioned in the Bible, and Theophrastus, the Greek, who lived in the fourth century B.C., wrote delightfully of saffron crocus and thyme growing on the Grecian hills and roadsides. He gives recipes for making perfumes and cosmetics which contain the same ingredients as are used today. Galen, another Greek who wrote about the medicinal use of plants, was the first to make cold cream. His writings

---

* Special articles on the subjects indicated by an asterisk (*) will be found at the words so marked.

Some examples of English knot gardens, now again in vogue among herb gardeners. All are from Leonard Meager's *The Complete English Gardener*, 1704.

and those of Dioscorides were transmitted by the monks, who copied books by hand, and were studied and followed until the Renaissance, as were the writings of the Roman country gentleman Pliny. *See* GARDEN BOOKS.

Although monks and educated people knew of these old formulae, the common people were unaware of them and used the herbs according to traditions handed down by word of mouth. The herb women still gathered the herbs from the woods and fields, probably to sell to people without gardens, but the thrifty housewife grew, dried and stored her own. Mothers, cooks and herb gatherers all made a tea of sage for sore throat, of balm leaves to cause sweating, of camomile flowers for indigestion, used anise water to cleanse the complexion, and the oils of lavender, rosemary and others for their stimulating and pleasant qualities. Besides their medicinal uses, these sweet-smelling herbs had for long been associated with religious and magical practices, also to flavor foods, and often to disguise the disagreeable odors of putrefaction. Fragrant oils were burned and carried through hospitals, partly to counteract unpleasant odors, but also for their supposed healing properties.

Charlemagne, about the year eight hundred, promulgated an order telling what vegetables to grow, and this gives us a picture of the gardens of his day, which, with few exceptions, contained what the European peasant grows in his combination vegetable-flower-and-herb garden today. In Charlemagne's time few flowers were grown for ornament, because the gardens were primarily practical. There would be lilies and violets, and, after the thirteenth century, the Damask and Provence roses. But there were always the flowers of hyssop, borage, opium poppies, the fennels, anise, the mints, sage and others. The cottage gardens were probably either a front or a back yard where the vegetables were grown, margined with neat lines of basil, chives or thyme.

INTRODUCTION INTO AMERICA

When the colonists came to North America they brought along the customs of their home lands. They carried seeds, roots and cuttings, of which many were herbs and simples. In the first newspapers were advertisements of herb seeds for sale, such as anise, caraway, chervil, fennel, mustard and savory.

The Indians showed the settlers where the native bee balms and wintergreen grew, and how to make teas from their leaves and medicines from other plants. The Indians used few flavorings in their food except the leaves of bee balm and of wild mint with the meats they dried for winter use. The roots of wild ginger (*Asarum canadense*) seasoned cakes made of hominy, and disguised the taste of meat and fish no longer fresh. They thought ginger was an antidote against the poison in decaying foods. The squaws gathered herbs and brought them into the New England villages until quite late. Some of these were used to flavor the Colonial beers, preserves and foods, as well as for medicine.

In time the colonists found wild onions, garlic, and strawberries and used them as they had the related plants growing at home. They also used the native artemisias for medicine, and the native angelica and rose hips.* By 1643 Adrian Van der Donck was growing in his Yonkers gardens such herbs as angelica, *Acorus calamus*, *Malva*, *Origanum*, geranium, *Althaea*, violet, iris, indigo, coriander and leeks.

Living in a wilderness, there was no other source of supply than one's own kitchen, and as it was essential for the colonial housewife to have a well-stocked larder, she grew her own herbs with her vegetables and fruits. There must have been a constant preserving and drying going on all through the growing season in the colonial kitchens. Many of the herbs were used to flavor the conserves, wines, and homemade drinks, as they had been in Europe, and the housewives often kept manuscript recipe books where the recipes which

* Special articles on the subjects indicated by an asterisk (*) will be found at the words so marked.

"Mother used to make" were handed down from one generation to the next.

Sassafras gave a special flavor to New Orleans Gumbo, rose water was in many recipes, thyme was popular with southern cooks, and the French colonists in the South flavored their food with saffron, bay leaves, thyme, cloves, garlic, cayenne pepper, mustard, tomato and parsley. The Spanish colonists in the West and Southwest were fond of the taste of marjoram and also used thyme, parsley, coriander, saffron, cumin, anise and sesame. Sesame, used for its oil in China and as a cereal throughout the Orient, was brought to the colonies by the negroes.

As the different nationalities came, each brought his favorite flavorings from home. Greeks were partial to sage, the Italians always flavor their soups and other dishes with basil. The French like chives, and the negroes, who are our best cooks, are fond of many herbs and use them well.

In time, new plants, unknown in Europe before the voyage of Columbus, took their places with the herbs of the Old World, such as the peppers from Central and South America. They were first used in the South and Southwest in the Spanish colonies. Peppers are said to be good for a sluggish stomach, for they stimulate the digestive juices. Nasturtium is a native of South America, and its seeds are often substituted for capers. Lemon verbena is another South American plant, the leaves of which have a lemon flavor. However, practically all of the herbs are native to the Old World, and the ones used here for flavoring are, with few exceptions, imported.

## Culture

There have been a few attempts to grow herbs for profit, the most extensive being that of the Shaker communities in Massachusetts and New York in the middle of the nineteenth century. Mint is grown commercially in the Middle West and in New York. There was a half-hearted attempt, in Florida, to raise fragrant-leaved geraniums commercially, which was not a success. At the present, it does not seem practical to grow them here on a large scale, but it is decidedly advantageous for the amateur, because home-grown and home-dried herbs and seeds are more fragrant than the ones which come from abroad.

The herbs are not difficult to grow. Most of them belong either to the parsley, the mint, or the composite families. On the whole, they germinate readily and can be raised without any special horticultural skill. Of course there are the usual exceptions, but they are few in number.

All but a few seem to thrive in a well-drained, sunny, friable* soil which is not too rich. The mints like a damp soil and after the frost has killed back the stems they can be cut down to the ground and the plants buried with compost which acts as a fertilizer. Tarragon likes a fairly rich soil and not too hot a sun. The bed for the herbs should be prepared as one does the soil for vegetables, except that no manure is applied. It should be trenched for eighteen inches or two feet and forked over several times to render it well aired and friable,* then smoothed down, leaving the top not too hard.

Seeds should be sown thinly. A bed measuring two by four feet is sufficient for each kind of herb for a private family, and seeds can cover the whole bed, being sown about half an inch apart. After sowing, cover the seeds by lightly strewing soil over them and press down with a board. For commercial growing the herbs can be planted in rows.

The young seedlings do not require watering, for most herbs are native of hot, dry regions. The weeds should be removed, if possible, by hand, because less damage is done that way, and as the season advances, a fine dust mulch around them will preserve the moisture in the soil. If the plants become too thick, they should be thinned, and, after cutting back the stems and leaves, it is a good plan to stir a little fertilizer around the roots so they will continue to produce more leafy stems. Too rich a soil, however, causes the plants to become leggy.* In herb culture a compact, bushy plant will produce more of the essential oil, and that is why a fairly lean soil is the best for them.

The annual members of the parsley family, such as coriander, cumin, anise, dill, and fennel all grow quickly and take from two to three months from seed time to harvest. If planted early in May out of doors, they will be bearing seeds in August or early September. All the annuals will ripen the first season, but a few, such as opium poppy and sesame, should have an earlier start than can be given them in northern gardens. It is a good plan to start them indoors, or in a hotbed or greenhouse, transplanting them into the garden after all danger of frost is past. Poppies are difficult to transplant because they have a slender taproot, but it can be done with skillful fingers. The best way is to prick out the seedlings into paper pots and plunge* the latter without disturbing the roots at all. From zone* 6 southward the poppies should be planted out of doors in February or March.

Annuals, such as the basils, summer savory and borage, can be started out of doors. There are eight sorts of basil, two of these have red leaves and one has twisted leaves. The two most attractive are the bush basil and sweet or common basil. Sweet marjoram and marigold should be started indoors in cold climates.

Caraway and clary are biennials and do not produce seeds until the second season. Angelica sometimes takes two years to flower, but dies after this. Parsley is a biennial, too, and germinates slowly, but since it is more often grown for its leaves than its seeds, it can be harvested the first season. It is not hardy in cold climates.

The perennials are all of them quite hardy except tarragon and rosemary. Tarragon may die in a very cold winter. Rosemary is generally hardy south of zone* 4, in the East. It comes so quickly from seed, however, that if started indoors in January, it will have grown into quite good-sized plants by May when it can be moved into the garden. Rosemary is one of the few herbs which do well in a pot over the winter. The thymes seem to live in pots, carried over in cold frames, better than they do in the garden, where they die back in cold winters, but they too can be easily replaced with new plants grown from seeds. The thymes and perennial savories like an exceedingly well-drained situation.

The sages die out after about four or five years and have to be replaced. Lavender reaches its optimum in the sixth or seventh year and should then be discarded. Damask roses should be replaced after five years. Most perennials are not permanent fixtures in the garden, although so many beginners think they are, but have a given life-span.

Fragrant-leaved geraniums, such as the rose, nutmeg and some forty others, are not hardy, nor is the lemon verbena. In southern climates they grow to be shrubs, but north of Washington have to be handled as pot plants.

## Herbs as Part of the Garden Picture

Herbs can be grown in a walled garden all to themselves, in small, rectangular beds. The beds of marjoram, hyssop, or rue can be outlined with chives, parsley, or basil. Or one can grow them in rows in a portion of the vegetable garden or in little beds strung together, separated by walks. Some of them are so decorative that they add to the charm of the herbaceous border. Among these are the hyssops, thymes, lavenders, winter savory, the artemisias, borage, the monardas, Florentine iris, rue, violet, and marigold. The anise and coriander are pretty in a dainty way, and angelica is a handsome plant with its lush leaves and ball-like inflorescence.

A few of the herbs, such as the mustards, are too weedy for the garden. The leaves of the young plants are peppery and tart in salads, but they are a fertile lot and growing them is courting an invasion. *Artemisia absinthium* makes a strong, shrubby growth and has to be cut to the ground once during the summer, for it spreads. Tansy is a strong grower and forms huge clumps. Camomile makes a mossy-looking ground cover and was so used in the gardens of Shakespeare's day and earlier, but it, too, will spread far and wide. There is an old saying that camomile keeps the garden healthy.

---

* Special articles on the subjects indicated by an asterisk (*) will be found at the words so marked.

The herb garden has a uniform fluffy, somewhat grayish, appearance, for so many of the herbs have a similar foliage and habit of growth. The basils, thyme, winter savory, the dwarf lavender and others are good edging plants. In the South, rosemary makes a fragrant and lovely edging for the garden. A dry wall, the chinks of which are filled with good garden soil, is a fine place in which to grow the thymes and savories. So are the spaces between steps and stone pavements.

## HARVESTING

It is important to harvest herbs when the plants are richest in essential oils. After the flowers have opened, there is less of the volatile oil present, so that the time to harvest plants to be used for their leaves and flowering branches is just as the buds are about to open or after the first one has unfolded its petals. The herbs should be cut while the dew is still on them, on the morning of what promises to be a hot summer's day. Carry your harvest indoors, where branches are washed and shaken dry, the leaves stripped from the stems, and the flowering truss cut off. Place the harvest scantily on trays of wire mesh and put in a shaded room, where the air can circulate around it. Every morning the leaves should be stirred about so all of them will be exposed to the air. In three or four days the plants should be thoroughly dry and ready to pack into air-tight containers. Of course damaged or diseased leaves or stems are thrown out. Hanging plants to dry from the rafters was an old custom, but is an excellent way to collect dust. Drying out of doors causes the leaves to shrivel and blacken.

Rose petals, violets, or lavender calyces are picked and dried in the same way. Rose petals should have their white claws* cut off. Pick early in the morning of the day they open and never if they have opened the day before. The lavender should be picked when the buds have formed, for the calyx is the most fragrant part.

Seeds are collected as soon as they are ripe and before they fall to the ground. They too are washed, dried and packed away for future use. Roots are dug either in the fall or spring, cut into small pieces and dried as one would apricots or peaches.

The leaves to be dried for teas should be kept whole, but many people crumble the other herbs into powders, which never look as pretty, for they do not show in the food. When herbs are used for flavoring in beans or rice pudding, it is attractive to see the little black specks or tiny stems. For making potpourris the herbs are dried this way too, but if it is intended to extract the oil from the plants, the fresh stems and leaves are used.

## HOW TO USE HERBS

Every perfume, sachet or potpourri has to have an element in it known as a fixative and, since Theophrastus's day and perhaps earlier, these have been ambergris, civet, musk and gum benzoin, all of them, except the last, expensive. The French perfumers have been using clary sage, which can be grown in the garden, as a fixative. Gum benzoin can be purchased at the druggist's. Salt is an adulterant of potpourris and not to be used. *See* POTPOURRIS.

HERB TEAS. In Colonial times there was an active propaganda for the use of herb teas. The people were called upon to drink home-made teas instead of those from China as a protest against the British tax. The following are only a few of the many Colonial herb teas: Sweet marjoram with a little mint; thyme and a little hyssop; sage with balm leaves, to which was added lemon juice; rosemary and lavender; clover and camomile; the leaves of a red rose and sweet myrtle; strawberry leaves and the leaves of sweetbrier; goldenrod and betony with honey; peppermint and yarrow.

Besides these, the following have been found to make pleasant teas: The leaves of costmary, balm, *Monarda fistulosa*, and fraxinella. Teas can be made from the flowers of camomile. As one becomes adept one can mix and combine different herbs into teas. All teas made of herbs are green, because the leaves are dried quickly and not allowed to ferment as are the leaves of black teas. Since these teas are green, they are not a dark color even when strong, but a pale green or yellow, so in brewing them the strength should be judged by the taste and not the appearance.

COOKING WITH HERBS. To cook with herbs no other implements than the usual cooking utensils are needed except for a mortar and pestle. When using them as a condiment, since their flavor is very penetrating, only a little of the herbs is required to give the dish the aromatic scent or taste. When infusing the herbs which have a peppery or spicy taste into a dish, very little salt and no pepper is needed. A dash of orange juice intensifies the flavor of some herbs. Dried herbs are just as potent as fresh ones if they have been properly stored, but they are not so pretty.

It has been found that butter, eggs, cheese, milk, or stock takes up the herb flavoring quickly. So first measure out any of these ingredients to be used and mix the herbs into them and if possible let them stand for a few hours before making up the dish. A few herbs such as coriander seeds and angelica seeds should be bruised in a mortar before using them. When flavoring soups, the dried herbs should cook in the soup for a while longer than the fresh ones, which should be put in just for a few minutes before serving. In flavoring cold fruit drinks or iced tea, the herbs should be boiled in the hot syrup first, which is then cooled before adding to the drink. After flavoring a soup with rosemary or thyme, it looks pretty to drop a tiny sprig of the herb in each plate.

Herbs make attractive garnishes. The basils, chervil, thyme, sage, rose geranium and lemon verbena are every bit as pretty as the ever-present parsley, but more difficult to obtain.

The French *fines herbes* consist of four different herbs combined variously according to the dish they flavor. Generally chives is one of them and parsley another, but any of the others, such as the savories, basils, chervil, sage or thyme can be added. Thyme, basil, summer savory and chives are a pleasant combination of *fines herbes* for omelettes, soups and meats. Chives with thyme, winter savory and fennel taste good in flavoring the butter sauce to go with fish. Basil, thyme, sweet marjoram and parsley are another delicious combination. Some people cannot digest chives and for them they must be omitted, but the good cook knows that members of the onion family are the best undertone for flavoring every dish except desserts. The French cooks rub the chives or garlic around the empty salad bowl before putting in the lettuce which they then dress in the bowl. The flowering tops and leaves of borage, which have a flavor of cucumber, are used for flavoring drinks, as are the leaves of spearmint, peppermint and of balm.

Tarragon has a very decided flavor, as has rosemary, and should preferably not be mixed with other herbs. Jellied eggs are flavored with tarragon by placing the leaves on the eggs before the jelly is poured over them. Vinegar is aromatized with tarragon and gives the flavor of the herb to the salad dressing. Vinegar can also be aromatized with fennel and dill. Tarragon leaves chopped and scattered over the salad give them a strong flavor. Rosemary flavors a chicken broth thickened with cream.

FINES HERBES. Stirred into cream or cottage cheese these make delicious sandwich fillings, as do mint leaves chopped finely, mixed with chives worked into butter with a little orange juice and sugar. The leaves of rose geranium, boiled, flavor custards, blanc mange and jellies, especially apple jelly. The juice of boiled mint leaves flavors jellies colored green to serve with roast lamb. Dill and fennel leaves flavor fish. In dishes where tomatoes are used, basil leaves give a delicate flavor. Thyme, sage, and marjoram have long been added to the stuffings and dressings for poultry, veal and pork. Sage is said to help digest the fat of certain meats and vegetables. Nowadays we flavor fruit salads with it, and iced tea, but as said above, the leaves should be boiled in the hot syrup and not scattered over the dish at the last moment.

---

* Special articles on the subjects indicated by an asterisk (*) will be found at the words so marked.

### Herb Recipes

#### Fruit and Herb Drink
Juices of 3 oranges and 2 lemons
½ cup of sugar syrup
1 cup of tea, very strong
1 sprig of balm, first pounded in a mortar
5 sprigs of borage
A bunch of mint
1 sprig of burnet
3 anise leaves
A pinch of salt

Pour the hot tea and syrup over the fruit juices and herbs. Cover the pitcher and allow the mixture to stand for an hour or more. Strain into another pitcher which is partly filled with ice. Add wine or White Rock and serve, first floating a few flowers of borage in the mouth of the pitcher.

#### Green Pea Soup with Mint
1 quart of fresh peas
1 onion
A few sprigs of mint
1 teaspoon of spinach juice
1 teaspoon of salt
1 teaspoon of sugar
2 tablespoons of butter
2 egg yolks
½ cup of cream

Boil the pods of the peas for two or three hours in water in which other vegetables have been cooked. Strain. To three pints of this strained water add the fresh peas, the onion, mint, salt and sugar. Cook until the peas are tender, then rub through a sieve, add butter, spinach juice, and bring to the boiling point. Season more if needed and just before serving add the egg yolk diluted with cream. Cook, stirring constantly, for five minutes but do not allow the liquid to boil. Strain and serve with croutons or fried bits of toast. This soup may also be made with one pint of dried peas which have been soaked.

#### Parsley Soup, also called Soupe à la Bonne Femme
2 cups of milk
1 cup of water
1 teaspoon of salt
2 tablespoons of butter
2 tablespoons of flour
1 medium-sized onion

Melt the butter, add flour and salt and the liquids and onion. Cook slowly for one hour. Remove the onion, add ½ cup of finely chopped, fresh parsley. Stir well and serve.

#### Eggplant Stuffed with Herbs
1 onion
A small bunch of parsley
A little thyme
1 cup of bread soaked in milk
1 egg
Salt and pepper
1 tablespoon of bread crumbs

Cook the eggplant in boiling water until it is soft, then cut off a piece from the top and remove the inside. Then add the onion which has been fried in butter, and mix all the ingredients together and put them back into the eggplant and scatter the bread crumbs on top. Put it in the oven for a half an hour until the top is brown. Then serve.

#### Cold Stuffed Eggs, for hors d'oeuvres
Hard-boiled eggs
Cold tomato ketchup
Salt and pepper
Basil and savory
Mayonnaise

Cut the eggs in half, remove the yolk and mix it with ketchup and other ingredients and put it over the top of half of the white. And over this put mayonnaise mixed with the ketchup.

#### Chopped Meat Balls
½ pound of chopped meat (beef, veal and pork)
1 teaspoon each of chopped chives, thyme, marjoram and parsley mixed
1 tablespoon of flour mixed with salt and pepper
Butter

Into the meat work the chopped herbs; form into balls; roll in seasoned flour; fry in butter until well browned.

#### Rose-Geranium Jelly
Prepare apples as for a usual jelly. Boil the juice from the pulp for twenty minutes. To each pint of juice add one pound of sugar and place in a kettle over the fire. Stir until all the sugar has melted, then add two or three rose-geranium leaves, bring to the boiling point and boil rapidly for two minutes, removing any scum which may rise to the surface. Turn into jelly glasses, removing the leaves, but place a fresh leaf in each glass. — H. M. F.

**HERB MERCURY** = *Mercurialis annua*.

**HERB OF GRACE.** See RUE.

**HERB PATIENCE** = *Rumex patientia*.

**HERB RECIPES.** See Recipes at HERB GARDENING.

**HERB ROBERT** = *Geranium robertianum*.

**HERB TEAS.** See How to Use Herbs at HERB GARDENING.

**HERCULES'-CLUB** = *Zanthoxylum clava-herculis* and *Aralia spinosa*.

**HERD'S GRASS** = *Phleum pratense*.

**HEREDITY.** Plants are described in terms of characters. Characters result from ancestrally inherited genes,* which may or may not express themselves under a given set of environmental conditions. In other words, by no means all of a plant's inheritance appears. Heredity is what a plant possesses from the beginning, at real birth, when egg and sperm unite. Environment is all that surrounds this inherited gift from conception to death. It is air, smoke, water, fertilizer, temperature, light, other living things, and myriads of different entities. Variations are simply differences, contrasts. They may be hereditary (germinal, mutations) or they may be environmental (see ENVIRONMENT). Thus we see that *environment,** *heredity* and *variation** are, in a sense, inseparable in an attempt to understand clearly their significance in breeding work.

The science of *genetics* is the study of these three phenomena and their interrelations. The most striking and fundamental fact in all genetics is that living things — both plants and animals — are made up of these independent units called genes,* and that these are transmitted through the succeeding generations in an orderly and predictable manner. It is upon this fact that all plant breeding rests. For the other factors involved see MUTATION, CROSSING, PLANT BREEDING, INBREEDING and SELECTION. — O. E. W.

**HERMAPHRODITE.** The normal condition of most garden plants and implying that both male (stamens*) and female (pistil*) organs of reproduction are within a single flower. Some plants, however, are polygamous, which means that they bear both hermaphrodite flowers and others which are only male or female, as in the ash and sumac. See also MONOECIOUS and DIOECIOUS.

**HERNIARIA** (her-nĭ-ā′rĭ-a). Herniary. A genus of prostrate or trailing herbs of the pink family, all from the Old World, two of the 15 known species of secondary garden interest. Both the hort. species are low, perennial, short-lived herbs with stalkless, small, opposite* leaves, and swollen joints, and usually much-branched. Flowers inconspicuous, greenish, without petals, and crowded in small clusters in the leaf-axils* (for details see CARYOPHYLLACEAE). Fruit a small capsule enclosed within the persistent calyx.* (*Herniaria* is from the Greek for hernia, in allusion to their supposed efficacy for rupture. The plants are sometimes called rupturewort or burstwort.)

Both species prefer a sandy soil as their original habitat

---
* Special articles on the subjects indicated by an asterisk (*) will be found at the words so marked.

is along the seacoast. They are sometimes used for carpet bedding or for covering rocks, and are of easy culture. While the flowers are too minute to be of interest, the foliage is attractive, and in warm regions persists through the winter and turns bronzy-red.

glabra. Prostrate, the stems not over 6 in. high, usually spreading over the ground. Leaves oblongish. Flowers greenish, in stalkless, leafy clusters in the leaf-axils. Eurasia.

hirsuta. Somewhat similar to *H. glabra* but the foliage hairy. Eu.

**HERNIARY.** See HERNIARIA.

**HERON'S-BILL.** See ERODIUM.

**HESPERALOE** (hes-per-ă'loe). A small genus of stemless desert plants of the lily family, found from Tex. to Mex. and suited only to similar climates or sometimes grown in the cool greenhouse. They differ from the closely related *Yucca* (which see) only in having rose-colored flowers. The only cult. species, **H. parviflora** of Tex., has basal, thread-margined leaves nearly 4 ft. long and about 1 in. wide. Flowers day-blooming (mostly night-blooming in *Yucca*), rose-pink, nodding, about 1½ in. long. The var. **engelmanni** has bell-shaped and smaller flowers. (*Hesperaloe* is from the Greek for western and *Aloe*, in allusion to their being New World representatives of the Old World aloe.)

**HESPERIDIUM.** See CITRUS.

**HESPERIS** (hes'per-is). Attractive, Old World, biennial or perennial herbs of the mustard family, comprising about 25 species, and generally called rocket or damewort. One is a widely grown flower-garden plant long known in cult. They are erect, branching plants with alternate,* usually finely toothed leaves, and showy purplish or white, fragrant flowers in long, terminal clusters (racemes*). Petals 4. Fruit a long, slender pod (silique*), contracted at intervals. (*Hesperis* is from the Greek for evening, in allusion to their marked fragrance at night.)

They should be grown as ordinary garden perennials or biennials, the seeds started a season before they are expected to bloom. *H. matronalis* is often a biennial and a supply should be kept to replace plants that die out after blooming.

matronalis. Dame's-rocket; called, also, dame's-violet and garden rocket. A branching herb 2-3 ft. high. Leaves lance-shaped or ovalish, 2-4 in. long, tapering at the tip, but nearly stalkless and broad towards the base. Flowers normally purple or lilac-purple. Pods 3-4 in. long, beaked. Eurasia. A double-flowered form is sometimes called, especially in England, the Whitsun gillyflower. White-flowered forms are also known, sometimes under the name *var. nivea*.

nivalis. A perennial herb up to 1 ft. high. Leaves oblongish, 1-2 in. long, without marginal teeth. Flowers pale, pure white, in a loose raceme.* An alpine species from the mountains of Persia, and little known in the U.S.

**HESPEROYUCCA** (hes-per-o-yuck'a). A single, Californian desert plant of the lily family, **H. whipplei**, there called the mountain queen or Quixote-plant, and formerly known as *Yucca whipplei*. It is almost stemless, but with a short, woody base from which arises a rosette of rigid, sword-like leaves 12-20 in. long and about ¾ in. wide, prickle-tipped and with fine, marginal teeth. Flowering stalk 10-12 ft. high, the cluster at the end branched. Flowers white, nearly 2 in. long, nodding. The plant needs the same conditions as for *Agave* (which see), and cannot be grown in frosty, wet regions. (*Hesperoyucca* is from the Greek for western, *i.e.* towards the sunset, and *Yucca*, in allusion to its far western range.)

**HETEROCENTRON** (het-er-o-sen'tron). Tropical American perennial herbs or under-shrubs of the family Melastomaceae, one of its 7 species a fairly common greenhouse plant, grown for its attractive flowers. Leaves opposite,* more or less lance-shaped and without marginal teeth. Flowers (in the hort. species) rose-pink or purple, in rather showy clusters (panicles*). Petals 4. Stamens 8, of unequal length. Fruit a 4-valved capsule.* (*Heterocentron* is from the Greek for unlike spurs, referring to the unequal anthers.*)

The only cult. species needs a warm, moist greenhouse and potting mixture* 3. It is an attractive pot plant with a profusion of small flowers. In frostless regions it can be grown outdoors.

elegans = *Schizocentron elegans*.
mexicanum = *Heterocentron roseum*.
roseum. Not over 2 ft. high (as cult.), the branches 4-angled. Leaves 1 in. long, conspicuously stiff-hairy on the margins. Flowers rose-pink (white in a hort. variety), about ½ in. long. Mex. Often known as *H. mexicanum*.

**HETEROMELES.** See TOYON.

**HETEROPHYLLA, -us, -um** (het-er-o-fill'a). With variously shaped leaves.

**HETEROSIS** or hybrid vigor. Crosses between different varieties or races of plants often increase the size, vitality, floriferousness and fruit yield of their immediate offspring. This phenomenon probably accounts for the vigor, general health and desirability of many cultivated plants asexually propagated, and its use is increasing in commercial pursuits, notably among tomato and sweet corn growers of canner's seed, among growers of fancy field corn seed, and to some extent in the lumber and wood-pulp trade.

In the last-mentioned fields, the use of heterosis is still experimental, but recent results with poplar (*Populus*) species crosses indicate a wide opportunity for commercial exploitation, as the natural wood-pulp stands decrease.

Many species crosses produce weak progeny, but in many cases the $F_1$ progeny exhibit remarkable hybrid vigor, as illustrated by Burbank's walnut species hybrids Paradox (California walnut × Persian) and Royal (California black × Eastern black), which grew several times more rapidly than the parents. Increased hardiness, greater longevity of life, greater ease of vegetative propagation and earlier maturity are other characters often associated with this phenomenon. Experimenters have often noticed higher percentage of germination among such crossed seed. The proverbial hardihood of the mule is a familiar example of heterosis in animals. In the application of heterosis to plant-breeding problems, a wide and little-exploited field, rich in possibilities, exists, particularly in regard to increasing yields, longevity, more rapid growth, and earlier maturity. — O. E. W.

**HETEROSPATHE** (het-er-o-spay'thee). A small genus of spineless feather palms from the islands of the Pacific and the Philippines, only **H. elata,** the sagisi palm, cult. in the U.S., mostly in the warmest parts of peninsular Fla. It has a slender, ringed trunk, 40-60 ft. high or more, usually quite erect. Leaves drooping, dark green, its many leaflets or segments drooping, ribbed, 2-3 ft. long, and tapering to a narrow tip. Flower cluster much-branched, from among the crown of leaves, the male and female flowers separate in the same cluster. Fruit pea-size, becoming white. Little-known as yet, but thriving on a variety of soils in southern Fla. (*Heterospathe* is from the Greek for unlike and spathe,* in allusion to the spathes of the flower cluster.)

**HEUCHERA** (hew'ker-a). Alumroot. Attractive, North American, perennial herbs of the family Saxifragaceae, comprising over 70 species, chiefly from the Rocky Mountain region. They have stout rootstocks and mostly basal, long-stalked, often roundish or lobed leaves. Stalk of the flower cluster arising from the rootstock, often leafy, and crowned with a narrow panicle* or raceme* of bell-shaped or saucer-shaped, green, white, red, or purple flowers. Petals small or narrow and inconspicuous, most of the color coming from the conspicuous 5-lobed calyx. Stamens* 5, attached to the petals. Fruit a 2-valved capsule.* (Named for Johann Heinrich von Heucher, German botanist.)

Coral bells (*Heuchera sanguinea*) is a very popular garden perennial suited to a variety of soils, but generally preferring some shade to full sunlight, as do most of the alumroots which are naturally woodland plants, preferring rocky cliffs. The most adaptable of all to general garden culture is *H. sanguinea*, the others being chiefly suited to the wild garden or rock garden. All may be propagated by division.

americana. Common alumroot; also called American sanicle. A woodland herb, the flowering stalk often 2 ft. high. Leaves roundish, mottled in youth, the marginal teeth rounded. Flowers greenish-white, the stamens protruding. Eastern N.A. June. Not suited to the open, and best grown in the shady part of the wild garden.

brizoides = *Heuchera lithophila*.
lithophila. A beautiful plant from the mountains of Calif., suited chiefly for the rock garden. Flowering stalk up to 28 in., the cluster a

---

* Special articles on the subjects indicated by an asterisk (*) will be found at the words so marked.

narrow panicle.* Flowers pinkish, about ⅓ in. long, very delicate. Sometimes offered as *H. brizoides.* Not certainly hardy in the East.

**micrantha.** A white-flowered plant, the stalk of the flower cluster not over 2 ft. high, sticky-hairy. Flowers small, but the cluster is beautifully light and airy. British Columbia to Calif. Not certainly hardy in the East.

**sanguinea.** Coral bells. Much the best known and easiest cult. of all the alumroots. It grows from 1–2 ft. high, the leaves all basal and shorter-stalked than in the other species. The flowering stalk is crowned at the top by a loose, often somewhat 1-sided, cluster of small, red, bell-shaped flowers that are scarcely ⅓ in. high. N. Mex., Ariz., and Mex. It is a perfectly hardy perennial, blooming most of the summer, well suited for the open (partly shaded) border. It is also commonly forced by florists and can be by the amateur. See FORCING. There are many popular varieties of this well-known favorite, among the best being: var. **gracillima**, which is more slender; var. **gracillima rosea**, slender and rose-pink; var. **alba**, white-flowered; var. **hybrida**, more robust. A good white-flowered named form is Perry's White.

**HEVEA** (he'vee-a). Amazon valley trees of the spurge family, of no hort. interest except as grown in extreme southern Fla. Even there it is neither hot nor moist enough to grow properly this leading rubber plant of the world as a commercial crop. It is **H. brasiliensis**, commonly called Pará rubber tree or seringera. It made millionaires of some Amazon River rubber dealers fifty years ago, but 90 per cent of the world's rubber is now from English and Dutch plantations in the Indo-Malayan region. The tree grows up to 60 ft. as cult. (much more in the Amazon Valley), and has a milky juice which is the source of rubber. Leaves alternate,* compound,* the 3 leaflets oblongish, 4–6 in. long (as cult.), rarely up to 1 ft. long. Flowers greenish, inconspicuous (for details see EUPHORBIACEAE). Fruit a capsule.* For another rubber plant see FICUS ELASTICA. (*Hevea* is a Latinized form of a Brazilian name for the tree.)

*HEXAGONA, -us, -um* (hecks-ag'o-na). Six-angled.

*HEXAGONOPTERA, -us, -um* (hecks-a-go-nop'ter-ra). With six wings or angles.

**HEXAGON PLANTING.** See Planting at FRUIT CULTURE.

*HEXANDRA, -us, -um* (hecks-an'dra). With six stamens.*

*HEXAPETALA, -us, -um* (hecks-a-pet'a-la). Six-petaled.

*HEXAPHYLLA, -us, -um* (hecks-a-fill'a). Six-leaved.

**HIBA ARBORVITAE** = *Thujopsis dolobrata.*

**HIBBERTIA** (hib-ber'tĭ-a; also hib-ber'shĭ-a). Rather showy, chiefly Australian, woody vines of the family Dilleniaceae, of its 100 species only **H. volubilis** of much garden interest. It is a high-climbing woody vine with alternate,* oblongish leaves 2–3 in. long, more or less clasping at the base and silky-hairy beneath. Flowers solitary, terminal, yellow, unpleasantly scented. Sepals 5. Petals 5, spreading and making rather an open flower. Stamens* numerous. Fruit a collection of 5 ripened carpels. Its culture is confined to southern Calif. (Named for George Hibbert, English patron of botany.)

*HIBERNICA, -us, -um* (hy-ber'ni-ka). From Ireland.

*HIBISCIFOLIA, -us, -um* (hy-bis-ki-fō'lĭ-a). With leaves like *Hibiscus.*

**HIBISCUS** (hy-bis'kus). An important genus of over 200 species of herbs, shrubs, and trees of the mallow family, of great hort. interest because it yields garden annuals, musky-seeded perfume plants, some foods, many showy perennials, a few shrubs, and some gorgeously colored tropical trees. Leaves alternate,* always with the veins arranged finger-fashion, sometimes lobed or parted. Flowers usually large, generally bell-shaped, of 5 petals and sepals, or sometimes the sepals united to form a 5-toothed calyx.* Stamens* united into a tubular structure which surrounds the style.* Fruit a dry, 5-valved capsule. The plants are generally called mallow or rose mallow, and, as in other genera of the Malvaceae, there is often a series of bracts* beneath the calyx.* (*Hibiscus* is Vergil's name for a mallow.)

The diversity of *Hibiscus* is so great that it is impossible to give general cultural notes that apply to all species. Those mentioned as annuals can be treated as hardy annuals and the seeds sown where wanted. For the others see the notes appended to each.

**abelmoschus.** The abelmosk or musk mallow. A tropical Asiatic annual or biennial hairy herb 2–6 ft. high. Leaves lobed, often deeply so, and the lobes toothed. Flowers nearly 4 in. wide, yellow but with a crimson eye.* Fruit oblongish, about 3 in. long, its seeds musky and used for perfume. India. Grown mostly for its seeds, and needs more summer heat than is found in most parts of the U.S., but it will flower in the North.

**esculentus.** Okra or gumbo. A garden-vegetable annual grown for its immature, mucilaginous pods. It is 2–6 ft. high, with 3–9-lobed or divided leaves that may be 1 ft. wide. Flowers solitary in the leaf-axils,* 2–3 in. wide, yellow, with a red eye.* Pods ribbed and beaked, 4–12 in. long. Old World tropics. For culture see OKRA.

**grandiflorus.** A southern representative of the next species, but with larger, pink, and red-eyed flowers. Ga., Fla., and Miss. Useful for seaside planting along the Gulf Coast and in Fla.

**moscheutos.** Rose mallow; called also swamp mallow and sea hollyhock, the latter in allusion to its normal salt-marsh habitat. The plant is also, incorrectly, called marshmallow, a name that properly belongs to *Althaea officinalis* (see HOLLYHOCK). A hairy, perennial herb, 3–7 ft. high. Leaves generally ovalish, sometimes slightly angled or lobed, 3–7 in. long, generally, in the wild form, white-felty beneath. Flowers 4–7 in. wide, useless for picking as they wilt within an hour, white or pink, but with no eye.* Fruit about 1 in. long. In brackish marshes, Mass. to Fla., rarely in fresh marshes westward to Mo. Aug.–Sept.

The rose mallow, while typically a salt-marsh plant, can be dug from the wild and transplanted directly to ordinary garden soil with complete success. Few grow it today because from it have been derived much finer plants, mostly the result of selection and crossing with other (non-hort.) species. These improved mallows, with hollyhock-like flowers often 6 in. wide, are of easy culture in most rich garden soils, but need plenty of room. They come in a variety of colors, ranging from pure white to deep crimson. Some have an eye.*

**mutabilis.** Cotton rose; also called Confederate rose, but a native of China. A shrub or sometimes tree-like. Leaves broadly ovalish, 4–8 in. wide, 3–5-lobed, the lobes triangular and round-toothed or scalloped. Flowers 3–4 in. wide, opening white or pink, but soon changing to deep red, hairy on the outside. Fruit globe-shaped, hairy, about 1 in. in diameter. A common bush in the South but not hardy north of zone* 7.

**oculiroseus.** White rose mallow. Perhaps not really distinct from *H. moscheutos*, but differing constantly in having a red eye.* Marshes, L.I. and Staten Is., to N.J. and D.C. An interesting plant and perhaps the source of the eye* in the improved mallows noted at *H. moscheutos*.

**rosa-sinensis.** Rose-of-China; called also China rose and shoeblack plant, the latter indicating the use of its flowers by tropical bootblacks, to polish shoes. A gorgeous, tropical Asiatic shrub, often 20–30 ft. in the tropics, less as widely grown in Fla. and southern Calif. It will stand no frost. Leaves broadly oval, 3–4 in. long, tapering at the tip, unlobed but often toothed. Flowers usually solitary in the upper leaf-axils,* 4–6 in. long, typically rose-red (but see below), flaring and spectacularly showy both on account of its petals and the long column of stamens.* Fruit egg-shaped, beaked.

The Rose-of-China is a familiar plant all over the tropical world, and is widely planted in frost-free parts of the U.S. There are many forms of it, some double-flowered, others with the petals cut or fringed, when, from a distance, the flowers suggest a huge scarlet spider. White-apricot, salmon-pink, and yellow-flowered forms are also known.

It is also grown in warm, moist greenhouses, where it needs rich feeding with liquid manure and potting mixture* 4. One of the glasshouse varieties has white- and red-splashed leaves.

**sabdariffa.** Roselle; called also red sorrel and Jamaica sorrel, although it is a native of the Old World tropics. An annual, 4–7 ft. high, much-branched from the base, and with reddish stems. Leaves (the upper ones) 3–5 parted, 3–4 in. wide. Flowers stalkless, solitary in the leaf-axils,* the petals yellow, longer than the thick, red calyx and its bracts,* for which the plant is grown.

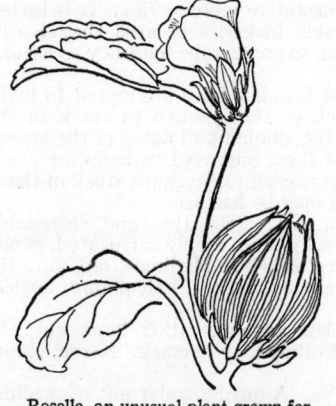

Roselle, an unusual plant grown for its acid calyx* and bracts.*

Roselle is a tropical annual, the cult. of which in the U.S. is confined to the warmest parts of the southern states. It may be grown in such places very much like eggplant (which see for details of spacing and cultivation). The immature calyx and its bracts are harvested for their much-prized acid, which supplies, in regions where the cranberry cannot be grown, a fair substitute. It is especially used for the making of acid jellies and drinks, but must be harvested before the parts become relatively juiceless and woody.

**syriacus.** Rose-of-Sharon; also called shrubby althaea, and sometimes listed as *Althea.* The only really hardy shrub of the genus and a valuable garden subject because of its late bloom. It is a shrub 5–15 ft. high with unlobed, ovalish leaves 2–5 in. long, sharply toothed. Flowers soli-

---

* Special articles on the subjects indicated by an asterisk (*) will be found at the words so marked.

tary, short-stalked, 3-5 in. long, red, purple, violet, or white, broadly bell-shaped and most showy on dark days. Fruit a 5-valved capsule. China. Aug.-Oct. Hardy from zone* 3 southward, and offered in many forms. Some of them have names like "coelestis" (lavender-blue), "totus-albus" (white), "monstrosus" (white with purple eye*), and several others, some double-flowered and some with variegated leaves. A good, double-flowered white form is Jeanne d'Arc, and a single white is Snowstorm.

**trionum.** Flower-of-an-hour. A flower-garden annual 18-24 in. high, the seed of which should be sown where wanted. Leaves 3-5 parted or lobed, the middle lobe much the largest. Flowers pale yellow or yellowish-white, with a dark eye.* Fruit a capsule, surrounded by the stiff-hairy, dark-striped calyx.* Central Af. Summer.

**HICKORY.** Valuable timber and nut trees comprising the genus **Carya** (kă'rĭ-a) of the walnut family, all of its 20 species North American except a single Chinese one. They are tall trees with alternate,* compound* leaves, the leaflets arranged feather-fashion with an odd, and usually larger, one at the end. Male and female flowers on the same tree but in different clusters, the male in pendulous catkins, without petals, and with 3-10 stamens. Female flowers also without petals, and consisting of an ovary enclosed by a 4-lobed involucre.* Fruit a fleshy drupe,* becoming hard and woody in age, and separating into 4 woody valves, within which is the usually edible nut (the hickory nut and pecan). The genus was long called *Hicoria*, a Latinized form of the old Indian name for the trees or their nuts. (Carya is from the Greek for the walnut, a related tree.)

For Culture see below.

**C. laciniosa.** Shellbark hickory; also called big shagbark. A tree up to 120 ft., its light gray bark shaggy. Leaflets 7-9, oblongish, 6-9 in. long, tapering at the tip, toothed, and hairy beneath. Nut nearly round, but obscurely 4-angled, pointed at the ends, its shell cracking with difficulty, the kernel sweet. N.Y. to Iowa, Tenn. and Okla.

**C. ovata.** Shagbark or shellbark hickory. Taller than the last and with more shaggy, gray bark. Leaflets usually 5 (rarely 7), oblongish, 4½-7 in. long, tapering at the tip, the margins decidedly fringed with hairs. Nut elliptic or inverted egg-shaped, slightly flattened and angled, the shell thinner than in *H. laciniosa*, the kernel sweet. Quebec to Minn., Fla. and Tex.

**C. pecan.** The pecan. A tree up to 130 ft., its bark deeply furrowed. Leaflets 11-17, short-stalked, oblongish, toothed, 5-7 in. long. Nut oblongish, 1¼-2½ in. long, the shell easily cracking, the kernel sweet. Central U.S. south to Ala., Tex., and Mex. For culture and varieties see PECAN.

### HICKORY CULTURE

There are many other wild species of hickory than the two listed above, but they have nuts too small, or too bitter, to be worth cult. Hickory cult. is scarcely a garden operation in any case, but much land too rough or hilly for gardens can appropriately be planted to these hardy trees. The pecan, which is less hardy, is considered elsewhere.

These two species of hickory, especially *C. ovata*, have been developed by nut breeders and there are now available various hort. varieties, most of them grafted trees. It is better to purchase such from a reliable dealer than to attempt the somewhat technical job of hybridizing these wind-pollinated trees and the subsequent isolation of desirable varieties by vegetative reproduction. It is useless to plant nuts of desirable hickories because they hardly ever come true from seed, so great is the tendency to natural hybridization.

VARIETIES. Most nut breeders have attempted to make the shell easier to crack or thin enough to crack in the fingers, and to increase the amount and flavor of the kernel. At present only a few of these improved varieties are available, because of the time needed to develop a stock of them. A few of the best which may be had are:

Hales. Originated in N.J. Shell thin and reasonably easy to crack. Kernel plump, deeply corrugated, sweet.

Kentucky. Originated in Ky. Medium-sized nut, the shell moderately easy to crack. Flesh plump, angled, rich, and sweet.

Kirtland. More or less angular, rather large nut, the shell thin and moderately easy to crack. Kernel plump and rich.

Vest. Originated in Va. A quadrangular nut of medium or small size, the shell thinner than in most hickories. Kernel deeply corrugated.

Weiper. Originated in Pa., probably from *C. laciniosa*. Nut elongated, the shell thick but reasonably easy to crack. Kernel plump and of good flavor.

Over 20 other varieties are known and improvements are to be expected yearly, so that it is advisable to get the latest catalogues of the specialists in nut culture before deciding upon which variety to choose. It naturally takes many years to correct an initial error.

Hickory trees have a deep taproot and care must be taken to see that they are planted with no injury to it. They do not transplant easily in any case. Put no manure in the hole which should be filled very carefully only with good topsoil. Never allow the roots to become dry, even for a few moments, or failure is pretty certain. Heel-in* or cover with wet bagging all trees waiting to be planted.

After planting, cut back the growth at least one third, and tie to a stout stake to prevent the wind from loosening the tree's hold on the soil. A swaying tree will probably die, at least the first year or two after planting. Water the young trees if there is a dry spell, but as they become established, this is no longer necessary.

Take particular care of the deep taproot in planting hickories and other trees with this root system.

If the trees are in a place where it can be done, it is advisable to cultivate the soil for the first year or two. Also, unlike some nut trees, hickories respond to an occasional mulch of well-rotted manure, especially when young, and during the summer. Remove or dig in the mulch before the winter, as it may harbor rodents who gnaw the bark.

INSECT PESTS. Insects include nut weevils, similar to those of chestnut, and several leaf pests, including the fall webworm (see PERSIMMON) and the walnut caterpillar (see WALNUT), a twig girdler (controlled by destroying fallen twigs as they drop), and several borers, beetle larvae (checked by keeping trees healthy). Hickory-bark beetles are very injurious; trees should be kept thrifty and infested parts removed and destroyed. See also PECAN.

DISEASES. The most destructive and conspicuous disease of hickory is the leaf blight. Symptoms vary from small spots to large patches of dead brown tissue involving one third or more of the total area of the leaf. Affected leaves are shed prematurely or remain clinging to the tree in a dried and shriveled state. Control by eradication of diseased, fallen leaves is suggested. Bordeaux mixture has been found generally effective against this disease. Leaf mildew of walnut and hickory is recognized by a white powdery fungus on the under side of the leaves, accompanied by a yellowing and dropping of the leaves. Twig infection sometimes results in witch's broom formation. The brooms should be cut off and the tree sprayed as for leaf blight, mentioned above.

**HICKORY FAMILY** = Juglandaceae.

**HICORIA** = *Carya*. See HICKORY.

**HIERACIUM** (hy-er-ray'see-um). A very large genus of showy herbs of the family Compositae, much grown abroad for their handsome flowers but here known only as extremely troublesome weeds, usually called hawkweed. Two of the worst are the orange hawkweed (*H. aurantiacum*) and the mouse-ear hawkweed (*H. pilosella*). For both see the list at WEEDS.

**HIEROCHLOË** (hy-er-rock'lō-e). A genus of grasses of little hort. interest except for the sweet-scented **H. odorata,** the vanilla grass, sometimes called holy grass or Seneca grass. It is a perennial grass with flat leaves and a terminal panicle* which may be 8-15 in. high and brownish. It is easily grown from division of its creeping rootstocks. While of little decorative value, it is hallowed in the memory of many from being strewn on the pavement of countless church doors on saints' days. It is wild throughout northern Eu., and in N.A. along the New England coast and about

---

* Special articles on the subjects indicated by an asterisk (*) will be found at the words so marked.

the Great Lakes. (*Hierochloë* is from the Greek for sacred and grass, in allusion to its chief use.)

**HIEROCHUNTICA** (hy-er-ro-chun′ti-ka). The original name of Jericho, hence the specific name for the Rose of Jericho or resurrection plant. See ANASTATICA.

**HIGAN-SAKURA.** See Japanese Flowering Cherries at PRUNUS.

**HIGH-BUSH BLUEBERRY** = *Vaccinium corymbosum*. For culture see BLUEBERRY.

**HIGH-BUSH HUCKLEBERRY** = *Gaylussacia baccata*. See HUCKLEBERRY.

**HIGH CRANBERRY** = *Viburnum trilobum*.

**HILL CLEMATIS** = *Clematis ligusticifolia*.

**HILL GOOSEBERRY** = *Rhodomyrtus tomentosa*.

**HILLOCK-TREE** = *Melaleuca hypericifolia*.

**HILLS-OF-SNOW** = *Hydrangea arborescens grandiflora*.

**HILUM.** The scar or mark (actually the navel) on a seed, showing its former point of attachment to the walls or partitions of the ovary.

**HIMALAICA, -us, -um** (him-a-lay′i-ka). From the Himalayas.

**HIMALAYA-BERRY** = *Rubus procerus*.

**HIMALAYAN FLEABANE** = *Erigeron multiradiatus*.

**HIMALAYAN MUSK ROSE** = *Rosa brunoni*.

**HIMALAYAN PINE** = *Pinus excelsa*. See PINE.

**HINOKI CYPRESS** = *Chamaecyparis obtusa*.

**HIP.** See ROSE HIP.

**HIPPEASTRUM** (hipp-e-ăs′trum). Amaryllis-like, tropical American, bulbous herbs, family Amaryllidaceae, comprising 70 or more species and many garden hybrids, the hort. sorts commonly called amaryllis and grown like them. They differ from the true *Amaryllis* chiefly in technical characters, but also in having a hollow stalk to the flower cluster. Leaves basal and, in the hort. kinds, strap-shaped. Flowers large, showy, lily-like, prevailingly red or sometimes white-lined, generally funnel-shaped and borne in a large, terminal umbel.* Fruit a globe-shaped capsule.* The plants are sometimes known under the name *Habranthus*. (*Hippeastrum* is from the Greek for horse and star, but of no known application here.)

The garden hippeastrums have been so much hybridized that it is doubtful if many of them are now referable to any particular wild species. Those below appear to be, however, the leading ones involved. For culture see AMARYLLIS.

equestre = *Hippeastrum puniceum*.

johnsoni. An old hybrid plant produced by a London watchmaker named Johnson. It may not now be in cult. in America, but is certainly the origin of many cult. varieties.

puniceum. One of the commonest species in cult. Bulb globe-shaped, the strap-shaped leaves produced from it after the plant has bloomed. Flowers few in the cluster, 4-5 in. long, red or salmon color, the throat greenish. Stamens* not protruding. Mex. and the W.I. to S.A. Often sold as *H. equestre*.

reginae. An old garden plant, the bulb globe-shaped and 3 in. in diameter. From it, after the plant blooms, develop the strap-shaped leaves which are 2 ft. long and about 1¾ in. wide. Flowers only 2-4 in a cluster at the end of a 2-ft. stalk. Corolla 4-5 in. long, bright red, but white-blotched in the throat. Mex. to Brazil.

vittatum. Much resembling the last, but the leaves fewer and the stalk of the flower cluster nearly 3 ft. long. Corolla 4-5 in. long, red, the short tube greenish. Brazil. One of the best known in cult. and with several hort. varieties, mostly minor variations in color.

**HIPPOCASTANACEAE** (hip-poe-cass-ta-nay′see-ee). The horse-chestnut or buckeye family (sometimes, but not here, called Aesculaceae), comprises only three genera. Two of them are Chinese, and not garden plants. The other, *Aesculus*, comprises the well-known horse-chestnut and the buckeyes. They are very ornamental trees or shrubs with compound* leaves, showy flowers in profuse clusters, and large seeds (horse-chestnuts) in a more or less prickly husk. See HORSE-CHESTNUT.

**HIPPOCASTANUM** (hip-po-kas′ta-num). The Latin name of the horse-chestnut.

**HIPPOPHAE** (hip-pof′fay-ee). Two Eurasian, spiny shrubs or small trees of the family Elaeagnaceae, one of them **H. rhamnoides,** the sea buckthorn, cult. for its foliage and the orange-yellow fruits. It is a shrub, sometimes tree-like, 10-25 ft. high. Leaves opposite,* lance-shaped or narrower, 1-3 in. long, and more or less silvery in youth, later greenish on the upper surface. Flowers yellowish, inconspicuous, the male and female on different plants, both without petals. Fruit fleshy, but somewhat hard, not quite egg-shaped, about ¼ in. long, orange-yellow and persistent for most of the winter. The shrub is tolerant of most kinds of soil, and is thoroughly hardy up to the limits of zone* 2. To ensure fruit, which is one of its most attractive features, it is necessary to plant both male and female kinds in close proximity. Propagated by seeds, cuttings, or layers. (*Hippophae* is an old Greek name for some spiny bush, but not certainly this one.)

*HIRCINA, -us, -um* (hir-sy′na). Goat-like, or smelling like one.

*HIRSUTA, -us, -um* (hur-sue′ta). Hirsute; *i.e.* more or less covered with stiff, coarse hairs.

*HIRSUTULA, -us, -um* (hur-su′tew-la). Somewhat stiffly hairy.

*HIRTA, -us, -um* (hur′ta). Hairy.

*HISPANICA, -us, -um* (his-pan′i-ka). From Spain.

*HISPIDA, -us, -um* (hiss′pi-da). Hispid; *i.e.* with bristly hairs.

*HISPIDULA, -us, -um* (hiss-pid′you-la). Somewhat bristly.

**HISTORY OF GARDENING.** See GARDEN HISTORY.

**HOARHOUND** = horehound.

**HOARY.** Covered with ashy-gray or whitish hairs.

**HOBBLEBUSH** = *Viburnum alnifolium*.

**HOE.** See TOOLS AND IMPLEMENTS, Section 1.

**HOEING.** One of the oldest skills in gardening, in fundamentals changing very little from the half-savage irritation of the soil to our modern tools for the same purpose. Some very skillful modern gardeners say that with a spade and a hoe they have the only two really essential tools, and if it must be only one, it is the hoe they would keep.

The reason is clear. With the ordinary hoe (see TOOLS AND IMPLEMENTS) many things can be done. Its sharp blade is set at an angle at the end of a long handle, and with the corner of it one can dig small holes or make a drill,* or dig deeper ones for planting potatoes. Its greatest use is for chopping down weeds or for any operation like hilling up corn or drawing the soil up around potatoes.

In cultivating with a hoe, and in fact with all operations of this essential tool, the action is a steady chopping *toward* one, hence its other name of draw hoe. Unless it is turned upside down, it is next to impossible to use a hoe for shoving soil *away* from the operator. For this reason, and for the more important one that a different sort of hoe would be better for cultivating, the D or Dutch hoe, sometimes called the English scuffle hoe, was developed.

Common hoe, often called a draw hoe

This tool (see TOOLS AND IMPLEMENTS) allows the operator to cultivate by pushing the blade *away* and towards

---

* Special articles on the subjects indicated by an asterisk (*) will be found at the words so marked.

# HOFFMANNIA

him. It is so set that the blade, by a series of short strokes, slides just beneath the surface, cutting off all weeds and leaving the soil in a good state of tilth.* The D hoe will not do as many things as an ordinary hoe, but it is one of the best all-round hand tools for cultivating. With it one can always see what one is doing, and it will reach into a broad bed without disturbing the plants.

The English scuffle hoe, often called a D or Dutch hoe

Whichever sort of hoe is used, an important point is not to walk over the hoed land. Begin at the end of a row and walk over the un-hoed land. For the reasons for this, and the general theory of cultivating with a hoe or any other tool, see CULTIVATION.

For large gardens hoeing is often too expensive an operation to be considered. To meet this condition there are various types of wheel hoes or machine cultivators, a description of which will be found at TOOLS AND IMPLEMENTS, Section 1.

**HOFFMANNIA** (hoff-man'ee-a). Tropical American foliage plants of the family Rubiaceae, a few of the 30 species grown in the greenhouse for their very showy leaves. They are herbs or under-shrubs with opposite* or whorled* leaves, which are usually more or less colored, especially along the veins. Flowers small, the corolla tubular, with mostly 4, blunt or narrow, lobes. Stamens 4. Fruit a many-seeded, oblongish berry. (Named for Georg Franz Hoffman, German botanist.)

These handsome foliage plants need a warm, moist greenhouse and should be grown in potting mixture* 3. Unless well grown, their leaves will not develop the fine color which is their chief attraction. Easily propagated by cuttings over bottom-heat.*

**discolor.** Hairy, not over 6 in. high, but generally drooping over the edge of the pot, the stems purplish. Leaves green above, purple or greenish-purple beneath, short-stalked, nearly 5 in. long. Flowers red and red-stalked, growing in long-stalked, curving clusters (racemes*). Mex.

**ghiesbreghti.** A smooth under-shrub, not over 4 ft. high, the stems 4-angled. Leaves oblongish, nearly 12 in. long, the base decurrent,* green above and very veiny, purplish-red beneath. Flowers yellow, but red-spotted, the short clusters crowded in the leaf-axils.* Mex. A hort. variety has handsomely mottled leaves.

**regalis.** A Mexican under-shrub, the stems 4-angled. Leaves roundish or ovalish, green above, purplish-red beneath. Flowers yellow, crowded in dense, stalkless clusters in the leaf-axils.*

**HOG CABBAGE PALM** = *Pseudophoenix vinifera*.

**HOGG, J.** See America at GARDEN BOOKS.

**HOG PLUM** = *Spondias mombin*.

**HOHERIA** (hoe-heer'i-a). New Zealand shrubs or trees of the mallow family, perhaps consisting of only one variable species, but cult. in Calif. under the three names below and possibly distinct. They have alternate,* stalked, toothed leaves, often differing in age and youth, and numerous small, white flowers in small clusters in the leaf-axils.* Petals 5, notched at the tip, oblique. Stamens* 20. Fruit of separate segments, each of which is winged. (*Hoheria* is a Latinized version of the N.Z. native name for these trees, meaning to bind a captive, in allusion to the use of the bark in making rope.) They are called ribbonwood and lacebark in N.Z.

The hoherias are grown only in Calif. in the U.S., and mostly in the San Francisco Bay region. They prefer well-drained, but moist soil, and partial shade. Propagated by hardwood cuttings or by seeds.

**angustifolia.** A tree up to 25 ft. Leaves oblongish or narrower, 1-2 in. long, the margins spiny-toothed. Flowers about ½ in. wide.

**populnea.** A little shorter than the last, the leaves ovalish, 3-5 in. long and doubly toothed. Flowers nearly 1 in. wide, in very profuse clusters, mostly on old wood. Aug.

**sexstylosa.** Usually about 25 ft. high, the leaves lance-shaped, 3-5 in. long, sharply toothed. Flowers about ¾ in. wide.

**HOLCUS** (hol'kus). Coarse Old World grasses, perhaps of only two species, but so long cult. for grain, syrup, brooms, and for forage that the varieties are many and the identity of the species most uncertain. They are tall, annual or perennial, quick-growing grasses with broad leaves and usually a very large terminal cluster (panicle*), the fruits of some of which have been important food plants for centuries. In others the branches of the panicle are commercially harvested for brooms. They have been assigned at different times to the genera *Andropogon* and *Sorghum*, the latter being also the common name of the leading species. (*Holcus* is Latin for some grain, but perhaps not this one.)

**halepensis.** Johnson grass; called also Means grass and Aleppo grass. A stout, perennial, forage grass of great value in warm regions, and much grown in the South, but prone to become a weedy nuisance in gardens. Stems up to 6 ft., leafy, the leaves 2 ft. long and 1 in. wide. Flowering cluster (panicle*) nearly 2 ft. long, its branches spreading. Mediterranean region, but naturalized and weedy in the southern states.

**lanatus** = *Notholcus lanatus*.

**sorghum.** Sorghum. A stout, annual grass, its pithy stem up to 12 ft. high and yielding in one variety a rich syrup. Leaves 2 ft. long and about 2 in. wide. Flowering cluster very variable as developed over the centuries in the widely different varieties listed below. Tropical Af. (probably). For culture of the typical form and the varieties see SORGHUM. Its most important varieties are:

*var.* **caffrorum.** Kafir. Taller and stouter than the type, producing no syrup, but grown for the edible grain of which there are white, red, and black forms. Called, erroneously, kafir corn (has nothing to do with corn). A tall form of it is known as African millet.

*var.* **caudatus.** Feterita. More slender, but 6-14 ft. high. Flowering cluster (panicle*) narrow, ultimately producing a nutritious, broadly elliptic, white, yellow, or red grain.

*var.* **drummondi.** Chicken-corn. Not over 6 ft. high, the flowering cluster (panicle*) pyramidal, 12-16 in. long, the ultimate grain oval, orange-yellow. Commonly grown in the South for chicken feed.

*var.* **durra.** Durra. An age-old cereal grain along the Nile, but little grown here. Flowering cluster (panicle*) compact, ovalish, more or less recurved, the grain nearly globe-shaped. A form of it is known as Jerusalem corn.

*var.* **roxburghi.** Shallu. A grain sorghum in India, but little known in the U.S. The stem is as tall as the type and somewhat waxy. Flowering cluster (panicle*) oblongish, dense, its branches erect. Grain elliptic.

*var.* **saccharatus.** Sorgho; also called sweet sorghum or sugar sorghum. The most important of all the varieties, because its rich, sweet sap is a commercial source of syrup. Its foliage also furnishes fodder. It grows 6-12 ft. high, and has a usually erect flowering cluster (panicle*), but sometimes it is recurved. It produces no edible grain.

*var.* **technicus.** Broomcorn. A stout grass 10-15 ft. high, grown for the very stiff branches of its large flowering cluster (panicle*). These rigid, stiff, slightly twisted branches may be 18-30 in. long in the largest sorts, and 12-20 in. in the smaller varieties. Both are commercially harvested for the making of brooms.

**sudanensis.** Sudan grass. Very like *H. halepensis*, but an annual, and somewhat used for forage in the southern U.S. It can only be grown in warm regions. Africa.

**HOLLAND BULBS.** See DUTCH BULBS.

**HOLLAND ELM** = *Ulmus hollandica*. See ELM.

*HOLLANDICA, -us, -um* (hol-lan'di-ka). From Holland.

**HOLLOW WALL GARDEN.** See WALLS AND WALL GARDENING.

**HOLLY.** Extremely valuable, mostly evergreen trees and shrubs comprising the genus **Ilex** (eye'lecks) of the family Aquifoliaceae. Of the 300 species, widely scattered in temperate and tropical regions, a few are among the most valuable of our broad-leaved evergreens, and a few others which drop their leaves are grown for their showy fruits. They have alternate,* sometimes spiny-toothed leaves, and inconspicuous white or greenish flowers usually in small clusters in the leaf-axils.* Sepals 3-6, and petals 4-5, both small. Fruit berry-like, often showy, actually a drupe* with a single seed. (*Ilex* is derived from the old Latin name of the holm oak, *Quercus ilex*.)

For the sea holly see ERYNGIUM. For the mountain holly see NEMOPANTHUS. For the California holly see TOYON.

---

\* Special articles on the subjects indicated by an asterisk (\*) will be found at the words so marked.

Culturally the hollies are divided between the evergreen and deciduous* species. The latter, which drop their leaves, are of simple culture in any good garden soil and present no difficulties in transplanting, although not all of them are hardy everywhere (see the notes at each species).

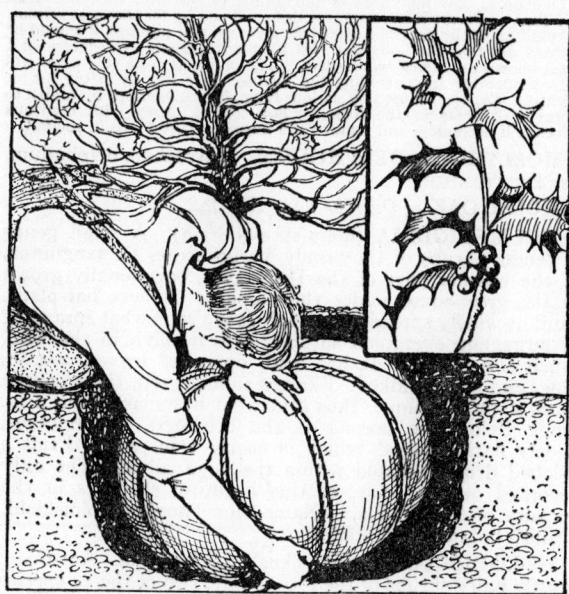

The evergreen hollies should be carefully packed with a ball and burlap, and in planting it is better to knock off most of their leaves, and prune severely.

The evergreen kinds are far more valuable and need greater care. Purchased plants will come with a ball of soil wrapped in bagging. Keep it moist until the specimen is planted. Most of the evergreen kinds are slow-growing and difficult to get established. Water them freely the first year or so after planting. If old plants are to be moved, most of their leaves should be knocked off before they are dug, and pruned freely after planting. A slow method of propagation is by seeds, but they must be stratified and even then usually take 2–5 years to germinate. A quicker method for the evergreen sorts is to make cuttings of ripe wood and plant them in sand in the cool greenhouse. They should root in a few weeks, but are slow to get really started. In spite of these difficulties, the evergreen hollies are very popular garden subjects, but expensive, as befits their worth and slow growth.

**I. aquifolium.** English holly. An evergreen tree up to 40 ft. high, usually much less in cult. in America. Leaves short-stalked, dark lustrous-green above, ovalish or oblong, 1½–2½ in. long, the margin wavy and with large, triangular, spiny teeth. Fruit nearly round, pea-sized, bright red, usually in clusters. Eurasia and northern Af. Precariously hardy in zone* 4, generally hardy southward, but it does not like hot, dry summers. It grows best in the U.S. in Ore. and Wash. Long cult. and found in many hort. varieties, especially in England. Two of the best are *var.* **albo-marginata**, with silvery-margined leaves, and *var.* **aureo-regina**, with yellow-margined, gray-mottled leaves. To ensure getting plants that will certainly produce fruit it is best to select a named form like the Van Tol or Dutch holly as it is called. It is a grafted variety and always fruits if given proper care.

**I. cassine.** Dahoon; called also, yaupon, but this is more correctly applied to the last species. An evergreen shrub or small tree up to 25 ft. Leaves oblongish, 2–3 in. long, shallowly toothed or without them. Fruit globe-shaped, red or yellowish, borne on the current season's twigs. N. Car. to Fla. and La. Hardy from zone* 6 southward.

**I. cornuta.** A handsome, Chinese relative of the English holly, the oblongish, evergreen leaves with 3 spines at the tip and one or two along the sides. Fruit globe-shaped, red, stalked, nearly ½ in. in diameter. Hardy from zone* 4 southward.

**I. crenata.** Japanese holly. An extremely handsome evergreen shrub with box-like habit and foliage. Leaves generally oblong, but broadest towards the tip, 1–2½ in. long, more or less wedge-shaped at the base, dark green and very finely toothed. Fruit black. Jap. Hardy from zone* 4 southward, sometimes in zone* 3 with protection. The *var.* **latifolia** has elliptic or oblongish leaves and is perhaps the most common form in cult.; *var.* **microphylla** has smaller leaves and is hardier than the type; *var.* **fortunei** is a trade name for typical *I. crenata*.

**I. glabra.** Inkberry; also called winterberry and bear-bush. Evergreen southward but only half-evergreen northward and then turning a rusty green in the late fall. Usually not over 6 ft. high, mostly 3–4 ft. Leaves oblongish, but broadest towards the tip, wedge-shaped at the base, 1–2½ in. long. Fruit pea-sized, stalked, black. Typically a bog shrub, native in eastern N.A., but growing in any reasonably good, sandy loam in the garden. Hardy from zone* 3 southward. A mulch of leaves is better than trying to cultivate the soil for this shrub.

**I. laevigata.** Smooth winterberry; called also, hoopwood. Not evergreen, and planted chiefly for its showy, orange-red fruits. It grows 5–8 ft. high, and has ovalish or narrower leaves 1½–2¾ in. long which are more or less wedge-shaped at the base and very finely toothed. Me. to Pa. and Va. Hardy from zone* 3 southward. Often mistaken for *I. verticillata*, but a more desirable plant than the latter.

**I. opaca.** American holly; called also, white holly. The New World cult. representative of the English holly, but not such a handsome plant. It is a spreading tree, up to 40 ft. Leaves evergreen, elliptic, 1¾–3 in. long, dull green above, yellowish-green beneath, the marginal teeth remote and spiny. Fruit usually solitary, pea-sized, red. Mass. to Fla. west to Mo. and Tex. Hardy from zone* 4 southward. It grows naturally in acid soils (pH 5–6; see ACID AND ALKALI SOILS) and is difficult to transplant. Its chief garden merit is that it is hardier than the much finer English holly.

**I. verticillata.** Black alder; also called winterberry and dogberry. Not evergreen, and usually a spreading shrub up to 8 ft. high, grown mostly for its bright red fruits, which are more profuse than in any other holly and persist over most of the early winter. Leaves ovalish or narrower, wedge-shaped at the base, 1½–2¾ in. long, very finely toothed. Eastern N.A. Hardy from zone* 3 southward.

**I. vomitoria.** The true yaupon; sometimes called cassena, and occasionally mistaken for *I. cassine* (the dahoon). It is an evergreen tree 15–25 ft. high, with short-stalked, elliptic or oblongish leaves about 1½ in. long, the margins wavy-toothed. Fruit scarlet, borne on the old wood. Va. to Fla. and Tex. Hardy from zone* 6 southward.

**HOLLY FAMILY** = Aquifoliaceae.

**HOLLY FERN** = *Cyrtomium falcatum*.

**HOLLYHOCK.** Old and popular flower garden plants belonging to the genus **Althaea** (al-thee′a) of the mallow family, and including, besides the garden hollyhock, the true marshmallow and the Antwerp hollyhock. The genus comprises only about 15 species of tall, leafy-stemmed annual, biennial, or perennial herbs, all from the temperate regions of the Old World. They have usually hairy, often felty, alternate* leaves and a terminal, spire-like cluster (mostly racemes*) of very showy flowers, the 5 petals usually notched, originally red or white, but variously colored in the hort. forms. Below the calyx* is a series of 6–9 bracts.* Fruit a collection of 1-seeded carpels, which are at first united in a circle, but ultimately separate from it and from each other. (*Althaea* is the Greek name of the marshmallow.)

For Culture see below.

**A. ficifolia.** Antwerp hollyhock. A biennial* herb related to the common hollyhock, but the leaves deeply divided into 7 narrow, irregularly toothed segments. Flowers showy, lemon-yellow or orange, in terminal spikes, double or single. Eu. Not much grown in the U.S., and it may be only a form or variety of the common hollyhock.

**A. officinalis.** Marshmallow; also called sweatweed. A perennial* herb 3–4 ft. high, more or less downy. Leaves sometimes unlobed but usually 3-lobed, generally ovalish or heart-shaped, the middle lobe much larger than the other 2. Flowers solitary or a few together in the leaf-axils,* not over 1 in. wide, pinkish. Eu., and naturalized in the salt marshes of the eastern U.S. Little grown here, but its roots yield a mucilage in Eu.

**A. rosea.** The common garden hollyhock. Originally a tall, Chinese, perennial herb, but grown mostly as a biennial and even as an annual (see below). It is erect, 5–9 ft. high, the stem leafy, spire-like and hairy. Leaves generally roundish, long-stalked, rough, wavy-angled on the margin or shallowly 5–7-lobed. Flowers essentially stalkless, in long, stiff, but wand-like, terminal clusters, typically single, and red or white, but the hort. forms of many colors and often double. It flowers from the bottom upwards. China.

A common misspelling for *Althaea* is *Althea*, and the latter is sometimes used in catalogues both for the hollyhock and for the Rose-of-Sharon. See HIBISCUS SYRIACUS.

### HOLLYHOCK CULTURE

The hollyhock had been cult. in China for perhaps a thousand years before it was introduced into England in 1573. Typically a short-lived perennial, it is now universally grown as a biennial or even as an annual.

Soon after the colonists reached America there are records of its cult. in their simple Colonial gardens, mostly red, pink, or white varieties with single flowers. Then, as now, it gave a note of aspiring and gay color to many otherwise bare places, especially fitting under windows, along picket fences, or against the walls of a house. It is better not to

---

* Special articles on the subjects indicated by an asterisk (*) will be found at the words so marked.

group hollyhocks in the general border. They are too striking and, if their lower leaves are too much shaded by surrounding vegetation, they do not thrive so well as out in the open sunlight.

CULTURE. Nearly any ordinary garden soil will suit hollyhocks. If they are to be treated as biennials, sow the seed in the frame or in flats outdoors in July or Aug. for plants to bloom next year. Prick out the seedlings and grow them along until frost time, when they should be lightly mulched and left in the frame or wherever they are growing, without any heat.

The following spring the seedlings should be moved to their permanent location. In planting, see that their naturally downward-pointing roots are left pointing downward; otherwise, they are much liable to frost heaving (see HEAVING) the following winter. Also plant them a little deeper than they were in the seed bed. Both these precautions should be taken to prevent their roots from becoming exposed, which they resent more than most plants, and to anchor properly such a tall, stately plant.

One of the best places for a planting of hollyhocks

Many of the newer strains of hollyhocks may be treated as tender annuals. Sow the seed in Feb.–March in the greenhouse or on a window ledge, and by the time outdoor planting arrives, the seedlings can be planted in their permanent place. Such plants will bloom the first season, but later than old ones and later than those started as biennials the season before.

VARIETIES. Because hollyhocks have been naturally and artificially much hybridized, the varieties of them are most unstable. This is especially true in the forms sold as annuals, which are also generally shorter than the normal biennial type. Of the annual sorts perhaps only 50% will come true from seed; also some will be single, some double, and some semi-double. A packet of annual hollyhock seed is therefore very much of a gamble.

It is somewhat less so with the sorts to be treated as biennials, although considerable instability is likely even in these. Named varieties are of fleeting permanence, but the following colors can usually be relied upon: crimson, pink, rose, salmon-pink, scarlet, yellow and white. As to form there is the common single-flowered type, double, and semi-double forms, and some with curled or fringed petals. Traditionally, hollyhocks were single-flowered and many prefer them so today, as they seem more fitting to the simplicity of the garden pictures than the newer types. In many catalogues these biennial hollyhocks are still listed as perennials, which, as we have seen, is historically correct, but horticulturally misleading.

INSECT PESTS. Several leaf-feeding caterpillars attack hollyhocks, and may be controlled with arsenicals. Red spiders attack the plant, and in the South it may serve as a winter host and source of spring infestation of other plants. Sulphur spray or dust will check these pests.

DISEASES. The hollyhock is susceptible to rust and leafspot. *Rust* (see Rust at PLANT DISEASES) is widespread and by far the most serious. In addition to the general suggestions given on rust diseases, it should be pointed out that the hollyhock rust fungus frequently overwinters on a weed known as *Malva rotundifolia*. The eradication of this weed will aid considerably in controlling the disease. (See No. 23 in the list at WEEDS.) *Leafspot*, caused by various fungi, is characterized by brown to white dead areas in the foliage. For control, spray with bordeaux mixture, if necessary, and remove and burn all plant debris in the fall.

**HOLLYHOCK DELPHINIUM.** A Wrexham delphinium. See DELPHINIUM.

**HOLM OAK** = *Quercus ilex*. See OAK.

**HOLMSKIOLDIA** (holm-skee-ol'dee-a). A small genus of tender shrubs of the family Verbenaceae, **H. sanguinea**, of the warmer part of the Himalayas, occasionally grown in the greenhouse under the name of Chinese hat-plant, from its widely spreading calyx.* It is a somewhat sprawling or straggling evergreen shrub, 10–30 ft. high in the wild, much less in cult. It has oval, opposite* leaves, 2–4 in. long, and short-stalked. Flowers tubular, red, the 5 corolla lobes slightly oblique, thus somewhat irregular, about 1 in. long. Below the corolla is the brick-red, membranous, widely flaring calyx* which is nearly 1 in. wide. Fruit a 4-lobed drupe,* seated within the large calyx.* The only recorded outdoor cult. of this beautiful shrub is in the vicinity of Miami, Fla. (Named for Theodor Holmskiold, Danish botanist and nobleman.)

**HOLODISCUS** (ho-lo-dis'kus). Spirea-like, American, mostly hairy shrubs of the rose family, two of the 14 species of secondary garden interest, and grown for ornament. They have alternate,* stalked, usually toothed leaves, sometimes slightly lobed. Flowers white, very small, but numerous in a branching cluster (panicle*). Calyx tube cup-shaped, the sepals 5. Petals scarcely longer than the sepals.* Stamens numerous, a little protruding. Fruit a collection of 5 achenes.* (*Holodiscus* is from the Greek for entire disk, in allusion to the disk of the flower.) Sometimes sold as *Schizonotus*.

Both the species below prefer open, sandy loams and full sunlight. The first is especially handsome in bloom, as its gracefully arching branches are a mass of creamy-white, spirea-like trusses. Propagated by seeds or by layers.

discolor. Cream bush. A spreading shrub 6–12 ft. high, its branches arching. Leaves oval, 2–4 in. long, white-felty beneath. Flower cluster about 9 in. long, very showy. British Columbia to Calif. and Mont. July. Hardy from zone* 4 southward. A variety with the leaves grayish-green beneath, instead of white, is the most likely form to be in cult.

microphyllus. Scarcely over 3 ft. high, the leaves elliptic, about ¾ in. long, more or less wedge-shaped at the base, white-silky beneath. Flower cluster about 3 in. long. Colo., Wyo., and Utah. July. Hardy from zone* 4 southward.

**HOLOSTEA** (ho-los'stee-a). Ancient Greek name for a chickweed-like plant. See STELLARIA.

**HOLY GHOST FLOWER** = *Peristeria elata*.

**HOLY CLOVER** = *Onobrychis viciaefolia*.

**HOLY GRASS** = *Hierochloë odorata*.

**HOMALOCEPHALA** (ho-mal-o-seff'a-la). A single species of cactus from Tex., N. Mex., and Mex., known there as manca caballo and to science as **H. texensis**. It is allied to *Echinocactus* and has the shape of a flattened orange, so that while it is only about 6 in. high, its width is nearly 12 in. The plant body has 13–27 ribs, and on them at intervals are spine clusters. There is one central and longer, erect spine and 6–7 shorter ones that divaricate. Flowers about 2 in. long, orange or scarlet below, but pink or even white at the tip, bell-shaped. Fruit fleshy, irregularly bursting. The plant is suited only to outdoor desert gardens in its own region or to greenhouse culture northward. See CACTI. (*Homalocephala* is from the Greek for like or similar and head, in allusion to the shape of the plant.)

**HOMALOCLADIUM.** See MUEHLEUBECKIA.

---

* Special articles on the subjects indicated by an asterisk (*) will be found at the words so marked.

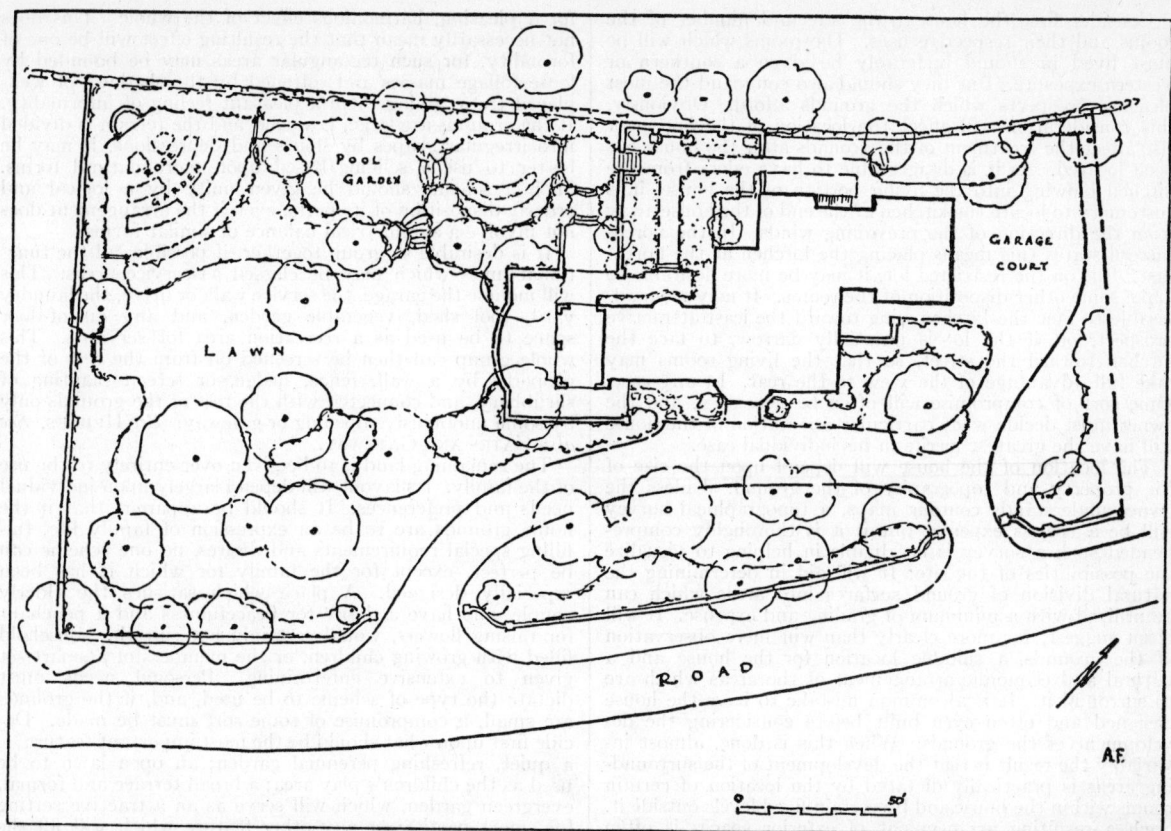

A plan for the intensive development of a small place. The apparent spaciousness of this acre suburban plot is achieved by organizing a series of related unit features. Note the privacy of the house and the area of lawn.

**HOME GROUNDS.** The home grounds are to be considered as the small- or medium-sized grounds of a suburban home, as distinguished from the backyard gardens of the city house and from the country estate. *See* BACKYARD GARDEN, COUNTRY ESTATE.

The above distinction is intended to be one of property size and surroundings rather than a classification of a type of homeowner. Even were it not for the fact that owners of suburban properties include many different classes and conditions of people, the variability of human needs and temperament would preclude laying down arbitrary rules for the development of such properties.

The primary consideration is to achieve an arrangement of the home grounds which will be aesthetically pleasing and economically sound, and, above all, which will satisfactorily fulfill the aims and desires of the individual owner and his family. In other words, a house and the grounds which surround it should express as fully as possible the life of the particular family which makes it their home. The problem is essentially an individual one, and the limitations of topography and surroundings make it even more so. This article then will attempt merely to point out the best procedure to follow in trying to solve individual problems, and will offer only such general advice and suggestions as may be widely applicable.

The best procedure, if a new and undeveloped lot has been acquired, is to visit the property several times, making notes of whatever special features it may possess — such as old trees, irregularities of the ground, views which may be taken advantage of, and objectionable or undesirable features to be removed or screened from sight. It is imperative to have a thorough knowledge of the site before attempting to make any plans. If possible the advice of a competent landscape architect should be obtained before proceeding with the plans. It is his business to visualize all the possibilities of a site, to know how to get the best use from all the available land, and to make the most of the attractive features. Even better than the architect, the landscape architect appreciates how greatly the exact location of a house may affect the possible treatment of surrounding areas, their aesthetic effect and usefulness, and incidentally the expense involved in developing them. A prospective home builder will be well advised to secure professional advice at the outset and obtain at least a sketch plan for the general development of the grounds. This will prevent the possibility of many blunders which are likely to arise from starting out without a well-considered, logical plan. A thoroughly organized arrangement of the entire grounds will give a reasonableness to the scheme which will enhance its aesthetic value as well as its usefulness.

Unless the land is very flat, it is almost essential to have a topographical survey made. From this survey and from notes taken upon the grounds, the landscape architect proceeds to work out a general plan of development. This plan later is tested upon the ground by staking out its main lines and seeing if any changes are advisable. It is at this stage that the architect should be called in, the two designers working in conjunction from then on.

### WITHOUT AN ARCHITECT?

For those who choose to carry out such planning themselves, it is necessary to have some understanding of the various factors which must be considered before a satisfactory solution can be arrived at. These will be taken up in the paragraphs following. Their relative importance, however, can only be determined in the light of personal tastes and requirements and the peculiarities of the individual property.

---

\* Special articles on the subjects indicated by an asterisk (\*) will be found at the words so marked.

Consider first the house — the size and number of the rooms and their respective uses. The rooms which will be most lived in should preferably be given a southern or western exposure. But they should also command the most pleasing prospects which the grounds afford. Obviously, this consideration will affect the location of the house, or else affect the treatment of the grounds after the house has been located. As it is disagreeable to have odors from the kitchen blowing into the living portion of the house, it is customary to locate the kitchen at the end of the house away from the direction of the prevailing winds. In the northeastern states this means placing the kitchen at the northeast. But on the restricted lot, it may be more desirable to make some other disposition of the rooms. It may seem advisable to face the kitchen wing toward the least attractive prospect, or, if the lot is unusually narrow, to face the kitchen toward the street, so that the living rooms may take full advantage of the view to the rear. In any case, some sort of compromise will often be necessary, and the owner must decide what particular orientation of the house will have the greatest merits in his individual case.

The location of the house will depend upon the size of the property and topography of the ground. Unless the owner understands contour maps, a topographical survey will be a useless expense; but if it is thoroughly comprehended such a survey is invaluable in helping to visualize the possibilities of the site: It will aid in determining the natural division of ground surfaces into areas which can be utilized with a minimum of grading and expense. It will often suggest, far more clearly than will mere observation of the grounds, a suitable location for the house and a natural and economic arrangement of the areas which are to surround it. It is a common mistake to have the house designed and often even built before considering the development of the grounds. When this is done, almost invariably the result is that the development of the surrounding areas is practically dictated by the location of certain rooms within the house and by certain fixed levels outside it. Such a resulting arrangement of exterior spaces is often unsatisfactory — a poor sort of compromise necessitated simply by lack of forethought. To obtain a truly satisfactory scheme under such conditions may be either excessively expensive or altogether impossible.

The owner, therefore, should seek a solution which embraces the greatest number of desirable features. He should weigh the respective merits of various possible locations and orientations of the house, both from the point of view of the interior arrangement of rooms, with their resultant views and exposures, and from the point of view of such exterior areas as the garden, lawn, approaches, play areas, and service areas. Let him then choose the location which will result in the greatest good to all in his household.

If, after the position of the house has been established, there remain any unattractive features of the neighborhood which must be obliterated, mark off on the plan, or upon the ground itself, an area to be planted with trees or shrubs which will successfully screen such objects from the view. These foliage masses may be sufficiently dominating to suggest some different arrangement of outdoor areas from that originally considered.

In deciding upon the shape, position, and relative size of any of the various outdoor units, it is advisable first to consider the grounds as a whole, and then to think of each individual area as a part of the whole. Otherwise some one unit may be given undue size and importance, detrimental to the other areas and to the unity of the general scheme. In a small lot, where the limits of the property are clearly visible as two sets of parallel lines perpendicular to each other, it is usually wise to choose some kind of rectilinear scheme of development. This is especially true if the family's needs require a division of the property into a number of smaller areas, for unless these areas are rectilinear, they cannot occupy all of the available land. Furthermore, with the use of a scheme based upon straight lines and rectangles it is easier to achieve that orderly, well-organized arrangement of shapes and spaces which makes for a pleasing, harmonious effect of the whole. This does not necessarily mean that the resulting effect will be one of formality, for such rectangular areas may be bounded by loose foliage masses and softened by the shadows of well-placed trees, giving them a pleasant feeling of informality. If the grounds are large, however, and the terrain is divided into irregular shapes by slopes and depressions, it may be better to use a scheme based upon more natural forms. Such a scheme should be given unity by a logical and orderly disposition of its parts, even if the arrangement does not involve a symmetrical balance of similar forms.

It is desirable to group together, if possible, all the functional units which may be classed as service areas. This will include the garage, the service walk or drive, the laundry yard, tool shed, vegetable garden, and any out-of-door space to be used as a recreation area for servants. This whole group can then be screened off from the rest of the property by a wall, fence, hedge, or screen planting of shrubbery, and connected with the rest of the grounds only by some unobtrusive opening or gateway. *See* HEDGES. *See also* GATES AND GATEWAY.

The remaining land is to be given over entirely to the use of the family. Its layout will depend largely upon individual needs and preferences. It should be apparent that if the home grounds are to be an expression of family life, fulfilling special requirements and desires, no one scheme can be perfect, except for the family for which it has been especially designed. A place which satisfies the elderly couple who have a desire for peacefulness and a penchant for raising flowers, would certainly not suit the household filled with growing children, or the members of a smart set given to extensive entertaining. Personal needs must dictate the type of scheme to be used, and, if the grounds are small, a compromise of some sort must be made. Decide first upon what should be the most important feature — a quiet, refreshing perennial garden; an open lawn to be used as the children's play area; a broad terrace and formal, evergreen garden, which will serve as an attractive setting for smart parties; or any other feature which will fill the greatest niche in family life. Let other considerations then follow in order of their importance. Terrace and garden may have to be small in order to make room for the children's play space, or some similar compromise made for the sake of the general good. But whatever area is most important should be featured and made attractive. *See* GARDEN ROOM, TERRACE.

Choice of architectural styles may also modify the design, as well as conditions of climate and the character of the general surroundings. Careful thought and good taste should guide all judgments not actually dictated by economic necessity. It is impossible in this limited space to give an adequate discussion of proportions, sizes and shapes of gardens, and similar areas. Such questions depend upon the character desired and the interdependent relationships in form, height, etc., of the areas involved; likewise, the question of materials for walls, fences, steps, hedges, etc. These are problems requiring personal judgment for each individual case. *See* the special articles on WALLS AND WALL GARDENING, HEDGES, FENCES, PATHS AND PAVING, GARDEN ROOM.

In general it is wise to strive for broad, simple effects. Interest in details may lead to lack of coherence and unity. It is better, for example, to use only one or two types of trees and two or three types of shrubs than to sacrifice a harmonious effect for the sake of using a greater number of plant materials. In the garden, too, a selection of a comparatively few types of vigorous, hardy plants is more apt to be successful in general effect, than the employment of a very wide range of varieties. Choose some fairly simple color scheme and enough plants of each of a few vigorous types to carry out this scheme effectively throughout the garden. The subtler color effects may be achieved with other less common plants used to fill in around the old standbys. *See* COLOR GARDENS.

Conditions vary so greatly that it is impossible to make definite recommendations that will apply to every property,

---

* Special articles on the subjects indicated by an asterisk (*) will be found at the words so marked.

especially in view of the great diversity in climate, taste, extent, and expense involved. Those who have read this article on the home grounds are advised to turn to the general article at LANDSCAPE ARCHITECTURE, and the specialized features there treated or referred to. Some of them will surely fit the needs of practically everyone faced with the development of a small home property. If your area is larger, see COUNTRY ESTATE; if smaller, see BACKYARD GARDEN.

### SOILS AND PLANTING

Whatever the final development of your place will be, there are two fundamentals which have nothing to do with design, but which must be determined before you can even start. They are soils and grading, and the plant materials you can use in different sections of the country.

There is no need to repeat here the details of soil management or of grading. See SOIL. See also GRADING LAND.

As to plants, by far the best plan for the home gardener is to study the following series of articles before deciding upon any planting plan:

| Trees | Border | Annuals | Water Garden |
| Shrubs | Perennials | Color Gardens | Rock Garden |
| Vines | Biennials | Seasonal Gardens | Garden Calendar |

If such a prospect seems too involved, there is no better plan than to call in a trained landscape architect and have him make a general plan for the development of your home grounds. From that you can deviate if you like, but it is at least a guide that, without special training or special needs, you will do well to follow. And by doing as much or as little as your purse or inclination may dictate, you will in a few years, by following such a plan, achieve a harmonious whole. — A. F. and B. J. L.

**HOME VEGETABLE GARDEN.** See KITCHEN GARDEN.

*HOMOLEPIS* (home-o'lep-is). Having structurally similar parts, as scales, leaves, buds, etc.

**HONESTY.** Two Eurasian herbs of the mustard family, long cult. for the satiny, parchment-like divisions of their pods, which are favorite winter decorations and are used in dried bouquets. See DRIED FLOWERS. They belong to the genus **Lunaria** (loo-nay'ri-a) of the mustard family. One is a biennial as cult., but it may be an annual; the other is a perennial. Leaves sometimes opposite,* most of them alternate,* more or less ovalish and stalked. Flowers violet-purple or white, in a terminal cluster (raceme*). Petals 4, long-clawed. Fruit a large, flat, roundish pod (silicle*), its valves falling away in age and leaving a satiny, paper-like remnant for which the plants are grown. (Named for the moon which the color and shape of the fruit suggest.)

The parchment-like partition of the pods of honesty

Of very easy culture in most ordinary sites. The first is treated as a biennial (see BIENNIALS), while the second is a perennial that may be increased by division of its roots.

**L. annua.** Honesty; moonwort, satinpod, or satin-flower. An annual, but grown as a biennial, from 18–30 in. high. Leaves coarsely toothed. Flowers fragrant, purplish, nearly 1 in. long. Pod thin and flat, nearly round, about 1½ in. wide. May–June. Much the best for dried bouquets.

**L. rediviva.** Perennial honesty. A perennial, the leaves sharply but finely toothed; otherwise as in the last, but the pods are oblongish, 2–3 in. long and not so showy as in the common honesty. May–June.

**HONEY BELL** = *Mahernia verticillata*.

**HONEY-BLOOM** = *Apocynum androsaemifolium*.

**HONEY-BUSH.** See MELIANTHUS.

**HONEY DEW.** In mid-summer it is common to find the leaves of certain plants, especially Norway maples, lindens, and roses, covered with a sticky exudation that is sometimes so plentiful as to fall off in minute drops. The condition, long thought to be a "bursting of the plant's vessels," is honey dew, so called because the sticky material is sweet, and in Calif. a source of honey for bees.

Honey dew is actually a rather complicated affair. In periods of intense heat and dryness, certain aphids and scale insects secrete this fluid more freely than in cooler and moister periods. The secretion furnishes an eagerly sought food for certain ants and for some fungi. The latter are not parasitic on plants but they form a fiber over the honey dew, which accounts for the fact that many leaves affected with honey dew look sooty. Before this happens, they look varnished, from the completeness of the film. Usually a rain or cool spell will clear up the trouble; otherwise, spraying must be resorted to as outlined for the plants involved.

**HONEYDEW MELON.** See MELON.

**HONEY-FLOWER** = *Melianthus major*.

**HONEY LOCUST.** Very thorny trees of the pea family, comprising the genus **Gleditsia** (gle-dit'si-a), which has only about a dozen species, chiefly American and Asiatic, but one in tropical Africa. They are usually tall trees, the trunks and branches of which are armed with often-branched thorns. Leaves compound,* the leaflets arranged feather-fashion and often irregularly wavy-toothed. Flowers not pea-like, usually greenish, polygamous (see HERMAPHRODITE), and mostly in racemes.* Petals 3–5, nearly equal. Fruit a large, usually flattened pod (legume*), sometimes sickle-shaped and twisted. (Named for G. Gleditsch, director of the Berlin Botanical Garden, but the generic name spelled as above by Linnaeus.)

The honey locusts are handsome trees, but do not compare with the common locust (which see) in the beauty of their flowers. The honey locust is not particular as to soils, but propagating it by seeds involves soaking them in hot (not boiling) water for a few hours to help their otherwise slow germination. For another plant sometimes called honey locust see MESQUITE. See also LOCUST. Those below flower in May–June.

**G. aquatica.** Water or swamp locust. A tree up to 60 ft. Leaflets 12–18, oblong, 1–2 in. long, usually notched at the tip. Occasionally there are leaves that are twice-compound. Pod long-stalked, thin, 1½–3 in. long, more or less ovalish and 1-seeded. S. Car. to Fla. and Tex. Hardy from zone* 4 southward.

**G. horrida.** A tree up to 75 ft. high, the thorns somewhat flattened and usually branched. Leaflets 16–20, oblongish, about 2 in. long. Pod a foot or more long, twisted and puckered. China and Jap. Hardy from zone* 5 southward. Sometimes sold as *G. japonica*.

**G. japonica** = *Gleditsia horrida*.

**G. triacanthos.** The common honey locust of the eastern U.S., often called black locust or three-thorned acacia. In maturity it may reach 130 ft., lower as usually cult., the trunk and branches armed with long, usually branched thorns. Leaflets 20–30, oblongish, 1–1½ in. long. Sometimes there are also twice-compound leaves with smaller leaflets. Pod sickle-shaped, twisted, nearly 18 in. long and persisting for months. Pa. to Neb., Miss., and Tex. Hardy from zone* 3 southward. The *var. inermis* has few or no thorns and is a more slender tree.

**HONEY MESQUITE** = *Prosopis juliflora glandulosa*. See MESQUITE.

**HONEY PLANTS.** See BEES AND BEE PLANTS.

**HONEYSUCKLE.** See LONICERA. The name is sometimes applied also to the swamp honeysuckle. See AZALEA VISCOSA. For the bush honeysuckle see DIERVILLA. For other plants occasionally called honeysuckle see TECOMARIA, HEDYSARUM, PASSIFLORA LAURIFOLIA.

**HONEYSUCKLE CLOVER** = *Trifolium pratense*. See CLOVER.

---

* Special articles on the subjects indicated by an asterisk (*) will be found at the words so marked.

**HONEYSUCKLE FAMILY.** A large family of mostly shrubs, trees, or vines such as the honeysuckle, elder, snowball, and *Abelia*, but it also contains, among cult. herbs, the twinflower and *Triosteum*. For the garden genera and their characteristics see CAPRIFOLIACEAE.

**HONEYWORT.** See CERINTHE.

**HOOKERA** or **HOOKERIA CORONARIA** = *Brodiaea coronaria*.

**HOOP ASH** = *Fraxinus nigra*. See ASH.

**HOOP-COOP PLANT** = *Lespedeza striata*.

**HOOP-PETTICOAT NARCISSUS** = *Narcissus bulbocodium*.

**HOOP PINE** = *Araucaria cunninghami*.

**HOOPWOOD** = *Ilex laevigata*. See HOLLY.

**HOP.** Valuable economic plants, but of secondary garden interest except as quick-growing but not very handsome vines. All belong to the genus **Humulus** (hew'mew-lus) of the family Cannabinaceae, and are rough-stemmed annual or perennial vines, all of the three known species being natives of the north temperate zone. Leaves opposite,* more or less lobed. Male and female flowers green, on separate plants, only the latter producing the hops used in beer-making. Male flowers in catkin-like racemes,* with a 5-parted calyx,* no petals and 5 stamens. Female flowers in pairs, each pair beneath a large bract,* the collection of which at maturity forms the cone-like body or "hop." It is the latter which contains lupulin, valued in beer-making. Fruit a small achene,* which is surrounded by the persistent calyx.* (*Humulus* is a Latin name of uncertain application to these plants.)

The first species, which is useless for the commercial production of hops, is an annual vine grown for a quick covering of unsightly objects. The second is the hop of commerce and is widely grown for brewing. Its culture, however, is an agricultural operation and scarcely a hort. subject for THE GARDEN DICTIONARY. In fact, where the common hop occasionally escapes, it can become a garden nuisance because of its rampant growth. For commercial culture trellises or poles must be provided, as it is a tall-growing vine. Commercial hop-yards are chiefly found in N.Y. and Ore.

**H. japonicus.** An annual, quick-growing, stem-climbing vine, useful for covering fences or unsightly buildings. Leaves rough, deeply 5-7-lobed, the lobes coarsely toothed, the stalk as long as the blade.* Male flowers in long, hanging clusters, 6–10 in. long. Fruiting cluster not much enlarged, the bracts* or scales long and narrow, and not resinous-dotted. Eastern As. See VINES.

**H. lupulus.** The hop of commerce and a native of Eurasia. A perennial, tall-growing vine, its leaves generally 3-lobed (rarely 5-7-lobed), the middle lobe larger than the others, rough above but less so beneath. Male flowers in a smaller cluster than in *H. japonicus*. Female flowers between bracts* that are much enlarged in fruit (the hop), the scales thin and ultimately light-colored and dotted with resinous glands which contain lupulin. The common green form, in some of its commercial varieties, is the plant of the hop-yards, although a yellow-leaved form is occasionally grown for ornament.

An interesting form of this has been called *H. americanus*, which differs only in minor characters from *H. lupulus*. It is supposed to be native in the central or western U.S., and is of interest chiefly because it has entered into some of the commercial varieties grown in Ore., especially the Oregon Cluster hop.

INSECT PESTS. A greenish caterpillar bores in the vine in some sections; when young it feeds in the tip, distorting the growth, and later bores in the vine below the ground. The distorted tips should be destroyed. In June the soil should be removed from the base of the plant to force the borers down into old roots, and replaced a week later.

The hop aphid, a green plant louse, feeds on plums in the spring, and on hop in the summer; nicotine sprays will control it on either host. Small larvae of moths, and larger spring larvae of butterflies, which sometimes eat the leaves, can be controlled with an arsenical applied early in the summer. Dusting or spraying with sulphur will control the red spider.

DISEASES. There are many diseases of hops, but the only two which the grower must actively combat are powdery mildew or blue mold, and downy mildew. The mold results in a white, talcum-like growth over all the succulent parts of the plant, later turning the hops brown and destroying their value. The downy mildew is even more destructive, dwarfing or killing the vines, and blackening the cones. The blue mold is combated by frequent applications of sulphur dust and the immediate destruction of all diseased refuse. Many farms are still free from the downy mildew, therefore every precaution should be taken to buy only healthy plants, and in other ways excluding it from the planting. When it once is present spraying at weekly intervals with bordeaux mixture will reduce the amount of injury. This should be accompanied by roguing* young diseased plants and burning of affected refuse.

**HOP-BUSH.** See DODONAEA.

**HOP-CLOVER.** See MEDICAGO.

**HOP FAMILY** = Cannabinaceae.

**HOP-HORNBEAM.** See OSTRYA.

**HOPPER-BURN.** See Diseases at POTATO.

**HOP TREE.** See PTELEA.

**HORAI-JIMA.** The Elysian Isle. See JAPANESE GARDEN.

**HORDEUM** (hor'dee-um). A genus of perhaps 20 species of annual or perennial grasses, widely distributed in temperate regions, the only two cult. species comprising a troublesome weed and the barley, which is only of agricultural interest. They have flat, grass-like leaves and terminal, more or less cylindric flower clusters, mostly dense spikes with conspicuous awns.* The individual spikelets are 1-flowered, three of the spikelets at each node* of the jointed stalk. Due to the infertility of some spikes, the resulting cluster may be 2-rowed or 4-rowed, an important feature in the barley. (*Hordeum* is the classical Latin name of barley.)

**jubatum.** Squirrel-tail grass. A perennial, seldom grown for ornament and more often a troublesome weed, usually 12–25 in. high, mostly unbranched. Leaves short, not over 5 in. long and about ⅛ in. wide. Spikes about 4 in. long, the awns* slender and nearly 3 in. long. North temperate zone.

**vulgare.** Barley. An annual cereal grass usually about 30 in. high. Leaves nearly 12 in. long and about ¾ in. wide. Flowering cluster almost 4 in. long, the long, bristly awns* nearly 6 in. long. Probably a cultigen* of Old World origin, and perhaps cult. for over 2000 years.

**HOREHOUND**; also spelled **HOARHOUND**. The common horehound is one of perhaps 40 species belonging to the genus **Marrubium** (mar-rew'bi-um) of the mint family, cult. for its aromatic oil. See HERB GARDENING. The only cult. species is **M. vulgare**, the common horehound, sometimes called the hound's-bane. It is a perennial, hairy, aromatic herb with square stems and opposite,* white-woolly, ovalish leaves ½–1¾ in. long, narrowed at the base to a short stalk. Flowers in profuse, nearly stalkless clusters in tight whorls* in the leaf-axils.* Calyx* tubular, the lobes with sharp teeth. Corolla irregular* and 2-lipped, whitish, and very small. Fruit a collection of small nutlets. The plant is Eurasian, but widely escaped* in N.A. For its culture and uses see HERB GARDENING. (*Marrubium* is the old classical name of the horehound and refers to its bitter flavor.)

*HORIZONTALIS, -e* (hor-rĭ-zon-tay'lis). Horizontal.

**HORIZONTAL TRAINING.** See Fruit Trees at TRAINING PLANTS.

**HORMINUM** (hor-my'num). A single species of perennial herb of the mint family, **H. pyrenaicum**, native in the Pyrenees and the Tyrol and occasionally grown in the rock garden (which see). It has a few basal leaves, but an essentially leafless stem about 10 in. high, the upper leaves reduced to bracts* among the usually 1-sided flower clusters. Corolla purple-violet, somewhat 2-lipped, scarcely protruding from the irregular* calyx. June–July. (*Horminum* is an old Greek name for sage (*Salvia*), which is a related plant.)

**HORNBEAM.** Hard-wooded, slow-growing, usually small trees or shrubs belonging to the genus **Carpinus** (kar-py'nus) of the birch family and cult. for ornament, although their flowers are inconspicuous. Of the 20 known Eurasian and North American species only 2 are of any hort. interest. They have smooth, gray, close-fitting bark and are twiggy enough, in the European cult. species, to make it a hedge subject. Leaves alternate,* but more or less 2-ranked, sharply toothed. Male and female flowers in different clusters on the same tree, both without sepals or petals. Male flowers in drooping, scaly catkins which are

---

* Special articles on the subjects indicated by an asterisk (*) will be found at the words so marked.

2-forked at the tip. Between each scale are 3-13 stamens.* Female catkins terminal. Fruit a ribbed nutlet, beneath and close to which is a flat, 3-lobed bract (it is more or less bladdery in the related hop-hornbeam; see OSTRYA). Both species bloom before the leaves unfold. (*Carpinus* is the ancient name of the hornbeam.)

The two below will grow in most ordinary garden soils, but the American species is a tree of the under-canopy of the forest, and hence prefers some shade and protection from wind. They are otherwise hardy but slow-growing trees. Propagated by stratified seeds, or the varieties by grafting on seedling stocks.

**C. betulus.** European hornbeam. A tree up to 50 ft., but much lower and more bushy as grown here, especially in the young state. Leaves ovalish to oblong, birch-like, 3-4 in. long. Female catkin 2½-4 in. long, the bract* beneath each nutlet nearly 2 in. long, the middle lobe much larger than the other two. Eu. to Persia. Hardy from zone* 3 southward, and suited for hedges if trained for it. See HEDGES. The var. **columnaris** has a column-like habit and is even more slender than var. **fastigiata**, where the branches are upright, forming a narrow, pyramidal tree. There are several other varieties of this long-cult. tree, some of them with deeply lobed leaves and another with the young foliage purplish.

**C. caroliniana.** American hornbeam; also called blue beech, ironwood, and water beech. Not very different from the last, but usually not tending to have a continuous trunk, the latter soon divaricating into several main branches, never over 30 ft. high, usually less. Leaves ovalish, or oblong, 3-4 in. long. Fruiting catkins 3-4 in. long, the bract* beneath the nutlet only about 1 in. long, the middle lobe of the bract* somewhat larger than the other two. Eastern N.A. but west to Tex. Hardy from zone* 3 southward.

**HORNED RAMPION.** See PHYTEUMA.

**HORNED VIOLET** = *Viola cornuta*.

**HORN POPPY.** See GLAUCIUM.

**HORNWORT; HORNWORT FAMILY.** See CERATOPHYLLUM.

*HORRIDA, -us, -um* (hor'ri-da). Horrid; usually horribly spiny.

**HORSE BALM** = *Collinsonia canadensis*.

**HORSE BEAN** = *Vicia faba* and *Parkinsonia aculeata*.

**HORSE BRIER** = *Smilax rotundifolia*.

**HORSE-CHESTNUT.** Highly prized street and lawn shrubs and trees belonging to the genus **Aesculus** (es'kew-lus)

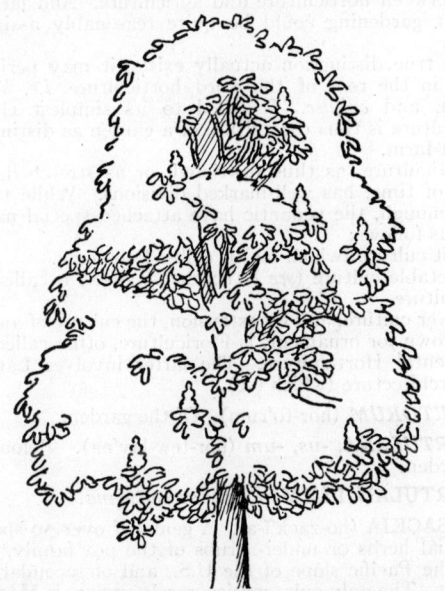

Scarcely any other tree casts so dense a shade as the horse-chestnut

of the family Hippocastanaceae, some of them called buckeye. Of the 25 known species, which are chiefly North American and Eurasian, several are much cult. and the common horse-chestnut is one of the most widely planted trees in the U.S. They have very scaly and, in the spring, gummy-coated buds, and large, compound,* long-stalked leaves, the 5-9 leaflets arranged finger-fashion (digitate*), and toothed. Flowers very showy in a large, many-flowered cluster (thyrse*), the calyx bell-shaped or tubular and 4-5-toothed. Petals 4-5, narrowed into long claws.* Stamens* 5-9. Fruit a large, 3-valved, often spiny capsule containing one or two very large seeds, the horse-chestnuts. (*Aesculus* is the classical Latin name of an oak that bears edible acorns, and applied to the horse-chestnut by Linnaeus, although its seeds are worthless.)

The common horse-chestnut casts the densest shade of almost any cult. tree. It is for this reason a welcome street tree, although many object to the litter of its many flowers and fruits. Few trees are so handsome in flower, especially some of the hort. forms. Most of those below are tolerant of all ordinary garden soils. They can be propagated by stratified seeds, and the shrubs also by mound layering, especially *AE. parviflora*. (See LAYERING.) Some of the shrubby species are extremely handsome specimen plants for the lawn, or in the shrubbery, but they need plenty of room. In Europe, especially in Paris and London, they are commonly called chestnut, a name here mostly restricted to *Castanea* (see CHESTNUT).

**AE. hippocastanum.** Common horse-chestnut. A tree up to 100 ft. high, usually broad and, in youth, dome-shaped. Leaflets 5-7, stalkless, wedge-shaped at the base, broader upwards, 5-9 in. long. Flowers white, tinged with red, about ¾ in. wide, the cluster 8-15 in. long, and very showy. Fruit about 2 in. thick, spiny. Balkans. May-June. Hardy from zone* 3 southward. There are hort. varieties or hybrids with variegated leaves, with deeply cut leaflets, with weeping branches, and one with flesh-colored or red flowers.

**AE. glabra.** Ohio buckeye. A tree not over 30 ft. Leaflets 5, elliptic or broadest towards the tip, 3½-5 in. long. Flowers pale yellowish-green, about ¾ in. long, the clusters 4-6 in. long. Fruit inverted egg-shaped, 1-2½ in. long. Pa. to Neb. and Ala. May. Hardy from zone* 4 southward, possibly in protected places in zone* 3.

**AE. octandra.** Sweet buckeye. A tree reaching 60 ft. or more. Leaflets 5, elliptic or broadest towards the tip, 4½-7 in. long. Flowers yellow, about 1¼ in. long, the cluster 4½-7 in. long. Fruit nearly globe-shaped, about 2¾ in. thick, without prickles. Pa. to Ga. and Ill. May-June. Hardy from zone* 3 southward.

**AE. parviflora.** A widely spreading shrub 8-12 ft. high. Leaflets 5-7, practically stalkless, elliptic to oblongish, but a little broader at the tip, 3½-8 in. long. Flowers white, about ½ in. long, the clusters cylindric, nearly a foot long. Stamens* pink, protruding and showy. Fruit inverted egg-shaped, about 1¾ in. high. S. Car. to Ala. and Fla. Aug.-Sept. Hardy from zone* 4 southward. A valuable lawn shrub and the latest of all the *Aesculus* to flower.

**AE. pavia.** Red buckeye. A shrub or more rarely a small tree 10-30 ft. high. Leaflets 5, short-stalked, oblongish, 3½-5 in. long. Flowers bright red (both the calyx and petals), the cluster loose, 4-7 in. long. Fruit roundish or egg-shaped. Va. to Fla. and La. June. Hardy from zone* 4 southward.

**AE. turbinata.** Japanese horse-chestnut. A tree 60-80 ft. high. Leaflets 5-7, more or less wedge-shaped, 9-14 in. long, pale beneath. Flowers about ¾ in. wide, yellowish-white, but with a red spot. Fruit pear-shaped, about 2½ in. thick, warty. Jap. June. Hardy from zone* 3 southward.

**HORSE-CHESTNUT FAMILY** = Hippocastanaceae.

**HORSE GENTIAN.** See TRIOSTEUM.

**HORSE GINSENG** = *Triosteum perfoliatum*.

**HORSEHEAL** = *Inula helenium*.

**HORSE MANURE.** See MANURE.

**HORSE MINT** = *Mentha rotundifolia*. See MINT. See also MONARDA.

**HORSE NETTLE** = *Solanum carolinense*. See list at WEEDS.

**HORSE-RADISH.** Perhaps the most pungent-rooted of garden plants, and belonging to the genus **Armoracia** (ar-more-ray'she-a) of the mustard family. There are only a few species of Eurasian perennial herbs in the genus and only the common horse-radish, *A. rusticana*, is cult. It is much grown near big cities, for there is a steady demand for the freshly grated root. The root is parsnip-like, but white, and always branched below. Stems coarse, 18-30 in. high, the leaves long-stalked and dock-like, often notched or more or less cut or fringed, especially the younger ones. Flowers scarcely ⅛ in. wide, white, borne in a long terminal

---

* Special articles on the subjects indicated by an asterisk (*) will be found at the words so marked.

cluster (raceme*). Fruit a short-oblong pod, often failing to mature and its seeds generally infertile. The plant has been called by many other names, among them *Radicula* and *Roripa armoracia*. (*Armoracia* is an old Latin name for the horse-radish.)

For centuries horse-radish has been grown to tickle the jaded appetites of the overfed. Because it habitually fails to set viable seed, and the deep perennial root is the part harvested, an unusual method of propagation has been practiced to perpetuate the plant. During spring and summer the plant goes on developing its stout root, the pungent qualities of which are best matured as cool or even cold weather sets in. The roots are then dug and must be marketed very soon, for their pungency is soon lost. Home gardeners can dig a few at a time, as the root is perfectly hardy if left in the ground all winter.

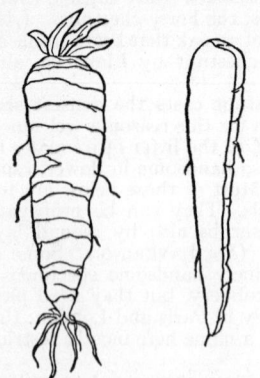

Horse-radish root and a piece cut for propagation

Next year's supply of plants comes from root cuttings. These are made lengthwise, the strips of cut root being 4–6 in. long and about ¼ in. thick. These should immediately be planted, the large end up (to plant them small end up means failure), about 12 in. apart. Such root cuttings will be ready to harvest a year hence. Cultivate and keep down the weeds, as with any other crop.

Horse-radish has no particular soil preferences, except that it does better in rich loam. It will not thrive on light, sandy soils. Also its roots during the summer are inferior or worthless, so that no roots should be dug until Oct. If a summer supply is wanted, store the fall-dug roots in a dark, cool root-cellar. See MUCKLAND GARDENING.

The plant is a weedy escape* in many parts of eastern N.A. Children are occasionally poisoned by eating the white root of the poke which grows in similarly moist places. The poke plant does not in the least resemble horse-radish, but the roots have a dangerous similarity. See PHYTOLACCA.

INSECT PESTS. Horse-radish is sometimes attacked by pests of radish, turnip, and cabbage, especially the harlequin bug (see CABBAGE). A black and yellow flea beetle ⅛ in. long, distinct from those on radish and turnip, attacks horse-radish; its larvae bore in the leaf stems. One or more applications of arsenicals when beetles appear will check them.

DISEASES. (See also CABBAGE DISEASES.) At least four different leafspots may destroy the foliage of this crop and thereby reduce the yield of roots. In addition there are two root rots that often cause much injury. Procuring healthy roots for transplanting, locating the bed on clean soil, and clipping the ends of the roots before planting to make sure that no diseased tissue is present are the only recommendations.

**HORSE-RADISH TREE** = *Moringa oleifera.*

**HORSE SUGAR.** See SYMPLOCOS TINCTORIA.

**HORSETAIL.** See EQUISETUM. See also the list at WEEDS.

**HORSETAIL CREEPER** = *Porana paniculata.*

**HORSETAIL FAMILY.** The Equisetaceae. See EQUISETUM.

**HORSETAIL TREE** = *Casuarina equisetifolia.*

*HORTENSIA, -us, -um* (hor-ten'si-a). A species name derived from the Latin *hortus*, a garden. *Hortensia* means literally a woman gardener, but as a specific name it has been applied to many, sometimes beautiful, plants. As a common name it is also widely used by gardeners for *Hydrangea macrophylla* (which see).

*HORTENSIS, -e* (hor-ten'sis). Of, or belonging to, the garden.

**HORTICULTURAL LITERATURE.** See GARDEN BOOKS and GARDEN MAGAZINES.

**HORTICULTURAL SOCIETIES.** There are scores of societies devoted to horticulture throughout the U.S. They range in importance from small groups of people who meet to discuss garden topics to the Massachusetts Horticultural Society with a large building of its own and perhaps the best horticultural library in the country. A few of the leading Horticultural Societies, all of which issue publications, are:

American Horticultural Society. Washington, D.C.
California State Board of Horticulture. Sacramento, Calif.
Horticultural Society of New York. 598 Madison Avenue, New York City.
Illinois State Horticultural Society. Normal, Ill.
Indiana Horticultural Society. Lafayette, Ind.
Iowa State Horticultural Society. Des Moines, Iowa.
Kansas State Horticultural Society. Topeka, Kan.
Kentucky State Horticultural Society. Lexington, Ky.
Massachusetts Horticultural Society. Boston, Mass.
Michigan State Horticultural Society. Fennville, Mich.
Minnesota State Horticultural Society. St. Paul, Minn.
New Jersey State Horticultural Society. Riverton, N.J.
Ohio State Horticultural Society. Newark, Ohio.
Pennsylvania Horticultural Society. Philadelphia, Pa.
Texas State Horticultural Society. College Station, Tex.
Wisconsin State Horticultural Society. Madison, Wisc.

Perhaps more important than any of them is the Royal Horticultural Society, Vincent Square, London, whose *Journal*, published for many years, is the leading horticultural periodical in the world.

**HORTICULTURE.** The main purpose of this book. It embraces the growing of plants whether for ornament or food, usually, but not always, upon a smaller scale than the production of field crops, which is the chief business of agriculture.

A large-scale, wholly horticultural, business like fruit-growing and an agricultural operation like the raising of cotton or corn often make it difficult to draw an inflexible line between horticulture and agriculture. And large-scale market gardening could be quite reasonably assigned to either.

If a true distinction actually exists, it may perhaps be found in the root of the word horticulture, *i.e. hortus*, a garden, and *culture*. Reduced to its simplest elements, horticulture is thus the culture of a garden as distinguished from a farm.

Horticulture, as thus restricted, or as stretched by the usage of time, has well-marked divisions. While they are plain enough, the pedantic have attached special names to them as follows:

Fruit culture (which see) is called Pomology.
Vegetable culture (*see* KITCHEN GARDEN) is called Olericulture.
Flower culture, and by extension, the culture of any plant grown for ornament, is Floriculture, often called Ornamental Horticulture. The latter involves Landscape Architecture (which see).

*HORTORUM* (hor-to'rum). Of the garden.

*HORTULANA, -us, -um* (hor-tew-lay'na). Belonging to the garden.

**HORTULAN PLUM** = *Prunus hortulana.*

**HOSACKIA** (ho-zack'i-a). A genus of over 50 species of perennial herbs or under-shrubs of the pea family, mostly from the Pacific slope of the U.S., and of secondary hort. interest. The only cult. species, rarely grown, is **H. gracilis,** the witch's-teeth, native from Wash. to Calif. It is a weak-stemmed herb about 12 in. high, with compound* leaves, its 3–7 oblongish leaflets arranged feather-fashion. Flowers pea-like, borne in small umbels* in leaf-axils. Corolla about ¾ in. long, rose-pink, but the upper petal yellow. Fruit an

---

* Special articles on the subjects indicated by an asterisk (*) will be found at the words so marked.

oblongish pod (legume*). (Named for David Hosack, New York physician and botanist, who founded the Elgin Botanic Garden, subsequently deeded to Columbia University and now the site of Radio City, New York.)

**HOSE.** See Section 1, Tools and Implements.

**HOSE-IN-HOSE.** That condition in a double flower, or one wherein the calyx and corolla are colored alike, resulting in one flower appearing to grow within another. It is found in some primroses, in certain Kurume azaleas, and in forms of the Canterbury bell.

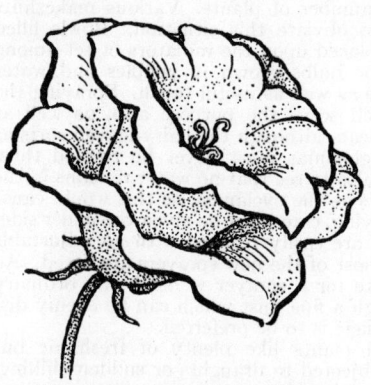

Hose-in-hose, or appearing as if one flower grew in another

**HOST.** A somewhat euphonious term for the victim of a parasite.* Among the flowering plants, hosts are usually plants infected by some parasitic disease (see Plant Diseases). But the oak is a common host to mistletoe, and there are several other parasitic flowering plants who live off their hosts, notably dodder and the broomrape.

**HOSTA.** See Plantain-lily.

**HOTBED.** A heated cold frame. See Cold Frame.

**HOTHOUSE.** See Greenhouse.

**HOTKAPS.** A trademarked, cone-shaped plant protector made of reasonably lasting, usually paraffined, paper, useful for covering tender seedlings or in hardening-off young plants.

**HOTTENTOT FIG** = *Mesembryanthemum edule*.

**HOUND'S BANE** = *Marrubium vulgare*. See Horehound.

**HOUND'S-TONGUE.** See Cynoglossum.

**HOUSELEEK.** Attractive and interesting succulent plants of the Old World belonging to the genus **Sempervivum** (sem-per-vy'vum) of the family Crassulaceae, many of them grown in the rock garden, in succulent collections in the greenhouse, and a few shrubby, tender species in Calif. All except the latter have dense rosettes of basal, thick, often gray or whitish leaves, and some of them produce many offsets,* by which they are readily propagated. Flowers yellow, red, or purple, mostly in terminal clusters (cymose panicles*), the often bracted* stalk of which arises at the leaf rosette.* Petals 6 or more, separate, but the flower often apparently tubular. Stamens* twice as many as the petals. Fruit a collection of 1-celled follicles.* (*Sempervivum* is Latin for live forever, in allusion to the lasting quality of some species.)

The houseleeks are primarily foliage plants, as their flowers are less showy than in the closely related sedums. All but a handful are stemless plants often used for elaborate carpet-bedding schemes in public parks, but widely grown also for the rock garden and for open, sandy places. They do not like too rich a soil nor too much moisture, especially in the winter. Some of them are very interesting plants. *S. tectorum*, the commonest species in cult., is often called the roof houseleek from the fact that it grows on the roof of many thatched cottages abroad. *S. arachnoideum*, the cobweb houseleek, has the rosette of leaves covered with a network of cobweb-like hairs, which the plant produces for no known cause.

The culture of most of them is simple, and those that need rock garden conditions are noted below. Most houseleeks are summer-bloomers.

*Sempervivum haworthi* and *S. spathulatum*, both from the Canary and Madeira Islands, are tender, shrubby species, not to be grown outdoors outside of southern Calif., where they are becoming popular in desert gardens. By some, these and related tender species are considered as belonging to the genus *Aeonium*, not here maintained.

**S. arachnoideum.** Cobweb houseleek. A small plant with about 50 leaves in a dense, globular rosette, the leaves about ⅝ in. wide and very cobwebby. Stalk of the flower cluster 3–4 in. high, leafy and hairy, forking at the top into a 9–12-flowered cluster. Flowers about 1 in. wide, red. Southern Eu. The *var.* **laggeri** has smaller rosettes. The *var.* **doellianum** has fewer leaves to a rosette and fewer cobwebby strands. For culture *see* Rock Garden.

**S. arenarium.** Rosettes globe-shaped and composed of 60–80, generally lance-shaped leaves, the outer ones about ¾ in. long and reddish on the back. Flowering stalk leafy and hairy, the cluster globe-shaped, nearly 3 in. thick, its flowers yellow. Tyrol.

**S. blandum.** Rosettes about 2 in. in diameter. Leaves bluish-gray, hairy on the margin, broadest above the middle, but generally ovalish, the tip with a soft prickle. Flowering stalk about 9 in. high, the flowers pale rose-pink. Transylvania.

**S. brauni.** Rosettes about 2 in. in diameter. Leaves about 1 in. long, sticky, slightly broader above the middle and with a soft prickle at the tip. Flowering stalk about 9 in. high, crowned with a close cluster nearly 4 in. wide. Flowers about 1 in. wide, yellow, but the petals green-keeled. Tyrol.

**S. calcareum.** Rosettes about 2 in. wide, the leaves very bluish-gray, slightly broader above the middle, but tipped with a reddish-brown, soft prickle. Flowering stalk about 12 in. high, the cluster 3–4 in. long. Flowers pale red, about ¾ in. wide. France. For culture *see* Rock Garden. Sometimes offered as *S. californicum*, but probably only a form of *S. tectorum*.

**S. californicum** = *Sempervivum calcareum*.

**S. fauconnetti.** Rosettes about 1½ in. wide, the leaves about ¾ in. long and tinged reddish-purple, and with a tuft of hairs at the tip. Flowering stalk about 8 in. high, the flowers nearly 1 in. wide, bright red. Eastern France in the Jura Mountains. For culture *see* Rock Garden.

**S. fimbriatum.** Rosettes about 1½ in. wide, the leaves broadest above the middle, the outer ones reddish, all tipped with a bunch of hairs. Flowering stalk about 10 in. high, the cluster open, the flowers bright red and about 1 in. wide. Pyrenees and the Tyrol.

**S. glaucum.** Rosettes about 3 in. wide, the leaves bluish-gray, with a brown spot towards the wider tip. Flowering stalk nearly 12 in. high, hairy, the cluster 3–4 in. long, the flowers about 1 in. wide and red. Central Eu.

**S. globiferum.** A plant of uncertain origin and identity. What commonly passes for it has rosettes about 3 in. wide, rather flattened in age, but globe-shaped in youth, the leaves gray-green and tipped with a soft prickle. Flowering stalk about 12 in. high, the flowers yellow and about 1 in. wide. Russia (?). Confused with *S. soboliferum*.

**S. haworthi.** A tender, shrubby species from the Canary and Madeira Islands, sometimes referred to the genus *Aeonium*. It has a shrubby trunk or stem 1–2 ft. high, with short, thick branches. Leaves thick, ovalish, but sharp-pointed. Flowers yellowish-rose, very numerous in a terminal cluster. Suited to outdoor culture only in southern Calif. and similar climates.

**S. mettenianum.** Rosettes about 2 in. wide, the leaves tipped and more or less blotched with red-brown. Flowering stalk about 6 in. high, the flowers rose-pink. Central Eu. For culture *see* Rock Garden.

**S. montanum.** Rosettes compact and scarcely 1¾ in. wide, the leaves about 1 in. long and hairy on the margins. Flowering stalk about 6 in. high, ending in a hairy cluster about 2 in. wide, the flowers mauve-red or purplish. Pyrenees and the Alps. For culture *see* Rock Garden.

**S. soboliferum.** A low plant with "globular rosettes forming pill-like offsets which are attached by short, slender threads which break and allow the offsets to roll away and form new colonies." This, *S. globiferum* and possibly *S. montanum* are sometimes confused in the catalogues. For culture *see* Rock Garden.

**S. spathulatum.** A tender, shrubby species from the Canaries and Madeira, and sometimes considered as of the genus *Aeonium*. Stems thick and woody, 1–2 ft. high, the leaves marked with red-brown. Flowers yellow in a profuse panicle.* Its outdoor culture is limited to southern Calif. and similar climates.

**S. tectorum.** The common houseleek and more widely cult. than all the others, often called roof houseleek (*see* above), hen-and-chickens, or old-man-and-woman, from its frequent offsets.* Rosettes 3–4 in. wide, the leaves many, wedge-shaped and tipped with a soft prickle. Flowering stalk about 12 in. high, dividing into 1-sided clusters of pinkish-red flowers that are about 1 in. wide, and have 12 petals. The stalk and branches of the cluster are hairy. Eurasia, and occasionally escaping* in the U.S.

**S. triste.** Perhaps only a form of *S. tectorum*, but with the upper part of the leaves reddish-brown, with the flowers bright red, and the cluster nearly 6 in. long. Origin unknown.

**HOUSE PLANTS.** Plants which are suitable for interior decoration must grow easily and satisfactorily in a residence without any special treatment other than ordinary care.

### Failure with House Plants

There are four primary causes to which failure with plants grown for home decoration generally may be attributed.

---

* Special articles on the subjects indicated by an asterisk (*) will be found at the words so marked.

LACK OF KNOWLEDGE OF PLANT NEEDS. Many difficulties connected with the successful growing of plants in the house may be overcome by a careful study of the actual requirements of the different kinds. Each plant requires food and water in certain proportions continually, the proper kind of soil, and sufficient light and heat necessary for its proper development.

UNSUITABLE PLANTS. Choosing plants which are not suited to the condition of the room in which they are to be grown and are not of a sturdiness commensurate with the skill of the grower, is ofttimes the cause of failure. Proper lighting in a room with little sun is difficult to achieve and varieties should be chosen which will do best with little or no sun. Moisture-loving plants should not be attempted in a dry or uneven atmosphere, nor those which require a high temperature, when there are facilities for growing cool house plants only.

NEGLECT. There are no hard and fast rules as regards growing conditions which apply equally to all plants, but there are certain fundamentals which must be observed with all plants if they are to survive. All specimens, regardless of type, must be given constant attention, particularly as to the proper amount of water at the proper time, additional fertilizer when needed, re-potting when necessary, and freedom from insect pests.

INJURIOUS GASES. Proper ventilation will to a large extent prevent loss of plants due to poisonous vapors. Some plant species are extremely sensitive to coal gas — the Jerusalem cherry, for example, dropping its leaves and fruit very quickly if coal gas is present. Illuminating gas does little harm to the tough-leaved varieties, such as rubber plants and aspidistras, but the tender kinds such as begonias, coleus, and geraniums are stunted and eventually killed. Primrose and carnation buds either fail to mature or the opened flowers close and then drop off, even in many cases where the amount of gas is so slight that the nose does not detect it.

## SUCCESS WITH HOUSE PLANTS

LIGHT. No other factor governing the growth of plants is so important as that of light. The amount required varies, of course, with different plants. The majority will do best in a window facing south or southwest, and moderately well in eastern light, but usually only foliage plants such as ferns, aspidistras, ivy and palms should be placed where they receive north light. Sunlight is absolutely essential to develop buds to maturity on such blossoming plants as begonias, fuchsias and geraniums. Unless, of course, you grow them under an electric light in the stands and brackets fitted with special lamps which are now on the market for this purpose. Earlier blooms may sometimes be obtained also in this manner. *See* ELECTROHORTICULTURE.

What happens when house plants are not turned every few days so that they do not become lopsided from one-sided illumination.

HEAT. Violent fluctuations in the temperature of a room in which plants are grown should be avoided as much as possible, as every plant has a definite range in which it makes its best growth. In general, a day-time heat of 60 to 70 degrees is best; plants which require a temperature of more than 70 degrees do not make satisfactory house specimens. During the night the plants must be cooler, as they would be normally after sunset if grown in their native habitat, but the drop should be about 10 or 15 degrees only. In extreme cold weather they might be given slight additional protection by covering with paper or some other non-conducting material.

HUMIDITY. Modern heating systems in new houses are often equipped with a humidifying device, or radiator covers contain water-holding compartments. But under ordinary conditions the atmosphere of most dwelling houses is too dry to suit a large number of plants. Various makeshifts may be employed to obviate this situation. Bowls filled with water may be placed upon the radiators or set among the potted plants, or bulbs grown in pebbles and water will add a decorative as well as useful touch. Spraying the foliage frequently will serve the purpose also, as well as keeping the plants clean, although the hairy-leaved sorts as African-violets and gloxinias must never be treated thus. Care must be taken also to see that no water remains in the crowns of such plants as the cyclamen, as this would cause them to rot. In spraying, care must be given the under sides of the leaves, which are easily reached with an adjustable nozzle, with which most of the new sprayers are fitted. An inexpensive substitute for a sprayer would be an ordinary bulb syringe, although a fine mist which can be evenly distributed over the foliage is to be preferred.

VENTILATION. All plants like plenty of fresh air but they must not be subjected to draughts or sudden chilling. Cold air blowing directly on many plants will cause them to lose their foliage and even, in the sensitive species, to die. Fresh air should be admitted gradually for a few minutes morning and afternoon, a good plan being to open a door or window in an adjoining room rather than in the one where the plants are kept. Even in very warm weather it is best not to open the windows directly beside them. Screen and canvas ventilators may be obtained which are adjustable to any size window.

WATERING. "When and how shall I water my plants?" one is frequently asked. And to this the reply must be "Whenever the plant is in need of water." No hard and fast rule can be given, but a good test is to rub some of the soil between the fingers. If it pulverizes without caking, it requires water; if it cakes, it requires none. During the dormant or rest period less water must be given than during their growing season, while in sunny weather they will dry out much more quickly than on moist, dull days. The type of pot

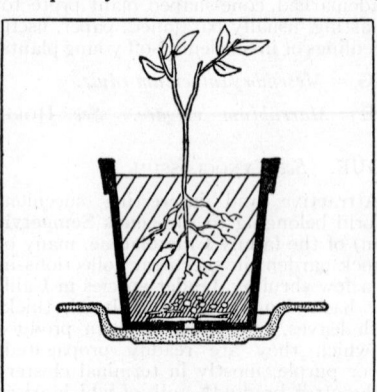

A house plant with saucer, allowing proper watering. The excess water rises by capillarity. Note the drainage crocks over the hole at the bottom.

must also be taken into consideration, as the unglazed varieties are porous, while the glazed ones hold all the moisture, unless they contain a drainage outlet. The latter containers retain so much moisture that the plant may often be watered as seldom as once a week.

When watering a plant, do it thoroughly — not just a little today and a little the next day — but a good, thorough soaking and then not again until you test the soil and find it actually needs it. The roots must be thoroughly soaked; the excess moisture will run out of the drainage hole in the bottom of the container and this excess must not be allowed to stand in the saucer, except in the case of plants which ordinarily grow in water. Standing water must never be allowed in jardinieres. If the plants are very dry or of extreme size, let the pots stand in water to within an inch or

---

* Special articles on the subjects indicated by an asterisk (*) will be found at the words so marked.

so of the brim; when the soil is thoroughly soaked remove them. Plants which cover the topsoil with leaves may be watered from below by keeping the saucer filled until the plant and soil refuses to take any more. Too warm or hot water should never be used, unless one desires to hasten growth, as with the calla lily. *See also* WATERING.

PRUNING AND TRAINING. House plants must be trained in much the same fashion as their relatives of the out-of-doors. If left to themselves most of them will develop certain undesirable traits such as lankiness, one-sidedness, weak growths or too many shoots. Spring is the best time to correct these faults. Prune back to within a few inches of the main stem all uneven growth in such plants as geraniums, flowering maples, fuchsias and hydrangeas. Pinch the top out of coleus and other foliage plants which have any tendency to tall, spindly growth.

PROPAGATION. The majority of plants reproduce easily in a number of ways. The one most often thought of is by means of seed sowing, but not all seed is easily procurable, in which case cuttings of stem, leaf or root may be substituted. Such plants as *Begonia semperflorens*, calceolaria, varieties of cactus, cineraria, cyclamen, Jerusalem cherry, petunia, primroses, dwarf and tall nasturtiums, and free-flowering vines of the order of morning-glories and *Cobaea scandens* are easily grown from seed. Certain cactus such as the common Christmas cactus, coleus, geraniums, poinsettia and the majority of the begonias are propagated usually from cuttings. The beefsteak type of begonia is best grown from root cuttings, as is the case with many ferns. Offsets and division are other methods of propagation; the first is used with the aloe and pandanus, while the latter is successful with ferns, aspidistras and other like plants. Air layering is the most successful method of securing new rubber plants. *See also* PROPAGATION.

SOIL AND FERTILIZERS. Although all plants will not do equally well in the same potting mixture, nearly all will thrive moderately well in any well-balanced soil by adapting themselves to the varying conditions that are forced upon them. For general potting, where a medium rich mixture is desired, use potting mixture* 3; this will do very well for all plants of the order of fuchsias, geraniums, palms and chrysanthemums. Many of the ferns, begonias and plants which require more humus are best grown in potting mixture* 4. When the plants are well established, additional fertilizer may be given to increase growth and strengthen the plant throughout. This may be mixed with the soil or applied in the form of liquid fertilizer; if the latter, be careful not to use it too strong, as there is danger of burning the roots with a strong solution. Fertilizer should never be applied when the soil is dry — always water well first — and should never be given to dormant plants, but only to those in which growth is well started. *See* LIQUID MANURE.

DRAINAGE. Next to light, perhaps the most important factor in the successful growing of house plants is drainage. Most pots, however small, have a drainage hole at the bottom which is to provide an escape for excess moisture. The best method is to put a piece of arched crock over the hole, which is all that is necessary in small pots. As the size of the pot increases, the amount of drainage will increase, so that in a ten-inch pot, for example, two or three inches of drainage, comprised of broken crock at the bottom with gravel, cinders or pebbles placed above the crocking, is not excessive. Some even advise putting a thin layer of sphagnum moss over the drainage material to prevent the soil washing down through the drainage openings, but it is not considered essential.

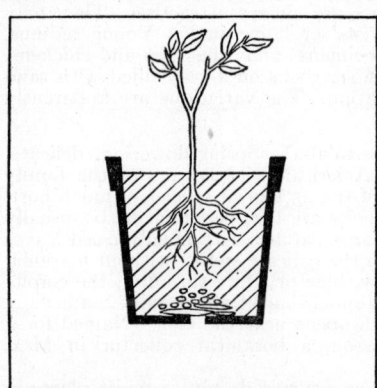

In potting house plants be sure to put broken crocks (potsherds) over the hole at the bottom. These allow proper drainage and aeration of the soil.

RE-POTTING. Most plants begin their most active season of growth in late spring, and the period just previous is, as a general rule, the best time for re-potting. The shock of re-shifting is then easily overcome during the summer outdoors. Examine the roots carefully before deciding to pot into a larger container. If the earth ball has a great number of fine roots on the outside of it, re-pot into a pot one size larger; if none are visible, there is a possibility that the earth has become sour and the roots are not in a healthy condition. In this case wash the earth carefully from the roots and re-pot in fresh soil in a pot one size smaller than its original pot. A good general rule is to use pots just large enough to hold the roots without crowding. Old pots should be thoroughly cleaned before using, while new pots must be washed and allowed to dry before using. When the plant is reset, place the main stem directly in the center of the pot; put the coarse soil above the drainage material, then fill in with the finer soil until it reaches about a half inch from the top. Firm the soil down well and tamp it carefully into place about the roots. If correctly done, the soil surface after settling should be just above the bottom of the rim at the top of the pot. The type of container used is not particularly important, so long as adequate drainage is assured. *See* POTTING.

REST PERIOD. All plants have a definite rest period, in a greater or lesser degree. During this time they require less light, heat and water than when in their period of active growth. Some plants do well during this dormant time in complete darkness, without water or food. Fertilizer should never be given to any plant during the rest period, as it forces it to unnatural growth at the sacrifice of health and vitality.

SUMMER CARE OF HOUSE PLANTS

During the warm summer months all house plants should be placed out-of-doors, either in the garden, in a window box, or even on a partially shaded porch.

PLUNGING. This is the best method of caring for house plants during the summer months. Sink the plants in their pots to the rim in the garden. Never remove the plant from the pot to plunge it directly into the ground, as by autumn the root growth would be beyond all bounds and would need drastic pruning to force it again within the confines of the pot. The reduced root system would not be able to care for the immense tops, which would be cut back in proportion, so that it would be months before the plant would be worth while as a house plant. Before sinking the pot, place a piece of crock beneath the drainage hole to prevent worms from entering. A shady location is best for ferns and foliage plants; a sunny place will be required for many of the flowering species, such as geraniums and heliotropes. Water must be given regularly, and the foliage sprayed to prevent insects.

PREPARATION FOR WINTER. Before frost all the plants must be lifted from the garden, removed from the pots and examined to make certain that drainage facilities are unimpaired. If possible, do not disturb the roots.

After they are established in their winter living quarters, special attention must be given to ventilation and spraying until they are thoroughly acclimated to the more dry, close atmosphere of the house. Even with all apparent precautions, some of the more delicate and sensitive plants will drop their leaves and blossoms. This will check them slightly, but will do no permanent damage if the cause is not continuous.

DISEASE. Plants as a rule, when grown indoors, are subject to few diseases, the most common being due to overwatering or allowing water to remain in the crown. *See* PLANT DISEASES.

INSECTS. Regardless of the kind of plant grown, even

---

* Special articles on the subjects indicated by an asterisk (*) will be found at the words so marked.

those that are healthy and well cared for may sometimes be subject to insect attack. Aphids, or plant lice, are the small black, green or white insects commonly seen on ferns and sometimes on ivy. See Insect Pests at ROSE, CHRYSANTHEMUM and CALLISTEPHUS.

Mealybugs look like tiny pieces of white cotton lodged in the joints of stems or leaf-axils* or even on the spines of cactus. See Insect Pests at BEGONIA, COLEUS and PALM.

Scale insects seem to be the special pests of foliage plants. See True Bugs at INSECT PESTS.

Red spider thrives only in a too dry atmosphere but is one of the worst of all the insect pests and requires courageous methods to remove it when once it has assumed control. See Insect Pests at CARNATION and CALCEOLARIA.

Whiteflies usually indicate a sour condition of the soil or, as is often the case, are a part of the life cycle of white worms which inhabit the earth. See Insect Pests at BEGONIA, COLEUS and AZALEA.

Commercial sprays suitable for these pests may now be bought especially to care for house plants. Many useless remedies have acquired a reputation as cure-alls for the ills of house plants. Chief among these are aspirin tablets, tobacco water, castor oil and beef capsules.

### VARIETIES OF FLOWERING AND FOLIAGE PLANTS AND BULBS

Inasmuch as not all homes or city apartments are blessed with a window with a southern exposure, it seems essential to divide house plants into those that require full sun to produce blossoms, those that will do well with partial sun, and the ones that are content with plenty of light, but little or no sun. Plants may be moved about to secure their requisite amount of light or sun, but this requires time and patience, and it seems to be better to grow only such species as are suited to their environment.

FULL SUN. The following list is not complete but is intended as a guide to the type of flowers which require at least five hours of sunlight each day. *Astilbe japonica*, Indica azalea, Cactus varieties, Calla lily, *Calceolaria*, Cape bulbs,* Cineraria, *Clivia*, Dutch bulbs, *Euphorbia splendens*, *Gardenia*, Geraniums, Heliotrope, *Hydrangea*, *Impatiens*, Jerusalem cherry, and *Poinsettia*.

PARTIAL SUN. Plants requiring two to three hours of sunlight each day: Begonias, *Coleus* (a few of the Cape bulbs might be included), Dracaena, *Anthurium*, Flowering maple, *Fuchsia*, *Cyclamen*, Primrose in varieties, Periwinkle, and any of the foliage plants in the following list.

LITTLE OR NO SUN. This list includes the foliage plants with inconspicuous or no flowers, such as ferns, palms, dracaena, pandanus, some succulents, vines such as Wandering Jew, and many others, also African-violet, *Aloe, Begonia Rex* and the tuberous-rooted varieties, Chinese evergreen, Hen-and-Chickens (*Sempervivum tectorum*), Norfolk Island pine (*Araucaria excelsa*), *Philodendron*, Rubber Plants, *Aspidistra*, also *Crassula portulacea*, and many sedums.

BULBS FOR FORCING. With careful planning in autumn it is possible to have a succession of blossoming bulbs from Thanksgiving Day past Easter. The Dutch bulbs, which include such as narcissus, hyacinth and tulips, remain in bloom for ten days to two weeks. Buy your bulbs early, so they may be potted at one time. Either soil or fiber can be used as a potting mixture, and these bulbs need a period of outdoor cult. before being brought into the house. See BULBS. Attractive pottery or glass bowls make excellent containers, or hyacinth pots or azalea pans may be used, if preferred. Easter lilies can be and are grown as house plants, but they require expert care. Lily-of-the-valley are easily grown and make lovely table decorations. Tropical bulbs, such as freesias, ixias and sparaxias, amaryllis, clivia, are more easily grown than the Dutch bulbs, as they require no period of cold before forcing.

Storage facilities in apartments are a problem, but bulbs are not expensive and it hardly pays to take the trouble to carry over forced bulbs. The hardy ones may be planted out in the garden. Cold frames are a good place to store potted bulbs.

### CARE OF HOLIDAY PLANTS

Ferns, palms, poinsettias, primroses, dracaenas, Jerusalem cherry, Christmas cactus and dozens of other plants are given each year as holiday gifts. Being forced plants the food supply in the soil will soon be exhausted and liquid fertilizer should be given every two or three weeks. Other care is the same as for ordinary house plants. Ferns in particular make excellent gifts. Among the best are the Boston, staghorn, bird's-nest, *Polypodium*, *Davallia*, *Cyrtomium* and the maidenhair. Ferns are fairly dormant in winter, will not tolerate wet feet, nor direct sunlight. Two excellent palms for the house are *Howea belmoreana* and *H. forsteriana*.

PLANTS THAT GROW IN WATER. We are not concerned here with the true aquatics (see AQUARIUM) but with those vines, bulbs and plants which will live and thrive in water. English ivy, once established, requires practically no care and will climb stucco walls or trail from a mantle with beautiful effects. Nasturtiums, cut before frost, will bloom indoors all winter if fertilizer is added to the water each week. Paper-white narcissus, Chinese sacred lily, Dutch and Roman hyacinths, and the Chinese evergreen (*Aglaonema modestum*) are all easily grown in water; add a little charcoal to sweeten.

DECORATIVE CENTERPIECES. Tiny, decorative scenes make ideal centerpieces, and in late years it is becoming the custom to give many of them as gifts. Tiny maidenhair ferns, placed on a pebble-filled tray or saucer, are exquisite; the holly ferns, crested and plain, do well in fern dishes if not overwatered. An inexpensive centerpiece is made by placing the upper section of two or three carrots in a dish of pebbles; fill with water and set in a light place. In a remarkably short time new green shoots will be replacing the old foliage with dainty, feathery sprays. Desert gardens composed of succulents are always attractive. They may be bought at the florists' or home-made. Young sedums, immature cactus specimens and the hen-and-chickens, placed attractively among rocks on a tray filled with sand make a good combination. The variations are apparently limitless. — C. H. M.

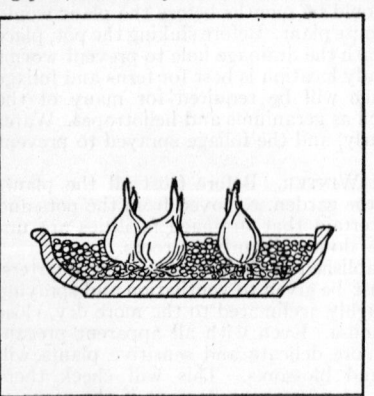

Cross-section of a gravel-filled dish and bulbs for forcing in the house. The line shows the level at which water should be kept.

**HOUSTONIA** (hoos-tō′nĭ-a). Spring-flowering, delicate, and beautiful North American wild flowers of the family Rubiaceae, only two of the 25 known species of much hort. interest. The cult. species are low, perennial herbs, usually tufted or growing in large patches with chiefly basal leaves but a few opposite* on the delicate stems, without marginal teeth. Flowers solitary, blue or white (in ours), the corolla regular, more or less funnel-shaped and small. Stamens 4. Fruit a capsule* which opens near the top. (Named for a Doctor William Houston, a botanical collector in Mex. and the W.I.)

Both the plants below are suited only to moist places in the wild garden. Few plants like to have their roots in cool water as much as these. They grow naturally on flat, wet rocks or in moist, grassy meadows. Easily propagated by division of the clumps which may also be dug from the wild.

**coerulea.** Bluets; also called Quaker ladies and innocence. Not over 7 in. high, usually about 5 in. Leaves scarcely ½ in. long, oblongish. Flowers usually pale blue, rarely violet or white, with a yellow eye,* solitary at the end of a slender stalk, not over ½ in. wide. Eastern N.A.

---

* Special articles on the subjects indicated by an asterisk (*) will be found at the words so marked.

**serpyllifolia.** Star violet. A perennial, the stems mostly creeping. Leaves nearly round, about ½ in. in diameter. Flowers deep blue, about ½ in. wide, the flowering stems usually about 8–10 in. high. In mountain meadows and along stream banks, Pa. to Ga. and Tenn.

**HOVENIA** (ho-veen'i-a). A single species of Chinese tree of the family Rhamnaceae, somewhat grown for its handsome foliage, although the Japanese, who grow it for the purpose, consider the fleshy fruiting stalks as edible. The only species is **H. dulcis,** the Japanese raisin tree, which grows about 25 ft. high and has alternate,* long-stalked, broadly oval leaves, 4–9 in. long, and 3-veined at the base. Flowers small, greenish, in cymes* that are terminal, or in the leaf-axils.* Fruit 3-celled, but drupe*-like, its stalks reddish, thick, and twisted at maturity. July–Sept. Hardy from zone* 3 southward, and prefers a sandy loam. Propagated by seeds or by root cuttings. (Named for David Hoven, a Senator at Amsterdam.)

**HOW?** Garden questions are as innumerable as the subjects of them. How to do this or that, or how large is an acre, or how do I increase the fertility or acidity of soil, or how do I prune roses — there is no end to such questions. The answer to all of them will be found in its proper place in THE GARDEN DICTIONARY, usually under such words as soil, pruning, etc., or the name of the plant involved.

If, in spite of looking at what seems the obvious entry, your query still remains unanswered, *see* GARDEN QUESTIONS, or the classified list of garden topics in the INTRODUCTION.

**HOWEA** (how'ee-a). Two feather palms, perhaps the most widely grown of all palms by florists, as they are better suited for decoration and house plants than almost any other (but *see* CHRYSALIDOCARPUS). Generally known as *Kentia*, the only two species of the genus are graceful, unarmed, ringed palms of medium height, crowned with a beautiful cluster of deep green, rather tough, gracefully curving leaves, made up of many slender, drooping leaflets or segments, their tips long-pointed but split at the extremity into two hanging ends. Flowers (never produced on small pot plants) from among the lowest leaves, the cluster with a long, usually unbranched, pitted stalk, within each pit 3 flowers, the central one female and the other two males. Stamens 30–100. Fruit more or less olive-shaped, but larger (pecan-sized), 1-seeded. (Named for Lord Howe's Island, east of Australia, where both species are native.)

The outdoor culture of these palms is nothing like so important as the use of them by florists. While grown in Fla. and Calif., many other palms are much more thought of than these kentias. As greenhouse subjects they range in size from small plants in 5-in. pots to large, tubbed specimens 20–30 ft. high. The dimensions given below are for full-sized mature plants which are rare in the U.S. For their culture *see* PALMS.

**belmoreana.** Curly palm. A tree not over 40 ft. high. Leaves about 7 ft. long, plumy, the many segments about 1 in. wide, abruptly rising from the main leafstalk, but ultimately hanging very gracefully at the tip, the whole leaf thus not flattish.

**forsteriana.** Flat palm. A tree up to 60 ft. Leaves about 10 ft. long, not so plumy as the last, the many segments about 1 in. wide, standing out horizontally from the main leafstalk, ultimately drooping more than in the last, but the leaf generally flattish.

**HOYA** (hoy'ya). A large genus of rather brittle, somewhat fleshy, tropical vines of the milkweed family, native from Asia to Australia, **H. carnosa,** the wax-plant, much grown in the greenhouse and outdoors in Fla. and Calif. *See* VINES. It is not hardy north of zone* 8. It is a vine 6–10 ft. high, climbing by many aerial* roots. Leaves opposite,* ovalish or oblong, short-stalked, very thick and fleshy, without marginal teeth, 2–4 in. long. Flowers white, pink-eyed, waxy and fragrant, about ½ in. wide, in small, nearly stalkless clusters in the leaf-axils.* Corolla wheel-shaped and within it is a crown of 5 fleshy scales. Stamens* united and covering the stigma* with their joined tips. Fruit a collection of smooth follicles.* Use potting mixture* 4 and grow in a warm (60°–70°), moist greenhouse, but reduce the heat and moisture during the dark winter months. (Named for Thomas Hoy, 18th-century gardener to the Duke of Northumberland.)

**HUAMUCHIL** = guamachil. *See* PITHECOLOBIUM DULCE.

**HUBAM CLOVER** = *Melilotus alba annua.*

**HUBBARD SQUASH.** A smooth-skinned, winter squash. For culture *see* SQUASH.

**HUCKLEBERRY.** Fruit-bearing, or ornamental evergreen, North American shrubs comprising the genus **Gaylussacia** (gay-loo-say'she-a) of the heath family, the fruiting ones commonly mistaken for the blueberry (which see), a far more valuable fruit. Leaves alternate,* usually without teeth, often resinous-dotted, evergreen in *G. brachycera*, but falling in all the rest. Flowers in small clusters (racemes*) mostly in the leaf-axils.* Corolla bell-shaped or urn-shaped, the 5 shallow lobes usually bent backward. Stamens 10. Fruit fleshy (a drupe*) with 10 seed-like nuts. While edible, it is not a true berry and lacks the fine flavor of the blueberry. (Named for J. L. Gay-Lussac, French chemist.)

The fruit-bearing species are scarcely worth cultivating, most of the fruit reaching the markets being collected from the wild. The exception is the nearly prostrate *G. brachycera*, an evergreen shrub with worthless fruit but valuable as a ground cover in shaded, peaty places. Except for the need for partial shade, the huckleberries need the same acid soil as the blueberry (which see).

**G. baccata.** Black huckleberry; also called high-bush huckleberry. A shrub not over 3 ft. high, the young growth sticky and resinous. Leaves oblongish, 1–3 in. long, yellowish-green above, resinous-dotted beneath. Flower clusters drooping, the corolla whitish-red, about ⅓ in. long. Fruit edible, black and shining, about ⅜ in. in diameter. Eastern N.A. May. Hardy from zone* 2 southward. Sometimes called *G. resinosa.*

**G. brachycera.** Box-huckleberry; also called juniper-berry. A nearly prostrate evergreen shrub, not over 18 in. high, the stems creeping but turning up at the tips. Leaves many, elliptic, ½–1½ in. long, smooth and not resinous-dotted. Flowers white or pink, about ¼ in. long. Fruit blue. In the mountains Pa. to Va. May. Hardy from zone* 3 southward.

**G. dumosa.** Bush huckleberry; also called gopher-berry. Not usually over 18 in. high, the twigs sticky-hairy. Leaves nearly stalkless, oblongish, 1½–2 in. long, resinous beneath. Flower cluster with several small leafy bracts.* Corolla white, pink, or red, about ⅜ in. long. Fruit insipid but edible, black. Newfoundland to Fla. and La., mostly in sandy bogs. May. Hardy from zone* 2 southward.

**G. frondosa.** Dangleberry (or tangleberry); also called blue huckleberry. A spreading shrub up to 6 ft. high, the twigs smooth. Leaves more or less elliptic, 1½–2½ in. long, green above, noticeably paler and hairy beneath. Corolla broadly bell-shaped, nearly ¼ in. long, greenish-purple. Fruit blue, with a bloom, nearly ½ in. in diameter, edible. N.H. to Fla. May. Hardy from zone* 3 southward.

**G. resinosa** = *Gaylussacia baccata.*

**HUCKLEBERRY FAMILY.** *See* ERICACEAE.

**HUERNIA** (hur'nee-a). A small genus of succulent, leafless herbs of the milkweed family, all African, only **H. penzigi** from the Nile region of any hort. interest. It somewhat resembles *Stapelia* and is a small succulent, scarcely 3 in. high, the stems angled and toothed, about ½ in. thick, the blunt teeth nearly ½ in. long. Flowers evil-smelling, blackish-purple, warty, about ¾ in. wide, mostly borne in small cymes* at the base of young shoots. The plant is suited to the desert gardens of southern Calif. or to the greenhouse. *See* SUCCULENTS. (Named for Justus Huernius, a collector of South African plants.)

**HUERNIOPSIS** (hur-nee-op'sis). A single species of South African succulent herbs of the milkweed family, **H. decipiens,** differing from *Huernia* in technical flower characters. It is a small, more or less prostrate, fleshy-stemmed, leafless plant, the stems club-shaped, not over 3 in. long, 4-angled and coarsely but bluntly toothed. Flowers evil-smelling, in clusters of 2–3, borne at the middle or toward the top of the stem, about 1 in. wide, yellowish-green, but streaked and spotted with purple on the outside, the inside brownish-red but yellow-spotted. Its outdoor cult. is confined to desert gardens in Calif., but it may be grown in the greenhouse elsewhere. *See* SUCCULENTS. (*Huerniopsis* means *Huernia*-like.)

**HUGO ROSE** = *Rosa hugonis.*

**HUISACHE** = *Acacia farnesiana.*

**HUISQUIL** = *Sechium edule.*

**HULL.** Loosely, the outer shell or covering of any fruit, often called its husk; specifically, the enlarged calyx* of the fruit of the strawberry.

* Special articles on the subjects indicated by an asterisk (*) will be found at the words so marked.

**HUMBLE PLANT** = *Mimosa pudica*.

**HUMEA** (hew'mee-a). Australian plants of the family Compositae, the only cult. species, **H. elegans,** often called amaranth-feathers from its mass of reddish disk flowers. It is a biennial herb 4–6 ft. high, the stems widely branching. Leaves oblongish, wrinkled, 7–10 in. long. Flowers of a cedar-like or strawberry-like fragrance, very numerous in long, feathery, drooping clusters (corymbs* or panicles*), the heads very small. Seed should be sown in the cool greenhouse in the late summer for next season's bloom. They should be grown, after the seedling stage, in potting mixture* 3 in flats or small pots and later transferred to 5-in. pots. Fill the pots nearly full of soil to prevent overwatering, which the plants will not stand, but they must not be allowed to dry out. As they approach flowering time they need plentiful applications of liquid manure. After warm weather has arrived, they may be put in the border or left as pot plants, as they make very decorative plants for porches or to set about a patio. (Named for Lady Hume.)

**HUMIDIGUIDE.** A trademarked, direct-reading hygrometer, useful for determining the relative humidity in a greenhouse.

**HUMIDITY.** The amount of moisture in the atmosphere, and of the greatest importance to plants. Except in the greenhouse (which see), and the living room (see HOUSE PLANTS), it is impossible to control humidity, which depends upon rainfall or proximity to a large body of water. See RAINFALL.

*HUMILIS, -e* (hew'mi-lis). Low-growing or dwarf.

**HUMMINGBIRD'S-TRUMPET** = *Zauschneria californica*.

**HUMOGRO.** A trademarked combination of humus* and commercial fertilizer with a 4-8-6 ratio (see FERTILIZERS).

**HUMULUS.** See HOP.

**HUMUS.** Humus is partly or thoroughly decomposed vegetable matter, but the simplicity of such a definition does not begin to state its importance to the gardener and the nation.

Perhaps no country, except China, has been so reckless in the destruction of such a priceless asset as our own. Forest fires have annually destroyed thousands of tons of rich woods soil, 80% of which is humus of the most valuable kind. In recent years the Forest Service has attempted to control these fires, well knowing that upon the maintenance of an adequate humus layer, the perpetuation of the forest depends. It is just as important to the gardener.

Ordinary mineral soil (the subsoil) is without any humus. Topsoil contains varying amounts of humus mixed with the mineral soil, while the humus layer under many forests may contain from 80–90% of vegetable matter. The implications of this to the gardener are important.

Moisture-holding capacity of soils. (A) A subsoil or inferior topsoil, holding 20% of water. (B) A fair garden topsoil, holding 60% of water. (C) Pure humus, which may hold several times its own weight of water. Black indicates the amount of humus in each sample.

Take some mineral soil, some topsoil, and some woods soil, or leaf mold as it is often called, and allow each to be dried (not burned) in an oven. When, by weighing, it is found that no more water can be driven out of any of them, weigh out exactly a pound of each of the oven-dry samples. Then allow each to soak up (by capillarity) as much water as it can, and weigh again. Under ordinary conditions, the mineral soil will absorb perhaps 20% of its own weight, the topsoil perhaps 60%, but the woods soil may easily, depending upon the sort of humus in it, absorb water from 300–500% of its weight.

Such a crude, simple experiment (the figures will vary much according to the soil type) demonstrates why humus is so important. Pure 100% humus is like a sponge for holding water, while mineral soils, except clay, give it off rather easily.

HUMUS IN THE GARDEN. Long before these fundamentals were understood, farmers plowed cover crops and vegetable refuse into the land. The humus so added enriches the soil far more than the chemical constituents of the plowed-under material might indicate, and this not only because the humus has raised the water-holding capacity of the soil. It does much more. For in the process of decay there is a whole series of microscopic organisms involved, which do things for the soil that nothing else will.

Ordinary garden topsoil contains a reasonable amount of humus, usually indicated by a darker color than the subsoil beneath it. If you use nothing but commercial fertilizers, some of which actually destroy humus, see to it that some cover crop is plowed in to overcome the deficiency (see GREEN MANURING), or else import humus and use it like manure.

COMMERCIAL HUMUS. Many firms today gather humus from different sources and sell it by the bag or carload for just this contingency. Some of them are baked, weed-free products of the greatest value. But in purchasing them one must be careful for what purpose they are wanted.

Thoroughly decomposed humus is usually black and is either neutral or only slightly acid (see ACID AND ALKALI SOILS). Such can be safely and most beneficially added to any ordinary garden soil. It is splendid too for potted plants in the house. Usually a layer about 1½ in. thick is enough and it should be worked into the existing soil. It is also good as a top-dressing for lawns. See LAWN.

If acid humus is needed, as it should be for rhododendrons, azaleas, many other plants of the heath family, and for a lot of places in the wild garden or bog garden, it is necessary to supply humus of a very different sort. Acid humus is usually not thoroughly decomposed and is apt to be brownish or tan in color. More important still, it should test to pH 4.5–5.5 (see ACID AND ALKALI SOILS). Dealers who know their business will be glad to meet these specifications. Several now produce acid humus baled up ready to use, and a very valuable grade is imported from Germany.

All of which shows that the intelligent gardener should not add "just humus" to his garden. Study the existing soil, the plants you wish to grow, and choose the sort of humus you need. Plowing in cover crops is the cheapest, but takes the most time. Manure always adds humus to the soil. The alternative is to supply commercial humus, according to one's needs. See also PEAT.

**HUNGARIAN BROME GRASS** = *Bromus inermis*.

**HUNGARIAN GRASS** = *Setaria italica nigrofructa*.

**HUNGARIAN LILAC** = *Syringa josikaea*. See LILAC.

**HUNNEMANNIA** (hun-nee-man'i-a). A single species of Mexican perennial herbs of the poppy family, generally known as Mexican tulip-poppy or golden cup, and to science as **H. fumariaefolia.** In the garden it is treated as a hardy annual (see ANNUALS), as it blooms the first year from seed. It is a showy herb 12–20 in. high, the leaves bluish-green and much dissected into blunt but narrow segments. Flowers 2–3 in. wide, yellow, but the many stamens orange and showy. Petals 4, sepals 2. Fruit a 2-valved capsule,* nearly ¼ in. long, splitting from the bottom upward. A popular flower garden annual, blooming from July 15 to Oct. and related to the California poppy. (Named for John Hunneman, English botanist.)

---
* Special articles on the subjects indicated by an asterisk (*) will be found at the words so marked.

**HUNNEWELL ARBORETUM.** See ARBORETUM.

**HUNTER'S ROBE** = *Scindapsus aureus*.

**HUNTINGDON ELM** = *Ulmus hollandica vegeta*. See ELM.

**HUNTSMAN'S-CUP** = *Sarracenia purpurea*. See PITCHER-PLANT.

**HUON PINE** = *Dacrydium franklini*.

*HUPEHENSIS, -e* (hoo-pay-en'sis). From Hupeh, China.

**HURA** (hew'ra). A genus of poisonous, milky-juiced, tropical American trees of the spurge family, **H. crepitans**, the sandbox tree, an interesting but horticulturally unimportant tree. It is spiny-trunked and reaches 80–100 ft. high and has alternate,* broadly ovalish, toothed leaves nearly 2 ft. long. Male and female flowers separate on the same tree, red, without petals, rather inconspicuous. Fruit a many-ribbed, woody capsule,* explosively splitting when ripe, sometimes with a loud report. It can only be grown in the warmest parts of southern Fla. (zone* 9), and prefers a light, sandy loam. (*Hura* is the South American name of the tree.) Its name of sandbox tree came from the sections of its fruit being used for the ink-drying sand that preceded modern blotters.

**HURSINGHAR** = *Nyctanthes arbor-tristis*.

**HUSK.** See HULL.

**HUSK TOMATO.** See PHYSALIS.

**HUTCHINSIA** (hut-chin'see-a). A small genus of Eurasian herbs of the mustard family, only **H. alpina** of any garden interest. It is a tiny, perennial, tufted herb, 1–4 in. high, suitable only to the rock garden (which see). Leaves mostly basal, ¾–1 in. long, divided into ovalish or oblong segments. Flowers very small, white, in a close raceme (see CRUCIFERAE for details). Fruit an ovalish or short-oblong pod (silicle*). (Named for a Miss Hutchins, an Irish student of flowerless plants.)

**HYACINTH.** See HYACINTHUS. For the grape-hyacinth see MUSCARI. See also SCILLA AMOENA, EICHHORNIA, and BRODIAEA LACTEA.

**HYACINTH BEAN** = *Dolichos lablab*.

**HYACINTH FAMILY** = Liliaceae.

*HYACINTHINA, -us, -um* (hy-a-sin-thy'na). Like a hyacinth.

**HYACINTHUS** (hy-a-sin'thus). A genus of perhaps 30 species of bulbous herbs of the lily family, chiefly from the Mediterranean region, and from tropical and South Africa. The chief hort. species is the common garden hyacinth, the other two below being more rarely grown. They have a deep, large bulb, narrow, basal, sometimes almost grass-like leaves without marginal teeth. Flowers fragrant in a showy, stiff, regular, terminal cluster (raceme*), each of the individual flowering stalks with a narrow bract* at the base. Corolla more or less bell-shaped, its 6 lobes or segments spreading or turned backwards. Stamens* 6. Fruit a 3-angled capsule.* (Named from the mythological character.) For Culture see below.

**amethystinus.** A slender, graceful, hardy, bulbous herb, 4–5 in. high, well suited for the rock garden, and providing a fine blue, early-flowering subject for the blue garden (which see). Its flowers are nodding, light blue, and bell-shaped. Spain.
**azureus.** Nearly 5 in. high, the leaves bluish-green and channeled. Flowers blue, in a dense, short cluster resembling the grape-hyacinth, but the lobes of the corolla not incurved. Mediterranean region. Sometimes offered as *Muscari azureum*. A good plant for the blue garden (which see).
**orientalis.** Common garden hyacinth. Flowering stalk up to 15 in., the leaves nearly 12 in. long and about ¾ in. wide. Flowers of many colors (see below) and sometimes double, blooming early in spring, always with a single cluster to each plant. Greece to Asia Minor. The var. **albulus,** mostly white (but see below), is the Roman hyacinth. It is a smaller plant, blooms earlier, and has several flower stalks to each plant, but these have fewer blooms and are not so stiff as the common hyacinth. It is not so hardy as the common sort.

### HYACINTH CULTURE

Garden hyacinths are all garden forms derived from *Hyacinthus orientalis*, and show what variation in color one may find within a single species. Although the bulb is reasonably hardy, it must be planted deeply (5–6 in.) and in good soil, rich in food. In the North a winter mulch, applied late in autumn, may be needed to protect the young shoots as they push through the soil. Given this care the plants are quite hardy and permanent.

As they come to market they are graded and sold as first and second sizes, which indicate not only the size of the bulb offered but also the size of the flower stalk that may be expected. Occasionally one may get an even larger size, sold as Exhibition size, which produces huge flower stalks. In color they range from white through lavender blues to deep blue-purple, through pale flesh-whites to crimson and reddish-purples, with a few yellows for good measure. King of the Blues, Oxford Blue and Grand Maître are porcelain blue; Queen of the Blues, darker; La Grandesse and L'Innocence, white; Orange Boven, pinkish-orange; Yellow Hammer, yellow; Roi des Belges, carmine; Gertrude, deep pink; Queen of Pinks, pure pink; General de Wet, palest pink; Moreno, rose-pink; and King of the Violets, violet-mauve.

Double-flowered forms of many of these can be had and are not as unattractive as might be thought, for the doubling adds a prim grace to the already formal flowers.

When planted in gardens, they should be used in clumps, not scattered singly or planted in lines and certainly never in the huge masses that once made livid blotches of color in our parks and filled the air too full with their delicious scent.

After their first flowering the bulbs usually send up several stalks of bloom each year with fewer flowers on each stalk and more graceful carriage. If these are admired, make no special effort to feed them and bring them back to their first size, but if only large spikes are wanted, feed generously and bring them back to their first size.

Hyacinths force well in pots, but must not be hurried until after their roots have filled the pots. They should be brought to the light later, and can often be kept on the floor or under the greenhouse bench, which will help to develop the flower stalk and prevent the opening of the flowers until the stalk is full size. They can also be grown in water, in hyacinth glasses, remembering the need for root development before the need of sunlight.

When it is hardy, the Roman hyacinth is useful, for it always gives many stalks with few bells. The variety commonly offered is white.

Through old southern gardens there are also other hyacinths that have the general appearance and behavior of Roman hyacinths, but are usually lavender or light purple, rarely pale pink. For a more informal planting these are invaluable, as they increase freely and yield annual displays of sweetly scented flowers. — B. Y. M.

DISEASES: Soft rot and yellow rot are the common diseases. *Soft rot*, a bacterial disease, is characterized by a malodorous rot of the basal part of the flower stalk and the upper portion of the bulb. For control, use clean soil, plant healthy bulbs, destroy affected plants and avoid overwatering. The typical symptoms of *yellow rot*, also caused by a bacterium, are yellow stripes in the foliage which later turn brown and die. Conspicuous rotted areas may also develop in the bulbs. Control is the same as for soft rot.

**HYBRID.** The offspring or progeny of a cross-fertilization between parents differing in one or more genes.* This definition makes hybrids much more common, and rightly so, than is generally appreciated. Hence the offspring of crosses between two individuals of the same variety or race (Shirley poppies), between different varieties, species and genera are hybrids. Hybrids may or may not breed true. Hybrids are often remarkably fertile; in other cases as remarkably sterile. Many, possibly the majority of our cultivated plants, have resulted either from artificial or natural hybridization. Striking results of artificial hybridization are found among roses (involving many species), gladioli, lilacs, and irises. For hybridization technique, see CROSSING. — O. E. W.

---

* Special articles on the subjects indicated by an asterisk (*) will be found at the words so marked.

*HYBRIDA, -us, -um* (hib'ri-da). Hybrid.

**HYBRIDIZING.** See CROSSING.

**HYBRID PERPETUAL ROSES.** See Group 4 at ROSE.

**HYBRID RUGOSA ROSES.** See Group 8 at ROSE.

**HYBRID TEA ROSES.** See Group 2 at ROSE.

**HYBRID VIGOR.** See HETEROSIS.

**HYDRANGEA** (hy-dran'jee-a). Important garden shrubs and woody vines of the family Saxifragaceae, many of the 35 species cult. for their showy flower clusters. Most of the garden sorts are Asiatic or North American, but the genus ranges to S.A. and Java. Leaves opposite,* stalked, usually toothed. Flowers small, prevailingly white, blue, or pink, arranged in dense, flat-topped or globe-shaped clusters, the outer flowers of the cluster often without stamens or pistils (sterile*) and with larger petals than the inner, fertile flowers. Petals usually 5, rarely 4. Stamens mostly 10, rarely 8-20. Fruit a 2-5-valved capsule* splitting at the top. (*Hydrangea* is from the Greek for water vessel, in allusion to the shape of the fruit.)

The common hydrangea (*H. paniculata grandiflora*) has been so much planted as to become tiresome to many. Its large masses of midsummer white bloom are very handsome, however, and its ease of growing and cheapness will make it popular long after the critics of it have turned to something else.

One of those below is a vine (*H. petiolaris*), little grown, but worth more attention by the gardener. A relative, also a vine, will be found at the genus *Schizophragma*.

Most of the others are shrubs, hardy as noted below, but the forms of *H. macrophylla*, widely called hortensia, demand notes on culture and uses. Originally a Japanese shrub, where it has been cult. for centuries and where there are many named varieties, it is now *the* hydrangea of the florists who force it in pots or tubs for spring bloom. While it will occasionally winter-kill in parts of zone* 4, it is perfectly hardy along the coast from N.Y. southward, and north of this if protected with straw or bagging. In the commonly cult. form it has huge globe-shaped clusters of blue or pink flowers, all of which are sterile. An occasional white-flowered form is found, and another with a flat-topped cluster in which only the marginal flowers are sterile. Pink-flowered, globe-shaped specimens may sometimes be changed to blue by putting bits of iron or alum in the soil.

The winter or early spring blooming of hortensia is from pot plants started from cuttings made the previous Feb. or March. Start them in shallow boxes or pans, over gentle bottom-heat,* and when rooted, plant them in small pots in potting mixture* 3. Plunge* the pots outdoors during the summer and re-pot as the plants increase in size. See that the plunged pots do not dry out and give them an occasional dose of liquid manure. By Sept. they are ready to be put in 8-in. pots, and after the first frost they should be brought into the cool greenhouse and kept there until Jan. Then increase the heat to 50°-60°, when they should be ready to flower by Easter. Just before flowering time, reduce the temperature again to harden them off, as forced plants may resent a sudden change to other conditions.

Large tubbed specimens of hortensia, widely used on porches and for accents along drives, should be left out until after the first frost has killed the leaves. Then move into a frost-free but cool pit, where they should be kept rather dry. In the spring re-pot them in fresh soil (potting mixture* 3) and put outdoors after hard frosts are passed. They need liberal watering and liquid manure during the growing season. The cult. species of *Hydrangea* are:

**arborescens.** Wild hydrangea; also called seven-bark. An upright but open, straggling shrub 3-5 ft. high. Leaves ovalish, more or less rounded or heart-shaped at the base, 3-6 in. long. Flowers white, the cluster 2½-5½ in. wide, flattish or a little rounded, all fertile except a few marginal, sterile flowers. N.Y. to Iowa and southward. June-July. Hardy from zone* 3 southward. The *var. grandiflora*, called hills-of-snow, has all the flowers sterile and in a ball-like cluster.

**bretschneideri.** A shrub 5-9 ft. high, the bark peeling and the twigs hairy. Leaves ovalish or elliptic, more or less wedge-shaped at the base, 3-5½ in. long. Flowers white, the cluster 4-7 in. wide, slightly arched, the sterile marginal flowers becoming purplish. China. July. Hardy from zone* 4 southward.

**hortensis; hortensia.** See HYDRANGEA MACROPHYLLA.

**macrophylla.** Hortensia, the common forcing hydrangea of the florists, and much grown in tubs. In the wild, a shrub up to 12 ft., less as usually grown. Leaves broadly oval, shortly tapering at the tip, 3-6 in. long, coarsely toothed, shining green above, lighter beneath. Flowers normally pink or blue (rarely white), all sterile in the form with globe-shaped clusters, only the marginal ones sterile in the form with flat-topped clusters. Jap. For hardiness and cult. see above. Sometimes known as *H. opuloides*. There are many varieties, of which the following are perhaps the best known:

*var. caerulea.* Flowers deep blue, or occasionally some marginal ones white.

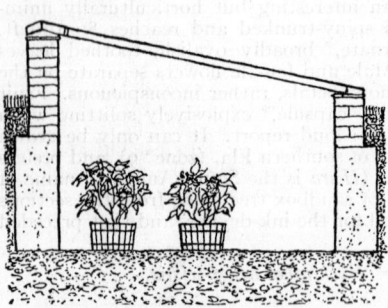

Wintering hortensia hydrangeas in a pit. Most growers do not put them in the pit until all the leaves have fallen.

*var. hortensia.* All flowers sterile, cluster globe-shaped, blue or pink. The most usual form in cult.

*var. mandshurica.* Stems dark purple or almost black. This form is sometimes catalogued as *H. opuloides cyanoclada*.

*var. otaksa.* A lower dwarf form.

*var. rosea.* A flat-clustered, pink-flowered form.

*var. veitchi.* Flowers a deep rose-pink.

**opuloides** = *Hydrangea macrophylla*.

**otaksa** = *Hydrangea macrophylla otaksa*.

**paniculata.** The commonest hardy hydrangea in cult., but almost universally grown in its *var. grandiflora*, which is commonly abbreviated to P.G. or even peegee. This form is a tree-like shrub 8-25 ft. high, the leaves elliptic or ovalish, rounded or wedge-shaped at the base, 3-5 in. long. Flower cluster 8-12 in. long, dense, white, later changing to pink and purple, long-persistent, nearly all the flowers sterile. Eastern As. Summer. Hardy from zone* 2 southward, possibly in zone* 1. It is better to prune the shrub a little each spring. It is still the best all-round, hardy hydrangea in cult.

**petiolaris.** Climbing hydrangea. A woody vine climbing by aerial rootlets up to 50-60 ft. Leaves broadly oval, more or less rounded or heart-shaped at the base, 2-4 in. long. Flower clusters loose, white, 6-12 in. wide, some of the marginal flowers sterile and thrice wider than the fertile ones. Eastern As. July-Aug. Hardy from zone* 3 southward. A fine vine for clinging to brick or masonry walls or to tree trunks. See VINES. Sometimes sold as *H. scandens* or *H. volubilis*.

**quercifolia.** A shrub not more than 6 ft. high, the twigs reddish and hairy. Leaves 3-7-lobed, almost oak-fashion, the lobes toothed, white-felty beneath. Flower cluster a panicle,* 4-10 in. wide, many of its flowers sterile, white and 2 in. wide. Later they turn purple. Ga. to Fla. and Miss. June. Hardy from zone* 5 southward, and perhaps in protected parts of zone* 4.

**scandens** = *Hydrangea petiolaris*.

**serrata.** Tea-of-heaven. A shrub 3-5 ft. high, the leaves elliptic or ovalish, 2-4 in. long, tapering at the tip, but wedge-shaped at the base. Flower cluster flat or slightly arched, 2-3½ in. wide, only a few of the flowers marginal and sterile, blue or white. Jap. and Korea. July-Aug. Hardy from zone* 4 southward.

**volubilis** = *Hydrangea petiolaris*.

**HYDRANGEACEAE.** See SAXIFRAGACEAE.

**HYDRANGEA FAMILY.** See SAXIFRAGACEAE.

*HYDRANGEOIDES* (hy-dran-jee-oy'deez, but see OÏDES). Like a hydrangea.

**HYDRASTIS.** See GOLDENSEAL.

**HYDRATED LIME.** See LIME.

**HYDRIASTELE** (hy-dre-ass'te-lee). A small genus of feather palms from Australia, only **H. wendlandiana** of hort. interest and its outdoor culture confined to extreme southern Fla. In cult. it is rarely more than 25 ft. high, with a terminal crown of leaves suggesting the common *Howea* of the florists. Leaves 4-5 ft. long, pale beneath, the leaflets or segments 20-30 in. long, about 2½ in. wide, more or less notched or toothed at the tip. Flower cluster much-branched, the flowers in threes, the middle one usually

*Special articles on the subjects indicated by an asterisk (*) will be found at the words so marked.

female. Stamens* 6. Fruit about ⅓ in. in diameter, reddish. In Fla. it does well on moist soils. It will stand no frost. (*Hydriastele* is from the Greek for water and column, the wild trees often found near springs.)

**HYDROCHARIS** (hy-drok'ar-is). Spongy-leaved, floating aquatic plants of the family Hydrocharitaceae, **H. morsus-ranae**, the frog's-bit, frequently grown in pools or aquaria. It is a Eurasian plant with very fine, thread-like and silky roots and floating stems with long-stalked, ovalish, spongy, thick leaves about 2 in. wide. Flowers minute, usually unisexual,* white. The plant dies outdoors over the winter, but may be propagated by cuttings of its runner-like stems, or by thickened winter buds which the plant produces in the fall. A graceful and interesting aquatic for the aquarium. (*Hydrocharis* is from the Greek for graceful water plant.)

**HYDROCHARITACEAE** (hy-dro-kăr-i-tay'see-ee). The frog's-bit family is wholly aquatic, all its cult. genera being submerged or floating water plants suited only to aquaria or pond culture. There are 14 genera and perhaps 85 species, found all over the world, some (non-hort.) in the sea.

In the four cult. genera the leaves are submerged and ribbon-like in *Vallisneria* (see EEL-GRASS), a popular aquarium plant, but scarcely ½ in. long in *Elodea*, where, however, they are very numerous. In *Hydrocharis* and *Stratiotes*, both floating aquatics, the leaves are thick and spongy.

Technical flower characters: The flowers are very small, inconspicuous and extremely simple. They have 3 minute sepals and 3 equally small petals, an inferior* ovary and 3–12 stamens. Fruit minute, nut-like.

**HYDROCLEIS** (hy'dro-cleez). Also spelled *Hydrocleys*. Brazilian, aquatic herbs of the family Butomaceae, one of the three known species cult. for the aquarium, for greenhouse pools, or outdoors south of zone* 7. The only cult. species is **H. nymphoides**, the water poppy, which is sometimes offered as *Limnocharis humboldti*. It has creeping stems which root in the mud and long-stalked, ovalish or narrower, floating leaves. Flowers on long stalks arising from joints of the stem, floating, about 2½ in. wide. Sepals 3, leathery and persistent. Petals 3, light yellow. Fruit a collection of 5–7 carpels which are not united. If grown in a tub, fill it about ⅔ full of potting mixture* 4 and plant the roots in it, covering them with a layer of sand about ½ in. thick. Fill the tub with water and put in a warm, sunny place. Only 2 or 3 roots are needed for each tub. Outdoor planting or that in a greenhouse pool may be directly in the mud, but not over 2½ ft. below the water surface, and preferably less. It will spread rapidly, but will stand no frost. (*Hydrocleis* is from the Greek for water and key, but the exact application here is unknown.)

**HYDROCYANIC GAS.** See FUMIGATION.

**HYDROGEN ION CONCENTRATION.** See ACID AND ALKALI SOILS.

**HYDROPHYLLACEAE** (hy-dro-fill-lay'see-ee). The waterleaf family comprises 18 genera and over 200 species of chiefly herbs, very abundant in N.A., but found widely elsewhere; all the cult. genera grown for ornament.

Leaves mostly opposite* (alternate in some nemophilas), often lobed or deeply cut. Flowers regular, but mostly in terminal or lateral, 1-sided clusters resembling a forget-me-not in aspect. They are showy in *Nemophila*, *Hydrophyllum*, *Phacelia*, *Nama* and *Emmenanthe*, all of which are herbs of outdoor culture. *Wigandia* is a tropical American, shrubby herb with small, tubular flowers, grown as a foliage plant, and *Romanzoffia* is a perennial herb from Calif. to Alaska with the habit of a saxifrage. The fruit of all genera is a 2-valved pod (capsule*).

Technical flower characters: Flowers hermaphrodite,* the united calyx 5-parted. Corolla regular,* mostly 5-lobed or 5-parted. Stamens chiefly 5, arising on the corolla and alternate with the lobes of it. Ovary superior,* mostly 1-celled. Styles 2.

**HYDROPHYLLUM** (hy-dro-fill'um). North American, mostly perennial herbs of the family Hydrophyllaceae, commonly called waterleaf, two of the six known species cult. in the wild garden. They have chiefly basal, divided or cut leaves, and terminal, 1-sided clusters (cymes*) of chiefly blue, lavender, or white flowers. Calyx* 5-parted, often with a small appendage between each lobe. Corolla more or less bell-shaped, but sharply 5-toothed or cleft. Stamens* (in ours) much-protruding. Fruit a 2-valved capsule,* its seeds globe-shaped. (*Hydrophyllum* is from the Greek for water and leaf, but of no known application here.)

These herbs are of simple culture if given a partly shaded place in the wild garden, preferably planted in rich woods soil. They can easily be increased by division, and they bloom in summer.

**canadense.** Waterleaf. Leaves with the segments arranged finger-fashion, the lobes 5–7, and more or less rounded, unequally toothed. Flowers white, the stalk of the cluster shorter than the leafstalks. The whole plant is about 18 in. high and nearly smooth. Eastern N.A.

**virginianum.** Waterleaf; also called Indian salad and Shawnee salad. A perennial herb about 18 in. high, the 5–7 leaf segments arranged feather-fashion, more or less oblongish, pointed, and sharply cut or toothed. Flowers white or violet-purple, the stalk of the cluster longer than the leafstalk. Eastern N.A.

**HYDROSME** (hy-dros'me). Tropical, very evil-smelling, rather fleshy herbs of the arum family, the few known species scattered in the East Indies, Africa, and Asia. Only one of them, **H. rivieri**, the snake palm (it is not a true palm) or devil's-tongue, is occasionally cult. in the tropical greenhouse under the name *Amorphophallus rivieri*. It is a rank-growing herb 3–4 ft. high. Leaves nearly 4 ft. high, the long, fleshy stalk spotted with brown and white. The leaf blade is divided, finger-fashion, into 3 main divisions, each of which is again divided into more or less triangular, irregularly cleft lobes. The leaves do not develop until the plant is through flowering. Flowers minute (see ARACEAE), crowded on a dense spadix,* which is set in the middle of a spathe* that suggests the calla lily, but dark red and carrion-scented, the whole inflorescence on a stout, fleshy stalk, 3–4 ft. high, dark-colored and red-spotted. The plant grows from a large, bulbous rootstock, and should be planted in potting mixture* 4 and given plenty of water. After it has flowered and leaved, it should be rested over the winter by reducing the water and lowering the temperature to about 50°. Re-pot and put in the tropical greenhouse about the end of March. Sometimes the pots may be plunged* outdoors in a shady place for the summer. (*Hydrosme* is from the Greek and apparently refers to its fondness for plenty of moisture.)

**HYDROSPEAR.** A patented implement used for applying water or liquid fertilizer to the roots of trees and shrubs, sold with directions for use.

*HYEMALIS, -e* (hy-e-may'lis). Relating to winter.

**HYGROMETER.** An instrument for measuring the humidity of the air. It is little used by gardeners, but foresters use it as a measure of the humidity of the forest floor conditions, which much affect the establishment of tree seedlings. The same factors also affect the growth of plants in the wild garden. Most ordinary garden plants are also affected by humidity, but less so than those of the forest.

**HYLOCEREUS** (hy-lo-seer'ee-us). Showy, tropical American, night-blooming cacti, mostly climbing and some tree-perching (epiphytic*), widely grown for their magnificent bloom, one of them commonly called night-blooming cereus (for others see SELENICEREUS and NYCTOCEREUS). They have long, 3-angled or 3-winged stems which bear aerial roots, but only a few, short, stout spines. Flowers large, white (in ours), the outside crowded with leaf-like scales, but without spines or wool as in some related genera. Fruit fleshy, edible in some species. (*Hylocereus* is probably from the Greek for matter, *i.e.* stuff-of or like, and *Cereus*, or *hylo* may refer to their woody stems.)

In Fla. these plants are very popular for covering low walls, or they will climb to a height of 25 ft. if given support. They are also used for hedges. Their immense, night-blooming flowers are among the showiest of the cacti, which *see* for culture in northern greenhouses. They root easily from cuttings of the stem, preferably with aerial* roots attached.

**tricostatus** = *Hylocereus undatus*.

**undatus.** The commonest of the plants known as night-blooming cereus, the stem high-climbing, its ribs or wings thin and wavy-margined. Flowers nearly 12 in. long, pure white, but the outer scales yellowish-

---

* Special articles on the subjects indicated by an asterisk (*) will be found at the words so marked.

green. Fruit oblongish, 4½ in. long, red, edible and often called strawberry pear or pitahaya. Tropical America.

**HYMENAEA** (hy-men-ee′a). Tropical American trees of the pea family, of little hort. interest, but one of them, **H. courbaril**, the West Indian locust, occasionally planted in zone* 9. It is a valuable tree in tropical America, yielding a copal or resin used in varnish, and grows about 60 ft. high, or less in cult. Leaves alternate,* compound,* the leaflets only 2, stalkless, very oblique, but generally oblongish, about 3 in. long. Flowers not pea-like, the sepals 4, the petals 5, not much longer than the sepals, about ¾ in. long, yellow, but purple-striped. Fruit an oblong, woody pod, 3-4 in. long, that does not split (see LEGUMINOSAE), filled with an acid pulp eaten by the Brazilian Indians. It is rare in cult. in the U.S. (*Hymenaea* is from the Greek for nuptial, in allusion to the paired leaflets.)

**HYMENOCALLIS.** See SPIDER-LILY.

*HYMENOSEPALA*, *-us*, *-um* (hy-men-o-see′pa-la). With membranous sepals.

**HYMENOSPORUM** (hy-men-o-spore′rum). A single species of Australian, evergreen shrubs or trees, family Pittosporaceae, **H. flavum** occasionally cult. for ornament in Calif., but unsuited to most sections of the country. It may reach 50 ft. in the wild, more often a shrub as cult. Leaves alternate,* without teeth, somewhat broader toward the tip, but generally ovalish, 4-6 in. long. Flowers yellow, nearly 1½ in. wide, more or less tubular and felty, and borne in a loose, terminal cluster (umbel*-like). Fruit a capsule about 1 in. long, its seeds winged. Its culture is the same as for the closely related genus *Pittosporum* (which see). (*Hymenosporum* is from the Greek for membrane and seed, in allusion to the winged seeds.)

**HYMENOXIS.** See BAERIA.

**HYOPHORBE** (hy-o-for′bee). Pignut palm. A small genus of feather palms from the Mascarene Islands, noteworthy because of their bulging trunks, hence their name of spindle palm or bottle palm. Two of them are sometimes planted outdoors in southern Fla. (zone* 9), but little known otherwise. They have handsome crowns of leaves, the many segments of which are set close together on the main leafstalk. Flowering cluster arising just below the crown of leaves, its many branches making a bushy cluster. Flowers small, 3-7 together, the lower 2 in each cluster female. Stamens 6. Fruit oblongish, purple, usually less than 1 in. long (a drupe*). (*Hyophorbe* is from the Greek for food for swine, in allusion to the fleshy fruits.)

As grown in Fla., both the species below make a reasonably rapid growth and thrive in both shade and sunshine on a variety of soils.

**amaricaulis.** Bottle palm; also called bitter-stem palm. Not usually over 40 ft. (higher in the wild), the trunk swelling near the base of the plant. Leaves 4-7 ft. long, the stalk about 1 ft. long, the segments or leaflets about 18 in. long, strongly veined.

**verschaffelti.** Spindle palm. As cult. usually 25-30 ft. high, the trunk swelling near the middle or toward the top of the trunk. Leaves 3-6 ft. long, the segments or leaflets about 2 ft. long, only the midrib prominent.

**HYOSCYAMUS** (hy-o-sy′ă-mus). Very poisonous (or medicinal), coarse and clammy herbs of the potato family from the Mediterranean region, **H. niger**, the henbane, and most dangerous of them, occasionally cult. It is a biennial or annual herb 18-30 in. high, with spindle-shaped roots. Leaves alternate,* oblongish, 5-7 in. long, more or less cut or toothed, and narrowed at the base into a clasping stalk. Flowers funnel-shaped, greenish-yellow, but black-veined, nearly stalkless in the leaf-axils,* or the upper ones in a small, leafy cluster. Fruit a capsule, enclosed by the persistent and much-enlarged calyx.* The plant is somewhat weedy, easily grown in almost any soil, and is occasionally naturalized in eastern N.A. (*Hyoscyamus* is from the Greek for hog and bean, in reference to its assumed poisoning of hogs.) See POISONOUS PLANTS.

**HYPANTHIUM.** See RECEPTACLE.

**HYPERICACEAE** (hy-perry-kay′see-ee). The St. John's-wort family, as here restricted, comprises only three genera, two of which, *Hypericum* and *Ascyrum*, are shrubby herbs, some of which are handsome garden plants of outdoor culture. By some the family is included within the Guttiferae (which see), but that family is here considered as including only tropical shrubs and trees with mostly edible fruit.

Plants of the Hypericaceae have opposite, mostly stalkless leaves, usually prominently spotted with resinous dots. They have regular flowers, mostly yellow or white (rarely pink), sometimes solitary, but typically in branched clusters (cymes*). In the only two cult. genera the sepals and petals are 4 in *Ascyrum*, but 5 in *Hypericum* (see ST. JOHN'S-WORT). Fruit a dry, many-seeded pod (capsule*).

Technical flower characters: Sepals 4 or 5 (see above). Petals 4 or 5. Stamens numerous, often in 3 or 5 distinct clusters. Ovary superior,* its styles 2-5.

*HYPERICIFOLIA*, *-us*, *-um* (hy-perry-si-fō′li-a). With leaves like a St. John's-wort (*Hypericum*).

*HYPERICOIDES* (hy-perry-koy′deez, but see OÏDES). Like a St. John's-wort (*Hypericum*).

**HYPERICUM.** See ST. JOHN'S-WORT (at Saint).

**HYPOCHAERIS** (hy-po-keer′is). Weedy, somewhat dandelion-like, chiefly Old World herbs of the family Compositae, one of the cult. species sometimes grown for ornament, the other a weed. They have mostly basal, cut or toothed, dandelion-like leaves and solitary or few heads of yellow flowers, all of which have only ray* flowers. Fruit a small, 10-ribbed achene,* plumed. (*Hypochaeris* is an old name of uncertain application here.)

There is no trouble about growing either of those below, but the first is sometimes a troublesome weed.

**radicata.** Cat's-ear; also called California dandelion (not native there) and gosmore. A coarse perennial herb, the stems nearly 2 ft. high, the leaves deeply toothed or lobed. Flower heads solitary, about 2 in. wide, deep-yellow. Eu., but common as a weed in N.A. See list at WEEDS.

**uniflora.** A perennial herb 12-18 in. high, and hairy. Leaves oblongish or narrower. Flower heads mostly solitary, about 1 in. wide, yellow. European mountains. Rare in cult.

*HYPOCHONDRIACA*, *-us*, *-um* (hy-po-kon-dry′a-ka). Morbid.

*HYPOGAEA*, *-us*, *-um* (hy-po-jee′a). Underground, or developing underground, as in the peanut.

*HYPOGLOTTIS*, *-e* (hy-po-glot′tis). With a swollen tongue.

**HYPOXIS** (hy-pocks′is). A large, widely distributed, but chiefly tropical genus of grass-like, perennial herbs, family Amaryllidaceae, commonly called star-grass. The only cult. species is **H. hirsuta**, the yellow star-grass, more often called yellow-eyed grass, and formerly known under the name of *H. erecta*. Its grass-like, ribbed leaves are nearly 12 in. long and about ⅙ in. wide, arising from a stout rootstock. Flowers yellow, star-like, about ½ in. wide, only a few in a terminal cluster on a leafless stalk, the outside of the flower greenish. Of very easy culture in open, sandy soil. July. (*Hypoxis* is the Greek name for some plant with sourish leaves, but probably not this one.)

**HYSSOP.** See HYSSOPUS.

**HYSSOP FAMILY** = Labiatae.

*HYSSOPIFOLIA*, *-us*, *-um* (his-sop-i-fō′li-a). With hyssop-like leaves.

**HYSSOPUS** (his-soap′us). A single species of Eurasian under-shrubs of the mint family, widely grown for ornament and as an herb for flavoring. The only species is **H. officinalis**, the hyssop. It is somewhat woody, 12-18 in. high, the stems 4-sided. Leaves opposite,* oblong or narrower, 1-2 in. long, without teeth. Flowers irregular,* 2-lipped,* about ½ in. long, blue, in 1-sided, terminal spikes 3-5 in. long. Fruit a collection of 4, egg-shaped, somewhat 3-angled nutlets. For culture and uses see HERB GARDENING. The *var.* **albus** has white flowers; *var.* **ruber,** red flowers; and the *var.* **grandiflorus** has considerably larger flowers. (*Hyssopus* is a very old name for the hyssop, but whether the sacred hyssop of the Jews is this plant or not is uncertain.)

*HYSTRIX* (hiss′tricks). Bristly, like a porcupine. It is also a generic name of a bristly (non-hort.) grass.

---

* Special articles on the subjects indicated by an asterisk (*) will be found at the words so marked.

**IBERICA**, *-us, -um* (eye-beer'i-ka). From Spain or Portugal.

**IBERIDIFOLIA**, *-us, -um* (eye-ber-id-i-fō'li-a). With leaves like a candytuft.

**IBERIS.** See CANDYTUFT.

**IBIDIUM** = *Spiranthes*.

**IBOLIUM PRIVET** = *Ligustrum ibolium*. See PRIVET.

**IBOTA** (eye-bo'ta). Japanese name for the ibota privet (*Ligustrum obtusifolium*). See PRIVET.

**IBOZA** (eye-bō'za). A genus of African shrubs or herbs of the mint family, I. riparia, cult. for ornament outdoors in zones* 8 and 9, sometimes under the name of *Moschosma*. It is a stout herb, 3–5 ft. high, with square stems, and opposite,* aromatic, broadly ovalish leaves 1–2 in. long, coarsely toothed and also notched at the base. Male and female flowers on separate plants, both very small, cream-white, numerous, in erect, terminal clusters (panicles*) which stand above the foliage. Corolla only slightly irregular, its limb 4–5-lobed. Stamens* 4. The plants should be cut to the ground after blooming. If grown under glass, give them a cool greenhouse, where they should bloom in winter. Propagated by cuttings. (Iboza is a Latinized version of a Kafir name for these plants.)

**ICACO** (ĭ-kă'ko). The Spanish name of the coco-plum. See CHRYSOBALANUS.

**ICELAND BUCKWHEAT** = *Fagopyrum tataricum*. See BUCKWHEAT.

**ICELAND POPPY** = *Papaver nudicaule*. See POPPY.

**ICE-PLANT** = *Mesembryanthemum crystallinum*.

**IDAEA**, *-us, -um* (eye-dee'a). From Mt. Ida, Asia Minor.

**IDAHO.** The state lies in zones* 2 and 3.

SOILS. The soil types of Idaho are as varied as its topography and climate, and exert an important influence on the character of the horticulture practiced in different parts of the state. Some of the glacial and residual soils of the northern panhandle, varying from fertile, deep silt loams and clay loams, to sand and gravel, are exceedingly productive; while others, of a morainic character, are so low in organic matter and natural fertility that they are unsuitable for crop production. The aeolian or "wind-blown" soils of the Palouse country are usually deep and fertile, and, where erosion has not been excessive, produce high yields of cereals, peas, and potatoes. The desert soils of the irrigated valleys and plateaus of southern Idaho are typified by the productive soils of the Boise-Payette region and the Snake River valley. Here the soils, mostly aeolian in origin, are often deep and fertile but sometimes are deficient in organic matter and nitrogen. Small, scattered areas of high alkali concentration, or "slick spots," within this region are unproductive. On the whole, the irrigated soils of the southern parts of the state are well adapted to the production of fruits, vegetables and alfalfa.

CHIEF GARDENING CENTERS. The Snake River from Saint Anthony to Weiser describes the arc of a semicircle that passes through, or borders on, the principal fruit and vegetable areas of Idaho. Apples comprise the most important fruit crop, with an average annual production of slightly over 4,000,000 bushels, produced principally in an area embracing Weiser, Caldwell, and Boise, and in the Twin Falls-Burley region. The Italian prune, marketed largely as a fresh fruit, is the second most important fruit crop, with an annual production of from 500 to 3000 cars, grown principally within the apple districts just outlined. Sweet cherries are grown on a limited scale in these southern districts, while both cherries and apples are produced in commercial quantities on the plateaus overlooking Lewiston, where the Snake River leaves the state border to enter

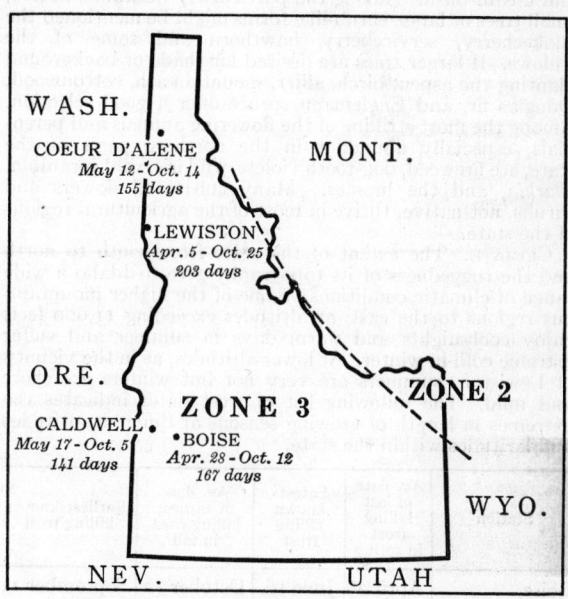

IDAHO

The zones of hardiness crossing Idaho are those shown on the colored map at ZONE, which should be consulted for details. The dates are the average latest killing frost in spring and the first one in the fall. The figures below the dates show the average length of the growing season. Annual rainfall near Salmon may not be over 10 in., while at Burke it is over 40 in.

Washington. Apples are now grown only to a limited extent under dry-land conditions in Latah and Kootenai counties, where, in earlier days, apples were a major crop. Peaches and pears are grown to a limited extent at Lewiston for local markets, and on bench lands in the Payette-Emmett region both for local markets and for a limited out-of-state trade. Strawberries, brambles, and American grapes are grown for home consumption in most parts of the state at altitudes of 6000 feet or less.

Head lettuce and onions are produced in abundance for distant and near-distant markets. The principal area for lettuce production centers in the Caldwell-Boise region, while onions are grown extensively both in that region and in the vicinities of Filer, Buhl, Twin Falls, and Rupert. A great variety of vegetables is grown for local markets in the fertile bottom lands or bench lands near Boise, Weiser, Caldwell, Twin Falls, Lewiston, Coeur d'Alene and other large towns and cities. Vegetable-seed production is coming to the fore as an important commercial industry, centering in Canyon County, near Caldwell. In general it might be stated that many kinds of vegetables and most of the temperate-zone fruits can be grown to perfection throughout extensive areas of southwestern Idaho.

In total income produced by Idaho farm products the potato ranks first. The region of greatest production extends along the banks and bench lands of the Snake River valley from near St. Anthony to the vicinity of Buhl. The higher altitudes of the northeastern end of this belt, together with isolated high-altitude districts in Lemhi and other eastern counties, supply large quantities of the best seed potatoes;

---

* Special articles on the subjects indicated by an asterisk (*) will be found at the words so marked.

while all of this belt, most of which is irrigated, yields heavy crops of market potatoes of excellent quality. Market potatoes are also grown commercially to some extent in all of the western counties of the northern panhandle.

BEST ORNAMENTAL PLANTS. With the exception of arid and semi-arid regions of the state, most parts of Idaho enjoy a wide variety of attractive native flowers, ornamental shrubs and trees. Outstanding among the ornamentals are the common wild rose (*Rosa nutkana*), mock-orange, snowberry, Oregon grape, red osier, golden currant, and cream bush. Among the particularly desirable, native, small trees or large, shrub-like forms might be mentioned the chokecherry, serviceberry, hawthorn and some of the willows. If larger trees are desired for shade or background planting the aspen, birch, alder, mountain ash, cottonwood, Douglas fir, and Englemann spruce offer a good selection. Among the most striking of the flowering annuals and perennials, especially abundant in the northern parts of the state, are fireweed, dog-tooth violets, wild iris, wild geranium, *Clarkia*, and the lupines. Many cultivated flowers and shrubs, not native, thrive in most of the agricultural regions of the state.

CLIMATE. The extent of the state from south to north and the ruggedness of its topography give to Idaho a wide range of climatic conditions. Some of the higher mountainous regions to the east, at altitudes exceeding 11,000 feet, enjoy cool nights and warm days in summer and suffer extreme cold in winter. At lower altitudes, as in the vicinity of Lewiston, summers are very hot but winters are short and mild. The following list of frost dates indicates the extremes in length of growing seasons at different altitudes and latitudes within the state.

| Station | Av. date of last killing frost in spring | Latest-known killing frost | Av. date of earliest killing frost in fall | Earliest-known killing frost |
|---|---|---|---|---|
| Boise | April 28 | June 16 | October 12 | September 11 |
| Caldwell | May 17 | June 9 | October 5 | September 14 |
| Lewiston | April 5 | April 29 | October 25 | October 5 |
| Coeur d'Alene | May 12 | June 12 | October 14 | August 31 |

Rainfall over much of the southern part of the state is deficient for crop production without irrigation. In many of the northern counties dry-land farming is practiced but only early-maturing crops are grown. Rainfall in the mountains is relatively high. Extremes between the arid and rainy regions are represented by Salmon with an annual rainfall of 9.6 inches, and Burke with an annual rainfall of 44.2 inches. Space does not permit discussion of seasonal distribution of rainfall, which varies so greatly among different locations that averages for the state have no meaning.

The address of the Agricultural Experiment Station, which has kindly supplied this information about Idaho, is Moscow, Idaho. The station is always ready to answer gardening questions.

IDAHO POTATO. *See* POTATO.

IDA-MAIA. *See* BREVOORTIA.

IGNEA, -us, -um (ig'nee-a). Colored like flame; fiery.

ILEX. *See* HOLLY. *See also Quercus ilex* at OAK.

ILICACEAE = Aquifoliaceae.

ILICIFOLIA, -us, -um (il-li-see-fō'li-a). With leaves like the holly (*Ilex*).

ILLECEBROSA, -us, -um (ill-le-see-brō'sa). Growing in the shade.

ILLICIUM (il-li'si-um). A genus of 20 species of shrubs and trees of the family Magnoliaceae, all of them natives of Asia, except two found in the southeastern U.S. They have aromatic, evergreen, alternate* leaves, usually short-stalked and without marginal teeth. Flowers yellowish or purplish-red, solitary or in few-flowered clusters in the leaf-axils.* Sepals (which soon fall away) 3–6. Petals 9 or more. Stamens numerous. Fruit a collection of woody, slowly splitting follicles,* sometimes star-like. (*Illicium* is Latin for something enticing, in allusion to their pleasant aroma.)

Neither of the plants below, both Asiatic, are hardy north of zone* 7, and in any case are little grown in the U.S. The native species, wild in Fla. and La., seem not to be in general cult. at all.

**anisatum.** A shrub or small tree, not over 12 ft. high. Leaves more or less elliptic, 2–3 in. long. Flowers about 1 in. wide, yellowish-green, the stalk bracted,* the petals many and narrow. Jap. Sometimes known as *I. religiosum*.

**religiosum** = *Illicium anisatum*.

**verum.** Star anise; also called Chinese anise. A shrub or small tree, usually 9 ft. high or less. Leaves elliptic or slightly broader at the tip. Flowers purplish-red, the petals about 10. Fruits making a star-shaped cluster (of follicles*), anise-scented, carminative, and generally known as badian. China. The plant is rare in cult. in the U.S.

ILLINOIS. The state is wholly in zones* 2, 3 and 4. The climate and soils are well adapted to the production of a wide range of horticultural plants, both from an amateur and a commercial standpoint.

SOILS. In characterizing the soils of Illinois one notes first the great profusion of varieties. No less than 214 distinguishable soil types have, to date, been identified by the State Soil Survey. These types represent all degrees of productiveness ranging from barren wastes to highly fertile land. Fortunately, the latter predominate.

Long-continued field experiments conducted in various parts of the state by the University of Illinois demonstrate the possibility of the economic improvement of most of the Illinois lands through proper practices of crop rotation and soil treatment.

The material most frequently required for soil improvement is limestone, in order to insure the successful growth of legumes. The legumes in turn provide the necessary nitrogen and organic matter for the soil.

Sufficient available phosphorus is frequently lacking and the application of some form of phosphate is often attended by profitable gains in crop yields. With the continuous removal of abundant crops from the soil, a growing need for available potassium is also becoming apparent.

The two outstanding problems connected with Illinois soils are, (1) the maintenance of fertility, and (2) the prevention of erosion.

CHIEF PRODUCTION CENTERS. Production of vegetables for local market is a well-developed industry in close proximity to each of the important cities of the state. Cook County, in which Chicago is located, is especially prominent in this type of production. Special vegetable crops for shipment to city markets are grown at several points in the state. The most prominent truck-growing region is in Union and adjacent counties in the southern end of the state. Here asparagus, tomatoes, cucumbers, string beans, spinach and sweet potatoes are especially important. Asparagus is also extensively grown in Madison, Ogle and La Salle counties. Watermelons thrive on the sandy soil along the Wabash, Illinois and Mississippi rivers, and muskmelons are grown to some extent in the same regions and also in certain other parts of the state. Sweet corn for canning is produced in large quantities in the central and northern parts of the state, as are peas.

Apples, peaches and pears are the principal tree fruits grown in Illinois. There are three well-defined commercial apple areas. In the extreme southern part of the state early apples predominate. In the area from Centralia to Olney, both fall and winter varieties are grown. In Calhoun and neighboring counties in the western part of the state, late varieties of apples predominate. Two distinct commercial peach regions are recognized. The southern region coincides with the region of early apple production. The more northerly region centers in Marion County, but includes several adjoining counties. The Elberta is the principal variety grown in both regions. Keiffer pears are produced extensively in Marion, Clay and Union counties.

Commercial grape production is most highly developed in Hancock and St. Clair counties. Strawberries are produced

* Special articles on the subjects indicated by an asterisk (*) will be found at the words so marked.

principally in Pulaski, Union, Fayette and Edgar counties. The red raspberry industry is especially developed in Pulaski County.

ORNAMENTAL PLANTS AND HOME GARDENS. The nursery business has been conspicuous in Illinois since an early date. Formerly fruit trees predominated, but more recently the production of ornamentals has been emphasized.

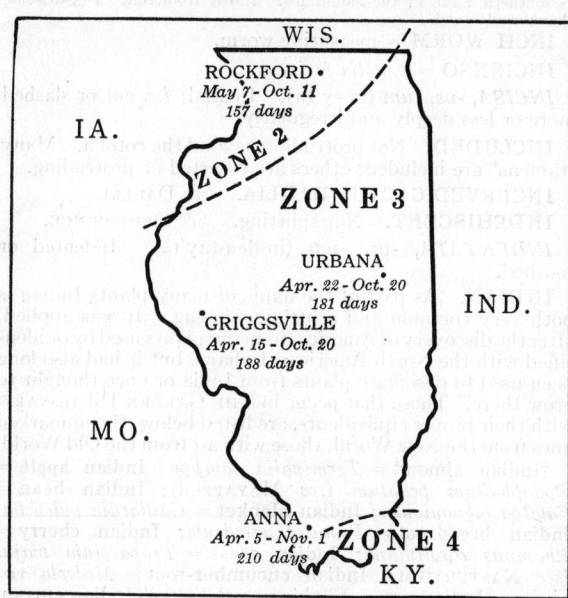

ILLINOIS

The zones of hardiness crossing Illinois are those shown on the colored map at ZONE, which should be consulted for details. The dates are the average latest killing frost in spring and the first one in the fall. The figures below the dates show the average length of the growing season. Rainfall is adequate.

The American elm is probably the most popular street tree in Illinois, and in the older towns many magnificent specimens are in evidence. The hard maple is also a favorite in some parts of the state. Shrubs and vines in wide variety enhance the beauty of the landscape in both public and private grounds. Flowering bulbs, herbaceous perennials and annual flowers thrive in great profusion wherever they are given proper care.

Home vegetable gardens are a source of pleasure and profit on Illinois farms and suburban places. The long-row farm garden, recommended by the College of Agriculture, University of Illinois, is especially well adapted to Illinois conditions.

CLIMATE. Since Illinois comprises an area nearly four hundred miles long, north and south, there is considerable difference in temperature and in the length of the growing season in different parts of the state. Frost data for four different locations are presented in the accompanying table.

DATES OF FROSTS IN FOUR ILLINOIS LOCALITIES

| Name of town | Average date of last killing frost in spring | Latest-known killing frost | Average date of earliest killing frost in fall | Earliest-known killing frost |
|---|---|---|---|---|
| Anna (Union County) | April 5 | May 1 | Nov. 1 | Sept. 30 |
| Griggsville (Pike County) | April 15 | May 7 | Oct. 20 | Sept. 22 |
| Urbana (Champaign County) | April 22 | May 25 | Oct. 20 | Sept. 14 |
| Rockford (Winnebago County) | May 7 | May 27 | Oct. 11 | Sept. 14 |

The mean annual temperature at Anna, in the southern part of the state, is 57.1° F., at Griggsville 53.9° F., at Urbana 51.5° F. and at Rockford 48.8° F. The average length of the growing season (that is, the period between the latest killing frost of spring and the earliest killing frost of fall) at Anna is 210 days, at Griggsville 188 days, at Urbana 181 days, and at Rockford 157 days.

The average annual rainfall is considerably greater in the southern than in the northern part of the state, being 46.67 inches at Anna and 33.51 inches at Rockford. However, a larger percentage of the total precipitation occurs during the period from April to September inclusive in the northern part of the state, being 62 per cent at Rockford, as compared with 55 per cent at Anna. Thus the average precipitation during the growing season is 20.97 inches at Rockford and 25.79 inches at Anna.

RAINFALL IN CERTAIN ILLINOIS LOCALITIES

|  | Total annual ||| April to Sept. incl. |||
|---|---|---|---|---|---|---|
|  | Ave. | High | Low | Ave. | High | Low |
| Anna | 46.67 | 64.93 | 32.75 | 25.79 | 35.63 | 13.14 |
| Griggsville | 37.07 | 57.36 | 24.09 | 23.59 | 45.92 | 12.08 |
| Urbana | 35.34 | 55.93 | 23.47 | 21.00 | 35.30 | 9.88 |
| Rockford | 33.51 | 43.30 | 22.87 | 20.97 | 30.17 | 13.41 |

The address of the Illinois Agricultural Experiment Station, which has kindly supplied this information about the state, is Urbana, Illinois. The station is always ready to answer gardening questions.

Garden Club activities in Illinois are extensive. There are several clubs of the Garden Club of America, the home office of which is 598 Madison Avenue, New York. The Garden Club of Illinois, Inc., also has over 120 chapters. For the address of your nearest one write to the Garden Editor, Houghton Mifflin Company, Boston, Mass. See also HORTICULTURAL SOCIETIES.

**ILLUMINATION.** See LIGHTING.

***ILLUSTRIS, -e*** (il-lus′tris). Brilliant or lustrous.

***ILVENSIS, -e*** (il-ven′sis). Described first as from the Island of Elba. Applied to *Woodsia ilvensis* (which see), now known to be a widely distributed fern.

***IMBRICARIA, -us, -um*** (im-bri-cay′ri-a). Imbricate.

***IMBRICATA, -us, -um*** (im-bri-kay′ta). Imbricate; *i.e.* overlapping as though shingled.

**IMMORTELLE.** An everlasting (which see); specifically often applied to *Xeranthemum annuum*.

**IMPATIENS** (im-pay′ti-enz). A genus belonging to the balsam family, represented by species widely distributed, found in As., tropical Afr. and N.A. They are tender, succulent annuals and perennials with irregular,* spurred* flowers which may be solitary or clustered in the axils* of the leaves. The fruit, a pod, will burst easily, often scattering the seeds, the plants deriving therefrom the names — touch-me-not, snapweed. (*Impatiens* is from the Latin for impatience, in allusion to the bursting of the pods.)

They are easily started from seeds. The species grown as house plants, or for bedding, are also propagated by cuttings, especially when varieties with striking colors have been developed, in order to assure their coming true.

**balsamina.** Tender annual, 24–30 in. tall, stiff and erect. Stem brittle and succulent, leaves smooth, lanceolate. Flowers of cultivated varieties of this species called lady's-slipper or garden balsam, come in brilliant colors, some very double or "camellia-flowered," in salmon-pink, old rose, scarlet, yellow, purple, white, the flowers being borne close to the stem. Seeds are started indoors or in frames in April, for planting out after the middle of May, in zones* 1 to 4, or are sown in the open in May. They succeed best in a good, rich soil, spacing the plants 18 in. apart for full development of the individual plant. Sub-tropical India and China.

**holsti.** Tender, fleshy sub-shrub to 3 ft. tall, the leaves ovate, about 3 in. long. Flowers scarlet, over 1 in. across, flat, with slender spur 1½ in. long. Tropical Af. Used as a pot plant indoors or for the garden during the summer. It is a more vigorous grower than *I. sultani*.

**roylei.** Annual, 4–5 ft. tall, very erect. Flowers purple, with short spur. Aug.–Sept. As.

* Special articles on the subjects indicated by an asterisk (*) will be found at the words so marked.

**sultani.** A native of Zanzibar, eastern Af., and therefore easily touched by frost and treated as a tender bedding plant in the garden. It is brittle, succulent, and 1–2 ft. high. Leaves smooth, alternate,* the upper ones sometimes whorled.* Flowers solitary or 2–3 on a short, slender stalk, 1–1½ in. across, with thin, long spur curving up. Bright scarlet in the original form, hybrids and sports in shades of pink, salmon, purple, white.

Jewelweed and snapweed are the names applied to N.A. species *I. biflora* and *I. pallida*, which are scarcely garden plants.

**IMPERATI** (im-per-ray'ti). Showy; imperial.

**IMPERFECT FLOWER.** One having stamens* or pistils,* but not both. See PERFECT.

**IMPERIALIS, -e** (im-peer-i-ā'lis). Fine or showy; imperial.

**IMPERIAL JAPANESE MORNING-GLORY.** See IPOMOEA NIL.

**IMPLEMENTS.** See TOOLS AND IMPLEMENTS.

**IMPREGNATION.** See FERTILIZATION.

**INARCHING.** See GRAFTING.

**INBREEDING.** When a plant is selfed,* and its progeny selfed, and so on for several generations, the procedure is called inbreeding, and the results are inbred plants or strains of plants. This example illustrates the most intense type of inbreeding. Where selfing is not possible or practicable, brother-sister crossing may be practiced, involving two closely related plants. Inbreeding is a matter of degree. Close inbreeding in many plants, especially normally cross-fertilized plants such as maize, often results in decreased vigor, size and yield, though this is not necessarily so. Actually, inbreeding tends to sort out pure breeding types, so that in a comparatively few generations the inbred lines cease to show any effect from inbreeding — the sorting process has stopped because everything is sorted. These sorted-out types may be good, poor or indifferent. Many of our very valuable plant varieties have resulted from crossing and subsequent inbreeding. — O. E. W.

**INCANA, -us, -um** (in-kay'na). Whitish or grayish-white.

**INCARNATA, -us, -um** (in-kar-nay'ta). Flesh-colored.

**INCARVILLEA** (in-kar-vil'lee-a). Tender herbaceous perennials belonging to the family Bignoniaceae. Leaves alternate,* 2–3-pinnate,* segments narrow. Flowers trumpet-shaped, five-lobed, spreading, somewhat irregular,* in terminal clusters, red to yellow. Species native of Tibet and China. Fruit a capsule. (Named for Father Incarville, French Jesuit in China.)

They should be given a sheltered position, in a sunny and warm spot in the garden. A well-drained soil, preferably sandy, enriched with humus, is best suited for their culture. They require special winter protection and are not hardy from zone* 3 northward.

**delavayi.** Semi-hardy perennial with graceful, pinnate leaves to 1 ft. long, each leaf with as many as 15–21 segments. Flower stalk to 2 ft. tall, rising above the foliage, bearing from 2 to 12 large, trumpet-shaped flowers, rosy-purple, the individual flower 1 to 2 in. long and as wide. Tube yellow inside and outside, the 2 upper lobes somewhat smaller than the 3 lower ones. Also called hardy gloxinia. Propagated by seeds and by division. Native of China.

**delavayi grandiflora** = *Incarvillea grandiflora.*

**grandiflora.** Similar to *I. delavayi*, but not as robust in growth. Leaflets shorter, the flowers fewer, but larger and with deeper trumpets. Deep rosy-red. The *var.* **brevipes** has brilliant crimson flowers.

**INCENSE CEDAR.** The incense cedars belong to the genus Libocedrus (lee-bo-see'drus), a small group in the pine family. They are handsome evergreen trees of pyramidal or spreading habit and with small, scale-like leaves on flattened branches; quite suggestive of arborvitae. Cones oblong, with 4–6 woody scales. (*Libocedrus* is from the Greek for drop, and cedar, referring to the oozing resin.)

Only one species can be grown outdoors in the North. Where hardy they are splendid ornamental trees, and in their native countries are widely used for their durable timber. A rather open, well-drained situation seems to be preferred. Propagation is mainly by seeds sown in the spring. See EVERGREENS.

**L. chilensis.** Alerce. Chilean arborvitae. A compact, pyramidal tree attaining 60 ft. Leaves small and spreading, glaucous, with a white line beneath; branchlets flattened. Cone oval, about ½ in. long. Chile. Hardy only in zones* 8 and 9.

**L. decurrens.** Incense cedar. White cedar. Columnar or narrow pyramidal tree growing 50–100 ft. high, occasionally higher. Bark red-brown, loose or scaly. Leaves small, scale-like, opposite, pressed close to the stem except at tip, dark glossy-green. Branches upright, flattened vertically. Cones ¾–1 in. long, oval or oblong. Ore. and western Nev. to southern Calif. in the mountains. Hardy from zone* 4 (3 in some places) southward.

**INCH WORM** = measuring worm.

**INCIENSO** = *Encelia farinosa.*

**INCISA, -us, -um** (in-sy'za). Incised; *i.e.* cut or slashed more or less deeply and irregularly.

**INCLUDED.** Not protruding beyond the corolla. Many stamens* are included; others are exserted or protruding.

**INCURVED CACTUS DAHLIA.** See DAHLIA.

**INDEHISCENT.** Not splitting. See DEHISCENCE.

**INDENTATA, -us, -um** (in-den-tay'ta). Indented or toothed.

**INDIAN.** As part of the name of many plants Indian is both very common and a little confusing. It was applied, after the discovery of America, to many plants used by or identified with the North American Indians, but it had also long been used to designate plants from India or once thought to grow there. Those that occur in THE GARDEN DICTIONARY, with their proper equivalents, are listed below, the unmarked ones from the New World, those with a † from the Old World.

†Indian almond = *Terminalia catappa;* Indian apple = *Podophyllum peltatum* (see MAYAPPLE); Indian bean = *Catalpa bignonioides;* Indian blanket = *Gaillardia pulchella;* Indian breadroot = *Psoralea esculenta;* Indian cherry = *Rhamnus caroliniana;* Indian cress = *Tropaeolum majus* (see NASTURTIUM); Indian cucumber-root = *Medeola virginiana;* Indian cup = *Silphium perfoliatum;* Indian currant = *Symphoricarpos orbiculatus;* Indian dye = *Hydrastis canadensis* (see GOLDENSEAL); Indian fig = *Opuntia ficus-indica;* †Indian hawthorn = *Raphiolepis indica;* Indian hemp = *Apocynum cannabinum;* Indian hippo = *Gillenia trifoliata;* †Indian jujube = *Zizyphus mauritiana;* Indian lettuce = *Pyrola americana* and *Montia perfoliata;* †Indian licorice = *Abrus precatorius;* †Indian millet = *Pennisetum glaucum;* †Indian mulberry = *Morinda citrifolia;* Indian paint = *Sanguinaria canadensis* (see BLOODROOT); Indian paint-brush = *Castilleja californica* and *C. parviflora;* Indian physic (see GILLENIA); †Indian pink = *Dianthus chinensis;* Indian pink = *Silene virginica;* Indian pitcher = *Sarracenia purpurea* (see PITCHER-PLANT); Indian poke = *Veratrum viride;* Indian plum family = Flacourtiaceae; Indian rice = *Zizania aquatica;* Indian sage = *Eupatorium perfoliatum;* Indian salad = *Hydrophyllum virginianum;* Indian sanicle = *Eupatorium urticaefolium;* Indian shot (see CANNA); †Indian strawberry = *Duchesnea indica;* Indian tea = *Ceanothus americanus;* †Indian tree cotton = *Gossypium arboreum;* †Indian trumpet-flower = *Oroxylon indicum;* Indian turnip = *Arisaema triphyllum.* See also PSORALEA.

**INDIANA.** The state lies wholly in zone* 3.

The soils of Indiana are divided into about five principal soil types, so far as fruits and vegetables are concerned. In northern Indiana are found several hundred thousand acres of muck soils. This same area contains a considerable quantity of sandy loam. South of this area is one of black prairie soil. In southwestern Indiana there is a sandy region in the valley of the lower Wabash and White rivers. A major portion of southern Indiana is made up of unglaciated clay soils. Southeastern Indiana contains a flat, poorly drained, whitish clay area.

The chief gardening centers are about the large cities, such as Indianapolis, Terre Haute, Fort Wayne, Evansville, South Bend, and Muncie.

The fruit sections include an apple and peach area in Knox County, near Vincennes, Indiana, and the lower Wabash Valley to Evansville. Other apple and peach areas are located near Salem, Indianapolis, and in the Lake Michigan territory, near South Bend and Elkhart. Small fruits are

---

* Special articles on the subjects indicated by an asterisk (*) will be found at the words so marked.

# Indiana

grown commercially near New Albany, just across the Ohio River from Louisville, Kentucky.

The muck soils of northern Indiana are producing several thousand cars of onions, a considerable quantity of potatoes, and a very high percentage of the peppermint of the United States. On the sandy soils of southwestern Indiana large

### INDIANA

The zones of hardiness crossing Indiana are those shown on the colored map at ZONE, which should be consulted for details. The dates are the average latest killing frost in spring and the first one in the fall. The figures below the dates show the average length of the growing season.

areas are devoted to melons, sweet potatoes, and early tomatoes. In a similar sandy soil in Jackson County, south of Indianapolis, we find the same crops being grown. A commercial potato acreage is distributed along the Ohio River, and tomatoes are produced for canning factories, mostly on central black soils and southern clay soils.

A wide range of flowers may be cultivated in Indiana. Many ornamental trees and shrubs will grow readily under Indiana conditions, including:

| TREES | SHRUBS |
|---|---|
| Oak | Viburnum |
| Hickory | Cercis canadensis |
| Maple | Cornus florida |
| Beech | Cornus stolonifera |
| Gum | Ostrya virginiana |
| Elm | Carpinus caroliniana |
| Sycamore | Philadelphus (see MOCK-ORANGE) |
| Tulip-tree | |

### FROST DATA

| Town | Average date of last killing frost in spring | Latest known killing frost | Average date of earliest killing frost in fall | Earliest known killing frost |
|---|---|---|---|---|
| South Bend | May 6 | May 28 | October 11 | September 20 |
| Indianapolis | April 16 | May 4 | October 19 | September 30 |
| Evansville | April 4 | April 21 | October 27 | September 30 |

The average annual rainfall for Indiana is 45.78 inches. Small areas along the Ohio River average more than 50 inches, with some sections in the north and northwestern parts of the state averaging less than 35 inches. The temperature lines cross the state from the northwest to the southeast.

The address of the Agricultural Experiment Station, which has kindly supplied this information about the state, is Purdue University Agricultural Experiment Station, West Lafayette, Indiana. The Station is always ready to answer gardening questions.

Garden Club activities in the state include over 30 branches of the Indiana Federation of Garden Clubs. For the one nearest to you write the Garden Editor, Houghton Mifflin Company, Boston, Mass. *See also* HORTICULTURAL SOCIETIES.

**INDIA WHEAT** = *Fagopyrum tataricum*. See BUCKWHEAT.

**INDICA, -us, -um** (in'di-ka). From India, but many plants described as from India were subsequently found in widely scattered regions, once generally called "the Indies."

**INDICA AZALEA.** See Culture at AZALEA.

**INDIGEN.** A native plant, then said to be indigenous.

**INDIGO.** See INDIGOFERA.

**INDIGOFERA** (in-di-goff'er-a). Herbaceous perennials and shrubs, belonging to the Leguminaceae, with about 300 species widely distributed through the tropical regions of the world, especially in As., Af. and the south of N.A. Leaves compound.* Flowers pea-like, in axillary racemes, fruits mostly cylindrical pods (*Indigofera* means indigo-bearing).

Most of them are not hardy in zones* 1 to 4 and are therefore treated as ornamental conservatory plants. Some species were formerly used in the manufacture of indigo dye by extracting the indigo from the herbage. Propagated by seeds and cuttings.

**gerardiana.** A low, much-branched shrub, 4-6 ft. high, with silvery-hoary branches. Leaves 1 to 2 in. long, the 9-17 pairs of leaflets about ¼ in. long, pale white, firm. Flowers rosy-red, hoary outside, in 13-21 flowered racemes.* Pod to 2 in. long. India.

**kirilowi.** Sub-shrub, 3-4 ft. high. Flowers in axillary racemes,* borne upright, longer than the leaf, bright rose-colored, individual flower ¾ in. deep. Leaves with 7-15 pairs of leaflets, which are about 1½ in. long. Propagated by division, suckers and cuttings. Does not produce seeds readily when in cultivation. Native of northern China and Korea. Hardy from zone* 4 southward. There is also a white-flowered form.

**potanini.** Shrub to 5 ft. high. Leaves 1½ in. long, the leaflets in 5-7 pairs. Flowers lilac-pink, about ⅓ in. deep, arranged in racemes,* which are longer than the leaves. China.

**INDIVISA, -us, -um** (in-di-vy'za). Undivided.

**INDURATA, -us, -um** (in-dew-ray'ta). Hardened.

**INERMIS, -e** (in-er'mis). Unarmed.

**INFERIOR.** As applied to flowers, the term indicates that the ovary is beneath the point of insertion of the calyx.* It occurs in many plants, notably in flowers of the rose family, in the blueberry, and in the amaryllis family. In the fruits of some of these the withered calyx persists on the apex of the fruit. See SUPERIOR.

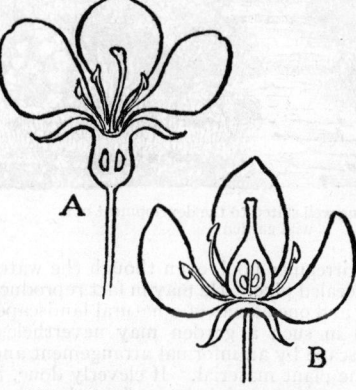

(A) An inferior ovary, the sepals and petals inserted above it. (B) A superior ovary, with the other organs inserted beneath it.

**INFLATA, -us, -um** (in-flay'ta). Inflated or swollen.

**INFLORESCENCE.** The arrangement of flowers in a cluster. It may be simple and solitary, as in the tulip. More often the cluster is compound and variously branched. Of the many types, the leading ones likely to be distinguished by the gardener are all described and figured at PANICLE, RACEME, SPIKE, THYRSE, CYME, CAT-

---

* Special articles on the subjects indicated by an asterisk (*) will be found at the words so marked.

KIN, and UMBEL. For a special sort of inflorescence, *see also* ARACEAE.

**INFORMAL GARDEN.** The informal, or naturalistic, garden, is laid out irregularly and modeled according to the forms and laws of nature, to express an appreciation of natural power and beauty. The true informal garden is essentially an inspiration, a sort of temperamental translation of nature, and the extent of its attractiveness is usually in direct relation to the amount of influence that nature has been allowed to exercise in bringing about the final result. The designer of the informal garden should therefore be primarily a lover of nature and be trained to accept as his model the best compositions among the many offered in a natural landscape.

The informal garden is most successful in a place where the designer can accept the beauty of a site and try to accentuate its characteristics. There are some occasions when the natural features are so dominating that they should be accepted as fixing the whole character of the work. All the designer has to do is to devise ways of making these gifts of nature more convincing, of amplifying them and perfecting their beauty.

Often, however, the site to be developed contains no features which can be of inspiration to the garden designer. Here his job is more difficult. He may develop an irregular, open lawn, surrounded by trees and shrubs, broken by two or three free-standing trees and decorated by irregular borders of the kind of flowers which look as though they belonged to the wild scene.

An informal setting well suited to the development of a wild garden

He may include an irregular pool, even though the water comes to it from a concealed pipe. He may in fact reproduce a few of the thousand and one effects of a natural landscape. The pictures created in such a garden may nevertheless suggest the wild landscape by an informal arrangement and by the character of the plant material. If cleverly done, it may seem to the owner more restful than a formal garden. The Japanese, who have acquired the art of being artificial without being affected, and of designing on nature's lines without being necessarily too realistic, are masters of an arrangement of this kind. The spirit of the Japanese garden exists in the best type of that informal garden called a rock garden, although the latter is primarily a setting for alpines and other small plants and should be so thoroughly enclosed as to be a unit completely apart. *See* JAPANESE GARDEN, ROCK GARDEN.

As the main purpose of the informal garden is to look as though it had grown up by a natural sequence of events rather than by human direction, the evidences of human occupation, such as paths, seats, steps, etc., should not be too important or emphatic; they should seem accidental and as if they had been brought in to enable the owner to enjoy the scene without too much exertion. Paths should be laid out where they would naturally be trodden by people passing over the ground; their course should not be arranged by any arbitrary system, but might best be determined by the necessity of avoiding some rock or impassable mass of shrubbery or of making an easy grade up a hill. They should be cleverly managed so that the wanderer can enjoy a series of the most beautiful pictures which the garden has to offer. They should never be forced to wriggle about, simply to avoid a straight line, in places where a straight or gently curving line would seem more logical.

Seats or a summer house should be put where the shade of a tree or the attractiveness of a view would naturally induce the wanderer to linger and rest.

A small, informal garden is often found near a house, and the smaller the house the better, for a man-made object should not dominate the naturalistic garden. If it threatens so to dominate, it should be softened by vines or partially hidden by trees. The garden is thus related to the house by the fact that the walls of the house and their adjacent planting form, as it were, one wall of the garden enclosure.

Such a small garden can often make no serious attempt to imitate exactly the natural landscape. It may have to remain obviously man-made and may include exotic plants and flowers.

Statuary may be perfectly in place in an informal setting, but it is true that many statues are not. The effect or suggestion of a statue must be in keeping with its location. A bronze, lead or weathered stone statue of a lion, for instance, may look well high up on a rock, whereas a marble bust of Benjamin Franklin would not.

The vice of artificiality is one to which the gardener is too apt to succumb. It appears frequently in the strange preference which many people have for rare and unusual plants which are often out of place in an informal or naturalistic garden; and it is shown too in an unaccountable dislike of the more familiar trees, shrubs and flowers. Underlying this is evidently an idea that there is some virtue in novelty for novelty's sake. Harmony of design is more important than aggressiveness of detail. By seeking after strange effects, rather than after simple beauty, and by using artifices which show misplaced ingenuity rather than a sincere desire to make the best use of the hints with which nature is so prodigal, the gardener convicts himself of incapacity to enter into the real spirit of the informal garden.

In the informal garden nothing should be done, as design or upkeep, to indicate that the designer has set up his own preferences against nature's intention. — R. L. F., Jr.

**INFUNDIBULIFORMIS,** -e (in-fun-dib-you-ly-for'mis). Funnel-shaped.

**INGA** (in'ga). A genus of over 150 species of chiefly tropical American, acacia-like, unarmed trees of the pea family, the two below somewhat grown for ornament in zones* 8 and 9, mostly in southern Calif. and Fla. Leaves compound,* the leaflets arranged feather-fashion, without an odd one at the end, and with a gland* between some of the larger leaflets. Flowers not pea-like, small, crowded in dense, ball-like clusters, the protruding stamens* conspicuous. Fruit a somewhat woody, 4-angled pod, thickened at the seams, splitting tardily or not at all, the pulp edible in some wild species. (*Inga* is a West Indian name for some species.)

The trees are little known in the U.S., but extensively planted for shading coffee plantations in the tropics.

**laurina.** Guama. A tree up to 50 ft. high. Leaflets 4-6. Flower heads white, fragrant, arranged in long, drooping clusters (racemes*). Pod about 6 in. long, flattish. Tropical America.

**vera.** Guaba. Not over 50 ft. high. Leaflets 8-12, the leafstalk

---

* Special articles on the subjects indicated by an asterisk (*) will be found at the words so marked.

winged. Flower heads white, arranged in short, dense spikes. Pod 4-6 in. long, more or less 4-ribbed. Tropical America.

**INGENHOUZIA** (in-gen-how'zee-a). Mexican undershrubs or perennial herbs of the mallow family, closely related to cotton, but without lint on the seeds. Only one of the two known species is cult., **H. triloba,** a smooth, perennial herb 4-10 ft. high, its branches purple-dotted. Leaves alternate,* more or less cut or parted, finger-fashion, nearly to the base. Flowers white, but soon turning pink, about 1 in. wide, solitary or in small clusters in the leaf-axils.* (For structure see MALVACEAE.) Fruit a capsule* about ½ in. long. The plant is rarely cult. in Calif. and similar climates, and needs the same general conditions as cotton (see GOSSYPIUM). (Named for Jean Ingen-Housz, Dutch plant physiologist.)

**INGENS** (in'jenz). Very large.

**INJURY.** For injury to trees see TREE SURGERY. For injury from insects see INSECT PESTS. For injury from disease see PLANT DISEASES. For injury caused by animals see ANIMAL INJURY.

**INKBERRY** = *Ilex glabra.* See HOLLY. The name is also applied, more rarely, to *Phytolacca americana* (which see).

**INK FOR LABELS.** See LABELS.

**INLAYING.** See GRAFTING.

**INNOCENCE** = *Houstonia coerulea.*

**INOCULATION.** See LEGUME INOCULATION.

**INODES** = *Sabal.*

*INODORA, -us, -um* (in-o-door'ra). Not fragrant.

**INSECT FRIENDS.** Insects pollinate many plants, and furnish food for useful animals, including birds, fish, poultry, and livestock. They produce some important commercial substances, including silk, honey, dyestuffs, wax, and shellac. It has been well said that a world without insects would be strangely lacking in many ways. Some insects perform an important service in killing injurious insects, and many pests are checked by their insect enemies.

The insects that attack other insects may be divided into two classes. Predators seize and devour insects as prey. Parasites lay eggs in, on, or near the insect host, and the larvae hatching from these eggs feed in or on the insect until it is destroyed.

The predators include a great variety of forms. The conspicuous praying mantis, the dragon flies, some true bugs or sucking insects, many beetles, some two-winged flies or their larvae, and some of the large wasps are predators. Among the most frequently observed predators are the lady-bird beetles, usually red with black spots, and their larvae, which look something like little lizards. Both adults and larvae do a useful work in feeding greedily on aphids. One of these insects may eat hundreds of aphids during its life.

Most parasites belong to two of the insect groups, the two-winged flies and the group containing the bees and wasps. The latter parasites are usually small, but on close inspection can be seen to resemble wasps. The different species of parasites vary in size according to the size of the host in which they develop. Even a little aphid may give forth an adult parasite, which has developed to full size inside it. Several small parasites may develop in one large host. A parasite often noticed is the one that affects the large green tomato worm and the caterpillar of the catalpa sphinx. A dead or sick larva may often be seen covered with white cocoons, which are the cocoons of little parasitic larvae that developed inside it. — F. M. W.

**INSECTICIDES** (Note: It is advisable to read INSECT PESTS in conjunction with this article). Great progress has been made recently in the field of insecticides, and new developments are being announced from time to time. Insecticides can be divided into four classes: (1) Stomach poisons, for biting insects; (2) contact insecticides, for sucking insects; (3) fumigants, for insects in inclosed spaces; and (4) repellents.

STOMACH POISONS

The principal stomach poisons are the compounds of arsenic, often called arsenicals. These are deadly to insects; there is, however, some danger of injury to the leaves. Some compounds are more injurious and some plants are more susceptible than others. The common garden, or snap, bean and the stone fruits, especially peach, are very sensitive to arsenicals. Nevertheless, arsenic compounds have been used with considerable success for more than 50 years. Small quantities will kill the insects, and washing by rain reduces the amount of poison remaining on the plants. In recent years, however, attention has been drawn to the danger in using such sprays on food crops. They must be used with care. They should not be applied to fruits or vegetables soon to be harvested, and they should be kept out of the reach of children. Residues can be removed from some crops, as by washing apples and removing the outer leaves of cabbage.

Lead arsenate is the most commonly used arsenical. It is of moderate cost, fairly poisonous to insects, has little tendency to injure the leaves of most plants, and remains on the plant for some time. The acid lead arsenate is the form that should be used rather than the less effective basic form. Lead arsenate was formerly sold as a paste, but now it is nearly always sold in the form of a fluffy white powder. It is usually applied as a spray at the rate of 1 pound to 50 gallons of water (1 ounce to 3 gallons), but it may be used at greater strength. It can also be applied as a dust, usually mixed with several times its weight of hydrated lime or some other carrier.

Paris green is well known to older gardeners, and is still in use. Originally a paint pigment, it was the first arsenic compound used against insects. Its chemical name is copper aceto-arsenite. It is more deadly to insects than lead arsenate, and is therefore useful against insects that are hard to kill, or in baits. As it has a strong tendency to burn leaves, it can only be used on crops, such as potatoes, which resist arsenic injury. It is sold in practically the original form, a rather heavy, bright green powder. As a spray it is used at the rate of about ½ pound to 50 gallons of water; the addition of a little lime will lessen its injury to leaves. For dusting it is usually mixed with about ten times its weight of hydrated lime.

Calcium arsenate has come into use in recent years. It is a fluffy white powder, effective against insects, and intermediate between lead arsenate and Paris green in its injury to crops. Since it is cheaper than either of these compounds, it is well suited for use when expense must be held down. Larger quantities of it are used than of any other arsenic compound, although lead arsenate is used on more kinds of plants. The cotton crop accounts for a large proportion of the amount used; it also has considerable use on truck crops. It is chiefly applied as a dust with lime or other carriers. As a spray it is applied at the rate of ¾ to 1 pound to 50 gallons of water.

Magnesium arsenate has recently had a limited use on beans, because it does not burn them so much as do other arsenicals. It is not so poisonous to the insects as the others. White arsenic and sodium arsenite are cheap and very poisonous; they are too injurious to plants for use in spraying, but are very good in baits.

Some other arsenic compounds have been used and proved less successful than those mentioned above; many others have been tested experimentally; but those discussed are the most important to the gardener.

Bran bait, useful against grasshoppers, cutworms, and other pests, is made by mixing ¼ pound of Paris green or white arsenic (*not* lead arsenate) with 5 pounds of bran, and making this into a moist, crumbly mash with ½ gallon of water in which 1 pint of cheap syrup is dissolved. The juice and chopped rind of an orange or lemon are often added. Syrup containing a little sodium arsenite will poison ants.

A few substances besides the arsenic compounds have given fairly good results as stomach poisons. Hellebore is one of the oldest insecticides, and is made from a plant. It is rather expensive, but has the advantage of not being

* Special articles on the subjects indicated by an asterisk (*) will be found at the words so marked.

dangerous to man and the higher animals, although poisonous to insects. It is sold as a powder, and loses strength with age. For spraying it may be made up with hot water, 1 or 2 ounces per gallon. It is too expensive for general spraying, but can be used on a few plants when a spray not dangerous to human beings is desired.

Several compounds of fluorine have been used with some success in the last few years. Sodium fluoride can be used against poultry lice and roaches, but not on plants. Sodium fluosilicate, barium fluosilicate, sodium fluoaluminate (cryolite), and other fluorine compounds are not so injurious to plants and have some use as sprays. They are used in about the same concentration as lead arsenate for dusting or spraying; some are on sale as proprietary preparations. As with arsenicals, there is some danger that fluorine compounds may leave a poisonous residue on food crops.

## Contact Sprays

The principal contact sprays can be classed as nicotine sprays, oil sprays, and sprays of sulphur or its compounds; but there are also other kinds.

Soap is one of the insecticides longest in use. A solution of soap at the rate of 1 pound to from 5 to 10 gallons of water kills plant lice; stronger solutions have been used against the more resistant scale insects. Soap is often hard to dissolve, tends to injure foliage, and if used in mixture with other insecticides may cause them to burn leaves or clog sprayers. Where the water is hard, some of the soap is precipitated by lime and rendered useless. Some special potash soaps are sold for spraying, and are better for this purpose than laundry soap. They include fish-oil soap and coconut-oil soap. Fish-oil soap (formerly replaced by whale-oil soap) is largely used as a scalecide in greenhouses, where it is applied as soapy water with a sponge. It is a good remedy also for mealy bug, especially on palm leaves.

Tobacco infusion or "tea" is another old-time spray that is of some value against plant lice; tobacco may also be used as a dust. However, we now have extracts of tobacco that are more reliable and easier to use. Most of these contain nicotine sulphate, which is 40% nicotine. Such extracts are effective against plant lice, thrips, and similar pests, when used at dilutions of 1 pint to 100 gallons of water (1 ounce to 6 gallons) or even higher. They do not injure most leaves. These concentrated extracts are very poisonous and should be kept in a safe place. In spraying with nicotine alone, a little soap (about 1 pound to 20 gallons) should be added to "activate" its killing power. Some activators to replace soap are now sold. In mixtures of several insecticides an activator is less desirable. Nicotine can also be used as a dust, bought ready made or mixed at home from the tobacco extract. In the latter case 5 to 7.5% of the 40% extract is added to hydrated lime or dusting sulphur, to give a finished product of 2 or 3% nicotine content. The mixture is put into a bucket or keg with some small stones, and the container is tightly covered and rolled until the material is mixed. Nicotine dust should be used while fresh, and nicotine extracts should be kept in tight containers.

The most important sulphur spray is lime-sulphur. The stock solution is made by boiling 40 to 50 pounds of freshly slaked lime and 80 to 100 pounds of sulphur in 50 gallons of water for an hour. This solution can be made at home, but it is now nearly always bought ready made. When tested with a hydrometer, it should give a reading of about 33° on the Baumé scale. This material is mixed at the rate of 1 part to 7 or 8 parts of water for a winter spray against resistant orchard scale insects; the trees must be dormant, as such a strong spray would injure them when in leaf. A much more dilute solution (1 part stock to 40 or 50 parts water) is used as a summer spray and is one of our principal fungicides. Dry preparations of lime-sulphur and similar compounds are on the market and are giving fairly good results as winter sprays at the rate of 15 pounds to 50 gallons, and as summer sprays at correspondingly weaker strengths. Several mixtures (not compounds) of sulphur and lime are used as fungicides. Uncombined sulphur is used against some fungous diseases and against mites. As a dust it is used without dilution or mixed with other insecticides; as a spray it may be used at the rate of 10 pounds to 50 gallons, with a little soap. Some sulphur is especially prepared to mix easily with water for spraying. Potassium sulphide, 1 ounce to 2 gallons, is used against some mites.

A number of oil sprays are in use. For spraying dormant trees against scale insects, strong oil sprays are used. In order to mix with water, an emulsifying agent is necessary, and this mixing is rather difficult. Insecticide companies sell ready-prepared stock emulsions, called miscible oils, with directions for dilution and use; these are very convenient, saving work in mixing, and are effective. They are usually sold under trade names. Home-made emulsions of lubricating oil have been developed lately. A good formula is oil (light grade) 1 gallon, water ½ gallon, and potash fish-oil soap 1 pound. The ingredients are poured together, brought to a boil, and pumped through a spray pump from one container into another until emulsified or mixed. This stock mixture is diluted with 20 or more times its volume of water for dormant spraying. Similar emulsions have been made of cold ingredients; calcium caseinate, strong bordeaux mixture, or some other emulsifier being used instead of soap. An emulsion has been made without water from 1 part of resin potash fish-oil soap to 9 parts of oil, stirred cold. Emulsions have been made with crude oil and with distillate oil. A little bordeaux mixture may be added to facilitate mixing these emulsion stocks with hard water. These dormant oil sprays, either miscible oil or home-made emulsion, usually injure trees in leaf, but they are often used in dilute form on citrus trees (which do not shed their leaves), and experiments in their use on deciduous trees during the growing season are going on. Highly refined petroleum oils (white oils) often sold under trade names, are least injurious to foliage.

Kerosene emulsion is an old-time contact spray which is still used occasionally, though it is difficult to use with hard water and sometimes injures plants. To prepare this emulsion, ½ pound of soap is dissolved in 1 gallon of water and heated to boiling, then mixed with 2 gallons of kerosene and pumped from one container to another until emulsified. For spraying, this stock is diluted with 6 to 12 times its volume of water. In all oil emulsions the oil and water tend to separate, and when this occurs the undiluted oil may injure the plants. Oil emulsions should therefore be used soon after they have been prepared.

Pyrethrum has been used for a long time as an ingredient of insect powders, and is also much used in sprays against houseflies (but should not be used on plants in this form). It is now being developed as a general contact spray. It is still rather expensive, but it is not injurious to plants, and is fairly effective against a number of soft-bodied insects. Preparations are sold under trade names, and are accompanied by directions for use. The unprepared pyrethrum powder may be used as a dust or made into an infusion for spraying (1 ounce to a gallon.)

A plant belonging to the genus *Derris* has recently been shown to contain the insecticidal substance rotenone, which gives promise as an effective contact spray. It has been experimented with extensively and is now sold commercially. Hop growers have long used another plant extract, called quassia, against plant lice. Corrosive sublimate in weak solution has some use against root maggots, and lately calomel has also been used against them.

## Repellents

The principal repellent spray is bordeaux mixture. It is also one of our most important fungicides, and has been mentioned as one of the emulsifiers used with oil. For its preparation see under Copper at Fungicides. Bordeaux mixture will quickly corrode iron, even if galvanized, but it does not affect brass. It repels leaf beetles and leafhoppers, and seems to keep young leafhoppers from thriving.

The common arsenic sprays have some repellent effect, especially on leaf beetles. Chinch bugs are repelled by a barrier of creosote, and the young bugs are thus kept out of cornfields.

---

\* Special articles on the subjects indicated by an asterisk (\*) will be found at the words so marked.

## COMBINATIONS

Materials are often combined for economy and efficiency against several pests. For example, lead arsenate combined with a fungicide is in regular use in orchard sprays, and nicotine is added if aphids are present. The arsenic compounds, when used as dusts, are often combined with some dust fungicide, such as a copper compound or sulphur, or with nicotine dusts, or both. Dormant sprays are not usually combined with others. Some sprays do not go well with others; soap or oil emulsions cannot be used with lime-sulphur, soap increases the tendency of arsenic compounds to injure leaves, and Paris green should not be used with lime-sulphur.

## FUMIGANTS

A number of gases have been used for fumigation. Some of them are only adapted for treating stored products, but several are used in connection with growing plants. These are discussed under FUMIGATION. — F. M. W. (See SPRAYING AND DUSTING for methods of applying the insecticides.)

**INSECTIVOROUS PLANTS.** Only a few plants are able to digest, directly, such nitrogenous substances as meat or the bodies of insects. The few that do so are not all closely related botanically, but they all have somewhat elaborate mechanisms for trapping insects and subsequently digesting them. Darwin devoted much time to studying the habits of these carnivorous or insectivorous plants before writing what is now the classic book *Insectivorous Plants*.

By no means all insectivorous plants are cult. Of those that are, the following will be found in THE GARDEN DICTIONARY, where notes on their culture should be sought: *Darlingtonia, Dionaea, Drosera, Nepenthes, Pinguicula, Sarracenia* (see PITCHER-PLANT), *Utricularia*.

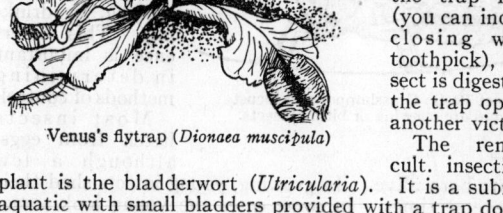

Pitcher-plants: Common pitcher-plant (*Sarracenia*) at the left, *Darlingtonia* in the center, and *Nepenthes* at the right.

As to their methods of catching insects the plants are easily divided into three categories: (1) Those that drown them, as in *Sarracenia, Nepenthes,* and *Darlingtonia*; (2) those that have sticky hairs in which the insect becomes enmeshed and is killed by a secretion of the plant, as in *Drosera* and *Pinguicula*; and (3) those that have trap-like or movable parts which imprison the insect as in *Dionaea* and *Utricularia*.

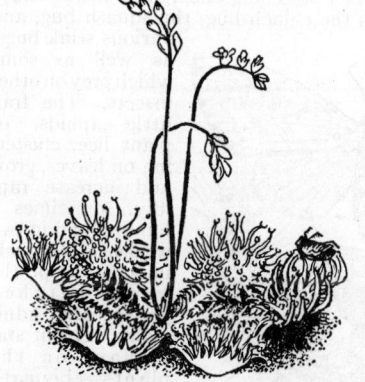

Sundew (*Drosera rotundifolia*)

The first group, which drowns its prey, are the plants usually called pitcher-plants, of which much the commonest here is *Sarracenia*. All agree in having the leaves modified into a pitcher-like organ, mostly fringed on the inside with down-pointing hairs. These allow the insect to crawl in but not out. At the bottom of the pitcher is a watery liquid in which the victim is drowned and finally digested and absorbed by the plant.

The insectivorous plants that rely upon sticky hairs are the sundews (*Drosera*) and the butterwort (*Pinguicula*), which, however, operate very differently. In the sundews the insect cannot get away because the foliage is covered with glistening, often reddish, very sticky hairs. Few small insects, who are attracted by the chance of food, can ever escape once they are caught. For the more they struggle, the greater number of hairs they touch, each making the victim more firmly entrapped. When all is over, the plant secretes enough digestive juices so that the insect is finally completely absorbed. In the butterwort (*Pinguicula*) the much more normal leaf is also covered with sticky hairs in which the insect becomes mired. But the leaf then rolls its margin over the victim and finally absorbs him by digestion much as in the sundews. The ability to roll the leaf margin seems to connect the butterwort with the third group which have trap-like parts or movements.

This third group of insectivorous plants is the most remarkable of all. *Dionaea*, or the Venus's flytrap, has the leaf divided into two hinged, valve-like segments, the inner face of which is beset with hairs. When an insect lands within these jaw-like valves, they close up and crush the insect, holding him, in the process, by the stiff hairs. Once the trap is shut (you can induce its closing with a toothpick), the insect is digested and the trap opens for another victim.

Venus's flytrap (*Dionaea muscipula*)

The remaining cult. insectivorous plant is the bladderwort (*Utricularia*). It is a submerged aquatic with small bladders provided with a trap door that cannot be opened from the inside. Minute water insects or other aquatic life push their way through the open door, which closes after them. It does not open until they have been digested. The plant is common in quiet pools and often grown in aquaria.

**INSECT PESTS AND THEIR CONTROL.** Injury by insects is one of the greatest problems of plant growing. About 10% of field crops and 20% of orchard and garden crops in the U.S. are destroyed by insects each year. It is estimated that the annual losses from ¾ of the leading insect pests amount to about a billion dollars.

Several hundred thousand species of insects are known to exist in the world, and several thousand kinds may be found in a single locality. Most of these are harmless and of little interest to man. Some are even helpful, for they perform such tasks as pollinating flowers, furnishing food for animals, producing honey, wax, silk, or shellac, and destroying harmful insects and noxious weeds. Many kinds, however, are injurious, and every plant species we value is attacked by some insects. Injury is done by the insects feeding on parts of the plant or its juices, and also, sometimes, by carrying plant diseases.

### INSECTS AND CLOSELY RELATED FORMS

Insects occur throughout the world, in many situations. They are of varied appearance and habits, and range in size

---

* Special articles on the subjects indicated by an asterisk (*) will be found at the words so marked.

# INSECT PESTS AND THEIR CONTROL

from almost microscopic to several inches, and in length of life from a few days or weeks to several years. However, all are built on the same basic pattern. They are an important class in the large group of animals with jointed bodies and a number of jointed legs, which have no true internal skeleton, but are supported by a stiff body wall on the outside. They are distinguished from other members of this group by having only three pairs of legs. Other characteristics are the possession of one pair of antennae or feelers, and usually a pair of compound eyes and one or two pairs of wings. Breathing is done through a number of pores, usually along the sides of the body, and air is carried through the body by a system of air tubes. Of other classes in this large group, one includes crabs, crayfish, and the common gray sowbug found on damp ground under boards; another includes the centipedes and millipedes (thousand-legs); and a third includes the spiders, mites, and ticks. The members of this third class have eight legs and no feelers, and some of them are very injurious. Certain kinds of mites are among our plant pests.

## IMPORTANT GROUPS OF INSECTS

Insects are divided by specialists into more than 20 groups, distinguished by the form of the wings, the mouth parts or jaws, and the method of growth. Some of these are of interest only to students; but a few of the important groups contain nearly all our plant pests.

In some the jaws are suited for biting or chewing food; in others the mouth parts are fitted together to form a tube or beak, for piercing, sucking, or drinking. This difference is important in determining methods of control.

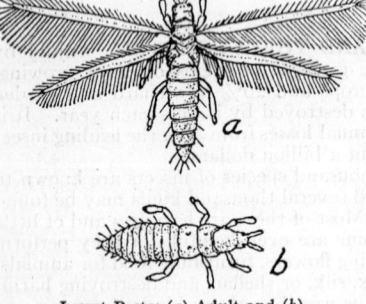

Insect Pests: Grasshopper and locust types are chewing or biting insects.

Most insects hatch from eggs, although a few kinds are born alive. In growing, young insects shed their skins several times. In some cases the young look something like their parents when hatched, and the resemblance increases with each molt, until after the last one they appear as adults. Such young are called nymphs and are active at all stages. This may be called development by gradual change. On other orders the young, called larvae, appear much different from their parents, and are worm-like until full grown, when they suddenly change to pupae, a quiescent form which does not move or eat; a little later the pupae give forth the adults. This may be called development by sudden change.

Seven orders contain most of the plant pests. These seven may be described briefly as follows:

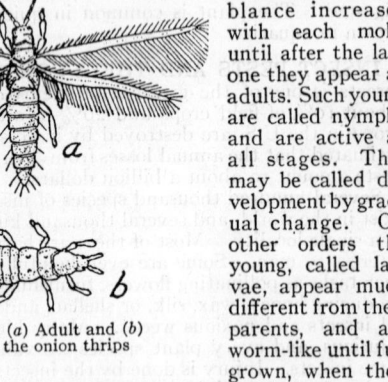

Insect Pests: (a) Adult and (b) nymph* of the onion thrips

(1) GRASSHOPPERS, CRICKETS, ROACHES, etc. Mouth parts suited for biting and chewing; front wings leathery, when present, covering hind wings, which are folded like fans; development gradual. This order has comparatively few kinds of pests, but some species of grasshoppers are among the most destructive insects known. They are especially injurious in the drier parts of the world.

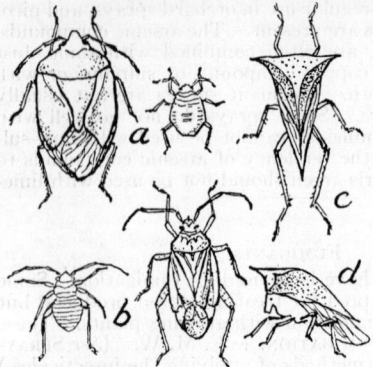

Insect Pests: The true bugs. (a) Green soldier bug and young nymph.* (b) Tarnished plant bug and nymph.* (c and d) Two views of a tree-hopper.

(2) THRIPS. Very small insects; wings fringed when present; mouth parts for rasping and sucking; development gradual. Several species are pests on leaves, flowers, or bark, either injuring the plants or spoiling their appearance.

(3) TRUE BUGS AND ALLIES. Piercing and sucking mouth parts; gradual development. In one division (true bugs) the front wings are leathery, fitted closely over the body, and most commonly with the front half thicker than the rear half. In the other division (plant lice, scale insects, leaf-hoppers, and others) the wings, when present, are held roof-like over the body. We may call this whole group the sucking insects. Adults and young have similar feeding habits. Some of the true

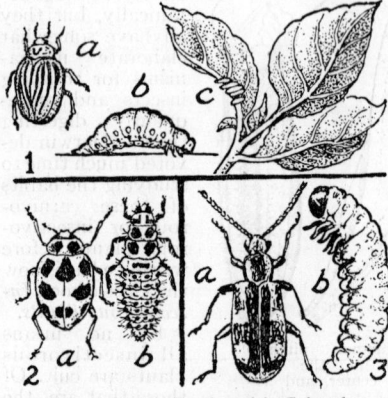

Insect Pests: Beetles. (1) Colorado potato beetle: (a) adult; (b) larva; (c) eggs. (2) Spotted ladybird beetle: (a) adult; (b) larva. (3) Asparagus beetle; (a) adult; (b) larva.

bugs are known by their sickening odor; they include such plant-feeding pests as the chinch bug, the squash bug, and various stink bugs, as well as some which prey on other insects. The frail little aphids, or plant lice, clustering on leaves, grow and increase rapidly, sometimes a hundredfold in two weeks. The scale insects, except the newly hatched young and adult males, remain stationary on the plants beneath scales which they form. The mealybugs are closely allied to the scales, but retain some

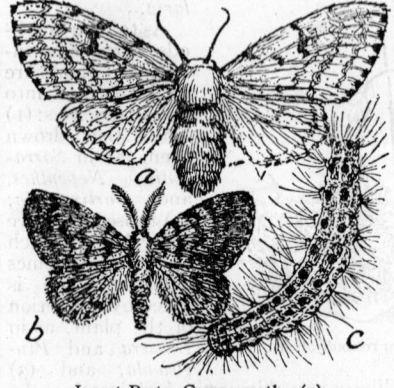
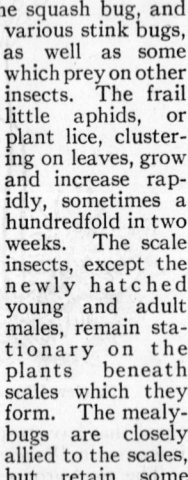

Insect Pests: Gypsy moth. (a) female; (b) male; (c) caterpillar.

power of motion. Whiteflies live within scales when young,

---

* Special articles on the subjects indicated by an asterisk (*) will be found at the words so marked.

but are active as adults. The active little leafhoppers and the larger cicadas are well-known insects of this group.

(4) BEETLES. Front wings hard and shell-like, fitted closely over body; development by sudden change, larvae grub-like; both adults and young with biting and chewing mouth parts. Either adult or larva may be injurious, but not always to the same plants. Sometimes one stage of a species is injurious while another stage is harmless or beneficial. Pests of this order are too numerous to mention, and there are also many harmless, colorful, and interesting forms. A few examples of the order are the leaf beetles, which include the Colorado potato beetle and the tiny flea beetles; the June bugs, whose young are the root-feeding white grubs; ladybird beetles, many of which feed on aphids and scale insects; blister beetles; wood borers; and snout beetles. The well-known Japanese beetle is of the June bug family, and the Mexican bean beetle is a plant-feeding ladybird beetle.

(5) MOTHS AND BUTTERFLIES. Wings large, with a velvety coating of scales; development by sudden change, larvae worm-like, called caterpillars; larvae with biting mouth parts, adult mouth parts in the form of a coiled tube suited only for drinking liquids. In this order are many handsome and conspicuous species sought by collectors. As a rule the pests are among the more inconspicuous forms. The butterflies differ from the moths in having feelers enlarged at the tips, and usually are slower fliers and active only by day.

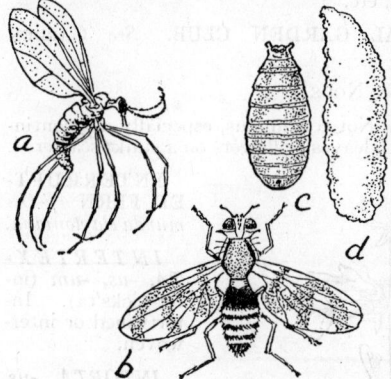

Insect Pests: Two-winged flies. (a) pear midge adult; (b) apple maggot fly; its pupa at (c), and the larva or maggot at (d).

The adults of moths and butterflies are not injurious, but the larvae are important plant feeders. Some are leaf miners, some bore into the stems or fruit, and many feed on the leaves or other parts of the plant. A number of larvae tie up leaves with web, thus making a protecting nest in which to feed. A few important pests of this order are the codling moth, oriental fruit moth, gypsy moth, bagworm, fall webworm, tomato worm, various species of cutworms, corn ear worm, cabbage worm, and European corn borer.

(6) TWO-WINGED FLIES, MOSQUITOES, AND GNATS. Front wings membranous, hind wings undeveloped; growth by sudden change, footless larvae called maggots; larval mouth parts suited for rasping and sucking; adult mouth parts tubular, suited for piercing and sucking in some species, only for drinking in others. Some adults bite or annoy man and animals. Larvae vary in habits; some feed in filth, some are useful parasites of insects, and some are plant feeders. The plant feeders include root maggots, leaf miners, gall formers, and fruit flies.

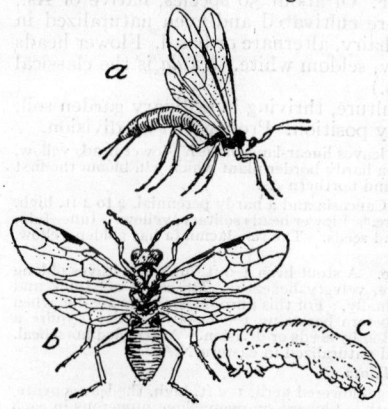

Insect Pests: (a) A minute parasite of the tent caterpillar; (b) rose-sawfly with its larva (c).

(7) BEES, ANTS, WASPS, SAWFLIES, etc. Four wings, membranous; development by sudden change; adults and larvae with mouth parts fitted for biting, but often modified for drinking also. The habits in this group are various; many species rear their young in nests, and many others are parasites which help hold destructive insects in check. The parasite lays its egg in or on the insect host, and the parasite larva develops in or on it, killing it. Some members of this order, especially the sawflies, are plant pests. Some of the sawfly larvae are borers, but most of them are leaf feeders.

The majority of the plant pests are included in three of these orders, sucking insects, beetles, and moths and butterflies. Some other orders of insects are dragonflies, mayflies, termites, bird lice, sucking lice, and fleas.

CONTROL OF INSECT PESTS

By control of a pest we mean reducing its numbers to such an extent that its injury becomes unimportant. In our struggles with insects we have learned how to check a great many of them, though our knowledge is far from complete. The value of a crop has much to do with the methods we can use. For a crop, such as wheat, raised on a large area with a low value per acre, we cannot use expensive methods. For crops, such as apples, tomatoes, or greenhouse flowers, with a high value per acre, more costly control methods can be used if necessary. Control methods include killing insects with poisonous substances, use of mechanical devices, modifications of ordinary farming operations, utilization of the insects' natural enemies, and the placing of quarantines.

NATURAL CONTROL. Nearly all insects have such a great power of increase that if not checked enormous numbers would result within a few generations. Their numbers are reduced by death from adverse weather, lack of food, disease, insect enemies, and other causes. A great many species are thus held down to small numbers all or nearly all the time, and even our bad pests are kept from increasing as much as they otherwise would. This is called natural control. Our efforts to control insects would be much harder if it were not for this natural control. Where valuable crops are involved, however, to depend entirely on such uncertain help would result in severe losses.

USE OF POISONS. This has been called chemical control. It will be discussed more in detail under the headings INSECTICIDES, SPRAYING, and FUMIGATION; only the basic principles will be mentioned here. The poisons used must be deadly to insects and do little or no harm to the plant. For chewing insects, which swallow solid pieces of plant tissue, the aim is to cover the plant with a thin coating of poison which the insect will swallow. Materials used for this purpose are called stomach poisons. Sucking insects, which pierce the plant surface and draw juice from the inside, do not swallow material from the outside of the plant, and are therefore not affected by stomach poisons. Against them sprays are used which kill by contact, by spreading over the body and entering the breathing pores. A third method of using poisons is by releasing a poison gas in a space that can be made air-tight, as in a greenhouse. This is called fumigation. A gas that will kill insects without harming the plants must be used. Sometimes materials are used which do not kill insects but which are so disagreeable to them that they do not feed on the plants; these are called repellents. With a few insects it is possible to put out a bait of some substance that they will eat mixed with a stomach poison. The use of poisons is rather expensive, as they usually require a special outlay for material, equipment, and extra labor.

MECHANICAL METHODS. Several simple control devices may be considered as mechanical. Collection and destruction of insects by hand is the oldest control method, and is still a good one where large, conspicuous insects are attacking a few prized plants. For example, tomato worms in small vegetable gardens or bagworms on a few shrubs can easily be controlled by hand picking. Barriers or traps are useful in checking the attacks of some in-

---

* Special articles on the subjects indicated by an asterisk (*) will be found at the words so marked.

sects. Sticky bands on trees will protect against cankerworms (see ELM INSECTS). Trap bands help in controlling the codling moth. Immature chinch bugs are kept out of cornfields by barriers such as dust furrows or lines of repellent material. Machines for collecting insects have had some use, chiefly against grasshoppers in the West. Some have been devised for use against the Colorado potato beetle and the pea aphid, but they have not been so satisfactory as some other methods. Plum-curculio adults can be jarred from trees onto a sheet.

Elms with sticky bands to prevent cankerworms crawling up

FARM PRACTICES. On farms the regular control operations can be carried on in such a way as to be unfavorable for insects. Rotation of crops is effective, especially where fields are large. Sometimes insect injury can be kept down by the use of resistant varieties of the plant. With some pests relief is obtained by slight modifications in time of planting the crop. The operations of draining and flooding cranberry fields can be conducted in such a way as to check cranberry insects. Early fall plowing reduces the numbers of some soil-inhabiting insects. Livestock and poultry sometimes aid in destroying pests. The most effective farm practices, however, consist of what is called "clean-up" practices — destroying plants after the crop has been picked, cleaning up trash which serves as winter shelter to the insects, and destroying wild plants on which pests will develop and spread to crops. In a home garden, radish plants that are going to seed may keep aphids alive to spread to young fall turnips. Outbreaks of the garden webworm may be traced to pigweeds growing near by. In southern orchards, cowpeas used as a cover crop foster stink bugs, which later damage fruits and pecans; some other cover crop should be used. Control by cultural practices is suited not only to field crops but also in horticulture, and this type of control is relatively inexpensive.

QUARANTINE. A large proportion of our worst pests were originally brought in from abroad, and insects in a new country or territory, away from their natural enemies, are often worse pests than in their old home. Public authorities try, by plant quarantine and inspection, to prevent new pests from coming in, and in certain cases, to hold back the spread of pests already here or to eradicate them. See QUARANTINE.

BIOLOGICAL CONTROL. This means the control of insects by their enemies, especially insect enemies, as well as disease, birds, and so forth. One way to increase this control would be to change the nature of the surroundings to give the enemies a better chance, but this has not been developed much as yet. Another way is to bring in new enemies from other countries, establish them in this country, and let them increase. This must, of course, be done by public authority. It has been very effective in the control of such pests as the cottony cushion scale and the gipsy moth. A third way is to increase the number of enemies already present. Ladybird beetles, which feed on pests, or tiny parasites, may be raised by mass-production methods and liberated among the crops. This has been done in a few cases by public authorities, and even undertaken commercially.

Our horticultural crops are of such value that we can usually afford the more expensive control measures, such as use of poisons, better than losses from insects, and these methods will be our main reliance. However, other methods should not be neglected; clean-up measures are helpful in preventing infestation, and mechanical methods are applicable in some cases. In all cases, watchfulness and prompt action will prevent loss and give full value for investments in control. — F. M. W.

*INSIGNIS, -e* (in-sig'nis). Distinguished or remarkable.

*INSITITIA, -us, -um* (in-si-tish'i-a). Grafted.

*INTEGRA, -us, -um* (in-tee'gra). Entire or whole; i.e. not cut.

*INTEGRIFOLIA, -us, -um* (in-tee-gri-fō'lĭ-a). With uncut leaves.

**INTERCROPPING.** See KITCHEN GARDEN.

*INTERMEDIA, -us, -um* (in-ter-mee'dĭ-a). Intermediate in color, form, habit, etc.

**INTERNATIONAL GARDEN CLUB.** See GARDEN CLUBS.

**INTERNODE.** See NODE.

**INTERRUPTED.** Not continuous, especially not continuously furnished with leaves or flowers on a stalk; scattered.

An interrupted flower cluster. Sometimes leaves are interrupted, as in the interrupted fern.

**INTERRUPTED FERN** = *Osmunda claytoniana*.

*INTERTEXTA, -us, -um* (in-ter-tecks'ta). Intertwined or interwoven.

*INTORTA, -us, -um* (in-tor'ta). Twisted.

*INTRICATA, -us, -um* (in-tri-kay'ta). Tangled; often densely branched.

*INTYBUS* (in'tĭ-bus). See ENDIVIA.

*INULA* (in'you-la). Hardy herbaceous perennials of rather coarse habit of growth, belonging to the Compositae, with daisy-like flowers ranging in color from yellow to orange. Of about 56 species, native of As., Eu., and Af., some are cultivated and even naturalized in N.A. Leaves mostly hairy, alternate or basal. Flower heads solitary or few, yellow, seldom white. (*Inula* is the classical name for these plants.)

They are of easy culture, thriving in ordinary garden soil, but preferring a sunny position. Propagated by division.

ensifolia. To 2 ft. tall, leaves linear-lanceolate. Flower heads yellow, 1½ in. across, July-Aug., a hardy border plant which will bloom the first year if sown early. Eu. and northern As.

glandulosa. Native of Caucasia and a hardy perennial, 2 to 4 ft. high. Leaves hairy, oblong, entire.* Flower heads solitary, yellow. June-July. Propagated by division and seeds. The *var.* laciniata has golden-yellow, fringed, drooping rays.

helenium. Elecampane. A stout herb 4-6 ft. high, the leaves oblong to 2 ft. long, rough above, velvety beneath. The roots are thick and coarse and are used medicinally. For this purpose the roots are dug when 2 years old, in August, before becoming too woody. They require a sunny position. Propagated by seeds or division. Also called horseheal. Native of Eu. and As. and naturalized in eastern N.A.

orientalis = *Inula glandulosa*.

royleana. A showy, large-flowered herb, 1-2 ft. high, the leaves ovate, 8-10 in. long, hairy beneath. Flowers orange-yellow, numerous in each head. It requires a sheltered place in the garden. Himalayas.

*INVOLUCRATA, -us, -um* (in-vol-you-kray'ta). Provided with an involucre (which see).

* Special articles on the subjects indicated by an asterisk (*) will be found at the words so marked.

**INVOLUCRE.** A collection, often whorled,* of small leaves or bracts.* It may be of several different forms. The most common one is the series of involucral bracts* which surround the base of the head or flower clusters of the daisy and related plants (see COMPOSITAE). In other plants it may be merely scale-like appendages between the otherwise naked cluster, as the involucre which covers the ovary in the female flowers of the hickory. And quite often the involucre is decidedly leafy, as in the leafy involucral bracts which surround the fruit of the hazel.

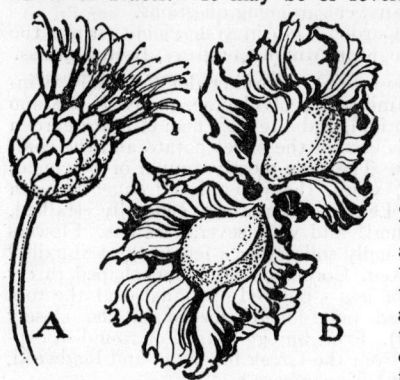

Two types of involucre. (*A*) The series of involucral bracts* on the head of a cornflower. (*B*) The leafy bracts* comprising the involucre around the hazelnut.

**IOCHROMA** (eye-o-krō′ma). Shrubs and small trees belonging to the family Solanaceae, and mostly native of Central and S.A., and therefore not hardy in zones* 1 to 6 of N.A. Leaves alternate,* or clustered, without teeth.* Flowers tubular or trumpet-shaped, showy. Fruit a pulpy berry. (*Iochroma* is from the Greek for violet-colored, in allusion to the color of some species.)

Grown in S. Cal. and as an ornamental in conservatories. Propagated by seeds and cuttings.

**fuchsioides.** Shrub with narrow leaves, almost smooth. Flowers orange-scarlet, in drooping clusters, the individual flower with long, cylindrical tube. Peru.

**lanceolata.** A hairy shrub 6–8 ft. high. Leaves sharp-pointed, oblongish or broadest towards the tip. Flowers nearly 2 in. long, deep purple-blue. Ecuador.

**tubulosa.** A hairy shrub 6–8 ft. high. Leaves ovalish, tapering to a sharp tip. Flowers about 1½ in. long, blue, the clusters drooping. Colombia.

***IOENSIS, -e*** (eye-o-en′sis). From Iowa.

***IONANTHA, -us, -um*** (eye-o-nan′tha). Violet-flowered.

**IONOPSIDIUM** (eye-on-op-sid′i-um). A single species of annual herbs of the mustard family. **I. acaule,** the only species, is from Portugal and is a very small rock garden herb, sometimes grown also in pots in the cool greenhouse. It is a creeping plant scarcely 3 in. high, the leaves alternate,* long-stalked, nearly round, and about ½ in. wide. Flowers minute, violet or white, at the end of slender thread-like stalks 3–4 in. long. Petals 4. Fruit an oblongish or globe-shaped pod (silicle*), slightly notched at the tip. For culture *see* ROCK GARDEN. (*Ionopsidium* is from the Greek for violet-like, in allusion to the flower color.)

**IOWA.** The state lies wholly in zones* 1, 2 and 3. All fruits, vegetables and flowers indigenous to these zones are commonly grown within the state. The vicissitudes of Iowa winters make it imperative that only hardy plants be used, especially in the northern half of the state.

SOILS. Iowa has a higher percentage of tillable land than any other state in the Union. Five distinct soil types are found within the state. They are either of glacial drift or wind-blown (loessal) origin. The loess* soils are mainly in southern Iowa and in general are excellent for fruit.

The topography of most of northern Iowa is level or gently rolling. The soil varies from a heavy muck to a light sandy loam. Many gravel deposits are found in the subsoil of this area. Certain areas are well adapted to vegetables but the soil is not so suitable for fruit growing.

FRUIT. Apples, Iowa's leading fruit, are grown in all sections of the state. Most of the commercial production, however, is in southern Iowa, along both the Missouri and the Mississippi rivers and around Des Moines. Jonathan is the leading variety, although Delicious, Grimes, Golden Delicious, Ben Davis and Northwestern Greening are also of commercial importance. Many other varieties are successfully grown in this area. Strawberries are the leading small fruit, being produced for home use in all sections of the state and commercially in extreme southeastern Iowa. Grapes are produced commercially, principally around Council Bluffs and Des Moines, and are grown for home use over all the state. Concord is the main variety, except in northern Iowa, where the more hardy varieties, such as Beta, are more successful. Most production of pears, cherries, plums and raspberries is for home use, although they are commercially produced in a few areas.

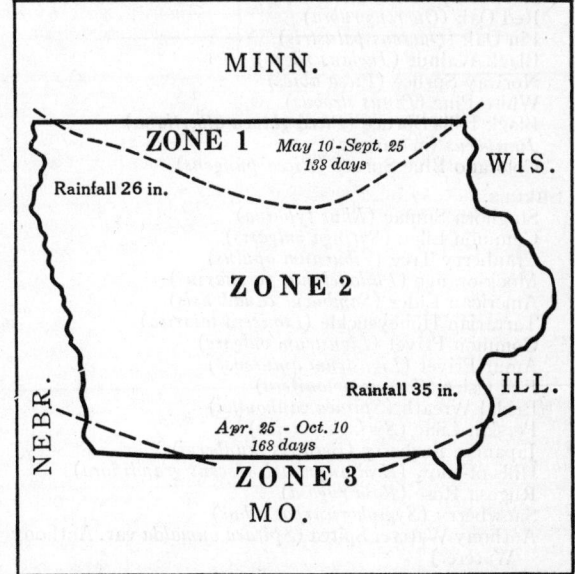

IOWA

The zones of hardiness crossing Iowa are those shown on the colored map at ZONE, which should be consulted for details. The dates are the average latest killing frost in spring and the first one in the fall. The figures below the dates show the average length of the growing season. The figures in inches show the total annual rainfall at the places indicated.

VEGETABLES. Returns from vegetables are greater than from any other horticultural crop grown in the state. Most farmers and many city and town dwellers have gardens. Potatoes are extensively grown for home use and are becoming increasingly more important commercially on the peat lands scattered through northern Iowa. Irish Cobbler, Rural and Ohio are the leading varieties grown. Cabbage and onions are grown commercially in several sections of northern and eastern Iowa. Melons and sweet potatoes are grown on some of the sandy soils, especially bordering the Mississippi River.

Iowa ranks second in the canning of sweet corn, some three million twenty-four-can cases being processed annually. Large quantities of tomatoes and pumpkins are also canned, with some of the 56 canneries processing other vegetables, such as asparagus, sauerkraut and string beans.

ORNAMENTALS AND FLOWERS. Since the first nursery was established in Iowa by Robert Avery, nearly 100 years ago, this business has grown until today, in value of products grown in nurseries, Iowa ranks eighth in the United States. The largest nursery centers are Shenandoah, Charles City, Hampton, Des Moines, Hamburg and Cedar Rapids.

Iowa's soil and climate are particularly adapted to the production of gladiolus bulbs, in which the state ranks third in number of bulbs planted. Two hundred and forty firms are engaged in the commercial greenhouse business, with nearly 5 million square feet of ground under glass.

Home gardening has been greatly stimulated during recent years by the garden club movement. At the present

---

* Special articles on the subjects indicated by an asterisk (*) will be found at the words so marked.

time, there are nearly 150 active clubs in the state, most of them affiliated with the Federated Garden Clubs of Iowa.

A wide range of ornamental plants may be successfully grown. Listed below are a few of the more commonly grown ornamentals that are hardy enough to withstand Iowa's rigorous winters. However, hundreds of other species can be and are used in decorating the outdoor living rooms of thousands of Iowa homes, school grounds, parks, streets and recreational centers.

STREET AND SHADE TREES.
- American Elm (*Ulmus americana*)
- Sugar Maple (*Acer saccharum*)
- Hackberry (*Celtis occidentalis*)
- Red Oak (*Quercus rubra*)
- Pin Oak (*Quercus palustris*)
- Black Walnut (*Juglans nigra*)
- Norway Spruce (*Picea abies*)
- White Pine (*Pinus strobus*)
- Black Hills Spruce (*Picea glauca albertiana*)
- *Juniperus* (in variety)
- Colorado Blue Spruce (*Picea pungens*)

SHRUBS.
- Staghorn Sumac (*Rhus typhina*)
- Common Lilac (*Syringa vulgaris*)
- Cranberry Tree (*Viburnum opulus*)
- Mock-orange (*Philadelphus coronarius*)
- American Elder (*Sambucus canadensis*)
- Tartarian Honeysuckle (*Lonicera tatarica*)
- Common Privet (*Ligustrum vulgare*)
- Amur Privet (*Ligustrum amurense*)
- Red Osier (*Cornus stolonifera*)
- Bridal Wreath (*Spiraea vanhouttei*)
- Persian Lilac (*Syringa persica*)
- Japanese Barberry (*Berberis thunbergi*)
- Hills-of-snow (*Hydrangea arborescens grandiflora*)
- Rugosa Rose (*Rosa rugosa*)
- Snowberry (*Symphoricarpos albus*)
- Anthony Waterer Spirea (*Spiraea bumalda* var. Anthony Waterer)

VINES.
- Virginia Creeper (*Parthenocissus quinquefolia*)
- Bittersweet (*Celastrus scandens*)
- Matrimony-vine (*Lycium halimifolium*)
- Riverbank Grape (*Vitis vulpina*)

PERENNIAL FLOWERS (Hardy).
- Dahlia
- Iris
- Peonies
- Hardy Phlox

BULBOUS PLANTS.
- Gladiolus
- Tulips
- Narcissus
- Lilies
- Dahlia
- Cannas

### CLIMATE

Iowa rainfall (including melted snow) averages 31.60 inches during the past 62 years. Of this, 38% falls in the three months, June, July and August, and 71% in the six months' period of April to September inclusive. The annual average ranges from less than 26 inches in the extreme northwest counties, to more than 35 inches in some southeast counties. The greatest variation in rainfall is in the central counties. More crop damage results from excessive heat than from deficient precipitation.

Damaging frost occurred somewhere in Iowa every month of the summer of 1863. It occurs occasionally in the peat beds of northern Iowa in June and August. The average date, for the whole state, of last killing frost in spring is May 2 and of first killing frost in autumn is October 5, giving an average of 156 frostless days per year. The average date of last killing frost in spring ranges from about April 25 in several southern areas, to about May 10 in several northern areas; and the average date of first killing frost in autumn ranges from about September 25 in the extreme northwest, to about October 10 in several southern areas.

The address of Iowa State College, which kindly furnished this information about the state, is Ames, Iowa. The College is always ready to answer gardening questions.

For the nearest Garden Club in your vicinity write the Garden Editor, Houghton Mifflin Company, Boston, Mass.

**IPOMOEA** (ip-po-mee'a). Morning-glory. Mostly twining vines of the family Convolvulaceae, many of the 400 species of tropical origin, and a few of them of much garden importance as the source of the sweet potato and the common morning-glory. They are mostly annual or perennial, often milky-juiced, vines, the perennials frequently with enormous roots. Leaves alternate,* generally stalked, simple,* or compound* and with several leaflets. Flowers large and showy, usually solitary or a few in the leaf-axils.* Calyx* lobed or parted. Corolla chiefly funnel-shaped, rarely bell-shaped, more or less 5-pointed or 5-angled at the top. Stigma* club-shaped or 2-lobed (forked in the closely related *Convolvulus*). Fruit an egg-shaped or roundish capsule.* (*Ipomoea* is from the Greek for worm and bindweed, and of no known significance here.)

The annual morning-glories, which are the chief ornamental kinds, are best sown where wanted. They are among our quickest and showiest of annual vines, and will grow easily in almost any soil. The perennial species are not always root-hardy in the North, as noted below. The roots of these tender sorts must be dug and stored over the winter in a cool, frost-free place, and planted outdoors when danger of frost is passed. Morning-glory seeds are very hard and germinate more readily if notched with a file.

**batatas.** Sweet potato. A sprawling perennial vine, rooting at the joints. Leaves lobed or unlobed, or sometimes divided finger-fashion, 4–6 in. long. Flowers rose-pink or violet-rose, about 2 in. long, but scarcely ever produced in the U.S. Probably tropical America. For culture see SWEET POTATO.

**bona-nox** = *Calonyction aculeatum*.

**coccinea** = *Quamoclit coccinea*.

**hederacea.** An annual, hairy, twining vine, the leaves ovalish or heart-shaped at the base, 2–3½ in. long, often 3-lobed. Flowers about 2 in. long, blue to pale purple, the sepals narrow and with recurved tips. Tropical America.

**hirsutula.** An annual, hairy, twining vine, the foliage resembling the last. Flowers bluish-purple or white, nearly 2½ in. long. Tropical America.

**horsfalliae.** A tropical perennial vine not hardy in the North (see above). Leaves compound,* finger-fashion, the leaflets* 5–7, thick, nearly 4 in. long. Flowers rose or pale purple, nearly 2½ in. long. The var. **briggsi** has crimson-magenta flowers.

**imperialis** = *Ipomoea nil*.

**leari.** Blue dawn-flower. Tropical American, perennial vine, its roots not hardy northward (see above). Leaves 6–8 in. long, generally ovalish or heart-shaped, sometimes 3-lobed, hairy beneath. Flowers 4–5 in. wide, very showy, blue but the tube white, ultimately turning pink.

**nil.** A tropical, hairy, perennial vine, the roots not hardy in the North (see above). Leaves broadly heart-shaped, 4–6 in. wide, more or less 3-lobed. Flowers about 4 in. wide, purple, blue, or rose-pink, often double. Sometimes offered as *I. imperialis*, and including among its many forms the Imperial Japanese morning-glories, which are larger-flowered and very bright-colored.

**pandurata.** Manroot; also called wild sweet potato and scammony. A native perennial vine, the root sometimes weighing 100 pounds and hardy in the North. Leaves broadly ovalish or heart-shaped, 4–6 in. long, rarely fiddle-shaped. Flowers nearly 4 in. wide, white, but the throat purple. Conn. to Fla. and Tex.

**purpurea.** The common morning-glory and an annual vine with a hairy stem. Leaves broadly oval or heart-shaped, 4–5 in. long, not lobed. Flowers nearly 3 in. long, purple, pink, or blue, the tube paler. There are forms with double flowers and with white flowers. Tropical America. Two especially fine hort. forms are Heavenly Blue and Rose Marie (pink). In Mex. there is also a double, yellow-flowered variety.

**setosa.** Brazilian morning-glory. A tropical perennial vine, the roots not hardy northward (see above), the stems covered with purplish and stiffish hairs. Leaves nearly 10 in. wide, 3-lobed and resembling the grape. Flowers about 3 in. long, rose-purple.

**tricolor.** A perennial, tropical American vine which blooms from seed the first year and can be grown as an annual. Leaves 4–5 in. long, unlobed, generally ovalish or heart-shaped. Flowers nearly 4 in. wide, purplish-blue, but the tip red before opening, the tube white.

**IPOMOPSIS** = *Gilia rubra*.

**IRESINE** (eye-re-sy'ne). Ornamental foliage plants (as grown) of the family Amaranthaceae, chiefly tropical. Of the 40 known species the two below are mostly grown as summer bedding plants. They will stand no frost and their winter care needs a greenhouse where they must be grown as is *Coleus* (which see). Leaves opposite,* stalked, generally ovalish. Flowers (rarely produced as grown) woolly,

---

* Special articles on the subjects indicated by an asterisk (*) will be found at the words so marked.

the parts rather chaffy or membranous, small, whitish, crowded in dense spikes* which are gathered in branched clusters (panicles*). Fruit 1-seeded, dry (utricle*). (*Iresine* is Greek for a woolly harvest garland, in allusion to the woolly flowers.)

As usually grown for bedding plants *Iresine* does not ordinarily produce flowers, and is propagated by cuttings wintered in the house or greenhouse. They are good, showy, summer-bedding, foliage plants. Florists often offer them under the name *Achyranthes*.

**herbsti.** Nearly 6 ft. high when full grown, the leaves 4–5 in. long, yellow-veined, but generally purplish-red, or green, notched at the tip. S.A.

**lindeni.** Leaves and stems mostly dark red, rarely green, the leaves pointed, not notched, more or less lance-oval, the veins prominent. Ecuador.

**IRIDACEAE** (eye-ri-day'see-ee). The iris family, often called the crocus or gladiolus family, is of outstanding garden importance. For besides these three popular favorites it contains the freesias and many other hort. genera of wide cultivation.

The family contains over 60 genera and perhaps 1000 species, scattered over most of the world, and of these over 20 genera are to be found in gardens or greenhouses throughout the country. All the garden genera are herbs, with chiefly basal, grass-like or sword-shaped leaves and usually very handsome flowers which arise from between 2 membranous bracts.* Nearly all the plants have an obvious stem, but *Crocus* is apparently (not actually) stemless.

The garden genera divide themselves, culturally, into three groups:
1. Hardy plants, wintering successfully in most regions: *Belamcanda, Crocus, Iris* (most species), *Lapeyrousia* (with protection) and *Sisyrinchium*.
2. Summer-blooming plants of warm regions, planted after danger of frost, and their underground parts lifted and stored over the winter; *i.e.* culture as for *Gladiolus*: *Acidanthera, Antholyza, Crocosmia, Gladiolus, Tigridia, Tritonia,* and *Watsonia*.
3. Tender plants of greenhouse culture or grown outdoors only in the frost-free (or nearly frost-free) South: *Aristea, Babiana, Dierama, Freesia, Ixia, Libertia, Moraea, Schizostylis* and *Sparaxis*.

The fruit in all genera is a 3-valved, many-seeded pod (capsule*).

Technical flower characters: (For *Iris*, see that entry.) Flowers otherwise regular in about half the genera, but very irregular in *Gladiolus* and its allies. Sepals 3, often petal-like and not easily distinguished from the 3 petals. The flowers in many genera are tubular, in others apparently (not actually) of separate petals. Stamens 3. Ovary inferior,* 3-celled, its usually 3 stigmas sometimes expanded and petal-like (*Iris* and *Moraea*).

**IRIDIFOLIA, -us, -um** (eye-rid-i-fō'lĭ-a). With iris-like leaves.

**IRIDIOIDES** (eye-rid-i-oy'deez, but see OÏDES). Iris-like.

**IRIS** (eye'ris). The genus *Iris* belongs to the family Iridaceae. Over 150 species were recognized by Dykes and since publication of his monograph (1913) further exploration has added to this number.

Irises are perennial herbs with long, narrow, mostly sword-shaped leaves, and rhizomes or bulb-like rootstocks. The flowers are in six segments and arise from spathe*-like bracts.* The three outer segments are reflexed (the "falls"), while the three inner ones are usually smaller and erect (the "standards"). Both have a narrow claw.* They are native mostly to north temperate zone. The sub-groups are many, and of them *Apogon* (the beardless irises) is the largest and the most widely distributed, extending through America, Europe, North Africa and Asia. *Pogoniris* (bearded irises), the second largest and the most important for gardens, is native to Central Europe and North Africa east to China. The fruit of all is a capsule.* (*Iris* was named for the goddess.)

The following species are of importance in American gardening either for their own beauty, or as parents of hybrids that are beautiful garden plants. Many others are known to fanciers, but are omitted here as not likely to interest the average grower.

### I. The Pogoniris Group (Bearded Iris)
#### A. Dwarf, Early

**pumila.** Austria to Russia and Asia Minor. Dwarf, hardy, early-blooming, almost if not entirely stemless, the wild types and hybrids having great range of color. Shallow-rooted, needs frequent transplanting.

**chamaeiris.** Southeastern France and northwestern Italy. A variable and much-confused species, with *I. pumila* the parent of most of the Dwarf Bearded Iris of commerce. It is distinguished from *I. pumila* by its stem which is from 1 to 3 inches long, and by greener, more rounded spathes* and its shorter tube. Its foliage is more persistent in winter than that of *I. pumila*.

#### B. Taller, Late

**pallida.** Southern Tyrol. Leaves 1 to 2 ft., the stems 2 to 3 ft. Spathe*-valves wholly membranous before the flowers expand. The tall, stout stems, with short branches near the center and above, and the broad foliage distinguish this species. Flowers are lavender-blue. It is the most, or one of the most, important parents of our garden Tall Bearded Irises. Dykes found this species and *I. variegata* growing together in two places in the mountains near the Adriatic Coast, and noted in each case innumerable wild hybrids between the two. Many earlier botanists had considered these hybrids as species. Here belong some of the plants formerly known as German Iris.

**variegata.** Austria east to southern Russia. The yellow standards and brown and purple falls readily distinguish this species from all others. Spathe*-valves not membranous. It is extremely hardy, its leaves dying away entirely in winter. With *I. pallida* it has proved a most important parent of garden irises, most of the yellow-brown and blended colors being derived from it. Here belong some of the plants formerly known as German Iris.

**trojana.** Troad, Asia Minor. This blue and red-purple species is distinguished by its branching habit and great size. This feature commended it to hybridists, and to it and the next species we owe the height, size and branching of many of our finest varieties. Spathes* green, flushed with purple, becoming membranous at tip, after the first flower has opened.

**mesopotamica.** Armenia, Syria. Lavender-blue. The flowers are so large and heavy that the long stems frequently sprawl instead of standing upright. This species has been much confused by botanists, but through its form *ricardi* it is now recognized as an important parent of garden varieties, particularly for mild climates like California.

### II. Apogon Group (Beardless Iris)
#### A. Sibirica Sub-section

**sibirica.** Central Europe and Russia. Tall, hollow stems, held well above foliage, flowers blue with network of veins, rather small. Spathes* membranous or brown.

**orientalis.** Manchuria and Japan. This eastern species differs from *I. sibirica* in having larger flowers on shorter stems, and broader foliage and spathes of red-purple. Most of the so-called Siberian irises now in the trade are hybrids between these two species.

#### B. Spuria Sub-section

**spuria.** Central and southeastern Europe. This species is variable and its exact relationship to other species or forms of the *I. spuria* sub-section is somewhat of a puzzle. Among the characteristics of the group is the way the branches of the stem rise perpendicularly and lie close to the main stem, the double-toothed stigma* and the semi-transparent, garment-like envelope which encloses each seed. The flowers are lilac in color and stand 2 to 3 ft. in height. The rhizomes are slender and tough.

---

* Special articles on the subjects indicated by an asterisk (*) will be found at the words so marked.

**ochroleuca.** Western Asia Minor. One of the tallest and most stately of iris, standing 3 to 5 ft. in good situations. Flowers are white with golden-yellow.

### C. Laevigata Sub-section

The four species of this sub-section have branching, leafy stems and smooth, flattened seeds.

**kaempferi.** Manchuria, Korea and Japan. Leaves with distinct midrib. Standards much shorter than falls. Capsules* broad, on long pedicels. Seeds thin and round. The above characteristics separate this species from *I. laevigata* with which it has been confused. The wild plants have red-purple flowers, their stalks about 2 to 2½ ft. high. The many gorgeous varieties of Japanese Iris are descended from this species.

**laevigata.** Eastern Siberia, Manchuria, possibly Japan. Leaves without raised midrib. Standards nearly as long as the falls. Capsules oblong, on short pedicels, the seeds thick. The wild plant is one of the finest of blue iris and there is also a wild, white form. They stand about 18 in. high.

**pseudacorus.** Europe, northern Africa to Siberia. This species, which is to be found in marshy spots all over Europe and even naturalized in this country, is characterized by splendid, clear yellow flowers borne on stems from 2 to 3 ft. high. The large rhizome is stout, tough and fibrous, and pinkish inside. It is the Fleur de Lys of France.

**versicolor.** Eastern N.A. The well-known Blue or Wild Flag of our eastern marshes and meadows. While it varies somewhat in color, it is practically a purplish counterpart of the yellow European *I. pseudacorus*, except that standards are a little more than half as long as the falls.

### D. Hexagona Sub-section

**hexagona.** Southeastern United States. Flowers lavender on 3-ft. stems. Like others of this section it is a marsh plant, but will grow in ordinary garden soil, although it is not reliably hardy north of Washington.

**foliosa.** Southeastern United States. This is a dwarf counterpart of *I. hexagona*, with similar flowers which are held below the leaves by a zigzag stem. It is much hardier. With *I. fulva* it is the parent of a number of fine hybrids. Many of the new species and forms discovered recently in Louisiana by Dr. John K. Small are closely related to *I. hexagona*, *I. foliosa* and *I. fulva*, and some of them may be hybrids or mere color forms.

**fulva.** Louisiana and other southern states. The best-known type of this species is one of the most distinct of all irises on account of its reddish flowers. Its six segments all droop outwards. It is hardy in the North but not always as free-flowering as in milder climates. Recently many color forms of this species have been discovered and they should make valuable additions to gardens.

### E. California Sub-section

The species of this sub-section are confined to the Pacific Coast states and are practically evergreen. The rhizomes are very slender and they have few root fibers, hence are exceedingly difficult to transplant. They should be grown from seeds and are exceedingly variable.

**tenax.** Washington and Oregon. A graceful, pleasing iris, hardy in the North. The 12- to 15-inch stems bear two lilac-purple flowers.

### F. Longipetala Sub-section

The species of this group are good garden plants but their names have been a good deal confused.

**missouriensis.** Rocky Mountains and western United States. This upland species has stems distinctly longer than the leaves, and a slender growth. It loses its leaves in autumn and remains dormant until spring. The capsule is thin-walled with 6 ribs and tapers toward either end. Seeds smooth, spherical, and brown. Flowers pale blue.

### Miscellaneous Beardless Irises

**unguicularis.** Algeria to Greece and Asia Minor. This species is not hardy north of Washington, D.C. It is of importance only in mild climates where it will bloom from December to February. The flowers are lilac and white, and most useful for cutting. Often offered as *I. stylosa*.

### III. Bulbous Iris Group

About twenty species of this group are cultivated in this country. They are valuable for their brilliant colors.

### A. Xiphium Sub-section

**xiphium.** Spain, Portugal and northern Africa. In the high mountains the plants are slender with small flowers blooming in August, but along the seacoast they are much larger and flower in April. The flowers are bluish and the leaves onion-like. This species is a parent of the garden race of Spanish Iris.

### B. Reticulata Sub-section

**reticulata.** Caucasia. This species has a network of fibers forming the outer coat of the bulb. The wild type is red-purple, only a few inches high, blooming in March and quite fragrant.

### C. Juno Sub-section

**orchioides.** Eastern Bokhara. The bulbs have light brown outer skins. Flowers with a narrow claw* to the falls, yellow or white, comparatively small, three or four in number produced singly on the axes of the outermost leaves. Seeds cubical.

### IV. Crested Iris Group

This small group is distinguished by a linear crest along the center of the claw.*

**cristata.** Southeastern United States. This species is distinct from the Asiatic members of the group in being practically stemless, the flowers being raised only three or four inches above the ground. They are borne singly, or in pairs, and are light lilac. Rhizome is slender and greenish.

**gracilipes.** Japan. A very slender, little species with slight wire-like stem 9 to 12 inches high. Flowers lilac or pinkish-mauve, with an orange crest. The spathe,* unlike all other irises, has but one valve.

**tectorum.** Central and southwestern China (but best known from Japan). The well-known Roof Iris of Japan, and a shallow-rooted plant. Leaves broad, about 18 inches long. Flower stalk branching, about 15 in. high, the flowers blue-purple.

### Alphabetical List of Iris Species
*With References to their Proper Group or Sub-section*
*(as above)*

| | | | | | |
|---|---|---|---|---|---|
| chamaeiris | I | A | ochroleuca | II | B |
| cristata | IV | | orchioides | III | C |
| foliosa | II | D | orientalis | II | A |
| fulva | II | D | pallida | I | B |
| germanica | A little-known plant long confused with *I. pallida* and *I. variegata* which include the "German" Iris, now better called Tall Bearded Iris. | | pseudacorus | II | C |
| | | | pumila | I | A |
| | | | reticulata | III | B |
| | | | sibirica | II | A |
| | | | spuria | II | B |
| | | | stylosa = *unguicularis* | | |
| | | | tectorum | IV | |
| gracilipes | IV | | tenax | II | E |
| hexagona | II | D | trojana | I | B |
| kaempferi | II | C | unguicularis | II | Miscellaneous Beardless |
| laevigata | II | C | | | |
| mesopotamica | I | B | variegata | I | B |
| missouriensis | II | F | versicolor | II | C |
| | | | xiphium | III | A |

### Iris Culture

Gardeners need not be greatly concerned about the vast number of *Iris* species, for some are unobtainable, some are comparatively unattractive, some thrive only under certain mild climatic conditions, and many are almost identical in general appearance. It is well, therefore, for the gardener to leave the consideration of most of the species to bota-

---
* Special articles on the subjects indicated by an asterisk (*) will be found at the words so marked.

## GARDEN IRIS

1 Kaempferi — Lavender
2 Kaempferi — Purple
3 Sibirica — Perry's Blue
4, 5 Cristata
6, 7 Shekinah (tall bearded)
8 Autumn King (tall bearded)
9 Xiphium (Spanish)

nists and to confine himself to choosing a reasonable number of species and varieties in each of the groups which will be enumerated here.

The two most important groups for the general gardener are, (1) the Bearded Iris group and (2) the Beardless Iris group. Following these in importance come (3) the Bulbous Iris group and (4) the Crested Iris group.

### (1) The Bearded Iris

For centuries this group has been the most important garden group of *Iris*, and there is no reason to suppose that the species and varieties of the other groups are likely to supplant the Bearded Iris in popularity, in wide distribution and in general garden usefulness. While it comprises over 20 species none of them are of garden importance because they have been superseded by the hybrid children of a few species of rather narrow geographical range.

All Bearded Irises have these distinguishing characteristics. The flower has the beard-like growth (from which the group gets its name) along the center line of the claw of the fall. The leaf is wide and sword-like. The rhizome is comparatively large, plump and smooth, is usually about half out of the ground, and has comparatively few and coarse roots (instead of many and fine as in the Beardless group). The plants demand good drainage, full sun and the warmest, driest situation. Because many of our native Beardless Iris grow in swamps, many gardeners injure or kill Bearded Iris with too much water. They like it dry, and given good drainage can be grown in practically every state of the Union, except perhaps Florida, and many of them thrive in even the coldest part of Canada.

Any good garden soil that will grow corn, potatoes, petunias or zinnias, will grow iris, but for the finest flowers the soil should be reasonably good. Add well-rotted cow manure or horse manure to the soil when making the bed. Top-dress occasionally with bone meal, acid phosphate (superphosphate) or wood ashes, or all three, but do not use any *fresh* animal manures or any strong nitrogen fertilizers, as they give a quick, soft growth which is easily attacked by disease. Very acid soil should be limed occasionally, but this is seldom really necessary and is often overdone.

Plant in early spring, or just after flowers are finished (June) (except in parts of the South subject to extreme summer drought), or in early fall (except in extreme North). In latitude of New York, spring and summer transplants do not require winter mulch, but fall-planted material should be covered with straw or marsh hay. North of New York and north and west of Chicago winter mulch is advisable for all *Iris*. Plant from 8 to 18 inches apart, according to effect desired. Divide and reset when plants become too crowded, which is usually between the third and fifth year. Do not transplant big clumps but divide down to strong, single rhizomes.

Bearded Iris may be roughly divided into Dwarf, Intermediate and Tall. The Dwarfs are hybrids of two species, *I. chamaeiris* and *I. pumila*, natives of Europe and the Caucasus respectively. They are four to twelve inches in height, early-blooming (April in latitude of New York City), not as vigorous-growing as the larger, later-blooming types, and are best grown on the edge of the herbaceous border or in the rock garden. The following varieties are good: Bride, white; Azurea, light blue; Black Midget, dark blue-purple; Socrates, red-purple; Orange Queen, yellow.

The Intermediate Bearded Iris bloom in mid-May in latitude of New York, and are from 12 inches to 30 inches or more in height. They are of two types: first, the wild types of Italy and Asia Minor, which are of confused botanical position and usually not given specific rank, but grouped together as the *germanica* group. (Note: the late Tall Bearded Irises are commonly but improperly called German Iris, but they are not directly related to this group and are descended from totally different species.) Included in this group are the well-known blue-and-purple flag, as well as a grayish-white one, and another with rich, deep purple flowers. The second type comprise man-made hybrids between the Dwarf and the later Tall Irises. Important varieties are: Ingeborg, white; Halfdan, pale yellow; Nymph, golden-yellow; and Prince Victor, blue and purple.

The most important of all irises are the late-blooming Tall Bearded hybrids. They grow from 2 to 4 ft. (even to 6 ft. in California) in height, and bloom in early June in the latitude of New York. At least five thousand varieties have been named in the past century. They constitute a most amazing horticultural development surpassed by no other hardy plant. The work of the many iris breeders — French, German, English and American, deserves a whole volume to itself but has been briefly covered in the bulletins of the American Iris Society.

Suffice it to say here that the varieties of the 19th century were descended mostly from the bluish *Iris pallida* of Italy and the yellow and brownish *Iris variegata* of Hungary and Bulgaria. Certain wild hybrids of these two species were brought into gardens more than a century ago and they and the resulting garden hybrids soon gave rise to the great color range which earned for the iris the name "rainbow flower." The breeders of the 20th century used not only these species, types and varieties, but also species, types and forms from Asia Minor, such as *I. trojana*, *I. mesopotamica*, and others, which gave additional height and size of flower and better branching of stalk. Some of these latter are not satisfactory garden plants in the North but their hybrid descendants have retained the hardiness of the *I. pallida* and *I. variegata* parents and are (with some few exceptions) well fitted to most American climates, particularly if extra care is taken to see that the drainage is good. Winter hardiness in *Iris* is often more a matter of resistance to excessive moisture and alternate freezing and thawing than to low temperature.

Probably over 1500 varieties of Tall Bearded Iris are offered in American catalogues today at retail prices ranging from 15 cents to $5, $10, $15, or even $50 apiece. Breeders and collectors and exhibitors are willing to pay high prices for fine new varieties but the average gardener need not concern himself with novelties but should stick to the good older varieties that can be had for 15 cents, 25 cents or 50 cents each. There is not and can never be any best list of 12, 25 or 50 varieties, as individual tastes vary so and varieties may vary in different soils and climates, but the following are all well tried and can be recommended without any hesitation:

WHITE (but sometimes marked with other colors): Fairy, White Knight, Chartier, Athene, True Charm, True Delight, Shasta, Rhein Nixe, Mildred Presby.
BLUE AND PURPLE: Corrida, Princess Beatrice, Queen Caterina, Ballerine, Lord of June, Baldwin, Souv. de Mme. Gaudichau.
PINK TO RED-PURPLE: Susan Bliss, Frieda Mohr, Rheingauperle, Seminole, Morning Splendor.
BLENDS: Afterglow, Quaker Lady, Jacquesiana, Ambassadeur, Ochracea, Dolly Madison.
YELLOW: Flavescens, Shekinah, Primrose, Gold Imperial.
YELLOW WITH BROWN AND PURPLE: Lorelei, Flammenschwert.

### (2) The Beardless Iris Group

This is the largest group botanically speaking, containing some fifteen sub-groups. It encircles the globe in the north temperate region and many species are to be found in each of the great continents of North America, Europe and Asia. In North America, Beardless Iris are found from Labrador to the Gulf of Mexico and west to the Rocky Mountains, and the Pacific Coast from northern Mexico to Canada.

All Beardless Irises have these distinguishing characteristics. The center line of the claw* of the falls lacks the so-called beard which is present in the Bearded Iris. The entire petal is smooth and "beardless." The flower, except in the Japanese Iris, is composed of narrower petals than those of Bearded Iris. The leaf is mostly narrower and grass-like, rather than sword-like. The rhizome is much smaller, more fuzzy, remains always underground and when dug the clump does not pull apart readily as does a clump of Bearded Iris,

---

* Special articles on the subjects indicated by an asterisk (*) will be found at the words so marked.

so that it has to be cut with a knife, spade or axe. It has many fine roots and they cannot be dried out with impunity in transplanting as can Bearded Iris rhizomes and roots. Transplanting must be done as carefully as with a delphinium or Sweet William or phlox, while a Bearded Iris clump may be torn carelessly apart, left lying on a path for a day or a week in the sun without fatal results.

Most Beardless Iris prefer a rather sour soil and they love lots of moisture. Some will stand drying out or even baking late in the season, but in the spring they flourish if constantly covered with water. Most of them grow successfully in the herbaceous border without artificial watering, but they will not give as large or as many flowers as those plants having their feet in water. They are gross feeders and should have a richer soil than other irises. Use cow manure freely when making the beds and as a summer dressing and winter mulch. They will stand more nitrogen than the Bearded Iris.

Transplanting is best done in early spring but can be done also after flowers are over if the new beds are kept well watered. Many people also transplant in autumn with success, but as severe losses occasionally result it is not recommended. Plants will need dividing in five or six years in most places. It is best not to make the divisions smaller than a good-sized fist. Most of the sub-sections bloom just after the Bearded Iris. The exceptions will be noted.

The following sub-sections are the most important:

(1) SIBIRICA. This sub-section includes about nine important species of which the species *I. sibirica* and its ally *I. orientalis* are the most important. The former, in spite of its name, is from Central Europe and Russia, the latter from Siberia. Grown in gardens they have produced many forms and hybrids of which Lactea and Snow Queen, white; Perry's Blue and Kingfisher Blue, pale blue; Emperor, deep purple; and Red Emperor, red-purple, may be mentioned. All are splendid plants and easily grown and deserve far greater recognition than they have had. Fine in the garden, they are superlative when naturalized in quantity on the edges of ponds and streams.

(2) SPURIA. This contains a dozen or more species and various wild and cultivated hybrids. Mostly they are not as vigorous or free-blooming as the *sibirica* sub-section, except on the Pacific Coast. The petals are narrower and rather stiffer and in this they resemble the Spanish Iris of the Bulbous group, and are often mistaken for them. *I. spuria* and *I. ochroleuca* are both tall, handsome garden plants. They bloom June 15th to 20th in New York.

(3) LAEVIGATA. This sub-section contains *Iris versicolor*, native from Labrador to the Gulf, and everywhere known as the blue or wild flag. Because it is so commonly seen in swamps untold thousands of Bearded Iris have been killed by kindly intentioned overwatering. Delightful in the wild or when naturalized along streams, I can scarcely recommend it for the small garden. This is true also of its close relative *Iris pseudacorus*, the Fleur de Lys of France, and native along water courses all over the continent of Europe, and stretching into the British Isles, into Siberia and into North Africa. It is a clear yellow and has escaped from cultivation in many places.

The most famous garden plant of this section or indeed of all Beardless Iris is *Iris kaempferi*, the Japanese Iris, which blooms in New York early in July and really winds up the iris season which began in March with *Iris reticulata* (to be mentioned later under Bulbous Iris). The flowers are sometimes a foot across and cover a great color range, from white through lavender-blue and lavender-pink up into rich, deep violet-purples and crimson-purples. There is no yellow. Persons talking of yellow Japanese Iris usually mean *I. pseudacorus* or some of the *spuria* section. The wild *Iris kaemepfri* is native to China and Japan and of a light magenta color. Our fine garden varieties are the result of generations and even centuries of cultivation and selection by Japanese gardeners. As in the case of the chrysanthemum, the Cherry and other famous Japanese flowers, little is known of the individuals who did this work, but often certain strains were for generations in the possession of single families or of small societies or guilds.

Unfortunately, the nomenclature of Japanese Iris has apparently always been and still is hopelessly mixed. Japanese dealers seem to have been very careless in their labeling, so that often the original plants reached this country under wrong names. Only recently has an attempt been made to assemble all varieties of Japanese Iris available in Japan, Europe and America, and to accurately describe them. This work will take many years and in the meantime it seems wiser for gardeners to buy their plants by color rather than by name. For those who wish to select by name, however, the following can be recommended:

WHITE: Gold Bound, Morning Mists.
BLUE: Blue Danube, Blue Jay.
PINK: Pink Progress.
RED-PURPLE: Helene Von Siebold, Mahogany, Orion, Paragon.

Japanese Iris (like most other Beardless Iris) are easily grown from seed, and if solid groups of colors or elaborate color schemes are not desired, this is the best way to start a garden of Japanese Iris. Buy the best quality seed and you should secure a good color range with both the single (or 3-petal) and the double (or 6-petal) forms.

(4) HEXAGONA. Before 1920 two species of this section, native to our southern states, *I. fulva* and *I. foliosa*, were to be seen occasionally in northern gardens, and also the hybrids Fulvala and Dorothy K. Williamson. Since 1920 the discoveries of Dr. John K. Small of the New York Botanical Garden, in Louisiana and other southern states have kept this sub-section in the limelight. About 100 new species and over 200 color forms have been named and described.

They have not found their way into many gardens and only a few kinds have been taken up by the nurserymen. Among these may be mentioned Vinicolor, Savannarum, Alba-spiritis, Kimballiae, *I. flexicaulis* and *I. rivularis*.

(5) CALIFORNIA. This sub-section comprises half a dozen or more species native to the California mountains and north into British Columbia. They get abundant spring moisture and then months of baking. While hardy in the North they have not made a great impression on our gardens because they resent transplanting and shipping. All should be grown from seed and treated as rock garden plants. *I. tenax* is the best known. They flower in May and June.

(6) UNGUICULARIS. The species of this sub-section are all tender in the North but thrive in California and other mild climates where they flower throughout the winter. The species *unguicularis* (more commonly called *I. stylosa*) is from Algeria and eastward.

### (3) THE BULBOUS IRIS GROUP

This really comprises two groups. First, the tiny *I. reticulata* and others from Asia Minor and the Caucasus, which bloom with the Crocus and are no larger. They belong in the rock garden. Second, the *Xiphium* group which are 18 to 24 inches in height, and bloom in May and June. Botanically, the latter group has half a dozen or more species, but in gardens, instead of growing these, we have three hybrid races, the Dutch and Spanish and English Irises, which bloom in the order named. All were developed in Holland from species native to the Mediterranean region.

All bulbous Iris should be planted in autumn like Tulips. The *I. reticulata* group are satisfactory at least as far north as Massachusetts in the rock garden and persist year after year if the tiny foliage isn't mistaken for garlic and pulled out. The varieties of the *I. xiphium* group will flower in the North the first season but usually tend to die out after that. They really should be lifted in late June and stored in a warm, dry place for the summer, and replanted in the autumn, but few gardeners will take the trouble to do this when bulbs cost but a few dollars a hundred.

South of Richmond and on the Pacific Coast they flourish and increase prodigiously. A variety of the Dutch Iris race is the one commonly forced by florists.

---

\* Special articles on the subjects indicated by an asterisk (\*) will be found at the words so marked.

### (4) The Crested Iris Group

The Crested Iris group is small but important for the rock garden. The name comes from the golden crest along the center of the claw.* The plants flourish in semi-shade, a very unusual characteristic with *Iris*. One species, *I. cristata*, is native to our southeastern states, while *I. gracilipes* and *I. tectorum* are from Japan. The latter grows easily from seed.

Like the Rose, the Dahlia, the Gladiolus and other popular flowers, the Iris has a special society devoted to its interests. The American Iris Society was organized in 1920 as a forum to bring together all persons interested in Iris, and to raise the quality of Irises in our gardens. The society publishes a quarterly bulletin of Iris news. It has conducted much research concerning Iris history, Iris cultivation, Iris breeding, Iris pests, etc. It has established more than a dozen great public collections of Iris and holds many exhibitions yearly.

All interested persons are welcomed as members. Full information can be secured by writing to the Garden Editor, Houghton Mifflin Company, Boston, Mass. — J.C.W.

INSECT PESTS. A large caterpillar, becoming 2 in. long, bores in the crowns and roots. Winter clean-up of weeds, trash, and iris foliage and summer destruction of infested parts of the plants are control measures. Spring sprays of lead arsenate, soap, and nicotine on new growth are of some value. Other pests are only incidental.

DISEASES. The principal diseases of iris are leafspot, soft rot and crown rot. When *leafspot* is present, the leaves exhibit brown, oval spots with water-soaked margins. Excellent control can be obtained by removing and burning all old leaves in the fall. With *soft rot*, a bacterial disease, a slimy, ill-smelling rot of the rhizomes and leaf bases is the typical symptom. Wounds are necessary for infection. For control, eradicate the iris borer, destroy severely infected plants, provide well-drained soil and adequate sunlight. In August, infected rhizomes should be dug and the rotted portions cut out. Then dip for ten minutes in corrosive sublimate, 1 ounce to 7½ gallons of water. *Crown rot* is characterized by a decay of the leaf- and flower-stalk bases. For control, destroy severely infected plants, use fresh or sterilized soil and avoid crowding of the plants. In cases of partial infection, treat the rhizomes with corrosive sublimate as suggested above.

**IRIS FAMILY.** Besides the iris itself this large family of plants produces many other garden favorites, among them gladiolus, crocus, freesia, blue-eyed grass, *Ixia*, and *Tigridia*. For the other cult. genera and a description of the family see IRIDACEAE.

**IRISH HEATH** = *Daboecia cantabrica*.

**IRISH JUNIPER** = *Juniperus communis hibernica*.

**IRISH YEW** = *Taxus baccata fastigiata*.

**IRONBARK.** See EUCALYPTUS SIDEROXYLON.

**IRON-TREE.** See METROSIDEROS.

**IRONWEED.** See VERNONIA.

**IRONWOOD.** Many hardwooded trees are so called in all parts of the world. Those in cultivation include: *Ostrya virginiana*, *Metrosideros*, *Carpinus caroliniana* (see HORNBEAM).

**IRREGULAR FLOWER.** A flower that is unsymmetrical, due to the parts being of different sizes, or because some part is lacking, but mostly because the flower is spurred or 2-lipped, as in the snapdragon. All orchid flowers are irregular. See REGULAR FLOWER.

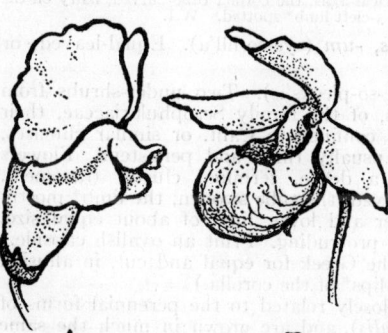

Two types of irregular flower. (*A*) Snapdragon. (*B*) Lady's-slipper.

**IRRIGATION.** Many places in the U.S. cannot be certain of growing crops without supplementing an inadequate or poorly distributed rainfall. While this applies chiefly to the region west of the 100th Meridian, there are many places in the East where summer droughts may be disastrous if a supplementary water supply is not forthcoming.

The remedy for such rainfall deficiency is irrigation, which for purposes of this discussion may be divided into overhead systems, and the sort used in the West, where the land itself is flooded. The latter system is in wide use in states where the annual rainfall is less than 10 in., and in many others where summer rainfall is almost lacking. See the name of your state for rainfall figures in your locality. There are many places, too, where a reasonably good winter rainfall (10-18 in.) will be followed by periods of from 130-250 days in which there is no effective rainfall, *i.e.* capable of wetting the soil. Growing anything but desert plants in such regions, without irrigation, is practically impossible, although their soils may be fertile enough. The Imperial Valley, much of the Calif. fruit areas, and the apple orchards at Wenatchee in Wash. are examples of irrigated districts that would be worthless without it.

WESTERN IRRIGATION. In regions such as these, large amounts of water must be brought to the garden or orchard during the growing season. It is impossible in a general article to specify whether driven wells, a local water company, or a state irrigation system will be the most economical source of supply. Sometimes irrigation water can be purchased for an agreed percentage of the final crop.

Assuming an adequate water supply, it must be conducted to every part of the garden or orchard, usually in tightly jointed iron pipes, but often in open ditches or by flumes, which are reasonably water-tight, V-shaped, wooden troughs. Whichever method is used, there must be provision for necessary outlets, so spaced that all parts of the plantation will be covered. In many irrigated districts the outlets are put 6-8 ft. apart for small crops, but 10-20 ft. apart for fruit trees.

No part of the irrigation system is more important than the ground level. If too steep, irrigation is impossible. If too flat, a large number of outlets are necessary properly to distribute the water over even such a small piece of land as an acre.

In moderately sloping land, a system of basins or ridges should be constructed which will hold enough water in comparatively small areas — a plan known as basin or check irrigation. But by far the best method is for the land to slope so gently in one direction that the water may flow directly but slowly between the rows of plants.

The amount and frequency of applying the water depend upon the kind and age of the crop, the kind of soil, the heat and the velocity of the wind, and the time since the last effective rain. They depend, also, in some states, upon the cost of the water. No definite rule can be given, but a few general principles should be understood.

When water is to be turned on, see that the whole area is thoroughly puddled, more for trees, of course, than for shallower-rooted crops. It may take an inch or 2 in. of water to do this, in some places more. When the soil is dry enough, cultivate* it thoroughly, for irrigation is not a substitute for cultivation, but an adjunct of it. Weeds must be kept down or they will steal some of the expensive water.

Many fruit growers plan to use, in rainless summers, about 4-5 applications of water, averaging 1½-2½ in. each. It is well known that too much or too frequent watering is harmful to the crop, and especially to the soil, which appears to lose some plant food by excessive water applications. See LEACHING. Again, no general rule is possible, but the rule of common sense and watching the crop and the weather always applies. See notes on irrigation at ARIZONA.

EASTERN IRRIGATION. Supplying gardens or trees with water on such a scale is never necessary in the East. But many shallow-rooted crops, like vegetables, are often caught by summer heat and droughts. And many commercial and private growers have found that some overhead sprinkling system more than pays for itself.

Since 1904 one of the best of these overhead watering plans is the device known as the Skinner system. It consists of galvanized pipes, elevated so as to throw a fine spray in

---

* Special articles on the subjects indicated by an asterisk (*) will be found at the words so marked.

both directions far enough to meet the spray of the next line of pipe. This means that the pipes are from 6–8 ft. above the ground level and must be supported about every 25 ft. with posts or iron pipe.

Water merely forced through holes in a pipe cannot be properly distributed. The merit of the Skinner system is that at each outlet (they should be 4 ft. apart) a patented nozzle is attached, and it is this that ensures a fine, mist-like spray. One can buy pipes already provided with the nozzles, or can drill the holes (with a patented drilling machine) and put the nozzles in. Also, when the system is moved, as it can be readily, a patented union for the piping is necessary.

In spite of the exclusive, patentable features of this system, it is not very expensive, varying from $90 to $150 per acre. It is by far the most effective system of overhead irrigation so far devised, for the water falls as in the finest rain. There is no soil washing, nor packing, and no injury to the crops, as may come from careless hosing. Sometimes insecticides or fungicides may be pumped into the system instead of water. There are, of course, several other systems in use.

Water must be kept at a definite pressure and the diameter size of the pipe varies with its length and with the pressure. For the most effective installation study the tables below:

SIZES OF PIPE FOR OUTDOOR NOZZLE LINES

Calculated on outdoor nozzles placed 4 ft. apart. If the nozzles are closer together larger pipe must be used.

| Nozzle No. | Length of line, ft. | No. ft. ¾-in. pipe | No. ft. 1-in. pipe | No. ft. 1¼-in. pipe | No. ft. 1½-in. pipe | No. ft. 2-in. pipe |
|---|---|---|---|---|---|---|
| No. 1 Outdoor | 150 | 150 | | | | |
| | 200 | 130 | 70 | | | |
| | 250 | 100 | 150 | | | |
| | 300 | 100 | 150 | 50 | | |
| | 400 | 90 | 160 | 150 | | |
| | 500 | 90 | 160 | 150 | 100 | |
| | 600 | 90 | 160 | 175 | 175 | |
| | 700 | 90 | 160 | 175 | 175 | 100 |
| No. 2 Outdoor | 150 | 115 | 35 | | | |
| | 200 | 100 | 100 | | | |
| | 250 | 90 | 100 | 60 | | |
| | 300 | 90 | 100 | 110 | | |
| | 400 | 80 | 100 | 120 | 100 | |
| | 500 | 75 | 100 | 120 | 120 | 85 |
| | 600 | 75 | 100 | 120 | 120 | 185 |

DISTANCE BETWEEN NOZZLE LINES FOR OUTDOOR IRRIGATION

| Nozzle No. | Pounds pressure | Distance between lines, feet | Nozzle No. | Pounds pressure | Distance between lines, feet |
|---|---|---|---|---|---|
| No. 1 Outdoor | 10 | 40 | No. 2 Outdoor | 45 | 60 |
| | 20 | 50 | | 75 | 60 |
| | 40 | 56 | | 80 | 56 |
| | 45 | 56 | | 100 and over | 50 |
| | 50 | 54 | | | |
| | 75 and over | 50 | | | |

There is still another system of irrigation better than any so far noted. It works upon the principle that in nature capillarity supplies the roots of plants with water drawn from below. Sub-irrigation does the same thing. It involves delivering water below the surface of the ground. For details of it see WATERING, as it is chiefly applied to greenhouse benches, frames, window-boxes, and hanging baskets (which see).

ISATIS (eye'sa-tis; also eye-say'tis). Rather unimportant herbs of the mustard family, chiefly from the Mediterranean region. Of the 50 known species only the two below are in cult., generally under the name of woad. Before the days of synthetic dyes they were of interest as the source of a blue dye. They are erect, usually branching herbs, with alternate,* often stem-clasping and mostly undivided leaves. Flowers small, in rather open, loose clusters (panicled racemes*), the 4 petals yellow. Fruit not splitting, key-like, hanging, oblongish or narrower, usually minutely notched at the tip. (*Isatis* is the classical name for some healing herb, but not necessarily of these plants.)

The first is a perennial, and seed of it should be sown the year before bloom is expected. *Isatis tinctoria* is a biennial and must also be sown the previous Aug.–Sept. for bloom the next season. Both are of easy culture in any garden soil.

**glauca.** A perennial herb 2–4 ft. high, the foliage very bluish-gray. Basal leaves blunt, oblongish, those of the stem nearly stalkless, the base narrowed and not stem-clasping. Flowers many, the terminal cluster large and branched. Fruit more or less oblongish, about ½ in. long. Persia and Asia Minor. June–July.

**tinctoria.** Common woad; also called dyer's woad. A biennial herb, 18–36 in. high. Basal leaves oblongish, usually without hairs and bluish-green, the stem leaves narrower, the base stem-clasping, with narrow auricles.* Flowers in compound racemes,* small. Fruit about ⅝ in. long, about ⅓ as wide. Eu. Once commonly raised for its blue dye.

**ISHI-BASHI.** A stone bridge. *See* JAPANESE GARDEN.

**ISLAND MYRTLE** = *Ceanothus arboreus*.

**ISLAY** = *Prunus ilicifolia*.

**ISMENE CALATHINA** = *Hymenocallis calathina*. *See* SPIDER-LILY.

**ISO-JIMA.** A rock island. *See* JAPANESE GARDEN.

**ISOLEPIS GRACILIS** = *Scirpus cernuus*.

**ISOLOMA** (eye-so-lō'ma). Tropical American herbs or shrubs of the family Gesneriaceae, comprising over 50 species, of which the two below, or hybrids of them and other species, are favorite greenhouse plants. They have creeping roots or rootstocks and opposite,* usually softly hairy and very handsome leaves. Flowers mostly scarlet or orange, borne singly or in small clusters in the leaf-axils,* or in a leafy terminal cluster (raceme*). Corolla more or less tubular, but somewhat swollen towards the top, its limb* not quite regular* and 5-lobed. Stamens 4, sometimes with an odd sterile one. Fruit a capsule.* (*Isoloma* is from the Greek for equal and throat, in allusion to the throat of the corolla.)

They should be grown in the warm-temperate greenhouse (see GREENHOUSE), in potting mixture* 4. Otherwise, their culture and propagation are the same as *Gloxinia* (which see).

**amabile.** A hairy, perennial herb 12–30 in. high. Leaves stalked, more or less oval, sharply toothed, more or less purple-veined and with scattered purple blotches. Flowers hanging, the corolla slightly curved, the tube purple-blotched and pale within, the limb* dark red, but purple-dotted. Colombia.

**hirsutum.** A hairy, shrubby plant 2–4 ft. high. Leaves short-stalked, ovalish or narrower, tapering at the tip, bluntly toothed. Flowers nodding, solitary in the leaf-axils, the corolla tube curved, hairy on the outside, purple, but the 5-cleft limb* spotted. W.I.

**ISOPHYLLA, -us, -um** (eye-so-fill'a). Equal-leaved; or with similar leaves.

**ISOPLEXIS** (eye-so-plecks'is). Two under-shrubs from the Canary Islands, of the family Scrophulariaceae, their outdoor cultivation confined to Calif. or similar climates. Leaves alternate,* usually thick and persistent. Flowers yellow, mostly in a dense, terminal cluster (raceme*). Corolla tubular, curved, the tube swollen, the limb* mostly 2-lipped,* the upper and lower lips* of about equal size. Stamens 4, slightly protruding. Fruit an ovalish capsule.* (*Isoplexis* is from the Greek for equal and cut, in allusion to the nearly equal lips* of the corolla.)

The plants are closely related to the perennial forms of the foxglove (*Digitalis*), and are grown in much the same way. *See* FOXGLOVE.

**canariensis.** A stiff, erect plant 3–4 ft. high, the leaves thick, lance-shaped, 4–6 in. long, and shining. Flower cluster (raceme*) nearly 12 in. long, the flowers about 1 in. long, yellowish-brown.

**sceptrum.** Resembling the last, but the leaves are larger, the flowers drooping, and the corolla not 2-lipped,* its 5 lobes nearly equal.

---

* Special articles on the subjects indicated by an asterisk (*) will be found at the words so marked.

**ISOPYRUM** (eye-so-py'rum). Dwarf herbaceous perennials, belonging to the Ranunculaceae. Of the 20 North American and Asiatic species only the false anemone, *I. biternatum*, is likely to be cult. Flowers white, solitary or in panicles, without petals, but with 5–6 sepals. (*Isopyrum* is the classical name of a *Fumaria*, and of no known application here.)

**biternatum.** False anemone. Leaves twice-compound,* the leaflets 3-lobed and with slender stalks. Flowers ¾ in. wide, the clusters appearing in spring. Ont. to Fla. and Tex. Suitable for the rockery in partial shade, and propagated by seed or by division.

**fumarioides** = *Leptopyrum fumarioides*.

**ITALIAN ASTER** = *Aster amellus*.

**ITALIAN BROCCOLI** = *Brassica oleracea italica*. For culture see BROCCOLI.

**ITALIAN CLOVER** = *Trifolium incarnatum*. See CLOVER.

**ITALIAN CORN SALAD** = *Valerianella eriocarpa*.

**ITALIAN CYPRESS** = *Cupressus sempervirens*.

**ITALIAN GARDEN.** See ARCHITECTURAL STYLE.

**ITALIAN HONEYSUCKLE** = *Lonicera caprifolium*.

**ITALIAN JASMINE** = *Jasminum humile*.

**ITALIAN KALE** = *Brassica rapa septiceps*.

**ITALIAN REED** = *Arundo donax*.

**ITALIAN RYE GRASS** = *Lolium multiflorum*.

**ITALIAN STONE PINE** = *Pinus pinea*. See PINE.

**ITALIAN WINE GRAPES.** See *Vinifera* var. at GRAPE.

*ITALICA, -us, -um* (i-tal'i-ka). From Italy.

**ITEA** (it'ee-a). A small genus of shrubs or trees of the family Saxifragaceae, one cult. for its showy flowers. Leaves alternate,* rather narrow. Flowers in clusters (racemes*), white, with five narrow petals and five persistent sepals.* Fruit a 2-valved capsule.* A few species in eastern As., one in N.A. (*Itea* is from the Greek for willow.)

**virginica.** Virginia Willow. A shrub 3–5 ft., sometimes 8 ft. high. Branches slender, upright, reddish when young. Leaves oval, 2–3 in. long, turning red in fall. Flowers fragrant, showy. June–July. N.J. to Fla. Hardy from zone* 3 southward. Prefers moist, good soil, but is adaptable; easily propagated by division.

**ITEACEAE.** See SAXIFRAGACEAE.

**IVY.** The ivy of tradition and history, as well as hort., is *Hedera helix* (which see). See also PARTHENOCISSUS. For other plants, in which ivy is part of their name, see SENECIO MIKANIOIDES, NEPETA HEDERACEA, CYMBALARIA MURALIS, CISSUS INCISA, and the next few entries.

**IVY FERN** = *Hemionitis palmata*.

**IVY GERANIUM** = *Pelargonium peltatum*.

**IVY GOURD** = *Coccinia cordifolia*.

**IXIA** (ick'si-a). South African bulbous herbs, belonging to the family Iridaceae, the corms producing grass-like leaves and flower spikes with pendulous, bell-shaped flowers. Leaves generally 2-ranked. Flowering stalk mostly longer than the leaves. Fruit a small capsule.* (*Ixia*, fr. the Greek for bird lime, possibly referring to the juice of some species.)

Hardy only in zones* 5 to 9. Elsewhere treated as greenhouse-bloomers, planting the corms of blooming size in 4- or 5-in. pots or pans in the fall, 4 to 7 to a pot, and treating them as crocus or grape hyacinths forced for early spring bloom. They grow readily out-of-doors in southern Calif., where they multiply quickly.

**columellaris.** Grows 2 ft. high. Flowers lilac or lavender, with blue throat. Corms 1 in. or less in diameter.

**maculata.** Leaves linear, ribbed, 6 to 12 in. long. Flowers bright yellow, in dense and erect spikes, with a black mark in the throat.

**speciosa.** Corm globose, small, fibrous. Leaves linear, about 6 from base. Flowers few, dark crimson, bell-shaped, on slender stalk.

*IXIOIDES* (icks-i-oy'deez, but see OÏDES). Like the genus *Ixia* (which see).

**IXIOLIRION** (ix-i-o-lir'i-on). A genus of Asiatic herbs of the amaryllis family, with blue or violet, spring-blooming flowers. They are little known in cult. and of uncertain identity.

*IXOCARPA, -us, -um* (icks-o-kar'pa). Sticky-fruited.

**IXORA** (icks-ō'ra). Tropical, mostly Asiatic shrubs and trees belonging to the family Rubiaceae, cultivated in the open only in Calif. and Florida, and grown as a conservatory plant elsewhere. Leaves opposite* or whorled.* Flowers red to white, in compact bunches, individual flower long-tubular, with 4–5 spreading lobes. Fruit a berry. (*Ixora* was named for a Malabar deity.)

Commonly grown for ornament and in a variety of soils, especially in Fla. For greenhouse culture use potting mixture* 4 and do not let the night temperature go below 65°. Some people confuse shrubs of this genus with *Hamelia erecta*. The most certain identification is through the fruit, which is 2-seeded in *Ixora*, but many-seeded in *Hamelia*.

**coccinea.** Flame-of-the-woods; called, also, jungle geranium. Evergreen shrub, the leaves oblong, 4 to 5 in. long. Flowers red, to 1¾ in. long, in dense clusters. East Indies.

**fulgens.** Shrub with narrow, oblong leaves 4–6 in. long, shiny above. Flowers orange-scarlet, to 1¾ in. long, in large, sessile bunches. India and in the East Indies.

**incarnata** = *Ixora coccinea*.

# J

**JABOTICABA** = *Eugenia cauliflora*.

**JABURAN** (jab'ur-ran). Oriental vernacular for *Ophiopogon jaburan*.

**JACARANDA** (jack-a-ran'da). Tropical American shrubs and trees of the family Bignoniaceae, comprising more than 50 species of which two are cult. for ornament, outdoors in zones* 8 and 9, and occasionally in the greenhouse. (It is not the genus yielding the valuable cabinet wood known as jacaranda, which is rosewood and derived from the non-hort. tree *Dalbergia nigra* of the pea family.) Leaves opposite,* twice-compound, the leaflets arranged feather-fashion, numerous, the foliage thus handsome. Flowers showy, blue or violet, the clusters (panicles*) terminal or in the leaf-axils.* Corolla tubular, its limb* slightly 2-lipped,* the flower thus a little irregular.* Stamens* 4, often with an odd sterile one. Fruit an oblongish or ovalish capsule.* (*Jacaranda* is the Brazilian name for these trees and for those yielding the cabinet wood mentioned above.)

The first species is one of the most popular flowering trees grown in Fla. and southern Calif. It stands many different sorts of soils, and even if hit by occasional frosts, it can be pruned back and used, in its young stages, as a handsome bedding shrub or as specimens on the lawn. It is widely so used in regions where it will not attain tree size. If grown under glass, put in the warm-temperate greenhouse and use potting mixture* 4. Propagated by cuttings of half-ripened wood.

**acutifolia.** A tree up to 50 ft. high, holding its leaves until early in the spring. Leaves hairy, fern-like, with 16 or more pairs of main divisions, each of these with 14–24 pairs of oblongish leaflets which are about ½ in. long. Flower cluster nearly 8 in. long, the flowers blue, about 2 in. long. Brazil. April–June (in Fla.). A very showy tree, sometimes known as *J. ovalifolia*.

**cuspidifolia.** Not usually over 30 ft. high, its leaves nearly 2 ft. long, smooth, and composed of 8–10 main divisions, each of which bears 10–15 pairs of leaflets which are about 1 in. long. Flowers bluish-violet, not over 1½ in. long. Brazil and the Argentine.

**JACK BEAN** = *Canavalia ensiformis*.

**JACKFRUIT** = *Artocarpus integrifolia*.

**JACK-IN-THE-PULPIT** = *Arisaema triphyllum*.

**JACK-IN-THE-PULPIT FAMILY** = Araceae.

* Special articles on the subjects indicated by an asterisk (*) will be found at the words so marked.

**JACK PINE** = *Pinus banksiana*. See PINE.

*JACOBAEA*, *-us*, *-um* (jack-o-bee′a). A specific name applied to several plants, perhaps named for Saint James or derived from the Latin *Jacobus* (James). See SENECIO and LOTUS.

**JACOBEAN LILY** = *Sprekelia formosissima*.

**JACOBINIA** (jack-o-bin′i-a). A genus of showy tropical American herbs and under-shrubs, of the family Acanthaceae, grown in the open only in warm climates, as those of zones* 7 to 9, but often grown as conservatory plants. They are closely related to *Justicia* and differ from it only in technical characters. Leaves opposite.* Flowers showy, irregular, 2-lipped, in dense, bracted* clusters. (*Jacobinia* is named for someone but for whom is unknown.)

*Jacobinia* and *Justicia* should be grown in the warm greenhouse, in potting mixture* 4, and given plenty of water. They root easily from cuttings.

**carnea.** A shrub 2–3 ft. high. Leaves ovalish or oblong, 6–7 in. long. Flowers rose-purple or flesh-colored, the dense, terminal heads nearly 4 in. long. Brazil. Often offered as *Justicia magnifica* and *Justicia carnea*.

**coccinea** = *Pachystachys coccinea*.

**pauciflora.** Sub-shrub to 2 ft. high, the leaves oblong to oval, about ¾ in. long. Flowers scarlet, tipped with yellow, ¾ in. long, solitary and nodding. Brazil. A floriferous plant, as easily grown as fuchsia.

**JACOB'S LADDER** = *Polemonium caeruleum*.

**JACOB'S ROD.** See ASPHODELINE.

**JACOB'S STAFF** = *Fouquieria splendens*.

**JACQUEMONTIA** (jak-kwe-mon′she-a). Twining, chiefly tropical American vines of the family Convolvulaceae, much resembling the morning-glory, but not so good as it. Only *J. pentantha* of the 70 known species is at all usual in cult., and it can only be grown outdoors in zones* 8 and 9, as it is native from Fla. to S.A. It is a perennial vine with a slightly woody base. Leaves alternate,* more or less ovalish or heart-shaped, 1½–2 in. long. Flowers blue, about 1 in. long, in clusters (cymes*), the stalk of which usually exceeds the length of the leaves. The plant differs only in technical characters (2 flattened stigmas*) from the closely related *Ipomoea*, and is grown like the tender species of that genus. (Named for Victor Jacquemont, French naturalist.)

**JAGGERY PALM** = *Caryota urens;* also *Arenga saccharifera*.

**JAK; JAKFRUIT** = *Artocarpus integrifolia*.

*JALAPA* (jal′a-pa). Latinized form of *jalap*, once thought to be derived from the four-o'clock (*Mirabilis jalapa*).

*JAMACARU* (ja-mack′a-roo). A Brazilian vernacular for a cactus from which the natives made their huts, and possibly a corruption of *mandacaru*. See CEREUS.

**JAMAICA COTTON** = *Gossypium punctatum*.

**JAMAICA GOLD FERN** = *Pityrogramma sulphurea*.

**JAMAICA HONEYSUCKLE** = *Passiflora laurifolia*.

**JAMAICA SORREL** = *Hibiscus sabdariffa*.

*JAMBOS.* Adaptation of the Hindu name for the rose-apple (*Eugenia jambos*).

**JAMBU** = *Eugenia jambos*.

**JAMESIA** (james′i-a). Three species of western American shrubs of the family Saxifragaceae, **J. americana** occasionally grown for its foliage, which turns bright orange and scarlet in the fall, and for its fragrant white flowers. It is an upright shrub 3–4 ft. high, with shreddy bark and opposite,* short-stalked, oval or elliptic leaves that are 1½–2½ in. long and white-felty beneath. Flowers white, or pinkish on the outside, in many-flowered clusters (cymes*) that are 1–3 in. long. Petals 5, hairy on the inside. Stamens* 10. Fruit a 3–5-valved capsule. The shrub is wild from Wyo. to Utah and N. Mex., and is hardy from zone* 4 southward. It prefers open, sunny sites and well-drained soils. Easily propagated by seeds or by cuttings of its ripe wood. (Named for Doctor Edwin James, botanical explorer of the Rocky Mountains.)

**JAMESTOWNWEED** = jimsonweed. See DATURA STRAMONIUM.

**JANUARY.** See GARDEN CALENDAR.

**JAPAN CEDAR** = *Cryptomeria japonica*.

**JAPAN CLOVER** = *Lespedeza striata*.

**JAPAN PLUM.** See LOQUAT.

**JAPANESE.** As part of the name of many plants or things that come from Japan or its vicinity, *Japanese* is common. Those that occur in THE GARDEN DICTIONARY, and their proper equivalents, are:

**Japanese anemone** = *Anemone japonica;* **Japanese angelica tree** = *Aralia elata;* **Japanese barberry** = *Berberis thunbergi;* **Japanese barnyard millet** = *Echinochloa crus-galli edulis;* **Japanese beetle** (see beetles at INSECT PESTS; see also Insect Pests at PEACH and ROSE); **Japanese black pine** = *Pinus thunbergi* (see PINE); **Japanese chestnut** = *Castanea crenata* (see CHESTNUT); **Japanese clematis** = *Clematis paniculata;* **Japanese evergreen oak** = *Quercus acuta* (see OAK); **Japanese fern** = *Cyclophorus lingua;* **Japanese flowering cherry** = *Prunus lannesiana, P. serrulata,* and *P. yedoensis;* **Japanese flowering quince** = *Chaenomeles lagenaria;* **Japanese garden** (see next main entry below); **Japanese hemlock** = *Tsuga diversifolia* (see HEMLOCK); **Japanese holly** = *Ilex crenata* (see HOLLY); **Japanese honeysuckle** = *Lonicera japonica;* **Japanese horse-chestnut** = *Aesculus turbinata* (see HORSE-CHESTNUT); **Japanese iris** (see IRIS); **Japanese ivy** = *Parthenocissus tricuspidata,* also *Hedera helix gracilis;* **Japanese larch** (see LARCH); **Japanese laurel** (see CRASSULA PORTULACEA); **Japanese lawn grass** = *Zoysia japonica;* **Japanese leaf** = *Aglaonema modestum;* **Japanese lily** = *Lilium speciosum;* **Japanese maple** = *Acer palmatum* (see MAPLE); **Japanese medlar** (see LOQUAT); **Japanese mint** = *Mentha arvensis piperascens* (see MINT); **Japanese morning-glory** (see IPOMOEA NIL); **Japanese pagoda tree** = *Sophora japonica;* **Japanese pear** = *Pyrus serotina;* **Japanese persimmon** = *Diospyros kaki* (see PERSIMMON); **Japanese plum** = *Prunus salicina* (see PLUM); **Japanese quince** = *Chaenomeles lagenaria;* **Japanese raisin tree** = *Hovenia dulcis;* **Japanese red pine** = *Pinus densiflora* (see PINE); **Japanese rose** = *Kerria japonica pleniflora;* **Japanese rubber-plant** (see CRASSULA PORTULACEA); **Japanese snowball** = *Viburnum tomentosum sterile;* **Japanese spurge** = *Pachysandra terminalis;* **Japanese white pine** = *Pinus parviflora* (see PINE); **Japanese wisteria** = *Wistaria floribunda;* **Japanese yew** = *Taxus cuspidata*.

**JAPANESE GARDENS.** A Japanese garden should not be judged by Western standards. Western gardens are designed as an attractive setting for flowers and shrubs. Japanese gardens are designed to represent natural scenery, complete without the aid of flowering plants — equally beautiful at all seasons of the year. But in the season when there are no flowers, Japanese gardens retain more beauty than Western gardens.

With the intense love of Nature possessed by the Japanese, it is impossible for them to live contentedly in crowded cities, without a suggestion of the out-of-doors. This passion for the beauties of Nature finds expression in a garden. The smallest space, back of a city house or shop, is used for a garden. The *Shō-ji,* or sliding doors, are pushed back, and before you is a glimpse of natural loveliness, too diminutive to walk about in, but sufficiently large to carry one's thoughts far from the city sounds and confusion. From these tiny gardens, like a natural landscape picture, developed the larger, rarely beautiful, gardens in temple enclosures, the *Cha-niwa,* or tea garden, surrounding the houses of the *Cha-no-yu,* or ceremonial tea masters, and the larger, more elaborately planned gardens, adjoining the old palaces, and on the old estates of noblemen and statesmen. The literary and artistic men, as well as the wealthy merchants, all plan and revere their gardens.

ENVIRONMENT. In Japan the placing of a garden does not depend on the character of the land. The garden may represent mountain scenery in a seaside environment, or the

---

* Special articles on the subjects indicated by an asterisk (*) will be found at the words so marked.

# JAPANESE GARDENS

designer of the garden may wish to reproduce some historical spot of beautiful scenery which he has mentally cherished, though years have passed since visiting this scene. This, to a Westerner, might seem incongruous, but placed in the same

**JAPANESE LANTERNS**

Kusuga, one of the standard variety, at the left. It takes its name from a Shinto deity. Snow-scene lantern or legged lantern, in the middle, wide-roofed to hold the snow. Enshu, named after Kobori Enshu, highest authority on tea ceremony. The form of this lantern suggests the long cranium of Fukurokuju, one of the seven gods of fortune.

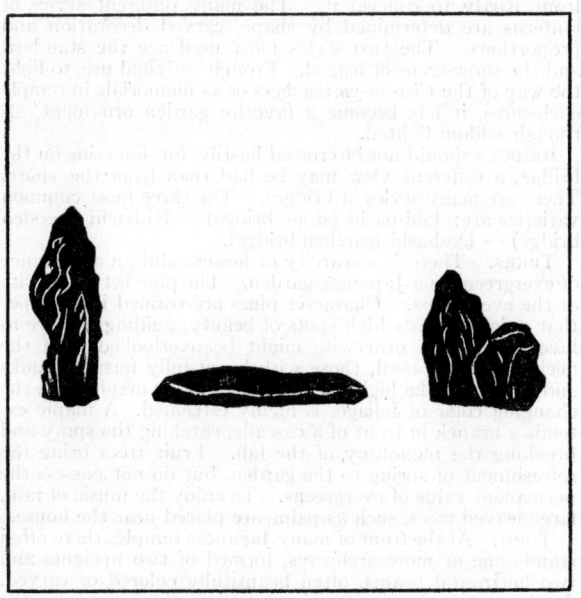

**STONES IN THE JAPANESE GARDEN**

Stone of Two Deities at the right, the Guardian Stone at the left, and the worshiping stone in the center

land, the garden fittings and style of construction are so typically Japanese that it appears most natural. There are many sections of New England, as well as in Westchester County, New York, in New Jersey and California, where a Japanese garden will fit perfectly into the environment. We have all seen marvelous natural gardens of iris and ferns combined with rock of such beauty that only a small degree of human aid will transform it into a perfect Japanese garden. Rocks do for lanterns and bridges, and there must be an abundance of water. However, there are many Japanese gardens in America which are so disturbingly out of place that they create in those who behold them a general dislike for all Japanese gardens.

THE OBJECT OF A JAPANESE GARDEN is to bring natural beauty to your very door; to refresh the mind by a complete change of outlook; to bring peace of mind by the contemplation of beautiful surroundings.

HISTORY. We know the existence in Japan of gardens as far back as the beginning of the third century A.D. As in all the arts, the making of gardens was imported either directly from China, or through Korea to Japan. Gardenmaking, coming from China, showed a strong Buddhist influence. Until the sixteenth century the gardens of Japan were Chinese in design, but at this period all foreign influence was thrown off. A style purely Japanese developed under the successive direction of the priests, the Cha-no-yu masters, of whom Kobori-Enshiu (1579–1647) was the greatest designer, and finally the Niwa-shi, or professional gardeners. Down to the present day the gardens of Japan hold an important place in the hearts of the people, reflecting their love of Nature, plus exquisite taste.

CLASSIFICATION. The many forms of Japanese gardens fall under two general heads:

TSUKI-YAMA, ARTIFICIAL HILLS, *and* HIRA-NIWA, LEVEL GROUND

*Shima*, meaning island, was the name applied to the ancient form of gardens. These gardens were without design, consisting merely of a lake, an island connected to the mainland by a bridge. The island is to give depth and variety to the garden. The one island multiplied to a large variety of islands, too numerous to enumerate, in spite of the interesting names by which they are distinguished. A few of these names follow, for although they sound poetical, they describe the form and character of the islands. The word *Shima* is changed to *Jima* for the sake of euphony. This happens frequently in the Japanese language. *Matsa-jima* (pine island) is much used even in a small lake. It frequently holds only one pine of beautiful form. *Iso-jima* (rock island) — the smallest of the islands often just a group of rocks placed in water to suggest an island and not connected to the mainland. *Kumo-gata-jima* (cloud-shaped island) — this island is formed completely of white sand, and gives the illusion of a cloud passing over the lake at that special point. *Horai-jima* (Elysian isle) is only seen in gardens of great dimension. This island is in the form of a turtle, and planted with pine trees.

LAKES, WATERFALLS, AND STREAMS. Lakes are important in making the garden appear larger and creating reflections. The earth dug out to make the lake, with some additional soil, should be used to make the hills. The lake should not be too regular in shape. Banks should be so curved that with the aid of trees, well planted, the full extent of the lake is not seen from any one position. Waterfalls form the central feature of many gardens. They should be located far from the main house, from which the garden is viewed. They are usually made to fall from a valley between hills, with higher hills or forest trees for a background. There must be a basin with rocks for the water to dash into. Streams — in the level gardens a spring is made to issue from among moss-covered rocks to form the origin of a stream. The direction of the stream should be determined by the grade of the land. It should flow between naturally curved banks and aid in the drainage. Even when there is no water available for a cascade — a rocky bed is made to give the appearance of the fall having dried up, which is apt to occur in Nature during a dry season. The natural forms of cascades have been closely studied. Every variety of fall is reproduced in the gardens of Japan: *Tsutai-ochi* (glide-falling) — the water falling down the surface of inclined rocks. *Nuno-ochi* (linen-falling), when it falls in a thin sheet; *Kata-*

---

* Special articles on the subjects indicated by an asterisk (*) will be found at the words so marked.

*ochi* (uneven-falling), in which the water falls more from one side than the other. The Japanese delight in placing these falls, when possible, where sunshine and moonlight enhance their beauty.

LANTERNS. One of the most striking features of a Japanese garden is the lanterns. They stand in the garden symbolizing light dispelling darkness. In placing, this should be kept in mind, and the lantern not considered only orna-

BRIDGES IN THE JAPANESE GARDEN
In the middle, Gangyo-bashi or stone bridge formed like a wedge of flying wild ducks. At the left, a bridge formed of one slab of stone. At the right, a wooden bridge used as an approach to temple or shrine.

STONES are too great a subject to be dealt with here. They are chosen for their size, shape, color, texture; according to their forms, they are divided into five varieties, "statue," "low-vertical," "flat," "recumbent," and "arching stones." A distinction of sex is applied to rocks and stones, which aids

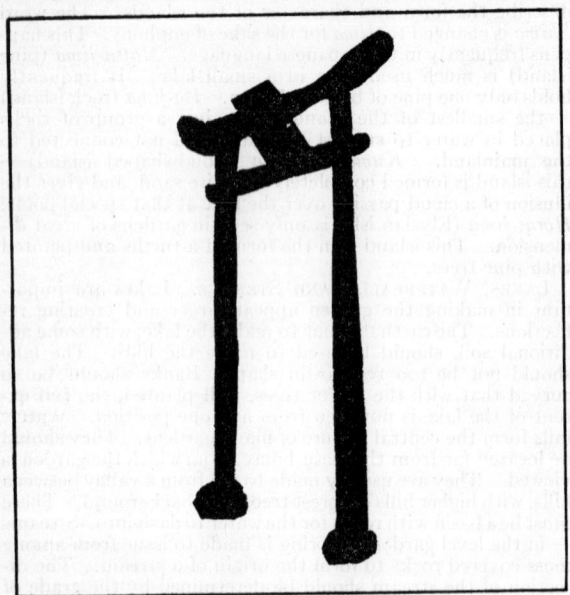

A torii. *See* text.

in obtaining a fitting contrast in grouping them. In a large garden there are as many as one hundred and thirty odd stones, each with its special name, and its own function to perform, in addition to a large number of others of secondary importance. In a small garden five rocks are sufficient, including always the "guardian stone," "stone of worship," "stone of two deities." These stones are illustrated.

mental. Lanterns are made of almost every kind of material, but those of stone are most popular. A lantern should not stand alone in full exposure. There should be set, close to it, a stone to step upon when putting in the light, and it should be guarded by a tree with a branch extending to the front partly to conceal it. The many different styles of lanterns are determined by shape, carved decoration and proportions. The two styles most used are the standard and the snow-scene or legged. From its original use, to light the way of the *Cha-no-yu* teachers or as memorials in temple enclosures, it has become a favorite garden ornament, although seldom lighted.

BRIDGES should not be crossed hastily, for, lingering on the bridge, a different view may be had than from the shore. There are many styles of bridges. The three most common varieties are: Ishi-bashi (stone bridge) — Ki-bashi (wooden bridge) — Do-bashi (earthen bridge).

TREES. There is a scarcity of flowers and an abundance of evergreens in a Japanese garden. The pine is the favorite of the evergreens. Character pines are trained into shapes that point towards high spots of beauty, guiding the eye to loveliness which otherwise might be overlooked. Of the deciduous trees used, those with beautifully formed trunks and branches take highest rank. *Momiji*, or maple, with the changing color of foliage, is highly esteemed. A maple extends a branch in front of a cascade, catching the spray and breaking the monotony of the fall. Fruit trees bring the refreshment of spring to the garden, but do not possess the permanent value of evergreens. To enjoy the music of rain, large-leaved trees, such as palm, are placed near the house.

TORII. At the front of many Japanese temples there often stands one or more archways, formed of two uprights and two horizontal beams, often beautifully colored or carved. As the name torii signifies, it was originally a perch for the birds offered to the gods, and was erected at any side of a temple, very rarely in the water.

With the introduction of Buddhism the original significance of a torii was forgotten, and they then came to be placed in front of temples and used as a gateway. Today, these interesting structures, which may be of stone, bronze, or wood, and sometimes painted red, are often a feature of larger Japanese gardens. — M. A.

* Special articles on the subjects indicated by an asterisk (*) will be found at the words so marked.

**JAPONICA, -us, -um** (ja-pon'i-ka). From Japan. *Japonica* is also a very common name for the camellia (which see), and is occasionally used for the dwarf Japanese quince. See Chaenomeles japonica.

**JARDINIERE.** A thoroughly misleading term, for it is from the French for a gardener, while most jardinieres work mischief to potted plants. It is no accident that experience has proved the benefit of clay flower pots, for plants need air and drainage at their roots. Jardinieres, as used by most people, defeat that aim. However beautiful and costly, they are all alike in being of some watertight and air-tight material. Into such a receptacle a pot is slipped, its shoulder often sealing the air at the top. And the bottom stands on the bottom of the jardiniere, often with fatal results. For excess water slowly rises from careless watering and soon the flower pot is standing in a puddle of foul water. With no fresh air from the top and with its feet in stagnant water, the plant soon responds by dying.

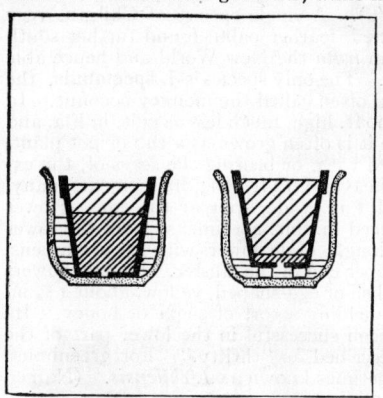

At the left, a water-soaked jardiniere; at the right, one properly arranged to prevent this. *See text.*

The remedy is to stand the pot upon an inverted saucer or piece of wood, so that the bottom of the pot will be at least an inch above the bottom of the jardiniere. Also see that the flower pot is small enough to allow at least a ¾ in. space between its rim and the edge of the container. With these precautions, only your taste and purse need limit the use of jardinieres. See House Plants.

**JASIONE** (jas-ee-ō'nee). European annual and perennial herbs of the Campanulaceae, useful for the rock garden and flower border. They have alternate,* simple leaves, and small white or blue flowers, borne in heads. Corolla cut into 5 very narrow segments, the heads thus resembling a composite, but *Jasione* is easily distinguished from the Compositae by having capsules for fruit. (*Jasione* is of no known application to these plants.)

Of easy culture in most garden soils if grown in full sun or in partial shade. Propagated by division and seeds.

**humilis.** A dwarf perennial, 6 to 9 in. high. Leaves linear. Flowers blue, on short stalks. July-Aug. Pyrenees.

**perennis.** Shepherd's-scabious, also called sheep's-bit. Perennial, herbaceous, to 1 ft. Leaves oblong-linear, entire. Flowers blue, in long-stalked, globose heads to 2 in. across. Southern Eu.

**JASMINACEAE** = Oleaceae.

**JASMINE.** See Jasminum. See also Gelsemium sempervirens. For other plants sometimes called jasmine, see Gardenia jasminoides, Mandevilla suaveolens, Trachelospermum, Stephanotis, Nyctanthes, and Androsace. Jasmine is often, more poetically, written *jessamine*, which is thus likely to be applied to any of the plants mentioned above.

**JASMINE TOBACCO** = *Nicotiana alata grandiflora*.

**JASMINOIDES** (jas-min-oy'deez, but see Oïdes). Jasmine-like.

**JASMINUM** (jas'mĭ-num). The jasmines, also called jessamines, comprise a large genus of shrubs or vines of the olive family, chiefly tropical and sub-tropical, found in Eurasia and Af., one in the New World. They are climbing or spreading shrubs with compound* opposite or alternate leaves (sometimes with only 1 leaflet), and often green, angled stems. Flowers generally about 1 in. across, in many-flowered clusters, yellow or white in ours. Calyx* bell-shaped. Corolla tubular, but with 4-9 spreading lobes. Fruit a small berry. (*Jasminum* is from the Arabic name for jasmine.)

Widely cultivated and esteemed for their attractive, fragrant flowers. They make fine conservatory plants and in mild climates may be grown outdoors, some species, mainly *J. nudiflorum*, *floridum* and *officinale*, are useful for training on walls. See Vines. They are of easy culture, preferring a sunny position and loamy soil. Propagated by layers* and cuttings* of nearly ripe wood.

**floridum.** Half-evergreen shrub with angled, smooth branches, upright and arching. Leaves alternate,* with 3-5 oval leaflets, ½-1½ in. long. Flowers golden-yellow in large terminal clusters. Calyx* lobes about ¼ length of corolla tube. Fruit a small black berry. China. July. Hardy from zone* 5 southward.

**gracillimum.** Graceful, sometimes climbing shrub from northern Borneo. Branches many from near the base, arching, hairy. Leaves opposite, about 1½ in. long, oval to heart-shaped, bright green above, hairy beneath. Flowers in large dense heads, white, fragrant, the corolla with about 9 lobes. Blooms in winter. Hardy from zone* 6 southward.

**grandiflorum.** Spanish Jasmine. Catalonian Jasmine. A species from India resembling *J. officinale*. More erect than most of the species though with arching, angled branches and growing about 4 ft. high. Leaves opposite* with 5 to 7 elliptic or oval leaflets. Flowers white, tinged crimson on the outside, freely borne and very fragrant. An excellent greenhouse plant and widely cultivated in Europe as an ornamental and for perfumery.

**humile.** Italian Jasmine. An evergreen or half-evergreen shrub with angled branches and of loose, spreading habit. Leaves alternate, composed of three to seven rather thick oblong leaflets that are dark green above, paler beneath and whose edges are slightly rolled under. Flowers bright golden-yellow, fragrant, summer or fall. Commonly cultivated in greenhouses and hardy outdoors where it is sometimes trained on walls as a vine. Hardy from zone* 5 southward. Much variation occurs in this species and the different forms are sometimes listed as *J. reevesi*, *J. revolutum*, *J. triumphans* and *J. wallichianum*. Tropical As.

**nudiflorum.** Winter Jasmine. Upright shrub with stiff, arching four-angled branches. Leaves opposite, dark green with 3 oval leaflets about 1 in. long, falling in autumn. Flowers yellow, ¾-1 in. across, solitary along branches of previous season, appearing in winter or spring before the leaves. China. Hardy from zone* 4 southward. In mild places blooms nearly all winter, but in north flower buds often frozen.

**officinale.** Common White Jasmine. Usually deciduous shrub with long spreading branches that require support. Sometimes reach 40 ft. Leaves opposite, leaflets 5-7, glossy, ½-2½ in. long, terminal one larger and stalked. Flowers white, very fragrant. Summer. Kashmir, Persia, China. Hardy from zone* 5 southward. Very attractive shrub cultivated for centuries.

**primulinum.** Primrose Jasmine. An evergreen shrub of rambling habit growing 6-10 ft. high. Branches green, four-angled; the leaves are opposite and composed of 3 rather thick and shiny leaflets, 1-2 in. long. Flowers are borne along branches of the previous season, yellow with darker eye, often double. Blooms in spring with the leaves. China. Hardy from zone* 5 southward. This species is closely related to *J. nudiflorum* and may be only a form of it.

**pubescens.** A climbing, hairy shrub with opposite somewhat heart-shaped leaves that are dark green and about 2 in. long. Flowers white with broad lobes, occasionally double, fragrant, about 1 in. across in many-flowered clusters; calyx lobes with spreading yellow hairs. India. August. Good conservatory plant.

**sambac.** Arabian Jasmine. Climbing shrub with angled, hairy branches. Leaves opposite or often in threes at the ends of the flowering branches, shiny, ovate, rounded or pointed at the tip. Flowers white, turning purple with age, borne in 3-12 flowered clusters, very fragrant and widely cultivated in the East on this account. There is a group with very double flowers sometimes known as *J. trifoliata*. India. Hardy only where there is no frost.

**JATROPHA** (jat'row-fa). A large genus of mostly tropical herbs, shrubs, or trees of the spurge family, having a milky, usually poisonous, juice. Of the 150 known species only the two below are of hort. interest, and both of secondary importance. They have alternate* leaves, usually long-stalked, and often somewhat lobed or divided finger-fashion. Male and female flowers separate, but on the same plant, with petals in the first species, without them in the second. Sepals 5, more or less joined at the base. Stamens* usually 10, in two series. Fruit a capsule.* (*Jatropha* is from the Greek for physician and food, in allusion to the medicinal value of some species.)

The first species is a tropical tree of easy culture, but only in zone* 9 or the most favored parts of zone* 8, and may be propagated by seeds or cuttings. *Jatropha texana* is a perennial herb suited to the southwestern states, but little known elsewhere.

**curcas.** Physic-nut; also called purging-nut and Barbados nut. A tree not usually over 20 ft., more often lower and shrubby. Leaves long-stalked, 3-5 in. wide, lobed and ivy-like. Flowers small, yellow or yellowish-green, and borne in branched clusters (cymes*). Petals present.

---

* Special articles on the subjects indicated by an asterisk (*) will be found at the words so marked.

Fruit olive-shaped, 1-1½ in. long, its 2 black seeds yielding a purgative oil dangerously poisonous in quantity. For these seeds the plant is cult. in the tropics, although in the U.S. the plant is mostly an ornamental, or used for informal hedges. Tropical America.

**texana.** A perennial herb 1-2 ft. high, bristly-hairy. Leaves deeply 3-5-lobed, nearly 6 in. wide, the lobes toothed or deeply cut. Flowers white, in small clusters. Petals none. Ark. to Tex.

*JAVANICA, -us, -um* (ja-van'i-ka). From Java.

**JAYS.** See BIRDS.

**JEFFERSONIA** (jef-fer-so'ni-a). Herbaceous perennial herbs, belonging to the Berberidaceae, native in eastern N.A. and As., one of the 2 known species used as an ornamental plant in the wild garden. The only cult. species is J. diphylla, the twin-leaf or rheumatism root. It is a woodland herb, 10 to 12 in. high, the leaves 2-parted into kidney-shaped, or lobed divisions. Flowers white, about 1 in. wide, with 4 sepals and 8 oblong, flat petals. Fruit a pear-shaped pod. (Named for Thomas Jefferson.)

**JEFFREY PINE** = *Pinus jeffreyi*. See PINE.

**JEQUIRITY BEAN** = *Abrus precatorius*.

**JERSEY ELM** = *Ulmus foliacea wheatleyi*. See ELM.

**JERUSALEM ARTICHOKE** = *Helianthus tuberosus*. See SUNFLOWER. It is neither an artichoke nor does it come from Jerusalem, being one of the few plants really cultivated by the North American Indians.

**JERUSALEM CHERRY** = *Solanum pseudo-capsicum*.

**JERUSALEM CORN.** A form of durra. See HOLCUS SORGHUM DURRA.

**JERUSALEM CROSS** = *Lychnis chalcedonica*.

**JERUSALEM DATE** = *Bauhinia monandra*.

**JERUSALEM OAK** = *Chenopodium botrys*.

**JERUSALEM SAGE.** See PHLOMIS.

**JERUSALEM THORN** = *Parkinsonia aculeata*; also *Paliurus spina-christi*.

**JESSAMINE.** See JASMINUM. For other plants so called see JASMINE, the spelling here preferred.

**JESUIT'S-NUT** = *Trapa natans*.

**JETBEAD** = *Rhodotypos tetrapetala*.

**JEW BUSH** = *Pedilanthus tithymaloides*.

**JEWELWEED.** See IMPATIENS.

**JEWELWEED FAMILY** = Balsaminaceae.

**JEW'S-APPLE.** See EGGPLANT.

**JEW'S-HARP** = *Trillium cernuum*.

**JEW'S MALLOW** = *Corchorus olitorius*.

**JEW'S MYRTLE** = *Ruscus aculeatus*.

*JEZOENSIS, -e* (ye-zo-en'sis). From Hokkaido (formerly Yezo), Japan.

**JIFFY-HOE.** See Section 1, TOOLS AND IMPLEMENTS.

**JIMSONWEED** = *Datura stramonium*.

**JIOTILLA** = *Escontria chiotilla*.

**JIPI-JAPA** = *Carludovica palmata*.

**JOB'S-TEARS** = *Coix lachryma-jobi*.

**JOCONOSTLE** = *Lemaireocereus stellatus*.

**JOE-PYE-WEED** = *Eupatorium purpureum*.

**JOHN EVANS ARBORETUM.** See ARBORETUM.

**JOHNNY-JUMP-UP.** See VIOLA TRICOLOR HORTENSIS.

**JOHNNY SMOKERS** = *Geum ciliatum*.

**JOHNS HOPKINS BOTANICAL GARDEN.** See BOTANIC GARDEN.

**JOHNSON GRASS** = *Holcus halepensis*.

**JOINT-FIR; JOINT-FIR FAMILY.** See EPHEDRA.

**JONATHAN.** An apple variety. See APPLE.

**JONQUIL** = *Narcissus jonquilla*. See also N. JUNCIFOLIUS and N. ODORUS.

**JOSEPHINE'S-LILY** = *Brunsvigia josephinae*.

**JOSEPH'S-COAT** = *Amaranthus tricolor*.

**JOSHUA TREE** = *Yucca brevifolia*.

**JUBAEA** (jew-bee'a). A single species of Chilean, very stout-trunked, unarmed, feather palm, found further south than almost any palm from the New World and hence able to stand a little frost. The only species is J. spectabilis, the coquito or wine palm, often called the monkey-coconut. In Chile it grows up to 90 ft. high, much less as cult. in Fla. and in greenhouses where it is often grown as a tub or pot plant. Trunk usually clothed with, or bearing the scars of, the expanded leaf bases. Leaves 6-12 ft. long, its segments many, about 2 ft. long and 1 in. wide, split at the tip. Flower cluster (rarely produced in cult. specimens) from the lower leaves, drooping and long. Male flowers with 15-30 stamens, and usually at the upper end of the cluster. Female flowers lower, the fruit roundish or egg-shaped, yellow, about 1½ in. long, its single seed yielding a sort of sugar or honey. Its culture in Fla. has been successful in the lower part of the state, where it is described as "thrifty." For greenhouse cult. see PALM. Sometimes known as *J. chilensis*. (Named for King Juba of Numidia.)

*JUBATA, -us, -um* (jew-bay'ta). Crested*; or with a mane-like crest.

*JUCUNDA, -us, -um* (jew-kun'da). Pleasing or agreeable.

**JUDAS TREE.** See REDBUD.

**JUGLANDACEAE** (jug-lan-day'see-ee). The walnut or hickory family, ours all trees, comprise only 6 genera and about 40 species, all confined to the temperate or warm regions of the northern hemisphere. There are only three cult. genera, one of them, *Juglans* (see WALNUT) of outstanding importance. The others are *Carya* (see HICKORY) and *Pterocarya* grown only for ornament.

Leaves alternate,* compound,* the leaflets arranged feather-fashion with an odd one at the tip. The male flowers are in drooping catkins, the female solitary or in clusters (racemes*). Both appear with or just after the unfolding of the leaves. The fruit in the walnut and hickory is fleshy (a drupe*), what is ordinarily called a nut, being the seed of this fruit. In *Pterocarya* the fruit is a true nut and is winged. All genera are wind-pollinated.

Technical flower characters: Flowers monoecious.* Male flowers with several stamens, no petals and sometimes with no sepals. Female flowers with a 3-5-lobed calyx. Ovary inferior,* mostly 1-celled.

**JUGLANS.** See WALNUT.

*JUJUBA* (jew-jew'ba). A Latinized version of the ancient vernacular for the jujube (*Zizyphus*).

**JUJUBE.** See ZIZYPHUS.

**JULIBRISSIN.** Persian vernacular for the silk tree (*Albizzia julibrissin*).

*JULIFLORA, -us, -um* (jew-li-flō'ra). With walnut-like flowers.

**JULY.** See GARDEN CALENDAR.

**JUMA.** An island. See JAPANESE GARDEN.

**JUNCACEAE** (jun-kay'see-ee). The rush family comprises grass-like herbs of which few are of any garden interest. The only cult. genus is *Juncus* (which see), and this is of minor hort. significance.

*JUNCEA, -us, -um* (jun'see-a). Rush-like.

**JUNCUS** (jun'kus). A very large genus, and the only cult. one, of the family Juncaceae (jun-kay'see-ee), known generally as rushes, and of little garden interest. They have grass-like, round or 3-sided leaves, often jointed, and compact clusters of small greenish or brownish flowers in spikelets. The only cult. species, of over 200 known, is J. effusus, the common, soft or bog rush. It is a tufted perennial, 2-4 ft. high, more or less pliant, its grass-like stems with a small

* Special articles on the subjects indicated by an asterisk (*) will be found at the words so marked.

cluster of brownish-green flowers near the tip, and apparently attached laterally. In marshy ground, throughout the north temperate zone, and suited only to similar sites. The fibrous stems are used to make mats. (*Juncus* is the classical name for the rushes.)

**JUNE.** See GARDEN CALENDAR.

**JUNE-BERRY.** See AMELANCHIER.

**JUNE BUDDING.** See BUDDING.

**JUNE BUG.** See Beetles at INSECT PESTS.

**JUNE DROP.** See ORANGE.

**JUNE GRASS** = *Poa pratensis*.

**JUNGLE GARDENS.** See Gardens at LOUISIANA.

**JUNGLE GERANIUM** = *Ixora coccinea*.

**JUNIPER.** See JUNIPERUS.

**JUNIPER-BERRY** = *Gaylussacia brachycera*. See HUCKLEBERRY.

**JUNIPERINA, -us, -um** (jew-nip-er-ry'na). Resembling a juniper.

**JUNIPERUS** (jew-nip'er-us). Juniper. The junipers form a large genus of evergreen trees and shrubs of the pine family. They vary in habit from low, prostrate shrubs to tall, slender trees, and are widely cultivated. The leaves are of two types: needle-shaped, and usually borne in 3's, and small, scale-like leaves that are opposite and pressed close to the twigs. On young plants and vigorous branches the needle-shaped leaves predominate, while the scaly leaves are characteristic of the adult plant. On older plants, however, both types are often found together and many species, especially in the *communis* group, retain the needle-like leaves permanently. The flowers are insignificant; male flowers borne

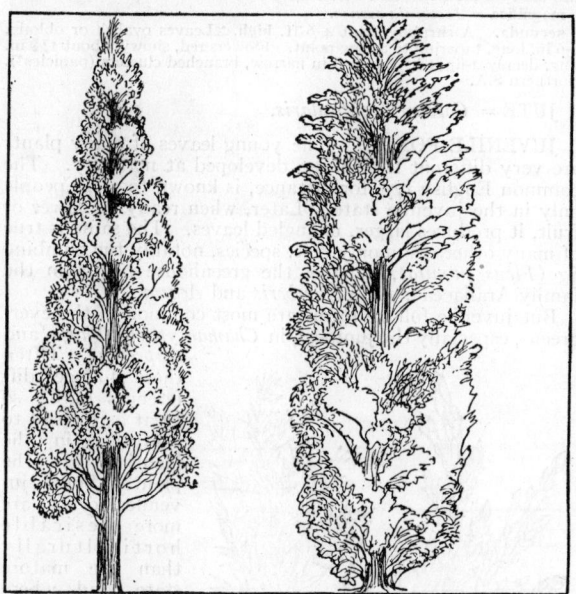

Common red cedar at the left (*Juniperus virginiana*), and at the right the columnar form of the Irish juniper (*J. communis hibernica*).

in small, oval clusters (catkins\*), the female flowers are composed of little scales on which the ovules are borne, these scales later become fleshy, grow together and form a berry-like fruit that takes 1–3 years to ripen, depending on the species. (*Juniperus* is the old Latin name for these plants.)

The junipers have a wide distribution in the northern hemisphere from the arctic regions to the sub-tropics. Their divers habits make them valuable ornamental plants; the tall, columnar types are conspicuous planted singly or in groups, while the low, spreading types are excellent for plantings around buildings. An aromatic oil is obtained from the berries and branchlets of certain species; the wood is durable and usually fragrant. Although a moderately moist, loamy soil is preferred, some species, as *J. communis*, will thrive in dry, rocky places. Propagation is by cuttings, seeds, layering and sometimes grafting. For cult. see EVERGREENS.

**bermudiana.** An irregular and rather widely branched tree growing about 70 ft. high, pyramidal when young, becoming round-topped and broader than high with age. The needle-like leaves are sharply pointed, nearly flat and whitish above, green beneath; the scaly leaves are blunt, overlapping and closely appressed. The thin gray bark peels off in long strips. Fruit dark blue, bloomy, about 1/4 in. across, broader than high. Bermuda, Barbados, Antigua. The most abundant and characteristic tree of Bermuda. Perhaps hardy in zone\* 8 or 9.

**chinensis.** Chinese juniper. A quite variable species ranging in habit from low, almost prostrate, shrubs to trees 60 ft. high. The linear leaves are spreading, sharply pointed, have two white lines above and are usually whorled; the scale-like leaves are obtuse and closely appressed. Male plants are usually of compact, upright habit, while the female ones are spreading, with slender branches. Fruit round, purplish-brown, about 1/3 in. across. China, Mongolia, Jap.

Many attractive forms are in cultivation; among them are var. **variegata**, a compact form in which the tips of the branchlets are often white; var. **aurea**, an upright form with the young branchlets golden-yellow; var. **mas**, a compact, upright shrub with usually linear leaves; var. **pyramidalis**, a narrow, pyramidal shrub with upright branches and glaucous, linear leaves; var. **pfitzeriana**, a very popular form with spreading, sometimes horizontal branches, roughly pyramidal in habit, and dark, dull green in color; will stand city conditions; var. **globosa**, a dwarf, compact form rather round in outline and with mostly scale-like leaves; var. **globosa aurea**, a form of var. *globosa* in which the branchlets are marked with yellow; var. **globosa alba**, a form of var. *globosa* in which the branchlets are marked with white; var. **japonica**, a dense shrub with low, spreading branches, leaves mostly needle-like, 2 white lines on upper surface, whorled.\*

**communis.** Common Juniper. An upright tree or shrub usually growing about 6–12 ft. high, though occasionally it attains 40 ft. The leaves are all needle-like, with a broad white band above, sharply pointed, spreading and in whorls. The fruit is about 1/4 in. in diameter, bluish-black, bloomy, used to flavor gin. N.A. south to Pa., Ill., and in the mountains of N. Mex. and northern Cal. Hardy from zone\* 1 southward.

This species is quite variable and has many good varieties. Var. **depressa**, the prostrate juniper, is a wide-spreading, low-growing form that rarely exceeds 3 or 4 ft. in height; it does well in dry, rocky soil; var. **depressa aurea** is a form of var. *depressa* in which the young growth is often yellow; var. **hibernica**, Irish juniper, a narrow, columnar form with upright, erect-tipped branches and rather short, dark green leaves, a good accent plant, often needs support; var. **oblonga-pendula**, a graceful, columnar shrub with narrow leaves and upright branches whose tips are pendulous.

**conferta.** A prostrate shrub with sharply pointed leaves, usually in threes, having a narrow white band and groove on the upper surface. Fruit black and bloomy, about 1/3 in. across. Japan, Saghalin. Hardy from zone\* 5 southward. Suited to sandy soils.

**excelsa.** Greek Juniper. A slender-branched tree of pyramidal habit growing about 60 ft. high. Leaves bluish-green, usually scale-like, pointed at tip opposite; the needle-like leaves are opposite and have two white bands on the upper surface. Fruit bloomy, purplish-brown. S.W. Eu., As. Minor, Caucasus. Hardy from zone\* 5 southward. Var. **stricta**. A narrow, upright form with glaucous, short, needle-like leaves; useful in the rock garden and as an accent plant. The plant sold in the U.S. under the name is not certainly the Greek juniper.

**horizontalis.** Creeping Juniper. A prostrate shrub with long, spreading branches. The leaves are glandular and of two types, needle-like and slightly spreading and on mature branches scaly and overlapping, bluish-green or gray-blue. Fruit on a short stem, blue, sometimes bloomy, about 1/3 in. across. Nova Scotia to British Columbia, south to N.J., Minn. and Montana. Hardy from zone\* 1 southward. Grows well in sandy, rocky soil, var. **douglasi**, Waukegan Juniper; a trailing form with blue-gray leaves that turn grayish-purple in the fall, var. **glomerata**, very low, dwarf form with short, compact branches and small, scale-like leaves.

**japonica** = *Juniperus chinensis japonica*.

**occidentalis.** Yellow Cedar. Western Juniper. A round-headed tree to 40 ft., occasionally 60 ft. high, sometimes a shrub. Leaves predominantly scale-like, in 3's, overlapping and pressed close to the stem, with a conspicuous gland on the back; needle-like leaves are about 1/6 in. long, sharply pointed and ridged on the back. Fruit rather oval, blue-black, bloomy, about 1/3 in. long. Wash. to southern Calif. Hardy from zone\* 4 southward.

**sabina.** Savin. Shrub with ascending or spreading branches, usually about 4–5 ft. high, though sometimes attaining 10–15 ft. Leaves dark green and of two types: needle-like in pairs, concave and glaucous\* above; on mature branches scale-like, rather thick and with a gland on the back. Fruit globular, about 1/4 in. long, brown covered with bluish bloom. Mts. of central and southern Eu., western As. to Siberia. Hardy from zone\* 3 southward. One of the handsomest dwarf evergreens, it stands city conditions and likes limey soil. The whole plant has a strong, slightly disagreeable odor, var. **cupressifolia**, a low, almost prostrate form, usually with overlapping, scale-like leaves; var. **tamariscifolia**, a low form in which the leaves are mostly needle-like and borne in 3's.

**scopulorum.** Western Red Cedar, also known as Rocky Mountain Red Cedar and Colo. Red Cedar. A round-topped tree, usually low, but sometimes growing 35–40 ft. high. Trunk short, often dividing near the ground; bark red-brown, shredding. Leaves of two types, mainly scale-like and opposite, pointed and closely pressed to stem. Male flowers with 6 stamens. Fruit blue, bloomy, about 1/3 in. across, ripening second

---

\* Special articles on the subjects indicated by an asterisk (\*) will be found at the words so marked.

year. British Columbia and Alberta south to Tex. and northern Ariz. in the mountains. Hardy from zone* 3 southward. The western representative of *J. virginiana*, from which it differs mainly in habit, bark and nature of fruit; stands dry and difficult situations; var. **argentea**, form with glaucous,* silvery leaves and of narrow, upright habit; var. **viridifolia**, habit upright, leaves bright green.

One of the best of all the prostrate junipers, *Juniperus chinensis pfitzeriana*

**squamata.** A low shrub with reclining, spreading branches that turn up at the ends. Leaves predominantly needle-like and in 3's, slender, pointed, slightly spreading, whitish above and grooved below. Fruit purple-black when mature, 1-seeded, oval, about ⅓ in. long, ripens second year. Himalayas and China. Hardy from zone* 3 southward. An attractive shrub with bluish leaves and compact habit; var. **meyeri**, a form with upright branches and very attractive, glaucous* leaves; becomes leggy with age; suited to the rock garden.

**virginiana.** Red Cedar. Tree, columnar or pyramidal when young, becoming broader and spreading with age, usually grows about 40-50 ft. high, though occasionally to 100 ft.; bark red-brown, peeling off in long strips. Leaves of two types: needle-like, glaucous* above, pointed, opposite or in 3's on young plants and branches, on mature branches and plants small and scale-like, pointed, overlapping. Male flowers with usually 12 stamens. Fruit oval, about ⅓ in. long, dark blue, slightly bloomy. A common tree in dry, rocky fields from Canada to Fla., east of the Rockies. Hardy from zone* 1 southward. The wood is fragrant and much used in pencils. A variable species with many varieties: var. **canaerti**, a form with dark green foliage and compact, pyramidal habit; var. **elegantissima**, in which the tips of the branches are golden-yellow; var. **glauca**, a form with silvery-gray foliage; var. **keteleeri**, a compact, upright form with dark green, scale-like leaves; var. **kosteri**, a low plant with spreading branches; var. **schoti**, a narrow, upright tree; var. **tripartita**, a low, rather dense shrub with spreading branches and mostly needle-like leaves; var. **venusta**, an upright form with shiny, dark leaves.

DISEASES. Juniper blight and canker is the most serious disease of young junipers, particularly nursery stock. Twigs are blighted and often whole plants are killed. The spread of the causal fungus is encouraged by moist conditions. Sanitation is suggested and copper fungicides have been used with some success. Where the disease is severe, resistant varieties are suggested. Juniper is a host for several rust fungi which also attack apples, hawthorn, quince, june-berry and related plants. Galls or slight swellings are formed on the leaves, twigs or branches. In the spring these galls bear gelatinous, orange-colored masses of spores. Principal symptoms on the alternate hosts are leafspots, yellowing and defoliation. Control obviously depends on the separation of the two hosts. Spraying with sulphur fungicides has given moderate control.

INSECT PESTS. Scale (see INSECT PESTS) and a webworm controlled by lead arsenate (see INSECTICIDES) are sometimes troublesome.

**JUPITER'S-BEARD** = *Centranthus ruber*.

**JUSSIAEA** (juss-si-ee'a). The cult. species of this chiefly tropical genus of the family Onagraceae are erect or creeping water plants or marsh herbs generally called primrose willow. Of the 50 known species only the two below are likely to be found in cult. They have alternate,* willow-like, toothed leaves and usually solitary, yellow flowers (in ours), found in the leaf-axils.* Petals 4-6, separate and spreading. Stamens* 8-12, in two rows. Fruit a round or 4-angled, many-seeded capsule.* (Named for Bernard de Jussieu, French systematic botanist and originator of a natural system of plant classification.)

The primrose willows will not stand frost, and are grown as summer-blooming, tender annuals. See ANNUALS. But their seeds must be sown in pans or shallow boxes, which must be kept an inch or so below water. Cover the seeds with a little sand to keep them from floating to the surface. After germination they should be potted up in small pots, which need not be submerged, but must be kept wet or at least very moist. They may be grown in the greenhouse or outdoors (in summer), but constant attention to their water needs is easier in the greenhouse.

**longifolia.** An erect, smooth herb with a 3-angled stem, not over 2 ft. high. Leaves lance-linear, 3-4 in. long, more or less glandular along the margins on the lower side. Flowers yellow, the petals faintly notched at the tip. Brazil.

**repens.** A prostrate herb, the creeping stems rooting at the joints. Leaves ovalish or spatula-shaped, 2-3 in. long. Flowers yellow, about ½ in. long. Tropics.

**JUSTICIA** (jus-tiss'i-a). A genus of rather showy-flowered herbs or under-shrubs of the family Acanthaceae, grown in the greenhouse for ornament. From the closely related *Jacobinia* they are separated only by technical characters. Their similarity to other genera has led to much confusion in the names of these plants (as shown below). They have opposite* leaves, without marginal teeth, and a showy, bracted,* terminal cluster of irregular,* 2-lipped* flowers. Stamens 2. Fruit a capsule.* Of over 200 species only *J. secunda* appears to be cult. (Named for James Justice, Scotch gardener.)

For culture see JACOBINIA.

**carnea** = *Jacobinea carnea*.

**coccinea** = *Pachystachys coccinea*. But the name *Justicia coccinea* is also used for another plant better known as *Odontonema stricta*.

**magnifica** = *Jacobinea carnea*.

**secunda.** A shrubby plant 4-6 ft. high. Leaves ovalish or oblong, 4-6 in. long, tapering to a long point. Flowers red, showy, about 1½ in. long, deeply 2-lipped,* grouped in narrow, branched clusters (panicles*). Northern S.A.

**JUTE** = *Corchorus capsularis*.

**JUVENILE FORMS.** The young leaves of many plants are very different from those developed at maturity. The common English ivy, for instance, is known to most people only in the juvenile state. Later, when ready to flower or fruit, it produces larger, unangled leaves. The same is true of many other commonly cult. species, notably the climbing fig (*Ficus pumila*), some of the greenhouse plants in the family Araliaceae, and in *Berberis* and *Acacia*.

But juvenile foliage forms are most common in the evergreens, especially the junipers, in *Chamaecyparis*, *Thuja*, and *Cupressus*. Often these foliage differences are so great as to lead to confusion in the identity of the plant. Some juvenile forms are more desirable horticulturally than the mature state, and where this is true, they are propagated by cuttings, layering, or other nonsexual methods. This results in millions of plants being produced, not one of which ever produces mature leaves, as in the usual forms of the English ivy (see HEDERA HELIX).

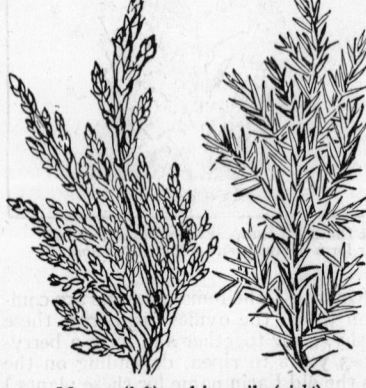

Mature (*left*) and juvenile (*right*) forms of juniper foliage

---

* Special articles on the subjects indicated by an asterisk (*) will be found at the words so marked.

FORMAL USE OF CLIPPED RED CEDAR (JUNIPERUS VIRGINIANA)

A part of the restored gardens of the Governor's Palace, Williamsburg, Virginia. The design is taken from a copper plate made about 1740 and found in the Bodleian Library. The dimensions were revealed by recent excavation.

# K

**KADSURA** (kad-soor'ra). A small genus of woody climbers, mostly from tropical Asia, belonging to the magnolia family. Only one species is hardy; this is a handsome climber, evergreen in the South but losing its leaves in northern winters. The flowers are inconspicuous, but when the heads of scarlet fruits are produced in the fall the plant is an arresting sight. It seems to prefer a sunny position and fairly good, loamy soil. Propagation is by cuttings. (*Kadsura* is the Japanese name for these plants.)

**japonica.** Climbs 10 ft. or more. Leaves alternate, thick, toothed, 2–4 in. long. Flowers yellow-white, with 9–15 sepals, and petals ½–¾ in. across, dioecious,* usually borne singly in the leaf-axils during summer. Fruit clustered, scarlet. Japan, Korea. Hardy from zone* 5 (possibly 4) southward.

**KAEMPFER'S AZALEA** = *Azalea obtusa kaempferi*.

**KAFIR** = *Holcus sorghum caffrorum*.

**KAFIR-BEAN TREE** = *Schotia latifolia*.

**KAFIR LILY** = *Schizostylis coccinea*. See also CLIVIA.

**KAIDO CRABAPPLE** = *Malus micromalus*.

**KAINIT.** See Potash at FERTILIZERS.

*KAKI* (kah'kee). Japanese vernacular for the persimmon.

**KALANCHOE** (kal-an-ko'ee). A large genus of succulent, sometimes woody herbs of the family Crassulaceae, many from South Africa, the others chiefly Asiatic. Of the 100 known species, **K. carnea** from South Africa is the chief one in cult. It is grown in desert gardens in warm regions, or in the greenhouse, and is an erect plant 12–24 in. high, with opposite,* ovalish leaves 3–4 in. long, thick, fleshy, and wavy-margined. Flowers fragrant, pink, about ½ in. wide, in a terminal, branched cluster (cyme*). Corolla with a longish tube, swollen at the base, the 4 lobes wide-spreading and sharp-pointed. Fruit a follicle.* For culture *see* SUCCULENTS. (*Kalanchoe* is thought to be derived from the Chinese name of one species.)

**KALE** (*Brassica oleracea acephala*). As its Latin name indicates, kale is a kind of cabbage that does not produce a head. There are at least three varieties of kale, one of them being collards, a sort that stands more heat than cabbage or ordinary kale, and is consequently grown in the South. Common kale has a profusion of erect, long, finely cut or curled or crisped leaves, the latter being preferred. In the home garden these may be harvested a few at a time, but for market the whole plant is cut. Its culture is the same as for cabbage (which see) and it is primarily a fall and winter vegetable which does not like heat. South of zone* 5, however, it can stand out all winter, furnishing a good supply of pot-herbs. Other names for it are borecole and cow cabbage.

A variety of it, known as Scotch kale, differs only in having light green and tightly curled leaves. Its culture is the same as for common kale, but it likes even less summer heat.

Kale

Collards is chiefly grown in the South. It, too, is a variety of kale, but is best treated as a biennial. Unlike true kale, it produces a short, trunk-like stem (10–30 in. high) which is crowned by a loose cluster of cabbage-like leaves that do not form a head. It may be grown as a winter annual by planting seeds in Sept. and transplanting the seedlings to the garden. Such plants stand out all winter in the South and the harvest of their leaves, a few at a time, begins in the spring. Or the seeds may be sown in the spring and the leaves harvested all the following fall and winter. See also SEA-KALE.

Collards

INSECT PESTS. Kale is affected by cabbage, radish, and turnip insects, especially aphids. These should be prevented from getting a start on young kale by spraying and by cleaning up old plants near by.

**KALMIA** (kal'mĭ-a). Shrubs, mostly evergreen, belonging to the heath family. The leaves are entire* and may be opposite,* alternate* or whorled.* Flowers purple, pink or white, usually showy and borne in terminal or lateral clusters, flat or cup-shaped, 5-lobed, with 10 slender stamens that are caught in the corolla and spring up when touched or disturbed, discharging their pollen. Fruit a round, 5-celled capsule.* (Named for Peter Kalm, a Swedish botanist who traveled in North America.) See POISONOUS PLANTS.

*Kalmia latifolia* is an exceptionally handsome plant when in bloom; it is splendid for massing or as a single specimen. The other species are of indifferent ornamental value, useful in wild plantings or mixed with other evergreens.

Kalmias prefer a somewhat shaded position in moist, peaty, decidedly acid, soil (*see* ACID AND ALKALI SOILS). They often grow well in comparatively dry and exposed places, but need a permanent mulch* of, preferably, oak or beech leaves. Propagation is usually by seed.

**angustifolia.** Sheep laurel, sometimes called lambkill and dwarf laurel. Evergreen shrub of thin, open habit, usually growing 2–3 ft. high. Leaves opposite or in 3's, oblong, 1–2 in. long, considered injurious to grazing animals. Flowers lavender-rose in lateral clusters. June. Labrador to Ga. Hardy from zone* 1 southward.

**carolina.** Closely related to the preceding species, it differs mainly in that the young growth and undersurface of the leaves are downy. Flowers pink or rose. June. Va. to S.C. Hardy from zone* 4 southward.

**glauca** = *Kalmia polifolia*.

**latifolia.** Mountain laurel, laurel, calico bush. Round-topped shrub usually growing 4–10 ft. high, though occasionally becoming a small tree. Leaves evergreen, oval, alternate or sometimes whorled, 2–4 in. long; Flowers rose to white, about ¾ in. across, in large, terminal clusters. May–June. New Brunswick to Fla. and Tenn. Hardy from zone* 3 southward. An excellent shrub for wild or formal plantings; sometimes forced. See FORCING.

**polifolia.** Swamp laurel; pale laurel. Low, thin shrub about 2 ft. high, branchlets 2-edged. Leaves opposite, almost stemless, oval or linear-oval, white beneath, ½–1½ in. long, the edges rolled under. Flowers rose-colored in terminal clusters. May–June. Labrador to Pa. and Minn. and from Alaska to Wash. Hardy from zone* 4 northward. Sometimes known as *K. glauca*, and suited only to the bog garden.

**KALMIAEFLORA**, *-us, -um* (kal-mĭ-ee-flō'ra). With flowers like the genus *Kalmia* (which see).

---
* Special articles on the subjects indicated by an asterisk (*) will be found at the words so marked.

**KAMTSCHATICA, -us, -um** (kam-chat′i-ka). From Kamchatka, Siberia.

**KANGAROO THORN** = *Acacia armata*.

**KANGRA BUCKWHEAT** = *Fagopyrum tataricum*. See BUCKWHEAT.

**KANSAS.** The state lies wholly in zones* 3 and 4. Its elevation increases gradually from 800 feet above sea level in the east central part to 3500 feet on the western boundary 400 miles away. Nearly 20 days are required for the march of spring across the state from south to north, about 200 miles.

Kansas has a great diversity of soils ranging from the thin, prairie soils of the famous "bluestem" region to the loessial (wind-blown) soils of the northeastern part of the state into which roots of apple trees penetrate to a depth of 20 feet. From a crop standpoint, Kansas soils are either uplands or the bottom lands along the water courses. Garden sites are numerous on both types, although the fruits range into the uplands much more extensively than do the vegetables or the flowers. Fifty years of crop production, combined with erosion losses, have greatly reduced the productivity of much of the uplands, but the better lying sites are still very productive when the rainfall is adequate.

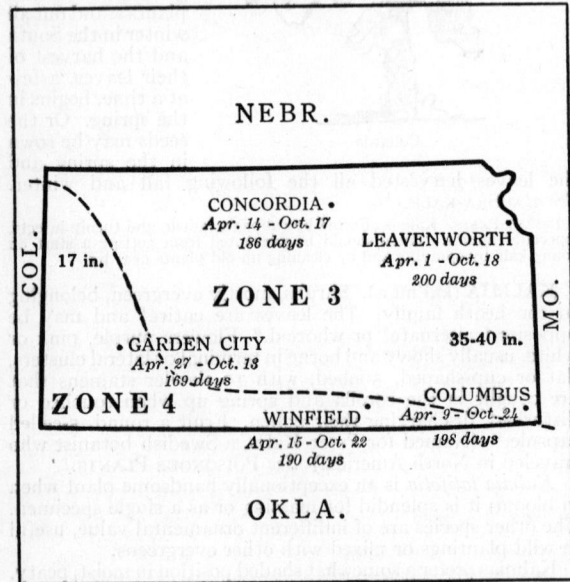

KANSAS

The zones of hardiness crossing Kansas are those shown on the colored map at ZONE, which should be consulted for details. The dates are the average latest killing frost in spring and the first one in the fall. The figures below the dates show the average length of the growing season. The figures in inches show the average annual rainfall in the eastern and western parts of the state.

Kansas has two well-developed orchard districts. The first of these lies in the eastern tier of counties from Johnson north to the state line, but the orchards are most concentrated in Doniphan County. The second follows the valley of the Arkansas River from Hutchinson to Arkansas City. The highest development in this district centers in Belle Plaine and Oxford. Fruit-growing could be greatly extended in the northeastern district, especially on the loess* soils along the Missouri River, and there are many well-adapted but unplanted sites in other parts of the state. Less extensive centers of fruit production are near Grantville, Council Grove, Lawrence, Fredonia, Strong City and other points. Of the tree fruits, the apple is pre-eminent, although there is considerable production of the sour cherry.

Grapes and small fruits are also grown in the tree-fruit localities and show extensive independent development in the southeastern part of the state, contiguous to the Ozark region.

Vegetables and flowers and ornamental nurseries are in the main confined to areas near centers of population. Kansas City, Wichita, Topeka, Hutchinson and Lawrence deserve mention among the cities around which these types of gardening assume considerable importance. In addition, certain truck crops are grown much more extensively than the local demand can consume in the valleys of the Kansas and Arkansas rivers. Potatoes, sweet potatoes and melons from the Kansas River Valley have a wide distribution. Melons are a crop of considerable importance in the valley of the Arkansas. A center of potato production, under irrigation, has developed recently in the "shallow water" district near Scott City.

Among the well-adapted flowering plants are the bulb group, and the iris, peony, gladiolus, rose, aster, snapdragon, in fact, nearly all of the flowers which can stand high summer temperatures and occasional drouths. Very few of the acid-loving plants can be grown. In the eastern third of the state nearly all of the ornamental trees and shrubs of the Mississippi Valley find a congenial home; the list is much abbreviated in the middle third, and only native plants or those imported from semi-arid regions can be grown in the high western third of the state.

The most outstanding characteristic of Kansas climate is its variability, "If you don't like it just wait an hour." Drouth and flood, heat and cold, sunshine and shadow follow in quick succession, with a strong tendency toward extremes. Destructive frosts occur in all parts of the state, but are no greater hazard to garden crops than in other sections of the country.

The following data show that there is a long growing season in all parts of the state.

KANSAS FROST DATA

| Town | Average date of last killing frost in spring | Latest known killing frost | Average date of earliest killing frost in fall | Earliest known killing frost |
|---|---|---|---|---|
| Leavenworth | April 1 | May 1 | Oct. 18 | Sept. 28 |
| Columbus | April 9 | May 9 | Oct. 24 | Sept. 29 |
| Concordia | April 14 | May 19 | Oct. 17 | Sept. 27 |
| Winfield | April 15 | May 20 | Oct. 22 | Sept. 26 |
| Garden City | April 27 | May 27 | Oct. 13 | Sept. 7 |

Except for two to five short periods, rarely of more than seven days' duration, Kansas winters are pleasant and favorable for plants. They have an abundance of sunshine. Such winter weather sometimes leads to severe winter injury to fruit and ornamental trees and to blossom buds. Prematurely active plant cells may then be killed by subsequent low temperatures.

Throughout the state the moisture supply, which falls in the form of rain or snow, is the principal determinant involved in yield of either field or garden crops. The month of lightest precipitation is January, after which there is an increase until June, the wettest month. Average precipitation varies from 35 or 40 inches in the eastern part of the state to about 17 inches on the western border. The fact that 70 per cent or more of this falls during the growing months, April to September, adds greatly to its value for crop production. Drouth during July or August is the most important crop hazard, climatic or biological.

The address of the Agricultural Experiment Station, which has kindly supplied this information about the state, is Manhattan, Kansas. The Station is always ready to answer questions relating to gardening.

Garden Club activities in the state include nearly 20 chapters of the Kansas Association of Garden Clubs. For the nearest one to your locality write the Garden Editor, Houghton Mifflin Company, Boston, Mass. *See also* HORTICULTURAL SOCIETIES.

---

* Special articles on the subjects indicated by an asterisk (*) will be found at the words so marked.

**KANSAS GAY-FEATHER** = *Liatris pycnostachya*.

**KAPOK.** See CEIBA PENTANDRA.

**KAPUKA** = *Griselina littoralis*.

**KARANDA** = *Carissa carandas*.

**KARO** = *Pittosporum crassifolium*.

**KATA-OCHI.** An uneven-falling waterfall. See JAPANESE GARDEN.

**KATSURA TREE** = *Cercidiphyllum japonicum*.

**KAURI PINE** = *Agathis australis*.

**KEEL.** The ridge, suggesting the keel of a boat, on the back of many petals and some leaves. In a more special sense the *keel* constitutes the two front and united petals in the flowers of the pea.

**KEEPING.** See STORAGE.

**KEG GARDENING.** See TUB GARDENING.

**KEI-APPLE** = *Dovyalis caffra*.

**KELP.** See MANURE.

**KEMP, E.** See America at GARDEN BOOKS.

**KENILWORTH IVY** = *Cymbalaria muralis*.

**KENNEDYA** (ken-ned'ee-a). Australian woody vines of the pea family, comprising perhaps a dozen species, but only the two below at all usual as cult. vines. They are grown for ornament south of zone* 7, otherwise, but rarely, in the cool greenhouse. Leaves alternate,* compound,* the leaflets generally 3 (sometimes only 1 in *K. nigricans*), the stalks hairy. Flowers red or purplish-black, showy, pea-like, one, or two, or a cluster in the leaf-axil.* Fruit a pod (legume*), flattened or roundish in section. (Named for Lewis Kennedy, English nurseryman.)

The outdoor culture of *Kennedya* does not present any difficulties so long as there is freedom from hard frosts. Under glass they should be grown in potting mixture* 4 and in the cool greenhouse. Propagated mostly by seeds, but also by cuttings.

**nigricans.** Stem hairy. Leaflets 3 (rarely 1), broadly ovalish, 2–4 in. long, without teeth but the tip often notched. Flowers in a 1-sided cluster (raceme*), the corolla about 1 in. long, purple-black, but green-blotched on the standard.* Pod flattened.

**prostrata.** Stems not very hairy or smooth. Leaflets 3, broadly ovalish or nearly round, scarcely 1 in. long. Flowers in clusters of 2-4 at the end of a long stalk, the corolla scarlet, about ¾ in. long. Pod round in cross-section. The *var.* **major** has larger flowers and its stem is more hairy.

**KENTIA.** A common Latin name for certain cult. palms, but of the true genus *Kentia* there appear to be none in cult. For plants called *Kentia* by the florists *see* the following:
Kentia belmoreana = Howea belmoreana.
Kentia canterburyana = Hedyscepe canterburyana.
Kentia forsteriana = Howea forsteriana.
Kentia macarthuri = Actinophloeus macarthuri.
Kentia sanderiana = Actinophloeus sanderiana.

**KENTUCKY.** The state lies wholly in zones* 3, 4 and 5.

The soils of the state range from sandy to medium clay and silt. An irregular area approximately 50 miles in diameter centering around Lexington is known as the Blue Grass section. The soils of this area contain large amounts of phosphorus, but in all other parts of the state the phosphorus content of the soil is rather low.

The chief garden centers are located around the larger cities, especially around Lexington and Louisville, where there are over 1500 acres of finely landscaped parks.

Among commercial vegetable crops, potatoes lead in importance with 30,000 acres grown. Sweet potatoes are second, and there are about 30 canneries scattered over the state for canning beans and tomatoes.

Orcharding is important in the counties adjacent to the Ohio River and particularly so in Boone, Jefferson, Henderson, Union, and McCracken counties, although orchards are found throughout the state. Apples and peaches are the principal tree fruits, but the strawberry is the leading fruit industry of the state. Most of the commercial acreage is located in the western or lower part of the state. Most of eastern Kentucky is mountainous.

Since the state lies midway between the North and the South a wide range of plants thrive in this climate. The number of native flowers, trees, and shrubs is exceeded by few other states. Notable are the bur oaks and elms in the vicinity of Lexington.

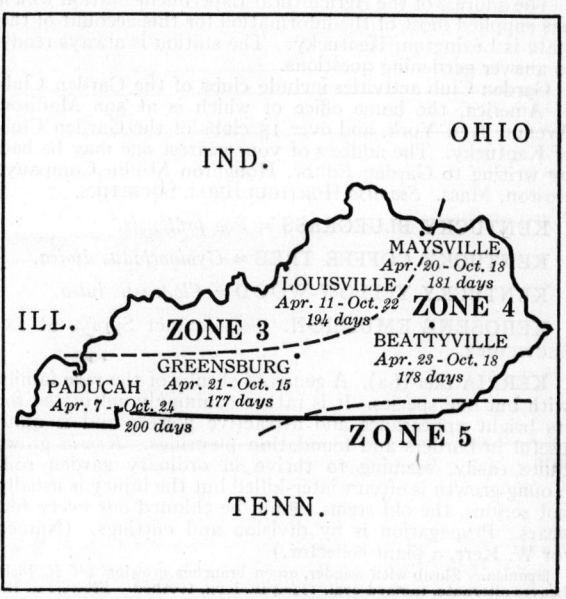

KENTUCKY

The zones of hardiness crossing Kentucky are those shown on the colored map at ZONE, which should be consulted for details. The dates are the average latest killing frost in spring and the first one in the fall. The figures below the dates show the average length of the growing season.

Among native shrubs and trees of decorative or economic value are willows (10 species), ash (6 species), hickories (7 species), oaks (19 species), elms (3 species), magnolia (3 species), and over 10 species of coniferous evergreens. In the mountains azalea and rhododendrons are especially fine. Persimmon, black walnut, and *Asimina triloba* (papaw) are all of importance, especially the walnut.

Important federal statistics (1930 census) which reflect the hort. possibilities of the state are: 64 nurseries (975 acres), 9 bulb specialists (31 acres), and 135 growers of flowers and vegetables (with 345 acres outdoors and over a million sq. ft. of greenhouses).

FROST DATA

Significant dates of the last killing frosts in spring and the first ones in autumn show the differences between the mountainous and lowland parts of the state, and dictate hort. operations accordingly.

| Name of town | Average date of last killing frost in spring | Latest-known killing frost | Average date of earliest killing frost in fall | Earliest-known killing frost |
|---|---|---|---|---|
| Beattyville | April 23 | May 10 | Oct. 18 | Sept. 26 |
| Maysville | April 20 | May 15 | Oct. 18 | Sept. 30 |
| Greensburg | April 21 | May 10 | Oct. 15 | Sept. 14 |
| Louisville | April 11 | May 14 | Oct. 22 | Sept. 26 |
| Paducah | April 7 | April 23 | Oct. 24 | Oct. 9 |

---

* Special articles on the subjects indicated by an asterisk (*) will be found at the words so marked.

# Kentucky Bluegrass

In eastern Kentucky the length of the growing season averages 176 to 188 days. In western Kentucky the length of the growing season averages 177 to 200 days.

## Rainfall

The annual rainfall averages 40 to 45 inches for the state. The average rainfall by months is well distributed throughout the year, but a dry period lasting from 4 to 6 weeks usually occurs some time between June 1 and Oct. 1, with occasional very dry summers such as those of 1930 and 1934.

The address of the Agricultural Experiment Station which has supplied most of the information for this account of the state is Lexington, Kentucky. The station is always ready to answer gardening questions.

Garden Club activities include clubs of the Garden Club of America, the home office of which is at 598 Madison Avenue, New York, and over 15 clubs of the Garden Club of Kentucky. The address of your nearest one may be had by writing to Garden Editor, Houghton Mifflin Company, Boston, Mass. See also HORTICULTURAL SOCIETIES.

**KENTUCKY BLUEGRASS** = *Poa pratensis*.

**KENTUCKY COFFEE TREE** = *Gymnocladus dioica*.

**KENTUCKY YELLOW-WOOD** = *Cladrastis lutea*.

**KEROSENE EMULSION.** See Contact Sprays at INSECTICIDES.

**KERRIA** (ker'ri-a). A genus of shrubs of the rose family with but one species. It is rather commonly cultivated for its bright appearance and attractive flowers and is quite useful in borders and foundation plantings. *Kerria* grows quite easily, seeming to thrive in ordinary garden soil. Young growth is often winter-killed but the injury is usually not serious, the old stems should be thinned out every few years. Propagation is by division and cuttings. (Named for W. Kerr, a plant collector.)

*japonica.* Shrub with slender, green branches growing 4–6 ft. high. Leaves alternate, tapered-oval, 1½–4 in. long, toothed. Flowers at the end of short, lateral branches, yellow, 5-petaled, ¾–1½ in. across. April–May. China. Hardy from zone* 3 southward. Sometimes listed under *Corchorus*. Var. *picta*. Usually lower and less robust, leaves edged with white. Var. *pleniflora*, the Japanese rose, is a taller, more vigorous form, with large, double flowers.

**KERRIOIDES** (ker-ri-oy'deez, but *see* OÏDES). Resembling the genus *Kerria* (which see).

**KETELEERIA** (kee-tel-eer'i-a). Evergreen Chinese trees of the pine family. The leaves are linear, flat or ridged, pale green below and often pointed on young trees, blunt on older ones. Cones 4–6 in. long, upright, the male flowers clustered. (Named for J. B. Keteleer, a French nurseryman.)

Handsome, tall trees suggestive of *Cunninghamia* (which see), pyramidal when young, becoming flat-topped with age. They are rare in cultivation and hardy only in mild climates.

*davidiana.* Tree, 100 ft. or more. Leaves linear, 1–2 in. long, rounded or notched at apex, midrib raised on both sides. Cones cylindric, upright, 4–8 in. long, scales recurved at tip. China. Hardy from zone* 6 southward.

*fortunei.* Tree, 90–100 ft. high. Leaves linear, ¾–1¼ in. long, ridged on both sides. Cones oval, 3–7 in. long. China. Hardy from zone* 6 (possibly 5) southward.

**KEWENSIS, -e** (kew-en'sis). From the Royal Botanic Gardens, Kew, England.

**KEY FRUIT.** See SAMARA.

**KEY LIME.** See Acid Lime at LIME (the citrus fruit).

**KHUS-KHUS** = *Vetiveria zizanioides*.

**KI-BASHI.** Wooden bridge. See JAPANESE GARDEN.

**KID-GLOVE ORANGE.** The tangerine. See CITRUS NOBILIS DELICIOSA.

**KIDNEY BEAN** = *Phaseolus vulgaris*. For culture *see* BEAN.

**KIDNEY VETCH** = *Anthyllis vulneraria*.

**KIDNEYWORT** = *Baccharis pilularis*.

**KIGELIA** (ky-gee'li-a). Two extraordinary tropical African trees of the family Bignoniaceae, one of them, **K. pinnata**, the sausage-tree, widely grown in warm regions for its odd fruit. It is a tree 20–40 ft. high with compound* leaves, the 7–9 oblongish leaflets 4–6 in. long. Flowers nearly 4 in. long, purplish-red, more or less bell-shaped, but slightly irregular,* or bent to one side. Fruit sausage-shaped, 1–2 ft. long, swinging on long, cord-like stalks. The fruits weigh 5–12 pounds each, and are so woody that they must be sawn open to find the many pale seeds which are embedded within. In Fla. it grows on a variety of soils, but only in the warmest parts of the peninsula. (*Kigelia* is a Latinized form of an African vernacular for the tree.)

Sausage-tree

**KILLWORT** = *Chelidonium majus*.

**KINDS OF CROPS.** There is no need to list here all the different plants in THE GARDEN DICTIONARY, but it may prove helpful to list the main cultural articles where most of the different classes of plants are treated.

FLOWERS: See ANNUALS, BIENNIALS, PERENNIALS, BORDER, BULBS, and ROCK GARDEN. See also FLOWERING SHRUBS, VINES, and the special articles on the culture of the important flowers, as at DAHLIA, CARNATION, SWEET PEA, PEONY, etc., etc.

FRUITS: See FRUIT CULTURE and the special articles on the culture of the important ones, as at APPLE, PEACH, APRICOT, PEAR, STRAWBERRY, etc., etc.

VEGETABLES: See KITCHEN GARDEN and the special articles on the culture of the important ones, as at BEAN, CABBAGE, PEA, TOMATO, etc., etc.

CULINARY HERBS: See HERB GARDENING.

MEDICINAL PLANTS: See MEDICINAL PLANTS.

And, particularly, look at the cross-references that originate at these main entries. These cross-references have been designed to lead the reader to many delightful garden genera and species which lend themselves better to individual than to group treatment.

Nor do the above exhaust the different sorts of specialized crops which one may care to grow. See also WATER GARDENING, CACTI, SUCCULENTS, GRASSES, PALM, MUSHROOM, GREENHOUSE.

**KING-CUP** = *Caltha palustris*. See MARSH MARIGOLD.

**KING ORANGE** = *Citrus nobilis*.

**KING'S CLOVER** = *Melilotus officinalis*.

**KINNIKINNICK** = *Arctostaphylos uva-ursi*.

**KITAMBILLA** = *Dovyalis hebecarpa*.

**KITCHEN GARDEN.** The kitchen garden is a valuable asset to any home, whether in the country or in the village and small cities. On the farm and in many small towns and villages fresh vegetables frequently are not available unless they are grown at home. Many vegetables are more tasty and more valuable from the dietary standpoint when fresh. One who has not eaten sweet corn within an hour or two after it has been picked knows little about the flavor of this product. As soon as sweet corn is picked its sugar begins to change to starch, thus resulting in loss in sweetness,

---
* Special articles on the subjects indicated by an asterisk (*) will be found at the words so marked.

The kitchen garden need not be kitchen-minded. An attractive vegetable garden in New England, modeled after the English plan.

increase in toughness of the skin of the kernel and a change in the consistency of the cooked product. Many other products decrease in quality after harvest owing to loss in sugar, increase in toughness, or a decrease in succulence.

A garden of one eighth of an acre well planned, well planted and well cared for will supply fresh vegetables for a family of four for a large part of the growing season and leave some for canning and storing. A garden of this size should yield a gross return of at least $50 and returns of $100 from an eighth of an acre are not unusual. Of course, the gardener should use retail prices when computing the value of his home-grown vegetables since this is the price he pays if he buys instead of produces them. For dimensions of gardens *see* Acre at WEIGHTS AND MEASURES.

It is frequently asserted that one can buy vegetables cheaper than he can produce them. This may be true under some conditions, if one has to rent the land and hire all of the labor for preparing the soil, planting and caring for the garden. For the indoor worker the kitchen garden offers good wholesome exercise in the fresh air and sunshine and, at the same time, gives a valuable return for the time spent. On the farm a good kitchen garden yields returns greater than most other enterprises, and, for most farms, is the only reliable source of fresh vegetables.

### PLANNING THE GARDEN

It is desirable, especially for the beginner, to make a garden plan on paper, and this should be done long in advance of the time of planting the garden. The plan should show what crops are to be grown, the space to be occupied by each, the direction of the rows, and the distance between the rows. Before making the plan one must decide on the direction of the rows. If the ground slopes much the rows should run across the slope, not up and down it. On level land the rows may run in any direction. Rows running north and south give equal sunlight to both sides, and this is desirable where the slope and the layout of the garden permit it. If the rows run east and west, tall crops, such as corn and pole beans, should be planted on the north side so that they will not shade smaller growing crops too much.

Should the rows run the long way or the short way of the garden? In a small garden, cultivated by hand, it makes little difference, but in a large garden, where horse cultivation is to be given, long rows are preferable to short ones. With rows running the long way of the garden there will be fewer rows, hence less space will be taken up in turning at the ends. For horse cultivation the garden should be relatively long and narrow, with the rows running the long way.

### ARRANGEMENT OF THE GARDEN

In deciding where to plant the various crops the following points should be given consideration:

1. Perennial crops, those that will remain in one place for several years, should be planted at one end or one side of the garden, so they will not interfere too much with plowing, harrowing and cultivation. Such crops are asparagus, rhubarb and perennial onions. If small fruits such as raspberries, blackberries, currants and gooseberries are to be grown in the garden, they should be planted at one side or one end also.

2. Tall crops and those that spread very much should be planted toward one side, where they will not shade or overrun smaller crops. These include sweet corn, pole beans, tomatoes, cucumbers, melons, winter squashes and pumpkins.

3. Small-growing crops and those that occupy the land about the same length of time should be grouped together, where convenient, so that the area occupied by them may be prepared as a unit for other crops succeeding them the same season.

4. Crops that occupy the land most or all of the growing season should be grouped together. Such crops include

---

\* Special articles on the subjects indicated by an asterisk (\*) will be found at the words so marked.

parsnips, salsify, chard, onions grown from seed and New Zealand spinach.

These points have been considered in the plans given, but it is not feasible in any one plan to follow all of them to the letter.

### Distance Between the Rows

If the garden is to be cultivated by horse-drawn cultivators the rows should be at least 2½ feet apart, and for large-growing plants greater spacing should be given. The distances between the rows, shown in the plan of the larger garden, are satisfactory for home gardens under most conditions and are given as a guide. Where hand cultivation is to be given the rows for most crops do not need to be as far apart as for horse cultivation. For small-growing crops, such as lettuce, spinach, onions, beets, carrots, parsnips, salsify, radish, turnip and others of similar size, a space of 15 to 18 inches between the rows is sufficient; for slightly larger crops, as snap beans, cabbage, small varieties of sweet corn and the like, 2 to 2½ feet spacing is sufficient; while for larger plants greater space is needed, as shown in the plan.

### What Crops to Grow

There are many things to consider in selecting the crops to grow in a home garden, the most important being (1) the size of the area available, (2) the relative returns for the space occupied, (3) the food value of the crops, (4) the likes and dislikes of those that are to consume the vegetables, (5) the soil and climatic conditions and the skill of the gardener. In small gardens it is better to plant small-growing crops, such as beets, carrots, lettuce and beans, rather than sweet corn, cucumbers and squashes. We should aim to have in the garden a continuous supply of the leafy crops, lettuce, spinach, chard, New Zealand spinach, cabbage and the like. These are rich in minerals and vitamins and add bulk to the diet. Snap beans, asparagus and peas are similar to the leafy crops in nutritive value. Carrots, beets, onions, turnips, parsnips or salsify, and, if the garden is large enough, peas, sweet corn and potatoes should be included. The tomato is one of the most important vegetable crops and should be grown in all kitchen gardens regardless of the size. Radishes and cucumbers have little food value but are eaten for their flavor.

The crops giving the highest returns in terms of nutritive value for the space occupied are snap beans, tomatoes, carrots, beets, parsnips, spinach, kale, chard, New Zealand spinach, lettuce and green onions. Peas, sweet corn and potatoes do not give high returns for the space occupied and should not be grown in the very small garden unless the gardener can obtain readily a supply of the other vegetables. Freshness is of such great importance with peas and sweet corn that the gardener may wish to sacrifice returns that might be obtained from other vegetables for high quality in these.

The climate of the region determines to some extent the crops that can be grown successfully. For example in zone* 1 the season is too short and too cool for muskmelons, watermelons, sweet potatoes, pole Lima beans, eggplant and peppers. The same is true of most of zone* 2 and even the cooler parts of zone* 3. However, in most of zone* 3, except in New England, New York and in the higher elevations of other parts of this zone, nearly all of the common vegetable crops can be grown. In the other zones there is practically no limitation, except that in parts of zone* 6 and in all of zones* 7, 8 and 9 the cool-season crops, such as spinach, kale, lettuce, celery, cabbage, peas, radishes, turnips, beets, carrots, parsnips, cauliflower and others, cannot be grown successfully in the hottest part of the summer. In fact, in the milder regions these crops are grown mainly in the winter.

### The Garden Plan

Detailed plans for gardens of two different sizes are given in the charts. The small garden, 50 by 100 feet, is suitable for a small family living in a village or a small city, while the larger one, 100 by 200, is suitable for a farm garden or for a small country estate. It is assumed that the small garden would be cultivated by hand and that the larger one would be cultivated by horse-drawn cultivators or by garden tractors. Some gardeners may wish to cultivate by hand the small-growing crops in the larger garden, in which case the rows do not need to be as far apart as is shown in the chart. In the event that these crops are planted for hand cultivation, several additional rows would be available for growing more kinds of crops, or more of some of the kinds included in the plan. Celery, cauliflower, kohl-rabi, Lima beans and other crops might be added to the list, or more space might be used for potatoes and other crops that keep well in storage.

It is not expected that the plans given here will be followed in detail and to the letter, but rather that they will serve as a guide. However, in making the plans there has been taken into consideration the quantities of vegetables of various kinds that would be needed for a family of 4 or 5 in the case of the small garden and what would be needed for 12 to 15 persons in the case of the larger garden. It is very important to have a planting large enough to provide sufficient at any one time for the number of persons that are to be served. This is particularly important with such crops as asparagus, beans and peas.

### Quantity of Seed and Number of Plants

A table is given showing the quantity of seed or the number of plants required for 100 feet of row, for a garden

TABLE SHOWING QUANTITY OF SEED AND NUMBER OF PLANTS FOR 100 FEET OF ROW, FOR A GARDEN 50 BY 100 FEET AND FOR A GARDEN 100 BY 200 FEET

| Kind of crop | For 100 feet of row | For garden 50 by 100 feet | For garden 100 by 200 feet |
|---|---|---|---|
| Asparagus | 60 plants | 120 plants | 200 plants |
| Beans, snap | ¾ lb. | 1½ lbs. | 4 lbs. |
| Beans, Lima | ½ lb. | | |
| Beets | 2 oz. | 2 oz. | ½ lb. |
| Broccoli | 50 plants | | 50 plants |
| Cabbage, early | 66 plants | 33 plants | 133 plants |
| Cabbage, late | 66 plants or 1 pkt. seed | 66 plants or 1 pkt. seed | 266 plants or 1 pkt. seed |
| Carrot | ½ oz. | ¾ oz. | 2 oz. |
| Cauliflower | 66 plants | | |
| Celery | 200 plants | | |
| Cucumber | ½ oz. | 1 pkt. | ½ oz. |
| Eggplant | 66 plants | | |
| Endive | 1 oz. | | |
| Kale | ¼ oz. | | |
| Lettuce | ¼ oz. | ¼ oz. | ½ oz. |
| Muskmelon | ½ oz. | | ½ oz. |
| Mustard | ¼ oz. | | |
| Onion sets | 2 lbs. | 3 lbs. | 4 to 8 lbs. |
| Onion seed | 1 oz. | | 2 oz. |
| Parsnips | ½ oz. | ¼ oz. | 1 oz. |
| Peas | 1 lb. | 2 lbs. | 4 lbs. |
| Peppers | 66 plants | 18 plants | 36 plants |
| Potatoes | 5 to 8 lbs. | 7 to 12 lbs. | 30 to 48 lbs. |
| Pumpkin | 1 oz. | | |
| Radish | 1 oz. | 1 pkt. | ½ oz. |
| Rhubarb | 35 roots | 10 roots | 30 roots |
| Rutabaga | ¼ oz. | | |
| Spinach | 1½ oz. | 1½ oz. | 2½ oz. |
| Spinach, New Zeal. | 1 oz. | 1 pkt. | 1 oz. |
| Squash, summer | ½ oz. | 1 pkt. | ½ oz. |
| Squash, winter | ½ oz. | | |
| Sweet corn | 2 oz. | 6 oz. | 1¼ lbs. |
| Swiss chard | 1 oz. | 1 pkt. | 1 oz. |
| Tomato, staked | 50 plants | 62 plants | 150 plants |
| Tomato, not staked | 33 plants | 40 plants | 100 plants |
| Turnip | ½ oz. | ½ oz. | 1 oz. |
| Watermelon | 1 oz. | | |

* Special articles on the subjects indicated by an asterisk (*) will be found at the words so marked.

50 by 100 feet and for a garden 100 by 200 feet. The quantities are based on the spacing recommended for vegetables grown in the home garden and for the number of feet of row of each crop as shown in the plans. In this table several crops are listed that are not included in the plans. Some gardeners may wish to grow other crops than those shown in the plans, or to make substitution in some cases. The information given in the second column of the table will enable the gardener to estimate the quantity of seed needed of any crop listed for any given length of row. Where only a very small quantity of seed of any one variety and kind is needed it is suggested that the gardener buy a standard seedsman's packet.

### Varieties of Vegetables for the Kitchen Garden

With many kinds of vegetables there are several good varieties, but there is no "best" variety for all localities and for all tastes and uses. The varieties in the following list are, in the main, of good quality and can be grown in nearly all sections where the particular crop is produced. There are, however, some exceptions to this. Some long-season varieties of tomatoes, muskmelons and watermelons cannot be grown successfully in regions having a short growing season. Note is made of this fact in connection with the varieties in question.

ASPARAGUS: Mary Washington.
BEANS:
  Snap, green-podded bush: Giant Stringless Green Pod, Tendergreen, Bountiful. Green-podded pole: Kentucky Wonder, Lazy Wife.
  Snap, wax-podded bush: Sure Crop, Pencil Pod, Davis Stringless, Wardwell.
  Lima, bush: Fordhook Bush Lima, Burpee Bush Lima, Burpee Improved, Henderson.
  Lima, pole: Leviathan, Challenge, King of the Garden, Sieva or Carolina.
BEETS: Crosby Egyptian, Detroit Dark Red.
BROCCOLI: Italian Green Sprouting or Calabrese.
BRUSSELS SPROUTS: Long Island Improved.
CABBAGE:
  Early: Early Copenhagen or Golden Acre, Jersey Wakefield, Charleston Wakefield.
  Mid-season: Glory, late strains of Copenhagen.
  Late: Danish Ballhead, Savoy (good edible quality).
CARROTS: Red Cored Chantenay, Nantes or Coreless, Danvers Half Long.
CAULIFLOWER: Snowball or Erfurt.
CELERY: Golden Self Blanching, Golden Plume or Wonderful, Easy Blanching or Newark Market, Giant Pascal, Utah, Salt Lake, Boston Market.
CHARD OR SWISS CHARD: Lucullus, Large Ribbed White or Silver Leaf.
CUCUMBER:
  Small pickling: Chicago Pickling, Snow Pickling, National Pickling.
  Slicing and large pickling: White Spine, Kirby, Early Fortune, Davis Perfect.
EGGPLANT: Black Beauty, New York Improved.
ENDIVE: Green Curled, White Curled, Broad-leaved Batavian.
KOHLRABI: Early Purple Vienna, Early White Vienna.
LETTUCE:
  Head: Big Boston, Unrivaled, White Boston, May King, Mignonette, New York or Wonderful.
  Leaf: Grand Rapids, Black-seeded Simpson, Prize Head.
MUSKMELON: Bender or Benders Surprise, Honey Rock, Hearts of Gold, Emerald Gem, Osage, Hales Best (in Southwest).
OKRA: Dwarf Long Pod Green, Perkins Mammoth, White Velvet.
ONIONS:
  Green bunching: Egyptian or Tree, any variety from sets.
  Mature bulbs: Danvers, Ebenezer, Yellow Globe, Riverside Sweet Spanish (large, mild slicing), Yellow Bermuda (mild).
PARSLEY: Moss Curled, Double Curled.
PARSNIP: Hollow Crown or Guernsey, Model.
PEAS:
  Early: Laxtons Progress, Peter Pan or Blue Bantam or Hundredfold, Thomas Laxton, Gradus.
  Late: Alderman or Dark Podded Telephone, Improved Telephone.
PEPPERS: World Beater, California Wonder, Harris Earliest, Ruby King, Sunnybrook or Squash or Tomato.
POTATOES:
  Early: Irish Cobbler, Bliss.
  Late: Green Mountain, Rural, Russet Rural, McCormick or Peachblow (grown in South).
PUMPKIN: Winter Luxury, Small Sugar, Connecticut Field, California Field.
RADISH: Scarlet Globe, Scarlet Turnip White Tip or Rosy Gem, Crimson Giant, Saxa or Rapid Red, Icicle, Ne Plus Ultra or Fireball.
RHUBARB: Victoria, Linnaeus or Strawberry, McDonald, Crimson Winter.
RUTABAGA: American Purple Top or Long Island Improved.
SALSIFY: Mammoth Sandwich Island.
SPINACH: Long Standing Bloomsdale, Savoy or Bloomsdale, Virginia Savoy (blight resistant), Old Dominion, King of Denmark, Princess Juliana, Prickly Seeded Winter (grown in California in winter).
SQUASH:
  Summer: Yellow Straightneck, Italian Marrow or Cocozelle, Zuchini, Early Bush Scallop.
  Winter: Green Hubbard, Blue Hubbard, Golden Hubbard, Boston Marrow, Quality, Delicious, Kitchenette, Table Queen or Des Moines.
SWEET CORN:
  Early and mid-season white: Early Market, Surprise, Whipple Early.
  Early and mid-season yellow: Extra Early Bantam, Sunshine, Golden Bantam, Golden Cross, Whipple Yellow, Black Mexican (mostly black).
  Late: Stowell Evergreen, Country Gentleman, Bantam Evergreen.
TOMATO: Bonny Best or John Baer or Chalk Jewel, Pritchard, Marglobe, Globe (long season), Stone (long season).
TURNIP: Purple Top White Globe, White Egg, Purple Top Strap Leaved.
WATERMELON: For short-season regions, Fordhook Early, Kleckley Sweet or Monte Cristo, Halbert Honey, Tom Watson, Stone Mountain. For long-season region, any of the above, Klondike, Florida Favorite, Irish Grey.

### Preparation of the Garden Soil

The soil for the kitchen garden should be thoroughly prepared before attempting to plant seeds or plants, for no amount of cultivation will make up for poor preparation. The soil should be plowed or spaded to the depth of 6 to 8 inches and the surface thoroughly pulverized and smoothed by harrowing or raking. Before sowing seed or setting plants the surface should be smooth, friable* and free from clods or lumps. A small garden, one-tenth acre or less, usually is spaded or dug by hand and then the surface is smoothed and prepared with a hand cultivator and a rake or with the rake alone. A garden larger than this ordinarily is plowed and harrowed, and even smaller ones sometimes are so prepared. After the soil has been plowed and harrowed, further preparation for planting can be done with hand tools. The surface soil should be kept loose and free from weeds until time for planting, and this requires frequent going over with the harrow, hand cultivator or rake. (See PLOWING, DIGGING, HARROWING and RAKING.)

---

* Special articles on the subjects indicated by an asterisk (*) will be found at the words so marked.

## PLAN OF A VEGETABLE GARDEN
100 × 50 feet

| Left column | Right column | Spacing |
|---|---|---|
| Asparagus | | 42 in. |
| Asparagus | | 42 in. |
| Asparagus | | 42 in. |
| Asparagus | Rhubarb | 42 in. |
| Sweet corn, third planting or late variety | | 36 in. |
| Sweet corn, third planting or late variety | | 36 in. |
| Sweet corn, third planting or late variety | | 36 in. |
| Sweet corn, first planting | Sweet corn, second planting | 30 in. |
| Sweet corn, first planting | Sweet corn, second planting | 30 in. |
| Sweet corn, first planting | Sweet corn, second planting | 30 in. |
| Tomatoes | Peppers | 42 in. |
| Tomatoes | | 42 in. |
| Tomatoes | | 42 in. |
| Cucumbers | Summer squash | 42 in. |
| Potatoes | | 42 in. |
| Potatoes | | 36 in. |
| Potatoes | | 36 in. |
| Potatoes | | 36 in. |
| Snap beans, first planting | | 30 in. |
| Snap beans, first planting | | 30 in. |
| Snap beans, second planting | | 30 in. |
| Snap beans, second planting | | 30 in. |
| Peas, early (followed by late cabbage) | | 30 in. |
| Peas, early (followed by late cabbage) | | 18 in. |
| Peas, later (followed by fall spinach or kale) | | 18 in. |
| Peas, later (followed by fall spinach or kale) | | 18 in. |
| Cabbage, early | | 30 in. |
| Parsnips or salsify | | 30 in. |
| Beets, early (followed by turnips) | | 18 in. |
| Carrots, early (followed by turnips) | | 18 in. |
| Beets, late | | 18 in. |
| Carrots, late | | 18 in. |
| Carrots, late | | 18 in. |
| Onion sets for green onions | | 18 in. |
| Onion sets for green onions | | 18 in. |
| Onion sets for bulb onions | | 18 in. |
| Onion sets for bulb onions | Radishes | 18 in. |
| Lettuce, early | | 18 in. |
| Spinach, kale or mustard, early (followed by lettuce) | | 18 in. |
| Spinach, kale or mustard, early | Turnips | 18 in. |
| New Zealand spinach or chard | | 18 in. |

← 50 feet →

100 feet

## PLAN OF A VEGETABLE GARDEN (200 × 100 feet)

| Row | Spacing |
|---|---|
| Asparagus | 48 in. |
| Asparagus | 48 in. |
| Rhubarb, horseradish | 48 in. |
| Bush fruits (raspberries, blackberries, currants) | 48 in. |
| Strawberries | 48 in. |
| Strawberries | 48 in. |
| Sweet corn, early variety | 36 in. |
| Sweet corn, early variety | 36 in. |
| Sweet corn, early variety | 36 in. |
| Sweet corn, second planting | 36 in. |
| Sweet corn, second planting | 36 in. |
| Sweet corn, second planting | 36 in. |
| Sweet corn, late, large variety | 36 in. |
| Sweet corn, late, large variety | 48 in. |
| Tomatoes | 48 in. |
| Tomatoes | 48 in. |
| Peppers, eggplant | 48 in. |
| Cucumbers | 48 in. |
| Melons or summer squash | 48 in. |
| Potatoes | 36 in. |
| Potatoes | 36 in. |
| Potatoes | 36 in. |
| Peas, early (followed by late cabbage) | 36 in. |
| Peas, second planting | 36 in. |
| Cabbage, early (followed by fall spinach) | 36 in. |
| Beans, snap, first planting | 36 in. |
| Beans, snap, second planting | 30 in. |
| Parsnips or salsify | 30 in. |
| Chard or New Zealand spinach | 30 in. |
| Beets, second planting | 30 in. |
| Sprouting broccoli | 30 in. |
| Carrots, second planting | 30 in. |
| Onion seed or sets for bulb onions | 30 in. |
| Onion sets for green onions (followed by late cabbage and lettuce) | 30 in. |
| Carrots, early (followed by fall spinach and lettuce) | 30 in. |
| Beets, early (followed by turnips) | 30 in. |
| Spinach, spring (followed by beans) | 30 in. |
| Spinach, spring | 30 in. |
| Lettuce, radishes | 30 in. |

100 feet wide, 200 feet long.

### Tools for the Kitchen Garden

Not many tools are needed for the small garden. A spade or spading fork, a hoe and a rake are essential, and a small hand weeder, a trowel and a garden line are desirable additions to any garden. A wheel hoe or hand cultivator is a great labor saver for either the small or the large garden and a hand sprayer or hand duster is very desirable. After the land is prepared for planting all labor can be done with the tools mentioned, even in a half-acre garden. On the farm, plows, harrows and horse-drawn cultivators are available and they are commonly used in the farm garden. Where plows and harrows are not used for other work than preparing the garden soil the home gardener should hire someone, who has the necessary equipment, to plow and harrow his garden. If a one-horse cultivator is not used for other work on the farm it is desirable to obtain one for the garden, since larger cultivators are not desirable or practical for the family garden. For a general list see Tools and Implements.

### Improvement of the Soil

It is seldom that the land available for the kitchen garden is entirely satisfactory for the purpose without improvement of the soil. Most areas are lacking in one or more fertilizing elements and many lack all of the three important ones, nitrogen, phosphorus and potash. Heavy soils, such as clays and clay loams, can be made lighter and more friable* by the addition of humus-forming material, and sandy soils are improved in texture and in their water-holding capacity by the same material. Stable manure supplies both humus and the common fertilizing elements. Where this material is available in sufficient quantities it might be applied at the rate of 20 tons to the acre. This should be supplemented with about 500 pounds of 16 per cent superphosphate to the acre, since manure is somewhat deficient in phosphorus.

Where manure is not available the texture of the soil can be improved by growing and turning under some soil-improving crop. Rye is a good crop to grow for turning under in most regions, but in regions of the South, where the soil-improving crop might be grown in the summer, cow peas may be planted to improve the soil. (See Green Manuring and Soil Management.) In addition to the soil-improving crop it is desirable to supply a complete fertilizer, which is one that contains nitrogen, phosphorus and potash. The quantity to apply should be governed to some extent by the natural fertility of the soil. On an infertile soil it is desirable to make an application of 1500 to 2000 pounds or more to the acre of a 5–10–5 or some similar fertilizer. (See Fertilizers.) This means 5 per cent nitrogen, 10 per cent phosphoric acid and 5 per cent potash. On a moderately fertile soil the application might be reduced and on a rich soil little or no fertilizer need be applied. Even where stable manure is used a light application of fertilizer is desirable. The most feasible method of applying fertilizer to the soil of the kitchen garden is to sprinkle it broadcast over the entire area after the soil is plowed or spaded. The fertilizer should then be mixed with the surface soil by harrowing or by raking. Coarse manure should be applied before the land is plowed or spaded and should be well turned under so as not to interfere with further preparation and with planting. Well-rotted manure may be applied after the land is plowed, in which case it should be harrowed in or raked in. (See Fertilizers.)

Most vegetable crops thrive best on a soil that is slightly acid, but many do not grow well on a very sour soil. Lime is used to correct soil acidity, but garden soil should not be limed unless it has been tested to show whether it is needed, and, if so, the quantity to apply. If spinach and beets grow well the soil probably does not need lime. (See Lime.)

### Growing Plants for Transplanting in the Garden

Several kinds of vegetable plants are practically always started in a specially prepared seed bed, from which they are later transferred to the garden. (See Seeds and Seedage.) These include cabbage, cauliflower, Brussels sprouts, celery, eggplant, pepper, tomato and sweet potato. Others, such as lettuce, onions, beets, muskmelons, watermelons and Lima beans, are sometimes started under protection in greenhouses and hotbeds. In regions having short growing seasons, or where an early crop is desired, seeds of these are generally sown under protection, as in a box in a sunny window of the dwelling house, in a cold frame, hotbed or in a greenhouse. (See Cold Frame.) In regions having a short growing season, as in all of zone* 1, in most of zone* 2 and in the cooler parts of zone* 3, good yields of tomatoes, eggplant and pepper cannot be obtained unless the plants are started under protection several weeks before it is safe to plant them in the garden. For an early crop of the other vegetables mentioned, it is desirable to start the plants under protection in these zones and in zones* 4 and 5 and in most of 6. In sections of the United States where the growing season is sufficiently long the plants for all of these crops might be started in a cold frame or even in a specially prepared bed in the open. Late cabbage, late cauliflower and late celery are nearly always started in open beds. See the name of your state or province for frost data.

When an early crop of cabbage, cauliflower, celery and lettuce is desired in regions where the winters are too severe to grow them in the open, seed should be sown 6 to 8 weeks in advance of the time to set the plants in the garden. In zone* 4 this should be from Feb. 1 to 15, in zone* 3 Feb. 15 to March 1; in zone* 2 March 1 to 15; and in zone* 1 March 15 to 30; in zone* 5 Jan. 15 to 30. In most of zone* 6 and in all of zones* 7, 8 and 9 the plants ordinarily would be grown in the open during the fall. Seeds of tomato, eggplant and pepper are usually sown 8 to 10 weeks in advance of planting in the garden. In zones* 1 to 5 the date of sowing seed of these crops should be 2 to 3 weeks later than for cabbage. In zone* 6 and the cooler parts of 7 seeds of these ordinarily would be sown in Feb. In the milder parts of zone* 7, as in the Gulf Coast region of Texas, and in zones* 8 and 9, these crops can be grown during the winter and spring, so that the time of sowing seed depends on the time the crop is desired.

It should be borne in mind that elevation and the proximity to large bodies of water modify the climate and, because of this, the dates given for starting plants in the various zones are only approximate. The reader should consult the name of his state or province where the dates of the last killing frost in spring, the first killing frost in fall and the length of the frost-free period are all given in detail.

In the growing of early plants for setting in the garden it is a common practice to transplant the seedlings once before they are taken to the garden. This is called pricking-out and is usually done when the plants develop their first true leaves and are from one to two inches tall. The purpose of this transplanting is to give the seedlings more space for development and to develop a more branched root system.

### Planting the Garden

The time for planting seeds or setting plants in the garden in most sections depends largely on the dates of the last killing frost in spring for the first planting and the last killing frost in fall for the latest safe date for planting. It is desirable to plant as early as possible in order to get a succession of crops. Some crops must be planted early to avoid hot weather, while others thrive best in warm weather. Some crops will grow before the soil gets warm and are not injured by light frosts, while others will not grow in a cool soil and are severely injured or killed by frost. The following grouping can be used to guide the gardener in planning his planting:

1. Crops that may be planted in the open 3 to 4 weeks before the last killing frost in spring are onion sets, spinach, radish, turnip, kale, mustard, lettuce (seed and plants), peas, early potatoes, asparagus and rhubarb roots. In most sections of northern United States these crops may be planted as soon as the ground can be prepared in the spring.

---

* Special articles on the subjects indicated by an asterisk (*) will be found at the words so marked.

In zone* 4 this would be about the middle of March, correspondingly later in zones* 2 and 1 and earlier in zones* 5 and 6. In the milder regions of zone* 6, in most of 7 and in all of zones* 8 and 9 these crops can be grown all winter.

2. Crops that may be planted a little before the last killing frost in spring are beets, carrots, chard, onion seed, parsnip, salsify, cauliflower plants, celery plants. In regions having severe freezes these may be planted about two weeks later than the group mentioned above, while in milder regions they may be planted at approximately the same time.

3. Crops to be planted after the danger of *killing* frost has passed are snap beans, sweet corn, New Zealand spinach. It may be worth while to take chances on a light frost with these crops.

4. Crops to be planted after *all* danger of frost is over and after the soil has become warm are tomatoes, eggplant, pepper, cucumber, muskmelon, watermelon, squashes and pumpkins, Lima bean and sweet potato. These crops are injured by light frosts and stunted by low temperatures even when there is no frost.

By consulting the frost data at the name of his state the reader can determine the approximate date of the last killing frost in spring in his locality. From this and from the suggestions given above the gardener can arrive at the time for making the first planting of the various crops.

In many sections of the South, as in most of zones* 5 and all of zones* 6, 7, 8, and 9, the cool-season crops do not thrive in the hottest part of the summer. This is true of spinach, turnips, kale and peas in most of zones* 2, 3 and 4. However, where the temperature is modified by elevation or by the cooling effects of large bodies of water these crops can be grown even in midsummer.

More than one planting should be made of many crops. There should be a continuous supply of snap beans, beets, carrots, cabbage, lettuce and sweet corn from the garden throughout the growing season, from the time the earliest is ready for the table until crops are killed by frost in the fall. This will require about three plantings of snap beans and three of sweet corn (or one planting each of an early,* a medium and a late variety); three or more of lettuce, two each of beets, carrots and cabbage. Two plantings of peas about two or three weeks apart, or one planting of an early and a late variety, will be sufficient in most regions, as this crop does not thrive in hot weather. Turnips, spinach and kale may be planted early in the spring and again in late summer and early fall for fall and winter use in most sections where they will not withstand winter weather. In milder regions where these crops are grown in the winter 3 or 4 plantings might be made to advantage. Two plantings of celery and cauliflower, one early and one late, are frequently made, one for early summer and the other for fall use. In most regions only one planting is made of Lima beans, cucumbers, eggplant, pepper, melons, summer squash, winter squash, pumpkin, parsnip, tomato, sweet potato, as these continue to bear until killed by frost, except in case they are destroyed by disease, insect or other means.

The garden plans suggest the arrangement of the plantings and the distance between the rows for gardens of two different sizes. (For details of the depth of planting, methods of planting and spacing of plants in the row *see* special articles on all the chief vegetable crops at CABBAGE, ONION, POTATO, PEA, etc.)

### CULTIVATION, HOEING AND WEEDING

Vegetable plants cannot compete successfully with weeds. The garden, therefore, should be given sufficient cultivation,* hoeing and weeding to keep weeds under control. The best time to destroy weeds is before they have become well established, for they can then be destroyed by shallow cultivation or hoeing, which merely breaks the crust and stirs the surface. By the proper use of the hand cultivator and hand hoe, pulling weeds by hand ought not to be necessary except to remove those near the plants. All cultivation and hoeing should be shallow in order to keep root destruction to the minimum. (For details *see* CULTIVATION, WEEDS, HOEING.)

### IRRIGATION

In arid and semi-arid regions irrigation is essential, and in humid regions artificial watering frequently is desirable, especially during periods of drought. In setting plants in the garden in any region it is the common practice to apply water around the plant unless the soil is well supplied with water. In irrigated regions water is always applied at the time of setting plants. The most common methods of applying water to the garden are by spraying or sprinkling from above and by trench or furrow irrigation between the rows. When water is applied it is desirable to apply enough to soak the soil to the depth of several inches and then withhold it until the crops need it again. Merely sprinkling the surface is useless. (For details *see* IRRIGATION.)

### DISEASE AND INSECT CONTROL

Diseases and insects cause large losses in home gardens where no control measures are employed. To be a successful gardener one must become acquainted with the common and most destructive pests and the methods of control. Good cultural practices and cleaning up the refuse greatly aid in controlling both diseases and insects. With some pests, however, other control measures are essential, such as spraying or dusting with the appropriate material. (For a general discussion *see* PLANT DISEASES and INSECT PESTS, and for specific crop pests *see* the special crop articles.)

### ROTATION OF CROPS

The term rotation or "crop rotation" means the systematic sequence of crops grown on the same land for a period of years. Rotation is important in vegetable growing in aiding in the control of diseases and insects and in equalizing the drain on the nutrients in the soil. In general, it is not desirable to grow the same crop or closely related crops on the same land year after year. For example, cabbage, cauliflower and broccoli should not follow each other since many of the same diseases attack all of them. Likewise cucumbers, muskmelons, watermelons and squashes and pumpkins should not follow each other. A good general plan is to follow foliage crops, celery, cabbage, lettuce, spinach and others, by root crops, such as beets, carrots and parsnips, and to follow these by fruit and seed crops, such as tomatoes, eggplant, peppers, beans and peas. However, in following such a system of rotation, care should be taken to avoid following a foliage crop with a root crop that is attacked by the same diseases. In a home garden it is seldom feasible to follow an ideal system of rotation because of the large number of crops grown and the difference in the size of the area devoted to the various ones. It is important, however, to keep in mind the general principles, and in case disease becomes serious on some crop this crop and others attacked by the same disease should be grown in a section of the garden that is free from the organism.

### SUCCESSION CROPPING

Succession cropping means the sequence of crops grown on the same land the same year, where more than one crop is so grown. The same general principles apply to succession cropping as apply to rotation. In planning the garden the cropping system for the entire season should be taken into consideration, and this has been done in the plans on pages 416 and 417. Where the area of land is limited, the garden should be planned so as to utilize it to the utmost throughout the season. The kind and number of crops to be grown are determined by the length of the growing season. As examples of succession cropping the following are given: (*a*) Early lettuce followed by snap beans or root crops, such as beets and carrots; (*b*) early cabbage followed by late potatoes, where the growing season is long enough; (*c*) early peas followed by late planting of beets, carrots or cabbage; (*d*) spring spinach or kale followed by tomatoes. In many regions three crops can be grown on the same land in one season.

---

* Special articles on the subjects indicated by an asterisk (*) will be found at the words so marked.

### Intercropping or Companion Cropping

When two or more crops are grown on the same land at the same time the system is known as intercropping or companion cropping. This may embrace succession cropping as in the planting of cabbage, lettuce and radishes at the same time on the same area. The radishes will mature and be harvested first and lettuce harvest will follow and both will be out of the way before the cabbage plants need all of the space. For intercropping to be successful there must be an abundance of nutrients and water.

In planning for intercropping the gardener should consider the time each crop is to be planted, the time each will mature and the space needed by each at various stages of growth. In nearly all plans small-growing, quick-maturing crops sometimes called catch crops, are planted with larger, later-maturing ones. One common plan is to plant lettuce plants between the rows of cabbage and also between the plants in the row. Radishes and carrots may be grown together, the former being planted between the rows of the latter. Many other combinations can be worked out by the thoughtful gardener.

### Harvesting Vegetables for Home Use

The garden has not one harvest time, but many. Crops are harvested throughout the growing season as they reach edible maturity and are either consumed at once or else are canned or otherwise preserved. There should remain in the fall crops to be stored for winter use. Some crops, as asparagus, peas and sweet corn must be harvested soon after they reach edible maturity or they deteriorate in quality. Asparagus spears branch out in a day or two after they come through the ground and peas and sweet corn lose sugar and become hard unless they are harvested soon after they reach edible maturity. Other crops, as snap beans, lima beans and tomatoes remain in edible condition for several days, while still others as beets, carrots, parsnips, cabbage, celery, eggplant and peppers remain in edible condition for several weeks. However, the length of time that any of these products remain in edible condition depends on the temperature. In general, the warmer the weather the shorter the time any of these products remain of good quality. Some crops, such as spinach, kale, New Zealand spinach, chard and lettuce may be harvested at any time after they reach sufficient size, until they become old and tough, or until they shoot to seed. The root crops, beets, carrots, parsnips and turnips, may also be harvested at any stage after they reach edible size until they become tough and woody. Frequently the home gardener allows these plants to grow thickly in the row until they reach sufficient size to use as food and then makes his early harvest a thinning process. Beets and turnips are often pulled for their foliage before the roots are large enough to use.

Summer squash should be harvested before the rind begins to harden, but may be harvested at any size desired. Winter squashes and pumpkins should be allowed to ripen completely in the field. Snap beans are best when harvested before the seeds develop to full size and lima beans should be harvested before the pods get yellow. Tomatoes should be left on the vines until color is well developed. Muskmelons and watermelons are of the highest quality when allowed to ripen on the vines. It is difficult to determine when a watermelon is ripe and only by experience can one become able to do so. The sound emitted when the melon is thumped with the finger is an index of maturity. A dull, dead sound is emitted when the melon reaches maturity, but varieties differ in this respect. One must, therefore, cut many melons before he can correlate the sound emitted on thumping with the stage of maturity. (For details of harvesting methods for the various vegetables see the special crop articles.) — H. C. T.

**KITTUL** = *Caryota urens*.

**KLEENUP.** A trademarked emulsified oil sold with directions for use as a dormant contact spray.

**KLEINIA.** *See* SENECIO.

**KNAPWEED** = *Centaurea*.

**KNAUR.** A burl.*

**KNAWEL** = *Scleranthus annuus*. *See* list at WEEDS.

**KNEELING PAD.** *See* Section 2, TOOLS AND IMPLEMENTS.

**KNIFFIN SYSTEM.** *See* Training at GRAPE.

**KNIPHOFIA** (nip-ho'fĭ-a). African, herbaceous perennials belonging to the Liliaceae, called torch lily, flame flower, or poker-plant. They have thick, fleshy roots, and long, linear, basal leaves. Flowers rising in long, red or yellow spikes or racemes,* above the leaves, and blooming from June to frost. Corolla drooping, tubular. Stamens* 6. Fruit a capsule.* (Named for J. J. Kniphof, German professor.) Often sold as *Tritoma*, and now found in many fine hort. forms, some with apricot-colored flowers.

For culture *see* the last species.

**foliosa.** Leaves broad, in a dense basal rosette. 3–4 in. broad at base, tapering into a long point. Flower stalk stout, erect, 2 to 3 ft. long. Flowers yellow, in a dense cylindrical raceme,* 6 to 12 in. long. Tropical and South Af.

**rufa.** Leaves to 1½ ft. long and ½ in. across. Flowers yellow, the upper ones tinged red. Stamens* protruding. June to frost. Natal.

**tucki.** Leaves to 1½ ft. high, about ¾ in. wide. Flowers about ½ in. long, yellow, tinged with red, the cluster nearly 6 in. long. South Af.

**uvaria.** Red-hot poker. A handsome plant 2–4 ft. high. Leaves nearly 3 ft. high. Flowers scarlet on the lower ones yellow, the cluster nearly 10 in. long. The *var*. *floribunda* flowers earlier; in *var*. **grandiflora**, the flowers are larger; and the *var*. **pfitzeri** blooms longer. Can be wintered over in the open in the north only if a heavy mulch of salt hay which does not mat down and cause rotting, is applied. Often wintered over in boxes in the cellar. Propagated by division, offsets and seeds.

**KNIVES.** *See* Section 5, TOOLS AND IMPLEMENTS.

**KNOB CELERY** = celeriac. For culture *see* CELERY.

**KNOT GARDENS.** The intricate patterns, once so well liked, in the arrangement of flower beds. They are scarcely ever seen today, except in some herb gardens which try to perpetuate the arrangement of many old gardens of herbs. *See* the illustration at HERB GARDENING for some examples of Knot Gardens.

**KNOTROOT** = *Stachys sieboldi*.

**KNOTWEED.** *See* POLYGONUM. *See also* the list at WEEDS.

**KOBUS** (kō'bus). Japanese name for *Magnolia kobus*.

**KOCHIA** (ko'kĭ-a). Of the 40–50 species of this chiefly Eurasian genus of the family Chenopodiaceae, only one is cult., but it is a widely grown tender annual valued for its bushy habit and brilliantly colored foliage. Usually called summer, standing or Belvedere cypress, it is known to science as **K. scoparia** of which the *var*. **tricophylla** is the one commonly grown. It is an erect, much branched, bushy herb, 20–36 in. high, sometimes nearly globe-shaped. Leaves extremely numerous, alternate,* often hairy, without teeth, very narrow, and nearly round in cross-section. They may be red, green, or yellow, but turn purple-red in the fall. Flowers greenish, inconspicuous, very small, and a few in the leaf-axils.* (For details *see* CHENOPODIACEAE.) Fruit a utricle.* The summer cypress is best treated as a tender annual (*see* ANNUALS), but seeds may be sown in place if delayed until the ground is warm. It is a showy plant for the border and holds its leaf color all summer. In the South it self-sows and is apt to become weedy. The Chinese make brushes from it. (Named for W. D. J. Koch, German botanist.)

**KOELREUTERIA** (kel-roo-teer'ĭ-a). A small genus of Asiatic trees of the family Sapindaceae; *K. paniculata* often grown for ornament, the yellow summer-blooming flower clusters being very handsome. Leaves alternate,* compound,* the leaflets arranged feather-fashion with an odd one at the end, all more or less irregularly toothed. Flowers in a large, terminal cluster (panicle), the corolla somewhat irregular.* Petals 4, with a claw* and with 2 upward-pointing appendages to each. Stamens 8 or fewer. Fruit a bladder-like 3-valved pod (capsule*) with black

---

* Special articles on the subjects indicated by an asterisk (*) will be found at the words so marked.

seeds. (Named for Joseph G. Koelreuter, German professor.)

The second species is not uncommon in the finer gardens but the first is scarcely known, and is not hardy in the North. They do well on a variety of soils but seem better suited to open sunshine than to shade. Propagated by stratified seeds, or by root cuttings.

**formosana.** A tree 30-50 ft. high, the leaves twice-compound, nearly 18 in. long. Leaflets ovalish or narrower, rather shallow-toothed. Pods nearly 2 in. long, papery. Formosa. Hardy only in zones* 8 and 9. Little known in the U.S.

**paniculata.** Pride-of-India; also called China-tree and varnish-tree. Not usually over 30 ft. high and of dome-like form. Leaves 9-14 in. long, the leaflets 7-15, ovalish-oblong and coarsely toothed, or even deeply cut near the base. Flower cluster 12-18 in. long, showy, each flower about ½ in. long. Pods about 2 in. long, papery. Eastern Asia. July-Aug. Hardy from zone* 3 southward.

**KOFUGEN.** See Japanese Flowering Cherries at PRUNUS.

**KOHLRABI** (*Brassica caulorapa*). This is a minor member of the cabbage tribe the erect stem of which is swollen just above the ground level. The swollen part, while still tender and juicy, has a fine flavor, liked by some, but later it becomes hard, bitter, almost woody, and useless. Kohlrabi (often called the turnip cabbage or turnip-rooted cabbage or even stem cabbage) is closely related to the turnip and by some considered superior.

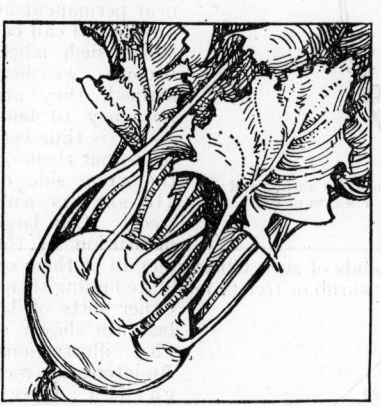
Kohlrabi

Its culture is exactly the same as for early cabbage (which see at CABBAGE) except that kohlrabi is set 8 in. apart in the row and the rows (except for horse or motor cultivators) can be 18 in. apart. Its insect and fungus pests are the same as cabbage. For their control see CABBAGE.

VARIETIES. The best varieties are Early Purple Vienna, Early White Vienna and Earliest Erfurt. As the names indicate, the vegetable is more popular abroad than here, where its use is largely among the foreign born.

Some, who want kohlrabi in the late fall, start a second crop exactly as late cabbage is grown. (See late cabbage at CABBAGE.) Whether early or late crops are grown, it is important to secure quick growth and to cut the whitish thickened stems before they become tough and woody. The plant will not stand great heat.

**KOIDZUMI** (koyd-zoo'mi). Native name in Formosa for *Pyracantha koidzumi*.

**KOLANUT** = *Cola acuminata*.

**KOLKWITZIA** (kolk-wit'zĭ-a). A single species of Chinese shrubs of the honeysuckle family, much cult. for its showy bloom under the name of beauty-bush. The only species, K. amabilis is a shrub 4-6 ft. high with opposite* ovalish leaves 2-3 in. long. Flowers in flattish clusters (corymbs*) nearly 3 in. wide, the corolla bell-shaped, pink, but with a yellow throat, about ½ in. long, the stalks and sepals* bristly. Fruit dry, both it and the stalk covered with bristly hairs. June. Hardy from zone* 3 southward. The plant is an attractive sight in bloom, which may be forced in the greenhouse weeks before outdoor flowering is due. See FORCING. Propagated by cuttings of green wood. (See CUTTINGS.) (Named for R. Kolkwitz, German professor of botany.)

**KOLOMIKTA** (ko-lo-mik'ta). Native name in Asia for *Actinidia kolomikta* (which see). It is here commonly called kolomikta vine.

**KONIGA.** See SWEET ALYSSUM.

**KORAIENSIS, -e** (kor-i-en'sis). From Korea.

**KOREAN AZALEA** = *Azalea yedoensis*.

**KOREAN CHRYSANTHEMUM.** See CHRYSANTHEMUM.

**KOREAN LAWN GRASS** = *Zoysia japonica*.

**KOREAN PINE** = *Pinus koraiensis*. See PINE.

**KOSTER'S BLUE SPRUCE** = *Picea pungens kosteriana*. See SPRUCE.

**KOUSA** (cow'sa). Japanese native name for *Cornus kousa*.

**KOWAHI.** See CLIANTHUS PUNICEUS.

**KRAUHNIA** = *Wistaria*.

**KRIGIA** (krig'ĭ-a). North American, dandelion-like, rather weedy herbs of the family Compositae, only of secondary garden interest. Leaves mostly basal, milky-juiced, somewhat lyre-shaped or toothed. Flower heads mostly small, yellow or orange, resembling the dandelion but the rays* not so spreading. Disk* flowers none. (Named for David Krieg, a German physician who collected plants in Md.)

These are not of much garden worth, but are occasionally grown in open sandy places. They bloom in spring.

**montana.** A perennial, usually branched herb, 8-12 in. high. Leaves very narrow, nearly 8 in. long. Flower heads bright yellow, about 1 in. wide. N. Car. to Ga. May be increased by division.

**virginica.** Dwarf dandelion. A usually unbranched annual, 3-5 in. high, the leaves chiefly basal, oblongish, 3-7 in. long, more or less toothed or cut. Flower heads about ½ in. wide, orange. Eastern U.S., mostly in sandy soils. Sow seeds where wanted. See SAND GARDENS.

**KUDZU-VINE** = *Pueraria thunbergiana*.

**KUMO-GATA-JIMA.** A cloud-shaped island. See JAPANESE GARDEN.

**KUMQUAT.** See FORTUNELLA.

**KUNZEA** (kun'zee-a). Generally heath-like, Australian shrubs of the family Myrtaceae, four of the perhaps 20 species grown for ornament outdoors in Calif., but little known elsewhere. Leaves small, often narrow, without teeth and alternate,* but often crowded. Flowers small, in terminal heads or spikes, their most conspicuous feature being the protruding stamens. (See MYRTACEAE for details of flower structure.) Fruits aromatic, fleshy, edible when cooked. (Named for Gustave Kunze, German botanist.)

Not much is known of the culture of these shrubs. They are related to *Callistemon* and the cultural notes there should be followed for these plants in the absence of more specific data.

**ambigua.** Related to K. peduncularis, and like it, but the flowers are stalkless.

**micrantha.** A low, erect shrub with line-like, stiff leaves scarcely ⅓ in. long. Flowers in close, terminal heads.

**peduncularis.** Mountain tea-tree. A tall, erect shrub, or even a small tree, the leaves lance-shaped or narrower, about ½ in. long. Flowers whitish, short-stalked, some in the leaf-axils,* others in terminal, leafy clusters.

**sericea.** A tall shrub, the twigs and foliage white-hairy. Leaves ovalish, but broader towards the tip. Male flowers in terminal clusters, the flowers containing both stamens* and pistils,* usually solitary.

**KURRAJONG** = *Brachychiton populneum*.

**KURUME AZALEA.** See AZALEA OBTUSA.

**KURUM OIL TREE** = *Pongamia pinnata*.

**KUSSAIE LIME.** See LIME (the citrus fruit).

**KWANZAN.** See Japanese Flowering Cherries at PRUNUS.

---

* Special articles on the subjects indicated by an asterisk (*) will be found at the words so marked.

# L

**LABELS.** For herbaceous plants or for those grown in pots or tubs, the best temporary label is the ordinary pot label as shown in the figure. They come in sizes from small ones useful for the smallest pots to larger ones that are a foot long and correspondingly wider. Anything written on their smooth wooden face with a soft lead pencil will usually last as long as such temporary labels are needed. They are cheap, well made, and in common use by all professional growers. On some better types of wooden labels (i.e. with better wood), India ink will last 4–6 years.

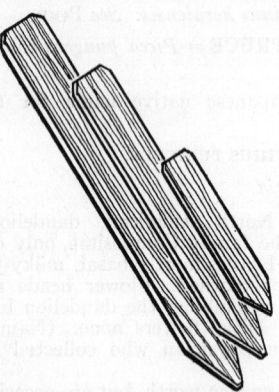

Wooden pot labels, useful also in the garden for temporary marking

If more permanent labels are needed for herbs or for marking varieties in the vegetable garden, they must be of metal, preferably of zinc. Such labels have, in the best forms, a channeled shank which anchors the label firmly in the ground, and a flattened, tilted upper part upon which the record is written. If such zinc labels are left out in the rain for a few days, the slightly oxidized surface can then be easily written upon with a soft lead pencil, and such writing will last for years. It will not last, however, unless the oxidizing is sufficient to coat the zinc with a whitish film which takes pencil marks very well.

**INK FOR LABELS.** The only objection to pencil marks on zinc labels is that they are sometimes hard to read. To overcome this difficulty an ink is preferred by many. One of the best is a formula used at the Missouri Botanical Garden. It is 1 dram acetate of copper, 1 dram ammonium sulphate, ½ dram lamp black, and 10 drams of water. Such an ink must be applied to the fresh, burnished metal (rubbed up with emory paper) and only a glass or quill pen can be used, or a fresh metal pen for each batch of labels. This ink etches an indelible record on zinc and can only be removed with sandpaper.

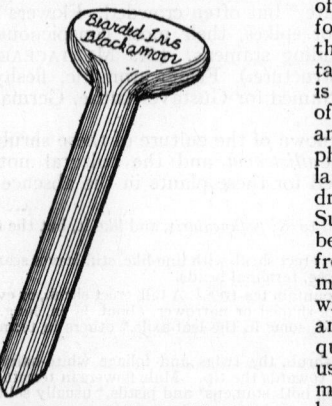

Permanent type of zinc label for herbaceous plants. About one-half of the shank should be in the ground.

**WOODY PLANTS.** All labels for woody plants must be wired to the twigs in such a way as to prevent girdling them as the twigs grow. Temporary wooden, wired labels, such as come on nursery stock, are all right for temporary marking, but their wires are usually twisted around the twigs too tightly and should be removed at planting time.

If the shrub or tree needs a permanent label, get one of the copper labels with an ample wire. Loop this as loosely but securely as possible around a twig, preferably between branchlets, so it cannot be blown away. The best type of copper labels are thin sheets of metal upon which the writing is dug into the metal with a stylus, preferably with a pad of paper under the label while printing it. Such etching is as near permanent as any record can be. When such labels become weather-stained, they are not easy to find, and it is thus better to put them on the same side of all shrubs and trees. One large institution in the country, with thousands of such labels, puts all of them on the south side of the shrub or tree to facilitate finding them.

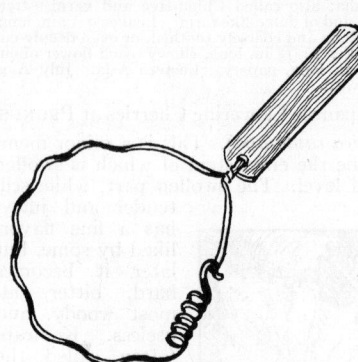

A wooden wired label for shrubs and trees; good for a season or two

Other sorts of labels are shown in the illustrations. An interesting rock garden label, known in England, consists of pieces of limestone, sandpapered smooth on one side, and painted with a fine brush. These are stuck in the ground and are more attractive in such a collection than wood or metal labels. They need re-touching from time to time.

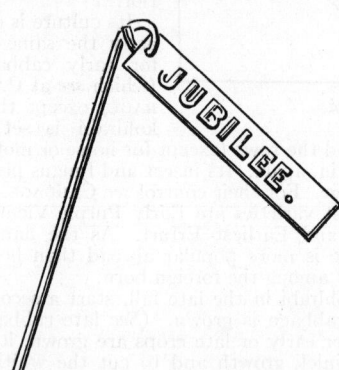

A metal wired label good for woody plants or herbs and lasting for years

**LABIATA, -us, -um** (lay-bee-ā′ta). Labiate; i.e. having flowers with a lip,* as in the mint family.

**LABIATAE** (lay-bee-ā′tee). The mint, hyssop, salvia or rosemary family is also, but not here, called the Menthaceae and Lamiaceae. It is an enormous group or family of plants comprising at least 160 genera and over 3000 species of mostly herbs (some tropical shrubs), nearly all with fragrant foliage and a square or at least 4-angled stem.

Leaves opposite* (rarely whorled*). Flowers always irregular,* commonly 2-lipped,* often arranged in tight, head-like clusters, but in many genera in open, branched clusters (spikes* and racemes*), the cluster often rather leafy in some of these genera. The fruit consists of 4 one-seeded nutlets, often, but incorrectly, called seeds, and are commonly found surrounded by the often persistent calyx.

The garden uses of the mint family are many. One group of genera are chiefly grown for the fragrant foliage, for seasoning, or in making various condiments. They are:

---

*Special articles on the subjects indicated by an asterisk (*) will be found at the words so marked.

*Hedeoma, Hyssopus, Lavandula, Majorana* (see SWEET MARJORAM), *Marrubium* (see HOREHOUND), *Melissa, Mentha* (see MINT), *Nepeta, Ocimum, Origanum, Rosmarinus* (see ROSEMARY), *Satureia* (see SAVORY), and *Thymus* (see THYME). For the uses of these *see also* HERB GARDENING.

The chief ornamental perennials (a few annual), of easy culture outdoors over most of the country, are: *Ajuga, Audibertia, Elsholtzia, Micromeria, Molucella, Monarda, Perilla* (foliage plant), *Phlomis, Salvia* (but *see* below for tender species), *Stachys* and *Teucrium* (some tender).

A secondary group of generally hardy genera are less grown, partly because they are often weedy. Some are adapted to the wild garden, others to the rock garden, and others only to the less desirable parts of the border. This group comprises (w = wild garden; r = rock garden; h = more or less weedy or coarse herbs): *Ballota* (h); *Collinsonia* (w); *Cunila* (h); *Dracocephalum* (w); *Horminum* (r); *Lamium* (w); *Leonurus* (h); *Lycopus* (h and w); *Monardella* (r); *Physostegia* (h); *Prunella* (h); *Pycnanthemum* (h); *Scutellaria* (w); and *Trichostema* which includes the bluecurls.

There are a few tropical shrubs or herbs, all tender. Some are grown only in the greenhouse or in frost-free parts of Calif. and Fla. Others, especially *Coleus* and the Mexican salvias, are used as summer bedding plants throughout the country. These valuable garden genera are: *Coleus* (foliage plant), *Colquhounia* (shrub), *Iboza, Leonotis, Prostanthera, Pycnostachys, Salvia* (but see above for hardy species) and *Sphacele*.

Technical flower characters: Flowers hermaphrodite.* Calyx regular* or 2-lipped,* usually 5-toothed or 5-parted, corolla irregular,* nearly always 2-lipped.* Stamens* 4, two longer than the others. Ovary superior,* deeply 4-lobed, ultimately separating into four 1-seeded nutlets.

**LABLAB.** Egyptian vernacular for the hyacinth bean (*Dolichos lablab*).

**LABRADOR TEA** = *Ledum groenlandicum*.

**LABRUSCA** (la-brus′ka). Latin name for a wild vine, but not necessarily for a grape to which it was applied. See VITIS LABRUSCA.

**LABURNOCYTISUS.** A bigeneric* hybrid between *Cytisus* and *Laburnum*. The only known case of it is the plant called *Laburnum adami*, which is of more scientific than hort. interest.

**LABURNUM** (la-bur′num). A small genus of deciduous trees or shrubs in the pea family. The alternate* leaves are composed of three leaflets. The flowers are pea-like, borne in terminal, usually pendulous clusters (racemes*) and followed by linear pods. (*Laburnum* is the Latin name used by Pliny.)

The trees are handsome objects in the spring when the clusters of bright yellow flowers are produced. They are of quite simple culture, growing even on rocky slopes and standing some shade, effective in shrub borders or as a single specimen. Seed usually germinates freely and is the simplest means of propagation. All parts of the plant, especially the young fruits and the seeds, are poisonous if eaten.

adami. See LABURNOCYTISUS.

alpinum. Small trees of stiff, upright habit growing about 20–30 ft. high. Leaflets 3, oval, 1½–2½ in. long, usually glabrous. Flowers yellow, about ¾ in. across in slender pendulous clusters sometimes to 15 in. long. June. Mountains of southern Europe. Hardy from zone* 3 southward.

anagyroides. Golden chain, or bean tree. Shrub or small tree growing about 20 ft. high, though occasionally higher; often branching close to the ground. Leaves composed of 3 leaflets, downy beneath. Flowers yellow, about ¾ in. across in racemes* 4–12 in. long; pod about 2 in. long. May–June. Southern Europe. Hardy from zone* 3 southward. This species has shorter racemes than the preceding and blooms perhaps two weeks earlier. The var. aureum is a form with yellow leaves.

vulgare = *Laburnum anagyroides*.

**LABYRINTH.** See MAZE.

**LACEBARK.** See HOHERIA.

**LACE BUG.** See Insect Pests at AVOCADO, AZALEA, and RHODODENDRON.

**LACE-FERN** = *Cheilanthes gracillima*.

**LACE-FLOWER.** See TRACHYMENE.

**LACE-LEAF** = *Aponogeton fenestralis*.

**LACERATE.** Torn into shreds or divisions.

**LACE-VINE** = *Polygonum auberti*.

**LACHENALIA** (lack-en-ā′li-a). South African greenhouse and bulbous herbs of the lily family, two of the 40 known species grown in pots for their showy flowers, and usually called Cape cowslip. Leaves 1 or 2, or few, basal and without marginal teeth. Flowers red and yellow, drooping (in ours), borne in a terminal cluster (spike or raceme*) at the end of a stalk that rises from the leaves. Corolla cylindric, tubular, its outer 3 segments shorter than the 3 inner. Stamens* 6. Fruit a 3-angled capsule.* (Named for Werner de Lachenal, Swiss professor.)

The culture of the Cape cowslips is the same as for *Freesia* (which see). They are propagated by offsets, and, more rarely, by seeds, but they may also be increased by leaf cuttings. See Leaf Cuttings at CUTTINGS.

pendula. A stouter plant than the next, the leaves nearly 2 in. wide. Flowers about 1½ in. long, the outer segments yellow below but red above, and nearly as long as the inner ones, which are red-purple at the tip.

tricolor. Not over 12 in. high, the leaves 2 to each plant, not over 1 in. wide, but as long as the flowering stalk, often purple-spotted. Flowers many in the cluster, the corolla about 1 in. long, its shorter outer segments yellow but green-tipped, the inner ones yellow but red-tipped. There is also a form, var. nelsoni, with yellow flowers, but with all of the segments green-tipped.

**LACHNANTHES** (lack-nan′theez). A single bog herb, the only species and only cult. genus of the family **Haemodoraceae** (hy-mo-door-ray′see-ee). It is **L. tinctoria,** the redroot, found in acid, sandy bogs from Cape Cod to Fla., and suited only to similar sites in the bog garden. It has mostly basal, narrow leaves with a few on the stem, which is grayhairy at the top. Flower cluster terminal, woolly, the flowers a dingy yellow. Corolla 6-parted nearly to the base, about ½ in. long. Stamens* 3, opposite the three larger and inner segments. Fruit a small, globe-shaped capsule.* The plant, sometimes known as *Gyrotheca*, is of only secondary hort. interest, but its red roots once furnished a dye. (*Lachnanthes* is from the Greek for wool and flower, in allusion to the woolly flower clusters.)

**LACINARIA** = *Liatris*.

**LACINIATA, -us, -um** (la-sin-ĭ-ā′ta). Laciniate; *i.e.* cut into narrow, almost fringe-like segments.

**LACINIOSA, -us, -um** (la-sin-i-ō′sa). Much torn or fringed.

**LACRYMA-JOBI** (lack-ri-ma-joe′bī). A specific name meaning Job's tears. See COIX.

**LACTEA, -us, -um** (lak′tee-a). Milk-white.

**LACTIFLORA, -us, -um** (lack-ti-flō′ra). With milk-white flowers.

**LACTUCA** (lak-too′ka). A large genus of milky-juiced herbs of the family Compositae, mostly from the north temperate zone, most of them weedy, but one species important as the source of lettuce. Leaves alternate* (except in the much-modified lettuce), usually cut or divided, often with the margin softly prickly. Flower heads small, usually nodding, mostly in large, terminal, branching clusters (panicles*), the florets all ray* flowers, yellow, pink, blue, or white (never produced in properly grown head lettuce). The bracts* beneath each head form a cylindric, apparently tubular involucre.* Fruit a flat achene* (the lettuce "seed"). (*Lactuca* is from the Latin for milk, in allusion to the milky juice.)

Except for lettuce, the genus comprises very weedy plants of no garden interest. One of them is the prickly lettuce, which is a common pest in gardens. See WEEDS.

perennis. A perennial, weedy herb 15–30 in. high. Leaves deeply lobed, the segments narrow, the upper leaves stem-clasping. Flower heads blue or pale violet, long-stalked. Southern Eu.

sativa. Lettuce. An annual herb, its flowering stalk 3–4 ft. high, but only produced after the common garden lettuce has produced its head of leaves. The lower leaves are normally long, narrow, or sometimes nearly roundish, but much modified in the crispy, curled leaves of the cult. lettuce. Flowers yellow. It is supposed to be a cultigen* of Eurasian origin. In its wild form the plant is practically unknown or rarely cult.

* Special articles on the subjects indicated by an asterisk (*) will be found at the words so marked.

by experts for breeding. So far as garden forms are concerned they fall into three varieties:
- var. **asparagina.** Asparagus lettuce. The thickened stem is used for food. Rare in cult.
- var. **capitata.** Common head lettuce. The leaves are in a compact head, actually it is a dense, shortened rosette.
- var. **longifolia.** Cos lettuce or Romaine lettuce. A form with long, loose, but rather columnar heads.

For culture see LETTUCE.

**scariola** = Prickly lettuce. See list at WEEDS.

**LACUNOSA, -us, -um** (lak-kew-nō'sa). Pitted.

**LADANIFERA, -us, -um** (la-da-nif'fer-a). Bearing labdanum, a dark-colored, soft, fragrant resin.

**LADIES'-TRESSES** = *Spiranthes cernua.*

**LADY BANK'S ROSE** = *Rosa banksiae.*

**LADYBIRD BEETLE.** See INSECT FRIENDS.

**LADY FERN** = *Athyrium filix-femina.*

**LADYFINGERS.** See Rish Baba, a *vinifera* grape at GRAPE.

**LADY-OF-THE-NIGHT** = *Brunfelsia americana.*

**LADY'S-BEDSTRAW** = *Galium verum.*

**LADY'S-EARDROPS.** See FUCHSIA.

**LADY'S-MANTLE** = *Alchemilla alpina.*

**LADY'S-SLIPPER.** See CYPRIPEDIUM and IMPATIENS.

**LADY'S-SMOCK** = *Cardamine pratensis.*

**LADY'S-THISTLE** = *Silybum marianum.*

**LADY'S-THUMB** = *Polygonum persicaria.* See list at WEEDS.

**LADY WASHINGTON GERANIUM** = *Pelargonium domesticum.*

**LAELIA** (lay'lĭ-a). Tropical American, tree-perching orchids, comprising perhaps 30 species, a few much grown in greenhouses for their showy flowers, and several others, together with many hybrids, prized by orchid fanciers. They have pseudobulbs* which are short, or longer and stem-like, and bear 1 or 2 stiffish, rather long leaves without marginal teeth. Flowers one, few, or several in a long-stalked cluster (raceme*). Sepals* nearly of equal length, free, and petal-like. Petals wider than the sepals, more spreading. Lip* more or less 3-lobed, the lateral ones smaller than the broad, expanded, central one. (*Laelia* is apparently named for someone, but it is unknown for whom.)

For culture see the epiphytic orchids among the greenhouse species at ORCHID.

**anceps.** Much the most widely grown and not uncommon in the florists' shops. Pseudobulbs* oblongish and flattened. Leaves 6–9 in. long, oblongish, thick and rather stiff. Flowering stalk arising at the end of the pseudobulb,* 18–30 in. long, more or less jointed and with a few bracts.* Flowers 2–5, rarely only 1, in a cluster, nearly 4 in. wide, very showy, and pale rose-purple, but the lip yellowish inside. The front lobe, also, is deep purple (and white-marked) and with a yellow keel.* Mex. Blooming Nov.–Jan. in the greenhouse. There are many named forms and hybrids.

**digbyana** = *Brassavola digbyana.*

**grandis.** Pseudobulbs* nearly 10 in. long, and bearing only 1 leaf nearly or quite as long. Flowers in pairs, nearly 6 in. wide, very handsome. The sepals and petals are both brownish-yellow. Lip wavy-toothed, generally white but veined or striped with violet. Brazil. Blooming April–June in the greenhouse.

**LAELIOCATTLEYA** (lay-lĭ-o-cat'lee-a). A group of bigeneric* hybrids between species of *Laelia* and *Cattleya*. Over four dozen of these showy orchids are known to orchid specialists, but they are not much grown by the average owner of a greenhouse.

**LAETA, -us, -um** (lee'ta). Bright or vivid.

**LAEVICAULIS, -e** (lee-vĭ-kaw'lis). Smooth-stemmed.

**LAEVIGATA, -us, -um** (lee-vĭ-gay'ta). Smooth.

**LAEVIS, -e** (lee'vis). Smooth.

**LAGENARIA** (laj-en-ā'rĭ-a). A single species of annual, Old World, tropical vines of the cucumber family, widely planted for its hard-shelled fruits commonly called calabash gourd (the source of calabash pipes), dipper gourd, and many other names. The only species, L. leucantha, the white-flowered gourd, is a musky-scented, quick-growing vine with a sticky-hairy stem and branched tendrils.* Leaves alternate,* broadly oval or kidney-shaped, 6–10 in. wide, not lobed or only faintly so. Male and female flowers separate but on the same plant, white, rather showy, usually withering by mid-day, 2–4 in. wide. Petals 5. Fruit very variable, 3–36 in. long, round or flattish, crooknecked, bottle-shaped, dipper-shaped, club-shaped, or like a dumb-bell, the hard rind used for many purposes in the tropics. The plant is easily raised from seed sown where wanted, but it needs heat and a long growing season to produce its fruits. See GOURDS. (*Lagenaria* is from the Latin for a bottle, in allusion to its fruit. *Lagenaria* is also a specific name at CHAENOMELES.)

**LAGER-BEER-PLANT** = *Aspidistra elatior.*

**LAGERSTROEMIA** (lay-ger-stree'mĭ-a). A genus of about 30 species of decorative shrubs and trees of the family Lythraceae, all from warm regions of the Old World, one widely cult. for its showy bloom. They have opposite* leaves, or the uppermost alternate,* without marginal teeth. Flowers in showy terminal clusters (panicles*), pink, purple (or white in some varieties), the calyx more or less turban-shaped. Petals 6, usually with a long claw,* the limb* crinkled or fringed. Fruit a capsule.* (Named by Linnaeus for his friend Magnus von Lagerstroem.)

For Culture see below.

**flos-reginae** = *Lagerstroemia speciosa.*

**indica.** Crape myrtle. A shrub or tree up to 20 ft., the twigs 4-angled. Leaves nearly stalkless, elliptic to oblongish, 1–2 in. long. Flowers pink, about 1¼ in. wide, the cluster 4–9 in. long. China. Blooms all summer. Hardy from zone* 6 southward. For Culture see below. There are several varieties, of which var. **alba** has white flowers; var. **purpurea**, purple flowers; and var. **rubra**, red flowers.

**speciosa.** Queen's-flower. A tree up to 50 ft. and extremely showy in bloom. Leaves ovalish to oblong, nearly 12 in. long, thick and leathery. Flowers purplish, almost 3 in. wide. India to Aust. Hardy only in zones* 8 and 9, and occasionally planted in Fla. and Calif.

### CRAPE MYRTLE CULTURE

Although crape myrtle blooms the first year from seed, it grows so readily from cuttings that the latter method of propagation is universally followed. Young cuttings set out in the fall often bloom profusely the following summer.

After the flowering season of young crape myrtles is over, they are cut back almost to the ground; otherwise, the next summer's bloom is likely to be sparse. As they grow older, the root system becomes strong enough to supply both foliage and flowers.

Crape myrtles flower from June to Oct.; usually they are at their peak the first 15 days in July.

If bloom of extraordinary quality and quantity is desired, superfluous shoots are cut out, tops pruned back, and in the spring when the growth has reached a height of about 1 ft., cow manure or commercial phosphate is worked into the soil around the shrubs.

Ordinarily the crape myrtle develops into a tree covered with little tufts of fine crepe. These trees are the type most commonly seen in the old South. Lately, however, a different sort of shrub has become popular. The crape myrtle shoots are pruned back and trained and produce long, drooping, lilac-shaped panicles of bloom at the end of each shoot. These shoots must be cut severely back every winter, else the symmetrical shrub will soon revert to a floriferous tree. — R. F. W.

**LAGUNARIA** (lag-you-nair'ĭ-a). A single species of Pacific Island and Australian evergreen tree of the family Malvaceae, of secondary hort. interest, although sometimes planted in southern Calif. for ornament. The only species is L. patersoni, often called tulip tree, although it has nothing to do with the native tulip tree (which see). It is a tree up to 50 ft. high with alternate,* oblongish or oval, thick leaves, 3–4 in. long, without marginal teeth, and grayish beneath. Flowers about 2 in. wide, pale rose-pink, mostly solitary in the leaf-axils.* (For structure see MALVACEAE.) Fruit a capsule* which splits into 5 parts. Propagated by cuttings, taken in the spring, over bottom-heat.* An attractive tree resembling hibiscus, but not hardy above zone* 7. (Named for Andres de Laguna, Spanish botanist.)

---

* Special articles on the subjects indicated by an asterisk (*) will be found at the words so marked.

(Courtesy of All Hallows Guild)

THE BISHOP'S GARDEN, WASHINGTON CATHEDRAL, MOUNT SAINT ALBAN, WASHINGTON, D.C.

**LAGURUS** (lag-you′rus). A single species of annual grass, **L. ovatus** of the Mediterranean region, commonly called hare's-tail grass or rabbit's-tail grass, and grown for dried bouquets. It is an erect grass 12–24 in. high, its narrow, grass-like leaves softly hairy. The flowering cluster is an oblongish head, 1–2 in. long, and comprised of many 1-flowered spikelets, all softly woolly, and with slender, protruding awns* about ½ in. long. Seed may be sown where wanted and culture is of the easiest. Sometimes grown in pots for its attractive, long-keeping flowering cluster. (*Lagurus* is Latin for a hare's tail.)

**LAMA** = *Maba sandwicensis*.

**LAMARCKIA** (la-mark′ĭ-a). A single species of annual grass, **L. aurea** of the Mediterranean region, commonly grown in the garden under the name of golden-top, for its handsome spikelets. It is a tufted grass about 12 in. high, the leaves numerous, flat, and grass-like, soft to the touch, its sheaths inflated. Spikelets golden-yellow, or even violet, crowded in dense, raceme*-like, drooping clusters which are grouped in a 1-sided cluster, 1–3 in. long. Seed may be sown where wanted, and the plant is of easy culture in any garden soil. It is sometimes offered as *Achyrodes*. (Named for J. B. Lamarck, French naturalist.)

**LAMBERT.** A cherry variety. *See* CHERRY.

**LAMBKILL** = *Kalmia angustifolia*.

**LAMB'S-EARS** = *Stachys lanata*.

**LAMB'S-QUARTERS** = pigweed. *See* list at WEEDS.

**LAMIACEAE** = Labiatae.

**LAMIUM** (lay′mĭ-um). Dead nettle. A genus of somewhat weedy Old World herbs of the mint family, of secondary garden interest, although two of its 40 known species are occasionally grown in the herbaceous border. They have opposite,* stalked leaves and a square stem. Flowers in close clusters (whorls*) crowded in the leaf-axils,* or terminal. Corolla irregular* and 2-lipped,* the lower lip 3-lobed. Stamens* 4. Fruit a collection of small nutlets surrounded by the withered calyx.* (*Lamium* is from the Greek for throat, in allusion to the shape of the corolla.)

Both the plants below are of the easiest culture in any ordinary garden soil. *Lamium maculatum* can be increased by division, while the seed of *L. purpureum*, an annual, may be sown where it is to stay.

**maculatum.** An erect or half-straggling perennial herb, the tips of its branches more or less upright. Leaves ovalish or heart-shaped, silver-marked, 1–2 in. long. Flowers purple-red, rarely white, nearly 1 in. long, the upper lip* of the corolla distinctly arched. Eu. June–Aug.

**purpureum.** Red dead nettle; also called French nettle. An annual, more or less sprawling herb 9–15 in. high. Leaves ovalish, ¾–1½ in. long. Flowers purple-red, about ½ in. long. Eurasia, but naturalized in N.A. Summer.

**LAMPRANTHUS.** *See* MESEMBRYANTHEMUM.

*LANATA, -us, -um* (la-nay′ta). Lanate, *i.e.* woolly or wool-like.

*LANCEOLATA, -us, -um* (lan-see-o-lay′ta). Lanceolate (which see).

**LANCEOLATE.** More or less lance-shaped; *i.e.* much longer than broad and tapering towards a slender, pointed tip. Typically lanceolate leaves are the peach or willow.

*LANCIFOLIA, -us, -um* (lan-sĭ-fō′lĭ-a). Having lanceolate* leaves.

**LANDSCAPE ARCHITECTURE.** How to apply the basic principles of garden design to each individual property is obviously outside the scope of this book and perhaps of any other. For this reason the general article below gives only the main features of what constitutes good planning. There is no substitute for taste and knowledge, and conditions over the country differ widely. So does people's ability to cope with the practical and financial implications of planning even a simple garden. In order to meet the needs of the greatest number of readers the practical applications of landscape architecture have been treated under the following special articles. All are in THE GARDEN DICTIONARY under the headings noted in the list below.

For all but the simplest gardens the beginner would do well to call in the services of a trained professional. He will avoid many mistakes. What you want him to do may well be suggested by the list of special articles below. And some of the problems treated at these articles, anyone with taste can do for himself.

SPECIAL ARTICLES ON PLANNING A GARDEN
OR ON PARTICULAR FEATURES OF IT

THE PLANNING OF DIFFERENT TYPES OF GARDENS
  Backyard Garden
  Country Estate
  Home Grounds (the small place)

GARDEN ORNAMENT AND STRUCTURES
  For Furniture, Pottery, Rustic Work, Seats, Statuary, Sundials, and Urns, *see* ORNAMENT AND FURNITURE
  For Garden Structures such as Gazebo, Pavilion, Pergola, Summer House, etc., *see* STRUCTURES
  For Night Illumination of the Garden, *see* LIGHTING

SPECIAL FEATURES IN THE GARDEN (*see*):
  Bridges, Drives, Fences, Gates and Gateways, Hedges, Paths and Paving, Steps, Terraces, Walls and Wall Gardening, Water

MINOR FEATURES WHICH MAY OR MAY NOT BE A PART OF ANY GARDEN (*see*):
  Accent Plant, Allée, Arbors and Arches, Banks, Bowling Green, Edging, Formal Garden, Foundation Planting, Informal Garden, Japanese Gardens, Maze, Modern Garden Design (modernistic), Patio Gardens, Penthouse Garden, and Service Yard

THE ART OF DESIGN

Landscape Architecture is the art of design by which grounds are arranged for practical and aesthetic enjoyment. Although the art of Landscape Design is akin to Architecture, Sculpture and Painting in its principles of composition, it is distinct in its use of natural materials.

Land, plants, water and space are the raw materials which the landscape designer composes either independently or in relation to architecture and sculpture to create landscape beauty. To create successful landscape design with these ever-changing living materials requires scientific as well as artistic ability. The landscape designer must know not only the art of pictorial composition but also the science of construction and planting.

From the other arts of design, painting, sculpture and architecture, Landscape Architecture derives its principles of pictorial composition, and from engineering and horticulture it derives its principles of construction and planting. Although these arts and sciences contribute their special knowledge to Landscape Architecture none of them individually possesses the complete knowledge essential to the landscape designer. Since Landscape Architecture aims to create beauty it is primarily an art, but because this beauty must be created with real three-dimensional materials it is also closely related to science.

Previous to the industrial era science and art had a common purpose — to create beauty. Had this purpose continued Landscape Architecture would probably never have developed as a specialized art. But, when horticulturists grew more interested in the culture of plants for their own sake rather than their function in design, when engineers began to ignore beauty, when architects and sculptors began to design on paper and model with little regard for the natural setting of their creations, a new type of designer called a Landscape Architect developed to revive the almost forgotten principles of landscape composition. The term Landscape Architect supplanted, in America, the older term Landscape Gardener (which see).

**DESIGN.** Landscape design begins with the study of the ground. Study means thought plus observation. Even the flattest piece of ground devoid of trees or any natural element

---

* Special articles on the subjects indicated by an asterisk (*) will be found at the words so marked.

of interest is bound to have some suggestion for the beginning of a design. Whether the ground is a rectangular lot in the heart of a city or a country estate of many acres the nucleus of a plan is there. Perhaps this nucleus is only a limited view, a particular orientation with the sun, or a condition of the soil. It may even be a suggestion that comes from the surrounding territory.

This inevitable suggestion that comes from the most nondescript plot of ground is called the potential design. Look for it; it is there. And from the recognition of this potential design comes all the variety and originality which makes landscape design so fascinating. The clever person will detect this natural individuality and develop from it a plan which expresses the character of his particular site.

The purpose in studying natural conditions is to design sympathetically, not destructively. Having studied sympathetically, the designer will naturally make no change where he cannot improve. Such changing and improving to create new beauty is the essence of landscape design, to which artists have directed their talents for many centuries. These changes, when skillfully done according to a well-composed plan, should produce an effect more beautiful than the natural condition.

There are a very few simple basic rules for creating landscape beauty which will produce results according to the artistic ability of the designer.

Regard the entire property as the complete picture. Within this picture such elements as the house, and other buildings, garden areas, service areas, walks and drives must be arranged. No one of these elements should be thought of in detail until they have all been logically related in an organized plan. Plan-organization in its preliminary stages is a process of trial and error, in which the various elements are shifted about until they fit the natural conditions and the proposed use. In this process the house is the controlling element.

There is no arbitrary rule about locating a house unless dictated by deed or building restrictions. It should command the most desirable views and exposure to the sun for the best rooms. Where choice of exposure is possible the north and south line should pass diagonally through the main rooms. This orientation provides the maximum year-round sun with a minimum direct glare into the rooms.

Location on the lot should conserve the greatest possible and most desirable space on the living side of the house. Where the lot is wide enough to allow anything but a central location the house should be pushed as close to the property line as possible on the service side, leaving only enough space to present a satisfactory appearance to the next neighbor.

Distance back from the main highway, unless controlled by restrictions, should be a minimum (30 ft.) necessary to present an attractive street picture. The highway frontage is rarely desirable or usable area in this motor age. Any area on the highway side is wasted as far as private use is concerned, and contributes very little to the rapidly passing public to whom a small area, if properly developed, can appear just as attractive as twice the space.

When an approximate house location is determined the garden, lawn, service, drive and walk areas should be blocked out roughly. Adjustments have to be made until they all fit logically together with the proportional amount of space required by each. In this adjustment ideas for better arrangement develop until the whole scheme seems to work perfectly.

To make a plan work perfectly it must first of all have unity, meaning it must tie together. If walks, buildings, walls or terraces break up the plan so that one part does not have a logical relation to the others the lack of unity will create an unpleasant sensation and always be disturbing. Simplicity of arrangement with the fewest possible divisions of area produces the greatest unity. For instance, a garden projected out into the middle of a lawn will break up the lawn into small areas which amount to nothing and destroy the quiet beauty of the area. The same garden placed at one side of the lawn could be arranged to preserve the unity of the whole scheme without sacrificing the garden. And so with walks; if they cut up the plan in unpleasant shapes they detract from the unity and are annoying to look at, while they should be arranged to bind the plan together with agreeable lines.

Quite as important as unity in design is harmony, which means consistency. A gazing globe or sun-dial stuck out in the middle of the front lawn is obviously out of harmony and inconsistent with its purpose. Not all questions of harmony are as obvious as this illustration. To be successful all materials used in landscape design should harmonize with each other in color, texture, and shape. A picket fence harmonizes with a Colonial frame house, while an elaborate brick wall, beautiful in itself, would be completely out of harmony. A simple test of the harmony of any element in design is whether or not it is conspicuous or whether it seems to take its place in relation to the complete scheme. Plants, color or architectural features which call attention to themselves, without any relation to other plants, color or architectural features, are out of harmony and do not belong.

Harmony in the size of things is called good proportion and all design is basically a matter of proportion. It is the relative size or proportion of the elements of a design which controls its beauty. A walk ten feet wide leading up to a modest cottage is out of proportion and would be ridiculous. Many equally ridiculous mistakes in proportion escape the designer merely because they are not so easily recognized.

Naturally, proportion varies with the effect desired and the size of one feature may be exaggerated to create a special effect. A sense of proportion is a matter of instinct or training and no rules can be made to take the place of such a sense. Questions of proportion can, however, be checked by comparing the size of elements in a proposed design to similar elements in a design which has already proved pleasing.

With the major elements of a design properly proportioned and arranged in a harmonious, unified plan, the details will fall logically into line. The arrangement and selection of trees, hedges, shrubs and flowers to serve their particular purpose is much simpler when their purpose relates to a well-conceived scheme. The modeling of lawns and design of walks, walls, terraces, pools, fountains or landscape features of any sort are all details which must be controlled by, rather than control, the basic design. All of these features take their logical place in the picture when they are used with definite knowledge of the effect they are to create.

In planning the broader, more natural landscape, where the house is not the controlling feature, there will be some other dominant feature to take its place, around which the development of a design progresses by the same process.

The ultimate proof of perfection in design is whether or not it serves the purpose for which it is intended, with nothing superfluous. Anything in the picture which seems to be there for no good reason, and contributes nothing to its interest or beauty, should be eliminated. Simplicity of arrangement, materials and form is essential to good design and characteristic of all beautiful landscape composition.

SELECTION OF A SITE. Since the design depends on the land chosen it is of fundamental importance that this choice be made in relation to the proposed use. There are ten questions to be considered in choosing a site for a definite purpose:
(1) Is the natural shape of the ground adaptable to the intended development?
(2) Is the existing plant growth of the right type and in the right location to help or hinder?
(3) Will the character of the soil permit the kind of planting anticipated?
(4) Does the land lie in the right relation to the sun and prevailing winds to make it usable for the proposed purpose?
(5) Are the climatic conditions favorable to the proposed use of the site?
(6) If the views and present surroundings are vital to the proposed development can they be preserved?
(7) Is the water supply adequate and protected?
(8) Is the access to the property practical and free from future obstruction?

---

* Special articles on the subjects indicated by an asterisk (*) will be found at the words so marked.

**THREE STAGES IN THE DEVELOPMENT OF A LANDSCAPE IDEA**
Above, the need for it; in the center, the vision of what to do; below, the outline of where the trees and shrubs should go to accomplish it.

STEPS IN A NATURALISTIC SETTING IN FRANKLIN PARK, BOSTON

(9) Is the surrounding community in harmony with the intended use of this land?

(10) If architectural structures are proposed and the character of the architecture has been predetermined, is it suitable to the site?

The fortunate selection of a site is a long step toward a successful result. Failure to consider all the aspects of a site as it may affect the intended use often leads to disappointment which might easily have been avoided by preliminary precaution.

When the site is dictated and there is no possibility of choosing a property to fit a particular use, then the use should be adapted to the existing conditions of the site. Having no choice in the selection of a site is not necessarily a handicap unless an attempt is made to fit some preconceived scheme to a site which is not adapted to that type of scheme. In other words, if a property is inherited in a neighborhood where the prevailing architecture is Colonial, with fairly level ground, and there is an ambition to have a Mediterranean style of house on a hillside, nothing but failure will result from insistence on trying to carry out such an ambition.

Either choose the site to fit an idea or shape the idea to fit whatever site is provided.

GARDEN PLANNING. The most beautiful gardens in the history of garden art are not necessarily celebrated show places. Mere size or elaboration does not constitute beauty. In every country and in all generations there have been gardeners who either by instinct or training have created masterpieces of garden art. These masterpieces have always achieved their distinction by recognition of the potential design supplied by nature. It was during the ages when men lived closest to nature and had leisure to contemplate her beauty that the finest gardens were created. The simple cottage garden of Europe owed as much to nature as it did to art for its inspiration. There was no quarrel between nature and art when designers understood that one was as essential as the other. It is only since art and nature have ceased to be a normal part of living that discussions have arisen about their relative value to garden art. Although habits of living have changed, garden design still relies on the same age-old principles. If garden design achieves real distinction nature cannot be detached from art nor art from nature.

The natural condition of the location chosen for garden development should suggest the design. If there is a preconceived idea of the type of garden desired then the location should be chosen to suit the idea. Preconceived ideas of gardens which have been formed by admiration of some other garden or by a desire to create a definite traditional type should never contradict the natural character of the location chosen. Gardens which inspire admiration are successful because they fit their location and use.

To copy a borrowed design on another site which does not have the same natural character is not design at all and rarely achieves a successful result. If admiration for some existing garden is based on an understanding of the reasons why this garden commands respect the same reasoning may be applied to other locations with comparable results. In other words, it is well to learn by observation, but it is necessary to discriminate in the selection of ideas to find those which can be carried out successfully in a different location. Since nature, personal taste and human ingenuity have provided the maximum opportunity for originality and individuality in gardening there can be very little excuse for stupid copying.

The entire outdoor surroundings of our living area are in a sense gardens. When grounds are considered in this sense the open lawns, terraces, utility areas and pleasure gardens are all a part of the garden. Considering any detached area as the garden independent of the rest of the property, and beautifying this area, leaving the other areas unattractive, is wasting an opportunity. It is quite as important that

---

* Special articles on the subjects indicated by an asterisk (*) will be found at the words so marked.

utility areas as well as those devoted to pleasure be made attractive. Someone must spend much of his time around the garage, the laundry yard or vegetable garden. Such areas can be quite as attractive as the pleasure areas if they are given equal thought in planning. If garden art occupied the same relation to complete living today that it did in past ages gardening would no longer be considered a privilege of the fortunate nor a leisure pastime; it would be considered an essential normal activity of good living.

To distinguish the area generally referred to as the "garden" from the garden conceived as a complete grounds, the term "pleasure garden" should be used. Compared to the other areas the pleasure garden is free from utility requirements and devoted entirely to enjoyment. *See* GARDEN ROOM.

There should be an agreeable merging of the interior plan of the house with the pleasure garden. This transition can be accomplished best by projecting vistas into the garden from the window or door openings. If the garden plan relates to the views from the interior rooms it serves the double purpose of providing a pleasant outlook as well as its own garden interest. *See* VISTA.

Houses are inevitably geometric and, therefore, formal in shape. Gardens connected with the house must harmonize with its architectural lines. Some transitional form of terrace must be used to harmonize the two. On small properties the terrace should be expanded into a terrace garden which is compact, convenient and easily maintained. Often limited space makes it impossible to plan a pleasure garden without crowding the property lines. In such cases it is much more satisfactory to concentrate the garden interest immediately around the house by use of terraces. The remainder of the property then becomes background and can successfully be screened for privacy. *See* TERRACES.

In working out from the house into the garden the dominant architectural lines should be projected into the garden plan and the architectural materials and general character of the garden should harmonize with the house. As the garden design recedes further from the influence of the house it may gradually become less architectural. If the house has a picturesque character with a rambling plan and informal materials it naturally requires less architectural treatment in the garden areas.

After the skeleton lines of the garden have been determined in relation to the house plan the development of the design on these basic lines depends on the intended use. If the garden is to serve primarily as a picture to be seen from the house it must be visualized like a painting. If it is to be used for outdoor living and entertainment it will require shade and open lawn in preference to flowers. If the objective is the growing of flowers for cutting or color effect, trees and lawn will be minimized. Perhaps the garden must serve all of these functions to some extent. It is not necessary to determine too arbitrarily just what the use of the garden shall be, but it is essential to anticipate exactly how the uses are to be unified in the design. Nothing but confusion can result from failure to plan for definite use. The available area, the natural shape of the ground, existing trees and means of access by steps and paths usually suggest the general scheme.

Not until the proposed scheme is fairly well visualized as to size, shape and general character should questions of detail be considered. Width and detailed shape of paths, height of walls, location and shape of pools or other architectural ornaments should not be the controlling features in the design but should gradually evolve as the major elements of the plan progress. Details of planting, color schemes and sculptural ornament should also be controlled by, rather than control, the general scheme.

The formation of a perfect snowflake is typical of the process by which garden design should evolve. From a center or controlling idea the design expands uniformly toward its ultimate shape, with major radiating lines gradually breaking up into more intricate patterns, but always according to a perfectly unified scheme in which every element contributes its proportional value to the completed design. Such a process prevents distortion of any one unit and avoids inconsistencies of function, scale, proportion, color or pattern. — R. E. G.

**LANDSCAPE GARDENING.** For centuries men who practiced what, in America, is called Landscape Architecture were proud of a profession which Wordsworth called the greatest of the arts. But they called themselves landscape gardeners, a term in disrepute among garden designers in America. They say that a landscape gardener here may be an itinerant laborer with a pushcart, a lawn mower, and a box of geraniums — scarcely a designer. It remains true, however, that in England, France, and Germany very talented designers of gardens still prefer to call themselves Landscape Gardeners. And so did Le Notre, the designer of Versailles, and the greatest of all landscape architects.

**LANDSCAPE MODELS.** *See* MODEL GARDENS.

*LANOSA, -us, -um* (la-no'sa). Woolly.

**LANTANA** (lan-tă'na). Tropical or sub-tropical shrubs of the family Verbenaceae, one of the 50 known species much planted outdoors from zone* 7 southward, and frequently grown as a pot plant by florists for its profuse bloom. They are generally opposite*-leaved shrubs, usually with a main stem. Flowers small, borne in dense clusters (spikes or heads) which may be terminal or in the leaf-axils.* Calyx minute. Corolla tubular, 4–5-parted, slightly irregular,* but not 2-lipped.* Stamens* 4. Fruit fleshy (a drupe*), with 2 hard seeds. (*Lantana* is an old name of uncertain application here; also applied as the species name of a *Viburnum*.)

The first species is a very ornamental shrub throughout the South and in Calif., where it thrives in every sort of soil. Northward it must be grown in the cool greenhouse in potting mixture* 3. It can be forced into bloom almost at any time by increasing the heat. *See* FORCING. Cuttings of softwood root easily. For a method of training it *see* Pinching at TRAINING PLANTS.

**camara.** Red or yellow sage. Not usually over 4 ft. high, much more in the tropics, occasionally prickly. Leaves ovalish or heart-shaped, 2–6 in. long, with rounded teeth, roughish above and hairy beneath. Flower clusters 1–2 in. wide, flat-topped, usually on stalks longer than the leafstalks. Flowers about ⅓ in. wide, yellow at first, then orange or red, sometimes all three colors simultaneously in a single cluster. Tropical America, north to Tex. and Fla. Hardy from zone* 7 southward.

**flava.** Common in some catalogues, but apparently a yellow-flowered form or state of *Lantana camara*.

**sellowiana.** A vine-like shrub (*see* VINES), but not tall-growing, and mostly used as a trailer. Leaves ovalish, about 1 in. long. Flowers pinkish-lilac, the clusters about 1½ in. wide. S.A.

**LANTERN-PLANT.** *See* PHYSALIS.

**LANTERNS.** *See* JAPANESE GARDEN.

*LANTOSCANA, -us, -um* (lan-tos-cay'na). From Lantosque in the Maritime Alps.

*LANUGINOSA, -us, -um* (lan-you-ji-nō'sa). Downy.

**LAPAGERIA** (lap-a-jeer'ĭ-a). A single species of showy Chilean vine of the lily family, *L. rosea,* the Chilean bellflower (for another *see* NOLANA). It is somewhat grown outdoors in Calif. and Fla., more rarely in the cool greenhouse. It is a tall-growing, handsome vine with alternate,* rather leathery, 3-veined, short-stalked leaves. Flowers rose-colored, solitary or a few together, 3–4 in. long, trumpet-shaped, but with separate segments. Fruit berry-like, beaked. There is a *var.* **albiflora** with white flowers, and another with red flowers. It needs partial shade and does not like open, sunny or windy places. Propagated by layering (which is the easiest method) or by seeds. (Supposed to be named for Tascher de la Pagerie who became the Empress Josephine.)

**LAPEYROUSIA** (la-pay-roo'sĭ-a). Also spelled *Lapeirousia*. South African bulbous herbs of the iris family, related to *Freesia,* but more hardy. They have small corms* and mostly basal, narrow, 2-ranked leaves. Flowers small, not fragrant, red or blue, summer-blooming, from between spathe*-like bracts.* Corolla tubular, slender, slightly swollen where the spreading, nearly equal segments diverge. Fruit a small, 3-valved capsule.* (Named for J. F. Galoup de Lapeyrouse, French naval officer.)

---

* Special articles on the subjects indicated by an asterisk (*) will be found at the words so marked.

Corms should be planted 3-4 in. deep in the spring, in any ordinary garden soil. The plants are perfectly hardy from zone* 5 southward, but north of this they should have a winter mulch of straw or litter. They should be divided every few years or they become too crowded.

**cruenta.** Leaves 6-10 in. long, thin and flat. Flowering stalk about as long, the few flowers in a 1-sided cluster (spike or raceme*). Corolla red, nearly 1½ in. long, the tube very slender.

**juncea.** Leaves 5-8 in. long and about ¾ in. wide. Flowering stalk 12-20 in. long, the few flowers in loose clusters (spikes). Corolla pale red, about ¾ in. long.

**LAPPA** (lap'pa). Classical name for a bur. See Burdock in the list at Weeds.

**LAPPONICA, -us, -um** (lap-pon'i-ka). From Lapland.

**LARCH.** Trees in the pine family belonging to the genus Larix (lar'icks). They have the typical pine habit, a cone-shaped head and more or less horizontal branches, but with leaves that are dropped in the fall. The leaves are narrow and needle-like; on actively growing branches they appear singly and are spirally arranged, on the short, lateral spur-like growths they are crowded into terminal clusters. The male and female flowers are borne separately on the same tree; the cone scales are woody and persistent. (Larix is the ancient name of the larch.)

The larches are valuable timber trees and are widely cultivated as ornamentals because of their attractive habit. They do well in almost any soil, preferring an open site where there is moisture and good drainage; the American larch usually grows in acid bogs. Propagation by seed is the best method. A rather serious insect trouble is the larch sawfly. It hibernates over the winter in cocoons in surface litter and in this stage is sure to be ignored. The sawflies appear in May or June and may strip the foliage. The best remedy is a spray of arsenate of lead (3 pounds of lead to 100 gallons of water) in late May.

**L. americana** = Larix laricina.
**L. dahurica** = Larix gmelini.
**L. decidua.** European larch. Tree of 100 ft. or more, the habit pyramidal when young, later becoming irregular. Branchlets, slender, yellow-gray, not downy. Leaves narrow, about 1 in. long, midrib raised on lower surface. Cones oval, to 1½ in. long with 40-50 rounded scales, downy on the back. Northern and central Europe. Hardy from zone* 2 southward.
**L. europaea** = Larix decidua.
**L. gmelini.** Dahurian larch. Tree of about 90 ft. with widespreading, horizontal branches; branchlets brown. Leaves narrow, an inch or more long. Cones small, ovoid, ¾-1 in. long with about 20 scales that are downy on the back; pink when young. Northern Asia. Hardy from zone* 1 southward; var. **japonica**, a form in which the branchlets are downy and usually red; northern Jap.; var. **principis-ruprechti**, cones larger, to 1½ in. long and with 30-40 scales; northern China.
**L. laricina.** American larch, often called tamarack or hackmatack. Tree of rather narrow, cone-shaped form growing 60 ft. or more. Young shoots brownish, glabrous and sometimes bloomy. Leaves slender, blunt, to 1½ in. long. Cones oval or rounded, to ¾ in. long, scales 12-15. Labrador south to Pa. and Ill. Hardy from zone* 1 southward.
**L. kaempferi.** Japanese larch. A tree up to 90 ft. high, its scaly bark leaving red scars. Leaves flattened, ¾-1½ in. long, blunt, bluish-green, white-banded below. Cones egg-shaped, ¾-1¼ in. long. Jap. Hardy from zone* 3 southward. A very handsome, quick-growing larch, sometimes offered as *L. leptolepis*, and occasionally confused with *Pseudolarix kaempferi* (which see).
**L. leptolepis** = Larix kaempferi.

**LARDIZABALACEAE** (lar-diz-a-ba-lay'see-ee). A small family of mostly woody vines, two genera of which, Akebia and Stauntonia are grown for ornament. Both are Asiatic. See also Vines.

Leaves alternate* and compound,* in both the cult. genera with the leaflets arranged finger-fashion. Flowers unisexual* or polygamous,* not very showy, without petals, but in *Akebia* attractive and brownish-purple, nearly always in racemes.* Fruit a berry in *Stauntonia*, but a fleshy, black-seeded pod in *Akebia*.

Technical flower characters: Sepals 6 in *Stauntonia*, 3 in *Akebia*, petal-like. Petals none. Stamens 6. Ovary superior,* usually with many ovules.

**LARGE-LEAVED CUCUMBER TREE** = Magnolia macrophylla.

**LARGE-LEAVED LINDEN** = Tilia platyphyllos. See Linden.

**LARGE-LEAVED TOMATO** = Lycopersicum esculentum grandifolium. See Tomato.

**LARGE-TOOTHED ASPEN** = Populus grandidentata.

**LARGER YELLOW LADY'S-SLIPPER** = Cypripedium parviflorum pubescens.

**LARICINA, -us, -um** (lar-i-sy'na). Larch-like.

**LARICIO** (lar-iss'i-o). An old name for some larch-like evergreen. See *Pinus laricio* at Pine.

**LARIX.** See Larch.

**LARKSPUR.** See Delphinium.

**LARREA** (lar're-a). A genus of four species of heavily scented desert shrubs from the southwestern states and adjoining Mexico, and the only cult. representatives of the family Zygophyllaceae (zy-go-fil-lay'see-ee). The family includes about 20 genera and over 150 species of herbs, shrubs, or trees, mostly from warm or tropical regions, usually with opposite* compound* leaves, the leaflets arranged feather-fashion. In the genus *Larrea*, only **L. tridentata**, the creosote bush or greasewood, is of any garden interest, and then only for desert gardens within its natural range. It is an evergreen, balsam-scented, much-branched and resinous shrub, 5-8 ft. high. Leaflets 2, stalkless, more or less oblique and ovalish, about ⅓ in. long. Flowers yellow, solitary, terminal, about ¼ in. long, the petals separate. Stamens* 8-10. Fruit a globe-shaped, white-felty, small capsule.* The plant needs a light sandy soil and intense sunlight. (Named for a Spaniard, Larrea, otherwise unknown.)

**LARVA** (plural larvae). The worm-like or grub-like and wingless stage in the life-history of many insects. The larvae of some moths and butterflies are among the most destructive of the garden pests, and in this stage are usually called grubs, maggots, or caterpillars. See Insect Pests.

**LASIACANTHA, -us, -um** (lay-si-a-kan'tha). Woolly-spined.

**LASIANTHA, -us, -um** (lay-si-an'tha). Woolly-flowered.

**LASIOCARPA, -us, -um** (lay-si-o-kar'pa). Woolly-fruited.

**LASTHENIA** (las-thee'ni-a). A small genus of Pacific Coast annual herbs of the family Compositae, one of them, **L. glabrata**, a tender annual, but not of primary hort. interest. It is a slightly fleshy herb 12-18 in. high, with opposite* narrow leaves, 1-2 in. long, the bases of which are joined around the stem. Flower-heads yellow, about 1 in. wide, composed of both ray* and disk* flowers. Below the head the bracts* are joined to form a cup-like involucre.* It should be grown as a tender annual. See Annuals. The var. **californica** (sometimes offered as *Lasthenia californica*) is a form in which the leaf bases are not united. (Named for a woman pupil of Plato.)

**LATANIA** (la-tay'ni-a). A small genus of medium-sized fan palms of the islands of the Indian Ocean, two of them occasionally grown in Fla. and Calif. for ornament. Florists also apply the name *Latania borbonica* to the Chinese fan palm, a widely cult. greenhouse plant better known as *Livistona chinensis* (which see). The true latanias have unarmed trunks, although the long, stiff leafstalks are occasionally prickly on young plants, as are also the leaf margins. The leaves are large, with many pointed segments. Flower clusters from among the crown of leaves, usually several feet long. Male and female flowers on separate trees, only the female fruiting. Male cluster comprised of dense spikes, the 15-30 stamens* in sunken pits. Female cluster looser-flowered. Fruit somewhat fleshy, yellow, 1-2½ in. long. (*Latania* is a Latinized version of an East Indian vernacular for these trees.)

For culture see Palm.

**borbonica** = *Livistona chinensis*, so far as the usual cult. plants are concerned. The true *L. borbonica*, is scarcely known in cult. The plant grown under that name is usually the next species.
**commersoni.** Not over 40 ft. high. Leaves nearly 5 ft. wide, the stalk and ribs crimson, especially on young plants. Leaf segments nearly 3 in. wide at the base (on old plants). Fruit nearly globe-shaped, ribbed. A

---

* Special articles on the subjects indicated by an asterisk (*) will be found at the words so marked.

very handsome but little cult. palm, occasionally planted in Fla. Mauritius.

**loddigesi.** A taller palm, but as cult. usually not over 10–20 ft. high. Leaves 3–5 ft. wide, bluish-green, the veins slightly reddish, especially on young plants. Leaf segments mostly less than 3 in. wide at the base, about 2 ft. long. The leafstalk is often spiny on young plants, merely hairy in age, 3–4½ ft. long. Fruit pear-shaped, 3-angled. Mauritius. Sometimes planted in Fla.

**LATE.** See EARLY.

**LATE BLIGHT.** See Diseases at POTATO.

**LATE LAWN MOWING.** See LAWN.

**LATERAL.** Borne on or at the side; not central nor terminal.

*LATERITIA, -us, -um* (la-ter-rĭ'she-a). Brick-red.

**LATEX.** See SAP.

**LATH HOUSE.** A "greenhouse" without glass and made of laths or slats so placed that there is ample circulation of air, but only about half the usual amount of light. The laths are usually about 1 in. apart. Lath houses are much used in tropical and sub-tropical regions for growing orchids and ferns, which find congenial quarters within the shaded, wind-free lath house. They are also used in temperate regions for plants needing shade, like the ginseng.

Lath house

**LATH SCREEN.** See TRELLISES.

**LATHYRUS** (lă'thi-russ). An important group of annual or perennial herbs of the pea family, comprising over 100 species chiefly from the north temperate zone. One of them is the ever-popular sweet pea, and several others are also widely grown for ornament. All our cult. species, except *L. vernus* and *L. splendens*, are tendril-bearing, vine-like plants, usually with winged or angled stems. Leaves alternate,* compound,* the leaflets usually few. Flowers typically pea-like, often very showy, especially in the cult. strains of the sweet pea. (For details of the typical pea flower see LEGUMINOSAE.) Fruit a flattish pod (legume*). (*Lathyrus* is an old Greek name for some plant of the pea family, but perhaps not for these.)

For the culture and varieties of *Lathyrus odoratus* see SWEET PEA. The perennial species (noted as such below) are of easy culture in most garden soils and bloom most of the summer. Some of them are very popular stem-climbing vines (see VINES) for covering porches. Two of them, *L. maritimus* and *L. littoralis*, are sea beach plants suited only to sandy soils. The easiest way to increase any of them is by seeds, but the young pods should be picked off the plants that are to produce the most and best flowers, leaving only a few pods for seed supply. All except *Lathyrus vernus* and *L. splendens* have only 2 leaflets. For the garden pea see PISUM. Some of the small species are occasionally called vetchling.

**grandiflorus.** Everlasting pea. A perennial, climbing by tendrils* up to 6 ft. or more. Leaflets ovalish, 1–1½ in. long. Flowers 2–3 together, on a long stalk, rose-purple, somewhat fragrant, nearly 1½ in. wide, very showy. Pod about 3 in. long. Southern Eu. See Stem Climbers at VINES.

**latifolius.** Perennial pea; also called everlasting pea. A perennial, climbing by tendrils up to 9 ft. or more. Leaflets ovalish or narrower, 2–4 in. long. Flowers several in a long-stalked cluster, rose-pink (or white or darker in some hort. forms), 1–1½ in. wide. Pod 3–5 in. long. Eu. A common garden plant coming in various colors.

**littoralis.** Beach pea (in Calif.). A sprawling, perennial seashore plant, suited chiefly to its native region from Wash. to Calif. Leaflets wedge-shaped or oblongish, silky-hairy. Flowers 2–6 in a cluster, about 1 in. wide, purple and white. See SAND GARDENS.

**maritimus.** Beach pea (along the Atlantic coast). A sprawling perennial, sand dune plant suited only to open sandy soils. Leaflets oblongish or ovalish, perfectly smooth. Flowers in clusters of 6–10, showy, about 1 in. wide, violet-purple. Coasts of the north temperate zone. See SAND GARDENS.

**odoratus.** The common sweet pea. An annual vine-like plant, 4–6 ft. high. Leaflets ovalish or oblong, 1–2 in. long, usually with a short, softly spiny tip. Flowers fragrant, 1–3, rarely 4, in a cluster, often 2 in. wide in some hort. varieties, of many colors as now cult., perhaps originally only purple. Pod about 2 in. long, hairy. Seeds nearly globe-shaped, hard, and grayish-brown. Italy. For culture and best varieties see SWEET PEA.

**splendens.** Pride-of-California. A perennial, more or less shrubby and not high-climbing. Leaflets ovalish or oblong, about 1 in. long, usually in 2–5 pairs. Flowers 6–12 in a stout-stalked cluster, pale rose-pink, or violet, or even magenta, very showy, about 1 in. wide. Pod 2–3 in. long, smooth and beaked. Southern Calif. and little known elsewhere.

**vernus.** Spring vetchling. A perennial herb, not climbing, and rarely over 2 ft. high, without tendrils.* Leaflets 2–3 pairs, ovalish, but tapering, 1½–3 in. long, prominently 2-veined. Flowers 5–8 in the cluster, nodding, bluish-violet, about ¾ in. long. Pod about 1½ in. long, smooth. Eu.

*LATIFLORA, -us, -um* (la-tĭ-flo'ra). With wide flowers.

*LATIFOLIA, -us, um* (la-tĭ-fō'lĭ-a). Broad-leaved.

*LATISQUAMA, -us, -um* (la-tĭ-skway'ma). Having broad, scale-like leaves or bracts.*

**LATTICE-LEAF** = *Aponogeton fenestralis.*

**LATTICE-PLANT FAMILY** = Aponogetonaceae. See APONOGETON.

**LAUNDRY YARD.** See SERVICE YARD.

**LAURACEAE** (law-ray'see-ee). The laurel, often called the cinnamon or sassafras family, is a very large one. Of its 45 genera and possibly 1000 species, nearly all are trees or shrubs of the tropics, a few of warm regions, and only a handful from the temperate zone. Of the latter the most familiar and widely cult. are *Sassafras, Benzoin, Umbellularia* (the California Laurel), and *Laurus* (the true laurel of the ancients, not the mountain laurel). The only other cult. genera are *Persea*, which yields the avocado or alligator pear, and *Cinnamomum*, which yields the cinnamon and camphor, both chiefly tropical.

All have alternate* leaves (some evergreen) and all are impregnated with a highly aromatic oil, hence the fragrant foliage of the Lauraceae. Flowers usually not very showy, more so in *Persea* and *Benzoin* than in the others, chiefly yellow or yellowish-green. Fruit fleshy, a berry* in *Persea*, a drupe* in most other genera.

Technical flower characters: Flowers perfect* (in *Persea* and *Umbellularia*), unisexual* (in *Sassafras* and *Benzoin*) or both in the other genera. Petals and sepals scarcely distinguishable as such, combined they usually total 6 more or less petal-like, or at least colored parts. Stamens 9 or 12, some often sterile. Ovary mostly superior.*

**LAUREL.** The laurel of history and hort. is *Laurus nobilis* (which see), commonly called the bay tree (not the bayberry). But laurel is also very frequently applied to other plants: see KALMIA, RHODODENDRON, UMBELLULARIA, LAUROCERASUS, DAPHNE LAUREOLA, and the next few entries.

**LAUREL CHERRY** = *Laurocerasus caroliniana.*

**LAUREL FAMILY.** A large group of generally aromatic shrubs and trees containing such diverse plants as the sassafras, spicebush, the true laurel (see LAUREL), the cinnamon, the avocado, and many others. For the cult. genera see LAURACEAE.

**LAUREL OAK.** Properly, *Quercus laurifolia*, but sometimes *Q. imbricaria* is so called. See OAK.

**LAUREL WILLOW** = *Salix pentandra.* See WILLOW.

**LAURELWOOD** = *Arbutus menziesi.*

*LAURIFOLIA, -us, -um* (law-ri-fō'lĭ-a). With leaves like the true laurel (*Laurus*).

*LAURINA, -us, -um* (law-ry'na). Like the true laurel (*Laurus*).

**LAUROCERASUS** (law-ro-se'ra-sus). Evergreen shrubs or trees of the rose family, often considered as part of the genus

---

* Special articles on the subjects indicated by an asterisk (*) will be found at the words so marked.

*Prunus* (the plums and cherries), but here kept separate for their hort. uses. They are usually called cherry laurel because their foliage is evergreen and suggests the true laurel, while no cult. plants of the genus *Prunus* are similarly endowed. Flowers white, in finger-shaped clusters (racemes*), which are leafless at the base. Fruit inedible, a more or less egg- or cone-shaped, 1-seeded drupe.* (*Laurocerasus* is a combination of the Latin names for laurel and cherry.)

These are handsome evergreen shrubs or trees prized for their lustrous green foliage even more than for the small white flowers. They are not hardy in the North, as noted below, but are favorite plants in suitable climates, where they grow well on a variety of soils. Propagated easily by seed or by cuttings of mature wood under glass.

**caroliniana.** Laurel cherry; also called mock-orange, cherry laurel, and wild orange (it is no orange). A tree up to 40 ft. high. Leaves oblongish or narrower, almost without marginal teeth. Flowers small, scarcely ¼ in. wide, the cluster slender, milky-white. Fruit black and shining, about ½ in. long. N. Car. to Tex. Hardy from zone* 6 southward. Often called *Prunus caroliniana*.

**lusitanica.** Portuguese cherry laurel. Much resembling the next, but with the toothed leaves shorter than the flower clusters; also it is a taller tree. Spain and Portugal. Hardy from zone* 5 southward. Often called *Prunus lusitanica*. The var. **variegata** has white-margined leaves.

**officinalis.** The common cherry laurel; sometimes called English laurel (but it is not the true laurel). An evergreen shrub or small tree up to 20 ft. high. Leaves oblongish, 2½–6 in. long, remotely or not at all toothed, short-stalked. Flowers fragrant, white, about ⅓ in. wide, the cluster shorter than the leaves. Fruit dark purple, about ½ in. long. Southeastern Eu. to Persia. Hardy from zone* 5 southward and a much-planted bush. The var. **angustifolia** has narrower leaves; var. **rotundifolia**, roundish ones; and the var. **pyramidalis** is a pyramid-shaped, almost cone-shaped form; var. **zabeliana** is one of the hardiest of all the varieties. There are many other forms of this very popular plant which has been cult. for centuries, often under the name of *Prunus laurocerasus*.

**LAURUS** (law'rus). A small but important genus of evergreen trees of the family Lauraceae, natives in the Mediterranean region. There are only two species, the cult. one being **L. nobilis,** the true laurel of history and the poets, but commonly called bay, bay tree, and sweet bay by gardeners. In Greece it is tree-like and from 40 to 60 ft. high. But as universally grown here it is perhaps the most popular of all tubbed evergreens, usually in the form of standards,* cones, pyramids, or any other shape, as it stands shearing very well. It has stiff, alternate,* oblongish leaves, 3–4 in. long, and without marginal teeth. Flowers small, inconspicuous (see LAURACEAE). Fruit a small berry. (*Laurus* is the classical name of the laurel.)

### BAY TREE CULTIVATION. (LAUREL)

While the laurel will stand considerable frost, it is not certainly hardy north of zone* 6, and is planted out as part of the shrubbery only south of this. Elsewhere it is grown, perhaps by the million, as a showy evergreen tub plant which needs winter protection. As a decorative, outdoor tub plant from April to October it is very widely used for porches, formal gardens, pools, courtyards, and public buildings, but it is not a good indoor subject as it dislikes dry heat.

Young plants should be potted up in potting mixture* and given plenty of water. As they grow they can finally be sheared into almost any desired shape and put into tubs of a size to be handled without too much effort — for all bay trees in the North must be moved twice a year. They are slow-growing and it takes several years to produce a specimen plant.

In the fall, before hard frosts are due (see the name of your state or province for the dates), the laurel tubs should be packed as closely together as they reasonably can be in a shed or deep pit, or in a heavily shaded greenhouse where the temperature can be kept between 38° and 45°. They need little water during the winter, but must not be allowed to dry out. Re-pot in the spring if necessary, but do not increase the size of the tub unless absolutely necessary. If the tops are kept sheared to the desired form, the only reason for re-potting is to renew worn-out soil.

The common green bay tree flourishes with considerable neglect, but it does best with plenty of moisture, and care must be taken to see that the tubs do not dry out during

Globe-shaped and conical forms of the bay tree, which may be easily sheared to any desired outline

the active growing season. Occasionally a variegated or crisp-leaved form is seen, but the common green laurel is the most popular.

**LAURUSTINUS** = *Viburnum tinus*.

**LAVANDULA** (la-van'dew-la). Lavender. Aromatic, Old World, perennial herbs or shrubs of the mint family, chiefly grown for their aromatic oil, although the flowers of some species are attractive. Of the 20 or more known species, the true lavender is the only one widely grown and it has been cult. for centuries. Leaves opposite,* without marginal teeth (in ours), and narrow. Flowers lavender or dark purple, crowded into dense clusters in the leaf-axils.* Corolla irregular,* the upper lip 2-cleft, the lower one 3-cleft. Stamens* 4, not protruding. Fruit a collection of dry nutlets. (*Lavandula* is from the Latin to wash, in allusion to its use in bath water.)

For the cult. and uses of the common lavender see HERB GARDENING. The only other cult. species is *Lavandula stoechas,* a shrub which is rarely grown in southern Calif., and is unsuited to most other regions.

**officinalis** = *Lavandula spica*.

**spica.** The common lavender. An under-shrub or woody herb 1–3 ft. high. Leaves narrow, lance-shaped or narrower, 1–2 in. long, often with smaller ones in the axils,* all white-felty and with rolled margins. Flowers about ⅓ in. long, the clusters interrupted.* Mediterranean region. For cult. and uses see HERB GARDENING. Sometimes known as *L. officinalis* and *L. vera*. This and the next are both known as French lavender.

**stoechas.** A shrub 2–3 ft. high, its foliage gray-felty. Leaves narrow and line-like, about ½ in. long. Flowers in dense clusters (spikes), among which are conspicuous purple bracts.* Corolla dark purple. Mediterranean region. Grown in southern Calif. Abroad it is known as stechados or French lavender.

**vera** = *Lavandula spica*.

**LAVANGA** = *Luvunga*.

**LAVATERA** (la-va-tee'ra). Tree Mallow. A genus of herbs of the family Malvaceae, mostly from the warmer regions of the Old World, a few grown for ornament in the flower garden. Of the 25 known species, the three below are annual, biennial, or perennial herbs, although others are shrubs or even trees. They have hairy stems and alternate,* somewhat maple-like, angled or lobed leaves. Flowers rather showy, pink or purplish in the cult. sorts, and below them a cluster of 3–9 bracts,* united to form an involucre.* Petals 5, notched or cut-off at the tip, the base with a claw.* Fruit a collection of beakless, dry, pod-like bodies (schizocarp*). (Named for the brothers Lavater, Swiss naturalists.) Cultural notes at each species.

---

* Special articles on the subjects indicated by an asterisk (*) will be found at the words so marked.

**arborea.** A biennial herb, but forming a tree or shrub-like plant 4-10 ft. high. Leaves 4-9 in. long, nearly as broad, long-stalked, with 5-9 rounded lobes and downy both sides. Flowers about 2 in. wide, pale purplish-red, but purple-veined at the base, borne in profuse, short, leafy clusters (racemes*). Eu. Seed should be started the season before bloom is wanted. *See* BIENNIALS. Perhaps the most commonly cult. form is *var.* **variegata,** with white-mottled leaves.

**assurgentiflora.** A perennial or shrubby plant 6-12 ft. high, confined to the islands off the southern Calif. coast and one of the few American species. It grows there, and in similar climates, nearly 6 ft. high and blooms the first season from seed. Leaves 3-6 in. wide, the 5-7 more or less triangular lobes coarsely toothed. Flowers about 2 in. wide, purple, stalked, 1-4 in the leaf-axil.* Petals with a tuft of hairs on the claw.* Not hardy outside of southern Calif., but used for temporary hedges there because of its quick growth.

**trimestris.** A widely grown, branching annual, 3-6 ft. high, especially in the *var.* **splendens,** which is an improved garden form of the wild species. Leaves irregularly round-toothed. Flowers usually solitary, nearly 4 in. wide, red or rose-pink, and very showy. Mediterranean region. A summer-blooming, hardy annual. *See* ANNUALS. There is also a *var.* **alba,** with white flowers.

**LAVENDER.** The true lavender is *Lavandula spica* (which see). But *see also* CHRYSANTHEMUM BALSAMITA. For the sea lavender *see* LIMONIUM.

**LAVENDER COTTON** = *Santolina chamaecyparissus.*

**LAVENDER GARDEN.** *See* GRAY AND LAVENDER GARDEN.

**LAWN.** There is no perfect substitute for a well-kept lawn, but there are many places in the U.S. where fine lawns are impossible. The different grasses that make up the standard lawn mixtures require far less annual rainfall than do trees and shrubs, but they do need an adequate supply during the growing season. If the total rainfall during the growing season falls below 18 or 20 inches, it is next to impossible to have a really fine lawn without more or less constant watering. A lawn of a sort one can have even in these unfavorable places, but it cannot be made of the grasses that are the basis of all the best lawn mixtures as outlined below. For such places there are special kinds of grasses, as there must be also for the South, where summer heat is too much for the best lawn grasses.

So important is this basic rainfall requirement for really fine lawns, that anyone contemplating the making of one should verify his local rainfall during the growing season. This is discussed toward the end of each article on the different states and will be found at the name of your state or province.

If your rainfall for the growing season is 18-20 in. or more, you are safe in assuming that you can have a fine lawn if you are willing to observe the few simple rules necessary to have one. If, on the other hand, you live in an unfavorable region, then your lawn must be made of hardier and coarser grasses, which are discussed later.

The basic requirements of a good lawn, assuming adequate rainfall or the ability to overcome an inadequate one by irrigation, are the right sort of soil and the proper mixture of lawn grasses.

### SOIL REQUIREMENTS

Any good garden loam will grow a good lawn. The best evidence for such a statement is that of over 200 soil types recognized and named by the U.S. Bureau of Soils, lawns are found on every one. The tolerance of lawn grasses for different sorts of soils stops, however, if they are markedly acid or predominantly sand. If the acidity of the proposed lawn soil is below pH 5.5, it would be foolish to seed down such a site without correcting that acidity. Usually all that is necessary is to broadcast enough agricultural lime just to cover the soil and thoroughly rake it in. If, after a rain or two, the soil still tests acid, it is better to treat it more heavily with lime, as outlined at Acid and Alkali Soils, where there is also a discussion on how to make the tests. The best of all lawn grasses is particularly intolerant of acidity, so that if your soil is even moderately acid, you should apply agricultural lime a little thicker — *i.e.* at about the rate of 7½ lbs. of agricultural lime or twice this amount of ground limestone to every 300 square feet.

Soils too high in sand are also unfavorable. They should be either avoided or else treated according to the articles on Green Manuring and Humus, for their humus content must be far better than that of sand to ensure the lawn's survival over a summer drought.

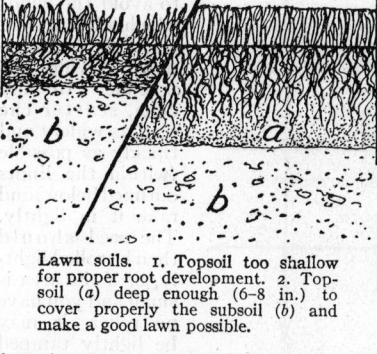

Lawn soils. 1. Topsoil too shallow for proper root development. 2. Topsoil (*a*) deep enough (6-8 in.) to cover properly the subsoil (*b*) and make a good lawn possible.

Assuming that you have neither acidity nor sand to contend with, there remains one of the major causes of lawn failure — inadequate depth of soil.

Many statements are made that as grasses are essentially shallow-rooted plants, 4 or 5 in. of good topsoil are all that are needed. If your summer rainfall is very high or you can sprinkle through all droughts, the statement is correct. But it is absolutely incorrect if your region is a more normal one, subject to summer droughts, and you have no facilities for lawn sprinkling. While it is true that most lawn grasses are comparatively shallow-rooted plants, it is much more nearly the truth to say that many thin-soiled sites drive them to be more shallow-rooted than they normally would be.

Good permanent lawns that will survive summer heat and dryness should be grown on not less than 7-8 in. of topsoil, and a foot will do no harm. In such a soil the grasses get a firm, deep hold, which means that their roots are in the coolest and moistest layer of the topsoil. It is impossible to over-emphasize the importance of this proper depth of topsoil. If you haven't got at least 7 in., it would be better to improve the soil by crop rotation or green manuring (which see), or else bring in enough topsoil from another place to make the site of the lawn at least 7-8 in. deep. An alternative is to top-dress with a good commercial humus. *See* HUMUS.

PREPARING THE SOIL. Given the proper depth of the right sort of topsoil, the next step is its preparation for the final seeding of the lawn mixture. If the site has been heavily cropped with vegetables or flowers, there is a fair chance that it is somewhat depleted of plant food. Stable manure, while it adds humus and plant food, is better kept out at this stage, as it will contain the seeds of many troublesome weeds. By far the best way to increase the humus content of the lawn soil is to cover it with 3 in. of prepared, weed-free, non-acid humus, and thoroughly dig or rake it in. *See* HUMUS.

While this adds an important ingredient to any lawn soil, humus is no substitute for plant food. After the humus is thoroughly mixed with the soil, top-dress it with a good commercial fertilizer with a 4-8-4 ration (*see* FERTILIZERS) at the rate of 1500-1800 lbs. per acre, or about 30 lbs. to 1000 sq. ft.

All of this should have been done 3-4 weeks before actual seed sowing, and it is assumed that the ground would have been spaded or plowed long before this, as in the preparation of any other soil for a garden crop. Such spading or plowing, especially in the case of preparing for a lawn, should be done carefully enough so that no coarse subsoil is brought to the surface.

PREPARATION OF SEED BED. Because of the nature of young grass shoots, lawn soil needs more final preparation than that of the vegetable garden. On large areas much time can be saved by disk-harrowing and following this with a spring-tooth or ordinary harrow (*see* HARROWING).

But neither of these will leave the land smooth or fine enough for a good lawn, and the only remedy is a final hand raking. See that all lumps are broken up and the soil left in as smooth and fine a condition as possible.

It is not advisable to rake a large area, perhaps leaving

---

* Special articles on the subjects indicated by an asterisk (*) will be found at the words so marked.

the seeding to a later date, because the seed will "take" better on freshly raked land. If the area is large, do the final hand raking in squares of about 50 × 50 ft., and seed immediately; then rake and seed another piece, and so on.

SOWING GRASS SEED. Grass seed is so fine that it cannot be sown on a windy day. Early-morning sowing is often practiced by experienced lawn makers to avoid the winds which often freshen enough later to make sowing impossible. In any case, scatter the seed as widely and thickly as possible (within the limits outlined below) and rake it in lightly. The seed should then be rolled lightly, or if the area is small and you have no roller, it may be lightly tamped with a board or the back of a spade.

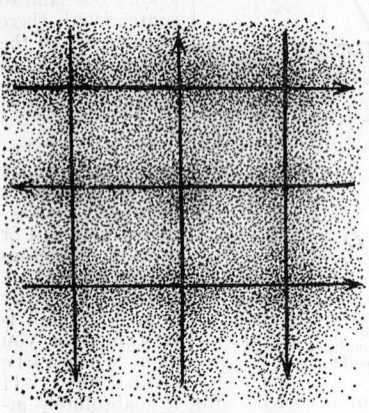

Sow grass seed in two lines, as shown by the arrows.

On a new lawn it is important to get as thick a stand of grass as possible. There is no better remedy or cure for the weeds that are bound to come up in a new lawn than for them to be crowded out by the grass itself. To help make the initial distribution of grass seed as thorough as possible, it is well to divide it in half. Walk in one direction while sowing the first half and then sow the other half on the same area, but walk in the opposite direction while sowing. Such a criss-cross sowing will be far more thorough than one done by simply walking in one direction.

The amount of seed necessarily differs on different soils and with different grass mixtures. For most soils in the North and using the standard mixtures as outlined below, at least 5 lbs. of seed should be used on 1000 sq. ft., and the cost of grass seed is so trifling that it would be better to use 7–8 lbs. on an area of that size. A niggardly policy in sowing grass seed is sure to bring much later trouble, especially in spring-sown seedings, which are most likely to be weed-infested, and this brings us to the preferred time of sowing.

There is no question that fall-sown seed has a better chance of making a good lawn than that sown in the spring. The reason is obvious enough. In the spring and early summer the young grass has to compete with all the weed seedlings that spring up with the grass. As summer heat comes along the scarcely established young lawn is in far from the best condition to withstand a possible drought or the competition of weeds. On small areas, which can be kept watered and hand weeded, there is, however, no objection to spring sowing. If this plan is followed, sow the seed somewhere between March 20 and May 1, the earlier the better.

Fall sowing should be done as soon as possible after really hot weather is over, which usually means about Sept. 15. Of course the seeded area should have been thoroughly cleared of the summer accumulation of weeds and just as thoroughly prepared as for spring planting. But it has the added advantage that the new lawn enters the winter with the young grass in practically exclusive possession of the soil. This is the ideal condition.

### LAWN MIXTURES

Unless lawn making is a large-scale operation of at least several acres, it scarcely pays to buy separately and mix the different species that make up the best lawn mixtures. The basis of all mixtures for regions of adequate summer rainfall is Kentucky bluegrass (*Poa pratensis*), sometimes known as June grass. Because this grass does not get thoroughly established the first season, it is mixed with other species of quick, though not lasting growth. The latter make a good showing the first year or two, but are ultimately crowded out by Kentucky bluegrass.

A good general purpose lawn mixture may contain something like the following percentages of the three leading grasses used:

| | |
|---|---|
| Kentucky bluegrass (*Poa pratensis*) | 80 % |
| Redtop (*Agrostis palustris*) | 10 % |
| Rhode Island Bent (*Agrostis capillaris*) | 10 % |

The exact proportions are of much less importance than purity of seed. Many cheap grass mixtures may be anywhere from $\frac{1}{5}$ to $\frac{1}{4}$ chaff, weed seeds, or undesirable grasses. Naturally only a poor lawn can be expected from the use of such. Buy the best and most expensive (*i.e.* cleanest) mixture you can get from a first-class dealer. The cost, except on large-scale operations, is trifling and failure pretty certain with cheap and dirty seed.

Whether or not you add common white clover to any mixture depends upon soil conditions partly and upon preference. It stains children's clothing much more than any grass, and is objectionable to many on this account. On most good garden soils it is not absolutely necessary, although it adds nitrogen to the soil, which no grass will do. If the soil is sandy, white clover should be used, at the rate of about 1½–2 ounces of clover seed for every 300 sq. ft. The seed is so heavy that it sinks to the bottom of any container of grass seed, and should therefore not be mixed with the grass seed and sown with it. Sow it separately, immediately after the grass seed, and then a reasonable distribution of the clover is more likely.

Such comparatively standard mixtures as the above, or trifling variations of them, are useful for nearly all regions (1) where there is adequate summer rainfall; (2) where the soil is not too acid; (3) where there is no shade; (4) which are not south of zone 6 or 7. For these specialized conditions it is necessary to use grasses of a different sort, because Kentucky bluegrass will not stand great heat, or shade, or an acid soil.

SHADE GRASSES. Most grasses are light-demanding and will not stand shade, even though there is adequate summer moisture. Under the shade of most trees a shade mixture can be used, however, so long as the trees are not evergreens, or those like the horse-chestnut and some lindens under which it is practically impossible to grow any grass. For such places other plants must be used. *See* GROUND COVER.

Another factor of importance in getting a lawn under the shade of trees is the immense amount of available water and plant food taken by the shallow-rooted trees at the expense of the grass. In such places watering and top-dressing with humus or occasional applications of commercial fertilizer are imperative. For the details *see* LAWN MAINTENANCE below.

Under moderate or even fairly heavy shade the best grasses are:

*Poa trivialis* (a relative of Kentucky bluegrass)
*Festuca ovina capillata*
*Poa compressa*
*Poa nemoralis*

Usually, for small-scale operations, it is better to buy prepared shade mixtures from a reputable dealer, as they will contain a reasonable mixture of the above and of a few other shade-enduring species.

ACID SOIL GRASSES. Where the soil is too acid to make Kentucky bluegrass a success, other species of lawn grasses are used. Small and perhaps temporary acidity or sourness can be corrected by using lime as outlined above. But over considerable sections of the country the whole soil reaction is sufficiently acid to make it better to adapt the grass to it rather than to try to change the acidity. (*See* ACID AND ALKALI SOILS for details of making the tests.)

---

\* Special articles on the subjects indicated by an asterisk (\*) will be found at the words so marked.

In places too acid for Kentucky bluegrass, by far the best lawn grasses are various kinds of creeping bent (*Agrostis maritima*, but often sold as *A. stolonifera*). This is the grass used also on fine putting greens, bowling greens, tennis courts, etc. Its great merit is that due to its habit and the way it is planted it will make a perfect lawn in 6–7 weeks. Its great defect is that it is very shallow-rooted, needs constant watering to survive droughts, and that its foliage is so thin and slender that only the closest mowing will keep it trimmed.

No finer turf in the world can be made than with creeping bent, of which there are several commercial varieties now on the market. But for ordinary lawn purposes it is advised only in acid-soil localities where Kentucky bluegrass will not grow. The maintenance, feeding, watering, etc., of a bent lawn must be as intensive as on a golf course where nightly watering of the greens is not unusual.

Creeping bent is not grown from seed, which is usually unavailable. The grass rootstocks creep all through the upper layers of the soil as do the stolons* along the surface. Bits of these vegetative pieces are planted instead of seed. The job is far more laborious than sowing grass seed, as each bit of the creeping bent must be slightly covered with soil, tamped down, and sprinkled. A usual interval is to plant the bits 3 × 4 in. apart, or 3 × 5 in. As in seeding, a niggardly policy is not economical in the long run, although creeping bent is far more expensive to buy and plant than ordinary grass seed. The results, however, are remarkable and quick. An even finer bent, still more expensive, is *Agrostis canina*, usually called dog or velvet bent. It is handled in the same way as creeping bent.

In regions where insect or other troubles make the keeping of a grass lawn impossible, an interesting substitute is the camomile (*Anthemis nobilis*), a rather weedy plant. But seed sown broadcast, as is grass seed, will soon produce an abundant growth. It will stand rolling and mowing, and if these are done regularly it makes a turf. While camomile lawns are rare in America, they were once common in England. They have been successful near Philadelphia, but they do not thrive in dry places, nor where it is too cold and windswept. *Thymus serpyllum* is also a possible grass substitute.

SOUTHERN LAWNS. In places of great heat or considerable drought, none of the grasses so far mentioned are of any use, unless constant watering is possible. Usually, as in most gardening operations, it is better to choose the plant for the site than to keep up a constant fight in order to maintain more desirable species.

The chief grasses for these unfavorable places are:

St. Augustine grass (*Stenotaphrum secundatum*).
Bermuda grass (*Cynodon dactylon*).
Centipede-grass (*Eremochloa ophiuroides*); also a variety of it known as St. Lucie grass.
Carpet grass (*Axonopus compressus*).

All of these are suited to warm, dry regions and will make a lawn, but none of them compare with Kentucky bluegrass. They are not mixed, but should be used alone, according to the sort of soil. In sandy, rather dry places it is better to use St. Augustine grass (also good for shade) or centipede-grass. In moist sand, carpet grass is the best; while for heavy or clayey soils Bermuda grass is preferable. The latter, in fact, will not generally tolerate a sandy soil.

In all of these grasses for the South it is better to plant bits of the stolons* than to try seed sowing. They may be planted as in the directions for creeping bent given above, but because of the heat, even greater care is needed until they become established. Do not let the bits of stolon* get dry either before or after planting. When established these lawns should be able to take care of themselves, except in periods of great drought. See also ZOYSIA.

There are, of course, many places in the U.S. where even these grasses will not grow, and a grass lawn is virtually impossible. The only remedy is to use some low-creeping plant such as those discussed at VINES and at GROUND COVER. See also LIPPIA.

CARE OF LAWNS

Once the lawn suited to your climate and soil is established, only about half the job is completed, for upon its subsequent neglect or care will depend the final result. Such care ranges from a mere mowing of the grass to the practice of that fanatical Englishman who prized his turf so highly that he lifted it each fall and carried it through the winter in the cool greenhouse. Reasonable care of a good lawn may be divided into (1) Mowing and Rolling; (2) Feeding and Watering; (3) Weeds and Repair.

Before taking these up in detail a word of caution about the initial treatment of a new lawn is necessary. When the new grass is about 3 in. high, mow it for the first time, leaving the mowings on the lawn. Thereafter follow the general directions under Mowing below. Also, no matter how well or carefully you have prepared the seed bed, it is certain to settle unevenly, and this should be corrected as soon as the first mowing is done. Fill up all depressions or holes with fine topsoil and re-seed immediately — this not only for the looks of the lawn but because every bare spot is a possible point for weeds to get ahead.

MOWING AND ROLLING. Throughout the region where there are alternate days of freezing and thawing in early spring, which is over a good part of the country, the minor heaving of lawns is inevitable. As the season advances these irregularities will tend to disappear, but before they do so are apt to leave some grass roots hung above the soil, when, of course, they will dry out. To avoid such troubles and for the general firming of the whole lawn it is better to roll it as soon as the season will permit. Never roll a thoroughly wet lawn, but wait until there is no danger of packing the soil into a cement-like layer. On reasonably well-drained sites this should be a day after a soaking rain.

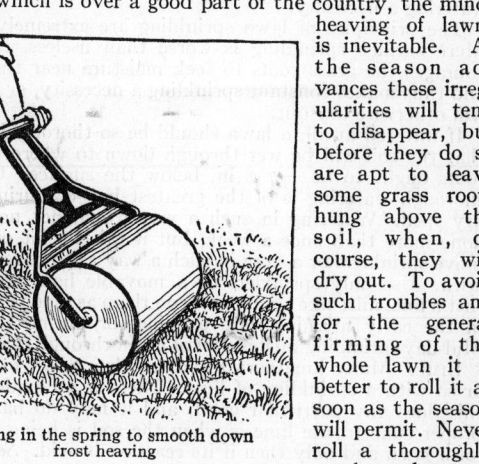

Rolling in the spring to smooth down frost heaving

Use a roller weighing 300–400 lbs. and roll the lawn only twice, once each way. This will take care of any frost heaving without packing the soil too much, a quite likely contingency if the soil is a heavy one with considerable clay or silt in it. See Section 3, TOOLS AND IMPLEMENTS.

As to mowing, no hard-and-fast rule can be given. During rainy spring weather it may have to be done every 5 days; later in the summer it had better be done only as often as absolutely necessary to keep a fine sward. This may bring mowings 9–15 days apart during a dry August.

Do not set the knives of the lawn mower too low. It is far better to have them set about 1 in. high than to cut too close. In the case of creeping bent, however, the machine cannot be set too low. But in ordinary lawns, cutting too close unnecessarily exposes the crown of the plant to too much direct sunlight, which does it no good. A good rule is to mow often enough so that a properly set mower will clip only about ½–¾ in. off the top. After such a cutting it is neither necessary nor desirable to rake the lawn, for the short mowings will filter down among the grass and help create a mulch over the roots. Properly managed lawns should thus need no raking. But if the grass has gone too long and the cutting is consequently heavy, it will have to be raked off or caught in one of the mowers fitted with a device to catch lawn mowings. See TOOLS AND IMPLEMENTS. In either case do not destroy the clippings, as they are valuable for the com-

---

* Special articles on the subjects indicated by an asterisk (*) will be found at the words so marked.

post pile. *See* COMPOST. The lawn should be mown as late in the season as growth continues.

FEEDING AND WATERING. Grass exhausts plant food just as do other crops. To overcome this it is well to top-dress the lawn twice a season with a 4–8–4 fertilizer (*see* FERTILIZERS), but do not use more than about 15 lbs. per 1000 sq. ft. Rake it in thoroughly, preferably before a rain. Top-dressing with even well-rotted stable manure is not recommended because it will be certain to bring in a lot of weed seeds. If the lawn needs humus, and few lawns don't, it is far better to cover it with about ¾ in. of a prepared, neutral, weed-free commercial humus. *See* HUMUS. Rake it in thoroughly, as its chief value is down at the base of the plant. Such humus is not a substitute for plant food — it simply does very well the job of creating a humus layer where the grass needs it most. Twice a season ought to be enough.

If you live in a region of adequate summer rainfall and have made your lawn on a proper depth of topsoil, it ought not to need watering except in some period of extreme summer heat and drought. Such a statement does not apply to any creeping-bent lawns, which need pretty constant watering to keep them in fine condition. It is also true that if the lawn is in the middle of a city or any other built-up area, the heat and dryness of such a condition may make watering a necessity.

The principles of lawn sprinkling are extremely simple. Mere surface sprinkling is worse than useless, for it encourages the grass roots to seek moisture near the surface and thus makes constant sprinkling a necessity, or the roots will otherwise dry out.

If watered at all, a lawn should be so thoroughly soaked that the soil will be wet through down to where the grass roots ought to be — 7–8 in. below the surface. One such thorough watering is of the greatest benefit during a long dry spell. Watering in such a way would not need to be done more than once a week, but it takes a lot of time to move sprinklers or a hose in such a way as to cover a whole lawn. Use only sprinklers or a movable hose nozzle that cast a fine, mist-like spray, and run them as much as possible in the early morning, late evening, or during the night. Mid-day sprinkling wastes a lot of water through evaporation.

LIME. Many amateurs top-dress their lawn every year or so with a sprinkling of lime. There is no evidence that this does any particular good, and it may do harm. The proper time to use lime is when the soil is being prepared for a lawn and only then if its reaction is acid. *See* the account of lawn soils above.

WEEDS AND REPAIR. A well-kept lawn, sown thickly enough to make a fine sward, ought to have no weeds — an ideal seldom, if ever, attained. Weed seeds will inevitably blow in and they must be coped with or they will soon make an unsightly place of the lawn.

All annual weeds are taken care of by constant mowing, which prevents their ever flowering or seeding unless they are the prostrate sorts that hug the ground so closely that no mower will reach them. Most perennials, unless they are of the prostrate type, are similarly prevented from seeding by constant mowing. Few weeds will stand steady mowing, but a few deep-rooted perennials will, and it is these that make the most trouble. Dock, dandelion, and any other weed with a deep taproot will not be starved by any number of mowings. Such should be cut off as deeply as possible below ground with an asparagus knife or an old carving knife. Fill up all holes so made with soil or, better yet, with the mixture mentioned below, for any general repairing of the lawn.

If weeds are numerous and of the broad-leaved type, some of the commercial weed killers may be used. *See* WEEDS AND WEEDING.

To repair holes made by removed weeds, or to fill up ruts made by careless motorists, it is well to keep in the tool house a dry mixture of ½ fine topsoil and ½ grass seed, thoroughly mixed. Fill up all depressions with this, tamp it down, and water it gently but thoroughly. There is no cure for weeds so good as more grass, and careful people keep this mixture handy and use it frequently.

Prostrate weeds that spread in spite of mowing often make patches in the lawn. The only real remedy is to rake or dig them out and re-seed. *See also* Lawn Troubles below.

LAWN TROUBLES

In spite of the greatest care there are still things that can make a lawn unsightly. A few of them and their remedies are suggested below.

BLACK ANTS. For control pour a teaspoonful of carbon bisulphide into small holes punched 2 in. deep, spaced about 12–18 in. apart, and plug with moist soil to prevent evaporation. Carbon bisulphide is poisonous and explosive.

GRUBS. The larvae of the common June bug often destroy considerable areas of turf before their presence is noted. For control apply, only when grass is dry, 5 lbs. of lead arsenate, mixed with 1 peck of dry loam to each 1000 sq. ft., and rake it in with a bamboo rake.

MOLES. These often make unsightly, ridged tunnels in even the finest lawns. Once they have been eradicated the ridges should be tamped down and depressions refilled before reseeding. To eradicate moles traps are the best of the older methods (*see* Moles at ANIMAL INJURY), but recently, chemical controls have proved useful, especially one or two trade-marked products which may be purchased from dealers.

SPOTS IN THE LAWN. Sometimes brownish spots from a foot across to several times that will appear in a lawn. If they first show in periods of drought, they are probably caused by a boulder too close to the surface or by some rubbish under the topsoil which destroys capillarity. The only remedy is to water such spots copiously.

If such spots appear in moist weather or after protracted watering, they are nearly always caused by a fungus disease, of which there is a general discussion at the end of the article on GRASSES.

MOSS IN THE LAWN. In some lawns, particularly partly shady ones, there are often encroachments of mosses which carpet the ground to the exclusion of grass. Often they are attractive enough to leave alone, but if they are to be replaced by grass, comb out all moss with a steel rake or dig it out. Fill in with fresh topsoil of which about ⅙ of its bulk is ordinary agricultural lime. Then re-seed thickly and be sure to water and look after such spots especially. Do not use on them any fertilizer containing much nitrogen, but instead sow some common white clover. If fertilizer is necessary — it should not be if fresh soil has been added — top-dress only with fertilizers containing mostly phosphoric acid. Later, when the trouble has been corrected, ordinary treatment can be resumed.

SLOPES. It is impossible to seed successfully slopes too steep to hold the soil while the grass is germinating. For such places sodding is the only remedy. For details of this *see* TURF. If the bank is too steep for sod, then some other plant will have to be used and the soil held in place while it captures the place. For details of this *see* BANKS. For a simple method of repairing holes or edges of lawns by turfing them *see* the illustrations at TURF.

**LAWN-BOY.** A patented power lawn mower.

**LAWNCOMB.** *See* Section 3, TOOLS AND IMPLEMENTS.

**LAWN GAMES.** For the minimum space requirements *see* BADMINTON, BOWLING GREEN, CROQUET and TENNIS.

**LAWN MIXTURES.** *See* LAWN.

**LAWN MOWER.** *See* Section 3, TOOLS AND IMPLEMENTS.

**LAWN MOWINGS.** *See* COMPOST.

**LAWN SAND.** A combination weed killer and fertilizer containing sulphate of iron. *See* WEEDS.

**LAWN SHEARS.** *See* Section 3, TOOLS AND IMPLEMENTS.

**LAWS OF HEREDITY.** *See* HEREDITY.

**LAWSONIA** (law-sō'nĭ-a). A single species of often spiny shrubs of the family Lythraceae, **L. inermis,** the mignonette-tree, the leaves of which are the source of henna. It is a native of northern Af., Asia, and Aust., and is virtually unknown as an outdoor plant in the U.S., but is sometimes

---

*Special articles on the subjects indicated by an asterisk (*) will be found at the words so marked.

cult. in greenhouses for interest. it has opposite,* short-stalked leaves, more or less lance-shaped and about 1 in. long. Flowers heavily fragrant, usually white but sometimes red or rose-pink, about ¼ in. wide, borne in a loose terminal cluster (panicle*). Fruit a capsule about ¼ in. in diameter. Can be grown outdoors only in zones* 8 and 9. (Named by Linnaeus for John Lawson, a traveler in N. Car. who was burned by the Indians.)

**LAXA, -us, -um** (lack'sa). Loose and open, as are many flower clusters.

**LAYERING.** Propagation by layering is the rooting of branches of woody plants while they are still attached to the parent plant. In nursery practice this method is used especially with varieties which have to be propagated vegetatively because they do not come true from seeds, and which are slow or unsatisfactory to grow from cuttings or grafts. For the amateur this simple and safe method is of particular importance, since it necessitates no special equipment and no great skill or experience is required to succeed with it.

There are only two main requirements, and both can be easily met in the garden. First: The soil, which in the various methods described below is used to cover the shoots which are to be rooted, must be loose and powdery so that it can be packed tightly without leaving air spaces; and it must be rich in humus to induce root formation. Second: The layered plants must be watered regularly in dry weather, since satisfactory root development will take place only in soil which is sufficiently moist.

PREPARATIONS. The nurseryman takes care of these needs by planting a special block of mother-plants which are used only for layering, and by selecting for them a low-lying place where rich humus soil is present. This place is plowed deeply in the fall after manure has been spread. In the spring healthy young plants are set out, far enough apart to allow ample room for the layering operation. The rows are carefully cultivated and weeded, for two or three years, after which the mother-plants will be strong enough to be ready for layering. The amateur, in most cases, will want to utilize an old established plant without moving it from its present locality. His practice will vary from that of the nurseryman also in that he will usually want to raise only a few layers from one shrub. Also he will not wish to ruin the shape and beauty of the mother-plant, while the nurseryman utilizes his mother-plants to the fullness of their capacity for a number of years; then he discards them and starts again with young plants. With most plants the best results are obtained only with strong one-year-old shoots. Where these are not present, their production must be induced. The nurseryman does this by cutting his mother-plants down to ground level and afterwards removing all weak growth which may develop. The amateur will always have a few suitable young shoots on his older plants, if he has pruned them regularly and has cared for them with proper feeding and watering. If neglected old shrubs, without suitable young growth, are the only specimens available for layering, they must first be restored to vigor by sharp pruning, cutting out all old and weak growth, and by feeding them liberally with manure.

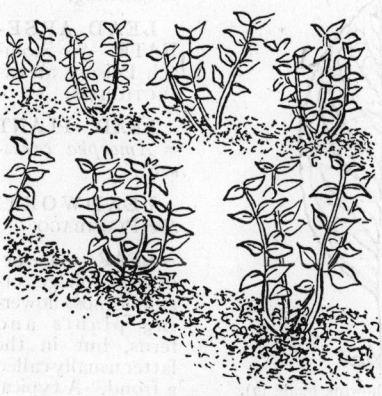

Preparing young shrubs for layering.
For details *see* text.

BEST TIME FOR LAYERING. True layering, for which the shoots of the previous season are used, always has to be done in the early spring, as soon as the ground can be worked and before growth has started. Mound or Stool Layering, as far as it uses the growth of the current season, has to wait until the young shoots are at least a few inches long.

### 1. TRUE LAYERING

SIMPLE LAYERING, which results in one plant from each layer. In this operation only the upper end of the shoot is buried in a slit in the ground which is made by inserting the spade about six inches deep and moving it back and forth a few times. The distance of the slit in the ground from the plant depends upon the length of the shoot. The shoot must be bent down as flat as possible. To avoid its tearing off at the base it is advisable to bend it in the opposite direction from that in which it grows and to twist it slightly when bending it. The shoot is anchored in the ground with a forked branch or a bent willow twig or a piece of wire.

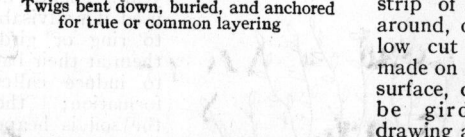

Twigs bent down, buried, and anchored for true or common layering

After that its tip is turned up sharply again and the slit in the ground is closed tightly over the bent shoot with a stamp of the foot. The tip should protrude at least three inches above the surface.

To facilitate rooting the shoot may be ringed by removing a narrow strip of bark all around, or a shallow cut may be made on its undersurface, or it may be girdled by drawing a piece of wire tightly around it. The best place at which to induce callus* formation by such an injury is — facing the plant — shortly behind the upward bend of the tip.

Strong shoots of the previous season are used in this method, which succeeds with a large variety of shrubs. Only with *Rhododendron*, *Azalea*, etc., which do not produce this type of shoot, are old branches bent to the ground. The two- to three-year-old twigs are then drawn into the soil and buried at least four inches deep, or to the base of the previous year's growth. In Europe, and sometimes here, the whole plant of rhododendron is dug up, replanted flat on the ground with the top spread fanwise, which provides much more layering material.

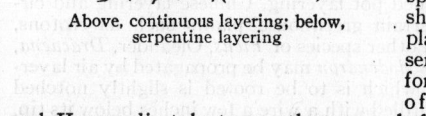

Above, continuous layering; below, serpentine layering

In the late fall of the same year the layered branches of most varieties will be rooted and should be severed from the mother-plant. The young plants, however, may be left where they are until spring, when they should be transplanted to the nursery. Some layers, for instance, those of *Rhododendron* and *Hamamelis*, take two or three years before they develop sufficient root system to make it safe to sever them from the parent plant.

---

* Special articles on the subjects indicated by an asterisk (*) will be found at the words so marked.

CONTINUOUS LAYERING, which results in several plants from each shoot. In this method, practiced in particular with varieties of *Acer negundo*, *Acer saccharinum* and some viburnums, the whole shoot is laid down flat in a shallow trench, running radially from the plant. The trench is left open until the buds have grown into 4–5 inch shoots, after which it is gradually filled with good humus soil. A shallow cut on the underside of the shoot at each node* will facilitate rooting.

SERPENTINE LAYERING, as practiced in particular with *Wistaria*, climbing honeysuckles, *Clematis* and other vines, is very similar to continuous layering. But in this case the shoot is not laid down flat but is bent up and down in a serpentine, always burying one node* and leaving the next above ground.

ARCHING LAYERS or TIP LAYERING is practiced especially with *Forsythia*, black raspberries and blackberries, which are by nature inclined to root at the tips of their branches. In their case all that is necessary is to peg the tips to the ground so that wind swaying cannot interfere with their rooting.

### 2. MOUND OR STOOL LAYERING

This method is employed mainly with low bushy shrubs, such as: *Ribes alpinum*, *Spiraea bumalda*, *Prunus glandulosa*, *Prunus nana*, Japanese quince, etc., but it is rather successful also with *Hydrangea paniculata*, *Aesculus parviflora*, *Tilia tomentosa*, *Cornus alba sibirica*, hybrid magnolias and for deciduous azaleas.

In mound layering, as contrasted with true layering, the shoots are not laid down but are left to grow upright, and in this position are buried eight to ten inches deep in rich humus soil. If last year's shoots are used, it is advisable to ring or girdle them at their base to induce callus* formation; then the soil is heaped up around and packed well between them. This operation is carried out in early spring before growth has started. The treatment of the rooted shoots is the same as recommended under true layering.

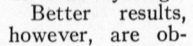
**Mound layering**

Better results, however, are obtained in this method with the shoots of the current season which have to be buried in three successive stages as they extend in length. Three or four inches of soil is added each time. No ringing is needed in this case.

STUMPING, as practiced, for instance, with the large-fruited blueberries, is very similar to mound layering. Old shoots are cut off at ground level, and a mixture of peat and sand is heaped over the stumps to a depth of four inches. The sand, through which the young shoots have to push their way, may be held in place with a board frame and must be kept continually moist to assure success.

### 3. AIR LAYERING

This is also called pot layering, Chinese layering and circumposition. Certain greenhouse plants such as crotons, rubber-plant and other species of *Ficus*, Oleander, *Dracaena*, etc. as well as *Rhododendron* may be propagated by air layering. The shoot which is to be rooted is slightly notched with a knife or girdled with a wire a few inches below its tip, and at this place sphagnum moss, which must be kept continually moist, is tied around it and is covered with oil-paper. One may also cut a flower pot lengthwise through the center, tie the two halves around the stem and fill them with peat moss or sphagnum. As soon as sufficient roots have developed, the moss is removed, the stem is severed below the new roots, and the young plant is potted in suitable soil. — H. T. See also PROPAGATION.

**Air layering.** *See text for details.*

**LAYIA** (lay'ĭ-a). A genus of mostly Californian herbs of the family Compositae, comprising perhaps 15 species, two of which are popular flower garden annuals grown for their showy flower heads. Leaves alternate,* generally without marginal teeth. Flower heads solitary, the stalks terminal. Ray* flowers handsome, 8–20, yellow or white and 3-toothed. Disk* flowers tubular. (Named for George T. Lay, a naturalist on Beechey's voyage.)

Both are hardy annuals and should be grown as such. See ANNUALS.

**elegans.** Tidy-tips. A branching, hairy herb, 1–2 ft. high in the wild, usually less in cult. Leaves very narrow, 1½–3 in. long. Heads showy because the usually yellow ray* flowers are each tipped with white. Calif. Summer.

**glandulosa.** White daisy. Not much branched, the stem sticky-hairy. Leaves lance-shaped or narrower, not over 1½ in. long. Flower heads nearly 1½ in. wide, the rays white or rarely pinkish-rose. British Columbia to Idaho and Mex.

**LAYING OUT AN ORCHARD.** *See* FRUIT CULTURE.

**LEACHING.** Rain-water has the power to dissolve out many chemical substances in the surface soil and carry them in solution to greater depth. While it is practically impossible to measure such losses, they should not be lost sight of in maintaining soil fertility, especially in irrigated districts. *See* IRRIGATION. Serious effects of leaching, however, are not experienced outdoors, but in potted or tubbed specimens. Few amateurs water such with sufficient care to prevent some water passing out of drainage holes at the bottom. Every scrap of such excess water carries with it some appreciable amount of plant food from the soil. Overwatering thus makes for soil exhaustion in potted plants, due wholly to leaching.

**LEAD ARSENATE.** *See* Stomach Poisons at INSECTICIDES.

**LEAD PLANT** = *Amorpha canescens*.

**LEADWORT.** *See* PLUMBAGO.

**LEAF.** The ordinary foliage organ of most flowering plants and ferns, but in the latter usually called a frond. A typical leaf comprises an expanded blade, a

A complete leaf showing blade (*a*), petiole or leaf stalk (*b*), and stipules (*c*).

stalk (the petiole*), and often a pair of small bract*-like, leafy organs at the base of the stalk known as stipules. Leaves may

---
* Special articles on the subjects indicated by an asterisk (*) will be found at the words so marked.

# LEAF-AXIL      439      LEECHEE

be simple* or compound,* depending upon whether there is a single blade or whether it is split into any number of leaflets (which see). The shape, veining, etc., of leaves have great value in the classification of plants as does their method of arrangement. Some, like the mint family, have only opposite* leaves. In others leaves are always alternate.* For the function of leaves and for their use in the garden see LEAVES.

**LEAF-AXIL.** See AXIL.

**LEAF BEET** = *Beta vulgaris cicla*. See BEET.

**LEAF BEETLE.** See Beetle at INSECT PESTS. See also Insect Pests at BLUEBERRY.

**LEAFBLIGHT.** See Diseases at CALCEOLARIA, STRAWBERRY, QUINCE, and CUCUMBER.

**LEAFBUD CUTTINGS.** See CUTTINGS.

**LEAF CURL.** See Diseases at PEACH and RASPBERRY.

**LEAF CUTTING.** See CUTTINGS.

**LEAFHOPPER.** See True Bugs at INSECT PESTS. See also the Insect Pests at GRAPE, CALLISTEPHUS, POTATO, and PEANUT.

**LEAFLET.** One of the ultimate segments of a compound* leaf. Typical examples are the leaflets of the ash, hickory, rose, or poison ivy. See COMPOUND.

**LEAF MINER.** See Two-winged Flies and Moths at INSECT PESTS.

**LEAF MOLD.** See HUMUS.

**LEAF MUSTARD** = *Brassica juncea*.

**LEAF NEMATODE.** See Diseases at BEGONIA.

**LEAF-ROLL.** See Virus Diseases at PLANT DISEASES, and see also Diseases at POTATO.

**LEAF ROLLER.** See Insect Pests at APPLE, CANNA, and STRAWBERRY.

**LEAF-SCORCH.** See Environmental Influences at PLANT DISEASES.

**LEAFSPOT.** See Diseases at CARNATION, CLEMATIS, DAHLIA, HOLLYHOCK, IRIS, LILY-OF-THE-VALLEY, and STRAWBERRY.

**LEAFSTALK.** A petiole.*

**LEAF TIER.** See Insect Pests at ANEMONE, CALCEOLARIA, CELERY, and CHRYSANTHEMUM.

**LEATHER BUSH** = *Dirca palustris*.

**LEATHERLEAF.** See CHAMAEDAPHNE.

**LEATHERWOOD** = *Fremontia californica*. See also DIRCA.

**LEAVES.** The functional importance of leaves cannot be overstated. Their green coloring-matter or chlorophyll is the only substance in the world that can make starch or sugar, both primary products in the economy of all plants as well as of man. Chlorophyll accomplishes this quite complicated chemical feat only in the presence of light, air, and the plant foods that have been derived from the soil. Leaves thus are of enormous importance to the gardener, quite apart from their beauty or diversity of coloring, for upon their proper functioning, free from wilting, disease, or smoke, depends all the subsequent transformations of the primary food they alone can make. In other words, flowers, fruits, seeds, wood, gums, resins, rubber, and hundreds of other plant products would be impossible without the normal functions of leaves. For the uses of fallen leaves in the garden see MULCH and COMPOST.

**LEBBEK** (leb'beck). Arabian vernacular for the siris (*Albizzia lebbek*).

**LECHEGUILLA** (letch-e-gweel'ya). Adapted from the Mexican vernacular *lechuguilla*, the name of a fiber-yielding *Agave*.

**LECHUGUILLA** (letch-ee-gweel'ya) = *Agave lechuguilla*.

**LECYTHIDACEAE** (les-i-thi-day'see-ee). Exclusively tropical trees, comprising 18 genera and perhaps 250 species. The family is of no garden interest, except for *Bertholletia* (the Brazil-nut) and *Barringtonia*, a handsome white-flowered tree from India. Both are rarely cult. in large greenhouses, or outdoors in the warmer parts of Calif. and Fla.

Leaves alternate,* but often crowded towards the ends of the branchlets. Flowers (in the cult. genera) in clusters (racemes*), white and showy in *Barringtonia*, less so in *Bertholletia*. Fruit a hard woody pod in *Bertholletia* with thick walls. Inside are 18–24 nuts (Brazil-nuts). The fruit of *Barringtonia* is a large berry with one oily seed.

Technical flower characters: Flowers regular.* Sepals 4 or 6, sometimes replacing lacking petals. Petals (when present) 4 or 6. Stamens numerous, in several series or groups. Ovary inferior,* 2 or more-celled.

**LEDIFOLIA, -us, -um** (lee-di-fō'lĭ-a). With leaves like the genus *Ledum* (which see).

**LEDUM** (lee'dum). A small but interesting genus of bog shrubs of the heath family, all the cult. species suited only to very acid sites in the bog garden. They have alternate,* evergreen, short-stalked leaves, without teeth, but with the margins often rolled, and generally sticky-hairy or felty on the under side. Flowers small, white, in umbel*-like, terminal clusters. Petals 5, spreading. Stamens* 5–10. Fruit a capsule.* (*Ledum* is the Greek name for the plants now put in the genus *Cistus*, very different plants from *Ledum*.)

All these can only be grown well in the bog garden, either in sphagnum moss or wet peat with an acidity reaction of pH 4.00–5.00 (see ACID AND ALKALI SOILS). All are shrubs of the colder parts of the north temperate zone and should not be grown in regions of long, hot summers. Propagated by spring-sown seeds or by division. The second and third species may often be transplanted from cold mountain bogs.

**columbianum.** A shrub 4–5 ft. high, the leaves oblong, 1½–2½ in. long, the margins only slightly rolled. Flowers white, the petals nearly round. Stamens* 5–7. Capsule* oblongish, under ½ in. long. May–June. Wash. to Ore. Hardy from zone* 5 and northward, but not in the East where the summers are too dry for it.
**groenlandicum.** Labrador tea. An upright bog shrub scarcely over 3 ft. high, its oblongish leaves 1½–3 in. long, rusty-hairy beneath and with the margins strongly rolled. Flowers about ¾ in. wide, white, the petals oblong. Capsule about ⅜ in. long. In cold bogs, Greenland to Pa. and westward. Hardy from zone* 4 northward. May–June. Often called *L. latifolium*.
**latifolium** = *Ledum groenlandicum*.
**palustre.** Wild rosemary; also called crystal tea. An upright bog shrub, never much over 3 ft. high. Leaves oblongish or narrower, ¾–2 in. long, the margins strongly rolled, the under surface rusty-hairy. Flowers ½–¾ in. wide, the petals oval. Fruit scarcely ⅓ in. long. Cold bogs throughout the north temperate zone and northward to the Arctic Circle. May–June. Hardy from zone* 3 northward. The var. **decumbens** is a more or less prostrate form with narrower leaves.

**LEEA** (lee'a). A small genus of tropical Old World shrubs and trees of the family Vitaceae, hence related to the grape but not vine-like. They are grown, only occasionally, in the greenhouse; still more rarely outdoors in zones* 8 and 9. Leaves alternate,* compound,* the leaflets arranged feather-fashion. Flowers greenish or yellowish, not showy, arranged in small clusters (cymes*). For details of flower structure see VITACEAE. Fruit a berry. (Named for James Lee, Scotch nurseryman.)

The plants are grown primarily for their beautiful foliage and need a tropical greenhouse (see GREENHOUSE) and potting mixture* 4. The chief growth is in spring and early summer; during the winter the plants should be partially rested by reducing their water and giving them less heat.

**amabilis.** Leaflets 5–7, more or less lance-shaped, toothed, green and bronzy, but white-striped and with white veins. Borneo. The var. **splendens** has red-marked leaves.
**sambucina.** Leaves twice-compound,* the ultimate leaflets toothed, bronzy but variegated or veined red. Aust. and tropical As.

**LEECHEE** = *Litchi chinensis*.

---
\* Special articles on the subjects indicated by an asterisk (*) will be found at the words so marked.

**LEEK** (*Allium porrum*). A hardy, onion-like plant, but milder than the onion and more hardy. Both the rather soft bulb and the leaves are used in cooking. It may be grown like the onion (which see), but in mild parts of the country it may stand out all winter and be harvested as needed. Often the lower part of the plant is blanched by hilling up the soil around it, especially at the approach of cold weather. If the weather gets very severe in the winter, leeks may be dug and stored in a cool, frost-free cellar, preferably being heeled-in.* See also HERB GARDENING for further details.

**LEGGY.** A common term in hort. for a plant that becomes gawky or "too long in the leg" from over-feeding, or often, in the greenhouse, from being too far from the glass. It is a common condition, too, among vegetable plants like tomatoes, which have been crowded too much in youth. The energy which should have produced a stocky plant has gone into making a spindling, leggy one. It can usually be corrected by pinching, or, in the greenhouse, by growing the plants nearer the glass.

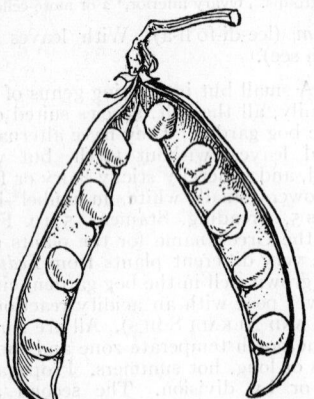

The common pea pod is a typical legume.

**LEGUME.** Typically a pea pod, a type of fruit that splits into two valves and has the seeds attached to the lower seam. See LEGUMINOSAE.

**LEGUME INOCULATION.** Many plants of the pea family will not grow satisfactorily unless the bacteria usually associated with their root tubercles is in the soil or can be put there. Often the organism is found in the soil due to the residue from a former crop. However, it is safer to buy cultures of the particular bacteria of each leguminous crop needing them. These cultures are sold by commercial firms and by some Experiment Stations, with specific directions for their use. They are particularly valuable for soils upon which, for the first time, the following crops are to be grown: soybeans, sweet clover, alfalfa, cowpea, and some clovers.

**LEGUMES.** A group name for many plants of the pea family or Leguminosae, usually and perhaps best restricted to those with edible pods or seeds like pea, bean, lentil, etc. It is often used to characterize any herbaceous plant of the pea family, such as vetch, clovers, alfalfa, etc. The legumes are often called pulse crops and they are of great economic importance. See LEGUMINOSAE for the different genera and their uses.

**LEGUMINOSAE** (le-gew-mi-nō'see). The pea family, as here considered, is perhaps the most important group of garden plants in the world. Its range and diversity are somewhat indicated by its having been variously called the bean, vetch, peanut, wisteria and locust family, while the botanists have, at times, called it Fabaceae and Papilionaceae.

Actually it includes three groups of plants, excluding non-hort. genera. All of these have been considered by some as separate families. They are the pea family itself, with typically pea-like flowers; the Mimosaceae, often called mimosa or acacia family, with small, not very pea-like flowers in dense clusters; and the Caesalpiniaceae, often called the senna, redbud, or tamarind family, which have nearly, but not quite, regular flowers. All of them have, as fruit, a pod or legume, of which the garden pea is the best example. But in many genera it is very small, in a few freakish genera it does not split (see HYMENAEA), and in many tropical trees it is an immense woody pod, although a true legume (which see).

Considering the Leguminosae as a whole there are over 450 genera and upwards of 10,000 species, worldwide in distribution and comprising (in the cult. genera) herbs, shrubs, vines and often gigantic trees. While the family is comparatively easy to recognize, the distinctions between even the cult. genera are mostly highly technical. The groups below are therefore wholly upon the basis of their use as garden plants for ornament or food, disregarding here the wide economic importance of the drugs, dyes, timbers, gums, oils, resins, etc., found in many non-hort. genera.

Leaves alternate* and typically compound* (sometimes reduced to a single leaflet) the leaflets arranged feather-fashion in some, as in wisteria, or finger-fashion in others like the lupines; sometimes twice- or thrice-compound, as in many acacias.

Three types of flowers in the pea family: acacia (*below*), sweet pea (*upper left*), and *Cassia* (*upper right*).

The flowers, usually very showy, are of three types. (1) Typically pea-like, with an upstanding petal (the standard* or vexillum*) two lateral ones (the wings) and two lower, more or less united petals which form the keel. (2) Not pea-like, but irregular enough to suggest it. This group comprises the genera formerly included in the Caesalpiniaceae. (3) Not pea-like, but small, regular* and often crowded in dense clusters. This group is considered by many as the family Mimosaceae.

There are technical differences between the three groups based upon the stamens. In (1) the 10 stamens are in two groups, a single one free and the other nine united into a tube (monadelphous*). In (2) there are 10 or less stamens, all free (not united). In (3) the stamens are usually more than 10 and all free or united in groups.

There are nearly a hundred cult. genera of the Leguminosae. All of them have root tubercles, which, with the aid of certain bacteria, allow the plants of this family to absorb free nitrogen from the air. It is this faculty which makes alfalfa, clover, vetch and some tropical genera such valuable cover crops. For centuries before this relationship was discovered, they had been plowed into the land for enrichment, a practice still as sound as when the Romans did it. See LEGUME INOCULATION, GREEN MANURING.

The genera below (not including some relatively unimportant ones entered at their proper place in the DICTION-

---

* Special articles on the subjects indicated by an asterisk (*) will be found at the words so marked.

ARY) are grouped wholly upon their use in the garden or for food. To help the student, each genus has a number, corresponding to the groups in the discussion of the flowers. They are:

(1) Pea tribe or family proper (the old Papilionaceae or Fabaceae)
(2) Senna tribe or family (the old Caesalpiniaceae)
(3) Mimosa or acacia tribe or family (the old Mimosaceae)

It will be noted that some genera are in two or more groups.

I. EDIBLE PLANTS.
  *Arachis* (1) (see PEANUT), *Cajanus* (1), *Cicer* (1), *Lens* (1) (see LENTIL), *Pachyrhizus* (1), *Phaseolus* (1), *Pisum* (1) (see PEA), *Psophocarpus* (1), *Vicia* (1), *Vigna* (1), *Ceratonia* (2) (see CAROB), *Tamarindus* (2).

II. FORAGE OR COVER CROPS GROWN MOSTLY FOR ANIMAL FOOD OR FOR SOIL IMPROVEMENT BY PLOWING IN.
  *Glycine* (1) (see SOYBEAN), *Lotus* (1), *Medicago* (1) (includes alfalfa), *Melilotus* (1), *Onobrychis* (1), *Trifolium* (1) (see CLOVER), *Vicia* (1), *Trigonella* (1).

III. GARDEN FLOWERS, MOSTLY ANNUALS* OR PERENNIALS.* Hardy outdoors over most of the country; but see individual genera for specific hardiness notes.
  *Anthyllis* (1), *Astragalus* (1), *Baptisia* (1), *Coronilla* (1), *Desmodium* (1), *Galega* (1), *Hedysarum* (1), *Lathyrus* (1), *Lespedeza* (1), *Lupinus* (1), *Ononis* (1), *Oxytropis* (1), *Petalostemon* (1), *Psoralea* (1), *Thermopsis* (1) and *Cassia* (2), but some of the latter are trees.

IV. SHRUBS, TREES OR WOODY VINES. Hardy outdoors over most of the country; but see some individual genera for specific hardiness notes.
  *Amorpha* (1), *Cladrastis* (1), *Colutea* (1), *Cytisus* (1) (see BROOM), *Laburnum* (1), *Maackia* (1), *Prosopis* (1) (see MESQUITE), *Robinia* (1) (see LOCUST), *Sophora* (1), *Spartium* (1), *Ulex* (1) (see FURZE), *Cercis* (2) (see REDBUD), *Gleditsia* (2) (see HONEY-LOCUST), *Gymnocladus* (2) and *Wistaria* (1).

V. VARIOUS TROPICAL PLANTS OF GREENHOUSE CULTURE, or grown outdoors only in zones* 8 and 9; mostly for ornament.
  *Adenocarpus* (1), *Abrus* (1), *Derris* (1), *Daubentonia* (1), *Dalbergia* (1), *Erythrina* (1), *Genista* (1), *Ormosia* (1), *Pueraria* (1), *Sesbania* (1), *Swainsona* (1), *Templetonia* (1), *Bauhinia* (2), *Cassia* (2), *Delonix* (2), *Hymenaea* (2), *Parkinsonia* (2), *Poinciana* (2), *Acacia* (3), *Albizzia* (3), *Leucaena* (3), *Mimosa* (3), and *Inga* (3).

For other genera, not mentioned above see: APIOS (1), CANAVALIA (1), CARAGANA (1), CENTROSEMA (1), CHORIZEMA (1), CLIANTHUS (1), CLITORIA (1), DOLICHOS (1), GLYCYRRHIZA (1) (see LICORICE), INDIGOFERA (1), RHYNCHOSIA (1), STIZOLOBIUM (1), ADENANTHERA (3) and PITHECOLOBIUM (3).

**LEGUMINOUS.** Bearing legumes* or belonging to the Leguminosae*; sometimes the term is used, rather loosely, for any pea-like plant.

**LEHIGH UNIVERSITY ARBORETUM.** See ARBORETUM.

*LEIMANTHOIDES* (lī-man-thoy'deez, but see OÏDES). Resembling the obsolete genus *Leimanthium* now referred to *Melanthium* (which see).

**LEIOPHYLLUM** (lȳ'o-fil'lum). Low, evergreen, North American shrubs of the heath family. They have small, glossy dark green leaves that may be opposite or alternate and attractive clusters of white flowers that are pink in bud. They are neat, compact shrubs worthy of cultivation, though sometimes difficult; suited to the rock garden or evergreen plantings. A moist, peaty and acid loam suits them well. Propagation by cuttings in midsummer or by seed. (*Leiophyllum* is from the Greek for smooth leaf, in allusion to the glossy foliage.) See WILD GARDEN.

**buxifolium.** Sand myrtle or sleek-leaf. Compact upright shrub about 18 in. high though sometimes more. Leaves usually alternate,* oval, smooth, to ½ in. long. Flowers white, in terminal clusters. They have 5 petals and 10 stamens. Fruit a many-seeded capsule. May to June. N.J. to Fla. Hardy from most parts of zone* 3 southward.

**lyoni.** Very much like the preceding species, and sometimes considered only a variety of it. It differs mainly in its low, dense and somewhat spreading habit; leaves usually opposite.* Mountains of N. Car. and Tenn.

**prostratum** = *Leiophyllum lyoni*.

**LEMAIREOCEREUS** (le-mare'ee-o-see-ree-us). A large genus of tree-like or shrubby, ribbed cacti, the plant body usually large, column-like, and mostly furnished with many stout spines. The group differs only in technical characters from *Cereus*. Flowers day-blooming, not very large, white, pink, or reddish, more or less bell-shaped or funnel-shaped, and not much flaring. Fruit fleshy, but in youth covered with spines. (Named for Charles Lemaire, Belgian student of the cacti, and *Cereus*.)

For culture see CACTI. All the cult. species, except *L. thurberi* need tropical desert conditions.

**griseus.** Trunk 1 ft. thick and 20–25 ft. high, or the plant sometimes branching from the base. Ribs 8–10, the spines needle-like. Flowers pinkish, about 3 in. long. Venezuela and islands in the vicinity.

**stellatus.** Joconostle. A shrub-like cactus 6–8 ft. high, mostly branching from the base, the branches 8–12-ribbed and bluish-green. Spines in clusters, the central ones longer and erect, the 10–12 lateral spines shorter. Flowers reddish, about 1½ in. long, slimly bell-shaped. Southern Mex.

**thurberi.** Pitahaya; also called sweet pitahaya. A tall cactus, 15–20 ft. high, usually branching from the base, the branches often 8 in. in diameter, and 12–17-ribbed. Spines long and needle-like. Flowers nearly 3 in. long, pinkish-purple, the petals white-margined. Southern Ariz. and Mex.

**weberi.** Cardon; also called candebobe. A huge cactus often 30 ft. high with innumerable erect branches which are mostly 10-ribbed. Spines in clusters of 1 central, erect, long spine and 6–12 smaller and lateral ones. Flowers nearly 4 in. long, white. Mex.

**LEMNA** (lem'na). Minute, floating, aquatic plants, commonly called duckweed, and the only cult. genus of the family **Lemnaceae** (lem-nay'see-ee). Outdoors they are frequently a nuisance as they may completely and rapidly cover the surface of a pool. They are, however, much prized in the aquarium (which see). They are minute stemless plants, without true leaves, these replaced by a tiny, floating, frond-like organ, beneath which are hair-like, short roots. Flowers and fruit practically microscopic. They are the smallest known flowering plants. (*Lemna* is an old Greek name for some water plant, but not certainly for this one.)

**LEMON.** Three kinds of lemons, all assigned to *Citrus limonia*, are grown in the United States; the common or acid lemon, the botanical variety or hybrid rough lemon, and the sweet lemon. The first named is the commercial fruit the culture of which is so important in California; the second is a vigorous-growing form much used for rootstock purposes in Florida; and the third, like the sweet lime with which it is often confused, is merely an interesting horticultural curiosity. The so-called Ponderosa, Chinese and Meyer lemons do not appear to be true lemons; the first two are probably lemon-citron hybrids, of little value, and the last a lemon-orange hybrid which is distinctly hardier to frost and also an acceptable substitute for the lemon.

COMMON OR ACID LEMON. The lemon, like the lime, is a tender evergreen sub-tropical tree which thrives in tropical and semi-tropical climates, and in true sub-tropical regions is grown only with the aid of irrigation. Its commercial culture is restricted to regions of sub-tropical climate because of the prevalence of diseases of the rind in regions of summer rainfall, and difficulties in "curing" the fruit; these result in a much lower quality of product. The lemon is slightly more frost-resistant than the lime but is distinctly tenderer than either the orange or grapefruit. While temperatures of 28° to 30° may apparently cause no injury, they are sufficient to occasion heavy shedding of the young fruits set from the fall bloom and this is the fruit which, maturing in spring and summer, normally brings the highest prices. Temperatures of 26° to 28° nearly always result in the killing of the young fruits and new growth; at lower temperatures the trees are seriously injured. For these reasons orchard heating is almost universal in the lemon districts of Cali-

---

* Special articles on the subjects indicated by an asterisk (*) will be found at the words so marked.

fornia (for details *see* FROST). The young fruits, and also those approaching maturity, are especially sensitive to sudden heat waves (temperatures of 95 to 100 degrees); with the former the effect produced is shedding, with the latter it is sunburn which may either destroy the fruit or render it virtually worthless. In this respect the lemon is even more sensitive than the lime. The rind of the fruit is easily bruised and the result is a scabby condition which detracts from its salability; for this reason comparative freedom from wind is necessary and wind protection is commonly employed (for details *see* WINDBREAKS). Because of its sensitiveness commercial culture of the lemon is restricted largely to the coastal region of southern California where the mild winters and cool summers make possible high yields and favor the production of fruit maturing in spring and summer.

Under favorable climatic conditions the lemon is almost everblooming and matures fruit continuously. There are two main periods of bloom, however, spring and fall, and two corresponding periods of peak production, winter and summer. The amount of fall bloom, and hence summer fruit, varies greatly and depends on the variety and climatic conditions. Many of the flowers are imperfect and non-functional, yet the number of normal flowers seems always to be sufficient to set satisfactory crops. There is no pollination problem for, like other citrus fruits, the lemon does not require seed formation for fruit-setting and development. Unpollinated flowers normally set seedless fruit; indeed the commercial varieties are seedless, or practically so, which is a highly desirable commercial characteristic.

PROPAGATION. The lemon is propagated by budding on seedling rootstocks; fall or dormant shield budding is the common and preferred method. The trees are usually planted as year old budlings, at which stage the root system ranges in age from 24 to 30 months. Until recently the rootstock most used has been the sour or Seville orange (*Citrus aurantium*), which is practically immune to the foot-rot and gummosis diseases. Widespread decline of young bearing trees of the Eureka variety in recent years, attributed to the use of this rootstock, has occasioned its virtual abandonment in favor of the sweet orange (*Citrus sinensis*), grapefruit (*Citrus paradisi*) and rough lemon rootstocks. There can be no doubt that all lemon varieties are somewhat dwarfed on the sour orange rootstock but satisfactory proof that it has caused the decline referred to is still lacking. The rough lemon rootstock appears very promising because of the vigor and early-bearing quality it confers on lemon varieties propagated on it, but must be regarded as still experimental in the absence of information concerning the longevity of the combination and the behavior of old trees. Sweet orange is today the safest rootstock to use. With all these rootstocks special precautions must be taken to prevent infection from the diseases above-mentioned; these include budding the rootstock seedlings high — 6 to 8 inches, the avoidance of planting too deep, special care in irrigation, and preventive soil treatments. The lemon topworks readily by budding or bark grafting, though the latter method is rarely used. For reasons as yet unknown lemon trees on sour orange rootstock are relatively short-lived when topworked to orange varieties.

SOILS. This fruit, like the other citrus fruits, has a wide range of soil adaptation, succeeding almost equally well on light soils and moderately heavy soils. Heavy and poorly-drained soils should be avoided because of its sensitiveness to excess moisture and the likelihood of root diseases. It is also highly sensitive to alkali salts and to borax, for which reason such soils should be avoided and only irrigation water of good quality be used. Because of its shallow root distribution, a depth of four feet of good soil, well-drained, will suffice.

PLANTING. Special care is required in the planting operations to prevent injury to the roots from desiccation. The use of balled nursery trees is almost universal in California and insures good results. Early spring is the best time for planting though it can be done at nearly any time of year, if balled trees are used. The best practice involves their heading, usually to a height of 24 to 30 inches, a few weeks before they are dug and balled. Planting distances range from 24 to 30 feet. *See* Ball and Burlap at PLANTING.

Irrigation and fertilization are the soil management practices of greatest importance. An adequate soil moisture supply must be maintained at all times and this usually requires from 4 to 10 irrigations per year; the amount applied per irrigation is approximately equivalent to 3 inches of rainfall. The total amount required is determined by the climate and the size and spacing of the trees; the period between irrigations depends on weather conditions and the nature of the soil. Both the furrow and basin methods are used; the former is the most widespread. *See* IRRIGATION. Fertilization is necessary to maintain satisfactory yields, and nitrogen is the only element the use of which has been shown to give results. Experience indicates that an adequate fertilization program consists of about 200 pounds of nitrogen per acre per year and 6000 pounds of decomposable organic matter. This represents an application of 10 tons of manure and 500 pounds of ammonium sulphate, or its equivalent as sodium or calcium nitrates. Winter green-manure crops are often grown; clover, vetch and mustard are the most common. Tillage is necessary only to turn under green-manure crops, weeds or fertilizers and to facilitate irrigation. The lemon requires more pruning than other citrus trees and is employed to provide a compact form, in order to minimize wind-injury, and to increase the amount of crop which reaches picking size while still immature. These are accomplished by shortening in to laterals and thinning.

The fruit is picked by clipping, while still immature and green, and held in storage until colored and ready for market. Coloring may be hastened by exposure to ethylene gas at high storage temperatures.

VARIETIES. The principal varieties in California are Eureka and Lisbon. The former is less vigorous but matures more of the crop during the spring and summer months. Villafranca is intermediate and of minor importance. The fruits are indistinguishable. Perrine, a lime-lemon hybrid of lemon characteristics, is now being planted in Florida.— R. W. H.

INSECT PESTS. Lemon is attacked by the same pests as are other citrus fruits, and control measures are similar (*see* ORANGE). Black scale, red scale, and mealybugs are especially important. For diseases, *see* ORANGE.

**LEMONADE SUMAC** = *Rhus trilobata.*

**LEMON BALM** = *Melissa officinalis.*

**LEMON DAYLILY** = *Hemerocallis flava.* See DAYLILY.

**LEMON GRASS** = *Cymbopogon citratus.*

**LEMON MINT** = *Monarda citriodora.*

**LEMON OIL.** A contact spray for aphis and scale insects; it is not one of those recommended at INSECTICIDES (contact sprays).

**LEMON-SCENTED GUM** = *Eucalyptus maculata citriodora.*

**LEMON THYME** = *Thymus serpyllum vulgaris.* See THYME.

**LEMON VERBENA** = *Lippia citriodora.*

**LEMON VINE** = *Pereskia aculeata.*

**LENS.** See LENTIL.

***LENTA, -us, -um*** (len′ta). Tough but pliant.

***LENTAGO*** (len-tā′go). Pre-Linnaean* name applied to the genus *Viburnum*; now the specific name of *V. lentago*.

**LENTEN ROSE** = *Helleborus niger.*

**LENTIBULARIACEAE** (len-tib-u-lair-ĭ-ā′see-ee). The bladderwort family, all aquatics or marsh herbs, comprises perhaps 10 genera and 250 species of widely distributed insectivorous plants. *Utricularia* is occasionally cultivated in aquaria or pools, mostly for its beautiful submerged foli-

---

* Special articles on the subjects indicated by an asterisk (*) will be found at the words so marked.

age, the fine flowers, or for its interesting method of catching insects. *Pinguicula*, which contains mostly marsh herbs, is sometimes grown in the rock garden. See INSECTIVOROUS PLANTS.

Leaves dissected into thread-like segments and submerged in *Utricularia*; more normal, but slimy and basal in *Pinguicula*, which is not submerged. Flowers, always produced above the water, showy, very irregular* and prominently 2-lipped.* Fruit a pod (capsule*). Stamens 2. Ovary superior,* 1-celled.

**LENTIL.** A pea-like, edible-seeded legume, much grown for food in Eu., but not often seen here. It belongs to the genus **Lens** (lenz′) of which there are only about a half-dozen species scattered along the Mediterranean region to western As. The only cult. species is the common lentil, **Lens esculenta**, a branching annual 10–18 in. high. Leaves compound,* the 4–14 leaflets arranged feather-fashion, oblongish or narrower, about ½ in. long. Flowers scarcely ¼ in. long, pea-like, whitish, usually only 1–3 on a slender stalk from the leaf-axil.* Pod (a legume*) nearly ¾ in. wide and long, its 2 seeds lens-like, dark-colored. Its culture is the same as for the pea (which see). (*Lens* is the classical name of the lentil, and the origin of the English word *lens*, so named from the shape of the seed.)

**LENT LILY.** See NARCISSUS.

**LEONOTIS** (lee-o-nō′tis). A genus of African herbs of the mint family, comprising a dozen species of which **L. leonurus**, the lion's-tail or lion's-ear, is the only one likely to be in cult. It is a shrub-like, perennial herb, 3–6 ft. high, or lower in a dwarf form, with a hairy stem and opposite,* oblongish or narrower leaves, 1–2 in. long, and coarsely toothed. Flowers (in ours) yellow or orange-red (white in a hort. form), in dense clusters (whorls*) in the leaf-axils.* Corolla irregular* and 2-lipped, the lower lip with 3 nearly equal lobes. Stamens* 4, generally curved. Fruit a collection of 4 nutlets, surrounded by the 8–10-ribbed, persistent calyx.* As an outdoor subject the plant is hardy only south of zone* 7, but it can be cult. outdoors northward all summer and then brought into the cool greenhouse, where it will flower in Nov.–Dec. If the latter plan is followed, it is better to make cuttings in the early spring and, when rooted, grow the plants outdoors until the fall, when they must be brought into the cool greenhouse. (*Leonotis* is from the Latin for lion's ear, which the flowers are supposed to resemble.)

**LEONTOPODIUM.** See EDELWEISS.

**LEONURUS** (lee-o-new′rus). Eurasian, rather weedy herbs of the mint family, of little hort. importance, but **L. cardiaca**, the motherwort or lion's-tail, occasionally grown in the informal border for ornament, although it is a commonly naturalized weed over much of N.A. It is a coarse, perennial herb, 3–5 ft. high, with opposite,* more or less coarsely toothed or divided leaves, 2–4 in. long, the upper ones decidedly narrower than the lower. Flowers small, woolly on the outside, white, crowded in dense clusters (whorls*) in the leaf-axils. Stamens* 4. Fruit a collection of 4 small nutlets. Of very easy culture in any ordinary garden soil, and readily propagated by division. (*Leonurus* is from the Greek for lion's tail, and a Pre-Linnaean* name for the plant now known as *Leonotis leonurus*, which see.)

**LEOPARD FOXGLOVE** = *Digitalis purpurea maculata superba*. See FOXGLOVE.

**LEOPARD LILY** = *Lilium pardalinum*. See also SANSEVIERIA.

**LEOPARD MOTH.** See Insect Pests at MAPLE, LILAC, and ELM.

**LEOPARD PLANT** = *Ligularia kaempferi aureo-maculata*.

**LEOPARD'S-BANE** = *Senecio doronicum*. See also DORONICUM.

**LEPACHYS** (lep′ack-is). Coneflower. A genus of North American, somewhat weedy, perennial herbs of the family Compositae, occasionally grown in the flower border. Leaves alternate,* more or less divided finger-fashion. Flower heads solitary, the rays* yellow and showy, the tubular disk* flowers brownish and on a rounded or arched disk.* The genus is sometimes known as *Ratibida*. (*Lepachys* is from the Greek for thickened scale, in allusion to the thickened tips of the chaff.)

Both the plants below are of the easiest cult. in any ordinary garden soil. They are not particularly choice garden subjects, but are sometimes dug from the wild in their native region. Propagated by division.

**columnaris.** Prairie coneflower. A rough-hairy, perennial herb, 1½–2½ ft. high, its leaf segments narrow and line-like. Flower heads nearly 2 in. wide, yellow, the disk* very prominent and columnar. Central U.S. south to Mex. Summer. The *var.* **pulcherrima** has brownish-purple rays.* There is also a double-flowered form, more showy than the typical plant.

**pinnata.** Often up to 5 ft., the stem rough-hairy. Segments of the leaf lance-shaped, the leaf 3–5 in. long. Flower heads nearly 5 in. wide, yellow, sunflower-like, but the disk* oblong. Eastern N.A. Summer. A coarse but showy plant.

**LEPARGYREA** = *Shepherdia*.

**LEPIDIUM** (lep-id′ĭ-um). Pepper-grass. Nearly 100 species of widely distributed, weedy herbs of the mustard family, of little garden interest except for **L. sativum**, the garden or upland cress, which is an Asiatic annual herb, 1–2 ft. high. It is grown occasionally as a sharp-flavored salad plant. Leaves alternate,* the basal ones more or less cut and toothed, the upper narrower and without teeth. Some of the hort. forms (the chief ones grown) have curled or crisped leaves. Flowers white or greenish, very small, in a terminal cluster (raceme*). Fruit a roundish, somewhat notched, flattish pod (silicle*), the cluster elongating in age. One of the numerous plants known as cress, and, to distinguish it from watercress, often called upland cress. (*Lepidium* is from the Greek for a little scale, in allusion to the small fruits.)

*LEPIDOPHYLLA, -us, -um* (lep-id-o-fill′a). Having scaly leaves.

*LEPORELLA, -us, -um* (lep-o-rell′a). A little hare.

*LEPTANDRA VIRGINICA* = *Veronica virginica*.

*LEPTINELLA* = *Cotula*.

*LEPTOCAULIS, -e* (lep-to-kaw′lis). Thin-stemmed.

*LEPTODACTYLON.* See GILIA CALIFORNICA.

*LEPTOLEPIS, -e* (lep-tol′ĕ-pis). Thin-scaled.

*LEPTOPA, -us, -um* (lep′to-pa). Having a thin or weak stalk or stem.

*LEPTOPHYLLA, -us, -um* (lep-to-fill′a). Thin-leaved.

**LEPTOPYRUM** (lep-to-py′rum). A single species of Asiatic annual herbs of the family Ranunculaceae, grown in the flower garden for its fine foliage and white flowers. The only species, **L. fumarioides**, is a spreading, hardy annual, 6–8 in. high, its stem smooth. Leaves basal or on the stem, twice- or thrice-compound,* the segments narrow and fumitory-like. Flowers small (⅛ in. wide), white, without petals, but with 4–5 petal-like sepals.* Fruit a collection of small follicles.* The plant is not much grown, and is sometimes known as *Isopyrum fumarioides*. (*Leptopyrum* is from the Greek for thin pear, in allusion to the small fruit.)

*LEPTOSEPALA, -us, -um* (lep-to-see′pa-la). With thin sepals.*

**LEPTOSIPHON.** See LINANTHUS.

**LEPTOSPERMUM** (lep-to-sper′mum). Tea-tree (but it has nothing to do with the tea plant). Australasian shrubs and trees of the family Myrtaceae, comprising over 25 species, several of which are widely cult. in Calif. and elsewhere below zone* 7. Leaves alternate,* small, rigid, often almost prickle-like. Flowers numerous, but solitary or 2

---

* Special articles on the subjects indicated by an asterisk (*) will be found at the words so marked.

or 3 together in the leaf-axils,* white or reddish in those below. Calyx* more or less bell-shaped, its lobes 5. Petals 5. Stamens* many, not protruding. Fruit a leathery capsule.* (*Leptospermum* is from the Greek for slender or thin seed.)

*Leptospermum* is a popular genus in Calif. In Aust. *L. laevigatum* is widely planted for reclamation of shifting sand. They are of easy cult. in the right climate and are propagated by seeds, or by cuttings. Some of them are grown in the cool greenhouse, where they need potting mixture* 3. They should be kept there until Feb.–March, when the temperature be raised to 55°–60°, which will force them into bloom. In Calif. *L. laevigatum* is by far the most widely grown, although fine specimens of *L. scoparium* are to be seen in Golden Gate Park.

**flexuosum** = *Agonis flexuosa*.
**laevigatum.** Australian tea-tree. A tree up to 30 ft., usually shrubby as cult. Leaves very numerous, blunt, about 1 in. long and ½ in. wide. Flowers white, about ¾ in. wide. Aust. Widely planted in Calif.
**pubescens.** A usually silky-hairy shrub or small tree. Leaves about ⅓ in. long, blunt. Flowers white, nearly ¾ in. wide. Aust.
**scoparium.** Tea-tree, and the best-known species in cult., but not so commonly planted in Calif. as *L. laevigatum*. A tall shrub or small tree, 12–25 ft. high, or occasionally dwarf and only 1–2 ft. high, the foliage silky when young. Leaves very numerous, about ⅓ in. long, almost prickle-tipped. Flowers about ½ in. wide, white. N. Zeal. and Aust. Several varieties are cult., of which *var.* **bullatum** has larger flowers; *var.* **juniperinum** has drooping branchlets and narrower leaves; *var.* **nichollsi** has carmine flowers and bronzy foliage.

**LEPTOSYNE.** See COREOPSIS.

**LESPEDEZA** (les-pe-dee′za). Bush clover. A large genus of annual or perennial herbs or shrubs of the pea family common in N.A. and As., a few in Aust. Some are grown for their showy flower clusters, while *L. striata* is grown in the South for forage and green manuring (which see). They have alternate,* compound* leaves, with mostly 3 leaflets that are without marginal teeth. Flowers small, but showy from the profuse clusters, of two kinds in many species. One set is pea-like, showy, and usually sterile*; the other without petals but fertile. Fruit a very short pod (loment*), usually reduced to 1 joint, half hidden in the persistent calyx,* and with a single seed. (Named for a Governor Lespedez, once Spanish governor of Fla., by his friend Michaux.)

*Lespedeza bicolor* and *L. formosa* are Asiatic shrubs valued for their late bloom. They prefer open, rather sandy soils and are not difficult to grow. Both are propagated by cuttings. *L. capitata* is a somewhat weedy North American herb which will grow in the poorest soils, and may be increased by division. *L. striata*, the Japan clover, is an annual, suited only to the South, where seed may be sown in the early spring as for clover.

**bicolor.** A shrub 6–9 ft. high. Leaflets 3, ovalish, ¾–1½ in. long. Flowers purple, or rose-purple, the clusters (racemes*) grouped in a large, showy, branching cluster (panicle*). Eastern As. Aug.–Sept. Hardy from zone* 3 southward.
**capitata.** Bush or dusty clover. A perennial herb 3–5 ft. high, the foliage silvery and silky. Leaflets 3, oblongish. Flowers purple-spotted, but generally yellowish-white, not showy, in dense, head-like clusters. Summer. Sandy soil in eastern N.A.
**formosa.** A shrub 3–7 ft. high, but often dying to the ground each winter, hence herb-like. Leaflets 3, oblong-elliptic, the middle one longer-stalked than the other two. Flowers rose-purple, the clusters (racemes*) long and drooping. Eastern As, Sept.–Oct. (see AUTUMN GARDEN). Hardy from zone* 4, possibly from zone* 3 southward.
**striata.** Japan clover; also called hoop-coop plant. An annual herb not over 18 in. high, grown for forage and as green manure in the South. Leaflets many, scarcely ¾ in. long, nearly stalkless. Flowers pinkish-purple, small, only 1–3 in each leaf-axil.* China and Jap., sometimes naturalized in the southern states.

**LESQUERELLA** (les-kwe-rel′la). Western North American annual or perennial herbs of the mustard family, often called bladder-pod, only **L. engelmanni** of any garden interest. It is a perennial, tufted herb 12–18 in. high, the leaves chiefly basal, oblongish, mostly in rosettes. Flowers small, yellow, but very profuse in dense clusters (corymbs*), rather showy. Fruit a somewhat inflated, rather long-stalked pod (silicle*). Native from Colo. to N. Mex. and Tex., and uncommon in cult. (Named for Leo Lesquereux, a botanist famous for work upon fossil plants and mosses.)

**LESSER WINTERGREEN** = *Pyrola elliptica*.

**LETCHWORTH PARK ARBORETUM.** See ARBORETUM.

**LETTUCE** (*Lactuca sativa* and varieties). Crisp, tender lettuce, the most desirable of all salad plants, can only be grown with the strictest attention to its moisture, soil, and climatic requirements. Originally a Eurasian annual* (unknown in the wild state), the plant has been developed into many strains or races each having dozens of named forms or varieties.

For the home gardener lettuce may be divided into three categories: (1) Tight, crisp, nearly white head lettuce with a cabbage-like head. (2) Loose, so-called leaf lettuce where, although there is a head, it is looser, and with many more outer green leaves. (3) Cos or Romaine lettuce, which is cylindric, has long, relatively loose leaves and forms (in some varieties) a head without being tied up, but often it has to be tied.

The order in which these types are listed is no accident. The first is by far the most desirable, but the most difficult to grow. The second is less desirable, but so much easier to grow that most beginners will do well to select one of its varieties. The third is the easiest of all and the only type that makes any pretense of standing summer heat.

And heat is what all the really desirable varieties will not stand. They can easily endure several degrees of frost, especially in the seedling stage, which greatly facilitates the handling of lettuce in the early spring. It is in this respect more hardy than cabbage. But midsummer heat, more than several other things to be mentioned presently, will throw the plant into flower. This ruins its chance of heading, because the tall flower stalk (18 in. or more) is forced up through what should be the head.

It is obvious from this that lettuce is a cool-season crop only (except Cos lettuce), and is consequently grown in early spring and late summer, or in favored localities where it is cool all the growing season. Lettuce commercially produced in the South and California is grown in their winter season when only greenhouse culture (widely practiced) is possible in the North.

VARIETIES. The home grower can ignore the many varieties that shipping requirements and adaptability to greenhouse culture have developed. All of them are highly specialized sorts much favored by commercial growers in different sections of the country. For ordinary garden uses the best varieties are:

(1) HEAD LETTUCE (*i.e.* with a cabbage-like head). These have relatively few outside green leaves, and a hard, solid, crisp, white head: Big Boston. Unrivaled. White Boston. May King. New York.

(2) LEAF LETTUCE. These have many more outer green leaves, the head is not so compact and is white only towards its center: Grand Rapids (much favored for

Types of lettuce: (*a*) Crisped type of head lettuce; (*b*) a typical non-crisped head lettuce; (*c*) Cos or Romaine lettuce.

greenhouse culture, also). Black-seeded Simpson. Prize Head.

(3) COS LETTUCE. With loose, oblong, head-like clusters of spoon-shaped leaves: Express Cos and Paris White

---

* Special articles on the subjects indicated by an asterisk (*) will be found at the words so marked.

Cos, both of which will form well-blanched, whitish, but rather loose heads without being tied up. Bath Cos is a variety that will not head without being tied up. Cos lettuce is little grown, but is useful for a summer supply or in regions too hot to grow the two first types. Often called Romaine lettuce.

SOILS AND FERTILIZERS. Any good garden soil will grow lettuce of a sort. But the most favored soils are rich, sandy loams. Some varieties, like Grand Rapids, do best on heavy soils with considerable clay in them. Some of the largest commercial growers in the country use reclaimed muck soils, not because they are particularly fertile (this is greatly augmented by fertilizers), but because muck soils usually have abundant soil moisture, easily available by capillarity with proper handling. Lettuce soils should not be acid. If they are they should be limed. See LIME; see also MUCKLAND GARDENING.

More important than the texture is soil moisture. If this is not available, do not attempt to grow lettuce unless you can supply the needed moisture by irrigation or an overhead sprinkling system. Both methods are widely used by commercial growers.

Plenty of soil moisture will help to induce quick growth, and no slow-growing lettuce is any good. But it will only do so if the soil is rich in plant food. To make it so, plow in liberal supplies of well-rotted stable manure (not filled with straw) at the rate of 15–20 tons to the acre (5 or 6 wheelbarrow loads to 100 ft. of row). In addition use 1500 pounds to the acre of a good general purpose commercial fertilizer (about 5 pounds to 100 ft. of row). If you can use only one of these, try to make it the stable manure, for it adds much humus to the soil and thus heightens its moisture-holding capacity as well as enriching it.

Needless to say, almost, is the necessity of getting these materials thoroughly plowed under and the soil brought to as mellow a condition of tilth* as possible. Once the plants are set out, especially the spring crop of the head lettuce type, it will be a race against the arrival of hot weather in any case. Soil moisture, plenty of plant food and perfectly worked soil will greatly help to force lettuce to head before summer heat makes heading impossible.

STARTING LETTUCE PLANTS. Sowing lettuce seed should be timed so that they are transplanted to the garden just as soon as the ground can be worked. You need not wait for the last (usually erratic) frost of spring in order to set out the seedlings, because, especially in their early stages, they will easily endure several degrees of frost. Count, as your possible outdoor planting date, the average date when the last frost in your locality occurs (see name of your state for frost dates).

Having determined your earliest safe date for outdoor culture, allow 8 or 10 weeks before this to begin indoor operations. Start by sowing the seed broadcast or in tiny drills in flats or boxes in a cool greenhouse or hotbed. If you have neither, put the box in the kitchen window (no gas stove). Cover the seeds with about ¼ in. of finely sifted soil. In a few days the plants will be up and as soon as they are 2 in. high, they must be pricked-out and spaced about 2 in. each way. A second and third shifting, each more amply spaced, is advisable but not obligatory. Mice are fond of the seedlings and should be coaxed away with corn soaked in strychnine solution.

Gradually harden off the plants by reducing the temperature to something like those they must meet when shifted outdoors. This can easily be done in the hotbed or cold frame.

OUTDOOR PLANTING. The young seedlings are then set out in the garden, preferably on a dull day, and in any case, they must be watered until they recover from the move. Put the plants 10 in. apart in the rows and have the rows 14 in. apart. Keep a few seedlings to replace some, more or less certain, failures. Cultivation and adequate moisture should then do the rest. If you have been thorough, this crop should supply you with head lettuce before warm weather.

In addition to this, it is advisable to sow lettuce seed directly in the garden at about the time, or just after, the indoor plants have been set out. It can be sown broadcast or in very shallow drills, in either case covered very lightly with the finest soil which the rake will pulverize.

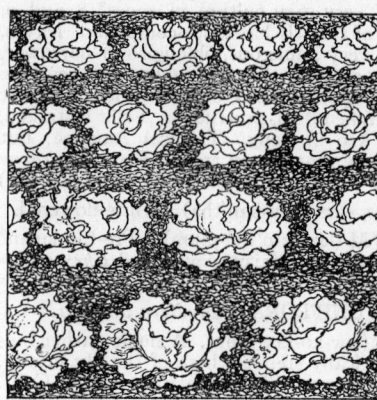

Good head lettuce, in rich soil, and properly spaced

Slightly tamp the soil and water it with a fine, mist-like spray (a hose stream without a fine nozzle will wash out the seeds). The plants will come up far too thick for permanent spacing. But as they grow they can be thinned to the intervals given above, and the thinnings are useful house greens.

In many favorable (i.e. cool) localities this outdoor-sown seed will provide good lettuce after the indoor plants have been harvested. And in especially cool regions a similar sowing may be made 12 days after the first. But in most regions summer heat puts a stop to all but one or two spring sowings.

For the fall crop exactly the same procedure is followed as for the early crop of indoor seedlings, except that the flats or boxes are put outdoors in a cool, shaded place. Young plants should be ready to set out about August 15 over most of the North.

In the Far North, lettuce may be grown throughout the brief, but cool growing season. This applies only to zones* 1 and 2, or to regions of great elevation and plenty of summer moisture (or irrigation). Both plants started indoors and outdoor-sown seed may be used, the latter sown about every 12 days for a succession.

For the preferred position and sequence of lettuce in your garden see KITCHEN GARDEN.

INSECT PESTS. Lettuce has few insect enemies, except general feeders. Leaf-feeding insects attack it occasionally. Arsenicals should only be used when the plants are very small, when there is no danger of poisoned leaves reaching the table. Derris or pyrethrum may be used on larger plants. Cutworms are sometimes troublesome; many kinds can be killed with bran bait sown thinly in the evening. In the greenhouse, aphids and other pests can be controlled by fumigation.

DISEASES. Lettuce drop, which manifests itself in a watery soft rot; bottom rot which destroys the lower leaves; and gray mold rot may be controlled in the greenhouse by sterilizing the soil with steam before planting. These and other maladies when occurring outdoors are more difficult to combat. Dusting an organic mercury compound on the ground, below the plants, two weeks before harvest will control bottom rot. Long rotations, destruction of diseased refuse, and getting seeds from healthy plants aid in controlling the other diseases. Some muck soils lack copper or other mineral which needs to be supplied for good growth of lettuce. In hotbeds downy mildew may be severe if proper ventilation is not arranged.

**LETTUCE FAMILY.** See COMPOSITAE.

**LEUCADENDRON** (lew-ka-den'dron). A large genus of South African shrubs and trees of the family Proteaceae, **L. argenteum,** the silver tree, widely planted in Calif. and similar climates for its beautiful silvery and silky foliage. Leaves scattered, without marginal teeth, but hard-tipped, 3–6 in. long, nearly stalkless. Male and female flowers on different plants, the male flowers numerous in dense, stalkless, head-like clusters, nearly 2½ in. wide. Female flowers in cone-like heads, beneath which is a series of woody bracts.* Both sorts of flowers have no petals, but 4 sepals. Fruit a nut. Propagated by seeds. (*Leucadendron* is from the Greek for white tree, in allusion to the silvery foliage. *Leucadendron* is also a specific name at *Melaleuca*.)

**LEUCAENA** (lew-see'na). Mostly tropical American shrubs and trees of the pea family, related to and somewhat

---

\* Special articles on the subjects indicated by an asterisk (\*) will be found at the words so marked.

resembling species of *Acacia*. The only cult. species, **L. glauca**, the white popinac, is an evergreen, spineless tree up to 30 ft. and of very easy culture in zones* 8 and 9, but not hardy north of this. It has twice-compound* leaves, the ultimate leaflets very numerous, oblongish or narrower, bluish-green or even grayish. Flowers white, not pea-like, crowded in a dense, globe-shaped cluster which is about 1 in. in diameter. Stamens* 10, protruding. Fruit a stalked, flat pod (legume*) 5–6 in. long. Tropical America, but naturalized and a somewhat weedy tree in Fla. (*Leucaena* is from the Greek for white, in allusion to the white flowers.)

**LEUCANTHA**, *-us, -um* (lew-kan'tha). White-flowered.

**LEUCANTHEMUM** (lew-kan'the-mum). Pre-Linnaean* name for the common white daisy, now called *Chrysanthemum leucanthemum*.

**LEUCOCORYNE UNIFLORA** = *Brodiaea uniflora*.

**LEUCOCRINUM** (lew-ko-kry'num). A single, rather bulbous-thickened, practically stemless herb of the lily family, **L. montanum**, the sand or star lily, native from Neb. to Calif. and Ore. It is not often seen in cult., but is occasionally transferred from the wild. It has a swollen, bulbous-thickened rootstock. Leaves basal, thick, flat, 4–7 in. long, scarcely ¼ in. wide. Flowers practically stalkless, borne at or near the ground, white and fragrant, the corolla funnel-shaped, partly buried. (*Leucocrinum* is from the Greek for white lily.)

**LEUCOJUM.** See SNOWFLAKE.

**LEUCONEURA**, *-us, -um* (lew-ko-newr'ra). White-veined.

**LEUCOTHOË** (lew-koth'o-ee). Ornamental shrubs of the heath family, only a few of which, from U.S. and Japan, can be considered hardy. The leaves are alternate* and deciduous or evergreen. In the hardy species the flowers are white, occasionally tinged pink, urn-shaped with 5 little teeth at the top and borne in clusters along, or at the tip of, the branches. The fruit is a dry, round, 5-celled capsule.* (Named for the daughter of Orchamus, mythological king of Babylonia.)

The leucothoës are handsome shrubs having good foliage and attractive flowers. The evergreen species (particularly *L. catesbaei*) are especially ornamental and desirable. They are of low habit, with graceful, arching branches and thick leaves that turn red or bronze in winter. For use with other evergreens, in foundation plantings, or borders they are invaluable. They grow well in light woods, and the sprays make very attractive winter bouquets.

Their chief cultural need is a moist, peaty soil or a sandy loam with plenty of humus. Propagation is by division, cuttings or seed.

**axillaris.** Evergreen shrub with arching branches, growing about 5 ft. high. Leaves leathery, ovoid-lance-shaped, 2–4 in. long, usually short-pointed and with a stalk of ¼–½ in. Flowers white, in clusters 1–2 in. long borne in the leaf-axils.* April–May. Va. to Fla. and Miss. Hardy from zone* 4 southward. Very similar to the following species, but is less hardy and has smaller, abruptly pointed leaves with shorter stalk.

**catesbaei.** Fetter-bush, also called dog-hobble. Evergreen shrub to 6 ft. high with slender, arching branches. Flowers white in drooping clusters along the branches. May. Va. to Ga. and Tenn. Hardy from most parts of zone* 3 southward. It is the hardiest of the evergreen leucothoës.

**keiskeri.** A Japanese evergreen shrub, the leaves ovalish or oblong, 1½–3½ in. long. Flowers white, larger than in any of the others, nodding, the clusters terminal or in the leaf-axils.* Hardy from zone* 4 (possibly from zone* 3) southward.

**racemosa.** Pepper-bush or white osier. Deciduous* shrub of upright, bushy habit growing 4–6 ft. or sometimes 12 ft. high. Leaves oblong or oval, toothed, 1–3 in. long. Flowers white, abundant, in clusters usually terminating short branches of the previous season. May–June. Mass. to Fla. and La. Hardy from zone* 3 southward.

**LEVANT COTTON** = *Gossypium herbaceum*.

**LEVERWOOD** = *Ostrya virginiana*.

**LEVISTICUM** (le-vis'ti-kum). A single species of perennial herb of the carrot family, **L. officinale** of southern Eu., the well-known lovage, which has been cult. for centuries for its aromatic fruits. It is a stout herb 3–6 ft. high, its leaves thrice-compound, the ultimate segments more or less wedge-shaped and coarsely toothed towards the tip. Flowers greenish-yellow, very small (see UMBELLIFERAE), but numerous in a compound cluster (compound umbel*). Fruit flattened and ribbed, the ribs more or less winged. For culture and uses see HERB GARDENING. (*Levisticum* is of uncertain origin.)

**LEWISIA** (lew-is'ĭ-a). A large genus of fleshy, perennial, practically stemless herbs of the family Portulacaceae, all from western N.A., a number cult. for ornament, mostly in the rock garden. They have thick, starchy roots and basal, narrow leaves in rosettes, usually club-shaped and without marginal teeth. Flowers solitary or in branched clusters at the end of a short stalk arising at the leaf rosette. Sepals* 2–8, mostly persistent. Petals 3–16. Fruit a many-seeded capsule.* (Named for Captain Meriwether Lewis of Lewis and Clark fame.)

The best known of all the species is the bitter-root, *L. rediviva*, which is grown in succulent collections. All of them need a gritty soil such as that in some sections of the rock garden (which see). The plants are not much grown as yet. The heights given are for the flowering stalk.

**columbiana.** About 12 in. high, the leaves narrow or spatula-shaped, 1–2 in. long. Flowers about ⅓ in. long, in loose clusters (panicles*), the 4–7 petals white or pink, but red-veined. Mountains of Wash. and Ore.

**cotyledon.** About 8–10 in. high, the leaves spatula-shaped, 2–3 in. long. Flowers about ½ in. long, in loose clusters (panicles*), the 7–10 petals white, but pink-veined. Calif.

**finchi.** About 12 in. high, the leaves 2–3 in. long and about half as wide. Flowers in a profuse cluster (cyme*), the petals pink, but white-margined. Calif.

**howelli.** About 6 in. high, the leaves oblong or ovalish. Flowers in cymes,* the 7–10 petals deep rose-red. Southwestern Ore.

**oppositifolia.** About 8 in. high, the leaves narrow, 1–3 in. long, sometimes with two opposite* ones on the flowering stalk. Flowers 2–4, long-stalked, the petals white or pink. Calif. and Ore.

**rediviva.** Bitter-root. A stemless, fleshy plant, the succulent leaves scarcely 1 in. long, the flowering stalk about as long. Flowers about 1 in. long, rose-pink or white. When through flowering, the plant is most inconspicuous and quite likely to be weeded out. It cannot stand much winter moisture and needs perfect drainage at all times. Its starchy root, edible in the spring, was once a food for the Indians, but by midsummer it becomes very bitter. Rocky Mountains to British Columbia.

**tweedyi.** Not over 4 in. high, the root very thick. Leaves more or less oblong, 2–4 in. long. Flowers 1–3, pink, about 2½ in. wide, showy. Alpine summits such as Mt. Ranier and others in Wash. Suited only to the rock garden.

**LEYCESTERIA** (ly-ses-teer'ĭ-a). Himalayan shrubs of the honeysuckle family, comprising only two species, one of them, **L. formosa**, cult. for ornament. It is a smooth shrub, 4–6 ft. high, with hollow stems and opposite,* stalked, broadly oval leaves, 2–7 in. long, and tapering at the tip. Flowers in drooping spikes, each flower from between purplish bracts.* Corolla funnel-shaped, purplish, ⅔–1¼ in. long. Stamens* 5. Fruit a many-seeded berry. A handsome shrub, blooming in Aug.–Sept. and hardy from zone* 6 southward. Chiefly conspicuous because of the showy bracts.* Little is known of its cultural requirements. (Named for William Leycester, a Bengal judge.)

**LIATRIS** (ly-ā'tris). A genus of perhaps 20 species of North American, rather weedy, but very showy, perennial herbs of the family Compositae, those below sometimes grown in open, sandy, or otherwise poor sites in the wild garden, or in informal borders. They are rather coarse plants with often resinous-dotted, alternate,* usually stiffish, narrow leaves and button-shaped heads of exclusively disk* flowers, the head close and surrounded by many, appressed,* greenish bracts.* The heads are borne in spikes or racemes,* and are handsome. All bloom in summer or early fall and are prevailingly rose-purple. The plants are commonly called button snakeroot and are sometimes offered under the name *Lacinaria*. (*Liatris* is of unknown origin.)

All are of the easiest culture in open, light soils, and may be increased by division. See SAND GARDENS.

**punctata.** A stout herb 12–20 in. high, with narrow, almost prickle-pointed leaves. Flower heads about ¾ in. long, numerous in a dense spike. Prairies of the central U.S.

**pycnostachya.** Prairie button snakeroot; also called Kansas gay-feather. A stout herb 3–5 ft. high, the stems wand-like. Leaves narrowly lance-shaped, becoming thread-like but stiffish toward the top. Flower heads about ½ in. long, in long, dense spikes. Prairies of the central U.S. July–Aug.

* Special articles on the subjects indicated by an asterisk (*) will be found at the words so marked.

**scariosa.** Gay-feather; also called rattlesnake master and blue blazing star. A hairy-stemmed herb, 3-5 ft. high, the leaves oblongish or narrower. Flower heads nearly 1 in. wide, but not numerous, bluish-purple, mostly in interrupted* racemes.* Eastern N.A. and west to the prairie states. July-Aug.

**spicata.** Gay-feather; called also prairie pine and devil's-bit. A very leafy-stemmed herb, 4-6 ft. high, the lower leaves 3-5-veined, narrow, and nearly 12 in. long, much diminishing upward. Flower heads about ½ in. long, the dense spike nearly 15 in. long. Eastern N.A. Sept.

**squarrosa.** Blazing star; also called rattlesnake master and colicroot. Not over 2 ft. high, the stem hairy. Leaves very narrow, nearly 6 in. long. Flower heads nearly 1½ in. long, not numerous, the cluster of them more or less interrupted. Eastern N.A. west to Tex.

**LIBANI** (lee′ba-ni). From Mt. Lebanon.

*LIBANOTICA, -us, -um* (lee-ban-nō′ti-ka). From Mt. Lebanon.

**LIBERIAN COFFEE** = *Coffea liberica.*

*LIBERICA, -us, -um* (ly-beer′i-ka). From Liberia, Africa.

**LIBERTIA** (li-ber′she-a). Little-grown plants of the iris family, chiefly Australasian, but the only cult. species, **L. formosa,** a native of Chile. It has a short, creeping rootstock and 2-ranked, rather rigid leaves, 12-18 in. long, the flowering stalk 2-3 ft. high. Flowers in nearly stalkless clusters (umbels*), of which there are many, the individual flowers about ⅝ in. long, white outside, greenish-brown within. Fruit a 3-valved capsule.* The plant is not hardy north of zone* 6, and requires a moist site. Propagated by division of the rootstock. (Named for Marie A. Libert, Belgian botanist.)

**LIBOCEDRUS.** *See* INCENSE CEDAR.

**LICHEN** (ly′ken). Curious flowerless plants of little interest to the gardener, but of unusual food habits. The common lichens which hug rocks and tree trunks consist of a flattish, usually brown plant body looking much like a patch. Within it is an alga and a fungus which live off each other. The process involves complicated chemical reactions, some of which result in the extremely slow disintegration of rocks into soil. Lichens are thus one of the first agencies in changing rock into soil. Sometimes used in terraria.*

**LICORICE.** This long-known cough remedy and flavor for tobacco is derived from the only cult. species of the genus **Glycyrrhiza** (gly-ki-ry′za) of the pea family, chiefly from the Mediterranean region. The only cult. species is **G. glabra,** the common or Spanish licorice, which is a perennial herb 2-3 ft. high, with compound* leaves having 4-8 pairs of ovalish leaflets. Flowers blue, pea-like, in short clusters (spikes or racemes*) in the leaf-axils.* Fruit a flattish pod (legume*), 3-4 in. long. The plant is suited only to Calif. and similar climates, but the harvest of its roots, which produce the licorice, is not certainly profitable in America. *See* MEDICINAL PLANTS. (*Glycyrrhiza* is from the Greek for sweet root.)

**LIFE PLANT** = *Bryophyllum pinnatum.*

**LIFTING.** The transplanting of specimens from one place to another. It is a planting operation and directions will be found at PLANTING.

**LIGHT.** The prime requisite for all garden plants; for, even with plenty of food and water, most plants will die without an adequate amount of light. While it is true that many forest plants have become shade-tolerant and in fact would perish in full sunlight, the fact still remains that only in the presence of light will leaves perform their function of making starch and sugar — a process absolutely essential to all plants with green leaves. *See* the work of chlorophyll at PLANT FOODS.

So important is solar influence to the growth of plants that much experimental work has been done on the composition of sunlight, and the effects of utilizing the different sorts of light rays found in it upon plants. Experimentally, plants can be made to do queer things by subjecting them to different kinds, amount, and duration of light (*see* ELECTRO-HORTICULTURE), but such experiments have more scientific than garden significance as yet.

One practical feature of the light question is the great improvement in glass now used for greenhouses (*see* GREENHOUSE). It allows more and better illumination for plants growing under it than the old type.

**LIGHTING.** The purpose of garden illumination is to reveal certain aspects of light by rendering visible out of the darkness of night subtle patterns in garden forms, textures, and colors. Light, a definite medium of visible expression, affords a subjective approach to creative design. Play of light and shade may interpret "song in light" as motifs modify the quality of light and control its distribution. As we sense values in shades and shadows, we become conscious of light, and as we discriminate certain objective illusions from more positive phases of subjective reality, we may discern that "light is the positive of dark," and subjective reality may shine forth as an overtone of optical illusion. Hence garden lighting may reveal in the quiet darkness of evening some hidden enchantment too elusive for the full boldness of day.

The general distribution of the sources of garden lighting and placement of light outlets are technical considerations of the utmost importance for successful illumination. In this matter there seem to be two schools of thought. First, those who prefer their light straight and direct and desire to maintain an obvious fixture and source of light; and second, those who are partial to indirect lighting. In a subtle combination of these two methods it is possible successfully to avoid tiresome stunts and trickiness. Reflected color, however, never has the power of direct color or light.

Where obvious source-lights are used the location and distribution of fixtures are dictated by the type of picture-patterns one is attempting to develop. They are subject to modifications affecting physical display, emotional appeal and intellectual stimulus. Source outlets to be considered for general installation cover such functions as guide lights to illuminate a pathway, sentinel lights along a vista, and specially featured light fixtures and outlets for spot and flood lighting.

Artificial lighting effects should be controlled to portray the dramatization of such distinctive features in the garden as may be worthy of special selection. It is assumed that only such areas would be featured as would lend themselves readily to this sort of dramatization.

The question of color is difficult and controversial. Warm, positive red may induce certain emotional reactions, whereas the cold and higher vibrational light of blue may be more soulful in appeal, but this all depends on local environment, both physical and psychological. Yellow — the golden mean — we have become psychologically adjusted to and have considered it as normal in our modern electric lighting systems. The wave length of red is about twice that of violet, and blue vibrates twice as fast as red. Blue, therefore, fades out the quicker, except at dusk when blue seems to be almost luminous. In the matter of color tones, warm, direct light causes cool shadows and cold light causes warm shadows. For natural lighting effects, structures such as walls and buildings are usually coldly lighted at night, whereas flowers and foliage masses take the complement to coldness — a warm light with an orange cast.

Light is the great revealer — constant, penetrating, and abstract — and we may eventually know its source and the significance of its integrating power through the right understanding of electrical phenomena. — A. F.

**LIGHT SOIL.** *See* SOIL MOISTURE.

**LIGHTWOOD** = *Acacia melanoxylon.*

**LIGNON-BERRY** = *Vaccinium vitis-idaea.*

*LIGNOSA, -us, -um* (lig-nō′sa). Woody.

**LIGULARIA** (lig-you-lay′ri-a). Handsome, Eurasian, perennial herbs of the family Compositae, cult. in the cool

---

* Special articles on the subjects indicated by an asterisk (*) will be found at the words so marked.

greenhouse or in the flower garden for their showy flower heads or (in a variety) for the variegated foliage. They have alternate,* or often basal and long-stalked leaves which are roundish or kidney-shaped, those on the stem sheathed and smaller. Flower heads usually nodding, arranged in branched or unbranched clusters (racemes* or corymbs*), the rays* usually yellow and strap-shaped. (*Ligularia* is from the root of *ligulate*, meaning strap-shaped, in allusion to the shape of the ray* flowers.)

The plants, which are closely related to *Senecio*, are of simple cultural requirements, doing well in ordinary garden soil. The leopard plant (*L. kaempferi aureo-maculata*) is chiefly grown for its foliage and is rather common as a window-garden plant. Propagated by cuttings or by division.

**clivorum.** A stout perennial, 3-4 ft. high, rusty-hairy in youth, ultimately nearly smooth. Lower leaves kidney-shaped or roundish, long-stalked, nearly 20 in. wide, sharply but remotely toothed. Flower heads numerous, orange-yellow, nearly 4 in. wide. China and Jap. Often sold as *Senecio clivorum*.

**kaempferi.** Rootstock prominent; and from it arise many roundish or heart-shaped or kidney-shaped leaves, 6-10 in. wide on slender, white-woolly stalks. Flower heads 1½-2 in. wide, light yellow, in branched clusters that are on white-woolly stalks 2-3 ft. long. Jap. Often sold as *Senecio kaempferi* or *Farfugium kaempferi*, but more commonly cult. in the var. **aureo-maculata** which has yellow, white, or occasionally pink-blotched leaves and is a favorite plant for window boxes; known as leopard plant, and not hardy over the winter above zone* 6.

**veitchiana.** A usually unbranched, stout perennial, 3-6 ft. high, the lower leaves more or less heart-shaped or kidney-shaped, nearly 12 in. wide and angularly toothed. Flower heads yellow, about 2½ in. wide, numerous. Jap.

**wilsoniana.** Nearly 5 ft. high, the basal leaves heart-shaped or kidney-shaped, sharply toothed and 12-18 in. long. Flower heads about 1 in. wide, yellow, in long, column-like spikes. China.

**LIGULATA, -us, -um** (lig-you-lay'ta). Strap-shaped.

**LIGULE** 1. A strap-shaped ray* flower in certain flower heads of the Compositae (which see).
2. A sheath-like organ found on the stems of some grasses and a few other plants.

**LIGUSTICIFOLIA, -us, -um** (ly-gus-ti-si-fō′lĭ-a). With leaves like the genus *Ligusticum*, which are weedy plants of the carrot family and of little hort. interest.

**LIGUSTRINA, -us, -um** (ly-gus-try′na). Privet-like.

**LIGUSTRUM.** See PRIVET.

**LILAC.** A large group of decorative shrubs and trees belonging to the genus **Syringa** (sir-ring′a) of the olive family. They are Old World plants with opposite,* usually unlobed leaves and showy clusters of flowers that are borne in spring and early summer, chiefly in thyrses.* The flowers are tubular, with 4 spreading lobes and 2 stamens.* They may be white, pink, lavender or purple and are often fragrant. The fruit is, in most cases, a brown, flattened, oval capsule.* (*Syringa* is probably from the Greek for pipe, and refers to the hollow stems of *Philadelphus* which was originally called *Syringa*.)

For Culture see below.

**S. josikaea.** Hungarian lilac. Shrub up to 12 ft. high. Leaves oval, 2-5 in. long, sometimes tapered at the ends, whitish beneath. Flowers deep lilac to violet, in slender clusters, slightly fragrant. June. Hungary. Hardy from zone* 3 southward. Late but not particularly showy.

**S. microphylla.** A spreading, slender-branched shrub, growing about 5 ft. high. Leaves ½-1½ in. long, roundish-ovate, hairy beneath. Flowers lilac, fragrant, small, in short clusters 1-3 in. long. May-June. China. Hardy from zone* 3 southward. A species distinguished by the small size of its leaves and flowers; a scattered bloom is often produced in the fall.

**S. oblata.** Shrub, occasionally tree-like, to 12 ft., resembling the common lilac in habit. The leaves are broad-oval to kidney-shaped, often broader than long and sharp-pointed, reddish when young and becoming red in the fall. Flowers pale lilac, in dense, rather broad clusters. Late April-May. China. Hardy from zone* 3 southward. One of the earliest lilacs to bloom. Var. **dilatata** is a form with oval, rather long-pointed leaves to 4½ in. long; and the flowers are more slender and the cluster less compact.

**S. persica.** Persian lilac. A compact shrub with slender, arching branches, usually about 5-6 ft. high though occasionally higher. Leaves lance-shaped, about 2½ in. long and sometimes lobed or divided. Flowers pale lilac, fragrant, in short, broad clusters about 3 in. long. May. Persia to northwestern China. Hardy from zone* 3 southward.

**S. pubescens.** A slender-branched shrub, sometimes round-headed, usually about 6 ft. high, rarely to 12 ft. Leaves broadly ovate, short-pointed, about 3 in. long, hairy on the veins beneath. Flowers fragrant, pale lilac, tube slender and petals narrow, clusters about 5 in. long. May. Northern China. Hardy from zone* 3 southward.

**S. reflexa.** Nodding lilac. An unusual and very handsome lilac that grows about 12 ft. tall and has nodding clusters, 4-8 in. long, of deep pink flowers. The leaves are 3-6 in. long, usually oval-oblong and tapered at the base. June. China. Hardy from zone* 3.

**S. sweginzowi.** An upright shrub with purplish-brown branches and oblongish or ovalish leaves, 2-4½ in. long. Flowers fragrant, reddish or paler lilac, the corolla about ½ in. long. Northern China. June. Hardy from zone* 3 southward. The var. **superba** is more profusely flowering. Of chief value because of its late bloom.

**S. villosa.** An upright, strong-growing shrub, attaining 9 or 10 ft. Leaves 3-6 in. long, more or less oval and pointed at the ends, whitish beneath. The flowers are lilac-pink or paler, and are borne in terminal clusters after most of the common lilacs have passed. May-June. China. Hardy from zone* 3 southward.

**S. vulgaris.** Common lilac. A handsome, widely cultivated shrub growing about 20 ft. high, sometimes becoming a small tree. The leaves are heart-shaped to oval, 2-6 in. long. The flowers are in clusters 6-8 in. long, very fragrant and usually lilac, though in many horticultural forms there are white, pink and purple flowers. Southeastern Europe. May. Hardy from zone* 2 southward. See below for the many hort. forms.

## LILAC CULTURE

*Syringa vulgaris*, *persica*, and *josikaea* from southern Eu. and northern As. contribute most of the common garden forms. The remaining species are found mostly in China or Korea and are largely of recent introduction. Among these are: *Syringa reflexa* with dull, rosy, pendulous flower clusters which are quite different than those of the better-known forms; *Syringa microphylla* which sometimes blossoms a second time in Aug. and has large, loose clusters of purple flowers. The first to bloom is *Syringa oblata* and its variety, *dilatata*. Although not over-conspicuous in the quality of their flowers, the fact that they bloom two to three weeks before the others makes them valuable. *Syringa villosa* with pale lavender flowers is the last of the shrubby types to show color. The only strong-scented lilac is *Syringa pubescens* with pale lavender flowers. The marked fragrance of this plant guarantees it a prominent place in any planting of the group. The Rouen Lilac, a hybrid between *S. persica* and *vulgaris*, is a large, spreading bush with purplish-lilac flowers. President Grevy is the largest growing of the garden forms and often reaches a height of sixteen feet.

Most of the garden varieties are forms of *Syringa vulgaris* and have come into being through seedling selection and plant breeding. Practically all the possible color combinations are available in either single- or double-flowered forms. A short list of some of the best of each is given here:

SINGLE-FLOWERED FORMS. Vestale, pure white; Mont Blanc, pure white; Marie Legraye, pure white; Jacques Callot, light lilac; Lamartine, mauve-pink; Lucie Baltet, rose-salmon; Wm. C. Barry, lavender; Crampel, bluish-lilac; President Lincoln, Wedgwood blue; Decaisnea, purplish-lilac; Volcan, purple; Diderot, claret-purple; Congo, deep purplish-red.

DOUBLE-FLOWERED FORMS. Miss Ellen Wilmot, white; Edith Cavell, creamy-white; Leon Gambetta, pinkish-lilac; Waldeck Rousseau, rosy-lilac; Belle de Nancy, satiny-rose; President Grevy, bluish-lavender; President Poincaire, claret-mauve; Wm. Robinson, violet-mauve; Colbert, clear purple; De Saussure, purple-red; Linne, lilac-red; Charles Joly, dark red.

CULTIVATION. The cultivation of the lilac is not difficult. Almost any well-drained soil will suffice but, if vigorous growth and good flowers are desired, the plant should be fertilized every two years. Well-rotted cow manure is best and may be applied in early spring. Cover an area about the plant four inches deep and equal in diameter to the height of small plants or about two thirds the height of mature specimens. Work the manure well into the soil and continue to spade this area every two or three weeks throughout the summer. Prepared fertilizers of a chemical nature should not be used, as they often stimulate woody growth to such an extent that the plant does not form flower buds for the next season.

Pruning is very important, especially if quality rather than quantity is desired in the flowers. In all cases the old

---

* Special articles on the subjects indicated by an asterisk (*) will be found at the words so marked.

blossoms should be removed as soon as they begin to fade.

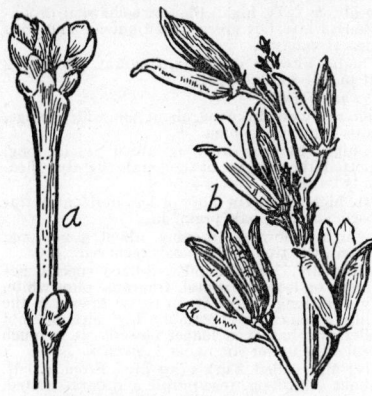

In pruning the lilac, allow flower buds (*a*) to remain, but prune away twigs with last year's fruits (*b*).

Pruning work may be done any time during the winter. Remove all weak wood which does not bear flower buds. Flowering branches are easily identified during the winter by the presence of several large buds at the tips. Only those branches which have vigorous buds should be left. If this method of pruning is carried out faithfully every three years a regular sequence of bloom will result.

The first year the quantity will be reduced but each cluster will be very large. The second season the flowers will increase in number and will be of good size. Finally, the third year will bring still more blossoms but smaller than those produced the first year. In many cases a two-year sequence of pruning is followed as it provides excellent quality of bloom at all times and requires the removal of less wood at each operation.

PROPAGATION. The lilac can be, and is, grown by almost every known method of propagation. The species are grown from seed, although asexual methods, such as grafting, are equally as common. Grafting is the most common method of propagating the varieties. Lilac seedlings or privet are used as stock and the work done in April and May. Budding on seedling lilacs in July is also practiced. None of these methods can be recommended, however, because of the constant trouble caused by the suckering of the stock. Root grafting on privet is more acceptable. The lilac cion is cleft grafted on a small piece of privet root in Jan. and stored in sand in the root cellar until spring. It is then planted out with the cion set deep in the ground. After three or four years a plant of sufficient size for permanent planting will result. Examination of the root at this time will generally show that the privet root has dried up and that the lilac is on its own roots. If the privet still persists it should be severed from the plant. Layering is the most simple method of propagation. The plant is cut back severely to induce suckering, and after one season each new branch is cut from the plant with a section of root attached and lined out in the nursery. Softwood cuttings are taken in late June and rooted in sand under glass. — A. D. S.

INSECT PESTS. A borer, similar to the caterpillar of the clear-winged moth on rhododendron, attacks lilac (*see* RHODODENDRON). A little caterpillar mines within the leaves, and when larger feeds on the outside; it can be controlled with nicotine spray. The oyster-shell scale, often injurious, may be checked with a dormant oil spray. The leopard moth is sometimes injurious (*see* MAPLE).

DISEASES. Powdery mildew of lilac, recognized by the powdery appearance of the dwarfed and yellowed foliage, may be eradicated by the use of sulphur fungicides. Bacterial blight, showing blackening and death of young shoots and tender parts, may be treated by removing and destroying all affected parts. Grafting of lilac on privet rootstocks gives rise to graft blight, characterized by sickly yellowish growth of 3-5-year-old plants. After about five years, plants either die or develop normal root systems and recover. *Phytophthora*\* blight of rhododendron and lilac occurs where these two plants are grown together. Control depends upon removal of suckers, which are particularly susceptible, combined with eradication of diseased wood and spraying, preferably with some copper-containing fungicide like bordeaux mixture.

**LILAC FAMILY** = Oleaceae.

***LILACINA, -us, -um*** (ly-la-sy′na). Lilac-like, either in form or color.

**LILIACEAE** (lil-ĭ-ā′see-ee). The lily family is of more garden importance than even its 200 genera and over 2000 species might suggest. It is sometimes called the aloe, hyacinth or tulip family, and it has been split by botanists into four families:

1. Lily family proper (Liliaceae)
2. Lily-of-the-valley family (Convallariaceae), often called Solomon's-seal or wakerobin family
3. Bunchflower family (Melanthaceae)
4. Smilax family (Smilaceae)

As here considered, all these are grouped in one big family, the Liliaceae. They are often bulbous herbs, but some are vines (*Smilax*), and woody or even tree-like plants occur in *Nolina*, *Yucca*, *Samuela*, *Hesperoyucca*, *Phormium*, *Cordyline*, *Dasylirion*, *Dracaena*, and *Aloe*, most of which come from warm regions. Garden vegetables are found in *Asparagus* and *Allium*. But the family is noteworthy for the showy bloom of most of its numerous garden genera, especially *Lilium*, *Brodiaea*, *Bulbocodium*, *Calochortus*, *Chionodoxa*, *Colchicum*, *Convallaria* (see LILY-OF-THE-VALLEY), *Eremurus*, *Erythronium*, *Fritillaria*, *Hemerocallis*, *Hosta*, *Hyacinthus*, *Kniphofia*, *Muscari*, *Ornithogalum*, *Scilla*, *Tulipa*, *Trillium*, *Urginea* and *Zygadenus*.

Some genera are chiefly greenhouse plants, notably *Agapanthus*, *Anthericum*, *Aspidistra*, *Chlorophytum*, *Eucomis*, *Gasteria*, *Gloriosa*, *Haworthia*, *Lapageria*, *Reineckia*, *Rohdea*, *Ruscus*, *Sansevieria* and *Schizobasopsis*.

There are, in addition, a few genera which contain native American plants, often in the woods in the East, and on prairies or the Pacific Coast in the West. They are suited to the wild garden, bog, or to other special sites. (See each genus for details.) They are: *Aletris*, *Androstephium*, *Bloomeria*, *Brevoortia*, *Camassia*, *Chamaelirium*, *Chlorogalum*, *Clintonia*, *Disporum*, *Hesperaloe*, *Helonias*, *Leucocrinum*, *Maianthemum*, *Medeola*, *Melanthium*, *Milla*, *Narthecium*, *Polygonatum* (see SOLOMON'S-SEAL), *Smilacina*, *Stenanthium*, *Streptopus*, *Uvularia*, and *Xerophyllum*. Many of these have attractive flowers and are well worth the gardener's attention, but they are not so widely grown as better-known genera.

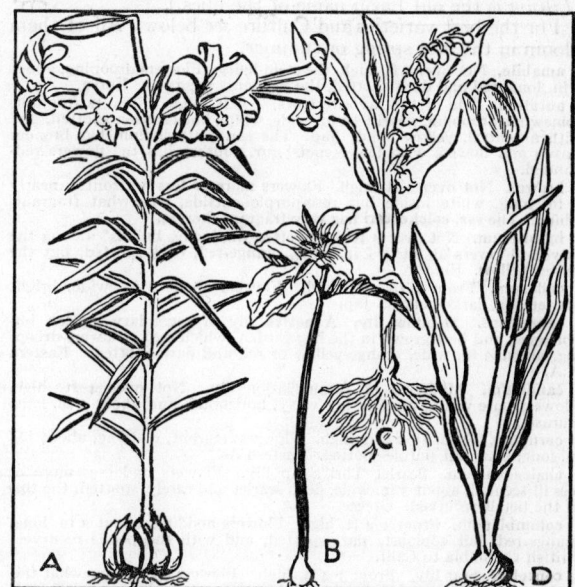

Four types of flowers in the lily family: (*a*) Easter lily; (*b*) trillium; (*c*) lily-of-the-valley; (*d*) tulip.

The only other plants of hort. interest are found in: *Asphodeline*, *Asphodelus*, *Galtonia*, *Lachenalia*, *Liriope*, *Ophiopogon*, *Paradisea*, *Puschkinia*, *Tricyrtis* and *Veratrum*.

The Liliaceae has alternate\* (whorled\* in some lilies) leaves, nearly always stalkless, generally without marginal teeth. In nearly all the herbs the stem arises from a bulb, very prominent in the onion and tulip, less so in some other

---

\* Special articles on the subjects indicated by an asterisk (\*) will be found at the words so marked.

genera, and replaced by a rootstock in many genera (*see* SOLOMON'S-SEAL).

Flowers nearly always very showy, typically of 6 segments, indistinguishable as to calyx or corolla, or in some genera tubular. While solitary flowers are not uncommon (tulip, *Erythronium*, etc.), generally the flowers are in clusters, the raceme* being the most common form of inflorescence. But umbels or umbel-like clusters occur in *Smilax*, *Allium* and several other genera. The ovary is superior* in all but two genera (*Liriope* and *Ophiopogon*), and this is the chief difference between this family and the Amaryllidaceae which has an inferior* ovary. Stamens* mostly 6, rarely 3. Fruit a berry or a capsule.*

**LILIAGO** (lil-ĭ-ā'go). An old, now obsolete, generic name for the St. Bernard's-lily. *See* ANTHERICUM.

**LILIASTRUM** (lil-ĭ-as'trum). Pre-Linnaean* name for *Paradisea liliastrum*.

**LILIFLORA**, *-us*, *-um* (lil-i-flow'ra). With lily-like flowers.

**LILIIFOLIA**, *-us*, *-um* (lil-ĭ-eye-fō'lĭ-a). With lily-like leaves.

**LILIUM** (lil'ĭ-um). A large genus of showy, bulbous herbs, the true lilies, the typical genus of the family Liliaceae, and of outstanding garden importance. There are perhaps 100 known species, mostly from the north temperate zone, over 60 of which are cult. in America, and of which those below are the best known. They are erect, perennial, leafy-stemmed herbs with deep, scaly bulbs. Leaves scattered or in whorls,* without marginal teeth, usually narrow. Flowers extremely showy, erect, horizontal or nodding, either solitary or in profuse clusters. Petals and sepals often colored alike and scarcely distinguishable as such, sometimes separate and clawed* or united, when the flower is more or less funnel-shaped. Stamens* 6. Fruit a many-seeded capsule.* (*Lilium* is the old Latin name of the lilies.)

For the best varieties and Culture *see* below. All of them bloom in the late spring or summer.

**amabile**. Not over 3 ft. high, the stem hairy. Flowers drooping, about 2 in. long, red and dark-spotted, the segments recurved. Korea.

**auratum**. One of the favorite sorts, 4–6 ft. high. Flowers fragrant, somewhat drooping, nearly 10 in. wide, white, but crimson-spotted, and with a central, yellow band. Jap. The var. **platyphyllum** has broader leaves and flowers with fewer spots; var. **rubrum** has the flowers red-banded.

**browni**. Not over 4 ft. high. Flowers more or less horizontal, nearly 9 in. long, white inside but rose-purple outside, somewhat fragrant. China. The var. **colchesteri** has very fragrant flowers.

**bulbiferum**. Not over 4 ft. high, often producing bulbils* among the leaves. Flowers about 3½ in. wide, orange-red, dark-spotted, but the center yellow. Eu.

**callosum**. From 1 to 2 ft. high. Flowers about 2 in. wide, bright scarlet, but dark-spotted. Jap.

**canadense**. Meadow lily. A native lily of secondary garden importance, and best grown in the bog garden (which see). Flowers drooping, about 3 in. wide, orange-yellow or red and dark-spotted. Eastern N.A.

**candidum**. Madonna or Annunciation lily. Not over 4 ft. high. Flowers pure white, more or less waxy, horizontal, and about 3 in. long. Eurasia.

**cernuum**. From 18–24 in. high. Flowers fragrant, nodding, about 1½ in. long, lilac, but purple-spotted. Eastern As.

**chalcedonicum**. Scarlet Turk's-cap lily. Flowers nodding, more or less ill-scented, about 3 in. wide, deep scarlet and rarely spotted, the tips of the petals recurved. Greece.

**columbianum**. From 3–4 ft. high. Flowers nodding, about 2 in. long, orange-red, but copiously dark-spotted, and with the petals recurved. British Columbia to Calif.

**concolor**. Star lily. From 3–4 ft. high. Flowers erect, somewhat fragrant, about 1½ in. wide, bright red, but unspotted. Jap. The var. **pulchellum** has somewhat spotted flowers.

**croceum**. Orange lily. Nearly 6 ft. high. Flowers erect, about 3 in. long, orange, but crimson-spotted. Mountains of southern Eu.

**dauricum**. About 3 ft. high. Flowers erect, sometimes 5 in. wide, orange-red, but dark-spotted. Siberia. There are forms with unspotted flowers and with the flowers brown-spotted.

**davidi**. Nearly 6 ft. high. Flowers nodding, about 3 in. long, red, but black-spotted. China.

**duchartrei**. Not over 4 ft. high. Flowers nodding, fragrant, about 3 in. long, white, but purple-spotted. Western China.

**elegans**. A very common lily in gardens, usually not over 2 ft. high. Flowers erect, nearly 6 in. wide, orange-red, somewhat dark-spotted. Jap. There are many cult. varieties or forms of this old favorite, some with larger, apricot-colored flowers, some with salmon and unspotted flowers, and some in other color patterns.

**giganteum**. An immense lily, 8–12 ft. high. Flowers somewhat drooping, fragrant, nearly 6 in. long, white, but green-tinged outside and with reddish-purple stripes inside. Himalayas.

**hansoni**. From 4–5 ft. high. Flowers drooping, fragrant, about 1½ in. long, orange-yellow, but purple-spotted. Jap.

**harrisi** = *Lilium longiflorum eximium*.

**henryi**. From 7–9 ft. high. Flowers drooping, about 3 in. wide, orange, but brown-spotted, the petals recurved. China.

**humboldti**. From 5–6 ft. high. Flowers drooping, about 3½ in. long, reddish-orange, but dark-spotted, the margins of the petals slightly rolled. Calif. The var. **magnificum** is larger.

**japonicum**. Not over 3 ft. high. Flowers more or less horizontal, fragrant, nearly 6 in. wide, rose-colored or pale pink. Jap.

**leichtlini**. From 4–6 ft. high. Flowers drooping, about 3 in. long, lemon-yellow, but dark-spotted, the tips of the petals recurved. Jap.

**longiflorum**. White-trumpet lily. An old and well-liked species, not over 3 ft. high. Flowers more or less horizontal, fragrant, pure white, trumpet-shaped and nearly 7 in. long. Jap. Much better known in the var. **eximium**, the Easter lily (often called "Bermuda lily" although not native there), which is taller and has even longer flowers. It is much forced for Easter bloom by florists under the name *L. harrisi*.

**martagon**. Martagon lily; also called Turk's-cap lily. From 4–6 ft. high. Flowers drooping, about 2 in. long, rose-purple and dark-spotted, the tips of the petals strongly recurved. Eurasia. The var. **album** has white flowers; and the var. **dalmaticum** has nearly black flowers.

**monadelphum**. Caucasian lily. Nearly 6 ft. high. Flowers drooping, almost 5 in. wide, golden-yellow, rarely spotted or tinged with purple, the tips of the petals recurved. Persia. Caucasus.

**myriophyllum**. Not over 4 ft. high. Flowers nodding, fragrant, about 1 in. long, greenish-white outside, but sometimes with a red keel,* yellowish inside. China. It often produces bulbils* among the numerous leaves.

**pardalinum**. Leopard lily. From 6–8 ft. high. Flowers drooping, about 4 in. wide, orange-red, but purple-spotted, yellow at the base, the tips of the petals strongly recurved. Calif. Suited to the bog garden (which see).

**parryi**. Not over 4 ft. high. Flowers more or less horizontal, fragrant, about 4 in. long, lemon-yellow, but spotted on the inside. Calif.

**parvum**. Sierra lily. A tall-growing, Pacific Coast lily, sometimes reaching a height of 5 ft. Flowers about 1¼ in. long, nearly erect, orange-red, but purple-spotted, and yellow at the base. Ore. to Calif.

**philadelphicum**. Wood lily. Mostly about 2 ft. high. Flowers erect, about 4 in. wide, the petals with long claws,* orange-red, but dark-spotted. Eastern U.S.

**philippinense**. Not over 18 in. high. Flowers more or less horizontal, fragrant, nearly 10 in. long, white, but greenish-tinged. Philippine Islands. A form from Formosa has flowers purple-tinged outside.

**regale**. Royal lily. From 4–5 ft. high. Flowers usually horizontal, fragrant, about 6 in. long, lilac or purplish outside, white inside but yellow at the base. Western China.

**rubescens**. Chaparral lily. Nearly 6 ft. high. Flowers erect, about 2 in. wide, at first pale lilac, ultimately rose-purple. Ore. to Calif.

**sargentiae**. Almost 6 ft. high. Flowers horizontal, fragrant, about 6 in. long, rose-purple outside but white inside. Western China.

**speciosum**. Japanese lily; an old garden favorite. About 4 ft. high. Flowers drooping, fragrant, about 4 in. long, white or blush, spotted with rose-red. Jap. There are many garden forms, especially var. **album** with nearly white flowers; and var. **rubrum** with carmine-pink flowers.

**superbum**. Turk's-cap lily of eastern N.A. From 5–8 ft. high. Flowers drooping, about 4 in. wide, orange-red, but dark-spotted, the tips of the petals recurved. Can be grown in the bog garden (which see).

**tenuifolium**. Coral lily. Not over 3 ft. high. Flowers nodding about 2 in. wide, bright scarlet and only occasionally spotted, the tips of the petals recurved. Eastern As.

**testaceum**. Nankeen (or Nankin) lily. From 5–7 ft. high. Flowers drooping, fragrant, about 3 in. wide, apricot-colored or yellowish, often pink-tinged, usually unspotted, the tips of the petals recurved. Of unknown origin, but once thought to be Japanese.

**tigrinum**. Tiger lily. From 4–6 ft. high. Flowers drooping, nearly 5 in. wide, orange-red or salmon-red, and black-spotted, the tips of the petals recurved. China and Jap. An old garden favorite and sometimes an escape* in eastern N.A. It often produces bulbils* among the leaves. There are many forms in cult. including the best being var. **fortunei** which has a densely hairy stem; var. **flore-pleno** has double flowers; var. **splendens** has more and larger flowers.

**warleyense** = *Lilium willmottiae*.

**washingtonianum**. Washington lily. From 4–6 ft. high Flowers horizontal, fragrant, about 4 in. long, white, but often purple-spotted. Ore. and Calif.

**willmottiae**. Not over 5 ft. high. Flowers drooping, about 3 in. wide, orange-red, but dark-spotted, the tips of the petals strongly recurved. China. Sometimes known as *L. warleyense*.

## LILY CULTURE

The lily, besides being a lovely flower for the garden because of its aristocratic beauty and exquisite perfume, has a long and interesting history. Its association with religious and mystical practices dates back to before the days of written history. The Madonna lily was used throughout the Dark and Middle Ages and into the Renaissance as the symbol of the annunciation of the Virgin. It is strange that

---

* Special articles on the subjects indicated by an asterisk (*) will be found at the words so marked.

today Easter decorations in churches are made of *L. longiflorum eximium*, now called Easter lily, as it comes from the Liukiu Islands near Japan. Perhaps it is partly due to the fact that *L. longiflorum* is easy to raise. Millions of them are grown in Bermuda to be shipped out for Easter.

## Propagation

Lilies are a difficult group to succeed with permanently, although quite easy to raise from seed. The difficulty consists in finding the right place for them to continue in, after they have been transplanted from the seed bed to the flower border.

Raising them from seed gives one a large number of bulbs to plant out in drifts or rows, whereas if the bulbs have to be purchased only a few would be possible to the average pocketbook. There are a few lilies, such as *L. giganteum*, which take a long time to flower from seed. *L. hansoni* and *L. tigrinum* do not set seed to their own pollen, and crosses do not come true to seed. If they are wanted, one has to buy the bulbs. Another reason for raising one's own lilies is that they are subject to mosaic and if a sick bulb enters the garden it may infect the whole plantation. This disease is not carried by the seeds, and therefore homegrown bulbs have a better chance for a healthy life than those purchased from other sources.

The safest way to raise them from seed, and the easiest, is to start the seeds indoors in a greenhouse in January or February. But it is not the only way, for the seeds will come up satisfactorily if sown in a cold frame, or even out in the garden, early in March or April, according to the locality. In those parts of the country where annuals are sown in the fall out of doors, lily seeds might also be sown in September or October, but in colder regions this is not safe, because the seeds may germinate and the young shoots be killed by the intense cold of the winter.

The soil for lily seeds consists of one part sand, one part loam and one part well-rotted leaves. This last gives a certain acidity to the soil, which is good for the lily seedlings. In a cold frame or garden this mixture need not be deeper than eight inches, but the ground under it should be well spaded and consist of good soil to the depth of at least a foot. It is absolutely essential in growing lilies that there should be perfect drainage. If the place where the seeds are to be sown is shaded it is helpful, but failing this the seedlings should be shaded with lathe or some other device until after the young shoots have been above the ground at least six weeks. Then the shade can be removed and the ground mulched with rotted leaves or peat moss. Out of doors in cold frames or in a bed the seeds should be sown far enough apart so that they will not have to be moved the first year; that is, about one inch in the row and each row about four inches from the next.

Indoors, of course, they are sown much closer. When the little bulbs are about ⅛ in. or ¼ in. long they can be transplanted into 2½-in. pots, and it will be found that potted plants grow much faster than those left in the ground, but of course this requires more work. The bulbs grown in flats or pots have to be moved as soon as they are large enough, for if not they will crowd together and their growth will be stunted. Out of doors the seedlings need not be moved until they have been in the ground two summers. Then they should be dug up, and it will be found that most of them will be large enough to transplant into the beds and borders of the flower garden. The small ones can be planted in a reserve bed for another year. Many lilies flower the second summer and nearly all do the third.

Lilies can also be propagated from the bulb scales, by pulling these off and planting them in sand. After a while a little bulb will grow onto the scale. Or they can be propagated from the bulbils* growing in the axils of the leaves of certain species such as *L. tigrinum*, *L. myriophyllum* and *L. bulbiferum*. A third way is to pull the stalk out of the bulb of *L. candidum* or *L. testaceum* after the flowers have faded and heel-in* the stem. In a few months little bulbs will form in the axils* of the leaves.

## Outdoor Culture

In the garden, lilies grow best in perfectly drained situations, like a little shade over the ground, and their flowering tops in a place where it is shady a few hours during the day. Some of them, such as *L. hansoni* and *L. henryi*, bleach unbecomingly in too bright a sunlight and keep their complexions bright and fresh only in partial shade. None of them will grow in deep shade. Some growers have advised planting lilies with low-growing, broad-leaved evergreens. This never seems a good idea, for lilies do not like being crowded. It is best to give them a ground cover which will not encroach upon them at all. *L. regale* does well with myrtle (*Vinca minor*), the dark glossy foliage of which matches the stem and leaves of the lily. And it is a foil to the white blossoms with golden throats and rosy markings. *Thalictrum* and columbine are good companion plants with *L. tenuifolium*, *L. amabile*, *L. elegans* and others. Their foliage comes out early in the season and will protect the young shoots of the lilies which come up out of the ground very early in spring. *L. tenuifolium* has raised its lacquer-colored, nodding blossoms up over a ground cover of forget-me-nots in one garden with a most pleasing effect. Lavender bushes are good with the creamy-colored *L. testaceum* and snowy *L. candidum*, and many of the herbs, such as winter savory and *Teucrium*, would go well with them. Strong perennials such as phlox, *Hemerocallis* and peonies, if grown with them, would smother them, but one can plant lilies behind these plants or to one side of them and produce an effect of companionship without actually intermingling the plants.

When planting lilies the bulbs should always be three times as deep in the ground as the height of the bulb. That is, if a bulb is two inches high, its base should be six inches below the surface of the soil. It is also a good precaution to surround the bulbs with sand, for this will keep away certain bacteria and also help with the drainage. Most lilies have stem roots, but need not be planted deeper on this account, for four inches of stem above a two-inch bulb will be sufficient for this, and as the bulb grows in size the contractile roots pull it farther down into the ground.

*Lilium candidum* is an exception to this and should have only one or two inches of soil above the top of the bulb. Bulbs which form mats such as *L. pardalinum* need not be planted quite so deeply either, nor does *L. testaceum*.

The best time of the year to plant lilies is when the foliage has died down and the plant is resting. But the roots should not be removed any more than they would be from any other perennial plant.

## The Best Kinds

The easiest lilies to grow in the United States are the Asiatic lilies which, on the whole, seem to thrive better in cultivation here than the native ones or than the European species.

South of Philadelphia *L. candidum* and *L. longiflorum* do exceedingly well and so ought *L. philippinense*, a white trumpet-lily valuable for its late blooming; especially its form known as *formosanum*.

*Lilium regale* is the hardiest of all and comes readily from seed and seems to like the garden; so do *L. tenuifolium*, *L. willmottiae*, *L. davidi*, *L. callosum*, *L. concolor*, *L. croceum* (a European), *L. dauricum*, *L. elegans*, *L. hansoni*, and *L. henryi*. The latter increases until it becomes almost bushlike, with innumerable tall stems carrying twenty to thirty flowers apiece.

Of the natives which like garden conditions, *L. superbum* seems to do best in eastern gardens. It grows to nine feet and has as many as 21 stems from one bulb. Others liking civilization are *L. humboldti*, which does very well in partial shade, and *L. pardalinum*. *Lilium canadense*, strangely enough, has a tendency to disappear. *L. philadelphicum* requires an exceedingly dry and partially shaded situation and is on the whole difficult in the garden. *Lilium columbianum* disappears from the eastern gardens and so do two lovely westerners of rosy tints, *L. washingtonianum* and *L. rubes-*

---

* Special articles on the subjects indicated by an asterisk (*) will be found at the words so marked.

*cens. Lilium parvum* is attractive, but it, too, disappears, as does the handsomest native of all, the yellow, fragrant *L. parryi.*

The tiger lilies are a hardy lot, also *L. elegans,* but it has now been discovered that they both have the mosaic (see diseases below) without showing any traces of it and can transmit it to other plants. Therefore it is advisable to keep these two lilies in a place some four hundred feet away from other plantings.

*Speciosum* lilies are quite hardy provided one obtains a clean stock and they increase in the garden; so is *L. auratum,* especially the variety *platyphyllum,* which grows to a gigantic height and stays in flower almost six weeks, one blossom opening slowly after another over this period.

Other attractive garden lilies which are a bit difficult are *L. chalcedonicum,* with a brilliant, glossy-scarlet, nodding flower, and *L. monadelphum,* of a good shade of light yellow. Also *L. leichtlini,* which is like a refined tiger lily, but without bulbils in the axils of its leaves. *Lilium cernuum* with its lavender flowers is not old in gardens, yet it seems to be hardy. So far *L. duchartrei,* a fairly recent introduction from Asia, has not proven an easy lily, and *L. brownii,* which is one of the handsomest, is a fleeting dweller in the garden, if north of zone* 4. *Lilium myriophyllum* is killed in the East in very severe winters, but stands milder conditions better.

Lilies, as all other plants, should be fed occasionally, and a well-rotted compost spread over them to the depth of an inch or so, will act as a winter mulch and replenish the ground at the same time. Most of them do not resent lime, but it is just as well not to give it to them. Rotted leaves make a good mulch and can be spaded into the ground in the spring. Some growers keep a mulch of leaves on their lilies all the summer, which prevents them from drying out too much. They should be watered if there is a drought just before their blossom time, but after flowering this is not necessary.

FORCING

Many amateurs like to force their lilies for Easter. To do this with several of the species one should pot them in fairly deep pots in September and sink them in the ground, as they need a chilling before forcing. (See RETARDING.) As soon as the pot is well filled with roots they can be brought indoors to flower in a cool greenhouse. — H. M. F.

INSECT PESTS. The principal pests of lily are those recorded as bulb pests (see BULBS). Occasional injury by stem borers and general feeders is noted.

DISEASES. Mosaic, yellow flat, *Botrytis* blight and brown tip are the common diseases. Lilies, when infected with *mosaic,* are stunted, produce distorted flowers and exhibit leaves patterned with light and dark green mottled areas. For control, propagate from seed, destroy infected plants and use nicotine or pyrethrum insecticides for control of aphids which transmit the disease. *Yellow flat,* another virus disease, is characterized by yellow, flattened plants with curled or distorted leaves. Control is the same as for mosaic. *Botrytis blight,* characterized by spots on the leaves, or flowers, can be controlled by applications of bordeaux mixture, the removal of infected leaves and the destruction of all plant debris in the fall. *Brown tip,* a non-parasitic disease in which the ends of the leaves are injured and turn red-brown in color, has been shown to be due to overdoses of nicotine or cyanide.

**LILY.** For the true lily *see* LILIUM. Many other lily-like plants are called lily, or the word occurs as part of their common name.

If you do not know the full common name of these plants, you will find them noted among the following genera:

| | | |
|---|---|---|
| Agapanthus | Erythronium | Leucocrinum |
| Amaryllis | Eucharis | Narcissus |
| Anthericum | Fritillaria | Nymphaea |
| Belamcanda | Gloriosa | Sprekelia |
| Brodiaea | Haemanthus | Victoria |
| Calochortus | Hedychium | Zantedeschia |
| Clivia | Hemerocallis | Zephyranthes |
| Cooperia | Hymenocallis | |
| Doryanthes | Kniphofia | |

Also the next few entries.

All the cult. plants of which lily is part of the name are also entered in THE GARDEN DICTIONARY under their preferred common names, such as adobe lily, Amazon lily, calla lily, Mariposa lily, etc., and the quickest way to find them is to turn at once to such entries, if you happen to know them. If not, the list of genera above may provide the clue for this most widely used and confusing of vernaculars.

**LILY FAMILY.** An immense group of very diverse plants, containing such well-known garden subjects as onion, lily, tulip, smilax, hyacinth, bunchflower, yucca, and the dracaenas. For all the garden genera and the characteristics of the family *see* LILIACEAE.

**LILY-FLOWERED TULIPS.** See Garden Tulips at TULIPA.

**LILY LEEK** = *Allium moly.*

**LILY-OF-THE-FIELD** = *Sternbergia lutea.*

**LILY OF THE NILE** = *Agapanthus umbellatus.*

**LILY-OF-THE-VALLEY.** A single species of very fragrant perennial herbs, constituting the genus **Convallaria** (kon-va-lair'i-a) of the lily family, found wild in Eurasia and in the higher mountains from Va. to S. Car. The only species, **C. majalis,** is cult. throughout the temperate world for its fine, persistent, but not evergreen foliage, but especially for its delicately scented, white, nodding flowers. Leaves all basal, from a horizontal rootstock, the blades oblong-oval, usually forming dense mats. Stalk of the flower cluster arising from the ground, 5–8 in. high, the cluster a loose, often somewhat 1-sided raceme of bell-shaped, white, nodding flowers, the tips of the corolla recurved. Stamens* 6, not protruding. Fruit a red berry about ¼ in. in diameter. The *var.* **fortunei** has larger leaves and flowers. Occasionally a pink-flowered or variegated-leaved sort is offered. (*Convallaria* is from the Latin for a valley.)

CULTURE

The lily-of-the-valley is primarily a shade plant. It can be made to grow in the open, will do fairly well in ground shaded for part of the day, but luxuriates best in places that are under the shade of trees. While very old plantations of it are often seen and they become solid, sod-like masses, the flowers are apt to be few and poor and most of the growth is foliage. The reason is that the plant gets too crowded if let alone for more than three years, when the bed should be dug up and re-planted with fresh pips (see below).

The lily-of-the-valley has a horizontal rootstock from which arises a small, upright, detachable portion containing a stout bud and plenty of roots. Commonly called *pips,* these propagative parts of the plant can be stored and are usually offered by dealers in the spring. They are the best material with which to start a bed. The pips should be planted close together, about 1½ in. deep, in good, rich garden soil. Such a bed, top-dressed in the late fall with well-rotted manure, will make a fine mat of foliage within a year or two and will provide plenty of flowers until the rootstocks become crowded.

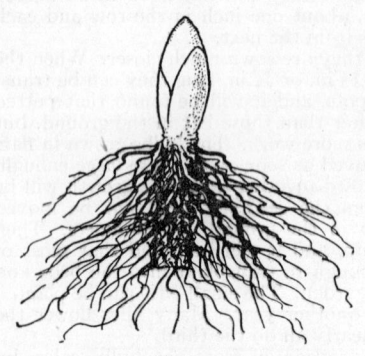

A pip of the lily-of-the-valley ready for planting

FORCING. The lily-of-the-valley is widely forced for winter bloom by the florists, and this can be done by anyone with a greenhouse. Pips are planted directly in the greenhouse bench in potting mixture* 1 or in pure sand.

---

* Special articles on the subjects indicated by an asterisk (*) will be found at the words so marked.

## GARDEN LILIES

1 Regale
2 Speciosum
3 Browni
4 Tenuifolium
5 Auratum

Keep the bench dark for the first 10–14 days by covering with boards, which should be removed gradually as the pips sprout.

Professional growers use only pips that have been stored for three months at a temperature of about 28°. Such do not need bottom-heat, and will be forced into bloom in about a month from planting time if the greenhouse is kept at about 65°. If you buy the ordinary pips sold by the average dealer, they will not have been held in cold storage and such pips, to force well, need bottom-heat (which see) of 70°–75°, and a greenhouse temperature of about 65°. In either case, they need plenty of water and, as they come to flowering, as much light as possible. The forcing can, of course, be done at any season of the year only if pips have been held in storage. Otherwise, they must be planted when available, which is usually in Feb.–March.

DISEASES. This plant is susceptible to a disease known as *leafspot*. The spots, occurring on the foliage, are purple-brown in color. The removal of infected leaves and sanitation* in the fall should give control.

**LILY-OF-THE-VALLEY FAMILY.** See LILIACEAE.

**LILY-TURF.** See OPHIOPOGON and LIRIOPE.

**LIMA BEAN** = *Phaseolus limensis*. For culture *see* BEAN.

**LIMB.** 1. The expanded flat part of an individual petal or of a united (*i.e.* gamopetalous*) corolla; sometimes called a blade.
2. One of the larger branches of a tree.

**LIMBER PINE** = *Pinus flexilis*. See PINE.

**LIME** = *Tilia*. See LINDEN.

**LIME.** There are two true limes, the acid lime (*Citrus aurantifolia*) and the sweet lime (*Citrus limetta*). Both are grown in the United States, the former giving rise to small but important, and now rapidly expanding, industries in Florida and California and the latter contributing a rare and interesting, though worthless, horticultural curiosity. In this same category also are to be grouped the so-called Rangpur and Kusaie limes which, though intensely sour and suitable as substitutes for the lime, are in reality mandarins. Mention should also be made of the limequat,* a hybrid of lime and kumquat parentage, which exhibits much of the acidity of the former and some of the hardiness of the latter, though a rather weak grower.

ACID LIME. Two botanical varieties or horticultural races of the acid lime are recognized; the Mexican, West Indian or Key lime and the Tahiti or Persian lime. The former bears smaller fruits, has foliage of lighter color and smaller size, and is decidedly less vigorous and hardy than the latter, which is one of the most beautiful of all citrus trees. At the present time the West Indian lime is more important than the Persian, a situation which seems destined to be reversed in the not distant future when the recently planted acreage of the latter comes into bearing.

The lime is a tender, evergreen, sub-tropical tree which thrives, unassisted, in tropical and semi-tropical climates, though in sub-tropical regions it requires irrigation. It is the commercial citrus fruit most tender to frost, which restricts its culture to regions of comparative freedom from even light frosts. Temperatures of 28° to 30° are sufficient to cause injury to the West Indian lime and temperatures slightly lower injure the Persian lime. It is also sensitive to sudden heat waves which, if severe, may cause dropping of the young fruit and burning of the rind of the ripe fruit. Comparative freedom from wind is required because of the fact that the rind of the fruit is easily injured and bruises result in a scabby condition which lowers the grade and hence adversely affects its salability. For these reasons the commercial culture of the lime in the United States is limited to Southern Florida and the areas of mildest winters in Southern California. Even there the frost hazard is often sufficient to result in occasional injury unless orchard heating is provided (for details *see* FROST).

Like its relative the lemon, the lime has several more or less overlapping periods of bloom and the result is that fruit ripens almost continuously throughout the year, though the heaviest production occurs during the winter and spring months. It also has the ability possessed by other citrus fruits to set and mature the fruits without the necessity of pollination. Such fruits are obviously seedless. As a consequence its culture presents no pollination problem.

SOILS. The lime has a very wide range of soil adaptation, succeeding about equally well on very light soils and moderately heavy soils. It thrives in the hard lime-rock soils of the Florida keys. Heavy and poorly drained soils should be avoided because of the intolerance of the roots to excess moisture and the likelihood of foot-rot and gummosis. It does about equally well under a range of soil reaction from moderately acid to slightly alkaline. Like other citrus trees, however, it is sensitive to even small concentrations of alkali salts, for which reason such soils should be avoided and only irrigation water of good quality be used. Because of its shallow rooting habit deep soils are not required; three to four feet of good soil with adequate drainage will suffice.

The bulk of the West Indian lime production in the United States still comes from the thickets of seedling trees on the Florida keys and this explains the notable variation in size and form of the fruit in the markets. The recent plantings, however, are nearly all of superior selections budded on rootstock seedlings, which has always been the practice with Persian lime varieties. The sour or bitter orange (*Citrus aurantium*) is the rootstock most employed, though the rough lemon (*Citrus limonia*) is used for the lighter soils in Florida. Experiments in California indicate that the sour orange rootstock exerts a moderate dwarfing effect on the trees of both kinds of limes in comparison with the sweet orange (*Citrus sinensis*), grapefruit (*Citrus paradisi*), and rough lemon when used as rootstocks. For heavy soils and regions of high rainfall the sour orange as a rootstock and budding the rootstock seedlings high, 8 to 12 inches, are recommended to avoid gummosis, a disease to which all citrus rootstocks other than sour orange are more or less subject. Nursery trees are propagated by shield-budding seedlings of suitable size, fall or dormant budding being preferred. The trees are usually planted as year-old budlings. The lime topworks readily by either budding or bark-grafting, though the latter method is rarely used.

PLANTING. The evergreen nature of the tree and the sensitiveness of its roots to desiccation require that special care be given to the planting operations, particularly in arid regions. In California the practice is almost universal of digging the nursery trees with a 20 to 30 pound ball of earth about the roots, which is held tightly in place by a burlap wrapping. This permits storing the trees under lath until conditions are favorable for planting and insures good results. Lime trees, like other citrus, should not be planted when the soil is cold, which prevents root growth. If balled trees are used and planting properly timed, the trees experience very little setback and start growth almost immediately. The best practice involves heading the trees, usually to a height of 24 to 30 inches, a few weeks before they are dug and balled. The West Indian Lime rarely attains large size and can safely be spaced at 15-foot intervals; the Persian lime reaches larger size and is usually planted 20 by 20 feet.

IRRIGATION. In arid regions irrigation is undoubtedly the most important soil management practice. The evergreen nature of the tree, its shallow rooting habit and relatively high water requirement, combine to produce the necessity for irrigation during the dry season; indeed the requirement of an adequate soil moisture supply at all times may necessitate irrigation at any time of year. The total amount of water required is dictated by the climate and the size and spacing of the trees; the period between irrigations depends on weather conditions and the nature of the soil. The method of irrigation is determined mainly by the slope of the land and nature of the soil. The furrow method is most widely used and the number of applications ranges from 4 to 10 annually. The ordinary irrigation is equivalent to about 3 inches of rainfall. *See* IRRIGATION.

---

* Special articles on the subjects indicated by an asterisk (*) will be found at the words so marked.

Fertilization is also important, for all the citrus fruits are high in nutrient requirement. Experience indicates that satisfactory yields can be maintained by annual applications of about 200 pounds of nitrogen per acre and that part of it can best be applied in the form of animal manures or leguminous straws which also provide organic matter. Sodium and calcium nitrates and ammonium sulphate are the principal chemical fertilizers used. Satisfactory evidence of benefits from phosphorus and potassium is lacking. Tillage is necessary only to turn under cover crops, weeds or fertilizers and to facilitate irrigation. Pruning is of minor importance and is confined to the removal of suckers and declined lower limbs and to light thinning of the bearing wood.

The fruit drops when ripe but should be removed by clipping, when the most desirable size is attained, and stored under cool, moist conditions. Within a few weeks it colors and the rind toughens. It is then ready for market. In California the fruit is wrapped and packed in cartons; elsewhere it is generally shipped loose in barrels.

There are no named varieties of the West Indian lime. Bearss, a seedless fruit, is the only named variety of the Persian lime. — R. W. H.

PESTS. Pests of limes are in general the same as those of other citrus fruits (*see* ORANGE).

**LIME.** Because calcium is an absolutely essential constituent of most plants, and because it helps in the availability of many other substances in the soil, some form of lime has been used by farmers since ages before the Christian era. The need for it is just as imperative today but it is still true that more money is wasted on useless liming, or in actually harmful liming, than ever, largely because the average gardener does not understand its true function nor the form in which lime should be applied.

WHAT LIME DOES. Rainwater is generally somewhat acid. It therefore tends to leach out of soil some of the necessary calcium, as well as other soluble materials. If too long continued, this process results in what the farmer calls a sour soil, unfit for clover and for many other crops, but, as we shall see below, often a boon to certain garden plants. If the region is one where there is a natural disintegration of limestone, the loss of lime by leaching is taken care of by the fresh addition of it from the minerals already in the soil which are slowly released. Such an area needs no lime added to it.

But where the basic soil materials cannot replace the leached lime, it is necessary to correct the loss, *but only* if the crop is one actually needing lime, which some do not. Generally speaking, sour soils are unfit for most vegetable or farm crops, but many cult. shrubs and trees are indifferent to moderate deficiencies of lime.

Besides the purely chemical action, lime of the right sort has the peculiar quality of making heavy clay or silt soils more workable. This action is apparently purely physical, for it results in the amalgamation of extremely fine soil particles into somewhat larger units, which allows far better aeration and drainage. On this score alone lime is of the greatest value.

DEFINITIONS. One of the chief wastes in the use of lime comes from the fact that lime is not "just lime." For garden or farm purposes it comes in many forms of greatly different value — all basically derived from limestone, oyster shells, or marl.

1. *Limestone.* The chief source of lime for many growers; useful, however, only when very finely ground. Its objections are its weight, the cost of hauling it from the lime quarry, and the fact that it has less value than hydrated lime which is made from it.

2. *Oyster shells.* Contain about the same amount of beneficial material as ground limestone, but are useful only when ground very fine. The objections are the lack of them except at a few favored places along the sea-coast, and the fact that, like ground limestone, they have less value than hydrated lime.

3. *Marl.* This is a mixture of lime, and, usually, fine silts or clays. The mixture is of uncertain amounts of these three substances, so that marl, unless found locally and at a cheap price, is the least effective way of applying lime.

4. *Chalk.* A poor form of lime. *See* CHALK.

For practical garden and farm use the hydrated lime manufactured from limestone is by far the best material to use, but only if its percentage of calcium oxide is at least 70%. Freshly burned limestone may contain as much as 90% calcium oxide or even more, but it comes in large lumps unfit for use. But hydrated (*i.e.* burned and slaked) lime is as fine as powder, comes in bags which keep well in a dry place, and is the best for all round use.

There is no honest objection to hydrated lime (70%), but much trickery has been practiced upon the gardeners and farmers by dealers who offer inferior products under the name of "Agricultural Lime." Sometimes these are made from an initially poor grade of limestone, and often they contain only mere sweepings of white dust, land plaster, and other relatively useless junk. In buying lime it is safer to specify hydrated lime of about 70% calcium oxide content. Some "agricultural lime" meets this specification but many do not.

### HOW TO USE LIME

The need for lime can be tested exactly as one tests for soil acidity (for details *see* ACID AND ALKALI SOILS). For most garden crops, except the important exceptions noted below, the soil needs lime if it shows a pH of much below 6.0, usually indicated by the presence of sour dock and other acid-tolerant weeds.

If lime is needed, it should be spread exactly as fertilizer is spread. Ordinarily, a coating enough to whiten the ground is sufficient. When hydrated lime is used, spreading is easy (not on a windy day) because the material is as fine as powder and spreads easily either by hand sowing or by a machine for spreading fertilizer.

It should be put on freshly harrowed land or on an area that is to be plowed or harrowed or raked over immediately. More important still is the necessity of spreading it thoroughly for lime works scarcely at all laterally and a poorly spread coating may leave many acid or sour places in an otherwise limed field.

AMOUNT NEEDED. A very usual application is a "ton of lime to the acre." But such an estimate loses sight of the fact as to what sort of lime is used. Generally speaking, such directions mean ground limestone. Translated into other sorts of lime, such directions mean:

2000 pounds of ground limestone
1571 pounds of hydrated lime
1384 pounds of burned lime, in lumps (not recommended)
2500 pounds of marl

For smaller plots figure that 1/20 of an acre is 33 × 66 ft. Such an application should not be repeated more than once in three or four years, unless the tests show that your soil needs more frequent applications.

### WHEN NOT TO USE LIME

Lime is not a fertilizer (which see); therefore, do not add it to the soil of growing crops. Never top-dress growing lawns with it (*see* LAWN). Keep it away from all rhododendrons, azaleas, and other plants of the heath family. Do not put any in the woods soil of the wild garden nor in the bog garden, nor in any other place where acid-tolerant plants are to be grown. (*See* the list of plants at ACID AND ALKALI SOILS.)

Do not add lime in any form to any manure heap, nor to a compost pile. It does more damage there than anywhere else for it greatly increases the loss of nitrogen. Never, for the same reason, mix it with any commercial fertilizer. It is sometimes permissible to mix and spread immediately (to save two operations) lime and phosphates, but such a time-saving operation is pure waste with a fertilizer containing nitrogen in any form.

There is no scientific evidence that lime is of any direct benefit to tree fruits, blackberries, gooseberries, currants, raspberries, or strawberries, and it may be positively harm-

---

* Special articles on the subjects indicated by an asterisk (*) will be found at the words so marked.

ful to many slightly acid potato lands. Moderate applications do have value for most garden plants of the pea family. It is, also, of great value for soils too acid to properly grow Kentucky bluegrass, but only if the application can be repeated every three or four years, which means plowing up the lawn and starting fresh. *See also* LIMESTONE PLANTS.

*LIMEANA, -us, -um* (ly-mee-ā'na). Relating to, or from, Lima, Peru; or relating to the lima bean.

**LIMEBERRY** = *Triphasia trifolia*.

**LIME-HATERS.** Plants that are acid tolerant. They do not "hate" lime, but appear to grow best in soils of a certain degree of acidity. For a list of such *see* ACID AND ALKALI SOILS.

**LIME-LOVING PLANTS.** *See* LIMESTONE PLANTS.

*LIMENSIS, -e* (ly-men'sis). From Lima, Peru.

**LIMEQUAT.** A hybrid citrus fruit derived from crossing the West Indian lime (*see* LIME) and the kumquat. It is more hardy than the common orange, but is not of much practical value. The fruit is light yellow, more or less oval, nearly 2 in. long, and with a very acid pulp. Its culture is the same as for orange (which see).

**LIMESTONE.** *See* LIME.

**LIMESTONE PLANTS.** While a considerable number of wild plants are, or are thought to be, confined to regions underlain by limestone, not many garden plants are especially restricted to such regions. The answer is perhaps found in the fact that the great bulk of the common garden plants have been successfully cult. for centuries in a great variety of soils.

There is, too, the question of how much the lime content of the soil is offset by the physical characteristics of it. While much experimental work is still necessary to get at the exact facts, it may be permissible to list most of the cult. species of *Clematis*, possibly *Prunus mahaleb*, *Aster amellus*, *Anthyllis vulneraria*, *Lithodora fruticosa*, and perhaps some of the scillas, as "limestone plants," a designation more common in the literature of gardening than specifically accurate. Another, and perhaps the most certain of all, is the hartstongue fern which appears to be confined, in America, to limestone ledges. Other garden plants which may be lime-tolerant are *Pellaea*, *Potentilla fruticosa*, *Teucrium marum*, many campanulas, *Daphne*, *Atropa*, and *Dianthus alpinus*.

**LIME-SULPHUR.** Used both in Fungicides (which see), and as a contact spray for insect pests. *See* INSECTICIDES.

**LIMNANTHACEAE** (lim-nan-thay'see-ee). The false mermaid family comprises only two genera of aquatic or marsh herbs of which only *Limnanthes* is cult. *See* this genus for the characters of the family.

**LIMNANTHES** (lim-nan'theez). A genus of 4 species of western North American herbs of the family Limnanthaceae, of which **L. douglasi**, the meadow-foam or marsh flower, is occasionally cult. in the flower garden. It is a spreading or sprawling annual, 4–8 in. high, and usually branching from the base. Leaves alternate,* compound,* the leaflets arranged feather-fashion and sharply lobed or toothed. Flowers solitary, long-stalked, fragrant, nearly 1 in. wide, white, or yellowish towards the base. Sepals* 3–5, persistent. Petals 3–5, usually notched at the tip. Stamens* twice as many as the petals. Fruit dry. The plant is best treated as a hardy annual (*see* ANNUALS) and its only requirement is a moist or nearly wet place. (*Limnanthes* is from the Greek for marsh flower, in allusion to its habitat.)

**LIMNOCHARIS** (lim-nock'a-ris). Tropical American aquatic herbs of the family Butomaceae, comprising only two species, of which **L. flava** (sometimes known as *L. emarginata*) is cult. in pools, tubs, or in aquaria for its yellow flowers. Leaves erect, standing 1–2 ft. above the water surface, velvety-green, blunt at the tip. Flowers in a stalked cluster (umbel*), the 3 sepals green and persistent, the 3 petals yellow and soon withering. Stamens* many, the outer ones sterile. Fruit a collection of small, splitting pods. The plant is of easy culture in reasonably shallow water and may be propagated by seeds or by the suckers that arise at the base of the flowering stalk. For the plant sometimes offered as *L. humboldti see* HYDROCLEIS NYMPHOIDES. (*Limnocharis* is from the Greek for marsh, in allusion to the habitat.)

**LIMODORUM TUBEROSUM** = *Calopogon pulchellus*.

**LIMONCITO** = *Triphasia trifolia*.

*LIMONIA* (ly-mō'nĭ-a). An obsolete generic name for certain citrus fruits, especially the lime and lemon.

**LIMONIUM** (ly-mō'nĭ-um). The sea lavenders or sea pinks comprise a genus of perhaps 180 species of the family Plumbaginaceae, mostly annual or perennial herbs, several of which are widely grown flower garden plants. They have mostly basal, often tufted, leaves. Flowers small, but numerous, in open loose clusters (panicles*) or in branching spikes, prevailingly lavender, rose-pink, or bluish, but sometimes yellow or white. Calyx* often membranous or colored, tubular. Corolla of 5 nearly separate and often clawed* petals. Fruit dry, enclosed by the persistent calyx. (*Limonium* is from the Greek for meadow, perhaps in allusion to the salt marsh habitat of many species.)

While mostly salt marsh plants in the wild state, the cult. sea lavenders are easily grown in the flower garden, preferably in somewhat sandy soils. They are of great use for dried bouquets as the chaffy flowers hold their color for a long time. Some of the more open-clustered sorts are especially fine for the feathery trimming of flower arrangements, suggesting the baby's-breath. The annuals should be sown where needed, while the perennials are easily increased by division. All bloom in summer or early autumn. Some of the species, especially *L. sinuatum*, are often grown in the cool greenhouse for the florist trade.

There is much confusion in the Latin name of these plants, which are often offered under the name *Statice*. The latter properly belongs only to the thrift (*see* STATICE), but many catalogues still list sea lavenders under *Statice* instead of *Limonium*.

**bonduelli.** An annual or biennial, 15–24 in. high. Leaves oblongish or oval, 4–6 in. long. Flowers yellow, in a branched cluster (panicle*), the branches winged. Algeria.

**latifolium.** A hairy perennial, 15–24 in. high. Leaves oblongish, 6–9 in. long. Flower cluster much branched, the calyx* white, but the corolla blue.* Eurasia. The *var.* album has white flowers, and the *var.* elegantissimum is a finer form with larger flowers.

**perezi.** Almost shrubby and nearly 3 ft. high. Leaves triangular, 4–6 in. long, square cut at the base, long-stalked. Calyx* bluish-purple, the corolla yellow. Canary Islands. Grown in Calif. and not certainly hardy except in similar climates.

**sinuatum.** A perennial or biennial, 15–24 in. high. Leaves lyre-like and cut, 6–8 in. long. Flower cluster (panicle*) much branched, the branches 3–5-winged. Calyx* blue, the corolla yellowish white. Mediterranean Region. One of the best for the outdoor garden, and often forced by florists.

**tataricum.** A perennial not over 12 in. high. Leaves ovalish, but broader towards the tip, 4–6 in. long. Flower cluster (panicle*) with the branches narrowly winged. Calyx* white, green-veined, the corolla red. Southern Eu. There is a fine dwarf variety.

**vulgare.** A perennial, 9–18 in. high. Leaves elliptic or oblongish, 4–6 in. long. Calyx* white, the corolla bluish-lilac. Mediterranean Region.

**LINACEAE** (ly-nay'see-ee). The flax family contains only two genera of garden interest, although 14 genera and over 150 widely distributed species are known. In the cult. genera *Linum* which is mostly hardy is herbaceous while *Reinwardtia* is a somewhat woody greenhouse plant from India.

Leaves usually alternate,* without marginal teeth in both the cult. genera. Flowers rather showy in both genera, prevailingly yellow or blue, but white or red in some species, always in clusters. In both the cult. genera the fruit is a dry pod (capsule*). *Linum* which yields linen and flax (also flaxseed oil) is the most important genus.

Technical flower characters: Flowers regular. Sepals 5 (rarely 4), usually not united, persistent. Petals opposite the sepals, in *Reinwardtia* somewhat connected at the base into a short tube. Stamens* usually 5, sometimes with 5 additional sterile ones. Ovary superior,* 2–5-celled.

---

* Special articles on the subjects indicated by an asterisk (*) will be found at the words so marked.

**LINANTHUS** (ly-nan'thus). A genus of about 12 species of western American annual herbs of the family Polemoniaceae, considered by some as belonging to *Gilia* and separated from that genus only by technical characters. They have opposite* leaves, divided finger-fashion, nearly to the base, into fine, thread-like segments. Flowers generally funnel-shaped. Fruit a 3-celled capsule.* (*Linanthus* is from the Greek for flax flower, but these plants are not like flax.)

*Linanthus grandiflorus* is an old flower garden favorite, but in recent years *L. parviflorus* is more generally grown. Both are of easy culture as hardy annuals, the seed of which should be sown freely where wanted. They make masses of bloom if sown thickly.

**densiflorus** = *Linanthus grandiflorus*.
**grandiflorus.** A sprawling annual herb, 1-2 ft. high. Flowers about 1 in. long, prevailingly lilac, but sometimes pinkish-white, borne in dense, head-like clusters. Calif. Frequently offered as *Gilia densiflora* and *Leptosiphon densiflorum*, and some catalogues call it California phlox (not a true phlox).
**parviflorus.** A popular annual, generally 4-8 in. high. Flowers about 1½ in. long, more salver-shaped than funnel-like, purplish-yellow, orange or pink, and borne in leafy clusters. Calif. Often offered as *Leptosiphon*, and under such names as "aureus," "hybridus," "luteus," etc., to designate the many different forms, all of which appear to be *L. parviflorus*.

**LINARIA** (ly-nay'ri-a). Toadflax. A genus of 100 species of annual or perennial herbs of the figwort family, all from the north temperate zone, a few grown for ornament in the flower garden or rock garden. They are rather slender herbs with opposite* or whorled* leaves, or the upper ones sometimes alternate.* Flowers usually showy, in terminal clusters (spikes or racemes*), the corolla irregular,* with a long tube, and also long-spurred.* Stamens* 4. Fruit a capsule.* (*Linaria* is from the Latin for flax, the leaves of which are like those of some species of toadflax.)

Toadflax is easily grown in most ordinary garden soils. Sow the annual species where wanted, and the perennials are readily increased by division. They may also be grown from seed and should bloom the second season.

**aequitriloba** = *Cymbalaria aequitriloba*.
**alpina.** A perennial, rock garden plant, 3-6 in. high, with very narrow leaves. Flowers blue and yellow, the spur about as long as the corolla. Alps. For culture see ROCK GARDEN.
**cymbalaria** = *Cymbalaria muralis*.
**dalmatica.** A perennial, border plant 2-4 ft. high, the leaves bluish-green and lance-shaped. Flowers yellow, the straight spur a little shorter than the corolla. Southeastern Eu.
**hepaticaefolia** = *Cymbalaria hepaticaefolia*.
**maroccana.** An annual suited to the rock garden, not over 18 in. high. Leaves very narrow and slender. Flowers red-purple or violet-purple, with a small yellow spot on the lower lip.* Spur about half as long as the corolla. Morocco. For culture see ROCK GARDEN.
**origanifolia.** A perennial, usually less than 12 in. high. Leaves oblong-ish or broader towards the tip. Flowers pinkish-purple or whitish, with a yellow patch on the lower lip.* Spur shorter than the corolla. Southern Eu.
**purpurea.** A showy flower garden perennial, 2-3 ft. high. Leaves lance-shaped or narrower. Flowers purple, but the lower lip somewhat white-bearded, the curved spur about equaling the corolla. Southern Eu.
**vulgaris.** Common toadflax; also called butter-and-eggs. A perennial Eurasian herb, often weedy throughout N.A., usually 12-15 in. high, sometimes double this. Leaves numerous, very narrow. Flowers yellow, the lower lip somewhat orange-bearded. Spur about the same length as the corolla, which is about 1 in. long.

**LINDELOFIA** (lin-del-ō'fī-a). Himalayan perennial herbs of the family Boraginaceae, comprising only two species, one of which, **L. longiflora** (sometimes offered as *L. spectabilis*), is occasionally grown in the rock garden. It is a leafy-stemmed, hairy herb, 12-18 in. high, with some basal and a few alternate* stem leaves, the upper more or less heart-shaped or stem-clasping. Flowers deep blue, about ¼ in. long, much resembling anchusa, but the stamens* protruding. Fruit a collection of nutlets, with hooked bristles. The plant is tolerant of many kinds of soils, but needs reasonably good drainage and protection from slush and wet feet in winter. (Named for Frederich von Lindelof, German patron of botany.)

**LINDEN.** Lime or basswood. A group of ornamental deciduous trees belonging to the genus **Tilia** (till'ĭ-a) of the family Tiliaceae. There are about 30 species native to the north temperate zone. The leaves are alternate,* toothed, usually heart-shaped at the base, and with one side longer than the other. The flowers are small, yellowish-white, fragrant and borne in long-stalked, drooping clusters; attached to the flower stalk for about half its length is a thin, oblong bract* that constitutes one of the prominent characteristics of this group. Fruit is the size of a small pea, dry and hard. (*Tilia* is the old Latin name of the linden.)

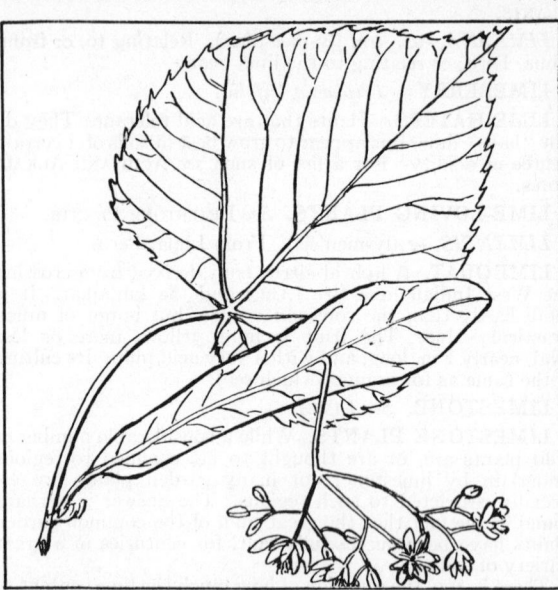

Leaf and flower cluster of the linden

The lindens are handsome trees of good habit and comparatively rapid growth. They make excellent shade trees and are much used along streets and avenues. Due to the abundant nectar the flowers attract many bees. The wood is light, easily worked and used in interior trim. Although not particular, they prefer a rich, moist soil and are liable to suffer during dry spells. Propagation is by seed, which is best sown soon after it ripens.

**T. americana** = *Tilia glabra*.
**T. argentea** = *Tilia tomentosa*.
**T. cordata.** Small-leaved linden. Shapely tree, 90-100 ft. high. Leaves rounded, 1½-3 in. long, heart-shaped at the base, with a short, tapered tip, toothed, dark green above, paler or whitish on the under surface, with tufts of brown hairs in the vein axils.* Flowers yellowish, fragrant, in late June or early July. Europe. Hardy from zone* 3, possibly zone* 2, southward.
**T. euchlora.** Tree to 50 ft. or more with somewhat pendulous branches. Leaves about 4 in. long, roundish-ovate and sharply toothed, heart-shaped at the base, with one lobe longer than the other, glossy on upper surface, paler below with tufts of brown hairs in the vein axils.* Flowers 3-7, in pendulous clusters. June. Hybrid origin. Hardy from zone* 3 southward. One of the most attractive lindens.
**T. europaea** = *Tilia platyphyllos*.
**T. glabra.** American linden. Tall tree sometimes to 120 ft. Leaves roundish-ovate, 4-8 in. long, heart-shaped at base, pointed at tip, coarsely toothed, dark green on upper surface, paler beneath with small tufts of hairs in the vein* axils. Flowers 6-15. June. Canada southward to Ala. and eastern Tex. Hardy from zone* 3 southward. Long known as *T. americana*.
**T. grandifolia** = *Tilia platyphyllos*.
**T. moltkei.** A handsome, vigorous tree with rather pendent branches. The leaves are broadly ovate, toothed, 4-7 in. long, downy beneath. Flowers 5-8, in compact clusters. June. Hybrid form. Hardy from zone* 3 southward.
**T. platyphyllos.** Large-leaved linden. A tall, shapely tree to 120 ft. Leaves round-ovate, 3-4 in. long, heart-shaped at base, toothed, dark green above, paler and usually hairy beneath, especially on the veins and midrib. Flowers whitish, in pendent, 3-flowered (rarely more) clusters. Fruit oval, 3-5-ribbed. June. Europe. Hardy from zone* 3 southward; var. **rubra.** A form with red branchlets; var. **laciniata.** The leaves of this variety are deeply cut into narrow sections.
**T. spectabilis** = *Tilia moltkei*.
**T. tomentosa.** Silver linden, also called white linden. A tree growing 90 ft. or more high, rather pyramidal in habit, with upright branches; young branchlets downy. Leaves 2-5 in. long, rounded, heart-shaped at base or straight across, sharply toothed, occasionally slightly lobed, dark green above, under surface covered with silvery-white down. Flowers whitish, 3-10. July. Eurasia. Hardy from zone* 3 southward.

---

* Special articles on the subjects indicated by an asterisk (*) will be found at the words so marked.

**T. vulgaris.** Common European linden, and a hybrid between *T. cordata* and *T. platyphyllos.* It closely resembles another hybrid, *T. euchlora,* and differs from it mostly in the leaves being dull green on the upper side. *T. vulgaris* is rare in cult. in this country, mostly being replaced by *T. cordata* and *T. platyphyllos.* Hardy from zone* 3 southward.

**LINDEN FAMILY** = Tiliaceae.

**LINDERA** = *Benzoin.*

**LINEAR.** Narrow, long, and with essentially parallel edges, as are many leaves.

*LINEARIFOLIA, -us, -um* (lin-ee-ā-rĭ-fō′lĭ-a). Narrow-leaved.

*LINEARIS, -e* (lin-ee-ā′ris). Linear.*

*LINEATA, -us, -um* (lin-ee-ā′ta). Lined or striped.

*LINGUA, -us, -um* (ling′gwa). A tongue; or tongue-like.

*LINGULATA, -us, -um* (ling-you-lay′ta). Tongue-like.

*LINIFOLIA, -us, -um* (ly-ni-fō′lĭ-a). With flax-like leaves.

**LINNAEA** (lin-nee′-a). Twinflower. One, or perhaps two, species of herb-like, woody, trailing evergreen plants of the honeysuckle family, found throughout the cooler parts of the north temperate zone, but extending north to Alaska and northern Siberia. They have opposite,* stalked, roundish leaves with shallowly scalloped margins. Flowers in pairs, at the end of slender, upright stalks. Corolla more or less bell-shaped, 5-lobed. Stamens* 4. Fruit dry, not splitting, 1-seeded. (Named for Linnaeus.*)

Whether there are one or two species is of little garden significance, although botanists are in opposite camps over the question. The twinflower requires partial shade, good drainage, and an acid humus of pH 5 (*see* ACID AND ALKALI SOILS), in order to thrive. It is thus suitable only to specially prepared places in the rock garden or wild garden, preferably north of zone* 4. *See* WILD GARDEN.

**americana.** Twinflower of N.A. The only real divergence from the traditional twinflower is in the leaf margins being hairy-fringed only near the base, and in the slightly longer, more tubular corolla. Labrador to the mountains of W. Va. westward to the Rocky Mountains, northern Calif. and to Alaska. Also known as deer vine and twin sisters.

**borealis.** Twinflower of Europe. Prostrate, its creeping stems slightly hairy. Leaves about 1 in. long, usually minutely hairy-fringed on the margin, and with a few scattered hairs on the upper surface. Flowers fragrant, rose-pink or white, about ⅓ in. long. Fruit yellow. Throughout northern and sub-arctic Eurasia, and possibly in Alaska. June-Aug.

**LINNAEUS.** Perhaps the most famous botanist in the world. While commonly called Linnaeus, he was a Swede whose real name was Karl von Linné, born 1707, died 1778. The great contribution which Linnaeus made was that, for the first time, he worked out a system for naming plants which is still the basis of our modern system. It discarded most of the Pre-Linnaean* complexities and substituted for every plant only two names — the first one for its genus, the second to designate its species. That is still the basis for naming all hort. plants, of which Linnaeus grew many in his now world-famous garden at Upsala, to which many make pilgrimages from all over the world.

His system of naming and classifying plants was contained in two of his books, *Species Plantarum,* 1753, and *Genera Plantarum,* 1754. Later he elaborated the plan in many other volumes, but from these two stem all the modern methods of naming plants. *See* PLANT NAMES.

**LINNET.** *See* Bird Nuisances at BIRDS.

*LINOIDES* (ly-noy′deez, but *see* OÏDES). Resembling flax (*Linum*).

**LINOMA** = *Dictyosperma.*

**LINOSYRIS** (ly-no-sy′ris). Old World perennial herbs of the family Compositae, the only cult. species being **L. vulgaris,** the goldilocks, grown for its numerous heads of late-blooming flowers. It is a smooth herb, 18–24 in. high, with alternate,* narrow leaves about 1 in. long. Flower heads about ½ in. wide, without rays,* pale yellow, and effective only because they are grouped in large, branching clusters (corymbs*). It is easily grown in any garden soil and may be propagated by division of its roots. (*Linosyris* is a combination of *Linum,* flax, and *Osyris,* a non-hort. genus.)

**LINSEED OIL.** *See* FLAX.

**LINUM** (ly′num). Flax. Nearly 100 species of rather slender annual or perennial herbs of the family Linaceae, all but one of the cult. species grown only for ornament. The single economic species is the common flax which yields linseed oil and linen. Leaves generally alternate,* stalkless, narrow and without marginal teeth. Flowers in generally terminal clusters (racemes* or cymes*), day-blooming and rather fleeting. Sepals and petals each 5, separate. Stamens* 5, alternating with the petals. Fruit a small, dry capsule.* (*Linum* is the classical name of the flax.)

The ornamental linums are of very simple culture. One of them, the flowering flax (*L. grandiflorum*), is a widely cult. hardy annual. Like other hardy annuals, its seed should be sown where the plants are to grow. The perennial species are propagated by division. The leaves of all species look so much alike as to make repetition of their characters useless for purposes of identification.

**alpinum.** A perennial 4–6 in. high. Flowers blue. Eu. *See* BLUE GARDEN.

**flavum.** Golden flax. A perennial, 1–2 ft. high. Flowers about ¾ in. wide, golden-yellow. Eu. Another plant, sometimes offered as *L. flavum,* is likely to be *Reinwardtia indica* (which see).

**grandiflorum.** Flowering flax. A widely grown hardy annual, 1–2 ft. high. Flowers nearly 1½ in. wide, red or pink or in shades of either. Northern Af. The var. **coccineum** with scarlet flowers, and the var. **rubrum** with bright red flowers are the two best-known forms.

**hirsutum.** A perennial, 1–2 ft. high. Flowers white or lilac. Southern Eu.

**lewisi.** Prairie flax. A perennial, 2–3 ft. high. Flowers about 1½ in. wide, blue. Western N.A.

**narbonense.** A perennial, 1–2 ft. high. Flowers about 1½ in. wide, sky-blue with a white eye.* Eu.

**perenne.** A perennial, 1–2 ft. high. Flowers about 1 in. wide, clear sky-blue. Eu. The var. **album** has white flowers.

**salsoloides.** Perennial, partly evergreen herb, 6–8 in. high. Flowers white with a purple eye.* Southern Eu.

**usitatissimum.** Common flax, and the source of linseed and linen. An annual perennial, 3–4 ft. high. Flowers about ½ in. wide, usually blue, sometimes white. Eu., but often established as an escape in N.A. *See* FLAX.

**viscosum.** A sticky-hairy perennial, 15–24 in. high. Flowers 1–1½ in. wide, pink, but violet-veined. Southern Eu.

INSECT PESTS. Flax species are recorded as attacked by general feeders; the commercial flax of the Northwest is especially injured by grasshoppers and cutworms. Grasshoppers are controlled with bran bait sown early in the morning; this is most successful as a community project. Some species of cutworms are killed by bait sown in the evening.

DISEASES. Wilt, anthracnose, and rust affect flax rather generally and may cause much loss. Recommended practices are the use of resistant varieties wherever possible, seed selection and cleaning, sowing early if rust is present, crop rotation, well-drained soil, and removal of old, diseased straw.

**LION'S-EAR** = *Leonotis leonurus.*

**LION'S-TAIL** = *Leonurus cardiaca;* also *Leonotis leonurus.*

**LIP; LIPPED.** That part of an irregular corolla which resembles a protruding lip, as in the snapdragon. The latter has an upper, erect, and 2-lobed lip, and a lower, spreading, and 3-lobed one. Such flowers are called 2-lipped. The lip is a common feature of many flowers, especially in the mint and figwort families, and in many orchids. It is, of course, never present in regular* flowers.

**LIPARIS** (lip′a-ris). Twayblade. A genus of orchids, widely distributed and growing in the ground, of secondary hort. interest, but two of the native species occasionally grown in the wild garden. They are erect, small, smooth, perennial herbs from a bulbous base, from which arise usually 2, chiefly basal, broad, rather thickish leaves (in ours). Flowers very irregular,* borne in a loose raceme* at the end of a slender stalk, prevailingly yellowish-green, or purplish. Sepals and petals nearly equal, narrow and spreading. Lip* nearly flat. Fruit a small capsule.* (*Liparis* is from the Greek for fat or shining, in allusion to the leaves.)

**liliifolia.** Twayblade. Usually about 6 in. high, the leaves ovalish, 3–5 in. long. Flowers 5–15 in the cluster, madder-purple, the lip* more or

---

* Special articles on the subjects indicated by an asterisk (*) will be found at the words so marked.

less wedge-shaped. Eastern U.S. June–July. It should be grown in a shady part of the wild garden in well-drained but good rich woods soil.

**loeseli.** Twayblade; called, also, fen orchis. Usually about 5 in. high. Leaves more or less elliptic, 2–4 in. long, more or less keeled.* Flowers 3–6 in the cluster, yellowish-green, the lip* oblongish. In bogs, meadows, and moist thickets, N.A. and Eu. June–July. Can only be grown in wet or moist places, but will stand open sunlight.

**LIP-FERN.** *See* CHEILANTHES.

**LIPPIA** (lip′pĭ-a). A large genus of often aromatic herbs or shrubs of the family Verbenaceae, nearly all tropical American, only two of much hort. interest. One is the popular old favorite, the lemon verbena, while the other is a widely used ground cover in Calif. and other warm regions where it often replaces lawn grasses. Leaves opposite* or whorled.* Flowers small, resembling those in *Lantana*, usually in small clusters (heads or spikes). Corolla slightly oblique, 4-lobed, or even 2-lipped.* Stamens* 4. Fruit 2 separate nutlets enclosed by the persistent calyx.* (Named for Dr. Auguste Lippi, French traveler.)

The lemon verbena is a favorite florists' plant and should be grown in the cool greenhouse in potting mixture* 4. It may be plunged* outdoors during the summer or used as a porch plant in pots. The first species is often mown like grass in Calif., where it is commonly called carpet grass or fog fruit. It is also a bee plant there. The best way to make a lawn of it is to plant sods of it at intervals. It grows rapidly and will usually smother all weeds, especially if kept mown.

**canescens.** A creeping, prostrate, rapidly spreading plant (see above). Leaves about ⅔ in. long, oblongish. Flowers lilac, but yellow-eyed, the head-like cluster scarcely ½ in. in diameter. S.A. Often offered as *L. repens*.

**citriodora.** Lemon verbena. A shrub 6–10 ft. high and much grown in greenhouses, usually as a pot plant and kept lower. Leaves prominently lemon-scented, especially when crushed, more or less lance-shaped, 2–3 in. long. Flowers white, generally in spikes, but the clusters sometimes branched. Chile and the Argentine. It is grown outdoors south of zone* 6, but northward as a greenhouse subject.

**repens** = *Lippia canescens*.

**LIQUIDAMBAR.** *See* SWEET GUM.

**LIQUID MANURE.** A mixture of cow or horse manure and water, very useful for feeding pot plants, hanging

A potato sack and butter tub method of making liquid manure.

baskets, house plants, or any others where constant watering tends to leach out plant food. Other manures such as guano or hen manure may be used, but usually they are not so easy to procure as cow or horse manure.

The danger in using liquid manure is that too much will be put on at a time or in too strong concentrations. To avoid this, follow the formulas below, and do not use the solutions more than once in ten days or two weeks. What are constantly referred to as "rich feeders" need far more liquid manure than others. No hard-and-fast rule can be given, but a general one is to feed generously the naturally quick-growing sorts, but give less liquid manure to slower-growing species. Most house plants would benefit by an application not oftener than once a month.

FORMULAS FOR LIQUID MANURES

Cow manure ½ bushel to 50 gallons of water (or 3 gallons of water to 1 dry quart of manure).
Horse manure ½ bushel to 40 gallons of water (or 2½ gallons of water to 1 dry quart of manure).
Guano or hen manure 10 pounds to 50 gallons of water (or 5 gallons of water to 1 pound of manure).
Sheep manure ½ bushel to 60 gallons of water (or nearly 4 gallons of water to 1 dry quart of manure).

In the case of cow and horse manure, some people prefer the water boiling, upon the theory that it kills many hibernating insects. But most busy gardeners use cold water. In any case, stir the mixture once a day for a week before applying. Use well-rotted horse or cow manure; the others can be used in the usual dried state in which they are sold.

Watering with liquid manure is exactly like ordinary watering, except that care must be taken to keep the solution off the foliage. Most housewives, too, prefer to have the operation done outdoors and the plants brought back after a few hours. Practical greenhouse men use liquid manure as part of their regular routine for many plants.

**LIQUID MEASURES.** *See* WEIGHTS AND MEASURES, 3.

**LIQUORICE** = Licorice.

**LIRIODENDRON.** *See* TULIP-TREE.

**LIRIOPE** (li-rĭ-ō′pe). Lily-turf. Asiatic, stemless, perennial herbs of the lily family, sometimes grown as ground covers in warm regions, as their thick but grass-like leaves are evergreen and very numerous. They have short, thickish rootstocks, and often spread by stolons* to form thick mats. Flowers in terminal clusters (spikes* or racemes*) at the end of stalks that are about as long as the leaves. Corolla small, white, blue, or violet. Stamens* 6. Unlike most plants of the family, *Liriope* has an inferior ovary. Fruit black and berry-like. (Named for the nymph.)

These plants are usually greenhouse subjects in the North, but can be used for ground cover south of Washington. For a more hardy lily-turf *see* OPHIOPOGON. *Liriope*, which is sometimes hardy in favorable places north of Washington, is best grown in the cool greenhouse in potting mixture* 3.

**graminifolia.** The plant passing as this is usually *Liriope spicata*, the true *L. graminifolia* being apparently unknown in cult.

**muscari.** Blue lily-turf. Leaves nearly 18 in. long, about ⅓ in. wide. Flowers lilac-purple, the stalk of the flower cluster about as long as the leaves. There are forms with fasciated* flower stalks. The var. **variegata** has the leaves yellow-striped. Often confused with *Ophiopogon jaburan*, which is more hardy.

**spicata.** Creeping lily-turf. Leaves grass-like, but thicker, about 8 in. long. Flowers pale lilac or nearly white, scarcely ¼ in. long, the cluster lax and open. There is a striped-leaved form.

**LITCHI** (lee′chee). A single species of Chinese tree of the family Sapindaceae, **L. chinensis**, variously called litchi, litchee, leechee, or lychee, and much cult. in warm regions for its fresh fruit. When this is dried it is the litchi-nut of the shops. It is a round-topped, medium-sized tree with compound* leaves, with 2–4 pairs of oblongish, pointed, leathery leaflets, which are shining green above but paler beneath. Flowers small, unisexual* or polygamous,* greenish-white, without petals, and in a large, loose, open cluster (panicle*) often a foot long. Fruit a drupe,* the fleshy aril* of its seed being the edible part of the fruit, which is so handsome that the tree is considered an ornamental by some. (*Litchi* is the Chinese name for the plant.)

---
* Special articles on the subjects indicated by an asterisk (*) will be found at the words so marked.

### Litchi Culture

Because of its susceptibility to cold injury, wherein sustained temperatures much below freezing are fatal, the litchi is sparingly grown in the U.S., and planting is limited to only the most frost-free sections of Fla. and Calif. Of the numerous Chinese varieties, few named ones are grown; most trees are seedlings or layers from unknown varieties. Bright red fruits, of about 1½ in. diameter and with a thin, tough, warty outer skin, are borne in clusters and ripen over a short season in early summer. The white, pulpy flesh has a pleasing flavor either as a fresh fruit or dried.

The trees thrive best in fertile, loamy soils having an acid reaction. Propagation is commonly by seeds or air layering, but may be accomplished by grafting, inarching and cuttings. They should be set 30–40 ft. apart, each way. — H. M.

**LITHOCARPUS** (li-tho-kar'pus). A large group of ornamental, evergreen trees of the oak family. They are Asiatic, with one exception, and can be cultivated only in warm climates. The only cult. species is **L. densiflora**, the tan oak, sometimes known as tanbark oak and chestnut oak, and is found from southern Ore. to northern Calif., where it is abundant along the coast. Under favorable conditions it grows 75–100 ft. high. Leaves leathery and evergreen, alternate,* toothed, more or less oblong, 3–5 in. long and densely covered on the under surface with matted hairs that eventually disappear. The flowers are in upright catkins, 2–4 in. long, with the male flowers toward the top of the catkin and a few female ones at the base. Fruit an acorn about 1 in. long. Possibly hardy from zone* 5 southward. The bark of this tree is of considerable importance for tanning leather. It likes a loamy soil, reasonably moist, is difficult to transplant and best propagated by seed. Long known as *Quercus densiflora*. (*Lithocarpus* is Greek for stone fruit, referring to the hard shell of the acorn.)

**LITHODORA** (lith-o-dō'ra). A small genus of rather shrubby plants of the family Boraginaceae from the Mediterranean region, of secondary garden importance. They are often included in *Lithospermum* (which see) from which they differ only in the shrubby habit. (*Lithodora* is from the Greek for rock-inhabiting, in allusion to the habitat of the leading species.)

*Lithodora fruticosa* should be grown in the rock garden where it will trail over rocks. It can be propagated by cuttings of old wood. In its native region the plant is tolerant of limestone, but does not appear to need it as grown here. The first species is not much known here, but is common in British rock gardens.

diffusa. A low, prostrate, evergreen under-shrub. Leaves narrowly lance-shaped. Flowers about ½ in. long, deep blue but striped with reddish-violet. Southern Eu. Sometimes listed as *Lithospermum prostratum* and *L. diffusum*.
fruticosa. A trailing, woody-stemmed, evergreen or persistent plant with narrow leaves having rolled margins and the under surface white-felty. Flowers blue. Southern Eu. Sometimes confused with *Lithodora diffusa*, and often listed as *Lithospermum fruticosum*.

*LITHOPHILA, -us, -um* (lith-ŏff'i-la). Rock-inhabiting.

**LITHOPHRAGMA** (lith-o-frag'ma). A small genus of herbs of the family Saxifragaceae, all from western N.A., but only **L. affinis**, the woodland star of Calif., of any garden interest. It is a slender-stemmed, sticky-hairy perennial, 8–15 in. high, with a tuberous rootstock, and chiefly basal, often bronzed, roundish leaves that are bluntly and shallowly lobed. Flowers small, white, in a terminal cluster (raceme*). For details of structure see SAXIFRAGACEAE. The plant is occasionally grown in the wild garden or rock garden, often under the name *Tellima affinis*. (*Lithophragma* is from the Greek for rock and fence, in allusion to the rocky habitat of some species.)

**LITHOSPERMUM** (lith-o-sper'mum). Gromwell; also called puccoon. A large genus of annual or perennial herbs of the family Boraginaceae, all from the north temperate zone, a few of them grown in the border or wild garden, but of secondary hort. importance. Leaves alternate,* without marginal teeth. Flowers yellow or blue (in ours), in leafy or bracted,* 1-sided clusters (spikes* or racemes*), the corolla funnel-shaped or salver-shaped, the throat sometimes crested. Stamens 5. Fruit a collection of small nutlets within the persistent calyx.* (*Lithospermum* is from the Greek for stone and seed, in allusion to the hard nutlets.)

The genus has been much confused as to names, as the list below shows very plainly. Shrubby species are to be looked for at *Lithodora*. The true gromwells are of easy culture in the wild garden or border, and may be raised from seed or increased by division.

angustifolium. Yellow puccoon. A diffusely branched perennial, 1–2 ft. high. Leaves very narrow. Earlier flowers bright yellow and about 1 in. long, the later flowers smaller and pale yellow. Central and western N.A. April–July. Sometimes known as *L. linearifolium*.
canescens. Orange puccoon. A hairy-stemmed or hoary perennial, 12–18 in. high. Leaves oblongish or narrower. Flowers orange-yellow, about ½ in. long, essentially stalkless in the cluster. Eastern N.A., but west to Tex. Sometimes known as alkanet.
diffusum = *Lithodora diffusa*.
fruticosum = *Lithodora fruticosa*.
graminifolium = *Moltkia suffruticosa*.
linearifolium = *Lithospermum angustifolium*.
petraeum = *Moltkia petraea*.
prostratum = *Lithodora diffusa*.
purpureo-coeruleum. A perennial herb with a creeping or procumbent stem which is 12–20 in. long. Leaves lance-shaped. Flowers about ½ in. wide, deep blue. Eu. Spring. For culture see ROCK GARDEN.

**LITHRAEA** (lith'ree-a). Evergreen South American trees or shrubs of the family Anacardiaceae, comprising only 3 species of which **L. molleoides** is planted for ornament in southern Calif. It is a shrub 8–12 ft. high, with compound* leaves, the 3–5 leaflets sharp-pointed, 1½–3 in. long, the stalks winged.* Flowers small, greenish-white, in clusters (panicles*) which are 2–3 in. long. Petals 5. Stamens* 10. Fruit a drupe,* but dry and with a hard, bony stone. The plant is closely related to the pepper-tree (*Schinus molle*), and requires similar culture. (*Lithraea* is from a Chilean vernacular for another species.)

**LITTLE PEACH.** A virus disease. See Diseases at PEACH.

**LITTLE PICKLES.** See OTHONNA.

*LITTORALIS, -e* (lit-to-ray'lis). Pertaining to the seashore.

*LITTOREA, -us, -um* (lit-tor'ee-a). Of the seashore or coast.

**LIVE-FOREVER** = *Sedum telephium*.

**LIVE OAK** = *Quercus virginiana*. See OAK.

**LIVERBERRY** = *Disporum lanuginosum*.

**LIVERLEAF.** See HEPATICA.

**LIVERWORT.** Applied to two very different plants. One is a flowerless plant known as *Marchantia polymorpha*, common in wet places, especially under greenhouse benches. See MARCHANTIA. The other liverwort is the common hepatica (which see).

**LIVING-ROCK** = *Ariocarpus*.

**LIVISTONA** (liv-i-stō'na). Popular, Old World fan palms, one of them widely grown by florists under the name of *Latania borbonica*, and perhaps the most cult. of all fan palms in America. Of over 20 species, only two others are occasionally grown outdoors in Calif. or Fla. All have more or less ringed trunks and a large crown of fan-like leaves, the stalks of which are sometimes prickly in youth. Otherwise the plants are unarmed. Flower clusters branched, appearing among the crown of leaves. Flowers small, perfect,* the stamens* 6. Fruit drupe-like, but the flesh thin, 1-seeded. (Named by Robert Brown in honor of P. Murray of Livistone, near Edinburgh.)

For culture see PALM.

australis. Australian fan palm. Taller than the next species and not so hardy. It may reach a height of 80 ft. Trunk slender, reddish-brown. Leafstalks spiny, especially on young leaves. Leaves 3–6 ft. wide, divided to the middle or below it into 30–50 segments that do not droop and are once- or twice-cleft at the tip. Fruit nearly round, about ⅝ in. diameter. Aust. As grown in Fla. it has not proved hardy in zone* 8, but is thoroughly hardy in zone* 9.
chinensis. Chinese fan palm; also called fan palm. In maturity

---
* Special articles on the subjects indicated by an asterisk (*) will be found at the words so marked.

30–40 ft. high, but much lower as a pot or tub plant in which form it is very widely grown in northern greenhouses. Leaves 3–6 ft. wide, divided ⅓ or ½ the distance to the center into many narrow and distinctly ribbed segments which droop at the tip and are also cleft nearly a foot. Fruit ovalish, about ½ in. long. Central China. Hardy from zone* 8, possibly in protected parts of zone* 7 southward. Commonly sold as *Latania borbonica*. *See* LATANIA.

**rotundifolia.** A slender-trunked palm 60–80 ft. high. Leaves 3–5 ft. wide, split into 60–90 narrow but short segments which are cleft at the tip, the leafstalk spiny on young leaves. Fruit nearly round, about ¾ in. in diameter. Malaya. Not hardy outside of zone* 9, and not much known here.

**LOAM.** *See* SOILS.

**LOASA** (low'a-sa). Tropical American herbs (in ours) of the family Loasaceae, usually provided with stinging hairs and of only secondary garden interest. Of 80 or more species only the two below are cult. Both are annual herbs with lobed or compound* leaves. Flowers prevailingly white or yellow, but often of additional colors as noted below, solitary in the leaf-axils* or in clusters (leafy racemes*). Petals 5, hooded or spreading and alternating with 5 hooded scales, which are bristly on the back. Stamens* many. Fruit a 3–5-valved capsule.* (*Loasa* is the South American name for some species.)

The two below should be grown as tender annuals. *See* ANNUALS.

**tricolor.** Not over 2 ft. high. Leaves opposite,* twice-compound, the leaflets arranged feather-fashion. Flowers yellow, but the hooded scales red and the stamens* white. Chile.

**vulcanica.** From 1–3 ft. high. Leaves simple,* but parted finger-fashion into 3–5 lobes. Flowers white, but the hooded scales yellow and barred red and white. Ecuador and Colombia.

**LOASACEAE** (low-a-say'see-ee). A family of 13 New World genera and about 200 species of herbs (rarely woody plants), four genera of which are of secondary garden interest. They are *Caiophora*, *Loasa*, *Mentzelia*, and *Blumenbachia*, all of which have stinging hairs, except *Mentzelia*, which is the most important hort. genus, and has merely barbed hairs.

Leaves opposite* in *Loasa* (mostly), *Caiophora* and *Blumenbachia*, but usually alternate* in *Mentzelia*. Flowers regular,* in various kinds of clusters, often showy in *Mentzelia*, the petals flat or hooded, often mixed with sterile, petal-like stamens. Fruit a dry pod (capsule*) in all the cult. genera.

Technical flower characters: Sepals usually 5, the margins overlapping, usually persistent. Petals usually 5, inserted on the receptacle.* Stamens* numerous, and usually mixed with many sterile, petal-like stamens. Ovary generally inferior,* 1-celled.

***LOBATA*, *-us*, *-um*** (lo-bay'ta). Lobed. *See* LOBE.

**LOBE.** A part or segment of an organ, especially the *lobes* of a petal or leaf. While there is no technical limit to the degree of division which constitutes a lobe, as usually understood a lobe is from ⅓ to ½ the depth of the whole. If the division extends more than half way to the center, the organ is better described as divided.

**LOBELIA** (lo-bee'lĭ-a). Showy-flowered perennial or annual herbs of the family Lobeliaceae, comprising over 250 species, some of the tropical sorts (not cult.) being trees. The garden kinds are popular for the border, some for the wild garden, and one a widely used edging plant. Leaves alternate.* Flowers in terminal, often very beautiful clusters (mostly spikes* or racemes*), which are sometimes leafy, or nearly always bracted.* Corolla irregular,* more or less tubular below, but split to the base, 3 of the lobes forming a lip, the other two erect or turned backward. Stamens* united by their anthers* into a ring around the style.* Fruit a 2-valved capsule.* (Named for Matthias Lobel, a Flemish father of modern botany.)

Except where noted, the lobelias are of easy culture in the open border. All except *L. erinus* are perennials which may be increased by division of the clumps in fall or spring. The edging lobelia (*L. crinus*) is a tender annual and should be grown as such. *See* ANNUALS.

**cardinalis.** Cardinal-flower; also called scarlet lobelia. An erect, stiffish perennial, 2½–5 ft. high. Leaves oblongish, 3–5 in. long, coarsely toothed, nearly stalkless. Flowers bright scarlet, about 1½ in. long. Eastern N.A. July–Sept. It needs a moist, shaded place in the wild garden for best development, but will stand some sun if planted in a moist place.

**erinus.** Edging lobelia. A tender annual, and one of the most popular of edging plants. *See* EDGING. It is a partly trailing herb 3–8 in. high, the leaves ovalish or narrower, somewhat broader towards the tip. Flowers ¼–¾ in. wide, blue (in the typical form), on very slender stalks. South Africa. The *var.* **alba** has white flowers. The *var.* **compacta** is lower and dense, and is the best form for edging. Other forms or named varieties (over a dozen) have variously colored or double flowers, and some have trailing stems and are useful for hanging baskets.

**fulgens.** A perennial, hairy herb, 2–3 ft. high. Leaves lance-shaped, usually bronzy. Flowers deep red, nearly 1½ in. long. Mex. Hardy from zone* 5 southward, but even there best mulched over the winter.

**laxiflora.** A hairy perennial, 3–5 ft. high. Leaves ovalish or narrower, toothed. Flowers about 1½ in. long, red and yellow, the stamens protruding. Mex. A plant for the cool greenhouse, especially for pot culture. Seeds sown in Feb. will produce bloom by autumn.

**syphilitica.** Blue or great lobelia. A hardy perennial, 2–3 ft. high, usually quite smooth. Leaves oblong-oval, tapering both ends, 3–5 in. long. Flowers about 1 in. long, deep blue or bluish-purple, very rarely white. Eastern U.S. A good late-flowering blue plant for the autumn garden. *See* BLUE GARDEN.

**LOBELIACEAE** (lo-bee-lĭ-ā'see-ee). The only four garden genera of the lobelia family are herbs, but some of its 20 genera and over 600 species are shrubs and trees in the tropics. Those of hort. interest are grown for their often showy, always irregular* flowers, some of which are 2-lipped.*

Leaves alternate* or basal, the plants often with an acrid or milky juice. Flowers rarely solitary, more often in various sorts of clusters, chiefly in spikes* and racemes.* Fruit a berry in *Centropogon*, but a dry pod (capsule*) in *Downingia*, *Lobelia* and *Palmerella*, the only other hort. genera.

Much the most important of these is *Lobelia*, which contains many fine garden plants, and some, like the cardinal-flower, suited to the wild garden.

Technical flower characters: Calyx united, its limb 5-lobed or 5-parted. Corolla irregular,* tubular, and mostly 2-lipped,* but the tube sometimes parted nearly to the base. Stamens five, the anthers often united around the style.* Ovary superior,* 2–5-celled, its stigma* fringed.

**LOBELIA FAMILY** = Lobeliaceae.

**LOBLOLLY BAY** = *Gordonia lasianthus*.

**LOBULARIA.** *See* SWEET ALYSSUM.

**LOCOWEED.** Many plants poisonous to stock on the western ranges are called locoweed. The only one of garden interest is *Oxytropis lamberti* (which see).

**LOCUST.** A small group of North and Central American deciduous trees and shrubs belonging to the genus **Robinia** (rō-bin'ĭ-a) of the pea family. The leaves are alternate* and compound,* the leaflets arranged feather-fashion. Flowers are pea-shaped, white, pink or purple, and borne in pendulous racemes.* Fruit a flat, many-seeded pod. (Named for J. and V. Robin, herbalists to Henry IV of France.) For the biblical locust, *see* CAROB.

The locusts are ornamental both in leaf and in flower. They do well in soil of moderate quality, often thriving in poor, sandy soil. Propagation is mainly by seed, though some may be multiplied by suckers; certain varieties are grafted. The tree species cast so little shade that grass can be grown under locusts easier than under most other trees.

**R. hispida.** Rose acacia, also called pink locust. A spreading shrub, usually 3–4 ft. high. The branches are brittle and covered with red bristles. Leaves composed of 7–13 oval or rounded leaflets about 1 in. long. Flowers rose-colored, in few-flowered clusters. Pods bristly, 2–3 in. long, seldom produced. May or June. Va. to Ala. Hardy from zone* 3 southward. One of the handsomest locusts; often suckers freely.

**R. kelseyi.** A handsome shrub or small tree growing about 10 ft. high. Leaflets 9–11, oval or narrow-oval, about 1 in. long. Flowers rose-colored, 1 in. across, in 5–8-flowered, bristly stalked clusters. May–June. N.C. Hardy from zone* 3 southward.

**R. neo-mexicana.** Thorny locust. Spiny, branched shrub or small tree 25–30 ft. tall. Leaflets 15–25, oval to ovate, 1–1½ in. long, downy beneath when young. June. Colo., Utah, N. Mex. and Ariz. Hardy from most parts of zone* 3 southward.

**R. pseudo-acacia.** Black locust, also called yellow locust and false acacia. Tree of 70–80 ft. with furrowed brown bark. Leaves 6–12 in. long, often with two spines at base, leaflets 7–19, oval, 1–2 in. long. Flowers white, fragrant, in many-flowered, pendulous racemes 3–5 in. long. Pods smooth, 3–4 in. long. June. Pa. to Okla. and often naturalized elsewhere in N.A. and also in Eu. Hardy from zone* 3 southward. The wood is strong and resists decay in contact with the soil; *var.* **bessoniana**, a slender-branched form developing a rather ovoid head; *var.* **decaisneana**, handsome, rose-colored flowers; *var.* **umbraculifera** develops a dense, rounded head.

**R. viscosa.** Clammy locust. Tree to 30 or 40 ft., the young twigs and leaf stems covered with sticky glands. Leaves 3–10 in. long, leaflets 11–25, ovate or oval, downy beneath when young. Flowers pink with a yellow blotch, not fragrant, in many-flowered clusters, 2–3 in. long.

* Special articles on the subjects indicated by an asterisk (*) will be found at the words so marked.

Pods about 3 in. long, somewhat sticky. May, June. N.C. to Ala. Hardy from zone* 4, and parts of 3, southward.

**LOCUSTA, -us, -um** (lo-kus'ta). Latin for locust, but of uncertain application to the corn salad (*Valerianella locusta*).

**LOCUST FAMILY.** See LEGUMINOSAE.

**LOESS.** Wind-deposited, usually very rich soils, covering many states in the central part of the U.S. They vary from fine, silt-like material to soils that are practically similar to rich garden loam.

**LOGAN, MRS. MARTHA.** See America at GARDEN BOOKS.

**LOGANBERRY** (*Rubus loganobaccus*). This bramble fruit, which has blackberry-like, but red, acid fruit is of uncertain origin. It was found or produced by a Judge J. H. Logan in Calif. in 1881. Whether it is a variety of the western dewberry or a hybrid of that species with the red raspberry is a disputed point, and one which may never be settled.

The plant is a vigorous grower and should be treated as a blackberry except for two points: (1) Its canes are so long and inclined to trail that the plant is best trained to wires, and is commercially so grown. The fence-like wire trellises should be about 6 ft. apart, and the plants spaced 8 ft. apart in the row. (2) Except on the Pacific Coast and in other places with mild winters, the loganberry is nearly sure to winter-kill,* or be killed outright, when the temperature drops to zero. This restricts its commercial cult. to Wash., Ore., Calif. and a few places along the Gulf of Mexico. Elsewhere, even with protection, it is not happy and produces far less fruit. Its pests are the same as those of the raspberry (which see).

A form known as Phenomenal, introduced by Burbank, is favored by some California growers in the region about Los Angeles, who claim it has richer, more raspberry-like fruit than the common loganberry.

**LOGANIACEAE** (lo-gan-i-ā'see-ee). Of the four cult. genera of this family only *Spigelia*, an American herb, is not woody. All the rest of the garden genera are shrubs, trees, or woody vines. Of its 30 genera and over 400 species many contain dangerous poisons in their juice, notably *Strychnos*, which yields strychnine. The other cult. genera are harmless, and comprise very beautiful shrubs in *Buddleia*. The ever-popular Carolina jasmine is in the genus *Gelsemium*.

Leaves opposite.* Flowers usually showy, always in clusters, these spike-like and very handsome in *Buddleia*. Fruit dry in all the cult. genera, except *Strychnos*, where it is somewhat fleshy.

Technical flower characters: Calyx united, its 4-5 lobes free but overlapping. Corolla more or less tubular or funnel-shaped, its limb 4-5-parted. Stamens alternating with the lobes of the corolla. Ovary superior,* 2-celled.

**LOGWOOD** = *Haematoxylon campechianum*.

**LOISELEURIA** (loy-zel-loor'i-a). A single species of prostrate, evergreen shrub of the heath family, **L. procumbens,** the alpine azalea or trailing azalea, which grows in cold regions throughout the north temperate zone. It rarely grows above 6 in. high, its trailing stems several times this length. Leaves opposite,* oval or oblong, about ¼ in. long, very numerous. Flowers in sparse terminal clusters, the corolla bell-shaped, scarcely ¼ in. long, white or pink. Fruit a 2-3-valved capsule, surrounded by the withered calyx. An attractive mat-forming evergreen, suited only to the rock garden from zone* 4 northward, and needing a gritty soil with a pH of about 5.0 (see ACID AND ALKALI SOILS). (Named for J. C. A. Loiseleur-Deslongchamps, French botanist.) See ROCK GARDEN.

**LOLIUM** (lō'li-um). Rye grass. A small genus of annual or perennial, Eurasian grasses, of little garden interest except as they are grown for meadow or pastures. They have erect or ascending, usually unbranched stems and flat grass-like leaves. Flowering spikes terminal, usually interrupted,* the spikelets flattened, the edge towards the stem. Some of them have short awns.* (*Lolium* is the Latin name of one species.)

They are not cult. for ornament, the seed being sown for pasture or meadow purposes.

italicum = *Lolium multiflorum*.

multiflorum. Italian rye grass, but called Australian rye grass in Calif. A perennial grass 15-30 in. high. Leaves nearly 8 in. long and about ⅓ in. wide. Flowering spikes nearly 1 ft. long, the spikelets awned,* and with 20-30 flowers. Eu., and naturalized in N.A. Sometimes offered as *L. italicum*.

perenne. Perennial rye grass; also called English meadow grass. A tufted, perennial grass 15-24 in. high. Leaves almost 5 in. long, about ⅙ in. wide. Spikes about 1 ft. long, the spikelets not awned, and with 5-10 flowers. Eurasia, and naturalized in N.A.

temulentum. Darnel; also called bearded darnel. An annual grass, 2-4 ft. high. Leaves about 10 in. long and ¼ in. wide. Spikes about 1 ft. long, the spikelets only 4-8-flowered, awned. Eu., and naturalized in N.A. Its seeds yield a narcotic poison.

**LOMA.** A trademarked fertilizer with a 5-10-4 ratio (see FERTILIZERS) for general use on lawns and gardens.

**LOMARIA** = *Blechnum*.

**LOMBARDY POPLAR** = *Populus nigra italica*.

**LOMENT.** A dry fruit, differing from a true legume* (pea) in being constricted between the seeds, the constrictions often being so deep that the loment may break into separable parts. See DESMODIUM and HEDYSARUM. Loments are confined to a few genera in the pea family.

**LONCHITIS** (lon-ky'tis). A generic name for a few non-hort. ferns; used as a specific name at *Polystichum lonchitis*, which is supposed to resemble the genus *Lonchitis*.

**LONDON PLANE** = *Platanus acerifolia*.

**LONDON PRIDE** = *Saxifraga umbrosa*.

*LONGA, -us, -um* (long'ga). Long.

**LONGAN** = *Euphoria longana*.

*LONGANA* (long-gan'a). Latinized version of longan. See EUPHORIA.

**LONGEVITY OF SEEDS.** See Viability at GARDEN TABLES II.

**LONGEVITY OF TREES.** See GARDEN TABLES III.

*LONGIFLORA, -us, -um* (lon-ji-flō'ra). With long flowers.

*LONGIFOLIA, -us, -um* (lon-ji-fō'li-a). With long leaves.

*LONGIPES* (lon'ji-peez). Long-stalked.

*LONGIPINNATA, -us, -um* (lon-ji-pin-nay'ta). Long-pinnate, that is with long compound* leaves, the leaflets of which are arranged feather-fashion.

*LONGISCAPA, -us, -um* (lon-ji-skape'a). With a long flowering stalk (scape).

*LONGISSIMA, -us, -um* (lon-jiss'i-ma). Longest.

**LONG MOSS** = *Tillandsia usneoides*.

**LONG PEPPER** = *Capsicum frutescens longum*.

**LONICERA** (lon-iss'er-ra). The honeysuckles comprise a group of 150 or more species of shrubs and woody climbers in the honeysuckle family. They are found throughout the northern hemisphere in both the Old World and America. Leaves opposite,* usually entire,* rarely evergreen. The flowers are tubular or bell-shaped, equally 5-lobed or more often 2-lipped,* the upper lip composed of four lobes and the lower of one. They are borne in pairs in the leaf-axils* or in clusters at the ends of the branches. Fruit a fleshy berry. (Named for Adam Lonicer, a 16th-century German naturalist.)

Practically all the honeysuckles are worthy of cultivation. The tall forms are fine for shrub borders and general use while certain of the lower ones are adapted to the rock garden. The often showy flowers are produced abundantly and are sometimes sweetly scented. The fruits are white, orange, red, blue or black, quite ornamental, and a favorite food for birds. They are of easy cultivation, thriving in almost any place, though a loamy soil, reasonably moist, is best. Propagation is by seeds or cuttings.

---

* Special articles on the subjects indicated by an asterisk (*) will be found at the words so marked.

**bella.** An upright shrub growing 9 or 10 ft. high with spreading branches that are a bit hairy when young. Leaves ovate to oblong, 1–2 in. long, sometimes hairy beneath. Flowers white to pink, fading yellow. Fruit red. May–June; fruit July–Aug. Hybrid origin. Hardy from zone* 3 southward. *Var.* **albida.** Flowers white; *var.* **rosea.** Flowers rosy-pink.

**caprifolium.** Common honeysuckle or Italian honeysuckle. A climbing vine sometimes attaining 20 ft. Leaves oval or elliptic, bluish-green beneath, 2–4 in. long, the upper 2 or 3 pairs fused, forming a cup or disk. Flowers in clusters at the ends of the branches, yellowish-white, sometimes tinged purple, about 2 in. long, 2-lipped,* tube slender. Fruit orange. May–June. Eu. and western Asia. Hardy from zone* 3 southward.

**chrysantha.** An upright shrub of 10–12 ft. The young branches are usually hairy but this character varies. Leaves oval or narrowly oval, pointed, 2–4 in. long. Flowers yellow, about ¾ in. long, tube swollen at base. Fruit red. May–June; fruit Aug.–Sept. Asia and Japan. Hardy from zone* 3 southward.

**dioica.** Small honeysuckle, sometimes called small woodbine. Shrub with spreading, sometimes twining, branches. Leaves oval or oblong, 2–4 in. long, the under surface conspicuously bloomy, the upper pairs grown together. Flowers in terminal clusters, yellow, sometimes tinged purple, about ¾ in. long, tube swollen at base. Fruit red. May–June; fruit July–Aug. Quebec to N.C. and Iowa. Hardy from zone* 2 southward.

**flava.** Yellow honeysuckle. Spreading, twining vine to 10 ft. Leaves elliptic, to 3 in. long, blue-green on under surface, upper pairs fused to form a disk. Flowers orange-yellow, fragrant, about 1 in. long, tube slender, not swollen at base. May–June. N.C. to Okla. Hardy from zone* 3 southward. Perhaps the handsomest of the American honeysuckles.

**fragrantissima.** Shrub growing 6–8 ft. high with spreading, somewhat recurved branches that form a rounded mass. Leaves oval, thick, 1–2 in. long, dark green above, paler beneath, evergreen in mild climates. Flowers creamy-white, very fragrant. Jan.–March. China. Hardy from lower part of zone* 3 southward. Valued for its good foliage and early flowers.

**heckrotti.** A low shrub with spreading, sometimes twining branches. Leaves oblong or oval, 1–2½ in. long, whitish beneath. Flowers 1½ in. long in terminal clusters, purple outside, yellow within, tube slender. June. Origin unknown, probably a hybrid. Hardy from zone* 3 southward. An attractive honeysuckle that blooms over a long period.

**henryi.** A free-growing, half-evergreen vine with slender, climbing or prostrate branches that are covered with stiff hairs. Leaves oblong, 1–4 in. long, pointed at the tip. Flowers borne in the leaf-axils,* purple-red, ¾ in. long. Fruit black. China. Hardy from zone* 3 southward. June–Aug.

**hirsuta.** Rough woodbine. Twining vine, the young branches covered with stiff hairs. Leaves oval, 2–4 in. long, downy on both sides, especially the lower, the upper pairs fused to form an elliptic disk. Flowers in terminal clusters, bright yellow, 1 in. long, the tube swollen at base. June–July. Quebec to Mich. and Pa. Hardy from zone* 3 southward.

**involucrata.** Twinberry. Shrub to 3 ft. with upright, slightly angled branches. Leaves elliptic-oval, 2–5 in. long. Flowers about ½ in. long with two large bracts at the base, yellow, tinged with red, borne on upright stalks. Fruit black, shiny. May–June. Quebec to Alaska and in the mountains to Mex. Hardy from zone* 1 southward.

**japonica.** Japanese honeysuckle. A vigorous, half-evergreen climber growing 20–30 ft.; branches slender, hairy. Leaves ovate to oblong, 1–3 in. long, pointed, usually downy beneath. Flowers white, tinged purple, fading to yellow, sweetly scented, 1–1½ in. long, 2-lipped,* the tube slender. Fruit black. June. Asia. Naturalized in eastern U.S. Hardy from zone* 3 southward. *Var.* **aureo-reticulata.** Leaves smaller and veined with yellow, tender; *var.* **chinensis.** Flowers to 2 in. long, reddish outside; leaves practically hairless except on the veins beneath. *Var.* **halliana.** Flowers white, fading to yellow, not tinged purple.

**korolkowi.** Spreading, graceful shrub 8–12 ft. tall. Leaves oval to ovate, pointed, about 1 in. long, hairy, especially beneath, bluish-green. Flowers pale rose, ⅔ in. long. Fruit red. May–June; fruit Aug. Hardy from zone* 3 southward. Attractive when in leaf because of its bluish cast. *Var.* **floribunda.** Flowers freely; leaves generally broader, not tapered at base.

**maacki.** A vigorous, wide-spreading shrub often 10–15 ft. high. Leaves ovate, with long, slender point, 1½–3 in. long, sometimes hairy. Flowers ¾ in. long, white, ageing yellow. Fruit red. May–June; fruit Sept.–Oct. Manchuria, Korea. Hardy from zone* 3 southward. One of the handsomest and largest honeysuckles, conspicuous in bloom and with bright red berries in the fall. *Var.* **podocarpa.** Hardly distinguishable from the type, leaves broader and habit more spreading.

**nitida.** An evergreen or half-evergreen shrub, rather low though sometimes to 6 ft. with slender branches. Leaves small, thick, glossy, oval to rounded, ¼–½ in. long. Flowers white, fragrant. Fruit purple. May; fruit Sept.–Oct. China. Hardy from zone* 5, and milder parts of 4, southward. Distinguished by its small, glossy leaves.

**periclymenum.** Woodbine. Twisted eglantine. A woody climber sometimes reaching 20 ft. Leaves variable, ovate to obovate, 1½–2½ in. long, bluish-green beneath, upper pairs almost stalkless but never fused. Flowers in terminal clusters, yellowish-white, often tinged with red, fragrant, about 2 in. long, tube slender. Fruit red. June–August; fruit Aug.–Sept. Eu., northern Africa, As. Minor. Hardy from zone* 3 southward.

**pileata.** Low, spreading, evergreen or half-evergreen shrub growing about 1 ft. or so high and having almost horizontal branches. Leaves ovate to oblong, ½–1½ in. long, glossy. Flowers white, fragrant, about ⅓ in. long. Fruit purple. April–May; fruit Oct. China. Hardy from zone* 5 southward. Adapted to use in the rock garden.

**ruprechtiana.** Shrub of good habit growing 8–10 ft. high. Leaves ovate to lance-shaped, pointed, 2–4 in. long, pale and downy beneath. Flowers white, turning yellow, ¾ in. long, not fragrant, tube thick, swollen at base. Fruit red or orange. May, June; fruit Aug., Sept. Manchuria, northern China. Hardy from zone* 3 southward.

**sempervirens.** Trumpet honeysuckle, also called coral honeysuckle. Climbing vine, evergreen in mild climates. Leaves oval to oblong, 1½–3 in. long, bluish-green beneath, and slightly downy, upper pairs united to form a disk. Flowers in terminal clusters, bright orange or red outside, yellow within, about 2 in. long, corolla lobes of almost equal length. Fruit orange to scarlet. May to Aug. Mass. to Fla. and Tex. Hardy from zone* 3 southward.

**standishi.** An upright, rather coarse shrub to 6 or 8 ft. with peeling bark and spreading branches that are bristly hairy when young; partly evergreen in mild climates. Leaves ovate-lanceolate, thick, 2–4 in. long, pointed, bristly hairy beneath, sometimes on upper surface. Flowers creamy-white, fragrant, ½ in. wide. Fruit red. March–April. China. Hardy from zone* 3 southward. Valued for its early flowers; inferior to *L. fragrantissima.*

**syringantha.** Graceful, spreading shrub 6–9 ft. high. Leaves oblong to oval, ½–1 in. long, smooth. Flowers rosy-lilac, sweetly scented. Fruit red. May–June. Hardy from zone* 3 southward.

**tatarica.** Tartarian honeysuckle, also known as garden fly honeysuckle and bush honeysuckle. An upright, vigorous shrub of pleasing habit growing 8–10 ft. high. Leaves oblong-ovate, pointed, 1–2½ in. long, pale beneath. Flowers white to pink, about ¾ in. long, 2-lipped.* Fruit red. May–June; fruit July–Aug. Russia and Siberia. Hardy from zone* 2 southward. The commonest of the bush honeysuckles; ornamental and easily grown. *Var.* **alba.** Flowers white; *var.* **grandiflora.** Flowers larger, white; *var.* **grandiflora rosea.** Flowers rosy-pink, larger; *var.* **rosea.** Flowers rosy-pink outside, paler within.

**thibetica.** Low, spreading shrub forming a rounded mass to 5 ft.; young shoots purplish and downy. Leaves oblong, pointed, ⅓–½ in. long, often in 3's, smooth above, white-hairy beneath. Flowers about ½ in. across, in pairs, often clustered at the joints, pale or rosy-purple, fragrant. Fruit red. May–June; fruit Aug. and Sept. Western China. Hardy from zone* 3 southward. A good, spreading or sprawling shrub, sometimes confused with *L. syringantha* but distinguished by the hairy under surface of the leaves.

**xylosteum.** European honeysuckle, bush honeysuckle. A bushy shrub growing about 10 ft. high. Leaves oval to obovate, pointed at tip, rounded or wedge-shaped at base, paler and hairy beneath. Flowers yellow, often tinged red, about ½ in. across, tube swollen at base. Fruit red. May–June; fruit Aug.–Sept. Eurasia. Hardy from zone* 3 southward.

**LOOFA.** *See* LUFFA.

**LOOSESTRIFE.** A name applied to several different groups of plants. *See* LYSIMACHIA, LYTHRUM, STEIRONEMA, and DECODON.

**LOOSESTRIFE FAMILY** = Lythraceae.

**LOPEZIA** (low-peez'ia). A small genus of tropical American herbs or under-shrubs belonging to the family Onagraceae, used chiefly as greenhouse plants, but not of much hort. importance. Leaves small, alternate,* broadly lance-shaped, the margin saw-like. Flower small, produced in clusters at the ends of the branches. Petals 5, the 2 upper bent upwards a little way from their base. At the bend there seems to be a drop of honey, in reality a dry, glossy piece of hard tissue which deceives flies. The real nectaries,* however, are at the base of the flower. Stamens* 2, one of which is fertile, the other petal-like. Fruit a small, round capsule* which splits into 4 cells containing the seeds. (Named for Thomas Lopez, a Spaniard who wrote on the history of the New World.)

Sow seeds in April, 1/16 in. deep, in the cool greenhouse, in fine potting soil.

**albiflora.** A soft-wooded perennial up to 2 ft. high. Leaves broadly lance-shaped, 1–1½ in. long. Flowers small, produced at the ends of the branches, the petals white, tinged pink near the center. Mexico. Sept.–Oct.

**coronata.** Annual and not over 1 ft. high. Flowers lilac, the 2 side petals red at the base. Mexico.

**lineata.** A shrubby perennial 1–3 ft. high. Stems and leaves slightly hairy, the leaves ovalish, short-stalked. Flowers small, in terminal clusters (racemes*), red. Mexico. Sept.–Nov.

***LOPHANTHA, -us, -um*** (lo-fan'tha). Having crested flowers.

**LOPHOSPERMUM SCANDENS** = *Maurandia lophospermum.* The word *lophosperma, -us, -um* (lo-fo-sper'ma) means having tufted or crested seeds.

**LOQUAT** (*Eriobotrya japonica*). The Chinese loquat, also commonly termed Japan plum and Japanese medlar, is grown in Calif., the Gulf states and Fla., but seldom fruits north of the citrus areas. The tree withstands temperatures of 10 to 15 degrees without material injury, but the fruit or blossoms, on the tree in midwinter, are damaged by a few degrees of frost. Commercial plantings are few, these mainly in Calif., although trees are frequently seen in yards

* Special articles on the subjects indicated by an asterisk (*) will be found at the words so marked.

and garden plantings since the attractive evergreen foliage and symmetrical growth habit make them desirable for ornamental planting even if fruiting is irregular. Fruit ripens from Feb. to May, the dates of maturity depending upon both variety and locality. Borne in large clusters, the fruit varies in shape from spherical to pyriform; in size, from 1 to 3 in. long; and in color, from pale yellow to deep orange. The flesh is firm and juicy with a pleasant, sprightly flavor, and while the fruit usually is eaten out of hand it is also cooked and makes a jelly of superior quality. The sugar content is from 10 to 13% and there is a difference in degree of acidity among varieties.

A wide range of soils, including sands and clays with either an alkaline or acid reaction, are adapted to loquat culture. A regular moisture supply, together with adequate drainage, is desirable, although the tree is quite drought-resistant. Amounts and kinds of fertilizers required will depend on soil type, the more fertile requiring little other than nitrogen, while the more sandy will need a complete mixture to insure greatest thrift and large-sized fruit. Addition of organic materials by mulching, leguminous cover-cropping, or application of stable manures is of benefit. Planting distances are from 12 × 24 ft. to 20 × 20 ft. The closer spacing tends to crowd the trees and is believed by some to increase fruit size. Little pruning is required other than shaping the young tree and later removal of excess branches and dead wood. Thinning of fruit is practiced to some extent to increase size.

The many introduced or locally developed varieties have been divided into two groups — the Japanese and Chinese, the differentiation based on fruit shape, color, size, flavor, and season of maturity. Those of the Japanese grouping are the smaller, juicier, less acid varieties with light-colored flesh (Early Red excepted) and spherical shape. In addition to numerous seedlings, the following are among varieties grown: Advance, Champagne, Thales, Early Red, Tanaka and Premier. Propagation is by seeds, grafting, shield budding and occasionally by cuttings. Loquat seedlings are preferred for stocks but quince may be used. — H. M.

INSECT PESTS. Few pests have been recorded; they include codling moth, green apple aphid, some scale insects, and general feeders. When injurious, they can probably be controlled as on apple and other hosts.

**LORDS-AND-LADIES** = *Arum maculatum*.

**LORETTE PRUNING SYSTEM.** See PRUNING.

**LORIFOLIA, -us, -um** (lor-ĭ-fō′lĭ-a). With strap-shaped leaves.

**LORO.** A trademarked liquid insecticide containing 50% of rhodanic acid salts and 40% sulphonated fatty acids; sold with directions for use against sucking insects.

**LOROMA** = *Archontophoenix cunninghamiana*.

**LOROPETALUM** (lor-o-pet′a-lum). A single, Chinese evergreen shrub of the family Hamamelidaceae, closely related to the witch-hazel but evergreen. Leaves alternate,* without marginal teeth. Flowers resembling the witch-hazel (see HAMAMELIS), but white and much more showy. The only species, **L. chinensis**, is a shrub 6–9 ft. high, with ovalish leaves 1–2 in. long. Petals strap-shaped, about 1 in. long. Fruit a woody capsule. The shrub is not much known in cult. and probably not hardy north of zone* 6, although it will stand some frost, if the wood is mature (see HARDINESS). Propagated by seeds or it may be grafted upon stock of the witch-hazel. It blooms in March–April. (*Loropetalum* is from the Greek for strap and petal, in allusion to the shape of the petals.)

**LOS ANGELES COUNTY ARBORETUM.** See ARBORETUM.

**LOTE BUSH** = *Zizyphus obtusifolia*.

**LOTIFOLIA, -us, -um** (lo-ti-fō′lĭ-a). With leaves like those of the genus *Lotus*.

**LOTUS.** The word *lotus* has many different meanings. The lotus of the lotus-eaters was probably derived from *Zizyphus lotus*, one of the non-hort. jujubes (see ZIZYPHUS). But *lotus* has also been applied to several water lilies (see NYMPHAEA and NELUMBIUM). And Linnaeus applied *lotus* to a group of plants of the pea family. This genus *Lotus* comprises perhaps 100 species of Old World, but largely European, herbs or under-shrubs with compound* leaves, composed of 3–5 leaflets, or sometimes apparently with several simple* leaves. Flowers mostly pea-like, solitary, or in pairs, or in small clusters (umbels*), yellow, white or purple. Fruit a cylindrical, several-seeded pod (legume*). (The name *Lotus*, as used by Linnaeus for these plants, has no connection with the classical lotus, nor has it any connection with the genus *Diospyros*, where it is a specific name.)

The only cult. species of the genus *Lotus* are of secondary garden importance, although the bird's-foot trefoil is a forage plant of wide use. The ornamental species are *L. jacobaeus* and *L. bertheloti*, neither of which is hardy in the East.

**bertheloti.** An under-shrub, 1–2 ft. high, its foliage silvery. Leaflets 3–7, narrow. Flowers showy, scarlet. Canary and Cape Verde Islands. Can be grown outdoors only in Calif. and similar climates, elsewhere in the cool greenhouse in potting mixture* 3.

**corniculatus.** Bird's-foot trefoil; also called ground honeysuckle, baby's-slippers, and bloom-fell. A perennial, rather sprawling herb, 1–2 ft. high. Leaflets 3, ovalish, but broadest towards the tip. Flowers yellow or sometimes red-tinged. Eurasia, and occasionally a troublesome weed in the U.S. See the list at WEEDS.

**jacobaeus.** St. James's-flower or St. James's-pea. A perennial herb, 2–3 ft. high. Leaflets 3–5, very narrow. Flowers black-purple, or yellow, or sometimes both colors on the same plant. Cape Verde Islands. Can be grown outdoors only in Calif. and similar climates.

**tetragonolobus.** Winged pea. A prostrate, annual herb grown (but not much here) for its edible pods and seeds. Leaflets 3, oval. Flowers purplish-red. Pods 4-sided. Southern Eu.

**LOUISIANA.** The state, at the apex of the Mississippi delta, enjoying a mild and equable climate, and exceptionally well watered, lies wholly in zones* 6 and 7.

SOILS. Louisiana belongs to the coastal plain province, rich alluvial plains extending its entire length and constituting the full area of many parishes (counties). Bluff lands, pine flats, pine hills, upland, prairie, wooded lowlands, marsh and coast marsh form the other agricultural soil divisions. The state is traversed by the valleys of the Mississippi, Red,

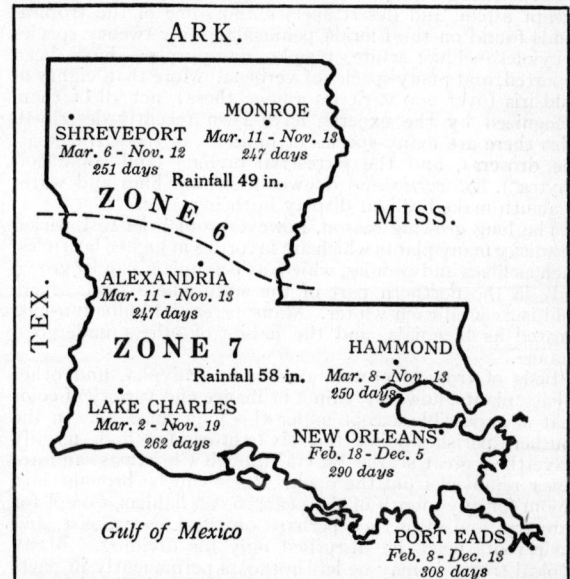

LOUISIANA

The zones of hardiness crossing Louisiana are those shown on the colored map at ZONE, which should be consulted for details. The dates are the average latest killing frost in spring and the first one in the fall. The figures below the dates show the average length of the growing season. The rainfall figures (in inches) are for total annual rainfall in the regions so indicated.

---

* Special articles on the subjects indicated by an asterisk (*) will be found at the words so marked.

Ouachita, and Sabine rivers, and covered with an intricate network of large water-basins and bayous. The sandy loam sloping back from the streams is easily cultivated. Much of this recent alluvial soil is of alkaline reaction, whereas the other areas tend to the acid side of the pH* scale. Black, heavier soil is found back from the streams, and the bluff lands of certain northern parishes are of yellowish-gray, but very fertile. Swamp reclamation has brought much new fertile soil into use.

FRUITS. As North Louisiana partakes largely of the continental climate and South Louisiana of maritime climate, almost all fruits may be grown. Most deciduous fruits do well in all but the extreme southern parishes, while these latter are well adapted to such as figs and citrus fruits. In cut-over pine lands of the Florida parishes, especially Tangipahoa and Livingston, the strawberry industry is large. Grapes, blackberries and dewberries are produced almost throughout the state on some commercial scale. Pecans are the only nuts harvested commercially. Date palms have not succeeded, but the phenomenon of a seedless date palm, producing up to 300 pounds of seedless dates every year, has been discovered in Orleans parish, thoroughly acclimated, and horticultural development from offshoots is hoped for.

VEGETABLES. Practically all vegetables may be and are grown in the state. Truck farming for winter and early spring markets of the North is a major industry in the southerly regions. Some vegetables in great local favor have not penetrated other markets, as the *mirliton*, or vegetable pear. Celery is a famous crop in the vicinity of New Orleans. Okra is produced in quantity, largely as ingredient for crab and chicken gumbos. Tomatoes are large and fine flavored, as are the eggplant, both shipped in quantity. Aromatics and condiments are raised for the local cuisine, and some for shipment, notably the peppers. Tabasco is grown for world markets in Iberia and its neighbor Acadian parishes. Cotton, corn, oats, and tobacco are grown in the northern and central parishes, sugar and rice becoming the great staples as the coast region is approached.

FLOWERS. Native flora embraces almost all genera of trees, shrubs, vines, and herbs common to the continent, except alpine and desert species and some of the tropical kinds found on the Florida peninsula. Over twenty species of violet — blue, white, purple, rose-purple — have been reported, and many species of verbena. More than eighty of wild iris (over 200 varieties among these), not all of them recognized by the experts, have been recently described. Also there are many species of hibiscus, of the sarracenias, the droseras, and the terrestrial orchids (and some epiphytes*). *Stewartia* and dogwood, swamp lilies and water hyacinth make brilliant display in their places.

The long growing season, however, and brief rest period handicap many plants which are favorites in higher latitudes, such as lilacs and peonies, which, as perennials, can be grown only in the northern part of the state where some severe cold is assured each winter. Many perennial bulbs must be treated as biennials, and the habits of others undergo a change.

Beds of tropical croton, caladium, acalypha, and other foliage plants, however, gain a brilliance and variety of color that is impossible except under this long sunshine. In the southern parishes poinsettias, six to fifteen feet high, usually wave their great scarlet bracts through Christmas, and are never removed from the open. Roses can be brought into bloom for any month of the year; so can dahlias, except for January, and even then perhaps on the Lower Coast, and their roots need be disturbed only for dividing. Many typical tropicals may be left outdoors permanently in parts of the state, with proper covering on approach of frost (carelessness in this is responsible for frequent disappointments). Most bulbs can be, or should be, left in the ground. The creole Easter lily, a form of *Lilium longiflorum*, greatly improved in size and number of blossoms, has been cultivated for generations, and the propagation of its bulbs is a large industry on the Lower Coast peninsula.

Azaleas, camellias, gardenias, pomegranates, redbuds, crape-myrtles, hydrangeas, altheas, night jasmine, are favored shrubs. Most evergreens do well in all sections, and many flowering vines add beauty, most conspicuously the perennial rosa montana which is always in blossom from early summer until frost. Chrysanthemums are raised in abundance, and the quantities of this flower used on All-Saints' Day almost surpass belief. A great many varieties of palms add to the tropical aspect of southern parishes (and suffer depredations on Palm Sunday), and a few hardier varieties can be grown throughout the state under selected conditions.

GARDENS. Almost every city or rural household has its flower garden, but gardening in Louisiana has been too easy a task to arouse the combative genius of the average householder. There is at present a strong tendency to landscaping, to specializing, and to scientific methods and study of effects. Gardening possibilities are almost unlimited, and the spread of the garden club movement has aroused new interest in horticultural work. Magnificent gardens always have existed in every part of the state. The most famous one at present is perhaps the Jungle Gardens of Iberia Parish, an old estate renowned for its flowers and birds, and chiefly for its unexcelled collections of camellias and iris. Active garden clubs exist in New Orleans, Alexandria, Baton Rouge, Bunkie, Lake Charles, Lecompte, Tallulah, Monroe, Hammond, Pineville, Ruston, Shreveport, St. Joseph, Vidalia, Newellton, Bernice, Houma, Jennings, Lafayette, Lake Providence, Mandeville, Mansfield, Montgomery, Natchitoches, New Iberia, Oak Grove, Pollock, and Minden.

CLIMATE. The climate is greatly modified by the 1500-mile, deeply indented coastline on the Gulf of Mexico, and by the 3097 square miles of water surface included in the 48,506 square miles of inland area. Annual average temperature for North Louisiana is 65.2°, for South Louisiana 68.2°. Mean minimum temperature for January ranges from 34.6° at Grand Cane to 49.8° at Burrwood; mean maximum temperature for July, from 95.1° at Antioch to 88.8° at Burrwood. Growing season averages from 209 days at Liberty Hill to 330 at Burrwood. Killing frost is frequently escaped in fall or spring, sometimes both, in South Louisiana, and is exceedingly rare on the Lower Coast and coastal belt, as also are the extreme high temperatures of summer. Growing season on the Lower Coast is practically 365 days, frost being reported at Burrwood in 12 out of 22 years.

FROST DATA

| Town | Average date of last killing frost in spring | Latest-known killing frost | Average date of earliest killing frost in fall | Earliest-known killing frost |
|---|---|---|---|---|
| Shreveport | Mar. 6 | April 9 | Nov. 12 | Oct. 20 |
| Monroe | Mar. 11 | April 9 | Nov. 13 | Oct. 10 |
| Alexandria | Mar. 11 | April 26 | Nov. 13 | Oct. 4 |
| Hammond | Mar. 8 | April 4 | Nov. 13 | Oct. 24 |
| Lake Charles | Mar. 2 | April 26 | Nov. 19 | Oct. 20 |
| New Orleans | Feb. 18 | Mar. 26 | Dec. 5 | Nov. 11 |
| Port Eads | Feb. 8 | Mar. 17 | Dec. 13 | Dec. 3 |

Average annual rainfall is 49.63 inches for North Louisiana, 57.95 for South Louisiana; ranging from 43.99 inches at Shreveport to 64.75 at Amite. For North Louisiana greatest precipitation is in December and March, for South Louisiana in June, July, and August. Relative humidity at New Orleans averages 84 per cent at 7 A.M., 64 at noon, 72 at 7 P.M. — P. Y.

**LOUSEWORT.** See PEDICULARIS.

**LOVAGE.** See LEVISTICUM.

**LOVE-APPLE.** The tomato.

**LOVE-IN-A-MIST** = *Nigella damascena*.

**LOVE-LIES-BLEEDING** = *Amaranthus caudatus*.

---

* Special articles on the subjects indicated by an asterisk (*) will be found at the words so marked.

**LOVE-VINE** = *Clematis virginiana*.

**LOWTHORPE SCHOOL.** See GARDEN SCHOOLS.

**LUBRICATING-OIL SPRAY.** See Contact Sprays at INSECTICIDES.

**LUCERNE** = *Medicago sativa*.

*LUCIDA*, *-us*, *-um* (lew'si-da). Bright or shining.

**LUCULIA** (loo-kew'lĭ-a). Himalayan shrubs of the family Rubiaceae, both the known species occasionally grown for ornament, generally in the cool greenhouse. They deserve to be much better known, for they are very handsome in bloom. They have opposite,* leathery leaves, and large, showy, terminal flower clusters (corymbs*) often nearly 12 in. wide. Corolla salver-shaped, its lobes rounded. Fruit a nearly woody capsule,* the seeds winged. (*Luculia* is probably a Latin version of a native name for them.)

These plants need a cool greenhouse and potting mixture* 3. They are winter-blooming and just before the buds begin to swell they will respond to liberal supplies of liquid manure. Plunge* outdoors in the summer, in partial shade, but bring them back to the cool greenhouse at the end of Aug. Keep the temperature around 50° at night, until they get ready to bloom when a night temperature of 55° should be provided.

**gratissima.** A shrub 10–15 ft. high (less as cult.), the leaves oval-oblong, 4–6 in. long. Flowers about 1½ in. wide, pink or rose-pink, the cluster about 6 in. wide. Himalayas.

**intermedia.** From 8–12 ft. high (less as cult.), the leaves oblongish, 4–6 in. long. Flowers nearly 2 in. wide, reddish, the cluster 6–8 in. wide. Himalayas.

**speciosa.** Probably not distinct from *L. gratissima* and considered a larger-flowered form of it.

**LUCUMA** (loo-kew'ma). Tropical American shrubs and trees of the family Sapotaceae, comprising over 50 species, but only **L. nervosa**, the canistel, ti-es, or eggfruit, of any hort. interest. It is a tree up to 25 ft. high, grown for its edible fruit in the tropics and only in the warmest parts of zone* 9 in Fla. Leaves alternate,* leathery, without marginal teeth, oblongish, 5–8 in. long. Flowers small, white (for details see SAPOTACEAE). Fruit fleshy (a berry), maturing in late summer, roundish, or egg-shaped, 2–4 in. long, orange-yellow, the pasty flesh orange-colored and sweetish. The tree is propagated by seeds and is indifferent as to soil. For a plant sometimes offered as *Lucuma mammosa* see ACHRAS ZAPOTA. (*Lucuma* is the Peruvian name for one of the species.)

**LUDWIGIA** (lud-wig'ĭ-a). False loosestrife. Swamp or aquatic, often rather weedy, herbs of the family Onagraceae, comprising perhaps 25 species of which only **L. mulertti** is of hort. interest, although several native species may be dug from the wild. This cult. species is a weak-stemmed aquatic herb, its stems rooting at the joints. Leaves opposite,* evergreen, without marginal teeth, oblongish or narrowed at the base to a stalk as long as the blade, green above, purple beneath. Flowers yellow (for details see ONAGRACEAE). Fruit a capsule, the top of which is crowned with the persistent calyx* lobes. The plant will not survive northern winters, but it is useful in greenhouse pools or in aquaria. (Named for C. G. Ludwig, German botanist.)

**LUFFA** (luf'fa). A small genus of tropical Old World gourds of the cucumber family grown chiefly for ornament or for their interesting fruits. They are tendril*-bearing, quick-growing, herbaceous, annual vines, with alternate,* 5–7-lobed leaves. Flowers yellowish or whitish, the male and female separate on the same plant. Male flowers in racemes,* the female solitary. Petals 5. Fruit with a dry or papery rind, the interior fibrous. The dried fibrous skeletons of the fruit, which are cucumber-shaped or club-shaped, are common in tropical markets where they are sold as though sponges, usually under the names of dishcloth gourd, vegetable sponge, rag gourd, or loofa. (*Luffa* is a Latinized version of the Arabic name for these gourds.)

The dishcloth gourds need the same culture as cucumbers, but they are even more sensitive to cold. As the vines, with plenty of heat and a rich soil, will grow 10–15 ft. high, they need the support of a trellis or post.

**acutangula.** Leaves very rough, not as large as in the next, and more angled than lobed. Fruit club-shaped, 9–12 in. long, ridged, the black seeds not margined.

**cylindrica.** The usual species in cult. and a strong-growing vine. Leaves 5–12 in. long, or nearly as wide and circular, with 3–7 lobes, the margins toothed. Fruit cucumber-shaped, 12–20 in. long, the black seeds margined.

**LUNARIA.** See HONESTY.

**LUNGAN** = *Euphoria longana*.

**LUNGWORT.** See PULMONARIA and MERTENSIA.

**LUPINE.** See LUPINUS.

**LUPINUS** (loo-pine'us). Lupine. A genus of many species belonging to the pea family. It is found in N.A., S.A., and on the shores of the Mediterranean Sea. All are hardy, and can be divided into three groups: the tree, herbaceous perennial, and annual lupines. The tree lupine is shrubby, growing 4–8 ft. Leaves compound,* finger-shaped, and covered with short, grayish hairs on upper and lower sides. Flowers showy, pea-like, in loose racemes* at the ends of the branches. Fruits, when ripe, are blackish, flattened pods about 3 in. long, containing 5 or 6 kidney-shaped, brown seeds. The perennials and annuals have herbaceous stems varying in height from 1–4 ft. Leaves like the tree group in shape, but sometimes bright green, especially on the upper side. Flowers pea-like, produced in dense terminal racemes.* Fruits similar to the tree group. (*Lupinus* is Latin for a wolf, implying that the plants tend to impoverish the soil.)

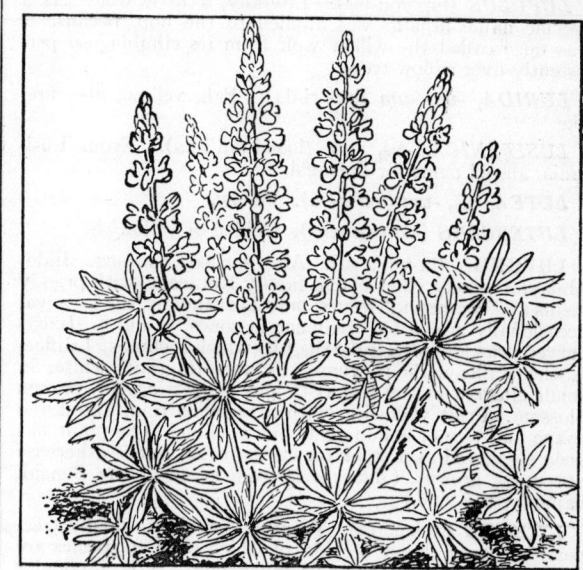

A garden lupine

Propagated from seeds, but the perennials may be divided in early spring. Sow in deeply dug, good garden soil in April–June, ½ in. deep, in permanent position, allowing plenty of space as roots are large. Good drainage is essential to carry plants through the winter. They will transplant, but do much better if let alone. However, as the perennials are sometimes long in germinating, it is advisable to sow them in a seed bed that can be left undisturbed until the following spring. There are many good hybrids of varying hues of blue, pink, yellow and white. They make good showy border plants. A few species are used for fodder. All are comparatively free from insect and fungus pests. The tree lupine is adaptable for training on sunny walls or a trellis. Annual varieties are much grown in greenhouses for early spring flowering. For greenhouse cult. sow seed in Aug.–Nov.

---

*Special articles on the subjects indicated by an asterisk (\*) will be found at the words so marked.*

**arboreus.** Tree lupine. Stems shrubby, 4-8 ft. high and slightly hairy. Leaves compound,* the leaflets finger-shaped, growing in a circle at the tip of a common stalk, hairy on both upper and lower sides. Flowers sulphur-yellow, fragrant, in loose racemes* at the ends of the branches. Calif. The var. **albus** has white flowers. There is also a purple-flowered form.

**cruckshanki** = Lupinus mutabilis cruckshanki.

**densiflorus.** Annual, handsome, shrub-like plant, up to 18 in. high. Leaves with both stalk and leaflets hairy. Flowers in closely packed, terminal racemes,* white, yellow, or rose. Calif.

**hartwegi.** Annual to 3 ft., really a perennial, but grown as an annual, very hairy and somewhat branching. Leaflets 7-9. Flowers blue, partially rose-colored. July-Sept. The vars. **albus, coelestinus, roseus** and **ruber** are color forms. Mex.

**mutabilis.** Annual to 4 ft. Leaves bright green. Flowers attractive. White with yellow or violet markings on upper petal, fragrant. The var. **cruckshanki** has bluish flowers, shaded violet; the vars. **roseus** and **versicolor** are color forms. S.A.

**nanus.** Annual, and not over 15 in. high, often branching from the base. Leaflets 5-7, hairy on both sides. Flowers in loose racemes,* on slender stalks, blue, with purple spots on the upper petal. Pods and seeds small. Particularly good grown in masses. Calif.

**perennis.** Quaker bonnets; the common wild lupine of eastern N.A., and 1-2 ft. high. Leaves and stem hairy. Flowers blue, varying to white. Eastern N.A. Prefers a sandy soil.

**polyphyllus.** A hardy perennial and a good garden species, to 5 ft. high, with stout, herbaceous stems. Leaves large and dark green. Flowers in long racemes.* Pods very woolly. Colors in shades of yellow, white, and blue. The var. **moerheimi** is more compact and considered the finest. The vars. **albus** and **roseus** are color forms. Western N.A.

**subcarnosus** = Lupinus texensis.

**texensis.** Bluebonnet, and the state flower of Texas. A showy, silky-hairy annual 8-12 in. high. Flowers blue, with a white or yellow spot. Pods about 1½ in. long and silky. Tex., and blooming there early in spring. May.

**LUPULINA, -us, -um** (lup-you-ly′na). Like a hop (Lupulus).

**LUPULUS** (lup′you-lus). Literally, a little wolf. As a specific name lupulus was applied to the hop, because it was once called the willow wolf from its climbing so persistently over willow trees.

**LURIDA, -us, -um** (lure′ri-da). Pale yellow; also fire-like.

**LUSITANICA, -us, -um** (loo-si-tan′i-ka). From Lusitania, an old name for Portugal.

**LUTEA, -us, -um** (loo′tee-a). Yellow.

**LUTESCENS** (loo-tess′senz). Golden or yellowish.

**LUVUNGA** (lu-vung′ga). Also spelled Lavanga. Indo-Malayan woody vines of the family Rutaceae, with prickly stems and compound* leaves, only **L. scandens**, the lavanga, occasionally grown for ornament in zones* 8 and 9. It has curved prickles in the leaf-axils,* by which it climbs. Leaflets 3, the stalks without wings. Flowers fragrant, white, in small clusters in the leaf-axil* and suggesting the orange blossom. Fruit yellowish, with a resinous rind, about the shape and size of a kumquat, but inedible. The plant has been suggested as a stock for citrus fruits, but is otherwise not much grown. (Luvunga is from lavanga, the Bengali name for the vine.)

**LYCASTE** (ly-kas′tee). Tropical American, chiefly tree-perching, very showy orchids, of which over 30 species are known, but only **L. skinneri** much cult. It is a popular greenhouse orchid with oblongish pseudobulbs* 3-5 in. long, bearing 1-3 long leaves which are oblongish, 9-15 in. long, folded like a fan in the bud, sheathing at the base, and much longer than the short stalk of the solitary flower. Flowers pink and white, 5-6 in. wide, waxy, the sepals and petals similar in shape but the petals shorter. Lip* oval, 3-lobed, spotted, but generally red-purple, the middle lobe bent backward. Guatemala. See Greenhouse orchids at ORCHID for culture. (Named for the daughter of Priam.)

**LYCHEE** = Litchi chinensis.

**LYCHNIS** (lick′nis). Catchfly. Campion. A large genus of herbs of the pink family, mostly from the north temperate zone and northward, some old garden favorites cult. for centuries. They are erect plants, annuals or biennials, but mostly perennial and often with sticky hairs. Calyx with 5 teeth. Petals 5, with a claw* at the base, the limb* rounded or sometimes 2-cleft or fringed. Stamens* 10. Fruit a capsule.* For closely related plants, also called catchfly or campion, see SILENE. (Lychnis is from the Greek for lamp, in allusion to the flame-colored flowers of certain species.)

The campions are of very simple culture in any ordinary garden soil. The perennials may be increased by division, and seed of the annuals sown where wanted. A few are biennials and should be grown as such. See BIENNIALS. Mostly summer-blooming, unless otherwise noted.

**alba.** Evening or white campion. A sticky-hairy biennial, or perhaps perennial, 1-2 ft. high. Leaves ovalish or oblong. Flowers about 1 in. wide, night-blooming, fragrant, in a few-flowered cluster (panicle*). Eu., sometimes naturalized along the Atlantic seaboard.

**alpina.** A smooth, tufted perennial 6-9 in. high, the leaves lance-shaped or narrower. Flowers about ⅓ in. wide, in a dense, terminal cluster (head). Arctic and alpine regions of the northern hemisphere, and best suited to the rock garden (which see).

**arkwrighti.** A hybrid species of garden origin, a perennial resembling L. haageana, but with scarlet flowers.

**chalcedonica.** Scarlet lychnis; also called Maltese or Jerusalem cross and scarlet lightning. A hairy, perennial herb 18-30 in. high, the leaves ovalish or lance-shaped, and usually clasping. Flowers about 1 in. wide, scarlet, in dense, terminal clusters (heads*). Siberia; often an escape* here. The var. **alba** has white flowers; and other color forms and a double-flowered sort are offered.

**coeli-rosa.** Rose-of-Heaven. A widely planted garden annual 12-15 in. high, the leaves very narrow. Flowers solitary, terminal, about 1 in. wide, rose-pink. Mediterranean region. It is sometimes sold as Agrostemma. There are forms with red or purple-eyed flowers and one with toothed petals.

**coronaria.** Mullein pink; also called dusty miller and rose campion. A white-woolly, biennial or perennial herb 18-30 in. high. Leaves ovalish or oblong. Flowers solitary, terminal, about 1 in. wide, crimson. Southern Eu. and often an escape* in the U.S. White and double-flowered forms are offered.

**flos-cuculi.** Cuckoo-flower; also called ragged robin. A hairy, perennial herb 12-20 in. high, sticky towards the top. Leaves narrowly lance-shaped, the upper ones smaller and stalkless. Flowers red or pink, in loose clusters (panicles)*, the petals with 4 narrow segments. Eurasia; naturalized in the eastern U.S. White and double-flowered forms are offered.

**flos-jovis.** Flower-of-Jove. A white-woolly, perennial herb 12-20 in. high. Leaves ovalish or oblong, more or less clasping. Flowers about ½ in. wide, in dense clusters (umbel*-like). Southern Eu., in the mountains.

**haageana.** A hybrid campion of garden origin, more or less hairy, usually not over 12 in. high. Flowers nearly 2 in. wide, usually in clusters of 2's or 3's, the petals 2-lobed and also with 2 teeth, usually orange-red or crimson.

**lagascae** = Petrocoptis lagascae.

**pyrenaica.** A rock garden, perennial species, not over 4 in. high, the basal leaves spatula-shaped and about 1½ in. long, the stem leaves heart-shaped. Flowers about ¼ in. wide, solitary and long-stalked, blush-pink. Pyrenees.

**vaccaria** = Saponaria vaccaria.

**viscaria.** German catchfly. A perennial herb 5-18 in. high, the stem smooth except beneath the flowers where it is sticky-hairy. Leaves long, narrow, tapering. Flowers red or purple, in interrupted* clusters, the petals somewhat notched. Eurasia. White and also double-flowered varieties are offered.

**LYCIUM** (liss′i-um). Matrimony-vine. A group of ornamental shrubs of the potato family. Though there are about 100 species in the temperate and sub-tropical regions of the world only a few are hardy. Their habit is often loose and the branches are frequently reflexed or arching and spiny. The flowers are small and borne singly or clustered in the leaf-axils.* Leaves alternate,* deciduous, small, not toothed. Fruit a berry, usually red. (Greek name for a spiny shrub from Lycias.) Sometimes called box-thorn.

The matrimony-vine, though ornamental, is often rank and coarse in growth and should be used only where it will have plenty of room in which to spread. It is adapted to arbors and fences and is excellent for covering piles of rocks and unsightly objects; planted closely it makes an impenetrable barrier.

Cultivation is simple, they seem to thrive in ordinary soil and prefer good drainage. Propagated by seeds, cuttings, layers or suckers.

**chinense.** A vigorous, strong-growing shrub with spreading or arching branches to 12 ft. long. Leaves quite variable in size and shape, usually ovate or lanceolate and about 1 in. long though sometimes to 3 or 4 in. Flowers purple. Fruit orange to scarlet. June-Sept.; fruit Aug.-Sept. Eastern Asia. Hardy from zone* 3 southward. Var. **ovatum.** Leaves broader and rhombic in shape, to 4 in. long; fruit larger, blunt at tip.

**europaeum.** An upright, bushy shrub growing about 6 ft. high, thorny. Leaves gray-green, lanceolate, rounded or pointed at tip. Flowers violet. Fruit red, oval. May; fruit Aug. Southern Eu. Hardy only in mild regions. Usually confused with L. halimifolium from which it differs in having a longer, more slender corolla, smaller leaves and being less hardy.

**halimifolium.** Shrub of 8 or 9 ft. with slender, spreading, sometimes

---

* Special articles on the subjects indicated by an asterisk (*) will be found at the words so marked.

spiny branches. Leaves variable, usually oval or narrow, 1½–2 in. long. Flowers dull purple, on slender stalks. Fruit oval, red, ⅔ in. long. June–July, and often again in Oct. Southeastern Eu. to western Asia. Hardy from zone* 3 southward.

vulgare = *Lycium halimifolium*.

*LYCOCTONUM* (ly-cock'to-num). Greek name for the wolfsbane, which was thought to poison wolves. See *Aconitum lycoctonum* at MONKSHOOD.

**LYCOPERSICUM.** See TOMATO.

**LYCOPODIACEAE.** See LYCOPODIUM.

**LYCOPODIUM** (ly-ko-pō'dĭ-um). Club moss. Evergreen, moss-like herbs, the only cult. genus of the family Lycopodiaceae (ly-ko-po-di-ā'see-ee) or club moss family, a few sometimes cult. in the wild garden, but best known for their much-to-be-deplored use in the making of Christmas wreaths. For the latter purpose there is a wide destruction of the wild plants annually. They have erect or creeping stems and tiny, scale-like, often overlapping leaves which are so numerous as to completely hide the stem. The club mosses are fern allies (which see) and thus produce no flowers. Instead they produce minute spores, often in special, club-shaped, stalked spikes, or occasionally in the axils* of the upper leaves. (*Lycopodium* is from the Greek for wolf and foot, assumed to be in reference to a fancied resemblance.)

The club mosses, some of which are called ground pine, are of far more historical than hort. interest. The ancestors of some of them were huge trees in the Carboniferous and helped to form the coal measures. Today they have dwindled to a few low herbs suited only to shady places in the wild garden, where they need rich woods soil (not especially acid) and plenty of moisture. Those below can easily be divided, and some of them root at the joints.

clavatum. Running pine; also called ground pine (not related to the true pines). A creeping herb, the stems often 8–9 ft. long, the very leafy branches ascending, but scarcely 3 in. high. Spore*-bearing spikes usually 1–4 in each stalk, each spike pencil-thick and 2–4 in. long. North temperate zone; common in woods in N.A.

complanatum. Ground cedar (not a true cedar). Not so long-trailing, the erect branches often divided fan-like. Spore*-bearing spikes 1–4 on each stalk, the spikes 2–5 in. long. North temperate zone and common in woods in N.A.

dendroideum = *Lycopodium obscurum*.

obscurum. Stems creeping underground, the ascending branches erect, bushy, almost tree-like, but not over 10 in. high, the scale-like leaves longer than in the other species and not hugging the stem. Spore-bearing spike nearly stalkless. Woods in N.A. and As.

**LYCOPUS** (ly'ko-pus). Mint-like herbs (without the mint odor) of the family Labiatae, comprising perhaps a dozen species of rather weedy plants of little garden interest. The only one likely to be cult. is **L. americanus**, the water horehound, an erect perennial 1–2 ft. high which spreads by stolons.* Leaves opposite,* toothed or even cut, stalked, 1–4 in. long. Flowers minute, crowded in dense stalkless clusters in the leaf-axils.* Corolla scarcely ⅙ in. long, pale purplish or whitish. In moist places throughout N.A. and suited only to such sites in the wild garden. (*Lycopus* is from the Greek for wolf and foot, in allusion to a fancied resemblance of the leaves to a wolf's foot.)

**LYCORIS** (ly-kō'ris). Asiatic, bulbous, amaryllis-like herbs of the family Amaryllidaceae, including perhaps 6 species, **L. squamigera** grown outdoors and in the greenhouse for its showy bloom. It has strap-shaped leaves about 1 in. wide which develop before the flowers appear. Flowers fragrant, nearly 3 in. long, the petals united below into a short tube, the segments crisped, lilac-pink or pink. Style* protruding but the stamens about the length of the petals. The flower cluster is a loose umbel* at the end of a solid stalk (scape*). The var. **purpurea**, with darker flowers, is in the trade. For culture in the greenhouse follow the directions for the plants mentioned at amaryllis. Its outdoor culture should be confined to the region south of zone* 5, and even then a light, strawy mulch is advisable. (Named for some Greek lady, but not the nymph.)

*LYDIA, -us, -um* (lid'ĭ-a). From Lydia, an ancient country in Asia Minor.

**LYGODIUM** (ly-gō'dĭ-um). Climbing fern. Vine-like ferns of the family Schizaeaceae, chiefly tropical but one native in the eastern U.S. Of the 30 known species the three below, and perhaps others, are cult. in greenhouses (or outdoors for *L. palmatum*) for their graceful habit and feathery foliage. They have long, climbing or trailing stems, or the stalk of the much-divided frond assuming the aspect and functions of a stem. In the latter case, what looks like leaves are actually segments of a many-times compound frond, which may have the ultimate segments arranged finger-fashion or feather-fashion. (*Lygodium* is from the Greek for flexible. in allusion to the slender, pliant stems.)

For the culture of the greenhouse sorts see FERNS AND FERN GARDENING.

japonicum. The leading greenhouse lygodium, and a slender plant with much-divided, pale green and soft-textured fronds. Ultimate segments arranged feather-fashion, about 1 in. long, variously toothed. Eastern Asia to Aust.

palmatum. Hartford fern. A hardy, native, climbing or sprawling fern. Fronds nearly round, 4–7-lobed, finger-fashion, the lobes not toothed. Eastern U.S. It should be grown in partly shady places in the fern garden or wild garden, and it needs an acid soil with a pH 4.00–5.00 (see ACID AND ALKALI SOILS).

scandens. A greenhouse lygodium, slender but more bushy and not so high-climbing as *L. japonicum*, and the foliage bluish-green. Ultimate segments 1–2 in. long, arranged finger-fashion, sometimes faintly lobed. Eastern As.

**LYME GRASS.** See ELYMUS.

**LYON BEAN** = *Stizolobium niveum*.

**LYONIA** = *Xolisma*.

**LYONOTHAMNUS** (ly-o-no-tham'nus). A single, evergreen shrub or small tree of the rose family, ornamental but tender. The one species, **L. floribundus**, the Santa Cruz ironwood or Catalina ironwood, is found only on Santa Catalina Island, and is suited only to similar climates. It has opposite,* lanceolate* leaves, 4–8 in. long, and small white flowers in flat, terminal clusters 4–8 in. across. Fruit a woody capsule. Considered difficult to propagate; cuttings of basal sprouts perhaps the best method. The var. **asplenifolius** is a form with deeply lobed leaves, and sometimes develops into a tree of 75 ft. (Named for W. S. Lyon, who sent specimens of this shrub to Asa Gray.)

**LYRATE.** Lyre-shaped, *i.e.* having a larger terminal and smaller lateral lobes, some of which are irregularly cut or divided.

**LYSICHITUM** (ly-sik'ĭ-tum). A single, evil-smelling, perennial herb of the arum family, **L. camtschatensis**, the yellow skunk-cabbage, found in western N.A. and eastern As. It differs only in technical characters from the common skunk-cabbage (which see) and needs similar conditions. Very early in the season the sheathing spathe* encloses the spadix* but the latter elongates and ultimately protrudes beyond the withered spathe.* (*Lysichitum* is from the Greek for free and cloak, in allusion to the spathe.*)

**LYSIMACHIA** (ly-si-mack'ĭ-a). Loosestrife (for other loosestrifes see LYTHRUM, DECODON, and STEIRONEMA). A large genus of widely distributed perennial herbs of the family Primulaceae, a few of them grown for ornament, although some are inclined to be weedy. Leaves without marginal teeth, variously arranged. Flowers solitary or in clusters, sometimes in the leaf-axils* or often terminal. Corolla more or less bell-shaped or wheel-shaped. Stamens* 5–6. Fruit a 5-valved capsule.* (Named for King Lysimachus.)

The loosestrifes are of secondary garden importance and should be grown in reasonably moist sites in the open border. All are erect herbs except *L. nummularia*, the moneywort, which is a good, creeping ground cover. Most of them bloom in the summer and all of them are easily increased by division in spring or fall.

ciliata = *Steironema ciliatum*.

clethroides. A somewhat hairy herb, 2–3 ft. high Leaves alternate,* more or less oblong or oval-lance-shaped, tapering at both ends, 3–6 in. long. Flowers about ½ in. wide, white, in narrow, terminal spikes. Eastern As.

---

* Special articles on the subjects indicated by an asterisk (*) will be found at the words so marked.

**japonica.** Not over 5 in. high, the stems more or less decumbent. Leaves more or less dotted, ovalish. Flowers solitary in the leaf-axils,* yellow. Eastern As. and the East Indies.

**nummularia.** Moneywort; also called creeping Charlie and creeping Jennie. A prostrate perennial with trailing stems that root easily at the joints. Leaves opposite,* nearly round, about ¾ in. in diameter. Flowers solitary in the leaf-axils, stalked, yellow. Eu., but commonly naturalized in eastern N.A. A good ground cover for moist, partly shady places, but it will also grow in full sunshine. See Creepers and Trailers at VINES.

**punctata.** An erect herb 2-3 ft. high. Leaves 3 or 4 at each whorl,* oval-lance-shaped. Flowers in whorls* in the leaf-axils,* the corolla yellow. Eu., but naturalized in the eastern U.S.

**vulgaris.** Golden loosestrife; also called willow-wort. A thick-set, bushy, erect perennial 3-5 ft. high. Leaves oval or lance-shaped, opposite* or in whorls.* Flower clusters (panicles*) leafy, the corolla yellow. Eurasia, but naturalized in eastern N.A.

**LYTHRACEAE** (lith-ray'see-ee). The loosestrife family comprises over 20 genera and 400 species of widely distributed herbs, shrubs and trees, a few of which, like the crape myrtle (*Lagerstroemia*), are of wide garden interest. Among the herbs are *Cuphea*, *Lythrum*, and *Decodon*, while *Lawsonia* (which yields henna) is, like the crape myrtle, woody.

Leaves generally opposite* (whorled* in some), without marginal teeth, flowers mostly in the leaf-axils,* solitary or in clusters, the individual flower stalks usually with 2 bracts.* They are very showy in *Lythrum*, *Decodon* and the crape myrtle, less so in *Lawsonia*, where, however, they are very fragrant. In *Cuphea* is the peculiar little cigar-flower, much grown in greenhouses and as a bedding plant. The fruit is a dry pod (capsule*), enclosed by the calyx.

Technical flower characters: Flowers regular* or irregular.* Calyx more or less bell-shaped, free from the ovary, mostly 4-6-toothed or lobed, and sometimes with secondary teeth between, sometimes petal-like. Petals 4-6, inserted at the throat of the calyx, sometimes (in the cigar-flower) none. Ovary superior.* Style 1.

**LYTHRUM** (lith'rum). Loosestrife (for other loosestrifes see LYSIMACHIA, DECODON, and STEIRONEMA). A group of annual or perennial herbs of the family Lythraceae, comprising two dozen widely scattered species, the three below often grown in moist places for their showy bloom. They have 4-sided stems and mostly opposite* leaves. Flowers in terminal clusters (spikes* or racemes*) or solitary in the leaf-axils,* purple or purplish-pink in those below. Calyx* tubular or cylindric, 8-12-ribbed. Petals 4-6 (in ours). Stamens* 4-12, some longer than the others. Fruit a 2-valved capsule,* enclosed by the calyx.* (*Lythrum* is from the Greek for blood, in allusion to the color of the flowers in some species.)

The ones below are best grown along the edges of pools or streams, although they may be grown in the open border. All are perennials of easy culture so long as the site is moist. They can be increased by division. They bloom in summer.

**alatum.** Milk willow-herb. An erect perennial 3-4 ft. high, the 4-sided stems narrowly winged. Leaves opposite* or some alternate,* stalkless, oblongish or narrower, about 1 in. long. Flowers solitary in the leaf-axils,* purple, scarcely ½ in. wide. Eastern U.S.

**salicaria.** Purple loosestrife; also called purple willow-herb and red Sally. A wand-like perennial 2-3½ ft. high, the base somewhat woody. Leaves willow-like, 3-4 in. long. Flowers in dense, showy, leafy, terminal spikes, the corolla bright purple and about ¾ in. wide. Eurasia, but commonly naturalized in the marshes of N.A. The *var.* roseum superbum has darker colored and larger flowers; *var.* tomentosum has white-felty foliage.

**virgatum.** Related to the last but with smaller flowers in leafy clusters (racemes*). Eurasia, but occasionally naturalized in New England.

# M

**MAACKIA** (mack'i-a). A small group of Asiatic trees of the pea family. Leaves opposite,* compound,* the leaflets arranged feather-fashion, 1½-3 in. long. The white pea-like flowers are borne in upright terminal clusters 4-6 in. long. Fruit a flat pod 2-3 in. long. (Named for R. Maack, a Russian naturalist.)

The maackias are hardy ornamental trees of good habit and with rather showy clusters of white flowers. They are not particular about soil, but like an open, sunny position. They are easily propagated by seeds.

**amurensis.** Tree of 40-45 ft. Leaves composed of 7-11 elliptic or oval leaflets, 2-3 in. long. Flowers white, in erect clusters (racemes*). Pods about 2 in. long. July or Aug. Manchuria. Hardy from zone* 3 southward.

**chinensis.** A tree eventually attaining almost 70 ft. Leaflets 11-13, oval to elliptic, 1-3 in. long, downy beneath. Flowers white, in terminal clusters. July-Aug. Central China. Hardy from zone* 3 southward. Very much like the above species but with shorter leaves and narrower, hairy leaflets.

**hupehensis** = *Maackia chinensis*.

**MABA** (mah'ba). Tropical or sub-tropical trees and shrubs of the family Ebenaceae, comprising over 60 species, of which the two below can be grown for ornament only in zones* 8 and 9. They have alternate* leaves without marginal teeth. Male and female flowers on different plants, the corolla small, more or less bell-shaped, greenish-yellow or yellowish-white, not conspicuous. Stamens* mostly 9. Fruit a berry. (*Maba* is the native name of some species.)

Not much is known of the culture of *Maba*, but the species have been grown on a variety of soils in southern Fla. and Calif.

**natalensis.** An evergreen shrub 12-20 ft. high. Leaves oblongish or ovalish, small. Fruit about ⅓ in. long, black, in small bunches. South Africa.

**sandwicensis.** Lama. A tree 30-40 ft. high. Leaves ovalish or oblong, 1-2 in. long, thick and leathery. Fruit about ⅓ in. long, reddish-yellow. Pacific Islands, especially Hawaii.

**MACADAMIA** (mac-a-dam'i-a). Slow-growing Australian trees of the family Proteaceae, only **M. ternifolia**, the Queensland nut, of hort. interest among its 5 known species. It is grown somewhat in zones* 8 and 9, both in Calif. and Fla., and is a tree up to 50 ft. high. Leaves in whorls* of 3 or 4, oblongish or narrower, nearly 12 in. long, bright green, remotely spiny-toothed and suggesting a long holly leaf. Flowers small (for details see PROTEACEAE), white, borne in pairs which are grouped in racemes* nearly 12 in. long. Fruit a hard drupe,* its edible seed globe-shaped, about 1 in. in diameter, very hard-shelled, and commonly (though incorrectly) called the nut. It grows very slowly and will not fruit for several years, preferring a moist, fertile soil. It may be increased from seeds, which must be stratified and then brought into the greenhouse and given gentle bottom-heat. Chiefly grown for its edible seeds. (Named for Doctor John Macadam, secretary of the Victoria Philosophical Institute.)

**MACARTNEY ROSE** = *Rosa bracteata*.

**MACHAEROCEREUS** (ma-kee-ro-seer'ee-us). A small genus of erect and bushy or prostrate, very spiny cacti, found in Lower Calif. and Mex. and cult. in desert gardens for ornament. They have usually long, ribbed branches, the central spine of each cluster dagger-like. Flowers day-blooming, not very large, yellow or purple (in ours). Fruit fleshy, edible in the second species, at first spiny, but the spines fall off as the fruit ripens. (*Machaerocereus* is from the Greek for sword or dagger, and *Cereus*, in allusion to the dagger-like central spines.)

For culture see CACTI.

**eruca.** A prostrate cactus, its radiating branches dying at one end and growing onward at the other, thus impossible to grow in a pot. Stems 3-7 in. diameter, densely spiny. Flowers more or less tubular, 4-5 in. long, yellow. Fruit about 2 in. in diameter, globe-shaped.

**gummosus.** Pitahaya (for others see LEMAIREOCEREUS, HYLOCEREUS, and ECHINOCEREUS). More or less bushy and erect, nearly 3 ft. high, sometimes clambering in age. Branches 7-9-ribbed, very spiny, the spines in groups of 15-20. Flowers 4-5 in. long, purple. Fruit scarlet, edible, somewhat acid, widely used as food by the natives. It is not easy to grow in the greenhouse, and flowers there only rarely.

**MACHINERY.** See TOOLS AND IMPLEMENTS.

---

* Special articles on the subjects indicated by an asterisk (*) will be found at the words so marked.

**MACKAYA** (ma-kay'ya). Four species of tender shrubs of the family Acanthaceae, three of them from India, the other, **M. bella**, from South Africa and grown outdoors in zones* 8 and 9 and in the greenhouse. It is about 4 ft. high and has opposite,* oblongish leaves, 3–5 in. long and toothed. Flowers tubular but widely flaring above, about 2 in. long, slightly irregular,* arranged in a 1-sided cluster (raceme*) and very showy. Stamens* 4. Fruit a capsule.* The greenhouse cult. of *Mackaya* is the same as for *Jacobinia* (which see). Outdoors it is planted in southern Calif. and Fla. (Named for James T. Mackay, Irish botanist.)

**MACLEAYA** (mack-lay'a). Showy, perennial, border plants of the poppy family, both the known species grown for ornament, often under the name of *Bocconia*. They are almost shrubby, erect herbs with stalked, alternate,* leaves which are deeply lobed, generally bluish-green or gray, especially beneath. Flowers small but very numerous in long terminal clusters (panicles). Sepals 2, petal-like and cream-colored. Petals none. Stamens* many and showy. Fruit an egg-shaped, stalked, 2-valved capsule.* (Named for Alexander Macleay, colonial secretary in Australia.)

The first species is a handsome, striking plant for the herbaceous border, but it needs plenty of space. They are rich feeders and need a good soil. Easily propagated by division.

**cordata.** Plume poppy; also called tree celandine. A stout perennial, 4–6 ft. high. Leaves nearly 8 in. wide, white on the under side, about 7-lobed. Flower cluster about 1 ft. long, very showy. Stamens* 24–30. China and Jap. June–July.

**microcarpa.** Somewhat similar but with the leaves merely hairy on the under side, and with only 8–12 stamens.* Central Asia.

**MACLURA** (ma-cloor'ra). A single species, **M. pomifera**, the Osage orange, or Bois d'Arc as it is sometimes called, is a spiny tree of about 50 ft., and belongs to the mulberry family, growing naturally from Ark. to Kansas. Leaves alternate,* ovate to oblongish, pointed, 1½–4 in. long, shiny above. The flowers are dioecious,* the male flowers small, greenish, and borne in pendulous clusters, the female flowers are also greenish but in dense heads. Fruit round, 2–5 in. across, greenish, somewhat suggestive of an orange, but worthless. Sometimes described as *Toxylon*. May, June; fruit Aug., Sept. Hardy from zone* 3 southward.

Although the osage orange is a tree it is often trained as a hedge, its spiny branches making an effective barrier. Growing naturally it forms an open-headed tree with spreading branches and furrowed orange-brown bark. The large fruits, though inedible, are odd and interesting. The trees are quite adaptable to ordinary conditions and are usually propagated by seeds. In the prairie states it makes a good windbreak (which see). (Named for W. Maclure, an American geologist.)

**MACNAB CYPRESS** = *Cupressus macnabiana*.

**MACOMBER.** See RUTABAGA.

*MACRADENA, -us, -um* (mak-ra-dee'na). With large glands.

*MACRANTHA, -us, -um* (ma-kran'tha). Large-flowered.

*MACROBOTRYS* (mak-ro-bō'triss). With a large, grape-like cluster.

*MACROCANTHOS* (mak-ro-kan'thos). With large spines or thorns.

*MACROCARPA, -us, -um* (mak-ro-kar'pa). Large-fruited. A variant is *macrocarpon*.

*MACROCEPHALA, -us, -um* (mak-ro-sef'fa-la). With large heads.

*MACROMERIS, -e* (ma-krom'er-is). With many parts, or large ones.

*MACROPHYLLA, -us, -um* (mak-ro-fil'la). Large-leaved.

*MACROPODA, -us, -um* (ma-krop'o-da). Large- or stout-stalked.

*MACRORHIZA, -us, -um* (mak-ro-ry'za). With large roots or rootstocks.

*MACROSPERMA, -us, -um* (mak-ro-sper'ma). Large-seeded.

*MACROSTACHYA, -us, -um* (mak-ro-stack'i-a). With large or long spikes.

**MACROZAMIA** (mak-ro-zay'mee-a). A small and dwindling genus of fern-like, Australian, woody plants of the family Cycadaceae, two of them occasionally grown in the cool greenhouse for interest rather than ornament. They belong to a family of remote geological antiquity, but now comprise only a relic of their former grandeur. They have underground, or partly underground, trunks, crowned with a large cluster of leathery, but fern-like, compound* leaves, the numerous leaflets or segments of which are arranged feather-fashion and are prominently lined or striped on the lower surface. Flowers in the hort. sense, none; the flower and fruiting cluster consisting of a cone-like, often large structure between the scales of which are borne the naked ovules. (*Macrozamia* is a compound of *macro*, large, and *Zamia*, a genus of cycads, which see.)

These are fern-like cycads, rare in cult. outside of botanic gardens. They need a cool greenhouse and potting mixture* 3. Some of them, besides being members of an ancient but dwindling group of plants, are destroyed by the Australians because they are poisonous to sheep. In a few years the cult. specimens may be the only survivors.

**flexuosa.** Trunk nearly all underground. Leaves in a large rosette,* the leaflets or segments about ¼ in. wide and about 7 in. long, without marginal teeth. New South Wales.

**spiralis.** Burrawang. Trunk partly underground, but sometimes above ground and 6 ft. high and 2 ft. thick. Leaves nearly 4 ft. long, rigid and stiff, the leaflets or segments nearly 10 in. long, a little decurrent,* the veins parallel on the under side. New South Wales.

*MACULATA, -us, -um* (mak-you-lay'ta). Spotted.

*MADAGASCARIENSIS, -e* (ma-da-gas-kar-i-en'sis). From Madagascar, an island off the east coast of Africa.

**MADAGASCAR JASMINE** = *Stephanotis floribunda*.

**MADAGASCAR PERIWINKLE** = *Vinca rosea*.

**MAD-APPLE.** See EGGPLANT.

**MADDER** = *Rubia tinctorum*.

**MADDER FAMILY.** A huge family of plants, all but a handful tropical shrubs and trees like coffee, cinchona, the gardenia, and the trees yielding ipecac. Among hardier sorts are the sweet woodruff, bluets, bedstraw, the partridge-berry, and the button-bush. For a complete list of the cult. genera and their characters see RUBIACEAE.

**MADEIRA-VINE** = *Boussingaultia baselloides*.

**MADEIRA-VINE FAMILY** = Basellaceae.

**MADIA** (may'di-a). Tarweed. A small genus of sticky-hairy, annual herbs of the family Compositae, all but one of them from western N.A., the remaining, Chilean. They are of secondary garden interest and little grown here. Leaves mostly alternate.* Flower heads yellow, composed of disk* and ray flowers, the latter 3-lobed. (*Madia* is the native Chilean name for the Chilean species.)

The cult. species are heavy-scented annuals, the seed of which should be sown where wanted. The flower heads are not particularly showy and close in full sunshine.

**elegans.** Not over 24 in. high, the leaves very narrow, 3–5 in. long. Flower heads long-stalked, about ¾ in. wide, generally yellow, but sometimes the head brown-eyed.* Ore. and Calif. to Nev.

**sativa.** Chilean tarweed. A coarse, stout annual, 3–4 ft. high, the leaves lance-shaped or narrower, 1–2 in. long. Flower heads scarcely ½ in. wide, brownish-yellow, essentially stalkless. Chile; but naturalized in Calif. and Ore.

**MADONNA LILY** = *Lilium candidum*.

**MADRAS THORN** = *Pithecolobium dulce*.

**MADRE DE CACAO** = *Gliricidia sepium*.

**MADROÑA** = *Arbutus menziesi*.

**MADWORT** = *Alyssum*.

**MAGAZINES.** See GARDEN MAGAZINES.

**MAGELLAN BARBERRY** = *Berberis buxifolia*.

---

* Special articles on the subjects indicated by an asterisk (*) will be found at the words so marked.

*MAGELLANICA, -us, -um* (ma-jel-lan'i-ka). From the Straits of Magellan, S.A.

**MAGGOTS.** For the control of maggots *see* the details on Insect Pests at APPLE, CHERRY, MANGO, WALNUT. For an account of the life-history of these destructive larvae *see* Two-winged Flies at INSECT PESTS.

**MAGIC TREE** = *Cantua buxifolia.*

**MAGNESIUM ARSENATE.** *See* Stomach Poisons at INSECTICIDES.

*MAGNIFICA, -us, -um* (mag-niff'i-ka). Magnificent or showy.

**MAGNOLIA** (mag-nō'lĭ-a). A genus of North American, West Indian, Mexican and Asiatic evergreen or deciduous trees or shrubs of the family Magnoliaceae, comprising about 30 species. Leaves alternate,* without marginal teeth, large. Flowers regular, solitary, usually large and showy, commonly white, yellow, rose, or purple, appearing with or before the leaves on the species not evergreen. Petals 6-15. Sepals* 3, often petal-like, the stamens numerous. The fruit is a cone-like brown or scarlet body, the seeds of which when ripe hang by thread-like cords. (Named for Pierre Magnol, a botanist of Montpelier.)

For Culture *see* below.

**acuminata.** Cucumber tree. A large handsome tree, reaching 100 ft. in height. Bark gray-brown, deeply ridged in mature trees. Small branches at first covered with soft hairs, later smooth, red-brown and shining. Leaves 6-10 in. long, somewhat oval or oblong, pointed at the end, soft-hairy and light green beneath. Flowers not showy, 2-3 in. high, cup-shaped. Petals 6. Sepals pointed, much smaller than the petals, soon turning back. Fruit somewhat oval or oblong, 3-4 in. long, becoming pink, or red. *Var.* **cordata** is found in Georgia. The branches are at first upright, then spreading, soft-hairy. Leaves not pointed, and hairy beneath. Flowers smaller than the type, canary yellow in color. N.Y. to Ga., west to Ill. May. Hardy from zone* 4 southward.

**conspicua** = *Magnolia denudata.*
**cordata** = *Magnolia acuminata cordata.*

**denudata.** Yulan. A tree becoming 50 ft. high, the branches spreading, young growth soft-hairy. Leaves oval, 4-7 in. long, 3-4 in. broad, tapering to the base, rounded at the end with a short point, light green and sparingly soft-hairy beneath. Flowers large, cup-shaped or broader, 5-6 in. across, white, fragrant. Petals and sepals alike, 9, fleshy. Fruit brownish, cylinder-shaped, 3-4 in. long. Central China. April-May. Hardy from zone* 3 southward.

**fraseri.** Mountain magnolia. A tree growing 50 ft. high with smooth young growth. Leaves broadly oval or narrower, 8-12 in. long, heart-shaped and eared at the base, smooth with a slight bloom* beneath. Flowers creamy-white, fragrant, 9-11 in. across. Petals 6-9, 4 to 5 in. long. Sepals 3, quickly-falling. Fruit 4 to 5 in. long, rose-red. Va. to Ga. and Ala. June. Hardy from zone* 3 southward.

**glauca** = *Magnolia virginiana.*

**grandiflora.** Evergreen magnolia; also known as bull bay and big-leaved magnolia. A large evergreen tree of noble proportions, becoming 100 ft. high. The branchlets and buds are rusty-woolly when young. Leaves 5-8 in. long, somewhat elliptic in shape, tapering both ways, leathery, shining above and rusty-woolly beneath. Flowers cup-shaped, coming out of great silky-hairy buds, 6-8 in. across, white, fragrant. Petals usually 6, rarely 9-12, fleshy. Sepals 3, petal-like. Fruit 4 in. long, heavy, rusty-woolly. *Var.* **lanceolata** has narrower leaves, and is of narrow pyramidal growth, and is sometimes known as *var. exoniensis.* N.C. to Fla. and Tex. May-June. Hardy from zone* 5 southward.

**kobus.** A hardy tree growing to 30 ft. high, but usually shrubby in cult. Branchlets smooth. Leaf and flower-buds soft-hairy. Leaves broadly oval, 2½ to 4 in. long, abruptly pointed, pale and almost smooth beneath. Flowers blooming in advance of leaves, 4-5 in. across, lily-shaped, white. Petals 6-9, thin with a faint purple line at the base outside. Sepals* 3, small and narrow, soon falling. Fruit 4-5 in. long, dark brown. *Var.* **borealis** is a pyramidal tree, very hardy, but not blooming freely when young. The leaves are larger than the typical form and the flowers pure creamy-white. Jap. April-May. Hardy from zone* 3 southward.

**liliflora.** A large tree-like shrub, the branchlets smooth except near the tips; buds soft-hairy. Leaves, somewhat oval, 3-7 in. long, light green and soft-hairy beneath when young, narrowing to a short point. Flowers, lily-shaped, slightly fragrant, white inside, purple outside, 8 in. across, on short stout stalks. Petals 6, 3-4 in. long. Sepals 3, shorter than the petals, soon falling. Fruit brown, oblong. China, much cult. in Jap. May-June. Hardy from zone* 4 southward. *Var.* **nigra** has larger flowers, darker purple outside and light purple inside, appearing partly with the leaves.

**macrophylla.** Large-leaved cucumber tree. A round-headed tree to 50 ft. high, with stout, spreading branches. Young growth, woolly. Leaves very large, oblong to somewhat oval, 1-3 ft. long, soft-hairy and with a slight bloom* beneath. Flowers opening with the leaves, cup-shaped, creamy-white, fragrant, 10-12 in. across. Petals 6, turned backward above the middle, purplish at base. Sepals* shorter than the petals. Fruit nearly round, rose-color when ripe. Ky. to Fla., west to Ark. and La. May-June. Hardy from zone* 4 southward.

**obovata.** A handsome tree growing up to 100 ft. high. Young growth smooth and purplish. Leaves broadly oval, 1 ft. or more long, bluntpointed, with a bloom* beneath when young. Flowers opening with the leaves, cup-shaped, 5-7 in. across, white, fragrant. Petals 6-9, leathery. Sepals* similar but shorter. Filaments* and pistils* bright crimson. Fruit 8 in. long, brilliant scarlet. Jap. May-June. Hardy from zone* 3 southward.

**parviflora.** A small tree growing 30 ft. high, with young growth covered with flattened soft hairs. Leaves 2-6 in. long, elliptic or broadly oval, bluntly pointed, soft-hairy and with a bloom* beneath. Flowers cup-shaped, fragrant, white, 3-4 in. across. Petals 6. Sepals shorter, pink. Fruit crimson, 1½ in. long. Jap. and Korea. June-July. Hardy from zone* 4 southward.

**salicifolia.** A slender tree becoming 30 ft. high. Branchlets and leaf buds smooth, with a slight bloom.* Flower buds densely soft-hairy. Leaves light green above, elliptic or narrower, 3-5 in. long, with a bloom beneath. Flowers blooming before the leaves, about 5 in. across, white or purple at base, fragrant. Petals 6, sometimes 7-13. Sepals narrow, half as long as petals, greenish-white. Fruit 3 in. long, rose-colored. Jap. April-May. Hardy from zone* 3 southward.

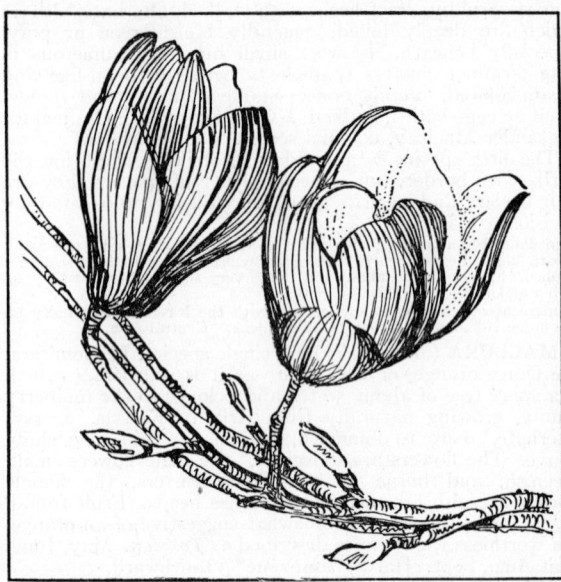

*Magnolia soulangeana*, one of the handsomest of spring-flowering trees

**soulangeana.** A large shrub or small tree, a hybrid between *M. denudata* and *M. liliflora.* Leaves broadly oval, slightly soft-hairy beneath. Flowers appearing before the leaves, cup-shaped, 6 in. across, purplish, seldom white, scentless or fragrant. Sepals usually petal-like, sometimes small and greenish. It originated in 1820. There are numerous forms among which are *var.* **alba superba** with pure white flowers, *var.* **alexandrina** with white flowers tinged purple outside toward the base, *var.* **lennei** with broader leaves and flowers white inside, rosy-purple on the outside. These forms are among the most popular and handsome of our flowering shrubs. May. Hardy from zone* 3 southward.

**stellata.** A much-branched spreading shrub or small tree, up to 15 ft. high, the young growth densely soft-hairy. Leaves broadly oval to oblong, 1½-4 in. long, smooth, dark green above, light green beneath. Flowers appearing before the leaves, white, fragrant, 3 in. across. Petals and sepals the same, 12-18, narrow, 1½ in. long, spreading and at length turned back. Fruit 2 in. long, red. Jap. March-April. Hardy from zone* 4 southward, but it flowers so early that its bloom is often destroyed by late frosts.

**tripetala.** Umbrella tree. A tree with spreading branches and open head, growing to 40 ft. high. Leaves oblong to broadly oval, 1-2 ft. long, pointed, pale green and soft-hairy beneath. Flowers appearing with leaves, cup-shaped, white, 10 in. across, of unpleasant, heavy odor. Petals 6-9. Sepals* shorter, soon turning back. Fruit 4 in. long, rose-pink. Pa. to Ala. and west to Ark. and Miss. May-June. Hardy from zone* 3 southward.

**virginiana.** Sweet bay; also known as white bay or swamp laurel. A deciduous* shrub, or half-evergreen tree, growing 60 ft. high in the south, but a shrub northward. Branchlets smooth. Buds soft-hairy. Leaves oblong or elliptic or narrower, pointed or blunt, with a bloom beneath, and at first silky soft-hairy, 3-5 in. long. Flowers appearing with the leaves, rounded, 3 in. across, white, very fragrant. Petals 9-12. Sepals shorter and thinner, spreading. Fruit 2 in. long, red. Mass. to Fla. and to Tex., near the coast. May-June. Hardy from zone* 3 southward, and generally a bog plant and preferring acid soils.

## MAGNOLIA CULTURE

Because certain members of the genus produce their flowers before the foliage is developed, a selection of species and varieties may be chosen which will offer flowering color

---

* Special articles on the subjects indicated by an asterisk (*) will be found at the words so marked.

from March until July and, quite often, well into Aug. The fruit ripens in Aug. and Sept. and appears in the form of long, colored, cone-like formations which split longitudinally at maturity, exposing scarlet-colored seeds.

The first species to show flower is *Magnolia stellata* which comes into bloom about the last week of March and is a shrubby plant hardy north of Boston. It is immediately followed by *Magnolia salicifolia, kobus, denudata, soulangeana*, and *liliflora* all of which produce their flowers before the development of the leaves. During the second week in June, *Magnolia acuminata, obovata, tripetala, fraseri, parviflora*, and *macrophylla* come into bloom. The last mentioned is not hardy north of Rochester, New York. Among the evergreen species are *Magnolia grandiflora* which is hardy only south of Washington, D.C. and *Magnolia virginiana* which although hardy throughout the U.S. retains its foliage only in the warmer sections of the country.

Good drainage rather than a rich soil is the prime essential for the successful cultivation of *Magnolia*. However, for best results it is recommended that some natural fertilizer such as well-rotted stable or cow manure be applied about the base of each plant every two or three years. All magnolias have fleshy roots which makes transplanting a tedious and painstaking operation. Whenever possible they should be left alone and not transplanted. Their root system cannot stand injury or drying out and, for this reason, all material should be carefully balled and burlapped when moved. For details see PLANTING.

Pruning of *Magnolia* is not necessary for the production of flowers and with few exceptions this operation may be dispensed with except as required for the occasional removal of dead or diseased wood.

Propagation is accomplished by several methods. The species are most commonly grown from seed. The hybrids and varieties are veneer-grafted on *Magnolia kobus*, the work being done in the greenhouse during Jan. Layering is an excellent method for the amateur. Vigorous shoots are selected near the base of the plant and, after having the bark scarred with a knife, are pegged to the ground and covered with a few inches of soil. After one or two seasons these shoots are severed from the plant and set out in good soil. After a few years a vigorous plant will result. Budding is also practiced and is perhaps superior to grafting. *Magnolia kobus* is used as a stock and the buds are tied from the top down, the opposite of the usual procedure in work of this kind. — A. D. S.

INSECT PESTS. The principal pest is a large, round, convex scale insect, which may be controlled with a dormant spray of miscible oil. A mealybug is sometimes troublesome; it is checked by the same dormant spray, and may be washed from the plant with a strong stream of water in summer.

**MAGNOLIACEAE** (mag-no-li-ā'see-ee). The magnolia family, geologically very ancient, contains some of our most beautiful garden shrubs and trees in its 10 genera and over 80 species, most of which, except *Magnolia, Kadsura*, and *Liriodendron* (see TULIP-TREE) are tropical.

Leaves alternate,* mostly without marginal teeth, the bud enclosed by the large, sheathing stipules.* Flowers very showy in *Magnolia* and *Liriodendron* (see TULIP-TREE), less so in *Michelia, Illicium, Kadsura* and *Schisandra*, the only other cult. genera. The fruit is peculiar in most genera, being a cone-like collection of dry fruits, which in *Magnolia* becomes fleshy (often scarlet) with the seeds suspended (for a brief time) on thread-like strings. All have perfect* flowers except *Kadsura*, a woody Asiatic vine with unisexual,* mostly solitary flowers, and berry-like fruit.

Technical flower characters: Sepals and petals often indistinguishable, when obvious the sepals 3, rarely 4, the petals 6 or more. Stamens many, spirally arranged. Ovary of many carpels (see PISTIL), superior,* 1-celled.

**MAGNOLIA FAMILY** = Magnoliaceae.

**MAGNOLIA GARDENS.** See SOUTH CAROLINA.

**MAHAGONI** (ma-ha-gō'nee). West Indian vernacular for the mahogany.

**MAHALA MAT** = *Ceanothus prostratus*.

**MAHALEB** (ma-hă'leb). Original Arabic name for *Prunus mahaleb*, the mahaleb cherry.

**MAHERNIA** (ma-her'ni-a). A genus of perhaps 30 species of chiefly South African herbs or under-shrubs of the family Sterculiaceae, only **M. verticillata**, the honey bell, of hort. interest. It is a sprawling shrubby plant, never over 6 in. high, the stems rough. Leaves alternate,* deeply cut into narrow segments. Flowers in pairs, nodding, yellow, fragrant, about ½ in. long. Calyx* bell-shaped, but the corolla of 5 separate, flat petals. Stamens* 5. Fruit a 5-valved capsule.* The honey bell is more widely grown in the cool greenhouse as a basket plant than outdoors where it is hardy only in southern Calif. It blooms in winter and early spring, and is sometimes offered as *M. odorata*. (*Mahernia* is an anagram of *Hermannia*.)

**MAHOBERBERIS** (ma-ho-ber'ber-is). A bigeneric* hybrid and including only a half-evergreen shrub of the family Berberidaceae, **M. neuberti**, a hybrid between *Mahonia aquifolium* and *Berberis vulgaris*. It is a shrub growing nearly 6 ft. high, without spines on the branches. Leaves 1–3 in. long, broadly oval to oblong, toothed or spiny, occasionally 3–5 leaflets, all on the same plant. It has not been known to bloom and is of secondary hort. interest. It is sometimes confused with *Berberis ilicifolia*.

**MAHOGANY.** The true mahogany is *Swietenia mahagōni* (which see). For other cult. plants sometimes called mahogany see EUCALYPTUS and CERCOCARPUS.

**MAHOGANY FAMILY** = Meliaceae.

**MAHOGANY GUM** = *Eucalyptus robusta*.

**MAHONIA** (ma-hō'ni-a). A genus of American and Asian evergreen, thornless shrubs, rarely small trees, comprising about 45 species. Leaves alternate,* compound,* the leaflets arranged feather-fashion (pinnate*), or rarely in 3's, spiny, often turning purplish in autumn. Petals 6. Sepals* 9, the flowers yellow, fragrant, in terminal clusters (racemes* or panicles*). Fruit a dark blue berry, usually covered with a bloom, rarely red or whitish. (Named for Bernard M'Mahon, an American horticulturist; see America at GARDEN BOOKS.)

Mahonias are handsome low-growing evergreens for the shrubbery border and foundation planting. They should be planted in sheltered positions or protected from the wind and sun in winter. Some of the western species do well as far north as Canada where they are protected by a heavy covering of snow all winter. They are increased by seeds and suckers, and by layers and cuttings of half-ripe wood under glass. They are sometimes listed as *Odostemon*.

**aquifolium.** Oregon grape. A shrub 3 to 10 ft. high. Leaflets 5–9, shiny, ovalish or oblong in shape, stiff, leathery, the marginal teeth spiny. Flowers yellow, in dense, erect terminal clusters (racemes*) 3 in. high. Fruit a small bluish berry, edible. British Columbia to Ore. April–May. Hardy from zone* 3 southward.

**bealei.** A shrub with stout, upright stems, sometimes 12 ft. high. Leaflets 9–15, round-oval, with a few large teeth on the margins, the end leaflet larger, bluish-green, with a slight bloom beneath, stiff and leathery. Flowers lemon-yellow, fragrant, in close-growing upright terminal clusters (racemes*) 6 in. high. Fruit bluish-black. China. March–May. Hardy from zone* 4 southward.

**japonica.** A shrub similar to *M. bealei*. Leaflets ovalish to oblong with a long spine at the end and with 5 or 6 strong spiny teeth on the margin, yellowish-green beneath and not as rigid-leaved as *M. bealei*. Flowers small, yellowish, in drooping, close-growing, terminal clusters. Fruit bluish-black. Cult. in Jap. and rarely seen in U.S. gardens.

**nervosa.** Oregon grape; also known as water holly. A shrub 2 ft. high, usually lower. Leaflets 11–19, oval to narrower, leathery, shiny above, pale beneath, with spiny teeth on the margin. Flowers bright yellow, fragrant, in erect terminal clusters 8 in. long. Fruit somewhat oval, dark blue with a bloom,* edible. British Columbia to Cal. May–June. Hardy from zone* 4 southward.

**pinnata.** California barberry. A shrub up to 12 ft. high. Leaflets 7–13, somewhat oval to narrower, spiny-toothed on the margins, slightly shiny and green beneath. Flowers pale yellow in terminal clusters in the axils* of the leaves. Fruit almost round, purplish-black. Cal. and N. Mex. to Mex. Hardy from zone* 6, and possibly from zone* 5 southward.

**repens.** Creeping barberry. A shrub with underground rooting stems, rarely more than 1 ft. high. Leaflets 3–7, roundish-oval, 1½–2½ in. long, dull bluish-green above, with a bloom* below, leathery, and with spiny marginal teeth. Flowers in terminal clusters (racemes*) at the ends of the branches. Fruit small, black, with a bloom.* British Columbia to N. Mex. and Cal. May. Hardy from zone* 3 southward.

---

* Special articles on the subjects indicated by an asterisk (*) will be found at the words so marked.

**trifoliolata.** Agarita; also known as algerita. A shrub sometimes 8 ft. high. Leaflets 3, oblong or narrower, with coarse marginal teeth, stiff. Flowers, few in a terminal cluster (raceme*). Fruit red, used in jelly. Occasionally planted in Tex. Tex., N. Mex. and Mex. Not certainly hardy north of zone* 6.

**MAHON STOCK** = *Malcomia maritima*.

**MAIANTHEMUM** (may-an'thee-mum). Generally woodland, low, perennial herbs of the lily family, two of them cult. in the wild garden, and suggesting the lily-of-the-valley, but far inferior as hort. subjects. They have creeping rootstocks and a short stem having only 2 or 3 leaves, and terminated by a short raceme of small white flowers. These are 4-parted, have 4 stamens,* and are followed by a somewhat speckled berry. (*Maianthemum* is from the Greek for May and flower, in allusion to their spring-blooming.)

They are of easy cult. in the wild garden, preferably in reasonably moist, partly shady places, where they will make large patches in a few years. Both species flower in early spring.

**bifolium.** Nearly 9 in. high and hairy. Leaves more or less triangular, but deeply heart-shaped at the base, the stalk about 1 in. long. Flower cluster about 1 in. long. Eurasia.

**canadense.** Wild lily-of-the-valley; also called Mayflower and bead-ruby. Usually about 5 in. high, rarely 7 in., the leaves only 1 or 2 on the stem, very short-stalked. Flowering cluster nearly 2 in. long. Eastern N.A. and west to N. Dak. In New England sometimes called Solomon's-seal.

**MAIDEN.** A one-year-old, single-stemmed fruit tree, used for budding or grafting in the production of trained fruit trees; often called a whip. See Fruit Trees at TRAINING PLANTS.

**MAIDENHAIR.** See ADIANTUM.

**MAIDENHAIR SPLEENWORT** = *Asplenium trichomanes*.

**MAIDENHAIR-TREE** = *Ginkgo biloba*.

**MAIDENHAIR-VINE** = *Muehlenbeckia complexa*.

**MAIDEN PINK** = *Dianthus deltoides*.

**MAIDEN'S-WREATH** = *Francoa ramosa*.

**MAINE.** The state lies wholly in zones* 2 and 3.

SOIL AND TOPOGRAPHY. Maine lies in a region of comparatively recent glaciation and as a result of this and the rugged topography of the state, marked soil variation exists. The "patchy" condition, together with factors related to topography, such as exposure to winds, air and water drainage, slope, etc., make the care in local selection of sites for vegetable and fruit production particularly important. Most areas are acid, and in many locations there is marked response by certain crops to lime application. Dolomitic limestone is preferred, particularly in the potato-producing area of Aroostook County, to overcome the deficiency of magnesium which frequently exists. The use of commercial fertilizers is essential to produce high crop yields, and marked response to phosphorus is usual.

VEGETABLE PRODUCTION. Commercial production of vegetables consists mostly of canning crops in the south central part of the state and of potatoes in Aroostook County, which is located in the northern part. Small truck-gardening areas lie in the southern portion near the coast and inland near the cities and in some lake regions that are summer resorts. Nearly all kinds of vegetables can be grown in the state. Some of the warm-season crops, such as melons, watermelons, peppers, and eggplant, can be grown satisfactorily only in the southern region and where soil and exposure are suitable. Cool-season crops such as members of the cabbage family, peas, and root crops are well adapted to the climate and develop excellent quality.

FRUIT PRODUCTION. Both small and tree fruits are grown in the state to supply local markets and to some extent for out-of-state trade.

The small fruits grown consist primarily of strawberries and raspberries, although other sorts are grown in home gardens to a limited extent. Only the southwestern part of Maine has a sufficiently mild climate for grape-growing, and this is limited to the hardier varieties for home use. Maine has, in recent years, become increasingly popular to tourists because of its summer recreational attractions, and this has resulted in increased demands for locally grown fresh fruits and vegetables. Good crops are obtained by those who exercise care in the selection of varieties, location and culture. Many of the larger growers of strawberries and raspberries find a ready market for their product by shipping to Boston and other cities in that vicinity. This is especially true of growers located in coastal towns where it is possible to ship by boat. The ripening season of strawberries and raspberries in Maine comes at a time when these fruits have little or no competition in markets farther south.

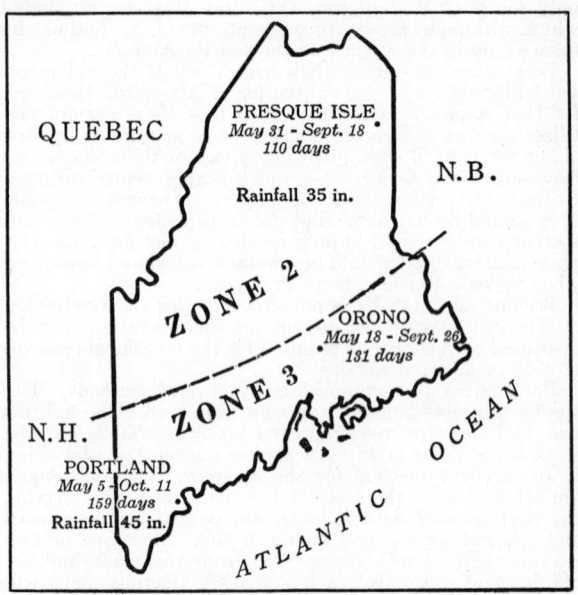

MAINE

The zones of hardiness crossing Maine are those shown on the colored map at ZONE, which should be consulted for details. The dates are the average latest killing frost in spring and the first one in the fall. The figures below the dates show the average length of the growing season. Rainfall figures (in inches) are for total annual rainfall in the regions so indicated.

Apples comprise the principal tree fruit grown for commercial production. Plums and cherries are grown to a limited extent for home use and for local market. Sweet cherries and peaches are only occasionally planted in home orchards in southern Maine, as the climate generally is considered too vigorous for these fruits. Northern Maine is too cold for any but the most hardy varieties of fruits. In fact, hardiness is an important factor to consider in the selection of varieties for almost any location in Maine, for either small or tree fruits. Certain apple varieties like MacIntosh and Northern Spy are admirably adapted to the soil and climatic conditions afforded in the state. Here, such varieties attain their maximum quality and attractiveness.

ORNAMENTALS. Many beautiful flower gardens are found on the estates of summer residents and also around homes of permanent residents. Annual flowers grow very well and have very brilliant coloring when grown along the coast, where the temperature and moisture are moderated by the cool, moist air from the ocean. Many herbaceous perennials succeed very well, especially where the snow cover remains throughout the winter. Occasional winters with little snow and frequent "thaws" cause more or less loss in this type of plant. Although a large number of shrubs are perfectly hardy, the greater part of the plantings consist of *Spiraea vanhouttei*, *Cornus stolonifera*, *Berberis thunbergi*, *Viburnum americanum*, *Syringa vulgaris*, and *Philadelphus coronarius*. A list of hardy shrubs would include all kinds of lilacs not

---

* Special articles on the subjects indicated by an asterisk (*) will be found at the words so marked.

grafted, mock-oranges, dogwoods except the flowering, spireas except *S. prunifolia*, viburnums, honeysuckles, laurels, rhododendrons, and most shrub evergreens. The American elm, some maples, and evergreens make up the majority of the ornamental trees used. Occasional nut trees are found, but for the most part fail to bear good crops.

MAINE FROST DATA

| Town | Average date of last killing frost in spring | Latest known killing frost | Average date of earliest killing frost in fall | Earliest known killing frost |
|---|---|---|---|---|
| Presque Isle | May 31 | June 29 | Sept. 18 | Sept. 6 |
| Orono | May 18 | June 5 | Sept. 26 | Sept. 2 |
| Portland | May 5 | June 3 | Oct. 11 | Sept. 11 |

The average annual rainfall varies between 35 and 45 inches from the northern inland part of the state to the coast regions, respectively. The mean precipitation during the growing season for these regions is from 18 to 21 inches, which is ample for most crops. Under certain conditions, some gardeners find irrigation practical. Proximity to the ocean, vast wooded areas, and about 2500 inland lakes all aid in minimizing crop damage by summer temperature extremes and drying winds.

The address of the Agricultural Experiment Station, which has kindly supplied this information about the state, is Orono, Maine. The Station is always ready to answer gardening questions.

Garden club activities include clubs of the Garden Club of America, the home office of which is at 598 Madison Avenue, New York. There are also over 15 clubs affiliated with the Garden Club Federation of Maine. For the nearest one to your locality write the Garden Editor, Houghton Mifflin Company, Boston, Mass.

**MAIZE.** See CORN.

*MAJALIS, -e* (ma-jay'lis). Literally May-time; usually meaning May-flowering.

*MAJOR, MAJUS.* Greater.

**MAJORANA.** See SWEET MARJORAM.

**MAKI** = *Podocarpus macrophylla maki*.

**MALABAR GOURD** = *Cucurbita ficifolia*.

*MALABARICA, -us, -um* (ma-la-bar'i-ka). From Malabar, India.

**MALABAR NIGHTSHADE.** See BASELLA.

*MALABATHRICA, -us, -um* (ma-la-bath'ri-ka). From Malabar.

**MALACEAE.** See ROSACEAE.

*MALACHODENDRON* (ma-lack-o-den'dron). Old name for plants now included in *Stewartia*.

*MALACOIDES* (ma-la-coy'deez, but *see* OÏDES). Softly mucilaginous.

*MALACOTHRIX* (mal'a-ko-thricks). A group of little-known herbs of the family Compositae, all from western N.A. and chiefly perennials, but the only cult. species annuals. The two below are essentially stemless, and have a basal rosette of much-divided leaves. Flower heads (in ours) bright yellow, composed only of ray flowers,* solitary in the first species, but the flowering stalk branched and with several heads in the second. (*Malacothrix* is from the Greek for soft hair, in allusion to the hairy foliage of some species.)

Treat both species as hardy annuals (see ANNUALS). They are natural inhabitants of sandy soils.

**californica.** Not over 12 in. high. Basal rosette of leaves woolly in youth. Leaves divided finger-fashion into narrow, line-like segments. Flower heads about 1¾ in. wide, somewhat dandelion-like. Calif. April-June (in Calif.), later when sown as a hardy annual.

**glabrata.** Similar to the above and perhaps only a variety of it, differing in the young leaves being smooth from the first, and the flowering stalk usually branched. Ore. to Calif. and Nev.

**MALANGA** = *Xanthosoma atrovirens*.
**MALAY JEWEL-VINE** = *Derris scandens*.
**MALCOLM STOCK** = *Malcomia maritima*.

**MALCOMIA** (mal-cō'mĭ-a). Commonly called Mahon, Malcolm or Virginia Stock. A small genus of low, grayish herbs belonging to the family Cruciferae, or mustard family. Stems branching profusely, making a compact plant. Leaves simple, alternate,* slightly cut. Flowers white, purple or reddish in a loose cluster at end of branches, the petals 4, long and narrow. Pods usually long and narrow, containing one or two rows of seeds. (Named for William Malcolm, an English horticulturist.) Propagated by seeds. Sow in permanent position, in masses in ordinary garden soil, in early spring, about 1/16 in. deep. The Virginia stock was much used in English cottage gardens in the Victorian era.

**flexuosa.** The plant so offered is usually *Malcomia maritima*.
**littorea.** Perennial to 12 in. The whole plant is covered with short, white hairs. Leaves narrow, lance-shaped. Flowers purple. It can be grown as an annual. Mediterranean region.
**maritima.** The Virginia Stock. An annual of spreading habit 6–12 in. high. Leaves simple, ovalish. Flowers reddish to white. The var. **alba** is a color form. Mediterranean region.

**MALE.** See FEMALE.
**MALE BAMBOO** = *Dendrocalamus strictus*.
**MALEBERRY** = *Xolisma ligustrina*.
**MALE FERN** = *Dryopteris filix-mas*.

**MALLOW.** See MALVA. For other plants sometimes called mallow see MALVASTRUM, SPHAERALCEA, CORCHORUS, ALTHAEA, HIBISCUS, and LAVATERA.

**MALLOW FAMILY** = Malvaceae.

**MALOPE** (ma-lō'pe). A genus of nearly a dozen smooth or hairy, annual herbs of the family Malvaceae, found in the Mediterranean region. Leaves alternate, without marginal teeth, occasionally 3-parted. Flowers showy, about 3 in. across, white, violet, or pink, surrounded by three heart-shaped bracts.* (*Malope* is a name used by Pliny for some kind of mallow.)

These plants are easily cultivated in any ordinary garden soil.

**grandiflora** = *Malope trifida grandiflora*.
**trifida.** Grows from 2–3 ft. high. Leaves smooth, 3-parted. The flowers grow on stalks, singly, from the axils* of the leaves; they are 2–3 in. across, rose or purple, blooming nearly all summer. Eu. and northern Africa. Var. **grandiflora** has larger, deep rosy-red flowers, and is sometimes known as *M. grandiflora*. Var. **rosea** has rose-colored flowers. See ANNUALS.

**MALPIGHIA** (mal-pig'ĭ-a). Tropical American shrubs and trees of the family Malpighiaceae, comprising over 40 species, only two of them of much garden interest. They have opposite,* short-stalked leaves, and not particularly showy flowers in short-stalked clusters (cymes* or umbels*) in the leaf-axils.* Petals 5, usually not quite equal. Stamens* 10. Fruit a drupe* with 3 stones. (Named for Marcello Malpighi, Italian naturalist.)

Neither species can be grown outdoors north of zone* 9, although they are apparently indifferent as to soils in Fla. The first is occasionally grown for ornament, while *M. glabra* is grown in the tropics, and to some extent in southern Fla., for its acid fruits used in preserves. Propagated by cuttings or by seeds.

**coccigera.** A West Indian shrub, rarely more than 3 ft. high. Leaves holly-like, spiny-margined, nearly ¾ in. long. Flowers about ½ in. wide, pink, the clusters few-flowered.
**glabra.** Barbados cherry. A shrub 5–10 ft. high, the leaves ovalish or narrower, 1–3 in. long, spiny, without marginal teeth. Flowers rose-pink. Fruit red, acid, about the size of a cherry. Southern Tex. to tropical America.

**MALPIGHIACEAE** (mal-pig-ĭ-ā'see-ee). A family of 55 genera and over 650 species of tropical shrubs, trees or vines, only three genera of which, *Malpighia*, *Thryallis* and *Stigmaphyllon* are of secondary hort. interest. The first two (in cultivation) are shrubby, while *Stigmaphyllon* comprises greenhouse vines.

Leaves mostly opposite.* Flowers not particularly showy,

---

* Special articles on the subjects indicated by an asterisk (*) will be found at the words so marked.

in various kinds of clusters, nearly regular,* the petals often fringed or toothed. Fruit usually separating into 3 nut-like segments, which are sometimes winged in *Thryallis* and *Stigmaphyllon*, but more or less fleshy in *Malpighia*.

Technical flower characters: Flowers hermaphrodite.* Sepals 5. Petals 5, usually unequal, and with a slender claw.* Stamens 10, some occasionally sterile, usually partly united. Ovary superior.* Styles usually 3.

**MALTESE CROSS** = *Lychnis chalcedonica.*

**MALUS** (may'lus). A genus of North American and Eurasian, mostly deciduous, trees or shrubs, of the rose family, rarely with spiny branches, but occasionally with spurs of the wild or escaped species becoming thorn-like. Leaves alternate,* toothed or lobed, folded or rolled in bud, with stipules.* Flowers, usually in advance of foliage, regular, white to pink or carmine, in umbel-like terminal clusters (racemes*). Petals 5, usually rounded, or broadly oval. Stamens* 15–20 or more. Fruit a true pome,* fleshy, often edible. Some of our most beautiful and valuable ornamental trees belong to this genus, as well as important fruit trees. Commonly known as apple; also as crabapple, crab, or crab-tree. The cultivated apple is *M. pumila.* For the culture, diseases, and insect pests of the apple and the ornamental species below, *see* APPLE. (*Malus* is the ancient Latin name of the apple.) All are early spring-bloomers, and many of them called *Pyrus* (which see). Next to the Japanese flowering cherries, the ornamental crabapples are among the finest of flowering trees.

**angustifolia.** Southern crabapple. A slender-branched tree growing to 25 ft. high, partially evergreen. Leaves 1–3 in. long, narrowly oblong, toothed or without marginal teeth, smooth and light green beneath. Flowers 1 in. across, pink or rose, fragrant. Fruit 1 in. or less in diameter, nearly round, depressed at both ends, yellow-green. *Var.* **rosea** has deeper rose-colored flowers. Va. to Fla. and Miss. Hardy from zone* 4 southward.

**arnoldiana.** A hybrid derived from crossing *M. floribunda* and *M. baccata.* A large bush or tree, 25 or more ft. high. Leaves 2–4 in. long; at first soft-hairy, then smooth, oblong, sharp-pointed, toothed. Flowers larger or lighter-colored than *floribunda.* Fruit also larger, yellow instead of red. Handsome bush, much used in shrubbery plantations or as a specimen on the lawn. Hardy from zone* 3 southward.

**atrosanguinea.** Carmine crabapple. A hybrid between *M. halliana* and *M. sieboldi.* A handsome, bushy shrub resembling *M. floribunda.* Leaves smooth, shining, toothed. Flowers rose-purple, not fading to white. Fruit red. Hardy from zone* 4 southward. Often known as *Pyrus atrosanguinea.*

**baccata.** Siberian crabapple. A round-headed tree sometimes growing 40 ft. high, with many smooth, slender, wiry branchlets. Leaves 2½–4 in. long, thin, smooth, somewhat oval, toothed, pointed. Flowers white, 1½ in. across. Fruit ¾ in. or less in diameter, yellow or red. Siberia and Manchuria and N. China. Common in cultivation. *Var.* **mandshurica** has soft-hairy leaves, flower stalks and calyx,* fragrant flowers, and larger fruit. *Var.* **jacki** is similar, but has smooth leaves and a smaller, bright red fruit. Hardy from zone* 2 southward.

**communis** = *Malus pumila.*

**coronaria.** American crab; often called sweet crabapple or garland crabapple. A twiggy, stiff-branched tree becoming 30 ft. high, foliage becoming quite smooth. Leaves thin, 2–3 in. long, nearly oval, sharp-toothed or sometimes notched. Flowers 1 in. or less across, rose, changing to white. Fruit 1 in. in diameter, flattened at ends. N.Y. to Ala. west to Mo. Hardy from zone* 3 southward. Sometimes known as *Pyrus coronaria.*

**dawsoniana.** A small tree, thought to be a cross between *M. fusca* and *M. pumila.* Leaves somewhat oval, 1½–3½ in. long, toothed, seldom lobed. Flowers 1 in. across, white. Fruit, yellow or green, flushed red. Both flowers and fruit twice as large as *M. fusca.* Hardy from zone* 3 southward. Also known as *Pyrus dawsoniana.*

**floribunda.** Showy crabapple. A large bush or tree with wide-spreading branches, becoming 25 or more feet high. Leaves dull green, somewhat oval in outline, 2 to 3 in. long, sharp-toothed. Flowers 1¼ in. across, rose or rose-red, fading white. Fruit ⅓ in. in diameter, red. Commonly supposed to be a hybrid between *M. baccata* and *M. sieboldi*, but probably a distinct species introduced from Jap., perhaps of Chinese origin. Hardy from zone* 3 southward. Sometimes known as *Pyrus floribunda.*

**fusca.** Oregon crabapple. A shrub or small tree sometimes 30 ft. high. Leaves somewhat oval, 3–4 in. long, sharply toothed, often 3-lobed, at first soft-hairy on both sides, later smooth above. Flowers white, ¾ in. across, 6–12 in a flat-topped cluster. Fruit oblong, ½–¾ in. long, yellow or green, flushed red. Northern Calif. to Alaska. Not often seen in cultivation, but interesting as supposed parent of *M. dawsoniana.* Hardy from zone* 2 southward. Sometimes listed as *Pyrus fusca.*

**halliana.** A shrub or tree with loose, open head, growing 18 ft. high. Young branchlets soon smooth, purple. Leaves shiny above, 2 to 3 in. long, somewhat long, oval, pointed, toothed, the midrib* purplish. Flowers deep rose, the calyx purple, 1–1½ in. across, on slender, purple stalks. Fruit ⅓ in. in diameter, purplish. Western China. *Var.* **parkmani** is a semi-double-flowered form. It was grown by Francis Parkman, the historian, near Boston. Hardy from zone* 3 southward. Also called *Pyrus halliana.*

**ioensis.** Prairie crabapple. A tree growing 30 ft. high, branchlets downy. Leaves somewhat oval or oblong, 2–4 in. long, toothed, occasionally lobed, sharp-pointed, sometimes downy beneath. Flowers 1–2 in. across, white or rose-tinted. Fruit almost round, sometimes angled, greenish, waxy. Betchel's crab is a double-flowered form. Ind. to Minn. and Mo. The double-flowered form is very handsome and often cult. as an ornamental shrub. Hardy from zone* 3 southward.

**kaido** = *Malus micromalus.*

**malus** = *Malus pumila.*

**micromalus.** Kaido crabapple. A small tree of upright habit, growing 25 ft. high. Leaves almost oblong, 2–4 in. long, narrowing to the base and long-pointed, shiny. Flowers deep pink, 1½ in. across. Fruit nearly red, hollowed at base. Perhaps a hybrid of *M. spectabilis* and *M. baccata.* Hardy from zone* 4 southward.

**nivalis** = *Pyrus nivalis.*

**prunifolia.** A small tree with young growth soft-hairy. Leaves 2–4 in. long, ovalish or elliptic, short-pointed, soft-hairy beneath, later smooth. Flowers about 1½ in. across, white. Fruit 1 in. in diameter, yellow or red, very abundant, and held long on tree. Northeastern As. *Var.* **rinki,** the Ringo crabapple, has leaves soft-hairy beneath, flowers pink and calyx* somewhat hairy. Eastern As. Hardy from zone* 3 southward. Sometimes known as *Pyrus prunifolia.*

**pumila.** The common apple. A round-headed, short-trunked tree growing 45 ft. high. The young branches are downy. Leaves 1¾–4 in. long, elliptic or ovalish, pointed, glossy above, downy beneath, bluntly toothed. Flowers 2 in. across, white and pink, appearing with first foliage. Fruit nearly round, yellow and red. Eu. and As. Cult. since ancient times. The parent of most of our cult. apples. Frequently known as *Pyrus malus* and as *Malus communis, sylvestris,* etc. *Var.* **niedzwetzkyana** has red bark, wood, leaves, flowers and fruit. Southwest Siberia and Turkestan. *Var.* **paradisiaca,** the Paradise apple, is a dwarf form. For apple cult. and best varieties *see* APPLE.

**purpurea.** A hybrid of *M. pumila niedzwetzkyana* and *M. atrosanguinea.* Young branchlets purple. Leaves when young purple, smaller than *M. pumila niedzwetzkyana*, shining. Flowers with oblong petals. Fruit small. *Var.* **aldenhamensis** is a small tree with leaves somewhat more oval, soft-hairy beneath or nearly smooth, veined and with purple rib. Flowers wine-red, partially double. Fruit deep purple-red. *Var.* **eleyi** has leaves reddish when unfolding, downy beneath, and a purple rib. The flowers are wine-red. Fruit conical-shaped, deep purple-red. Hardy from zone* 4 southward.

**sargenti.** A low, bushy, much-branched, spiny shrub, 3–5 ft. high. Young growth downy. Leaves 2–3 in. long, ovalish or elliptic, short-pointed, toothed, turning orange and yellow in autumn. Flowers pure white, 1 inch across, 5 or 6 in a cluster, the petals oval, overlapping. Fruit nearly round, ½ in. or less in diameter, dark red with a slight bloom.* Jap. Hardy from zone* 3 southward.

**scheideckeri** = *Malus floribunda.*

**sieboldi.** Toringo crabapple. A shrub with spreading branches, and up to 15 ft. high. Young growth soft-hairy. Leaves 1–2½ in. long, broadly oval, with coarse marginal teeth, or 3- or 5-lobed. Flowers pink or deep rose in bud. Fruit pea-shaped, ⅓ in. in diameter, red or brownish yellow. This is the cult. dwarf mountain form. Jap. *Var.* **arborescens** is a graceful tree growing about 30 ft. high, with larger, less soft-hairy and less deeply lobed leaves than the typical form and with flowers nearly white. This is the common wild form. Hardy from zone* 3 southward. Also known as *Pyrus sieboldi.*

**spectabilis.** A small ornamental tree up to 25 ft. high. Leaves 2–4 in. long, narrower than those of the common apple, stiff, shiny, short-pointed. Flowers 1½–2 in. across, deep rose-red in bud, fading to blush, semi-double or single. Fruit ¾–1 in. in diameter, yellowish, sour and bitter. China, but not known in the wild. Often listed as *Pyrus spectabilis. Var.* **albiplena** has double white flowers and is one of the handsomest crabapples when in bloom, though the fruit is not showy. A hort. form has double rose-pink flowers *Var.* **riversi** has larger leaves, and larger double pink flowers. Hardy from zone* 3 southward.

**sylvestris** = *Malus pumila.*

**theifera.** A small tree about 20 ft. high with stiff, spreading branches. Young growth soft-hairy, soon becoming smooth. Leaves 2–4 in. long, with sharp marginal teeth, pointed. Flowers 3–7 in a cluster, white or pinkish, fragrant. Fruit ⅓ in. across, greenish-yellow with red cheek. China and the Himalayas. Sometimes called *Pyrus theifera.* Hardy from zone* 3 southward.

**toringoides.** A beautiful shrub or small tree, 25 ft. high. Young growth soft-hairy, soon becoming smooth. Leaves, 1–3 in. long, with sharp marginal teeth, often 3-lobed. Flowers 1 in. or less across, 6–12 in a cluster, white or pinkish. Fruit ½ in. in diameter, yellow, usually with red cheek. Western China. Frequently listed as *Pyrus toringoides.* Hardy from zone* 3 southward.

**trilobata.** A shrub or tree growing to 18 ft. high. Young growth soft-hairy. Leaves 3-lobed, with fine saw teeth on margin, 2–3 in. long, shining, bright green above. Flowers 1 in. across, 6–8 in a cluster, white. Fruit ¾ in. in diameter, longer than broad. Western As. Often known as *Pyrus trilobata.* Hardy from zone* 3 southward.

**zumi.** A pyramidal tree, 20 ft. high. Similar to *M. sieboldi arborescens.* Leaves somewhat oval or oblong, 1½–3½ in. long, pointed, with marginal teeth, or lobed. Flowers 1 in. across, pink in bud, but becoming white. Fruit about ½ in. in diameter, round, red. Jap., but considered a hybrid between *M. baccata mandshurica* and *M. sieboldi.* Hardy from zone* 3 southward.

**MALVA** (mal'va). Mallow. About 30 species of widely distributed herbs of the family Malvaceae, several grown for ornament, but some rather weedy. They have alternate,* usually angled, lobed, or dissected leaves. Flowers mostly in the leaf-axils,* solitary or clustered, most of them with 3 or 2 involucre*-like bracts beneath them. Calyx* united, but 5-cleft. Petals 5, with a notch at the tip, mostly

* Special articles on the subjects indicated by an asterisk (*) will be found at the words so marked.

pink or white. Fruit a collection of ultimately separable, but at first united, carpels, joined to form a depressed, cheese-shaped cluster. (*Malva* is from the Greek for emollient, in allusion to the mucilaginous juice of some species.)

These mallows are far less satisfactory than those found in the closely related genus *Hibiscus* (which see). But *Malva* is of easy culture in any ordinary garden soil. The annuals may be sown where needed, as they are hardy annuals (see ANNUALS). The perennials are also of very simple cult., and may readily be divided in spring or fall. Besides the ones below there are several others which are mere weeds, although only *M. rotundifolia* is really a serious weed.

**alcea.** Vervain mallow; called also European mallow. A perennial resembling *M. moschata*, but its leaves only once-parted, each of the 5 parts not again divided. Eu.; sometimes an escape* in N.A.

**chinensis** = *Malva verticillata*.

**crispa.** Curled mallow. A rank-growing, unbranched annual, 4-10 ft. high, occasionally much more, the thick, nearly tree-like, stem leafy throughout. Leaves 5-7-lobed, the margins crisped or curled. Flowers scarcely ¼ in. wide, white, in dense clusters in the leaf-axils.* Eu., often persisting in old gardens and sometimes an escape.*

**moschata.** Musk mallow; also called musk rose. A hairy, perennial herb 1-2 ft. high. Stem leaves 5-parted, the divisions cleft or divided into narrow segments. Flowers pink or white, nearly 2 in. wide, mostly confined to the upper leaf-axils.* Fruit downy. Eu., but sometimes an escape in N.A. The var. **alba** always has white flowers.

**pulchella** = *Malva verticillata*.

**rotundifolia.** The common mallow, often called cheeses from the shape of its fruit. A common, prostrate herb, usually a pest and one of our worst weeds. Eurasia. See the list at WEEDS.

**verticillata.** Curled mallow. An annual or perennial, rather weedy herb, not very different from *M. crispa*, but usually lower and with pink, stalkless flowers. Eurasia. Sometimes known as *M. pulchella* and *M. chinensis*.

DISEASES. Rust and leafspot are the common diseases. For *rust, see* Rust at PLANT DISEASES. *Leafspot*, caused by various fungi, can be controlled by destroying infected leaves and by burning all plant debris in the fall.

MALVACEAE (mal-vay'see-ee). The mallow family is of much garden interest, for it contains many showy herbs, some foods, cotton, and a few shrubs and trees among its 45 genera and perhaps 1000 species, which are scattered all over the world.

Leaves alternate,* the main veins arising from the base of the blade, many of the leaves deeply lobed or cut, sometimes dissected. Flowers showy in many genera, especially in *Althaea* (see HOLLYHOCK), *Callirhoë*, *Hibiscus*, *Lavatera*, *Malope*, *Malvaviscus*, and *Sidalcea*. A common characteristic in most genera is a ring of bracts* just beneath each flower, sometimes very near the calyx.

Among tropical plants are *Abutilon*, *Hoheria*, *Ingenhousia*, *Lagunaria*, *Plagianthus*, and *Thespesia*, some of which are grown outdoors in frost-free parts of Calif. and Fla., or in the greenhouse. *Gossypium* is the cotton. *Malva* contains both decorative plants and weeds. *Malvastrum*, *Pavonia*, and *Sphaeralcea* complete the genera of garden interest.

Technical flower characters: Flowers regular* and hermaphrodite,* usually with 5 petals and 5 sepals, both free, or the sepals sometimes united. Stamens numerous, united to form a tube which surrounds the styles. Ovary superior,* its often separate segments forming a dry fruit, the segments of which fall separately; rarely berry-like.

MALVAEFLORA, -us, -um (mal-vee-flō'ra). With mallow-like flowers.

MALVASTRUM (mal-vas'trum). A large genus of American and South African, summer-blooming herbs of the family Malvaceae, comprising over 80 species of which the most common in cult. is **M. coccineum**, the red false mallow or prairie mallow. It is a woody-based, perennial herb, 8-12 in. high, usually silvery-hairy, with the alternate* leaves parted into narrow segments. Flowers brick-red, about 1 in. wide, mostly in close, terminal clusters (racemes*). It is practically a weed in central N.A., but is sometimes grown in the flower garden, where it is of very easy cult.; propagated by division. (*Malvastrum* is from *Malva*, in allusion to the similarity to that genus.)

MALVAVISCUS (mal-va-vis'kus). Hairy, tropical American shrubs or shrubby herbs of the family Malvaceae, a few of the dozen species grown for ornament outdoors in zones* 8 and 9, rarely in the greenhouse northward. They have alternate,* more or less heart-shaped, somewhat lobed leaves. Flowers showy, red, somewhat resembling a fuchsia, because the petals do not spread, and are more or less erect. Below each flower are 7-12 narrow bracts.* Stamens* protruding. Fruit berry-like and sticky at first, ultimately dry and separating into segments. (*Malvaviscus* means sticky mallow, in allusion to the fruit.)

Out of doors in Fla., the Gulf Coast, and in Calif., these plants, sometimes called Turk's-cap, are of easy cult. in a variety of soils. In the greenhouse they need potting mixture* 3 and a warm-temperate house. The Latin names are in some confusion, especially as to the identity of the commonest species in cult.

**arboreus.** Monacillo. A low shrub, not very different from *M. mollis*, with which it is often confused. It has smaller leaves than *M. mollis* and its leaves are not velvety as in that species. Tropical America. Sometimes sold as an abutilon.

**conzatti.** A shrub, the leaves more or less heart-shaped or ovalish, not usually lobed, but with rounded marginal teeth. Flowers nearly 2 in. long, red. Mex. and Guatemala. The plant offered as this is usually *M. grandiflorus*.

**grandiflorus.** A shrub 10-12 ft. high, the ovalish-oblong leaves scarcely lobed, but toothed. Flowers almost 2½ in. long, red. Mex. This is a showy shrub, perhaps more commonly cult. in the Far South than any of the other species.

**mollis.** A low shrub, the leaves more or less angled or lobed, the margins wavy or toothed, velvety, especially on the under side. Flowers about 1½ in. long, scarlet. Mex. to northern S.A. Often grown in the South and in northern greenhouses, usually under the name of *M. arboreus*.

MAMEY = *Mammea americana*. See also ACHRAS.

MAMEY FAMILY = Guttiferae.

MAMMEA (mam'mee-a). A small genus of tropical trees of the family Guttiferae, only **M. americana**, the mamey or mammee-apple, of any hort. interest. It is cult. in the tropics for its edible fruit, but only to a very limited extent in the warmest parts of southern Fla. It is a tree 40-60 ft. high, with opposite,* thick, glossy leaves 6-8 in. long. Flowers white, about 1 in. wide, fragrant (for details see GUTTIFERAE). Fruit a drupe,* nearly round, the rind russet, the flesh yellow, sweet in the best varieties, somewhat acid in the poorer ones. The fruit is nearly 6 in. in diameter and contains 1-4 large seeds, by which the plant is propagated. (*Mammea* is derived from mamey, the W.I. name for the cult. species.) For another plant, with a very different fruit, but also called mamey, see ACHRAS.

MAMMEE-APPLE = *Mammea americana*.

MAMMILLARIA = *Neomammillaria*.

MAMMOSA, -us, -um (mam-mō'sa). With breasts or nipples.

MAMMOTH CLOVER = *Trifolium pratense serotinum*. See CLOVER.

MAMONCILLO = *Melicocca bijuga*.

MANAGEMENT OF SEEDLINGS. See SEEDS AND SEEDAGE.

MANCA CABALLO = *Homalocephala texensis*.

MANDACARU = *Cereus jamacaru*.

MANDARIN ORANGE = *Citrus nobilis deliciosa*.

MANDEVILLA (man-de-vil'la). Tropical American, woody vines of the family Apocynaceae, comprising perhaps 50 species, of which **M. suaveolens**, the Chilean jasmine, is the only species of hort. interest. It is a high-climbing, woody vine with opposite,* oblong or heart-shaped leaves, 1-3 in. long, and pale bluish-green beneath. Flowers fragrant, showy, white or pinkish, more or less funnel-shaped, nearly 2 in. wide, mostly in loose clusters (racemes*). Fruit consisting of 2 pods (follicles*). The plant is scarcely known as an outdoor subject in the U.S. If grown in the greenhouse, it needs a warm-temperate house (see GREENHOUSE), and should be planted direct, not in a pot or tub. It is recorded as needing a peaty, sandy loam, and as being propagated by cuttings over bottom-heat. While called Chilean jasmine, it is a native of the Argentine. (Named for Henry J. Mandeville, British minister at Buenos Aires.)

MANDIOCA = *Manihot esculenta*.

MANDRAGORA (man-drag'o-ra). A genus of stemless perennials of not much importance, belonging to the potato

* Special articles on the subjects indicated by an asterisk (*) will be found at the words so marked.

family. They have thick, tuberous roots, divided into 2 leg-like branches, hence the name mandrake. Leaves growing from the tips of the roots, simple,* undivided, but with wavy margins. Flowers purple, cup-shaped, borne in clusters on stems rising between the leaves. Fruit an oblong, juicy berry which contains the seeds. (*Mandragora* was the name used by Hippocrates, said to mean that the plant is hurtful to cattle.) Mandrake in America means the mayapple (*Podophyllum*).

There are many superstitions connected with this plant, some say it is the dudaim mentioned in Genesis. It is related to the belladonna, has poisonous qualities, and is not usually cultivated.

**autumnalis.** A small form of the next, with violet flowers and smaller roots and leaves. Southern Eu. and northern Af.
**officinarum.** Common mandrake. Height about 1 ft., the roots spindle-shaped, often branching root. Leaves ovalish, nearly 1 ft. long. Flowers greenish-yellow, about 1 in. long. Southern Eu.

**MANDRAKE.** Traditionally mandrake is *Mandragora officinarum* (which see), but in America the name is often applied to the mayapple (*Podophyllum peltatum*). See MAYAPPLE.

**MANDSHURICA, -us, -um** (mand-sure′i-ka). From Manchuria.

**MANETTIA** (ma-net′ti-a). Tropical American, woody vines of the family Rubiaceae, two of the 40 known species grown for ornament. Leaves evergreen, opposite* (in ours). Flowers yellow and red (in ours), the corolla more or less tubular, the lobes spreading or slightly recurved. Stamens* 4-5. Fruit a 2-valved, many-seeded capsule.* (Named for Xavier Manetti, a Florentine botanist.)

The two below are often grown as greenhouse vines, as they will clamber over rafters, trellises, etc. They need a cool greenhouse and potting mixture* 3, and may be propagated by cuttings over bottom-heat. Outdoors their cult. must be confined to zones* 8 and 9, but they are not much grown either in Calif. or Fla.

**bicolor.** A smooth vine with nearly stalkless, lance-shaped leaves. Flowers solitary, about ¾ in. long, red below but yellow-tipped, the lobes of the calyx* more or less erect. Style* protruding. Brazil.
**inflata.** Resembling the last, but the stems hairy and the leaves hairy on the veins beneath. Flowers also similar, but the lobes of the calyx* recurved, and the style* not protruding. Paraguay and Uruguay.

**MANETTI ROSE** = *Rosa chinensis manetti*.
**MANETTI-VINE** = *Boussingaultia baselloides*.

**MANFREDA** (man-fre′da). A small genus of fleshy, bulbous herbs belonging to the family Amaryllidaceae. Leaves basal. From the center of the leaf rosette there usually arises the long flowering stem, 3-6 ft. high. Leaves thin, lance-shaped, usually with teeth-like margins, dying off in the winter. Flowers, which open at night, are greenish or purplish-white, tubular, splitting into 6 segments at the tip, the style* and stamens* protruding. Fruit a 3-celled capsule.* (Named for an ancient Italian writer.)

For cultivation see AGAVE, to which it is closely allied.

**virginica.** False aloe; also called rattlesnake master. Leaves green, narrow to 2 ft. in length. Flower stems 3-5 ft. high. Flowers short-stalked, about 2 in. long, fragrant, greenish-yellow. The tube is 3 times as long as the segments. The *var.* **tigrina** has mottled leaves. Southern U.S. and Mexico.

**MANGANAR.** A copyrighted powdered insecticide, containing 68% manganese arsenate; used as a stomach poison for chewing insects.

**MANGEL-WURZEL.** See BEET.

**MANGIFERA.** See MANGO.

**MANGO.** Asiatic or Indo-Malayan fruit trees, comprising the genus **Mangifera** (man-jif′fer-ra), of the sumac family, comprising perhaps 30 species, of which **M. indica**, the common mango, is of world-wide cult. throughout the tropics, and, as noted below, to a limited extent in the U.S. It is a splendid, round-headed tree up to 90 ft. high, with lance-shaped, alternate* leaves, 8-14 in. long. Flowers small, pinkish-white, scarcely ⅓ in. long, usually in terminal clusters (panicles*) and sometimes polygamous.* Fruit large, fleshy, aromatic (often with a turpentine odor), drupe*-like, usually red or yellowish-orange, very juicy, and not long-keeping. (*Mangifera* is from *mango*, the original vernacular for the best-known species, and from the Latin to bear, in allusion to the fruit.)

MANGO CULTURE

The mango is among the oldest and most highly esteemed of cult. fruits, and because of its excellent quality and widespread usage has been termed the "apple of the tropics" and "king of fruits." Native to tropical As., it is now found throughout the tropics in plantings of few to many irregularly planted trees and is seldom grown in numbers in regular orchard form. Strictly tropical in requirements, the tree endures but little frost, and is grown in the U.S. only in southern Fla. and in a very limited way in Calif. Although first introduced into Fla. over one hundred years ago, the past quarter-century has seen the greatest development in its culture and the fruit is now produced in fair quantity.

The smooth-skinned, ovoid-pointed fruits, yellow to red in color, are most attractive in appearance. Choice grafted varieties are not to be confused with the more common "turpentine" sorts. The former are rich, sweet and spicy, with flesh of melting texture and free of objectionable fibers; the latter, although quite edible, have a fibrous flesh and distinct turpentine flavor. There is much variation in shape and size of the fruit, that of common seedlings usually being small, while better varieties may weigh to 3 lbs. or more. Ripe fruits contain from 11 to 19 per cent sugar — in the form of sucrose, ½ to 1 per cent protein, little or no starch, and are a source of vitamins A and C. Served principally as a dessert, the fruit also may be used in the preparation of chutneys and preserves.

But few of the hundreds of named varieties are grown in Fla. These include for the most part the Haden, Paheri, Cambodiana, Cecil, Pico, Sandersha, Langra Benarsi and Amini. The Haden, because of its quality, large size, attractive color and free-bearing habit, is most widely planted. Beginning in May, the season of maturity extends with a few varieties into late fall.

Although thriving on some of the poorest of sandy soils, the trees attain their greatest size on more fertile types. They are symmetrical in growth habit and are planted extensively for their shade and ornamental value. The large size in maturity requires wide spacing for maximum development, usually not less than 30 × 30 ft. Fertilizers are of value, but an excess of nitrogen may stimulate too much vegetative growth at the expense of fruit production. Bearing age is reached in 5 to 7 years, and the trees are exceptionally long-lived.

Propagation is commonly by seeds and inarching, and to some extent by shield budding and crown grafting. Seeds of most of the Philippine varieties will come true to seed. — H. M.

INSECT PESTS. Red spider mites, several scale insects, and thrips are injurious in Fla. One or two winter applications of lubricating-oil emulsion, diluted 1-70, with nicotine sulphate added, will check all these pests; lime-sulphur, 1-60, is best for mites alone. Fruit-fly maggots, injurious in the tropics, are not generally present in the U.S.

**MANGO FAMILY** = Anacardiaceae.

**MANGO MELON.** See MELON.

*MANGOSTANA* (man-go-stan′a). Latinized form of mangostan, the Malayan name for the mangosteen.

**MANGOSTEEN.** See GARCINIA.

*MANICATA, -us, -um* (man-i-kay′ta). Long-sleeved; often applied to flowers with a long, tubular calyx.*

**MANIHOT** (man′i-hot). A very large, chiefly Brazilian genus of herbs, shrubs, and trees of the family Euphorbiaceae, of far more economic than hort. significance, at least in the U.S. They have alternate,* often lobed or cut, but simple* leaves and a milky juice. In some, especially the herbs, there is an immense starchy root, poisonous in the most important species until treated, but yielding a farina used as a staple food by all Brazilian natives who call it manioc or mandioca. Elsewhere, and the plant is now grown all over the tropical world, it is called cassava and is the chief

---

* Special articles on the subjects indicated by an asterisk (*) will be found at the words so marked.

MANILA HEMP 477 MANITOBA

source of tapioca. Other species, all trees, produce an inferior sort of rubber. Flowers greenish-yellow, the male and female in different clusters on the same plant, both without petals. (For details see EUPHORBIACEAE.) Fruit a capsule.* (*Manihot* is a native Brazilian name for these plants.)

The only species of any importance in the U.S. is *M. esculenta*, the common cassava, which is grown in Fla. more for stock food than anything else. It is occasionally grown in northern greenhouses, where it needs a warm but dry house. All the species are easily propagated by cuttings over bottom-heat.

**carthaginensis.** Yuquilla. A medium-sized tree, the leaves 5–7-lobed, the lobes again parted or divided. Flowers in small clusters (racemes*), the calyx* about ½ in. long. A desert tree ranging from southern Tex. to S.A.; little known in cult.

**dulcis.** Sweet cassava. A shrubby herb 3–12 ft. high, perhaps not distinct from the next, but its root smaller and not initially poisonous. Brazil. There are several varieties cult. in the tropics, but the plant is little known here.

**esculenta.** Cassava or tapioca-plant; in Brazil called manioc or mandioca. A woody herb or a shrub, 3–9 ft. high, the leaves 3–7-parted, the lobes narrow, tapering, 4–8 in. long. Flowering cluster a panicle,* the calyx less than ¼ in. long. Brazil. The poisonous roots, which may weigh 20 pounds, are rendered wholesome by a process of maceration, pressure to squeeze out some of the juice, and finally heat to drive off the rest. The plant is also known as *M. utilissima*.

**utilissima** = *Manihot esculenta*.

**MANILA HEMP** = *Musa textilis*.

**MANILA TAMARIND** = *Pithecolobium dulce*.

**MANIOC** = *Manihot esculenta*.

**MANITOBA.** The province lies wholly in zone* 1.

SOILS. A wide range of soil types, from light sand to heavy gumbo clay, including acid peat, is to be found. In general, the northern and eastern portion is of granite formation, tending to somewhat acid reaction, whereas the southwestern or prairie section is considered as of limestone formation and is usually neutral or slightly alkaline. The Red River Valley is, to large extent, heavy clay.

### GARDENING CENTERS

VEGETABLE GARDENING on an extensive scale is found chiefly near the city of Winnipeg, and there notably on the silty clay soil near the Red and Assiniboine rivers. The produce of the market gardeners is known widely for its quality excellence. Cauliflower, tomatoes, sweet corn, cabbage, celery, cucumbers, beans, peas, muskmelons, and root crops are grown under auspicious conditions. The canning industry has specialized in peas and beans. There is a growing development in commercial vegetable gardening for local trade near other cities and large towns.

SMALL FRUITS. The culture of small fruits has recently spread over a considerable territory from the Brokenhead River on the east, and Dauphin on the north, to near the Saskatchewan boundary on the west. Raspberries and strawberries are mostly grown. Gooseberries are considered a reliable crop, but there is only moderate market demand for these and currants. It is considered highly desirable to have facilities to water artificially during periods of dry weather.

TREE FRUITS. Apples, plums, and sand cherry (*Prunus besseyi*) hybrids are grown in home gardens as far north as Swan River, but commercial plantations are chiefly in southern Manitoba, near the eastern slope of the Pembina Mountains, but to some extent also on the eastern slope of, or near the eastern side of, the Riding Mountains, and in the Turtle Mountains.

The apples grown are Russian varieties, hardy productions from the Central Experimental Farm, Ottawa, and from the Experiment Stations of Minnesota and South Dakota, and seedlings of these which have been developed around Morden.

Recommended plum varieties are limited nearly altogether to select natives, and to hybrids which carry some blood of native plums or sand cherries. *Prunus nigra* is found growing in the woodlands as far north as the Duck Mountains, and the sand cherry as far as Hudson Bay Junction.

Cherries are mostly of Russian Morello types and *Prunus tomentosa*. These are planted for home use.

Pears are in the early experimental stage.

Grapes of eastern early-maturing varieties are ripened successfully in southern areas, but require winter mulching of the vines. The native *Vitis vulpina* is fairly common in the Riding Mountains.

GREENHOUSE CROPS. Tomatoes and cucumbers are grown under glass in some bulk near Winnipeg. However, most Manitoba glass is reserved for growing cut flowers, pot plants, and bedding stock.

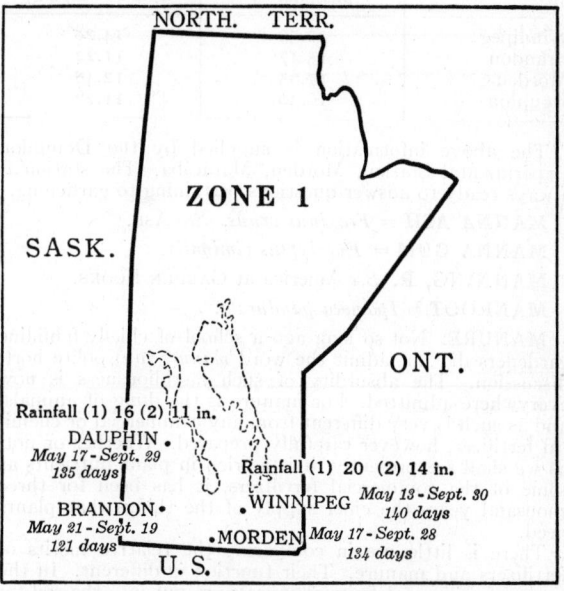

MANITOBA
The zones of hardiness crossing Manitoba are those shown on the colored map at ZONE, which should be consulted for details. The dates are the average latest killing frost in spring and the first one in the fall. The figures below the dates show the average length of the growing season. Rainfall figures (in inches) show (1) the total annual rainfall and (2) the amount falling in the growing season at the places indicated.

ORNAMENTAL TREES AND FLOWERS. The prairies are featured by considerable air movement, and a first consideration of the farm home is tree shelter. Materials mostly used are *Caragana*, green ash, white spruce, box-elder, willow, poplar, and Scotch pine. See WINDBREAKS.

Ornamental trees in popular favor include native mountain-ash, white birch, Colorado spruce, Swiss stone pine, Amur maple, hackberry, basswood, Russian olive, and Ohio buckeye. Shrubs most used are *Caragana*, lilacs, honeysuckle, spireas, dogwoods, hawthorns, viburnums, elder, sumac, tamarisk, dwarf willows, buffaloberry, *Cotoneaster*, golden currant, flowering plum, Russian almond, and bush roses. The better classes of roses require soil mulch for winter protection. Woody vines in common use are native grape, bittersweet, Virginia creeper, hardy clematis, and climbing honeysuckle.

An extensive list of herbaceous perennials are grown effectively. Those esteemed include peony, iris, delphinium, lilies, *Gypsophila*, *Dianthus*, asters, monkshood, spireas, hollyhock, hardy phlox, sedums, campanulas, daisies, and tulips.

A number of nursery firms catering to the prairie trade are located at different centers.

CLIMATE. Manitoba horticulture is limited by comparatively low winter temperatures and uncertain summer precipitation. These disadvantages are lessened by establishing a shelter belt with snowtrap and a local system of irrigation.

---

* Special articles on the subjects indicated by an asterisk (*) will be found at the words so marked.

### Frost Data

| Town | Average date of last frost of 29° F. or lower | Latest-known killing frost | Average date of earliest frost of 29° | Earliest-known killing frost |
|---|---|---|---|---|
| Winnipeg | May 13 | May 27 | Sept. 30 | Sept. 13 |
| Brandon | May 21 | June 21 | Sept. 19 | Aug. 28 |
| Morden | May 17 | June 7 | Sept. 28 | Aug. 26 |
| Dauphin | May 17 | May 23 | Sept. 29 | Sept. 12 |

### Rainfall

| Town | Total annual precipitation | Total precipitation April 1 to Sept. 30 |
|---|---|---|
| Winnipeg | 20.59 | 14.28 |
| Brandon | 15.47 | 11.22 |
| Morden | 17.65 | 12.48 |
| Dauphin | 16.30 | 11.22 |

The above information is supplied by the Dominion Experimental Station, Morden, Manitoba. The station is always ready to answer questions pertaining to gardening.

**MANNA ASH** = *Fraxinus ornus.* See Ash.

**MANNA GUM** = *Eucalyptus viminalis.*

**MANNING, R.** See America at Garden Books.

**MANROOT** = *Ipomoea pandurata.*

**MANURE.** Not so long ago a school of chiefly feminine gardeners did not admit the word *manure* into polite hort. discussion. The absurdity of such fastidiousness is now everywhere admitted. For manure is the dung of animals, and as such is very different from any commercial or chemical fertilizer, however carefully prepared. Whether or not, as we shall see presently, it is as rich in plant nutrients as some of the commercial fertilizers, it has been for three thousand years the chief supply of the things that plants need.

There is little use in comparing the relative merits of fertilizers and manure. Their function is different. In the case of fertilizers definite chemicals are put into the soil for a relatively quick and sure return so far as the immediate crop is concerned. That result is fairly certain, other things like good cultivation, the proper climate, and freedom from pests being assumed. But it must never be forgotten that commercial fertilizers add little permanent value to the soils, and it is exactly this thing which most manures accomplish. Long periods wherein the soil has been treated only with commercial fertilizers, while it may yield good crops, often result in leaving the soil fagged or tired. Such terms may not be in the scientific jargon of the soil scientists, but the fact remains that soil cannot be indefinitely treated as a laboratory to produce crops and only that percentage of nutrients added to it that chemical analyses show to be the chief needs of the crops. Because manure, or the dung of animals, adds much more than this to the soil, it always will, or should, have an important place in any permanent garden scheme.

Nowhere is the contrast between manure and fertilizers so well illustrated as in China and the U.S. We have used perhaps millions of tons of fertilizers, but our yields per acre are very nearly the lowest in the world. China, without commercial fertilizers or only a negligible amount of them, has been successfully farming for forty centuries. Why? The answer is that in China thousands of men carry out to their fields the night soil (human excrement) which has accumulated during the day in a densely populated country. Their yields per acre, due to this and intensive, largely hand, cultivation, are extraordinarily high. Such material is forbidden in most urban centers of the U.S., but we annually waste millions of dollars by such a restriction. In the country, if it is properly buried, there is still a chance to use it, to the lasting value of the land and the crops. It is utilized, under restriction, in the region near Philadelphia and Baltimore.

Night soil being a banned commodity for most of us, the other sources, really no less offensive, are the animal excrement of horses, cows, sheep, chickens and other poultry, as well as guano (the excrement of Peruvian, oceanic birds), and such supplies of nitrogenous matter as come from the commercial utilization of sewage and urine. A comparison of the value of these is necessary for any gardener, whether he keeps chickens, cows, horses, or not. The chief chemical value of all of them is the amount of available nitrogen they contain. But apart from the immediate benefit to the crop is the value of manure to the soil itself.

Manure is much more than a chemical analysis of it shows. The processes of digestion, combustion, and final evacuation of the food of the manure-producing animals leave much undigested vegetable matter in the excrement. In the case of bedded animals, like cows and horses, the bedding (usually straw or sphagnum moss or sawdust) is naturally mixed with the excrement, so that what we call manure is a compound of partly decomposed vegetable matter (the bedding) and the nutrients contained in the excrement itself. In fresh manure the strawy material predominates, but in well-rotted manure the straw is much reduced and, by weight or volume, the well-rotted manure is thus far more valuable and consequently much more expensive.

### Comparison of Common Manures

While manure is used as a definite crop stimulator, its greatest value is that it not only does this, but adds a large proportion of humus to the soil. The great item of its value in this regard is that while commercial fertilizers add not one scrap to the moisture-holding capacity of a soil, manure adds a great deal. *See* Humus.

Apart from this humus content, manures differ in their chemical constituents, and a comparison of the leading sources of manure should be known to all prospective purchasers of it. The U.S. Department of Agriculture has published the following figures:

### Average Composition of Fresh Manures per Ton

| Source | Nitrogen | Phosphoric acid | Potash | Value† |
|---|---|---|---|---|
|  | Pounds | Pounds | Pounds |  |
| Hen | 20 | 16 | 10 | $4.40 |
| Hen, air-dried | 40 | 30 | 19 | 8.45 |
| Sheep | 20 | 9 | 17 | 4.30 |
| Sheep, air-dried | 45 | 20 | 40 | 9.75 |
| Hog | 13 | 7 | 10 | 2.80 |
| Horse | 11 | 6 | 13 | 2.60 |
| Cow | 9 | 6 | 8 | 2.05 |
| Mixed | 10 | 5 | 10 | 2.25 |

† Values are figured on the cost of plant food in fertilizers with nitrogen at 15 cents per pound, phosphoric acid, 5 cents, and potash, 5 cents.

**Horse Manure.** The leading source of manure and the most valuable, as it is the quickest to decompose. If not used fresh, a practice which is not advisable in small, handworked gardens, because of the straw in fresh manure, it can be stacked in heaps, never more than 4 ft. deep, and allowed to decompose. It will take about 6-8 months of handling to produce well-rotted manure, during which time it should be turned two or three times and kept pretty wet to prevent spontaneous combustion. The wetting or rainfall should not be allowed to leach out the valuable constituents of this farmyard product. It is common sight, on poorly managed farms, to see coffee-colored water running away from badly constructed or inadequately covered manure piles. Such a procedure is simply wasting the most valuable, because most soluble, constituents of the manure. Lime in any form should never be added to the manure pile.

Horse manure, in intensively cultivated crops, can be spread 3 in. deep and plowed or harrowed into the soil. Commercial growers often use it at the rate of 50 tons per acre. If you purchase it, see that your bids are for cubic yards, not tons, as the latter method of purchase often means paying for water hosed into the pile the day before.

---

* Special articles on the subjects indicated by an asterisk (*) will be found at the words so marked.

Fresh horse manure generates more heat than any other kind, and is the only one useful to put in the pit of a hotbed.

COW MANURE. Slower acting than horse manure but usually less strawy, and it can often be applied directly to the soil without composting. It is especially valuable in making liquid manure (which see). Many growers prefer it for water lilies, and when it is dried and easier to handle than in the fresh state, it is widely used by experienced gardeners for greenhouse potting soil. See POTTING MIXTURE.

Rain and run-off take most of the value from manure piled like this.

HOG MANURE. Not widely available, but, as the table shows, it is a valuable source of plant food. Many commercial market gardeners find it profitable, but its foul odor makes it unsuited to most home gardens.

HEN AND POULTRY MANURE. Because of its ease of handling and its richness in plant food, chicken manure is one of the most valuable of all manures for the small garden. If you cannot purchase it and wish to use it from your own poultry (hens, ducks, or turkeys), see that the dropping boards are covered with a thin layer of acid phosphate to which a little dry soil or sand has been added. Clean the boards once a week and allow the mixture to dry a little before using. Hen manure is especially valuable because it contains not only nitrogen but large percentages of phosphoric acid and potash. Guano is about as valuable as chicken manure, but must always be purchased.

Properly piled manure, dished at the top to collect rain. Without a pit, this is the best method of storage.

SHEEP MANURE. This, when fresh, will produce nearly as much heat as horse manure. But few gardeners have access to it in this state and it is better to buy it, dry, from dealers. Its value is approximately that of hen manure, so that its use should be dictated by cost and availability.

### OTHER MANURES

Besides the more usual sources of manure, there are a few special plant foods, usually classed as manures, although they are not so, strictly speaking.

FISH. The Indians used fish for the cultivation of their corn. It is still used along the coast by fishermen who combine fishing and gardening. Used chiefly for its nitrogen and phosphoric acid, fish has only about half, or even less, of these substances than manure. Because of its odor and relatively low value as fertilizer, fish should only be used where it is very cheap. Its use is forbidden in some sections due to the odor when decomposing. The only way to avoid this is to follow the old Indian plan of burying the fish.

SEAWEED. Along the coasts there are many gardeners who use seaweed, wrack, and sometimes salt marsh ooze for fertilizer or manure. The only value of such material beyond, of course, its humus content, is in the potash it contains. Compared to stable manure it is low in nitrogen and especially in phosphoric acid. If you live near a source of supply, it should be remembered that seaweed is best collected in Jan.–March and plowed under as soon as possible. If stacked for long, it becomes simply a slimy mass with which nothing can be done. Eel-grass, however, can be stacked, as it is not a seaweed and has more fiber. It is, however, of less fertilizing value than seaweed.

The commercial harvesting of the giant kelp of the Pacific Coast is done for the potash extracted from it. Kelp, one of the largest seaweeds in the world, cannot be put on the land directly. *See also* COTTONSEED MEAL.

SYNTHETIC OR ARTIFICIAL MANURE. Since the World War there has been, with much reason, a tremendous amount of interest in a discovery made at the Rothamsted Experiment Station in England. It involves the use of straw, leaves, crop remains, grass cuttings, or other refuse vegetable matter. To this certain chemicals are added, under the conditions noted below, and the result is what is widely known as artificial or synthetic manure. The process was patented in England and here under the trade name of Adco.*

Since then many American Experiment Stations have published formulas for the production of synthetic manure, which compares very favorably with stable manure. The Agricultural Experiment Stations of N.Y., Pa., Iowa, and R.I. have all worked on this wholly new development in manure, well knowing that the passing of the horse and the increasing cost of stable manure make a serious situation for gardeners. The consensus of opinion on the production of artificial manure gives the following directions:

Make a pile of vegetable refuse (*see* above), not over 4–6 ft. high. Make the pile of 6 in. layers which should be tramped or packed down, thoroughly watered, and on which should be sprinkled the salts to be described presently. Keep on packing the 6 in. layers and following the plan until the pile is the desired height, making the top with a central depression to hold all rain-water. Do not fail to water each layer nor to put the salts on it, as the process is only effective when these details have been carefully attended to.

Water the pile with a hose frequently, and if it shows a tendency to heat up, the pile must be forked over. Fermentation, however, is what is desired, and if directions have been followed it should begin within a week. At ordinary summer temperatures (slower in cool weather) the refuse will in three or four months resemble well-rotted horse manure in texture and composition.

In calculating the amount of straw, etc., figure that 1 ton of dry straw will make about 3 tons of synthetic manure, fermentation and the large amount of water explaining the increase. For one ton of dry straw about 150 pounds of salts will be needed, divided as follows: about 70 pounds of ammonium sulphate, 60 pounds of ground limestone, and 20 pounds of superphosphate. Those who do not want to bother with this mixing can use Adco.*

When completed, the synthetic or artificial manure can be used like well-rotted stable manure.

### HOW TO USE MANURE

There is little danger of using too much manure so long as it is plowed under and the land left without planting for two or three weeks. Manure is so expensive that it is necessary to know how little to use rather than caution one not to use too much.

A generous allowance of well-rotted stable manure is 32 tons to the acre, but half this amount will often produce 80% of the crop that would have developed if the 32 tons had been used. In other words, doubling the manure does not necessarily double the crop, and in fact it very rarely does. Manure being costly, it is better to use it sparingly, and for most gardens 16–20 tons per acre is ample. (For small gardens calculate that a plot 33 × 66 ft. is exactly 1/20 of an acre.)

---

* Special articles on the subjects indicated by an asterisk (*) will be found at the words so marked.

For stable manure much the best plan is to spread it early in the season and plow it under a week or two before planting time. Fresh manure needs a longer period between plowing under and planting time, preferably two or three months.

The manures from hens, sheep, guano, etc., while higher in plant food than stable manure, contain far less humus. This fact and their cost limit their use to sprinkling them between the rows of vegetables and working them into the soil with a hoe or wheel cultivator. They are strong and should not touch the plants nor be sown in the drills unless thoroughly covered with soil.

For those who cannot get manure, there is a very good substitute provided by the use of fertilizers and by what is called green manuring. *See* FERTILIZERS, GREEN MANURING, HUMUS. *See also* LIQUID MANURE.

**MANURE FORK.** *See* Section 1, TOOLS AND IMPLEMENTS.

**MANZANITA.** *See* ARCTOSTAPHYLOS.

**MAPLE.** About 115 species of American and Old World, mostly deciduous trees, rarely shrubs, constituting the genus Acer (ā'sir) of the family Aceraceae. The leaves are opposite,* simple and lobed, or compound.* The flowers commonly unisexual,* small, in terminal clusters (panicles*) or flat-topped clusters (corymbs*). Fruit a two-winged key (samara*). (*Acer* is the ancient Latin name of the maple.)

Many of the maples are grown as shade trees, also for their ornamental foliage which often assumes brilliant hues in the fall, and for timber. They have a watery juice, in some species used to make syrup and sugar. For Culture see below.

**A. buergerianum.** A small tree, the young growth smooth. Leaves 3-lobed, 1–2 in. across, lobes triangular, margins toothed, dark green above, pale beneath. Flowers small, in a compound, soft-hairy, terminal cluster (panicle*). Fruit smooth, the wings parallel. Eastern China and Jap. May. Hardy from zone* 4 southward.

**A. campestre.** A round-headed tree 50 ft. or more high, the branches slightly corky. Leaves 3–5-lobed, 2–4 in. across, dull green above, soft-hairy beneath, turning yellow in autumn. Flowers greenish, in erect, flat-topped clusters (corymbs*). Fruit usually soft-hairy, the wings spreading horizontally. Eurasia. May. Hardy from zone* 2 southward.

**A. cappadocicum.** A tree 50 ft. high. Leaves 5–7-lobed, heart-shaped at base, 3½–5½ in. across. Flowers pale yellow, small, in smooth, flat-topped clusters (corymbs*). Fruit with wings spreading at a wide angle. Caucasus, Western As. to Himalayas. May–June. Hardy from zone* 4 southward.

**A. circinatum.** Vine maple. Small, round-headed tree 40 ft. high, more usually a wide-spreading shrub with handsome foliage, beginning to color red and orange in late summer and early autumn. Branches smooth, slender. Leaves 7–9-lobed, 4–5 in. across, with marginal teeth. Flowers small, smooth, in 6–20 flowered, flat-topped clusters (corymbs*). Petals white, the sepals purple and larger. Fruit with wings spreading almost horizontally. British Columbia to Calif. April–May. Hardy from zone* 3 southward.

**A. dasycarpum** = *Acer saccharinum.*

**A. ginnala.** A shrub or tree 20 ft. high. Branches smooth and slender. The leaves 3-lobed, 1½–4 in. long, the end lobe usually much longer than the side ones, with marginal teeth, dark green and shiny above, light green beneath. Flowers yellowish-white, fragrant, in compound, terminal clusters (panicles*). Fruit smooth with wings nearly parallel. Central and North China, Manchuria and Jap. May. Hardy from zone* 3 southward.

**A. japonicum.** Shrub or small tree. Leaves light green, turning crimson in autumn, smooth, 7–11-lobed, 3–5½ in. across, with marginal teeth or lobes. Flowers purple, in flat-topped clusters (corymbs*). Fruit with wings spreading almost horizontally. Jap. May. Hardy from zone* 4 southward.

**A. macrophyllum.** Oregon maple. A large, stately tree, growing 100 ft. high. Leaves deeply 3–5-lobed or cut, 1 ft. or more across, dark green, almost leathery, pale green beneath, turning brilliant yellow or orange in fall. Flowers yellow, fragrant, in narrow, hanging compound clusters (panicles*) 5 in. long. Fruit with wings of key spreading at right angle or nearly upright, the nutlet with stiff, yellow hairs. Alaska to Calif. Often planted as a shade tree where native. May. Hardy from zone* 4 southward.

**A. negundo.** Box-elder. A quick-growing tree 70 ft. high. Leaves compound,* the 3–5 leaflets arranged feather-fashion (pinnate*), bright green, 2–4 in. long. Flowers before the leaves, yellowish-green, the male in flat-topped clusters (corymbs*), the female in hanging, terminal clusters (racemes*). Fruit with wings set at an acute angle and usually incurved. The typical form from New England and Ontario to Minn., Neb., Kans., Tex., and Fla. Very hardy and frequently planted for shelter belts in the Northwest. March–April. Hardy from zone* 1 southward.

**A. palmatum.** Japanese maple. Small, graceful tree to 25 ft. or a shrub. Branchlets smooth and slender. Leaves 5–9-lobed or divided, 2–4 in. across, the lobes with marginal teeth and pointed, smooth, turning bright red in fall. Flowers purple, small, in small, flat-topped clusters (corymbs*). Fruit with wings spreading at an obtuse angle and incurved, the nutlet smooth. Korea and Jap. Introduced about 1820. There are many horticultural varieties, of which the leaves are of many forms and colors. *See* below. Hardy from zone* 3 southward.

**A. pennsylvanicum.** Moosewood; also known as striped maple. A small tree, sometimes 40 ft. high. Branchlets green, striped with white lines, conspicuous in winter. Leaves round to broadly oval, 3-lobed at point, 4–7 in. long, the lobes long-pointed, rusty, soft-hairy beneath when young, turning bright yellow in fall. Flowers yellow, in drooping, terminal clusters (racemes*), 7 in. long. Fruit with wings spreading at a wide angle. Quebec to Wis., south to northern Ga. May–June. Hardy from zone* 2 southward.

**A. platanoides.** Norway maple. A smooth tree, attaining 100 ft. in height. Leaves 5-lobed, 4–7 in. across, bright green, with marginal teeth, turning yellow in autumn. Flowers greenish-yellow, in erect, many-flowered, stalked, flat-topped clusters (corymbs*). Fruit drooping with horizontally spreading wings. There are many varieties. Eu. and Caucasus. Long cultivated, and blooming before the leaves unfold. April–May. Hardy from zone* 2 southward.

**A. pseudo-platanus.** Sycamore maple. A large, vigorously growing tree, sometimes 100 ft. high. Leaves 5-lobed, 3½–6½ in. across, dark green and smooth above, with a slight bloom* beneath. Flowers yellowish-green, in drooping, compound, terminal clusters (panicles*). Fruit with wings spreading at acute or at right angle. Eu. and western As. Cult. for centuries. There are many varieties. May. Hardy from zone* 2 southward.

**A. rubrum.** Red maple. A large tree attaining a height of 120 ft., valuable as an ornamental tree in parks or as shade tree on the street. Leaves 3–5-lobed, 2–4 in. long, shiny above, with bloom beneath, turning brilliant scarlet and yellow in autumn. Conspicuous red flowers before the leaves. Fruit bright red when young, smooth on a slender stalk, wings of key spreading at a narrow angle. Newfoundland to Fla., west to Minn., Iowa, Okla. and Tex. March–April. Hardy from zone* 2 southward.

**A. saccharinum.** Silver maple. A large tree 120 ft. high. Leaves deeply 5-lobed, 3–6 in. across, lobes long-pointed, and with marginal teeth, bright green above and silvery-white beneath, turning yellow in fall. Flowers short-stalked without petals. Fruit soft-hairy when young, the wings widely spread and sickle-shaped. Quebec to Fla., west to Minn., Nebr., Kans., and Okla. There are several varieties, one of them (*var.* wieri), with deeply dissected, narrow leaf lobes, being the popular Wier's cut-leaved maple. Feb.–March. Hardy from zone* 2 southward.

**A. saccharum.** Sugar maple. A tall tree, often up to 120 ft., the bark furrowed or shaggy in age. Leaves 3–5-lobed, resembling the Norway maple, but without the milky juice, 4–6½ in. wide. Flowers greenish-yellow, appearing before the leaves unfold. Fruit with widely divergent keys. Eastern N.A., west to Tex. The leading source of maple sugar. April. Hardy from zone* 2 southward.

**A. tataricum.** A shrub or tree to 20 ft. high. Leaves broadly oval to almost oblong, with marginal teeth, 2–4 in. long, long-pointed, bright green, turning yellow in autumn. Flowers greenish-white, in upright, compound, terminal clusters (panicles*). Fruit bright red, conspicuous in late summer, the wings of the key nearly parallel with the nutlet. Southeastern Eu. and western As. May. Hardy from zone* 2 southward.

## MAPLE CULTURE

Maples are among the most desirable of deciduous trees for garden ornamentation. *Acer saccharum*, so popular in the East as a street and shade tree and succeeding as it does in a variety of soils, appears to offer little hope of success in the humid coastal regions of the Pacific Coast. The silver maple, *Acer saccharinum* and its varieties, is undoubtedly tolerant of a wide range of soil and climatic conditions, but the unpromising behavior of the sugar maple in the Pacific Coast region has made nurserymen shy of the silver maple. It is practically certain that this desirable tree would succeed in the gardens of the Pacific Coast.

*Acer rubrum* and its varieties are hardly known in the Far West, but like the silver maples have suffered through the failure of the sugar maples. *Acer platanoides*, the Norway maple, is frequently planted as a street tree, but its low, round head, so valuable as a specimen lawn tree, makes it undesirable as a street tree, unless pruned. The Norway maple and its varieties are very hardy and succeed in any soil where crops can be grown.

The hardiest maples appear to be *Acer platanoides*, *Acer platanoides schwedleri*, *Acer ginnala*, *Acer negundo*, *Acer palmatum* and *Acer palmatum atropurpureum*. *Acer negundo* thrives in semi-arid regions, attains the stature of a forest tree, and is good for windbreaks, but in humid coastal regions it is to be heartily condemned, owing to the fact that the branches become very weak. *Acer macrophyllum* has suffered in reputation on the Pacific Coast by frequently being used as a street tree, where it is unsuitable. This is the best park tree native to the West Coast, but when planted as a street tree is far too vigorous and its roots inevitably lift the pavement.

*Acer circinatum* is a desirable low tree or shrub, but grown as a standard is valuable to produce avenue effects on small places. *Acer palmatum*, the Japanese maple, has given rise to many striking varieties of great garden value. The forms

---

* Special articles on the subjects indicated by an asterisk (*) will be found at the words so marked.

One of the numerous leaf forms of the Japanese maple

of *Acer palmatum* with red, purple or varigated foliage and any forms with divided or much-cut leaves provide for a wide range of garden uses. Perhaps the most striking use that can be made of Japanese maples is that of mound planting, in mixed groups, with a carpeting of crocuses, scillas or chiondoxas. Another very effective use is in beds carpeted with violas, to contrast with the foliage. When used this way it is desirable to keep them dwarfed by heading-in. A further use is as pot plants for conservatory decoration; any variety may be used and can be forced as desired. See FORCING.— T. R. A.

INSECT PESTS. Such leaf feeders as cankerworms, tussock moths, tent caterpillars, bagworms, and green-striped maple worms succumb to arsenicals. Mites causing leaf galls are checked with early spring dormant sprays of lime-sulphur. Plant lice are controlled with nicotine sprays. The large, white, cottony maple scale and other scales can be controlled on red maple by miscible oil sprays applied early in the spring; summer sprays of nicotine are better on sugar maple, which is injured by oil. In the East larvae of the leopard moth start boring in small limbs and work into large ones; destroying the small limbs at first sign of injury will check them. Several other borers occur; sometimes they can be cut out.

DISEASES. The most fatal disease of maple is the wilt, caused by a fungus parasitic in the sapwood. Norway maples are particularly susceptible. Whole trees or parts of trees suddenly wilt, the leaves remaining on the tree, and the affected parts die. When the wood is examined, bright green streaks are found in the sapwood. These and the wilt constitute an absolute diagnosis. Affected trees must be destroyed by burning.

Anthracnose is a leaf disease caused by a fungus invasion. It is more severe in wet weather, when the irregular dead spots may appear almost over night. Spraying with bordeaux mixture, beginning as soon as the lesions appear, will check its development. Leaf scorch superficially resembles anthracnose, but the lesions are more regular. The dead areas usually extend from the margin inward, and are rather uniform on all the leaves on a given branch. Drouth, poor soil and exposure to hot winds bring about scorch. In order to effect control, adverse conditions should be relieved by watering, mulching and protecting from winds.

**MAPLE FAMILY** = Aceraceae. See MAPLE.

**MARANTA** (ma-ran'ta). Tropical American foliage plants of the family Marantaceae, grown mostly for ornament in the greenhouse, but one cult. in warm countries for its starchy root, the source of arrowroot. Leaves mostly basal, sometimes a few on the fleshy stem, wholly without marginal teeth, always with a more or less sheathing leafstalk. In some species the leaves are beautifully colored, in which case they are grown only for the foliage. Flowers (when produced) in racemes* or panicles,* more or less tubular, but usually enlarged or with a 1-sided swelling at the base, the upper part slightly unequal. Stamens,* or some of them, petal-like. (Named for B. Maranta, Venetian botanist.)

Many plants commonly called *Maranta* by the florists actually belong to the genus *Calathea* (which see), and some plants offered as *Calathea* belong here, especially the plant often offered as *Calathea bicolor*. Both *Maranta* and *Calathea* require the same greenhouse treatment as *Caladium* (which see), although the latter does not belong to the same family as either of the others. *Maranta* needs a rich soil and frequent applications of liquid manure.

arundinacea. Arrowroot. A slender, branched herb 2-6 ft. high, grown in tropical regions for its starchy root which yields arrowroot (sometimes called Bermuda arrowroot, but not native there). It is cult. for ornament in the greenhouse mostly in the *var.* **variegata** which has yellow- or white-marked leaves which are oval-oblong, 6-8 in. long, tapering at the tip but rounded at the base. Flowers white. Tropical America, but naturalized in Fla.

bicolor. Not over 1 ft. high, and the leading cult. plant grown for its handsome foliage. Leaves oblongish or elliptic, wavy-margined, purple beneath, but pale bluish-green above, but with a pale band along the midrib, and dark-blotched between this band and the margins. Brazil. Often, or usually, offered as *Calathea bicolor*.

leuconeura. Not over 1 ft. high, and a handsome foliage plant for the greenhouse. Leaves broadly elliptic, blunt or short-tapering, grayish- or bluish-green above, but with white bands along the veins above, purplish or grayish beneath. Brazil. The *var.* **kerchoveana** has the leaves red-spotted on the under side; and the *var.* **massangeana** has smaller leaves which are rich-purple beneath.

**MARANTACEAE** (ma-ran-tay'see-ee). The arrowroot family is almost wholly tropical, but one of its cult. genera, *Thalia*, extends into the swamps and marshes of the southeastern U.S. The family comprises about 30 genera and possibly 260 species of herbs, most of which have tuberous rootstocks, from one of which, *Maranta*, arrowroot is derived. The other cult. genus is *Calathea*, which, with *Maranta*, furnishes many handsome foliage plants of greenhouse culture.

Leaves without marginal teeth, mostly basal and two-ranked,* usually narrowed into a more or less sheathing leafstalk, often (in hort. varieties) variegated or with a metallic sheen. Flowers (rarely produced in cult. greenhouse plants) very irregular,* not showy, mostly in head-like clusters, the whole surrounded by sheathing bracts.* Fruit dry or a berry. This and several other related families were once included within the Scitamineae (which see).

Technical flower characters: Sepals 3. Petals 3, usually joined to form a tube or one forming a hooded structure. Ovary inferior,* 3-celled. Style and stigma 1 each.

**MARCH.** See GARDEN CALENDAR.

**MARCHANTIA** (mar-kan'ti-a). A curious group of flowerless plants without true leaves, commonly called liverworts, and of little garden interest except as they become naturalized in moist places, as under greenhouse benches or occasionally on wet rocks. The plant body, which hugs the soil, consists of a leaf-like thallus* 4-5 in. long and about 1 in. wide. From the thallus* arise small, stalk-like bodies which bear the sexual organs. **M. polymorpha** is the commonest of the many known species and is often seen in greenhouses. It is never cult., but appears as if spontaneously.

**MARECHAL NEIL.** See ROSA NOISETTIANA.

*MARGARITA*, -us, -um (mar-gar-ri'ta). Pearly in color or texture.

*MARGARITACEA*, -us, -um (mar-gar-i-tay'see-a). Pearly in color or texture.

*MARGARITIFERA*, -us, -um (mar-gar-i-tiff'e-ra). Bearing pearls, or as if bearing them.

*MARGINALIS*, -e (mar-jin-a'lis). Margined; usually with a different color or texture, as are some leaves.

*MARGINATA*, -us, -um (mar-jin-a'ta). Margined or striped.

**MARGUERITE** = *Chrysanthemum frutescens*.

**MARIA** = *Calophyllum antillanum*.

*MARIANA*, -us, -um (mar-i-a'na). Named for the Virgin Mary.

**MARIHUANA.** See CANNABIS.

**MARIGOLD.** The name marigold is commonly applied to several different kinds of plants. One is the pot marigold (see CALENDULA), which has scentless leaves; another is

---

* Special articles on the subjects indicated by an asterisk (*) will be found at the words so marked.

Tagetes (tay-gee′teez), the subject of this article. Still other plants in which marigold is part of their name should be looked for at *Bidens, Dimorphotheca, Mesembryanthemum,* and at marsh marigold.

*Tagetes,* which includes the African and French marigold, is neither French nor African, but comprises a group of tender annual herbs of the family Compositae, all native from N. Mex. to the Argentine. They have strong-scented foliage, the leaves mostly opposite* and usually finely dissected. Flower heads showy, solitary or clustered. Below each head is a series of involucral bracts,* united into a cup-like base. (*Tagetes* may be named for Tages, an Etruscan god, but this is not certain.)

For Culture see below.

**T. erecta.** African marigold (long thought to be native there), better called Aztec or big marigold. An erect, rather bushy herb 18–24 in. high and branched. Leaves finely divided, the segments narrow and toothed. Flower heads 2–4 in. wide, yellow or orange, the rays with a long claw* or even quilled in some forms. The stalk of the head is swollen just below the cluster. Mex.

**T. lucida.** A sweet-scented marigold from Mex., really a perennial, but grown as a tender annual. It has undivided, nearly stalkless leaves and usually grows only about 1 ft. high. Flower heads scarcely ½ in. wide, in dense clusters, the rays only 2–3 to each head, orange-yellow.

**T. patula.** French marigold. A much-branched annual, rarely over 1 ft. high, the leaves divided, the segments narrow and toothed. Flower heads about 1½ in. wide, the numerous rays yellow but with red markings. Mex. There are many hort. forms, ranging from pure yellow to nearly pure red, and some are double-flowered. There is also a dwarf variety useful for edging.

**T. tenuifolia.** An annual, cult. chiefly in the *var.* pumila, which is a dwarf form scarcely 12 in. high, with very small heads of clear yellow flowers. Mex. The variety is an attractive window box plant.

### Marigold Culture

Marigolds of the type of *Tagetes lucida* and the African marigold are best suited to the open border, for they are erect, relatively branchy plants without the compact habit of the French marigold. The latter is a valuable bedding plant because of its compact, bushy habit. It also flowers very well from the middle of June until frost.

All marigolds are good for cutting, with the exception of *T. lucida,* which has less showy flowers than the other three, but this is offset by its pleasantly scented foliage, which the other three lack. Some people do not like either the French or African marigold as a cut flower because of the strong odor of the foliage. All leaves should be cut from the submerged part of flowering stalks.

These marigolds, for early bloom, are best treated as tender annuals (see ANNUALS), and they thrive better if the last shift from the bed where they were raised is into pots. Sometimes the seed is sown directly where wanted, especially that of the African marigold, but this delays bloom far behind those raised from seed indoors and subsequently planted outdoors. They all need summer heat, so should not be put outdoors until cool weather has passed.

*MARILANDICA, -us, -um* (mar-i-lan′di-ka). From Maryland.

**MARINE IVY** = *Cissus incisa.*

**MARIPOSA LILY** = *Calochortus.*

*MARITIMA, -us, -um* (ma-rit′i-ma). In the sea or on seashores.

**MARJORAM.** The word is applied to two wholly distinct plants. For the common or pot marjoram, sometimes called wild marjoram, see ORIGANUM VULGARE. For the other marjoram see SWEET MARJORAM.

**MARKET GARDENING.** See VEGETABLE GARDENING.

**MARL.** See LIME.

**MARLBERRY** = *Ardisia paniculata.*

**MARMALADE BOX.** See GENIPA AMERICANA.

**MARMALADE PLUM** = *Achras zapota.*

*MARMORATA, -us, -um* (mar-more-ray′ta). Mottled.

*MAROCCANA, -us, -um* (ma-rock-kay′na). From Morocco.

**MAROON GARDEN.** See RED GARDEN.

**MARRAM** = *Ammophila arenaria.*

**MARRUBIUM.** See HOREHOUND.

**MARSHALL, C.** See America at GARDEN BOOKS.

**MARSHALLIA** (mar-shall′i-a). A small genus of North American plants of the family Compositae, usually tufted,* about 1 ft. high, and the leaves without marginal teeth. Flowers in heads, without rays,* suggesting the scabious. **M. trinervia,** sometimes known as Barbara's buttons, has a stalk usually leafy halfway up. Flowers purplish, whitish, or pink. Treated as an ordinary outdoor perennial in the border. Va. and southward. (Named for Humphrey Marshall, author of the first American work on trees.)

**MARSH FERN** = *Dryopteris thelypteris.*

**MARSH FLOWER** = *Limnanthes douglasi.*

**MARSHMALLOW** = *Althaea officinalis.* See HOLLYHOCK. See also HIBISCUS MOSCHEUTOS.

**MARSH MARIGOLD.** Marsh, or swamp, perennial herbs constituting the genus **Caltha** (kal′tha) of the buttercup family, growing in the north temperate and arctic zones. There are about 20 species. The stem is hollow, the leaves roundish, heart- or kidney-shaped, without teeth. The flowers are 1 to 2 in. across, without petals, but having pink, white or yellow petal-like sepals.* The fruit is a collection of small, dried pods (follicles*). (*Caltha* is the old Latin for marigold and applied by Linnaeus to this genus.)

**C. leptosepala.** A perennial herb growing 1 ft. high. The leaves oval, 3–4 in. long. Flowers white, tinged blue on the outside, growing singly. In marshes from New Mexico to Alaska.

**C. palustris.** Cowslip, and the common marsh marigold of N.A.; also called king-cup, May-blob and gools. From 1–2 ft. high. Leaves 3–6 in. wide. Flowers bright yellow, several together. Growing in marshes or by brooks in eastern U.S. Easily transplanted to the wild garden, or it will grow in rich, moist soil in the border if given partial shade. Increased by division or by seeds.

**MARSH TREFOIL** = *Menyanthes trifoliata.*

**MARSILEA** (mar-sill′ee-a). Aquatic or marsh herbs, and the only cult. genus of the family **Marsileaceae** (mar-sill-ee-ā′see-ee), the pepperworts, which are flowerless plants classed with the fern allies (which see). They are of little hort. importance, but the two below are often found in aquaria, or, in the case of *M. quadrifolia,* in outdoor pools in the North. They have 4-parted or compound,* cloverlike, floating leaves, which arise from long runners. The spores are borne in small cases near the base of the leafstalk in the second species, but, in the first, on short stalks which bear nothing else. (Named for Giovanni Marsigli, Italian botanist.)

The pepperworts are of very easy culture in aquaria and pools. The first species is not hardy and can only be grown in greenhouse pools or aquaria or outdoors in the Far South. But *M. quadrifolia* is naturalized in several places in the U.S. and may completely choke the surface of a pool unless kept in check.

**drummondi.** Nardoo. An Australian aquatic suitable for aquaria or greenhouse pools, the four leaflets wavy-margined and more or less white-hairy.

**quadrifolia.** A Eurasian perennial, aquatic herb, naturalized in several places in the U.S. and often a local pest. Leaflets or the 4 clover-like segments not hairy and not notched.

**MARSILEACEAE.** See MARSILEA.

*MARTAGON* (mar′ta-gon). A specific name derived from the Italian martagone, a kind of turban, and applied to the lily *Lilium martagon.*

**MARTHA WASHINGTON.** See ASPARAGUS.

**MARTIN.** See BIRDS.

**MARTINEZIA** (mar-ti-nee′zi-a). A small genus of very spiny, tropical American, feather palms, of which only **M. caryotaefolia,** from Colombia, is likely to be cult., mostly in the warmest parts of southern Fla. It has a solitary, ringed trunk, 40–60 ft. high (less in cult.), but not usually more than 6 in. thick, and covered with long, needle-like,

---

* Special articles on the subjects indicated by an asterisk (*) will be found at the words so marked.

black spines. Leaves 4–6 ft. long, also spiny, the segments or leaflets 7–12 in. long, each segment broadest towards the tip and there more or less cut or jagged after the fashion of the fish-tail palms. Flowering cluster not over 18 in. long, its sheath (spathe*) very spiny, the male and female flowers separate, but in the same cluster. Fruit yellow, 1-seeded, about ¾ in. long, more or less egg-shaped. In Fla. it grows equally well in shade or open sunlight. (Named for Archbishop B. J. Martinez Compañon, of Peru, who collected plants there.)

**MARTYNIA** = *Proboscidea*.

**MARTYNIACEAE.** See PROBOSCIDEA.

**MARUM** (mar'rum). An old and unexplained name for *Teucrium marum*.

**MARUMI KUMQUAT** = *Fortunella japonica*.

**MARVEL-OF-PERU** = *Mirabilis jalapa*.

**MARYLAND.** The state lies mostly in zones* 4 and 5, but zone* 3 just crosses the northern edge of the state, and zone* 6 extends up to the region around Eastville, Va.

In a state like Maryland where the altitude of the crop land varies from a few feet above sea level to more than 2000 feet, topography becomes an important factor in determining the character of the soil, the facility and economy of cultivation, and in the range of climate.

The state forms a portion of the Atlantic slope and is divided into three important divisions: (1) The Coastal Plain, (2) The Piedmont Plateau, and (3) The Appalachian Region.

The Coastal Plain, comprising nearly half the area of the state, is divided into two sections by the Chesapeake Bay, the eastern portion being known commonly as the Eastern Shore, while the western part is spoken of as Southern Maryland. This region is characterized by broad, level stretches increasing in elevation as it joins the Piedmont Plateau on the west.

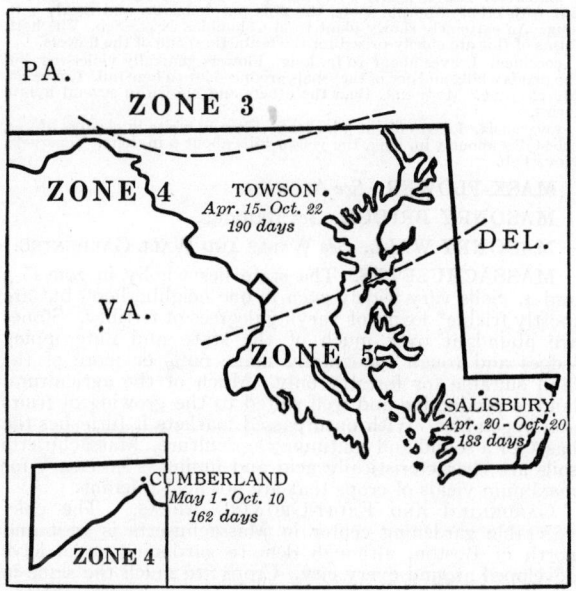

MARYLAND

The zones of hardiness crossing Maryland are those shown on the colored map at ZONE, which should be consulted for details. The dates are the average latest killing frost in spring and the first one in the fall. The figures below the dates show the length of the growing season. Rainfall is adequate.

The soils of the Coastal Plain are generally sandy in character, although several areas are fine-textured and often poorly drained. The soils of the area are lacking in organic matter which results in their being light in color. Phosphoric acid seems to be the element most needed in the soils of this region, although a complete fertilizer will generally give best returns.

The Piedmont Plateau, extending from the southwest to the northwest, occupies the North-Central portion and includes about one fourth of the area of the state. The region is undulating in topography, and the northern highland section has an average elevation of 800 to 900 feet.

The soils for the most part are fine-textured, consisting mainly of brown or yellowish-brown friable* loams. They are naturally well supplied with potash but respond to additional supplies of nitrogen and phosphoric acid. Because of the rolling character of the land, surface drainage is often excessive and erosion results where soil is improperly handled.

Western Maryland is a part of the Appalachian Region and includes the highest, roughest, and most densely forested, sections of the state. It is divided into the Blue Ridge District on the east, the Greater Appalachian Valley in the center, and the Allegany Plateau on the west.

The eastern section consists of typically limestone valleys with fine-textured loam soils and with many limestone outcrops. The soils are brown, dark brown, or reddish brown in color and phosphoric acid seems to be the element most needed. Much of the remaining portion of this area is unfit for agricultural crops because of its mountainous character.

In a general way the chief garden centers include the Eastern Shore and the North-Central portions of the state.

FRUITS. The apple and the strawberry are the two leading fruits grown and these represent more than three fourths of the total production of fruit in the state. Approximately half of the apple production is centered in Washington County, with other counties of the Piedmont Plateau contributing the bulk of the remainder. Wicomico, Worcester, and Talbot Counties of the Eastern Shore and Anne Arundel County in Southern Maryland are important producing centers.

The commercial production of strawberries is located largely on the Eastern Shore, Somerset, Wicomico, Worcester and Caroline Counties leading in the production of this fruit. Anne Arundel and Prince Georges Counties in Southern Maryland contribute about one tenth of the total production.

Washington County leads in the production of peaches. Most of the counties of the Piedmont Plateau and Worcester, Wicomico, Anne Arundel, Talbot, and Dorchester Counties in the Coastal Plain comprise important producing areas.

The production of cherries and plums is relatively unimportant and confined mainly to Washington County and the Piedmont Plateau. Kent County in the upper section of the Eastern Shore is the largest area producing pears.

Grapes are grown mostly in the North-Central region. Raspberries are also grown in this area, although the heaviest production occurs in the Hagerstown valley. Blackberries and dewberries are grown mostly in the central part of the Coastal Plain although considerable quantities are produced in Washington and Allegany Counties.

POTATO. The white potato is one of the most important crops grown in the state. The early crop which constitutes more than one half the total production is produced almost entirely on the Eastern Shore, with Worcester and Somerset Counties contributing the major share of the production. Irish Cobbler is the principal early variety grown. The late crop is more generally distributed with about 70 per cent of the farms reporting some production.

Sweet potatoes are produced mainly on the lighter soils of the Coastal Plains with Wicomico County furnishing two thirds of the total production.

VEGETABLES. Approximately 150,000 acres are devoted to the production of vegetables, this being 8.9 per cent of the total crop area. This does not include vegetables produced in home gardens to the value of over $2,000,000. A large variety of types are grown; yet the major portion is concerned with only a relatively few crops. In order of their relative importance the following eleven crops represent 94.4 per cent

---

* Special articles on the subjects indicated by an asterisk (*) will be found at the words so marked.

of the total value of all vegetables exclusive of white and sweet potatoes: tomatoes, sweet corn, beans (snap), cantaloupes, spinach, peas, cucumbers, cabbage, asparagus, beans (lima), and watermelons.

The census figures of 1929 give the value of the tomato crop for that year as $4,732,401. The tomato is grown quite generally over the Eastern Shore and in the northeastern section of the North-Central area.

The greatest production of sweet corn is in Harford, Baltimore, Carroll, Frederick, and Talbot Counties with scattered production in other areas.

Baltimore, Somerset, Anne Arundel, Carroll, and Wicomico Counties furnish three fourths of the total production of string beans, while the production of lima beans is concentrated mainly in Wicomico, Talbot, Somerset, and Dorchester Counties of the Eastern Shore.

The production of cantaloupes and muskmelons centers in Anne Arundel, Wicomico, and Dorchester Counties.

Baltimore County furnishes the major portion of the spinach crop although substantial quantities are grown in Prince Georges and Harford Counties.

Peas which are grown primarily for canning are produced mainly in Carroll, Caroline, Talbot, Baltimore, and Dorchester Counties. A new production center is developing in Garrett County. Alaska is the variety principally grown.

Wicomico County produces more than three fourths of the cucumbers grown in the state. Carolina, Anne Arundel, and Dorchester Counties are other producing centers.

Two thirds of the cabbage is produced in Baltimore County, with Prince Georges and Anne Arundel Counties furnishing a considerable proportion of the remainder.

Most of the asparagus is grown in the Eastern Shore Counties. Baltimore County is, however, an important producing area.

Wicomico County is the largest producer of watermelons, although a considerable acreage is planted also in Dorchester, Anne Arundel, and Caroline Counties.

ORNAMENTAL PLANTS. With the exception of the western mountainous section of the state, the climatic conditions are favorable to the development of a wide variety of ornamental trees, shrubs, and flowers.

Characteristic deciduous trees are the elm, red maple, tulip-tree, oaks, wild cherry, black gum, sweet gum, beech, dogwood, redbud, and sassafras. In the mountain section the sugar maple is common.

A characteristic slender, columnar form of the red cedar is common in the lower altitudes. Other common evergreens include the pines, hemlock and the American holly.

Many native shrubs and wild flowers are to be found in many sections although some forms are rapidly disappearing.

In the last decade there has been a notable extension in the number and acreage of nurseries, particularly those devoted to the production of plants for ornamental purposes. The rapid development of garden clubs also indicates a widespread interest in ornamental plants. A feature of the area in general is the overlapping of northern and southern types of plants. This contributes to the wide variety of forms to be met with in the state.

*Climate.* The climate of the state is equable with mild winters and warm summers usually tempered by cool spells originating in more northern latitudes. Spring and autumn are both delightful seasons.

FROST DATA

| Average date of last killing frost in spring | Latest known killing frost | Average date of earliest killing frost in fall | Earliest known killing frost |
| --- | --- | --- | --- |
| Cumberland, May 1 | May 17 | Oct. 10 | Sept. 6 |
| Towson, April 15 | May 12 | Oct. 22 | Oct. 7 |
| Salisbury, April 20 | May 12 | Oct. 20 | Oct. 8 |

The growing season or frost-free period for the eastern half of the state is remarkably long, averaging 180 days.

. The rainfall is generally well distributed and averages 40.93 inches. The amount falling during the growing season is about 28 inches, which is ample.

The address of the Agricultural Experiment Station, which has kindly supplied this information about the state, is College Park, Maryland. The station is always ready to answer gardening questions.

Garden Club activities in the state are extensive. They include clubs of the Garden Club of America, the home office of which is 598 Madison Avenue, New York, N.Y. There are also over 25 clubs belonging to The Federated Garden Clubs of Maryland. For the address of the nearest one to your locality write to Garden Editor, Houghton Mifflin Company, Boston, Mass.

**MARYLANDICA**, *-us, -um* (mare-ĭ-lan'di-ka). From Maryland.

**MARYLAND DITTANY** = *Cunila origanoides.*

**MARY WASHINGTON.** *See* ASPARAGUS.

**MAS.** A species name at *Juniperus* and *Cornus*, implying male, or male flowers.

**MASCARENE GRASS** = *Zoysia tenuifolia.*

**MASDEVALLIA** (mas-de-vall'ĭ-a). Tropical American, tree-perching orchids (epiphytes*), with grotesque and rather showy flowers, a few of the 150 species cult. in greenhouses, but not widely. They have no pseudobulbs,* the thick, sheathing leaves somewhat swollen at the base. Petals small. Calyx greatly enlarged and thus the most prominent part of the flower. Some of the calyx-lobes are often cut into long drooping tails. (Named for Joseph Masdevall, Spanish botanist.)

These orchids, which appear to have no common name, should be grown as epiphytes.* See the section on the culture of epiphytic orchids at ORCHID. The times given are the blooming period in the greenhouse.

**bella.** Leaves about 7 in. long. Flowers yellow, but brown-spotted, solitary, the stalk about 7 in. high, the tails nearly 4 in. long. Colombia. Jan.–May.

**chimaera.** Leaves nearly 1 ft. long. Flowers in clusters of 2–6, yellow, but with crimson-purple spots, the tails purple-brown and nearly 1 ft. long. An extremely showy plant from Colombia. Nov.–Feb. The hort. forms of this are chiefly prized for the fantastic shape of the flowers.

**coccinea.** Leaves about 10 in. long. Flowers generally violet-red, but the petals white, and one of the sepals produced into a long tail. Colombia. March–June. More cult. than the others and known in several hybrid forms.

**tovarensis.** Leaves about 5 in. long. Flowers white in clusters of 2–4, the stalks about 5 in. long, the yellow tails about 6 in. long. Venezuela. Nov.–Feb.

**MASK-FLOWER.** *See* ALONSOA.

**MASONRY BRIDGE.** *See* BRIDGES.

**MASONRY WALL.** *See* WALLS AND WALL GARDENING.

**MASSACHUSETTS.** The state lies wholly in zones* 3 and 4. Soils vary widely even in one neighborhood but are mostly friable* loams of varying degrees of fertility. Stones are abundant over most of the state and outcropping ledges and rough topography make 60% or more of the land suitable for forestry only. Much of the agricultural land is productive and well suited to the growing of fruits and vegetables. With unsurpassed markets it furnishes the basis for a sound and continuing agriculture. Massachusetts soils are characteristically acid and liming is necessary for maximum yields of crops that are not acid tolerant.

GARDENING AND FRUIT-GROWING AREAS. The chief vegetable gardening center in Massachusetts is west and north of Boston, although definite gardening areas have developed around every city. Crops are much the same in all districts and include asparagus, beans, beets, cabbage, carrots, cauliflower, celery, cucumbers, lettuce, onions, parsnips, peas, peppers, radishes, rhubarb, spinach, sprouting broccoli, tomatoes, squash, and sweet corn.

The greenhouse vegetable industry is nearly all within twenty-five or thirty miles of Boston. The chief greenhouse crops are tomatoes, cucumbers, lettuce, and rhubarb. Mansfield is the location of an intensive greenhouse development mostly devoted to cucumbers.

Aside from districts centering about the cities, there are

---

* Special articles on the subjects indicated by an asterisk (*) will be found at the words so marked.

# MASSACHUSETTS

more isolated sections on Cape Cod and in the Connecticut Valley which grow specialized vegetable crops, often on a large scale. The principal vegetable crops on Cape Cod are asparagus and rutabagas. In the Connecticut Valley where onions and tobacco are the main crops, asparagus, root crops and other vegetables are grown on an increasing acreage. Both Cape Cod and the Connecticut Valley are within easy trucking distance of Boston and other marketing centers.

Apples are grown for market in almost every part of the state. Good fruit soils and orchard sites are abundant over most of the state and the industry is growing steadily. The most intensive district lies in western Middlesex and eastern Worcester Counties, where deep, well-drained soils afford splendid conditions for tree growth.

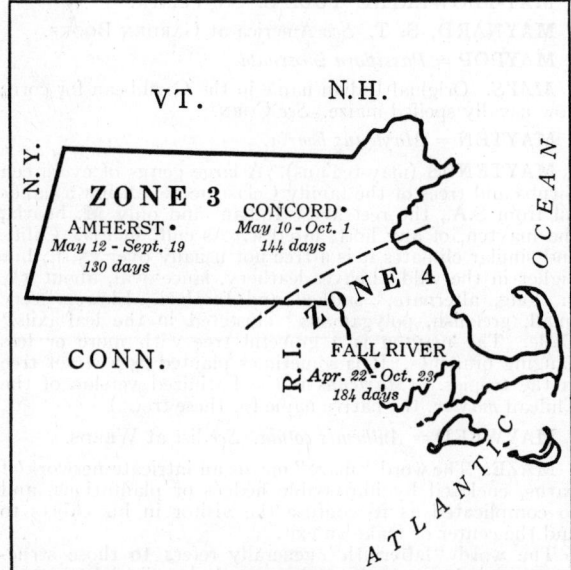

### MASSACHUSETTS

The zones of hardiness crossing Massachusetts are those shown on the colored map at ZONE, which should be consulted for details. The dates are the average latest killing frost in spring and the first one in the fall. The figures below the dates show the length of the growing season. Rainfall is adequate.

Massachusetts lies on the northern edge of the commercial peach belt and peach growing is confined to the more favored sites. Destructive spring frosts are much less common than in many districts further south but the intense cold of midwinter sometimes kills peach fruit buds, and protected sites with good air drainage are almost a necessity for profitable peach production. The industry is scattered and lies mostly in Hampden, southern Worcester, Middlesex, Plymouth, and Bristol Counties.

Pear orchards lie mostly in the eastern half of the state but pears are grown, at least for home use, in all parts of the state. Plums are grown widely for home use but not extensively for market.

Strawberries are grown for market more or less around every city. Aside from this there are important producing centers in the Falmouth district on Cape Cod, in Bristol County around Dighton, and a smaller district south of Boston in Abington and Marshfield. Grapes are grown everywhere for home use and there are small commercial vineyards near every city. There are, however, no centers of grape production.

Raspberries are profitable and are widely grown, especially in the eastern half of the state. The nearest approach to a center of production is the New Salem district in eastern Franklin County.

*Climate.* Winters are often severely cold but unbroken by thaws and therefore less trying to plant life than some milder climates. The summers usually afford good growing conditions for northern plants and prolonged drought is rare. The following data is from the records of the United States Weather Bureau:

| Town | Average date of last killing frost in spring | Latest known killing frost | Average date of earliest killing frost in fall | Earliest known killing frost |
|---|---|---|---|---|
| Amherst | May 12 | June 8 (1932) | Sept. 19 | Aug. 22 (1894–5) |
| Concord | May 10 | June 21 (1918) | Oct. 1 | Sept. 2 (1886) |
| Fall River | April 22 | May 12 (1907) | Oct. 23 | Sept. 17 (1889) |

The average total annual precipitation for Massachusetts is 42.72 inches. The average total precipitation for the crop growing season, April to September inclusive, is 21.10 inches.

The address of the Massachusetts Agricultural Experiment Station, which has supplied this information about the state, is Amherst. The station is always ready to answer gardening questions.

Garden Club activities include several clubs of the Garden Club of America, the home office of which is 598 Madison Avenue, New York, N.Y. There are also over 80 clubs affiliated with the Garden Club Federation of Massachusetts. For the address of your nearest one write the Garden Editor, Houghton Mifflin Company, Boston, Mass. See also HORTICULTURAL SOCIETIES.

**MASTACANTHUS** (mas-ta-kan'thus). An old, and now obsolete, name for *Caryopteris*.

**MASTERWORT** = *Heracleum lanatum*. See also ASTRANTIA.

**MASTICA.** A plastic material for use on greenhouse glass and hotbed sash, in place of putty. *See* Section 6, TOOLS AND IMPLEMENTS.

**MASTIC-TREE** = *Schinus molle*.

**MAT BEAN** = *Phaseolus aconitifolius*.

**MATHIOLA** (ma-thy'o-la). Stocks belong to a genus of the mustard family containing 50 species of Old World annuals, perennials, or subshrubs, only two species in common cultivation. Leaves alternate,* without marginal teeth, or wavy, or cut into segments. Flowers in terminal clusters (racemes*), lilac, purple, or white, with many variations. Petals 4, with a long claw.* Fruit, a pod. (Named for Peter Andrew Matthioli, 1500–1577, Italian writer on plants.) Sometimes spelled *Matthiola*.

Common garden and florist flowers, grown in ordinary garden soil. For culture, *see* STOCK.

*bicornis.* Evening stock. Low growing annual or biennial herb, much branched. Leaves 1½ to 3 in. long, narrow, with or without marginal teeth. Flowers small, scattered, purple, very fragrant, opening in the evening. Fruit, a two-horned pod. Eurasia.

*incana.* Stock, also called Brompton stock and gillyflower. They are biennial or perennial herbs, with many intermediate races, growing erect from 1 to 2 ft. Leaves felty, usually oblong, 2½ to 4 in. long. Flowers white, blue, purple or reddish, blush, or yellowish, fragrant, usually double, though some of the single forms are most desirable. Fruit, a pod without horns. Southern Eu. *Var.* **annua,** the ten-weeks stock, is less woody at the base. It is grown from seeds started in late winter or early spring in the house or greenhouse; usually handled as a half-hardy annual. It makes a fine house plant from seeds started in summer (*see* STOCK).

**MATILIJA POPPY** = *Romneya coulteri*.

**MATRICARIA** (ma-tri-cay'ri-a). An Old World genus of the Compositae, closely related to *Chrysanthemum*, with which it is often confused. It contains about 50 species of annuals, biennials and perennials. The leaves are finely cut, often strong-scented. Flowers in heads, the disk* flowers yellow, the rays* white, or lacking. They are known as wild camomile, false camomile or matricary. Some of them are used in the garden, others have been introduced as weeds. The cultural requirements are similar to the hardy species of *Chrysanthemum*. (*Matricaria* is derived from the Latin for mother, in allusion to its use in sickness.)

---

* Special articles on the subjects indicated by an asterisk (*) will be found at the words so marked.

**capensis** = *Chrysanthemum parthenium*.

**chamomilla.** German camomile; also called sweet false camomile. An annual growing from 1 to 2 ft. in height, smooth, branched. Leaves finely cut. Flower heads 1 in. across with 10 to 20 ray* flowers. Eu. and northern As. Sometimes an escape* in eastern U.S. Occasionally called simply camomile, but that name properly belongs to *Anthemis nobilis*. See HERB GARDENING.

**inodora.** Scentless camomile; also called corn mayweed. An annual growing about 2 ft. high, much-branched, the foliage scarcely scented. Leaves much cut. Flower heads 1½ in. across, with 20 to 30 white rays. Eurasia. *Var.* **plenissima** has large, double white heads. It is common in gardens, sometimes under the name of Bridal Rose.

**parthenoides** = *Chrysanthemum parthenium*.

**MATRICARY.** See MATRICARIA.

**MATRIMONY-VINE.** See LYCIUM.

*MATRONALIS, -e* (ma-tro-nay'lis). Matronly; sedate; as used for plants it often implies that they are hoary.

**MATS.** See Mats and Shutters at COLD FRAME.

**MATSA-JIMA.** A pine island. See JAPANESE GARDEN.

**MATTEUCCIA** = *Pteretis*.

**MATTHIOLA** = *Mathiola*.

**MATTOCK.** See Section 1, TOOLS AND IMPLEMENTS.

**MAUL OAK** = *Quercus chrysolepis*. See OAK.

**MAURANDIA** (mau-ran'di-a). Mexican perennial, more or less climbing, herbs of the family Scrophulariaceae, three of the 6 known species cult. for their showy, gloxinia-like flowers. They have mostly alternate,* rather angular and usually coarsely toothed leaves. Flowers in the leaf-axils,* the corolla showy, slightly irregular, somewhat swollen at the base, the throat bearded in lines. Stamens* 4. Fruit a many-seeded capsule.* (Named for a Professor Maurandy of Cartagena, Spain, a promoter of botany.)

These showy herbs can be grown as perennials in climates like Calif., or occasionally as biennials. But most of them will bloom from seed the first year if treated as tender annuals (see ANNUALS). They will also flower in the cool greenhouse during the winter. To get the best results from seed, sow in potting mixture* 3, cover the pot or pan with glass, and keep as near 60° as possible. Greenhouse specimens may also be increased by cuttings taken in January.

**barclaiana.** Leaves halberd-shaped, but without marginal teeth, about 1 in. long. Flowers velvety-purple outside, about 1½ in. long, the sticky sepals* long-tapering. A very showy plant from Mex.

**erubescens.** Foliage sticky-hairy, the leaves more or less triangular, toothed, 3-4 in. long. Flowers nearly 3 in. long, rose-red, the sepals* leafy. Mex. Often grown as *M. scandens*.

**lophospermum.** Closely related to the last, but the corolla tube is not hairy on the outside as in that species; also the sepals are sharper-pointed than in *M. erubescens*. Mex. Sometimes offered as *Lophospermum scandens*.

**scandens** = *Maurandia erubescens*.

*MAURITANICA, -us, -um* (mau-ri-tay'ni-ka). From Mauretania, an old name for Morocco and part of Algiers.

*MAURITIANA, -us, -um* (mau-ri-she-a'na). From the island of Mauritius.

**MAURITIUS HEMP.** See *Furcraea gigantea*.

**MAUVE CUSHION.** See MICHAELMAS DAISY.

**MAX.** A specific name for the soybean. See GLYCINE.

*MAXIMA, -us, -um* (macks'i-ma). Large or largest.

**MAY.** See GARDEN CALENDAR.

**MAYAPPLE.** Woodland, perennial herbs constituting the genus **Podophyllum** (po-do-fil'lum) of the family Berberidaceae, all but one of the 5 known species Asiatic, the other North American. They have a creeping rootstock from which springs a forked stem. Leaves of two sorts, one solitary, shield-shaped, and with the leafstalk attached to the center of the 3-7-lobed blade, the others in pairs. Flowers cup-shaped, nodding, white or pinkish, waxy, usually short-stalked in the fork of the stem. Petals and sepals colored alike. Fruit a berry. (*Podophyllum* is from the Greek for foot and leaf, in allusion to the stout leafstalks.)

These should be grown only in good rich woods soil in shady or partly shady parts of the wild garden. They can easily be propagated by division of the rootstocks, which in the native species are medicinal. See MEDICINAL PLANTS.

**P. emodi.** A little-known plant from the Himalayas, the leaves 3-5-lobed, bronzy in youth. Flowers white or pale pink. Fruit red.

**P. peltatum.** The common mayapple of eastern N.A., called also Indian apple, Mayflower, and mandrake (for the true mandrake see MANDRAGORA). Not over 18 in. high, the leaves nearly 12 in. wide, generally 5-7-lobed, and green. Flowers white, rather unpleasantly scented, nearly 2 in. wide. Fruit yellow, about 1 in. long, edible. May.

**MAY-BLOB** = *Caltha palustris*. See MARSH MARIGOLD.

**MAYFLOWER.** Many plants have been so called. Two of the best-known Mayflowers are hepatica and trailing arbutus (see both terms). For other Mayflowers in THE GARDEN DICTIONARY see MAIANTHEMUM CANADENSE, MAYAPPLE, and CLAYTONIA VIRGINICA. There is no one plant to which Mayflower should be restricted.

**MAY-FLOWERING TULIPS.** See TULIPA.

**MAYNARD, S. T.** See America at GARDEN BOOKS.

**MAYPOP** = *Passiflora incarnata*.

**MAYS.** Original Indian name in the Caribbean for corn; now usually spelled maize. See CORN.

**MAYTEN** = *Maytenus boaria*.

**MAYTENUS** (may-tee'nus). A large genus of evergreen shrubs and trees of the family Celastraceae, all but a handful from S.A., the rest West Indian, and only **M. boaria**, the mayten, of any hort. interest. As cult. in Fla., Calif., and similar climates it is a tree not usually over 25 ft., but higher in the wild. Leaves leathery, lance-oval, about 1¼ in. long, alternate,* stalked and toothed. Flowers very small, greenish, polygamous,* clustered in the leaf-axils.* Chile. The mayten is a graceful tree with more or less hanging branches. It is sometimes planted as a street tree in the tropics. (*Maytenus* is the Latinized version of the Chilean *mayten*, the native name for these trees.)

**MAYWEED** = *Anthemis cotula*. See list at WEEDS.

**MAZE.** The word "maze" means an intricate network of paths, enclosed by impassable hedges or plantations, and so complicated as to confuse the visitor in his efforts to find the center or make an exit.

The word "labyrinth" generally refers to those structures, entirely or partly underground, described by writers of antiquity.

Both words imply a mental and physical hazard.

Pliny mentions four famous labyrinths of antiquity:

1. The Egyptian — a large building containing many chambers, half of which were underground and probably used for sepulchral purposes.

2. The Cretan — famous for its connection with the legend of the Minotaur.

3. The Lemnian — similar to the Egyptian. Remains of it existed in Pliny's time.

4. The Italian — a series of chambers in the tomb at Clusium, below which was a series of confused passages.

There is considerable speculation as to how the typical labyrinth form first came into existence. Many labyrinthine designs are found in Roman pavements, dating from the fourth century A.D. and later, and the idea was adopted by the early Christian Church and used as an ornament in walls and pavements.

In gardening there were several kinds of mazes used in the Middle Ages and in early Renaissance times in Europe. One had a goal at or near the center, consisting of an open space in which was a seat, statue, or fountain. Another consisted of alleys only, so that when the farther end was reached the visitor had only to travel back again. Some of these older designs avoided closely parallel walks and, where space permitted, consisted of winding ways carried through thick plantations called "wildernesses." The famous old maze at Versailles (destroyed in 1775) was one of the latter. Any plant thick enough and high enough to be above eye level was used.

In England there were few hedge mazes, like the old one at Hampton Court, but many "turf mazes." These turf

---

* Special articles on the subjects indicated by an asterisk (*) will be found at the words so marked.

mazes are thought to have been cut by the monks as a penance and were connected with old churches.

As a garden favorite, the maze has had its day. The labor involved in its maintenance is probably a guarantee that it will never again return to general use. — R. L. F., Jr.

**MAZUS** (may'zus). A small group of low, prostrate, perennial herbs of the family Scrophulariaceae, two of the six known species grown in the rock garden or as ground covers. All are from Asia, Indo-Malaya, or Australasia. They have alternate* or opposite* leaves, or sometimes only basal ones, all stalked, toothed or cut. Flowers blue or white, sometimes yellow-eyed, in terminal, slightly 1-sided clusters (racemes*). Corolla irregular* and 2-lipped, the upper lip erect and 2-lobed, the larger, lower lip 3-lobed and with 2 ridges in the throat. Stamens* 4. Fruit a capsule. (*Mazus* is Greek for teat, in allusion to the ridges on the corolla.)

The plants are not difficult to grow and are easily increased by division. *M. pumilio* is not hardy north of zone* 5 and should be mulched even there over the winter. They are good plants for covering bare ground, neither species being erect. Both are evergreen in mild climates.

**japonicus.** A prostrate perennial, only the flowering branches erect and sometimes 6–9 in. high. Leaves ¾–2 in. long, coarsely but bluntly toothed. Flowers blue, about ⅝ in. long, the ridges on the lower lip brown-spotted, and bearded. Eastern As. Sometimes known as *M. rugosus*. May–June.

**pumilio.** A prostrate perennial, the underground stems creeping. Leaves nearly 3 in. long, coarsely toothed or sometimes without teeth. Flowers white or bluish, about ⅓ in. long, sometimes yellow-eyed. Australasia. June–July.

**MAZZARD CHERRY.** See PRUNUS AVIUM.

**McINTOSH.** An apple variety. See APPLE.

**McMAHON, B.** See America at GARDEN BOOKS.

*MEADIA* (meed'i-a). The specific name for a shooting star (*Dodecatheon*), named for Ricnard Mead, an English doctor.

**MEADOW-BEAUTY.** See RHEXIA.

**MEADOW-BEAUTY FAMILY** = Melastomaceae.

**MEADOW FESCUE** = *Festuca elatior*.

**MEADOW-FOAM** = *Limnanthes douglasi*.

**MEADOW FOXTAIL** = *Alopecurus pratensis*.

**MEADOW LILY** = *Lilium canadense*.

**MEADOW PINK** = *Dianthus deltoides* and *Habenaria fimbriata*.

**MEADOW RUE.** See THALICTRUM.

**MEADOW SAFFRON.** See COLCHICUM.

**MEADOW SALSIFY** = *Tragopogon pratensis*.

**MEADOWSWEET** = *Spiraea alba* and *S. latifolia*. See also FILIPENDULA.

**MEALY BELLWORT** = *Uvularia perfoliata*.

**MEALYBUG.** See True Bugs at INSECT PESTS. See also the Insect Pests at ORANGE, LEMON, BEGONIA, COLEUS, and many other greenhouse plants.

**MEASURES.** For sizes, volumes, capacity, etc., see WEIGHTS AND MEASURES. For the number of plants per acre, amount of seed, height of trees, longevity of seed, etc., see GARDEN TABLES.

**MEASURING WORM.** The larva of any moth, often very destructive to all sorts of garden plants. For a description of their life history and methods of control see INSECT PESTS.

**MECONOPSIS** (me-kō-nop'sis). A genus of about 30 species of annual or perennial herbs of the poppy family, single-stemmed or branched and with a yellow juice. Leaves alternate,* without marginal teeth, divided or cut, short-stalked or stalkless. Flowers borne singly, or in flat-topped or branching, terminal clusters, yellow, reddish or blue. Petals 4, sometimes 5 to 9. Fruit, a pod (capsule*), oblong or club-shaped. As., N.A., western Eu. (*Meconopsis* is derived from the Greek for *poppy-like*.)

A number of species of *Meconopsis* have recently become popular in the border and in the rock garden. They are mostly hardy and grow readily from seed sown in the open in the spring, or they may be started in the house or greenhouse and transplanted. In order to have the annual or biennial sorts blossom the second year the seedlings should be carried on in pots over summer and planted out in the autumn.

**baileyi** = *Meconopsis betonicifolia baileyi*.

**betonicifolia.** A perennial herb growing as high as 6 ft. Leaves 6 in. long, somewhat oval or oblong, with large marginal teeth, or nearly divided to the center, covered with bloom on the under side. Flowers blue-violet or purple, 2 in. across, in broad, flat-topped clusters (cymes*). China. The *var*. **baileyi** differs only in the ovary* being covered with yellowish bristles instead of being smooth, as in the typical form.

**cambrica.** Welsh poppy. A pale green, slightly hairy, perennial herb growing 2 ft. high, and forming large tufts. Leaves 4–6 in. long, cut feather-fashion (pinnate*), the parts of the leaf with sharp marginal teeth, and having a bloom beneath. Flowers pale yellow, 2 in. across, borne singly, high above the finely cut foliage. Rocky woods and shady places in western Eu.

**heterophylla.** Wind poppy. A smooth, slender, annual herb, 1 to 2 ft. high. Leaves 4–6 in. long, cut irregularly feather-fashion. Flowers brick-red, with purple center, 2 in. across, satiny in texture, borne singly on slender stalks. An attractive plant from western N.A.

**pratti.** An annual herb growing 3 ft. high. Leaves 3½–5½ in. long and 1 in. wide. Flowers blue, sometimes tinged with purple, in long terminal clusters (racemes*). China.

**wallichi.** Satin poppy. A perennial from 3 to 6 ft. high, making a mound of attractive foliage, covered with a bloom. Leaves cut feather-fashion (pinnate*), covered with rusty hairs. Flowers pale blue, satiny, crinkled, with rounded petals. Central As.

**MEDEOLA** (me-dee'o-la). A perennial, woodland herb of the lily family, growing in eastern N.A. There is but one species, **M. virginiana**, known as Indian cucumber-root, because of the taste of the edible root. It grows 2 ft. high. The leaves are 3–5 in. long and about 2 in. wide, growing in two widely separated whorls.* Flowers small, greenish, nodding, in an umbel,* surrounded by the upper circle of leaves. The fruit is a purple berry. It is found mostly in damp soil and suited mostly for the wild garden. (Named for the sorceress *Medea*, because of its supposed medicinal virtues.)

*MEDIA, -us, -um* (mee'di-a). Intermediate.

**MEDIACID.** A soil term for acid soils with a pH of 5.0. For the details see ACID AND ALKALI SOILS.

**MEDIC.** See MEDICAGO.

*MEDICA* (med'i-ka). From the ancient country of Media, now part of Persia.

**MEDICAGO** (med-i-kă'go). A genus of about 50 species of annual and perennial herbs, rarely shrubs, of the pea family. Leaves alternate, the leaflets arranged feather-fashion, in threes, and toothed. Flowers small, pea-like, yellow or violet, in terminal clusters, or in heads from the axils* of the leaves. The fruit is a spirally twisted, unsplitting pod, smooth or spiny, 1- to few-seeded. Commonly known as medic or hop-clover. Old World plants and naturalized in N.A. (Named from Media, the country from which alfalfa is supposed to have come.)

Some of the annual species are grown for ornament and are easily propagated from seed in any ordinary garden soil. Other species are important forage and bee plants.

**arabica.** Spotted medic. A downy, spreading annual. The flowers 3 to 5, yellow. The pods spiny. Eu. naturalized in N.A.

**hispida.** Bur clover. A nearly smooth annual, similar to *M. arabica*, but pods having a thin, sharp edge, and furrowed. Eurasia, and naturalized in N.A.

**lupulina.** Black medic; also known as nonesuch, and one of the plants that passes for shamrock. An annual, deep-rooted herb, much-branched, the branches 2½ to 3 ft. long. Flowers small, light yellow. The fruit, a nearly smooth pod, becoming black. Eu., widely naturalized. Often confused with clover, but the heads of flowers are smaller. It is of no garden value, but is sometimes used for forage.

**sativa.** Alfalfa; also known as lucerne, purple medic, Burgundy trefoil, or, in California, as Spanish trefoil. A smooth perennial, from 1 to 3 ft. high, and having a long taproot. The leaflets are small, and have distinct marginal teeth. Flowers purplish, in short terminal clusters (racemes*), from the axils* of the leaves. The pods are slightly downy and twisted. Eu., now widely grown for a forage plant, especially in western N.A. It is an important bee plant in Calif. If grown for the first time on a site

---
* Special articles on the subjects indicated by an asterisk (*) will be found at the words so marked.

it needs the right sort of bacteria inoculation. *See* LEGUME INOCULATION.

**MEDICINAL PLANTS.** The collection and cultivation of plants useful in healing is far older than the growing of ornamentals. Our earliest gardens and botanical writings were by men who studied the wild flora more from the medical than the strictly botanical viewpoint. That interest, well over three thousand years old, has never waned, but the U.S. has been singularly out of the picture so far as the cult. of medicinal plants is concerned.

Not one of the really important plant drugs is grown here. The climate is wholly unsuited to cinchona (quinine) or to the cocaine. And the culture, from the drug standpoint of the plants that produce opium, digitalis, belladonna, henbane, ephedrine, aconite, camphor, and several other standard drugs, has not so far been a commercial success, but *see* EPHEDRA. The causes of the failure are twofold.

Cheap labor abroad is available for the exacting cultural demands of these plants. All of them can be and most of them are grown in various parts of the U.S., chiefly as ornamentals or for interest. But some of them have been experimented upon by the U.S. Department of Agriculture, and by several large pharmaceutical firms. It was soon found that merely growing the plant is one thing and getting it to produce a yield of its active constituents is quite another. Still more difficult is doing this more economically than foreign growers who are long practiced in the art.

Unless, and until, we are prepared to duplicate the long, intelligent, and very successful experiments of the Dutch with their cinchona plantations in Java, there is little hope of this country's becoming a source of even a few of the world's major drugs. Much the nearest attempt at Dutch perfection has been made in Calif. upon belladonna. But even in this case the alkaloidal content of the plant (*Atropa belladonna*) is still far from what it should be.

There is no doubt that with our diversity of climate and soils, especially in a state like Calif., drug plants like the ones mentioned above (except camphor) can some day be grown upon a commercial basis. But much needs to be known about their cultural demands, especially soil and climatic requirements, before that end will be accomplished.

No one should think of undertaking the culture of such plants without a thorough study of them in the regions where they are known to be productive. All of them have long been in cult., and some varieties are far better than others, and a productive variety under one set of conditions may be worthless in another country, or even in the same one, with different handling. The most dramatic instance of this is that out of 10 pounds of the seed of a certain cinchona tree, the English lost all the seedlings derived from 9 pounds, and upon the remaining pound the Dutch built a world monopoly in quinine. Tests for other standard medicinal plants show only 5% germination, while others show only 12-20%, and a few as high as 80% germination.

What, then, can be grown in this country? A few things of value in medicine and pharmacy, mostly plants native in the temperate regions of N.A. It is upon these that any intelligent grower should concentrate. But even in this restricted field there are pitfalls. One must be certain that the plant selected cannot be collected cheaper from wild plants, because this is still an industry of very considerable proportions in this country and Canada. Before starting the culture of any drug plant, study the current prices in lists of wholesale dealers in them.

Among plants of medicinal value, those apparently most worth cultivating are the following:

†Arnica (*Arnica montana*)
†Cascara sagrada (*Rhamnus purshiana*)
Castor-oil plant (*Ricinus communis*)
Goldenseal (*Hydrastis canadensis*)
†Licorice (*Glycyrrhiza glabra*)
Mayapple (*Podophyllum peltatum*)
Senega snakeroot (*Polygala senega*)
Virginia snakeroot (*Aristolochia serpentaria*)
Wild ginger (*Asarum canadense*)

Those marked with a dagger (†) are suited only to the specialized, rather dry sections of Calif. and should not be attempted, for drug production, elsewhere. All of them can be grown as ornamentals in many other parts of the country. All are entered elsewhere in THE GARDEN DICTIONARY and further information about them should be sought for under their names.

The third plant in the list is a common summer-bedding foliage plant all over the country (*see* CASTOR-OIL PLANT), but the production of oil from its seeds is at present confined to tropical regions. It can, however, be grown for oil in southern Calif., Tex., and in southern Fla. But no one should start such an enterprise without careful study of varieties suited to these regions.

The rest of the plants in the list are native American woodland plants of which the goldenseal is by far the most valuable from the medicinal standpoint. All of them, except cascara sagrada, can be grown under the same conditions as ginseng. *See* GINSENG. The latter is not a real medicinal plant at all, the very large trade in it being based upon the ignorance and superstition of the Chinese, to whom practically all ginseng is sent. Most of them can also be grown in the shadier parts of the wild garden. *See* WILD GARDEN. This location obviates the need for lath shade as in most ginseng plantations. Cascara sagrada is a shrub the cult. of which, should not be undertaken far away from its native region. *See* RHAMNUS PURSHIANA.

Even in this rather meager list of medicinal plants worth growing, there are two things to remember: one is the danger of collected sources producing a cheaper product than you can grow; the other, and much more serious, thing is the fact that only a comparatively small amount of any of them, except goldenseal, is needed. In other words, wholesale production would depress the market for any of them. The growing of medicinal plants is thus a very interesting pastime, but can rarely be a serious hort. operation.

No mention is made here of scores of medicinal plants, mostly weedy herbs, for which there is always a steady market. They are grown or collected on a considerable scale, largely by Italians. But their average price ranges from 3-20 cents per pound (dried), and either growing or collecting them is scarcely a profitable undertaking to any busy gardener.

Many plants grown for their fragrant foliage or flowers, and usually classed as "herbs," also yield medicines; some, like mint, on a considerable scale. These are all treated at the article on HERBS AND HERB GARDENING, and the information about them need not be repeated here. Some of the old wives' remedies made from such plants were known as simples, but their use is often local and traditional rather than medicinal.

**MEDIEVAL GARDEN.** *See* GARDEN HISTORY.

**MEDINILLA** (med-in-nil'la). A genus of over 125 species of handsome, Old World, greenhouse shrubs and trees of the family Melastomaceae, two of which are occasionally grown for ornament. They have attractive, generally opposite* leaves with 3-9 main veins. Flower clusters very showy in the first species because of the highly colored bracts.* Flowers white or rose, in long, branching clusters (panicles*). Petals 5 (in ours). Stamens 8-10. Fruit a berry crowned by the lobes of the persistent calyx.* (Named for Jose de Medinilla, Governor of the Ladrones.)

Plant in potting mixture* 4, provide plenty of water and a warm greenhouse for these showy plants of the tropical forests of the East Indies, where both the cult. species are native. *M. magnifica* is a very striking plant when in bloom, but is not much grown. Both of them want a good light greenhouse, but protection from the direct rays of the sun.

**amabilis** = *Medinilla teysmanni*.

**magnifica.** An evergreen shrub or small tree (about 10-15 ft. as cult.), the stems 4-angled. Leaves ovalish or oblong, nearly 12 in. long. Flowers about 1 in. long, and with striking, pinkish bracts.* Philippines.

**teysmanni.** Stems 4-angled, the leaves ovalish or oblong, nearly 12 in. long. Flowers about 2 in. long, the cluster erect, about 1 ft. long, and without bracts.* Petals red. East Indies.

**MEDITERRANEA**, *-us*, *-um* (med-i-ter-ray'nee-a). From the region bordering the Mediterranean Sea.

---

\* Special articles on the subjects indicated by an asterisk (\*) will be found at the words so marked.

***MEDIUM.*** A Pre-Linnaean* name for certain species of bellflower (*Campanula*). See also MEDIA.

**MEDLAR.** See MESPILUS.

**MEEHAN, T.** See America at GARDEN BOOKS.

***MEGACANTHA, -us, -um*** (meg-a-kan'tha). Large-spined.

**MEGASEA** = *Bergenia*.

***MEGASTIGMA, -us, -um*** (meg-a-stig'ma). With a large stigma.*

**MEIWA KUMQUAT** = *Fortunella crassifolia*.

**MELALEUCA** (mel-a-lew'ka). Bottle-brush. Tea-tree. A genus of Australian trees and shrubs of the myrtle family, comprising 100 species, closely allied to the genus *Callistemon*. Leaves mostly alternate,* simple. Flowers red, white or yellow in spikes or heads, the stamens* so much protruding that the flowers resemble a bottle-brush. Fruit a capsule. (*Melaleuca* is from the Greek for black and white, in allusion to the black trunk and white branches of one species.)

These shrubs and trees are freely planted in Calif. and in other warm regions, some as ornamental shrubs, others to fix muddy shores, and others for timber. They grow well in almost any type of soil. They are propagated by cuttings of ripened wood and by seeds. The capsules are gathered in summer and allowed to ripen on sheets of paper or in boxes. They can also be grown in the cool greenhouse in potting mixture* 4.

**armillaris.** Shrub or small tree, sometimes 30 ft. high. Leaves crowded, very narrow, 3/4 in. long, 1/16 in. or less wide, smooth, pointed and often curved at the tip. Flowers white, the spike-like cluster 2 in. long.
**decussata.** Large shrub or small tree up to 20 ft. high. Leaves opposite,* small and narrow, 1/2 in. long and 1/6-1/8 in. wide, sharp-pointed. Flowers lilac, the spikes 1 in. or less long.
**ericifolia.** A large shrub or small tree. Leaves narrow, 1/2 in. or less long. Flowers yellowish-white, in spikes 1 in. long. Sterile flowers in nearly round, terminal heads.
**hypericifolia.** Hillock-tree. Tall, smooth shrub. Leaves mostly opposite,* oblong or narrower, 1 1/2 in. long and 1/4 in. wide, blunt or abruptly pointed. Flowers rich red, in dense spikes 2-3 in. long.
**leucadendron.** Cajuput tree; also known as punk-tree or paper bush. Large, conspicuous tree, with spongy bark, shredding in wide strips. Leaves 2-4 in. long, 1/2-3/4 in. wide, tapering at both ends. Flowers creamy-white, in terminal spikes 2-6 in. long.

***MELANOCARPA, -us, -um*** (mel-an-o-kar'pa). Black-fruited.

**MELANOSE.** See Diseases at ORANGE.

***MELANOXYLON*** (mel-an-ox'ee-lon). Having black or dark-colored wood.

**MELANTHACEAE.** See LILIACEAE.

***MELANTHERA, -us, -um*** (mel-an'ther-ra). With black anthers.

**MELANTHIUM** (mel-an'thi-um). Unimportant garden plants of the lily family, found in bogs from R.I. to Fla. and suited only to the bog garden. Less than half a dozen species are known, of which **M. virginicum**, the bunch-flower, is the only one likely to be cult. It is a stout plant with a thickish rootstock and mostly basal leaves in a dense, rosette-like cluster, the leaves narrow and about 12 in. long. Flowering stalk nearly 4 1/2 ft. high, crowned at the top with a large, branching cluster (panicle*). Flowers small, greenish-white, often unisexual* or polygamous.* Fruit a 3-valved, many-seeded capsule.* (*Melanthium* is from the Greek for black flower, perhaps in allusion to the dark-colored flowers of some species.)

**MELASTOMA** (me-las'to-ma). Asiatic or Pacific Island shrubs or trees of the family Melastomaceae, two of them occasionally grown in the greenhouse or outdoors in zone* 9 and protected parts of zone* 8. Leaves opposite,* without marginal teeth. Flowers solitary or in small, terminal clusters, the 5 petals rather large and usually of unequal size. Fruit a leathery or fleshy berry. (*Melastoma* is from the Greek for black and mouth, from the stain left in the mouth by the berries.)

The melastomas are not much grown, and sometimes the plants so offered belong to the genus *Miconia* (which see for culture).

**malabathrica.** Not over 8 ft. high. Leaves hairy, scarcely 2 1/2 in. long, and about half as wide. Flowers nearly 2 in. wide, mauve-purple. India.
**molkenboeri.** A shrub or small tree 10-15 ft. high. Leaves nearly 4 in. long, about 1 1/2 in. wide, hairy. Flowers about 2 in. wide, mauve. Java. The *var.* **alba** has white flowers.

**MELASTOMACEAE** (me-las-toe-may'see-ee). The meadow-beauty family comprises, among its cult. genera, chiefly tropical trees and shrubs, except the meadow-beauty (see RHEXIA), which is a native herb in the bogs and marshes of eastern U.S. There are over 170 genera and nearly 3000 species, some of great beauty as to flowers or leaves, often both. Practically all are tropical, the Amazon valley being especially rich in them.

Leaves opposite* (sometimes whorled*), the chief veins often running from the base to tip in strikingly arched curves, sometimes handsomely colored. Flowers often very showy and in magnificent clusters, sometimes also, with brightly colored bracts.* Fruit a berry, or dry, enclosed in the often persistent calyx.

The family furnishes some of our most beautiful greenhouse plants, but they are not much cult. except *Melastoma*, *Tibouchina*, *Medinilla*, *Miconia*, *Tococa* and *Phyllagathis*, all trees or shrubs. Tropical, herbaceous plants, chiefly grown for their strikingly handsome foliage include: *Bertolonia*, *Sonerila*, *Heterocentron*, *Schizocentron* (a vine-like plant with purple flowers) and *Centradenia*. All are occasionally grown outdoors in frost-free, warm regions with plenty of moisture.

Technical flower characters: Flowers regular.* Calyx united into a tube which is 4-5-lobed at the tip, and often joined to the mostly inferior* ovary. Petals 4-5. Stamens* 4-5 or 8-10, sometimes alternating as to length.

***MELEAGRIS, -e*** (mel-ee-ā'gris). Speckled like a guinea-hen.

**MELIA** (mee'li-a). A genus of Asian or Australian, deciduous or half-evergreen trees of the family Meliaceae. About a score have been described, but only one is in common cult. in this country, **M. azedarach**, the China-tree, also known as Chinaberry. It has alternate,* compound leaves, the leaflets arranged feather-fashion (pinnate*) and toothed. Flowers conspicuous, in compound, terminal clusters (panicles*), from the axils* of the leaves, white or purple. It is a mostly deciduous tree of spreading habit, sometimes growing 50 ft. high, with furrowed bark. Flowers purple or lilac, fragrant, in loose, compound, terminal clusters (panicles*). The fruit is nearly round, yellow, 3/4 in. across, hanging after the leaves fall. Himalayas. Cult. since the 16th century and naturalized in all warm-temperate and tropical regions around the world. The *var.* **umbraculiformis**, the Texas umbrella tree, has drooping foliage, on erect, crowded branches which spread from the trunk like spokes, thus giving an umbrella-like effect. It originated before 1860. (*Melia* is an ancient Greek name given the genus by Linnaeus.)

**MELIACEAE** (mee-li-ā'see-ee). The mahogany family is of little garden interest, none at all if it were not for the widely cultivated China-tree (see MELIA). Of the other two cult. genera, *Swietenia* (the mahogany) is tropical and so are most of the species of *Cedrela*, except the hardy *C. sinensis*. The family has over 40 genera and 600 species, nearly all tropical shrubs and trees.

Leaves mostly alternate* and compound,* often very large, the leaflets arranged feather-fashion. Flowers not showy (except in *Melia*), usually in many-branched clusters. Fruit fleshy and colored in *Melia*, a somewhat leathery pod (capsule*) in the other cult. genera.

Technical flower characters: Calyx 4-5-cleft, the edges of the lobes overlapping. Petals 4-5, free, or united to the stamens. Stamens* 8-10, usually united into a tube. Ovary superior,* mostly 2-5-celled.

**MELIANTHACEAE** (mee-li-an-thay'see-ee). A family of African trees and shrubs with only 3 genera and about 20 species, having two cult. genera, *Greyia* and *Melianthus*,

---
* Special articles on the subjects indicated by an asterisk (*) will be found at the words so marked.

somewhat grown for ornament in warm regions or, rarely, in greenhouses.

Leaves alternate,* compound* in *Melianthus*, simple* in *Greyia*. Flowers very irregular* in *Melianthus*, but regular* in *Greyia*, borne in terminal clusters (racemes*) in both genera, or the clusters sometimes in the leaf-axils.* Fruit a dry pod (capsule*).

Technical flower characters: Flowers hermaphrodite*; by the twisting of flower stalks each flower is inverted. Sepals 4 or 5. Petals 4 or 5, one of them, in *Melianthus*, abortive and long-clawed.* Stamens* 4 in *Melianthus*, 10 in *Greyia*. Ovary superior.*

**MELIANTHUS** (mee-lee-an'thus). Honey-bush. Strong-scented, handsome, evergreen, South African shrubs of the family Melianthaceae, rather popular in southern Calif. for outdoor cult. but little grown elsewhere. Of the six known species only **M. major**, which is sometimes called the honey-flower, is of hort. interest. It grows 7–10 ft. high, and has alternate,* compound* leaves which are nearly 1 ft. long. Leaflets arranged feather-fashion, toothed, the stalks winged. Flowers about 1 in. long, reddish-brown (for details *see* MELIANTHACEAE), the showy cluster nearly 1 ft. long. Fruit a papery capsule.* (*Melianthus* is from the Greek for honey and flower, in allusion to the sweet flowers.)

**MELICOCCA** (mel-i-cock'a). Two tropical American species of trees of the family Sapindaceae, one of them, **M. bijuga**, the genip (also called mamoncillo or Spanish lime), cult. for its fruit in Fla., where it fruits best near Key West, although it is hardy as far north as Palm Beach. It is a tree up to 50 ft. high, the leaves alternate,* compound,* the leaflets only 2 pairs, more or less elliptic and 2–4 in. long, the stalks winged. Flowers fragrant, small, greenish-white, the male and female on different trees, or occasionally polygamous.* Fruit fleshy (a drupe*), about 1 in. in diameter, the flesh yellow, juicy, rather sweet, but well liked. Care must be taken to see that there are ample supplies of both male and female trees, in the absence of which there will be no fruit. Some plantations have failed because this has not been looked after. (*Melicocca* is from the Greek for honey and berry, in allusion to the taste of the fruit.)

**MELILOT.** *See* MELILOTUS.

**MELILOTUS** (mel-li-lō'tus). Melilot or sweet clover. Weedy herbs of the pea family, all from the Old World, and of no garden interest except as planted for forage, soil improvement, or as bee plants. They are annual, biennial, or perennial herbs with rather sweet-smelling foliage, and have compound* leaves with only 3, essentially stalkless, leaflets. Flowers very small, pea-like, in narrow, spire-like clusters (racemes*) which may be terminal or in the leaf-axils.* Fruit a small, egg-shaped pod, with only 1 or 2 seeds, not pea-like and scarcely splitting. (*Melilotus* is from the Greek for honey and lotus, in allusion to the fragrance of the foliage and its similarity to the genus *Lotus*.)

The sweet clovers are of very simple requirements and are more often roadside waifs than cult. plants. But any of them are useful as green manure, and the white melilot is much liked by bees. If grown for green manure, for the first time on a particular site, it is a good plan to provide a culture of the bacteria usually associated with their roots. *See* LEGUME INOCULATION.

**alba.** White melilot; also called Bokhara clover. A Eurasian biennial herb, widely naturalized in the U.S. It grows from 5–8 ft. high and is very bushy. Flowers white. Summer. The *var. annua*, the Hubam clover, is used for forage. It matures in a single season.

**caerulea** = *Trigonella caerulea*.

**indica.** A Eurasian perennial, not over 3 ft. high, found as an occasional weed over the eastern U.S. but grown as a cover crop on the Pacific Coast. Leaflets wedge-shaped, but slightly notched at the tip. Flowers yellow.

**officinalis.** Yellow melilot; also called King's clover. Resembling *M. indica*, but the leaflets larger, nearly oval, and not notched. Flowers yellow, larger than in *M. indica*.

**MELISSA** (me-lis'sa). Lemon-scented Eurasian herbs of the mint family, comprising only 3–4 species, of which only **M. officinalis**, the lemon or bee balm, is in cult. It is an erect perennial, with opposite,* broad, toothed leaves and a square stem. Leaves 1–3 in. long. Flowers irregular,* 2-lipped, not over ½ in. long, white, arranged in small, close clusters in the leaf-axils.* It is widely grown for its value in seasoning; for its culture *see* HERB GARDENING. A variegated-leaved form is sometimes grown for ornament in the border. Both bloom in late summer, and the common form is occasionally naturalized in eastern N.A. (*Melissa* is Greek for bee, perhaps in allusion to the shape of the flower or to the sweet odor of the plant.) It may become a pest from self-sown seed, which is very plentiful.

**MELLIFERA, -us, -um** (mel-lif'er-ra). Honey-bearing.

**MELO** (mee'lo). Old Latin for melon. *See* CUCUMIS.

**MELOCACTUS** (me-lo-kak'tus). A genus of tropical American, largely Caribbean cacti, grown for interest rather than ornament, outdoors only in the warmest parts of the U.S. and in greenhouses devoted to succulents. Of the 18 known species only the 3 below are of much hort. interest. The plant body is melon-shaped, globular, or cylindric, or sometimes like a flattened orange, with 9–20 prominent ribs, upon which are borne clustered spines. Flowers not large or showy, usually pinkish or red, mostly opening in the middle of the afternoon, and borne on a terminal, cushion-like or hairy structure, often colored and turban-like (hence the common name of Turk's-cap cactus for one of them). Fruit fleshy. (*Melocactus* is from the Latin for melon and *Cactus*, in allusion to the shape of the plants.)

For culture *see* CACTI.

**communis.** Turk's-head or Turk's-cap cactus. Plant body cylindric or roundish-cylindric, not over 12 in. high (less as cult.), the terminal, fezz-like, flower-bearing part tawny red. Ribs 10 or 11, the spines needle-like. Flowers about 1½ in. long, red. Jamaica.

**intortus.** Plant body nearly globular and nearly 3 ft. high, the terminal, flower-bearing part a densely woolly head, often 8–9 in. high. Ribs 14–20, the yellowish-brown spines about 3 in. long. Flowers about ¾ in. long, pinkish. W.I.

**macrocanthos.** Plant body depressed-globular (*i.e.* orange-shaped), but 8–11 in. high, the terminal, flower-bearing part 8–10 in. long. Spines of 2 sorts, the outer ones of each cluster needle-like and flattened, the central ones stouter and erect. Flower pinkish, about ¾ in. long. Curacao and neighboring islands.

**MELON.** The term as commonly used includes the fruits of two distinct genera of the family Cucurbitaceae — *Cucumis melo*, the cantaloupe or muskmelon, honey dew, casaba, and related varieties; and *Citrullus vulgaris*, the watermelon and citron (*see* WATERMELON).

Cucumis Melo. A warm-temperate annual, with trailing or climbing, soft, hairy vines. The fruit varies greatly in the many cult. forms or botanical varieties. Native to Persia or Cent. As. *Var. reticulatus*: Netted or nutmeg melons. Includes Amer. varieties of cantaloupes and muskmelons. Fruit with netted skin, shallow sutures* and ribs, and flesh varying from light green to reddish-orange, with a musky odor. *Var. cantalupensis*: Eu. cantaloupe. Fruits have hard rinds and are rough, warty, or scaly. Not grown in N.A. *Var. inodorus*: Winter melons.

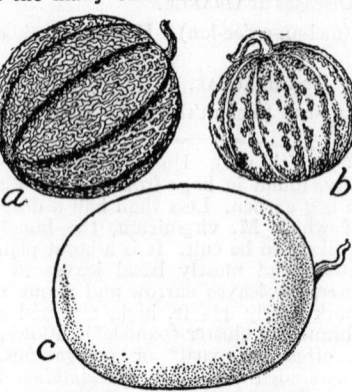

(a) Netted or nutmeg melon; (b) a European type of cantaloupe; (c) the winter melon, to which belong the casaba and honey dew melon.

Fruits lack musky odor, ripen late, and keep well. Skin smooth, ridged, or corrugated; flesh whitish, light green, or orange. Casabas, honey dews. *Var. flexuosus*: Snake melon. Long, slender, crooked, non-netted fruits. Inedible. A novelty in N.A. *Var. chito*: Mango melon, vegetable orange, vine peach. Fruits size and shape of orange; yellow or greenish; flesh white, not fragrant, cucumber-like.

---

* Special articles on the subjects indicated by an asterisk (*) will be found at the words so marked.

Used for making preserves and pickles. *Var.* **dudaim:** Pomegranate melon, Queen Anne's Pocket melon. Small, round, very fragrant, inedible. Used in U.S. only for ornamental purposes.

The development of the commercial cantaloupe industry in U.S. originated with the introduction of the Netted Gem variety from France in 1881. From this the varieties shipped from large growing sections of southwestern U.S. have been developed, particularly in the Rocky Ford district of Colo. Prior to 1895 muskmelons, lacking quality, uniformity, and ability to withstand shipping, were available locally for only a few weeks each summer: high quality melons are now available from May to October.

CULTURE. For successful culture cantaloupes require a long, warm growing season. In eastern and northern sections of U.S., to secure a sufficiently long season, plants must be started under protection and transplanted to the field when frost danger is past. In Imperial Valley of Calif. the earliest crop is secured by planting in Nov. and Dec. and protecting the individual plants with glassine paper covers or Hotkaps, until frost danger is past. Additional protection is given a small acreage by "brushing" or placing strips of heavy paper along the north side of each row. Hotkaps and brush are removed as early as the season allows.

Melons thrive on any well-drained, friable,* fertile soil: for early crops a light, sandy loam is preferred. Excessive alkali should be avoided. Manures or fertilizers are not generally used in the principal producing regions, the fertility being maintained by rotation and the use of green-manure crops. For market and home gardens the use of 3 to 5 tons of well-rotted manure or 200 to 300 pounds of complete fertilizer per acre, applied directly below each hill, is recommended. For small gardens figure that an area 33 × 66 ft. is exactly 1/20 of an acre.

A melon vine. Note the unforked tendrils,* which are forked in the watermelon.

Where irrigation is necessary, *i.e.* the semi-arid Southwest, melons are grown on raised beds, with a smooth slope preferably facing south; in regions of summer rainfall, on level ground. Seed is drilled in rows with a seeder or planted in hills by hand just above the water mark on the south slope of the bed. If planted on the level, the field is marked in checked rows, and seed planted in hills at intersections. Rows or beds should be 6 to 8 ft. apart, and hills 3 to 5 ft. in the row, with 2 or 3 plants per hill.

When transplanting is necessary, the plants are started in a hotbed or greenhouse. Plant bands or pots are used and the plants set in the field while quite small, without disturbing the root system, as melons and other plants of the cucumber family transplant with difficulty. When seed is planted directly to the field, the soil must be warm and frost danger past; the seed germinates best at about 80° F. and will rot in a cold, damp soil; 6 to 12 days are required for germination. If field conditions are not favorable for germination, the seed may be soaked overnight, germinated on moist cloth or paper, and put in the ground when the root is an inch long.

Edibility of cantaloupes and related melons depends on texture, flavor, and sweetness. During ripening the flesh softens, due to change of pectic substances to soluble form; sugars increase up to the "full slip" stage, then decrease. There is no reserve of starch; sugars decrease after removal from vine and will not increase if picked green. The expressed juice should contain at least 8% soluble solids; high-quality fruits contain 12 to 15%. In certain varieties the fruit stalk is naturally detached at maturity or "slips"; in others, not. Yellowing of the skin and softening of the blossom end of the fruit accompany maturity. Flavor depends on variety and growing conditions.

Melons for distant markets are shipped under refrigeration; they should be brought to the temperature of the car as soon after harvest as possible. Precooling by forced air circulation in the car for 8 to 24 hours is practiced to an increasing extent, especially with "full slip" or hard-ripe fruit. Melons in general do not keep well in cold storage; at 50° to 55° and 75% to 85% relative humidity, cantaloupes and muskmelons remain in good condition 1 to 3 weeks, honey dews 3 to 4 weeks, and casabas 4 to 8 weeks. Lower temperatures induce a disagreeable flavor and higher humidities cause decay. Melons deteriorate rapidly when removed from storage. Melons grown for local market are handled in open crates or barrels. They are sold soon after harvest and should be picked at the hard-ripe stage.

Principal varieties for shipping: Hale's Best (several strains), Perfecto, Heart of Gold, Emerald Gem (orange flesh); Pollock 10–25 (salmon-tint flesh); Honey Dew, Honey Ball (green flesh). The Persian, a large, coarse, orange-fleshed variety, and Golden Beauty casaba, white-fleshed, are shipped to some extent from California.

Principal varieties for local market and home garden (in addition to above): Tip Top, Bender's Surprise, Osage, and Persian, Armenian, Turkish, and Japanese melons (orange or salmon flesh); Hackensack and Montreal Market (green flesh); Golden Beauty, Winter Pineapple and Santa Claus casabas (white flesh). Varieties grown adjacent cross readily; saving of fruits for seed is not recommended unless fruit is of unusual merit. Contrary to popular belief the presence of squash or pumpkin vines has no effect whatever on the flavor of adjacent melons. — G. W. S. For Diseases *see* WATERMELON.

MELONS IN THE GREENHOUSE. Growing melons under glass should be attempted only by those who can devote a whole greenhouse to them, for the temperature demands are exacting. The night temperature must not be below 70° and the day temperature 80°–85°. Seed may be planted in potting mixture* 4, to which an extra amount of well-rotted manure should be added. If grown in the bench, the soil need not be over 6 in. deep, or the seed may be planted in boxes of the same depth. Some growers prefer to start the plants in pots and transfer them later to the permanent place. They should be started in small pots and gradually potted-on until they need a 5-in. pot, when they are ready for planting out in the greenhouse.

The vines must be trained to grow as near the glass as possible and, of course, all female flowers must be hand-pollinated, preferably on clear, bright days. As the fruit sets and increases in size, a net must be attached firmly to the roof of the house and the maturing fruit cradled in it; otherwise, the weight of the fruit will tear the vine from its support.

Growing melons so as to get fruit in winter is not easy,

* Special articles on the subjects indicated by an asterisk (*) will be found at the words so marked.

because the vines must be kept in active growth, which means plenty of water and frequent applications of liquid manure. Keeping up such a program during the dull or relatively dark days of winter is apt to provoke disease unless the houses are watched very carefully. Keeping the proper atmospheric moisture in the house demands wetting down the floors twice during the night as well as during the day.

The best varieties for forcing (nearly all English) are: 1. (Green-fleshed) Sutton's Ringleader, Perfection, Windsor Castle; 2. (Scarlet-fleshed) Sutton's A-1, Sutton's Scarlet; 3. (White-fleshed) Royal Favorite, Hero of Lockinge.

INSECT PESTS. The principal pests are the cucumber beetles and the melon aphid (see CUCUMBER). Because of the longer life of the melon vine, control of these pests is more important than on cucumber. The greenish pickle worm, a moth larva about ¾ in. long, bores in melons in the southern and sometimes in the eastern states. If a few summer squashes are planted in the field, many worms will congregate on the squash blossoms, which can be destroyed. Derris dust applied at 10-day intervals in summer shows promise as a means of control. The melon worm is similar to the pickle worm, but is found only in the South.

**MELON FAMILY** = *Cucurbitaceae*.

**MELONGENA** (mel-on-gee′na). Pre-Linnaean* name for the eggplant or some relatives of it. See SOLANUM.

**MELON PEAR** = *Solanum muricatum*.

**MELON SHRUB** = *Solanum muricatum*.

**MELON WORM.** See Insect Pests at MELON.

**MELOPEPO** (mee-lo-pee′po). A specific name derived from the old names for melon and pumpkin, signifying a melon-like pumpkin. See CUCURBITA.

**MELOTHRIA** (me-lō′thrĭ-a). Tropical or sub-tropical, herbaceous vines of the cucumber family, comprising over 70 species, of which the two below are the only ones of hort. interest and these are of secondary importance. They are annual or perennial vines with unbranched tendrils,* and alternate,* lobed leaves (in ours). Flowers small, greenish or whitish, the male and female separate on the same plant. Male flowers in clusters (racemes*), the female solitary. Corolla shortly bell-shaped. Fruit (for which they are chiefly grown) berry-like, pitted or rough. (*Melothria* is of unexplained application to these plants.)

The first species is a perennial and can be left outdoors only in the warmer parts of U.S. over the winter. Elsewhere the root should be dug out and stored in a cool, dark, and frost-free place for next spring's planting, or it can be grown as a window-garden plant if the top is cut back when dug in the fall. *Melothria scabra* is an annual and it will fruit, from April-sown seeds, before frost.

punctata. A perennial, herbaceous vine, the root thick. Leaves more or less ovalish or heart-shaped, obscurely 3-5-lobed or angled. Fruit brown, somewhat pitted, about ¼ in. in diameter. Tropical Africa.

scabra. An annual (or perhaps a perennial grown as an annual) vine. Leaves triangular or ovalish, but lobed, rough above. Fruit about 1 in. long, not pitted, but spotted with green. Mex.

**MEMORIAL ROSE** = *Rosa wichuraiana*.

**MENDEL.** Gregor Mendel (1822–1884) experimented with garden peas for eight years in an Augustinian cloister garden in Brünn, Czechoslovakia. In 1865 he presented his results and interpretations before the local scientific society, which in 1866 published them. They attracted no attention until 1900, when similar results, obtained independently by several scientists, brought them into prominence, and Mendel soon became known as the father of genetics, or the modern study of heredity, variation, environment and their interrelations.

Mendel thought of the character differences between true-breeding pea varieties as occurring in pairs — tall *vs.* dwarf varieties, colored *vs.* white-flowered varieties, round *vs.* wrinkled-seeded varieties. From experiments and studies on seven pairs of such characters, he arrived at certain conclusions, which have become known as Mendel's laws. These are three in number — dominance, segregation, and independent assortment.

Mendel found that when a true-breeding tall variety of pea was crossed with a true-breeding dwarf variety, the offspring ($F_1$)* were all tall. Because only the tall character appeared, he called it *dominant*.* Since the dwarf character was not expressed, though potentially inherited, he called it *recessive* (see DOMINANT). All characters, he thought, were either dominant or recessive, but we know now that, in many cases, both are partially expressed, resulting in characters intermediate between those of the parents. Whichever variety was used as pollen parent, the same results were obtained.

Pollinating any one of these $F_1$ tall plants with their own pollen (self-pollinated), the seed obtained produced approximately 3 tall plants to 1 dwarf. Self-pollinating these plants, Mendel found the dwarfs produced only dwarfs, whereas the talls were of two kinds — 1 tall out of 3, bred true, while the remaining 2 talls each had offspring approximately three fourths of which were tall, and one fourth dwarf. Mendel thought of these characters as being represented in the pollen grains and egg-cells. Diagrammatically, the above described three generations may be shown thus:

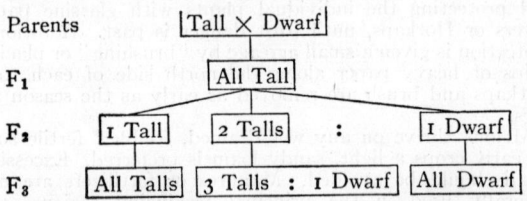

Combining tall and dwarf in an $F_1$ hybrid, only tall shows. Segregation takes place, and both the grand-parental types (tall and dwarf) reappear in a definite, predictable ratio.

The third contribution Mendel made to an understanding of heredity is "independent assortment," which simply means that any two of these pairs of characters previously described, when present in the same $F_1$ plant, are inherited as though they were associated purely by accident or chance. The result is that a tall, colored-flowered race crossed with a dwarf, white-flowered race would produce only tall, colored-flowered offspring, which when selfed* would give a predictable ratio — in this case — 9 tall colored : 3 tall white : 3 dwarf colored : 1 dwarf white — which is only another way of saying (3 talls + 1 dwarf) × (3 colored + 1 white).

Since 1900, experiments testing these laws have been performed on thousands of varieties of hundreds of species of plants involving many different kinds of characters, and although many new so-called laws have been discovered which add complications, Mendel's contributions have been abundantly confirmed. With these aids, plants can be more and more written in terms of formulas, as chemists do with their compounds. In plants such as maize, peas, tomatoes, sweet peas and others, on which research has been very extensive, one can quite definitely predict the result of many crosses, as chemists do when combining compounds.

To plant breeders, an understanding of Mendel's laws saves time, does away with much useless labor, makes desired results more certain and shows the limitations of what can be expected. Such knowledge provides a lighted road as against an unlighted pathway. — O. E. W. See also PLANT BREEDING.

**MENDEL TULIPS.** Rather early-flowering tulips, derived from crossing the Duc van Thols with the Darwins. See Garden Tulips at TULIPA.

**MENISPERMACEAE** (men-i-spur-may′see-ee). The moonseed family, mostly woody vines in 63 genera and over 200 species, is chiefly tropical, but the only two cult. genera, *Cocculus* and *Menispermum*, are hardy over considerable areas of the U.S. They do not have very showy flowers, but are considerably grown for the handsome foliage and bluish-black or red fruit which often hangs in profuse clusters.

Leaves alternate.* In some species of *Menispermum* the leafstalk arises from the middle of the blade or near it, instead of from the base. Male and female flowers on separate

---

* Special articles on the subjects indicated by an asterisk (*) will be found at the words so marked.

plants, usually in clusters or small bunches in the leaf-axils.* Fruit small, fleshy, the stone usually sculptured.

Technical flower characters: Sepals* 6, in two series; or 10. Petals 6, (in our genera) mostly smaller than the sepals. Stamens* 6 or more. Ovary superior.*

**MENISPERMUM** (men-i-spur′mum). Moonseed. A genus of North American and Asian, twining, woody vines of the family Menispermaceae, comprising 2 species. Leaves alternate,* shield-shaped, 3-7-lobed. Flowers small, white or yellow in terminal clusters (racemes*) or compound terminal clusters (panicles*). Sepals 4-10. Petals 6-9. Fruit a drupe.* (*Menispermum* is from the Greek for moon and seed.)

Moonseed vines have attractive foliage and are suitable for outdoor culture in the North. They are easily grown from seed or cuttings of ripened wood, or the East Asian species spread by suckers. Only the female plants produce fruit.

**canadense.** Canada moonseed; also called yellow perilla. Climbing to 12 ft. Leaves round-oval, 4-8 in. long, not toothed, occasionally lobed, soft-hairy beneath when young. Fruit black, resembling grapes. Quebec to Ga. and Ark. May-June. Hardy from zone* 3 southward.

**dauricum.** Twining to 12 ft. Leaves round-oval, 2½-5 in. long, usually toothed, lobed, pointed, smooth, with a bloom beneath. Flowers in slender-stalked, umbel*-like, compound terminal clusters (panicles*). Fruit black, about ⅜ in. across, in dense clusters. Eastern As. June. Hardy from zone* 3 southward.

**MENTHA.** See MINT.

**MENTHACEAE** = Labiatae.

**MENTZELIA** (ment-zee′li-a). A genus of the Loasaceae, containing about 50 species of American, annual or perennial herbs, shrubs or trees, usually with barbed but not stinging hairs. Leaves usually alternate,* without marginal teeth, cut into lobes or cleft almost to the center. Flowers white, yellow or red, often showy, borne singly, or in terminal clusters (racemes*), or in flat-topped clusters (cymes*). Petals usually 5. Stamens* numerous. Fruit a pod (capsule*), opening at the top. (Named for Christian Mentzel, a German botanist.)

A few species are easily cultivated in the flower garden from seeds sown where the plants are to grow.

**aurea** = *Mentzelia lindleyi*.

**decapetala.** Prairie lily; also known as gumbo lily. A biennial herb 1 ft. or more high, the leaves much cut. Flowers white or yellow, 3-5 in. across, the stamens protruding, opening toward night, and very fragrant. South Dakota to Texas.

**laevicaulis.** Blazing star. A stout, perennial herb growing from 2 to 3½ ft. Leaves long, narrow, 2 to 8 in. long, the edges wavy, with marginal teeth. Flowers light yellow, 2½ to 4 in. across, the petals pointed. Wyo. to Calif.

**lindleyi.** An annual, 1 to 4 ft. high, single-stalked, or branched and straggling. Leaves 2 to 3 in. long, coarsely toothed or cleft. Flowers 1½ to 2½ in. across, bright yellow, opening in the evening and closing the following morning, very fragrant. Calif. Sometimes offered as *Bartonia aurea*.

**MENYANTHACEAE.** See GENTIANACEAE.

**MENYANTHES** (men-yan′theez). A single species of bog or marsh perennial herbs of the gentian family, found in the cooler parts of the north temperate zone and not uncommon in many parts of N.A. The only species, **M. trifoliata**, the buckbean (also called bogbean and marsh trefoil), is a sprawling, rather fleshy herb with creeping rootstocks and long-stalked, compound* leaves with 3 oblongish leaflets without marginal teeth. The leafstalk is sometimes as long as 10 in. and sheathing at the base. Flowers in terminal, 10-20-flowered, long-stalked clusters (racemes*). Corolla shortly funnel-shaped, about ½ in. long, usually white (rarely purplish), bearded on the inside, blooming from May-July. Fruit a slowly splitting capsule,* nearly ¾ in. long. The plant can be grown only in the bog garden (which see). (*Menyanthes* is from the Greek, perhaps signifying month flower, but of uncertain application to the buckbean.)

**MENZIESIA** (men-zee′si-a). A genus of American and Asian, small, deciduous shrubs of the heath family comprising about 7 species. Leaves alternate,* without marginal teeth. Flowers in terminal clusters, bell- or urn-shaped. Stamens 5-10, not protruding. Fruit a leathery capsule.* (Named for Archibald Menzies, an English surgeon and naturalist.)

They are of no particular ornamental value, but are very hardy in the North and often planted in the rock garden. They are easily propagated by seeds, by layers, and by cuttings of mature wood under glass. The only cult. species is:

**pilosa.** Minnie-bush. A shrub sometimes growing 6 ft. high. Leaves twice as long as wide or longer, abruptly sharp-pointed, soft-hairy above and fringed with hairs. Flowers bell-shaped, ¼ in. long, yellowish-white or pinkish, few, drooping. Capsule somewhat oval, covered with glandular* bristles. Pa. to Ga. and Ala. on the mountains. May-June. Hardy from zone* 3 southward. For a plant listed as *M. polifolia* see DABOECIA CANTABRICA.

**MERATIA** (mer-ră′ti-a). A genus of Chinese deciduous or evergreen shrubs of the family Calycanthaceae, comprising only 2 species, one of which is cult. for ornament. Leaves opposite,* smooth, without marginal teeth. Flowers appearing before the leaves, the sepals* numerous, overlapping, yellow. Petals none. Stamens* 5-6. (Named for François Victor Merat, French physician and botanist, 1780-1851.)

These shrubs are propagated by layering in the autumn or by seeds in the spring.

**praecox.** A shrub growing 9-10 ft. high. Leaves 4-6 in. long, ovalish or longer, long-pointed. Flowers fragrant, about 1 in. across, the outer sepals yellow, the inner striped purplish-brown. China. Often listed as *Chimonanthus fragrans*. Not hardy above zone* 6, possibly in zone* 5 with protection, and in the South blooming nearly all the winter, and very fragrant.

**MERCURIALIS** (mer-cure-i-āl′is). Mediterranean herbs or under-shrubs of the spurge family, of little hort. significance, the only one of garden interest being **M. annua**, the herb mercury, an annual weedy plant once, and sometimes still, grown for its medicinal qualities. It is a sprawling herb, 1-2 ft. high, the leaves opposite,* ovalish or narrower and usually toothed. Male and female flowers on different plants and usually without petals and inconspicuous. Fruit a capsule.* The plant is a native of E. and northern Af., but is common as a naturalized weed in many parts of the U.S. (Named for Mercury.)

**MERCURIC CHLORIDE; MERCURIC OXIDE.** See Mercury at FUNGICIDES.

**MERCURY.** See Mercury at FUNGICIDES.

**MERTENSIA** (mer-ten′si-a). Bluebells. Lungwort. Showy, mostly shade-enduring, and in ours, perennial herbs of the family Boraginaceae. Of the 40 known species, all from the north temperate zone, many, and the two below, are native in N.A. They often have bluish-green foliage, the leaves alternate,* often dotted. Flowers usually drooping, in terminal, rather loose, somewhat 1-sided clusters (racemes* or cymes*). Corolla more or less funnel-shaped, blue or purplish (in ours), sometimes bearded in the throat. Stamens* 5. Fruit a collection of 4 nutlets. (Named for Franz Carl Mertens, German botanist.)

Besides the two below, a number of native lungworts are apt to be dug from the wild and planted in the wild garden, especially in the Rocky Mountain region, where there are several species. Both the ones below need partial shade and a moist site for best development, although *M. virginica* can be grown in the open border. As they can be divided only with great difficulty, it is best to raise new plants from seed, which should be sown as soon as harvested. Mertensias die down early in the season.

**ciliata.** A Rocky Mountain herb with pale or grayish-green foliage; not over 2 ft. high. Leaves ovalish or oblong. Flowers bright blue, about ½-¾ in. long. Spring.

**virginica.** Virginia cowslip; called also American lungwort. A smooth herb up to 2 ft. high, the foliage pale green. Leaves elliptic or oblongish, long-stalked, decurrent* at the base, 3-7 in. long. Flowers about 1 in. long, the tube purplish, but blue when the corolla expands. In rich, moist woods, N.Y. to Tenn. April-May. There is also a pink-flowered form.

**MESA OAK** = *Quercus engelmanni*. See OAK.

**MESCAL BEAN** = *Sophora secundiflora*.

**MESEMBRYANTHEMUM** (me-sem-bri-an′thee-mum). Fig-marigold. As originally, and here, understood, the fig-marigolds comprise a huge genus of fleshy-leaved, annual or perennial, mostly desert herbs (rarely shrubby) of the

---

* Special articles on the subjects indicated by an asterisk (*) will be found at the words so marked.

family Aizoaceae. All but a handful of nearly 1000 species are South African, and all the cult. species come from there, although some of them are naturalized escapes* in Calif. Systematic botanists, mostly South Africans, have divided this huge aggregation of plants into many other genera, some of which apply to the species below; notably *Aptenia, Carpanthea, Carpobrotus, Cryophytum, Dorotheanthus,* and *Lampranthus.* While such segregated genera may be essential for a systematic botanical understanding of these plants, they have long been grown by gardeners under the name *Mesembryanthemum,* which is here retained for the cult. species below.

While some non-hort. species have condensed, almost cactus-like and generally leafless plant bodies, closely simulating the desert stones among which they grow, the cult. sorts have usually fleshy leaves, mostly without marginal teeth (some spiny-margined). In a few species the leaves are covered with glittering dots, hence the name ice-plant for some of them. Flowers large and showy, often with a superficial resemblance to a daisy, from the great number of petals and stamens,* mostly white, red, or yellow. Calyx* with 5 rather leafy lobes. Fruit a many-seeded capsule,* but fleshy in one species. (The name is from the Greek for midday-flower, from the opening of the flowers in sunshine and their closing at night and during cloudy weather.)

In growing the plants below it must not be forgotten that all of them are inhabitants of hot, dry deserts and consequently heat is essential to proper development. The annuals can be grown as such (*see* ANNUALS), provided there is a long, warm, and not too moist growing season. The perennials cannot be grown outdoors north of zone* 7, and even south of this their need for heat and dryness is better provided for in southern Calif. than in Fla. In the former state the plants are popular, and dealers or fanciers have many other species than the ones here noted. To include all those known to be in cult. in the U.S. would be to devote more space to *Mesembryanthemum* than they are worth — at least to most American gardeners. Their greenhouse culture is the same as for any other succulent (which see). *See also* SAND GARDENS.

**aurantiacum.** A perennial, much resembling *M. aureum,* but the flowers about 1½ in. wide, orange, and the petals in about 3 series.

**aureum.** A perennial herb, woody at the base and not over 2 ft. high. Leaves fleshy, more or less bluish-green, 1-2 in. long, narrow and 3-angled. Flowers usually solitary, long-stalked, golden-yellow, about 2 in. wide, the petals in many series.

**blandum.** A shrubby perennial, with stiffish, erect branches, about 2 ft. high. Leaves in distant, opposite pairs, united at the base, 3-angled, but flattish, 1-2 in. long. Flowers in 3's (rarely solitary or in 2's), pale rose-color, the stalks about 2 in. long, the head nearly 3 in. wide.

**cordifolium.** A perennial 1-2 ft. high, branched, not very fleshy, minutely warty. Leaves more or less heart-shaped, flat, opposite,* usually stalked, scarcely 1 in. long. Flower purple, solitary, not over ½ in. wide, short-stalked. A good window-garden plant.

**criniflorum.** An interesting annual, somewhat resembling *M. lineare,* but with larger, daisy-like flowers, ranging from pink and apricot to buff, tan, and crimson.

**crystallinum.** Ice-plant; called also sea fig and sea marigold, especially in Calif. The most commonly grown of all the species and an annual (or grown as such). Foliage covered with glistening dots. The plant is prostrate, with alternate,* flat, fleshy leaves that are ovalish, but clasping at the base. Flowers nearly stalkless, white or pale pink, about ¾ in. wide. Much grown for its glistening foliage, both as a garden annual and as a pot plant. Naturalized along the Calif. coast, and much cult. there. Reported as a pot herb with edible leaves used like spinach.

**edule.** Hottentot fig. A prostrate or sprawling perennial, with a woody base, sometimes used to cover banks in Calif. Leaves 3-4 in. long, opposite* and joined at the base, 3-sided and fleshy. Flowers yellow, short-stalked, about 3 in. wide, very showy. Fruit fleshy and edible (in Africa). It is sometimes an escape* or even naturalized in Calif.

**gramineum** = *Mesembryanthemum lineare.*

**lineare.** An annual with little or no stem, the branches prostrate, and making a dense clump 6-8 in. wide, the whole plant warty. Leaves 2-3 in. long, opposite and joined at the base. Flowers very numerous, about 1¼ in. wide, solitary on stalks 1-4 in. long, pink with a red center, or white, pink, or red throughout. Should be grown as a flower garden annual. Sometimes sold as *M. gramineum* or *M. tricolor.*

**multiradiatum.** A somewhat woody perennial, 1-2 ft. high, the foliage bluish-green. Leaves numerous, narrow, 3-angled, hardly joined at the base, the tips curving inward, about 1 in. long. Flowers about 1½ in. wide, rose-pink, usually in 3-5-flowered clusters, the petals in 2 series, and 2-toothed.

**pomeridianum.** A branching, nearly erect annual. Leaves about 2 in. long, more or less spoon-shaped or lance-shaped, somewhat 3-angled, narrowed into a channeled stalk. Flowers about 1½ in. wide, yellow, the stalk hairy. A good flower garden annual. In South Africa it is called vetkousie and is used like spinach.

**tricolor** = *Mesembryanthemum lineare.*

**MESOPOTAMICA, -us, -um** (me-so-po-tay'mi-ka). From Mesopotamia.

**MESPILUS** (mes'pĭ-lus). A genus containing one small, deciduous, Eurasian tree, sometimes thorny, of the rose family, **M. germanica,** the medlar, growing 20 ft. or more high. Leaves oblong or narrower, alternate,* short-tapering, pointed, 3-5 in. long, short-stalked, slightly soft-hairy and dull green above, soft-hairy beneath. Flowers solitary, white or blush, 1½-2 in. across, appearing after the foliage. Stamens* 30-40, the anthers* red. Fruit apple-shaped, open-topped, 1-2 in. across, edible after frost or when almost rotten; sometimes used in preserves. Propagated by seeds or by grafting on seedling stock, or on pear, quince or hawthorn. Long cultivated. *Var.* **gigantea** has much larger fruit, and *var.* **abortiva** is a seedless form with small fruit. (*Mespilus* is the old Latin name for the medlar.)

**MESQUITE.** A genus of tropical or sub-tropical thorny trees or shrubs belonging to the pea family, comprising about 25 species, and known as **Prosopis** (pro-soap'is). Stems with or without spines. Leaves twice-compound, leaflets small, not toothed. Flowers not pea-like, greenish, small, in roundish spikes, growing from the axils* of the leaves. Pod very narrow, leathery, not splitting. (*Prosopis* is from the Greek, but the meaning is obscure.)

The mesquite is usually a thorny shrub, only a few feet high in the desert, where it is of great economic importance as a forage plant throughout the southwestern states.

**P. juliflora.** Honey locust; also known as algaroba. A West Indian species with many pairs of leaflets close together, thin, elliptic to oblong, the ends and base blunt and round. *Var.* **glandulosa** is the common species with more rigid, narrow leaflets. It is an important bee plant in Calif., Tex., N. Mex., southern Calif. and Mex., but otherwise of little hort. significance, outside of the desert garden.

**METROSIDEROS** (met-tro-sĭ-deer'os). Iron-tree. Ironwood. Very hardwooded trees of the family Myrtaceae, comprising 20 species, all from Australasia and the Pacific Islands, the only two commonly cult. species from N. Zeal. They are tall trees with chiefly opposite* leaves and showy red flowers in mostly terminal clusters (cymes*). Calyx more or less turban-shaped. Petals 5. Stamens many, long-protruding, and most conspicuous. Fruit a leathery capsule.* (*Metrosideros* is from the Greek for heart and iron, in allusion to the hard wood.)

Both species, especially the first, are planted in zones* 8 and 9 for ornament. They are not hardy elsewhere, and their cult. is mostly confined to southern Calif. They can be propagated by cuttings.

**robusta.** Rata. A round-headed tree 60-100 ft. high, less as usually cult. Leaves 1-1½ in. long, smooth, ovalish, or oblong. Flowers dark red, the clusters dense. Fruit about ¼ in. long. In N. Zeal. the tree starts as an epiphyte.*

**tomentosa.** Lower than the last and much-branched. Leaves 2-4 in. long, broadly oblong, mostly white-felty on the lower surface. Flowers dark red. Fruit about ½ in. long.

**METALLICA, -us, -um** (me-tăl'li-ka). With a metallic sheen.

**METCALFE BEAN** = *Phaseolus metcalfei.*

**METEL** (me'tel). An Arabic name for *Datura metel.*

**MEXICAN.** As an adjective *Mexican* is linked to many plants from Mexico or the region once included in it (most of our Southwest and Guatemala). Those that occur in THE GARDEN DICTIONARY and their proper equivalents are:

**Mexican apple** = *Casimiroa edulis;* **Mexican avocado** = *Persea americana drymifolia;* **Mexican bean beetle** (*see* Insect Pests at BEAN); **Mexican blue palm** = *Erythea armata;* **Mexican bush sage** = *Salvia leucantha;* **Mexican cotton** = *Gossypium mexicanum;* **Mexican fire-plant** = *Poinsettia heterophylla;* **Mexican ground cherry** = *Physalis ixocarpa;* **Mexican ivy** = *Cobaea scandens;* **Mexican lime,** see Acid Lime at LIME (the citrus fruit); **Mexican orange** = *Choisya ternata;* **Mexican rubber-tree** = *Castilla elastica;* **Mexican star** = *Milla biflora;* **Mexican stone pine** = *Pinus cembroides* (*see* PINE); **Mexican tea** = *Chenopodium am-*

---

\* Special articles on the subjects indicated by an asterisk (\*) will be found at the words so marked.

*brosioides* (see list at WEEDS); **Mexican tulip poppy** = *Hunnemannia fumariaefolia*.

**MEXICANA, -us, -um** (meck-si-kay'na). From Mexico.

**MEYER LEMON.** See LEMON.

**MEZEREON** = *Daphne mezereum*.

**MEZEREON FAMILY** = Thymelaeaceae.

**MEZEREUM** (me-zeer'ee-um). Native Persian name for *Daphne mezereum*.

**MICE.** See ANIMAL INJURY.

**MICHAELMAS DAISY.** The name applied to late summer and fall-blooming, hardy, perennial asters. In Europe, especially in England, these plants are greatly valued for garden adornment and cut flowers, and some specialists in hardy plants list more than 100 named varieties in their catalogues. The majority of these varieties have been derived by selection and hybridization of North American wild asters. The New York Aster (*Aster novi-belgi*) is a species most prolific in the production of garden forms — over 80 named varieties being ascribed to this species. Among other native asters which have been developed by European cultivators are: the New England Aster (*A. novae-angliae*), *A. cordifolius*, *A. ericoides*, and a few others. Varieties of *A. amellus*, a Eurasian species, are commonly included in lists under the heading of "Michaelmas Daisies." It is doubtful if this species and its derivatives should be included, as their earliness of bloom (August), habit of growth, and type of flowers, single them out from the general appearance of this group.

The fall-blooming asters vary in color from white to almost red, and from pale lavender to deep purple. In size they range from 1 ft. in the case of Snow Sprite to the 6 ft. or more in the Climax types. In habit there are spreading kinds such as Mauve Cushion, and the upright-growing forms of the *novae-angliae* group.

Doubts have been expressed as to whether any real improvement over wild types has been effected by the hybridization and seedling selection effected by European growers. A prominent English horticulturist says that in his opinion "almost any of the wild asters, if accorded the cultural treatment given to the garden forms, would equal the beauty of the named varieties." While not subscribing to this statement, nevertheless it must be admitted that most of the wild asters do respond with larger flowers and more vigorous growth when given liberal treatment in the flower garden.

American nurserymen, in general, list only a tithe of the varieties offered in the European trade, and restrict their offerings to the *amellus*, *novae-angliae* and *novi-belgi* groups. Following is a selection from the varieties available in this country:

AMELLUS VARIETIES:
  elegans, 1–2 ft. Aug. Long sprays of soft lavender flowers.
  King George, A.M., R.H.S. Aug. Individual flowers up to 3 in. in diameter. Bluish-violet rays and golden-yellow disc.
NOVAE-ANGLIAE VARIETIES:
  Barr's Pink, A.M., R.H.S., 4–5 ft. Brilliant rose-pink. Last well as cut flowers.
  Mrs. J. F. Rayner, 3 ft. Large, rosy-red flowers.
NOVI-BELGI VARIETIES:
  Blue Gem, 5 ft. Deep blue, semi-double, free-flowering.
  Climax, 6 ft. Light, lavender-blue. Individual flowers up to 3 in. under favorable conditions.
  Elsa, A.M., R.H.S., 3 ft. Pale lilac, semi-double, free-flowering.
  Gray Lady, 3 ft. Opal-gray, semi-double.
  Lady Lloyd, 3 ft. Loose sprays of rose-pink flowers.
  Queen Mary, 3–4 ft. Rich blue, tinted with lavender. Flowers up to 2½ in. in diameter; pyramidal inflorescence.
  Robinson V. C., A.M., R.H.S., 3–4 ft. Bluish-mauve, double flowers in long sprays, suitable for cutting.
  San Banham. Similar to "Climax," but white.
  Snow Sprite, 1–2 ft. Compact, bushy habit, with semi-double, white flowers.
  Mauve Cushion. A dwarf, spreading type, said to be of Japanese origin.
  Recently introduced varieties, not exceeding a foot in height, include: Countess of Dudley, Lady Henry Maddocks, Marjorie, Nancy, Ronald, and Victor.

CULTIVATION. To get best results with Michaelmas daisies, deep, moist, rich soil must be provided and annual division of clumps practiced. The *novae-angliae* kinds will thrive in wet situations. Some of the best English growers of these plants trench* the ground 3 ft. deep and set out in early spring young plants that were rooted from cuttings made the preceding fall and carried over winter in cold frames. Good success is also obtained by separating the clumps every fall or spring, and planting only the strongest divisions (each of 2 or 3 shoots*) obtained from the outside of the clump. These divisions in the case of the strong varieties should be set from 3–4 feet apart and the smaller kinds from 2–3 feet apart. Not more than three or four shoots should be allowed to develop from each clump. To overcome the sparse effect in spring of such wide spacing, they may be interplanted with early-blooming and maturing bulbous plants, such as daffodils.

Strangely enough, many of the improved forms of wild asters have not been very successful under American cultivation. They are subject to mildew, and also to a wilt disease. The beauty of this group and their value in the perennial border, in beds by themselves, and as cut flowers, are such that it is well worth while to make special efforts to grow them. Mildew may be kept under control by the use of sulphur preparations, and it is possible that the wilt disease could be overcome by propagation with short cuttings in fall and rotation of planting situations. — M. F.

**MICHAUXIA** (me-show'i-a). A small genus of herbs of the family Campanulaceae, all from Asia Minor, the only cult. species being **M. campanuloides**, a perennial herb sometimes grown in the border for its rather showy, drooping flowers. It is a stout herb, 3–5 ft. high, with alternate,* lance-shaped, irregularly toothed and bristly leaves. Flowers more or less bell-shaped, about 2 in. long, white, but tinged with purple, the 8–10 lobes of the corolla somewhat recurved. July. While a perennial, it can be raised as a biennial (see BIENNIALS), and is more suited to Calif. than to regions with cold, slushy winters. (Named for André Michaux, famous French botanist in America.)

**MICHELIA** (me-chel'i-a). A genus of Asiatic trees or shrubs of the Magnoliaceae, comprising 12 species. They resemble *Magnolia*, but the flowers come from the axils* of the leaves. Flowers solitary, sepals and petals similar, 9–15, or more. Fruit a long spike of leathery carpels. (Named for P. A. Micheli, a Florentine botanist.)

Michelias are propagated by seed sown immediately when ripe, or stratified, or by ripe-wood cuttings, bearing one or two leaves, started under glass with bottom-heat. An excellent greenhouse plant for the North, where it needs a cool house and potting mixture* 5.

**fuscata.** Banana-shrub. A shrub attaining a height of 10–15 ft. Young growth covered with a brownish wool. Leaves elliptic or narrower, smooth in maturity. Flowers 1–1½ in. across, brownish-yellow, edged with light carmine, and having a strong banana fragrance. China. Hardy outdoors from zone* 7 southward, and popular in Calif.

**MICHIGAN.** The state lies wholly in zones* 1, 2, and 3.

All of Michigan was glaciated, and much of the western portion of the Lower Peninsula was subsequently under water. Many depressions have subsequently accumulated deposits of peat and muck, some of which are acid and some mixed with marl. Moraines are common. The soils used for fruit growing are generally low in fertility; in many cases they are sandy and many of them are subject to water and wind erosion when kept under clean culture. The peat and muck soils contain the greater portion of the celery, onion, cabbage and carrot acreage.

FRUIT. The greatest concentration of fruit production, and of melons and tomatoes, is in southwest Michigan, where climatic advantages combine with proximity to the

---

* Special articles on the subjects indicated by an asterisk (*) will be found at the words so marked.

Chicago market. Berrien County is one of the leading counties in the United States in peach production. This crop is grown extensively in Van Buren and Allegan counties, and to a lesser extent farther north. Occasional plantings occur in the southern tiers of counties reaching across the state, but these are chiefly for supplying local markets. Commercial pear growing is almost entirely confined to the three counties mentioned; Bartlett is the principal variety, though many Kieffers are produced for canneries. The principal grape acreage is in Van Buren County; Concord is the chief variety, with Delaware a remote second. A ponderable fraction of the crop is manufactured into unfermented grape juice. Sour-cherry production is heaviest along the Lake Shore from Oceana to Grand Traverse counties; Montmorency is nearly the sole variety grown, and most of the crop is canned. The sweet cherry is grown in a limited way along the Lake Shore. Apple production is widely diffused along the Lake Shore and across the southern half of the Lower Peninsula; Northern Spy, Baldwin, Fameuse, McIntosh and Rhode Island Greening comprise the greater portion of the bearing acreage; newer plantings contain few Baldwins and more Jonathan and Delicious. Tree-fruit production in the Upper Peninsula is confined almost entirely to the hardier varieties of apples, such as Wealthy and McIntosh. Raspberries, dewberries and strawberries are produced extensively in the southwestern counties, and red raspberries rather extensively around Manistee, Onekama and Cheboygan. The most serious pests are leaf-spot in cherries, leaf-curl and virus diseases in peaches, fire-blight in pears, and, in apples, codling moth and apple scab. Most of these are amenable to control by proper spraying, but present difficulties which discourage production of fruit in small gardens, where spraying equipment is usually inadequate.

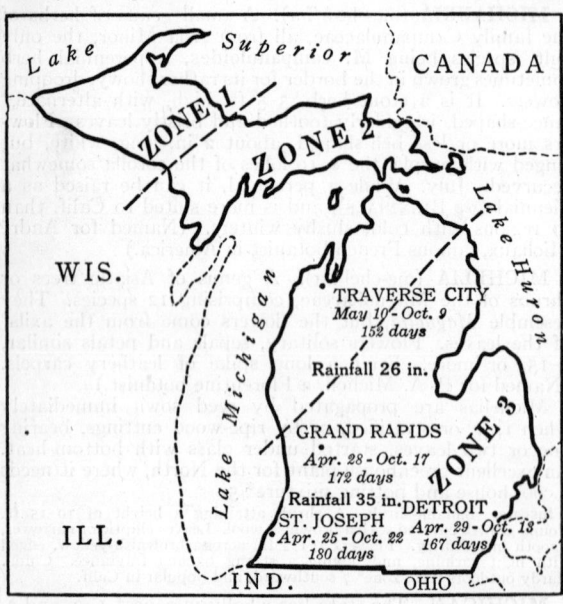

MICHIGAN

The zones of hardiness crossing Michigan are those shown on the colored map at ZONE, which should be consulted for details. The dates are the average latest killing frost in spring and the first one in the fall. The figures below the dates show the length of the growing season. Rainfall figures (in inches) show the total annual rainfall in the regions so indicated.

VEGETABLES. The seven leading vegetables grown in the state, based upon the 1929 acreage, are as follows: sweet corn, cucumbers, green peas, green beans, cabbage, onions (dry), and tomatoes. The seven leading crops based upon the acre value, however, are: celery, onions (dry), tomatoes, cucumbers, cabbage, sweet corn, and muskmelons.

The commercial tomato and muskmelon areas are south of the Saginaw Bay–Muskegon line, with the heaviest plantings in the southwest and southeast portions. Berrien County leads in the production of both these crops. Sweet corn is grown in nearly every county of the state, but the largest plantings are concentrated on the eastern side of the lower half of the Lower Peninsula. With the exception of eight or ten counties in the northeastern part of the Lower Peninsula, cucumbers for pickling and green beans are distributed over the remaining counties. The green-pea area is the east-central portion of the Lower Peninsula, with the heaviest plantings being in the Thumb district.

Celery, onions and carrots are now grown largely on muck soils. Most of the celery is grown in seven counties in the southwest portion of the state. The leading counties, based upon their 1929 average, are Ottawa, Van Buren, Kalamazoo, Allegan and Kent. The onion acreage is largely concentrated in the same muck sections, but the plantings spread out into some of the counties east and north. The leading onion-growing counties in 1929 were Allegan, Barry, Ottawa, Newaygo, Van Buren and Washtenaw. Carrots, parsnips, beets and spinach are grown in these muck areas also. Cabbage is grown all over the lower half of the Lower Peninsula, but the heaviest plantings are in these muck sections. See MUCKLAND GARDENING.

The cool-season vegetables are being grown more extensively on muck soils, but the warm-season crops such as tomatoes, peppers, eggplant, melons, cucumbers, and pumpkins and squash are not recommended for muck soils because of the frost hazard.

ORNAMENTAL PLANTS. There are about 800 florists in the state, and approximately 6,800,000 square feet of glass devoted to the production of cut flowers and plants. About 30 per cent of the florists are located in the Detroit area. Mt. Clemens is the principal producing area in the state, while Ann Arbor and the Grand Rapids–Kalamazoo sections are of considerable importance also.

The most important breeder of new chrysanthemums in the United States is located at Adrian, Michigan. The growing of strawflowers is of some importance in the vicinity of Lansing. The production of cyclamen seeds is centered at Sturgis, Michigan.

Michigan ranks first of all states in the production of gladiolus bulbs, with about 500 acres devoted to this crop. The state ranks third in tulip production, sixth in bulbous iris, and eighth in narcissus. Since 1930 the commercial culture of dahlias has increased in importance. The estimated commercial plantings for 1935 total 100 acres. There are several large producers of peonies in the state.

This large commercial production of ornamental plants is, of course, merely a reflection of the high degree to which gardening has been developed in the state. Near some of the larger cities are some of the finest private estates in America. Also in this state is the interesting development of horticulture and industrial life sponsored by Henry Ford.

CLIMATE. For a state with relatively small differences in altitude, Michigan presents an unusual variety of climate. Lake Michigan exercises a moderating effect on temperatures in a narrow belt along its eastern shore, producing the rather curious phenomenon of a "fruit belt" extending north and south, while land a few miles to the east is subjected to more extreme temperatures, particularly in winter. The mean minimum for February at Traverse City is 11° F.; at Grayling, almost due east, it is 4.6° F. In the Upper Peninsula similar influences are evident; the mean minimum for February at Eagle Harbor, the most northerly station, but on Lake Superior, is 9° F., while at Iron River, considerably south, but in the interior, the figure is −1.3° F.

In spring vegetation awakens later and spring frosts cease earlier along the Lake Michigan shore than at comparable points in the interior, thus decreasing the frost hazard. In the Lower Peninsula the frost-free season ranges from 180 days at St. Joseph to 114 at Grayling; in the Upper Peninsula from 153 days at Calumet to 78 at Ewen. Frost dates for points of horticultural significance are shown in tabular form.

---

\* Special articles on the subjects indicated by an asterisk (\*) will be found at the words so marked.

| Town | Average date of last killing frost in spring | Latest known killing frost | Average date of earliest killing frost in fall | Earliest known killing frost |
|---|---|---|---|---|
| Grand Rapids | April 28 | May 28 | Oct. 17 | Sept. 23 |
| Detroit | April 29 | May 31 | Oct. 13 | Sept. 23 |
| St. Joseph | April 25 | May 11 | Oct. 22 | Sept. 15 |
| Traverse City | May 10 | May 31 | Oct. 9 | Sept. 17 |
| Lansing | May 6 | May 30 | Oct. 8 | Sept. 19 |

The mean annual rainfall in the Lower Peninsula ranges from 26.73 in. at Traverse City to 35.10 at Kalamazoo. The monthly distribution is rather uniform, though the rainfall for the six warm months is generally somewhat higher than that of the six cold months. Along the Lake Michigan shore the summer precipitation is rather light, making control of fungous diseases generally somewhat easier.

Cloudiness is high in winter, sunshine being less than 20 per cent of the possible amount in January, thus presenting problems to greenhouse men, but in July sunshine is 10 per cent greater in western Michigan than in Ohio and Indiana. Prevailing winds are westerly, with a prevalence of southwest winds in the southern half, and of northwest winds in the northern half, of the Lower Peninsula.

The address of the Agricultural Experiment Station which has supplied this information is East Lansing. The Station is always ready to answer gardening questions.

Garden Club activities in Michigan include clubs of the Garden Club of America, the home office of which is 598 Madison Avenue, New York. And there are over 70 clubs affiliated with The Federated Garden Clubs of Michigan. For the nearest one to your locality write the Garden Editor, Houghton Mifflin Company, Boston, Mass. *See also* HORTICULTURAL SOCIETIES.

**MICHIGAN PEAT.** See SOIL SPONGE.

**MICONIA** (my-kō'nĭ-a). A genus of tropical American shrubs or trees of the family Melastomaceae, comprising nearly 600 species. Leaves opposite,* usually stalked, with or without marginal teeth. Flowers rather small, white, rose, purple, or yellow. Petals 4–8, spreading or turned back. Calyx lobes 4–8, short. Fruit a dry, leathery berry. (Named for D. Micon, Spanish physician.)

Miconias are often grown in the warm-temperate greenhouse for their handsome foliage. They should be given fibrous soil, plenty of water, and shaded from direct sunlight. They are propagated by cuttings of ripened wood over bottom-heat.

magnifica. A shrub several ft. high when cult. Leaves broadly oval, 2–2½ ft. long, with wavy margins, shining green above, reddish-bronze below, with prominent white or light green veins. Flowers inconspicuous, in compound terminal clusters (panicles*). Mex.

**MICRAMPELIS** = *Echinocystis*.

*MICRANTHA, -us, -um* (my-kran'tha). Small-flowered.

**MICROBE.** See BACTERIA.

*MICROCARPA, -us, -um* (my-kro-kar'pa). Small-fruited.

*MICROCEPHALA, -us, -um* (my-kro-seff'a-la). Small-headed.

**MICROCITRUS** (my-crow-sit'rus). A genus of 4 Australian, very spiny shrubs, or small trees of the family Rutaceae. Leaves broadly oval, sometimes wedge-shaped. Flowers very small. M. australasica, the finger-lime, is the only cult. species. It is a tree 30–40 ft. high. Young leaves very small, the mature leaves 1–1½ in. long, broadly oval. Fruit yellow, longer than broad, 4 in. long by 1 in. thick, the juice acid. Much hardier than the lemon or lime, otherwise the culture is similar. It has already been crossed with *Citrus mitis*, the Calomondin or Panama orange. The young plants are quite ornamental, and likely to be useful for a hedge in warm climates because of the dense, spiny growth. (*Microcitrus* is from the Latin for *small*, and *Citrus*.)

**MICROMALUS** (my-kro-may'lus). A small apple or crabapple. See MALUS.

**MICROMERIA** (my-kro-meer'ĭ-a). A large genus of herbs of the mint family, mostly from the north temperate zone, a few grown in the rock garden or for their fragrant foliage (*see* FRAGRANCE). They are mostly trailing or prostrate plants with small, opposite* leaves and angled or square stems. Flowers small (none over ¼ in. long), irregular* and 2-lipped, mostly crowded in the leaf-axils,* sometimes solitary there, or in terminal spikes. Fruit a collection of tiny nutlets, hidden by the persistent calyx.* (*Micromeria* is derived from *micromeris*.*)

The plants are of reasonably easy culture in the rock garden or border, except the first species which is not well suited to regions of cold, wet winters. Best propagated by division of the roots in spring.

chamissonis. Yerba Buena. A Pacific coast trailing perennial, its branches rooting at the tips, hence making close patches. Leaves roundish, nearly 1 in. long, hairy, and wavy on the margins. Flowers mostly solitary, white.

piperella. Not over 6 in. high and sprawling or trailing. Leaves smooth, more or less ovalish. Flowers in small clusters, reddish-purple. Southern Eu.

rupestris. A low-growing, dense, heath-like perennial, its prostrate stems turning up at the ends. Leaves like pennyroyal in odor, very numerous and small. Flowers white, but lavender-spotted, blooming from July to frost. Southern Eu. and a fine plant for the rock garden or border.

*MICROMERIS, -e* (my-kro-mee'ris). Having few or small parts — petals, sepals, etc.

*MICROPETALA, -us, -um* (my-kro-pet'a-la). With small petals.

*MICROPHYLLA, -us, -um* (my-kro-fil'la). Small-leaved.

**MIDDLETON PLACE GARDENS.** See SOUTH CAROLINA.

**MIDGE.** See Insect Pests at CHRYSANTHEMUM.

**MIDRIB.** The principal vein or rib of a leaf.

**MIGNON.** See DAHLIA.

**MIGNONETTE.** Erect or reclining herbs, sometimes woody at the base, constituting the genus **Reseda** (re-zee'da), family Resedaceae. It contains 50 or 60 species, of which only a few are cultivated. M. odorata, the common mignonette, is of the greatest horticultural interest. It has a number of varieties, especially *var*. grandiflora arborea, a large garden form. They are erect or declining herbs, annual or biennial. The leaves are alternate* or clustered. The flowers are small in terminal clusters or spikes, the petals 4 to 7, toothed or cleft. The fruit is a capsule, usually 3–6-horned or angled, and opening at the top when ripe. Mediterranean region and the Red Sea. (*Reseda* is the Latin name of a plant, from the word meaning to heal or assuage.)

Mignonette, although not showy, has such a delightful fragrance that it is extensively grown as a garden flower. The outdoor culture is very simple. The seeds should be sown where the plants are to grow and the seedlings thinned, as mignonette is exceedingly difficult to transplant. A first sowing should be made in late April in the North and another in July to extend the season of bloom. The soil should be rich, and the bed should be, in shade part of the day.

For a number of years mignonette has been popular as a cut flower in winter. It is successfully cult. under glass in about the same manner as carnations are treated. Use potting mixture* 4 about 5 in. deep on the benches, over an in. of well-rotted manure. Three sowings of seed are made, one in July, one in August and one in September, and the soil lightly watered. After the plants have formed a number of true leaves they are thinned to stand a few inches apart. They should be grown in a cool house, the temperature ranging between 45° and 65°. Mignonette must never be allowed to dry out, but never over-watered; water on the foliage will often cause spotting. It should be kept constantly growing. When the flower-shoots are well set it is well to apply a mixture of 1 part sheep manure and 2 parts loam, or an application of weak liquid manure water. The

* Special articles on the subjects indicated by an asterisk (*) will be found at the words so marked.

side shoots should be pinched back to throw vigor into the central stalks and the mature plants supported by wire rings. *See* Pinching at TRAINING PLANTS.

Mignonette is grown in pots also, but this is attended with more difficulty. Fill 2½-in. pots with potting mixture* 4, similar to that used in the benches. Plant several seeds in a pot, and after plants have developed three or more leaves, remove all but the sturdiest. Instead of pinching the side shoots as in bench culture, in pot-grown mignonette the center shoot is pinched back, thus developing a bushy, symmetrical growth of side shoots. Never allow plants to become pot-bound, transplanting when necessary until the plants are in 7–8-in. pots. Water carefully and support the mature plants with stakes.

**MIGNONETTE FAMILY** = Resedaceae.

**MIGNONETTE-TREE** = *Lawsonia inermis*.

**MIGNONETTE-VINE** = *Boussingaultia basselloides*.

*MIKANIOIDES* (my-kay-nĭ-oy′deez, but *see* OÏDES). Like the climbing hempweed (*Mikania*), a weedy vine scarcely worth cult.

**MILDEW.** *See* Fungi at PLANT DISEASES. *See also* the Diseases at ONION.

**MILFOIL** = *Achillea millefolium*.

*MILIACEA, -us, -um* (mil-ĭ-ā′see-a). Relating to millet.

**MILKMAIDS** = *Cardamine pratensis*.

**MILK PURSLANE** = *Euphorbia corollata*.

**MILK THISTLE** = *Silybum marianum*.

**MILK VETCH.** *See* ASTRAGALUS.

**MILKWEED.** Milky-juiced, rather showy, but sometimes rather weedy, perennial herbs constituting the genus Asclepias (as-klee′pĭ-as), of the family Asclepiadaceae, and including over 150 species chiefly from the New World, but a few African. The cult. species are chiefly North American plants for the wild garden, but two of those below are tropical and must be grown in the greenhouse in the North. Leaves opposite* or in whorls,* rarely alternate,* without marginal teeth. Flowers regular,* often showy, especially in the tropical species, usually in close, roundish clusters (umbels*), but sometimes in few-flowered clusters in the leaf-axils. Corolla deeply 5-cleft. Stamens* with the filaments joined in a circle around the style.* (*See* ASCLEPIADACEAE.) Fruit a pair of follicles,* the many seeds with a tuft of hairs, often beautifully silky. (*Asclepias* is the classical Greek name of these plants.)

The native species are of very simple culture in the right kind of site, which is indicated for each. The tropical species, *A. curassavica*, can only be grown in the greenhouse northward. It is a more showy plant than any of the native species and is often forced by florists. *A. mexicana* can be grown outdoors in mild sections of the country, but not in the East north of zone* 6.

**A. curassavica.** Blood-flower. From 2–4 ft. high, the stem smooth or nearly so. Leaves opposite,* oblongish or narrower, 3–5 in. long. Flowers about ¼ in. high, brilliant orange-red. Fruits 1½–4 in. long, essentially smooth. Tropical America, and a weed there, but the showiest of all the milkweeds.

**A. incarnata.** Swamp or rose milkweed. A stout, rather coarse herb, 3–4 ft. high. Leaves oblongish or narrower, 4–7 in. long, tapering at the tip. Flowers rose-purple, about ¼ in. wide, the cluster ball-like and nearly 3 in. thick. In swamps and wet places, eastern N.A. and west to Colo. Summer.

**A. mexicana.** From 3–5 ft. high, the leaves opposite* or in whorls,* narrowly lance-shaped, 4–6 in. long. Flowers small, greenish-white, sometimes tinged with purple. Ore. to Mex. and not suited to outdoor cult. in the East, north of zone* 6.

**A. tuberosa.** Butterfly-weed; also called pleurisy-root and orange milkweed. The showiest of all the native milkweeds and thriving in dry, sandy soil. It is a rough-hairy herb, 1–3 ft. high, erect or sprawling. Leaves coarse, oblong or lance-oblong, 2–6 in. long, usually short-stalked. Flowers about ¼ in. wide, bright orange, the cluster very showy. Aug.–Sept.

**A. verticillata.** Whorled milkweed. A slender-stemmed, leafy herb, usually 12–20 in. high. Leaves in whorls* of 3–7, smooth, narrow, the margins slightly rolled. Flowers greenish-white, the clusters rather loose. In dry places, often in the woods, eastern N.A. and westward to New Mex. and Alberta.

**MILKWEED FAMILY.** Besides the true milkweeds, this family includes many herbs, shrubs, and woody vines, nearly all with a milky juice. It also includes some cactus-like succulents belonging to the genus *Stapelia* and others, mostly from South Africa. For a complete list of the hort. genera and the characters of the family *see* ASCLEPIADACEAE.

**MILK WILLOW-HERB** = *Lythrum alatum*.

**MILKWORT.** *See* POLYGALA.

**MILKWORT FAMILY** = Polygalaceae.

**MILLA** (mil′la). A single species of bulbous herbs of the lily family found from New Mexico and Arizona to Mexico, and grown for ornament. The only species is **M. biflora**, the Mexican star, often cult. under the name of *Bessera elegans*. It has basal, grass-like leaves and fragrant, white flowers nearly 2½ in. wide. The flowers are in a loose cluster of 3–5 blooms at the end of a naked stalk 12–18 in. high. Corolla salver-shaped, its separate segments 3-veined. Stamens* 6. Fruit a stalkless capsule.* (Named for J. Milla, Spanish gardener at the Madrid court.)

The plant can be grown in pots for winter or early spring bloom. Put several bulbs in a pot, using potting mixture* 3, and grow in a cool greenhouse, allowing about 3 months from planting until bloom is wanted. For outdoor culture treat exactly as with gladiolus (which see), as the bulbs will not stand outdoors in severe climates. For the plant sometimes advertised as *M. uniflora see* BRODIAEA UNIFLORA.

*MILLEFOLIA, -us, -um* (mil-lee-fō′lĭ-a). Literally "thousand-leaved"; as a specific name usually indicating finely dissected leaves, as in *Achillea millefolium*; or leaves with many leaflets.

**MILLEPEDES.** *See* Insect Pests at CINERARIA.

**MILLET** = *Panicum miliaceum* or *Setaria italica*, the latter usually called foxtail millet. For other plants to which the name millet is sometimes applied, *see* ELEUSINE, PENNISETUM, ECHINOCHLOA, and PANICUM TEXANUM.

**MILLETTIA** = *Wistaria*.

**MILTONIA** (mil-tō′nĭ-a). Little known, but very handsome, tree-perching, South American orchids, comprising over 20 species, several of which are in the collections of orchid fanciers, the 2 below somewhat more generally grown, but still rare in cult. They differ only in technical characters from *Odontoglossum* and from *Oncidium*. They have short pseudobulbs* bearing one or two leaves at the top and others sometimes at the base. Flowers 1 to several at the end of a stalk arising from the base of the pseudobulb.* Sepals and petals very similar, but the petals a little broader. Lip large, sometimes 2-toothed, but not lobed, and usually expanded. (Named for Viscount Milton, a patron of horticulture.)

For culture *see* Greenhouse Orchids at ORCHID.

**roezli.** Pseudobulbs* oblongish, nearly 2 in. long. Leaf solitary, nearly 1 ft. long, very narrow. Flowers 2–3, the stalk about 6 in. long, each flower 3–5 in. wide, flattish, white, but with a purple blotch or band at the base of each petal, the lip brownish at the base. Colombia. It usually blooms in the winter and again in the spring.

**vexillaria.** Resembling the last, but with broader leaves and larger flowers which are rose-pink, but the lip streaked with yellow and red. Ecuador and Colombia. Blooms from April–June.

**MIMBRE** = *Chilopsis linearis*.

**MIMOSA** (my-mo′sa). An immense genus of mostly tropical American herbs, shrubs, and trees of the pea family, some of the 300 species planted for ornament in the tropics, but only the two below much known in cult. in the U.S. They have alternate,* twice-compound* leaves, the leaflets numerous, usually very small, arranged feather-fashion, and very sensitive in the first species. Flowers not pea-like, small, more or less tubular, in dense, ball-like clusters, and rose-purple or lavender in those below. Stamens protruding. Fruit a flat pod (legume*), ultimately separable into 1-seeded

---

* Special articles on the subjects indicated by an asterisk (*) will be found at the words so marked.

joints. (*Mimosa* is from the Greek for mimic, in allusion to the sensitive collapse of the leaves of some species.)

The first species is one of the most extraordinary plants grown in the greenhouse. It is a roadside weed in the tropics. Upon the slightest irritation all the leaflets immediately fold up face to face, and the whole leaf collapses, and if the shock is sufficient, all the leaves on the plant will do likewise. Much nonsense has been written about the "nerves" of this plant, but the fact remains that its reaction to shock (or cloudy weather) is one of the most remarkable cases of physiological response known in the plant world. It must be grown in a warm greenhouse in potting mixture* 4. The second is a spiny shrub, also chiefly grown in the greenhouse, but cult. outdoors in zones* 8 and 9, especially in southern Calif.

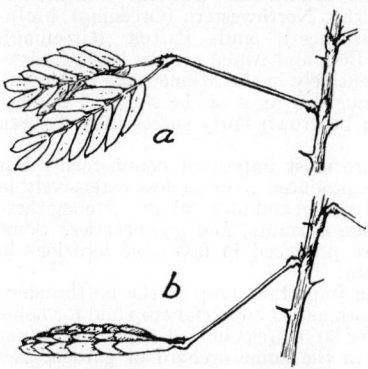

The sensitive plant (*Mimosa pudica*) before (*a*) and after (*b*) the shock to its leaves has caused them to collapse.

**pudica.** Sensitive plant; also called humble plant. A low, somewhat woody perennial, more or less hairy and slightly spiny. Leaflets very small, sensitive (see above). Flowers rose-purple or lavender, the ball-like clusters long-stalked in the leaf-axils. Tropical America, and naturalized in Fla. and along the Gulf.

**spegazzini.** A spiny shrub, 4–6 ft. high. Leaflets larger than in the last and far less sensitive. Flowers rose-purple, the ball-like clusters dense. Argentina. Grown for ornament in southern Calif. and occasionally in the greenhouse.

**MIMOSACEAE.** See LEGUMINOSAE.

**MIMOSA FAMILY.** See LEGUMINOSAE.

**MIMULUS** (mim′you-lus). A genus of about 115 declining or erect annual or perennial herbs, or sometimes subshrubs, of the figwort family. Plants smooth or hairy, often sticky or clammy. Leaves opposite,* with or without marginal teeth. Flowers showy, 2-lipped,* often spotted, giving the effect of a face (hence the name monkey-flower), growing singly from the axils* of the leaves, or in terminal clusters (racemes*). Fruit an oblong or very narrow pod. Found in North and South America, As., Aust., South Af. and very numerous in western N.A. These plants are sometimes called *Diplacus*. (The name is derived from the Latin for a little mimic, from the grinning face.)

A few species of monkey-flowers are grown in the garden and in the greenhouse, and some of the large kinds in gardens in California. Those cultivated by florists in the greenhouse are grown from seed sown from January in potting mixture* 3; they are also increased by cuttings and division. In the open they require semi-shade and plenty of water. Though perennials they are generally treated as annuals. *M. luteus*, which often has spotted flowers, is the main source of most of the cult. types.

**cardinalis.** A perennial, sticky and hairy herb, with weak or erect stems, 1 ft. high. Leaves 4½ in. long with sharp marginal teeth. Flowers red, occasionally yellow, 2-lipped,* 2 in. long, the stamens* protruding. Utah to Ore. and Lower California.

**guttatus.** A smooth perennial herb, 1½ ft. high. Leaves nearly oval, with small marginal teeth. Flowers yellow, generally with red or brown dots on the throat, 2-lipped, 1½ in. long. Calyx* much swollen in fruit. Alaska to Mex. Easily transplanted, or grown from seed in the wild garden.

**langsdorfi** = *Mimulus guttatus*.

**lewisi.** A perennial, sticky and hairy herb, nearly 2½ ft. high. Leaves oblong, about 2½ in. long, with very fine marginal teeth. Flowers rose-red or rose-purple. *Var.* **alba** has white flowers. British Columbia to Calif. and Utah, in mountain meadows, and in shady, moist ground at lower elevations.

**luteus.** A smooth or slightly downy, perennial herb with a declining stem 1 ft. high, larger forms 2 to 4 ft. high. Leaves almost oval, 4 in. or more long, with sharp, marginal teeth. Flowers deep yellow, commonly with dark spots within, 1½ in. long, growing in loose terminal clusters (racemes*). Chile.

**ringens.** A branching herb 1 to 4 ft. high, perennial from rootstocks, the stems 4-angled. Leaves oblong or narrowly lance-shaped, 3–4 in. long, sharply cut on the margins. Flowers violet, occasionally white. Growing in wet places in eastern N.A. A common native plant, easily established in colonies in the wild garden.

**MINER'S LETTUCE** = *Montia perfoliata*.

*MINIATA, -us, -um* (min-ĭ-ā′ta). Vermilion.

**MINIATURE DAHLIA.** See DAHLIA.

**MINIATURE GARDENS.** For living ones, *see* TERRARIUM. For small models of landscape or garden, *see* MODEL GARDENS.

*MINIMA, -us, -um* (min′i-ma). Smallest.

**MINIMACID.** A term for slightly acid soils with a pH of about 6.0. For details *see* ACID AND ALKALI SOILS.

**MINIMALKALINE.** A term for soils that are neutral or slightly alkaline, with a pH of 7.00–8.00. For details *see* ACID AND ALKALI SOILS.

**MINNESOTA.** The state, north-centrally located, lies almost wholly in zone* 1. Kandiyohi County, a few miles west of the Twin Cities, is the approximate geographical center of North America, exclusive of Alaska.

The drainage of the state empties into three great systems. The northeastern part drains into the Atlantic Ocean through the Great Lakes and St. Lawrence River system; the northwestern into Hudson Bay through the Red River of the North system; and the remainder of the state, approximately two-thirds, into the Gulf of Mexico through the Mississippi River system.

Recurring glaciations and stream erosion have given Minnesota a diversified topography. Although the altitude varies from 602 to 2230 feet, the greater portion of the state is level or gently rolling without strong reliefs. Nearly 7 per cent is covered by lakes, a great many of them occupying basins among moraine ridges and knolls and on outwash plains.

The native vegetation of the state is also diversified, varying from that of the typical prairie in the western and southwestern parts, through the hardwood forest area bordering the prairie to the coniferous forest area comprising, approximately, the northeastern third of the state. The flora is composed of about 6500 species of plants. Among them are found about 1900 species of flowering plants and 65 species of ferns and fern allies, which provide much horticultural material for use in its natural state and in the development of new horticultural varieties.

SOILS. The soils of Minnesota are widely diversified. A small portion of the state's surface is made up of rock outcrops and wind-blown sand which is unsuited to horticulture. Limited areas are covered with stream deposits and large areas by lake deposits, both glacial and modern. Loess* covers an extensive area in southeastern Minnesota. There are about 7,000,000 acres of peat in the state, much of which has been and is being put into production, a considerable portion being devoted to the production of potatoes and vegetable crops. The soils of the remainder of the state are clayey in nature, intermixed with gravelly or sandy moraine and outwash plain deposits. As a general rule, Minnesota soils are fertile and productive.

HORTICULTURE. Minnesota produces a wide variety of vegetable, fruit and ornamental crops, but does not produce enough of some of them to meet the needs of its people. The chief gardening centers are Minneapolis, St. Paul and Duluth. These are areas of general production. While they are the most important centers, there are numerous centers specializing in certain specific crops.

VEGETABLES. Certain varieties of all the commonly grown vegetable crops can be produced in nearly all sections. A large part of the vegetable production is confined to market gardens in the vicinity of the larger cities and towns and to home gardens, but there are considerable areas devoted to the production of truck crops for shipment both within and outside the state.

---

\* Special articles on the subjects indicated by an asterisk (\*) will be found at the words so marked.

Minnesota is one of the leading states in the production of potatoes. While practically every farmer grows some potatoes, the major areas of production of the main crop are in the Red River Valley section and on numerous peat developments throughout the state. One of the most important of these peat areas is at Hollandale, near Albert Lea, where a bog, some 18,000 acres in extent, is in cultivation and devoted largely to potato production. Early potatoes are produced to a large extent on the lighter soils of Anoka, Hennepin and surrounding counties. Hollandale also produces considerable quantities of celery and onions.

MINNESOTA

The zones of hardiness crossing Minnesota are those shown on the colored map at ZONE, which should be consulted for details. The dates are the average latest killing frost in spring and the first one in the fall. The figures below the dates show the length of the growing season. Rainfall figures (in inches) show (1) the total annual rainfall and (2) the amount falling in the growing season at the places indicated.

Large areas are devoted to the production of celery, head lettuce, and cauliflower in the Meadowlands and Fens regions near Duluth. Considerable areas are devoted to the production of cabbage in the vicinity of Dodge Center and Plainview. Minnesota is one of the leading states in the production of rutabagas. Most of these are grown near Askov. New Brighton, near the Twin Cities, is the squash-producing center of the state and large quantities of squash move from there into inter-state commerce. Other vegetable crops are grown on a commercial scale in various parts of the state but they are not of as great economic importance as the preceding.

Minnesota has forged ahead considerably in the canning of peas and corn and ranks high among the states in their production. This industry is centered largely in the southeastern part of the state, principally in the Minnesota River Valley. Considerable areas are devoted to the production of pickling cucumbers in other sections. No appreciable amount of any other vegetable is canned.

FRUITS. The principal fruits produced in Minnesota are raspberries, strawberries, apples, and grapes. While raspberries and strawberries are grown throughout most of the state for local consumption, the chief production centers are in the vicinity of the Twin Cities, Duluth, Aitkin, Rochester, Owatonna, and La Crescent. The most important varieties are listed. RED RASPBERRIES: Latham, Chief and King. BLACK RASPBERRIES: Cumberland, Older and Plum Farmer. JUNE-BEARING STRAWBERRIES: Premier, Dunlap, Beaver and Minnehaha. EVER-BEARING STRAWBERRIES: Mastodon, Progressive, Wayzata. Apples are also grown in home orchards in most parts of the state but the most important centers of production are the Twin City area and southeastern Minnesota. The more important varieties are the Wealthy, Northwestern (Greening), McIntosh, Oldenburg (Duchess), and Patten (Greening). Grapes, of which the Beta and Alpha are the leading varieties, are produced intensively in the Minnetonka region and to a lesser extent throughout most of the state. A number of other varieties can be grown fairly successfully if given winter protection.

The above fruits are most important commercially but many other fruits are produced more or less extensively in the home orchard and garden and for local use. Among these are plums, blackberries, currants, and gooseberries. Some pears and cherries are produced in favorable locations in southeastern Minnesota.

The blueberry is an important crop in the northeastern quarter of the state, both as a commercial crop and for home use. It grows wild over large areas in that region and is not found to any extent in the home orchard or garden. See BLUEBERRY.

ORNAMENTAL HORTICULTURE. Gardening plays a very important part in the lives of the people of Minnesota, both from the commercial and the aesthetic viewpoint. With the wealth of native material available, much of this has been adapted to such uses, although considerable numbers of species and varieties have been introduced. To provide material for ornamental uses, as well as fruit and vegetable plants and seeds, an extensive nursery and greenhouse industry has developed. Nearly 200 nurseries are located throughout the state, the largest ones being in the vicinity of the Twin Cities and in southeastern Minnesota. Extensive greenhouses are located in metropolitan areas and many smaller ones in smaller cities and towns.

While the number of species and varieties of plants used in ornamental horticulture is too numerous to mention here, a few of the most hardy and most commonly used ones are listed.

*Evergreen trees:* Black Hills, Blue, and White spruce; Norway, Mugho, White, Scotch and Austrian pine; Douglas fir; Red cedar; arborvitae and the junipers.

*Deciduous trees:* American and Chinese elms; Poplars, Maples, Ash, Linden, Hackberry, Mountain-ash.

*Shrubs: Spiraea*, Mock-orange, *Hydrangea*, Honeysuckle, Hardy roses, Japanese barberry, Dogwood, *Viburnum*, *Euonymus*, Pea tree, Flowering plum, Sumac, Flowering almond, Ninebark, and the Button-bush.

*Fruiting shrubs:* Cranberry tree, Elderberry, Snowberry, Juneberry, Buffaloberry, Wild crabapple, Sand cherry, and the ornamental plum hybrids.

*Vines:* Virginia creeper, Trumpet honeysuckle, Matrimony-vine, *Clematis paniculata* and Bittersweet.

*Hedges:* Buckthorn, Alpine currant, Japanese barberry, Lilac, Tartarian honeysuckle, Arborvitae, and Pea tree.

*Ornamental herbs: Delphinium*, peonies, irises, *Phlox*, columbine, hollyhock, *Gaillardia, Coreopsis*, daisies, New England aster, bellflower, *Pentstemon*, baby's-breath, poppies, flax, daylily, meadowrue, bleeding-heart, pinks, violas, *Alyssum, Achillea*, and speedwell.

CLIMATE

Minnesota has a mid-continental climate which is characterized by warm summers and cold winters. Wind directions are very variable and there are no prevailing winds from one direction over long periods of time. The sun never shines with equatorial directness and there are no large mountain ranges or large bodies of water, except Lake Superior, to affect the climate. The rainfall is fairly uniform and the average annual precipitation varies from about 20 inches in the northwestern to about 32 inches in the southeastern part. The mean annual temperature varies from 35° F. in the northeastern to 45° F. in the southeastern.

---

* Special articles on the subjects indicated by an asterisk (*) will be found at the words so marked.

### Frost in Minnesota

| Station | Date of last killing frost in the spring - Average | Date of last killing frost in the spring - Latest | Date of first killing frost in the fall - Average | Date of first killing frost in the fall - Earliest |
|---|---|---|---|---|
| Moorhead | May 10 | June 8 | Sept. 25 | Aug. 25 |
| Two Harbors | May 19 | June 17 | Sept. 27 | Sept. 7 |
| Virginia | May 29 | June 23 | Sept. 14 | Aug. 16 |
| Rochester | May 11 | May 30 | Sept. 27 | Aug. 30 |
| St. Paul | April 24 | May 23 | Oct. 8 | Sept. 18 |
| Winona | May 1 | May 25 | Oct. 5 | Sept. 10 |
| Fergus Falls | May 11 | June 6 | Sept. 24 | Sept. 6 |
| Morris | May 14 | June 7 | Sept. 27 | Sept. 5 |
| Worthington | May 10 | June 6 | Sept. 30 | Sept. 7 |

### Rainfall in Minnesota

| Station | Average precipitation in inches - Annual | Average precipitation in inches - (Approximate) During growing season |
|---|---|---|
| Moorhead | 22.87 | 12 |
| Two Harbors | 26.66 | 15 |
| Virginia | 27.59 | 14 |
| Rochester | 28.43 | 16 |
| St. Paul | 27.17 | 16 |
| Winona | 30.00 | 20 |
| Fergus Falls | 24.09 | 13 |
| Morris | 23.78 | 12 |
| Worthington | 27.43 | 15 |

The address of the Agricultural Experiment Station, which has kindly supplied this information about the state, is the Minnesota Agricultural Experiment Station, University Farm, St. Paul, Minnesota. The station is always ready to answer gardening questions.

Garden Club activities include clubs of the Garden Club of America, the home office of which is at 598 Madison Avenue, New York. There are also chapters of the Federated Garden Clubs of Minnesota, and the nearest one to your locality can be had by writing to the Garden Editor, Houghton Mifflin Company, Boston, Mass. *See also* HORTICULTURAL SOCIETIES.

**MINNIE-BUSH** = *Menziesia pilosa*.

**MINOR, -us** (my'nor). Smaller.

**MINT.** Strong-scented perennials, 25 to 30 in number, constituting the genus **Mentha** (men'tha) of the family Labiatae. They have square stems and opposite,* undivided, aromatic leaves. Flowers small, purple, pink or white, clustered in the axils* of the leaves, in terminal spikes, or in heads. The fruit is a collection of small, smooth nutlets.* Native in northern Eurasia and N.A., but several are naturalized in N.A. (*Mentha* is derived from the Greek Minthe, a nymph.)

These herbs are occasionally grown for ornament, but more frequently for their essential oils, present in all their parts. They are easily grown from seed or propagated by cuttings or by division, and they soon become established and tend to run wild.

**M. arvensis.** Corn mint; also called field mint and wild pennyroyal. A perennial herb, the stem erect, 2 ft. high and producing runners 2 ft. in length. The leaves are slightly downy, 1 to 2 in. long, rounded at the base. The flowers grow in circles in the axils* of the leaves. This species in various forms is widely distributed. Eurasia and N.A., frequently naturalized. *Var.* **piperascens**, the Japanese mint, is a larger plant, 3 ft. high, with leaves longer, 1½ to 3 in., narrowed at the base with sharp marginal teeth. The var. produces much more oil.

**M. citrata.** Bergamot mint. A smooth, perennial herb, stalk 2 ft. in length, reclining on the ground, much-branched, with underground, rooting stems. The leaves are 2 in. long, broad or narrow, with a pointed tip. The flowers are in the upper axils* of the leaves or in spikes 1 in. long. Eu., naturalized in N.A.

**M. piperita.** Peppermint; also known as brandy mint. A perennial herb 1 to 3 ft. high, characterized by its strong, pungent oil, reproducing by underground stems, or by rooting branches. Leaves about 3 in. long, narrow, with marginal teeth. Flowers purple, seldom white, in terminal spikes, nearly 3 in. long. Eu. For culture and uses *see* HERB GARDENING. Much grown commercially in Indiana (which see).

**M. pulegium.** Pennyroyal. A perennial herb with prostrate, much-branched stems. Leaves downy, round-oval, with small marginal teeth. Flowers small, bluish-lilac, in circles in the axils* of the leaves. Eurasia.

**M. requienii.** A small, creeping herb with thread-like stalks and very small, round leaves. Flowers mauve or pale purple, growing in whorls* in the leaf-axils.* The plant is peppermint-scented. Corsica. For culture *see* ROCK GARDEN.

**M. rotundifolia.** Horse mint; also known as apple mint. A downy, occasionally sticky, perennial, reproducing by leafy, underground stems. The latter are sometimes unbranched and at other times branching, and 20 to 30 in. high. Leaves oval, 1–2 in. long. Flowers purple, in dense spikes, 2–4 in. long. Eu., naturalized in N.A.

**M. spicata.** Spearmint; also known as common garden mint or green mint. A smooth herb 1–2 ft. high, perennial by underground, rooting stems. Leaves 1–2½ in. long, having marginal teeth. The flowers in interrupted* spikes, the central spike higher than the others. Eurasia, extensively naturalized in old gardens in N.A. For culture and uses *see* HERB GARDENING.

INSECT PESTS. Few insects attack mint. The most important one in the north central states is a flea beetle, the larvae of which feed on the roots in the spring, and the adults attack leaves late in the summer. Control suggestions include rotation, use of insect-free planting stock, cleanup of infested material, and the use of arsenical dust after harvest.

**MINT-BUSH.** *See* PROSTANTHERA.

**MINT FAMILY.** A very large group of plants, difficult to identify as to species, but nearly all having the family characters of aromatic herbage, opposite* leaves, and square stems. The flowers are so various that the garden genera are hard to distinguish, as they include, besides the true mint, plants like coleus, rosemary, sage, savory, basil, thyme, and the scarlet salvia. For the complete list of the hort. genera and their differences *see* LABIATAE.

**MINT GERANIUM.** The costmary. *See* CHRYSANTHEMUM BALSAMITA.

*MINUTA, -us, -um* (my-new'ta). Very small.

**MIRABILIS** (mi-ră'bil-is). Tropical American perennial herbs of the family Nyctaginaceae, one of them, the common four-o'clock, widely grown as a tender annual. Of the 12 known species only this one, and sometimes *M. longiflora*, are of garden interest. They have (in their native region) thickened or tuberous roots and opposite,* generally stalked leaves. Flowers solitary or a few from a calyx*-like involucre,* the true calyx corolla-like, tubular, and variously colored (red, yellow, or white). Petals none. Stamens* 5–6. Fruit a leathery ribbed achene.* (*Mirabilis* is from the Latin for wonderful.)

The common four-o'clock and *M. longiflora* are both easily grown as tender annuals (*see* ANNUALS), or if later bloom is desired, they can be sown where wanted. They are so popular that, especially in the four-o'clock, there are many hort. forms, such as compact, dwarf, or even variegated sorts. From Washington southward they are permanent, either as perennials or by self-sown seed.

**jalapa.** Four-o'clock; also called Marvel-of-Peru. A perennial (grown as a tender annual) 14–30 in. high, quick-growing. Leaves ovalish, smooth, the stalk about half the length of the blade. Flowers nearly 1 in. wide, the tube 1–2 in. long, usually solitary in the involucre,* red, yellow, or white. Tropical America. Aug.–Oct. Flowers open late in the afternoon.

**longiflora.** A sticky-hairy herb 2–3 ft. high, the leaves more or less heart-shaped. Flowers 3 or more in the involucre, fragrant, the tube nearly 5 in. long and white, the expanded limb often rose or violet. Mex. Flowers open after sundown. If desired, the roots of this may be dug in the fall, stored, and planted again in the spring. It is not hardy in the North.

**MIRLITON** = *Sechium edule*.

**MISCANTHUS** (mis-kan'thus). A genus containing about 6 tall, perennial grasses, of the Old World, grown for their decorative effect on the lawn or in the border. The species most commonly grown is **M. sinensis**, usually called *Eulalia*. The leaves are grass-like, 1 in. wide and 2–3 ft. long, with a prominent, whitish, central line, usually growing in heavy clumps. Flowers in beautiful, feathery, compound, terminal clusters (panicles*), 2 ft. in length, the whole plant 4 to 10 ft. high. China and Japan, and an occasional escape* in N.A. *Var.* **variegatus** has leaves striped white or yellowish; *var.* **zebrinus**, the zebra-grass, has banded leaves. (*Miscanthus* is from the Greek for a stem and flower, in allusion to the stalked spikelets.)

**MISSISSIPPI.** The state lies wholly in zones* 5, 6, and 7. The soils of Mississippi can be divided into 10 more or less

---

* Special articles on the subjects indicated by an asterisk (*) will be found at the words so marked.

distinct areas. These are the Delta, Loess,* Gulf Coast, Longleaf Pine, Central Prairie, Shortleaf Pine, Flat Woods, Pontotoc Ridge, Northeast Prairie, and Northeast Highlands.

The Delta area lies between the Mississippi and Yazoo rivers, and is characterized by a relatively flat topography and fertile, alluvial loam and clay loam soils. The Loess* area is a belt 30 to 40 miles wide on the eastern border of the Delta area. The soils are yellow to dark brown, fine-textured and moderately fertile silt loams. The Gulf Coast area is a strip 15 to 20 miles wide on the coast. It consists mostly of level areas of fine silt loam, generally low in organic matter.

The Longleaf Pine area occupies a major portion of the southern part of the state. It is gently rolling and consists of gray, brown and yellow sandy loams, which are open textured, well drained and low in organic matter. They are generally adapted to the growing of horticultural crops when well fertilized.

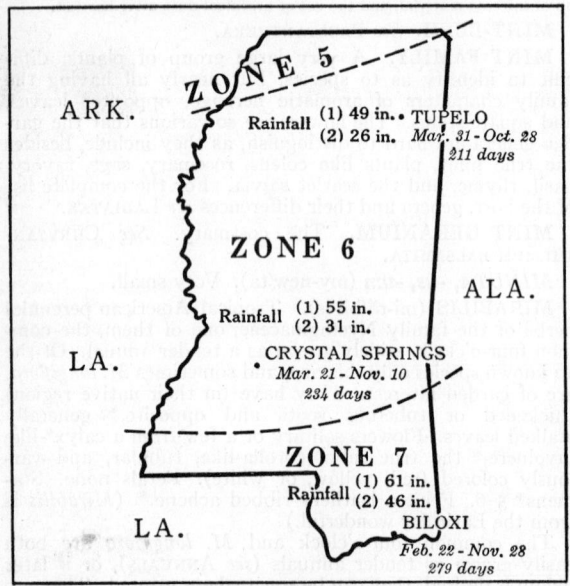

MISSISSIPPI

The zones of hardiness crossing Mississippi are those shown on the colored map at ZONE, which should be consulted for details. The dates are the average latest killing frost in spring and the first one in the fall. The figures below the dates show the length of the growing season. Rainfall figures (in inches) show (1) the total annual rainfall and (2) the amount falling in the growing season at the places indicated.

The Central Prairie is a narrow belt of clay loam soils about 20 miles wide on the northern border of the Longleaf Pine area. The Shortleaf Pine area, of sandy loam soils, lies north of the Central Prairie and east of the Loess area. Rather high ridges between the streams are characteristic features.

The Flat Woods, Pontotoc Ridge, Northeast Prairie and Northeast Highlands are narrow strips extending north to south and situated in the northeastern portion of the state. The Flat Woods area is mostly flat. The Pontotoc Ridge consists of a series of ridges which form the divide between the Tombigbee and Mississippi rivers' drainage systems. The Northeast Prairie is gently rolling to undulating and the Northeast Highlands is comparatively hilly and rugged. These soils are sandy loams and clay loams.

The principal garden-crop areas are as follows: The tomato and cabbage trucking area in the vicinity of Hazlehurst and Crystal Springs and the watermelon section in the vicinity of Water Valley and Coffeeville.

In the Hazlehurst-Crystal Springs section, about 10,000 acres of tomatoes, 4000 acres of cabbage, 2000 acres of peas and 1300 acres of string beans are grown. In the Water Valley section, about 2000 acres are used for the production of watermelons.

String beans (about 6000 acres) are grown for early market throughout the southern portion of the state. Irish potatoes (9000 acres) are grown for early market, and sweet potatoes (about 70,000 acres) are grown for late market and home consumption. The Irish and sweet potato acreage is distributed quite generally throughout the state.

The following fruits are grown throughout Mississippi for home use and local markets, with no large commercial districts: peaches, plums, pears, bunch grapes, muscadine grapes, blackberries, and dewberries.

Apples are best adapted to northeast Mississippi, but are grown throughout the north half of the state for home use and local markets. Figs are planted for home use and to a limited extent for local markets throughout the south half of the state, and sparingly in north Mississippi.

Plantings of named varieties of pecans are most extensive in the coast counties and adjoining counties. Native trees have been top-worked to named varieties throughout the state, especially in the vicinity of Natchez. See PECAN.

Strawberries are widely grown, with commercial production centering around Sanford in south Mississippi, Marion in the central area, and Shannon and Amory in the northeast.

The satsuma orange is grown in the Coast area. The largest planting — about 9000 acres — centers around Picayune and Carriere.

There are approximately 25,000 acres of tung-oil trees in the Coast area; mostly in Pearl River County, and set out largely during the past five years.

Outstanding native trees are the longleaf pine, live oak, magnolia, sweet gum, black gum, elm, hackberry, pecan, shell-bark hickory, bald cypress, and holly. Ornamental small trees include redbud, dogwood, yaupon, deciduous holly, and fringe-tree. Many species of shrubs and wild flowers are common, such as: wild azalea, callicarpa, iris, ageratum, perennial asters, and violets.

CLIMATE

| Part of state | Town | Ave. date of last killing frost in spring | Latest-known killing frost | Ave. date of earliest killing frost in fall | Earliest-known killing frost |
|---|---|---|---|---|---|
| North | Tupelo | March 31 | April 17 | Oct. 28 | Oct. 11 |
| Central | Crystal Springs | March 21 | April 25 | Nov. 10 | Oct. 21 |
| South | Biloxi | Feb. 22 | March 26 | Nov. 28 | Oct. 30 |

The average annual rainfall is 61.02 inches at Biloxi; 55.21 at Crystal Springs; and 49.93 at Tupelo. During the growing season the rainfall at Biloxi ranges from 2.93 to 6.8 per month with a total of 46.58; at Crystal Springs from 3.11 to 5.81 with a total of 31.30; and at Tupelo from 2.59 to 4.44 with a total of 26.20. In spite of these apparently large amounts of rainfall, drouths may occur at any time during the growing season, due to the fact that the rainfall for an entire month may fall in one or two rains.

The address of the Agricultural Experiment Station which has kindly supplied this information about the state is State College, Mississippi. The station is always ready to answer gardening questions.

Garden Club activities include over 30 clubs affiliated with the Garden Club of Mississippi. For the one nearest your locality write the Garden Editor, Houghton Mifflin Company, Boston, Mass.

**MISSISSIPPIENSIS, -e** (mis-sis-sip-pĭ-en′sis). From the state of Mississippi, or from the Mississippi River region.

**MISSOURI.** The state lies wholly in zones* 3 and 4 and is located near the center of the United States. It includes an area of 68,727 square miles, or 43,985,280 acres. Most of the unimproved land is found in the southern Ozark region and the southeastern lowlands.

SOILS. For soil varieties, few states are comparable to Missouri, which is often called the meeting ground of all the important soil regions of the Mississippi Valley. Its extensive glacial and loessial soils in the northern counties

* Special articles on the subjects indicated by an asterisk (*) will be found at the words so marked.

are much like those of the Great Plains and the regions to the north. Limestone soils of the Ozarks are closely related to those of similar origin in Arkansas, Kentucky, and Tennessee. The southeastern lowlands represent the northern extension of the great alluvial soil belt along the Mississippi River from Cape Girardeau to the Gulf.

The loess* soil along the Missouri and Mississippi rivers is generally considered very desirable for the growing of fruits and vegetables. It is distinctive for its depth, mellowness, fertility, and silty nature, while the subsoil is characterized as a silty clay, open, friable, and very deep. Its texture readily frees it from excessive moisture and yet retains enough to successfully produce horticultural crops.

CHIEF GARDENING CENTERS. Practically all of the common vegetables and truck crops may reach their highest development in Missouri. The geographical position makes it possible to grow varieties of both the South and the Far North. Because of the great diversity of soils, an opportunity is given producers to choose those best adapted to their particular needs and requirements. The growing of these crops on a commercial scale is mainly confined to the areas near the larger cities. This is especially true for St. Louis and Kansas City, while St. Joseph, Springfield, Joplin, Hannibal, and other cities have extensive garden areas located near by.

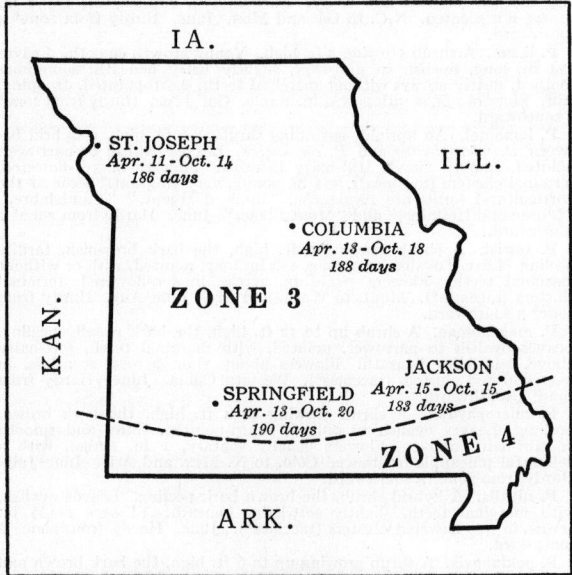

MISSOURI

The zones of hardiness crossing Missouri are those shown on the colored map at ZONE, which should be consulted for details. The dates are the average latest killing frost in spring and the first one in the fall. The figures below the dates show the average length of the growing season.

Recently, due to favorable soils, climate, and transportation facilities, large areas of southeast Missouri have been devoted to garden and truck crops. Watermelons attain their best growth here, as they do in other bottom or alluvial soil, and thus cause the state's production to rank among the first in the Union. Sweet potatoes are another important crop, and early Irish potatoes are being grown more extensively as a cash crop. In fact, this region is often called the garden section of the state.

The Orrick district in Ray County, near Kansas City, is synonymous with early Irish potato production. The crop has been grown extensively and profitably for more than a score of years. Consequently, other counties having similar soil types and climatic conditions are large producers. These are Jackson, Clay, Carroll, St. Louis and others.

The Sarcoxie district in southwest Missouri specializes in peony culture. While the flower growing here dates back more than half a century, it has reached commercial proportions only within the last fifteen to twenty years. Originally peonies were grown only for the sale of roots, but now, with better culture and pre-cooling methods, thousands of buds are shipped annually to distant markets throughout the United States.

Horticultural crops of all kinds produce millions of dollars of wealth each year. Missouri apples rank high for their fine flavor and quality and easily merit the compliments paid them and the efforts made to secure greater consumption. The many different fertile and adaptable soil types have extended their production and cause them and other fruits common to the central states area to be profitable in each of the 114 counties.

Commercial apple production in the Ozark region of southwest Missouri centers near Marionville in Lawrence County. In addition to Lawrence, other leading counties are Green, Newton, Barry, Jasper, McDonald and Webster. Another extensive apple-growing district extends along the Mississippi River from Cape Girardeau to Hannibal, and along the Missouri River from St. Louis to St. Joseph. This area includes the famous loess region, and some of the counties leading in production are Buchanan, Jackson, Lafayette, Pike, Marion, Jackson, Howard, Lincoln, and Cooper.

Grape culture in the Missouri and Mississippi river regions is assuming a commercial status, while the group of counties in southwest Missouri listed for apple production are also important grape-producing areas. Small fruits, particularly strawberries, blackberries, and dewberries, are grown profitably here. Missouri strawberries are known everywhere and the chief producing center is Monett. In this same region, tomato and sweet potato growing is extensive, having developed into an important source of income for the producers. Peaches also constitute one of the most valuable crops of the south central and southeastern areas and along the Mississippi River as far north as St. Louis County.

CLIMATE. A mean temperature in winter of 33° and in summer of 75° makes it safe to grow many varieties of the different horticultural crops. The rainfall averages 40 inches per year and is therefore sufficient for the highest development of fruits and vegetables. Also, about half of this, or over 16 inches, occurs in the spring and summer, from March through June, the season when it is most needed.

The wide range of latitude, extending from approximately 37 to 41 degrees, makes it possible to grow successfully ornamental trees, shrubs, and flowers of the Far North and South. Furthermore, with altitudes ranging from 229 feet in extreme southeast to 1625 feet in the Ozarks of the southwest, ideal locations may be found for practically all species common to the temperate zone. Significant frost information and dates for four different parts of the state which are very representative follow:

| City | Average date of last killing frost in spring | Latest-known killing frost | Average date of earliest killing frost in fall | Earliest-known killing frost |
|---|---|---|---|---|
| Springfield | April 13 | May 19 | Oct. 20 | Sept. 21 |
| Columbia | April 13 | May 9 | Oct. 18 | Sept. 18 |
| Jackson | April 15 | May 14 | Oct. 15 | Sept. 13 |
| St. Joseph | April 11 | April 28 | Oct. 14 | Sept. 26 |

The address of the Agricultural Experiment Station which has kindly supplied this information about the state is Mumford Hall, Columbia, Missouri. The station is always ready to answer gardening questions.

At St. Louis is the Missouri Botanical Garden, the oldest and one of the most important of the gardens in this country. Founded by Henry Shaw in 1860, it contains remarkable collections of plants of interest to any gardener. See BOTANIC GARDEN.

**MISSOURI BOTANICAL GARDEN.** See BOTANIC GARDEN.

---

* Special articles on the subjects indicated by an asterisk (*) will be found at the words so marked.

*MISSOURIENSIS*, *-e* (miz-zur-i-en'sis). From Missouri.

**MISSOURI GOURD** = *Cucurbita foetidissima.*

**MISSOURI PRIMROSE** = *Oenothera missouriensis. See* EVENING PRIMROSE.

**MIST** = *Gypsophila paniculata.*

**MIST-FLOWER** = *Eupatorium coelestinum.*

**MISTLETOE.** This is not a garden plant and cannot be cultivated, as it is a parasite* on trees, in America, usually upon oaks. The common mistletoe of the eastern U.S. is *Phoradendron flavescens*, found from N.J. to the Gulf. In the West other species, and even genera, furnish mistletoe, but none can be cultivated. The mistletoe of history and legend is *Viscum album*, an Old World parasite unknown in America.

**MISTLETOE CACTUS** = *Rhipsalis cassytha.*

**MITCHELLA** (mit-chel'la). A single species of evergreen, rather woody, prostrate herbs of the family Rubiaceae, found in woods over most of the eastern half of N.A. The only species, **M. repens,** the partridge-berry, also called twinberry, squawberry, and teaberry, is a wild garden plant for shady places and good, rich, woods soil, not especially acid. It has slender stems, not usually over 15 in. long, rooting easily at the joints and making flat patches. Leaves opposite,* nearly round, about ¾ in. wide, green, but sometimes with white lines. Flowers borne in united pairs, at the end of a short stalk. Corolla funnel-shaped, white, about ½ in. long. Fruit a showy, scarlet, berry-like drupe,* usually with 8 nutlets. It is one of the best plants for a winter terrarium, and is often used for a centerpiece decoration, but it does better under a glass, as it does not like the heat and dryness of a room. (Named for John Mitchell, a Virginia botanist.) *See* WILD GARDEN.

**MITELLA** (my-tell'a). A small genus of North American and Asiatic, delicate, perennial, woodland herbs of the family Saxifragaceae, usually having alternate* leaves. **M. diphylla,** commonly called mitrewort, bishop's-cap, or fairy-cap, grows about 1½ ft. high. Leaves stalkless, heart-shaped, with marginal teeth, growing in pairs. Flowers small, white, in a terminal cluster 6–8 inches long, the petals deeply cut. Fruit a pod, soon widely splitting. Quebec to N. Car. and Mo. Excellent in the shaded rock garden or in the wild garden. (*Mitella* is the diminutive of *mitra*, a cap, in allusion to the shape of the fruit.)

**MITES.** *See* Insect Pests at BLACKBERRY, CHERRY, DATE, FIG, CYCLAMEN, BOX, and HAZEL.

*MITIS*, *-e* (my'tis). Mild or gentle.

**MITRA** = *Astrophytum myriostigma.*

**MITREWORT** = *Mitella diphylla.* For false mitrewort *see* TIARELLA.

**MIXED BORDER.** *See* BORDER.

**MIXTURE OF SOILS.** *See* POTTING MIXTURES.

**M'MAHON, B.** *See* America at GARDEN BOOKS.

**MOCCASIN FLOWER** = *Cypripedium acaule.*

**MOCK CUCUMBER** = *Echinocystis lobata.*

**MOCK-ORANGE.** A genus of North American and Eurasian deciduous shrubs, mostly erect, but with curved or drooping branches, of the family Saxifragaceae, known as **Philadelphus** (fil-a-del'fus) and comprising about 40 species, having solid white pith, and close or flaky bark. Leaves opposite,* with or without marginal teeth. Flowers white, rarely purple near the base, solitary or in small clusters, often fragrant. Sepals and petals 4. Stamens* numerous. Fruit a capsule* with numerous small seeds. They are variously known as mock-orange or sweet syringa. Mock-orange is also applied to *Laurocerasus carolinianum.* (*Philadelphus* is the name given by Linnaeus, from King Ptolemy Philadelphus, 3d century B.C.)

These shrubs and their numerous hybrids are widely planted in the shrubbery border. They bloom in late spring and are very showy. Pruning should be done immediately after blossoming, for they flower from wood of the previous year. They are propagated from cuttings, seeds, layers, and suckers. Cuttings are usually made from mature wood, but softwood cuttings may be started in frames in summer.

**P. brachybotrys** = *Philadelphus pekinensis brachybotrys.*

**P. coronarius.** Common mock-orange; also known as sweet mock-orange; or false syringa. A shrub to 10 ft. high. Bark dark brown and peeling off on last year's growth. Leaves ovalish to oblong, pointed, 1½–4 in. long. Flowers creamy-white, very fragrant, in 5–7-flowered, terminal clusters (racemes*). Eu., southwest As. *Var.* **aureus** has leaves bright yellow when young, later greenish-yellow. *Var.* **dianthiflorus** and *var.* **floro-pleno** have double flowers. June. Hardy from zone* 2 southward.

**P. falconeri.** A shrub to 8 ft. high. Leaves ovalish to narrower, 2–3 in. long, slightly hairy on veins beneath, those on young shoots broadly oval and toothed. Flowers 3–7 on slender, smooth stalks or in 7-flowered, flat-topped terminal clusters 1½ in. across, pure white and fragrant. Possibly a hybrid between *P. coronarius* and *P. laxus.* Hardy from zone* 3 southward.

**P. gordonianus.** A shrub 9–12 ft. high. Bark yellowish-gray, not peeling off. Leaves ovalish to oblong, pointed, coarsely toothed, soft-hairy beneath. Flowers 1½–2 in. across, fragrant in 7–9, rarely 11-flowered clusters (racemes*). British Columbia to northern Calif. June–July. Hardy from zone* 4 southward.

**P. inodorus.** A handsome, upright shrub, with arching branches and peeling bark. Leaves ovalish to broader, 3–5 in. long, pointed, occasionally toothed, smooth and shiny. Flowers 1–3, cup-shaped, 1½–2 in. across, not scented. N.C. to Ga. and Miss. June. Hardy from zone* 4 southward.

**P. laxus.** A shrub growing 4 ft. high. Young growth smooth. Leaves 2–3 in. long, ovalish to narrower, slightly hairy beneath, sometimes toothed, nearly always without marginal teeth, sharp-pointed, drooping, stiff. Flowers 1–3, scentless, 1½ in. across. Ga. June. Hardy from zone* 5 southward.

**P. lemoinei.** An upright, spreading shrub, 4–6 ft. high, a hybrid between *P. microphyllus* and *P. coronarius.* Leaves ovalish to narrower, pointed, smooth above, stiff-hairy beneath. Flowers in 3–7-flowered, terminal clusters (racemes*), 1½ in. across, very fragrant. Some of the horticultural forms are Avalanche, "Boule d'Argent," "Candelabre," "Manteau d'Hermine," and "Mont Blanc." June. Hardy from zone* 2 southward.

**P. lewisi.** A shrub growing 6 ft. high, the bark brownish, tardily peeling. Leaves ovalish to oblong, 1–3 in. long, pointed, with or without marginal teeth. Flowers 1–1½ in. across, in 5–9-flowered, terminal clusters (racemes*). Mont. to Wash. and Ore. June–Aug. Hardy from zone* 3 southward.

**P. magdalenae.** A shrub up to 12 ft. high, the bark usually peeling. Leaves ovalish to narrower, pointed, with marginal teeth, soft-hairy above, stiff-hairy beneath. Flowers about 1 in. across, scentless, in 7–11-flowered clusters (racemes*). Western China. June. Hardy from zone* 3 southward.

**P. microphyllus.** A shrub growing to 4 ft. high, the bark brown, peeling. Leaves ovalish to oblong, sharp-pointed, shiny and smooth or stiff-hairy above. Flowers usually solitary, 1 in. across, with a delightful pineapple fragrance. Colo. to N. Mex. and Ariz. June–July. Hardy from zone* 4 southward.

**P. nivalis.** A hybrid shrub, the brown bark peeling. Leaves ovalish, with marginal teeth, slightly soft-hairy beneath. Flowers 1–1½ in. across, in 5–9-flowered clusters (racemes*). June. Hardy from zone* 2 southward.

**P. pekinensis.** A shrub growing up to 6 ft. high, the bark brown and peeling. Leaves oblong or ovalish, smooth except beneath, stalks purplish. Flowers 1–1½ in. across, creamy, fragrant, in 5–9-flowered clusters (racemes*). North China to Korea. *Var.* **brachybotrys** has grayish-brown bark, not readily peeling. Leaves usually sparingly stiff-hairy on both sides, stalks green. Flowers in a 5-flowered, short, thick cluster (racemes*). June. Hardy from zone* 3 southward.

**P. virginalis.** Probably a hybrid between *P. lemoinei* and a variety of *P. nivalis.* Bark brown and peeling or gray-brown and slightly peeling. Leaves ovalish, 2½–3 in. long, slightly toothed, soft-hairy beneath. Flowers semi-double or double, in 3–7-flowered clusters (racemes*). Useful for forcing (which see). Some horticultural forms are "Argentine," "Glacier," and "Virginal."

**P. zeyheri.** A spreading shrub up to 6 ft. high, the bark brown, and peeling. Leaves ovalish, 3½–4 in. long, tapering-pointed, slightly toothed or not, smooth except on veins beneath. Flowers 1½–2 in. across, in 3–5-flowered clusters. Of hybrid origin. June. Hardy from zone* 3 southward.

**MOCK STRAWBERRY** = *Duchesnea indica.*

**MODEL GARDENS.** For flower-show exhibits and sometimes in the development of an extensive estate, it is often desirable to make a model of the property, showing grading, buildings, planting, and lawn. Such models are far easier to understand than an architect's drawing or specifications, and they can be made most attractive if carefully done to scale and colored in harmony with the finished design.

* Special articles on the subjects indicated by an asterisk (*) will be found at the words so marked.

Because they are gardens in miniature, with no living material in them, various substitutes for trees, shrubs, lawns, etc., have been devised, the handling and placing of which in the model require considerable skill and knowledge.

The foundation must come first and it should be of plasteline or it can be of newspapers boiled to a pulp, to which flour paste or glue is added. While still workable, either of these materials can be moulded to any desired topography, but before they "set," trees, shrubs, or models of buildings must be placed, because after the foundation becomes hard it is difficult to add such features.

Coloring material for tinting soil, plants, stones, buildings, etc., may be ordinary house paint, pastel crayons, Tintex, or aniline dyes. If shiny effects are needed, use enamel paints, or, for dull finish, add turpentine to paints.

To make grass, use freshly mixed plasteline stippled with a stiff-bristled brush, and then colored. Or grass may be made with terry cloth, ratiné, or bath-towel material.

For making paths, green sawdust, sandpaper, Wheatena, Cream of Wheat, or roofing paper, all appropriately colored, will simulate gravel, sand, or paved walks. For walls, use bits of painted laths, cartons, or cardboard.

In making miniature hedges or formal, clipped evergreen plantings like box, use rubber sponge, ordinary sponge, or fine baby sponge, cut and colored in accordance with your plan. Use aniline dyes for ordinary sponge and a water paint for rubber sponge. For low, evergreen edging, use pussy-willow catkins dyed with Tintex.

The most difficult operation is making shrubs and trees that look effective in the model. The trunk and main branches should be dried twigs, roots upside-down (for the crown), broom bristles, twisted wire (usually covered with tire tape, linen, etc.) or pipe-cleaners. This framework must all be shellacked and twisted into shape before any "foliage" is added. Just before the shellac is put on, mineral wool, Brillo, lamb's wool or similar material should be drawn through the shrub or tree to make a base upon which the "foliage" is put. The latter consists of feathery bits of moss, cut-up bits of cotton or linen, raffia, velvet, dyed cereal grits, sawdust, sponge, feathers, or tiny segments of fern fronds, depending on what the nature of the tree may be. Sometimes a whole "tree" can be made from one dried plant or part of it, as an elm tree from goldenrod, or a spruce from ground pine (see LYCOPODIUM).

For flowers it is usually best to use those described at DRIED FLOWERS, coloring them to suit your composition.

To simulate water, use sheets of cellophane or some clear celluloid substitute. Pools can be made by letting into the ground shallow trays covered with cellophane. For foam use shaving soap, and for a meandering stream use silver paper.

Miniature ornaments can be made from clay, pencil erasers, soap, or even from bread, all colored to your design. Buildings, steps, and other architectural features can be cut from soap, made of cardboard, or of plaster mixed with cotton batting held together with glue. Often kindergarten toys or the ten cent store will provide many useful accessories.

Model gardens cannot, of course, be made without a good deal of deftness and skill. In addition to the items already mentioned, the following equipment will be found useful: fine brads, sharp knives and scissors, rubber gloves (for aniline dyes), orange sticks, tweezers or forceps, toothpicks, green thread, putty, clay, upholstery needles, and liquid glue.

When made, the models are very fragile and must be packed with the greatest care if it is necessary to ship them. The foundation should be screwed to the bottom of a tight box and all possibly loose structures (fences, buildings, etc.) held in place by tire tape.

**MODERN GARDEN DESIGN.** Tendencies toward the future are very apparent in modern garden design. It is undergoing the changed attitude toward nature that is manifested one way or another in all the philosophy and effort of civilization. Throughout the childhood of mankind, nature was the enemy, and was hated and feared. This was evident in thought and art until well into the 18th century, and relics persisted in aesthetics until Ruskin finally bottled and labeled them "sublime," "mysterious" and "supernatural."

We no longer fear nature in her normal moods. The completed change of feeling is obvious today, when we check rivers in sublime mountain gorges to make a garden in the desert, and harness the mysterious tides to light a farmhouse. Nature, to the average man, now means little more than a farm, a garden or a picnic ground.

Gardening for many centuries was concerned with the attempt of man to control nature in his immediate environment, and shut out all that he could not discipline. In his irregularly disposed chaos, the obvious order was symmetrical balance on axis and cross-axis. This principle of design is static and had largely two-dimensional results, notwithstanding the classic French law that a garden must have a floor of water or of earth, walls of marble or verdure, and ceiling of sky.

When dread evaporated, it was discovered that nature was beautiful. The landscape-gardening school arose in 18th-century England, with a violent reaction against symmetrical axial balance and rigid architectural embellishment. Occult balance and irregular distribution of meadows, streams and vegetation in the manner of a pleasantly composed country park became the fashion and has many adherents today. The two schools quarreled, and until recently the only compromise was to formalize the ground immediately about the dwelling and thence to modulate, as well as might be, into irregular natural scenes in the distance.

A modernistic terrace garden on two levels at Neuilly, France. Plants are subordinated to the texture and color of floor materials and to furniture.

The modern garden designer sweeps aside both schools and their compromise as unnecessary limitations. He fuses the two and goes beyond either. He is more abstract in his conceptions. He designs in volumes rather than surfaces. He studies with far more care than was used in the past not only sizes and proportions of his foliage and architectural masses, but also the shape of the air spaces between them. This has led him to experiment with vertical planes, sinking, raising and sloping garden floors and walls till they are almost indistinguishable. To emphasize the sense of definite volume, he pushes ceilings out from walls or carries the garden in under buildings. The garden pattern more and more includes the house, covering terraces on different floors and finally the roof itself.

He is interested in color, size and texture of both archi-

---

* Special articles on the subjects indicated by an asterisk (*) will be found at the words so marked.

tectural and plant material, more as part of the garden structure than for their intrinsic beauty or apparent fitness. Some colors approach, others recede from the eye. This means more to him than harmonious combinations, though pleasure in color also has its place.

In this connection it must be remembered, however, that most of the experimenting along new lines has been done by Frenchmen or by designers influenced by the French school. In France interest in the usefulness of plants has always seemed to outweigh love of pure horticulture. So it is natural that, in the new work, the French point of view with regard to the placing and importance of flowers remains as of old. When the new design grows common in America, it is inevitable that the difference, if not greater interest, in plants and flowers here, will mean quite a different racial use.

The modern designer of gardens is no longer satisfied with strictly static axial balance, nor with the more lively but limited picturesqueness of park-like, "natural" compositions. He groups so-called "formal" or architectural planes and masses with subtle irregularity around an axis that skips, turns and is sometimes lost. He grades land in frankly sculptural rather than natural forms. Does he not practice an art? Why should he shut his eyes to the possibility of sculpture on a grand scale as is intimated by the chance beauties of engineering?

One element in the making of gardens is altogether new in our own day. Electric illumination belongs uniquely to our own time and to the future. Its possibilities in garden design are scarcely yet conceived. We only know that light can be used in intricate design that is beautiful in itself; and it can be used to illuminate other objects, bringing out new and unexpected beauties. It can also, by emphasis or neglect, quite alter the sizes, shapes and proportions of things at night from what is apparent by daylight. Modern garden designers have begun to work with electricity and marked development is now under way. In light we have the excitement of anticipation. *See* LIGHTING.

Aesthetics aside, there is a marked tendency toward the creation of small places, intensively developed. The cost and bother of maintaining a large country estate is discouraging. Farm, stables and some sports excepted, there is nothing in the way of home comforts and gardens that cannot be provided on a place of five acres or even considerably less. The constant improvement in mechanical devices which simplify maintenance can easily be installed on a small place. So instead of the great houses and expanses of open land that were formerly the hope of the ambitious, one begins to find small houses with grounds in proportion, designed to take advantage of every minor possibility that art or comfort can suggest. Obviously the small garden, constantly observed and criticized, must approach perfection in proportion, scale and detail. There is a growing demand for such gardens, which tax the ingenuity and imagination of designers.

All experience is grist for the artist's mill, and the garden designer who expresses the time in which he lives will not turn away from anything modern, even though it be ugly or unpleasant. It is his job to find everywhere the inspiration with which he proceeds to create beauty. — F. S.

**MOHAWKWEED** = *Uvularia perfoliata*.

**MOHRODENDRON** = *Halesia*.

**MOISTURE.** *See* SOIL MOISTURE.

**MOLD.** *See* SOILS. *See also* Fungi at PLANT DISEASES.

**MOLDAVICA**, *-us*, *-um* (mol-dā'vi-ka). From Moldavia, now part of Rumania. *See* DRACOCEPHALUM for a plant so named.

**MOLES.** *See* ANIMAL INJURY.

**MOLINIA** (mo-lin'ĭ-a). A small genus of rather unimportant, tufted, perennial, Eurasian grasses, one of them, **M. coerulea**, occasionally planted for ornament. It is a stiff, smooth grass, 3–5 ft. high, with somewhat stiff, grass-like leaves 6–12 in. long. Flowering cluster (panicle\*) 7–15 in. long, its branches mostly erect, bearing the 2–4-flowered, sharp-pointed, greenish or purplish spikelets which are without awns.\* Eu., but naturalized in the U.S., and sometimes known as *Aira coerulea*. It is of simple culture in any soil. A lower, variegated-leaved form is sometimes used for edging. (Named for J. Molina, Chilean botanist.)

**MOLLEOIDES** (mol-lee-oy'deez, but *see* OÏDES). Like something softly hairy.

**MOLLIS**, *-e* (mol'lis). Softly hairy.

**MOLLISSIMA**, *-us*, *-um* (mol-liss'i-ma). Very softly hairy.

**MOLLUGO** (mol-lew'go). A specific name derived from the genus *Mollugo*, which is of no garden interest.

**MOLTKIA** (molt'kĭ-a). A genus of Eurasian, hairy, perennial herbs of the family Boraginaceae, containing about 6 species, 2 or more of which are used as alpines in the rock garden. It is closely allied to *Lithospermum* and often listed under that name. Leaves alternate,\* undivided, hairy or downy. Flowers blue or yellow, somewhat funnel-shaped, the stamens\* protruding, usually growing in terminal or flat-topped clusters (racemes\* or cymes\*). Fruit a collection of small nutlets. (Named for Count Joachim Gadske Moltke, Denmark.)

graminifolia = *Moltkia suffruticosa*.
petraea. A somewhat woody, perennial herb, growing 6 to 12 in. high. Leaves 1½ in. long, very narrow, covered with a thick, white down. Flowers deep violet-blue, ½ in. long, generally in flat-topped clusters. Eu. Also known as *Lithospermum petraeum*.
suffruticosa. A somewhat woody perennial growing 1½ ft. high. Leaves very narrow, covered with white down beneath. Flowers purple-blue, ½ in. long. Italy. Also known as *Lithospermum graminifolium*.

**MOLUCCA BALM** = *Molucella laevis*.

**MOLUCELLA** (mol-lew-sell'a). Two species of aromatic, Old World, annual herbs of the mint family, both found in old-fashioned gardens, but not widely cult. They have opposite,\* stalked, generally toothed leaves. Flowers very small, in whorls\* in the leaf-axils,\* the tiny, irregular, white or pinkish corolla scarcely or not at all exceeding the bristly or prickly calyx.\* Fruit a collection of 4 nutlets, nestled in the shell-like, persistent calyx\* in the first species. (*Molucella* is a diminutive of *Molucca*, but neither plant is known from this East Indian island.)

Both species are best grown as tender annuals (*see* ANNUALS) and are of easy culture.

laevis. Molucca balm; also called shell-flower. A simple\* or branching herb 2–3 ft. high. Leaves roundish or heart-shaped, ¾–1½ in. long. Flowers fragrant, very numerous, the calyx with 5 small prickles, but expanding in fruit and the nutlets nestled in it; hence the name shell-flower. Western As.
spinosa. An annual (or perhaps a biennial) 5–7 ft. high, the stems brownish-red. Leaves ovalish, deeply cut or toothed. Calyx with 8 long prickles or spines. Southern Eu. and Syria.

**MOLY** (mō'lee). An ancient name for some reputedly medicinal plant of great value. *See* ALLIUM.

**MOMBIN** (mom'bin). Tropical American native name for *Spondias mombin*.

**MOMIJI.** A maple tree. *See* Trees at JAPANESE GARDEN.

**MOMORDICA** (mo-more'di-ka). A genus of over 40 species of tropical Asian or African, tendril\*-bearing vines of the cucumber family, two of them grown for ornament mostly in warm regions. Both are annuals of quick growth. Leaves alternate,\* compound\* or deeply divided. Male and female flowers separate, sometimes on different plants or on the same one, both solitary (in ours), yellow or white, stalked, the stalk bearing a prominent bract.\* Corolla bell-shaped or more open, parted nearly to the base. Fruit oblongish or globe-shaped, tardily splitting, the seeds with a showy aril\* (in some). (*Momordica* is from the Latin to bite, in allusion to the jagged seeds of some species.)

Being tropical vines they are best treated, in the North, as tender annuals (*see* ANNUALS). In the South they make quick growth and will soon cover a porch or screen. The second species is very handsome in fruit.

---

\* Special articles on the subjects indicated by an asterisk (\*) will be found at the words so marked.

**balsamina.** Balsam apple. A high-climbing, herbaceous vine, the tendrils* unbranched. Leaves 2–4 in. wide, 3–5-lobed, the lobes pointed. Flowers yellow, the center darker, about 1 in. wide in the male flowers, smaller in the female. Fruit egg-shaped, about 2 in. long, slightly warty, orange, its seeds flat, gray or brown, usually scalloped on the edges. Old World tropics.

**charantia.** Balsam pear. A taller-growing vine than *M. balsamina* and with larger, more deeply lobed leaves. Flowers very similar, but the bract* on the flower stalk without teeth. Fruit oblongish or oval, 4–8 in. long, more warty than in the balsam apple, orange-yellow, when split showing the bright scarlet arils* of its seeds. Old World tropics.

**MONACILLO** = *Malvaviscus arboreus*.

**MONADELPHOUS.** Having the stamens* united by their filaments* into a single group, as in many plants of the pea family. See LEGUMINOSAE.

**MONANDRA, -us, -um** (mo-nan'dra). Having one stamen.*

**MONANTHES** (mo-nan'theez). A genus of the Crassulaceae containing about 10 fleshy, small, perennial, tufted herbs, usually glandular*-hairy. Leaves opposite* or alternate,* nearly always in rosettes. Flowers usually solitary, or in terminal clusters (raceme*) or in flat-topped clusters (cymes*). Petals 6 to 12, with petal-like scales. The species most commonly grown, **M. atlantica**, is a native of the Canary Islands and Morocco. The branches are 1 to 3 in. long, lying on the ground and bearing at the ends rosettes of 20 or more fleshy leaves, each about ⅙ of an inch in length. Flowers golden-yellow, spotted with red on the back, growing on stalks from the ends of the branches. For culture see SUCCULENTS. (*Monanthes* is from the Greek for solitary and flower, in allusion to the often solitary flower.)

**MONARDA** (mo-nar'da). A North American genus of the mint family including 12 to 18 species of annual or perennial aromatic herbs, some of which are grown for their showy flowers. Leaves opposite* and with marginal teeth. Flowers rather large, white, red, purplish, yellow or mottled, 2-lipped,* often with showy, colored bracts* beneath the flower clusters, which are terminal or in the leaf-axils.* They are known as horse mint and bergamot. (Named for Nicolas Monardes, a Spanish botanist and physician.)

The monardas are rather coarse plants, but often very brilliant in color. Those of striking color should be grown in masses along the banks of a stream or in a corner of the woods. They are easily cult., growing readily in any good soil. They spread quickly and should be divided often, spring division being much more successful than fall, as the fall-divided clumps often winter-kill.

**citriodora.** Lemon mint. An annual herb growing about 1 ft. high. Leaves oblong or narrower, with small marginal teeth. Flowers white or pinkish, not spotted, growing in heads from the axils* of the leaves, or at intervals on a spike. Whole plant delightfully lemon-scented. Ill. to Neb. and Tex.

**didyma.** Bee-balm; also called Oswego tea or red balm. A perennial herb, somewhat hairy, with a sharply 4-angled stem, growing 3 ft. high. Leaves 3 to 6 in. long, slightly longer than oval, pointed. Flowers scarlet, nearly 2 in. long, in terminal clusters, surrounded with red-tinged bracts.* Quebec to Ga. and Tenn. *Var.* **alba** has white flowers; *var.* **rosea**, rose-colored flowers, and there are improved, scarlet forms. See also HERB GARDENING.

**fistulosa.** Wild bergamot. A softly hairy or smooth, perennial herb, growing 3 ft. high. Leaves narrowly oval, 4–6 in. long. Flowers lilac to purple, 1½ in. long, growing in terminal clusters, the surrounding bracts* whitish or purplish. Me. to Fla. and La. Easily transplanted to the wild garden, in dry situations, and is sometimes effectively used in combination with perennial phlox in the hardy border. *Var.* **alba** has white flowers. See HERB GARDENING.

**punctata.** Horse mint; also called rignum. A perennial herb, slightly downy, growing 3 ft. high. Leaves narrow, 2–3 in. long. Flowers yellowish, spotted with purple, the bracts* white or purplish. N.Y. to Fla. and Tex. Adapted to naturalizing in dry, sandy soil.

**MONARDELLA** (mo-nar-del'la). About 15 species of aromatic, mostly Californian herbs of the mint family, not much known in the garden, but **M. villosa**, the coyote mint, occasionally grown for ornament. It is a perennial, 12–18 in. high, the foliage hairy, its leaves more or less oval, about 1 in. long, and opposite.* Flowers purple, pink, or white, about ½ in. long, in dense, terminal, head-like clusters. It differs only in technical characters from *Monarda*. It is of easy culture in Calif., and can be increased by division in the spring. Eastward its availability is not certain. (*Monardella* is a diminutive of *Monarda*, which these plants resemble.)

**MONASTERY GARDEN.** See GARDEN HISTORY.

**MONDO** = *Ophiopogon*.

**MONESES** (mo-nee'seez). A genus of perennial, evergreen herbs of the heath family, growing in N.A. and Eurasia, having only one species, **M. uniflora**, known as one-flowered wintergreen. Stem prostrate, the leaves roundish, toothed, about 1 in. long, clustered near the base of the stem. Flower solitary, on a drooping stalk, 5 or 6 in. long. Corolla white or pink, fragrant, about ¾ in. across, the petals 5, and spreading. Fruit a capsule,* about ¼ in. across. The one-flowered wintergreen grows in moist, cool woodlands, and should only be grown in shady places in the wild garden. (*Moneses* is from the Greek for single delight; alluding to the pretty solitary flower.)

**MONEYWORT** = *Lysimachia nummularia*.

**MONGREL.** See CROSS-BREED.

**MONIMIACEAE.** See PEUMUS.

**MONKEY-COCONUT** = *Jubaea spectabilis*.

**MONKEY-FLOWER.** See MIMULUS.

**MONKEY-POD.** See SAMANEA SAMAN.

**MONKEY-PUZZLE** = *Araucaria araucana*.

**MONKEY'S-BREAD.** See ADANSONIA DIGITATA.

**MONKSHOOD.** The aconites, or, as some of them are called, the wolfsbanes, are mostly showy, perennial herbs comprising the genus **Aconitum** (ak-ko-ny'tum) of the buttercup family. Of over 100 species, nearly all from the north temperate zone, only a handful are of garden interest, and one of them, *A. napellus*, the common monkshood, yields the drug aconite, of world-wide use as a heart sedative. All are dangerously poisonous (not to the touch). They have usually thickened or even tuberous roots and leaves that are cleft or divided finger-fashion, but not compound.* Flowers very irregular,* mostly in terminal clusters (panicles* or racemes*), prevailingly blue or purple, but white or yellow in some. Sepals* 5, petal-like, one of them large, hood-shaped (hence monkshood) or helmet-like. Petals 2–5, two of them spur-like and contained in the hood, the others small or wanting. Stamens* numerous. Fruit a collection of many-seeded follicles.* (*Aconitum* is the ancient classical name of the monkshood.)

The monkshoods are showy garden plants (but children should be warned against the poisonous juice). They prefer partial shade and a rich soil. The taller sorts need staking, as they are somewhat weak-stemmed plants. They are fine plants for late summer and early autumn gardens, and some of the blue-flowered sorts are particularly valuable for the blue garden (which see). All the cult. kinds are best treated as perennials, and bloom the second or third year from seed. They may also be increased by division, but generally they dislike being moved. Their foliage superficially resembles the closely related larkspurs (see DELPHINIUM), but the latter does not have the helmet-shaped flowers of the monkshoods.

**A. anthora.** Not over 2 ft. high, the divisions of the leaf very narrow. Flowers with the helmet extended into a short beak, pale yellow. Southern Eu. July-Aug.

**A. autumnale.** A Chinese perennial, 4–5 ft. high, the leaves 5-lobed. Flowers generally blue, sometimes whitish or lilac, the helmet nearly closed. There is doubt as to the true identity of the plant usually offered as *A. autumnale*, as it may be a form of *A. fischeri*.

**A. cammarum.** A perennial, 3–4 ft. high, the lobes of the much-divided leaf blunt. Flowers in a loose cluster, purple, the helmet nearly closed. Hungary. The plant is sometimes offered as *A. exaltatum*.

**A. exaltatum** = *Aconitum cammarum*.

**A. fischeri.** One of the most popular of the garden monkshoods and from 4–6 ft. high. Leaves 3-lobed, the lobes often notched. Flowers generally blue (rarely white), the helmet extended into a spur-like visor.

---

* Special articles on the subjects indicated by an asterisk (*) will be found at the words so marked.

MONK'S PEPPER-TREE

A very handsome plant from eastern Asia, badly confused as to identity and names, as many gardener's names appear to be referable to this species. Sept.–Oct.

**A. lycoctonum.** Wolfsbane. A perennial, 4–6 ft. high, the leaves with 3–9 broadish segments which are toothed. Flowers yellow or creamy-white, in spike-like racemes.* The upright helmet is constricted below the top. Eurasia.

**A. napellus.** The common monkshood and the source of the drug aconite (see MEDICINAL PLANTS), but cult. here for ornament. It is not over 4 ft. high, the leaves twice- or thrice-divided into narrow segments. Flowers blue, the broad helmet with a beak-like visor. Eu. An extremely poisonous plant. There is a white-flowered variety and the var. sparksi, with pale blue flowers, is fine for the blue garden (which see).

**A. uncinatum.** Wild monkshood. A native perennial, weak, partly climbing, but not over 5 ft. high. Leaves 3–5-lobed, the lobes again divided or deeply toothed. Flowers blue. In rich, moist woods, especially along streams, Pa. to Ga. and Wisc. Best suited to shady, moist places in the wild garden. June–July.

**MONK'S PEPPER-TREE** = *Vitex agnus-castus.*

**MONOCOTYLEDON.** A plant having only one cotyledon* or seed leaf. Monocotyledonous plants usually have parallel-veined leaves and the parts of their flowers (petals, stamens, etc.) in threes or multiples of three. Common examples of monocotyledonous plants are grasses, lily, palm, iris, tulip, gladiolus, crocus, and the orchids. *See* DICOTYLEDON.

**MONOECIOUS** (mo-nee'shus). Having the male and female flowers separate, but on the same plant, as in many members of the cucumber family, some palms, and in all the walnuts and oaks. *See* DIOECIOUS.

*MONOGYNA, -us, -um* (mo-noj'y-na). Having one pistil.*

**MONOHYDRATED COPPER DUST.** *See* Copper at FUNGICIDES.

*MONOPHYLLA, -us, -um* (mo-no-fil'la). Single-leaved; sometimes used for plants with only one leaflet.

*MONOSPERMA, -us, -um* (mo-no-sper'ma). One-seeded.

**MONOTYPIC GENUS.** *See* GENUS.

**MONSTERA** (mon-steer'ra). A genus of tropical American aroids, comprising perhaps 30 species, of which **M. deliciosa**, the ceriman, is cult. in northern greenhouses for its remarkable foliage, and in tropical regions and southern Fla. for its fruit. It is a strong-stemmed, climbing plant with many cord-like, aerial roots. Leaves 2–3 ft. long, nearly as broad, much cut into large, rounded lobes, the body of the blade plentifully perforated with oblong or elliptic holes, some of which may be 3–4 in. long. Leafstalk long, stout, sheathing at the base and channeled. Flowers borne on a dense, club-shaped spadix,* which is 8–10 in. long and about 2 in. thick, ultimately developing into a cone-like mass of fleshy, sweet fruits, which are aromatic and flavored somewhat like a mixture of banana and pineapple. For details of its flower structure *see* ARACEAE. In greenhouses it needs a stout support, potting mixture* 4, plenty of water and a warm, moist greenhouse. Under these conditions it will often fruit in the greenhouse. It will stand no frost. In southern Fla. the fruits are occasionally to be found in the markets, but the plant is chiefly grown for its extraordinary foliage. (*Monstera* is of unknown origin.) The plant is sometimes known as *Philodendron pertusum.*

*MONSTROSA, -us, -um* (mon-stro'sa). Large or monstrous.

**MONTANA.** The state lies wholly in zones* 1, 2, and 3. Within the zone limits, however, Montana presents a great variation, due to the fact that it is a mountainous state. Horticultural crops are found being produced through a range in elevation from less than 2000 feet to around 7000 feet. Some of the mountain valleys furnish extremely favorable conditions. The part of the state west of the continental divide is to quite an extent adapted to many of the crops found in the states farther west. The area east of the divide is essentially a part of the plains area and has more severe conditions than does the western part.

SOIL. A wide range of soil types prevails in the state.

Within limited areas the soil types vary and even small valleys may show a number of soil types. As an example, we may refer to one of the valleys of western Montana. The west side of this valley has a soil very low in lime, formed from granite formations. The east side has a calcareous soil, very high in lime in some portions. A river marks the definite line between the two types. Physically, the soil in various sections is adapted to a wide range of horticultural crops.

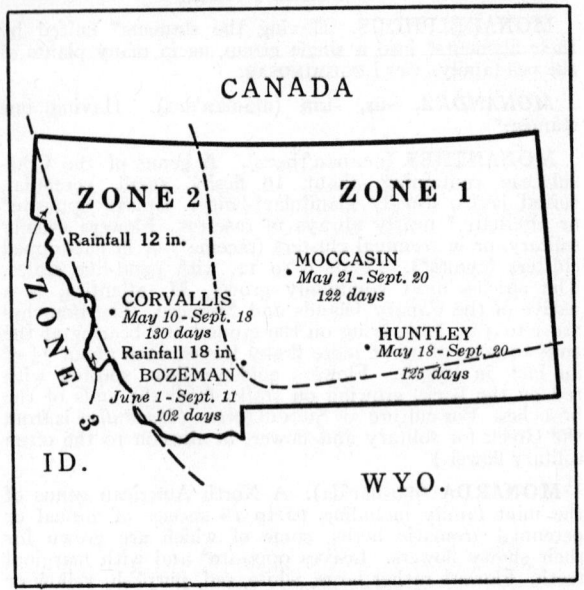

MONTANA

The zones of hardiness crossing Montana are those shown on the colored map at ZONE, which should be consulted for details. The dates are the average latest killing frost in spring and the first one in the fall. The figures below the dates show the length of the growing season. Rainfall figures (in inches) are for total annual rainfall in the regions so indicated.

Commercial fruit crops are primarily found in western Montana, west of the continental divide, and in south central Montana. In the Bitter Root Valley one finds the commercial apple orchards and the sour cherry. The McIntosh apple prevails as to apples, and here it finds conditions where it can be produced to advantage. The Montmorency and English Morello cherries are grown extensively for canning purposes. In the Flathead Valley, on the east shore of Flathead Lake, is found an extensive and growing sweet cherry section, and varieties such as Bing and Lambert are produced for carlot shipment to distant markets. Crop failures of this sweet cherry section due to weather factors are rare, due to the protection from the Mission Range and Flathead Lake. The commercial possibilities are accented by the fact that the crop ripens late, after practically all other sweet cherry sections have harvested and marketed their crops.

Apples and sour cherries constitute the main tree-fruit possibilities in the south central part.

Extensive commercial plantings of red raspberries and strawberries are also found in western Montana. Special emphasis is placed on the everbearing types and August and September are the heavy crop periods.

Vegetable production occurs in western Montana and considerable commercial production is found also in other parts of the state, chiefly around Great Falls and Billings, and in various favored locations in close proximity to other cities of the state.

Commercial production of head lettuce is distinctly on the increase. High elevations make possible the cutting and marketing of head lettuce during August and early September, at times when high summer temperatures

---

* Special articles on the subjects indicated by an asterisk (*) will be found at the words so marked.

curtail production in many sections. Such development has particularly occurred in southern Montana, near West Yellowstone.

Ornamental horticulture is found flourishing in all parts of the state. A wide range of tree and shrub selections is possible in some parts, but is restricted in other places by length of growing season and sudden temperature changes. In these latter areas, selections must necessarily be made from the hardier trees and shrubs. Poplars, birch, green ash, elm, Russian olive, willows, and the various evergreens are universal over much of the state. Maple, oak, walnut, locust, and a variety of other trees in turn are grown in addition in some other sections. The same is true of shrubs, limited to hardier species in some sections and a wide range in others.

CLIMATE. Climatic conditions in Montana are so variable that a study of one or two locations does not in any way represent the state. The wide range in elevation and the location of mountain ranges are responsible. Some sections record the last spring frost in April; other sections have the last killing frost occurring in June. And a like spread occurs in the fall, with average dates of first killing frost ranging from early September to October. Summer temperatures are also variable. The length of the growing season is therefore variable over the state.

MONTANA FROST AND RAINFALL

|  | Bozeman | Corvallis | Huntley | Moccasin |
|---|---|---|---|---|
| Elevation | 4900 ft. | 3575 ft. | 3026 ft. | 4300 ft. |
| Annual rainfall | 18.68 in. | 12.56 in. | 13.67 in. | 15.54 in. |
| Apr. to Sept. rainfall | 11.50 in. | 5.86 in. | 8.80 in. | 11.25 in. |
| Last spring frost | June 1 | May 10 | May 18 | May 21 |
| First fall frost | Sept. 11 | Sept. 18 | Sept. 20 | Sept. 20 |
| Average frost-free period | 102 days | 131 days | 125 days | 122 days |

The amount of rainfall varies materially in different parts of the state. Also the season in which moisture falls varies. A comparison of figures in the table shows a lower percentage of moisture during the growing season in western Montana than in eastern parts of the state. Most commercial horticultural enterprises depend on irrigation.

The address of the Agricultural Experiment Station, which has kindly contributed this account of the state, is Bozeman, Mont. The Station is always glad to answer gardening questions.

*MONTANA, -us, -um* (mon-tay'na). Growing on a mountain or in a mountainous region.

**MONTANOA** (mon-ta-nō'a). Tropical American shrubs and trees of the family Compositae, comprising perhaps 20 species, only those below of garden interest and little known outside of warm regions. The cult. species are shrubby and have opposite* leaves. Flower heads small or medium-sized, composed of both ray and disk flowers, white in those below. (Named for Don Luis Montana, Mexican naturalist.)

They can be grown as greenhouse pot plants, or outdoors as bedding plants in zones* 8 and 9. They need a warm-temperate greenhouse and potting mixture* 3. As they are winter-blooming, they are useful as sub-tropical bedding plants.

bipinnatifida. Not over 8 ft. high, and a strong-growing, erect, shrubby plant. Leaves more or less deeply cut feather-fashion, hairy. Flower heads white, nearly 3 in. wide. Mex.

hibiscifolia. Shrub 10–15 ft. high, the leaves divided finger-fashion nearly to the middle, and 9–12 in. wide. Flower heads about 1½ in. wide, white. Guatemala and Costa Rica. A striking plant with very showy leaves.

**MONTBRETIA.** See TRITONIA.

**MONTEREY PINE** = *Pinus radiata*. See PINE.

*MONTEVIDENSIS, -e* (mon-te-vi-den'sis). From Montevideo, Uruguay.

**MONTEZUMA CYPRESS** = *Taxodium mucronatum*.

**MONTIA** (mon'ti-a). A genus of about 18 small, annual or perennial North American herbs of the family Portulacaceae. Leaves usually opposite,* small, smooth, fleshy. Flowers usually very small, nodding, the 3 petals more or less joined, white or pale rose-color. Flowers are solitary or in loose terminal clusters (racemes*). Fruit a 3-seeded pod. (Named for Giuseppe Monti, professor of botany at Bologna.)

These herbs are grown for ornament, one as an interesting salad or pot herb. They are very easily cultivated, for the seed may be sown in spring or summer in the ground where the plants are to stand.

parviflora. A slender green herb, often covered with a bloom.* Leaves basal, spoon-shaped or very narrow. Flowers white or rose. Western N.A.

perfoliata. Winter purslane; also called Indian lettuce, or miner's lettuce. An annual herb, coarse, green, often reddening with age. Basal leaves 1 to 3 inches broad. Flowers small, white on stalks 1 ft. high, beneath them 2 disk-like stem leaves. Western N.A. Often used as a salad or pot herb, and it has been introduced into many other regions and countries.

*MONTICOLA, -us, -um* (mon-tick'o-la). From mountains.

**MONTMORENCY.** A sour cherry. See CHERRY.

**MOONFLOWER** = *Calonyction*.

**MOONLIGHT BROOM.** See *Cytisus scoparius* at BROOM.

**MOONSEED.** See MENISPERMUM and COCCULUS.

**MOONSEED FAMILY** = *Menispermaceae*.

**MOONWORT** = *Botrychium*. See also HONESTY.

**MOOR MYRTLE** = *Myrica gale*.

**MOORPARK.** See APRICOT.

**MOORWORT** = *Andromeda polifolia*.

**MOOSEWOOD** = *Acer pennsylvanicum*. See MAPLE.

**MORACEAE** (more-ray'see-ee). The mulberry or fig family is of interest chiefly for its edible fruits. But it contains some hardy and tropical trees of ornamental value among its 55 genera and possibly 1000 species, many of which are tropical. Part, or all, of this family is by some called the Artocarpaceae.

Rubber is derived from *Castilla*. Fruits are found in *Ficus* (figs), *Artocarpus* (breadfruit), and *Morus* (see MULBERRY). *Maclura* (the Osage orange) and *Broussonetia* are grown for ornament outdoors over most of the U.S., while *Cecropia* is a tropical tree grown outdoors in southern Fla. Nearly all genera have milky juice, and all cult. genera are woody plants.

Leaves alternate*; in *Artocarpus* and some species of *Ficus* often much cut or lobed, but simple.* Flowers small and inconspicuous, the male and female ones separate, sometimes (*Maclura* and *Cecropia*) on separate trees.

The fruit of this family is complicated (see FIG). The other genera have fleshy fruit formed from the amalgamation of the ovaries of several flowers, sometimes embedded in the fleshy remains of ripening flower parts other than the ovary. (See SYNCARP.)

Technical flower characters: Flowers regular,* without much distinction between petals and sepals, which together usually total 4. Ovary superior,* 1–2-celled.

**MORAEA** (more-ee'a). Also spelled *Morea*. Iris-like, and in ours, South African herbs of the family Iridaceae, comprising over 60 species. They bear corms* or rootstocks and have basal, sword-shaped or narrower, leaves. Flowers almost exactly like *Iris* which this genus replaces in the southern hemisphere. Unlike *Iris*, *Moraea* is not hardy outdoors in the North, and should be grown in the cool greenhouse with much the same conditions as for *Freesia* (which see). With protection the second species is occasionally hardy as far north as zone* 4. They are unlike *Iris*, also, in that their flowers last only a day, consequently they are poor substitutes for iris when the two can be grown. (Named for J. Moraeus, Swedish physician, whose daughter married Linnaeus.)

iridioides. Leaves in fan-like, basal rosettes, arising from a creeping rootstock. Flowers nearly 3 in. wide, borne on the end of a bracted*

---

* Special articles on the subjects indicated by an asterisk (*) will be found at the words so marked.

stem, white, the claws* streaked or marked with yellow. Can be grown outdoors in Calif., where it blooms from early spring to Nov.

**pavonia.** Peacock Iris. A corm*-bearing herb with narrow, usually softly hairy leaves. Flowers orange-red, with a dark spot at the base of each petal or segment, without claws.* There are several color forms, as yellow, purple, or white, but most of them are dark-spotted at the base of the petals. Often offered as *Pavonia*.

**MORAINE GARDEN.** See ROCK GARDEN.

**MOREA** = *Moraea*.

**MORETON BAY CHESTNUT** = *Castanospermum australe*.

**MORETON BAY FIG** = *Ficus macrophylla*.

**MORETON BAY PINE** = *Araucaria cunninghami*.

*MORIFOLIA, -us, -um* (more-ĭ-fō′lĭ-a). Mulberry-leaved.

**MORINA** (more-ry′na). Rather unimportant, Asiatic, somewhat thistle-like herbs of the family Dipsacaceae, related to the teasel, but the flowers in whorls, forming interrupted* spikes. Of the 10 known species only **M. longifolia,** sometimes called whorl-flower, is in cult. It is a Himalayan, hardy perennial, 3–4 ft. high, the foliage usually hairy, thistle-like, but handsome. Leaves nearly 6 in. long, about 1 in. wide. Flowers white, but later pink or red, the corolla tubular and surrounded by the 2-lobed, slightly irregular, spiny calyx.* June–July. It is a stout plant, useful in the border, but little known here. (Named for Louis Morin, French botanist.)

**MORINDA** (more-rin′da). Tropical shrubs or trees, rarely vines, of the family Rubiaceae, two of the 60 species sometimes grown for ornament in zones* 8 and 9, little known as cult. plants otherwise, except in India. Leaves mostly opposite.* Flowers small, crowded in dense heads, these solitary in the leaf-axils* or sometimes clustered. Corolla more or less tubular, white (in ours), and joined to each other at the base. Stamens* mostly 5. Fruit fleshy. (The name is a combination of *Morus* (mulberry) and *indica*, in allusion to the Indian mulberry.)

The plants are of easy culture in a variety of soils in Calif. and Fla., and they are scarcely known elsewhere. The first species yields red and yellow dyes.

**citrifolia.** Indian mulberry. A small tree with somewhat 4-angled branches. Leaves shining, short-stalked, more or less elliptic, 7–10 in. long. Flower heads solitary, short-stalked, in the leaf-axils,* the corolla tube about ½ in. long. Fruit nearly 2 in. long, yellowish. India to Australasia.

**royoc.** Wild mulberry; called also yaw-weed. A West Indian, erect or vine-like shrub, not over 4 ft. high, commonly naturalized in southern Fla. Leaves narrowly oblong, 2–4 in. long. Flowers in heads. Fruit yellow, about 1 in. wide.

**MORINGA** (more-ring′ga). Tropical Old World trees, and the only genus of the family **Moringaceae** (more-ring-gay′see-ee), of which the only cult. species is **M. oleifera,** the horse-radish tree, so named from its pungent, edible root. It is a small, softwooded tree, not over 25 ft. high, with corky bark and thrice-compound,* very feathery leaves. The whole leaf may be 2 ft. long, but its ultimate leaflets are very numerous and small. Flowers white, fragrant, nearly an inch wide, in loose clusters (panicles*) in the leaf-axils.* Fruit a 9-ribbed, cylindric pod, often 15 in. long, its seeds 3-angled and winged. The tree is hardy only in zones* 8 and 9, but has become established as an escape* in southern Fla. Its seeds yield ben oil (oil of ben), used for lubricating watches. (*Moringa* is the Latinized version of the Malay name for this tree.)

**MORNING-GLORY.** See IPOMOEA.

**MORNING-GLORY FAMILY.** All the garden genera are vines, which vary in uses from the showy morning-glory to the sweet potato. Some are pernicious weeds. For the hort. genera see CONVOLVULACEAE.

**MORRIS ARBORETUM.** See ARBORETUM.

*MORSUS-RANAE* (more-sus-ray′nee). Frog's bite.

**MORUS.** See MULBERRY.

**MOSAIC.** See Virus Diseases at PLANT DISEASES. See also the Diseases at LILIUM, NARCISSUS, ROSE, SWEET PEA, TULIPA, BEAN, and POTATO.

*MOSAICA, -us, -um* (mo-zay′i-ka). With a pattern-like difference in color.

*MOSCHATA, -us, -um* (mos-kay′ta). Musky or musk-scented.

*MOSCHEUTOS* (mo-shoo′tos or mos-kew′tos). Pre-Linnaean* name for some mallow. See HIBISCUS.

**MOSCHOSMA** = *Iboza riparia*.

**MOSQUITO BILLS** = *Dodecatheon hendersoni*.

**MOSQUITO-PLANT; MOSQUITO-TRAP** = *Cynanchum acuminatifolium*. See also CASTOR-OIL PLANT.

**MOSS.** The true mosses are flowerless plants scarcely cult., except in the wild garden and when used to line hanging baskets. For covering old logs, wet rocks, and moist, shady banks, nothing is finer than moss, which must be collected from the woods. See also SPHAGNUM, LYCOPODIUM. For flowering moss see PYXIDANTHERA. For Spanish or Long Moss see TILLANDSIA.

**MOSS CAMPION** = *Silene acaulis* and *S. schafta*.

**MOSS IN THE LAWN.** See LAWN.

**MOSS ON FLOWER POTS.** See FLOWER POTS.

**MOSS PINK** = *Phlox subulata*.

**MOSS ROSE** = *Rosa centifolia muscosa*. See Group 5 at ROSE.

**MOSSY-CUP OAK** = *Quercus macrocarpa*. See OAK.

**MOSSY STONECROP** = *Sedum acre*.

**MOTH BEAN** = *Phaseolus aconitifolius*.

**MOTHER BULB.** The old bulb around which bulblets* are formed.

**MOTHER-OF-THOUSANDS** = *Saxifraga sarmentosa*.

**MOTHER-OF-THYME** = *Thymus serpyllum*. See THYME.

**MOTHER SPLEENWORT** = *Asplenium bulbiferum*.

**MOTHERWORT** = *Leonurus cardiaca*.

**MOTH MULLEIN** = *Verbascum blattaria*.

**MOTH ORCHID.** See PHALAENOPSIS.

**MOTHS.** See Moths at INSECT PESTS.

**MOTTLING OF LEAVES.** See Virus Diseases at PLANT DISEASES.

**MOULD.** Both the disease known as such and the garden soil are often so spelled, but THE GARDEN DICTIONARY prefers *mold*.

**MOUND LAYERING.** See LAYERING.

**MOUNTAIN.** As an adjective *mountain* has been linked with the names of many plants that grow, or were once thought to grow, upon mountains. Those in THE GARDEN DICTIONARY and their proper equivalents are:

**Mountain-ash** (see first main entry below); **Mountain avens** (see DRYAS); **Mountain azalea** = *Azalea canescens*; **Mountain bluet** = *Centaurea montana*; **Mountain camellia** = *Stewartia pentagyna*; **Mountain cranberry** = *Vaccinium vitis-idaea minus*; **Mountain creeper** = *Thunbergia fragrans* and *Porana paniculata*; **Mountain currant** = *Ribes alpinum*; **Mountain ebony** = *Bauhinia variegata*; **Mountain fetter-bush** = *Pieris floribunda*; **Mountain fleece** = *Polygonum amplexicaule*; **Mountain fringe** = *Adlumia fungosa*; **Mountain hemlock** = *Tsuga mertensiana* (see HEMLOCK); **Mountain holly** = *Nemopanthus mucronata*; **Mountain holly**

---

* Special articles on the subjects indicated by an asterisk (*) will be found at the words so marked.

fern = *Polystichum lonchitis;* **Mountain laurel** = *Kalmia latifolia;* **Mountain leatherwood** = *Fremontia californica;* **Mountain magnolia** = *Magnolia fraseri;* **Mountain mahogany** (see CERCOCARPUS); **Mountain mint** (see PCYNANTHEMUM); **Mountain pine** (see DACRYDIUM); **Mountain queen** = *Hesperoyucca whipplei;* **Mountain rose bay** = *Rhododendron catawbiense* (for the common rose bay see R. MAXIMUM); **Mountain sage** = *Artemisia frigida;* **Mountain sandwort** = *Arenaria groenlandica;* **Mountain saxifrage** = *Saxifraga oppositifolia;* **Mountain snow** = *Euphorbia marginata;* **Mountain starwort** = *Arenaria groenlandica;* **Mountain tea-tree** = *Kunzea peduncularis.*

**MOUNTAIN-ASH.** A genus of Eurasian and North American deciduous trees or shrubs of the rose family called **Sorbus** (sor′bus), comprising perhaps 80-100 species. Leaves alternate,* simple* or compound,* the leaflets arranged feather-fashion (pinnate*), sharply toothed. Flowers white, many and showy, in terminal, branching, flat-topped, leafy clusters (corymbs*). Petals 5, broad or narrow, clawed.* Stamens* 15-20. Fruit a small, berry-like pome.* (*Sorbus* is the ancient Latin name.)

Most of the species of *Sorbus* may be grown easily even in dry soil. Rare kinds are propagated by grafting on *S. americana* or *S. aucuparia.* Others increased by seeds or by layers.

**S. americana.** American Mountain-ash. A smooth tree becoming 30 ft. high. Leaflets 13-15, bright green, narrow, taper-pointed, with sharp marginal teeth. Flowers white, ⅓ in. across, in compound terminal clusters (corymbs*). Berries round, bright red. Common in woods Labrador to Manitoba, south in the mountains to N.C. and westward. May-June. Hardy from zone* 2 southward.

**S. aria.** Whitebeam. A broad-headed tree, sometimes 50 ft. high, remaining a shrub on poor lands. Young growth soft-woolly. Leaflets elliptic or ovalish, 2-5 in. long, with marginal teeth, sharp-pointed or blunt, usually wedge-shaped, bright green and smooth above, white, soft-woolly beneath, leathery. Flowers in flat-topped terminal clusters (corymbs*), 2-3¼ in. across. Fruit orange-red or scarlet with mealy flesh. Eu. long cult. May. Hardy from zone* 3 southward.

**S. aucuparia.** Rowan tree; also known as European Mountain-ash. A tree 50 ft. or more high. Leaflets 9-15, 1-2 in. long, oblong or narrower, pointed or blunt, dull green above, with a bloom beneath, hairy or smooth. Flowers ⅓ in. across, in compound terminal clusters (corymbs*), 4-6 in. across. Fruit round, bright red. Eu. to western As. and Siberia. Long cult. *Var.* **pendula** has long, drooping branches. June. Hardy from zone* 2 southward.

**S. decora.** A tree 30 ft. high, or shrubby. Leaves of 11-17 leaflets from 2½-3 in. long, with spreading teeth, smooth and dark green above. Flowers white, ⅓ in. across, in flat-topped clusters (corymbs*). Fruit bright red. Labrador to Minn., southern N.Y. and Vt. May. Hardy from zone* 2 southward.

**S. domestica.** Service tree. A tree with scaly bark, reaching 60 ft. Leaves with 11-21 leaflets, narrow-oblong, pointed and with sharp marginal teeth, smooth above, woolly-haired beneath. Flowers ½ in. across, in dense, pyramidal terminal clusters, 2½ to 4 in. across. Fruit apple- or pear-shaped, yellowish-green or brownish, tinged with red. Southern Eu., North Africa, western As. May. Hardy from zone* 3 southward.

**S. hybrida.** A tree attaining 40 ft. Leaves ovalish or longer, 3-5 in. long, with 1-4 pairs of leaflets at the end, the leaflets toothed, and woolly beneath. Flowers ½ in. across, in compound, flat-topped, terminal clusters (corymbs*), 2½-4 in. across. Fruit nearly round, red. Of hybrid origin. Scandinavia. May. Hardy from zone* 3 southward.

**S. quercifolia** = *Sorbus hybrida.*

**MOUNT MORGAN WATTLE** = *Acacia podalyriaefolia.*

**MOUNT VERNON.** For the trees planted by General Washington, see Mount Vernon at TREES.

**MOURNING BRIDE** = *Scabiosa atropurpurea.*

**MOURNING CYPRESS** = *Cupressus funebris.*

**MOUSE-EAR CHICKWEED** = *Cerastium vulgatum.* See list at WEEDS.

**MOUSE-EAR HAWKWEED** = *Hieracium pilosella.* See list at WEEDS.

*MOUTAN* (moo′tan). The Chinese name of the tree peony.

**MOVING TREES.** See Moving Trees at TREES.

**MOXIEBERRY** = *Chiogenes hispidula.*

**MUCKLAND GARDENING.** In many sections of the country, especially in the glaciated part of N.A., there are large deposits of muck or peat, popularly supposed to be the most productive soils in the U.S. With proper treatment they may be, but millions of dollars have been lost in unwise attempts at reclamation of such land, notably in N.Y., Minn., Ohio, Wisc., and Mich.

These great failures, long since corrected, were due to a lack of understanding of the real nature of muckland. And to avoid repeating such errors it is necessary to record here the essentials of successful muck management.

If you have on your property a tract of real swamp or a bog, a simple way to determine whether its draining and reclamation are worth considering is to study the existing wild vegetation. Generally speaking, if the trees are hardwoods like maple, tupelo, black ash, or elm, the muck will probably be productive without too great an initial cost for rectifying it. But if the trees are tamarack, arborvitae, black spruce, or if there are none and the area is covered with large patches of sphagnum moss and typical bog shrubs like *Chamaedaphne calyculata, Andromeda polifolia,* or *Ledum,* the venture may be doubtful.

For the successful utilization of muckland is based upon two things: (1) Regulation of its water level; and (2) its acidity or alkalinity, which is roughly indicated by the wild vegetation as outlined above. But the acidity or alkalinity needs closer study than merely observing the native flora.

(1) REGULATION OF WATER LEVEL. All mucklands are accumulations of vegetable matter which grew in, or were supplied with, plentiful amounts of water. In their present untouched state they are usually saturated with far too much water to make gardening possible. Furthermore, the muck may be anywhere from 75% to 90% decayed vegetable matter, which is like a sponge for holding water. Study the levels and see if by ditching or draining it is possible to get the permanent water table about 2½ ft. below the finished ground level. This makes an ideal condition, because the success of muckland gardening depends upon capillarity bringing up from this permanent reservoir of water enough for crop needs. If the water table is too near the surface, the roots will be drowned; if it is too deep, the upper layer of muck will become powder dry and failure will be certain. Of course one could put in an overhead irrigation system (see IRRIGATION), but in a properly managed muck scheme no money should be spent on irrigation, for mucklands are used precisely because they have ample supplies of water. For details of draining see DRAINING.

(2) ACIDITY OR ALKALINITY. Most failures in muckland gardening have come from neglect of this. To test the muck for acidity or alkalinity, collect samples from many different parts of the area and from depths ranging from the surface to 2 ft. down. Take care that no perspiration from the hands, tobacco ash, or other alkaline substances gets into your samples, and see that the containers are of some neutral material — a flower pot is excellent. Then run a series of tests exactly as described in the article ACID AND ALKALI SOILS to determine the pH value of your samples.

If the muck tests from pH 6.0 to 7.5, there is little that needs to worry you about its availability, for most crops will grow perfectly within this range, provided you can manage the water table as outlined above. But if the muck tests from pH 5.5 down to 4.0 or even 3.8, a serious problem is presented at once. For no ordinary garden crop will grow in such an acid muck.

Muck soils with a pH of 3.9-5.5 must be treated, preferably with ground limestone, at the rate of 9 tons per acre (1/20 of an acre = 33 × 66 ft.), and this treatment must be repeated whenever the acidity shows a tendency to return, which is likely after the second or third year. Whether you decide to use such a site is really a question of whether the money spent for limestone will be repaid by the admittedly high yields from good muckland. Some commercial growers use the limestone, but most prefer to seek a more neutral site.

The third possibility, much more rare than the other two, is that the muck is definitely alkaline, that is, it tests from pH 7.5 to 8.5 or even higher. In such a place aluminum

---

* Special articles on the subjects indicated by an asterisk (*) will be found at the words so marked.

sulphate at the rate of about 8 tons to the acre (1/20 acre = 66 × 33 ft.) would have to be applied. Such application is as doubtful a venture as the application of limestone for the too acid site.

MUCKLAND CROPS. Assuming proper soil acidity and water conditions, there are several vegetables that show tremendous yields on muckland. In order of their especial value for muck soils these are: celery, carrots, onion, horse-radish, lettuce, Chinese cabbage, potatoes, and spinach. And among flowers, the common garden aster (*Callistephus*) and the sweet pea do well on muck.

The effect of muckland on celery

Plants that require a long, warm growing season will usually not do well on muck, because it is late in warming up and, in wet weather, mucks may be cold. Such plants as beans, melons, eggplants, peppers, and tomatoes should not be planted in muck.

Muck soils lose moisture so slowly that, especially in wet spring weather, they are hard to manage. Keep off them until implements such as a plow or harrow can be used without becoming clogged with soggy soil. And in summer heat see that they are thoroughly cultivated to keep from evaporating the constant supply of capillary water which rises in all muck soils and is their chief value.

Contrary to popular opinion, muck soils are not permanently fertile without the addition of plant food. Because they are so high in humus, there is little need for stable manure, and none at all for green manuring. But most regularly cropped muck soils will repay an application of commercial fertilizer with a 2-8-10 ratio (see FERTILIZERS) at the rate of about 1½ tons per acre (1/20 of an acre = 66 × 33 ft.). Half this is applied at the time of spring plowing; the rest is top-dressed in the rows during the summer. And some growers, especially on lettuce and spinach, use nitrate of soda for the second application, but not more than 400 pounds per acre.

For the use of swamp land, without rectifying the soil, as a site for a wild or swamp garden see SWAMP.

*MUCOSA, -us, -um* (mew-kō′sa). Mucilaginous or slimy.

MUCRO. See MUCRONATA.

*MUCRONATA, -us, -um* (mew-kro-nay′ta). Having a mucro; *i.e.* a short, sharp point, as in many leaves.

MUDDING = puddling. See PLANTING.

MUEHLENBECKIA (mew-len-beck′ĭ-a). Somewhat woody, shrub-like or vine-like plants of the family Polygonaceae, all from the south temperate zone, three of the 15 known species grown more as oddities than for ornament. They have wire-like or flattened, usually greenish, and sometimes leafless stems. Leaves, when present, alternate,* small, with sheathing stipules.* Flowers small and inconspicuous, in small clusters in the leaf-axils.* Petals none, the sepals chaffy or becoming fleshy in age. Fruit a 3-angled achene.* (Named for H. G. Muehlenbeck, an Alsatian physician.)

The muehlenbeckias can be grown outdoors in Calif. or Fla., but are rather rare in cult., except *M. complexa*. In the greenhouse they need potting mixture* 3 and a cool, dry house. The first two species are occasionally used for hanging baskets, as their prostrate or sprawling, wire-like stems are very hardy if they happen to be neglected. *M. platyclados* is a curious, essentially leafless, erect shrub. The plants are sometimes known under the names of *Calacinum* and *Homalocladium*.

**axillaris.** A sprawling or prostrate, bushy plant, its wire-like stems forming a compact mass, but not over 1 ft. long. Leaves scarcely ¼ in. long. New Zealand. Sometimes known as *M. nana*.

**complexa.** Wire-vine; also called maidenhair-vine. A twining, green-stemmed vine with wire-like stems. Leaves nearly circular, about ½ in. in diameter. New Zealand. Often planted in Calif.

**nana** = *Muehlenbeckia axillaris*.

**platyclados.** Ribbon-bush; also called Centipede-plant. An erect shrub, 6–9 ft. high (half this in cult.), with ribbon-like, jointed, green branches about ½ in. wide, leafless at flowering time and sometimes for months. Leaves (when present) lance-shaped, about 1 in. long. Fruit apparently a red or purplish berry, but this is merely a covering for the achene* within. Solomon Islands.

*MUGO* (mew′go). A native name in the Alps for the Swiss mountain pine (*Pinus mugo*).

MUGWORT = *Artemisia vulgaris*.

MULBERRY. These fruit-bearing trees, one of them widely grown in the Far East as food for silkworms, comprise the genus Morus (more′us) of the family Moraceae, all the cult. species of which are Asiatic except a native American one. They have alternate,* often lobed leaves, and small, greenish flowers in stalked, hanging catkins,* the male and female separate, sometimes on different trees. Petals none, the sepals usually 4. Fruit edible, berry-like, but actually an aggregate* fruit, resembling a blackberry, consisting of a dry fruit (achene*) covered with the fleshy sepals from several flowers. (*Morus* is the old Latin name of the mulberry.)

For Culture *see* below.

**M. acidosa.** A small tree, not over 25 ft. high, often shrubby. Leaves slightly rough above, more or less ovalish, toothed or lobed, 4–6 in. long. Fruit sweet, dark red, about ½ in. long. Eastern Asia. Hardy from zone* 3 southward. Sometimes known as *M. japonica*.

**M. alba.** White mulberry. The tree (or a form of it) cult. in eastern Asia for its leaves, the food of silkworms. It is not over 50 ft. high. Leaves broadly oval, 3–5 in. long, usually lobed, and coarsely toothed, bright green above. Fruit insipid, sweetish, nearly 1¾ in. long, usually white, sometimes pinkish-violet. China. Hardy from zone* 1 southward. The *var.* **tatarica**, the Russian mulberry, is smaller, more hardy, and usually has red fruit. The commonly grown weeping mulberry is grown as a standard upon which is grafted a pendulous-branched variety. There are many other varieties of this tree, which has been grown in Eu. since 1596, and for two thousand years before this in China.

**M. japonica** = *Morus acidosa*.

**M. multicaulis.** Perhaps only a variety of the white mulberry, but with larger leaves, and usually only shrub-like in habit. It is of little hort. interest here, but is considered the best mulberry for silkworm culture in China, and was once planted in an attempt to introduce that industry into the U.S. — a failure.

**M. rubra.** Red or American mulberry. A tree up to 60 ft. high, with scaly, brown bark. Leaves ovalish, softly hairy beneath, 4–6 in. long, sharply toothed and sometimes irregularly lobed. Fruit red or purplish-red, about 1 in. long. Eastern U.S., west to Tex. Not much planted for ornament, but rather common on old properties, where its fruit is eaten by chickens, hogs, and children.

### MULBERRY CULTURE

As ornamental trees the mulberries are practically unknown except for the very popular weeping mulberry, one of the most satisfactory weeping trees for the lawn known in this country. Derived from the Russian mulberry, it is extremely hardy. It originated in Carthage, Mo., about

---

* Special articles on the subjects indicated by an asterisk (*) will be found at the words so marked.

1883. The Russian mulberry (*M. alba tatarica*) is also widely planted in wind-swept, bleak regions as a windbreak, as is the closely related Osage orange.

As fruit trees mulberries suffer from the fact that their fruit is either too sweet or too insipid to have won much favor. Furthermore, the fruit is difficult to keep or ship and is thus rare in the markets. Most mulberry cult. is thus local, for home consumption only. There are, however, several well-known hort. varieties for fruit-bearing mulberries, notably Black English, Downing, Hicks, and New American. Anyone contemplating the planting of mulberries would do well to use one of these varieties rather than the species from which they have been derived, mostly *M. alba* and *M. rubra*. All mulberry fruits are much loved by birds.

There is no trouble about growing mulberry trees, for their soil tolerance is large. Any ordinary farm or garden soil will do. If they are to be planted as an orchard (some are for hog feed), space the trees about 30 ft. apart each way.

For the French mulberry see CALLICARPA AMERICANA. For the paper mulberry see BROUSSONETIA.

INSECT PESTS. Mulberry is only occasionally attacked by insects. Red spiders injure foliage as on many other plants; they may be controlled with a sulphur spray, such as summer-strength lime-sulphur. Bagworms (see SPRUCE) may be controlled by hand-picking cocoons or with arsenicals. The fall webworms attack mulberry (see PERSIMMON).

**MULBERRY FAMILY** = Moraceae.

**MULCH AND MULCHING.** Mulching is a practice that does at once what nature would ultimately do to any piece of ground that was bare. After being prepared by digging or cultivating, nature would produce a crop of something, ranging from green scum to trees, without human assistance.

One theory of mulching is that, by covering the soil in the vicinity of growing plants during the early stages of growth, and especially during warm weather, moisture will be retained in the soil and thus be available to the plants.

The winter use of a mulch has the same idea of retaining moisture. It is much better for plants to freeze wet than dry, and the mulch helps this.

DUST MULCH. The process of shallow surface cultivation is known as the dust mulch. This is especially valuable in the cultivation of long rows, of either vegetables or flowers on light soil. By forming a layer of dust on the surface, the moisture that ordinarily would rise to the surface and evaporate is checked and the plants are benefited. See CULTIVATION.

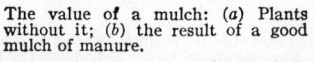

The value of a mulch: (*a*) Plants without it; (*b*) the result of a good mulch of manure.

MULCHING MATERIAL. Leaves, rotted cow and horse manure, straw, salt hay, grass cuttings, peat moss, pine needles, coconut fiber, burlap and prepared paper are the principal materials used for mulching purposes.

From the point of view of their initial purpose, that of holding surface moisture, they rank about equally, but they vary considerably as to their desirability. No hard-and-fast rules as to their usage can be laid down that will apply universally. Soil, climate, and the conditions of any vicinity vary so rapidly that what might work out all right in one place fails in another.

Nature's own mulch — leaves — when available in quantity, are excellent for mulching rhododendrons, azaleas, evergreens, deciduous shrubs, and all native woodland plants. They are also useful on perennial borders and rock gardens. One objection to them is that they blow away so easily. They can, however, be worked into the soil and thus become available as plant food, but the roots of rhododendrons and azaleas should not be disturbed in working in a leaf mulch.

Thoroughly rotted cow and horse manure is excellent for mulching ornamental and fruit trees, shrubs and berry bushes; rose and asparagus beds, perennial borders and rock gardens. They also serve the dual purpose of providing plant food.

PLAIN STRAW will serve in place of leaves or rotted manure, when they are not available. It is also specially used for mulching strawberry beds. The principal function in this case is to keep the fruit clean; though it also serves as an aid to the runners.

SALT HAY has come into vogue as a general mulch in recent years. As a winter covering it provides a light, yet dense mulch and is largely used by commercial growers of pansies to cover their beds. It has no plant food value and must be raked off and either stored in stacks for future use, used for bedding, or burned.

GRASS CUTTINGS make a temporary mulch during the summer, but disappear quickly under extremes of heat and moisture.

PEAT MOSS has a tendency to form a waterproof covering, thus during a dry spell it sheds much available moisture. This neutralizes its value for conserving moisture, but it is an excellent mulch for all acid-soil plants.

COCONUT FIBER has qualities similar to peat moss.

PINE NEEDLES make a natural mulch for pine trees and could be used for other conifers, but they are too acid for general garden purposes.

BURLAP is used in the germination of seedlings and would do all that mulch paper does. It is rather expensive for this purpose, however.

PAPER MULCH, recently marketed, is the most efficient mulch for large-scale planting in rows. It is made up in rolls of various widths and stands up to the weather better than ordinary paper. Originally used on Hawaiian pineapple fields, it is now widely used where none of the above materials are available, and, by some, in preference to all of them. There is no doubt that black mulching paper, spread in the row, conserves much moisture. But caution must be used as to the kind selected, as some have shown a tendency to leach undesirable material into the soil. Only mulching paper

Paper mulch, showing the method of laying it, and (*in the inset*) a crop after it has matured with a paper mulch.

guaranteed against this should be used. For smaller-scale paper mulching the material is also sold in squares, provided with a slit in the center for slipping over individual plants. — R. M. C.

**MULE-EARS.** See WYETHIA.

**MULE-FAT** = *Baccharis viminea*.

**MULLEIN.** See VERBASCUM. For Cretan mullein see CELSIA CRETICA.

**MULLEIN PINK** = *Lychnis coronaria*.

**MULTICAULIS, -e** (mul-ti-cau'lis). Many-stemmed.

---

\* Special articles on the subjects indicated by an asterisk (\*) will be found at the words so marked.

**MULTICAVA, -us, -um** (mul-tĭ-cay'va). Much-hollowed.

**MULTIFIDA, -us, -um** (mul-tiff'i-da). Multifid; i.e. much-divided or parted.

**MULTIFLORA, -us, -um** (mul-tĭ-flō'ra). Many- or profusely flowered.

**MULTIFLORA BEAN** = *Phaseolus coccineus*.

**MULTIFLORA ROSE.** See ROSA MULTIFLORA.

**MULTIJUGA, -us, -um** (mul-tĭ-jew'ga). In many yokes or pairs; applied to leaflets.

**MULTIPLIER ONION** = *Allium cepa solaninum*. See ONION.

**MULTIRADIATA, -us, -um** (mul-tĭ-ray-dee-ā'ta). Many-rayed, as are the heads of some daisies; sometimes with many petals, as are the flowers of *Mesembryanthemum*.

**MULTISCAPOIDEA, -us, -um** (mul-tĭ-skay-poy'dee-a). With many scapes or stalks.

**MUM.** Florist's slang for chrysanthemum.

**MUMMY BERRY.** See Diseases at BLUEBERRY.

**MUNG BEAN** = *Phaseolus aureus*.

**MUNGO** (mung'go). Latinized version of *mung*, the name in India of the black gram (*Phaseolus mungo*).

**MUNICIPAL ROSE GARDENS.** See ROSE GARDENS.

**MUNITA, -us, -um** (mew-ny'ta). Armed or fortified.

**MURALIS, -e** ('mew-ray'lis). Growing on walls.

**MURIATE OF POTASH.** See Potash at FERTILIZERS.

**MURICATA, -us, -um** (mure-ĭ-kay'ta). Roughened with hard points.

**MURRAYA** (mur'rie-a). Also spelled *Murraea*. A small genus of aromatic, Indo-Malayan shrubs or small trees of the family Rutaceae, sometimes known as *Chalcas*. The only cult. species is **M. exotica**, the orange jasmine, frequently planted in Fla. and Calif. for its handsome evergreen leaves and beautifully fragrant, white flowers. It is a tree-like shrub 10–12 ft. high with no spines and alternate,* compound* leaves consisting of 3–9 ovalish, shining leaflets, 1–2 in. long. Flowers more or less bell-shaped, about ¾ in. long, the 5 petals pointed. Stamens* 8–10. Fruit an egg-shaped, red berry, usually a little less than ½ in. long. India. A very handsome ornamental, which blooms several times a year. Not hardy north of zone* 8. (Named for J. A. Murray, an English editor of some of the works of Linnaeus.)

**MUSA** (mew'sa). Giant herbs chiefly from the Indo-Malayan region and belonging to the family Musaceae, their huge, fleshy, tree-like stems formed of the tightly packed sheathes of the leaf bases. They have usually large rhizomes from which springs the single, trunk-like stem which flowers only once and then is replaced by suckers from the base. Leaves very large, without teeth, having a single, stout midrib* from which diverge many parallel, transverse veins along which the leaves split into ribbons in the wind (seldom in the greenhouse). Flower cluster terminal, appearing amongst the crown of leaves. It consists of a long, usually drooping spike composed of colored, tightly overlapping bracts, between each of which is a flower. These are highly irregular* and consist of a tubular calyx which splits down one side, and a single petal. Stamens* 6, one of them sterile and petal-like. Fruit long, berry-like, regularly seedless and sterile in the common banana, but producing seeds in some others. The collection of the fruits forms the familiar "hand" of bananas. (Named for Antonio Musa, physician to the first Emperor of Rome.)

For culture see BANANA.

**cavendishi.** Dwarf, Cavendish, or Chinese banana. Not over 6 ft. high and cult. chiefly for ornament, the stems 5–6 in. thick. Leaves 2–4 ft. long, about half as wide, bluish-green, often colored or spotted when young. Flowering spike drooping, with reddish-brown bracts,* the calyx yellowish-white. Fruits very numerous, often 200 in the cluster, 6-angled, 4–5 in. long, somewhat curved and fragrant, mostly seedless, edible. Southern China. This does not produce the small, edible banana which is a variety of *M. sapientum*. The dwarf banana is widely planted for bedding in warm regions. For cult. see BANANA.

**ensete.** Abyssinian banana. A huge, tree-like herb 20–40 ft. high, the stem swollen at the base. Leaves 10–20 ft. long, about 2–3 ft. wide. Flowering spike erect, its bracts* reddish-brown, the flowers whitish. Fruit inedible, dry, 2–3 in. long, bearing a few large black seeds. Abyssinia.

**paradisiaca.** Plantain. Closely resembling the common banana, but the fruit larger, green when ripe, good only when cooked, and a staple food for millions of poor people in the tropics. The fruit is seedless. India.

**sapientum.** The common banana. A tree-like, fleshy-stemmed herb 15–30 ft. high. Leaves 5–10 ft. long, 18–24 in. wide. Flowering spike drooping, 3–5 ft. long, its bracts purplish-violet or brownish, the flowers yellowish-white. Fruits usually 100 or less in the whole cluster, yellow when ripe, sweet, and edible without cooking, seedless. India. Cult. for centuries and now found in innumerable varieties. Two of the best-known are the small, red-skinned sort, and another small-fruited kind known as lady-finger banana, with a very thin skin. For culture see BANANA.

**textilis.** Abaca; the plant yielding Manila hemp. Not over 20 ft. high, its leaves scarcely 2 ft. long, their stalks containing the finest cordage fiber in the world (Manila hemp). Flowering spike drooping. Fruit inedible, about 3 in. long, with many black seeds. Philippine Islands, and grown there as a major industry; little cult. otherwise.

**MUSACEAE** (mew-zay'see-ee). The banana family comprises the largest herbs in the world, often of tree-like stature, but true herbs, except in the extraordinary traveler's-tree of Madagascar (see RAVENALA). There are only 6 tropical genera and perhaps 70 species found in the family, which, with some others, were once included in the Scitamineae.

Four genera are in cult. *Musa* (the banana and plantain) is a world-wide tropical fruit. *Heliconia*, *Strelitzia*, and *Ravenala* are grown in greenhouses or tropical regions for their strikingly beautiful flowers, among them the bird-of-paradise flower (see STRELITZIA).

Leaves gigantic, without marginal teeth, usually with long, channeled and sheathing leafstalks (holding much water in the huge, fan-like crown of *Ravenala*). Flowers in clusters from between sheathing bracts* (spathes*) which are often highly colored, hence very showy. Fruit various; a seedless berry in the cult. varieties of the common banana, but with seeds in the other species, a woody capsule in *Ravenala*, often dry or fleshy in the other cult. genera.

Technical flower characters: Sepals 3, free or united. Petals 3, usually 3. Stamens* 6, one of them abortive or sterile. Ovary inferior,* 3-celled.

**MUSAICA, -us, -um** (mew-zay'i-ka). Banana-like.

**MUSCADINE** = *Vitis rotundifolia*.

**MUSCARI** (mus-cay'ree). Grape-hyacinth. Small bulbous, herbaceous, perennials comprising about 45 species of the lily family, natives of the Mediterranean region, and early spring-flowering. Leaves 4–6, long and narrow, green. Flowers on a leafless stalk, in a terminal raceme,* blue, blue and white, or pink. The individual flower is urn-shaped and drooping, segments of the corolla ending in 6 teeth-like points, or they may be much cut. Stamens* 6. Fruit, a 3-celled capsule. (*Muscari* is from the Latin for musky, in allusion to the musky odor of some of them.) They are occasionally called baby's-breath.

For Culture see below.

**azureum** = *Hyacinthus azureus*.

**botryoides.** Bluebells; called also starch hyacinth. Grows to a height of 9 in. Leaves ¼ in. wide. Flowers about ¼ in. high, blue, the lower flowers fertile, having both stamens and pistil, the upper flowers sterile. A great garden favorite. *Var.* **album** (white), and *var.* **carneum** (pink), are color varieties. Southern Eu.

**comosum.** Tassel-hyacinth. Leaves 1 in. wide. Flowers blue or violet. Eurasia. *Var.* **monstrosum**, commonly called the feather-hyacinth, also blue, but the corolla lobes much cut and feathered.

**conicum.** Grows to a height of 6 in. Leaves ¼ in. wide. Flowers violet-blue. Southern Eu.

**moschatum.** A musk-scented perennial 6–8 in. high. Leaves ½–¾ in. wide. Flowers purplish at first, ultimately yellowish or brownish. Asia Minor.

GRAPE-HYACINTH CULTURE

The grape-hyacinths are among the spring's most valuable bulbous plants, easy to grow and making fine spreads of color. They thrive and increase rapidly in sunny situations where the soil is deep and rich and somewhat sandy. Many kinds make a fall growth, and should be planted in September or early October, 3 in. deep and 3 or 4 in. apart in generous quantities. Certain species are very sweet-scented.

* Special articles on the subjects indicated by an asterisk (*) will be found at the words so marked.

Among these are *M. conicum* and *M. moschatum*. Planted thickly beneath Japanese flowering cherries, the variety Heavenly Blue makes a lovely show. The feather-hyacinth, *M. comosum monstrosum*, is frequently forced indoors. *M. botryoides* will hold its own and increase when planted in grass. All the species are useful for massing along the edges of shrubbery borders or in colonies between perennials. They do not require frequent lifting and replanting but will look after themselves without attention. The flowering of the different species covers many weeks of the spring, beginning after the snowdrops and scillas have come to an end. Propagated by seeds and offsets. — L. B. W.

**MUSCATEL.** See *vinifera* varieties at GRAPE.

**MUSCIPULA,** *-us, -um* (mus-kip'you-la). A mouse-trap or like one. See DIONAEA.

**MUSCOSA,** *-us, -um* (mus-ko'sa). Moss-like.

**MUSHROOM.** Of many wild species of edible fungi (see FUNGUS) only the common mushroom (*Agaricus campestris*) can be considered as a cultivated plant. The subterranean truffle, perhaps the greatest delicacy in the fungus world, is unknown in America, its collection or cultivation being confined chiefly to southern France.

The common mushroom, which is often spontaneous on lawns and fields, is much safer to grow than to collect. Wild plants, which are not uncommon in August and September, if moisture conditions are right, closely resemble very deadly relatives of the common mushroom. No absolutely safe method can be given to distinguish the edible mushroom from very similar poisonous toadstools, and none will be attempted here. Amateur attempts to make the distinction result in many deaths every year.

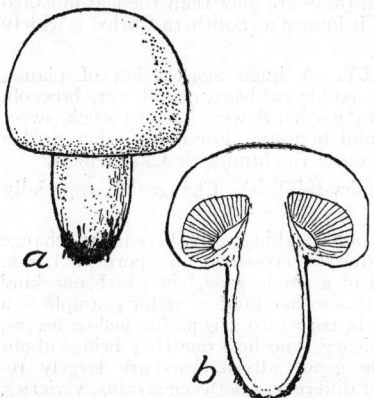

Common mushroom (*Agaricus campestris*). (a) The mature plant and (b) a cross-section showing its gills.

NATURE OF THE PLANT. *Agaricus campestris* is one of the fleshy fungi with a stout stalk and, in maturity, an umbrella-shaped cap or crown. It produces no flowers nor seeds, but as in other fungi, is reproduced by spores* — a somewhat technical process of which only one stage is of interest to the grower, as we shall see presently. Like most other fungi it is never green (produces no chlorophyll*) and thus does not manufacture plant food as do all normal green plants. But the mushroom does make a very nutritious and palatable food for us from the material in which it grows — manure. Living upon organic matter and having no green coloring substance in its makeup dictates the sort of place in which the mushroom is best grown. It should be dark, and no better organic matter has ever been found than stable manure. Darkness, manure, temperature, and moisture are the four essentials of mushroom growing and they are all important.

The darkness may be secured in any convenient cellar, cave (there are acres of artificial mushroom caves under Paris), quarry, or in a covered pit. Securing darkness is usually easier than providing the other three essentials of mushroom growing.

MANURE. Well-rotted manure is useless for the mushroom bed. Fresh, hot, steaming horse manure, in which there is plenty of straw, is absolutely necessary to start the process outlined below. Manure where the animals have been bedded with shavings, sphagnum moss, salt hay, or almost any other form of bedding should be rejected, as should the synthetic or artificial kinds. *See* MANURE. No stable manure that has been disinfected or to which fly dope has been added can be used.

Pile up the fresh, straw-laden manure in a heap of sufficient size so that it will not dry out. Small piles of a bushel or two are nearly useless. Preferably the pile should not be less than 4 ft. deep. Wet the pile thoroughly and let it stand for a few days until fermentation starts. Turn the pile over thoroughly after a few days, as the manure must not "burn." Wet it down again and let it stand for a few more days. During the first three turnings of the pile the temperature of the manure will probably be between 130° and 150°, which is satisfactory at this stage.

After each turning and wetting, a process that should be continued for 23–35 days, the temperature of the manure will gradually fall, and nearly all of the foul odor will go. When the temperature at the center of the pile reaches 70°–75°, the manure is ready to be put in the mushroom beds.

MAKING THE BEDS. The manure compost, having reached about 70°, is then put into layers 6–8 in. deep on the benches or ledges, upon which the plant will be grown or sometimes on the floor. It should be packed down reasonably but it should not be tamped or rammed down. To save space some growers build benches one above another, which, as light is not needed, is a good plan, provided that temperature and moisture conditions can be controlled.

Planting should not begin until the temperature of the manure in the bed has fallen to between 58° and 65°, and the air temperature of the house should be kept at about this. If over 75° air temperature is permitted for 24 hours, failure may result, and if air temperature falls below 50° the crop, while it is not killed, will be much delayed. Once the mushroom bed starts into activity the air temperature of the house must be kept as nearly as possible to 56°–58°. At this stage air temperatures below 50 or above 60 are detrimental or may be fatal.

PLANTING. Mushrooms are started from spawn, which comes in spawn bricks or in cartons. Whichever is used the principle is the same. They both consist of the dried state of a certain stage in the life-history of the mushroom which is held in a dormant condition. Planting this material in beds prepared as outlined above provides the opportunity for the plant to complete another stage of its life history — which is the mushroom as we know it. The heat and moisture conditions of the bed and house are such that the plant should begin to grow about 10–15 days after planting.

Pieces of spawn about 2 in. square should be planted in the bed 10 in. apart in both directions. The pieces of "brick" should be pressed into the manure compost not more than 1–2 in. deep. At this stage it is important to see that little or no water is added to the bed. If it is drenched, failure is certain. If air temperature has been properly managed, there should be enough moisture in the manure to permit the spawn brick to grow. If, on the other hand, the manure shows a tendency to dry out, water it very gently with a fine-rose watering pot, using tepid water. On no account use cold water from a hose.

After the spawn has been in the bed 10–15 days, the first sign of activity will be a series of white, thread-like ramifications which will spread in all directions from each piece of spawn. In about 3 weeks from planting the manure should be pretty completely infested with these threads (mycelium, *see* next illustration). Then the final planting operation should be completed. This consists of covering the whole bed about 1 in. deep with good garden loam, free of stones, fertilizer, weeds, or any residue of insecticides or fungicides. Some growers prefer the virgin soil immediately beneath freshly stripped sod.

SUBSEQUENT CARE. After the beds have been covered with the layer of soil, it will be from 6–7 weeks before the first small mushrooms appear above the surface. If all conditions are right, the bed should then bear continuously for two or three months or even more, after which the "spent" manure should be removed, never again to be used for mushrooms, although it is valuable material to add to the

---

* Special articles on the subjects indicated by an asterisk (*) will be found at the words so marked.

compost pile, or to use as ordinary manure. Being "spent," it is useless, of course, for a hotbed.

During the period of waiting for the mushrooms to appear, and while the bed is in production, the utmost care must be taken about temperature and moisture. The air temperature must be kept as near 56°–58° as possible. The beds must never be allowed to dry out, but they *must not be soaked*. Water the surface layer of soil just enough to keep it moist (not muddy). Use tepid water (rain water is fine) and sprinkle very lightly with a fine-rose watering pot.

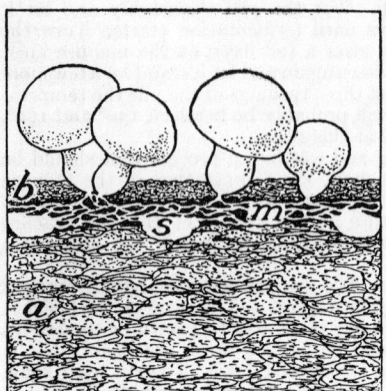

Cross-section of mushroom bed.
a) Six to eight in. of manure.
b) About ¾ in. of good soil.
s) A piece of mushroom spawn.
m) The growth of mushroom mycelium (*see* text) from which the crop springs.

The moisture conditions of the air are equally important. If you use a hygrometer,* see that humidity is kept as near 70–75 per cent as possible. If you have no instrument, the moisture condition can be gauged roughly by keeping the air just as moist as possible without drops collecting on the roof or walls. There must be no drip on the beds. In warm regions care must also be taken to see that the room is not too dry. If it is, the walls should be lightly sprayed. The only really safe guide is a daily hygrometer* reading.

HARVESTING. It is purely a matter of taste whether you prefer little "button" mushrooms, or larger ones. At first there will be an obvious first crop, usually at the places where the spawn bricks were planted. Later and successive crops will be more generally distributed. When the crop finally decreases to nearly zero, it is questionable whether it is better to try and induce a fresh crop or treat the stoppage as final. Some growers induce an apparently spent bed to produce a final crop by one thorough soaking of the bed with tepid water. But the plan often fails.

When the bed is finally cleared of spent manure, the whole house should be thoroughly hosed out, disinfected, dried off, and allowed to rest a few weeks before a fresh lot is started.

### OTHER METHODS

This somewhat elaborate technique of mushroom growing is not the only one, but it is the only sure one for quantity production. Many thoughtful readers are no doubt wondering why the need for darkness, considering that the plant is rightly called *Agaricus campestris*, that the latter word means *of the field*, and that mushrooms are not uncommon on lawns.

Darkness is not necessary for the final stage of the life-history of the mushroom, but it is for other phases of it. And conditions of temperature and moisture are better controlled in a dark cellar or cave than in open sunlight. For certain and quantity production there is no doubt about the need for darkness. But if a reasonable amount of failure can be tolerated, one very troublesome operation can be avoided and a crop may still be fairly sure.

When the manure is fresh, before stacking, separate out the straw and mix the pure dung with good garden loam, using ⅔ manure and ⅓ soil. Mix thoroughly and put in the beds immediately. Thereafter the process of planting and subsequent care must follow rigidly the directions given for the more usual method.

Still another short-cut, with a higher proportion of failure, is to use a cold frame or hotbed. Fill in with the mixture exactly as outlined for the regular method, but keep the bed covered with a 6-in. layer of straw or mats. Moisture and temperature conditions are hard to control in such a makeshift, but if it is on the north side of the house, and the weather is not too hot, some sort of a crop is fairly sure. Follow, as nearly as possible, the planting directions for the regular method.

The final, most hazardous, but by far the easiest, method is to plant 2-in. squares of spawn brick about 2 in. deep in the lawn. Moisture conditions will often be unfavorable and no crop will result that year. But if the moisture conditions are nearly right, a crop may be expected in late August or early September, and once planted, the chances of several annual crops are not very remote.

**MUSK MALLOW** = *Malva moschata* and *Hibiscus abelmoschus*.

**MUSKMELON.** See MELON.

**MUSK ROSE** = *Rosa moschata* and *Malva moschata*.

**MUSQUASH-ROOT** = *Cicuta maculata*.

**MUSTARD.** As a plant name *mustard* is applied to many weedy, chiefly annual herbs of the family Cruciferae, some of them serious pests. The true mustards all belong to the genus *Brassica* (which see), especially *B. juncea*, *B. nigra*, and *B. alba*. Varieties of the first species are sometimes grown as greens, but the genus *Brassica* contains much more important plants, like the cabbage, cauliflower, brussels sprouts, etc. While all these are finer than the leaf mustard (*B. juncea*), a form of it known as Southern Curled is widely grown for greens.

**MUSTARD FAMILY.** A huge aggregation of plants, containing besides the edible cabbage, cauliflower, broccoli, radish, and cress, many garden flowers like the stock, sweet alyssum, candytuft, and honesty. For many other garden genera and a description of the family see CRUCIFERAE.

*MUTABILIS, -e* (mew-tab'il-is). Changeable, especially as to color.

**MUTATION.** Simply speaking, any hereditary change in a character not due to crossing — a sport or break. Usually an alteration of a single gene,* in which one kind of gene is changed into another kind — as for example — a gene for green leaves in corn into a gene for yellow leaves, or a blue-flowered chicory gene into one that brings about white flowers. These gene* alternations are largely responsible for character differences between strains, varieties, species, and still larger plant groups.

They are the variations* that the plant breeder looks for in examining thousands of plants of a wild or a cultivated species. They are the off-types of a given variety. In a bed of seedlings, just one often of thousands has crinkled leaves, wavy flower petals, dwarf stature, yellow foliage, marked change in leaf or flower shape, earlier flowering period, increased yield, greater disease resistance and so on. These are often mutations. By saving them a new variety comes into being.

Mutations occur more commonly among seedlings, but there are many records of bud mutations — variations in which a part of the plant such as a branch is altered so as to yield a different type of fruit, or an ever-blooming race of flowers. The Starking sport of the Delicious apple, involving an earlier and richer red coloring of the fruit, appeared as a branch on an ordinary Delicious tree. Many other cases of this type in apples have been found, several of which have high commercial value. The New Dawn rose illustrates another valuable bud mutation. The well-known June-flowering Dr. van Fleet climbing rose produced a branch which flowers more or less continuously through the summer and fall. Cuttings from this branch gave rise to New Dawn.

Flower color bud sports or mutations often arise on dahlias, monthly roses, chrysanthemums and azaleas. Talisman has given rise to several that are commercially propagated. Presumably most plant species mutate, but some mutate more often than others. Contrast asparagus and lily-of-the-valley (rare) with corn and dahlias (common).

---

* Special articles on the subjects indicated by an asterisk (*) will be found at the words so marked.

Generally speaking, mutations occur more often among seed-propagated plants than those multiplied by asexual methods, such as cuttings, grafting, budding, tubers, corms, bulbs, etc.

Mutations seemingly occur among all sorts of characters — size, color, stature, flavor, yield, odor, etc. Their appearance is unpredictable. The majority of them will breed true in respect to the altered character on selfing.* Many of them require more coddling than the type from which they arise, although this by no means follows.

Mutants have been experimentally produced through the use of changes in temperature, ageing of seed, X-rays and radium. Some of these are new, and many are similar to those occurring naturally. In the latter case, the process is speeded up. In time, such efforts may result in valuable new types, especially among plants that are commonly asexually propagated. — O. E. W. See also VARIATION.

**MUTISIA** (mew-tiss'ĭ-a). A genus of evergreen, flowering shrubs, of about 50 species of the tropical Andes, belonging to the family Compositae, few of which are in cultivation and these few mostly climbers. Leaves alternate* and compound,* the leaflets ovalish. The leafstalk is prolonged into a tendril by which means the plant climbs. Flowers in large heads, composed of both ray* and disk* flowers, the ray flowers purple; rose or yellow. (Named for Jos. C. Mutis, a South American botanist.)

Mutisia can be grown in a cool greenhouse or outside where the temperature does not drop below 40°. Propagation by cuttings of half-ripened shoots in sand under a bell-jar or in a propagating frame in a temperature of 55°–65°, preferably in May or June. As soon as rooted pot into a compost 3 parts loam, 1 part leaf mold and 1 part sand. When the plants begin to grow, water freely, and apply liquid manure before flowering. Prune slightly after flowering. They are suitable for training up rafters or trellis. If grown outside, plant in sheltered position in good, rich soil.

**clematis.** A good, cool greenhouse climber, the rather woody stem hairy. Leaflets 4–5 pairs, ovalish. Flower heads about 2 in. across, with bright red ray flowers. Peru.

**MYCELIUM.** See the second illustration at MUSHROOM.

**MYOPORACEAE** (my-o-pore-ray'see-ee). A family of chiefly Australian and Pacific Island shrubs and trees of secondary garden interest. Of its 5 genera and 90 species, only *Myoporum* (chiefly from Australasia and the Pacific Islands) is in cult., mostly in greenhouses.

Leaves alternate,* opposite* or scattered, usually without marginal teeth, sticky in *Myoporum*. Flowers regular* in *Myoporum*, in not particularly showy clusters. Fruit fleshy.

Technical flower characters: Calyx more or less tubular, 5-parted or cut. Corolla tubular or funnel-shaped and regular* in *Myoporum*. Stamens 4, two longer than the others, and with a fifth one sterile. Ovary superior,* 2-celled, or sometimes 2–10-celled.

**MYOPORUM** (my-o-pore'rum). Somewhat heath-like shrubs or trees, comprising perhaps 30 species, and the only cult. genus of the family Myoporaceae (which see for their characters). Only three are cult. for ornament, mostly in the greenhouse, and otherwise little known. (*Myoporum* is from the Greek implying that the leaves are dotted.)

They should be grown in the cool greenhouse in potting mixture* 4. Hardy outdoors only in zones* 8 and 9. Propagated by cuttings.

**acuminatum.** A shrub with alternate,* resinous-dotted leaves, about 3 in. long, generally narrow or lance-shaped. Flowers white, about ⅓ in. long, nearly bell-shaped, bearded within. Fruit nearly globe-shaped. Aust.

**laetum.** A shrub or small tree, not over 15 ft. high. Leaves shining, bright green, thickish, generally lance-shaped, 2–4 in. long. Flowers about ½ in. long, white, but with purple spots. N. Zeal.

**sandwicense.** Bastard sandalwood; called also naio. A tall tree in its native region of Hawaii, sometimes 60 ft. high. Leaves mostly crowded at the ends of the twigs, oblongish, 4–6 in. long, mostly sticky when young. Flowers white or pink, in clusters of 5–8. Fruit white.

*MYOSOTIDIFLORA*, *-us*, *-um* (my-o-so-ti-di-flō'ra). With flowers like those of the next genus.

**MYOSOTIDIUM** (my-o-so-tid'ĭ-um). A perennial herb of the Chatham Islands (N. Zeal.), of only one species of the family Boraginaceae. The only species, **M. hortensia**, grows to a height of 12–18 in. Leaves broad at the base, narrowing to a point, becoming smaller as they approach the top of the plant, covered with stiff, gray hairs. Flowers dark blue, becoming lighter towards the center, in dense cymes,* the individual flowers ½ in. across. Propagate from seeds, sown in early spring where intended to bloom, ⅛ in. deep in ordinary soil. Treat as an annual. Several sowings may be made during the summer as it produces flowers from seeds in 8–10 weeks. See BLUE GARDEN. The plant is sometimes offered as *M. nobile*. (*Myosotidium* is from the Greek for like forget-me-not, to which this genus is closely related.)

**MYOSOTIS.** See FORGET-ME-NOT.

**MYRIAD-LEAF** = *Myriophyllum verticillatum*.

**MYRICA** (mir-ī'ka). Shrubs or trees, often pleasantly aromatic, belonging to the family Myricaceae, and comprising about 35 species, three of which are sometimes cult. in specialized places. They have alternate* leaves and small, greenish, inconspicuous flowers, without sepals or petals, the male and female separate and often on different plants, mostly in catkins.* Fruit fleshy or nut-like, covered with an aromatic wax or resin. (*Myrica* is an old Greek name for some shrub, probably the tamarisk, and of no real significance here.)

The first two species are admirable shrubs for very dry, sandy soils, as both grow naturally in such places. Both species are commonly called bayberry, but neither is the true bayberry (which see). *Myrica gale* is a bog shrub and should be grown in the bog garden. All are easily propagated by seeds, especially the first species.

**carolinensis.** Bayberry. A shrub 3–8 ft. high, the leaves ultimately falling, but often holding on until early winter. Leaves very aromatic, more or less elliptic or broadest towards the tip, 3–4 in. long. Fruit conspicuously grayish-waxy, very aromatic, and used in making bayberry candles. Eastern N.A., mostly along the coast. Hardy from zone* 2 southward.

**cerifera.** Wax myrtle; called also bayberry and tallow-shrub. A tall shrub or small tree, never more than 35 ft. high. Leaves evergreen or very persistent, more or less lance-shaped, 1–3 in. long. Fruit grayish-waxy, aromatic. Southern N.J. to Fla. and Ark. Hardy from zone* 4 southward.

**gale.** Sweet gale; also called moor or bog myrtle. A bog shrub, not usually over 4 ft. high. Leaves deciduous,* lance-shaped or broadest towards the tip, 1–2½ in. long. Fruit resinous-dotted, in dense catkins. Northern N.A. and northern Eurasia. Hardy from zone* 4 northward. It grows naturally in cool bogs almost to the Arctic Circle, but southward, in the mountains, to Va. Useful only in acid sites in the bog garden.

**MYRICACEAE** (mi-ri-cay'see-ee). Commonly called the bayberry family, although the true bayberry (*Pimenta*) does not belong here. The Myricaceae contains only two genera, both of secondary importance as garden shrubs and trees, and both having resinous-dotted, aromatic foliage. One is *Myrica*, containing the bayberry or wax myrtle, the other *Comptonia* or sweet fern.

Leaves alternate.* Male and female flowers on separate twigs or even on separate plants, small, and inconspicuous. Fruit a small often waxy nut, or fleshy. Both the genera furnish shrubs for more or less specialized conditions (dry sand or bogs).

Technical flower characters: Petals and sepals wanting; the rudimentary flowers in small catkins.* Stamens 2–16. Ovary 1-celled.

**MYRICARIA** (mi-ri-cay'ri-a). Tamarisk-like shrubs of the family Tamaricaceae, not much known in cult., but **M. germanica**, a native of Eurasia, occasionally grown for ornament. It is somewhat more hardy than the closely related *Tamarix*, from which it is separated only by technical characters. Leaves extremely small and scale-like, practically clothing the wand-like stems which are 4–6 ft. high. Flowers pinkish, very small, but numerous, in dense spire-like clusters (racemes*), which are terminal or in the leaf-axils.* Fruit a 3-valved capsule.* May–July. Hardy from zone* 3 southward. (*Myricaria* is derived from *Myrica*, the old Greek name of the tamarisk.)

**MYRIOPHYLLUM** (mi-rĭ-o-fill'um). Water-milfoil. Widely dispersed, fresh-water aquatic herbs of the family Haloragidaceae, two of the 20 known species popular plants

---

* Special articles on the subjects indicated by an asterisk (*) will be found at the words so marked.

for pools and aquaria. They have hair-like submerged leaves, but sometimes above-water leaves that are broader, toothed or sometimes without teeth, especially in some of the native, non-hort. species. Flowers extremely minute, lacking sepals* or petals, or both. Fruit a collection of small nutlets, sometimes roughened on the back and not splitting. (*Myriophyllum* is from the Greek for myriad-leaved, in allusion to the many, fine, thread-like leaves.)

The plants are of the easiest culture in any aquarium, where cuttings may be planted in mud or sand. In large pools, especially southward, they may become a nuisance as they grow quickly and may choke a pool in a season or two.

**proserpinacoides.** Parrot's-feather. An extremely graceful aquatic with a weak stem, about 6 in. of which grows above the water, the rest submerged. Leaves feathery, composed of 10–25 hair-like divisions. Chile and Uruguay. The commonest and best species for aquaria.

**verticillatum.** Myriad-leaf. Plant nearly all submerged, the under-water leaves in whorls* of 3, the segments hair-like. The above-water leaves (when produced) more or less lance-shaped and deeply cut or divided, but not hair-like. North temperate zone.

**MYRIOSTIGMA, -us, -um** (mi-ree-o-stig'ma). With many stigmas.*

**MYROBALAN PLUM** = *Prunus cerasifera* and *Terminalia catappa*.

**MYRON STRATTON ARBORETUM.** See ARBORETUM.

**MYRRH.** See MYRRHIS.

**MYRRHIS** (mir'ris). Myrrh. A hardy, perennial, aromatic herb, of only 1 species belonging to the carrot family and a native of Eu. It is the common myrrh, **M. odorata**, also known as sweet cicely of Eu. It grows 2–3 ft. high. Leaves compound,* the leaflets lance-shaped, finely divided, having a fern-like appearance, fragrant, and chiefly grown for this. Flowers small, whitish, inconspicuous, produced in compound umbels.* Fruit a capsule of about 1 in. long, strongly ribbed. A graceful plant, used in the olden times as a flavoring. Propagated by seeds sown outdoors in ordinary soil ½ in. deep, in open sunny border, in Sept. or April, but preferably as soon as seeds are ripe. The roots may be divided in Oct. or March. (*Myrrhis* is from the Greek for perfume.)

**MYRSINACEAE.** See ARDISIA.

**MYRSINITES** (mir-sin-eye'teez). A Pre-Linnaean* name for several quite different plants. See PACHISTIMA, EUPHORBIA.

**MYRSIPHYLLUM** = *Asparagus asparagoides*.

**MYRTACEAE** (mir-tay'see-ee). The myrtle, allspice or guava family, comprising 72 genera and nearly 3000 species of chiefly tropical, aromatic shrubs and trees, is of outstanding interest to gardeners in warm regions, and to many florists. Among the cult. genera are *Eucalyptus*, *Eugenia*, *Leptospermum*, *Melaleuca*, *Callistemon*, and *Metrosideros*, all, and some very widely, grown for ornament, especially outdoors in Calif. and Fla. and also in greenhouses. *Callistemon* is especially fine as a greenhouse shrub.

Fruit-yielding or economic genera are *Psidium* (see GUAVA), *Feijoa*, *Pimenta* (allspice and the true bayberry) and *Rhodomyrtus*.

*Myrtus* contains the classical myrtle, and the other cult., mostly ornamental genera, are: *Agonis*, *Angophora*, *Calothamnus*, *Kunzea*, *Syncarpia* and *Tristania*.

Leaves mostly opposite* and evergreen, usually without marginal teeth. Flowers often very showy, solitary or in clusters, quite often with a few or many bracts* in the clusters. Fruit very various, a nut, pod, berry or drupe.*

Technical flower characters: Flowers hermaphrodite* and regular.* Sepals 4 or 5, usually free, but their bases merged with the fleshy receptacle, which is joined to the ovary in most genera. Petals 4–5. Stamens* very numerous, conspicuous and furnishing most of the flower color in some genera (*Callistemon* and *Melaleuca*). Ovary inferior,* 1-many-celled. The fruit is usually surrounded by the persistent calyx-lobes.

**MYRTIFOLIA, -us, -um** (mir-ti-fō'li-a). With leaves like the myrtle (*Myrtus*).

**MYRTILLOCACTUS** (mir-til-lo-kak'tus). A small genus of chiefly Mexican, very spiny, tree-like cacti, of which **M. geometrizans**, the garambullo, is grown for oddity or interest in desert gardens in the Southwest. It is a much-branched, tree-like plant up to 15 ft. high, the branches about 4 in. thick, 5–6-ribbed and bluish-green. Spines usually 6 at each cluster, the central one erect and dagger-like, the other 5 diverging, and more slender. Flowers not over 1 in. wide, day-blooming, purplish. Fruit about the size of an olive, purplish and edible. For culture *see* CACTI. (*Myrtillocactus* means a myrtle-like cactus, perhaps in reference to the fruit, as the habit is very unlike a myrtle.)

**MYRTLE.** The true myrtle is *Myrtus communis* (which see). But several other plants are occasionally called myrtle. *See* LAGERSTROEMIA, RHODOMYRTUS, ANGOPHORA, VINCA MINOR, LEIOPHYLLUM, and MYRICA CERIFERA.

**MYRTLE FAMILY.** An immense family of chiefly tropical shrubs and trees, generally aromatic, and including the guava, eucalyptus, allspice, and the true myrtle (not the creeping myrtle or periwinkle). For a list of all the garden genera and a description of the family *see* MYRTACEAE.

**MYRTUS** (mir'tus). Myrtle. Tropical or sub-tropical shrubs or trees of the family Myrtaceae, comprising over 100 species, from the Old and New World, only a handful of any garden interest, one of them the classic myrtle of legend and history and widely grown for ornament. They have opposite,* simple leaves without marginal teeth, very aromatic in some species. Flowers white or pink (in ours), solitary in the leaf-axils* or in few-flowered clusters, neither large nor showy. Petals 4–5. Stamens* numerous, longer than the petals but not conspicuously protruding. Fruit a berry, crowned with the persistent calyx-lobes. (*Myrtus* is the classical Greek name of the myrtle.)

The first species is widely planted throughout zones* 7, 8, and 9 for its handsome evergreen foliage. Northward it is a common greenhouse pot plant, much grown by florists for decoration. It needs a cool greenhouse and potting mixture* 4. Propagated by cuttings of half-ripened wood under glass; or by seeds. The other two species are little grown.

**communis.** The true myrtle. An evergreen, aromatic shrub 3–9 ft. high. Leaves ovalish to lance-shaped, 1–2 in. long, shining green, almost stalkless. Flowers about ⅝ in. wide, white or pinkish. Fruit about ½ in. long, bluish-black, or white in a hort. form. Mediterranean region and western As. The var. **microphylla** has smaller and much more numerous, nearly overlapping leaves; var. **flore-pleno** is double-flowered; var. **variegata** has variegated leaves. There are many other hort. forms differing mostly in stature or leaf-form.

**ralphi.** A shrub or small tree, not over 15 ft. high. Leaves ovalish, ¾–1 in. long. Flowers pinkish, about ½ in. wide. Fruit about ⅓ in. long, dark red. N. Zeal.

**ugni.** Chilean guava. A shrub or small tree, not over 20 ft. high. Leaves shining green above, whitish beneath, leathery and more or less oval. Flowers rose-pink, and beneath them are 2 persistent bracts.* Fruit about ½ in. in diameter, purplish-red, pleasant-flavored and edible.

---

* Special articles on the subjects indicated by an asterisk (*) will be found at the words so marked.

# N

**NADEN.** See Japanese Flowering Cherries at PRUNUS.

**NAEGELIA** (nay-ge′li-a). A small genus of tropical American, herbaceous, tuberous-rooted perennials, of the family Gesneriaceae, often referred to as *Gesneria* to which they are closely allied. Leaves opposite,* soft, velvety and heart-shaped. Flowers tubular, red or yellowish-white, in terminal clusters. Fruit a dry capsule.* (Named for Karl von Naegeli, a Munich professor of botany.)

Cultivated in greenhouses and propagated by seeds, tubers or offsets. Sow seeds on surface of well-drained pots of sandy peat in temperature of 75° in March or April. Cuttings of young shoots should be inserted in pots of sandy peat in temperature 75°–85° in spring. Tubers may be divided before starting the plant into growth after resting period. Plant 1 in. deep, singly in 5 in. pots or 1–2 in. apart in larger sizes. Use a potting compost of 2 parts fibrous peat, 1 part loam, 1 part leaf mold with a little decayed cow manure and silver sand. Water moderately until plants are 3–4 in. high, then water freely. Apply liquid manure once a week when flower buds appear, but after flowering gradually reduce water until foliage dies down, then keep dry during winter months. A good place is under the bench* as they should not be stored in too dry a place.

**cinnabarina.** Grows to 2 ft. high. Leaves covered with red or purplish hairs. Flowers about 1½ in. long, drooping, tubular, red on upper side, and the throat spotted with white. A fine winter-blooming plant. Mexico.

**multiflora.** Grows to 1½ ft. Leaves with long hairs, also velvety. Flowers numerous, hanging, white, or cream-colored, the tube narrow. Mexico.

**zebrina.** Grows to 2 ft. Leaves densely hairy, having distinctly marked veins of purple, red, or dark brown. Flowers red, with yellow spots, 1½ in. long, the tube contracted at the base. Particularly good for fall flowering. Brazil.

**NAGAMI KUMQUAT** = *Fortunella margarita*.

**NAIL-HEAD RUST.** See Rust at PLANT DISEASES.

**NAIO** = *Myoporum sandwicense*.

**NAKED FLOWER.** One without petals or sepals* as in the willow and *Myrica*.

**NAMA** (nay′ma). American herbs or sub-shrubs of the family Hydrophyllaceae, comprising 36 species, of which the only one of garden interest is **N. parryi**, a native of Cal. It is a shrubby perennial, 3–6 ft. high, the stem ½ in. in diameter. Leaves alternate,* without stalks, dark green, long and narrow. Flowers violet-blue in small lateral clusters, funnel-shaped, about ½ in. long. May–July. Cult. in Calif., but almost unknown elsewhere. (*Nama* is from the Greek for stream or spring, in allusion, possibly, to the moist site of some species.)

**NAMES OF PLANTS.** See PLANT NAMES.

*NANA, -us, -um* (nay′na). Small.

**NANDIN** = *Nandina domestica*.

**NANDINA** (nan-dy′na). A single species of evergreen shrub of the family Berberidaceae, native in China and Japan, hardy outdoors only from zone* 7 southward. The only species is **N. domestica,** the nandin, sometimes called sacred bamboo, although it has nothing to do with any bamboo. It is an attractive shrub, 6–8 ft. high, with alternate,* twice- or thrice-compound* leaves, the ultimate leaflets narrow, 1–2 in. long and very handsome in their fall, red color. Flowers small, white, not showy, but the clusters (panicles*) nearly a foot long and handsome. Sepals* numerous, in series of 3, gradually passing into the white petals. Stamens* as many as the petals. Fruit a red, 2-seeded berry about ½ in. in diameter, very handsome when ripe, and the chief attraction of the plant. The shrub is not particular as to soil, but it prefers a reasonably moist site, failing which it should be regularly watered. North of zone* 7 it is often hardy in protected places, where, if the top should be winter-killed, the roots may survive, especially if they are well mulched.* June–July. (*Nandina* is the Latin version of the Japanese name for this shrub.)

**NANKEEN** (or Nankin) **LILY** = *Lilium testaceum*.

*NANKINENSIS, -e* (nan-kin-en′sis). From Nankin, China.

**NANNYBERRY** = *Viburnum lentago*.

**NAPELLUS** (na-pel′lus). Literally a little turnip; as a specific name used to designate small turnip-like roots, as in *Aconitum napellus*. See MONKSHOOD.

**NAPOBRASSICA** (nay-po-brass′i-ka). Literally a "turnip-mustard" or a "rape-mustard"; used as a specific name for the rutabaga (*Brassica napobrassica*).

**NAPOLEON.** A cherry variety. See CHERRY.

*NAPUS* (nay′pus). A Pre-Linnaean* name for the rape (*Brassica napus*).

*NARBONENSIS, -e* (nar-bon-en′sis). From Narbonne, France.

**NARCISSUS** (nar-sis′sus). Important, chiefly hardy, bulbous plants of the family Amaryllidaceae, most of them European, very widely grown for ornament or fragrance, and including such well-known plants as the daffodil, jonquil, paper-white, the Chinese sacred lily, and the poet's narcissus. All bear bulbs. Leaves generally rush-like or more or less terete in cross-section in the jonquil and its relatives, but flat or nearly so in the common daffodil, basal in all sorts, and usually about the length of the flowering stalk. Flowers prevailingly white or yellow, often nodding. Calyx and corolla not separable as such, but modified in two ways: (1) The flower having a central crown (corona) which is long and tubular (in the trumpet narcissus or daffodil); or (2) the central crown (corona) reduced to a shallow, ring-like cup (as in the jonquil and poet's narcissus). Outside of this central corolla-like organ are the six segments which comprise the petals and sepals. In the group with a long tubular corona there is the typical hose-in-hose* effect of one flower growing within another. Stamens* 6, usually hidden in the crown. Fruit a 3-lobed, many-seeded capsule.* The species have been much hybridized so that those below are somewhat uncertain as to exact botanical identity, although they represent the chief sorts in cult. (*Narcissus* is named for the mythological youth so fond of his own reflection that after long gazing at it he was changed into the flower.) They are sometimes called Lent lilies.

For the garden uses and Culture *see* below.

**barri.** A group of plants of hybrid origin, presumably derived from crossing *N. incomparabilis* and *N. poeticus*. They have solitary yellow flowers, the crown about ⅓ as long as the segments, and somewhat wavy-margined.

**bulbocodium.** The petticoat or hoop-petticoat narcissus (or daffodil). Leaves channeled or nearly round in cross-section, usually longer than the flowering stalk, which is 4–12 in. high. Flowers solitary, yellow or white, the crown longer than the tubular corolla. Southern France and Morocco. For cult. see ROCK GARDEN.

**cyclamineus.** A little known species from Portugal, with solitary flowers having a very short tube and recurved, lemon-yellow segments, which are shorter than the orange-yellow crown and strongly turned upward. For culture *see* ROCK GARDEN.

**incomparabilis.** Leaves flat, about 12 in. long and ¼ in. wide. Flower solitary, the corona about half the length of the tube, wavy-edged. Southern Eu.

**jonquilla.** The common jonquil. Leaves nearly 18 in. long, rush-like and nearly terete. Flowers in clusters of 2–6, fragrant, yellow, the tube about 1 in. long, the corona less than half as long as the segments. Southern Eu. and northern Af. Double-flowered forms are known.

**juncifolius.** A little known jonquil, its rush-like leaves scarcely 6 in. long. Flowers 1–4 in the cluster, yellow, the tube about ½ in. long, the corona about half the length of the segments, darker yellow and wavy-edged. Double-flowered forms are known.

---

* Special articles on the subjects indicated by an asterisk (*) will be found at the words so marked.

**leedsi.** A group of hybrid narcissus with flat leaves and white, solitary flowers, the wavy edges, yellow, but with a white- or pink-tinted crown which is nearly as long as the segments in some giant forms.

**minor.** A yellow, trumpet narcissus. Perhaps merely a form of N. pseudo-narcissus. It has yellow flowers, the corona sulphur-yellow, and the whole plant is scarcely more than 5 in. high. The *var.* **minimus** is still smaller, and rarely grows over 3 in. high. Both are rock garden species. *See* ROCK GARDEN for culture.

**moschatus.** White trumpet narcissus. Perhaps merely a form of N. pseudo-narcissus, but with cream white flowers, the segments slightly twisted, sulphur-yellow-tinged in youth, ultimately white, the corona as long as the segments and pure white.

**odorus.** Campernelle jonquil. Leaves about 12 in. long, very narrow or rush-like. Flowers in clusters of 2–4, fragrant, yellow, the tube about ¾ in. long, the wavy or lobed corona about half as long as the segments. Double-flowered forms are offered.

**poetaz.** Poetaz narcissus. A group of hybrids between the poet's narcissus and the polyanthus narcissus. They have clusters of 2–6 flowers, which are more fragrant than in the polyanthus narcissus (*N. tazetta*). See notes at Culture below.

**poeticus.** Poet's narcissus. Leaves about 18 in. long, and ¼ in. wide, flat and grass-like. Flowers very fragrant, white, the tube about 1 in. long, the corona very shallow, much shorter than the segments, the edges wavy and conspicuously red-margined. Southern Eu. The *var.* **ornatus** is earlier-flowering. Double-flowered forms are also known.

**pseudo-narcissus.** The common trumpet narcissus or daffodil. A stout, long cult. plant now of many forms and coming in innumerable named garden types. Leaves flat, 12–18 in. long, usually just reaching the flowers. Corolla about 2 in. long, typically pale yellow, the segments and corona mostly of a slightly different shade. Corona very long, deeply wavy or even slightly fringed. Eu. There are many forms, some with double flowers.

**tazetta.** Polyanthus narcissus. Leaves flat, about 18 in. long and nearly ¾ in. wide. Flowers generally white, fragrant, usually in clusters of 4–8, the tube about 1 in. long, the corona much shorter than the segments and usually pale yellow. Eurasia and in the Canary Islands. Long cult. and the origin of many popular hort. forms, but not hardy outdoors in frosty regions, for it is normally autumn-growing. Among the best known is the Paper White narcissus forced on a great scale by florists for winter bloom. As the name indicates, it is pure white. The *var.* **orientalis**, the Chinese sacred lily, has pale yellow segments and a darker yellow crown about ⅓ the length of the segments. Commonly grown in bowls of pebbles and water in the house. For notes on culture *see* below.

**triandrus.** Leaves about 12 in. long, rush-like or nearly round in cross-section. Flowers pure white, the tube about ¾ in. long. Corona cup-like, with the margins not crisped or wavy, about half the length of the segments. Southwestern Eu. For culture *see* ROCK GARDEN.

## NARCISSUS CULTURE

KINDS. From the gardener's point of view all narcissus may be divided into two sections, the small group of species that are of value in rock gardens and the edges of borders, and the great collection of horticultural forms that have been derived from relatively few species.

The first group contains the small yellow trumpets, *N. minor* and its var. *minimus;* the white trumpets, mostly *N. moschatus;* the hoop-petticoats, forms of *bulbocodium* in white and various hues of yellow; *cyclamineus,* a trumpet with characteristically reflexed petals; the forms of *triandrus;* and several small forms of jonquil. For the culture of most of these *see* ROCK GARDEN.

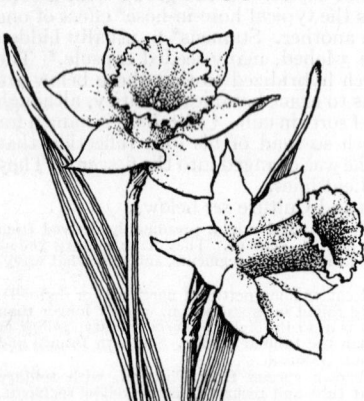

Trumpet narcissus (daffodil)

The second group contains the selected and hybrid forms of trumpet narcissus, commonly called daffodil, and of *N. poeticus,* together with the hybrids that have resulted from these two, and from hybrids between the hybrids. In the South and on the Pacific Coast, the bunch-flowered *N. tazetta,* which grows during the winter and flowers very early in the spring, may be useful. In the North only the hybrids resulting from *poeticus* × *tazetta,* known as Poetaz forms, may be used safely to represent this section.

Because of the great number of these garden forms, it has been convenient to divide them into groups based on the form and color of their flowers, as well as the size of their parts. In late years, due to the wide interbreeding between these groups, it is increasingly difficult to make sharp lines of demarcation.

Jonquil

The trumpet section embraces all those flowers in which the central trumpet is as long as or longer than the surrounding six petals that form the perianth.* In this group are both yellow and white examples, as well as a wide range of forms in which the perianth is white and the trumpet yellow, varying from pale to deep golden-yellow. This group, in its pale forms, very closely approaches the white trumpets which are pure white only in some of the more modern varieties.

The *N. incomparabilis* group resembles the trumpet group in general character except that the central crown is either a short trumpet or a bowl-shaped cup, in rare cases flattened somewhat but never flat like the eye of *N. poeticus*. The color patterns may be pure yellow, or have a yellow perianth with a red margin to the yellow cup, white perianth with a pure yellow cup, or white perianth with a yellow cup variously suffused or bordered with color. Recent seedlings sometimes referred to as Giant Incomparabilis resemble the type of the group but usually have trumpet rather than bowl-shaped crowns. In no case, however, may the depth of the cup equal the length of the perianth* segment.

The petals may be either white or yellow and the cup is always yellow more or less suffused, if not entirely covered, with some hue of red. In general style these varieties more closely resemble their *poeticus* ancestor.

The *N. leedsi* group parallels the *N. incomparabilis* group in all features save color. Here the petals are never yellow and the cup or crown is never solid yellow but always white tinted with yellow that often fades out as the flower ages, leaving a white cup. In some modern forms there is often a pinkish or apricot suffusion in the cup or on its margin.

Poet's narcissus

In this section there are many of the Giant *leedsi* type which are usually most effective garden plants.

The *N. barri* group usually has rather smaller flowers than any of the preceding, with a smaller central crown that is more or less flattened.

In the poet's narcissus, *N. poeticus,* the petals are always glistening white, the cup or eye is small, usually flat or saucer-shaped, and yellow in color with a margin of gold. This margin is usually narrow and well defined, but sometimes diffused and in some modern sorts diffused over the entire eye. All forms in

---

* Special articles on the subjects indicated by an asterisk (*) will be found at the words so marked.

this group have a sweet and very characteristic fragrance.

The Poetaz group is the result of crossing the poet's narcissus with the bunch-flowered *N. tazetta* and forms two sections, one with many small flowers on a stalk, and another with two or three larger flowers on a stalk. The first group more closely resembles *N. tazetta*, and the second *N. poeticus*. All have a strong fragrance, combining the perfumes of the two parents. The bunch-flowered narcissus are variations of *N. tazetta*, with many small, highly perfumed flowers on each stalk. In color they may be self yellow, pure white, yellow with orange cups, white with yellow cups. In no case is there a suggestion of red.

The jonquils are for the most part species, chiefly *N. jonquilla*, *juncifolius*, and *odorus*, with rush-like leaves, several to many small flowers on a stalk, little color variation and a very characteristic scent. In recent years jonquil hybrids have appeared, usually the result of jonquil pollen on a trumpet, that resemble the parents in their scent, the clarity of their yellow color, and differ in the flatter leaves and fewer flowers on the stalk.

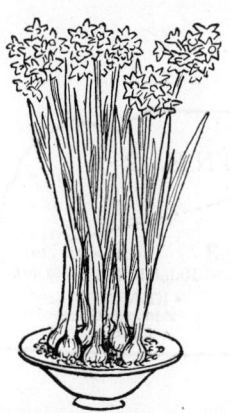

The Chinese sacred lily (*Narcissus tazetta orientalis*), and the popular paper white, can be grown in a bowl of pebbles and water.

PLANTING. Narcissus are suited to a wide range of climatic conditions but not all do equally well in all places. The farther north they are planted, the less well trumpet narcissus and their derivatives do, and chief use must be made of *N. poeticus* and its hybrids. *N. tazetta* and any other winter-growing sorts should be used only in the South.

The bulbs must be planted deeply at least two and one half times the depth of the bulb, erring to deeper rather than to more shallow planting. The soil must be well drained so that no stagnant moisture can bring decay to the plants at the base of the bulb from which the roots spring. Food should be put well below the bulb and no animal manure should ever touch the bulbs, although the annual roots may grow into it. In preparing the soil, a layer of sand or soil should cover the deep compost before the bulbs are set.

As the bulbs increase they should be lifted, divided and replanted, taking care not to injure the base of the bulb in division. This is necessary every three or four years but is done annually with fine stock. If longer intervals between division and resetting are wanted, plant more deeply as this retards increase.

All narcissus may be forced, using potting mixture* 4 with bone meal substituted for cow manure. Nearly all may also be grown in bowls of pebbles and water. The surest results come from the *tazetta* varieties, especially the Chinese sacred lily, but the trumpets, and *N. leedsi* and *incomparabilis* varieties, force well if the bulbs are held late into the winter before using.

For the details of forcing *see* BULBS. At the same article will be found the description of how to treat narcissus when naturalized in the lawn. There is no more effective way to mass them. — B. Y. M.

DISEASES. The more important diseases of *Narcissi* are nematodes, basal rot, leafspot and mosaic. When *nematodes* are present, the bulbs exhibit an internal brown discoloration. Infected leaves are stunted, yellow, twisted and covered with small swellings. For control, use hot water treated bulbs (*see* BULBS). Discard infected plants and sterilize the soil. *Basal rot* is characterized by dwarfed plants with rotted roots and bulbs. Use clean bulbs, dip bulbs in Ceresan* one pound to eight gallons of water for one to two minutes, discard infected plants and practice crop rotation. *Leafspot*, caused by various fungi, can be controlled by applications of copper fungicides and the burning of all plant debris in the fall. *Mosaic*, a virus disease, is characterized by leaves mottled with dark and light green areas. The immediate removal of infected plants is the only effective means of control.

**NARDOO** = *Marsilea drummondi*.

*NARDUS* (nar'dus). Latin equivalent for the old Asiatic nard, the name for the grass *Cymbopogon nardus*, and its aromatic oil.

**NARTHECIUM** (nar-thee'si-um). Called by some *Abama*. Hardy perennial herbs of the lily family, not very common in the bogs and swamps of East Asia, Eu., and N.A., and comprising only about 6 species, the following being the only ones of garden interest. Leaves grass-like. The flowering stalk rises from the center of the leaves and is crowned by a raceme* of yellowish-green flowers. Petals 6. Stamens* 6. Fruit a 3-celled capsule,* its seeds with a little tail at each end. (*Narthecium* is from the Greek word *narthex* meaning a rod, but of uncertain application here.)

Propagated by seeds sown in March or April, or by division of roots in Oct. or March. The plants must be grown in acid soil or boggy peat. Moist beds, borders or margins of ponds are only tolerably suitable places, as naturally the plants are often found growing in sphagnum moss.

**americanum.** Bog asphodel; called also yellow grass. A rare plant confined to the pine-barren bogs of N.J. and Del. Leaves 3–8 in. long, the upper shorter. Flower cluster dense, 1–2 in. long, gray-hairy. Pods gray. June–Sept.

**californicum.** Leaves iris-like, but only about ⅙ in. wide and 4–8 in. long. Flower cluster 3–4 in. long. Pods salmon color. Calif.

**NASEBERRY** = *Sapota achras*.

**NASTURTIUM.** The common garden nasturtium comprises the genus **Tropaeolum** (tro-pee'o-lum), the only one of the family **Tropaeolaceae**, with about 45 species of annual or perennial, soft-stemmed herbs, most of which are climbing. They are natives of the cooler parts of S.A. The perennial species have tuberous underground stems but in all other respects resemble the annuals. Leaves alternate,* more or less round, light green, with strongly marked veins radiating from the center from which the stalk arises. Leaf stalk fleshy and sensitive, curling round any object with which it comes in contact enabling the tall kinds to climb as much as 10 ft. Flowers are showy and solitary, growing from the axils* of the leaves, pale yellow, orange, scarlet, crimson or dark red. Sepals 5, joined at the base, 3 prolonged into a spur at the back of the flower. Petals usually 5, broad, suddenly narrowing at the base into a kind of stalk where they join the sepals. Stamens* 8, curving towards the back of the flower. Fruit 3-celled, with 1 seed in each cell. (*Tropaeolum* is from the Greek for trophy, in allusion to the shield-shaped leaves.)

Easily cultivated from seeds or cuttings. Sow seeds where plants are required to bloom, 1 in. deep, in April or they may be sown in pots or boxes in the cool greenhouse and transplanted. Soil should not be too rich or plants will produce lots of foliage and few flowers. Cuttings may be made from the young shoots at any time, they should be about 4 in. in length and inserted in sand, in shady part of the cool greenhouse or cold frame, where they will root in a few days. Cuttings rooted in Sept. make excellent pot plants for flowering in the cool greenhouse and can be used for house window plants. Nasturtiums make excellent coverings for trellis, posts and rocks. The flowers make very attractive decorations when cut.

**T. lobbianum** = *Tropaeolum peltophorum*.

**T. majus.** Common nasturtium or Indian cress, so called because the young flower buds and fruits are used as seasoning. (*See* HERB GARDENING.) Strong-climbing annual, growing to a height 8–12 ft. Leaves round, on long stalks. Flowers 2½ in. across, yellow-orange sometimes striped and spotted with red. The *var*. **nanum** (Tom Thumb) is a dwarf form, *vars*. **atropurpureum** (dark red), **coccineum** (scarlet) and **heinemanni** (chocolate) are color forms. S.A. A beautiful, low-growing, late-flowering, yellow form is known as Golden Gleam.

**T. minus.** Dwarf nasturtium. Of scrambling habit and smaller than *T. majus*. Flowers 1½ in. or smaller. S.A. *See* HERB GARDENING.

**T. peltophorum.** A climbing annual, slightly hairy except under sides of leaves which are long-stalked. Flowers 1 in. long, and long-spurred, orange-red. S.A.

**T. peregrinum.** Canary-bird flower. An annual of tall climbing habit. Leaves round, but deeply cut into 5 finger-like sections. Flowers pale

---

* Special articles on the subjects indicated by an asterisk (*) will be found at the words so marked.

yellow, 1 in. long. A particularly dainty type used in English cottage gardens. Peru.

**NASTURTIUM-AQUATICUM.** *See* RORIPA.

**NASTURTIUM FAMILY** = Tropaeolaceae.

*NATALENSIS, -e* (nay-tal-en'sis). From Natal, South Africa.

**NATAL GRASS** = *Tricholaena rosea.*

**NATAL ORANGE** = *Strychnos spinosa.*

**NATAL PLUM** = *Carissa grandiflora.*

*NATANS* (nay'tanz). Floating.

**NATIONAL ARBORETUM.** *See* ARBORETUM.

**NATIONAL BOTANIC GARDEN.** *See* BOTANIC GARDEN.

**NATIONAL COUNCIL.** Short for National Council of State Garden Club Federations. It is an amalgamation of the garden club federations of over 33 states, and the central office is R.C.A. Building, Rockefeller Center, New York City. It includes most garden clubs that are not affiliated with the Garden Club of America.

**NATIONAL FLOWERS.** There is no national floral emblem for the U.S., although many suggestions have been put forward, notably mountain laurel, columbine, flowering dogwood, and rose. Perhaps only the latter is found in some form in every state in the Union, but it is already the national flower of England, and is not peculiarly American, as is the mountain laurel. But the latter is not found wild west of Ohio and Tenn., and is therefore scarcely "national" in distribution. *See also* STATE FLOWERS.

The floral emblems of the leading foreign countries are:

| | | | |
|---|---|---|---|
| Canada | Sugar maple | Egypt | Egyptian lotus (water lily) |
| England | Rose | | |
| France | Fleur-de-lis | Scotland | Thistle |
| Germany | Cornflower | Ireland | Shamrock |
| Italy | Lily | Wales | Leek |
| Spain | Pomegranate | China | Narcissus |
| Newfoundland | Pitcher-plant | Japan | Chrysanthemum |
| Chile | Chilean bellflower | Australia | Wattle |

**NATIVE FUCHSIA.** *See* CORREA.

**NATIVE PLANTS.** *See* WILD GARDEN.

**NATIVE ROSE.** *See* BAUERA.

**NATURAL ORDER.** *See* PLANT FAMILY.

**NAVEL ORANGE.** A usually seedless orange in which the ovary is abortive and appears as a small, secondary fruit within a fruit, mostly just beneath a pointed or depressed section of the rind. It originated as a bud-sport* in a monastery garden in Bahia, Brazil, from whence it was imported into the U.S. in 1870. From it has come the Washington Navel, one of the most widely grown varieties in Calif. *See* ORANGE.

**NAVELWORT** = *Cotyledon umbilicus.* *See also* OMPHALODES.

*NEAPOLITANA, -us, -um* (nee-a-pol-i-tay'na). From Naples.

**NEAPOLITAN VIOLET.** The Parma violet. *See* VIOLA ODORATA.

**NEBRASKA.** The state lies wholly in zones* 2 and 3. It reaches from the Missouri River on the east to the foothills of the Rocky Mountains on the west, with the altitude ranging from less than 1000 feet to over 5000 feet.

SOILS. In the eastern end of the state the soils are of loessial origin — the pure loess* of the Missouri River hills* often being 50 feet or more in depth. There are also some evidences of glaciation in this section. The sandhill area includes most of the territory north of the Platte River in the central part of the state. Soils of alluvial nature are found along the Platte and Republican River valleys while in the panhandle section high tablelands are the general rule. The fertility, aside from the sandhill area, is reasonably good. Acid soils are seldom found, but in some areas alkali is becoming a problem.

Nebraska agriculture has developed primarily along agronomic and stock-raising lines. Widespreading wheat and corn fields and large cattle herds are common sights. Horticulture, always a very intensive occupation, came in only incidentally over the greater portion of the state. This has been due partially to lack of demand for horticultural crops (there are few large centers of population) and partially to climatic limitations, which are listed later. Treeless prairies greeted the early pioneer who, dissatisfied with their appearance, began to plant trees. Governor Robt. W. Furnas, Prof. C. E. Bessey, Isaac Pollard, and J. Sterling Morton were leaders in such work, the latter being responsible for the establishment of Arbor Day.*

NEBRASKA

The zones of hardiness crossing Nebraska are those shown on the colored map at ZONE, which should be consulted for details. The dates are the average latest killing frost in spring and the first one in the fall. The figures below the dates show the average length of the growing season. Rainfall figures (in inches) are for total annual rainfall in the regions so indicated.

Protection given by such plantings encouraged the planting of fruits, vegetables and ornamental species, but large plantings of any sort are seldom found outside the eastern third of the state except it be a favored valley or under irrigation.

FRUIT GROWING. This is limited very largely to the Missouri River counties which lie south of Omaha. Some 5000 acres of apple trees (generally less than 20 years of age) are found in the section with Nebraska City and Shubert being the centers of largest acreage. Over 350 acres of sour cherries are found near Nebraska City, with some acreage of grapes and other small fruits near Brownville, Omaha and Nebraska City. Scattered plantings extend to the north and west, particularly along the Platte River.

VEGETABLES. These are of consequence throughout the Platte Valley, particularly where irrigation water is available. Tomatoes, sweet corn, beans and other canning crops are grown in considerable quantity in the territory adjacent to canning plants at Nebraska City, Plattsmouth, Blair, and Norfolk, and considerable market gardening is carried on near Lincoln and Omaha, and in the Platte Valley within trucking distance of these points. Conditions in the extreme western end of this valley are quite favorable for vegetable production, but the distance to market is a limiting factor. From the total value standpoint the Irish potato is the most valuable vegetable crop in the state. These are produced both under irrigation and on dry land

---

* Special articles on the subjects indicated by an asterisk (*) will be found at the words so marked.

# Nebulosa 523 Negundo

as a late crop in the high altitude region and as an early crop in the eastern part of the state. Excellent quality certified Triumph seed potatoes are grown and hundreds of carloads are shipped south each year.

ORNAMENTALS. These cover the intermediate range — that is, tender ones suffer somewhat, but often can be grown with special care. Soils of neutral or alkaline reaction naturally exclude the growth of certain species. Hot, dry summers also make survival of certain species rather problematical. Among the perennials, iris does very well and Hans and Jacob Sass, in their gardens near Omaha, have been able to produce some wonderful new varieties by hybridization.

Elms, maples, lindens, hackberry and poplars are the more common deciduous tree species, while spruce, fir, juniper and pine represent the evergreen type. Most all of the common shrub species are found and also a wide list of herbaceous perennials and annuals. Wild forms of many of the cultivated varieties are found here in their native habitat.

### CLIMATE

As in all other states, climate has a very decided influence upon horticultural crops in Nebraska. The average annual mean temperature varies from 53° in the southeast to 44.1° in the western end of the state. The range is from about 23° in January to around 75° in July. Maximum temperatures of 100° or more usually occur several times each year and zero or lower from 15 to 25 times each year. Minima of −30° or even −40° are not unknown in the west end, but are seldom recorded at other points. The average number of frost-free days varies from approximately 175 in the southeast to 120 or less in the northwest. Frost data for three points are given below.

### KILLING FROST DATA

| Town | Average in spring | Latest in spring | Average in fall | Earliest in fall |
| --- | --- | --- | --- | --- |
| Omaha | April 14 | May 19 | Oct. 16 | Sept. 18 |
| Kearney | April 29 | May 17 | Oct. 5 | Sept. 12 |
| Alliance | May 12 | June 2 | Sept. 25 | Aug. 25 |

Precipitation is a most important factor, directly affecting all plant growth in this state. Total precipitation varies rather uniformly from an average of 32 inches in the extreme southeast to 16 inches in the west. Extremes are from 10 to 40 inches annually. From 75 to 80% generally falls during the growing season, with June being the wettest month. The winters usually are dry, with February and March having the heaviest snowfall.

Nebraska sunshine is sufficient for all plant needs, since during the summer nearly ¾ of the daylight hours are free of clouds and approximately ½ during the winter.

Destructive hailstorms sometimes occur, particularly as one goes west, and southeast summer and northwest winter winds are often strong enough to be damaging to vegetation, in addition to having a drying effect on the soil.

The address of the Agricultural Experiment Station, which has kindly supplied this information about the state, is Lincoln, Nebraska. The station is always ready to answer gardening questions.

**NEBULOSA, -us, -um** (neb-you-lō′sa). Indefinite or obscure. Sometimes applied to flowers that make a cloud-like mass.

**NECK.** The stem-like but thickened extension at the tip of some tuberous roots or bulbs, notably in the onion, rutabaga and in some amaryllises.

**NECKLACE ORCHID** = *Coelogyne dayana*.

**NECKLACE TREE.** See ORMOSIA.

**NECTAR; NECTARY.** A very sweet substance, chiefly water and sugar, secreted by the nectary of many flowers, and the chief source of honey. Nectaries are usually near the base of a flower, often near the base of a petal or stamen. This forces the insect visitor to get deep down in most flowers in order to reach the nectar. In the process the insect usually becomes dusted with pollen, so that nectar contributes directly to the cross-pollination of flowers. See POLLINATION.

While the nectaries of most flowers are simple glands for secreting nectar, and are usually near the base of the flower, they are often elaborately contrived. In the common toad-flax and columbine the nectaries are borne in the ends of the spurs. In the grape they are distinctly swollen receptacles between the base of the stamens, while in the buttercup the nectaries form scales on the petals. Most remarkable of all are the nectaries of orchids, some of which are very beautifully concealed.

A special form of nectary, not borne in the flower, is often found on leaf stalks or near the base of them. Such nectar as is secreted by these glands is apparently of no value in ensuring cross-pollination by insects. But in certain tropical trees this non-floral nectar often attracts ants, which actively repel leaf-eating insects. The latter might defoliate the tree if this helpful association of ants and nectar were not in operation.

**NECTARINE.** A smooth-skinned, hairless peach. Known for over 2000 years, nectarines are not yet well known in the U.S., and seldom grown. Their culture is the same as for the peach (which see).

While there are no constant differences, except lack of a fuzzy coat, between the nectarine and peach, the flavor of the former is thought by some to be richer and sweeter than that of the peach. Nectarines, like peaches, have clingstone and freestone* varieties.

The origin and repeated re-appearance of nectarines on peach trees and peaches on nectarine trees is one of the most interesting phenomena known in the fruit world. It occurs everywhere, often in the absence of the other tree, and is not due to cross-pollination. Darwin, who studied the problem for years, came to the conclusion that it was caused by bud mutations, or, as some call them, bud-sports. No competent plant breeder or pomologist is willing to hazard even a guess as to the cause of these bud mutations. Much nonsense has been written about them, but the fact remains that their occurrence remains essentially unexplained.

Nectarines, on the whole, do better west of the Rocky Mountains than east of them. The only varieties likely to be met are: Hunter, Kentucky, Red Roman, Sure Crop and Quetta (sometimes known as Persian). The latter was introduced by the U.S. Department of Agriculture and is now in commercial production. Occasionally some of these are grown in the greenhouse. See Fruit at GREENHOUSE.

**NEEDLE PALM** = *Rhapidophyllum hystrix*.

**NEGLECTA, -us, -um** (neg-lek′ta). Neglected; often used as a specific name for a garden plant of negligible value.

**NEGLECTED ORCHARDS.** If long neglected, weedy, ridden by pests, and with pretty old trees in them, most orchards do not pay for renovation. It is quite another matter, however, to try to re-invigorate a favorite tree or even a few of them.

Study the cultural articles on all the leading fruits, especially, of course, the particular one on your own tree. Get rid of weeds, trim out all dead or diseased wood, and then prune according to the direction given at your particular fruit. Top-dress with a good layer of well-rotted manure, and keep up a steady program of spraying for insects and disease.

These operations are all relatively expensive, and with the quick-bearing, small trees of the modern nurseryman so cheap, the renovation is by no means a profitable operation. For old apple-tree renovation see APPLE.

**NEGUNDO** (nee-gun′do). Specific name for the box-elder (*Acer negundo*) which was once thought to belong to a genus called *Negundo*. See MAPLE.

---

* Special articles on the subjects indicated by an asterisk (*) will be found at the words so marked.

**NEILLIA** (nee'li-a). Asiatic, spirea-like shrubs of the rose family, 3 of the 10 known species sparsely grown for ornament. They have alternate,* simple leaves, usually lobed, and doubly toothed. Flowers small, but showy, as the cluster (raceme* or panicle*) is often very handsome. Calyx* bell-shaped to tubular, its 5 lobes erect. Petals 5, white or pink. Stamens* 10-30, in 1-3 series. Fruit a small, dry pod, enclosed by the persistent calyx. (Named for Patrick Neill, Scotch botanist.)

These attractive little shrubs are of easy cult. in a variety of soils, and have proved hardy in many regions of long winters and bitter winds. They may be propagated by cuttings of green wood under glass, or by seeds.

**sinensis.** Not over 6 ft. high, usually about half this. Leaves ovalish or oblong, 1¾-3½ in. long, more or less lobed. Flowers pinkish, nodding, about ¾ in. long, the cluster (raceme*) about 2 in. long. China. May-June. Hardy from zone* 2 southward.

**thibetica.** Not usually over 5 ft. high, often less. Leaves ovalish, but long-tapering at the tip, 2-3½ in. long, sparingly lobed. Flowers pink, short-stalked, about ¾ in. long, the cluster (raceme*) nearly 3 in. long. China. Hardy from zone* 3, perhaps from zone* 2, southward.

**thyrsiflora.** Not usually over 4 ft. high, occasionally up to 6 ft. Leaves ovalish, 3-lobed, 1¾-4½ in. long. Flowers white, short-stalked, the cluster terminal, branched, nearly 3 in. long. Himalayas. Aug.-Sept. Hardy from zone* 3 southward.

**NELUMBIUM** (nee-lum'bi-um). Lotus. A genus of 2 species of strong-growing water plants of the family Nymphaeaceae, one a native to N.A., the other to the Orient. They are chiefly distinguished by their large leaves, growing from 3-6 ft. above the water, the flowers growing even higher than the leaves, sometimes as much as 5 ft. above the water. Flowers at the top of strong, leafless stalks, showy, solitary, cup-shaped, 5-10 in. across, with many petals, closing at night. Fruit a large capsule* with a flat top which when ripe has many openings like a pepper-pot through which the seeds are dispersed. (*Nelumbium* is the Latin version of *nelumbo*, the old Ceylonese name for this plant.)

They are of easy cultivation, and very attractive for shallow pools in formal gardens, but plenty of space must be allowed for their strong-growing rootstocks. Propagation by division of the rootstocks in May. Plant in shallow tubs, boxes or baskets, in a mixture of turfy loam and cow manure, 2 in. deep, covering the top of the containers with ½ in. clean sand to keep the water clean. Place in water so that the tops of the containers are 8 in. below surface. The water should be in the pool several days before planting, as the plants will fail to grow if water is too cold. After growth commences water may be added a further 6 in. The pool should be in bright sunlight. In Oct. the Oriental variety, which is tender, should have the water drained off and containers, for convenience, gathered together in one part of the pool. Cover them completely with 3 ft. of salt hay or strawy manure, where they can safely be left until the following spring. Where only 1 or 2 plants are in question they can be lifted from the pool and stored in a frost-proof place, in which case they must not be allowed to become dry. If the water is deep enough to prevent the rootstocks from freezing, the East Indian lotus can be left out all winter. It has been naturalized for many years at Bordentown, N.J., and, with sufficient depth of water, may be left out all winter up to zone* 4.

**luteum.** American lotus or water chinquapin. Leaves usually 1-2 ft. above water surface, cup-shaped, 1-2 ft. wide. Flowers pale yellow, 1-2 ft. above the surface, 8-10 in. across. Suitable for natural ponds where water is deep enough to prevent freezing of rootstocks in mud during the winter. Eastern N.A.

**nelumbo.** East Indian lotus, or more commonly called the Egyptian lotus. Rootstock long and jointed, with small, scale-like leaves. The true leaves, growing 3-6 ft. above the water, are large and round, the leafstalk being joined to the middle of under side, slightly grayish in color due to a waxy covering. Flowers, which grow higher than the leaves, are 4-10 in. across, pink or rose, and sweet-scented. Petals many, usually in 2 rings. Many varieties in cultivation varying in color from white to red. The *var*. **pygmaea** is a dwarf form, rosy-pink in color, very suitable for smaller pools. Southern As. to Aust.

**nuciferum** = *Nelumbium nelumbo*.

*NELUMBO* (nee-lum'bo). An old generic name for plants now included in *Nelumbium*.

**NEMATODES.** See Root Knot at PLANT DISEASES. See also Diseases at NARCISSUS.

**NEMESIA** (ne-mee'she-a). Tender, African, annual or perennial herbs or sub-shrubs, comprising 50 species, belonging to the family Scrophulariaceae. The annuals are the only ones of garden interest. Stem square, and grooved. Leaves simple,* lance-shaped, not stalked, in alternating pairs, becoming smaller towards the top. Flowers in terminal clusters. Corolla short and tubular, the expanded limb wide, flat, and 2-lipped, the base of the lower lip forming a small spur, the upper being cut into 4 segments. Colors yellow, brown, crimson, pink, blue, white, often showing 2 colors in one flower. (*Nemesia* was used by Dioscorides for some kind of snapdragon.)

Nemesia makes a very dainty garden plant, especially if planted in masses. It is easily propagated from seed sown in boxes of sandy loam in a cool greenhouse or cold frame in Feb. or early March for flowering in June, July, or Aug. When planting out allow 8 in. between plants. It is essential for them to have an early start so as to make as much growth as possible before summer heat. They are often grown as greenhouse plants. Seeds should be sown the end of Aug. and grown in a cool greenhouse. They will make good pot plants for Feb. and March flowering. They are much improved by pinching. See Pinching at TRAINING PLANTS.

**strumosa.** Grows to a height of 2 ft. Leaves 2-3 in. long. Flowers white, yellow or purple, deeply marked on the outside. The *var*. **suttoni** is much superior, having larger flowers and a better range of colors, which come very true from seed. See BLUE GARDEN.

**NEMOPANTHUS** (nee-mo-panth'us). A single species of not particularly handsome shrubs of the holly family, much more attractive in fruit than in flower. The only species is **N. mucronata**, the mountain holly or prick-timber, which is wild in the forests of eastern N.A. It is scarcely over 6-8 ft. high, with alternate,* short-stalked, elliptic leaves, ¾-1¾ in. long. Flowers small, inconspicuous, greenish-white, mostly unisexual,* with mostly 5 sepals and 5 petals. Fruit a dull red drupe* about ¼ in. in diameter. The shrub prefers cool, moist woods and should not be planted in dry, open places. Its foliage turns yellow in autumn. Hardy from zone* 2 southward. (*Nemopanthus* is from the Greek for thread and flower, in allusion to the slender flower stalks.)

**NEMOPHILA** (nem-off'i-la). A North American genus, comprising 18 species of annual herbs of the family Hydrophyllaceae, few of which are of garden interest. Some are climbing, while others are dwarf or trailing plants. All are hairy. Leaves usually much cut, alternate* or opposite.* Flowers showy, growing at the tips of the branches in clusters. Corolla bell-shaped, blue, white, purple, or spotted. Calyx of 5 spreading sepals* with additional leafy growths alternating, the latter increasing in size when fruiting. Fruit a dry capsule.* (*Nemophila* is from the Greek for grove, and love, in allusion to the plants liking a shady place.)

Propagation is by seeds sown in ordinary garden soil in early spring in masses where intended to bloom. Position must be partly shady.

**aurita.** Fiesta-flower. Of scrambling habit, climbing by means of prickles on the stems to a height of 3-6 ft. Leafstalks embracing the stem. Leaves deeply cut. Flowers 1 in. wide, violet, lighter on the outside. In low, shady grounds, Sacramento Valley to San Diego, Calif.

**insignis.** Baby blue-eyes. Grows to a height of 6 in. Leaves cut into 7-9 segments. Flowers bell-shaped, bright, clear blue, ½-1 in. across. There are white, and also blue and white forms. A garden favorite. Calif. See ROCK GARDEN.

**maculata.** Five-spot. Grows to a height 6 in. Leaves lyre-shaped, cut into 5-9 segments, blunt at the tip. Flowers bell-shaped, white, with a purple spot at the base of each petal. Western and central Calif.

*NEMORALIS*, -*e* (nem-o-ray'lis). In groves or woods.

*NEMOROSA*, -*us*, -*um* (nem-o-rō'sa). Growing in shady woods.

**NEOMAMMILLARIA** (nee-o-mam-mill-ā'rī-a). Pincushion cactus. A genus of over 150 species of globe-shaped, depressed, or shortly cylindric cacti, chiefly from the deserts of N.A., a few of them widely cult. in desert gardens and as house plants. The plant body is prominently tubercled instead of being ribbed, the tubercles arranged in loose spirals and between them (*i.e.* in the pits) there is usually a small

---

* Special articles on the subjects indicated by an asterisk (*) will be found at the words so marked.

tuft of hairs, wool, or bristles. At the tip of most tubercles is a collection of spines. Flowers day-blooming, somewhat bell-shaped, not large but often brilliantly colored. Fruit berry-like. The plants are sometimes known as *Mammillaria*. (*Neomammillaria* is from *neo*, new, and *Mammillaria* [an old name for them], in allusion to the nipple-like tubercles.)

Cactus fanciers and specialists are known to grow over 50 species of these popular succulents, but of these only a few are likely to interest the average grower. Many plants, often credited to *Neomammillaria* (and to *Mammillaria*) are now credited to other genera. Those admitted to The Garden Dictionary should be sought at Coryphantha, Epithelantha, Escobaria, Pediocactus, and Strombocactus.

For culture *see* Cacti.

**compressa.** Usually growing in small clumps, the plant body more or less cylindric, bluish-green. The pits between the tubercles are woolly. Spines usually 4 to a cluster. Flowers about ½ in. long, pink. Central Mex.

**geminispina.** A bright green, somewhat cylindric cactus, woolly between the tubercles and very spiny. Spines 16–24 in each cluster, 2–4 erect, all the rest spreading, all bright-colored but with black tips, hence very striking. Flowers dark red. Central Mex.

**lasiacantha.** Plant body not much over 1 in. in diameter, nearly globe-shaped, extremely spiny, the pits between the minute tubercles not woolly. Spines 40–60 at each cluster, hairy, scarcely 1/10 in. long. Flowers nearly ½ in. long, pinkish. Western Tex. and northern Mex.

**plumosa.** Feather-ball. Plant body very small, usually growing in clusters, the whole completely hidden by the mass of short white spines, underneath which is the white wool of the tubercle-pits. Flowers about ¼ in. long, white. N. Mex. and northern Mex.

**rhodantha.** Plant body more or less cylindric, nearly 10 in. high, the pits of the roundish tubercles bristly. Spines 15–26 at a cluster, white, 4–6 in the center erect, the rest divergent. Flowers about ½ in. wide, rose-pink. Mex.

**spinosissima.** Plant body more or less cylindric, 9–12 in. long and about 4 in. thick, the tubercles not prominent, the pits bristly. The whole plant is covered with spines, of which there are about 28 at each spine-cluster. Flowers about ½ in. long, purplish. Central Mex.

**NEO-MEXICANA, -us, -um** (ne-o-mecks-i-kay′na). From New Mexico.

**NEOWASHINGTONIA** = *Washingtonia*.

**NEPALENSIS, -e** (ne-pal-en′sis). From Nepal, India.

**NEPENTHACEAE.** See Nepenthes.

**NEPENTHES** (ne-pen′theez). Pitcher-plant. Climbing, often tree-perching, or bog herbs, sometimes a little woody at the base, and the only genus of the family **Nepenthaceae** (ne-pen-thay′see-ee). Chiefly East Indian, but extending into Madagascar, these Old World pitcher-plants are among the showiest of all insectivorous plants, useful only in the greenhouse, as indicated below. Leaves alternate,* usually longish, but prolonged at the tip into a long tendril* which is terminated by a hollow, pitcher-like, winged structure with a thickened rim, a lid, and, on the inside of the pitcher, several honey-glands. Usually the pitchers are suspended (upright) at the end of the long tendril,* and the bottom of the pitcher contains water into which an insect slips and is drowned. See Insectivorous Plants. Flowers inconspicuous, the male and female on different plants, without petals, and 3–4 sepals. Male flowers with 4–16 united stamens.* Fruit a leathery capsule,* the seeds tailed. (*Nepenthes* is from the Greek for removing all sorrow, whether because of the often beautifully colored pitchers, or in allusion to assumed narcotic properties is uncertain.)

The species below are often replaced by named hybrid forms, of which scores were offered when there was a craze for growing these interesting and often beautifully colored plants. Some of these hybrids are also included. Now they are chiefly confined to the larger greenhouse collections, although florists occasionally display them in their windows. For Culture *see* below.

**domini.** A hybrid; the pitchers beautifully mottled with green and purple, its wings fringed.

**hookeriana.** Pitchers nearly 6 in. long and 3 in. in diameter, green, but purple-marked, its wings broad and double-fringed, or sometimes unfringed. Borneo.

**masteriana.** A hybrid; pitchers dark crimson, or greenish-crimson, often purple-spotted, its wings small, sometimes fringed.

**phyllamphora.** Pitchers nearly 6 in. long, about 1½ in. in diameter, reddish-green or red, its wings narrow and cord-like. East Indies and southern China.

**veitchi.** Pitchers almost 8 in. long and 3 in. in diameter, hairy, yellowish-green to reddish, its wings fringed. Borneo.

### Culture of Nepenthes

Nepenthes are grown from seeds or cuttings, requiring at all times heat, moisture, and shade. The hybrids developed in cultivation are generally showier and easier to grow. Seeds germinate in a month or less if sown on the moist surface of fine sphagnum and peat, under a bell-jar in a temperature of 80°–85°. Mature shoot cuttings root readily early in the year, if stuck through empty inverted pots over sphagnum or fiber in a close, moist case, with bottom-heat of 80°. When rooted, pot in equal parts peat-fiber and sphagnum, with a dash of fine charcoal and sharp sand, replacing in the case, for a few days, to encourage a good start. Later, they grow best in orchid-baskets suspended from a hothouse roof in a minimum temperature of 65°–70°, using similar compost as before, only coarser.

Nepenthes in an orchid basket

Syringe daily and water freely when actively growing. Removing the growing point after several leaves have formed gives finer pitchers. Flowering is prevented unless seed is required. Leggy* plants may be cut back in Feb., and inert soil replaced with fresh compost. — H. E. D.

**NEPETA** (nep′e-ta). Perennial and annual herbs found throughout the Northern Hemisphere, comprising about 150 species of the mint family. Tall and erect, or dwarf and trailing, generally aromatic, and more or less hairy. Stems square. Leaves mostly heart-shaped, the margins toothed. Flowers in close clusters on the stems, often in whorls,* blue or white. Corolla 2-lipped, the upper composed of 2 lobes, the lower 3, joined at the base and forming a narrow tube. Stamens* 4, 2 longer than the others. Fruit a 2-celled capsule, which when ripe splits into 4 parts. (*Nepeta* is probably Latin from *Nepete*, an Etrurian city.)

They are easily cultivated in ordinary soil. Usually propagated from seeds, sown during spring or summer, or by division of roots, but sometimes from the runners which creep along the ground.

**cataria.** Commonly known as catnip or cat-mint, owing to its attraction for cats. Perennial, with sturdy, straight stems, growing 2–3 ft. high. Leaves grayish-green, heart-shaped, hairy. Flowers white or lilac, ¼ in. long, produced in several clusters towards the tip of the branches. Eurasia, but naturalized in N.A. For another plant attractive to cats, see Actinidia polygama.

**glecoma** = *Nepeta hederacea*.

**hederacea.** Ground Ivy, Gill-over-the-Ground, Field-Balm. A creeping perennial, with low-growing, branching, prostrate stems which make a dense mat, every joint producing roots from which new plants may grow. Leaves roundish, with scalloped margins, 1–2½ in. across, dark green. Flowers light to dark blue, about 1 in. long, in scattered clusters. Will grow either in sunny or shady places. Suitable for ground cover or hanging over rocks. The var. *variegata*, with variegated leaves, is sometimes used as an edging plant. Eurasia, but naturalized in N.A. See also the list at Weeds.

**mussini.** A perennial growing to 2 ft., covered with rough, whitish hairs, giving the whole plant a light gray appearance. Branches many. Leaves lance-shaped, 1–2 in. long, slightly wrinkled. Flowers blue, with dark spots, ½ in. long, in loose clusters forming a long raceme.* A great garden favorite used either as a border or rock plant, or for bedding (which see). Caucasus. Persia.

**nuda.** A perennial, growing to 4 ft. high. Leaves lance-shaped, 2 in. long, light green. Flowers in clusters, white, spotted purple, about ½ in. long. Southern Eu.

**ucranica.** A perennial growing to 2 ft. high, slightly hairy. Leaves lance-shaped. Flowers blue, small, inconspicuous, in loose clusters. Eastern Eu. and western As.

---

* Special articles on the subjects indicated by an asterisk (*) will be found at the words so marked.

**NEPHROLEPIS** (nee-froll'e-pis *or* neph-ro-lee'pis). Sword fern. An extremely important genus of ferns of the family Polypodiaceae, all tropical or sub-tropical. Nearly half its dozen known species are grown for ornament, one of them having given rise to the Boston fern, easily and deservedly, the most popular house fern in the U.S. They grow in the ground, or some are tree-perching (epiphytes*), and have long, not usually compound, fronds, which are variously cut, mostly feather-fashion, into many segments. In some recent forms of the Boston fern the fronds have become extremely fine and feathery. Spore cases on the upper forks of the veins, on the lower side of the segments, more or less kidney-shaped. (*Nephrolepis* is from the Greek for kidney and scale, in allusion to the shape of the spore cases.)

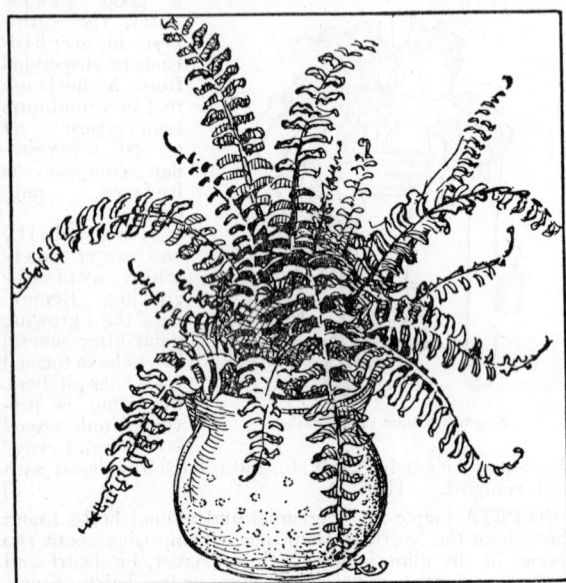

The Boston fern was a chance sport (mutation) originating in Philadelphia.

For culture (except the Boston fern) see Greenhouse Ferns at FERNS AND FERN GARDENING.

The Boston fern (*Nephrolepis exaltata bostoniensis*) is comparatively recent, having originated, by chance, in a lot of plants of *Nephrolepis exaltata* sent from Philadelphia to Boston about 1894. One of the shipment had more gracefully drooping, somewhat broader fronds, and it grew faster than the common *N. exaltata*. Subsequently it was given the varietal name *bostoniensis*, has been grown by the million, traveled to every country in the world, and is the best of all house ferns. This is partly due to the fact that it endures house conditions better than most ferns, to its fairly quick growth, and also because even with some neglect it will ultimately grow into an immense, bushy fern. If grown on a pedestal, its fronds will often become several feet long (in some varieties).

While the Boston fern will endure house conditions, it responds to decent treatment like any other fern. As it gets larger, re-pot in potting mixture* 4. During the summer put the plant outdoors, preferably plunged* if the fronds are not too long, or at any rate in the shade.

Because it is a quick-growing, active plant, it needs plenty of water. If possible, plunge the pot in a pail of water whenever the plant gets anywhere near dry. If you cannot tell how dry it is, because the pot is crammed with roots and frond bases, tap the pot smartly with the knuckles. If it gives off a sharp, ringing sound, the plant needs water. If, on the other hand, the tap sounds dead or sodden, there is pretty sure to be enough soil moisture for the present. It will grow in ordinary room temperatures, but it will not stand frost. On many days, if outdoor temperature is above 45°, it can profitably be put outdoors during a rainy day.

While scores of varieties of the Boston fern have been developed since 1900, the most popular is still the common sort, and it appears to be the best for house conditions.

The species of sword fern are:

**acuminata.** Fronds nearly 3 ft. long and a third as wide, drooping, the segments narrowly lance-shaped and coarsely toothed. The plant produces many runners. Malaya.

**biserrata.** Fronds 2-4 ft. long, 6-10 in. wide, the segments thick, the frond stalk scurfy. Segments rather distant, 2-6 in. long, the margins faintly round-toothed, and eared at one side of the base. Malaya. The *var. furcans* has the segments forked.

**cordifolia.** Tuber fern. An erect fern, the rootstocks bearing tubers. Fronds about 24 in. long and 2½ in. wide. Segments about 1½ in. long, numerous or crowded, bright green and sharply toothed. Tropics. There are several varieties in cult., especially a low, compact one, and another with plumy fronds. Some are variegated.

**exaltata.** Sword fern. Fronds stiff and erect, 3-5 ft. long and nearly 6 in. wide. Segments numerous, close together, 2-3 in. long, obscurely toothed or without teeth. Tropical regions generally (except India). Very little known in cult., having been almost wholly supplanted by *var. bostoniensis*, the Boston fern (*see* above). It has narrower, and, in maturity, drooping and much longer fronds. It produces abundant runners. The Boston fern has been the origin of over 50 named forms, differing in the amount and degree of fineness of the segments. For house plants the original Boston fern is still the best, however, the recent variations of it being more ingenious than horticulturally important.

**pectinata.** Basket fern. A compact, small, grayish-green fern, the fronds less than 18 in. long and about 1 in. wide. Segments numerous, close together, about ½ in. long and toothed. Tropical America. A good fern for the hanging basket.

**NERIIFOLIA, -us, -um** (neer-ee-i-fō'lĭ-a). With leaves like the oleander (*Nerium*). It is sometimes spelled *nereifolia*.

**NERINE** (ne-ry'ne). A genus of South African bulbous herbs of the family Amaryllidaceae, two of the 15 known species cult. for their handsome fall and early winter bloom. Leaves all basal, strap-shaped. Flowers funnel-shaped, in a close terminal cluster (umbel*) on a solid stalk. Corolla with practically no tube, its segments scarcely separable as to petals or sepals, red, often crisped on the margins. Stamens* 6, sometimes protruding, but 3 shorter than the others. Fruit a 3-valved capsule.* (Named after the nereids, or perhaps for one of them, the daughter of Nerius.)

These are best grown, in the North, in pots in the cool greenhouse, where they flower in the late fall, or they may be forced almost any time if the bulbs have been rested for four or five months before planting. Bulbs started in Oct. will bloom at Christmas, if given plenty of water. Use potting mixture* 3. When the plant is through blooming, after which the leaves develop, the water should gradually be reduced, and stopped altogether when the bulbs are resting. During the resting period, the time for which is indicated by the yellowing of the leaves, the pots should be turned on their sides, in the sun, and left there without water until the plants are to be started into growth. In Calif. and similar climates they may be grown outdoors, but from about May to Aug. the bulbs are better lifted and stored in a cool, dry place, and planted again in Sept.

**curvifolia.** Flowers scarlet, the petals not much crisped. Stamens* scarcely protruding. Leaves (appearing after the bloom) usually 6, about 12 in. long, curved and thick. Not so much grown as the *var. fothergilli*, which is the best of the nerines for forcing. It is a more robust plant than the type and the cluster bears more flowers.

**fothergilli** = *Nerine curvifolia fothergilli*.

**sarniensis.** Guernsey lily (not native there, but grown there after its importation from South Africa). Flowers crimson, about 10 in the cluster. Corolla about 1½ in. long, its segments somewhat crisped, the stamens* protruding. Leaves (appearing after the bloom) about 12 in. long, ¾ in. wide, not curved. There are several varieties, mostly slight variants as to flower color, which ranges from rose-pink to deeper scarlet.

**NERIUM.** See OLEANDER.

**NERO'S-CROWN** = *Tabernaemontana coronaria*.

**NERTERA** (ner'ter-ra). Tender, creeping, perennial herbs of the family Rubiaceae, comprising 6 species. Natives of the Andes, N. Zeal., Aust., Hawaii and Malaya. (*Nertera* is from the Greek for lowly, in allusion to the habit.)

The only cult. species is propagated by seeds, or by division of the rootstocks. Sow seeds in spring in the greenhouse or cold frame. Plant out in June in cool, shady spots in

*Special articles on the subjects indicated by an asterisk (*) will be found at the words so marked.*

rich, sandy soil, or grow as a pot plant for greenhouse decoration or house plant. It is used as a ground cover in Calif., if the ground is moist and shady.

**depressa.** Bead-plant. Grows to a height 6-10 in. Stems square. Leaves short-stalked, small, ⅛ in. long, ovalish, leathery. Flowers solitary, inconspicuous, and greenish. Fruit a showy, orange-colored, transparent berry the size of a pea, which persists for months. Tasmania and N. Zeal.

*NERVOSA, -us, -um* (ner-vō′sa). Nerved or veined.

**NEST BOXES.** See BIRDS.

**NESTING SITES.** See BIRDS.

**NETTED MELON.** See MELON.

**NETTLE.** Stinging herbs of no interest to the gardener, except to uproot them (with gloves on). Those below belong to the genus **Urtica** (ur′ti-ka; ur-ty′ka) of the family Urticaceae. There are over 30 species of nettles, mostly annual or perennial herbs with opposite, stalked, usually toothed leaves, covered, sometimes not very obviously so, with stinging hairs. Flowers small, without petals, greenish, in loose or head-like clusters, the male and female separate, sometimes on different plants. Fruit dry (an achene*), enclosed by the persistent sepals. (*Urtica* is the Latin name of the nettles and is from *urere*, to burn.)

**dioica.** Stinging or great nettle. A very bristly and stinging herb, 15-30 in. high. Leaves ovalish or heart-shaped, deeply toothed, often nearly 5 in. long and 3 in. wide. Flower cluster forked. Eurasia; naturalized in N.A. The thrifty Scotch use the young foliage like spinach.

**pilulifera.** Roman nettle. An annual herb, 1-2 ft. high. Leaves ovalish or heart-shaped, 1-3 in. long. Male flower clusters branched, the female in close heads. Southern Eu.

**NETTLE FAMILY** = Urticaceae.

**NETTLE TREE** = *Celtis occidentalis*. See HACKBERRY.

**NEUTRAL.** A soil term applied to those soils which are neither acid nor alkaline. See ACID AND ALKALI SOILS.

**NEVADA.** The state lies wholly in zones* 3, 4, 5, and 6, which because of the mountains, turn sharply northward, instead of running east and west as in most of the country.

SOILS. The soils in Nevada are variable. In the western valleys, along the east side of the Sierra Nevada range, the soils are generally composed of decomposed granite and other igneous rocks. They have a fair supply of organic matter and are, on the whole, relatively free from alkali. Soils suitable for gardening are usually readily found.

The soils in the central valleys farther to the east are generally more alkaline, heavier in texture, and lower in organic matter. Here greater care must be exercised in selecting a site for a garden. Farther east toward the headwaters of the Humboldt River the soils, while variable, improve in quality.

The soils of the southern half of the state are nearly always of limestone origin, and are apt to contain harmful amounts of alkali in their native condition. They are normally low in organic matter. Garden soils in this area must be selected with extreme care.

CHIEF GARDENING CENTERS. Reno and vicinity is the chief gardening center in the western valleys. Here hardy vegetables and fruits, including potatoes, tomatoes, peas, beans, sweet corn, squash, carrots, onions and other common garden vegetables are grown in great variety for the local market.

Fallon, in the lower Carson Valley, is a center for the growing of cantaloupes. The Mason Valley is noted for its potatoes.

The Moapa Valley in the extreme south has a mild climate and is noted for its early spring vegetables and its summer melons. The vegetables include asparagus, radish, lettuce, spinach, carrots and green onions. Cantaloupes and watermelons are marketed in July. Many millions of tomato plants are grown for shipment to Utah.

A little farther north the Pahranagat Valley is becoming important as a general gardening area, growing a wide range of vegetables similar to those of the Reno area. The climate is milder than that of Reno and the growing season is longer.

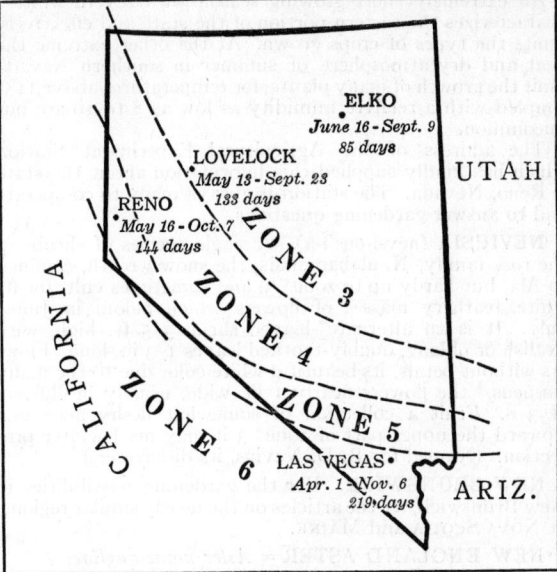

NEVADA

The zones of hardiness crossing Nevada are those shown on the colored map at ZONE, which should be consulted for details. The dates are the average latest killing frost in spring and the first one in the fall. The figures below the dates show the average length of the growing season. For rainfall *see* text.

FLOWERS AND SHRUBS. Roses are perhaps the most universally grown of all flowers. They do well nearly everywhere in the state. The tall-bearded iris is also widely grown and thrives in most localities. Many bulbs adapted to a short-growing season, such as narcissus, hyacinths, tulips, and gladioli, are quite satisfactory. The dahlia does well in certain areas, but is not suitable for general use over the state. Most of the short-season annuals can be grown any place in the state where the soil is suitable. In the extreme South, stocks, larkspur, and snapdragon are favorites.

In the western valleys there is some English ivy; the Virginia creeper is a common vine, growing extremely well. Hops, morning-glory, perennial pea, and, to some extent, sweet peas, are commonly used for climbing vines in the colder zones. Virginia creeper is used to some extent in the extreme South, though the German ivy is better. Wild grapes and certain European grapes, as Thompson's seedless and Muscat, are grown in arbors in this area.

FROST DATES

| Town | Average date of last killing frost in spring | Latest known killing frost | Average date of earliest killing frost in fall | Earliest known killing frost |
|---|---|---|---|---|
| Reno | May 16 | June 13 | Oct. 7 | Sept. 13 |
| Lovelock | May 13 | June 13 | Sept. 23 | Sept. 5 |
| Elko | June 16 | July 14 | Sept. 9 | Aug. 7 |
| Las Vegas | April 1 | May 12 | Nov. 6 | Oct. 4 |

The rainfall over the state is scant, averaging about 9 inches per year. In the valleys where the crops are grown, the rainfall is only about half the average for the state as a whole, and in the extreme South it is still less, averaging about 3½ inches per year at Las Vegas. The heaviest storms are normally received during the winter when deep snows are deposited on the mountains. From this source comes the water which supplies the streams from which irrigation water is drawn for the valleys. Successful cropping is impossible without ample irrigation water, and the precipitation received during the growing season is of little practical benefit to crops.

---

* Special articles on the subjects indicated by an asterisk (*) will be found at the words so marked.

An extremely short growing season with severe winters characterizes the eastern portion of the state and effectively limits the types of crops grown. At the other extreme the heat and dry atmosphere of summer in southern Nevada limit the growth of many plants; for temperatures above 115° coupled with a relative humidity as low as 8 to 10 are not uncommon.

The address of the Agricultural Experiment Station which has kindly supplied this information about the state is Reno, Nevada. The station is always ready to co-operate and to answer gardening questions.

**NEVIUSIA** (nev-ĭ-ous'ĭ-a). A single species of shrubs of the rose family, **N. alabamensis,** the snow wreath, confined to Ala. but hardy up to zone* 3, and sometimes cult. for its white, feathery masses of flowers which bloom in June–July. It is an alternate*-leaved shrub 3–5 ft. high, with ovalish or oblong, doubly-toothed leaves 1–3 in. long. Flowers without petals, its beautiful white color due to the many stamens,* the flowers nearly 1 in. wide, usually in clusters of 3–8. Fruit a collection of somewhat fleshy achenes.* Toward the upper part of zone* 3 it may need winter protection. (Named for R. D. Nevius, its discoverer.)

**NEW BRUNSWICK.** For the gardening possibilities in New Brunswick, *see* the articles on the nearly similar regions, at Nova Scotia and Maine.

**NEW ENGLAND ASTER** = *Aster novae-angliae.*

**NEW HAMPSHIRE.** The state lies wholly in zones* 2 and 3. Commercial horticulture is largely taken up with the culture of apples in the southern part of the state and potatoes in the northern area. Both the climate and the soil in southern New Hampshire are ideal for the culture of the McIntosh and the Baldwin apples, and these two varieties grow to perfection there, taking on a color and a finish that cannot be obtained in the more southerly apple sections. Of other fruits, hardly enough is grown for home use, partly on account of the short growing season and partly on account of the relatively cool summers.

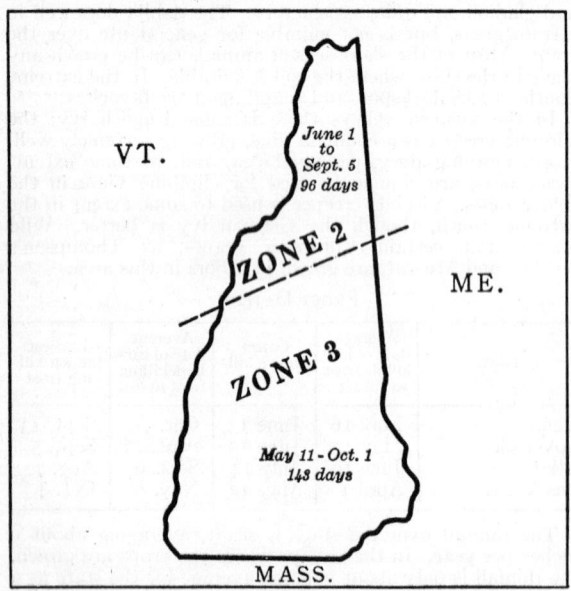

NEW HAMPSHIRE

The zones of hardiness crossing New Hampshire are those shown on the colored map at Zone, which should be consulted for details. The dates are the average latest killing frost in spring and the first one in the fall. The figures below the dates show the average length of the growing season.

Potatoes, on the other hand, may be grown in any section of the state, but the culture of this crop finds its highest development in northern New Hampshire in Coos County. In this region the potatoes are seldom planted before June first, while the first killing frost often comes as early as September 1 to 10, thus making potatoes a 90- to 100-day crop. But a rich soil and a cool climate, together with a liberal use of high-grade commercial fertilizers, cause potatoes to grow so fast that yields of 400 bushels per acre are not unusual.

It has been proven experimentally that certified potatoes outyield home-grown potatoes for seed by many bushels. Since it is almost necessary to grow certified seed in 100 days or less, this northern New Hampshire country presents ideal conditions for the culture of this crop.

Commercial vegetable culture in the state is limited almost wholly to the production of seasonal vegetables for the local market. However, with the exception of a few hot-weather long-season vegetables, like sweet potatoes, practically all others are grown in considerable quantity. Vegetables, like corn, string beans, celery, peas, and the root crops, like carrots and beets, grow exceptionally well during the comparatively cool nights of New Hampshire's summer season and possess very high eating quality.

The farm garden has been developed to a very high degree of excellence, and the value of $70 per garden, as given by the U.S. census figures, is the highest of any state in the Union. It is perhaps higher than necessary and indicates that a considerable amount of vegetables are grown for the roadside trade, to supply the large summer tourist population.

As for flowers, quality again is the important factor, rather than quantity. Certain flowers, like asters and gladiolus, are shipped to the New York markets, and command a premium price because of the intensity and the freshness of the colors of the flowers. The glare of the sun is tempered by the relatively high humidity of the atmosphere, thus preventing the burning out or fading of the more delicate shades.

Large numbers of summer residents are attracted to the state by its mountains, lakes and seashore. Many of these have built estates of considerable size, and the landscaping of these estates and many of the summer hotels and golf clubs is extremely attractive.

CLIMATE. The average date of the last killing frost in the spring is May 11 for the southern part of the state, and June 1 in the extreme north. In the autumn the first killing frost may be expected about Sept. 5 in the extreme north, and about Oct. 1 in the vicinity of Concord. All figures, of course, are much changed at elevations along the Presidential Range, where the frost-free period is sometimes not over 60 days. Rainfall is adequate over all the state, averaging 40–45 in. per year.

The address of the Agricultural Experiment Station which has kindly supplied this information about the state is Durham, N.H. The station is always ready to answer garden questions.

Garden Club activities, because of the large number of summer residents, are extensive. There are clubs of the Garden Club of America, the home office of which is 598 Madison Avenue, New York. There are also over 20 chapters of the New Hampshire Federation of Garden Clubs and 15 clubs affiliated with the United Garden Clubs of New Hampshire. For the one nearest your locality write the Garden Editor, Houghton Mifflin Company, Boston, Mass.

**NEW JERSEY.** The state lies wholly in zones* 3, 4, and 5.

SOILS. The soils of the state are of wide range of texture and fertility. The state has been divided into 5 soil zones, the borders of which run practically parallel and in a NE–SW direction. Soil zone 1, in the northwest corner of the state, is bounded by a line from the New York state line near Quarryville to the Delaware River above Belvidere. The land is hilly and mountainous and the soils are typically relatively heavy. Soil zone 2 is bounded in the southeast by a line from Cresskill to the Delaware River between Phillipsburg and Frenchtown. This, too, is a rolling, hilly and mountainous section where the soils are predominantly heavy loams, well-drained, of granitic derivation in the

* Special articles on the subjects indicated by an asterisk (*) will be found at the words so marked.

highlands, while limestone soils occupy the valleys. In this region are many lakes of glacial formation and large areas of muck soils. Soil zone 3 is bounded on the southeast by a line from Perth Amboy to the Delaware River at a point just above Trenton. This is the Piedmont section, gently rolling country with low, stony ridges. On the ridges is a rather heavy soil derived from the dense traprock; but the prevailing soils are the red soils derived from red shale and sandstone. The first two and the northern half of the third zone are glaciated. The fourth soil zone is bounded by a line from Raritan Bay to Port Morris on Delaware Bay. This is the heavy coastal plain belt, the soils being predominantly loams and sandy loams, sometimes containing green sand marl. The fifth soil zone is the light coastal plain belt, containing very sandy loams and light sands. In this belt are the pine barrens and much bog land.

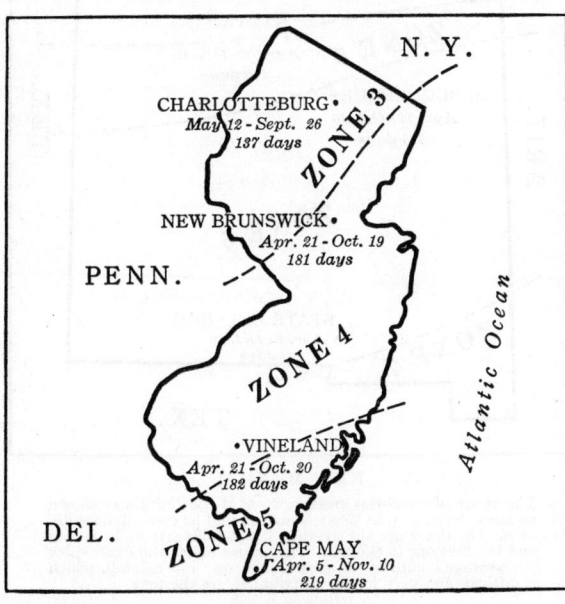

NEW JERSEY

The zones of hardiness crossing New Jersey are those shown on the colored map at ZONE, which should be consulted for details. The dates are the average latest killing frost in spring and the first one in the fall. The figures below the dates show the average length of the growing season.

CHIEF GARDENING CENTERS. New Jersey has long been known as the Garden State, because, lying as it does between two of the largest markets in the country, New York and Philadelphia, its soil resources have been devoted to the production of vegetable and other horticultural crops for these markets, as well as for its own citizens.

### VEGETABLES

Because of the topography and the fairly open nature of the soil, a section in the northeastern part of the state (Hudson and parts of Passaic, Bergen and Morris counties) is adapted to the growing of early spring truck crops, such as spinach, lettuce, early beets, carrots, and so on. In the northwestern part are large muck areas devoted to the culture chiefly of lettuce, onions and celery. A considerable area in soil zones 2 and 3 is devoted to late truck, such as late sweet corn and cabbage. In Monmouth County is an area devoted to general vegetable crops, especially asparagus. Soil in zone 4 is particularly favorable for the production of potatoes and the southern half to tomatoes. In middle soil zone 4 are large acreages of early sweet corn. Sweet potatoes are grown extensively in the southern part of soil zone 5, as well as large quantities of peppers and other truck.

### FRUITS

Apples are grown to some extent in soil zones 1 and 2, where conditions are favorable for winter apples, such as Baldwin, Greening and Stayman. Another apple district is located in soil zone 4 in the neighborhood of Freehold, and summer apples are grown extensively in the middle part of soil zone 4 in Burlington, Camden and Gloucester counties. Peaches are most extensively grown in the southern and southwestern section. Bush fruits and strawberries are the chief fruit of parts of Atlantic and Cumberland counties; while cranberries and cultivated blueberries occupy bogs and drained bogs in Atlantic, Burlington and Ocean counties.

### ORNAMENTAL HORTICULTURE

The whole of the northeastern section of the state (Hudson, Bergen, Passaic, Essex, Union, and parts of Somerset, Middlesex and Monmouth counties) are very thickly populated because of their proximity to New York City, and the same is true to a lesser extent of parts of Burlington, Camden and Gloucester counties in relation to Philadelphia. In consequence of this large suburban population and the nearness of these two metropolitan markets, New Jersey has always been among the leading states in the production of nursery and florists' products.

COMMERCIAL ASPECTS. In New Jersey are more than six hundred nurseries that are registered with and inspected by state agencies. Some of these produce special plants, such as roses, rhododendrons, azaleas, peonies, rock garden plants; while others deal in a general line of woody or herbaceous, perennial plants. The state is especially noted for the origination and dissemination of dahlia varieties. One of the largest producers of aquatic plants is located in this state.

The production of cut flowers and potted plants has always been a large industry located mainly in the suburban districts. The neighborhood of Madison is famous for its rose culture under glass. Bound Brook is becoming a center of gardenia production. In the northeastern section are grown large quantities of pot plants of all descriptions, and a general line of miscellaneous cut flowers is produced here. In New Jersey are collected, also, osmunda* peat for the culture of orchids and the sphagnum* moss that is used so extensively in floriculture. In addition, there are large deposits of peat moss and of cultivated peat or humus,* which are used for soil improvement.

GARDENING ORGANIZATIONS. That the interest in gardening is great is attested by the fact that there are about 150 organized garden clubs in the state, with one county federation consisting of 25 clubs and a state federation of 66 clubs. There are also clubs of the Garden Club of America. Many of the Federated Women's Clubs have very active garden club sections. There are two state-wide special crop societies — the Dahlia Society of New Jersey and the New Jersey Gladiolus Society. The New Jersey State Horticultural Society is devoted solely to pomology and vegetable gardening. Commercially and professionally there is a New Jersey Florists' Association, a number of local florists' organizations and several local organizations for private gardeners.

NATIVE PLANTS. The great laurel (*Rhododendron maximum*) is abundant in the northern part of the state and to some extent on the ridges along the Delaware River, as far south as Burlington County. Mountain laurel is plentiful in the southern part of the state. American holly is found on the coastal plain section. Oaks of various species are standard trees in all parts of the state. Sugar and swamp maple and white ash contribute to autumnal effect. Sycamores are found near streams, and red gum or sweet gum is abundant in the south-central part. The pine barren area has a peculiar flora of its own.

CULTIVATED PLANTS. Because of the variation in topography and climate, a very wide range of plants can be grown in the various sections of the state. In the extreme northern portion, conditions are favorable for plants hardy

---

* Special articles on the subjects indicated by an asterisk (*) will be found at the words so marked.

in the neighborhood of Boston; while in the southern portion, plants considered hardy up to Washington, D.C., may be successfully established. Along the southern part of the coast, *Hydrangea macrophylla otaksa* is used extensively for foundation plantings and as a garden shrub. In the neighborhood of Salem, crape myrtle and *Poncirus trifoliata* are seen as well-established plants. Even *Albizzia julibrissin* has been established in a favorable locality.

The heavier soils of the state are very favorable for the culture of iris, peonies and roses. The state has long been known for its dahlias, which are cultivated for commercial, as well as for garden and show purposes. Delphiniums do well in the northern part, as well as in gardens on the northern part of the coast. Since a considerable part of the state is urban or suburban, there is a great interest in home gardens and, in consequence, a very wide range of herbaceous material is grown, both annual and perennial.

Conditions are very favorable in certain sections for alpine and rock gardening. Along the seacoast, especially the upper section, very successful gardens are cultivated under great difficulties, such as soil texture and the salty breezes.

### CLIMATE

Because of the form and geographical location of the state, a difference of more than a month in season is observed in a study of the frost data:

#### FROST DATA

|  | Elevation | Average date of last killing frost in spring | Latest-known killing frost | Average date of earliest killing frost in fall | Earliest-known killing frost |
|---|---|---|---|---|---|
| Cape May | 17 | April 5 | April 22 | Nov. 10 | Oct. 22 |
| Vineland | 109 | April 21 | May 22 | Oct. 20 | Sept. 22 |
| New Brunswick | 110 | April 21 | May 17 | Oct. 19 | Sept. 22 |
| Charlotteburg | 719 | May 12 | June 21 | Sept. 26 | Sept. 11 |

#### RAINFALL

|  | Elevation | Average annual rainfall | Average rainfall in growing season |
|---|---|---|---|
| Cape May | 17 | 40.30 | 23.43 (April to Oct.) |
| Vineland | 109 | 45.08 | 26.68 (April to Oct.) |
| New Brunswick | 110 | 46.52 | 28.73 (April to Oct.) |
| Charlotteburg | 719 | 49.57 | 22.08 (May to Sept.) |

The address of the Agricultural Experiment Station is New Brunswick, N.J. The station is always ready to answer gardening questions.

**NEW JERSEY TEA** = *Ceanothus americanus.*

**NEW MEXICO.** The state lies wholly in zones* 4, 5, 6 and 7.

While a considerable percentage of the area of New Mexico is occupied by mountains, many of which, especially in the southern half of the state, are craggy and have little vegetation, there are millions of acres of good agricultural land. The soils are usually of a loamy nature, deep, and, on the whole, retain moisture well. Dry-farming is practiced extensively in some regions, particularly in eastern New Mexico. As a rule, in the western part, except in the higher mountainous areas, irrigation is necessary. There are extensive irrigation projects in southern, central, northwestern and southeastern New Mexico. It is chiefly in these districts that the horticultural operations are centered; especially near Albuquerque, Las Cruces, Roswell, and Carlsbad.

Practically all horticultural operations in the state are carried on under irrigation. Wherever water is available for irrigation many of the temperate zone fruits and vegetables are cultivated for both commercial and home purposes. While practically all temperate zone fruits grow, those planted for commercial purposes are generally apples, pears, peaches, plums, and grapes. These, on the whole, are the surest fruits under New Mexico conditions. Apricots, Japanese plums, sweet cherries and many varieties of peaches are frequently injured by late spring frosts, which are an important limiting factor in the production of these fruits.

Varieties of the *vinifera* grape are better suited for the lower and irrigated districts, while those of the American type are grown more extensively in the higher and more northern districts. The largest fruit-growing areas are found in the San Juan, Espanola, Albuquerque, Las Cruces, Roswell, Carlsbad, and Fort Sumner areas. Apples and pears are the two leading fruits.

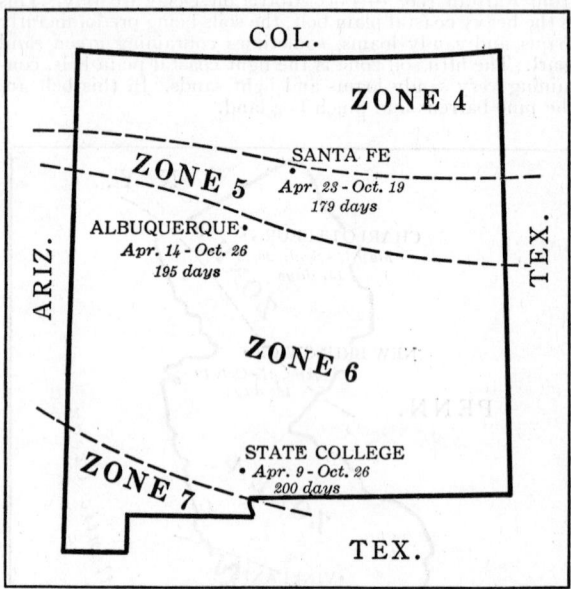

NEW MEXICO

The zones of hardiness crossing New Mexico are those shown on the colored map at ZONE, which should be consulted for details. The dates are the average latest killing frost in spring and the first one in the fall. The figures below the dates show the average length of the growing season. For rainfall, which is critical, and very locally distributed, *see* the text.

Many different kinds of vegetables are grown in the irrigated areas. In the home gardens a large variety of vegetables are planted both in the lower and higher irrigated areas of the state. In some of the southern irrigated valleys, cantaloupes, sweet potatoes, tomatoes, peppers, asparagus, cabbage and onions are grown on a large enough scale for shipping outside the state. In the higher altitudes and northern regions, sweet potatoes, melons, peppers and tomatoes are planted on only a small scale, but excellent vegetables of the cool-season type are grown. Irish potatoes are raised in many parts of the state where there is enough moisture either from rain or irrigation. In southern New Mexico, the Irish Cobbler is the favorite variety. It usually matures the first of July. At Tres Piedras and Tusas the Peachblow has been one of the favorite sorts.

Onions are well adapted to New Mexico conditions. In the southern irrigated valleys they are harvested from the last of June on through September. In the northern areas the growing season is shorter; the onions are planted later and are not harvested until September or the first of October. The Early Grano, Valencia, White Globe, and Crystal Wax are the popular varieties.

Beans are raised extensively, especially the dry beans. These are produced mostly under dry-farming conditions in the central and eastern parts of the state. The Pinto is the variety raised for commercial purposes.

Aside from growing vegetables for eating fresh or canning in the home, an industry in seed production is being started. Onion, spinach, carrot, and beet seed are the principal seed crops. These can best be grown in the southern and warmer

* Special articles on the subjects indicated by an asterisk (*) will be found at the words so marked.

irrigated valleys, where the seed can be planted the last of August or first of September and will produce seed the following July, as a rule. There are only a few commercial canneries, and these quite small, in the state.

Practically all flowers and ornamental trees and shrubs of the temperate zone flourish under irrigation. Even many of the humblest homes have flowers, if nothing more than a few geraniums and cactuses. Dozens of species of cactus, some of them very beautiful, are indigenous to this part of the Southwest, and they, the salt cedar and the bird-of-paradise bush (*Poinciana gilliesi*) require comparatively little water, after once started. Many species of wild flowers, including columbine, the Indian paint brush, several pentstemons, and asters of numerous sorts, abound; some in the higher altitudes and others at the lower elevations. A large percentage of the wild flowers of New Mexico have yellow blossoms; about 90 per cent of the aster family being of some shade of this color.

A native acacia has small, yellow blossoms that are very fragrant; while the desert willow, locusts, and other ornamental trees and shrubs, as well as some of the wild roses and vines indigenous to the state, have very attractive flowers. Some of the yuccas are often transplanted to the home grounds; also an occasional agave. Native cottonwoods; conifers, both native and introduced; elms; mulberries; maples; willows; Virginia creepers; honeysuckles; privets; and in recent years the pecan tree, have wide use as shade trees or ornamentals. An attractive and striking plant that is frequently seen about the yard is pampas grass.

Cosmos, zinnias, petunias, hollyhocks, dahlias, chrysanthemums and roses are often found around homes in the irrigated valleys; while an *Amaranthus*, one of the foliage plants, sometimes escapes and tends to grow as a weed under irrigation.

The varied climatic and soil conditions make the growing of a large assortment of flowers, vegetables, ornamental shrubs and trees feasible, though the arid or semi-arid climate usually requires that irrigation be practiced for satisfactory results.

CLIMATE. This is characterized by an unusually high percentage of clear days, a dry atmosphere and cool nights. Frost data for Albuquerque, Santa Fe and State College will be found below:

FROST DATES

| Town | Average date of last killing frost in spring | Latest known killing frost | Average date of earliest killing frost in fall | Earliest known killing frost |
|---|---|---|---|---|
| Albuquerque | April 14 | May 1 | Oct. 26 | Sept. 17 |
| Santa Fe | April 23 | May 18 | Oct. 19 | Sept. 25 |
| State College | April 9 | May 8 | Oct. 26 | Oct. 1 |

The average annual precipitation is about 15 inches, but varies from less than 6 inches at the lower elevations in northwestern New Mexico to more than 34 inches near the tops of some of the higher mountains. About two thirds of it generally falls during the growing season. In some regions, plant growth is at times retarded more or less in the spring by strong winds and, in some instances, by the cool nights.

The address of the Agricultural Experiment Station, which has kindly supplied this information regarding the state, is State College, New Mexico. The station is always ready to answer gardening questions.

NEW PLANTS. Fresh stock of existing plants can only come from seed or from their propagation by some method of vegetative increase, mostly by cuttings, grafting, division, or layering. If you are uncertain as to which applies (all are the subject of special articles) turn to the general article on PROPAGATION.

NEWPORT PINK. See DIANTHUS BARBATUS.

NEW SPECIES AND VARIETIES. For the production of wholly new species and varieties, as distinguished from the increase of old ones, see PLANT BREEDING.

NEW YEAR'S GIFT = *Eranthis hyemalis*.

NEW YORK. Nearly all of New York State, except Long Island, lies wholly within zones* 2 and 3. Long Island and Staten Island are on the northern edge of zone* 4, which also includes most of the City of New York. Most of the horticultural crops common to the temperate zone are grown successfully within the borders of the state. This does not mean that all of these crops can be grown successfully in all parts of the state. In some regions the growing season is too short for many long-season, heat-loving plants, such as melons, lima beans, eggplant and peppers, and the winters are too cold for tree fruits.

New York is one of the leading horticultural states. In 1929 she ranked fourth in value of fruits with a value of about $27,000,000; second in vegetables (including potatoes) with a total value of about $61,000,000; and first in cut flowers and potted plants with a value of about $12,000,000. In value of nursery products New York also ranks high with a value of about $7,000,000.

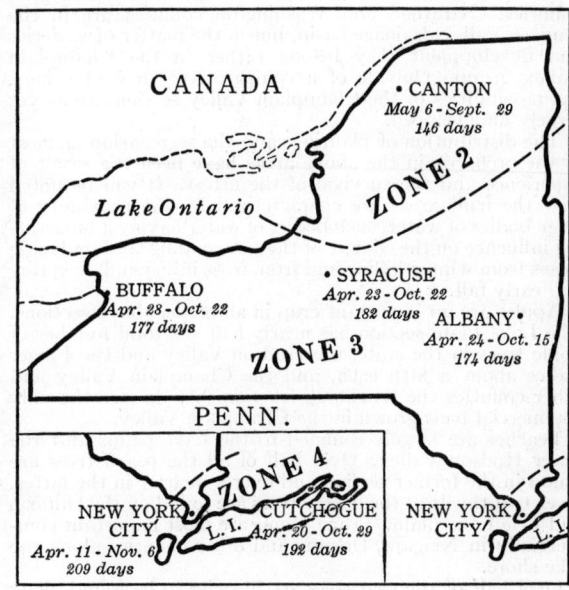

NEW YORK

The zones of hardiness crossing New York are those shown on the colored map at ZONE, which should be consulted for details. The dates are the average latest killing frost in spring and the first one in the fall. The figures below the dates show the average length of the growing season.

New York is outstanding in the beauty of its home surroundings, whether they are large private estates, or small urban, suburban or rural homes. Climatic conditions are such that herbaceous and woody ornamental plants, native over wide areas, grow freely, and in the southern sections of the state many species that are native of the South survive normal winters. There is, however, a comparatively small area where acid-soil plants, such as azaleas, rhododendrons, and others, find naturally favorable conditions for growth. Such areas are in the Adirondack and Catskill Mountains, along the Hudson River, and extending some distance along the northern shore of Long Island Sound and also on Long Island.

SOILS

The soils of New York cover a wide range of classes, including clay, clay loam, silty-clay loam, silt loam, gravelly

---

* Special articles on the subjects indicated by an asterisk (*) will be found at the words so marked.

silt loam, loam, sandy loam, fine sandy loam, fine sand, and organic or muck soil. All of the mineral soils are used for a wide range of crops, including fruits, vegetables, and ornamental plants. The organic soils that are under cultivation are used mainly for the production of celery, onions, lettuce, potatoes, carrots, and a few other vegetables. Such soils are considered almost ideal for celery, lettuce, and onions, and a large part of the acreage of these crops grown in New York is produced on muck soil. *See* MUCK GARDENING.

## CHIEF HORTICULTURAL CENTERS

The fruit sections of New York State may be designated as the Ontario and Erie Lake plains, comprising the northern part of the territory embraced by the counties of Oswego, Wayne, Monroe, Orleans, Niagara, Erie, and Chautauqua; the Finger Lakes, including parts of Genesee, Ontario, Steuben, Schuyler, Yates, Tompkins, Seneca, Cayuga, and Onondaga counties; the Hudson Valley, including the river slopes and the adjacent uplands of the more important counties of Albany, Rensselaer, Columbia, Greene, Ulster, Dutchess, Orange and Rockland, and the Champlain Valley, comprising a more or less narrow belt along the main waterway in Clinton, Essex, Warren, Saratoga, and Washington counties. Saratoga and Washington counties are in the Hudson Valley drainage basin, but in the matter of varieties and development they belong rather in the Champlain Valley group. Outside of a comparatively few plantings, the possibilities of the Champlain Valley section are as yet largely undeveloped.

The distribution of plantings and the segregation of most of the orchards in the above areas have been the result of experience and the survival of the fittest. It will be noted that the fruit areas are characterized by the proximity of large bodies of water, such bodies of water having a moderating influence on the climate of the surrounding land, reducing losses from winter-killing and from frost injury in late spring and early fall.

Apples are an important crop in all of the above sections. The Lake Plain section has nearly half the total number of apple trees in the state, the Hudson Valley and the Finger Lakes about a fifth each, and the Champlain Valley and other counties the remaining fraction. Apples are the only commercial fruit grown in the Champlain Valley.

Peaches are largely confined to the Lake plains and the lower Hudson Valley. Over half of all the peach trees are found in the former section and over a quarter in the latter. Over two-thirds of the cherry trees are found on the Ontario and Erie Lake plain. Prune plums are most important commercially in Niagara, Orleans and other counties along the lake shore.

Over half of the pear trees are likewise to be found along the two Great Lakes and about a fourth in the Hudson Valley.

The Erie shore is the predominating grape section, containing approximately three-fourths of the total number of vines. Grapes are also of commercial importance in the Finger Lakes region and the Hudson Valley.

Small fruits are of some commercial importance in all three sections.

Vegetables are grown for home use and, to some extent, for market, in practically all of the agricultural regions of the state. The principal commercial vegetable-producing areas are on Long Island and in Erie, Chautauqua, Niagara, Genesee, Orleans, Monroe, Ontario, Livingston, Wayne, Onondaga, Madison, Oneida, Oswego, and Albany counties. This production includes intensive market gardening around the important cities of New York, Albany, Schenectady, Syracuse, Rochester, and Buffalo, as well as more specialized types of vegetable growing in various areas.

One of the specialized types of production is the growing of celery, lettuce, onions, carrots and other special crops on the muck soils in Genesee, Orleans, Monroe, Livingston, Wayne, Onondaga, Oswego, Madison and Orange counties. Another type is the growing of cauliflower in Suffolk, Delaware, and Erie counties, and the production of cabbage as a general farm crop in Ontario, Monroe, Orleans, Niagara, Wayne, Onondaga, and Cortland counties.

A third type of vegetable growing is the production of crops for the canning factory. The important canning-crop regions are in Chautauqua, Erie, Niagara, Orleans, Monroe, Livingston, Genesee, Ontario, Wayne, Madison, Oneida, and Cortland counties. The principal crops grown for canning are tomatoes, sweet corn, peas, and snap beans. Tomatoes for canning are grown mainly in the counties bordering Lake Erie and Lake Ontario and those immediately adjoining them where the growing season is relatively long. Sweet corn for canning is grown mainly in Livingston, Erie, Monroe, Ontario, Onondaga, and Oneida counties. All of these counties, as well as Genesee, Orleans, Madison, Steuben, Wayne, Wyoming and Yates are important in the production of peas for canning. Madison County is the principal producer of peas for market. Snap beans for canning are grown mainly in Erie, Wayne, Oneida and Chautauqua counties.

The growing of flowers and other ornamental plants is widespread. Commercially the cut-flower industry is most important in the southeastern section, especially on Long Island, but in the vicinity of all important cities cut flowers and potted plants are grown for sale. The principal kinds of cut flowers grown are roses, carnations, chrysanthemums, snapdragons, sweet peas, and calendulas. More and more interest is being manifested in the growing of flowers out-of-doors for sale, and cloth houses are coming into rather wide use. The improved quality of the flowers grown in cloth houses makes the growing of asters, gladioli, snapdragons, sweet peas and others of similar nature for cut-flower sales remunerative during the summer (*see* CLOTH). Soil and climatic conditions in some sections, particularly on Long Island, are especially favorable for the production of bulbs. At the present time there are approximately 128 bulb farms in the state, which have an annual production valued at over six hundred thousand dollars.

The growing of nursery products is fairly widespread, but the most important areas of production of ornamental woody plants are in the north central section.

In both rural and suburban sections there is increasing interest in home beautification by the use of native plant materials. There is a growing appreciation of the beauty and appropriateness in the use of such native trees as beech, birch and maples in the deciduous group and hemlock, cedars, pines and spruces in evergreens. Native shrubs, such as dogwoods, viburnums and similar types, are being fairly generally planted, not only about homes but around public properties, such as school buildings, libraries, churches and in village squares. Wild flower gardens are also popular where areas suited for their growth are available.

## CLIMATE

New York State has a great diversity of climate due to difference in latitude, in altitude, and in distance and direction from large bodies of water. In general, the average annual temperature decreases about one degree F. for each degree of latitude. New York State lies between 41° and 45° north latitude. Altitude is more important than latitude, since for every rise of 300 feet there is an average decrease in temperature of about one degree F. The land surface in New York ranges from sea level to more than 5000 feet. The elevated sections also have a higher rainfall than do the lower areas. Land heats and cools faster than does water, therefore temperatures over water areas are more uniform than those over land areas, and, in general, regions near large bodies of water are not subject to sudden changes in temperature that are experienced farther inland. The climate of the regions lying along the Great Lakes and near the Atlantic Ocean is influenced greatly by the proximity of these bodies of water. These regions have a longer growing season, and a larger percentage of sunshine for the growing season than any other portion of the state.

The average date of the last killing frost in spring and the

---
\* Special articles on the subjects indicated by an asterisk (\*) will be found at the words so marked.

first killing frost in fall for several locations in the state is given in the following table:

FROST DATES

| Station | Last killing frost in spring |  | First killing frost in fall |  |
|---|---|---|---|---|
|  | Average | Latest | Average | Earliest |
| Albany | April 24 | May 30 | Oct. 15 | Sept. 15 |
| Binghamton | May 4 | May 29 | Oct. 8 | Sept. 14 |
| Buffalo | April 28 | May 23 | Oct. 22 | Oct. 3 |
| Canton | May 6 | June 2 | Sept. 29 | Sept. 11 |
| Cutchogue, L.I. | April 20 | May 12 | Oct. 29 | Oct. 4 |
| Ithaca | May 4 | June 9 | Oct. 9 | Sept. 11 |
| Jamestown | May 14 | June 20 | Oct. 6 | Sept. 15 |
| New York City | April 11 | April 30 | Nov. 6 | Oct. 15 |
| Rochester | April 27 | May 27 | Oct. 22 | Sept. 14 |
| Setauket, L.I. | April 13 | April 26 | Nov. 9 | Oct. 21 |
| Syracuse | April 23 | May 5 | Oct. 22 | Sept. 21 |

The average length of the growing season varies from 90 days in portions of the Adirondack Mountains to 200 days on the western end of Long Island. In the regions along Lake Erie and Lake Ontario the growing season varies from about 170 to 180 days and decreases eastward and southward from the lakes. Likewise, the length of the growing season decreases northward and westward from the Atlantic Ocean.

The mean sunshine, expressed in percentage of the possible sunshine, for the growing season, varies from 50 to 62, the regions of greatest sunshine being along the shore of Lake Ontario and near the Atlantic Ocean. The percentage of sunshine decreases eastward and southward from Lake Ontario and northward and westward from the ocean. The region of lowest sunshine, 50 to 54 per cent, embraces the area bounded by a line from the southwest corner of Steuben County on the west diagonally across the state to Warren and Washington counties and then southwestward through Albany, Greene, Ulster and Sullivan counties.

There is a wide variation in the annual and growing-season (April–August) precipitation in New York State. The average annual precipitation varies from less than 30 to more than 50 inches, and the growing-season rainfall from less than 12 to more than 20 inches. In general, the regions of heaviest precipitation are: (1) the Adirondack Mountains and surrounding areas, including most or all of Madison, Oneida, Lewis, Herkimer, and Hamilton counties and parts of Fulton, Montgomery and Otsego counties; (2) southeastern New York south and east of a line running through Columbia, Greene and Sullivan counties; (3) Chautauqua and Cattaraugus counties.

The address of the Agricultural Experiment Station which has kindly supplied this information about the state is Cornell University Agricultural Experiment Station, Ithaca, New York. There is also another important station at Geneva, N.Y., which has specialized on fruits. Both stations are always willing to answer gardening questions.

Garden Club activities are more extensive than in any other state. There are several clubs of the Garden Club of America, the home office of which is at 598 Madison Avenue, New York City. In addition there are over 170 clubs affiliated with the Federated Garden Clubs of New York State, Inc. For the one nearest your locality write the Garden Editor, Houghton Mifflin Company, Boston, Mass. See also HORTICULTURAL SOCIETY.

At the Grand Central Palace, New York City, is held an annual spring flower show, perhaps the most extensive in the country. Recently a permanent exhibit of interest to gardeners has been opened as "Gardens of the Nations" at Rockefeller Center. See also BOTANIC GARDEN.

**NEW YORK ASTER** = *Aster novi-belgi.*

**NEW YORK BOTANICAL GARDEN.** See BOTANIC GARDEN.

**NEW ZEALAND BUR** = *Acaena microphylla.*

**NEW ZEALAND FLAX** = *Phormium tenax.*

**NEW ZEALAND ICE-PLANT.** = NEW ZEALAND SPINACH.

**NEW ZEALAND SPINACH.** A good hot-weather substitute for spinach, belonging to the genus **Tetragonia** (tet-ra-gō′nĭ-a) of the family Aizoaceae. Of the 25 known species, mostly from the southern hemisphere and eastern Asia, only **T. expansa,** the New Zealand spinach, is of interest to the gardener. It is a stout, annual herb with prostrate, thickish stems often several feet long. Leaves alternate,* more or less triangular or ovalish-triangular, 2–4 in. long, thickish, somewhat glistening with minute dots (hence its other name of N. Zeal. ice-plant). Flowers very small, 1 or 2 in the leaf-axils, yellowish-green, without petals. Fruit dry, small, more or less 4-angled, top-shaped and horned. (*Tetragonia* is from the Greek for four-angled, in reference to the fruit.)

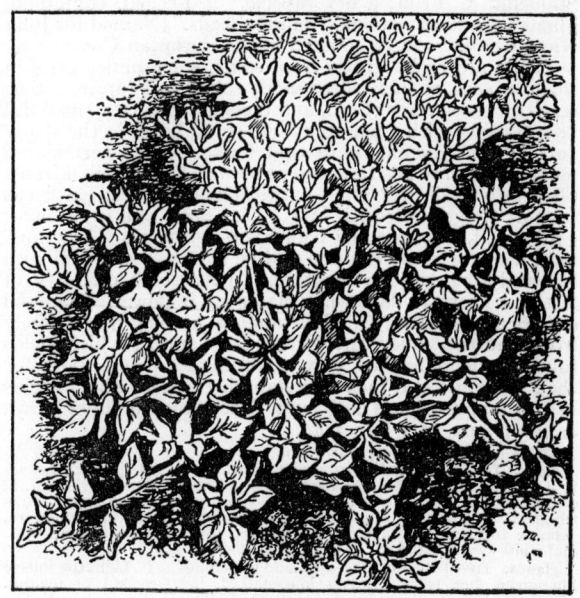

New Zealand spinach

New Zealand spinach can be grown whenever or wherever the heat is too great for ordinary spinach. Usually the plant sprawls so much that it makes large round patches, so that planting in hills is more satisfactory than in rows. The seed germinates slowly and it is best to soak the seed for a few hours in very hot water before planting. The hills should be 3–4 ft. apart. Sow 3 seeds at each hill, thinning them to a single plant later. Some growers prefer to start plants in the hotbed and transplant outdoors when warm weather has arrived. While the plant is commonly called N. Zeal. spinach and is native there, it is also native in Jap., Aust., and S.A. The young new leaves are far better than old ones; the latter sometimes become strong-tasting.

**NEW ZEALAND WINEBERRY** = *Aristotelia racemosa.*

**NICANDRA** (ny-kan′dra). Strong-growing, annual herbs from Peru, comprising 2 species of the family Solanaceae, one of garden interest. It is now seldom seen, although it has escaped* from cultivation and become naturalized in tropical America. (It is believed to be named for an ancient poet of Colophon.)

Propagated by seeds, sown ⅛ in. deep in pots or boxes of light soil in temperature 55°–65° in March. Transplant the seedlings, 3 ft. apart, outdoors, in May, in ordinary soil. Seeds may also be sown outdoors in April, transplanting the seedlings in June.

**physalodes.** Apple-of-Peru. A strong, spreading, annual herb, growing to a height of 4 ft. Leaves alternate,* ovalish, the margins toothed. Flowers solitary, tubular, blue, 1–2 in. across and on curving stalks.

---

* Special articles on the subjects indicated by an asterisk (*) will be found at the words so marked.

**Fruit**, a 3–5-celled, many-seeded berry enclosed in an inflated calyx. Occasionally offered under the name "shoofly."

**NICO-FUME.** A trade-marked nicotine preparation sold with directions for use in fumigation.

**NICOTIANA** (ni-ko-she-ā′na). Herbaceous annuals and perennials, occasionally shrubby or tree-like, mostly tropical and comprising 45 species of the potato family, all American except for one found in Aust. They grow 2–20 ft. high, and have mostly large soft leaves, the whole plant more or less covered with short sticky hairs. Stems branching, sometimes fasciated (see FASCIATION). Leaves alternate,* simple, the juice having narcotic or poisonous properties. Flowers in clusters at the ends of the branches, sweet-scented, mostly opening from 5 P.M. to 8 A.M. but remaining open on sunless days, white, greenish-yellow or purple. Calyx* of 5 partly united, green sepals. Corolla tubular or funnel-shaped. Stamens* 5. Fruit, a dry capsule,* 2–4-celled, containing numerous and exceptionally minute seeds. (Named for John Nicot who introduced tobacco to the European Courts.)

Plants are easily grown from seeds, sown under glass in shallow boxes of finely sifted sandy soil in early spring. Sow seeds on the surface of soil, and press down with a small flat board, water with a fine spray and stand boxes in the shady part of cool greenhouse or cold frame. When germinated move to a sunny position, and as soon as large enough transplant into small pots or boxes, transplanting to the garden as soon as danger of frost is over. They grow well in ordinary garden soil, but lime and potash are beneficial. They must have a warm sunny position and be kept well supplied with water during hot dry weather. Apply small quantity of fertilizer every 10 days when plants are in flower. Perennial species are usually treated as annuals, as they flower freely from seed the same year. Except for 1 species which yields tobacco, nicotianas are very useful border plants, both for their fragrance and their long flowering period, which begins in July and continues until frost. They are sometimes grown as pot plants, in 6–8 in. pots.

**affinis** = Nicotiana alata grandiflora.
**alata.** Tender perennial, growing to 5 ft., erect and slender. Leaves to 4 in. long, not stalked, the tip blunt or pointed. Flowers fragrant, in a loose raceme,* the tube white within, violet without, the limb yellowish-green, 2 in. across. Brazil, Uruguay, Paraguay. The var. **grandiflora**, jasmine tobacco, has much larger flowers, the tube being more open and white (see ANNUALS). It often seeds itself on L.I.
**glauca.** Tree Tobacco. Tree-like, and sometimes 20 ft. high, the foliage blue-green, not hairy. Leaves long-stalked, heart-shaped or ovalish. Flowers in loose terminal bracted clusters. Calyx tubular, its 5 teeth-like lobes slightly hairy. Corolla yellow, 1½ in. long, constricted, its lobes oval. S.A., but naturalized in Tex. and Calif. Grown for its stately habit and blue-green foliage.
**sanderae.** A hybrid annual of bushy habit, growing to 3 ft. Leaves spoon-shaped to 1 ft. long, short-stalked. Flowers to 3 in. long, the tube greenish-yellow, tinted rose, becoming carmine-rose as it expands, its lobes pointed. Originated by Sander and Sons, St. Albans, Eng.
**sylvestris.** Herbaceous perennial growing to 5 ft. Leaves not stalked, broad, spoon-shaped, wrinkled, partly clasping the stem. Flowers drooping, in clusters. Calyx short, slightly swollen, its lobes pointed. Corolla white, fragrant, the tube 3–3½ in. long. Argentina.
**tabacum.** Tobacco. Herbaceous annual growing to 6 ft. and covered with short sticky hairs. Leaves thin, not stalked, partly clasping the stem, 1 ft. or more long, broadly lance-shaped. Flowers stalked, in bracted clusters (racemes*). Corolla 2 in. long, the tube white, whitish, rose, or purplish-red, its lobes pointed. Grown as an agricultural product but it is a striking garden plant. Tropical America. See TOBACCO.
**tomentosa.** Shrubby perennial, growing to 20 ft. high and covered with short, whitish, sticky hairs. Leaves 10–19 in. long, 4–6 in. wide, stem-clasping, pale green, with a conspicuous mid-rib. Flowers ½ in. long, in loose terminal racemes* nearly a foot long. Calyx ½ in. long, smooth and green, its lobes narrow. Corolla tube short, pale green, hairy on the outside, and yellow, tinged with red, inside, the limb spreading. Brazil.

**NICOTINE.** A widely used insecticide. See Contact Sprays at INSECTICIDES. See also FUMIGATION.

**NICOTROL.** A trade-marked nicotine preparation ready mixed and sold with directions for use as a contact spray.

**NIDULARIUM** (nid-you-lay′rĭ-um). Showy, Brazilian, tree-perching plants of the family Bromeliaceae, comprising perhaps 20 species of which the two below are grown in the greenhouse for the handsome foliage and brilliantly bracted* flowers. The ones below have practically no stems and a dense basal rosette* of broad-based, but otherwise strap-shaped, often spiny-toothed leaves. Flower cluster almost stalkless, nestled in the center of the leaf rosette, but just beneath it a cluster of brilliantly colored, leaf-like bracts,* joined into a sort of involucre.* Corolla, in ours, whitish, more or less tubular. Sepals* not united. Fruit a berry. (Nidularium is from the Latin for nest, in allusion to the nest-like position of the flower cluster.)

Should be grown in pots or orchid baskets with a mixture composed of ⅓ potting mixture* 3 and ⅔ chopped fern fiber or coir. They need a warm moist greenhouse with a night temperature of about 65°, and plenty of water during their active growing season (March–Aug.). During the winter they need much less water, often a light sprinkling of the foliage being sufficient. Propagated by the usually frequent suckers which arise below the rosette of leaves.

**amazonicum** = Canistrum amazonicum.
**fulgens.** Leaves about 12 in. long and nearly 2 in. wide, mostly spotted with dark green. Flowers white, but the bracts beneath the dense head-like cluster, brilliant scarlet. The plant is sometimes offered as N. pictum.
**innocenti.** Leaves about 12 in. long, scarcely over 1 in. wide, green but tinted red or brown. Flowers white, the bracts beneath the dense head-like cluster, red.
**pictum** = Nidularium fulgens.

**NIDUS** (ny′dus). Latin for a nest. See ASPLENIUM NIDUS.

**NIEREMBERGIA** (near-em-berg′ĭ-a or -ber′jĭ-a). Cup-flower. Tropical American perennial herbs or under-shrubs of the potato family, comprising about 25 species, of which 3 are grown for their attractive tubular flowers. They are inclined to sprawl or creep, and have alternate* somewhat scattered leaves without marginal teeth. Flowers white or pale violet, mostly near the ends of the twigs. Calyx more or less bell-shaped, 5-parted. Corolla long-tubed, the 5-lobed limb abruptly expanded, yellow in the throat in ours. Stamens* 5, protruding, one shorter than the others. Fruit a 2-valved capsule.* (Named for J. E. Nieremberg, a Jesuit professor of natural history at Madrid.)

While these plants are hardy or very nearly so up to zone* 4, it is safer to dig them up for the winter and plunge* in a cold frame. They may also be grown in the cool greenhouse where N. frutescens will bloom almost continuously. They can be propagated by seeds, by cuttings in the fall (wintered in the greenhouse) or by division of the rooting stems of N. rivularis.

**filicaulis** = Nierembergia gracilis.
**frutescens.** A well-known one in cult. and more erect than sprawling, often 1–3 ft. high. Leaves very narrow, usually about 1 in. long, scattered. Flowers nearly 1 in. wide, white, or lilac or blue-tinted, the limb of the corolla saucer-shaped. Chile. Can be grown in the border or in the greenhouse. Forms are offered with purple or with larger flowers.
**gracilis.** More or less sprawling and not over 6–8 in. high. Leaves very narrow, scarcely ½ in. long, the upper ones a little hairy. Flowers white, but purple-tinged or veined towards the center, the limb somewhat convex. Argentina. Sometimes offered as N. filicaulis.
**rivularis.** Creeping and rooting at the joints, forming a dense mat. Leaves oblongish, nearly 1 in. long, stalked. Flowers cream-white, sometimes rose- or blue-tinged, the bell-shaped limb 1–2 in. wide. Argentina. Perhaps the best known of the three. For cult. see ROCK GARDEN.

**NIGELLA** (ny-jell′a). Herbaceous annuals, comprising about 12 species, mostly natives of the Mediterranean Region, belonging to the buttercup family. Stems erect, branching. Leaves alternate,* often of lace-like appearance owing to their being finely divided in thread-like segments. Flowers blue or white, produced at the ends of the branching stems, each flower enclosed by much-branched, thread-like bracts* growing from the base. Petals 5–8, notched. Stamens* indefinite in number. Pistils* usually 5–10, separated at the top, but united at the base. Fruit an inflated capsule, containing many hard black seeds which are dispersed through openings at the top. The seeds were at one time used as pepper. (Nigella is from the Greek for black, in reference to the black seeds.)

Sow seeds ⅛ in. deep, where required to bloom, in ordinary soil, in sunny beds or borders. Plants do not require much attention except to thin out to 8 in. apart.

**damascena.** Love-in-a-mist; also called devil-in-the-bush. Height 12–18 in., much branched. Leaves lace-like, bright green. Flowers light blue or white, 1½ in. across, set in the midst of thread-like bracts. Fruit, a globe-shaped capsule.* Southern Eu. See BLUE GARDEN.
**sativa.** Fennel-flower. Height 1 ft., branching. Leaves lance-shaped, not cut. Flowers blue, solitary, not enclosed in lace-like bracts. Fruit

---

* Special articles on the subjects indicated by an asterisk (*) will be found at the words so marked.

an inflated capsule. Seeds sometimes used for seasoning. **Mediterranean Region.** See HERB GARDENING.

**NIGER** (ny'jer). Black.

**NIGGER-TOES.** See BERTHOLLETIA EXCELSA.

**NIGHT-BLOOMING CEREUS.** As now understood, none of the plants known as night-blooming cereus belong to the genus *Cereus*. For the three best-known ones, all called night-blooming cereus, see HYLOCEREUS UNDATUS. SELENICEREUS PTERANTHUS, and NYCTOCEREUS SERPENTINUS. The first is the most widely cult. of the three. All are at their best after midnight.

**NIGHT-BLOOMING FLOWERS.** See NOCTURNAL FLOWERS.

**NIGHT GARDENS.** See LIGHTING.

**NIGHT JASMINE** = *Nyctanthes arbor-tristis* and *Cestrum nocturnum*.

**NIGHTSHADE.** See SOLANUM. See also BASELLA.

**NIGHTSHADE FAMILY** = Solanaceae.

**NIGHT SOIL.** See MANURE.

**NIGHT TEMPERATURES.** The best night temperatures to maintain in the different sorts of greenhouses are:
Cool greenhouse . . . . . . . . . . . . . . . . . . . 45–50°
Warm-temperate greenhouse . . . . . . . . 50–55°
Tropical greenhouse . . . . . . . . . . . . . . . . 60–65°

In certain cases the tropical house will have to be kept warmer than this through the night, especially for some plants of the pineapple family and for some aroids. See GREENHOUSE for the details.

*NIGRA, -us, -um* (ny'gra). Black.

*NIGRICANS* (ny'gri-kanz). Black.

*NIGROFRUCTA, -us, -um* (ny-gro-fruck'ta). Black-fruited.

**NIKAU PALM** = *Rhopalostylis sapida*.

**NIKKO FIR** = *Abies homolepis*. See FIR.

**NIKOTEEN.** Trade-marked nicotine preparations, including a liquid, powder, and "punk," sold with directions for use in spraying, dusting, and fumigation.

**NIL.** Arabic vernacular for a morning-glory. See IPOMOEA NIL.

**NINEBARK.** See PHYSOCARPUS.

**NIOBE.** See PLANTAIN-LILY.

*NIPPONICA, -us, -um* (nip-pon'i-ka). From Japan.

*NITIDA, -us, -um* (nĭ'tĭ-da). Shining.

**NITRATE OF SODA.** See FERTILIZERS.

**NITRATES.** See FERTILIZERS.

**NITROGEN.** One of the essentials for plant growth. For the sources of it and its use as an ingredient of fertilizers see FERTILIZERS. For the role of nitrogen in the chemical composition of plants see PLANT FOODS.

*NIVALIS, -e* (niv-vay'lis). Snowy; *i.e.* white.

*NIVEA, -us, -um* (niv'e-a). Snowy; *i.e.* white.

*NIVOSA, -us, -um* (niv-vō'sa). Snowy; *i.e.* white.

**NIWA-SHI.** A professional Japanese gardener. See JAPANESE GARDEN.

*NOBILIS, -e* (nō'bil-lis). Famous or renowned; sometimes, also, noble.

*NOCTURNA, -us, -um* (nock-tur'na). Night-blooming.

**NOCTURNAL FLOWERS.** While most flowers bloom in daytime, and many close at night, there are an appreciable number that bloom at night and are apt to be closed or nearly so in bright sunshine.

By far the greatest number of these night-blooming flowers are tropical. They are often white, sometimes very fragrant, and the presumption is (not always verified) that they are pollinated only by night-flying insects, mostly moths. The most spectacular of these nocturnal flowers is, of course, the night-blooming cereus, the blooms of which are nearly 12 in. long, extremely fragrant, and usually come to perfection after midnight. They mostly open only once and then wither. But several other tropical flowers bloom for several nights, notably the night jasmines (see NYCTANTHES and CESTRUM). Many other tropical plants do this, but they are not usually cult. plants.

Among hardy garden flowers that bloom at night, or at least do not begin to bloom until toward or after sunset, perhaps the outstanding belong to the genus *Nicotiana*. Also night-blooming are the evening primroses. A brief list of other plants mostly blooming at night would include the following plants, all of which are entered in THE GARDEN DICTIONARY under the names given below:

| | |
|---|---|
| Akebia quinata | Mirabilis |
| Brunfelsia americana | Nymphaea (some tropical sorts) |
| Cooperia | |
| Gladiolus tristis | Petunia axillaris |
| Hemerocallis thunbergi | Saponaria |
| Hesperis | Schizopetalon walkeri |
| Lonicera heckrotti | Silene noctiflora |
| Lychnis alba | Yucca (some species) |
| Manfreda virginica | Zaluzianskya |
| Mathiola bicornis | |

While all of these may flower in the day, especially towards evening, their finest flowering is always at night, and their greatest fragrance comes long after sundown. Any of them may flower during the day if the weather is overcast.

**NODDING LILAC** = *Syringa reflexa*. See LILAC.

**NODDING TRILLIUM** = *Trillium cernuum*.

**NODE.** The place at which a leaf, bud, or other organ (sometimes the branch of a flower cluster) joins the stem to which it is attached; a joint. The space between such joints is sometimes, but incorrectly, called a node. Properly, it is an internode.

**NODULE.** See TUBERCLE.

*NODULOSA, -us, -um* (nod-you-lō'sa). Tubercled. See TUBERCLE.

**NOISETTE ROSE** = *Rosa noisettiana*.

**NOLANA** (no-lay'na). Prostrate perennial herbs, grown as annuals, comprising about 20 species of the family Nolanaceae, and natives of Chile and Peru. Stem angular, sometimes spotted and streaked, smooth or sticky, the much branched ends turning upwards. Leaves usually in pairs, spoon-shaped. Flowers bell-shaped, solitary stalked, borne in the axils* of the leaves, blue or purple, rarely white or rose. Stamens* 5. (Nolana is from the Latin for a little bell, in reference to the shape of the flower.)

Suitable for rock gardens or barren hillsides, as they like light sandy soil and sunny position. They can also be utilized for hanging baskets. Propagate by seeds, sown in patches in April, thinning out to 4 in. apart. It is not much in cultivation, the Chilean bellflower being the best-known.

**atriplicifolia.** Chilean Bellflower. Stems spotted and streaked with purple on the upper side, spreading from the root, and about 1 ft. long. Leaves spoon-shaped, fleshy. Flowers blue with white and yellow throat, 2 in. across. The *var.* violacea has violet flowers.

**lanceolata.** Whole plant covered with white hairs. Leaves lance-shaped, 4–6 in. long. Flowers deep blue, with the throat spotted creamy-white, 2 in. across.

**paradoxa.** *Nolana atriplicifolia.*

**prostrata.** Resembles *N. atriplicifolia*, but the flowers are smaller, and with a purple-veined throat. Peru. It may be only a form of the first species.

**NOLANACEAE** (no-lan-ā'see-ee). A small family of South American herbs or under-shrubs, containing only 3 genera, of which *Nolana* is the only one of hort. interest. See NOLANA.

**NOLINA** (no-ly'na). Bear grass. Strictly desert plants of the lily family, found in the southwestern U.S., but most abundant in Mex., two (or perhaps more) occasionally cult. in desert gardens. They are related to *Dasylirion* (which

---

* Special articles on the subjects indicated by an asterisk (*) will be found at the words so marked.

see). For years they may have no stem and a basal rosette* of leaves, but in the 2 below they ultimately form a trunk-like stem, the leaf rosette then terminal. Leaves tough, strap-shaped or sword-shaped, usually rough on the margins, usually very numerous in the rosette. Flowers small, whitish, in a terminal cluster (panicle*). Fruit a papery capsule.* (Named for C. P. Nolin, French agriculturist.)

Neither plant can be grown outdoors much beyond its wild range, for it cannot stand cold, wet winters. Sometimes grown in the greenhouse where they should be treated as succulents (which see).

**longifolia.** Trunk (ultimately) 8–10 ft. high, swollen at the base, sometimes branched at the top. Leaves nearly 3 ft. long, about 1½ ft. wide, usually drooping over the trunk. Flower cluster nearly stalkless among the leaves, the flowers about ¼ in. long. Mex. The roasted trunks serve as food to the Mexican Indians.

**parryi.** Trunk (ultimately) about 6 ft. high, unbranched. Leaves about 3 ft. long and ¾ in. wide. Stalk of the flower cluster about 2 ft. long, its branches stout. Southern Calif.

**NOMENCLATURE.** See PLANT NAMES.

**NONE-SO-PRETTY** = *Silene armeria*.

**NONESUCH** = *Medicago lupulina*.

*NONSCRIPTA, -us, -um* (non-scrip′ta). Undesignated or undescribed.

**NOODLE-PLANT.** A trade name for a small decorative gourd.*

**NOOTKA CYPRESS** = *Chamaecyparis nootkatensis*.

*NOOTKATENSIS, -e* (noot-ka-ten′sis). From Nootka, near Vancouver.

**NOPAL** = *Opuntia lindheimeri*, but *see also* NOPALEA.

**NOPALEA** (no-pay′lee-a). Six species of *Opuntia*-like, Mexican cacti, one of which, **N. cochenillifera,** the cochineal plant, was once the most important economic cactus in cult., now grown mostly for interest or ornament. Upon it fed the cochineal insect, the source of a famous dye, now largely replaced by synthetic products. It is a tree-like, branched cactus, 10–15 ft. high. Joints fleshy and leaf-like, oblongish, 15–20 in. long, and generally spineless. Unlike most other cacti, there are often produced small, nearly terete leaves, which soon drop off, and may often be wanting. Flowers scarlet, about 2 in. long. Fruit a red, juicy, edible berry, nearly 2¼ in. long. The cochineal plant can only be grown in frostless regions, or northward in the greenhouse. *See* CACTI. For centuries the plant and its insect were very important commercially, and were known to the Aztecs long before the conquest. They called it nopal, of which *Nopalea* is the Latin version.

**NORCROSS.** A trade-marked cultivator with curved, blade-like teeth at the end of a long handle; useful for cultivating or weeding.

**NORDMANN FIR** = *Abies nordmanniana*. *See* FIR.

**NORFOLK ISLAND PINE** = *Araucaria excelsa*.

**NORTH BORDERS.** *See* Shady Border at BORDER. *See also* SHADY GARDEN.

**NORTH CAROLINA.** The state lies wholly in zones* 5 and 6. The production of horticultural crops and the development of horticultural industries in North Carolina are closely identified with the climate and soil of the four natural subdivisions of the state commonly known as the Coastal Plain, Sandhill, Piedmont, and Mountain sections.

The Coastal Plain includes a belt bordering on the Atlantic Ocean and extending about 150 miles westward to the Piedmont and Sandhill sections. This area is characterized by soils of a light, sandy texture, mostly underlaid with clay, varying from coarse sands to sandy loams and fine, sandy loams. These soils warm up quickly, are easily cultivated, and are therefore valuable for vegetable growing. The winter and early spring temperatures are usually very mild, making this region especially adapted to the production of early vegetable crops for shipment to northern markets. The city of Wilmington lies in the center of the most intensive truck-growing area of the state. The winter temperature at Wilmington seldom goes below 20° F. under normal conditions.

The most important truck crop grown in the Coastal Plain is the early Irish potato. Other vegetable crops that are grown more or less generally throughout the area are sweet potatoes, string beans, lima beans, peas, tomatoes, squash, cucumbers, watermelons, cantaloupes, mustard, kale, cabbage, collards, turnips, peppers, onions, okra, beets, carrots, radishes, and corn. In the Wilmington area the chief market crops are lettuce, cucumbers, string beans, lima beans, peas, early turnips, cabbage, spinach, radishes, sprouting broccoli, beets, and carrots. Here the growing season is so long that it is often possible to grow three different crops successively on the same piece of land during one season.

NORTH CAROLINA

The zones of hardiness crossing North Carolina are those shown on the colored map at ZONE, which should be consulted for details. The dates are the average latest killing frost in spring and the first one in the fall. The figures below the dates show the average length of the growing season.

In the vicinity of Wilmington a considerable acreage is now being devoted to the growing of bulbs — narcissus, Dutch iris, tulips, and gladiolus. These flowers come into bloom so early in the spring that the shipment of cut flowers has become an important item as a side line of the bulb industry. This section of the state is also noted for its great variety of native evergreens, trees and flowers, chief among which are pines, cypress, holly, yaupon, inkberry, cherry laurel, leucothoë, dogwood, fringe-tree, tulip-tree, live oak, magnolia, sweet bay, smilax, Spanish moss, and the rare Venus's-flytrap. Gardenias, camellias, and the more tender *indica* azaleas can be successfully grown along with the more hardy shrubbery.

Strawberries, blueberries, dewberries, figs, Muscadine grapes and, to a lesser extent, peaches, are the fruit crops grown commercially in the Coastal Plain. However, adapted varieties of practically all the common fruits can be grown for home use.

The Sandhill section is a small area in the south central part of the state, the name being indicative of the prevailing soil types, with sands and sandy loams, light in color and of a porous, open structure, predominating. This section is the most important peach- and dewberry-producing area. Muscadine grapes are also an important crop. On account of the general infertility of the soil most vegetable crops are not of importance except for home use.

The Piedmont section is a wide belt extending from the

* Special articles on the subjects indicated by an asterisk (*) will be found at the words so marked.

Coastal Plain and Sandhills on the east to the Mountains on the west. The Piedmont soils are of the Cecil clay series, in which the clays predominate. Toward the east they are more or less blended with the sandy types of the Coastal Plain. This section of the state is primarily a general farming area. Any or all of the common vegetable crops may be grown here for home use and near-by markets, but the section cannot generally compete with the Coastal Plain section in the production of truck crops for market. The season is somewhat later and the soils heavier and therefore harder to work.

The Piedmont is well adapted to the growing of fruits, chief of which are apples, peaches, grapes, pears, and red raspberries along the western edge of the area. Strawberries, blackberries, plums, and cherries may also be grown. Of the native shrubs, flowering dogwood, the various haws, crabapples, viburnums, and redbud are distinctive of this area. Here also are the hardwood forests.

The Mountain section of North Carolina includes approximately the western one-sixth of the state, extending from the edge of the Blue Ridge on the east to the Great Smoky range on the west. The soils of this area are mostly clay loams and sandy loams of the Porter series. This area is of great horticultural importance. The Irish potato, for seed purposes and eating stock, is the most important truck crop. Cabbage, snap beans, dry beans, lima beans, onions, rhubarb, sweet corn, tomatoes, turnips, rutabagas, celery, spinach, lettuce, beets, and carrots thrive in this section.

The leading fruit of the Mountain section is the apple. Pears, peaches, plums, cherries, raspberries, blackberries, strawberries, and grapes are grown to a lesser extent.

The native shrubs and trees are characteristic of the section. Here we find hemlock, balsam, white pine, chestnut, sourwood, cucumber tree, sugar maple, black walnut, serviceberry, hardy azaleas, rhododendron, mountain laurel, leucothoë, galax, trailing arbutus, wintergreen, ginseng, goldenseal, and many kinds of ferns. Dahlias and other flowers requiring a cool, moist climate reach perfection in the mountains.

### CLIMATE

The climate of North Carolina varies greatly from the Coast, where it is tempered by the Gulf Stream, to the Mountains where the high altitudes give a climate comparable to the New England states.

The following table gives frost data for various points in the state:

| Name of town | Average date of last killing frost in spring | Latest known killing frost | Average date of earliest killing frost in fall | Earliest known killling frost |
|---|---|---|---|---|
| Wilmington | March 22 | May 1 | Nov. 14 | Oct. 16 |
| Edenton | April 2 | April 26 | Oct. 31 | Oct. 12 |
| Pinehurst | April 7 | April 26 | Nov. 1 | Oct. 12 |
| Winston-Salem | April 14 | May 15 | Oct. 24 | Oct. 2 |
| Hendersonville | April 24 | | Oct. 20 | |

The average length of the growing season from the above table is 237 days for Wilmington, located on the Coast, 193 days for Winston-Salem, in the Piedmont, and 178 days for Hendersonville, in the Mountains. In the higher altitudes of the Mountain area the growing season is somewhat shorter.

A word should be said about thermal belts. They are belts, more or less indefinite in width, where the minimum temperatures average higher than at either base or summit of the ridge, free from the frost of the valley and from the freezes of the higher levels. Within this belt foliage is often fresh and green when that above and below has been killed by frost. A number of these thermal belts are found in the North Carolina mountains and are of great importance to the fruit grower.

The annual rainfall of the state will average approximately 50 inches for the Coastal area, 47 inches for the Piedmont and 54 inches for the Mountains. One station, Highlands, in the Mountain area, has an average annual rainfall of approximately 80 inches.

The address of the Agricultural Experiment Station which has kindly supplied the information about the state is State College Station, Raleigh, N.C. The station is always ready to answer gardening questions.

Garden Club activities include clubs of the Garden Club of America, the home office of which is 598 Madison Avenue, New York, N.Y. There are also nearly 50 clubs affiliated with the Garden Club of North Carolina. For the address of the nearest one to your locality, write the Garden Editor, Houghton Mifflin Company, Boston, Mass.

**NORTH DAKOTA.** The state lies wholly in zone* 1.

The soil of eastern North Dakota counties lies in what was formerly the bed of Glacial Lake Agassiz. This is known as the Red River Valley and is an extremely fertile, level area. Between the Red River Valley and the Missouri River, the soil is of glacial origin. Because of this, there is considerable local variation in elevation and in the nature of the soil. South and west of the Missouri River, the land is not glaciated, but is the result of disintegration of the residual rock. Where erosion has taken place to a marked degree, we have what is known as the Bad Lands.

The chief gardening centers lie in the neighborhood of the larger cities such as Grand Forks, Fargo, Bismarck, Minot and Jamestown. Gardening in these areas is largely for local market.

There is only one horticultural crop of commercial importance, and that is potatoes, which are raised in large quantities, the chief producing area being in the north end of the Red River Valley.

With the proper selection of varieties it is possible to raise satisfactorily nearly all kinds of vegetables and most kinds of fruits and flowers for home ornamentation and use.

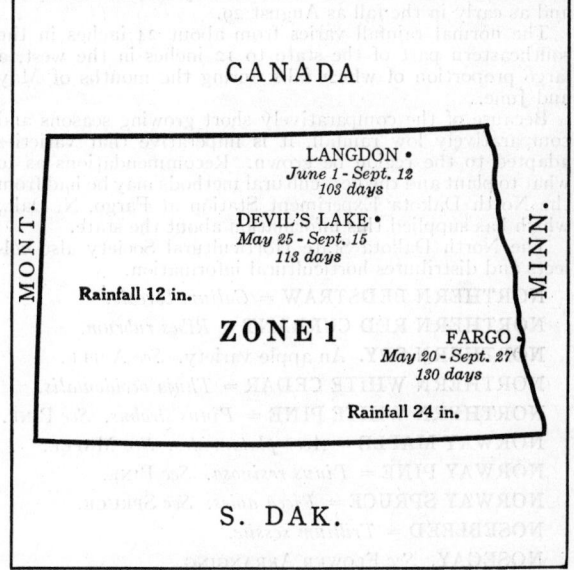

NORTH DAKOTA

The zones of hardiness crossing North Dakota are those shown on the colored map at ZONE, which should be consulted for details. The dates are the average latest killing frost in spring and the first one in the fall. The figures below the dates show the average length of the growing season. Rainfall figures (in inches) are for total annual rainfall in the regions so indicated.

Because of short summers and long days with a comparatively cool temperature, it is possible to raise many things in North Dakota which cannot be raised farther south where the rainfall is greater.

---

* Special articles on the subjects indicated by an asterisk (*) will be found at the words so marked.

The reason why North Dakota can produce better crops with the same amount of moisture than farther south is partly accounted for by a comparatively short growing season, during which the average temperature is comparatively cool. It is only during these summer months that the rate of evaporation is high. Hence, 15 inches of rain will give a much greater effect in a 100-day growing season than in a 200-day growing season. Coupled with this more efficient use of moisture there are extremely long growing days. In midsummer there will be 16 hours of sunshine. This extra day length makes plants grow very much more rapidly than would be the case with shorter days. Hence, a variety of sweet corn may produce roasting ears in 49 days from the date the seed was sown.

Ornamental plants which are particularly adapted to North Dakota climate are the peony and the gladiolus. There are a number of peony and gladiolus shows held in the cities and small towns of the state.

The principal native ornamental trees are elm, box-elder, poplar, bur oak and willows among the deciduous trees, and bull pine and red cedar among the evergreens.

In general, there is a difference of about five degrees in average summer temperature between the northern and southern parts of the state. The longest frost-free season is found in the southeastern part of the state and along the Missouri River. Fargo, Devils Lake and Langdon are selected as towns representing variations in climate.

| Town | Average date of last killing frost in spring | Average date of earliest killing frost in fall | Average length of frost-free season |
|---|---|---|---|
| Fargo | May 20 | Sept. 27 | 130 days |
| Devils Lake | May 25 | Sept. 15 | 113 days |
| Langdon | June 1 | Sept. 12 | 103 days |

At Fargo frost has occurred as late as June 10 in the spring and as early in the fall as August 29.

The normal rainfall varies from about 24 inches in the southeastern part of the state to 12 inches in the west, a large proportion of which falls during the months of May and June.

Because of the comparatively short growing seasons and comparatively low rainfall, it is imperative that varieties adapted to the region be grown. Recommendations as to what to plant and the best cultural methods may be had from the North Dakota Experiment Station at Fargo, N. Dak., which has supplied this information about the state.

The North Dakota State Horticultural Society also collects and distributes horticultural information.

**NORTHERN BEDSTRAW** = *Galium boreale.*

**NORTHERN RED CURRANT** = *Ribes rubrum.*

**NORTHERN SPY.** An apple variety. See APPLE.

**NORTHERN WHITE CEDAR** = *Thuja occidentalis.*

**NORTHERN WHITE PINE** = *Pinus strobus.* See PINE.

**NORWAY MAPLE** = *Acer platanoides.* See MAPLE.

**NORWAY PINE** = *Pinus resinosa.* See PINE.

**NORWAY SPRUCE** = *Picea abies.* See SPRUCE.

**NOSEBLEED** = *Trillium sessile.*

**NOSEGAY.** See FLOWER ARRANGING.

**NOTHOLCUS** (no-tholl'kus). Perennial or annual, ornamental grasses comprising about 8 species, natives of Europe and North Africa. The only one of garden interest is the velvet grass. (*Notholcus* is from the Greek for false and *Holcus*, which see.)

Propagation is by division of rootstocks in Oct. or April. Usually grown in clumps, in any ordinary garden soil.

**lanatus.** Velvet grass. Erect, perennial grass, growing up to 3 ft., the whole plant covered with soft, velvety hairs. Leaves 6 in. long, ½ in. wide, with spear-like points. Spikelets produced at the tips of the stems, in clusters 4 in. long, arranged in pairs, slightly spreading from the main stem, pale green. The plant is also known as *Holcus lanatus.* There is a variegated form with white-striped leaves. Eu., but naturalized in N.A.

**NOTHOPANAX** (no-tho-pay'nacks). Indo-Malayan or Australasian, evergreen shrubs and trees of the family Araliaceae, all those below from N. Zeal., and without prickles. The genus is, and has been for many years, in the utmost confusion as to its exact identity, and as to the validity of the species names. The four below are sometimes grown outdoors in Calif., but elsewhere are little known as cult. plants. Much of the confusion of identity is due to the fact that the leaves may be simple,* or compound,* or sometimes both on the same shrub, simultaneously, or at different ages of the plant. Flowers small, usually greenish or greenish-white, often not produced for years, and unknown in some cult. plants. They are borne in simple or compound umbels.* Fruit fleshy. (*Nothopanax* is from the Greek for false and *Panax*, in allusion to their relationship to the ginseng.)

Nothing definite is known about their soil preferences or propagation.

**anomalum.** A shrub 8-12 ft. high. Leaves compound* and with 3 leaflets in young plants, but simple, nearly round, and about ⅔ in. long on older ones. Flowers in simple umbels.* Fruit blotched.

**arboreum.** A tree up to 25 ft. high. Leaves generally compound,* or deeply divided into 5-7 oblong, toothed segments that are nearly 7 in. long, and arranged finger-fashion. Umbels* compound. Fruit black.

**colensoi.** A shrub or small tree 10-15 ft. high. Leaves compound,* the 3-5 oblongish leaflets somewhat broader toward the tip, about 6 in. long and toothed. Umbels* compound.

**simplex.** A tree 20-25 ft. high in maturity with lance-shaped, simple leaves 3-5 in. long. In the young state the leaves may be lobed or deeply parted or even compound, feather-fashion. Umbels compound.

*NOVAE-ANGLIAE* (no-vee-ang'li-ee). From New England.

**NOVA SCOTIA.** The climate of Nova Scotia is favorable for the growth of all the principal garden crops. In general the last spring frost is not later than the 24th of May and there is rarely fall-frost injury until the latter part of September. The seeding of tender vegetables such as corn and beans is usual around the 20th of May, at which time the soil has warmed up sufficiently for good germination. It is possible to mature early-maturing field beans and corn. The planting of tomatoes, eggplants, and peppers started under glass is general the last week in May and early in June, and in the more favored sections, with favorable soil, early kinds will mature practically a full crop. The province lies within zones* 2 and 3.

The summers usually are fairly dry, and in some years the precipitation may not be sufficient for continued vigorous growth on light, sandy soils. The autumns are generally ideal, although in some years the precipitation is greater than required, and unusual rains in September and October may hamper crop harvesting. Because of the maritime situation the air is high in humidity, and for this reason the rainfall required is not so great as that required at more inland locations. The average mean summer temperature is around 63°, and rarely does the highest day temperature exceed 83°. The winter is not low in temperature and a drop to below zero is of short duration and happens only a few times during the winter.

The soil is a sandy loam for the most part, and such soils are available for gardening on almost any farm. The market for garden produce is limited because of the small population. Market gardeners are located adjacent to all the large centers of population, and can fully supply the market during the growing period for the staple vegetable crops. Vegetables such as root crops, cabbage, pumpkins, squash, and potatoes are stored on the farms in various sections and shipped to markets in the winter when prices are better.

There has been considerable trade in the rutabaga from Nova Scotia to New England markets in the past. Certified potatoes for seed purposes are grown quite extensively for the West Indies market, but this trade is limited. Cuba some years ago took considerable table-stock potatoes, but this market has largely gone to the Maine or other United States growers.

From the foregoing it will be noted that no country offers better opportunity for the general culture of most vegetable

---

* Special articles on the subjects indicated by an asterisk (*) will be found at the words so marked.

crops, and their culture is general on all farms. Asparagus of excellent quality is produced. Celery of excellent quality is readily grown. Sweet peppers and eggplants have been mentioned previously. Spinach, lettuce, and peas are of the excellent quality possible only under moderate climatic conditions.

A climate suitable for vegetable crops is also suitable for all small fruits, of which strawberry and raspberry are the most important. Apples, plums, pears, and cherries are extensively grown, and in very protected situations peach trees of early sorts mature fruit. Grapes are perfectly hardy, but the summer temperature and length of season make maturity difficult except of early varieties such as Moyer.

NOVA SCOTIA

The zones of hardiness crossing Nova Scotia are those shown on the colored map at ZONE, which should be consulted for details. The dates are the average latest killing frost in spring and the first one in the fall. The figures below the dates show the average length of the growing season.

Needless to say, a climate suitable for fruits and vegetables is also excellent for both annual and perennial flowering plants. The tender annuals are started under glass and transplanted the last of May. Many of the hardy annuals are handled this way also and give earlier bloom. The various perennials, such as iris, peony, columbine, delphinium, and similar plants, grow to perfection. The dahlia does exceptionally well and the canna is readily grown. All bulb plants, including lilies and gladioli, do well. The leading ornamental shrubs grow and bloom to perfection.

With canning plants now being established offering an outlet for surplus crops at paying prices, more attention will be given to special canning crops such as peas, beans, beets, carrots, asparagus, corn, and tomatoes. These canneries will also greatly increase the small-fruit plantings through being able to use all such surplus crops.

**NOVEBORACENSIS, -e** (no-ve-bor-ra-sen′sis). From New York.

**NOVELTIES.** The procession of horticultural novelties is endless. In the last 20 years thousands of new varieties or forms of existing species have been put forward — flowers, fruits, vegetables, and ornamental shrubs and trees. How many exist five or ten years after their launching?

The desire to produce them is laudable, for progress in horticulture can only come from those willing to breed, select, and ultimately disseminate novelties of promise.

Reputable dealers, and all the national societies devoted to special plants (dahlia, rose, sweet pea, iris, gladiolus, etc.) have for years tried to set up standards as to just what a novelty should be. In part they have been successful, but hosts of plants put out as novelties are mere trivial variations of existing plants. Such "novelties" are not worth the time to grow them, and emphatically the gardening public should be put on its guard against them.

Guarding against fraud is perhaps more difficult in the field of hort. than in any other. The number of existing forms of plants is so huge that no one person, nor even a group of specially interested judges, can be absolutely sure that the proposed novelty is really new — let alone know the future value of it.

Perhaps the most significant event in this much-debated field is the comparatively new plan of having novelties of worth registered and patented at the U.S. Patent Office. See PLANT PATENTS. Of the hundreds that apply for such registration less than a hundred and fifty have so far been allowed. That is a pretty fair criterion of the worth of many plants offered for registration as novelties.

For the average gardener or visitor to the larger flower shows where novelties are yearly offered in profusion, the attitude should be a keen appreciation of the effort to launch them, tempered with a reasonable degree of skepticism for the often extravagant claims. At first the novelties are always expensive. And a good rule to follow might be this: If you are impatient and experimental and rich, try all that interest you. But if your gardening budget is limited, wait and watch. Real novelties of worth survive the fanfare of their launching, just as the Shirley poppy and Boston fern have done. And some day they will be as cheap.

**NOVEMBER.** See GARDEN CALENDAR.

**NOVI-BELGI** (no-vi-bel′ji). From New Netherlands; i.e. New York.

**NOZZLE.** See Section 3, TOOLS AND IMPLEMENTS.

**NUCIFERA, -us, -um** (new-sif′fer-ra). Nut-bearing.

**NUDA, -us, -um** (new′da). Naked.

**NUDICAULIS, -e** (new-di-cau′lis). Naked-stemmed.

**NUDIFLORA, -us, -um** (new-di-flō′ra). Naked-flowered.

**NUMMULARIA, -us, -um** (num-mew-lay′ri-a). Coin-like; i.e. round and thin.

**NUMMULARIFOLIA, -us, -um** (num-mew-lay-ri-fō′-lee-a). With coin-shaped leaves.

**NUNO-OCHI.** A waterfall. See JAPANESE GARDEN.

**NUPHAR** = *Nymphozanthus*.

**NURSE-ROOT GRAFTING.** See GRAFTING.

**NURSERY.** An establishment where young plants are propagated and grown until they are ready for permanent planting. Few private owners have room for a nursery, but many would profit from having one. For in no other way can new stocks be obtained so easily and cheaply.

For most of us a nursery is a commercial establishment, and for purposes of the U.S. Census a nursery is defined so as to exclude bulb growers, growers of flowers and fruits under glass, and seed raisers. This pretty closely coincides with the general idea that a nursery is a place for propagating and growing herbs, shrubs, trees, and vines.

Few realize the extent of the industry. The 1930 census (the first to show horticultural products and industry) reported 7208 nurseries in the country and an annual business of over 58 million dollars. As in so many garden activities Calif. leads all other states. A few of the leading states and the number of nurseries in each are:

| California | 832 | Texas | 418 |
| Ohio | 520 | Pennsylvania | 330 |
| Florida | 487 | Illinois | 292 |
| New York | 479 | Washington | 272 |
| Michigan | 462 | New Jersey | 248 |

In the value of the stock sold N.Y. leads all other states,

* Special articles on the subjects indicated by an asterisk (*) will be found at the words so marked.

Calif. is a close second, and the others follow in the order of Ohio, N.J., Pa., Tex., Ill., Mass., Mich., and Iowa.

Such a purely commercial criterion of hort. does not, of course, tell us anything about the development of gardening in any of these states, but it is a reflection of the needs of their population for nursery stock. To the average home grower the catalogues of these firms, many of them full of sound information, are of never-failing interest. *See* CATALOGUES.

**NUT.** Technically, a nut is a hard, bony, one-celled fruit that does not split. A typical example is an acorn, or a hazelnut. Horticulturally, the term *nut* is more inclusive, and includes almond, pecan, hickory-nut, coconut, peanut, and the Brazil-nut, all of which are technically seeds borne in a fruit that is not a nut at all. For nuts in the hort. sense *see* NUTS AND NUT CULTURE.

*NUTANS* (new'tanz). Nodding.

**NUTHATCH.** *See* BIRDS.

*NUTKANA*, *-us*, *-um* (noot-kay'na). From or near Nootka Sound, British Columbia.

**NUTLET.** A small nut (in the technical sense of nut\*).

**NUTMEG.** The Moluccan spice tree producing this (and mace) is not known to be in outdoor cult. in the U.S. For the California nutmeg *see* TORREYA CALIFORNICA.

**NUTMEG GERANIUM** = *Pelargonium odoratissimum*.

**NUTMEG MELON.** *See* MELON.

**NUT PINE** = *Pinus cembroides edulis*. *See* PINE.

**NUTS AND NUT CULTURE.** The food value of nuts is so high and their use is so much on the increase that the production of them has become an important business in the U.S. Nut growing is possibly not a garden operation at all and should thus be excluded from a book devoted to gardening. For, as a serious crop, they are mainly grown on land unsuited to gardening. Nuts are ideal crops for rough hillsides, or to replace second-growth or poor forests, and in such places the cost of the preparation of the land need be no more than for any forestry project. There are, however, nut crops that need as much care as any fruit orchard, and, especially in Calif., the production of them is a highly organized hort. operation.

Some of the major nut-producing plants, their best varieties, and how to grow them, are dealt with in detail in special articles in THE GARDEN DICTIONARY. For an account of them *see*:

| | |
|---|---|
| †Almond | Hickory |
| Butternut (*see* WALNUT) | †Litchi |
| Chestnut | †Peanut |
| †Coconut | †Pecan |
| Filbert (*see* HAZEL) | Pignut (*see* HICKORY) |
| Hazelnut (*see* HAZEL) | †Walnut |

*Note:* Those with a † are best suited to the warmer sections of the country. The rest are hardy, in some of their varieties, over most of the U.S.

While the above list includes the more important plants cult. in this country for their nuts (in the hort. sense), there are many other plants in THE GARDEN DICTIONARY which yield edible products to which the term nut is generally applied. In the list below some of these plants may be of interest to those seeking new or little-known sources of food, or oils, or industrial applications of plant products. A few of them are already important in highly specialized fields. Those suited only to warm or tropical sections of the country are marked with a †. Because some of them may be known only by their technical or common name both are included, the one in black-face type being the entry word which should be sought for additional information about them.

†Areca catechu. Betelnut.
Beech. *Fagus*.
†Betelnut. **Areca catechu.**
†Cashew. **Anacardium occidentale.**
Chinquapin (*Castanea*). **Chestnut.**
Chufa. **Cyperus esculentus.**
Cobnut (*Corylus*). **Hazel.**
†Cohune. **Attalea cohune.**
Earthnut. **Cyperus esculentus.**
Groundnut. **Apios tuberosa.**
Groundnut. **Peanut.**
†Kolanut. **Cola acuminata.**
†Physic-nut. **Jatropha curcas.**
†Pistachio. **Pistacia vera.**
†Tung-oil tree. **Aleurites fordi.**
Water chestnut. **Trapa natans.**

**NUT WEEVILS.** *See* Insect Pests at PECAN.

*NUX-VOMICA* (nucks-vom'i-ka). A specific name meaning the vomiting nut, or one that causes it. *See* STRYCHNOS.

**NYCTAGINACEAE** (nick-ta-ji-nay'see-ee). The four-o'clock family has only three genera of garden interest, but they include the beautiful *Bougainvillaea* of the tropics, the popular four-o'clock (*Mirabilis*) of all old-fashioned gardens, and the genus *Abronia*, often called sand verbena on the Pacific Coast, where they are very popular.

The 25 genera and over 350 species, predominantly tropical American, are mostly shrubs and trees (a few herbs) with simple\* leaves having no marginal teeth. Flowers without petals, but usually (especially in *Bougainvillaea*) very showy, from the profusion of colored bracts\* which may be separate or united. In the four-o'clock the calyx is tubular and petal-like. Fruit small, dry (an achene\*), grooved or winged. The magnificent *Bougainvillaea* is perhaps the most showy vine in cult., but suited only to the warmer regions of Fla. and southern Calif. The family is sometimes called Allioniaceae.

Technical flower characters: Flowers regular,\* usually hermaphrodite.\* Colored bracts present and showy, usually below the petal-like, often tubular calyx. Petals none. Stamens\* 1–many. Ovary superior.\* Style 1.

**NYCTANTHES** (nick-tan'theez). A single species of jasmine-like tree of the olive family, a native of India, and cult. in zones\* 8 and 9, or in greenhouses northward, for its very fragrant, night-blooming flowers. The only species is **N. arbor-tristis**, the night jasmine, called, also, the hursinghar, tree-of-sadness, and sad tree. It is a shrub (or small tree in India) with opposite,\* ovalish, short-stalked, roughish leaves and 4-angled twigs. Flowers in a close head, the latter grouped in branched clusters (cymes\*). Corolla white, its tube orange. Fruit a nearly round capsule,\* about ¾ in. long. It needs a warm-temperate greenhouse and potting mixture\* 4 if grown under glass. In Fla. it thrives on a variety of soils. Propagated by cuttings of half-ripened wood over bottom-heat. (*Nyctanthes* is from the Greek for night flower, in allusion to its nocturnal blooming.)

**NYCTOCEREUS** (nick-to-seer'ee-us). A small group of mostly Mexican or Central American, climbing cacti, with magnificent, fragrant, night-blooming flowers, one of them commonly called night-blooming cereus (they once belonged to the genus *Cereus*). They are at first erect, but ultimately climb 6–8 ft. high. The branch-like stems are many-ribbed and the spines are numerous. Flowers white, the outer segments bract-like and spiny. Fruit red, berry-like, black-seeded. (*Nyctocereus* is from the Greek for night and *Cereus*, in allusion to the nocturnal bloom.)

For culture *see* CACTI. For other cacti known as night-blooming cereus *see* HYLOCEREUS and SELENICEREUS.

**guatemalensis.** Not so well known as the next, but very similar. The chief differences are that the plant is shorter and that its branches (without support) are apt to root at the downward-curving tip. Guatemala.

**serpentinus.** One of the plants commonly cult. as night-blooming cereus. Stems ultimately 6–8 ft. high, the ribs low and the branches somewhat weak. Ribs 10–13. Flowers about 6 in. long. Mex.

**NYMPH.** The immature state of certain insects. They occasionally do some damage. *See* Insect Pests.

**NYMPHAEA** (nim-fee'a). Water Lily, also called nymphea. A genus of herbaceous water plants of about 40 species distributed through tropical and temperate regions of the world, and belonging to the water lily family (Nym-

---

\* Special articles on the subjects indicated by an asterisk (\*) will be found at the words so marked.

The flowers of hardy water lilies usually lie float, while the tender sorts often stand out of the water.

phaeaceae). They have beautiful showy flowers in various shades of white, red, pink, yellow and blue, some species opening only at night but the majority during the day. The under-water perennial stems are usually thick and fleshy, sometimes tuberous, and are embedded in the mud. They grow horizontally or erect, and from them the leaves and flowers are produced. Leaves roundish, green on the upper side, sometimes purplish on under side, floating, or growing 3-4 in. above the water when crowded. Leaf stalk long, thick and flexible, composed of loosely packed tissue, having small air cavities which help the leaves to float. Flowers solitary, on long, cord-like stalks, the calyx of four or more long, green sepals* which completely enclose the petals when flower is closed. When open they lie flat on the water exposing the petals and stamens,* or in some species the flowers stand out of the water. Petals many, arranged in a closely packed spiral, though apparently on the same level, giving the flower a cup-like appearance. Stamens* many, with yellow or purplish anthers.* Ovary many-chambered, many-seeded, splitting when the seeds are ripe. (Named for *Nympha*, a Greek and Roman nature goddess.) Sometimes known as *Castalia*.

For culture and a discussion of the many beautiful hybrids see WATER GARDEN.

**alba.** European white water lily. Strong and hardy. Leaves crowded on the rootstocks, roundish, 4-12 in. across, red when very young. Flowers white, 4-5 in. across, open most of the day. Petals broad and ovalish. Seeds small. Eu. and northern Af. *Var.* **candidissima** has yellow leaves when young and pure white flowers. It is the first to bloom in spring, continuing until early fall.

**caerulea.** Blue Lotus of Egypt, also called Egyptian lotus. Tropical. Leaves ovalish, the under surface green with dark purple splotches, 12-16 in. across. Flowers 3-6 in. across. Sepals marked with black lines and dots. Petals light blue, dull white at the base. Flowers freely but is not showy. Egypt and Central Af.

**capensis.** Cape Blue water lily. Sub-tropical. Leaves ovalish, 12-16 in. across. Flowers rich sky blue, 6-8 in. across. Sepals green outside, whitish inside. Petals blue, white at the base. A very beautiful species.

South Af. The *var.* **zanzibariensis** has somewhat smaller leaves and larger flowers of deep blue, 6-12 in. across. Sepals green outside, deep purplish-blue within, and on the margins. The forms *zanzibarensis azurea* and *rosea* are color forms.

**flavovirens.** Tropical. Leaves shield-shaped, 15-17 in. across, the under side pure green. Flowers white, 6-8 in. across. Sepals pure green. Petals pointed. Mexico. Sometimes known as *N. gracilis*.

**gracilis** = *Nymphaea flavovirens*.

**lotus.** Egyptian white lotus. Tropical. Leaves 12-20 in. across, dark green on upper side, brownish on under side. Flowers 5-10 in. across, white with the outer petals pinkish. Sepals green. Opens at night until nearly noon next day. Egypt.

**marliacea.** A series of hardy hybrids, many of which are yellow.

**mexicana.** Yellow water lily. Sub-tropical. Rootstock erect and tuberous. Leaves oval, 4-8 in. across, green but blotched brown on the upper side, crimson-brown, with black spots on the under side. Flowers 4 in. across, standing above water. Petals canary-yellow, gradually getting smaller toward the center and merging into the stamens. Fla. to Mexico.

**odorata.** White water lily; toad lily and our common white water lily of N.A. Hardy. Leaves 3-10 in. across, roundish, leathery, thick, purplish-red when young, dark green above, purplish-red beneath. Flowers white, fragrant, 3-5 in. across, opening in early morning and until noon. Sepals green, tinged with reddish-brown. Petals broadly lance-shaped. Stamens yellow, numerous, the outermost becoming petal-like and white. Eastern U.S. The hardy *var.* **rosea**, found at Cape Cod, is pink-flowered; the *var.* **gigantea** is tropical, and has pure white flowers, 4-7 in. across; the *var.* **minor** is hardy, and has smaller leaves and flowers, 2¼-3¼ in. across, the sepals definitely purple, and is a shy bloomer; the *var.* **sulphurea** is a hort. form, the leaves 4-6 in. across, like *odorata*, but blotched with brown, the flowers pale yellow, 4-5 in. across, open in the morning.

**ovalifolia.** Tropical. Leaves 10 in. long and 6 in. wide, having brown blotches above, but plain green beneath. Flowers deep blue, closed in dull weather. Tropical Af.

**pygmaea** = *Nymphaea tetragona*.

**tetragona.** Hardy. It is the smallest species in cultivation and has been much used for hybridization. Leaves reddish-brown beneath, 3-4 in. across. Flowers white, 1½-2½ in. across, opening only in the afternoon. Grows readily from seed and is a shy bloomer. Siberia to Japan, and in northern Idaho and Ontario.

**tuberosa.** Hardy. The rootstocks have tubers, 1-3 in. long, that easily become detached. Leaves green, the leafstalks with longitudinal brown stripes. Flowers 4-9 in. across, pure white, the sepals green, opening in the morning. N.A. The *var.* **maxima** is a small form found in N.J.; the *var.* **richardsoni** has more petals and is ball-like when fully open.

* Special articles on the subjects indicated by an asterisk (*) will be found at the words so marked.

**NYMPHAEACEAE** (nim-fee-ā'see-ee). The water lily family, all aquatic plants, comprises about 8 genera and perhaps 60 species, widely distributed, especially in the tropics. Besides the common water lily (see NYMPHAEA) it includes the showy plants known as lotus (see NELUMBIUM) and the magnificent *Victoria*, the largest water lily in the world, which grows in S.A. Less important cult. genera are *Brasenia* and *Nymphozanthus*. All of these except *Brasenia* have broad, sometimes immense, leaves and extremely showy flowers. The remaining cult. genus *Cabomba*, an aquarium plant, has finely dissected submerged leaves and minute flowers. It and *Brasenia* are sometimes considered as constituting a separate family, the Cabombaceae (then called the fanwort or water shield family), but not here kept separate.

Most of the water lily family have thick rootstocks which creep in the mud and from which arise long-stalked leaves and flowers, some floating, others erect above the water surface. In many of them the floral parts are very numerous and the transition from green sepals to colored petals, and to often sterile, petal-like stamens is very gradual. Fruit various: of separate carpels in *Cabomba* and *Brasenia*; berry-like in *Nymphaea*, *Victoria*, and *Nymphozanthus*; but in *Nelumbium* there is a fleshy, pitted receptacle that stands far above the water, its pits containing the large seeds. For the culture of all these see WATER GARDEN.

**NYMPHEA** = *Nymphaea*.

**NYMPHOIDES** (nim-foy'deez, but see OÏDES). Widely distributed, floating aquatic plants of the family Gentianaceae, three of the 20 known species grown in pools or tubs for their attractive yellow or white flowers. Leaves alternate,* floating, more or less ovalish or roundish, or deeply heart-shaped at the base. Flowers borne in the leaf-axils,* sometimes stalked. Calyx* 5-parted. Corolla somewhat wheel-shaped, its deeply 5-parted lobes often fringed. Stamens* 5. Fruit a capsule.* (*Nymphoides* means nymphaea-like; *i.e.* like a water lily.)

The cult. is the same as for water lily. See WATER GARDEN. All bloom in midsummer.

**indicum.** Water snowflake. Leaves nearly round, 2–6 in. in diameter, with a deep split at the base, the margin otherwise entire.* Flowers about ¾ in. wide, in short-stalked umbels,* white, but yellowish toward the center. Tropical regions. Not hardy northward, and suited to greenhouse or warm-region pools. There is a form with dark yellow or golden flowers.

**lacunosum.** Floating heart. Leaves about 2 in. wide, ovalish or roundish, purple beneath. Flowers white, about ½ in. wide, in small clusters (umbels*) in which are occasional small tubers. N.A. and perfectly hardy over the winter.

**peltatum.** Leaves nearly round, about 4 in. wide, the stalk attached to the middle of the blade. Flowers yellow, about 1 in. wide, very numerous and showy. Eurasia, sparingly naturalized in the eastern U.S. and perfectly hardy up to zone* 4. A very handsome aquatic, but spreading rapidly and often hard to hold in check.

**NYMPHOZANTHUS** (nim-fo-zan'thus). Often known as *Nuphar*. Coarse aquatic plants of the family Nymphaeaceae, comprising several species of which the best known is the common spatterdock (often called yellow pond lily or cow lily) and known to science as **N. advenus**. Leaves large, thick, nearly 12 in. long, more or less ovalish, some submerged, others floating and some on erect stalks above the surface. Flowers yellow, never fully opened, more or less globe-shaped, about 2½ in. thick, standing above the surface, and much less attractive than in the closely related water lilies. Its culture is easy in any pool, and it often chokes them with its coarse, profuse foliage. N.A. (*Nymphozanthus* is from the Greek meaning a yellow-flowered nymphaea; *i.e.* water lily.)

**NYSSA** (nis'sa). A small genus of North American and Asiatic trees of the dogwood family, two (both American) cult. for ornament, especially for their fine autumnal foliage. They are generally known as tupelo or sour gum, and *N. sylvatica* has perhaps the most distinctive branching of any native tree. Leaves alternate,* practically or wholly without marginal teeth. Flowers small, greenish, not showy, borne in small, head-like clusters, unisexual* or polygamous.* Fruit an oblong, 1-seeded drupe,* black-purple in both those below. (*Nyssa* is from the Greek and is variously assigned to the word for post, *i.e.* a trunk, or to the name of a nymph, in allusion to the moist or swampy site of the native species.)

Both species are hard to transplant and still more difficult to dig from the wild. Nursery-grown trees, properly root-pruned and delivered with a ball and burlap, are the safest. Or they may be raised from seed, but it must be fresh and stratified at once. Both will do best in low, moist sites.

**aquatica.** Tupelo gum; also called bay poplar, cotton gum, and sour gum. A swamp tree 70–100 ft. high, not much cult. Leaves slightly toothed, oblongish, 5–7 in. long, green above, paler beneath. Fruit usually solitary, about 1 in. long. Southern Ill. and Va. to Fla. and Tex. Hardy from zone* 5, possibly from zone* 4 southward.

**sylvatica.** Sour gum; called, also, pepperidge, black gum, and tupelo. A tree 60–90 ft. high, its branches horizontal but drooping very gradually and gracefully at the ends. Leaves 3–5 in. long, somewhat broader toward the pointed tip, mostly without any marginal teeth. Fruit usually in clusters of 1–3, about ⅔ in. long. Eastern N.A., but more common along the coast southward than northward. Hardy from zone* 3 southward. In the autumn its foliage turns first a dull, brick red, later a brilliant scarlet. One of the finest native trees for moist sites.

**NYSSACEAE.** See CORNACEAE.

# O

**OAK.** The finest hardwood timber trees in the temperate world, and also furnishing many species of great beauty for planting on lawns, parks, street, or for the home woodlot. All oaks, as here restricted, belong to the genus *Quercus* (kwer'kus) of the family Fagaceae. The genus comprises perhaps 200 species, nearly all from the north temperate zone, a few outliers in mountainous regions in the tropics. By far the larger number are evergreen, especially the Asiatic species, and the group as a whole just misses being evergreen in N.A., where many species have leaves, usually withered, that persist over most of the winter. In the list below, however, only those whose leaves stay green through the winter are designated as evergreen. All others are deciduous.*

Leaves alternate,* stalked, variously lobed, toothed or divided in most species, but unlobed and without teeth in a few. In those that are lobed or toothed, about a third have the lobes or teeth bristle-pointed (the black oak group) but the rest have no bristles on the lobes or teeth (the white oak group); but this character does not hold in the evergreen species. Flowers unisexual,* but on the same tree, the male in drooping catkins,* the female in short spikes, or solitary, both without petals. Most of them flower very early in the spring. Fruit a true nut (the acorn) set in a cup-like involucre,* which may surround the nut only at the base, or partly or completely cover it; the cup sometimes fringed. In some species the acorns are edible and others furnish large quantities of food for hogs. (*Quercus* is the classical Latin name for the oak.)

For other trees sometimes called oak, or where oak is part of the name see CASUARINA, GREVILLEA, LITHOCARPUS, and RHUS. For a weedy herb known as Jerusalem oak see CHENOPODIUM BOTRYS.

For the culture and uses of the true oaks see below. Over 60 species are known to be in cult. of which the following are most likely to be met.

**Q. acuta.** Japanese evergreen oak. A small evergreen tree. Leaves not lobed, and without teeth, sometimes wavy-margined. Acorn-cup hairy. Jap. Possibly hardy from zone* 5 southward.

**Q. agrifolia.** California live oak; called, also, Coast live oak and encina. Evergreen tree 60–90 ft. high, often shrubby in cult. Leaves

---

* Special articles on the subjects indicated by an asterisk (*) will be found at the words so marked.

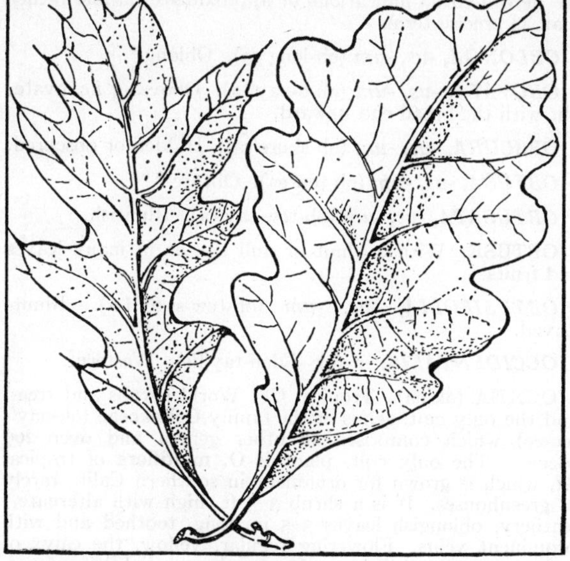

Leaves of the black oak group (*left*) and the white oak group (*right*)

with wavy-bristle-pointed teeth, generally elliptic, 2–3 in. long. Cup of the acorn hairy. Calif. Hardy only from zone* 6 southward.

**Q. alba.** White oak. A magnificent round-headed tree (in the open) 60–100 ft. high. Leaves broadest toward the tip, bluntly 5–9-lobed, the lobes not bristle-tipped. Cup of the acorn only ¼ its length. Eastern U.S. Hardy from zone* 2 southward. Probably the largest of all the native oaks, old specimens being over 20 ft. in circumference.

**Q. bicolor.** Swamp white oak. Not over 70 ft. high, usually less. Leaves somewhat broader toward the tip, 4–6 in. long, coarsely toothed or lobed nearly to the middle, the lobes not bristle-tipped, whitish beneath. Cup of the acorn about ⅓ the length of the nut. Eastern N.A. Hardy from zone* 2 southward.

**Q. borealis.** *See* QUERCUS RUBRA.

**Q. cerris.** Turkey oak. A tree up to 100 ft. high, less as cult. here. Leaves oblongish, 3–5 in. long, with 4–9 pairs of sharp-pointed lobes, which are without teeth. Cup of the acorn roughish, covering about ½ of the nut. Eurasia. Hardy from zone* 4 southward.

**Q. chrysolepis.** Cañon live oak; also called maul oak. An evergreen tree 50–80 ft. high. Leaves elliptic, 2–4 in. long, the margins rolled or toothed, but not lobed, white-felty beneath. Cup of the acorn felty, only about ¼ the depth of the nut. Ore. to Lower Calif. Hardy from zone* 6 southward.

**Q. coccinea.** Scarlet oak. An upright, more or less cylindric tree 50–80 ft. high. Leaves oblongish, 4–6 in. long, shining green, sharply and deeply 7–9-lobed, the lobes bristle-tipped. Cup about ⅓ the length of the nut. Eastern U.S. Hardy from zone* 2 southward. Turns brilliant scarlet in the fall.

**Q. densiflora** = *Lithocarpus densiflora.*

**Q. dumosa.** California scrub oak. An evergreen shrub not over 8 ft. high. Leaves scarcely 1 in. long, without lobes, but often spiny-toothed, green above, paler beneath. Cup about ½ the length of the acorn. Calif. Hardy from zone* 6 southward.

**Q. engelmanni.** Evergreen white oak; also called mesa oak. An evergreen tree 40–60 ft. high. Leaves oblongish, 1–2 in. long, not lobed, but sometimes toothed. Cup of the acorn about ½ its length. Southern Calif. Probably not hardy in the East.

**Q. ilex.** Holm oak. An evergreen tree 40–60 ft. high, with prickly holly-like leaves 2–3 in. long, and yellow-felty beneath. Cup of the acorn about ½ its length. Southern Eu. Hardy from zone* 6 southward.

**Q. ilicifolia.** Scrub oak. Much resembling *Q. prinoides*, but with sharper, bristle-tipped lobes to the leaves. Eastern N.A. Very hardy everywhere and good for dry, sandy soils.

**Q. imbricaria.** Shingle or laurel oak. A tree 40–60 ft. high. Leaves oblongish, 4–6 in. long, without lobes, teeth or bristles. Cup of the acorn a little less than half its length. Pa. to Ga. and Ark. Hardy from zone* 3 southward.

**Q. laurifolia.** Laurel oak. A half-evergreen tree 40–60 ft. high. Leaves oblongish, 4–6 in. long, unlobed or sometimes faintly lobed, without teeth or bristles. Cup only ¼ the length of the acorn. Va. to Fla. and La. Hardy from zone* 6 southward.

**Q. lobata.** Valley or California white oak. A tree up to 100 ft. Leaves about 2½ in. long, with 7–11 blunt lobes, gray-felty beneath, the lobes not bristle-tipped. Cup about ⅓ the length of the acorn. Calif. Hardy from zone* 6 southward.

**Q. macrocarpa.** Bur oak; also called mossy-cup oak. A tree up to 100 ft. Leaves 7–10 in. long, deeply lobed, the terminal lobe larger than the others, none of them bristle-tipped. Cup about ½ the length of the acorn and conspicuously fringed. Eastern N.A. and west to Tex. Hardy from zone* 2 southward.

**Q. montana.** Chestnut oak; also called rock chestnut oak. A tree up to 100 ft. high. Leaves chestnut-like but not bristle-tipped, yellowish-green above, 5–7 in. long. Cup about ⅓ the length of the acorn. Me. to S. Car. and Ala. Hardy from zone* 2 southward. Long mistaken for *Q. prinus*, a more southern form of it.

**Q. nigra.** Water oak. Not over 80 ft. high. Leaves bluish-green, about 3 in. long, without lobes or 3-lobed at the tip. Cup about ⅓ the length of the acorn. Del. to Fla. and Tex. Hardy from zone* 4 southward.

**Q. palustris.** Pin oak. Not over 80–90 ft., usually less in cult., the branches conspicuously horizontal. Leaves more or less elliptic, 4–5 in. long, sharply and deeply 5–9-lobed, shining green, the lobes bristle-tipped. Cup scarcely ⅓ the length of the acorn. Mass. and Del. to Ark. Hardy from zone* 3 southward and a valuable street or lawn tree. *See* below.

**Q. phellos.** Willow oak. Not over 60 ft. high. Leaves narrowly oblong, 4–5 in. long, without teeth, lobes or bristles. Cup about ¼ the length of the acorn. Staten Island, N.Y., to Fla. and Tex. Hardy from zone* 4 southward.

**Q. prinoides.** Scrub oak. A shrubby oak, usually not over 6 ft. high, often less. Leaves oblong, 3–5 in. long, bluntly toothed but not bristle-tipped. Acorns small, the cup about ½ the length of the nut. Me. to Ala. and Tex. Hardy from zone* 2 southward.

**Q. prinus.** *See* QUERCUS MONTANA.

**Q. robur.** English or British oak. A round-headed tree, not over 80 ft. high. Leaves 3–5 in. long, broadest toward the tip, with 6–14 rounded lobes, without bristles. Cup about ⅓ the length of the acorn. Eurasia and northern Af. Hardy from zone* 3 southward. Many hort. forms are known, mostly in Eu.; one, the *var.* **fastigiata,** has a columnar habit. Others have variegated or even dark purple foliage.

**Q. rubra.** Red oak. Botanists consider that there are two forms of this native oak. The more northerly one is called *Q. borealis*, has leaves pale green on the under side, and grows from Nova Scotia to Pa. and westward. For the more southerly form, native from N.J. to Fla. and westward, they retain the name *Q. rubra*, and this tree is "tawny or grayish pubescent beneath." Most gardeners consider them all as *Q. rubra*, the red oak. It is a tall, relatively quick-growing oak with 3–11 (usually 5–7) sharp-pointed lobes that are bristle-tipped. Acorn-cup from ⅛ (in the southern) to ⅓ (in the northern) the length of the nut. Hardy from zone* 3 southward, for the northern form, which is the better of the two and widely planted for ornament. The southern form is hardy from zone* 4 southward and is not so widely known.

**Q. stellata.** Post oak. A round-headed tree, sometimes 100 ft. high, usually about half this. Leaves lobed lyre-fashion, leathery and roughish, 6–8 in. long, the lobes blunt and rounded, without bristles. Cup of the acorn from ⅓ to ½ the length of the nut. Mass. to Fla., especially common along the edges of the salt marshes and even on the dunes, where it becomes a picturesque, wind-wrenched, bushy tree. Hardy from zone* 3 southward.

**Q. suber.** Cork oak. Its bark, harvested every 10–15 years, is the source of cork (mostly in Spain and Portugal). A tree not over 40 ft. high, its outer bark thick and corky. Leaves evergreen, ovalish, or oblong, without lobes but coarsely toothed, green above, gray-felty beneath. Cup about ⅓–½ the length of the acorn. Southern E. and northern Af. Hardy from zone* 6 southward.

**Q. velutina.** Black or yellow oak; called, also, quercitron. A columnar tree 100–125 ft. high, its inner bark conspicuously yellow-orange. Leaves 7–9 in. long, ovalish or oblong, 7–9-lobed, the lobes sharp-pointed and bristle-tipped. Cup of the acorn ½ or more the length of the nut. Me. to Fla. and west to Tex. Hardy from zone* 3 southward.

**Q. virginiana.** Live oak. An evergreen tree, usually round-headed and not over 70 ft. high, often draped with the Spanish moss in the southern part of its range. Leaves elliptic or oblong, 3–5 in. long, without lobes, very rarely toothed, and with no bristles, green above, white-felty beneath. Acorn-cup felty, about ¼ the length of the nut. Va. to Fla. and Mex. Hardy from zone* 6 southward.

## OAK CULTURE

The oak is one of the largest hardwooded groups of deciduous trees hardy in the temperate sections of the U.S. Although somewhat slow-growing when compared to many other trees, it develops at a sufficient rate to permit good size in plantings of moderate age and its longevity is surpassed by no other ornamental tree. Both deciduous and evergreen types are in cultivation but only the former are hardy throughout the colder parts of the country.

The value of the oak in ornamental work lies in its massive, shapely habit and beautiful, lustrous, green foliage. In some of the forms, such as *Quercus macrocarpa* and *montana*, the foliage coloring is further enhanced by a silvery sheen on the under side of the leaves. Although all of the oaks are beautiful in autumn, *Quercus coccinea* and *palustris* are especially planted for their autumn effect. Their leaves turn a beautiful scarlet during October and, in the species *coccinea*, remain on the tree until spring. *Quercus prinoides* and *ilicifolia* are shrubby and form effective plantings when used in quantity in light soil. *Quercus ilex* and *suber* are both evergreen and are commonly cultivated in Europe. In this country, they are hardy only in the South. Among the native evergreen species are: *Quercus virginiana*, from the Southeast; and *chrysolepis* and *agrifolia*,

* Special articles on the subjects indicated by an asterisk (*) will be found at the words so marked.

from California. *Quercus palustris* is often grown as a street tree because of its pyramidal habit and rapid growth.

The oaks like a rich soil. Some of the species, among them *Quercus rubra, stellata, coccinea,* and *imbricaria*, prefer a light, sandy loam. *Quercus bicolor, nigra, alba,* and *phellos* will do best in a heavy, damp clay.

Some care is necessary in transplanting certain species of the oak. *Quercus alba,* the white oak, is not easily moved except while young and where large specimens are desired, the red, black, or pin oaks will transplant more easily. Oaks are excurrent trees; that is, they have a single main trunk extending their entire length. For this reason, pruning operations during transplanting should be restricted, if possible, to heading back the lateral branches and preserving the main stem. This will prevent the formation of several main branches and a stubby head which generally result when the original single leader is damaged or removed.

Propagation is usually by seed which is planted in the fall immediately after it is gathered. If planting at this time is impossible, the seed should be stratified in damp sand or moss until spring. Sprouting may occur while in storage but no harm will be done if the seed is not permitted to dry out after planting. The number of hybrid oaks is innumerable and many varieties are known. Few, however, are commonly grown. Propagation of the hybrids and varieties is by grafting in the greenhouse during Jan. Cleft and tongue grafts are used with *Quercus rubra* or *velutina* for stock in the black oak group and *Q. robur* for the white oak group. In Europe, some of the evergreen forms are increased by layering and cuttings, but such methods are seldom employed in this country.—A. D. S.

INSECT PESTS. In New England leaf-feeding caterpillars of the gypsy and brown-tail moths are serious pests. The former is controlled by destroying the oval, yellow egg masses in the winter; the latter, by destroying the winter webs on the tips of the branches. Both may be killed by arsenicals in summer. A number of leaf feeders occur, but they are seldom important. Scale insects can be controlled with dormant miscible-oil spray, as can spider mites. Gall-forming insects are noticeable but seldom important. Borers include the leopard moth (*see* MAPLE) and the two-lined borer (*see* CHESTNUT).

DISEASES. Anthracnose is a leaf disease of oaks, particularly destructive on the white oak varieties. It also attacks the leaves and twigs of sycamore, causing similar symptoms. Irregular, dead patches occur in the green leaves and cankers and blight on the twigs. Bordeaux mixture, applied beginning with the opening of the buds and repeated at intervals of ten to fourteen days, is usually effective in checking this disease, although its complete control depends upon the eradication of fallen affected leaves and removal of diseased twigs from the tree. *Strumella* canker is caused by a fungus infection of the bark of oak trees. It is usually found on the trunk, where the long, regular outline of the infection is quite typical and easily recognized. Another canker of more irregular shape, the *Nectria* canker, is also frequently found on oak. In valuable shade trees these cankers may be eradicated by surgical methods. With age, oaks become affected with various wood rots. Remedial measures are rarely justified and protection of young trees from wounds is a better safeguard against these rots.

**OAKESIA.** *See* UVULARIA SESSILIFOLIA.

**OAK FAMILY** = Fagaceae.

**OAK FERN** = *Dryopteris linnaeana*.

**OAT.** *See* AVENA.

**OAT GRASS.** *See* ARRHENATHERUM.

**OBASSIA** (o-bas'si-a). Native Japanese name for *Styrax obassia*.

**OBCONICA,** *-us, -um* (ob-kon'i-ka). Inverted cone-shaped.

**OBEDIENT PLANT** = *Physostegia virginiana*.

**OBLATA,** *-us, -um* (ob-lay'ta). Oblate; *i.e.* flattened at the ends.

**OBLIQUA,** *-us, -um* (ob-ly'kwa). Oblique or lop-sided.

**OBLONG.** A common descriptive term in botanical literature and throughout this book. Technically an oblong is a rectangle with parallel edges, two of which are longer than the other two. In plants, especially in leaves, to which the term is mostly applied, a perfect oblong is so rare as to be almost unknown. Hence, *oblong* and *oblongish* are here used as indications of approximate outline rather than as precise terms.

**OBLONGA,** *-us, -um* (ob-long'ga). Oblong.*

**OBOVATA,** *-us, -um* (ob-o-vay'ta). Obovate; *i.e.* ovate, but with the broad end upward.

**OBSCURA,** *-us, -um* (ob-skure'ra). Hidden or obscured.

**OBTUSA,** *-us, -um* (ob-tew'sa). Obtuse.*

**OBTUSATA,** *-us, -um* (ob-tew-say'ta). Bluntish.

**OBTUSE.** With a blunt or dull tip, as in many leaves and fruits.

**OBTUSIFOLIA,** *-us, -um* (ob-tew-si-fō'lĭ-a). Blunt-leaved.

**OCCIDENTALIS,** *-e* (ok-si-den-tay'lis). Western.

**OCHNA** (ok'na). Tropical Old World shrubs and trees, and the only cult. genus of the family **Ochnaceae** (ok-nay'-see-ee) which comprises 16 other genera and over 200 species. The only cult. plant is **O. multiflora** of tropical Af. which is grown for ornament in southern Calif., rarely in greenhouses. It is a shrub 3–5 ft. high with alternate,* leathery, oblongish leaves 3–5 in. long, toothed and with prominent veins. Flowering regular, yellow, the calyx of 5 separate, petal-like sepals; petals 5, slightly twisted. Fruit fleshy (a drupe*). Propagated by cuttings of partly ripened wood, in late summer. (*Ochna* is from the Greek for a pear tree, in allusion to the pear-like leaves.)

**OCHNACEA,** *-us, -um* (ok-nay'see-a). Resembling the genus *Ochna*.

**OCHNACEAE.** *See* OCHNA.

**OCIMUM** (os'si-mum). Aromatic annual or perennial herbs, rarely shrubs, of the mint family, comprising over 60 widely distributed species, of which one is cult. for its fragrant foliage. Leaves opposite.* Flowers small, irregular,* crowded in whorls* which are grouped in branching clusters (often racemes*). Corolla very small, usually not exceeding the toothed calyx,* the lobes or teeth recurved in fruit. (*Ocimum* is from the Greek for an aromatic plant, possibly for the basil.)

The basil (*O. basilicum*) is the only one of much hort. importance. For its varieties and culture *see* HERB GARDENING.

**basilicum.** Basil; also called sweet basil. A much-branched annual (or often grown as such) 1–2 ft. high. Leaves purplish, oval, 1–2 in. long. Flowers white- or purplish-tinged, about ¼ in. long. Tropical Old World and the Pacific Islands. *See* HERB GARDENING.

**minimum.** Bush basil. This may be only a lower, more woody form of *O. basilicum*. Not much known in cult.

**OCOTILLO** = *Fouquieria splendens*.

**OCTANDRA,** *-us, -um* (ok-tan'dra). Having eight stamens.

**OCTOBER.** *See* GARDEN CALENDAR.

**OCTOPETALA,** *-us, -um* (ok-to-pet'a-la). Having eight petals.

**OCULIROSEA,** *-us, -um* (o-kew-ly-rō'zee-a). Crimson-eyed.

**OCYMOIDES** (o-sy-moy'deez, but *see* OÏDES). Resembling a plant of the genus *Ocimum* (which see).

**ODESSANA,** *-us, -um* (o-des-say'na). From Odessa, in the Ukraine.

**ODONTIODA** (o-don-tĭ-ō'da). A little-known group of bigeneric* orchids. They include crosses between the genus *Odontoglossum*, which is fairly well known in cult., and *Cochlioda*, a genus scarcely known except to orchid fanciers, who are the only people interested in *Odontioda*.

* Special articles on the subjects indicated by an asterisk (*) will be found at the words so marked.

**ODONTOGLOSSUM** (o-don-to-gloss'um). A large genus of tree-perching (epiphytic*), tropical American orchids, 3 of its 100 species cult. in the greenhouse for their odd, showy flowers. They have short, rather broad pseudobulbs* which bear 1-3 leaves. From the base of the pseudobulb* arises a slender, long-stalked flower cluster (panicle* or raceme*). Petals and sepals generally similar, the petals sometimes a little broader. Lip* lobed, the middle one with a fleshy crest near the base, the two side lobes smaller and erect. (*Odontoglossum* is from the Greek for tooth and tongue, in allusion to the teeth-like crest on the central lobe of the lip.)

Besides the species given below there are many others, and numerous hybrids, but they are known mostly only to orchid fanciers. The odontoglossums need a relatively cool greenhouse because they grow far up on tropical mountains. For general culture *see* Greenhouse Orchids (epiphytes) at ORCHIDS.

**citrosmum** = *Odontoglossum pendulum*.
**crispum.** Leaves 12-16 in. long, 2-3 from each pseudobulb. Flowers nearly 3 in. wide, the cluster with 8-20 blooms, white, but brown-spotted, the lip wavy-margined, the throat yellow. Colombian Andes.
**grande.** Leaves about 12 in. long and 3 in. wide, usually 2 to each pseudobulb. Flowers nearly 5 in. wide, yellow but brown-spotted, the lip wavy. The flowers are mostly in clusters of 3-6. Guatemala.
**pendulum.** Leaves about 12 in. long and 3 in. wide. Flowers about 3 in. wide, white or rose-pink, the lip rose-colored. The cluster is a many-flowered raceme* nearly 16 in. long. Mex. Sometimes known as *O. citrosmum*.

**ODONTONEMA** (o-don-to-nee'ma). Tropical American herbs or shrubs of the family Acanthaceae, **O. strictum**, the only one of its 20 species likely to be much found in cult. It is an erect shrub 4-6 ft. high with opposite,* oblongish leaves 4-6 in. long and without marginal teeth. Flowers crimson, about 1 in. long, borne in a terminal, small-bracted* spike-like cluster. Corolla nearly regular, 5-lobed. Stamens* 4, two of them sterile. Fruit a capsule.* It can be grown outdoors only in zones* 8 and 9, where it is rather widely planted for ornament, sometimes under the incorrect name of *Justicia coccinea* which is also an incorrect name for *Pachystachys coccinea*. Its greenhouse cult. is the same as for *Jacobinia* (which see). (*Odontonema* is from the Greek for thread and tooth, in allusion to the toothed filaments* of the stamens.*)

**ODONTONIA** (o-don-tō'nĭ-a). A group of bigeneric* orchids, resulting from the crossing of *Odontoglossum* and *Miltonia*. They are little known except to orchid fanciers.

**ODONTOSORIA** (o-don-to-sa'rĭ-a). Chiefly Old World tropical ferns of the family Polypodiaceae, resembling *Davallia* and separated from it only by technical characters. Of the 20 known species, **O. chinensis** is sometimes grown in the greenhouse. It is a graceful, small fern, its fronds about 18 in. long and half as wide, and thrice-compound,* the ultimate segments wedge-shaped, toothed, scarcely ⅛ in. long, the foliage thus very delicate and feathery. For culture *see* FERNS AND FERN GARDENING. (*Odontosoria* is from the Greek for teeth, in allusion to the toothed frond-segments.)

**ODOR.** For plants fragrant in the garden *see* FRAGRANCE. For those cult. chiefly as a source of perfume *see* PERFUME PLANTS.

*ODORA, -us, -um* (o-do'ra). Fragrant.

*ODORATA, -us, -um* (o-do-ray'ta). Fragrant.

*ODORATISSIMA, -us, -um* (o-do-ra-tiss'i-ma). Most fragrant.

*ODORIFERA, -us, -um* (o-do-rif'fer-ra). Having or bearing fragrance.

**ODOSTEMON** = *Mahonia*.

**OEDEMA.** *See* Diseases at PELARGONIUM.

**OENOTHERA.** *See* EVENING PRIMROSE.

*OFFICINALIS, -e* (off-fi-si-nay'lis). Producing, or thought to produce, a medicine.

*OFFICINARUM* (off-fi-si-nay'rum). Of the apothecaries.

**OFFSCAPE.** A little-used term among landscape architects for the region in the offing; distant from the immediate landscape.

**OFFSET.** A short lateral shoot, arising at or near the base of a plant, usually rooting at the tip and thus producing a new plant. It is common in the house-

Offsets (on the short stems) of the houseleek

leek, some crinums, and in many agaves, and provides one of the easiest methods of propagation. *See also* RUNNER, STOLON.

**OHIO.** The state lies wholly in zones* 3 and 4.

SOILS. The soils in the western half of Ohio developed from limestone materials and have a reaction much more favorable for the growth of horticultural crops than the soils of eastern Ohio which developed from sandstone and shales and are as a rule distinctly acid.

As a result of the favorable reaction these western Ohio soils developed an organic matter content of approximately ten per cent. These black soils conserve moisture, retain their desirable physical state more easily, and supply more fertilizing materials upon decay than do the light-colored soils in the eastern half of the state which contain an average of only two per cent organic matter.

The fifty thousand acres of muck scattered throughout the northern part of the state are used largely for vegetable production. *See* MUCKLAND GARDENING.

CHIEF VEGETABLE-GROWING CENTERS. The largest acreages of vegetables are grown in the vicinities of the four largest cities, *i.e.* Cleveland, Cincinnati, Toledo and Columbus. Onions, potatoes, carrots, beets, turnips, celery and parsnips are grown extensively on the muck in Hardin, Stark, Summit, Mohoning, Wayne, and Lorain counties. Early tomatoes, cabbage, cucumbers, and sweet corn are grown for trucking in Washington and Lawrence counties. Tomatoes and sweet corn for canning are grown in the central and western portions of the state. Cabbage for kraut is grown in the north central counties of Huron, Lorain and Erie.

Approximately 115,000 acres of potatoes and 100,000 acres of other vegetables are grown in the state each year.

WOODY ORNAMENTAL TREES AND SHRUBS. Ohio is well adapted to the production of nursery stock. Approximately 1600 nurserymen are licensed in the state but about half of these are growers of bulbs, berry plants or fruit trees only. Some 15,000 acres of land are devoted to nursery production in the state, the largest centers being in Lake, Hamilton, Cuyahoga, Miami, Montgomery and Clark counties.

The nurserymen devoted to the production of woody ornamentals grow a wide range of plant materials. The northeastern section is especially fortunate in that the climate is comparatively cool and moist. Some of the evergreens, such as the firs and hemlocks, are not entirely satisfactory in the southern part of the state, but here many of the more tender broad-leaved evergreens can be grown and used to good advantage. With few exceptions, the deciduous ornamental plants can be produced advantageously in Ohio.

FLOWERS. The majority of annual and perennial flowers

---

* Special articles on the subjects indicated by an asterisk (*) will be found at the words so marked.

# OHIO

offered for sale by the many seedsmen and nurserymen are hardy and satisfactory throughout Ohio. Those normally considered half-hardy or tender may usually be grown along the Ohio River without any difficulty. The production of perennial plants commercially is largely confined to the nursery producing section but are especially grown in the Lake County territory.

The commercial florist industry is one of the largest in the country due to the large industrial centers scattered throughout the state. Over 12,000,000 square feet of glass being devoted exclusively to flower crops with sales of over 5½ million dollars yearly. Large amounts of glass are found around Cleveland, Cincinnati, Akron, Youngstown and other large cities. Many small wholesale ranges are scattered through the rural areas of the northern half of the state. Many of these specialize on certain crops such as geranium, hydrangeas and cyclamen.

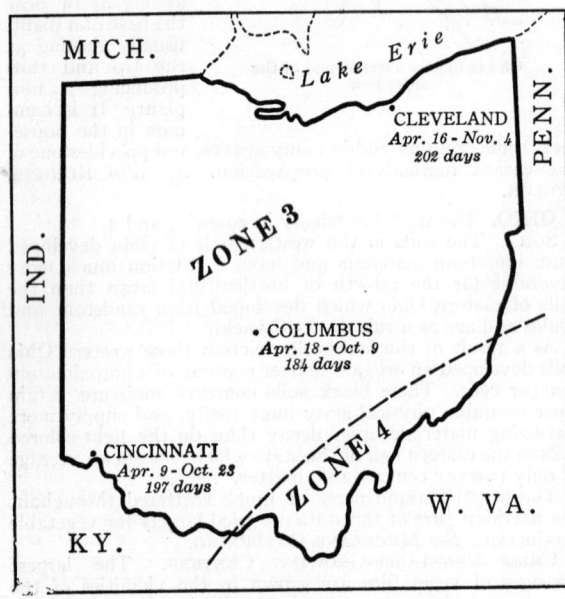

OHIO

The zones of hardiness crossing Ohio are those shown on the colored map at ZONE, which should be consulted for details. The dates are the average latest killing frost in spring and the first one in the fall. The figures below the dates show the average length of the growing season.

The amateur gardener's interest in flowers, although of relatively recent development, extends into practically every county, urban and rural area alike.

FRUIT. The fruit district of major importance in Ohio is on favorable sites in the counties bordering Lake Erie, including Ottawa, Erie, Sandusky, Lorain, Huron, Cuyahoga, Lake, Geauga, and Ashtabula counties. This region also embraces the commercial grape-growing district of Ohio and in addition, a considerable quantity of grapes are produced on the Islands of Lake Erie, where the climate is favorable for the ripening of Catawba and Delaware varieties. The sour cherry industry centers around Clyde in Sandusky County. Apples, peaches, plums, pears and small fruits are widely grown on favorable sites throughout this district. A considerable planting of apples is found in the Columbiana-Mahoning district of eastern Ohio. On favorable sites in southeastern Ohio — in Lawrence, Jackson, Gallia and Washington counties, a considerable acreage of apples is found and in this region Rome Beauty is the predominating variety. A large number of apple orchards are found on favorable sites throughout the state, particularly in localities where local marketing can be developed. Scattered counties with important fruit interests are — Clermont, Ross, Fairfield and Licking. Strawberries are grown rather widely over the state for local marketing. Black raspberries are produced in considerable quantity around Lucasville in Scioto County; around Clyde in Sandusky County and throughout the northern and eastern Ohio fruit belt. There is a scattered planting of peaches on favorable sites throughout the fruit counties of Ohio, with a trend toward location of orchards on sites that permit local marketing.

CLIMATE. The average length of the crop-growing season is 190 days near Lake Erie and in the southwestern part of the state. The average length of the growing season is 160 days for the north central portion of the state, 150 days for the northeastern tier of counties and from 160 to 190 days for the south central counties. The average dates for frosts in Cleveland, Cincinnati and Columbus are shown in the following table:

| Town | Average date of last killing frost in spring | Latest known killing frost | Average date in earliest killing frost in fall | Earliest known killing frost |
|---|---|---|---|---|
| Cleveland | April 16 | May 21 | Nov. 4 | Oct. 2 |
| Columbus | April 18 | May 17 | Oct. 19 | Sept. 21 |
| Cincinnati | April 9 | April 26 | Oct. 23 | Sept. 30 |

RAINFALL. The average rainfall is about 34 inches in northern, 35 inches in central, and 39 inches in southern Ohio. The percentage of possible sunshine is 49 at Cleveland, 54 at Columbus and 57 at Cincinnati. The prevailing winds are from the southwest although in the Cleveland area the winds come from the southeast almost as frequently.

The average rainfall is about 4.4 inches for May, 5.3 inches for June, 5.9 inches for July, 4.9 inches for August, 3.5 inches for September, and 2.1 inches for October.

The address of the Agricultural Experiment Station which has kindly supplied this information about the state is Wooster, Ohio. The station is always ready to answer gardening questions.

Garden Club activities in Ohio, due to the high development of ornamental hort. are extensive. The Garden Club of America, whose home office is at 598 Madison Avenue, New York, has clubs in Cincinnati, Cleveland, Dayton, and other places. There are also over 72 clubs of the Garden Club of Ohio and over 150 of the Ohio Association of Garden Clubs. For the one nearest your locality write the Garden Editor, Houghton Mifflin Company, Boston, Mass. See also HORTICULTURAL SOCIETIES.

**OHIO BUCKEYE** = *Aesculus glabra*. See HORSE-CHESTNUT.

**OHIO STATE UNIVERSITY.** See BOTANIC GARDEN.

**OÏDES.** A very common Greek suffix in the botanical and hort. names of plants meaning *like* or *resembling*. It is commonly, but not properly, pronounced oy′deez (exactly as in toy′deez). The Trojans correctly called it o-eye′deez, a three-syllable effort which is apparently beyond the patience of most gardeners. *Oïdes* occurs in such words as *ulmoides* (elm-like), *betuloides* (birch-like), *cerastioides* (chickweed-like), and many others.

**OIL OF BEN.** See MORINGA OLEIFERA.

**OIL SPRAYS.** See Contact Sprays at INSECTICIDES.

**OKLAHOMA.** The state lies wholly in zones* 4, 5, and 6.

SOILS. About eighty per cent of the surface soils in Oklahoma are fine sandy loams with friable* sandy clay or compact clay subsoils. Enough clay occurs in some soils to produce an unfavorable physical condition. The depth of the surface soil is a very important factor in determining plant adaptation. Most of the soils in the eastern half of the state are deficient in phosphorus. About thirty per cent of the soils in this area are very acid. The majority of Oklahoma soils are deficient in organic matter.

---

* Special articles on the subjects indicated by an asterisk (*) will be found at the words so marked.

OKLAHOMA 547 OKLAHOMA

Fertilizers such as 4–8–6, or 4–12–4 (see FERTILIZERS), which are used on garden soils, may also be applied to areas where flowers or shrubs are grown. The rate of application should be about one to two pounds for every one hundred square feet of soil. Cottonseed meal applied in early spring at the rate of two to four pounds for each one hundred square feet of area and thoroughly worked into the surface of the soil is one of the best fertilizers for most purposes.

FRUITS AND NUTS. Fruits and nuts produced in Oklahoma are, in order of importance, as follows: pecans, apples, strawberries, peaches, blackberries and dewberries, grapes, pears, cherries, plums, walnuts. Pecans are found growing wild along the streams in practically all sections of the area, being much more abundant in the southern half than in the northern half of the state. Considerable quantities of nuts are annually harvested each year, the most important producing counties being Lincoln, Carter, Jefferson, Garvin and Love.

Apples, as well as other fruits, are produced in many different sections of the state. As a rule, the producing areas are rather scattered, the greatest concentration for apples being found in the following counties: Cherokee, Adair, Delaware, Pottawatomie, Mayes, Ottawa, Oklahoma, Sequoyah, and Craig.

In the western part of the state there are some very interesting orchards which are located in the sandy type of sub-irrigated soil usually found along the rivers and streams in Major, Dewey and Woodward counties. Some of the

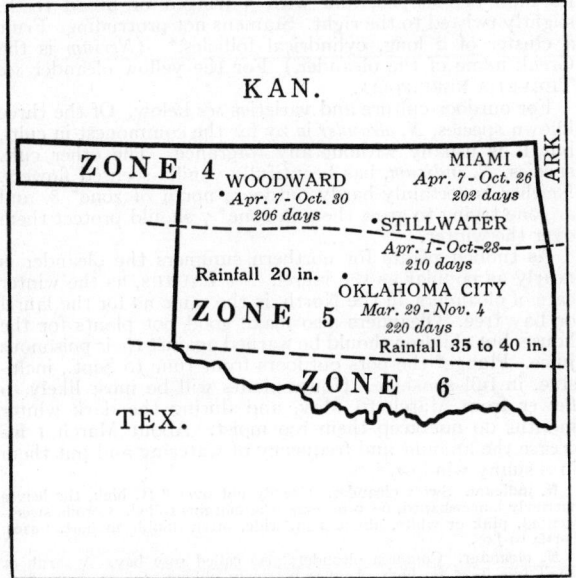

OKLAHOMA

The zones of hardiness crossing Oklahoma are those shown on the colored map at ZONE, which should be consulted for details. The dates are the average latest killing frost in spring and the first one in the fall. The figures below the dates show the average length of the growing season. Rainfall figures (in inches) are for total annual rainfall in the regions so indicated.

best apples produced in the state are grown in that area, usually in rather isolated orchards. The most profitable phase of apple orcharding in Oklahoma is probably the production of early-ripening varieties.

Strawberries are produced for market in most of the eastern counties of Oklahoma, particularly those located in the northern tier of eastern counties. The following counties have a large acreage of strawberries: Adair, Sequoyah, Delaware, Cherokee, Ottawa, Craig, Muskogee, LeFlore and Tulsa.

Peaches have in the past been planted in practically all sections of Oklahoma. However, due to late spring frosts the orchards are being discontinued in many of the older sections of the state, and production is increasing in the southeastern section of the state where crops are not so frequently lost. At the present time some of the most important counties are Logan, Tulsa, LeFlore, Grady, McCurtain, Beckham and Cherokee.

Blackberries and dewberries are produced in all parts of Oklahoma. They are widely grown, being produced for commercial purposes in rather an intensive way in the following counties: Pottawatomie, Major, Caddo, Oklahoma, Grady, Stephens, Hughes, and Cleveland.

Many different varieties of grapes succeed in Oklahoma, some varieties being used in one section of the state, others in another. The most important grape counties are Adair, Grady, Cherokee, Oklahoma, Tulsa, Delaware, Pottawatomie, Craig.

Other fruits are produced more or less uniformly over the state in scattered tracts of small areas.

VEGETABLES. The vegetable crops are produced in large quantities in Oklahoma, many sections of the state being especially well suited to the production of some of the leading types. In order of importance the following vegetables are produced in Oklahoma. Early potatoes, sweet potatoes, watermelons, tomatoes, cantaloupes, onions, beans, sweet corn, cabbage.

The most important potato counties are Muskogee, LeFlore, Wagoner, McCurtain, Sequoyah, Okfuskee, Choctaw, Haskell, Pittsburg, McIntosh, Johnston, Hughes, Oklahoma, Pontotoc, Tulsa, Pottawatomie, Caddo.

The most important sweet potato counties are Tulsa, Grady, Okfuskee, McCurtain, LeFlore, Stephens, Muskogee, Canadian.

The most important watermelon counties are Gray, Grant, Tulsa, Pottawatomie, Oklahoma, LeFlore, Adair, Canadian, Kay, Caddo, Seminole.

The most important tomato counties are Adair, Oklahoma, Tulsa, Grant, McCurtain.

The most important cantaloupe counties are Carter, Tulsa, Oklahoma, Muskogee, Creek.

The most important onion counties are McIntosh, Tulsa, Oklahoma, Pottawatomie. The most important bean counties are Adair, Sequoyah, Tulsa, Oklahoma, Cleveland. The most important sweet corn counties are Tulsa, Okmulgee, Oklahoma, Muskogee, Greer. The most important cabbage counties are LeFlore, Oklahoma, Tulsa, Logan, Kay Creek.

ORNAMENTALS. While greenhouses are found in most parts of Oklahoma the industry has centered around Ardmore, Muskogee, Oklahoma City, and Tulsa, producing the usual greenhouse crops as roses, carnations, chrysanthemums, minor cut-flower crops, and to some extent general pot plants and early vegetable and bedding plants for spring.

Nurseries of ornamentals are found predominately in these sections of the state. Conditions are much more suitable and favorable in the eastern and southern parts of the state for the production of nursery stock.

CLIMATE. The accompanying tables indicate the range of Oklahoma weather conditions. In a general way the eastern part of the state receives approximately 35 to 40 inches of rainfall, while the central portion of the state receives about 30 inches of rainfall. The western portion of the state receives approximately 20 inches of rainfall. The detailed figures, which show an ample annual supply, except at Kenton, are:

| Town | Yearly rainfall in inches |
| --- | --- |
| Oklahoma City | 31.1 |
| Woodward | 24.7 |
| Kenton | 17.6 |
| Okay | 39.3 |
| Stillwater | 33.6 |
| Miami | 43.5 |

* Special articles on the subjects indicated by an asterisk (*) will be found at the words so marked.

# OKRA 548 OLEANDER

### Frost Data

| Town | Average date of last killing frost in spring | Date of latest known frost in spring | Average date of killing frost in fall | Date of earliest known frost in fall |
|---|---|---|---|---|
| Oklahoma City | March 29 | April 30 | Nov. 4 | Oct. 7 |
| Woodward | April 7 | May 8 | Oct. 30 | Sept. 26 |
| Kenton | April 23 | May 15 | Oct. 19 | Sept. 27 |
| Okay | | | | |
| Stillwater | April 1 | May 1 | Oct. 28 | Oct. 8 |
| Miami | April 7 | April 22 | Oct. 26 | Oct. 10 |

Garden Club activities in the state include nearly 90 clubs affiliated with the Oklahoma Association of Garden Clubs. For the club nearest your locality write the Garden Editor, Houghton Mifflin Company, Boston, Mass.

**OKRA** (*Hibiscus esculentus*). A tall, annual, Old World herb cultivated for the peculiar, mucilaginous taste of its immature pods, commonly called gumbo.

It is primarily a tropical crop, but can be grown here where cucumbers or tomatoes are hardy. To produce the best crop, however, it wants much summer heat and therefore does better south of zone* 6 than north of it.

The plant is a tall, rank grower, and the rows should not be less than 4-5 ft. apart. The seeds should not be sown until the ground is definitely warm. Sow the seeds 1 in. deep and space them every few inches, but thin out the seedlings so that the plants will be at least 2 ft. apart as they mature. Some dwarf, but not so prolific, varieties can be planted closer than this.

Okra is successful on a variety of soils in the South, where it is chiefly grown, and it requires no other attention than cultivation to keep down weeds. Like any other crop it grows better on good land than on poor soil, but too heavily fertilized soils may produce more herbage than pods.

The best varieties are: Perkins, Mammoth, Dwarf Green Prolific, White Velvet, and Lady Finger. It is important to pick the pods while young and tender, and to allow ripening only in those pods to be saved for seed. Old pods are unfit for food. It takes about an ounce of seed for 75 ft. of row.

INSECT PESTS. A green caterpillar, crawling with looping motion, sometimes eats the leaves in the South; lead arsenate will control it. Some general feeders attack the plant.

DISEASES. Two types of soil fungi may cause the plants to wilt and die. Another fungus is found commonly as a pod spot. Mosaic also has been reported. Crop rotations, healthy seed, and destruction of disease-plant refuse are worth-while recommendations.

**OLD-FASHIONED FLOWERS.** The flowers common in cultivation two hundred years ago are sometimes called old-fashioned flowers, but with little real reason. Many of our best-known garden flowers have been cult. for over two thousand years, among them the rose, chrysanthemum, peony, hollyhock, narcissus, lily, marigold, foxglove, and many flowering shrubs and trees.

But old-fashioned flowers do seem to mean, in America at least, those that were cult. in the pre-Revolutionary gardens of our ancestors. Among them were the hollyhock, pansy, marigold, foxglove, lily-of-the-valley, some lilies, tulip, narcissus, iris, Virginia stock, and candytuft. Much remains to be done on the definite date of introduction of many common flowers into America. Even less is known as to when some of the Mexican plants like dahlia and cosmos first came northward, but they were certainly here about the time of the Revolution or before.

**OLD MAN** = *Artemisia abrotanum*.

**OLD-MAN-AND-WOMAN** = *Sempervivum tectorum*. See HOUSELEEK.

**OLD-MAN CACTUS** = *Cephalocereus senilis*.

**OLD-MAN'S-BEARD** = *Chionanthus virginica*. See also CLEMATIS VITALBA and C. VIRGINIANA.

**OLD WOMAN** = *Artemisia stelleriana*.

**OLD WOOD.** Ripened wood suitable for making hardwood cuttings.

**OLEA.** See OLIVE.

**OLEACEAE** (o-lee-ā'see-ee). The olive, ash or lilac family comprises one of the more important groups of garden shrubs and trees, for it includes *Fraxinus* (see ASH), *Forsythia*, *Ligustrum* (see PRIVET), *Jasminum*, and *Syringa* (see LILAC), all of outstanding importance in the garden. There are only 20 genera and perhaps 500 species in the family, which is widely distributed over the earth. The most important genus is *Olea* (see OLIVE), and the other hort. genera, besides those above, most of them ornamental, are *Chionanthus*, *Fontanesia*, *Forestiera*, *Nyctanthes*, *Osmanthus*, and *Phillyrea*. The family is sometimes called Jasminaceae.

Leaves prevailingly opposite,* mostly without marginal teeth, evergreen in several genera (olive, *Osmanthus*, *Phillyrea* and several privets). Flowers extremely handsome and showy in the lilac, *Jasminum*, *Forsythia*, *Chionanthus* and some other genera, but small and inconspicuous in the olive and ash which has (usually) no petals. Fruit a true drupe* in the olive, dry and winged (a samara*) in the ash, and a fleshy or dryish berry in several other genera.

Technical flower characters: Flowers regular,* prevailingly hermaphrodite,* usually borne in profuse clusters. Calyx 4-lobed or none. Corolla tubular and 4-lobed, or of four separate petals or none. Stamens* usually 2. Ovary superior,* mostly 2-celled.

**OLEANDER.** Widely cult. ornamental, evergreen shrubs or small trees comprising the genus **Nerium** (neer'ĭ-um) of the family Apocynaceae, all of them with a dangerously poisonous juice. Leaves opposite* or more usually in whorls* of 3, rather thick and leathery, without teeth. Flowers in showy terminal clusters (cymes*). Corolla funnel-shaped, its limb bell-shaped, and with 5 fringed or broad teeth, slightly twisted to the right. Stamens not protruding. Fruit a cluster of 2 long, cylindrical follicles.* (*Nerium* is the Greek name of the oleander.) For the yellow oleander see THEVETIA NEREIFOLIA.

For outdoor culture and varieties *see* below. Of the three known species, *N. oleander* is by far the commonest in cult., but it is usually without any fragrance. The other cult. species, *N. indicum*, has beautifully vanilla-scented flowers. Neither is certainly hardy outdoors north of zone* 8, and anyone trying to grow them in zone* 7 should protect them over the winter.

As tubbed plants for northern summers the oleander is nearly as popular as the laurel. See LAURUS, as the winter care of oleanders, in the North, is the same as for the laurel or bay tree. Oleanders also make good pot plants for the house, but children should be warned against their poisonous juice. Plunge* the pots outdoors from June to Sept., inclusive, in full sunshine. House plants will be most likely to flower from March to May, and during the dark winter months do not keep them too moist. About March 1 increase the amount and frequency of watering and put them in a sunny window.

**N. indicum.** Sweet oleander. Usually not over 8 ft. high, the leaves narrowly lance-shaped, 6-10 in. long, the margins rolled. Corolla sweet-scented, pink or white, about 2 in. wide, often double in hort. forms. Persia to Jap.

**N. oleander.** Common oleander; also called rose bay. A shrub or small tree 8-25 ft. high. Leaves narrowly oblong, 4-8 in. long, dark green above, paler, and with a prominent midrib beneath. Flowers white, red, pink, or purple, about 2¼ in. wide, often double in hort. forms. Southern Eu. and northern Af., but cult. throughout the tropical and sub-tropical world and often naturalized there. For its many varieties see below.

### Outdoor Oleander Culture

Besides the favorite rose-colored double oleander — the most used for southern boulevard planting, for it is the most persistent bloomer of all — and the pure white single, which is, perhaps, the hardiest, there are newer varieties. One is a deep cream; another, a variegated-leaved, pink-flowered, sometimes having part-cream blossoms; still another a velvety deep crimson, very beautiful with cultivation, but not quite as resistant to neglect as the others; and perhaps the most appealing of all, a starry single, a lovely shade of delicate peach-blossom pink. This variety often makes a tall, slender tree about 25 ft. in height.

Nothing makes better informal flowering hedges, sidewalk or boulevard plantings than the oleanders, and certainly no

---

* Special articles on the subjects indicated by an asterisk (*) will be found at the words so marked.

truly southern garden should be without these gracefully decorative shrubs. They are very well adapted to town planting, making a good appearance during hot, dry, windy, dusty weather when other shrubs wilt and droop.

The oleander is readily grown from layers or from cuttings made from soft or hard wood. In olden times the French women of New Orleans stuck oleander cuttings in fruit jars of water until tiny rootlets were formed; then the cuttings were set out in the garden. Modern nurserymen, using material cut in pruning mature plants, set their cuttings out in sandy soil; these cuttings are started from Dec. to March.

Sunny situations suit oleanders best. They prefer sandy soil, and, though they live and bloom through absolute neglect, when old manure or commercial fertilizer is added to the soil, with cultivation and thorough watering now and then, they respond with an unbelievable abundance of flowers. Watering is discontinued after the flowering period so that the plants may rest.

Oleanders grow rapidly and may be pruned into any height and shape desired — a small, graceful shrub, a symmetrical giant 20 ft. tall and as many ft. across, or a formal, round-topped tree.

Coming into bloom in March in the tropical South, through May and the latter part of June in the more temperate territory, and flowering off and on during the summer and fall, usually until late in Oct., these shrubs for pictorial value are unsurpassed. Through hot weather and drought they appear fresh and varnished-looking, holding aloft their graceful sprays of showy blossoms. They are much subject to scale insects and need frequent spraying with contact sprays to keep them clean. See Contact Sprays at INSECTICIDES. — R. F. W.

**OLEARIA** (o-lee-ā'rĭ-a). Tree aster or daisy tree. Mostly Australasian shrubs and trees of the family Compositae, with aster-like flowers. Of the 100 or more known species over 20 are in occasional cult. in Calif., of which the three below are by far the best known. Leaves mostly alternate, nearly always white-felty beneath. Flower heads aster-like, the ray flowers in a single row, white or violet (in ours). The heads are usually grouped in clusters (corymbs* or panicles*), but sometimes solitary. (*Olearia* is variously explained as named for Adam Olearius, a German traveler, for J. G. Olearius, a German botanical author, and as derived from *Olea*, because of the olive-like foliage of some species.)

The outdoor cult. of olearias is mostly confined to Calif., and of the three below *O. haasti* is the most hardy. Propagated by cuttings of half-ripened wood or by seeds.

**haasti.** A bushy shrub 6–8 ft. high. Leaves oblongish, about 1 in. long, without marginal teeth. Flower heads white, about ½ in. wide, in long-stalked clusters (corymbs*). N. Zeal. The hardiest species, but not safe above zone* 7 or possibly 6.
**forsteri** = *Olearia paniculata*.
**paniculata.** A shrub or small tree 15–20 ft. high. Leaves oblongish or ovalish, 2–3 in. long, the margins wavy. Flower heads white, about ⅓ in. wide, in a branched cluster (corymb*). N. Zeal. Suited only to zones* 7 and 8. Sometimes known as *O. forsteri*.
**stellulata.** A shrub, not over 5 ft. high. Leaves oblongish or narrower, 2–3 in. long, wavy-toothed. Flower heads violet, showy, mostly in branched clusters (panicles*). Australia. Suited only to zones* 7 and 8.

**OLEASTER** = *Elaeagnus angustifolia*.

**OLEASTER FAMILY** = Elaeagnaceae.

**OLEIFERA, -us, -um** (o-le-if'fer-ra). Oil-bearing or oily.

**OLERACEA, -us, -um** (o-ler-ā'sĭ-a). Of the vegetable garden; used in cooking.

**OLERICULTURE.** See VEGETABLE GARDENING.

**OLITORIA, -us, -um** (o-li-to'rĭ-a). Pertaining to the vegetable garden or to vegetable gardeners.

**OLIVE.** Evergreen shrubs and trees of the Old World comprising the genus **Olea** (ō'lee-a) of the ash family, one of its 40 known species cult. for centuries for its fruit (the olive). It is a tree 25–70 ft. high (usually less as cult. in Calif.), with opposite* leaves having no marginal teeth. Flowers small, white (*see* below). Fruit a true drupe* (the common olive is the only edible one). (*Olea* is the classical Latin name of the olive.)

**O. europaea.** The common olive. Branches thornless (but a wild thorny variety is known). Leaves elliptic or oblongish, 1–3 in. long, green above, silvery and somewhat scurfy beneath. Flowers fragrant, in clusters (panicles*) shorter than the leaves. For fruit *see* below. Native throughout the Mediterranean region, but only in the hottest parts of it. For hardiness *see* below.

For the false olive *see* ELAEODENDRON. For the Russian olive *see* ELAEAGNUS ANGUSTIFOLIA. For the tea olive *see* OSMANTHUS.

### OLIVE CULTURE

The olive was brought to N.A. from Spain, and to Calif. from Mex. by the Mission fathers. It is a hardy sub-tropical evergreen of high heat requirement, the commercial culture of which in this country is limited to the Pacific Southwest. Remarkably resistant to heat and drought, for satisfactory bearing it requires moderate water supply. Northward distribution is limited by cold; as the tree suffers injury at 15° and fruit at 28°. It succeeds in Gulf Coast states, but high atmospheric humidity prevents setting of the fruit. Because of late blooming and the amount of heat necessary to mature it, the fruit requires a long, hot, growing season. It does not ripen until late fall even in the hottest regions. Commercial culture is restricted, therefore, to interior valleys of Calif. and warmer portions of Ariz. Principal climatic hazards in its culture are early fall frosts, before harvest, and desert winds during blooming and fruit-setting period.

The olive tree is remarkably tenacious of life and one of the longest-lived and most beautiful of all fruit trees. In Calif. some of the original trees are still in existence; in the Mediterranean trees are known many centuries old (*see* Age of Trees at GARDEN TABLES III). Under favorable conditions it attains great size. Most varieties exhibit a tendency toward alternate bearing, and two large crops are rarely produced in succession. Correction of this habit is one of the principal production problems. All varieties appear self-fruitful to a reasonably satisfactory degree, though in occasional seasons advantages of cross-pollination are evident.

The flowers are small and inconspicuous, and extremely numerous; many of them are imperfect, however. Borne only on growth of the previous season. Pollen produced in abundance. Fruit small, rarely exceeding 2 in. in length and 1¼ in. in diameter; and the form ranges from apple-shaped to football-shaped. When fully ripe the color ranges from reddish-purple to black. Ripening season extends from Oct. to Dec. 15. In some varieties, when pickled, the flesh separates readily from the seed, in others not. The principal constituent of the fruit is oil; when extracted and clarified known as olive oil. It occurs in seed and flesh, though the latter gives the best quality. Fresh fruit never edible because of bitter principle contained in the flesh, which gives a most unpleasant taste. This substance is removed in most processing or pickling treatments. Range in oil content varies from 15 to 30 per cent of fresh weight.

The olive propagates readily from cuttings, either hardwood or softwood tip cuttings; the latter are employed mainly in Calif. Also it top-works easily, principal methods being bark-grafting and patch-budding.

The tree has a wide range of soil adaptation, but requires good drainage. It has no special cultural requirements, but the high premium paid for large-sized fruit makes important those practices which promote attainment of this objective. Among these are irrigation, pruning and fruit thinning. Moderately severe pruning increases the size of the fruit, but at expense of both size of crop and tree. Fruit thinning not only increases the fruit size but also materially assists in overcoming the alternate bearing tendency. While expensive this practice is increasing. Evidence indicates that this fruit responds to fertilization only on soils of low fertility and that nitrogen is the element which increases yields.

Increase in yield is usually associated with smaller size of fruit, and the yield is unquestionably restricted by shading. It is necessary, therefore, to provide proper spacing or to regulate the size of trees by pruning.

Fruit for pickling is harvested by hand and must be handled carefully for high quality. It is usually picked to color, and several pickings are required because of unevenness

---

* Special articles on the subjects indicated by an asterisk (*) will be found at the words so marked.

in ripening. It is best picked in baskets or buckets, the latter sometimes containing water to prevent bruising. If processing plant is remote from the orchard, fruit is shipped in barrels containing light brine.

While grown abroad primarily for extraction of the oil, in this country the industry is based entirely on pickling or processing the fruit, oil extraction providing merely an outlet for fruit of small size or inferior grade. The American oil, however, equals the best imported product. At the pickling plant the fruit is hand graded, mechanically sized and placed in wooden or concrete vats where it undergoes one of several pickling processes, following which it is packed in cans or bottles, depending on the nature of the process. Most of the crop is handled by the Calif. ripe olive process, which turns out a uniform dark-colored fruit with a rich, nutty flavor and high food value. Succession of lye treatments and washings removes the bitterness, and aeration provides uniform dark color necessary for standardization of product.

The fruit is then canned in light brine and sterilized at 240° F. for one hour. It is one of the safest of all canned products. Small quantities are pickled green, some by the method just described and some by lactic-acid process employed for the imported product. Some fruit is also processed by curing in heavy brine or ground rock salt, without lye.

Practically all the commercial production is located in Calif., the principal centers being Tulare and Butte counties; the acreage is approximately 35,000 and the production 15,000 to 25,000 tons. A major fruit as grown in the Mediterranean basin, where Spain and Italy are the principal countries, with approximately nine million acres. Olive oil and Spanish processed olives are imported into the U.S. in large quantities.

The major varieties in Calif., and their countries of origin, are as follows: Mission, Manzanillo, Sevillano (Spain), Ascolano (Italy), Barouni (Tunisia), Redding Picholine (France), and Nevadillo (Spain). Sevillano, Ascolano, and Barouni are large-fruited varieties, sometimes called Queen olives. The first three comprise most of the acreage. — R. W. H.

INSECT PESTS. The black scale of orange is an olive pest of some importance (see ORANGE). The olive fly, a serious pest in Europe, has not yet become established in the U.S.

DISEASES. Olive knot or tuberculosis of the olive occurs throughout most of the Mediterranean olive-growing districts, and has been observed in California. The disease causes conspicuous swellings on the trunk, limbs, twigs, and leaves. Only in extreme cases are affected parts of the tree killed. The knots should be removed as soon as they show. If much pruning is required, the task should be delayed until winter. Bordeaux mixture has been suggested as of value when applied during the winter and very early spring. Root rot caused by the honey fungus is sometimes present. In the first stages the affected parts may be pruned away, but after the disease has invaded whole roots or a big share of the base of the stem, the tree should be removed and destroyed. Leafspot and fruit rot occasionally may be present. The spraying suggested above, together with good practices in keeping the trees thrifty, will overcome most of these minor diseases.

**OLIVE FAMILY.** Shrubs and trees, many of them of great garden importance, are found in the olive or ash family. Among them are the olive, privet, lilac, jasmine, ash, and *Forsythia*. For a complete list of the commonly cult. genera and the characters of the family *see* OLEACEAE.

**OLIVERANTHUS** (ol-i-ver-ran'thus). A Mexican perennial herb, the only one of the genus, and belonging to the family Crassulaceae. The only species, **O. elegans,** is an erect herb to 20 in. high. Leaves fleshy, broad at the tip, narrowing to the base, crowded near the tip of the stems. Flowers 1–2 at the ends of branches, bright red, tipped with yellow, 1 in. long. Petals free nearly to the base. Pistils* 5, separate. It is sometimes offered as *Cotyledon elegans*. (Named for G. W. Oliver of the U.S. Dept. of Agriculture.)

It is an attractive summer-flowering plant, not hardy north of Washington, D.C. It does well in sandy soil, in sunny positions, and is suitable for rock gardens or borders. Propagated from seeds and by stem and leaf cuttings.

*OLIVIFORMIS, -e* (ol-iv-i-for'mis). Olive-shaped.

*OLYMPICA, -us, -um* (o-lim'pi-ka). From or near Mount Olympus, Greece.

*OMORIKA* (o-more-ree'ka). Servian vernacular for the spruce *Picea omorika.*

**OMPHALODES** (om-făl-lō'dez). Navelwort. Low, annual or perennial herbs, comprising about 20 species, closely allied to *Cynoglossum* of the forget-me-not family, which they resemble, and natives of Eu. and As. Stems smooth or slightly hairy. Basal leaves long-stalked, lance-shaped or heart-shaped, the stem leaves smaller, fewer, and alternate.* Flowers blue, sometimes pinkish, arranged in loose, one-sided racemes.* Calyx joined halfway down. Corolla united to form a short tube, usually white, but with vein-like markings radiating from the center, giving it a star-like appearance. Stamens* 5, not protruding. Fruit 4-celled, when ripe splitting into 4 separate parts, each containing one or more seeds. (*Omphalodes* is from the Greek for navel-shaped, in allusion to the seeds.)

The annual species should be sown where required to flower, in ordinary garden soil, in moist, half-shady position. Sow the seeds ⅛ in. deep. Seeds sown in spring will flower the same season, and if sown in Sept. will flower in early spring. Hardy. Perennial species require the same treatment, but seeds should be sown in spring. They may also be propagated by division of roots in Sept. or April. All grow best in a cool, partially shaded position, where the soil is neutral or slightly alkaline. *Omphalodes* is not much in cultivation, but is sometimes used as ground cover or in the rock garden.

**cappadocica.** A perennial, 6–10 in. high. Leaves usually heart-shaped, with prominent veins, and soft-silky hairs, the lower leaves stalked. Flowers bright, clear blue, with markings at the throat. One of the best for shady spots in the rock garden. Spring. Asia Minor.

**cornifolia** = *Omphalodes cappadocica.*

**linifolia.** Annual, up to 1 ft., the foliage light green. Lower leaves wedge-shaped, the upper spear-like, with slightly hairy margins. Flowers white, the corolla tube twice as long as the calyx.* The var. **caerulescens** is a color form, having blue flowers. This species can be grown on dry or stony ground. Spring or summer. Spain and Portugal.

**verna.** Creeping forget-me-not. A perennial, growing to 8 in. high, the main stems prostrate, but with erect, flowering stems. Leaves ovalish, the lower ones long-stalked. Leaves on flowering stems short-stalked and spear-like. All are pointed. Flowers borne in pairs, in loose racemes,* the individual flowers about ½ in. across. Often used as a ground cover. Spring. Eu.

**ONAGRACEAE** (o-na-gray'see-ee). The evening primrose family, sometimes called the fuchsia family, includes many herbs with showy flowers, a few tropical genera, and one or two aquatic or mud-loving herbs. There are over 30 genera and about 470 species, most common in the temperate parts of the New World.

From the garden standpoint *Fuchsia* is perhaps the best-known plant. It is prevailingly tropical American and needs greenhouse culture. The other tropical genera are *Jussiaea* (treated as a tender annual) and *Lopezia* (Mexican herbs or shrubs). All the other cult. genera are herbs, often with very fine bloom, and easily grown outdoors over most of the U.S., the exception being *Zauschneria*, which is native in Calif. The herbaceous genera of relatively easy culture are: *Clarkia, Epilobium, Eucharidium, Gaura, Godetia,* and *Oenothera* (see EVENING PRIMROSE). *Ludwigia* and *Trapa*, like *Jussiaea,* are aquatic or mud-loving.

Leaves alternate* or opposite.* Flowers usually showy and regular,* but appearing irregular in *Fuchsia*, sometimes solitary, more often in handsome clusters. Fruit a dry pod (capsule*), often with silky-haired seeds in some genera, fleshy and berry-like in others.

Technical flower characters: Calyx 2–6 (typically 4)-lobed, its tube joined to the inferior* ovary. Petals 4, mostly clawed.* Stamens 4 or 8, inserted on the throat of the calyx tube. Ovary 2–4-celled.

**ONCIDIUM** (on-sid'i-um). Very beautiful, tropical American, tree-perching (epiphytic*) orchids, comprising over 300 species and many hort. varieties of which a great number are grown by orchid specialists, but few are in general cult. They have small pseudobulbs* from which arise 1 or 2 leaves that are usually long, narrow, and without teeth. Flowers not usually large, but the long, slender, branched cluster very handsome. Corolla very irregular,* although the sepals are usually uniform, but sometimes two of them are united or partly so. Petals similar to the remaining sepal. Lip various,

---

* Special articles on the subjects indicated by an asterisk (*) will be found at the words so marked.

often beautifully colored, spreading at nearly right angles to the column, its crest swollen or tubercled. (*Oncidium* is from the Greek for tubercle, in allusion to the swollen crest of the lip.)

For culture see the epiphytic orchids at the article ORCHID (greenhouse species).

**papilio.** Butterfly-orchid. Leaf only 1, usually red-mottled, about 8 in. long and 2 in. wide. Flower nearly 2½ in. wide, solitary on a slender stalk nearly 3 ft. long. Petals and sepals narrow, brown but yellow-spotted. Lip yellow but brown-margined. Venezuela. Blooming most of the year in the greenhouse.

**varicosum.** The commonest species in cult. and often seen in florists' windows. Leaves 2, nearly 9 in. long and very narrow, but tough. Flowers about 1 in. wide, very numerous in a long, slender, branched, usually drooping cluster nearly 5 ft. long. Sepals and petals greenish-yellow, but spotted with red-brown. Lip, the only really showy part of the bloom, golden-yellow, its crest toothed or tubercled, sometimes blotched with red-brown. Brazil. Blooming Oct.-Jan. in the greenhouse. The var. **rogersi** has flowers (mostly the lip) nearly 2 in. wide, yellow, but with showy red bars.

**ONE-FLOWERED WINTERGREEN** = *Moneses uniflora*.

**ONION** (*Allium cepa*). The underground stem (a bulb) of this pungent, strong-smelling plant has been extremely popular for many centuries. Today there are two main types that interest the gardener. They are the young, green or white, bunching sorts eaten fresh and before the mature bulb has formed. The other and much more widely grown sort develops a large, coated bulb with a papery skin. These are used fresh (rarely, for they are pretty strong), or more often boiled or fried. Certain varieties of them can be easily stored for considerable periods.

VARIETIES. *For bunching and eating green:* Egyptian or Tree. These are raised from sets or multiplier-onions (*see below*). *For mature bulbs:* Danvers, in several strains. Ebenezer. Yellow Globe. Yellow Bermuda (a poor keeper). Prizetaker (a good keeper). The Yellow Bermuda is one of the mildest for slicing and eating fresh.

SOILS AND FERTILIZERS. Onions require a rich, well-drained soil, but any good vegetable-garden soil will be satisfactory so long as it is not too stony. The bulbs need a loose, friable* soil in which to expand. To be sure it is rich enough use a pound of well-rotted manure to each square foot of soil and in addition use 4-5 pounds of a fertilizer with a 4-8-10 ratio (*see* FERTILIZERS) to each 100 square ft. (approximately a ton to the acre). Stable manure should always be used if it is the only enrichment the onion soil will have.

The soil must be moist, as the plant will not thrive in dry sites. It is grown successfully in nearly all but the desert states, but it thrives best in the comparatively cool North. Commercial production in Fla. and Calif. is based upon using their comparatively cool winter and early spring months. *See also* MUCKLAND GARDENING.

METHOD OF STARTING. There are three ways of raising onions: by seeds, by sets, and by the multipliers or potato-onions that often develop among the flower clusters.

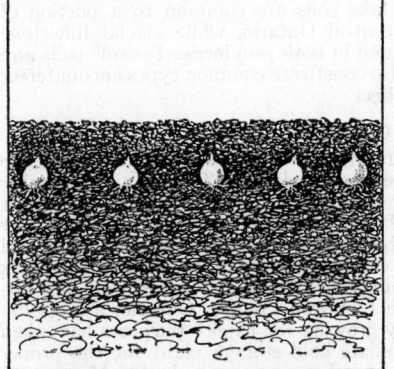

Cross-section of an onion bed, showing the sets planted about 2 in. apart and 2 in. deep.

For most home gardeners raising onions from seed is a tedious failure more often than a success. Seedling plants, raised by the expert dealers, are inexpensive and far easier to handle. These seedlings are one of the most satisfactory methods of starting an onion patch.

Onion sets are also very inexpensive in the amounts needed by the average household. The "set" consists of a small, dried, immature bulblet* which has been harvested from a large bulb grown for the purpose. These immature bulblets will each produce a mature onion during the season. Sets are used almost exclusively for the bunching type of spring onion eaten fresh. They are also used by many for mature onions, because of the ease of planting and from the fact that while seedlings may wilt, the young sets scarcely ever fail.

The third method of starting is peculiar. Many plants of the genus *Allium* (onion and its relatives) occasionally produce bulbils* among the flower cluster. These are not true bulbs like the sets, but an aerial, bulb-like organ from which a new plant will grow. Because of this curious character such plants are often called multiplier- or potato-onions. They may be bought at the dealers and their use is largely confined to the onions to be bunched and eaten fresh.

Whichever method is used, it is of the greatest importance to secure true stock, authentic as to variety and from a most reliable dealer. Cheap stock, especially in sets, will very likely end in relatively costly failure.

PLANTING. We may safely disregard growing onions from seed. It is so troublesome that many large commercial growers prefer to buy seedlings ready to plant, or sets.

If sets are used, they may be planted about 10 days before it is safe to put out seedlings. Sets should be planted, one to a hole, about 2 in. deep. Or you can plant them in a 2-in. drill. In either case, the space between bulblets should be four inches for the onions you expect to grow to maturity, and 1½ in. for the bunching type, which will soon be pulled out. Keep the rows 15 in. apart (more if horse or motor cultivator is to be used).

If seedling plants, instead of sets, are used, they should be planted upon the same intervals as those already given for sets. Plants may be set out whenever reasonably warm weather has arrived. A fair criterion for your neighborhood is when the common lilac has just passed out of bloom.

Some growers, especially those using the easily stored sets, will plant a succession of onions so as to ensure a crop until frosty weather arrives. But it should be remembered that mature onions take from 120 to 160 days to develop, so that successional sowings will very likely have to be harvested before maturity or as bunching onions.

CULTIVATION. The onion is, in spite of its bulb, a shallow-rooted crop, and its bulbs are very easily injured by implements. It is necessary to cultivate enough to keep down weeds and conserve moisture, but the cultivator or hoe should not go more than an inch or two below the surface, and no bulbs must be disturbed. On small patches the scuffle hoe is much the safest tool to use. Keep the soil pulverized at all times.

If it is available, sow between the rows, about a month after the plants have been set out, enough chicken manure to make a thin covering of the center of the space between the rows. Gently and shallowly work it into the soil. Its high nitrogen content makes poultry manure an exceedingly valuable fertilizer for onions. Some growers use two applications of it about five weeks apart. It must not touch the plants.

HARVESTING. There are few crops where you can plan with such exactitude for your needs as with onions grown from sets. Plant only as many as your present or winter needs demand. When the tops turn yellow and begin to wilt it is time to pull up the bulbs. Some, not mature, but perfectly satisfactory for immediate use, can be harvested before this. But for those you expect to store, it is better to allow them to come to full maturity.

The tops should be cut off the pulled onions about an inch above the bulb and the bulbs spread out on the barn floor or upon racks to dry off thoroughly the surface moisture. This will take from 10-14 days. A sane guide as to their proper curing is that the neck or cut-off stem is no longer green and plump but more or less shriveled. When this stage is reached, onions may safely be stored, preferably in airy crates or net sacks, in a cool, well-ventilated, dry room.

For the preferred position and sequence of onions in your garden *see* KITCHEN GARDEN. For the sea onion *see* URGINEA MARITIMA.

---

* Special articles on the subjects indicated by an asterisk (*) will be found at the words so marked.

INSECT PESTS. The onion thrips, only 1/25 in. long and hardly visible, cause whitish spots on leaves and stems, and weaken the plants. A strong spray of nicotine, 1 to 500, with soap, will reduce the numbers, but they will build up quickly again, and spraying onions is difficult and expensive. Sweetened derris spray has recently given better results. Crop remnants should be cleaned up.

Onion maggots feed on roots and in bulbs in the North; corrosive sublimate has been used in control (see CABBAGE). Good results have been obtained by spraying young plants with bordeaux mixture to which has been added 1 part in 30 of stock lubricating-oil emulsion. Several applications are made, a week apart.

DISEASES. The onion bulb furnishes an excellent diet for a dozen or more fungi. Onions that are to be stored therefore should be free of blemishes, thin-necked, mature, dry, and placed in bins where moisture and temperature can be governed. Seed onions sometimes are affected with a mold that can be controlled by weekly dusting with copper-lime. Most old onion soils in northern areas contain smut spores. Running formaldehyde (1 part in 128 parts of water), 200 gallons to the acre, in the furrow with the seed, will protect the plants during their stage of susceptibility.

The *bulb nematode* kills the onion plants, beginning in a small circle. Treating these beginning infection areas with steam is the only means of eradication. *Mildew* in cool, wet weather may destroy the crop. Planting healthy seeds or sets, avoiding wind barriers, destroying diseased plant refuse, and long rotations aid in avoiding the trouble, as well as reducing certain other diseases, as white rot, and pink root. *Yellow dwarf* may be reduced by planting only tested sets.

**ONION HOE.** See Section 1, TOOLS AND IMPLEMENTS.

**ONOBRYCHIS** (o-no-bry'kiss). Perennial, Eurasian herbs or spiny shrubs, comprising about 80 species of the pea family. Leaves compound,* the leaflets entire,* lance-shaped, opposite,* the main leafstalk ending in a leaflet. Flowers pea-like, deep rose to light pink, in racemes* or spikes. Calyx of 5 sepals, sometimes prickly and joined at the base. Stamens* 10, 9 joined by their stalks, 1 free. Fruit a pod which does not split. (*Onobrychis* is from the Greek for food of asses, in allusion to the use for forage.)

Cultivated generally for its fodder value, especially in Europe, but occasionally used in the flower border, and planted in masses. Propagated from seeds sown in spring or summer for flowering the following year. Sow seeds ½ in. deep where intended to bloom in ordinary soil. They will grow in poor or sandy soil.

**crista-galli.** Height 1 ft. Leaflets small. Flowers flesh-colored. Pods hard and dry. Mediterranean region.
**viciaefolia.** Sainfoin or Saintfoin, also called holy clover. It usually grows to a height of 2 ft. Leaflets many, ovalish, 1 in. long, slightly hairy on the under side, light green on the upper. Flowers pale pink or white. Pods curved on the lower edge, with teeth-like margins, sometimes prickly. This is the species used for fodder. Eu. and northern As.

**ONOCLEA** (o-no-klee'a). A single species of hardy, rather coarse ferns of the family Polypodiaceae, common in moist thickets and meadows throughout N.A., Eu., and As., and sometimes grown in such sites in the fern or wild garden. The only species, **O. sensibilis**, is the sensitive fern, so called because its leaflets are supposed to, and sometimes do, fold up slightly when picked. Its foliage fronds are 2-4 ft. high, more or less triangular-oval, leafy, twice-compound,* its ultimate segments oblongish, slightly lobed or unlobed. The spores are borne on special spore-bearing fronds which are about 2½ ft. high, twice-compound, the ultimate segments rolled into berry-like or bead-like bodies. For culture *see* FERNS AND FERN GARDENING. (*Onoclea* is of no application here, being originally applied to a borage by Dioscorides.)

**ONONIS** (o-no'nis). Restharrow. Hardy, herbaceous perennials and deciduous* shrubs, comprising 70 species, belonging to the pea family, chiefly natives of Eu. and northern Af. Leaves compound,* but usually with only 3 clover-like leaflets. Flowers butterfly-shaped, yellow, purple or light pink, rarely white, solitary or 2-3 in short racemes.* Calyx bell-shaped, deeply cut into 5 lobes. Stamens* 10, joined or free. Fruit a swollen pod with few seeds. (*Ononis* is from the Greek for ass and to delight, in allusion to its being asses' fodder in Eu.)

They are easy of cultivation in ordinary garden soil. Propagated by seeds or division. Sow seeds 1/16 in. deep in semi-shady position, outdoors in April or in boxes in cool greenhouse or cold frame in March. As soon as large enough plant out where intended to bloom, in sunny banks or borders or in the rock or wild garden. Flower stems should be cut down in Oct., and the plants mulched with manure during winter.

Lift and divide plants every 4-5 years. Prune shrubby species into shape after flowering.

**arvensis** = *Ononis hircina*.
**cenisia.** Perennial, growing to 10 in. high, the stem slightly woody. Flowers solitary, rose-pink. Southern Eu.
**hircina.** The common restharrow, and a shrubby herb 15-24 in. high. Leaflets oblongish or narrower. Flowers usually in pairs, red and white. Eu. Summer.
**rotundifolia.** Attractive shrubby plant, growing to 18 in. high. Leaflets 3, ovalish, with teeth-like margins. Flowers bright rose, 2 or 3 together, produced on short stalks in the axils* of the leaves. Upper petal shaded deeper rose. Southern Eu.

**ONOPORDON** (o-no-por'don). Coarse-growing, annual or biennial, European, spiny herbs, comprising 12 species of the family Compositae, generally grayish in color. Stems ridged and ragged. Leaves large, as long as 1 ft., alternate,* the veins radiating from the midrib, the margins prickly spined. Leaf blade much decurrent,* thus giving the ragged appearance to the stem. Flower heads borne in a cup-shaped ring of prickly or cobwebby bracts,* solitary or in clusters, generally in globe-shaped heads, purple or white. (*Onopordon* is an old Greek name derived from ass and to consume, in allusion to its being asses' fodder.)

They are not much in cultivation, but suitable for a sunny position where plants can be given a dark background. Propagated by seeds, sown ⅛ in. deep in sunny position in April. When large enough plant out in well-drained, sunny borders, singly or in groups of 3, allowing plenty of space.

**acanthium.** Scotch thistle or cotton thistle. Biennial, and 3-9 ft. high. Lower leaves as much as 1 ft. long, silver-white, and spiny. Flower heads pale purple, cobwebby, generally solitary, to 2 in. across, globe-shaped. Eu.
**bracteatum.** Tall, cottony, much-branched biennial. Lower leaves broadly lance-shaped, with shallow lobes and tipped with stout, yellow spines. Upper leaves much smaller. Flower heads large and globe-shaped, the ring of bracts round the head curving outwards. Mediterranean region.
**tauricum.** White and hairy, growing to 6 ft. high. Leaves narrow and long, the margins wavy and spiny. Flower heads in clusters. Southern Eu.

**ONOSMA** (o-nos'ma). Little-known Eurasian herbs of the family Boraginaceae, comprising over 80 species of which few are cult., and only **O. stellulatum** likely to be seen here. It is a hairy, perennial herb 6-8 in. high, with alternate,* very narrow leaves. Flowers yellow, tubular, nodding, about 1 in. long, borne in 1-sided, forked clusters (cymes*). In this country less known than the *var.* **tauricum** (sometimes offered as *O. tauricum*) which has the leaf margins rolled and larger flowers. The plant needs a light, open, sunny exposure, preferably with somewhat sandy soil. It is sometimes grown in the rock garden. (*Onosma* is from the Greek for ass and scent, in allusion to the fancied resemblance in the odor of some species to that animal.)

**ONTARIO AND QUEBEC.** These provinces lie wholly in zones* 1, 2 and 3.

SOILS. The soils of the above area vary much from windblown sands to mucks and heavy clays, with all the intergradients. Glacial lake soils are common to a portion of southwestern and central Ontario, while glacial limestone soils are quite common in both provinces. Podsol* soils and brown forest soils also constitute common types encountered, particularly in Quebec.

### Gardening Centers

VEGETABLE GARDENING AND SMALL FRUIT CENTERS are located near all large towns and cities. There is a considerable development of vegetable gardens near Montreal, much of it on muck and peat lands; around Ottawa on muck and light loam; in considerable area in the vicinity of Toronto and London. Large developments have taken place in the Essex Peninsula at Leamington, Chatham, Port Rowan and adjacent territory. In Lambton County, Ontario, a large development of celery growing for export purposes has taken place and an up-to-date cold storage plant for the proper handling of the crop has been constructed. *See* MUCKLAND GARDENING.

GREENHOUSE CROPS. The development of greenhouses has largely taken place in the milder regions of the two provinces where fuel costs are reduced. The large development

---

* Special articles on the subjects indicated by an asterisk (*) will be found at the words so marked.

at Brampton, Ontario (near Toronto), mainly devoted to floriculture, is one of the largest in existence, but there are numerous other glasshouse developments, particularly near London, Ontario, and in the Niagara Peninsula; in the environs of Toronto and in the Essex Peninsula, large areas are devoted to the production of out-of-season vegetables like lettuce, tomatoes and cucumbers. All large towns and cities have their quota of such glasshouses, Montreal having a considerable area devoted to vegetable growing.

FRUIT CROPS. Owing to the tremendous variation in climate the fruit regions of these two provinces vary a great deal in the kinds and varieties of fruits to be recommended. In the Niagara Peninsula where the influence of the Great Lakes makes for a mild climate the commercial production of grapes, sweet and sour cherries, peaches and plums is carried on extensively. Peaches, one of the tenderest of fruits, may also be grown in the Essex Peninsula with a considerable degree of success. Other fruits, such as apples,

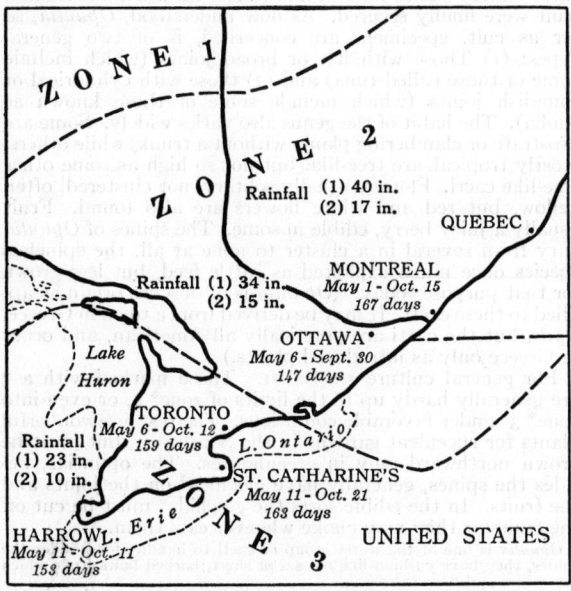

ONTARIO AND QUEBEC

The zones of hardiness crossing Ontario and Quebec are those shown on the colored map at ZONE, which should be consulted for details. The dates are the average latest killing frost in spring and the first one in the fall. The figures below the dates show the average length of the growing season. Rainfall figures (in inches) show (1) the total annual rainfall and (2) the amount falling in the growing season at the places indicated.

pears, strawberries and raspberries, are grown more extensively throughout Ontario. Large apple areas are found in the counties of Norfolk, Lambton, Wentworth, Durham, Northumberland, Grenville and Dundas and in the region around Collingwood on the Georgian Bay.

In Quebec the only tree fruit of commercial production is the apple, which is being grown in increasing amounts in the regions within forty or fifty miles of Montreal, in the counties of Rouville, Bagot; Hyacinth, Missisquoi; Chateauguay and Huntingdon. Small fruits, such as strawberries and raspberries, are very extensively produced in Ontario in the region between Toronto and Hamilton and in the Niagara Peninsula and in the Essex Peninsula. In Quebec, aside from the widespread growth of these throughout the province, there is a unique development on the Island of Orleans, close to the city of Quebec, where extensive developments have taken place.

FLOWERS AND ORNAMENTAL TREES. While there is a very wide range of ornamental trees, shrubs and herbaceous perennials which may be grown throughout the entire area, the following trees are of particular importance: Birch; Sugar Maple; Weir's Cut-leaved Maple; White Birch; Weeping Birch; American Elm; Mountain-ash, and Red Oak, among the deciduous; with White Pine, Swiss Stone Pine, Red Pine, White Spruce, Norway Spruce and American Arborvitae, among the evergreens. Larch is common and very useful, the European form being quite at home. Shrubs of most common use are *Spiraea vanhouttei* and *arguta*; *Syringa villosa* (see LILAC); *Philadelphus*; *Caragana*; *Lonicera tatarica*; Elder; Japanese barberry; Privet; *Weigela*. In herbaceous perennials the Peony and Iris are the most universally grown, but most herbaceous material succeeds, being well protected by snow. Roses grow without protection in the Niagara Peninsula, Essex Peninsula around Toronto and London; in most other regions some winter protection is essential.

CLIMATE. Great variation in climate exists in these two provinces, and below is a table setting forth some data from four centers. These are all located in what might be termed regions with commercial horticulture. Northern Ontario and Quebec would be more severe in temperature, and for comparative purposes could be compared with Manitoba.* Generally speaking, lack of moisture in these regions is not a factor and in this respect northern Ontario and northern Quebec would compare favorably with the above records.

FROST DATA

| Town | Average date of last killing frost in spring | Latest known killing frost | Average date of earliest killing frost in fall | Earliest known killing frost |
|---|---|---|---|---|
| Toronto | May 6 | May 22 | Oct. 12 | Sept. 23 |
| Montreal | May 1 | May 20 | Oct. 15 | Sept. 29 |
| Harrow | May 11 | May 25 | Oct. 11 | Sept. 26 |
| St. Catharine's | May 11 | May 27 | Oct. 21 | Oct. 8 |
| Ottawa | May 6 | May 29 | Sept. 30 | Sept. 3 |

RAINFALL

| Town | Total annual precipitation | Total precipitation during growing season† |
|---|---|---|
| Toronto | 32.33 | 14.37 |
| Montreal | 40.67 | 17.22 |
| Harrow | 23.72 | 10.26 |
| St. Catharine's | 27.94 | 12.47 |
| Ottawa | 34.34 | 15.80 |

† Total precipitation includes snowfall.

The address of the Experimental Station which has kindly supplied this information is Horticultural Division, Experimental Farm, Ottawa, Ontario. The station is always ready to answer questions pertaining to horticulture.

**ONYCHIUM** (ō-nick'ĭ-um). A small genus of widely distributed ferns of the family Polypodiaceae, sometimes called claw-fern, of which the only cult. species is **O. japonicum**, a little fern admirably suited to the conservatory or for centerpieces on the table. Fronds very graceful and fragile, thrice- or even more compound,* the ultimate segments oblongish, about ½ in. long, toothed or divided, the divisions again toothed; the foliage of great delicacy. For culture see FERNS AND FERN GARDENING. (*Onychium* is from the Greek for claw, in allusion to the shape of the lobes of the ultimate frond segments.)

*OPACA, -us, -um* (o-pay'ka). Opaque or pale.

**OPAL.** See ANCHUSA AZUREA.

**OPHIOGLOSSACEAE** (o-fī-o-gloss-ā'see-ee). The adder's-tongue family comprises a small group of ferns of little garden interest except, possibly, in the rock garden or wild garden. Of the 3 genera and 50 species, two are in cult. — *Botrychium* and *Ophioglossum*.

* Special articles on the subjects indicated by an asterisk (*) will be found at the words so marked.

They are delicate ferns having simple* leaves without marginal teeth in *Ophioglossum*, but compound* or dissected ones in *Botrychium*. The spores* are borne on a separate, leaf-like organ, often branched, and not on the back of ordinary fronds as in most forms. *See* both genera for further notes on these little-grown plants.

*OPHIOGLOSSOIDES* (o-fĭ-o-glos-soy'deez, but *see* OÏDES). Resembling the adder's-tongue (*Ophioglossum*).

**OPHIOGLOSSUM** (o-fĭ-o-gloss'um). Adder's-tongue fern. A genus of 30 species of small, widely distributed ferns of the family Ophioglossaceae, only one, **O. vulgatum**, the common adder's-tongue, occasionally planted in the fern or wild garden. It bears two sorts of fronds. The foliage fronds are usually solitary, erect, narrowly ovalish, about 12 in. long, without teeth, lobes, or divisions, the blade a little shorter than the stalk. Fertile fronds, which bear the spores,* are about 2 in. long, the stalk 8–10 in. long. The plant grows mostly in moist meadows or thickets and has little decorative value. (*Ophioglossum* is from the Greek for serpent and tongue, in allusion to the shape of the foliage fronds.)

**OPHIOPOGON** (o-fĭ-o-pō'gon). Lily-turf. Useful ground-covering plants of the lily family, sometimes known by the name *Mondo*. All of the few species are natives of eastern Asia and are hardy up to the edge of zone* 3. They prefer moist, shady banks and make admirable plants for ground cover under trees. Leaves all basal, grass-like, but much thicker, growing in such masses as to suggest turf. Flowers small, nodding, usually borne in small clusters that do not exceed the foliage. Corolla small, not over ¼ in. long, and, unlike nearly all plants of the lily family, with an inferior* ovary. Fruit berry-like. (*Ophiopogon* is from the Greek for snake and beard, in somewhat fanciful allusion to the shape of the flower cluster.)

There is also another plant known as lily-turf. *See* LIRIOPE. From the latter *Ophiopogon* differs only in technical characters, but the two species below are generally more hardy than *Liriope* and more widely used for ground cover under shade. They are evergreen, almost sod-forming plants, easily increased by division.

**jaburan.** Jaburan. Leaves up to 15 in. long, usually less, and arising from a mass of cord-like roots. Flowers white, about ½ in. long. Fruit violet-blue, oblong. Jap. The *var.* **variegatus** has white-striped leaves.

**japonicum.** The best as a sod-forming ground cover, the leaves dark green, 8–10 in. high and arising from underground stolons,* the roots bearing small tubers. Flowers light lilac, about ¼ in. long. Fruit pea-sized, blue. Eastern As.

*OPHIUROIDES* (o-fĭ-your-roy'deez, but *see* OÏDES). Like a plant of the genus *Ophiurus*, which is scarcely of garden interest.

**OPIUM POPPY** = *Papaver somniferum*. *See* POPPY.

**OPLISMENUS** (o-plis'me-nus). Tropical or sub-tropical, mostly weak or sprawling, sometimes climbing grasses, comprising 15 species, of which **O. compositus**, the basket grass, is often cult. for ornament, often under the name *O. hirtellus*. It is a perennial from tropical Africa and America, not hardy northward, and has prostrate, weak stems that root at the joints. Leaves flat, 2–4 in. long, ½–1 in. wide, sheathed at the clasping base, usually velvety beneath. Flower cluster of alternate* and somewhat distant racemes,* the spikelets awned.* The plant is often used for edgings in the South, and for hanging baskets or grown under the greenhouse bench in the North, often in the *var.* **vittatus**, which has white- and pink-striped leaves. (*Oplismenus* is from the Greek for awned,* in allusion to the awned* spikelets.)

**OPPOSITE.** Having the point of attachment, as of leaves, twigs, etc., precisely opposite each other; not alternate. *See* ALTERNATE.

*OPPOSITIFOLIA, -us, -um* (op-pos-i-ti-fō'lĭ-a). Opposite*-leaved.

**OPULASTER** = *Physocarpus*.

*OPULIFOLIA, -us, -um* (op-you-li-fō'lĭ-a). With leaves like the guelder rose.

*OPULOIDES* (op-you-loy'deez, but *see* OÏDES). Like the guelder rose, an old name for which was *Opulus*. *See* VIBURNUM OPULUS STERILE.

**OPULUS** (op'you-lus). An interesting specific name. *Opulus* is the same as *Populus* (the poplars). But Linnaeus,* without apparent reason, used *opulus* as a specific name for a *Viburnum*, which has nothing to do with a poplar. *See* VIBURNUM OPULUS.

**OPUNTIA** (o-pun'tĭ-a; also o-pun'she-a). Prickly pear, some of them also called tuna and cholla. A very large genus of cacti, spread from New England to the Argentine or Tierra del Fuego and comprising over 250 species, of which over 40 are grown in the collections of various cactus specialists, but only those below in even general cult. The group is in much confusion as to its naming, perhaps due to its diverse habit and the fact that many species have been described before the flowers or fruit were known, and many of these turned out to be well-known species when flowers and fruit were finally secured. As now understood, *Opuntia*, so far as cult. specimens are concerned, is of two general types: (1) Those with flat or broad joints (which include some of those called tuna) and (2) those with cylindrical or roundish joints (which include some of those known as cholla). The habit of the genus also varies widely. Some are prostrate or clambering plants without a trunk, while others, mostly tropical, are tree-like, but not so high as some other tree-like cacti. Flowers usually solitary, not clustered, often yellow, but red and white flowers are also found. Fruit usually a juicy berry, edible in some. The spines of *Opuntia* vary from several in a cluster to none at all, the spineless species once much exploited as cattle feed, but less grown for that purpose today. (*Opuntia* is of obscure origin as applied to these cacti. It may be derived from a town in Greece, *Opus*, but the cacti are practically all American, and occur in Greece only as introduced plants.)

For general culture *see* CACTI. Those marked with a † are generally hardy up to the limits of zone* 4, or even into zone* 3, under favorable conditions. The rest are wonderful plants for succulent gardens in the Southwest, but must be grown northward only in greenhouses. The opuntias, besides the spines, generally have glochids* on the joints and the fruits. In the edible sorts the glochids* must be cut off the fruits or they may choke whoever eats them.

*Opuntia* is one of the worst group of cacti to handle, for besides the spines, they have cushion-like masses of short, barbed hairs from which the spines and flowers arise.

**†compressa.** The common and only wild prickly pear of the northeastern U.S. Joints flat, oblong or ovalish, 3–5 in. long, the whole plant prostrate. Spines 1–2 at each cluster, often lacking. Flowers yellow, 2–3 in. wide. New England and Ontario to Ala. and Mo. Long known as *O. vulgaris*.

**engelmanni.** A flat-jointed cactus, sometimes bushy in Mex., but without a definite trunk. Joints oblongish to nearly round, usually 6–8 in. long, but sometimes as much as 1 ft. long. Spines 3–4 at each cluster (10 in old plants), or sometimes none in young joints. Flowers yellow, often 3–4 in. wide. Fruit red, about 2 in. long. Tex. and Ariz. to Mex.

**ficus-indica.** Indian fig. A flat-jointed cactus, bushy or tree-like and sometimes 15 ft. high. Joints oblongish, 15–25 in. long, and usually spineless. Flowers yellow, nearly 4 in. wide. Fruit juicy, red, edible, 2–3½ in. long, pear-shaped. Probably central Mex., but cult. throughout the tropical world, the markets of which nearly always have Indian figs for sale.

**leptocaulis.** Tasajillo. A bushy or tree-like cactus, the trunk 2–3 in. in diameter. Joints cylindric. Spines slender, solitary on young joints, but 2–3 in a cluster on old plants. Flowers about ¾ in. wide, greenish-yellow. Southwestern U.S. and adjacent Mex.

**lindheimeri.** Nopal; also called cacanapa. A tree-like, flat-jointed cactus, 8–12 ft. high and with a trunk, or sometimes merely spreading. Joints ovalish or broader, sometimes nearly circular and 8–10 in. in diameter, bluish-green. Spines 1–6 in each cluster. Flowers yellow or red, about 3 in. wide. Fruit purple, pear-shaped, about 2 in. long. La. to Tex. and Mex.

**megacantha.** Tuna. A tree-like cactus, 10–15 ft. high, and with an obvious trunk. Joints flat, oblongish or wider, 14–24 in. long. Spines white, 1–5 in a cluster. Flowers yellow or orange, nearly 3 in. wide. Fruit pear-shaped, red, about 3 in. long and edible. Mex. and much cult. there for its juicy fruit, which is the chief tuna in the market.

**phaeacantha.** A low, nearly prostrate, flat-jointed cactus. Joints 4–6 in. long, less than half as wide. Spines 1–4 in each cluster. Flowers about 2 in. wide, yellow. Fruit about 1½ in. long, contracted at the base. Tex. and Ariz. to N. Mex. and Mex.

**†polyacantha.** A low, nearly prostrate, flat-jointed cactus, the joints nearly circular and about 3½ in. wide. Spines 5–9 in each cluster. Flowers about 2 in. wide, pale yellow on the inside, but reddish-tinged on the

---

* Special articles on the subjects indicated by an asterisk (*) will be found at the words so marked.

ORACH

outside. N. Dak. to Wash., south to Tex. and Ariz. Probably hardy up to zone* 2.

**tuna.** Tuna. A low, prostrate, flat-jointed prickly pear, the joints oblongish, 3-6 in. long. Spines yellow, 2-6 in a cluster. Flowers about 2 in. wide, yellow but tinged with red. Fruit red, pear-shaped, about 1½ in. long. Jamaica, and the leading tuna in the W.I., where it is cult. for its edible fruits.

**vulgaris** = *Opuntia compressa*.

**ORACH** = *Atriplex hortensis*. It is also sometimes applied to *A. patula*, for which see Orach in the list at WEEDS.

**ORANGE.** For the true orange *see* the next entry. For various other plants to which the name of orange is sometimes applied *see* CHOISYA, CITROPSIS, STRYCHNOS, LAUROCERASUS CAROLINIANA. See also MOCK-ORANGE and MACLURA.

**ORANGE.** The orange is much the most important of all the citrus fruits and its culture provides major fruit-growing industries in both Florida and California. There are two principal species: the sweet or common orange (*Citrus sinensis*), the production of which comprises the industries mentioned, and the sour or Seville orange (*Citrus aurantium*), which is used in this country primarily as a rootstock. The mandarins (including the tangerine), which belong to the species *C. nobilis*, are often incorrectly referred to as oranges. Likewise, the fruit of the species *C. bergamia* is commonly called the bergamot orange, though it is actually a close relative of the lemon.

SWEET ORANGE. The sweet orange, like other citrus fruits, is a tender, sub-tropical evergreen, which is subject to injury by frost. It is much hardier than the lime, however, and considerably more so than the lemon, though less hardy than the grapefruit and sour orange. Temperatures of 25 to 26 degrees cause injury to the fruit and young growth and at 20 degrees severe tree injury occurs. Because of the high average value of the crop and the comparative infrequency of severe frosts orchard heating is profitable and extensively employed; in California approximately one-fourth of the acreage is protected. (For details *see* FROST.) Unlike the lime and lemon, the orange requires a high total amount of heat to ripen the fruit, though the variation in amount of heat necessary for different varieties is notable. This gives rise to early-ripening, mid-season, and late-ripening varieties. In regions of cool summers and mild winters, such as the coastal area of southern California, varieties of high-heat requirement (late-maturing), such as Valencia, ripen in the summer of the year following bloom, a season when they experience no competition with oranges from other states. This explains the apparent ever-bearing characteristic of this variety: at the period of bloom the crop of the previous season is approaching maturity; at other seasons the trees regularly carry the crops of two succeeding blooms. In regions of hot summers, however, varieties of lower heat requirement, such as Hamlin, Parson and Washington Navel, ripen in the fall or winter of the year of bloom and hence carry but one crop of fruit. A proper combination of varieties and climatic zones, therefore, permits a marked extension of the shipping season. In California one early and one late variety, grown in three climatic zones differing in amount of heat, provide an all-year marketing season; this situation seems not to occur elsewhere.

The orange thrives in tropical climates, but the color and quality are poor. Its commercial culture is restricted to semi-tropical and sub-tropical regions; in the latter irrigation is required to supplement the rainfall. Sudden heat waves during the fruit-setting period in early summer are likely to cause excessive shedding of the young fruits, known as "June drop"; the navel* varieties are especially affected. Desiccating winds accentuate loss from this cause. Comparative freedom from wind, or wind protection, is required for satisfactory yields and quality, though the orange is less sensitive to this factor than either the lime or lemon.

The sweet orange has a much wider range of climatic adaptation than the lime and lemon, but its commercial culture in the United States is limited to central and south Florida, the lower Rio Grande Valley of Texas, and areas of mild winters in Arizona and California. The principal climatic hazards are: for the Gulf Coast states frost and cyclonic winds, and for California and Arizona frosts, desiccating winds and early summer heat waves.

The orange, like other citrus fruits, does not require pollination for fruit-setting, and hence there is no pollination problem in its culture. Unpollinated fruits are seedless, which is a desirable commercial character. The fruits vary greatly in seediness, depending on variety and the opportunity for pollination. Three classes are recognized — seedless, commercially seedless, and seedy. The first class, represented by Washington navel, is seedless when planted in solid blocks, because it produces virtually no functional pollen; in mixed blocks, where pollination occurs, it rarely produces seeds because it normally has few or no functional ovules. The commercially seedless varieties — Valencia, Hamlin, Enterprise and others — produce viable pollen in abundance, but have few functional ovules.* The seedy varieties have many functional ovules* and plenty of viable pollen.

The orange fruit exhibits a pronounced tendency to doubling, and this frequently results in the production of a navel, a small, rudimentary secondary fruit embedded in the apical end of the primary fruit. Many varieties exhibit this phenomenon occasionally, some frequently, a few regularly. The latter are known as navel oranges; one of these, the Washington navel, is an important commercial variety. A few varieties, known as blood oranges, regularly have the juice red-colored and exhibit a reddish blush on the rind. This coloration is not constant, however; in some localities and seasons it is much more pronounced than in others.

PROPAGATION. The orange, like other citrus fruits, is propagated by budding on seedling rootstocks; fall or dormant shield-budding is the common and preferred method. The seed is planted shallow in seedbeds, usually under partial shade provided by lath, as early in spring as the soil becomes warm enough, usually March or April. The seedlings remain there until a year later, when they are transplanted to nursery rows. They usually attain suitable size for budding by the end of the second growing season. The trees are usually planted as year-old budlings, though they may be allowed to grow in the nursery another year. The rootstock most used is the sour orange, though the sweet orange succeeds about equally well on several other rootstocks. The trifoliate orange (*Poncirus trifoliata*) commonly, though not always, dwarfs sweet orange varieties and is very little used. Both the sweet orange and grapefruit (*Citrus paradisi*) are satisfactory, but their greater susceptibility to root and bark diseases is against their use. Rough lemon (*Citrus limonia*), a vigorous, disease-resistant kind of lemon (*see* LEMON) is used only where other rootstocks do not thrive. It should be avoided where possible because of its effects on the quality of the fruit; the color is paler, the rind thicker, the juice and acid content lower, and the fruit tends to drop from the trees when full maturity is attained. The sweet orange top-works readily by budding or bark grafting; the former is employed in arid regions, the latter in Florida.

PLANTING. The evergreen nature of the tree and the sensitiveness of the roots to injury from desiccation require that special care be used in handling and planting nursery trees, particularly in arid regions. In California the use of balled nursery trees is almost universal; in Florida the high atmospheric humidity favors planting the trees bare-rooted. The trees should not be planted when the soil is cold, for citrus roots have a high-temperature requirement for growth. Late spring is the preferred time for planting in California; in Florida early spring or fall. The best practice involves heading the trees a few weeks before they are dug; higher heading is practiced in California, 24 to 30 inches, than in Florida. In arid regions newly planted trees require frequent but light irrigation and should be protected against sunscald* by whitewashing or wrapping. For the first two or three winters they should be protected against frost; in arid regions this is best done by tying cornstalks about the trunks, in humid regions by mounding earth up to the heads. Planting distances range from 20 to 25 feet.

SOILS. Like other citrus trees, the orange has a wide range

---

* Special articles on the subjects indicated by an asterisk (*) will be found at the words so marked.

of soil adaptation and succeeds almost equally well on light and moderately heavy soils. It is sensitive to both high lime content and excess moisture, for which reason such soils should be avoided. Excellent drainage is a requirement and reduces the likelihood of root diseases. A soil reaction from moderately acid to slightly alkaline seems to give equally satisfactory results. Like other citrus trees, however, the orange is sensitive to even small concentrations of alkali salts and only soils free from alkali, and irrigation water of good quality should be used. Because of its shallow rooting habit deep soils are not required; three to four feet of good soil, adequately drained, will suffice.

IRRIGATION. In arid regions irrigation is the soil-management practice of greatest importance. An adequate soil-moisture supply must be maintained at all times, for the tree is evergreen and active to some degree throughout the year. In hot climates this may require 10 to 15 irrigations; in the cool coastal belt of southern California 3 or 4 may suffice. The amount of water applied at an irrigation is usually equivalent to 3 inches of rainfall. The total amount of water required depends upon the climate and the size and spacing of the trees; the period between irrigations depends on weather conditions and the water-storing capacity of the soil in the rooting zone. The method of irrigation is determined mainly by the slope of the land and porosity of the soil. The furrow method is most widely used, followed by the basin method.

The maintenance of satisfactory yields requires regular and heavy fertilization. Nitrogen is the only element which has been demonstrated to give results. An adequate fertilization program in California consists of about 200 pounds of nitrogen per acre per year and 3 tons dryweight of decomposable organic matter. Approximately half the nitrogen is supplied in chemical form — 500 pounds of ammonium sulphate, or its equivalent in calcium or sodium nitrate. The balance is provided in bulky organic form — 10 tons of dairy manure, or its equivalent in bean straw, alfalfa hay or similar substances. Somewhat less total nitrogen is used in Florida, where complete fertilizers are applied two or three times per year. Green-manure crops, winter in California and summer in Florida, are widely grown to provide organic matter. For the most part tillage operations are employed to turn under green-manure crops, weeds or fertilizers, and to facilitate irrigation. Pruning is of very minor importance and is confined to the opening-up of the trees for better penetration of light and to the removal of dead or dying branches.

When ripe the fruit should be clipped from the tree; this tends to prevent decay. Coloring may be hastened, if desirable, by exposure to ethylene gas at high storage temperatures.

Because of widely differing climatic conditions, the appearance of the orchards, the characteristics of the fruit, and the nature of the orchard-management problems and practices differ markedly in Florida and California. Since irrigation is not necessary, complete clearing, leveling and grading of land are not required in Florida; indeed large areas require drainage, usually provided by ridging and open ditches. In California the land must be completely cleared, graded and leveled, and sometimes contoured or terraced. The high atmospheric humidity and even temperature of Florida cause the fruit to be thinner skinned, juicier, lower in acid content and paler in color; the consequence is less attractive appearance and inferior shipping quality. Summer cover crops are grown in Florida; in California the winter cover crop predominates. In Florida fertilization involves the use of chemical fertilizers; in California manures are of chief importance. Relatively clean culture is the practice in California; little cultivation is employed in Florida, weed competition being controlled, if at all, by mowing. The purpose of pruning in California is to regulate light penetration, in Florida to control disease. The insects and diseases are mostly different.

Valencia, a commercially seedless, late-ripening sort of wide range of climatic adaptation, is the most important variety in both states. Washington navel, early-ripening and seedless, is next in importance and is grown in California and Arizona. It is restricted in climatic range and produces low yields of poor-quality fruit in semi-tropical climates. Parson and Hamlin are important early varieties in Florida, and Pineapple, Homosossa, and Jaffa are the principal mid-season varieties. In California there are two relatively unimportant mid-season varieties, St. Michael and Mediterranean Sweet. Florida still produces quantities of unnamed seedling sorts. — R. W. H.

INSECT PESTS. One of the most serious pests of citrus trees in Calif. is the black scale, a round, convex scale about ⅛ in. across. An unsightly black mold grows on its excretions. It has been controlled by hydrocyanic-acid fumigation under tents in the fall, but in some places this has not been fully effective recently. An oil emulsion containing a special grade of oil and a non-soap emulsifier has been developed for it. When diluted to 1 or 2 per cent, sometimes with the addition of lime-sulphur 1-65 to 1-100, and calcium caseinate 1 pound to 100 gallons, and applied as a spray in the fall, it has been effective.

The red scale, resembling the San Jose scale except in color, is injurious in Calif.; a similar species occurs in Fla. In Calif. it is usually controlled by fumigation, but, like the black scale, it has recently shown some resistance to cyanide. It can also be controlled with lubricating-oil spray, stock diluted 1-65.

The purple scale, resembling the oyster-shell scale, is more important in Fla. than in Calif.; an oil-emulsion spray late in the spring and another in the fall will check it. Other scales are controlled by similar measures.

Whiteflies are small insects that look as if they have been dusted with flour; the young look like tiny scale insects. They are especially injurious in Fla., but are controlled with the sprays for purple scale.

Mealybugs are slow-moving insects, covered with mealy-white wax filaments. They are most injurious in Calif. Oil emulsions especially prepared for summer spraying control them.

The little red spiders destroy the leaf surface and form strands of web under which they work. They are best combated by lime-sulphur, 1-50, applied early in the growing season. The tiny rust mite, which blemishes the fruit, is controlled with the same spray, and if abundant another application may be given late in the fall.

Thrips injure tender growth and blossoms; lime-sulphur will control them. In warm weather, sulphur dust has been found effective.

DISEASES. The list of diseases which attack citrus fruits is a very long one, and the percentage of the crop injured is extremely large. Among those troubles which occur on grapefruit and oranges, *melanose* is one of the more serious ones. It produces small, circular, brown, roughened spots on the leaves, twigs, and fruit. In severe cases the foliage may be much distorted and the fruit entirely covered with the spots.

A *stem-end-rot* also may occur when conditions are favorable for the fungus. *Scab* is another common disease that attacks leaves, twigs, and fruit of most types of citrus fruit, and causes roughened, wart-like malformations. When *citrus canker* was introduced into the Gulf states, its potential losses were so appalling that a drastic campaign of eradication was undertaken, with the result that the disease seems to have been wiped out from these southern states. Canker affects most parts of the tree above ground. *Foot-rot*, as the name indicates, attacks the bark of the crown roots, and base of the trunk, usually near the surface of the soil. If the disease is severe enough to girdle the trunk, the tree dies. Mushroom root-rot and collar-rot have somewhat the same appearance and results as foot-rot. *Gummosis* is another dreaded trouble which causes cracks in the bark and oozing of a pale-colored liquid gum. *Scaly bark* or *nail-head rust* is a disease chiefly confined to the sweet orange. Spotting is produced on nearly all parts of the tree above ground. Withertip and anthracnose are present on many citrus plants, and may cause much loss by injury to the twigs and spotting or russeting of the fruit. In addition there are *fly-speck*, *sooty-blotch*, and a large number of fruit decays.

In the control program for all these troubles on citrus trees the first requisite is having the planting in suitable soil, which is well drained, properly fertilized and contains sufficient humus. The handling of the grove should be such that the trees are kept in a thrifty state of growth. Care should be taken that the roots and trunks are not injured, and all dying parts removed and destroyed at once. Spraying with bordeaux-oil emulsion mixture or lime-sulphur may at times be required. The concentrations to use and the time of applications are dependent upon the season and the locality; therefore the recommendations of the local plant pathologist should be followed closely. Since the control of fruit rots depends upon keeping the fruit uninjured, the greatest precautions should be taken in picking, handling, packing, shipping, and cooling the fruit so that it is kept in excellent condition until it reaches the consumer.

**ORANGEBERRY** = *Triphasia trifolia*.

**ORANGE CONEFLOWER** = *Rudbeckia fulgida*.

**ORANGE-EYE BUTTERFLY-BUSH** = *Buddleia davidi*.

**ORANGE GARDEN.** See YELLOW GARDEN.

**ORANGE GUM** = *Angophora lanceolata*.

**ORANGE HAWKWEED** = *Hieracium aurantiacum*. See list at WEEDS.

**ORANGE HORSE GENTIAN** = *Triosteum aurantiacum*.

**ORANGE JASMINE** = *Murraya exotica*.

**ORANGE LILY** = *Lilium croceum*.

---

* Special articles on the subjects indicated by an asterisk (*) will be found at the words so marked.

FOUR TYPES OF HARDY ORCHIDS
(*Left to right*) fringed orchis (*Habenaria*), lady's-slipper (*Cypripedium acaule*), showy orchis (*Orchis spectabilis*), and arethusa (*Arethusa bulbosa*).

**ORANGE MILKWEED** = *Asclepias tuberosa*. See MILKWEED.

**ORANGE MILKWORT** = *Polygala lutea*.

**ORANGE PUCCOON** = *Lithospermum canescens*.

**ORANGE SUNFLOWER** = *Heliopsis scabra*.

*ORBICULATA, -us, -um* (or-bick-you-lay′ta). Round.

**ORCHARD.** See FRUIT CULTURE.

**ORCHARD GRASS** = *Dactylis glomerata*.

**ORCHID.** There are thousands of species of orchids, of which many hundreds are in cult. For a complete list of all the genera of orchids in THE GARDEN DICTIONARY, see ORCHIDACEAE, at which entry will also be found an account of their flower structure.

Here we are concerned only with their uses as garden or greenhouse plants, and as such they are culturally divided into two groups: (1) those that are hardy outdoors and grow mostly in the ground (terrestrial orchids), and (2) tropical orchids suited only to the greenhouse in the North or in lath houses in frost-free regions.

### HARDY ORCHID CULTIVATION

The terrestrial orchids are beautiful and are well worth cultivation in the rock garden or wild garden, or in the bog. Most of the species are easily grown if proper attention is given to their requirements and they will thrive if a few important details are followed in reference to their culture. Usually they are transplanted at the wrong season, that is, just as the flowers are opening. This method is to be condemned, as then the plant is developing the tuber for the following year, and if injury results from the lifting, the plant dies. (*Cypripedium acaule* is a good example of this.) The correct method is to mark the plants when in flower, allowing them to develop until September or October. By this time the tubers will have matured, and the risk of transplanting will have been reduced to the minimum, providing the plant is taken up with a ball of soil attached to the roots.

The next problem is the one of soil, and too much emphasis cannot be laid on the importance of proper soil conditions for the plant. Nearly all the native orchids require a soil with an acid base, and most prefer a soil of a fibrous loam or peaty character with ample moisture throughout the entire season. See ACID AND ALKALI SOILS.

The woodland plants do best if given the protection and partial shade of vegetation such as trees or shrubs. Up to the present very little has been accomplished relative to the raising of native orchids from seed and their propagation has been neglected. Most of the plants are purchased from the many dealers in native plant material, they being collected by thousands from the wild. The colonies of plants are rapidly being destroyed, and unless someone takes up the commercial propagation from seed, the species will disappear from all but the most inaccessible places.

Some of the hardy orchids inhabit bogs, some are at home on sandy plains, while others prefer the companionship of the meadow grasses where the soil is cool and moist. It is therefore essential to take into consideration their native habitat when they are to be transplanted into the garden. The conditions under which they grow are very important if the best results are to be achieved.

Protection during winter is another factor of importance. This can best be accomplished, after freezing weather sets in, by covering the plants with a mulch of leaves to the depth of about four inches, or two inches of peat moss may be used.

KINDS TO GROW. The species designated by a dagger are bog orchids; for culture *see* BOG GARDENING. Other species are humus plants of the woods and should be grown in ac-

---

\* Special articles on the subjects indicated by an asterisk (\*) will be found at the words so marked.

cordance with the suggestions made above. A few are dealt with in more detail at the article on WILD GARDEN.

| † *Arethusa bulbosa* | Dragon's-mouth |
| † *Calopogon pulchellus* | Swamp pink |
| *Cypripedium acaule* (see WILD GARDEN) | Moccasin flower |
| † *Cypripedium arietinum* | Ram's-head lady's-slipper |
| † *Cypripedium parviflorum* | Small lady's-slipper |
| *Cypripedium parviflorum pubescens* (see WILD GARDEN) | Large yellow lady's-slipper |
| *Cypripedium reginae* | Showy lady's-slipper |
| † *Habenaria blephariglottis* | White fringed orchis |
| † *Habenaria ciliaris* | Yellow fringed orchis |
| *Habenaria fimbriata* | Purple fringed orchis |
| † *Habenaria psycodes* | Pink fringed orchis |
| *Orchis spectabilis* | Showy orchid |
| *Orchis rotundifolia* | Shin-plasters |
| † *Pogonia ophioglossoides* | Rose pogonia |

Other hardy orchids, not quite so showy as those above, will be found at APLECTRUM, EPIPACTIS, and LIPARIS. — D. L.

### GREENHOUSE ORCHIDS

In view of the peculiar conditions under which tropical orchids grow in their native habitat, the grower should know something of the general natural surroundings before starting to grow them himself. The most fertile collecting fields for the common *Cattleya* group is in the Andes of South America, where they grow most abundantly at from four to six thousand feet elevation. Here the temperature is relatively constant, between 60° and 70°. We usually consider orchids as tropical, which is true as far as latitude goes for at least 85% of them; but their elevation puts them distinctly among the temperate plants, and the amateur is wrong to shy off from them as being out of place except in a tropical greenhouse.

Since the orchids most commonly grown under cultivation are the epiphytic,* or tree-perching type, it will be well to give a more detailed account of their habits of growth. They are attached to the trees, and are sometimes thought to be parasitic. This, however, is a mistaken idea, since they use the tree only for support, and not for nourishment. They usually have large, fleshy roots, in nature sometimes attaining a length of three or four feet. To exist during the dry season, when the only moisture is obtained from the very heavy morning dews and mists, the plants are equipped with much-thickened stems and leaves, the stems being referred to as pseudobulbs, in view of their bulb-like appearance. These act as reservoirs for food and water, to be released at the need of the plants. During the wet season, of course, the air is constantly saturated with moisture, and the exposed roots, in the furrows of the bark of the tree where the orchid is suspended, readily absorb both food and moisture from the air.

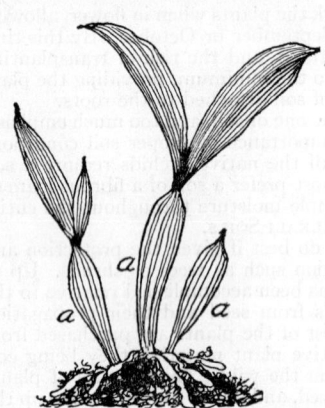

A tropical orchid with its pseudobulbs (*a*)

Their location in the trees is such that they are protected from the sun between eleven A.M. and about three P.M. The remainder of the day they receive plenty of sun. From this casual study of the orchid in its native surroundings, we gather several important facts. In the first place, most of the orchids obtained from dealers will be of the epiphytic* type, which in nature are found suspended from trees. If possible, they should be suspended even in cultivation. Secondly, the temperature in nature for most of them is temperate, between 60° and 70° F. Thirdly, since it is impossible to repeat accurately the wet and dry seasons of their tropical home, it will be necessary to keep in mind their aerial root system and keep them from drying out. Lastly, protect them from the burning sun, as nature does in their tree-top homes. With these few facts in mind, we may proceed to the cultural details.

A greenhouse is desirable in growing orchids, but it is not absolutely necessary. Of recent date, there are a number of amateurs in the Middle Western states in this country who are successfully growing orchids in sun parlors or in Wardian cases (see TERRARIUM) which have been especially constructed to accommodate several plants. During the summer orchids may be placed out-of-doors, so the chief object of a greenhouse is to keep them at a moderate temperature during the winter, in a location where they may receive the small amount of sun necessary for their growth.

SUNLIGHT AND TEMPERATURE. During the summer the plants should be shaded the greater portion of the day, and even in winter the burning sun should be kept from them. When the days are long and sunlight is plentiful, it is advisable to shade them from about nine A.M. to four P.M. The early-morning and late-afternoon sun will be sufficient for their needs. This time will be changed, of course, in winter, but the same general rules will apply.

Temperature may vary considerably, but it is good to remember that below 60° is the danger line. If your plants have been placed out-of-doors during the summer, they should be brought inside while the windows are still left open in the fall — before the temperature drops below 65°, the exact date being governed by the geographical location. If a controlled temperature is possible indoors, keep them between 60° and 70°.

MOISTURE AND LOCATION. During the summer, the best results will be obtained by placing the plants out-of-doors, if you do not have a greenhouse; suspending them from a tree, and watering them morning and evening. In a greenhouse, suspended plants should hang at least two feet below the roof glass. Even during the winter the plants do best when suspended. If this is impossible, stand them on inverted pots in shallow tanks of water. Moisture in a sun parlor may be further controlled by vaporizing cans on the radiators.

Don't over-water orchids in winter. When watering is necessary, dip the plant in a tub or bucket of water until it is thoroughly soaked. Then remove it, and don't water again until the peat becomes a light brown. Watch carefully, however, to be sure that a sufficient water supply is maintained to prevent any shriveling of stems or roots.

LIST OF SUGGESTED ORCHIDS. The most common commercial varieties are epiphytic,* or plants which grow naturally suspended from trees. There are, however, a few terrestrial varieties obtainable from the growers, which grow very successfully under much the same conditions as the epiphytes if they are given sod-soil instead of the usual orchid peat. It is not necessary to suspend them. Otherwise the treatment is the same for both epiphytic* and terrestrial plants. The following list gives the most common genera, species of which are handled by the orchid growers and are available for amateur cultivation.

EPIPHYTES.* To be grown in orchid peat.
    Cattleya group
        Hybrid Cattleyas
        Hybrid Laelias
        Laeliocattleyas
        Brassocattleyas
    Cypripediums (Tropical Species)
    Oncidium
    Dendrobiums
TERRESTRIAL.* To be grown in sod-soil.
    Cymbidiums (Have also been grown in orchid peat)
    Calanthe
    Phaius

---

* Special articles on the subjects indicated by an asterisk (*) will be found at the words so marked.

GREENHOUSE ORCHIDS
(A) *Dendrobium*; (B) *Oncidium*; (C) *Odontoglossum*; (D) *Cattleya*

TRANSPLANTING. An amateur should purchase only well-developed plants at first, and it is best to buy them in the late spring, when they are usually making growth. At first it will be unnecessary to do anything but give them the usual care as to water, light and temperature, but if the plant is large, one season's growth may necessitate transplanting it. After the orchid becomes established, it should be transplanted every two years.

The plants will go through each year a period of growth, of blooming, then resting and finally the forming of new pseudobulbs.* These pseudobulbs, or thickened stems, then send out new shoots. When these new shoots have grown to such an extent that they are approaching the edge of the pot or basket, it is time to think of transplanting.

The exact moment for transplanting, once this stage is reached, will be determined by the appearance of roots on the base of the new shoots. In order to avoid breaking these roots, it is necessary to transplant before they attain any great length.

DIVIDING. A newly purchased clump may not need dividing at the first transplanting, but eventually, when six or seven pseudobulbs* have been formed, it is advisable to cut off the three oldest pseudobulbs, or back-bulbs as they are called. These have dormant eyes at their base which will form new plants when stimulated by the division.

POTTING. Potting an epiphytic orchid is an entirely different process from that of the ordinary plant, where soil is used as the potting medium. The usual potting process consists of pressing down the soil around the roots of the plant. This is satisfactory for a terrestrial orchid, but when an epiphytic orchid is the subject, the potting medium is soft and spongy, and consequently cannot be pressed down and expected to hold the plant in place. The slabs of orchid peat must be inserted vertically, like the cells of a storage battery, being tightly forced in so that there is no possible chance for the orchid to become loose in its pot or basket.

Orchid peat is composed of fern roots (*see* OSMUNDA),

Potting an orchid in orchid peat (osmunda fiber). Most tree-perching sorts are best grown in these wooden cribs (orchid baskets).

and comes in large clumps which must be chopped into pieces about two inches thick. These pieces are then thoroughly soaked to a sponge-like consistency. If a pot is used, be sure it is large enough to accommodate the plant; and cover the bottom with an inch of broken crockery for drainage. Insert enough of the potting material to fill half of the pot or basket when held firmly with your hand. Then take the orchid plant, with a generous ball of the old peat around the roots, and hold it firmly in the middle of the pot, against the peat already inserted. Insert layer after layer of peat in front of the plant, forcing in the last piece with a pointed stick or dibber. The sides are also filled in firmly, and the final test is to take the plant up after this operation and give it a careful shake. If it stays solidly in place, the transplanting has been successful. Many growers prefer an orchid-basket (which see).

In securing the desired depth of planting, be careful to

---

* Special articles on the subjects indicated by an asterisk (*) will be found at the words so marked.

keep the connecting stem or rhizome between the pseudobulbs on the surface of the peat. Be certain, also, that you have left a generous space at the top of the pot for adequate watering.

LIST OF "DONT's"

Don't attempt to raise orchids from seeds. It is a highly specialized task and should be left to the experts.

Don't experiment with fertilizers. Transplanting every two years will provide sufficient nutriment.

Don't forget to clean the leaves of your orchids with a soapy water. The pores must be kept open and free from all dust or soot.

Don't keep orchids entirely shaded. They must have some light to produce blooms. See directions above.

Don't permit scale insects to spread. They are apt to get under the bracts covering the pseudobulbs, in which case, entirely remove the bracts. These were formed as a protection for the young shoots, and after they turn white on the old pseudobulbs they are no longer necessary, serving only to harbor pests.

Don't over-water orchids in winter. See directions above.

Don't look for flowers on the genera listed until your young shoot has developed into a thickened stem or pseudobulb. The flowers will appear from the base of the leaf enclosed in a green sheath, from which the bud pushes itself out. Different species bloom at different times, and by properly choosing your varieties you can literally have orchids all year long. — G. H. P.

DISEASES. Leafspot, anthracnose, gray mold and rot are the common diseases of orchids. *Leafspot* is confined to the foliage in the form of dead, discolored lesions. With *anthracnose*, infection occurs on the stems as well as the leaves. The lesions are dark brown to black in color. Both diseases are controlled in the same manner. Remove infected leaves, increase air circulation, reduce the humidity and spray with bordeaux mixture, if necessary. *Gray mold* causes spotting of the flowers. For control, remove infected blossoms, avoid careless watering and reduce the humidity within the greenhouse. *Rot* may occur at the base of the pseudobulb. For control, cut out the rotted portion, increase the air circulation and provide better drainage.

**ORCHIDACEAE** (or-kid-day'see-ee). The orchid family probably has the most spectacularly beautiful flowers in the world. It is an enormous group of perhaps 450 genera and over 7500 species, possibly many more, scattered all over the world, but most frequent and most showy in the tropics. All are herbs, varying from the relatively large epiphytes* of the tropical forest to tiny plants growing in the ground in temperate regions, where many of them are bog plants. Most tropical genera grow attached to trees (see EPIPHYTES*), while most temperate-region genera grow in the ground, usually in forest, humus or in bogs, a few in meadows, and some in dry, sandy woods. See ORCHID for directions as to how to grow both groups.

The tropical orchids often have leaves with a swollen base (a pseudobulb) which stores water over the dry season, and from which the blade often falls away in droughts. Temperate genera do not have pseudobulbs. In all genera there are no marginal teeth. They may have thickened, thread-like, or bulbous roots, or fleshy, brittle ones, but in all genera there is a bacterial relationship between the roots and the plant food absorbed by them. In many tropical genera the air roots of the epiphytes are covered with a whitish film that absorbs atmospheric moisture (see VELAMEN).

The flowers of orchids present extreme specialization to insect fertilization (Darwin devoted two volumes to it). They also present extreme difficulty in separating the different genera, even considering only the small number in cult. The typical orchid flower is highly irregular* and composed of 3 outer segments (sepals*), usually similar, and often not showy. There are three inner segments (petals), two of which may be more or less alike, but the third forms a lip or spur of infinite variety of shape and color in the different genera. Sometimes the spur may be a foot long (see ANGRAECUM). Again there is no spur, but the lip will be bag-like, twisted, or contorted. The stamens and pistil are joined into a single organ (the gynandrium), sometimes called the column. The structure and shape, and contents of this gynandrium are of endless variety.

The leading cultivated genera of orchids are easily divided (but difficult to distinguish) upon the basis of their habitat. They form two groups.
1. TROPICAL GENERA OF GREENHOUSE CULTURE.
    (a) The leading and most showy are: *Calanthe, Cattleya* ("the" florist's orchid), *Coelogyne, Cymbidium, Cypripedium* (also temperate), *Dendrobium, Epidendrum, Laelia, Lycaste, Odontoglossum, Oncidium, Phaius, Sobralia, Stanhopea,* and *Vanda*.
    (b) Secondary tropical orchid genera, often very beautiful, but less grown: *Aerides, Angraecum, Brassavola, Gomesa, Miltonia, Phalaenopsis, Peristeria, Renanthera* and *Zygopetalum*.

There are a few other tropical cult. genera, among them vanilla, almost the only orchid of economic importance.
2. TEMPERATE GENERA MOSTLY GROWN IN THE GROUND, often in rich woods humus or in bog gardens.
    *Aplectrum, Arethusa, Calopogon, Calypso, Cypripedium* (some tropical), *Epipactis, Habenaria, Liparis, Orchis, Pogonia* and *Spiranthes*.

See all these genera for further notes on them.

**ORCHID BASKET.** A crib-like basket, usually square and about 4–5 in. deep. Its sides and bottom are made of stout slats about ½ in. square, and usually there is a space of about ½ in. between the slats. Such a basket will not hold soil, but it is admirable for holding orchids or other air plants potted chiefly in fiber or orchid peat. See illustration on page 559.

**ORCHID FAMILY** = Orchidaceae.

**ORCHID PEAT.** See Potting Greenhouse Orchids at ORCHID.

**ORCHID TREE** = *Bauhinia variegata*.

**ORCHIOIDES** (or-kĭ-oy'deez, but *see* OÏDES). Orchid-like.

**ORCHIS** (or'kiss). Woodland, hardy orchids, comprising over 70 widely distributed species of which the two native ones are sometimes cult. in the wild garden. They have tuberous roots, mostly basal leaves, and not especially showy flowers in terminal clusters (racemes*). Flowers very irregular, magenta or white, and magenta-spotted (in ours). Sepals similar, free or united, usually larger than the petals. Lip turned downward, generally spurred below. (*Orchis* is the old Greek name for these plants.)

They require rich woods soil and the partial shade of the wild garden. See WILD GARDEN.

rotundifolia. Shin-plasters. Leaf solitary, nearly circular, 6–7 in. long, almost as wide. Flowers magenta, the stalk of the cluster naked. Lip white, but magenta-spotted, 3-lobed. Quebec to N.Y. and westward, mostly in the mountains. June–July.

spectabilis. Showy or gay orchis. Flowering stalk nearly 12 in. high, the cluster bracted.* Leaves 2, basal, shining, oblongish, 3–7 in. long, 2–4 in. wide. Flower purple-magenta, the petals and sepals united to form a hood. Lip white, but violet-blotched. Eastern N.A. May–June.

**ORDER.** See PLANT FAMILY.

*OREGANA, -us, -um* (o-ree-gay'na). From Oregon.

**OREGON.** As part of the name, *Oregon* has been applied to many plants native to Oregon or to the region near it. The hort. species so named and found in THE GARDEN DICTIONARY are:

Oregon cedar = *Chamaecyparis lawsoniana;* Oregon cluster. A variety of hop (which see); Oregon crabapple = *Malus fusca;* Oregon grape = *Mahonia aquifolium* and *M. nervosa;* Oregon laurel = *Arbutus menziesi;* Oregon maple = *Acer macrophyllum* (see MAPLE).

**OREGON.** The state lies wholly in zones* 3, 4, 5, and 6, which, due to the proximity of the mountains and the sea, extend approximately north and south instead of east and west as they do over much of the country.

SOILS. The chief truck and vegetable gardening soils are found in the following series in western Oregon, including the Willamette Valley and the coast: Chehalis, Newberg, Columbia, Peat (Beaverdam), Willamette, Sifton, Coquille. In

---

* Special articles on the subjects indicated by an asterisk (*) will be found at the words so marked.

southern Oregon, the Neal and Columbia are among the best. In eastern Oregon, Wind River, Milton, Onyx, and Columbia are outstanding.

Among the fruit soils in the Willamette Valley of western Oregon the following are best: Aiken, Olympia, Willamette, Powell, Chehalis, and Newberg. In southern Oregon, Columbia, Kerby, Corning, Medford, and Meyer series are among the best. In eastern Oregon, the Underwood, Columbia, Wind River, Milton, Catherin, and Alicel are excellent soils.

The chief gardening centers are around the city of Portland, in the northern part of the state. In addition to this section, the Milton-Freewater district, in Umatilla County, in the northeastern part of the state, produces tomatoes for shipment and watermelons also. Near The Dalles, in Wasco County, on the Columbia River, early market vegetables are produced, which are chiefly early tomatoes, peppers, cu-

OREGON

The zones of hardiness crossing Oregon are those shown on the colored map at ZONE, which should be consulted for details. The dates are the average latest killing frost in spring and the first one in the fall. The figures below the dates show the average length of the growing season. Rainfall figures (in inches) show (1) the total annual rainfall and (2) the amount falling in the growing season at the places indicated.

cumbers, eggplant, seed corn, lettuce, and cantaloupe. In the Hermiston district of northern Oregon, asparagus and watermelons are produced for eastern shipments. Near Troutdale and Fairview, in Multnomah County, there is grown a wide variety of vegetables, and particularly cauliflower, cabbage, celery, pickle cucumbers, and general market vegetables, supplying Portland. Near Milwaukie, in Clackamas County, celery is produced in large quantities, also some general marketing vegetables. In the Oswego district of Clackamas County, cabbage, cauliflower, and broccoli are the leading vegetables. Near Hillsboro, in Washington County, large quantities of cannery vegetables are produced. In the vicinity of Tualatin and throughout the valley of that name, a large production of commercial onions is found. Near Salem, the state capital, in Marion County, onions, onion sets, celery, lettuce, mint, and general peat-land crops are found. In the vicinity of Eugene, in Lane County, large quantities of cannery vegetables are raised. Stayton and West Stayton, in Marion County, produce cannery beans. Roseburg, in Douglas County, specializes in winter cauliflower (broccoli). Near Medford and Ashland, in southern Oregon, cannery vegetables, especially tomatoes, are featured. In the coastal counties of Coos, Lincoln, and Clatsop, green peas are produced for shipment. In Klamath Falls, Klamath County, and near Redmond and Bend, in Deschutes County, large quantities of potatoes are raised.

FRUIT. Most of the fruit of Oregon is produced in four sections. The Hood River district, lying just east of the Cascade Mountains, bordering on the Columbia River, is known all over the world for the quality of its apples. It is coming to be recognized also as a producer of first-quality winter pears. It raises large acreages of sweet cherries and of strawberries, and some other kinds of fruits are produced in more limited quantity.

The Medford district, in Jackson County, southern Oregon, produces the largest tonnage of winter pears in the state of Oregon. In addition, it produces very good Bartlett pears. The pear production of this district is about 3500 cars a year. Yellow Newtown apples of fine quality are produced here also.

In the extreme northern part of the state, in Umatilla County, is located a district near Milton-Freewater where a wide diversity of fruit is produced, chiefly for eastern shipments. The list of fruits includes sweet cherries, prunes, apples, peaches, and some pears. The Willamette Valley, embracing some 9 counties in western Oregon, is noted chiefly for its dried prunes, for its excellent peaches, for some apples and pears, large acreages of sweet cherries, some sour cherries, nearly all of the walnut and filbert plantings of the state, and for most of the strawberries, loganberries, black raspberries, red raspberries, and blackberries of the state which are used for canning and barreling purposes.

CLIMATE. Oregon has a wide range of climatic conditions. East of the Cascade Mountains the high plateau region is too cool for fruit growing, except in protected situations. West of these mountains is a region of rather heavy rainfall during the winter, with a long, rather dry summer. Climatic data have been assembled for three of the most prominent localities interested in fruit growing — Milton, Hood River, and Medford. The temperatures affecting fruit growing in these three districts are as follows:

| Town | Average date of last killing frost in spring | Latest known killing frost | Average date of earliest killing frost in fall | Earliest known killing frost |
|---|---|---|---|---|
| Milton | April 17 | May 26 | Oct. 24 | Sept. 12 |
| Hood River | April 20 | May 22 | Oct. 20 | Sept. 7 |
| Medford | May 7 | May 31 | Oct. 14 | Oct. 3 |

The annual rainfall and the rainfall throughout the six months of growing season are, in inches, as follows:

|  | Milton | Hood River | Medford |
|---|---|---|---|
| Annual | 14.41 | 32.11 | 18.08 |
| Six months | 5.18 | 5.36 | 4.25 |

The Pacific Ocean on the west and the Columbia River on the north both exert considerable influence on the fruit-growing possibilities of the counties adjoining them.

The coastal part of Oregon is particularly well suited climatically to the culture of garden flowers that like summer coolness. Roses are especially fine, as are larkspurs, snapdragons, foxglove and sweet peas. Broad-leaved evergreens, such as the English holly, also flourish there.

The address of the Oregon Agricultural Experiment Station which has supplied this information is Corvallis, Oregon. The station is always ready to answer questions concerning gardening and fruit growing.

Garden Club activities include clubs of the Garden Club of America, the home office of which is at 598 Madison Avenue, New York, N.Y. There are also over 30 clubs affiliated with the Oregon Federation of Garden Clubs. For

* Special articles on the subjects indicated by an asterisk (*) will be found at the words so marked.

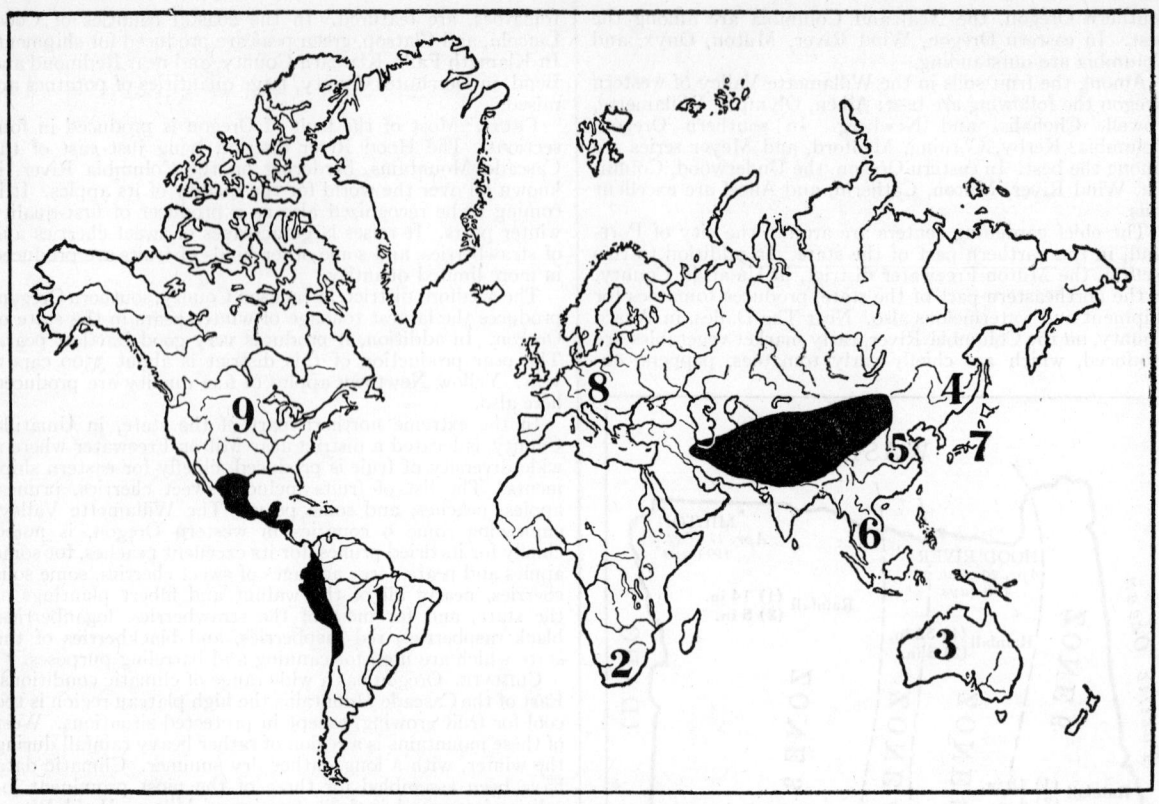

**ORIGIN OF SOME CULTIVATED PLANTS**

The black area in Mexico and southward is the region where the Aztecs grew Indian corn, tobacco, guava, vanilla, dahlia, marigold, cosmos, and many other New World plants. The black area in northwestern S.A. gave us the potato, quinine, cocaine, and many Peruvian, Bolivian, and Chilean ornamentals. The black area in Central Asia gave us the common Old World vegetables and fruits listed in the article below and many garden flowers. The figures on the map show the approximate origin of the following:
1. Chocolate, Lima bean, Pará rubber, peanut, tomato, sweet potato, many orchids and palms.
2. Garden geranium, gladiolus, freesia, and many Cape Bulbs (which see).
3. *Eucalyptus, Banksia,* and many other plants popular in Calif. originated in Aust. and neighboring islands. (*See* AUSTRALIAN.)
4. Ginkgo, many chrysanthemums, and a great variety of trees and shrubs came from various parts of China. (*See* CHINESE.)
5. Most citrus fruits.
6. Sugar and banana, and, to the eastward, the coconut palm, many palms and orchids.
7. Many ornamental garden plants. (*See* JAPANESE.)
8. Europe is far less important in the origin of cult. plants than the other regions mentioned. (*See* EUROPEAN.)
9. Among ornamental plants, temperate N.A. has given us sunflower, many bulbous plants, besides shrubs and trees. For lists *see* AMERICAN, CANADA, INDIAN, CALIFORNIA, etc.

the one nearest your locality write the Garden Editor, Houghton Mifflin Company, Boston, Mass.

**ORELLANA, -us, -um** (o-rel-lay'na). Named for a branch of the Amazon River.

**ORGANENSIS, -e** (or-gan-en'sis). From the Organ Mountains, Brazil.

**ORGAN-PIPE CACTUS** = *Pachycereus marginatus.*

**ORGYALIS, -e** (or-jee-ā'lis). About six feet long.

**ORIENTAL ARBORVITAE** = *Thuja orientalis.*

**ORIENTAL FRUIT MOTH.** *See* Moth at INSECT PESTS. *See also* Insect Pests at PEACH and QUINCE.

**ORIENTALIS, -e** (or-ee-en-tay'lis). From the Orient; eastern.

**ORIENTAL PLANE** = *Platanus orientalis.*

**ORIENTAL POPPY** = *Papaver orientalis. See* POPPY.

**ORIGANIFOLIA, -us, -um** (or-rig-gan-i-fō'li-a). With marjoram-like leaves.

**ORIGANOIDES** (or-rig-ga-noy'deez, but *see* OÏDES). Like a marjoram (*Origanum*).

**ORIGANUM** (or-rig'a-num). A small genus of Eurasian perennial herbs of the mint family, of which the only cult. species is O. vulgare, the pot or wild marjoram, sometimes called winter-sweet. (It is not the sweet marjoram.) The pot marjoram is a hardy, perennial herb with aromatic foliage and creeping or horizontal rootstocks. Leaves opposite,* broadly oval, about 1 in. long. Flowers small, irregular,* 2-lipped, purplish-pink, borne in spike-like clusters. The plant is often naturalized in N.A. For its culture and uses *see* HERB GARDENING. For a plant sometimes offered as *O. majorana, see* SWEET MARJORAM. (*Origanum* is thought to be the old Greek name for the plant and means delight of the mountains.)

**ORIGIN OF CULTIVATED PLANTS.** All cultivated plants must, of course, have originated from wild ancestors. Sometimes, in fact most often, the process of passing from a weedy ancestor to a definitely cultivated plant is lost in the past. Reconstructing such histories is one of the most fascinating of the many problems of the historical botanist, but little space can be given to it here.

From such studies, however, the gardener may glean much of historical interest. It is not perhaps of much practical importance to the average gardener to know where his chief crop plants have come from, but it adds much of cultural and educational interest. So much is this true that a brief record of some of the facts of the origin of cultivated plants is worth recording here.

---
* Special articles on the subjects indicated by an asterisk (*) will be found at the words so marked.

All scientists are pretty well agreed that there have been two main regions responsible for the origination of most of our commonly cultivated plants — Asia and Asia Minor in the Old World, and the region from central Mexico to Chile in the New.

Let us take the American one first. It is hard now to realize what the voyage of Columbus was to mean to the history of cultivated plants. In 1492 the Old World had never heard of the potato, sweet potato, corn, peanut, tobacco, pineapple, chocolate, guava, cinchona, rubber, cocaine, string bean, Lima bean, tomato, dahlia, cosmos, marigold, upland cotton, nor vanilla, every one of which was well known to the Aztecs or the Incas, but not often to both of them. Besides these and many more, there are whole families of plants, some of them enormous, that are wholly American, and were unknown before the conquest. The two most notable are the pineapple family with about 1000 species and the cactus family with over 1300.

Perhaps 2000 years before Columbus arrived, some of these purely American plants had already split up into any number of horticultural forms, notably corn, chocolate, tobacco, and potato, around which an immensely rich and varied civilization had grown up in Mexico or Peru. So highly developed had these people become that the Spanish conquerors were astounded. Such a degree of culture was, and must always be, built upon the basis of a stable agriculture. But, before Columbus, that agriculture did not include one major cereal (except corn), few of our common vegetables, no sugar, and others to be mentioned presently.

The Old World had existed for nearly 1500 years without American plants, and probably for countless centuries before that. Most commonly grown European vegetables have been in cultivation over 2000 years, some much longer. But few of them are really European in origin, any more than most of the people appear to be. Sometimes a wild ancestor of a commonly cult. vegetable will be a European plant, but the origin of the vegetable as a cult. crop is more often Asiatic.

Somewhere in the vast reaches of central Asia which stretch from Pamir to China, there must have been a primitive agriculture for a very long period. For somewhere in this region it appears certain that the following plants became real cultivated plants for the first time:

| Apple | Cherry | Plum |
| Artichoke | Cucumber | Quince |
| Asparagus | Lettuce | Rhubarb |
| Barley | Oats | Rice |
| Beet | Onion | Rye |
| Cabbage | Pea | Turnip |
| Carrot | Peach | Wheat |
| Celery | Pear | |

While this is an impressive list, it is mostly of plants of the temperate zone and is by no means complete. And it does not include such flowers as peony, hollyhock, narcissus, chrysanthemum, foxglove, or dozens of others — all from the Old World. And if the tropical and sub-tropical Old World is counted, as it should be, we must add the coconut palm, banana, sugar cane, date, all citrus fruits, tea, coffee, the watermelon, and most of the important drug plants except cocaine and quinine.

Among purely ornamental plants eastern Asia is also outstanding for the greatest concentration of species in the barberry, oak, rhododendron, fir, spruce, pine, azalea, and flowering cherries. Far more than in the New World, these Asiatic primitive people seem to have originated many varieties of ornamental plants. The Incas and the Aztecs spent more effort on creating varieties of corn, tobacco, chocolate, and the potato.

**ORIGIN OF NEW PLANTS.** See PROPAGATION.

**ORIGIN OF NEW SPECIES AND VARIETIES.** See PLANT BREEDING.

**ORIOLE.** See BIRDS.

**ORMOSIA** (or-mō′sĭ-a). Little-known tropical trees of the pea family, comprising over 40 species, of which only O. monosperma, the necklace tree, appears to be in cult. It is hardy only in zone* 9, or possibly in zone* 8, and is a large tree with compound* leaves. Leaflets arranged feather-fashion, usually of 5 pairs and an odd one at the end. They are oblongish, 3–4 in. long. Flowers pea-like, blue, about ¾ in. long, in large, showy clusters (panicles*) which are rusty-hairy. Fruit a 1-seeded, leathery pod (legume*), not over 1½ in. long, the seeds scarlet, with a black patch. (Ormosia is from the Greek for necklace, in allusion to the use of the seeds for making necklaces.)

**ORNAMENTAL GRASSES.** See GRASSES.

**ORNAMENTAL TREES.** See TREES.

**ORNAMENT AND FURNITURE.** The three most important features to be considered in garden furnishing are comfort, good design, and durability. It is vital to have furniture that is placed out-of-doors made of the best possible material so that it may withstand sunshine, snow, wind, and rain, all the cause of disintegration.

In the selection of furniture for outdoors, consideration should be given to the purpose for which it is to be used and its suitability for the location in which it is to be placed. A bench, chair, or table that is intended to be an adjunct of a formal garden should be more restrained in design than the more casual type used in the garden of a country cottage or the rustic furniture which is suitable either for summer camps or the decoration of a woodsy nook. There are two types of furniture, one which becomes a permanent part of the garden and which is not intended to be moved, such as a settee to mark the end of a vista, and the other which is intended for incidental living and should therefore be of lighter weight and easy to transport.

There are many mediums which can be used out-of-doors. Stone benches, seats, tables, and the like, and iron furniture of heavy proportions are the more permanent types. Also combinations of iron and wood or iron laced with rawhide or iron slung with awning material. Swedish iron is a more expensive and less adulterated composite which can be counted upon not to rust. To insure protection for the average iron that is used in American gardens, it should be treated with red lead and subsequently painted or parkerized, a process in which the metal is submerged in acid. This treatment is relatively costly, but it is the more permanent of the two methods to prevent rusting.

Wood is also an attractive material for furniture for the garden. Of the many kinds that are available, teakwood is the hardest and most durable. Hard cypress is also satisfactory. Hickory, oak, and redwood are also fairly permanent, but to insure a long life chairs and tables that are made of these woods should be rubbed frequently with linseed oil or, better still, painted. If they are not subjected to this treatment or are not painted, they are apt to check. All wooden furniture should be pinned together with wooden pegs; glue should not be used and joinings of metal are apt to rust and to cause an eventual disintegration of the wood itself. In the construction of wooden furniture, the material should be so selected that as little cross-wood as possible is exposed. The joints, too, should be so designed as to prevent moisture getting into them. It is also advisable to consider the problem of draining so that water will not settle on the seats of chairs, and this can be accomplished by having them slightly tilted or made of slats. Slatted table tops are also useful for the same reason.

Many attractive and satisfactory examples of furniture which is suitable for uncovered terraces are made of wire. This material lends itself to varied designs, either classic or modern in form. In recent years furniture has also been constructed of aluminum which, being of light material, has the advantage of making it easily transportable. There are two schools of thought, one which maintains that aluminum is a satisfactory weather-resisting material and one which believes it will disintegrate after several years of usage.

Reed, rattan, and stick willow, either painted or shellacked, fill another need and supply a great degree of comfort. The life of these materials when left in the open is of

---

* Special articles on the subjects indicated by an asterisk (*) will be found at the words so marked.

course limited, but given proper care, such as frequent applications of shellac, these mediums are excellent for porches and terraces which have a reasonable degree of protection.

Chair cushions and pillows used to complete the reed and rattan type, as well as incidental cushions which are employed to add comfort to other classes of furniture, should be covered with a water-resistant material. Of these, fabricoid, which is a rubberized material, is perhaps the best, although awning material is also durable. There is a suède cloth on the market which is attractive, but does not have a long life. Indentone is a cotton material treated chemically, which also has the reputation of being sunfast. Linens, too, can be treated for outdoor usage by a process called cravenetting, which fills the open weave so as to make it semi-water-resistant and also to set the color of material, thereby making it less susceptible to the sun.

In considering the selection of chairs, benches, seats, and gliders, the question of color, as well as design, is one that should be considered. If these accompaniments of outdoor living are to be placed in or near a brilliant, perennial border, it is advisable to keep them in an inconspicuous tone, lest they distract from the beauty of the garden itself. Tables for outdoor dining are frequently made with glass tops so as to be easy to clean in case of dust or unexpected showers.

For the protection of the dining terrace or as a shield against the sun, awnings can perform the function of being both decorative and useful. These can be constructed with a roller device which permits the awning to be closed or opened at will, and which, when the roller is up, neatly encases it in a metal hood, thus increasing its life span. The awning which is used as a permanent fixture is usually stretched over metallic piping or is supported by tubing frequently crowned with a decorative form.

There is also the transportable awning with wheels attached which can be moved about at will to insure shade on any part of the porch or terrace or well-graded lawn. The awning material of these devices is woven duck. There is also a painted canvas which is available in many attractive colors. A new invention is a fireproof awning which is particularly useful in city backyards or penthouse terraces where matches or cigarette butts may be thrown on it from near-by windows. This awning is treated with a chemical process.

Umbrellas are also a useful and gay adjunct for protection against the sun. Many of them are constructed with a tilting device, and can be supported by a table top which is perforated by the pole of the umbrella, or else fixed permanently by a metal device inserted in the terrace floor or held in a small, inconspicuous, iron or concrete block sunk in the grass itself.

## Ornament

A garden without ornamentation seems incomplete. The use of potted plants is something that enhances the beauty of tiled or brick terraces or where no plants could otherwise be grown. These pots are made of terra cotta, both high and low glaze, lead, iron, and stone. Many of the composition stone pots are strengthened by wire bands inserted in them to prevent chipping and breakage. Ornamental pots are available and are specially suitable if they contain growing plants or small evergreens, or unornamented, which is more desirable if one relies upon the color of the plant itself for decorative purposes. For more formal locations, such as a terminal of walls, etc., urns form an excellent decorative feature.

Trellises and brackets of wood or iron fulfill the function of wall decoration and are recommended for garden use. These should be specially designed to carry out the general architectural feeling of the house or terrace which they decorate and can be constructed along either classic or modern lines. There are many lead ornamental flower boxes, commonly used in England, which are adaptable to our contemporary needs. Lead leaders are also available and can be placed so as to form attractive wall fountains.

Wall fountains and spitters are eminently suited for garden decoration and are available in types varying from the simplest to the most formal and ornate. In the planning of a garden, a place should be reserved for them, as the sound of water dripping into a pool gives a lively interest to garden design and creates a feeling of coolness even on the hottest of days. Basins of lead, brick, and bronze, or even of concrete, can be designed to receive the water from fountain heads. If antique lead fountains or spitters seem difficult to secure, the contemporary sculptor will gladly create a figure suitable in size and design for the location in which the fountain is to be placed. These designs may take the form of either human or animal faces or the stylization of flowers. Seahorses, fish, and the like have also been successfully adapted for this purpose.

Sundials and bird baths are interesting garden ornaments, and of these a generous supply of old and modern is available for garden lovers. Both wall and armillary sundials must be carefully placed so as to receive the rays of the sun at an angle which records the correct time. They can be placed either on decorative pedestals or against a flat surface of the terrace or house wall. *See* SUNDIAL.

Bird baths which attract the bird life give a constant source of joy to garden owners. These should not be too deep and should be so constructed that the bird will have a walk on which to sun himself before and after bathing. It is an advantage to have the bird bath set on a pedestal high enough to protect it from the encroachment of cats, although many bird baths which are located in the woods or near garden pools have to be on the ground level. Stone, bronze, concrete, lead, and iron are mediums employed for the creation of bird baths. Many of these are decorated with high sophistication, and others which find placement in informal locations are created with design suitable for this location. *See* BIRDS.

In selecting sculpture for the garden, great care should be taken, as, next to the tree itself, sculpture is perhaps the most permanent feature in the garden. Sculpture to fulfill its purpose should be regarded as a unit of garden design. It must fit its location in scale and feeling and should emphasize a focal point. It should never be placed casually without a definite reason, such as marking the end of a vista or an accent in the shrubbery. Another use for sculpture is for terminals of walls or guard dogs by a gate of a residence. Also a sculptured figure, such as a fountain set in a niche. Mediums are lead, iron — which is specially popular in Sweden — bronze, marble, stone, and composition stone. The quality of the sculpture should be considered in the location in which it is to be placed. The type of garden governs the type of sculpture that is to be placed in it. Next to its suitability and location, the question of size is of the most vital importance. Figures that look large when exhibited in a gallery frequently appear to shrink in size when placed out-of-doors. Too detailed a type of sculpture is also not satisfactory when placed in the open. Vigorous sculpture with plane value is the best, as it is enhanced by the resultant quality of light and shadow that nature provides.

Of various mediums that are available marble and bronze are the most formal. Marble shows to great advantage when placed against a background of green foliage. In this placement the white figure becomes the dominant note. Bronze is a handsome and durable material and one of the most expensive. If a bronze figure is placed against trees or shrubbery, it is apt to be absorbed and may cease to fulfill the very function for which it was intended. Lead has for years been one of the most popular garden mediums. It is reasonable in price and takes on a beautiful patina as it becomes weathered. The English leads are perhaps the best known, although in both the French and Dutch gardens large lead figures were at one time extremely popular. The Italian leads are combined with antimony which makes the figures darker in quality and gives the feeling of greater rigidity, as in bronze. Many leads are now available that have been made in the old molds. However, in the executing of lead, sand casting seems to be the most satisfactory method, as it avoids any ridges showing where the molds join.

Stone is a very suitable medium and weathers beautifully, and it has the added charm that it is cut by the sculptor him-

---

* Special articles on the subjects indicated by an asterisk (*) will be found at the words so marked.

**GARDEN ORNAMENTS AND FURNITURE**

self. Abastone is a new type of artificial stone which has recently become available. It decreases the cost of massive figures and has an established reputation for being weatherproof. This stone is made from marble dust with a chemical binder and can be tooled by the sculptors after the molds are cast. — R. A. M.

**ORNATA, -us, -um** (or-nay′ta). Ornamental or ornate.

**ORNITHOGALUM** (or-ni-thog′a-lum). Hardy or tender, bulbous herbs of the lily family, comprising about 70 species, the hardy ones natives of Europe and western Asia, the tender species of Africa. Bulbs rather small. Leaves narrow or broad, tapering to a point at the tip. Flowers in clusters (racemes*) on leafless stems, sometimes as high as 3 ft. Individual flowers stalked, and with a small, leafy bract. Petals 6, separate, spreading, white, yellow, or orange-red. Stamens* 6. Fruit a dry, 3-valved capsule* (*Ornithogalum* is from the Greek, for bird and milk, in allusion to the egg-like color of some species.)

The outdoor species are generally used for wild gardens, as the bulbs increase so quickly as to become a nuisance in beds or borders. Propagate by offsets* removed from old bulbs when dormant. They require no attention. The tender species may be grown as border plants in the South or in cool greenhouses or sunny windows in temperate regions. They should be planted in a compost of 2 parts sandy loam, 1 part leaf mold and sand. Plant the bulbs Sept.–Feb., 1 in. deep, in pots, bowls or boxes with good drainage. Water moderately when growth begins, freely when in full growth, gradually withholding water when foliage begins to turn yellow. Apply liquid manure when flower buds appear. Bulbs can be dried and stored for use the following year.

**arabicum.** Bulb oval. Leaves 5–8, pale green, 1–1½ ft. long, ¾ in. wide. Flower stem 1–2 ft. Flowers 6–12, white, 1 in. long, with prominent black pistils.* Makes good pot plant. Mediterranean region.

**nutans.** Star-of-Bethlehem. Bulbs oval, 1 in. in diameter, producing offsets freely. Leaves pale green, 1–1½ ft. long, ¼–½ in. wide. Flower stalks 8–12 in. long. Flowers 3–12, white inside, green outside, with a white margin, nodding. This species can be used for naturalizing. Asia Minor.

**thyrsoides.** Bulbs globe-shaped, 1½ in. thick. Leaves 5–6, 1–2 in. wide, 6–12 in. long, the margins slightly hairy. Flower stem 6–18 in. long. Flowers 12–30 in a dense raceme,* white or yellow. South Africa. Not hardy north of zone* 6.

**umbellatum.** Star-of-Bethlehem; also called summer snowflake and Sleepy Dick. Bulbs round, 1 in. thick. Leaves 6–12 in. long, ¼–½ in. wide, veined or spotted white. Flowering stem 6–8 in. long. Flowers 12–20 in the cluster, star-like, white, the 3 outer segments having green margins. Common in American gardens. Mediterranean region, and widely naturalized in eastern N.A.

**ORNUS** (or′nus). An ancient name for the mountain-ash.

**ORONTIUM** (or-ron′she-um). Golden club, also called floating arum, and water dock. Hardy water plant of northeastern America, the only species being O. aquaticum, of the arum family. It is a strong-growing aquatic plant, found in shallow pools and ponds or sides of slow-moving streams, and of little garden importance, but sometimes used in the bog or wild garden. Rootstocks thick and fleshy. Leafstalks 10–20 in. long. Leaves floating or erect, depending on the depth of the water, 2–5 in. wide, 6–12 in. long. Leafblade with no central midrib, but strongly marked with numerous parallel veins. Flowers arranged in a closely packed cluster (the spadix*), enclosed in a long, yellow cylindrical, club-shaped spathe.* See ARACEAE. (*Orontium* was adopted from the Greek by Linnaeus, but is of uncertain application to this plant.)

**OROXYLON** (or-rox′i-lon). A single species of Indo-Malayan tree of the family Bignoniaceae, O. indicum, the Indian trumpet-flower, cult. for ornament in Calif. and Fla., and hardy only in zones* 8 and 9. It is a tree up to 40 ft. high with very striking foliage. Leaves 2–4 ft. wide, thrice-compound, its leaflets very numerous, ovalish, 4–5 in. long, without teeth, glossy-green. Flowers bell-shaped, about 3 in. wide, white or purplish, its fine lobes crisped. Stamens* 5, slightly protruding. Fruit a slender, flattened pod, 2–3 ft. long, about 2½ in. wide. The tree needs a rich soil, plenty of moisture, and may be propagated by seeds or by cuttings over bottom-heat. (*Oroxylon* is from the Greek for mountain tree, although the plant grows also in lowlands.)

**ORPINE** = *Sedum telephium*.

**ORPINE FAMILY.** A very large group of mostly succulent plants suited to dry places. Besides the orpine, it includes the stonecrops, houseleeks, and many other plants with thick leaves or stems. For a list of the garden genera see CRASSULACEAE.

**ORTHOCARPUS** (or-tho-kar′pus). A genus of New World annual or perennial herbs of the family Scrophulariaceae, generally called owl's-clover in Calif., where some species are native. The only plant of garden interest is O. purpurascens, the escobita, which is an annual scarcely 12 in. high. Leaves alternate,* much cut into thread-like segments, the upper ones bract*-like, colored, and among the flower clusters. The latter are usually spikes and very showy, nearly 4 in. long. Flowers irregular, 2-lipped,* about 1 in. long, purple or crimson, the lower lip white but with yellow or purple streaks. Bracts* in the flower cluster tipped with red. The escobita can be treated as a hardy annual. See ANNUALS. (*Orthocarpus* is from the Greek for erect fruit, in allusion to the upright, small pods.*)

**ORTHOL K.** A trademarked emulsified oil of light grade, suitable for summer use, and sold with directions for use as a contact spray.

**ORYZA.** See RICE.

**OSAGE ORANGE.** See MACLURA.

**OSIER WILLOW** = *Salix viminalis*. See WILLOW.

**OSMANTHUS** (oz-man′thus). Tea olive; also called sweet olive (not a true olive). Evergreen shrubs or small trees of the olive family, all but one of the 10 known species Asiatic or Polynesian, but the devilwood (O. americanus) a native of the southeastern U.S. Leaves opposite,* spiny-toothed or with none. Flowers often very fragrant, not showy, usually unisexual or polygamous,* and borne in terminal clusters (cymes* or panicles*), or these sometimes in the leaf-axils.* Calyx* short and 4-lobed. Corolla tubular, but short, 4-lobed at the summit. Stamens* mostly 2, not protruding. Fruit fleshy, egg-shaped, a drupe* with a single stone. (*Osmanthus* is from the Greek for fragrance and flower, in allusion to the most fragrant species, O. fragrans.)

The tea olives, especially O. fragrans, are very popular shrubs in the warmer sections of the country, where they are grown in a variety of soils. Occasionally they are grown under glass in the North and need a cool greenhouse and potting mixture* 4. Propagated by late-summer cuttings of half-ripe wood, rooted under glass, more rarely by seeds which are scarce and take nearly two years to germinate.

**americanus.** Devilwood. A tree 20–40 ft. high. Leaves elliptic or narrower, 4–6 in. long, without marginal teeth, shining green above. Flowers fragrant, greenish. N. Car. to Fla. and Miss. Hardy from zone* 6 southward. May.

**aquifolium** = *Osmanthus ilicifolius*.

**fortunei.** A fragrant, hybrid shrub, 4–6 ft. high, derived by crossing O. fragrans and O. ilicifolius. Leaves ovalish, 3–4 in. long, spiny-toothed on the margin.

**fragrans.** The most common in cult., and a shrub or small tree sometimes up to 25 ft. high. Leaves ovalish or oblong, 2–4 in. long, slightly toothed or without any teeth. Flowers white, very fragrant, the corolla divided nearly to the base. Southeastern As. Hardy from zone* 7 southward, but also grown in northern greenhouses. April. It is sometimes offered as *Olea fragrans*.

**ilicifolius.** A shrub 15–20 ft. high. Leaves oblong to ovalish, 1½–2½ in. long, the margins with a few spiny teeth. Flowers fragrant, white, the corolla divided almost to the base. Jap. Hardy from zone* 5 southward. June–July. There are several hort. forms, mostly with variegated, golden, or purplish foliage. The plant makes a good hedge subject where hardy. See HEDGES.

**OSMARONIA** (oz-ma-rō′nĭ-a). A single species of shrub of the rose family found on the Pacific Coast from British Columbia to Calif. and cult. for ornament. The only species, O. cerasiformis, the osoberry, is an upright shrub 10–15 ft. high, its branches erect. Leaves alternate,* stalked, oblongish, 2–4 in. long, without marginal teeth. Male and female flowers on different plants, sometimes polygamous,* greenish-white, fragrant, mostly in short clusters (racemes*), the individual flower stalks with two bractlets. Petals oblongish. Stamens* 15, five shorter than the other 10.

---

* Special articles on the subjects indicated by an asterisk (*) will be found at the words so marked.

Fruit a collection of small, bluish-black drupes,* about ½ in. long. The plant blooms in April–May, and prefers partial shade and a moist site. Propagated by fresh or stratified seeds or by suckers. (*Osmaronia* is of doubtful origin.)

**OSMUNDA** (oz-mun'da). Coarse, stiffish, easily grown ferns, the only cult. genus of the family **Osmundaceae** (oz-mun-day'see-ee), all those below mostly from the north temperate zone, but a few others tropical. They have erect fronds that are cut, divided, compound,* or twice-compound,* usually in large basal clusters. The foliage fronds are usually different from the spore*-bearing ones, but in other species some of the leaf segments are modified to bear spores.* (Named for *Osmunder*, a Saxon name for the god Thor.)

For culture see FERNS AND FERN GARDENING. Much of the orchid peat used for potting orchids is derived from the fibrous roots, etc., of the first two species, much collected for this purpose, and often called osmunda fiber.

**cinnamomea.** Cinnamon fern. Foliage fronds taller than the spore*-bearing ones, the stalks rusty-woolly. Blades deeply cut or divided into narrowly lance-shaped segments, the ultimate divisions also deeply cut, but the frond not compound.* Spore-bearing frond similar, but smaller, brownish, contracted and soon withering. In wet, low woods or thickets, N.A., Eurasia, and southward to Brazil.

**claytoniana.** Interrupted fern; also called Clayton fern. An upright fern, the fronds 2–4 ft. high, sometimes even more. Fronds deeply divided, but not compound,* the divisions with many deeply cleft segments. Most of the outer leaves are exclusively foliage fronds, but some of the inner leaves have, toward the center of the frond, a few divisions that are brownish and wholly spore*-bearing. In wet or moist places, eastern N.A., also in eastern As.

**regalis.** Royal fern. Fronds long-stalked, twice-compound,* the ultimate segments somewhat distant, oblongish, 2–3 in. long, without teeth or divisions. Some of the main divisions of the compound leaf are wholly spore-bearing, brown, and much narrower than the foliage segments. Throughout the U.S. in moist places, usually in the open, but widely distributed in tropical America, Eurasia, and Af.

**OSMUNDACEAE.** See OSMUNDA.

**OSOBERRY** = *Osmaronia cerasiformis*.

**OSTEOMELES** (os-tee-om'e-leez). Three species of Asiatic or Polynesian shrubs of the rose family, the two below somewhat grown for ornament in the South, but not hardy northward. They have alternate,* compound* leaves, the leaflets arranged feather-fashion, and without marginal teeth. Flowers rather showy, white, in terminal clusters (corymbs*). Petals 5. Stamens* 15–20. Fruit small, bony but apple-like, crowned with the persistent calyx.* (*Osteomeles* is from the Greek for bone and apple, in allusion to the fruit.)

They thrive best in the open, and in a well-drained soil. They are best propagated by cuttings, started under glass, or by grafting on *Cotoneaster*.

**anthyllidifolia.** An evergreen shrub, 4–6 ft. high. Leaflets silky beneath, about ½ in. long, usually 13–19 comprising the whole leaf. Flowers about ½ in. wide, the loose cluster 2–3 in. wide. Fruit hairy. May–June. South Pacific Islands and Hawaii. Reported as hardy in "parts of N.Y.," but certainly so only south of zone* 6.

**schwerinae.** A partially evergreen or deciduous shrub 6–9 ft. high. Leaflets about ⅓ in. long, grayish-hairy beneath, usually 15–31 comprising the whole leaf. Flowers about ½ in. wide, the loose cluster 2–3 in. wide. Fruit smooth. Western China. May–June. Hardy from zone* 5 southward, possibly in zone* 4 with protection.

**OSTERDAMIA** = *Zoysia*.

**OSTRICH FERN** = *Pteretis struthiopteris*.

**OSTROWSKIA** (os-trow'ski-a). A single perennial species of central Asiatic herbs of the family Campanulaceae. The only species, **O. magnifica**, is a tall herb resembling a giant bellflower (*Platycodon*), to which it is closely related, differing in having whorled* leaves. The plant grows 4–6 ft. high. Leaves ovalish, 4–6 in. long, toothed. Flowers blue, nearly 3½ in. wide, in a sparse, terminal cluster, usually not more than 4–5 blooms in all, but very showy. The plant is apt to die out in a year or two, and it needs winter protection north of zone* 5. Propagated by division or by cuttings of young shoots. (Named for N. Ostrowski, a Russian botanist.)

**OSTRYA** (os'tri-a). Hop-hornbeam. A genus of 7 species of American or Eurasian hardwooded trees of the birch family, **O. virginiana**, the American hop-hornbeam (also called ironwood and leverwood), cult. for ornament and native in eastern N.A. It is a moderately ornamental tree, usually about 30 ft. high, but often taller in the wild. Leaves alternate,* ovalish, 3–5 in. long, sharply and double-toothed. Male and female flowers separate, on the same tree, greenish and inconspicuous, the female clusters ultimately forming bladdery, fruiting bracts, between which are the nutlets. The tree is closely related to *Carpinus* (see HORNBEAM). The fruiting cluster is the most attractive feature of the hop-hornbeam, as its flowers bear neither petals nor sepals. Hardy from zone* 2 southward. (*Ostrya* is an old Greek name for some tree with hardwood, but not for this one.)

**OSWEGO TEA** = *Monarda didyma*.

**OTAHEITE APPLE** = *Spondias cytherea*.

**OTAHEITE GOOSEBERRY** = *Phyllanthus acidus*.

**OTAHEITE ORANGE** = *Citrus taitensis*.

**OTAKSA** (o-tak'sa). Japanese name for the hortensia (*Hydrangea macrophylla otaksa*).

**OTHAKE SPHACELATA** = *Polypteris hookeriana*.

**OTHONNA** (o-thon'na). South African succulent shrubs or herbs of the family Compositae, comprising over 80 species, of which **O. crassifolia** (also known as *O. capensis*) is often grown in greenhouses or in hanging baskets. It is a drooping or trailing perennial herb with alternate,* fleshy or pulpy, cylindrical leaves nearly 1 in. long (hence sometimes called "little pickles"). Flower heads solitary, bright yellow, about ½ in. wide, at the ends of slender stalks 3–6 in. long, thus standing far above the essentially prostrate foliage. They bloom only in sunlight. The plant is a rampant grower in any well-drained soil, preferably potting mixture* 3. It needs a cool greenhouse, and, as a basket plant, will stand considerable neglect. (*Othonna* is a Greek name of no known application to this genus.)

**OUNCE.** See WEIGHTS AND MEASURES, 4.

**OUR LADY'S THISTLE** = *Cnicus benedictus*.

**OUVIRANDRA.** See APONOGETON.

**OVAL.** Broadly elliptic; usually about 1½ times as long as broad and rounded at the ends. The term is often confused with ovate (which see).

**OVAL FLOWER BED.** For the number of plants needed for an oval flower bed see GARDEN TABLES IV.

*OVALIFOLIA, -us, -um* (o-val-i-fō'li-a). Oval-leaved.

*OVALIS, -e* (o-vay'lis). Oval.

**OVAL KUMQUAT** = *Fortunella margarita*.

**OVARY.** The usually swollen base of a pistil, containing one or more ovules, which, after fertilization, become the seeds. In most flowering plants the ovary and/or its attendant parts become the fruit. See FLOWER, FERTILIZATION.

*OVATA, -us, -um* (o-vay'ta). Ovate (which see).

**OVATE.** Egg-shaped in outline with the broader end downward, usually applied to surfaces. The technical distinction between ovate and oval is clear enough, but it often breaks down in hort. and botanical descriptions, because leaves, to which it is mostly applied, may well be ovate or oval on the same plant. In such cases the common term is oval, although many leaves so designated are slightly egg-shaped.

**OVER-POTTING.** A common fault of amateur growers, which results in plants being grown in pots too big for them. For details see POTTING.

*OVIFERA, -us, -um* (o-vif'fer-ra). Ovule-bearing; literally egg-bearing.

*OVINA, -us, -um* (o-vy'na). Relating to sheep; woolly or sheep-like. In plant names it also signifies sheep fodder.

**OVOID.** Egg-shaped (ovate); usually applied to solids.

**OVULE.** The usually minute body (often numerous) within the ovary,* which becomes the seed, after the ovule

---

* Special articles on the subjects indicated by an asterisk (*) will be found at the words so marked.

has been fertilized. In the pine and its relatives the ovule is naked (see GYMNOSPERM). See FERTILIZATION.

**OWLS.** See BIRDS.

**OWL'S-CLOVER.** See ORTHOCARPUS.

**OWL'S-CROWN** = *Gnaphalium sylvaticum*.

**OWN-ROOT.** A common term in hort. and applied to those plants that are budded or grafted upon roots of the same or closely related species or varieties. Own-root roses are preferred by some growers, while many lilacs are grown upon privet stock, and such would not be own-root plants.

**OXALIDACEAE** (ox-al-i-day'see-ee). The wood sorrel family does not mean much in the gardening world, but two of its 10 genera, *Oxalis* and *Averrhoa*, are somewhat grown for ornament. *Oxalis*, while partly weedy, contains some beautiful herbs for the wild garden (the wood sorrel) as well as some greenhouse species. *Averrhoa* comprises tropical evergreen trees with edible fruit and can be grown outdoors only in zone* 8 or 9.

Leaves compound,* the leaflets arranged finger-fashion in *Oxalis*, but feather-fashion in *Averrhoa*. Flowers not very showy (but fine in some species of *Oxalis*), usually in clusters. Fruit a dry pod (capsule*) in *Oxalis*, but fleshy and edible in *Averrhoa*.

Technical flower characters: Flowers regular* and hermaphrodite.* Sepals 5. Petals 5, sometimes slightly united at the base. Stamens* 10. Ovary superior,* 5-celled, the styles separate.

**OXALIS** (ox'a-lis; *also* ok-sal'is). Wood sorrel. A very large and interesting group of sour-juiced herbs, the chief genus of the family Oxalidaceae, producing somewhat woody cushion plants in the Andes, edible tubers in Mexico, some beautiful wild flowers in our woods, and several rather weedy, yellow-flowered roadside weeds. Of the over 300 species, which are most abundant in the Andes and South Africa, only a few are of any hort. interest. All have compound,* clover-like leaves, the leaflets always arranged finger-fashion, folding up at night or in dark weather (hence described as "going to sleep"). Flowers solitary, or more often in few-flowered clusters, white, pink, red, or yellow. Sepals and petals 5 each. Stamens* 10, 5 longer than the others. Fruit a capsule.* (*Oxalis* is from the Greek for sour, in allusion to the sour juice of most species.)

The species of *Oxalis* come from such widely different regions that no general cultural directions will apply. See the different species for notes on culture. All are low herbs (3–6 in.) except *O. ortgiesi*. For the blue oxalis see PAROCHETUS.

**acetosella.** Common wood sorrel; called, also, sleeping beauty and sheep sorrel. It is also one of the plants known as shamrock.* A woodland, stemless, perennial herb. Leaflets 3, notched. Flower solitary, about ¾ in. wide, at the end of a short stalk. Petals white, but pink-veined, blunt, but not notched. Northern Eu. and N.A. A June-blooming plant needing rich woods soil and shade. Suitable for the wild garden.

**adenophylla.** A perennial herb with tuberous roots. Leaflets 12–22, notched, about ½ in. long, bluish-green. Flowers pink, but veined with deeper pink. Chile. A winter-blooming greenhouse plant. Grow in potting mixture* 3, in a cool greenhouse, and when through flowering the tubers should be lifted and stored in a cool, dark place, and planted again in the autumn.

**bowieana.** A perennial herb with a thickened rootstock and scaly bulbo-tubers. Leaflets 3, notched. Flowers nearly 2 in. wide, rose-purple, blooming late in summer and in the autumn. South Africa. It is not hardy over the winter and its tubers should be grown exactly as are gladioli (which see).

**cernua.** Bermuda buttercup (neither native in Bermuda nor a buttercup, but naturalized there). A bulbous, South African herb with 3 notched leaflets. Flowers yellow, about 1½ in. wide, nodding. Hardy in the Far South, but in the North to be treated the same as *O. adenophylla*.

**corniculata.** The common yellow wood sorrel of our roadsides. A perennial herb, the leaflets 3, notched. Flowers about ½ in. long, yellow, in few-flowered clusters. Eu., but widely naturalized in N.A. More a weed than a garden plant.

**enneaphylla.** A perennial herb with tuberous roots. Leaflets 9–20, notched, bluish-green. Flower solitary, white, but purple-veined. Falkland Islands. To be grown as in *O. adenophylla*.

**ortgiesi.** A leafy-stemmed, perennial herb, 12–18 in. high. Leaflets 3, cut fishtail-fashion at the tip. Flowers yellow, but veined darker yellow, usually in long-stalked clusters (cymes*) from the leaf-axils.* Peruvian Andes. To be grown as in *O. adenophylla*.

**rosea** = Generally, *Oxalis rubra*.

**rubra.** A perennial herb, the leaflets 3, notched. Flowers in a cluster (umbel*) which is higher than the leaves. Petals rose-pink, but darker-veined, sometimes lilac or even white. Brazil. Sometimes grown in the window garden or in the greenhouse, or outdoors far southward. Should be handled as in *O. adenophylla*.

**valdiviensis.** A perennial herb with a bulbous root. Leaflets 3, notched. Flowers in long-stalked clusters (umbels*), the petals bright yellow, but brown-striped within. Chile. While this is a true perennial, it will bloom from seed in a single season if treated as a tender annual. See ANNUALS.

**violacea.** Violet or purple wood sorrel. A perennial, woodland herb. Leaflets 3, notched at the tip. Flowers several in a cluster, the stalk of which arises from the ground. Petals rose-purple, rarely pinkish-white. In rich woods, Mass. to Fla. and west to the Rocky Mountains. Culture is the same as for *O. acetosella*.

**OXERA** (ok'ser-ra). Australian shrubs or woody vines of the family Verbenaceae, only *O. pulchella* of the 15 known species likely to be cult. here. It is a woody vine grown for ornament in southern Calif. and scarcely hardy elsewhere. Leaves opposite,* oblongish, 3–5 in. long, without marginal teeth. Flowers white, trumpet-shaped, about 2 in. long, in forked clusters (cymes*). Calyx* showy, greenish-yellow. Corolla 4-lobed. Stamens protruding. Fruit fleshy. A very handsome climber, useful also in the warm-temperate greenhouse, although little known here. (*Oxera* is of uncertain application to these plants.)

**OXEYE.** See BUPHTHALMUM and HELIOPSIS.

**OXEYE CAMOMILE** = *Anthemis tinctoria*.

**OXEYE DAISY** = *Chrysanthemum leucanthemum*.

**OXLIP** = *Primula elatior*.

**OXYACANTHA, -us, -um** (ok-si-a-kan'tha). Sharp-spined.

**OXYCOCCUS.** See VACCINIUM.

**OXYDENDRUM** (ok-si-den'drum). A single species of beautifully white-flowered trees of the family Ericaceae, found wild from Pa. to Fla. and La. and cult. for ornament up to the limits of zone* 3. The only species, **O. arboreum**, the sourwood or sorrel-tree, is 30–50 ft. high. Leaves alternate,* stalked, bitter-tasting, oblongish, 6–8 in. long, brilliantly scarlet in the fall. Flowers small, not over ⅓ in. long, in drooping clusters (racemes*) 8–10 in. long, very handsome in midsummer. Fruit a gray-hairy capsule.* While the tree is hardy north of its wild range, it is of slow growth, and few cult. specimens reach the dimensions given. (*Oxydendrum* is from the Greek for sour and tree, in allusion to the acid foliage.)

**OXYTROPIS** (ox-it'ro-pis). Perennial herbs and shrubs comprising about 230 species of the pea family, mostly natives of Asia, but about 18 species found in the Rocky Mountains. They are not of much garden interest, but occasionally used in the rock garden. (*Oxytropis* is from the Greek for sharp, and a keel, in allusion to the shape of the flower.)

Easily propagated by seeds or division, the only cult. species prefers a dry, sandy loam, in a sunny position.

**lamberti.** Locoweed, so called because it poisons sheep and cattle. A tufted perennial with strong taproot. Height to 1½ ft. Leaves compound,* the leaflets 7–14 pairs and covered with silky hairs on the under side. Flowers on leafless stalks, twice as high as the leaves, pea-like, arranged in short, dense spikes, usually purple or violet. Fruit a leathery pod, covered with silky hairs. There are hort. color forms. Great Plains from Canada to New Mex.

**OYSTER PLANT.** A name applied to several plants, but commonly and most correctly to *Tragopogon porrifolius*, the salsify (which see). For the Spanish oyster plant *see* SCOLYMUS. The name oyster plant is also applied to *Rhoeo discolor* (which see), and the name of vegetable oyster is applied to the common oyster plant (*Tragopogon porrifolius*).

**OYSTER SHELLS.** See LIME.

**OYSTER-SHELL SCALE.** See Insect Pests at APPLE, BOX, LILAC, and ELM.

---

* Special articles on the subjects indicated by an asterisk (*) will be found at the words so marked.

# P

$P_1$, $P_2$. *See* $F_1$, $F_2$, $F_3$.

***PABULARIS, -e*** (pab-you-lay'ris). Suitable for pasture; fodder.

**PACHIRA** (pa-ky'ra). Tropical American, very showy trees of the family Bombacaceae, comprising about a dozen species of which only **P. aquatica,** the Guiana chestnut, is occasionally cult. in zone* 9, rarely in greenhouses because of its size. Leaves compound,* the 5–7 leaflets arranged finger-fashion, nearly stalkless, without marginal teeth, and 5–10 in. long. Flowers 8–12 in. long, the calyx* tubular, the petals fringed, pink or purple. The filaments* of the stamens* are nearly as long as the petals, red or scarlet, and very striking. Fruit a 5-celled capsule* about 1 ft. long and 3 in. in diameter. An extraordinarily showy tree, its immense flowers blooming in early spring in southern Fla. It will stand no frost. S.A. (*Pachira* is a Latinized version of a native name for some of them in Guiana.)

**PACHISTIMA** (pa-kiss'ti-ma). A genus of the staff-tree family (Celastraceae) comprising two North American species. They are low evergreen shrubs, with small opposite* leaves and inconspicuous flowers that are borne in the leaf-axils.* (*Pachistima* is from the Greek for thick stigma.)

They are fairly ornamental, forming neat evergreen tufts, and adapted to the rock garden or borders of low evergreen plantings. They prefer a sandy, somewhat peaty soil, but are not particular so long as the situation is well drained. Propagated by seeds, cuttings or layers. The name is sometimes spelled *Pachystima.*

**canbyi.** Rat-stripper. Low shrub growing about 1 ft. high, with trailing, rooting branches. Leaves ½ to 1 in. long, linear or narrowly oblong, toothed toward the tip, the margins turned under. Flowers tiny, reddish, on slender stems from the leaf-axils.* May. Open rocky slopes of the mountains in Va. and W. Va. Hardy from zone* 3 southward.

**myrsinites.** Spreading shrub with stiff branches, sometimes to 2 ft. high. Leaves narrow-oblong or elliptic, ⅓–1¼ in. long, toothed toward the tip, the margin slightly turned under. Flowers white to reddish. May to Aug. In the woods from British Columbia to Calif. and N. Mex.

**PACHYCEREUS** (pack-i-seer'ee-us). Mostly Mexican, tree-like or columnar cacti, comprising perhaps 10 species which differ from *Cereus* only in technical characters. They have tall, deeply ribbed stems, and are definitely trunk-like and woody at the base, often branched at the top. Flowers day-blooming, not very showy, often scaly or spiny on the outside. Fruit bur-like, dry. (*Pachycereus* is from the Greek for thick and *Cereus,* in allusion to the huge stems.)

The two below are suited only to tropical desert gardens, and are too big for greenhouse culture northward. *See* CACTI.

**marginatus.** Organ-pipe cactus. Stems not usually branched, 15–20 ft. high, 5–7-ribbed, the ribs white-cushioned along the ridge. Spines 5–8 at each cluster, one central and erect, the others spreading, none over ¾ in. long. Flowers about 1½ in. long, funnel-shaped, brownish-purple. Mex.

**pecten-aboriginum.** Hair-brush cactus. A stout cactus, the trunk 6 ft. long and 12 in. in diameter, crowned with many erect, ribbed branches up to 30 ft. high. Ribs 10–11. Spines in clusters of 8–12, one or two central and erect, the others spreading, usually ½ in. long or less. Flowers about 2 in. long, white inside, but purplish outside. Fruits bur-like, used by the Indians as combs, hence *pecten-aboriginum.* Mex.

**PACHYPHYTUM** (pack-i-fy'tum). Little-grown, Mexican succulent plants of the family Crassulaceae, **P. bracteosum** sometimes found in greenhouses or in desert gardens in frost-free regions. It is a bluish-green herb, 8–12 in. high, with very thick leaves borne in rosettes on the stem. Leaves broadest above the middle. Flowering stalk curved at first, ultimately erect, and bearing a 1-sided cluster (raceme*) of red flowers. Mex. For culture *see* SUCCULENTS. (*Pachyphytum* is from the Greek for thick plant, in allusion to the thick leaves.)

**PACHYRHIZUS.** *See* YAM BEAN.

**PACHYSANDRA** (pack-i-san'dra). Low-growing, perennial herbs or sub-shrubs comprising 5 species of the family Buxaceae and natives of N.A. and eastern As. Stems fleshy. Leaves alternate,* simple, spoon-shaped, the upper half with teeth-like margins. Flowers greenish-white, in spikes, the lower flowers fertile, having 4 sepals and a pistil,* the upper having 4 sepals, 4 stamens* and a rudimentary pistil,* and not fertile. Fruit a small, whitish, oval berry. (*Pachysandra* is from the Greek for thick and men, in allusion to the stamens.)

*Pachysandra* can be grown readily in ordinary soil, making admirable ground cover for either shady or sunny positions, particularly useful under large trees or on steep banks. *P. terminalis* is especially useful for this purpose. Easily propagated by cuttings taken in July or Aug., planted in a mixture of ½ sand and ½ soil, in a cold frame which should be well watered and shaded until cuttings are rooted. For making a quick ground covering they should be planted 8–12 in. apart.

**procumbens.** Alleghany spurge. Evergreen in the South, deciduous* in the North. Stems trailing at first and then becoming erect. Leaves alternate,* ovalish, dingy green, 2–4 in. long. Flowers white or purplish in spikes produced from the leaf-bearing stems. Grown mostly for its early spring flowers. West Va. to Fla.

**terminalis.** Japanese spurge. Growing to 1 ft., the stems beneath the surface of the soil sending out underground runners or stolons,* hence its quick-spreading habit. Leaves thick, dark, glossy-green, spoon-shaped, alternate. Flowers white in terminal spikes, 3–4 in. long. Jap. One of the best evergreen ground covers for partly shady places.

**PACHYSTACHYS** (pack-i-stack'is; *also* pack-iss'tack-is). Tropical American shrubs comprising 6 species of the family Acanthaceae, the one below the only plant of hort. interest. They differ only in technical characters from *Jacobinia.* (*Pachystachys* is from the Greek for thick spike, in allusion to their dense flower clusters.)

Grown chiefly as a greenhouse plant, sometimes grown outdoors in the southern states. Propagated from cuttings of young shoots in early spring. If grown as pot plants, No. 5 potting mixture* should be used.

**coccinea.** Also known as *Jacobinia coccinea, Justicia coccinea,* and *Odontonema strictum,* to which it is closely allied. Grows to 9 ft. Leaves simple, ovalish, to 8 in. long, margins sometimes wavy. Flowers in dense terminal heads, scarlet, 2 in. long. Calyx of 5 sepals. Corolla tubular, widely 2-lipped. Stamens* 4. Fruit a 2-celled, many-seeded capsule. S.A.

**PACHYSTIMA** = *Pachistima.*

***PACIFICA, -us, -um*** (pa-siff'i-ka). From the Pacific, usually from the islands of the Pacific; sometimes from our Pacific Coast.

**PACIFIC DOGWOOD** = *Cornus nuttalli.*

**PACKING.** CUT FLOWERS. The container should either be a shallow box of light wood or cardboard only deep enough to hold one layer of flowers or, if deeper, be fitted with trays, each to hold one layer of flowers.

The boxes must be lined with oiled paper, and the paper must be arranged in such a way as to fold over the top to prevent side drying. Wet paper must be packed around the stems to prevent their drying out, and to provide a humid atmosphere. There must be sufficient space between the lid and the flowers to prevent heating. If on a regular flower route, it may be sufficient to have paper packing over the stems to make a tight lid contact, but it is far safer to lace the flower stems to the bottom of the box by means of a packing needle and string. Orchids, camellias, and gardenias are kept apart by means of cotton batting to prevent mechanical injury — in the case of orchids it is imperative to sew the stems to the bottom of the box. Flowers should be in water over night before packing.

POTTED PLANTS. Plants may be packed upright one layer deep or horizontally in several layers. The plants must be wet at the roots, the plants firmly staked and tied. Cover the top of the soil with damp moss and tie on firmly to prevent the shaking out of the plant; sometimes banding with

* Special articles on the subjects indicated by an asterisk (*) will be found at the words so marked.

paper is necessary. Moist moss or excelsior must be between the pots and over the bottom of the crate. It is advisable to cleat in the pots by passing over them inch strips of wood and nailing to the sides.

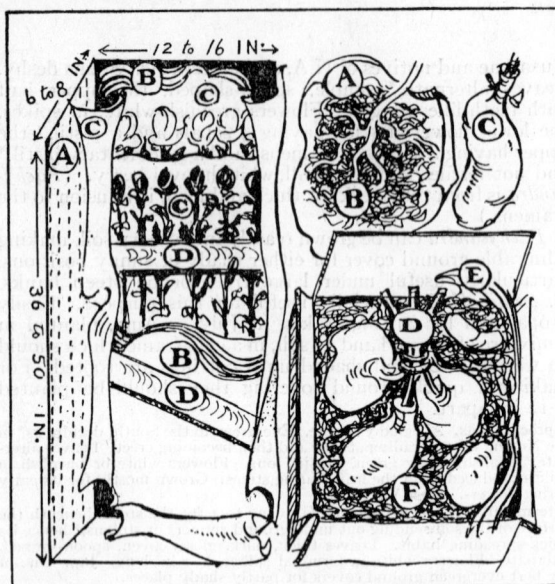

PACKING FLOWERS (*left*) AND HERBACEOUS PLANTS (*right*) FOR SAFE SHIPMENT

*At the left:* (*A*) Four to six layers of flowers in the box. (*B*) Wet newspapers between the layers, with wax paper (*C*) separating the layers. (*C*) Wax paper for outer packing of all. (*D*) Nailed cleats to keep flowers in place.
*At the right:* (*A, B,* and *C*) Wax paper surrounding moist sphagnum* and roots, the whole tied securely. (*D*) Stalks, if several, tied with raffia.* (*E* and *F*) Moistened layers of paper around all, and excelsior or paper packing between bundles to prevent shifting.

Horizontal packing is by tiers at both ends of the crate. The pots are laid on their sides and cleated in front. Ventilation is provided through the sides.

Nursery stock is balled in moist moss and packed tight in crates. — T. R. A.

**PAEONIA.** See PEONY.

**PAGODA TREE** = *Sophora japonica* and *Plumeria acuminata*.

**PAINTED-CUP.** See CASTILLEJA.

**PAINTED LADY.** See CHRYSANTHEMUM COCCINEUM, PHASEOLUS COCCINEUS, and PHLOX PANICULATA.

**PAINTED-LEAF** = *Poinsettia pulcherrima*.

**PAINTED TRILLIUM** = *Trillium undulatum*.

**PAK-CHOI** = *Brassica chinensis*.

*PALAESTINA, -us, -um* (pal-ees-ty′na). From Palestine.

**PALAQUIUM** (pa-lay′kwee-um). Indo-Malayan, milky-juiced trees of the family Sapotaceae, of far more economic than hort. interest, as one of them, **P. gutta**, is the gutta-percha tree, which is occasionally cult. for interest in zone* 9. It is hardy nowhere else in the U.S. Not over 40 ft. high. Leaves alternate,* leathery, ovalish, 3–4 in. long, rusty beneath. Flowers small, white, in short-stalked clusters in the leaf-axils.* Corolla scarcely ⅓ in. long. Fruit a small, egg-shaped berry. (*Palaquium* is a Latinized version of a Philippine Island vernacular for one of the species.)

**PALE CORYDALIS** = *Corydalis sempervirens*.

**PALE LAUREL** = *Kalmia polifolia*.

**PALIURUS** (pal-i-your′us). A small genus of Eurasian, usually spiny shrubs or small trees of the family Rhamnaceae,

**P. spina-cristi**, the Christ's-thorn or Jerusalem thorn, sometimes cult. more for legendary interest than ornament. By some it is supposed to be the plant from which the Crown of Thorns was made. It is a shrub or small tree 10–20 ft. high, with both hooked and straight spines. Leaves alternate,* ovalish, 1–1½ in. long, prominently 3-veined and finely toothed on the margin. Flowers very small, greenish-yellow, in small clusters (cymes*). Fruit nearly 1 in. in diameter, brownish-yellow, leathery. Southern Eu. to northern China. June–July. Hardy from zone* 5 southward. It is easily grown in open, sunny places, preferably in well-drained soil. (*Paliurus* is the old Greek name for these plants.)

*PALLIDA, -us, -um* (pal′lid-a). Pale.

**PALM.** Decorative foliage plants, widely grown both in greenhouses and outdoors in suitable climates, for their striking habit and beautiful leaves. As usually cult. their flowers and fruits are of secondary interest and are often not produced at all. As hort. subjects they lend themselves to all sorts of fine groupings, both outdoors as in Calif. and Fla., and as florists' pot or tub plants for indoor ornament.

There is no need to repeat here the kinds and characters of all the palms entered in THE GARDEN DICTIONARY. A complete list of the genera and an account of the characters of the family will be found at the next entry, PALMACEAE.

Coconut palms in Florida

Of the 45 genera which appear to represent the leading palms in cult. in the U.S. many are little known or rarely grown and will not be dealt with here. The ones below have been selected because of their availability, their ability to stand cultivation, and their decorative value. The list includes the most important palm genera in cult. here, and all are entered in their proper alphabetical sequence. Those with a † are also widely grown by florists for indoor decoration, and usually make good house plants, or are used as tubbed specimens for porches or patios.

FAN PALMS (*i.e.* THE LEAVES PALMATE*)

| | |
|---|---|
| †Chamaerops | Serenoa |
| Coccothrinax | Thrinax |
| †Livistona | Trachycarpus |
| Rhapidophyllum | Washingtonia |
| Sabal | |

---

* Special articles on the subjects indicated by an asterisk (*) will be found at the words so marked.

FEATHER PALMS (*i.e.* THE LEAVES PINNATE\*)

| | |
|---|---|
| Actinophloeus | †Hedyscepe |
| Archontophoenix | †Howea |
| †Arecastrum | †Phoenix |
| Caryota | Pseudophoenix |
| †Chamaedorea | Roystonea |
| †Chrysalidocarpus | †Syagrus |
| Cocos | |

There are, also, especially attractive palms to be found in the genera *Balaka, Ceroxylon, Erythea, Jubaea,* and *Latania*, but most of them are more cult. outdoors than in the greenhouse.

Of the few palms native in the U.S. only *Sabal* and *Washingtonia* are outstanding hort. subjects, the first being commonly planted from N. Car. to the Gulf, while *Washingtonia* is a valuable Californian native plant widely grown there for avenue planting and as a specimen on the lawn. In Fla. another native palm, *Pseudophoenix vinifera,* is widely planted for ornament, while *Serenoa*, also a native, is less popular. Other native palms for outdoor cult. will be found in the genera *Thrinax* and *Coccothrinax*.

Within the U.S. the coconut palm is of no economic importance. It is somewhat planted in Fla. but only for ornament. Its real home is in the Old World tropics and the commercial exploitation of it is chiefly in regions warmer than any part of the U.S. (*see* COCONUT). The only cult. palm of real economic importance in the U.S. is the date palm (*Phoenix dactylifera*). See DATE. There are also valuable decorative palms in the genus *Phoenix*, especially *P. canariensis* which is widely planted in Calif. for ornament.

While the outdoor cult. of most palms must be limited to frost-free regions, there are certain of them that will stand occasional frosts and such relatively hardy palms are much planted. The chief genera containing such plants are *Brahea, Chamaedorea, Chamaerops, Coccothrinax, Erythea, Jubaea, Sabal, Serenoa, Trachycarpus,* and *Washingtonia*. *Sabal*, particularly, contains species hardy as far north as the coast of N. Car., and the only palm native in Eu., *Chamaerops humilis,* is perhaps the hardiest of all palms. Not one of these, however, is really hardy north of zone\* 6 in the East.

INDOOR CULTURE. Outdoors any of the palms cult. in the U.S. will ultimately produce a trunk, flowers, and fruit, but as cult. in the greenhouse or as house plants, they rarely, if ever, do so. In other words, practically all palms in the greenhouse are cult. only in the juvenile state. Of these the feather palms in the genera *Chrysalidocarpus, Howea, Phoenix,* and *Syagrus* are by far the most important. For many people these constitute all the palms they ever see because these contain the palms one sees in the florists' windows. And of these, two species of *Howea*, commonly called *Kentia*, are probably the most widely cult. palms in America.

For the culture of *Chrysalidocarpus* (and of *Areca* and *Arenga*) see CHRYSALIDOCARPUS. For the culture of many other genera, which require less heat than *Chrysalidocarpus*, the best greenhouse temperature is 55°–60° at night, and about 10° warmer during the day. Use potting mixture\* 4 and be careful not to use too large a pot. A common fault among householders is to over-pot palms, thus reducing their chances of continuous growth and inviting too great an accumulation of water in the pot. This results in slacking of growth and often leads to yellowing of the foliage.

The ideal should be to keep all potted palms on the edge of being pot-bound.\* Water them freely during their most active growing season (April–Oct.), but reduce the amount of water during the winter when most palms are merely marking time. This is especially true of house palms, which due to relative darkness are practically dormant. Such plants need only just enough water to keep from drying out. After all danger of frost is passed, all house palms are better plunged\* outdoors, in the shade, and then they should be watered liberally; every third week with liquid manure (which see).

In the greenhouse most of the commonly cult. palms need the glass shaded, either by paint or by roller shades, as most palms will burn badly if exposed to the sun through clear glass.

A mature specimen of the dwarf fan palm (*Chamaerops humilis*), one of the hardiest of all palms

For those who may not know the different genera of palms the list below may be useful in identifying any particular one known only by its common name. It includes most of the common cult. palms of the U.S. and all will be found at their proper generic names in the body of THE GARDEN DICTIONARY. To save space the word palm is omitted in the list, but it applies to most of them; *i.e.* Betel = Betel palm.

African hair = *Chamaerops*
African oil = *Elaeis*
Areca = usually *Chrysalidocarpus*
Australian fan = *Livistona*
Betel = *Areca*
Bitter-stem = *Hyophorbe*
Bluestem = *Sabal*
Bottle = *Hyophorbe*
Buccaneer = *Pseudophoenix*
Cabbage = *Sabal, Roystonea, Pseudophoenix*
California fan = *Washingtonia*
Cane = *Chrysalidocarpus*
Chinese fan = *Livistona*
Cluster = *Actinophloeus*
Coconut = *Cocos*
Cohune = *Attalea*
Coquito = *Jubaea*
Curly = *Howea*
Date = *Phoenix*
European fan = *Chamaerops*
Everglade = *Acoelorraphe*
Fiji fan = *Pritchardia*
Fish-tail = *Caryota*
Flat = *Howea*
Fountain = *Livistona*
Gachipaes = *Guilielma*
Gomuti = *Arenga*
Ground rattan = *Rhapis*
Guadalupe = *Erythea*
Hemp = *Trachycarpus*
Hog cabbage = *Pseudophoenix*
Jaggery = *Arenga, Caryota*
Kentia = *Howea*
Kittul = *Caryota*
Mexican blue = *Erythea*
Monkey-coconut = *Jubaea*
Needle = *Rhapidophyllum*
Nikau = *Rhopalostylis*
Palma dulce = *Brahea*
Palmetto = *Sabal, Thrinax, Coccothrinax*
Palmiste = *Roystonea*
Panama-hat = *Carludovica* (not a palm)
Pejibaye = *Guilielma*
Pignut = *Hyophorbe*
Pindo = *Butia*
Plumy coconut = *Arecastrum*
Porcupine = *Rhapidophyllum*
Queen = *Arecastrum*
Raffia = *Raphia*
Royal = *Roystonea*
Sabal = *Sabal*
Sagisi = *Heterospathe*
Sago = *Cycas* (not a palm)
Sargent = *Pseudophoenix*
Saw-cabbage = *Acoelorraphe*
Saw palmetto = *Serenoa*
Silvertop palmetto = *Coccothrinax*
Spindle = *Hyophorbe*
Sugar = *Arenga*
Thatch = *Coccothrinax, Thrinax*
Toddy = *Caryota*
Umbrella = *Hedyscepe*
Wax = *Ceroxylon*
Wild date = *Phoenix*
Windmill = *Trachycarpus*
Wine = *Caryota, Jubaea*

\* Special articles on the subjects indicated by an asterisk (\*) will be found at the words so marked.

INSECT PESTS. Palms in greenhouses are attacked by mealybugs and by several varieties of scale insects. Lubricating-oil emulsion, diluted 1–65, and miscible oils have given good control of both mealybugs and scales. Calcium cyanide fumigation is also useful. Outdoors, palms suffer less from pests. (See COCONUT, which is a species of palm.)

**PALMACEAE** (pal-may'see-ee). The palm family, sometimes called the Arecaceae, are the most distinctive and noble foliage plants of the tropics. They range from stemless plants of pot culture to the magnificent royal palm (*Roystonea*) which, in many tropical cities, notably in Rio de Janeiro, makes imposing avenues of feathery foliage. While their hort. uses are extensive their economic importance is still greater, notably the coconut (*Cocos*), the date (*Phoenix*), and the African oil palm (*Elaeis*). Many other palms are of wide use in the arts and industries for fiber, food, drugs, resins, wood, etc., and are also cult. for ornament. Among these are species of *Arenga, Butia, Caryota* (the fish-tail palms), and *Raphia* (raffia).

The great mass of its 140 genera and more than 1200 species are real denizens of the tropics, but some of the cult. genera will stand considerable frost (see PALM).

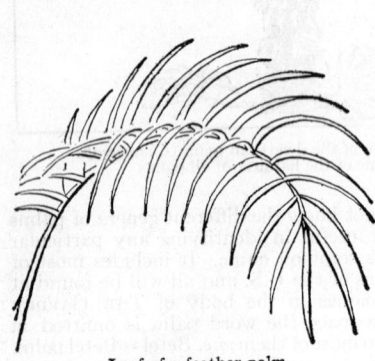

Leaf of a feather palm

All the palm family are easily (but not technically) divided into two groups by their leaves—the feather palms, with pinnate (*i.e.* arranged feather-fashion) leaflets, and the fan palms, with palmate (*i.e.* arranged finger-fashion) leaflets or segments to the otherwise undivided leaf. In both sorts the leaf is usually long-stalked.

The fan palms in the remaining hort. genera (not including those already mentioned) are: *Brahea, Chamaerops, Coccothrinax, Erythea, Latania, Livistona* (the chief fan palm of the florists), *Pritchardia, Rhapidophyllum, Rhapis, Sabal, Serenoa, Thrinax, Trachycarpus, Trithrinax* and *Washingtonia*. All the rest of the cult. genera (not including those already mentioned) are feather palms, of which the outstanding genera for decorative use by florists are: *Arecastrum, Chrysalidocarpus, Howea* (usually called *Kentia*), *Syagrus,* and some (not the date) species of *Phoenix*.

Most palms have a single trunk with a crown of leaves at the top. Some of these leaves are of huge size (65 ft. long) in their native regions, but much smaller in cult. Large-leaved feather palms

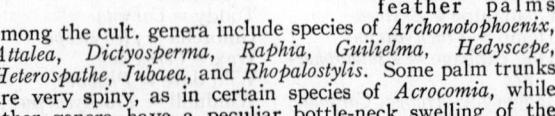

Leaf of a fan palm

among the cult. genera include species of *Archonotophoenix, Attalea, Dictyosperma, Raphia, Guilielma, Hedyscepe, Heterospathe, Jubaea,* and *Rhopalostylis*. Some palm trunks are very spiny, as in certain species of *Acrocomia*, while other genera have a peculiar bottle-neck swelling of the trunk, as in *Hyophorbe*. The rattan palms (*Calamus*), scarcely in cult. in America, are climbing vines with stems, in Ceylon, hundreds of feet long.

Because of their beauty and decorative value there is no limit to the number of palm genera that may be in cult. in America. Some special collections (see Brett and the Montgomery collections at ARBORETUM) have a tremendous variety. But for most gardeners in Fla. or Calif., or the Gulf Coast between them, the genera so far mentioned and the few to follow constitute the chief plants of interest in the palm family. The remaining genera (all feather palms) are: *Acoeloraphe, Actinophloeus, Areca, Balaka, Chamaedorea, Ceroxylon, Hydriastele, Martinezia, Ptychosperma,* and *Pseudophoenix*.

The individual flowers of the palms are small and inconspicuous, but the cluster in which they are normally crowded is often large and handsome. Typically this unopened cluster is enclosed between sheathing bracts* (a spathe*) from which it issues at blooming time. The spathe may be persistent, woody, and boat-shaped in some genera. Flowers perfect* or unisexual,* with 3 petals and 3 sepals, or the 6 indistinguishable as either, generally greenish or yellowish. Stamens usually 6, but many more in some genera, notably *Howea*. Ovary superior,* 3-celled. Fruit various, often a very hard nut or fleshy (see COCOS).

Because few greenhouse palms ever produce either flowers or a trunk their exact identification is most difficult. The technical characters in this family are mostly in the flowers and fruit, neither of which is normally produced until the plant has grown a trunk. For cult. and hort. uses see PALM.

**PALMA CHRISTI** = *Ricinus communis*. See CASTOR-OIL PLANT.

**PALMA DULCE** = *Brahea dulcis*.

**PALMA SAMANDOCA** = *Samuela carnerosana*.

*PALMATA, -us, -um* (pal-may'ta). Palmate.*

**PALMATE.** With leaflets, or with the lobes or veins of a simple leaf, radiating from one point. *Digitate* and *palmate* are often used interchangeably, *digitate* being more often applied to leaflets, as in the horse-chestnut, and *palmate* to the lobes or veins of a simple leaf, as in a maple. See PINNATE.

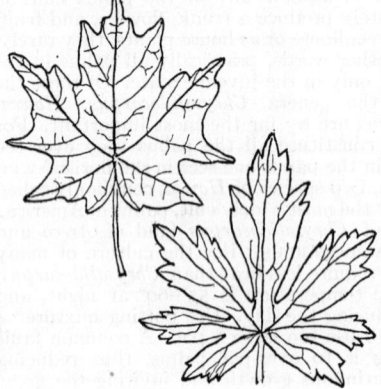

Palmate leaves, showing the palmate arrangement of veins (*left*) and leaf lobes (*right*).

**PALMERELLA** (pal-mer-rel'la). A small genus of perennial herbs of the family Lobeliaceae, found in Mex. and southern Calif., P. debilis sometimes cult. in the border for ornament, but of uncertain hardiness in the North. It is a slender herb, 1–2 ft. high, with alternate,* narrow leaves, 2–3 in. long, and without marginal teeth. Flowers tubular, about ¾ in. long, the tube white, the 2-lipped* limb bluish, the cluster a terminal raceme.* Fruit a capsule. The *var*. serrata has sharply toothed leaves. (Named for Dr. Edward Palmer, American botanist.)

*PALMETTO* (pal-met'to). A variant of the Spanish *palmito,* a little palm. See SABAL. For the saw or scrub palmetto see SERENOA. For the silvertop palmetto see THRINAX and COCCOTHRINAX. For the cabbage palmetto see SABAL.

---

* Special articles on the subjects indicated by an asterisk (*) will be found at the words so marked.

**PALM FAMILY** = Palmaceae.

**PALM GRASS** = *Setaria palmifolia*.

*PALMIFOLIA, -us, -um* (pal-mi-fō'li-a). With palm-like leaves.

**PALMISTE** = *Roystonea oleracea*.

**PALO-VERDE** = *Cercidium torreyanum*.

*PALUSTRIS, -e* (pa-lus'tris). Growing in a marsh.

**PAMPAS GRASS.** See CORTADERIA.

**PAN.** See FLOWER POTS.

**PANAMA-HAT PLANT** = *Carludovica palmata*.

**PANAMA ORANGE** = *Citrus mitis*.

**PANAMA RHUBARB.** See RHUBARB.

**PANAX** (pay'nacks). Perennial Asiatic or North American herbs of the family Araliaceae, their only hort. interest being that two of the species yield ginseng and another is a delicate little spring-blooming plant for the wild garden. They have stout, sometimes forked rootstocks (the ginseng "root" in the first two species), and compound* leaves, the leaflets arranged finger-fashion and toothed. Flowers small, greenish or white, unisexual* or polygamous,* the petals 5. Fruit berry-like. (*Panax* is from the Greek for all-healing, in allusion to the reputed medicinal value of the ginseng.)

For the culture of the first two species *see* GINSENG. The third species is native in the U.S. and needs a shady, moist place in the wild garden with good, rich woods (not too acid) soil.

**quinquefolium.** Ginseng (of America). A smooth herb 10-18 in. high, the rootstock spindle-shaped and often forked. Leaflets 5, oblongish, 3-5 in. long, thin and sharply toothed. Flower cluster (umbel*) solitary. Fruit red, about ½ in. in diameter. June. Quebec to N.Y. and southward in the mountains to Ga., west to Mo. For cult. *see* GINSENG.

**schinseng.** Ginseng (of China). An Asiatic representative of the above, and perhaps not distinct from it, but with leaves more finely toothed. Manchuria and Korea. For cult. *see* GINSENG.

**trifolium.** Dwarf ginseng (it yields no ginseng). A slender, perennial herb, not over 4 in. high, the rootstock globular. Leaflets 3-5, usually 3, ovalish and stalkless, not over 1 in. long. Flowers very small, white, the globe-shaped cluster (umbel*) usually solitary and long-stalked. Fruit 3-angled, yellow. Nova Scotia to Ga. and westward, mostly in moist wood. Suited only to the wild gardens.

**PANCRATIUM** (pan-kray'shĭ-um). Little-known, bulbous, Old World herbs of the family Amaryllidaceae, with mostly narrow, strap-shaped, basal leaves. Of the 14 known species only **P. maritimum** of the Mediterranean region is likely to be much cult. It has a globe-shaped bulb which tapers into a neck,* from which arise the bluish-green leaves that are about 2 ft. long. Flowers white, lily-like, fragrant, 5-10 in a terminal cluster (umbel*) on a stout, solid, somewhat flattened stalk. Fruit a 3-valved capsule.* The culture of *P. maritimum* is the same as for amaryllis (which see). For the plant sometimes offered as *P. calathinum*, *see Hymenocallis calathina* at SPIDER-LILY. (*Pancratium* is from the Greek for all-powerful, in reference to reputed medicinal value of some species.)

**PANDANACEAE** (pan-dan-nay'see-ee). The screw pine family comprises only one hort. genus, *Pandanus*, which see for the characters of the cult. Pandanaceae.

**PANDANUS** (pan-day'nus). Screw pine. A large genus of chiefly Indo-Malayan shrubs or trees of the family Pandanaceae, only a very few of its 250 species cult. for ornament, but two of them very popular as house plants and widely grown by florists. In maturity they have a distinct trunk, but as cult. for pot plants this is rarely developed. Many large tubbed specimens in greenhouses and outdoor plants in the South develop considerable trunks, but in the tropics these plants may well be 30-60 ft. high in some species and palm-like in the huge, terminal crown of leaves which in most species, especially in maturity, are conspicuously spirally arranged. In some species there are large prop roots, especially in old specimens. Flowers (rare in cult. specimens) without petals or sepals, the naked pistils* and stamens* separate and scattered over the cluster (mostly heads* or spikes*). Fruit aggregate,* often ball-like or cone-like, and heavy. (*Pandanus* is a Latinized version of a Malayan name for some species.)

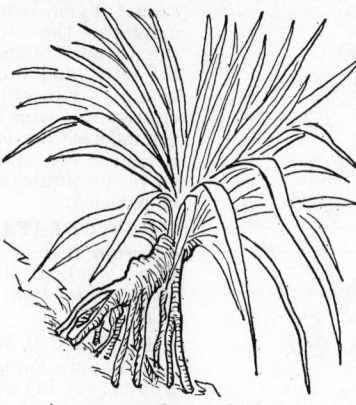

A mature pandanus, with its prop roots

The cult. screw pines, especially *P. veitchi*, are very good house plants. For perfect growth, however, they need a tropical greenhouse, plenty of moisture, and are best grown in potting mixture* 3. In the greenhouse their culture is very much the same as for palms, and do best when the glass is partly shaded. For the household management of *P. veitchi*, one of the most widely grown of florists' plants, *see* HOUSE PLANTS.

**pygmaeus.** A small screw pine, the trunk, if produced, not over 2 ft. high. Leaves 1-2 ft. long, scarcely ⅓ in. wide, spiny on the margins and on the midrib below. Madagascar.

**sanderi.** Possibly only a form of *P. veitchi*, but the leaves narrower and golden-banded instead of silver-banded. It is also a more densely tufted plant than *P. veitchi*. Timor, Dutch East Indies.

**utilis.** In the tropics up to 60 ft. high, its prop roots often arising 15-20 ft. from the ground. Leaves bluish-green, 1-3 ft. long, about 3 in. wide, its spines red. An immense, striking, very spiny Madagascan plant, commonly planted outdoors in frost-free regions, and sometimes in greenhouses.

**veitchi.** A very popular pot or house plant, the leaves 2-3 ft. long, about 2½ in. wide (less in young plants), usually arching, prominently white or silver-banded, spiny-margined. Probably from Polynesia, but its identity, as well as that of the related *P. sanderi*, is still in doubt.

**PANDORANA** = *Pandorea*.

**PANDOREA** (pan-door'ee-a). Tropical Old World, showy, woody vines of the family Bignoniaceae, three of the 5 known species somewhat grown for ornament in zones* 8 and 9. They have opposite,* compound,* evergreen leaves, the leaflets arranged feather-fashion, with an odd one at the end. Tendrils* none. Flowers pink or white, the corolla funnel-shaped. Stamens* 4, not protruding. Fruit an oblong pod, its seeds winged. (*Pandorea* and *pandorana* are both derived from Pandora, the sister of Prometheus.)

The pandoreas are not much grown in the U.S. They need an open, sunny site, rich, well-drained soil, and may be propagated from greenwood cuttings under glass. Not hardy north of zone* 7.

**jasminoides.** Bower plant. Leaflets 5-9, practically stalkless, ovalish or narrower, 1-2 in. long. Flowers white, or pinkish in the throat, 1½-2 in. long, the lobes of the corolla scalloped. Australia. Sometimes known as *Tecoma jasminoides*.

**pandorana.** Wonga-wonga. Leaflets 3-9, elliptic or ovalish, 1-2½ in. long. Flowers white or yellowish-white, but violet-spotted in the throat, not over ¾ in. long, but showy from the profuse clusters. Australia. Also offered as *Tecoma australis*.

**ricasoliana.** Leaflets 7-10, short-stalked, ovalish, about 1 in. long. Flowers about 2 in. long, pink but red-striped. Pod 10-12 in. long. South Africa. Sometimes offered as *Tecoma ricasoliana*.

*PANDURATA, -us, -um* (pan-dure-ray'ta). Fiddle-shaped.

**PANIC GRASS.** See PANICUM.

**PANICLE.** A loose, open flower cluster which blooms from the center or bottom toward the edges or top of it.

---

* Special articles on the subjects indicated by an asterisk (*) will be found at the words so marked.

The main stalk (axis) is never terminated by a flower. Strictly, a panicle is a compound raceme.* Typical examples are the oat, the Adam's-needle, the olive, and the catalpa. Flower clusters in which the inflorescence is a panicle are said to be paniculate or panicled.

Panicle

**PANICULATA, -us, -um** (pan-ick-kew-lay'ta). Panicled. See PANICLE.

**PANICUM** (pan'i-kum). Panic grass. A large genus of annual or perennial grasses found in all parts of the world, but mostly in the tropics. They are of creeping or erect habit, and vary considerably in height and the size of the leaves. The flowers are usually in light feathery clusters, in which the upper flowers are fertile and the lower flowers rarely so. (*Panicum* is from an old Latin name for Italian millet.)

A few of these grasses are grown for grain or fodder and occasionally for ornament (*see* DRIED FLOWERS). Propagated from seeds, but the perennials may be divided. Annuals can be used in the garden. Sow in patches ⅛ in. deep, in early spring, thinning plants out when 1 in. high to 3 in. apart. Perennials may be divided in Oct.

**barbinode.** Pará grass. Strong-growing perennial, which has both creeping and erect stems, the creeping ones rooting in the soil at every joint and spreading 10–20 ft., the erect stems growing to 10 ft. Leaves to 1½ ft. long and ½ in. wide, rough edge, more or less hairy. Flower clusters 8–12 in. long. Used as forage in the tropics.

**maximum.** Guinea grass. Perennial growing to 8 ft., in bunches. Stems stout. Leaves to 2 ft. long, ½ in. wide with light central vein. The flower clusters 1–2 ft. are arranged in spreading whorls, the clusters shiny. Used for forage in the South. Africa.

**miliaceum.** Millet. Broomcorn millet. Annual, 3–4 ft. high. Leaves to 10 in. long, 1 in. wide, soft. Flower clusters of drooping habit, about 1 ft. long, the stalks slender and crowded. The smooth, shiny seed is almost white. Cultivated from earliest times for fodder and grain. East Indies.

**texanum.** Texas millet. Colorado grass. Annual, to 3 ft., of creeping habit and softly hairy. Stems stout, to 4 ft. high. Leaves 6–8 in. long, about ¾ in. wide. Flowers in one-sided, crowded clusters. It is not much cultivated. Tex.

**virgatum.** Switch grass. Strong perennial, to 6 ft. high. Leaves 12–15 in. long, ½ in. wide, with rough margins. Flower clusters to 18 in. long, the stalks spreading. Sometimes grown as an ornamental grass. Me. to Central America.

*PANNOSA, -us, -um* (pan-nō'sa). Tattered.

**PANS.** See FLOWER POTS.

**PANSY.** (*Viola tricolor hortensis.*) Pansies are universal favorites, their adaptability to the large and small gardens making them one of the most useful plants in cult. They may be planted as edging plants, or in masses of mixed or separate colors, in the flower border or in beds. Used as a ground cover between roses or tulips they make a beautiful display from mid-April to June, some excellent color combinations being made this way. Planting between tulips should be done early in Oct., tulips should, however, be planted first, then the pansies 8 in. apart. They will then make a complete carpet the following spring, without injury to the bulbs which will grow up through them.

VARIETIES. There are many excellent varieties on the market, some of the best for size and substance being of American origin, Calif. and N.J. having produced some of the finest strains. It is wise to procure seeds from specialists as home-saved seeds soon degenerate. Unusual strains are Mastodon, strong-growing, with large flowers, beautifully marked and shaded in many colors (Calif.); Ullswater Blue, large flower of cornflower blue with blue-black center (Eng.); Crimson Queen, wall-flower red with dark center. Clear white and yellow forms may be obtained, but pansies are generally admired for their color variations or their waved or frilled petals.

Winter-flowering varieties, where only very slight frosts occur, will flower outside all winter. These can be grown in a cold frame or cool greenhouse. A strong strain with flower stalk to 10 in. and large flowers, for greenhouse cult., has also been distributed recently with great success.

SOILS. Pansies do well in any good garden soil, but prefer cool, moist conditions, their roots never being allowed to become dry at any time. They are best raised from seed every year as the old plants become straggling and the flowers small, often dying completely during the hot summer months. Not allowing seeds to form prolongs the flowering considerably. They are very hardy and will withstand 15° or more, but in northern localities should have a light covering of salt hay or strawy manure from late fall until early spring.

The new crop of seeds is usually obtainable early in Aug. and this is the best time for sowing. If plants are required to bloom the same fall, seed should be sown in July. Prepare a cold frame or seedbed outdoors by digging and well pulverizing soil, leveling with rake and making surface very fine, water thoroughly and allow surface to dry until soil will not cling to the fingers. Then sow seeds thinly, ⅛ in. deep, in rows. This is easily done by making slight depressions with back of iron rake or with a pointed stick. After sowing they should be watered with a fine spray and shaded from strong sunlight until germinated, when the shading should be gradually reduced. This may be done by removing shades from 4 P.M.–10 A.M., thus shading only during the hottest part of the day. Never allow the seeds to become dry. As soon as large enough, transplant to nursery bed or permanent position as the plants must not be allowed to become crowded in the seedbed. Seeds may also be sown in Sept. or early Oct. in a cold frame, but must then remain there during winter, transplanting in the spring.

Pansies root easily from cuttings made from the tips of young shoots, which are produced after the flowering season. The cuttings should be put in a cold frame in ½ sand, ½ soil, keeping sashlights closed, and shaded from strong sunlight for 4 weeks, then admitting light and air gradually. — H. R. M.

DISEASES. Wilt, root rot and leafspot are the common diseases. With *wilt*, affected plants wilt and die suddenly. Discoloration of the stem at the ground line is a typical symptom. When *root rot* is present, the infected plants are stunted, the leaves are yellow and the roots exhibit a black rot. For control, destroy diseased plants and practice crop rotation. *Leafspot* can be controlled by bordeaux spray and by gathering and burning all old leaves in the fall.

**PAPAVER.** See POPPY.

**PAPAVERACEAE** (pap-pa-ver-ray'see-ee). The poppy or bloodroot family contains a few genera of outstanding garden interest. The chief favorite is *Papaver* (see POPPY), but in California it may well be *Platystemon* (see CREAMCUPS), or the California poppy (*Eschscholtzia*), or the beautiful Matilija poppy (*Romneya*). *Sanguinaria* (see BLOODROOT) is a wild garden favorite in the East; *Stylophorum* somewhat less so.

The family contains about 25 genera and over 100 species of herbs (rarely shrubs) that are most common in the north temperate zone. *Argemone* and *Hunnemannia*, however, are largely Mexican, and *Dendromecon* is a Californian shrub. The other cult. genera are *Eomecon, Glaucium, Macleaya* and *Meconopsis*, while *Chelidonium* is somewhat weedy. Most of these plants have a milky juice or colored juice, and alternate* or basal leaves, which are often lobed or divided.

The flowers in most genera are extremely showy, but often wither rapidly when picked, and in some genera the petals fall naturally within a day or two. Fruit a dry pod (capsule*), the juice of the unripe pod of *Papaver somniferum* yielding opium.

Technical flower characters: Flowers regular* and hermaphrodite.* Sepals usually 2, soon falling. Petals 4–6, the margins overlapping, soon

---

* Special articles on the subjects indicated by an asterisk (*) will be found at the words so marked.

falling in many genera, and wrinkled in some. Stamens* many. Ovary superior.* Style* short or none.

**PAPAW** = *Carica papaya* and *Asimina triloba*.

*PAPAYA* (pap-py′ya). Tropical American vernacular for the papaw. See CARICA.

**PAPERBARK** = *Melaleuca leucadendron*.

**PAPER BIRCH** = *Betula papyrifera*. See BIRCH.

**PAPER BUSH** = *Edgeworthia papyrifera* and *Melaleuca leucadendron*.

**PAPER MULBERRY** = *Broussonetia papyrifera*.

**PAPER MULCH.** See MULCH.

**PAPER POTS.** See FLOWER POTS.

**PAPER TREE** = *Edgeworthia papyrifera*.

**PAPER WHITE.** See NARCISSUS TAZETTA.

**PAPHIOPEDILUM.** See CYPRIPEDIUM.

*PAPILIO* (pap-pill′i-o). A butterfly. See ONCIDIUM.

**PAPILIONACEAE.** See LEGUMINOSAE.

**PAPILIONACEOUS.** Having pea-like flowers. For a description and picture of them see LEGUMINOSAE.

**PAPOOSE-ROOT** = *Caulophyllum thalictroides*.

**PAPPUS.** See COMPOSITAE.

*PAPYRACEA, -us, -um* (pap-i-ray′see-a). Papery.

*PAPYRIFERA, -us, -um* (pap-i-rif′fer-ra). Paper-bearing.

**PAPYRUS** = *Cyperus papyrus*.

**PARADICHLOROBENZENE.** See FUMIGATION.

**PARADISE.** A dwarf variety of apple (*Malus pumila paradisiaca*), used for grafting stock of dwarf apple trees. See APPLE.

**PARADISEA** (par-a-di′see-a). St. Bruno's-lily. Herbaceous, hardy perennials of only one species, belonging to the family Liliaceae and a native of the Pyrenees, Apennines, Alps and Juras. (Origin of name obscure, but believed so named as being worthy of Paradise.)

It is of easy cultivation either from seeds or division. Seeds may be sown in spring in a cool greenhouse or cold frame, and transplanted to partially shaded border of soil rich in leaf mold and decayed cow manure.

liliastrum. Leaves basal, about 12 in. long, narrow. Flowers, 2–10, borne on slender, leafless stem, 12–18 in. high, in loose racemes, the corolla fragrant, white, funnel-shaped, and about 2 in. long. May–June.

**PARADISE-FLOWER** = *Solanum wendlandi*.

*PARADISI, PARADISIACA, -us, -um* (par-a-di-si-ā′ka). Of parks or gardens.

*PARADOXA, -us, -um* (par-a-dock′sa). Strange or paradoxical.

**PARÁ GRASS** = *Panicum barbinode*.

**PARÁ NUT** = *Bertholletia excelsa*.

**PARÁ RUBBER-TREE** = *Hevea brasiliensis*.

**PARASITE.** A plant that steals all its food from another, to which it is attached. No true parasites can therefore be garden plants, although many tree-perching orchids, aroids, ferns, and plants of the pineapple family are often incorrectly called parasites. Actually, they are epiphytes (which see). Parasites are most frequent among the fungi. See PLANT DISEASES, MISTLETOE.

**PARASOL TREE** = *Firmiana simplex*.

*PARDALINA, -us, -um* (par-da-ly′na). Spotted like a leopard.

**PARIS DAISY** = *Chrysanthemum frutescens*.

**PARIS GREEN.** See Stomach Poisons at INSECTICIDES.

**PARKERIACEAE.** See CERATOPTERIS.

**PARKINSON, J.** See Herbals at GARDEN BOOKS.

**PARKINSONIA** (par-kin-sō′nĭ-a). Tropical, usually spiny, shrubs or trees of the pea family, only one of the 5 known species likely to be met. It is the Jerusalem thorn or ratama (or retama), sometimes called the horse bean, and known to science as **P. aculeata,** and probably a native of tropical America. It is grown in zones* 8 and 9 for ornament, and is a tree up to 30 ft., its spines nearly 1 in. long. Leaves thrice-compound,* the ultimate leaflets very numerous, scarcely ¼ in. long, but the whole leaf nearly 12 in. long and drooping. Flowers not pea-like, yellow, fragrant, in clusters 4–6 in. long. Petals 5,* some larger than the others. Fruit a legume,* constricted between the seeds, nearly 5 in. long. The tree, which in the young state makes a good hedge plant, is much grown in Fla. and Calif. (Named for John Parkinson, herbalist.)

**PARMA VIOLET.** See VIOLA ODORATA.

**PARMENTIERA** (par-men-tĭ-ee′ra). A small genus of tropical American shrubs or trees of the family Bignoniaceae, comprising only two species, one of which, **P. cerifera,** the candle tree from Panama, is occasionally planted for ornament in the warmest parts of Fla. (zone* 9). It is a medium-sized, spiny tree with compound* leaves, the 3 leaflets broadest toward the tip, and 1–2 in. long. Flowers funnel-shaped, but slightly irregular, about 3 in. long, white, but with a conspicuous, brownish calyx.* Fruit a hanging, candle-like, smooth, yellowish-white pod, nearly 3–4 ft. long. A striking tree in fruit, but little known in cult. (Named for A. A. Parmentier, French horticulturist.)

**PARNASSIA** (par-nass′i-a). Grass-of-Parnassus. Low-growing herbaceous perennials comprising about 25 species of the family Saxifragaceae, found in wet or damp, and shady places, throughout the northern hemisphere. Growing from 6 in. to 2 ft. high, they have a graceful, showy appearance. Leaves basal, with long stalks, the blades smooth, ovalish or kidney-shaped and green. The flower stalk bears 1 stalkless leaf. Flowers solitary, white or yellow, strongly veined with green. Calyx* of 5 sepals, joined at the base, green. Corolla of 5 petals. Fertile stamens 5, alternating with the petals. Ovary 1-celled, many-seeded. (*Parnassia* was named from Mt. Parnassus.)

Not of much garden interest except for cool, very damp, shady places, such as the sides of bogs, lakes or rivers. Propagated by seeds or division. Seeds should be sown in moist, boggy peat in shady position outdoors in fall or spring.

californica. A Californian representative of a European plant. Height to 16 in. Leaves ovalish, kidney-shaped at base, 1–2 in. long. Leaf on flower stalk above the middle. Flowers 1½ in. across. Mountains of Calif.

caroliniana. Height 1–2 ft. Leaves ovalish, sometimes heart-shaped at base, 1–2 in. long. Leaf on flower stalk clasping, below the middle. Flowers 1½ in. across. This species is the most suitable for cultivation. Swamps and bogs, eastern N.A.

fimbriata. Height to 1 ft. Leaves kidney-shaped, 1–1½ in. long. Leaf on flower stalk partly clasping at middle. Petals fringed. Western N.A.

**PARNASSIACEAE.** See SAXIFRAGACEAE.

**PAROCHETUS** (par-o-key′tus). Attractive herbaceous perennial of trailing habit, of only one species, belonging to the pea family, and a native of the mountains of Asia and East Africa. (*Parochetus* is derived from the Greek for near and a brook, in allusion to its wild habitat.)

communis. Shamrock-pea, blue oxalis. Grows 2–3 in. high, the root-like stems creeping. Leaves compound*; leaflets 3, similar to the shamrock, except that they are marked deeply at the base with a brown crescent and have no stalk. Flowers produced in the leaf-axils,* pea-shaped, upper petal cobalt blue, 2 side petals pink. Fruit a pod, 1 in. long. Propagated by seed sown 1/16 in. deep in light, sandy soil in March or April, or by division of plants in March. Plant out in ordinary garden soil in margins of sunny borders or rockeries. They can also be used for hanging baskets.

**PARROT-BEAK** = *Clianthus puniceus*.

**PARROTIA** (par-rō′tĭ-a). A single species of shrub or small tree of the family Hamamelidaceae, **P. persica,** a native of Persia, and with foliage resembling the witch-hazel. It is not over 20 ft. high, the leaves alternate,* ovalish or oblong, 3–4 in. long, coarsely toothed toward the tip, turning scarlet, orange, or yellow in the fall, and long-persistent. Flowers in dense heads nearly ½ in. in diameter,

---

* Special articles on the subjects indicated by an asterisk (*) will be found at the words so marked.

blooming before the leaves unfold, the head surrounded by rusty-hairy bracts.* Petals none. Fruit an egg-shaped, beaked capsule.* March–April. Hardy from zone* 3 southward. (Named for F. W. Parrot, German naturalist.)

**PARROT'S-BILL** = *Clianthus puniceus*.

**PARROT'S-FEATHER** = *Myriophyllum proserpinacoides*.

**PARROT TULIPS.** An old race of garden tulips with flaked or feathered petals, which are fringed or notched on the edges. *See* Garden Tulips at TULIPA.

**PARSLEY.** This best-known plant for garnishing is the only cult. species of the genus **Petroselinum** (pet-ro-se-ly'-num) of the carrot family, which comprises only 6 species of European herbs. The common parsley, **P. hortense**, is a biennial or soon-failing perennial which should be planted every other year or so to secure a steady supply, though it will sometimes persist without re-planting. It is a much-branched herb, 10–15 in. high, the leaves thrice-compound,* the ultimate segments wedge-shaped, and with crisped margins in one of the commonest hort. forms. Flowers very small, greenish-yellow, in compound umbels* (for details *see* UMBELLIFERAE). Fruits ribbed, about ⅛ in. long. The common parsley is best raised from seed, which, however, is of slow and uncertain germination. The latter can be hastened by soaking the seeds in warm water for a few hours before planting. For family needs only a small patch is required and this can often be started from the roots that are frequently on parsley as purchased from the store. Simply cut off the leaves and plant the roots. Such roots, planted in pots kept on the kitchen window-sill will yield a crop of leaves through the winter, as will well-mulched plants outdoors. The diseases of parsley and their control are the same as for celery (which see). For culture and uses of parsley *see* HERB GARDENING. The *var.* **radicatum**, the turnip-rooted or Hamburg parsley, is a form grown mostly in Eu. for its parsnip-like, much-thickened root. (*Petroselinum* is from the Greek for rock parsley.) The insect pests of parsley are the same as for celery and carrot. See both for methods of control.

**PARSLEY-FERN** = *Cryptogramma acrostichoides*.

**PARSNIP.** The common garden parsnip is the only cult. species of the genus **Pastinaca** (pas-ti-nay'ka), (family Umbelliferae), which comprises about a dozen species of Eurasian biennial or perennial herbs. **P. sativa**, the cult. parsnip, is a strong-scented, robust biennial with a much-thickened taproot, often 10–18 in. long and 3½ in. in diameter at the apex. Stems 3–5 ft. high (at flowering time), branching, grooved and becoming hollow with age. Leaves twice-compound,* the leaflets coarse, ovalish or oblong, usually toothed or lobed or both. Flowers small, greenish-yellow in a large, compound umbel* (for details *see* UMBELLIFERAE). Fruit flattened, ribbed, the margins winged. (*Pastinaca* is from the Latin for food, in allusion to the edible root.)

### PARSNIP CULTURE

As a root crop parsnips require a deep, rich, but not too heavy soil. Stony land or those soils with too much clay or silt are not suited to growing good parsnips. Sandy, but rich, soils produce the best roots.

Seed should be sown as early in the spring as the ground can be worked, as a full season is required for growth, and in any case the parsnip is primarily a fall and winter vegetable. Rows should be about 14 in. apart (more if a tractor or horse cultivator is to be used), and the drills need be no more than ½ in. deep. The seed germinates slowly and poorly so that plenty of seed should be sown to allow the plants to be thinned to about 4½ in. apart. Because germination is so slow it is a good plan to sow radishes in the same drill; they will come up and mark the row long before the parsnips are up. This also allows for one or two cultivations of the soil before the parsnips have germinated.

More than almost any other vegetable parsnips are improved by cold, or even by freezing. They may be harvested all through the fall and some may be left in the ground all winter. But they should be mulched to prevent alternate thawing and freezing, which soon spoils the roots, and to facilitate digging. If it is desired to dig them all up in the late fall, the dug roots can be buried or put in a cold but frost-free pit.

A variety known as the turnip parsnip is only rarely grown in this country, but is comparatively well liked in Eu. It has a turnip-shaped root.

While some people object to the strong taste of parsnips, they are among the most nutritious of the root crops, and their flavor is always better after prolonged cold weather. The plant is thus unsuited to the warmer parts of the country. The best varieties of the common parsnip are Hollow Crown and Guernsey.

INSECT PESTS. A caterpillar sometimes webs up flower heads of seeding parsnip, celery, etc.; arsenicals will control it. Celery and carrot pests often attack parsnip.

DISEASES. Dusting the leaves weekly with copper-lime protects the plants against leafspots, mildew, and white mold, and helps to reduce soft rot of the roots.

**PARSNIP FAMILY** = Umbelliferae.

**PARSONS, S.** *See* America at GARDEN BOOKS.

**PARSONS, S. B.** *See* America at GARDEN BOOKS.

**PARTED.** Cleft or divided nearly, but not quite, to the base; applied mostly to leaves, more rarely to petals.

**PARTERRE.** *See* BEDDING.

**PARTHENIUM** (par-thee'nĭ-um). New World herbs or under-shrubs of the family Compositae, of more economic than garden interest. The only cult. species, **P. argentatum**, the guayule, a native of the southwestern U.S. and adjacent Mex., was once widely and is still somewhat cult. for the pustules of rubber found in its tissue, but guayule is of less economic interest than formerly. It is a much-branched, desert under-shrub, 2–3 ft. high, with alternate,* narrow, silvery leaves 1–2 in. long. Flower heads not over ¼ in. wide, the tiny ray flowers white. The plant has little decorative value, and for commercial cult. the plants are raised from seed and planted in rows 2–3 ft. apart, set out in March. No one should contemplate such a planting with commercial exploitation in mind, for over 30 million dollars have been lost in guayule. It was well known to the Aztecs, but has been largely supplanted by plantation rubber from the East Indies. (*Parthenium* is an old Greek name for a plant with white ray flowers and has been variously applied. It is a specific name at *Chrysanthemum*.)

*PARTHENOIDES* (par-thee-noy'deez, but *see* OÏDES). Like a plant of the genus *Parthenium*.

**PARTHENOCISSUS** (par-thenn-o-sis'sus). All the members of this genus, which is in the grape family and sometimes called *Psedera*, are woody climbers from eastern Asia and N.A. They are grown chiefly for their good foliage and the fact that most of them cling firmly to walls and trees by means of disk-tipped tendrils.* The leaves are alternate* and composed of 3–5 leaflets. Flowers small, inconspicuous, in clusters opposite the leaves. Fruit small, dark blue or almost black. (*Parthenocissus* is from the Greek meaning virgin ivy.)

These vines are widely used on brick, stone or wooden surfaces where they cling firmly and form a dense cover. They are adapted to city conditions and some forms assume brilliant colors in the fall. They are not particular about soil, but grow more vigorously in a fairly moist loam. They may be propagated by seeds, cuttings or layers.

henryana. A handsome but tender species whose leaflets are 1½–3 in. long, narrowly ovate or sometimes broader above the middle, toothed only toward the tip, velvety or bronze above with silvery markings, and reddish beneath. Flowers in slender panicles* 3–6 in. long. Fruit blue. July. China. Possibly hardy from zone* 5 southward. Also known as *Ampelopsis henryana*.

quinquefolia. This species, commonly called Virginia creeper, woodbine or American ivy, is a vigorous, tall-growing vine. Leaflets 5, elliptic to oblong, 2–5 in. long, pointed, toothed. Flowers inconspicuous. Fruit blue-black, bloomy. July. New England to Mexico. Hardy from zone* 3 southward. Also known as *Ampelopsis quinquefolia*. Leaves become scarlet in the fall; *var.* **engelmanni**, a form with smaller leaves; *var.* **hirsuta**, young growth usually hairy and red when young, leaves hairy beneath;

---

* Special articles on the subjects indicated by an asterisk (*) will be found at the words so marked.

*var.* **saint-pauli,** leaflets oblong-obovate with spreading teeth, the young growth hairy; short rootlets sometimes appear on the branches.

**tricuspidata.** Boston ivy or Japanese ivy. Climbs high and clings firmly. Leaves either of 3 leaflets or simple* and 3-lobed, to 10 in. long, usually shiny on both sides. Flowers inconspicuous. Fruit blue-black, bloomy. July. Japan and China. Hardy from zone* 3 southward. Also known as *Ampelopsis tricuspidata.* Hardy and ornamental; foliage colors well in the fall; *var.* **lowi,** a form with leaves ¾–1½ in. long, simple or with 3 leaflets; of slower and more restrained growth, not dense; *var.* **purpurea,** leaves purple; *var.* **veitchi,** smaller leaves, purple when young.

**vitacea.** This species does not have the adhesive disks on the tendrils and is usually low and rambling. Leaflets 5, elliptic to oblong, 2–5 in. long, toothed. Flowers yellowish, inconspicuous. Fruit blue-black, bloomy. June. New England to Tex. Hardy from zone* 2 southward. Also known as *Ampelopsis vitacea.*

**PARTRIDGE-BERRY.** See MITCHELLA.

*PARVIFLORA, -us, -um* (par-vi-flow′ra). Small-flowered.

*PARVIFOLIA, -us, -um* (par-vi-fō′lĭ-a). Small-leaved.

**PASPALUM** (pas′pa-lum). Annual or perennial grasses comprising about 150 species of the grass family, found throughout temperate and warmer regions of the world, but mostly in America. The flowering spikelets are arranged in 1-sided racemes.* (*Paspalum* is from the old Greek name for millet.)

These grasses are not of much garden interest, although their other uses are diverse. A few are grown for ornament, while 1 species is sometimes used for lawns in place of Bermuda grass, and yet another is grown for its fodder value in Argentina.

**dilatatum.** A coarse-growing perennial, up to 5 ft. high. Leaves to 1 ft. long, and ½ in. wide. Flowers in loose, 1-sided clusters to 5 in. long. Argentina, but naturalized in the southern states.

**racemosum.** An annual of creeping habit, with stems to 3 ft. high. Leaves 5 in. long, about 1 in. wide. Flowers numerous in clusters 6 in. long. Colombia and Peru.

**PASQUE-FLOWER.** See PULSATILLA.

**PASSIFLORA** (pass-i-flow′ra). The passion-flowers are tendril*-climbing vines, and comprise the only cult. genus of the family **Passifloraceae** (pass-i-flow-ray′see-ee). All but a few of the 300 species are natives of the New World, and several are cult. for ornament, while a few tropical sorts yield edible fruits like the granadilla. Leaves alternate,* stalked, lobed or undivided. Flowers often showy, regular, the 3–5 sepals often petal-like, and sometimes tubular. Petals 3–5, or sometimes none. Within the flower is a usually fringed, often differently colored corona* or crown composed of many free filaments, or sometimes tubular and fringed at the top. Stamens* mostly 5, the filaments* united. Fruit a berry, edible in some. (*Passiflora* is Latin for passion-flower, in allusion to the flowers suggesting the Crucifixion.)

Some of the passion-flowers are handsome, stem-climbing vines (*see* VINES), but useful only from zone* 7 southward, and some of them are really suited only to the warmest regions of the country.

The granadilla and related species which yield widely used tropical fruits are scarcely known outside extreme southern Calif. and Fla., and are not commercially grown in the U.S., as the fruits are too perishable to ship. They make delicious soft drinks and sherbets in tropical countries, and jam and marmalade are also made from them.

The most widely grown of the ornamental sorts is the maypop or wild passion-flower (*P. incarnata*), which is native from Va. to Tex. It is a strong-growing vine, which dies down each winter. Few of the others will stand any frost. All have rather striking flowers.

**alato-caerulea.** A hybrid passion-flower with 3-lobed leaves. Flowers nearly 4 in. wide, fragrant, white outside, pink inside, the crown purple, blue and white. Fruit not edible.

**caerulea.** Leaves 5-lobed, the lobes narrow. Flowers nearly 4 in. wide, pink, but the crown white and purple. Fruit about 1½ in. long, yellow. Brazil. There are forms with even larger flowers, and one known as Constance Elliott has white flowers.

**edulis.** Purple granadilla. Leaves deeply 3-lobed, the lobes toothed. Flowers about 2 in. wide, white, the crown white and purple. Fruit edible, dark purple, nearly 3 in. long. Much grown in the tropics for the fruit. Brazil.

**incarnata.** Maypop or wild passion-flower. The hardiest of the lot. Leaves 3-lobed, the lobes toothed. Flowers 1½–2 in. wide, white, the crown purplish-pink. Fruit edible, yellow, about 1½ in. long. Va. to Fla. and Tex.

**laurifolia.** Yellow granadilla; also called water lemon and Jamaica honeysuckle. Leaves unlobed. Flowers nearly 4 in. wide, white but red-spotted, the crown white and violet. Fruit edible, yellow, 2–3 in. long. Tropical America.

**manicata.** Leaves 3-lobed, the lobes ovalish and toothed. Flowers almost 4 in. wide, scarlet, the crown blue. Fruit yellowish-green, not edible. Northwestern S.A. Cult. for its extremely showy flowers. It climbs to the tops of trees in southern Calif.

**mollissima.** Leaves 3-lobed, the lobes toothed, and the leaf hairy on the under surface. Flowers about 3 in. wide, rose-pink, the tube of the calyx* nearly 5 in. long. Fruit yellow, not edible. Andes.

**quadrangularis.** Granadilla or giant granadilla. The leading passion-flower cult. for its fruit which is greenish-yellow, edible, and nearly 10 in. long. It is a strong-growing vine with winged stems and unlobed leaves. Flowers fragrant, about 3 in. wide, white, the crown purple and white. Tropical America. Often cult. also for ornament. There is a variegated-leaved variety.

**PASSIFLORACEAE.** See PASSIFLORA.

**PASSION-FLOWER.** See PASSIFLORA.

**PASTINACA.** See PARSNIP.

**PASTURE ROSE** = *Rosa carolina.*

*PATAGONICA, -us, -um* (pat-a-gon′i-ka). From Patagonia.

**PATCH BUDDING.** See BUDDING.

*PATENS* (pay′tenz). Spreading.

**PATENTS.** See PLANT PATENTS.

**PATHOGENE.** An organism, usually microscopic, causing disease in plants. The pathogene may be carried by wind, water, animals, or insects. See PLANT DISEASES, VECTOR.

**PATHOLOGY.** See PLANT DISEASES.

**PATHS AND PAVING.** The number, arrangement, length and width of walks in a garden will obviously depend on its plan. If the walks must be narrow, 18 in. is a sufficient width to enable one person to walk comfortably. For two persons a width of about 4 ft. 9 in. is necessary.

Flagstone paving

Garden paths are usually made of grass, flags, slates, bricks, gravel or pebbles.

Where the traffic is not sufficient to wear bare spaces, grass walks in gardens may be attractive, economical to make and not difficult to maintain. Stepping stones, so popular nowadays, were probably used to take up the wear and tear of feet-abrading spaces in the grass, and the transition was not very far to a pavement of flagstones, squared or irregular, with grass or other dwarf plants growing between them. Grass walks through meadows are common

---

* Special articles on the subjects indicated by an asterisk (*) will be found at the words so marked.

in England and may be used here, especially where grass is allowed to grow in order to allow naturalized spring bulbs to ripen.

FLAGS. If flags or slates are laid with mortar joints the best practice is to set them on a bed of concrete 4 in. thick laid over a bed of sand, gravel or cinders 6 in. deep, so that the thickness of the walk construction is 11 to 12 in. or more. The flags (or slates), whether of rectangular or irregular shapes, should be cut so that their joints, although they may not be quite even, do not have the wide variations permissible in flags laid in the ground with grass or other plants between. Such flags, laid flush with the general surface, are the most generally useful and popular and the least expensive. Considerable variety in the size and shape of the stones adds to the interest of the pattern: but no stone should be laid small enough to rock when trodden on.

Spaces between stones may be very varied in form and width, according to the stones available, and these should not be broken or trimmed more than is really necessary. Skill and patience are necessary to set stones of different thickness on a firm bed with a true upper surface.

If stepping stones only are required, they may be set with their centers 2 ft. 3 in. or less apart. If the flags are rectangular they may be of different sizes, the openings between to be 2–4 in. wide. Concrete* slabs may be used, cast either in the ground or not. It is quite practicable to make a good-looking surface of concrete by using a cinder aggregate and floating off some of the surface cement, and even by adding some flattish pebbles. But to produce a good piece of work of this class requires a skilled and interested workman willing to make experiments.

BRICKS. Bricks may be laid in mortar with a foundation as described for flags. Or they may be laid dry, *i.e.* on a bed of sand or cinders 4 in. or more deep, with or without sand between the joints. A very wide sand joint between bricks (as much as ½ in.) is sometimes desirable, and it is even practicable, by mixing some soil with the sand joint, to grow small plants such as arenarias between or, in shady, damp places, moss. Bricks laid in mortar may be set flat or on edge, but bricks laid dry are better on edge. For garden walks they should be of a good quality dark red and

Stepping stones let into the sod

not too smooth. Bricks are usually laid in walks in rows at right angles to the line of the walk or in a herringbone pattern. In a narrow walk this pattern may be used to advantage with the bricks parallel and at right angles to the walk line. Other and more complex patterns may be worked out by those preferring them.

There are also walks made in "crazy" patterns of bricks or any pieces of stone that can be arranged to make a surface reasonably easy to walk on. Construction as for bricks or flags laid in mortar. The design must depend on the designer and his materials, and it is advisable to piece together an experimental pattern before starting to lay it in mortar.

GRAVEL. Gravel walks (of mixed sand and pebbles) are useful in districts where there are gravels with natural binders. They may be laid 2–3 in. deep, or more, on a broken stone or cinder foundation or on the bare ground. In the latter case, the gravel should be deep enough to prevent the growth of weeds, at least 4 in. or more.

PEBBLE SURFACE. Pebble-surface walks are made of reinforced pebble concrete on a bed of sand or cinders having the surface so manipulated that the close-set pebbles are exposed. While the mortar is still wet, it is treated with a chemical which prevents the surface mortar from setting, so that it can be brushed off, leaving the surface of the stones exposed. It is not advisable to attempt the construction of this kind of walk without the aid of a professional.

Various kinds of oil-bound aggregate walks with specially treated surfaces are found: and anyone interested should consult an expert or one of the companies furnishing the materials.

DRAINAGE. Drainage of garden walks is sometimes important, and this does not differ in principle from that of drives (which see). — H. A. C.

**PATIENTIA** (pay-tee-en'shi-a). Latin for patience; applied to the herb patience (*Rumex patientia*) by Linnaeus.

**PATIO GARDENS.** A patio, in its simplest form, is a hollow square, uncovered, surrounded by the four walls of the house. Variations of the patio, commonly used as a family living room, are found in all hot-climate countries. It is made gay and attractive with potted plants and vines, and cool and refreshing by water trickling in fountains and pools. There may be from one to a dozen or more of these patio gardens opening one into the other, connected by an arch or a door through the wall, like the rooms of a house. Rarely are they built upon the same level, a step or two leading either up or down. This form of architectural gardening was introduced into the southwestern United States by the Spaniards, after their conquest of Mexico.

Due to the present-day vogue of penthouses, set-backs, open-air cafés, and small, city backyard gardens, this type of gardening, so suited to California and the South, is adaptable in modified form for the North and Middle West. All gardens should harmonize with their surroundings, regardless of where situated, but the planting schemes, some of the plants, the tiled and pebbled pavings, the fountains, the pots, and many of the ornamental accessories of these southern-type gardens, fit easily and naturally into small spaces. If desired, brick or stepping stones might be substituted for tile, apple or pear trees for orange trees, and hardy shrubs for oleanders and crape myrtle. Frost-proof tile now is being made in this country, as is also ornamental iron for grille work.

Grass in a hot, dry climate is a luxury, and seldom looks well, but the ground may be covered instead with a paving of black and white pebbles, tiles, cobblestones or flags. Colored pebbles, in harmonizing tints, also may be skillfully combined with architectural details. They come in a variety of colors such as Belgian black, red and yellow verona, emerald and oak-leaf green, mother-of-pearl, jet black, and pure white. Pebbles used in the making of paths should be set in cement, never left loose to roll under foot, while those used for conventionalized designs are kept in position in the beds by means of steel or wood curbings. If preferred, a ground cover may be clipped close, to resemble grass.

Pansies, violets, myrtle, portulaca, sedums, crassula, dwarf cotoneasters, English ivy, or *Lippia canescens* are all desirable plants for this purpose. Space for soil beds is usually totally absent or very limited. This introduced the

---

* Special articles on the subjects indicated by an asterisk (*) will be found at the words so marked.

custom of placing plants in individual containers at strategic points. If flowering plants are used they can be shifted around for different color effects and are easily replaced with fresh ones when the blossoms fail.

If soil beds are to be used, a good plan is to have four paths start at the center of the patio at right angles to each other, thus forming four rectangles. These may be subdivided in the same manner, if the garden is a large one, and so on. Plantings may be in true Oriental manner, all types of plants and colors mixed together, or in the more formal French and English fashion. A vivid effect can be obtained by the use of annuals such as the larkspur, African marigolds, candytuft, nigella, *Phlox drummondi*, nasturtium, blue salvia, verbena and certain of the California wild flowers, such as lupines, godetias, clarkia, nemophila, cream-cups and California poppies in shades of pink, rose, cream and the original golden-yellow. The beds might be edged with spring bulbs, such as *Tulipa clusiana* and *T. kaufmanniana*, or freesias, crocus and scilla.

Another good planting scheme is to place a shrub or small tree in the center of each bed and cover the ground with low-growing foliage plants, or even a ground cover of English ivy, creeping juniper, or some other shade-tolerant plant. For a four-bed planting, two shrubs of one kind and two of another might be placed diagonally across from each other; a variety of the Indian hawthorn, *Raphiolepis delacouri*, with pale pink blossoms, is especially recommended in combination with camellias, or streptosolen, with its wealth of small, trumpet-shaped flowers of reddish-yellow. Gardenias and rosebushes, unpruned, especially tea roses and small-sized wild lilacs (*Ceanothus*), are also good in conjunction with each other. For a very small patio garden a single tree or shrub is planted, usually in the center, for accent. The tamarisk is one of the most beautiful as well as one of the most useful shrubs for this purpose. Against soft-toned plaster walls it resembles a mist of green and rose, with its feathery leaves and flowers, withstands salt spray and makes an excellent windbreak. For general utility purposes *Pittosporum tobira*, with small, fragrant, white blossoms resembling daphne, is generally satisfactory. It blooms in winter when flowers are scarce, has beautiful rich foliage and prunes well. The beds are edged, as a rule, with tile or brick, although box may be preferred. Garden paths may be of pebbles, tile, hard-trodden earth or stepping stones, this latter especially in northern localities.

The center square of a patio garden usually contains a well, pool, or fountain, without which it would not be complete. It is made of cement, tiles, generally Talavera or maiolica, or of painted wood lined with tile in a contrasting color, and the shape and size are optional with the whim of the owner. Aquatics are sometimes planted directly in the pool, and potted plants in gay tile or clay containers are grouped around the curbing or set upon the ledge. Tropical water lilies in shades of rose, cerise, pink, yellow and white, both the day- and night-blooming sorts, may be used in the large pools, but the tendency in the smaller ones is to leave the surface of the water clear. Tiny little pools are often sunk at the intersections of paths, with a rim of polychrome tile rising a few inches above the surface. The water spouts up from the center and falls back into the pool itself.

Other pools are built high on pedestals which may stand two or even three or more feet above the ground, the water overflowing from the basin being carried off in shallow-tiled or cement channels. The walls which surround the wells are usually two and a half to three feet high and either circular, six- or eight-sided. They are made of whitewashed brick, tiles, or painted wood, usually with a maiolica rim made all in one piece, known as "brocales." Wall fountains are set into niches or built into tiled panels, occasionally directly into the garden wall itself. Heads of animals, flowers, and modernistic designs are cast in bronze or carved and used as water spouts.

Swimming pools are now becoming a part of many large patios, with the bathhouse and background forming a decorative part of the garden itself. The best of these have the rim flush with the ground, with the water level just a few inches below. They are usually lined with colored tile. The walks around the pool may be of the same paving as the rest of the patio, with small-sized trees, such as orange trees, flowering crabapples and cherries, or fragrant-leaved shrubs forming the background. Green hedges planted close to the pool side will serve to darken the color of the water, while tall-growing, white flowers (in tubs, to secure a succession of bloom) will serve to lighten the color. Colored lights are often used for night effects. A garden house is often built near the pool, although not necessarily in connection with it.

Next to tiles the most characteristic feature of any patio garden is the potted plants. They are used as accents,* to outline a pool or the beds and borders of walks; they encircle the well-tops, stand singly on stairways, hang from the balconies around the patio, and grace the *balcóns* above the street; they are placed casually against a green bit of shrubbery, march across the rooftops in serried ranks, and stand in close formation on the pavement tiles. In other words, wherever there is a level spot or a niche in the garden walls. Aside from the purely decorative, their most useful purpose is as fillers-in. This applies to both North and South, as one can move them about and compose a brilliant garden today and a cool green one for tomorrow. Color schemes may be built around the flower pots, such as pale blue patio walls, clothed with espalier orange trees, black-and-white-tiled flooring, and blue-and-white-tiled pots filled with orange zinnias. Tree ferns with delicate fronds like lace, dwarf palms, heliotrope, azaleas, calla lilies, tuberoses, myrtle, rose geranium, and bamboo and papyrus are grown in pots for a variety of purposes.

Hedges of living plants, rather than walls of tile or cement, are often used to divide the patios one from the other, with a door or opening cut through to the next garden. Climbing roses, jasmine, cereus and tall shrubs such as oleanders, crape myrtle, camellias, gardenias and poinsettias are used for this purpose. Box is often allowed to grow unchecked, with pots of bright flowers interspersed at irregular intervals. Sweet olive, although the blossoms are inconspicuous, is an excellent and very fragrant hedge plant, as are also certain of the mimosas and magnolias. *See also* COURTYARD GARDEN. — C. H. M.

**PATTYPAN.** *See* CUCURBITA PEPO MELOPEPO.

**PATULA, -us, -um** (pat'you-la). Spreading.

**PAUCIFLORA, -us, -um** (pau-si-flow'ra). Few-flowered.

**PAUCIFOLIA, -us, -um** (pau-si-fō'li-a). Few-leaved; also, sometimes, small-leaved.

**PAULLINIA** (paul-lin'i-a). A large genus of tropical American and African woody vines of the family Sapindaceae, only P. thalictrifolia of the 140 known species of any hort. interest. While a Brazilian vine of considerable size, it is grown as a greenhouse pot plant and should be kept pinched back to induce plenty of stocky growth and foliage, for which the plant is chiefly grown. Leaves thrice-compound,* 4–9 in. long, the ultimate segments small, bronze-tinted, the whole leaf very feathery and fern-like. Flowers very small, pink, with 4 petals and 4 sepals, mostly unisexual,* and borne in small clusters (corymbs*). Fruit a somewhat fleshy, 3-valved capsule.* A related, non-hort. species yields the famous Brazilian tonic, guaraná. *P. thalictrifolia* needs a tropical greenhouse, plenty of moisture, and should be grown in potting mixture* 4. (Variously credited as named for Simon Paulli, a Danish botanist, or for C. F. Paullini, German botanist.)

**PAULOWNIA** (paul-ō'ni-a). A small group of deciduous Chinese trees of the figwort family (Scrophulariaceae). They are ornamental and vigorous, but only two species can be considered hardy. The leaves are opposite* and variable in size and shape, usually entire,* but sometimes lobed, suggesting the catalpa. The flowers are tubular, resembling the foxglove, white to violet and borne in terminal clusters (panicles*), sometimes before the leaves. Fruit an ovoid,

---

* Special articles on the subjects indicated by an asterisk (*) will be found at the words so marked.

pointed capsule* containing a great many small winged seeds. (Named for Princess Anna Paulowna of the Netherlands.)

The paulownias are handsome trees when in bloom, making good lawn specimens. The flower buds are exposed during winter, and north of Philadelphia they often fail to develop due to frost injury. Plants are sometimes cut to the ground in the spring so that vigorous, large-leaved shoots will be thrown up. They seem to prefer a rich, loamy soil and sheltered situation. Propagation is by seeds, or by stem or root cuttings.

**fortunei.** A sparsely branched tree growing 60–70 ft. Leaves broadly ovate, 6–12 in. long, heart-shaped at base and ending in a slender, pointed tip. Flowers pale lilac with yellow throat, 3 in. long, in erect, terminal clusters. Capsule ovoid, pointed. June. China. Hardy from zone* 5 southward.

**imperialis** = *Paulownia tomentosa*.

**tomentosa.** Tree of 30–50 ft. with thick, stiff branches, rather open in habit and becoming round-topped. Leaves hairy, more or less ovate, entire* or lobed, varying in size from 5–10 in. on ordinary growth, to 2 ft. or more on vigorous shoots. Flowers pale violet, about 2 in. long. May or June. China. Hardy from milder parts of zone* 3 southward. Escaped from cultivation in the eastern states from N.Y. to Ga.; *var.* **lanata**, leaves more densely hairy beneath; *var.* **pallida**, flowers whitish-violet.

**PAUL WOHLERT.** See Japanese Flowering Cherries at PRUNUS.

**PAUROTIS WRIGHTI** = *Acoelorraphe wrighti*.

*PAVIA* (pay′vi-a). A specific name derived from the genus *Pavia*, once used for the buckeye and its relatives. See HORSE-CHESTNUT.

**PAVILION.** See STRUCTURES.

**PAVING.** See PATHS AND PAVING.

*PAVONIA* (pa-vō′ni-a). Evergreen herbs or shrubs, comprising about 150 species of the family Malvaceae, found in the warm and tropical regions of the world. They grow sometimes as high as 20 ft. Leaves alternate,* sometimes cut. Flowers yellow, pink or purple, solitary or in clusters, usually having conspicuous bracts* in united pairs. (Named for J. Pavon, part author of a book on Peruvian and Chilean flora.) For a very different, bulbous plant sometimes known as *Pavonia*, see MORAEA PAVONIA.

They are not of much garden interest, except for a few species, which are used as hothouse plants in the North and grown outdoors in warmer climates. Propagated by seeds or cuttings in early spring, using potting mixture* 4.

**hastata.** Shrubby perennial, growing to 6 ft. high. Leaves halberd-shaped, the margins toothed. Flowers solitary, pink with a dark spot at base of the petals, about 1 in. long. S.A.

**multiflora.** Shrubby perennial. Leaves alternate,* lance-shaped. 6–10 in. long, and narrow, the margins toothed. Bracts* 1½ in. long, narrow and pointed, whorled, covered with red hairs. Flowers purple, 1½ in. long, in terminal clusters. Stamens* 2½ in. long. Brazil.

**spinifex.** Shrub to 20 ft. Stems slender, sparsely branched. Leaves ovalish, slightly hairy on both sides. Flowers yellow, 1 in. long, solitary. Tropical America; naturalized in southern U.S.

*PAVONINA, -us, -um* (pa-vo-ny′na). Like a peacock.

**PAWPAW** = papaw.

**PEA.** For the common garden pea *see* the next main entry. There are many other plants to which pea has been applied, or where it is part of their name. Those in THE GARDEN DICTIONARY and their proper equivalents are:

**Asparagus pea** = *Psophocarpus tetragonolobus*; **Black pea** (*see* LATHYRUS); **Butterfly pea** (*see* CENTROSEMA and CLITORIA); **Chick-pea** (*see* CICER); **Glory-pea** (*see* CLIANTHUS); **Pigeon pea** = *Cajanus cajan*; **Rosary pea** = *Abrus precatorius*; **Sweet pea** = *Lathyrus odoratus* (*see* SWEET PEA); **Winged pea** = *Lotus tetragonolobus*.

There are also many others, some of them of minor importance. See also the genera LATHYRUS, PISUM, VIGNA, and DOLICHOS.

**PEA.** The garden pea is the most important species of the genus **Pisum** (py′sum) which belongs to the Leguminosae or pea family.

The genus comprises six or seven annual or perennial herbs, mostly native in the Mediterranean region and western Asia, only the following of any garden importance. It has compound* leaves, the leaflets arranged feather-fashion,* and the main leafstalk always ends in a branched tendril.* At the base of the main leafstalk are two prominent, leaf-like organs (much-developed stipules*). The flowers are typically pea-like (for a description *see* LEGUMINOSAE). The fruit is the well-known pea pod, a legume,* the seeds of which furnish the common pea. In one variety (*see* below) the pod is also eaten. (*Pisum* is the classical name of the pea.) The only cult. species is:

**P. sativum.** Here belongs the tall-growing pea, which needs brush for support. It grows from 3–6 feet high, has smooth foliage and oval or oblong leaflets about 1½ in. long. The stipules (*see* above) are mostly larger than the leaflets. Flowers usually white. Pod 2–4 in. long, the seeds wrinkled or smooth. The plant has several varieties: (1) *var.* **arvense**, the field pea, with pinkish-purple flowers. Grown only for forage and of no garden interest; (2) *var.* **humile**, the early dwarf pea (the common low sort of the garden), which grows only from 8–24 in. high and has shorter pods than the tall type; (3) *var.* **macrocarpon**, the edible-podded or sugar pea. This has soft pods with little or none of the papery lining common in the other sorts. The pods, as well as the seeds, are used (mostly in Europe). This variety is little known in America.

Tall peas grow well on brush, but many prefer to use chicken wire. See text.

### PEA CULTURE

Tall sorts = *Pisum sativum*

Dwarf sorts = *Pisum sativum humile*

The garden pea combines two features of great value. It is not only very nutritious and rich in Vitamins A, B, and C, but provides many advantages of a green vegetable. Hence its first-rate importance as a garden crop. Unfortunately for the home gardener, it is a cool-season plant, or an all-season crop for only the coolest climates, as in zones* 1 and 2, or for high altitudes elsewhere. Occasionally, in proximity to cool sea water, as along the coast of Maine and the Maritime Provinces, it can also be grown all through the growing season.

Elsewhere peas must be grown between the time when the ground is workable and the heat of summer, which they will not tolerate. Some growers try to utilize the coolness of autumn by making late sowings, but such crops are rarely satisfactory. For most of the home gardeners the pea must be a spring crop. Its all-the-year-round presence in the markets is due to the great value of the crop and the fact that somewhere in such a large country there is always a period of a few cool weeks in which to grow them. The tall sorts mature in 60–80 days, the low or bushy types in about 55 days.

SOILS AND FERTILIZERS. Any good garden soil will grow peas. If it has been manured the autumn previous, that is a help. If manuring is left until just before planting, it is

---

* Special articles on the subjects indicated by an asterisk (*) will be found at the words so marked.

essential that only well-rotted manure be used, as fresh manure is dangerous for this crop. Although the pea is a legume, and consequently absorbs nitrogen from the air (*see* LEGUMINOSAE), it does not begin doing so until some time after germination. It is consequently of advantage to use a commercial fertilizer with a ratio of 4-8-8 (*see* FERTILIZERS), at the rate of 500 pounds to the acre (about 2 pounds per 100-ft. row).

If the manure or fertilizer is thoroughly plowed in and the soil raked smooth, planting may begin.

PLANTING PEAS. Almost no garden crop is so easy to start as peas. Seed of the low sorts should be planted just as early as the ground can be worked. You need not wait for the last erratic late frost. Choose a time approximating the average day when the last frost in your region may be expected (*see* the name of your state for frost dates). Plant on that day or even a little before it. Planted pea seeds are not injured by the surface soil being touched by frost, and the earliest possible planting date is always the best. Sowing pea seed should be practically the first spring activity in the vegetable garden. The tall varieties are better planted about 10 days later than the low sorts.

For the first plantings of low varieties make the drills about 2 in. deep (in a light, sandy soil) or 1 in. deep if the soil is heavy and has much clay in it. Later plantings should be in drills about twice this depth, but only half filled at first. As the plants grow the trench is gradually filled up. The object of this deeper drill, for later plantings, is to secure greater coolness and moisture for the roots of plants that will have to face greater heat.

In planting low varieties the seed should be scattered rather freely in the drill, certainly not less than an inch apart, and some very competent growers prefer less space between the seeds. As the plants come up they may be thinned so that the final plants will be 2-3 in. apart. If left at the one-inch intervals, the plants will be too crowded. It takes about 1 pound of seed for 100 ft. of row for the dwarf varieties. Rows should be 18 in. apart.

Tall varieties are planted somewhat differently. The rows should be about 30-36 in. apart and the seeds are planted in double rows. Make two parallel drills about 6 in. apart (or one trench 6 in. wide) and about 4 in. deep. Plant the seeds about 2½ in. apart (closer if expense does not matter) in each drill, or on the outer edges of the 6-in. trench if this method is easier. Cover the seeds with only enough soil to half fill the drills or trench, putting in the rest of the soil as the plants come up.

The object of this double row, with 6 in. between the plants, is that the space between will be occupied by the brush or wire needed for the support of these tall varieties. It should be set before the seed is covered (*see* below). Use a pound or pound and a half of seed for each double row of 100 ft., but see that the ultimate stand is spaced (by thinning) about 4 in. apart.

CULTIVATION. Peas need only sufficient cultivation to keep down weeds. If your garden is a reasonably kept one, the space between the double-rowed tall sorts should be fairly free of weeds, due to the growth of the pea plants. If not, hand weeding is the only remedy.

VARIETIES. Most low varieties have smooth seeds and shorter pods, and are less desirable as to yield and flavor than the usually wrinkled-seeded, larger-podded, tall sorts. The great merit of the low sorts is their quicker maturity, and the freedom from the bother of supports. According to their classes, the home grower will find most satisfaction in using the following varieties:

LOW OR BUSH PEAS (needing no support). Laxtons Progress. Blue Bantam. Thomas Laxton. Hundredfold. Alaska (for canning, especially in Md.).

TALL PEAS (for later planting and needing support). Alderman Improved Telephone. Dark-podded Telephone. Lincoln.

SUPPORTS FOR TALL VARIETIES. These should be placed at planting time. Twiggy brush (with the bark on) is perhaps the best, but not always available. It should be about 4-5 ft. high after the stems are sunk in the ground enough to make it a stout support. It should also be close enough together so that no wandering tendril will fail to find a support.

Many prefer to use ordinary chicken wire 4-5 ft. high. Stretch it as tightly as possible between stout posts at each end of the row. Then tie it to dahlia stakes set at 6-foot intervals for greater stiffening. The advantage of the wire is that, after cleaning, it may be rolled up, posts and all, and stored for next season, whereas the brush is not so easy to manage once the pea season is over.

HARVESTING AND YIELDS. It is easy to see when peas are ready for picking. The younger they are, the better. And, for the home gardener, they should never be picked more than an hour or two before they are cooked.

Yields vary greatly, depending on the variety used, the soil, and especially upon the amount of heat that is encountered by later sowings. Some put in several sowings of the dwarf sorts at 10-day intervals. But some of the later lots may be overtaken by the heat and yield little or nothing. Only one planting of the tall sorts is advisable unless your summers are consistently cool.

For the average family of 5, the yield from 2 pounds of pea seed, split about half between tall and low varieties, should be ample. If only low varieties are used, gambling on several succession plantings at 10-day intervals will give you an ample supply until heat ends the pea season.

For the preferred position and sequence of peas in your garden *see* KITCHEN GARDEN.

INSECT PESTS. The pea aphid, a rather large (⅙ in.), green, plant louse, attacks peas, clover, etc., becomes numerous, and saps the plants. In small gardens strong nicotine dust or spray may be used, or aphids may be shaken from the vines onto paper. In large fields control is more difficult, but some success has been had with nicotine dust.

DISEASES. The most troublesome diseases of peas are those grouped as root rots. The crop is very susceptible to many soil fungi, and when these are present in large numbers, as they are likely to be in gardens or in fields where peas are grown intensively, the entire harvest may be lost. The root rots cause the plants to yellow and die prematurely.

Control measures include long rotations with unrelated crops, extra-early planting, well-drained soil, treating the seed with organic mercury or red copper oxide, and obtaining seed from the far Northwest, where pea diseases are not so prevalent.

Almost the same symptoms are made manifest when peas are affected with wilt. This is caused by another soil organism that persists so long after it once is introduced into a field that crop rotations are of little value. In some of the areas where wilt is troublesome, resistant strains have been bred and these should be planted when necessary. The bacterial blight and anthracnose may cause dying of young plants, or later spotting of the pods and leaves. The control measures are the same as those suggested for root rots.

PEACH (*Amygdalus persica*). The peach is second only to the apple as a money-making orchard crop in America. Perhaps there are more elements of chance in growing peaches for the market than with any other tree fruit, but gambling with the crop makes peach culture all the more attractive in the speculative business of growing fruit. To the gardener and the owner of a home orchard, the pleasure of good peaches and the fields of adventure into which peach growing leads him make the charm of the peach irresistible.

The peach can be grown in any part of North America north of sub-tropical Florida where winter temperatures do not drop lower, except in an occasional cold winter, than 15° F. Where there are long periods of excessive heat in the summer, as in the lowlands of the Gulf states, the quality of the fruit suffers. In northeastern America, the peach is grown successfully, for the most part, only near large bodies of water — the ocean, the Great Lakes, or the Finger Lakes of New York. Heat absorbed by bodies of water in the spring retards blooming and cuts down danger from frost. The release of heat during winter moderates the temperature and prevents wood and bud injury from freezing.

SOILS. The peach thrives upon a great diversity of soils, provided two conditions be present, good drainage and soil warmth. Perhaps no other tree fruit is so impatient of an excess of moisture as the peach. The tree will stand droughts but never a flooded soil. The peach delights in a warm soil; therefore the best peaches are grown on sandy, gravelly, and stony soils. Upon such soils the trees make a firm growth, the wood matures early and thoroughly, and

---

* Special articles on the subjects indicated by an asterisk (*) will be found at the words so marked.

the fruit is highly colored and well flavored. Still, good peaches are grown on clays, especially in the South, and on moderately heavy loams.

High, rolling, or hilly lands are good peach lands because they are naturally well drained and because in such locations there is less danger from winter and the spring frosts which are everywhere so disastrous to this fruit. Even moderate success cannot be expected in low, level lands or in pockets between hills where the air is bagged up and stagnates. In locations where the air does not circulate freely, fungous diseases, especially the dreaded brown-rot, take great toll.

PLANTING. At planting time, the peach tree should be one year old from the bud, vigorous but not succulent from overgrowth, well rooted and free from crown gall. Peach trees in America are practically always budded on seedlings grown from the pits of wild peaches — at least such was the case until recent years when cannery pits have been substituted by some for the wild pits. Planting distances depend upon the suitability of the soil for the peach and on the variety. On poor soils trees may be set as close as 18 ft. apart each way, but on rich soils 20, 22, and even 24 ft. are distances none too great. Different varieties vary greatly in the size of trees, some being very compact growers and others widespreading, factors affecting distances.

When the trees are set they should be headed back to about 24 in. and either pruned to a whip or left with three or four scaffold branches evenly spaced, the lowest one a foot or thereabouts from the ground. The crotches should not be too acute, as later the tree will split. The peach does not stand transplanting well, and this cutting back to a whip or to stubs of branches should be done to prevent excessive transpiration.*

PRUNING. Subsequent pruning and training resolve themselves into two rather distinct problems: To increase the vigor of the tree; and to train the tree to a form that will make orchard operations easy and give a maximum amount of fruit-bearing wood. At best the peach is a short-lived tree, 20 years in an orchard being a long span of life, and most growers want a short life and a productive one for their trees, say 16 or 18 years, and prune to secure this objective. This means a greater amount of pruning for the peach than for any other tree fruit. In general, this rule should guide peach pruners: Varieties weak in growth must be pruned severely; strong-growing sorts are pruned rather lightly.

A start is made to form the top in the year after the tree has been set in the orchard. Two shapes of the treetop are open to choice: the vase-formed or open-centered tree; and the globe-shaped or close-centered tree. In the vase-shape, the tree consists of a short trunk surmounted by three, four, or five main branches ascending obliquely and no central trunk. In the globe-shape, the trunk is continued above the branches, forming the center of the tree, and later, being "headed in," a globe-like head is formed.

A few years ago the vase-shape was more common, but now the globe-shape is oftener found for the reasons that it gives more bearing surface, the trees are less likely to split, live longer, and are more easily trained. Perhaps the peaches on the vase-shaped trees are a little larger and better colored and flavored, since they are more exposed to the sun. In training to the vase-shape shorten the branches the second year the trees are in the orchard from ⅓ to ½, cutting to upper and inner buds so that the oblique ascending position of the branches is maintained. The pruning for succeeding years is much the same, except that more is done, and more interior branches are removed, thus opening up the head to air and sunshine.

When the globe-shaped tree is chosen, little pruning is needed until the tree has borne two or three crops, when some of the branches will become naked at their bases and spread too far from the tree. In such cases these long branches must be headed back to vigorous lateral shoots. Such pruning not only rejuvenates the tree but keeps the bearing surface closer to the trunk, thereby making orchard operations easier. Another result is that the crop is thinned and the remaining fruits are larger and better. Unless branches are headed back, also, the fruit is borne mostly on terminals and there is much breakage in years of full crops. In training to this shape, in particular, interior branches should be removed to let in sun and air.

CULTIVATION. However fruit-growers differ as to soil management for other tree fruits, all agree that a peach orchard must be tilled. An untilled peach orchard is the desolation of desolation — trees "sod-yellow," scraggly, sparse in fruit and foliage, and fruits small and gnarly. Never put a peach orchard down to grain nor sow the orchard to grass except for a cover crop. The orchard should be plowed in late fall or early spring, after which there should be frequent cultivation until late July, when a cover crop of some legume or cereal should be sown. Annual applications of from 300 to 500 pounds of nitrate of soda usually meet all fertilizer requirements.

A problem that every northern peach-grower must face is that of avoiding injury from frosts and freezes. To secure the greatest possible hardiness inherent in the peach, plant on warm, well-drained soils. Either extreme of moisture, too wet or too dry, gives favorable conditions for winter-killing. Small-growing varieties with compact heads are hardier than free-growing sorts with large heads. The most effective treatment to avoid winter injury is to sow cover crops which cause the trees to ripen their wood thoroughly, protect the roots from cold, and assist in regulating the supply of water. Peach trees are more likely to suffer from cold if not thrifty than if thrifty. Late fall growths are susceptible to winter injury. Testimony is unfavorable to windbreaks as a protection against cold. Some varieties are much hardier than others.

THINNING. Good peaches can seldom be grown without thinning the crop. This work is best done as soon as possible after the "June drop." The fruits should be thinned to stand 5 or 6 in. apart. Without thinning, the fruits are small, unattractive, and inferior in quality, and the trees suffer in vigor and often break from overloading.

Peaches are nearly all self-fruitful, and in planting most varieties cross-pollination need receive no attention. Two notable exceptions among major varieties are Mikado and J. H. Hale, which should be interplanted with other varieties which bloom at the same time.

Perhaps three-fourths of all of the peaches grown in commercial orchards east of the Rocky Mountains are Elbertas. Out of a half-hundred other meritorious varieties, gardeners can supply about every need and find sorts for all peach regions among the following choicely good varieties, very generally adapted to all peach localities in zones* 3, 4, 5, and 6. These are named in order of seasons.

### VARIETIES

MIKADO. Fruit yellow, blushed, handsome, flesh yellow, semi-clinging, good quality, earliest yellow peach. Tree hardy, productive, and healthy. Requires cross-pollination.

GREENSBORO. Fruit white, bright blush, medium in size, white flesh, quality fair, semi-cling. Tree very vigorous, healthy and productive.

MARIGOLD. Fruit medium in size, yellow, blushed, flesh yellow, good quality, freestone. Tree hardy, healthy, and productive.

ORIOLE. Fruit yellow, large, yellow flesh, stone free, excellent quality. Tree vigorous and productive.

ROCHESTER. Fruit yellow, very pubescent,* rather small, flesh yellow, stone free. Tree hardy and productive, but it and its fruits are susceptible to brown-rot.

CARMAN. Fruit white, blushed, round, medium in size, flesh white, stone free, quality good. Tree satisfactory in all characters.

VALIANT. Fruit yellow with bright blush, large, round, flesh yellow, stone free, quality excellent. Tree productive and healthy, but lacks somewhat in size and vigor.

SOUTH HAVEN. Fruit yellow, bright blush, large, fuzzy, flesh yellow, stone free, good flavor. Tree rather small, but satisfactory.

VETERAN. Differs from Valiant chiefly in ripening a few days later and in greater vigor of tree.

CHAMPION. Fruit yellowish-white, bright blush, large,

---

* Special articles on the subjects indicated by an asterisk (*) will be found at the words so marked.

flesh white, nearly free, excellent quality. Tree one of the best in the peach family.

BELLE. Fruit creamy-white with handsome crimson cheek, large stone free, flesh white, good. Tree very satisfactory.

EARLY CRAWFORD. Fruit yellow with beautiful blush, medium size, flesh yellow, with red rays at pit which is free, excellent quality. Tree large, vigorous, but late and uncertain in bearing.

J. H. HALE. Fruit yellow with handsome blush, very large, flesh yellow, stone free, fair in quality. Tree vigorous but uncertain in bearing. Requires cross-pollination.

ELBERTA. Fruit yellow, large, handsome, stone free, medium quality. Splendid in all tree characters. Standard for commercial orchards.

CROSBY. Fruit yellow, dull blush, very fuzzy, small, flesh yellow, stone free, red at pit, quality good. Tree small and compact, but possibly hardier than that of any other variety. — U. P. H.

For the greenhouse cult. of the peach, see Fruit at GREENHOUSE.

### WEST OF THE ROCKY MOUNTAINS

Peaches may be successfully grown in many areas in the states west of the Rocky Mountains where there is sufficient rainfall and the winter temperatures do not become too cold nor the occurrence of late spring frosts is too frequent. While the quality of the fruits of the peach tree seems to be rather definitely influenced by climatic conditions, there are no areas in these states where peaches of excellent quality cannot be grown when the above limitations are considered.

The young trees are propagated by budding on seedlings grown from seeds obtained from local dry yards or canners. The nurseryman sells them as one-year-old trees, or as June-budded trees. The latter are trees which have been budded in the early summer following the spring in which the seeds have been planted. These trees are smaller than the one-year-old trees at the time of buying, but will usually produce as good a tree as those bought at one year of age.

Peach trees will show a definite response to a lack of available water in the size of the tree and the size and quality of the fruit. In planning the orchard, the grower should bear this in mind in areas where there is a deficiency of rainfall. If only a few trees are to be planted, basins can be thrown up around the trees by hand, and they can be watered by means of a hose or pipe. If very many trees are to be planted, it will be found advisable to use some type of irrigation system. This should be decided upon and the ground properly leveled and prepared prior to the planting of the trees. See IRRIGATION.

In these states, peach trees may be planted in the winter or early spring. In the sections where the winters are quite mild, the trees may be planted any time during the period the young trees are dormant. A common practice is to wait until after there has been sufficient winter rainfall to moisten the ground thoroughly before planting. In the sections where considerable freezing occurs during the winter, it will be advisable to delay the planting until spring.

After planting, the trees should be headed back to 24 to 30 inches. In most cases, the side branches which have developed in the nursery will not be desirably located for permanent scaffold* branches, so it will be necessary to remove them. These should be cut back, leaving a stub about a quarter of an inch long. Whitewashing to prevent sunscald* during the first summer is desirable. Pruning at the end of the first summer should consist in the selection of three branches for the permanent scaffolds. These should be at different levels on the trunk, 6 or 8 inches apart and equally spaced around the trunk. All other branches should be removed and the permanent scaffolds lightly headed back. At the end of the second summer, the secondary scaffolds, 5 to 7 in number, should be selected and all other branches removed. Pruning the bearing peach tree consists in removing objectionable branches, and sufficiently heavy cutting to maintain a desirable balance between new growth and the crop borne by the tree.

Some form of cultivation will be necessary for the successful production of good trees and fruit. The frequency of cultivation, however, may vary widely and will depend almost entirely upon the availability of water. If there is an abundance of water, the only cultivations necessary are those required to incorporate the cover crop, either of weeds or one that has been planted, into the soil. If there is not an abundance of water, more frequent cultivations are necessary to remove the competition of the weeds for the moisture supply.

VARIETIES. Certain varieties have been developed in these states which are especially adapted for canning or drying. The canning varieties are firm-fleshed, of a golden-yellow color without red at the pit, of a good symmetrical size and ripen uniformly throughout. They are picked when the flesh has reached its full yellow color, but before softening has begun. A variety that is suitable for drying should preferably be a freestone with a small pit, the flesh should be sweet in taste, of a clear yellow color with no red at the pit, of a firm texture, and have a low drying ratio. For drying, the fruit is allowed to become fully mature before picking. After removal of the pit, the halves are placed on trays, with the cut surface up, exposed to the fumes of burning sulphur for three to four hours and then either dried in the sun or in a dehydrating plant.

The varieties used for canning in order of ripening are as follows: Tuscan, Hauss, Johnson, Palora, Peak, Gaume, Sims, Phillips Cling. All these are clingstone varieties. The Muir and the Lovell are the two chief varieties used for drying, although the Elberta is dried in smaller amounts than the others. The Muir ripens about a week after the Elberta and about two weeks ahead of the Lovell.

The varieties grown for fresh fruit are the same as those already listed for the region east of the Rocky Mountains. — L. D. D.

INSECT PESTS. The San Jose scale is a serious pest of peach trees, and is controlled with dormant sprays of oil or lime-sulphur (see APPLE). The round, convex terrapin scale is controlled with a stronger oil emulsion (stock diluted 1-16).

Peach borers, yellowish caterpillars about 1 in. long, work under the bark near the ground and sometimes kill trees. Paradichlorobenzene may be used against young borers in the fall. The soil around the trunk is smoothed, and the white crystals are put in a ring about 1½ in. away and covered with several inches of soil, which is then packed. The soil covering is removed in 4 to 6 weeks. One tree requires ½ to 1½ ounces of paradichlorobenzene, depending on its size. Trees less than 3 years old may be injured by the treatment. It is applied in the last two weeks of Sept. in the Middle States, in Oct. in the South.

The plum curculio affects the fruit. It is controlled with a spray or dust of lead arsenate with several times its weight of lime as the petals fall, another 10 days later, and sometimes a third 4 weeks before harvest. Dropped fruits should be cleaned up, for they contain larvae. Sprays must be used carefully, as peach is easily injured.

The peach twig borer is a minor pest, worst in the West (see APRICOT).

The oriental fruit moth, in the eastern half of the U.S., bores in twigs in the spring and in fruit later; control is still in the experimental stage.

The handsome greenish Japanese beetles, ½ in. long, swarm over peaches and many other plants, attacking foliage and fruit. They are repelled by arsenicals.

Bark beetles are injurious to trees of poor vigor (see APPLE).

Spray schedules against peach insects call for dormant spray when needed, and several mild fungicide applications beginning at blossom fall, the first, and sometimes others, containing lead arsenate for control of curculio.

DISEASES. Leaf curl is a very striking disease of the peach foliage. The leaf surface becomes puckered along the midrib and the lateral veins, the thickness of the leaf often is doubled, and the green color may be replaced by pretty shades of yellow or red. The fungus causing leaf curl probably lives over winter between the bud scales and attacks the leaf as soon as the bud swells sufficiently in the spring to permit the pathogene to enter between the scales. The tree may then be defoliated, and even a second crop of leaves destroyed. This weakens the tree to such an extent that it easily succumbs to winter injury.

Spraying once with lime-sulphur (1-15), either late in the fall or early in the spring before the buds swell, eradicates the fungus.

Another very important disease of peach is brown-rot, which causes the fruit to decay with a subsequent ashen-colored mold over the surface, and in severe cases causes a limb canker. The fungus lives over winter mostly in the old fruits either on the ground or the mummied fruit left hanging on the tree. Lime-sulphur cannot be used on peach trees during the summer without the possibility of injury; therefore some form of wettable sulphur, as dry-mix sulphur-lime spray or a sulphur dust is used. The applications should be (first) when blossoms show pink, (second) when shucks fall, (third) two to three weeks later, and (fourth) two to four weeks before the fruit ripens.

Peach scab which causes freckles on the skin of the peach is so commonly present that it sometimes is considered a normal coloring. It dwarfs the fruit, destroys the flavor, and reduces the size of the crop. It may also attack the leaves. Spraying or dusting as for brown-rot control is recommended.

---

* Special articles on the subjects indicated by an asterisk (*) will be found at the words so marked.

The same spray schedule also holds in check powdery mildew, blight, and bacterial spot, although lately zinc*-lime spray has been suggested for the bacterial disease.

Yellows, little peach, rosette and phony peach, are virus troubles, which can be held in check only by rigid orchard inspection, and destruction of trees as soon as symptoms are apparent. Healthy young trees should be procured from the nursery both in regard to these virus maladies and crowngall which may cause big swellings on the roots.

**PEACH BELLS** = *Campanula persicifolia.*

**PEACH FAMILY.** *See* ROSACEAE.

**PEACH TWIG BORER.** *See* Insect Pests at APRICOT, PEACH, and PLUM.

**PEACOCK-FLOWER** = *Delonix regia.*

**PEACOCK IRIS** = *Moraea pavonia.*

**PEA FAMILY.** Perhaps the most important family of plants to the gardener because it includes pea, bean, clover, vetch, peanut, soybean, and many other crop plants. Among ornamental favorites are acacia, wisteria, genista, broom, lupine, gorse, locust, laburnum, and the redbud. And it also yields many drugs, such as licorice, and some poisons. For its many cult. genera, and a description of its flowers and fruits, *see* LEGUMINOSAE.

**PEANUT.** Brazil is the native home of the peanut, which belongs to the genus **Arachis** (ă'ra-kis) of the pea family. Of the 10 known species only the common peanut, **A. hypogaea**, sometimes called goober or groundnut, is cult., but this species is of wide economic importance. It is an annual herb 12–18 in. high, with alternate,* compound* leaves, its 4 ovalish leaflets 1½–2½ in. long, without marginal teeth. Flowers of two kinds: one set showy, yellow, pea-like, and sterile; the others, also yellow, but fertile and on recurved stalks which touch the ground, penetrate it, carrying the fertilized ovary beneath the surface where it ripens (the peanut). Unlike nearly all other fruits of the pea family, this one does not split. Seeds oily and nutritious. (*Arachis* is from the Greek for some pea-like plant, but of very uncertain application to the peanut.)

Peanut and its underground fruit

### PEANUT CULTURE

As an interesting, annual, economic plant the peanut can be grown anywhere in the U.S. below zone* 3, but it needs far more heat to ripen its underground fruit than it usually finds north of zone* 5. Consequently, its commercial cult. is confined to the warmer parts of the country and from zone* 6 southward is its preferred climatic region in the U.S. It is widely grown in most tropical countries.

In zones* 3 and 4 an occasional long hot summer will permit fruit to ripen, but in the North generally the peanut is mostly an interesting curiosity because of its extraordinary fruiting habits.

In its own climatic region the seeds, removed from the pod if the latter is hard to split, are sown in drills about 30 in. apart, the plants to be spaced 8–10 in. apart in the row. Do not sow them until warm weather is assured, because the plant does not like coolness and is killed outright by frost.

Warm, sandy loams are the best for the peanut, and its commercial culture, which is more a large-scale agricultural operation than a hort. one, is confined to such soils. Like any other crop it needs to be cult. to keep down weeds and conserve soil moisture. But the plant will stand much heat and considerable drought.

There are two general types of peanut grown. One is the runner peanut in which the vine-like plant is apt to sprawl, consequently needing more space than the second form known as the bunch peanut. In the latter the plant is bushier and essentially erect. The bunch peanut is mostly grown by those who harvest the tops for forage. For the runner peanut the spacing should be more than that given above, which is for the bunch type.

Harvesting is like that of any root crop — the peanuts must be dug or plowed out when ripe. Usually the whole plant is plowed out and, with the peanuts attached, stacked on frames off the ground for curing and drying. They should be stacked in such a way that the nuts are covered by the foliage while curing, as the peanut will discolor if exposed to the weather while curing.

INSECT PESTS. This crop is not seriously attacked by insects. The potato leafhopper sometimes yellows the foliage by its feeding; bordeaux spray will control it, but the injury and crop value seldom justify a spray. The corn-ear worm sometimes feeds on the plant late in the season. This and other occasional leaf feeders may be checked with arsenicals, but spraying would probably not pay.

DISEASES. Leaf blights, sclerotium blight, southern root rot, wilt, chlorosis, and fruit rots are in part controlled by having long rotations with crops belonging to the grass or grain families, destruction of diseased refuse, selecting soil that is not too acid or too alkaline, and planting healthy seed.

**PEANUT FAMILY.** *See* LEGUMINOSAE.

**PEAR.** For the common pear *see* the next main entry. For other plants to which the name pear is also applied *see* PSIDIUM (for alligator pear), MOMORDICA (for balsam pear), OPUNTIA (for prickly pear), and SECHIUM (for vegetable pear).

**PEAR.** Because the pear is more suited to the Pacific Coast than to the East, the chief cultural notes on this fruit will be grouped under the first section of this article.

### ON THE PACIFIC COAST

With few exceptions, pear varieties of high quality grown in America are of European origin. These sorts belong to the species *Pyrus communis* or European pear. The Japanese cultivate many varieties of *Pyrus serotina* or Japanese pear, not pleasing to the occidental palate, because of the number of stone cells in the flesh. Hybrids between these species, which are intermediate in quality, are grown to a certain extent in all parts of America. *P. serotina* strains, either pure or hybrid, tend to resist pear blight, undoubtedly the greatest single factor limiting the growth and production of pears. *See* below.

Pears are grown successfully under many conditions. Warm, dry summers apparently favor high quality, especially in certain varieties. Although some pears are as sensitive to cold as peaches, winters should be chilly enough to break the "rest period." In general, pears will withstand about the same winter temperatures as the rather tender Baldwin apple. The pear blooms relatively late and so can be planted more widely than almonds, apricots, and peaches; frosty locations, however, should be avoided. Artificial heating of pear orchards is economically questionable. Windy locations should be avoided, as fruit often scars even if not blown from the tree.

SOILS. A well-drained, deep clay loam is probably best for pears, although they are grown on many soils. Adequate moisture should be available either from rainfall, or from irrigation.* Most orchards are clean cultivated, although many, especially in Wash., have a permanent cover crop such as alfalfa. Pear trees grown in sod or in soils low in fertility may benefit from the application of nitrogenous fertilizers. If the ground is clean cultivated, barnyard manure is perhaps the best source of additional fertility. At all events, the effect of the addition of fertilizers should be determined first on a few trees before treatment of the whole plantation. Excessive vegetative growth, especially in bearing trees, whether induced by fertilization or irrigation, is undesirable: it encourages development of pear blight.

Although pear trees are long-lived and may eventually

---

* Special articles on the subjects indicated by an asterisk (*) will be found at the words so marked.

reach great size, this fruit will do well when the trees are planted relatively close. Many old orchards are as close as 16 × 16 ft. When grown as dwarfs (on quince roots), 12 × 12 ft. is a good spacing; possibly the most popular distance is 20 × 20 ft. for standard trees.

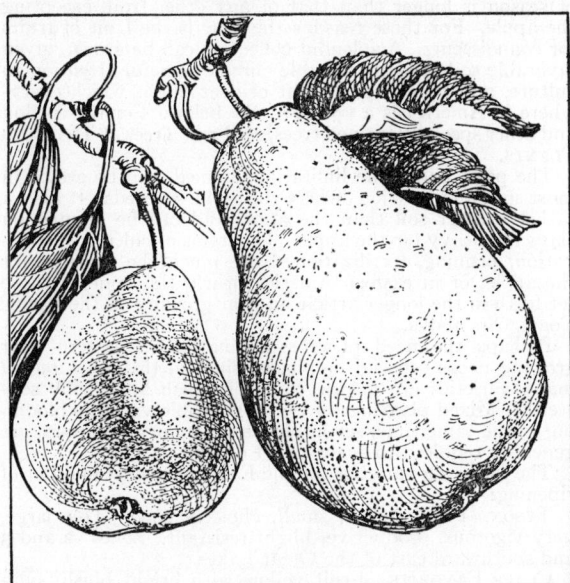

Bartlett (*right*) and Seckel (*left*) pears

The most common root for pears is the French (*P. communis*). Though it suckers rather badly and is susceptible to pear blight and pear root aphis, it is adaptable to various soil conditions, vigorous, long-lived, and partially resistant to oak fungus; and produces splendid fruit.

The Japanese root (*P. serotina*), widespread on the Pacific Coast, especially in Calif., is resistant to pear root aphis, but only partially resistant to pear blight. After 20 years' experience, Calif. orchardists have concluded — as did South African growers 30 or more years ago — that this root is highly unsatisfactory. It is poorly adapted to soils having high moisture or lime content. After 12 to 15 years, the trees often stop growth. Probably the most serious drawback, however, is the "Black End" or "Hard End" affecting much of the crop. Often the calyx end is hard and black, or merely hard. The fruit is ruined for fresh consumption, canning and drying. There is apparently no causal organism, nor any correlation with soil, climate, or culture condition. This disease has never appeared on quince stock, and but rarely on French-rooted trees.

With quince (*Cydonia oblonga*), sometimes used as a dwarfing stock for pears, double-working is often necessary. Hardy is universally satisfactory as the intermediate variety. Several plantings of Bartletts in Calif. now 75 years old were thus propagated. The resultant fruit is excellent. With good soil and culture, the trees are only semi-dwarfs. The quince root is particularly well adapted to moist, heavy soils.

PLANTING. Usually a one-year-old whip, 4 to 6 feet high, with a caliper of ½ inch at the base, is planted and immediately headed to about 30 inches. This planting is generally done in the spring when the soil is moist and before the young tree has started root or top activity. Whitewash the entire tree at planting to prevent sunscald.* Some growers prefer the use of tree protectors for this purpose. At the end of the first summer, three branches are selected so that a good spacing up and down the trunk is secured, all others are removed. This spacing is more important than balancing the growth around the stem, since the next season's shoots take care of this problem. The distance between the origin of the branches on the trunk never changes during the life of the tree. If possible, space these main scaffolds* 6 to 8 in. apart and head back moderately to encourage the appearance of secondary scaffolds during the second summer. At the end of the second season in the orchard, the new shoots are thinned out and a few (4–5) saved and lightly headed. Follow the same procedure during the next few years, heading only where a new branch is desired and thinning out superfluous shoots. After the tree comes into bearing, the pruning given will necessarily vary with the variety and growing conditions. Maximum crops and abundant replacement wood do not go hand in hand. The crop should be limited by removal of wood sufficient to induce a new shoot growth of from 12 to 18 inches over the periphery of the tree. Pruning for size of fruit is often profitably supplemented by thinning the fruit. In windy locations, this practice is often desirable to prevent scarring of the fruit.

The pear is well adapted to espalier and cordon training, and is thus grown in many European fruit gardens. These methods of handling should more often be used by the amateur fruit-grower in this country, and the pear tree lends itself particularly well to these practices. *See* TRAINING PLANTS.

Cross-pollination is needed by most pear varieties, including Bartlett, except in especially favorable locations, such as the interior valley pear sections of Calif. Any two pear varieties that blossom at the same time will successfully cross-pollinate each other. Efficient pollinations may be secured with the minimum number of pollinators by planting these as every third tree in every third row. This gives one tree in nine to the pollinating sort.

PICKING. Pears ripen to better quality off the tree. Unless picked early, they develop more stone* cells and a coarser texture. Whether for shipping, canning, or drying, therefore, they are not harvested tree ripe. Pears may be stored at temperatures down to 32° F., but thereafter should be ripened at above 60° F.

Pears for drying — ripened, halved, with calyx and stem removed — are exposed on trays to the fumes of burning sulphur from 6 to 24 hours, and then placed in the sun to dry. After a day or so, the trays are stacked and the drying slowly completed. About 5 pounds fresh makes 1 pound dry.

VARIETIES. Most of the varieties of pears raised in the United States either by the amateur or commercial grower are of European origin. A definite effort was made, particularly in Belgium and France, for more than a century (1730–1850) to secure improved varieties. Many of our better

Kieffer (*right*) and Beurre Bosc (*left*) pears

---
* Special articles on the subjects indicated by an asterisk (*) will be found at the words so marked.

varieties thus originated. Little attention has been given to systematic pear breeding in America, and the general prevalence of pear blight has undoubtedly killed many natural seedlings. Many of the better pear varieties now growing in this country originated as chance seedlings. A few of the best varieties will be discussed in the approximate order of their ripening. Those marked with a † are also suited to the East. *See* below.

† BARTLETT. This is the most important variety in the U.S. Of English origin, it is known, except in U.S., as the Williams Bon Chretien. Trees large and productive. Fruit large to very large, clear yellow, often with blush. Excellent quality. Best flavor and texture developed when grown where summer temperatures are high. Suitable for dessert, canning and drying. Susceptible to pear blight. Season, September in N.Y.; last of June to September in western U.S.

BEURRE HARDY. A French variety originated about 1850. Makes satisfactory union with quince root. Trees grow to large size and produce heavy crops. Fruit large, greenish-yellow under a light russet. Very good quality. A popular variety on the English market. Somewhat less susceptible to pear blight than Bartlett.

KIEFFER. An American hybrid between a European variety and a Japanese. Trees vigorous, reaching good size, productive. Fruit large to very large, rough, blushed with brownish-red. Flesh granular, often gritty, juicy, below medium quality. Because of partial resistance to pear blight, widely grown in warm, humid sections in southeastern U.S. and Mississippi Valley.

† SECKEL. Of Penn. origin. Tree vigorous, productive. Fruit very small, yellowish-brown, often lightly russeted; sweet and of best quality. An excellent sort for the home garden. More resistant to pear blight than most varieties.

† BEURRE D'ANJOU. This old French variety is vigorous. The trees reach large size and are irregular in productivity. Fruit large, greenish to yellow; very good in quality. Unless well grown, fruit often subject to internal breakdown known as "Anjou spot." Trees are moderately susceptible to pear blight.

† BEURRE BOSC. A Belgium variety of great vigor, but straggly growth, especially as a young tree. Of medium productivity. Fruit large to very large with long, tapering neck; greenish-yellow, often overlaid with very heavy russet. When well grown of highest quality, especially on heavy soils. Trees are very susceptible to pear blight.

DOYENNE DU COMICE. A French variety of good vigor. Irregular to shy in productivity. Fruit large, yellow with faint reddish-brown russet. Quality excellent. Moderately susceptible to pear blight.

† WINTER NELIS. An old Belgian variety, slow in growth, but eventually reaching great size. Trees difficult to train when young due to twisting habit of growth. Fruit small to medium, yellow-green, often completely overlaid with russet; very good in quality; an excellent storage variety. The most resistant of the European varieties to pear blight. — W. P. T.

### EAST OF THE ROCKY MOUNTAINS

The pear reaches perfection in few places east of the Rocky Mountains for the reason that the climate in this great region is uncongenial to it. Pears are at their best only in equable climates and do not endure well the sudden and extreme variations in weather to which all parts of North America excepting the Pacific states are subject. In the region under consideration commercial pear culture is confined to favorable localities between the Atlantic and the Great Lakes. A few varieties, hybrids with the Japanese pear, can with difficulty be grown in the Gulf states and the states of the plains.

The reasons given above, and the further one that of all fruits the varieties of this one are most variable in quality, keep the fruit from being a favorite with those who grow fruits for home use. Gardeners do not like to grow varieties that should produce fruits of high quality and then harvest a crop indifferent in flavor, color, and texture because of some slight uncongeniality in soil or climate.

On the other hand, those who love choicely good fruits find the charm of individuality more marked in the pear than in any of its orchard associates. The fruits of varieties of pears are, perhaps, more varied in size, shape, texture, and flavor than those of any other hardy tree fruit. The length of season is longer than that of any other fruit, excepting the apple. For these reasons the pear is the fruit of fruits for connoisseurs. A splendid collection can be grown, given favorable soil, a fairly equable climate, careful attention to culture, and drastic treatment of pear blight which everywhere in America is a scourge. *See* below. For the cordon and other specially trained trees, *see* Fruit Trees at TRAINING PLANTS.

The pear, under the limitations named, can be grown in most soils and locations where the apple succeeds. It likes a rather heavier soil than the apple and can be planted on clays too heavy for the apple. The items of culture — cultivation, pruning, fertilization — are much the same as for the apple, or in eastern America nearly the same as those set forth in the longer article on pear growing on the Pacific Coast. *See* above.

Perhaps the need of cross-pollination in eastern pear growing needs especial emphasis, since in this great region many varieties are grown, some of which are wholly self-sterile. Mixed plantings of two compatible varieties blooming at the same time, set in blocks of two or three rows, are generally required to ensure a set of fruit.

The following varieties for the East are named in order of ripening:

TYSON. Fruit yellow, small, choicely good. Tree large, very vigorous, productive, blight-resistant. Zones* 2 and 3 and southward east of the Great Lakes.

CLAPP FAVORITE. Fruit yellow with bright blush, symmetrical, quality fair, softens at center quickly. Tree large, vigorous, fairly productive, very susceptible to blight. Zones* 2 and 3 and southward east of the Great Lakes.

BARTLETT. For description *see* above. All parts of zones* 2 and 3 and southward where pears can be grown.

GORHAM. Fruit yellow, large, Bartlett type and flavor but ripens 2 weeks later. Tree like that of Bartlett but blight-resistant. Succeeds wherever Bartlett is grown.

SECKEL. For description *see* above. Zones* 2 and 3 and southward in all parts where pears are grown.

CAYUGA. A seedling of Seckel with much larger fruits which otherwise are similar. Tree similar with the same adaptations.

BEURRE BOSC. For description *see* above. Favored localities in zones* 2 and 3 and southward east of the Great Lakes.

BEURRE D'ANJOU. For description *see* above. Zones* 2 and 3 and southward where pears can be grown.

WINTER NELIS. For description *see* above. Suceeds only in very favorable localities in zones* 2 and 3. — U. P. H.

INSECT PESTS. Most pests of apple attack pear. The San Jose scale and the codling moth are controlled as on apple. The pear slug, a sawfly larva, is easily checked by arsenicals (*see* CHERRY). The pear leaf blister mite injures young leaves and fruit; the dormant sprays for scale control it. The pear psylla, an aphid-like sucking insect, 1/10 in. long, is often injurious. A delayed-dormant spray of oil emulsion on mild days in spring will kill over-wintered adults as they become active. The tiny pear thrips injure buds and flowers; delayed-dormant oil spray with nicotine added, or a spray of nicotine with soap, as buds open, and sometimes again as blossoms fall, is recommended.

DISEASES. The extent to which pears may be grown depends entirely upon the success in combating the dreaded disease, fire-blight. This is caused by a bacterium which enters the tip of young shoots and quickly kills the tissue as it progresses downward through the host.* When the trunk is once invaded, the tree is soon girdled and dies. The dried leaves persist on the branches, giving somewhat the appearance of having been injured by fire. Apple and quince also may be seriously affected. The only effective control measure is complete eradication of diseased parts. Each commercial orchard should be patrolled daily during heavy infection periods, and infected twigs removed and burned. It may be necessary in extreme cases to remove large limbs or even an entire tree to destroy centers of inoculum. In California surface treatment of cankers with a zinc chloride solution has proved effective, but has not been so successful under other conditions. The larger wounds are disinfected with a solution of one part each of mercuric chloride and mercuric cyanide in 500 parts of water.

Susceptible varieties of pears frequently are much injured by pear scab. This has the appearance of scab on apple, but is caused by a different species of the fungus. The leaves and fruit are affected with a black, mold-like growth, and when affected early may be much distorted. The fungus lives over winter in the old leaves on the ground, from where it is splashed to the new foliage in the spring. Scab may be controlled by spraying. When the blossom buds have separated in the cluster, a lime-sulphur spray.

---

* Special articles on the subjects indicated by an asterisk (*) will be found at the words so marked.

PEAR FAMILY. *See* ROSACEAE.

PEAR HAW = *Crataegus tomentosa*.

PEARL BUSH = *Exochorda racemosa*.

PEARL MILLET = *Pennisetum glaucum*.

PEARLWORT. *See* SAGINA.

PEARLY EVERLASTING = *Anaphalis margaritacea*.

PEAR SLUG. *See* Insect Pests at CHERRY.

PEAR TOMATO = *Lycopersicum esculentum pyriforme*. *See* TOMATO.

PEA SHRUB. *See* CARAGANA.

PEAT. A word of widely different significations in hort. Peat, in the technical sense, consists of the partially or wholly decomposed remains of plants; in other words, peat is the first stage in the process of the formation of coal. Old, but unconsolidated peat, is really muck, and its hort. use is discussed at MUCKLAND GARDENING.

Long before peat has reached the muck stage of decomposition its uses to the gardener are various, depending upon its origin and its stage of rotting. The only partially decomposed roots and rootstocks of many ferns are gathered on a great scale for what is known as orchid peat, because it is used for potting up orchids. For that use *see* the Greenhouse Orchids at ORCHID. *See also* OSMUNDA.

When the peat is wholly of upland origin, derived from the partial or complete decomposition of the leaves, twigs, or trunks of trees and shrubs, it is usually called leaf mold or humus and may be very acid or almost neutral. Acid peat is usually brownish, what the foresters call raw, and in this state is very valuable for plants of the heath family and for certain wild flowers, but not for all. *See* ACID AND ALKALI SOILS. *See also* HUMUS. Much later, as the woodland peat becomes older and nearly black, it usually loses its acidity, and in this stage it is typical rich woods soil, of the greatest use in the wild garden.

By far the largest amount of peat, outside of that derived from the forest floor, is derived from bog mosses of the genus *Sphagnum*. In its fresh-growing state sphagnum moss is intensely acid. And even when partially decomposed, sphagnum peat is still so acid that it is the best material for use in the bog garden. Much later (perhaps 200–500 years) it is in the process of becoming muck which may or may not be acid, depending on conditions of decomposition. *See* MUCKLAND GARDENING.

The value of peat, like any other humus, is largely its great water-holding capacity. In woods soil and in the bog it provides an ideal environment for microscopic organisms upon which many wild plants depend, at least in part, for getting their food.

PEAT-LOVERS. A common, but misleading term in hort. literature. Some plants *grow* in peat, especially acid peat, not because they "love" such sites, but because they must. To call such plants peat-lovers is more picturesque than truthful. Actually they are acid-tolerant plants. For a list of them *see* the list at ACID AND ALKALI SOILS.

PEAT MOSS. A popular mulch prepared from the peat of ancient sphagnum bogs. *See* MULCH AND MULCHING, and SPHAGNUM.

PEA TREE = *Caragana*; also *Agati grandiflora*.

PECAN (*Carya pecan*). Millions of pecan trees are wild or have been planted in the southern states and up the Mississippi and its tributaries as far north as Iowa. The pecan is now grown far beyond the wild range of the original species, which covered the region from Iowa and Ind. to Ala., Tex. and Mex. Today there are in Tex. over 70 million bearing trees, most of them wild. Thomas Jefferson brought the first pecan trees from the Mississippi Valley to Va. and gave George Washington some of them. He planted them March 25, 1775, and three of them are still at Mount Vernon.

The wild population of pecan trees is very erratic as to the size of the nut and yields, and the tree rarely comes true from seed. These two facts have made it necessary to bud or graft really fine varieties upon existing trees. And thousands of relatively old trees have been thus top-worked. But millions of seedling are raised every year, not to be allowed to grow until bearing age, for the crop may be worthless. The year-old seedlings are simply used as stock upon which fine varieties are budded. *See* BUDDING.

Most non-commercial growers will not care to bother with the somewhat elaborate technique of top-working old trees, or to wait for the slow process of budding. It is far better to purchase trees from a reliable dealer, and of the variety suited to your region. Pecan varieties, more than in most nut trees, are extremely important, as some are suited only to special conditions or regions.

VARIETIES. While the pecan will stand many degrees of frost, and some varieties have stood temperatures as low as 20° below zero, the tree is primarily a southern one. And, while some varieties will stand winter cold, they need a lot of summer heat to produce good nuts. The northern limit of pecan culture is about zone* 3, and in this region the following varieties are the best: Busseron, Butterick, Green River, Indiana, Niblack, and Posey. Not all dealers will have all these varieties, but most of them are available at least from a few dealers.

South of zone* 3, especially in the lowlands of the Mississippi, other and better pecan varieties are available. The tree is also cult. throughout the southern states, far outside its wild range, and certain varieties seem best adapted to these areas while some do better in the drainage area of the lower Mississippi. For the latter region, the real center of wild distribution, the best varieties are: Stuart, Schley, Van Deman, and Curtis. In the East, that is, from N. Car. to Fla. and Ala., the best varieties are: Bradley, Curtis, Moneymaker, President, and Stuart, and in eastern Tex. the same varieties are also suitable.

More than 100 named varieties of pecan are in the trade, but many of them are relatively useless because of poor yield, thick shells, or climatic restrictions. Those selected above have stood the test of the comparatively few years since pecan varieties have been even partially standardized. Many others of promise are constantly coming forward. The prospective planter will do well to visit the nursery where such are offered and get a complete history of the parent tree. It is useless to plant seeds of it, and only guaranteed budded or grafted trees should be accepted. There are now hundreds of thousands of relatively useless pecan trees throughout the South, due to the ignoring of these simple essentials.

PLANTING. The young pecan tree has a deep (3-4 ft.), stout taproot. It *must* be carefully handled, for upon the taproot will depend its chance of successful transplanting. During the first year few or maybe no lateral roots will develop, so it is important to dig a deep hole and see that the taproot has good soil, well packed in. Also it must be remembered that the mature tree will have a root spread twice as great as its spread of branches, which means that, for orchard planting, pecan trees must be at least 80 ft. apart each way, or within 25 years their root systems will be touching.

The rooting habits of the pecan have an important bearing upon its cultivation. Once the young tree is established it begins sending out in all directions many long, lateral roots. These are all in the upper layers of the soil, many of them scarcely 12 in. below the surface, and sometimes only 6 in. If cultivation is to be done, and it should be in all extensive plantings, it must be with a shallow cultivator, not with the plow. Cultivation is most beneficial to keep down weeds which otherwise would rob such shallow-rooted trees too much. To avoid the trouble of cultivation some growers keep the pecan orchard in sod or weeds, but it is not a good plan.

YIELDS. Mature pecan trees yield from 100–600 pounds

---

* Special articles on the subjects indicated by an asterisk (*) will be found at the words so marked.

of nuts a year. But it takes many years for the trees to get to such a prolific stage of bearing, and few ever reach the higher figure. Some top-worked trees have been very good yielders. One of them, in Mississippi, the whole top of which was changed to the variety Stuart, had the following record:

| Pounds of nuts | | Pounds of nuts |
|---|---|---|
| 1st year | 5 | 7th year | 75 |
| 2nd " | 20 | 8th " | 110 |
| 3rd " | 20 | 9th " | 210 |
| 4th " | 35 | 10th " | 240 |
| 5th " | 60 | 11th " | 250 |
| 6th " | 100 | 12th " | 350 |

This was, of course, a mature but undesirable tree when its top was grafted with Stuart cions. Young budded or grafted trees would not reach such bearing for many years. Perhaps a fair average for young trees would be 6–20 pounds in ten years after planting.

INSECT PESTS. A round, gray, obscure scale may be controlled with dormant sprays of oil; aphids, with sprays of nicotine and soap or bordeaux late in the spring and in summer. Several small caterpillars attack pecan. The nut case bearer lives in a little case that it makes for itself and attacks young shoots and nuts; satisfactory control has not yet been found. The leaf case bearer on buds and leaves can be controlled with a midsummer arsenical spray. The shuckworm is partially controlled by burning old hulls. Leaf feeders (fall webworm, walnut caterpillar, etc.) are easily checked by arsenicals. Nut weevils are partly controlled by early destruction of infested pecans and hickory nuts. The southern green stink bug is kept down by using velvet bean instead of cowpeas as cover crop. Twig girdlers and several borers occur (see HICKORY).

Spray schedules call for the dormant spray and 4 applications of bordeaux (fungicide), applied 3 weeks apart, beginning when the nuts set; nicotine or arsenical may be added to any of these applications if needed.

DISEASES. Pecan scab is the disease most dreaded by the commercial grower of this crop. The small, black spots on the veins, on the under side of the leaves, and on the twigs and fruits appear at first to be of little importance, but as they increase in size and number they cause great damage. Control is accomplished by the use of bordeaux spray of the formula 3-4-50. From three to five applications are necessary. Brown leaf spot and leaf blotch, caused by different organisms, both damage the leaves and cause early defoliation. These diseases are controlled as in pecan scab. Pecan rosette is caused by abnormal conditions of nutrition associated with deficiency of available zinc. This element when added to the soil in some soluble form serves to correct the condition.

**PECK.** See WEIGHTS AND MEASURES, 3.

**PECTEN-ABORIGINUM** (peck-ten-ab-o-rij'i-num). Native's comb. See PACHYCEREUS.

**PECTINATA, -us, -um** (peck-ti-nay'ta). Comb-like.

**PEDALIACEAE.** See SESAMUM.

**PEDATA, -us, -um** (pe-day'ta). Pedate (which see).

**PEDATE.** Palmate,* with the lateral or side lobes cleft or divided; usually applied to leaves.

**PEDICEL.** See PEDUNCLE.

**PEDICULARIS** (pe-dick-you-lay'ris). Wood-betony. Lousewort. A large genus of annual or perennial herbs, comprising about 250 species of the family Scrophulariaceae, scattered through the northern hemisphere, but a few found in S.A. Mostly erect, 3 in.–3 ft. high. Leaves alternate* or whorled, or sometimes in opposite pairs, generally finely cut into many segments. Flowers purplish, red, rose or white, borne in the axils of bracts* in a terminal raceme.* Corolla 2-lipped, tubular. Stamens* 4, 2 long and 2 short. Fruit a capsule*; seeds few. (*Pedicularis* is from the Latin for louse, in allusion to the supposed effect on sheep eating it.)

Propagated by seeds and division. Sometimes difficult to grow owing to its being partially parasitic on roots of other plants, therefore not a favorite, and suited mostly to the wild garden.

canadensis. Herbaceous hairy, perennial, growing to 18 in. high. Leaves 5 in. long, segmented. Flowers yellow, often tinged red, ¾ in. long. Fruit 3 times as long as the persistent calyx.* April–June. Eastern N.A., in the woods.

lanceolata. Smooth, herbaceous perennial to 3 ft. high. Leaves to 5 in. long, slightly segmented. Flowers yellow, ¾ in. long. Fruit when ripe same length as calyx. Sept.–Oct. New Eng. to Va. and westward.

**PEDILANTHUS** (ped-i-lan'thus). Tropical American, cactus-like, succulent plants of the spurge family, comprising over 30 species, only one of which is much cult. It is the redbird cactus, also called slipper-flower and Jew bush, and known to science as **P. tithymaloides**. It is a shrubby plant 4–6 ft. high, with fleshy, milky-juiced, zigzag stems, with ovalish leaves 2–4 in. long, keeled on the midrib beneath, and toothed. Flowers minute, bright red, in dense clusters (cymes*), the colored involucre spurred (hence slipper-flower). Fruit a capsule, about ¼ in. long. It is native from Fla. to Venezuela, and is often grown in the greenhouse northward. For its indoor cult. see SUCCULENTS. (*Pedilanthus* is from the Greek for slipper-flower.)

**PEDIOCACTUS** (ped-i-o-kak'tus). A single species of globe-shaped or orange-shaped cactus, **P. simpsoni**, the snowball cactus, so called because in the young state the plant is densely covered with white wool, most of which is lost in age. The plant body is about 6 in. thick, tubercled, and densely spiny. Spines 15–20 in a cluster, needle-like, 5–7 of the center ones erect and stouter than the diverging lateral spines. Flowers pinkish, about 1 in. long, funnel-shaped, and borne among tufts of white wool at the top of the plant. Fruit dry. It is one of the hardier species of cacti, being native from Kan. to Wash. and N. Mex. For culture see CACTI. It does not take kindly to transfer from the wild. (*Pediocactus* is from the Greek for plain and *Cactus*, in allusion to its growing on the Great Plains.)

**PEDUNCLE.** The stalk of a solitary flower, or the main stalk of a flower cluster. Each of the flowers in a cluster may have its own individual stalk, which is then properly called a pedicel.

**PEDUNCULARIS, -e** (pe-dunk-you-lar'is). Having a stalk or peduncle.*

**PEDUNCULATA, -us, -um** (pe-dunk-you-lay'ta). Having a stalk or peduncle.*

**PEEGEE.** An abbreviation, and often the trade vernacular, for *Hydrangea paniculata grandiflora*, sometimes written in the catalogues *Hydrangea p. g.*

**PEENTO.** A Chinese variety or race of rather tender peaches having flattish fruit. In the U.S. they are grown only in sub-tropical parts of the Gulf states.

**PEEPUL** = *Ficus religiosa*.

**PEJIBAYE** = *Guilielma gasipaes*.

**PEKINENSIS, -e** (pee-kin-en'sis). From Pekin (now Peiping), China.

**PELARGONIUM** (pee-lar-gō'ni-um). Garden geranium. Stork's-bill geranium. A large genus of South African, tender, perennial herbs and shrubs of the family Geraniaceae, their habits being very diverse in the different species. Stems strong-growing or trailing, herbaceous or woody. Leaves alternate,* stalked, simple, entire* and roundish, or much cut and often fern-like, some deeply marked on the upper side, smooth or hairy, a few fragrant. Flowers in umbel-like clusters growing on a leafless stalk from the axils* of the leaves. Individual flowers showy, varying from pure white, pink, crimson and bright scarlet in color, irregular. Calyx* of 5 sepals joined at the base. Petals 5. Stamens* 10. Ovary 5-celled, splitting into 5 sections when ripe, each containing 1 seed. (*Pelargonium* is from the Greek for a stork, in allusion to the shape of the fruit.)

crispum. Growing to 3 ft. with erect, thin, woody-wiry stems, having many upright branches, slightly hairy. Leaves alternate,* in 2 rows, short-stalked, small, roundish, 3-lobed, margins crinkled, lemon-scented. Umbels 1–3-flowered. Flowers pink, 2 upper petals lined deeper pink, 3 lower petals long and narrow.

denticulatum. Weak-growing, erect, to 1 ft. high. Leaves with long, finger-like lobes, the lobes deeply toothed, flat, smooth on the upper side, rough-hairy on the under side, and with balsamic odor. Umbels 3–4-flowered, with short, hairy stalks. Flowers lilac-rose or purple, 2 upper petals 2-lobed with dark markings.

domesticum. Show geranium. Fancy geranium. Lady Washington geranium. These common names are perhaps not properly associated with the true *domesticum* but have been classed under this species. Growing to 2 ft., of straggling habit. Stems soft, fleshy and hairy when young, lower part becoming hard and woody in age. Leaves 2–4 in. across, roundish, slightly lobed, toothed. Umbels few- to many-flowered. Flowers large, white, pink, or red, 2 upper petals usually blotched darker.

fragrans. Erect habit, growing to 1 ft., lower branches woody. Leaves numerous, roundish, hairy, margins wrinkled, lower leaves long-stalked, upper leaves without stalks. Umbels 4–8-flowered. Flowers whitish with pink veins. Closely allied to *odoratissimum*.

* Special articles on the subjects indicated by an asterisk (*) will be found at the words so marked.

**graveolens.** Rose geranium. Growing to 3 ft., woody. Leaves roundish in outline, 5-7-lobed, lobes toothed, fragrant. Umbels 5-10-flowered, flowers rose-pink. *See* HERB GARDENING.

**hortorum.** Fish geranium. Growing 1-6 ft. high, the stems strong and fleshy. Leaves 3-5 in. across, roundish, generally having a deep horseshoe-shaped marking or zone on the upper side, the margins scalloped. The plant has a faint, fish-like odor. Umbels many-flowered. Flowers red, salmon-pink, or white.

**odoratissimum.** Nutmeg geranium. The apple geranium is probably a variety. Stems erect, at first weak and spreading, up to 18 in. high. Leaves small, roundish, covered with soft, short hairs, hence grayish, the margins scalloped. Nutmeg-scented. Umbels 5-10-flowered. Flowers white, 2 upper petals veined deep pink.

**peltatum.** Ivy geranium. Stems trailing to 4 ft. long, fleshy when young, becoming woody below in age, angled at the joints. Leaves ivy-shaped, 5-pointed, bright glossy-green. Umbels 5-7-flowered. Flowers white to deep rose, upper petals having dark markings.

For other, quite different, and mostly hardy plants also called geranium *see* the genus GERANIUM.

### GARDEN GERANIUM CULTURE

Gardeners for convenience divide the pelargoniums into 4 groups, each differing in its method of culture, and each having its own particular use in the greenhouse or garden. They are all known as geraniums both by gardeners and the general public, although botanically they are not geraniums, but this name has been in use so long that it is doubtful if it will be discontinued. All are tender and can only be grown outside all year round in frost-free localities. Most pelargoniums in cultivation are hort. varieties.

GROUP 1. This type known as the Show or Fancy pelargoniums (Lady Washington geranium) have the largest individual flowers of the genus. They make very showy pot plants either for cool greenhouse or house plants, in a sunny window. Propagated from cuttings of firm shoots 3-4 in. long in July, inserted in a mixture of ½ sand, ½ soil in 2-in. pots, watering well after planting. They should then be placed in a cold frame or greenhouse in an airy position and shaded from strong sun.

As soon as rooted pot into 4-in. pots in potting mixture* 3, keeping plants near the glass to promote sturdy growth. When 6 in. long pinch out tip of shoots to make plant branch, more flowers being obtained by this method. In early Jan. re-pot into 6-in. pots, keeping in a cool, airy place, and water sparingly during winter months. Temperature should be 45°-60°. Water well from March-June, and when flower buds appear give small quantity of a general fertilizer once a week until first flowers open.

After flowering prune back to within 4 in. of the base, stand plants outdoors in full sun until new shoots appear, then take out of pots and remove most of the old soil. Re-pot into smaller pots, placing them under glass in Sept. Large specimens can be made by pruning old plants less, using 5-in. pots when re-potting and potting on into 7- or 8-in. pots. Good drainage and firm potting are essential. *See* POTTING.

GROUP 2. This type known as Zonal or Fish geraniums is the one so much used at one time for garden and window-box decoration and is still one of the best for continuous bloom from early summer to late fall. Included in this group are the variegated forms with white and green leaves, others with gold and bronze-shaded leaves, used for edging or color contrasts. Propagated from cuttings 3-5 in. long of young, short-jointed shoots in early Sept., avoiding sappy growths. Insert in mixture of 2 parts soil and 1 part sand, placing 5 round the edge of 5-in. pot. Water and stand in shady position outside or in cool greenhouse for 2 weeks, by which time a callus* will have formed.

They must then be moved to a sunny position in greenhouse or cold frame. When well rooted pot singly into 3-in. pots, using potting mixture* 3. Re-pot in Feb. or early March into 5-in. pots in which they should remain until planted out in the garden toward the end of May. Plants grow best when pots are standing on a bed of coal ashes or fine gravel with sufficient space between for air to circulate freely. Water sparingly during winter or stems will develop stem rot and die. Temperature should be 45°-60°. Flower buds should be picked off until April.

This type grows well in ordinary garden soil, if not too rich in nitrogen, which makes the plants develop fleshy stems and leaves, but few flowers. Plant in light, sunny position, never in complete shade. In frost-free localities they may be grown outside all year, plants often growing 6-8 ft. when trained on a trellis or wall.

An easy method of rooting a cutting of garden geranium

GROUP 3. This type, known as Ivy-leaved geraniums, having weak stems, ivy-shaped leaves, and many flowers, is admirably adapted for hanging baskets, ornamental vases or for window-box planting. Large specimens can be made by growing several in a large box or tub and training on wires to any desired shape. They may also be planted in beds 1 ft. apart and allowed to trail over the ground, forming a good ground cover with many flowers. Propagate the same as Fish geraniums, except in the young stages smaller pots may be used. When grown close together, in winter, each plant should be staked, when plants are about 8 in. high.

GROUP 4. This type, known as scented-leaved geraniums, are general favorites, due to their varied fragrance. There are over 200 varieties in cult., the best known being the lemon, rose, cinnamon, nutmeg and apple. Grown entirely for their leaves, they make good window plants, or may be grown outside in summer, when they will grow rapidly. Their stems are useful and fragrant decorations. Propagate as for Fish geranium. — H. R. M.

A good selection of garden geraniums should include: S. A. Nutt, semi-double, dark crimson; La Favorite, double, pure white; Mme. Récamier, white; Dryden, cherry-red, but white-eyed; and Beauté Poitevine, salmon-pink.

INSECT PESTS. Most pests of fuchsia attack geranium, as do some leaf feeders, which are controlled with arsenicals. Slimy, dark slugs occurring in greenhouses are checked by arsenicals when on plants, by tobacco when on soil, and also by bran bait.

DISEASES. Leafspot, gray mold, oedema and cutting rot are the common diseases. Caused by various fungi and bacteria, the *leafspots* can be controlled by removing infected leaves, reducing the humidity, avoiding crowding and keeping the plants dry. *Gray mold* occurs on the flowers, where spotting and blight are typical symptoms. Control is the same as for *leafspot*. *Oedema* first appears on the leaves as water-soaked spots which later turn brown and corky. The corky swellings may also appear on the leafstalks and stems. Increase ventilation, lower the humidity and avoid overwatering. *Cutting rot* is characterized by a black rot of the young cuttings. Use clean or sterilized sand and take cuttings from healthy plants.

**PELECYPHORA** (pell-e-siff′o-ra). A single species of low, tubercled, Mexican cactus, P. aselliformis, the hatchet-cactus, sometimes cult. in desert gardens or in greenhouses northward. The plant body is cylindric, not over 4 in. high,

---

* Special articles on the subjects indicated by an asterisk (*) will be found at the words so marked.

about 2 in. in diameter, its strongly flattened tubercles arranged in prominent spirals, each tubercle crowned with a solitary spine. Flowers about 1 in. wide, bell-shaped, purple, or the outer segments whitish. For culture *see* CACTI. (*Pelecyphora* is from the Greek for hatchet-bearing, in allusion to the fancied resemblance of the flattened tubercles to a hatchet.)

**PELICAN-FLOWER** = *Aristolochia grandiflora.*

**PELLAEA** (pell-ee'a). Cliff Brake. A large, widely distributed genus of ferns of the family Polypodiaceae, a few grown in the greenhouse or outdoors for ornament. They are mostly rock-inhabiting ferns, most of them inhabiting limestone. Fronds simply compound,* or in some species twice- or thrice-compound,* the stalks sometimes brown-hairy and chaffy, but usually polished and dark-colored. Spore* cases oblongish or circular, usually near tips of free veins, and often covered by the rolled edge of the segment. (*Pellaea* is from the Greek for dusky, in allusion to the usually dark frond stalks.)

The last two species are not hardy in the North and should be grown in the cool greenhouse. *P. atropurpurea*, a native plant, can be grown in the fern garden, preferably on a dry limestone wall. For cult. and propagation *see* FERNS AND FERN GARDENING.

**atropurpurea.** A hardy fern, not over 1 ft. high, the fronds tough, leathery, only once-compound,* the stalks dark purple and polished. Segments of the frond about 2 in. long and ⅜ in. wide. Eastern N.A. A plant for the hardy fern garden.

**densa** = *Cheilanthes densa.*

**rotundifolia.** Fronds not over 1 ft. long, once-compound,* the stalks shaggy and brown-hairy. Ultimate segments alternate, oblongish or rounder, the terminal one arrow-shaped, all faintly angled or toothed, or the margins entire. New Zealand. A greenhouse fern.

**viridis.** Fronds nearly 2 ft. long, the brown, shining stalk rather stiff and stout. Fronds twice- or thrice-compound,* each main division again compound, the ultimate segments varying from narrow to broad or even oval or arrow-shaped. Africa. A greenhouse fern.

**PELLIONIA.** Plants sometimes offered as of this genus are usually referable to *Ruellia* (which see). The true genus *Pellionia* is of no interest to American gardeners.

**PELLUCID.** Having the tissue transparent, as in many water plants.

**PELTANDRA** (pel-tan'dra). Arrow-arum. North American bog or water herbs of the arum family, one of the two known species occasionally cult. in the bog garden or along the edges of pools. It is the green arrow-arum, sometimes called poison arum and known to science as **P. virginica.** Leaves large, coarse, arrow-shaped, the stout, sheathing stalk about 3 times as long as the blade. Spathe* elongated, ultimately leathery and partly enclosing the green, berry-like fruit when ripe. Flowers minute, the male above the female, completely covering the spadix (*see* ARACEAE). There is no difficulty about growing arrow-arum in any wet place, and it will grow well nowhere else. (*Peltandra* is from the Greek for disks and flowers, in allusion to a technical character of the male flowers.)

**PELTARIA** (pel-tay'ri-a). Shieldwort. A small and rather unimportant genus of perennial herbs of the mustard family, **P. alliacea** occasionally grown for ornament, although it has an unpleasant onion odor. It is a smooth, branching herb, 12–18 in. high, the leaves alternate,* without marginal teeth, the upper leaves stem-clasping. Flowers small, white, in terminal clusters (racemes*), each flower with a very slender stalk. Fruit a flat, nearly round, papery pod (silicle*), splitting very tardily. The plant is easily raised from seed, and will bloom the second year. It can also be increased by division. (*Peltaria* is from the Greek for little shield, in allusion to the shape of the fruits.)

*PELTATA, -us, -um* (pell-tay'ta). Peltate.*

**PELTATE.** Having the stalk attached away from the margin of a leaf blade, and often in the center of it. Peltate leaves are apt to be shield-shaped, as in the common garden nasturtium and in the water shield (*Brasenia schreberi*).

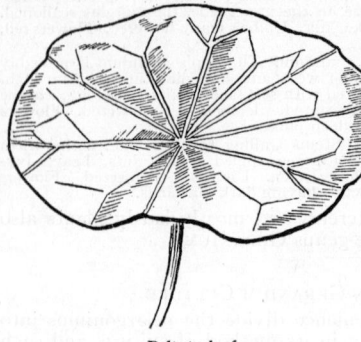

Peltate leaf

**PELTOPHORUM** (pell-toff'o-rum). A genus of tropical trees of the pea family, sometimes known as *Baryxylum*, only one of the species, **P. inerme**, of much hort. interest. It is an Indo-Malayan, quick-growing tree, up to 50 ft. high, occasionally planted for ornament in Fla. and throughout the tropics. It has twice-compound,* rusty-hairy leaves, the ultimate leaflets about ¾ in. long, and in 10–20 pairs. Flowers yellow, fragrant, not pea-like, the 5 petals nearly equal. Pod flattish, not splitting. The tree is hardy only in zone* 9, and resembles the royal poinciana except for the yellow flowers. (*Peltophorum* is from the Greek for shield-bearing, in allusion to the shape of the stigma.*) Sometimes offered as *P. ferrugineum*.

*PENDULA, -us, -um* (pen'dew-la). Hanging.

*PENDULIFLORA, -us, -um* (pen-dew-li-flow'ra). With hanging flowers.

**PENETROL.** A trademarked activator and spreader for nicotine sprays, sold with directions for use.

**PENICILLIUM ROT.** *See* Diseases at GLADIOLUS.

**PENIOCEREUS** (pen-i-o-seer'ee-us). A single species of cactus from western Tex., Ariz., and Mex., **P. greggi**, the deerhorn cactus, cult. in desert gardens for its curious habit, and showy, nocturnal, white flowers. It has a huge, turnip-like root, nearly 2 ft. in diameter, from which arise angled, leafless stems, 6–10 ft. long and about 1 in. in diameter, erect or sprawling. Spines small, black, 6–11 in a cluster, the central one or two erect, the rest divergent. Flowers nearly 8 in. long, white, but reddish on the outside. For culture *see* CACTI. There is one other species from Lower Calif. (*Peniocereus* is from the Greek for phalloid and *Cereus*, in allusion to the shape of the branches.)

*PENNATA, -us, -um* (pen-nay'ta). Same as *pinnata.*

**PENNISETUM** (pen-i-see'tum). A genus of 50 species of chiefly tropical grasses, some economic, and a handful grown for ornament in the border. They are annual or perennial grasses with erect stems (tall in the pearl millet) and grass-like leaves, sometimes colored in the hort. forms. Flowering cluster a spike-like panicle,* the spikelets having beneath them bristles, sometimes plumed, which are often longer than the spikelets. Fruit a grain in the pearl millet and edible. (*Pennisetum* is from the Greek for feather and bristle, in allusion to the often plumed bristles of some species.)

The pearl millet (*P. glaucum*) is a tropical annual, grown in the tropics for its grain which is used as food. In the U.S. it is suited only to the South and is little grown except for forage. *P. alopecuroides* and *P. ruppeli* are ornamental, hardy perennials grown in the border for ornament. They are of easy cult. and may be increased by division.

**alopecuroides.** A slender-stemmed grass, 2–4 ft. high, hairy as far up as the spike. Leaves bright green. Flowering spike 2–6 in. long, silvery, the anthers* purplish. Bristles of the spikelet long and conspicuous. China. Sometimes known as *P. japonicum*.

**americanum** = *Pennisetum glaucum.*

**glaucum.** Pearl millet, also known as Indian and African millet. A tall, annual, tropical grass of unknown origin, the stems stout, 6–10 ft. high. Leaves 2–3 ft. long, rough on the edges and on the veins. Flowering spike cat-tail-like, 12–18 in. long, with a leaf-like, spreading bract.* Spikelets with plumed bristles. Fruit an egg-shaped, bluish or whitish grain about

---

* Special articles on the subjects indicated by an asterisk (*) will be found at the words so marked.

PENNSYLVANIA 591 PENNSYLVANIA

⅛ in. long, which usually bursts the enclosing envelope. Occasionally known as *P. americanum*, but probably not American.

**japonicum** = *Pennisetum alopecuroides*.

**ruppeli**. Fountain grass, and the leading ornamental species. A gracefully arching, perennial grass 3–4 ft. high. Leaves many, 15–20 in. long, about ⅛ in. wide, sometimes with the margins rolled, green (or variously colored in the hort. forms). Spikes 6–10 in. long, curved or nodding, the bristles of the spikelets about 1 in. long. In the most popular cult. forms the spikes and foliage may be rose-purple, or, in the *var.* **cupreum**, coppery. A handsome ornamental grass native in Abyssinia, but hardy over most of the country.

**PENNSYLVANIA.** The state lies wholly in zones* 3 and 4.

Soils. Pennsylvania soils vary widely in every possible manner, with the result that the state contains some of the best and considerable areas of the poorer soils in northeastern United States. Soils not adapted for growing any specific class of plants are under a severe handicap. It should be recognized, however, that a particular soil, unsuited for the commercial production of any given crop, may often be successfully utilized in an amateur way, where the gardener is not dependent for revenue on the produce, and where he feels it worth while in results obtained to go to more trouble and expense to make artificially an area suitable for his purposes than could ever be justified commercially.

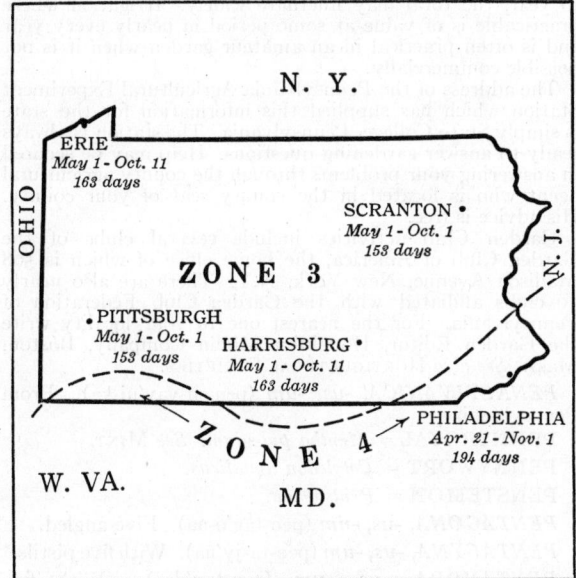

PENNSYLVANIA

The zones of hardiness crossing Pennsylvania are those shown on the colored map at Zone, which should be consulted for details. The dates are the average latest killing frost in spring and the first one in the fall. The figures below the dates show the average length of the growing season.

Chief Gardening Centers. These are in general located in and about the larger cities of the state and in the more densely populated counties such as Pittsburgh, Philadelphia, Scranton, and Harrisburg.

Main Fruit and Vegetable Areas. The principal grape area is in Erie County. Apples and peaches are grown chiefly in the southern and eastern parts of the state, although the former are produced to some extent in every county. Small fruits of all kinds are usually grown near the cities and towns where they are marketed.

Canning crops are produced principally in south central Pennsylvania. The greenhouse industry is located mainly in northwestern Pennsylvania near the Ohio line. Sweet corn, one of the most important vegetables, is most plentiful in Allegheny County near Pittsburgh, although it is grown in varying amounts near practically all the cities and boroughs. There is an intensive area in Chester and Delaware counties devoted to mushroom culture.

The principal market-gardening area is in Philadelphia, Bucks and Montgomery counties. Other areas extend along the Delaware River about as far as Trenton and on the flood plains of the Susquehanna River.

Cabbage, ranking with sweet corn in importance, is produced as a field crop in many parts of the state.

Ornamental Plants

The ornamental trees and shrubs which have been found adapted to Pennsylvania conditions are as follows:

Shrubs:
  *Abelia grandiflora.*
  *Amelanchier canadensis.*
  *Aronia arbutifolia* — Red chokeberry.
  *Azalea viscosa* — Swamp honeysuckle.
  *Azalea calendulacea* — Flame azalea.
  *Azalea nudiflora* — Pinxter-flower.
  *Azalea arborescens* — Tree azalea.
  *Berberis thunbergi* — Japanese barberry.
  *Berberis thunbergi minor* — Box barberry.
  *Chaenomeles lagenaria* — Japanese flowering quince.
  *Chionanthus virginica* — Fringe-tree.
  *Cornus florida* — Flowering dogwood.
  *Cornus mas* — Cornelian cherry.
  *Cotoneaster divaricata.*
  *Cotoneaster dielsiana.*
  *Daphne cneorum.*
  *Deutzia gracilis.*
  *Euonymus patens.*
  *Euonymus radicans vegetus.*
  *Euonymus alatus* — Winged spindle-tree.
  *Exochorda racemosa* — Pearl bush.
  *Forsythia suspensa* — Weeping golden bell.
  *Forsythia intermedia spectabilis.*
  *Ilex verticillata* — Winterberry.
  *Kolkwitzia amabilis* — Beauty-bush.
  *Laburnum anagyroides* — golden chain.
  *Ligustrum amurense* — Amur privet.
  *Ligustrum obtusifolium regelianum* — Regel's privet.
  *Lonicera fragrantissima.*
  *Lonicera maacki.*
  *Lonicera tatarica* — Tartarian honeysuckle.
  *Philadelphus virginalis* — Mock-orange.
  *Rhododendron maximum* — Great laurel.
  *Rhodotypos tetrapetala* — Jetbead.
  *Spiraea trichocarpa.*
  *Spiraea vanhouttei* — Bridal wreath.
  *Stephanandra incisa.*
  *Syringa vulgaris* — Lilac.
  *Syringa persica* — Persian lilac.
  *Viburnum carlesi.*
  *Viburnum dentatum* — Arrow-wood.
  *Viburnum dilatatum.*
  *Viburnum prunifolium* — Black haw.
  *Viburnum tomentosum.*
  *Viburnum tomentosum sterile* — Japanese snowball.

Deciduous Trees:
  *Acer saccharum* — Sugar maple.
  *Acer pennsylvanicum* — Striped maple.
  *Acer ginnala.*
  *Betula pendula* — Weeping form.
  *Betula populifolia* — Gray birch.
  *Betula papyrifera* — Canoe birch.
  *Cercidiphyllum japonicum* — Katsura tree.
  *Cercis canadensis* — American redbud.
  *Cercis chinensis* — Asiatic redbud.
  *Crataegus crus-galli* — Cockspur thorn.
  *Crataegus phaenopyrum* — Washington thorn.
  *Crataegus oxyacantha* — English hawthorn.
  *Elaeagnus angustifolia* — Russian olive.
  *Fagus sylvatica cuprea* — Copper beech.
  *Fraxinus americana* — White ash.
  *Ginkgo biloba* — Ginkgo or Maidenhair-tree.
  *Koelreuteria paniculata* — Pride-of-India.

---

* Special articles on the subjects indicated by an asterisk (*) will be found at the words so marked.

# PENNSYLVANIA

*Liquidambar styraciflua* — Sweet gum.
*Malus atrosanguinea* — Carmine crabapple.
*Malus floribunda* — Showy crabapple.
*Malus ioensis* (fl. pl.) — Bechtel's crab.
*Malus sargenti.*
*Oxydendrum arboreum* — Sourwood.
*Platanus acerifolia* — London plane.
*Quercus palustris* — Pin oak.
*Quercus rubra* — Red oak.
*Sophora japonica* — Japanese pagoda tree.
*Sorbus aucuparia* — European mountain-ash.
*Ulmus americana* — American elm.
*Ulmus parvifolia* — Chinese elm.

CONIFEROUS EVERGREENS:
*Abies concolor* — White fir.
*Abies veitchi.*
*Chamaecyparis obtusa* — Hinoki cypress.
*Chamaecyparis pisifera plumosa.*
*Juniperus chinensis pfitzeriana.*
*Juniperus communis depressa* — Prostrate juniper.
*Juniperus communis hibernica* — Irish juniper.
*Juniperus horizontalis douglasi* — Waukegan juniper.
*Juniperus sabina tamariscifolia.*
*Juniperus squamata meyeri.*
*Juniperus virginiana* — Red cedar.
*Juniperus virginiana glauca.*
*Larix decidua* — European larch.
*Picea engelmanni* — Engelmann's spruce.
*Picea pungens kosteri* — Koster's blue spruce.
*Pinus resinosa* — Red pine.
*Pseudotsuga taxifolia* — Douglas fir.
*Taxus baccata repandens.*
*Taxus cuspidata* — Japanese yew.
*Taxus cuspidata capitata.*
*Taxus cuspidata nana.*
*Thuja occidentalis* — Arborvitae.
*Tsuga canadensis* — Hemlock.

The flowers recommended for Pennsylvania conditions are as follows:

Roses — Hybrid Tea, Hybrid Perpetual, Ramblers and Climbers, Polyanthas, and many species types. *See* ROSE.
Gladiolus.
Peony.
Dahlia.
Iris — mostly tall bearded types. *See* ROSE.
Tulips.
Narcissus, and practically all types of spring-flowering bulbs such as

| | |
|---|---|
| Scilla | Galanthus |
| Chionodoxa | Fritillaria |
| Muscari | Crocus |

ANNUALS:

| | |
|---|---|
| Aster | Hollyhocks |
| Pansy | Sweet alyssum |
| Petunia | Calendula |
| Snapdragon | Bachelor's button |
| Sweet pea | Sweet sultan |
| Zinnia | Clarkia |
| Gypsophila | Coreopsis |
| Dianthus | Cosmos |
| Lupine | Candytuft |
| Forget-me-not | Feverfew |
| Poppy | Stock |
| Phlox | Four-o'clock |
| Portulaca | Mignonette |
| African daisy | Salpiglosis |
| Gaillardia | Scabiosa |
| Impatiens | Marigold |
| Lobelia | Verbena |
| Celosia | |

PERENNIALS. Practically all the types of perennial garden flowers grow in the state. *See* PERENNIALS.

# PENTHOUSE GARDEN

FROST DATES

| Town | Average date of last killing frost in spring | Date when chance of killing frost in spring falls to 10 per cent | Average date of earliest killing frost in fall | Date when chance of killing frost in fall rises to 10 per cent |
|---|---|---|---|---|
| Philadelphia | Apr. 21 | May 1 | Nov. 1 | Oct. 11 |
| Pittsburgh | May 1 | May 21 | Oct. 1 | Sept. 21 |
| Erie | May 1 | May 21 | Oct. 11 | Sept. 21 |
| Scranton | May 1 | May 21 | Oct. 1 | Sept. 21 |
| Harrisburg | May 1 | May 21 | Oct. 11 | Oct. 1 |

The above dates are for the Weather Bureau Stations only. Because of local topography or some other reason, wide variations in the frost dates, hence the length of the growing season, frequently occur in neighboring areas.

RAINFALL

The average total annual precipitation for Pennsylvania varies only slightly with the locality from 36 to somewhat over 40 inches. The rainfall during the growing season from May to September, inclusive, is from 16½ to 18½ inches on the average. However, for any given month from year to year, the total may fluctuate widely. Irrigation where practicable is of value at some period in nearly every year and is often practical in an amateur garden when it is not possible commercially.

The address of the Pennsylvania Agricultural Experiment Station which has supplied this information for the state is simply State College, Pennsylvania. The station is always ready to answer gardening questions. Help may be secured in answering your problems through the county agricultural agent who is located in the county seat of your county. His advice is free.

Garden Club activities include several clubs of the Garden Club of America, the home office of which is 598 Madison Avenue, New York, N.Y. There are also nearly 70 clubs affiliated with the Garden Club Federation of Pennsylvania. For the nearest one to your locality write the Garden Editor, Houghton Mifflin Company, Boston, Mass. *See also* HORTICULTURAL SOCIETIES.

**PENNSYLVANICA**, *-us, -um* (pen-sil-vay'ni-ka). From Pennsylvania.

**PENNYROYAL** = *Mentha pulegium.* See MINT.

**PENNYWORT** = *Cotyledon umbilicus.*

**PENSTEMON** = *Pentstemon.*

**PENTAGONA**, *-us, -um* (pen-tag'o-na). Five-angled.

**PENTAGYNA**, *-us, -um* (pen-ta-jy'na). With five pistils.*

**PENTANDRA**, *-us, -um* (pen-tan'dra). With five stamens.*

**PENTANTHA**, *-us, -um* (pen-tan'tha). Five-flowered.

**PENTAPHYLLA**, *-us, -um* (pen-ta-fil'la). Five-leaved; or often, with five leaflets.

**PENTAS** (pen'tas). Chiefly African herbs or undershrubs of the family Rubiaceae, P. lanceolata the only one of the 10 known species of hort. interest. It is a somewhat woody herb 1–2 ft. high, with opposite,* ovalish leaves 4–6 in. long. Flowers tubular, about 1 in. long, pale purple, hairy in the throat, usually stalkless or nearly so in a close cluster (cyme* or corymb*). Stamens* usually 5. Fruit dry. This is an attractive greenhouse plant for the North or may be used as a bedding subject in the Far South. It needs a tropical greenhouse and potting mixture* 5 in the North, and can be propagated by cuttings of partly ripened wood over bottom-heat. It is sometimes offered as *P. carnea*, and comes also in white and in red flowers. (*Pentas* is from the Greek for five, in allusion to most of the floral parts being in fives.)

**PENTHOUSE GARDEN.** The modern penthouse garden has its origin in the zoning laws which require set-backs in the upper stories of tall buildings, thus providing terraces on which man can exercise his gardening ingenuity. In planning for the garden, however, it is wiser to content

---

* Special articles on the subjects indicated by an asterisk (*) will be found at the words so marked.

PENTHOUSE GARDEN ON A ROOF MADE FOR IT
See text for the management of roof gardens where such a weight of soil and water is impossible.

oneself with creating the illusion of a garden, by using only a minimum of city-proof plants in a pleasant setting of good architectural backgrounds and accents.

One of the chief reasons for choosing architectural rather than horticultural treatment for the penthouse garden is the presence of conditions inimical to the growth of plants. The handicaps of insufficient soil, high winds, lack of moisture, and constant deposit of soot and dirt on the leaves, make it difficult for even the hardiest plants to survive. These difficulties can be overcome to a certain extent by installing windbreaks of glass or lattice fences, where building restrictions permit, by artificial irrigation systems, and in the case of new buildings, by constructing the building so as to permit the additional load of topsoil, two to three feet deep, properly drained, over the terrace area. Without these rather expensive, and often impracticable aids to horticulture, the penthouse gardener has the alternative of resigning himself either to the exclusive use of privet, ailanthus, and wisteria, or to the annual replacement of all his plant material. With the windbreak, irrigation, and proper soil depth it is possible to enlarge greatly the planting list. One can then grow Japanese flowering cherries (*Prunus subhirtella* is the best), flowering crabapples (*Malus floribunda, coronaria, theifera, sieboldi*), lilacs, forsythia, Rose-of-Sharon (*Hibiscus syriacus*), *Pieris japonica*, Rhododendron *carolinianum* and *maximum*, hawthorns (*Crataegus phaenopyrum, crus-galli, intricata, oxyacantha*), and others of the hardier flowering shrubs and trees. In general, it is better to choose plants with smooth, even shiny leaves, rather than those with rough, hairy ones, as the soot and dirt are more easily removed.

Flower bloom in the penthouse garden is restricted to very few disease-resistant perennials and annuals. Iris, peonies, chrysanthemums, among the perennials, and petunias, lobelia, lantana, zinnias and French marigolds, among the annuals, make the list of successful plants on the roof. Provision should be made for a foot of well-enriched soil, at least a half-day's sun and daily, thorough watering. All soil should be fertilized with bone meal and shredded cow manure, or a well-balanced commercial fertilizer every year. The flowers should be grown either below the parapet wall or with a windbreak of hedge or trellis behind them. The high, persistent wind on most terraces will snap off stems and dry up the leaves almost immediately unless the plants are well sheltered.

The most satisfactory blooms in the penthouse garden are the spring-flowering bulbs. Tulips, narcissus, hyacinths, planted in the fall, give a mass of color in April and May. The bulbs should be renewed each fall for full success, and the soil refertilized before planting them. A covering of peat moss and evergreen boughs for the winter is advisable over all bulb plantings.

Aside from the difficulty of making plants live and thrive, the architectural treatment is advisable from purely aesthetic standpoints. In the first place the flat planes of the house walls, the parapet, and the adjoining buildings are made into a more harmonious whole by utilizing them in the decorative scheme, and combining them with allied or identical shapes and materials. The house walls may be covered by perspective trellis in interesting pattern, with an occasional vine tracery against it. Where it is desirable to block out part of a neighboring building or to frame an interesting view of the skyline, the parapet wall (usually rather ugly, with its copper flashing and heavy coping) may be concealed by trellis work extended to the necessary height and designed to reveal or obliterate neighboring objects.

---

\* Special articles on the subjects indicated by an asterisk (\*) will be found at the words so marked.

Where the terrace extends around two sides of the penthouse, an illusion of distance and spaciousness is gained by an open arch or gateway through which one catches a glimpse of the garden beyond. *See* the picture at MODERN GARDEN DESIGN.

The use of running water in a city garden does much to make it enticing and interesting. A simple wall fountain, with a shallow basin below, is possible at a very little expense. An old lead cistern or a shallow stone pool basin may be made into a mirror pool with a figure or a fountain jet for accent opposite a door or window. Where the terrace construction makes piping difficult or prohibitively expensive a small pipe run from the hose connection can be concealed behind the planting and will be ample for the small amount of water needed for a pool supply.

In making the penthouse garden the wisest initial expenditure is for suitable, well-designed, permanent, architectural background and accent, with provision for protection from wind and dirt, adequate water supply and rich soil. With these basic elements provided and an allowance for refurnishing the planting each year, the penthouse garden, whether a tiny terrace outside the living room or a great expanse of gardens and allées surrounding a large penthouse, may be a source of enjoyment and outdoor activity throughout the year, with an expenditure in keeping with the size of the property and the tastes of the owner. — M. D. L. *See also* the illustration at MODERN GARDEN DESIGN.

### FURNITURE AND ORNAMENT

Furniture on the penthouse terrace must be of a sturdy type to withstand the constant exposure to weather conditions. In many of the European terraces this has been planned for at the time the building is erected — and tables and benches of concrete are made as an integral part of the structure. It should also be made of a material heavy enough to be wind-resistant. Stone and iron benches are the most practical if not the most comfortable penthouse furniture, and can be kept clean in city conditions where soot is prevalent by turning the hose on them. But when comfort is desired iron, with wooden-slatted backs and seats, or wooden furniture forms a good compromise. Terrace furniture of a less formal nature, of iron laced with rawhide, or seats slung with awning material make for a greater degree of informality and are suitable if a casual outdoor living room is desired. Stick-willow chaises and chairs, with cushions covered with water-resistant material, add to the comfort and livable quality of the terrace.

As many penthouse terraces are lived on in summer, and looked at in winter, it is desirable to furnish them with permanent decorations such as trellises and iron wall brackets which support vines or contain pots for plants. These should be made to conform to the general architectural character of the building itself. In many instances fences and gates are necessary for the insurance of privacy and protection. These if made of grilled iron can be designed to harmonize with the wall brackets and trellises that are in use. Wood picket fences are also a desirable medium, although frequently discouraged because of fire laws.

Pots of all varieties are definite terrace ornaments, but should be made of material heavy enough to have a wind resistance, such as concrete, iron, lead and other metals. Pots of flowers add color and charm to a terrace and have the advantage of being easily moved so that the effect of flower planting can be placed wherever a touch of color is needed according to season. These potted plants can also be brought into the house when the cold days come so that an investment in plant material is not lost.

For protection against rain and sun the terrace awning is an important feature. Awnings are of the type that are regulated by a roller device and when closed are protected by an overhanging guard. What are perhaps more satisfactory are those supported by structural piping over which the awning is permanently stretched. As a preventive against fire hazard there is now available a fireproof awning material which is impervious even to a lighted cigarette thrown from an upper window or from sparks blown from adjacent chimneys.

Perhaps one of the most interesting and neglected features in terrace decoration is the use of sculpture. Sculptured figures are a delight to the eye in wind and rain, and also when weighted with snow. These figures should be selected with great care both from the quality of design and from point of view of proper scale. They should be placed at some focal point which fits in with the general landscaping scheme of the terrace or where they can be equally enjoyed when looked at from the room adjoining the terrace itself. It is important that sculpture, particularly if placed on a parapet, be securely attached to its base so there may be no fear of any danger of its falling on passers-by. The more formal and decorative type of sculpture seems to fit in well with the average architectural rigidity that surrounds it. Carved stone, bronzes and lead, and if the terrace is lavish and formal, possibly marble, are the best mediums for figures that perform this decorative function. — R. A. M.

**PENTSTEMON** (pent-ste′mon). Beardtongue. A large genus of perennial herbs (rarely shrubs) of the family Scrophulariaceae, one of them Asiatic, all the rest of the 150 species North American, chiefly from the western U.S. They have opposite* or whorled* leaves, and showy, 2-lipped,* tubular flowers, mostly in terminal clusters (racemes* or panicles*) that bloom in summer. Calyx* 5-parted. Corolla with the lower lip 3-lobed, the upper lip 2-lobed. Stamens 5, 4 of them fertile, the fifth sterile and often bearded. Fruit a capsule. (*Pentstemon* is from the Greek for 5 stamens,* which the genus has, although one is sterile.)

The beardtongues include attractive border plants, some rock garden species, and a few of uncertain hardiness in the eastern states north of zone* 4, especially in the case of those species native along the Pacific Coast. The cult. of the species grown chiefly in the rock garden will be found at ROCK GARDEN. The others, all perennials, will often flower rather quickly from seed, some the first year, especially forms known as *P. gloxinioides*. Generally, the beardtongues can be grown in full sunshine, but they tend to die out in a year or so if kept there. Most of them do better if given a light mulch in winter, especially those from the Pacific Coast. Many of the species are important bee plants in the West.

**acuminatus.** St. Joseph's-wand. Stems smooth, bluish-green, 1–2 ft. high. Leaves ovalish, 2–3 in. long, without teeth. Flowers about ¾ in. long, blue, the sterile stamen* bearded. Wash. and Ore.

**alpinus.** Stems smooth, not over 1 ft. high. Leaves lance-shaped, 2–4 in. long, without teeth. Flowers about 1 in. long, bluish-purple, the sterile stamen* not bearded. Rocky Mountains. For cult. see ROCK GARDEN.

**angustifolius.** Stems smooth, bluish-green, not over 12 in. high. Leaves lance-shaped or narrower, 1½–2½ in. long, without teeth. Flowers about ¾ in. long, blue, the sterile stamen* bearded. Prairies from S. Dak. to Mont. and N. Mex. Sometimes known as *P. caeruleus*.

**antirrhinoides.** A shrub, 3–6 ft. high, not hardy eastward. Leaves oblongish or narrower, about ½ in. long. Flowers about ⅝ in. long, yellow, the sterile stamen* bearded. Southern Calif., and not certainly hardy except in similar climates.

**barbatus.** A stout perennial 4–6 ft. high, the stems smooth. Leaves narrow. Flowers about 1 in. long, red, the lower lip* bearded, the sterile stamen* not bearded. Utah to Mex. A good pink hort. form is Pink Beauty.

**caeruleus** = *Pentstemon angustifolius*.

**centranthifolius.** Scarlet bugler. Stems 2–3 ft. high, bluish-green. Leaves thick, ovalish or narrower, 1½–2½ in. long, without teeth. Flowers about 1 in. long, red, the sterile stamen* not bearded. Calif. to Ariz.

**cobaea.** A hairy-stemmed perennial 1–2 ft. high. Leaves oblong or wider, 3–5 in. long, toothed. Flowers nearly 2 in. long, purplish, not much 2-lipped, the sterile stamen* bearded. Prairies, Mo. to Tex.

**cordifolius.** A shrub, half erect or climbing, the stem hairy. Leaves oval, 1–2 in. long, toothed. Flowers about 1 in. long, scarlet, the sterile stamen* bearded. Southern Calif. and not hardy in colder regions.

**diffusus.** A bushy, hairy perennial, 1–2 ft. high. Leaves ovalish or narrower, 1½–2½ in. long, deeply toothed. Flowers blue or purple, about ¾ in. long, the sterile stamen* bearded. British Columbia to Ore.

**digitalis.** Foxglove beardtongue. A nearly smooth herb, 3–5 ft. high. Leaves ovalish or narrower, 4–6 in. long, toothed. Flowers about 1 in. long, white (rarely pink), the tube dilated, the sterile stamen* bearded. Me. to Va. west to S. Dak. and Tex.

**glaber.** A smooth-stemmed perennial, 1–2 ft. high. Leaves oblongish, or broadest toward the tip, 4–6 in. long, without teeth. Flowers about 1 in. long, blue or purple, the sterile stamen* not bearded but somewhat hairy. N. Dak. to Wyo. For cult. see ROCK GARDEN.

**gloxinioides.** A race or group of garden hybrids thought to be derived from crossing *P. hartwegi* and *P. cobaea*. They are found in many colors and will generally bloom the first year from seed.

**grandiflorus.** A stout, upright perennial, 4–6 ft. high, the stems smooth. Leaves ovalish or broader toward the tip, 1½–2½ in. long. Flowers

---
* Special articles on the subjects indicated by an asterisk (*) will be found at the words so marked.

lavender-blue, about 2 in. long, the sterile stamen* bearded. Prairies, Ill., N. Dak. and Wyo.

**hartwegi.** Not over 4 ft. high, the stems nearly smooth, purplish. Leaves ovalish or narrower, without teeth. Flowers very showy, the clusters drooping, the corolla nearly 2 in. long, slightly curved, brilliant scarlet. Colder parts of Mex. and uncertainly hardy northward, even with winter mulch.

**heterophyllus.** A smooth shrub 3–5 ft. high. Leaves lance-shaped or narrower, 1½–2½ in. long, without teeth. Flowers about 1½ in. long, purple, the sterile stamen* smooth. Calif. For cult. *see* ROCK GARDEN.

**hirsutus.** A sticky-hairy perennial, 2–3 ft. high. Leaves oblongish or narrower, 3–4½ in. long, toothed. Flowers purple or violet, about 1 in. long, the sterile stamen* and the throat densely bearded. Me. to Fla. and Tex.

**laevigatus.** A nearly smooth perennial, 2–3 ft. high. Leaves oblongish or narrower, 4–6 in. long, toothed. Flowers about 1 in. long, purple, the sterile stamen* bearded. Pa. to Fla. and westward.

**menziesi.** A woody-based perennial, 4–6 ft. high, the leaves oblong or ovalish, not over ¾ in. long. Flowers violet-blue or purple, about 1 in. long, the sterile stamen* bearded. May. British Columbia to Ore.

**ovatus.** A hairy-stemmed perennial, 2–4 ft. high. Leaves broadly oval, 2–3 in. long. Flowers about ¾ in. long, first blue then purple, the sterile stamen* bearded. Ore. to British Columbia.

**rattani.** Not over 18 in. high. Leaves oblong or triangular-oval, 1½–2¼ in. long, toothed. Flowers about 1 in. long, lavender, the sterile stamen* not bearded but slightly hairy. Calif.

**rupicolus.** A shrubby, rock garden plant, not over 5 in. high, the stems hairy. Leaves ovalish or nearly round, bluish-green, not over ½ in. long. Flowers about 1½ in. long, crimson, the sterile stamen* smooth. Wash. For cult. *see* ROCK GARDEN.

**spectabilis.** A smooth, bluish-green perennial, 4–6 ft. high. Leaves ovalish or narrower, 2–3½ in. long, toothed. Flowers rose-purple or lilac, about 1 in. long, the sterile stamen* smooth. Ariz. and Calif.

**torreyi.** Perhaps not more than a variety of *P. barbatus*, but with scarlet flowers and the lower lip not bearded. Colo. to northern Mex.

**unilateralis.** Not over 2 ft. high, the stems smooth. Leaves narrowly lance-shaped or broadest toward the tip, 3–4 in. long. Flowers about ¾ in. long, blue, the sterile stamen* smooth, the flower cluster 1-sided. Wyo. to Utah. For cult. *see* ROCK GARDEN.

**PEONY.** These outstandingly beautiful garden flowers are all derived from perennial herbs (one woody) of the genus **Paeonia** (pee-ō'ni-a) of the buttercup family, which comprises about 25, chiefly Asiatic, species. Of these the five below, with their varieties and derivative hybrids, make up most of the garden peonies of today, although other species are to be found in the collections of fanciers and are used chiefly in making new crosses. All are erect herbs from tuberous or thickened roots, the leaves large, some basal, others on the stem, all compound,* sometimes thrice-compound* or with dissected segments. Flowers large, showy, usually solitary and terminal, rarely a few in a cluster, variously colored (*see* below). Sepals 5. Petals 5–10, but much more numerous in some of the hort. varieties (especially the double-flowered types). Stamens numerous, some of them sterile and petal-like. Fruit a collection of dried pods (follicles*), the seeds fleshy. (Named, or thought to be, for a Greek god of healing, Paian.)

For culture *see* below. All are spring-blooming.

**P. albiflora.** The chief source of the Chinese or common peony (*see* below). Root a collection of narrow tubers. Stems erect, unbranched and with one flower, or branched and with 2–5 flowers, usually 2–3½ ft. high. Leaves twice-compound,* the ultimate segments often red-veined, not lobed or dissected, usually oblongish or narrower. Flower stalk long, stout, often bracted.* Petals 8, or much more in some hort. sorts. Stamens* golden-yellow. Fruit usually smooth. Jap., China, and Siberia. The *var.* **festiva** has large, white, double flowers. The *var.* **sinensis** has double, very large crimson flowers. The latter is sometimes offered as *P. sinensis.*

**P. lutea.** A somewhat shrubby perennial, 2–3 ft. high. Leaves compound, the ultimate segments oblongish, cut or lobed. Flowers nearly 4 in. wide, golden-yellow. Fruit smooth. China.

**P. moutan** = *Paeonia suffruticosa.*

**P. officinalis.** Not over 3 ft. high. Leaves twice-compound,* the oblongish ultimate segments lobed. Flowers nearly 4 in. wide, crimson, white, or yellowish. Fruits white-felty. Southern Eu. and western As. For its many varieties *see* (3) below.

**P. sinensis** = *Paeonia albiflora sinensis.*

**P. suffruticosa.** Tree Peony. A much-branched shrubby plant 4–6 ft. high, often less as cult. Leaves twice-compound,* the ultimate segments 3–5-lobed and pale beneath. Flowers sometimes 12 in. wide, rose-red or white. Fruit densely hairy. China. There are many color forms and varieties (*see* below).

**P. tenuifolia.** Not over 18 in. high, and with creeping rootstocks. Leaves thrice-compound,* the ultimate segments narrow and fern-like. Flowers 3–4 in. wide, crimson or purple. Fruit hairy. Southeastern Eu. and western As.

### PEONY CULTURE

1. CHINESE PEONIES. The so-called Chinese peonies of our gardens are the descendants of a plant, *Paeonia albiflora*, or its variety *sinensis*, found still growing wild in northeastern Asia. When Chinese peonies were first brought to Europe, about 1800, there were more than a hundred distinct varieties already existing in Chinese gardens. We should probably regard all varieties in this group as simply mutations* from the original wild plant rather than as hybrids with any other species.

Chinese peonies soon became popular in Europe and from there came over to America; so that from about 1800 to the present day horticulturists have busied themselves with raising plants from seed for the purpose of getting new and improved varieties. Several thousand of such have been named and put on the market, and the stream shows no sign of abating.

PEONIES FROM SEED. Peonies are easily raised from seed; it should be sown in autumn in an open frame where a few may germinate the following spring, but most the spring after that. The young seedlings in the second year of their growth may be lifted and set into well-prepared ground. This transplanting should be done either very early in spring, or else in July or later, when the leaves have grown resistant. The young plants if well cared for may bloom within two or three years more. They will not "come true"; *i.e.* most of them will be unlike the parent in color and form. If the seed was gathered from fine varieties a fair percentage of the new plants will yield flowers of satisfactory quality, but none of them are likely to be distinct or in any way superior to named kinds already in existence. The hope of producing fine novelties lies either in an immense mass production of seedlings or else in careful intercrossing between chosen parents of the highest quality.

PROPAGATION. When a seedling of merit appears and it seems desirable to propagate it, the plant should be grown on, until it is large enough to produce about half a dozen stems. Then in autumn the clump may be lifted and cut up into sections, each of which must have one or more pieces of root attached to a portion of the crown carrying a bud or buds. The ideal division will have a good strong attachment from the roots to the crown fragment, the roots themselves being cut down to about six inches. It is a good procedure in dividing precious plants to cut back all the roots as soon as the plant is dug; this makes it easier to handle. It should then be washed to facilitate the actual dividing. The process may be repeated at intervals of about three years. It is usually quite useless in dividing Chinese peonies to save and replant the root fragments which have been broken off and which have no buds attached. Most varieties in this group do not possess the power of developing buds on root fragments, though there seem to be occasional, and very rare, exceptions to this rule.

CULTURE. Peony plants should be set so that the buds are two or three inches below the surface of the soil. New plants should never be set in ground from which established peony clumps have been recently removed. The peony likes rich ground, but the roots must not be placed in contact with manure. The best method of preparing the soil is by deep digging and deep manuring, leaving a sufficient depth of sweet clean loam in which to set the roots. A peony well set in a strong soil should not require further fertilization for 25 years. The roots are almost always set in autumn, from September to November. Spring transplanting is risky. Peonies may be planted either in full sun or in partial shade. Some protection from sunlight helps the flowers to retain the full delicacy of their coloring, which fades out in bright sunlight. On the other hand, the peony detests having its ground invaded by tree roots. Hence elm trees are particularly bad neighbors for a peony bed.

TYPES. The three main types of bloom among the Chinese peonies are (1) singles, (2) Japanese, (3) doubles. The singles may not have more than one or two rows of "guard" petals, with true pollen-bearing stamens in the center. The flowers of the Japanese type have also one or two rows of guard petals, but the stamens are here transformed into narrow petal-like blades, short or long, flat or twisted, white, yellow, pink, red, or striped, but with no pollen, or very little. The doubles are a further transformation, in which the stamens are replaced by broad petals so that the differentiation between guard petals and central petals is often lost.

* Special articles on the subjects indicated by an asterisk (*) will be found at the words so marked.

### Varieties

The following list includes some of the best of the Chinese peonies of the different types. The doubles are arranged under color, the varieties under each color being placed roughly in the order of their blooming.

WHITE. La Rosière, Le Cygne, Primevère, Alice Harding, Kelway's Glorious, Marie Jacquin, Avalanche, Baroness Schroeder, Marie Lemoine.

VERY LIGHT PINK. Lady Alexandra Duff, Madame Jules Dessert, La Perle, Madame Emile Gallé, Milton Hill, Solange.

PINK. Silvia Saunders, M. Jules Elie, Eugénie Verdier, Thérèse, Walter Faxon, Venus, Mabel Franklin, Georgiana Shaylor, Kelway's Queen, Sarah Bernhardt, Rosa Bonheur, President Wilson, Grandiflora.

RED. Adolphe Rousseau, M. Martin Cahuzac, Cherry Hill, Félix Crousse, Karl Rosenfield, Auguste Dessert, Longfellow, Lora Dexheimer.

JAPANESE TYPE (beautiful and much to be recommended). Isani-gidui (white), Aureolin (white and yellow), Tamatbaku (pink), Ama-no-sode (pink), Fuyajo (red), King of England (red), Mikado (red).

SINGLES. La Fiancée (The Bride) (white), Le Jour (white), Helen (pink), Black Prince (dark red).

2. TREE PEONIES. Tree Peonies are descendants of a wild plant, *P. suffruticosa*, usually called *P. moutan*, native to western China. This plant makes a permanent woody growth above ground, whereas the herbaceous kinds die to the ground every autumn. The Chinese have cultivated and admired the tree peony for many centuries, and the best of the commercial sorts today are of Chinese or Japanese origin. It is called by the Chinese the "King of Flowers," and it is in truth not only the grandest of all the peonies, but one of the most beautiful of all garden plants. The single and semi-double forms which have originated in the East are generally preferred by connoisseurs to the more lumpy doubles of European origin.

As it is almost impossible to get varieties true to name, it would be useless to give a list of names; but almost all singles or semi-doubles in white or light pink are sure to be beautiful. The tree peony has been neglected in America during the past forty years, but there are signs now of a re-awakening interest, and it is at present possible to get plants of fine sorts from several sources.

The best method of propagation is by grafting, which should be done upon the roots of the Chinese peony, never on *P. officinalis* which forms buds on root fragments. Practically all the commercial stocks in this country are grafted on *P. albiflora*.

A very remarkable race of hybrids has been produced by crossing the tree peony with the yellow *P. lutea*. This work was begun in France but has also been carried on in America. Among the best of these hybrids, which bear large single or double flowers in clear yellow or yellow stained with red, are Souvenir de Maxime Cornu, La Lorraine, Chromatella, Argosy.

3. OFFICINALIS VARIETIES. The European species *P. officinalis* has been in cultivation for several centuries, and has yielded through mutations a few varieties worthy of a place in our gardens. *Rubra plena, rosea plena, rosea superba plena, sabini*, Ophia, Charmer, may all be recommended; and as they begin to bloom about ten days before the Chinese peonies they make a welcome extension to the rather short season of peony bloom.

4. HYBRID HERBACEOUS PEONIES. Of late years the attention of breeders has turned toward the almost unexplored possibilities in crosses between the various species of *Paeonia*. Some years ago Lemoine in France produced a few fine varieties by crossing *P. albiflora* with *P. wittmanniana*. These are in commerce, as are also the crosses already mentioned between tree peonies and *P. lutea*. In America the cross between the *albiflora* varieties and the forms of *officinalis* has been much worked with in very recent years, and has yielded a race of very fine hybrids which have attracted much attention at the annual exhibitions of the American Peony Society.

This organization, which exists to further public interest in the peony, publishes a quarterly bulletin and organizes an annual peony show. Anyone specially interested in peonies might find it worth while to enroll as a member. In 1928 the society published a Manual of the Peony, which is now the standard work on the subject. For information about the society write the Garden Editor, Houghton Mifflin Company, Boston, Mass.

It would seem that the future of the peony must lie in the development of hybrid strains, and in the popularizing of the tree peony, for the Chinese peony itself has now reached a stage of development where any further substantial progress seems unlikely. — A. P. S.

DISEASES. The important diseases of the peony are root knot, blight and leafspot. For *root knot*, see Root Knot at PLANT DISEASES. Although *blight* may be caused by two different fungi, the symptoms are practically identical. Young shoots may wilt and die, due to decay close to the soil line. In other instances, infection may start at the tip and progress downward. Bud rot and brown blotches on the leaves may also result from blight. For control, remove infected shoots, spray with bordeaux mixture, cut all tops close to the ground in the fall and burn, avoid applications of manure around the stems and remove any mulching material early in the spring. *Leafspot* can be satisfactorily controlled by sanitation.

**PEONY DAHLIA.** See DAHLIA.

**PEONY FAMILY** = Ranunculaceae.

**PEPEROMIA** (pep-er-ō′mi-a). A huge genus of tropical, often fleshy herbs of the family Piperaceae, only **P. sandersi** of the 500 known species in general cult. It is a Brazilian, stemless herb very widely grown as a foliage plant by florists, both in the typical form and in the *var.* **argyreia,** which has lighter-colored patches between the veins of its leaf. Leaves thick, fleshy, ovalish, 3–5 in. long, without teeth, the thick, red stalk usually attached away from the margin (peltate*). Flowers minute, crowded on a dense, slender, usually curving spike. For details see PIPERACEAE. This very popular little pot plant requires a tropical greenhouse, plenty of moisture, and benefits from fortnightly applications of liquid manure. It roots easily from cuttings (or even from cut leaves) in sand over bottom-heat. While it is a plant of the moist Brazilian forests, it is also a good pot plant for the living room. See HOUSE PLANTS. (*Peperomia* is from the Greek for pepper-like, in allusion to its close relationship to the true pepper.)

**PEPINO** = *Solanum muricatum*.

**PEPO** (peep′o). Pre-Linnaean* name for the pumpkin. It is also the modern botanical name for the specialized type of berry found in most plants of the cucumber family. It is a fleshy fruit that does not split and usually has a hard rind. Common examples are the watermelon, melon, pumpkin, and the gourds.

**PEPPER.** For the true pepper (the spice) see PIPER. For the red, Cayenne, green, and other fleshy-fruited peppers see CAPSICUM.

**PEPPER-BUSH** = *Leucothoë racemosa*. For the sweet pepper-bush see CLETHRA.

**PEPPER FAMILY** = Piperaceae.

**PEPPER-GRASS.** See LEPIDIUM.

**PEPPERIDGE** = *Nyssa sylvatica*.

**PEPPERMINT** = *Mentha piperita*. See MINT.

**PEPPERMINT GUM** = *Eucalyptus amygdalina*.

**PEPPER-ROOT.** See DENTARIA.

**PEPPER-TREE.** The tree that produces ordinary pepper (the spice) is *Piper nigrum* (which see). For the plant commonly called pepper-tree in Calif. and elsewhere see SCHINUS MOLLE.

**PEPPER-VINE** = *Ampelopsis arborea*.

**PEPPERWORT.** See MARSILEA.

**PERAMIUM** = *Epipactis*.

**PERCENTAGE OF SEED GERMINATION.** See GARDEN TABLES II.

---

* Special articles on the subjects indicated by an asterisk (*) will be found at the words so marked.

**GARDEN PEONIES**

La Fiancée (The Bride)
Walter Faxon
Mikado

Tree Peony
Félix Crousse
Le Cygne

**PEREGRINA, -us, -um** (pe-re-gry′na). Foreign or exotic.

**PERENNIAL.** Lasting through more than two seasons' growth, often much more. Perennial is usually applied, especially by gardeners, only to herbs, but all woody plants are, of course, perennial in their growth. For the uses of perennial herbs in the garden see PERENNIALS. See also ANNUAL, BIENNIAL.

**PERENNIAL CANDYTUFT** = *Iberis sempervirens*. See CANDYTUFT.

**PERENNIAL HONESTY** = *Lunaria rediviva*. See HONESTY.

**PERENNIAL PEA** = *Lathyrus latifolius*.

**PERENNIAL PHLOX** = *Phlox paniculata*.

**PERENNIAL RYE GRASS** = *Lolium perenne*.

**PERENNIALS.** A perennial is a nearly ever-living plant. It forms the background of all gardens in temperate climates. It is the encouragement of the beginning gardener; it is the stay of the advanced one. Its growth, generous and fine, means that it may be divided and shared, thus giving it a true social value; and its beauty for gardens great or humble is undisputed. William Robinson and Miss Jekyll have earned the undying homage of all good gardeners, the one for his re-introducing of perennials into gardens, the other for her pictures of high beauty in their use.

LIST. A partial list of the more important perennials follows:

Alyssum, arabis, hardy aster in variety, astilbe, aubrietia, avens, betony, bluebells, boltonia, bugle, bugloss, campanula in variety, campion, candytuft, cerastium, Christmas rose, chrysanthemum in variety, cinquefoil, clematis, coreopsis, evening primrose, gaillardia, gas-plant, globeflower, globe thistle, gypsophila, incarvillea, iris in variety, larkspur in variety, lily in variety, mallow, nepeta, pea, pentstemon, peony in variety, pink, plantain-lily, plume poppy, polemonium, poppy, rock cress, St. John's-wort, sneezeweed, speedwell, spiderwort, sunflower, thermopsis, thrift, torch lily, valerian, wild indigo, wormwood in variety, yarrow and yucca.

But what a poor substitute for description are the words "in variety" here. This list tells nothing of the loveliness of the newer hardy asters, it gives no hint of the pearl-like buds of wormwood, *Artemisia vulgaris lactiflora*, of the soft effect of *Artemisia albula*, Silver King, so useful as a "between plant" in the border. Such alyssums as Silver Queen (*A. saxatile*), such candytufts as Queen of Italy, such irises as those from the early *I. pumila* to the latest Japanese varieties, with the great range of beautiful flowers between — all come to mind as the generic names are written. Delphiniums are in marvelous colors today, of many types and even of many heights. Among larkspurs, *Delphinium grandiflorum* is one of the best of all perennials, 2–4 ft. high and of a pure cobalt blue. And the tall kinds are now so familiar as to need no heralding. From lily-of-the-valley and *Lilium tenuifolium*, which is perhaps the smallest of all lilies, to *L. regale*, *L. speciosum* and the great *L. auratum*, this family is now widely spread over the gardens of the world.

### PROPAGATION

The simplest ways of raising perennials in one's own garden are from seed, by division and by root cuttings. There is no such interesting gardening as this; there is none so economical. We sow in July a few lines of a precious variety of delphinium from some foreign source or from our own good plant; we almost forget the existence of the row of seedlings; suddenly in the following year a rarely lovely spire of blue shows itself on a two-foot plant, and we remember that in this place last summer we carefully put in seed. For seeding the earth should be of good quality and finely worked, and if the soil is heavy, mix sand with it. Partial shade is a help to quick germination.

Sow the seed thinly in the row, cover to about three times its own thickness and firm the earth down with a board. If the weather is dry after sowing in the open border or bed, sprinkle every other day. Keep weeds down after the seedlings are large enough so that weeding will not disturb their roots, and cultivate when the plants are strong enough to bear this. In a northern climate, do not transplant seedlings till the spring after they are started; in milder airs it is well to move little perennials to their permanent places in early autumn, say mid-Sept. Such is the variety of American climates and soils, however, that minute directions cannot be given for this procedure.

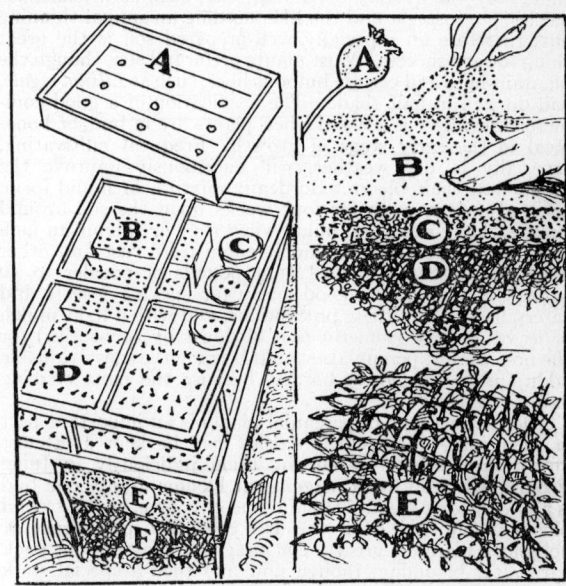

RAISING PERENNIALS FROM SEED

*At the left:* A flat (*A*) and the young seedlings in flats or pots (*B*, *C*, and *D*) in a hotbed. Note the depth of soil (*E*) and manure (*F*) in the hotbed.

*At the right:* Planting poppy seeds directly where they are shed (*A*). Sow them broadcast (*B*), give very shallow covering of soil and press in firmly with the hands or a board. The upper layer of soil (*C*) should be finely pulverized, and the soil thoroughly spaded below this (*D*). Cover the seedbed with brush (*E*) and water very gently every other day.

Propagation by cuttings or by dividing is a quick and interesting method of increasing the stock of perennials. Nothing is more amusing than to see how quickly a row of two-inch-long cuttings of roots of the hardy phlox, *Phlox suffruticosa*, set in rows in a seedbed in Sept., will send up leaflets. Take up a root with a sharp knife or scissors, cut any or all of the rootlets into two-inch lengths, and plant them in well-prepared ground in an upright position, with the top about half an inch below the surface. Growth will soon start. Oriental poppies, arabis, Japanese anemone and gypsophila, and *Anchusa azurea*, may also be increased in this manner. *Iris variegata* and the other tall bearded irises and hybrids should be taken up very soon after blooming, say in July, the earth shaken from their rootstocks and these pulled gently apart, leaving at least three rootlets to every rhizome. They may be cut apart with a sharp knife or spade, but pulling is better. *Arabis alpina* (the double-flowered form), so much finer than the single variety, may be increased by taking cuttings of the young growth in June and growing them in sand.

Most gardeners divide perennials at the end of three years, as they begin to show signs of straggling or thinning out. In the colder climates dividing is much better done in spring than in autumn, but it should take place early, when the leaves are not more than two in. high. In the case of Michaelmas daisies or hardy asters which increase tremendously in favorable seasons, the whole root should be lifted, and the ring of plantlets surrounding the old central root should be the only parts used. In hardy phloxes the

---

\* Special articles on the subjects indicated by an asterisk (\*) will be found at the words so marked.

plant may be cut with a sharp spade into as many small sections as desired. To divide herbaceous peonies (the tree peony cannot be divided), lift and wash the root and separate the tubers with a sharp knife.

### Care and Cultivation

Set perennials in well-spaded and well-manured ground. As a rule perennial plants stay in one position for a long time, only the quickly spreading ones, such as Michaelmas daisies, physostegia and the like, needing an annual thinning out; therefore an especially well-prepared soil is the great thing toward success. Most plants prefer full sun, though the plantain-lilies and certain bulbous lilies, such as *Lilium regale*, will do well in half shade. The application of a good commercial fertilizer is advised when plants are in bud, or bonemeal in the early stage of growth. Frequent cultivating, especially in dry weather, will enormously improve the plants and their bloom. Bordeaux mixture in liquid form, sprayed once a week for four weeks upon the soil around peonies, hollyhocks and phlox when they are about an inch high, should assure a certain freedom from rust and other troubles. Arsenate of lead (1½ pounds of powder to 50 gallons of water) is a good spray for sucking insects and caterpillars. With these precautions, and with a light mulch of leaves or hay (sometimes held down by cornstalks) for the first winter, perennials should become the most valuable additions to the flower border, because the most striking and permanent.

The cutting back of perennial plants is an important part of their care. Michaelmas daisies may be kept at almost any desired height by cutting them judiciously in June. Peonies will send forth magnificent blooms if only one bud is allowed to one stem. Delphiniums, of course, have a second bloom if cut back after the first one. The persistence of hollyhock plants is greatly encouraged if they are cut back hard after blooming, though now and then a special stalk may be reserved for seed. Such low-growing subjects as the hardy alyssums and the dwarf veronicas should be cut back hard after flowering and well fertilized to give strength for next year's bloom.

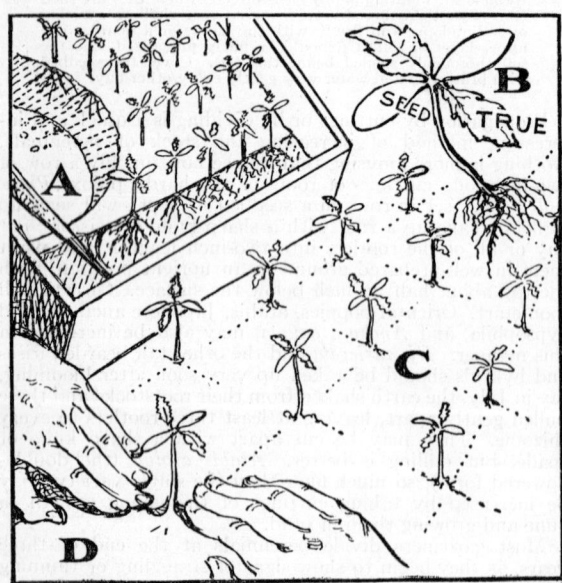

PRICKING-OUT PERENNIAL SEEDLINGS

(*A*) Loosen soil around roots with pointed stick. (*B*) The time for the first move is when the seedlings have developed the first pair of true leaves. (*C*) Do not overcrowd the seedlings as they will soon be growing rapidly. (*D*) Be sure to firm the soil around each plantlet so that it will not have air pockets (*i.e.* no soil) around its roots.

### Winter Protection

It is often forgotten that the real danger to perennial plants does not come in winter but in spring, with its alternate freezing and thawing. For that reason, with plants that must be protected, leaves should not be closely packed around their roots or crowns; some light framework, such as evergreen boughs or tree branches, should first be placed over the plants and the leaves laid upon these, thus keeping the plants beneath dry. No covering should be done until the ground is frozen.

The longevity of perennials is touched upon constantly in garden writing, but few records seem to have been kept. There is known, however, a plant of dictamnus which has lived in a New England garden through four generations. The perennials observed as hardy in northeastern N.Y., after the rigors of two unusually severe winters, are: peonies, iris, pinks, certain campanulas, *Pentstemon glaber*, iberis, arabis, delphinium, phloxes in variety, lily-of-the-valley, veronica, lilies, such as *Lilium candidum, regale*, and *elegans*, also *Nepeta, Thalictrum, Platycodon, Heuchera, Sidalcea, Anchusa*, columbine, *Statice, Thermopsis, Hemerocallis* and sedum.

### Grouping

A vast and most pleasurable aspect of this subject is the grouping of perennials, but it can be only lightly touched upon here. As to variety of perennials in one border, it is safe to say that all may be used together, provided that enough gray-leaved plants such as *Stachys lanata* and *Cerastium tomentosum* for the front of the border, *Eryngium amethystinum* and the ornamental thistles, and such plants as *Aruncus sylvester*, boltonia, hardy asters, *Artemisia vulgaris lactiflora* and thalictrums, are placed among other flowers of brighter colors. These plants, of more or less subdued color, harmonize the other hues, and the result may be as beautiful as an old Persian rug. For contrasts in color, either in planting or for cutting — and nothing is so fine as the right tall tulip or the right perennial in flower before a shrub which has proved itself a beautiful companion — there are these one or two suggestions: *Iris variegata*, Sachem below the lilac (*Syringa sweginzowi superba*); iris Monsignor or Archevêque with *Veronica teucrium* Royal Blue near by; tree peony Argosy near a Persian Yellow Rose. *Tripterygium* fronted by a damask rose, or golden-leaved privet with a foreground of the hardy alyssum Basket of Gold, will illumine even a shaded border in early spring. *Elsholtzia stauntoni* is charming in early Sept. with dwarf hardy asters below its racemes of lavender.

A good juxtaposition of perennials for July would be *Thalictrum glaucum* with a tall delphinium near by, such as Isla, the new beauty from England, or some of the light blue Lyondel delphiniums, or *Clematis recta* and *Salvia nemorosa* below all these. This results in a nice picture of pale yellow, light blue, cream white and deep violet flowers in one and the same spot. *Iris sibirica* Perry's Blue — the bluest of irises — with one of the new varieties of daylilies below it, or again, the same iris beside a blooming plant of peony Thérèse, make two excellent combinations. Rose Frau Karl Druschki, one of the hardiest of the family, with *Salvia farinacea* below and around it makes a picture worth creating, though the salvia is hardy only in the warmer parts of the country. *Lilium elegans*, its orange-red blooms against masses of common elder, delphinium (larkspur), near the rich pink of clematis Ville de Lyon grown against a wall, these complement each other unusually well. Endless is the variety in placing, lovely are the pictures that ensue when the perennial plant is a part of a good composition in gardens. — L. Y. K.

**PERENNIS, -e** (per-en'nis). Perennial.*

**PERESKIA** (per-res'ki-a). Tropical American, tree-like, shrubby or vine-like cacti, unlike all others in bearing true, flat, alternate* leaves. Of the 20 known species the two below have long been grown for their fruit or for ornament, especially in the tropics. They have woody, branching stems which are spiny. Spines in pairs, without sheaths and with-

---

* Special articles on the subjects indicated by an asterisk (*) will be found at the words so marked.

out the cushion of barbed bristles found in the closely related genus *Opuntia*. Flowers in small clusters (in ours), the stamens* numerous. Fruit fleshy, juicy, often edible. (Named for N. Claude Fabry de Peiresc, French scientist.)

For cult. *see* CACTI. They can only be grown in frost-free regions, and are not generally grown in the greenhouse.

**aculeata.** Barbados gooseberry; also called lemon vine and blade-apple. Ultimately a woody vine 10–20 ft. long, at first shrubby and erect. Leaves oblongish, 2–3 in. long, short-stalked. Spines usually 2 to a cluster, curved. Flowers about 1½ in. wide, fragrant, white, yellowish or pink, mostly in clusters (corymb* or panicle*). Fruit about ¾ in. in diameter, yellow. Tropical America. There is a variety with crimson, yellow, and green leaves. The plant was once called *Pereskia pereskia*.

**bleo.** A shrub or tree 10–30 ft. high, the trunk often 4 in. thick and spiny. Leaves oblongish, 3–6 in. long. Spines solitary, straight. Flowers 1½–2 in. wide, rose-purple. Fruit pear-shaped, 1–2 in. long. Brazil. Often cult. under the name *P. grandifolia*.

**grandifolia.** Usually the plant cult. as this is *P. bleo*.

**PERESKIOPSIS** (per-res-ki-op'sis). A small genus of cacti differing from *Pereskia* only in having cushions of barbed bristles. Of the 10 known species, all from Mex. and Guatemala, **P. spathulata,** the only cult. sort, is of minor importance. It is a branching shrub 4–6 ft. high, bearing true leaves which are spatula-shaped, 1–2½ in. long, thick and fleshy. Spines 1 or 2 at each cluster, white-based. Flowers red. For cult. *see* CACTI. (*Pereskiopsis* means *Pereskia*-like.)

**PEREZIA** (pe-ree'zi-a). A relatively unimportant, New World genus of perennial herbs of the family Compositae, two of them occasionally planted for ornament. They have alternate,* leathery leaves that are cut or toothed on the margin. Flower heads small, wholly of disk* flowers, blue, purple, or white (in ours), the heads not showy, but the clusters (panicles* or corymbs*) attractive. (Named for Lazarus Perez, Spanish apothecary.)

Little is known of the best method of growing the two below. They are related to *Mutisia* (which see).

**microcephala.** Not over 3½ ft. high. Leaves stem-clasping, oblongish, or broader, 3½–7 in. long, the margins toothed. Flower heads white or purplish, about ½ in. long, grouped in panicles.* Calif.

**multiflora.** Not over 18 in. high. Leaves spiny-margined, 4–6 in. long, cut into triangular divisions. Flower heads in dense clusters (corymbs*), blue. Andes.

**PERFECT.** As to flowers, those that bear both male (stamens*) and female (pistils*) organs of reproduction. *See* COMPLETE and ESSENTIAL ORGANS.

*PERFOLIATA, -us, -um* (per-fo-li-ā'ta). Perfoliate; *i.e.* with the stem passing through the leaf, as in some honeysuckles.

**PERFUME PLANTS.** The cultivation of plants from which volatile and aromatic oils are commercially extracted is not to be undertaken lightly by anyone, for it is very much in the same category as the cultivation of medicinal plants. In other words, the risks are great and the production of these oils abroad is an old, established art.

Comparatively few plants are used in the art of perfumery on a scale to make their cult. worth while, for many very sweet-smelling flowers are useless when it comes to holding their odor long enough to be worth cult. for perfumery. For the leading sorts *see* FRAGRANCE. *See* also CANANGA.

Plants actually used in perfumery, such as the rose, violet, and lavender, are all but unknown in this country as commercial sources of their beautiful odors. The cult. of them for this purpose is practically confined to southern Eu. and Asia Minor.

Of the plants containing volatile oils in sufficient strength to be worth extracting, only the following are of possible significance in the U.S.

| Peppermint | Tansy | Lavender |
| Spearmint | Wormseed | Rosemary |
| Wormwood | Rose geranium | Thyme |

Of these the rose geranium, which yields an oil indispensable in perfume manufacture, is by far the most important, but the chief source of it, commercially, is still Turkey and northern Africa. And this illustrates as well as any other on the list the difficulty of growing such plants here in competition with old and practiced growers.

Climate, soil, the time of harvesting, and special strains or varieties of these plants, all make it a decidedly expert business to grow any of them for the perfume trade. The quality and quantity of the oil vary from season to season, and especially from youth to age of the plant. Most of them appear to be at their most fragrant stage about the time of blooming.

The extraction of the oil is a highly technical chemical problem needing expert training. All of which means that growing perfume plants may be a very pleasant, fragrant pastime for the gardener, but except, possibly, in Calif. it cannot be considered much else. The sole exception is, of course, the large-scale extraction of peppermint and spearmint oil in Mich., but neither are real perfume plants.

While the commercial extraction of perfumes is thus a rather technical process, anyone may experiment in home-made perfume making by following the directions below:

Put at the bottom of a stone jar a layer of cotton batting about 1 in. thick, thoroughly soaked in pure olive oil. Upon the oil-soaked cotton place a thin layer of whatever flower you desire, preferably picked early in the morning of the day you begin the operation. Pull off all green parts of the flower (calyx* or bracts*), and if the petals are thick, detach them. Over the layer of flowers sprinkle a little common salt. Repeat the process until the jar is filled with alternate layers of oil-soaked cotton and salt-sprinkled petals — all well pressed down. Then tie a piece of oiled paper over the jar and put it in the sun for two days.

This is usually long enough for nearly all the fragrance of the flowers to have passed into the oil-soaked cotton. Put the latter into a clean cheesecloth bag and squeeze out all the oil that you can into stoppered bottles. Such a mixture will make a surprisingly delightful homemade perfume.

**PERGOLA.** *See* STRUCTURES.

*PERGRACILIS, -e* (per-gras'il-is). Very slender.

**PERIANTH.** Collective term for the calyx* and corolla,* especially when they are more or less indistinguishable, as in many lilies and other monocotyledons.*

**PERICARP.** The ripened wall of the ovary,* usually much modified in the mature fruit; sometimes fleshy, or even bony as in nuts.

*PERICLYMENUM* (pe-ri-cly'men-um). Pre-Linnaean* name for the woodbine (*Lonicera periclymenum*).

**PERIGYNOUS.** Having the calyx,* stamens,* etc., inserted around the ovary and not below it. A common example is the apple blossom, which has an inferior* ovary, the stamens,* calyx,* etc., being inserted around it, hence *perigynous*.

**PERILLA** (per-rill'a). A small genus of tender, herbaceous annuals of the mint family, natives of eastern Asia. Leaves green, or dark reddish-brown, in opposite* pairs, inversely heart-shaped. Flowers small, in pairs, borne in the axils* of bracts in terminal racemes.* (Origin of name obscure.)

They are suitable for beds or borders where color contrasts are required. Propagated by seeds or cuttings. Seeds should be sown under glass in Feb. or March, in a temperature of about 60°, in finely sifted, sandy soil, ⅛ in. deep. Transplant to pots or boxes in potting mixture* 2, and transfer outdoors at the end of May. Cuttings may be made in Aug. and kept through the winter in a warm greenhouse, from which cuttings may be taken again in spring for planting out in May. It frequently self-sows in warmer parts of the country.

**frutescens.** Leaves green on both sides, occasionally marked reddish-brown, opposite, slightly wrinkled, inversely heart-shaped, the margins slightly toothed, 3–6 in. long. Flowers 3–8 in a raceme,* the corolla white, sometimes tinged red, and small. India and Jap. The *var.* **crispa** is the form generally cult. in gardens, its leaves of dark reddish-brown with bronzy sheen, being particularly handsome. This variety rarely grows more than 2 ft. high.

**nankinensis** = *Perilla frutescens crispa.*

**PERIPLOCA** (per-ip'lo-ka). Silk vine. A small genus of Old World, milky-juiced, woody vines of the milkweed family, one of them, **P. graeca,** of southern Eu. and western As., a stem-climbing vine grown for ornament from zone* 5

---
* Special articles on the subjects indicated by an asterisk (*) will be found at the words so marked.

southward. It may climb up 25-40 ft. high, and has opposite,* oblongish, stalked leaves, 2-4½ in. long, without marginal teeth, dark shining green above, paler beneath. Flowers about 1 in. wide, greenish-brown, in long-stalked terminal clusters (cymes*), the corolla wheel-shaped, its lobes oblong, softly hairy and spreading. Fruit a collection of narrow, smooth pods (follicles*) 3-5 in. long. It is easily propagated by seeds or by layering. (*Periploca* is from the Greek for twine and about, in reference to the twining habit.)

**PERISTERIA** (pe-ri-ster'i-a). Tropical American orchids, the genus mostly South American, with evergreen foliage and large pseudobulbs.* The only cult. species is P. elata, a remarkable, waxy-flowered orchid from Panama, variously called Holy Ghost flower, dove flower, and dove orchid. It has 3-5, large, plaited leaves to each pseudobulb,* the blade nearly 3 ft. long and about 6 in. wide. Flowering spike nearly 5 ft. high, composed of 15-25 flowers that are about 2 in. wide, fragrant, white, but the lip* spotted with red inside, the whole flower cup-shaped and very beautiful. July-Aug. For cult. see Greenhouse Orchids at ORCHID. (*Peristeria* is Greek for dove, in allusion to the shape of the flower.)

**PERISTROPHE** (per-i-strō'fe). A genus of 15 species of chiefly tropical, Old World herbs or under-shrubs of the family Acanthaceae, two of them somewhat grown in the greenhouse for ornament. Leaves opposite,* without marginal teeth. Flowers in few-flowered clusters, each surrounded by a series of bracts* which are longer than the 5-lobed calyx. Corolla irregular,* the tube expanded, the limb 2-lipped,* the lower lip 3-lobed or 3-toothed. Stamens* 2. Fruit a capsule. (*Peristrophe* is from the Greek for belted around, in allusion to the involucre*-like bracts beneath the flowers.)

They should be grown in the warm-temperate greenhouse in potting mixture* 4, and need plenty of moisture, but not too moist air. Easily propagated by cuttings, but the first species is usually grown as an annual.

**angustifolia.** Probably an annual and usually grown as such, much-branched, weak but ultimately erect. Leaves lance-shaped, 2-3 in. long, tapering both ends. Flowers red, the bracts* hairy-margined. Java. Chiefly grown in the var. **aureo-variegata**, which has yellow-variegated leaves.

**speciosa.** An erect or perennial, somewhat woody under-shrub, 2-3 ft. high, the stems more or less swollen at the joints. Leaves ovalish or elliptic, 4-5 in. long. Flowers violet-purple, about 2 in. wide and long, the stamens* protruding beyond the lower lip. India.

**PERIWINKLE** = Vinca minor.

**PERNETIANA ROSE.** See Group 2 at ROSE.

**PERNETTYA** (per-net'ti-a). Evergreen shrubs of the heath family, ranging from Mex. to Tierra del Fuego, only P. mucronata of its 25 known species of any hort. interest. It is a low, much-branched shrub, not over 2 ft. high. Leaves alternate,* short-stalked, ovalish, about ¾ in. long, usually bristly-toothed. Flowers about ¼ in. long, solitary, nodding, the corolla urn-shaped, white or pinkish. Fruit a many-seeded red berry, but lilac in the var. **lilacina**; bright red in the var. **coccinea**; and white in the var. **alba**. May-June. Chile. Grown chiefly for the attractive, winter-persisting fruit. Hardy from zone* 5 southward, and preferring a moist, sunny, rather acid soil. (Named for A. J. Pernetty, who wrote "A Voyage to the Falkland Islands.")

*PERPUSILLA, -us, -um* (per-pew-sil'la). Very small.

**PERRINE.** A lemon variety. See LEMON.

**PERSEA** (per'see-a). Tropical or sub-tropical trees and shrubs, usually aromatic, belonging to the family Lauraceae, all but one of the 50 known species American, the other from the islands of Canary, Madeira, or Azores. The chief hort. species is P. americana, the avocado; the other two cult. species are grown for ornament. Leaves alternate,* without marginal teeth. Flowers small, greenish, the petals and sepals similar, usually totaling 6. Stamens* 12. Fruit a berry (large in the avocado). (*Persea* is an ancient name for some Persian or Egyptian tree, and of no known application to these.)

For the culture and varieties of the avocado *see* AVOCADO. The other two species are grown for their evergreen, ornamental foliage which suggests the true laurel (*Laurus*). They can be propagated by seeds or cuttings.

**americana.** Avocado; also called alligator pear. A tree, usually 40-60 ft. high (less in cult. varieties) and much-branched. Leaves ovalish or elliptic, 4-8 in. long. Flowers in dense, terminal clusters, greenish, very small. Fruit pear-shaped, or nearly round, 3-6 in. long, green at first, but yellowish in maturity, the yellow, oily flesh of delicious flavor. Seed 1, large. Tropical America. The var. **drymifolia**, with anise-scented foliage and thinner-skinned fruit, is the Mexican avocado. For the cult. of both kinds *see* AVOCADO.

**borbonia.** Red bay; a so called bull bay. An evergreen tree 30-40 ft. high. Leaves oblongish or a little narrower, 4-6 in. long, faintly bluish-green. Fruit about ½ in. long, blue or blue-black, red-stalked. In low places, Del. to Fla. Hardy from zone* 5 southward. Not much planted, but an ornamental tree, especially in the winter with its red-stalked fruit.

**indica.** A small, evergreen tree, with oblong, leathery leaves, 4-6 in. long. Flowers very small, in few-flowered clusters in the leaf-axils.* Fruit about ¾ in. long, scarcely fleshy. Azores, Madeira, and Canary Islands. Hardy only in zones* 8 and 9, and planted for its fine evergreen foliage in Fla. and Calif.

**PERSIAN BUTTERCUP** = *Ranunculus asiaticus*. See BUTTERCUP.

**PERSIAN LILAC** = *Syringa persica*. See LILAC.

**PERSIAN LIME.** See Acid Lime at LIME (the citrus fruit).

**PERSIAN MELON.** See MELON.

**PERSIAN WALNUT** = *Juglans regia*. See WALNUT.

**PERSIAN YELLOW** = *Rosa foetida persiana*.

*PERSICA, -us, -um* (per'si-ka). From Persia.

*PERSICARIA* (per-si-cay'ri-a). A now obsolete generic name for plants here included in *Polygonum*. See the lady's-thumb at WEEDS.

*PERSICIFOLIA, -us, -um* (per-si-si-fō'li-a). With peach-like leaves.

**PERSIMMON.** The persimmon belongs to the large, chiefly tropical and sub-tropical genus **Diospyros** (dy'os-py'-ros) of the ebony family. Although this genus includes about 200 species only 4 can be considered hardy. The leaves are usually alternate* and entire. The male and female flowers, both inconspicuous, are borne on separate trees. Fruit a large fleshy berry containing 1-10 flat seeds; the calyx continues to grow after the corolla has fallen and is conspicuous at the base of the fruit. (*Diospyros* is from the Greek for Jove's grain, in allusion to the edible fruit.)

The persimmons are of some ornamental value, having glossy leaves of good color, and though the flowers are hardly noticeable the orange or yellow fruits are quite decorative. The Chinese persimmon, D. kaki, is cultivated in the southern states and Calif., and its large fruits are of commercial importance.

For cultivation *see* below.

**D. kaki.** Japanese persimmon. Deciduous tree attaining 40 ft. or more. Leaves more or less oval, 2-6 in. long or longer, glossy above, somewhat downy beneath. Flowers yellowish. Fruit 3 in. long, orange, variable in size and color. June. China, and early introduced into Jap., hence the common, but not strictly correct name of Japanese persimmon. Hardy from zone* 5 southward.

**D. lotus.** Date plum. Deciduous tree of about 40 ft. Leaves oval, tapered at ends, 2-5 in. long, glossy above, hairy on veins beneath. Flowers reddish or greenish. Fruit globular, about ¾ in. long, yellow or purplish, variable in size and shape. June. Fruit in Nov. Himalayas, China, and Asia Minor. Hardy from zone* 3 southward.

**D. virginiana.** The common persimmon, sometimes called American persimmon, is a tree of 50 ft., occasionally to 100 ft., with somewhat pendulous branches and thick bark that is deeply cut into squares or rectangles. Leaves oval to ovate, pointed at tip, broader and more rounded at base than in *D. lotus*, glossy above, paler beneath and often hairy along midrib. Flowers yellowish-white, bell-shaped, with 4 lobes, male flowers in 3's, female flowers solitary. Fruit globular, to 1½ in., orange. May-June. Conn. to Tex. Hardy from zone* 3 southward.

## PERSIMMON CULTURE

There are two principal kinds: American (*Diospyros virginiana*) and Japanese (*D. kaki*), the latter the chief persimmon of commerce. *Diospyros lotus*, a small-fruited Old World species, is employed as rootstock for grafting.

AMERICAN PERSIMMON. A warm-temperate, deciduous fruit found wild in the eastern states; can be grown as far north as R.I. and the Great Lakes. Small tree in the open,

---

* Special articles on the subjects indicated by an asterisk (*) will be found at the words so marked.

but under forest conditions often much larger. The sexes usually separated, requiring male trees for satisfactory bearing. Fruit 1–2 in. diameter, round, yellow to yellowish-red, until ripe highly astringent. Astringency is usually lost during ripening, but this is not dependent upon the action of frost. Ripening season Aug. to Dec. Propagated by whip-grafting or budding young seedlings. Large trees may be cleft-grafted. Transplanting young trees is difficult because of long taproot, although the tree has a wide range of soil adaptation and no special cultural requirement. Best-known good varieties: Early Golden, Miller, Ruby.

JAPANESE PERSIMMON. A hardy, sub-tropical, deciduous fruit of Chinese origin, but introduced into this country from Jap. Withstands 10° F., but usually injured at 0°. It has a wide range of climatic adaptation, but the quality is best in regions of mild summer and freedom from prevailing winds. Moderately small, spreading tree.

The principal varieties bear only female flowers and ordinarily do not require pollination, the fruit being seedless. If pollinated, seedy fruits result; in some varieties seed formation causes dark coloration of the flesh, in others not. Some varieties bear flowers of both sexes, and fruit is then normally seedy. Still others bear male flowers sporadically. Perfect flowers are occasionally found. It is safest, though usually unnecessary, to plant both male and female varieties.

Fruit small to large (3–4 in. long, 4–5 in. diameter), tomato-shaped to conical, yellow to red. Ripening season Sept. to Dec. With exception of the Fuyu variety, the immature fruits are astringent. Astringency disappears in dark-fleshed fruits before softening, in others with softening. It can be removed by freezing, prolonged immersion in warm water, or subjection to alcoholic fumes, smoke, carbon dioxide or ethylene. This last is practiced commercially in Calif.

Propagated by whip-grafting or budding on seedlings of the American, Japanese or *lotus* species, the two latter preferred in Calif. It has a wide range of soil adaptation and no special cultural requirements.

Commercial culture of the Japanese persimmon is important in China and Jap.; but in this country, it is confined mainly to Calif. where there are approximately 3000 acres of it, mostly in Los Angeles area. There is also a small production in Gulf Coast states.

Principal commercial varieties: Hachiya (outstanding), Tanenashi, Hyakume, Triumph, Tamopan, and Fuyu.— R. W. H.

INSECT PESTS. The fall webworm, a moth larva, frequently attacks persimmon as well as other trees. The hairy caterpillars feed in summer in colonies, each colony under an unsightly web. They can be killed by arsenicals or by pruning off the branch tips with the webs. A twig girdler also attacks persimmon (*see* HICKORY).

**PERSIMMON FAMILY** = Ebenaceae.

**PERSISTENT.** Hanging on, even though withered, as do some oak leaves and many fruits. *See* EVERGREEN.

*PERSOLUTA, -us, -um* (per-so-lew'ta). A garland, or garland-like.

*PERULATA, -us, -um* (per-you-lay'ta). Pocket-like.

*PERUVIANA, -us, -um* (pe-roo-vi-ā'na). From Peru.

**PERUVIAN BARK.** *See* CINCHONA OFFICINALIS.

**PERUVIAN DAFFODIL.** *See* SPIDER LILY.

**PERUVIAN LILY.** *See* ALSTROEMERIA.

**PERUVIAN MASTIC** = *Schinus molle.*

*PESTIFER* (pes'ti-fer). A pest; pestiferous.

**PESTS.** For the main garden pests *see* Insect Pests, Plant Diseases, Animal Injury, and Bird Nuisances at BIRDS.

**PETAL.** One of the usually colored segments of a flower, distinct and separate in some, but united and forming a gamopetalous* corolla in others.

**PETALOID.** Petal-like in color or texture, as are some sepals and sterile stamens.*

**PETALOSTEMON** (pet-a-los-tee'mon). Also spelled *Petalostemum.* Prairie clover. American, mostly western, perennial herbs comprising about 27 species of the pea family. Leaves compound,* the leaflets unequal, lance-shaped, the margins rolled on the upper edge when young. Flowers pea-like in short or long spikes, white, purple or violet. Fruit a short pod (legume). (*Petalostemon* is from the Greek for petal and stamen, in allusion to the way in which these are joined.)

Petalostemons are not much in cultivation, but may be used in the rock or wild gardens, as their low, bushy habit is attractive.

**candidum.** White tassel-flower. Grows to 2 ft. high, the stems erect and smooth. Leaves compound,* the leaflets 5–9, lance-shaped, about 1 in. long. Flowers white, growing in the axils* of awl-shaped bracts,* in slender spikes to 4 in. long. Seed pods hairy. Mid-western states.

**decumbens.** Slightly hairy the stems erect or trailing, 1–2 ft. long. Leaves compound,* the leaflets 5–7, lance-shaped, ¾ in. long. Flowers pink, the short, thick spikes about ¾ in. long. Ark. to Tex.

**purpureum.** Red tassel-flower. Smooth or slightly hairy, growing up to 3 ft. high. Leaves compound,* short-stalked, the leaflets 3–5, spear-shaped, ¾ in. long. Flowers violet or purple, the dense clusters about 2 in. long. Central N.A.

**PETASITES** (pet-a-sy'teez). Butterbur. Hardy perennial herbs comprising about 20 species of the daisy family (Compositae), found throughout the northern hemisphere. They have thick, fleshy rootstocks from which grow numerous underground runners, spreading rapidly. Leaves appearing in early spring after the flowers, basal, large, covered with matted, wool-like hairs on the under side. Flowers white-purple, in heads, borne on a stalk which has numerous, scale-like bracts.* Calyx of individual flowers is represented by a ring of hairs to which the seeds are attached. The seeds may be carried by the wind for considerable distances. (*Petasites* is from the Greek for a broad-brimmed hat, in allusion to the large, broad leaves.)

They are of little garden interest, but useful covering for stony or unsightly banks where more choice plants will not grow. Easily propagated from seeds or division of roots.

**fragrans.** Winter heliotrope. Sweet coltsfoot. Evergreen, growing 6–12 in. high. Leaves roundish, smooth and green on the upper side, fine-matted with hairs on the under side, the margins toothed. Flower heads small, fragrant, dirty-white to purple, blooming in early spring. Mediterranean region.

**japonica.** Grows to 6 ft. high. Leaves roundish, 3–4 ft. across, with wavy margins. Flower heads several, borne at the top of a common flowering stalk, arranged in an upright cluster. Island of Sachalin.

*PETIOLATA, -us, -um* (pet-i-o-lay'ta). Having a petiole (leafstalk).

**PETIOLE.** A leafstalk. Sometimes the stalk is winged, as in the orange, when it is called a winged petiole.

*PETRAEA, -us, -um* (pe-tree'a). Rock-inhabiting.

**PETREA** (pe'tre-a). A small genus of tropical American shrubs or woody vines of the family Verbenaceae, **P. volubilis,** the purple wreath or queen's-wreath, much grown for ornament in Fla. in zone* 9, and also in the greenhouse. It is a handsome woody vine, often growing 15–20 ft. high. Leaves evergreen, opposite,* leathery, more or less oblong, 3–6 in. long, usually wavy-margined. Flowers blue, showy, in terminal clusters (racemes*) that may be 8 in. long. Calyx tubular, its blunt, colored lobes much longer than the tube. Corolla funnel-shaped. Fruit a 2-celled drupe,* completely hidden by the persistent, colored, and showy calyx. The plant is often grown in the warm-temperate greenhouse, preferably planted out. Its profuse bloom in early spring is most attractive. In Fla. it can only be grown in absolutely frost-free regions. (Named for Baron Robert James Petre, a patron of botany.)

**PETROCOPTIS** (pet-ro-cop'tis). A small genus of herbaceous perennials, found in the Pyrenees, belonging to the pink family, comprising only 3 species. Leaves basal, narrow, in clusters or rosettes. Flowers pale pink-rose, in branching clusters. They are closely related to *Lychnis.* (*Petrocoptis* is from the Greek for cleft and rock, in allusion to their rooting in the clefts of rocks.)

A charming little plant for the rock garden, easily propagated from seeds sown in spring in the cold frame, transplanting later to ordinary garden soil.

**lagascae.** Grows 2–4 in. high. Leaves smooth, shiny, lance-shaped.

* Special articles on the subjects indicated by an asterisk (*) will be found at the words so marked.

Leaves on flowering stem arranged in 2 rows. Flowers pale rose, with white center, ¾ in. across. Seeds woolly. Also known as *Lychnis lagascae*.

**PETROSELINUM.** See PARSLEY.

**PE-TSAI** = *Brassica pekinensis*. For cult. see CHINESE CABBAGE.

**PETTICOAT NARCISSUS** = *Narcissus bulbocodium*.

**PETUNIA** (pe-too'ni-a). An important group of garden flowers, the petunias comprising the genus *Petunia* which has about a dozen species of annual or perhaps perennial, weak, straggling, clammy or sticky herbs, nearly all from the Argentine. They have soft, flabby leaves, without marginal teeth, alternate* below but the upper opposite.* Flowers variously colored (see below), the corolla funnel-shaped, its limb often slightly irregular* or even obscurely 2-lipped.* Stamens* 5, 4 in pairs, the odd one smaller, rudimentary, and sterile. (*Petunia* is a Latinized version of a South American vernacular for them.)

For Culture see below.

**axillaris.** A white-flowered ancestor of the garden petunia, about 18 in. high, the flowers dull white, about 2 in. long, nocturnally fragrant. Argentina. Not much cult. now, but often seen persisting in old gardens.

**hybrida.** Common garden petunia. A sticky-hairy annual, derived from crossing the first and last species. It has a weak, but usually erect stem, 8-18 in. high. Leaves variable. Flowers (depending on the strain) from 2-4½ in. wide, sometimes fringed, double, or crisped and ranging from white to red-purple, often striped, barred, or otherwise marked. For cult. and hort. varieties see below.

**violacea.** Stems very weak and slender, sticky-hairy. Leaves ovalish, short-stalked, those near the flowers in pairs. Flowers about 1½ in. long, violet or rose-red, the limb of the corolla slightly unequal. Argentina.

### PETUNIA CULTURE

The garden petunias (*Petunia hybrida*) are very popular tender annuals, widely used for bedding, window boxes, pot plants, or for the border. They are all best treated as tender annuals, the seed started indoors or in the greenhouse 7-8 weeks before the plants are to be put outdoors. This should not be done until warm weather is settled. Nearly all the strains are summer bloomers and will stand no frost. For the details of handling tender annuals see ANNUALS. Those who do not wish to start the plants indoors can sow seed (after warm weather has come), but such plants will be delayed in flowering.

Unfortunately, petunias, while often self-sown in some of the strains, are quite likely to revert to a wild type, so that self-sown seedlings are pretty sure to deteriorate, which means that for the finest types fresh seed from a reliable dealer should be started every year.

The petunia has been much hybridized and now comes in many colors, notably white, pink, blue, red, some self-colored, others edged with white, some with a vari-colored eye,* and many with a star-like center.

As to form, the flowers are either single and funnel-shaped (the usual sort) or, in some of the finer strains, ruffled, doubled, or crisped. All the latter are unstable when it comes to raising them from seed, but may be increased by cuttings wintered in the greenhouse. While petunias, as grown here, are treated as tender annuals, their wild ancestors were most probably perennials.

For different purposes the petunia has been bred into at least two types of habit. The relatively dwarf, bushy types, such as Rosy Morn, Heavenly Blue, or Violet Queen are best for bedding. For window boxes those sometimes called balcony petunias, which have weaker and almost trailing stems are most useful. One of the best is Balcony Blue. Other fine varieties are Exquisite, Pink Beauty, and Pride of Portland. See PINK GARDEN.

**PEUMUS** (pe-you'mus). A single species of Chilean, evergreen trees, and the only cult. genus of the family **Monimiaceae** (mo-nim-i-ā'see-ee), which comprises about 30 genera of tropical trees with opposite* leaves, rather small, inconspicuous flowers with many stamens, and dry or fleshy fruits. The only cult. species is **P. boldus**, the boldo, which is cult. in Calif. for its evergreen, fragrant foliage. It is about 20 ft. high, the leaves leathery, warty, rough, more or less ovalish. Male and female flowers on different trees, neither showy, white, and grouped in small clusters (panicles*). Fruit a collection of 2-5 small, stalked, edible drupes.* While a valuable economic tree (wood, charcoal, fruit, dyes, and medicine) in Chile, it is little known here outside of Calif., where it is cult. only for ornament. (*Peumus* is the Chilean name for it.)

**P.G.** Same as peegee.

**pH.** A symbol for the hydrogen ion concentration (acidity and alkalinity) of soil solutions. For the details see ACID AND ALKALI SOILS.

**PHACELIA** (fa-see'li-a). American herbaceous annuals, or occasionally perennials found mostly in the northwestern states, comprising about 114 species of the family Hydrophyllaceae. Leaves simple or compound,* alternate,* fleshy, sometimes hairy, the veins prominent on the under side. Flowers blue, purple or white, arranged in rolled, one-sided racemes,* the raceme unrolling as the flowers open. Individual flowers on short stalks. Calyx* of 5, narrow sepals, widening toward the apex, but joined at the base. Corolla bell-shaped, the petals 5, sometimes having sterile anther* lobes between the petals, at the top of the tube. Stamens* 5, conspicuous. (*Phacelia* is from the Greek for a bundle, in allusion to the flowers.)

Phacelias are important bee plants and easily cult. (see ANNUALS). They require open, sunny positions and are best planted in masses.

**campanularia.** Californian bluebell. Annual, to 8 in. high, the stem and leaves fleshy, leafstalk reddish, and grooved on the upper side. Leaves simple, ovalish and wrinkled, the margins bluntly lobed, the upper surface covered with short hairs that are like velvet to the touch. Flowers in one-sided racemes,* deep blue, bell-shaped, marked with 5 white sterile anther-lobes between the petals. Deserts of southern Calif.

**grandiflora** = *Phacelia whitlavia*.

**tanacetifolia.** Fiddleneck. Annual, growing to 3 ft. high, erect, covered with rough hairs. Leaves divided into 9-17 narrow leaflets. Flowers in one-sided racemes,* blue or pale lilac. Stamens* and style* conspicuously protruding. Calif.

**viscida.** An annual, not over 2 ft. high. Leaves ovalish and toothed. Flowers deep blue, the center purple or whitish. Calif. Sometimes offered as *Eutoca*.

**whitlavia.** Californian bluebell. Annual, to 1½ ft. high, loosely branching, hairy. Leaves ovalish, the margins toothed. Flowers blue or purple, bell-shaped, in one-sided racemes,* the tube of corolla 1 in. long, the lobes spreading. Southern Calif. The *var.* **gloxinioides** has white flowers with blue center, while *var.* **alba** has entirely white flowers.

*PHAEACANTHA, -us, -um* (fee-a-kan'tha). Dark-spined.

**PHAEDRANTHUS** (fee-dran'thus). A single Mexican species of showy woody vines of the family Bignoniaceae, **P. buccinatorius**, the clarin, widely grown there for ornament, but suited here only to the warm-temperate greenhouse. It is an extremely handsome, evergreen vine with opposite,* compound* leaves, the leaflets 2, the terminal one usually replaced by a branched tendril. Flowers in drooping terminal clusters (racemes*), the corolla tubular or funnel-shaped, nearly 4 in. long, bright red, but yellow at the base. This vine, sometimes known as *Bignonia buccinatoria*, is practically unknown as an outdoor plant in the U.S., but should be hardy over most of zone* 8 and all of zone* 9. In the greenhouse it should be planted out. (*Phaedranthus* is from the Greek for splendid flower, in allusion to the showy bloom.)

*PHAENOPYRA, -us, -um* (fee-no-py'ra). Literally, with spiny pears; *i.e.* fruit.

**PHAIUS** (fay'i-us). Sometimes spelled *Phajus*. Very showy, large, Old World, tropical orchids, some terrestrial, the rest tree-perching (epiphytes*), comprising 20 species, of which the two below, especially *P. grandifolius*, are often cult. in the greenhouse for their showy bloom. Both the cult. species are tree-perching and bear pseudobulbs,* from which spring 2-6 large, sometimes spotted leaves. The flowering stalk is leafless but sheathed, often 3-4 ft. long, and bears a cluster (raceme*) of 7-20 flowers. Sepals and petals nearly alike, free, usually spreading. Lip* usually swollen, sometimes spurred behind, 3-lobed. (*Phaius* is from the Greek for swarthy, in allusion to the dark-colored flowers of some species.)

For culture see Epiphytic Greenhouse Orchids at ORCHID.

**flavus.** Leaves 2-3 at each pseudobulb,* yellow-spotted, 15-24 in. long.

---

* Special articles on the subjects indicated by an asterisk (*) will be found at the words so marked.

Flower cluster with 7-10 blooms, the flowers about 3 in. wide, yellow, but the tip of the lip brownish-yellow and wavy. Malaya. Blooming in April-May in the greenhouse.

**grandifolius.** The common species in cult. Leaves 4-6 at each pseudobulb,* 2-3 ft. long, green. Flower cluster with 12-18 blooms, the flowers 3-4 in. wide, silvery-white outside, yellowish-brown within, the lip purple, margined with yellowish-brown. China and Aust.

PHALAENOPSIS (fal-ee-nop'sis). Moth Orchid. Indo-Malayan, tree-perching (epiphytic*) orchids comprising over 50 species and many hort. hybrids, and including some of the finest of cult. greenhouse orchids. They have leafy stems, no pseudobulbs,* the leaves oblong, thick, and leathery, sometimes mottled. Flower clusters drooping (panicles*), the flowers generally white, but often tinged rose or purple. Sepals spreading, almost equal, usually shorter than the petals. Lip* variously shaped, but not spurred, sometimes marked or with appendages at the tip. (*Phalaenopsis* is from the Greek for moth-like, in allusion to the flowers.)

For culture see Epiphytic Greenhouse Orchids at ORCHID.

**amabilis.** A widely grown and very popular greenhouse orchid. Leaves oblongish, 7-15 in. long, pale green. Flowers 3-5 in. wide, pure, but dull white, stained with yellow blotches, the lip with a few purple spots. Philippine Islands and Malaya. Oct.-Dec. There are many forms or varieties known to orchid fanciers, most of them with variously colored lips.

**aphrodite.** Possibly a distinct species, but considered mostly as a variety of *P. amabilis*. It has smaller flowers and the lip* is darker-colored at the base. Philippine Islands. Sometimes known as *P. sanderiana*.

**sanderiana** = *Phalaenopsis aphrodite*.

**stuartiana.** Leaves mottled when young, 8-12 in. long, nearly 5 in. wide. Flower cluster drooping, the flowers about 2 in. wide, generally white but spotted with reddish-brown, the lip* yellow and similarly spotted. Philippine Islands. Nov.-Feb.

PHALARIS (fal'ar-ris). Ornamental and seed-yielding grasses found in the north temperate zone, cult. for the sometimes variegated foliage and one of them a source of bird seed. They are annual or perennial grasses with flat, grass-like leaves. Flower cluster terminal, usually a narrow spike or panicle,* its spikelets flattened but not awned.* (*Phalaris* is an old Greek name for some of the species.)

The first species is a perennial and a popular border plant, especially in the striped-leaved variety. It is of easy culture in any ordinary garden soil and may be increased by division of the clumps. The Canary grass is an annual, the seed of which should be sown where wanted.

**arundinacea.** Reed Canary grass. A stout perennial grass, 4-6 ft. high. Leaves about 12 in. long and ¾ in. wide. Flowering cluster (panicle*), nearly 8 in. long, dense, its branches erect. North temperate zone. Much more widely grown is the *var.* **picta**, known as ribbon-grass or gardener's-garters. It has white-and-yellow-striped leaves, and is sometimes known as *P. variegata*.

**canariensis.** Canary grass. An annual, 18-24 in. high. Leaves about 6 in. long and ¼ in. wide. Flowering cluster (spike) more or less egg-shaped, about 1½ in. long, its ripe seeds, for which it is grown, shining and straw-colored and a favorite feed for birds. Eu., but naturalized in the U.S.

**variegata** = *Phalaris arundinacea picta*.

PHANEROGAM. Any plant producing flowers and seeds in the ordinary garden sense of those terms. It includes all garden plants except those mentioned at CRYPTOGAM, and is a botanical rather than a hort. term. Flowering plants are thus said to be phanerogamous; i.e. having the reproductive organs and functions manifest. See CRYPTOGAM.

PHASEOLUS (fa-see'o-lus). Bean. A very large genus of annual or perennial, mostly tropical herbs of the family Leguminosae, of outstanding garden importance because it contains the string bean, the lima bean, the scarlet runner, and several others used in warm regions for food or forage. They are chiefly twining plants (bushy in some dwarf hort. sorts), with compound* leaves, mostly with 3 leaflets. Flowers pea-like, but the keel coiled, variously colored. Fruit a somewhat flattened or cylindrical pod (legume*), edible in the string bean, but grown for the highly nutritious seeds in the lima bean and many others. (*Phaseolus* is the Latin name of the bean.)

While a few of the beans, like the scarlet runner, are grown for ornament, the most important are the string bean and lima bean, grown for food. For their culture *see* BEAN.

Most of the others are forage plants, or grown for their seeds in warm countries, and not much planted in the U.S.

**aconitifolius.** Mat bean; also called Moth bean. A low, more or less trailing annual. Leaflets 3, cut or divided into 3-5 narrow segments. Flowers yellow. Pod nearly cylindrical, 1-2 in. long, its seeds gray, sometimes black-mottled. India(?). Much cult. in India for edible seeds and for forage, but little known in the U.S.

**acutifolius latifolius.** Tepary bean. An annual, twining when robust but bushy on poor soils. Leaflets ovalish or narrower, pointed, 2-3 in. long, without marginal teeth. Flowers white or light violet, about ⅓ in. long. Pod beaked, flattened, 2-3 in. long. Seeds yellow, brown, white or bluish-black. Mex. and Ariz. It is a drought-resistant food plant suited to dry regions.

**angularis.** Adzuki bean. Annual and bushy, 1-2½ ft. high. Leaflets 2-3½ in. long, sometimes shallowly lobed. Flowers yellow. Pod 2½-5 in. long, cylindric, its seeds variously colored, the pod usually constricted between them. As. Much grown there for food and somewhat cult. in this country.

**aureus.** Mung bean; also called gram, and green or golden gram. Resembling the black gram (*P. mungo*) but the seeds not usually blackish, the pod short-hairy, and usually taller than the black gram. India(?), and much cult. there for food, also in the Philippines, Jap., etc., but not much grown here.

**calcaratus.** Rice bean. Weakly climbing annual, 3-6 ft. high. Leaflets broadly oval, 2½-3½ in. long, usually pointed, very rarely 3-lobed. Flowers yellow. Pod usually curved, 3-5 in. long, short-beaked, the seeds red, black, brown, or straw-colored. Asia, and cult. there for food (seeds), but little known in the U.S.

**caracalla.** Snail-flower; also called corkscrew-flower. A tender, perennial vine, 10-20 ft. high, cult., but rarely, for ornament in the greenhouse or outdoors in Calif. Leaflets ovalish, pointed. Flowers fragrant, yellowish or purplish, the keel shaped like a snail's shell. Tropics, probably of the Old World.

**coccineus.** Scarlet runner; also called *multiflora* or flowering bean, and painted lady. A tall-growing vine, actually a perennial, but grown as an annual for ornament. Leaflets broadly oval. Flowers scarlet, showy. Pod nearly 1 ft. long, its seeds nearly 1 in. wide. Tropical America. The scarlet runner is grown for ornament, but it is probably the original of the beans grown by the Aztecs. A modern *var.* **albus**, called the White Dutch runner, or Dutch case-knife bean, has white flowers and is grown for its edible seeds. Both it and the scarlet runner should be grown the same as pole beans. *See* BEAN. There is also a dwarf, bushy form of the White Dutch runner.

**limensis.** Lima bean. A tropical American perennial herb, grown as an annual in the North, its stems climbing. Leaflets broadly oval, sharp-pointed. Flowers yellowish-white. Pods 3-5 in. long, about 1 in. wide, flattened, the seeds ½-¾ in. long. The *var.* **limeanus** is the bush or dwarf lima bean. For the culture of both *see* BEAN.

**metcalfei.** Metcalfe bean. A perennial herb of the southwestern U.S. and adjacent Mex. and grown there mostly for forage. It has long, trailing stems and a large, fleshy root. Leaflets oblongish or broader, 2-3 in. long, blunt. Flowers reddish-purple. Pod flat, 1½-2½ in. long, slightly curved, the seeds brownish-black.

**multiflorus** = *Phaseolus coccineus*.

**mungo.** Black gram; also called urd and gram. A hairy, spreading annual, 1-3 ft. high. Leaflets ovalish, 2-4 in. long, sharp-pointed. Flowers scarcely ¼ in. long, yellow. Pod nearly terete, 1½-2 in. long, covered with long hairs, the short beak hooked. Seeds black, but with a white spot. India(?), and grown there for food. Not much known in the U.S.

**vulgaris.** The common string bean; called also kidney bean (England), haricot (France), and often snap bean here (the wax, butter, and stringless beans are forms of it). A tall, twining annual, the stem hairy. Leaflets broadly oval, pointed, 4-6 in. long, not lobed. Flowers yellowish-white (rarely purplish), ½-¾ in. long. Pod slender, slightly curved, 4-8 in. long (longer in some English forms), its beak curved. Seeds oblongish, of many colors in numerous hort. forms. Probably tropical American. The *var.* **humilis** is the common bush or dwarf bean. An interesting form is the Pinto bean, with mottled seeds, and grown for them in the southwestern U.S. For culture and varieties *see* BEAN.

PHEASANT'S-EYE = *Adonis annua*.

PHEGOPTERIS (fee-gop'ter-is). An old generic name for certain ferns here placed in *Dryopteris*.

PHELLODENDRON (fell-o-den'dron). Cork-tree. A genus of 8 or 9 species of deciduous, Asiatic trees of the rue family. They are ornamental and often picturesque. Leaves opposite,* compound,* with leaflets arranged feather-fashion. Leafstalks swollen at the base, and concealing the buds. Male and female flowers are borne in terminal clusters on separate trees; they are greenish-yellow, small and inconspicuous. Fruit black, berry-like. (*Phellodendron* is the Greek name for a cork-tree, but not the one producing cork, for which *see* OAK.)

The cork-trees are of rapid growth when young, developing into shapely, round-headed trees. They make good lawn specimens. The foliage is dark green, decorative and turns yellow in the fall; although the flowers are not showy they are followed by clusters of black fruits that hang on the tree for several months and are interesting in winter. Both leaves and fruit are strongly aromatic when crushed. The trees will grow in almost any soil and may be propagated by seeds.

**amurense.** Amur cork-tree. Tree of 40-50 ft. with gray, deeply fissured, corky bark. Leaves 10-15 in. long with 5-13 ovate or oval leaflets, 2-4 in. long. Flowers yellow-green, small, in clusters 2-3 in. across. Fruit black,

---

* Special articles on the subjects indicated by an asterisk (*) will be found at the words so marked.

berry-like. June. Northern China, Manchuria. Hardy from zone* 2 southward.

**chinense.** Tree growing 20-35 ft. high with thin, slightly fissured, brown bark. Leaves to 15 in. long, with 7-13 leaflets 3-5 in. long, hairy beneath. Flowers yellowish-green in compact, hairy clusters that are higher than broad. Fruit black. June. China. Hardy from zone* 2 southward.

**PHELLOS** (fell'os). An old name for a group of oaks that includes the willow oak (*Quercus phellos*). See OAK.

**PHENOGAM** = Phanerogam.

**PHENOLOGY.** An absorbingly interesting science having to do with the relation of climate to the periodic response to it, and, in the garden, best manifested in the time of flowering and fruiting.

Herbs, shrubs, and trees come into flower with enough regularity so that their blooming is often rather accurately predictable. The annual progression of bloom in the garden is well enough known to make a rough timetable of plants in flower for every month of the year. The details of that are not repeated here for they will be found under each month in the GARDEN CALENDAR.

All gardeners should keep yearly records for at least a few woody plants and herbs. Such tabulations from different parts of the country would be very valuable if correlated with weather data, especially temperature. But contrary to popular opinion, it is not always temperature that dictates the time of blooming. Recent studies on the length of the day (*i.e.* the number of hours of sunshine per day) indicate that illumination even more than temperature is a determining factor in phenology. In any given locality the blooming of some plants, but not all, comes with such regularity that its occurrence seems more certainly connected with the length of the day (a constant factor) than it is with temperature, which is always erratic. Phenology is well worth study by any thoughtful gardener.

**PHENOMENAL BERRY.** A form of the loganberry (which see).

**PHILADELPHICA, -us, -um** (fill-a-del'fi-ka). From Philadelphia.

**PHILADELPHUS.** See MOCK-ORANGE.

**PHILIPPINENSIS, -e** (fill-i-pin-en'sis). From the Philippine Islands.

**PHILLYREA** (fill-i-ree'a). Four species of evergreen shrubs or small trees of the olive family, native to the region about the Mediterranean. The opposite* leaves are toothed or entire. Flowers 4-lobed, small and white or greenish, in axillary clusters; male and female on separate plants. Fruit globular or oval, black. (*Phillyrea* is the ancient Greek name for these plants.)

The phillyreas have rather ornamental foliage and are useful in mixed evergreen plantings. They are dependably hardy only in the southern states, where they seem to prefer a sunny situation and to thrive in soil of average quality. Propagation is by seeds or summer cuttings.

**angustifolia.** A dense evergreen shrub growing about 10 ft. high. Leaves linear, to 2½ in. long and about ⅜ in. wide, tapered at both ends, usually entire.* Flowers white, fragrant. Fruit black, round or oval, ¼ in. May-June. Southern Eu. and northern Africa. Hardy from parts of zone* 5 southward.

**latifolia.** Shrub or occasionally a small tree to 30 ft. high. Leaves 1-2½ in. long, variable in shape, usually ovate or rounded ovate, toothed. Flowers dull white, in small clusters. Fruit blue-black, rounded or oval, ¼ in. long. May-June. Southern Eu., Asia Minor. Hardy from milder parts of zone* 5 southward.

**PHILLYREOIDES** (fill-i-re-oy'deez, but see OÏDES). Like a plant of the genus *Phillyrea* (which see).

**PHILODENDRON** (fill-o-den'dron). Handsome, tropical American foliage plants of the family Araceae, often grown in greenhouses for ornament, more rarely outdoors in zone* 9. They often climb many feet in the tropics and some are tree-perching. Most of them need support as grown in the greenhouse. Of over 200 species only the few below are of hort. interest. They have (in maturity) rather woody stems and thick, fleshy, very variable leaves with sheathing, usually channeled, leafstalks. Flowers minute, unisexual* (see ARACEAE), crowded on a spadix* which rarely exceeds the boat-shaped, often colored spathe.* Fruit fleshy. (*Philodendron* is from the Greek for tree-loving, in allusion to their nearly universal habit of climbing up trees.)

As cult. greenhouse plants the philodendrons need a warm, moist house and potting mixture* 3, to which about ⅓ its bulk of orchid peat or other fiber (like coir) has been added. They grow rapidly and need plenty of space. During the bright sunny months the glass should be shaded. Propagated by cuttings or division of the woody stems.

**devansayeanum.** Not high-climbing, the stem short and thick. Leaves ovalish or heart-shaped or nearly round, reddish in youth, long-pointed at the tip, 12-20 in. long, the stalk purplish in youth, round in cross section. Spathe* nearly 6 in. long, the tube white, the limb red-margined. Peru.

**giganteum.** High-climbing, often with hanging, whip-like roots. Leaves 2-3 ft. long, the stalk 3-4 ft. long, the blade ovalish or heart-shaped, sharp at the tip, deeply split near the base. Spathe* 6-10 in. long, the tube purplish, the limb yellowish-green. W.I.

**lindeni** = *Philodendron verrucosum*.

**pertusum** = *Monstera deliciosa*.

**verrucosum.** Stems swollen at the joints, angled, grayish-green. Leaves oval or heart-shaped, pointed at the tip, deeply split at the base, green but pale-lined above, pale green but salmon-lined beneath, the stalks red, both bristly and hairy. Spathe* purplish. Central and South America.

**PHLEBODIUM AUREUM** = *Polypodium aureum*.

**PHLEUM** (flee'um). Perennial grasses, comprising 10 species of the grass family, found throughout the temperate regions of the world. They are of no garden interest, but one species is valuable agriculturally, being extensively grown for hay, but it does not make good permanent pasture. (*Phleum* is from the Greek for a kind of reed.)

**pratense.** Timothy. Herd's grass. Grows to 5 ft. high, but varies according to conditions under which it is grown. Leaves 12 in. long, ¼ in. wide. Flowers in cylindrical spikes 3-6 in. long. Eurasia; naturalized in N.A.

**PHLOMIS** (flō'mis). Jerusalem sage. Strong-growing perennial herbs or sub-shrubs, comprising about 70 species of the mint family, found in the Mediterranean region and as far east as China. Not of much garden importance, a few species are grown in wild gardens for the large flowers. Stems coarse, and square, 1½-6 ft. high. Leaves large, ovalish or heart-shaped, opposite.* Flowers yellow, purple, or white, in whorls in the axils* of leafy bracts.* Corolla 2-lipped, the upper lip* hairy. Stamens* 4, 2 long and 2 short. Fruit 2-celled, when ripe splitting into 4 parts, each containing a seed. All of them are more or less woolly. (*Phlomis* is an old Greek name for the mullein and of no application here.)

Easily propagated by seeds, cuttings or division of tubers.

**alpina.** Perennial, growing to 1½ ft. high. Leaves heart-shaped, about 8 in. long, and 6 in. across. Flowers numerous, in whorls.* Siberia.

**fruticosa.** Jerusalem sage. A many-branched sub-shrub, 2-4 ft. high, and covered with yellowish, matted hairs. Leaves ovalish, to 4 in. long, wrinkled. Flowers yellow, numerous in whorls.* Southern Eu.

**tuberosa.** Herbaceous perennial with thick tuberous roots. Stems 4-6 ft. high, smooth or slightly hairy. Leaves heart-shaped, 6-8 in. long. Flowers purple, in 30-40 flowered whorls.* Southern Eu. and As.

**PHLOX** (flocks). Perennial and annual, usually hardy herbs, comprising about 50 species of the family Polemoniaceae, found mostly in N.A., but a few Asiatic. Growing from a few inches to 4 ft. high, some are strong and erect, others trailing. Stems sometimes becoming slightly woody at base. Leaves lance-shaped, opposite,* and in pairs, or alternate,* smooth or slightly hairy. Flowers in terminal, loose or closely packed clusters. Individual flowers showy, ranging in color from pure white to bright red, pale lilac or purple, usually having a conspicuous eye-like marking at the opening of the corolla tube. Calyx of 5 sepals united half-way down. Corolla of 5 united petals, forming a short, narrow tube, the lobes opening salver-wise. Stamens* 5, usually enclosed in the corolla tube. Fruit a 3-celled capsule,* usually only 1 seed in each cell maturing. (*Phlox* is from the Greek for flame, in allusion to the flowers.)

Phloxes are general garden favorites for the border or rock garden and should be grown in full sun. Their easy culture and long flowering periods make them particularly useful. Propagated from seeds, cuttings and division of roots. Annuals are grown from seeds sown in early spring

---

* Special articles on the subjects indicated by an asterisk (*) will be found at the words so marked.

in cool greenhouse or cold frame, or they may be sown a little later outdoors where required to bloom. Sow ⅛ in. deep, in well-pulverized soil. If sown in greenhouse or cold frame they must be transplanted when 2 in. high where required to bloom, and set 8 in. apart. They may be grown as pot plants.

Perennials are usually grown from cuttings or division of roots to enable the gardener to keep the true plant. They should be taken up and divided every 3 years. Cuttings for the spring-flowering, trailing species should be made July–Aug., from the tips of young shoots, 2–3 in. long. Insert in ½ sand and ½ soil, in well-shaded cold frame, keeping sashlights closed during day and opened slightly at night for 3–4 weeks. When rooted sashlights should be removed. Old plants, after flowering, may be trimmed back and roots divided and replanted. Cuttings for the tall, summer-flowering species should be made in Sept. or as soon as young growths appear in early spring. Follow the same culture as the trailing types, using a cool greenhouse in the fall if more convenient. They grow well in any ordinary garden soil, but better results will be obtained by using rich soil and well watering during dry periods. Division of roots may be made in early spring.

**adsurgens.** A spreading perennial, the stems 3–6 in. high. Leaves ovalish, 1 in. long. Flowers rose or pale pink, 1 in. across, in dense clusters. Spring. Ore.

**amoena.** Spreading perennial to 1 ft. high. Leaves numerous, broadly lance-shaped, 2 in. long. Flowers purplish-red, ¾ in. across, in close terminal clusters. Spring. See ROCK GARDEN. Va.–Fla. Sometimes known as *P. procumbens.*

**arendsi.** A hybrid, perennial, growing to 2 ft. Leaves broadly lance-shaped, to 4 in. long. Flowers lavender or mauve, 1 in. across, in large, loose clusters. June–July. Miss Lingard is a white form, and Louise is useful for the gray garden.

**argillacea** = *Phlox pilosa.*

**carolina** = *Phlox ovata.*

**diffusa.** A spreading perennial, growing to 4 in. high. Leaves lance-shaped, ½ in. long. Flowers white, ½ in. long, solitary. British Columbia to Calif.

**divaricata.** Blue phlox. Wild Sweet William. Erect perennial, growing to 18 in., with creeping, flowerless stems which root, thus increasing the size of the plant rapidly. Leaves broadly lance-shaped, 2 in. long. Flowers mauve, to 1 in. across, in loose clusters. Spring. Eastern N.A. The var. *alba* (white) and *laphami* (violet-blue) are color forms.

**douglasi.** Perennial, and spreading to 10 in. wide. Leaves spear-like, ½ in. long. Flowers solitary, small, white or lavender. Western N.A. For culture see ROCK GARDEN.

**drummondi.** Annual phlox. Drummond phlox. Texan pride. Erect annual, growing to 1½ ft. Leaves broadly lance-shaped, to 3 in. long. Flowers ranging from white to purple, also buff, 1 in. across, in umbel-like clusters. Tex. The var. *cuspidata* has fringed petals, while the var. *stellaris,* the star phlox, has star-shaped flowers, the petals being deeply cut and pointed. May–Aug.

**maculata.** Wild Sweet William. Erect perennial, growing 3 ft. high, the stems purple-spotted. Leaves lance-shaped, 3–5 in. long. Flowers pink or purple, ½ in. across, in loose racemes.* June–July. Eastern N.A.

**ovata.** A perennial, growing to 2 ft. high, spreading at first, then becoming erect. Leaves broadly lance-shaped, 1–2 in. long. Flowers purple, 1 in. across, in small, loose clusters. May–June. Pa. to Ala. Sometimes known as *P. carolina.*

**paniculata.** Garden phlox. Perennial phlox. Strong stems, growing to 4 ft. high. Leaves broadly lance-shaped, thin, 3½–5 in. long, with prominent veins. Flowers varying in color, 1 in. across, in large, spreading clusters. Varieties of this species are much cult. July–Aug. Southern U.S. Here belong many popular garden forms. Besides the white varieties, the following will be found useful. RED: Africa, Debs, Coquelicot, Firebrand and Goliath. PINK: Annie Cook, Elizabeth Campbell, Enchantress, Johnson's Favorite, Jules Sandeau (a dwarf), Mme. Paul Dutrie, Painted Lady, Peachblow and Rheinlander.

**pilosa.** Prairie phlox. Slender, erect perennial, up to 18 in. high. Leaves lance-shaped, narrow, 2–3 in. long. Flowers varying in color from white to purple, ¾ in. across, in small clusters. June. Eastern U.S. Also offered as *P. argillacea.*

**procumbens.** See PHLOX AMOENA.

**reptans** = *Phlox stolonifera.*

**stolonifera.** Perennial, growing to 1 ft. high, with creeping, flowerless stems which root and cause the plant to increase. Leaves broadly lance-shaped, 2–3 in. long, covered with short hairs. Flowers purple or violet, ¾ in. across, in dense clusters. For culture see ROCK GARDEN. June. Pa. to Ala.

**subulata.** Ground pink. Moss pink. Flowering moss. Evergreen, creeping perennial forming a dense mat. growing to a height of 6 in. Leaves crowded, needle-like, ½ in. long. Flowers bright purple, pink, or white, ¾ in. across, in dense clusters. Especially useful in the rock garden. See ROCK GARDEN. May. N.Y. to N.C. The varieties E. T. Wilson (blue), and Vivid (pink) are the best in their respective colors.

**suffruticosa.** Early perennial phlox. Growing to 3 ft. high. Stems slightly woody at the base. Leaves broadly lance-shaped, thick, 3–5 in. long. Flowers purple, sometimes rose or white, ¾ in. across, in loose clusters. Mostly cult. in hort. forms. June–July.

DISEASES. Mildew, root knot, leafspot and stem nematode are the common diseases. For *mildew* and *root knot* see Mildew or Root Knot at PLANT DISEASES. *Leafspot,* characterized by brown lesions on the foliage, appears first on the lower leaves and in cases of severe infection may cause death. Spraying with bordeaux mixture and a thorough cleanup of all plant debris in the fall will afford control. *Stem nematodes,* when present, cause a serious disease. Infected plants are stunted and exhibit swollen or cracked stems. The leaves are markedly distorted or aborted and flowering is inhibited. Diseased plants should be removed and destroyed immediately.

**PHLOX FAMILY** = Polemoniaceae.

**PHOEBE.** See BIRDS.

*PHOENICEA, -us, -um* (fe-ni'see-a). From Phoenicia.

*PHOENICOLASIA, -us, -um* (fee-nick-o-lay'zi-a). Purple-haired.

**PHOENIX** (fee'nix). An important genus of feather palms, including the date, and several others widely grown for ornament. There are scarcely a dozen known African and Asiatic species, at least five of which are of hort. importance. Spineless, except for the spine-like lower segments on the leaves of some species. Trunk not usually tall (as cult.), nor woody, often consisting merely of the woody bases of old leaves. Leaflets or segments long and narrow, the midrib replaced by a ridge, along each side of which are two prominent veins. Male and female flowers on different plants, rarely blooming in cult. (except on the date palm). Flowers small, yellowish, borne on long, drooping, branched stalks. Stamens* 6. Fruit a fleshy drupe,* its seed with a single groove. (*Phoenix* is an old Greek name for the date.)

For the cult. of the ornamental species (all but the date) see PALM. See also DATE.

**canariensis.** A handsome, ornamental palm 50–60 ft. high in the wild, much less as cult. Leaves 15–20 ft. long, the leaflets or segments very numerous, standing at different angles from the main leafstalk, narrow, long-pointed, the lower ones spiny. Fruiting cluster often drooping, 3–8 ft. long, the fruit egg-shaped or roundish, yellowish-red. Canary Islands. A deservedly popular palm, more hardy than many others and widely planted throughout zones* 8 and 9, sometimes even hardy in protected places in zone* 7. Much used for avenue planting in Calif.

**dactylifera.** Date or date palm. A tall palm, usually producing suckers at the base. Leaves erect when young and stiffish, drooping in age, the segments or leaflets 12–18 in. long, bluish-green, the lower ones spiny. Fruit oblongish, 1–3 in. long, the pulp sweet. Western Asia or northern Africa, but exact native uncertain. It has been cult. for perhaps 4000 years. For culture and varieties see DATE.

**reclinata.** Trunks usually several in a clump, 10–20 ft. high. Leaves cottony beneath when young, losing it in age. Leaflets recurved at the tip, often in pairs or 3's, not over 12 in. long, the lower ones replaced by long spines. Fruit about ¾ in. long, brown or reddish. Africa. Widely planted for ornament, but not so hardy as *P. canariensis.*

**roebelini.** A dwarf, very slender-leaved palm, not over 4–6 ft. high, and widely used as a very desirable pot plant, or outdoors in zones* 8 and 9. Stems usually several, sometimes with a swollen base. Leaves very graceful, drooping, the segments very narrow, rather soft, generally opposite,* a few of the lower ones replaced by weak spines. Fruiting cluster scarcely 12 in. long, the fruit about ½ in. long. Cochin-China(?).

**sylvestris.** Wild date. Trunk up to 50 ft. high (less as cult.), solitary. Leaves drooping, bluish-green or even grayish, the leaflets or segments very numerous, rigid, borne in small groups and at divers angles from the main leafstalk. Fruit about 1 in. long, oblongish, orange-yellow. India. Commonly planted in Calif. and about as hardy as *P. canariensis.*

**PHOENIX-TREE** = *Firmiana simplex.*

**PHONY PEACH.** A virus disease of the peach. See Diseases at PEACH.

**PHORADENDRON.** See MISTLETOE.

**PHORMIUM** (for'mi-um). A genus of only two species of large perennial herbs of the lily family, grown for ornament in Fla. and Calif., but for the valuable fiber of one of them in N. Zeal., where they are native. They have basal, distichous,* very tough, long and sword-shaped leaves, without marginal teeth or spines. Flowering stalk usually exceeding the leaves, the upper part with alternate* and bracted* branches upon which the flowers are borne. Flowers red or yellow, 1–2 in. long, tubular, somewhat curved, the 6 stamens* protruding. Fruit a 3-celled capsule. (*Phormium* is from the Greek for basket, in allusion to the fiber of the leading species.)

They can be grown outdoors only in zones* 8 and 9, where their culture presents no difficulties. Seeds sown in early spring will germinate in time for plants to be set out that year, or they may be increased by dividing the roots.

---

* Special articles on the subjects indicated by an asterisk (*) will be found at the words so marked.

Their fine long foliage, especially when planted in clumps, is a striking object on any lawn or in the border, but in the latter place they need plenty of space.

**colensoi.** Leaves 5–7 ft. long, about 2 in. wide, and not so rigid as in *P. tenax*. Flowers nearly 1½ in. long, yellow. N. Zeal. Sometimes offered as *P. cookianum*.

**cookianum** = *Phormium colensoi*.

**tenax.** New Zealand flax; also called flax lily. An important cordage fiber plant in N. Zeal., but cult. here for its striking leaves which may be 15 ft. high, about 5 in. wide, very tough and leathery, usually red-margined and shreddy at the tip. Flowers about 2 in. long, dull red, the whole cluster well above the foliage. The *var.* **variegatum** has white- and yellow-striped leaves. There are also forms with reddish-purple, and with white-striped leaves.

**PHOSPHORIC ACID.** *See* FERTILIZERS.

**PHOSPHORUS.** *See* PLANT FOODS.

**PHOTINIA** (fō-tin′i-a). Most of the species of *Photinia*, which belong to the rose family and come from northern Asia, are ornamental. They are deciduous or evergreen shrubs or trees with alternate,* often leathery leaves. The flowers are white, have 5 petals, and are borne in clusters (corymbs* or panicles*). Fruit round or oval (a pome*), red, about ¼ in. long. (*Photinia* is from the Greek for shining, in allusion to the glossy leaves.)

The photinias are excellent ornamental shrubs, the deciduous species have attractive white flowers and red fruits and the leaves turn red and scarlet in the fall, while the evergreen species have, in addition, handsome, shiny foliage. They like a sunny place in well-drained, loamy soil. Propagation is by seeds and cuttings.

**arbutifolia.** *See* TOYON.

**glabra.** Evergreen shrub 8–10 ft. high. Leaves elliptic to oblong-obovate, 2–3½ in. long, wedge-shaped at base, finely toothed. Flowers white, in clusters (panicles*) 2–4 in. across. Fruit red. May–July. Jap. Hardy from zone* 5 southward.

**serrulata.** An evergreen shrub or sometimes a small tree of 30–40 ft. Leaves oblong, shiny, reddish when young, finely toothed, 4–8 in. long. Flowers white in clusters 4–6 in. across. Fruit red. May–July. China. Hardy from zone* 5 southward. A very handsome shrub.

**villosa.** Deciduous shrub or small tree to 15 ft. Leaves obovate to oblong-obovate, 1–3 in. long, pointed at tip, finely toothed, hairy beneath. Flowers white, in clusters 1–2 in. across, stems warty. Fruit red. June. Jap., China and Korea. Hardy from zone* 3 southward.

**PHOTOSYNTHESIS.** As the etymology of the word suggests, photosynthesis is an activity of plants carried on in the light. It is incomparably the most important function of all leaves, for it is the name for the process by which they manufacture starch and sugar, a feat which the chemists have never yet duplicated.

Upon photosynthesis depends all other activities of plant life. It involves the action of sunlight upon the green coloring substance (chlorophyll) in all leaves. This action, in the presence of food brought from the roots, water, and certain gases, results in the manufacture of starch, then sugar. For the details of the process *see* PLANT FOODS.

**PHRAGMITES** (frag-my′teez). Tall, perennial, mostly marsh grasses, natives in the north temperate zone and in S.A., one of the three known species cult. for its handsome foliage and its beautifully plumed fruiting cluster. The only cult. species, **P. communis**, the common reed grass, is a striking plant, 10–15 ft. high. Leaves 12–20 in. long and about 2 in. wide. Flower cluster terminal, 6–12 in. long, much-branched, its spikelets, especially in fruit, beautifully silky from its many soft hairs. While growing naturally in marshes it is readily cult. in ordinary garden soil, preferably somewhat moist. Its plumy panicles make fine winter decorations. Eurasia and N.A. There is also a variegated leaved form. (*Phragmites* is from the Greek for hedge-like, in allusion to its hedge-like growth along ditches.)

**PHRAGMOPEDILUM.** *See* CYPRIPEDIUM.

**PHU** (fu). Arabic name for *Valeriana phu*.

**PHYGELIUS** (fy-jee′li-us). South African, rather small, smooth shrubs of the family Scrophulariaceae, comprising only two species, one of them, **P. capensis**, the Cape fuchsia (not a real fuchsia) grown for ornament, but only rarely. It is not over 4 ft. high, has a 4-angled stem, and usually opposite,* ovalish or narrower, toothed leaves, 3–5 in. long. Flowers scarlet, drooping, in terminal clusters (panicles*), 9–18 in. long. Corolla tubular, a little curved, about 2 in. long, the five lobes almost equal, the four stamens protruding. Fruit a capsule.* The Cape fuchsia can be grown in the cool greenhouse northward, in potting mixture* 4, or it may be grown outdoors from zone* 6 southward, and perhaps in protected parts of zone* 5. Propagated by seeds or from autumn-taken cuttings. (*Phygelius* is from the Greek for sun flight, in allusion to its supposed need for shade.)

**PHYLLAGATHIS** (fill-ag′a-this). A baker's dozen of mostly Indo-Malayan or tropical Chinese, greenhouse shrubby plants of the family Melastomaceae, only **P. rotundifolia** of Sumatra of much hort. interest. It is a shrubby plant, 1–2 ft. high, with a 4-angled stem and large, showy, opposite,* ovalish leaves, 5–7 in. long, faintly toothed, green and plaited above, metallic and blue- or purplish-red beneath. Flowers rose-red, about ½ in. wide, crowded in a dense, head-like, short-stalked cluster, beneath which are 5–6 purple bracts. A showy, handsome plant for the tropical greenhouse, needing high temperatures from spring to autumn and plenty of moisture. Use potting mixture* 3. Propagated by cuttings, taken in early spring, over bottom-heat. (*Phyllagathis* is from the Greek, and probably refers to the bracts* beneath the flower cluster.)

*PHYLLAMPHORA, -us, -um* (fil-am′for-a). A specific name applied to a species of *Nepenthes* and meaning a cavity leaf; *i.e.* a pitcher. *See* NEPENTHES.

**PHYLLANTHUS** (fill-an′thus). A genus of 50 species of mostly trees and shrubs (a few non-hort. species are herbs) of the spurge family, widely distributed over the earth, but chiefly tropical. The only plant of much hort. significance is **P. acidus**, the Otaheite gooseberry or gooseberry-tree, a native of India and Madagascar, now naturalized in Fla. It is a tree up to 20 ft. high, occasionally grown in Fla. for its acid fruit used for preserving. Branches scarred with the remains of deciduous, leaf-bearing branchlets. Leaves alternate,* but distichous,* ovalish, 2–3 in. long. Flowers small, red, without petals, crowded in small clusters (panicles*), these sometimes in the leaf-axils.* Fruit a berry, angled, about ⅝ in. long. Propagated by seeds or by cuttings. For the plant sometimes known as *P. nivosus see* BREYNIA NIVOSA. (*Phyllanthus* is from the Greek for leaf-flower, some non-hort. species bearing their flowers on apparent leaves.)

**PHYLLITIS** (fill-eye′tis). A small genus of rather leathery-fronded, hardy ferns of the family Polypodiaceae, one of them, **P. scolopendrium**, the hartstongue fern, occasionally grown in the outdoor fern garden. It is a widely scattered evergreen fern found in Eu. and at a few sporadic localities in N.A., most of them limestone regions. Fronds undivided, strap-shaped, 7–18 in. long, without lobes or teeth, but sometimes wavy-margined. Spore* cases long, usually in pairs and standing at nearly right angles to the midrib, numerous. Suited only to the outdoor fern garden and apparently, in America, a limestone plant. In Eu., and among fern specialists here, there are many forms with divided, crisped, dwarf, or crested fronds. (*Phyllitis* is from the Greek for leaf, and is also the old Greek name for the hartstongue fern.)

**PHYLLOCACTUS.** *See* EPIPHYLLUM and ZYGOCACTUS.

**PHYLLODIUM** (plural phyllodia). An expanded, leaf-like leafstalk. While leaf-like, there is no true leaf blade. Phyllodia, among cult. plants, are chiefly confined to certain species of *Acacia* (which see).

**PHYLLODOCE** (fill-od′o-see). A small group of low, evergreen shrubs, of the heath family (Ericaceae), found in N.A. and northern Eurasia. The leaves are alternate* and linear, the margins often rolled under. Flowers urn-shaped or bell-shaped on slender, nodding stems. Fruit a dry, 5-celled capsule.* (*Phyllodoce* — a sea nymph.)

These attractive little shrubs are adapted to the rock garden, but somewhat difficult to grow. They like a cool,

---

* Special articles on the subjects indicated by an asterisk (*) will be found at the words so marked.

moist, shaded place and peaty soil. Propagation is by seed, cuttings and layers.

**breweri.** Dwarf evergreen shrub of tufted habit growing about 1 ft. high. Leaves linear, ½–¾ in. long, the margin rolled under. Flowers saucer-shaped, ½ in. long, 5-lobed, purplish-rose, on slender stalks forming a terminal cluster, but growing from the leaf-axil.* May. Calif. Hardy from zone* 4 southward.

**coerulea.** Mountain heath. A low, much-branched, evergreen shrub growing about 6 in. high. Leaves linear, ¼–½ in. long, finely toothed. Flowers urn-shaped, ⅓ in. long, bluish-purple, borne singly or clustered, on nodding stalks. June–Aug. Northern N.A. and Eurasia. Hardy from zone* 1 southward.

**empetriformis.** A rather dense and tufted shrub, growing 6–9 in. high. Leaves ¼–½ in. long, narrow. Flowers bell-shaped, reddish-purple, ¼ in. long on slender stalks. April–May. British Columbia to Calif. Hardy from zone* 3 southward. Probably the most adaptable of the group.

**glanduliflora.** Related to P. coerulea, but about twice as high, and the flowers sulphur-yellow. Alaska to Mont. and Ore. For cult. see WILD GARDEN.

**PHYLLOSTACHYS** (fill-o-stack'is). Bamboo-like, Asiatic, woody-stemmed grasses, generally more hardy than the true bamboos. Of the 25 known species several are grown for ornament. They have moderately tall, hollow, flattened or grooved stems and creeping rootstocks. Leaves grass-like, but relatively broad, short-stalked, and usually checkered. Flowering cluster a terminal, mostly leafy panicle,* the spikelets with protruding stamens,* and plumy stigmas.* (Phyllostachys is from the Greek for leaf and spike, in allusion to the leafy inflorescence.)

For culture see GRASSES. For related and other bamboo-like grasses see BAMBOO.

**aurea.** Golden bamboo. Erect, yellow-stemmed grass, 9–15 ft. high, the upper leaf-joints distant and with a swollen band beneath them. Leaves 2½–5¼ in. long, about ¾ in. wide, the sheath bristly, dark green above, bluish-gray beneath. China and Jap. Hardy from zone* 5 southward.

**bambusoides** = Phyllostachys reticulata.

**nigra.** Leafy-stemmed, and very woody grass, 15–20 ft. high, the stems green at first, later black, the stems white-banded just below each joint. Leaves 2½–5 in. long, about ¾ in. wide, minutely toothed on the margin (i.e. a cutting edge), bluish-green below. China and Jap. Hardy from zone* 5 southward.

**reticulata.** Upright, often 18 ft. high, sometimes as much as 35 ft., more or less bloomy below the leaf-joints. Leaves 4–6½ in. long, about 1¾ in. wide, bluish-green below, the sheaths bristly. China. Hardy from zone* 5 southward.

**PHYLLOXERA.** See Insect Pests at GRAPE.

**PHYMOSIA** = Sphaeralcea.

**PHYSALIS** (fiss'a-lis). Husk tomato. Ground cherry. Annual or perennial herbs, found throughout warm and temperate regions, but mostly American, comprising about 75 species and belonging to the family Solanaceae. Leaves alternate,* ovalish, or heart-shaped. Flowers 1–2, produced in the axils* of the leaves, inconspicuous, blue, or whitish-yellow. Calyx* after fertilization has taken place becomes inflated and colored, enclosing the round, yellow or green, 2-celled, sometimes sticky berry containing the seeds. (Physalis is from the Greek for bladder, in allusion to the inflated calyx.)

Mostly grown for the ornamental calyx* which becomes pale yellow to deep orange in the fall. When cut these will keep for weeks in the house. A few are grown for their edible fruits. Easily propagated by seeds or division of the roots, but usually treated as tender annuals. Sow seeds in early spring in cool greenhouse or cold frame in sandy soil. As soon as large enough to plant out transfer to permanent position, planting 1 ft. apart. They will grow in ordinary garden soil, but prefer open, sunny position. Division of roots may be made in early spring.

**alkekengi.** Winter cherry. Chinese lantern-plant. Strawberry tomato. Hardy perennial, growing to 2 ft. high, with long, creeping, underground stems that quickly increase size of plant. Leaves ovalish, 2–3 in. long, the margins hairy. Flowers whitish. Fruit a small red berry, enclosed in large, orange-red inflated calyx.* Southeastern Eu. to Jap.

**edulis** = Physalis ixocarpa.

**francheti** = Physalis alkekengi.

**ixocarpa.** Tomatillo. Mexican ground cherry. Tender annual, growing 3–4 ft. high. Leaves ovalish, 2–3 in. long, the margins toothed. Flowers ¾ in. across, yellow, with 5 blackish spots in the throat. Fruit a bluish, sticky berry enclosed in an inflated calyx which has purple veins. Mex.

**peruviana.** Cape gooseberry. Tender perennial, growing 1–3 ft. high. Leaves heart-shaped, covered with soft hairs. Flowers pale yellow, ½ in. long, the throat purple. Fruit an edible, yellow berry, enclosed in a long-pointed calyx.* Tropics.

**pruinosa.** Strawberry tomato. Strong-growing hardy annual, dwarf, with angular, erect and spreading stems, covered with gray hairs. Leaves ovalish, 3–4 in. long, coarsely toothed. Flowers dull yellow. Fruit an edible, greenish-yellow berry, enclosed in a large, hairy calyx. N.A.

**PHYSALODES** (fiss-a-low'deez). An old generic name for the apple-of-Peru, now included in Nicandra.

**PHYSIC-NUT** = Jatropha curcas.

**PHYSOCARPUS** (fy-so-kar'pus). Ninebark. Attractive, white-flowered, spirea-like shrubs of the rose family, all the 13 species North American except a single Asiatic one. They have shreddy or peeling bark, and alternate,* stalked, toothed, and often 3-lobed leaves. Flowers small, white in the cult. species, crowded in dense terminal clusters (corymbs*), the sepals and petals 5 each. Stamens* 20–40. Fruit a collection of inflated follicles,* the seeds shining and yellowish. (Physocarpus is from the Greek for bladder and fruit, in allusion to the inflated follicles.*)

The ninebarks (sometimes known as Opulaster) are of easy culture in any ordinary garden soil. Their flowers, while small, are attractive from the profusion of their clusters. Propagated by seeds or cuttings. Both species flower in June.

**monogynus.** Not over 3 ft. high, the leaves broadly kidney-shaped, rather deeply 3–5-lobed. Flower clusters sparse, white, but sometimes pinkish. Fruits 2 to a cluster, hairy and united to about the middle. Central U.S. Hardy from zone* 3 southward.

**opulifolius.** An erect or arching shrub 5–8 ft. high. Leaves ovalish or rounded, 2½–3½ in. long. Flower cluster profuse, nearly 2 in. wide, the individual flowers scarcely ¼ in. wide. Fruits usually 5 to a cluster, smooth. Eastern N.A. Hardy from zone* 2 southward.

**PHYSOSTEGIA** (fy-sos-stee'gi-a). North American, hardy perennials of the mint family, comprising only 3 species, one of them, **P. virginiana**, the false dragonhead or obedient plant, often cult. in the open border. It is a tall (4 ft.), wand-like herb with 4-sided stems and opposite,* oblongish, toothed leaves, 3–5 in. long. Flowers usually purple-red, rarely rose-pink or even lilac, in a terminal, leafy cluster (spike*), nearly 8 in. long and showy. Corolla tubular, inflated upward, 2-lipped,* but the lips small. Fruit a collection of small nutlets, seated in the much-inflated fruiting calyx. The var. **alba** has white flowers; var. **gigantea** grows up to 7 ft. high; and the var. **grandiflora** has bright pink flowers. All are rather commonly cult. in the flower border and are of easy culture. They may be propagated by division of the clumps. Eastern N.A. Summer. Sometimes known as Dracocephalum virginianum. (Physostegia is from the Greek for bladder and covering, in allusion to the fruit being covered by the inflated calyx.*)

**PHYTEUMA** (fi-tew'ma). Rampion; also called horned rampion. Eurasian perennial herbs of the family Campanulaceae, comprising about 40 species, the few cult. ones mostly suited to the rock garden, and not widely grown. They are upright herbs with basal and alternate* stem leaves, some of them narrow enough to be grass-like. Flowers in dense terminal clusters (mostly head-like), prevailing blue, but sometimes whitish. Corolla not opening very much, sometimes its 5 narrow segments remaining closed. Flower buds long, curved and horn-like. Fruit a capsule,* crowned by the persistent calyx-lobes. (Phyteuma is an old Greek name for any plant, but of no significance as applied to these.)

For culture see ROCK GARDEN.

**hemisphaericum.** Not over 6 in. high and tufted. Leaves very narrow, without marginal teeth. Flowers blue, rarely whitish, in dense, ovalish, head-like clusters. Alps.

**scheuchzeri.** Erect and 10–18 in. high. Leaves oblongish or narrower, toothed. Flowers in a dense, globe-shaped cluster about 1 in. thick, violet-blue, below it a series of narrow, long bracts.* Southern Eu.

**spicatum.** Erect and 2–4 ft. high. Basal leaves long-stalked, the stem leaves ovalish to much narrower, toothed. Flower clusters dense, oblong spikes, the flowers white but green-tipped. Eu.

**PHYTOLACCA** (fy-to-lak'ka). Pokeweed or pokeberry. Mostly tropical trees and shrubs, a few perennial herbs of the temperate zone, belonging to the family Phytolaccaceae, and of very diverse hort. interest. They have alternate,* simple* leaves without marginal teeth. Male and female flowers on separate plants in P. dioica, but the flowers perfect* in the common poke. Flowers small, in terminal clusters (racemes*), without petals, the 4–5-parted calyx

---

* Special articles on the subjects indicated by an asterisk (*) will be found at the words so marked.

corolla-like. Fruit a usually staining berry, edible in some (non-hort.) species. (*Phytolacca* is from the Greek for plant and the French or Italian for *lac*, in allusion to the staining berries.)

For cultural notes *see* each species.

**americana.** Poke or pokeweed; also called scoke and inkberry. A dangerous, strong-smelling, weedy herb 6–10 ft. high, common as a wild plant in eastern N.A., especially in wet places and among coastal sand dunes. Its root, which resembles horse-radish, is violently, perhaps even deadly, poisonous. Leaves oblong-oval, 6–9 in. long, often red-veined or red-stalked. Flowers white. Fruit a blackish-red berry. Not much cult., although a handsome plant. All children should be warned about its dangerous roots, although the foliage is used by some for spring greens.

**decandra** = *Phytolacca americana*.

**dioica.** Umbra. An evergreen, handsome tree, much grown for ornament in southern Calif. and similar climates (not hardy elsewhere). Leaves elliptic or ovalish, its midrib projecting beyond the tip. Flowers white. It is a tree of very rapid growth and specimens scarcely 50 ft. high may (in Calif.) have a trunk diameter of 6 ft.

**PHYTOLACCACEAE** (fy-toe-lak-kay'see-ee). The pokeweed family is of secondary garden interest. Of its 22 genera and perhaps 100 species of herbs, shrubs and trees, only *Phytolacca* and *Rivina*, mostly tropical, are of the least garden significance. The former, largely weedy, contains one quick-growing tree that is cult. outdoors in Fla. and southern Calif., while *Rivina* is fairly common as a greenhouse plant.

Leaves alternate,* without marginal teeth. Flowers in racemes,* either terminal or in the axils* of the leaves, not very showy and without petals. Fruit a fleshy berry in both the cult. genera.

Technical flower characters: Flowers regular* and hermaphrodite.* Calyx more or less tubular, 4–5-parted at the top, petal-like. Petals none. Stamens* 4 and alternate with the calyx lobes in *Rivina*, more numerous in *Phytolacca*. Ovary superior.*

**PHYTOPHTHORA BLIGHT.** A series of destructive blights caused by microscopic fungi of the genus *Phytophthora*. For control *see* the Diseases mentioned at LILAC, RHODODENDRON, and POTATO.

**PIAROPUS** = *Eichhornia*. *See* WATER HYACINTH.

**PICEA.** *See* SPRUCE.

**PICH** = *Calliandra portoricensis*.

**PICKAX.** *See* Section 1, TOOLS AND IMPLEMENTS.

**PICKERELWEED.** *See* PONTEDERIA.

**PICKERELWEED FAMILY** = Pontederiaceae.

**PICKLE WORM.** *See* Insect Pests at MELON.

**PICOTEE.** *See* CARNATION.

*PICTA*, *-us*, *-um* (pick'ta). Painted; *i.e.* often variegated.

*PICTURATA*, *-us*, *-um* (pick-ture-ray'ta). Variegated.

**PIECE-ROOT GRAFTING.** *See* GRAFTING.

**PIE-PLANT.** *See* RHUBARB.

**PIERIS** (py-ear'is). Valuable, broad-leaved evergreen shrubs or small trees, of the heath family, very widely planted for ornament, comprising only 8 species from N.A. and eastern As., two of which are the chief hort. species. They have generally alternate,* stalked, toothed leaves. Flowers in terminal clusters (narrow panicles*), the buds very obvious all the winter previous to blooming. Corolla white, urn-shaped, its 5 lobes short. Stamens* 10. Fruit a dry capsule.* (Named for the Greek Muse.)

The uses of *Pieris* in the garden are many. They are fine for gateway plantings, as accent plants in the shrubbery, and for the rock garden. They should be grown in peaty, somewhat sandy and moderately acid soils (*see* ACID AND ALKALI SOILS) and should be kept mulched with leaves. They are slow-growing, rather expensive, but very handsome shrubs, propagated by seeds or by layers.

**floribunda.** Mountain fetter-bush. An erect shrub, 3–4 ft. high. Leaves elliptic or ovalish, 1½–3½ in. long, pointed, minutely hairy on the margin. Flowers nodding, the cluster upright, 2–4½ in. long. Va. to Ga. April–May. Hardy from zone* 4 southward, and in sheltered places in zone* 3. Sometimes known as *Andromeda floribunda*. It is a useful plant for forcing (which see).

**japonica.** A splendid evergreen shrub 3–8 ft. high, or even more in age. Leaves oblongish, 1½–3½ in. long, dark shiny green. Flower clusters hanging, 3–5 in. long, the corolla about ⅜–⅝ in. long. Jap. April–May. Hardy from zone* 4 southward. Often sold as *Andromeda japonica*.

**lucida** = *Xolisma lucida*.

**mariana** = *Xolisma mariana*.

**PIGEONBERRY** = *Duranta repens* and *Cornus alternifolia*.

**PIGEON GRAPE** = *Vitis aestivalis*.

**PIGEON PEA** = *Cajanus cajan*.

**PIGNUT.** Various inferior hickory-nuts are classed as pignuts, but they are scarcely worth cultivating. For the hickories worth attention *see* HICKORY.

**PIGNUT PALM.** *See* HYOPHORBE.

**PIGWEED** = *Chenopodium album*. *See* the list at WEEDS.

**PILEA** (py'lee-a). Also known as *Adicea*. American annual or perennial herbs, mostly tropical, comprising about 150 species, and belonging to the family Urticaceae. Stems fleshy, much-branched and spreading. Leaves opposite,* small, fleshy, and ovalish. Flowers greenish, inconspicuous, produced in small clusters in the axils* of the leaves. In some plants the flowers have stamens* only, in others pistils* only, while some have both stamens* and pistil.* Fruit, which does not split, 1-celled, 1-seeded. (*Pilea* is from the Latin for cap, in allusion to the flowers.)

Not of much garden importance, but one species cult. in the greenhouse for the neat, fern-like habit and the interesting manner in which the pollen is discharged explosively when dry. It is this which explains the common name of artillery-plant. It is easy of cult., and propagated by cuttings inserted in sharp sand, in a temperature of 65°. As soon as rooted they should be put in 2-in. pots in potting mixture* 2. Re-pot when necessary, in 5-in. pots, and use potting mixture* 3. They should be watered plentifully at all times.

**microphylla.** Artillery-plant. Annual, of spreading habit, to 1 ft. high. Leaves small, fleshy, broadly lance-shaped, about ¼ in. long. Flowers bear both stamens* and pistil.* Tropical America.

**muscosa** = *Pilea microphylla*.

**serpyllifolia** = *Pilea microphylla*.

*PILEATA*, *-us*, *-um* (py-lee-ā'ta). Having a cap.

**PILLAR ROSES.** *See* Group 6 at ROSE.

**PILOCEREUS** = *Cephalocereus*.

*PILOSA*, *-us*, *-um* (py-low'sa). Pilose; *i.e.* hairy, with long, soft hairs.

*PILOSELLA* (py-low-sell'a). Pre-Linnaean* name for the mouse-ear hawkweed. *See* the list at WEEDS.

**PILOTWEED** = *Silphium laciniatum*.

*PILULARIS*, *-e* (pill-you-lay'ris). Globule-like, or bearing minute globules.

*PILULIFERA*, *-us*, *-um* (pill-you-lif'fer-a). Globule-bearing.

**PIMELEA** (py-mee'lee-a). Rice-flower. Tender Aust. and N.Z. shrubs comprising about 80 species of the family Thymelaeaceae. Leaves opposite* and crowded on the stem, rolled when young, ovalish. Flowers showy, small, white or pink, in heads or clusters surrounded by reddish bracts.* Fruit like a very small plum. (*Pimelea* is from the Greek for fat, in allusion to the fleshy seeds.)

A few grown as cool greenhouse plants. Propagated by seeds or cuttings. Seeds should be sown ⅛ in. deep, in light, sandy soil in temperature 55°–65°, Feb.–May. Cuttings of young shoots, 2–3 in. long, should be inserted in 1 part peat, 2 parts sharp sand, in temperature 55°–65° in March or April. Transplant when rooted to 2-in. pots and potting mixture* 2. As the plants increase in size, re-pot firmly, in 5-in. pots, and use potting mixture* 3. After flowering trim back and re-pot. Shoots should be pinched back to induce bushy growth. Plants should be grown in humid atmosphere and shaded from the sun in summer months. They are subject to red spider if conditions are too dry. Some dealers list these plants under *Banksia*, with which they have nothing to do.

---

* Special articles on the subjects indicated by an asterisk (*) will be found at the words so marked.

PIMENTA 609 PINE

decussata = *Pimelea ferruginea.*
  **ferruginea.** Much-branched shrub, 2–3 ft. high. Leaves ovalish, ½ in. long. Flowers rose-pink, in round heads surrounded by colored bracts.* Western Aust.

**PIMENTA** (pi-men'ta). Aromatic, tropical American trees of the family Myrtaceae, two of the five known species of far more economic than ornamental value. They have opposite,* leathery, usually thick leaves. Flowers small, white (in ours), in compact clusters (cymes*), the petals and sepals separate. Fruit a fleshy, berry-like drupe.* The genus differs only in technical ovary characters from the closely related *Eugenia*. (*Pimenta* is the Latinized version of the Spanish pimento, which is now the English name for the fruit of *P. officinalis*, and should not be confused with pimiento.)

Both species can only be grown in zone* 9 as they will stand no frost. *P. officinalis* is somewhat grown in Fla. but only for ornament, as the production of allspice has not been found profitable.

**acris.** The true bayberry; also called bay rum tree and wild clove. A very aromatic tree, 30–45 ft. high, its fragrant oil yielding bay rum. Leaves elliptic or broadest toward the tip, 4–6 in. long. Flowers small, white. Fruit about ⅓ in. long, dark brown. W.I. and in northern S.A. Scarcely known in cult. in the U.S.

**officinalis.** Allspice; also called pimento. An aromatic tree 20–40 ft. high. Leaves oblongish, 5–7 in. long. Flowers small, white. Fruit about ¼ in. long, dark brown. W.I. and Central America. Its dried fruits are the pimento (not pimiento, for which *see* CAPSICUM) or allspice.

**PIMENTO** = *Pimenta officinalis*. Sometimes, incorrectly, pimento is mistaken for pimiento (which see).

**PIMIENTO.** The fruits of certain peppers of the genus *Capsicum* (which see).

**PIMPERNEL** = *Anagallis*.

**PIMPINELLA.** See ANISE.

*PIMPINELLIFOLIA*, *-us*, *-um* (pim-pi-nel-li-fō'li-a). With anise-like leaves.

**PINACEAE** (py-nay'see-ee). The pine, fir or spruce family might properly be called also the larch or hemlock family. It contains in its 33 genera and over 250 species the greatest group of ornamental evergreen shrubs and trees in the world, most of them suited to outdoor culture in all parts of the U.S. with adequate rainfall (*see* individual genera for details). The trees are commonly called conifers, because of their coniferous (cone-bearing) type of flower and fruit (*see* below). Many of the genera are resinous and aromatic, and their timber, or turpentine, or gums are of great economic importance.

A few genera are wholly tropical or sub-tropical so far as their cult. species are concerned. *Agathis*, *Araucaria*, *Callitris*, *Cunninghamia* (one species nearly hardy northward), *Fitzroya* and *Keteleeria* are grown outdoors only in southern, relatively frost-free regions, or in greenhouses. *Araucaria excelsa* (the Norfolk Island pine) is a very common plant in florists' windows.

By far the most important hort, genera, however, are those of wide outdoor cultivation for their beautiful evergreen foliage, and of these the pines, spruces, firs, umbrella pine, and hemlock are the most important. *See* these terms and *Thuja*, *Chamaecyparis* and *Juniperus* for the really important plants of chief hort. interest. The larch (*Larix*), *Pseudolarix*, and *Taxodium* are not evergreen, but included here for their cone-bearing habit. They shed their leaves in the fall, unlike the other, truly evergreen, cult. genera.

A group of perhaps secondary garden interest in America comprises the genera *Cedrus*, *Cupressus*, *Libocedrus* and *Thujopsis*. Many beautiful trees are found in them, such as the incense cedar and the funereal cypress of the Old World, but they are more widely cult. in Europe than here. The two remaining cult. genera are noteworthy. *Sequoia* contains the famous big tree of Calif. and the redwood, while forests of *Pseudotsuga* (the Douglas fir) are one of the great timber assets of Washington and Oregon. Both these genera, especially *Pseudotsuga*, are also widely cult. for ornament.

Leaves generally evergreen, more or less needle-like or awl-shaped in the pines, spruces, firs, hemlock, larch, *Pseudolarix*, *Cedrus* and a few other genera, but scale-like and pressed tightly into twig-like or fan-shaped clusters in *Juniperus* (mostly), *Thuja*, *Thujopsis*, *Chamaecyparis*, *Cryptomeria*, *Cupressus*, and *Libocedrus*.

The flowers and fruit of the Pinaceae differ from most other garden plants. There is no flower in the garden sense of that term. Instead there are naked male and female organs of reproduction borne above or below but always between small, often woody scales. It is the conical aggregation of these scales of the female flowers that results in the cone, best typified by the common pine cone. Sometimes the cone-scales are prickle-tipped, and in some pines the cone is enormous, while in *Sequoia* and the hemlock the cones are small. In some genera the cone is scarcely recognized as such, notably in the berry-like fruits of the juniper. (*See* also TAXACEAE.)

In most genera the male and female flowers are on different twigs and in some on different trees, but the female cone, which ultimately bears the seed, is the only permanent one. The male flowers produce much pollen (almost cloud-like masses in the pines), always wind-borne.

Between mature scales of the female cone the naked, often winged seed develops. Upon sprouting it sends up more than two seed leaves or cotyledons, and the plants are thus said to be polycotyledons — almost unique in the plant world, which otherwise has only one or two seed leaves.

**PINCH OFF.** See PRUNING. See also DISBUDDING.

**PIN-CLOVER** = *Erodium cicutarium*.

**PINCUSHION.** See SCABIOSA.

**PINCUSHION CACTUS.** See NEOMAMMILLARIA and CORYPHANTHA.

**PINCUSHION-FLOWER** = *Hakea laurina*.

**PINDO PALM** = *Butia capitata*.

**PINE.** For the true pine *see* the next main entry. Many other plants have been called pine, or the word is part of their name. For those found in THE GARDEN DICTIONARY see AGATHIS, ARAUCARIA, CALLITRIS, CASUARINA, DACRYDIUM, LYCOPODIUM, PANDANUS, and SCIADOPITYS.

**PINE.** Magnificent evergreen trees, constituting the genus **Pinus** (py'nus) of the family Pinaceae, of outstanding value both for timber and as widely cult. ornamentals. There are about 80 known species, nearly all from the north temperate zone, a few outliers in Mex., and the W.I. and in Malaya. In nearly all pines the trunk is (without injury) continuous, and has whorls* or tiers of branches, seldom with sporadic branches outside the whorl. Leaves (the permanent ones) needle-like, borne in sheathed clusters of 2–5, very rarely solitary, the sheaths parchment-like or pellucid and only enclosing the bases of the leaves. There are, in addition, small, scale-like leaves, which soon fall and are rarely noticed. Male flowers consisting of naked, catkin-like or cone-like masses of anthers* which produce much pollen (dust-like clouds of it in some species). Female flowers consisting of naked ovules between the bases of woody scales, the collection of the latter forming the familiar pine cone. Scales of the cone, in some species, tipped with a recurved prickle. Seeds, edible in some species, usually winged. The trees are all wind-pollinated. (*Pinus* is the old Latin name for the pine.)

There are probably over 50 species of pine in cult. in different parts of the U.S., many of them known only to specialists in these evergreens. The ones in the list below have been selected because of their availability, their ease of culture, or their beauty in the landscape. Many valuable timber trees have been omitted because their culture is largely a forestry project outside the scope of this book. Even among those admitted only some are of outstanding hort. importance and these especially desirable species are marked with a †. Only the characters of the leaves and cones are of significance in determining the identity of the different pines, and all other characters are omitted below.

Because of the arrangement of pine needles in bundles of usually 2, 3, or 5 in each sheath, the different species are

---

* Special articles on the subjects indicated by an asterisk (*) will be found at the words so marked.

Bigcone pine (*Pinus coulteri*), a handsome Californian evergreen

often spoken of as two-leaved, three-leaved, or five-leaved pines. Only the latter group, often generally called white pine, is subject to blister rust (*see* Diseases below).

For Culture of the pines *see* below.

† = Especially desirable hort. species.

**P. austriaca** = *Pinus nigra*.

**P. banksiana.** Jack pine; also called scrub or gray pine. A shrubby tree, rarely more than 60 ft., usually less. Leaves 2 in. long, stiff, twisted, 2 in each sheath. Cones oblongish, 1–2 in. long. Northeastern N.A. west to Minn. Hardy from zone* 2 southward. Sometimes known as *P. divaricata*, and useful for northern dune planting.

†**P. cembra.** Swiss stone pine. A slow-growing tree 40–75 ft. high. Leaves 4–5 in. long, 5 in each sheath. Cones more or less egg-shaped, about 3½ in. long, the seeds edible. Eurasia. Hardy from zone* 3 southward.

**P. cembroides.** Mexican stone pine, there called piñon. A low tree, not usually over 25 ft. high. Leaves about 2 in. long, 2 or 3 in each sheath. Cones nearly globular, about 2 in. long, the seeds edible. Ariz. to Mex. The *var.* **edulis**, the nut pine, is a hardier form found from Wyo. to New Mex. The species is hardy from zone* 6 southward, while *var.* **edulis** is hardy as far north as zone* 4 and perhaps beyond.

**P. coulteri.** Coulter pine; also called bigcone pine. A magnificent forest tree, up to 75 ft. high. Leaves stiffish, 8–12 in. long, bluish-green, 3 in each sheath. Cone cylindric, drooping, nearly 14 in. long and 4 in. thick. Calif. Hardy from zone* 4 southward.

†**P. densiflora.** Japanese red pine. A round-headed tree up to 90 ft. high. Leaves bluish-green, 3–5 in. long, 2 in each sheath. Cones oblongish, about 2 in. long. There are several hort. forms with white- or yellowish-tipped leaves, and the *var.* **umbraculifera**, the tanyosho, is a dwarf form with an umbrella-shaped head. Jap. Hardy from zone* 3 southward.

**P. divaricata** = *Pinus banksiana*.

**P. edulis** = *Pinus cembroides edulis*.

†**P. excelsa.** Himalayan pine. A wide-spreading, handsome tree up to 120 ft. Leaves drooping, 6–8 in. long, bluish-green or even grayish-green, 5 in each sheath. Cone cylindric, nearly 10 in. long. Himalayas. Hardy from zone* 4 southward.

**P. flexilis.** Limber pine; also called white pine (in the West). Not over 70 ft. high, usually half that. Leaves stiff, dark green, 2–3 in. long, 5 in each sheath. Cones egg-shaped, 4–6 in. long. Western N.A. Hardy from zone* 4 southward.

†**P. halepensis.** Aleppo pine. A round-headed, open tree up to 60 ft. high. Leaves light green, 3–4 in. long, 2, or rarely 3, in each sheath. Cones egg-shaped or conical, about 3 in. long. Mediterranean region. Hardy from zone* 6 southward, and considerably planted in Ariz. for ornament.

†**P. jeffreyi.** Jeffrey pine. An immense forest tree, up to 180 ft. high. Leaves 5–8 in. long, pale bluish-green, 3 in each sheath. Cones conical or egg-shaped, 9–12 in. long. Ore. to Calif. Hardy from zone* 4 southward.

**P. koraiensis.** Korean pine. A pyramidal tree 50–80 ft. high. Leaves dark green, 3–4 in. long, 5 in each sheath. Cones oblongish, 4–6 in. long. Korea and Jap. Hardy from zone* 3 (in sheltered places) and zone* 4 southward.

**P. laricio** = *Pinus nigra*.

**P. montana** = *Pinus mugo*.

†**P. mugo.** Swiss mountain pine. Shrubby or nearly prostrate, rarely a tree up to 25 ft. Leaves numerous, bright green, 1½–2 in. long, 2 in each sheath. Cones egg-shaped, about 2 in. long. Southern Eu., but high up in the Alps. Hardy from zone* 2 southward. An extremely valuable evergreen for low, massed plantings. There are many varieties, especially the commonest form which is a prostrate shrub.

†**P. nigra.** Austrian pine. A pyramidal tree up to 90 ft. high. Leaves dark green, 4–6½ in. long, 2 in each sheath. Cones egg-shaped or conical, about 3 in. long. Southern and central Eu. and in Asia Minor. Hardy from zone* 3 southward. Long known as *P. austriaca* and *P. laricio*, it is one of the most widely cult. pines in the country, and, with *P. thunbergi*, the best for city conditions. There are also many hort. varieties, one of them being *var.* **calabrica**, the Corsican pine, which forms a narrower crown than the typical species.

**P. parviflora.** Japanese white pine. In the cult. state, usually a grafted tree, low, and with wide-spreading branches. Leaves about 1 in. long, twisted, 5 in each sheath, usually crowded near the ends of the twigs, thus appearing in dense, small tufts. Cones egg-shaped, 2–3 in. long. Jap. Hardy from zone* 3 southward.

**P. pinea.** Italian stone pine. A tree up to 80 ft. high. Leaves bright green, stiff, 6–8 in. long, 2 in each sheath. Cones egg-shaped, nearly 5 in. long. Southern Eu. and northern Af., there cult. for its edible seeds. Hardy from zone* 6 southward.

**P. ponderosa.** Western yellow pine; also called bull, yellow, or ponderosa pine. A magnificent timber pine, often 150 ft. high, less important as a cult. tree. Leaves dark green, 8–11 in. long, 3 in each sheath. Cones oblongish, nearly 6 in. long. British Columbia to Tex. and Mex. Hardy from zone* 4 southward. The *var.* **scopulorum**, the Rocky Mountain yellow pine, is a lower tree, hardy as far north as zone* 3. Both are more planted in the western states than eastward.

**P. radiata.** Monterey pine. An irregular-headed, extraordinarily picturesque tree, confined to the coast of southern Calif. and not certainly hardy elsewhere. Leaves bright green, 4–6 in. long, 3 in each sheath.

†**P. resinosa.** Red or Norway pine, the latter name said to originate from Norway, Me., where the tree is common. A very valuable, quick-growing tree, useful for timber or in ornamental plantings. It makes a pyramidal tree up to 100 ft. high. Leaves glossy-green, 4–6 in. long, 2 in each sheath. Cones egg-shaped or conical, about 2 in. long. Newfoundland to Pa. and west to Minn. Hardy from zone* 1 southward.

**P. rigida.** Pitch pine. A scraggly, often picturesque tree, worthless for timber, firewood, and most hort. uses, but an excellent tree for exposed, wind-swept dunes along the Atlantic Coast. Leaves dark green, stiff, 4–5 in. long, 3 in each sheath. New Brunswick to Ga. and inland to Ky. Hardy from zone* 2 southward.

†**P. strobus.** White pine; also called northern white pine and (in Eng.) the Weymouth pine. One of the outstanding timber pines of N.A. and perhaps the most beautiful of all the eastern species, often reaching 150 ft. in maturity. Leaves soft, bluish-green, 4–5 in. long, 5 in each sheath. Cones cylindric, 4–6 in. long. Eastern N.A. Hardy from zone* 2 southward. There are many hort. forms of this most popular pine, some with variegated foliage, others dwarf, and one with a columnar, erect habit (fastigiata).

†**P. sylvestris.** Scotch pine. In age an irregular, round-topped tree up to 75 ft., the bark cinnamon-brown. Leaves stiff, twisted, bluish-green, 2–3 in. long, 2 in each sheath. Cones egg-shaped or conical, about 2 in. long. Eurasia. Hardy from zone* 2 southward. There are many hort. forms with variously colored foliage (white, golden, yellow, variegated) and one with pendulous branches. There is also a columnar form (*var.* **fastigiata**).

†**P. thunbergi.** Japanese black pine. Perhaps only a form of the Austrian pine, but with somewhat shorter, darker-colored leaves, that are rarely over 4 in. long, 2 in each sheath. Cones not over 3 in. long. Jap. Hardy from zone* 3 southward, and far quicker-growing than the Austrian pine which it bids fair to replace as one of the most satisfactory of cult. pines from the Old World.

## PINE CULTURE

Contrary to popular belief, the pine does not require a really rich soil and, for the most part, will do quite well in a rather light soil. Drainage is by far the most important consideration, for few pines will succeed in wet soil. Exposure and winter sun are great enemies of the pine. In the summer a drying wind will do far greater damage than dry soil, for this group of plants are so constituted that their roots reach far into the earth and exact from it whatever moisture there may be present. The leaves cannot withstand dry, scorching wind resulting in excessive transpiration which, in severe cases, browns the foliage. A warm winter's sun, such as may be received from a direct southern exposure, often causes a similar effect. Late in winter it is not uncommon for the sun's heat to become quite intense during the middle of the day, although the temperature at night may be at the lowest point of the year. This alternate changing of temperature causes an expansion and contraction of the cellular structure of the leaves which damages the tissues and causes the well-known browning of the foliage. The best cure for these conditions is to arrange the plant in a sheltered location. A northern slope is excellent for most conifers because it removes the danger of sun scorching and, to a large extent, the effect of our westerly drying winds.

The roots of the pine cannot stand exposure to the air and, for this reason, it is necessary to remove them with a ball of earth when transplanting. The pine is one of the few conifers which forms a more or less distinct taproot

---

* Special articles on the subjects indicated by an asterisk (*) will be found at the words so marked.

and, hence, it becomes a considerable task to move large specimens, although it is by no means an impossibility. Commercial growers make a practice of systematic root pruning to prevent undue taproot development and to encourage the growth of fibrous roots.

White pine (*Pinus strobus*), of eastern North America, one of our finest evergreens

Pruning the pine for shape and form is a painstaking task and must be carefully planned. If a plant becomes misshapen or unbalanced do not use a cutting instrument unless the malformation is very pronounced, in which case it is probably too late to practice corrective pruning. Select those branches which are too long or unsymmetrical and examine the tip. Except during the early summer months, there will be seen a cluster of buds which will develop during the coming season. If the branch is too long, pick out the center bud. This operation will stop terminal growth for one year and the remaining buds will develop lateral branches of considerable vigor. Dead or diseased parts are, of course, removed in the customary way.

Propagation is accomplished by seed and grafting. The species are raised from seed planted in the spring after all danger of frost has passed. The varieties and forms are veneer-grafted. Seedlings of a hardy species closely related to the variety are used as stock. The forms of the five-needled group are grafted on white pine seedlings, while the pines having less than five needles to a cluster employ seedlings of the Scotch or Austrian pine. — A. D. S.

INSECT PESTS. Larvae of the white pine weevil tunnel in terminal shoots in summer in the Northeast; dormant lime-sulphur spray in spring and pruning infested leaders are advised. Larvae of several moths feed or bore in shoots; planting insect-free stock and cutting out infested shoots will check them. Sawfly larvae and similar feeders will yield to arsenical sprays. The whitish, pine-needle scale yields to miscible-oil spray early in the spring; the woolly pine bark aphid, to a dilute oil spray with nicotine added in May. Bark beetles are very injurious in pine forests but not so important on ornamental pines if the trees are kept in a vigorous condition.

DISEASES. White pine blister rust is the best known and most destructive disease of young white pines. Cankers occur on the stem and branches, characterized at certain times by the production of copious masses of orange spores. Girdling and death result. To complete its life cycle the rust fungus requires another host plant, a currant or gooseberry, wild or cultivated. The complete elimination of all the currants and gooseberries for a distance of 900 feet will protect the pines, except that the cultivated European black currant should be removed for one mile.

Other rust diseases affect other kinds of pine. The southern pine species are attacked by a rust which causes large galls on the stem. The alternate host is some species of oak, a tree which is so common in that country that its elimination is in most cases out of the question. Leaf blister rust of red or Norway pine alternates to aster or goldenrod. It may be controlled by sulphur fungicides.

Many pines suffer from the leaf cast disease in which the needles are killed and fall from the tree. When the disease becomes serious, as in nurseries, sanitation and spraying with bordeaux mixture are suggested. Pines growing in shallow soil or where the roots tend to develop near the surface in heavy or wet soils are especially liable to winter injury. The symptoms are very general and the evidence often obscure. Death of a part of the root system results in a sickly looking tree with no further sign of disease. Heavy mulching with well-rotted manure will do much to protect trees from injury to the roots by cold. Older pines are affected with heart rot which enters broken tops or branches. When once established, this type of decay cannot be eradicated. Prevention of wounds exposing the heartwood is the most effective way to guard against heart rot.

**PINEA** (py-nee′a). Latin for pine cone.

**PINEAPPLE.** The common pineapple comprises a single species of the genus **Ananas** (a-nă′nas) of the family Bromeliaceae, perhaps originally from the Amazon Valley, but certainly confined to tropical America, known as **A. sativus**. Besides being a delicious fruit, it is botanically an extraordinarily interesting one. What we call the fruit (the ordinary pineapple) is actually a syncarp,* composed partly of the thickened, very fleshy stalk of the inflorescence (the juicy part of the mature fruit) and the sterile ovaries which form berries (the angular segments embedded in the fruit). No other cult. fruit has the stem passing through it, as in the pineapple — a stem prolonged beyond the top of the fruit and bearing the familiar tuft of scaly leaves. This crown of leaves, if detached, will grow into a new plant.

Leaves sword-shaped, spiny-margined, borne in a dense basal rosette, from the center of which rises the flowering, bracted, and leafy stalk, bearing at the top a tuft of leaves (these subsequently form the crown of the fruit). The flowering stalk is 2–4 ft. high. Flowers stalkless, violet or reddish, completely sterile in the common cult. varieties, but functional in the wild plant, where the coalescence of parts forming the fruit (*see above*) is not so complete, and the "fruit" may be more open, bear flowers, and subsequently true berries, which are abortive and buried

A young pineapple fruit; for development *see* text.

in the flesh of the cult. pineapple. The plant suckers freely from the base (*i.e.* forms ratoons*). It is never epiphytic.* (*Ananas* is the Latinized version of the South American vernacular for the plant.) A variegated-leaved form is sometimes grown for ornament.

While *Ananas sativus* is usually considered to be the only species, some authorities recognize 4 others. But the plant has been so long cult. (before the Spanish conquest) that these species may well be mere forms of *A. sativus*.

### PINEAPPLE CULTURE

The pineapple, originating in tropical America, has become common in most tropical countries and, either fresh or canned, is known and highly prized as a dessert fruit nearly everywhere. Since the time when Fla. ceased to be a factor in production, America's supply has been almost wholly from the West Indian and Hawaiian Islands. Southern Fla. at one time had some 5000 acres producing over 1,000,000 crates annually but, due to soil depletion, nematode attack and other factors, the industry has gradually declined to a production of only a few thousand crates. Within recent years the acreage has again slightly increased. The plants cannot be grown elsewhere in the U.S. on account of their temperature requirements.

Porous, thoroughly drained soils are required. In Fla., two types are planted, the deep "scrub pine" or "hickory

---

* Special articles on the subjects indicated by an asterisk (*) will be found at the words so marked.

scrub" sands and flatwoods pine-land. The former, though quite sandy and requiring rather heavy fertilization, has comprised the major part of the acreage. Fertilizers are used in annual amounts ranging from 1 to 2 tons per acre, in 3 or 4 applications; the formulae approximate a 4-6-6 ratio for younger plants and 5-5-10 for the fruiting crop (see FERTILIZERS). Plants are grown for the most part in open fields, but slat sheds, about 7 ft. high and giving half-shade, are used to some extent — mainly for the Smooth Cayenne variety on flatwoods soils. Plants are commonly set 22 × 22 in. in 6-row beds and to a lesser extent 10 × 12 in. in 2-row beds with wide spacing between. According to spacing, 8 to 12 thousand plants are set to the acre. Planting is usually in Aug. or early Sept.

Propagation is mostly by slips (stem suckers), although ratoons* (basal suckers) and the crowns (fruit tufts) are sometimes used. Old plantings are perpetuated by allowing the ratoons* from the matured plant to develop in place. Seeds are seldom planted except in the effort to develop new varieties. Slips are set in the soil 2-4 in. and suckers somewhat deeper. Fruit is matured in the second year after setting the slips, and annually thereafter in the old planting which may continue to produce satisfactorily for several years. The main season of fruit maturity is from May into July. At no stage of growth does the fruit contain more than a trace of starch, so that plant-ripened fruits, containing more sugar, are nearly always superior in flavor to those picked partially immature. Ripe fruit contains from 8 to 15 per cent sugar and is a source of vitamins A, B and C.

Varieties grown include mainly the Red Spanish, a few Smooth Cayenne, and Abachi and a few others in negligible quantity. — H. M.

INSECT PESTS. Mealybugs, attended and fostered by ants, do direct injury and spread disease. The use of insect-free planting stock and measures to reduce ant numbers aids in controlling them. A spray of kerosene-carbolic acid emulsion has been advised for mealybugs on pineapple; it is made and diluted as described for kerosene emulsion under INSECTICIDES, except that a pint of crude carbolic acid is included in the stock emulsion.

**PINEAPPLE CACTUS** = *Coryphantha robustispina*.

**PINEAPPLE FAMILY** = Bromeliaceae.

**PINEAPPLE-FLOWER** = *Eucomis punctata*.

**PINEAPPLE GUAVA** = *Feijoa sellowiana*.

**PINEAPPLE SQUASH.** A type of smooth-skinned summer squash. See SQUASH.

**PINE FAMILY.** Evergreen, cone-bearing trees and shrubs of first-rate timber and hort. importance. The most important groups are the pines, spruces, firs, cypress, cedar (see these terms), and many others. For the other cult. genera and a description of the family see PINACEAE. See also EVERGREENS and TAXACEAE.

**PINE SISKIN.** See Bird Nuisances at BIRDS.

**PIN-EYED.** A tubular flower in which the protruding stigmas* are visible in the throat of the corolla, but the stamens* are hidden within it. If the anthers* are visible but the stigmas* hidden within the tube, the flower is said to be thrum-eyed.

**PINGUICULA** (pin-gwick'you-la). Butterwort. Insectivorous herbs, comprising over 30 species of the family Lentibulariaceae, found in damp places throughout the northern hemisphere and in S.A. They often grow in sphagnum moss. Leaves basal, generally in rosettes, fleshy, the upper side covered with a greasy secretion to which small insects adhere. Flowers white, purple or yellow, solitary, on leafless stalks 6-12 in. high. Corolla 2-lipped,* and long-spurred* at the base. Fruit a capsule.* (Named from the Latin *pinguis* for fat, in allusion to the leaves.)

Pinguiculas are not of much garden importance, but are sometimes grown for their novelty. Propagated by seeds or division of plants. Seeds should be sown on the surface of shallow pans, filled with equal parts of chopped sphagnum moss, peat and sand and be kept moist in a temperature of 55°-65° under a bell-jar. March-April. They should be transplanted into pans filled with equal parts of fibrous peat and sphagnum moss with broken crocks at the bottom. These pans should be stood in saucers of water on inverted pots covered with bell-jar and stood in shade. Bell-jar should be removed ½ hour each day. Divisions of plants may be made in spring.

**grandiflora.** Grows to 8 in. high. Leaves basal, ovalish, 2-3 in. long, in rosettes, pale green in color. Flowers violet, 1 in. long, ¾ in. across, the lobes wavy. Weste n Eu.

**vulgaris.** Common bog violet or butterwort. Sheepweed. Grows to 6 in. high. Leaves basal, in rosettes, ovalish, to 2 in. long. Flowers violet-blue, ½ in. long and broad. Northern hemisphere. See INSECTIVOROUS PLANTS.

**PINGUIN** (pin'gwin). West Indian native name for *Bromelia pinguin*.

**PINK.** As a general term *pink* is best restricted to plants of the genus *Dianthus* (which see). But it is widely used for many other plants, especially in the related genera *Silene* and *Lychnis*, and for still others from which it should perhaps be excluded. But popular usage has applied pink to plants in the genera *Helonias, Limonium, Lobelia, Phlox,* and *Spigelia* (see these genera).

**PINK CALLA LILY** = *Zantedeschia rehmanni*. See CALLA LILY.

**PINK CORYDALIS** = *Corydalis sempervirens*.

**PINK FAMILY.** A very large family of plants, all herbs having opposite* leaves and swollen joints, and usually with handsome flowers. Besides the carnation and pink, it contains the baby's-breath, catchfly, chickweeds, and the bouncing bet. See CARYOPHYLLACEAE.

**PINK FRINGED ORCHIS** = *Habenaria psycodes*.

**PINK FRITILLARY** = *Fritillaria pluriflora*.

**PINK GARDEN.** In borders or gardens composed chiefly of pink, blush, rose-colored or carmine flowers the inclusion of numerous plants having gray foliage is helpful in bringing about a pleasant effect, and as foils a few white flowers, as well as those of pale yellow or lavender coloring, may be introduced. Stone walls make a good background for flowers in this color scale, or such features as are made of wood as trellis-work, fences, gates, arbors or seats may be painted silver-gray, pure white or prussian blue.

SHRUBS OR SMALL TREES TO BE USED AS BACKGROUND OR ACCENTS

SPRING-FLOWERING. *Azalea nudiflora* 5-8 ft.; *A. schlippenbachi* 5-8 ft., *A. vaseyi* 5-10 ft.; *Cornus florida rubra* to 20 ft.; *Crataegus oxyacantha plena* 15 ft.; *Kolkwitzia amabilis* 5-6 ft.; *Malus floribunda* 15-20 ft., *M. halliana* 15-20 ft., *M. ioensis* (Betchel's Crab) 10-15 ft.; *Prunus glandulosa rosea* (Flowering Almond) 4-5 ft., *Amygdalus persica* (double-flowering Peach) to 20 ft., *Prunus sieboldi, P. subhirtella* to 20 ft., *P. triloba* 6 ft.; *Rhododendron carolinianum* 3-6 ft.; many hybrid rhododendrons, blush to deep pink, 3-8 ft.; *Viburnum carlesi* 3-5 ft., *Deutzia rosea* 1-3 ft., *D. scabra* (pink form) 6-10 ft.

SUMMER-FLOWERING: *Hibiscus syriacus* to 12 ft.; *Kalmia latifolia* 4-8 ft.; *Robinia hispida* 6-7 ft.; *Rosa blanda* 3-6 ft., *R. nitida* 1-2 ft., *R. spinosissima* Stanwell Perpetual 5-6 ft.; *Weigela florida* 6 ft.; *Tamarix africana* to 10 ft.

AUTUMN-FLOWERING: *Lespedeza formosa* to 10 ft., *Spiraea bumalda* Anthony Waterer 2 ft.

TALL PLANTS FOR USE IN BACKGROUND

SUMMER-FLOWERING: *Althaea rosea* (Hollyhock) double and single, blush to carmine; *Boltonia latisquama;* dahlias; *Lavatera trimestris splendens* (annual).

AUTUMN-FLOWERING: *Aster novae-angliae* (pink form); *Cosmos,* pink form (annual); dahlias, blush to carmine.

PLANTS OF MEDIUM HEIGHT

SPRING-FLOWERING: *Aquilegia* pink vars.; *Centranthus ruber; Dicentra eximia, D. spectabilis; Pulmonaria saccharata.*

SUMMER-FLOWERING: *Antirrhinum,* blush to carmine

---
* Special articles on the subjects indicated by an asterisk (*) will be found at the words so marked.

(annual); *Callistephus*, annual asters, blush to carmine; *Astilbe davidi* vars. America, Gloria, Gruno, Meta Immink, Queen Alexandra, Rose Pearl, *A. japonica;* *Boltonia latisquama nana; Centaurea cyanus*, pink form; *Chrysanthemum coccineum* (pyrethrum) blush to carmine; *Clarkia elegans* Salmon King; *Dianthus barbatus; Gladiolus* pale to deep pink and rose; *Gypsophila elegans carminea; Iris* (pink forms); Larkspur (annual) blush to carmine; *Lilium speciosum rubrum; Lupinus polyphyllus moerheimi; Malva alcea, M. moschata; Monarda didyma; Papaver* (annual) single and double, blush to cherry; *Papaver orientale* vars. Mrs. Perry, Queen Alexandra, Victoria Louise; *Paeonia* (double and single pink vars.); *Pentstemon barbatus* Pink Beauty; *Phlox paniculata* vars. Annie Cook, Elizabeth Campbell, Enchantress, Johnson's Favorite, Jules Sandeau (dwarf), Mme. Paul Dutrie. Painted Lady, Peachblow, Rheinlander; *Potentilla nepalensis willmottiae; Sidalcea malvaeflora* Rosy Gem; Stocks (annual); *Veronica spicata rosea; Zinnia* (annual) blush to carmine.

LOW-GROWING PLANTS FOR FOREGROUND

SPRING-FLOWERING: *Aster alpinus ruber; Aubrietia*, rose vars.; *Statice armeria laucheana, S. plantaginea; Bellis perennis* (Pink); *Crucianella stylosa; Hyacinthus orientalis* (bulb); *Myosotis*, pink forms; *Papaver nudicaule* Coonora Pink; *Phlox amoena, P. subulata* (Pink); *Saponaria ocymoides; Scilla hispanica* Rosalind, *S. nonscripta* Blush Queen (bulbs); *Tulipa clusiana*, Tulips, many vars. early, Cottage, Darwin, etc. (bulbs).

SUMMER-FLOWERING: *Antirrhinum* (annual) dwarf forms, blush to carmine; *Dianthus caesius, D. deltoides*, hybrid pink vars., *D. chinensis* (pink form); *Iberis umbellata* (annual) blush to rose; *Petunia* (annual) vars. Exquisite, Pink Beauty, Pride of Portland, Rosy Morn; *Phlox drummondi* (annual) blush to rose; *Silene pendula rosea* (annual), *S. schafta; Tunica saxifraga; Verbena* Miss Willmott.

CLIMBERS

*Clematis montana rubens* (spring); *Convolvulus* (annual pink); Roses, many climbing and pillar varieties (summer); Sweet Peas (spring). — L. B. W.

**PINK LADY'S-SLIPPER** = *Cypripedium acaule.*

**PINK LOCUST** = *Robinia hispida*, and *R. pseudoacacia decaisneana.* See LOCUST.

**PINKROOT** = *Spigelia marilandica.*

**PINKSTER-FLOWER** = *Azalea nudiflora.*

**PINK VINE** = *Antigonon leptopus.*

**PINNA.** One of the ultimate divisions or leaflets of a compound* leaf which is pinnate (which see). *Pinna* is most often applied to fern fronds.

*PINNATA, -us, -um* (pin-nay'ta). Pinnate.*

**PINNATE.** With leaflets, or with the veins of a simple* leaf, arranged as are the segments of a bird's feather, *i.e.* opposite or alternate from each other along a common axis, not radiating from one point. Compound leaves which are pinnate are thus, and often in this book, said to have their leaflets arranged featherfashion. See PALMATE.

**PINNATIFID.** Cut or divided (but not compound*), as in the segments of a bird's feather. See PINNATE.

**PIN OAK** = *Quercus palustris.* See OAK.

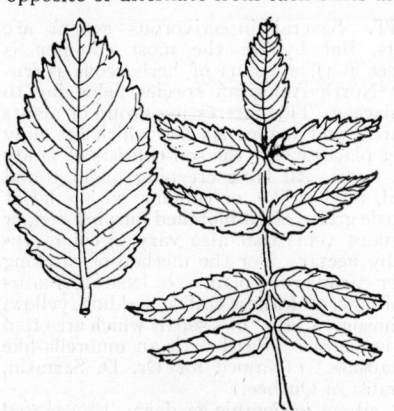

Leaves, showing pinnate veining (*left*) and pinnate arrangement of leaflets(*right*)

**PIÑON** = *Pinus cembroides.* See PINE.

**PINT.** See WEIGHTS AND MEASURES, 3.

**PINTO BEAN.** A variety or form of the common string bean (*Phaseolus vulgaris*) with mottled seeds. It is grown chiefly in the southwestern states, both for its seeds and for the herbage used as forage.

**PINUS.** See PINE.

**PINXTER-FLOWER** = Pinkster-flower. See AZALEA NUDIFLORA.

**PINYON** = Piñon. See *Pinus cembroides* at PINE.

**PIP.** The raised crown or individual rootstock* of a plant, as distinguished from a mass of rootstocks. Pips are sometimes valuable for propagation purposes, especially in the lily-of-the-valley (which see for an illustration of a pip), and are found occasionally in other plants. *Pip* is also colloquial for a small seed.

**PIPER** (py'per). A huge genus of mostly tropical herbs, shrubs, woody vines or even trees of the family Piperaceae, very largely aromatic and of little hort. but much economic interest. Of over 700 species only the three below are likely to be found in cult., the first two (cubeb and pepper) grown here mostly for interest, the last an ornamental greenhouse climber. All the cult. species are climbers (in youth at least) with alternate* leaves. Flowers extremely simple, minute, unisexual, crowded on catkin-like spikes, without petals or sepals. Fruit a small, fleshy, or dry berry. (*Piper* is the classical Latin name for the plant.)

These are only grown in the greenhouse, their outdoor culture in the U.S. being practically impossible for lack of heat and moisture, although they may be hardy in zone* 9. They need a tropical greenhouse, plenty of water, and should be grown in potting mixture* 4. In the early stages all need support, but *P. cubeba* becomes tree-like in age. An interesting non-hort. species, *P. betel*, is widely grown in Indo-Malaya for its leaves, used to wrap the betelnut. See ARECA CATECHU.

**cubeba.** Cubeb. A woody vine, ultimately tree-like. Leaves elliptic or ovalish, or narrower, pointed at the tip, unequally heart-shaped at the base. Fruit nearly ¼ in. in diameter, brownish, yielding the cubebs of commerce. East Indies.

**nigrum.** The true pepper (but *see* CAPSICUM). A woody vine, with aerial roots. Leaves broadly oval or nearly round, unequally heart-shaped at the base. Fruit about ¼ in. in diameter, yellowish-red when ripe. The dried whole fruit yields black pepper, but when the outer shell is taken off the resulting product is white pepper. East Indies.

**ornatum.** An ornamental greenhouse climber grown for its handsome foliage. Leaves ovalish or nearly round, 2½–5 in. long, the upper side at first pink-spotted, ultimately white-spotted, the stalk attached to or near the middle of the leaf blade. Celebes.

**PIPERACEAE** (py-per-ray'see-ee). The pepper family is only of value because it contains the plant yielding common black pepper (*see* PIPER), a very different plant from the kitchen garden pepper (*Capsicum*). The family also includes the genus *Peperomia* which contains one foliage plant of greenhouse culture that is widely grown for ornament. The family comprises 9 genera, and perhaps 1200 species, nearly all tropical. Most of them are herbs or shrubs with jointed stems.

Leaves alternate* (rarely opposite* in *Peperomia*), often thick or fleshy and usually minutely, but distinctly spotted with small dots, always without marginal teeth. Flowers minute, without petals, crowded on slender, usually pencil-thick spikes. Fruit berry-like, often aromatic, in *Piper* yielding both pepper and cubeb.

Technical flower characters: Sepals and petals none, the flowers unisexual* in *Piper*, hermaphrodite* in *Peperomia*, regular* in both. Stamens (in the cult. genera) 1–4. Ovary superior,* 1-celled and with a single ovule.

*PIPERASCENS* (py-per-ras'senz). Like peppermint.

*PIPERELLA* (py-per-rel'a). A little pepper-tree, or like one.

*PIPERITA, -us, -um* (py-per-ry'ta). Pepper-like, or like the pepper-tree (*Piper nigrum*).

**PIPEVINE** = *Aristolochia durior.*

* Special articles on the subjects indicated by an asterisk (*) will be found at the words so marked.

**PIPSISSEWA** = *Chimaphila umbellata.*

**PIQUERIA** (py-queer'i-a). Also known as *Stevia.* Tropical American herbaceous and shrubby perennials, comprising about 20 species, and belonging to the family Compositae, only one of garden interest. Leaves opposite,* toothed, broadly lance-shaped, with short stalks. Flowers fragrant, white, in small heads arranged in clusters growing from the axils* of the leaves. (Named for A. Piquer, a Spanish physician of the 18th century.)

Easily propagated from seeds or cuttings and they require little attention. Seeds should be sown in light, sandy soil in cool greenhouse in March, or cuttings made in Feb. or March inserted in sand. When rooted, pot in 2-in. pots in potting mixture* 2, transferring later to larger pots and potting mixture* 3. Pots should be transferred outdoors when danger of frost is over, plunged* in beds of coal ashes, where they can remain until early Oct. They should then be removed to greenhouse for Dec. flowering. Plants may be used in the garden in frost-free localities, but they are of a straggling habit and should be kept staked and tied.

**trinervia.** Called by nurserymen *Stevia serrata.* Perennial, growing to 4 ft. high. Leaves broadly lance-shaped, toothed, and with prominent veins on the under side. Flower heads arranged in clusters, white, fragrant. Useful for cutting in winter. Central America. The var. **variegata** has leaves with broad white edges and is sometimes used as a bedding plant for color effects.

*PISIFERA, -us, -um* (py-sif'fer-a). Literally, pea-bearing; as a specific name it usually indicates plants bearing merely small, pea-like fruits or seeds.

**PISTACHE, PISTACHIO.** See PISTACIA.

**PISTACIA** (pis-tash'i-a). Aromatic shrubs or trees of the family Anacardiaceae, most of the 8 species Eurasian, but one from the Canary Islands and another from Calif. and Mex. Only the two below are of hort. interest, one of them being grown for its seeds which yield pistache. They have alternate,* compound* leaves, the leaflets arranged feather-fashion, in ours without an odd one at the end. Male and female flowers on separate plants, small, inconspicuous, without petals, and mostly in lateral clusters (panicles*). Fruit a dry drupe, its seeds, in *P. vera,* the pistachio nut of commerce. (*Pistacia* is the Latin name of the pistachio.)

The second species can only be grown outdoors in regions suited to the olive, which fact confines its cult. mostly to Calif. The first is planted mostly for ornament or for grafting stock for *P. vera,* which is often grown upon it. The pistachio should be planted about 25 ft. apart each way, and for every 20 female trees it is necessary to interplant 4 male trees to be sure of pollination.* Propagated mostly by budding or grafting, especially for *P. vera.*

**chinensis.** Chinese pistachio. A tree up to 60 ft. high, not evergreen. Leaflets in 5–6 pairs, more or less lance-shaped. Fruit flattened, about ¼ in. long, dark scarlet at first, ultimately purplish. China. Grown for ornament, and as grafting stock for the next, in Calif. and Fla., its foliage handsomely colored in the autumn. Hardy from zone* 6 southward.

**vera.** Pistachio. Not over 30 ft. high. Leaflets in 1–5 pairs, generally oval, but tapering at the base. Fruit oblong or egg-shaped, red and wrinkled, about 1 in. long, the kernel of its stone rich, oily, green or yellowish-green and the source of pistache. Mediterranean region and the Orient. Hardy only in zones* 8 and 9, but unsuited to this region in Fla. because of excess moisture. It is somewhat grown commercially in Calif.

**PISTIA** (piss'ti-a). A single, free-floating, aquatic plant of the family Araceae, found in nearly all tropical countries and also in Fla. and Tex., and widely used in aquaria or in pools. It will stand no frost, and should have a water temperature 70°–75°. The only species is **P. stratiotes,** the water lettuce, which has a rosette of roundish or ovalish, thick, spongy leaves, 2½–5½ in. long, from the floating mass of which hang (beneath the surface) many feathery, hair-like roots. Flowers extremely minute, in the axils* of the leaves (*see* ARACEAE). Fruit fleshy, minute. (*Pistia* is said to be from the Greek for liquid, in allusion to the aquatic habit.)

**PISTIL.** The complete female organ of reproduction in flowers. The typical pistil consists of a usually swollen base (the ovary) containing the ovules (which will become seeds after fertilization), a shank-like stalk (the style), and a club-shaped or variously divided tip (the stigma). Upon the latter pollen is deposited and begins the process ending in fertilization (which see).

A pistil may have only one chamber or several, and in the latter case is called a compound pistil. Whether of one or more chambers or cells, a pistil is technically considered to be a much-modified leaf, rolled to form the chamber. Such a leaf is known as a carpellary leaf and a 1-celled pistil is then also properly called a carpel. When the ovary is several-celled (*i.e.* a compound pistil), it is conceived as being formed of several carpellary leaves, and thus to be (theoretically) composed of several carpels. That such a concept of a pistil is more than a theory is proved by those fruits which split into component and often separable carpels, as in *Magnolia,* the Trochodendraceae, *Brachychiton, Zanthoxylum,* and in many plants of the mallow family.

**PISTILLATE.** Bearing only pistils.* See FEMALE.

**PISUM.** See PEA.

**PIT.** A very useful adjunct in any garden of more than simple requirements, because pits make the best winter storage for tubbed hortensia hydrangeas, bay trees, oleanders, orange trees, and a lot of other tubbed plants that need freedom from severe frosts, but no winter heat. *See* illustration at HYDRANGEA.

The best type of pit should be nearly all below ground, at least 6–8 ft. deep (more if taller plants are to be wintered) and preferably with brick or concrete walls and floor. The walls may extend above the general ground level a few inches, but more than this invites too much exposure to cold.

The roof should have just enough pitch to allow rain to drain off. If the pit is of any size, the roof should be of removable shutters, the size of a hotbed sash, and of solid wood if there must be no light in the pit during winter. Otherwise hotbed sash can be used. The shutters should overhang the pit-walls enough to keep rain from draining into the pit, which should be dry all winter.

Some elaborate pits are made with steps down into them. But this is not necessary and may let in too much cold. The theory of a pit is that the tubs are put far below the level of frost penetration, and with proper covering (extra mats may be needed in zero weather), they make snug quarters for plants needing this sort of winter care.

**PITAHAYA.** The name in Spanish America for many cacti with edible fruit. Those in THE GARDEN DICTIONARY will be found at *Machaerocereus gummosus, Lemaireocereus thurberi, Hylocereus undatus,* and *Echinocereus polyacanthus.*

**PITANGA** = *Eugenia uniflora.*

**PITCHER-PLANT.** Insectivorous plants with their leaves modified into variously shaped, pitcher-like organs. For the common pitcher-plant of eastern N.A. *see* the next entry. For other pitcher-plants *see* NEPENTHES and DARLINGTONIA.

**PITCHER-PLANT.** Several insectivorous genera are called pitcher-plants, but by far the most common is **Sarracenia** (sar-ra-see'ni-a), a genus of herbaceous perennials, comprising 7 North American species belonging to the family Sarraceniaceae. This interesting group of plants consists of both hardy and tender species which are only found in bogs or wet places where the soil consists of sandy peat, or sphagnum moss. All have creeping underground stems. Leaves basal, pitcher-like, or tubular, with a lid at the top. Some are pale green, often blotched purplish-red, or white, with conspicuous veins that also vary in color. Insects are attracted by nectar. For the method of catching insects and for other carnivorous plants *see* INSECTIVOROUS PLANTS. Flowers solitary, on leafless stalks, nodding, yellow, purplish-green or crimson. Calyx* of 5 sepals which are often colored. Stamens* numerous. Pistil with an umbrella-like stigma.* Fruit a capsule.* (Named for Dr. D. Sarrasin, physician and naturalist of Quebec.)

Not much in cult. except in botanic gardens. Propagated by seeds or division of rootstocks in March or April. They

---

* Special articles on the subjects indicated by an asterisk (*) will be found at the words so marked.

must be grown in acid peat or sphagnum.* See also DARLINGTONIA and NEPENTHES.

**drummondi.** Tender perennial. Leaves to 4 ft. high, upright, green, deeply purplish-veined. Lid ovalish, nearly erect, with a wavy margin. Flowers purplish, 2-4 in. across. One of the most showy of the species. Bogs, Ga., Fla., and Ala.
**flava.** Trumpets. Yellow pitcher-plant. Trumpet-leaf. Tender perennial. Leaves to 3 ft., yellow-green with crimson throat, sometimes entirely crimson, with prominent veins. Lid bent over the opening. Flowers yellow, 2-4 in. across. Va. to Fla.
**purpurea.** Common pitcher-plant. Sidesaddle-flower. Huntsman's-cup. Indian pitcher. Hardy perennial. Leaves to 1 ft. long, green or dark purple. Lid almost upright. Flowers purplish, to 2 in. across. Labrador to Fla. and the Rocky Mountains. The floral emblem of Newfoundland.

**PITCHER-PLANT FAMILY** = Sarraceniaceae.

**PITCHER SAGE** = *Sphacele calycina*.

**PITCH PINE** = *Pinus rigida*. See PINE.

**PITHECELLOBIUM** = *Pithecolobium*.

**PITHECOCTENIUM** (pith-e-cock-tee′ni-um). Tender, evergreen, woody vines, comprising about 20 species of the trumpet-creeper family (Bignoniaceae), natives of Central and South America. Leaves compound,* the leaflets 2-4, the main leafstalk prolonged into a tendril by means of which the plant climbs. Flowers white, sometimes yellowish, bell-shaped, in terminal clusters or racemes. Fruit a prickly capsule.* (*Pithecoclenium* is from the Greek for monkey's comb, in allusion to the spiny fruit.)

It is only cult. in warm and tropical regions. Propagated by seeds and cuttings.

**cynanchoides.** Stems slightly ribbed when young. Leaves opposite,* the leaflets ovalish, 1-2 in. long. Flowers white, 1-2 in. long, funnel-shaped, in loose racemes.* Corolla slightly hairy outside. Fruit a large capsule, to 2½ in. long, covered with yellowish spines. Seeds many, arranged in rows. Argentina. Uruguay.

**PITHECOLOBIUM** (pi-thee-ko-lō′bi-um). A genus of over a hundred tropical trees and shrubs of the pea family, a few cult. for ornament in zone* 9 or the most protected sites in zone* 8. They have alternate,* twice-compound* leaves, and white flowers in globe-shaped, acacia-like heads, or in dense spikes in some non-hort. species. Corolla not pea-like, its stamens much-protruded. Fruit a flattish pod (legume*), variously twisted or coiled. (*Pithecolobium* is from the Greek for monkey and ear-ring, in allusion to the coiled pods.) Sometimes spelled *Pithecellobium*.

**dulce.** Guamachil (sometimes spelled huamuchil); called also Manila tamarind and Madras thorn. A tree up to 50 ft. high, the leafstalks often with a pair of thorns to replace the stipules.* Leaflets very numerous, blunt, oblongish, about 1 in. long, very one-sided. Flower clusters finely hairy, the white, globe-shaped flower clusters about ¾ in. in diameter. Pods 5-6 in. long, spirally twisted, its black seeds shining. Mex., but early taken to the eastern tropics and long thought to be native in the Philippines. It needs staking in its early stages as growth is rapid and sometimes unsymmetrical without support. Widely used as an avenue tree in Fla.
**saman** = *Samanea saman*.
**unguis-cati.** Cat's-claw; also called Florida cat's-claw and black bead. A spiny shrub or small tree, not over 15 ft. high. It resembles the first species, but the flower clusters are smooth, the heads greenish-yellow and the red, spirally twisted pods 2-4 in. long. Fla., the W.I., and northern S.A.

**PITTOSPORACEAE** (pit-toss-spor-ray′see-ee). The tobira family, largely Australian, includes four genera of secondary garden interest. *Hymenosporum*, *Pittosporum* and *Bursaria* include shrubs and trees, while *Sollya* is a beautiful, flowering, woody, almost climbing shrub often grown as a vine. There are 9 genera and over 150 species in the family. All the cult. genera can be grown outdoors only in warm regions. *Pittosporum* and *Sollya* are not uncommon greenhouse plants, especially the former, which is the only cult. genus that is found, also, outside Australia.

Leaves alternate,* often leathery or thick. Flowers rather showy, especially in *Pittosporum* and *Sollya*, nearly always regular,* and in various sorts of clusters. Fruit (in the cult. genera) a dry pod (capsule*), but berry-like in some (non-hort.) genera.

Technical flower characters: Sepals* 5. Petals 5, clawed, the claws* sometimes united at the base. Stamens* 5. Ovary superior.* Style 1.

**PITTOSPORUM** (pit-toss′por-rum). Australian laurel. Chiefly Australasian evergreen shrubs and trees of the family Pittosporaceae, comprising over 100 species, of which several are grown for ornament in zones* 8 and 9, especially in southern Calif., and one in the greenhouse. They have alternate, or on young twigs apparently whorled* leaves, wavy-margined and faintly toothed or without teeth. Flowers in clusters or solitary, usually terminal, but sometimes in the leaf-axils.* Sepals* 5, usually distinct. Petals 5, mostly clawed and more or less joined at the base, free above. Fruit a capsule,* its seeds sticky. (*Pittosporum* is from the Greek for resinous and seed, in allusion to the sticky seeds.)

The Australian laurels and the related genus *Hymenosporum* cannot be grown outdoors with safety north of zone* 8, but they are very popular shrubs and trees in Calif., Fla., and along the Gulf Coast. They are of easy culture in a variety of soils and are propagated by seeds, by cuttings of half-ripened wood or by grafting on *P. undulatum*, all preferably in a cool greenhouse. *P. tobira* and a variegated-leaved form of it are often grown as pot plants in the cool greenhouse. It needs potting mixture* 4 and is a handsome plant.

**crassifolium.** Karo. A shrub or small tree, not over 25 ft. high. Leaves 2-3 in. long, ovalish or broader toward the tip, shining green above, white-felty beneath. Flower clusters terminal, the corolla red, about ½ in. wide. Fruit about 1¼ in. long, densely hairy. N. Zeal.
**eugenioides.** Tarata. A tree up to 40 ft. high. Leaves 2-4 in. long, wavy-margined, elliptic but pointed. Flower clusters (compound umbels*) terminal, the corolla about ¼ in. long, yellowish and fragrant. N. Zeal. There is also a variegated-leaved variety.
**phillyraeoides.** Butter-bush. A small tree (up to 20 ft.), the branches drooping. Leaves 3-4 in. long, lance-shaped or narrower. Flowers yellow, about ⅓ in. long, solitary or in small clusters in the leaf-axils.* Fruit about ½ in. long, yellow. Aust.
**rhombifolium.** Diamond-leaf laurel. A tree 60-80 ft., usually less in cult. Leaves 3-4 in. long, ovalish or diamond-shaped, rather coarsely toothed above the middle. Flowers in terminal clusters (corymbs*), the corolla white, about ¼ in. long. Fruit orange-yellow, about ¼ in. long. Aust.
**tenuifolium.** Tawhiwhi or black mapau. A tree 20-30 ft. high. Leaves 1½-2½ in. long, oblongish, wavy-margined. Flowers solitary or in small clusters in the leaf-axils,* the corolla dark purple, about ½ in. long. N. Zeal. There is also a variegated-leaved form.
**tobira.** Tobira. A shrub 6-10 ft. high, useful for hedges in Calif. and Fla., and often grown as a pot plant in greenhouses. Leaves thick and leathery, ovalish but blunt toward the tip, 3-4 in. long. Flower clusters terminal, the corolla fragrant, greenish-white, about ½ in. long. Fruit densely hairy, about ½ in. long. China and Jap. The var. *variegatum* has white marked leaves. Both are hardier than any other *Pittosporum*.
**undulatum.** Victorian box; also called cheesewood. A tree 30-40 ft. high. Leaves oblongish or narrower, 4-6 in. long, wavy-margined, tapering at the tip, shining green. Flower clusters terminal, the corolla fragrant, white, about ½ in. long. Fruit about ½ in. long. Aust.
**viridiflorum.** A shrub 15-20 ft. high. Leaves leathery, shining green, more or less ovalish, 2-3 in. long, the margins rolled. Flower clusters dense, terminal. Corolla yellowish-green, about ¼ in. long. Fruit about ¼ in. long. South Africa.

**PITYROGRAMMA** (pi-ti-ro-gram′a). Gold Fern. Silver Fern. Known to gardeners as *Gymnogramma*. American, mostly tropical, evergreen ferns comprising about 90 species belonging to the family Polypodiaceae. Some have creeping underground stems. Fronds dark green, twice-compound,* the ultimate segments broad at the base, narrowing at the tip, cut or dissected. Spore* cases on under side of fronds, on the veins. Leafstalk and under side of fronds covered with white or yellow powdery substance. (*Pityrogramma* is from the Greek for bran-like, in allusion to the powder on the fronds.)

Easily grown in the greenhouse, in temperatures not below 55°. They are commonly used as house plants. Propagated by spores sown on the surface of fine, sandy peat under a bell-jar in temperature 75°-85° at any time. Division of the plants may be made in Feb. They should be grown in potting mixture* 4.

**sulphurea.** Jamaica gold fern. Leafstalks shorter than the leaves. Leaves to 1 ft. long, 5 in. wide. Under side covered with pale yellow, powder-like substance. Leaflets much cut. West Indies.
**triangularis.** California gold fern. Leafstalks to 1 ft. Leaves 7 in. long, to 6 in. wide. Under side covered with deep yellow, powder-like substance, occasionally white. Calif. to British Columbia.

**PLAGIANTHUS** (pla-ji-an′thus). Australasian trees or shrubs, comprising about 12 species of the family Malvaceae. Hardy only in sheltered places from zone* 7 southward. The cult. species are trees to 60 ft. high, or shrubs to 12 ft. Leaves simple, alternate.* Flowers white, with 5 petals; some having stamens* and pistil,* others stamens only or

---

* Special articles on the subjects indicated by an asterisk (*) will be found at the words so marked.

pistil only. (*Plagianthus* is from the Greek for oblique flower.)
Not much in cult.; two grown in southern Calif.

**betulinus.** Ribbonwood. Growing to 60 ft. with trunk to 3 ft. across. Leaves 1–3 in. long, ovalish, coarsely toothed. Flowers small, yellowish-white, in loose axillary clusters. N. Zeal.

**pulchellus.** Shrub 9–12 ft. Leaves lance-shaped, 1–3 in. long, coarsely toothed. Flowers white, small, in long, loose clusters, growing from the axils* of the leaves. Aust.

**PLANA,** *-us, -um* (play'na). Flat.

**PLANE.** See PLATANUS.

**PLANERA** (play'ner-ra). A single species of elm-like tree belonging to the family Ulmaceae, commonly called water elm or planer tree and known to science as **P. aquatica.** It grows from southern Ill. to Fla. and Tex. and is not hardy north of zone* 4. Leaves alternate,* ovalish, 2–2½ in. long, somewhat oblique. Flowers small, unisexual* or polygamous,* without petals, the male flowers with 4–5 stamens, the perfect* flowers 1–3, in the axils* of the young leaves. Fruit a small drupe, with fleshy, irregularly crested ribs. The tree is little known in cult. and sometimes is mistaken for a small-leaved species of elm. (Named for J. J. Planer, German professor of medicine.)

**PLANER TREE** = *Planera aquatica*.

**PLANE TREE.** See PLATANUS.

**PLANE TREE FAMILY** = Platanaceae. See PLATANUS.

**PLANIFOLIA,** *-us, -um* (play-ni-fō'li-a). Flat-leaved.

**PLANK DRAG.** See Section 3, TOOLS AND IMPLEMENTS.

**PLANNING.** See LANDSCAPE ARCHITECTURE.

**PLANTAGO.** See Plantain in the list at WEEDS.

**PLANTAGINEA,** *-us, -um* (plan-ta-gin'i-a). Plantain-like.

**PLANTAGO-AQUATICA** (plan-tay-go-a-kwat'i-ka). A specific name derived from an old genus *Plantago-aquatica*, not used here for the water plantain (*Alisma plantago-aquatica*).

**PLANTAIN.** The true plantain is *Musa paradisiaca*, a world-wide tropical vegetable. See MUSA. But the word plantain is also applied to weeds of the genus *Plantago*. See the list at WEEDS. For other plants to which the name plantain is sometimes applied see ALISMA, EPIPACTIS, ERIGERON, and HELICONIA.

**PLANTAIN-LILY.** Perennial, widely cult. garden herbs of the genus **Hosta** (hos'ta) of the lily family, often known under the names of *Funkia* and *Niobe*. Of the 10 known species, all from China and Jap., most are in common cult., especially those below. They are tufted plants, grown both for their handsome, conspicuously ribbed, basal leaves, and their white, lilac, or blue flowers in terminal clusters (spikes or racemes*) terminating a usually bracted stalk that arises from the leaves. Flowers tubular, usually expanded at the summit, the six lobes not distinguishable as petals and sepals, all petal-like. Stamens 6. Fruit an elongated capsule,* rarely produced in some species. (Named for N. T. Host, Austrian botanist.)

Plantain-lilies are of the easiest culture and are common in old-fashioned gardens, especially under partial shade and in moist sites. They will, however, grow perfectly in the open border and are readily increased by spring or fall division of the clumps. They are sometimes known as daylily, but the latter name is better restricted to the related genus *Hemerocallis* (see DAYLILY).

**H. caerulea.** Leaves broadly oval, narrowed to a winged stalk, the blade 4–9 in. long, the foliage standing 18–24 in. high. Flowering cluster slightly taller, pale or deep blue, the corolla 1½–2 in. long. Summer.

**H. fortunei.** Leaves 4–5 in. long, oval-heart-shaped, pale bluish-green. Flowering cluster much exceeding the foliage, the corolla about 1½ in. long, pale purple or white. June–July.

**H. japonica.** Leaves oval-lance-shaped or narrower, tapering both ends, the blade 4–6 in. long, the stalk much longer. Flowering stalk 18–24 in. high, the corolla 1½–2 in. long, pale lavender or lilac. Summer. The *var.* **albo-marginata** has white-margined leaves; and the *var.* **tardiflora** blooms in autumn. Sometimes known as *H. lancifolia*.

**H. lancifolia** = *Hosta japonica*.

A plantain-lily

**H. plantaginea.** Leaves very strongly ribbed, oval-heart-shaped, 6–10 in. long, 4–6 in. wide, long-stalked. Flowering stalk 18–24 in. high, the corolla white, fragrant, 4–5 in. long. Aug.–Oct. One of the most common in old gardens, and sometimes known as *H. subcordata*.

**H. sieboldiana.** Leaves oval-heart-shaped, 6–10 in. long, the leafstalk so long as to overtop the flowering stalk. Flowers thus half-hidden by the foliage, numerous, pale lilac, 2–2½ in. long. June–July.

**H. subcordata** = *Hosta plantaginea*.

**H. undulata.** The tallest of all the cult. species, the flowering stalk often 3 ft. high. Leaves broadly ovalish, sometimes heart-shaped at the base, 6–8 in. long, the stalk a little longer. Corolla about 2 in. long, funnel-shaped, pale lavender, the flowers numerous. June–July, but usually following *H. sieboldiana* and *H. fortunei*.

**PLANT BREEDING.** This is an old practice, but a real understanding of its principles is very new. Three primary proceedings are involved — selection,* inbreeding,* and hybridization or crossing.* Selection is the simplest and the oldest. Far back beyond historic records man has noted wild plants of a species better than the average, just as today small boys often know about special persimmon, papaw or wild plum trees. Primitive man, having noted these more desirable representatives, next transferred them to his home surroundings, either by transplantation, conscious or accidental planting of their seeds, or by offshoots. Pride and appreciation in his discovery eventually led to further selection, through choice of superior seedlings.

This illustrates both selection and a kind of crude unconscious inbreeding, through relative isolation. Selection* and inbreeding* are still just as simple in everyday practice, except for the greater understanding many of us have as to what we are doing, and consequent refinement in methods. Now we plant bushels of seed, and hunt for these variations. Now we protect these highly desirable variants with various devices that prevent them from making mesalliances, and we realize that it is worth our while to take special care of them and their offspring — even at times the weakest — rather than let them struggle and compete in unfavorable environments with their less desirable wild types.

The third plant-breeding practice is hybridization or crossing.* Natural crossing has undoubtedly given man — even primitive man — many of his most desirable types of cultivated plants, and until very recently he has been practically unconscious of this fact. Corn and bread wheat are both now suspected to have arisen in this fashion. Probably the same thing is true of potatoes, bananas, tomatoes, and tobacco. Natural hybrids are by no means uncommon even in the wild. The collection of many types, varieties, and species,

---

* Special articles on the subjects indicated by an asterisk (*) will be found at the words so marked.

in nurseries, test gardens, arboretums, botanic gardens, and estate and palace surroundings has undoubtedly greatly facilitated natural hybrid production, and this went on before historic records began, even as it does today among relatively primitive peoples.

Many of our best varieties of plums, apples, berries, flowers and other cultivated plants have originated as chance seedlings, but with an observer standing by, so to speak, who knew "beans when the bag was open," and saved them for posterity. These chance seedlings very often represented some type of hybrid, and from their progeny, through selection, inbreeding and further crossing have come still more desirable types, of which Golden Bantam sweet corn and the Early Rose potato are examples.

Conscious plant hybridization, in which the worker had some idea of what he was doing, is a little over 200 years old, while scientific hybridization is very much younger. In the former one crosses varieties having desirable characters that are to be combined, and grows the progeny of the cross, hoping to find among it the type with, or approaching, the desired combination. In many cases, he does; in many others, he does not, in which case he tries again, if he is persistent. No particular attention is paid to the ancestry of the parents, and no great precautions are taken as to labeling or prevention of contamination from undesirable pollen. The actual parentage is often more or less a guess, especially as regards the pollen parent. Again, seeds of known hybrids of such plants as irises and roses and apples are planted, the progeny grown and selection practiced.

Little knowledge of the fundamental principles of variation* and inheritance are necessary in this method of plant breeding, but one needs to be thoroughly familiar with the nature and kinds of material, and as persistent and enthusiastic as an artist. This method often wastes time and produces discouragement because of failure in attempting the impossible. The varieties produced by this method, which last, are largely chance combinations, "winning numbers in a living lottery." For every individual saved, thousands are destroyed.

The scientific method often provides short-cuts by decreasing the time element, lessening the amount of work involved, sustaining enthusiasm by pointing out the road and the limitations of what can and cannot be done. Through its use in some cases, and this will be increasingly true, one can definitely calculate the difficulties and possibilities of obtaining the desired type. In other words one can come near to making a new desired type to order, by shuffling the available characters through crossing, selection, re-crossing, and again selecting. This has been done in obtaining disease-resistant beans and wheat, and more desirable types of tobacco and sweet corn. — O. E. W. *See also* MUTATION.

**PLANT DISEASES.** The causes of diseases in plants are analogous to those which produce maladies in the human or animal bodies. Fortunately, however, none of the organisms which affect plants are capable of producing distinct diseases in man. There is a further distinction in that molds, or more properly fungi, are the biggest group of parasites on plants, while this group is of less importance so far as animal diseases are concerned. The following list of causal agents is given somewhat in the order of their importance: fungi, viruses, bacteria, slime-molds, and lower forms of animal life, particularly nematodes. In addition certain nutritional or environmental factors may produce serious maladjustments in the plant organs.

ROOT KNOT is caused by nematodes or eelworms, which, as the name implies, are eel-shaped and for the most part microscopic in size. They are world-wide in their distribution. They enter the plant either above or below the ground and cause swellings or dead areas in the invaded tissue. Severely infected plants may be killed, particularly when young, while in cases of moderate infection the plants are sickly and stunted with a tendency to wilt in dry weather. When the host* is absent the organism may survive by assuming a heavy covering, or encysting, until favorable conditions return for feeding and reproduction.

In general, root knot is more prevalent on light, sandy soils. Low temperatures are not favorable to the parasite, and for this reason root knot, as a rule, is not serious out of doors in temperate regions. In the northern United States, the disease is more common on plants grown under glass.

Infected plants should be removed and burned. In cases where the nematodes are known to be present in the soil, sterilization with steam is essential. Under field conditions, the nematode population can often be reduced by crop rotations in which non-susceptible plants are used, such as barley, millet, corn, nearly all types of grasses, rye, velvet beans, wheat, winter oats, and certain resistant varieties of cowpeas.

SLIME-MOLDS. The lowest group of parasites* in plants is the slime-molds, which are nothing more than minute, naked masses of protoplasm, resembling somewhat the white of an egg. At maturity this mass breaks up into an unbelievably large number of pellets, far too small to be seen by the unaided eye. These globular, wall-enclosed bodies are known as spores,* which take the place of seeds found in higher plants. The spores may lie free in the soil for years waiting for the presence of a host* to stimulate them into germinating. The small mass of living matter liberated from the spore gains an entrance into the plant tissue and there reproduces itself. Among the diseases caused by slime-molds are clubroot of crucifers* and powdery scab of potatoes.

BACTERIA. It has not been many years since investigators argued that bacteria could not live in the acid sap of plants and, therefore, were incapable of producing plant diseases. But every year new bacterial diseases are now being added to the very long list already in existence.

Bacteria are of many forms and types, but so far only rod-shaped, non-spore-forming types have been found associated with diseases in plants. This is of much practical importance to growers, for spores* of bacteria are very resistant to heat or other killing agencies, while the bacteria without spores are relatively easy to destroy. The life history of a bacterium is quite simple. It reproduces by growing smaller in the middle until finally the cell divides into two. This division continues at an extremely rapid rate when environmental conditions are favorable. It may live in a dormant stage on or in plant seeds, plant refuse, hibernating insects, or soil during the winter, and then be splashed or carried to susceptible crops when the weather is optimum for its entrance into the plant parts. It may cause spots, cankers, rots, swellings, or other symptoms. Among some of the common diseases caused by bacteria are fire-blight of fruit trees, crown-gall of many plants, and bacterial blight of beans.

VIRUS DISEASES. The true nature of a virus is not yet known. Some investigators believe that the active agent is some form of plant or animal life too small to be seen by the highest known power of the microscope, while others are equally insistent that it must be some chemical substance which is soluble in the cell sap. Virus diseases have been recognized as distinct maladies for relatively only a few years and this no doubt accounts for the lack of knowledge regarding them.

Nearly all plants appear to be susceptible to some virus. The principal symptoms of the affected host are mottling, variegation, rolling of leaves, yellowing, foliage corrugation, distortion, and dwarfing. Because of the symptoms the names generally applied to such diseases are mosaic, leaf-roll, yellows, and streak. Sometimes characteristic symptoms are caused by the combining of two or more viruses in the same host.

Each virus usually is specific for a given host* or a narrow group of hosts, although in some cases, as in aster yellows and curly top of beet, the viruses affect an extremely large number of plants. Since the virus cannot be cultured, it must be classified by the symptoms it causes on the plant, the length of time it will remain alive in expressed sap, the amount of heat required to make it inactive, the plants it will infect, and the insects which act as carriers. In most cases it gains entrance into the plant when sucking insects, which transmit it, are feeding. Aphids and leaf-hoppers are common vectors,* as the insect carriers are named. In

---

* Special articles on the subjects indicated by an asterisk (*) will be found at the words so marked.

certain cases, as in bean mosaic, it is carried in the seed, or in the tubers, as in the potato.

FUNGI are found everywhere and frequently are of vital importance to man's well-being. A large number of the species, however, are important enemies to cultivated crops. There probably is no plant in the universe that is not susceptible to some one of this immense group of lower plants. Among the fungi are listed such well-known types as mildews, rusts, smuts, toadstools, and molds. The life history of these organisms sometimes is rather complicated and must be studied carefully by the grower if intelligent control measures are to be applied. The body of the fungus usually consists of thread-like wefts which resemble cobwebs.

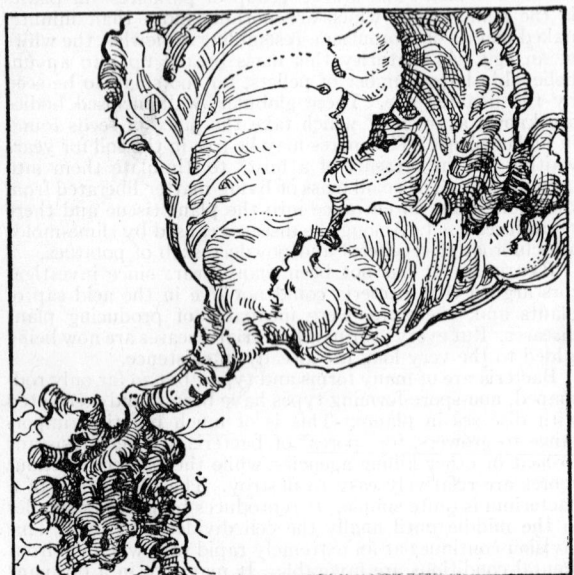

Clubroot of cabbage. For control see Diseases at CABBAGE.

Various types of fruit bodies arise from these threads and serve as a means of identification to the specialist who deals with such lower forms. The important point to the grower is that many of the fungi have two types of fruiting, a sexual and an asexual. The one type may enable the parasite to live through the winter or during unfavorable weather periods, while the other aids in rapid reproduction and infection when the crop is growing. In nearly all cases the control recommendations are based on a knowledge of these two stages.

Some of the fungous diseases, such as rust and powdery mildew, react so nearly alike on all hosts and their control is so similar that they can be treated in this general discussion of diseases.

RUST DISEASES occur on a wide variety of plants. In general, however, any given rust is rather specific in its host* range. Many rusts have several kinds of microscopic spores.* With such forms, the fungus may infect two entirely different plants living part of the year on one host and the remainder of the year on the other. The presence of a rust disease can always be determined by the appearance of yellow, orange or reddish-brown powdery pustules on the leaves, stems, or buds of infected plants. The spores produced in these pustules are carried by splashing rain or air currents to near-by healthy plants where new infections occur.

Since all of the rust fungi over-winter on infected plant parts, it is very important to rake up and burn all debris in the fall. The removal of early-spring infections will also aid materially in preventing rapid spread of the disease later on during the summer. The spores of the rust fungi may be carried on the seeds; consequently it is important to obtain seeds only from healthy plants.

Dusting sulphur has proved to be the most effective fungicide for diseases of this sort. The first application should be made before infection has occurred, since rust is difficult to control once it has gained much headway. With certain ornamentals such as asters and snapdragons, the use of dusting sulphur on the blooms will cause burning and bleaching. For this reason, a strenuous attempt should be made to control the disease before the plants begin to flower.

POWDERY MILDEW, a fungous disease, commonly affects many herbaceous and woody plants. Although there are various kinds of mildews, with many of them specific to certain hosts,* the symptoms are similar in all cases. The disease can be recognized by the white, talcum-like, or gray moldy patches of fungous growth on the leaves, stems or buds. Infected plants are weakened, turn yellow, and drop their leaves prematurely. In many cases the leaves and flowers are curled and distorted.

The mildew diseases are more prevalent toward the end of the summer when aging of the foliage and cool, damp nights with heavy dews combine to make conditions optimum for infection.

Frequent applications of very fine dusting sulphur will give excellent control of powdery mildew. The fungicide should be applied with a duster when the leaves are dry. Heavy applications are not necessary for maximum control. If spraying is preferred, colloidal or wettable sulphur sprays are also effective against the disease.

Since the fungus over-winters on fallen infected leaves, all plant debris should be carefully raked up and burned after the killing frosts. In setting out susceptible plants, sufficient space should be provided to promote free circulation of the air and shady or low, damp situations should be avoided.

### DISSEMINATION OF PARASITES

The means by which all the disease-producing organisms are disseminated also is important in any control program. For instance, if a parasite can be kept from a country or any localized area, the cost of protecting each plant or eradicating the invading organism can be eliminated. Consequently the grower should be much interested in the manner in which these lower plant forms are spread from one field to another.

Wind is one of the important agents in spore dissemination. Luckily many spores are so dried by the air currents which carry them that they are not viable when they finally land on their favorite host. Rust spores,* among others, however, may be carried long distances by prevailing winds and probably account for unexpected epidemics that arise seemingly from nowhere.

The chief method of dissemination from one plant to another is by the splashing of rain. A raindrop may land on a spore mass which includes thousands of individuals. This drop may then be washed into a puddle, the water of which in turn is splashed into a distant puddle, and so on throughout the field. During rainstorms rivulets of water flow from an infested field to a neighboring one, thereby infesting soil that may never have grown a diseased crop. Flooding, too, disseminates organisms that otherwise might have been confined to a small area. Shallow wells and ponds from which water is drawn for greenhouses are breeding places for some of the fungi that kill seedling plants or cause rots on recently potted cuttings.

Contaminated soil is an important source for later infection of plants. A field that has grown one diseased crop may retain the parasite for one year or possibly for many years. If such contaminated soil is carted into the greenhouse, or is left clinging to roots of seedlings that are transplanted, the harmful organism may be spread into many fields. In a similar way plants imported from other countries may have clinging to their roots soil that harbors parasites which have never before been introduced into the country. Some soils when wet are sticky, so that when a drove of animals walk through a contaminated field during a rainy day, they may convey enough infested mud to adjoining fields to cause a serious outbreak of some plant disease the following season.

It is a common practice to drop undesirable plant parts

* Special articles on the subjects indicated by an asterisk (*) will be found at the words so marked.

in the garden where the crop is grown or toss them into a heap for humus the following year. If such trash is not thoroughly composted, disease-producing organisms may remain alive in the affected plant tissue and serve as a source of infection when the same or a related crop is grown there again. It seems fitting, also, to throw rotted plant parts on to the manure pile, but the practice becomes dangerous if the manure is spread over the fields for fertilizer, and susceptible plants grown on this same soil. The presence of the manure may stimulate the growth of the fungus as well as that of the plant, as in the case of corn smut.

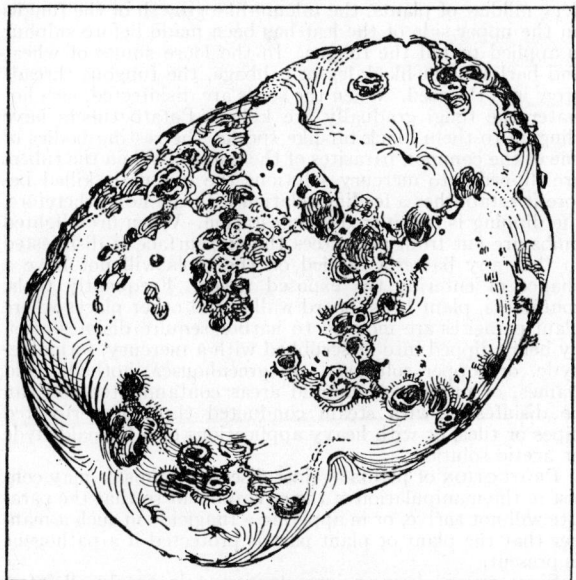

Potato scab. For control *see* Diseases at POTATO.

Every grower has learned to his sorrow that plant parasites may be transmitted in seeds, bulbs, tubers, cuttings, and other living plant parts. Many of our most obnoxious pests were introduced into this country in this manner. Such transmission is so common that the careful grower is ever attempting to find sources of seeds or other propagating plant parts that are free from fungi, bacteria, and viruses.

Insects are responsible for the spread of many diseases. Plant lice and leaf-hoppers are generally associated with virus transmission. In some cases, such as the bacterial wilt of cucurbits, bacteria cannot over-winter except in the presence of beetles. The spores of many fungi may cling to bodies of migrating insects, and thus be carried long distances. Higher animals may also serve as carriers. For instance birds are supposed to have disseminated the chestnut blight fungus so widely that eradication methods became useless.

### ENVIRONMENTAL INFLUENCES

No control measures of plant diseases are wholly adequate, if environmental conditions have not been taken into consideration. The organisms which cause diseases are affected favorably or adversely by much moisture or little moisture in the air or soil, high or low temperatures, amount of sunlight, type of soil, acidity or alkalinity of the soil, humus content of the soil, and sometimes even by the kind and quantity of the fertilizer.

Unfavorable environmental conditions for the plant may produce types of disease without the intervention of parasites. Tip-burn or leaf-scorch, which is prevalent on many cultivated and forest crops, has been shown to be caused, in part at least, by lack of potash in the soil (tip-burn of cabbage, leaf-scorch of currants). If tomatoes are grown too rapidly in their seedling stage and are then transplanted into fairly dry soil lacking humus, the resulting fruit may be seriously injured by a blossom-end rot. Very seriously stunted plants grown in unproductive muck may be restored to normal vigor by an application of copper sulphate or in some cases manganese to the soil. An extensive literature has come into existence regarding the effects on the growth and appearance of plants when some mineral food element is lacking.

In storage and in greenhouses, plant parts frequently are badly damaged by gases which escape from the cooling system or are liberated for fumigation purposes. A very small amount of ammonia gas in a cold-storage room may produce lesions that simulate closely disease-produced cankers. Cyanide gas used for killing insects may cause extreme injury to living plant parts. Chemicals spilled in freight or express cars or over containers may cause considerable loss of crops during transportation.

Lack of proper ventilation or temperature control may cause typical types of injury in stored tubers or roots. Thus when potatoes are placed in tight bins and the temperature permitted to rise, the centers of the tubers become black (black-heart). If the temperature is permitted to drop too low, the various degrees of chilling will manifest themselves in the plant tissue by slight to severe discoloration, and by slight hardening to advanced stages of softening.

### CONTROL MEASURES

EXCLUSION. Diseases of plants may be controlled by preventing the introduction of disease into uninvaded areas. Exclusion may be effected by intercepting the pathogene* en route to the uninvaded area; by eliminating the pathogene* from the carrier before admitting the latter to the area; or by prohibiting the introduction of natural carriers of the parasites from known or suspected centers of distribution.

After much opposition the National Government finally passed the Plant Quarantine Act. *See* QUARANTINE.

ERADICATION is the removal, elimination, or destruction of the pathogene in certain areas where it already is established. The removal of diseased plants from among the healthy is a very common method of eradication. It is known as *roguing*, and is applicable to all stages in plant growth. Many of the virus diseases can in part at least be controlled in this manner. It is almost the only way in which woodlots can be kept free from affected timber. When cankers or twig blights are present, it usually is not necessary to remove the entire tree, for the trouble can successfully be combated merely by the removal of the affected parts, that is, by *pruning*. This applies generally to shade and fruit trees.

The removal of infested plant refuse is a type of eradication by elimination which might be employed advantageously more often than it is at present. It consists primarily in the collection and removal of fallen parts of plants which are infested with pathogenes.* Fallen leaves, fruits, and twigs often harbor the pathogene or serve for its saprophytic development just where it will be in the best position for inoculation of new growth the next season. Raking and burning, removal and composting, or burying are some of the ways of getting rid of dangerous debris, and therefore of eliminating the parasites which have been harbored there. For the same reason, it may be necessary occasionally to remove old infested soil from greenhouses, even though at a big expense, and carting in soil free from obnoxious organisms.

Another means of elimination is the extirpation of weeds or other plants that act as hosts* for the same parasites that affect any given cultivated crop. A long list of such examples might be given. Some rather common diseases which are controlled, either completely or in part, in this manner are: cucumber and tomato mosaic, the virus of which remains active during the winter in the roots of such perennial plants as milkweed, ground cherry, pokeweed, and catnip. Many of the rusts have alternate hosts and when one of these hosts is eradicated the rust disappears. Among these are the white pine blister-rust whose alternate hosts are the

---

* Special articles on the subjects indicated by an asterisk (*) will be found at the words so marked.

currant and gooseberry family, the apple rust, which spends part of its life on the cedar tree, and to a lesser degree, the black-rust of cereals, one stage of which requires the common barberry for reproduction. On farms where care is taken to keep out all wild mustard and related weeds, clubroot of cabbage can be controlled more successfully.

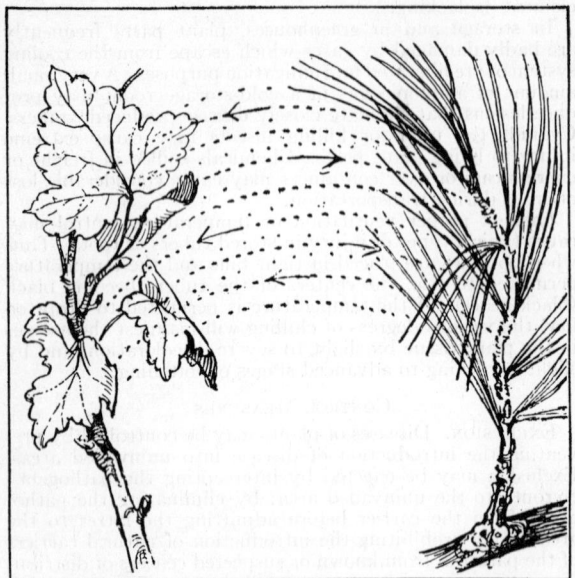

Some diseases live partly on one host* and partly on another. In the white pine blister rust (*above*) the spores, as shown by the arrows, may travel in either direction between the evergreen and a currant bush. Another alternate-host* disease is the notorious wheat rust which leads half its life on barberry bushes. *See* BERBERIS.

Cultivation helps in eradication of the parasite in at least two ways. The stirring of the soil tends to dry the surface and make it unfavorable for the growth of the molds and bacteria that so frequently are present near the base of susceptible plant stems. Thus young seedlings may sometimes be protected from damping-off* molds by keeping the surface soil well stirred. The more common effect of cultivation, however, is to turn under diseased plant refuse so deeply that the parasite cannot get an opportunity of causing infection, at least until the crop is mature enough to withstand the injury.

If the old apple leaves, bearing the winter stage of scab, or cherry leaves carrying the leafspot fungus, are turned under deeply, much of the early spring inoculum is destroyed. Most of the leafspots or blights on cultivated crops are reduced in intensity if the previous affected crop is plowed under. Summer cultivation, also, may destroy weed hosts.

Nearly every grower knows the importance of crop rotation, but seldom practices it sufficiently. When a dangerous fungus or bacterium once becomes established in a field, there is almost no way in which it can be eradicated unless it can be starved out by growing plants which are immune to the organism. In the corn-wheat country one of the common pathogens affects both crops, so that it is necessary to have in the rotation hay or other crops which are not affected by the fungus. The black-leg fungus of cabbage lives as long as three years in the soil, thus requiring at least a four-year rotation with other crops to starve it out completely. Nearly every cultivated plant is affected by one or more parasites, which get into soil, and require rotation of crops for their eradication. It is true, however, that some fungi, especially those that cause wilts, may remain alive so long that crop rotation cannot be depended upon to reduce the amount of inoculum. Furthermore some crops cannot well occur in the same rotation with others. For instance, cabbage, susceptible to clubroot, requires soil with plenty of lime, while potatoes cannot be grown in such soil for fear of being disfigured by common scab. Similarly strawberries and watermelons require a fairly acid soil for best growth while alfalfa would not thrive under such conditions.

DISINFECTION AND DISINFESTATION. These are both of extreme importance in the eradication of plant pathogens. The term disinfection usually is applied to the killing of a parasite after it once has established a relationship with the host, while disinfestation is the killing of organisms that may be clinging to any host parts. Thus in the case of powdery mildew of plants, the talcum-like growth of the fungus on the upper side of the leaf has been made before sulphur is applied to kill the fungus. In the loose smuts of wheat and barley or in black-leg of cabbage, the fungous threads grow into the seed. When the seeds are disinfected with hot water the fungi gradually are killed. Potato tubers have clinging to them black tar-like specks, the resting bodies of one of the common parasites of the potato. When the tubers are dipped into mercury solutions the fungus is killed before it establishes a feeding relation with the host; therefore, the dipping is considered disinfestation. When fire-blighted limbs are cut from pear trees the cut surface is disinfested so that any bacteria carried on the tools will not have a chance of entering the exposed tissue. Frequently tools, containers, plant beds, board walks, and other places where plant parasites are inclined to harbor require disinfestation by being dipped into or scrubbed with a mercury, formaldehyde, or copper solution. In greenhouses, hotbeds, cold frames, or other very limited areas contaminated soil can be disinfested with steam conducted through perforated pipes or tiles, or with heavy applications of a formaldehyde or acetic solution.

PROTECTION of plants against disease organisms may consist in the manipulation of the environment so that the parasite will not thrive, or in applying a fungicide in such a manner that the plant or plant part is protected if a pathogene is present.

Since water plays an important part in nearly all infection processes, the governing of the moisture about the plant is one of the practical means of protection. Air drainage, which in turn affects the amount of humidity, needs attention for nearly all crops. The movement of the air through the crop tends to hasten evaporation and removes the moist air from the vicinity of the plants. In humid regions where rains, dews, and fogs are of frequent occurrence, it is necessary in disease control that free water on the plants should be evaporated quickly. Air drainage is accomplished by the selection of a location for planting where air currents are not retarded.

Hillside plants have in most cases a natural air drainage, for cool air tends to flow downward. Low places in a field, high, thick hedgerows, the presence of high weeds, plants crowded too closely together, and poorly pruned trees all tend to hinder air currents, so that dew or rain may stand in droplets on the leaves for a few hours longer than would be true otherwise and thus permit parasites to gain an entrance into the host.

In greenhouses, plants can sometimes be kept dry and infection avoided by applying all the water to the soil through sub-irrigating pipes or tile.

SOIL MOISTURE in excess may be as harmful, so far as plant diseases are concerned, as heavily moisture-laden air. It is a general observation that late-blight rot of potatoes is common in wet soil. Nearly all kinds of root rots are increased by water-holding soil. The trouble can be avoided either by changing the crops to different types of soil, or by soil drainage. Tile drainage tends to remove heavy rainfalls quickly and so restore the aerated condition of the soil necessary to the health of roots. Soil moisture sometimes can be decreased by frequent cultivation or stirring of the surface layer. This is practiced in seedbeds where various fungi that cause damping-off live in the very topmost soil.

In some cases plant troubles may be caused by too dry soil, such as the blossom-end-rot of tomatoes. Each year

---

* Special articles on the subjects indicated by an asterisk (*) will be found at the words so marked.

sufficient humus in some form should be added to keep the water-holding capacity of the soil to its optimum.

TEMPERATURE is closely related to the severity of attack by many parasites. In the field the temperatures cannot be governed but the time of planting may sometimes be altered to such an extent that the crop is not subjected to the temperature favorable for the parasite. Several of the pathogenes on peas thrive best in warm soil. Therefore if the crop is planted very early the dry, hot weather of midsummer is avoided. Similarly, early potatoes may avoid late blight because they mature before the arrival of cool nights in the autumn.

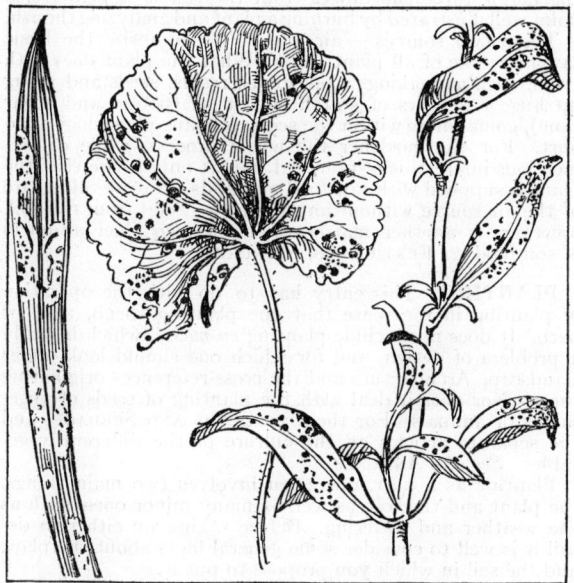

Rust symptoms on leaves of carnation (*left*), hollyhock (*center*) and snapdragon (*right*). For control *see* the disease notes at each crop.

A quick way to warm a soil is to drain it well, for it takes much more of the sun's energy to heat water than it does dry soil. It is for this reason that some parasites are found only in wet soils.

In greenhouses where the temperature may be raised or lowered almost at will it is possible to protect the plants by growing them in a temperature unsuitable for the growth of the pathogenes.* Raising the night temperature reduces the ravages of white rust of radish, the anthracnose of lettuce and gray mold rot of many plants. Lowering the temperatures hinders the growth of still other parasites.

STORAGE. The most obvious application of lowering temperatures to protect plant parts is cold storage. All kinds of perishable plants can be kept for months if the temperature is lowered sufficiently to stop completely the development of pathogenes.* Each crop may require a slightly different temperature for best results. The watery mold rot of celery is kept in check only when the storage is maintained at slightly below 32° F. Potato tubers acquire a sweetish taste if held much below 37° F., while sweet potatoes and squashes can be kept well at still higher temperatures. In order to insure further the keeping qualities of the crops placed in cold storage, they should not be subjected to high temperatures between harvesting and storage, they should be placed in clean containers, and the storage-room walls and floors should be washed with a fungicide to remove the refuse from previously contaminated crops.

Tomato and sweet corn seed grown in the northern states usually is more nearly free from disease organisms than is that grown in the middle states where the temperature is high enough to permit the rapid development of some of the worst parasites on these crops.

Much of the sunscald* and winter injury found on fruit trees are due to sudden changes, particularly on sunny days in early spring. The sun warms the trunk on one side several degrees higher than the opposite side. If then the temperature drops quickly at night injury results. Setting the trees so that they lean toward the southwest, and being careful not to over-prune help in reducing the chances for such type of sunscald. For a similar reason rose bushes and certain shrubbery are wrapped with straw during the winter to minimize the injury from too sudden changes in the temperature. *See* PROTECTING PLANTS.

Sometimes when apples are placed in storage the volatile gases excreted may be confined in the bin until scald of the fruit results. It has been found that oiled wrappers will absorb these gases, and prevent the scald.

Modifying the acidity or alkalinity of the soil for the protection of plants has only recently been receiving major attention. Clubroot of cabbage and other crucifers* can be controlled if a few weeks before planting enough hydrated lime is added to the soil to raise the reaction slightly above neutral. On the other hand, when common potato scab is very prevalent, the disease has been controlled by growing other cultivated crops for a few years to leach out excess lime from the soil, turning under green cover crops, fertilizing liberally with ammonium sulphate, and in the worst cases adding sulphur to the soil. The ground rot and scurf of sweet potato are held in check by a similar acidifying of the soil. *See* ACID AND ALKALI SOILS.

A further means of protecting plants from diseases is to interfere with the dissemination of the parasite either by the erection or introduction of direct barriers or by the elimination of the agent which transmits the inoculum. Direct barriers are of varied sorts, such as wrapping fruit when placed in storage, hilling potatoes to avoid late-blight rot, growing plants in glasshouses or cheesecloth tents which tend to bar floating spores of fungi, or to make use of hedgerows, intervening tall crops like corn, or other barriers that do not permit the pathogenes to reach the susceptible host. In view of the fact that insects so often carry the inoculum, the plants frequently may be protected by growing related crops so far apart that the carrier cannot fly from one field to the other. The application of the proper insecticide may reduce the insect population to such an extent that infection is avoided.

APPLICATION OF CHEMICAL PROTECTANTS. If wounds of any considerable size on woody parts of trees are left exposed, rots may set in before a protective callus has time to form. Consequently, wound dressings are used on flat wound surfaces, or in cavities made in the removal of diseased wood from trunks or limbs. These act as barriers in preventing the invasion of the numerous wood-destroying fungi.

The most common method of applying chemical protectants is spraying or dusting. The materials used generally are bordeaux mixture or lime-sulphur for spraying and copper-lime dust or superfine sulphur for dusting. There now are many modifications of these fungicides on the market, and to a slight extent even new chemicals are applied. *See* FUNGICIDES and SPRAYING AND DUSTING.

The important diseases of the leading plants in the DICTIONARY and their control follow the culture of them at each entry. *See also* DAMPING-OFF. — C. C.

**PLANT FAMILY.** A family of plants is a group of related genera (*see* GENUS), united by the botanists because they all have a family resemblance, although quite distinct one from another.

A simple illustration is the poppy family, known to science as the Papaveraceae, a family name composed of *Papaver* (the poppy) and *aceae*\* (belonging to). The poppy family comprises about 25 genera, of which over a dozen are garden plants, among them the poppy itself, the California poppy, the prickly poppy, etc. (for the list of them *see* PAPAVERACEAE). These genera of the poppy family are included within it because of similar flower or fruit structures, which are also the basis for the identity and scope of all the other plant families.

---

* Special articles on the subjects indicated by an asterisk (*) will be found at the words so marked.

Some plant families have such a strong family likeness that even the uninitiated will at once pick out plants belonging to them — such, for instance, as the grass family (Gramineae), daisy family (Compositae), pea family (Leguminosae), mint family (Labiatae), or the lily family (Liliaceae). But other plant families, based upon more technical characters, will only be recognized by the expert.

While the grouping of plants into families is essential for purposes of systematic classification, few gardeners take as much notice of what family their favorites belong to as they should. Because of this, and to give the users of this book a quick method of tracing related plants, all of the families of cultivated plants are entered and described in THE GARDEN DICTIONARY at their proper alphabetical position, and at each family is a list of all the cult. genera in it. And at every genus the name of the family is always mentioned. This double-entry of all generic and family names makes comparison and cross-referencing as simple as it can be.

There are 190 families of cult. plants included in the book, and space forbids repeating a list of them here. From the hort. standpoint the twenty most important are:

Gramineae (grass family)
Liliaceae (lily family)
Iridaceae (iris family)
Palmaceae (palm family)
Orchidaceae (orchid family)
Fagaceae (beech family)
Caryophyllaceae (pink family)
Ranunculaceae (buttercup family)
Cruciferae (mustard family)
Rosaceae (rose family)
Leguminosae (pea family)
Rutaceae (rue family)
Euphorbiaceae (spurge family)
Malvaceae (mallow family)
Myrtaceae (myrtle family)
Umbelliferae (carrot family)
Ericaceae (heath family)
Labiatae (mint family)
Scrophulariaceae (figwort family)
Compositae (daisy family)

Some confusion exists in older books, and in some modern ones in England, between the words *family* and *order*. In modern botany and hort. there need not be, for a family is what has been outlined above, while an order is a group of families — a botanical classification which has no place in a book like this. But for many years *order* and *natural order* were used loosely to designate what is now called a plant family; hence the confusion. See also GENUS and SPECIES.

**PLANT FOODS.** There are but two sources for the food of most garden plants, the air and the soil. From the former they absorb various gases, the use of which will be apparent presently, while from the soil plants absorb water and various substances carried in solution in water. The sole exceptions to these general statements are certain tropical tree-perching plants which absorb moisture from the air (no other plants do), and the peculiar insectivorous plants which are the only ones to digest directly nitrogenous materials. See INSECTIVOROUS PLANTS.

For simplicity it will be convenient to separate the discussion of plant foods into those derived from the air and those from the soil. We should not forget that the plant makes no such distinction. What happens in an ordinary leaf on a sunny day is actually a perfect balance of chemical and physical factors, whether from the air or soil. The source of the materials, while very different, is of little significance to the leaf which can carry on its function only by combining all materials, including light.

FROM THE AIR. An ordinary green leaf, with its cells distended with water from the roots (*i.e.* turgid), stands out with its blade surrounded by air and its surface exposed to sunlight. Ordinary air is roughly composed of 78% nitrogen, 20% oxygen, 1% argon, and only about .03 of 1% carbon dioxide. But it is the latter that is of incomparably the greatest importance to the leaf. Through its pores it absorbs the air, with the minute fraction of carbon dioxide, the latter being absorbed by the cells of chlorophyll (the green coloring matter of leaves).

By a process not yet thoroughly understood, this chlorophyll, in the presence of water, carbon dioxide, and sunlight, transforms the first two into starch — the first end product of the whole process. Nothing else in the world has this power of manufacturing starch, which is soon, however, in most plants changed to various kinds of sugars.

FROM THE SOIL. The process outlined above can only be carried on when there is a regular supply of water and the substances soluble in water. These are absorbed by the roots and travel through the stem, leafstalk midrib, the finest ramifications of the veins, and finally to the individual cells of chlorophyll. What reaches the chlorophyll is never pure water, but water containing the various plant foods found in the soil. These are phosphorus, potash, and nitrogen (often in the form of ammonia or nitrates), and a few other substances of minor importance. The plant's need of the major three substances from the soil is imperative, a point well illustrated by burning a plant and analyzing the ash.

These two sources — air and soil — comprise the basic raw materials of all plant foods. What the plant does with them, such as making wood, gums, resins, seeds and piling up huge reservoirs of starch and sugar (potato and sugar cane), comes more within the scope of plant physiology than hort. For the gardener the whole process, while of tremendous interest, is of practical import only to see that the plant is supplied with raw food materials. Nature takes care of the air source without any thought. Food from the soil, however, is another matter. For the two chief adjuncts of soil food see FERTILIZERS, MANURE.

**PLANTING.** This entry has to do with the operation of planting in the sense that one plants a shrub, tree, or herb. It does not include planting *en masse*, which is really a problem of design, and for which one should look under Landscape Architecture and the cross-references originating there. Nor does it deal with the planting of seeds of vegetables or annuals. For these see SEEDS AND SEEDAGE, and the separate articles on the culture of the different vegetables. See also ANNUALS.

Planting as a hort. operation involves two main things, the plant and the soil, as well as many minor ones, such as the weather and watering. Before taking up either in detail it is well to consider some general facts about the plant and the soil in which you propose to put it.

In any planting operation the shock of moving a living organism from one place to another should never be forgotten. The moment you dig up a rooted plant, whether herb, shrub, or tree, you break, for a briefer or longer time, the continuity of its food and water supply. Hence, as general principle number one, never make this period of transition from one home to another a moment longer than it must be. Even with the greatest care and the least possible loss of time, there is still a large element of shock in any planting operation, and to reduce this, general rule number two is practiced by all skillful gardeners. It is to reduce by about ¼–⅓ the top of the planted specimen of all woody plants except evergreens. In other words cut back drastically all such plants at the time of planting. Such pruning reduces by ¼ or ⅓ the number of leaves for the first season after planting and by so much reduces the water requirements of the newly planted specimen. This may seem drastic, but long experience has proved it the only safe rule. It cannot always be followed with herbs because at planting time they usually have no tops, and in any case they suffer less than do woody plants from shock.

It may be objected that some woody plants, such as privet, spirea, willow, forsythia, and quite a few others, are moved with great ease and begin almost at once to grow in their new home. While this is partly true of such plants, it is not so generally true that the average planter can afford to ignore either of the main principles outlined above. To follow them usually means at least 90% of success, while to ignore them, even for easily transplanted specimens, may mean failure.

BALL AND BURLAP (usually abbreviated to B & B in the catalogues). Most evergreens, azaleas, rhododendrons, magnolias, box, sour gums, some oaks, and most of the broad-leaved evergreens are far more difficult to plant than the average run of nursery stock. In other words, they resent the breaking of the continuity of their food and water

---

* Special articles on the subjects indicated by an asterisk (*) will be found at the words so marked.

supply so much that special planting methods are necessary to overcome this hazard.

All competent nurserymen dig such plants with a ball of soil in which (because of root pruning) there are many small feeding roots. The ball of soil is immediately tied up, pudding-fashion, in tightly roped or sewn burlap or canvas. This keeps the roots in constant contact with the soil and the bagging or canvas is not taken off until planting time. For most small plants burlap is used, and as it rots quickly, it can usually be left on and planted with the ball, especially if it is slit in one or two places just before planting. Canvas, which is used for all larger plants, is often a somewhat elaborately stitched affair for which a renting charge is made. It should, therefore, and also because it rots too slowly, be removed at the last moment before planting, and returned to the nurseryman, together with a board platform to which all good-sized ball and burlap trees will be roped.

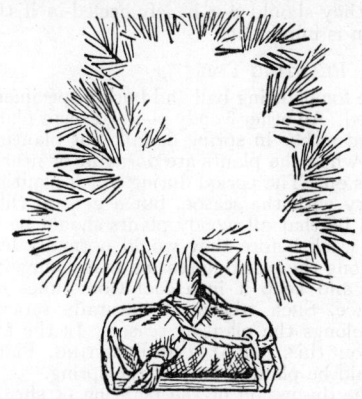

An evergreen showing the ball and burlap method of protecting its roots while awaiting planting.

The object of the ball and burlap method is to keep the roots free from wind and dry air. If the specimens arrive before you are ready to plant, put them under a tree or in a cool shed, and water the balls thoroughly until you are ready to plant them.

The best season for planting ball and burlap plants is early in the spring, and from Aug. 15–Sept. 15 over all the country north of zone* 5. South of this their planting season is less important, but they should never be put into cold, wet soil just before frosty weather, as they need a period of a few weeks, in the fall, to get a fresh start.

### The Soil

In any sort of planting it is of the greatest importance to see that the soil is suitable. We need not repeat here the differences in the value of topsoil and subsoil, nor discuss the relative merits of clay, loam, sandy loams, etc. All these details you will find at Soils and the cross-references originating there. And if you need to enrich the soil see Fertilizers and Manure for the details of these operations.

But a few general soil directions should not be forgotten. If the planting operation is a small one, or expense no object, dig the holes for the plant and cart away all the subsoil, replacing it with good topsoil. Of course separate the subsoil and topsoil when digging the hole, retaining the latter for planting.

If the planting operation is a large one, or the expense of hauling in enough topsoil is prohibitive, follow this procedure: Dig a hole the desired size, separating the excavated soil into three piles: (1) the best topsoil; (2) the best of the subsoil; and (3) the worst of the subsoil. In planting put some of the topsoil in the bottom of the hole and the rest around the roots of the plant. Then fill in with the best of the subsoil and put the worst of the subsoil at the top. Large-scale plantings, managed this way at no cost for fresh topsoil, and well mulched with manure for a season or two, will often not have 5% of failure.

The only objection to such a method is that the plants will not grow quite so fast nor so well for the first year or so as they would in good topsoil, which should always be used if it is available.

Sometimes the soil is underlaid by an impervious belt of hardpan or by rocky ledges. Such a site would make planting impossible if it were not for dynamite (which see). See also Hardpan.

### Planting

In digging holes for any planting it is essential to make them deep and wide enough to amply take care of the roots, or ball if the specimen is a ball and burlap plant. No specific depths or widths can be given, for plants vary so much. But a general rule should be to make the hole about ⅓ deeper and wider than the spread of roots on the new plant. This will allow ample space.

It is quite useless to put the roots at the bottom of a hole on the freshly exposed subsoil. Fill in the hole with enough topsoil to bring it up to the desired height. The final depth of the partly filled hole is determined by the old soil line on the stem of the specimen to be planted. Most shrubs and trees should be set at their old level, but a few, like box and privet, should be set a trifle deeper.

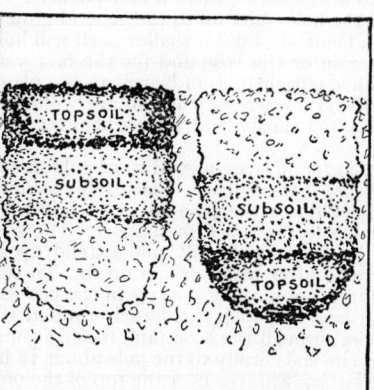

Putting topsoil (right) where it will do most good. At the left the natural layers of topsoil and subsoil. For details see The Soil (just above).

In filling in with topsoil, before the specimen is planted, don't merely throw the soil in and smooth it off. Jump in the hole several times until the topsoil is well packed down, and on this firmed-down layer place the roots of the plant. If the soil under the roots is not well tamped, settling will inevitably leave air pockets in which feeding roots will dry out, and if there are enough of such air holes the plant will be what the gardeners call "hanged," i.e. killed or crippled, even though planted, for lack of its feeding roots being in contact with the soil. So important is this that many gardeners, especially in England, follow the process of

Puddling (sometimes called mudding). Because it was well known that it is not the large roots that matter most in a planting operation, but the small feeding roots, the puddling method was devised centuries ago. Its object is to coat all the roots with a thin film of wet soil just before planting. They are dipped in a slimy mixture of good fine loam and water and then planted. This insures closer contact of the fine feeding roots than is possible without it, even with the greatest care in filling in the hole. There is no doubt that puddling, especially in dry weather, is a beneficial method. Its objections are that it is a troublesome, messy job, and on large-scale plantings often cost too much so to be worth it.

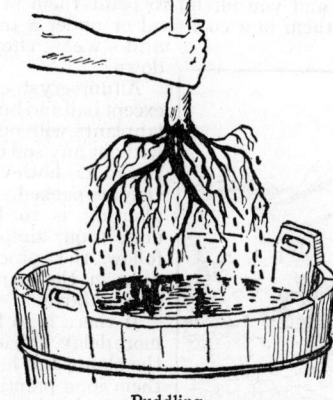

Puddling

Roots. In all woody plants it will be found that there are some large roots and many smaller ones. At planting time the larger ones are of the least importance. If any are

---

* Special articles on the subjects indicated by an asterisk (*) will be found at the words so marked.

broken or bruised, cut them off, making a clean diagonal cut with a knife or pruning shears. Such cut roots will almost certainly put out a lot of fine feeding roots, which is exactly what the newly planted specimen most needs. Even if there are no broken or injured roots, it is a good plan to cut off the ends of the largest roots just to induce the production of feeding roots. See ROOT.

All being now ready, the hole properly filled, the roots cared for, and the specimen cut back as outlined above, the final planting should be done. It is by far the quickest of the whole series of operations. See that the specimen is straight and gradually fill in the soil, using the feet or a rammer so that the topsoil will be thoroughly packed around the roots. In other words, leave no air pockets.

Do not at first fill the hole quite up to the general ground level, but about 2 in. below it. Such a shallow well will hold water whether from rain or the hose and for the first year such a depression, while unsightly, is of benefit to the plant. You can, however, avoid its necessity if you are willing to water your newly planted shrubs and trees whenever they need it.

Remember, also, that for all trees, a good stout pole should be set in the hole *before* it is filled up. Place the specimen in the hole, then drive down the pole so as to injure no roots, and deep enough to make a firm support. The pole should be about 4 in. from the trunk, and extend up at least 6 ft. above ground after being driven down. To this pole wire the young tree, not girdling the tree in the process. Cut up pieces of old hose and loop this loosely around the trunk. Run stout wire through the hose (and hence around the trunk) and secure its ends firmly to the pole about 18 in. below the top of the latter. From or near the top of the pole stretch three tight guy wires fastened to stakes driven firmly in the ground, each of the stakes from 4–5 ft. from the trunk. Leave this staking on the tree for the first two years, and see that the guy wires are kept tight. Without these the wind will so loosen the feeding roots that successful tree planting is sometimes long delayed, and the tree may die if shaken too violently by the wind. Most shrubs will not need staking.

MULCHING. Most shrub and tree plantings will be benefited by a mulch of manure put on just after planting. For the details of this see MULCH AND MULCHING. For special plants like rhododendron, azalea, and broad-leaved evergreens the mulch should be of leaves. For details *see* these three entries.

### HEELING-IN

It is often impossible to plant shrubs and trees the moment they arrive. If they are packed in sphagnum moss or if the bundle of roots is tied up in burlap (not balled and burlapped, *see* above), and you intend to plant them in a day or so, simply put them in a cool shed or under a tree and wet them down.

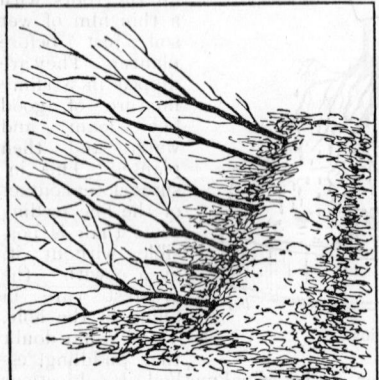

Heeling-in. For details *see* text.

All nursery stock, except ball and burlap plants, will come without any soil on the roots, however they are packed. If planting is to be done soon, simply follow the procedure in the paragraph above.

If there is to be more delay, unpack the plants and heel them in, a practice universal with all experienced gardeners. Heeling-in simply consists in temporary planting. Dig a trench long enough to take care of your shipment, and deep enough to cover completely all roots when the trench is filled. Pack the plants as closely together as possible without injuring the roots, and tip the tops at an angle of about 45°. Then fill in the trench as quickly as possible, and do not worry about all the details of actually filling in for a planted specimen. Simply see that no roots are left exposed and such heeled-in specimens will keep perfectly for a week or two, but they should not be left heeled-in if the active growing season is imminent.

### PLANTING TIME

The preferred time for planting ball and burlap specimens has already been noted. All other woody plants, except plane trees, may be planted either in spring or fall, but planting should only be done when the plants are dormant or nearly so; *i.e.* without leaves on. The period during which planting can be done will vary with the season, but a general rule, in the spring, should be that all woody plants should be in the ground about a week before they would normally leaf out. In order to prolong the planting season, many nurserymen dig their stock and keep it in a cool (sometimes refrigerated), dark place. Such treatment naturally retards development and prolongs the planting season. In the fall there is no trouble about this. See AUTUMN PLANTING. Plane trees (*Platanus*) should be planted only in the spring.

Before we leave the discussion of the planting of shrubs and trees, reference should be made to stagger, quincunx, and hexagon planting. These are methods of planting orchard fruits to save space. For the details *see* Planting at FRUIT CULTURE and the diagram there.

### HERBACEOUS PLANTING

The planting of herbs is much less troublesome than the details outlined above, chiefly because they are shallow-rooted. Because of this they rarely extend their roots below the layer of topsoil, and the operation of planting them is comparatively easy. Some gardeners prefer to reduce the roots of herbaceous plants, as shown in the illustration.

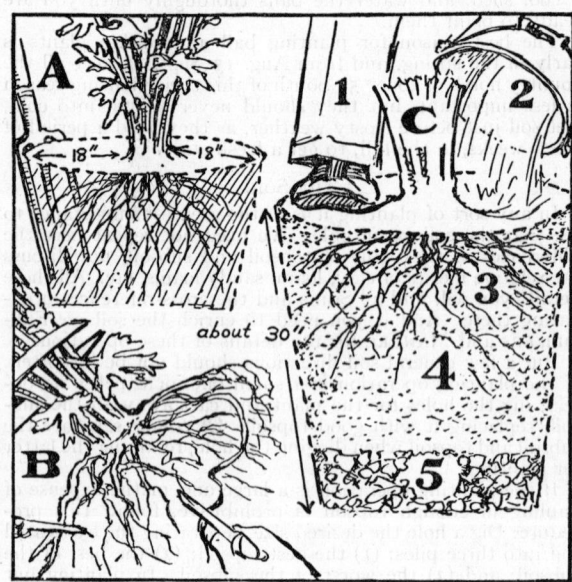

MOVING HERBACEOUS PERENNIALS

(*A*) Insert spading fork deeply so as not to cut roots. (*B*) Lift out carefully and cut back the top and any broken or very long roots. (*C*) The plant in its new site: (1) Firm the soil with foot or spade handle; (2) water it plentifully; (3) see that the roots are well spread; (4) be sure the soil around and just below the roots is good topsoil, enriched with well-rotted manure if possible; (5) if the subsoil is clay or hardpan,* remove it and fill in with coarse gravel for better drainage.

The only caution is to see that they are firmly planted so that there will be no air pockets about their roots. And in the case of fleshy-rooted herbs especial care must be used

---

* Special articles on the subjects indicated by an asterisk (*) will be found at the words so marked.

to prevent their heaving. In fact, this heaving, caused by the alternate thawing and freezing of the soil, is often a source of a lot of trouble. The only remedy is deep, firm planting or a mulch. See HEAVING.

There remain two other sorts of planting, both the subject of special entries. For the spring and fall planting of bulbs see BULBS. For the planting of greenhouse material in pots or tubs see POTTING.

**PLANTING TABLES.** See GARDEN TABLES I.

**PLANT LICE.** See True Bugs at INSECT PESTS. For control see Contact Sprays at INSECTICIDES.

**PLANT NAMES.** Unhappily for all gardeners and botanists, plants are cursed with two sets of names, the Latin ones of science, and the vernacular names of common speech.

Because the latter are much better known than technical Latin names, a special effort has been made to include in this book as many valid common names as possible. Something over 4400 common names are entered, far less than the 4800 species in THE DICTIONARY. Many cult. plants have no common name, and for such none have been entered, their Latin name having to suffice and being far preferable to so-called common names manufactured by the bookish. The really valid common names of plants come from the people to the books, not the other way around. But many well-known plants have several, and in some cases, alas, dozens of vernacular names. Those that are obscure, or too local, or purely colloquial have had to be excluded. But the 4500 that are entered have wide usage behind them in some part of the country. THE DICTIONARY contains more valid common names than any other garden publication, and a word here may help the reader to find them.

As in any other Dictionary, they are entered in strict alphabetical sequence. Look for **red** oak, **New England** aster, **white** spruce, **black** oak, **pink** lady's-slipper, etc., under the boldface word, not under oak or spruce or lady's-slipper or aster. You will, of course, find them under oak or spruce or lady's-slipper or aster, but much more quickly and directly (*i.e.* referred to the exact species) by going to the first word of names that contain two. For all others the strictly alphabetical entry needs no explanation.

LATIN NAMES. While common names are better known than technical ones, the Latin names are far more precise and comprise the only universal method of plant naming (nomenclature). In the vast majority of cases, garden plants have only two names, thus: *Dianthus deltoides*. The first name tells us that the plant belongs to the genus *Dianthus*, the pinks, while *deltoides* tells us that it is the maiden pink. The first name is thus the generic name and is applied to all other plants in the genus *Dianthus*, while *deltoides* is a specific name applied only to this particular species of *Dianthus*.

In some cases it becomes necessary to designate still further a plant which already has a generic and specific name. This third name, also in Latin, is a *varietal* one (*i.e.* it designates a particular variety of a species). Such varietal names appear as the third of a trio thus: *Dianthus deltoides glaucus*, which tells us that this is a variety (hence the abbreviation *var.*) of the maiden pink, with bluish-green foliage.

Because specific and varietal names are in Latin (usually derived from Greek) and their meanings may be unknown to many owners of THE DICTIONARY, all such names used in this book have been entered at their proper alphabetical place, pronounced and defined. Nearly 2200 such specific and varietal names are entered, the only ones omitted being those based on the names of persons and hence obvious; *i.e. grayi, wilsoni, thunbergi*. See also SPECIES, GENUS, VARIETY.

SYNONYMS. Because many authors in widely scattered parts of the world and of many degrees of competence have had a hand in christening plants with Latin names, it happens pretty frequently that a plant acquires several, to the permanent confusion of everyone. Unfortunately, the literature of botany and hort. is strewn with thousands of these invalid Latin names, for, of course, a plant can have only one that is really valid. All others are invalid or untenable and may be grouped here under the general term of *synonyms* (there are several technical interpretations of the term). In most books synonyms, which are more confusing to the amateur than almost any other feature of nomenclature, follow the valid name, always in parentheses. A typical illustion is:

*Plumeria acuminata (P. acutifolia).*

This indicates to the initiated that *P. acutifolia* is, for some reason, an untenable name for *P. acuminata;* in other words, a synonym for it. The obvious question is why not omit all reference to the untenable *P. acutifolia* and thus avoid future confusion? The answer is that while technically invalid it may have been once widely current in any number of books or other printed records, especially nurserymen's catalogues.

Wherever synonyms have had sufficiently wide usage to demand notice they have been entered in THE GARDEN DICTIONARY, but not in the technical way above cited, because few of our readers may understand its significance. Instead all synonyms are added separately, under some such phrase as "known also as ——," "sometimes offered as ——."

**PLANT PATENTS.** Long-continued agitation preceded the eventful development of a copyright law through which mental property in the written word is now protected. Similarly, and following equivalent agitation, there now exists Federal protection of mental property in plant origination. On May 23, 1930, certain amendments to the general patent laws were adopted constituting what is generally known as the "Plant Patent Act," despite the fact that it is wholly supplementary to the laws relating to mechanical processes and gadgets.

Approximately 125 plant patents have been granted, predominantly to roses. Other subjects patented are carnations, chrysanthemums, freesias, fruits, etc.

The life of a plant patent is seventeen years, during which time the owner may legally defend against infringement. He may sell or lease the patent plants or propagating rights, or he may even refuse to permit the introduction of the plant. He may make licenses of any sort, or arrange for a royalty.

His patent rests on a claim of novelty in color, form, habit, hardiness, or any other distinction established to the satisfaction of the Patent Office authorities. He may patent a new seedling, or the variation from an existing variety called a "sport." No foreign country yet has similar laws, though plants of foreign origin can be patented in the U.S.

The method of obtaining a plant patent and a statement as to its cost are given in the following:

Application for a plant patent must be filed within two years after such plant is introduced to the public or described in public print. To apply for a plant patent, the necessary blanks must be obtained, preferably through a patent attorney, from the office of the Commissioner of Patents in Washington, and these, including a complete and detailed description of the plant, must be sworn to. With them must go duplicate color representations of the new plant, conforming to specified requirements.

The Patent Office charges a filing fee of $30, payable with the application. There then follows a $30 final fee, payable if and when the patent is granted, with a further fee of $3 if the patent is to be assigned to any other than the patentee. There are, in some cases, slight additional Patent Office fees. These fees do not cover the attorney's fee, which usually approximates $75. Much detailed and persistent attention is requisite to meet the requirements of the Patent Office. — J. H. McF.

**PLANT PATHOLOGY.** See PLANT DISEASES.

**PLANT PHYSIOLOGY.** This is scarcely a hort. subject, although the plant's response to its environment dictates our success or failure in growing it. This is especially true of the reaction of plant cells to moisture, cold, wind, and light. The details of such reactions comprise the sub-

---

\* Special articles on the subjects indicated by an asterisk (\*) will be found at the words so marked.

ject of plant physiology, but they lie outside the scope of this book.

**PLANT QUARANTINE.** See QUARANTINE.

**PLANTS PER ACRE.** For the number needed at different intervals from 1 × 1 in. to 100 × 100 ft., see GARDEN TABLES I.

**PLASH.** See PLEACH.

**PLATANACEAE.** See PLATANUS.

*PLATANIFOLIA*, *-us*, *-um* (pla-tan-i-fō'li-a). With leaves like the plane tree (*Platanus*).

*PLATANOIDES* (pla-ta-noy'deez, but see OÏDES). Like a plane tree (*Platanus*).

*PLATANTHA*, *-us*, *-um* (pla-tan'tha). With broad leaves.

**PLATANUS** (plă'ta-nus). Plane, plane tree, or buttonball tree. Valuable forest trees, one a hybrid and perhaps the best all-round street tree, and the only genus of the family **Platanaceae** (pla-ta-nay'see-ee), and comprising only 6 or 7 species from N.A. and Eurasia. They have large, long-stalked, alternate* leaves, lobed and veined finger-fashion. Flowers small, inconspicuous, in dense, ball-like, stalked clusters, the male and female separate on the same tree. The female clusters mature into a persistent, ball-like mass (a syncarp*) of small nutlets, the fruiting cluster conspicuous most of the winter in the London plane. The outer bark of all species peels off in large plates, exposing the much lighter inner bark. (*Platanus* is the classical Greek name for the plane tree.) One of the leading arias in Handel's opera *Serse* is *Ombra mai Fù*, which is an ode to a plane tree. This soprano aria is the familiar "and preposterous arrangement now known as Handel's Largo." (Philip Hale.)

The first species, the London plane, is a hybrid between the second and third species. It is the most widely planted street tree in London, Paris, and most American cities in the temperate region. It stands abuse, smoke, dust, and windy streets better than any other tree. The second species, the American buttonwood or sycamore, while probably the largest deciduous tree (in girth) in the U.S., does not take so kindly to city cult. The third species is scarcely, or not at all, known in cult. in America, but commonly listed — all the nurserymen's trees being actually *P. acerifolia*.

The London plane, the only important cult. one, should not be planted in the autumn north of zone* 5. Otherwise, its culture is easy.

**acerifolia.** London plane. A tall, widely spreading tree up to 140 ft. Leaves 3-5-lobed, cut off at the tip, 5-9 in. wide. Fruiting clusters in groups of 2, bristly, about 1 in. in diameter, winter-persisting. A hybrid between *P. occidentalis* and *P. orientalis.* Hardy from zone* 3 southward.
**occidentalis.** Buttonwood; also called sycamore (but not the true sycamore of the Bible which is a non-hort. species of *Ficus, F. sycomorus*). A very large forest tree, the trunk with an immense girth in maturity. Leaves 5-9 in. wide, commonly 3-lobed, but sometimes 5-lobed. Ball-like fruiting clusters nearly always solitary, rarely 2, about 1½ in. in diameter, not bristly. Eastern N.A., reaching its greatest known girth (42 ft. 3 in.) in bottom-lands near Worthington, Ind. Hardy from zone* 3 southward, and a good tree for country planting, but not for city streets.
**orientalis.** Oriental plane. Not so tall as the other two. Leaves 5-7-lobed, 4½-8 in. wide. Ball-like fruiting heads in clusters of 2-6, about 1 in. in diameter, bristly. Eurasia, and cult. there, but rare or unknown in cult. in America. Hardy from zone* 6 southward. All plants offered as this in the U.S. are sure to be *P. acerifolia*.

**PLATE BUDDING.** See BUDDING.

*PLATYCENTRA*, *-us*, *-um* (plat-i-sen'tra). With a broad center.

*PLATYCERAS* (plat-i-see'ras). Having broad horns.

**PLATYCERIUM** (plat-i-seer'i-um). Also known as *Alcicornium*. Staghorn fern. A small genus of large, strong-growing ferns found growing on branches, or trunks of trees, or on wet rocks in tropical Af., As. and Aust., and belonging to the family Polypodiaceae. They have two kinds of fronds; one sterile, large, round, and plate-like, enclosing the roots and clasping the support on which it grows. The base of this frond is thick, as this is where the plant stores its water; the outer portion thin and membranous, wavy in outline. The other kind of frond is 1-6 ft. long, narrow at the base, widening out and branching into lobes like a stag's horn. These lobes droop, the under sides being partially covered with large, brown patches where the spores* are produced. The plant gets part of its moisture from the air but also by catching the rain. The roots are embedded in humus formed by the decaying sterile leaves and sometimes penetrate the bark of the tree on which the plant is growing. (*Platycerium* is from the Greek for broad horn, in allusion to the leaves.)

Generally cult. in greenhouse, in temperature not less than 60°. Propagated by spores or division of plants, usually the latter. Pieces of plant are wired onto a piece of wood hung on the side of a damp greenhouse. Shade and dampness essential.

**bifurcatum.** Grayish-green, the fertile fronds, 2 or 3 together, hairy, drooping, 1-3 ft., branching into 6-8 narrow lobes with brown patches (spores) on under side extending to the tips. Sterile leaves have wavy margins. Aust. and Polynesia.
**stemmaria.** Grayish-green. Fertile fronds drooping, to 3 ft. long, covered with short, white hairs on the under side. Lobes 4, spore patches not extending to the tips. West tropical Af.
**willincki.** Grayish-green, thinly covered with small, branching hairs when young. Fertile fronds growing 3 together, to 3 ft. long, branching into two about ⅔ of their length, one branch continuing entire and narrow, the other branching into numerous lobes all bearing spore patches nearly to the tips. Java.

*PLATYCLADOS* (plat-i-clay'dos). With broad branches.

**PLATYCODON** (plat-i-kō'don). A single, Eurasian, showy, perennial herb of the bellflower family, *P. grandiflorum*, commonly called balloon-flower, and widely cult. for ornament. It is an erect herb, 18-30 in. high, the leaves alternate,* ovalish or narrower, 2-3 in. long. Flowers usually solitary, long-stalked, broadly bell-shaped or deeply saucer-shaped, 2-3 in. long, dark blue (or pale or white in some hort. forms). Fruit a 5-celled capsule, splitting at the top. There are dwarf (var. **mariesi**) forms, and one with the 10 lobes of the corolla making it appear star-like (var. **japonicum**). There are also double and semi-double flowered forms. A handsome border plant, summer-blooming, and of easy cult. in most garden soils. Increased by division in spring. (*Platycodon* is from the Greek for broad bell, in allusion to the shape of the corolla.)

*PLATYNEURON* (plat-i-new'ron). With broad nerves or veins.

*PLATYPETALA*, *-us*, *-um* (plat-i-pet'a-la). With broad petals.

*PLATYPHYLLA*, *-us*, *-um* (plat-i-fill'a). Broad-leaved. Sometimes written *platyphyllos*.

**PLATYSTEMON.** See CREAM-CUPS.

**PLEACH.** A method of pruning and training trees to produce a hedge-like wall. The trees are planted about 6-8 ft. apart, and most of the front and back branches are removed. The side branches are more or less interwoven (pleached, also called plashed), and as the tree grows, the narrow hedge-like effect is very striking. A pleached allée* can be an imposing feature in any garden, but it takes time and patience to produce it. One of the finest pleached allées in the world is at the Schönbrun Palace, Vienna, made of the London plane.

Pleached trees

**PLEASANCE.** See GARDEN HISTORY.

---

* Special articles on the subjects indicated by an asterisk (*) will be found at the words so marked.

**PLEIOGYNIUM** (ply-o-gy′ni-um). A genus of Australian, evergreen trees of the family Anacardiaceae, the only species being **P. solandri**, the Burdekin plum. It grows 40–60 ft. high, with a trunk 2–3 ft. in diameter. Leaves compound,* the leaflets 7–9, ovalish, not cut, 2–4 in. long. Flowers greenish, in dense clusters produced in the axils* of the leaves. The clusters of the male flowers are longer than the clusters bearing female flowers. The male flower has 10 stamens.* Fruit plum-like, 1½ in. across, used for preserves. Cult. in Calif. and Fla., but little known. (*Pleiogynium* is from the Greek for many wives, but of unknown application here.)

*PLEIONEURA*, *-us*, *-um* (ply-o-new′ra). Many-veined.

*PLENA*, *-us*, *-um* (plee′na). Double; usually double-flowered.

*PLENIFLORA*, *-us*, *-um* (plen-i-flow′ra). Double-flowered.

*PLENISSIMA*, *-us*, *-um* (plen-iss′i-ma). Most doubled.

**PLEURISY-ROOT** = *Asclepias tuberosa*. See MILKWEED.

*PLICATA*, *-us*, *-um* (ply-kay′ta). Plaited or folded in plaits.

**PLINY.** See Early Romans at GARDEN BOOKS.

**PLOUGHING** = plowing.

**PLOW.** See Section 1, TOOLS AND IMPLEMENTS.

**PLOWING.** One of the oldest agricultural operations in the world, having for its object the turning over of soil needed for planting. Volumes have been written on the evolution of the plow from a crude wooden device, not much more effective than a pointed stick, to the modern power-driven plow with the cutting tools in gangs.

In spite of modern methods, the operation of plowing is still very much what it was in the olden time, the only real exception being that some machines are now made that can throw the furrow in either direction. As will be explained presently, this avoids all but one of the blind furrows that are inevitable in ordinary plowing.

In the latter operation there are two ways of starting: (1) The first is to start at the edges, proceeding around the plot, and this results in one dead (or blind) furrow in the center. The blind furrow results from two parallel journeys of the plow, one throwing the soil to the left, the return journey also throwing its soil to the left, thus making a deep trench in the center — the blind furrow. The advantage of this method is that there is only one blind furrow to be filled up. The disadvantage is the obvious one that at the beginning of the operation there is much useless walking or driving along the ends of the field, without plowing at all. (2) The second method is to plow the land in strips of 15–20 ft. width, which avoids much useless walking around the edges of the field, but results in as many blind furrows as you have strips.

In the modern plow with a moldboard adjusted so it will throw the soil in either direction there will only be a single blind furrow — the last one. In this sort of plowing, start at one end of the field and upon reaching the end of the furrow, reverse the moldboard and return directly, this time throwing your furrow in the desired direction. Keep on reversing the moldboard at the end of each row, and at the end of the field you will have only one blind furrow, and will, in addition, have taken no extra steps; *i.e.* with an idle, dragging plow.

Plowing is only necessary if your garden is larger than 25–50 ft., and some enthusiasts still prefer to dig, bit by bit, a garden as large as 50 × 50 ft. For anything larger a spring and preferably a fall plowing are essential. In areas with thin topsoil care must be taken to see that the subsoil is not thrown on top of the topsoil.

Another feature of plowing most necessary to watch is in turning under cover crops for green manuring. They should not be allowed to grow until too long to be completely buried. But even if plowed under at the right stage (6–8 in. high), some careless plowers will leave the herbage half-exposed. It should be completely buried even if the operator is forced to plow more furrows (*i.e.* ones closer together) in order to accomplish complete coverage by soil. Taller cover crops are sometimes mown and then plowed under. See GREEN MANURING. See also SOIL OPERATIONS.

**PLUM.** For the common plum see the next main entry. For other genera to which the name is also applied, or in which *plum* is part of the name *see* ACHRAS, CARISSA, CHRYSOBALANUS, COCCOLOBIS, DIOSPYROS (at Persimmon), FLACOURTIA, PLEIOGYNIUM, and SPONDIAS. See also PRUNUS.

**PLUM.** Four groups of plums are grown in America, all derived from different species of *Prunus*. These are: the Domesticas or European plums; the Insititias or Damsons; the Salicinas or Japanese; and a diverse group evolved from several wild species. The status of these groups in America must be briefly set forth.

The European plum is represented in America by many varieties quite distinct in the characters which make them desirable as cultivated fruits. Culture of the Domesticas is restricted in eastern America to a few favored regions near the Atlantic westward to the Great Lakes.

Damson plums are second in importance to the Domesticas in eastern America. In the main the two groups are grown in the same region and are given the same orchard treatment. The Damsons, however, are adapted to a somewhat greater variety of soils and stand extremes of heat and climate a little better.

The Japanese plums, introduced more than a half-century ago, were for a time over-praised and over-planted in eastern America. A few varieties are still very popular and rightly so. The qualities which commend Japanese plums are: a wide range of adaptability to soils and climates; great productiveness; and immunity to black-knot, leaf-blight and curculio. Faults are: early blooming; susceptibility to brown-rot; tenderness to cold; poor quality; clinging stones; and soft flesh.

Varieties of native species are grown only in the Middle West where they meet the demand for hardiness to cold and heat. A great number of hybrids between native species and the Japanese plums have enriched pomology with valuable new varieties.

Some varieties of these four species of plums may be grown on most of the soils suited to general farm crops in eastern America where climate permits plums to grow. The several species, however, have very decided preferences for soils. The Domesticas and Damsons grow best on clays and heavy loams. The Japanese sorts grow best on light loams and sands and in general thrive wherever the peach is at home. Some variety of the several species of native plums can be found for every farm or garden in America. As with every other fruit, soils for plums must be well drained and slopes are better than flats.

The plum has been grown in eastern America on at least six stocks. The New York Agricultural Experiment Station long ago started an experiment to determine which of the six is best. After a test of 20 years the results clearly show that the Myrobalan stock (*Prunus cerasifera*) is far and away the best. Fortunately nurserymen find this the cheapest stock upon which to grow the many varieties of the several species and all plums offered by them are on this stock.

Two-year-old trees from the bud should be set in the spring. Varieties differ greatly in size of tree so that distances apart vary. For small-growing varieties of Damsons, Japanese, and native plums, 18 ft. usually suffices; 20 ft. is better for the Domesticas, and on fertile soil perhaps 22 or 24 ft. apart each way would repay for the use of the land. The usual precautions should be taken in planting to have the hole large enough to take the roots when spread out, to have the tree set as deep as it stood in the nursery row, and to firm the soil about the tree. See PLANTING.

CULTIVATION. In common with all fruits, plums do best under tillage — sod-mulch culture should be the exception, never the rule. Tillage consists of plowing in the spring,

---

* Special articles on the subjects indicated by an asterisk (*) will be found at the words so marked.

followed by frequent cultivation until late July when a cover crop of clover, oats, barley, buckwheat or other succulent crop should be planted to be plowed in late autumn or early spring. It may be assumed that if the trees are vigorous and bearing well fertilizers are not needed. When the foliage is light in color, the growth scant, and the fruits small, nitrate of soda might be tried at the rate of 3 to 5 pounds per tree. In garden culture, where most often trees are kept in sod, the grass should be cut and used as a mulch supplemented by manure or straw. Trees so grown nearly always respond to nitrate of soda or its equivalent in some other nitrogenous fertilizer.

Plums cult. under sod (*right*) and under cultivated soil (*left*). A tree under sod produced 65 pounds of fruit, while a tree of the same variety with soil cultivation yielded 83 pounds.

PRUNING. Usually plum trees are trained about a central leader, but some Japanese varieties do well trained to the vase shape. Superfluous branches, those that cross, and one making an acute crotch should be cut out. Pruning should humor the natural growths of the exceedingly variable plum. The Japanese sorts usually require heavy pruning; Domesticas and Damsons, comparatively little; native sorts much to train the scraggling wayward growths.

Many plums do not set fruit even though the trees bloom abundantly. This self-infertility is remedied by planting in neighboring rows varieties which bloom at the same time which will furnish pollen for the sterile variety. Japanese sorts, in particular, are self-sterile. Varieties of the same species are required for cross-pollination.

Out of a hundred or more plums that might be grown east of the Rocky Mountains perhaps 18 may be selected as the best. Seven of these are Domestica sorts; 2 Insititias; 5 Japanese; and 4 Natives. Varieties of the four groups are described in order of ripening.

### DOMESTICAS

WASHINGTON. Fruit light yellow, round-oval, sweet, excellent quality. Tree medium in size, hardiness, and productiveness; home use. Zone* 3 eastward from the Great Lakes.

IMPERIAL EPINEUSE. Fruit purplish-red, prune shape, medium size, very sweet, delicious. Tree large, vigorous, hardy, productive. Zone* 3 eastward from the Great Lakes.

STANLEY. Fruit dark blue, heavy bloom, prune shape, freestone, excellent quality. Tree large, vigorous, hardy, zone* 3 eastward from the Great Lakes.

ITALIAN PRUNE. Fruit purple-black, medium in size, freestone, excellent for culinary use. Tree large, vigorous, hardy. Zone* 3 eastward from Great Lakes.

REINE CLAUDE. Fruit large, yellow, round-oval, sweet, very good. Tree medium in size, hardiness, and productiveness. Zone* 3 eastward from the Great Lakes.

HALL. Fruit dark purple, large, very good, semi-cling. Tree excellent in all characters. Zone* 3 eastward from the Great Lakes.

ALBION. Fruit purple-black, delicate bloom, large, deep suture, clingstone. Tree large, vigorous, hardy, productive. Zone* 3 eastward from the Great Lakes.

### DAMSONS

SHROPSHIRE. Fruit purple-black, heavy bloom, oval, excellent for culinary uses. Tree vigorous, hardy, enormously productive. Zone* 3 eastward from the Great Lakes.

FRENCH. Very similar to Shropshire but fruits larger and of better quality; tree smaller and not so productive. Thrives in the same territory.

### JAPANESE

BEAUTY. Fruit dark red, round-conic, flesh tinged red, excellent quality, clingstone. Tree large, vigorous, productive. Zone* 3, 4, and 5 east of the Mississippi.

ABUNDANCE. Fruit red, roundish, sweet, juicy, good, poor keeper. Tree large, well-formed, hardy, productive. Zones* 3, 4, and 5.

BURBANK. Fruit red, medium size, good. Tree large, but sprawling in habit, hardy, productive. Zones* 3, 4, and 5.

FORMOSA. Fruit very large, oval, sweet, good, clingstone. Tree characters good. Zones* 3, 4, and 5.

SANTA ROSA. Fruit reddish-purple, large, prune-shaped, flesh tinged with red, very good. Tree characters best of all the species. Zones* 3, 4, and 5.

### NATIVES

POTTAWATTOMIE. Fruit medium in size, currant-red, round-oval stone clinging, very good. Tree dwarfish, very productive, very hardy. Zones* 1, 2, 3, 4, and 5 in the Great Plains states.

DE SOTO. Fruit yellow-red, rather large, oval, stone nearly free, very good. Tree small, vigorous, productive. Best of the natives. Zones* 1, 2, 3, 4, and 5 in the Great Plains states.

SURPRISE. Fruit dark red, medium size, round, clingstone, very good. Tree large, vigorous, very productive, hardy. Zones* 1, 2, 3, 4, and 5 in the Great Plains states.

WOLF. Fruit dull crimson, medium size, round-oval, semi-free, sweet, astringent at pit, good. Tree large, vigorous, hardy, productive. Zones* 1, 2, 3, 4, and 5 in Great Plains states.

Planted singly or in groups, the native plums are beautiful ornamentals. No other native plant furnishes so great an abundance of white when in blossom nor so much red when in fruit. — U. P. H.

### PLUMS
#### WEST OF THE ROCKY MOUNTAINS

Although the American species of plums (*Prunus americana*) have wide distribution, commercial production west of the Rockies is confined primarily to rather well-defined areas or districts of California, Oregon, Washington, and Idaho, where the European (*Prunus domestica*) and the Japanese (*Prunus salicina*) types can be grown successfully. Production in California, the principal plum state of the Pacific Coast, is for two primary purposes: for shipping as fresh fruit, and for drying (*see* PRUNE). A small proportion of the crop is canned.

The purpose for which the fruit is produced largely determines both the varieties and the districts in which it is grown. Heaviest production of shipping varieties in California centers in Placer county in the Sierra Foothills, in Sacramento, Solano, and Yolo counties of the Sacramento Valley, in San Joaquin, Tulare, Kern, and Fresno counties in the San Joaquin Valley. These sections are relatively

---

* Special articles on the subjects indicated by an asterisk (*) will be found at the words so marked.

free from spring frosts and fogs. Summer temperatures are usually high. Drying and canning varieties are grown primarily in cooler districts subject to coastal influences. A long growing season and high yields are essential rather than earliness. The Santa Clara Valley, south of San Francisco, is the most important section. Napa and Sonoma counties, north of San Francisco Bay; Tehama, Butte, Glenn, Colusa, and Sutter counties, in the Sacramento Valley; and Tulare County, in the San Joaquin Valley, are also important areas for prune varieties.

In Washington and Oregon, the principal areas for shipping plums are confined primarily to the irrigated valleys with the more important centers adjacent to Yakima and Walla Walla, Washington, the Milton-Freewater section in Washington and Oregon, and the Weiser-Emmett-Boise section in Idaho. The larger production centers in Oregon and Washington are devoted to prune varieties. In the former state, these include the cultivated areas between the Cascade Mountains and the Coast Ranges, while in Washington, production is confined almost exclusively to Clarke County.

VARIETIES. California produces a succession of varieties, ripening from June until September. Of some 25 or more shipping varieties, the more important ones, listed in their approximate order of ripening, are: Beauty, Tragedy, Formosa, Climax, Santa Rosa, Duarte, Wickson, Diamond, Gaviota, Kelsey, Giant, Grand Duke, and President. These vary greatly in size, color, shape, and flavor. The Japanese type and some of their hybrids, represented by Kelsey, Wickson, and Climax, are characterized by large size and by their typical heart shape. Kelsey usually remains a dark green color even when ripe. Duarte possesses red flesh similar to Satsuma. Yellow Egg, Washington, and Jefferson, yellow or green varieties, are preferred for canning. For drying varieties, see PRUNES. Oregon and Washington produce some of the above-named varieties, but most plantings in these states and in Idaho are the Italian prune or Fallenberg, grown both for shipping and for drying.

POLLINATION. Many varieties of plums are unfruitful when pollinated with their own pollen. A few varieties are intersterile. Thus, to insure satisfactory yields, provision should be made for suitable cross-pollination. Varieties may be mixed in the tree rows, or several rows of one kind may alternate with others of similar blooming period. As pollination is affected largely by bees, western orchardists often arrange for colonies to be placed in or near the orchard during the period it is in bloom.

IRRIGATION. Irrigation is desirable in all plum-growing districts and is necessary in most of them. Water is applied either in basins about the trees, or by means of a system of furrows made between each two rows of trees. In hilly foothill sections furrows are most frequently run on the cross-slopes, rather than up and down the hill. The type of soil, topography of the land, the amount of irrigation water available, and its cost largely determine the method of application. Flooding is best adapted with large heads of water on medium to light soil and on flat grades. From 2 to 8 applications may be given annually. Light or shallow soils demand more frequent applications than those more retentive of moisture. The total quantity of water used during a season varies in California from 15 to 30 inches per acre. The chief essential in irrigation practice is to secure good penetration and even distribution.

CULTURE. Cultural operations in most districts on the Pacific Coast are a combination of cultivation, irrigation and cover crops. Where irrigation is practiced these operations are closely related and one may depend upon the other. In most instances the winter cover crop is first plowed or disked under in the spring and the soil pulverized with a disk or spike-toothed harrow. Many of the heavier or adobe soils must be worked at just the proper time, as plowing or disking either too early or too late results in a hard, lumpy soil which remains in this condition throughout the summer.

With the soil put in good condition early in the spring, the frequency of subsequent cultivations will depend primarily upon weed growth and the frequency of irrigations. Cultivations, however, may or may not follow each application of water, this depending largely upon the number of irrigations and the nature of the soil.

In non-irrigated orchards, cultivation for the control of weed growth, particularly the western morning-glory (*Convolvulus arvensis*) is of great importance in maintaining soil moisture. Rank-growing legumes, such as vetch, melilotus, Canada field peas, horse beans, and bur clover, are among the important annual crops. In some of the irrigated orchards of eastern Oregon, eastern Washington, and Idaho, alfalfa is grown as a perennial cover crop. In these orchards the system of management is similar to that described for apples.

PRUNING. At the time of planting, plum trees are usually headed at a height of 18–24 inches. Usually 3–5 main branches are allowed to develop, each of these in turn giving rise to secondary branches. Subsequent training consists of both thinning out and cutting back. Varieties of upright growing habit are thinned to admit sufficient light and to maintain the vigor of the fruit spurs. Upright branches are frequently headed to outside laterals to induce greater spread. Other varieties must be pruned to encourage a more upright growth. With bearing trees, the main function of pruning is to maintain a proper balance between wood growth and fruit production. Because most Japanese varieties set more fruit than can be properly sized or the tree can support, pruning is relatively severe.

THINNING. Although the size of the crop is reduced by severe pruning, hand thinning is also usually necessary in order to secure large-size fruit of even color. Thinning generally follows the so-called "June drop," individual fruits usually being spaced so as to be from 1–3 inches apart when mature. European varieties require less thinning than the Japanese sorts, while prune varieties are rarely thinned.

HARVESTING. The perishable nature of plums necessitates harvesting in the most careful manner, and avoiding unnecessary delay between the time of picking and using. Although handled under refrigeration, considerable ripening takes place in transit and, as from 10–15 days are usually required to deliver the fruit to the consumer after it is harvested, most plums must be picked before they attain their characteristic color. — F. W. A.

For the culture and management of espalier and other forms of trained plum trees, see TRAINING PLANTS.

INSECT PESTS. Control problems are somewhat like those of peach. The San Jose scale and sometimes other scales cause serious injury; they are controlled with dormant sprays. The plum curculio is controlled as on peach; when there are a few trees, something may be accomplished by jarring the beetles from the trees to a sheet early in the morning in spring. Several kinds of aphids, green and brown, attacking plum in the spring may be controlled with nicotine sprays.

The prune plums of the Pacific Coast are attacked by the peach twig borer (see APRICOT) and by several kinds of mites, which are controlled by dormant sprays or by summer sprays of lime-sulphur. The pear thrips, sometimes injurious, can be controlled with a delayed-dormant oil spray with nicotine added. The peach borer sometimes attacks plums (see PEACH). Various leaf feeders are readily controlled with arsenicals. The bark beetles offer the same problems as on apple and peach.

DISEASES. The diseases of the plum are the same as for the cherry (which see for control).

***PLUMARIA, -us, -um*** (ploo-may′ri-a). Plumed.

**PLUMBAGINACEAE** (plum-ba-ji-nay′see-ee). The plumbago family contains among its 10 genera and 300 widely distributed species many plants that have long been favorites among gardeners. Chief among them is *Statice* (the thrift) and *Acantholimon* which is a favorite among rock gardeners. *Limonium* contains both the sea lavender of our salt marshes and other garden plants widely used for dry bouquets. *Ceratostigma* and *Plumbago*, partly shrubby, are plants of warmer climates.

Plants apparently stemless and with basal leaves in a rosette* in *Statice*, *Acantholimon* and *Limonium*, but with obvious stems and alternate* leaves in the other cult. genera. Flowers usually rather showy and regular,* in dense button-like clusters in *Statice* and *Acantholimon*, more open and spreading in the other genera. Fruit dry, usually enclosed by the persistent calyx.

Technical flower characters: Flowers hermaphrodite.* Calyx tubular or funnel-shaped, 5-toothed, bracted* at the base, sometimes colored.

* Special articles on the subjects indicated by an asterisk (*) will be found at the words so marked.

Corolla tubular or of 5, partly united petals. Stamens* 5. Ovary superior,* 1-celled.

**PLUMBAGINOIDES** (plum-ba-ji-noy'deez, but see OÏDES). Resembling a plant of the genus *Plumbago* (which see).

**PLUMBAGO** (plum-bay'go). Leadwort. A genus comprising about 12 species of sub-shrubs or herbs, sometimes climbing or trailing, mostly perennial, of the family Plumbaginaceae, and natives of southern Eu., Af., As. and tropical America. Stems slender. Leaves alternate,* simple, not cut, broadly lance-shaped. Flowers in terminal spikes or clusters, blue, white or red. Individual flower has calyx of 5 sepals sometimes colored. Corolla long, narrow, tubular, with 5 lobes which open saucer-like. (*Plumbago* is from the Latin for lead, but the allusion seems to be obscure.)

Grown mostly in a cool greenhouse, but may be used in the garden in summer months. They make excellent pot plants. Propagated by seeds or cuttings. Seeds should be sown on the surface of sandy peat, slightly covered with sand, in temperature 65°–75° in Feb. or March. Cuttings may be made of young side shoots, 2–3 in. long, inserted in equal parts of sand and peat in propagating frame or under bell-jar in Feb. or Aug. When rooted transplant to potting mixture* 1, finally to potting mixture* 3. If old flowering shoots are cut back, the plants will bloom all summer. They should be allowed to become partially dry through Dec.–Jan., when plants may be cut back, old soil shaken out and re-potted. They should then be kept in a temperature of 65°, when they will soon start into growth.

**capensis**. Tender shrub of spreading habit growing to 8 ft. or more. Leaves alternate, lance-shaped, smooth and thin in texture, 2–3 in. long. Flowers in terminal clusters, azure-blue. Corolla tubular, narrow, to 1½ in. long. Petals 5, spreading saucer-like, ¾ in. across. S. Af. The var. **alba** is a white form. This species most general in cult.
**indica**. Tender shrub of spreading habit. Leaves ovalish, 2–4 in. long. Flowers in long terminal spikes, reddish-purple. Corolla tube 1 in. long. Southern As.
**larpentae** = *Cerastostigma plumbaginoides*.
**scandens**. Toothwort. Tender shrub of spreading habit, rarely vine-like. Leaves broadly lance-shaped, to 5 in. long. Flowers white, the corolla tube ½–¾ in. long. Tropical America.

**PLUMBAGO FAMILY** = Plumbaginaceae.

**PLUMCOT.** A hybrid between the plum and apricot, of more scientific than hort. importance. It was originated by Burbank in 1901 and in 1909 he had 75 thousand seedlings of it at his nursery in Santa Rosa, Calif. Little is heard of it today, although two hort. varieties of it are offered by a few nurseries. The original was named Rutland plumcot by Burbank, and the only other one is a variety called Apex. The fruit is fuzzy-skinned like an apricot, but the flesh is deep red and slightly acid. Little is known of its culture, but it has been grown in Calif., N.Y., and N.J., and thus appears to have a wide climatic tolerance. The fruit is of no commercial importance.

**PLUM CURCULIO.** See Insect Pests at CHERRY, PEACH, and APRICOT.

**PLUME GRASS.** See ERIANTHUS.

**PLUMELESS THISTLE.** See CARDUUS.

**PLUME POPPY** = *Macleaya cordata*.

**PLUMERIA** (ploo-meer'i-a), also spelled *Plumiera*. Frangipani or temple tree. Tropical American, very handsome shrubs and trees of the family Apocynaceae, widely cult. in zone* 9 for their showy, funnel-shaped, fragrant flowers. They have a milky juice, thick, fleshy branches, and alternate* leaves which are feather-veined but also have a prominent marginal vein, without marginal teeth. Flowers in terminal, stalked clusters (cymes*), each flower with bracts* beneath it which soon fall. Corolla lobes slightly twisted, the slender tube long. Stamens* 5. Fruit a pair of leathery pods (follicles*). (Named for Charles Plumier, French botanist.)

Of the 50 known species of *Plumeria*, only four are in common cult. and of these *P. acuminata* is the best known. They flower mostly when leafless, but occasional flowers are produced over a period of several months. The plants are popular in southern Fla., especially the first and last species. They are propagated by cuttings in early spring.

**acuminata**. Pagoda tree. A handsome tree, but not over 20 ft. high. Leaves oblong, 12–16 in. long, about 3 in. wide. Flowers very fragrant, white with a yellow base, the lobes of the corolla longer than the tube. Mex. Sometimes known as *P. acutifolia*.
**acutifolia** = *Plumeria acuminata*.
**alba**. A tree up to 35 ft. high. Leaves lance-shaped or narrower, 7–10 in. long, not over ½ in. wide, the margins rolled, the under surface white-hairy. Flowers white, about 1 in. wide, the lobes of the corolla about as long as the tube. W.I.
**emarginata**. A tree, usually less than 20 ft. high. Leaves ovalish, 5–7 in. long, 2–3 in. wide, slightly notched at the tip, hairy on the under side. Flowers white, the corolla lobes rounded and about 1 in. long. Cuba.
**rubra**. Red jasmine. A shrubby tree, not over 15 ft. high. Leaves oblongish or broadest toward the tip, 12–16 in. long, 3–4 in. wide, pointed. Flowers very fragrant, pink or reddish-purple, about 2 in. long, the blunt lobes of the corolla longer than the tube. Mex. to Venezuela.

**PLUM FAMILY.** See ROSACEAE.

**PLUMIERA** = *Plumeria*.

**PLUMOSA, -us, -um** (ploo-mō'sa). Plumose; i.e. plumed, usually feathery or with fine, silky hairs.

**PLUM TOMATO.** See TOMATO.

**PLUMY COCONUT** = *Arecastrum romanzoffianum*.

**PLUM-YEW.** See CEPHALOTAXUS.

**PLUNGE.** To bury the flower pot in which a plant is growing up to its rim in the soil outdoors or in ashes or sand or moss on the greenhouse bench. Many tender plants are plunged outdoors in the summer, and do far better than if the pot were standing on the surface. The advantages of plunging are that the plant does not dry out as much as if the pot were exposed and that while getting this benefit of growing in the ground, it can still be lifted in the fall without the shock of transplanting or re-potting.

A plant plunged outdoors for the summer

Plunging is a very common hort. operation, especially useful to gardeners forced to leave house plants neglected for a time. If plunged they will often survive without watering for considerable periods, provided they are grown in common, not glazed pots and plunged in the shade. The plants most often plunged are chrysanthemums, calla lily, some alpine plants, *Maranta*, many ferns, camellias, and any other pot plant.

**PLURIFLORA, -us, -um** (plur-i-flow'ra). Many-flowered.

**PNEUMONANTHE** (new-mo-nan'thee). A specific name derived from the genus *Pneumonanthe*, which is scarcely of hort. interest. See GENTIANA.

**POA** (pō'a). Annual and perennial grasses found throughout the temperate and cold regions, comprising about 100 species. They have no decorative value, but are very useful for lawn mixtures or for permanent pastures. (*Poa* is an old Greek name for grass.)

For culture and uses see LAWN.

**compressa**. Canada bluegrass. Wire grass. Perennial, growing to 2 ft. with creeping rootstocks. Leaves bluish-green, to 4 in. long, ⅛ in. wide. Flowers in short, loose clusters. Useful on poor soils and in shady places. Eu., but naturalized in N.A.
**nemoralis**. Wood meadow grass. Coarse perennial, to 3 ft. high, but with spreading habit. Leaves to 5 in. long, ⅛ in. wide. Flowers in long, narrow clusters. Used in shady places for pasture and lawn. Eurasia.
**pratensis**. Kentucky bluegrass. June grass. Perennial to 3 ft. with creeping rootstocks. Stems spreading, hairy at base. Leaves 4–7 in. long, ¼ in. wide. Flowers in pyramidal clusters to 8 in. long. Best lawn or

---

\* Special articles on the subjects indicated by an asterisk (\*) will be found at the words so marked.

pasture grass, and much used in lawn-grass mixtures. Eurasia, and naturalized in N.A. *See* LAWN.

**trivialis.** Perennial to 3 ft. Stems spreading at the base. Leaves to 7 in. long, ¼ in. wide. Flowers in loose clusters 6 in. long. Good for shade mixtures for lawn or pasture (*see* LAWN). Eu., naturalized in N.A.

POACEAE = Gramineae.

**POCKET GOPHERS.** *See* ANIMAL INJURY.

**POCKET PLANTING.** *See* BANKS.

**POD.** Technically, any dry fruit that splits open, as a pea pod. But *pod* and *seed pod* have long lost any technical significance among gardeners, to whom a pod is pretty much any dry fruit that contains seeds.

***PODAGRARIA*** (po-da-gray'ri-a). Greek for foot and chain; *i.e.* the gout. *See* AEGOPODIUM.

**PODALYRIA** (pō-da-lir'i-a). South African evergreen shrubs comprising about 20 species, belonging to the pea family. Leaves alternate,* simple,* ovalish, to 2 in. long. Flowers pea-like, solitary, or in 2–3-flowered clusters, produced in the axils* of the leaves, purple, pink or white. Fruit a roundish pod, covered with silky hairs. (Named for Podalyrius, son of Aesculapius.)

Propagated from seeds sown under glass in early spring and later grown in potting mixture* 3. They are grown outdoors in the southern states, and in Calif.

**calyptrata.** Shrub to 6 ft. Leaves 1–2 in. long, 1 in. wide, hairy on both sides. Flowers pink.

**sericea.** Grows 4–6 ft. high, but of spreading habit. Whole plant covered with soft, silvery hairs. Leaves broadly lance-shaped. Flowers purple.

***PODALYRIAEFOLIA, -us, -um*** (po-da-lir-i-ee-fō'li-a). Having leaves like a plant of the genus *Podalyria*.

***PODOCARPA, -us, -um*** (po-do-kar'pa). Having stalked fruits.

**PODOCARPUS** (po-do-kar'pus). Handsome evergreen trees or shrubs of the family Taxaceae, mostly from the southern hemisphere (one Asiatic) and chiefly from the mountainous parts of it. Of the 60 known species only a few are in cult. in the U.S., mostly in Calif., the Gulf Coast and Fla., and they are doubtfully hardy elsewhere. Leaves alternate,* mostly narrow or ovalish, but not scale-like or needle-like, and not suggesting the foliage of a coniferous evergreen. Male and female flowers on different plants, the male flowers consisting of naked, catkin-like masses of anthers,* the female consisting of a solitary, naked ovule between 1 or 2 small bracts. Fruit fleshy-stalked, mostly plum-like, or berry-like. (*Podocarpus* is from the Greek for foot and fruit, in allusion to the prominent stalk to the fruit.)

The four below grow in a variety of soils and present no difficulties beyond the fact that they will not stand severe frosts. Any area north of zone* 7 is dangerous except possibly for *P. alpina* which is hardier than the others. Occasionally *P. elongata* is grown in the cool greenhouse as a foliage plant. It needs potting mixture* 4, to which a little acid peat should be added.

**alpina.** A densely branched shrub or small tree, not over 15 ft. high. Leaves narrow, about ½ in. long, blunt, dull green above, but paler beneath. Fruit egg-shaped, about ⅓ in. thick, red. Aust. and Tasmania.

**andina.** A tree 15–30 ft. high, densely branched. Leaves practically stalkless, about 1 in. long, narrow, green above, but with 2 whitish bands beneath. Fruit egg-shaped, yellowish-white, about 1 in. long. Chile.

**elongata.** A tree up to 70 ft. high in the wild, much less as cult. and mostly prized in Calif. for its young state, and as a foliage plant. Leaves narrow, 2–3 in. long, pointed and rather thin. Fruit globe-shaped, about ⅓ in. in diameter. Mountains of South Africa and tropical Africa.

**macrophylla.** Much the commonest in cult. in the U S., and a tree 40–60 ft. high. Leaves lance-shaped, 3–4 in. long, dark green above, paler beneath. Fruit egg-shaped, about ½ in. long, greenish-purple, the fleshy stalk purple. Jap. The *var.* **maki,** the maki of the Chinese and Japanese, is usually only a shrub and has smaller, more crowded leaves. China. Less hardy than the typical *P. macrophylla.*

**PODOLEPIS** (pō-doll'e-pis). Australian annual or perennial herbs, comprising about 16 species, found in the family Compositae. Leaves alternate,* long and narrow, covered with short, cotton-like hairs when young. Flowers in terminal heads, yellow, pink or purple. The flower head is surrounded by a ring of numerous, overlapping, thin, transparent bracts,* usually colored. (*Podolepis* is from the Greek for foot and scale, in reference to the bracts.)

In cult. *Podolepis* is usually a half-hardy annual. Propagated by seeds, sown in sandy soil, ⅛ in. deep, in temperature of 55°–65°, under glass. Transplant to porous soil and sunny position outdoors end of May. They may also be sown outdoors at the end of April. When transplanting, space 4 in. apart. Suitable for the rock garden. They can also be used as pot plants, using potting mixture* 4.

**aristata.** Annual, growing to 1 ft. high. Leaves long and narrow, partly clasping the stem. Flower heads solitary, yellow, 1 in. across, surrounded by a whorl of numerous, thin, transparent bracts.*

**PODOPHYLLUM.** *See* MAYAPPLE.

**PODSOL.** White or gray, somewhat ashy soil, found in many regions, its color and texture due to the weathering of organic matter, mostly the litter of the forest. Many podsols ultimately become good garden soils.

**POETAZ NARCISSUS** = *Narcissus poetaz.*

**POET'S NARCISSUS** = *Narcissus poeticus.*

**POGONIA** (po-go'ni-a). Beautiful, mostly bog-inhabiting orchids of the north temperate zone, the only North American cult. species, **P. ophioglossoides,** the rose pogonia, adder's-mouth, or snakemouth being also the only cult. one. It is a 3-leaved bog plant, usually with a single, long-stalked basal leaf, and one or two essentially stalkless stem leaves, 1–3 in. long, and oblongish. Flower solitary, fragrant, nodding, pale rose-purple, with a single bract beneath it. Petals and sepals nearly equal, about 1 in. long. The hanging lip* is beautifully crested and fringed. Eastern N.A. Suited only to the bog garden. June–July. (*Pogonia* is from the Greek for bearded, in allusion to the lip.*)

**POGONIRIS.** *See* IRIS.

**POINCIANA** (poin-si-ā'na). Showy tropical trees or shrubs of the pea family, widely cult. for ornament in warm regions, but in the U.S. their outdoor cult. must be confined to zones* 9 or 8 and the most favorable parts of zone* 7. Both the commonly cult. species are shrubs with alternate,* twice-compound* leaves, the very numerous leaflets arranged in pairs, feather-fashion, and without an odd one at the end. Flowers not pea-like, the 5 broad, separate, showy petals slightly unequal. Stamens* 10, distinct and protruding. Fruit a narrow, flattened pod (legume*). (Named for M. de Poinci, a governor of the French W.I.) For the tree known as the royal poinciana, probably the most showy of all cult. trees, *see* DELONIX.

The two below are cult. throughout most of Fla., the Gulf states, and in Calif. While not as spectacular as the royal poinciana (*see* DELONIX), they are extremely handsome shrubs. Propagated by seeds, which are best soaked in warm water for several hours, as they germinate with difficulty. Later they should be grown along in pots, but may be planted out when a foot or two high. They grow well in a great variety of soils.

**gilliesi.** Bird-of-paradise bush. A shrub or small tree, the branches straggling and sticky-hairy. Leaflets very numerous and small, the foliage thus graceful and feathery. Flowers yellow, the bright red stamens* protruding 4–5 in. and very showy. Pods 3–4 in. long. S.A. Sometimes offered as *Caesalpinia gilliesi.*

**pulcherrima.** Barbados pride; also called Barbados flower-fence and dwarf poinciana. A prickly shrub 6–10 ft. high. Leaflets very numerous, ½–¾ in. long. Flowers orange-yellow, the bright red stamens protruding 2–2½ in. Pods about 4 in. long. Tropical regions and widely cult. there, often under the name of *Caesalpinia pulcherrima.*

**regia** = *Delonix regia.*

**POINSETTIA** (poin-set'ti-a). Tropical American herbs or shrubby plants of the spurge family, two of them widely grown for their gorgeously colored bracts* (often mistaken for flowers). They have a milky juice and alternate,* often lobed, thin leaves. Flowers small, colored, but not very conspicuous because of the brilliantly colored bracts* beneath the small, nearly stalkless cluster. (For flower structure *see* EUPHORBIACEAE.) Fruit a capsule* separating into 3 carpels. (Named for Joel R. Poinsette of S. Car.)

For the culture of the common poinsettia of the florists, which is *P. pulcherrima* and its varieties *see* below. The only

* Special articles on the subjects indicated by an asterisk (*) will be found at the words so marked.

other cult. species, *P. heterophylla*, is mostly grown as a tender annual in warm regions.

**heterophylla.** Mexican fire-plant. A showy annual herb, 1-3 ft. high. Leaves varying from ovalish and unlobed to lobed or fiddle-shaped. The upper leaves pass into the bracts which are red at the base or mottled red and white. In the Mississippi Valley from southern Ill. to Fla. and southward to Peru. Sometimes known as *Euphorbia heterophylla*.

**pulcherrima.** The common poinsettia of the florists; sometimes called painted-leaf. In the wild a shrub 2-10 ft. high or even more; as cult. a handsome winter-blooming pot plant, usually 2-4 ft. high, grown in the greenhouse or outdoors as indicated below. Leaves ovalish or elliptic, 3-6 in. long, usually shallowly lobed or wavy-margined and weakly toothed, the upper leaves passing into the brilliantly colored, vermilion bracts.* Flowers and attendant structures green and yellow. Tropical America. Often known as *Euphorbia pulcherrima*. For the hort. varieties and cult. see below.

### Poinsettia Culture

This showy plant has become a symbol of Yuletide. In southern California and in much of tropical America, it grows luxuriantly out of doors. The typical species has scarlet bracts,* beneath the rather uninteresting greenish-yellow flowers. The double variety is very distinct, having a double series of bracts. There is also a variety with pink bracts and still another with white ones. Some varieties have oak-like leaves, while others have egg-shaped leaves.

Poinsettia is grown in pots singly, or several in one pot. Late-rooted plants are adapted for making an attractive basket if, around early September, a number, established in small-sized pots, can be worked out through the wires of the basket.

Store away in January in a temperature of 50° minimum and keep dry until May, when they may be stood in a temperature of 60° and given water. They may be rooted from the end of June until early September. It is important that the cuttings do not wilt. When taken from the parent plant, prepare for insertion in the propagating bench by cutting below a node* and removing unnecessary leaves. Have water handy to submerge them, thus reducing transpiration.*

Dibble them tightly into sand that has been pounded firmly into the bench, in a house in which the atmosphere is moist and not inclined to airiness. Water thoroughly when inserted and soak every morning after. Spraying the foliage in the late afternoon should be avoided to forestall the appearance of fungous diseases. The glass should have a permanent shading, and on very hot and bright days a further shading of cheesecloth or paper should be used. In from two to three weeks these cuttings will have made sufficient roots to be potted into 2½-in. pots in potting mixture* 1. Shade a few days until the roots have gotten a hold of the soil. Later re-pot in potting mixture* 3 as the demand arises. After the pots are filled with roots, feed twice a week with weak liquid manure. This will be particularly useful, when the bracts are being formed, but cease feeding when the actual flowers begin to show.

For bench growing, plant in potting mixture* 3, about August 15, those that are established, in 4-inch pots.

Poinsettias are sun-loving plants and never form their bracts well if at all shaded. Grow as near the glass as possible and during the summer months the ventilators should always be open. When fall approaches guard against the temperature dropping below 60° and avoid drafts or a too dry condition at the roots, which would result in a losing of foliage. — J. G. E. For the management of gift plants in the house see HOUSE PLANTS.

DISEASES. This plant is susceptible to a disease known as *collar rot*. Yellowing, wilting and death may result from infection. A dark, wet decay of the stem close to the soil line will be noted. Destroy infected plants and use clean or sterilized soil.

**POINSETTIA FAMILY** = Euphorbiaceae.

**POISON ARUM** = *Peltandra virginica*.

**POISON BAIT.** This is used in the control of two sorts of pests. For the bait for insects see Stomach Poisons at INSECTICIDES. For the poison bait used against animal nuisances see ANIMAL INJURY.

**POISON BULB** = *Crinum asiaticum*.

**POISON BUSH.** See SWAINSONA.

**POISON HAW** = *Viburnum molle*.

**POISON HEMLOCK.** Two horticulturally unimportant, Eurasian, biennial herbs comprising the genus **Conium** (ko-ny'um; also kō'ni-um) of the carrot family, the only cult. species **C. maculatum** (sometimes called "winter fern"), a dangerously poisonous plant, and the hemlock that killed Socrates. It is a rank-growing herb, 2-4 ft. high, with finely cut, twice-compound* leaves, the ultimate segments toothed or cut. Flowers minute, white, in many small clusters (umbels*) which are grouped in a compound umbel. Fruit small, flattened, 5-ribbed. It is of no garden interest, but children should be taught to know and avoid it. (*Conium* is the ancient Greek name for it.) For a related, somewhat similar, and also poisonous plant see CICUTA.

**POISON IVY.** The common poison ivy is *Rhus toxicodendron* (which see), and is one of the few native plants that are poisonous by contact. For the difference between poison ivy and Virginia creeper, sometimes confused with it, see the picture at the left. A similar Calif. species, also poisonous, is *Rhus diversiloba*. The plants differ also in their fruit, the poison ivy having small, white, berry-like fruits, while those of the Virginia creeper are black or blackish-purple.

The irritating, non-volatile oil which is secreted upon the leaves of the poison ivy is

Poison ivy (*upper left*) and the Virginia creeper (*lower right*), the leaves of which confuse many.

the cause of the painful, itching skin eruption. If you know you have touched its foliage and can take steps within a few minutes, the best home remedy is to smear the affected part with a paste made of the cheapest laundry soap available. If this is impossible and the skin irritation has already begun, it is advisable to consult a physician at once. While the skin irritation may be no more than a nuisance, it can become serious, and in rare cases fatal. For the eradication of it see Poison Ivy in the list at WEEDS. A related plant is the poison sumac (*Rhus vernix*) of the swamps of eastern N.A. It is a tall shrub with reddish twigs, 7-13 leaflets and white fruits resembling those of poison ivy. It is even more poisonous than poison ivy and the remedies for it are the same as those given above.

**POISONOUS PLANTS.** Fortunately, not many garden plants are dangerously poisonous. Of course any medicinal plant may be poisonous if a considerable amount of it is eaten, and in fact many relatively harmless plants can cause trouble if taken in too large quantities. The only caution needed for such plants is a little common sense and moderation, but no amount of either will save one from the effects of really poisonous plants.

Of the common garden plants or weeds, listed in THE GARDEN DICTIONARY, only the following are really serious. They may be divided into those poisonous by contact, and those which must be eaten. For a description of them turn to the names in the list below.

#### Contact Poisons

POISON IVY and POISON SUMAC. There are at least three poisonous species of *Rhus*: *toxicodendron*, *diversiloba*, and *vernix*. See POISON IVY.

CYPRIPEDIUM. The pink lady's-slipper is occasionally somewhat poisonous.

---

* Special articles on the subjects indicated by an asterisk (*) will be found at the words so marked.

PRIMULA. One greenhouse species is very irritating to some people. It is *Primula obconica*.

URTICA. The nettles have more nuisance value than actually poisonous qualities. The stinging sensation which they cause is usually not lasting.

### POISONOUS ONLY IF EATEN

This group contains all the really serious poisons, some of them deadly. They will be found, with descriptions of their leaves, flowers, and fruit, in the body of THE GARDEN DICTIONARY under the names in boldface type in the list below. If there is the least suspicion that any of them have been eaten by children, who are apt to do much casual nibbling, send for a physician at once. The poisonous part of each is in parentheses.

Aconitum napellus. **Monkshood** (all parts very dangerous).
**Arum maculatum.** Lords-and-ladies (all parts dangerous).
**Atropa belladonna.** Belladonna (all parts deadly).
**Cicuta maculata.** Water hemlock (all parts dangerous).
Conium maculatum. **Poison hemlock** (all parts deadly).
**Datura stramonium.** Jimsonweed (all parts deadly).
**Delphinium.** Most of the larkspurs (foliage).
Digitalis. **Foxglove** (foliage dangerous).
**Helleborus niger.** Christmas rose (root a violent heart poison).
**Hyoscyamus niger.** Henbane (the juice is deadly).
**Kalmia.** Both the native laurels (foliage).
**Laburnum anagyroides.** Golden chain (seeds dangerous).
Nerium oleander. **Oleander** (all parts very dangerous).
**Phytolacca americana.** Poke (root dangerous).
**Prunus serotina.** Wild black cherry (wilted foliage very dangerous). Also the related *P. virginiana*.
**Rhododendron.** All species (foliage).
Ricinus communis. **Caster-oil plant** (seeds deadly).
**Solanum nigrum.** Deadly nightshade (wilted foliage deadly).
**Taxus baccata.** Yew (leaves and fruits dangerous).

These do not exhaust all the poisonous garden plants, but the list includes the worst of them. There are also several very deadly toadstools. See MUSHROOM.

WHAT TO DO. Amateur doctoring for such serious poisons is worse than folly because prompt, expert care may save life. Some of the narcotics may give little indication that their baleful effects have already begun; they cause the so-called "sleep of death." The moment the patient shows the least symptoms (pain, headache, vomiting, drowsiness, or convulsions), send for a doctor at once, and if possible, show him a specimen of the plant causing the trouble.

While some authorities give what are called "home remedies" for various poisonous plants, they are omitted from this book because of the danger from the unskilled use of them. The antidotes to really serious poisons are as dangerous as the poisonous plant itself, and should be given only by a physician.

**POISON SOIL.** See SOILS.

**POISON SUMAC** = *Rhus vernix*. See POISON IVY.

**POKE, POKEBERRY.** See PHYTOLACCA.

**POKER-PLANT.** See KNIPHOFIA.

**POKEWEED.** See PHYTOLACCA.

**POKEWEED FAMILY** = Phytolaccaceae.

**POLECAT-WEED.** See SKUNK-CABBAGE.

**POLEMONIACEAE** (pole-ee-mo-ni-ā'see-ee). The phlox family needs no introduction to most gardeners, and would need none at all if it did not contain several other less-known plants among its 12 genera and over 270 species which, while widely distributed, are most common in N.A. Besides *Phlox*, which is perhaps more widely grown than any other garden flower, the following genera are all hardy: *Collomia*, *Gilia*, *Linanthus*, and *Polemonium*. The only other cult. genera are *Cobaea*, a tendril-climbing vine, and *Cantua*, which is an aromatic shrub. Both are greenhouse plants, the former widely grown as a quick-blooming annual.

Leaves alternate* or opposite,* simple* or compound.* Flowers, especially in the hort. forms of *Phlox*, very showy and profuse, nearly always in clusters, often in corymbs.* Fruit a dry pod (capsule*).

Technical flower characters: Flowers regular* and hermaphrodite.* Calyx often bell-shaped, its lobes 5. Corolla tubular or funnel-shaped, its lobes or teeth 5. Stamens* 5, alternating with the lobes of the corolla and attached to it. Ovary superior,* usually 3-celled, its style 1, but usually 3-branched.

**POLEMONIUM** (pō-lee-mō'ni-um). Hardy perennial, rarely annual, herbs comprising about 20 species belonging to the phlox family, and natives of N.A. or a few found in Eu. and As. Stems fleshy, and ribbed. Leaves alternate,* compound,* long, and with many leaflets opposite,* narrow and lance-shaped, giving the leaves a ladder-like appearance. Flowers in loose, branching clusters, blue, purple, yellow or white. Calyx* of 5 sepals* joined halfway down. Corolla broadly bell-shaped, composed of 5 lobes joined at the base, forming a short tube. Stamens* 5. Fruit a dry, 3-celled capsule which becomes erect when the corolla has withered. (The origin of the name is obscure.)

Propagated by seeds or division of rootstocks. Seeds should be sown in sandy soil, in a cold frame or cool greenhouse in early spring, and transplanted to permanent position as soon as large enough to handle. They will grow in ordinary garden soil. Plant 9–12 in. apart. Division of rootstocks, with the exception of *P. caeruleum*, should be made in March or April, for *P. caeruleum* in Sept. or Oct.

caeruleum. Greek valerian. Jacob's ladder. Charity. Strong-growing, to 3 ft. Leaves crowded at the base, and longer than the stem leaves. Leaflets many. Flowers blue, 1 in. across, drooping, in large clusters. A good border plant. Eu. The *var*. album has white flowers.
carneum. Loosely branching, to 2 ft. Leaflets to 1½ in. long, broadly lance-shaped. Flowers in clusters, salmon-pink, fading to purple, 1½ in. across. Calif. and Ore.
humile. Low-growing, to 9 in. high, with creeping, underground stems. Leaflets small and ovalish. Flowers blue or purple, ½ in. across, in clusters. Suitable for the rock garden and blue garden (*see* BLUE GARDEN). Arctic regions. Sometimes known as *P. richardsoni*. The *var*. pulchellum has violet or white, usually smaller, flowers. It is sometimes offered as *P. pulchellum*.
pulchellum = *Polemonium humile pulchellum*.
reptans. Bluebell. American abscess-root. Growing to 1 ft. of spreading habit, not creeping. Leaflets broadly lance-shaped. Flowers light blue to ¾ in. long, in loose clusters. N.A.
richardsoni = *Polemonium humile*.

**POLIANTHES.** See TUBEROSE.

*POLIFOLIA*, *-us*, *-um* (po-li-fō'li-a). With the whitish leaves of the poly (*Teucrium polium*), a European herb of no garden interest.

*POLITA*, *-us*, *-um* (po-ly'ta). Polished.

**POLLARD.** A tree so pruned that all its main branches are cut back to the trunk. Pollarding is a brutal sort of pruning, sometimes practiced to induce a dense, globe-like mass of foliage. It probably originated for the production of osiers, which are very plentiful on willow trees that have been pollarded. See *Salix viminalis* at WILLOW.

**POLLEN.** The male element in the process which culminates in the fertilization of the ovule in all flowering plants. It is borne by the anther* and is usually a mass of yellow, dust-like or sticky particles, the pollen grains. Each pollen grain, if deposited upon a receptive stigma,* may result in the fertilization of an ovule. For some interesting figures on the viability of pollen, *see* CROSSING. See also POLLINATION and FERTILIZATION.

**POLLEN TUBE.** See FERTILIZATION.

**POLLINATION.** The act or process by which pollen is transferred from an anther* to a stigma.* It is the first step in fertilization, but far from the completed impregnation of the ovule. See FERTILIZATION.

The main agents in pollination are insects, which carry

---

* Special articles on the subjects indicated by an asterisk (*) will be found at the words so marked.

from flower to flower a considerable cargo of pollen. Often the visit of the insect is not for the pollen but for nectar,* which it uses in the making of honey. But in the process of getting the nectar most insects get pollen-dusted, which means that they are ready to act as pollen carriers. Another very usual method of pollination is by the wind, which carries the pollen of all grasses, sedges, pines, and most catkin-bearing trees. Among aquatic plants, the water, especially in submerged species, acts as a pollen carrier. In the tropics bats and snails also carry pollen. The last, and from the breeding standpoint, the most important method is artificial pollination. Upon the ability of the plant breeder to accomplish this depends the making of hybrids or crossing. For the details of artificial pollination see CROSSING. See also BEES AND BEE PLANTS.

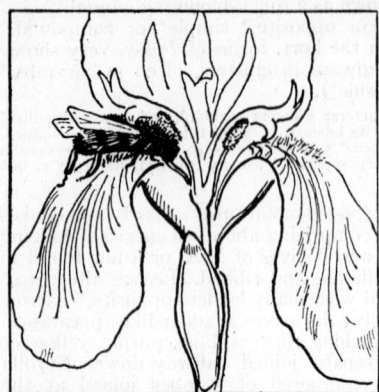

Bees and butterflies are the most common agencies of pollination, but wind, water, snails, and bats are also pollinators.

**POLYACANTHA**, *-us, -um* (pol-i-a-kan'tha). Many-spined.

**POLYANDRA**, *-us, -um* (pol-i-an'dra). With many stamens.

**POLYANTHA**, *-us, -um* (pol-i-an'tha). With many flowers.

**POLYANTHA ROSES.** See Group 3 at ROSE.

**POLYANTHEMOS** (pol-i-an'thee-mos). Many-flowered.

**POLYANTHUS NARCISSUS** = *Narcissus tazetta*.

**POLYCOTYLEDON.** A plant sprouting with more than two seed leaves (cotyledons), as the pine and its relatives. Most garden plants have one seed leaf (monocotyledonous) or two seed leaves (dicotyledonous).

**POLYGALA** (pol-lig'a-la). Milkwort. A large genus of hardy or tender, annual and perennial herbs or sub-shrubs, a few tree-like, comprising over 500 species of the family Polygalaceae, found throughout the world, about 40 species in N.A. Leaves alternate,* lance-shaped. Flowers in terminal clusters, or spikes, in some species showy. Colors various. Calyx* of 5 sepals,* 3 small, 2 large, sometimes colored. Petals 4–5. Fruit a 2-celled capsule, sometimes winged. (*Polygala* is from the Greek for much milk, in reference to a superstition that some species increased the supply of cow's milk.)

The tropical species are unusual in cult. Propagate by cuttings taken in spring. Cuttings should be inserted in sandy peat in temperature of 55°–65°, under a bell-jar in shady position. When rooted pot into potting mixture* 2, potting on in potting mixture* 3. After final potting water freely and stand outdoors in summer months. The tender one below can also be grown outdoors in the southern states and in Calif. Hardy species are propagated by seeds and cuttings. Seeds may be sown in fall or early spring in sandy soil in a cold frame and transplanted to permanent position as soon as large enough to handle. Cuttings should be made in Sept., inserted in sandy peat in a cool greenhouse or cold frame.

**dalmaisiana.** Tender hybrid shrub, 3–6 ft. high. Leaves ovalish, to 1 in. long, not stalked. Flowers in terminal racemes,* purplish-red, the lower petal whitish. Long flowering period.

**lutea.** Orange milkwort. A very showy hardy annual. Flowers yellow, in dense terminal cluster. Suited only to the bog garden (which see). L.I. to Fla. near the coast. Summer.

**paucifolia.** Flowering wintergreen. Fringed polygala. Gay-wings. Trailing perennial 3–6 in. high. Lower leaves small and scale-like, upper leaves clustered, ovalish, 1½ in. long. Flowers reddish-purple, sometimes white, in 1–4 flowered clusters. Corolla conspicuously fringed. New Brunswick to Ga. in rich woods, and suited only to the wild garden. May.

**senega.** Seneca or senega snakeroot. Perennial, 1–1½ ft. high. Leaves lance-shaped, to 2 in. long. Flowers small, greenish-white in terminal spikes. June. Roots used medicinally. See MEDICINAL PLANTS.

**POLYGALACEAE** (pol-lig-a-lay'see-ee). The milkwort family comprises about 10 genera and over 700 species of herbs, shrubs, and trees, some of them found nearly throughout the world, but wanting in N. Zeal. and a few other places. The only cult. genus is *Polygala*, which see for the characters of the garden Polygalaceae.

*POLYGAMA*, *-us, -um* (pol-lig'a-ma). Polygamous; *i.e.* with both perfect* and imperfect flowers. See HERMAPHRODITE.

**POLYGONACEAE** (pol-lig-o-nay'see-ee). The buckwheat or rhubarb family is important because of these two plants, rather than for its genera of plants with showy flowers. Among its perhaps 35 genera and over 800 species of herbs, shrubs, vines, and trees, of very wide distribution, only a handful are grown for ornament. Of these *Antigonon*, which is a showy tropical vine, is easily first. *Eriogonum* comes perhaps second, and comprises many herbs from the western U.S. *Polygonum*, except for a few species, is largely weedy, and *Rumex* (the dock) is chiefly a pest (see the list at WEEDS).

The two economic genera are *Rheum* (see RHUBARB) and *Fagopyrum* (see BUCKWHEAT). The only other cult. genera are tropical. They are *Muehlenbeckia* and *Coccolobis*, both shrubs or trees of little garden interest.

Most of the plants have jointed stems. Leaves simple,* but very various as to arrangement and shape, their stalks, however, always surrounded by a split, membranous or chaffy sheath near the base. True flowers scarcely showy, without petals, but often grouped in relatively handsome clusters, the color of which is due to bracts* or wing-like structures in the flower. Fruit small, dry (an achene*), sometimes surrounded by remains of the flower, occasionally fleshy, or prominently winged.

Technical flower characters: Flowers mostly hermaphrodite.* Sepals 2–6, sometimes united and colored, but scarcely petal-like, often merely chaffy. Petals none. Stamens* 2–9. Ovary superior,* usually 1-celled.

**POLYGONATUM.** See SOLOMON'S-SEAL.

**POLYGONUM** (pol-lig'o-num). Smartweed. Knotweed. Erect, trailing or climbing, annual or perennial herbs, the climbing species sometimes woody, comprising about 200 species of the family Polygonaceae. They are found throughout the world, their habits being very diverse. Stems angled, swollen at the joints where leaf base clasps the stem, sometimes spotted or streaked brown. Leaves alternate* and simple. Flowers small, in terminal spikes or loose racemes. Calyx of 5 sepals generally colored pink or white. Corolla absent. Stamens* 3–9. Fruit dry, triangular, 1-celled, 1-seeded. (*Polygonum* is from the Greek for many-jointed, in allusion to the stems.)

Easy of cult., but only a few species worth it, these generally being climbers which are grown for their foliage and flowers. All are useful bee plants. Propagated by seeds, cuttings and division of rootstocks. Annuals are propagated from seed (*see* ANNUALS). Perennials may be propagated from seeds sown in cool greenhouse or cold frame in early spring, transplanting to permanent positions as soon as large enough to handle. Cuttings of the woody species may be made by taking pieces of the hard wood about 8 in. in length, in Dec. Insert them in sand to ½ their length in a cold frame, where they should be left until the following April, when callus will have formed. They may then be planted in permanent position in ordinary garden soil in sun or shade. Perennial rootstocks may be divided in March or April. Perennials should be given manure annually.

**affine.** Hardy perennial with creeping rootstock. Leaves basal, lance-shaped, brownish in color, 6 in. or more long, margins finely toothed. Flowering stalk to 1¾ ft. Flowers in dense spikes, 2–3 in. long, bright rose in color. Fall. For cult. see ROCK GARDEN. High Himalayas.

* Special articles on the subjects indicated by an asterisk (*) will be found at the words so marked.

**amplexicaule.** Mountain fleece. Hardy perennial, with spreading rootstock, which is also woody. Stems green, growing to 3 ft. Leaves ovalish, margins wavy. Upper leaves clasping the stem, lower leaves short-stalked. Flowers in terminal spikes, to 6 in. long, rose or white. July. Good border plant. High Himalayas.

**auberti.** Silver-lace vine. Fleece-vine. Chinese fleece-vine. Lace-vine. Hardy, twining, woody perennial with slender stems growing to 25 ft. Leaves to 2½ in. long, alternate, broadly lance-shaped. Flowers greenish-white, fragrant, in long, erect or drooping clusters, growing from the axils* of the leaves near top of plant. Aug. Excellent for pergola or trellis (see VINES). Western China and Tibet.

**aviculare.** Knotweed. See list at WEEDS.

**baldschuanicum.** Similar to *P. auberti*, but with larger rose-colored flowers, in numerous, dense clusters. Aug. Bokhara.

**convolvulus.** Black bindweed. See list at WEEDS.

**cuspidatum.** Strong-growing, hardy perennial, to 8 ft. high. Leaves roundish, and sharply pointed, base of leaf clasping stem, to 5 in. long. Flowers small, greenish-white, numerous, in loose clusters growing from the axils* of the leaves. Late summer and early fall. Jap. Often offered as *P. sieboldi* or *P. zuccarini*. The *var.* **compactum** is a dwarf form about 2 ft. high.

**orientale.** Prince's-feather. Annual growing to 6 ft. high, hairy, much-branched. Leaves ovalish, 6-10 in. long, base of leaf clasping the stem. Flowers pink or rose, in branching spikes, to 3 in. long. Flowers clustered on the spikes. Fall. As. and Aust., naturalized in N.A.

**persicaria.** Lady's thumb. Annual to 2 ft. Leaves lance-shaped, with dark brown spot near the middle. Flowers pink, sometimes greenish in dense spikes 2 in. long. Summer. A garden weed (see list at WEEDS). Eu., naturalized in America.

**sieboldi** = *Polygonum cuspidatum*.

**zuccarini** = *Polygonum cuspidatum*.

**POLYLOPHA, -us, -um** (pol-i-lō'fa). Much-crested or much-tufted.

**POLYMORPHA, -us, -um** (pol-i-mor'fa). Many- or variously formed.

**POLYPETALOUS.** With separate petals. See the illustration at GAMOPETALOUS.

**POLYPHYLLA, -us, -um** (pol-i-fil'la). Many-leaved.

**POLYPODIACEAE** (pol-i-po-di-ā'see-ee). The polypody family comprises most of the common ferns of cult., both hardy and tropical. For the others (largely tree ferns and a few unimportant genera) see CYATHEACEAE, OPHIOGLOSSACEAE, OSMUNDACEAE and SCHIZAEACEAE.

The ferns have simple or much-dissected, or compound leaves, usually called fronds, of the greatest diversity of shape, but widely cult. because of their beauty. For the hort. uses and culture of ferns see FERNS AND FERN GARDENING. All the ferns agree in having their young leaves start in a crossier-like coil, which in some tropical genera is very large and striking, often being clothed with a shaggy or velvety sheath. Scarcely any have a distinct trunk, as do the tree ferns, but some are woody at the base and many have very stout rootstocks.*

The family is a huge one, comprising in its many genera and over 5000 species perhaps three-quarters of all known forms, which in former geological periods were far more numerous than now. None produce flowers. For a description of the organs that replace flowers and for the function of the dust-like spores found on the back of many fern fronds see FERNS AND FERN GARDENING.

Because the characters that differentiate the ferns are wholly technical (residing in the microscopic spores* and how they are borne) the following cult. genera are grouped mostly upon how they are grown. Some of the genera are in more than one group due to the great diversity of geographical range in which they grow.

1. **Fern genera mostly for the outdoor fern garden or for the wild garden.**
   *Adiantum, Asplenium, Athyrium, Camptosorus, Cheilanthes, Cryptogramma, Cystopteris, Dennstaedtia, Dryopteris, Onoclea, Pellaea, Phyllitis, Polypodium, Polystichum, Pteridium, Pteretis, Woodsia* and *Woodwardia*.

2. **Fern genera in which some or all of the species require greenhouse culture, some needing much heat and moisture.**
   *Adiantum, Asplenium, Blechnum, Coniogramme, Cyclophorus, Cyrtomium, Davallia, Doodia, Dryopteris, Elaphoglossum, Hemionitis, Nephrolepis, Odontosoria, Onychium, Pityrogramma, Platycerium, Polypodium, Polystichum* and *Pteris*.

3. **Fern genera containing the most widely grown greenhouse species.**
   Used as decorative plants by florists, for centerpieces, window boxes, house plants, etc.
   *Adiantum, Cyrtomium, Davallia* (for hanging baskets and fern balls), *Doodia, Nephrolepis* (includes the Boston fern), *Odontosoria, Onychium, Pityrogramma,* and *Pteris*.

From these three groups, and from the cultural notes at FERNS AND FERN GARDENING, the enthusiast can make a selection to suit his fern needs. See also each of the genera for description of the species and for further notes.

**POLYPODIOIDES** (pol-i-po-di-oy'deez, but see OÏDES). Resembling a polypody.

**POLYPODIUM** (pol-i-pō'di-um). Polypody. An immense genus of ferns of the family Polypodiaceae, scattered all over the world, and of such diverse habit that some are hardy ferns of our woodlands, some tropical tree-perchers (epiphytes*), and one is commonly called the resurrection fern. Nearly all have a creeping rootstock (rhizome) from which the frond stalks arise, and upon which they leave a scar when falling off. While the genus contains hundreds of species, only a handful are in cult. and none is of first-class hort. importance. They have simple or compound* fronds upon the back of which are the conspicuous, round, naked spore* cases. (*Polypodium* is from the Greek for many feet, in allusion to the often branched rhizome.*)

The first and second species are greenhouse ferns, the hare's-foot polypody being rather widely cult. as it is a good house plant. For their culture see FERNS AND FERN GARDENING. The common polypody (*P. vulgare*) is useful only in the outdoor fern garden, preferably in the shade and in a moderately acid soil.

**aureum.** Hare's-foot fern; also called golden polypody. A stout, rather coarse fern 2-4 ft. high, its copious rootstock brown and scaly and very apt to creep out of the pot in which it is grown. Fronds long-stalked, the blade simple,* oblong, 12-18 in. long, the margins deeply cut on the lower half of the frond, the segments 6-12 in. long and about 1 in. wide, the whole frond green or deep bluish-green. Tropical America, and the source of several hort. forms, some of them prominently bluish-green. There are also crested, or fringed or wavy-leaved forms (*P. mandaianum*), probably originating as mutations. Often offered as *Phlebodium aureum*.

**polypodioides.** Resurrection fern. A drought-resistant fern, mostly growing on trees, and the most abundant of all epiphytic* ferns in Fla. Fronds 5-7 in. long, 1-2 in. wide, cut into oblong segments, evergreen.

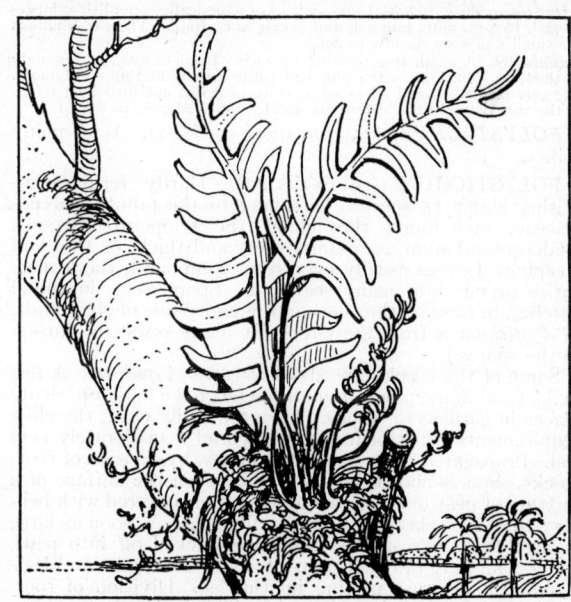

The resurrection fern (*Polypodium polypodioides*) in its growing state. When dry it curls up into a ball-like mass.

* Special articles on the subjects indicated by an asterisk (*) will be found at the words so marked.

In the dry season the fronds are coiled so that the plant is a mere ball of apparently dead leaves, but in moist conditions opening and continuing growth — hence its name of resurrection fern. (For an account of a still more extraordinary resurrection plant see ANASTATICA.) Southeastern U.S. southward to tropical America.

**vulgare.** The common polypody of European woodlands; also called wall fern. A very common fern (the North American form sometimes designated as *P. virginianum*) with fronds practically evergreen, 1–2 ft. long, 3–5 in. wide, deeply cut into segments that are 1½–2 in. wide, the segments near the middle of the frond longer than the lower ones. Eurasia. N.A., and common on banks, rocky ledges, or even on trees in the South. Of easy culture in woods soil.

**POLYPODY.** See POLYPODIUM.

**POLYPODY FAMILY** = Polypodiaceae.

**POLYPTERIS** (pol-lip'ter-is). North American herbs comprising 4 species belonging to the family Compositae, of erect branching habit, to 4 ft. high. Leaves alternate,* simple. Flowers purplish, rose or pale pink, in loose, clustered heads. Heads surrounded by 2 whorls of bracts,* generally colored at the tips. Ray flowers showy. Fruit 4-sided. (*Polypteris* is from the Greek for many-winged, in allusion to the pappus.)

Not of much garden importance, only *P. hookeriana* in cult. It is a hardy annual (see ANNUALS). *Polypteris* likes sandy soil and sunny positions.

**hookeriana.** Also known as *Othake sphacelata*. Strong-growing annual, to 4 ft. high, slightly hairy and sticky. Leaves lance-shaped, to 4 in. long. Flower heads 1 in. or more across. Ray florets reddish, deeply divided into 3 segments, to ½ in. long. Whorls of bracts tipped purple. Neb. to Tex.

**POLYSCIAS** (pol-lis'i-as). A large genus of tender, showy shrubs and trees of the family Araliaceae, with handsome foliage. They are natives of tropical Af., India and the Pacific Islands. Leaves compound,* variable in shape and color. Flowers inconspicuous, whitish-green in clustered umbels*; rarely seen in cult. Fruit small, berry-like. (*Polyscias* is from the Greek for many and shade, in reference to the abundant foliage and shade.)

Chiefly grown as greenhouse foliage plants, although grown outdoors in the South. They need potting mixture* 5, a warm, moist greenhouse and plenty of water. The color of the foliage is best produced under partial shade. Most of what the florists call aralias belong here.

**balfouriana.** Densely branched, spreading tree to 25 ft. Stem grayish-green. Leaves long-stalked, swollen and clasping at the base. Leaflets generally 3, roundish, to 4 in. across, coarsely toothed, sometimes white at the margins. New Caledonia.

**filicifolia.** Strong-growing shrub, to 8 ft. Leaves varied in form. Leaflets to 1 ft. long, many, sometimes deeply cut into many segments, or entire,* even on the same plant. Pacific Islands.

**fruticosa.** Shrub to 8 ft. Leaves with 3 or more leaflets, ovalish or lance-shaped, to 4 in. long, toothed, and deeply cut. India. The *var.* **plumosa** has small and very narrow leaflets.

**guilfoylei.** A small tree growing to 20 ft. Leaflets ovalish, remotely toothed, to 5 in. long, often blotched white on the margin. Polynesia. The *var.* **laciniata** has leaflets with white margins, cut into long teeth. In the *var.* **victoriae** the leaflets are divided into many segments.

*POLYSTACHYA, -us, -um* (pol-i-stack'i-a). With many spikes.

**POLYSTICHUM** (pol-lis'ti-kum). Hardy ferns, comprising about 15 species, belonging to the family Polypodiaceae, and found throughout the temperate regions. Underground stem, sometimes short and thick, or thin and creeping. Leaves usually evergreen, compound, the leaflets entire or cut into many segments. Spore cases in round patches, in rows on the veins on the under side of the fronds. (*Polystichum* is from the Greek for many rows, in allusion to the spores.)

Some of the species are also known as *Aspidium*. A few make good house plants, but all can be grown in damp, shady places in gardens or woods. They are easily cult., the chief requirements being plenty of water and a moderately acid soil. Propagated from spores,* but a few by division of rootstocks. Spores should be sown in pans on the surface of a mixture of peat moss, sand and loam, then covered with bell-jar and shaded, keeping damp at all times. As soon as large enough to handle, plants should be pricked off into pans, using a mixture of equal parts of sand, loam, peat and leafmold. Finally, use potting mixture* 5. Division of rootstocks may be made in early spring. This is also the best time for making new plantings.

**acrostichoides.** Also known as *Dryopteris acrostichoides*. Dagger fern. Christmas fern. A hardy, evergreen fern, the fronds to 2 ft. long, in dense clusters growing from the crown of the stem. Fertile leaves, that is, those bearing spores have shorter leaflets than the sterile leaves. Leaflets lance-shaped, 1–2 in. long, slightly toothed. Suitable for house plant. Eastern U.S.

**brauni.** Prickly shield fern. Rootstock thick, growing obliquely. Leaves to 2 ft., forming a ring round crown of stem. Leafstalks covered with hair-like scales. Leaflets in pairs, narrow and pointed, the margins toothed. Leaves die down in fall. N.A. and Eu.

**falcatum** = *Cyrtomium falcatum*.

**lonchitis.** Mountain holly fern. Hardy, evergreen, the fronds nearly 2 ft. long, stiff and leathery. Leaflets lance-shaped, to 1½ in. long. N.A., Eu. and As.

**munitum.** Giant holly fern. Hardy, evergreen, the leafstalks to 1 ft. long, covered with chaffy scales. Leaves to 3½ ft. long, the leaflets long and narrow, sharply toothed, sometimes cut into segments. Western N.A.

**tsus-simense.** Small. Leaves to 18 in. long, thin, dark green. Leaflets narrow. Suitable for fern dishes or hanging baskets. Jap.

**POMACEAE.** See ROSACEAE.

**POMADERRIS** (pō-ma-der'ris). Tender shrubs and trees, found in Aust., N.Z., and the South Pacific Islands, comprising about 22 species, belonging to the family Rhamnaceae. Leaves alternate,* simple.* Flowers in loose clusters, growing from the axils* of the leaves, near the ends of the branches. Individual flowers numerous, small. Calyx greenish-white. Corolla none. Fruit, a small 3-celled capsule.* (*Pomaderris* is from the Greek for lid and skin, in allusion to the capsule covering.)

Only one species is cult., grown in the southern states and Calif. for ornament. Propagated by cuttings of half-ripened shoots in July, inserted in a mixture of sandy peat under glass.

**apetala.** Tainui. A small tree to 20 ft. Leaves ovalish, 3–4 in. long, with white-woolly hairs on the under side, brownish on the veins. Flowers greenish-white, in long, loose clusters, 3–7 in. long. Aust. and N.Z.

**POMARIUM.** An old name for a fruit orchard. See FRUIT CULTURE.

**POMATO.** A true chimera,* produced by grafting tomato cions on potato stock, and more of a scientific curiosity than a hort. subject. It has fragrant, tomato-like, juicy fruit, used as is the tomato. See CHIMERA. It was originally called potomato, and the grafts were made either way. In those in which potato was the stock and the tomato the cion, it was thought that the resulting plant would produce potatoes under ground and tomatoes in the air — an illusory hope.

**POME.** Typically, the fruit of an apple, pear, quince, hawthorn, and related plants. It is technically a fleshy fruit without a stone, but having several seeds, usually within a papery or bony chamber at the center, which is all that remains of the ripened ovary. The fleshy, juicy part of a pome is mostly the much-enlarged receptacle.*

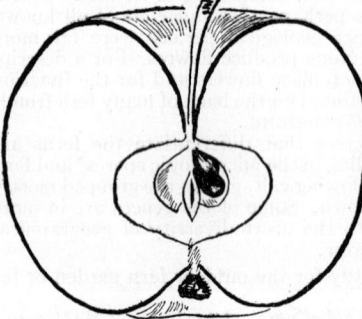

Cross-section of an apple (pome). For details see text.

**POMEGRANATE.** A delicious, but little-known fruit in the U.S., and thought by some to be insipid here, but prized for centuries abroad. It is derived from the only cult. species of the genus **Punica** (pew'-ni-ka) of the family Punicaceae. The common pomegranate is **P. granatum**, an Asiatic shrub or small tree, 10–20 ft. high, and hardy outdoors only in zones* 7, 8 and 9. It often has spiny-tipped branches and opposite,* short-stalked, oblongish or oval-oblong, shining leaves, 1½–3 in. long. Flowers in small clusters of 1–5, at the ends of short shoots borne in the

---

* Special articles on the subjects indicated by an asterisk (*) will be found at the words so marked.

leaf-axils.* Calyx leathery, partly tubular, the 5-7 lobes persistent on the fruit. Corolla of 5-7 separate, wrinkled, orange-red petals, the flowers about 1¼ in. wide. Stamens* numerous. Fruit a fleshy, several-chambered, brownish-yellow or red berry, orange-sized, the juicy flesh crimson and slightly acid. (*Punica* is the old name for Carthage, the pomegranate having once been called the apple of Carthage.)

### Pomegranate Culture

The pomegranate, one of the oldest of cultivated fruits and well known to Theophrastus, is not much grown in the U.S., where its outdoor cult. is confined to zones* 7, 8, and 9. Calif. and Fla. are best suited to it, but in the latter state it is chiefly grown for home use or for ornament.

The trees, if grown for the best fruit, should be set 15-20 ft. apart each way, and the numerous shoots from the base should be cut out in order to make the plant more compact and tree-like. It will grow well in a great variety of soils, and where not grown for fruit, makes an extremely attractive hedge, as its flowering period may last several weeks (April-May), and the showy fruit ripens in July-Aug.

The easiest method of propagation is to use the numerous shoots that spring up around all pomegranate trees.

If fruit is the desired aim, the best varieties are Wonderful, Sweet, Acid, and Dwarf. If the plant is grown mostly for ornament, and it is very decorative, the best varieties are Double Dwarf, Double Acid, Double Red, and several other double-flowered sorts that do not produce edible fruit. Some of these decorative forms, and even the fruiting pomegranate, are occasionally grown in the cool greenhouse for ornament. They are then kept pruned and make handsome plants for pot or tub. Use potting mixture* 4.

**POMEGRANATE FAMILY** = Punicaceae.

**POMEGRANATE MELON.** See MELON.

**POMELO** = *Citrus paradisi*. See GRAPEFRUIT.

**POMERIDIANA, -us, -um** (po-mer-id-i-ā′na). Flowering in the afternoon.

**POMICULTURE** = Fruit culture.

**POMME BLANCHE** = *Psoralea esculenta*.

**POMO-GREEN.** Trademarked insecticides and fungicides sold with directions for use against leaf-eating insects and various plant diseases.

**POMOLOGY.** Fruit culture; and especially the study of various varieties of fruit.

**POMPELMOUS** = *Citrus maxima*.

**POMPON.** A hort. term for button-like heads of flowers, much smaller and usually more compact than the ordinary flower heads of the plant. Pompons are found among varieties of chrysanthemum and dahlia, and in a few other groups. See CHRYSANTHEMUM, DAHLIA.

**PONCIRUS** (pon-sy′rus). A single, spiny, deciduous* species of Chinese trees of the family Rutaceae and the hardiest of all the citrus fruits, although its fruit is inedible. The only species is **P. trifoliata** (sometimes known as *Citrus trifoliata*), the hardy or trifoliate orange, grown for ornament from zone* 4 southward, where it forms impenetrable, defensive hedges. It is also used as grafting stock for the more tender citrus fruits. The tree, sometimes called the trifoliate orange, is rarely over 20 ft. high, its spines mostly about ¾ in. long. Leaves alternate,* compound,* its 3 leaflets oval or oblong, 2-3 in. long, the stalk winged. Flowers white, nearly 2 in. wide, flattish, the 5 petals oblongish and longer than the sepals. Stamens* 8-10. Fruit orange-like, but scarcely over 2 in. in diameter, its flesh dryish, very acid, but fragrant. (*Poncirus* is from the French *poncire*, for a kind of citron.)

**POND-APPLE** = *Annona glabra*.

**PONDEROSA, -us, -um** (pon-der-rō′sa). Heavy or massive.

**PONDEROSA LEMON.** See LEMON.

**PONDEROSA PINE** = *Pinus ponderosa*. See PINE.

**PONDS.** See WATER.

**PONGAMIA** (pon-gay′mi-a). A genus of only one species of trees of the pea family, found in tropical As. and Aust. and cult. in southern Fla. and Calif. for ornament. The only species is **P. pinnata**, the Kurum oil tree, or Poonga oil tree, which grows up to 40 ft. Leaves compound,* bright green, leathery, strongly aromatic. Leaflets 5-7, in pairs, ovalish. Flowers pea-shaped, reddish-pink to white, in loose racemes 5 in. long growing from the axils* of the leaves. Fruit a short pod, 1 to 2 in. long and 1 in. wide, woody and flat, its one seed containing a thick, reddish-brown oil. (*Pongamia* is a Latinized version of a Malayan name for the tree.)

**PONTEDERIA** (pon-te-deer′i-a). Pickerelweed. American, hardy, perennial aquatic herbs of 2 or 3 species of the family Pontederiaceae. They have strong-growing rootstocks, creeping horizontally in the mud of shallow pools. Leaves long-stalked. Flowers blue, in spikes. Individual flowers funnel-shaped, 2-lipped,* both the upper and lower lips being divided into 3 lobes. Blooms profusely but fades quickly. (Named for G. Pontedera, an Italian botanist.) Useful for shallow pools, edges of ponds, slow-moving streams and for the bog garden. Propagated by division of rootstocks in early spring.

**cordata.** Pickerelweed; called also alligator wampee. Grows to 4 ft., usually in clumps. Leaves roundish, arrowhead-shaped at base, to 10 in. long, and 6 in. wide. Base of leafstalk sheathed. Flowers in spikes, blue, with 2 yellow or white spots on the upper lip. There is also a narrow-leaved form. Eastern N.A.

**PONTEDERIACEAE** (pon-te-deer-i-ā′see-ee). The pickerelweed family includes only two cult. genera, *Pontederia*, the pickerelweed, and *Eichhornia* (see WATER HYACINTH). Both are aquatic, the first native in America and very showy in pools with its midsummer bloom. The water hyacinth, often a pest in tropical rivers, is a beautiful floating plant suitable for greenhouse pools or for outdoor culture in the summer. The family comprises only 6 genera and perhaps 20 species, found throughout the world except Eu.

Leaves spongy and floating in *Eichhornia*, erect and narrow or heart-shaped in *Pontederia*. Flowers irregular,* crowded in spikes, very showy in both genera. Fruit dry, a 1-seeded utricle* in *Pontederia*, and a dry pod (capsule*) surrounded by the withered flower parts in *Eichhornia*.

Technical flower characters: Flowers with the six segments colored alike, hence not easily separable into sepals or petals, more or less funnel-shaped, but irregular.* Stamens* 3 or 6, often long-protruding, of unequal length. Ovary superior,* 3-celled.

**PONTICA, -us, -um** (pon′ti-ka). From Pontus, an old name for a region south of the Black Sea in Asia Minor.

**POOLROOT** = *Eupatorium aromaticum*.

**POOLS.** See WATER.

**POONGA OIL TREE** = *Pongamia pinnata*.

**POOR MAN'S-MANURE.** See SNOW.

**POOR MAN'S-ORCHID.** See SCHIZANTHUS.

**POOR MAN'S-WEATHERGLASS.** The scarlet pimpernel. See the list at WEEDS.

**POOR ROBIN'S-PLANTAIN** = *Erigeron pulchellus*.

**POPCORN** = *Zea mays everta*. See CORN.

**POPINAC** = *Acacia farnesiana*. For the white popinac see LEUCAENA GLAUCA.

**POPLAR.** For the true poplars see POPULUS. For another tree sometimes called poplar see TULIP-TREE.

**POPPLE.** See POPULUS.

**POPPY.** For the true poppies (*Papaver*), see the next main entry. Many other plants also have *poppy* as part of their names. Those in THE GARDEN DICTIONARY are: Argemone, Dendromecon, Eomecon, Eschscholtzia, Glaucium, Hunnemannia, Hydrocleis, Macleaya, Meconopsis, and Romneya.

---

* Special articles on the subjects indicated by an asterisk (*) will be found at the words so marked.

# POPPY

**POPPY.** The true poppies all belong to the genus **Papaver** (pap'a-ver), and comprise a large group of annual or perennial herbs of the family Papaveraceae, found mostly in the temperate regions of Eu. and As. and a few in western N.A. They vary in height from 6 in. to 4 ft. Leaves basal, generally many and usually deeply segmented and hairy. Flowers solitary, on a long, flowering stalk, when in bud nodding but straightening as the flower opens. Calyx* of 2 sepals,* which fall when the petals open. Corolla of 5 petals, vividly colored red, violet, yellow or white, sometimes blotched at the base. Stamens* numerous. Fruit a capsule,* 4–20-celled, with numerous minute seeds. The capsule is covered with a shield-like cap, underneath which small pores are formed, through which the seeds are dispersed. Any part of the plant if cut or broken exudes a milky substance. (*Papaver* is the classical Latin name of the poppy.)

For Culture see below.

**P. alpinum.** Alpine poppy. Hardy perennial, with short stem, 1–2 in. above the ground, from which the numerous leaves and flower stalks are produced. Leaves 4–6 in. long, grayish-green, cut into 2–3 deep lobes, which are again cut into many segments. Flowers on stalks to 10 in. high, white or yellow, fragrant. Fruit an oblong capsule. Alps.

**P. bracteatum.** Hardy perennial, growing to 3 ft. high, the whole plant covered with stiffish hairs. Leaves to 1 ft. long, and 4 in. across, segmented almost to midrib, the lobes opposite and toothed. Flower stalk with leafy, toothed bracts.* Flowers red. Mediterranean region.

**P. glaucum.** Tulip poppy. Annual, growing to 2 ft. Stem leaves bluish-green, cut into deep lobes which are opposite each other. Flowers cup-shaped, scarlet, inside marked at the base. This species produces numerous flowers. Syria. Persia.

**P. nudicaule.** Iceland poppy. Hardy perennial to 1 ft. high. Leaves smooth or hairy, cut into equal lobes. Flowering stalk to 15 in. high, hairy. Flowers 1–2 in. across, sweet-scented, the colors ranging through white, red, yellow and orange. Arctic regions. A good pink hort. form is Goonora Pink.

**P. orientale.** Oriental poppy. Strong-growing, hardy perennial, 3–4 ft. high, with stout, deeply growing rootstocks. The whole plant is covered with stiffish hairs. Leaves to 18 in. long, segmented almost to midrib, the lobes being opposite and sharply toothed. Flowering stalks have leafy, segmented bracts,* which get smaller toward the top. Flowers showy, to 6 in. across, scarlet, the petals marked at the base purplish-black. Mediterranean region. There are many fine hort. forms, among the red ones being Beauty of Livermore, Goliath, Olympia and Taplow Scarlet.

**P. pavoninum.** Annual to 1 ft., hairy. Leaves lobed and sharply toothed. Flowers scarlet, to 1 in. across. Petals have a dark spot at base. Turkestan and Afghanistan.

**P. pilosum.** Perennial to 3 ft. Leaves irregularly segmented, covered with soft hairs. Flowering stalk branched. Flowers brick-red, to orange, about 2 in. across. Mt. Olympus in Asia Minor.

**P. rhoeas.** Corn poppy. Annual to 3 ft. Stems branching and wiry. Leaves irregularly lobed, sometimes entire, deep green in color. Flowers red, deep purple, scarlet or occasionally white, 2 in. across. Eu. and As., naturalized in N.A. The Shirley poppy was originated from this species by the Rev. W. Wilks at Shirley, Eng., and has become a great garden favorite. The common corn poppy is the one immortalized in Flanders during the World War.

**P. somniferum.** Opium poppy (see HERB GARDENING). Strong-growing annual, 3–4 ft. high. Leaves grayish-green, coarsely lobed and toothed. Stem leaves clasping. Flowers white, pink, red, or purple, 3–4 in. across. Greece and Orient. It is the juice of the unripe pod which yields opium, but not commercially in the U.S. See MEDICINAL PLANTS.

## POPPY CULTURE

Most poppies are of easy culture. They need (1) light loam or sandy soil containing humus, (2) sun, (3) ample room for development.

Annual poppies dislike transplanting. Seed of these should be sown in autumn unless the winters are exceptionally severe, in which case sow seed in early spring. Seed of perennials and biennials may be sown under glass or in cold frames, transplanted to small pots of potting mixture* 2, and planted in the early spring, with as little disturbance as possible, in the permanent locations. Cover all poppy seed very lightly. Annual poppies will grow in poor soil, but if given a better soil will pay for it with increased size and greater beauty. Perennial poppies will flourish in rich loam with good drainage.

The brilliant red oriental poppy of the Mediterranean region (*P. orientale*) is a most satisfactory large plant for the perennial border. It should be staked before the bloom matures and should remain undisturbed for several years to develop its full beauty. Mulch* in autumn with old manure and dig this in in spring. The plant makes an autumn growth. The easiest method of propagation is to dig up the long taproot, when dormant in August, cut it into small pieces and start these in light, sandy loam. Some of the newer

The Iceland poppy, a beautiful hardy perennial from the Far North

hybrid oriental poppies are superior to the type and come in rich orange, pink, salmon and claret shades, and in white.

The yellow and orange Iceland poppy (*P. nudicaule*), from Arctic regions, is one of the best smaller perennial poppies. It requires light soil and perfect drainage. Without this it will rot off at the collar and die, often when at its best. It blooms the first year from seed and often self-sows freely. The last ten years have brought many interesting hybrid Iceland poppies in shades of pure pink, as well as stronger strains with larger flowers and long stems.

*Papaver pilosum* is somewhat similar to *P. nudicaule*, a perennial, self-sows freely, and thrives in light soil. It has long-stemmed flowers about the size of the Iceland poppy, generally in shades of orange, or brick-red.

The alpine poppy (*P. alpinum*) is a most satisfactory rock garden poppy. It likes good drainage and light, gritty soil, and seeds freely. The flowers, on stems a few inches high above gray cut foliage, are of white, orange and shades of pink. The modern varieties of alpine poppy are especially good. Although a perennial it is satisfactory when treated as an annual.

The opium poppy (*P. somniferum*) and the Shirley poppy, tall annuals, both need plenty of room in which to grow. If the plants are not thinned, results will be poor. Both these poppies will flourish in either sandy soil or loam. The opium poppy has smooth, gray foliage, large flowers, double or single, and grows several ft. tall. There are two main strains, one with fringed (the so-called carnation poppies) and the other with unfringed petals. The colors run through all shades of purple, crimson, red, and pink, to white. The Shirley poppy, developed from the common scarlet, black-centered corn poppy of Eurasia (*P. rhoeas*), has single flowers in shades of scarlet, pink and salmon, and white, all without the black center of the original type. When given plenty of room the Shirley poppy will make a plant two or three ft. across, with many flowers of great beauty.

The tulip poppy (*P. glaucum*) of Syria and Persia is an annual, or in mild climates, a biennial. It thrives in loose, gravelly soil and is a branching plant with gray foliage and single, cup-shaped, scarlet flowers. — L. R.

**POPPY ANEMONE** = *Anemone coronaria*.

**POPPY FAMILY.** A medium-sized family of chiefly herbaceous plants, including, besides the poppy, the California poppy, bloodroot, cream-cups, and the tree poppy.

---

* Special articles on the subjects indicated by an asterisk (*) will be found at the words so marked.

For the cult. genera and a description of the family see PAPAVERACEAE.

**POPPY MALLOW.** See CALLIRHOË.

*POPULIFOLIA, -us, -um* (pop-you-li-fō'li-a). With leaves like a poplar (*Populus*).

*POPULNEA, -us, -um* (pop-pull'nee-a). Poplar-like.

**POPULUS** (pop'you-lus). Poplar; some of them also called cottonwood, aspen and popple. A genus of quick-growing, softwooded trees of the willow family, comprising about 30 species from the north temperate zone (a few in warmer parts of northern Africa). They have alternate,* stalked, usually ovalish leaves. In some species (the quaking aspens) the leafstalk is compressed or slightly twisted or both, causing the leaves to shiver or quake in the slightest wind. Male and female flowers on separate trees, both in hanging catkins which bloom before the leaves unfold (in ours), the individual flowers minute, without petals or sepals. Fruit often silky, the small 2–4-valved pod ripening before the leaves are fully grown. (*Populus* is the classical Latin name of the poplar.)

For Culture see below. All of them bloom early in the spring. Many recent hybrids or clones* have been developed for reforestation and pulpwood, but they are scarcely hort. trees.

**alba.** White, or silver-leaved poplar. From 30–70 ft. high, or even more. Leaves not quaking, 3–5 in. long, lobed or cut finger-fashion, prominently white beneath. Eurasia. Hardy from zone* 2 southward. The *var.* **nivea** has leaves still whiter beneath; *var.* **pyramidalis** is a valuable accent* plant with a columnar habit. The latter variety is sometimes known as *P. bolleana*.

**balsamifera.** Cottonwood; also called balsam poplar. A stout tree up to 90 ft. high. Leaves quaking, 5–7 in. long, somewhat heart-shaped at the base. Eastern N.A. and hardy everywhere. The tree has had many names in the past, among them *P. deltoides* and *P. monolifera*. In the South some authors recognize the *var.* **pilosa**, and the *var.* **missouriensis**.

**berolinensis.** Certinensis poplar. A very hardy poplar of hybrid origin, admirably suited for cult. in the northern prairie states and for windbreaks.* It is a columnar tree, resembling the Lombardy poplar, but much hardier. It has yellowish-gray, hairy twigs and angularly ovalish, long-pointed leaves. Hardy from zone* 1 southward.

**bolleana** = *Populus alba pyramidalis*.

**canadensis.** Carolina poplar, but not native there and thought to be a French hybrid (in 1750) between *P. balsamifera* and *P. nigra*; only male trees are known. A tall tree, 50–90 ft. high. Leaves quaking, ovalish or triangular, 3–4 in. long, usually broad-based and minutely hairy on the margins. The *var.* **eugenei**, the Eugene poplar, has a narrowly pyramidal habit. See Culture below. There are also several other habit-varieties, one of them fastigiate. Hardy from zone* 2 southward.

**candicans.** Balm-of-Gilead; also called balsam poplar. A tree up to 90 ft. high; only female trees are known. Leaves not quaking, broadly oval or triangular, broad but heart-shaped at the base, coarsely blunt-toothed, 4–6½ in. long, whitish and hairy beneath. Buds sticky. Of unknown, but possibly of hybrid, origin, and considered by some to be a clone.* Hardy from zone* 3 southward.

**deltoides** = *Populus balsamifera*.

**eugenei** = *Populus canadensis eugenei*.

**grandidentata.** Large-toothed aspen. A somewhat weedy tree, 40–60 ft. high. Leaves quaking, 3–4 in. long, coarsely toothed, at first whitish beneath, later smooth. Eastern N.A. Hardy from zone* 2 southward.

**monolifera** = *Populus balsamifera*.

**nigra.** Black poplar. A wide-spreading tree, 40–90 ft. high. Leaves quaking, broadly triangular-oval, or wedge-shaped, 3–4 in. long, nearly as wide, finely blunt-toothed. Eurasia. Hardy throughout the country, but much less planted than the *var.* **italica**, the Lombardy poplar, with a columnar fastigiate habit. Many consider *P. alba pyramidalis* a tree superior to the Lombardy poplar, which has been perhaps over-planted in the U.S.

**simoni.** A narrow-headed tree, 20–36 ft. high. Leaves not quaking, ovalish or squarish, 3–5 in. long, white or pale green beneath. China. Hardy from zone* 2 southward. There are also fastigiate and weeping varieties available.

**termula.** European aspen. A round-headed tree rarely up to 90 ft. high, usually less than half this, the twigs a little sticky. Leaves quaking, thin, roundish or ovalish, 2–3 in. long, the teeth large. Eurasia and northern Africa. Hardy throughout.

**tremuloides.** Quaking aspen. A tree up to 90 ft. high. Leaves quaking, ovalish or nearly round, broad at the base, finely toothed, the teeth glandular. N.A. and hardy throughout. The *var.* **pendula** has drooping branches.

### POPLAR CULTURE

The hardiness and fast growth of the poplar make it a valuable ornamental and economic tree. It will thrive under almost all conditions, but prefers a damp soil and lowland. When compared with other trees of similar size and habit, it is short-lived, and, wherever possible, its use should be restricted to situations where other materials will not succeed. In this way, the present over-planting and stereotyped use of this group will be lessened. In many localities, the poplar is employed for street planting. This cannot be recommended because of its relatively short life, brittle branches, and vagrant root system which often causes trouble by growing into sanitary and drainage systems.

Lombardy poplars. See also POPULUS ALBA PYRAMIDALIS.

*Populus alba pyramidalis*, known also as *Populus bolleana*, is an excellent form of upright habit and is commonly used for windbreaks.* It is less formal and more graceful than the more common Lombardy poplar (*Populus nigra italica*). Where a large, somewhat spreading tree is desired, the Eugene poplar (*Populus canadensis eugenei*) is most desirable. *Populus balsamifera* and several fast-growing hybrids are now being grown in large numbers for reforestation purposes. The fast growth of the poplar prevents soil erosion and its timber is available in a short time for pulpwood.

Propagation by hardwood cuttings is the usual method. The cuttings are taken in the fall and buried over winter in sand. Because the group hybridizes freely, seed is not commonly used. The several weeping forms are grafted six to eight feet high on standards. For this work, *Populus grandidentata* is most often used. — A. D. S.

INSECT PESTS. Several species of leaf beetles, metallic blue or spotted, and their grub-like larvae, eat leaves of poplar and willow; they can be killed with arsenicals. Various other leaf feeders (fall webworms, bagworms, tent caterpillars, etc.) can be similarly controlled. Larvae of several beetles bore in the trees; they can sometimes be cut out and killed. Badly infested parts of the tree should be removed and destroyed.

DISEASES. (Most poplar diseases also affect willow.) Poplar is subject to several canker diseases on the trunk and on the twigs. All are best controlled by removing and burning affected parts. Poplar and willow scab frequently becomes important in ornamental trees. Control is accomplished by several applications of bordeaux spray. Poplar suffers at an early age from wood rots. Avoidance of wounds and prompt attention to unavoidable injuries will reduce damage of this nature.

**PORANA** (por-ray'na). A genus of 15 species of tropical, Old World, twining herbs of the family Convolvulaceae, one of them, **P. paniculata**, the mountain creeper or horsetail creeper, occasionally grown for ornament in zones* 8 and 9, mostly in Fla. It is a tall-climbing (30 ft.), herbaceous vine, with alternate,* ovalish or heart-shaped leaves, 4–6 in. long, and white-hairy beneath. Flowers resembling the morning-glory, but small, not over ⅓ in. wide, white, in profuse clusters (panicles*). India. Sometimes known as "white corallita" in Fla., but that name is better applied to *Antigonon*. (*Porana* is the native name for these plants.)

---
* Special articles on the subjects indicated by an asterisk (*) will be found at the words so marked.

**PORCUPINE PALM** = *Rhapidophyllum hystrix*.

*PORRIFOLIA*, *-us*, *-um* (por-ri-fō'li-a). With leek-like leaves.

*PORRUM* (por'rum). Latin for the leek.

**PORT.** For wine making *see vinifera* varieties at GRAPE.

**PORTIA TREE** = *Thespesia populnea*.

**PORTLAND CIVIC ARBORETUM.** See ARBORETUM.

**PORT ORFORD CEDAR** = *Chamaecyparis lawsoniana*.

**PORTO RICAN ROYAL PALM** = *Roystonea borinquena*.

*PORTORICENSIS*, *-e* (por-to-ri-sen'sis). From Porto Rico.

**PORTUGUESE CYPRESS** = *Cupressus lusitanica*.

**PORTUGUESE LAUREL** = *Laurocerasus lusitanica*.

**PORTULACA** (por-tew-lăk'a). Purslane. Low-growing, mostly trailing annual or perennial herbs, comprising about 40 species of the family Portulacaceae, and found in tropical and temperate regions. Stems soft and fleshy, often reddish in color. Leaves alternate,* small, thick, entire, often spoon-shaped, 1-2 in. long. Flowers usually terminal, opening only in full sunlight, sometimes inconspicuous, sometimes showy. Calyx* of 5 sepals.* Corolla of 5 petals, in varying colors. Stamens* numerous. Fruit a small capsule,* containing many seeds, splitting transversely. (*Portulaca* is the Latin name of the purslane.) Only 1 species of garden importance. Propagated by seeds sown in June where required to bloom in sunny places.

**grandiflora.** Rose moss. Garden portulaca. Sun moss. Wax pink. Trailing annual, to 1 ft., much-branched and fleshy. Leaves simple, spoon-shaped, to 1 in. long. Flowers terminal, showy, 1 in. across, ranging in color from white, pink, yellow, red or purple. Suitable for dry, sunny rockeries, dry banks or border edges. Brazil.

**oleracea.** Purslane. Pussley. Trailing annual with reddish, fleshy stems, the joints of which produce roots when in contact with the soil. Leaves thick and fleshy, spoon-shaped, to 2 in. long. Flowers small, bright yellow. Persistent garden weed. *See* list at WEEDS.

**PORTULACACEAE** (por-tew-lă-kay'see-ee). The purslane family, notorious because it contains the pestiferous "pussley," also comprises several very beautiful garden plants among its 18 genera and 180 species. They are mostly herbs, but some tropical genera are shrubby, especially the African *Portulacaria*, a greenhouse plant with fleshy leaves. All the family have a tendency toward thick or fleshy leaves.

The most popular of the garden genera is *Portulaca*, in spite of its weedy members. Some of the garden forms are among the gayest-colored of all flowers. *Montia* is sometimes

fading in most, and opening only in sunlight in a few. Fruit mostly a dry, 3-valved pod (capsule*).

Technical flower characters: Sepals* 2. Petals 4 or 5, sometimes slightly united at the base, often notched at the tip. Stamens* of an indefinite number. Ovary superior,* except in *Portulaca*.

**PORTULACARIA** (por-tew-lak-cay'ri-a). Fleshy-leaved, little-known, South African shrubs or small trees of the family Portulacaceae, **P. afra**, the purslane tree, somewhat grown in Calif. for interest more than ornament, and also in the cool greenhouse northward. It is a stout-stemmed, softwooded tree, 8-12 in. high, with opposite, very fleshy, blunt leaves mostly less than ½ in. long. Flowers pink, scarcely 1/10 in. wide, clustered (panicled*) in the upper leaf-axils.* Fruit dry, 3-winged, scarcely or only tardily splitting. The tree should be grown as a succulent (which see). It will not stand much frost. (*Portulacaria* means similar to *Portulaca*.)

*PORTULACEA*, *-us*, *-um* (por-tew-lay'see-a). From *Portulaca*, the old Latin name of the purslane; hence any thick-leaved plant.

**POSOQUERIA** (po-so-queer'i-a). Tropical American shrubs or small trees, comprising about 15 species of the family Rubiaceae. Leaves simple,* opposite,* leathery, ovalish, the stipules* (leafy growths at the base of the leafstalks) 2, large. Flowers in terminal clusters, fragrant, white, pink, or red. Calyx* of 5 sepals.* Corolla 5-lobed, tubular. Stamens* 5. Fruit a large, fleshy berry. (*Posoqueria* is derived from a native name for these trees in Guiana.)

Not much in cult., except as a tropical greenhouse plant, but grown outdoors in southern Fla. Propagated by cuttings.

**latifolia.** Tree to 20 ft. Leaves dark green, shiny, 8-10 in. long. Flowers to 6 in. long, white, tubular, the lobes opening salver-like. Fruit a yellow, globe-shaped berry 2 in. across. Mex. to S.A.

**POST OAK** = *Quercus stellata*. See OAK.

**POTASH.** For its use in fertilizers *see* FERTILIZERS. As part of the food of plants *see* PLANT FOODS.

**POTASSIUM CYANIDE.** See FUMIGATION.

**POTASSIUM PERMANGANATE.** See Aid of Chemicals at CUTTINGS.

**POTASSIUM SULPHIDE.** See Contact Sprays at INSECTICIDES.

**POTATO.** For the culture of the common potato *see* the next main entry. *See also* DIOSCOREA, SWEET POTATO, APIOS, ALLIUM CEPA SOLANINUM, and SOLANUM JASMINOIDES, for other plants sometimes called potato.

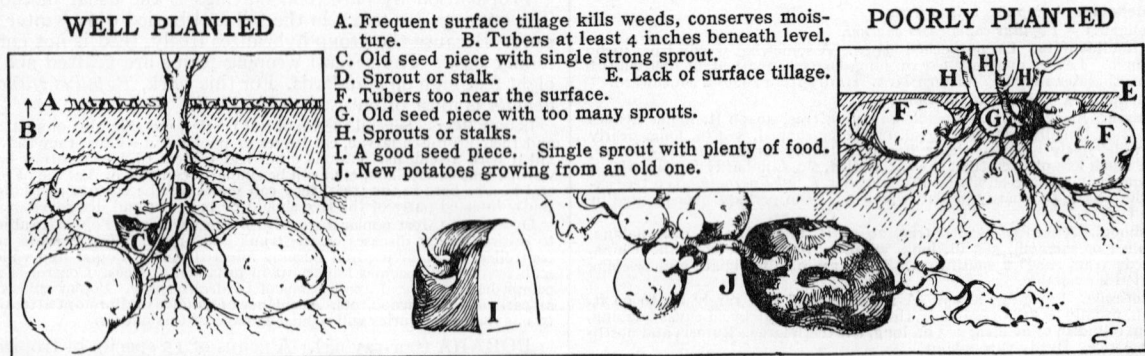

WELL PLANTED — POORLY PLANTED

A. Frequent surface tillage kills weeds, conserves moisture. B. Tubers at least 4 inches beneath level.
C. Old seed piece with single strong sprout.
D. Sprout or stalk. E. Lack of surface tillage.
F. Tubers too near the surface.
G. Old seed piece with too many sprouts.
H. Sprouts or stalks.
I. A good seed piece. Single sprout with plenty of food.
J. New potatoes growing from an old one.

grown as a salad. *Calandrinia* comprises a few rather important species with quick-fading flowers. *Claytonia* (the spring beauty) is chiefly for the wild garden. *Talinum* and *Lewisia* (largely for the rock garden species) are somewhat widely cult., while *Spraguea*, largely Californian, is suited only for the rock garden.

Leaves alternate* or opposite,* always without marginal teeth. Flowers regular, showy in some genera, but quickly

**POTATO** (*Solanum tuberosum*). This upland Peruvian plant has become the staple vegetable crop of the temperate world within the last 150 years. Its high starch content and food value make it a most important garden plant, but one not to be undertaken if your garden is too small for the space potatoes need. *See* KITCHEN GARDEN for plan and details.

The earliest Spanish chronicler of the potato told us that it originally grew far up in the Andes, where the Incas valued

* Special articles on the subjects indicated by an asterisk (*) will be found at the words so marked.

it highly. It is a region where it freezes, at least a little, during every month in the year. Potatoes have never gotten over their fondness for that ancient coolness, and that is why their culture is limited, or should be, to regions having a long cool spring for the early varieties, and a reasonably cool summer for the later sorts, which are usually stored for winter use.

The best potato regions are in the North, especially Maine and the states along the Great Lakes. Enormous yields are harvested on eastern Long Island, where proximity to cool sea water makes a very favorable environment. Thousands of acres are planted within a few hundred feet of the ocean, just behind the dunes. Similarly favored localities are rare, but the potato is planted successfully all over the U.S. by utilizing the coolest season for the early varieties. Late potatoes are not successful in regions of great summer heat.

The commercial production of early potatoes follows the waning winter from Florida northward in the East. In California, where crops are very heavy, they utilize the relatively brief cool season of favored localities with great success. Of course all mountain states can grow it easily, the elevation bringing just the conditions potatoes need. See COLORADO.

SOILS AND FERTILIZERS. Most good garden soils are suitable for potatoes. Many indications, especially in the soils of Long Island, point to a somewhat acid soil being the most favorable. And soils with a pH value of 5 or 6 are often very prolific (see ACID AND ALKALI SOILS for details of making the tests and controlling the soil acidity). Other regions produce good crops with a normal, nearly neutral soil.

The soil, however, must be very rich, and not too stony to permit proper tuber development. Fresh stable manure is to be avoided, and even well-rotted stable manure had better be plowed under the autumn before spring planting. If manure is used, allow 15–20 tons per acre (10 wheelbarrow loads for a 100-ft. row). Most commercial growers rely upon special potato mixtures (available at all dealers) of commercial fertilizers. These are drilled into the trenches in which the plants will grow, at the rate of 3000 pounds per acre (about 12 pounds per 100-ft. row). If commercial fertilizer is used, it is imperative that none of it touches the planted "seed" (see below).

PLANTING. The ordinary seed of the potato, resulting from its blossom, is never used (except for breeding experiments). Potatoes are propagated and universally grown by cutting up an ordinary potato tuber, allowing one or two "eyes" (really buds of the underground stem) to each piece. Cut the pieces so that there will be as much flesh as possible for the eyes, as the plant will live on this stored food while sprouting.

It is essential, in view of the disastrous diseases to which the potato is subject (see below) that only certified, disease-free tubers (commonly called seed) be purchased from a thoroughly reliable dealer. They cost a little more, but their use may prevent failure. After the tubers have been cut, it is well to allow them to callus* slightly before planting. They will do this naturally if spread thinly in a cool, dry place for 24 hours. Some growers dust them over with fine, powdery soil. For treatment of seed before planting see Diseases (below).

Make the trenches or drills about 5 in. deep, and put a piece of cut potato tuber every 12–14 in. The rows should be 2 ft. apart for the early varieties and 2½–3 ft. apart for the late sorts. Cover the tubers thoroughly. They will take nearly three weeks to sprout above ground.

The date for planting is important. All the early varieties should be planted at least 10 days or two weeks before the date of the average last killing frost in your region (see the name of your state for frost data). Even considerable frost after planting will not harm the buried seed, and an early start is essential if heat and disease are to be avoided.

Late varieties (see below) are planted about 6 weeks after the early sorts. Except in the most favorable regions, with long, cool summers, their use is to be avoided by most home gardeners. Their diseases and harvesting are very difficult nuts to crack over much of the country. They are, however, as in Maine, eastern Long Island, Michigan, and Idaho, grown (mostly commercially) with great success.

It takes about 5–8 pounds of tubers (depending on their size and the frequency of their "eyes") to plant 100 ft. of row, the final yield of which should be about a bushel. Commercial yields average 400–550 bushels per acre on Long Island and in Maine, much less over most of the country. A single favorable Long Island acre has yielded over 900 bushels. The American record appears to be 1145 bushels, on a high-altitude Colorado farm. See COLORADO.

CULTIVATION. Clean, frequent cultivation is essential, especially in the early stages. No weeds and a dust mulch should be the rule for the first few weeks. As the plants get bushy it will be more difficult to cultivate, but it must be kept up until the tops show signs of withering, as they always do when the tubers are approaching maturity. See CULTIVATION.

It is, of course, necessary to cultivate with sufficient care so as not to disturb the tubers, which, as the crop approaches harvesting, will occupy much more space than the original width of the trench. At the last or next to the last cultivation, the soil should be hoed, or plowed, over the plants on both sides so as to make a ridge or mound about 10 in. high, through which the tops will keep on growing until the end.

HARVESTING. When the tops have finally withered, potatoes may be dug. The early varieties can be left in the ground for a short period after they are ready to dig, if the weather is not too warm and wet.

The late varieties are quite safe to leave in the ground for 4–6 weeks after the tops have withered, and some growers risk leaving early potatoes for considerable periods.

After digging, the potatoes must only be dried enough to remove soil moisture and loose soil (a few hours in the sun is enough). They must then be stored in a cool, perfectly dark place. For winter storage of the late varieties the best temperature is about 37°. If light strikes the stored tubers, they will become green, and possibly poisonous. If the temperature is too high (room temperature), they will sprout.

VARIETIES: For early potatoes the best varieties are Irish Cobbler, Bliss, Early Rose.

For late potatoes use Green Mountain, Rural, Russet Rural, or in the warmer areas, Peachblow.

The so-called Idaho potato, a variety unknown to the experts, but widely publicized, is Netted Gem or Russet Burbank — both late potatoes.

INSECT PESTS. The yellow-and-black-striped Colorado potato beetle and its red, slug-like larvae are known over most of the United States. Both stages are injurious, but they are easily controlled with arsenicals, especially in the larval stage. Small, black, jumping flea beetles make small holes in the leaves in the spring; they can be checked with arsenicals. In the north central states a small green leafhopper causes the leaves to dry in the summer and shortens the life of the plant. Bordeaux mixture controls this pest and also checks diseases. In the Northeast, green and pink aphids sometimes injure potatoes; nicotine dust or spray will control them. The tiny caterpillar of the potato tuber moth mines in leaves, stems, and tubers of potato. It continues to work in stored tubers. It is injurious in Calif. and sometimes in the South. Potatoes should be well hilled where it occurs, and old vines should be cleaned up. Carbon disulphide fumigation can be used on stored potatoes. Stalk borers, which sometimes work in potato, can be kept down by cleaning up old vines and weedy borders. Blister beetles, slender, active, and gray, black or striped, often invade gardens and feed on potatoes and other plants; they are partially controlled with arsenicals.

DISEASES. More than sixty diseases of potato have been listed, many of which are of minor importance. A small number of them, however, are serious throughout the entire world. When the air is moist and cool, the vines may be killed in a few days by early blight. Later the *tuber rot* due to the dreaded *late blight* disease may appear. When the air is warm and relatively dry, tip-burn and hopper-burn, which destroy the foliage, may cause as much damage as late blight. *Early blight* causes target spots on the leaves, and in a humid climate may destroy them entirely, and also produces a shallow lesion on the tuber. All these diseases may be controlled by spraying carefully with bordeaux mixture or dusting with copper-lime, beginning when the plants are about four inches tall and repeating the applications at ten-day intervals.

On many seed potatoes are small, black, tar-like specks, which are the resting bodies of the fungus, *Rhizoctonia*, which kills the sprouts, girdles large plants, and causes many small, ill-shapen tubers. The same fungus also hibernates in the soil, and is able to attack many kinds of plants. Treating the seed one and one-half hours with corrosive sublimate (1/1000) or with various other mercury compounds, reduces the amount of disease. Common scab causing the corky, roughened spots is produced by a bacterium that thrives best in soil that tends to be alkaline. Avoiding the use of lime, wood ashes, and other alkaline-producing substances, and in severe cases applying sulphur to the soil, will aid in growing smooth potatoes.

So many names have been applied to the various degeneration diseases that all of them cannot be enumerated here. Most of them dwarf the plant, distort the leaf, yellow the foliage, and reduce the yield. Among these are the mosaics, leaf-roll, spindle-tuber, and yellow-dwarf. Seed certification aids in locating healthy stock, which should always be planted.

---

* Special articles on the subjects indicated by an asterisk (*) will be found at the words so marked.

*Black wart* has been found in a few mining towns and is present in much of Europe. Plant quarantines and the growing of resistant varieties are the only remedies.

The potato crop should be stored in small bins, with the temperature at 37° F. to ensure against the various storage rots.

**POTATO BEAN** = *Apios tuberosa*.

**POTATO FAMILY.** A huge family of plants of outstanding hort. importance, containing foods, drugs, poisons, narcotics, and some garden flowers. It comprises herbs, shrubs, vines, and trees from all over the world, and includes the potato, tomato, pepper (not the common black pepper), tobacco, petunia, matrimony-vine, henbane, and many others. For an account of them *see* SOLANACEAE.

**POTATO HOE.** See Section 1, TOOLS AND IMPLEMENTS.

**POTATO-LEAVED TOMATO** = *Lycopersicum esculentum grandifolium*. See TOMATO.

**POTATO ONION** = *Allium cepa solaninum*. See ONION.

**POTATO VINE** = *Solanum jasminoides* (not the true potato).

**POT-BOUND.** A plant growing in a pot or tub, with the roots so closely packed that there seems little room for further growth. Some plants, however, bloom best when pot-bound, and many others grow more thriftily under such conditions, notably the palms. *See* POTTING.

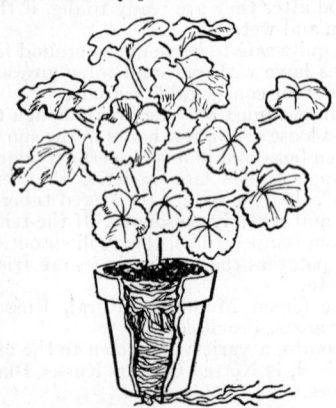

A pot-bound plant which needs re-potting. For details *see* POTTING.

**POTENTILLA** (pō-ten-till'a). Cinquefoil. Perennial, rarely annual herbs, or small shrubs, comprising over 200 species of the rose family, found in temperate and arctic regions mostly in the North. Stems creeping or erect, the creeping species rooting at the joints. Leaves compound.* Leaflets 3 or many, more or less hairy. Flowers in numerous small, loose clusters, yellow, white or red. Calyx* of 5 sepals,* joined at the base, forming a cup. Corolla of 5 petals growing on the calyx rim. Stamens* numerous. Fruits several, dry, one-seeded. (*Potentilla* is the diminutive of Latin *potens*, powerful, in allusion to supposed medicinal properties.)

Only a few of the perennials are in general cult. Among the hybrids are very good double-flowered varieties, and Gibson's Scarlet is a good red-flowered form. Easily propagated by seeds or division of rootstocks. Seeds should be sown in sandy soil, ⅛ in. deep, in shallow pans, in temperature of 55°–65° in cool greenhouse or cold frame in early spring. Seedlings may be transplanted outdoors as soon as large enough to handle, in ordinary garden soil. Rootstocks may be divided in Sept. or March and April. Herbaceous potentillas should be lifted and divided every 3 years. Shrubby species may be propagated from cuttings of half-ripened wood in Sept. and Oct.

**argyrophylla.** Herbaceous perennial. Stem to 18 in. Leaves compound*; basal leaves long-stalked. Leaflets 3, coarsely and sharply toothed, the under side covered with matted, whitish hairs. Flowers in loose, long-stalked clusters, yellow, 1 in. across. Commonly cult. and a good border plant. June–Aug. Himalayas.

**atrosanguinea.** Similar to *P. argyrophylla*, but with larger leaves and dark purple or red flowers. Himalayas.

**fruticosa.** Shrubby cinquefoil. Hardhack. Small, much-branched shrub, 1–4 ft. high. Leaves small. Leaflets 3–7, lance-shaped to 1 in. long, covered with short, silky hairs, the margins slightly rolled. Flowers numerous, showy, bright yellow, in small clusters. June–Aug. Tolerates a limey soil. Eu., As. and northern N.A. The *var.* **purdomi** has smaller leaflets, is less hairy and has pale yellow flowers. In *var.* **veitchi** the leaflets are not hairy; flowers creamy-white. *P. fruticosa* and its varieties make some of the finest flowering shrubs for the garden.

**glandulosa.** A sticky-hairy perennial, not over 2 ft. high. Leaflets 7–9, toothed. Flowers about ½ in. wide, yellow, in profuse clusters. S. Dak. to Calif. Sometimes known as *Drymocallis glandulosa*.

**grandiflora.** Herbaceous perennial, 6–15 in. high. Leaflets 3, hairy and toothed, to 1 in. long. Flowers showy, golden-yellow, to 1 in. across, in branching few-flowered clusters. July–Aug. Good border plant. Eu.

**hybrida.** A group of hybrid cinquefoils derived from crossing *P. argyrophylla* and *P. nepalensis*. They are showy garden plants with generally purple flowers. June.

**multifida.** Herbaceous, spreading plant, to 4 in. high. Leaflets deeply cut into narrow segments, with short, white hairs on the under side. Flowers small, yellow, 2–3 in a cluster. For cult. *see* ROCK GARDEN. Eu.

**nepalensis.** Strong-growing, herbaceous perennial to 2 ft. Basal leaves to 12 in. long. Leaflets of stem leaves 2–3 in. long, toothed, green on both sides, slightly hairy. Flowers showy, rose-red, to 1 in. across, long-stalked, in branching clusters. July–Aug. For cult. *see* ROCK GARDEN. Himalayas. The *var.* **willmottiae** is a dwarf free-flowering form, with magenta-rose flowers.

**pyrenaica.** Strong-growing, herbaceous perennial, 4–12 in. high. Leaflets 5. Stem leaflets small, to ¾ in. long, finely toothed toward the tip. Flowers golden-yellow, to 1 in. across, in loose clusters. July–Aug. Pyrenees.

**russelliana.** A hybrid cinquefoil derived from crossing *P. nepalensis* and an unknown species. It has scarlet flowers. June–July.

**tonguei** = *Potentilla multifida*.

**tridentata.** Three-toothed cinquefoil. Herbaceous perennial, growing to 1 ft. Leaves mostly basal. Leaflets 3, dark shiny green on upper side, with 3 teeth at the tip. Flowers small, white, in loose clusters. July–Aug. For cult. *see* ROCK GARDEN. Eastern N.A.

**POTERIUM** (po-teer'i-um). Southern European under-shrubs, comprising only 1 species of the family Rosaceae, *P. spinosum*. It may be propagated from seeds sown in the spring or from cuttings of half-ripened shoots in late summer. It is a small, deciduous, spiny under-shrub with compound* leaves. Leaflets small, 7–15, hairy. Flowers in short spikes of 2 kinds, sterile and fertile, small. Calyx of 5 sepals, greenish, petals none. Fruit red, berry-like. Not of much hort. interest. (*Poterium* is the Greek name for some plant, but not certainly for this one.)

For the plant known as *P. canadense, see* SANGUISORBA CANADENSIS. For *P. sanguisorba, see* SANGUISORBA MINOR.

**POT HERBS.** A somewhat general name for any herbs cooked in a pot, as spinach, kale, collards, chard, etc. For a more specialized use of certain herbs used in seasoning, and sometimes called pot herbs, *see* HERB GARDENING.

**POTHOS** = *Scindapsus*, so far as hort. species are concerned.

**POT LAYERING** = Air layering. *See* LAYERING.

**POT MARIGOLD** = *Calendula officinalis*.

**POT MARJORAM** = *Origanum vulgare*.

**POTOMATO** = Pomato.

**POTPOURRI.** Of the many ways of making potpourri, the most usual are the dry and the moist. As the latter method is very tedious and perhaps no better, only the dry method will be noted.

Take two quarts of rose petals and buds — of course, the sweet-smelling varieties only should be used. Put them on sheets of paper in an airy room to dry, which should take about twenty-four hours. Sprinkle with a thin layer of table salt (some people prefer to add a little benzoic acid to the salt). Add sweet geranium or lemon verbena leaves, a few bay leaves, lavender, heliotrope, mignonette, jasmine, garden pinks, carnations, Parma violets, orange or lemon blossoms, any sweet-smelling flowers you have, and any sweet-smelling herb, such as rosemary, basil, marjoram, anise, etc. A bit of cedar leaf and some balsam needles can be added, but always keep in mind that roses must predominate. The leaves should be dried before mixing with the rose petals.

As you add the other flowers to the rose petals, add more salt. When all the flowers are thoroughly dry, add a spice mixture made of one-quarter ounce each of powdered cloves, mace, cinnamon, and allspice; one-eighth ounce each of crushed coriander, cardamon seeds, powdered gum storax, and powdered gum benzoin; and one ounce of violet sachet powder. Mix the flowers thoroughly with the spice mixture, then dampen with a bit of brandy. A drop or so of attar of rose will enhance the fragrance. Leave the potpourri in a tightly covered crockery jar for some weeks, stirring occa-

---

* Special articles on the subjects indicated by an asterisk (*) will be found at the words so marked.

sionally. When ready for use, put in bowls, to give a delicious scent to the rooms.

If powdered storax and benzoin are not easily procurable, use a small amount of gum storax and tincture of benzoin, and rub in the various spices until dry. — M. C.

**POTS.** *See* FLOWER POTS.

**POTSHERDS.** A very old term, spanning from the Book of Job to the modern gardener, for broken pottery. In modern hort. it nearly always indicates merely broken flower pots or crocks used for drainage. Potsherds are put over the hole in the bottom of a pot to keep water from washing out the soil and to allow air to get into it.

**POTTERY.** *See* ORNAMENT AND FURNITURE.

**POTTING.** The practice of supplying, within a flower pot or tub, the room for root development as the needs of the plant demand. Clean flower pots should always be used, as the tender roots do not freely circulate around the pot if they have to contend with remnants of soil left over by a previous occupant. Also the plants will not readily slip out of a dirty pot, when they must be re-potted. Proper drainage is of the utmost importance to ensure healthy plants. A piece of broken pot or crock, as it is popularly called, should be placed over the hole and sufficient rough material, such as the refuse from sifted soil, be placed over this according to size of pot used. Pots above 6 in. may have 3 or 4 in. of drainage, the smaller sizes less.

Potting mixtures* are fully discussed at another entry, but where much potting is done a compost heap is of the greatest importance. This should be made of top sod taken from a rich pasture and stacked up for future use as follows: Place two feet of sod with the grass side down, on this put 8 in. of cow or barnyard manure and continue to build this up to any size or height, finishing with a layer of manure. When used cut a slice from the front of the stack all the way down. This will give you a good rich loam to put under the potting bench for general use, to which can be added the necessary sand, peat, leaf mold, or fertilizer to produce any of the described potting mixture formulas.

Provided the proper mixture is used and the soil is in the right condition, neither too wet nor too dry, a plant should be potted firmly, but as a general rule softwooded plants, like cinerarias, primulas, calceolarias, geraniums, etc., do not require such hard potting, and the soil can be pressed in quite firmly with the fingers. But hardwooded plants, like azaleas, camellias, ericas, boronias, genistas, rhododendrons, chorizemas, acacias, etc., should be hard-potted by the use of a potting stick, usually a piece of broom handle 18 in. long and wedge-shaped on one end. Never court disaster by using a cracked pot, as it always breaks at the wrong time.

### How to Pot a Plant Properly

Put the plant in the center of the pot in which has been previously placed the necessary soil mixture — to about half full. Do not depress the roots, but rather build up a small mound and place the plant on top. In this position the roots will fall downwards, and when the pot has been filled with soil and pressed down firmly the roots will be in a natural position. This refers more particularly to plants being potted for the first time. When potting vigorous-growing plants, such as *Pandanus, Areca, Livistona,* or *Phoenix,* a generous pruning of the roots is necessary, as these plants have such a strong root system that they may raise the plant out of the pot. This treatment also permits keeping the plant in a pot most suitable to its size.

A small shift, *i.e.* to only a slightly larger pot, is always advisable, and very firm potting is necessary. Keep the soil as level as possible, finishing 1 in. below the rim of the pot to allow for proper watering. The process of potting is simple if a few rules are observed. At the second and subsequent pottings the plant should be carefully removed from the pot, the edge around the ball should be removed and also any drainage material which adheres to the ball of earth. Then place the plant in the new pot, filled about ⅓ with proper soil, including free drainage. With a light pressure center it upright in the pot, fill in with soil and press firmly all around, filling to just below the rim of the pot, finishing as level as possible. By gradually turning the pot and using the thumbs a sufficient pressure can be given for

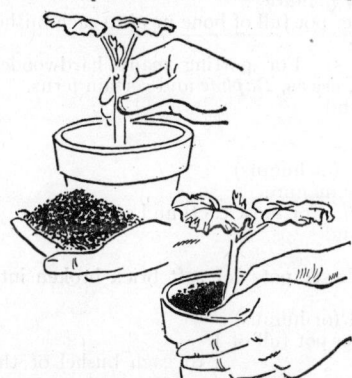

The correct steps in a potting operation. Be sure the soil is firmed about the roots, and that the drainage hole at the bottom is covered by crocks or gravel.

For larger specimens it is best to use a potting stick. It ensures the soil being well packed around the roots.

the potting of most softwooded plants without the use of the potting stick, but hardwooded plants require very firm potting, and a potting stick is indispensable.

When a plant has become pot-bound, *i.e.* the pot entirely filled with roots, a condition which is sometimes necessary to induce flowering, no harm will result, if attention is given to feeding at this time. But unless relieved by potting-on, in the case of foliage plants and palms, the plant becomes hard and stunted and will eventually turn yellow and lose its foliage. At this stage the roots should be reduced by chopping about ⅓ of the ball and the remaining roots loosened out with a pointed stick. Use a pot one size

Reduce the root system of a pot-bound plant before re-potting. For details *see* text.

larger than the old one, pot firmly and keep in a close atmosphere until root action begins.

The roots of palms may be cut down without injury to the plant, so that a reduced size of pot can be used. There is always danger of over-potting, which should be carefully guarded against. A plant that is not doing well will often respond by being put into a smaller pot.

The time for potting plants must largely be decided by their condition. The best time is after the plant has just started into growth, or just before growth is completed. In the first case the growing plant is full of energy and able to stimulate the newly disturbed roots into immediate activity. In the second case the ripening process being nearly completed, the tendency is for the plant to increase its root action and store up the vital energies contributed by sun and air

---

\* Special articles on the subjects indicated by an asterisk (\*) will be found at the words so marked.

for the maturing of the plant. So this time is ideal for shifting plants, but the operation should not be delayed until too near maturity, or root action will become dormant and inactive and take hold of the new soil too slowly.

Considerable judgment must be used in the class of plants to be potted, and the purpose for which they are grown. Some softwooded plants may need potting once a month, while hardwooded plants may only need potting once in two years. Foliage plants whose objective is fine foliage should be shifted to larger pots and be potted oftener than flowering plants where matured growth is the basis of perfect flowering.

The condition of the roots is the best indication of the needs of the plant. When the roots reach the side of the pot and hunt around for food, then is the time to give it additional space, but so long as the roots are not freely developed on the outside of the ball there is sufficient room for further growth without re-potting. Potting must be entirely controlled by the condition of the roots, and frequent systematic potting will prevent the plants from becoming pot-bound.

After potting foliage plants a genial temperature should be maintained, moderation in watering, and a closer atmosphere with gentle syringing of the foliage. All these assist in getting root action started. Plants usually respond quickly to this treatment, but it may be necessary to give slight shade for a few days.

Never pot a plant when it is dry. The new soil will absorb all the water, and the old ball of soil will not get sufficient for the need of the plant, which will eventually turn yellow and growth will be retarded. A good plan is to water the plants the day before you are to handle them. On the other hand if the soil is too wet it is apt to fall away from the plant and so damage the roots. A good gardeners' test for soil of the proper moisture content is to squeeze it in the hand and if it forms a close ball it is too damp, but if it just retains the form of the hand it is right for potting. Never use finely sifted soil for potting, but when the compost is being mixed break up all lumps of soil and manure with the back of the spade, removing all stones. After it has been turned over a few times it will be fine enough for all ordinary potting. Always endeavor to pot the plant as firmly as the old ball, and be sure the new soil is evenly packed down, leaving no empty spaces, so that the roots can take hold of the new soil quickly. It will be impossible to pot hardwooded plants hard enough, without the use of a potting stick to ram the soil well down, even in the small sizes, and it is essential that only sound pots be used or they will not stand the hard potting.

### Potting Shed

A good potting shed is very important in greenhouse work, and should be constructed to make potting material easily available at all times and keep it in condition for immediate use whenever necessary. A good potting bench should be the first consideration, the top of which should be laid with 2-in. plank to make it rigid for potting, and a back at least 12 in. high. In a large range of glass it should run the whole length of the shed and be plentifully supplied with light. Bins should be placed underneath for storage of soil, sand, leaf mold, peat, drainage material, manure and pots, with an 8- or 10-in. board nailed to the front on the floor, this will prevent the material from working out on the floor, and also serve as a foot rest for the person doing the potting. The bench should not be less than 4 ft. wide, which will allow room for mixing batches of soil, and also for storage and to be used as a table for surplus plants while potting. One compartment underneath the bench should be used for the storage of insecticides, sprayers, or tools, and should be supplied with doors to add to the neatness of the shed. The bench should be about 3 ft. from the floor for comfortable working.

### Flower Pots

Pots are a vital necessity in horticultural practice, and are used for growing plants, by confining the roots for the more ready application of special soil. They also permit greater convenience of handling, transportation, and minimize any serious check to transplanted specimens. Pots are made in many sizes to suit the great variety of plants for which they are used. See FLOWER POTS for sizes. The common clay pots are the best, and at the present time, by a mixture of suitable clays, the manufacturers have produced a standard pot, neither too hard nor too porous.

Many fancy glazed pots are on the market, and while these may be more ornamental and easily kept clean, they have never become popular. Plants can be well grown in these, though they require much less water and more ample drainage. Not being so porous they cannot receive the same amount of aeration as from an unglazed pot. See JARDINIERE. Pots made of glass are not recommended, as plants do not generally thrive in them. They have been experimented with for orchids and other plants with but limited success.

New flower pots should always be well soaked and allowed to dry before using, otherwise the pot will absorb all the moisture from the soil and the plant suffer in consequence. Pots that have been washed should never be used while wet. — A. J. L.

**POTTING MIXTURES.** Nearly all plants grown in pots, tubs or window boxes, have rather definite soil requirements. These may vary with the age of the plant, its ancestral home, and many other things. Fortunately, most of these requirements can be reduced to the six standard potting mixtures, the preparation and uses of which are listed below. Throughout THE GARDEN DICTIONARY the preferred potting mixture for all potted plants, and for many others, is indicated by the numbers one to six, and these mixtures should be prepared in accordance with the following:

POTTING MIXTURE 1. For potting up rooted cuttings taken from sand.
 2 Parts sharp sand
 1 Part loam
 1 Part leaf mold (or peat moss for acid-tolerant plants)

POTTING MIXTURE 2. For transplanted seedlings and for cuttings when moved from Mixture No. 1.
 1 Part sharp sand
 1 Part loam
 1 Part leaf mold

POTTING MIXTURE 3. For general potting, especially for such plants as the garden geranium (*Pelargonium*), fuchsias, chrysanthemums, *Sansevieria*, *Pandanus*, palms, etc.
 1 Part sharp sand
 2 Parts loam
 1 Part leaf mold (or humus)
 ½ Part dried cow manure
 1 Five-inch flower pot full of bone meal to each bushel of the mixture

POTTING MIXTURE 4. For plants requiring more humus than in Mixture No. 3, such as begonias, many ferns, primulas, etc.
 2 Parts sharp sand
 2 Parts loam
 2 Parts leaf mold (or humus)
 ½ Part dried cow manure
 1 Five-inch flower pot full of bone meal to each bushel of the mixture

POTTING MIXTURE 5. For potting many hardwooded plants such as azaleas, ericas, *Daphne* and certain ferns.
 2 Parts sharp sand
 2 Parts loam
 2 Parts peat moss
 1 Part leaf mold (or humus)
 ⅓ Part dried cow manure

POTTING MIXTURE 6. For most cacti and **succulents**.
 2 Parts sharp sand
 2 Parts loam
 1 Part broken flower pots (or soft brick broken into small pieces)
 ½ Part leaf mold (or humus)
 1 Five-inch flower pot full of bone meal } to each bushel of the
 1 Five-inch flower pot full of ground limestone } mixture.

**POTTING-ON.** The gradual increase of the size of the flower pot to take care of increased root development. Potting-on requires several shifts or re-potting operations. For details see POTTING.

*POUKHANENSIS, -e* (poo-ka-nen'sis). From Poukhan, China.

**POULTRY MANURE.** See MANURE.

**POUND.** See WEIGHTS AND MEASURES, 4.

**POWDERY MILDEW.** See Powdery Mildew at PLANT DISEASES. See also Diseases at GRAPE and PEACH.

**POWDERY SCAB.** See Slime-molds at PLANT DISEASES.

**POWER SPRAYER.** See SPRAYING AND DUSTING.

*PRAEALTA, -us, -um* (pree-al'ta). Very tall.

*PRAECOX* (pree'cocks). Very early.

*PRAESTANS* (pree'stanz). Excellent or distinguished.

**PRAIRIE.** As an adjective prairie has been used as part of the name of many plants of plains and prairies, mostly from the central part of N.A. Those in THE GARDEN DICTIONARY and their proper equivalents are:
Prairie button snakeroot = *Liatris pycnostachya;* Prairie clover (see PETALOSTEMON); Prairie coneflower = *Lepachys columnaris;* Prairie crabapple = *Malus ioensis;* Prairie flax = *Linum lewisi;* Prairie gentian = *Eustoma russellianum;* Prairie lily = *Mentzelia decapetala* (see also COOPERIA); Prairie mallow = *Malvastrum coccineum;* Prairie phlox = *Phlox pilosa;* Prairie pine = *Liatris spicata;* Prairie rose = *Rosa setigera;* Prairie smoke = *Geum ciliatum.*

*PRATENSIS, -e* (pra-ten'sis). Growing in meadows.

*PRAVISSIMA, -us, -um* (pra-viss'i-ma). Very crooked.

**PRAYING MANTIS.** See INSECT FRIENDS.

*PRECATORIUS* (pre-ka-tor'i-us). One who prays; hence applied to plants yielding seeds used as rosaries. See ABRUS.

**PRE-LINNAEAN.** As applied to Latin plant names, pre-Linnaean indicates the existence of the name before the publication by Linnaeus of his *Species Plantarum* in 1753. Many pre-Linnaean names were adopted by Linnaeus and are in common use today, especially as specific names. A few examples (the pre-Linnaean name in boldface) are: *Campanula* **medium**, *Cardiospermum* **halicacabum**, *Hibiscus moscheutos*, and *Leonitis* **leonurus**. See LINNAEUS.

**PRESERVING MELON** = *Citrullus vulgaris citroides.* See WATERMELON.

**PRETTY-FACE** = *Brodiaea ixioides.*

**PRICKING-OUT.** See SEEDS AND SEEDAGE.

**PRICKLE.** See SPINE.

**PRICKLY ASH.** See ZANTHOXYLUM.

**PRICKLY COMFREY** = *Symphytum asperum.*

**PRICKLY LETTUCE** = *Lactuca scariola.* See list at WEEDS.

**PRICKLY PEAR.** See OPUNTIA.

**PRICKLY PHLOX** = *Gilia californica.*

**PRICKLY POPPY.** See ARGEMONE.

**PRICKLY SHIELD FERN** = *Polystichum brauni.*

**PRICKLY THATCH** = *Thrinax microcarpa.*

**PRICKLY THRIFT** = *Acantholimon.*

**PRICK-TIMBER** = *Euonymus europaeus* and *Nemopanthus mucronata.*

**PRIDE-OF-CALIFORNIA** = *Lathyrus splendens.*

**PRIDE-OF-INDIA** = *Koelreuteria paniculata.*

**PRIDE-OF-ROCHESTER.** See DEUTZIA SCABRA.

**PRIM** = *Ligustrum vulgare.* See PRIVET.

**PRIMROSE.** For the true primrose *see* PRIMULA. For other plants to which the name primrose is often applied *see:* ARNEBIA CORNUTA, EVENING PRIMROSE, and STREPTOCARPUS.

**PRIMROSE FAMILY** = Primulaceae.

**PRIMROSE JASMINE** = *Jasminum primulinum.*

**PRIMROSE WILLOW.** See JUSSIAEA.

**PRIMULA** (prim'you-la). Primrose. A large genus of over 300 species of low-growing, herbaceous perennials and a few biennials, of the family Primulaceae, chiefly natives of the northern hemisphere, and found mostly in alpine and cool localities. Stem short, or none. Leaves crowded, stalked, long and narrow, or roundish or tufted, the midrib generally prominent on the under side. Flowers on leafless stalks, sometimes with leafy bracts,* solitary, or in loose umbels,* or whorled in tiers, or in rounded heads. Flowers in various shades of yellow, white, red, blue, pink, and purple. Calyx* of 5 sepals,* joined halfway, usually slightly inflated, generally pale green. Corolla of 5 lobes, tubular at the base, opening salver-wise. Stamens* 5, not protruding. In some species the stamens are prominent at the opening of the corolla tube (thrum-eyed) and in others the pin-headed stigma* is conspicuous (pin-eyed*). Fruit a dry, many-seeded capsule. (*Primula* is a diminutive of *primus*, first, in allusion to the spring bloom.)

For Culture *see* below.

**acaulis** = *Primula vulgaris.*

**auricula.** Auricula. Hardy perennial, to 8 in. high. Leaves basal, 2–4 in. long, thick and fleshy, ovalish, grayish-green, smooth, or white-powdery, toothed. Flowers varied in color, but usually with a conspicuous eye, in many-flowered umbels. April–May. Alps. Suitable for rock garden (see ROCK GARDEN), beds or borders.

**beesiana.** Strong-growing perennial, to 2 ft. high. Leaves basal, to 6 in. long, narrow, wrinkled, irregularly toothed. Flowers rose-red, with a yellow eye, in several whorls on each stalk. June. China. Good bog garden plant.

**bulleyana.** Strong-growing perennial, to 2½ ft. high. Leaves broadly lance-shaped, thin, margins sharply toothed. Flowers deep yellow, in several whorls* on each stalk, with small leafy bracts* under each whorl.* June. Suitable for bog garden and rock garden (see ROCK GARDEN). China.

**capitata.** Stiff-growing perennial, to 19 in. high. Leaves basal, broadly lance-shaped, 3–5 in. long, grayish on under side, margins finely toothed. Flowers lavender, in a dense, many-flowered, rounded head. April–May. Suitable for rock garden, beds or borders. Himalayas.

**cortusoides.** Hardy perennial, to 1 ft. high. Leaves basal, ovalish, heart-shaped at the base, 2–4 in. long, slightly hairy and lobed. Flowers rose-color, in loose, many-flowered umbels.* May–June. Suitable for rock garden (which see for cult.). Siberia.

**denticulata.** Hardy perennial, 10–15 in. high. Leaves basal, broadly lance-shaped, 2–5 in. long, thin, usually white-powdery. Flowers lilac, in dense clusters. Flower clusters surrounded by small, leafy bracts.* May. Himalayas. The *var.* **cachemiriana** (or **cashmeriana**) has more powdery leaves and flowers of rich purple, with a yellow center. Both suitable for the rock garden. See ROCK GARDEN, also GRAY AND LAVENDER GARDENS.

**elatior.** Oxlip. Hardy perennial, to 8 in. high. Leaves basal, ovalish, 2–4 in. long, wrinkled, slightly hairy on under side, midrib prominent on under side. Flowers yellow, showy, in many-flowered umbels.* April–May. Suitable for rock garden, border, or naturalizing. Eu. and western As.

**farinosa.** Bird's-eye primrose. Strong-growing perennial, to 1 ft. high. Leaves basal, broadly lance-shaped, 4–6 in. long, white-powdery on the under side. Flowers lilac, with yellow throat and eye, small, in many-flowered umbels.* May–June. Suitable for rock garden and border. Alpine regions of Eu. and As.

**florindae.** Strong-growing perennial, to 4 ft. high. Leaves basal, ovalish, with heart-shaped base, 8 in. or more long, with reddish-brown stalk. Flowers sulphur-yellow, drooping, in loose, many-flowered, mealy clusters. June–July. Suitable for the bog garden. Tibet. Not hardy in severe climates.

**forbesi.** Baby primrose. Slender-growing, tender perennial, to 15 in. high. Leaves basal, ovalish, with heart-shaped base, 1–2 in. long, slightly white-hairy. Flowers lilac or rose in several whorls on each stalk. Feb.–April. Grown in greenhouse. China and Burma.

**frondosa.** Dwarf-growing perennial, to 5 in. high. Leaves basal, small, thin, spoon-shaped, usually white-powdery on under side, the margins slightly toothed. Flowers, lilac, in many-flowered umbels.* April–May. Suitable for rock garden or border. Balkans.

**japonica.** Strong-growing perennial, to 2 ft. high. Leaves broadly lance-shaped, 4–6 in. long, thin, the margins slightly toothed. Flowers purple, pink, or white, glistening, in several whorls on each stalk. There are small, green, leafy bracts* under each whorl. June–July. Suitable for rock garden. Many hort. color forms. Japan.

**malacoides.** Fairy primrose. Tender perennial, to 1½ ft. high. Leaves basal, numerous, with long, slender stalks, the blade ovalish, with heart-shaped base, thin, slightly hairy, the margins deeply lobed and toothed. Flowers lilac or pink, small, in several whorls on each stalk. Jan.–April. Grown in greenhouse. China.

**obconica.** Tender perennial, to 1 ft. high. Leaves basal, stalked, ovalish, to 4 in. long, slightly covered with short, sharply pointed hairs, which when handled by some people cause a poisonous irritation. Flowers lilac or pink, in many-flowered umbels.* Jan.–April. Grown in greenhouse. China. Many good hort. forms.

**polyantha.** A group of garden, hybrid primroses, probably derived from the oxlip, cowslip, and the English primrose. They average about 1 ft.

---

* Special articles on the subjects indicated by an asterisk (*) will be found at the words so marked.

# PRIMULA

high and their leaves are narrowed into winged stalks. They are found in many colors and the cluster is usually profuse. May.

**pulverulenta.** Hardy, strong-growing perennial to 3 ft. high. Leaves basal, broadly lance-shaped, to 16 in. long, thin, margins irregularly toothed. Flowers purple, with orange eye, in several whorls on each stalk. There are small leafy bracts below each whorl. Flower stalks silvery. May-July. Suitable for the bog garden. China.

**sikkimensis.** Hardy, strong-growing perennial, 1-2 ft. high. Leaves basal, narrow, 4-5 in. long, wrinkled, margins sharply toothed. Flowers yellow, slightly drooping, in many-flowered umbels.* Calyx powdery. Small, leafy bracts surround the umbels.* May-June. Suitable for the bog garden. Himalayas. Not hardy in severe climates.

**sinensis.** Chinese primrose. Tender perennial, to 10 in. high. Whole plant covered with short hairs. Stem 1-4 in. high, slightly woody. Leaves crowded on the stem, fleshy, stalked, roundish, lobed, the margins prominently veined on the under side. Flowers large, in several colors, with conspicuous eye, in large umbels.* Jan.-April. Grown in greenhouse. China. The *var.* **stellata**, the star primrose, has smaller star-shaped flowers.

**stellata** = *Primula sinensis stellata*.

**veris.** Cowslip (see HERB GARDENING). Hardy perennial to 8 in. high. Leaves basal, wrinkled, broadly lance-shaped, 3-4 in. long, slightly hairy on under side. Flowers yellow, with orange eye, fragrant, in nodding umbels.* Calyx pale green, slightly inflated. May. Suitable for rock garden, border or naturalizing. Eurasia. There are double-flowered forms.

**vulgaris.** English primrose. Hardy perennial, to 6 in. high. Leaves basal, broadly lance-shaped, 3-5 in. long, wrinkled, the margins crinkled. Flowers numerous, or solitary, on slender, slightly hairy stalks, usually yellow. April-May. Suitable for the rock garden (see ROCK GARDEN), border or for naturalizing. Eu. Often called *P. acaulis*. There are many color forms, the *var.* **caerulea** being suitable for the blue garden. There are double-flowered forms. See BLUE GARDEN.

## PRIMULA CULTURE

The hardy species of *Primula*, with their early spring to early summer blooming period, deserve a place in every garden. The conditions under which the various species grow being so diverse, even the smallest garden will provide conditions suitable for one or more species. All require shade during the summer months. Some of the places in which they may be grown are the rock garden where they do not overrun other plants; the bog garden, which provides a splendid location for many of the showy, strong-growing species which when once established are not harmed if the roots are completely under water during the winter. In such a position they will often naturalize themselves, but only in regions of mild winters.

Flower beds and borders are suitable for the shorter species. The naturalizing of *P. vulgaris*, *P. veris*, and *P. elatior* under deciduous trees or in the grass is particularly beautiful in the early spring. These three species prefer cool, moist positions.

Propagated by seeds or division. Seeds are best sown as soon as ripe, Sept.-Oct., in a cool greenhouse or cold frame or they may be sown in early spring. Soil should be finely sifted and composed of 1 part loam, 1 part leaf mold, and ½ part sand. Seeds should be sown ⅛ in. deep, watered and shaded from the sun. If seeds are sown in the fall they should be carried through the winter in cool greenhouse or cold frame and transplanted as soon as danger of frost is over, to permanent positions. Leaf mold added to the soil where permanent plantings are made is beneficial. The hardy primulas are best not covered in winter except while young.

The tender species of *Primula* make admirable pot plants grown in the cool greenhouse for winter flowering. They are generally treated as annuals. Propagated by seeds or division. Seeds should be sown in March or April, 1/16 in. deep, in well-drained pans. Soil should be the same as for the hardy species. Pans must be covered with glass until seeds have germinated to prevent drying out, and be kept in temperature of 55°-65°. When the plants have 3 leaves, they should be transplanted 2 in. apart in the same mixture. When large enough pot into 3-in. pots, using potting mixture* 4. As plants increase in size they should be transplanted into larger pots as necessary, using the same mixture.

They should be kept in a cold frame during the summer months, shaded from sunlight, keeping the sash-lights on, but allowing plenty of air. This may be accomplished by resting the sash-lights on 4- or 5-in. flower pots. Good drainage is essential, but the plants must never be allowed to become dry. On returning plants to cool greenhouse they should be kept in a temperature of 45°-55°. These tender primulas make good house plants, and if kept in a cool room will last for many months.

Double varieties do not produce seeds and are propagated by division of rootstocks or cuttings in early spring.

The cowslip (*Primula veris*)

Contrary to popular belief, primulas do not set up a skin irritation, with the exception of *P. obconica*, and then not always so. See POISONOUS PLANTS. For rock garden conditions suitable for primulas, see ROCK GARDEN. — H. R. M.

DISEASES. Primulas are susceptible to root knot, gray mold and leafspot. For *root knot*, see Root Knot at PLANT DISEASES. *Gray mold* and *leafspot* are diseases characterized by spots on the foliage. Control can be obtained by spraying with bordeaux mixture and by burning all dead leaves in the fall.

**PRIMULACEAE** (prim-you-lay'see-ee). The primrose family, all herbs, comprises 30 genera and 700 widely distributed species, most abundant in the north temperate zone, and contains many old garden favorites. Of these the chief is easily *Primula*, comprising not only the primrose and cowslip, but several greenhouse plants of wide cult. and many rock garden species. *Cyclamen*, a favorite pot plant, needs greenhouse culture, but nearly all the rest of the family are plants of the open border, the rock garden or the wild garden, while a few are marsh or semi-aquatic species. *Anagallis* is largely weedy.

*Trientalis* and *Dodecatheon* are most suited to the wild garden. *Androsace*, *Soldanella* and *Douglasia* are chiefly for the rock garden, while *Lysimachia* (which includes creeping Charlie) and *Steironema* are of easy cult. in the open border.

The leaves are alternate* or opposite,* or even whorled,* and in many genera in a basal rosette. Flowers regular,* solitary or in various sorts of clusters (often in umbels*), very showy in *Cyclamen*, although the flower is solitary. Fruit a dry pod (capsule*) splitting into 5 or 10 segments.

Technical flower characters: Calyx more or less tubular or bell-shaped. Corolla funnel-shaped, or tubular and abruptly expanded above, mostly 5-lobed. Stamens 5, opposite the corolla lobes and borne on them. Ovary generally superior,* 1-celled, with many ovules. Style and stigma 1.

**PRIMULINA, -us, -um** (prim-you-ly'na). Primrose-like.

**PRIMULOIDES** (prim-you-loy'deez, but see OÏDES). Like a primrose (*Primula*).

**PRINCE'S-FEATHER** = *Polygonum orientale*, and *Amaranthus hybridus hypochondriacus*.

**PRINCE'S-PINE** = *Chimaphila umbellata*.

**PRINCIPLES OF HEREDITY.** See HEREDITY.

* Special articles on the subjects indicated by an asterisk (*) will be found at the words so marked.

*PRINOIDES* (pry-noy'deez, but *see* OÏDES). Like a plant of the obsolete genus *Prinus*, which included plants now classed among the hollies.

**PRINSEPIA** (prin-see'pi-a). A small genus of spiny, Asiatic shrubs of the rose family, only **P. sinensis** likely to be cult. and little grown outside the collections of fanciers. It is an attractive, arching shrub, 4-6 ft. high, its spines slender but sharp, about ¾ in. long. Leaves alternate,* oval-lance-shaped, long-pointed, 2-3 in. long, bright green and minutely hairy on the essentially entire* margin. Flowers yellow, about ½ in. wide, in clusters of 1-4. Petals 5, nearly round. Stamens* 10. Fruit purplish, about ⅓ in. long (a drupe*), its stones slightly sculptured. March-April. Hardy from zone* 3 southward. Propagated by seeds sown when ripe or by cuttings of green wood under glass. Manchuria. (Named for Macaire-Prinsep, Swiss botanist.)

*PRINUS* (pry'nus). *See* PRINOIDES. *Prinus* was once used as a specific name for the chestnut oak, but this is now called *Quercus montana. See* OAK.

**PRITCHARDIA** (prit-chard'i-a). Erect, spineless, Pacific Island fan palms, comprising half a dozen species, of which **P. pacifica**, the Fiji fan palm, is planted in Fla. for ornament, but is hardy only in zone* 9. It has a smooth trunk, 15-30 ft. high, with a crown of handsome, fan-shaped leaves at the top. Leaves 3-4 ft. wide, green both sides, cut rather shallowly into about 90 narrow, stiffish segments, which are long-pointed. Leafstalk about 3 ft. long, spineless. Flowers small, greenish, the cluster shorter than the leaves. Fruit about ½ in. in diameter, globe-shaped. Other species may be known to fanciers in Calif., some of them under the name *Styloma*. (Named for W. T. Pritchard, British consul in Polynesia.)

**PRIVET.** Best known as hedge plants, privet comprises many other species of the genus **Ligustrum** (ly-gus'trum) of the olive family. Of the 50 known species, all from the Old World, those below are of chief hort. interest. They are shrubs, or rarely trees, with opposite,* generally ovalish, often persistent or evergreen, or half-evergreen leaves, without marginal teeth. Flowers small, white, sometimes malodorous, mostly in terminal clusters (panicles*), often not produced on clipped hedge specimens. Corolla short-tubular, its 4-lobed limb* spreading. Stamens* 2. Fruit a small, berry-like drupe,* usually black or bluish, 1-4-seeded. (*Ligustrum* is the classical Latin name of the privet.)

For Culture and uses *see* below. All those not specified as persistent, half-evergreen, or evergreen, drop their leaves in the autumn. Practically all are without autumnal color.

**L. acuminatum.** A shrub 4-6 ft. high, its branches upright. Leaves 2-3 in. long, more or less wedge-shaped at the base, hairy on the midrib beneath. Flower clusters nearly 2 in. long, the stamens* protruding. Jap. June. Hardy from zone* 3 southward. The *var.* **macrocarpum** is more stiffly erect and has larger fruit.

**L. amurense.** Amur privet. A shrub 10-15 ft. high, its branches erect. Leaves half-evergreen, 1¾-2½ in. long, hairy on the midrib beneath. Flower cluster almost 2 in. long, the corolla with a longer tube than lobes. Northern China. June-July. Hardy from zone* 3 southward. Resembles the California privet (*L. ovalifolium*), but is hardier, and not so suited for hedges.

**L. coriaceum** = *Ligustrum japonicum rotundifolium*.

**L. ibolium.** Ibolium privet. A hybrid derived from crossing *L. ovalifolium* with *L. obtusifolium*, and a useful, but not much grown, hedge plant. It is an upright shrub, hardier than the California privet (*L. ovalifolium*), the leaves hairy on the midrib beneath. Flower cluster slightly and softly hairy. Aug. Hardy from zone* 3 southward.

**L. ibota.** A rare and little-known privet, long mistaken for *L. obtusifolium* (the true ibota privet). It is a shrub 4-6 ft. high, the branches spreading. Leaves 1-2 in. long, hairy on the midrib beneath. Flower clusters head-like, 4-8-flowered, scarcely over ⅔ in. long. Jap. June. Hardy from zone* 3 southward, but one of the least decorative of the privets.

**L. japonicum.** Wax privet. An evergreen shrub 7-10 ft. high. Leaves oblong-oval, leathery, 3-4 in. long, smooth. Flower clusters 4-6 in. long, the tube of the corolla only slightly longer than the lobes. Jap. and Korea. July-Sept. Hardy from zone* 6 southward, perhaps in protected parts of zone* 5. A useful hedge plant. The *var.* **rotundifolium** (sometimes offered as *L. coriaceum*) is a lower, more compact shrub, with lustrous, dark green, more numerous leaves.

**L. lucidum.** An evergreen shrub or even a small tree, up to 30 ft. high. Leaves pointed, 4-6 in. long, shining and smooth. Flower cluster nearly 10 in. long, the tube and lobes of the corolla about of equal length. Jap. and China. Aug.-Sept. Hardy from zone* 6 southward. Occasionally planted as a street tree, especially in central and northern Fla.

**L. massalongianum.** An evergreen shrub, not over 3 ft. high. Leaves narrowly lance-shaped, 2-3 in. long, smooth. Flower cluster 2½-3½ in. long, slightly hairy. Himalayas. July-Aug. Hardy from zone* 6 southward.

**L. nepalense.** An evergreen shrub or small tree, the twigs hairy. Leaves oblong or oval-oblong, pointed, 2-5 in. long, hairy on the under side. Flower clusters broad, furnished with stalked bracts.* Himalayas. July-Aug. Hardy from zone* 7 southward, and used for hedges in Calif.

**L. obtusifolium.** Ibota privet (but *see L. ibota*). A spreading or arching shrub, 6-10 ft. high. Leaves elliptic or oblongish, 1½-2½ in. long, hairy beneath. Flower clusters nodding, not over 1½ in. long, the corolla tube thrice longer than its lobes. Jap. July. Hardy from zone* 3 southward and long known, incorrectly, as *L. ibota*. A widely cult. shrub with profuse flowers and black, slightly bloomy fruit. The *var.* **regelianum,** Regel's privet, is lower and has horizontally spreading branches.

**L. ovalifolium.** California privet, really a native of Jap., and less used in Calif. for hedges than in the East. A compact, half-evergreen shrub, 5-20 ft. high, easily the most widely used hedge plant in the U.S. Leaves 2-2½ in. long, shining, without any hairs. Flower cluster 3-4 in. long, the corolla tube longer than its lobes. July. Surely hardy from zone* 4 southward, but in zone* 3 sometimes killed to the ground or outright by severe winters such as 1917-18 and 1933-34. There are many hort. forms, mostly with variegated or variously margined leaves, marked either with yellow or white. The common green form is the best for hedges.

**L. quihoui.** A Chinese privet, 4-6 ft. high, the branches spreading and somewhat rigid. Leaves elliptic or oblongish, 1-2½ in. long. Flower cluster hairy, the spikes in a branched cluster 5-8 in. long. Aug.-Sept. Hardy from zone* 6 southward.

**L. sinense.** A Chinese privet up to 12 ft. high, the branches spreading. Leaves elliptic or oblongish, 1½-3 in. long, hairy on the veins beneath. Flowers in a loose, hairy, branching cluster (panicle*) 3-5 in. long. July. Hardy from zone* 6 southward.

**L. vulgare.** Common privet or prim. Next to *L. ovalifolium* the most widely grown of all hedge privets, because it is hardier than *L. ovalifolium*, but its leaves are not half-evergreen over most of the country, sometimes so southward. It is a shrub 6-15 ft. high. Leaves oblong-oval, 1¾-2½ in. long. Flower cluster not over 2 in. long, the corolla tube shorter than or about the length of, its lobes. Eu. and northern Af., sometimes naturalized in the U.S. July. Hardy from zone* 3 southward. There are many hort. forms, with golden, variegated, white-margined or otherwise marked foliage. There is also a variety with yellow fruit.

### PRIVET CULTURE

No shrubs grow so easily as privet, and many professional gardeners scorn the whole group as being decidedly weedy shrubs. One of the most famous of them wrote "the meanest of all mean shrubs, but popular beyond all others, its weed-like facility of increase making it dear to those to whom something growing with a fungus-like rapidity is a treasure." There is also what he calls their "vile and sickly odor."

While the fact of rapidity of growth and malodorous flowers is true, it remains that the privets contain some ornamental shrubs, particularly among the really evergreen species. Of these the best are *Ligustrum japonicum, L. lucidum, L. massalongianum*, and *L. nepalense*, none of them, unfortunately, hardy in the North.

For hedge plants the outstanding one is the California privet (*L. ovalifolium*), followed closely by *L. vulgare*, and as fair substitutes, *L. ibolium* and *L. amurense*. For their use as hedge plants *see* HEDGES. The rest of the species are moderately decorative shrubs for the border, their chief attraction being their fruits.

Most of the commonly grown privets will stand more smoke, dust, wind, and even sea spray than any other shrubs. In other words, they are of the easiest culture in a variety of soils and in the most unfavorable sites. All of them are easily increased from slips rooted in moist sand, and the hedge species will often root in any garden soil. Most of them are also easily raised from seed.

INSECT PESTS. Small scale insects infesting privet can be controlled with a dormant oil spray. Mites are controlled with sulphur sprays.

DISEASES. Anthracnose may seriously damage European privet. Small cankers on the twigs or larger lesions on the lower stem and roots lead to death of twigs and sometimes whole plants. Eradication by removal and burning of affected parts is the best control known. California privet is immune to this disease but very susceptible to winter injury.

**PRIVET ANDROMEDA** = *Xolisma ligustrina*.

**PRIZES.** *See* EXHIBITIONS AND SHOWS.

**PROBOSCIDEA** (pro-bos-sid'i-a). Curiously fruited annual (in ours), clammy or sticky herbs, and the only cult. genus of the family **Martyniaceae** (mar-tin-i-a'see-ee), which comprises 2 other genera and about 10 species, all from the tropics or sub-tropics. The only cult. species is **P. louisianica** (often known as *P. louisiana* or *Martynia louisianica* or, wrongly, as *P. jussieui*), the unicorn-plant, also called pro-

---

* Special articles on the subjects indicated by an asterisk (*) will be found at the words so marked.

boscis-flower. It is a sprawling annual, with alternate* or nearly alternate, roundish-oval, thick, soft leaves that are 7–10 in. wide, and heart-shaped at the base. Flowers bell-shaped or funnel-shaped, the limb slightly 2-lipped,* yellowish-purple, in few-flowered clusters in the axils. Corolla about 1½ in. long. Stamens* 4, jointed by the anthers.* Fruit a hanging, woody, curved and beaked capsule,* the body of which is about 3 in. long. Beak splitting when dry and forming 2 hooked appendages, nearly 3 in. long. In the South the young and still green fruits are used like pickling cucumbers. The plant is a tender annual needing the same conditions for culture as the tomato (which see), but should be set at least 5 ft. apart each way. The plant is native in the southeastern U.S. (*Proboscidea* is from the Greek for snout, in allusion to the long-beaked fruit.)

**PROBOSCIS-FLOWER** = *Proboscidea louisianica*.

*PROCERA*, -*us*, -*um* (pro'ser-ra). Tall.

*PROCUMBENS* (pro-kum'benz). Procumbent; *i.e.* trailing, but not rooting. See RUNNER.

**PROFIT IN GARDENING.** See ACCOUNTS.

**PROLIFERATION.** The horticulturally useful attribute of many plants to produce offsets,* bulbils* or other vegetative means of propagation. Proliferous organs and the tendency of some plants to proliferation are of the greatest value to the gardener who uses such parts to increase his stock, notably in the houseleek (offsets), some onions (bulbils), and in begonia (a proliferating leaf).

Quite often the ability to produce a new plant on an existing growing one furnishes the most interesting cases of proliferation. Sometimes a new plant will sprout directly from a growing leaf, as in *Asplenium bulbiferum*. And in at least one case a whole new crop of young plants will start from the leaf margin, as in the air plant (*see* BRYOPHYLLUM PINNATUM). While proliferation can be induced by an injury, as in making a leaf cutting of begonia, the causes of natural proliferations are wholly unknown.

*PROLIFICA*, -*us*, -*um* (pro-liff'i-ka). Prolific, as to flowers or fruit.

**PRONG BUDDING.** See BUDDING.

**PROPAGATION.** The increase of new plants from existing ones. For the origin of really new plants (*i.e.* new species and varieties) *see* PLANT BREEDING. It is unnecessary to repeat here the best method of propagating the different plants in this book, for at every entry the preferred method has been mentioned. Here we are concerned chiefly with the principles of propagation and with guiding the gardener to the proper articles where the details will be found.

The propagation of plants falls into two very different categories: (1) Those raised from seeds or spores,* the production of both of which involves sexual union, hence called sexual reproduction; (2) those propagated vegetatively, in ways to be discussed presently, without the intervention of sexual union, hence called asexual reproduction or vegetative propagation.

SEEDS AND SPORES. How these are produced will be found at FERTILIZATION (for seeds) and at FERNS AND FERN GARDENING (for spores). At the latter entry also there is a description of how young ferns are raised from spores.

Raising new plants from seed, still the commonest form of propagation, is treated in detail at SEEDS AND SEEDAGE, and need not be repeated here.

VEGETATIVE PROPAGATION. Some plants will not come true from seed; others, like the banana, pineapple, and the navel orange, ordinarily have no seeds; and for many others the increase of new plants is much quicker and easier without using seeds. The Greeks knew this well, and Theophrastus wrote a description of the making of cuttings.

Whatever method is used it involves two different principles. One is the ability of plants to send out roots from an injured (*i.e.* a cut) surface, and sometimes without any cutting; the other is the ability of the tissue of related plants to weld and grow as one when properly united.

In the first category the gardener finds the ability to root from a cut surface of the greatest use. In hundreds of plants he makes a cutting or slip which when inserted in the proper medium will ultimately produce roots and a new plant. For the details of this extremely common method of vegetative propagation *see* CUTTINGS.

In the second category, the gardener, instead of detaching the injured (*i.e.* cut) member, leaves it on the parent plant. When properly handled and covered with soil this will root, after which it is detached and grows into a new plant. Some, in fact many, plants will root at the joints without injury so long as the stem is covered with soil. In any case propagation by this method usually involves laying a stem down so it can be covered with soil, hence the operation is known as LAYERING, which see for the details.

In both cuttings and layering the production of new roots is the object sought. But in the remaining forms of vegetative propagation very different tactics are followed. Both of them are based upon the ability of properly joined tissue to weld or grow together. But mere welding would be of no value if the piece brought to the union did not contain one or more buds which would ultimately flourish. It is upon the ability of detached buds, or of a single one, to grow, once the welding process is accomplished, that the remaining methods are based. One of them, because it uses only a single bud, is known as BUDDING; the other, using several buds, is known as GRAFTING. For the details and management of both *see* BUDDING, GRAFTING.

Budding, grafting and layering, while not exclusively so, are largely means of propagating woody plants. Cuttings may be made of both woody and herbaceous plants. But the last method of propagation, by division or separation of the existing clump, is used practically always upon herbaceous perennials. For the details of this *see* DIVISION. *See also* OFFSETS, RUNNER.

**PROPHET-FLOWER** = *Arnebia echioides*.

**PROP ROOT.** A root that acts as a prop or support. Prop roots originate from stems, but ultimately penetrate the soil, serving both as anchors and food gatherers. Corn produces them (*see* CORN), and many other plants do also. The most notable are the screw pines (*see* PANDANUS) which, in the tropics, may produce prop roots far up the trunk. These diverge from it, ultimately penetrate the soil many feet from the trunk, and make large, stem-like prop roots.

*PROSERPINACOIDES* (pro-ser-pin-a-koy'deez, but *see* OÏDES). Resembling a plant of the genus *Proserpinaca*, which does not contain cult. plants. See MYRIOPHYLLUM.

**PROSOPIS.** See MESQUITE.

**PROSTANTHERA** (pros-tan'ther-a). Mint-bush. Tender Australian shrubs or small trees, comprising about 40 species, belonging to the mint family. Leaves simple,* opposite,* ovalish or lance-shaped, scented. Flowers in whorls or terminal clusters, white, red, or purple. Calyx* of 5 sepals, joined halfway down. Corolla broadly tubular, dividing into 2 lips.* Stamens* 4, in pairs, 2 long, and 2 short. Fruit 2-celled when young, when ripe splitting into 4, each part containing 1 seed. (*Prostanthera* is from the Greek for add to and anther, in reference to a technical feature of the anthers.)

Sometimes grown in the greenhouse, but can be grown outside in the southern states and in Calif. Propagated from cuttings of young shoots taken in the early spring. When grown as a pot plant use potting mixture* 5.

nivea. Handsome shrub 3–6 ft. high, and of shiny appearance. Stems slender and much-branched. Leaves simple,* small, narrow, to 1½ in. long, entire, margins slightly rolled. Flowers in axillary whorls,* pure white or tinged blue.

rotundifolia. Shrub 3–7 ft. high. Leaves small, ovalish, to ½ in. long, the margins entire or slightly cut into rounded teeth. Flowers purplish-blue, ⅓ in. long, in terminal clusters (racemes*).

*PROSTRATA*, -*us*, -*um* (pros-tray'ta). Lying flat; prostrate.

**PROSTRATE JUNIPER** = *Juniperus communis depressa*.

**PROSTRATE PIGWEED** = *Amaranthus blitoides*. See list at WEEDS.

---

* Special articles on the subjects indicated by an asterisk (*) will be found at the words so marked.

**PROSTRATE VINES.** See VINES.

**PROTEACEAE** (pro-tee-ā'see-ee). The Australian Oak family is very large, comprising over 50 genera and perhaps 1000 species of trees and shrubs, mostly Australian, but found also in South Africa, Asia, and South America. The six hort. genera are ornamental shrubs and trees, grown outdoors in southern Calif. and Fla., or in greenhouses where some of them are rather widely grown, especially *Leucadendron* (the silver tree), *Banksia, Hakea* and *Grevillea*. The other two cult. genera are *Macadamia*, with an edible nut (the Queensland nut), and *Dryandra*, which comprises mostly shrubby Australian plants popular in Calif.

Leaves alternate* or scattered (whorled* in some), sometimes tiny and awl-shaped or needle-like, always without marginal teeth, expanded and very silvery in *Leucadendron*. Flowers usually in dense clusters, without petals, male and female on different plants in *Leucadendron*. Fruit various, usually a nut, capsule,* or drupe.*

Technical flower characters: Sepals 4, united or more or less tubular. Petals none. Stamens* 4, opposite the sepals, and borne on them. Ovary superior,* the style 1 and undivided.

**PROTECTING PLANTS.** Most people infer that winter protection of plants is an effort to keep the plants warm by wrapping them up, just as we clothe ourselves in a fur coat during the winter. This, however, leaves out of consideration the fact that a plant has no body warmth which might be preserved by a warm covering, and that within a few hours it will be just as cold as if it had no protection. A plant which dies from the effect of frost at a temperature near the freezing point — as, for instance, most tropical plants — cannot be kept alive outdoors with any amount of covering. Only artificial heat in a greenhouse or room will sustain it over the winter.

Those who reason this far not infrequently reach the conclusion that there is therefore no sense in covering plants at all; that either they are hardy and need no covering, or they are not hardy and covering will not save them, hence they are better not raised at all. This, however, is as much a mistake as it is an illusion that we cover plants in order to keep them warm.

For what reason then do we cover them? This question cannot be answered without explaining that hardiness is by no means only the ability to withstand low temperatures. It includes also the capacity to stop and start growth at the most opportune time in fall and spring, and to resist effectively the fatal loss of moisture which may be caused when the winter sun or drying winds act upon the frozen twigs, buds, or evergreen leaves.

Hardiness further implies the ability to remain dormant, or at rest, during prolonged warm spells in the later part of the winter; and to send the roots down deeply enough to reach beyond the destructive influence of violent fluctuations of temperature which are frequent in the upper, exposed layers of the soil.

If these facts are understood, it is easy to understand also in what manner a covering may assist a plant in its struggle against the hardships imposed upon it by the winter; and this understanding, again, will help us to apply the covering most effectively.

### How to Apply a Winter Covering

A heavy covering, applied with the wrong notion that it has to keep the plant warm, may easily smother and kill an otherwise hardy plant. At any rate, it will do more harm than good. A light covering, on the other hand, which simply protects the plant against the drying effect of sun or wind, or which, if applied to the ground around the plant, will prevent violent fluctuations of temperature and preserve the moisture content of the soil, may be the deciding factor between life and death.

A covering of the ground around the plant — called mulch by the gardener, and consisting of leaves or straw or well-decayed manure — if applied after a heavy freezing, and especially if accompanied by shading of the upper parts of the plant, will also serve to prevent certain plants from starting into growth during warm spells in February or early March. This early growth usually suffers serious injury from later frosts. Such covering, then, actually serves to keep the plant cool instead of warm. See MULCH.

### Plants Which Need Protection

A covering, which mainly consists in shading, either in the form of burlap, stretched on a wire frame over the whole plant — as generally practiced with Boxwood — or in the form of a screen, made from laths, straw mats or burlap and set up in particular on the east and south sides of the plant, can be recommended for most broad-leaved evergreens and for many conifers, if they have been planted in an exposed place. This same type of plant will also be greatly benefited by a mulch of leaves or well-decayed manure applied in the fall. The necessity for a sun-screen may in many instances be circumvented if the plants are given the right exposure in the beginning and are located in such a manner that they receive natural shelter from the south and east.

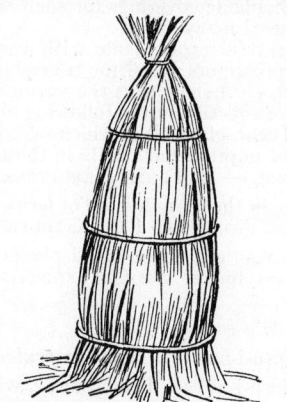

This plant is not tied up to keep it warm. For reasons see text.

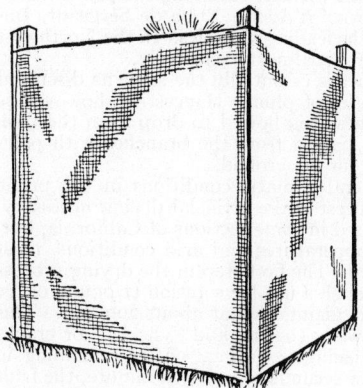

Useful burlap-covered frame for protecting box or evergreens. In severe climates it is often filled with dried leaves or straw.

The most beautiful of the climbing roses will suffer serious winter injury in many parts of the northern United States if they are not taken down from their trellises, bundled up with straw and covered with soil. The hybrid Tea roses need protection only to their crown, which is achieved by heaping soil over them to a height of about one foot.

Most rock garden plants are benefited by a dressing of stone chips, which will prevent moisture from stagnating at their crowns. Since from their native haunts these plants usually are accustomed to a snow covering, which with us they frequently do not get, we have to provide for many of them a protection which in some manner will take the place of the missing snow. Pine branches have been found to be most effective for this purpose, since they will shed moisture quickly and will never pack down tightly. All moisture-holding litter must be avoided on alpine plants.

Sunscald* of trunks or frost-splitting of recently planted trees may be prevented by wrapping the trunks in burlap during the winter months. For the methods of fighting cold in orchards see FROST and FROST CONTROL.

### Spring Frosts

Often an untimely late frost will apparently kill some freshly started seedlings. A good method is to sprinkle such lightly before sunrise, which will often save them. Such a

---

* Special articles on the subjects indicated by an asterisk (*) will be found at the words so marked.

plan is only effective after light frosts in late spring, and sprinkling while the temperature is below freezing will do more harm than good.

If you anticipate a late spring frost, you may reduce the loss of heat through radiation from the ground by covering the garden at sundown with cheesecloth, or even better, by paper pegged down. And in the case of individual plants, a paper bag slipped over them will do the job. There are also several waxed paper or cellophane coverings for such emergencies, and they may be used many times.

Some recent and very careful experiments with various kinds of individual plant protectors (used for transplanted seedlings of tomato, melon, etc.) show that the various devices sold by the dealers are effective in the following order: waxed paper, glassene, and cel-o-glass, all of which saved the plants under them, while of unprotected plants in the same row 92% were killed by frost. — H. T. See HARDINESS.

**PROTHALLUS.** A stage in the reproduction of ferns. See Spores and Reproduction at FERNS AND FERN GARDENING.

**PROTOPLASM.** The living cell tissue of all plants and animals, and assuming many forms. See CHLOROPHYLL for one of the most important.

**PROVENCE ROSE** = *Rosa gallica*.

*PRUINATA, -us, -um* (pru-i-nay′ta). Same as *pruinosa*.

*PRUINOSA, -us, -um* (pru-i-nō′sa). Pruinose; *i.e.* with a whitish, hoary bloom.*

**PRUNACEAE.** See ROSACEAE.

**PRUNE.** Prunes are merely certain varieties of plums which, on account of their firm flesh and high sugar content, can be successfully dried without removing the pit. In California the French (Prune d'Agen), Robe de Sergeant, Imperial, and Sugar are the leading varieties. In the Northwest the Italian prune is grown almost exclusively.

The culture of prunes is essentially the same as discussed for the shipping varieties of plum. Harvesting, however, is different, in that prunes are allowed to drop from the tree, or after fully mature, jarred from the branches with poles and then picked up from the ground.

Fall rains and general climatic conditions in the prune sections of the Northwest make artificial drying necessary. Dehydration is also used in some sections of California, but, with high summer temperatures and arid conditions, most of the crop is sun-dried. The first step in the drying process is to put the fruit through a hot lye solution (1 pound of lye to 20 gallons of water, maintained at about 200° F.). This removes the natural waxy coating and "checks" or cracks the skin in order to facilitate drying. After remaining in the solution from a few seconds to nearly a minute, the fruit is removed, rinsed, and then placed on shallow, wooden trays for drying.

In sun-drying, the trays are usually placed directly on the ground in a dry-yard where they are left fully exposed to the sun for from 10 days to 2 weeks. Frequent turning of the fruit is necessary to secure even drying in some varieties. Drying is usually considered complete when a handful of fruit may be squeezed together without mashing. When dehydrated under rapidly circulating air at temperatures of 120°–165° F., the time required for drying is reduced to a period of 20–36 hours.

After drying, the prunes are usually placed in storage bins, where they are allowed to "sweat" for about 3 weeks to equalize their moisture content before packing. — F. W. A.

**PRUNELLA** (pru-nell′a). Low-growing, hardy, perennial herbs, comprising 6 species of the mint family, and natives of Eu. and As. Stems square. Leaves simple,* opposite,* the veins prominent on the under side, margins generally toothed. Flowers purple or violet-blue, in dense heads or spikes. Calyx* of 5 sepals* joined halfway down, enclosing the ripened fruit. It closes and points upwards in dry weather but opens and stands horizontally in damp weather. Corolla short and tubular, 2-lipped.* Stamens* 4, in pairs, 2 long, and 2 short. Fruit 2-celled when young, but splitting into 4 parts when ripe, each part containing 1 seed. (*Pru-*

*nella* is believed to be from a German word for the quinsy, for which these plants were considered a specific.)

Not much in cult., as most species are garden weeds, but can be used for damp and shady places in the rock or wild garden. Easily propagated from seeds or division of rootstocks. Seeds should be sown in early spring, in cool greenhouse or cold frame, and transplanted to permanent positions as soon as large enough to handle. Seeds may be sown outdoors in April, when division of rootstocks also may be made.

**grandiflora.** Hardy perennial, to 9 in. high. Leaves ovalish, margins toothed or entire. Flowers purplish-blue, 1 in. long. June–July. Suitable for the blue garden (see BLUE GARDEN). Eu. There are several hort. color forms.

**incisa** = *Prunella vulgaris*, probably the *var. laciniata*.

**vulgaris.** Self-heal. Heal-all (*see also* the list at WEEDS). Hardy perennial, to 2 ft. high, of spreading habit. Leaves ovalish to lance-shaped, to 4 in. long, margins toothed or entire. Flowers violet, ½ in. long. June–Oct. Eu.; naturalized in N.A. The *var.* **laciniata** has cut leaves.

*PRUNIFOLIA, -us, -um* (pru-ni-fō′li-a). With cherry-like leaves.

**PRUNING.** The practice of cutting or trimming existing growth on woody plants for the benefit of that left on the tree, shrub or vine, done mostly to promote flower and fruit production, or to make the plant more shapely.

### FRUIT TREES

The object of pruning, which in horticultural parlance means to cut or trim, is manifold. With fruit trees, while in the young state, it is done to shape the trees according to one's desires, that is to say, by proper and careful pruning one lays the foundation of a tree, whether it is to be a standard, bush, espalier or any other type of tree. As a rule, the gardener buys his fruit trees when their form is already established, from the nurseryman who has done the preliminary pruning. From that time on, the purpose of pruning is to keep the trees shapely and to make them fruitful. Left to their own devices after planting, young fruit trees will more or less run wild and make much useless wood before reaching the fruiting stage, which in itself naturally steadies future growth.

If one aspires to grow his own fruit trees from the start, he must either bud or graft the desired varieties on the proper rootstocks, or buy one-year-old trees known as whips, which are upright stems with practically no branches. If to be grown on as a standard* or half-standard, the young tree must be allowed to run upward to the desired height before it is topped to make it branch. Standards have usually a six-foot stem or trunk, half-standards three to four feet. Any shoots that appear on the lower part of the stem should be cut away clean, but until the top is removed and the desired branches are definitely under way, the stem should not be trimmed too closely, as all the leaves possible are needed to stimulate root growth. Bush trees usually have a short leg, and the one-year-old whips should therefore be cut back to the desired point, and the succeeding shoots carried forward as branches. Trained types of trees are similarly treated at the start and afterward dealt with as described in the entry on TRAINING PLANTS.

The groundwork of the tree secured, the pruning that follows is to encourage fruitfulness, as well as to keep the tree shapely. Whether the tree has one or two stems only, as in cordons, or six or more main branches, as in a bush, it is natural for such stems or branches to push forth lateral growths, particularly from the upper portions. These branchlets or laterals theoretically are the fruiting parts of the tree. Whatever the type of tree, the stems or branches must be encouraged to branch from the base up. The cordon stem or the branches of a bush tree may in the first year grow a yard, and if this growth is permitted to stand unpruned, the following spring it will probably push laterals from the upper eyes, the lower ones remaining dormant, resulting in after years in a tree with blank spaces. As a rule, it is good policy to cut back all main stem growths made the previous year about one-third; that is, when a tree is in the making, no matter what its shape, the leaders should be so cut back early in the spring to induce the emis-

---

* Special articles on the subjects indicated by an asterisk (*) will be found at the words so marked.

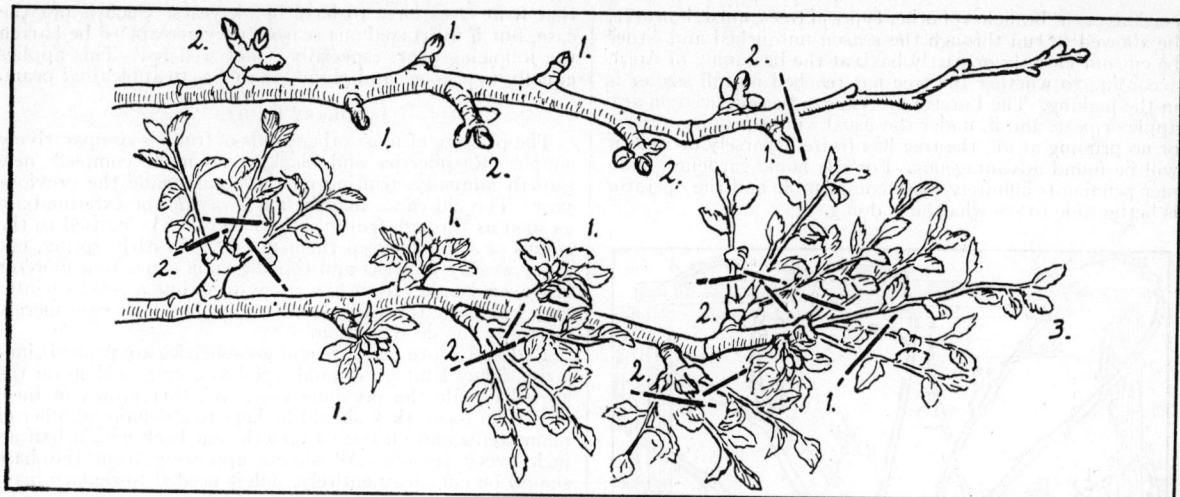

LORETTE SYSTEM OF PRUNING
(As Illustrated by the Apple)

The upper, dormant branch shows at (1) the natural fruit spurs and at (2) the growth buds of sterile shoots to be pruned in June (see below). Note the long terminal leader which should be cut back to the point indicated early in April.

The lower figure is the same branch in June, before pruning. (1) The natural fruit spurs showing fruits just beginning to set. (2) The sterile spurs with their new growth, which should be cut back as indicated when 12 inches long (usually in June) to induce formation of fruit buds for next season. At (3) is shown the leader which should be allowed to grow during this season, but cut back next April as shown in the upper figure.

sion of laterals fairly close together. This cutting back one-third should be done each year until the tree has attained the size and height wanted, by which time it should be fruiting; after that, all the leaders should be cut back entirely every season, the vigor of the tree being maintained by the laterals it makes, and feeding. These remarks, in the main, relate to apples and pears. Cherries and plums are apt to make fruiting laterals and spurs rather more readily, and as a rule they are kept to standard or bush forms. When once they start fruiting, little pruning is needed, except in the way of removing wild shoots that threaten to spoil the shape of the tree. Plums respond well to espalier training if they are to be grown on a wall. Peaches, usually grown in bush form, require but moderate pruning after they attain fruiting size, the removal of shoots that tend to crowd being all that is necessary.

WHEN TO PRUNE. In the small or moderate-sized garden apples and pears are the most valuable fruits because they can be kept within any desired limits, especially when on dwarfing stocks. In the orchard, where large trees are permissible, the customary time for pruning is during the late fall or even in the winter when the weather is fairly mild. If summer pruning is done at all, the usual plan, if the trees are of bush type, is to cut back the strongest laterals halfway, completing the pruning during the winter. For the home garden, and even in orchards where the trees have been kept to a low stature, we favor the Lorette system of pruning, a system devised by a noted French specialist for pears, but which is also applicable to apples and to some extent to other fruits.

One of the great failings of stereotyped fruit pruning is that it encourages much useless growth. We have seen garden trees pruned year after year with sedulous care, yet the desired fruit has been sparse or entirely absent; particularly is this the case if trained trees are not on dwarfing stocks. It should be understood that apples and pears produce their fruits on spurs or short laterals, not direct from the trunks or branches. As stated, the main stems or branches persistently produce laterals every season, and the natural reaction to cutting away these laterals is the production of still more wood. A tree naturally will settle down to fruiting in due time if left alone, but the gardener, unlike the orchardist, wants small trees to fruit,

and if he follows the usual winter pruning custom he is apt to be disappointed.

The Lorette system, in effect, is quite technical and requires intense study, but one can follow the general principles quite readily. Instead of the usual pruning practice, which is to cut back all laterals during the winter to the last bud or two, as well as the leaders if the tree has reached full size, Lorette pruning entails all summer and no winter pruning, and the heading back of the leaders in early April. Scientific study has shown that the fruit buds are formed by the end of June or thereabouts, at least in Europe. It is, therefore, useless to assume that winter pruning can bring about fruit buds. There are instances where obvious fruit buds have in the spring changed to growth buds and vice versa, but in a general way it is definitely known that fruit buds are set during the middle of the year, and if they are not there in embryo no winter pruning will create them; in fact, the only effect of such pruning is to make the eyes left push forth more strong growths, and so on *ad infinitum*.

The modern summer pruning entails the removal of all laterals above 12 inches in length at the end of June or thereabouts, sharp pruning shears being used so that the shoots are cut clean back to the base, leaving only the basal cluster of leaves where the dormant, invisible eyes are situated. During the balance of the summer, the remaining laterals, when they lengthen out, are so cut back, whether they emanate from the spurs or from the branch itself. Those that do not reach 12 inches may be cut back in late fall unless they carry plump-looking buds at the tips. It is quite common for shoots six inches or so in length to bear fruit buds at the tips, some varieties of apples being essentially tip bearers. As a rule, however, it is good policy to keep the spurs fairly short. Spurs are short, stubby branchlets that should each carry one or more clusters of fruit buds. Some varieties make natural spurs fairly freely, especially after they have started fruiting, but in the main, artificial spurs have to be encouraged by pruning as outlined.

Contrary to what one might expect, the hard cutting back of the laterals during the summer does not encourage all the basal eyes to start into growth. A few may, and they can be cut back in late fall. The old-time summer system of pruning the laterals half back, on the other hand, excites quite a mass of new growths. The leaders, that is, the top growths of

* Special articles on the subjects indicated by an asterisk (*) will be found at the words so marked.

cordons or the branches of other types of trees, must, however, be allowed to run through the season untouched and either be cut out entirely or partly back at the beginning of April, according to whether the tree has reached its full size or is in the making. The Lorette system can be practiced on any apple or pear, and if, under the usual winter pruning system or no pruning at all, the tree has fruited sparsely or well, it will be found advantageous. For the home gardener, summer pruning is infinitely more comfortable and the operator is better able to see what he is doing.

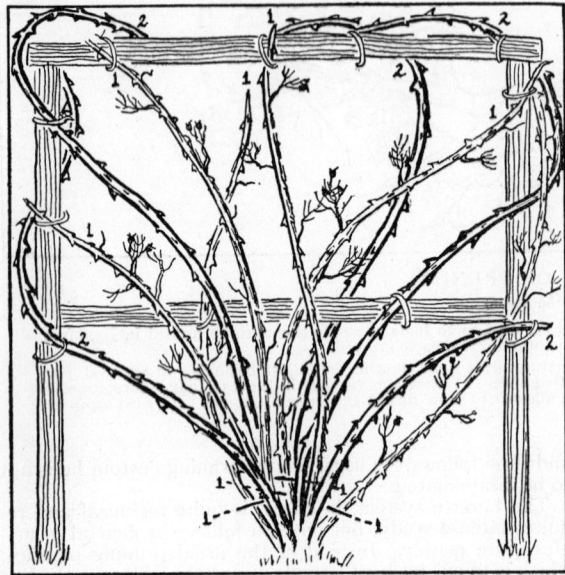

CORRECT PRUNING OF RAMBLER ROSE
(1) Cut back to the base growths that have flowered when bloom is finished; (2) retain the new shoots which will produce flowers the following year.

Reverting to the term spurs, these, as stated, are the fruit-bearing branchlets. Natural spurs may extend only an inch or two from the main branch. Artificial spurs, induced by repeated pruning, may extend much farther, especially on old trees that have been fruiting over a long period. These artificial spurs perforce carry growth eyes and produce laterals each season. A tree must produce a requisite amount of foliage to ensure healthiness, and only by producing laterals can it make the necessary leaves. Summer pruning as outlined does not of course denude the tree of foliage beyond the safety margin, but it does check some of the food supply to the roots, and after pruning it is, therefore, good policy then to give the trees a good dressing of fertilizer and water if conditions are dry. The reason for not heading back the leading growth or growths is that these keep the sap active so that the roots are not entirely robbed of support. Left to carry on the major part of the work, these leaders usually grow quite vigorously. As stated, the heading back must not be done until early April when the trees are preparing to make new growths.

THINNING. When fruit trees, particularly apples, pears and peaches, have reached full bearing, it is desirable to disbud if the trees appear to be carrying too many fruits over a given area. It may look well to see a branch laden heavily, and an apple or pear may set several fruits on each spur, but if the spurs are six inches or so apart it is too much to expect choice, large fruits if several hang on each spur. It is sometimes desirable to remove some of the flower clusters when they are overabundant, but ordinarily the thinning out can best be done as soon as the fruitlets are set. Too heavy a set of fruit allowed to remain invariably means a light or no crop the following year. It is often assumed that fruit trees have to have blank years. Such is not the case, but if overtaxed one season, they are apt to be barren the following year, especially if not well fed. This applies equally to peaches and plums, as well as to apples and pears.

### BERRY FRUITS

The pruning of most other kinds of fruits is comparatively simple. Raspberries and blackberries make complete new growth annually, fruiting on the stems made the previous year. The old canes may be cut away at the extreme base as soon as through fruiting, the new canes being tied to the stakes or wires to keep them upright. In early spring, cut away weakly growths and top the main canes to a more or less even height, from five to six feet; but a severe winter may kill back the tops considerably, in which case merely cut away the dead portion.

Red and white currants and gooseberries are pruned similarly. They fruit on the old wood as a rule, seldom on the growths made the previous year. Whether grown in bush or cordon form, they should be kept to a definite number of main stems and all lateral growths cut back within half an inch every season. All shoots appearing from the base should be cut away entirely, unless needed to replace main stems that have become weakened by age or borers. To permit sun and air to reach the main branches, cut back the longest laterals halfway during July, and complete the pruning after the foliage has dropped. Black currants are not spur fruiters. They fruit on both old and new wood and need only have the oldest stems cut away after fruiting.

Grapevines can be pruned in varying degrees according to the position they occupy. For the different systems used for the *vinifera* and common varieties see GRAPE.

### ORNAMENTAL TREES AND SHRUBS

The pruning of trees and shrubs is for two purposes: to keep them shapely, and, in the case of flowering subjects, to encourage better quality blooms. Young trees, whether for shade purposes or for ornamental use, have all undergone more or less pruning and trimming at the hands of the nurseryman, and, aside from the removal of lower branches to give more stem length as they increase the heads, they require only occasional attention to prevent crowding. Flowering trees of all kinds, too, require but a moderate amount of trimming or pruning, mainly to keep them

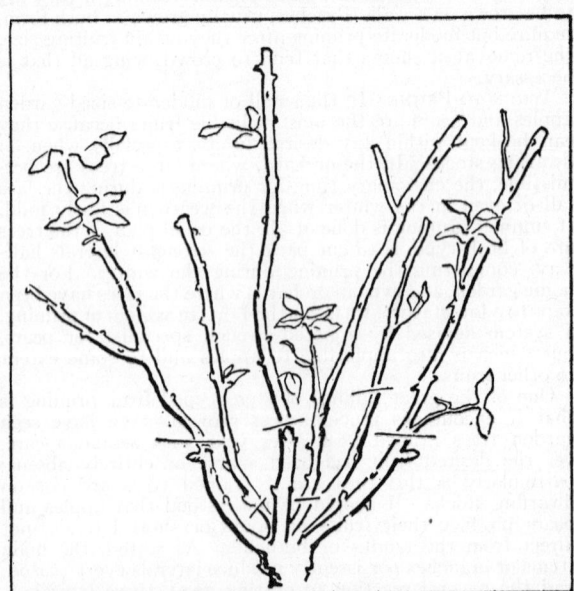

DORMANT ROSEBUSH IN APRIL
Prune where the cuts are shown, leaving not more than 3–6 buds on strong shoots, and cutting weak shoots to the base.

* Special articles on the subjects indicated by an asterisk (*) will be found at the words so marked.

shapely, as when once they reach flowering age pruning has but little influence upon flower production, and only in exceptional instances is it necessary to disbud. As a rule, the more flowers an ornamental tree bears, the more it is appreciated, whether it be a dogwood, *Magnolia*, flowering crab, cherry or plum. Some ornamental trees, such as the cherry, crab and plum, flower largely on natural spurs; the redbud (*Cercis canadensis*) blooms directly on the branches and stems, while the *Magnolia* and sundry others flower on the points of the previous year's growth.

Flowering shrubs come under two headings, those that flower in the spring, and those that bloom any time after June. The late bloomers, when pruning is necessary, must be subjected to the knife only in winter or early spring. For the most part they flower largely on the wood made the same season. By trimming or pruning in the spring, new wood that will duly flower is encouraged. Spring-bloomers, on the other hand, largely flower on the wood made the previous season. To prune any time after the leaves fall would mean the removal of much flowering wood. Immediately after flowering is finished is the time to prune or trim spring-flowering shrubs.

Examples of spring-flowering shrubs, to be pruned after flowering, are: Azalea, *Cercis*, Dogwood, *Diervilla*, *Kalmia*, *Kerria*, *Leucothoë*, *Philadelphus*, *Pieris*, *Rhododendron*, *Rhodotypos*, *Spiraea*, *Syringa* (lilac) and *Viburnum*. Late-flowering shrubs, to be pruned while dormant, are: *Buddleia*, *Clethra alnifolia*, *Caryopteris*, *Hibiscus syriacus*, *Hydrangea*, and *Vitex*. Of these, *Buddleia*, *Caryopteris* and *Vitex* are often cut back to the ground each season in any case, especially where they are doubtfully hardy.

It should be understood that the pruning of shrubs is mainly for the purpose of keeping them shapely and within bounds. They should not be trimmed like a privet hedge, and if they are naturally tall growers it must not be assumed that constant trimming will keep them dwarf, except at the expense of flowering. The habit of each shrub must be studied. If naturally prone to sending up new growths from the base, cut away old wood near the ground line. Shrubs with a branching habit should be pruned less vigorously, but at the same time sufficiently to prevent overcrowding of the growths. All deciduous trees and shrubs should be well cut back or pruned at planting time. Damaged and long, straggly roots should also be trimmed off clean. See ROOT PRUNING.

Shearing is a form of pruning practiced on hedges to keep them dense and compact. In northern climates the last shearing should be done sometime in July, otherwise the growths made later will not have time to ripen, and severe damage may be done by hard freezing. The shearing of coniferous evergreens at no time is to be recommended unless formal-shaped trees are desired. To encourage growths and keep them shapely, junipers, *Thuja*, etc., may be pruned any time between May and July, the work being done with the knife or sharp pruning shears otherwise known as secateurs. Short lengths of growth only should be removed. If the size is to be kept to definite limits, the leader must be stopped and the side branches frequently gone over. Conifers cannot be cut hard back like deciduous subjects, as the old wood lacks power to make new growth.

### PERENNIALS AND ANNUALS

The term pruning is not applicable to herbaceous perennials and annuals, but both can be benefited by disbudding or disshooting. Perennials, such as *Phlox*, *Helenium*, *Aster*, *Artemisia vulgaris*, *Delphinium*, etc., after the first season are apt to produce too many stems for the area the roots occupy, and if all are allowed to remain the flower clusters will be curtailed in size however well the plants are fed. Exhibition flowers of this class are usually grown on single-stemmed plants specially propagated, but in the garden roots up to three or four years old will give superb results if in May the gardener goes over his plants and removes all but the strongest shoots. Two or three is enough for *Delphinium* and not more than six for the others. With *Delphinium* the shoots should be cut out low; in other cases it is often possible to pull out the weak growths. Annuals, such as China asters, African marigolds, zinnias, etc., by disbudding, can be made to produce larger and finer flowers. These plants usually branch naturally after the center flower bud starts to develop. The side branches in turn develop a bud and make laterals. By pinching out the surplus laterals the leading flowers are much benefited.

Dahlias, if well grown, also require disshooting and disbudding. If a *Dahlia* plant with one stem has the top pinched out when it is 12 inches or so tall, it will send out several laterals, each of which will duly produce a cluster of three buds. The best of the three only is retained, assuming a fine large flower is wanted. In the meantime, several stems will start pushing forth laterals at the upper leaf joints. These are duly nipped out, only those at the base being allowed to develop. Thus, if a plant originally has six stems, six to 12 more will take their places after the flowers are cut, and unless unduly late or frost comes early, these will likewise flower. Constant disshooting and the removal of portions of foliage are necessary if high-class flowers are desired.

Outdoor chrysanthemums of the Pompon class require no disshooting, and disbudding, unless rigorously done, is not worth while. Large-flowered sorts, however, whether outdoor or under glass, must not be allowed to have more than two or three stems and only one flower bud on each stem is permissible. All side shoots that develop after the flower bud shows must be removed. — T. A. W. *See also* ROOT PRUNING.

**PRUNING KNIFE.** *See* Section 5, TOOLS AND IMPLEMENTS.

**PRUNING SAW.** *See* Section 4, TOOLS AND IMPLEMENTS.

**PRUNING SHEARS.** *See* Section 4, TOOLS AND IMPLEMENTS.

**PRUNUS** (proo'nus). A large and immensely important genus of shrubs and trees of the rose family, nearly all from the north temperate zone, a few reaching to the Andes. It comprises over 150 species and includes all the plums, cherries, and apricots, and some consider it as including still other closely related plants like the peach and almond (including the flowering almond) here kept separate in the

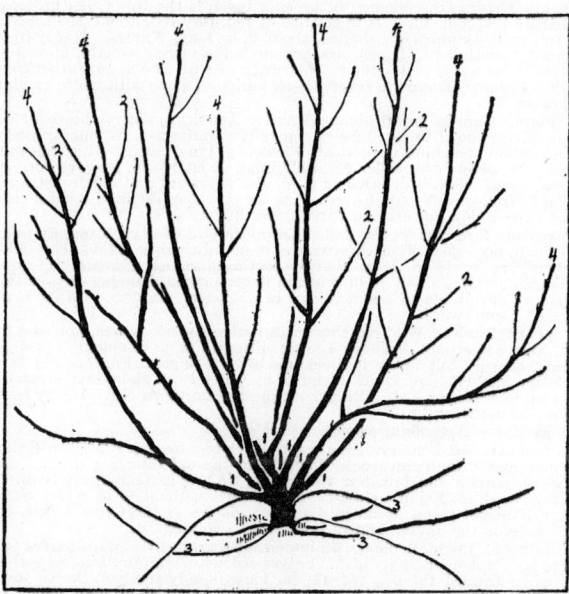

**PRUNING CURRANT OR GOOSEBERRY BUSHES**
(1) Fruiting main stems, to be retained; (2) lateral branches, to be cut back halfway at the end of June; (3) basal shoots, to be removed at any time; (4) the leaders, to be headed back each fall to keep the bushes about 4 ft. high.

* Special articles on the subjects indicated by an asterisk (*) will be found at the words so marked.

genus *Amygdalus* (which see). A few evergreen species, considered by some as belonging to *Prunus*, are here assigned to *Laurocerasus* (the cherry laurels).

Besides the outstanding importance of the fruit trees in *Prunus*, it contains all the Japanese flowering cherries (*see* below) and many other superb flowering shrubs and trees, the fruit of which is generally inedible and often wanting.

All, or nearly all, deciduous trees and shrubs with alternate,* never compound* leaves which are nearly always sharply toothed. Flowers in clusters (corymbs* or racemes), or sometimes few or only one, white, pink, or red (in some hort. forms), typically with 5 sepals, 5 petals, and many stamens. In some of the hort. forms there is much doubling of the petals and sometimes no functional stamens and no fruit. The latter is typically a drupe,* that is, a fleshy fruit with a single stone, hence often called stone fruits. The stone is generally flattish and grooved in the plums, but round and ungrooved in the cherries. (*Prunus* is the classical Latin name of the plum tree.)

For culture of the important edible species *see* CHERRY, PLUM, and APRICOT. *See also* PEACH and ALMOND for the culture of trees sometimes included in *Prunus*. For the ornamental, flowering species *see* below. Those especially desirable for their bloom or foliage, and usually grown for no other purpose, are marked with a dagger (†). All bloom early in the spring, some before the leaves expand.

**americana.** Wild or yellow plum. A native American tree 20–30 ft. high, usually less as cult. Leaves willow-like, 3–4 in. long, about 1 in. wide. Flowers white, 2–5 in a cluster, about 1 in. wide. Fruit about 1 in. in diameter, mostly yellow, sometimes red. Eastern N.A. Hardy from zone* 3 southward.

**amygdalus** = *Amygdalus communis.*

**angustifolia.** Chickasaw plum. A native American, twiggy shrub or small tree, usually not over 12 ft. high. Leaves trough-like, lance-shaped, 1–3½ in. long. Flowers 2–4 in a cluster, white, about ⅝ in. wide. Fruit nearly round, about ½ in. in diameter, red or yellow. Southeastern U.S. Hardy from zone* 4 southward. The *var.* **watsoni,** the sand plum, from Kansas and vicinity, is a low bush with zigzag twigs.

**armeniaca.** Apricot. A tree 15–25 ft. high. Leaves roundish or heart-shaped, hairy on the veins beneath, 2–4½ in. long. Flowers solitary, about 1 in. wide, blooming before the leaves unfold, white or pink. Fruit smooth-skinned (in maturity), nearly stalkless, about 1¾ in. in diameter. Western Asia. For culture and varieties *see* APRICOT. Its flowers are so attractive that it is sometimes cult. for ornament. Hardy from zone* 5 southward, but its blossoms often killed by late spring frosts, except in the region of commercial cult., *i.e.* Calif.

**avium.** The common sweet cherry. A tall tree with birch-like outer bark. Leaves oblongish or broader toward the tip, 2½–6 in. long. Flowers white, 3–6 in a cluster (umbel*). Fruit nearly globe-shaped, stalked. Eurasia, and of very ancient culture. Hardy from zone* 3 southward, or north of this for many hort. varieties. It is often an escape, and is then sometimes known as the Mazzard cherry, used mostly as grafting stock. The *var.* **duracina** is the Bigarreau or hard-fleshed cherry (*see* CHERRY); *var.* **juliana** is the heart cherry; and the *var.* **regalis** is the Duke cherry. The Duke cherry is called by some *P. effusus.* For culture and best varieties *see* CHERRY.

**besseyi.** Sand cherry. A low shrub with often prostrate stems. Leaves elliptic or ovalish, 1–2½ in. long. Flowers 2–4 in a cluster, white, about ⅓ in. wide. Fruit nearly round, about ½ in. in diameter, black, edible, and sweet. Central N.A. Hardy from zone* 1 southward, and sometimes used for grafting stock to increase hardiness.

**caroliniana** = *Laurocerasus caroliniana.*

**cerasifera.** Cherry plum; also called myrobalan plum. A slender tree not over 25 ft. high. Leaves thin, bluntly oval, finely toothed, 1½–2 in. long. Flower solitary, or in clusters of 2 or 3, white, about ¾ in. wide. Fruit sweet, juicy, globe-shaped, red or yellow, about 1 in. in diameter. Southeastern Asia. Hardy from zone* 3 southward. The chief value of the myrobalan plum is for grafting stock for the apricot and other kinds of plums. There are, however, several hort. varieties cult. for ornament, notably *var.* **divaricata,** which has smaller but more profuse flowers, blooming as the leaves unfold; and *var.* **pissardi,** which has purple leaves and larger, pink flowers and wine-red fruits.

**cerasus.** Sour cherry. A round-headed tree not over 35 ft. high, inclined to sucker from the base. Leaves elliptic-oval, rather stiff, pointed, 2–3½ in. long, doubly toothed. Flowers white, about 1 in. wide, in profuse clusters. Fruit sour, scarcely ¾ in. in diameter, red. Eurasia. Hardy from zone* 3 southward. For culture and best varieties *see* CHERRY.

**communis** = *Amygdalus communis.*

**†dasycarpa.** Purple apricot. A very showy small tree, never over 25 ft. high, the twigs purplish. Leaves elliptic-oval, 1½–2½ in. long, long-pointed, finely toothed, hairy on the veins beneath. Flowers white, about 1 in. wide, very numerous and blooming before the leaves expand. Fruit (rarely produced) dark purple, hairy, acid, nearly globe-shaped, about 1½ in. in diameter. Thought to be a hybrid between the apricot and cherry plum; unknown as a wild tree. Hardy from zone* 3 southward.

**†davidiana** = *Amygdalus davidiana.*

**domestica.** Common plum. A round-headed tree, not usually over 25–30 ft. high. Leaves elliptic or broadest toward the tip, 2¼–4½ in. long, the margins coarsely but bluntly toothed. Flowers greenish-white, about ¾ in. wide, the clusters sparse, but very numerous and blooming before the leaves expand. Fruit, from long cult. and many hybrid races, various, but typically oblongish or egg-shaped, bluish-black, sweet, and with a free stone (clingstone in some hort. forms). Eurasia. Hardy, in some of its forms, nearly throughout the country. The *var.* **insititia,** the damson plum or bullace, considered by some as a separate species (*P. insititia*), has larger, pure white flowers and a clingstone fruit. For culture and best varieties of both the common plum and damson, *see* PLUM.

**effusus.** *See* PRUNUS AVIUM REGALIS.

**†glandulosa.** Flowering almond (but it is not a true almond, for which *see* AMYGDALUS COMMUNIS). A very showy shrub, not over 5 ft. high. Leaves ovalish-oblong, or narrower, 1½–4 in. long. Flowers very numerous, but in clusters of 1 or 2, blooming before the leaves unfold, white or pinkish, about ¾ in. wide. China and Jap. Hardy from zone* 3 southward. There are several hort. varieties, among the best being *var.* **rosea** with pink flowers; *var.* **sinensis** with double pink flowers; and *var.* **alboplena** with double white flowers. Few of the varieties produce fruit, but in the typical form it is red and about ⅓ in. in diameter.

**hortulana.** Hortulan plum. A native American plum, and the basis of several cult. varieties (*see* PLUM). A tree not over 30 ft. high. Leaves oblong-oval or elliptic, long-pointed, 3½–5½ in. long. Flowers 2–4 in each cluster, white, about ½ in. wide. Fruit (in the wild form) about 1 in. in diameter, reddish-yellow. Ky. to Tenn., Iowa, and Okla. Hardy from zone* 3 southward. For culture and best varieties *see* PLUM.

**†ilicifolia.** Islay; also called evergreen cherry. A handsome, evergreen shrub or small tree, native from San Francisco to southern Calif. and Lower Calif., not over 30 ft., usually much less as cult. Leaves holly-like, 1–2 in. long, spiny-toothed. Flowers white, about ⅓ in. wide, in finger-shaped clusters (racemes*). Fruit red or black, about ⅔ in. in diameter, the flesh edible but scanty. Hardy from zone* 7 southward.

**insititia** = *Prunus domestica insititia.*

**†lannesiana.** Japanese flowering cherry; or often called simply flowering cherry. A tree, not over 30 ft. high, the twigs smooth. Leaves oval or oval-oblong, 2½–5 in. long, sharply and doubly toothed, the teeth bristly. Flowers 2–5 in a cluster, pink in the typical form, but white, red, or double-flowered in many of the hort. forms, fragrant, usually in a raceme*-like, leafy-bracted* cluster. Fruit (often wanting) small, black, shining. Jap. Hardy from zone* 4 southward. For its culture and varieties *see* below.

**†laurocerasus** = *Laurocerasus officinalis.*

**†lusitanica** = *Laurocerasus lusitanica.*

**mahaleb.** Mahaleb or St. Lucie cherry. A Eurasian tree of no value for its fruit, but widely used for grafting stock for better cherries. It is a loose-headed tree, with the young twigs hairy. Leaves broadly oval or roundish, 1¼–2½ in. long, bluntly round-toothed. Flowers in finger-shaped clusters (racemes*), 6–10 in a cluster, white and fragrant. Fruit about ¼ in. in diameter, black. Hardy from zone* 3 southward. For its use as grafting stock *see* CHERRY.

**maritima.** Beach plum. A native American shrub found on coastal dunes and rocky shores from Me. to Va., not over 6 ft. high, the lower branches often decumbent. Leaves ovalish or elliptic, 2–3½ in. long, sharply toothed, often riddled by leaf miners. Flowers pure white, about ¾ in. wide, in clusters of 2–3, but very numerous. Fruit globe-shaped, dull purple or blackish, bloomy, its flesh delicious, suggesting the guava in flavor. Hardy from zone* 3 southward, but rarely cult.

**†nana.** Dwarf Russian almond (not a true almond, for which *see* AMYGDALUS COMMUNIS). A shrub scarcely over 4½ ft. high, cult. for ornament. Leaves lance-shaped or broader toward the tip, 1½–3 in. long, sharply toothed. Flowers in clusters of 1–3, rosy-red, about ¾ in. wide. Fruit hairy-skinned, egg-shaped, about ¾ in. long. Eurasia. Hardy from zone* 3 southward. Sometimes, and probably more correctly, known as *Amygdalus nana*, as its affinity appears to be with that genus rather than with *Prunus*. There are several hort. varieties, some with white or pink flowers.

**nigra.** Canada or red plum. A native American, narrow-headed tree, rarely over 30 ft. high. Leaves generally elliptic, 3–5 in. long, coarsely and doubly, but bluntly toothed. Flowers 3–4 in a cluster, white but fading pink, about 1 in. wide. Fruit ellipsoid, about 1½ in. long, red or yellowish-red. New Brunswick to N.Y. and westward and northwestward. Hardy from zone* 1 southward. It is the parent or origin of several cult. fruit trees. For culture and varieties *see* PLUM.

**padus.** Bird cherry; also called European bird cherry. A tree up to 40 ft. high, not especially decorative and of no fruit value. Leaves elliptic or oblongish, 3–5½ in. long, sharply toothed, grayish beneath. Flowers fragrant, white, about ½ in. wide, in finger-shaped, hanging clusters (racemes). Fruit black, about ¼ in. in diameter. Eurasia. Hardy from zone* 2 southward.

**pennsylvanica.** Wild red cherry. A native American tree, not over 30 ft. high, sometimes shrubby. Leaves oblongish or lance-oblong, 3–5½ in. long, sharply but finely toothed, the tip prolonged. Flowers 2–5 in a cluster (umbel*-like), white, about ¾ in. wide. Fruit globe-shaped, about ⅓ in. in diameter, red. Throughout most of northern N.A. Hardy from zone* 2 northward.

**persica** = *Amygdalus persica.*

**†pumila.** Sand cherry. An attractive, white-flowered, American shrub, sometimes 6 ft. high, usually lower, and the old branches decumbent. Leaves narrow, but broadest toward the tip, 2–3 in. long, finely toothed. Flowers white, 2–3 in a cluster, very numerous, about ½ in. wide. Fruit purple-black, about ⅓ in. in diameter. Shores of the Great Lakes, especially on the dunes. Hardy from zone* 1 southward.

**salicina.** Japanese plum. An important source of many fruit trees (*see* PLUM). Not over 25 ft. high. Leaves oblong or elliptic, but somewhat broader toward the tip, 2½–4½ in. long, doubly toothed, the tip prolonged. Flowers mostly 3 in a cluster, white, about ¾ in. long, yellow or reddish, sometimes pointed at the tip. China, but early introduced into Jap. Hardy from zone* 3 southward. For culture and varieties *see* PLUM.

**serotina.** Wild black cherry; also called choke cherry. An important American timber tree in parts of its range, elsewhere very weedy and widely planted by birds along fence-rows. In maturity, and in the forest, up to 90 ft. high, less as usually seen. Leaves oblongish, or narrower,

*** Special articles on the subjects indicated by an asterisk (*) will be found at the words so marked.**

2½–5½ in. long, its numerous marginal teeth incurved. Flowers white, fragrant, sometimes unpleasantly so, about ¼ in. wide, in long, hanging, finger-shaped clusters, blooming long after the leaves expand. Fruit round, about ⅓ in. in diameter, ultimately black, sour. Throughout eastern N.A. and hardy everywhere. The juice of its wilted foliage is dangerously poisonous.

†**serrulata.** Flowering cherry. Japanese flowering cherry. Typically, a tree up to 30 ft. high, much smaller in some of the numerous hort. varieties. Leaves ovalish or narrower, 2¾–5½ in. long, long-pointed, toothed or doubly toothed, the teeth short-bristly. Flowers typically white, 3–5 in a cluster (raceme*-like), the cluster with a few leafy bracts.* Fruit (often wanting) black. Jap., China, and Korea. The most commonly cult. variety is white and double-flowered. For this and many others see below. Hardy from zone* 3 southward.

†**sieboldi.** Resembling *P. serrulata*, but the twigs and under side of the leaves softly hairy. Flowers generally pink or white, single or double. Unknown as a wild tree, but long cult. in Jap., where it is one of the flowering cherries. Hardy from zone* 3 southward, but not much known in the U.S.

**spinosa.** Sloe. Blackthorn (for an American plant known as black thorn see CRATAEGUS TOMENTOSA). A thorny shrub or small tree, freely suckering at the base, usually less than 12 ft. high. Leaves numerous, small, scarcely over 1½ in. long. Flowers 1 to a cluster, but very numerous, blooming before the leaves unfold, white, about ⅔ in. wide. Fruit nearly round, about ¾ in. in diameter, bluish-black and with a bloom, but the flesh reddish, tart, and used to flavor sloe gin. Eurasia. Hardy from zone* 3 southward. The source of most Irish blackthorn walking-sticks.

†**subhirtella.** Rosebud cherry. A very showy Japanese tree, 20–30 ft. high, rarely shrubby. Leaves ovalish or oblong-oval, 1½–3 in. long, often doubly toothed, hairy on the veins beneath. Flowers 2–5 in a cluster, but very numerous, nearly 1 in. wide, light pink, the petals notched. Fruit about ⅓ in. in diameter, black. Jap. Hardy from zone* 3 southward. A particularly fine form is the *var.* **pendula**, with gracefully hanging branches, and more cult. than the typical form. The *var.* **autumnalis** is fall-flowering.

**tomentosa.** A shrub or small tree (cherry), not over 10 ft. high, cult. chiefly for ornament. Leaves numerous, rather crowded, more or less elliptic, 2½–3½ in. long, unequally toothed. Flowers 1–2 in a cluster, white or pinkish-white, about 1 in. wide. Fruit nearly round, about ¾ in. in diameter, red and edible. China. Hardy from zone* 1 southward.

†**triloba.** Flowering almond. Usually a shrub, rarely a tree up to 10 ft. high. Leaves broadly oval, sometimes 3-lobed, coarsely double-toothed, 1½–2½ in. long, a little hairy beneath. Flowers 1 or 2 in an essentially stalkless cluster, pinkish, nearly 1¼ in. wide, appearing before the leaves expand. Fruit hairy, red, about ½ in. in diameter, often lacking. China. Hardy from zone* 3 southward, but most cult. in the *var.* **flore-pleno**, a double-flowered pink shrub of great beauty. The flowering almond has been so long known to gardeners as *P. triloba* that it seems best to retain that name here, although its hairy fruit and other characters reveal the fact that it belongs with the almond and peach and technically should bear the name *Amygdalus*. It is usually, however, grafted on plum stock.

**virginiana.** Choke cherry. A shrub-like counterpart of *P. serotina*, rarely over 10 ft. high, still more rarely tree-like and 20 ft. high. The simplest way to distinguish its foliage from *P. serotina* is by the divaricate marginal teeth, which in *P. serotina* are incurved. Fruit dark purple-black, sour. Throughout northern N.A. and hardy everywhere. Of little decorative value, but children should be warned against the dangerously poisonous juice of its wilted leaves.

†**yedoensis.** Flowering cherry. Japanese flowering cherry. A very showy tree up to 40 ft. high, the young twigs slightly hairy. Leaves elliptic or broader toward the tip, 2½–5½ in. long, strongly double-toothed. Flowers 5–6 in a cluster (short and raceme*-like), white or pink, faintly fragrant. Fruit round and black, often wanting. Unknown as a wild tree, but long cult. in Jap. and supposed to have originated there by crossing *P. subhirtella* and *P. lannesiana*. Hardy from zone* 3 southward, and widely cult. in some of the many named Japanese forms (see below).

ORNAMENTALS

The shrubs and trees grouped under the general names of flowering cherry, Japanese flowering cherry, flowering plum, flowering apricot, and flowering almond are among the most decorative plants in cult. Most of the species from which such plants have been derived are marked with a dagger (†) in the above enumeration. But there are innumerable named forms, especially among the Japanese flowering cherries, nearly all derived from *Prunus lannesiana*, *P. serrulata*, and *P. yedoensis*, although other species could with equal justice be called Japanese flowering cherries, notably *P. sieboldi* and *P. subhirtella*, the latter usually called the rosebud cherry.

JAPANESE FLOWERING CHERRIES. The Japanese, who have grown these plants for centuries, have assigned hundreds of Japanese vernacular names to them, but most such names are more a source of confusion here than a help in identifying them. The following Japanese named forms, however, are widely grown under their Japanese varietal names. Some of the best are: Higan-sakura (also a fall-flowering form of it); Shidare-higan-sakura (a weeping form of Higan-sakura); Somei-yoshino-sakura (derived from *P. yedoensis*); Fujisan-sakura (white-flowered); Asahi-Botan (a dwarf variety suitable for the rock garden); Amanogawa (resembling a Lombardy poplar in habit, flowers rose-pink); Naden (derived from *P. sieboldi;* a good shade tree); Kofugen (similar to Naden, but flowers deeper pink); and Shirofugen (resembling Kofugen, but flowers ultimately white). Kwanzan is one of the best double-flowered sorts, with deep rose-pink bloom. Two other varieties, without Japanese names, are Paul Wohlert (semi-dwarf with deep pink flowers) and Ruth Wohlert (with double, deep pink flowers).

A Japanese flowering cherry tree and its blossom

The culture of these ornamentals presents no greater difficulties than are found among the fruit trees. See PLUM, CHERRY, APRICOT, PEACH, and ALMOND, the two last belonging to the genus *Amygdalus*, but closely related. All appear to favor well-drained soils and open sunlight. The shrubs do not need much space, but the tree-like, Japanese flowering cherries should be planted at least 20–25 ft. apart each way. Their magnificent bloom in early spring is helped by a good winter mulch of well-rotted manure. The finest collection in the country is that at the Tidal Basin, Washington, D.C., presented by the City of Tokio in 1912. They usually bloom during the first two weeks in April.

For the pests of the ornamental species of Prunus see those mentioned at CHERRY, PLUM, APRICOT, and PEACH.

*PRURITA, -us, -um* (pru-ry′ta). Itching; or causing it.

*PSEDERA* = *Parthenocissus*.

*PSEUDACORUS* (sood-ak′o-rus). False sweet flag. See IRIS.

**PSEUDERANTHEMUM** (soo-der-ran′thee-mum). A large genus of widely distributed tropical plants of the family Acanthaceae, a few grown in the greenhouse for their sometimes colored foliage or for their variously colored flowers. They are shrubby or herbaceous plants with opposite* leaves, having no marginal teeth (in ours), but the margins wavy in one of the cult. species. Flowers white or purplish in those below, the corolla tubular, its 5 lobes very nearly regular, sometimes 2 of them smaller than the other 3. Stamens* 4, 2 of them infertile. Fruit a stalked, oblong capsule.* (*Pseuderanthemum* is from the Greek for false and *Eranthemum*, a closely related genus.)

The culture is the same as for *Eranthemum* (which see).

**atropurpureum.** A smooth-stemmed shrub, 3–4 ft. high. Leaves broadly oval, 3–6 in. long, purple or pinkish-purple, usually blotched (rarely green or yellow-spotted). Flowers white, but with rose-purple center and spots, or purplish throughout, the corolla tube short, the lobes spreading and about 1½ in. wide. Polynesia (?).

---

* Special articles on the subjects indicated by an asterisk (*) will be found at the words so marked.

**bicolor.** A smooth-stemmed shrub 2-3 ft. high. Leaves narrowly ovalish, 4-8 in. long, tapering both ends, dark green. Flowers stalkless, in spikes which arise in the leaf-axils.* Corolla with a slender tube, the limb salver-shaped, about 1½ in. long, white, but the lower lobes purple-spotted. Polynesia (?).

**reticulatum.** A smooth-stemmed shrub, 2-3 ft. high, the branches angled. Leaves oval-lance-shaped, 6-10 in. long, tapering at the tip, the margins wavy, dark green but the veins golden. Flowers short-stalked in small clusters (panicles*), the corolla tubular, white, but the throat purple and one of the lobes purple-spotted. The tube is about ½ in. long, the expanded lobes about 1½ in. wide. Polynesia (?).

*PSEUDO-ACACIA* (soo-do-a-kā′sha). False acacia.

**PSEUDOBULB.** The swollen, stem-like, often grooved base of many orchids. It usually stores water and food upon which the plant thrives during the dry season. Pseudobulbs usually bear one or more leaves at the top, and the flowering stalk from the base. See ORCHID.

*PSEUDO-CAPSICUM* (soo-do-kap′si-kum). Pre-Linnaean* name for the Jerusalem cherry, meaning false pepper.

**PSEUDOLARIX** (soo-do-lar′ricks). Golden larch. A single species of Chinese, cone-bearing trees of the pine family, resembling the true larch in dropping its leaves in the fall. The only species, **P. kaempferi** (often known as *P. amabilis*), is a popular ornamental tree, 60-100 ft. high or more (in the wild), its branches in tiers. Leaves narrow, line-like, 1¼-2¾ in. long, scattered on long shoots, but clustered or whorled on the short, lateral spurs, turning bright golden-yellow in autumn. Male and female flowers separate on the same plant, the male flowers catkin-like, the female flowers solitary and consisting only of a naked ovule between the scales of the cone. Mature cone egg-shaped, reddish-brown, 2¾-3½ in. long, its woody scales notched at the tip. The golden larch is of simple culture in most garden soils, except those derived from limestone which should be avoided. (*Pseudolarix* is from the Greek for false and *Larix*, the closely related true larches.)

**PSEUDOPHOENIX** (soo-do-fee′nicks). One or perhaps more species of West Indian feather palms, the only cult. species, **P. vinifera**, also a native of a few keys in Fla., and much cult. there from Miami southward. It is known as the hog cabbage palm, buccaneer palm, and in Miami as the Sargent palm (perhaps because it was once named *Pseudophoenix sargenti*). It does not grow over 25 ft. high, the trunk about 12 in. in diameter, and usually bulged near the middle. Leaves in a terminal crown, the leaf about 4-6 ft. long, the larger leaflets or segments 16-18 in. long, less than this towards the top and bottom of the leaf. Fruits cherry-like, about ¾ in. in diameter, orange-red. It grows well in the sandy soils of Fla., and is often used as a substitute for the royal palm, although it is far less decorative than the latter. (*Pseudophoenix* is from the Greek for false and *Phoenix*, the date.)

*PSEUDO-PLATANUS* (soo-do-plat′a-nus). Literally, a false plane tree (*Platanus*); used as a specific name for the sycamore maple (which see).

**PSEUDOTSUGA** (soo-do-soo′ga). Magnificent evergreen trees of the pine family, comprising four species from western N.A. and eastern As. The only commonly cult. species is **P. taxifolia**, the Douglas fir, which is one of the most valuable timber trees of the Northwest, reaching a height of nearly 300 ft. and trunk diameters of 10-12 ft. This, the typical form of the coast ranges from British Columbia to Calif., is not a satisfactory evergreen in the eastern states, but a form of it from the Rocky Mountains does well in the East and should be specified when ordering. Leaves spirally arranged, straight, rarely curved, line-like, about ¾ in. long, with 2 pale bands beneath. Cones egg-shaped, 2½-4½ in. long, hanging, its scales rounded and concave. Seeds 2 under each scale. The Rocky Mountain form is hardy from zone* 4 southward; it grows more slowly than the timber tree of the Northwest. Of the several hort. varieties, two of the best are *var.* **fastigiata**, a pyramidal form, the branches upright; and *var.* **glauca** with bluish-green foliage, and also known in a form with pendulous branches. The Douglas fir was long, and is still sometimes known by the name *P. douglasi*. (*Pseudotsuga* is from the Greek for false and *Tsuga*, the hemlock, to which it is closely related.)

DISEASES. Douglas fir suffers particularly from heart rot. Avoidance of wounds and prompt attention to unavoidable injuries that involve the heartwood are the most efficient methods of control of heart rot. Mistletoe* is a serious pest on Douglas fir in the West. Isolated trees are especially susceptible.

**PSIDIUM.** See GUAVA.

**PSOPHOCARPUS** (so-fo-kar′pus). Tender, twining, annual herbs comprising about 5 species, belonging to the pea family, and found in tropical Af. and As. Roots strong, tuberous. Stems twining. Leaves compound,* the leaflets 3, ovalish or lance-shaped. Flowers pea-like, blue or lilac, in racemes.* Fruit a 4-angled pod. (*Psophocarpus* is from the Greek for noise and fruit, in allusion to its exploding when dry.)

One species grown in tropical and sub-tropical regions for its edible roots and young pods.

**tetragonolobus.** Goa bean. Asparagus pea. Stems smooth, twining. Leaflets ovalish, to 6 in. long. Flowers in loose racemes,* bright blue, 1 in. long. Pods to 9 in. long. India.

**PSORALEA** (so-ray′lee-a). Scurfy pea. Indian turnip. Tropical and sub-tropical herbs, shrubs or sub-shrubs, comprising about 115 species (about 30 of which are North American), belonging to the pea family. They are annuals, biennials or perennials, usually marked with transparent black spots, and strongly fragrant. Roots sometimes tuberous. Leaves compound,* the leaflets ovalish or lance-shaped. Flowers in clusters or spikes, terminal, or growing from the axils* of the leaves. Individual flowers pea-like, blue, purplish or white, the keel darker. Fruit a short, 1-seeded pod. (*Psoralea* is from the Greek for warty, in reference to the spots.)

Not of much garden importance, but the shrubby species sometimes cult. as greenhouse plants. The herbaceous species may be propagated by division of the roots in early spring.

**cuspidata.** Herbaceous perennial, growing to 2 ft. high, the roots tuberous. Leaflets 5, ovalish. Flowers blue, in dense spikes. May-June. S. Dak. to Tex.

**esculenta.** Indian breadroot. Pomme blanche. Herbaceous perennial, to 1½ ft. high, with edible, tuberous roots. Leaflets 5, ovalish. Flowers bluish, in dense spikes. May-July. Prairies, east of the Rocky Mountains.

**PSYCHOTRIA** (sy-kō′tri-a). An enormous group of tropical shrubs and trees of the family Rubiaceae, related to coffee, but only a handful of the 500 known species in occasional cult. for ornament. The one most likely to be met is **P. capensis**, the wild coffee, which is rarely cult. in southern Fla. and not hardy elsewhere. It is an evergreen shrub or small tree, with ovalish, shining, opposite* leaves, a little broader towards the tip, 3-5 in. long. Flowers yellow, very small, tubular, in branched clusters (corymbs*), the ends of the branches each with an ultimate umbel*-like cluster. Fruit black, shining, fleshy (a drupe*). Little is known of its cultural requirements. South Africa. (*Psychotria* is from the Greek for life-preserving, in allusion to the medicinal properties of some non-hort. species.)

*PSYCODES* (sy-kō′deez). Fragrant.

*PTARMICA, -us, -um* (tar′mi-ka). Greek for sneeze-producing. See ACHILLEA.

*PTARMICOIDES* (tar-mi-koy′deez, but *see* Oïdes). Resembling the sneezewort (*Achillea ptarmica*).

**PTELEA** (tee′lee-a). Perhaps 3 species of North American shrubs or small trees of the family Rutaceae, of secondary hort. interest, although **P. trifoliata**, the hop-tree or wafer ash, is occasionally planted for ornament. It is a coarse shrub or small tree, not over 20 ft. high, with strong-smelling foliage. Leaves alternate,* compound,* the 3 leaflets elliptic or oblong, essentially stalkless, 2-4½ in. long, usually faintly dotted. Flowers greenish-white, about ⅓ in. wide, inconspicuous. (For details *see* RUTACEAE.) Fruit a dry, notched, veiny samara* about ¾ in. long, nearly round, its 2 seeds plump. N.Y. to Fla. and westward. Hardy from zone* 3 southward and of easy cult. if grown in a moist, partly shady

---

* Special articles on the subjects indicated by an asterisk (*) will be found at the words so marked.

place. Propagated by autumn-sown seeds. (*Ptelea* is the Greek name for the elm tree and of uncertain application to the hop-tree.)

*PTERANTHA, -us, -um* (ter-ran'tha). With winged flowers.

**PTERETIS** (ter-ree'tis). A small genus of Eurasian and North American hardy ferns of the family Polypodiaceae, two of them occasionally cult. in the outdoor fern garden. They have twice-compound foliage fronds which are borne in a circle that surrounds the fertile or spore-bearing fronds. The latter have the ultimate segments contracted and pod-like, and surround the spore* cases. Both those below are rather bold, coarse ferns suited to shady places. (*Pteretis* means *Pteris*-like.) The plants are sometimes known as *Matteuccia*.

For culture see FERNS AND FERN GARDENING.

**nodulosa.** The ostrich fern of N.A. A tall, robust fern, the foliage fronds 6–10 ft. long (stalks 8–14 in. long), broadly lance-shaped, the ultimate segments usually with a rolled margin, narrow and deeply cut. Spore*-bearing, *i.e.* fertile, fronds shorter, the pod-like segments almost necklace-like, brown. Eastern N.A. Often offered under the name of the next species.

**struthiopteris.** The ostrich fern of Eu. Similar, but the foliage fronds 3–5 ft. long, the stalk 3–5 in. long. Eu.

**PTERIDIUM.** See BRAKE.

*PTERIDOIDES* (ter-ri-doy'deez, but see Oïdes). Resembling a form of the genus *Pteris*.

**PTERIS'** (teer'is). Mostly tropical ferns of the family Polypodiaceae, probably comprising over 150 species, a few of which are very commonly grown in greenhouses and for fern dishes under the name of brake, although the true brake or bracken is *Pteridium* (see BRAKE). They have once- or twice-compound* fronds, the ultimate segments of which have usually rolled margins beneath which are the spore* cases. The foliage of all the cult. species is very feathery, but lasting, and they are hence good plants for the home. (*Pteris* is from the Greek for wing, in reference to the feathery fronds.)

For culture see Greenhouse Ferns at FERNS AND FERN GARDENING. The two best known and most useful are the forms of *P. cretica* and *P. serrulata*.

**cretica.** A widely distributed tropical and sub-tropical fern, its fronds not over 12 in. high, the stalks slender and straw-colored. Fronds once-compound,* the ultimate segments about ¼ in. wide, the lowermost often deeply cut. Commonly grown for fern dishes and centerpieces, especially in some of the crested or much-divided hort. forms.

**ensiformis.** A slender fern, the foliage fronds erect, 15–20 in. high, once-compound, the ultimate segments about ¼ in. wide. Spore*-bearing fronds shorter, the segments nearly ⅜ in. wide. Indo-Malaya and Aust.

**multifida** = *Pteris serrulata*.

**serrulata.** A slender fern, widely grown for fern dishes and centerpieces, the fronds nearly 18 in. high and 12 in. wide in maturity, usually half this as cult. Fronds once-compound,* the ultimate segments long and very narrow, the main stalk winged. Some of the lower segments are 2–3-forked. China and Jap. There are many crested, dwarf, or variegated hort. varieties. The plant is sometimes offered as *P. multifida*.

**wimsetti** = A crested form of *P. cretica*.

**PTEROCARYA** (teer-o-kar'i-a). Horticulturally unimportant Asiatic trees of the family Juglandaceae, comprising 6 species of which **P. stenoptera** is occasionally cult. for ornament. It is a tree up to 100 ft. high (in the wild), with alternate,* compound* leaves, the leaflets arranged feather-fashion and with an odd one at the end, the main stalk winged. Leaflets 11–23, oblongish, 3–4 in. long. Male and female flowers separate on the same tree, both in catkins. Fruit an oblong, winged, 1-seeded nutlet, arranged in racemes, 8–14 in. long. China. Hardy from zone* 4 southward, and propagated by seeds or by layers. (*Pterocarya* is from the Greek for wing and *Carya*, the hickory, in allusion to the winged nut.)

**PTEROSTYRAX** (teer-ro-sty'racks). Three species of Asiatic shrubs or trees of the family Styracaceae, two of them sometimes cult. for ornament, but of secondary garden importance. They have alternate,* stalked leaves and fragrant white flowers in large clusters (panicles*). Petals 5, separate. Stamens* 10. Fruit an oblongish, dry drupe,* ribbed or winged. (*Pterostyrax* is from the Greek for wing and *Styrax*, a closely related genus.)

The two below prefer a reasonably moist site. The second species should be better known, for it is handsome during June when its fragrant, hanging clusters of flowers are in bloom. Propagated by seeds or by layers.

**corymbosa.** A shrub or small tree, the leaves elliptic or ovalish, 3–5 in. long, finely toothed, the teeth bristly. Flower cluster (a corymbose panicle*) 3–5 in. long, the stamens* unequal. Fruit densely hairy, 5-winged. Jap. and China. Hardy from zone* 3 southward.

**hispida.** Epaulette-tree. A tree up to 45 ft. high, the leaves oblongish, 5–7 in. long, minutely toothed, the teeth not bristly. Flower cluster hanging, 7–10 in. long, the flowers white, fragrant, nearly stalkless in the cluster. Fruit bristly, 10-ribbed. China and Jap. June. Hardy from zone* 3 southward.

**PTYCHOSPERMA** (ty-ko-sper'ma). East Indian or Australasian feather palms, comprising perhaps 20 species, only one, **P. elegans**, in cult., and this little known. It is a slender, ringed, unarmed palm with a solitary trunk not over 20 ft. high, the terminal crown of leaves rather sparse. Leaves 3–5 ft. long, bright green, the ultimate segments 18–24 in. long and 1⅓–3 in. wide, narrowed at the base but broader towards the oblique, cut-off, or deeply jagged tip. Flower cluster not over 20 in. long. Fruit about ¾ in. long. Eastern Aust. Rarely cult. outdoors and hardy only in zone* 9 or the warmest parts of zone* 8. For culture see PALM. Several other plants are credited to this genus but belong elsewhere. They are: *P. alexandrae* = *Archontophoenix alexandrae*; *P. macarthuri* = *Actinophloeus macarthuri*; *P. seemani* = *Balaka seemani*. (*Ptychosperma* is from the Greek for folded seed, in allusion to a technical character of the seed.)

*PUBENS* (pew'benz). Downy or sparsely soft-hairy.

*PUBERULA, -us, -um* (pew-ber'you-la). Somewhat hairy.

*PUBESCENS* (pew-bes'senz). Pubescent.*

**PUBESCENT.** Covered with soft hairs.

**PUBLIC ROSE GARDENS.** See ROSE GARDENS.

**PUCCOON.** See LITHOSPERMUM.

**PUDDING-PIPE TREE** = *Cassia fistula*.

**PUDDLING.** See PLANTING.

*PUDICA, -us, -um* (pew'di-ka). Bashful or retiring.

**PUERARIA** (poo-er-ray'ri-a). A genus of Asiatic and East Indian, rapid-growing vines of the pea family, **P. thunbergiana**, the kudsu-vine of China and Jap. often cult. for ornament. It is a somewhat woody, hairy-stemmed vine often climbing to a great height, not certainly hardy north of zone* 5, and often killed to the ground south of this, but growing again from its thick, starch-yielding root. Leaves compound,* the 3 leaflets broadly oval or nearly round, 3–6 in. long, hairy, with a small point. Flowers pea-like, purple, about ⅝ in. diameter, fragrant, in dense, upright clusters (racemes*) nearly 10 in. long. Pod (legume*) hairy, flat, oblongish, 1¾–4 in. long. The vine (sometimes known as *P. hirsuta*) is a quick grower and useful for making a dense shade over arbors. More useful for temporary than permanent planting, but widely grown in the South. Propagated by division or by seeds. (Named for M. N. Puerari, Swiss botanist.)

*PUGIONIFORMIS, -e* (pew-ji-o-ni-for'mis). Dagger-shaped.

**PUKA** = *Griselina lucida*.

*PULCHELLA, -us, -um* (pull-kell'a). Beautiful, or merely pretty.

*PULCHER* (pull'care). Beautiful.

*PULCHERRIMA, -us, -um* (pull-ker'ri-ma). Most beautiful.

**PULMONARIA** (pul-mo-nay'ri-a). Lungwort. Low-growing, perennial herbs, comprising about 10 species of the family Boraginaceae, and natives of Eu. They have creeping rootstocks, and are more or less hairy. Basal leaves long-stalked, broadly lance-shaped, sometimes mottled. Upper leaves few and alternate.* Flowers blue or purplish, in terminal, coiled clusters, which straighten as the flowers

---

* Special articles on the subjects indicated by an asterisk (*) will be found at the words so marked.

open. Calyx of 5 sepals.* Corolla funnel-shaped, sometimes with a hairy throat. Stamens* 5, not protruding. Fruit 2-celled when young, splitting into 4 parts when ripe, each part containing 1 seed. (*Pulmonaria* is from the Latin for lung, in allusion to the plants being a supposed remedy for diseases of the lungs.)

Pulmonarias make useful spring-flowering, border plants. Easily cult. in ordinary garden soil. Propagated by division of roots in Sept., or early spring, or by seeds sown in a cold frame or outdoor seedbed in early spring. They may be transplanted to permanent positions as soon as large enough to handle.

**angustifolia.** Grows 6–12 in. high. Leaves lance-shaped. Flowers blue. April–May. Useful border plant. The *var. azurea* is a hort. form.

**officinalis.** Grows 6–12 in. high. Basal leaves with long stalks, tufted, lance-shaped, mottled, and covered with coarse hairs. Flowers purplish-red, in terminal, branching clusters.

**saccharata.** Bethlehem sage. Grows to 1½ ft. high. Basal leaves broadly lance-shaped, mottled, white. Flowers white or reddish-purple, in terminal clusters. April–May. Prefers shade.

**PULQUE AGAVE** = *Agave atrovirens*.

**PULSATILLA** (pul-sa-till′a). Pasque-flower. Anemone-like herbs of the buttercup family, by some included in the genus *Anemone*, but here kept separate largely because of their plumy, silky fruit-appendages which are even more showy than the flowers. They are perennial herbs with basal, long-stalked, much-divided leaves, the divisions often cut into fine segments. Petals none, but the sepals petal-like. Fruit a dense head of achenes,* each tipped with the long, plumy style.* (The origin of *Pulsatilla* is unknown.)

The pasque-flowers are hardy perennials to be grown in the same way as the hardy species of *Anemone* (which see). The cult. of *P. vulgaris* is discussed at ROCK GARDEN.

**patens.** Not much over 6 in. high, but the flowering or fruiting stalk twice this. Leaves of 3 main divisions, each of which is divided into many narrow segments. Flower bluish-purple, about 2 in. wide, blooming before the leaves develop. April–May. N.A. This is the pasque-flower of N.A., sometimes called *Anemone patens*.

**pulsatilla** = *Pulsatilla vulgaris*.

**vernalis.** Not over 6 in. high. Leaver divided feather-fashion, silky-hairy. Flowers about 2 in. wide, the 6 sepals purple outside but white inside. Eu. April. The pasque-flower of Eu. and often called *Anemone vernalis*.

**vulgaris.** Nearly 12 in. high, the leaves divided feather-fashion and appearing with the flowers, which are blue or reddish-purple, bell-shaped and about 2 in. wide. Eu. April. There are also some hort. forms with lilac or red flowers and one with variegated foliage. For culture *see* ROCK GARDEN.

**PULSE CROPS.** *See* LEGUMES.

**PULVERULENTA, -us, -um** (pull-ver-you-len′ta). Dusty or powdered.

**PUMILA, -us, -um** (pew′mi-la). Small.

**PUMILIO** (pew-mill′i-o). Small or dwarf.

**PUMMELO** = *Citrus maxima*.

**PUMPKIN.** The common field pumpkin, which is too sprawling for the average garden, is derived mostly from *Cucurbita pepo* (which includes the common sort), *C. maxima* (which includes very large squashes that often pass as pumpkins), and *C. moschata* (large-fruited varieties of squash that also pass as pumpkins). For the technical differences between these *see* CUCURBITA.

The common sort of pumpkin often develops huge fruits which differ from the closely related winter squashes in not keeping over the winter and in being usually orange in color, and furrowed. But all the plants in this series have been much hybridized so that their exact identity is often in doubt.

From the garden standpoint all are grown in the same way. They are plants of tropical origin and must be grown only in our warmest season. Two or three seeds can be planted about 2 in. deep, in hills that are at least 6 ft. apart each way, or they may be inter-planted with corn as most farmers do. They will stand any amount of heat, but are retarded by cool weather. In other words, do not plant them until the ground is really warm.

For those who want especially large fruits a good plan is to sow pumpkin seeds on hills made over the spent manure from a mushroom bed or from a hotbed. The plants are rich feeders, but if grown in manure the rank excess of vine should be pinched back or more foliage will be produced than fruit.

Some people prefer the bushy sorts, but they do not produce such large fruits as the normal, widely sprawling, prostrate vines. If you live in zone* 3 or north of it, pumpkin seeds are best planted in paper pots in the hotbed or greenhouse and transplanted to the open ground when warm weather arrives. Otherwise, they may not finish fruit ripening before the first frost.

INSECT PESTS. The insects of pumpkin are in general the same as those attacking squash. The striped cucumber beetle, the squash bug, and the squash borer are the most injurious. *See* SQUASH.

**PUMPS.** *See* SPRAYING AND DUSTING.

**PUNCTATA, -us, -um** (punk-tay′ta). Punctate; *i.e.* dotted or spotted.

**PUNCTILOBULA, -us, -um** (punk-ti-lob′you-la). With dotted or spotted lobes.

**PUNGENS** (pun′jenz). Pungent.*

**PUNGENT.** Sharp-pointed; also with a sharp or acrid taste.

**PUNICA.** *See* POMEGRANATE.

**PUNICACEAE** (pew-ni-kay′see-ee). The pomegranate family consists only of the genus *Punica*, which comprises only 2 species. One of them is *P. granatum*, the pomegranate, while the other is a little-known plant from the island of Socotra. For a description of *P. granatum* see POMEGRANATE.

**PUNICEA, -us, -um** (pew-niss′ee-a). Purplish-red.

**PUNK-TREE** = *Melaleuca leucadendron*.

**PUPA** (plural pupae). An intermediate, usually inactive stage in the life history of many insects. While most insect pests do little damage during the pupal stage, that period is often the best one in which to destroy them. The cocoon of the butterfly is a common example of the condition of an insect while it is still a pupa. *See* INSECT PESTS.

**PURGING-NUT** = *Jatropha curcas*.

**PURPLE.** As an adjective *purple* is used as part of the name of many plants or animals that are of interest to the gardener. Those in this book, and their proper equivalents, are:

**Purple apricot** = *Prunus dasycarpa*; **Purple beech** = *Fagus sylvatica atropunicea* (see BEECH); **Purple boneset** = *Eupatorium purpureum*; **Purple cane** (see RASPBERRY); **Purple cestrum** = *Cestrum elegans*; **Purple chokeberry** = *Aronia atropurpurea*; **Purple coneflower** (see ECHINACEA); **Purple coral-pea** = *Hardenbergia monophylla*; **Purple daisy** = *Echinacea angustifolia*; **Purple finch** (see Bird Nuisances at BIRDS); **Purple foxglove** = *Digitalis purpurea* (see FOXGLOVE); **Purple fringed orchis** = *Habenaria fimbriata*; **Purple granadilla** = *Passiflora edulis*; **Purple loosestrife** = *Lythrum salicaria*; **Purple medic** = *Medicago sativa*; **Purple mombin** = *Spondias purpurea*; **Purple mullein** = *Verbascum phoenicum*; **Purple ragwort** = *Senecio elegans*; **Purple rock cress** (see AUBRIETIA); **Purple scale** (see Insect Pests at GRAPEFRUIT, ORANGE); **Purple trillium** = *Trillium erectum*; **Purple willow-herb** = *Lythrum salicaria*; **Purple wood sorrel** = *Oxalis violacea*; **Purple wreath** = *Petrea volubilis*.

**PURPURASCENS** (pur-pure-ras′senz). Purplish.

**PURPUREA, -us, -um** (pur-pure′ee-a). Purple.

**PURPUREO-COERULEA, -us, -um** (pur-pure-ee-o-see-roo′lee-a). Purplish-blue.

**PURSHIA** (pur′shi-a). A single species of straggling, rather unimportant, western American shrubs of the rose

---

* Special articles on the subjects indicated by an asterisk (*) will be found at the words so marked.

family, of little hort. interest, although **P. tridentata**, the antelope-brush, is occasionally grown for ornament. It is a silvery-foliaged shrub, 4–6 ft. high, with alternate,* very small, stiff, narrow leaves that are ¼–⅝ in. long and 3-toothed at the tip. Flowers yellow, solitary, about ½ in. wide, the 5 petals thin, not showy. Stamens* about 25. Fruit a hairy achene,* longer than the persistent calyx. Rocky Mountain region to Ore. and Calif. May. Hardy from zone* 4 southward. The *var.* **glandulosa** has even smaller and sticky leaves, is little known in cult., and not so hardy as the typical form. (Named for F. T. Pursh, a German botanist who traveled in, and wrote much about the plants of N.A.)

**PURSLANE** = *Portulaca*. *See also* the list at WEEDS. For the winter purslane *see* MONTIA.

**PURSLANE FAMILY** = Portulacaceae.

**PURSLANE TREE** = *Portulacaria afra*.

**PUSCHKINIA** (pus-kin′i-a). A small genus of spring-blooming, bulbous herbs of the lily family, comprising two species, one of which, **P. scilloides**, the striped squill, is cult. for ornament (for culture *see* below). It has basal leaves, about 12 in. long and 1 in. wide, and small, striped, bluish, bell-shaped flowers, about ½ in. long in a terminal cluster (raceme*) at the end of the flowering stalk, not very showy. Asia Minor. (Named for a Count M. Puschkin.)

### PUSCHKINIA CULTURE

The striped squill is not a showy garden ornament, but it very distinctly has its uses. These small cousins of *Scilla*, with their pale striped bells gathered in dense trusses on the slender 4 to 6 in. stems, are capable of making a modest but charming display. Planted in close colonies on a sunny plain in the rock garden, with a foreground of pink *Arabis*, they show to advantage. If used in a border it should be in large numbers if they are to be effective, and they should not be placed in competition with coarse growths. They bloom in early April. The bulbs are quite hardy as far north as Canada. They should be planted 3 in. deep and 3 in. apart in September or early October. A sandy, nourishing soil is the best for them, and they thrive equally well in sun or half shade. The bulbs need not be disturbed for several years, unless flowering is falling off, when they may be dug up after the foliage has fully ripened and replanted in fresh soil. The bulblets may then be detached from the old bulbs for purposes of propagation. — L. B. W.

*PUSILLA, -us, -um* (pew-sill′a). Very small or dwarf.

**PUSSLEY** = purslane. *See* the list at WEEDS.

**PUSSYTOES** = *Antennaria*.

**PUSSY WILLOW.** *See* WILLOW.

**PUTTY BULB.** *See* Section 6, TOOLS AND IMPLEMENTS.

**PUTTYROOT** = *Aplectrum hyemale*.

**PUYA** (pew′ya). Mostly Chilean, desert plants of the family Bromeliaceae, comprising over 25 species of spiny, rather large herbs, two or three occasionally grown in the cool greenhouse. They inhabit cool, dry, stony slopes of the upper Andes and, while herbs, have stout, somewhat woody stems in maturity. Leaves in a dense rosette, spiny-tipped and spiny-margined, stiff, long, and narrow. Flowers blue or greenish-yellow in those below, in terminal spikes or racemes,* the cluster bracted.* Flower segments mostly free. Fruit a somewhat fleshy, 6-valved capsule.* (*Puya* is the Chilean vernacular of some of the species.)

For culture *see* SUCCULENTS.

**alpestris.** Nearly stemless, the leaves 18–24 in. long, about 1 in. wide, pale on the under side. Flowers blue, about 1½ in. long, with a metallic sheen, the anthers* orange. Flower cluster much-branched. Chile.

**chilensis.** With a distinct, stout stem, 3–5 ft. high. Leaves nearly 4 ft. long, very narrow, bluish-green. Flowers greenish-yellow, about 2 in. long, the cluster branching. Chile.

**PYCNANTHEMUM** (pick-nan′thee-mum). Mountain mint. North American, hardy, herbaceous perennials, comprising about 18 species of the mint family. Leaves fragrant, simple,* entire, opposite,* smooth or hairy. Flowers white or purple, small, in many-flowered whorls, with numerous bracts,* forming small terminal heads. Calyx of 5 sepals.* Corolla 2-lipped. Stamens 4, in pairs, 2 long and 2 short. Fruit 2-celled when young, splitting into 4 parts when ripe. (*Pycnanthemum* is from the Greek for dense and blossom, in allusion to the dense flower heads.)

They are not of much garden importance, but sometimes grown as border plants. Easily propagated from seeds, which may be sown in a cold frame or outdoor seedbed in early spring. They may be transplanted to permanent positions as soon as large enough to handle, in ordinary garden soil.

**flexuosum.** Slender-growing herb, to 2½ ft. high. Leaves narrow, 1–2 in. long. Flowers in small, crowded heads. Fields, eastern N.A.

**incanum.** Grows to 3 ft. high. Leaves to 3 in. long, and 1½ in. wide, covered with white hairs on the under side. Flowers in loose clusters, 1½ in. across. Eastern N.A.

**virginianum.** Strong-growing, to 3 ft. high. Leaves to 2 in. long, lance-shaped. Flowers in small, dense heads. Eastern N.A.

*PYCNOCARPON* (pick-no-kar′pon). With densely crowded or many fruits.

*PYCNOSTACHYA, -us, -um* (pick-no-stack′i-a). Thick-spiked.

**PYCNOSTACHYS** (pick-no-stack′is). Chiefly African, perennial herbs of the mint family, comprising over 40 species, of which only **P. dawei** is of any hort. interest. It is a stout herb, 4–6 ft. high, with opposite, lance-shaped, toothed and hairy leaves, 9–12 in. long. Flowers blue, very irregular* and 2-lipped,* in a dense spike, 3–5 in. long. Corolla about ¾ in. long. Stamens* 4. Fruit a group of small nutlets, hidden by the persistent calyx, the teeth of which become somewhat spiny. Tropical Africa. Not much known in cult., and suited only to the tropical greenhouse, where it needs potting mixture* 3. (For origin *see* PYCNOSTACHYA.)

*PYGMAEA, -us, -um* (pig-mee′a). Small.

**PYRACANTHA** (py-ra-kan′tha). Fire-thorn. A small genus of Asiatic, evergreen, thorny shrubs of the rose family, most of the species cult. for their fine foliage and ornamental fruits. They have alternate,* short-stalked leaves, and small, white flowers in branched clusters (compound corymbs*). Petals 5, nearly round. Stamens* 20, the anthers* yellow. Fruit fleshy (a pome*), red or orange, usually crowned with the persistent calyx. (*Pyracantha* is from the Greek for fire and thorn, in allusion to the thorny twigs and showy fruit.)

The fire-thorns are closely related to *Cotoneaster* and need the same general culture. But several of them are not hardy everywhere, and the notes on hardiness should be studied carefully. For the best method of propagation *see* Softwood Cuttings at CUTTINGS.

**angustifolia.** A shrub 8–12 ft. high, its branches sometimes prostrate. Leaves narrowly oblong, or wedge-shaped at the base, sometimes notched at the tip, 1½–2 in. long, ashy beneath. Flower cluster densely felty. Fruit orange or brick-red, about ⅓ in. in diameter. China. May. Hardy from zone* 6 southward.

**coccinea.** Everlasting thorn. The best-known species in cult., and a shrub 12–20 ft. high. Leaves ovalish, 1–1½ in. long, toothed, ultimately without hairs. Flower cluster hairy. Fruit bright red, about ⅓ in. in diameter. Eurasia. May. Hardy from zone* 4 southward. The *var.* **lalandi** has the leaves less deeply toothed, and bears orange-red fruit. It is hardier and more vigorous than the typical form. Both do well when trained against a wall, especially the *var.* **lalandi**. *See* VINES. Also called *Cotoneaster pyracantha*.

**crenulata.** A shrub, or even a small tree, 12–20 ft. high. Leaves oblongish, but blunt toward the bristly tip, 1–2 in. long, finely blunt-toothed. Flower cluster not hairy. Fruit about ⅓ in. in diameter, orange-red. Himalayas. May. Hardy from zone* 6 southward.

**formosana** = *Pyracantha koidzumi*.

**gibbsi.** A shrub not over 9 ft. high, the leaves elliptic or oblongish, 2–3 in. long, shining above and without hairs, often wavy-toothed on the margin. Fruit nearly ½ in. in diameter, coral-red. China. May. Hardy from zone* 5 southward. The *var.* **yunnanensis** has blunter leaves than the typical plant and may be hardier. It is the usual form of *P. gibbsi* offered by nurserymen.

**koidzumi.** A shrub, the leaves mostly clustered at the ends of the twigs. Leaves oblongish, or broader toward the tip, about 1 in. long, without marginal teeth, hairy and pale on the lower side. Flower cluster nearly without hairs. Formosa. May. Hardy from zone* 7 (?) southward. Sometimes known as *P. formosana*.

**yunnanensis** = *Pyracantha gibbsi yunnanensis*.

---

* Special articles on the subjects indicated by an asterisk (*) will be found at the words so marked.

**PYRAMIDALIS, -e** (pir-ra-mi-day'lis). Like a pyramid.

**PYRAMID FRUIT TREES.** See TRAINING PLANTS.

**PYRENAICA, -us, -um** (py-re-nay'i-ka). From the Pyrenees.

**PYRETHRUM.** A very old garden name, and also once a generic name, but of confused application. As now understood, the common garden pyrethrum is *Chrysanthemum coccineum* (which see). Most plants once credited to the genus *Pyrethrum* are now included in *Chrysanthemum* or *Matricaria*.

**PYRETHRUM POWDER.** See Contact Sprays at INSECTICIDES.

**PYRIFOLIA, -us, -um** (py-ri-fō'li-a). With pear-like leaves.

**PYRIFORMIS, -e** (py-ri-for'mis). Pyriform; *i.e.* pear-shaped.

**PYROLA** (pī'ro-la). Shinleaf. Hardy, low-growing perennials of the northern hemisphere, comprising about 15 species of the family Ericaceae. Rootstocks spreading. Basal leaves in clusters, evergreen, roundish. Flowers nodding, whitish, green, or purplish, solitary or in terminal racemes,* on a (talk having scale-like bracts.* (*Pyrola* is a diminutive of *Pyrus*, the pear, in allusion to supposed resemblance of leaves.)

Pyrolas are not of any garden importance, and can be used only in the wild garden. They are not easy of cult. as they do not like being transplanted and are near to being saprophytes.* They thrive best in sandy peat or in rich woods soil, in a shady position.

**americana.** Consumption-weed. Indian lettuce. Canker lettuce. Strong-growing, to 12 in. high. Basal leaves roundish, to 2 in. long, with leafstalk longer than the thick, dark, glossy, green leaf blade. Flowers numerous, white, waxy, sweet-scented, in loose terminal racemes. Aug. Eastern N.A.

**elliptica.** Lesser wintergreen. Grows 8-10 in. high. Leaves ovalish, with leafstalk shorter than the thin, dull, olive-green leaf blade. Flowers greenish-white, waxy, fragrant, in loose 5-10-flowered clusters. June-July. N.A.

**rotundifolia** = *Pyrola americana*.

**PYROLACEAE.** See ERICACEAE.

**PYROSTEGIA** (py-ro-stee'gi-a). Extremely showy, South American, tendril*-bearing, woody vines of the family Bignoniaceae, comprising only 4 species, of which **P. ignea**, the flame-vine of Brazil, is cult. for ornament outdoors in zone* 9 and the most protected part of zone* 8. It is a quick-growing, high-climbing, evergreen vine, its tendrils 3-forked and clinging to stone or wood. Leaves compound,* the 2-3 leaflets ovalish, 1 in. long, pointed at the tip. Flowers in dense clusters, tubular, nearly 3 in. long, reddish-orange, slightly 2-lipped,* the lobes of the corolla turned backward, and white-margined with hairs. Fruit a long, slender pod, 8-12 in. In Fla. it blooms profusely for several weeks in mid-winter, and often again in summer, but more sparsely, and is considered to be, next to *Bougainvillaea*, the finest vine in cult. there. (*Pyrostegia* is from the Greek for fire and roof, in allusion to the color of the flowers.) Often known as *Bignonia venusta*.

**PYROTE.** A trademarked insecticide containing pyrethrum and rotenone, sold with directions for use as a contact spray.

**PYRUS** (py'rus). Pear. An Old World genus of trees (rarely shrubs) of the rose family, of outstanding hort. importance because it contains the pear and a few other, mostly ornamental, plants, or trees used as stock for pear grafting. There are about 20 known species, of which only 4 are in common cult., and of these the fruit tree is far the most important. They have alternate,* stalked leaves and white flowers in umbel-like clusters which bloom with or before the expanding of the leaves. Petals 5, nearly round, but narrowed to a claw.* Stamens* 20-30, the anthers red or dark-colored. Fruit a pear-shaped pome,* technically differing from the closely related apple only in the possession of stone or grit cells in the flesh. (See STONE CELLS.); (*Pyrus* is the classical Latin name [spelled *Piris*] of the pear tree.)

For the cult. of the pear and the trees related to it see PEAR.

For the many other plants once, and sometimes still, credited to *Pyrus* see below.

**calleryana.** A Chinese tree, showy when in bloom, but of chief interest as possible grafting stock for the common pear. Leaves ovalish or broader, 1½-3½ in. long, bluntly toothed. Flowers nearly 1 in. wide. Fruit nearly globe-shaped, brown-spotted, ⅓-½ in. in diameter. April. Hardy from zone* 3 southward.

**communis.** Common pear tree. A broad-headed, sometimes long-lived tree, up to 45 ft. high, rarely somewhat higher. Leaves roundish or ovalish, a little wedge-shaped at the base, rather hard-textured, 1-3½ in. long. Flowers nearly 1 in. wide, appearing with the leaves. Fruit pear-shaped, but very variable in the cult. sorts. Eurasia. April. Hardy from zone* 3 southward, and in some hort. forms hardy to zone* 2. For culture and best varieties see PEAR. Old and escaped trees are sometimes a little spiny.

**nivalis.** Snow pear. A small, often white-felty tree with ovalish, pointed leaves, 2½-3¾ in. long, wedge-shaped at the base. Flowers showy, nearly 1½ in. wide. Fruit nearly globe-shaped, 1-2 in. in diameter. Eastern Eu. and Asia Minor. April. Hardy from zone* 3 southward. Somewhat planted for ornament and its fruit used for making pear cider. Also known as *Malus nivalis*.

**pyrifolia** = *Pyrus serotina*.

**serotina.** Japanese pear; also called sand pear. A Chinese tree (long cult. in Jap.) with oval-oblong, pointed leaves, 3-5½ in. long, sharply bristly toothed. Flowers about 1¼ in. wide, appearing with or just before the leaves. Fruit apple-shaped, brownish, the flesh hard. April. Hardy from zone* 2 southward, and the origin of many cult. varieties, the Kieffer among them. For the place that Japanese pears have made in American fruit culture see PEAR. Formerly known as *Pyrus pyrifolia*.

### PYRUS AND ITS ALLIES

The ancient Greeks and Romans distinguished two distinct genera to include the apples and pears. To the first they gave the name *Malus*, and to the pears, *Pyrus*. In modern times some botanists have included all these plants in *Pyrus*, a proceeding not followed here; others have included some in *Malus*, others in *Aronia*, and in still other genera. The confusion in naming is thus very great. The four species listed above are the only ones here considered as properly assigned to the genus *Pyrus*.

But many other plants will be found in various catalogues, books, Experiment Station bulletins, etc., under the name *Pyrus*. So far as these are in THE GARDEN DICTIONARY, they should be looked for as indicated below:

Pyrus arbutifolia = Aronia arbutifolia.
Pyrus atropurpurea = Aronia atropurpurea.
Pyrus atrosanguinea = Malus atrosanguinea.
Pyrus coronaria = Malus coronaria.
Pyrus dawsoniana = Malus dawsoniana.
Pyrus floribunda = Malus floribunda.
Pyrus fusca = Malus fusca.
Pyrus halliana = Malus halliana.
Pyrus ioensis = Malus ioensis.
Pyrus kaido = Malus micromalus.
Pyrus malus = Malus pumila.
Pyrus melanocarpa = Aronia melanocarpa.
Pyrus micromalus = Malus micromalus.
Pyrus nigra = Aronia melanocarpa.
Pyrus prunifolia = Malus prunifolia.
Pyrus purpurea = Malus purpurea.
Pyrus sargenti = Malus sargenti.
Pyrus sieboldi = Malus sieboldi.
Pyrus spectabilis = Malus spectabilis.
Pyrus theifera = Malus theifera.
Pyrus toringoides = Malus toringoides.
Pyrus trilobata = Malus trilobata.
Pyrus zumi = Malus zumi.

**PYSECT.** A trademarked pyrethrum insecticide, sold with directions for use as a contact spray.

**PYSOL.** A trademarked insecticide, containing derris, and sold with directions for use as a contact spray.

**PYXIDANTHERA** (pix-i-dan'ther-ra). A single species of evergreen, cushion-forming, prostrate plants of the family Diapensiaceae, commonly called pyxie or flowering moss,

---

* Special articles on the subjects indicated by an asterisk (*) will be found at the words so marked.

and known to science as **P. barbulata.** It grows in moist, sandy, somewhat acid soils, from the pine-barrens of N.J. to N. Car., and is only suited to such sites in the rock garden or wild garden. Leaves alternate,* crowded, very narrow, scarcely ¼ in. long. Flowers not clustered, very numerous, but actually solitary, white or pinkish, bell-shaped, scarcely ⅛ in. wide. Fruit a tiny, globe-shaped capsule.* April. An attractive, evergreen, trailing plant for specialized sites, but unsuited to the ordinary garden. (*Pyxidanthera* is from the Greek for a small box and anther,* in allusion to the lid-like opening of the latter.) Some consider the form found in N. Car. as a distinct species.

**PYXIE** = *Pyxidanthera barbulata*.

**PYXIE FAMILY** = Diapensiaceae.

# Q

**QUACK GRASS** = *Agropyron repens*. See list at WEEDS.

*QUADRANGULARIS, -e* (kwad-rang-you-lar′is). Four-angled.

*QUADRANGULATA, -us, -um* (kwad-rang-you-lay′ta). Four-angled.

*QUADRICOLOR* (kwad-rick′o-lor). Four-colored.

*QUADRIFIDA, -us, -um* (kwad-riff′i-da). Cut into four segments.

*QUADRIFOLIA, -us, -um* (kwad-ri-fō′li-a). Four-leaved, or with four leaflets.

**QUAIL-BRUSH** = *Atriplex breweri*.

**QUAKE GRASS** = *Bromus brizaeformis*.

**QUAKER BONNETS** = *Lupinus perennis*.

**QUAKER LADIES** = *Houstonia coerulea*.

**QUAKING ASPEN** = *Populus tremuloides*.

**QUAKING GRASS.** See BRIZA.

**QUAMASH** (kwa′mash). Probably the original, and Indian, form of camas. See CAMASSIA QUAMASH.

**QUAMASIA** = *Camassia*.

**QUAMOCLIT** (kwam′o-klit). Tropical American, annual or perennial vines, comprising about 10 species of the family Convolvulaceae, with tall-growing, climbing stems. Leaves alternate,* simple or compound.* Flower clusters in the axils* of the leaves, long-stalked, sometimes branching. Individual flowers red or yellow, the corolla salver-shaped. Fruit a dry capsule.* (*Quamoclit* is from the Greek for dwarf kidney bean, in allusion to its climbing habit.)

They are useful climbers, as they can be grown as annuals and used as a covering for trellises or screens. Easily propagated from seeds sown in a cool greenhouse or cold frame in early spring. They may be transplanted to permanent position as soon as danger of frost is over. Mostly planted in the southern states, and in Calif.

**coccinea.** Star ipomoea. An annual vine growing to 10 ft. high. Leaves simple,* heart-shaped, 4–6 in. long, sometimes angularly lobed. Flowers about 1½ in. long, scarlet, but with a yellow throat. Tropical America; naturalized in the southern states. Sometimes known as *Ipomoea coccinea*.

**lobata.** Strong-growing perennial, growing 15–20 ft. high. Leaves heart-shaped, to 3 in. across, divided into 3 lobes. Flowers on opening crimson, fading to pale yellow, to ¾ in. wide, with a short tube. Stamens* prominent. July–Sept. Mex.

**pennata.** Cypress-vine. Annual, growing to 20 ft. high. Leaves compound.* Leaflets opposite, many, and thread-like. Flowers scarlet, funnel-shaped, to 1½ in. long. Tropical America, but naturalized in the southern states, and widely planted in Calif.

**sloteri.** Cardinal climber. A hybrid vine derived from crossing *Q. coccinea* and *Q. pennata*. It has leaves deeply lobed, the segments 7–15, and scarcely ½ in. wide. Flowers nearly 2 in. long, scarlet without, but the throat white. July–Sept.

**QUANTITY OF SEED.** For the amount of seed needed for different crops and different sized gardens see GARDEN TABLES I.

**QUARANTINES.** In November of 1918 the U.S. Department of Agriculture, after several public hearings, passed a plant quarantine act which provided that on and after June 1, 1919, certain restrictions would be enforced regarding the entry of plant material from foreign countries into the U.S. The purpose of the act was to protect the existing plants in this country from infestation by insect and plant disease pests that had not already been introduced. Its great objective was the preservation of many agricultural crops, and also ornamentals, from the ravages of foreign pests.

The main feature of the quarantine so far as ornamental plants are concerned was the exclusion from the country of all ball and burlap nursery stock. The soil by which such material is surrounded is reasonably sure to carry spores* or dormant states of insect pests, and when the stock is unpacked and grown, the pests are sure to spread, and many times have become very serious. Such restriction stopped the importation of azaleas, rhododendrons, box, evergreens, many broad-leaved evergreens, and all other shrubs and trees whose roots must be surrounded by soil while in transit. The quarantine also provided for the exclusion of many other plants, or propagative parts of them, because of specific dangers. And for some plants importation, while permitted, is allowed only under permit and upon rigid inspection by the government experts. The exact details of what can and cannot be imported is a complicated document of interest and importance only to importing, mostly commercial interests, which are obliged to keep posted as to the modifications of the quarantine which the authorities find necessary to issue. They hardly concern the average home grower. But everyone should understand that importation

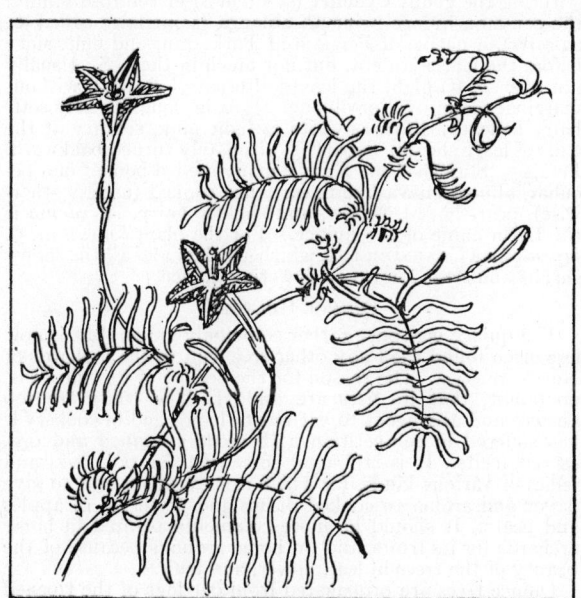

Cypress vine (*Quamoclit pennata*)

* Special articles on the subjects indicated by an asterisk (*) will be found at the words so marked.

of plants with balls of earth about their roots is still prohibited, and probably will always be so.

From time to time the authorities revise the quarantines in order not to make them more burdensome than they must be, and because certain pests are under control, or no longer serious. The latest general revision, effective January 14, 1935, allows many importations heretofore prohibited, but confirms a previous rule that, because of the Dutch Elm Disease, the importation of all elm seeds from Europe is forbidden. The new rule provides:

The following nursery stock, other plants and parts of plants, including seeds, which are governed by special quarantines and other restrictive orders now in force, nor such as may hereafter be made the subject of special quarantines, may be imported, without limitation as to quantity or use, from countries which maintain inspection under permit, upon compliance with these regulations:

(1) Bulbs, corms, or rootstocks (pips) of the following genera: *Lilium* (lily), *Convallaria* (lily-of-the-valley), *Hyacinthus* (hyacinth), *Tulipa* (tulip), and *Crocus*; and, until further notice, *Chionodoxa* (glory-of-the-snow), *Galanthus* (snowdrop), *Scilla* (squill), *Fritillaria*, *Muscari* (grape-hyacinth), *Ixia*, and *Eranthis* (winter aconite); and, on and after December 15, 1936, *Narcissus* (daffodil and jonquil).

(2) Cuttings, cions, and buds of fruits or nuts: *Provided*, That cuttings, cions, and buds of fruits or nuts may be imported from Asia, Japan, Philippine Islands, and Oceania under certain restrictions. (Stocks of fruits or nuts may not be imported, under permit or otherwise.)

(3) Rose stocks, including Manetti, *Rosa multiflora* (brier rose), and *R. rugosa*.

(4) Nuts, including palm seeds for growing purposes: *Provided*, That such nuts or seeds shall be free from pulp.

(5) Seeds of fruit, forest, ornamental, and shade trees, seeds of deciduous and evergreen ornamental shrubs, and seeds of hardy perennial plants: *Provided*, That such seeds shall be free from pulp: *Provided further*, That citrus seeds may be imported only through specified ports subject to disinfection: *Provided further*, That mango seeds may be imported under permit or otherwise, except from the countries of North America, Central America, and South America, and the West Indies.

Importations from countries not maintaining inspection of nursery stock, other plants and parts of plants, including seeds, the entry of which is permissible under this regulation, may be made under permit upon compliance with these regulations in limited quantities for public-service purposes only, but this limitation shall not apply to tree seeds.

Those going abroad or intending to bring plants into the country by importation should first find out whether such entry is permitted, under permit or without one. The rules, to meet sudden emergencies, are changed whenever the authorities see the need. Unless you obtain the necessary permission and permits, it is likely that your stock will be refused entry. For the latest regulations write to the Chief, Bureau of Entomology and Plant Quarantine Control, U.S. Department of Agriculture, Washington, D.C.

In addition to these Government regulations, nearly every state has special or local quarantines. They change frequently and if you contemplate moving plant material from one state to another it is wise to write to the Experiment Stations of both states for the latest regulations. See the name of your state for the address of the Experiment Station.

**QUART.** See WEIGHTS AND MEASURES, 3.

**QUASSIA.** See Contact Sprays at INSECTICIDES.

**QUA-SUL.** A trademarked fungicide useful for mildew and other plant diseases of rose bushes.

**QUEBEC.** See ONTARIO.

**QUEEN ANNE'S-LACE.** See CARROT.

**QUEEN ANNE'S POCKET MELON** = Pomegranate melon. See MELON.

**QUEEN-OF-THE-MEADOW** = *Filipendula ulmaria* and *Spiraea salicifolia*.

**QUEEN-OF-THE-PRAIRIE** = *Filipendula rubra*.

**QUEEN OLIVE.** Large-fruited olives derived from the varieties Sevillano, Ascolano, and Barouni. See OLIVE.

**QUEEN PALM** = *Arecastrum romanzoffianum*.

**QUEEN'S-FLOWER** = *Lagerstroemia speciosa*.

**QUEENSLAND NUT** = *Macadamia ternifolia*.

**QUEEN'S-WREATH** = *Petrea volubilis*.

**QUEEN VICTORIA ARBORVITAE** = *Thuja occidentalis alba*.

**QUENOUILLE TRAINING.** A French system of pruning and tying to produce, in ornamental shrubs and trees, a nearly perfect cone-shaped outline. It is little known in the U.S., and involves patient and laborious tying down of lower branches and pruning of upper ones. For training fruit trees see TRAINING PLANTS.

Quenouille training

*QUERCIFOLIA, -us, -um* (kwer-si-fō'li-a). With leaves like the oak (*Quercus*).

**QUERCITRON** = *Quercus velutina*. See OAK.

**QUERCUS.** See OAK.

**QUESTIONS.** See GARDEN QUESTIONS.

**QUICK SOILS.** See SOILS.

**QUILLAJA** (quill-ā'ya). A small genus of South American, evergreen trees of the rose family, comprising only 3 or 4 species, of which **Q. saponaria**, the soapbark tree, is occasionally cult. in zones* 8 and 9, especially in Calif., for ornament. It is a tree up to 60 ft. high, with alternate,* shining, ovalish, toothed leaves 1½–2 in. long. Flowers white, unisexual,* polygamous* or the sexes on different trees in rare instances, usually in terminal, sparse clusters. Petals 5, small. Stamens* 10. Fruit a collection of 5 leathery follicles,* united by their bases. Chile. Little known outside of southern Calif., but interesting because of its saponaceous (i.e. lathering) bark. Propagated by cuttings under glass. (*Quillaja* is from the Chilean vernacular *quillai*, meaning to wash, in allusion to the saponaceous bark.)

**QUINA.** See CINCHONA OFFICINALIS.

*QUINATA, -us, -um* (kwi-nay'ta). In fives.

**QUINCE.** A single species of medium-sized trees, constituting the genus **Cydonia** (sy-dō'ni-a) of the rose family, the common quince being **C. oblonga** (sometimes called *C. vulgaris*), a native of Persia and Turkestan, and cult. since before the Christian era, but not much in the U.S. Usually not over 25 ft. high, the leaves alternate,* stalked, without marginal teeth, oval or oblong, 2½–4 in. long, densely soft-hairy beneath. Flowers white or light pink, solitary at the ends of leafy shoots. Sepals* 5, ultimately turned backward. Petals 5. Stamens* 20. Fruit a many-seeded pome,* of a peculiar, almost guava-like flavor when cooked (useless otherwise), pear-shaped, yellow, and slightly hairy. (*Cydonia* is the Latin name of the quince.) For the plant known as *C. japonica* see CHAENOMELES, which also includes all the showy shrubs and trees known as flowering quince.

### QUINCE CULTURE

The quince was once rather commonly grown, but is now less often found than any other tree fruit in the orchards of North America. The reason for the decline of its culture is, no doubt, that its uses are limited. The fruits are too austere and astringent to eat out of hand, and in cookery it has suffered in competition with modern canned and preserved fruits. It is still used somewhat for preserves and jellies of various kinds, for which it is excellent, and to give flavor and aroma to cooked dishes and preserves of apples and pears. It should be more commonly planted in home orchards for its fruits, and on home grounds because of the beauty of the trees in leaf, flower, and fruit.

Quince trees are propagated from cuttings of the ripened wood or pieces of root; or better from mound layers, in which

---

* Special articles on the subjects indicated by an asterisk (*) will be found at the words so marked.

case the old plant is cut back to encourage sprouts from the crown which are then layered. Nursery trees, which are usually best, are budded on the Angers quince, grown by layerage. Trees should be two years old when set in the orchard.

The best soil for quinces is a heavy, moist, retentive clay loam which should be well drained, quite contrary to popular opinion that this fruit grows well on wet land. Quinces grown on light soils are not long-lived and do not produce well.

Usually quinces are planted a rod apart each way, but on good soils they should have a little greater distance and on light soils a little less. The trees begin to bear two or three years after planting, and are in full fruitage for twelve or fifteen years, and from then on produce well for a quarter of a century. The quince is shallow-rooted and the trees should not be deeply set, and in after years the cultivation should be shallow; or, perhaps better, they may be left in sod with the grass cut for a mulch. On good soils fertilization is not much needed, and if so the requirements are the same as for the apple and the pear.

The quince may well be left to grow in its natural shape with little pruning to train the tree. The habit of growth is crooked and scraggly and some heading-back is required to correct these natural tendencies. Interfering and superfluous branches should be removed. The trees bear year in and year out and sometimes overbear, in which case pruning may be used to thin the crop and stimulate greater growth. Pruning should be done only in winter or early spring.

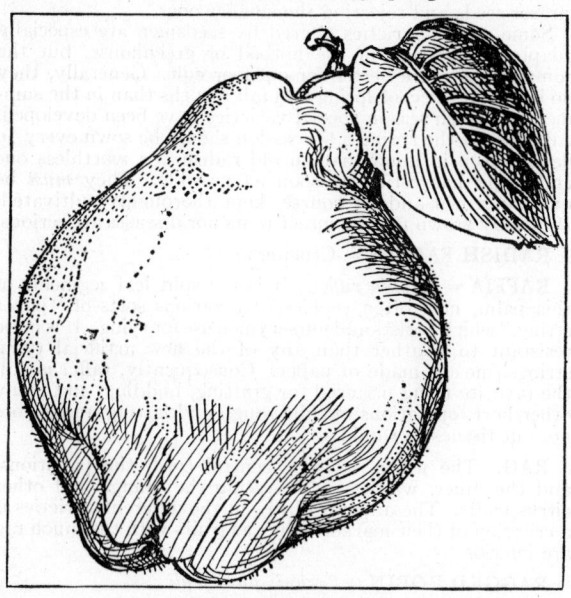

Quince fruit and foliage

The quince fruit has a delicate skin which shows bruises easily, to the great detriment of the clear golden color. The fruits must, therefore, be handled with much care in picking and storing. Usually the fruits may be kept for six weeks or two months after the harvest. They keep best in small receptacles and are sent to market in 20-pound baskets. The fruits are exceedingly variable in size and shape and must, therefore, be graded carefully for marketing. Because of the pronounced aroma, readily imparted to apples and pears, quinces ought not to be stored in storerooms with these fruits.

Although quinces have been grown since fruit growing had its beginning in the Old World, there are but few varieties, nor are new sorts being added to quince lists. The varieties differ chiefly in shape of fruit; thus, there are varieties with fruits shaped like oranges, apples, and pears. There are some but not great differences in season and keeping qualities. Texture and flavor vary. Perhaps a score of kinds have been offered by American nurserymen, of which probably not more than three or four can now be purchased. One kind will probably succeed as well as another in the several plant zones of the country. Orange is the most commonly grown variety and is the best. Champion, Rea, and Meach give variations in season and slight differences in fruits. — U. P. H.

INSECT PESTS. The quince is attacked by a number of apple pests. The codling moth, San Jose scale, and leaf feeders are controlled as on apple. The round-headed apple tree borer is reported as attacking quince severely. The oriental fruit moth infests the fruit heavily, late in the season (see PEACH). The quince curculio, a small snout beetle, differing somewhat from the plum curculio, attacks it, and the larvae feed in the fruit. One or two sprays of lead arsenate, applied a week or two after blossoms fall, are prescribed as control; jarring may be useful (see PLUM).

DISEASES. (See PEAR diseases for fire-blight, which is one of the serious troubles on quince trees.) Next to fire-blight, leafblight is probably the most serious disease of quince. It causes circular, reddish spots which coalesce and soon kill the entire leaf. The whole tree may be defoliated, and so weakened that winter-injury later kills it. The fruit, too, may be much spotted. Spraying at ten-day intervals with lime-sulphur, 1-40, beginning when the blossoms show pink, will protect the trees. Quince rust may cause much damage in areas where red cedar trees grow adjacent to the quince orchard. The rust fungus must have the two hosts* for the development of its complete life history. Spraying has not helped much in controlling the rust, but in areas where the cedar trees can be removed, the disease is no longer troublesome.

**QUINCE FAMILY.** *See* ROSACEAE.

**QUINCULA** (kwin'kew-la). A single species of little-known and hort. unimportant perennial herbs of the potato family, the only one being **Q. lobata,** a prostrate or spreading, scurfy herb found from the central U.S. to Calif. and Mex. It has alternate,* wavy-margined or faintly lobed, oblongish leaves, 3-4½ in. long, the base tapering into a long stalk. Flowers solitary or in pairs, the stalk arising in the leaf-axils.* Corolla flat, bell-shaped, purplish, about 1 in. wide, the anthers* orange. Fruit consisting of a few, kidney-shaped seeds, enclosed by the veiny, much-enlarged, 5-angled calyx. The plant is of little garden interest, as the related species of *Physalis* are much more desirable, but it is suited to dry, sandy, hot sites. (The origin of *Quincula* is unknown.)

**QUINCUNX.** A method of spacing orchard trees to save space. *See* the details at Planting in the article on FRUIT CULTURE.

**QUININE.** *See* CINCHONA.

**QUININE BUSH** = *Garrya elliptica.*

**QUININE TREE.** *See* CINCHONA.

*QUINQUEFOLIA, -us, -um* (kwin-kwe-fō'li-a). With 5 leaves or 5 leaflets.

*QUINQUENERVIS* (kwin-kwe-ner'vis). Five-veined.

**QUISQUALIS** (kwis-kwā'lis). A small genus of woody vines of the family Combretaceae, the only cult. species being **Q. indica,** the Rangoon creeper from Indo-Malaya and the Philippines, which is grown for ornament in southern Fla. (hardy outdoors, nowhere else). It is a quick-growing vine, without tendrils, having oblong, stalked, abruptly pointed, opposite* leaves, 3-5 in. long. Flowers showy, blooming all summer (in Fla.), the long-tubed calyx green, the fragrant corolla white, changing to pink or red. Fruit a dry, leathery, 5-angled capsule,* not over 1 in. long. Propagated by seeds or cuttings over bottom-heat. (*Quisqualis* means, literally, who or what for, and is without known application here.)

**QUIXOTE-PLANT** = *Hesperoyucca whipplei.*

* Special articles on the subjects indicated by an asterisk (*) will be found at the words so marked.

# R

**RABBITS.** See Animal Injury.
**RABBIT'S-TAIL GRASS** = *Lagurus ovatus*.
**RACCOON GRAPE** = *Vitis cordifolia*.
**RACE.** See Variety.
**RACEME.** An elongated flower cluster, blooming from the bottom upward, with a single main stalk, from which arise the stalks of the individual flowers. The main stalk is never terminated by a flower, and when branched, the cluster is known as a compound raceme. Typical examples are the currant, mustard, honey locust, fireweed, squill, and lily-of-the-valley. See Panicle and Spike.

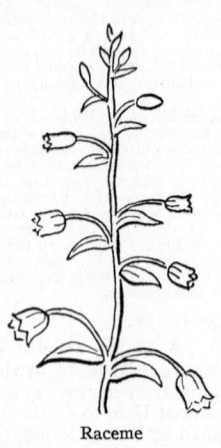

Raceme

*RACEMIFLORA, -us, -um* (ra-see-mi-flow'ra). Having flowers in racemes.*

*RACEMOSA, -us, -um* (ra-see-mō'sa). See Raceme.

**RACHIS** (ray'kiss). The main stalk of a flower cluster or the main leafstalk of a compound* leaf.

*RADIATA, -us, -um* (ray-di-ā'ta). Radiate; i.e. rayed, often having spreading rays or petals. See Compositae.

**RADICAL.** Having to do with the root; as *radical* leaves are basal or root leaves.

*RADICANS* (rad'i-kanz). Rooting, especially along the stem.

*RADICATA, -us, -um* (rad-i-kay'ta). Rooted; often strongly rooted.

**RADICLE.** The first young root put forth from a seed; or, among gardeners, a similar initial root put forth from a tuber* or rootstock.*

**RADICULA.** A much-abused generic name, variously applied to several different plants. For the only important garden application of it *see* Horse-radish.

**RADISH.** This is the easiest of all vegetables to raise, and all the cult. varieties of it belong to the genus **Raphanus** (raf'an-us) of the mustard family, comprising 8–10 Eurasian herbs of which only one, **R. sativus** and its varieties, is of any garden interest. This, the common radish, is an annual or biennial herb with a thick, fleshy, pleasantly pungent root, for which it is grown in the typical variety, although the cult. varieties of it have many forms, some of which are grown for the pods. Leaves mostly basal, lyre-like, or cut featherfashion, but not usually compound.* Flowers (not produced in ordinary, harvested plants), rather showy, white or lilac, in terminal clusters (racemes*), the spongy pod 1–3 in. long (a silique*), more or less constricted between the seeds and long-beaked. The above applies only to the commonly cult. radish, but there are at least two well-marked varieties, neither of which is much grown in the U.S. They are *var.* **caudatus** (sometimes called *R. caudatus*), the rat-tailed radish, which bears no edible root, but a long, curved, often twisted pod, 8–12 in. long, used as are common radishes; and *var.* **longipinnatus**, the Chinese radish, which has leaves 1–2 ft. long, with 8–12 leaflets, and bears long, durable and hard roots, which are usually cooked. It is sometimes known as the winter radish and is little known here. The Japanese call it daikon. The typical species, *R. sativus*, is a cultigen,* unknown in the wild, and may be derived from *R. raphanistrum*, a European herb now widely distributed in N.A. as a naturalized weed. (*Raphanus* is the classical Latin name of the radish.)

### Radish Culture

The common radish will germinate in 4–5 days and, if grown properly, will have useful roots ready to harvest in 28–40 days. If it takes longer than this, the roots will be spongy, acrid, or woody — hence, useless. The secret of getting crisp, delicious radishes is quick growth. For this they need a rich soil in good tilth* and free of stones. Sow the seeds about ⅓ in. deep in drills not over 8–12 in. apart. Small, quick-growing roots (the only kind worth harvesting) can be secured by early planting, preferably sifting out the largest seeds and rejecting the smaller ones.

Some of the varieties offered by seedsmen are especially adapted to forcing in the hotbed or greenhouse, but the common sorts are better for outdoor cult. Generally, they do better in the cool spring and fall months than in the summer, for which season special varieties have been developed. All through the spring a succession should be sown every 10 days. Keep in mind that an old radish is a worthless one and begin harvesting as soon as possible. They *must* be quickly grown and, of course, kept thoroughly cultivated. If quickly grown neither insect pests nor diseases are serious.

**RADISH FAMILY** = Cruciferae.

**RAFFIA** = *Raphia ruffia*. It is the split leaf segments of this palm, now often replaced by various sorts of "paper string," which florists and nurserymen use for tying. It is more resistant to weather than any of the new artificial tying strings, mostly made of paper. Consequently, raffia is still the favorite tying material for grafting, budding, and many other hort. operations. While tough and lasting, raffia does not cut tissues as would string.

**RAG.** The white, stringy, central cord, the partitions, and the inner, white skin investing the orange and other citrus fruits. The amount of rag in the different varieties is a criterion of their market value, as fruits with too much rag are inferior.

**RAGGED ROBIN** = *Lychnis flos-cuculi*.

**RAG GOURD.** See Luffa.

**RAGWEED** = *Ambrosia elatior*. See list at Weeds.

**RAGWORT.** See Senecio.

**RAILINGS.** See Fences.

**RAINFALL.** Few statistics issued by the Weather Bureau are of more importance than those on rainfall, which includes both rain and melted snow in all annual summaries.

Rainfall is the only practical source of soil moisture and the amount of rainfall thus dictates what can be grown in any particular region. From the crest of the Alleghenies to the Atlantic the annual rainfall varies from 35–50 in. per year, which is ample for the growth of heavy forest, and for practically all garden crops. Summer droughts may retard or even ruin shallow-rooted garden plants, but generally, the rainfall is adequate for most garden needs.

From the Alleghenies westward there is a gradual reduction of rainfall. In the Great Plains states it falls to such a

---

* Special articles on the subjects indicated by an asterisk (*) will be found at the words so marked.

figure that forest is no longer possible and is replaced by grassland. The cult. of many evergreens and broad-leaved evergreens in such a region is impossible or very difficult. Still farther west, and throughout the region from western Tex. to southern Calif., there is not enough rainfall for even grassland to survive, and we have instead the desert or semi-desert of the cactus country. Such regions may have fertile soil, but without irrigation (which see) they are useless for most garden plants.

In the extreme northwestern coastal region there is the heaviest rainfall in the U.S., resulting in the magnificent coniferous forests of British Columbia, Wash., Ore., and northern Calif., and making of this region a place as favorable for gardening as England.

So important are these rainfall figures, especially the amount that falls in the growing season, that they have been included in the account of each state and Canadian province. See the name of your state or province for the significant rainfall data of your locality. See also DRIP.

Many experienced gardeners always water greenhouse plants with rain water rather than tap water. The various chemical and bacteriological safeguards which municipal water systems must set up, do things to tap water which are not found in pure rain water. Hence the frequency of the old-fashioned rain barrel in some very extensive greenhouse ranges.

**RAIN LILY.** See COOPERIA.

**RAIN TREE** = *Samanea saman*.

**RAISIN.** The dried, sweet fruit of certain varieties of grapes. For the best varieties of grapes for raisin-making and the conditions necessary to produce them *see vinifera* varieties at GRAPE. For the Japanese raisin tree *see* HOVENIA DULCIS.

**RAJANIA** (ra-jay'ni-a). Yam-like, West Indian, herbaceous vines of the family Dioscoreaceae, comprising about 6 species, only **R. pleioneura**, the guayabo or gunda, of any hort. interest. It is sometimes grown for ornament in extreme southern Fla. and is a rather shrubby vine arising from a large tuberous root. Leaves alternate,* roundish or heart-shaped, 2-5 in. wide, usually abruptly long-pointed at the tip. Flowers small, greenish, inconspicuous, the male and female on different plants. (For details *see* DIOSCOREACEAE.) Fruit key-like, winged, oblongish and blunt. Cuba. The plant often produces aerial* tubers which are irregular and cockscombed. (Named for John Ray, famous British botanist.)

**RAKE.** See Section 1, TOOLS AND IMPLEMENTS.

**RAKING.** The smoothing and pulverizing of soil before seeding. There is no better tool for it than the common steel-toothed rake, the teeth of which should be kept sharpened. As in cultivating or hoeing, the only instruction necessary is to so arrange your work that you never have to walk over raked soil. Where the area is too large (*i.e.* half an acre or more), hand raking is too expensive and a harrow should be used (*see* HARROWING). But for the final touches only raking will put the soil in the finest shape, especially if the ground is being prepared for a lawn (which see). See also SOIL OPERATIONS.

To make soil friable* there is no substitute for raking.

**RAMERO** = *Trichostema lanatum*. See BLUECURLS.

**RAMIE.** See BOEHMERIA NIVEA.

**RAMONA.** See AUDIBERTIA.

**RAMONDIA** (ray-mon'di-a); also spelled *Ramonda*. Delicate little perennial herbs from the mountains of Eu. and among the only hardy representatives of the family Gesneriaceae (for the others *see* HABERLEA). Of the 10 known species the two below are grown for ornament, mostly in rock gardens where their culture requires considerable care. They are nearly stemless herbs, covered with reddish, soft hairs. Leaves chiefly basal. Flowers typically purple or bluish-lavender (white in a hort. form), flat-bell-shaped, almost without a tube, and borne sparsely at the end of a leafless stalk. Fruit an oblong, rather pointed capsule.* (Named for L. F. E. von Ramond de Carbonnieres, French botanist.)

For culture *see* ROCK GARDEN.

**nathaliae.** Low herb with oval, wavy-toothed, hairy leaves. Flowers lavender-blue, but yellow-eyed, the corolla 4-lobed. Serbia and Bulgaria.

**pyrenaica.** Not over 3 in. high, the ovalish leaves hairy and deeply toothed. Flowers purple, about 1 in. wide, the corolla 5-lobed. Pyrenees. There is also a white-flowered hort. form.

**RAMONTCHI** = *Flacourtia indica*.

*RAMOSA, -us, -um* (ra-mō'sa). Branched.

*RAMOSISSIMA, -us, -um* (ra-mo-siss'i-ma). Much-branched.

**RAMPION.** See PHYTEUMA.

**RAM'S-HEAD LADY'S-SLIPPER** = *Cypripedium arietinum*.

**RANCHO SANTA ANA.** See BOTANIC GARDEN.

**RAND, E. S.** See America at GARDEN BOOKS.

**RANDOM FLAG WALKS.** See PATHS AND PAVING.

**RANGOON CREEPER** = *Quisqualis indica*.

**RANGPUR LIME.** See LIME (the citrus fruit).

**RANUNCULACEAE** (ra-nun-kew-lay'see-ee). The buttercup or crowfoot family, often, and with equal reason, called the peony or hepatica family, is horticulturally important as well as being a large natural group of herbs (a few are vines). There are about 30 genera and perhaps 1200 known species, nearly all of which come from the cooler parts of the north temperate zone.

By far the most important garden genus is *Paeonia* (*see* PEONY), but *Delphinium, Anemone, Aquilegia* (*see* COLUMBINE), *Clematis, Pulsatilla,* and *Aconitum* (*see* MONKSHOOD) are extremely popular garden plants, some of them with very showy flowers. Some of the genera are of comparatively easy cult., but see each of them for further notes.

A perhaps secondary group of garden genera, some of which, however, are very old garden favorites are: *Adonis, Anemonopsis, Eranthis, Helleborus, Leptopyrum, Nigella, Trollius* and *Trautvetteria*. More suited to the wild garden and nothing like so showy are: *Actaea, Anemonella, Caltha* (*see* MARSH MARIGOLD), *Cimicifuga, Coptis, Hepatica, Hydrastis* (*see* GOLDENSEAL), *Isopyrum,* and *Zanthorhiza* which is somewhat shrubby. For *Ranunculus see* BUTTERCUP, and for the meadow rue *see* THALICTRUM.

Leaves alternate* or opposite,* but basal in many genera, usually divided or even compound,* but undivided in some. Flowers very various. In the peony they are larger than in any other genera in the family, in some hort., double-flowered forms often 5 in. across, or more. In all the rest of the garden genera the flowers are smaller, but sometimes, as in *Delphinium*, in spectacular clusters. In two genera the flowers are very irregular* and more or less spurred* (*see* DELPHINIUM and MONKSHOOD). They are spurred,* but regular, in *Aquilegia* (*see* COLUMBINE). All the rest of the cult. genera have regular* flowers but some, like *Hepatica* and *Thalictrum*, lack petals.

Most of the garden plants are perennials, but most *Clematis* and *Zanthorhiza* are woody plants. The fruit is dry and in most genera made up of separable follicles* or achenes,* but berry-like in *Actaea* and in some other genera.

---

* Special articles on the subjects indicated by an asterisk (*) will be found at the words so marked.

Technical flower characters: Sepals 3-15, sometimes petal-like, in other genera hooded and irregular. Petals 3-5, sometimes lacking, in a few genera prominently spurred or hooded. Stamens* many. Ovary superior.*

**RANUNCULUS.** *See* BUTTERCUP.

*RAPA* (ray'pa). Classical name of the turnip.

*RAPACEA, -us, -um* (ra-pay'see-a). Rape-like or turnip-like.

**RAPE** = *Brassica napus.*

**RAPHANUS.** *See* RADISH.

**RAPHIA** (ray'fi-a). Chiefly tropical African or Madagascan feather palms of no hort. interest except for *R. ruffia* which yields raffia, a very widely used tying fiber. The raffia palm is practically unknown in cult. in the U.S. outside of the collections of a few specialists, but it could be grown in southern Fla. It has a trunk 25-30 ft. high, crowned with perhaps the largest known leaves in the world. These stand straight upward, are often 65 ft. long, the stalks about 10-15 ft. long. There are a tremendous number of leaflets which are stiffish, 2-5 ft. long, and grayish beneath. It is from them that raffia is harvested. Fruit oblongish, beaked, 1-2 in. long. Tropical Af., but chiefly Madagascar, where most raffia fiber comes from. (*Raphia* is from the Greek for needle, in allusion to the short, sharp beak of the fruit.)

**RAPHIOLEPIS** (ra-fi-ol'e-pis). Asiatic, handsome, evergreen shrubs of the rose family, comprising only half a dozen species of which two are widely planted for ornament from zone* 7 southward, more rarely in the cool greenhouse northward. They have alternate,* thick, fleshy, short-stalked leaves and white or pink flowers in rather showy terminal clusters (panicles* or racemes*). Petals 5. Stamens* 15-20. Fruit a bluish-black or purplish-black, generally round pome* with 1-2 seeds. (*Raphiolepis* is from the Greek for needle and scale, in allusion to the scale-like bracts* in the flower cluster.)

All the species are popular in Calif. and along the Gulf Coast, where they can be grown in a variety of soils. While they will stand some frost they cannot be grown safely north of zone* 7, and do best south of this. If grown in the greenhouse, use potting mixture* 5 and keep in the cool house. Propagated by seeds or by cuttings of ripe wood, under glass.

**delacouri.** A hybrid between the second and third species, but having toothed leaves and pink flowers. It forms a compact, showy shrub, often used in southern patios. *See* PATIO GARDENS.
**indica.** Indian hawthorn. Not over 5 ft. high. Leaves oblongish, or narrower, 2-3 in. long, bluntly toothed. Flowers pinkish-white, about ½ in. wide, the clusters loose and without hairs. Southern China.
**umbellata.** Yeddo hawthorn. A shrub, often low and spreading, but occasionally 8-10 ft. high. Leaves very thick, 2-3 in. long, slightly toothed, the margins rolled. Flowers white, about ¾ in. wide, fragrant, the clusters dense and hairy. Jap. The *var.* ovata has broader leaves without marginal teeth.

*RAPUNCULOIDES* (ra-pun-kew-loy'deez, but see OÏDES). Resembling a *Rapunculus*, an obsolete name for some bellflowers.

**RARERIPE** = Ratheripe.

*RARIFLORA, -us, -um* (rare-ri-flow'ra). With a few, or with loosely clustered, flowers.

**RASPBERRY.** Four groups of raspberries, each with many varieties, are grown in North America. These are in order of introduction to cultivation: The European red raspberry, derived from the wild red raspberry of Europe; the American red raspberry, the cultivated form of the American wild red raspberry; the black raspberry, or blackcap, also a cultivated native; and the purple-cane raspberries, hybrids between varieties of the two reds and the black raspberry. The culture of these four groups differs only in minor details, possibly most in method of propagation. All belong to the genus *Rubus*, which see.

Red raspberries are propagated from suckers that spring up from the roots of fruiting plants. These suckers may be set in the field as they are taken from the mother plants, or they may be grown for a year in nursery rows, a procedure not often warranted. Black and purple raspberries are propagated by tipping. Late in the summer, the snake-like tips of canes which have dropped to the ground develop roots. Under cultivation, the tips are buried to prevent whipping by the wind. By the following spring roots have formed and the tipped plants are set in the field or for a season in the nursery row.

SOILS. Raspberries are not choosers as to soil but seem to be most at home, especially the reds, in warm, sandy loams, while the blacks and purples take to heavier, moister loams and even to clays. Some variety may be found for any good garden soil. In soils too moist the plants "run to wood" and bear little fruit so that good drainage is imperative. A soil on which potatoes grow well is ideal for the reds; one on which corn grows well, for the blacks and purples. Whether soils are acid or alkaline, matters little to raspberries — lime applied to raspberry soils is wasted; so, for most part, are commercial fertilizers, but organic matter from stable manure or cover crops is a prime requisite.

The dotted lines show how much terminal growth should be pruned from raspberry canes.

Climate plays an important part in the selection of sites. Raspberries are tender to both cold and heat and withstand either extreme rather less well than, say, the apple. The blacks are more easily hurt by cold and less easily by heat than the reds. European reds are tender, alike, in American winters and summers. Varieties of all four groups vary in what they will stand from climate. All like climates tempered in winter and summer by bodies of water.

CULTURE. Raspberries of any of the four types are grown either in hills or solid rows. Red raspberries are set 5 × 5 ft. in the hill system; black and purple need a little more room and are often set 6 × 6 ft. apart. In the hedge-row system, the rows for reds are 6 or 7 ft. apart and plants in the row 2 or 3 ft. apart. Blacks and purples need at least a foot greater distance each way.

Spring is the time to plant. Before planting, the canes should be cut back to 4 to 6 in. Cultivation should be begun as soon as the ground can be worked in the spring and continued until after picking, when a cover crop should be sown.

Raspberry canes are biennial and the fruiting canes should be cut out as soon as the crop is harvested. Black and purple varieties naturally run to long, sprawling canes difficult to manage. To prevent this, the shoots should be pinched in June when they have reached the desired height; red raspberries should not be so pinched. Spring pruning of red raspberries consists in cutting back the fruiting canes to a height of 4 or 5 ft. depending on the vigor of the variety; weak canes

---

* Special articles on the subjects indicated by an asterisk (*) will be found at the words so marked.

# RASPBERRY

should be removed. At the spring pruning lateral branches on the black and purple types should be shortened to 6 or 8 in. Spindling canes bear little fruit and rob stronger ones; thin these out, leaving 5 or 6 strong canes to each plant.

Raspberries are tender fruits and require careful handling. The fruit should be picked every other day during the height of the season and always when berries are free from moisture. Overripe berries spoil quickly. Raspberries are marketed and should be picked in pint and quart baskets which are marketed in crates holding 32 baskets. Picking should be done in the cool of the morning and the berries should be kept in a cool place until consumed.

VARIETIES. The three groups are described in order of ripening. Red varieties may be grown in Zones* 1, 2, and 3; black and purple varieties, in Zones* 2, 3, and 4.

### RED RASPBERRIES

JUNE. Fruit large, bright red, firm, good quality, very early. Plants vigorous, productive; easily kept free from mosaic.

NEWBURGH. Fruit very large, firm, bright red, good. Plants vigorous and very productive; nearly immune to mosaic.

VIKING. Fruit large, bright red, firm, good. Plants vigorous, very productive; susceptible to mosaic.

CUTHBERT. Fruit bright red, medium size, firm, of highest quality. Plants productive but not very vigorous; susceptible to mosaic.

LATHAM. Fruit large, bright red, firm, crumbles, fair quality. Plants productive and fairly resistant to mosaic.

### BLACK RASPBERRIES

KANSAS. Fruit medium in size, glossy, firm, mild subacid, good. Plants very productive and relatively free from mosaic.

BLACK PEARL. Fruit large, glossy, quality very good. Plants vigorous, productive, and very hardy.

PLUM FARMER. Fruit large, heavy bloom, highest quality; ships well. Plants vigorous and productive but susceptible to mosaic.

NAPLES. Fruit large, glossy, mild subacid. Plants vigorous and very productive; relatively free from mosaic.

### PURPLE RASPBERRIES

COLUMBIAN. Fruits large, dark purple, high quality. Plants very productive, but susceptible to mosaic.

SHAFFER. Similar to Columbian, with the same zone adaptabilities with larger berries and earlier, but plants not so good except hardier.

### EUROPEAN RED RASPBERRIES

Berries of the European reds are better in quality than those of the American, but the plants are less hardy. Gardeners might grow Lloyd George for its splendid fruits.

LLOYD GEORGE. Berries dark red, very large, excellent quality, early. Plants medium in productiveness, vigor and healthfulness. — U. P. H.

INSECT PESTS. The insect pests of raspberry are much the same as those of blackberry. The cane borers, controlled by pruning out injured canes; the rose scale, controlled by dormant spray if present; the green sawfly larvae, controlled by arsenicals when abundant; the tree crickets, controlled by arsenical spray in early summer; are noted under blackberry. Red raspberries in the North are sometimes injured by the raspberry fruitworm, the adult of which is a brown beetle about ⅛ in. long. The adults eat the leaves and the whitish larvae later feed within the fruit. It is controlled by killing adults with an early summer arsenical spray. Aphids should be controlled because they spread plant diseases.

DISEASES. The virus diseases of raspberries have in late years sprung into exceptional prominence and in some cases have limited the growing of the crop. The red and the yellow mosaics are found everywhere and are recognized by leaf mottling, corrugation, yellowing, and dwarfing of the plant. Leaf curl manifests itself in dark green foliage and rough leaves that are curled downward. It is not so common as mosaic, but causes very severe injury to the plantings in which it does occur. Mild and severe streak cause dark streaks in the plant, which later may die.

Other names for these two diseases are rosette or eastern bluestem. These viruses are usually disseminated by means of certain aphids which inhabit raspberry bushes.

Next to the virus troubles, anthracnose probably causes more injury than most of the other raspberry diseases. It causes small circular, to oval, sunken spots on the stems. When these become very numerous, the stem may be girdled and the plant dies. The fungus causing it frequently is transmitted to new plantings on the stumps of canes that have been cut off some distance above the ground.

Crown-gall also is carried from infested nurseries and causes large swellings on infected plants. Orange and yellow rusts when present are so conspicuous on the foliage that they cannot be missed.

Spur and cane blights cause reddish or bluish cankers on the stems, and when large enough to girdle the plant, cause its death. Several leaf spots are common on some varieties, root rots have been found, and powdery mildew may be present.

In most intensive berry sections, inspected nursery stocks relatively free from virus diseases, crown-gall, and other troublesome maladies are available and should be planted. The new planting should be some distance from older plantings and also from wild bushes. The rows should be far apart, and the weeds kept down so that air currents can quickly dry the foliage after rains. Each planting should be rogued carefully, the affected plants first being treated with a blow torch to kill the aphids which otherwise might scatter and carry virus diseases.

All old diseased canes should be removed promptly, and without leaving stubs. The plants should be sprayed during the dormant stage with lime-sulphur, 1-10, if anthracnose has been present. Since raspberries are very susceptible to spray injury, it is doubtful whether any summer application should be recommended. In all cases where resistant or disease-escaping plants are available, they should be planted if at all possible.

**RASPBERRY FAMILY.** See ROSACEAE.

**RATA** = *Metrosideros robusta*.

**RATAMA** = *Parkinsonia aculeata*.

**RAT CORN.** A trademarked poison bait, sold with directions for use against small vermin.

**RATHERIPE.** Maturing earlier than the rest of the fruit on a tree; sometimes called rareripe. Neither term is in much use in this country, but will be heard in England.

**RATIBIDA.** See LEPACHYS.

**RATOON.** A basal sucker used for propagation in the pineapple, sugar-cane, and banana. Other plants produce ratoons, which, because they already have roots, make useful material for propagating plants that ordinarily do not set seeds. The term is more commonly heard in the tropics, and is also used as a verb, as to *ratoon* a pine-apple field; *i.e.* propagate by using ratoons.

**RAT-POISON PLANT** = *Hamelia erecta*.

**RATS.** See ANIMAL INJURY.

**RAT-STRIPPER** = *Pachistima canbyi*.

**RAT-TAIL CACTUS** = *Aporocactus flagelliformis*.

Ratoon of pineapple

**RAT-TAILED RADISH** = *Raphanus sativus caudatus*. See RADISH.

**RATTAN.** The plants yielding rattan belong to the genus *Calamus*, which, in Ceylon, are climbing palms with stems several hundred feet long. They are scarcely known in cult. here. For a cult. palm called ground rattan see RHAPIS EXCELSA.

**RATTLEBOX.** See CROTALARIA.

**RATTLE-BUSH** = *Baptisia australis*.

**RATTLESNAKE FERN** = *Botrychium virginianum*.

**RATTLESNAKE MASTER.** A name applied to several North American plants thought to have some efficacy against the poison of rattlesnakes. Those found here are: *Eryngium aquaticum*, *Manfreda virginica*, *Liatris scariosa* and *L. squarrosa*, and *Habenaria ciliaris*.

**RATTLESNAKE PLANTAIN** = *Epipactis pubescens*.

**RATTLESNAKE-WEED** = *Cimicifuga racemosa*.

---

* Special articles on the subjects indicated by an asterisk (*) will be found at the words so marked.

RAVENALA (ra-ven-nay′la). Extraordinary, banana-like plants of the family Musaceae, one Brazilian, the other the famous traveler's-tree of Madagascar, R. madagascariensis, often cult. for its very striking habit in regions where the banana is hardy. In maturity it has a stout, palm-like trunk, 20–40 ft. high, crowned with a tuft of immense, banana-like leaves so arranged (i.e. two-ranked) that the foliage stands in one plane like a gigantic fan. Leaves 20–30 ft. long, the channeled, sheathing stalks holding much

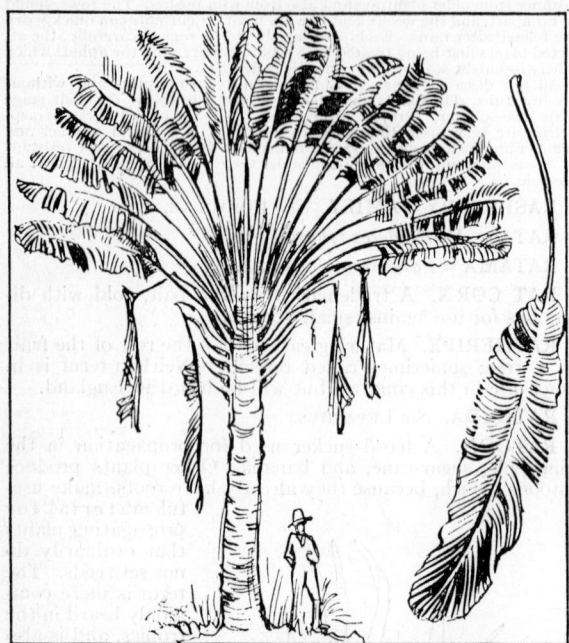

The traveler's-tree of Madagascar

water at the point of insertion. For flower characters see Musaceae. The fruit is quite unlike the closely related banana in being a 3-celled, woody capsule.* In southern Fla. (it is hardy nowhere else in the U.S.) the leaves are, like the banana, often torn by the wind, but with little or no damage. Fla. plants do not usually reach the dimensions given above, but plants up to 30 ft. high are not uncommon. (*Ravenala* is a Latinized version of the Madagascan name for the tree.)

**RAVENNA GRASS** = *Erianthus ravennae*.

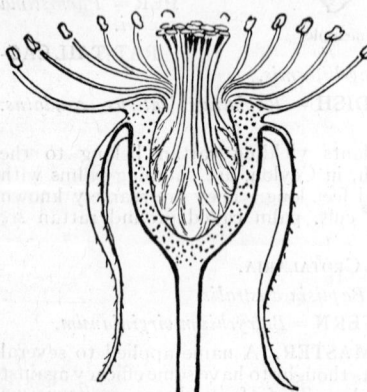

Cross-section of the receptacle (dotted) of a rose flower. It ultimately forms the rose hip.

**RAY.** Loosely, any narrow, spreading petal, or the outer and sometimes sterile flowers in an umbel.* Correctly, a ray is one of the flat, marginal flowers in a head of the aster, sunflower, daisy, etc., as distinguished from the central disk flowers. See Compositae.

**RECEPTACLE.** A term of several meanings in botany and hort., although all of them originate in the basic fact that a receptacle is the much-modified stem-end upon which a flower is borne; an alternative term for it is *torus*.

It takes many forms to which special terms are applied. In some plants of the rose family the receptacle and part of the united calyx are fused into what is known as the hypanthium, which later provides most of the fleshy, juicy part of apple and pear fruits. Most, or perhaps all, of a rose hip is the enlarged receptacle. In other families it is often mistaken for a true fruit (i.e. a ripened ovary), especially in the fleshy "fruits" of *Elaeagnus* and some plants of the Trochodendraceae. Perhaps the most familiar receptacle is the strawberry, the fleshy part of which is all receptacle, the only real fruits being what are commonly called the seeds embedded in the surface.

The disk, upon which is inserted the head of flowers in the Compositae or daisy family, is another familiar example of a receptacle.

**RECESSIVE.** See Dominant.

*RECLINATA, -us, -um* (reck-li-nay′ta). Reclinate; *i.e.* bent backwards.

*RECTA, -us, -um* (reck′ta). Upright or straight.

**RECTANGULAR TANKS.** For contents see Weights and Measures, 5.

**RECTIFIED.** A term applied to certain flowers, especially tulips, which have unusual color markings, presumably produced by disease, and probably by a mosaic disease. The term is more common in England than here.

*RECURVA, -us, -um* (re-ker′va). Recurved; *i.e.* bent backwards.

*RECURVATA, -us, -um* (re-ker-vay′ta). See Recurva.

**RECURVED CACTUS DAHLIA.** See Group 8 at Dahlia.

**RED.** As part of a name, *red* is applied to many garden plants and things. Those that are found in The Garden Dictionary and their proper equivalents are:

Red A. (see first main entry below); **Red Arrow** (see second main entry below); **Red ash** = *Fraxinus pennsylvanica* (see Ash); **Red Astrachan** (see Apple); **Red balm** = *Monarda didyma*; **Red baneberry** = *Actaea rubra*; **Red bay** = *Persea borbonia*; **Red beech** = *Fagus grandifolia* (see Beech); **Red-berried elder** = *Sambucus racemosa* (see Elder); **Redberry** = *Heteromeles arbutifolia* (see Toyon); **Red birch** in the East, *Betula nigra*, in the West, *Betula fontinalis* (see Birch); **Redbird cactus** = *Pedilanthus tithymaloides*; **Red box** = *Eucalyptus polyanthemos*; **Red buckeye** = *Aesculus pavia* (see Horse-chestnut); **Redbud** (see third main entry below); **Redbug** (see Insect Pests at Apple); **Red cabbage** = *Brassica oleracea capitata* (for culture see Cabbage); **Red calla lily** = *Zantedeschia rehmanni* (see Calla Lily); **Red cedar** (in the East, *Juniperus virginiana*, in the West, *J. scopulorum*, also applied to *Thuja plicata*); **Red chokeberry** = *Aronia arbutifolia*; **Red clover** = *Trifolium pratense* (see Clover); **Red cluster pepper** = *Capsicum frutescens fasciculatum*; **Red cohosh** = *Actaea rubra*; **Red cuprous oxide** (see Copper at Fungicides); **Red date scale** (see Insect Pests at Date); **Red dead nettle** = *Lamium purpureum*; **Red dogwood** = *Cornus florida rubra*, also *C. sanguinea*; **Red elder** = *Sambucus pubens* (see Elder); **Red false mallow** = *Malvastrum coccineum*; **Red fescue** = *Festuca rubra*; **Red Garden** (see fourth main entry below); **Red gum** = *Eucalyptus rostrata*; **Red haw** = *Crataegus mollis*; **Red-heart** = *Ceanothus spinosus*; **Red-hot poker** = *Kniphofia uvaria*; **Red ironbark** = *Eucalyptus sideroxylon*; **Red jasmine** = *Plumeria rubra*; **Red kowahi** = *Clianthus puniceus*; **Red larkspur** = *Delphinium nudicaule*; **Red mahogany** = *Eucalyptus resinifera*; **Red maids** = *Calandrinia caulescens menziesi*; **Red maple** = *Acer rubrum* (see Maple); **Red mombin** = *Spondias purpurea*; **Red mosaic** (see diseases at Raspberry); **Red mulberry** = *Morus rubra* (see Mulberry); **Red oak** (see *Quercus rubra* at Oak); **Red osier** = *Cornus stolonifera*; **Red pepper** (see Capsicum); **Red pine** = *Pinus resinosa* (see Pine); **Red plum** = *Prunus nigra*; **Red raspberry** = *Rubus idaeus strigosus*; **Red ribbons** = *Eucharidium concinnum*; **Redroot** = *Lachnanthes tinctoria*; **Redroot** = *Ceanothus americanus*; **Redroot** = San-

---

* Special articles on the subjects indicated by an asterisk (*) will be found at the words so marked.

# Red A 669 Regular Flower

*guinaria canadensis* (see BLOODROOT); **Red sage** = *Lantana camara;* **Red Sally** = *Lythrum salicaria;* **Red sandalwood** = *Adenanthera pavonina;* **Red scale** (see Insect Pests at ORANGE); **Red shanks** = *Geranium robertianum;* **Red sorrel** = *Hibiscus sabdariffa* (the roselle); **Red spider** (see Insect Pests at AVOCADO, FIG, ORANGE, CALCEOLARIA, CARNATION, and HOLLYHOCK); **Red tassel-flower** = *Petalostemon purpureum;* **Redtop** = *Agrostis palustris;* **Red trillium** = *Trillium sessile;* **Red turtlehead** = *Chelone lyoni;* **Red valerian** = *Centranthus ruber;* **Redwood** = *Sequoia sempervirens;* **Red whortleberry** = *Vaccinium vitis-idaea;* **Red wine grapes** (see *vinifera* varieties at GRAPE).

**RED A.** A trademarked soap, specially prepared for contact spraying and sold with directions for use.

**RED ARROW.** A trademarked insecticide, containing pyrethrum, derris, and soap, and sold with directions for use as a contact spray.

**REDBUD.** Very attractive shrubs or small trees constituting the genus **Cercis** (sir′sis) of the pea family, three of the 7 known species often grown for their showy flowers, which bloom in early spring, mostly before the leaves expand. Unlike most plants of the pea family, the leaves are not compound,* but simple and usually roundish or heart-shaped, stalked, and with the veins arranged finger-fashion. Flowers small, but usually numerous, pea-like or nearly so, rose-pink or rose-purple in the cult. sorts. Stamens* 10, not united. Fruit (a legume*) flat, thin, and narrowly winged, its seeds flattened. (*Cercis* is the ancient Greek name for the European species.) The redbud is often known as Judas-tree.

They are of easy cult. in open, rather sandy loams, but do not like heavy, moist sites, and are hard to move when mature. They may be propagated by seeds, by layers, or by greenwood cuttings, preferably under glass, except for the layers. Their very early bloom, usually about peach-blossom time, makes them useful for color in the shrubbery while most plants are still dormant.

**C. canadensis.** American redbud. A small, round-headed tree, not usually over 30 ft. high, mostly half this. Leaves broadly oval or nearly round, heart-shaped at the base, 3–5½ in. long, pointed at the tip. Flowers about ½ in. long, rosy-pink, in clusters of 4–8, but the clusters very numerous. Pod about 3 in. long. N.Y. and Ontario to Fla. and Tex. Hardy from zone* 3 southward. There is also a white, and a double-flowered form.

**C. chinensis.** Asiatic redbud. Much resembling the last, but with leaves more deeply heart-shaped at the base, larger and more numerous, rosy-purple flowers, and slightly longer pods. Central China. A finer cult. shrub or small tree than the American redbud, but not quite so hardy, and doubtfully safe north of zone* 4. As cult. this is more apt to be shrubby than tree-like, and flowers when younger than does *C. canadensis*. It is sometimes offered as *C. japonica*.

**C. japonica** = *Cercis chinensis*.

**C. siliquastrum.** A tree up to 30 ft. high, usually less as cult. Leaves rounded or notched at the tip, generally roundish, 3½–5½ in. long. Flowers rose-purple, nearly ¾ in. long, in clusters of 3–6. Pods nearly 4 in. long. Eurasia. Not certainly hardy much above zone* 5 or the most protected parts of zone* 4. There is also a white-flowered form.

**RED GARDEN.** Pure red or scarlet flowers are not uncommon, but a garden or border planted solely with them would be crude and garish, unless relieved by the use of many white flowers and white accessories. A softening influence is furnished by the introduction of flowers of blue-gray coloring. Dark red and maroon are admirable in toning down the sharp scarlets. Example: Maroon Sweet William used with *Lychnis chalcedonica*. In a red garden the brilliant autumn coloration of certain shrubs and trees may be made use of if desired as well as such as have conspicuous red berries. See AUTUMN FOLIAGE.

### SHRUBS AND SMALL TREES

*Chaenomeles japonica* (Japanese flowering quince), 6 ft., spring; *Ribes sanguineum*, 8 ft., spring; *Weigela hybrida* Eva Rathke, 8 ft., June; *Rhododendron* vars.; Rose vars. June.

### TALL PLANTS FOR USE IN BACKGROUND

SUMMER AND AUTUMN FLOWERING: *Althaea rosea* (Hollyhock), red and maroon; *Dahlia* vars.; *Gladiolus*, Dr. F. E. Bennett, Pfitzer's Triumph, Aflame, etc.; *Helenium autumnale rubrum;* *Lilium bulbiferum, L. chalcedonicum, L. super-* *bum, L. tigrinum; Lychnis chalcedonica; Pentstemon torreyi; Phlox* Africa, Goliath, Firebrand, Debs, Coquelicot, etc.; *Salvia splendens* vars. (annual); *Kniphofia uvaria grandiflora; Zinnia* vars. (annual).

### PLANTS OF MEDIUM HEIGHT

SPRING FLOWERING: *Aquilegia canadensis, A. skinneri; Brevoortia ida-maia* (bulb); *Fritillaria imperialis* vars., *F. recurva* (bulbs); *Tulipa eichleri, T. fosteriana, T. gesneriana, T. greigi, T. ingens, T. praestans, T. sprengeri;* also Darwin, Cottage, and Breeder tulips in red varieties (bulbs). See TULIPA.

SUMMER AND AUTUMN FLOWERING: *Alonsoa warscewiczi* (annual); *Antirrhinum* vars.; Balsam (annual); Carnation, hardy border strains; *Centranthus ruber; Clarkia* Vesuvius; *Delphinium nudicaule; Gaillardia* Burgundy; *Geum chiloense* Mrs. Bradshaw; *Heuchera; Lilium canadense, L. elegans* vars., *L. philadelphicum; Linum grandiflorum; Lobelia cardinalis, L. fulgens; Lychnis haageana; Monarda didyma; Tritonia* James Coey, Lord Nelson, Princess, etc.; *Papaver* annual vars., *P. orientale* Beauty of Livermore, Goliath, Olympia, Taplow Scarlet; *Paeonia officinalis rubra, P. tenuifolia*, and red-flowered hort. forms. See PEONY; *Physalis alkekengi; Potentilla* Gibson's Scarlet.

### LOW-GROWING PLANTS

SPRING, SUMMER AND AUTUMN FLOWERING: *Antirrhinum*, dwarf (annual); *Dianthus cruentus; Dianthus* annual vars.; *Eschscholtzia* Geisha (annual); *Helianthemum* red vars.; *Primula* red vars.; *Silene virginica; Tulipa linifolia, T. montana; Verbena* Etna, Spectrum Red (annual); *Zinnia* dwarf vars.

### CLIMBERS

*Clematis texensis; Lonicera sempervirens;* Nasturtiums (annual); Rose, climbing, red-flowering vars. See ROSE; Scarlet Runner Beans (annual); Sweet Peas (annual); *Campsis chinensis* (30 ft. tender north of zone* 5); *C. radicans*, 20 ft., see TRUMPET-CREEPER.

### TENDER BEDDING PLANTS

Begonias (tuberous-rooted); Geraniums; Cannas, Fuchsias. — L. B. W.

**REDIVIVA, -us, -um** (re-di-vi′va). Restored to life; freshened.

**REDWOOD** = *Sequoia sempervirens*.

**REED CANARY GRASS** = *Phalaris arundinacea*.

**REED GRASS** = *Phragmites communis*.

**REED MACE** = *Typha latifolia*. See CAT-TAIL.

**REFLEXA, -us, -um** (ree-fleck′sa). Reflexed; i.e. bent backward.

**REFRACTA, -us, -um** (ree-frak′ta). Broken.

**REFRIGERATION.** See STORAGE.

A regular (i.e. symmetrical) flower

**REGALIS, -e** (ree-gay′lis). Royal.

**REGEL'S PRIVET** = *Ligustrum obtusifolium regelianum*. See PRIVET.

**REGIA, -us, -um** (ree′ji-a). Royal.

**REGINAE** (ree-jy′nee). Pertaining to a queen.

**REGULAR FLOWER.** One that is essentially symmetrical, because its petals or other organs are of uniform size, not twisted, and regularly arranged. Most flowers are regular, but many, as the

---

* Special articles on the subjects indicated by an asterisk (*) will be found at the words so marked.

snapdragon, salvia, azalea, and all the peas and orchids, are not. Instead they have irregular* (*i.e.* unsymmetrical) flowers, which are often 1-sided, 2-lipped,* twisted, or, in the orchids, of fantastic irregularity.

**REHMANNIA** (ray-man′i-a). Showy, Asiatic, somewhat sticky, perennial herbs of the family Scrophulariaceae, two of the half-dozen known species grown for ornament, outdoors from zone* 7 southward, elsewhere in the cool greenhouse. They have tall, sparsely leaved stems, which usually branch from the base, and alternate,* oblongish, coarsely toothed or lobed leaves. Flowers irregular,* 2 in. or more long, 2-lipped,* the front lobe 3-cleft, the other lobe 2-cleft. Stamens* 4, not protruding. Fruit a broad, many-seeded capsule,* surrounded and half-hidden by the bell-shaped calyx.* (Named for Joseph Rehmann, Russian physician.)

These very showy herbs may be grown in most garden soils or in potting mixture* 3 in the cool greenhouse. If raised from seed they will bloom the second year and may then be propagated by cuttings.

**angulata.** Not over 3 ft. high. Leaves with numerous sharp teeth, or with a few toothed lobes. Flowers red, the upper lip* scarlet-margined, the lower lip orange-dotted. Corolla about 2 in. long. China. The *var.* **tigrina** has spotted flowers; *var.* **tricolor** has purple flowers which later become violet-rose, the whitish throat purple-spotted.

**elata.** Nearly 6 ft. high, the leaves few-lobed, the lobes not toothed. Flowers 2–3 in. long, generally rosy-purple, but the yellow throat red-dotted. China.

**REINECKIA** (ry-neck′i-a). A single species of Asiatic herbs of the lily family, **R. carnea** of China and Japan, with creeping underground stems and somewhat grass-like, but fleshy, basal leaves, 12–18 in. long and less than ½ in. wide. Flowers small, almost stalkless, flesh-colored, borne in small, short clusters (racemes*) which are much exceeded by the leaves. Corolla bell-shaped, its lobes recurved. Fruit a small, nearly globe-shaped berry. The foliage closely resembles *Ophiopogon* and *Liriope*, but these do not have the pink flowers of *Reineckia* and bear capsular fruits instead of a berry. (Named for J. Reinecke, a German gardener.)

**REINE HORTENSE.** A cherry variety. *See* CHERRY.

**REINWARDTIA** (rine-wardt′i-a). Two East Indian under-shrubs of the family Linaceae, one of them, **R. indica,** the yellow flax, grown in the warm-temperate greenhouse or outdoors in zones* 7, 8, and 9 for ornament. Not over 4 ft. high, and best kept compact by frequent pinching. Leaves alternate,* without marginal teeth, more or less elliptic, with a sharp tip. Flowers yellow, 1–2 in. wide, solitary or in few-flowered, close clusters, the 5 petals (somewhat united below) soon falling. Fruit a round, 6–8-valved capsule.* Use potting mixture* 3. Often grown under the name *R. trigyna* or *Linum flavum*. (Named for K. G. K. Reinwardt, Dutch scientist.)

**REJUVENATION.** The restoration of vigor to old or neglected orchard trees. For a discussion of its desirability and methods *see* NEGLECTED ORCHARDS.

*RELIGIOSA, -us, -um* (re-li-ji-ō′sa). Sacred or religious.

**REMBRANDT TULIPS.** Darwin tulips in which the color is broken, *i.e.* not all one color. *See* Garden Tulips at TULIPA.

**REMONTANT.** Having a second blooming season, as do many roses, some delphiniums, and various other plants. In some of them it is induced by cutting back, or by extra feeding, after the first crop of bloom.

**REMONTANT ROSES.** *See* ROSA BORBONIANA.

**RENAISSANCE GARDEN.** For the history of renaissance gardens *see* GARDEN HISTORY. *See also* ARCHITECTURAL STYLE.

**RENANTHERA** (re-nan′ther-ra). Indo-Malayan, tree-perching orchids, comprising over 20 species, but only **R. imschootiana** of much interest to most growers. It is a leafy-stemmed orchid, about 12 in. high, without pseudobulbs,* the oblongish leaves about 3 in. long and 1 in. wide. Flowers red and yellow, nearly 2 in. wide, borne in a drooping, branched, red-stalked cluster, 12–18 in. long, usually in Feb.–April in the greenhouse. Petals and sepals nearly similar, but the petals a little shorter than one of the sepals. Lip* small, scarlet, its crest yellow. For culture *see* the epiphytic Greenhouse Orchids at ORCHID. (*Renanthera* is from the Greek for kidney-shaped and anther,* in reference to a technical anther character of another species.)

**RENEALMIA NUTANS** = *Alpinia speciosa*.

*RENIFORMIS, -e* (re-ni-for′mis). Reniform; *i.e.* kidney-shaped.

**RENOVATE.** To prune, usually gradually, all the old wood from a shrub, thus inducing new, fresh growths. In this sense *see* PRUNING. Renovate is also used to describe the process of rejuvenating worn-out or neglected orchard trees. In this sense *see* NEGLECTED ORCHARDS. One can also renovate worn-out lawns or borders.

*REPANDENS* (ree-pan′denz). Wavy-margined.

*REPENS* (ree′penz). Creeping.

*REPTANS* (rep′tanz). Creeping.

**REPUBLICAN.** A cherry variety. *See* CHERRY.

**RESCUE GRASS** = *Bromus unioloides*.

**RESEDA.** *See* MIGNONETTE.

**RESEDACEAE** (res-e-day′see-ee). The mignonette family comprises 6 genera of herbs of the Mediterranean region, the only one of garden interest being the mignonette. The cult. plants are annual or biennial herbs with alternate leaves and very fragrant, irregular flowers. Fruit a capsule.* For culture and description of species *see* MIGNONETTE.

*RESINIFERA, -us, -um* (rez-i-niff′e-ra). Resin-bearing.

*RESINOSA, -us, -um* (rez-i-nō′sa). Resinous.

**RESTHARROW.** *See* ONONIS.

**RESTING LAND.** *See* FALLOW LAND.

**RESTING PLANTS.** Plants are said to be resting when they are in a quiescent period, and fail to develop growth, even though provided with heat and moisture and subjected to good cultural treatment. We speak of the resting period of plants, in the fall of the year, when the trees and shrubs complete their annual growth and, in the case of the deciduous ones, lose their leaves after bud development has taken place. They become inactive so far as is revealed by their exterior conditions. Such plants then go into their rest period, and under natural conditions remain at rest for periods of weeks or months.

In temperate climates these periods of quiescence, to a marked degree, coincide with the winter cycle. From this it is easy to assume that the rest period has been brought about in response to temperature conditions. But in plant material growing in the tropics we find a similar condition, and the various trees and plants go through a period of growth and quiescence.

When woody plants such as roses, lilac, *Prunus*, etc., are brought into the forcing house, they show little activity for a time, a longer or shorter period elapsing before growth is noticeable. This varies to a large extent with the species of plant and its treatment before being transferred to the forcing house. Many species, after having been subjected to frost, respond to forcing treatment quite readily. As an example take lily-of-the-valley; the new crop pips are worthless to the forcer unless they have been subjected to chilling by frost or to cold-storage treatment. This treatment also is favorable to the forcing of lilacs, roses, etc. As is indicated this quiescence is an internal factor and not a factor related to temperature and other external conditions.

It has been shown that treatment with chemical vapors such as ether or chloroform would break this dormant period and permit the buds to develop normally. Not only ether and chloroform but a number of other chemicals, including ethyl bromia, ethyl iodid, carbon tetrachlorid, etc., could be successfully used in breaking the rest period of plants.

---

* Special articles on the subjects indicated by an asterisk (*) will be found at the words so marked.

As an example of resting, let us take the grapevine *Vitis vinifera* as grown under glass, after the crop has ripened and the bunches of fruit have been cut. The ventilators of the house are kept open, night and day, allowing an abundance of air to circulate among the vines. Waterings are gradually reduced and full sun is allowed to reach the plants. In the course of very few weeks the vines will enter the quiescent stage. This period is known to the horticulturist as the resting period, preceding as it does the period of activity or growth. While many experiments have been conducted to influence the continuity of growth in plants, these have not been successful.

Take again plants growing in the tropics. The orchid *Cattleya trianae*, for example, in order to produce flowers, is required to pass through a quiescent period. Nearly all epiphytic* orchids are subject to a period of rest, growth taking place during the rainy season, while their resting period occurs during the dry season. This prepares the plants for the blossoming period and at the same time prevents them from making weak and puny growths which would take place if nature attempted to keep them in a period of activity throughout the year.

Success with forcing the various bulbous plants such as hyacinths, tulips, narcissus, amaryllis, gloxinias, nerines, and the like, is more dependent on the resting period, which is the ripening period of the bulbs, than for the good cultural treatment the bulbs are subject to when being forced.

It seems apparent then that this law of nature is exacting. It requires that a plant go through a period of rest and dormancy in order to prepare it for the mission it has to fulfill; namely, to grow, flower, and fruit. — D. L. *See also* DORMANCY.

**RESURRECTION FERN; RESURRECTION PLANTS.** At least three different plants in general cult. have the ability to assume, during a dry period, the appearance of death, mostly by coiling up their foliage into a dense, brownish mass. But they retain the ability to renew growth when water is available, and may repeat this alternate dormancy and growth many times. By far the most famous resurrection plant is *Anastatica hierochuntica* (which see). For the resurrection fern *see* POLYPODIUM POLYPODIOIDES. For the third resurrection plant *see* SELAGINELLA LEPIDOPHYLLA.

**RETAMA** = *Parkinsonia aculeata*.

**RETARDING.** Retarding the growth in plants has been practiced by growers for many years. We may speak of it as the direct antithesis of forcing (which see), and it should in no way be confused with resting. The functions of resting and retarding being quite distinct operations.

Growers of azaleas and Easter lilies well know the value of retarding. In fact, it would not be possible to time and bring into flower large houses of Easter lilies for Easter Day were it not for the fact that the plants can be forced and retarded at the will of the grower. Sunny or sunless days as well as the earliness or lateness of Easter Day are important factors to consider in lily forcing. The bulbs of lilies do not develop growth simultaneously; therefore, the ones making more rapid growth would have to be retarded in some manner while those slow to start would need encouragement by being forced at a higher temperature. With azaleas, as the natural period of flowering arrives, the buds begin to swell and soon burst into flower unless in some way or other their growth is retarded. If the Easter festival is late many of the early and free-flowering varieties are apt to be at their best several days or weeks in advance of the festival.

On many private estates and commercial establishments, sheds, houses, and deep pits are to be seen. These structures are largely used for retarding purposes.

RETARDING HOUSE

A particularly useful structure from a practical standpoint for retarding plants is one built in the manner of an even-span greenhouse with a rather low roof running east and west. The roof is shingled, save for ventilators (sash 3 × 4 feet) placed at intervals on the north side of the house. No other light is available. The house is benched* in similar manner to a greenhouse. This structure proves an ideal house in which to retard the flowering period of plants or to hold them when in flower for several days before being marketed. Azaleas, hydrangeas, cherries, lilacs, astilbe, lilies, bulbs, and various other plant material are kept in an inactive condition. The plants are watered as occasion requires, and the house is held at a temperature of 40° to 42° F. at night, an abundant amount of air being administered throughout the day. Humidity is controlled by moistening the sand under the benches with water. In the case of some species of plants the dormancy is extended for several weeks.

COLD STORAGE. In the case of *Lilium longiflorum* and its varieties, used so much for cut-flower work by the florist, the bulbs on their receipt from Japan or other countries are placed in cold storage to retard growth. They are taken out in numbers as required and forced. Lilies may be had the full cycle of the year by this method of retarding growth.

PITS. The cold pit is much used for the purpose of retarding plant growth. It is virtually a deep hotbed frame with or without sash but without any heat. It can also be used to carry bedding plants through the winter and shrubs and bulbs for forcing. When used as a retarding medium the glass is shaded with whiting and gasoline, or lath screens are placed over the glass, sometimes cheesecloth is all that is needed to give the necessary shade in mild regions. *See* PIT.

COOL GREENHOUSE. Half-span greenhouses having a northern aspect may function as retarding houses for many native or exotic flowering plants. By vigilant attention regarding air, shading, and watering this structure is capable of retarding plant material for a great length of time.

An example of nature's retardation is best exemplified in what is known as a late spring. The cold weather and low temperatures are the factors involved. The principles governing the holding of plant material in a state of retardation beyond their natural period of lethargy are largely those of temperature, shade, and moisture. — D. L.

*RETICULATA, -us, -um* (re-tick-you-lay′ta). Reticulated; *i.e.* netted, especially netted-veined.

**RETINISPORA.** *See* CHAMAECYPARIS. It is sometimes spelled *Retinospora*.

*RETORTA, -us, -um* (ree-tor′ta). Twisted backwards.

**RETROFLEXA TULIPS.** Lily-flowered or cottage tulips with recurved outer petals. *See* Garden Tulips at TULIPA.

*RETUSA, -us, -um* (ree-too′sa). Notched.

**REVERSE T-BUDDING.** *See* Shield Budding at BUDDING.

**REVIVING WILTED FLOWERS.** *See* WILTING.

*REVOLUTA, -us, -um* (rev-o-lew′ta). Revolute; *i.e.* rolled backwards or downwards; applied especially to leaf margins so rolled.

**REX BEGONIA.** *See* BEGONIA REX.

**RHAGODIA** (ra-gō′di-a). A comparatively unimportant genus of Australian shrubs or herbs of the family Chenopodiaceae, the only cult. species being **R. nutans,** one of the plants called saltbush (for others *see* ATRIPLEX). It is a perennial herb, 1–2 ft. high or more or less prostrate, with mostly alternate,* arrowhead-shaped or lance-shaped leaves, ¾–1 in. long. Flowers small, inconspicuous, greenish-white, without petals, mostly polygamous,* and in a nodding terminal cluster. Fruit a small berry. The plant is occasionally cult. in Calif. and similar climates, but is little known otherwise. (*Rhagodia* is from the Greek for berry-like, in allusion to the fruit.)

**RHAMNACEAE** (ram-nay′see-ee). The buckthorn family is of secondary garden importance in spite of its 45 genera and over 550 species. All are trees, shrubs or woody vines, rather spiny in *Paliurus, Colletia* and *Zizyphus* (which yields the jujube), and more showy in *Ceanothus* than in the few

---

* Special articles on the subjects indicated by an asterisk (*) will be found at the words so marked.

other cult. genera. *Rhamnus*, of little or no decorative value, is chiefly grown for its medicinal qualities (cascara sagrada, etc.). *Berchemia* is a woody vine. *Hovenia* is Asiatic and hardy from zone* 4 southward, while *Pomaderris* is Australasian and more tender.

Leaves mostly alternate,* and simple. Flowers regular,* usually small, whitish or greenish, of little decorative value except in some species of *Ceanothus*, and mostly in clusters. Fruit dry and winged in some genera, in others fleshy.

Technical flower characters: Sepals 5, the margins touching, rarely 4. Petals 4 or 5 (wanting in some species of *Rhamnus*). Stamens* 4 or 5, opposite the petals. Ovary inferior* or superior,* mostly 2-3-celled. Styles* 2-4.

**RHAMNOIDES** (ram-noy'deez, but see OÏDES). Like a buckthorn (*Rhamnus*).

**RHAMNUS** (ram'nus). Buckthorn. A large group of horticulturally unimportant, but medicinally significant, shrubs or trees of the family Rhamnaceae, most of the 100 known species from the north temperate zone, a few from Brazil and South Africa. The cult. species are chiefly shrubs, often somewhat thorny, with alternate* or opposite* leaves. Flowers small, greenish, unisexual* or polygamous, often without petals and never showy. Fruit a nearly round drupe.* (*Rhamnus* is the old Greek name for the buckthorn.)

The buckthorns have no decorative value as flowering shrubs or trees. *Rhamnus purshiana* is the only source of cascara sagrada and is cult. for that purpose on the Pacific Coast (see MEDICINAL PLANTS). Also in Calif. *R. californica*, an evergreen, is a relatively important bee plant. The others, sometimes cult. for ornament, are indifferent hort. subjects, with no very special soil requirements, except that most of them prefer moist to dry sites. Some, like *R. caroliniana*, have red fruits for a time, but most of them ultimately are black-fruited.

**californica.** Coffeeberry. An evergreen shrub, 4-6 ft. high. Leaves oblongish, 1½-2½ in. long, finely toothed. Flowers small, greenish, in umbels.* Fruit red, ultimately black. Calif. May-July. Ore. to Calif. Not hardy north of zone* 5; planted as a bee plant in Calif.

**caroliniana.** Yellow bush. Indian cherry. A shrub, or even a small tree up to 25 ft. high. Leaves elliptic or oblongish, 4-6 in. long, without marginal teeth or very finely toothed. Flowers in small umbels,* not showy. Fruit red at first, ultimately black, about ⅜ in. in diameter. Southeastern U.S., west to Tex. and Neb. May-June. Hardy from zone* 4 southward.

**cathartica.** Common buckthorn. A shrub, 10-25 ft. high, the twigs often thorny. Leaves ovalish, 2-3 in. long. Male and female flowers on different plants. Fruit black. Eurasia, but often escaped* in the eastern U.S. May-June. Long cult., sometimes under the names of Hart's thorn, Waythorn or Rhineberry, and useful in the informal shrubbery or as an informal hedge plant. Hardy everywhere.

**frangula.** Alder buckthorn. A shrub or small tree, not over 18 ft. high. Leaves ovalish, or broadest toward the tip, 1½-2½ in. long. Flowers in clusters (umbels*) of 2-10. Fruit red at first, ultimately black. Eurasia and northern Af., naturalized sporadically in the U.S. May-July. Hardy everywhere. One of the best from the hort. standpoint because of its lustrous leaves that turn bright yellow in autumn.

**purshiana.** Cascara sagrada; also called bearberry and shittimwood. A tall shrub, or occasionally a tree to 40 ft. high. Leaves elliptic to oblongish, 6-8 in. long, finely toothed. Flowers in small, hairy clusters (umbels*). Fruit purplish-black. British Columbia to northern Calif. and Mont. May-June. Hardy from zone* 5 southward. See MEDICINAL PLANTS.

**RHAPIDOPHYLLUM** (ra-pid-do-fill'um). A single species of low, spiny fan palms, **R. hystrix**, the needle or porcupine palm, found in low, moist places from the coastal plain of S. Car. to Fla. and Miss. It is a nearly stemless palm, the base horribly armed with the needles of the leaf-sheaths, the needles 7-15 in. long. Leaves 2½-3½ ft. wide, cut into many stiff, narrow, prominently ribbed segments, which are 2-toothed or cut at the tip, and about 1½ in. wide. Flowering and fruiting cluster smothered in the leaf-sheaths and needles near the base of the plant. Fruit somewhat fleshy, egg-shaped, about 1 in. long. In Fla. it grows in dense, low masses. (*Rhapidophyllum* is from the Greek for leaf and *Rhapis*, in allusion to the leaves being like those of *Rhapis*.)

**RHAPIS** (ray'pis). A small genus of Asiatic, somewhat reed-like, low, mostly tufted fan palms, two of the 5 known species very widely grown as tub palms for indoor decoration and for patios, also outdoors in zones* 8 and 9. They are usually several-stemmed and fibrous, and have fan-like, much-parted leaves on slender, unarmed stalks. Male and female flowers on different plants, the calyx and corolla 3-toothed. Stamens* 6, in the male flowers, replaced by 6 infertile stamens* in the female ones. Fruit 1-seeded and berry-like. (*Rhapis* is from the Greek for needle and of unknown application here.)

For culture and uses see PALM.

**excelsa.** Ground rattan. Stems thin, several or numerous, conspicuously fibrous, 5-6 ft. high. Leaves fan-shaped, sometimes with 3-7 segments, usually with 10, green both sides, notched at the tip, the stalks flattened and somewhat fibrous at the base. China (?). Long grown as *R. flabelliformis*, and widely cult. for ornament by florists.

**humilis.** A lower palm than *R. excelsa*, and practically stemless. Leaves fan-like, the segments mostly 9 or more, some of them spreading or pointing backwards. China.

**RHAPONTICUM** (ray-pon'ti-kum). Literally, the sour rhubarb; the name *rhaponticum* derived from the Pontic rha or rhubarb.

**RHEA** = *Boehmeria nivea*.

**RHEUM.** See RHUBARB.

**RHEUMATISM-ROOT** = *Jeffersonia diphylla* and *Chimaphila maculata*.

**RHEXIA** (rex'i-a). Meadow-beauty. Pretty little North American perennial herbs, of the family Melastomaceae, which is otherwise largely tropical and woody. Of the dozen or so known species only the two below are of any hort. interest. They are attractive little wild flowers, suited only to the bog garden, and needing acid (see ACID AND ALKALI SOILS), preferably moist, sand. Leaves essentially stalkless, opposite,* rather prominently 3-5-veined. Calyx* 4-lobed, bell-shaped at the base. Petals 4, oblique, rather showy, purplish in those below. Stamens* 8. Fruit a 4-valved capsule.* (*Rhexia* is from the Greek for breaking and of no known application here.)

Suited only to the bog garden (which see).

**mariana.** A slender, hairy-stemmed plant, 1-2 ft. high. Leaves narrowly oblong, 1-1½ in. long. Flowers about 1 in. wide, pale purple, the clusters (cymes*) few-flowered. In pine-barren bogs, southeastern U.S., west to Tex. June-Sept.

**virginica.** Deer grass; also called handsome Harry. A nearly smooth-stemmed herb, 9-15 in. high, the stem angled. Leaves ovalish, 1½-2 in. long, the margins hairy-fringed. Flowers nearly 1½ in. wide, purple, in few-flowered clusters (cymes*). In sandy bogs along the coast, Me. to Fla. and La. July-Sept.

**RHINEBERRY** = *Rhamnus cathartica*.

**RHIPSALIS** (rip'sa-lis). Willow cactus; also called mistletoe cactus (they strongly resemble mistletoe). A curious genus of mostly tree-perching (epiphytic*) cacti, comprising over 60 species scattered from Fla. to the Argentine, a few supposed to be native in Madagascar, but doubtfully so. They are leafless cacti, the slender, usually rope-like stems provided with hairs, bristles or wool, but no spines. Branches cylindric or slightly flattened. Flowers small, not showy, stalkless on the edges of the branches. Fruit mistletoe-like. (*Rhipsalis* is from the Greek for wicker-work, in allusion to the mass of branches which usually grow much mixed up together.)

*Rhipsalis* and the closely related *Hatiora*, while true cacti, do not inhabit deserts. They grow mostly on trees in tropical forests and should be grown in orchid baskets in the warm-temperate greenhouse, preferably suspended from the roof. Use ½ potting mixture* 6 and ½ orchid peat. They are chiefly grown for their interesting mistletoe-like aspect, and have otherwise little or no decorative value.

**cassytha** (sometimes spelled *cassutha*). The common mistletoe cactus. A much-branched plant, the stems cylindric, pencil-thick, usually 3-4 ft. long (sometimes 10 ft. in Brazil), the branchlets about 1 ft. long. Flowers scarcely ¼ in. wide. Fruit very like that of the mistletoe. Common throughout tropical America, and naturalized in the Old World tropics.

**salicornioides** = *Hatiora salicornioides*.

**RHIZOCTONIA.** See Diseases at POTATO.

**RHIZOME.** A rootstock.*

**RHIZOPHYLLA, -us, -um** (ry-zo-fill'a). A specific name meaning, literally, root-leaved; usually applied to plants in which the leaves are all basal.

---

* Special articles on the subjects indicated by an asterisk (*) will be found at the words so marked.

**RHODANTHA**, *-us, -um* (ro-dan'tha). With flowers like a rose.

**RHODANTHE.** See HELIPTERUM MANGLESI.

**RHODE ISLAND.** The state lies wholly in zone* 4.

SOILS. The soils of Rhode Island have been submitted to such extreme glaciation that few large areas of any one soil type are to be found. The predominating soil types are Gloucester stony loam, Merrimac stony loam, and Warwick sandy loam. The larger areas of Gloucester stony loam are quite heavily wooded and do not easily support agriculture. The Merrimac stony loam is well adapted to intensive truck farming. Smaller areas of Merrimac silt loam are found in Washington County. This soil type is well suited to intensive farming operations and sizable potato fields are located there. In common with the soils of New England, high fertilization is necessary, and due to the extreme acidity, caused by long ages of leaching, it is necessary for the Rhode Island farmer to use much lime on his fields.

VEGETABLE AREAS. The excellent markets which exist within very short distances have brought about the development of intensive market-gardening areas within the state. These are located chiefly in the towns of East Providence,

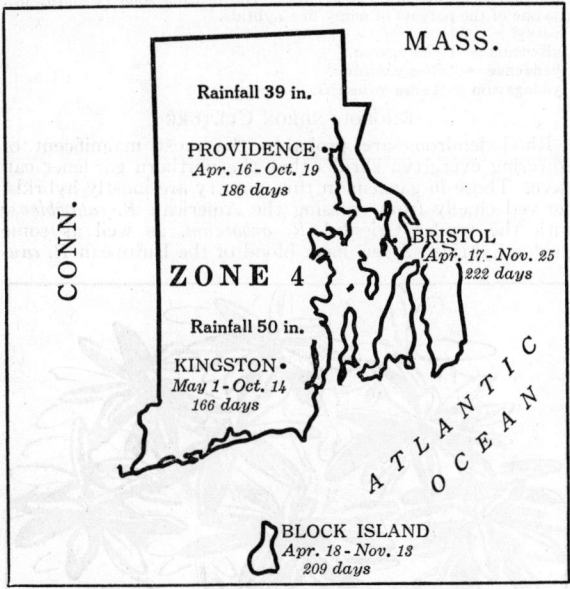

RHODE ISLAND

The zones of hardiness crossing Rhode Island are those shown on the colored map at ZONE, which should be consulted for details. The dates are the average latest killing frost in spring and the first one in the fall. The figures below the dates show the average length of the growing season. Rainfall figures (in inches) are for total annual rainfall in the regions so indicated.

Barrington, Cranston, and Warwick, all of which are within a few miles of the Providence market. Additional truck-growing areas are found in the town of Westerly, where the growers market their produce in Westerly and near-by shore resorts, and the town of Portsmouth, with the cities of Newport and Fall River as market centers. In all these towns, a general selection of vegetables is grown. In particular, due to climatic and soil conditions, East Providence produces tomatoes, cabbage, celery and lettuce; Cranston and Warwick, sweet corn and melons; and Barrington, asparagus, sweet corn, and melons. Considerable quantities of potatoes are grown in Middletown, Portsmouth, Cranston, and North Kingston.

FRUITS. The largest acreages of fruit production are found in the northwestern part of the state and consist in the main of apple orchards. The towns of Smithfield, Gloucester and Burrillville produce the largest quantities of apples. These towns are well suited, by reason of soil and climate, for apple growing, since they lie at higher altitudes than some other parts of the state, and at the same time are hilly in nature, giving good air drainage and, on the average, freedom from early spring frosts. In some localities, pears are also grown. Among the small fruits considerable acreages of grapes are found south of Providence, and due again to the excellent market, raspberries and strawberries are produced in quantity near the cities of the state.

FLOWERS, ORNAMENTAL TREES AND SHRUBS. Due to the proximity of the Atlantic Ocean and Narragansett Bay, the climate of certain portions of Rhode Island is such that flowers, trees, and shrubs not ordinarily found in northern latitudes may be grown with ease. Among the flowers, roses, lilies, and bulbous plants, in particular daffodils, grow readily in areas close to Narragansett Bay and along the coast in Washington County. The ocean fogs help to provide the conditions suitable for ornamental trees and shrubs, rhododendrons, azaleas, laurels, and dogwoods are found in the swamps and uplands as a part of the native flora. Many less hardy, flowering, deciduous shrubs and members of the rose family, such as flowering quince, almond, crabapple, and others, are easily cultivated. Ornamental evergreens are readily grown.

CLIMATE. While the state of Rhode Island covers a relatively small area, there are marked variations in climatic conditions, due to the many miles of ocean and bay shoreline. Thus, considerable differences as to the growth of horticultural plants are found. Frost data showing significant differences are given.

| Town | Average date of last killing frost in spring | Latest known killing frost | Average date of earliest killing frost in fall | Earliest known killing frost |
|---|---|---|---|---|
| Block Island | April 18 | April 26 | Nov. 13 | Oct. 11 |
| Bristol | April 17 | April 29 | Nov. 25 | Oct. 14 |
| Kingston | May 1 | May 16 | Oct. 14 | Sept. 11 |
| Providence | April 16 | April 24 | Oct. 19 | Oct. 9 |

There is considerable variation in rainfall between various localities within the state. This is observed particularly between the northern and southern counties and is shown by the total average annual rainfall in three locations:

Block Island — 41.3 inches
Kingston — 50.8 inches
Providence — 39.2 inches

The Rhode Island climate allows a growing period of approximately seven months and extends from April to October inclusive. The average precipitation for this seven-month period varies as follows:

Block Island — 22.6 inches
Kingston — 27.6 inches
Providence — 21.9 inches

In addition to temperature and precipitation differences, as one goes inland from the ocean, quite marked differences are found in snowfall and fog. More snow is to be expected in the northwest portion of the state than in the easterly areas. Ocean fogs are also very common in the areas adjacent to the coastline. Both of these climatic factors play roles of considerable importance in determining the types and density of natural flora and cultivated crops.

In the region around Newport there is one of the finest developments of ornamental horticulture to be found in the country. This, in spite of the fact that much of the land upon which these estates were developed was originally thin and poor. Time, money and taste have made some of these gardens almost world-famous. Also, at Peacedale, is a famous old garden with one of the finest collections of rhododendrons in the country.

Garden Club activities are, for such a small state, very extensive. They include several clubs of the Garden Club of America, the home office of which is 598 Madison Avenue, New York, N.Y. There are also nearly 20 clubs affiliated

---

* Special articles on the subjects indicated by an asterisk (*) will be found at the words so marked.

with the Rhode Island Federation of Garden Clubs. For the one nearest your locality write the Garden Editor, Houghton Mifflin Company, Boston, Mass.

**RHODE ISLAND BENT** = *Agrostis capillaris*.

**RHODE ISLAND GREENING.** An apple variety. See APPLE.

**RHODE'S-GRASS** = *Chloris gayana*.

**RHODODENDRON** (ro-do-den'dron). A very large genus of evergreen or deciduous shrubs, rarely trees, of the family Ericaceae, chiefly from the north temperate zone, a few on the high mountains of the Old World tropics, but none in Mex. Considered by some authorities as including *Rhododendron* proper, *Azalea*, and *Rhodora*; the two latter are here kept separate because of the long tendency of gardeners to separate them from *Rhododendron*. See AZALEA and RHODORA.

The rhododendrons, as here limited, are chiefly evergreens (many azaleas and rhodora are deciduous), with alternate* leaves, which are mostly stalked, always without marginal teeth. Flowers very showy, mostly tubular or funnel-shaped, the 5-lobed limb slightly irregular.* Stamens* 5-10. Fruit a capsule.* (*Rhododendron* is from the Greek for rose and tree, and is the old Greek name for the oleander, but applied by Linnaeus to these plants.)

For Culture see below.

While gardening practice keeps *Azalea*, *Rhodora*, and *Rhododendron* separate, there are no technical characters that warrant such separation. Because of this all the names of *Rhododendron* species (taken in its broad sense), admitted to this book, are listed below. Those belonging to *Azalea* or *Rhodora* are cross-referenced to those genera and descriptions and culture of them should be sought there. All those described here are considered true rhododendrons in the garden sense.

**amoenum** = *Azalea obtusa amoena*.
**arborescens** = *Azalea arborescens*.
**arboreum**. A tall evergreen shrub, 18-30 ft. high. Leaves nearly 7 in. long, white-felty or rusty beneath. Flowers about 1¼ in. wide, red, pink, or white, bell-shaped, sometimes spotted. Himalayas. March-May. Hardy from zone* 6 southward.
**calendulaceum** = *Azalea calendulacea*.
**californicum**. An evergreen shrub, 6-10 ft. high. Leaves 4-6 in. long. Flowers nearly 2½ in. wide, rose-purple but brown-spotted. British Columbia to Calif. May-June. Hardy from zone* 5 southward. Another plant sometimes known as *R. californicum* should be sought at *Azalea occidentalis*.
**canadense** = *Rhodora canadensis*.
**canescens** = *Azalea canescens*.
**carolinianum**. An evergreen shrub, 4-6 ft. high. Leaves 2-3 in. long, rusty and scaly beneath. Flowers bell-shaped, nearly 1½ in. wide, pale rose-purple to whitish. Mountains of N. Car. May-June. Hardy from zone* 3 southward. Used as a tubbed or potted plant for penthouse gardens, as well as for the border. An extremely handsome plant.
**catawbiense**. Mountain rose bay. A magnificent evergreen shrub 12-18 ft. high. Leaves 3-5 in. long, shining green above, paler beneath. Flowers bell-shaped, nearly 2½ in. wide, lilac-purple. Mountains from Va. to Ga. May-June. Hardy from zone* 3 southward. The parent of many of the finest hort. forms of rhododendron. See below.
**caucasicum**. A dwarf evergreen shrub, never over 2 ft. high. Leaves 2-4 in. long, brownish beneath. Flowers narrowly bell-shaped, nearly 2 in. wide. Caucasus. May. Hardy from zone* 4 southward, but rare in cult. Of chief interest as one of the parents of many hybrid rhododendrons. See below.
**ferrugineum**. A low evergreen shrub, not over 3 ft. high. Leaves 1-2 in. long, shining green above, rusty and scaly beneath. Flowers funnel-shaped, about ½ in. wide, pink or carmine. Central European mountains. July-Aug. Hardy from zone* 4 southward. For cult. see ROCK GARDEN.
**gandavense** = *Azalea gandavensis*.
**griffithianum**. An evergreen shrub, 6-8 ft. high. Leaves 8-12 in. long. Flowers fragrant, bell-shaped, nearly 3 in. wide, pure white. Himalayas. Little known in cult. but one of the parents of many fine, hardy, hybrid forms.
**hinodegiri** = *Azalea obtusa hinodegiri*.
**indicum**. See AZALEA INDICA.
**japonicum** = *Azalea japonica*.
**kaempferi** = *Azalea obtusa kaempferi*.
**lapponicum**. A beautiful, little, alpine evergreen shrub, 6-12 in. high. Leaves scarcely ¾ in. long, rusty and scaly beneath. Flowers bell-shaped, about ¼ in. long, rose-purple. Arctic and alpine regions of the northern hemisphere. June-July. Hardy from zone* 4 far northward, but suited only to the rock garden (which see).
**ledifolium** = *Azalea mucronata*.
**macranthum** = *Azalea macrantha*.

**maximum**. Great laurel. Rose bay. A splendid evergreen shrub, rarely a tree, 10-25 ft. high, or even more. Leaves 7-10 in. long, densely hairy beneath. Flowers bell-shaped, about 1½ in. wide, rose-pink but green-spotted. Eastern N.A. June-July. Hardy from zone* 3 southward. A very handsome evergreen shrub, but its showy flowers much hidden by the foliage. See below.
**minus**. An evergreen, usually straggling shrub, 4-5 ft. high or sometimes more. Leaves 2-4 in. long, scaly on the under side. Flowers funnel-shaped, about 1¼ in. wide. S. Car. to Ga. and Ala. June-July. Hardy from zone* 4 southward.
**molle** = *Azalea mollis*.
**mucronatum** = *Azalea mucronata*.
**nudiflorum** = *Azalea nudiflora*.
**obtusum** = *Azalea obtusa*.
**occidentale** = *Azalea occidentalis*.
**ponticum**. An evergreen shrub, 6-10 ft. high. Leaves 4-6 in. long, pale on the under side. Flowers narrowly bell-shaped, nearly 2 in. wide, purple but brown-spotted. Spain, Portugal, and Asia Minor. May-June. Hardy from zone* 4 (with protection) southward. Little grown as a species, but one of the parents of many fine varieties.
**poukhanense** = *Azalea yedoensis poukhanensis*.
**roseum** = *Azalea rosea*.
**schlippenbachi** = *Azalea schlippenbachi*.
**smirnovi**. An evergreen shrub 12-18 ft. high. Leaves 4-6 in. long, densely brown-hairy beneath. Flowers narrowly bell-shaped, nearly 3 in. wide. Caucasus. May. Hardy from zone* 3 southward. An interesting, but somewhat straggling shrub, one of the parents in many hybrid forms.
**ungerni**. An evergreen shrub 15-20 ft. high. Leaves 4-6 in. long, densely brown-hairy beneath. Flowers broadly bell-shaped, nearly 2 in. wide, pinkish-white. Caucasus. May. Hardy from zone* 3 southward. It is one of the parents of many fine hybrids.
**vaseyi** = *Azalea vaseyi*.
**viscosum** = *Azalea viscosa*.
**yedoense** = *Azalea yedoensis*.
**yodogavum** = *Azalea yedoensis*.

### RHODODENDRON CULTURE

Rhododendrons are probably the most magnificent of flowering evergreen shrubs that the northern gardener can have. Those in gardens in this country are mostly hybrids, derived chiefly from crossing the American *R. catawbiense* with the tender Oriental *R. arboreum*, as well as some garden hybrids. A few have blood of the European *R. cau-*

A rhododendron with an oak leaf mulch*

*casicum* and some others are hybrids of *R. smirnovi* and of *R. griffithianum*. All are plants requiring acid soil, rich in humus and abundantly supplied with moisture, especially during the growing season which usually follows flowering. Although sunlight is essential to full flowering, the plants will grow in shade and, in all cases, some shade should be provided as protection from the early morning sunlight during winter. (General cultural notes as for *Azalea*, which see, remembering particularly the constant need of a deep, well-rotted, acid humus mulch.*)

---

* Special articles on the subjects indicated by an asterisk (*) will be found at the words so marked.

Native rhododendrons in this country are mountain plants, with the dwarf *R. carolinianum* and *R. minus* and the taller *R. catawbiense* and *R. maximum* as the conspicuous plants in many parts of the Alleghenies, and *R. californicum* from California to British Columbia on the Pacific Coast. Although the first two are commonly referred to as dwarf, in nature they may reach a height of five or six feet. In cultivation they are much more likely to make a more spreading plant with lesser stature. They have small leaves of fine dark green color that cover the rather twiggy growth of the bushes. The flowers come in crowded heads, usually white with greenish dots on the upper lobes in *R. minus*, and pale pink in *R. carolinianum*. Because of this more delicate growth and smaller foliage, these plants make excellent contrast with the more robust *R. catawbiense* and *R. maximum*.

In *R. catawbiense* the typical flower color is lilac-purple, but there is considerable variation toward rose-purples, and albinos are known and cultivated. Possibly this has been of more value as a parent than for itself, for from it have come the gorgeous hybrids such as Mrs. C. S. Sargent, Kettledrum, Gomer Waterer, Amphion, Parson's Gloriosum and the like. In *R. maximum* the chief value is in the growth and the foliage, for the flowers are often hidden by the young growths that surround them, as they do not open until all the other native species have finished their blooming. As they are essentially white, sometimes pink-tinted, the floral display is not comparable to that of some other sorts. The foliage, however, is superb enough to warrant use of the plant for foliage alone.

On the Pacific Coast the native species somewhat resembles *R. catawbiense* both in habit and in flower.

Europe contributes the rather tender lavender *R. ponticum*, once largely used for stocks in grafted rhododendrons, the pinkish or yellowish-white *caucasicum*, rose-colored *smirnovi*, and more rarely the pink and white *ungerni* to the large shrubbery. All of these save the first are hardy and tolerant of both summer heat and winter cold.

The real home of the rhododendron, however, is the Orient, with the greatest number of species and forms in China. Although many of these have been introduced into this country, they have not yet been grown under a sufficiently wide range of climatic conditions to justify any particular assurances as to their final usefulness. In these forms there is the greatest diversity of stature, habit and color, from the many low, thicket-forming species of the high mountain ranges in China to the tall, tree-like species of Burma. From such trials as have been made, cold does not seem to be the sole determining factor. Apparently light has much to do with success, for many species seem to suffer most if they do not have long periods of gray weather and abundant moisture in the air. These are conditions that are somewhat difficult to supply in cultivation and limit the general use to seacoast regions where fogs contribute to their happiness.

Like azaleas, rhododendrons are easily raised from seed, although the tall species come more slowly to flowering. Propagation is also possible by layers and piece-root grafts in winter, as well as the usual grafting methods. — B. Y. M.

The named forms of rhododendrons are legion, practically all of them of hybrid origin. Not all of them are worth the expense and time for long trials. In the list below are named forms, which, over a period of many years, have been a magnificent success. They were selected from over two hundred varieties, tested for two decades at the estate of the late Lowell M. Palmer, Esq., at Stamford, Conn., not far from L.I. Sound. All proved perfectly hardy there.

| | |
|---|---|
| Album elegans | Everestianum |
| Album grandiflorum | F. D. Godman |
| Atrosanguineum | Giganteum |
| Bacchus | Guido |
| Bluebell | Hamlet |
| Boule de Neige | Hannibal |
| Caractacus | Henrietta Sargent |
| Charles Dickens | H. H. Hunnewell |
| Delicatissimum | H. W. Sargent |
| Edward S. Rand | James Bateman |
| James Macintosh | Mrs. R. S. Holford |
| James Nasmyth | Mrs. Shuttleworth |
| Kettledrum | Mrs. S. Simpson |
| King of the Purples | Old Port |
| Lady Armstrong | Picturatum |
| Madame Carvalho | Purity |
| Maximum Wellsianum | Purpureum elegans |
| Maxwell T. Masters | Purpureum grandiflorum |
| Mirandum | Ralph Sanders |
| Mrs. Charles Sargent | Roseum elegans |
| Mrs. Harry Ingersoll | Scipio |
| Mrs. John Clutton | Sefton |
| Mrs. J. P. Lade | Sherwoodianum |
| Mrs. Milner | Silvio |
| Mrs. R. G. Shaw | Sir Thomas Seabright |

The list includes 50 varieties which may be considered among the most satisfactory of all rhododendrons. As to their culture at Stamford, Mr. Palmer left the following notes: "They do not like lime, nor do they like a heavy clay soil. Most important of all they do not want disturbance of their roots, so mulch them with leaves, and do not take the leaves off in the spring. Merely add to the mulch each autumn enough leaves to replace those lost through decay or by the wind. The leaf-mulch should be eight to ten inches thick."

As to shade: many rhododendrons grow naturally under complete or partial shade of a forest canopy. If that is not available, one may still plant rhododendrons, but shade should be provided for the first three years. A simple method is to make slat screens, the slats being one and a quarter inches apart. Put the screens on posts so that they are about three feet above the tops of the plants. These should be left out continually, but after the second summer remove alternate slats which will let through twice the amount of light. One more summer's protection, with this increased amount of sunshine, and the plants are ready to grow without protection, except for a winter covering of evergreen boughs, or if these are not available, dried cornstalks will do. If neither is to be had, the lath screen may be put back. Some protected places need no winter covering, but it is safer to put it on anywhere north and east of New York City.

INSECT PESTS. A lace bug, similar to the one on azalea, attacks rhododendron (see AZALEA). A caterpillar of a clear-wing moth bores in the stems. Another borer is a beetle larva. The infested parts of the plant should be removed and destroyed late in the summer.

DISEASES. Wilt is the most serious disease of *Rhododendron* nursery stock, especially *R. ponticum*. The causal fungus appears to be unable to survive the winter in fallow, unprotected soils as far north as New Jersey. It carries over, however, in infected seedlings in protected beds or in greenhouse plants. Symptoms are yellowing and wilting of foliage, accompanied by some dead roots and a streak of brown in the cambium (see BARK) region of the root or lower stem.

Early removal of infected plants with surrounding soil is the best method of control. Leaf spots are caused by various fungi. Control may be obtained by strict sanitation, which means removal of diseased parts as soon as they appear, spraying with bordeaux mixture 4-5-50, and pruning of infected twigs.

Twig blight or die-back of *Rhododendron* and lilac is discussed fully at LILAC. *Rhododendron* and *Kalmia* suffer from nutritional troubles, many of which may be attributed to improper acid conditions in the soil. These plants require a good, well-drained loam soil, free from lime or other materials which tend to make soil sweet. Mulching with well-rotted oak leaf mold maintains acidity and also protects plants from excessive drying.

**RHODOMYRTUS** (ro-do-mir'tus). Tropical Australian, Asiatic or East Indian shrubs and trees of the family Myrtaceae, **R. tomentosa**, the Hill gooseberry or downy myrtle, occasionally grown in nearly frost-free regions for its berry, used for jam. It is a shrub 3-5 ft. high, with opposite,* short-stalked, blunt, more or less elliptic leaves 1-2½ in. long. Flowers 1-3 in each cluster, rose-pink, about ¾ in. wide, the 5 petals densely hairy on the outside. Fruit a globe-shaped, purplish berry about ½ in. in diameter. Tropical Asia and the Philippines. In Fla. it can be grown up to zone* 8 on a variety of soils and will stand an occasional frost. Propagated by seeds. (*Rhodomyrtus* is from the Greek for rose myrtle, in allusion to the myrtle-like, rose-pink flowers.)

**RHODOPENSIS, -e** (ro-do-pen'sis). From Rhodope, Bulgaria.

---

* Special articles on the subjects indicated by an asterisk (*) will be found at the words so marked.

**RHODORA** (ro-doe′ra). A small genus of azalea-like shrubs of the heath family, the only cult. species being the beautiful **R. canadensis,** the rhodora immortalized in Emerson's poem. It is a shrub 2–3 ft. high, with alternate,* dark green, deciduous* leaves, 1½–2 in. long, without marginal teeth, gray-hairy beneath. Flowers irregular,* 2-lipped, very showy, about 2 in. wide, rose-purple. Newfoundland to N.Y. and Pa., mostly in the mountains. March–April. Flowering before the leaves expand. Hardy from zone* 4 northward. Its cult. is the same as for *Azalea* (which see). (*Rhodora* is from the Greek for a rose, in allusion to the rose-purple flowers.)

**RHODOTYPOS** (ro-do-ty′pos). A single species of hardy, Asiatic shrubs of the rose family, **R. tetrapetala,** variously known as jetbead, white kerria, and corchorus. It is a handsome shrub, 4–6 ft. high, with opposite,* short-stalked, doubly toothed leaves which are more or less oblongish, 3–4 in. long. Flowers pure white, nearly 2 in. wide, the 4 petals suggesting a single rose. Sepals* 4, toothed, alternating with 4 small bracts.* Fruit a collection of 4 shining, black, dry drupes set in the persistent calyx. China and Jap. Hardy from zone* 2 southward and widely grown both for attractive flowers and fruit. May. Of easy cult. in any ordinary garden soil and propagated by seeds or cuttings. Sometimes known as *R. kerrioides* and *R. scandens.* (*Rhodotypos* is from the Greek for rose and type, in allusion to the flowers resembling a single rose.)

**RHODY-LIFE.** A trademarked preparation, sold with directions for increasing the acidity of soil for rhododendrons and other plants of the heath family.

*RHOEAS* (ree′as). The Latin name of the corn poppy (*Papaver rhoeas*). See POPPY.

**RHOEO** (ree′o). A single species of Mexican and West Indian, fleshy, short-stemmed perennial herbs of the family Commelinaceae, **R. discolor,** sometimes, but most unfortunately, known as oyster plant. It has densely overlapping, narrow leaves, nearly 12 in. long, purplish on the under side, the bases sheathing. Flowers white, the sepals 3 and the petals 3, the latter soon withering, the flowers borne in a dense umbel* which is enclosed by 2 boat-shaped bracts.* The common form in cult. is the *var. vittatus,* which has the leaves purple both sides, but yellow-striped above. The plant is naturalized in Fla. and is occasionally grown in sub-tropical gardens, more often as a pot plant in the warm-temperate greenhouse. It needs potting mixture* 4 and plenty of moisture. (The origin of *Rhoeo* is unknown.)

*RHOMBIFOLIA, -us, -um* (rom-bi-fō′li-a). With rhomboid leaves. See RHOMBOIDEA.

*RHOMBOIDEA, -us, -um* (rom-boy′dee-a). Rhomboid; *i.e.* with oblique angles but parallel sides.

**RHOPALOSTYLIS** (ro-pal-o-sty′lis). A few feather palms from N. Zeal. and vicinity, one of them, **R. sapida,** the nikau palm, cult. for ornament in southern Calif. It is the only native palm of N. Zeal., grows up to 25 ft. high, with an unarmed trunk up to 8 in. in diameter. Leaves very handsome, more or less erect, 6–8 ft. long, the segments or leaflets very numerous, 2–3 ft. long, 1–2 in. wide, the stalk with a sheathing base. Flower cluster from just below the leaf-crown, 12–15 in. long, the fruit red, egg-shaped, about ½ in. long. Scarcely known outside of Calif. Sometimes offered as *R. baueri.* (*Rhopalostylis* is from the Greek for club and style, in allusion to the club-shaped style.*)

**RHUBARB.** A group of deep-rooted, perennial, acid-juiced herbs constituting the genus **Rheum** (ree′um) which comprises perhaps 25 species of stout, Asiatic herbs of the family Polygonaceae. They have basal, long-stalked leaves, which are divided or veined finger-fashion, the leafstalks channeled or sheathed. Flowers small, greenish-white, at the end of a stout central stalk which bears numerous flowers in dense, panicled clusters. Fruit a strongly winged achene.* (*Rheum* is from the old Greek word for rhubarb.)

For the culture of the common garden rhubarb *see* below.

The only other cult. species, *R. palmatum,* is mostly grown for its striking foliage. It is easy to grow in any rich garden soil and is a handsome, hardy foliage plant.

**R. palmatum.** Resembling the common rhubarb, but the leaves deeply lobed. Northeastern As. Chiefly grown in the *var.* **atrosanguineum,** which has reddish flower clusters; and the *var.* **tanguticum,** which has longer leaves, not so deeply lobed.

**R. rhaponticum.** Common garden rhubarb; also called pie-plant, and wine plant. A stout perennial herb, cult. for its pleasantly acid, wholesome leafstalks which are 12–30 in. long, green or red. Leaf blade roundish, not lobed, about 18 in. wide, often wavy-margined. Flowering stalk 4–6 ft. high, hollow. Siberia.

### RHUBARB CULTURE

One of the most permanent crops in the vegetable garden is rhubarb. It must, like asparagus, be put in a position so that annual plowing or harrowing will not disturb it, and once established it should not be moved. If the directions given below are followed, a row of rhubarb will continue to bear for many years. Ten or fifteen roots will be enough for a small family, but twice that many are needed if the family is large, or more frequent cuttings are wanted, or if it is to be used for wine making.

SOIL PREPARATION. Rhubarb will grow in most ordinary garden soil, but to get the best results it is necessary to do much more than merely plant the roots in such a soil. The chief value of the crop is the length and succulence of the leafstalks, both of which demand quick growth in the early spring.

Rhubarb plants should be allowed to develop fully in the summer.

To be sure of getting such a growth it is better to dig a trench about 1 ft. wide and 2½ ft. or even 3 ft. deep. Save all the topsoil from the excavation, but cart away all the subsoil. Fill in the trench with old, well-rotted cow manure up to within 1 ft. of the top. Pack the manure well, filling in enough to bring the level of manure 1 ft. below finished grade after all shrinkage or settling. Then use enough topsoil to cover the manure about 8 in. deep, the topsoil level then being 4 in. below the general soil level. Pack down the topsoil well, adding enough to make it 4 in. below finished grade when settled.

At this stage of preparation you have a rich, deep trench, filled in as directed, and ready for planting. The stout rhubarb roots should be planted 4–5 ft. apart in the trench, covered with the final 4 in. of topsoil, and well firmed in the soil. If more than one row is needed, 4–5 ft. apart.

In such a trench rhubarb will grow well. It must be kept cultivated, both to conserve moisture and to keep down weeds. During the first season after planting no stalks should be cut, but cutting, or rather pulling, the stalks may begin the second season and continue every spring.

Even after the harvesting is over for the season, the plant must be well taken care of, for it is during the summer that it is storing in its roots the food that will make next year's stalks. Every fall the plants should be mulched with strawy manure, which should be dug in early in the spring.

If you want rhubarb during the winter and have the proper sort of cellar, it can be forced by following the directions given at CELLAR GARDENING.

The so-called Panama rhubarb is a variety of the common sort with longer, nearly stringless, sweet stalks, grown in Calif. and other warm regions.

INSECT PESTS. A brownish snout beetle about ½ in. long sometimes punctures and blemishes the stalks. Hand picking, and destroying the wild food plant, dock, is advised. Other insect injury is only occasional.

---
* Special articles on the subjects indicated by an asterisk (*) will be found at the words so marked.

DISEASES. A few plants affected with foot-rot may be removed carefully. When the disease becomes general, healthy plants should be set in a new field. Leafspots and more rarely, mildew, may be present. Destroying the diseased plant parts in the fall, and in severe cases spraying is recommended.

**RHUBARB FAMILY** = Polygonaceae.

**RHUS** (rus). Sumac. A large genus of shrubs and trees of the family Anacardiaceae, the 150 species scattered very widely. Among them are several plants, notably the poison ivy and poison sumac, which are the only serious contact poisons in our native flora, but they are not garden plants. See POISON IVY for a description of them and for remedies. The juice of a related, non-hort., Asiatic tree, still more poisonous, yields lacquer.

The cult. sumacs, none of which are poisonous, are shrubs or small trees with compound* leaves, the leaflets arranged feather-fashion and with an odd one at the end. Flowers small, greenish, perfect or polygamous,* the petals, sepals, and stamens* each 5. Fruit a small drupe, clustered, red and hairy in all the cult. sumacs, but smooth and white or gray in the poisonous but not cult. poison ivy and its relatives. (*Rhus* is from the old Greek name for the sumac.)

The cult. sumacs are of little decorative value until the autumn, when their foliage turns a more brilliant red than almost any other shrubs or trees. Their fruits are also handsome. They are easily grown in any garden soil, or even in dry sand or on rocky hillsides, and may be readily raised from seed.

**aromatica** = *Rhus canadensis*.
**canadensis.** Fragrant sumac. A sprawling shrub 18-36 in. high. Leaflets 3, ovalish, 2-3 in. long, coarsely toothed, the foliage aromatic. Flowers greenish-yellow, borne in small spikes and blooming before the leaves expand. Eastern N.A. March-April. Hardy from zone* 2 southward.
**copallina.** Dwarf sumac. A shrub or small tree, 7-15 ft. high. Leaflets 9-21, oblong or narrower, not toothed, 3-4 in. long, the main leafstalk conspicuously winged. Flowers greenish, in a dense, terminal, branched cluster. Eastern U.S., especially common in dry, sandy soils. July-Aug. Hardy from zone* 3 southward, and will stand smoke, sand or even cinders.
**cotinoides** = *Cotinus americanus*.
**cotinus** = *Cotinus coggygria*.
**diversiloba.** A Calif. relative of the poison ivy (which see).
**glabra.** Smooth sumac. A shrub or small tree 8-20 ft. high, wholly without hairs. Leaflets 11-31, oblongish or narrower, 4-5 in. long, toothed. Flowers green, in a dense terminal cluster (panicle*). Eastern N.A. June-July. Hardy from zone* 2 southward. It has showy, red-hairy fruits.
**hirta** = *Rhus typhina*.
**toxicodendron** = Poison ivy (which see).
**trilobata.** Squaw-bush; also called lemonade sumac. Somewhat resembling *R. canadensis*, but the foliage ill-scented and smaller. Leaflets 3, ovalish, coarsely toothed, ¾-1¼ in. long. Flowers greenish, in small spikes blooming before the leaves expand. Ill. and Tex. to the Pacific Coast. March-April. Hardy from zone* 3 southward. Not so showy as *R. canadensis* and more upright.
**typhina.** Staghorn sumac. A shrub or small tree, 10-30 ft. high, the twigs densely brown-hairy. Leaflets 11-31, oblong-lance-shaped, 4-5 in. long, toothed. Flowers greenish in a large, terminal cluster (panicle*). Eastern N.A. June-July. Hardy from zone* 3 southward. The *var.* laciniata has the leaflets attractively and finely cut into narrow segments. The staghorn sumac is by far the best from the hort. standpoint, as both its showy fruiting cluster and gorgeous autumnal foliage are most attractive. It was long known as *R. hirta*.
**vernix** = Poison sumac. See POISON IVY.

**RHYNCHOSIA** (rin-kō'zi-a). Little known, tropical, chiefly trailing or prostrate vines of the pea family, the two below occasionally grown for ornament in zones* 8 and 9. They have compound* leaves, with 3 leaflets. Flowers pea-like, yellow, mostly in small clusters (racemes*) borne in the leaf-axils. Fruit a flattish pod (legume*). (*Rhynchosia* is from the Greek for beak, in allusion to the shape of the keel.)

**minima.** A slender, vine-like herb, usually trailing. Leaflets more or less ovalish or obliquely angled. Flowers about ¼ in. long. Pods ½-¾ in. long. Tropical regions, but extending northward to Tex. and Fla.
**puberula.** A prostrate or somewhat climbing vine, its small branches or twigs weak and numerous. Leaflet oblongish. Flowers about ⅓ in. long. Pods nearly ¾ in. long. South Africa.

**RHYTIDOPHYLLA, -us, -um** (rit-i-do-fill'a). With wrinkled leaves.

**RIB.** Any vein or nerve in a leaf. The main one is the midrib.*

**RIBBON BED.** See BEDDING.

**RIBBON-BUSH** = *Muehlenbeckia platyclados*.

**RIBBON-GRASS** = *Phalaris arundinacea picta*.
**RIBBONWOOD.** See HOHERIA and PLAGIANTHUS.

**RIBES** (ry'beez). A large genus of sometimes prickly shrubs, mostly from temperate regions, belonging to the family Saxifragaceae, and of first-rate hort. importance because it includes the currant, gooseberry, and several related shrubs grown for ornament. There are over 150 species, but beyond the few below most of them are not in general cult., except in a few collections of specialists. Leaves alternate,* simple,* but usually lobed finger-fashion. Flowers prevailingly greenish, yellowish, or reddish, the sepals usually colored and larger than the petals, which are sometimes very small or lacking. Stamens* 5. Fruit a true, juicy berry, bristly in the gooseberry. The individual flower stalks are jointed in the currants, but not jointed in the gooseberries, for which some retain the name *Grossularia*; the gooseberries are also usually spiny, the currants without spines. (*Ribes* is a Latinized version of an Arabic name for a plant with an acid juice.)

For the culture and uses of the fruit species see GOOSEBERRY, also CURRANT. The other, ornamental, species are of easy culture and may be propagated by layering, cuttings, or by seeds. All bloom early in the spring and fruit in midsummer. The genus provides an alternate host for white pine blister rust, especially the common gooseberry and the black currant. Neither should be planted within 900 ft. of any of the white pines. See Diseases at PINE.

**alpinum.** Mountain currant. An ornamental shrub, 5-8 ft. high. Lobes of the leaf toothed. Flowers in upright clusters (racemes*) greenish-yellow, the male and female on different plants. Fruit scarlet, smooth. Eu. Hardy from zone* 5 northward.
**aureum.** Golden or flowering currant. A widely cult., showy, unarmed shrub, 4-6 ft. high. Lobes of the leaf only slightly toothed. Flowers yellow, fragrant, in drooping clusters (racemes*), ultimately reddish. Fruit purplish-brown, smooth. Western N.A. Hardy everywhere. Sometimes confused with *R. odoratum* (which see).
**gordonianum.** A hybrid between the buffalo currant (*R. odoratum*) and the flowering currant (*R. sanguineum*). It resembles the former, but has yellow flowers which turn red, and are somewhat sticky. Hardy from zone* 4 southward. Popular as an ornamental currant.
**grossularia.** The garden or English gooseberry. A spiny shrub, 3-4 ft. high, the twigs bristly. Lobes of the leaf blunt-toothed. Flowers in clusters of only 1 or 2, green. Fruit acid, generally bristly, or at least glandular*-hairy, typically green, but yellow or even red in some forms. Eurasia and northern Af. Hardy from zone* 6 northward. For culture and varieties see GOOSEBERRY.
**nigrum.** Black currant; also called European black currant. An unarmed shrub 4-6 ft. high. Lobes of the leaf irregularly toothed. Flowers greenish-white, the clusters (racemes*) drooping. Fruit black, smooth, of fine flavor. Eurasia. Hardy from zone* 6 northward. There are many varieties, some of them, with the species, the source of the garden black currants. In all of them the bruised foliage has a heavy odor. For culture and varieties see CURRANT.
**odoratum.** Buffalo currant. An ornamental, unarmed shrub, 4-6 ft. high. Lobes of the leaf coarsely toothed. Flowers yellow, fragrant, the clusters showy and drooping. Fruit black, smooth, edible, especially in a variety known as Crandall which is sometimes grown for the fruit. Central U.S. Hardy from zone* 6 northward. One of the finest ornamental currants and closely related to *R. aureum* with which it is often confused. The only constant difference is that the latter species has sepals more than half the length of the calyx tube, while *R. odoratum* has sepals less than half as long as the tube of the calyx.
**rubrum.** Northern red currant. An unarmed shrub, 4-6 ft. high. Lobes of the leaf toothed. Flowers greenish-brown, the clusters drooping. Fruit red, edible. Eurasia. Hardy from zone* 6 northward; scarcely cult. in America, but commonly so in northern Eu.
**sanguineum.** Flowering currant. A very ornamental and widely cult., unarmed shrub, 8-10 ft. high. Lobes of the leaf irregularly toothed. Flowers red, the sticky, drooping, many-flowered clusters (racemes*) very showy. Fruit bluish-black, with a bloom. Northwestern N.A. Hardy from zone* 6 northward. An extremely popular bush, useful for the red garden, but found in many hort. forms, some with pink, white, deep red, or with double flowers.
**sativum.** Common garden currant. An unarmed shrub 3-5 ft. high. Lobes of the leaf toothed. Flowers greenish-purple, the profuse clusters (racemes*) drooping. Fruit normally red, smooth, juicy. Western Eu. Hardy from zone* 6 northward. For culture and varieties see CURRANT.

**RICCIA** (rick'si-a). A large genus of very simple, free-floating aquatic plants of no interest to the gardener, except for one or two that are used on the surface of aquaria. They are minute, flowerless plants, without differentiation of stem and leaf, microscopic sexual organs, and usually grow in masses on the water surface, hence looking like green scum. They resemble *Lemna*, which, however, is a flowering plant.

**RICE.** A widely grown cereal grass, and the only cult. species of the genus **Oryza** (o-ry'za), which comprises about

---
* Special articles on the subjects indicated by an asterisk (*) will be found at the words so marked.

6 species of chiefly marsh grasses from the East Indies. The common rice is **O. sativa**, next to wheat the most important cereal in the world and probably the staple food of more people than rely upon wheat. Typically, it is a water-inhabiting grass, 3–4 ft. high, with smooth, angled stems mostly hidden in the long leaf-sheaths. Leaves grass-like, flat, 6–12 in. long, about ½ in. wide, roughish. Flowering cluster terminal, branched (a panicle*), usually curved to one side, the spikelets flat and ribbed. Fruit the familiar rice grain, normally yellowish, but white when polished. There are cult. varieties with red grains, and several adapted to upland cultivation. (*Oryza* is a Latinized version of an Arabian name for rice.) For the wild rice *see* ZIZANIA.

### RICE CULTURE

Rice cult., which is an agricultural rather than a hort. operation, is apparently on the decrease in the U.S., the 1920 acreage being nearly one million, while the 1930 census shows only about 740 thousand acres of rice, practically all of which are confined to La., Ark., Tex., and Calif. And La. now raises twice as much as any other two states.

Many years ago rice cult. in S. Car. was a large and profitable industry, based upon the fact that there were lowlands capable of irrigation or flooding. But similar lands in La., much greater summer heat, and a longer growing season, have almost, but not quite, driven rice cult. from the Atlantic seaboard to the delta of the Mississippi.

The plant needs level ground which can be cheaply covered with water at certain seasons. The number of streams, or cheaply drilled wells, for this water supply are better provided in southern La. than anywhere else.

Most planters sow the seed broadcast early in April or late in March, on land from which the water has been withdrawn the autumn before. The seed should be harrowed in, much as oats are. When the seedlings are a few inches high the soil is gradually moistened and then made soaking wet by allowing irrigation water to flow over it. When the plants reach a good height the water is kept about 8 in. deep over the whole patch. And it is better not to let the water become stagnant. Professional growers keep a steady but almost imperceptible flow of water through the fields throughout the growing season. When the plants are ready to harvest the water is completely drained off and the crop cut like any cereal.

The growing of upland varieties of rice, without irrigation, while possible, is not recommended. Several varieties of upland rice are grown in India, China, and Jap., and could be grown here. But they are inferior in quality and yield to our irrigated sorts, one of which, a variety known as "gold seed," is considered a finer rice than that grown in any other country. Other varieties for irrigated districts are Honduras and Japanese.

INSECT PESTS. A stink bug, ⅓ in. long, attacks rice, sucking the forming grains. It can be checked by keeping down grass around the fields. Larvae of a snout beetle, which feed on the roots, are controlled by the same measure. Several stem borers, larvae of moths, are checked by cleaning up grass, plowing rice stubble in the fall, and planting rice at some distance from corn. Chinch bugs in Ark. are controlled by flooding young rice fields. Clean-up measures and rotation are most helpful against rice pests in the South. Calif. is comparatively free from rice insects.

DISEASES. Rice is subject to many maladies, among which are blast, rotten-neck, foot-rots, smuts, leaf stripes, chlorosis, stack-burn, and stem rot. The soil should be slightly acid, well aerated, and have proper watering and fertilizing. The crop should be rotated and grown from healthy seed or the seed treated with hot water (15 minutes at 139° F).

**RICE BEAN** = *Phaseolus calcaratus*.

**RICE-FLOWER.** *See* PIMELEA.

**RICE-PAPER TREE** = *Tetrapanax papyriferum*.

**RICH-MAN'S CABBAGE.** *See* CAULIFLOWER.

**RICHWEED** = *Collinsonia canadensis* and *Eupatorium urticaefolium*.

*RICINIFOLIA, -us, -um* (ri-sin-i-fō'li-a). With leaves like the castor-oil plant (*Ricinus*).

**RICINUS.** *See* CASTOR-OIL PLANT.

**RICOTIA** (ri-kō'she-a). Unimportant, annual herbs of the mustard family, found in the Mediterranean region, one of them, **R. lunaria**, sometimes grown for ornament. It is a low, spreading, much-branched herb with alternate leaves cut feather-fashion. Flowers with 4 petals, lilac, the cluster a loose, terminal raceme,* each flower scarcely more than ½ in. wide. Fruit a drooping, flat, thin silique,* about 1 in. long. Syria and Egypt. Rarely grown in the rock garden. Treat as a hardy annual (*see* ANNUALS). It should bloom in 2 months from seed sowing. (Named for a M. Ricot, a French botanist.)

**RIDGING OUT.** *See* TRENCHING.

**RIESLING.** For the best grapes for making this Rhine wine *see vinifera* varieties at GRAPE.

*RIGENS* (ry'jenz). Stiff or rigid.

*RIGIDA, -us, -um* (ri'ji-da). Stiff or rigid.

**RIGNUM** = *Monarda punctata*.

**RIMU** = *Dacrydium cupressinum*.

**RIND GRAFTING** = Bark Grafting. *See* GRAFTING.

**RING.** To girdle a tree; *i.e.* remove a complete circle of its outer bark and cambium, usually resulting in the death of the tree. *See* BARK.

*RINGENS* (rin'jenz). Ringent; *i.e.* gaping; used mostly to describe certain 2-lipped corollas. *See* MIMULUS.

**RING-NECKED PHEASANTS.** *See* BIRDS.

**RINGO CRABAPPLE** = *Malus prunifolia rinki*.

*RIPARIA, -us, -um* (ry-pay'ri-a). Of river banks.

**RIPE.** As usually understood a fruit is ripe when it is ready to eat. Properly, however, *ripe* signifies that the fruit has matured to the point where its seeds are ready for germination.

A common hort. use of *ripe* describes the condition of the wood of a cutting, cion, etc., indicating that they are in fit condition for propagation. Ripe wood is thus wood that will root well or, in grafting, is ready for a perfect union.

**RIP-RAP.** *See* BANKS. For rip-rap walls *see* WALLS AND WALL GARDENING.

*RITRO* (rit'ro). Native name in southern Eu. for *Echinops ritro*.

**RIVER ASH** = *Fraxinus pennsylvanica*. *See* ASH.

**RIVERBANK GRAPE** = *Vitis vulpina*.

**RIVER BIRCH** = *Betula nigra*. *See* BIRCH.

**RIVER SUNFLOWER** = *Helianthus decapetalus*. *See* SUNFLOWER.

**RIVINA** (ri-vy'na). Weak-stemmed, tropical American, perennial herbs of the family Phytolaccaceae, one of the three known species, **R. humilis**, the bloodberry or rouge-plant, grown for ornament. It is a spreading herb, 1–3 ft. high, with alternate,* ovalish leaves, 2–4 in. long and without marginal teeth. Flowers small, white or pinkish, without petals, the 4-parted calyx petal-like. The clusters are erect or weak racemes,* far more attractive in fruit than in flower. Fruit a pea-sized, red berry. The plant, sometimes known as *R. aurantiaca*, is common throughout Fla. and the Gulf states and is also cult. there. It is also grown, but not commonly, in the warm-temperate greenhouse northward. Use potting mixture* 4. (Named for A. Q. Rivinus, a German botanist.)

*RIVULARIS, -e* (riv-you-lar'is). Growing in or near brooks.

**ROADSIDE IMPROVEMENT.** One of the best activities of garden clubs has been the improvement and preservation of roadsides. It is still true, however, that thousands of miles of American highways remain painfully hideous. Hot-dog stands, gas stations, and the billboards still disfigure miles of what should be restful and pleasant highways. The elimination of the billboards and the restriction of the two other causes of disfigurement are best illustrated by the superb parkways radiating from some of our larger cities,

---

* Special articles on the subjects indicated by an asterisk (*) will be found at the words so marked.

notably those in Westchester and Long Island, near New York. Such parkways are the best of all solutions of highway beautification. They are so costly, however, that only public money makes them possible.

The local garden club can, on a small scale and often very inexpensively, adopt the principle of parkway development for a country road. Its activities should take two main channels: (1) Encouraging better-looking and adequately planted gas stations and refreshment stands, and (2) Planting of bare spots along the edges of the roads.

(1) The vested right of anyone to set up a stand or gas station, however hideous, cannot be legally denied. But the garden club often can and should offer to advise or even help in planting the surroundings of such. They can perhaps appoint a committee to pass on the plans for such structures. No compulsion need be exercised, but it does lie in the club's power to encourage and patronize owners who co-operate in such a scheme for roadside improvement. Most of the large oil companies already maintain good-looking gas stations. But the local dealers' stations and the refreshment stands remain a problem. Without legal compulsion, the garden club and civic improvement societies are often the only agencies that can deal with this purely local problem. And prizes and patronage are more potent arguments for co-operation than anything else.

(2) Roadside Planting. In many places the widening or straightening of roads leaves ugly scars, which, left to themselves, become mere thickets or patches of weeds. Permanent planting of shrubs and trees, and even seeding level places to lawn is advised. But the latter should be done only if there is provision for permanent care.

Masses of shrubbery or trees, however, especially on country roads, can be planted with the expectation of their needing little subsequent care beyond spraying. While it is sometimes desirable to plant the sorts native in the region, there is nothing against the use of any shrub or tree material that is hardy and suitable. The fetish that foreign plants are "unnatural" and out of place has worn a bit thin, because the inherent artificiality of all roads makes the use of native or exotic plants equally welcome in beautifying them. See TREES, STREET TREES, FLOWERING SHRUBS.

Unless there is adequate provision for permanent care, it is unwise to use ordinary perennials, although on really woodland roadsides it is often possible to make attractive displays of native wild flowers and hardy ferns. See WILD GARDEN, FERNS AND FERN GARDENING.

**ROADWAYS.** See DRIVES.

**ROBIN.** See BIRDS.

**ROBINIA.** See LOCUST.

**ROBIN'S-PLANTAIN** = *Erigeron pulchellus*.

*ROBUR* (rō'bur). Old name for the oak of England. See *Quercus robur* at OAK.

*ROBUSTA, -us, -um* (ro-bus'ta). Stout or robust.

*ROBUSTISPINA, -us, -um* (ro-bus-ti-spy'na). Stout-spined.

*ROCHEA* (rō'kee-a). South African succulent herbs or under-shrubs of the family Crassulaceae, **R. coccinea** a popular florist's plant grown for its showy red bloom. It has usually several stems, 12–18 in. high, with many opposite,* simple, fleshy, ovalish leaves about 1 in. long and so numerous as to be overlapping. Flowers tubular, nearly 2 in. long, brilliant scarlet, fragrant, crowded in a dense, terminal, head-like cluster, somewhat resembling a phlox. The limb of the corolla is expanded, and about ½ in. wide. Fruit dry. A good pot plant, useful for house decoration, as its bloom is lasting. For cult. see SUCCULENTS. It is sometimes sold as *Crassula coccinea*. (Named for François de la Roche, Swiss botanist.)

**ROCHESTER, N.Y.** See ARBORETUM.

**ROCK ASTER** = *Aster alpinus*.

**ROCK BORDER.** See Rock Border at BORDER.

**ROCK BRAKE.** See CRYPTOGRAMMA.

**ROCK CHESTNUT OAK** = *Quercus montana*. See OAK.

**ROCK CRESS** = *Arabis*.

**ROCK ELM** = *Ulmus racemosa*. See ELM.

**ROCKERY.** A passé term for a rock garden.

**ROCKET.** See HESPERIS.

**ROCKET CANDYTUFT** = *Iberis amara*. See CANDYTUFT.

**ROCKET LARKSPUR** = *Delphinium ajacis*.

**ROCKET SALAD** = *Eruca sativa*.

**ROCKFOIL.** See SAXIFRAGA.

**ROCK GARDEN.** Rock gardens furnished with alpine and saxatile* plants are a comparatively recent development in horticulture. Alpine plants, according to Paxton, have been grown in England since the 16th century, but in those early days they were grown as pot plants in cold frames, or planted out in the flower border, and not in rock gardens.

The use of rockwork in gardens was introduced to the western world towards the close of the 17th century — the idea coming from China and Japan. Unfortunately the motive that inspired the Chinese and Japanese in the construction of their rockwork was not imported with the practice and the result was that in many European gardens grottoes, cascades, caves and rockeries consisting of meaningless jumbles of rocks interspersed with soil were erected. Examples of a good idea gone wrong are still in evidence in so-called rock gardens that are nothing more than rock piles planted with unsuitable material.

Apparently it was not until about the middle of the 19th century that it occurred to anyone that alpine plants and rockwork could be in any way connected. Nowadays it is so obviously an ideal combination that it seems unbelievable that the connection should have been missed for so long. F. Dawtrey Drewitt in his book "The Romance of the Apothecaries' Garden at Chelsea" states that a rock garden was constructed there in 1772 for the growth of alpine plants, but whether Mr. Drewitt just assumed that alpines were grown in it or whether he has real evidence on this point does not appear. This rock garden had its inception in the fact that Sir Joseph Banks, on his return from Iceland in 1772, brought with him a quantity of lava which was supplemented by forty tons of stone from the Tower of London. Later, someone donated a quantity of flints and chalk. Brain coral, bricks, and conch shells also had a place in this rock garden. Many of the early rock gardens exhibited a similar lack of perception, on the part of the builders, of the desirability of a certain amount of unity, and the importance of avoiding incongruities in rock garden construction. Even in the famous rock garden of the Royal Botanic Gardens at Kew, as late as 1910, broken masonry, and portions of brick piers, could be seen substituting for rocks.

During the past thirty years or so, considerable progress has been made in the art of rock garden construction, so that today in this country, as well as in Europe, where rock gardening is most highly developed, rock gardens may be seen which are artistically correct and well adapted to the cultivation of alpine and rock plants.

### THEORY OF ROCK GARDENS

It is correct to assume that the ideal rock garden is one capable of supporting a healthy growth of alpine and rock plants. In order to display them in an appropriate setting, and to provide proper cultural conditions, in part at least, approximating those under which they grow in nature, a rock garden is necessary.

Apart from their value in providing a picturesque and natural setting, the rocks in a rock garden have several distinctly utilitarian functions to perform. They help to keep the ground cool; they conduct moisture to the roots of the plants and prevent, in part, its loss by evaporation. As many alpine plants grow in situations where the soil is constantly moistened, during the growing season, with ice

---

* Special articles on the subjects indicated by an asterisk (*) will be found at the words so marked.

or snow water, the importance of providing a cool root run is immediately obvious. The rocks serve to give shade and shelter and aid in promoting the efficient drainage which is so necessary. Also they hold up the soil, making it possible to provide a variety of contours in the garden.

One of the difficulties in growing alpine plants under lowland conditions is the great difference in the length of the growing season compared with what they experience when growing wild. In the vicinity of New York the growing season (between the last frost of spring and the first frost of autumn) is 210 days; whereas in their natural habitats the growing season is about half this length. For the length of the growing season in your region *see* the frost dates at the name of your state or province.

As long ago as 1857 the late Dr. Regel, in a paper on the Swiss alpine flora and the culture of alpine plants, advanced the theory that alpine plants require a much poorer soil under cultivation than they do when they are growing under natural conditions. The reason given is that when alpines are planted in poor soil it slows up their rate of growth and in a measure compensates for the long growing season they experience under lowland conditions. Whether or not Dr. Regel's theory is tenable it is generally agreed that an over-rich soil is not good for alpine and rock plants under cultivation. In the first place it is liable to stimulate their growth so that they no longer possess the characteristic compactness of habit which is one of their charms. Another disadvantage of a rich soil and consequent lushness of growth is that the plants are likely to "damp off" during the hot, humid periods in summer, or die from the effects of the winter.

For a good example of a rock garden see the colored plate. The picture was taken in July at "Cronamere," the rock garden of Mrs. C. I. DeBevoise at Greens Farms, Conn.

## Types of Rock Gardens

The forms that rock gardens take are many and varied, ranging from the many-pocketed erection made solely for the purpose of growing a large collection of alpine and rock-inhabiting plants, to the type designed purely as a landscape feature, in which the plants are merely incidental decorative material. The ideal garden lies between these extremes and consists of a construction in which the rocks are arranged artistically — usually with some relation to what one might find in nature, and placed in such a way that a reasonably large collection of plants may be cultivated.

A type that is satisfactory when the general surroundings permit of its construction is in the form of a winding ravine. Such a garden affords every conceivable aspect, a desideratum when dealing with the more capricious alpines.

Then there is the mound type formed by building up above the surrounding level over a central core made up largely of drainage material. This kind of a garden, because it quickly dries out, is more likely to be satisfactory in sections which have considerable rainfall evenly distributed throughout the growing season.

Some rock gardens consist of a series of raised rocky beds from one to three feet in height with winding walks between. Such construction is good when the main object in view is the cultivation of a collection.

A sloping bank may afford opportunity for the construction of an interesting rock garden and in some instances a rock garden has been effectively used in place of the usual turf of a terrace slope.

Some purely formal types of rock garden are in existence and are quite appropriate if the home is formal in architecture and the garden has to be placed near it. In such cases the garden may consist of raised beds supported by almost vertical stone walls laid up without cement and planted. (*See* Walls and Wall Gardening.) Walks of flagstone of random sizes with rock plants growing in the crevices between the stones form an appropriate concomitant.

When the garden supplements existing rocky outcrops it is important that the new construction should be in harmony with them. These outcrops may appear to be ideal as a nucleus for rock garden construction (and sometimes they really are), but appearances are often deceptive and the soil pockets in the vicinity of the rocks may be too shallow to admit of the cultivation of the plants it is desired to grow.

In order to be correct and to avoid a jarring note the rock garden must be in harmonious relation with its surroundings. If the architecture of the house is formal and it is necessary to place the rock garden in its proximity it is a mistake to attempt a replica of wild mountain scenery.

When the house and surroundings are informal, more especially if the plot has sharp contours, the rock garden that partly imitates and partly idealizes nature should be constructed.

If the plot and general environment present a level surface a rock garden that rises much above the general level looks like an excrescence and entirely out of place. When it is desired to make a rock garden under such conditions it is a good plan partially to screen it with a shrub planting which will also serve as a background for the rock garden. Diversity of contour in a garden of this kind may be obtained by excavating a winding walk and using the soil thus obtained to provide height along the sides.

## Site and Aspect

As a general rule the site of the rock garden should be in the open, not subjected to the drip from trees or to competition from their roots.

Preferably the subsoil should be of a porous nature, permitting the rapid drainage of surplus moisture. This is true despite the fact that some alpines thrive in boggy situations.

No matter what the aspect of the garden may be some rock plants can be found that will thrive in it. But, in order to provide varied cultural conditions for a large collection of plants it is well to have many aspects. When the bulk of the collection is to be made up of alpine plants the garden should face, in the main, north or northeast. Although many of our choicest alpines are exposed to blazing sunshine in their native haunts they appreciate a little shade during the hottest part of the day when grown in lowland regions of the temperate zone. This shade can be provided by the conformation of the rock garden and by large individual rocks.

## The Kind of Rock to Use

As a general rule the stone available locally should be used even though it may not be ideal for the purpose. By using local stone there is less danger of constructing a garden that looks incongruous in its setting. The use of imported rocks may result in a better-looking garden *per se*, but if it introduces a jarring note into the general surroundings it is artistically inadmissible. The use of alien material may be permissible when it is possible to construct and screen the rock garden so that it can only be seen as a unit and not in relation to surrounding topography.

Weather-worn limestone of irregular shapes is perhaps the most pleasing material for construction and the easiest to work with. But weathered rocks of almost any kind can be used to advantage provided they are angular and blocky in form, of a neutral color, and of pleasing appearance. Stratified rocks, when they are not too thin, permit the construction of picturesque effects in the way of ledges, cliffs, and bold promontories.

The kind of rock that is commonly known as "tufa," because of its porosity, cavities, and lime content, is admirable from the standpoint of providing ideal cultural conditions for certain groups of lime-loving rock plants, but its color and general appearance are against its extended use.

Other things being equal, rocks that are sufficiently porous to absorb considerable moisture, but sufficiently dense so that they do not crumble when exposed to the weather are to be preferred.

Glacial boulders may be used in rock garden construction if they are of varied size and not too spherical in outline. They should be used sparingly, and the general idea in mind when making the garden should be the simulation of

---

* Special articles on the subjects indicated by an asterisk (*) will be found at the words so marked.

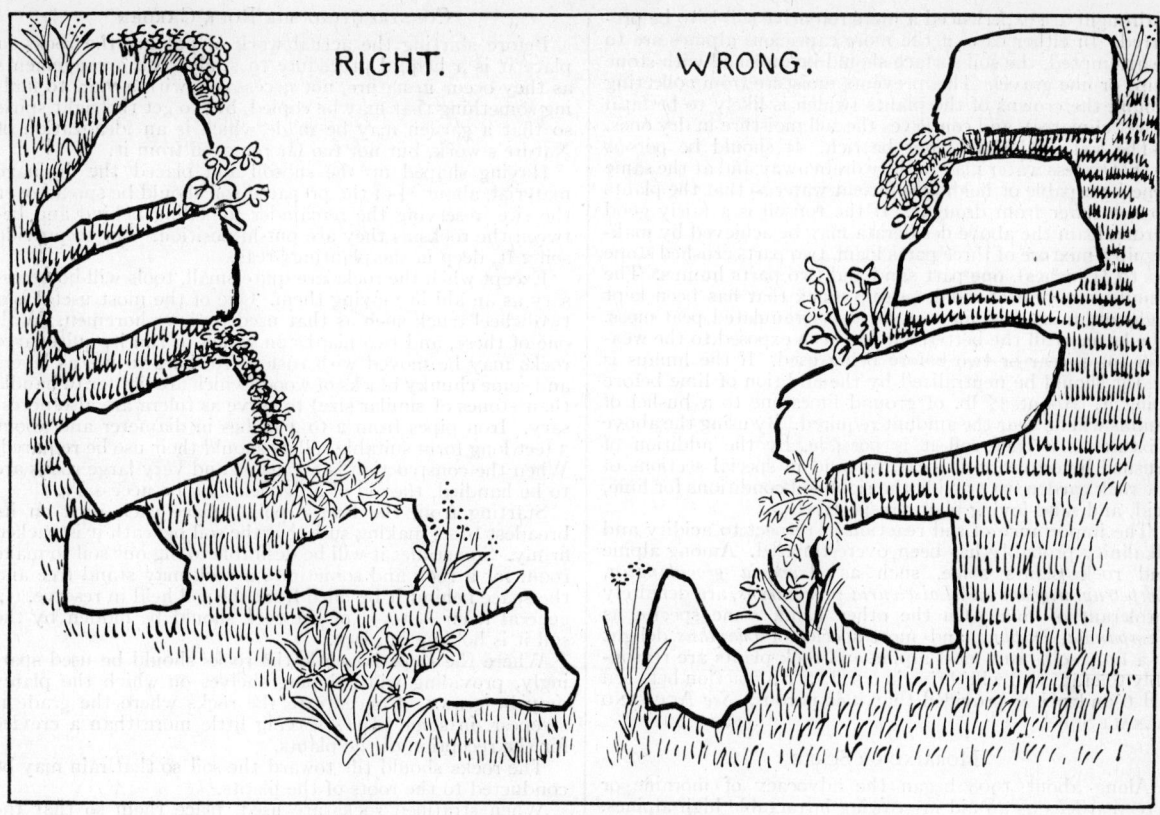

THE RIGHT AND WRONG WAYS TO BUILD A ROCK GARDEN
The rocks should always be placed so that moisture runs into, not out of, the garden.

a boulder-strewn slope, such as one might be expected to find on a terminal moraine.

The worst kind of rocks to work with are small, spherical boulders. If these are the only kind available it would be well to give up the idea of a rock garden. But if they are used it should be with the sole idea of making it possible to grow alpines and rock plants in such a manner that they will hide most of the rocks.

Only in exceptional cases should more than one kind of rock be used in the rock garden. It has many times been said, and it is worth repeating here, that a rock garden is a rock garden, and not a collection of geological specimens.

### Water in the Rock Garden

Although ornamental water in the form of a cascade, brook, or pool is not absolutely necessary, it does add movement, interest and attractiveness to the rock garden. Furthermore, in its immediate vicinity it affords opportunity to provide special cultural conditions for certain groups of plants. It should not, however, be introduced unless it can be done convincingly with a natural appearance. A "spring," whose source is the city water main, gushing from the top of a hill, does not look quite right. See WATER.

### Grading

Having decided on the location and knowing the kind and amount of rock available, the next step is to remove the topsoil from the area that is to be the rock garden. This topsoil with the modifications to be described below is the medium in which the rock plants will be planted. For convenience in handling later on, part of the topsoil should be placed on the walk and part on the outskirts of the rock garden.

Having removed the topsoil, the subsoil should be shaped up so that its contours roughly conform to the configuration the rock garden is to assume. If the garden is being built on sloping ground, it will probably be desirable to dig into the bank at strategic points and use the excavated soil to heighten near-by areas to obtain more rugged effects.

When the site of the rock garden is level the best plan is to make a valley by digging out the area where the walk is to be and use the excavated material to gain height on the sides. In gardens made in this way it usually is necessary to provide a drain or drains at the lowest points to carry off surface water, otherwise after a rainstorm the walks may be knee-deep in water.

### Drainage

When the subsoil has been graded the next step is to provide ample drainage. If the subsoil is naturally gravelly and porous no artificial drainage will be necessary, but if it is impervious to moisture, provision must be made to carry excess water quickly away from the roots of the alpines. This should be done even though drainage is not so important in most parts of this country as it is in rainy England.

It has been found that a 12-inch layer of coarse coal ashes, underneath the rock garden soil, works admirably. Preferably, ashes should be used which have been exposed to the weather for six months or more so that injurious compounds have had an opportunity to leach out. If ashes are not available, brickbats, small rocks or similar material can be substituted.

### Soil

The nature of the climate has an important bearing on whether one should lean toward porosity or retentiveness in making up a soil mixture. In a rainy section extreme porosity is a desideratum, but in a region where long periods

---

* Special articles on the subjects indicated by an asterisk (*) will be found at the words so marked.

of drought are experienced a more retentive soil is to be preferred. In either case, if the more capricious alpines are to be attempted, the soil surface should be mulched with stone chips or fine gravel. This prevents moisture from collecting around the crowns of the plants (which is likely to be fatal in wet climates), and conserves the soil moisture in dry ones.

The soil used should not be rich. It should be porous so that excess water may rapidly drain away and at the same time be capable of holding sufficient water so that the plants do not suffer from drought. If the topsoil is a fairly good garden loam the above desiderata may be achieved by making up a mixture of three parts loam, two parts crushed stone (⅛ to ⅜ inches), one part sand and two parts humus. The humus may be leaf mold, swamp muck that has been kept high, and fairly dry, for two years, or granulated peat moss. The latter is all the better if it has been exposed to the weather for a year or two before being used. If the humus is acid it should be neutralized by the addition of lime before using it. About ½ lb. of ground limestone to a bushel of humus will be near the amount required. By using the above mixture as a base soil it is possible, by the addition of crushed limestone, acid peat, or sand in special sections of the rock garden, to provide the right soil conditions for lime, acid, and sand-loving plants respectively.

The importance of soil reaction in respect to acidity and alkalinity probably has been overestimated. Among alpine and rock plants some, such as *Arenaria groenlandica*, *Empetrum nigrum* and *Loiseleuria procumbens*, are definitely intolerant of lime. On the other hand, some species as *Campanula*, *Daphne*, and most species of *Dianthus* delight in a limy soil. But most alpine and rock plants are reasonably tolerant and will thrive in a soil with a reaction between pH 6 and pH 8, provided that it is porous. *See* ACID AND ALKALI SOILS.

## MORAINE OR SCREE

Along about 1908 began the advocacy of moraine or scree gardens as an aid in growing intractable high alpines. A moraine or scree in rock gardener's parlance consists of a bed of stones, two feet or more deep, with or without a small proportion of soil and humus, and watered either from above or below. One conception of a moraine is of a watertight basin two feet deep and of any convenient length and breadth filled with a mixture made up of 5 parts crushed stone (½ in. and smaller), 1 part sand and 1 part sifted leaf mold. Water is supplied during the growing season through a pipe at the upper end and the surplus drawn off by an outlet at the other end *1 ft. below the surface*. Another outlet is necessary at the bottom of the basin to drain off all water during the winter. The theory back of this practice is that there is a constant supply of cool water running through the rooting medium, thus supplying the moisture and cool root run that high alpines delight in; while comparatively dry conditions are provided during the winter when the plants are at rest.

Many growers prefer not to bother with subirrigation in the moraine and rely on rainfall or occasional overhead watering. In the rock garden of the Brooklyn Botanic Garden a moraine of this type with the soil mixture described above has been fairly successful; such plants as *Silene acaulis*, *Geranium argenteum* and some of the encrusted saxifrages taking very kindly to this treatment.

Almost indefinite changes can be made in the character of the stony mixture. It may be of limestone, sandstone, or granite; with varying portions of sand and humus. An experimenter in Ireland using dozens of different mixtures found that pure limestone chips, including the dust just as it came from the crusher, gave best results, whereas a neighbor 5 miles distant found that limestone and soil, 3 to 1, was the most satisfactory mixture.

In order to give an air of verisimilitude to the moraine it might be well to construct it so that it seems to be pouring out from between two rocks on a slope and broadening out, more or less fan-shaped, toward the base. A few flattish rocks placed here and there will serve as stepping stones and help mitigate the gravel-walk appearance that is inevitable.

## CONSTRUCTING THE ROCK GARDEN

Before starting the actual work of putting the rocks in place it is a helpful procedure to study rock arrangements as they occur in nature, not necessarily with a view to finding something that may be copied, but to get the right spirit so that a garden may be made which is an idealization of Nature's work, but not too far removed from it.

Having shaped up the subsoil and placed the drainage material, about ¾ of the prepared soil should be spread over the site, reserving the remainder for filling behind and between the rocks as they are put in position. Try to provide soil 2 ft. deep in the planting areas.

Except when the rocks are quite small, tools will be necessary as an aid in moving them. One of the most useful is a two-wheel truck such as that used by longshoremen. With one of these, and two planks on which to run it, quite large rocks may be moved with ease. Crowbars to use as levers and some chunky blocks of wood (which are lighter to handle than stones of similar size) to serve as fulcra are also necessary. Iron pipes from 2 to 4 inches in diameter and about 3 feet long form suitable rollers should their use be required. When the construction is extensive and very large rocks are to be handled, the aid of a derrick may be necessary.

Starting from the lowest point, place each rock on its broadest base, making sure that the soil beneath it is packed firmly. Sometimes it will be desirable to dig out soil to make room for a rock and sometimes a rock may stand free and the space behind it be filled from the soil held in reserve. In general from ⅔ to ¾ of the rock should be hidden by the soil it is holding in place.

Where the slope is gentle the rocks should be used sparingly, providing wide, sloping shelves on which the plants may be grown. Concentrate the rocks where the grade is steepest, in some places leaving little more than a crevice for the reception of the plants.

The rocks should tilt toward the soil so that rain may be conducted to the roots of the plants.

When stratified rocks are used, place them so that the stratification lines lie in one plane. As a general rule the strata should be slightly off horizontal. If placed vertically and the rocks are of a crumbling nature the effects of weather may cause them to disintegrate more rapidly than is desirable. Of course if neighboring rock formations exhibit vertical strata the rock garden should be made to correspond.

If the rocks are too small to gain the desired height when used singly it is sometimes possible by careful matching to place several rocks together giving the appearance, when planted, of a single fissured rock.

## WALKS

Walks in the rock garden may be of turf, gravel, or flat stones. Turf walks, although pleasing in appearance and suggesting alpine meadows, present a problem in upkeep owing to the difficulty of mowing in proximity to rocks. The invasion of the planting areas by grass stolons* is also a disadvantage. Furthermore, in wet weather it is not too easy to get around a turf walk in comfort to view the rock plants.

Gravel walks are permissible in gardens where there is considerable traffic, providing their color harmonizes with the general surroundings; but for most rock gardens flat rocks interplanted with dwarf carpeting plants are to be preferred. In small gardens where the traffic is light these walks may take the form of irregular stepping stones with plants between.

Whichever kind of walk is chosen ample under-drainage must be provided so that there is no standing water during rainy periods. *See* PATHS AND PAVING.

## PLANTING

Rock plants may be set out in early fall or spring. In general in an established rock garden, hardy, early-blooming subjects should be planted in the fall. As most of the nurserymen specializing in rock garden plants grow a good proportion of their stock in pots it is possible to obtain material

---

* Special articles on the subjects indicated by an asterisk (*) will be found at the words so marked.

A CONNECTICUT ROCK GARDEN IN JULY

(Courtesy of Mrs. C. I. DeBevoise)

that may be planted at any time during the growing season without checking growth.

When planting, the soil should be packed firmly about the roots, taking care to leave no air spaces. When crevices between rocks are to be planted it is better to do so as the work of construction proceeds, since it is a difficult and tedious task properly to spread out the roots and pack soil around them in existing crevices. A natural appearance should be aimed at in planting the rock garden. Avoid setting the plants in straight lines.

As a general rule all the plants of one variety should be grouped together rather than to spot them all over the rock garden. It may be desirable to depart from this practice when it is necessary to find the right cultural conditions for a species that is known to be difficult.

Although the alpine plant enthusiast as a rule pays little attention to grouping plants with reference to their color values, being quite content with a kaleidoscope so long as his plants are healthy, those who find pleasure in harmonizing color schemes have plenty of scope for their efforts in planting the rock garden.

### General Care

In the spring as soon as the frost is out of the ground and the winter covering has been removed it is necessary to look carefully over the garden and restore to earth any roots that have been heaved out by the action of frost. It is good at this time to apply a mulch of equal parts of stone chips and leaf mold. Prostrate plants such as mountain avens seem to benefit greatly from a mulch of this kind worked among their prostrate stems.

It is important to ensure that the plants do not suffer from lack of moisture during spring. A drought in May when the plants are actively growing may injure them.

A careful watch must be kept at all times for weeds. As it is seldom possible to use a hoe, weeding in the rock garden is largely a matter of finger and thumb work, with a hand fork or small cultivator to help remove the stubborn weeds, and to loosen the surface soil. In connection with weeding it should be remembered that the most beautiful plant may become a weed if it is growing in the wrong place, therefore keep a close watch on the more exuberant rock plants so that they may be restrained should they show signs of overwhelming weaker, choicer material.

### Watering

Most alpines and rock plants require abundant water when they are actively growing. Some authorities recommend subirrigation by means of perforated water pipes, but this is expensive to install and quite likely to get out of order. The simplest way to water the rock garden is by means of sprinklers throwing a fine spray. These should be left in one position long enough to soak the ground thoroughly. Some plants such as the silvery-leaved milfoils and some of the more difficult high alpines are likely to suffer from too much overhead watering. These should be segregated and water supplied by pouring water into a short length of porous drain tile, or even an ordinary flower pot, permanently sunk in the ground beside them. A promising method of applying water that may solve the problem of watering the rock garden as a whole, as well as those plants which object to overmuch water on their leaves, is by means of portable, perforated, flexible pipes, or cloth hose from which the water may drip or ooze upon the ground in the vicinity of the plants.

### Winter Protection

In sections of the country where the rock garden is covered with a thick layer of snow all winter there is no need to worry about winter protection. It is in those regions where frost and thaw alternate that protection is needed — not to keep the plants warm, but to keep the ground frozen, to shade the plants from late winter sunshine, and prevent them from starting into premature growth which may suffer from late frosts.

The kind of covering used must be light and of such a nature that it will not mat down into a soggy mass as a result of exposure to rain. Evergreen boughs such as fir or pine are the best possible covering. Salt hay or oak leaves may be used if evergreen boughs are not available. In localities where considerable rain is experienced during the winter it may be necessary to protect from overhead moisture, by placing over them a pane of glass on suitable supports, such plants as the silvery-leaved milfoils, and any woolly-leaved high alpines. The covering should not be put on until the ground has been frozen sufficiently to stop all growth for the season.

### Propagation

BY SEEDS. The seeds of most rock plants germinate readily if planted in a cool greenhouse in March. Some kinds apparently need a period of after-ripening at low temperatures to ensure a good stand. Seeds of this nature may be planted in the fall and left out of doors. A plan that is followed successfully in England and one that would probably be equally successful here is to plant the seeds in late fall or early winter and place the seed pots or flats in a cold frame which is filled with snow as soon as it is available. When the snow has melted, the seeds are brought into a slightly heated greenhouse when germination usually is prompt. Those kinds which mature their seeds early may be planted as soon as they are ripe.

BY CUTTINGS AND DIVISION. Plants of garden origin such as *Phlox subulata* varieties or hybrids, and species which seldom set seeds should be propagated vegetatively. Cuttings of young shoots from 1 to 3 inches long may be made and inserted in sand in a shaded cold frame in July and August.

Species which bloom and make their growth early in the spring may be taken up and divided in late summer. Those which start into growth and bloom late in the season may be divided in spring. The divisions should be planted in soil that is somewhat more porous than that in which the parent plant is growing and kept watered and shaded until new roots are formed. In the case of many alpine and rock plants procumbent shoots are produced which root as they grow. These may be dug up for propagation purposes without disturbing the parent plant.

### Where Rock Gardens May be Made

If we except mountainous regions, the places in North America where rock gardens are likely to be most successful (in the sense of being able to grow without too much trouble the alpine plants that are considered ideal rock garden material) are Oregon, Washington and British Columbia. Many rock gardens, furnished with a large proportion of alpine plants, are in existence in the eastern states from Philadelphia northwards. There is considerable interest in rock gardening in many of the southern states, and in the high-lying sections there is no reason why some at least of the alpine plants should not be grown. In the Middle West, particularly in Ohio, where there is a successful Rock Garden Society, rock gardening is in great favor and fair collections of the more tolerant alpines are grown.

The cultivation of most high alpines is certain to be attended with almost insuperable difficulties except in regions having a low summer temperature and a growing season of 140 days or less.

But rock gardens can be made and furnished with other than what we normally think of as rock garden material. If anyone is fortunate enough to possess a wooded, rocky ravine on his property, there is offered an opportunity to develop it as a charming wild flower garden by utilizing for planting our native woodland flowers.

In some of the northeastern states rocky outcrops are common which could be converted into pleasing landscape features by a judicious planting of such subjects as dwarf junipers and cotoneasters.

Unfortunately, the human race is prone to want "what is not," and garden makers, instead of making full use of natural features, seem to prefer to blast out the rocks and make a level greensward if they are in a rocky region, and import

---
\* Special articles on the subjects indicated by an asterisk (\*) will be found at the words so marked.

rocks at great expense to make a rock garden if they live on the great plains.

Rock gardens should not be attempted in rockless regions, more especially if the climate is such that it does not admit of the cultivation of alpine plants. But there are many parts of the country where picturesque rock formations abound, and these may appropriately be embellished with whatever plant material is available.

### Plants for the Rock Garden

Sufficient has already been said to indicate that the preferred plants for the rock garden are alpines or other plants which exhibit a similar dwarf or compact habit of growth.

In general, species which thrive as well in flower border or shrubbery as they do in the rock garden should be used with reluctance and looked upon as mere fillers, tolerated only until more suitable material is obtainable.

Crevice plants for the rock garden: *Saxifraga macnabiana* (foreground) and candytuft

Bedding plants, such as begonia, pelargonium, petunia, heliotrope, and lantana, are absolutely taboo. Annuals, in the opinion of this writer, should be used very sparingly, resolutely avoiding commonplace varieties, such as portulaca and sweet alyssum. The chief use of annuals in the rock garden is to cover bare ground left by the dying down of early spring bulbs.

Dwarf evergreens may be planted with discretion to give accent* and provide some variety in height. If properly chosen and placed, they look in keeping with the rest of the plants. Evergreens are occasionally of value to hide errors in construction.

The importance of carefully choosing the plants for the rock garden cannot be overemphasized. If the wrong material is used, the rock garden loses its air of distinction and becomes merely a flower garden in which there are rocks.

The following plants, except where noted, will grow in the soil mixture previously described without overmuch coddling.

Except where otherwise indicated, the plants should be grown in open, sunny situations. Light shade during the hottest part of the day is desirable in regions having high temperatures, except for those kinds whose indicated preference is for hot, dry situations.

Those recommended for beginners are marked with a dagger (†).

**Achillea ageratifolia.** Gray, toothed foliage. Daisy-like flowers on 8-in. stems.

**A. argentea.** Silvery leaves, flowers as above, on 4-in. stems.

†**A. tomentosa.** Green, woolly leaves, flowers yellow on 8-in. stems.

The achilleas mentioned above thrive best in sunny situations and rather poor, stony soil.

**Aethionema coridifolium.** Sometimes sold as *Iberis jucunda*. Blue-gray, glaucous foliage smothered with dense heads of pink flowers 4 in. in height.

**A. grandiflorum.** Makes a graceful bush, 12 in. high, with loose spikes of pink flowers.

**A. pulchellum.** Drooping, and much-branched. Flowers rose-pink. About 8 in. high.

Aethionemas are a much-hybridized race. Exceptionally good forms should be propagated by cuttings of young shoots in summer. As they tend to be short-lived under cultivation, a few should be propagated every year. They require a sunny spot and well-drained soil mixed with crushed limestone.

†**Alchemilla alpina.** Grown for its beautiful foliage; shining green above, and silvery with silken hairs below. The flowers are dowdy and should not be allowed to form.

†**Alyssum alpestre.** Prostrate, with hoary foliage; yellow flowers produced over a long period in spring.

**A. argenteum.** Grayish leaves, golden-yellow flowers, 18 in. high.

†**A. saxatile.** Its myriads of yellow flowers, surmounting the hoary leaves, are showy. It is a sprawly plant about 1 ft. high.

**Androsace carnea.** Tufts of green foliage, heads of pink flowers on 2–3-in. stems.

Increase the amount of humus and stone chips for the above. Light shade during the hottest part of the days is desirable.

**A. lanuginosa.** Makes long, trailing shoots with silvery leaves. Umbels of rose-lilac flowers in succession in late summer. Splendid when seen draping dark-colored rocks.

†**A. sarmentosa.** Foliage in rosettes. Plant spreads by runners similar to those of strawberry. Flowers in pink umbels* on 6-in. stems. Does well in moraine, but will grow in normal rock garden soil.

**Anemone** (*see also* Pulsatilla).

†**A. hupehensis.** Of comparatively recent introduction. Like a small edition of the Japanese anemone, with reddish-mauve flowers. Part shade.

**A. sylvestris.** Flowers white on 8-in. stems. This species needs a cool, moist, shady spot and plenty of humus in the soil.

†**Aquilegia alpina.** Flowers large, of deep, clear blue, with golden stamens, on 18-in. stems.

†**A. canadensis.** Flowers cinnabar-red and yellow. Height from one to two ft. or more, dependent on soil. Plant in poor, rocky soil for best results. It becomes coarse and weedy-looking in rich soil.

†**A. coerulea.** Flowers lavender-blue and white on one- to two-ft. stems.

†**A. flabellata nana.** Quite dwarf — about 9 in. Flowers white, leaves glaucous.

Aquilegias will grow in full sun, but seem to prefer partial shade.

†**Arabis albida.** Gray, woolly leaves and 8-in. spikes of white flowers. The double-flowered form is unobjectionable, and indeed preferable, because of its long blooming period. This species is often sold under the name *A. alpina*.

**A. alpina.** Greenish leaves, and smaller flowers than the preceding.

**A. aubrietioides.** Grayish, hairy leaves in close tufts, surmounted by 6-in. spikes of pink flowers. Not very permanent.

**A. kellereri.** Makes a mat of silvery foliage closely hug-

---

* Special articles on the subjects indicated by an asterisk (*) will be found at the words so marked.

ging the ground. Heads of small white flowers. Plant in moraine or very gritty soil.

**Arenaria balearica.** When happy, covers soil and rocks with a ¼-in. carpet of bright green, studded in spring with pure white flowers, on 2-in. stems. It needs a cool, moist, well-drained spot, and porous rocks over which to spread. Although sometimes a troublesome weed in English rock gardens, it is difficult to establish here.

†**A. grandiflora.** Green, pointed leaves. Flowers pure white on 6-in. stems.

**A. montana.** A trailing species with grayish leaves, and large white flowers. In England it may ramble happily through the walls (of brick laid up without mortar) of a cold frame.

†**Aster alpinus.** Daisy-like, purple flowers on 8-in. stems. There are many forms, including a white one — not so good, but the variety known as *speciosus* is very good indeed.

†**Aubrietia.** This genus forms one of the standbys in European gardens. When exposed to the hot sun of American gardens the flowering period is considerably shortened. Good varieties are: Bridesmaid, soft pink; Lavender Queen, Crimson King; Dr. Mules, dark purple; Moerheimi, gray foliage and pale pink flowers. These varieties must be propagated by cuttings or division to keep them true to type. Many American nurserymen raise them from seed and offer under color only.

**Campanula bellardi.** According to Farrer this is the name by which *C. pusilla* should be known. It is a variable plant with quivering, bell-shaped flowers on slender 4-in. stems. It has a habit of flowering itself to death. Plant in moraine or very gritty soil.

†**C. carpatica.** A strong and "easy to grow" kind. The ft.-long stems tend to flop and may smother any choice plant in their vicinity.

There are many forms ranging in color from white to deep blue.

**C. excisa.** Violet-blue, narrow, bell-shaped flowers. Grow it in moraine or gritty soil from lime.

**C. garganica** has a central tuft of leaves and spreading, prostrate branches. The flowers are flat and starry, ranging in color from white to slaty-blue.

†**C. portenschlagiana.** One of the easiest of the dwarf campanulas. It has violet-blue flowers and grows 4–5 in. high.

*Campanula* is a genus that contains a large number of species suitable for rock gardens. Space does not permit mention of the dozens of fine species available.

**Cymbalaria aequitriloba.** A trailer built along the lines of the Kenilworth ivy but much smaller in all its parts. Farrer calls it "a Tiny Tim of extraordinary charm." Fine for crevices.

**Dianthus alpinus.** Perhaps the best of all the mountain pinks. It forms a mat of glossy, green foliage, surmounted by rose-pink flowers the size of a 50-cent piece, on 3-in. stems. It needs ample drainage with a liberal supply of limestone chips in the soil.

†**D. caesius.** Bluish foliage, and fringed, pink flowers delightfully fragrant.

†**D. deltoides.** Forms dense mats of green foliage and small, deep-pink blooms abundantly produced.

**D. neglectus.** Grassy tufts of foliage, pink flowers with a satiny-buff reverse, on 5-in. stems. Good for the moraine.

Almost any of the dwarf dianthuses look well in the rock garden. The commoner kinds should be prevented from seeding, for otherwise there is certain to be a crop of self-sown seedlings which are liable to run out choicer plants.

†**Dicentra eximia.** Fern-like foliage and racemes of rose-pink flowers.

**Dodecatheon radicatum.** A shooting star from the West, which in May sends up a flower stem of about 14 in. surmounted by a cluster of pale lilac-rose flowers. Needs light shade, a moist situation, and loamy soil.

**Douglasia vitaliana.** (Sometimes sold as *Androsace*.) Forms flat mats of narrow, greenish-gray leaves, at blooming time almost completely hidden by the clear, citron-yellow flowers. It should receive moraine treatment.

**Draba aizoides.** Forms dense tufts of spiny-looking rosettes with yellow flowers on stems 2–3 in. high.

**D. olympica.** Similar, with golden-yellow flowers 4 in. high.

The drabas are well adapted for crevice planting — preferably in limestone.

**Dryas octopetala.** A prostrate shrub, its branches clothed with evergreen, tiny, oak-like leaves. The flowers are creamy-white, on 2–3-in. stems, looking something like those of *Anemone sylvestris*. It should be top-dressed in spring with a half-and-half mixture of leaf mold and stone chips.

†**Epilobium nummularifolium.** A carpeting plant 1 in. high with tiny, round, bronzy leaves. The flowers are insignificant. It is a valuable plant to cover the ground where spring-flowering bulbs are planted.

**Erinus alpinus.** A tufted plant with 3–4-in. stems of rosy-purple flowers. It is a biennial or short-lived perennial. Plant in partial shade. Suitable for crevices. There is a form with carmine flowers, and one that is white.

†**Genista sagittalis.** A dwarf shrub which makes a mat of trailing branches with erect, curiously winged twigs, surmounted by yellow pea-like blossoms. It needs a hot, dry situation.

**Gentiana acaulis** has now been divided into five or more distinct species. The segregate known as *G. gentianella* is the one most amenable to cultivation. It requires a deep, rich, well-drained soil and abundance of crushed limestone. The flowers are enormous, of true gentian blue, arising, stemless, from a tuft 1 in. high of deep green foliage. It blooms in May.

†**G. septemfida.** This species, and its many forms, are among the most tolerant of the worth-while gentians. It grows happily in well-drained but rather moist soil, in sun or partial shade. In August it produces clusters of flowers of soft, clear blue, on rather weak 8-in. stems.

This genus contains some of the most valued of alpine plants. The most desirable species are ofttimes difficult of cultivation, while the dowdy, weedy kinds, as usual, will thrive anywhere.

**Gypsophila cerastioides.** A dwarf (2–3 in.), tufted* plant with white flowers, marked with purple lines. It comes from the Himalayas.

†**G. repens.** A trailing species with gray-green foliage, and airy sprays of white, or rose-tinted, small flowers.

†**Helianthemum nummularium.** Sometimes sold as *H. vulgare* and *H. chamaecistus*. There are many garden varieties offered under such names as: *grandiflorum, cupreum, tomentosum, venustum, roseum, stamineum, macranthum*, etc.; all of which are good rock garden plants in sections where the winters are not too severe. Their hardiness is dubious north of Philadelphia. Helianthemums are shrubs of more or less prostrate habit, some with gray and some with green foliage. The individual flowers are fleeting, but are produced in succession over a long period. The color range includes white, yellow, pink, copper, and crimson. They require a well-drained soil, well limed; and a sunny situation. When flowering is over the plants should be lightly sheared to promote a more compact habit. North of Philadelphia the bushes should be protected by covering with evergreen boughs. It is a good plan to root cuttings of young shoots in midsummer and carry them over winter in a cold frame, as a measure of insurance against winter losses, and to replace specimens that have grown too large or become worn out. They may readily be raised from seeds but the seedlings are likely to be variable.

**Hypericum** (*see* St. John's-wort).

---

* Special articles on the subjects indicated by an asterisk (*) will be found at the words so marked.

**H. polyphyllum.** Makes a tuft of slender shoots 6 in. long clothed with small bluish-gray leaves and topped with golden flowers.

**H. reptans.** One of the loveliest. It makes a trailing mat of vivid green with large golden flowers in succession throughout the summer. It comes from Sikkim and sometimes winter-kills* in the vicinity of New York.

**Iberis** (*see* CANDYTUFT).

†**I. sempervirens.** A sprawling evergreen shrub, showy when its white flowers are displayed in May. Admirable for draping over large rocks. Should be lightly sheared after blooming.

†**Iris cristata.** A dwarf, with creeping rhizomes. The leaves are pale green, about 6 in. long. Flowers of pale blue on 3–4-in. stems. There is a white form that is desirable. *I. cristata* does best in partial shade.

**I. gracilipes.** Forms a tuft of narrow, curving leaves, and pinkish-lavender flowers on graceful stems. Give it a gritty soil, with lots of humus, and partial shade.

**I. tectorum.** Rather large for the small rock garden. Strong clumps of leaves with bright lilac flowers on 18-in. stems. Plant in well-drained soil, in sun.

Edelweiss (*Leontopodium alpinum*) in a congenial setting

†**Leontopodium alpinum** (*see* EDELWEISS).

This easily grown plant is reputed to be responsible for many Alpine tragedies, when climbers have lost their footing in the endeavor to pluck its flowers. Its bracts, which look like gray flannel, are said to become white when planted in a soil that is rich in lime. It will grow in any well-drained soil.

**Mentha** (*see* MINT).

†**M. requieni.** A tiny creeper which closely hugs the ground. The leaves are small, orbicular, and emit an aromatic fragrance when bruised. The flowers are almost microscopic, violet in color, produced in late June. A good carpeting plant for a moist spot.

†**Nierembergia rivularis.** A low-growing plant spreading by underground stems. The flowers, almost 2 in. in diameter, 2–3 in. high, white, with a yellow throat, are produced from June until the fall. This sometimes fails to survive the winter out-of-doors in the vicinity of New York. To be on the safe side portions should be dug up and kept in the cold frame over the winter.

**Pentstemon glaber.** Glaucous, bluish leaves; flower spikes 1–2 ft. with large, bright blue or purplish flowers.

**P. heterophyllus.** Green leaves, lance-shaped and linear. Flowers on slender stems 2 ft. or more high. Opalescent, pink, and rose-purple.

**P. rupicolus.** A dwarf (3–6 in.), creeping species from the Cascade Range. Small, blue-green, leathery leaves. Comparatively large red flowers. Needs gritty soil and shade during the hottest part of the day.

**P. unilateralis.** Glaucous, bluish-green leaves; flower stems up to 2 ft. with the blue flowers arranged mostly on one side.

There are many other species of *Pentstemon* suitable for rock garden planting. In general they require gritty soil, and object to moisture during winter. Many of them are not long-lived under cultivation and it is a good plan to propagate a few every year so as to have vigorous young plants coming along to replace those that succumb to the effects of winter.

**Phlox adsurgens.** A westerner with prostrate stems and glossy leaves. The flowers are large, varying from white to deep pink or a combination of these colors. Good drainage and partial shade.

†**P. amoena.** A low, spreading plant with rosy flowers on 6–8-in. stems in early spring.

†**P. divaricata.** Flowers blue in cluster on 12–18-in. stems. The varieties, *laphami* and "Perry's variety," have a longer blooming season. They should be grown in light shade, in soil well supplied with humus.

**P. douglasi.** Forms a small tuft of narrow, pointed leaves, with lilac or white flowers. It is not easy to grow. In wet regions a well-drained, gritty soil and protection from moisture during winter are probably desirable.

†**P. stolonifera.** Makes a trailing mat of light green foliage, spreading by means of reddish runners which root as they grow. Flowers purple in loose, sparse clusters on 6–12-in. stems. Partial shade.

†**P. subulata.** A well-known and easily grown species. The color of the flowers in some forms is rather overwhelming. The varieties: *lilacina*, pale lilac; *alba*, white; and "Vivid" salmon pink are unobjectionable.

**Phyteuma hemisphaericum.** Tufts of grassy foliage, tiny blue flowers in almost globular heads on 3–6-in. stems.

**P. scheuzeri.** Heads of blue flowers on 1-ft., slender, bare stems.

**Polygonum affine.** A trailing species from the Himalayas with evergreen, attractive foliage which assumes bronzy tints in the fall. The deep pink flowers are produced from August to Oct. in dense spikes on 6-in. stems.

†**Potentilla nepalensis.** A species from the Himalayas growing about 2 ft. high, with rose-crimson flowers produced from July to the fall. Its variety *willmottiae* is dwarfer.

†**P. tridentata.** An evergreen about 6 in. high with deep green, leathery leaves, and small white flowers in summer. Sun or shade.

†**P. verna.** Makes a dense mat of foliage, with golden flowers in early spring 3–6 in. high. Needs a sunny, dry situation, and stony soil.

†**Primula auricula.** Thick, mealy leaves, and yellow flowers, with a ring of meal in their throats. Plant in partial shade and mix crushed limestone in the soil. A very variable species.

**P. bulleyana.** A strong-growing species, with leaves like those of Cos lettuce, and red-gold flowers in candelabra tiers on 2-ft. stems in July. Needs a rich, damp, deep soil and light shade.

†**P. denticulata.** Rosettes of strong foliage and rounded heads of soft lilac flowers on 10-in. stems in early spring. Damp, well-drained soil in sun or light shade.

**P. frondosa.** Crinkly leaves, gray with meal on the under sides. Pink flowers in loose heads on 3–4-in. stems. Partial shade.

†**P. japonica.** A "lettuce-leaved" type with tiers of flowers, on 2-ft. stems. The color varies from white to magenta.

---

* Special articles on the subjects indicated by an asterisk (*) will be found at the words so marked.

The deep crimson forms are most desirable.

If the soil is really wet they grow well in full sun; otherwise they should be planted in partial shade.

Primula is one of the largest alpine genera. There are hundreds of species suitable for rock gardens, but unfortunately many of them are difficult under cultivation.

†**Pulsatilla vulgaris.** Often sold under the name of *Anemone pulsatilla*. It has large, rich purple flowers, with masses of golden stamens.* Each flower is surrounded by a lacy ruff of gray-green, hairy bracts.* Its achenes* with long feathery styles prolong its attractiveness after the blossoms have fallen. It is more in keeping with the rest of the rock garden plants if grown in poor soil with plenty of crushed limestone — in rich soils it grows too lush.

**Ramondia nathaliae.** Rosettes of glossy green; flowers lavender-blue with four-lobed corolla.

**R. pyrenaica.** Rosettes dull green, with many rufous hairs; flowers purple, corolla with five lobes.

The ramondias are among the choicest alpine plants. They should be planted in rock crevices, facing north in deep, peaty soil, with the rosettes flat against the rocks so that no water may lodge in the centers of them.

†**Saponaria ocymoides.** A trailing species with myriads of pink flowers. Valuable for draping rocks in full sun. Needs a well-drained soil.

†**Saxifraga aizoon.** A species, with lime-encrusted leaves, which runs into dozens of varieties, with white, pink-spotted, or yellowish flowers and silvery leaves.

Plant in gritty soil on a north slope or in shade of large rocks.

**S. apiculata.** This forms a cushion made up of innumerable tiny rosettes of evergreen, strap-shaped leaves. The flowers, of primrose yellow, are in loose heads on 3–4-in. stems. Shade during hottest part of day. Moraine soil with ⅓ humus; plenty of water in early spring.

**S. cochlearis.** One of the "encrusted" group, with rosettes of reflexed, silvery leaves, and 6–8-in. sprays of pure white blossoms. Plant on north side of large rock in deep soil mixed with crushed limestone.

†**S. decipiens.** A variable species, with many garden hybrids. Flowers of the type are white — the hybrids vary from white to crimson. It is one of the "mossy" saxifrages. This group requires a deep, gritty soil with ⅓ humus and partial shade. Small stones should be laid on the soil about the plants to conserve moisture and keep the ground cool. Keep a stock of young plants coming along — propagating them by taking off rosettes in Aug. and inserting them in sand and humus in a shaded cold frame.

†**S. hosti.** When happy, forms cushions made up of rosettes of silvery, encrusted leaves. The flowers are white on 12–18-in. stems.

†**S. macnabiana.** It has a 12–18-in. panicle* of white flowers, speckled with crimson dots. One of the easiest of this group to grow. *See* illust., page 684.

**S. moschata.** A dwarf, spreading "mossy" with many varieties ranging in color from creamy-white to red.

**S. oppositifolia.** Makes prostrate mats of tiny foliage with flowers that, in many varieties, tend toward magenta in color. Here in the vicinity of New York it is difficult to grow it beyond the seedling stage. It needs cool conditions, a stony soil and lots of water in spring.

There are hundreds of species and varieties of *Saxifraga* suitable for rock gardens. Such species as *S. hosti* and *aizoon* run into scores of varieties and hybrids. With the increasing interest in rock gardening in America, and more knowledge concerning their culture in our varied climate, considerably more than the sixty or so varieties now offered by some specialists may be expected to be listed in their catalogues.

†**Sedum acre.** Dwarf, fleshy, bright green leaves and golden flowers. Should be used with discretion as it is potentially a pernicious weed, because any portion of the plant that is broken off and left lying on the ground is liable to form a new colony.

†**S. album.** Evergreen ground cover with tiny sausage-like leaves and pure white flowers in July.

†**S. dasyphyllum.** One of the most delightful sedums. Compact clusters of almost globular, blue-gray leaves on 2–3-in. stems. It has loose heads of white or rose-tinted flowers. Will thrive in a shallow soil.

†**S. reflexum.** Mats of narrow, fleshy leaves, with 8-in. stems surmounted by heads of yellow flowers in July.

†**S. sarmentosum.** Too vigorous and invasive a grower for the small garden. Trailing shoots, clothed with fleshy, green leaves. The flowers are yellow. Will grow in part shade.

†**S. sexangulare.** Stems 2–3 in. high, densely clothed with narrow, cylindrical leaves. Flowers yellow.

†**S. spurium.** A trailing evergreen with flat leaves and pinkish flowers. The deeply colored var. *coccineum* is preferable.

**Sempervivum** (*see* HOUSELEEK).

†**S. arachnoideum.** The small rosettes are covered with woolly strands. Attractive at all times and especially so when displaying its starry red flowers on 6–8-in. stems. The size attained by this and other species is determined largely by the character of the soil in which they are growing. In poor, stony soil the rosettes are small, and increase in size if planted in rich, porous earth.

†**S. calcareum.** Bluish-green rosettes 2 in. in diameter — each leaf tipped with reddish-brown. Flowers light red on stems up to 1 ft. A distinct species.

†**S. fauconnetti.** A small edition of *S. arachnoideum* but not so cobwebby. In poor soils the rosettes may be not more than ⅛ in. in diameter.

†**S. soboliferum.** Globular rosettes with numerous pill-like offsets* attached by short, slender threads which break and allow the offsets to roll away and form new colonies.

According to Correvon, Dr. Jordan of Lyons, France, claimed to have in his garden 6000 different forms of *Sempervivum*.

**Silene acaulis.** Forms dense cushions of tightly packed rosettes of tiny, pointed leaves. Collected plants from the Italian Alps may have the foliage almost completely hidden by the rose-pink flowers, but it is a shy bloomer under cultivation. Plant in moraine.

†**S. alpestris.** Low, dense masses of shining green foliage and myriads of pure white flowers on branching stems 6 in. high. A grand plant for sun or partial shade.

†**S. schafta.** Leafy tufts, with rose-pink flowers produced over a long period in late summer and early fall.

†**Thymus serpyllum.** A useful, fragrant ground cover for sunny situations, especially in limy soils. The flowers vary in color from white to rose-purple on erect stems a few inches high. A distinct form known as var. *lanuginosus* with gray, woolly leaves is desirable.

†**Tunica saxifraga.** A tufted* plant with airy foliage on thin, wiry stems which are surmounted by tiny, pink, dianthus-like flowers. It is in bloom from May to Nov. and is especially valuable in poor soils in hot, dry situations.

†**Veronica gentianoides.** A strong-growing kind with low, leafy tufts of glossy green foliage and foot-high spires of large, pale blue flowers. Does best in fairly good soil.

†**V. incana.** Has silvery-gray leaves and 8–12-in. spikes of small violet-blue flowers. Worth growing for foliage alone. Dryish, well-drained soil.

†**V. pectinata.** Prostrate mats of hoary, deeply toothed leaves. There is a rose-colored form and one that has blue flowers. Grows well in partial shade.

†**V. repens.** A creeper barely 1 in. high with small, egg-

---

* Special articles on the subjects indicated by an asterisk (*) will be found at the words so marked.

shaped, glossy leaves. Pale blue, almost white flowers arising just above the foliage. A delightful, tolerant plant which, however, prefers partial shade and moist soil.

†**V. spicata.** A variable species in general appearance similar to *V. incana* but with green leaves.

†**V. teucrium.** Grows rather too large (20 in.) for the small rock garden. It is a handsome, lush-looking plant with profuse spikes of large, rich blue flowers. There is a form commonly sold as *rupestris* (probably referable to *V. teucrium dubia*) which is preferable for rock garden planting. This forms low mats with spikes of flowers 3–4 in. high which may be almost any color from white to rose and deep blue.

†**Viola cornuta.** An alpine pansy of which there are many garden varieties. The flowers of pale violet are produced throughout the summer. The *var.* George Wermig has deep violet flowers and the *var.* **alba** has pure white flowers. Rich, well-drained soil and partial shade.

BULBS, CORMS, AND TUBERS. Many of the smaller growing bulbs, which are difficult to accommodate in the flower border, find ideal quarters in the rock garden, and may with propriety be used there. *Colchicum, Crocus, Erythronium,* etc., contain alpine representatives. Following is a list of kinds which are not difficult.

**Chionodoxa luciliae**
**C. sardensis**
  Beautiful and easy; among the first flowers of spring.
**Colchicum autumnale**
**C. speciosum**
  Valuable for their fall blooms. The foliage, which appears in spring, is coarse and unattractive.
**Crocus** (spring-flowering)
  **C. biflorus**
  **C. susianus**
**Crocus** (autumn-flowering)
  **C. speciosus,** and varieties. These are the showiest of the fall crocuses.
  **C. zonatus**
  Fall-blooming crocuses should be planted as soon as the corms are obtainable in Aug. or Sept. They are valuable because they bloom at a time when rock garden flowers are scarce.
**Eranthis hyemalis**
**Erythronium americanum**
  **E. johnsoni**
  **E. revolutum**
  Erythroniums should be planted in shade in well-drained soil, rich in humus.
**Fritillaria meleagris.** The curious, checkered, pendent flowers are interesting and beautiful.
**Galanthus nivalis.** *See* SNOWDROP.
**G. elwesi**
  Valuable for giving early bloom in partially shaded places.
**Leucojum vernum.** *See* SNOWFLAKE.
**Lilium.** The small lilies, such as *L. tenuifolium,* may be used to advantage.
**Muscari botryoides**
  **M. botryoides album**
  **Muscari** Heavenly Blue
**Narcissus bulbocodium**
  **N. cyclamineus**
  **N. minor**
  **N. minor minimus.** This grows only 3 in. high.
  **N. triandrus** and varieties.
  The above are all good rock garden plants. Strong-growing varieties of *Narcissus* should be kept to the flower border or naturalized.
**Scilla sibirica.** When planted in masses provides sheets of deep blue color.
**Sternbergia lutea.** Bright yellow goblet-like flowers in Sept. Needs a well-drained, sunny, sheltered spot.

**Tulipa.** Most of the small wild tulips may be used in the rock garden. The following are desirable species:
  T. clusiana
  T. dasystemon
  T. kaufmanniana
  T. linifolia
  T. persica

DWARF TREES AND SHRUBS
Evergreen:
  **Arctostaphylos uva-ursi.** Trailer, 4–5 in.; sandy soil.
  **Berberis verruculosa**
  **Chamaecyparis obtusa compacta**
  **Cotoneaster dammeri.** Prostrate habit.
  **Daphne cneorum**
  **Erica carnea**
  **Euonymus radicans minimus.** Low, sprawly climber.
  **Hedera helix conglomerata.** A dwarf, semi-upright form of English ivy.
  **Juniperus excelsa stricta.** Upright.
  **J. horizontalis douglasi.** Trailing.
  **J. squamata meyeri.** Spreading.
  **Picea glauca conica.** *See* SPRUCE.
  **Pieris floribunda.** Peaty soil.
  **Pinus mugo.** *See* PINE.
  **Rhododendron ferrugineum**
  **Thuja occidentalis ellwangeriana**
  **T. orientalis sieboldi**
  **Vaccinium vitis-idaea.** Peaty soil.

DECIDUOUS
  **Cotoneaster adpressa**
  **C. horizontalis.** For large rock gardens.

ANNUALS
  **Androsace lactiflora**
  **Ionopsidium acaule**
  **Linaria maroccana**
  **Mesembryanthemum lineare**
  **Nemophila insignis**
  **Sanvitalia procumbens**
  **Sedum coeruleum**
  **S. hispanicum**

All of the plants in the lists will be found at their proper entries elsewhere in THE GARDEN DICTIONARY, and should be sought there for additional information. The recently organized American Rock Garden Society welcomes members interested in the growing of these charming plants of the mountains and rocky ledges. It may be addressed through the Garden Editor, Houghton Mifflin Company, Boston, Mass. — M. F.

**ROCK GOLDENROD** = *Solidago canadensis.* See GOLDENROD.

**ROCK JASMINE** = *Androsace.*

**ROCK PHOSPHATE.** See Phosphoric Acid at FERTILIZERS.

**ROCK PINK** = *Talinum calycinum.*

**ROCK PURSLANE.** See CALANDRINIA.

**ROCKROSE.** See CISTUS.

**ROCKROSE FAMILY** = Cistaceae.

**ROCK SAXIFRAGE** = *Saxifraga virginiensis.*

**ROCK SPRAY** = *Cotoneaster microphylla.*

**ROCKWORK.** See ROCK GARDEN.

**ROCKY MOUNTAIN BEE-PLANT** = *Cleome serrulata.*

**ROCKY MOUNTAIN FIR** = *Abies lasiocarpa.* See FIR.

**ROCKY MOUNTAIN FLOWERING RASPBERRY** = *Rubus deliciosus.*

---

\* Special articles on the subjects indicated by an asterisk (\*) will be found at the words so marked.

**ROCKY MOUNTAIN RED CEDAR** = *Juniperus scopulorum.*

**ROCKY MOUNTAIN YELLOW PINE** = *Pinus ponderosa scopulorum.* See PINE.

**ROD.** See WEIGHTS AND MEASURES, 2.

**RODGERSIA** (rod-jer'si-a). Hardy herbaceous perennials comprising about 8 species of the family Saxifragaceae and natives of China and Japan. They have spreading rootstocks which are thick and black. Leaves, long-stalked, large, alternate,* simple or compound,* bronze-green in color. Leaves of some species are cut into finger-like segments, while others have leaflets in pairs. Flowers small, numerous, greenish-white, in large, showy, terminal clusters to 1 ft. long, similar to *Astilbe.* Calyx of 5 sepals, usually greenish-white. Corolla usually absent. Stamens* 10. Fruit a dry capsule. (Named for a Commodore Rodgers, U.S.N.)

These strong-growing plants, with their feathery flower clusters make good plants for the half-shady border where they must be allowed plenty of space. Though considered hardy in the northern states they are benefited by a light covering in the winter. They require plenty of water and prefer peaty soil. Propagated by division of the rootstocks in March or April.

**podophylla.** Strong-growing plant to 5 ft. high, with scaly rootstocks. Leaves large, divided into 3 finger-like lobes with toothed margins. Flowers small, yellowish-white, in terminal clusters, 1 ft. long. China.

**tabularis.** Grows to 3 ft. Leaves long-stalked, roundish, the margins being deeply cut into teeth-like segments. Flowers white, numerous, in terminal clusters. China.

**ROGUE, ROGUING.** In a population of normal plants there are often a few non-typical ones. Usually, as *rogue* has come to be used, these are inferior or diseased or stunted or otherwise undesirable. Getting rid of them is called *roguing,* a very common practice among plant breeders, pathologists, and done every day by ordinary gardeners. It is a process of selection by elimination. See Eradication at PLANT DISEASES.

**ROHDEA** (rō'dee-a). Tender perennials comprising only one species, but of many varieties, from Japan and China, belonging to the family Liliaceae. Much interest is shown in these plants in China and Japan, where they are cult. extensively. They make useful house plants if kept in a cool position. The only species is **R. japonica,** with a long and round rootstock. Leaves basal, green, leathery, upright, 18–24 in. long, and 3 in. wide, 9–12 arranged in a rosette. Flowers on a short, thick, leafless stalk, in short dense spikes, hidden by the leaves. Fruit a berry, with red pulp, usually 1-seeded. (Named for Mich. Rohde, physician and botanist of Bremen.) Grown chiefly as a foliage plant, as its flower cluster is inconspicuous and resembles an aroid.*

**ROLFS, P. H.** See America at GARDEN BOOKS.

**ROLLER.** See Section 3, TOOLS AND IMPLEMENTS.

**ROLLING.** An agricultural operation, rarely used in the garden, having for its object the smoothing of the harrowed land, and especially designed to break up lumps of soil. Such rolling needs a power or horse roller of at least 1000 pounds weight. For lawn rolling see LAWNS.

**ROLLING OF LEAVES.** Many diseased leaves show a tendency to have their margins rolled, mostly the result of a virus disease. See Virus Diseases at PLANT DISEASES. See also REVOLUTA.

**ROMAINE LETTUCE** = *Lactuca sativa longifolia.* For culture see LETTUCE.

**ROMAN GARDENS.** See GARDEN HISTORY.

**ROMAN HYACINTH** = *Hyacinthus orientalis albulus.*

**ROMAN NETTLE** = *Urtica pilulifera.* See NETTLE.

**ROMAN WORMWOOD** = *Artemisia pontica.*

**ROMANZOFFIA** (ro-man-zoff'i-a). A small genus of low, perennial herbs of the family Hydrophyllaceae, found in western N.A., one of them, **R. sitchensis,** providing an attractive white-flowered plant for edging. It is scarcely over 6 in. high, the rootstock bearing small tubers. Leaves mostly basal, roundish or heart-shaped. Flowers small, white, borne in a small terminal cluster (raceme*) at the end of a stalk which arises from the ground. Easily grown in any ordinary garden soil and propagated by division of the rootstocks. (Named for Count Nicholas Romanzoff, a Russian nobleman.)

**ROME BEAUTY.** An apple variety. See APPLE.

**ROMNEYA** (rom'nee-a). Tender perennial herbs or subshrubs, comprising 2 species from Calif. and Mex., belonging to the poppy family. They grow to 8 ft. high, have spreading rootstocks and branching stems. Leaves in pairs, stalked, broadly lance-shaped, deeply lobed, to 4 in. long. Flowers solitary, at the ends of the branches, white, to 6 in. across. Calyx of 3 sepals. Corolla of 6 petals, all alike. Stamens* numerous. Fruit a many-seeded capsule.* (Named for T. Romney Robinson, who discovered the species below.)

Romneyas make beautiful garden plants, but are difficult to establish, unless grown in pots and transplanted without too much disturbance of the roots. They are sometimes grown as greenhouse plants in the northern states. May be propagated by seeds, which are best sown as soon as ripe. Seeds should be sown on the surface of a mixture of fine, sandy peat in well-drained pans under a bell-jar in a temperature of 55°–60°. As soon as large enough to handle they should be transplanted into separate pots containing a similar mixture. Roots should be disturbed as little as possible. When well established they may be transplanted to permanent positions in sunny, well-drained borders, which have been treated with peat and sand. To move well-established plants, cut well down.

**coulteri.** Matilija poppy. California tree poppy. Grows to 8 ft., much-branched above. Leaves thin, paper-like. Flowers white, to 6 in. across, solitary. Calif. and Mex.

**RONDELETIA** (ron-de-lee'shi-a). A genus of over 80 species of tropical American, evergreen shrubs and trees of the family Rubiaceae, the two below (and perhaps others) grown for ornament. They have generally opposite* leaves, rarely in whorls of 3. Flowers tubular, the limb 5-lobed (in ours), showy, crowded in dense clusters mostly from the leaf-axils.* Stamens* 4–5. Fruit a many-seeded capsule.* (Named for William Rondelet, French naturalist.)

The rondeletias are handsome shrubs, well-liked in zones* 8 and 9 for their profusion of orange or red or pink flowers, and handsome foliage. They grow well outdoors in a variety of soils and may be propagated by cuttings of half-ripened wood. They are also to be grown northward in the warm-temperate greenhouse (see GREENHOUSE), in potting mixture* 5.

**cordata.** A shrub, 5–7 ft. high. Leaves oblongish or ovalish, 3–5 in. long, practically without hairs. Flowers pink or rose-red, about ¼ in. wide, hairy on the outside, the throat yellow-bearded. Guatemala.

**odorata.** A shrub 4–6 ft. high. Leaves ovalish or oblong, 1–2 in. long, the margins rolled. Flowers about ½ in. wide, orange-red, but yellow-throated. Panama and Cuba. The best known of the rondeletias and sometimes offered as *R. speciosa.*

**speciosa** = *Rondeletia odorata.*

**ROOF GARDEN.** For an account of the development of the ancient roof gardens see GARDEN HISTORY. The modern development of gardens on the roof, or on terraces, has come mostly in cities where the height of buildings has forced "set-backs" every ten stories or so. The use of such terraces and the roof itself as a garden site has been widely adopted in most large cities. For the details of planting, design, maintenance, etc., of such gardens see PENTHOUSE GARDEN.

**ROOF HOUSELEEK** = *Sempervivum tectorum.* See HOUSELEEK.

**ROOF IRIS** = *Iris tectorum.*

**ROOM PLANTS.** See HOUSE PLANTS.

---

* Special articles on the subjects indicated by an asterisk (*) will be found at the words so marked.

**ROOT.** The organ that gathers most of the food of the plant from the soil, and, in epiphytes,* some from the air (*see also* VELAMEN). From the gardening standpoint, the root is the underground food-gathering organ, but technically, and also practically, it is much more. A proper understanding of its function and structure may avoid many common garden mistakes, especially in dealing with woody plants.

A much magnified root showing the root hairs, which are the real food gatherers.

Practically all the larger, easily seen ramifications of roots are functionally inactive as food gatherers. They are of greatest use, however, as conductors of the food gathered by parts of the root system not so easily seen, and as anchors. The food gatherers are the tiny root hairs or tips, most of which are provided with a relatively hardened root cap. The latter more easily penetrates the soil than the root hair itself, but it is the root hair that functions as the actual absorber of plant food.

It is for this reason that nurserymen root prune woody plants. By reducing the amount of mere conducting roots (the larger ones) they force the plant to produce a greater number of root hairs. This relatively compact mass of small roots, with their much greater profusion of food-gathering root hairs, greatly eases the shock of transplanting woody plants. For tuber and tuberous root see TUBER.

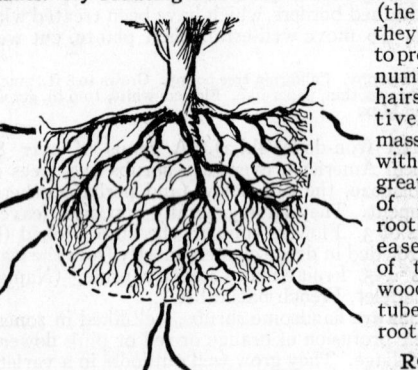

Root pruning. The roots beyond the dotted line should be cut off to promote the growth of feeding roots near the stem.

**ROOT-BOUND** = Pot-bound.

**ROOT CAP.** See ROOT.

**ROOT CROPS.** Among the common root crops, all the subjects of special articles, are carrot, turnip, parsnip, onion, beet, potato, and sweet potato. The term thus includes underground crops other than those derived from true roots, because the potato is a tuber, and the onion a bulb. Popular usage, however, will continue to call these underground crops *root* crops, whether true roots or not. Other less known root crops are salsify* and skirret.*

**ROOT CUTTING.** See CUTTING.

**ROOT DIVISION.** See DIVISION.

**ROOTERY.** A somewhat fanciful name for an uprooted tree, the roots and soil of which are used as a planting site.

**ROOT GALL.** An abnormal swelling on the roots of plants usually caused by disease or nematodes. See Root-knot at PLANT DISEASES. There are many plants, especially in the pea family, that bear tubercles or nodules that may be mistaken for root galls. But tubercles or nodules of this sort are beneficial.

**ROOT GRAFTING.** See GRAFTING.

**ROOT HAIR.** See ROOT.

**ROOT HARDY.** Hardy only because the root survives. Many plants, killed to the ground every year, survive because their roots only are hardy. See HARDINESS.

**ROOT-KNOT.** See Root-knot at PLANT DISEASES. See also the diseases at PEONY.

**ROOT MAGGOTS.** For a description of these pests *see* Two-winged Flies at INSECT PESTS. They are controlled by corrosive sublimate. For the details see Contact Spray at INSECTICIDES.

**ROOT PRUNING.** Root pruning scarcely needs explanation, and in the garden it is rarely necessary to practice it, except where ornamental trees have become too rapacious by invading flower borders or the vegetable garden. The maple, for example, is apt to send out masses of fibrous roots fairly close to the surface, and assuming these roots get beyond the legitimate bounds, the gardener, in defense of his cherished plants, must from time to time put a check upon their ramifications, especially if the offending tree happens to be in a neighboring garden or lot. By digging a trench 18 or 24 inches deep, six or more feet from the tree, any thong-like roots from which the fibrous mass is produced may be cut and the unwanted fibers afterwards taken out. To stop further invasions a corrugated iron or cement barrier may be set in the trench.

Root pruning of fruit trees to make them fruitful is an old-time practice, and where an established tree of some size is not responsive to fair treatment except in the way of making wild and useless wood, it may be assumed that the tree has more roots than are good for it. As a rule such a tree has a tap or central root and none too many fibrous roots near the surface. By carefully excavating around the tree one can find whether there are any large anchor roots. The severing of these should be accomplished so that the cut surface is uppermost, but with large trees this should not be done close to the tree. Do not damage any thin or fibrous roots. Failure to find any fair-sized roots around the tree is almost a sure indication that a wild tap root must be got at and severed. This work should be done in the late fall. The arduous task of root pruning is not recommended unless the tree is worth the effort, as the Lorette system of pruning (*see* PRUNING), will in a season or two make the tree see the error of its ways.

Root pruning of ornamental trees and shrubs is a more common, and truly essential practice in nurseries, inasmuch as all the stock grown is for future sales. Anyone who has attempted to lift cedars, dogwoods and other trees from the wild will have noted that the roots are disproportionate to their size compared with well-grown nursery stock of the same size. Indeed, there is but a slim chance of wildings above two or three feet surviving. The reason is that wildings have stood from the seed stage in one spot undisturbed, and consequently have made a few heavy roots rather than a mass of fibrous ones. The nursery stock, raised from seed, cutting or graft, is encouraged to make fibrous roots by the process of lining out in the field. A year or two later the young plants are lifted and set further apart, and before they reach specimen size they may be shifted several times, or, if set wider apart in the first place to avoid transplanting, they are treated to a root-pruning process by means of a machine, the blade of which passes beneath them at a certain depth and severs all delving roots. This lifting or root-pruning process is carried on with both evergreen and deciduous material until of specimen size. Deciduous trees cannot profitably be lifted and transplanted after they reach a large size, and they become a liability unless they can be taken up with a ball of soil by special machines. Temperamental deciduous trees, like magnolias and dogwoods, must also be lifted with a ball after they are three or four years old, and all evergreens, both coniferous and broad-leaved, after the lining-out stage are invariably lifted with a ball. The more shifts such plants undergo, the more matted is the root ball. See Ball and Burlap at PLANTING. See also the second illustration at ROOT.

---

* Special articles on the subjects indicated by an asterisk (*) will be found at the words so marked.

In the garden, most evergreens, even after being established some years, still retain the matted ball of roots and may be shifted with such if the facilities for moving such heavy weights are available. Deciduous shrubs of movable size can be prepared for transplanting to a new spot by forcing a sharp spade around and fairly close to the stems. Done during summer, this will encourage more fibrous roots and make shifting in the fall rather easier. Moving very large specimens, however, is not a practical proposition for the gardener, while it is practically useless to attempt shifting large magnolias. — T. A. W.

**ROOT ROT.** *See* Diseases at CALLA LILY, PANSY, PEA, and SWEET PEA.

**ROOTSTOCK.** The word has two distinct meanings to the gardener. Most fruit culturists and those interested in grafting use *rootstock* as the term for the underground *stock* upon which a desirable variety has been grafted.

Much more commonly, a rootstock is the usually swollen, but more or less elongated underground stem of a perennial herb, common examples being the rootstocks of the iris and Solomon's-seal. Botanists usually call a rootstock a rhizome.

Because a rootstock is usually an underground organ, many people mistakenly call it a root. But it is a storage organ and not a food gatherer, and therefore not a root. Most rootstocks have quite obvious roots attached to them.

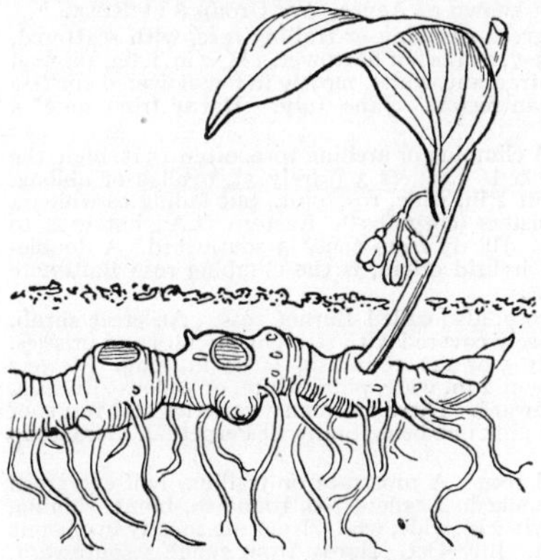

A rootstock is an underground stem provided with eyes (buds) for next season's growth, and with roots for food gathering.

The practical garden advantage of a rootstock is great. Most of them can be easily divided in the spring or fall, thus serving as the easiest method of propagation. This is possible because all rootstocks (being stem organs) bear buds from which the new plant will sprout. Roots bear no buds so that divided roots will usually not produce new plants.

All underground stems are not rootstocks. *See* BULB, CORM, and TUBER.

**ROOT TIP.** *See* ROOT.

**ROOT WORM.** *See* Insect Pests at CRANBERRY and ROSE.

**ROPE BARK** = *Dirca palustris.*

**ROQUETTE** = *Eruca sativa.*

**RORIPA** (ror'ri-pa). A large genus of botanically much confused herbs, chiefly Eurasian, and belonging to the mustard family. Of the 50 known species only **R. nasturtium-aquaticum,** the watercress, is of any hort. interest. It is a creeping or floating aquatic perennial, growing mostly in cold waters, its foliage furnishing a pleasantly pungent salad. Leaves deeply cut or even compound,* the terminal leaflet or segment larger than the others. Flowers white, very small, in long terminal clusters (for details *see* CRUCIFERAE). Fruit a curved, slender pod (silique*), the tip beaked. For cult. *see* WATERCRESS. For a plant sometimes called *Roripa armoracia see* HORSE-RADISH. (*Roripa* is an unexplained name.)

**ROSA** (rō'za). Rose. A genus of shrubs or vines, comprising all the true roses, and typifying the family Rosaceae. According to the usual concept of them there may be 200 true species of roses, but one authority has credited to Eurasia alone over 4000 species. In any case, the differences between species, even the few below, are mainly technical, and it seems better here to direct attention only to their more obvious characters. They have been selected from over 75 species known to be cult. in America, with two things in mind. (1) Their beauty, or ease of cult.; or (2) Because they have entered into the main hort. groups of roses treated at ROSE. At the latter entry also is grouped all information on rose culture, and there also is a list of the best-known forms or horticultural varieties. The number of these forms runs into the thousands, but many are little known today, some are worthless, and a few, while popular for a year or two, are probably destined to oblivion.

*Rosa*, as a genus, comprises prickly shrubs or vines with alternate,* compound* leaves, the leaflets arranged feather-fashion, and always with an odd one at the end. The prickles may be hooked or straight. Flowers solitary or in small clusters, typically with 5 petals in wild, single roses, but much doubled in most of the hort. forms, nearly always fragrant. Stamens* numerous. Pistils* numerous, enclosed at the base in a cup-shaped receptacle,* which enlarges in fruit, becomes fleshy and berry-like (the familiar rose hip) and encloses the true fruits which are bony achenes.* (*Rosa* is the old Latin name of the rose.)

For culture *see* ROSE. All the species below have single flowers unless otherwise noted. They represent wild species of roses from which, with others, all the beautiful horticultural forms have been derived, mostly by a complicated history of breeding and selection. Some of them are not hardy in the North, although their hort. descendants are often perfectly so, due to selection or breeding. Wherever possible the hort. forms, which have originated from any of the species are noted, although the parentage of some of our finest cult. varieties is in much confusion. Even the wild species below are known to hybridize naturally. Mostly May or June flowering, unless otherwise noted.

**alba.** A hybrid rose of unknown origin, 4–6 ft. high, the prickles hooked. Leaflets usually 5, broadly elliptic, 2–2½ in. long. Flowers usually double, about 3 in. wide, white or pinkish. The unusually fragrant *var.* **suaveolens** is little known here but is the chief source of attar of roses in southern Eu., for which it is much cult.

**anemoneflora.** A climbing rose with few, small and hooked prickles. Leaves almost evergreen, the 3–5 leaflets narrowly ovalish, 2–3 in. long. Flowers about 1½ in. wide, white and double, the inner petals shorter than the outer ones. China. Hardy from zone* 5 southward.

**arvensis.** A trailing rose with scattered prickles. Leaflets generally 7, ovalish, 1–1½ in. long. Flowers about 1½ in. wide, white, not fragrant, in small clusters. Eu. June–July. Hardy from zone* 3 southward. The *var.* **ayreshirea**, the Ayreshire rose, is a more vigorous plant. Double-flowered plants, sometimes classed as Ayreshire roses, are apparently hybrids.

**banksiae.** Banks or Lady Bank's rose. A beautiful, climbing, evergreen rose, often 15–20 ft. high, with a few hooked prickles or none. Leaflets 3–5 (rarely 7), elliptic-oval, 1½–2½ in. long. Flowers in profuse clusters (umbels*), a little fragrant, white or yellow, not over 1 in. wide. China; naturalized in the southern states. June–Aug. Hardy from zone* 6 southward. *See* Group 7 at ROSE.

**blanda.** A native rose, 4–6 ft. high, its slender stems mostly without prickles, but often bristly. Leaflets 5–7 (rarely 9), elliptic-oblong, 1½–2½ in. long. Flowers pink, about 2 in. wide, usually solitary, but sometimes in few-flowered clusters. Eastern N.A. Hardy from zone* 2 southward.

**borboniana.** Bourbon rose. A famous hybrid rose, derived from crossing the Provence with the China rose, and since, with successive crossing, the origin of many Hybrid Perpetual or Remontant roses. It is an upright shrub with prickly and bristly stems. Leaflets 7, ovalish or narrower. Flowers usually purple, double or nearly so, about 3 in. wide. July–Sept. Hardy, at least in some of its forms, from zone* 3 southward. *See* Group 5 at ROSE.

**bracteata.** Macartney rose. A trailing or partly climbing, evergreen rose, with stout, hooked prickles. Leaflets 5–9, elliptic or broader toward the tip, 1½–2 in. long, shining above. Flower solitary, white, about 3 in. wide, beneath it a series of conspicuously toothed bracts.* China, but naturalized from Va. to Fla. and Tex. Aug. Hardy from zone* 6 southward. *See* Group 7 at ROSE.

**brunoni.** Himalayan musk rose. A partially climbing rose with stout, short, hooked prickles. Leaflets 5–7, elliptic or oblongish, 2–2½ in. long. Flowers white, very fragrant, nearly 2 in. wide, in many-flowered clusters (corymbs*). Himalayas. June–July. Hardy from zone* 6 southward. Often mistaken for, and offered as, the true musk rose (*R. moschata*).

**canina.** Dog rose. A shrubby rose 6–9 ft. high, the stems arching, and furnished with stout hooked prickles. Leaflets 5–7, ovalish or elliptic, 1–1½ in. long. Flowers nearly 2 in. wide, white or pink, solitary or in few-flowered clusters. Eu. Hardy from zone* 4 southward. The plant is much used for propagating stock.

**carolina.** Pasture rose. A native rose, the erect stems not usually over 3 ft. high, bristly and with slender, straight prickles. Leaflets 5 (rarely 7), ⅝–1¼ in. long. Flowers usually solitary, rose-pink, about 2 in. wide. Eastern U.S. June–July. Hardy from zone* 3 southward. One of the best of our native roses and good for the shrub border.

* Special articles on the subjects indicated by an asterisk (*) will be found at the words so marked.

**cathayensis.** A Chinese rose, considered by some as only a variety of *R. multiflora*, but important as the source of several widely grown hort. forms. It is a climbing or somewhat trailing rose with hooked prickles. Leaflets mostly 5–7, oblongish, ¾–1½ in. long. Flowers about 1¼ in. wide, numerous, in many-flowered, flattish clusters, pink or rose, and fragrant. China. June–July. Hardy from zone* 3 southward. The *var.* **platyphylla** has larger leaflets, deeper pink flowers, and is the probable origin of the Seven Sisters Rose and the Crimson Rambler (but *see* R. MULTIFLORA). *See* Group 6 at ROSE.

**centifolia.** Cabbage rose. An upright rose, 4–6 ft. high, with creeping rootstocks, the stems both prickly and bristly. Leaflets mostly 5, hairy both sides, 1½–2 in. long. Flowers double, nearly 3 in. wide, solitary, nodding, pink and fragrant. Caucasus. June–July. Hardy from zone* 3 southward. A very old rose, known since ancient times, and found in many varieties. One of them is the *var.* **muscosa,** the moss rose, which has the flower stalk and calyx* sticky and mossy.

**cherokeensis** = *Rosa laevigata.*

**chinensis.** China rose; also called the Bengal rose. An upright, partly evergreen rose, not over 3 ft. high, the stems with a few, somewhat hooked prickles, occasionally unarmed. Leaflets 3–5, broadly oval, 2–2½ in. long, shining green above, paler below. Flowers usually solitary, rarely long-stalked, about 2 in. wide, crimson to pink or even white. China. July–Oct. Hardy from zone* 6 southward. An important species because it is the origin of many hort. forms. The *var.* **manetti,** the Manetti rose (by some considered a variety of *R. noisettiana*) has been widely used as stock for many tea roses. The *var.* **minima,** the fairy rose, is a dwarf shrub, rarely over 18 in. high with small, single or double, rose-red flowers. From this and other plants has come the Baby Rambler. The *var.* **semperflorens,** the Chinese monthly rose, has usually solitary, crimson or deep pink flowers. The *var.* **viridiflora,** the green rose, has its petals and sepals transformed into green leaves. *See* Group 5 at ROSE.

**cinnamomea.** Cinnamon rose. An erect shrub 4–6 ft. high, with short, hooked prickles, or unarmed. Leaflets 5–7, elliptic or oblongish, 1–1½ in. long, densely hairy beneath. Flowers about 2 in. wide, fragrant, purplish-red, solitary or only a few in the cluster. Eurasia, occasionally an escape* in the eastern U.S. Hardy from zone* 3 southward.

**damascena.** Damask rose. An erect shrub, 5–7 ft. high, the stems with hooked prickles and sometimes also bristly. Leaflets 5 (rarely 7), ovalish or oblong, 2–2½ in. long. Flowers double, pink or red, fragrant, mostly in loose clusters (corymbs*). Asia Minor (?). June–July. Hardy from zone* 4 southward. Cult. in Eu. as a source of attar of roses. *See* HERB GARDENING. The *var.* **versicolor,** the York and Lancaster Rose, has white-striped, semi-double flowers, or some white and some pink flowers on the same bush. It gets its name from the houses of York and Lancaster who wore the contrasting colors in their Wars of the Roses.

**eglanteria.** The eglantine or sweetbrier. A much-branched shrub, 5–8 ft. high, with pleasantly aromatic foliage, the stems bristly, and with strongly hooked prickles. Leaflets 5–7, nearly round or broadly oval, about 1 in. long, sticky. Flowers nearly 2 in. wide, pink, generally solitary. Eu., commonly naturalized in the U.S. Hardy throughout. Long known as *R. rubiginosa.*

**foetida.** Austrian brier. An erect or arching shrub, 7–10 ft. high, the stems with straight prickles. Leaflets 5–9, broadly ovalish, 1–1½ in. long. Flowers nearly 3 in. wide, deep yellow, unpleasantly scented. Western As. Hardy from zone* 3 southward. The *var.* **bicolor,** the Austrian copper brier, has the flowers orange-scarlet or coppery inside. The *var.* **persiana,** the Persian Yellow, has double, yellow flowers.

**gallica.** Provence or French rose. An upright shrub 3–4 ft. high, the rootstock creeping, the stems densely prickly and bristly. Leaflets 3–5, broadly elliptic, 2–2½ in. long. Flowers nearly 3 in. wide, solitary, pink, or crimson. Eurasia. Hardy from zone* 3 southward. *See* HERB GARDENING.

**glauca.** Related to the dog rose (*R. canina*) but more prickly, and with bluish-green foliage. Flowers rose-red, the upright, lobed sepals long-persistent. Eurasia. Hardy from zone* 4 southward.

**hugonis.** Hugo rose, often called Father Hugo's rose. A handsome, free-flowering shrub, 6–8 ft. high, the branches drooping, beset with flattened, straight prickles and bristles. Leaflets 5–13, ovalish or elliptic, ½–¾ in. long. Flowers solitary, about 2 in. wide, yellow. China. Hardy from zone* 3 southward and one of the best single, yellow roses in cult. *See* Group 7 at ROSE.

**laevigata.** Cherokee rose. A Chinese rose, widely naturalized in the southern states. It is an evergreen, climbing rose, often 15 ft. high, with scattered, hooked prickles. Leaflets 3 (rarely 5), elliptic-oval, 1¾–2½ in. long, shining. Flowers nearly 3½ in. wide, white, fragrant, and solitary. Hardy from zone* 7 southward. It is the origin of a much more hardy, very popular climbing rose known as Silver Moon. *See* Group 6 at ROSE.

**moschata.** Musk rose. An arching or partly climbing rose with straight or slightly curved prickles. Leaflets 5–7, oblongish, 1½–2 in. long. Flowers musk-scented, white, nearly 2 in. wide, in usually 7-flowered clusters (corymbs*). Mediterranean region. Hardy from zone* 6 southward, but not much grown, most of the plants under the name of *R. moschata* being *R. brunoni.*

**multiflora.** Multiflora rose. A climbing or trailing rose with stout, hooked prickles. Leaflets 5–9, generally oblongish, 1–1½ in. long. Flowers about ¾ in. wide, fragrant, often double, in many-flowered clusters (panicles* or corymbs*). Jap. and Korea. July–Aug. Hardy from zone* 3 southward. With *R. cathayensis,* the source of many important climbing or prostrate, hort. varieties, and possibly entering into the variety known as Crimson Rambler. *See* Group 6 at ROSE.

**nitida.** A low native rose, rarely over 18 in. high, the stems densely bristly and with slender, straight prickles. Leaflets 7–9, oblongish, about 1 in. long, shining. Flowers generally solitary, about 2 in. wide, rose-pink. Newfoundland to Conn. Hardy from zone* 2 southward.

**noisettiana.** Noisette rose, also called Champney rose. A widely grown hybrid rose derived from crossing *R. chinensis* with *R. moschata.* It is an erect shrub 7–10 ft. high, the prickles hooked and reddish. Leaflets 5–7, oblong to ovalish. Flowers white, pink, red, or yellow in many-flowered clusters (corymbs*). Hardy from zone* 6 southward. Widely used as a stock for tea roses and for China roses. A climbing form of it is the well-known Marechal Neil rose, with yellow flowers.

**nutkana.** A native American rose, 3–5 ft. high, the dark brown, upright stems with large, straight prickles. Leaflets 5–9, broadly elliptic, 1½–2 in. long. Flowers solitary, nearly 2 in. wide, mostly rose-pink. Alaska to Wyo., Idaho, and Calif. June–July. A good rose for the Rocky Mountain states and the Pacific Coast.

**odorata.** Tea rose. An evergreen, tea-scented, partially climbing rose with hooked prickles. Leaflets 5–7, ovalish or oblong, 2–3 in. long, shining above. Flowers solitary or 2 or 3 in a cluster, nearly 3 in. wide, usually double, white, pink, or yellow. China. June–Oct. Hardy from zone* 6 southward. Little cult. in its original form, but entering widely into many hort. forms.

**palustris.** Swamp rose. A native rose, the upright stems 4–6 ft. high, often reddish, armed with straight prickles and bristles. Leaflets mostly 7, narrowly oblong, 1½–2 in. long. Flowers about 2 in. wide, pink, in few-flowered clusters (corymbs*). Eastern U.S. June–Aug. Hardy from zone* 2 southward.

**polyantha.** Polyantha roses. A group of horticultural hybrids derived from crossing *R. multiflora* (or *R. cathayensis*) with *R. chinensis.* They are mostly upright, low shrubs with many, rather small, double flowers. The polyantha group has entered into many hort. forms. *See* Group 3 at ROSE.

**rubiginosa** = *Rosa eglanteria.*

**rugosa.** An upright shrub, 4–6 ft. high, ultimately making large patches (10–20 ft. in diameter). Stems densely bristly and prickly, the prickles straight. Leaflets 5–9, more or less elliptic, 1½–2 in. long, very rough and veiny on the upper surface, shining. Flowers usually solitary, nearly 3½ in. wide, red or white. Jap. and China. July–Aug. Hardy from zone* 3 southward, and rather commonly escaped, especially near the seashore in the eastern U.S. There are many hort. varieties, some with double flowers, a good one being the form known as Agnes. *See* Group 8 at ROSE.

**sempervirens.** An evergreen climbing or trailing rose, with scattered, hooked prickles. Leaflets 5–7, ovalish or narrower, 1½–2 in. long, shining. Flowers almost 2 in. wide, fragrant, white, mostly in few-flowered clusters (corymbs*). Mediterranean region. June–July. Hardy from zone* 5 southward.

**setigera.** Prairie rose. A climbing or arching rose, often 15 ft. high, the prickles scattered and hooked. Leaflets 3 (rarely 5), ovalish or oblong, 3–4 in. long. Flowers about 2 in. wide, rose-pink, but fading to whitish, mostly in few-flowered clusters (corymbs*). Eastern N.A., but west to Neb. and Tex. June–Aug. Hardy from zone* 3 southward. A double-flowered form, perhaps of hybrid origin, is the climbing rose Baltimore Belle. *See* Group 6 at ROSE.

**spinosissima.** Scotch rose; also called Burnet rose. An erect shrub, 2–3 ft. high, the stems densely covered with straight prickles and bristles. Leaflets mostly 7–9 (rarely 5 or 11), roundish, ½–¾ in. long. Flowers solitary, but numerous, about 2 in. wide, pink, white, or yellow. Eurasia. Hardy from zone* 3 southward. There are many varieties and forms of this long-cult. rose, a good pink one being Stanwell Perpetual. *See* Group 7 at ROSE.

**wichuraiana.** Memorial rose. A prostrate or trailing, half-evergreen rose, the strong prickles hooked. Leaflets 7–9, roundish, blunt, shining, ¾–1 in. long. Flowers nearly 2 in. wide, white, fragrant, mostly in clusters (corymbs*). Eastern Asia. July–Oct. Hardy from zone* 3 southward. The origin of many valuable roses useful for covering walls and banks (*see* Wall-top Tumblers at VINES). One old favorite is Dorothy Perkins. *R. wichuraiana* is also involved in the parentage of Dr. Walter Van Fleet, a fine climbing rose with peach-pink flowers. *See* Group 6 at ROSE.

**xanthina.** An Asiatic shrub related to *R. hugonis,* but with double or semi-double yellow flowers as usually cult., although the wild form is single-flowered. China and Korea. Hardy from zone* 3 southward. *See* Group 7 at ROSE.

***ROSACEA, -us, -um*** (ro-zay'see-a). Rose-like.

**ROSACEAE** (ro-zay'see-ee). The rose family is one of the two or three most important plant families to the gardener. It is often called the strawberry, raspberry or spirea family, but besides these it includes many other genera of outstanding value to the flower enthusiast, the fruit culturist and to the grower of some of our most decorative shrubs and trees.

As here considered the rose family is a tremendous aggregation of herbs, shrubs and trees, comprising about 100 genera and well over 2000 species of very wide distribution. They have not always been considered as of one big family, but as three. The segregation of these three families (here considered as tribes) has considerable cogency, as will be seen from the tabulation below. In order to aid the student all the genera of the Rosaceae will be numbered in accordance with that tabulation.

1. Rose tribe or rose family proper (the Rosaceae in the old restricted sense). Fruit not like the plum or apple, usually dry, but *see* STRAWBERRY.
2. Apple tribe or family, often called the pear or quince family (the Malaceae or Pomaceae). Here are grouped the fleshy-fruited, largely edible genera typified by the apple, *i.e.* with the fruit a pome,* and an inferior* ovary.
3. Peach tribe or family, often called the plum, almond or cherry family (the Amygdalaceae, also called the Drupaceae or Prunaceae). Here are grouped the

* Special articles on the subjects indicated by an asterisk (*) will be found at the words so marked.

fleshy-fruited, largely edible genera typified by the peach or plum or cherry, *i.e.* with the fruit a drupe* and with a superior* ovary. Quite generally called the stone fruits.

While many gardeners will disregard these distinctions, they have much hort. basis, and still more botanical significance. Because of this all the genera below will be indicated by number as to their proper tribe in accordance with the above tabulation.

The garden genera of the whole rose family may be grouped, culturally, as follows:

I. GROWN PRIMARILY FOR FRUIT.
   *Amygdalus* (3), *Cydonia* (2) (see QUINCE), *Chrysobalanus* (3), *Eriobotrya* (2), *Fragaria* (1) (see STRAWBERRY), *Malus* (2), *Pyrus* (2), *Prunus* (3), *Rubus* (1).

II. TROPICAL OR SUB-TROPICAL GENERA grown for ornament, outdoors mostly from zone* 7 southwards, elsewhere in greenhouses.
   *Heteromeles* (2) (see TOYON), *Quillaja* (1), *Lyonothamnus* (1), *Osteomeles* (2), *Raphiolepis* (2) and *Laurocerasus* (3) (some hardy).

III. ORNAMENTAL SHRUBS, TREES AND VINES of outdoor culture over a good part of the country (but *see* individual genera for specific details). A few genera also contain herbs.
   *Acaena* (1), *Adenostoma* (1), *Amelanchier* (2), *Aronia* (2), *Cercocarpus* (1), *Chaenomeles* (2), *Cotoneaster* (2), *Crataegus* (2), *Exochorda* (1), *Holodiscus* (1), *Mespilus* (2), *Kerria* (1), *Neviusia* (1), *Osmaronia* (3), *Physocarpus* (1), *Photinia* (2), *Prinsepia* (3), *Pyracantha* (2), *Purshia* (1), *Prunus* (3), *Rhodotypos* (1), *Rosa* (1), *Sibiraea* (1), *Sorbaria* (1), *Sorbus* (2) (see MOUNTAIN-ASH), *Spiraea* (1) and *Stranvaesia* (2).

IV. ANNUAL OR PERENNIAL HERBS FOR THE BORDER, ROCK GARDEN or wild garden, of outdoor culture over most of the country (but *see* individual genera for specific details). A few genera also contain woody plants.
   *Alchemilla* (1), *Aruncus* (1), *Dalibarda* (1), *Dryas* (1), *Duchesnea* (1), *Filipendula* (1), *Geum* (1), *Gillenia* (1), *Potentilla* (1), *Poterium* (1), *Sanguisorba* (1) and *Waldsteinia* (1).

Among these lists are such outstanding fruits as the pear, apple, quince, plum, peach, almond, apricot, strawberry, blackberry, raspberry. See these terms for the culture and hort. varieties of each.

By far the most important decorative material will be found in Group III (the ornamental shrubs and trees), which includes such old favorites as the rose, spirea, hawthorn, shadbush, flowering quince and all the splendid flowering cherries, and many other fine shrubs and trees. The herbaceous plants (Group IV) are much less important, some of the genera being suited only to the wild garden.

Leaves alternate,* compound* in several genera (*Rosa*, *Rubus*, etc.) but often simple.* For the fruits *see* tabulation above. The flowers of the Rosaceae have typically 4–5 sepals and petals, but these are inserted on the edges of a hypanthium (see RECEPTACLE). This is of various shapes. In the rose it forms the rose hip, and in the blackberry it is the cone-shaped structure that is left on the bush when the fruit is picked. Stamens* usually numerous. Ovary superior* or inferior.*

**ROSA MONTANA** = *Antigonon leptopus*.

**ROSARIUM.** An old name for a rose garden.

**ROSARY PEA** = *Abrus precatorius*.

**ROSA-SINENSIS** (ro-za-sy-nen′sis). Rose of China. *See* HIBISCUS.

**ROSA SOLIS** = *Drosera rotundifolia*.

**ROSE.** A nozzle for a hose or the perforated end of the spout of a watering pot. *See* Section 3, TOOLS AND IMPLEMENTS.

**ROSE.** For the culture and varieties of the garden rose *see* the next main entry. The word *rose*, however, has been applied to many other plants. Among the most important, and their proper equivalents, are:

Bridal Rose = *Matricaria inodora plenissima*
California rose = *Convolvulus japonicus*
Christmas Rose = *Helleborus niger*.
Confederate Rose = *Hibiscus mutabilis*.
Cotton Rose = *Hibiscus mutabilis*.
Guelder Rose = *Viburnum opulus sterile*.
Native Rose. See BAUERA.
Rose-apple = *Eugenia jambos*.
Rose Bay. See RHODODENDRON and OLEANDER.
Rose Mallow = *Hibiscus moscheutos*.
Rose Milkweed = *Asclepias tuberosa*. See MILKWEED.
Rose Moss = *Portulaca grandiflora*.
Rose-of-China = *Hibiscus rosa-sinensis*.
Rose-of-Heaven = *Lychnis coeli-rosa*.
Rose-of-Jericho = *Anastatica hierochuntica*.
Rose-of-Sharon = *Hibiscus syriacus*.
Rose Pink. See SABBATIA.
Rose Pogonia = *Pogonia ophioglossoides*.
Rockrose = *Cistus*.
Sun-rose = *Helianthemum*.
Tuberose. See TUBEROSE.

**ROSE.** This best-loved garden flower pervades the civilized world, reaching its greatest development in the north and south temperate zones. Its recorded world history reaches back to pre-Babylonian times. The name itself is almost identical in the languages of civilization.

In the discussion which follows, constant reference is made to the classes of roses dominantly in American gardens. These have originated over generations of time by natural and artificial hybridization, bringing together the native roses of the temperate zones. These may be broadly classified into 8 groups.

1. TEA ROSES. Seldom growing over two feet in height, of branching habit. They have reasonable vigor, attractive foliage, bear many large flowers, usually with the fragrance which the name implies. They definitely belong in the southern part of the U.S. along the Gulf Coast, and in California. About the old Calif. Missions there are Tea roses, brought in generations ago, which are of enormous size. They are less well adapted to general culture only because they yield more easily to low temperatures. Nevertheless, they have high value for many parts of the U.S. in which the Hybrid Tea roses (*see* group 2 below), sometimes substituted for them, do not provide equal persistence of bloom.

Unfortunately, their color range is relatively limited, and is without positive red varieties and permanently yellow sorts. The flowers tend to hang their heads. They do particularly well, however, during the winter months in the South, having no disposition to "rest" where the temperature and conditions warrant continuous blooming.

Once very numerous in the rose catalogues, there are now available in the U.S. barely twenty-five varieties. It was the sudden rush of European hybridizers two generations ago toward the then new Hybrid Tea class that checked the improvement of both the Teas and the Hybrid Perpetuals (*see* group 4 below).

Varieties of Tea roses that may be had in the U.S. include Mrs. Foley Hobbs, Mrs. Herbert Stevens, The Bride, William R. Smith, with white or creamy flowers; Alexander Hill Gray, Blumenschmidt, Etoile de Lyon, Lady Hillingdon, Mlle. Franziska Krüger, Marie van Houtte, Perle des Jardins, in various shades and tints of yellow; Comtesse du Cayla (a China rose), Safrano, Souv. de Pierre Notting, Sunset, in shades of apricot; Catharine Mermet, Duchesse de Brabant, Maman Cochet, Mme. Lambard, Mrs. B. R. Cant, Papa Gontier, in shades of pink and carmine.

The culture of Tea roses, and indeed of all roses here mentioned, is relatively simple. Thorough soil preparation is requisite to good results. Soil that is capable of growing good peas, potatoes, or other vegetable crops to kitchen-garden satisfaction, will grow good roses. It needs to be deeply dug, not less than two spades or eighteen inches deep above any required drainage, for roses will not endure "wet feet." An admixture of well-rotted animal manure, to the extent of even twenty-five per cent, is desirable, as roses are strong

---

* Special articles on the subjects indicated by an asterisk (*) will be found at the words so marked.

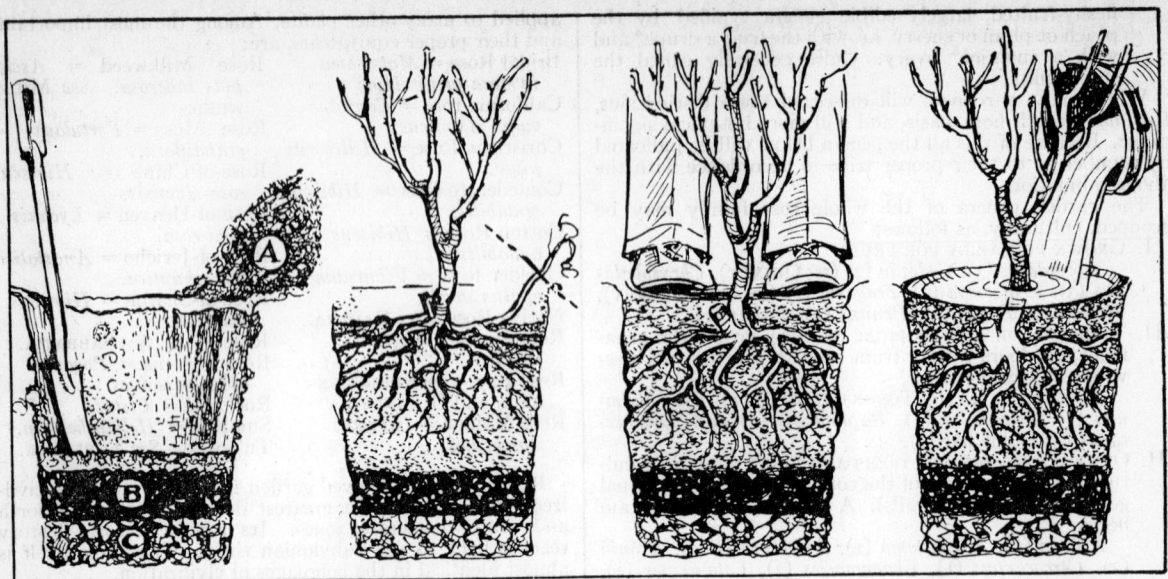

FOUR STEPS IN CORRECT ROSE PLANTING

A = Topsoil. B = Manure. C = Drainage material. From left to right: Dig an ample hole and use good topsoil for planting. See that all roots are well spread out and covered, cutting off old ones (as shown by dotted line). Be sure to firm the soil thoroughly around the roots, and, finally, water the plant.

feeders. In the absence of animal manure, a prepared commercial complete fertilizer (see FERTILIZERS), used as directed by the manufacturers, can be substituted. If the ground is rough and hard, humus is a valuable adjunct, and this can be in the shape of rotted leaves, usually called leaf mold, or of commercial forms of humus (see HUMUS). In some cases it is desirable to use humus in which dried animal manures have been incorporated, or which has been used as stable bedding.

When Tea roses, and Hybrid Tea roses particularly, have bloomed freely, summer fertilization may be provided by the use of liquid manure (which see), about a pint to a plant, with clear water preceding or following.

Roses should not be forced to compete with other plants; weeds must be kept down. In recent years roses have been found in America to do better in partial shade. They may be planted in borders or near trees or hedges, if care is used to avoid the possibility of direct root interference.

In planting roses it is well to provide that when the rose reaches partial maturity it quite well shades the ground. The distances for the various classes that follow, therefore, will be in some cases as much as three feet apart, and from that down to eighteen inches or less.

Pruning for Tea roses, for the Hybrid Tea and the Polyantha classes (see group 3 below), is largely a matter of preference. The fewer buds that are left on the plants in the spring (save for the Polyantha group) the fewer, but larger, will be the flowers to follow. In general, spring pruning for all these classes should include the removal of interfering, winter-damaged or weak shoots. Generally the plant may be re-shaped as desired with each annual pruning. After a severe winter, some roses are perforce pruned almost to the ground, or to the "bud" just above the ground, but these usually make new shoots and bloom the same season.

The Hybrid Perpetuals can well be kept to not more than three feet in height, unless a special purpose is in mind. The Polyantha roses are better if but little growth is removed. As before stated, pruning is largely a matter of preference, and the thoughtful grower will soon discover how best to accomplish the results he has in mind.

Summer pruning of these classes is usually accomplished satisfactorily, as roses are cut for use with liberal stems.

The pruning of the Hardy Climbing roses is referred to later. The shrub and the species roses need pruning only to remove dead or interfering twigs.

2. HYBRID TEA ROSES include the largest percentage of varieties planted in America. Combining to a certain extent the easy growth and recurrent bloom habits of the Tea roses, they also add a portion of the vigor and the stature with the greater hardiness and the richer flower characteristic of the Hybrid Perpetuals. All the colors normal to the rose are found among the Hybrid Teas. The varied forms of the rose, from single to very double, with bud forms pointed, tapering, ovoid, globular or urn-shaped, are included. Some varieties tend to cluster blooming, and some provide the long, single, slender stems beloved of the florist. The Pernetiana group introduces a most fortunate warmth and richness of color.

The plants are generally vigorous, and have frequently endured zero weather without protection, while with protection they may be carried through anywhere in America.

The Hybrid Teas are the bedding roses *par excellence*. With the knowledge concerning their habits in various parts of the country annually made available through the published experiences of members of the American Rose Society, they afford the closest approximation to the aim of that Society, which is "A rose for every home, a bush for every garden."

In the Hybrid Tea class there tend to arise, from time to time, sports or mutations. Thus, the important variety Radiance has given rise to Mrs. Charles Bell, a lighter pink, and to Red Radiance, of a distinct crimson color. These sports usually retain most of the characters of growth and bloom-habit of the variety from which they have arisen.

A restricted list of Hybrid Tea varieties, based upon the reports of impartial inquirers gathered annually, includes Mme. Jules Bouché and Caledonia as to white varieties. Among pink sorts are Betty Uprichard, Edith Nellie Perkins, Impress, Mme. Butterfly, Mrs. Henry Bowles, Radiance. Red are the blooms of Étoile de Hollande, Margaret McGredy, Mrs. J. D. Eisele, National Flower Guild, Red Radiance, The General. Shades of yellow are Golden Dawn, Lucie Marie, Mrs. Dunlop Best, Mrs. E. P. Thom, Soeur Therese, Souvenir. Apricot, salmon and orange are found in Autumn, Luis Brinas, Mme. Edouard Herriot, President Herbert Hoover, Talisman.

The same culture recommended for Tea roses applies to Hybrid Tea roses, which are usually of somewhat stronger

---

* Special articles on the subjects indicated by an asterisk (*) will be found at the words so marked.

GARDEN ROSES

Betty Uprichard
Kaiserin Auguste Viktoria

Golden Dawn

President Herbert Hoover
Etoile de Hollande

and more upright growth. In the southern part of the United States, Hybrid Tea roses tend to make rather large bushes, and must, consequently, be planted farther apart than in the Middle states, where it is excellent practice to set them eighteen inches apart. Clean culture is at all times desirable. Some rosarians find it advantageous to mulch* the rose beds with peat moss, buckwheat hulls, ground cork waste, or other substances that will tend to keep the ground cool and to restrain weeds.

3. POLYANTHA ROSES come next among the bedding roses. Quite generally of lower stature (under two feet save for certain exceptions), they serve admirably as border plants for the beds of taller-growing sorts. They have, too, the high

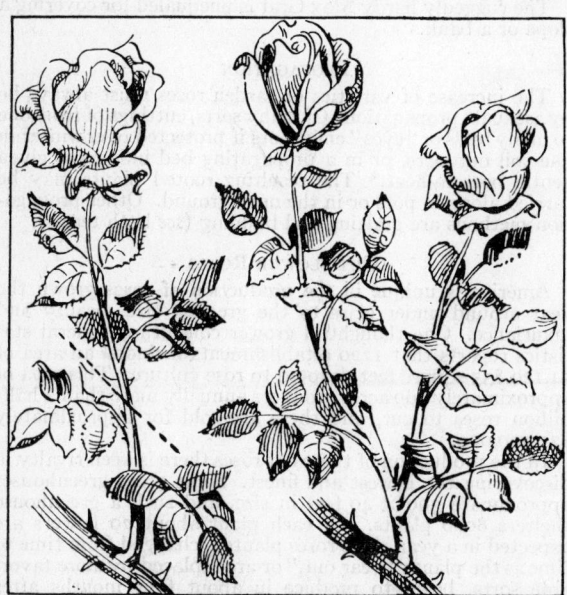

The right way to cut a rose (*left*) and the result of it (*right*) which is to produce more flowers.

merit of long retaining their blooms in good order, and of recurrent blooming as they grow. They are, in the average American garden, more nearly everblooming than any other class. Of hardiness fully equal to that of the Hybrid Teas, they have also, as a class, a pleasantly compact habit of growth.

The Polyantha roses may be used to add flashes of color in the shrubbery border. In front of beds of the tall Hybrid Perpetuals they serve to hide their sometimes naked stems.

Desirable Polyantha varieties of the smaller-flowered group are Eblouissant, Ideal, Jessie, Orleans, Scarlet Button, in red; Aennchen Müller, Bébé Blanc, Dorothy Howarth, Katharina Zeimet, La Marne, Maman Turbat, Marie Pavic, Yvonne Rabier, in white to light pink. Larger-flowered sorts are Clotilde Soupert, Gruss an Aachen, Marie Pavic, Mrs. R. M. Finch, in the lighter shades; Chatillon, Lafayette, Mme. Anth. Kluis, in deeper pink; Else Poulsen, Kirsten Poulsen, of taller growth, in shades of carmine.

Culture of this class does not differ materially from that previously recommended for the Tea and Hybrid Tea roses.

4. HYBRID PERPETUAL ROSES, often cited as Remontant, bloom heavily in June or July, and certain of them bloom recurrently. Assuredly they are hybrids as to parentage, for they include a mingling of China, Bourbon, French and Damask blood. (See the list of rose species at ROSA.)

The Hybrid Perpetuals are generally taller, stronger in growth and bolder in effect than the Hybrid Teas. They are frost-hardy in all but the coldest locations, and are quite permanent when once established. The flowers, largest of all, and including nearly all the forms of the rose, range in color from purest white to deepest crimson and scarlet, but with, so far, only approximate yellows and shades of orange.

The varieties in the Hybrid Perpetual class were once almost innumerable. Among those now available in the U.S. the famous American Beauty is first mentioned, though it is not important outdoors. Candeur Lyonnaise and Frau Karl Druschki are white; Baroness Rothschild, Clio, George Arends, Magna Charta, Mme. Albert Barbier, Mrs. John Laing are various shades of pink; Captain Hayward, General Jacqueminot, J. B. Clark, Suzanne-Marie Rodocanachi, Ulrich Brunner are crimson and near-scarlet; Soleil d'Or and St. Ingeberg have shades of primrose and apricot.

Because the Hybrid Perpetuals are stronger-growing roses, as well as of quite permanent character, their culture should involve somewhat more liberal ground preparation.

Some of the Hybrid Perpetuals can be planted as close as two feet apart, but those intended to reach full maturity need double this distance. All the other previous statements with respect to fertilization are in point. These roses can be tied down to make a hedge effect with resulting bloom advantages.

5. MOSS ROSES, BOURBON and BENGAL ROSES are here included as Bedding Roses. The first named are now returning to the gardens from which their fragrance and charm have too long been absent. In growth they are generally similar to the Hybrid Perpetuals. The flowers, mostly in light shades, are fragrant, and of open, cupped form. It is the buds that show the mossy growth so much admired, and this "moss" is itself fragrant in some varieties. The plants are easily subject to powdery mildew, and need good soil. The few varieties available include Blanche Moreau, white; Crested Moss and Salet, pink; Henry Martin, crimson; Golden Moss, primrose.

The China, Bourbon and Bengal roses include survivors of the days before the "modern" roses usurped the garden. Mostly of growth between the Hybrid Tea and the Hybrid Perpetual, they tend to bloom freely and frequently. The China varieties are the most important, and include Hermosa as a particularly floriferous clear pink, and Beauty of Rosemawr, Ducher and Fabvier, all in shades of pink.

All these roses require planting and culture about as previously cited, with special reference to the permanent quality involved in those last above mentioned; this meaning, as with Hybrid Perpetual roses, adequate and liberal ground preparation and fertilization.

The rose classes previously mentioned are frost-hardy without special protection as far north as the Mason and Dixon line. Beyond that winter protection is desirable in the shape of any loose material which will permit air circulation, will not encourage the burrowing of rodents, but nevertheless will serve to keep off the sun and the wind of late winter. An excellent protection practice is that of drawing up about the base of each plant six inches of loose soil. In the event of frost damage this gives a basis from which a new plant structure may be built.

6. HARDY CLIMBING ROSES. No roses, save certain tropical species that "climb" by hooked prickles or thorns, are truly climbing in habit. Those we so designate are really varieties of vigorous growth that will easily accept attachment to any support, or that will trail over a fence, a slope, a wall, or similar surface. Certain of them — especially of the Multiflora class, typified by the familiar cluster-flowered Crimson Rambler — are particularly upright in their habit, while the larger group, relating more closely to the Japanese *R. wichuraiana* as one parent, tends in a few varieties actually to trail or creep, and in most to a moderate growth, producing large flowers in richer colors.

These two groups include most of our modern climbers. There are also many so-called climbing forms — that is, taller-growing — of the Hybrid Tea sorts, otherwise known as climbing sports, thus, Climbing Talisman, Climbing Radiance. There are also some Climbing Hybrid Teas of direct hybridization, such as the lovely Australian roses, Daydream, Countess of Stradbroke, and others. A few important varieties arise from other bases, as the superb, fragrant, thornless Bourbon hybrid, Zephirine Drouhin, and the exquisite Mermaid, a constant-blooming hybrid of *R. bracteata*.

It is difficult to distinguish between the Multiflora and

---

* Special articles on the subjects indicated by an asterisk (*) will be found at the words so marked.

Wichuraiana hybrids. While both classes are primarily once-blooming — in June or July — there are some sorts that bloom recurrently. The superb Dr. W. Van Fleet, probably the finest of all American hardy climbers, has provided us with a recurrent-blooming sport in the patented New Dawn, and Blaze is assumed to be a continuous-blooming Paul's Scarlet Climber. An entirely new race of super-hardy climbers, resting on the native *R. setigera* as its base, is now coming into use.

Disregarding separate classification, there may be mentioned as satisfactory white climbing varieties Mme. Alfred Carriere, Purity, Silver Moon. Pink shades include Alida Lovett, American Pillar, Dr. W. Van Fleet, Ile de France, Mme. Gregoire Staechelin, New Dawn, Nora Cuningham; in yellow shades are Emily Gray (not always hardy), Ghislaine de Feligonde, Jacotte, Golden Climber, La Reve, Mrs. A. C. James; brightly red are Bess Lovett, Dr. Huey, Excelsa, Kitty Kininmonth, Royal Scot, Paul's Scarlet Climber. *See* colored plate at Vines.

These Hardy Climbing roses are admirably used for hedges of any height up to eight feet or more, if the proper sorts are selected. They also provide garden objects of great beauty when trained as pillars on any suitable support. In one successful use, the climbing rose is planted close to a post, which may be of wood or metal, being then trained to the top of the support, which, in some cases, may be eight to ten feet above the ground. Posts of seven or eight feet in height six feet apart can have a simple but very beautiful arch provided by a strap-iron support between the posts on which the roses may be trained. Climbing roses are also trained to follow ropes between two posts, thus reversing the arch.

In general, climbing roses are of easy culture. They should be planted in a hole dug at least two feet square and deep, and it is wise to have a liberal admixture of well-rotted manure added at the bottom of this small pit, with any necessary drainage if the ground is soggy. If manure is lacking, an admixture of ground bone tends to provide continuing prosperity.

The summer treatment of these roses is simple. The Multiflora types, as well as Crimson Rambler and Dorothy Perkins, for example, need the removal each year at their base of old canes immediately after flowering. The plant then renews itself with new canes. Others of Wichuraiana parentage, and those known as Climbing Hybrid Teas, together with such varieties as Dr. W. Van Fleet and Mermaid, need little pruning save the removal of objectionable shoots or those actually dead.

For most of the U.S. these roses are actually winter-hardy. Where the climate is particularly severe, with long winter exposures of sub-zero temperatures to 25 or 30 degrees, it is sometimes found necessary to take them down from the supports and protect them with soil or with other loose material in which mice cannot burrow. *See* the colored illustration at Vines.

7. Shrub or Species Roses. These include all the native or species roses. Most of them provide flowers of much beauty in their season, maintaining, as well, varied and attractive foliage, and, in some cases, equally attractive thorns, seed hips and twig color which give distinction in the winter months. Some of the hardy climbing roses may also be allowed to scramble in the shrubbery with little or no support.

The border line between roses grown in beds and those which are advantageously used in the shrubbery, in park planting, for isolated specimens in well-ordered gardens, and not infrequently as background material, is quite indefinite. It includes certain species native to various continents.

Thus American gardens have been greatly enriched in recent years through the introduction, mostly from Asia, of effective native species. *R. hugonis* and *R. xanthina* have given us admirable shrub forms with abundant once-blooming yellow inflorescence, and attractive distinctness in habit and foliage. The fine old Scotch form, *R. spinosissima*, has a rounded garden beauty, and as naturally varied, produces flowers of white and those with slight color admixture. The American natives, *R. setigera, R. carolina, R. palustris,* and *R. nutkana,* each has distinction and beauty. In the South three Asian immigrants have naturalized. The Cherokee rose (*R. laevigata*) runs wild over miles of fences. The Lady Bank's rose (*R. banksiae*) and the Macartney rose (*R. bracteata*), none frost-hardy in the North, are highly esteemed.

8. Hybrid Rugosa Roses, some of which send up ten-foot straight shoots in one season, make very different and distinct shrubs. These roses also are hedge material of value if sufficient courage is exercised in pruning them to the determined height and form. Useful sorts are Blanc Double de Coubert and Schneezwerg in white, Conrad Ferdinand Meyer and Sarah Van Fleet in pink, Agnes and Vanguard in apricot and salmon, with F. J. Grootendorst (excellent for hedges) and Ruskin in red.

The ruggedly hardy Max Graf is unequaled for covering a slope or a bank.

### Propagation

The increase of varieties of garden roses must always be by asexual* propagation. Of many sorts, cuttings of from one to many buds or "eyes" emit roots if protected over winter in fine soil outdoors, or in a propagating bed indoors if given gentle bottom-heat.* The resulting rooted plants may be carried along in pots or in the open ground. Other propagation methods are grafting and budding (*see* both terms).

### Cut-flower Roses

America is unique in the production of roses grown the year around under glass to the greatest size, beauty and luxuriance. One thoughtful grower consulting Federal statistics reports that 1220 establishments included an area of 34,129,855 square feet devoted to rose culture. This area of approximately 800 acres produces annually more than a half-billion roses to cut, and these are sold for approximately $21,000,000.

In the production of these cut roses there is keen rivalry in discovering the newest and finest. Some great greenhouses approximate 300 × 40 feet in size, and such a greenhouse shelters 8000 plants. Of each plant about 20 flowers are expected in a year. The roses planted, changed from time to time as the plants "wear out," or are replaced by more favorable sorts, begin to produce in about four months after planting, but are at their best in a year or more, lasting approximately three and a half to four years until a change is needed.

By far the larger portion of the approximately twenty million rose plants annually produced in the U.S. are propagated by budding.* The same effect is much less extensively secured by the grafting process.

Virtually all roses forced under greenhouse conditions are Hybrid Teas. Among the varieties at present in large use are Briarcliff, Hollywood, Premier Supreme, in pink; Double White Killarney; Joanna Hill, Souvenir de Claudius Pernet, Talisman, in yellow and shades; E. G. Hill, Mrs. F. R. Pierson, in red.

Reference has previously been made to the American Rose Society, an organization of several thousand earnest amateurs which maintains constant intercommunication between its members all over America through correspondence, pilgrimages and publications. Its *American Rose Annual* keeps its members posted as to new varieties as well as to the best methods of rose nurture. This Society may be addressed at Harrisburg, Pa. — J. H. McF.

Insect Pests. Outdoor roses are attacked in the spring by green aphids, which are controlled by thorough spraying or dusting with nicotine. Greenish sawfly larvae devouring leaves are easily killed with arsenicals. Japanese beetles, rose chafers, and other beetles eating foliage in summer can be checked by lead arsenate spray, 1 pound to 10 gallons. The same treatment will check the curculio, a snout beetle puncturing buds, and leaf-feeding caterpillars. Stem borers are checked by destroying infested stems. The rose scale (*see* Blackberry) is controlled with dormant sprays.

In the greenhouse, aphids are checked by nicotine spray or fumigation, leaf tiers and other caterpillars by arsenicals, and the red spider by lime-sulphur (or derris spray if the roses are blooming). Larvae of the rose midge feed in buds; clean stock should be planted, and the soil covered with tobacco dust if injury occurs. The root worm is also controlled with tobacco dust, and its small adult beetles may be killed with arsenical spray.

Diseases. Roses are susceptible to a considerable number of diseases, among the more important of which are rust, mildew, root-knot, black

---

* Special articles on the subjects indicated by an asterisk (*) will be found at the words so marked.

spot, brown canker, leafspot, crown gall, and mosaic. For *rust, mildew,* and *root-knot* see Rust, Mildew and Root-knot at Plant Diseases. *Black spot* is chiefly a foliage disease, although in some instances cane infections have been observed. It is characterized by black, somewhat circular spots with radiating margins. Affected leaves turn yellow and fall prematurely. For control, all fallen leaves should be carefully raked up and burned in the autumn. Frequent applications of dusting sulphur will serve to hold the disease in check.

*Brown canker,* characterized by large cinnamon-buff, oval dead areas on the canes, is particularly severe on Hybrid Tea varieties. Cut out all cankers early in the spring, apply lime-sulphur as a dormant spray and follow during the summer with frequent applications of dusting sulphur. These suggestions should also be followed for other canker diseases of roses. *Leafspot,* caused by various fungi, is more prevalent on the climbing roses. Control is the same as for black spot.

*Crown gall,* a bacterial disease, produces galls usually at the crowns of the plants, although they may also occur on the aerial parts and roots as well. Infected plants are stunted and lack vigor. In most instances, the galls occur at places where the plants have been wounded. For control, remove and destroy diseased plants. When the roses are growing out of doors, the surrounding soil may be drenched with a corrosive sublimate solution, 1-1000.

*Mosaic* is a recently discovered virus disease. Infected plants are stunted, lack vigor and produce few flowers. Distinct yellow areas which result in distortion of the leaves are the typical symptom. The effects of the disease are more serious under glass than out of doors. When possible, infected plants should be discarded before planting. If the disease appears after planting, the mosaic-infested plants should be destroyed and replaced with healthy individuals.

**ROSEA, -us, -um** (rō′zee-a). Rose-colored.

**ROSE ACACIA** = *Robinia hispida.* See Locust.

**ROSE-APPLE** = *Eugenia jambos.*

**ROSE BAY.** A name applied to at least three very different plants. The two most important are the oleander and *Rhododendron maximum.* See also Epilobium Angustifolium, and Tabernaemontana coronaria.

**ROSEBUD CHERRY** = *Prunus subhirtella.*

**ROSE CAMPION** = *Lychnis coronaria.*

**ROSE CHAFER.** See Insect Pests at Rose and Grape.

**ROSE-COLORED GARDEN.** See Pink Garden.

**ROSE FAMILY.** Rose relatives are legion, including herbs, shrubs, and trees. Few are as showy, individually, as the rose itself, but among the many garden groups are spirea, pearl bush, jetbead, ninebark, hawthorns, the mountain-ash, and all the showy flowering cherries and crabapples. Besides these ornamentals, the rose family contains such important fruits as the strawberry, blackberry, raspberry, peach, plum, apple, pear, and quince. For a complete list of the many genera *see* Rosaceae.

**ROSE GARDENS.** Two broad divisions of this subject appear. Both private and public rose gardens need to be discussed. There are many hundreds of private rose gardens in the U.S., some of which are accessible, under certain restrictions and at certain times, to the general public. It may be said in general that these private gardens are of wide range and scope, and constitute definite proof of the universality of the rose in America. While gardens made and maintained at great expense are to be found, many interesting private gardens are those of smaller area.

Thus, one woman has gathered in Maryland a large collection of what are known as "old roses," meaning those that have survived from colonial days, often of forms, colors and habit very different from the conventional roses of twentieth-century commerce. Access to this garden by any interested visitor is permitted. A similar garden in Monterey, Calif., includes precious old roses from the famed Spanish Missions of the Coast. In Portland, Oregon, world-famous for roses along the streets, there are many great private rose gardens, open to the public on certain days. One such has 17,000 plants.

Three gardens, one in a Worcester, Mass., backyard, another in Point Loma, Calif., and the third in Chevy Chase, Md., emphasize the effectiveness of shade in obtaining the best results.

Of recent years there have been constructed in the vicinity of Boston a number of elaborate and very beautiful private rose gardens, designed and planted through the combined work of several competent landscape architects and one woman of real rose genius. These superb gardens are usually opened in rose-time to the public under reasonable restrictions as to dates, hours and numbers. One similar and quite extensive rose garden blooms in beauty near Detroit, at the home of a famous automobile manufacturer.

At Phoenix, Ariz., a private rose garden proves that roses can be grown under peculiar conditions, while another amateur in Kan. develops in her garden a process of obtaining success with roses under conditions of scanty rainfall.

A Texas garden keeps its roses "on probation" for the information of the owner and her friends. A Mich. rose-lover is ready to show how he can overcome the dangers of bitter winter weather in his garden. Similarly a Colo. garden defies climatic limitations, and similar successes are noted in rose gardens in Maine and other states and provinces that have plenty of winter's chill.

Public Rose Gardens

The public or so-called municipal rose garden is probably the finest and most efficient expression in America of the park spirit, which tends so definitely toward maintaining good order and content. (Men and women enjoying roses growing in public parks do not require expensive policing. They do not commit crimes!) These gardens are broadly of two characters. The municipal show-garden is designed to provide the utmost bloom for the longest time, displayed in the best arranged masses in divisions and groups available for easy view by the largest number of people. The public test-garden, on the other hand, while not infrequently operated in conjunction with the show-garden, aims to try out impartially as many rose varieties as possible, with the thought of providing information and suggestion to the general public, and thus extending the advantages of home gardening.

Reference is here made to certain of the municipal rose gardens, and that reference is confined to those open throughout the year. A locked rose garden in a park is not a "public" garden.

The first municipal rose garden in America, and probably the first of its type in the world, is in Elizabeth Park, Hartford, Conn. It includes less than two acres in its area, and was designed, constructed and planted in 1904 at a cost of $2,682.96. To keep it going costs less than $2,000 annually. Approximately one million visits are made to it each year. Its design has been adapted of late years not only to the convenience of those who inspect the roses in its more than one hundred beds, but to the pleasure of those who drive about its roads in automobiles enjoying the mass, color, fragrance and freshness of the display.

Also in Connecticut, New Haven enjoys a rose garden in East Rock Park, and Waterbury maintains one in Hamilton Park.

Boston provides two municipally maintained rose gardens, one in the Fenway, and another, of larger extent, in Franklin Park. Roses are also adequately used in other portions of the city's great park system.

New York City, in the Botanical Gardens in Bronx Park, has several thousand roses in some 400 varieties. In the Brooklyn Botanic Garden is an admirably designed garden showing some 3000 roses in 300 varieties. In Buffalo several thousand roses flourish in Delaware Park, framed by tall trees. Syracuse has in Thornden Park the Dr. E. M. Mills Rose Garden, which, after its establishment in 1924, was necessarily doubled in size to meet the public demand. In Rochester a "Rose Bowl" precedes, at this writing, the establishment of a considerable and complete municipal garden. Niagara Falls enjoys a garden of some 1700 roses in Hyde Park.

Providence, R.I., has an important rose garden of some 6000 plants in Roger Williams Park, surrounded on three sides by a 15-foot arbor of climbing roses.

Pennsylvania, with many beautiful private gardens, has few municipal rose gardens. One of distinguished quality is in Allentown, where two acres include some 6500 roses in Cedar Creek Park. Bethlehem, not far away, has 4500 roses in 107 varieties in West Side Park.

Washington, the Federal capital, has a rose garden in Po-

---

* Special articles on the subjects indicated by an asterisk (*) will be found at the words so marked.

tomac Park, visited by many thousands on foot, and easily viewed from automobile driveways.

In Ohio there are creditable public rose gardens in Cincinnati, in Wade Park of Cleveland, and in Ottawa Park of Toledo.

In Indiana, Fort Wayne has a rose garden in Lakeside Park, in connection with a sunken garden and a lily pond. There are also fine rose plantings in Garfield Park.

Chicago includes many public rose plantings, the major one being in Humboldt Park, and gardens of high merit also in Garfield Park and in Douglas Park. Other Illinois municipal rose gardens are in Highland Park, in Rockford, and in East St. Louis.

Kansas is distinguished by the Reinisch Municipal Rose Gardens in Topeka, including more than 16,000 roses planted amid most impressive surroundings.

Minnesota has municipal rose garden representation in Lyndale Park, of Minneapolis, designed by the same man who installed the original municipal rose garden in Hartford. Also in Minn., in Isanti, is a small but very interesting rose garden.

Missouri has a municipal rose garden in Jacob L. Loose Memorial Park of Kansas City. In St. Louis, excellent models of small rose gardens are shown for the encouragement of backyard gardeners at the Missouri Botanical Gardens, open always to the public.

In Colorado, Denver cares for roses in Arlington Park and on several parkways, including altogether some 10,000 plants in more than six acres. Pueblo shows a rose garden of 1000 roses in Mineral Palace Park.

The Pacific Northwest is distinguished for its extraordinary roses. In Seattle's Woodland Park there is a two-acre rose garden. In Tacoma, Point Defiance Park shows many roses. In Bellingham a rose garden of 5000 plants is open.

Portland, Ore., above-mentioned as notable for the planting of roses on its streets, as well as for its show and International Test-Gardens in Washington Park, has also a great show of roses at Peninsula Park, including some 14,000 plants. There is likewise a considerable rose garden at the U.S. Veterans' Hospital.

California has roses in the public eye — even a railroad yard is fenced with them — from end to end. In San Francisco Golden Gate Park has a beautiful rose garden. Oakland has established in Linda Vista Park a rose garden unusual in character by reason of its interesting slopes. In Monterey the rose garden is near the center of the city in connection with a sunken lily pool. In the five-acre rose garden in Exposition Park of Los Angeles are some 15,000 plants. Near-by Pasadena has 5000 roses on the banks of its famed "Rose Bowl." San Diego has in Balboa Park a considerable rose planting. In San José five acres of city park land are being developed into a magnificent rose planting.

Texas, in the eastern portion of which millions of rose plants are grown annually for shipment north, has many interesting rose gardens. Fort Worth includes two park rose gardens; Dallas is similarly advantaged. Houston has a great planting of Radiance roses in Hermann Park. El Paso shows 4200 plants in Washington Park. At Arlington is a small but beautiful rose garden which recently obtained a national prize. At Port Arthur, on Lake Shore Drive, is a municipal rose garden of 2000 plants.

In Oklahoma, at Enid and at Mangum are creditable municipal rose gardens.

In Mississippi, both Jackson and Long Beach care for rose gardens.

In Georgia there are gardens in Atlanta, Cordele, Waycross and other communities, mostly under control of Garden Clubs or similar organizations.

North Carolina has begun in Charlotte the construction of a municipal rose garden.

Florida, with great climatic possibilities for the rose, has as yet but one public garden, that in Eola Park, Orlando.

Admittedly this survey of municipal rose gardens is incomplete, as it must be at any time because of the rapid spread of the idea and because rose love is growing even more rapidly. It is probable that barely one-fourth of the existing municipal rose displays have been here mentioned.

### Test-gardens

Test-gardens under public or semi-public control (as in connection with a college or agricultural experiment station) are not so numerous as they are notable. At the South Dakota Experiment Station, in Brookings, a persistent and patient investigator has established a State Rose Garden of 20 acres in which he breeds roses that will stand blizzard conditions. In Portland, Ore., the International Rose Test-Garden in Washington Park receives, cares for and observes new varieties from all the rose world. Its awards are highly cherished.

Counting with this garden in importance is a Canadian test-garden at Guelph, Ontario, in connection with the Ontario Agricultural College.

The Federal Department of Agriculture has tested rose under-stocks extensively at Beltsville, Md., and at Shafter, Calif.

Rose variety tests were long maintained at Cornell University, Ithaca, N.Y. Here also have been conducted investigations in promotion of under-glass rose-growing, and an intensive study of the control of rose diseases. The famous Boyce Thompson Institute, at Yonkers, N.Y., has promoted rose garden success in many ways, especially in germination tests.

Important private test-gardens, in addition to those previously referred to, are at Rutherford, N.J.; West Grove, Pa.; Harrisburg, Pa.; Chevy Chase, Md. While these gardens are privately owned and maintained, they are really open to the interested public. — J. H. McF.

**ROSE GERANIUM** = *Pelargonium graveolens*.

**ROSE HIP.** The much-enlarged, fleshy, berry-like receptacle* of the rose. It is not technically a fruit, although commonly called so. Actually, it encloses the true fruits of the rose, which are bony achenes.* See Rosa.

**ROSELLE** = *Hibiscus sabdariffa*.

**ROSE MALLOW.** See *Hibiscus moscheutos*.

**ROSEMARY.** Hardy perennial evergreen shrubs comprising the genus **Rosmarinus** (ros-ma-ry′nus) which has only one species, a native of the Mediterranean region, and belonging to the mint family. These shrubs are general garden favorites, owing to their strongly scented leaves and flowers. The only species is **R. officinalis**. It grows up to 6 ft., and is of upright habit, much-branched. Leaves small, lance-shaped, to 1 in. long, grayish-green on the upper side, covered with short white hairs on under side. Flowers light blue, in clusters growing from the axils* of the leaves. Calyx of 5 sepals. Corolla tubular, 2-lipped,* upper lip consisting of 2 lobes, lower lip of 3 lobes. Stamens* 4, in pairs, 2 long, 2 short. Fruit 2-celled when young, splitting into 4 parts when ripe. Mediterranean region.

Propagated from cuttings. Cuttings should be made in Sept. of young shoots about 6 in. long, which should be inserted in a mixture of ½ sand and ½ soil, in a cool greenhouse or cold frame. After rooting they should be planted in potting mixture* 2, and left in cold frame during winter months. See Herb Gardening. In the northern states they require sheltered positions. They make good hedge plants in the southern states. (*Rosmarinus* is from the Latin for sea-dew, in allusion to its being found on the sea cliff of southern France.)

**ROSEMARY FAMILY** = Labiatae.

**ROSE MILKWEED** = *Asclepias tuberosa*. See Milkweed.

**ROSE MOSS** = *Portulaca grandiflora*.

**ROSE-OF-CHINA** = *Hibiscus rosa-sinensis*.

**ROSE-OF-HEAVEN** = *Lychnis coeli-rosa*.

**ROSE-OF-JERICHO** = *Anastatica hierochuntica*.

---

* Special articles on the subjects indicated by an asterisk (*) will be found at the words so marked.

**ROSE-OF-SHARON** = *Hibiscus syriacus;* also *Hypericum calycinum.* See St. John's-wort at SAINT.

*ROSEO-PICTA, -us, -um* (ro-zee-o-pick'ta). Rose-blotched or rose-marked.

**ROSE PINK.** See SABBATIA.

**ROSE POGONIA** = *Pogonia ophioglossoides.*

**ROSE POT.** See FLOWER POTS.

**ROSE SCALE.** See Insect Pests at ROSE and BLACKBERRY.

**ROSETTE.** See Diseases at PEACH and RASPBERRY.

**ROSETTE.** A usually radiating cluster of basal leaves, common in many herbs, especially plants like the houseleek and in most saxifrages. Rosettes are common also as the first-year stage of many biennials. While rosettes are usually basal, they are sometimes terminal, as in the sago palm (*Cycas revoluta*), and in many other plants.

A terminal rosette (*above*) is not so common as the basal rosette found in houseleek and many other plants.

**ROSETUM.** A rose garden.

**ROSINWEED.** See SILPHIUM. See *also* CHRYSOPSIS VILLOSA.

**ROSMARINUS.** See ROSEMARY.

*ROSTRATA, -us, -um* (ros-tray'-ta). Beaked.

**ROSY MILFOIL** = *Achillea millefolium roseum.*

**ROTATE.** Applied to flowers which have a very short tube and a flat, expanded, more or less wheel-shaped limb.* A typically rotate corolla is the moneywort or creeping Charlie; also in many flowers of the genus *Solanum* (potato, etc.).

**ROTATION OF BLOOM.** A continuous succession of plants in bloom is perhaps more desired than almost anything else in the garden. A list of one thousand of the commonest ornamental plants, arranged by the months in which they flower, will be found at GARDEN CALENDAR. From such a list anyone can plan a garden for a continuous rotation of bloom.

**ROTATION OF CROPS.** An agricultural and horticultural practice of very ancient use, based upon the fact that too long occupancy of one site by a single crop is neither good for it nor for the soil in which it grows. Where it is impossible to allow land to lie fallow,* some of the benefits of fallow land may be accomplished by a definite system of rotation of crops.

Such a plan, which should operate over a period of years to be effective, should be so arranged that the same kind of crop never occupies the same soil for two successive years. The advantages of this are that over-wintered diseases or insect pests will not have the same crop upon which to feed. Also soils are at least thought to get "tired" of the one-crop occupancy. Whether or not they really do so is a disputed point among the experts. In any case, rotation can do no harm, and for centuries it has been most beneficial by actual test.

It is usually impossible to follow any rotation scheme in ornamental plantings, except, of course, for annuals and bulbs which should be rotated if possible. But in the vegetable garden rotation is to be strongly recommended. For the details of several rotation schemes *see* KITCHEN GARDEN.

**ROTECIDE.** A trademarked derris insecticide, sold with directions for use as a contact spray.

**ROTENONE.** See Contact Sprays at INSECTICIDES.

**ROTOFUME.** A trademarked derris insecticide, sold with directions for use as a contact spray.

**ROTTEN-NECK.** See Disease at RICE.

**ROTTEN WOOD.** See WOOD ROT.

**ROTUND.** Circular; orbicular.

*ROTUNDIFOLIA, -us, -um* (ro-tun-di-fō'li-a). Round-leaved.

**ROTUNDIFOLIA GRAPES.** Another name for Muscadine grapes, derived from *Vitis rotundifolia.* See GRAPE.

**ROUEN LILAC.** See Lilac Culture at LILAC.

**ROUGE-PLANT** = *Rivina humilis.*

**ROUGH LEMON.** See LEMON.

**ROUGH WOODBINE** = *Lonicera hirsuta.*

**ROUND FLOWER BEDS.** For the number of plants needed see GARDEN TABLES IV.

**ROUND KUMQUAT** = *Fortunella japonica.*

**ROUND TANKS.** For contents see WEIGHTS AND MEASURES, 5.

**ROWAN TREE** = *Sorbus aucuparia.* See MOUNTAIN-ASH.

**ROYAL.** An apricot variety. See APRICOT.

**ROYAL ANN** = Napoleon, a cherry variety. See CHERRY.

**ROYAL DUKE.** A cherry variety. See CHERRY.

**ROYAL FERN** = *Osmunda regalis.*

**ROYAL HORTICULTURAL SOCIETY.** See HORTICULTURAL SOCIETIES.

**ROYAL LILY** = *Lilium regale.*

**ROYAL PALM.** See ROYSTONEA.

**ROYAL POINCIANA** = *Delonix regia.*

**ROYAL WATER LILY** = *Victoria regia.*

*ROYOC* (roy'yock). Tropical American vernacular name of *Morinda royoc.*

**ROYSTONEA** (roy-stone'ee-a). Royal Palm. Magnificent feather palms from tropical America (one extending

Royal palm

---

* Special articles on the subjects indicated by an asterisk (*) will be found at the words so marked.

into extreme southern Fla.), planted throughout the tropical world. Three of the four known species are planted for ornament in Fla., but only in zone* 9 or the southernmost part of zone* 8. Some tropical cities, notably Rio de Janeiro, have magnificent avenues of these royal palms, most of which are native in the West Indies. They are tall, single-stemmed, unarmed palms, the trunks sometimes bulging, crowned with an immense tuft of large, gracefully drooping leaves, the stalk of which is usually concave or convex in cross section. Male and female flowers separate in the same cluster which arises just below the crown of leaves. Fruit scarcely over ½ in. in diameter, generally roundish and bluish. (Named for General Roy Stone, American engineer in Porto Rico.)

The royal palms are scarcely known in greenhouses and they have never been successfully grown outdoors in Calif. In Fla. by far the most commonly planted and hardiest is *R. regia*. Taller and more tender is *R. oleracea*, suited only to zone* 9. Also very tender is the Porto Rican *R. borinquena*. It is lower than the other two but does better on light sandy soils than either of the other royal palms.

**borinquena.** Porto Rican Royal Palm. Not usually over 35 ft. high as cult., the trunk swollen about ¾ of the way to the top, tapering above and below the swelling. Leaves about 10 ft. long, its many segments or leaflets about 2–2½ ft. long, 2 in. wide, tapering to a fine point. Fruit egg-shaped or roundish, yellowish-brown. Porto Rico and St. Croix.

**oleracea.** Barbados Royal Palm; also called palmiste and cabbage palm. A slender-stemmed palm, sometimes 120 ft. high, the swelling of the trunk near the base. Leaves 10–15 ft. long, more or less ascending at first, ultimately drooping. Fruit oblong-roundish, the cluster hanging far below the leaves. W.I. A magnificent avenue palm.

**regia.** Cuban Royal Palm. Usually not over 70 ft. high, the trunk swelling near the middle or just above it, tapering above and below the swelling. Leaves 10–15 ft. long, usually drooping from the first, and generally covering the flower and fruit cluster. Fruit nearly round, scarcely ½ in. in diameter. Cuba, Panama, and perhaps elsewhere in tropical America; also native on some of the Fla. Keys and in the Everglades. Widely planted in southern Fla.

**RUBBER-PLANT.** The common rubber-plant of the florists, and a good house plant is *Ficus elastica* (which see). It does not now produce rubber commercially, all of which is derived from *Hevea brasiliensis* (which see).

**RUBBER-TREE** = *Hevea brasiliensis*.

**RUBBISH.** Rubbish may be placed roughly into two classes — combustible and non-combustible. The former includes organic matter such as leaves, grass, weeds, branches from shrubs and trees, mulch and paper; the latter, inorganic matter such as stones, metallic objects, glass and vegetable refuse that is not readily dried.

Leaves from deciduous trees and lawn clippings may be used as mulch* or put into the compost* heap and permitted to rot. With the addition of Adco, a commercial preparation, at the rate of two pounds to a wheelbarrow load of vegetable refuse, a clean, odorless manure may be secured in three to four months. It would be well, however, not to include in this vegetable manure any weeds whose seed is partially or fully matured, as germination may not be totally destroyed by rotting. See Synthetic Manure at MANURE. However, some part of the vegetable refuse is unfit for the compost heap, vegetable manure, or for mulching and must be disposed of in some other manner, preferably by incineration.

Of the two methods of incineration, the open fire with its ever-present "fire hazard," and the small portable incinerator, the latter is to be preferred. Large branches of trees or shrubs and flower stalks such as hollyhocks, dahlias, delphiniums, and other refuse too bulky to be placed in the portable incinerator, are best destroyed in small open fires. It is better to do this on a windless day. The fire should be placed at an adequate distance from trees or shrubs, so that any change in the air current would not cause scorching of the branches or foliage. Small fires to which refuse may be added from time to time are to be preferred to large fires that may easily get beyond control and do irreparable injury to the surrounding vegetation.

The small portable incinerator consists of a metallic frame covered with a wire mesh, either rectangular or circular in shape and with or without a cover for the top. They are comparatively inexpensive and may be purchased from supply houses or hardware stores. With a little mechanical ingenuity a serviceable incinerator may be constructed at home. Ten or fifteen feet of band iron and a few yards of wire mesh are all that is required. Even a steel oil drum perforated on the bottom and sides and raised a few inches from the ground makes a serviceable incinerator. All light refuse should be burned in these appliances which may easily be moved from place to place. An added advantage is that they can be used on windy days with perfect safety, as the fire is confined by the wire mesh and burning pieces of light rubbish cannot be scattered by the wind.

All other rubbish of mineral or vegetable origin that cannot be destroyed by incineration must be disposed of by hauling to the public dump, or, if in small quantities, by burial in a pit or trench. In the case of metallic objects the disintegration after burial will be hastened if they are first put into the incinerator to burn off the protective coating.

All too frequently the first vacant lot, open field, or patch of woodland becomes the unwilling recipient of a load of rubbish, deposited there by persons either too careless or too lazy to dispose of it otherwise. The presence of the first load is a distinct invitation for others to follow, inevitably the adjoining landscape is covered with wind-blown pieces of paper or light rubbish, while the cans, bottles and heavier refuse remain in heaps to become breeding places for mosquitoes, flies and other vermin. Many persons who pride themselves on their own neat homes and gardens, have no hesitancy in making use of the so-called "public dump." Certainly the natural beauty of any landscape is not enhanced by heaps of rubbish, paper scattered to the four winds and disintegrating skeletons of defunct automobiles. In addition to this, the litter left behind by picnic parties, who, however neat they may be at home, still think the wide open spaces are merely places to be defiled with debris of all descriptions, have ruined places of beauty for those who appreciate Nature more than the hand of man. See also COMPOST PILE.

*RUBER* (roo'ber). Red.

*RUBESCENS* (roo-bess'senz). Reddish.

**RUBIA** (roo'bi-a). Perennial herbs of about 40 species; of the family Rubiaceae, found distributed throughout the temperate and tropical regions of the world. Leaves generally in whorls* of 4–8, narrowly lance-shaped, sometimes stalked, smooth or covered with prickly hairs. Flowers small, greenish-yellow or white in terminal clusters, or in the leaf-axils.* Fruit a small berry. *R. tinctorum* has red, fleshy roots. (*Rubia* is from the Latin for red.) These plants are not of much garden importance, although *R. tinctorum* is grown for its dye, which is obtained by grinding the roots.

**tinctorum.** Common madder. Growing to 4 ft., of spreading habit. Leaves in whorls of 4–6, lance-shaped, 2–4 in. long, with prickly hairs on midrib and margins. Flowers greenish-yellow, small, in branching clusters. Southern Eu. and As.

**RUBIACEAE** (roo-bi-ā'see-ee). The madder or coffee family while a very large one (350 genera and 4500 species) is more important commercially than from the garden standpoint. It includes herbs, shrubs and trees, most of them tropical, and a few of worldwide importance, like *Coffea* and *Cinchona* (quinine). Only a handful are suited to outdoor culture in frosty regions. Of these, herbs (sometimes slightly woody) are found in *Asperula, Galium, Houstonia, Mitchella*, and *Rubia*, while the only generally hardy, woody plant is *Cephalanthus* (see BUTTON-BUSH).

All the rest of the cult. genera are shrubs, vines, or trees of tropical or sub-tropical regions to be grown outdoors only in frost-free parts of the country or in greenhouses. These tender genera, mostly of secondary garden importance, are *Bouvardia, Coprosma* (some nearly hardy), *Hamelia, Hoffmannia* (a greenhouse foliage plant), *Ixora, Luculia, Manettia* (vines), *Morinda* (includes the Indian mulberry), *Nertera* (tender ground cover), *Pentas* (nearly herbaceous), *Posoqueria, Psychotria, Rondeletia*, and *Serissa*. Two other tropical genera are far more important. One is *Gardenia*

---

* Special articles on the subjects indicated by an asterisk (*) will be found at the words so marked.

which includes the florists' flower of that name, the other is *Genipa* with edible fruit (the genipap).

Leaves opposite* (or whorled* in a few genera), usually without marginal teeth. Flowers mostly regular, very showy in some of the tropical genera (*Ixora*, *Hamelia*) and attractive in *Cephalanthus*, mostly in various sorts of clusters, but in pairs in *Mitchella*. Fruit fleshy or dry.

Technical flower characters: Calyx* more or less united, 2–6-cleft or parted. Corolla united, 4–6-lobed, the edges of the lobes touching (not overlapping). Stamens* 4–6, borne on the corolla. Ovary inferior,* mostly 2-celled, the style* 1.

**RUBIOIDES** (roo-bi-oy'deez, but *see* OÏDES). Resembling the madder (*Rubia*).

**RUBRA, -us, -um** (roo'bra). Red.

**RUBROFRUCTA, -us, -um** (roo-bro-fruck'ta). Red-fruited.

**RUBUS** (roo'bus). An immense genus of shrubby, usually prickly, plants of the rose family, including all the wild brambles, the cult. blackberry, dewberry, and raspberry, and a few others grown for ornament. Nearly all the 500 species are from the north temperate zone, but a few outliers are found on tropical mountains, in the southern hemisphere, and a small group of species extends to or beyond the Arctic Circle. They are erect or trailing plants, many of them with biennial canes (*i.e.* leafy the first year, but flowering and fruiting the second year and then dying). The first-year canes, bearing only leaves, are known as turions. Some species bear perennial canes.

Leaves alternate,* simple and lobed, or more usually compound* and the leaflets arranged finger-fashion (rarely feather-fashion). Flowers prevailingly white, but purplish-pink in a few, the 5 petals often rounded, sometimes small or even wanting. Stamens* numerous. Fruit (in ours) a collection of small, sometimes dryish drupelets,* the "berry" (*i.e.* the edible part) of two sorts: (1) In the blackberry and dewberry the mass of fleshy drupelets (commonly called seeds) adheres to the fleshy receptacle* which is part of the "berry" and eaten with it; (2) in the raspberry (including the blackcap) the mass of drupelets,* or what is incorrectly called the berry, parts from the receptacle* when picked, and the "fruit" is hollow. In other words we eat the receptacle* in blackberries but leave it on the plant in the raspberry. The loganberry, of hybrid origin, is usually considered as having fruits of the blackberry type, although one of its parents is a raspberry. (*Rubus* is the old Latin name of the brambles.)

Perhaps no genus of plants, except *Crataegus*, is in such a chaotic condition as to Latin names and identities as the brambles. While there are supposed to be 400–500 species, some authorities recognize nearly twice this number. In addition, there are hundreds of natural and induced hybrids. All that can be done here is to list a few of the more important species that appear to or may be involved in the production of the four major fruit crops, and a few others grown for ornament or interest. The major fruit crops, all the subjects of separate articles which should be consulted for varieties and culture, are: BLACKBERRY, DEWBERRY, RASPBERRY, and LOGANBERRY. The species involved in the production of the common cult. blackberry are omitted from the list below because they are unknown. It seems to have been derived from a group of North American species or hybrids of wild brambles. While over 60 species of *Rubus* are recorded as being cult. in the U.S., the inclusion of all of them here does not seem to be warranted, nor have we included the scores of wild brambles.

Turion as used below means a first-year cane bearing leaves only. Plants bearing perennial canes are noted as perennials.

**deliciosus.** Boulder raspberry. Rocky Mountain flowering raspberry. A perennial, shrubby plant, the stems without prickles or bristles. Leaves simple,* roundish, shallowly 5–7-angled, irregularly toothed, about 2 in. wide. Flowers white, nearly 2 in. wide. Fruit (a raspberry) dark reddish-purple, worthless. Colo. May. Hardy from zone* 4 southward. Grown for ornament.

**flagellaris.** Dewberry. A trailing blackberry, the very prickly, but not sticky stems rooting at the tip. Leaflets 3–5, ovalish or triangular, toothed.

Flowers white, not numerous, in a forking cluster. Fruit (a blackberry) nearly round or oblongish, black. Eastern N.A. May–June. Hardy from zone* 3 southward, but seldom grown in the wild form here noted. For the cult. and varieties of the common dewberry, apparently derived from this species, and notes on hardiness *see* DEWBERRY. *See also* RUBUS TRIVIALIS.

**hispidus.** Swamp dewberry. A perennial, prostrate, vine-like plant, with 3 leaflets, no prickles, but bristly stems. Leaflets partly evergreen, toothed, blunt. Flowers small, white, few and inconspicuous. Fruit (a blackberry) sour and relatively worthless. Eastern N.A. May. Hardy everywhere. Planted only for ground cover in moist, shady places.

**idaeus.** European raspberry. An erect, shrubby plant with biennial, prickly or bristly stems. Leaflets 3 (5 on the turions), toothed, gray-white. Flowers white and small. Fruit (raspberry) conical or thimble-shaped, mostly red. Eurasia. Scarcely known here, but the source of some cult. red raspberries. The var. **strigosus**, a closely related form from N.A. and eastern As., has fruit which is flatter or hemispherical and is the source of most of the red raspberry varieties. *See* RASPBERRY.

**illecebrosus.** Strawberry-raspberry; also called balloon-berry. An arching, very prickly plant, its stems practically herbaceous, about 4 ft. high and forming patches. Leaflets 5–9, narrow, long-pointed, 3–4 in. long. Flowers white, about 1 in. wide, fragrant. Fruit (a raspberry) scarlet, large, but insipid or sour, sometimes used cooked. Jap. July–Sept. Hardy from zone* 3 southward. Planted for ornament.

**laciniatus.** Cutleaf or Evergreen blackberry. An arching or trailing blackberry, its perennial canes prickly, or ultimately smooth. Leaflets 3–5, evergreen or nearly so, cut into fine, toothed segments. Flowers white or pinkish, in branched clusters (panicles)*. Fruit (a blackberry) small, nearly round, black and sweet. Eu., but naturalized on the Pacific Coast. June–July. Hardy from zone* 4 southward. Grown mostly for ornament, although it may be the part origin of some cult. blackberries.

**loganobaccus.** Loganberry. A vigorous blackberry-like, prickly plant, the canes bluish-green, somewhat vine-like. Leaflets 3 (5 on turions), ovalish or wider, toothed, gray-felty beneath. Flowers white, nearly 2 in. wide, sometimes double. Fruit nearly 1¼ in. long, acid, red. For origin and culture *see* LOGANBERRY (which also includes a variety known as Phenomenal).

**occidentalis.** Blackcap raspberry. Thimbleberry. An erect, prickly plant, the stems very bluish or even bluish-purple, ultimately arching over and rooting at the tip, hence making impenetrable thickets unless controlled. Leaflets 3, ovalish but tapering, doubly toothed, conspicuously

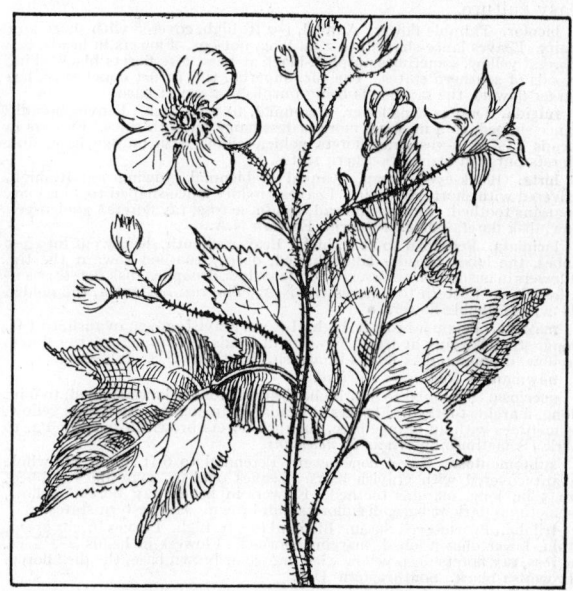

Flowering raspberry (*Rubus odoratus*)

white-felty beneath. Flowers whitish, small, in dense, prickly clusters. Fruit (a black raspberry) black, but with a slight bloom. Eastern N.A. May–June. Hardy from zone* 2 southward. The source of several hort. varieties. Its cult. is the same as for raspberry (which see).

**odoratus.** Flowering raspberry. A showy shrub with perennial, bristly or sticky, but not prickly stems, 4–6 ft. high, the bark shreddy. Leaves simple,* broadly heart-shaped, 4–8 in. wide, generally 5-lobed, irregularly toothed, green and hairy both sides. Flowers purplish or rose-purple, nearly 2 in. wide, showy. Fruit (a raspberry) red, dryish, and worthless. Eastern N.A. June–Aug. Hardy from zone* 2 southward. Planted for ornament, but best suited to partial shade in the informal shrub border, as it ultimately makes large patches.

**phoenicolasius.** Wineberry. An upright, shrubby plant, the canes arching and ultimately rooting at the tip, densely covered with red, sticky hairs and a few weak, straight prickles. Leaflets mostly 3, purple-veined, white-felty beneath. Flowers small, pinkish or white, the calyx large and red-bristly. Fruit (a raspberry) red, small, edible, but insipid. Jap. and

* Special articles on the subjects indicated by an asterisk (*) will be found at the words so marked.

China, often running wild from old gardens in eastern N.A. July-Aug. Hardy from zone* 3 southward. Rather ornamental, but making impenetrable thickets if let alone.

**procerus.** Himalaya-berry (not from the Himalayas). A woody, perennial-stemmed, creeping or clambering blackberry, the stems 20-30 ft. long and very prickly. Leaflets 3-5, densely white-felty beneath, partly persistent, doubly toothed. Flowers white, the clusters white-felty. Fruit (a blackberry) thimble-shaped. Eu. Introduced into the U.S. about 1890 and somewhat grown for fruit in Calif. It needs trellis or fence-like support and the general cult. methods followed for dewberry (which see).

**trivialis.** Southern dewberry. A creeping or trailing blackberry, the stems very prickly and often with sticky bristles. Leaflets partly evergreen, 3-5, narrowly oblongish, toothed, smooth. Flowers white or pinkish, in long clusters (panicles*). Fruit (a blackberry) oblong, black. Va. to Fla. and Tex. April-May. For the cult. and varieties *see* DEWBERRY. Other plants are involved in the production of the cult. dewberry, notably *R. flagellaris.*

**RUBY GRASS** = *Tricholaena rosea.*

**RUDBECKIA** (rood-beck'i-a). Coneflower. North American hardy perennial, annual or biennial herbs, comprising about 30 species, of the family Compositae. Leaves usually alternate,* simple or compound,* in some species much cut and lance-shaped, the veins prominent, the margins deeply toothed toward the tip. Flowers in terminal or axillary heads, generally yellow, in some species the disk florets* being brown or black. Fruit dry, 1-celled, 1-seeded. (Named for two Professors Rudbeck, father and son.)

Rudbeckias are useful border plants, easily cult. Propagated by seeds or division of rootstocks. Seeds should be sown thinly, ⅛ in. deep in early spring in the cool greenhouse or cold frame or later in outdoor seedbed. They may be transplanted to permanent positions as soon as large enough to handle. Division of rootstocks may be made in March or April. One of the most popular of all perennials is the Golden Glow, a variety of *R. laciniata*, which is of very easy culture.

**bicolor.** Thimble flower. Annual, 1-2 ft. high, covered with short, stiff hairs. Leaves lance-shaped, to 2 in. long, not cut. Flowers in heads, ray florets* yellow, sometimes purplish-black at base, disk florets black. Pine woods of southern states. The *var.* **superba**, the Erfurt coneflower, has larger flowers, the ray florets being purplish-brown at base.

**fulgida.** Orange coneflower. Perennial, to 2 ft. high. Leaves broadly lance-shaped, to 4 in. long, more or less hairy on both sides. Flowers in heads 1½ in. across, ray florets golden-yellow with orange base, disk florets purplish-black. Southern states.

**hirta.** Black-eyed Susan. Annual or biennial growing 1-3 ft. high, covered with short, stiff hairs. Leaves broadly lance-shaped to 5 in. long, margins toothed. Flowers in head, 3-4 in. across, ray florets* golden-yellow, disk florets purplish-brown. Eastern N.A.

**laciniata.** Perennial to 12 ft. high. Leaves smooth, deeply cut into 3-5 lobes, the lobes broadly lance-shaped, deeply toothed toward the tip. Flowers in heads 4 in. across, ray florets yellow, drooping, disk florets greenish-yellow. Eastern to midwestern N.A. The *var.* **hortensia**, the golden glow, has double flowers.

**maxima.** Perennial to 9 ft. high. Leaves grayish-green, ovalish, to 1 ft. long, stem-clasping at base. Flowers in heads 5-6 in. across, ray florets yellow, drooping, disk florets brownish. Southern U.S. July-Aug.

**newmani** = *Rudbeckia speciosa.*

**speciosa.** Perennial to 3 ft. high. Leaves broadly lance-shaped, to 6 in. long, margins toothed. Flowers in heads 3-4 in. across, ray florets yellow, sometimes with an orange base, the disk florets brownish-purple. Pa. to Ark. Sometimes known as *R. newmani.*

**subtomentosa.** Sweet coneflower. Perennial to 6 ft. high, the whole plant covered with grayish hairs. Leaves ovalish, sometimes 3-lobed, to 5 in. long, margins toothed. Flowers in heads; ray florets* yellow, sometimes dark at base, disk florets dull brown. Midwestern states.

**triloba.** Brown-eyed Susan. Biennial to 5 ft. high. Leaves bright green, thin, lower ones 3-lobed, margins toothed. Flowers in heads 2-2½ in. across, ray florets deep yellow with orange or brown base, the disk florets brownish-black. Southeastern U.S.

**RUDIS, -e** (roo'dis). Wild, not cultivated; the word means, literally, of the rubbish pile.

**RUE.** Aromatic, perennial herbs or under-shrubs, comprising the genus **Ruta** (roo'ta) of the family Rutaceae, all the 40 known species from Eurasia or the Canary Islands. The common rue, **R. graveolens**, is usually the only one in cult. It is an evergreen under-shrub or woody herb, with twice-compound,* alternate* leaves, the ultimate leaflets small. Flowers dull yellow, about ½ in. wide, in a terminal cluster (a loose cyme*). Petals 5, concave, fringed on the margin. Stamens* 8-10. Fruit a 4-5-lobed capsule.* Southern Eu. Cult. for centuries, and once called herb of grace because it was associated with repentance. For cult. *see* HERB GARDENING. (*Ruta* is the old Latin name of the rue.) For meadow rue *see* THALICTRUM.

**RUE ANEMONE** = *Anemonella thalictroides.*

**RUE FAMILY.** Tropical or warm-region trees, like the bael and all the citrus fruits, comprise most of the cult. plants in the rue family. But some trees or under-shrubs or even herbs of cooler regions are found in the family, such as the rue itself, the gas-plant, the prickly ash, and the genus PHELLODENDRON. For a complete list of the cult. genera *see* RUTACEAE.

**RUELLIA** (roo-ell'i-a). Tender and hardy perennial herbs or under-shrubs, comprising about 200 species, belonging to the family Acanthaceae, and found throughout the world. Leaves simple, opposite.* Flowers solitary, or in clusters, generally in blue or purple shades, sometimes white or red. Calyx* of 5 sepals,* joined at the base. Corolla of 5 lobes, funnel-shaped or salver-shaped. Stamens* 4, in pairs, 2 long, 2 short. Fruit a capsule,* which explodes when seeds are ripe. Seeds possess surface hairs which when wet, swell and stick to the ground. (Named for Jean de la Ruelle, French botanist.)

They are not much in cultivation, but a few species are grown as warm-greenhouse plants in the northern states or in the open garden in the South. *Ruellia ciliosa*, though hardy and attractive, is rarely seen. Propagated by cuttings or seeds. Cuttings of young shoots should be made in late spring or early summer, in a temperature of 75°-85°. Some plants offered as *Pellionia* are apt to belong to *Ruellia.*

**amoena.** Perennial from 1-2 ft. high. Leaves broadly lance-shaped, to 5 in. long, margins wavy. Flowers bright red, 1 in. long, in long-stalked, axillary clusters. S.A.

**ciliosa.** Hardy herbaceous perennial, from 1-2½ ft. high. Leaves broadly lance-shaped. N.J. to Fla. and Tex. Flowers light blue, funnel-shaped, to 2 in. long in loose clusters. N.J. to Fla. and Tex.

**devosiana.** Sometimes known as *Pellionia.* Low-growing, tender perennial, to 18 in. high. Leaves roundish, to 2 in. long, with white veins on the upper side, and the under surface purple. Flowers small, solitary, white, veined lilac-blue, to 1¾ in. long. This species makes a good greenhouse plant for the hanging basket. Brazil.

*RUFA, -us, -um* (roo'fa). Red.

**RUFFIA.** Tropical African name for the palm yielding raffia. *See* RAPHIA.

*RUGOSA, -us, -um* (roo-gō'sa). Rugose; *i.e.* rough.

**RUMEX** (roo'mecks). Dock or sorrel. Perennial herbs, comprising about 100 species of the family Polygonaceae, found throughout the world. They have strong roots with simple, basal, or stem leaves. Flowers in long, branching clusters, small, usually greenish-white. Flowers on same plant are sometimes of 2 kinds, some bearing stamens* only, others pistils* only. Calyx* of 6 sepals. Corolla absent. Stamens* 6. Fruit a 3-sided capsule, often winged. (*Rumex* is the Latin for sorrel.)

They are not much in cultivation, as most species are garden weeds. A few, however, are grown for their leaves, which are edible, and a few for decoration. Easily propagated from seeds, which may be sown outdoors in early spring.

**abyssinicus.** Spinach-rhubarb. Strong-growing perennial to 9 ft. high. Leaves arrow-shaped to lance-shaped, to 7 in. long. Flowers of 2 kinds, stamens only or pistil only. Leaves sometimes used as spinach and leaf-stalks as rhubarb. Abyssinia.

**acetosa.** Sorrel. Erect-growing perennial to 3 ft. high. Stems ridged. Basal leaves ovalish, arrow-shaped at base, thin, light green in color, to 5 in. long. Stem leaves narrowing to a sharp point. Flowers of 2 kinds, stamens only, or pistil only. Leaves used as "greens." Eu. and As., naturalized in N.A. The *var.* "Large Belleville" is the form generally cult.

**acetosella** = sheep's-sorrel. *See* list at WEEDS.

**crispus** = curled dock. *See* list at WEEDS.

**hymenosepalus.** Canaigre. Perennial to 3 ft. high, with clustered tuberous roots, from which tannin is obtained. Leaves broadly lance-shaped, to 1 ft. long. Flowers in clusters 1 ft. or more long. Okla. to Calif.

**patientia.** Herb patience. Spinach-dock. Strong-growing perennial to 6 ft. high. Basal leaves 8-10 in. long, tapering both ends, margins wavy. Stem leaves broadly lance-shaped. Flowers in branching clusters, 2 ft. long. Basal leaves excellent for "greens" if used in spring. Eu., naturalized in N.A.

**RUNNEL.** A tree that has been pollarded. *See* POLLARD.

**RUNNER.** A weak, usually prostrate shoot that roots at the joints, as in the strawberry. Runners afford a very

---

* Special articles on the subjects indicated by an asterisk (*) will be found at the words so marked.

easy method of propagation in those plants that produce them; all that is necessary for propagation is to detach the rooted joints. *See also* STOLON *and* PROCUMBENS.

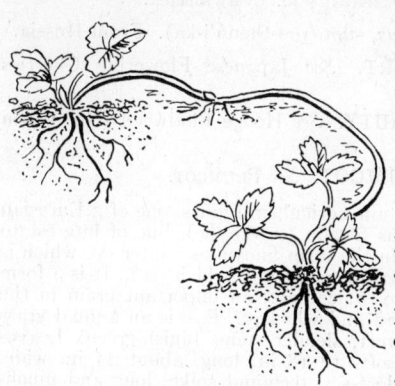

Runner of the strawberry

**RUNNER PEANUT.** *See* PEANUT.

**RUNNING BIRCH** = *Chiogenes hispidula*.

**RUNNING MYRTLE** = *Vinca minor*.

**RUNNING PINE** = *Lycopodium clavatum*.

**RUNNING STRAWBERRY-BUSH** = *Euonymus obovatus*.

*RUPESTRIS, -e* (roo-pes'tris). Rock-inhabiting.

*RUPICOLA, -us, -um* (roo-pick'o-la). Growing on ledges or cliffs.

**RUPTUREWORT.** *See* HERNIARIA.

*RUSCIFOLIA, -us, -um* (rus-ki-fō'li-a). Having leaves like the butcher's-broom (*Ruscus*).

**RUSCUS** (rus'kus). A small genus of low shrubs belonging to the lily family, found from Madeira to the Caucasus, one of them, *R. aculeatus*, the butcher's-broom or Jew's-myrtle, widely cult. for its foliage which is often colored for winter decoration (*see* DRIED FLOWERS). It is a prickly, stiff, evergreen shrub, 2–3 ft. high, without obvious leaves but with leaf-like branches (cladophylls*) that are ovalish, ¾–1¼ in. long, thick, and leathery, and prickle-tipped. Male and female flowers on different plants, small, greenish, inconspicuous, borne in the middle of the leaf-like branches. Fruit a bright red (rarely yellow) berry about ⅜ in. in diameter. Very widely grown by florists for the Christmas trade, and dyed red. Useful for winter decoration, as the leaf-like branches do not fall as would true leaves. Also grown outdoors from zone* 7 southward. Eu. If grown outdoors (it is popular in Calif.), it is important to get both male and female plants or there will be no fruit. In the greenhouse it needs potting mixture* 4 and a cool house. (*Ruscus* is the old Latin name of this plant.)

**RUSH.** *See* JUNCUS. For Flowering Rush *see* BUTOMUS.

**RUSSELIA** (rus-see'li-a). Tender, tropical American shrubs, comprising about 20 species of the family Scrophulariaceae. Stems much-branched and slender, often pendulous. Leaves opposite* or in whorls,* small, sometimes scale-like. Flowers showy, red, in branching clusters, the individual flower growing from scale-like bracts.* Calyx* of 5 sepals joined at the base. Corolla tubular, opening into 2 lips,* upper lip 2-lobed, lower lip 3-lobed. Stamens* 4, in pairs. Fruit a dry, many-seeded capsule.* (Named for Alexander Russell.)

Russelias make good warm-greenhouse plants, but may be grown outdoors in the South. Easily propagated by cuttings. Cuttings should be made in spring and inserted in clean sand in a temperature of 75°. When rooted they may be transplanted into small pots using potting mixture* 2. In final potting, use potting mixture* 3.

elegantissima. A supposed hybrid between *R. equisetiformis* and *R. sarmentosa*.

equisetiformis. Fountain-plant. Coral plant. Shrubby, much-branched plant, growing to 4 ft. high. Branches slender and smooth, square, drooping. Leaves small, bract*-like toward the top, broadly lance-shaped, the margins toothed. Flowers in clusters, 1–2-flowered. Mex., naturalized in Fla.

juncea = *R. equisetiformis*.

sarmentosa. Resembling *R. equisetiformis*, but with no scale-like leaves, and the flower clusters more profuse. Mex.

**RUSSIAN ALMOND** = *Prunus nana*.

**RUSSIAN MULBERRY** = *Morus alba tatarica*. *See* MULBERRY.

**RUSSIAN OLIVE** = *Elaeagnus angustifolia*.

**RUSSIAN THISTLE** = *Salsola pestifer*. *See* the list at WEEDS.

**RUSSIAN TURNIP** = Rutabaga.

**RUSSIAN WORMWOOD** = *Artemisia sacrorum*.

**RUST DISEASES.** *See* PLANT DISEASES.

*RUSTICANA, -us, -um* (rus-ti-kay'na). Relating to the country.

**RUSTIC BRIDGE.** *See* BRIDGES.

**RUSTIC WORK.** *See* ORNAMENT AND FURNITURE.

**RUST MITE.** *See* Insect Pests at ORANGE.

**RUSTY GUM** = *Angophora lanceolata*.

**RUTA.** *See* RUE.

**RUTABAGA** (*Brassica napobrassica*). Rutabagas, also called Macomber, Swede, and Swedish, Russian, and Winter turnips, are very similar to but hardier than the common turnips, although they do not resemble them in appearance, having smooth, shiny foliage of a bluish-green and a tuber with a long, leafy neck.* They require longer to mature than turnips, and to secure heavy crops of large roots for stock-feeding the seed should be sown in the North from June 15th to July 1, in rows two to two and a half feet apart. They make one of the best winter feeds available for sheep. One ounce of seed will sow four hundred feet of drill; one to two pounds of seed are required per acre when sown in drills; and four to five pounds per acre if sown broadcast. The plants should be spaced about one foot apart. They will reach their full growth by October and should be harvested after a frost but not allowed to freeze, as this would interfere with their keeping qualities.

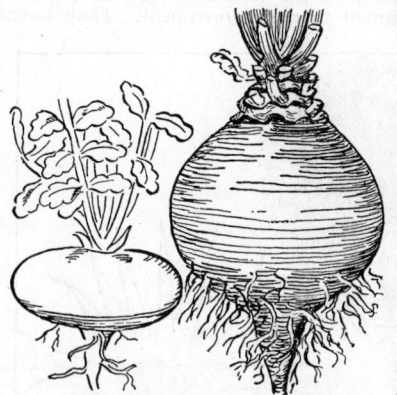

Common turnip (*left*) and the rutabaga (*right*). The latter is often called yellow turnip.

They are splendid for table use and as they are a late season crop are highly valued. They have firmer flesh than turnips and can be stored in the cellar in moist sand or in pits for use during the winter and well into the spring. For table use seed should be sown about July 15 or even later in the season. These late-planted rutabagas will be of better quality, although not so large. The soil should be rich and moist.

Although the yellow varieties were formerly considered the best, the new white rutabagas of the Macomber strain are of finer quality than the old yellows, as the flesh is very sweet and fine-grained. For fall home or market use seeds may be sown two or three weeks earlier than those for storing purposes. Good yellow varieties for table use are Golden Heart, Golden Neckless, Improved Purple-top, and Perfection Swede. Larger, heavier yielding sorts, like the Improved Long Island and American Purple-top, are best for stock-feeding purposes.

---

* Special articles on the subjects indicated by an asterisk (*) will be found at the words so marked.

**RUTACEAE** (roo-tay'see-ee). The rue or citrus family comprises a few unimportant genera of little cultural value, and a group of perhaps the most important fruit trees in the country (orange, grapefruit, lime, lemon, etc.) — the citrus fruits. The family is a large one (120 genera and about 1000 species), mostly tropical, but the following shrubs and trees, mostly Eurasian or North American, are cult. outdoors in most of the U.S.: *Evodia, Phellodendron, Poncirus* (a hardy, inedible orange), *Ptelea,* and *Zanthoxylum, Ruta* and *Dictamnus,* largely herbaceous, are plants for the open border.

The rest of the cult. genera are all tropical or sub-tropical and are grown outdoors only in essentially frost-free parts of the country, or in greenhouses. Of these, *Citrus* and its related or pertinent genera (*Citropsis, Fortunella* and *Microcitrus*) are by far the most important, because of their fruit, but edible fruit are also found in *Casimiroa.*

Other cult. genera, grown mostly for ornament, are: *Boronia, Choisya* (some nearly hardy northward), *Correa, Diosma, Luvunga, Murraya, Severinia, Skimmia* and *Triphasia.*

Leaves mostly alternate,* simple* or compound* (in *Citrus, Phellodendron,* etc.), usually with resinous or aromatic glands in them, which explains the generally fragrant odor of the crushed foliage. Flowers often very fragrant (orange blossom), but not often particularly showy, sometimes greenish and inconspicuous. Fruit various, a berry in the orange and its relatives, a dry pod (capsule*) in several genera, and sometimes with a winged fruit (*Ptelea*).

Technical flower characters: Flowers mostly regular*; dioecious* in *Phellodendron* and *Zanthoxylum.* Sepals* 4–5, often partly united. Petals 4–5, sometimes none. Stamens* 8–10. Ovary superior.*

**RUTHENICA, -us, -um** (roo-thenn'i-ka). From Russia.

**RUTH WOHLERT.** *See* Japanese Flowering Cherries at PRUNUS.

**RUTLAND BEAUTY.** *See* Hedge Bindweed (No. 17) in the list at WEEDS.

**RUTLAND PLUMCOT.** *See* PLUMCOT.

**RYE.** An important agricultural grass, one of 3 Eurasian species of the genus **Secale** (see-kay'le), but of interest to the gardener only in the form known as winter rye which is a useful plant for green manuring (which see). It is a form of the common rye, **S. cereale,** an important grain in the making of rye bread and whiskey. Rye is an annual grass 3–5 ft. high, its erect, slender stems bluish-green. Leaves grass-like, rather soft, 12–18 in. long, about ½ in. wide. Flower cluster a close-set, terminal spike, long and much-awned,* the spikelets on a tiny zigzag stalk. Fruit the familiar grain of rye, oblongish, about ⅓ in. long and minutely grooved. The common rye is unknown as a wild plant, but is probably a cultigen* derived from one of the European species. (*Secale* is an old Roman name for some cereal, but not certainly of this one.) For wild rye *see* ELYMUS.

**RYE GRASS.** *See* LOLIUM.

# S

**SABAL** (say'bal). Palmetto. New World fan palms, comprising about 20 species, a few native in the southeastern U.S. and much planted there for ornament. They have

The palmetto (*Sabal palmetto*) is one of the commonest wild and cult. palms in the southeastern states.

moderately tall trunks in *S. blackburniana* and *S. palmetto,* but none in *S. minor* and in several other (non-hort.) species where the trunk is buried or altogether lacking. Leaves fan-like, but only in *S. minor* with the stalk ending at the blade. In the other two the leafstalk appears as though continued through the blade. Flower cluster from among the leaves, branched, usually drooping, the flowers small, greenish-white. Sepals and petals 3 each. Stamens* 6. Fruit a roundish or pear-shaped, dark-colored drupe.* (*Sabal* may be derived from a native name from a South American species.)

*Sabal* is one of the hardiest genera of palms, the common *S. palmetto* being native from N. Car. to Fla., mostly along the coast. They are of the easiest cult. and thrive on the sandy soils of the coastal plain. *S. palmetto* is not certainly hardy north of the coastal region of N. Car., and the other two are not safe north of the limits of zone* 8 or 7. All the cult. species were once included in the genus *Inodes.*

**blackburniana.** Bermuda palmetto. A stout palm, the trunk sometimes 35 ft. high, usually shedding the old leaf bases. Leaves 5–9 ft. wide, green both sides but checkered beneath, cut nearly halfway by its many segments which are 1–2 in. wide, usually with a single, stout fiber at each cleft. Flower cluster large, and much-branched. Fruit nearly round, about ½ in. in diameter, black. Bermuda. Not hardy north of zone* 8.

**glabra** = *Sabal minor.*

**minor.** Dwarf palmetto; also called bluestem. An apparently stemless palm, the leafstalks arising from the ground. Leaves bluish-green or pale green, stiffish, the central segments divided about half the depth of the blade, the others more deeply cleft. Flower cluster about as long as the leaves, much-branched. Fruit round, about ⅓ in. in diameter. Ga. to Fla. and Tex., and preferring moist sites. Not particularly showy. Hardy up to zone* 7.

**palmetto.** The common palmetto of the southeastern states, often called cabbage palmetto. In maturity its trunk may be 70–90 ft. high, and is usually long, clothed with the persistent leaf bases, but ultimately bare of them below. Leaves not very numerous in the terminal crown, green, 5–8 ft. or more wide, conspicuously fibrous. Central segments cleft more than halfway to the center, the other segments more deeply cleft, all the tips curving or drooping. Flower cluster much-branched, usually longer than the leaves, hence hanging below the withered but persistent leaves. Fruit round, black, nearly ½ in. in diameter. N. Car. to Fla., mostly near the coast.

**SABBATIA** (sab-bay'she-a). American centaury; also called sea pink and rose pink. A genus of 15 species of annual or biennial, mostly weak herbs of the gentian family, found in eastern N.A. and of little hort. interest except for **S. dodecandra.** It is a pretty little salt marsh herb, 7–15 in. high, the leaves narrowly lance-shaped or even line-like. Flowers pink (rarely white), the corolla with a very short

---

*Special articles on the subjects indicated by an asterisk (*) will be found at the words so marked.

tube, its limb expanded into 9–12 rather showy, rounded lobes. Stamens* 4–12, the anthers* coiled. Fruit a small, egg-shaped or roundish capsule.* Useful only in seaside gardens in moist, salty sand or in salt marshes. New England to Fla., along the coast. July–Sept. (Named for L. Sabbati, an Italian botanist.)

**SABDARIFFA** (sab-da-riff'a). Turkish vernacular name for the roselle (*Hibiscus sabdariffa*).

**SABINA** (sa-by'na). An old generic name (derived from the Sabines) for certain plants now included in *Juniperus*.

**SABRE BEAN** = *Canavalia gladiata*.

**SACASIL** = *Wilcoxia poselgeri*.

**SACCHARATA**, *-us, -um* (sack-a-ray'ta). Sugary or sweet.

**SACCHARIFERA**, *-us, -um* (sack-a-riff'er-ra). Bearing sugar.

**SACCHARINA**, *-us, -um* (sack-a-ry'na). Sweetish.

**SACCHAROIDES** (sack-a-roy'deez, but *see* OÏDES). Like sugar or the sugar cane (*Saccharum*).

**SACCHARUM** (sack-kar'rum). Woody-stemmed, tall grasses, chiefly East Indian, of no garden interest, but **S. officinarum**, the sugar cane, of world-wide economic importance. It is a solid-stemmed plant 10–15 ft. high, the stem green or purplish, conspicuously ringed, its juice the source of sugar. Leaves very like common corn but longer, and with rough or cutting edges. Flower cluster terminal, usually a branching panicle 15–30 in. long, the branches plume-like but drooping, rarely produced except in the tropics and often infertile there. Probably a cultigen,* as sugar was cult. centuries before it was known in Eu. or America (early 16th century). Most of the profitable varieties need more heat than is found in the U.S., but some sorts are grown in La. See SUGAR CANE. (*Saccharum* is an old Greek word for sugar, and is used also as a specific name for the sugar maple.)

**SACRED BAMBOO** = *Nandina domestica*.

**SACRORUM** (sack-ror'rum). Sacred.

**SADDLE GRAFTING.** See Splice Grafting at GRAFTING.

**SAD TREE** = *Nyctanthes arbor-tristis*.

**SAFFLOWER** = *Carthamus tinctorius*.

**SAFFRON CROCUS** = *Crocus sativus*, often called simply saffron, which it yields. For the false saffron *see* CARTHAMUS TINCTORIUS.

**SAGE.** For the common sage *see* SALVIA. For other plants to which the name sage is sometimes applied *see* PULMONARIA SACCHARATA and PHLOMIS FRUTICOSA.

**SAGINA** (sa-jy'na). Pearlwort. Slender annual or perennial herbs, often tufted* or matted, belonging to the pink family, all the dozen known species from the north temperate zone. The only one of much garden interest is S. subulata, a Corsican perennial evergreen herb, sometimes grown in the rock garden or border for its prostrate, moss-like foliage and profusion of tiny white flowers. It is a tufted plant with very small but numerous leaves. Flowers very small, the petals 5. Stamens* 5. Fruit a tiny, 5-valved capsule. Of easy culture and readily propagated by division. (*Sagina* is an old Greek name for spurry, a weedy, non-hort. plant also found in this genus.)

**SAGISI PALM** = *Heterospathe elata*.

**SAGITTALIS**, *-e* (sa-ji-tay'lis). Arrowhead-shaped or arrow-like.

**SAGITTARIA** (sa-jit-tair'i-a). Arrowhead. Hardy and tender perennial aquatic or marsh herbs, comprising about 30 species of the family Alismaceae, found in temperate and tropical regions throughout the world, except Af. and Aust. They are of erect habit, or a few with submerged leaves. Rootstocks thick and tuber-like. Under-water leaves ribbon-like, the floating leaves ovalish, those growing above the surface of the water, arrow-shaped. Flowers in whorls,* on leafless stalks, of 2 kinds, usually on the same plant. Male flowers above the female ones, or in some cases perfect* flowers are produced, having both stamens* and pistils* in the same flower. Sepals* 3, small, greenish-white. Petals 3, white or spotted. Stamens* and pistils* numerous. (*Sagittaria* is from the Latin for arrow, in allusion to the arrow-shaped leaves.)

Sagittarias are useful for shallow water, bogs or aquariums. Easily cult. but subject to aphis. Propagated by seeds sown ¼ in. deep in rich soil in boxes placed in shallow water, or by division of the tuber-like roots in March or April.

**engelmanniana.** Grows to 18 in. high. Leaves arrow-shaped, 6–8 in. long. Flowers white, to 1 in. across. Mass., Conn. and R.I.

**latifolia.** Common arrowhead. Wapatoo. Grows to 4 ft. high. Leaves arrow-shaped, variable in width. Flowers pure white, to 1½ in. across. N.A. Its edible roots were the tule potatoes of the Indians in Oregon.

**montevidensis.** Giant arrowhead. Tender. Growing to 6 ft. high. Leaves arrow-shaped, lobes at the base of leaf as long as the blade. Flowers 2 in. or more across, with brownish spot at the base of the petals. S.A., naturalized in southern U.S.

**sagittifolia.** Grows to 4 ft. high. Leaves arrow-shaped, variable in width. Flowers white, about 1 in. across, spotted purple at the base of the petals. This species produces underground tubers which are edible. Eurasia. The var. flore-pleno with double flowers is the form usually cult.

**SAGITTATA**, *-us, -um* (sa-ji-tay'ta). Sagittate; *i.e.* arrowhead-shaped.

**SAGITTIFOLIA**, *-us, -um* (sa-ji-ti-fō'li-a). With arrowhead-shaped leaves.

**SAGO PALM.** See CYCAS REVOLUTA.

**SAGO PALM FAMILY** = Cycadaceae.

**SAGUARO; SAHUARO** = *Carnegiea gigantea*.

**SAILOR CAPS** = *Dodecatheon hendersoni*.

**SAINFOIN** = *Onobrychis viciaefolia*.

**SAINT.** Many plants were named for the saints during the Middle Ages, long before Latin names were invented for them. Those in this book and their proper equivalents are:

St. Andrew's-cross = *Ascyrum hypericoides*; St. Augustine grass = *Stenotaphrum secundatum*; St. Barbara (see BARBAREA); St. Bernard's-lily = *Anthericum liliago*; St. Brigid (see ANEMONE CORONARIA); St. Bruno's-lily = *Paradisea liliastrum*; St. Dabeoc's-heath = *Daboecia cantabrica*; Saintfoin = *Onobrychis viciaefolia*; St. James's-flower = *Lotus jacobaeus*; St. James's-lily = *Sprekelia formosissima*; St. James's-pea = *Lotus jacobaeus*; St. John's-bread = *Ceratonia siliqua* (see CAROB); St. John's-wort (see first main entry below); St. John's-wort family = Hypericaceae; St. Joseph's-wand = *Pentstemon acuminatus*; St. Lucie cherry = *Prunus mahaleb*; Saintpaulia (see second main entry below); St. Thomas tree = *Bauhinia tomentosa*.

**SAINT JOHN'S-WORT.** The St. John's-worts comprise a useful group of herbs or under-shrubs constituting the genus **Hypericum** (hy-per'i-kum) of the family Hypericaceae. While most of the 200 known species, nearly all from the north temperate zone, are somewhat weedy, those below are popular for the border or rock garden. Some are occasionally known as tutsan. Leaves generally opposite,* mostly resinous-dotted, without marginal teeth or lobes. Flower yellow (in ours), in clusters (cymes*), or solitary. Petals 5, somewhat oblique. Stamens* many, usually conspicuous. Fruit a capsule* (in ours). (*Hypericum* is an old Greek plant name of uncertain application here, perhaps meaning under, or among, the heather.)

The St. John's-worts are of simple culture, except for the rock garden species which are discussed at ROCK GARDEN. Some, as indicated below, do better in partial shade. They may be propagated by division or by seeds.

**H. aureum.** Shrub, not over 3 ft. high, the bark reddish and peeling. Leaves oblongish, bluish-green, 2–3 in. long. Flowers nearly 2 in. wide, solitary or few. Southeastern U.S. July–Aug. Hardy from zone* 4 southward.

**H. buckleii.** An under-shrub, not over 12 in. high, the stems 4-angled, decumbent or ascending. Leaves elliptic or broader toward the tip.

---
* Special articles on the subjects indicated by an asterisk (*) will be found at the words so marked.

½–¾ in. long. Flowers few, nearly 2 in. wide. N. Car. to Ga. June–July. Hardy from zone* 4 southward. Suitable as ground cover or for the rock garden.

**H. calycinum.** Rose-of-Sharon. An evergreen under-shrub, not over 12 in. high. Leaves oblongish, 3–4 in. long, pale beneath. Flowers few or solitary, about 2 in. wide. Southeastern Eu. and Asia Minor. July–Sept. Hardy from zone* 4 southward. A good ground cover in shady places and for sandy soils. *See* SAND GARDENS.

**H. coris.** An under-shrub, not over 12 in. high. Leaves very narrow, about 1 in. long, in whorls* of 4–6. Flowers about ¾ in. wide, in clusters (cymes*). Southern Eu. July–Aug. Hardy from zone* 5 southward.

**H. densiflorum.** An evergreen shrub, 4–6 ft. high, the branches 2-angled. Leaves narrowly oblong, 1–2 in. long. Flowers in dense clusters (cymes*), not over ½ in. wide. N.J. to Fla., west to Mo. and Tex. July–Sept. Hardy from zone* 4 southward.

**H. kalmianum.** An evergreen under-shrub, 2–3 ft. high, the stems 4-angled. Leaves narrowly oblong, 1½–2½ in. long. Flowers few, about 1 in. long. Quebec to Ill. Aug. Hardy from zone* 3 southward.

**H. moserianum.** Gold-flower. A hybrid under-shrub, not over 2 ft. high, the stems reddish; one of the best cult. species. Leaves ovalish, 1–2 in. long. Flowers nearly 2½ in. wide, solitary or in few-flowered cymes.* The *var.* **tricolor** has white-variegated leaves edged with red. Both are hardy from zone* 5 southward and bloom in mid-summer.

**H. olympicum.** An under-shrub, not over 12 in. high. Leaves oblongish or narrower, 1–1½ in. long. Flowers nearly 2½ in. wide, in terminal clusters (cymes*). Southeastern Eu. and Asia Minor. Hardy from zone* 6 southward.

**H. patulum.** An evergreen shrub, 2–3 ft. high. Leaves ovalish or oblong, 1½–2½ in. long. Flowers about 2 in. wide, solitary or in sparse clusters (cymes*). Jap. July–Sept. Hardy from zone* 5 southward. The *var.* **henryi**, from China, is a more vigorous, larger-flowered plant, hardy up to zone* 4 and possibly zone* 3.

**H. polyphyllum.** A perennial herb with ascending stems, not over 12 in. high. Leaves elliptic or narrower, not over ⅓ in. long. Flowers nearly 2 in. wide, in terminal clusters (cymes*). Armenia. For culture *see* ROCK GARDEN.

**H. prolificum.** Bush broom. An evergreen shrub, 4–5 ft. high, the branches 2-edged, the bark peeling. Leaves oblongish or narrower, 2–3 in. long. Flowers about ¾ in. wide, in terminal clusters (cymes*). N.J. to Iowa and southward. July–Sept. Hardy from zone* 4, possibly from zone* 3 southward.

**H. repens.** A prostrate, perennial herb. Leaves oblongish or much narrower, scarcely ½ in. long. Flowers about 1 in. wide, in terminal clusters (cymes*). Southeastern Eu. and Asia Minor. Not certainly hardy north of zone* 5.

**H. reptans.** A prostrate shrub, rooting at the joints. Leaves oblongish or elliptic, about ½ in. long. Flowers solitary, about 1 in. wide. Himalayas. For culture *see* ROCK GARDEN. Not certainly hardy north of zone* 5.

**SAINTPAULIA** (saint-paul′i-a). Very beautiful, tropical African, stemless herbs of the family Gesneriaceae, two of the four known species often grown in the warm-temperate greenhouse for their handsome flowers. They are hairy plants with long-stalked basal leaves which form an open rosette. Flowers very showy, generally violet, in long-stalked, few-flowered clusters (cymes*). Corolla with a short tube, its lobes beautifully 2-lipped.* Fertile stamens* 2; also there are 2 infertile ones. Fruit a 2-valved, oblong capsule.* (Named for Baron Walter von Saint Paul, who discovered the first species.)

Fine pot plants needing plenty of moisture, and a warm-temperate greenhouse. Use potting mixture* 3. The first species is the most widely grown, and is sometimes grown in window boxes, but it does not like too much sun and wind. Propagated by leaf cuttings (*see* CUTTINGS).

**ionantha.** African or Usambara violet. Leaves forming a wide rosette, the blades roundish or ovalish, blunt-toothed, not over 1½ in. long. Flowers nearly 1 in. wide, in clusters of 1–6. Capsule* narrow, oblongish. The *var.* **grandiflora** has larger, deeper violet flowers. The *var.* **variegata** has yellow and white markings on its leaves.

**kewensis.** Somewhat similar to the above, but the leaves white-hairy and without marginal teeth. Capsule broader than in *S. ionartha*.

**SALAD BURNET** = *Sanguisorba minor.*

**SALAD CHERVIL.** *See* ANTHRISCUS.

**SALAD PLANTS.** In its original sense a salad plant was one in which the leaves were eaten raw. Of these probably the most universally popular is lettuce. In varying combinations with cucumbers, tomatoes, onions, and sweet peppers it forms the year-round salad dish. Unfortunately for the home gardener, it does not stand heat well. But other salad plants may be substituted, or combined with each other.

Corn or field salad is one of the earliest of all the raw salad materials. Fall-sown plants are hardy and in much demand for winter use. Both leaves and stems are chopped together, with the outer stalks of celery added, for a green salad. Endive is popular for autumn and winter use. It should not be cut before frost, as frost improves the flavor. The heart portion makes the best salad. French endive or Witloof chicory is a European delicacy now in common use in this country. *See* CELLAR GARDENING. The large, tender, white sprouts thrown out by the roots are the parts used. Chinese cabbage, also called celery cabbage, makes a good salad. The large midribs of the leaves are white, crisp and very tender, with a delicate flavor.

Finnochio or Florence fennel is in general appearance and use much like celery, although the top is different. The enlarged leafstalk blanches easily, is crisp and tender, and the heart is used for salads. Celeriac or knob celery may be used either raw or cooked. If cooked it is usually sliced and served with French dressing. The blanched main stalks only of cardoon are used for salad, answering the same purpose as celery. Jerusalem artichokes are sliced and served raw, with dressing, or baked like potatoes.

Leek, blanched and pulled young, is sliced and used alone as a salad or as garnishing. Double curled chervil, like parsley, is chopped fine and used with other raw salad materials. The chopped leaves of chives are a good seasoning for green salads. The seeds are used to season cooked salads. Cress and water cress are excellent garnishings or eaten alone with a dressing. Dandelions are eaten raw or cooked, while mustard may be used like lettuce or with other salads. For the culture of these plants *see* the special articles devoted to them. *See also* HERB GARDENING.

**SALAL** = *Gaultheria shallon.*

**SALICACEAE** (say-li-kay′see-ee). The willow family comprises only *Salix* (*see* WILLOW) and the poplars (*see* POPULUS), which together total 200 species. Except for the weeping willow and Lombardy poplar, they are mostly trees and shrubs of secondary garden importance, most of them being rather short-lived. But the willows are often useful bushes along water courses or pond edges, and the osiers are used for basket making.

Leaves always alternate* and undivided. Flowers in catkins* (the pussywillow is an example), appearing with or before the leaves unfold, the male and female catkins on different trees. Fruit a small, splitting pod (capsule*), the seeds surrounded by silky tufts.

Technical flower characters: Flowers minute, each flower (in the catkin) in the axil* of a minute bract.* Sepals and petals none. Stamens* 2–many. Ovary 1-celled.

**SALICARIA**, **-us**, **-um** (sal-i-care′i-a). Resembling a willow.

**SALICETUM.** A growing collection of willows.

**SALICIFOLIA**, **-us**, **-um** (sal-i-si-fō′li-a). With willow-like leaves.

**SALICORNIOIDES** (sal-i-kor-ni-oy′deez, but *see* OÏDES). Resembling a plant of the genus *Salicornia*, which are salt marsh herbs of no garden interest.

**SALIGNA**, **-us**, **-um** (sa-lig′na). Willow-like.

**SALIX.** *See* WILLOW.

**SALLOW** = *Salix caprea*. *See* WILLOW.

**SALOMONIA** = *Polygonatum*. *See* SOLOMON'S-SEAL.

**SALPICHROA** (sal-pi-crow′a). Tropical South American, perennial shrubs or herbs, sometimes climbing, comprising about 10 species of the family Solanaceae. Leaves long-stalked, alternate,* generally small, ovalish. Flowers solitary, 2–3 in. long, tubular or urn-shaped, white or yellow. Calyx* of 5 sepals, sometimes tubular. Corolla of 5 petals. Stamens* 5. Fruit a 2-celled berry, with numerous seeds. (*Salpichroa* is from the Greek for tube and skin, in allusion to the texture of flowers.)

Not much in cultivation, but sometimes grown in the warm greenhouse or outdoors in the southern states. Succeeds well when fully exposed to the sun, and grown in alkali soil. Propagated by cuttings of half-ripened shoots, inserted in sand under a bell-jar in temperature of 75°. They may also be grown from seeds if obtainable.

---

* Special articles on the subjects indicated by an asterisk (*) will be found at the words so marked.

**rhomboidea.** Tender, rapid-growing climber, with fleshy roots that have a strong odor. Stems thin and flexible. Leaves ovalish, ¾ in. long. Flowers drooping, white, urn-shaped, to ½ in. long. Berry yellowish or white, edible, known as cock's-eggs. Argentina.

**SALPIGLOSSIS** (sal-pi-gloss'is). Chilean half-hardy annual or perennial herbs, comprising about 8 species, of the family Solanaceae, mostly covered with short, sticky hairs. Leaves alternate,* broadly lance-shaped, the margins wavy or slightly cut. Flowers in loose terminal clusters growing from the axils* of small, leafy bracts.* Individual flowers large, showy, varying in color through purple, blue, brown, yellow and cream, all having a velvety appearance and generally veined with gold. Calyx* of 5 sepals, joined ¾ of their length. Corolla funnel-shaped, widely open at the throat, the 5 lobes notched. Stamens* 5, 2 long, 2 short, and 1 sterile. Fruit a 2-celled capsule. (*Salpiglossis* is from the Greek for tube and tongue, in allusion to the form of the corolla.)

These plants are beautiful for the garden, and make useful cut flowers. They can also be grown in the greenhouse for April flowering. Easily cult. as tender annuals. See ANNUALS. Salpiglossis must be sown early in Feb. in cool greenhouse or in March in cold frame so as to enable them to make good growth before warm weather. For greenhouse culture they should be sown Aug.–Sept.

**grandiflora** = *Salpiglossis sinuata*.
**sinuata.** Half-hardy annual, growing to 3 ft. high, and of branching habit. Leaves broadly lance-shaped, margins bluntly toothed. Flowers large, funnel-shaped, with wide, open throat, in various colors. Chile.

**SALSIFY** (*Tragopogon porrifolius*). As now utilized in the U.S., salsify is one of the secondary root crops, less known than it should be. It has a delicious flavor and, in the main, can be grown somewhat like parsnips. In the markets it is often called oyster plant or vegetable oyster. For a related plant known as black salsify, with a similar, but black-skinned root, see SCORZONERA. For another closely related plant, usually called Spanish oyster-plant, see SCOLYMUS.

Salsify is an all-season crop and needs even a longer growing season than the parsnip to produce good roots, which are long, tapering, and white-skinned. Consequently, it cannot be grown where there is a short growing season, and north of zone* 3 it may not mature before frost. It is comparatively hardy and seed can be sown as soon as the ground is workable in the spring. Sow the seeds in drills about ½ in. deep and keep the rows about 12 in. apart (twice this if motor or horse cultivation is to be used).

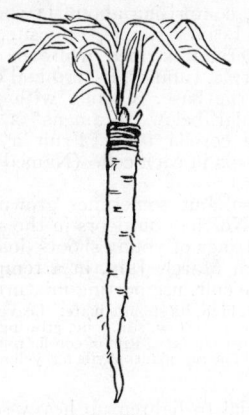
Salsify

The soil must be deeply dug or plowed, at least a foot of pulverized or friable* loam being necessary for proper root development. It does best on somewhat sandy loams, and if the soil is heavy (*i.e.* too much clay or silt) it should be lightened by the addition of sand, or better yet by liberal applications of well-rotted stable manure. The plant is a rich feeder and responds well to manure, or if this is lacking, to a good all-round fertilizer with a 5-8-5 ratio (see FERTILIZERS). Coarse, fresh, and rough manure should not be used as it is apt to make the roots rough and prongy.

Most families will find a 50-ft. row of salsify enough. The plants should stand, after thinning, about 4 in. apart in the rows, and they should be regularly cultivated (see CULTIVATION), but, as in other root crops, care must be used not to injure the roots. Plants may be harvested as needed in the fall, and the roots may be left in the ground all winter if the row is mulched (see MULCH), and dug as wanted. Or, if the winters are too severe for this, the roots may be dug in the fall and stored (see STORAGE). The best variety is Sandwich Island.

**SALSOLA PESTIFER** = Russian thistle. See the list at WEEDS.

**SALSOLOIDES** (sal-so-loy'deez, but *see* OÏDES). Resembling a plant of the weedy genus *Salsola* for which see Russian Thistle in the list at WEEDS.

**SALTBUSH.** See ATRIPLEX and RHAGODIA NUTANS.

**SALT CEDAR** = *Tamarix gallica*.

**SALT PLANTS.** See SEASIDE GARDENS.

**SALT TREE** = *Tamarix articulata* and *Halimodendron halodendron*.

**SALVER-SHAPED.** As applied to flowers, salver-shaped means having a slender tube and an abruptly expanded limb,* as in phlox.

**SALVIA** (sal'vi-a). Sage. Annual, biennial, or perennial herbs, under-shrubs or shrubs, comprising about 500 species, belonging to the mint family, and distributed throughout the tropical and temperate world. Stems usually square. Leaves in pairs, opposite,* simple, ovalish or lance-shaped, sometimes hairy, the margins toothed or deeply cut into segments, smaller toward the top. Flowers in whorls,* the clusters 2- to many-flowered, growing from the axils* of small, leafy bracts and arranged in terminal spikes or racemes.* Colors varying from scarlet, purple, blue to white and pale yellow. Calyx 5-lobed, joined about ½ way down. Corolla 2-lipped,* 3 lobes in the lower lip and 2 in the upper lip. Stamens* 4, in pairs, 2 long, 2 short. Fruit 2-celled when young, splitting into 4 parts when ripe. (*Salvia* is from the Latin to be healthy, in reference to the medicinal properties of some species.)

Salvias are grown for their flowers and for their leaves, the leaves of some species being used for seasoning. Easily propagated from seeds, division of rootstocks or by cuttings. Seeds should be sown in the early spring in the cool greenhouse or cold frame and transplanted to permanent positions as soon as large enough to handle. Tender species may not be planted out until danger of frost is over. Division of rootstocks should be made in Sept. or March–April. Cuttings should be made in Sept. or early spring. Salvias require open, sunny positions and plenty of water in dry weather. Many of the cult. and wild species are important bee plants.

**argentea.** Silver sage. Half-hardy biennial growing to 4 ft. high, covered with white-woolly hairs. Basal leaves broadly ovalish, 6-8 in. long, cut into lobes. Flowers in interrupted, 6-10-flowered whorls.* Individual flower showy, upper lip longer than lower, whitish-yellow or purplish. Mediterranean region. June.

**azurea.** Perennial growing 4-5 ft. high. Leaves green, smooth, lance-shaped, slightly toothed. Flowers blue or white in interrupted, 6-flowered whorls.* Calyx slightly hairy. S.C. to Fla. and Tex. Aug. The *var.* offered as **grandiflora** is *Salvia pitcheri*.

**coccinea.** Texas sage. Perennial to 2 ft. high, slightly woody at base, covered with short, soft hairs. Leaves ovalish, 2-3 in. long, margins toothed. Flowers scarlet, to 1 in. long, in 6-10-flowered whorls. S.C. to Fla. and Tex., and tropical America. July to frost.

**farinacea.** Perennial to 3 ft. high, covered with whitish, short hairs, and mealy. Leaves stalked, lance-shaped to 4 in. long, bluntly toothed. Flowers 1 in. long, in many-whorled* racemes, violet-blue. Flower-stalks sometimes bluish. Tex. See BLUE GARDEN. Good for cutting. Summer.

**leucantha.** Mexican bush sage. Small-growing shrub to 2 ft. high. Leaves lance-shaped, to 6 in. long, covered with white-woolly hairs on the under side, the margins toothed. Flowers white, ¾ in. long, in whorled* racemes. Calyx covered with short, lavender hairs. Mexico. June.

**mellifera** = *Audibertia stachyoides*.

**nemorosa.** Violet sage. Strong-growing, much-branched perennial, growing to 3 ft. high. Leaves lance-shaped, to 4 in. long, wrinkled, hairy on the under side, margins toothed. Flowers purplish-violet, to ½ in. long, in whorled, slender spikes to 16 in. long. Eu. and western As. The *var.* **alba** is smaller, and has shorter spikes of white flowers.

**officinalis.** Garden sage. See HERB GARDENING. Hardy under-shrub, growing to 2 ft. high. Branches and leaves covered with short, white hairs. Leaves stalked, broadly lance-shaped, 2-3 in. long, wrinkled,

---

* Special articles on the subjects indicated by an asterisk (*) will be found at the words so marked.

slightly toothed. Used for seasoning. Flowers purplish-blue or white, in many-flowered whorls, in short racemes. Mediterranean region.

**patens.** Half-hardy perennial, growing to 2½ ft. high and covered with short, sticky hairs. Leaves stalked, arrow-shaped margins toothed. Flowers gentian-blue, 2 in. long, in pairs, in widely spaced racemes.* See BLUE GARDEN. Mountains of Mexico. Summer.

**pitcheri.** Half-hardy perennial, growing 4-5 ft. high and covered with short, grayish hairs. Leaves lance-shaped, slightly toothed. Flowers deep violet-blue or white, 1 in. long, in many-flowered whorls,* in long racemes. Midwestern states. Aug.-Sept. Often offered as *S. azurea grandiflora*.

**pratensis.** Hardy perennial growing to 3 ft. high. Leaves ovalish or heart-shaped, wrinkled, slightly spotted with red, the margins toothed. Flowers bright bluish-purple, 1 in. long, in interrupted,* whorled* racemes. Eu. Summer.

**sclarea.** Clary. Clear-eye. Hardy biennial growing to 3 ft. high. Leaves broadly ovalish, to 9 in. long, covered with grayish hairs, the margins toothed. Bracts* thin, colored, white at the base, rose at the tip. Flowers bluish-white, 1 in. long in loose, whorled* racemes. Southern Eu. Aug. See HERB GARDENING.

**splendens.** Scarlet sage. Tender shrub, growing to 8 ft. high, but when grown as an annual, usually not over 3 ft. Leaves stalked, bright green, wrinkled, ovalish, to 3½ in. long, the margins toothed. Bracts* colored. Flowers scarlet, 1½ in. long in whorled* racemes. Calyx scarlet. Brazil. Summer. This is the common red salvia so widely used for summer bedding. For this purpose it must be grown as a tender annual. See ANNUALS.

### SALVIA FAMILY = Labiatae.

**SALVINIA** (sal-vin′i-a). Free-floating, small, aquatic plants of the family Salviniaceae, one of them, **S. auriculata,** of tropical America, a popular aquarium plant and useful for greenhouse pools or in the open in the South. It will stand no frost. It is a fern ally, hence producing no flowers and reproduced by spores.* The plant grows usually in masses on the surface of the water and consists of nearly round leaf-like fronds, about ⅜ in. wide, from which are suspended hair-like, feathery, and very graceful roots (beneath the surface). The under side of the fronds is usually pimply or hairy. The plant is sometimes known as *S. natans*, but the true *S. natans* is a hardy, non-cult. species with oblong fronds. (Named for Antonio M. Salvini, Italian professor.)

**SALVINIACEAE** (sal-vin-i-ā′see-ee). A small family of free-floating, very small, aquatic plants, its two genera, *Azolla* and *Salvinia*, both grown for aquaria and in greenhouse pools. They are extremely simple plants (fern allies), without flowers or seeds, and reproduced by spores.* For this process *see* FERNS AND FERN GARDENING.

The leaves of *Salvinia* are about ½ in. long and not cut, while *Azolla* grows in moss-like, feathery masses on the water and has much-divided foliage.

**SAMAN** (sam′an). Central American vernacular for the rain tree (*Samanea saman*).

**SAMANEA** (sa-mā′nee-a). Tropical American trees of the pea family, comprising over 30 species, one of them, **S. saman,** planted throughout the tropical world for shade and ornament, but cult. in the U.S. only in extreme southern Fla. (zone* 9). It is commonly called rain tree, perhaps because its innumerable leaflets fold at night and at the approach of cloudy or rainy weather. Much nonsense has been written about its "causing" rain. Other names for it are saman (or zaman) and, in Hawaii, monkey-pod. It is a flat-topped tree, usually 40–70 ft. high, but the canopy often 100 ft. wide. Leaves thrice- or twice-twocompound,* the ultimate leaflets very numerous, roundish, and about 2 in. long. Flowers yellowish, acacia-like, packed in dense, ball-shaped clusters, from which the numerous, light crimson stamens* protrude thrice the length of the corolla. Fruit a straight, thickish pod, 6–8 in. long, which does not split, its seeds surrounded by a pulp. The plant is sometimes known as *Pithecolobium saman*, but in *Pithecolobium* the pods are usually twisted or curved. (*Samanea* is derived from saman.)

**SAMARA.** A one-seeded fruit which does not split, and is provided with a more or less membranous wing. Common examples are found in the fruits of ash, maple, and elm. Often known as key fruits, especially in the maple.

*SAMBAC* (sam′bac). Native name in India for *Jasminum sambac*.

*SAMBUCINA, -us, -um* (sam-bew-sy′na). Elder-like.

**SAMBUCUS.** *See* ELDER.

**SAMUELA** (sam-you-el′a). Yucca-like plants of the lily family, comprising only a few species from the southwestern U.S. and Mex., two of them cult. for interest or ornament in desert gardens but not hardy north of zone* 7. They have stout, tree-like trunks, crowned with a mass of narrow, sword-shaped, sharp-pointed leaves, the margins of which bear conspicuous fibers. Flowers white, more or less tubular, but widely expanded above, generally larger and more showy than in *Yucca*. The cluster (a large panicle*) is borne at the end of a long stalk. Fruit a capsule.* (Named for Sam F. Trelease, American botanist.)

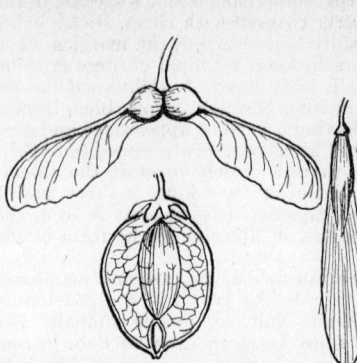

Samaras of maple (*above*), elm (*lower left*), and the ash

The two below are considerably planted in western Tex., N. Mex., Ariz. and southern Calif., the first species especially. In Mex. the natives use the pulp of the trunk for stock feed. Both the flowers and fruit are eaten by the Mexicans.

**carnerosana.** Palma samandoca. Trunk 10–18 ft. high, usually unbranched. Leaves 12–18 in. long, 2–3 in. wide. Flowers nearly 4 in. wide, the tube about 1 in. long. Fruit 2–3 in. long. Mex.

**faxoniana.** Trunk 9–15 ft. high, often branched near the top. Leaves 3–4 ft. long, 2–3 in. wide. Flowers almost 4 in. wide, the tube usually less than ½ in. wide. Fruit 2–3 in. long. Western Tex.

**SANCHEZIA** (san-key′zi-a). Tropical South American, perennial herbs or shrubs, comprising about 11 species, of the family Acanthaceae. Leaves simple, opposite,* large, ovalish, shiny green sometimes striped white or yellow. Flowers orange, red, or purple, tubular, in terminal clusters. Calyx 5-lobed, joined at the base. Corolla with 5 lobes, rounded at the top, tubular below. Stamens* 2 perfect, 2 sterile, inserted on the corolla tube. Fruit a 2-celled capsule,* with usually 4 seeds in each cell. (Named for Jos. Sanchez, Spanish professor.)

Not much in cultivation, but sometimes grown in the tropical greenhouse in the North or outdoors in the southern states. Propagated by cuttings of young shoots, inserted in sand under a bell-jar, from March–July, in a temperature of 60°–70°. For greenhouse cult. use potting mixture* 5.

**nobilis.** Shrub growing to 5 ft. high, its stems square. Leaves broadly lance-shaped, to 1 ft. long. Flowers yellow, 2 in. long, growing from the axils* of bright red bracts,* in loose clusters. Rim of corolla rolled under. Stamens* prominent. Ecuador. The *var.* **glaucophylla** has yellow or white markings along the leaf veins.

**SAND.** The best material to lighten up heavy soils (*i.e.* those with too much clay or silt), and for the cutting bench. Sharp sand is rather coarse, has no loam or silt in it and is the best for hort. purposes. The value of sand is that there is nothing in it to decay, and when coarse (*i.e.* sharp) it allows better aeration than any other rooting medium.

Ordinary builders' sand fills all hort. requirements and is the only sort to be used in the mixing of concrete or cement. If for the latter purpose, or for the rooting of cuttings, it is necessary to avoid sea sand as it usually contains too much salt for either purpose. Sand from the back of the dunes may sometimes be used, but it is safer to soak a quart of it in 2 quarts of distilled water for an hour and taste the extract. If it is brackish, the sand should be avoided. For technical definition, and the size of the particles of sand *see* SOILS.

---

* Special articles on the subjects indicated by an asterisk (*) will be found at the words so marked.

**SANDALWOOD.** The true sandalwood (*Santalum album*), is a partially parasitic tree from India, unknown in cult. in the U.S. For the bastard sandalwood *see* MYOPORUM SANDWICENSE. For red sandalwood *see* ADENANTHERA PAVONINA.

**SAND BINDER.** Along the coast it is often necessary to stop shifting dunes from inundating the garden. In New Zealand and France millions of acres of pasture and farm land have been rescued from such a fate.

In the U.S., and nearly throughout the world, the best plant for this purpose is the marram grass. *See* AMMOPHILA for description and details of planting this grass. When marram has completed the first step in transforming a shifting dune to a stable one, other herbs and finally shrubs and trees can complete the process.

For later details of planting, once the sand has stopped being wind-blown, *see* the plants mentioned at SAND GARDENS.

**SANDBOX-TREE.** *See* HURA.

**SANDBUR** = *Cenchrus tribuloides.* *See* list at WEEDS.

**SAND CHERRY** = *Prunus besseyi* and *P. pumila.*

**SAND GARDENS.** In many sections of the country there are sandy areas that seem unpromising from the garden standpoint. Not many of the finer hort. plants will grow in pure sand, or if they do, it is only just to survive.

Assuming that your sandy area is not made up of shifting dunes (if it is *see* SAND BINDER), and that it is not salty (if it is *see* SEASIDE GARDENS), the problem is one of selecting plants that will grow in pure sand, and tolerate the often intense midday heat of the sand during the summer. Temperatures of the upper inch of the sand on a clear day may be as high as 120°, even in regions otherwise comparatively cool. Desert sands in the Southwest are much hotter. Not many plants, wild or cult., will stand such conditions. But some will, notably the cacti (which see), and a few others listed below. All are entered at their proper places elsewhere in THE GARDEN DICTIONARY. Notes on their hardiness will be found at these entries and will not be repeated here. All those below will grow without more water than rainfall, if in a region where the annual rainfall is 30 in. or more. *See* the name of your state for rainfall figures. For places with more heat and less rainfall than 20–25 in. it is better to use species mentioned at DESERT GARDENS.

LOW PLANTS. One of the best sand plants is the bearberry (*Arctostaphylos uva-ursi*), which is really a prostrate woody vine. Two others, especially suited to intense heat and the white sands of the pine barren regions, are *Eupatorium hyssopifolium* and *Euphorbia corollata.* Among other genera which contain sand-tolerant herbs or low shrubs the most useful are:

| | |
|---|---|
| *Aralia nudicaulis* (wild sarsaparilla) | *Desmodium canadense* (bush trefoil) |
| *Arenaria* (sandwort) | *Eupatorium* (boneset) |
| *Artemisia stelleriana* (dusty miller) | *Euphorbia* (spurge) |
| *Asclepias* (milkweed) | *Hypericum* (see ST. JOHN'S-WORT) |
| *Atriplex* (orach) | *Krigia* (dwarf dandelion) |
| *Calluna* (heather) | *Lathyrus* (beach pea) |
| *Cerastium* (chickweed) | *Liatris* (button snakeroot) |
| *Chrysopsis* (golden aster) | *Mesembryanthemum* (fig-marigold) |

TALLER SHRUBS AND TREES. There are fewer woody plants able to withstand the conditions in pure sand. By far the best are:

| | |
|---|---|
| *Myrica carolinensis* | *Salix tristis* |
| *Prunus maritima* | *Sophora viciifolia* |
| *Prunus pumila* | *Ulex* (see FURZE) |
| *Rhus copallina* | |

Besides these the vines found among the wild species of *Smilax* and the Virginia creeper (*Parthenocissus*) all do well in pure sand. So will the pitch pine (*Pinus rigida*) and the Jack pine (*P. banksiana*) among coniferous trees.

There are many other native plants suited to the sand garden. Most of them are not considered hort. subjects and so cannot be had from the dealers. The only way to get them is by digging from the wild. It will be found that this is no easy task, as many sand plants have deep taproots,* sometimes 3 ft. long, although the top may be only a small herb. Quite often too, as in *Arenaria* and *Euphorbia*, the taproot is very brittle, so that digging it out uninjured is a slow job. *See also* DESERT GARDENS.

**SAND LILY** = *Leucocrinum montanum.*

**SAND MYRTLE** = *Leiophyllum buxifolium.*

**SAND PEAR** = *Pyrus serotina.*

**SAND PLUM** = *Prunus angustifolia watsoni.*

**SAND VERBENA** = *Abronia.*

*SANDWICENSIS, -e* (sand-wi-sen'sis). From the Sandwich (Hawaiian) Islands.

**SANDWORT** = *Arenaria.*

**SAN FRANCISCO, CALIF.** *See* ARBORETUM. *See also* CALIFORNIA.

*SANGUINALE, -is* (san-gwi-nay'le). Blood-red.

*SANGUINARIA.* *See* BLOODROOT.

*SANGUINEA, -us, -um* (san-gwin'ee-a). Blood-red.

**SANGUISORBA** (san-gwi-sor'ba). Burnet. Hardy perennial herbs of the north temperate regions, comprising about 35 species, belonging to the rose family. Leaves alternate,* compound.* Flowers small, crowded in short spikes at the top of long flowering stalks. Flowers may be male (stamens* only) or female (pistil* only) or both. Calyx of 4 sepals, petal-like, spreading. Corolla absent. Stamens many. Fruit 1-celled, 1-seeded, enclosed in the dry, persistent calyx. (*Sanguisorba* is from the Latin for blood, and drink up, in allusion to supposed medicinal remedies.)

Not much in cultivation, but sometimes grown in the border, or for their leaves which are used for flavoring. Easily cult. Propagated by seeds sown in early spring or by division of rootstocks in Sept., March or April.

**canadensis.** Also known as *Poterium canadense.* Strong-growing perennial to 6 ft. high. Leaves compound, leaflets 5–17, opposite,* broadly lance-shaped, to 3 in. long, margins toothed. Flowers white, numerous, in spikes to 6 in. long. Eastern N.A.

**minor.** Salad burnet. Toper's-plant. Hardy perennial, growing to 2 ft. high. Leaves compound, leaflets 7–19, opposite, ovalish, ¾ in. long, deeply toothed. Flowers greenish, in short spikes, ½ in. long. Leaves edible. *See* HERB GARDENING. Eurasia, naturalized in N.A. Sometimes offered as *Poterium sanguisorba.*

**SANITATION.** As a hort. term sanitation means the destruction or deep plowing-under of diseased plants so that future healthy ones may escape infection.

**SAN JOSE SCALE.** A serious scale insect pest of woody plants. For its control on the crops it most infests *see* Insect Pests at APPLE, APRICOT, CHERRY, PEACH, PEAR, and COTONEASTER. *See* illust., page 714.

**SAN SEBASTIAN** = *Cattleya skinneri.*

**SANSEVIERIA** (san-se-veer'i-a). Bowstring-hemp; also called snake plant and leopard lily, especially in the florists' shops. Tender, herbaceous perennials, comprising about 54 species of the lily family, natives of Af. and India. They have short, thick rootstocks, with thick, erect, basal leaves, which may be flat or con-

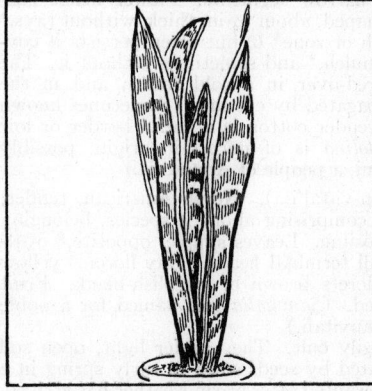

*Sansevieria thyrsiflora*, the common snake plant

---

* Special articles on the subjects indicated by an asterisk (*) will be found at the words so marked.

cave. Leaves long and narrow, often variegated, or mottled. Flowers on leafless stalks, in a long, cylindrical raceme or spike, white or pale yellow in color, showy, but often wanting in cult. Individual flowers, tubular, with 3 petal-like sepals, and 3 petals. Stamens* 6. Fruit a 3-celled capsule.* (Named for Raimond de Sangro, Prince of Sanseviero.)

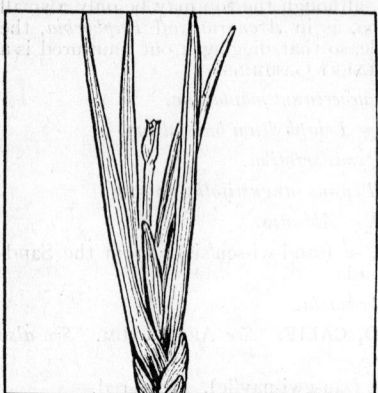
*Sansevieria cylindrica*, a bowstring hemp less commonly cult.

These plants are easily cult. and make excellent house plants (which see), as they do not require much sunlight. Often grown outdoors in the southern states. Propagated by division of the rootstocks in early spring, or leaves may be cut into pieces about 3 in. long and inserted in sand, in a temperature of 55°–60°, when a new rootstock will form.

**cylindrica.** Leaves to 5 ft. long, cylindric, thick, often banded across with light, grayish-green. Flower stalks shorter than the leaves, the flowers white, sometimes tinged pink, numerous, in a raceme to 1 ft. long. Tropical Af., especially in the deserts of Abyssinia.

**guineensis** = *Sansevieria thyrsiflora*.
**laurenti** = *Sansevieria trifasciata laurenti*.
**thyrsiflora.** Leaves 1½ ft. long, 3½ in. wide, flattish, banded across with pale green, the margins yellow. Flowers greenish-white, fragrant, 1½ in. long, the cluster 10–12 in. high. S. Af. This is the common snake plant of the shops and stands more abuse as a house plant than almost any other. If given reasonably good care it often blooms in Aug. in the living room.
**trifasciata laurenti.** Similar to *S. zeylanica*, but with yellow-striped leaves. Belgian Congo.
**zeylanica.** Leaves to 2½ ft. long, and 1 in. wide, concave, banded across with pale green, and lined on the back. Flowers white, 1¼ in. long, in spikes. Ceylon. The leaves are sometimes nearly cylindrical.

**SANTA ANA CAÑON.** *See* BOTANIC GARDEN.

**SANTA CRUZ IRONWOOD** = *Lyonothamnus floribundus*.

**SANTA CRUZ WATER LILY** = *Victoria cruziana*.

**SANTA MARIA TREE** = *Calophyllum antillanum*.

**SANTA MARTA** = *Heliocereus speciosus*.

**SANTOLINA** (san-to-ly′na). Evergreen, aromatic undershrubs of the family Compositae, most of the 8 species from the Mediterranean region. The only commonly cult. one is S. chamaecyparissus, the lavender cotton, a silvery-gray plant not over 20 in. high. Leaves alternate,* finely divided feather-fashion into narrow segments. Flower heads solitary, yellow, globe-shaped, about ¾ in. thick, without rays.* It is not hardy north of zone* 6, but often persists if covered with a strawy mulch,* and sometimes without it. The plant can be wintered-over in a cold frame, and in the spring it can be propagated by cuttings. Sometimes known as *S. incana*, the lavender cotton is a useful border or low edging plant. (*Santolina* is of uncertain origin, possibly named for the Santoni, a people of Aquitania.)

**SANVITALIA** (san-vi-tal′i-a). North American, tender, herbaceous annuals, comprising about 4 species, belonging to the family Compositae. Leaves simple, opposite,* ovalish. Flowers in small terminal heads. Ray florets* yellow or white, the disk florets brown or purplish-black. Fruit dry, 1-celled, 1-seeded. (*Sanvitalia* was named for a noble Italian family, the Sanvitali.)

Sanvitalias are easily cult. They prefer light, open soil in full sun. Propagated by seeds sown in early spring in a cold frame, or where wanted after warm weather has arrived.

**procumbens.** Trailing annual, growing about 6 in. high, covered with short hairs. Stems much-branched. Leaves ovalish, about 1 in. long.

Flower heads numerous, to 1 in. across. Ray florets yellow, disk florets purplish-black. Mex. *See* ROCK GARDEN.

**SAP.** Popularly, the juice of plants. But *sap* comprises *crude* sap, an upward stream which carries soluble salts absorbed by the roots, and *elaborated* sap, which is the result of what has happened to crude sap in the leaves. It is the elaborated sap, usually a downward stream, which contains sugar (as sugar cane, sugar maple, some palms, etc.). From the elaborated sap also the plant manufactures the highly complex gums, oils, resins, and often a milky juice (latex). It is from the coagulated latex we get rubber, gutta-percha, chicle, and many other products. Technically, latex is not sap, although commonly so called. Some of the gums produced from elaborated sap are useful to trees in sealing wounds.

**SAPIDA,** -*us,* -*um* (sap′i-da). Of pleasing taste.

**SAPIENTA,** -*us,* -*um* (say-pee-en′ta). Pertaining to wise men; or to authors.

**SAPINDACEAE** (sap-in-day′see-ee). The soapberry family means little to the average northern gardener. Although it comprises 120 genera and over 1000 species of shrubs and trees, most of them are tropical and only *Sapindus* (some species), *Xanthoceras* and *Koelreuteria*, are much grown outdoors in the North. The latter is somewhat extensively grown for ornament. The family is also called Dodonaeaceae.

In the tropics (less so in Fla. and southern Calif.) the family is much more important because of its fruit: *Blighia* (the akee), *Euphoria* (the longan) and *Litchi* (the litchi) and *Melicocca* are the chief genera with useful fruit. The remaining cult. genera, grown mostly for ornament in frost-free regions or in greenhouses, are: *Cardiospermum* (a summer, annual vine), *Cupania*, *Dodonaea* and *Paullinia*.

Leaves alternate,* undivided or compound,* with or without an odd leaflet at the end, sometimes thrice-compound. Flowers nearly regular, never very showy, nearly always in clusters (cymes* or panicles*), mostly unisexual.* Fruit various; dry or fleshy, a drupe,* nut, or sometimes winged.

Technical flower characters: Sepals 4–5. Petals 4–5, or wanting, usually with scales or hairs at the base. Stamens* 8 or 10, in two distinct series. Ovary superior,* mostly 3-celled.

**SAPINDUS** (sa-pin′dus). Soapberry. Chiefly tropical American trees of the family Sapindaceae, of secondary hort. importance, but the two below native in Fla. and occasionally planted for interest or ornament. They have alternate,* compound* leaves, the leaflets arranged feather-fashion, and with an odd one at the end. Flowers very small, greenish or whitish, inconspicuous, borne in a large terminal cluster (panicle*). Petal 4–5. Stamens* 8–10. Fruit a fleshy or somewhat leathery berry, the pulp easily lathering like soap, the seeds bony and black. (*Sapindus* is partly Latin for soap, combined with *Indian*, in allusion to the Indians' use of the berries for soap.)

*Sapindus marginatus* drops its leaves during the winter, although it is considered as a satisfactory shade tree in Fla., in spite of the lack of showy flowers. *S. saponaria* is evergreen. They grow well in dry, sandy soil. Propagated by seeds.

**marginatus.** A tree up to 30 ft. high. Leaflets 7–13, stalked, narrowly oblong, pointed both ends, 4–5 in. long. Fruit inverted egg-shaped, yellow, about 1 in. long, keeled on the back, ripening in late summer. The pulp is reported to have about 30% of saponin. Fla. and Tropical America. Hardy in zones* 8 and 9, perhaps in the southern part of zone* 7.
**saponaria.** Not over 30 ft. high. Leaflets 7–9 in. long, elliptic or oblong, 2½–3½ in. long, evergreen. Fruit nearly round, about ⅝ in. in diameter, orange-brown, ripening in early summer or spring. Southern Fla. to the W.I. and Tropical America. Hardy only in zone* 9.

**SAPIUM** (say′pi-um). A large genus of poisonous-juiced, tropical trees of the spurge family, only one of the hundred known species likely to be cult. This is **S. sebiferum**, the Chinese tallow-tree, also called vegetable tallow, a native of southern China and Jap. and naturalized from S. Car. to Fla. and La. It grows up to 50 ft. high (less as cult. here), and has alternate,* ovalish or angled leaves 1–3 in.

---

* Special articles on the subjects indicated by an asterisk (*) will be found at the words so marked.

long, slenderly long-stalked, the stalks ultimately red. Flowers not showy, without petals (see EUPHORBIACEAE), in terminal spikes, 2-4 in. long. Fruit a 3-lobed capsule,* about ½ in. wide, the seeds white. It is for the latter that the plant is grown in many regions, the waxy covering yielding a tallow-like substance used for soap and candles. In the U.S. cult. for ornament, but not hardy north of zone* 7. It is somewhat poplar-like and grows in a variety of soils. Propagated by seeds or cuttings, or sometimes by grafting. (*Sapium* is the old Latin name for the genus.)

**SAPODILLA** = *Sapota achras*.

**SAPODILLA FAMILY** = Sapotaceae.

**SAPONARIA** (sap-o-nair'i-a). Hardy annual, or perennial herbs, comprising about 20 species, belonging to the pink family, and found in the north temperate zone, but chiefly in the Mediterranean region. Leaves simple, opposite,* more or less lance-shaped, smooth or hairy. Flowers showy, in loosely branched clusters, pink or white in color. Calyx 5-lobed, tubular. Corolla of 5 petals, alternating with the sepals. Stamens* 5. Fruit a dry, 2-3-celled capsule.* (*Saponaria* is from the Latin for soap, the bruised leaves and stem of some species forming a lather in water.)

Saponarias make useful plants both for the border and rock garden. Easily propagated by seeds, division of the rootstocks or by cuttings. Seeds should be sown in early spring, ⅛ in. deep, in a mixture of sandy loam, in a cool greenhouse or cold frame. Division of the rootstocks may be made in Sept., March or April. Cuttings of young shoots taken in Aug.-Sept. should be inserted in a mixture of half sand and half soil, and shaded from sun until rooted.

**ocymoides.** Trailing, much-branched perennial, growing to 9 in. high and covered with soft hairs. Leaves broadly lance-shaped. Flowers bright pink, in loose clusters. Calyx purple. Suitable for rock or pink garden. Central and Southern Eu. May-Aug. There is a white-flowered variety.

**officinalis.** Bouncing Bet. Soapwort. Strong-growing perennial, to 3 ft. high, not much-branched. Leaves broadly lance-shaped to 3 in. long. Flowers pink or white, about 1 in. long, in dense clusters. Western As., naturalized in N.A. May-Sept., mostly blooming at night. The var. **flore-pleno**, with double flowers, is the form usually grown. Both are useful border plants.

**vaccaria.** Cowherb or cockle. Also known as *Lychnis vaccaria*. Annual, growing to 3 ft. high. Leaves smooth, broadly lance-shaped. Flowers deep pink, ¾ in. across, in loose clusters. Eu., naturalized in N.A., and often a weed in the fields, although a desirable garden plant. There is a white-flowered form.

**SAPOTA** (sa-pō'ta). A single species of densely foliaged, tropical American trees of the family Sapotaceae, commonly called sapodilla or naseberry, and known to science as **Sapota achras** (sometimes called *Achras zapota*, but *Achras* includes the sapote or marmalade-tree). The sapodilla, hardy only in zone* 9, is very widely grown throughout the tropical world for its fruit, but even more important is the milky juice harvested in Yucatan and neighboring regions for chicle used in chewing gum, hence often called chicle-tree. Not over 60 ft. high, its alternate,* leathery, oblongish, evergreen leaves 4-6 in. long, without marginal teeth. Flowers solitary in the leaf-axils, short-stalked, white, about ½ in. wide or less. Sepals* hairy on the outside, usually 6, in 2 series. Corolla urn-shaped. Stamens* 6, alternating with 6 sterile, petal-like stamens. Fruit an apple-shaped berry, russet and scurfy on the outside, the flesh yellowish, granular, sweet, and delicious. Seeds 1- several, black. Can only be safely grown in extreme southern Fla. Fruit ripening is scattered through most of the year. Propagated by shield budding in May, or by grafting. Seeds may also be sown, but the results are uncertain. (*Sapota* is a native name in tropical America for this and several related trees.)

**SAPOTACEAE** (sa-pō-tay'see-ee). The sapodilla family scarcely touches the northern garden except for the genus *Bumelia*, shrubby plants of the southeastern U.S. and southward. All the rest of the 30 genera and over 400 species are tropical shrubs and trees, mostly with a milky juice. In one of them, *Sapota*, the coagulated milky juice yields chewing gum, and in another, *Palaquium*, it yields gutta-percha.

Some genera furnish tropical fruits little known in the North: *Achras* (marmalade plum), *Chrysophyllum* (see STAR-APPLE), and *Lucuma*, the canistel. See these, and *Argania*, the only other cult. genus, for details of their use in the U.S.

Leaves alternate,* without marginal teeth, often rather thick and leathery. Flowers never very showy, often solitary or a few clustered in the leaf-axils.* Fruit a berry, often edible.

Technical flower characters: Sepals 4-6, separate, and mostly in two series. Corolla united, its lobes with small appendages or slightly fringed. Stamens* as many as the lobes of the corolla, and opposite them, often with some sterile. Ovary superior.*

**SAPOTE** = *Achras zapota*. For the white sapote see CASIMIROA EDULIS.

**SAPROPHYTE.** A plant that lives on the dead remains of other plants, as does the Indian pipe and a few other wild flowers. Naturally such plants can be cultivated only with rare success. They get their food with the aid of various microscopic organisms of decay (fungi and bacteria), which help to decompose the material upon which saprophytes live. This means that the few cult. saprophytes which can be grown thrive only in woods soil impregnated with the organisms upon which they rely for getting their food. See also PARASITE. The whole subject of saprophytism, while of absorbing interest to the botanist, really lies outside the scope of gardening.

**SARCOCOCCA** (sar-ko-kok'a). A small group of Asiatic and Malayan, evergreen shrubs of the family Buxaceae, closely related to the box, but with alternate,* and longer leaves. Two of the 6 known species are occasionally planted for ornament, but they are not certainly hardy north of zone* 5. Leaves stalked, without marginal teeth, rather leathery. Flowers small, whitish, without petals, the male and female separate on the same plant. Fruit a black or dark red, fleshy, berry-like drupe* with 1 or 2 seeds. (*Sarcococca* is from the Greek for fleshy and berry, in allusion to the fruit.)

Their culture is the same as for box (which see). Propagated by seeds.

**hookeriana.** A shrub 4-6 ft. high. Leaves lance-shaped or oblong, 2-3 in. long, pointed at the tip, wedge-shaped at the base. Fruit nearly round, about ⅓ in. in diameter, black. Himalayas. Sept.-Feb.

**ruscifolia.** A shrub 4-6 ft. high in the wild, usually less as grown here and a useful ground cover for partially shady sites. Leaves ovalish or elliptic-oval, 2-3 in. long, shining green above. Flowers white, fragrant. China. Sept.-Feb.

**SARDENSIS, -e** (sar-den'sis). From Sardinia.

**SARGENT PALM** = *Pseudophoenix vinifera*.

**SARMATICA, -us, -um** (sar-mat'i-ka). From Sarmatia, an obsolete name for the region north of the Black Sea; also for Poland.

**SARMENTOSA, -us, -um** (sar-men-tō'sa). Sarmentose; i.e. bearing runners.

**SARNIENSIS, -e** (sar-ni-en'sis). From the Channel Island of Guernsey.

**SARRACENIA.** See PITCHER-PLANT.

**SARRACENIACEAE** (sar-ra-see-ni-ā'see-ee). The pitcher-plant family is of chief interest because of its insect-catching, and its ability to digest them. See also NEPENTHES, DROSERACEAE and UTRICULARIA.

There are only two cult. genera in this group of insectivorous plants. *Sarracenia* (see PITCHER-PLANT) and *Darlingtonia*, the California pitcher-plant, are both cult. as curiosities, and the former has some species with very handsomely colored pitchers.

Leaves mostly in a basal rosette. They are modified so that they are more or less shaped like a bent pitcher, hold considerable water and the inside of the pitcher slippery or so furnished with hairs that the insect can get in but not out. Both genera are bog plants, and both have more or less of a lid or flap to the pitcher.

Technical flower characters: Petals and sepals 5. Stamens* many. Ovary superior.* Fruit a capsule.*

---

* Special articles on the subjects indicated by an asterisk (*) will be found at the words so marked.

**SARSAPARILLA.** The true sarsaparilla (various tropical American species of *Smilax*) is not a cult. plant in the U.S. For the wild sarsaparilla *see* ARALIA NUDICAULIS.

**SASA.** *See* ARUNDINARIA and BAMBUSA.

**SASH.** *See* COLD FRAME.

**SASKATCHEWAN.** For the garden possibilities of this province *see* the accounts of the generally similar conditions in MANITOBA, MONTANA and NORTH DAKOTA.

**SASSAFRAS** (sass'a-frass). Three species of deciduous trees of the family Lauraceae, two of them Asiatic or Formosan, the third, S. variifolium, the common sassafras of eastern N.A. It is usually a small, slender tree, but specimens up to 100 ft. high, and a girth of over 12 ft., are known on Gardiner's Island, L.I. Leaves alternate,* without teeth, but often irregularly and lopsidedly lobed, or regularly 3-lobed, the lobes rounded, or some leaves (even on the same twig) unlobed, generally ovalish, 3–5 in. long. Flowers often unisexual, yellow (*see* LAURACEAE), usually in racemes* that bloom before the leaves unfold, delightfully fragrant. Fruit bluish-black, with a bloom, on fleshy, bright red stalks. While it grows in a wide variety of soils it is not of the easiest cult. Almost no native tree has such gorgeous scarlet foliage in the fall. April–May. (*Sassafras* is from the Spanish *salsafras*, in reference to the medicinal value of its root bark.)

**SASSAFRAS FAMILY** = Lauraceae.

**SATIN-FLOWER.** *See* HONESTY, SISYRINCHIUM and GODETIA.

**SATINLEAF** = *Chrysophyllum oliviforme*. *See* STAR-APPLE.

**SATINPOD.** *See* HONESTY.

**SATIN POPPY** = *Meconopsis wallichi*.

*SATIVA, -us, -um* (sa-ty'va). Cultivated.

**SATSUMA ORANGE** = *Citrus nobilis unshiu*.

**SATUREIA.** *See* SAVORY.

**SAUCERS.** *See* FLOWER POTS.

**SAUERKRAUT.** The fermented, shredded leaves of cabbage. While almost any variety of cabbage will serve, the best one is a late variety known as Wisconsin All Season (*see* CABBAGE for culture). The process of making sauerkraut is troublesome and must be done with care. Cut the heart or core out of the head, and shred the leaves into fine slivers. Into a crock or beer keg put about a 4-in. layer of shredded leaves and sprinkle a little common salt over them. They must then be rammed with a wooden plunger until thoroughly macerated. At this stage, the juice of the mass should rise to the surface. When it does so (induced by vigorous tamping), put in another 4-in. layer of shredded leaves and salt, and renew the tamping. Continue this process until the crock or keg is within 3–5 in. of being full. Then cover the mass with cheesecloth or cabbage leaves, but only if there is enough juice to reach the surface. If there isn't, continue to tamp. When the juice has risen, fit a tight lid (wood or crock) over the cheesecloth. The lid must be small enough to slip inside the crock or keg, for it is to act as a plunger or piston when a heavy weight (at least 60 pounds) is finally put on top of the lid. No water is to be added, the fermentation being wholly of cabbage juice.

Allow the keg or crock to stand, with the weight on the lid-like piston, in a room kept as near 75°–80° as possible. Drain off the scum which will form from time to time. Depending upon conditions, the sauerkraut should be ready to use in from 10 to 25 days.

**SAUSAGE-TREE** = *Kigelia pinnata*.

**SAUTERNE.** For the best wine grapes for sauterne *see vinifera* varieties at GRAPE.

**SAVIN** = *Juniperus sabina*.

**SAVING SEED.** *See* SEED COLLECTING.

**SAVORY.** The summer and winter savory are fragrant herbs, which, with others, constitute the genus **Satureia** (sat-you-ree'a) of the mint family. The name is sometimes spelled *Satureja*. They are hardy annual, or perennial, aromatic herbs or small shrubs, comprising about 160 species distributed through the warm regions of the world. Stems usually square. Leaves opposite,* ovalish or lance-shaped, the margins sometimes toothed. Flowers pink, white, or purplish, in whorls,* in axillary or terminal racemes.* Calyx 5-lobed, usually tubular. Corolla a narrow tube opening into 2 lips, upper lip 2-lobed and flat, the lower lip 3-lobed and widely flaring. Stamens 4, in pairs, 2 long, 2 short. Fruit 2-celled when young, splitting into 4 parts when ripe, each containing a seed. (*Satureia* is the old Latin name for the savory.)

Grown chiefly for their leaves which are used for flavoring. Sometimes grown in the border for their flowers. Easily cult. in ordinary garden soil. Propagated by seeds, division of rootstocks or by cuttings. Seeds should be sown ⅛ in. deep, outdoors, in early spring. Division of rootstocks may be made in Sept. or early spring. Cuttings of young shoots may be made in spring, they should be inserted in a mixture of ½ sand and ½ soil, in a cold frame, and kept shaded until rooted.

**alpina.** Alpine savory. Much-branched perennial, shrubby at the base, growing to 6 in. high. Leaves small, ovalish, ½ in. long, slightly toothed. Flowers purple. Whorls* 4–6-flowered, in terminal spikes. Mediterranean region.

**hortensis.** Summer savory. *See* HERB GARDENING. Annual, growing to 18 in. high. Leaves lance-shaped, 1½ in. long. Flowers pink, lavender or white, in loose whorls,* in spikes. Eu., naturalized in the U.S.

**montana.** Winter savory. Small shrub, growing to 15 in. high. Leaves rigid, lance-shaped, to 1 in. long. Flowers white or purplish, in loose whorls,* in spikes. Eu. and N. Af. *See* HERB GARDENING.

**SAVOY CABBAGE.** *See* CABBAGE.

**SAWARA CYPRESS** = *Chamaecyparis pisifera*.

**SAW CABBAGE-PALM** = *Acoelorraphe wrighti*.

**SAW FERN** = *Blechnum serrulatum*.

**SAWFLY.** For a description of it *see* Bees at INSECT PESTS. It attacks blackberry, cherry, strawberry, and pansy, at all of which are notes on the control.

**SAW PALMETTO** = *Serenoa repens*.

**SAXATILE.** Inhabiting rocks, or growing in rocky places.

*SAXATILIS, -e* (sacks-at'i-lis). Saxatile.*

**SAXIFRAGA** (sacks-iff'ra-ga). Saxifrage. Rockfoil. Annual or biennial, but mostly perennial, herbs, comprising about 400 species of the family Saxifragaceae, found chiefly in the temperate regions of Europe and America. They are of very diverse habit, but usually low-growing, spreading or creeping, the rootstocks spreading by offsets* or runners.* Leaves thick and fleshy or soft and moss-like, sometimes arranged in a rosette, the shapes of the leaves varying from roundish or spoon-shaped to ovalish. Margins generally toothed, often encrusted as with lime, hence silvery. Flowers pink, white, purple or yellow, in clusters. Calyx* of 5 sepals, spreading. Corolla of 5 or more petals. Stamens* 10 or more. Fruit a 2-celled capsule,* many-seeded. (*Saxifraga* is from the Latin for stone and to break, in allusion to supposed medicinal remedy for gallstones.)

Saxifragas and the genus **Bergenia** make useful plants for the rock garden or border, as they seldom run over the other plants. The foliage changes color with the seasons and so gives great variety. The alpine species can be planted in the clefts of rocks. For best results in growing saxifragas, plant in positions shaded from midday sun, in gritty soil with lime. Easily propagated from seeds, division of the rootstocks, or by runners and bulblets,* the latter being found in some species. Seeds should be sown ⅛ in. deep, in sandy soil, in a cool greenhouse or cold frame, in early spring. As soon as large enough to handle, they should be pricked-off into pans, until well established, when they may be transferred to permanent positions. Division of the

---

* Special articles on the subjects indicated by an asterisk (*) will be found at the words so marked.

rootstocks, runners and bulblets* may be made in spring or summer. *See* ROCK GARDEN.

**aizoon.** Strong-growing perennial, to 20 in. high. Leaves basal, in dense rosettes, narrowly spoon-shaped, 1¼ in. long. Margins toothed and encrusted. Flowers in clusters, creamy-white, with purple markings, ½ in. across. Arctic N.A., Eu. and As. Summer. The *var.* **baldensis** has short, thick, gray leaves, with whitish flowers. The *var.* **brevifolia** has white flowers. The *var.* **flavescens** has clear yellow flowers. The *var.* **lagaveana** is a dwarf form with silvery-gray leaves and reddish stems, the flowers creamy-white, wax-like. The *var.* **pectinata** has silver-margined leaves, with white flowers spotted with red. All good for border or rock garden (which see).

**altissima.** Strong-growing perennial, to 2 ft. high. Leaves basal, thick, to 4 in. long, rounded at the apex. Margins toothed, the teeth tough. Flowers white, but marked with purple, to ½ in. across, in clusters. Flower stalks slightly hairy. Tyrol. Summer.

**andrewsi.** A hybrid between *S. aizoon* and a European species. It grows up to 6 in. high. Flowers white, marked red. Useful rock garden plant.

**apiculata.** A hybrid saxifrage, and a dwarf perennial, to 3½ in. high, forming a dense mat. Leaves inversely spoon-shaped, with small, open pores round the margins. Flowers yellow, in small, loose clusters. For cult. *see* ROCK GARDEN.

**caespitosa.** Dwarf perennial, strong-growing, to 6 in. high, and of tufted* habit. Leaves deep green, 3-lobed, about ½ in. long. Flowers white, to ½ in. across, in loose clusters. Northern N.A. and Eurasia. Spring.

**cartilaginea.** Perennial, to 9 in. high. Leaves in rosettes, narrow, to 1 in. long, the margins with tough teeth. Flowers white, rose, or purple, to ½ in. across. Asia Minor.

Three saxifrages: (*A*) *Saxifraga sarmentosa;* (*B*) *S. aizoon;* (*C*) *S. oppositifolia*

**cochlearis.** Perennial, to 9 in. high, growing in thick tufts.* Leaves narrowly spoon-shaped, to 1 in. long, the margins with tough teeth. Flowers white, to ¾ in. across, in loose clusters. Alps. Spring. For cult. *see* ROCK GARDEN.

**cordifolia** = *Bergenia cordifolia.*

**crassifolia** = *Bergenia crassifolia.*

**cuneifolia.** Perennial, to 1 ft. high. Leaves broadly lance-shaped, to 1½ in. long, in rosettes. Margins toothed at the apex. Flowers white, yellow at the base, ¼ in. across, in loose clusters. Eu. Summer.

**decipiens.** Perennial, 6–12 in. high, growing in dense tufts.* Leaves wedge-shaped, cut into 3–5 narrow lobes. Flowers white, to ½ in. across. There are many hort. varieties with larger or differently colored flowers. Eu. Spring. For cult. *see* ROCK GARDEN.

**elizabethae.** A hybrid saxifrage, and a dwarf perennial, 2–3 in. high, growing in small, cushion-like tufts.* Leaves in rosettes, deep green. Flowers yellow, large, in 3–5-flowered clusters. Summer.

**godseffiana.** A hybrid saxifrage, and a perennial, to 4 in. high, growing in small tufts.* Leaves prickly margined. Flowers deep yellow. Early summer.

**hosti.** Strong-growing perennial, to 2 ft. high. Leaves in rosettes, about 4 in. long, rounded at the tip. Margins wavy and encrusted as with lime. Eu. Spring. For cult. *see* ROCK GARDEN.

**lantoscana** = *Saxifraga lingulata lantoscana.*

**ligulata** = *Bergenia ligulata.*

**lingulata.** Perennial, to 1 ft. high, growing in tufts.* Leaves narrow and spoon-shaped, to 3 in. long. Margins rolled under and encrusted. Flowers white, ½ in. across, in loose, many-flowered clusters. Pyrenees. Summer. The *var.* **lantoscana** has shorter and blunted leaves.

**macnabiana.** A hybrid saxifrage growing to 18 in. high. Leaves basal, in rosettes, 2–3 in. long. Margins toothed and encrusted. Flowers white, spotted purple, in long loose-branching clusters. Summer. For cult. *see* ROCK GARDEN and illust., page 684.

**moschata.** Perennial, to 5 in. high, growing in tufts.* Leaves narrow, sometimes cut in 2–3 lobes. Flowers greenish-yellow, occasionally purple or white. Eu. Spring. For cult. *see* ROCK GARDEN.

**oppositifolia.** Mountain saxifrage. Perennial, to 2 in., spreading and forming dense mats. Leaves ovalish, ¾ in. long, slightly hairy. Flowers rose or purple, ½ in. across, in small, loose clusters. Eurasia and northern N.A. For cult. *see* ROCK GARDEN.

**sarmentosa.** Strawberry geranium. Beefsteak saxifrage. Mother-of-thousands. Trailing perennial, growing to 2 ft. long, sending out runners* like the strawberry. Leaves basal, long-stalked, roundish, heart-shaped at base, to 4 in. across, hairy, dark green, marked with white on upper side and reddish on under side. Margins coarsely toothed. Flowers white, ¾ in. across, in loose racemes. Useful basket or pot plant for the house. Eastern As. Summer.

**umbrosa.** London Pride. Perennial, growing to 1 ft. Leaves basal, in rosettes, thick, ovalish, to 2½ in. long, often reddish on the under side. Margins with tough teeth. Flower stalks reddish. Flowers small, white, with numerous pink spots, in loose-branching clusters. Often used for an edging plant in Eng. Eu. Early summer.

**virginiensis.** Early saxifrage. Rock saxifrage. Perennial, growing to 1 ft. high. Leaves basal, in rosettes, ovalish, to 3 in. long, the margins toothed. Flowers white, about ¾ in. across. Eastern N.A. May.

**SAXIFRAGACEAE** (sacks-i-fray-gay'see-ee). The saxifrage family is a large and important one to gardeners, to fruit growers and especially to lovers of its many decorative shrubs. While it is a large and natural family (about 80 genera and perhaps 1000 species), many botanists have split it into several smaller families, not here considered as such. For reference they are listed here:

Hydrangeaceae or hydrangea family
Grossulariaceae or gooseberry family
Escalloniaceae
Iteaceae
Parnassiaceae

As here treated, all these are considered as one big family, the Saxifragaceae, which contains many genera of wide cult. The only important fruit is found in *Ribes* (currant and gooseberry).

The most important decorative shrubs are in the genera *Deutzia, Philadelphus* (*see* MOCK-ORANGE) and *Hydrangea,* but other woody genera yielding fine decorative shrubs, trees or woody vines are: *Decumaria, Schizophragma, Carpenteria* and *Itea,* all of which are more or less hardy in the North. *Bauera* and *Escallonia* are more tender and sometimes grown in the cool greenhouse or outdoors in warmer regions southward.

In perennial, or rarely annual, herbs for the open border, wild garden or rock garden the family is very rich. Those mostly suited to the open border are *Heuchera* (also for the wild garden, and one or two for the greenhouse), *Bergenia, Astilbe, Jamesia* and *Rodgersia.* The wild garden genera are best exemplified by *Heuchera, Mitella, Tellima* and *Tiarella,* while those most suited to rock gardens are *Saxifraga, Tolmiea* and *Lithophragma.* The only two remaining cult. genera are *Francoa,* a somewhat tender herb from Chile, and *Parnassia,* which are largely bog plants.

Leaves various, often in a basal rosette* in the herbs, but alternate* or opposite* in the trees and shrubs. Flowers regular,* very showy and profuse in many of the shrub genera (*Deutzia, Philadelphus* and *Hydrangea,* especially), smaller but most attractive in many of the rock garden saxifrages and in some wild garden plants. Fruit dry in most genera, but a berry in *Ribes* and some others.

Technical flower characters: Sepals and petals 4 or 5. Stamens* 4 or 5, or 8 or 10. Ovary inferior* or superior,* of 2–5 segments which are usually wholly or partly united, but sometimes separate.

**SAXIFRAGE.** *See* SAXIFRAGA.

**SAXIFRAGE FAMILY** = Saxifragaceae.

**SAXIFRAGE PINK** = *Tunica saxifraga.*

**SAYERS, E.** *See* America at GARDEN BOOKS.

**SCAB.** *See* Diseases at APPLE, ORANGE, POTATO, PEACH, and GLADIOLUS.

***SCABER*** (skay'ber). Rough.

***SCABERRIMA, -us, -um*** (skay-ber'ri-ma). Very rough.

* Special articles on the subjects indicated by an asterisk (*) will be found at the words so marked.

**SCABIOSA** (skay-bi-ō′sa). Scabious. Pincushion. Hardy annual or perennial herbs, comprising about 70 species of the family Dipsaceaceae, found mostly in the temperate regions. Leaves simple, opposite,* ovalish or lance-shaped, often lobed or deeply cut. Flowering stalk long. Flowers in terminal heads, surrounded by 2 rows of small, leafy bracts,* blue, purple, brownish-black, reddish-brown, pink, cream or white. Calyx represented by bristles. Corolla tubular, sometimes 2-lipped,* with lower lip greatly extended. Stamens 4. Fruit a 1-celled capsule* which does not split. (*Scabiosa* is from the Latin for itch, in allusion to the medicinal use of some species.)

Scabiosas make good garden plants, the flowering period being long. Easily cult. in ordinary garden soil. Propagated by seeds or division of rootstocks. Seeds should be sown in a cold frame as early as possible in spring. Perennial species sometimes flower the first year. Division of rootstocks should be made in March or April. Established plants should be taken up every 3 years and the soil well dug with manure before re-planting.

**atropurpurea.** Sweet scabious. Mourning bride. A tender annual growing 2–3 ft. high and of branching habit. Basal leaves broadly lance-shaped, cut in lyre-shaped lobes. Margins coarsely toothed. Flowers dark purple, pink, or white, the heads to 2 in. across. Eu. The *var.* **candidissima** has white flowers which are sometimes double. The *var.* **flore-pleno** has double flowers. The *var.* **grandiflora** has larger flower heads.

**caucasica.** Hardy perennial, growing to 2½ ft. high. Basal leaves narrowly lance-shaped, entire.* Stem leaves lance-shaped, cut into narrow segments. Flowers in flattish heads, light blue, to 2–3 in. across. The *var.* **alba** has white flowers. The *var.* **magnifica** has large deep lavender-blue flowers. See GRAY AND LAVENDER GARDEN. Caucasus, in the mountains.

**japonica.** Perennial, of tufted habit, growing to 2 ft. high. Leaves broadly lance-shaped, divided into many narrow lobes. Flowers violet-blue, in heads to 2 in. across. Jap. See GRAY AND LAVENDER GARDEN.

*SCABIOSAEFOLIA*, *-us*, *-um* (skay-bi-o-si-fō′li-a). Having leaves like the scabious (*Scabiosa*).

**SCABIOUS.** See SCABIOSA. For the shepherd's-scabious see JASIONE PERENNIS.

*SCABRA*, *-us*, *-um* (skay′bra). Rough.

**SCABROUS.** Rough to the touch, as are many leaves.

**SCAFFOLD.** The lateral branching caused by initial pruning of fruit trees to produce the desired shape and branching of the canopy. See PRUNING.

**SCALE.** A small, often dry, leaf or bract.*

**SCALECIDE.** A trademarked miscible oil, sold with directions for use as a dormant contact spray.

**SCALE INSECTS.** Very troublesome garden pests, the young of which suck the juices of plants. For a description of scale insects see True Bugs at INSECT PESTS. Various sorts of scale insects attack important hort. plants. Some of the most important and the control measure for each will be found at the discussion of the Insect Pests at APPLE, AVOCADO, DATE, GRAPEFRUIT, LOQUAT, MANGO, OLIVE. They are often troublesome in the greenhouse, where sponging with whale-oil soap is usually the best remedy.

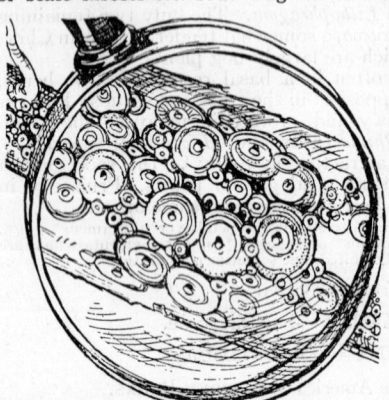

San Jose scale, one of the most destructive of the scale insects, shown also (magnified) as it occurs on twigs.

**SCALE-O.** A trademarked miscible oil, sold with directions for use as a dormant contact spray.

**SCALLION.** A young onion, the base somewhat swollen, but without a true bulb, or pulled before the bulb develops. Scallions are grown for bunching and eating green. See ONION for culture. *Scallion* is also sometimes used for the leek and for shallot (see both terms).

**SCALLOP SQUASH.** See CUCURBITA PEPO MELOPEPO.

**SCALY BARK.** See Diseases at ORANGE.

**SCAMMONY** = *Ipomoea pandurata*.

*SCANDENS* (skan′denz). Climbing.

**SCAPE.** A flower stalk, usually leafless, that arises at the ground. Scapes often, however, bear small scales or bracts.* Scapose plants are common in the garden, such as tulip, bloodroot, most primroses, and many others.

**SCARBOROUGH LILY** = *Vallota speciosa*.

**SCARECROW.** See BIRDS.

*SCARIOLA* (scare-i-ō′la). An old generic name for the prickly lettuce and its relatives now included in *Lactuca*. See Prickly Lettuce in the list at WEEDS.

*SCARIOSA*, *-us*, *-um* (scare-i-ō′sa). Scarious; *i.e.* with leaf-like, usually small bracts or other organs, which are thin, nearly transparent, or membranous, and not green.

**SCARLET.** As an adjective *scarlet* is linked with the names of many plants or objects in the garden. Those in this book and their proper equivalents are:

Scarlet bloom = *Eucalyptus ficifolia*; Scarlet bugler = *Pentstemon centranthifolius*; Scarlet-bush = *Hamelia erecta*; Scarlet clematis = *Clematis texensis*; Scarlet eggplant = *Solanum integrifolium*; Scarlet-flowered gum = *Eucalyptus ficifolia*; Scarlet fritillary = *Fritillaria recurva*; Scarlet garden (see RED GARDEN); Scarlet larkspur = *Delphinium cardinale*; Scarlet lightning = *Lychnis chalcedonica*, also *Centranthus ruber*; Scarlet lobelia = *Lobelia cardinalis*; Scarlet lychnis = *Lychnis chalcedonica*; Scarlet oak = *Quercus coccinea* (see OAK); Scarlet pimpernel = *Anagallis arvensis* (see list at WEEDS); Scarlet plume = *Euphorbia fulgens*; Scarlet runner = *Phaseolus coccineus*; Scarlet sage = *Salvia splendens*; Scarlet Turk's-cap lily = *Lilium chalcedonicum*.

**SCENTLESS CAMOMILE** = *Matricaria inodora*.

*SCEPTRA*, *-us*, *-um* (sep′tra). Pertaining to a scepter.

*SCHAFTA* (shaff′ta). A species name for a *Silene*; of uncertain origin, but supposed to be a "country appellation for the plant" (in Russia).

**SCHAUERIA** (shau-er′i-a). Tropical under-shrubs or perennial herbs of the family Acanthaceae, all but one of the 10 known species from tropical America. The only cult. sort is *S. flavicoma*, of Brazil, often grown in the warm-temperate greenhouse for its showy, yellow flowers. It is a woody under-shrub, 2–4 ft. high. Leaves opposite,* without marginal teeth, ovalish or oval-lance-shaped, 4–6 in. long, broad at the base, but tapering to the tip. Flowers about 1½ in. long, light yellow, in a dense, close, head-like cluster. Corolla tubular below, but 2-lipped,* the lower lip with 3 segments. Fruit a slender-stalked capsule. It needs plenty of moisture and should be grown in potting mixture* 4. (Named for J. C. Schauer, a German professor.)

**SCHINSENG** (shin′seng). The Chinese name for the plants known to us as ginseng.

**SCHINUS** (sky′nus). Chiefly South American, resinous trees of the family Anacardiaceae, comprising perhaps 15 species, the two below much grown for ornament in Calif. and Fla., usually under the name pepper-tree, although neither is a true pepper. (See PIPER and CAPSICUM.) They have alternate,* and in ours compound* leaves, the leaflets stalkless and with an odd one at the end. Male and female flowers on different trees, small, white, in branched clusters (panicles*). Petals 5. Stamens 10. Fruit a berry-like, reddish drupe.* (*Schinus* is Greek for the true mastic-tree, which these resemble in being resinous.)

---

* Special articles on the subjects indicated by an asterisk (*) will be found at the words so marked.

SCHISANDRA 715 SCHIZOCENTRON

The first species is one of the most popular shade trees in Calif., being hardy from San Francisco southward, except in the mountains. As part of its attractiveness is the fruit, care must be taken to ensure this by planting both male and female trees. The other species is more commonly planted in Fla. where *S. molle* does not do so well. Both grow in a variety of soils, and are of simple cult., but *S. molle* is often attacked by scale and should be carefully sprayed as detailed at Insect Pests. Both are easily raised from seed.

**molle.** Pepper-tree; also called California pepper-tree (not native there), Peruvian mastic-tree, or simply mastic-tree. An evergreen tree, 20-30 ft. high, its branches gracefully drooping. Leaflets numerous, narrowly lance-shaped, toothed or sometimes without teeth. Flowers in a much-branched terminal cluster, yellowish-white. Fruit rose-red, about ¼ in. wide, persisting most of the winter. Peru, but widely planted throughout the tropical world. *Molle* is not Latin (*see* MOLLIS), but from the Peruvian vernacular *mulli*.

**terebinthifolius.** Brazilian pepper-tree. Christmas-berry tree. An evergreen, small tree or shrub, its branches not drooping. Leaflets 5-9, about 2 in. long, dark green above. Flowers in a denser cluster than in *S. molle*. Fruit bright red, smaller than in *S. molle*. Brazil. Hardy in zones* 8 and 9, and especially popular in Fla. where its bright red berries persist over the winter months.

**SCHISANDRA** (sky-zan'dra). Also spelled *Schizandra*. Aromatic woody vines of the family Magnoliaceae, all its 13 species Asiatic except for one (non-hort.) in the southeastern U.S. The only commonly cult. species is **S. chinensis,** a high-climbing vine with the male and female flowers on different plants so that both sexes must be planted to ensure fruit. Leaves alternate,* ovalish or broader towards the tip, 3-4 in. long. Flowers white or pink, about ½ in. wide, in few-flowered, stalked clusters in the leaf-axils.* Sepals and petals alike, totaling 7-12. Stamens* 5-15. Fruit a collection of berry-like, ripened carpels, in a spike-like, drooping mass. China and Jap. May-June. Hardy from zone* 3 southward, and very attractive in fruit (Aug.-Sept.). Easily propagated by seeds or layers. (*Schisandra* is from the Greek for cleave and man [stamen], in allusion to the cleft anthers* of one species.)

**SCHISMATOGLOTTIS** (skiz-mat-o-glott'is). Tender perennial herbs from the Malay Archipelago, comprising about 75 species of the family Araceae. Rootstocks thick and branching, sometimes showing above the ground. Leaves lance-shaped, heart-shaped or arrowhead-shaped, often variegated. Flowers in a spike on a long leafless stalk enclosed in a large green or colored spathe,* similar to Jack-in-the-pulpit. Flowers of 2 kinds, male (stamens only) on the upper portion, and female (pistil only) on the lower portion. Fruit a small berry. (*Schismatoglottis* is from the Greek for falling tongue, in allusion to the spathe.*)

These plants are grown mostly for their leaves, and can only be grown where a temperature of about 70° is available through the winter. Sometimes used as house plants. Propagated by cuttings of pieces of the stem about 2 in. long, inserted in sandy soil under a bell-jar, in a temperature of 75°-85° in early spring. For pot culture use potting mixture* 4.

**picta.** Leafstalk to 1 ft. long. Leaves ovalish, heart-shaped at base, to 8 in. long, and 5 in. wide, light green, marked with white spots. Spathe* enclosing the spadix,* greenish-yellow, 2½ in. long. Java. A handsome, but very tender, foliage plant.

**SCHISTOSA, -us, -um** (shiss-tō'sa). Easily cleaved or divided.

**SCHIZAEA** (sky-zee'a). A genus of about 20, chiefly tropical species of very small ferns of the family Schizaeaceae, only **S. pusilla,** the curly-grass, likely to be cult. and then only in moist sand or sphagnum moss with a strongly acid reaction. (*See* ACID AND ALKALI SOILS.) Localized in bogs in Nova Scotia, Newfoundland, and the pine-barrens of N.J., the curly-grass looks more like a tiny grass than a fern. Fronds of two sorts, the spore*-bearing ones slightly longer than the sterile fronds, not over 5 in. high, both narrow, hair-like, or grass-like, slightly twisted. The fertile fronds are minutely divided, feather-fashion toward the summit, the tiny segments bearing the spores.* Of no decorative value, but sometimes grown for interest. (*Schizaea* is from the Greek for cleft, in allusion to the cleft fronds of some species.)

**SCHIZAEACEAE** (sky-zee-ā'see-ee). A small and horticulturally unimportant family of ferns, comprising only 4 genera and about 100 species, nearly all tropical. The only cult. genera are *Schizaea*, a very small and unfern-like bog plant of northeastern N.A. and *Lygodium* which includes climbing ferns (both hardy and greenhouse) somewhat grown for ornament. *See* both these genera for further details.

**SCHIZANDRA** = *Schisandra*.

**SCHIZANTHUS** (sky-zan'thus). Fringe-flower. Butterfly-flower; also called poor man's-orchid. Chilean, half-hardy, brittle annuals, comprising about 7 species of the family Solanaceae. Leaves alternate,* broadly lance-shaped, usually cut into many fern-like, light green segments. Flowers showy, in terminal, loose, many-flowered clusters, of many colors. Corolla margins usually of contrasting colors or shades, with streaks and spots of another color or shade at the base. Calyx* 5-lobed, joined at the base. Corolla a short tube opening widely into 2 lips,* the upper 2-lobed, the lower 3-lobed. Stamens* 2, prominent. Fruit a small, 2-celled capsule.* (*Schizanthus* is from the Greek, for split and flower, in allusion to the corolla.)

Fringe-flowers are best grown as pot plants in the cool greenhouse for winter or spring flowering, but make very attractive garden plants where the temperature is moderate. Propagated by seeds. For winter flowering, seeds should be sown Aug.-Sept. ⅛ in. deep, in sandy soil, in temperature of 60°-70°. When large enough to handle, plants should be pricked-off into pans, using potting mixture* 2, then moved into 3-in. pots, and use potting mixture* 4, continuing with this mixture when re-potting into larger pots until final potting. Throughout their growing period they should be kept in a temperature of 45°-55°. For a method of improving the bloom *see* Pinching at TRAINING PLANTS.

For the garden, seeds should be sown ⅛ in. deep, in sandy soil, in cool greenhouse or cold frame in Feb. or March, in a temperature of 50°-60°, following the same procedure as for greenhouse culture, planting out in the garden as soon as danger of frost is over.

**grahami.** Strong-growing, to 5 ft. high. Flowers, lilac or rose, the middle of the upper lip* marked orange or yellow.

**pinnatus.** Strong-growing, to 4 ft. high. Flowers 1½ in. across, lower lip lilac or purplish, upper lip usually paler, lower part of upper lip marked yellow which is again spotted or marked purple toward the base. The colors vary considerably. Stamens* prominent.

**retusus.** Grows to 2½ ft. high. Flowers to 1¾ in. across, usually deep rose, the upper lip* marked orange, except for the margin.

**wisetonensis.** Hybrid between *S. pinnatus* and *S. grahami*. Growing to 4 ft. high. Flowers white, blue, pink or brownish, the middle of the upper lip* streaked yellow.

**SCHIZOBASOPSIS** (sky-zo-ba-zop'sis). Also known as *Bowiea*. South African bulbous plants of the lily family, comprising only one species, **S. volubilis,** which is a perennial with a thick underground bulb about 5 in. across which produces offsets.* The center of the bulb sends up each year a long, twining, much-branched, green stem, with a few scale-like leaves that quickly drop off. Flowers greenish-white. It is an interesting plant for the greenhouse or may be grown outdoors in the South. It requires a dry atmosphere and should be grown in potting mixture* 6. Propagated by seeds or division of the bulb. Bulbs should be dried off during the summer months and re-potted in Oct. when they should be kept well watered. The plant is one of the most perfectly adapted drought-resistant species known. Its large bulb has been known to put forth an annual growth, while stored on a museum shelf, for four consecutive years. (*Schizobasopsis* is from the Greek meaning like the genus *Schizobasis*, which is of no hort. interest.)

**SCHIZOCARP.** A dry fruit, really a compound fruit composed of several 1-seeded fruits which do not split themselves, but split from each other. Many plants in the mallow family bear schizocarps.

**SCHIZOCENTRON** (sky-zo-sen'tron). Mexican creeping perennial herbs of the family Melastomaceae, comprising

---

* Special articles on the subjects indicated by an asterisk (*) will be found at the words so marked.

only one species, **S. elegans** (also known as *Heterocentron elegans*). It is a much-branched, creeping perennial, which roots at the joints, forming thick mats. **Leaves** stalked, small, ovalish, to ½ in. long. Flowers solitary, on short, slender stalks, purple, 1 in. across. Not of much garden importance, but sometimes grown as a basket plant in the greenhouse. Propagated by seeds or cuttings, and grown in potting mixture* 3. (*Schizocentron* is from the Greek for split and spur, in allusion to a technical character of the anthers.*)

**SCHIZOCODON** (sky-zo-kō'don). Japanese, hardy, evergreen shrubs, comprising 1-2 species of the family Diapensiaceae, and growing only a few inches high. Leaves basal, stalked, roundish-heart-shaped at base, sometimes bronzy, leathery, the margins wavy and coarsely toothed. Flowers deep rose, pink or white, 4-6 borne on leafless stalks, nodding. Calyx of 5 sepals. Corolla funnel-shaped and fringed. Stamens* 5. Fruit a 3-celled capsule. (*Schizocodon* is from the Greek for cut and bell, in allusion to the fringed corolla.)

These plants are rarely seen in gardens, but make useful rock garden plants in partially shaded positions. Propagated by division of roots in April. They should be grown in equal parts of sandy peat and leaf mold and watered freely in dry weather. They should be protected during winter.

**soldanelloides.** Fringed galax. Tufted* plant growing only a few inches high. Leaves basal, stalked, roundish, leathery, the margins coarsely toothed. Flowers to 1 in., nodding, deep rose, shading to white at edges. Early spring.

**SCHIZONOTUS.** See HOLODISCUS and SORBARIA.

**SCHIZOPETALON** (sky-zo-pet'a-lon). Chilean, half-hardy annuals, comprising about 5 species, of the family Cruciferae of erect habit, growing 1 ft. or more high. Leaves alternate,* ovalish, the margins wavy or deeply cut into lobes. Flowers white or purple, almond-scented, in long racemes, each flower stalk in the axil* of a leafy bract. Calyx of 4 sepals. Corolla of 4 petals, fringed. Stamens* 6, 2 short, 4 long. Fruit a 2-celled capsule.* (*Schizopetalon* is from the Greek for cut and petals, in allusion to the fringed petals.)

These plants are sometimes grown in the cool greenhouse or as tender annuals in the border, for their fragrant, mostly night-blooming, white flowers. Propagated by seeds. See ANNUALS.

**walkeri.** Growing to 1 ft. high, of weak habit. Leaves ovalish, 4-5 in. long, rough, margins wavy and cut. Flowers white, almond-scented, in terminal racemes.

**SCHIZOPHRAGMA** (sky-zo-frag'ma). Asiatic woody vines of the family Saxifragaceae, only **S. hydrangeoides** of the three known species likely to be cult. It much resembles *Hydrangea petiolaris* and is often mistaken for that plant. It is a high-climbing vine, often 30 ft. long, with opposite,* nearly round leaves, 3-4 in. wide, pale on the under side and toothed. Flowers white, in loose, terminal, more or less flat-topped clusters (corymbs*). Central flowers fertile, small, composed of 4-5 sepals, 4-5 petals, and 10 stamens.* Outer marginal flowers showy, sterile, consisting of only 1 large white sepal. (*Hydrangea petiolaris* has several sepals in its sterile marginal flowers.) Jap. July. Hardy from zone* 3 southward. The vine climbs by aerial rootlets, but it needs support or it will trail on the ground and do poorly. Propagated by seeds or by layers. (*Schizophragma* is from the Greek to cleave and wall, in allusion to the splitting of its capsules.*)

**SCHIZOSTYLIS** (sky-zo-sty'lis). South African, tender, perennial herbs, comprising 2 species, belonging to the Iris family. Rootstocks thick and fleshy. Leaves narrow, sword-shaped. Flowers red, borne at the top of stalk about 1 ft. long, enclosed in a large membranous bract (spathe*). Fruit a 3-celled capsule. (*Schizostylis* is from the Greek for to cut and style, in allusion to the thread-like segments of the style.)

Not much in cultivation, but can be grown in the greenhouse for late autumn flowering. Propagated by division of the rootstocks in early spring. After flowering, rootstocks should be dried off and stored until March. They require plenty of water during growing period.

**coccinea.** Crimson flag. Kafir Lily. Growing 1-2 ft. high. Leaves 18 in. long and narrow. Flowers red to 2 in. across, the tube nearly straight and about 1 in. long.

**SCHOENANTHA,** *-us, -um* (skee-nan'tha). With a reed-like flower.

**SCHOENOPRASA,** *-us, -um* (skee-no-pray'za). Rush-like or reed-like.

**SCHOLAR-TREE.** See SOPHORA JAPONICA.

**SCHOOL GARDENING.** In a wide sense, a school garden is that part of the school grounds which can support plant life. However, in many schools, the school garden is the plot, preferably on school grounds, which has been set aside and equipped for the intensive study and cultivation of a variety of plants by the pupils of the school.

Children's Gardens are land areas on public or private property cultivated by the qualified children in the given community and conducted by social organizations other than schools.

The first purpose of the school garden is to provide a school laboratory in nature education. Fundamentally, the school garden is educative. Healthy exercise, knowledge of industry, production of food, home and community beautification, are also worthwhile aims.

AREA AND LOCATION. A school garden should be a plot no larger than can easily be cultivated by a single class of pupils. A garden 750 square feet in area (25 ft. by 30 ft.) is a minimum size. The area of a school garden of a single school should be rarely more than 7500 square feet.

A school garden should be located in the sunniest portion of the school grounds, provided it is at the side or rear of the school building. The grounds in the front of the school building should be lawns, planted with herbaceous perennials, shrubs, and trees as a landscape feature.

PLAN. The plan of the school garden should express the cultural factors of real gardening as a proper ideal for pupils. In a small school garden, vegetables should be massed in straight rows usually in the central plots on either side of a wide central path. An entire class of pupils may assemble and be instructed on this path. Around the vegetable masses, borders five to seven feet in width, should be planted in irregular flower masses of perennials and annuals. Many deciduous and evergreen shrubs may be introduced.

Depending on the size of the garden, a limited amount of garden furniture and garden features may be introduced, such as a pergola, rose arch, sundial, bird bath, bird house, weather vane, garden seats, a lily pool, fountain, and rock garden. See ORNAMENT AND FURNITURE; STRUCTURES.

In gardens larger than one-half acre, children may be assigned to individual plots about eight by ten feet or eighty square feet in area. Each child's plot should grow a variety of plants. Allowing liberally for paths and borders, an acre will accommodate from 400 to 500 children. The size of the plot should be increased with the age and efficiency of the pupil gardener. The individual plot plan is especially recommended for all children's gardens conducted by social groups.

EQUIPMENT. As a general rule, it is best to surround a school garden on school grounds with a cyclone wire fence twelve feet high. This protects the garden from flying balls on the playground, as well as from many other depredations. However, a few gardens are so located on school grounds and in selected neighborhoods that a fence is unnecessary.

Every school garden should have a tool house, water outlets, provision for locking, compost pit, cold frame, potting benches, fertilizer bins and metal seed containers.

Annually, school gardens should be supplied by the Board of Education with fertilizers, seeds, garden tools;—based on one-third annual replacement.

The seeds for beginners are those listed below as plants. The number of plant varieties should be increased annually. Certain woody and herbaceous perennials, a working set of tools, as hoe, rake, spading fork, trowel, weeder, watering can, garden line, shovel, wheelbarrow, should be furnished

---

* Special articles on the subjects indicated by an asterisk (*) will be found at the words so marked.

each year. Other garden tools, seeds and plants should be supplied as the work develops.

PLANTS. Educationally the aim of a school garden should be to introduce the child to as many species of plants as the garden can support and the pupils can find time to study. However, the best vegetables to begin a school garden with are: radish, lettuce, bean, beet, carrot, kohlrabi, and Swiss chard. The best annual flowers are: marigold, cosmos, calendula, zinnia, portulaca, petunia, alyssum, ageratum, and California poppy.

As proficiency in the garden work increases, an average school garden may easily contain one hundred species of plants.

The teacher in charge of a school garden should be the one best equipped for that work in a given school. The head garden teacher in each school should be held responsible for the success of the garden. The intensive gardening should be done largely by the class of this head garden teacher. It is most important that one skilled leader be placed in charge of any children's garden.

School vacations, especially during the summer, call for special garden organization. Each school should form a garden club of selected pupils for summer garden care. This club should work at least two hours daily in medium-sized gardens under a skillful teacher throughout the entire summer vacation.

The instruction in a school garden should be given following a definite program, as in all other school laboratories. Many small garden projects, as making cuttings, seedlings in cold frames, and transplanting, may be given to individual pupils. The garden instruction should be planned for each grade so as to cover the all-important applications of nature teaching. Garden Fairs exhibiting flowers, produce and projects are profitable, especially during June and September.

It is important to apply the principles of landscape gardening to school gardens. Every school garden should be beautiful as well as practicable. The aim should be to introduce a great variety of plants in an artistic manner.

The school garden in the city is a little oasis where the child of the tenement can work and play. Such a garden is well worth the support of the Garden Clubs or Settlement Workers. — V. E. K.

**SCHOOL OF HORTICULTURE FOR WOMEN.** *See* GARDEN SCHOOLS.

**SCHOTIA** (shot′i-a). An unimportant genus of African shrubs or small trees of the pea family, but the two below grown in Fla. and similar climates for ornament, but not widely. Leaves alternate,* compound,* the leaflets arranged feather-fashion, without an odd one at the end. Flowers not pea-like, the 5 petals slightly unequal, and sometimes shorter than the colored calyx.* Stamens* 10, nearly free. Fruit an oblongish pod (legume*). (Named for Richard Schot, who traveled with Jacquin when the latter was exploring in America.)

Both those below are grown on a variety of soils in Fla. and southern Calif. Their rather large clusters (panicles*) of pink or red flowers, in early spring, are handsome.

**brachypetala.** A small tree, not over 20 ft. high. Leaflets 8-10, oblongish. Flowers crimson, most of the color coming from the calyx, which exceeds the small petals. South Africa.

**latifolia.** Kaffir-bean tree. A tree 20-30 ft. high. Leaflets 4-8, ovalish or roundish, 1-2½ in. long, the main leafstalk narrowly winged. Flowers pinkish, the clusters much-branched, the petals longer than the calyx.* South Africa.

**SCIADOPITYS.** *See* UMBRELLA PINE.

**SCILLA** (sill′a). Squill. A large genus of bulbous herbs of the lily family, most of the 80-90 known species from the temperate regions of Eurasia, and several cult. for their cheery, mostly early spring bloom. Leaves narrow, almost grass-like in some species, basal, usually appearing with the bloom. Flowers small, blue, white, or purple, bell-shaped, in a terminal cluster (raceme*) at the end of a naked stalk which arises from the leaf cluster. Corolla segments 6, not actually joined but apparently so. Stamens* 6. Fruit a 3-lobed or 3-angled capsule.* (*Scilla* is the old Latin and Greek name for these plants.) *See also* URGINEA.

For Culture *see* below.

**amoena.** Star hyacinth. Not over 6 in. high, the leaves nearly ¾ in. wide. Flowers blue or whitish, nearly ¾ in. wide, usually only 4-6 in the cluster. Central Eu.

**campanulata** = *Scilla hispanica.*

**hispanica.** Spanish bluebell. Spanish jacinth. At least 12 in. high, sometimes more, the leaves nearly 1 in. wide. Flowers blue, nearly 1 in. wide, and a fine plant for the blue garden (which see) in the typical form. Clusters 12-15-flowered. Spain and Portugal. The *var.* alba has white flowers. A good pink-flowered form is the variety Rosalind. *See* PINK GARDEN. Other fine hort. forms are Blue King, Blue Queen, Excelsior, La Grandesse and Rose Queen. *Scilla hispanica* is sometimes called *S. campanulata.*

**nonscripta.** The common Bluebells of England, also called wood hyacinth. Not over 1 ft. high, the leaves about ½ in. wide. Flowers blue, in 6-12-flowered clusters, the corolla more or less cylindric, about ½ in. wide. Eu. Often known as *S. nutans*, and a fine plant for the blue garden (which see). Blush Queen is a good pink-flowered hort. variety. *See* PINK GARDEN.

**nutans** = *Scilla nonscripta.*

**peruviana.** Cuban lily. A showy squill from the Mediterranean region, but mistakenly named as from Peru. Leaves nearly 1 in. wide. Flowers purple or reddish (white in a hort. variety), about ½ in. long, in handsome clusters of 50 or more flowers.

**sibirica.** Siberian squill. About 4-6 in. high, the leaves about ½ in. wide. Flowers nodding, deep blue, about ½ in. wide, rarely more than 3-5 to a cluster. *See* BLUE GARDEN. Eurasia. A good, early-flowering bulb for the rock garden.

**verna.** Sea onion. Not over 6 in. high. Leaves nearly ¾ in. wide. Flowers about ½ in. wide, blue, fragrant, the clusters (racemes*) branched. Western Eu.

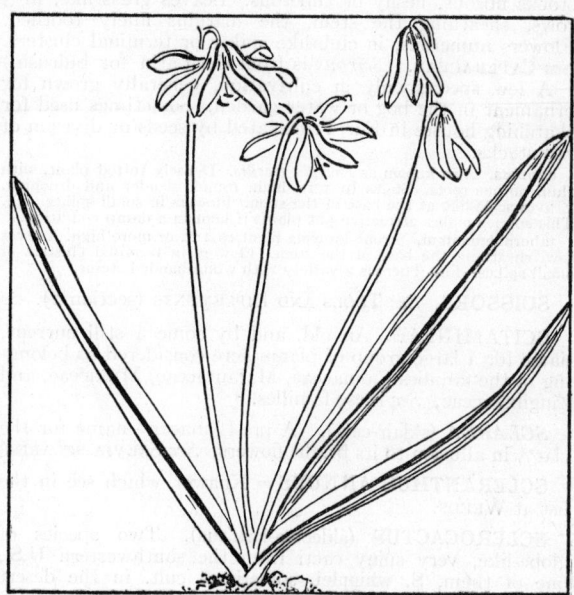

*Scilla sibirica*

SQUILL CULTURE

Scillas are easily grown and increase rapidly in rich, sandy soil, preferably in partial shade. The low-growing, early kinds, such as *S. sibirica*, should be planted in hundreds or thousands beneath spring-flowering, deciduous shrubs and trees, at the edge of woodland or in the rock garden. *S. sibirica* will thrive under evergreen trees where little else will survive. The tall, late-blooming bluebell type, forms of *S. nonscripta* and *S. hispanica*, are fine in wide plantations in open woodlands or set along the edges of fern borders. They also make good carpet plants for beds of May tulips. Plant from September through October, setting the bulbs three times their own depth in the soil and 3 or 4 inches apart. The different species flower from March well into May. They are easily increased by bulblets* from the older bulbs taken in autumn. An occasional top-dressing of old manure or good soil is beneficial in the fall. — L. B. W.

**SCILLOIDES** (sill-loy′deez, but *see* OÏDES). Like a squill (*Scilla*).

---

* Special articles on the subjects indicated by an asterisk (*) will be found at the words so marked.

**SCINDAPSUS** (sin-dap′sus). Also known as *Pothos*. Tender, climbing, perennial herbs, comprising about 20 species of the family Araceae, natives of the East Indies and Malaya. They have small roots on their stems, similar to the English ivy, by means of which they climb. Leaves simple, roundish, or heart-shaped, 6–18 in. long, usually variegated and lobed. Flowers in spikes enclosed in a spathe.* For details see ARACEAE. Fruit a berry. (*Scindapsus* is an old Greek name for some other plant.) The second species is rather widely cultivated, and should be grown in the warm greenhouse. Propagated by rootstocks in Feb. or March. Soil should be composed of equal parts of rough peat, sphagnum* moss, charcoal and coarse sand.

**aureus.** Hunter's robe. Colombo agent. Tall, climbing plant. Leaves ovalish or broadly lance-shaped, to 18 in. long and 12 in. wide, sometimes lobed. Marked pale yellow. Flowers in spikes enclosed in a spathe.* Solomon Islands.

**pictus.** Growing to 40 ft. high. Leaves ovalish to 6 in. long and 3 in. wide, one side of the blade larger than the other, bright green, with darker green spots. Flowers in spikes enclosed in a white spathe,* about 3 in. long. East Indies. The var. **argyraeus,** the silver vine, has heart-shaped leaves marked with silvery-white spots on the upper side. It is the usual form in cult.

**SCION** = Cion.

**SCIRPUS** (skir′pus). Bulrush. Aquatic, or marsh, perennial, grass-like herbs, comprising about 200 species of the family Cyperaceae, found throughout the world. Rootstocks fibrous, fleshy or tuberous. Leaves grass-like, in 3 rows, sheathing the stem, the margins finely toothed. Flowers numerous, in club-like spikes or terminal clusters. See CYPERACEAE. (*Scirpus* is from the Latin for bulrush.)

A few species only in cultivation, generally grown for ornament in the bog or water garden. Sometimes used for thatching houses in Eu. Propagated by seeds or division of rootstocks.

**cernuus.** Also known as *Isolepis gracilis*. Densely tufted plant, with thin, fibrous roots. Stems to 1 ft. high, round, slender and drooping. Leaves scale-like at the base of the stem. Flowers in small spikes. Eu. This species makes attractive pot plants if kept in a damp condition.

**tabernaemontani.** Strong-growing plant to 2 ft. or more high. Leaves few, sheathing the base of the stem. Flowers in terminal clusters of small spikes. Eu. There is a variety with white-banded stems.

**SCISSORS.** See TOOLS AND IMPLEMENTS (section 2).

**SCITAMINEAE.** An old, and by some a still current, name for a large group of plants here considered as belonging to the families Cannaceae, Marantaceae, Musaceae, and Zingiberaceae. See these families.

*SCLAREA* (sklair-ee′a). A pre-Linnaean* name for the clary, in allusion to its bright flowers. See SALVIA SCLAREA.

**SCLERANTHUS ANNUUS** = Knawel, which see in the list at WEEDS.

**SCLEROCACTUS** (skleer-o-kak′tus). Two species of globe-like, very spiny cacti from the southwestern U.S., one of them, **S. whipplei,** sometimes cult. in the desert garden, or in the greenhouse. The plant body is nearly globe-shaped, about 3 in. wide, occasionally nearly cylindric and 4–6 in. long. There are 13–15 ribs, each furnished with clusters of spines. Spine-clusters with usually 4 central, sometimes hooked spines, and 7–11 divaricate spines which are not hooked. Flowers about 1½ in. wide, purple or lavender. Fruit scaly and fibrous. Colo., Utah, and northern Ariz. (*Sclerocactus* is from the Greek for hard or tough, and *Cactus,* apparently in allusion to the fibers on the fruit.)

**SCLEROTIUM-BLIGHT.** See Diseases at PEANUT and SORGHUM.

**SCOKE** = *Phytolacca americana*.

*SCOLOPENDRIUM* (sko-lo-pen′dri-um). An old generic name for the hartstongue fern. See PHYLLITIS.

**SCOLYMUS** (skoll′i-mus). Annual, biennial or perennial herbs, comprising 3 or 4 species of the family Compositae, found in the Mediterranean region. They are strong-growing and have a thick, sometimes edible, taproot.* Stems much-branched. Leaves alternate,* much-cut, with spiny margins. Flowers in heads, ray and disk florets all long, yellow. Fruit 1-celled, 1-seeded. (*Scolymus* is the old Greek name for the species below.)

Not much in cultivation, but *S. hispanicus* is grown for its roots which are similar in flavor to the oyster plant. Propagated by seeds sown where required to mature, ⅛ in. deep, thinning out to 12 in. apart.

**hispanicus.** Spanish oyster plant. Golden thistle. Strong-growing biennial, to 2½ ft. high. Root to 1 ft. long and 1 in. thick. Stems much-branched. Leaves lobed, the margins spiny and thistle-like. Flowers in small heads, yellow. S. Eu. For a related, also edible plant, see SALSIFY.

*SCOPARIA, -us, -um* (sko-pair′i-a). Broom-like.

*SCOPULORUM* (skop-you-lor′um). Of the rocks; sometimes used as a specific name for plants from the Rocky Mountains.

**SCORPIOID.** Coiled, and with the flower cluster usually 1-sided, as in many forget-me-nots; coiled like a scorpion's tail.

*SCORPIOIDES* (score-pi-oy′deez, but see OÏDES). Scorpion-like; *i.e.* scorpioid.*

**SCORPION GRASS.** See FORGET-ME-NOT.

**SCORPION SENNA** = *Coronilla emerus*.

**SCORZONERA** (skor-zo-neer′ra). A genus of over 100 species of chiefly perennial, Old World herbs of the family Compositae, only one, **S. hispanica,** the black salsify, of any garden interest. It is a secondary root vegetable, the foliage also sometimes used for salad. It is a perennial herb, 15–24 in. high, with a deep, tapering, white-fleshed, but black-skinned root, used as is common salsify, and thought to be superior to it by some. Stems much-branched. Leaves alternate,* clasping, more or less lance-shaped, or narrower, often dissected or lobed. Flower heads solitary, long-stalked, yellow (lavender in common salsify). Eu. The plant, introduced into England in 1576, is little known in the U.S. and is grown much like common salsify (which see), but is more difficult to raise. While a true perennial it is raised as an annual or biennial, the seeds being sown only after the ground is warm. (*Scorzonera* is from an old French word for serpent, the black salsify being a reputed cure for snake bites.)

**SCOTCH.** As an adjective *Scotch* has been applied to several things of garden interest. Those in this book and the proper citations to where they are noted in detail are:

**Scotch broom** = *Cytisus scoparius* (see BROOM); **Scotch crocus** = *Crocus biflorus;* **Scotch curlies** = Scotch kale (see KALE); **Scotch heath** = *Erica cinerea;* **Scotch kale** (see KALE); **Scotch marigold** = *Calendula officinalis;* **Scotch pine** = *Pinus sylvestris* (see PINE); **Scotch pink** = *Dianthus plumarius;* **Scotch rose** = *Rosa spinosissima;* **Scotch soot** (see SOOT); **Scotch thistle** = *Onopordon acanthium*.

**SCOURING RUSH** = *Equisetum hyemale*.

**SCREE.** See Moraine at ROCK GARDEN.

**SCREEN PLANTING.** If the area to be screened and the space available for screen planting are small, as on a city or suburban lot, the most effective planting screen may be a high hedge (see HEDGES). On larger spaces the screen should be a mass planting of conifers or mixed conifers and deciduous trees. Conifers have the advantage of making an effective screen at all seasons of the year, and pines, with their rounded tops, make a more solid mass to the limit of their height than spiry-topped firs or spruces. See EVERGREENS. If the screen is to serve as a windbreak, a very important question in many localities, and especially near the seashore, blue spruce and Austrian pines are favorites and, in some localities, the Japanese black pine has proved to have remarkable resisting power to ocean winds. In similar conditions it is likely that *Cryptomeria* would be a good windbreak if its cost did not prohibit its use in sufficient quantities.

In many localities windbreaks are necessary to protect houses, orchards, or crops. Deciduous trees make good windbreaks where there is room to plant enough of them, more especially as a windbreak, to be efficient, is not necessarily

---

* Special articles on the subjects indicated by an asterisk (*) will be found at the words so marked.

What screen planting can do for an unsightly prospect.

tight. Two rows of trees staggered in any convenient alignment and 15 ft. or more apart, depending on the growth of trees and time allowed for the windbreak to become effective, may serve, but it would be better to plant more rows, especially as the trees protect each other from the winds. Trees native to the region are usually desirable as being acclimated. Windbreaks* should not be planted so as to interfere with a normal circulation of air. See TREES.— H. A. C.

**SCREW PINE.** See PANDANUS.

**SCROPHULARIA** (skroff-you-lair'i-a). Figwort. Annual or perennial herbs, comprising about 150 species of the family Scrophulariaceae, found throughout the northern hemisphere, generally in damp places. They are of erect habit, growing from 2–10 ft. high, usually strong-smelling. Leaves generally opposite,* simple, ovalish, the margins toothed. Flowers small, greenish-yellow or purple, in loose, terminal branching clusters. Calyx of 5 sepals. Corolla tubular, slightly irregular. Stamens* 2 long, 2 short, and 1 sterile (staminode*). Fruit a 2-celled capsule,* the seeds dispersed through pores. (*Scrophularia* was named from its supposed use in the cure of scrofula.) Not generally cult. as it is regarded as a weed, or a wild garden plant. Propagated by seeds or division of roots.

aquatica. Strong-growing perennial to 4 ft. high, with square stems. Leaves smooth, shiny, ovalish, but heart-shaped at base. Flowers purple, in loose-branching clusters, to 2 ft. long. Wet places, Eu. and W. As.
lanceolata. Strong-growing perennial, to 6 ft. high, covered with fine hairs. Leaves broadly lance-shaped, short-stalked. Margins sharply toothed. Flowers green or purplish, in long branching clusters. Northern U.S.
leporella = Scrophularia lanceolata.
marilandica. Perennial growing to 8 ft. high, the stems smooth and grooved. Leaves broadly lance-shaped, about 5 in. long, with thin stalks. Flowers greenish-purple, ¾ in. long, in long branching clusters. Eastern U.S.

**SCROPHULARIACEAE** (skroff-you-lair-i-ā'see-ee). The figwort, snapdragon, or foxglove family (180 genera and over 3000 species) contains many hardy garden plants, a few shrubs and trees, and several plants extensively grown for ornament in greenhouses. It contains no fruits or vegetables, but many are poisonous (not to the touch), and a few yield valuable medicines, notably *Digitalis* (see FOXGLOVE).

Among its more notable, mostly herbaceous, genera for the outdoor garden are: *Antirrhinum* (see SNAPDRAGON), which is also forced, *Alonsoa, Celsia, Chelone, Collinsia, Digitalis* (see FOXGLOVE), *Erinus, Hebenstretia* (treated as annuals), *Linaria, Nemesia* (tender annuals), *Mimulus, Pentstemon, Scrophularia, Synthyris, Torenia* (tender annuals), *Verbascum* (some weedy), *Veronica* (includes, also, tender shrubs from New Zealand), *Wulfenia* and *Zaluzianskya* (tender annuals). Another group of herbs of somewhat difficult culture comprises *Castilleja, Orthocarpus* and *Pedicularis.*

The leading genera for greenhouse culture (or for frost-free regions outdoors) are: *Angelonia, Calceolaria* (a popular florists' flower), *Cymbalaria* (the Kenilworth ivy), *Diascia* (also outdoors), *Isoplexis, Maurandia, Phygelius, Rehmannia, Russelia,* and *Veronica* (the tender New Zealand shrubs).

The only other cult. genera are *Mazus,* which are low, mat-forming herbs, and *Paulownia,* the only hardy tree of the family in the North.

Leaves opposite,* alternate* or whorled. Flowers mostly irregular,* often notably so, and 2-lipped,* usually very showy, and mostly in clusters, rarely solitary. Many of the cult. genera are extremely handsome, especially the foxglove, *Calceolaria,* snapdragon and a number of greenhouse plants. Fruit nearly always a dry pod (capsule*), usually many-seeded.

Technical flower characters: Flowers hermaphrodite.* Calyx more or less tubular, 4-5-toothed or divided. Corolla united, its 4-5 lobes nearly equal in a few genera, but notably 2-lipped in many others; nearly always more or less irregular.* Stamens* 4, two shorter than the others. Ovary superior,* mostly 2-celled.

**SCRUB OAK** = *Quercus ilicifolia, Q. prinoides,* and *Q. dumosa.* See OAK.

**SCRUB PALMETTO** = *Serenoa repens.*

**SCRUB PINE** = *Pinus banksiana.* See PINE.

**SCUFFLE HOE.** See TOOLS AND IMPLEMENTS (section 1).

**SCUM.** The green scum which frequently disfigures the surface of pools or ponds is caused by microscopic algae (see ALGA), uncounted millions of which constitute the floating scum. Several chemicals will destroy them, but the danger is considerable of destroying gold fish or desirable aquatic plants, unless the chemicals are used in minute concentrations.

Copper sulphate (blue vitriol) is the best, but it must be used with care. The algae are peculiarly sensitive to it and will disappear if a cotton bag containing copper sulphate (a dangerous poison) is dragged through the water. If at all possible, estimate the number of gallons of water to be treated (a gallon is 231 cubic inches, which is approximately a cylinder 7 in. in diameter and 6 in. high).

In using copper sulphate, put the fresh crystals in a cotton bag and tow it in a boat, making several criss-cross passages through the scum-infested water. Note, from the table below, the minute concentrations of copper sulphate that will be effective for the scum. Increasing the concentration may kill fish or valuable plants, neither of which will be in the least injured if the table is followed carefully.

| Gallons of water | Drams of copper sulphate needed (16 drams = 1 ounce) |
|---|---|
| 555 | 1/10 |
| 1,110 | ⅕ |
| 2,777 | ½ |
| 5,555 | 1 |
| 11,110 | 2 |
| 55,550 | 5 |
| 88,880 | 16 (i.e. 1 oz.) |

While it is difficult to estimate the number of gallons in irregularly shaped pools, and pools of irregular depths, the following table may serve as a guide:

| Size of square pools, in feet | Depth 3 ft. Gallons | 4 ft. Gallons | 5 ft. Gallons |
|---|---|---|---|
| 6 × 6 | 807 | 1077 | 1346 |
| 8 × 8 | 1436 | 1914 | 2393 |
| 10 × 10 | 2244 | 2992 | 3740 |
| 12 × 12 | 3231 | 4308 | 5385 |

* Special articles on the subjects indicated by an asterisk (*) will be found at the words so marked.

**SCUPPERNONG** = *Vitis rotundifolia*.

**SCURFY PEA.** See Psoralea.

**SCURFY SCALE.** See Insect Pests at Apple and Elm.

**SCURVY-GRASS.** See Cochlearia; also Barbarea verna.

**SCUTCH GRASS** = *Cynodon dactylon*.

**SCUTELLARIA** (skew-te-lair'i-a). Skullcap. Annual or perennial herbs or small shrubs, comprising about 140 species of the mint family, found throughout the world, but chiefly in the temperate regions. Leaves opposite,* simple, sometimes cut into lobes. Margins often toothed. Flowers blue, violet, scarlet or yellow, 2-lipped,* growing in the axils* of bracts, and arranged in spikes. Calyx bell-shaped, 5-lobed. Corolla tubular, opening into 2 lips. Stamens 4, in pairs, 2 long, 2 short. Fruit 2-celled when young, splitting into 4 nutlets when ripe. (*Scutellaria* is from the Latin for dish, in allusion to the calyx.)

Not generally cult., but sometimes grown in the border or rock garden. Propagated by seeds or division of rootstocks. Seeds should be sown in early spring, in sandy soil, ⅛ in. deep, in a cool greenhouse or cold frame, and transplanted to permanent positions as soon as large enough to handle. Division of the rootstocks should be made in March or April.

**alpina.** Spreading perennial about 10 in. high, with creeping stems that root at the joints. Leaves small, ovalish, to 1 in. long, slightly toothed. Flowers white and purple, 1 in. long, in thick, terminal racemes.* Eu.

**baicalensis.** Spreading perennial, to 1 ft. high. Leaves lance-shaped. Flowers blue, in racemes.* Eastern As. The *var.* **coelestina** has large, bright blue flowers, 1 in. long.

**SCYTHIAN LAMB** = *Cibotium barometz*.

**SEA BUCKTHORN** = *Hippophaë rhamnoides*.

**SEA CAMPION** = *Silene maritima*.

**SEACOAST GARDENS.** See Seaside Gardens.

**SEA DAHLIA** = *Coreopsis maritima*.

**SEA FIG** = *Mesembryanthemum crystallinum*.

**SEAFORTHIA ELEGANS.** See Archontophoenix cunninghamiana.

**SEA GRAPE** = *Coccolobis uvifera*.

**SEA HOLLY.** See Eryngium.

**SEA HOLLYHOCK** = *Hibiscus moscheutos*.

**SEA-ISLAND COTTON** = *Gossypium barbadense*.

**SEA-KALE** (*Crambe maritima*). A little-known vegetable in the U.S., the young, blanched shoots of which are used like asparagus. It is a seacoast perennial from Eu., and with proper care should yield an annual crop for 6–10 years, when the plants should be renewed.

Like rhubarb, it should be put in a part of the garden where it will not be disturbed by spring plowing, as it does not like to be moved once it becomes established. The plants should be at least 3–4 ft. apart each way, as after the cutting season they have a wide spread due to their conspicuous, bluish-green leaves.

The season for sea-kale is very early in the spring, as the young shoots appear above ground long before the leaves expand. They must be blanched before cutting, and the easiest way to accomplish this is by heaping loose earth over the shoots as they appear. Some growers prefer to cover the shoots with boxes or flower pots, with a cork in the hole in the bottom of the pot. All light must be excluded or blanching will not be complete and the stalks are apt to be tough. (See Blanching.) Properly grown and blanched sea-kale is delicious. The shoots, which are the young leafstalks, should be about 12 in. high when cut.

The plant needs a deep, rich, heavily manured soil and a reasonable degree of moisture. Its handling is very much the same as for rhubarb (which see). While seeds of it are offered by most dealers, the quickest way to propagate it is by root cuttings. Strong root cuttings, planted in the spring, if given good cultivation, should be ready for harvesting the following spring. Plants raised from seed, which is easily done if they are handled like early cabbage (which see), will not produce plants fit for cutting short of three years.

Sea-kale

The cutting season for sea-kale must stop once the leaves begin to expand. When this happens, the soil used for blanching should be smoothed off and the plant allowed to grow as it will, which means there will be a mass of tough, long, cabbage-like leaves and a cluster of white flowers up to 3 ft. high. During this stage the plant needs no attention beyond cultivation to keep down the weeds and to conserve moisture. Do not cut the foliage down until fall, when the plants should be given a light mulch of strawy manure. The summer growth is important, as upon it depends the growth of the following spring. See also Kale.

**SEA LAVENDER.** See Limonium.

**SEALWORT** = *Polygonatum biflorum*. See Solomon's-seal.

**SEA LYME GRASS** = *Elymus arenarius*.

**SEA MARIGOLD** = *Mesembryanthemum crystallinum*.

**SEA ONION** = *Urginea maritima* and *Scilla verna*.

**SEA PINK.** See Sabbatia, Statice, and Limonium.

**SEA POPPY** = *Glaucium*.

**SEA PURSLANE** = *Atriplex hortensis*.

**SEASIDE DAISY** = *Erigeron glaucus*.

**SEASIDE GARDENS.** Gardening near the sea, to be successful, requires taking into consideration four important factors — wind, sand, salt spray and salt fog.

If flowers other than typical salt, shore or strand plants are desired, windbreaks of evergreen shrubs and hardy growth should be used as a protective barrier. Shade trees, shrubs, buildings and even natural slopes will, to some extent, protect the plants from intense light and heat. The sandy, porous soil should be mixed with heavier earth, and well-rotted manure added, in order that they may obtain proper nourishment and moisture. If a lawn is desired, a special mixture of "Seashore" lawn grass, composed of deep-rooting varieties, must be used. See Lawn. Ordinary lawn grass will not thrive in sandy soil. Four inches of good garden soil, above a two-inch layer of heavy clay, will keep the lawn in good condition. Perennials, such as hollyhocks, foxgloves, Canterbury bells, iris, Oriental poppies, delphiniums, phlox and peonies, do well in mixed beds or borders. Annuals may be used as fillers-in or to provide brilliancy of color. Cornflowers, nasturtiums, petunias and portulaca, all of which are sun-loving and drought-resistant plants, do well near the shore without protection or special bedding. Roses, hydrangeas and other shrubs may be grown if well protected from high winds and salt spray.

Chief consideration in this article, however, is given to such planting materials as are suited to seashore gardens,

---

* Special articles on the subjects indicated by an asterisk (*) will be found at the words so marked.

without the necessity of preparing special soils and planting conditions.

EASTERN ATLANTIC COAST. Plants must fit both soil and environment, so that each type of seacoast — sand dunes, coastal strip, or brackish marshes, will require a different floral planting, with the exception of such flowers as thrive in more than one kind of soil.

Making a garden near the sea must begin with a protecting plantation to shut off high winds and salt spray.

Beach grass makes an excellent sand binder for the dunes and coastal strips, as does also sea lyme grass. Holly, black oak, beach plum, wild cherry, California privet, tamarisk, Jack pine, with its twisted, wind-blown branches, and Japanese black pine may be used for hedges and windbreaks, on dunes or beach. Pitch pine may be planted as a hedge or mixed with Jack pine as a forest. One of the best of all trees, almost on the dunes, is the London plane. Flowering or fruiting plants for the shore are *Cornus baileyi*, bayberry, the common barberry, elderberry, and sumac. Farther back may be planted high-bush blueberry, sweet pepperbush, arrow-wood, and wild roses. If the coastal strip is low and moist, white swamp honeysuckle may be planted where it has some protection. Other moist ground plants with a fair resistance to salt spray and fog are pin oaks, red maple, viburnum, and witch-hazel. Mugo pines do well in practically all soil conditions along the shore and are easily naturalized.

Among herbs the sandworts are useful for dry, sandy spots where, if allowed to spread, they will form thick mats closely covered in spring and summer with small, white blossoms. Dusty miller thrives on sand and gravel alike. Sea pinks (*Statice*) or sea lavender (*Limonium*), in shades of white, yellow, rose, lavender and blue, require the usual culture for annuals and perennials. But they make excellent cut flowers and may be dried for use with everlastings. In the East, sand verbenas must be treated as annuals, doing best near the shore when sown in the open. Both the yellow and pink may be used. Sea poppies (*Glaucium*), with their golden or orange blossoms, grow wild in a few places in the eastern coastal section.

Brackish marshes are lovely with plantings of Turk's-cap lilies, sea goldenrod, rose mallow and blue chicory. Bracken and marsh ferns require plenty of moisture and not too much salt. Hardy buckthorn may be planted along the edge of a marsh.

PACIFIC COAST. Due to the difference in climatic conditions, many plants are available for naturalization on the seacoasts of the Pacific that are too tender to stand the rigors of an eastern winter. Likewise hedges for protection are desirable, but not absolutely essential. Privet, *Rosa rugosa* (also hardy eastward), the common barberry, sea buckthorn, and many native shrubs may be used as hedges. The beach grass makes an excellent soil binder. Sand verbenas, beach pea (*Lathyrus littoralis*), seaside daisy or beach aster, cerastiums, native sedums, and California wild flowers of many sorts, planted as annuals, may be used as sand plants. *Coreopsis maritima*, the sea dahlia, also likes sandy places. A creeping rock spray (*Cotoneaster horizontalis*) is beautiful when covering a rocky coast. Sea campion (*Silene maritima*) is a hardy perennial which gives best results when used in the rock garden or border. *Mesembryanthemum crystallinum*, the ice plant, is commonly naturalized along the shores of southern California, but may be grown as an annual farther north.

SUB-TROPICAL. This includes the south Atlantic Coast, the Gulf shore region, and southern California. Among the many trees and shrubs for seaside gardens are seaside mahoe, *Ficus aurea*, *Pittosporum tobira*, coconut palm and silver palmetto, the sea grape, the sea urchin, and the cajuput- or punk-tree, which is one of the most easily naturalized. Good hedge material is the coco plum, the hardy orange (*Poncirus trifoliata*), the Australian pines (*Casuarina*), and in California, especially for windbreaks and ornament, *Atriplex breweri* and *Lavatera assurgentiflora*. A fine, southern rose mallow (*Hibiscus grandiflorus*) is a good plant for the coastal lowlands, while centipedegrass will quickly cover the sandy places with thick, mat-like growth. This requires no cutting. The sea dahlia likes a sandy spot, while the sea holly is an excellent border plant. *See* the body of THE DICTIONARY for cultural notes and hardiness of the plants suited for seaside gardens. *See also* SAND GARDENS. — C. H. M.

**SEASIDE GOLDENROD** = *Solidago sempervirens*. See GOLDENROD.

**SEASIDE LAUREL** = *Xylophylla speciosa*.

**SEASIDE MAHOE** = *Thespesia populnea*.

**SEASIDE PAINTED-CUP** = *Castilleja latifolia*.

**SEASIDE PLUM** = *Coccolobis uvifera*.

**SEASONAL GARDENS.** Planning the flower garden so that most of the bloom will come at definite seasons is necessary for those who spend more time in the country during one season than another. For the convenience of such seasonal gardeners, the more important plants flowering at each season have been grouped under the headings SPRING GARDEN, SUMMER GARDEN, AUTUMN GARDEN, and WINTER GARDEN. *See* these special articles, or, if you want particular data for any one month, *see* GARDEN CALENDAR.

**SEASONAL WORK.** See GARDEN CALENDAR.

**SEA SQUILL** = *Urginea maritima*.

**SEATS.** See ORNAMENT AND FURNITURE.

**SEA URCHIN** = *Hakea laurina*.

**SEAWEED.** For its use as manure *see* MANURE.

**SEA WORMWOOD** = *Artemisia canadensis*.

**SEBESTEN** = *Cordia sebestena*.

**SEBESTENA** (seb-es-tee′na). An Arabic name for an evil-smelling plant.

**SEBIFERA, -us, -um** (seb-biff′er-ra). Tallow-bearing.

**SECALE.** See RYE.

**SECATEURS.** See Section 4, TOOLS AND IMPLEMENTS.

**SECHIUM** (seek′i-um). A single, rather important species of tendril-bearing, perennial, tropical American vines of the family Cucurbitaceae, known to science as **S. edule**, but widely grown for its edible fruit or young root tubers under a variety of names of which the chief are chayote and

---

* Special articles on the subjects indicated by an asterisk (*) will be found at the words so marked.

huisquil. Other names for it are chuchu, Christophine, cahiota, vegetable pear, and, in La., mirliton. It is a quick-growing vine with herbaceous stems, and alternate,* broadly triangular or ovalish leaves, 7-10 in. long, and shallowly lobed. Flowers small, whitish, unisexual* (for details see CUCURBITACEAE), the male flowers in clusters, the female solitary or two, in the leaf-axils.* Fruit generally pear-shaped, furrowed, green or white, 3-4 in. long, fleshy, enclosing a single seed, 1-2 in. long. (*Sechium* is from the Greek for a pen or fold and of uncertain application here.)

### CHAYOTE CULTURE

The plant can be grown as a perennial, which it really is, if the ground does not freeze more than an inch or two. This confines its cult. as a perennial mostly to zones* 7, 8, and 9. It may be grown as an annual farther north, but it needs heat and a long growing season and may not mature fruit if planted too far north.

It is a scrambling vine for which a support must be provided, and the plants should not be closer than 10 ft. apart each way. Sometimes it produces only male or only female flowers, so it is safer to have several vines together rather than one, which may turn out to be of one sex only, although this is not usual.

If planted in good, rich soil, each vine will produce from 50-100 fruits in a single season. They are mostly used boiled, like squash, and are very popular throughout the tropics. Where the plant is really perennial, and there is continuous growth, as in the tropics, the large tuber produces smaller ones which are harvested and used like potatoes.

The chayote may be started from seed, the whole 1-seeded fruit usually being planted, the stem end being left slightly exposed. Plant the fruit where the vine is to stand if in the region where chayote may be left out all the year.

**SECKEL.** A pear variety. See PEAR.

**SECUNDA**, -*us*, -*um* (see-kun'da). Secund; *i.e.* one-sided; applied to flower clusters, or sometimes to leaves, when the flowers or leaves are arranged only on one side of the stalk.

**SECUNDATA**, -*us*, -*um* (see-kun-day'ta). See SECUNDA.

**SECUNDIFLORA**, -*us*, -*um* (see-kun-di-flow'ra). With a 1-sided flower cluster.

**SEDGE.** See CAREX.

**SEDGE FAMILY** = Cyperaceae.

**SEDUM** (see'dum). Stonecrop. Low-growing, annual or perennial, fleshy herbs, chiefly perennial, comprising about 300 species, belonging to the family Crassulaceae, found through the temperate and colder regions of the northern hemisphere. They are diverse in habit, some creeping, with the stems rooting at the joints or trailing, some tufted,* others in rosettes, while still others are upright. Leaves alternate,* or opposite* or in whorls.* Margins sometimes cut. Flowers white, yellow, pink, red or blue in terminal clusters. Calyx of 4-5 sepals. Corolla of 4-8 petals. Stamens* double the number of petals. Fruits of 4-5, 1-celled follicles,* each with several seeds. (*Sedum* is from the Latin to sit, in allusion to the way they grow on rocks and walls.)

Sedums and the related genus *Gormania* are particularly adapted to the rock garden, but a few species can be used in the flower border. Easily cult. in ordinary garden soil. Good drainage is essential with most species, as they do not thrive in wet positions during winter. Propagated by seeds, division of roots, cuttings and leaves. Seeds should be sown ⅛ in. deep, in sandy soil, in the cool greenhouse or cold frame in early spring. Division of the roots should be made in Sept., March or April. Cuttings may be made during spring and summer. These should be inserted in sandy soil in cold frame or cool greenhouse. It is not necessary to shade from sun except for the species having thin leaves.

**acre.** Wall pepper. Mossy stonecrop. Golden moss. Gold-dust. Low, evergreen, creeping perennial, to 5 in. high, forming a carpet. Leaves alternate, small, triangular to ⅛ in. long, fleshy, crowded on the stem. Flowers bright yellow in terminal clusters. Specially suitable for dry places. Eu. and As. June. The *var.* **aureum** is a weaker plant, the leaves of which are yellow in the spring. See ROCK GARDEN.

**aizoon.** Strong-growing perennial, to 18 in. high. Rootstocks thick and tuberous. Stems upright, not branched. Leaves alternate,* broadly lance-shaped, to 3 in. long. Margins sharply toothed. Flowers yellow to orange, to ½ in. across, in terminal branching clusters. Siberia and Jap. June-Aug.

**album.** Worm-grass. Creeping evergreen, to 8 in. high. Leaves alternate,* fleshy, cylindrical, to ½ in. long. Flowers white, to ¼ in. across, in terminal branching clusters. Mediterranean region. July. The *var.* **murale** has purplish leaves and pale pink flowers. See ROCK GARDEN.

**anglicum.** Creeping evergreen, forming a carpet, to 2 in. high. Leaves alternate,* fleshy, cylindrical, to ¼ in. long. Flowers white, to ½ in. across. Western Eu. Summer.

**arboreum.** See CRASSULA PORTULACEA.

**caeruleum.** Annual, to 4 in. high. Leaves alternate,* fleshy, ovalish, to ¾ in. long. Flowers blue, marked white at base, to ¼ in. across. Mediterranean region. Summer. See ROCK GARDEN.

**dasyphyllum.** Tufted* evergreen, with slender branches, to 1 in. high. Leaves opposite,* fleshy, cylindrical, to ⅛ in. long. Flowers flesh-color, tinged yellow at the base, ¼ in. across. Eu. and northern Af. June. For cult. see ROCK GARDEN.

**ewersi.** Perennial, growing to 1 ft. high. Leaves opposite,* ovalish, ¾ in. long. Flowers purplish-pink, to ½ in. across. Himalayas and Mongolia. Summer.

**forsterianum** = *Sedum rupestre forsterianum.*

**glaucum** = *Sedum hispanicum minus.*

**hispanicum.** Perennial, but treated as an annual, and growing to 6 in. high. Leaves grayish-green, becoming reddish, crowded on the stem, to ½ in. long. Flowers flesh-pink, to ½ in. across. Southern Eu. and western As. The *var.* **minus** has bluish foliage. July. For cult. see ROCK GARDEN.

**kamtschaticum.** Erect perennial, growing to 9 in. high. Leaves alternate* or opposite,* ovalish, to 2 in. long, the margins toothed. Flowers orange-yellow, to ¾ in. across. Northeastern As. July-Aug.

**lydium.** Creeping evergreen, to 3 in. high. Leaves crowded on the stem, fleshy, cylindrical, to ¼ in. long. Flowers white, ¼ in. across. Asia Minor. June.

**maximowiczi** = *Sedum aizoon.*

**middendorffianum.** Perennial, of tufted* habit, to 1 ft. high. Leaves alternate,* lance-shaped, to 1½ in. long, the margins toothed. Flowers yellow, to ¾ in. across. Siberia and Manchuria. June-July.

**obtusatum** = *Gormania obtusata.*

**oppositifolium** = *Sedum spurium.*

**oreganum** = *Gormania oregana.*

**pruinatum.** Evergreen, of spreading habit, to 6 in. high. Leaves grayish-green, alternate,* narrow, fleshy, to ¾ in. long. Flowers pale yellow, to ¾ in. across. Portugal. Summer.

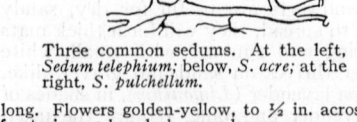

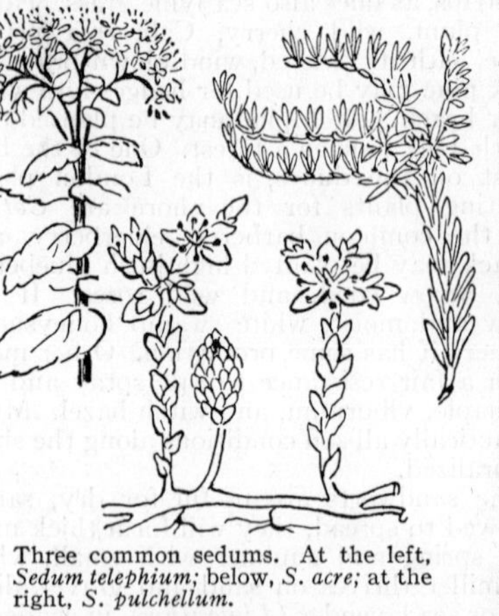

**pulchellum.** Widow's-cross. Flowering moss. Evergreen, growing to 1 ft. high. Leaves crowded on the stems, fleshy, narrow, cylindrical, to ¾ in. long. Flowers purplish, to ½ in. across. Eastern U.S. June-July.

**reflexum.** Yellow stonecrop. Creeping evergreen, forming a carpet. Leaves crowded on the stem, fleshy, narrow, cylindrical, to ½ in. long. Flower stalks to 1 ft. Flowers golden-yellow, to ½ in. across. Eu. Summer. For cult. see ROCK GARDEN.

**rupestre.** Creeping evergreen, forming a carpet. Leaves crowded on the stem, gray-green, narrow, to ¾ in.

Three common sedums. At the left, *Sedum telephium*; below, *S. acre*; at the right, *S. pulchellum*.

long. Flowers golden-yellow, to ½ in. across. Eu. Summer. The *var.* **forsterianum** has dark green leaves.

**sarmentosum.** Trailing evergreen. Leaves in whorls* of 3, broadly lance-shaped, to 1 in. long. Flowers bright yellow, to ½ in. across. Northern China and Jap. Summer. For cult. see ROCK GARDEN.

**sexangulare.** Creeping evergreen, to 4 in. high, forming a carpet. Leaves crowded on the stem, arranged in a spiral, narrow, to ¼ in. long. Flowers yellow, to ¼ in. across. Eu. Summer. For cult. see ROCK GARDEN.

**sieboldi.** Trailing perennial, to 1 ft. high. Leaves in whorls* of 3, grayish-green, reddish towards the margin, roundish, to 1 in. across. Flowers pink, to ½ in. across. Jap. Late fall. See AUTUMN GARDEN.

**spectabile.** Strong-growing perennial, to 2 ft. high. Leaves in whorls of 3, grayish-green, ovalish. Margins of upper part toothed. Flowers pink, to ½ in. across. Jap. and Central China. Aug.-Sept. See AUTUMN GARDEN.

**spurium.** Strong-growing, creeping evergreen, to 6 in. high. Leaves opposite,* ovalish, 1 in. or more long. Flowers pale pink, to ½ in. across. Caucasus. Summer. For cult. see ROCK GARDEN.

**stahli.** Evergreen, growing to 8 in. high, slightly hairy. Leaves oppo-

---

* Special articles on the subjects indicated by an asterisk (*) will be found at the words so marked.

# Seed 723 Seeds and Seedage

site,* roundish, to ½ in. across. Flowers yellow, to ½ in. across. Mex. Summer and fall.

**stoloniferum.** Creeping evergreen, to 6 in. high. Leaves opposite,* spoon-shaped, to 1 in. long. Flowers pink, to ½ in. across. Southwestern As. Early summer.

**telephium.** Orpine. Live-forever. Strong-growing perennial, to 18 in. high. Leaves ovalish, to 3 in. long, the margins toothed. Flowers reddish-purple. Eurasia. Late summer.

**SEED.** The ripened, fertilized ovule* of a flower, usually in some sort of a fruit (which see), but naked in the pines and related plants. The essential part of a seed is the embryo.* For raising plants from seed *see* SEEDS AND SEEDAGE.

**SEEDAGE.** *See* SEEDS AND SEEDAGE.

**SEEDBED.** *See* SEEDS AND SEEDAGE.

**SEED COLLECTING.** Saving seed from favorite plants or from especially good strains is often desirable, but should be undertaken with an understanding of its potentialities. Many garden flowers will not come true from home-grown seed collections, this being especially true of horticultural varieties among annuals and certain perennials. Most shrub and tree seeds, on the other hand, are reasonably sure to come true to type, and so will some vegetables. But in the latter there is the constant danger of foreign pollen* adulterating the population. Only trial and error can tell you which seeds are worth saving and which will probably bring disappointment.

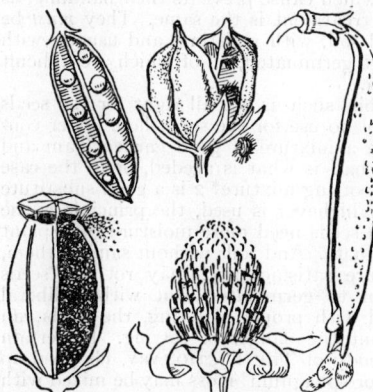

Seed pods of sweet pea (*right*), iris (*upper center*), rose-of-Sharon (*upper left*), poppy (*lower left*), and the fruiting head of zinnia (*lower center*).

If seeds are to be saved, select the healthiest and finest blooms and allow only these to set seeds. All other flowers on the plant should be pinched off, thus throwing to those that will produce seed all the nourishment possible.

When the fruit is ripe, it should be harvested and brought into a warm, dry place, ready for pulling and cleaning the seed. This should be done as soon after the fruit will easily release its seeds as possible. The seeds should then be stored in paper packets, or in stoppered bottles if they are to be kept for a long time, and it should be remembered that vermin are fond of most seeds. If paper packets are used, they had better be stored in tin boxes.

A simple, home-made seed packet, easily made from a piece of paper 3 × 5 in.

The harvesting of seeds from fleshy fruits is a troublesome business. The seeds must be cleaned of pulp or flesh mechanically or by soaking in water. This is often a long and messy job, but essential if the seeds are to be kept. Uncleaned seeds with fleshy parts still clinging to them are pretty apt to rot. After the flesh has been removed, the seeds should be washed in cold water and spread out on papers to dry. When thoroughly dry they may be stored as those above.

For planting seed, and the process known as stratification, *see* SEEDS AND SEEDAGE.

**SEED-GERM.** *See* EMBRYO.

**SEEDLINGS.** *See* SEEDS AND SEEDAGE.

**SEED PAN.** *See* FLOWER POTS.

**SEED POD.** *See* POD.

**SEEDS AND SEEDAGE.** Most plants are raised from seed in spite of many other methods of propagation (which see). The reasons for this are that no other means of increasing one's stock is so easy, and that seeds, because most of them will endure a reasonably long period of dormancy, can be stored and used as wanted, while most cuttings and other methods of vegetative reproduction must be fitted to the seasonal demands of such operations.

While seeds can be kept, they cannot be kept indefinitely and still retain the power to sprout. Much work has been done on the viability of seeds after storage for briefer or longer periods. It is unnecessary to repeat this data here, for it will be found at GARDEN TABLES II. Nor are we here concerned with the number or percentage of average germination of the different sorts of seeds. Few of them have 100% germination chances, and in planting it is always best to allow enough extra seed to take up the inevitable failure of a certain percentage of nearly all varieties to sprout. *See* GARDEN TABLES II.

Nor is it necessary to repeat here the details of the amount of seed needed per acre or for 100 ft. of row in the vegetable garden. All such data will be found at GARDEN TABLES I, where, also, will be found further statistical information on the number of seeds to an ounce or pound.

Here we are concerned with seeds chiefly as they provide the easiest method of increasing or propagating plants — in other words, with their power to germinate.

### GERMINATION

Most seeds need moisture and darkness in order to sprout, and ordinary soil provides the easiest method of supplying both. But there are times when moisture can be too great or when because of the fineness of the soil particles, the circulation of air through them is retarded. In ordinary garden soil the conditions seem nearly perfect for the germination of most seeds, especially when these are not too small. But there are certain seeds that will not sprout without much more attention than merely planting them. These are described in detail below.

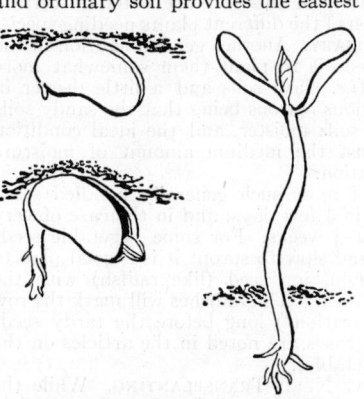

Germination of a bean seed, the final stage being the production of the first pair of leaves (*at right*).

From the practical gardening standpoint we must distinguish among at least three main methods of managing seeds: (1) Those that grow where planted, as do most vegetable and annual flower seeds; (2) those that are planted with the expectation that their seedlings will be several times transplanted before being finally planted; and (3) those seeds that must be stratified.

(1) SEEDS PLANTED WHERE THEY ARE TO STAY. This applies to nearly all the common vegetables and to the seeds of those flower garden annuals which are sown where needed — in other words, the hardy annuals. Tender an-

---

* Special articles on the subjects indicated by an asterisk (*) will be found at the words so marked.

nuals (see ANNUALS) come under the second category, i.e. those that will be several times transplanted before final planting, and their handling will be described under (2).

For those sown where needed the chief thing to remember is the *depth* to plant. Very fine and small seeds must never be sown with more than a thin layer of soil over them — barely covered, in fact. A good plan is to see that the upper layer of soil for such seeds is finely pulverized, then scatter the seeds, and merely rake them in very gently. Such a method will leave some seeds only partly covered, some shallowly covered, and some not covered at all. Then lightly tamp the soil with the back of a spade or a board and this will firm the seeds in the soil (even the uncovered ones) enough so that they will germinate.

These fine seeds are hard to manage as to their early water needs, especially before and just after germination. Being so shallowly planted, they are very likely to become dried out, and to prevent this they should be watered with a very gentle, fine spray, preferably in the late afternoon. A heavy downpour, or water from a hose, will, of course, wash them out. But a fine spray from a fine-rose watering can or syringe will be just what they need.

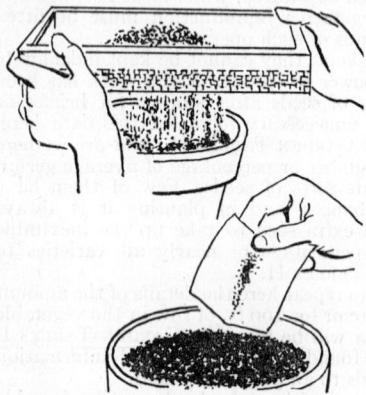

Sifting soil for fine seeds and a method of sowing those too small to be handled with the fingers.

For the usual run of more ordinary and larger seeds there is much less trouble about the depth to plant them. A fair general rule is to plant them 2–3 times as deep as their own diameter, whether in drills* or sown broadcast. Variations from this rule are noted in certain cases at the description of the different plants needing special depths in this DICTIONARY. Another general caution in the usual handling of seeds is to plant them somewhat more shallowly in heavy (*i.e.* clay) soils and a little deeper in sandy ones. The obvious reasons being that the sandy soils are drier and heavy soils moister, and the ideal condition we are seeking is just the medium amount of moisture necessary for germination.

The germination of most such generally handled seeds will ordinarily occur in a few days, and in the case of very tardy ones in from 2–3 weeks. For some vegetable seeds that are both small and slow to sprout it is a good plan to plant a quickly germinating seed (like radish) with the slow one in the same drill.* The radishes will mark the row (for purposes of cultivation*) long before the tardy seeds are up. Several such cases are noted in the articles on the culture of special vegetables.

(2) SEEDLINGS THAT NEED TRANSPLANTING. While the usual run of vegetable and annual flower seeds are sown where wanted and therefore come under the methods described under (1), there are many others that are sown with the understanding that their seedlings must be several times transplanted before being put in their final location. The chief plants needing such attention are:

Tender Annuals (see ANNUALS).
Vegetable Plants, such as tomatoes, peppers, the cabbage tribe, celery, and many others noted in the special articles on the culture of vegetables. See *also* KITCHEN GARDEN.
Flower Garden Perennials.
Many Greenhouse Plants.
Many Shrubs and some Trees.

While the details of handling such a miscellaneous lot of seeds will naturally vary, the main fact that applies to all of them is that the seeds are started in flats, pots, or boxes, or in a specially prepared seedbed. After germination they are several times transplanted, and for the details of this *see* the section below on the management of seedlings.

For large-scale operations a seedbed is prepared, usually in the hotbed or cold frame, or under a lath screen outdoors, or sometimes in a propagating bench in the greenhouse. And in some cases the latter must be supplied with bottom-heat (which see), but seeds needing this are noted at their proper entries throughout THE GARDEN DICTIONARY. For all others, the seeds, whether planted in seedbeds or in boxes, pans, or flats, need the following general conditions.

The reason for their special requirements is that they germinate with difficulty or that immediately after germination they are unfit to cope with the conditions they will finally meet as growing plants. It does not matter, in their initial management, which cause prevents their handling, as in (1), because their treatment is the same. They *must* be provided with special soil, with moisture, and usually with shade, until they have germinated, all of which are difficult to control in the open.

Ordinary garden soils such as are all right for the seeds discussed at (1) are of no use for the seeds here under consideration. For them a mixture of good garden loam and sand mixed half and half is what is needed, or in the case of greenhouse plants potting mixture* 2 is a good substitute for many of them. Whichever is used, the principle is the same. It is that such seeds need more moisture than plant food in order to germinate. And soils without sand in them, while holding moisture satisfactorily, may rot the seeds before allowing them to germinate. But with a liberal mixture of sand, and with proper watering, the seeds can be kept moist without the danger of rotting. In certain cases, noted in the body of THE DICTIONARY, chopped-up osmunda* fiber, coir, or sphagnum* moss may be mixed with the sand or even replace it. But for most seeds under consideration in this section, sand should make up about ½ of the material in which they are planted.

The depth to plant these seeds is the same as discussed under (1), but the conditions of moisture and the necessity for shade are very different. As for most home gardeners such seeds will be planted in pots, pans, flats, or boxes, it is necessary to point out that these must be provided with perfect drainage, so that while plenty of water can be used, it will never stagnate at the bottom of the container. The only way to be sure of this is to fill ⅕ or ¼ of the pot or box with pieces of broken flower pots or crocks, and in the case of flats to put a layer of sphagnum moss about ¾ in. thick under the soil.

While water is a prime necessity, it is usually inadvisable to keep up a steady and sometimes harmful excess of watering. To avoid the necessity of this and still keep the seed pans or boxes moist, it is usually better to shade them. Depending on the scale of your operations this may be accomplished by lath screens, by cheesecloth, paper, or in the greenhouse propagating bench by shading the glass.

The object in all cases is the same: to preserve a moist atmosphere just over the soil in

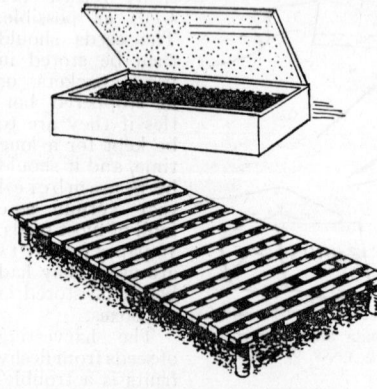

A glass cover (raised) for a seed box, and a lath shade for a seedbed. Both are used to keep the air and soil moist.

which your seeds are planted. Sometimes a sheet of ground glass over a flower pot is all that is necessary, or several flats

---

* Special articles on the subjects indicated by an asterisk (*) will be found at the words so marked.

may be put in a cold frame and cheesecloth frames made to replace glass sash. Or in the nursery seedbed, a light brush screen, put about 5 in. above the soil, will give the same result, or a lath screen may be used. The danger in all such methods of shading is that too much moisture will accumulate, which is just as fatal as to let the seedbed or containers dry out. Specific directions for the daily maintenance of proper moisture conditions are impossible to describe. The thing to keep in mind is that shade and moisture (and of course watering) must be so regulated that the seeds are never without sufficient moisture, that they get enough fresh air (but no drying wind), but that stagnation of soil moisture or air does not invite the condition known as damping-off (which see).

Some growers in order to avoid these difficulties never water their seeds directly at all. They plant them in the usual way in a flower pot which is set in a larger flower pot.

Seedlings in an inner pot which is surrounded by wet sphagnum* moss from which they absorb enough moisture to avoid direct watering of the seedlings.

The space between the inner and outer pot is packed with sphagnum* moss and this is watered freely and regularly. The inner pot (it must not be glazed) absorbs what moisture is needed from the sphagnum and keeps its seeds in just the right condition of moisture, provided the whole contrivance is covered with a sheet of ground glass until the seeds have sprouted.

When the seeds have germinated they must be grown along for a longer or shorter period, depending on the variety, and are then required for, and in fact demand, special handling. *See* the section below upon the management of seedlings.

A few seeds, in spite of every care, will not germinate within a reasonable time, say 1–6 weeks. They have such slow germination that the grower is apt to think they have died. This may be so, but it is better to carry such pans or flats along for 10–15 months (even 2 years in extreme cases) before throwing their contents away. Such notoriously slow germinations are noted at their proper entries in the body of the book, so you will be on your guard in such cases.

There are, too, a few seeds, also noted specially at their proper entries, which will not germinate without soaking in warm water, or filing their husks, or soaking in acids, or planting in specially acid soils, but such are the exceptions. Much more common are those that come under the third method of handling seeds.

(3) STRATIFIED SEEDS. The stratification of seeds is an attempt to imitate the natural conditions of those trees and shrubs which drop their seeds in late summer but which do not germinate them until the following or even the second spring. Many trees naturally do this, especially nut trees, while others, like most evergreens, sprout their seeds as soon as dropped.

Those that retard germination for 6 or for 18 months (*i.e.* the first or second spring after falling) are naturally kept from drying out and dying, and in the process nature does three things to them. Merely by letting the litter of the forest floor cover them they are kept in the dark, kept from drying out, and throughout most parts of the country they are more or less frozen, although the experts are undecided whether actual freezing is a necessity or not. There is no doubt that such seeds need a prolonged chilling even if not frozen.

The nursery practice of imitating these conditions is known as stratification. It consists of planting such seeds as soon as harvested in boxes of pure sand, often in wire cages if rodents are a pest, and then burying the boxes about 6 in. deep, in the shade, preferably on a well-drained slope. If the region is a reasonably moist one, the stratified seeds need no further attention until they are taken up and planted according to the directions given at (2).

Stratified seeds

All seeds needing stratification are so indicated in the body of THE GARDEN DICTIONARY, and should be handled as described above. Some very small ones may be placed between layers of cheesecloth buried in sand to facilitate finding them in the spring. Or some prefer to put fine seeds in bags of mosquito wire before burying. But most stratified seeds are big and easily sifted out of the sand when needed.

Before considering the management of seedlings, it is necessary to point to two special sorts of seedage described elsewhere. One is the seeding of lawns, which will be found at LAWN. The other is the reproduction of fern spores.* The latter are not true seeds, but their handling approximates the methods mentioned at (2). For the details *see* FERNS AND FERN GARDENING.

MANAGEMENT OF SEEDLINGS

Much depends upon the careful growth of a tiny seedling as soon as it is germinated and commences life on its own account. All through its early stages it is subject to the dangers incident to life in nature, and we must care for these tender seedlings so that we may reap the benefits to be derived from the germination methods described above.

Seedlings are nature's own way of propagation, and most plants have the power of reproduction by seed, but many kinds under cultivation require considerable care to bring the seedlings to maturity. Attention must be given the seedling as soon as germination takes place, as neglect at this stage means ruin.

As soon as the seedling makes its second leaf it must have attention or it will become weak and spindly, and while perhaps too small to handle with the fingers, a pointed stick may be used to transfer the young plants to flats, which is generally known as pricking-off or pricking-out. Flats should be made about 3 in. deep, 14 in. wide, and 24 in. long. This is a good size to handle, and will accommodate 42 plants spaced 2 × 3 in. If 12-in. ends are used and 3-in. stock, it will leave openings in the bottom,

Water pricked-off* seedlings **very** gently, with as fine a spray as possible.

just wide enough for perfect drainage. The soil for flats should be reasonably fine and sifted only to remove stones

---

* Special articles on the subjects indicated by an asterisk (*) will be found at the words so marked.

and large lumps, and be a little lighter than the plants will ultimately need.

Drainage can be assured by covering the bottom of the flat with strawy manure which also acts as a stimulant when the young roots reach it. Or sphagnum* moss may be used for the lowest layer. Assuming the proper soil has been prepared, the flat properly drained, filled, pressed down around the outer edge and leveled off, not too dry or too wet, it is ready to receive the plants.

With a pointed stick dig out a small batch of seedlings, separate them and transfer to the flat individually, gently pressing each one in place. When these touch each other, in a week or two, they are ready for transferring to pots or for planting into permanent quarters. Some seed germinates very slowly and the seedlings appear at irregular intervals. In such cases the seedlings should be pricked-off several in a pot as they appear.

Pricking-off young seedlings. For directions *see* text.

The greatest menace to raising seedlings is their tendency to damping-off after they appear. This is caused by insufficient air and the right conditions of heat and moisture to encourage the growth of a fungus which spreads with alarming rapidity. If not checked damping-off will eventually spread over the whole seedbed and destroy every seedling. Modern research has recently discovered many preventives for damping-off. But most of them have yet to stand the test. The most recent method to prevent damping-off is the use of formaldehyde dust incorporated with the soil according to directions. Semesan is also used for the same purpose, and in both cases directions should be closely followed to avoid trouble. Should the fungus appear, however, in spite of all precautions, the affected part should be carefully removed and the surface dusted with powdered charcoal. This will usually retard its further development. *See also* DAMPING-OFF.

After the seedlings are pricked-off they should be given a good watering to settle the soil around the plants, shaded from direct sunlight for a few days, and kept in a closer and warmer atmosphere. Little water will be required until growth commences, and great care is needed to prevent a saturated condition of the soil which would cause it to become sour. But a light sprinkling for a few days will freshen them up and not wet the soil too much. After the seedlings have recovered their slight check they may be allowed plenty of light and air and strong, sturdy plants will result. If the plants are allowed to remain in the flats too long, they ripen up and start flowering, and at the best become drawn, leggy* and weak, so as soon as ready they should be planted out or potted-on (*see* POTTING-ON) as the case demands. — A. J. L.

**SEED-SOWING MACHINE.** *See* Section 1, TOOLS AND IMPLEMENTS.

**SEGETA, -us, -um** (se-get′a). Growing in cornfields.

**SEGMENT.** One of the divisions of a leaf, petal, or sepal. Segments are not properly parts of a compound leaf, although leaflets are quite generally called segments. *See* LEAFLET.

**SEGREGATION.** Hybridization or crossing brings together two characters belonging to different strains, races, varieties, species, etc. It creates new combinations at once of already existing characters, and these first-generation hybrids can be propagated by various asexual* methods such as cuttings, grafts, etc. But the new combinations are relatively few if one stops at the $F_1$* generation — only one per cross in many cases. If these $F_1$'s* are selfed or backcrossed on the recessive parent, many more new combinations are obtained, amounting to hundreds if the original parents were distinct in a large number of characters and genes.*

This is what segregation brings about. In other words, when the hybrid plant produces its reproductive cells, segregation separates the character determiners brought together by crossing, and produces an opportunity for many new combinations and rearrangements of characters to take place. Thus, in a cross between some tall yellow and certain white four-o'clock races, the immediate offspring would be all tall light yellow, which is new and could be asexually propagated, but by selfing this hybrid, six kinds would be obtained — tall yellow, dwarf white, tall white, dwarf yellow, tall light yellow and dwarf light yellow — four of them new and all could be propagated by root division. This is a very simple illustration of what occurs in practice, since the forms crossed often have many hereditary qualities that one does not notice or are not expressed, except through hybridization. Thus two white-flowered races of sweet peas produce colored flowered offspring; two dwarf types of corn produce talls, certain self-colored bean varieties produce mottled progeny, some four-o'clock species hybrids are more cold-resistant than either parent. — O. E. W.

**SEGUINE** (se-gwin′e). Tropical American vernacular for the dumb cane (*Dieffenbachia seguine*).

**SELAGINELLA** (see-laj-i-nell′a). Annual or perennial herbs of fern-like habit, and related to the ferns, comprising about 400 species of the family Selaginellaceae. They are distributed mostly through tropical regions, generally in damp places in forests, but sometimes in desert places. They are of very diverse habits; — some small and creeping, others erect, while still others are climbing. Leaves small, scale-like in various shades of green, sometimes with metallic shadings. They are crowded on the stems, opposite* in pairs, one being smaller than the other, the smaller pressed against the stem, so giving an alternate* appearance. They do not bear flowers, but the tips of the shoots bear scale-like leaves of equal size, in the axils* of which the spores* are produced. (*Selaginella* is from the Latin *selago*, an old name of a club moss.)

These plants are usually grown in the greenhouse. They make useful pot plants for table decoration. Easily cult. in potting mixture* 4. Shade and plenty of water are essential. Propagated by pieces of the plant which can be inserted in permanent pans or pots, as they do not need transplanting. Several pieces will quickly cover a pan. They can be used for covering unsightly places under greenhouse benches.

**emmeliana.** Erect-growing perennial, to 1 ft. high, much-branched. Leaves bright green. Tropical America.

**flabellata.** Erect perennial, of stiff habit, growing to 8 in. high, branching above. Leaves green, ovalish, one side of blade larger than the other. Sub-tropical and tropical regions.

**kraussiana.** Creeping, moss-like perennial, with stems that root at the joints. Leaves bright green. Azores to South Af. Excellent for pans or pots.

**lepidophylla.** Resurrection plant. Desert perennial, growing to 4 in. high, in dense tufts.* Stems curling inwards when dry, giving plant a ball-like appearance. *See* ANASTATICA. Leaves ovalish, one side of blade larger than the other, green, paler on the under side. Tex. to S.A.

**rupestris.** Perennial, of tufted* habit, growing 4–5 in. high. Stems much-branched. Leaves white-tipped. In damp places, eastern U.S.

**SELAGINELLACEAE** (see-laj-i-nel-lay′see-ee). A family of flowerless, moss-like plants, the only genus of which is *Selaginella*, which see for the characters of the family.

**SELECTION.** Many wild plant species are genetic mixtures (the sum of many strains) and the same statement is true of many cultivated varieties and strains. This is especially true of plants such as corn and sugar beets which are commonly cross-fertilized, and much less true of self-fertilized plants such as peas, beans and sweet peas. Cross-fertilized plants represent more hybridity than self-fertilized types. In sugar beets the thrip insect is the cross-pollinator. In corn, it is the wind.

---

* Special articles on the subjects indicated by an asterisk (*) will be found at the words so marked.

Wild sugar beets contain 7 to 14% sugar. By saving seed only from the sweetest beets for two generations, Vilmorin obtained types with 21% sugar. This illustrates selection. What Vilmorin did was simply to separate out by selection high sugar strains. The genes* for these were already in the wild species. No new ones were produced by selection. Once the desired result is attained through selection, the strain or variety remains thus, barring mutation* and providing crossing is prevented. Selection among self-fertilized plants is less apt to produce results. In the past selection has probably been the largest factor in producing new, desirable types, and every observant gardener practices it today. — O. E. W. See PLANT BREEDING, MUTATION.

**SELENICEREUS** (se-len-i-seer'e-us). Beautiful night-blooming, mostly climbing or trailing cacti, comprising about 16 species found from Tex. to the Argentine, one of them widely grown in greenhouse or outdoors in the Far South as a night-blooming cereus. They have ribbed or angled stems with many aerial* roots which help them to climb. Spines few and small. Flowers white, usually very large, the outside scaly and often with tufts of hair, the outer segments often greenish or brownish.

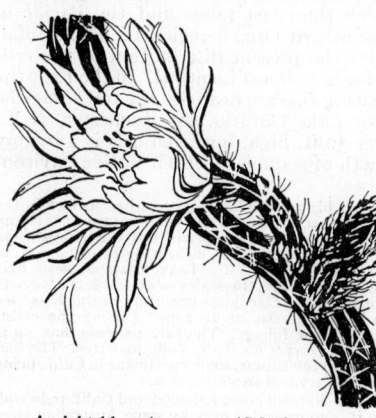

A night-blooming cereus (*Selenicereus pteranthus*)

Fruit berry-like, but covered at first with bristles, hairs, and spines. (*Selenicereus* is named for the moon goddess and *Cereus*.)

For culture see CACTI.

**grandiflorus.** Stems stoutish, 7–8-ribbed or the ribs fewer. Spines needle-like, usually mixed with white hairs. Flowers about 7 in. long, white, but salmon-colored on the outside. Cuba and Jamaica.

**pteranthus.** Night-blooming cereus. Stems 1–2 in. thick, rather strongly 4–6-angled, the spines 1–4 at each cluster. Flowers 10–12 in. long, remarkably sweet-smelling, white. Mex. Widely grown in greenhouses and frequently used in hybridizing with *S. grandiflorus* and with *Heliocereus speciosus*. See also HYLOCEREUS and NYCTOCEREUS.

**SELENIPEDIUM.** See CYPRIPEDIUM.

**SELFED.** See SELF-POLLINATION.

**SELF-FERTILIZATION.** The fertilization of an ovule by its own pollen; often called close fertilization. See FERTILIZATION. See also CLEISTOGAMOUS FLOWERS.

**SELF-HEAL** = *Prunella vulgaris*. See also the list at WEEDS.

**SELF-POLLINATION.** The process by which a flower is pollinated by its own pollen, or, more broadly, by pollen from any other flower on the same plant. Such a flower is said to be selfed. See CROSSING.

**SELF-STERILITY.** In the flowering plants, the inability of normal pollen from any given plant to fertilize its own flowers. This occurs in over 100 different species involving 50 plant families. It is more frequent in some families than in others. Among these are the rosaceous fruits — sweet cherries, plums, almonds, apples, pears and Japanese quince. It is also a striking phenomenon among hippeastrums, gladioli, avocados, carnations, poppies, cabbage, rye, Cornelian cherries, and muscadine grapes.

Many of the plants mentioned are asexually propagated and very often planted without considering this aspect. They flower profusely, look healthy, but fail to set fruit. This is especially true of small home garden plantings of the rosaceous fruits. Not all varieties of economic plants nor of a given species behave thus. Many are self-fertile, but in those varieties in which it does occur, it is emphatically hereditary, and interplanting with suitable varieties is the only practical remedy. (*See also* CROSS-STERILITY.) — O. E. W.

**SEMESAN.** A trademarked fungicidal material sold with directions for use in disinfecting the seeds of cacti, the soil in which they are planted, for control of damping-off, and like purposes.

**SEMI-CACTUS DAHLIA.** See DAHLIA.

*SEMIDECANDRA*, *-us*, *-um* (sem-i-de-kan'dra). With five stamens.

*SEMPERAURESCENS* (sem-per-or-res'senz). Always golden.

*SEMPERFLORENS* (sem-per-flow'renz). Ever- or continuously flowering.

*SEMPERVIRENS* (sem-per-vy'renz). Ever- or always green.

**SEMPERVIVUM.** See HOUSELEEK.

**SENECA.** A cherry variety. See CHERRY.

**SENECA GRASS** = *Hierochloë odorata*.

**SENECA SNAKEROOT** = Senega snakeroot (*Polygala senega*). See SENEGA.

**SENECIO** (sen-ee'si-o). Groundsel. Ragwort. Annual, biennial or perennial herbs, shrubs or small trees and a few climbers, comprising about 1250 species of the family Compositae, found throughout the world. Leaves alternate* or basal. This genus being among the largest and therefore having diverse habits is difficult to define, the chief difference being in the rings of bracts which surround the head. These do not overlap each other, and the lower bracts are scale-like,* giving a calyx-like appearance to the upper ring of bracts.* The flower heads are generally yellow, but sometimes purple, red, blue or white, solitary or in clusters. The heads are often showy, composed of ray* and disk florets,* but the ray florets are sometimes absent. (*Senecio* is from the Latin for old man, in supposed allusion to the pappus.)

Comparatively few of these species are in cultivation, but a few are used for the border. The chief hort. species is *S. cruentus*, the cineraria of the florists, and a useful decorative plant for the house.

Some of the species below are occasionally credited to the genus *Cineraria*. See that entry for an explanation of its varied use. Some are also known as *Kleinia*, a genus not here maintained.

**aureus.** Golden ragwort. Strong-growing, hardy, herbaceous perennial, to 2 ft. high, sometimes slightly hairy. Basal leaves stalked, ovalish, heart-shaped at base, to 6 in. long, purplish on the under side. Margins toothed. Stem leaves smaller, cut into lobes almost to midrib. Flowers yellow, in heads to ¾ in. across, in many-headed, branching clusters. Eastern N.A. June–July.

**cineraria.** Dusty Miller. Hardy, branching, herbaceous perennial, growing to 2½ ft. high, covered with long, white, matted hairs. Leaves alternate,* thick, cut into narrow, rounded lobes. Flowers yellow or cream, in heads to ½ in. across, in small terminal clusters. Mediterranean region.

**clivorum** = *Ligularia clivorum*.

**cruentus.** Low-growing, herbaceous perennial, sometimes covered with white-woolly hairs. Leaves alternate,* large, long-stalked, ovalish or heart-shaped. Margins wavy and toothed. Flowers in heads, in clusters. Canary Islands. This species is the parent of the cineraria of the florists. For cult. see CINERARIA.

**doronicum.** Leopard's-bane. Hardy, herbaceous perennial to 2½ ft. high, slightly hairy. Leaves alternate,* with thick, fleshy stalks and veins, broadly lance-shaped, to 7 in. long. Margins sometimes toothed. Flowers showy,* orange or yellow, in heads 2½ in. across, 2–3 heads on each stalk. Bracts surrounding heads black-tipped. Useful border plant for spring-flowering. S. Eu.

**elegans.** Purple ragwort. Tender annual, growing to 2 ft. high, covered with sticky hairs. Leaves broadly lance-shaped, to 3 in. long, either lobed or toothed. Flowers in heads, disk florets yellow, ray florets purple or red. Heads in loose branching clusters. S. Af. Can be grown in the border or as a cool greenhouse plant. See ANNUALS.

**jacobaea.** Tansy ragwort. Perennial, growing to 4 ft. high. Basal leaves to 8 in. long, cut into lyre-shaped lobes, stalked. Stem leaves broadly lance-shaped, to 6 in. long, cut into 2–3 lobes. Flowers yellow, in heads ½ in. across, numerous, in branching clusters. Eu., naturalized in N.A. Useful border plant. Can be used for cutting.

**kaempferi** = *Ligularia kaempferi*.

---

* Special articles on the subjects indicated by an asterisk (*) will be found at the words so marked.

**mikanioides.** German ivy. Tender, herbaceous, climbing perennial, smooth and shiny. Stems woody at base. Leaves alternate,* fleshy, bright green, ovalish, cut into 4-5 pointed lobes. Flowers yellow, in small heads, in few-headed clusters, of disk florets only. South Af. Suitable for window boxes, and a good house plant.

**pulcher.** Strong-growing perennial, to 4 ft. high, covered with long, fine, white hairs. Leaves lance-shaped, to 10 in. long, slightly lobed, with rounded teeth. Flowers in heads to 3 in. across, ray florets reddish-purple, disk florets yellow. Uruguay and Argentina. Hardy if grown in well-drained soil.

**scandens.** Climbing perennial, with woody stems, hairy when young. Leaves gray-green, ovalish or broadly lance-shaped, often lobed at the base, covered with short hairs. Flowers yellow, in heads, in loose, branching clusters. China.

**succulentus.** A low, succulent, South African shrub with fleshy stems and clustered, thick leaves which are cylindrical, about 1¼ in. long and bluish-green. Flowers yellow, the heads about ½ in. wide, in few-flowered clusters (corymbs*). South Africa.

**SENEGA** (sen'e-ga). Latinized form of Seneca, and now perpetuated in Senega snakeroot, first known as a medicinal plant by the Seneca Indians.

**SENEGA SNAKEROOT** = *Polygala senega*.

**SENILIS, -e** (sen'i-lis). Senile; usually old and white-haired.

**SENNA.** See CASSIA. For other plants sometimes called senna see COLUTEA and CORONILLA EMERUS.

**SENNA FAMILY.** See LEGUMINOSAE.

**SENSIBILIS, -e** (sen-sib'i-lis). Sensitive.

**SENSITIVE FERN** = *Onoclea sensibilis*.

**SENSITIVE PLANT** = *Mimosa pudica*.

**SEPAL.** One of the separate parts of a calyx (which see).

**SEPARATION.** See DIVISION.

**SEPIUM** (see'pi-um). Found along hedges or fences.

**SEPTEMBER.** See GARDEN CALENDAR.

**SEPTEMFIDA, -us, -um** (sep-tem-fid'a). Cut into seven segments.

**SEPTICEPS** (sep'ti-seps). Seven-headed.

**SEQUENCE.** For the sequence of bloom in the garden see GARDEN CALENDAR.

**SEQUOIA** (see-kwoy'ya). Magnificent relics of a once widely distributed genus of coniferous trees of the pine family. Today there are only two species localized in Calif. and remnants of an ancient group which have been found as fossils in many parts of the world. The survivors include only the giant sequoia or big-tree and the California redwood, both gigantic evergreens. Leaves small, decurrent,* mostly 2-ranked, narrow, more or less hugging the twigs in the big-tree. The trees are without flowers in the ordinary sense of that term, the male flowers consisting of bunches of spirally arranged stamens* in clusters in the leaf-axils,* the female in cone-like clusters with 5-7 naked ovules between the cone scales. The ovules and cones ultimately ripen into a small, woody cone with 5-7 winged seeds at each cone scale. (Named for Sequoiah, a Georgia Indian and the inventor of the Cherokee alphabet.)

Neither the big-tree nor the Calif. redwood takes kindly to cult. in the East. Climatic conditions in their native habitat are practically impossible to imitate in the East. The big-tree grows high up in the Sierras, while the California redwood is found between the coast range and the Pacific in northern Calif. and southern Ore., a region of high rainfall and much fog. In fact the present distribution of the redwood and that of the fog are almost identical. In the East the only places approximating this are near the sea and along the shores of Lake Erie or Lake Ontario. At Rochester, N.Y., there is a sequoia over 50 ft. high, but even this is a pygmy compared to the growth of sequoias in their native environment.

**gigantea.** Giant sequoia or big-tree. The largest coniferous tree in the world (for deciduous trees of huge girth see PLATANUS OCCIDENTALIS and ADANSONIA DIGITATA). The largest known specimen is the famous General Sherman tree in Sequoia National Park, measuring nearly 320 ft. in height, and with a trunk diameter of 35 ft. Leaves narrow, scale-like, scarcely ½ in. long. Cones 2-3 in. long, the scales woody. Sierra Nevada Mountains of Calif. above 7000 ft. Hardiness uncertain in the East (see above), but occasionally it will persist up to zone* 4 along the coast. The *var.* **glauca** has bluish-green foliage. The *var.* **pendula** has more drooping branches and in cult. forms a narrow, columnar tree. The big-tree may well be the oldest of living things, some specimens in Calif. being over 2500 years old, but see TAXODIUM MUCRONATUM.

**sempervirens.** Redwood; also called coast redwood and Calif. redwood. Extreme height up to 340 ft. and exceeded only by some Australian trees of the genus *Eucalyptus*. The trunk diameter is less than the big-tree, not exceeding 28 ft. and usually 10-20 ft. Leaves nearly 1 in. long, more spreading than in *S. gigantea*. Cones scarcely 1 in. long. Northern Calif. and southern Ore. in the fog belt. Scarcely adapted to the East, but making magnificent forests in its own region, far more extensive than the big-tree, and an important source of valuable timber. For hardiness notes see above; it is certainly not hardy in the East above zone* 5. The *var.* **glauca** has bluish-green foliage. There is also a form with pendulous branches. The burls of the redwood are often sold by florists. They make interesting growths when put in water. See BURL.

**SERBIAN SPRUCE** = *Picea omorika*. See SPRUCE.

**SERENOA** (ser-en-ō'a). A single species of small, horticulturally rather unimportant fan palms found from S. Car. to Fla. and Tex., sometimes cult. for ornament, but very common throughout its range. The only species is S. **repens**, the scrub or saw palmetto, which is usually nearly stemless and forms large patches. Leafstalks prickly, the blades fan-shaped, 2-2½ ft. wide, divided or cleft to or below the middle into about 20 rather stiff segments which are 2-toothed at the tip. Flower clusters usually longer than the leafstalks, branched, the flowers perfect.* Fruit ½-¾ in. long, egg-shaped or roundish, black, 1-seeded. The plant is of easy culture in many types of soil and spreads rapidly. It generally has creeping stems, but some are erect and several feet high. For the plant sometimes called *S. arborescens* see ACOELORRAPHE WRIGHTI. (Named for Sereno Watson, American botanist.)

**SERICEA, -us, -um** (ser-riss'ee-a). Silky.

**SERICOFERA, -us, -um** (ser-i-kō'fer-a). Silky or bearing silk.

**SERINGERA** = *Hevea brasiliensis*.

**SERISSA** (se-riss'a). A single species of Japanese shrubs of the family Rubiaceae, S. **foetida**, sometimes cult. for ornament in the cool greenhouse or outdoors from zone* 7 southward. It is a low shrub, 15-24 in. high with opposite,* nearly stalkless, ovalish leaves, nearly ½ in. long and evil-smelling when bruised. Flowers white, about ⅜ in. long, in rather floriferous clusters, or solitary, on small flowering twigs. Corolla funnel-shaped, its 4-6 lobes bluntly 3-lobed.

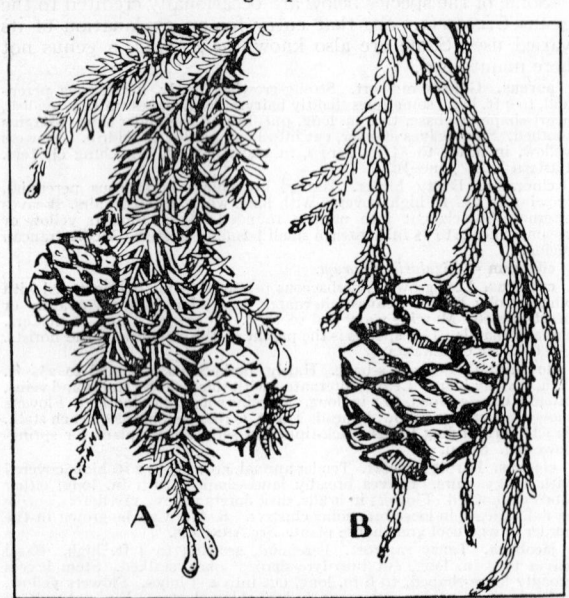

Foliage and cones of the redwood (A), and the giant sequoia (B)

* Special articles on the subjects indicated by an asterisk (*) will be found at the words so marked.

Corolla tube hairy on the inside. Fruit a nearly round drupe.* (*Serissa* is a Latinized form of the native name for the plant.)

**SEROTINA, -us, -um** (ser-rot'i-na). Tardily flowering or fruiting.

**SERPENTARIA** (ser-pen-tair'i-a). An old and now obsolete name for certain species of *Aristolochia* (which see).

**SERPENT GOURD** = *Trichosanthes anguina*.

**SERPENTINA, -us, -um** (ser-pen-ty'na). Snake-like.

**SERPENTINE LAYERING.** See LAYERING.

**SERPYLLIFOLIA, -us, -um** (sir-pill-i-fō'li-a). Having leaves like the thyme, an ancient name for which was serpyllium.

**SERRATA, -us, -um** (sir-ray'ta). Serrate.*

**SERRATE.** Having teeth like those of a saw.

**SERRATIFOLIA, -us, -um** (sir-rat-i-fō'li-a). Having serrate* leaves.

**SERRULATA, -us, -um** (sir-roo-lay'ta). Serrulate; *i.e.* having minute, saw-like teeth.

**SERVICEBERRY** = *Amelanchier*.

**SERVICE TREE** = *Sorbus domestica*. See MOUNTAIN-ASH.

**SERVICE YARD.** There are few places, even quite small ones, where it is not of advantage to provide a screened or sheltered place in which to wash the car, dry clothes, keep the ash and garbage cans, and perhaps a tool box. Often it is possible to combine such a service yard with the garage and at the same time provide space in which to turn a car. The latter is the most space-demanding.

If a two- or three-car garage, and the necessary space for turning the cars is to be provided, the total area cannot be less than 40 × 40 ft. and for comfort had better be more than this. Sometimes it is necessary to save space by combining the needed area for cars with that necessary for drying

A PRACTICAL AND ATTRACTIVE SERVICE YARD

(*A*) Ash and garbage cans, well screened. (*B*) Wheelbarrow, tools, etc. (but *see* TOOL HOUSE). (*C*) Clothes reel. (*D*) Drive to garage. (*E*) Entrance from kitchen door. (*F*) Children's wading pool. (*G*) Garden. (*H*) Hedge surrounding the yard.

clothes. If this is done, clothes poles are, of course, impossible, and a single-pole, 4-5-arm drier must be used. These are set in a socket flush with the ground and can be folded up and removed when not needed.

Whichever type of service yard your needs demand, it is essential that such activities be screened from the house and from other parts of the garden; the higher and thicker the screen, the better. If your space must be limited you may not have room for the necessary depth of planting to make the most desirable type of screen. The best and most costly screen planting would be evergreens, but very satisfactory screens can be made of deciduous shrubs and trees. For the necessary space and the preferred plants for either type of screen *see* SCREEN PLANTING.

If the space available will not permit of screen planting, the next best thing to do is to plant a stout hedge around the service yard. For the space needed for this, the planting, and the best hedge plants, *see* HEDGES.

Upon the assumption that you are still too cramped to permit the use of a hedge, the final solution for hiding the service yard is a trellis with some large-leaved or dense-growing vines over it. For the details of these *see* TRELLIS and VINES.

Where it is possible to keep the service yard proper separate from the garage and turning space, there arises the question of whether lawn or pavement is the best floor for a service yard. Unless there is much traffic through the service yard, it is cooler and far more attractive to keep it in lawn. But if this is impossible, it may be paved, at least along the lines of clothes-hanging. *See* PATHS AND PAVING. The latter plan also has winter advantages, because when such paths are kept clear of snow, pavement takes little damage from alternate freezing and thawing. But a much-used grass track around the clothes lines may become a muddy path.

**SESAL VEGETAL.** See BLIGHIA SAPIDA.

**SESAME** = *Sesamum orientale*.

**SESAMUM** (ses'a-mum). Tropical African and Asian herbs of the family **Pedaliaceae** (ped-al-i-ā'see-ee) which includes 13 other genera and perhaps 50 species of herbs or shrubs, all from the Old World and all of them with generally opposite,* usually somewhat slimy leaves. The only cult. species of *Sesamum* is *S. orientale* (long known as *S. indicum*), the sesame, the seeds of which are the benne (or benny) of commerce, known in Africa as sim-sim, and used as food and for their oil. The plant is a rough-hairy herb, 1-2 ft. high, with oblongish or narrower leaves, 3-5 in. long, the lower often 3-parted, the upper sometimes alternate.* Flowers about 1 in. long, white or pink, solitary in the leaf-axils.* Corolla tubular, its limb 2-lipped,* the upper lip 2-lobed and shorter than the 3-lobed under lip.* Fruit an oblongish capsule.* Little grown in the U.S. and suited only to zones* 8 or 9, but can be grown as an annual northward. The commercial production of benne is chiefly African and Indian. (*Sesamum* is the Greek version of the Arabic name for the sesame.)

**SESBANIA** (sez-ban'i-a). Widely distributed tropical herbs or shrubs of the pea family, comprising perhaps 20 species, of which only **S. exaltata**, native in the southern U.S., is of any garden interest. It is a coarse annual, 8-12 ft. high, grown chiefly as a cover crop or for green manure in its native region and in Calif. Leaves compound,* the leaflets arranged feather-fashion, without an odd one at the end, usually about ¾ in. long. Flowers showy, pea-like, yellow but purple-spotted, mostly in clusters (racemes*) that are 3-4 in. long. Fruit a flattish pod (legume*) 7-9 in. long. It is only used as an annual, warm-country cover crop sown in early spring, and is sometimes known as *S. macrocarpa*. For the plant occasionally called *S. punicea* see DAUBENTONIA PUNICEA. For *S. grandiflora* see AGATI GRANDIFLORA. (*Sesbania* is the Latinized version of the Arabian name for a related species.)

**SESQUIPEDALIS, -e** (ses-kwi-pe-day'lis). Literally, one and one-half a foot's length; *i.e.* 18 in.

**SESSILE.** Stalkless.

---

* Special articles on the subjects indicated by an asterisk (*) will be found at the words so marked.

***SESSILIFOLIA, -us, -um*** (ses-sil-i-fō′li-a). With stalkless leaves.

***SESSILIS, -e*** (ses′si-lis). Stalkless.

**SET.** A common but rather indefinite garden term used in several senses. As a verb usually implying that an ovule has been fertilized and the ovary is on the way to producing a fruit; as in the phrase — a tree has *set* fruit.

Used as a noun *set* means some small propagative part of a plant, the most common application being to an onion *set*, which, in the plural, are small bulblets* used for the planting of onions. *See* ONION.

**SETARIA** (see-tair′i-a). Chiefly agricultural, warm-country, annual or perennial grasses, comprising over 60 species, only two of them here admitted, and one of these chiefly a forage or fodder grass. They have grass-like leaves and a large, spike-like terminal cluster (panicle*), each spikelet having beneath it a long bristle which persists after the spikelet has fallen. Fruit an edible grain in the first species. (*Setaria* is from the Latin for bristle.) They are sometimes known under the name *Chaetochloa*.

The first species and its several varieties is only of agricultural interest and is grown as an annual grass. The second, grown for ornament, is found in greenhouses and sometimes is spontaneous there. Its chief value is the handsome foliage.

**italica.** Foxtail millet. An annual grass 3–5 ft. high, mostly unbranched. Leaves grass-like, rough, about ¾ in. wide, the basal sheath fringed with hairs. Flowering cluster 2–10 in. long, about 1¼ in. thick, the bristles green, purplish or brown. Cult. for forage or hay. Probably a cultigen.* The *var.* **nigrofructa,** Hungarian grass, has nearly black grains; *var.* **rubrofructa,** Siberian or Turkestan millet, has the grain reddish-orange; and the *var.* **stramineofructa,** the German or Golden Wonder millet, has large spikes and yellow grains

**palmifolia.** Palm grass. A slender, perennial grass, 4–6 ft. high. Leaves grass-like, but nearly 1 in. wide at the middle and tapering to a fine point at the tip, the sheathing base strongly hairy on the margins. Flower cluster 8–12 in. long, not usually continuous. East Indies. There is also a form with variegated leaves, usually in stripes.

***SETIGERA, -us, -um*** (see-tij′er-a). Bristly.

***SETISPINA, -us, -um*** (see-ti-spy′na). With bristly spines.

***SETOSA, -us, -um*** (see-tō′sa). Bristly.

**SETTLEMENT GARDENING.** *See* SCHOOL GARDENING.

**SEVEN-BARKS** = *Hydrangea arborescens.*

**SEVEN SISTERS ROSE.** *See* ROSA CATHAYENSIS PLATYPHYLLA.

**SEVEN-STARS** = *Ariocarpus retusus.*

**SEVEN-TOP TURNIP** = *Brassica rapa septiceps.*

**SEVERINIA** (sev-er-in′i-a). A single species of spiny shrubs or small trees of the rue family, **S. buxifolia** of southern China and Formosa, occasionally grown for ornament or for hedges south of zone* 7, but little known. It has simple,* alternate* leaves, ovalish, about 1 in. long, somewhat resembling box, but with a spine on each side of the buds. Flowers solitary or few in the leaf-axils,* white and small, with 5 petals and 10 stamens.* Fruit a pea-sized, shining, black berry. (Named for M. A. Severino, an Italian professor.)

**SEVILLE ORANGE** = *Citrus aurantium.* For culture *see* ORANGE.

**SEWAGE.** *See* MANURE.

***SEXANGULARIS, -e*** (sex-ang-you-lar′is). Six-angled.

***SEXSTYLOSA, -us, -um*** (sex-sty-lō′sa). With six styles.*

**SEXUAL REPRODUCTION.** The production of new plants as the result of fertilization, as in seeds and spores. *See* PROPAGATION.

**SHADBLOW.** *See* AMELANCHIER.

**SHADBUSH** = *Amelanchier.*

**SHADDOCK** = *Citrus maxima.*

**SHADE.** The ability of some plants to tolerate shade, the necessity for shade in certain specialized gardens, the need for shading seedlings, and the erection of lath screens to provide shade — all are different phases of the response of plants to light, and what we must do to meet that response. It seems best here to separate the different ways in which shade is a garden factor as follows. All the subjects below are treated as special articles under the headings or cross-references noted below:

Shaded Lawn. *See* LAWN for grasses suited for shade.

Shade Plants. For those that are shade-enduring *see* SHADY GARDEN. *See also* WILD GARDEN.

Shade Trees. *See* TREES.

Shading. See the article SHADING for the best methods of providing shade for the plants that need it.

**SHADING.** There are several reasons for shading outdoor plants. Seedbeds in the open must be given some shade. Seedlings newly transplanted must be protected

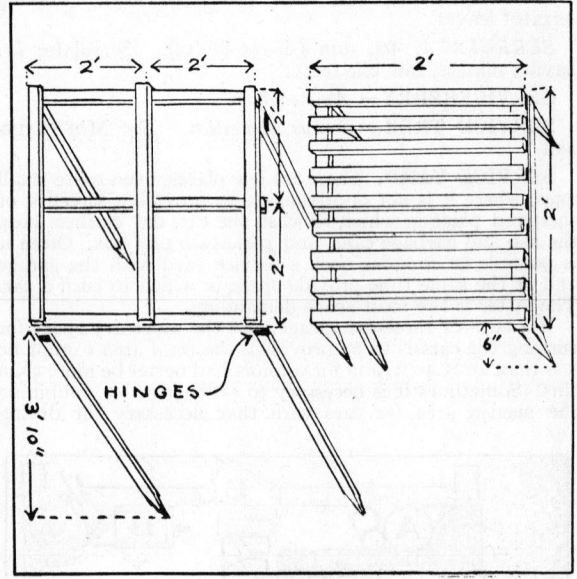

SHADING

At the right, a practical, movable lath shade for plants, or small areas. At the left, a wooden frame for taller plants. It can be covered with cheesecloth or burlap. The hinged legs allow it to be folded up and easily stored.

from hot sun and wind. Shades are used to prevent burning of tender plants which must be watered in full sun. Large plants which have been moved must be shaded until established in the new quarters. Flowers grown for cutting purposes, which fade in strong light, must be shaded at certain times. Shade is sometimes necessary to regulate the flowering time of plants intended for flower-show exhibit.

Shades are for temporary use and must be portable. Plants needing constant shade should be planted in permently shady outdoor places, or in the shade of a pergola, lath house or greenhouse. The simplest way to shade a single small plant is an inverted flower pot. This can be used only temporarily and under constant inspection, as it admits insufficient light and air and is a harbor for slugs and woodlice. An ideal portable shade for seedbeds and transplanted seedlings is made of laths nailed two in. apart across a flat square or oblong frame of light wood mounted on four strong but slender legs tall enough to hold the frame above the level of the plants. Handy sizes for this type of shade are 2 ft. × 2 ft. and 4 ft. × 18 in. Several small shades, which can be placed close together, are better than one large one which is clumsy to handle. If denser shade is needed, sacking or newspapers can be laid on top of the laths.

For taller plants a light wooden frame 4 ft. × 4 ft. square, strengthened by two narrow cross-strips and covered with

---

* Special articles on the subjects indicated by an asterisk (*) will be found at the words so marked.

heavy cheesecloth or light unbleached muslin is very satisfactory. It is supported by four legs, 1 in. × 1 in. × 3 ft. 10 in. These are pointed at the bottom and hinged at the top to the corners of the square frame, like a card table. This type of shade, giving protection, with plenty of light and air, is particularly good for flowers in the cutting garden and for shade-loving plants during a period of intense heat.

A satisfactory device for shading late-sown sweet peas and all tall flowers grown in rows is as follows. Make a temporary frame by setting firm stakes at the four corners of the row and others at 3-ft. intervals down both sides, and screw a metal eye into the top of each corner stake. Take a strip of heavy cheesecloth or light unbleached muslin the length of the row, tack each end of it to a stick (preferably round) and screw a hook fitting the eyelets on the corner stakes into each end of each stick. This cloth can then be stretched along the top of the temporary frame, hooked to the corner stakes and supported by the side stakes. It will be needed only during the hottest part of the day and can easily be unrolled and rolled up. A stitched hem along each side will strengthen the cloth. If the exposure is windy strings should also be attached every 3 ft. to tie into additional eyelets screwed into the side stakes. If permanent shelter is necessary, as well as temporary shade, a strip of cloth can also be stretched vertically along the exposed side of the row and tacked to the stakes to hold it in position.

Espaliered fruit trees and vines trained against a wall or fence can be protected from a dangerously hot sun by strips of unbleached muslin tacked to round poles and dropped from the top of the fence or wall in the manner of window shades. — L. R.

**SHADOW BOX.** A shadow box is an individual box or container which permits exhibitors at flower shows greater scope in arrangements, backgrounds and colors without conflicting with other compositions. The boxes are made of wood with space approximately two feet seven inches high, two feet wide and ten inches deep. These should be placed about two feet from the wall. Architects' cloth is stretched across the front of the frame, which is hinged to make it easier to stage the exhibit. In the large boxes the light, preferably a 60-100 watt and adjustable as to height, should hang at the back about six or eight inches from the floor. In small boxes concealed lights are often placed at the front edge to allow proper lighting. The chief drawback to shadow boxes is the heat caused by the electric lighting. Fragile blossoms only last one day and must be replaced if the show is of longer duration.

Shadow box

**SHADY GARDEN.** To the theory that a garden is necessarily composed of flower beds, many a tree was once sacrificed to provide needed light and sun for massed bloom, and corners full of potential serenity and repose were neglected as garden areas. As realization awoke that flowers were but incidentals in the plan, the green garden was evolved, form and texture taking precedence of color. Next came the discovery that only a modicum of sun was needed for many species, so waste dark spots were reclaimed, and the garden of shade took its place among other specialized developments.

Success lies not only in using suitable materials, but in following certain tenets, many of them suggested by Nature herself. Provide good drainage, as soil stagnation comes easily in dusky places. Lighten heavy earths with sand. Delay spring housecleaning and let it be scant. Many of the plants resent poking, make late appearances, and in order to have any semblance of luxuriance, should be allowed to bring forth their seedlings when and where it strikes their fancy. The shady garden is an excellent spot for seed germination, especially those needing many months and an interim of cold for fulfillment. An abundance of water is necessary at all times, and a mulch to conserve the dampness. Evaporation will not be great, especially under trees, but they rob soil moisture quickly. As conditioning fertilizers are better than quick stimulants, a high proportion of phosphorus is needed, especially bone meal or superphosphates. Lime well areas not demanding acid soils, and enrich with pulverized sheep manure. While dogmatic statements are unwise, the following notes are pertinent.

Seldom replace a failure with the same plant; it is usually waste effort. Expect no masses of bloom, but enjoy each flower for its own beauty. White varieties of any plant family do best. When a plant self-sows and colonizes its tribe, it is an indication that the location is to its liking. Accept it, whether it is a favorite or not. The shady garden is seldom one of early frosts, but it is one of early coolness. Many inmates, both bulbs and plants, become biennial in bloom, requiring two seasons instead of one for recuperation.

There are various degrees of shade. The solitude of some country spot where the sun is excluded merely by trees or occasional buildings, with a fair circulation of untainted air, presents fewer obstacles than a hemmed-in city or suburban section, where the atmosphere is laden with dust or fumes, and the tree drip, always pernicious to many plants, becomes deadly from factory or chimney deposits.

### Shade-tolerant Plants

All species in these lists are described under their proper entries elsewhere in The Garden Dictionary, to which reference should be made for a description of them and for notes on their hardiness. Those marked with a dagger (†) are especially adapted to the shade condition found in cities. The others are more suited to the ordinary country atmosphere and to the shade of trees. Those with a double dagger (††), will stand the dense shade and drip of maple trees.

ANNUALS. Expect little, and disappointment will be less keen. Start seeds in heat; transplant seedlings.

    Ageratum          Nicotiana
    Alyssum           Petunia
    Calendula        Zinnia

BULBS. Small varieties of early spring yield well, as they bloom and mature before the days of deep shadows.

    †Chionodoxa.
    Eranthis.
    Fritillaria meleagris alba.
    †Galanthus.
    Lilium. Many types make a fine display the first year, then wane and disappear. Annual plantings are advised.
      candidum. Madonna lily.
      croceum. Orange lily.
      elegans.
      †hansoni.
      longiflorum. White-trumpet lily.
      martagon album.
      speciosum. Japanese lily.
    Muscari.
    Narcissus. Seldom bloom the second year. There is neither light nor warmth for leaf maturing. White varieties are best.
    †Scilla. Plant among lilies-of-the-valley.
    Tulips. Yield bloom, but the stems are weak. Cottage varieties most satisfactory. None permanent, treat as annuals.

EVERGREENS. Coniferous and broad-leaved evergreens.
    Background.
    ††Rhododendron.
    ††Taxus cuspidata. Japanese Yew.

---

* Special articles on the subjects indicated by an asterisk (*) will be found at the words so marked.

Tsuga canadensis. Hemlock.
Tsuga caroliniana. Spruce Pine.
*Medium.*
Azalea.
††Euonymus radicans.
Leucothoë catesbaei.
††Taxus canadensis. Ground Hemlock.
GROUND COVERS. The following will be found useful, but there are others, some doing well in partial shade. *See* GROUND COVER.
Ajuga reptans. Bugle.
†Hedera helix. English ivy. Put in young plants closely together.
Lonicera japonica halliana, pegged down.
Lycopodium obscurum.
Lysimachia nummularia. Moneywort.
†Nepeta hederacea. Ground-ivy.
††Pachysandra terminalis.
†Vinca minor. Periwinkle.
PERENNIALS.
*Tall.*
Aconitum. In variety. Few flowers, foliage good.
††Cimicifuga racemosa. Black snakeroot.
Delphinium. Needs good staking. Flowers few, color good.
††Eupatorium urticaefolium. White snakeroot.
†Thalictrum. All varieties.
*Medium.*
††Astilbe japonica.
Campanula persicifolia. Peach bells.
†Dicentra. All varieties.
†Hosta. All varieties.
††Mertensia virginica. Virginia cowslip.
††Myrrhis odorata.
Paeonia. Single.
Phlox divaricata. Blue Phlox.
Phlox Miss Lingard.
†Tradescantia virginiana. Spiderwort.
*Low.*
†Astilbe simplicifolia.
†Convallaria majalis. Lily-of-the-valley.
Corydalis. All varieties.
Geranium ibericum.
Heuchera sanguinea. Coral bells.
Iris pumila.
Oenothera fruticosa youngi.
†Polemonium reptans. Bluebell.
Primula vulgaris. English primrose.
††Tiarella cordifolia. Foam flower.
SHRUBS. Abundant foliage is all that can be depended upon. If blooms come they are the more appreciated for their fickleness. The best species or variety for shade growing is given. Heights will differ in shade from those attained in sun.
*Background.*
††Amelanchier canadensis.
Crataegus crus-galli.
†Forsythia suspensa. Weeping Golden bell.
††Hamamelis virginiana. Witch-hazel.
††Hydrangea arborescens. Wild Hydrangea.
††Hydrangea paniculata.
Lonicera fragrantissima.
Syringa. Lilac.
*Medium.*
Kerria japonica.
Kolkwitzia amabilis. Beauty-bush.
†Ligustrum amurense.
Lonicera henryi.
†Rubus odoratus. Flowering Raspberry.
Spiraea japonica.
Spiraea vanhouttei.
Stephanandra incisa.
Viburnum acerifolium. Dockmackie.
*Low.*
††Zanthorhiza apiifolia. Yellowroot.
TREES. Two of value to the shady garden both in foliage form and habit of growth.

Koelreuteria.
††Ailanthus. Difficult to start, but the best of all trees for city backyards with little sun. Plant a small seedling, or a sucker.*
VINES. Good foliage but few flowers are all that can be expected. Three-year roots should be bought with a surplus of vigor to spend in becoming established.
††Actinidia. All species.
Aristolochia durior. Dutchman's-pipe.
††Celastrus scandens. Bittersweet.
†Humulus japonicus. Called an annual, but springing up from the roots each year, in perennial fashion.
Lonicera japonica.
†Polygonum auberti. Silver-lace vine.
Pueraria thunbergiana. Kudzu-vine.
Wistaria. If the runners are pegged down it makes a good ground cover.
Cobaea scandens.
Echinocystis lobata. Wild balsam apple. Self-sows, thus becoming persistent. These last two are annuals. *See also* VINES.
WILD FLOWERS AND FERNS. Many of these are adapted through their natural habits to shade conditions. *See* WILD GARDEN. *See also* FERNS AND FERN GARDENING.
In the city when plants are under trees, the oil and soot deposits on the tree leaves are washed down upon them and form an added menace to the naturally obnoxious drip. The plant foliage becomes coated, transpiration is checked, and the plant slowly suffocates. In small gardens it is possible to keep the large-leaved types such as rhododendrons sponged off with soap and water, and others well and continuously washed off with the hose spray. The conifers are especially grateful for this treatment. *See* DRIP. — H. M. C.

**SHAGBARK HICKORY** = *Carya ovata* and *C. laciniosa*. *See* HICKORY.

**SHALLON** (shall′on). Original Indian vernacular for the salal (*Gaultheria shallon*).

**SHALLOT** (*Allium ascalonicum*). An onion-like plant, often called eschallot, and grown for the small, pointed, grayish bulbs, sometimes called cloves.* These are the separable parts of the parent bulb and are used for cooking or for flavoring and are considerably milder than onions. They are more popular in Eu. than here and are little grown.
Shallot is grown by planting the small bulbs, just as onion sets are planted (*see* ONION), and their subsequent care and cultivation are the same. But unlike the onion, the maturing bulb of shallot separates into sections (cloves) which are harvested in the fall and will keep, when dried as are onions, for several months.

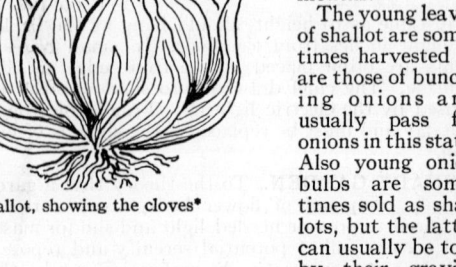

Shallot, showing the cloves*

The young leaves of shallot are sometimes harvested as are those of bunching onions and usually pass for onions in this state. Also young onion bulbs are sometimes sold as shallots, but the latter can usually be told by their grayish color, and by the fact that they are pointed and more or less angular. The shallot is sometimes called cibol, but that name is better restricted to the Welsh onion (*Allium fistulosum*). The insect pests of shallot are the same as for the onion.

**SHALLU** = *Holcus sorghum roxburghi*.

---

* Special articles on the subjects indicated by an asterisk (*) will be found at the words so marked.

**SHAMROCK.** In different seasons and in different regions at least three cult. plants pass as "shamrock." The most common and perhaps the true shamrock, if there is one, is the common white clover (*Trifolium repens*). Another plant often sold as shamrock is the hop clover (*Medicago lupulina*). The third is a wood sorrel (*Oxalis acetosella*). Which is the true shamrock might be left to the Irish, if they agreed, but they do not. In the U.S. the shamrocks sold on the streets are certainly seedling plants of the white clover. The seeds are sown in flats in the cool greenhouse in Sept. and are ready, as small potted plants, by the following March.

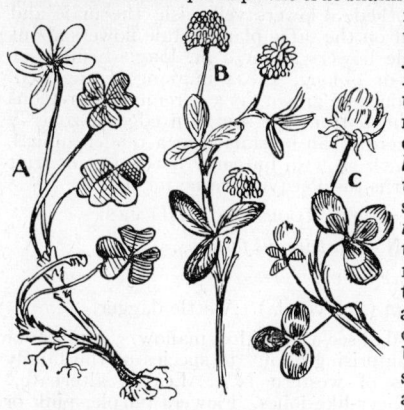

Three plants that pass as shamrock: (A) *Oxalis acetosella*; (B) *Medicago lupulina*; (C) *Trifolium repens*.

**SHAMROCK PEA** = *Parochetus communis*.

**SHASTA CYPRESS** = *Cupressus macnabiana*.

**SHASTA DAISY.** A large-flowered, handsome form of *Chrysanthemum maximum* (which see).

**SHAWNEE SALAD** = *Hydrophyllum virginianum*.

**SHEATH.** Any tubular or sheathing organ, often leaf-like or membranous, which surrounds the base of a stalk or helps to form one. Sheaths are common in the grasses, in some plants of the family Polygonaceae and on many flower stalks. Some bracts* are sheathing, notably in the palms, and the sheathing leaf bases of the banana make up its stem.

**SHEEPBERRY** = *Viburnum lentago*.

**SHEEP-LAUREL** = *Kalmia angustifolia*.

**SHEEP MANURE.** See MANURE.

**SHEEP'S-BIT** = *Jasione perennis*.

**SHEEP'S-FESCUE** = *Festuca ovina*.

**SHEEP SORREL** = *Oxalis acetosella*.

**SHEEP'S-SORREL** = *Rumex acetosella*. See list at WEEDS.

**SHEEPWEED** = *Pinguicula vulgaris*.

**SHELLBARK HICKORY** = *Carya ovata* and *C. laciniosa*. See HICKORY.

**SHELL-FLOWER** = *Chelone glabra*, *Molucella laevis*, and *Alpinia speciosa*.

**SHELTER TREES.** See WINDBREAK.

**SHE-OAK.** See CASUARINA.

**SHEPHERDIA** (shep-her′di-a). Three species of very hardy, North American shrubs of the family Elaeagnaceae, two of them in rather common cult., the third evergreen and known mostly in the wild. They are spreading shrubs, one of them prickly, with opposite,* stalked leaves, and inconspicuous, small, yellowish flowers, the male and female on different plants. Petals none. Calyx* or sepals* petal-like. Stamens* 8. Fruit fleshy, drupe-like, really a dry fruit enclosed by the fleshy calyx, edible in the first species. The genus was once, and is sometimes still called *Lepargyrea*. (Named for John Shepherd, a curator of the Liverpool Botanic Garden.)

Both species are among the hardiest shrubs in cult., being perfectly at home far up into zone* 1. They will stand dry, wind-swept sites, stony soils, and much abuse, especially the first species, which is sometimes planted for hedges in places where no other hedge plant will survive. Easily propagated from seed. If fruit is wanted, both sexes must be planted.

**argentea.** Buffaloberry; also called wild oleaster and silverleaf. A spiny or thorny shrub or small tree, 10–18 ft. high, the foliage silvery both sides. Leaves oblongish, ½–2½ in. long, more or less wedge-shaped at the base. Fruit egg-shaped, yellowish or red, about ⅓ in. long, sour, but prized for jellies. Central N.A. far northward. April–May.

**canadensis.** Buffaloberry. Not over 8 ft. high and without spines or thorns. Leaves elliptic or ovalish, ¾–1½ in. long, green above, silvery beneath. Fruit egg-shaped, yellowish-red, about ⅓ in. long, nearly tasteless. Throughout northern N.A. and northward to Alaska. April–May.

**SHEPHERD'S-PURSE** = *Capsella bursa-pastoris*. See list at WEEDS.

**SHEPHERD'S-SCABIOUS** = *Jasione perennis*.

**SHERRY.** For the best wine grapes for sherry *see vinifera* varieties at GRAPE.

**SHEUGH.** An old term for heeling-in, which see at PLANTING.

**SHIDARE-HIGAN-SAKURA.** See Japanese Flowering Cherries at PRUNUS.

**SHIELD BUDDING.** See BUDDING.

**SHIELD FERN.** See DRYOPTERIS.

**SHIELD GRAFT.** A side graft. See GRAFTING.

**SHIELDWORT.** See PELTARIA.

**SHIMA.** An island. See JAPANESE GARDEN.

**SHINGLE OAK** = *Quercus imbricaria*. See OAK.

**SHINLEAF.** See PYROLA.

**SHINLEAF FAMILY.** See ERICACEAE.

**SHIN-PLASTERS** = *Orchis rotundifolia*.

**SHIRLEY POPPY.** See *Papaver rhoeas* at POPPY.

**SHIROFUGEN.** See Japanese Flowering Cherries at PRUNUS.

**SHITTIMWOOD.** A name applied to two cult. plants. See BUMELIA LANUGINOSA, which is perhaps better called chittamwood. See also RHAMNUS PURSHIANA.

**SHOEBLACK PLANT** = *Hibiscus rosa-sinensis*.

**SHOOFLY** = *Baptisia tinctoria*. See also NICANDRA PHYSALODES.

**SHOOT.** Any, usually lateral, growth from a bud, which diverges from a main axis or stem. A shoot may, and often does, produce both flowers and leaves, but many leafy shoots do not produce flowers until the second season.

**SHOOTING STAR.** See DODECATHEON.

**SHORE PLANTS.** See SEASIDE GARDENS.

**SHORTIA** (short′i-a). Low-growing evergreen herbs, comprising 2 species of the family Diapensiaceae, and natives of the mountains of N.C., S.C., and Jap. They have creeping, underground stems, and basal, roundish, or heart-shaped, shining green, stalked leaves, the margins wavy. Flowers white, solitary, on leafless stalks to 8 in. high. Calyx* of 5 sepals surrounded by a few scaly bracts.* Corolla of 5 petals, bell-shaped. Stamens* 5, growing on the petals, alternating with 5 sterile stamens. Fruit a 3-celled capsule. (Named for Dr. Charles W. Short, Kentucky botanist.)

The plant below is especially adapted for the rock garden but must be grown in shade, in soil composed of sandy peat and leaf mold. It is difficult to establish, so should not be moved more than necessary. Propagated by division in April.

**galacifolia.** Leaves basal, long-stalked, roundish, sometimes heart-shaped at base, the margins wavy. Flowering stalk slender, to 8 in. high. Flowers white, to 1 in. across, nodding. Mountains of N.C.

**SHOT-HOLE.** See Diseases at CHERRY.

**SHOT-HOLE BORER.** See Insect Pests at APPLE.

**SHOVEL.** *See* Section 1, TOOLS AND IMPLEMENTS.

**SHOW GERANIUM** = *Pelargonium domesticum*.

---

* Special articles on the subjects indicated by an asterisk (*) will be found at the words so marked.

**SHOWY CRABAPPLE** = *Malus floribunda.*

**SHOWY LADY'S-SLIPPER** = *Cypripedium reginae.*

**SHOWY ORCHIS** = *Orchis spectabilis.*

**SHOWY PRIMROSE** = *Oenothera speciosa.* See EVENING PRIMROSE.

**SHRUB.** The distinction between a tree and shrub is difficult to make and breaks down in many commonly cult. plants. Generally a shrub is a low, woody plant that has several stems instead of a single trunk, as most trees have. But quite a few trees bear several trunks or branch rather low down and are hence shrub-like, while some shrubs tend to have only one main stem and are then tree-like.

For garden purposes shrubs are of infinite variety. There is no need to repeat here all those found in THE GARDEN DICTIONARY. Those that are particularly showy will be found listed at FLOWERING SHRUBS. Some beautiful evergreen sorts are noted at BROAD-LEAVED EVERGREENS. See also AZALEA, RHODODENDRON. For the uses and care of shrubs see Shrub Border at BORDER. See also PRUNING.

**SHRUB.** A common name for *Calycanthus.*

**SHRUBBERY.** A shrub border or a planting of shrubs. See BORDER.

**SHRUB BORDER.** See BORDER.

**SHRUB COLLECTIONS.** See ARBORETUM.

**SHRUB YELLOWROOT** = *Zanthorhiza apiifolia.*

**SHRUBBY ALTHAEA** = *Hibiscus syriacus.*

**SHRUBBY BITTERSWEET** = *Celastrus scandens.*

**SHRUBBY CINQUEFOIL** = *Potentilla fruticosa.*

**SHRUBBY FERN** = *Comptonia asplenifolia.*

**SHUCK.** The outer husk of a fruit, as in the hickory, or the husks of corn. A more unusual use for *shuck* is a specialized one. In the flower of the peach the calyx* becomes gradually drier and is ultimately pushed off by the expanding fruit. Such a shed calyx is known as a shuck.

**SHUCKWORM.** See Insect Pests at PECAN.

**SHUTTERS.** See COLD FRAME.

**SIBERIAN CRABAPPLE** = *Malus baccata.*

**SIBERIAN IRIS.** See IRIS ORIENTALIS and I. SIBIRICA.

**SIBERIAN LARKSPUR** = *Delphinium grandiflorum.*

**SIBERIAN MILLET** = *Setaria italica rubrofructa.*

**SIBERIAN SQUILL** = *Scilla sibirica.*

**SIBERIAN TEA** = *Bergenia crassifolia.*

**SIBERIAN WALLFLOWER** = *Erysimum asperum.*

**SIBIRAEA** (sy-bi-ree'a). Low-growing, deciduous shrubs of only 2 species, belonging to the rose family, and natives of As. and southeastern Eu., and very similar to *Spiraea.* Leaves simple,* alternate,* broadly lance-shaped, bluish-green or silvery-gray. Flowers greenish-white or yellow, small, in spikes in terminal branching clusters, 3–5 in. long. Individual flowers of 2 kinds, male (stamens only) and female (pistil only). Calyx* of 5 sepals. Corolla of 5 petals. Stamens* 10. Fruit a 2-celled capsule. (*Sibiraea* is derived from Siberia, where the one below is native.)

Not usually cult. Propagated by seeds sown in spring or by layers.

**laevigata.** Also known as *Spiraea laevigata.* Low-growing shrub to 5 ft. high. Branches erect. Leaves broadly lance-shaped, to 3½ in. long, bluish-green, shining. Flowers greenish-white, the male and female being borne on different plants and the male flowers showier. Siberia. May. Hardy from zone* 4 southward.

*SIBIRICA, -us, -um* (sy-bir'i-ka). From Siberia.

**SICANA** (si-kay'na). Tropical American, tendril*-bearing, fleshy-stemmed vines of the family Cucurbitaceae, comprising only three species, one of them, **S. odorifera,** the cassabanana or curuba, grown for its fragrant, ornamental fruit which is also edible. It is a perennial, high-climbing vine (to 40 ft.), with angled stems and branched tendrils.* Leaves alternate,* nearly round, 7–12 in. wide, conspicuously lobed, heart-shaped at the base, the margins shallowly angled or wavy-toothed. Flowers yellowish, the male and female separate, but on the same plant. Male flowers about ½ in. long. Female flowers about 2 in. long. Fruit very fragrant, cylindric or oblong, 15–24 in. long, orange-red. Brazil (?). It can only be grown, as a perennial, in regions of strong summer heat, from the southern edge of zone* 7 southward. Elsewhere it can be started as a tender annual, and will make a quick growth, but may not flower or fruit northward. (*Sicana* is the Peruvian name for it.)

**SICKLE.** See Section 3, TOOLS AND IMPLEMENTS.

**SICKLE THORN** = *Asparagus falcatus.*

**SICK SOILS.** See SOILS.

*SICULA, -us, -um* (sick'you-la). A little dagger.

**SIDALCEA** (sy-dall'see-a). False mallow. Annual or perennial herbs, comprising about 30 species of the family Malvaceae, natives of western N.A. Leaves alternate,* simple,* cut into finger-like lobes. Flowers purple, pink or white, in terminal spikes. Calyx* of 5 sepals. Corolla of 5 petals. Stamens* in groups united by their filaments.* Fruits, kidney-shaped, several, united at first, ultimately separable. (*Sidalcea* is a compounded word derived from *Sida* and *Alcea,* both of which are non-hort. genera.)

Sidalceas make good border plants, and only the perennial species are in cult. Easily propagated by seeds or division of roots. Seeds should be sown in a cold frame in ordinary garden soil in early spring. They may be transplanted as soon as large enough to handle. Division of roots may be made in Sept., March or April. Plants should be lifted every 3 years and soil well manured before re-planting. They are sometimes rather short-lived and behave more like biennials than perennials.

**candida.** Perennial, growing to 3 ft. high, the foliage bright shining green. Lower leaves roundish, heart-shaped at base. Margins deeply cut, with rounded lobes. Upper leaves cut into 5–7 finger-like lobes. Flowers white, to ¾ in. across, in terminal spikes. Rocky Mountains.

**malvaeflora.** Wild hollyhock. Checkerbloom. Erect-growing perennial to 2 ft. high. Lower leaves bluntly lobed. Upper leaves cut into narrow segments. Flowers rose, to 1½ in. across, in many-flowered spikes. Calif. A good pink form is Rosy Gem. See PINK GARDEN.

**parviflora.** Strong-growing perennial, to 4 ft. high, the foliage bright green, slightly hairy. Leaves cut into finger-like segments. Flowers rose, to ½ in. across, in long, slender spikes. S. Calif.

**SIDE GRAFTING.** See GRAFTING.

**SIDE OATS.** See AVENA SATIVA.

*SIDEROXYLON* (si-der-rock'si-lon). A specific name derived from the genus *Sideroxylon* which is scarcely of hort. interest; it means hard wood. See EUCALYPTUS.

**SIDESADDLE-FLOWER** = *Sarracenia purpurea.* See PITCHER-PLANT.

**SIDE-WHIP GRAFT.** See Root Graft at GRAFTING.

**SIERRA LILY** = *Lilium parvum.*

**SIERRA SHOOTING STAR** = *Dodecatheon jeffreyi.*

**SIGHTWORT** = *Chelidonium majus.*

*SIKKIMENSIS, -e* (sick-kim-en'sis). From Sikkim, India.

**SILENE** (sy-lee'ne). Catchfly. Campion. Tender and hardy, annual, biennial or perennial herbs, comprising about 350 species, belonging to the pink family, and distributed throughout the world. They are of erect, tufted or spreading habit, and the stems or calyx are sometimes sticky. Leaves opposite,* simple, without teeth. Flowers solitary or in loose-branching clusters, white, pink or red. Calyx tubular, its 5 lobes teeth-like. Corolla of 5 separate petals. Stamens* 10. Fruit a capsule.* (*Silene* is from the Greek name of one of Bacchus's companions.)

Silenes are useful rock garden or border plants, although not many of the species are in cultivation. Easily propagated from seeds, by division or by cuttings. The seeds of the annual species may be sown in the fall or spring. Seeds

---

\* Special articles on the subjects indicated by an asterisk (\*) will be found at the words so marked.

should be sown ⅛ in. deep, where plants are required to bloom. Seeds of perennial species should be sown ⅛ in. deep, in the cold frame, in early spring. They may be transplanted when large enough to handle. Division of plants may be made in Sept., March or April. Cuttings of young shoots may be taken in July, and inserted in sandy soil in a cold frame, shading from sun until rooted. Perennials once established should not be moved but may be topdressed each year with a mixture of soil and manure.

**acaulis.** Cushion pink. Moss campion. Tufted* perennial, to 2 in. high. Leaves lance-shaped, ½ in. long. Flowers purplish-red, solitary, ½ in. across. Eu. and N.A. June-Aug. For cult. see ROCK GARDEN.

**alpestris.** Alpine catchfly. Spreading perennial, to 6 in. high, with sticky stems. Leaves lance-shaped. Flowers satiny-white, ½ in. across, in loose clusters. Mountains of Eu. Summer. It is best grown in the moraine. See ROCK GARDEN. The var. **flore-pleno** has double flowers.

**armeria.** Sweet William catchfly. None-so-pretty. Erect, bright green annual, growing to 2 ft. high. Leaves broadly lance-shaped, to 3 in. long. Flowers light or deep pink, ½ in. across, in terminal clusters. Southern Eu., naturalized in U.S. Summer.

**compacta.** Bright green biennial, growing to 2 ft. high. Leaves ovalish, to 2 in. long. Flowers pink, in densely clustered heads, to 3 in. across. Heads surrounded by a ring of leafy bracts.* Eastern Eu. and Asia Minor. June.

**fortunei.** Perennial, growing to 3 ft. high, the lower part of the stem woody. Leaves narrowly lance-shaped. Flowers white or pink, to ½ in. across, in short clusters. Calyx tube 1 in. long. Petals 2-lobed. China. Sept.

**hookeri.** Low-growing perennial, to 5 in. high. Leaves ovalish, to 2 in. long. Flowers white or pink, solitary, to 2 in. across, with fringed petals. Calif. and Ore.

**lerchenfeldiana.** Low-growing, bright green, tufted perennial. Leaves lance-shaped. Flowers deep pink, in terminal clusters. Petals slightly notched. Southeastern Eu.

**maritima.** Sea campion. Perennial, growing to 1 ft. high, grayish-green. Leaves broadly lance-shaped. Flowers white, ¼ in. across, in 1-4-flowered clusters. Calyx inflated. Petals lobed. Eu. June.

**noctiflora.** Erect annual, growing to 2 ft. high. Leaves lance-shaped. Flowers pale pink, opening at night, in small clusters. Petals 2-lobed. Eu.

**orientalis** = *Silene compacta*.

**pendula.** Spreading annual, growing to 10 in. high, covered with soft hairs. Leaves broadly lance-shaped. Flowers flesh-pink, to ½ in. across, in loose-branching, hanging clusters. Petals 2-lobed. Mediterranean region. The var. **rosea** has rose-colored flowers. See PINK GARDEN.

**saxifraga.** Tufted perennial of shrubby habit, growing to 10 in. high. Leaves narrowly lance-shaped. Flowers greenish white, solitary, or in 2-3-flowered clusters. Petals 2-lobed. Eu. and Asia Minor.

**schafta.** Moss campion. Perennial, of spreading habit, growing to 6 in. high, covered with short, soft hairs. Leaves small, lance-shaped, in rosettes. Flowers rose or purple, 1-2 flowers on each stalk. Petals notched. Caucasus. For culture see ROCK GARDEN.

**virginica.** Fire-pink. Indian pink. A showy, native perennial, 6-10 in. high. Leaves thin, oblongish or spatula-shaped. Flowers few, in a loose cluster (cyme*), the petals deep crimson, 2-cleft. In sandy woods, eastern N.A. June-Aug.

**SILICLE.** See SILIQUE.

*SILIQUA, -us, -um* (sil-li'kwa). A silique.*

*SILIQUASTRUM* (sil-li-kwas'trum). Bearing a silique* or a fruit like it.

**SILIQUE.** The dry, pod-like fruit of plants of the mustard family. It splits down both seams, leaving a parchment-like center. The term silique is properly restricted to those that are long and slender, as in the mustards. When, as in honesty and the shepherd's-purse, the fruit is short or nearly roundish, it is called a silicle. See CRUCIFERAE.

Silique (*right*) and a silicle (*left*)

**SILK-COTTON TREE.** See CEIBA.

**SILK-COTTON TREE FAMILY** = Bombacaceae.

**SILK-OAK** = *Grevillea robusta*.

**SILK-TASSEL TREE** = *Garrya elliptica*.

**SILK TREE** = *Albizzia julibrissin*.

**SILK VINE.** See PERIPLOCA.

**SILKWEED** = *Asclepias*. See MILKWEED.

**SILKY.** Covered with fine silky hairs, as are the leaves, and sometimes other parts, of many plants.

**SILKY CAMELLIA** = *Stewartia malachodendron*.

**SILKY CORNEL** = *Cornus amomum*.

**SILPHIUM** (sill'fi-um). Rosinweed. Hardy, herbaceous perennials, comprising about 25 species of the family Compositae, natives of N.A. They are tall, strong and coarse herbs, the leaves opposite,* alternate* or in whorls,* the blades sometimes encircling the stem and holding water. Leaf margins sometimes lobed or toothed. Flower heads usually yellow, similar to the sunflower. Bracts* surrounding the head, leaf-like. Ray florets fertile, disk florets sterile. (*Silphium* is a Greek name for some resinous plant, but not of these, although adopted by Linnaeus for them.)

Easily cult., growing well in full sun. Propagated by seeds or division of roots. Seeds should be sown ¼ in. deep, in good garden soil, in cold frame or outdoor seedbed, in spring or early summer. Division of roots may be made in Sept., March or April.

**laciniatum.** Compass-plant. Pilotweed. Growing to 12 ft. high, the stems and leaves covered with short, stiff hairs. Leaves broadly lance-shaped, to 1 ft. long, cut in 1-2 lance-shaped lobes. Upper leaves clasping the stem. Flower heads to 5 in. across. Midwestern states. July-Sept.

**perfoliatum.** Cup-plant. Indian cup. Growing to 8 ft. high, with square stems. Leaves ovalish, to 1 ft. long. Upper leaves clasping the stem. Flower heads to 3 in. across. Eastern N.A. July-Sept.

**SILT.** See SOILS.

**SILVER BEET** = Swiss chard. See BEET.

**SILVER-BELL TREE.** See HALESIA.

**SILVERBERRY** = *Elaeagnus argentea*.

**SILVER FERN.** See PITYROGRAMMA.

**SILVER FIR** = *Abies alba*. See FIR.

**SILVER KING ARTEMISIA.** See ARTEMISIA ALBULA.

**SILVER-LACE VINE** = *Polygonum auberti*.

**SILVERLEAF** = *Shepherdia argentea*.

**SILVER-LEAVED POPLAR** = *Populus alba*.

**SILVER LINDEN** = *Tilia tomentosa*. See LINDEN.

**SILVER MAPLE** = *Acer saccharinum*. See MAPLE.

**SILVER MOON.** See ROSA LAEVIGATA.

**SILVER MORNING-GLORY.** *Argyreia splendens*.

**SILVER-ROD** = *Solidago bicolor*. See GOLDENROD.

**SILVER SAGE** = *Salvia argentea*.

**SILVERTOP PALMETTO** = *Coccothrinax argentea* and *Thrinax microcarpa*.

**SILVER TREE** = *Leucadendron argenteum*.

**SILVER VINE** = *Scindapsus pictus argyraeus* and *Actinidia polygama*.

**SILVER VINE FAMILY** = Dilleniaceae.

**SILVER WATTLE** = *Acacia decurrens dealbata*.

**SILVERWEED** = *Thalictrum dioicum*.

**SILVERY.** Covered with silvery hairs or scales, as are the leaves of many of the plants in the list of "silver" entries above this one. Other genera in which there are plants with a silvery sheen will be found at *Santolina*, *Potentilla*, *Helianthemum*.

**SILVERY SPLEENWORT** = *Athyrium acrostichoides*.

**SILVICULTURE.** The growing of trees, *en masse*, for timber, firewood, or other use, as distinguished from the growing of trees for ornament. Silviculutre is thus scarcely a garden operation, but as it affects some estates and farmers with a woodlot to manage, it is treated briefly at FORESTRY.

---

*Special articles on the subjects indicated by an asterisk (*) will be found at the words so marked.

**SILYBUM** (sil-ly′bum). Annual or biennial herbs, comprising only 2 species of the family Compositae, natives of Eu., Af., and As. Leaves alternate,* with white spots and veins on the upper side, the margins lobed and spiny. Flower heads purplish, solitary and nodding. Bracts* surrounding the head, many, forming a globe-shaped receptacle for it. (*Silybum* is an old Greek name applied by Dioscorides to thistle-like plants.)

Grown sometimes as an ornamental plant for the silvery leaves. Also grown as a vegetable, roots, leaves and flower heads being edible. Easily cult. Propagated from seeds. Seeds should be sown ⅛ in. deep, in ordinary garden soil where required to mature. If sown early they will bloom the first year.

**marianum.** Lady's-thistle. Milk thistle. Annual, sometimes biennial, growing to 4 ft. high. Leaves to 2½ ft. long, glossy, the margins wavy and spiny. Flower heads purplish-red, to 2½ in. across. Bracts* surrounding heads curved and spiny. Mediterranean region, naturalized in Calif.

**SIMAROUBACEAE** (sy-mar-roo-bay′see-ee). A family of over 30 genera of chiefly tropical shrubs and trees with alternate,* compound* leaves, the leaflets arranged feather-fashion. They have mostly small flowers, sometimes unisexual* and drupe-like fruit. The only genus of cult. interest is *Ailanthus*, which see for further particulars of the family Simaroubaceae.

**SIMPLE.** In a leaf, having only one blade to the main leafstalk; not compound.* For the sense in which a flower cluster is said to be simple, see INFLORESCENCE.

As a noun, *simple* is used for a medicinal herb or the medicine made from it, but this use of simple is passing with the passing of much old medical lore regarding the supposed or real medicinal virtue of many plants, always, in the old days, called simples.

*SIMPLEX* (sim′plecks). Unbranched.

*SIMPLICIFOLIA, -us, -um* (sim-pliss-i-fō′li-a). With simple,* not compound* leaves.

**SIM-SIM** = *Sesamum orientale*.

*SINENSIS, -e* (sy-nen′sis). From China.

**SINGLE DAHLIA.** See DAHLIA.

**SINGLE EYE CUTTINGS.** See CUTTINGS.

**SINGLE FLOWERS.** See DOUBLE FLOWERS.

**SINNINGIA.** See GLOXINIA.

*SINUATA, -us, -um* (sin-you-ā′ta). Sinuate; *i.e.* wavy-margined.

**SINUS.** Any recess or depression between two lobes; as the sinus of an oak leaf, or the usually sharper sinus of a maple leaf.

*SIPHO* (sy′fo). A tube or pipe.

**SIRIS** = *Albizzia lebbek*.

**SISAL** = *Agave sisalina*.

*SISALINA, -us, -um* (sy-sa-ly′na). From Sisal, an abandoned seaport on the coast of Yucatan. See AGAVE SISALINA.

**SISARUM** (sy-sair′rum). Greek name for some plant with an edible root, of uncertain application as applied to *Sium sisarum*.

**SISSOO** (sis′soo). East Indian vernacular name for *Dalbergia sissoo* (which see).

**SISYRINCHIUM** (sis-i-rink′i-um). Blue-eyed grass. Low-growing, American, half-hardy or hardy perennial herbs, comprising about 150 species of the iris family, of grass-like habit, and with short rootstocks. Leaves erect, long and narrow, parallel-veined, pale green, or bluish-green, mostly shorter than the flowering stalk. Flowers reddish-purple, blue or yellow, in terminal umbels* enclosed in 1-2 bracts* (spathe*). Calyx of 3 colored sepals, the corolla of 3 petals, alternating with the sepals, widely open. Stamens* 3. Fruit a 3-celled capsule.* (*Sisyrinchium* is an old Greek name, at one time applied to another plant.) Sometimes known as satin-flower.

Not usually cult., but they make attractive flower border plants if planted in clumps, especially in damp places. They can also be used for naturalizing in the wild garden. Easily cult. Propagated by seeds or division of roots. Seeds should be sown ⅛ in. deep, in a cold frame in early spring. They may be transplanted as soon as large enough to handle. Division of roots should be made in Aug. or Sept.

**angustifolium.** Hardy perennial, growing to 1 ft. high. Leaves narrow, pale bluish-green. Flowering stalk flat and twisted. Flowers deep blue, with a 6-pointed white, star-like center, accented with golden-yellow, in 3-4-flowered umbels.* U.S. May-Aug. See BLUE GARDEN.

**californicum.** Golden-eyed grass. Half-hardy perennial, growing to 1 ft. or more. Leaves many, erect, to 10 in. high, and ⅓ in. wide. Flowering stalks flat, and winged. Flowers bright yellow with brown markings, in 3-6-flowered umbels.* Ore. to Calif.

**grandiflorum.** Hardy perennial, to 1 ft. high. Leaves short, sheathing the stem. Flowers reddish-purple, sometimes white, in 3-4-flowered umbels.* Western N.A. June.

*SITCHENSIS, -e* (sit-chen′sis). From Sitka, Alaska.

**SITE.** While few gardeners can choose what might be considered a perfect site, there are a few things about site and exposure that are worth consideration. The purely aesthetic aspect of site, such as the utilization of distant scenes or vistas, the planting-out of objectionable objects, or the screening-out of the noise and dust of the street — these are part of landscape design and are discussed at Landscape Architecture and the articles there mentioned.

Here we are concerned mostly with site as it affects planting, and thoughtful gardeners will do well to study their site thoroughly before making any plans. The two most important things about a site are its exposure and topography.

Exposure to bitter winter winds, or to the still more trying winds from the South in March and April — such a site should be avoided for evergreens, if possible. A site so situated should be protected by dense screen planting. Another site which is difficult to control is exposure to steady sea breezes. But some very fine gardens have been made directly back of the dunes by molding the sand and planting dense groves of the London plane or the Japanese red pine. Such an ambitious changing of the fundamentals of a site is not always possible. But what every gardener can do is to consider site as pretty much fixed by local topography and plant with relation to his site.

Such common-sense procedure involves the planting of things out of the direct wind, if possible. It avoids the lowest places for the most tender of the woody plants, because of cold-air drainage to such places. And it sees that every advantage is taken of topography, soil condition, and water supply, rather than the reverse.

**SITFAST** = *Ranunculus repens*. See Creeping Buttercup in the list at WEEDS.

**SITKA CYPRESS** = *Chamaecyparis nootkatensis*.

**SITKA SPRUCE** = *Picea sitchensis*. See SPRUCE.

**SIUM** (si′um). A genus of 10 species of perennial herbs of the family Umbelliferae, mostly from the north temperate zone, only *S. sisarum,* the skirret, of any garden interest, and a root crop of secondary importance. It is a tuberous-rooted, perennial herb, 1-3 ft. high, with compound* leaves, the leaflets arranged feather-fashion, usually in 1-3 pairs, narrow and toothed. Flowers very small, white, in a terminal, much-divided, compound umbel.* Fruit flattened, dry, 3-ribbed on the face and ribbed on either edge. The roots, which are used like salsify, need most of the season for development. Seeds should be sown in drills in the spring (or late fall southward). Germination is slow and poor and allowance should be made for this and for the fact that the plants will have to be thinned to 8 in. apart in the row. The roots may be harvested in the fall or left in the ground all winter. In the latter case a light mulch of straw or leaves will facilitate digging. The skirret came from eastern As., and is little known here. (*Sium* is an ancient Greek name for a marsh plant, most of the genus growing in such places.)

---

* Special articles on the subjects indicated by an asterisk (*) will be found at the words so marked.

**SKEWERWOOD** = *Euonymus atropurpureus*.

**SKIMMIA** (skim′i-a). Somewhat tender, Asiatic, evergreen shrubs of the family Rutaceae, two of the 9 known species grown for ornament. They have alternate,* short-stalked, dotted leaves, without marginal teeth, decidedly aromatic when crushed. Flowers small, white, some of them perfect,* others polygamous,* and in the first species the sexes on different plants. The male flowers are larger than the others, very fragrant, and borne in larger clusters (panicles*). Female flowers usually with 4-5 sterile stamens.* Fruit red, berry-like, but actually a drupe* with 2-5 stones. (*Skimmia* is the Latin version of a Japanese native name for some species.)

The skimmias are handsome evergreen shrubs, occasionally grown in the cool greenhouse northward, where they should be given potting mixture* 4 and preferably plunged* during the summer. Their chief value is for outdoor plantings in the South, as indicated below. In the first species care must be taken to plant both male and female shrubs if the attractively colored fruits are desired. Propagated by seeds or by cuttings over bottom-heat.

**fortunei** = *Skimmia reevesiana*.
**japonica.** A low, densely branching shrub, 3-5 ft. high, or often less. Leaves more or less crowded at the ends of the twigs, elliptic or oblongish, 3-5 in. long, yellowish-green. Male and female flowers usually on different plants, yellowish-white, about ⅓ in. wide. Fruit nearly round, about ⅓ in. thick, bright red. Jap. April-May. Hardy from zone* 6 (with protection) or from zone* 7 southward.
**reevesiana.** Similar to *S. japonica*, but about half as high, and with narrower and shorter leaves. Flowers generally perfect* or polygamous,* whitish. Fruit inverted egg-shaped, dull crimson. China. April-May. Hardy from zone* 5 southward. Sometimes known as *S. fortunei*.

**SKINNER IRRIGATION.** A trademarked, overhead watering system for gardens. For details *see* IRRIGATION.

**SKIRRET** = *Sium sisarum*.

**SKULLCAP.** *See* SCUTELLARIA.

**SKUNK-CABBAGE.** A single species of foul-smelling marsh herbs constituting the genus **Symplocarpus** (sim-plo-kar′pus) of the family Araceae, common in wet places in eastern N.A. and of little garden interest, except as occasionally transferred to shady, wet places in the wild garden. The only species, S. foetidus, the common skunk-cabbage, also called swamp cabbage and polecat-weed, is a coarse herb with a very large, deep root. Leaves large, handsome, nearly round, the blades 8-12 in. in diameter, all basal, long-stalked, and appearing after the flowers. The latter appear in late Feb. or March in a closed, beautifully colored, sheath-like spathe,* within which is the club-shaped spadix* (*see* ARACEAE for details). Fruit an aggregate of beautifully scarlet, berry-like units. The plant is also known as *Spathyema*. For a Pacific Coast skunk-cabbage *see* LYSICHITUM. (*Symplocarpus* is from the Greek for connection and fruit, in allusion to the coalescence of the ovaries into an aggregate fruit.)

**SKUNK SPRUCE** = *Picea glauca*. *See* SPRUCE.

**SKY-FLOWER.** *Duranta repens* and *Thunbergia grandiflora*.

**SLATY GUM** = *Eucalyptus tereticornis*.

**SLEEK-LEAF** = *Leiophyllum buxifolium*.

**SLEEPING BEAUTY** = *Oxalis acetosella*.

**SLEEPY DICK** = *Ornithogalum umbellatum*.

**SLIME-MOLDS.** *See* PLANT DISEASES.

**SLIP.** A cutting. *See* CUTTINGS. The word slip is also applied, occasionally, to the ratoons* of the pineapple.

**SLIPPER-FLOWER** = *Pedilanthus tithymaloides*.

**SLIPPERWORT.** *See* CALCEOLARIA.

**SLIPPERY ELM.** In the East, *Ulmus fulva* (*see* ELM). In the West, *Fremontia californica*.

**SLOE** = *Prunus spinosa*. The fruit is used to flavor sloe gin; its wood is the blackthorn.

**SLUGS.** *See* ANIMAL INJURY.

**SLUGSHOT.** A trademarked insecticide sold with directions for use as a dusting powder.

**SMALLER YELLOW LADY'S-SLIPPER** = *Cypripedium parviflorum*.

**SMALL FRUITS.** *See* BUSH FRUITS.

**SMALL HONEYSUCKLE** = *Lonicera dioica*.

**SMALL-LEAVED LINDEN** = *Tilia cordata*. *See* LINDEN.

**SMALL PLACE.** *See* HOME GROUNDS.

**SMALL SOLOMON'S-SEAL** = *Polygonatum biflorum*. *See* SOLOMON'S-SEAL.

**SMALL WOODBINE** = *Lonicera dioica*.

**SMARTWEED.** *See* POLYGONUM.

**SMILACEAE.** *See* LILIACEAE.

**SMILACINA** (smy-la-see′na). False Solomon's-seal. Perennial herbs, comprising about 25 species of the lily family, natives of North America and temperate Asia, with thick rootstocks. Leaves simple,* alternate,* broadly lance-shaped, with parallel veins. Flowers greenish-white in racemes* or terminal branching clusters, sometimes fragrant. Calyx of 3 colored sepals. Corolla of 3 petals alternating with the sepals. Stamens* 6 in 2 whorls.* Fruit a 3-celled berry. (*Smilacina* is a diminutive of *Smilax*, to which these plants are related.)

Not much in cultivation, but can be used in the hardy border or wild garden. Easily propagated by division of roots. They can be raised from seed, but period before flowering time would be several years.

**racemosa.** Wild spikenard. Treacleberry. Growing to 3 ft. high. Leaves alternate,* ovalish, to 6 in. long. Flowers greenish-white in terminal, branching clusters, to 4 in. long. Fruit a red berry. Shaded places N.A.
**stellata.** Starry Solomon's-seal. Growing to 20 in. high. Leaves broadly lance-shaped, to 5 in. long, clasping the stem. Flowers greenish-white in short racemes.* N.A.

**SMILAX** (1). The term has two distinct hort. meanings. The common smilax of the florists, widely used for decoration, is usually *Asparagus asparagoides*, the culture of which is discussed at SMILAX (2). But *Smilax*, as a genus of plants, comprises the common catbriers or greenbriers, and they are the plants here considered. The genus *Smilax*, which belongs to the lily family, comprises over 200 species of herbaceous or woody, usually prickly vines, widely distributed in both tropical and temperate regions. All climb by tendrils,* borne in pairs in the leaf-axils.* The lower leaves are reduced to scales, but the upper ones produce proper blades, which are without marginal teeth, but sometimes slightly lobed, with 3-9 main veins, and sometimes blotched with white. Male and female flowers always on separate plants, small, greenish-yellow or white, mostly in small, stalked umbels* in the leaf-axils.* Sepals and petals totaling 6, alike, soon falling. Male flowers with 6 stamens.* Fruit a small berry. (*Smilax* is the ancient Greek name for these vines.)

The plants of the genus *Smilax* are of the easiest culture, and the only real difficulty is to prevent them from making impenetrable, prickly thickets as they always do in the wild. For such a purpose they are surpassed by almost no other cult. plants. Elsewhere they easily become a nuisance. They grow in all sorts of soils, but most often in sandy, poor ones. Only a very few are cult. Some tropical species yield sarsaparilla.

**herbacea.** Carrion-flower. Stems not prickly or only slightly so, usually dying down at the end of the season. Leaves not evergreen, ovalish to narrower, 3-5 in. long, generally heart-shaped at the base. Fruit bluish-black, in rather handsome, long-stalked umbels.* Eastern N.A. May.
**lanceolata.** A prickly vine, the stems with strongly hooked prickles. Leaves evergreen, thin, ovalish or lance-shaped, 2-4 in. long, wedge-shaped at the base, 5-7-veined. Fruit dark red. Southeastern U.S. June. Hardy from zone* 6 southward. Little grown, but it is sometimes harvested from the wild and passes as the florist's smilax or "southern smilax." *See* SMILAX (2).
**laurifolia.** A high-climbing, very prickly vine, the prickles straight. Leaves evergreen, thick and leathery, oblongish, 2½-5 in. long, 3-veined; dark green above, paler beneath. Fruit black, usually produced the second season. N.J. to Fla. and westward. July-Aug. Hardy from zone* 4 southward.

---

* Special articles on the subjects indicated by an asterisk (*) will be found at the words so marked.

rotundifolia. Common catbrier; also called horse brier. A green-stemmed, wiry vine, prickly, but the prickles never at the joints. Leaves nearly round, shining, green both sides, more or less heart-shaped at the base, 2-4½ in. wide. Fruit bluish-black. Eastern N.A. June. Often a prickly nuisance on estates, and difficult to eradicate, as it has numerous, long-creeping rootstocks.

**SMILAX** (2) (*Asparagus asparagoides*). Smilax is propagated from seeds. Seeds should be sown thinly in flats during the month of February. When the plants are from 2 to 3 inches high, pot off into 2¼-in. pots in a soil composed of loam, 3 parts, well-decayed cow manure, 1 part. In early May the plants should be shifted into 4-inch pots, and by the middle of June they will be ready for benching. See BENCH.

Grow in a well-drained, solid bed containing a soil the texture of a rose soil. Plant at a distance 10 × 7 in. In training place a wire close to the soil near the plant and a wire parallel to this near the roof of the greenhouse, and at each plant run up a string of silkaline. Keep the bed cultivated and train the new growths as they develop.

Above, the smilax of the florists (*Asparagus asparagoides*); below, the common catbrier (*Smilax rotundifolia*)

Smilax, when established, makes rapid growth; therefore, liberal waterings are necessary. Syringe to keep down red spider and fumigate with tobacco occasionally to destroy aphids. Water sparingly after cutting until new growth appears, then top-dress with a good, rich soil. A temperature of 60°-65° gives best results. The house should be shaded during the early spring and summer.

While the usual smilax of the florists is this plant, there occasionally appear on the market lots of *Smilax lanceolata* (see SMILAX (1)) from the South. They are often called southern smilax. — D. L.

INSECT PESTS. A small, black, jumping bug, the garden flea hopper, injures smilax and other plants in greenhouses and outdoors. Nicotine spray and clean-up of weedy borders are valuable control measures.

**SMILING WAKEROBIN** = *Trillium undulatum*.

**SMOKE.** For most city gardeners and for many suburban ones smoke is a serious cause of failure or at least the explanation for poor and stunted plants. Smoke is of different sorts and degrees of harmfulness to plants. The worst of all are the industrial smokes from smelters and gas works, which are usually fatal if long continued. They definitely poison the air and prevent the normal interchange of gases in leaves, as described in the article Plant Foods.

Ordinary chimney smoke, mostly from soft coal or anthracite, while harmful, is chiefly so from the sooty deposit left on leaves, especially in foggy weather. Still more likely to stick to foliage is the ever-increasing amount of smoke from oil-burning furnaces, and perhaps from your own. In this connection, it pays to study weather charts for the prevailing direction of the wind, and try to keep your choicer plantings to windward of this menace.

The smoke deposit derived from these non-industrial chimneys can, in small gardens, be removed by frequent syringing, or even sponging off the leaves of broad-leaved plants. But such a task becomes too much of a steady chore, and if there is no escape from the smoke it is better to choose relatively smoke-resistant plants.

SMOKE-ENDURING SHRUBS, VINES, AND TREES

After many years of experiment the plants most likely to endure smoke have been found to be the following. For a description of each, turn to the names listed, and in the body of THE GARDEN DICTIONARY will be found notes on their general culture and hardiness. Especially fine smoke-endurers are marked with a dagger (†).

Acanthopanax sieboldianum
†Ailanthus altissima
Aralia spinosa
Aucuba japonica
Berberis thunbergi
†Campsis radicans
†Catalpa bignonioides
Chaenomeles japonica
Cornus mas
Cornus sanguinea
†Deutzia scabra
†Elaeagnus multiflora
Elder (*Sambucus canadensis*)
Forsythia (most species)
†Hibiscus syriacus
†Hydrangea paniculata
†Lonicera tatarica
†Lycium halimifolium
Mock-orange (*Philadelphus coronarius*)
Mulberry (*Morus alba*)
Physocarpus opulifolius
†Platanus acerifolia
†Privet (most species)
†Rhamnus cathartica
Rhodotypos tetrapetala
†Rhus copallina
†Spiraea vanhouttei
†Symphoricarpos (all species)
Viburnum opulus

From such a collection it is possible to choose plants for a border screen that may strain out a lot of the deposit from smoke fumes. Behind such a protective planting it is often feasible to grow a fairly good garden, but only if most of the smoke can be sifted out by these smoke-enduring species.

Besides the plants listed above there are others which are fairly hardy under city conditions of shade, wind, and smoke. See the plants listed at BACKYARD GARDEN. For the only beneficial effects of smoke see FUMIGATION. See also SMUDGES.

**SMOKE-TREE.** See COTINUS.

**SMOKING BEAN TREE.** See CATALPA.

**SMOOTH ALDER** = *Alnus rugosa*. See ALDER.

**SMOOTH-LEAVED ELM** = *Ulmus foliacea*. See ELM.

**SMOOTH SUMAC** = *Rhus glabra*.

**SMOOTH WINTERBERRY** = *Ilex laevigata*. See HOLLY.

**SMOTHER CROP.** Sometimes fallow land, or a lawn being plowed up for re-seeding, or a part of the vegetable garden, will suddenly become invaded by a crop of noxious weeds. The quickest way to stop this, if it is not desired to keep the land cultivated, is to plant a smother crop. As the name implies, the crop, if properly planted, will smother out the weeds.

If the invaders are mostly low weeds, Dutch clover or buckwheat are as good smother crops as any. They must be sown broadcast, and very thickly, as the object is to get as thick and dense a stand as possible. If the weeds are higher, it is better to use oats or rye as the smother crop. When they have accomplished their purpose, smother crops should be plowed under (with the remains of the weeds). In the case of the grains, they will have to be harvested when ripe and only the stubble turned under. Smother crops are more often used on farms, but they may be equally useful in the garden on a smaller scale.

**SMUDGES.** It was long thought that smoky fires, so managed that they covered the orchard with a pall of

* Special articles on the subjects indicated by an asterisk (*) will be found at the words so marked.

smoke, were the best method of frost control. It is now known that the application of direct heat, smokeless or nearly so, is by far the most effective. See FROST.

**SMUTS.** See Fungi at PLANT DISEASES. See also the Plant Diseases at CORN.

**SNAIL-FLOWER** = *Phaseolus caracalla*.

**SNAILS.** See ANIMAL INJURY.

**SNAILSEED.** See COCCULUS.

**SNAKE EGGPLANT.** See SOLANUM MELONGENA SERPENTINUM.

**SNAKE GOURD** = *Trichosanthes anguina*.

**SNAKE GRASS** = *Tradescantia virginiana*. See SPIDERWORT.

**SNAKE-HEAD** = *Chelone glabra*.

**SNAKE LILY** = *Brodiaea volubilis*.

**SNAKE MELON.** See MELON.

**SNAKEMOUTH** = *Pogonia ophioglossoides*.

**SNAKE PALM** = *Hydrosme rivieri*.

**SNAKE PLANT.** See SANSEVIERIA.

**SNAKEROOT.** More than 20 different plants have had the name snakeroot applied to them. Two of the best known, among cult. plants, will be found at *Cimicifuga* and *Asclepiadora decumbens*. For other plants to which the name snakeroot is sometimes, or in part, applied, see ARISTOLOCHIA, ERYNGIUM, EUPATORIUM, LIATRIS, POLYGALA.

**SNAKE'S-HEAD** = *Fritillaria meleagris*.

**SNAKEWOOD** = *Cecropia palmata*.

**SNAP BEAN.** The string bean (*Phaseolus vulgaris*). For culture see BEAN.

**SNAPDRAGON.** Very popular garden and florists' flowers all belonging to the genus **Antirrhinum** (an-tir-ry'-num) of the family Scrophulariaceae. They are hardy, herbaceous perennials or annuals, comprising about 32 species, and natives of the northern hemisphere. Erect, climbing or of spreading habit, sometimes covered with short, sticky hairs. Leaves alternate,* lance-shaped or ovalish, with heart-shaped base, sometimes bluntly lobed. Flowers solitary or in long terminal racemes,* the individual flower growing from the axil* of a small, leafy bract,* white, yellow, pink, red or purple. Calyx* of 5 sepals. Corolla tubular, pouched, forming a mouth, the upper lip* 2-lobed, the lower lip 3-lobed, the lips turning outwards. Stamens* 5, 4 fertile growing inside the corolla tube, 1 sterile. Fruit a dry, 2-celled capsule,* many-seeded. Seeds dispersed through pores. (*Antirrhinum* is from the Greek for like a nose, in allusion to the shape of the flower.)

For Culture see below.

**A. asarina.** Perennial, of spreading habit, covered with short, sticky hairs. Leaves ovalish, heart-shaped at base, cut into 5 rounded lobes. Flowers solitary, white or pale pink, to 1½ in. long. Southwestern Eu.

**A. coulterianum.** Chaparral snapdragon. Bright green, erect or climbing annual, to 3 ft. high. Leaves ovalish, to 1½ in. long. Flowers purple to white, with yellow hairs in throat of corolla, ½ in. long, in racemes. Calif.

**A. majus.** Common snapdragon, also called toad's-mouth. Bright green perennial, growing to 3 ft. high. Leaves lance-shaped, to 3 in. long. Flowers reddish-purple, sometimes white, to 1½ in. long, in long terminal racemes.* Mediterranean region. There are many hort. color forms in this species. See below.

### SNAPDRAGON CULTURE

Snapdragons are among the finest flowering plants for the garden. The hort. varieties which have been derived from the species *A. majus* can be obtained in so many colors from pure white through various shades of yellow, pink, orange, flame, red and purple, that planted in masses they make a great show for the most humble gardener.

They are roughly divided into 3 groups, the dwarf, growing to 9 in., the intermediate, growing to 20 in., and the tall, growing to 4 ft. All three have their place in the flower border or colored gardens, while the dwarf and intermediate

Snapdragon

can be used to advantage for bedding. They can also be grown for cut flowers in the greenhouse or outdoors, the tall-growing usually being used for the greenhouse. The following are some of the best varieties for this purpose:

Amber Queen (yellow).
Geneva pink (rose-pink).
Jennie Schneider (light pink).
Philadelphia pink (pink).
Navajo (canary-yellow).
Golden West (deep yellow).
Newport yellow (rich yellow).
White Rock (pure white).
Shasta (white with yellow throat).
Afterglow (light bronze shades).
Orlando (light bronze shades).
Penn Orange (orange).
Yosemite (lilac-purple).
Gloria (rose-red).
Empress (crimson).
Purity (white).

The flowering period of the snapdragons can be extended by sowing seeds at different periods and by keeping the seed pods picked off. They are easily cult., but thrive best when grown under cool conditions. Propagated by seeds or cuttings.

For outdoor culture, seeds should be sown in light, sandy soil 1/16 in. deep, in a cold frame or in flats in a cool greenhouse in Aug. or Sept. As soon as large enough to handle they should be pricked-off into a cold frame, continuing in light, sandy soil, about 3 in. apart, where they should be allowed to stand through the winter. They must be protected from hard frost, and this can be done by covering the sash with mats or old straw or hay. Air must be admitted every day when the temperature is above freezing. They must not be allowed to become dry.

In the spring the sash should be taken off every day and gradually left open at night so as to harden the plants off. They will stand a little frost if this treatment is given gradually. After this, they should be planted out where required to flower as early as possible so as to get well established before the hot weather. Seeds may also be sown in Jan. or Feb. in pans in cool greenhouse, pricked-off into flats, and then removed to cold frame for hardening, before planting out in the garden. These plants will bloom a little later. In localities where there is not more than 15° of frost, they may be entirely grown out-of-doors.

---

* Special articles on the subjects indicated by an asterisk (*) will be found at the words so marked.

For greenhouse culture, for winter- and spring-flowering, seeds should be sown from June–Aug. in pans in the coolest part of the greenhouse or in a cold frame, where they should be shaded from the sun until they have germinated. They should then be pricked-off into flats and placed in the cold frame.

When 4 in. high they should be potted into 4-in. pots, using potting mixture* 3, still keeping them in the cold frame. After 2 weeks the tips should be pinched back to make them bushy. They may remain in these pots until a bench* has been prepared from Sept.–Jan., according to the time when they are required to flower. For instance, if sown in June and benched in Sept. they should flower the end of Dec. Benches should not be less than 4 in. deep, 6 in. is better. Soil for the bench should be old pasture loam and cow manure which has been lying for 6 months, and should be well mixed before filling the bench.*

Seedlings should be planted 10 in. apart and watered thoroughly to settle the soil round the roots. They should then be kept rather on the dry side until strong growth begins, in temperature of 45° at night and 55°–60° during the day. Four to six of the strongest shoots should be selected for flowering and all others pinched out. As the flowering stems grow, all side shoots must be kept pinched off. When plants are about 15 in. high, a light dressing of artificial manure should be given every week until the first flower opens.

Cuttings are only taken when it is desired to keep a particular variety or color, as plants do not always come true from seed. Cuttings root readily if inserted in sand and shaded from sun at any time.

Ants are very partial to snapdragon seeds, which are very small, and unless precautions are taken will carry them all away. To prevent this the seed pans should be placed on inverted pots in saucers of water, so making it impossible for the ants to reach the newly sown seeds. After germination the ants will not do any harm. — H. R. M.

INSECT PESTS. Common greenhouse pests, such as aphids, leaf tiers, whiteflies, mites, and thrips, attack snapdragon (see CHRYSANTHEMUM, CARNATION, and BEGONIA). A black stink bug injures flowers outdoors (see Tarnished Plant Bug at DAHLIA).

DISEASES. Rust, root-knot, leafspot and blight are the common diseases. For *rust* and *root-knot*, see Rust or Root Knot at PLANT DISEASES. *Leafspot*, associated with various fungi, is characterized by round or oval, brown dead areas on the foliage. For control, take cuttings from healthy plants, remove infected plants or leaves, spray with bordeaux mixture, avoid overhead watering, and burn all plant debris in the fall. When infected with *blight*, sudden wilting and death of the plants may occur. Dead areas on the foliage and cankers on the stems are other typical symptoms. Remove infected plants, spray with bordeaux mixture and burn all plant debris in the fall. Some of the newer strains are nearly or quite rust-resistant.

**SNAPDRAGON FAMILY** = Scrophulariaceae.

**SNAPWEED.** See IMPATIENS.

**SNAROL.** A trademarked poison bait sold with directions for use against insects that bite or chew leaves.

**SNEEZEWEED.** See HELENIUM.

**SNEEZEWORT** = *Achillea ptarmica*.

**SNOUT BEETLES.** See Beetles at INSECT PESTS. They are rather common pests on various garden plants. For their control see the Insect Pests at RHUBARB, SWEET POTATO, PEPPER (*Capsicum*), APPLE, BANANA, QUINCE, STRAWBERRY, and ROSE.

**SNOW.** An apple variety. See APPLE.

**SNOW.** The white blanket of snow is a valuable protection to all perennial crops, but it is effective generally only from zone* 3 northward, as south of this, snow cover is either erratic or lacking altogether. The places of greatest snowfall in the U.S. are in the coast ranges in Ore., Wash., and northern Calif., where an annual accumulation of 8–10 ft. is not uncommon.

Besides its value as a winter protection to the plants it covers, snow is also of great value to plowed land. Hence comes its name of "poor-man's manure." It does not, of course, add any more plant food than rain does, but on many soils its accumulation and gradual thawing do help the physical texture of the soil.

**SNOWBALL** = *Viburnum opulus sterile*. See also V. TOMENTOSUM STERILE.

**SNOWBALL CACTUS** = *Pediocactus simpsoni*.

**SNOWBERRY** = *Symphoricarpos albus*. For the creeping snowberry see CHIOGENES.

**SNOW BUSH** = *Breynia nivosa*.

**SNOWDRIFT** = Sweet Alyssum.

**SNOWDROP.** Pretty little spring-blooming, bulbous herbs, comprising the genus **Galanthus** (ga-lan′thus) of the family Amaryllidaceae, all Eurasian, and 3 of the 10 known species cult. for their handsome, very early bloom. They have small bulbs, a solid flowering stalk, and only 2–3, narrow, basal leaves. Flowers solitary at the end of the stalk, usually nodding, the outer segments white, the inner green or greenish, without a tube. Stamens* 6. Fruit a 3-valved capsule.* (*Galanthus* is from the Greek for milk and flower, in allusion to the white bloom.) They are sometimes called Candlemas bells.

For Culture see below.

G. byzantinus. Leaves broader than in the other 2 species, bluish-green, the margins recurved. Flowers about ¾ in. long, oblongish, the inner segments green, the outer white. Southeastern Eu. Jan.–March.

G. elwesi. Giant snowdrop. Flowering stalk 10–18 in. high, the leaves about 7 in. long, ¾ in. wide, very bluish-green. Flowers nearly 1¼ in. long, the inner segments partly green, the outer white. Asia Minor. Dec.–April.

G. nivalis. Common snowdrop. Flowering stalk 7–12 in. high, the leaves 6–8 in. long and not over ¼ in. wide. Flowers about ¾ in. long, the inner segments partly green, the outer white. Eu. and southwestern As. Jan.–April. There is also a double-flowered form.

### SNOWDROP CULTURE

The flowering of the different snowdrop species covers many weeks of the early year. They are the first flowers to make their appearance and as such are very welcome. Most of the kinds flourish in light, rich soil beneath deciduous trees and shrubs, and in such positions the rotting leaves supply all the nourishment they require. But *G. elwesi* prefers a sunny situation and sandier soil, and a mulch of well-decayed manure may be given every other autumn.

Snowdrops should be planted in hundreds or thousands to make an effective display. If happy they increase freely and may be left undisturbed for years to form large, close colonies. It is of prime importance to get the bulbs planted early, in August if possible, certainly in September. Set them 3 in. deep and 3 in. apart. They may be combined with winter aconites, chionodoxas, snowflakes, *Scilla sibirica*, the early *Crocus* species, *Hyacinthus azureus* and Christmas roses. Pussy willow bushes set about with snowdrops and Christmas roses provide the earliest garden picture of the year. — L. B. W.

**SNOWDROP TREE.** See HALESIA.

**SNOWDROP WINDFLOWER.** See ANEMONE SYLVESTRIS.

**SNOWFLAKE.** Spring- or autumn-flowering, bulbous herbs, comprising the genus **Leucojum** (lew-kō′jum) of the family Amaryllidaceae, three of the 10 known species often cult. in the flower garden. All are natives in Eu. They have small bulbs and a hollow flower stalk which usually exceeds the basal, narrow leaves. The leaves appear with the spring-flowering species, but after the bloom in the fall-flowering sorts. Flowers not tubular, mostly nodding, the inner and outer segments alike, but often differently colored, generally white and tinged with red or green. Stamens* 6. Fruit a 3-valved capsule,* its seeds nearly globe-shaped. (*Leucojum* is from the Greek for white violet, perhaps in allusion to the white flowers.) For the water snowflake see NYMPHOIDES INDICUM.

For Culture see below.

L. aestivum. Flowering stalk 9–12 in. high, the leaves as long or a little longer, and about ½ in. wide. Flowers in clusters of 2–8, each flower about ¾ in. long, white, but green-tipped, on a slender, individual stalk. Eu. Late spring.

---

* Special articles on the subjects indicated by an asterisk (*) will be found at the words so marked.

**L. autumnale.** Flowering stalk 7–9 in. long, the shorter, thread-like leaves appearing after the fall bloom. Flowers 1–3 together, on slender, drooping, individual stalks, the corolla about ½ in. long, white, but red-tinged. Southern Eu. and northern Af. Fall.

**L. vernum.** Flowering stalk 9–12 in. high, the leaves a little less and about ½ in. wide. Flowers solitary, white, but green-tipped, nodding, about ¾ in. long. Central Eu. Early spring.

### Snowflake Culture

The snowflakes are perfectly hardy and flourish in rich garden soil of a somewhat sandy character. Planted in bold clumps between shrubs, in borders of ferns or in the rock garden they are very effective. Once planted, 4 or 5 in. deep and about 4 in. apart, they need not be disturbed for years. They are easily propagated by bulblets,* which may be detached after the leaves have withered. The finest of the genus is *L. vernum.* Its large blossoms are very showy and quite fragrant. Grouped with *Chionodoxa luciliae* it makes a cheerful early picture. — L. B. W.

**SNOW-IN-SUMMER** = *Cerastium tomentosum.*

**SNOWMOLD.** See Diseases at GRASSES.

**SNOW-ON-THE-MOUNTAIN** = *Euphorbia marginata.*

**SNOW PEAR** = *Pyrus nivalis.*

**SNOW POPPY** = *Eomecon chionantha.*

**SNOW SPRITE.** See MICHAELMAS DAISY.

**SNOW TRAP.** See WINDBREAK.

**SNOW TRILLIUM** = *Trillium nivale.*

**SNOW WREATH** = *Neviusia alabamensis.*

**SOAP.** See Contact Sprays at INSECTICIDES.

**SOAPBARK TREE** = *Quillaja saponaria.*

**SOAPBERRY.** See SAPINDUS.

**SOAPBERRY FAMILY** = Sapindaceae.

**SOAP PLANT** = *Chlorogalum pomeridianum.*

**SOAPWORT.** See SAPONARIA.

**SOBOLE.** A sucker arising from the ground, often developing into a stem as important as the main one, especially in some palms which are then said to be soboliferous. Such plants appear to grow in clumps, but may be only a single one with several soboles.

**SOBRALIA** (so-bray′li-a). Reed-like, leafy-stemmed, tropical American orchids with very showy flowers. They grow in the ground and comprise perhaps 30 species, of which **S. macrantha,** of Mex. and Guatemala, is by far the most popular in cult., although others are known in collections of fanciers. It has leafy stems 6–7 ft. high, the leaves tapering, 6–9 in. long, strongly veined, somewhat folded like the leaves of a fan. Flowers several, in a short terminal cluster (raceme*), generally short-lived. Flowers very irregular,* 5–6 in. wide, the petals and sepals spreading, pinkish-purple, the lip large, wavy-margined, deep purple. An extremely showy plant in bloom (May–July in the greenhouse), but the flowers not good for cutting, as they do not last. For culture see the terrestrial orchids at Greenhouse Orchids at ORCHID. (Named for a Spanish botanist, Sobral, otherwise unknown.)

*SOCOTRANA, -us, -um* (so-ko-tray′na). From the island of Socotra, in the Indian Ocean.

**SOD.** See TURF.

**SOD CULTURE; SOD MULCH.** An alternative to open cultivation of the soil under fruit trees, or to the use of cover crops under them. For a discussion of the merits of each method of handling orchard soils see Cover Crops at FRUIT CULTURE.

**SODIUM FLUORIDE.** See Stomach Poisons at INSECTICIDES.

**SOD LIFTER.** See Section 3, TOOLS AND IMPLEMENTS.

**SOFT ROT.** See Diseases at CALLA LILY, HYACINTHUS, IRIS, and PARSNIP.

**SOFT RUSH** = *Juncus effusus.*

**SOFT SCALE.** A scale insect with a very soft body. They are sometimes very destructive. One of the worst is the terrapin scale. For its control see Insect Pests at PEACH.

**SOFTWOOD CUTTINGS.** See CUTTINGS.

**SOIL.** The source of all food which the plant does not get from the atmosphere, and the only food supply which can be controlled or at least ameliorated by the gardener. Being the basic material in which most plants are rooted, it is natural that the soil has been much studied by the experts, both its physical make-up, its chemical composition, and its greatly varying response to fertilizers, manure, and lime. Such a body of information is essential to the soil scientists, and much of what they have discovered is now translated into the common practice of the farmer and gardener.

For the latter there are two phases of soil that should be considered: (1) What it is, what kinds of soil there are, and their chemical make-up. All of this basic information is grouped under the general article SOILS (or at the articles cross-referenced from there). (2) What we do *with* soils, a topic which has for its scope the common garden skills such as plowing, digging and the like. These are all summarized at the article SOIL OPERATIONS (or at the special cultural articles cross-referenced from it).

There still remains the much-debated question of soil acidity and alkalinity. All the information on this is at the entry ACID AND ALKALI SOILS.

The subject of soils is so important that we summarize here all the leading articles on it in THE GARDEN DICTIONARY. They will be found in the body of the book as they are listed below:

Soils (general, including kinds and texture).
Soil Moisture (general). *See also* special articles on DRAINING, IRRIGATION, MUCKLAND GARDENING.
Soil Management.
Soil Operations (general). *See also* special articles on CULTIVATION, DIGGING, HARROWING, HOEING, PLANTING, PLOWING, RAKING.
Fertility (brief). *See also* the articles on FERTILIZERS, MANURE, LIME.
Acid and Alkali Soils.

**SOIL ACIDITY.** See ACID AND ALKALI SOILS.

**SOIL CULTIVATION.** See CULTIVATION.

**SOIL FERTILITY.** See FERTILITY.

**SOIL FUMIGATION.** See FUMIGATION.

**SOIL HEAVING.** See HEAVING.

**SOIL IMPROVEMENT.** See GREEN MANURING.

**SOIL INOCULATION.** See LEGUME INOCULATION.

**SOIL MANAGEMENT.** The year-by-year management of cultivated soils requires a little thought and planning. For more than two thousand years it has been known that continuous cropping of any one area will ultimately deplete its fertility unless something is done to overcome the annual loss of plant food. And even more disastrous is the continued use of one kind of crop upon the same land.

To overcome these difficulties two things are obvious but are quite often ignored. One is to let the land lie idle; the other is to practice a rotation of crops. In small places it is often impossible to let land be idle (*i.e.* fallow land) for a season or two, although the advantages of such a plan are so great that many good farmers manage to have *some* land fallow every year.

When conditions make this impossible the next best plan is to practice a rotation of crops. This means so planning your garden that exactly the same crop does not occupy exactly the same piece of land in two successive years. This is impossible, of course, in permanent ornamental plantings, but it can be easily accomplished in the vegetable garden. Several suggestions for such rotations will be found in the section Rotation of Crops at KITCHEN

---

* Special articles on the subjects indicated by an asterisk (*) will be found at the words so marked.

GARDEN. It can often be done in the flower garden, especially with annuals and biennials, and when re-planning the perennial border it is well to keep the rotation principle in mind.

The reasons for rotation and for fallow land are not thoroughly understood. It appears, in both cases, to be a highly complex adjustment as between soil fertility, the phenomenon known as "sick soils" (*i.e.* tired of one crop), and the more obvious fact that insects and diseases are left without their favorite food if the crop is elsewhere. So many destructive organisms winter-over in the soil that changing crops is one of the best ways to starve out such pests. *See also* CULTIVATION, DRAINING.

**SOIL MIXTURES.** For the natural mixtures of soils as they occur in the garden *see* SOILS. For the mixtures suitable for potting and window boxes *see* POTTING MIXTURES.

**SOIL MOISTURE.** The only source of soil moisture is rainfall, but what the physicists call "free water" (*i.e.* not held by the soil particles) is of little or no use to plants, except aquatics. In other words, the only soil moisture of any use to the gardener is that known as *capillary* water, a film of which surrounds each soil particle. By capillarity such soil moisture is constantly rising from the permanent ground water and most of it is either used by the plant or is lost by evaporation.

Two things are indicated by this fact — increase if possible the water-holding capacity of your soil, and try to stop or retard its evaporation from the surface. The latter is best accomplished by creating a dust mulch upon the surface, the details of which will be found at CULTIVATION. Another way to conserve soil moisture is by a mulch, the details for which will be found at MULCH AND MULCHING.

Increasing the moisture-holding capacity of garden soils is often necessary and sometimes imperative. Ordinary garden soils vary greatly in their capacity to hold water, the light (*i.e.* sandy and gravelly) ones holding too little, and some heavy clay and silt soils holding too much. The latter condition can be relieved by adding sand to small areas and often lime to large ones. *See* LIME.

But light, sandy soils need particular attention when it comes to their moisture-holding capacity, especially in view of the ease with which they lose water during summer droughts. The reason they do so is because the coarseness of their soil particles allows too much space for air and too little opportunity for the retention of capillary water.

The remedy for this condition is the addition of humus, the moisture-holding capacity of which is far higher than any mineral soil. There are two ways of getting humus into soils deficient in it. The first and most expensive is by direct addition of commercial humus. For the details of this *see* HUMUS. The second, slower, but much less expensive method is to grow crops upon the soil and plow them under. For this method *see* GREEN MANURING.

**SOIL OPERATIONS.** The operations necessary for the proper preparation of garden soils are governed by several factors, the most important of which are: the type of soil under consideration (its physical and mechanical condition); the purpose for, or the object of its preparation; and the size of the plot to be prepared. These factors govern the proper methods of procedure, and the selection of suitable implements to be employed. All the main sections below are also the subjects of special articles, where the details of the various soil operations should be sought. Here they are merely summarized.

For all gardening purposes a well-drained, deep, fertile topsoil is essential. This soil should contain a liberal amount of available plant food; it must warm readily; be rich in humus; be porous and friable,* yet absorbent and retentive of moisture for the best growth and development of plant life.

Where space permits, tractor or horse-drawn implements may be used in the preparation of the soil, though, in some instances, especially the home grounds or gardens, space is limited and hand tillage must be resorted to.

### DRAINING

Proper drainage should receive first consideration, for plants will not thrive in wet, soggy soils. Sandy or gravelly soils seldom require artificial drainage, therefore we are more concerned with the heavy soils, or those having clay or "hard-pan" subsoils. Drainage, where necessary, may be accomplished by providing furrows or open ditches, covered ditches, by tiling, subsoiling, or by deep wells. The method must be governed by the requirements of the individual case. *See* DRAINING.

Good drainage ensures better germination of seeds; more vigorous growth; earlier maturity and greater productivity by improving the mechanical and physical condition of the soil; encourages bacterial development, making plant food more easily and quickly available; aids in warming the soil; makes it more porous, thus keeping it in a sweet and friable* condition; and makes it more absorbent and retentive of moisture. Weed seeds do not germinate as readily, for they require an abundance of moisture, and insect pests are not so liable to harbor in well-drained soils. Also all soil operations are more efficiently and economically facilitated.

### PLOWING

Proper drainage having been provided, turning the soil, either by plowing or digging (spading), is the next consideration. The object is to stir the soil; to incorporate or work into it humus or organic matter, either in the form of stable manure, or green cover crops; to loosen or aerate it, thereby increasing the chemical action of bacteria,* which is very essential to proper plant growth and development; to turn under trash, etc. Plowing or turning the soil, especially when humus in some form has been turned under, increases its moisture-holding capacity and encourages stronger and deeper root development.

The proper time to plow depends greatly upon the composition of the soil. Soils containing much clay give best results when plowed in the fall, for frost action which breaks up the lumps or clods, mellows it. Soils of a light or sandy nature, which have a tendency to run together during the winter, after having been plowed or spaded in fall, should be plowed in spring for best results. Turning the soil to a depth of 5 to 8 in. is advisable with most soils for nearly all purposes. *See* PLOWING.

### DIGGING

Digging or spading is another method of turning the soil and must be resorted to where space is limited. Though the method differs, the object of and the results secured are practically identical with plowing. Hand digging must be practiced where flower and shrub beds or borders, or other small areas are to be spaded or turned. *See* DIGGING.

### HARROWING AND RAKING

Preparation of the soil after plowing is best done by harrowing or raking, which pulverizes the clods, and levels and firms the seedbed. The fine surface soil thus formed acts as a blanket, preventing the escape of soil moisture through cracks.

Frequent harrowing ventilates the soil; kills vast numbers of weed seedlings; aids capillary attraction or the movement of soil fluids; hastens the decomposition of manurial or vegetable matter, thus making plant food more readily available; increases bacterial development, and encourages deep, vigorous root growth. It also kills or checks insect pests, especially grubs and cutworms.

We must resort to hand raking where space is limited or where an exceptionally fine seedbed is desired, as in the building of lawns, flower beds, etc., and also in their maintenance. The object of or results secured by raking are identical with harrowing, excepting that a more exacting finish and a finer surface are obtained. In the preparation

---

* Special articles on the subjects indicated by an asterisk (*) will be found at the words so marked.

of the soil, harrowing or raking should be done after every rain, but never when the ground is wet or sticky.

### ROLLING

The seedbed should be firmed by rolling after the surface has been well pulverized. Horse- or tractor-drawn roller may be used, space permitting; otherwise, hand-rolling must be resorted to.

Rolling prevents the rapid escape of soil moisture; reveals inequalities of the surface; firms the seedbed; assures quicker and better germination; and allows soil fluids to be brought up by capillary attraction which would otherwise be lost to growing plants.

Injury to crops and lawns caused by heaving or frost action can be overcome or partially corrected by rolling lightly early in spring, thereby pressing the raised plant roots back into the soil.

### CULTIVATION

Though ideas and methods of cult. vary greatly, an understanding of certain conditions is necessary to apply them properly.

Cultivation should be practiced often and thoroughly during the early part of the growing season, to keep down weeds; to prevent excessive evaporation of soil moisture by forming a dust mulch; to stimulate the capillary movement of air and moisture in the soil, necessary to the life of the bacteria which make plant food available.

Many types of cultivators are in use — tractor- or horse-drawn where space permits, and hand cultivators for limited areas. Proper selection depends upon local conditions. *See* CULTIVATION, TOOLS AND IMPLEMENTS.

### HOEING

The garden hoe is most suitable where space is limited, and for most purposes — to cult. flowers or shrubs, etc.; between plants in the row; to furrow out rows for seeding or planting; to eradicate weeds; to loosen the soil, etc. The object of hoeing and the benefits derived are almost identical with cult. in most soil operations. *See* HOEING.

### TOP-DRESSING

Top-dressing, as generally understood by the average person, applies to the fertilization of lawns. It is just as beneficial for flowers and vegetables, trees or shrubs, etc. The materials used as top-dressing may be in the form of compost, peat moss, manure, bone meal, tankage, or commercial fertilizers.

The purpose is to supply an immediate source of available plant food to growing plants, and, in most instances, organic matter as well.

Top-dressing aids in the absorption and retention of moisture; the suppression of weeds; the development of soil bacteria; and aids capillary movement. It also increases the yield and improves the quality of plants or crops so treated. *See* TOP-DRESSING.

### TRENCHING

Trenching, practiced where surface soils are very poor, or where a very deep, fertile soil is required, consists of mixing or working manure into the soil to a depth of 18 in., applying the manure as the earth is being turned, after first having removed some of the soil from the trench to the required depth, to facilitate mixing.

Another method is to remove the soil entirely from the space to be trenched to a depth of 12 to 18 in., then putting 6 in. of well-rotted manure in the bottom of the trench and filling in with good topsoil.

Trenching promotes deep, vigorous root growth; prevents injury by drought; and assures an abundant supply of plant food for many years. *See* TRENCHING.

### HEAVING

Heaving of the soil, caused by frost action, is more severe in moist soils, especially in soil depressions, where water stands. It tears the fibrous roots of the plants, causing them to winter-kill. Severe heaving may be overcome by providing proper soil drainage, and the injury to plants lessened by applying a mulch, either in the form of manure, peat moss, marsh hay, straw, leaves, or evergreen boughs. The injury to lawns and other crops may be lessened or corrected by rolling in the early spring, when the surface of the soil is dry. *See* HEAVING. — E. P. E.

**SOILS.** The soil is a mixture of weathering rock and organic matter which covers the earth in a thin layer. It is a medium from which all plants and animals draw, directly or indirectly, a large part of their sustenance. The soil is the home of the plant roots and the storehouse of the mineral elements and of water.

The term soil, as used here, includes both the topsoil or surface soil and the subsoil down to the parent material. The soil is composed of solids, liquids and gases. The solid portion of most soils is composed of minerals and organic matter, both in all stages of decomposition. In all except the organic soils (mucks and peats) the mineral part predominates. The spaces between the soil particles are normally occupied by air and water, the proportion of each depending on the character of the soil and the conditions under which it is functioning. As the water increases the air decreases and vice versa. A representative silt-loam soil, when in good condition for plant growth, contains approximately 50% solid and 50% pore space. At optimum moisture about half of the pore space is occupied by water and half by air. The 50% solid matter represents roughly 45% mineral and 5% organic matter, by volume.

### ORIGIN OF SOILS

Mineral soils are formed from the breakdown of rocks at the earth's surface by mechanical disintegration and by chemical action. The kind of rock (limestone, granite, sandstone and shale) determines to a large extent the character of the soil. Mechanical disintegration of the rock material is brought about by erosion, by differential expansion of the minerals, by frost action and by plants and animals. Chemical decomposition is hastened by the action of water, oxygen and carbon dioxide. In humid, sub-tropical and tropical climates chemical soil weathering is intense and continuous. Biological activity also goes on rapidly under these conditions and the organic matter is quickly reduced to carbon dioxide and other simple substances.

Organic soils (see HUMUS and MUCKLAND GARDENING) are formed from the remains of plants and animals, deposited under water. Drainage waters and other transporting agencies bring in mineral matter which becomes incorporated with the organic materials.

Mineral soils (the solid part) vary in organic matter content from a trace to 12 to 15%. So-called organic soils contain from 20 to 90 or 95% of organic matter. Representative types of organic soils contain 70 to 80% of organic matter.

### SOIL PROFILE AND SOIL HORIZON

A **soil profile** is a vertical section of the soil from the surface into the underlying unweathered material. A profile having characteristics common to the soils of a broad geographical region is known as a **regional profile.** A profile that is definitely representative of a soil series is called a **typical profile,** and a characteristic profile that has developed under conditions that have remained relatively uniform throughout the period of development is called a **normal profile.**

A soil **horizon** is a layer of the soil profile approximately parallel to the surface and distinguished by more or less well-defined characteristics. In American literature on soil science three distinct horizons are recognized, A, B and C. **Horizon A** is the upper horizon, the surface soil, from which material has been removed by percolating waters. **Horizon B** is the layer to which materials have been added by percolating waters and is immediately below horizon A. **Horizon C** is the relatively unweathered material underlying horizon B.

---

\* Special articles on the subjects indicated by an asterisk (\*) will be found at the words so marked.

### Surface Soil and Subsoil

The term **surface soil** or topsoil is applied to the upper or surface layer, horizon A. In cultivated soils the term refers to the portion that is modified by tillage and by the decomposition of organic matter. In other cases, where the color of the upper portion is modified by accumulation of organic matter, the term is applied to the full depth of the color horizon.

The **subsoil** is the layer immediately beneath the surface soil. In many cultivated mineral soils the subsoil is lighter in color than is the surface soil and, if composed of the same material, is always more compact.

### Classification of Soils

Soils are classified in various ways and with many divisions, but only the soil type and the soil class (textural grade) will be considered here.

**Soil Type.** A soil which, throughout the extent of its occurrence, has relatively uniform profile characteristics, represents a **soil type**. A name unmodified may refer to the dominant or **key** type of the series. Any particular soil of a series is designated by its textural name, as **sandy loam, clay, clay loam,** etc. To this is added the series name. The type name is, therefore, made up of two parts, the first designating the series and the second the individual within the group. Examples are Dunkirk clay loam, Norfolk sandy loam and Carrington silt loam. The first word in each of these type names designates the series and the others the textural grade or class. All of them taken together is the name of the soil type.

**Soil Class (Textural Grade).** The **soil class** or **textural grade** is a classification based on texture alone. **Texture** is a term used to indicate the coarseness or fineness of the soil. The textural composition is determined by a mechanical analysis, which is a laboratory process. The system used by the United States Department of Agriculture separates the soil into seven sizes as shown below.

#### United States Department of Agriculture Classification of Soil Particles

| Name of soil | Size in millimeters (1 millimeter = .0397 inch) |
| --- | --- |
| Fine gravel | 2 to 1 |
| Coarse sand | 1 to 0.5 |
| Medium sand | 0.5 to 0.25 |
| Fine sand | 0.25 to 0.10 |
| Very fine sand | 0.10 to 0.05 |
| Silt | 0.05 to 0.005 |
| Clay | 0.005 and below |

Soils are divided into three groups determined by the proportion of the several sizes as given in the table. These three groups, **sandy soils, loamy soils** and **clayey soils,** are separated into classes as follows:

| Sandy soils | Loamy soils | Clayey soils |
| --- | --- | --- |
| Gravelly sands | Coarse sandy loams | Gravelly clays |
| Coarse sands | Medium sandy loams | Sandy clays |
| Medium sands | Fine sandy loams | Clays |
| Fine sands | Very fine sandy loams | Heavy clays |
| Very fine sands | Silt loams | |
| | Silty clay loams | |
| | Clay loams | |

**Sandy Soils.** A **sandy soil** is loose and single-grained. The individual grains can be seen and felt readily. If squeezed in the hand when dry it will fall apart when the pressure is released. When moist a sandy soil can be formed into a ball, but it will crumble readily when touched. Soils classed as sandy contain less than 15% of silt and clay. The different classes of sandy soils are separated on the basis of the proportion of the various sand separates making up the soil. **Coarse sands** contain 35% or more of fine gravel and coarse sand, and less than 50% of fine sand or very fine sand. **Medium sands** contain 35% or more of fine gravel, coarse and medium sand, and less than 50% of fine or very fine sand. **Fine sands** contain 50% or more of fine and very fine sand, while **very fine sands** contain 50% or more of very fine sand. Sandy soils are known as "early soils" because they dry out early in the spring and warm up earlier than other soils. They are naturally infertile soils since they are leached readily. They are considered valuable for very early crops which do not require a long season. The sands are not retentive of moisture, and are not, therefore, suitable for long-season crops, or those that are grown during the drier part of the season, unless they are irrigated. The moisture-holding capacity of sands can be increased by the addition of organic matter in the form of manure and soil-improving crops. *See* Manure and Green Manuring.

**Sandy Loams.** A **sandy-loam soil** is one that contains much sand, but which has enough silt and clay to make it hold together somewhat. The individual grains of sand can be seen and felt. If sandy loam is squeezed when moist it will form a cast that will bear careful handling without breaking. These soils contain from 20 to 50% of silt and clay. The four classes of sandy loams are separated on the basis of the percentage of the various separates as follows: **Coarse sandy loams** 45% or more of fine gravel and coarse sand; **medium sandy loams** 25% or more of fine gravel, coarse sand and medium sand, and less than 35% of very fine sands; **fine sandy loams** 50% or more of fine sand, or less than 25% of fine gravel, coarse and medium sand; **very fine sandy loams** 35% or more of very fine sand.

Sandy loams are more retentive of moisture and of nutrients than are the sands and are considered better for general garden purposes. They are not as early* as are the sands, but are earlier than the silts, silt loams, clays and clay loams. They are considered almost ideal soils where earliness is of prime consideration. Both the sands and sandy loams may be worked soon after rains or after irrigation and this is a great advantage in early preparation of the soil and in keeping weeds under control by cultivation.

**Loam Soils.** A **loam** is a soil having a relatively even mixture of the different grades of sand and of silt and clay. It is mellow, has a somewhat gritty feel and is plastic when moist. If squeezed in the hand when dry it will form a cast that will hold together when handled carefully, while a cast made of moist loam can be handled freely without breaking. Loams contain less than 20% of clay, from 30 to 50% of silt and from 30 to 50% of sand. Such soils are more retentive of moisture and nutrients than are the sands and sandy loams and are considered good for general purposes.

**Silt Loams.** Silt loams contain less than 20% of clay, 50% or more of silt and less than 50% of sand. These soils have a moderate percentage of the finer grades of sand and only a small percentage of clay, with half or more of soil made up of the size called "silt." When dry silt loam breaks up it is cloddy or lumpy, but the lumps can be readily broken down, and when pulverized it feels smooth and soft. When wet it runs together, and when either dry or wet it will form a cast when squeezed.

**Clay Loams.** This group contains from 20 to 30% of clay. A soil in this group that contains less than 30% silt and from 50 to 80% sand is called a **sandy clay loam;** one with from 20 to 50% silt and from 20 to 50% sand is known as **clay loam,** while one containing from 50 to 80% of silt and less than 30% sand is known as **silty clay loam.** A clay loam is fine-textured and usually breaks up into clods and lumps that are hard when dry. The moist soil is plastic and will form a cast that will stand much handling without breaking. When the moist soil is pressed between the thumb and fingers it will form a thin ribbon which will break readily. Clay loams are more retentive of moisture than the soils of coarser texture, but they are difficult to prepare and are not as good for early crops. The physical condition is improved by freezing and thawing, by the addition of organic matter and to some extent by liming. *See* Lime.

**Clays.** These contain 30% or more of clay. **Sandy-clay soils** contain from 30 to 50% of clay, less than 20% silt, and from 50 to 70% sand; **clay soils** contain 30% or more of clay, less than 50% silt, and less than 50% sand; **silty clay soil** contains from 30 to 50% of clay, from 50 to 70% silt, and less than 20% sand. A clay soil is fine-textured

---

* Special articles on the subjects indicated by an asterisk (*) will be found at the words so marked.

and usually forms hard lumps when dry. It is plastic and sticky when wet. When the wet soil is pinched between the thumb and fingers it will form a long, flexible ribbon. In general, heavy clays are not well suited to gardening, but they can be improved as mentioned for clay loams. Clay and clay loams both puddle badly if plowed, harrowed or cultivated when wet. Well-drained clay and clay loams are very productive when properly managed.

### Rich versus Poor Soil

In general, a **rich** or **fertile** soil is one that contains an abundance of organic matter. The organic matter is the most active portion of the soil. Through the action of bacteria and fungi the tissues of the organic matter are broken down to humus, and, in this process, organic acids are set free, which act on the mineral portion of the soil. Thus a soil well supplied with organic matter is likely to be richer in available nutrients than are similar soils low in organic matter.

A **poor** or **infertile** soil is one that is deficient in organic matter and in available nutrients. If a soil is well supplied with organic matter it is not likely to be deficient in available nutrients. Coarse-textured soils deficient in organic matter are low in water-holding capacity and for this reason are unproductive unless irrigated, even though nutrients are supplied in abundance. A soil may be well supplied with organic matter and with the common mineral elements and yet be unproductive. Lack of drainage, consequently lack of aeration; an excess of compounds that are toxic to plants; or lack of some minor element, such as iron, zinc, copper or manganese, may render a soil unproductive when it is well supplied with organic matter and the common nutrients. A soil may be unproductive for certain crops when it contains parasitic organisms that attack those crops. Many areas, infested with nematodes that cause root-knot, for example, are unproductive as far as the crops seriously attacked are concerned. Soils so affected are sometimes called "sick soils," but the term may be applied to soils that are unproductive because of the presence of substances that are toxic to plants. *See also* Manure, Fertilizers. — H. C. T.

**SOIL SPONGE.** A trademarked variety of acid peat from Michigan, useful for acid-tolerant plants.

**SOIL STERILIZATION.** In certain greenhouse soils or potting mixtures, and sometimes in the soil for hotbeds or cold frames, it is necessary to sterilize the soil, because of the danger of eggs or spores* which may breed disease or insect pests. When sterilization is necessary, the best method is to force steam into the soil.

If steam is not available, small quantities of soil can be baked in an oven for two hours at 160°–180°. If an oven is also unavailable, a good wood fire under a sheet of tin will answer. Simply pile a layer of soil about 4 in. thick and start the fire. Stir the soil occasionally and do not let it burn. All that is needed is enough heat to kill insect eggs or spores,* not enough to burn out any of the humus in the soil.

**SOIL TESTING.** For acid and alkali tests *see* Acid and Alkali Soils. For testing for fertility *see* Fertility.

**SOIL TEXTURE.** *See* Soils.

**SOIL WASHING.** *See* Erosion.

**SOJA MAX** = *Glycine max*. *See* Soybean.

**SOLANACEAE** (so-la-nay'see-ee). The potato family, often called the tobacco or tomato family, is easily one of the leading hort. groups of plants, for it includes vegetables of world-wide cultivation, narcotics, drugs, tobacco and a large number of garden flowers. There are over 75 genera and perhaps 2000 species, most abundant in the tropics, but common, also, in temperate regions.

Vegetables dominate the leading cult. genera. *Solanum* includes the potato and the eggplant, as well as many tropical shrubs and trees. For *Lycopersicum see* Tomato. The common garden peppers (both green and red) are found in *Capsicum*.

Tobacco (*see* Nicotiana) comes second in importance among the cult. genera (some decorative), followed by *Atropa*, which yields belladonna.

The genera cultivated mostly for ornament are readily divided into the tropical sorts needing greenhouse protection and the genera that are hardy outdoors over most of the country.

The leading tropical genera cult. for ornament are: *Brunfelsia, Cestrum, Cyphomandra, Fabiana, Grabowskia, Iochroma, Schizanthus* (also for outdoor cult.), *Solanum* (many species), *Solandra*, and *Streptosolen*. Many of these are grown outdoors in the South or in Calif.

There are, also, several important genera of garden plants, all perennials or tender annuals, and some very widely grown for ornament. They are *Browallia, Nicandra, Nierembergia, Petunia, Physalis, Quincula*, and *Salpiglossis*. The only other genera of garden interest are *Lycium* (shrubs), *Datura* (tropical trees and weeds), *Mandragora* (the true mandrake) and *Salpichroa* (a vine from the Argentine). Many of the plants contain poisonous alkaloids, some deadly. *See* Hyoscyamus.

Leaves alternate.* Flowers regular,* or rarely irregular,* solitary in a few, but mostly in various sorts of clusters, showy in some genera, especially in *Datura, Nicotiana* and *Petunia*. Fruit a dry pod (capsule*) or a berry, sometimes surrounded by a brightly colored, persistent and bladdery calyx (*see* Physalis).

Technical flower characters: Flowers hermaphrodite.* Calyx 5-lobed, sometimes persistent. Corolla usually with a short tube, but expanded upward into a flattish, wheel-shaped flower. Stamens* 5, alternate with the corolla lobes, often connected by the anthers. Ovary superior,* usually 2-celled, with many ovules.

**SOLANDRA** (so-lan'dra). Tropical American, woody, climbing plants, comprising about 4 species of the potato family. Leaves alternate,* ovalish and leathery. Flowers large, solitary, greenish-white or yellow. Calyx tubular, 5-lobed. Corolla funnel-shaped, its limb 5-lobed. Stamens* 5. Fruit a 2-celled berry. (Named for Daniel C. Solander, Swedish naturalist.)

Not much in cultivation, but can be grown in the greenhouse where the temperature does not drop below 50°, or outdoors in zones* 8 and 9. Propagated by cuttings, inserted in a mixture of sand and peat and then grown in potting mixture* 3. As these plants are winter-flowering they require plenty of water from Oct.–April, but should not be given much water during the summer, to ensure the wood being well ripened.

**grandiflora.** Climbing to 30 ft. high. Leaves simple, alternate,* ovalish, to 5 in. long, thick and bright green. Flowers solitary, fragrant, yellowish-white. Calyx 2–3 in. long. Corolla 6–7 in. long. W.I. Popular in Calif. for outdoor cult.

**guttata.** Chalice vine. Of shrubby habit, more or less climbing, growing to 20 ft. high, and covered with short downy hairs. Leaves ovalish, to 6 in. long, hairy on the under side. Flowers fragrant, solitary, white, turning yellow with age, marked purple, to 9 in. long. Mex.

*SOLANINA, -us, -um* (so-la-ny'na). Potato-like.

**SOLANUM** (so-lay'num). A huge genus of herbs, shrubs, vines, and sometimes trees, typifying the family Solanaceae, comprising over 1200 species, and of nearly world-wide distribution, but overwhelmingly tropical. Some of them are of outstanding garden importance, for the genus includes the potato and eggplant; others are decorative plants for the greenhouse or outdoor culture in the South; some are pernicious weeds; and the juice of the wilted leaves of some species is deadly. The common name of the whole genus is nightshade, but several of those below are scarcely ever so called.

Leaves alternate,* the juice of the wilted leaves deadly in some species, suspect in most others. Flowers often borne in the leaf-axils* or near them, often solitary or in few-flowered clusters. Calyx* united. Corolla regular, shallowly bell-shaped or wheel-shaped (rotate), the 5 stamens* usually inserted on its throat. Fruit a berry, edible in some species, deadly poisonous in others. (*Solanum* is thought to be from the Latin for quieting, perhaps in allu-

---

* Special articles on the subjects indicated by an asterisk (*) will be found at the words so marked.

sion to the dangerously narcotic properties of some species.)
  The genus is so variable that it is impossible to give general cultural directions. For the culture of the two most important garden crops *see* POTATO and EGGPLANT. The cult. of the others is noted at each species. Over 40 kinds are in cult. in the U.S., but the following are most likely to be met.
  **auriculatum.** A beautiful, velvety, unarmed shrub, 12-18 ft. high. Leaves ovalish or oblong, 5-8 in. long, without marginal teeth, often bearing smaller, roundish leaves in the axils.* Flowers bluish-white or violet, about ½ in. wide, mostly in small clusters (corymbs*). Fruit about ¾ in. thick. Tropical As. and Am. Suited only to zones* 8 (with protection) and 9. A very handsome shrub.
  **capsicastrum.** False Jerusalem cherry. An unarmed shrub, not over 2 ft. high, and generally resembling the true Jerusalem cherry (*S. pseudo-capsicum*), but with grayish foliage and less persistent fruit. Brazil. Its culture is the same as for *S. pseudo-capsicum*.
  **carolinense.** Horse nettle. A perennial and pernicious weedy herb, both the leaves and stem armed with yellow, straight prickles. Flowers violet. Berries orange-yellow. Eastern N.A., and west to Tex. A troublesome weed. *See* Horse nettle in the list at WEEDS.
  **dulcamara.** The traditional bittersweet (for the plant so called in America *see* CELASTRUS); also called withywind and climbing nightshade. A scrambling, vine-like herb, often climbing up to 8 ft. high, more often prostrate or nearly so. Leaves 2-4 in. long, ovalish-oblong, but sometimes lobed at the base. Flowers in loose clusters, the corolla violet, but green-spotted, about ½ in. wide. Fruit scarlet, about ½ in. thick. Eurasia, but commonly naturalized in N.A. Scarcely cult., but all should be warned against its dangerously poisonous berries and the juice of its wilted leaves.
  **integrifolium.** Scarlet or tomato eggplant (not the true eggplant). A hairy and prickly annual herb, 2-3 ft. high, grown for its ornamental fruit. Leaves oblong-ovalish, shallowly lobed, 6-8 in. long. Flowers about ¾ in. wide, white, in sparse clusters. Fruit furrowed, nearly round, scarlet or yellow, about 2 in. thick. Af. It should be grown as a tender annual. *See* ANNUALS.
  **jasminoides.** Potato vine (not the true potato). A very handsome, tender, woody vine, 8-10 ft. long, smooth and without prickles. Leaves ovalish or narrower, 2-3 in. long, simple,* or the lower ones with a tendency to be compound.* Flowers showy, about 1 in. wide, white, but blue-tinged, star-like, in handsome, branched clusters. Brazil. Hardy only in comparatively frost-free regions, but a popular ornamental in Fla. and Calif.

*Solanum jasminoides*

  **lycopersicum** = *Lycopersicum esculentum*. *See* TOMATO.
  **melongena.** A hairy, perennial herb or under-shrub from tropical Africa and Asia, scarcely known in cult. except for the *var. esculentum*, the eggplant, which is grown as an annual in the U.S. It is a stout herb 2-4 ft. high, the angled or lobed leaves 10-15 in. long. Flowers violet-purple, nearly 2 in. wide, usually nodding. Fruit a large berry, usually dark purple and shining, but sometimes white, yellow or striped, 6-10 in. long. For cult. *see* EGGPLANT. There is a dwarf variety with smooth leaves and smaller fruit. The *var. serpentinum*, the snake eggplant, has nearly cylindrical fruit about 1 in. thick and a foot long, coiled or curved at the tip.
  **muricatum.** Pepino. Melon pear. Melon shrub. A little-known perennial herb or under-shrub, 2-3 ft. high, grown in warm regions for its edible fruit. Foliage spiny. Leaves oblongish or narrower, 4-6 in. long, the margins sometimes wavy. Flowers about ¾ in. wide, bright blue. Fruit egg-shaped, 4-6 in. long, yellow, but marked with purple. Peru.
  **nigrum.** Black or deadly nightshade. A weedy, very variable annual herb, found in some of its forms throughout the temperate and tropical zones, 1-2 ft. high, its foliage clammy. Leaves ovalish-lance-shaped, 3-5 in. long, often somewhat angled. Flowers about ½ in. wide, white, mostly in sparse, drooping clusters. Fruit black (in the wild form), about ¼ in. thick. The juice of the wilted leaves is dangerously poisonous. The fruit, in some improved garden forms, known as garden huckleberry, sunberry, and wonderberry, is used locally for making pies. The fruit is poisonous in some wild forms. The plant is easily grown, as an annual, in any garden soil.
  **pseudo-capsicum.** Jerusalem cherry. A popular greenhouse pot plant, much grown by florists for its persistent, scarlet or yellow fruits, which are globe-shaped and about ½ in. in diameter. It is an unarmed shrub, 2-4 ft. high, with oblongish, wavy-margined leaves 3-4 in. long, and shining green, at least above. Flowers about ½ in. wide, white. Old World. Both this and *S. capsicastrum* should be grown in potting mixture* 4 in the warm-temperate greenhouse, and may be propagated by seeds or cuttings.

*Solanum pseudo-capsicum*

  **seaforthianum.** A smooth, unarmed, woody vine, 8-10 ft. long. Leaves generally compound,* nearly 7 in. long, the leaflets of unequal size. Flowers about 1 in. wide, star-like, blue or purple, in small clusters (cymes*). Fruit pea-size, scarlet. Tropical America, and hardy only in zone* 9, or possibly protected parts of zone* 8.
  **tuberosum.** Potato; also called white or Irish potato. A weak, unarmed, but sticky herb with edible tubers. Leaves compound,* the leaflets of irregular size. Flowers about 1 in. wide, white, lavender or pinkish-lavender. Fruit globe-shaped, about ¾ in. thick, yellowish or green, often not produced in the cult. varieties. Originally a native of the high Andes of old Peru (modern Ecuador, Peru, and Bolivia), in a region "where it freezes a little every month of the year," according to the first chronicler of the potato, Pedro de Cieza de Leon (1538). For culture and varieties *see* POTATO.
  **wendlandi.** Costa Rica nightshade; also called paradise-flower. A climbing, prickly shrub, but not hairy. Leaves compound,* the terminal leaflet larger than the others, or sometimes the upper leaves simple.* Flowers showy, about 2 in. wide, lilac-blue, in handsome, branched clusters. Costa Rica. Hardy only in zone* 9, and possibly in protected parts of zone* 8, and a popular ornamental in Fla.

**SOLDANELLA** (sol-da-nell'a). Low-growing, hardy, perennial herbs, comprising 6 species of the family Primulaceae, natives of the mountains of Eu. They have short rootstocks, and basal, long-stalked leaves, roundish and with a heart-shaped base. Flowering stalk slender, 6-15 in. high. Flowers solitary or in umbels,* blue, violet or rose, to ¾ in. across. Calyx of 5 sepals. Corolla tubular, opening salverwise. Stamens 5.* Fruit a 5-celled capsule.* (*Soldanella* is from the Latin for a small coin, in reference to the shape of the leaves.)
  Soldanellas are seldom seen in American gardens as they are difficult to establish. They are suitable for the rock garden or border. Propagated by seeds or division of roots.

---

* Special articles on the subjects indicated by an asterisk (*) will be found at the words so marked.

Seeds should be sown in March or April in pans, 1/16 in. deep, in a mixture of sandy loam and peat. Pans should be placed in the cold frame and shaded from the sun. As soon as plants are large enough to handle they should be pricked-off into cold frame and still shaded from the sun. When large enough plant in permanent positions in damp, shady places, using same mixture of soil throughout.

**alpina.** Grows to 6 in. high. Leaves roundish, to 1½ in. across. Flowers pale blue, in 1–3-flowered umbels.* Blooms in early spring. Most suited to the rock garden (which see).

**SOLDANELLOIDES** (sol-dan-nel-loy'deez, but *see* OÏDES). Like a plant of the genus *Soldanella* (which see).

**SOLDIER'S-PLUME** = *Habenaria psycodes*.

**SOLIDAGO.** See GOLDENROD.

**SOLID BULB.** A corm.*

**SOLITARY.** Borne singly, but not necessarily alone. Many flowers and fruits are described as being solitary, *i.e.* one to a single main stalk, and thus not part of a cluster. But such solitary flowers may be borne on a shrub or tree in great profusion, as in the sloe (*see* PRUNUS SPINOSA).

**SOLLYA** (soll'ya). Australian evergreen twining shrubs, comprising about 3 species of the family Pittosporaceae. Leaves alternate.* Flowers blue, nodding, in loose, terminal, few-flowered clusters. Calyx of 5 sepals. Corolla spreading, of 5 petals. Stamens* 5. Fruit a 2-celled capsule. (Named for Richard Horsman Solly, English naturalist.)

Sollyas are not much in cultivation, but are sometimes grown in the greenhouse or outdoors in the South. Seeds should be sown ⅛ in. deep, in light, sandy soil, in the cool greenhouse, in early spring. Cuttings of young shoots may be taken in March or April and inserted in sand in a temperature of 65°–75°. Both seedlings and cuttings when rooted should be potted into potting mixture* 1, and later into No. 3.

**heterophylla.** Australian bluebell creeper. Grows to 6 ft. high or more, with slender, twining stems. Leaves narrowly lance-shaped, to 2 in. long, light green on the under side. Flowers blue, about ½ in. long, in terminal clusters. Western Aust. Grown extensively in Calif.

**SOLOMON'S LILY** = *Arum palaestinum*.

**SOLOMON'S-SEAL.** Generally hardy, herbaceous perennials, often growing in moist places, and constituting the genus **Polygonatum** (po-lig-o-nay'tum) of the lily family. There are about 60 species distributed throughout the northern hemisphere. Rootstocks thick and branching, about 2 in. below the surface of the soil, and from them the aerial stems are produced each spring, and dying down in the fall. Stems erect at first, then slightly bending. Leaves on the upper part of the stem only, in 2 rows, alternate,* simple, broadly lance-shaped or ovalish, parallel-veined. Flowers white or greenish-white, in hanging, 1–many-flowered clusters growing from the axils* of the leaves. Flower tubular, 6-lobed. Stamens* 6. Fruit a 3-celled berry. (*Polygonatum* is from the Greek for many knees, in allusion to the many joints of the rootstocks.) Sometimes known as *Salomonia*.

These plants are useful in the damp or half-shady places in the garden. Easily cultivated in ordinary garden soil. Propagated by division of rootstocks in Oct., March or April. Rootstocks should be planted about 2 in. below the surface of the soil. The species *P. multiflorum* is sometimes grown as a pot plant in the cool greenhouse for early spring flowering. For false Solomon's-seal see SMILACINA. In New England Solomon's-seal is sometimes applied to *Maianthemum canadense*.

**P. biflorum.** Grows to 3 ft. high. Leaves broadly lance-shaped, to 4 in. long, slightly hairy on the under side. Flowers greenish-white, ½ in. long, in 1–4-flowered umbels.* Eastern N.A. May.

**P. commutatum.** Strong-growing, to 8 ft. high. Leaves ovalish, to 6 in. long, bright green. Flowers ¾ in. long, in 1–8-flowered umbels. N.A. June.

**P. multiflorum.** Grows to 3 ft. high. Leaves broadly lance-shaped, bright green. Flowers greenish-white, ¾ in. long, in 2–8-flowered umbels.* Eurasia.

**SOLOMON'S-SEAL FAMILY.** See LILIACEAE.

**SOMEI-YOSHINO-SAKURA.** See Japanese Flowering Cherries at PRUNUS.

*SOMNIFERA, -us, -um* (som-niff'er-a). Causing sleep.

**SONCHUS OLERACEUS** = Sow thistle, which see in the list at WEEDS.

**SONERILA** (sohn-er-rill'a). Tender, perennial herbs, or small shrubs, comprising about 75 species of the family Melastomaceae, natives of India and the Malay Archipelago. Leaves opposite,* generally ovalish, with purplish veins, variously spotted on the upper side, often scarlet or purplish on the under side. Flowers usually rose, sometimes purple, in spikes or racemes.* Calyx of 3 sepals. Corolla of 3 petals. Stamens 3. Fruit a 3-celled capsule. (*Sonerila* is a Latinized version of a native name for some species in India.)

Sonerilas are not of garden interest except as greenhouse plants, where they are grown for their ornamental foliage. Difficult of cultivation, as they require a temperature not below 75°, shade, and atmospheric moisture. Plants do not like water on their leaves. Propagated by seeds and cuttings. Seeds may be sown and cuttings taken from Jan.–May. Soil should be composed of equal parts of fibrous peat, sphagnum moss, charcoal and sand. Good drainage essential.

**margaritacea.** Grows to 12 in. high. Leaves broadly lance-shaped, with pearl-white spots in rows on upper side. Under side purplish. Flowers rose. Java. Summer.

*SONGARICA, -us, -um* (son-gar'i-ka). From Songchin, Korea.

**SOOT.** This smutty, black nuisance in most large cities is detrimental to the growth of plants and is one of the greatest hazards of city gardens. See SMOKE.

Much old, and chiefly English, garden literature abounds with references to the value of soot as a fertilizer, and soot still has its adherents today, even in America. Its older advocates were perhaps justified, for it does contain small quantities of plant nutrients, which were worth considering in the days when standard fertilizer mixtures were unavailable. At the present time soot has no place in the garden.

A possible exception is Scotch soot, a kind derived from the burning of peat. As peat fuel is little known in the U.S., Scotch soot is scarce, unless imported in bags. In any case, it is really a form of wood ashes, and not so high in potash as the latter. See ASH AND ASHES.

**SOOT DEW.** An unimportant disease of plants caused by a fungus, which covers the leaves with a black, smutty coating.

**SOOTY-BLOTCH.** See Diseases at ORANGE and APPLE.

**SOPHORA** (so-for'ra). Handsome, profusely flowering shrubs or trees of the pea family, most of the 20 known species Asiatic, but a few in N.A. Leaves compound,* the leaflets arranged feather-fashion, with an odd one at the tip. Flowers pea-like, usually in showy clusters (panicles* or racemes*). Fruit a stalked pod (legume*) constricted between the seeds, splitting very slowly if at all. (*Sophora* is the Latin version of an Arabian vernacular for a tree with pea-like leaves.)

They do well on a variety of soils and can be propagated by greenwood cuttings or by layering. Seeds germinate very slowly.

**davidi** = *Sophora viciifolia*.

**japonica.** Pagoda tree; also called Japanese pagoda tree and Chinese scholar tree. A spreading, round-headed tree, 40–60 ft. high, sometimes more. Leaflets 7–17, stalked, ovalish or narrower, 1–2 in. long. Flowers about ½ in. long, yellowish-white, the clusters (panicles*) loose, 12–15 in. long, very showy. Pods 2–3 in. long. China and Korea. July–Sept. Hardy from zone* 3 southward. The *var.* **pendula** is a very picturesque form with drooping branches.

**secundiflora.** Mescal bean. An evergreen shrub or small tree, the shining leaflets 1½–2½ in. long. Flowers fragrant, about 1 in. long, violet-blue, the terminal cluster (raceme*) nearly 4 in. long. Pod 6–8 in. long. Tex. and N. Mex. to northern Mex. Not hardy north of zone* 7.

**viciifolia.** A shrub 6–8 ft. high. Leaflets 13–19, elliptic, nearly ½ in. long, slightly notched at the tip. Flowers about ⅝ in. long, bluish-violet or paler, in clusters (racemes*) with 8–12 flowers. Pods 1½–2 in. long. China. June. Hardy from zone* 3 southward. Useful for dry, sandy places. Sometimes offered as *S. davidi*.

---

* Special articles on the subjects indicated by an asterisk (*) will be found at the words so marked.

**SOPHROCATLAELIA.** A trigeneric* hybrid derived from crossing the orchid genera *Sophronitis, Cattleya,* and *Laelia,* and known only to orchid specialists.

**SOPHRONITIS** (so-fro-ny'tis). Tender Brazilian orchids, comprising about 6 species. They are small plants growing on the branches of trees or pieces of wood, with thick, fleshy rootstocks and small, bulb-like stems, at the top of which grow 1-2 narrow leaves. Flowers showy, rosy-red with yellow, scarlet or violet markings, solitary or in short terminal racemes.* Sepals and petals similar to each other except 1, which forms the lip* which has 1 center wide lobe, and 2 smaller erect side lobes. (*Sophronitis* is from the Greek for modest, in allusion to the pretty flowers.)

Grown in the greenhouse in a moist atmosphere, in shade, preferably in shallow pans with good drainage, osmunda* fiber and charcoal. Keep a winter temperature of 55°-65° and a summer temperature of 65°-80°. They require little water during winter months. See ORCHID.

**coccinea.** Leaves narrow, to 3 in. long. Flowers solitary, bright scarlet, to 4 in. across, lip marked yellow at the base.
**grandiflora** = *Sophronitis coccinea.*

**SORBARIA** (sor-bair'i-a). False spirea. Tender or hardy, Asiatic deciduous shrubs, similar to *Spiraea,* comprising about 8 species, and belonging to the rose family. Leaves alternate,* compound,* the leaflets in odd numbers, lance-shaped with toothed margins. Flowers white, small, numerous, in large, branching clusters. Calyx* of 5 sepals. Corolla of 5 petals. Stamens* many. Pistils 5, joined at the base. (*Sorbaria* is derived from *Sorbus,* in allusion to the resemblance of the leaves.)

These plants are grown for their clusters of white flowers. Useful for the shrubbery or wild garden. They should not be associated with choice low-growing shrubs, as they spread rapidly. Easily propagated by seeds, hardwood or root cuttings. They are sometimes known as *Schizonotus.*

**aitchisoni.** Also known as *Spiraea aitchisoni.* Strong-growing, to 10 ft. high. Stems not much branched. Leaves large, leaflets 15-21, lance-shaped, bright green. Flowers white, in branching erect clusters, to 10 in. long. Western As. July-Aug. Hardy from zone* 4 southward.
**arborea.** Grows to 18 ft. Leaflets 13-17, lance-shaped, to ½ in. wide, hairy on the under side. Flowers white, in loose branching clusters, to 1 ft. long. China. The *var.* **glabrata** has bright, shining green leaflets. July-Aug. Hardy from zone* 4 southward.
**sorbifolia.** Also known as *Spiraea sorbifolia.* Hardy shrub, to 6 ft. high. Leaflets 13-21, lance-shaped, sometimes hairy on the under side. Flowers white, in dense, erect, branching clusters. Northern As. June-July. Hardy from zone* 1 southward.

**SORBARONIA.** A bigeneric* hybrid derived from crossing plants of the genera *Sorbus* and *Aronia.* Two such crosses are known, but they are of little garden interest.

**SORBOPYRUS.** A bigeneric* hybrid derived from crossing plants of the genera *Sorbus* and *Pyrus.* They are not much grown in the U.S., but one such cross has long been cult. in Eu.

**SORBEX.** A trademarked, pulverized peat moss useful to increase the humus content of potting soils.

*SORBIFOLIA, -us, -um* (sor-bi-fō'li-a). With leaves like mountain-ash (*Sorbus*).

**SORBUS.** See MOUNTAIN-ASH.

**SORGHO** = *Holcus sorghum saccharatus.*

**SORGHUM** (*Holcus sorghum* and varieties; see HOLCUS). The sorghums are very stout, corn-like grasses, of more commercial than hort. interest. Their culture is mostly a large-scale agricultural operation, although their plumy tassels are handsome.

From a practical standpoint the varieties listed at *Holcus* may be divided into three groups: (1) Those grown for the sweet juice, and often generally called sugar sorghums or sorgho. They yield a widely marketed, honey-like syrup; (2) the broom corns, grown commercially for the bristle-like branches of the inflorescence, used in the making of whisk brooms; and (3) forage grasses of which the best-known is Johnson grass, sometimes a pernicious weed.

All the sorghums should be grown in regions of long, hot summers, preferably south of zone* 4, although some varieties will fruit north of this. They should be grown like field corn, but the rows should be 6-8 ft. apart, as several varieties are as tall as sugar cane (8-15 ft.).

They thrive on the sandy soils of the coastal plain region of southeastern U.S., but will also grow in the richer loams of ordinary garden soil. Like corn they need cultivating to keep down weeds, but as they do not usually produce prop roots it is not necessary to hill up around them as in corn.

INSECT PESTS. The small gray chinch bug and its reddish nymphs injure corn and sorghum in the Corn Belt and a little farther west. Winter burning of wild bunch grasses and clean-up of Sudan grass stubble will kill many. A creosote barrier will stop nymphs in their migration from ripening wheat to corn and sorghum. The sorghum midge occurs in the Southwest; its little larvae feed on developing grains. It may be checked by crop rotation, by keeping down Johnson grass, and by roguing* or destroying heads of early-flowering sorghum plants.

DISEASES. Among the more serious diseases of sorghum are rusts, smut, and fungous and bacterial leafspots. Long rotations, destruction of diseased refuse, choosing suitable types of soil for the crop, selecting seed from a healthy crop, and dusting it with some fungicide, as copper-carbonate (3 ounces for each bushel), are recommended control measures.

**SORREL.** See RUMEX. For Jamaica sorrel see HIBISCUS SABDARIFFA. For wood sorrel see OXALIS.

**SORREL-TREE** = *Oxydendrum arboreum.*

**SORUS** (plural *sori*). The collection of spore cases under or in which are the spores* of ferns. The sori usually occur on the under side of fern fronds, and resemble small fruiting bodies, hence sometimes called (incorrectly) fruit dots. For the reproduction of ferns see FERNS AND FERN GARDENING.

**SOTOL.** See DASYLIRION.

**SOUR CHERRY** = *Prunus cerasus.* For culture see CHERRY.

**SOUR GUM.** In the North, *Nyssa sylvatica;* in the South, *N. aquatica.* See NYSSA.

**SOUR ORANGE** = *Citrus aurantium.* For culture see ORANGE.

**SOURSOP** = *Annona muricata.*

**SOURWOOD** = *Oxydendrum arboreum.*

**SOUTH AFRICAN PLANTS.** Within recent years many South African plants not generally in cult. have become popular in American gardens. They fall into four main categories: (1) Succulents; (2) Bulbous plants; (3) Annual and perennial herbs; and (4) Shrubs and trees. See the various genera mentioned below for special cultural directions or notes on related species. Not all of them can be grown outdoors in the North.

(1) SUCCULENTS. The desert regions of South Africa offer even a wider choice of succulents than is found among the cacti, an American group of plants unknown in South Africa. Among the leading Cape succulents are plants of the genus *Euphorbia,* some of which greatly resemble our tree-like cacti.

Other succulent plants, mostly belonging to the lily, milkweed, or orpine family, will be found at the following genera:

| | |
|---|---|
| Cotyledon | Aloe |
| Crassula | Haworthia |
| Rochea | Gasteria |
| Portulacaria | Senecio |
| Schizobasopsis | Stapelia |
| Mesembryanthemum | Huerniopsis |

Also from South Africa comes the plant commonly called asparagus fern (see ASPARAGUS), which although not a succulent, has its leaf area reduced in response to semi-desert conditions. See also SUCCULENTS.

(2) BULBOUS PLANTS. Scarcely any region in the world has yielded so many valuable garden bulbs as South Africa. Among the most valuable are *Gladiolus* and many relatives of it in the iris and lily families. The following genera are

---

* Special articles on the subjects indicated by an asterisk (*) will be found at the words so marked.

either exclusively South African or contain species from that country:

| | |
|---|---|
| Lachenalia | Watsonia |
| Crinum | Clivia |
| Brunsvigia | Gloriosa |
| Moraea | Haemanthus |
| Sparaxis | Antholyza |
| Acidanthera | Dierama |
| Lapeyrousia | Schizostylis |

Very different from any of these is the beautiful *Zantedeschia rehmanni*, which is closely related to the common calla lily of the florists' shops. For this and related species *see* CALLA LILY.

(3) ANNUALS AND PERENNIALS. While many American gardeners will not care to go to the trouble of raising South African succulents, and some may not care to grow many of the bulbous plants, anyone can grow the annuals or perennials, not a few of which will bloom from seed the first year.

While most South African annuals ought to be tender and thus need to be started under glass some weeks before they can be put outdoors, many of them may be sown where wanted.

All the genera below are noted in the body of the DICTIONARY, and whether they are to be treated as tender or hardy annuals is noted at each entry. If you don't know the difference in the culture of hardy and tender sorts *see* ANNUALS.

The following genera contain some of the most beautiful South African wild flowers and are to be had as seeds from many dealers. Some are a little woody, and others are usually grown only in the greenhouse.

| | |
|---|---|
| Arctotis | Charieis |
| Felicia | Dimorphotheca |
| Gazania | Gerbera |
| Heliophila | Nemesia |
| Ursinia | Venidium |
| Anchusa | Streptocarpus |
| Pelargonium | Zaluzianskia |

(4) SHRUBS AND TREES Nearly all woody plants from South Africa are plants of greenhouse culture in the northern states, but are popular for outdoor culture from zone* 8 southward. The list of shrubs, trees, and vines from the Cape is far too long to cite here. Notable among the genera containing South African species grown in American gardens are:

| | |
|---|---|
| Erica | Acacia |
| Leucadendron | Phygelius |
| Tecomaria | Gardenia |
| Podalyria | Podocarpus |

Of these, by far the most important, as hort. subjects, are the South African heaths (*see* ERICA), and these are widely grown both in the greenhouse and outdoors.

**SOUTH CAROLINA.** The state lies wholly in zones* 6 and 7.

In the upper half or the Piedmont section of the state the soil is largely clay loams and in the lower half or Coastal Plain section sands and sandy loams predominate. Both types of soils vary greatly in fertility and in adaptability to various crops.

In the upper Coastal Plain an area crosses the state in a line with Hamlet, North Carolina, and Augusta, Georgia, about thirty-five miles in width, which is known as the Sandhills, and there the soil is largely coarse to fine sandy. The extreme northwestern corner of the state is mountainous, the Piedmont section is gently to steeply rolling while the Coastal Plain is gently rolling to flat.

All deciduous fruits can be grown in some part of the state and in the southeastern corner even Satsuma and round oranges as well as a few grapefruit trees are grown in home orchards.

The main fruit areas are in Spartanburg, Greenville and Laurens counties in the Piedmont section. Peaches, apples and grapes are the principal fruit grown. In the Coastal Plain Chesterfield, Richland and Saluda counties grow peaches and dewberries. Horry County grows most of the strawberries, although they can be grown throughout the state. Peaches are adapted to all parts except the lower coastal plain and certain varieties of grapes can be grown in all counties. The Muscadine grapes are largely grown in the Coastal Plain and *labrusca* and other American species in the Piedmont. Pecans are best adapted to the middle coastal plain, although they are grown throughout the state.

SOUTH CAROLINA

The zones of hardiness crossing South Carolina are those shown on the colored map at ZONE, which should be consulted for details. The dates are the average latest killing frost in spring and the first one in the fall. The figures below the dates show the average length of the growing season.

Vegetable production is largely centered in the Coastal Plain. The main crops grown are asparagus, lima and snap beans, beets, cabbage, cantaloupes, cucumbers, lettuce, peas, peppers, Irish potatoes, sweet potatoes, spinach, squash, tomatoes and watermelons. Charleston and Beaufort counties are the chief commercial areas for Irish potatoes, cabbage, string beans, tomatoes, beets, carrots, etc.; Hampton, Allendale, Bamberg and Barnwell counties, watermelons; Barnwell, Allendale, Charleston and Orangeburg counties, cucumbers; Barnwell, Saluda, Edgefield and Aiken counties, asparagus; Barnwell, Bamberg, Allendale counties, cantaloupes and cucumbers; Florence, Orangeburg and Williamsburg counties, peas.

On account of high temperatures during July and August few vegetables are grown during those months except in the extreme northwestern part. It is the usual practice to grow two crops each year of many vegetables in most of the state, while some crops, such as cabbage and lettuce, in the Coastal Plain are grown throughout the winter. The gardener throughout South Carolina can truly have a "year round" garden whether it be vegetables or flowers and flowering shrubs.

Market gardening is most developed around the cities and larger towns, Charleston. Columbia, Greenville, Spartanburg, Florence, Sumter and Anderson.

Many varieties and species of flowers, ornamental trees and shrubs are adapted to the entire state, a complete list of which would be too lengthy for this article. The following are the chief flowers and ornamental plants.

ORNAMENTAL PLANTS FOR SOUTH CAROLINA GARDENS

ANNUALS: Sweet peas, larkspur, *Cosmos, Salvia, Petunia*, marigolds, zinnias, nasturtiums, pansies, poppies.

HARDY PERENNIALS: Columbine, carnation, Sweet William, bleeding-heart, foxglove, blanket-flower, sunflower, phlox,

---

* Special articles on the subjects indicated by an asterisk (*) will be found at the words so marked.

snapdragons (biennial), dahlias (all types), peonies (all standard sorts), roses (all standard sorts), chrysanthemums (all standard sorts).

BULBS: Tulips (all types), hyacinths (standard sorts), narcissus (daffodils, jonquils), iris (all standard types), hardy lilies (all standard types), crocus, snowdrops, oxalis, grape hyacinth, gladiolus.

DECIDUOUS SHRUBS: *Azalea calendulacea, Chaenomeles lagenaria, Exochorda racemosa, Forsythia suspensa, Hydrangea paniculata grandiflora, Lagerstroemia indica, Lonicera fragrantissima, Spiraea vanhouttei, Spiraea thunbergi, Weigela rosea.*

BROAD-LEAVED EVERGREENS: *Abelia grandiflora, Azalea indica, Buxus sempervirens, Camellia japonica, Elaeagnus pungens simoni, Ilex opaca, Ilex vomitoria, Ligustrum lucidum, Nandina, Photinia glabra.*

TREES: *Acer palmatum atropurpureum, Albizzia julibrissin, Cercis canadensis, Cornus florida, Cornus florida rubra, Liriodendron tulipifera, Magnolia soulangeana, Quercus alba, Quercus nigra, Quercus palustris.*

CONIFERS: *Cedrus deodara, Chamaecyparis lawsoniana, Chamaecyparis pisifera squarrosa, Cryptomeria japonica, Juniperus chinensis pfitzeriana, Juniperus sabina, Juniperus communis, Juniperus chinensis globosa, Thuja orientalis aurea nana, Thuja orientalis aurea compacta.*

Near Charleston and Summerville are found the world's famous Magnolia, Middleton Place and Cypress Gardens, and large numbers of azaleas, camellias and many other ornamental plants have been growing in these gardens for many years. Other gardens of a similar nature have been planted near various towns in the Coastal Plain in recent years.

CLIMATE

The number of growing days per year varies from 221 in the northwest corner of the state to 294 at Charleston.

| Town | Average date of last killing frost in spring | Latest known killing frost | Average date of earliest killing frost in fall | Earliest known killing frost |
|---|---|---|---|---|
| Charleston | Feb. 20 | April 2 | Dec. 11 | Nov. 8 |
| Columbia | Mar. 17 | April 17 | Nov. 18 | Oct. 30 |
| Greenville | Mar. 30 | April 21 | Nov. 6 | Oct. 10 |

The yearly rainfall for the whole state has averaged 47.74 inches for the past 48 years. The rainfall is well distributed throughout the year, although November, December, January average slightly less precipitation than the other months. Occasionally very heavy rains occur in a few hours in small areas. The average number of clear days is 175; partly cloudy days, 95; and cloudy, 95 days.

The address of the Agricultural Experiment Station which has kindly supplied this information about South Carolina is Clemson. The station is always ready to answer gardening questions.

Garden Club activities in the state comprise over 25 clubs affiliated with The Garden Club of South Carolina. For the one nearest your locality write the Garden Editor, Houghton Mifflin Company, Boston, Mass.

**SOUTH DAKOTA.** The state lies wholly in zones* 1, 2 and 3. The variation in the vegetative growth from south to north is typical of the change in latitude. The change in type of vegetation from east to west is much more marked. In the eastern border of the state the vegetation is characteristic of the northern prairie. Westward it gradually changes to one of Great Plains character. Along the western edge of the state the Rocky Mountain type of vegetation is found.

SOILS. The soils east of the Missouri River are of glacial origin and consist largely of glacial till types. West of the Missouri River the soil is of sedimentary origin and consists of several different types.

CHIEF GARDENING CENTERS. The possibilities of horticulture in South Dakota are somewhat difficult, due to cold and frequently open winters, protracted drought periods during the growing season, and the drying southwest winds. However, if suitable sites and soils are chosen, hardy kinds and varieties selected, and the plants given proper care, the home gardener should be successful in growing fruits, vegetables, flowers and ornamental plants. The commercial horticultural sections of the state are located in the southeastern and Black Hills regions. Horticultural enterprises are carried on in home gardens over the entire state.

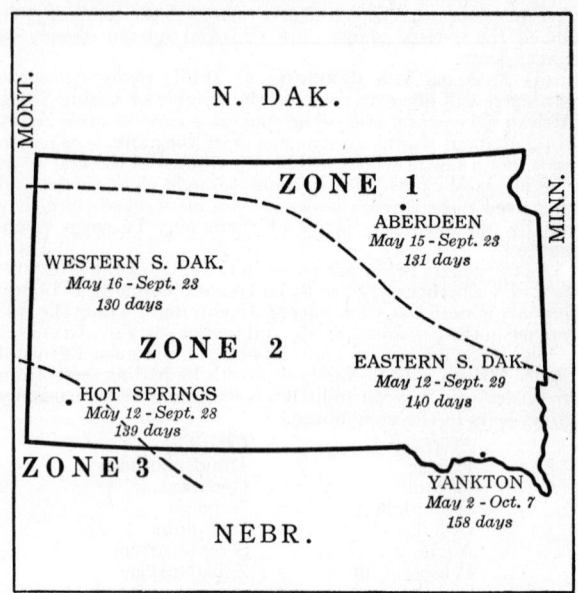

SOUTH DAKOTA

The zones of hardiness crossing South Dakota are those shown on the colored map at ZONE, which should be consulted for details. The dates are the average latest killing frost in spring and the first one in the fall. The figures below the dates show the average length of the growing season. Annual rainfall is about 20 in. per year.

MAIN FRUIT AND VEGETABLE AREAS. The principal fruit crops are the apple, plum, currant, gooseberry, and red raspberry. The principal vegetable crops are the potato, melons and other vine crops, cabbage, onion, tomato, sweet corn, pea, bean, carrot, beet, asparagus, and rhubarb.

FLOWERS, ORNAMENTAL TREES AND SHRUBS. The principal perennial flowers are the peony, iris, hollyhock, larkspur, daisy, and many others. There are over one hundred native species of shrubs, namely: *Mahonia*, hazel, currant, spirea, juneberry, chokecherry, lead-plant, prickly-ash, burning bush, shrubby cinquefoil, sumach, buffaloberry, dogwood, *Viburnum* and *Symphoricarpos* species. There are nearly as many native species of trees, namely: American elm, green ash, box-elder, basswood, bur oak, hackberry, black walnut, black cherry, canoe birch, hawthorn, honey locust, silver maple, willow, poplar, cottonwood, Black Hills spruce and pine, red cedar and juniper. There are many exotic species of trees and shrubs that are adapted to the state, namely: Colorado spruce, white fir, Austrian pine, Chinese elm, *Caragana*, Russian olive, lilac, honeysuckle, *Cotoneaster*, and barberry. There are a number of vines commonly grown in the state, namely: Virginia creeper, wild grape, clematis, bittersweet, matrimony-vine.

CLIMATE. Due to the fact that the state lies a great distance from any large bodies of water, and to its altitude, the daily, monthly, and annual ranges of temperature are variable. Killing frosts are liable to continue until about the middle of May and to occur in the autumn during the last week in September. The average length of the growing season is one hundred and thirty-five days.

* Special articles on the subjects indicated by an asterisk (*) will be found at the words so marked.

The average annual precipitation for the state is 19.98 inches. Three-fourths of this falls within the crop-growing season, April 1 to September 30. The normal amount, if properly distributed, will produce good crops. Drought sufficient to reduce crop production occurs occasionally, but a real crop failure due to drought is rare.

|  | Average date of last killing frost in spring | Latest known killing frost | Average date of earliest killing frost in fall | Earliest known killing frost |
|---|---|---|---|---|
| Yankton | May 2 | May 24 | Oct. 7 | Sept. 14 |
| Aberdeen | May 15 | June 21 | Sept. 23 | Aug. 20 |
| Hot Springs | May 12 | June 7 | Sept. 28 | Sept. 6 |
| Western S. Dak. (Av. of 42 sta.) | May 16 | June 7 | Sept. 23 | Sept. 2 |
| Eastern S. Dak. (Av. of 47 sta.) | May 12 | June 8 | Sept. 29 | Sept. 4 |

The address of the Agricultural Experiment Station which has kindly supplied this information about the state is Brookings, South Dakota. The station is always ready to answer gardening questions.

**SOUTHERN CANE** = *Arundinaria macrosperma.*

**SOUTHERN CRABAPPLE** = *Malus angustifolia.*

**SOUTHERN CURLED.** A form of leaf mustard with crisped leaves, grown for greens. See BRASSICA JUNCEA.

**SOUTHERN CYPRESS** = *Taxodium distichum.*

**SOUTHERN DEWBERRY** = *Rubus trivialis.*

**SOUTHERN SMILAX.** See SMILAX LANCEOLATA. See also SMILAX (2).

**SOUTHERN WHITE CEDAR** = *Chamaecyparis thyoides.*

**SOUTHERNWOOD** = *Artemisia abrotanum.*

**SOWBUGS.** See Insect Pests at CINERARIA and SWEET PEA.

**SOWING.** For the sowing of ordinary garden seeds, both vegetables and flowers, see SEEDS AND SEEDAGE, at which entry will also be found a description of the special methods needed for sowing some seeds. For the sowing of grass seed see LAWN.

**SOW THISTLE** = *Sonchus oleraceus.* See list at WEEDS.

**SOYBEAN.** Of over 40 species of the genus **Glycine** (gly-sy'ne) only G. **max**, the soybean, is of any hort. importance. Like the rest of the species it is a native of the Old World and is more of a farm than garden crop. It is the mainstay of the agriculture of Manchuria, in which country and in Jap. it is native. It is an erect, bushy annual, 3-6 ft. high, with alternate* compound leaves composed of 3 ovalish leaflets 3-6 in. long and without marginal teeth. Flowers pea-like but inconspicuous, white or purplish. Pods (legumes*) short-stalked, drooping, 2-3 in. long, about ½ in. wide, hairy and brownish. Seeds globe-shaped, variously colored in the many varieties now in cult. (*Glycine* is from the Greek for some plant with edible parts, but not certainly this one.) The plant was long known as *Soja max.*

### Soybean Culture

While soybeans have been grown as a food crop in China and Jap. for thousands of years, their use in the U.S. is chiefly as forage and for green manuring. It is an annual requiring a warm summer for maturity, but it will also stand considerable drought, and is thus admirably adapted to some of the prairie states and is widely grown there, sometimes under irrigation. Before planting, its seeds should be sprinkled with a culture of bacteria, sold for the purpose. See LEGUME INOCULATION. It does well on warm, well-drained soils and should be planted, after warm weather starts, in drills 3 ft. apart, the plants spaced 18-20 in. apart in the row. They need frequent cultivation until the sometimes sprawling plants shade the ground, when cultivation must stop.

The seeds of soybeans are extremely nutritious and vary in color from green through yellow and brown to black. Besides their high food value, their oil is widely used in the paint trade, in the making of linoleum and soap, and the vinegar from one variety is the basis of Worcestershire sauce. Soybean mash as prepared for industrial uses is highly inflammable.

INSECT PESTS. In the Southeast the soybean is sometimes injured by the green clover worm, the larva of a small moth. Calcium arsenate dust, about 5 pounds per acre, will control them. Blister beetles are often injurious in the South; a dust of sodium fluosilicate, 15 pounds per acre, will give control. Grasshoppers sometimes injure soybeans severely, working in from the edge of the field. Bran bait sown thinly around the border of the field early in the morning is effective. A snout beetle that lives on clover often eats seedlings of soybeans on ground recently in clover. Such ground should not be put into soybeans, unless cultivated thoroughly and planted late.

DISEASES. Soybeans, like other legumes, are affected by many diseases. Some of the more common ones are blight, wilt, bacterial pustule, bacterial blight, mildews, sclerotium blight, mosaic and leafspots. In many localities resistant strains have been developed and should be grown. Otherwise the seed should be obtained from as far north as possible where certain maladies do not occur. In addition the usual crop sanitation recommendations of rotations, and care in handling diseased refuse, should be followed.

**SPADE.** See Section 1, TOOLS AND IMPLEMENTS.

**SPADING.** See DIGGING.

**SPADING FORK.** See Section 1, TOOLS AND IMPLEMENTS.

**SPADIX.** The thick, usually fleshy and crowded spike of flowers in members of the arum family. In a few other plants. A common example is the central "Jack" (spadix) in the Jack-in-the-pulpit, surrounded by the pulpit, which is a spathe. See ARACEAE. Spathes may be of many shapes and are found in other plants than the aroids.* In some palms the spathe may be several feet long, boat-shaped, and woody.

**SPAGHETTI-PLANT.** A trade (usually hawker's) name for a small decorative gourd. See GOURDS.

**SPANISH BAYONET** = *Yucca aloifolia* and *Y. filamentosa.*

**SPANISH BLUEBELL** = *Scilla hispanica.*

**SPANISH BROOM** = *Spartium junceum* and *Genista hispanica.* For related plants see BROOM.

**SPANISH BUTTONS** = *Centaurea nigra.*

**SPANISH CEDAR** = *Cedrela odorata.*

**SPANISH CHESTNUT** = *Castanea sativa.* See CHESTNUT.

**SPANISH DAGGER** = *Yucca aloifolia* and *Y. gloriosa.*

**SPANISH GARDEN.** The type of gardening introduced into America by the Spaniards and really based upon the art of the Moors. Its outstanding characteristic is the use of the patio, and the necessity of making gardens in regions of intense heat, bright sunshine, and deficient rainfall.

Many beautiful gardens of this type are to be found in N. Mex., Ariz., Calif., Fla., and, most of all, in Latin America. See PATIO GARDENS. See also America at GARDEN BOOKS.

**SPANISH IRIS.** See IRIS.

**SPANISH JACINTH** = *Scilla hispanica.*

**SPANISH JASMINE** = *Jasminum grandiflorum.*

**SPANISH LICORICE** = *Glycyrrhiza glabra.* See LICORICE.

**SPANISH LIME** = *Melicocca bijuga.*

**SPANISH MOSS** = *Tillandsia usneoides.*

**SPANISH NEEDLE** = Beggar-ticks, which see in the list at WEEDS.

**SPANISH OYSTER PLANT** = *Scolymus hispanicus.*

---

* Special articles on the subjects indicated by an asterisk (*) will be found at the words so marked.

**SPANISH PLUM** = *Spondias purpurea.*

**SPANISH TREFOIL** = *Medicago sativa.*

**SPARAXIS** (spa-racks'is). Wand-flower. South African perennial herbs with bulbous corms, comprising about 3 species, belonging to the iris family. Spring-flowering plants, closely allied to *Ixia*. Leaves basal, narrow, sword-shaped, with parallel veins. Flowers yellow, rose, red or purple often tinged brown, in short spikes, each flower enclosed in a cut or fringed spathe.* Calyx* of 3 colored sepals. Corolla of 3 petals alternating with the sepals. Stamens* 3. Fruit a 3-celled capsule.* (*Sparaxis* is from the Greek for torn, in allusion to the torn spathe.*) For cult. see IXIA.

**grandiflora.** Leaves narrow, to 1 ft. long. Flowering stalk to 1 ft. high. Flowers yellow, or purple, 1 in. or more long, solitary or in few-flowered spikes.

**pulcherrima** = *Dierama pulcherrima.*

**tricolor.** Growing to 18 in. high, similar to *S. grandiflora*, except that flowers are variable in color, usually having 3 distinct colors, but the throat always bright yellow.

**SPARMANNIA** (spar-man'i-a). Tender African shrubs, or small trees, comprising about 5 species, of the family Tiliaceae, usually covered with erect, soft, silky hairs. Leaves alternate,* heart-shaped, toothed, or sometimes lobed. Flowers white, in numerous terminal clusters (umbels*). Calyx* of 4 sepals. Corolla of 4 petals. Stamens* many. Fruit a prickly capsule.* (Named for Andreas Sparmann, Swedish naturalist.)

Sparmannias are very attractive and showy, even after the flowering period. They can be grown outdoors in frost-free localities, and make good greenhouse pot plants for winter flowering. Propagated by cuttings. Cuttings of the tips of young shoots, taken in early spring, will flower the following winter. They should be grown in potting mixture* 3. They like plenty of light and air at all times. After flowering they may be cut back, re-potted and grown on for flowering the next year.

**africana.** Growing to 20 ft. high. Leaves to 9 in. long, heart-shaped at base, cut into 5–7 lobes, the margins toothed. Flowers white, to 1½ in. across, with prominent yellow stamens.* Fruit spiny, ½ in. across. The *var.* flore-plena has double flowers.

**SPARROWS.** See Bird Nuisances at BIRDS.

**SPARTIUM** (spar'shi-um). A single species of essentially leafless shrubs of the pea family, *S. junceum*, the Spanish or weaver's broom, often grown for its profusion of yellow bloom. It has grooved, rush-like stems, 6–8 ft. high, with alternate,* simple* leaves (when produced). Flowers fragrant, pea-like, yellow, about 1 in. long, mostly in terminal clusters (racemes*) that may be 15 in. long, hence very showy. Fruit a flattened pod (legume*), about 4 in. long and hairy. A handsome shrub in bloom, otherwise of indifferent aspect. Southern Eu. May–Sept. (or all year in Calif.). Hardy from zone* 6, possibly from zone* 5 (with protection), and southward. Much planted in Calif. on a variety of soils. Propagated by cutting or by seeds. (*Spartium* is from the ancient Greek name for the plant.) See BROOM and GENISTA for closely related plants.

**SPATHE.** A leaf-like or often colored bract* which surrounds or encloses a flower cluster. A common example is the "pulpit" which surrounds and hoods the spadix* in the Jack-in-the-pulpit. See ARACEAE. But many other plants than the aroids* bear spathes, which surround or are just below the flower clusters in most of the iris family, many palms, the banana, and in some plants of the lily and amaryllis family. Sometimes a spathe may be papery or membranous, but in many palms it is hard, woody, and boat-shaped.

**SPATHIPHYLLUM** (spath-i-fill'um). Tropical American perennial herbs, comprising about 25 species of the family Araceae, having thick rootstocks and basal leaves. Leafstalks to 2½ ft. long, sheathing at the base. Leaves large, broadly lance-shaped, thin, with strong-marked midrib. Flowers in a spadix,* enclosed in a large leafy bract (spathe*) similar to Jack-in-the-pulpit. Flowers of 2 kinds, male (stamens* only) on the upper part of the spadix, and female (pistil* only) on lower part. (*Spathiphyllum* is from the Greek leaf and spathe, in allusion to the leaf-like spathe.*) They are not much in cultivation, but sometimes grown in the warm greenhouse for their foliage. Propagated by division of the rootstocks. They should be grown in potting mixture* 4.

**floribundum.** Leafstalk to 6 in. long. Leaves lance-shaped, to 6 in. long, and 2½ in. wide, one-half of the leaf blade larger than the other, dark green on upper side, paler green on under side. Flowers greenish-yellow, enclosed in a white spathe* 2½ in. long. Colombia.

**patini.** Leafstalk to 1 ft. long. Leaves lance-shaped, to 10 in. long, and 2½ in. wide. Flowers enclosed in a whitish spathe.* Colombia.

**SPATHODEA** (spath-ō'dee-a). Tropical African, evergreen trees, comprising about 3 species, of the family Bignoniaceae, growing 20–70 ft. high. Leaves compound,* bright green. Leaflets unequal in number, sometimes only 3, the margins without teeth. Flowers scarlet, in loose terminal clusters. Calyx of 5 sepals, joined together, but splitting on one side to the base, exposing the corolla. Corolla large, bell-shaped, its limb 5-lobed. Stamens* 4, in pairs, 2 long, 2 short. Fruit a woody capsule to 8 in. long. (*Spathodea* is from the Greek for spathe*-like, in allusion to the shape of the calyx.*)

Spathodeas are only grown in sub-tropical or tropical areas, as they do not flower until they become large trees. Propagated by seeds or cuttings.

**campanulata.** Large evergreen tree, growing to 70 ft. Leaves compound, to 1½ ft. long, bright green. Leaflets 9–19, lance-shaped, to 4 in. long, slightly hairy on the under side when young. Flowers scarlet, to 4 in. long, in many-flowered, loose, terminal clusters. Calyx tough and leathery. A popular, quick-growing, very handsome tree, considerably planted in the warmer parts of Fla.

*SPATHULATA, -us, -um* (spath-you-lay'ta). Spatulate; *i.e.* spoon-shaped.

**SPATHYEMA.** See SKUNK-CABBAGE.

**SPATTERDOCK** = *Nymphozanthus advenus.*

**SPATULATE.** Spoon-shaped.

**SPAWN.** See MUSHROOM.

**SPEAR.** A young shoot; as of asparagus.

**SPEARFLOWER** = *Ardisia.*

**SPEAR LILY.** See DORYANTHES.

**SPEARMINT** = *Mentha spicata.* See MINT.

**SPECIAL COLOR GARDENS.** See COLOR GARDENING.

**SPECIES** (plural species). A group of individual plants more like each other than anything else and all belonging to a single genus.* Sometimes the genus has only one species in it, as the giant cactus is the only species in the genus *Carnegiea*, the bloodroot the only species in the genus *Sanguinaria*, the castor-oil plant the only one in *Ricinus*, and so on.

Such species are easily recognized by everyone, for they have no near relatives with which they may be confused. Genera containing only one species (usually called monotypic genera) are, however, comparatively rare. Much the most usual case is presented by genera like *Aster, Rosa, Solanum, Rhododendron,* or *Chrysanthemum.* They may contain anywhere from two to over one thousand species, and it is in such cases, by far the most numerous in this book, that the validity and usefulness of *species* is evident.

For grouped around each species (as a concept) are a lot of individual plants more like each other than like any similar group or species in that genus. To recognize and delimit this category of individuals, botanists, and perforce gardeners, have applied to each species a *specific* name.

These species names, of which there are over two thousand in this book, are all defined and pronounced at their proper alphabetic entry (*see* EGLANTERIA, CANINA, MOSCHATA for those used in *Rosa* below), unless they happen to be derived from people's names such as *grayi, wendlandiana, wilsoni*, and hence of obvious origin and meaning.

Species names are usually, but not always, supposed to indicate some feature of the particular plant. Hence *alba* for

---

* Special articles on the subjects indicated by an asterisk (*) will be found at the words so marked.

white, *rubra* for red, *canadensis* for from Canada, etc. The meaning of all such species names will be found throughout the book, as many of them have not only an interesting history but actually help to describe the plant. Some species names are misleading, however, because the person who christened a particular plant may have mistaken its origin or have been mixed up as to its true identity. The species name cannot be changed, however, once the plant is properly christened, which accounts for occasional names that are confusing. All such have been noted wherever they occur.

Throughout botanical and hort. literature this specific or species name (always in Latin or Greek), in italics, follows the name of the genus, which tells us at once that it not only belongs to that genus but is a specified and limited part of it. To illustrate:

*Rosa* is the genus name of all the roses, and *Rosa* contains many species. Each of them has its own specific name such as,
*Rosa eglanteria* for the sweetbrier.
*Rosa canina* for the dog rose.
*Rosa moschata* for the musk rose.

In each case the second name is the species or specific name and must always be used if one needs to specify exactly to which of many members of the genus *Rosa* the particular plant belongs. Often, in this book and throughout hort. literature, you will find *Rosa* (or of course other generic names) written out in full when first used, but abbreviated afterwards. This is done merely to save space; and the three species of rose mentioned above would then be written
*Rosa eglanteria, R. canina,* and *R. moschata*
not
*Rosa eglanteria, Rosa canina,* and *Rosa moschata.*

Throughout THE GARDEN DICTIONARY, also to save useless repetition, even the initial *R.* is omitted, once the genus name is clearly stated, as at *Rosa* and all the other genera in the book. See ROSA where the species are listed alphabetically (without the abbreviation *R.*). See also GENUS, PLANT NAMES, VARIETY.

*SPECIOSA, -us, -um* (spee-si-ō'sa). Showy.

**SPECKLED ALDER** = *Alnus incana.* See ALDER.

*SPECTABILIS, -e* (speck-tab'i-lis). Remarkably showy.

**SPECULARIA** (speck-you-lair'i-a). Hardy, annual herbs, comprising about 10 species of the family Campanulaceae, found in the northern hemisphere, with one in Australia. They are low-growing, erect, or of spreading habit, the leaves alternate,* lance-shaped, the margins sometimes toothed. Flowers blue, purple or white, in 1-3-flowered clusters, growing from the axils* of the leaves. Calyx tubular. Corolla widely open to ¾ in. across, its limb 5-lobed. Stamens* 5. Fruit a 3-celled capsule. (*Specularia* is from *speculum-veneris,* which see.)

Useful annual for the border or rock garden. Easily cult. Seeds may be sown in fall or early spring where required to bloom, or may be sown in a cold frame and transplanted.

**speculum-veneris.** Also known as *Campanula speculum.* Venus's-looking-glass. Growing to 15 in. high, and of erect habit. Leaves broadly lance-shaped, to 1½ in. long, the margins toothed. Flowers deep blue, or white, to ¾ in. across, in 1-3-flowered clusters. Sepals curved. Mediterranean region.

*SPECULUM-VENERIS* (speck-you-lum-ven'er-is). The looking-glass of Venus. See SPECULARIA.

**SPEEDWELL.** See VERONICA. See also the list at WEEDS.

**SPERGULA ARVENSIS** = Spurry. See the list at WEEDS.

*SPHACELATA, -us, -um* (sfa-see-lay'ta). Withered or diseased.

**SPHACELE** (sfa-see'le). A little-known genus of shrubs or under-shrubs of the mint family, found in Calif., Hawaii, and S.A., and comprising perhaps 20 species. The only one of hort. interest is **S. calycina,** the pitcher sage of Calif., somewhat grown there for ornament, or occasionally in the cool greenhouse in frosty regions. It is a hairy shrub, 3–5 ft. high, with opposite,* ovalish or oblong, toothed leaves, 3–4 in. long. Flowers about 1 in. long, white or pinkish, usually solitary in the axils* of bracts, the collection of them forming a leafy cluster (raceme*). Fruit of 4 small nutlets hidden in the inflated calyx.* (*Sphacele,* an old Greek name, is of uncertain application to these plants, as it was used originally for a salvia.)

**SPHAERALCEA** (sfee-ral'see-a). Globe mallow. Shrubs or perennial herbs, comprising about 65 species of the family Malvaceae, mostly natives of tropical and sub-tropical America, but a few found in South Africa. Leaves alternate,* lance-shaped or roundish and lobed, the margins sometimes toothed. Flowers large and showy, lilac, pink, or red, solitary or in clusters, terminal or growing from the axils* of the leaves, with 3 small, scale-like bracts* beneath each flower. Calyx* of 5 sepals. Corolla of 5 petals. Stamens* many. Fruits many, growing in a ring at the top of the disk-like receptacle.* (*Sphaeralcea* is from the Greek for globe, and *Alcea,* which see.) They are sometimes offered as *Phymosia.* Sometimes cult. in the warm greenhouse or grown outdoors in the South. Propagated by seeds or cuttings made from the tips of young shoots.

**rosea.** Shrub, growing to 12 ft. high. Leaves roundish and lobed. Flowers rose, in clusters. Bracts* on flower stalks united at the base. Guatemala.

**umbellata.** Shrub, growing to 15 ft. high. Leaves roundish, slightly cut into 7 lobes. Flowers scarlet, to 2 in. across, in axillary clusters, the petals white-marked at the base. Mex.

**vitifolia** = *Sphaeralcea rosea.*

*SPHAEROCARPA, -us, -um* (sfeer-o-kar'pa). Round-fruited.

*SPHAEROCEPHALA, -us, -um* (sfeer-o-seff'a-la). Round-headed.

**SPHAGNUM** (sfag'num). A large group of generally bog mosses, mostly with pale or ashy foliage and of little cult. importance, but widely used for packing plants and for other purposes.

Dried sphagnum, which comes in large bales, has many uses, for its ability to hold water makes it a good medium for rooting plants which are air-layered. See LAYERING.

Coming mostly from bogs, sphagnum is generally acid, often very much so. It is consequently of the greatest use in the bog garden, where some orchids and insectivorous plants grow better in wet sphagnum than in anything else.

Commercial preparations of sphagnum, baked to kill weeds, and with the acid removed, and sometimes mixed with dried cow manure, are extremely useful forms of humus (which see).

**SPHENOGYNE.** See URSINIA.

*SPICA, -us, -um* (spy'ka). A spike (or ear) of grain.

*SPICANT* (spy'kant). Spiked or spike-like.

*SPICATA, -us, -um* (spy-kay'ta). Spiked; or having flowers in a spike.*

**SPICEBERRY** = *Gaultheria procumbens.*

**SPICEBUSH.** In the East, *Benzoin aestivale;* in Calif., *Calycanthus occidentalis.*

**SPICE TREE** = *Umbellularia californica.*

**SPICEWOOD** = *Benzoin aestivale.*

*SPICULIFOLIA, -us, -um* (spick-you-li-fō'li-a). Having sharp-pointed leaves.

**SPIDERFLOWER** = *Cleome spinosa,* but see also TIBOUCHINA.

**SPIDER-LILY.** Rather showy, chiefly tropical American bulbous herbs, comprising the genus **Hymenocallis** (hy-men-o-kall'is) of the family Amaryllidaceae. Of the 40 known species only two are of much cult. interest, although there are wild species, found from S. Car. to Fla., which are sometimes transferred to grounds in their own region. They have narrow, strap-shaped, basal leaves and few-

---

* Special articles on the subjects indicated by an asterisk (*) will be found at the words so marked.

flowered clusters (umbels*) of white flowers at the end of a stout, solid stalk. Corolla white, cylindric and united below, broadening at the top and with narrow segments. Stamens* 6, their filaments* much broadened and united at the base into a white, cup-like structure which is very conspicuous. Fruit a 3-valved capsule.* (*Hymenocallis* is from the Greek for beautiful membrane, in allusion to the cup-like base of the stamens.*) Also called Peruvian daffodil.

The spider-lilies are popular plants for outdoor culture in tropical gardens. In the North they need greenhouse care and should be planted in large pots or small tubs, as their bulbs become large in age. Use potting mixture* 4 and grow in the warm-temperate house. *Hymenocallis caribaea* blooms in the winter, and its bulbs should be rested in the summer (see RESTING PLANTS). *H. calathina* is a summer-bloomer and should be rested during the winter. The plants are closely related to *Pancratium*, of which they are considered American representatives by some.

**H. calathina.** Basket-flower. Bulb with a long, stout neck* from which arise the 6–8 leaves which are nearly 2 ft. long and 2 in. wide, two-ranked. Flowers nearly 8 in. long, tubular for about half this length, the segments narrow. The cup-like base of the stamens nearly 2 in. wide, fringed, the stamens protruding beyond it about ½ in. Peruvian and Bolivian Andes. Often offered under the names *Pancratium calathinum* and *Ismene calathina*.

**H. caribaea.** Bulb with little or no neck. Leaves 12–20, usually 12–20 in. long, nearly 3 in. wide, not 2-ranked. Flowers fragrant, about 6 in. long, tubular for about half this length. Cup-like base of the stamens about 1 in. wide, the stamens protruding beyond it nearly 2 in. Fla. and W.I.

**SPIDER ORCHID.** See BRASSIA.

**SPIDER PLANT.** See CHLOROPHYTUM ELATUM.

**SPIDERWORT.** Rather weak-stemmed, watery-juiced, perennial herbs constituting the genus **Tradescantia** (tray-des-kan′ti-a) of the family Commelinaceae, all the 40 known species American, and mostly tropical. Two are occasionally cult. in the hardy border, and one is an extremely popular greenhouse plant for hanging baskets — the wandering Jew (for another plant so called see ZEBRINA PENDULA). Leaves (in ours) long and narrow, or ovalish and stalkless, without marginal teeth. Flowers white or bluish-purple, or even pinkish, rather ephemeral. Sepals 3, often green or colored. Petals 3, separate. Stamens* 6. Fruit a 3-valved capsule.* (Named for John Tradescant, gardener to Charles I.) The plants are sometimes known as widow's-tear.

The hardy spiderworts (*H. bracteata* and *H. virginiana*) are of easy cult. in most garden soils, preferring some moisture and partial shade to open, dry sites. They can easily be divided in the spring, or detached joints of their stems will usually root in any sandy soil. The wandering Jew also roots easily from cuttings or even broken bits of stem. It is common in greenhouses and often runs wild under the benches. It is a useful plant for hanging baskets, where, because of its drooping habit, it soon covers the sides of the basket.

**T. bracteata.** A hardy perennial, not over 12 in. high. Leaves narrowly lance-shaped, 6–8 in. long. Flowers blue or purplish-blue, the 2 bracts* beneath them wider than the leaves and boat-shaped. Central U.S. June–Aug.

**T. dracaenoides** = *Spironema fragrans*, usually. The true *T. dracaenoides*, rare or little known in cult., is a Mexican plant with tuberous roots, hairy-margined leaves, and rose-pink flowers.

**T. fluminensis.** Wandering Jew. A prostrate or trailing plant, the leaves ovalish, 2–2½ in. long, pointed both ends, essentially stalkless. Flowers white. S.A., but naturalized in warm sections of the U.S. A very common plant in greenhouses, widely used for hanging baskets, and useful as a house plant, as it will grow in almost any soil so long as it is kept moist. The var. **variegata** has white-striped leaves and is even more common in cult. than the normal green form. There are also yellow-marked varieties. See also ZEBRINA PENDULA.

**T. virginiana.** Common spiderwort, sometimes called snake grass. A hardy perennial, 2–3 ft. high. Leaves 12–15 in. long, scarcely 1 in. wide, often channeled. Flowers violet-purple or bluish. Eastern U.S., west to Ark. May–Aug. The var. **alba** has white flowers.

**T. zebrina** = *Zebrina pendula*.

**SPIDERWORT FAMILY** = Commelinaceae.

**SPIGELIA** (spy-gee′li-a). Tender or hardy American annual or perennial herbs, comprising about 50 species of the family Loganiaceae. Leaves opposite,* ovalish or broadly lance-shaped, thin. Flowers red, yellow or purple, in one-sided, branching clusters. Calyx* narrowly tubular. Corolla tubular, its limb 5-lobed. Stamens* 5, growing on the corolla tube. Fruit a 2-celled, flattish capsule. (Named for Adrian von der Spigel, Dutch botanist.)

These plants are not much in cultivation, a few species grown in the greenhouse, and the one below as a border plant. Propagated by division of roots in March or April. Soil should be deeply dug, and a little leaf mold added to it. They prefer half-shady positions and plenty of water in hot weather.

**marilandica.** Pinkroot. Worm-grass. Star-bloom. Hardy perennial, growing to 2 ft. high. Leaves ovalish, to 4 in. long. Flowers tubular, red with yellow throat, to 2 in. long in terminal one-sided clusters. N.C., Fla. and Tex. Summer. It yields a remedy for intestinal worms.

**SPIKE.** A raceme*-like cluster in which the individual flowers are stalkless or nearly so (they are stalked in a raceme*). Common examples of a spike are found in the true pepper (see PIPER), the prince's-feather (*Polygonum orientale*), the mignonette, and in the hyssop.

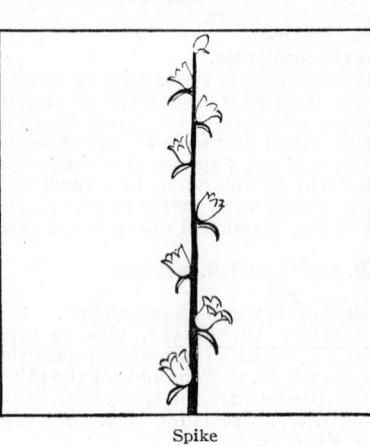

Spike

**SPIKED ALDER** = *Clethra alnifolia*.

**SPIKE GRASS** = *Demazeria sicula*.

**SPIKE HEATH** = *Bruckenthalia spiculifolia*.

**SPIKELET.** A small spike,* especially one of the small spikes which make up the inflorescence of the grasses.

**SPIKENARD** = *Aralia racemosa*.

**SPIKE-TOOTH HARROW.** See Section 1, TOOLS AND IMPLEMENTS.

**SPILANTHES** (spy-lan′theez). Perennial herbs, comprising about 40 species, of the family Compositae, distributed throughout the world, mostly in the tropical regions. They are of creeping or erect habit, and have opposite,* ovalish leaves, with toothed margins. Flowers in long-stalked, terminal heads, the ray florets yellow or white, the disk* florets yellow or brownish. (*Spilanthes* is from the Greek for spot and flower, in allusion to the brown disk florets of some species.)

They are not of much garden importance, the majority of the species being tropical weeds. The one below is sometimes grown for its leaves which are edible, or for its odd-shaped flower heads.

**oleracea.** Of spreading habit, much-branched. Leaves ovalish, the margins wavy-toothed. Flower heads ovalish, to 1 in. long, greenish-yellow, of disk florets* only. Tropical America. Late summer.

**SPINACH.** The garden spinach is one of only 3 or 4 species of Asiatic annual herbs constituting the genus **Spinacia** (spin-ach′i-a), of which **S. oleracea** is the common spinach. They belong to the goosefoot family (Chenopodiaceae). Leaves alternate,* mostly basal or nearly so, ovalish, or ovalish-oblong, or in some cult. varieties roundish, usually crinkly margined. The stem leaves (not usually produced on harvested plants) are smaller and narrower. Flowers small, unisexual* (for details see CHENOPODIACEAE). Fruit an utricle,* surrounded by a small, prickly, capsule-like body (commonly but incorrectly called the seed). There is also a variety, little known, where the fruit is invested with a covering that is not spiny. (*Spinacia* is from the Latin for spine, in allusion to the husk of the fruit.) See also NEW ZEALAND SPINACH.

---

* Special articles on the subjects indicated by an asterisk (*) will be found at the words so marked.

## Spinach Culture

Spinach is a cool-season annual grown as a pot herb or for greens. No spinach will stand extreme summer heat without "shooting" seed stalks. For this reason the seed must be sown early in the spring or late in the summer, to avoid the danger of the crop maturing in July or August. For spring and summer use sow as early as the ground can be worked, and make successive plantings every two weeks until May fifteenth. The leaves will be ready for use four or five weeks after sowing; however, it should not be used much later than the middle of June. For autumn use sow seed about August first. The spinach will grow very large and can be cut from the first of September until the ground freezes.

To winter-over, and have extra early spring spinach, seed should be sown in early September. Although the plants are hardy in well-drained soil as far north as New York, and probably considerably farther north, it is best to give a winter protection of straw or leaves. Uncover gradually in the spring when danger of severe freezing is past. For home use during the winter seed may be sown in the hotbed, or young plants transplanted to frames in the fall and covered to secure good green leaves.

The best results are obtained with spinach which is grown on soil containing an abundance of plant food, especially nitrogen. The ground cannot be too rich and the pH should preferably be between 8.0 and 6.0, but not less than 6.0. (See ACID AND ALKALI SOILS.) Nitrate of soda or ammonium sulphate in solution should be applied as a fertilizer. Two or more applications should be made; a sprayer, used as an applicator, provides for even distribution. About one ounce of nitrate of soda to two gallons of water makes a full-strength solution. Ammonium sulphate is slower to take effect upon the plants but contains more nitrogen than nitrate of soda and the effect is longer lasting.

For home consumption seed should be sown in drills about twelve inches apart and covered to a depth of not more than one inch. If grown for commercial purposes the rows should be at least two feet apart, to allow proper cultivation either by power or horse tillage. One ounce of seed will sow one hundred feet of drill.

Certain types of spinach, such as the Nobel and Savoy, are excellent for both market and home use. Of these Long Standing Bloomsdale Savoy, Viking, King of Denmark, and Old Dominion are good varieties. For fall sowing, Virginia Blight Resistant Savoy; for canning, medium-sized Thickleaf; and for wintering-over, Eskimo, which is hardy and stands cold well.

INSECT PESTS. A bluish jumping flea beetle with yellow neck, nearly ¼ in. long, attacks seedlings in the spring; the larvae add to injury by feeding on the leaves. Very young plants may be protected by arsenicals, but the poison should not be applied to leaves soon to be harvested. A green aphid feeds on spinach and may injure the plant or lower its value. Nicotine dust has been found effective. A fly larva sometimes mines in the leaves. Spinach pests may develop on pigweed, which should therefore be kept down. These pests will also attack beet and chard.

DISEASES. Spinach seedlings are very susceptible to damping-off.* Treating the seed with red copper oxide, one teaspoonful shaken up with each pound of seed will sometimes give big increases in yield and stand. The mature plants in cool, moist weather often are destroyed by mildew. No sure means of control are available. Planting in well-drained soil, long rotations, and with the rows far enough apart to permit air currents to dry the leaves, will aid in diminishing the loss.

Blight or mosaic is one of the serious diseases, especially late in the summer. It is caused by the cucumber mosaic virus transmitted by aphids, and results in the dwarfing and yellowing of the entire plant. At least two varieties have been bred for resistance to this disease, and should be planted where blight has caused much trouble. Among other diseases present are black mold, smut, leafspots, anthracnose, and rust. Only general recommendations of sanitation* and crop rotation can be given for these.

**SPINACH-BEET** = Swiss Chard. See BEET.

**SPINACH-DOCK** = *Rumex patientia*.

**SPINACH FAMILY** = Chenopodiaceae.

**SPINACH-RHUBARB** = *Rumex abyssinicus*.

*SPINA-CHRISTI* (spy-na-kriss'ti). Christ's-thorn. See PALIURUS.

**SPINACIA.** See SPINACH.

**SPINDLE PALM** = *Hyophorbe verschaffelti*.

**SPINDLE-TREE.** See EUONYMUS.

**SPINDLE-TUBER.** See Diseases at POTATO.

**SPINDLING.** Inclined to produce more stalk and foliage than flowers or fruit. It may be caused by too rich a soil, or by crowding. It is often caused, in greenhouses, by growing plants too far from the glass. A more common garden term for spindling is leggy.*

**SPINE.** A strong, often woody, very sharp-pointed body arising from the wood or other tissue, but not usually from a bud. A weak or slender spine is usually called a prickle, such as those commonly found on the rose or blackberry. But spine is more often applied to the armature of plants like the cacti. See THORN.

**SPINESCENT.** Somewhat spiny.

*SPINIFEX* (spin'i-fecks). Spiny or prickly.

**SPINK** = *Dianthus deltoides*.

*SPINOSA, -us, -um* (spy-nō'sa). Spiny.

*SPINOSISSIMA, -us, -um* (spy-no-siss'i-ma). Very or most spiny.

*SPINULOSA, -us, -um* (spin-you-lō'sa). Weakly spiny.

**SPIRAEA** (spy-ree'a). Spirea (the preferred spelling for the common name; see SPIREA for other plants so called). An important and valuable genus of handsome flowering shrubs of the rose family, comprising over 80 species, mostly from the north temperate zone, but a few southward to Mex. and the Himalayas. All are deciduous* shrubs with alternate,* mostly toothed or lobed leaves, rarely altogether without teeth, nearly always stalked. Flower clusters usually showy, mostly of umbel-like racemes,* sometimes of panicles* or corymbs.* Individual flowers small, prevailingly white or pinkish-purple, the sepals and petals 5 each. Stamens* 15–60. Fruit a dry pod (follicle*), splitting along the inner seam. (*Spiraea* is from the Greek for a wreath or garland, for which some species were probably used.)

Of the 80 known species, and many hybrids, over 55 are known to be in cult. in the U.S., but only a selection of the best of them can be included here. Fortunately, the garden spireas are of the simplest culture, as they thrive in a variety of soils and under all sorts of exposures. Of course they repay attention as do any other flowering shrubs, but they thrive with less attention than many others. If they have a preference, it is for open sunshine and a reasonably moist site.

Such is the popularity of spireas that they are perhaps more widely planted than any other flowering shrubs, especially the early-blooming sorts like *S. arguta*, *S. vanhouttei*, *S. prunifolia*, *S. crenata*, and *S. trilobata*, some of which include the sorts commonly called Bridal Wreath. Scarcely less popular are the later-blooming forms like *S. bumalda*, *S. japonica*, *S. salicifolia*, *S. tomentosa*, and the especially popular *S. billiardi*. Most of these require little pruning, unless they happen to winter-kill.

Most of them are easily propagated by seeds, sown when ripe or stratified, or by cuttings of green wood in the greenhouse, and many of them can be easily layered, as some tend to arch over and root at the tips.

As will be seen below the genus *Spiraea* once included many species now considered to belong to other genera.

aitchisonia = *Sorbaria aitchisoni*.

**alba.** Meadowsweet. An upright shrub, 4–6 ft. high. Leaves short-stalked, oblongish, 1–2½ in. long. Flowers white in leafy, pyramidal clusters (panicles*). Fruit smooth. Eastern U.S. July-Aug. Hardy from zone* 3 southward.

**arguta.** A hybrid shrub derived from crossing *S. thunbergi* with another hybrid. It resembles *S. thunbergi*, but is a little taller, more vigorous, and much more freely flowering. May. Perhaps the most profusely blooming of all white-flowered early spireas.

aruncus = *Aruncus sylvester*.

astilboides = *Astilbe astilboides*.

**billiardi.** A very popular hybrid spirea, 4–6 ft. high, derived from cross-

---

* Special articles on the subjects indicated by an asterisk (*) will be found at the words so marked.

ing *S. douglasi* with *S. salicifolia*. Leaves oblongish, 2–3½ in. long, often doubly toothed, but without teeth toward the base, grayish beneath. Flowers bright rose-red, in narrow, dense clusters (panicles*). Fruits smooth. July–Aug. Hardy from zone* 3 southward.

**blumei.** The plant usually offered as this is *S. trilobata*, the true *S. blumei* being rare in cult.

**bumalda.** A very widely cult. and popular spirea, derived from crossing *S. japonica* and another Japanese species not much known in cult. Not over 2 ft. high, the twigs striped. Leaves ovalish or lance-shaped, doubly toothed. Flowers white to dark pink. July. Not much grown in the typical form, as the *var.* **froebeli**, a taller plant with bright crimson flowers, is more likely to be in the nurseries. So is the *var.* **Anthony Waterer**, perhaps the most popular of all late-flowering spireas. It is more compact than the typical species, has narrower leaves, and bright crimson flowers. All bloom in late June or July and are hardy from zone* 3 southward.

**callosa** = *Spiraea japonica*.

**camtschatica** = *Filipendula camtschatica*.

**cantoniensis.** An arching shrub, not over 5 ft. high. Leaves somewhat angularly oblongish, wedge-shaped at the base, 1–2½ in. long, pale beneath, deeply toothed. Flowers white, in dense, smooth clusters (umbels*). China and Jap. June. Hardy from zone* 4 southward. Known also as *S. reevesiana*.

**crenata.** A slender shrub scarcely over 3 ft. high. Leaves oblongish or narrower, wedge-shaped at the base, ¾–1¾ in. long, distinctly 3-veined. Flowers white in dense, slightly hairy clusters (umbels*). Eurasia. May. Hardy from zone* 3 southward.

**douglasi.** A beautiful, Pacific Coast spirea, 5–8 ft. high, its twigs reddish, hairy, and striped. Leaves narrowly oblong, 1½–4 in. long, whitefelty beneath, unequally toothed toward the tip. Flowers deep rose-red, in showy, densely hairy clusters (panicles*) which may be 4–7 in. long. British Columbia to Calif. July–Aug. Hardy from zone* 4 southward.

**filipendula** = *Filipendula hexapetala*.

**fortunei** = *Spiraea japonica fortunei*.

**froebeli** = *Spiraea bumalda froebeli*.

**japonica.** An upright shrub, 4–6 ft. high. Leaves ovalish or oblong, wedge-shaped at the base, ¾–2¾ in. long, hairy on the veins beneath. Flowers pink, in much-branched, rather loose clusters (panicles*). Jap. June–July. Hardy from zone* 3 southward. The *var.* **fortunei** is somewhat taller, has leaves smooth beneath, and incurved, doubly toothed leaf teeth. It is found in China. The *var.* **macrophylla** has much larger and puckered leaves but smaller flower clusters. It is of hort. origin. Plants offered as *S. callosa* are *S. japonica*.

*Spiraea vanhouttei* (above), one of the bridal wreaths. Below, the Anthony Waterer variety of *S. bumalda*.

**laevigata** = *Sibiraea laevigata*.

**latifolia.** Meadowsweet. An upright shrub 3–7 ft. high, the twigs reddish-brown and angled. Leaves broadly elliptic, pointed both ends, 1½–3 in. long, coarsely toothed. Flowers white or pinkish, in broadly pyramidal clusters (panicles*). Northeastern N.A. June–Aug. Hardy from zone* 5 northward.

**margaritae.** A handsome, hybrid spirea, 3–5 ft. high, the twigs purple-brown. Leaves narrowly elliptic, or somewhat broader, abruptly pointed at the tip, wedge-shaped at the base, 2–3½ in. long, coarsely and doubly toothed. Flowers bright pink in large, leafy, slightly hairy clusters (corymbs*). July, and also, less profusely, in late Aug.–Sept. Hardy from zone* 3 southward.

**opulifolia** = *Physocarpus opulifolius*.

**prunifolia.** Bridal Wreath (a name also applied to *S. vanhouttei*). Not much cult. in the typical, wild form, but in the *var.* **plena**, one of the most widely cult. of all spireas. It is a slender shrub, 4–6 ft. high, with arching, somewhat angled branches. Leaves elliptic or elliptic–oblong, pointed both ends, ¾–2 in. long, finely toothed. Flowers pure white, double, very numerous, but in 3–6-flowered, nearly stalkless clusters (umbels*). Eastern As. April–May. Hardy from zone* 3 southward.

**reevesiana** = *Spiraea cantoniensis*.

**salicifolia.** Queen-of-the-meadow; also called bridewort. A rather stiffly erect shrub, 4–6 ft. high, the twigs slightly angled and yellowish-brown. Leaves oblongish or narrower, pointed both ends, 2–3½ in. long, sharply and closely toothed. Flowers rose-pink, in slender, pyramidal, hairy clusters (panicles*). Eurasia. June–July. Hardy from zone* 3 southward.

**sorbifolia** = *Sorbaria sorbifolia*.

**thunbergi.** A handsome, twiggy spirea, 3–5 ft. high, its foliage orange-scarlet in the fall. Leaves narrowly lance-shaped, ¾–1¾ in. long, sharply toothed, bright green. Flowers pure white, very numerous, but in 3–5-flowered, nearly stalkless clusters (umbels*). China and Jap. April–May. Hardy from zone* 3 southward.

**tomentosa.** Hardhack; also called steeplebush. A stiff, upright shrub, its branches brown-felty. Leaves ovalish, 1½–2½ in. long, unequally toothed, densely gray or brownish-felty beneath. Flowers rose-purple, in narrow, densely brown-felty, spire-like clusters (panicles*). Fruit hairy. Eastern N.A. July–Sept. Hardy from zone* 2 southward.

**trichocarpa.** An erect shrub, 4–6 ft., the branches spreading. Leaves oblongish, 1–2 in. long, pointed at the tip, few-toothed. Flowers white, very numerous, in a branched, hairy cluster (umbel*-like). Fruits hairy. Korea. June. Hardy from zone* 3 southward. Some of the plants passing as Bridal Wreath may belong here.

**trilobata.** A shrub much resembling the far more popular *S. vanhouttei*, but smaller in all its parts, and the leaves somewhat blunter. As. May–June. Hardy from zone* 3 southward. Some of the plants offered as *S. blumei* belong to this species.

**ulmaria** = *Filipendula ulmaria*.

**vanhouttei.** Bridal Wreath. By far the most commonly cult. spirea in America, and standing smoke and city conditions better than most. It is a hybrid between *S. cantoniensis* and *S. trilobata*, and is a slender shrub 4–6 ft. high, with beautifully arching branches. Leaves somewhat angularly ovalish, pointed at the tip, ¾–1¾ in. long, pale beneath. Flowers pure white, very numerous, in many-flowered clusters (umbels*). May–June. Hardy from zone* 3 southward. A good spirea for forcing (which see).

**SPIRALIS, -e** (spy-ral'is). A spiral; or spirally arranged.

**SPIRANTHES** (spy-ran'theez). A genus of over 60 species of delicate, terrestrial orchids, mostly from the north temperate zone, about 18 of them scattered in meadows or bogs over N.A. They are small plants with clustered, rather fleshy roots, bracted* flowering stalks and chiefly basal, narrow, almost grass-like leaves. Flowers very small, irregular,* white, arranged in spirals from the twisting of the main flower stalk. They are of little hort. importance except for **S. cernua**, the ladies'-tresses, one of the largest-flowering of the American species. It is a meadow plant, usually hidden among grass or other herbs in the wild, 7–18 in. high. Leaves very narrow, about the height of the flower stalk, without marginal teeth. Flowers about ¼ in. long, turned downward, the spiral cluster (spike*) 3–5 in. long. Other native species are likely to be transferred to the wild garden where they need moist, meadow-like conditions or the sphagnum of the bog garden. All were once called *Ibidium*. (*Spiranthes* is from the Greek for coil or curl, in allusion to the spirally twisted flowering stalk.)

**SPIRE.** An old, and now unusual, term for a shoot or sprig; also, as a verb, to become spindling.

**SPIREA.** Properly, spirea is the preferred common name of shrubs belonging to the genus *Spiraea*. But spirea is much used for other plants which resemble *Spiraea*. The common potted spirea of the florists may be *Aruncus sylvester*, an *Astilbe*, or a *Filipendula*. Other plants to which the name spirea is applied will be found at *Caryopteris* and *Sorbaria*.

**SPIREA FAMILY.** See ROSACEAE.

**SPIRONEMA** (spy-ro-nee'ma). A single species of Mexican, weak-stemmed herbs of the family Commelinaceae, **S. fragrans**, usually grown under the name *Tradescantia dracaenoides*. It is a greenhouse plant for the hanging basket, with trailing stems 1–2 ft. long, and transparent foliage. Leaves oblong or narrower, sheathing at the base, pointed at the tip, prominently parallel-veined. Flowers waxy-white, fragrant, the petals diaphanous, the sepals green. Stamens* 6. Not much grown. (*Spironema* is from the Greek for spiral thread, in allusion to the stalks of the anthers.*)

**SPITTLE INSECTS.** See Insect Pests at BLUEBERRY.

---

* Special articles on the subjects indicated by an asterisk (*) will be found at the words so marked.

**SPLEENWORT.** See ASPLENIUM and ATHYRIUM.

*SPLENDENS* (splen'denz). Splendid or showy.

**SPLICE GRAFTING.** See GRAFTING.

**SPODIUM.** A charcoal derived from burning bones or other animal refuse, and used in the manufacture of certain superphosphate fertilizers.

**SPONDIAS** (spon'di-as). Tropical fruit trees of the sumac family, grown for their fleshy, edible fruits, which are usually called ciruela, and are little esteemed in the U.S. Leaves alternate,* compound,* the leaflets arranged feather-fashion, with an odd one at the end. Flowers small, often polygamous,* mostly in branched clusters (panicles* or racemes*). For details see ANACARDIACEAE. Fruit a fleshy drupe, its single large stone covered with many spines which penetrate the fleshy, yellow pulp and make separation of it difficult. (*Spondias* is an old Greek name for a plum-like fruit, in allusion to the fleshy drupes.*)

The first species and *S. mombin* are somewhat grown in zone* 9 in Fla., and are hardy nowhere else. Less known is *S. purpurea*, the purple mombin, which is also very tender. All are of simple culture on a variety of soils, so long as the region is frost-free. Easily propagated by seeds.

**cytherea.** Otaheite apple; also called vi-apple and ambarella. A tree up to 60 ft. high. Leaflets 11–13, oblongish, slightly toothed or without teeth, about 3 in. long. Flowers whitish. Fruit resembling a large yellow plum, 2–3 in. long, the flesh acid or sweetish, not highly regarded and used mostly for preserves. It ripens in winter in Fla. Society Islands.

**lutea** = *Spondias mombin*.

**mombin.** Yellow mombin; also called hog plum. A very common tree throughout tropical America and elsewhere, and cult. in extreme southern Fla.; often up to 60 ft. high. Leaflets 7–17, ovalish or narrower, 3–4 in. long, essentially without teeth. Flowers purplish-green. Fruit egg-shaped, 1–1½ in. long, yellow, sweetish or slightly acid, ripening in late summer and considered inferior to *S. purpurea*. Tropical regions generally. Also known as *S. lutea*.

**purpurea.** Purple or red mombin; also called Spanish plum. A tree scarcely over 30 ft. high. Leaflets 7–23, oblongish, about 1 in. long. Flowers greenish. Fruit yellowish-red or red at maturity, 1–2 in. long, its flesh highly prized in tropical America, either raw or cooked, but little known in Fla. Tropical America.

**SPONGE TREE** = *Acacia farnesiana*.

**SPORE.** The microscopic organ upon which ferns, mosses, lichens, fungi, and algae depend for reproduction. Spores are far smaller than even the smallest seeds, contain no embryo, and are functionally very different. But in the reproductive processes of the flowerless plants they replace seeds. For the germination and subsequent life history of the only spores of garden interest see FERNS AND FERN GARDENING. Many spores also provide a quick and easy method of spreading disease. See PLANT DISEASES.

**SPORT.** See MUTATION.

**SPOT.** See Bacteria at PLANT DISEASES.

**SPOTBLIGHT.** See Diseases at GRASSES.

**SPOTS IN THE LAWN.** See LAWN.

**SPOTTED CALLA LILY** = *Zantedeschia albo-maculata*. See CALLA LILY.

**SPOTTED COWBANE** = *Cicuta maculata*.

**SPOTTED MEDIC** = *Medicago arabica*.

**SPOTTED SPURGE** = *Euphorbia maculata*. See list at WEEDS.

**SPOTTED WINTERGREEN** = *Chimaphila maculata*. The plant is also called rheumatism-root and dragon's-tongue; it may be a partial saprophyte.*

**SPRAGUEA** (sprague'ee-a). Summer-blooming, delicate, perennial herbs of the family Portulacaceae, comprising perhaps only 2 species, one of them, **S. umbellata**, from the mountain summits of Calif. and northward, a rare rock garden plant. It has several stiff, erect stems, 2–9 in. high, and mostly basal, fleshy, oblongish leaves, a few smaller leaves on the stem. Flowers small, white or rose-tinged, borne in small spikes, grouped in a close, dense cluster (umbel*). Petals 4. Stamens* 3. Fruit a membranous, 2-valved capsule. It needs a sandy or gritty soil, and rock garden cult. (Named for Isaac Sprague, American botanical draughtsman.)

**SPRAYING AND DUSTING.** Important insecticides and their action are discussed under INSECTICIDES and INSECT PESTS. In spraying or dusting the aim is to give a uniform but light coating of poison, not only to prevent injury to the plants, but to keep down the expense. With stomach poisons the entire surface of the plant should be covered; with contact sprays the aim is to cover all the insects. Dusting is easy and rapid, and it does away with the weight of the large volume of water which handicaps spraying. However, against many pests the results are not so dependable as in spraying. Spraying is the more general practice, although dusting is used where it has been found to be effective.

### METHODS OF APPLICATION

In spraying, the light coating of insecticide desired is obtained by diluting it with water and directing it onto the plant as a fine mist, through a nozzle under pressure developed by a pump. In dusting, the material is applied in the form of a light cloud.

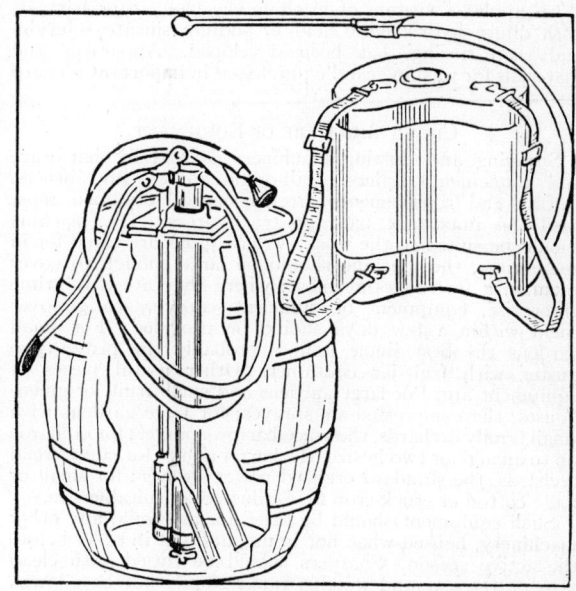

A practical barrel and knapsack spraying outfit for liquid insecticides

The applications should be thorough, and should be made in time to check the pest. Sprays are applied to low-growing crops at the rate of 100 to 200 gallons per acre, and to orchard trees at 2 to 25 gallons per tree. Dusts are used at only a few pounds per acre, or ¼ pound to 2 pounds per tree. Most insecticides are poisonous to man and animals, and must be kept out of reach of children and livestock. Spraying or dusting should not be done during or just before a rain, for insecticides wash off easily when first applied, and spraying should not be attempted in freezing weather. Dormant-strength sprays should not be used when trees are in leaf, as they may then be injurious to them, but they may be used when buds are just beginning to open (delayed-dormant). Stomach poisons should not be used on trees in bloom, lest they kill the orchardist's friends, the bees.

Sometimes a substance is added to a spray to increase its spreading power, and to wet smooth leaves, such as those of cabbage. Such materials are called spreaders; soap

---

* Special articles on the subjects indicated by an asterisk (*) will be found at the words so marked.

is one, and calcium caseinate is another. Spreaders are not needed in ordinary spraying.

Nicotine, soap, and lime-sulphur are dissolved or emulsified in water and will not settle; but arsenic compounds, bordeaux mixture, oils, and uncombined sulphur are only in suspension, and will settle out if not kept stirred during the spraying.

Pressures of 200 pounds or more per square inch, such as are given by power sprayers, are desirable for effective spraying. Hand sprayers work with lower pressure, often below 100 pounds, but with care fairly good results may be obtained.

It has been noted under INSECTICIDES that the principal insecticides are often combined with fungicides or with each other for economy in application. Some of our orchard fruits, especially apple, are so beset by pests that a definite planned schedule of spray combinations for the season is advised for them. The schedules vary in different localities, and are discussed under each fruit. Sometimes the major pest, such as the codling moth, is closely observed to determine the best time to spray.

The danger of eating fruits and vegetables that have been sprayed with arsenic compounds has been much stressed recently. Care is necessary in spraying, especially products grown for sale. Applications should not usually be made after the fruit or edible part has grown to any size. With apples a system of washing the fruit, after harvest, with dilute hydrochloric acid or sodium silicate solution, and then rinsing, has been developed. Apparatus and materials for washing can be purchased in important orchard districts.

### Choice and Care of Equipment

Spraying and dusting machinery is sold by hardware and implement dealers, mail-order houses, and others. Outfits and replacements are, of course, obtained most easily in important fruit or truck areas. The machine should be suited to the work. Where crops are cared for in spare time, the machine should be large enough to cover them in a few hours at most; where they are a full-time enterprise, equipment of sufficient capacity to go over them within a few days should be provided. For small gardens the best single unit is probably the piston-type duster with fruit-jar container. Other useful pieces of equipment are: For large gardens and small fruit, or greenhouses, the compressed-air sprayer; for large gardens with small family orchards, the wheelbarrow sprayer; for orchards up to an acre or two in size, the barrel pump; for commercial orchards, the standard orchard power sprayer; for small or large cotton or truck-crop fields, dusters of suitable size.

Such equipment should be cared for as should any other machinery, housed when not in use, and put in order before the active season. Sprayers should be rinsed with clean water after use, and wooden tanks should not be allowed to dry out.

### Spraying Machinery

Sprays can be applied by pouring them from a sprinkler or shaking them from a brush. Such crude methods, however, are more laborious and less effective than dusting with homemade devices. For effective spraying a real sprayer is needed. Any sprayer includes a tank for holding the liquid, a pump for forcing it out, one or more nozzles to break it into a mist, and some connections between the pump and the nozzle.

Large sprayers have wooden tanks, small sprayers metal ones. Brass tanks are more expensive, but more durable, than galvanized-iron tanks. Pumps are of a cylinder type, to be operated by hand or power; the large ones have more than one cylinder. The parts to be exposed to liquid should be of brass or bronze; an air chamber to equalize pressure, and some provision for agitating the liquid, should be included. Pressure gauges are useful items of equipment. Nozzles are usually of brass, of the disk type, and give a hollow cone of spray. They should be held within a couple of feet of the surface to be sprayed. Sometimes large nozzles, called spray guns, set on a short piece of pipe, are used. They can be adjusted for a fine spray or for a coarse spray which can be thrown 10 feet or more. They can only be used with powerful pumps. Rubber hose secured by clamps is generally used to connect pump and nozzle; it varies in length from a few feet for hand sprayers up to 25 or 50 feet for power sprayers. Nozzles should not be placed at the end of the hose, but set on an extension pipe to allow the operator to keep away from the spray and also to give him a greater spraying range. These extensions are furnished with large sprayers, but not always with small ones, although they always should have them. Shut-offs in the extension

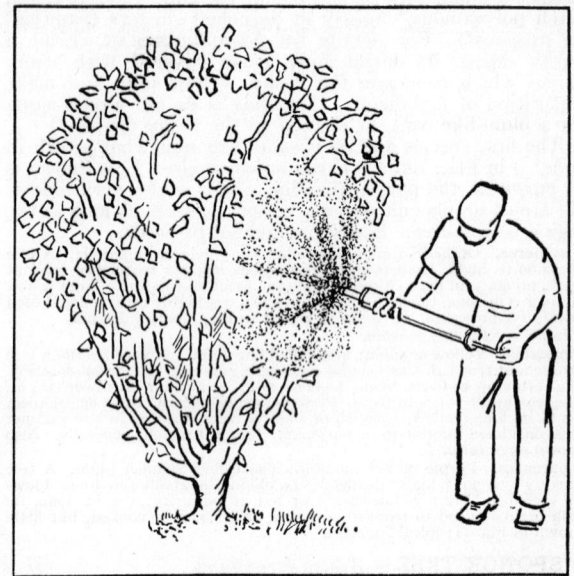

In dusting it is essential to get the leaves thoroughly covered.

pipes are convenient. Nozzles should be set at an angle of 45° from the pipe, to allow both upper and under sides of the leaves to be sprayed easily.

Atomizers cost less than a dollar, but they are not suitable for use on anything more than a few house plants. Several kinds of small spray pumps are on the market. Bucket pumps are arranged to be placed in a bucket or tub, which serves as the tank, and are operated by hand. Compressed-air sprayers cost from $5 to $10, and hold about 3 gallons of liquid. The operator partly fills one, pumps until the pressure is high, opens the shut-off, and sprays without pumping until the pressure becomes too low. They do not have agitators, and should be shaken occasionally. Wheelbarrow sprayers are mounted on a frame like that of a wheelbarrow, and have a metal tank holding about 15 gallons and a hand pump. They are about the largest hand sprayers that can be handled by one man. The barrel pump resembles a well pump, and is either installed in a barrel or arranged to clamp into one, the barrel serving as the tank. It must be carried on a wagon or sled, and pumped by one man while another sprays. The last two types cost from $15 to $25. A larger hand pump is a double-action, horizontal pump, to be used on a wagon with a barrel or tank.

For large jobs power sprayers are preferred. The typical orchard sprayer is mounted on a truck, has a tank in front, a gas engine operating a 2- to 4-cylinder spray pump in the rear, and a high platform on which a man may stand to spray the upper parts of trees. The engine in large sprayers is from 3 to 12 horsepower, and the pump delivers from 10 to 30 gallons per minute at a pressure of 300 pounds or more. A pump and hose to fill the tank and an agitator are included in the equipment. Such outfits cost from $300

---

* Special articles on the subjects indicated by an asterisk (*) will be found at the words so marked.

to $800. Two or more leads of hose are often used, and sometimes two nozzles to a lead. Unless spray guns are to be used, the sprayers are equipped with extensions, 6 feet or more long, of brass pipe within bamboo sticks. Still more powerful sprayers are used for tall park trees.

Some progress has been made in use of stationary spray outfits, with pipes to distribute spray material under pressure through orchards. For work in vineyards and on low-growing crops, such as truck crops, special types of sprayers are sold, with nozzles usually fixed on supply pipes to cover the plants from different angles. The combination of supply pipes and nozzles is called a boom. Such a sprayer may be operated by a gas engine or by power supplied by gears from the wheels of the truck; the former is more satisfactory. An orchard sprayer may be used for row crops by attaching a boom.

### DUSTING EQUIPMENT

Against some pests, and when only a few plants are involved, the dust may be shaken onto the plants through a cloth bag or a bucket with a perforated bottom; this will not, however, reach the under sides of the leaves. Dusters usually consist of a container for the insecticide, a device for blowing air into the container, and a discharge pipe through which the cloud of dust is forced out. Discharge pipes are larger than used on sprayers, of light metal, and have a flattened opening which sends out the cloud of dust in the direction desired.

An effective type of hand duster uses as a blower a piston pump, as a container an ordinary mason jar screwed into place, and with the aid of several feet of discharge pipe with an elbow, will dust the under sides of leaves and apply fungicides, contact dusts, and stomach poisons. It can be bought for as little as a dollar. Other small hand dusters have either pistons or bellows. Large hand dusters have fan blowers turned by a crank, and with them several acres can be covered in a day.

Horse-drawn dusters are manufactured in a number of forms. In truck-crop and cotton fields, traction dusters, with fan geared to the wheels, are often used; with some others the power is supplied by gas engines. Dusting machines are also designed for orchard and vineyard work. Dusting by airplane has been very successfully done and is practical where several thousand acres are to be dusted, as hundreds of acres can be covered in one hour. — F. M. W. See also FUMIGATION, INSECTICIDES, and FUNGICIDES.

**SPREADER.** Any oil emulsion, soap, or other substance added to an insecticide or fungicide, which spreads the desired ingredients over the foliage more effectively than they could be distributed without the spreader. The term is also used as an equivalent of filler* in fertilizers.

Spreader, as an implement, is a horse- or motor-driven machine for spreading manure, and is an agricultural rather than a garden implement.

**SPREADING DOGBANE** = *Apocynum androsaemifolium*.

**SPREKELIA** (spreck-kee′li-a). Tender, Mexican, bulbous herbs of family Amaryllidaceae, comprising only 1 species, **S. formosissima**, the St. James's-lily or Jacobean lily. It is also known as *Amaryllis formosissima*. Bulb ovalish. Leaves few, narrow, thick, to 1 ft. long. Flowers solitary, on a leafless stalk, to 1 ft. high, which appears before the leaves. Flower about 4 in. long, enclosed in a membranous spathe.* Calyx of 3 sepals, bright red, cylinder-like. Corolla of 3 petals, narrow and erect, bright red, alternating with the sepals. Stamens 6. Fruit a 3-celled capsule.* For cult. see AMARYLLIS. (Named for J. H. von Sprekelson, who introduced the genus to Linnaeus.)

**SPRIG.** A young shoot.

**SPRIG BUDDING.** An erroneous term for a form of grafting (which see).

**SPRIG GRAFTING.** See Side Grafting at GRAFTING.

**SPRING.** As an adjective spring has been applied to many garden plants or operations. Those that occur in this book and their proper equivalents are:

**Spring beauty** (*see* CLAYTONIA); **Spring garden** (*see* second main entry below); **Spring heath** = *Erica carnea;* **Spring lily** = *Erythronium albidum;* **Spring meadow saffron** = *Bulbocodium vernum;* **Spring onion** = *Allium fistulosum;* **Spring planting** (*see* second main entry below); **Spring starflower** = *Brodiaea uniflora;* **Spring vetch** = *Vicia sativa;* **Spring vetchling** = *Lathyrus vernus;* **Spring work** (*see* GARDEN CALENDAR).

**SPRING FROST.** See PROTECTING PLANTS.

**SPRING GARDEN.** It is not always possible or desirable to devote a special area of the grounds to a single season. There are times, however, when it is both practicable and advantageous to do this. A garden planted wholly with spring-flowering bulbs, shrubs and hardy plants may be a charming feature, especially if it is possible to so place it that it need be on view only when in its prime. Or in cases where the owner later removes to another locality for the summer months there is every reason to devote the entire planting space to early-flowering subjects.

One of the advantages of a sequestered spring garden is that in it the taste for bulbs may be freely indulged, without provision being made to hide their subsequent untidy dying off. Lovely and informal spring gardens are contrived in light woodland, where bulbous things thrive exceedingly, or a wide irregular border may be laid out against a bank of early-flowering shrubs and evergreens. Again a spring garden may be enclosed in a hedge of evergreens or some flowering shrub, such as hawthorn or Japanese quince, or by espaliered fruit trees on a wall of brick, stone or stucco.

The plan of such a garden would probably be in the form of a pattern of little beds, perhaps edged with dwarf box, with a straight border following the line of the enclosure, and some formal feature, such as a sundial, a well-head or bit of statuary, used as a focal point. The planting of such a garden will necessarily be somewhat formal, the beds filled with evenly spaced bulbs floored over with a ground cover of *Arabis*, English daisies, violas, wallflowers or forget-me-nots, but the outer border may be more unconventional and permit the use of shrubs and a few flowering trees, underplanted with irregular groups and drifts of bulbs and hardy plants in harmonious color relation.

If the spring garden is in a wood or along a bank of shrubs, its planting may be wholly informal, and in the case of the border, if it runs from sun into shade, the range of available material will be greatly increased.

The furnishings of any spring garden will largely consist of bulbous things and shrubs, but a judicious intermingling of certain hardy plants that qualify for admission by reason of their forehanded blossoming, or because of the beauty of their young foliage, brings about a fuller and more interesting effect. The happiest results are secured if the planting is done in long, irregular drifts of a single kind of plant or bulb, rather than in small groups, which are apt to appear spotty and restless. The plants and bulbs should be selected and placed with due consideration for a pleasing color harmony with each other and with the flowering trees and shrubs also made use of. If space permits, the pewter-gray trunks of beech trees, and groups of white-stemmed birches and red-stemmed dogwoods enhance the early spring scene. Trees and shrubs with conspicuous catkins are also valuable and, in the shaded sections, the uncurling fronds of ferns add much interest.

A choice of material for a spring garden would include species and varieties of the following:

BULBS: *Brodiaea; Calochortus; Camassia; Chionodoxa; Eranthis; Erythronium; Fritillaria; Galanthus; Hyacinthus azureus, H. amethystinus; Iris reticulata; Leucojum; Muscari; Narcissus; Ornithogalum; Puschkinia; Scilla; Trillium; Tulipa; Uvularia;* and *Zygadenus.*

HARDY PLANTS: *Adonis amurensis, A. vernalis* (yellow); *Ajuga reptans metallica crispa* (foliage); *Alyssum saxatile citrinum* (yellow); *Anemone quinquefolia* (white); *Aquilegia*

---

* Special articles on the subjects indicated by an asterisk (*) will be found at the words so marked.

(foliage); *Arabis albida* (white or rose, single or double); *Asarum* (foliage); *Aubrietia* vars. (purple, lavender, rose); *Bellis* (pink, rose, white); Bloodroot (white); *Brunnera macrophylla* (blue); *Erysimum asperum* (orange); *Claytonia virginica* (pink and white); *Clintonia* (greenish-white); *Corydalis cheilanthifolia* (yellow), *C. lutea* (yellow); Cowslips (yellow); *Dicentra eximia* (rose), *D. spectabilis* (pink); *Dianthus plumarius* (foliage); *Doronicum* (yellow); *Epimedium* (foliage); *Euphorbia epithymoides* (yellow); Ferns (foliage); *Festuca ovina glauca* (foliage); *Geranium ibericum* (violet); *Helleborus orientalis* (rose, cream, greenish); *Hepatica* (blue, white, pink); *Heuchera* (foliage); *Iberis* (white, mauve); *Iris pumila* vars. (blue, violet, white, yellow), *I. cristata* (lavender); Lavender Cotton (foliage); Lily-of-the-valley (white); *Mertensia virginica* (blue); *Phlox divaricata* (lavender), *P. amoena* (pink), *P. subulata* (lavender, white, pink); *Polemonium caeruleum* (blue), *P. reptans* (blue); Polyanthus Primroses (yellow, white, orange, etc.); *Polygonatum commutatum* (cream); *Primula vulgaris* vars. (yellow, white, rose, blue), *P. denticulata* (mauve, white); *Pulmonaria angustifolia* (blue), *P. saccharata* (blue); *Bergenia ligulata* (pink); *Smilacina racemosa* (white); *Thalictrum glaucum* (foliage); *Viola blanda* (white), *V. cornuta* vars. (lavender, rose, purple, yellow, white), *V. gracilis* (purple), *V. odorata* (mauve, white, purple); Wallflowers (yellow, orange, brown).

SHRUBS AND TREES: *Berberis* vars.; *Corylopsis* vars.; *Cercis canadensis*, *C. siliquastrum*; Japanese Flowering Cherry; Crabapples (*Malus baccata*, *M. coronaria*, *M. floribunda*, *M. halliana*, *M. ioensis*, *M. sargenti*, *M. theifera*); *Daphne cneorum*, *D. mezereum*; Dogwoods (*Cornus florida*, *C. kousa*, *C. mas*, *C. nuttalli*); Ericas; Flowering Almond; *Forsythia*; Hawthorns; Japanese Quince; Kalmias; *Kolkwitzia amabilis*; *Laburnum*; Lilacs; *Lonicera*; Magnolias; Peach, double-flowering vars.; *Philadelphus* vars.; *Pieris floribunda*, *P. japonica*; *Prunus cerasifera pissardi*, *P. tomentosa*, *P. triloba*; *Azalea obtusa amoena*, *A. obtusa kaempferi*; *Rhododendron ferrugineum*; *Rhodora canadensis*; *Azalea yedoensis poukhanensis*; *Ribes* (Flowering Currant); *Spiraea*; *Viburnum carlesi*.

CLIMBERS: *Akebia quinata*; *Clematis montana* and var. *rubens*; *Jasminum nudiflorum*; Wistarias, white and purple vars.

The culture of these spring garden plants, and the hardiness of them (most are perfectly hardy over much of the country), will not be repeated here. All the plants in the lists are entered in THE GARDEN DICTIONARY at their proper alphabetical places, and should be sought there by anyone planning a spring garden. — L. B. W.

**SPRING PLANTING.** There is every advantage in getting as much planting done in the spring as possible, except one. That is the onrush of spring itself. The daily march of increasing sunshine, longer days, and greater heat, all contribute to making the spring planting season a hectic one for most gardeners, but of great value to the plants.

Of course the planting of vegetable and flower seeds can be varied a little, one way or the other, by circumstances other than the march of spring. Such variations may mean earlier or later crops. The preferred or proper time for sowing such seeds will not be repeated here, for it is stated at the cultural notes on all the more important crops, whether flowers or vegetables.

The chief difficulty about spring planting lies in those crops which, because they are fast coming out of winter dormancy, *must* be planted before it is too late. This applies to all woody plants, whether fruit trees, ornamental shrubs, trees, or vines, and to the division of many perennial herbs.

The advantages of planting these in the spring are obvious. If you complete the job in time (*i.e.* before they have leaved out), such plants get a full season's growth before they enter their first winter after transplanting. But sometimes, due to other imperative spring work (for which *see* the spring months at GARDEN CALENDAR), it is simply impossible to complete planting before it is too late.

Except for plane trees, and a few others noted at their proper entries, this need not disturb the gardener. For most woody plants can just as well be planted in the fall, which, because of a waning season, is a far more leisurely planting time. *See* AUTUMN PLANTING.

Plane trees and magnolias should only be planted in the spring. Evergreens* and broad-leaved evergreens (which see) may be planted in the spring, but if that is impossible, their second planting period over much of the country should be between Aug. 15 and Sept. 15. For the actual details of planting shrubs, trees, vines, or perennial herbs *see* PLANTING. If you are equipped so that you can retard the normal growth of nursery stock, you can, of course, greatly prolong the spring planting season. For the details of this *see* RETARDING. *See also* SEEDS AND SEEDAGE.

**SPRING-TOOTH HARROW.** See Section 1, TOOLS AND IMPLEMENTS.

**SPRINKLER.** See Section 3, TOOLS AND IMPLEMENTS.

**SPRINKLING CANS.** See Section 1, TOOLS AND IMPLEMENTS.

**SPROUTING BROCCOLI** = *Brassica oleracea italica*. For culture *see* BROCCOLI.

**SPROUTS.** Short for Brussels sprouts (which see).

**SPRUCE.** Usually majestic, sometimes gigantic evergreen trees, comprising the genus **Picea** (py-see′a, py′see-a) of the pine family, of first-rate hort. importance, also widely used for timber and in the making of paper pulp. Only 39 species of spruce are known, all from the northern hemisphere, and generally from the cooler and moister parts of it. They have (without injury and ignoring some dwarf hort. forms) a single, unbranched trunk, with tiers or whorls of branches, and often the outline of the trees is almost exactly the shape of a candle flame. Leaves small, very numerous, needle-like, each on a tiny foot-like cushion or stalk, from which it falls away very readily when dry. The leaves are rarely, if ever, flat, generally being somewhat 4-sided in cross-section. Flowers, in the garden sense, none, being composed in the male flowers only of naked anthers,* and in the female of naked ovules between the scales of what is ultimately the cone. The latter are mostly drooping in fruit, the scales becoming somewhat woody, but not really woody or prickly as in many pines. Seeds 2 under each scale, the seeds winged. (*Picea* is the classical Latin name of the spruce.)

For Culture and uses *see* below. Some people confuse the spruces with the firs, but this is not necessary if a few facts are kept in mind:

| SPRUCE (*Picea*) | FIR (*Abies*) |
|---|---|
| Leaves generally 4-sided. | Leaves flat. |
| Leaves easily falling; hence a poor tree for Christmas greens. | Leaves persistent even when dead; hence the best of all trees for Christmas greens. |
| Cones generally drooping. | Cones always erect. |

Over 30 species and scores of hort. varieties are known to be in cult. in the U.S. Those below have been selected as the most representative, readily available, and generally hardy of the cult. spruces.

**P. abies.** Norway spruce, and probably the most widely cult. evergreen tree in America. A pyramidal tree up to 150 ft. high, the mature bark reddish-brown, the branches pendulous at the end. Leaves about ¾ in. long, shining, dark green. Cones 5–7 in. long. Eu. Hardy from zone* 2 southward. Many hort. forms of the typical tree (which is sometimes known as *P. excelsa*), have been developed for special purposes. Some differ in habit or stature, others in the color of the young or mature foliage. The leading ones are:

*var.* **argentea.** Leaves variegated with white.

*var.* **aurea.** Leaves, or the young ones, golden-yellow.

*var.* **compacta.** A low, dense, nearly globe-shaped dwarf; also in variegated form.

*var.* **conica.** A low, dwarf form with conical habit.

*var.* **gregoryana.** A dwarf form, not over 2 ft. high, its branchlets crowded and pale.

*var.* **maxwelli.** A dwarf, flattish form, not over 2 ft. high, the branchlets short and thick; very dense.

*var.* **nana.** A dwarf, 1–2 ft. high, with orange-yellow foliage.

*var.* **pendula.** Medium-sized plant with hanging branches.

*var.* **procumbens.** Prostrate form with bright yellow twigs.

---

* Special articles on the subjects indicated by an asterisk (*) will be found at the words so marked.

**var. pygmaea.** Dwarf, dense, not over 1 ft. high.
**P. ajanensis** = *Picea jezoensis*.
**P. alba** = *Picea glauca*.
**P. alcockiana** = *Picea bicolor*.
**P. bicolor.** Alcock spruce. A pyramidal evergreen, up to 75 ft. high, the bark grayish-brown. Leaves about ¾ in. long, with 2 white bands on the upper side. Cones cylindric, 3-4 in. long. Jap. Hardy fron zone* 3 southward. Sometimes known as *P. alcockiana*.
**P. canadensis** = *Picea glauca*.
**P. engelmanni.** Engelmann's spruce. A splendid evergreen tree up to 150 ft. high, its whorls* of branches numerous and rather close. Leaves nearly 1 in. long, bluish-green, slightly curved, and a little flattish. Cones 2-3 in. long. British Columbia to Ore., Ariz., and N. Mex. Hardy from zone* 1 southward. One of the finest and hardiest of the cult. spruces. The *var.* **argentea** has silvery leaves; *var.* **glauca**, blue leaves; and the *var.* **fendleri** has drooping branchlets and slightly longer leaves.
**P. excelsa** = *Picea abies*.
**P. glauca.** White or skunk spruce. A tree nearly 100 ft. high, the branches ascending, but the branchlets drooping. Leaves about ¾ in. long, bluish-green. Cones cylindric, 1½-2 in. long. Northern N.A. Hardy from zone* 1 southward, and a very handsome tree. The *var.* **albertiana**, the Black Hills spruce, has shorter cones and more crowded leaves. It is especially suited to states like Minn. and Iowa, where, as well as in neighboring states, it is preferred to the typical form. The *var.* **caerulea** has the leaves still more blue-green. The *var.* **conica** is a dwarf, conical form, useful as an accent* plant or for the rock garden. *Picea glauca* has been, at different times, called also *P. alba* and *P. canadensis*.
**P. jezoensis.** Yeddo spruce. A tree up to 150 ft. high, the bark grayish and scaly. Leaves more or less flattened, nearly ¾ in. long, dark green beneath, silvery above. Cones 2½-3½ in. long. Northern As. and Jap. Hardy from zone* 3 southward.
**P. mariana.** Black spruce. A native spruce, usually not over 50 ft. high, and often growing in bogs. Leaves scarcely ¾ in. long, dull green. Cones ¾-1½ in. long. Throughout northern N.A. and south to Va. Hardy from zone* 1 southward.
**P. omorika.** Serbian spruce. An evergreen tree up to 100 ft. high, the branches ascending. Leaves somewhat flattened, scarcely ½ in. long, dark green beneath, but with 2 white bands above. Cones 2-2½ in. long. S. Eu. Hardy from zone* 3 southward and a very satisfactory spruce for the eastern states.
**P. orientalis.** A magnificent evergreen, sometimes reaching 180 ft. in height, but much less in cult., the branches ascending, but the branchlets often drooping. Leaves glossy-green, scarcely ½ in. long. Cones 2-3½ in. long. Caucasus and Asia Minor. Hardy from zone* 3 southward, but of rather slow growth.
**P. polita.** Tigertail spruce. An evergreen tree up to 120 ft. high, the bark gray and rough. Leaves very stiff, spreading, prickly, nearly 1 in. long, dark glossy-green. Cones 4-5 in. long. Jap. Hardy from zone* 3 southward.
**P. pungens.** Blue spruce; also called Colorado blue spruce. A beautiful, American evergreen tree, often 140 ft. high in the wild, less as cult., the whorls of branches rather remote. Leaves rigid, stiff, prickle-pointed, nearly 1¼ in. long, bluish-green. Cones 3-4 in. long. Rocky Mountain region. Hardy from zone* 1 southward. Much cult., but still more so in the *var.* **kosteriana**, Koster's blue spruce, which is one of the most popular of all blue spruces for lawn planting. It differs from the typical tree in having still more bluish foliage and in the pendulous branches. The *var.* **compacta** is a low, dense form with twiggy branchlets. There are also several other color forms, one with green leaves.
**P. sitchensis.** Sitka spruce. A magnificent tree, sometimes up to 180 ft. high, less as cult., the branches horizontal, but forming a majestic, pyramidal tree. Leaves somewhat flattish, prickle-tipped, nearly 1 in. long, dark glossy-green below, silvery above. Cones 3-4 in. long. Alaska to Calif. Hardy from zone* 4 southward, but not in the East, as it demands more summer moisture than is found along the Atlantic seaboard.

While the above constitute the true spruces, there are other evergreens to which the name is occasionally applied. *See* HEMLOCK.

### SPRUCE CULTURE

The spruce is without doubt the most versatile of our cultivated conifers, and offers a wide selection of material, ranging in size from small shrubby plants to huge forest specimens. The dwarf forms are particularly adapted to foundation plantings and several of the really diminutive varieties of the Norway and Oriental spruce may be well employed in the rock garden. Because of its dense habit, the spruce lends itself admirably to protective plantings such as hedges and windbreaks. Whether the hedge be for purposes of protection or purely ornamental, there is an excellent choice of materials. *Picea polita*, the tigertail spruce, so-called because of its sharp needles, has long been planted as a protective barrier and, as such, equals the effectiveness of a barbed entanglement. For the ornamental hedge there is a selection of narrow upright forms ranging in height from less than fifteen inches to more than twenty feet.

Like all of the conifers, the spruce must be carefully transplanted. The roots react quickly to drying out and, hence, should always be moved with a ball. The root system of this group lies close to the surface and spreads horizontally. The absence of a distinct taproot facilitates moving, although this operation will be easier if root pruning is practiced to stimulate short fibrous growth.

Specimen plantings of the spruce seldom require pruning other than the occasional removal of dead or diseased wood. The habit of growth is dense, and the general outline sufficiently symmetrical, so that little or no pruning for form is required. Where some corrective shaping is desired it is best to disbud rather than use the knife. Disbudding consists of the removal of the terminal bud on those branches which are growing out of place or are developing too fast and thus giving the specimen a thin, lanky appearance. In the case of hedges, a knife or shears may be employed, in order to obtain a dense growth within exact limits. All pruning work should be done in August.

The spruce, like most conifers, is not over-particular as regards soil, although it will do best in a light, sandy loam.

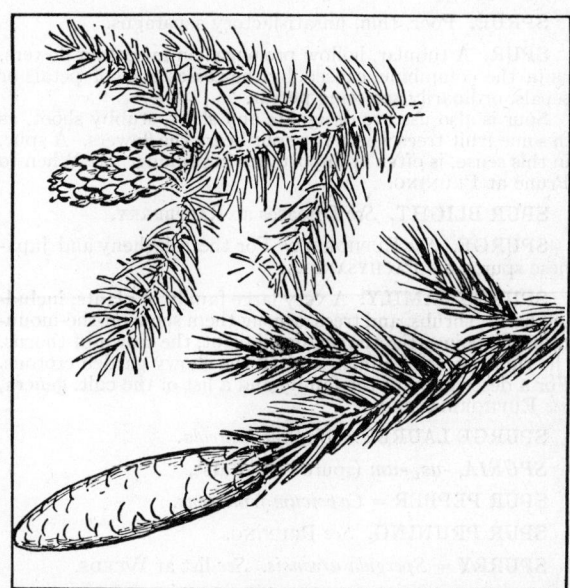

Foliage and cones of Norway spruce (*below*) and the Colorado blue spruce (*above*)

Its requirements for moisture are far more exacting and it will thrive neither in a really dry nor in a poorly drained soil. A well-drained, cool, deep soil should be provided. Few conifers are more susceptible to exposure than the spruce, and drying winds and strong winter sun must be avoided. Because it does not mind partial shade, it is often possible to secure protection from the elements without resorting to planting on northern slopes, the most common method of natural protection.

Propagation is accomplished by seed, grafting, and cuttings. The species are grown mostly from seed sown late in spring and carefully watered and shaded during the first year to prevent damping-off.* Most of the forms are propagated commercially by veneer grafting on *Picea abies* in the greenhouse during Jan. The well-known Koster's blue spruce is now grafted in large numbers on potted seedlings of *Picea pungens* during Aug. It is safe to say that any spruce can be grown from cuttings, although varieties of *Picea abies* and *P. glauca* root easier than most of the others. Cuttings are made from hardwood taken with a heel* and set in washed sand during Dec. They are kept under glass at a temperature of seventy degrees for at least six weeks, after which time root action will generally have commenced. After two or three months they are taken from the sand and potted in a light, rich soil. They are generally set out in the propagating beds late in the spring. — A. D. S.

INSECT PESTS. Gall-forming aphids, sawfly larvae, and spruce budworms are often injurious (*see* FIR). Mites injuring foliage can be checked

---

* Special articles on the subjects indicated by an asterisk (*) will be found at the words so marked.

by dormant oil spray or summer sulphur spray. Bagworms are often abundant; they live in cases of web and trash, and can be controlled by hand-picking or with arsenicals.

DISEASES. Ornamental spruces, especially Norway and Colorado blue spruce, are frequently attacked by a fungus which causes the death of the branches. Small cankers appear accompanied by a copious pitch flow from the affected region. Unless checked the disease spreads upward in the tree. Prompt eradication of all affected parts is the first consideration in control. The use of bordeaux spray will supplement this. Spruce suffers from scorch or wind burn during very warm days in early spring while the ground is still frozen. Deep mulching with well-rotted stable manure will tend to alleviate this condition. Older spruce trees under cultivation, particularly the Norway spruce, tend to slow growth and deterioration after about 50 years. No definite cause of this is known. Wood rots play an important part in the degeneration of older trees and the proper cleaning-out of broken tops and branches is an important consideration in the care of such trees.

**SPRUCE BUDWORM.** *See* Insect Pests at FIR.

**SPRUCE FAMILY** = Pinaceae.

**SPRUCE PINE** = *Tsuga carolinianc*. *See* HEMLOCK.

**SPRUE.** Poor, thin, unsatisfactory asparagus.

**SPUR.** A tubular, hollow prolongation in certain flowers, as in the columbine, caused by the coalescence of petals or sepals, ordinarily secreting nectar.

Spur is also used to designate any short, stubby shoot, as in some fruit trees where the spur bears the flowers. A spur, in this sense, is often of importance in pruning. *See* When to Prune at PRUNING.

**SPUR BLIGHT.** *See* Diseases at RASPBERRY.

**SPURGE.** *See* EUPHORBIA. For the Allegheny and Japanese spurge *see* PACHYSANDRA.

**SPURGE FAMILY.** A very large family of plants, including herbs, shrubs, and trees, among them snow-on-the-mountain, the poinsettia, the castor-oil plant, the crown-of-thorns, the rubber-tree of Brazil, and all the showy garden crotons. For a description of the family and a list of the cult. genera, *see* EUPHORBIACEAE.

**SPURGE LAUREL** = *Daphne laureola*.

*SPURIA, -us, -um* (spure′i-a). False.

**SPUR PEPPER** = *Capsicum frutescens*.

**SPUR PRUNING.** *See* PRUNING.

**SPURRY** = *Spergula arvensis*. *See* list at WEEDS.

*SQUALIDA, -us, -um* (skwal′i-da). Squalid; often evil-smelling.

*SQUAMATA, -us, -um* (skwam-may′ta). With scale-like, very small leaves or bracts.\*

*SQUAMIGERA, -us, -um* (skwam-mij′er-a). Scaly.

*SQUAMOSA, -us, -um* (skwam-ō′sa). Scaly.

**SQUARE FLOWER BED.** For the number of plants needed *see* GARDEN TABLES IV.

**SQUARE MEASURE.** *See* WEIGHTS AND MEASURES, 2.

**SQUARE TANKS.** For contents *see* WEIGHTS AND MEASURES, 5.

*SQUARROSA, -us, -um* (skwa-rō′sa). Squarrose; *i.e.* with spreading or recurved tips.

**SQUASH.** The botanical identity of the various garden and farm plants that go under the name of squash and pumpkin is discussed at *Cucurbita*, to which all of them belong. For practical purposes it does not matter what their origin may be, and in fact it is often unknown. Here we are concerned only with the garden types of squashes and how to grow them.

The common garden squashes (some of them are in reality pumpkins, which see) are best divided into two main types, depending on the use of their fruits — summer squashes and winter squashes. Color of the rind does not always indicate ripeness, and in the summer squashes the rind should be soft enough to prick with the thumb nail before picking.

SUMMER SQUASHES. These comprise several forms, but they all agree in having fruits that are used soon after harvesting and generally the fruits do not, or are not, kept through part of the late fall and winter, as are the winter squashes.

Of the summer squashes there are two well-marked forms or types — the crookneck, usually called summer crookneck squash, and the pineapple, Pattypan, or scallop squashes. The illustrations show the fruit forms of these, but their qualities cannot be illustrated. In the summer crookneck squash the outer skin is much puckered or furrowed, in addition to the crooked neck of the fruit, and the flesh is yellow. The Pattypan or scallop squashes, including what the English and some here call the vegetable marrow, are not crooknecked, the outer skin is smooth, and the flesh is generally greenish or greenish-yellow. While the ancestral types of all these were probably vine-like, the modern varieties are without tendrils,\* or very few, and because they are compact, bushy plants are usually called bush squashes (or pumpkins, for some of them belong to the pumpkin affinity.)

AUTUMN AND WINTER SQUASHES. These are also divided into those that have a crooked neck, as in the winter crookneck squash, and those varieties, usually with a much larger fruit, that are smooth-skinned. Some of the latter produce huge fruits, nearly all yellow, which pass for pumpkins. An old and well-known variety of these winter squashes is the Hubbard. Here, also, belong the variety known as Boston Marrow and the forms known as Turban squash or "squash-within-a-squash" (*see* CUCURBITA MAXIMA TURBANIFORMIS).

### CULTURE

Whatever type of squash is grown, they must be treated as extremely tender annuals, especially the winter and autumn varieties, which in some northern regions will ripen their fruits uncertainly, due to lack of heat and a short growing season. There is generally, except in the coldest regions, no difficulty about raising summer squashes, but all sorts repay quick growth and plenty of heat.

If you have space and prefer to grow the vine-like forms, the hills should be at least 8 × 8 ft. apart, but if space requirements make the bush forms imperative, and they are far easier to grow, cultivate and harvest, the hills can be about 30 in. apart each way.

It is useless to put squashes in a heavy, wet soil, for they grow too slowly in such places. It is better to select a warm, sandy loam upon which they thrive if it can be made rich enough. Being spaced so far apart, there is no use in a program of general soil enrichment for squashes, but every reason for concentrating the fertilizer or manure under the hills. A good plan is to dig out about 2 ft. of indifferent soil and fill in with a half-and-half mixture of sandy loam and well-rotted manure. Or if this is lacking, mix about 1 pound of a good commercial fertilizer with the soil.

For the summer squashes, of the bush type, unless your soil warms up very slowly, the seeds should be planted directly in the hills, 4–5 seeds to a hill, which should ultimately be thinned to 2 or 3 plants to a hill, depending upon their vigor and the ravages of the cutworms.

If your season is short or the soil slow to warm up, the seeds can be started in the hotbed, sown in paper pots or old strawberry baskets about 1 month (no longer) before outdoor planting is possible. When really warm weather has come, 3–4 seedlings should be planted at each hill. The objection to starting plants ahead of time is that they are apt to prematurely flower and fruit soon after transplanting — usually with a single flower or fruit. If they do so, and if you want more and later fruit, the premature flower should be pinched off as soon as it forms.

For the winter squashes or for any that have long, sprawling vines, it is better to start them in the hotbed, as outlined above, if you live in a region with a short growing season. Otherwise, some of the late fruits will be caught by frost before maturity. In any case, the vine-like ones should be watched to see that all the growth does not run to vine and leaf at the expense of fruit. This is especially likely in rich soils or in ones that get extra top-dressings of fertilizer.

If you are out for a record-sized fruit (and many of the large kinds of winter squash habitually pass as pumpkins), the top-

---

\* Special articles on the subjects indicated by an asterisk (\*) will be found at the words so marked.

dressing with fertilizer is a good plan. The only caution is to keep such vines well pinched back, and also to pinch off all but one, or at most two, fruits. Also top-dressing should not include nitrate of soda, but a mixture of fertilizers containing more phosphoric acid and potash than nitrogen (see FERTILIZERS). See also PUMPKIN.

INSECT PESTS. The dark brown squash bug, ⅔ in. long, appears late in the spring, and its grayish nymphs are abundant in summer; it is injurious and difficult to kill. Adults may be hand-picked early in the season; strong soap and nicotine sprays will kill many nymphs.* Crop remnants should be cleaned up early in the fall. The squash borer, a white caterpillar, tunnels the stems and sometimes kills the vines. The borer may be killed by making a small slit in the stem and crushing it; old vines should be destroyed.

Cucumber beetles are serious pests of young plants, and must be checked with arsenicals. Aphids are only minor pests (see CUCUMBER). Pickle worms attack squash (see MUSKMELON). The squash ladybird resembles the Mexican bean beetle; it is easily controlled with arsenicals.

DISEASES. (See also diseases at CUCUMBER.) A disease known as black-rot is very common on squash, especially in storage. The control measures suggested are: seed from healthy fruits, seed disinfection with corrosive sublimate, crop rotations, delaying harvest until the squash are mature, care in not scratching or bruising fruits, placing the crop in storage as soon as harvested; and proper care of storage in ventilation, temperature, and sanitation.* In extreme cases the fruit may be dipped in formaldehyde (1 part in 50 parts of water) before they are put away for the winter.

**SQUASH BUG.** See True Bugs at INSECT PESTS, and the insect pests at SQUASH.

**SQUASH FAMILY** = Cucurbitaceae.

**SQUAWBERRY** = *Mitchella repens*.

**SQUAW-BUSH** = *Rhus trilobata*.

**SQUAW-ROOT** = *Caulophyllum thalictroides*.

**SQUAW WATERWEED** = *Baccharis pilularis*.

**SQUIBB, R.** See America at GARDEN BOOKS.

**SQUILL.** See SCILLA. See also URGINEA.

**SQUIRREL.** See ANIMAL INJURY.

**SQUIRREL-CORN** = *Dicentra canadensis*.

**SQUIRREL'S-EAR** = *Epipactis repens*.

**SQUIRREL'S-FOOT FERN** = *Davallia bullata*.

**SQUIRREL-TAIL GRASS** = *Hordeum jubatum*.

**SQUIRTING CUCUMBER.** See ECBALLIUM.

**ST.** The abbreviation for Saint (which see for all names beginning St.).

**STACHYOIDES** (stack-i-oy'deez, but see OÏDES). Like a betony of the genus *Stachys*.

**STACHYS** (stack'iss). Betony. Woundwort. Annual or perennial herbs, comprising about 270 species of the mint family, distributed throughout the world, but chiefly in the temperate zones, and mostly in damp or wet places. Generally they have fibrous roots and erect stems, but *S. sieboldi* has tuberous, edible roots. Leaves opposite,* smooth or hairy, ovalish or broadly lance-shaped, the margins entire* or toothed. Leaves on the upper part of the stem reduced to leafy bracts.* Flowers purple, scarlet, yellow or white, in 2–many-flowered whorls,* arranged in terminal spikes. Calyx joined about ¾ of its length. Corolla tubular, opening into 2 lips.* Stamens* 4, in pairs, 2 long, 2 short. Fruit 2-celled, splitting into 4 parts when ripe. (*Stachys* is a Greek name used by Dioscorides for another genus.)

A few species are useful in the flower border and one in the kitchen garden. Easily cult. in ordinary garden soil. Propagated by seeds sown in early spring or by division of roots in Sept., March or April. The edible species *S. sieboldi*, the Chinese artichoke, is the one grown as a vegetable. Tubers should be planted in April, 4–6 in. deep, in rows 18 in. apart. They may be dug as required in the fall.

ciliata. Perennial, growing to 6 ft. high, slightly hairy. Leaves ovalish, to 6 in. long, the margins toothed. Flowers reddish-purple, to 1 in. long, in terminal, whorled* spikes, to 8 in. long. British Columbia to Ore.

corsica. Annual, and of sprawling habit, covered with short, soft hairs. Leaves bluntly ovalish, to ½ in. long, with rounded teeth. Flowers pinkish-white, to ¾ in. long, in distant 2–4-flowered whorls.* Mediterranean region.

grandiflora. Hardy perennial, growing to 3 ft. high, slightly hairy. Leaves ovalish, heart-shaped at the base, with rounded teeth. Lower leaves long-stalked. Flowers violet, showy, to 1 in. long, in 20–30-flowered whorls.* Asia Minor. The *var.* **superba** has bright mauve-purple, or white flowers.

lanata. Lamb's-ears. Hardy perennial, growing to 1½ ft. high, covered with soft, white, woolly hairs. Leaves large, 4–8 in. long, broadly lance-shaped, the margins entire.* Flowers small, purple, in densely flowered whorls.* Caucasus and Persia. Often seen in English cottage gardens.

sieboldi. Chinese artichoke. Chorogi. Knotroot. Erect, slightly hairy perennial, growing to 18 in. high, producing numerous small, white, edible tubers underground. Leaves broadly lance-shaped. Flowers small, white or pink in small spikes. China. and Jap. For cult. see above.

**STAFF-TREE.** See CELASTRUS.

**STAFF-TREE FAMILY** = Celastraceae.

**STAG BUSH** = *Viburnum prunifolium*.

**STAGGER-BUSH** = *Xolisma mariana*.

**STAGGER PLANTING.** See Planting at FRUIT CULTURE.

**STAGHORN FERN.** See PLATYCERIUM.

**STAGHORN SUMAC** = *Rhus typhina*.

**STAKES AND STAKING.** Plants are staked for protection from wind and storm and to preserve their symmetry and beauty. Only experience, which often comes too late to prevent damage, will convince the amateur grower of the necessity of staking. It is especially needed by: weak-stemmed and top-heavy plants; tall plants surmounted by tall leafless flowering stems; tall plants in isolated positions; plants which have been disbudded, thus losing the natural support of the side branches; flowers which are grown for cutting, especially when a long stalk is desired. Specific kinds generally needing staking are the taller snapdragons, delphiniums, dahlias, lilies, chrysanthemums, the taller campanulas, climbing plants. Many plants such as Michael-

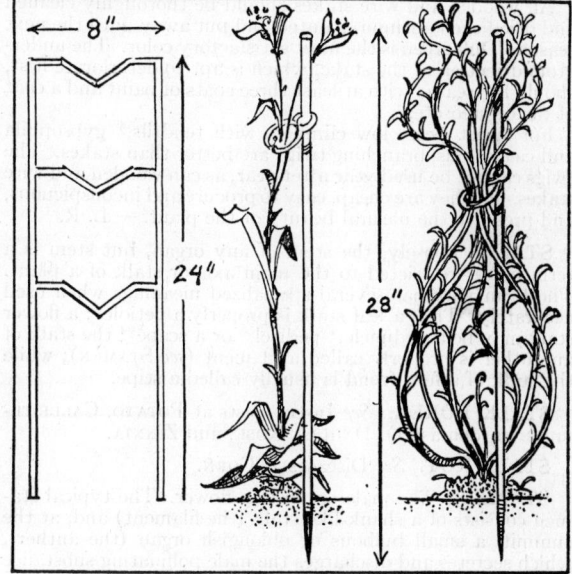

STAKES AND STAKING

At the left, a simple wire contrivance for staking annuals. Use two of them connected by 2 or 3 cross-wires. In the center, the right way to stake a larger plant. At the right, a wrong but common method of staking.

mas daisies will, if the center growth is pinched out, take on a lower, bushier form and make their own support. The shelter of a fence or house-wall will take the place of staking with hollyhocks.

The essentials of staking are: (1) sinking the stakes firmly, for weak staking is useless; (2) staking before the need is apparent; (3) staking inconspicuously. Early staking is concealed by the later growth of the plant, especially if the

* Special articles on the subjects indicated by an asterisk (*) will be found at the words so marked.

stakes are placed as near as possible to its center and the tying done carefully. This is particularly true of bushy plants with soft outlines, such as peonies and gypsophila, which do not need such tall stakes as chimney campanulas, for instance. If plants, especially annuals and climbers, remain unstaked too long, no amount of skill can hide the mistake.

Stakes can be made and painted at home or bought ready-made. Home-made ones are often more satisfactory. Stakes should be a little shorter than the final height of the plant. For annuals, light bamboo canes or #4 wire stakes are best. For shrubs with heavy stems use 2 in. $\times$ 2 in. lumber in short lengths which will support the lower part of the stem where bending is most likely. Iron rods are also good for this purpose. Between these two extremes are a number of stake sizes. For chrysanthemums use ⅞ × ⅞ in. thick and 2 to 3 ft. long. For dahlias and delphiniums use slightly thicker stakes, 4½ to 5½ ft. long. All wood stakes should be pointed at the foot.

Plants with many stalks of heavy-headed flowers, such as peonies, need either many stakes or an encircling wire to which the upper parts of the flower-stems are tied. Or separate wire supports made of two uprights connected by two or three cross-pieces can be set round the plant. Both these devices are on the market. For plants needing slight restraint but not firm tying, use an upright with a loop of wire attached. Secure the wire to the upright with a twist, curve the two ends round the flower-stem and hook them together.

For tying use a soft string which will not cut, green or natural color raffia or green silkaline thread. In tying, first fasten the string or raffia firmly to the stake, then pass it round the flower stem, tying firmly enough to prevent friction, but not so tightly as to check the growth. The knot should be on the inner side, where it shows least. Use plenty of stakes. Never economize by trying to control a plant of several stems with one stake.

All wooden and wire stakes should be thoroughly cleaned and dried each autumn, painted and put away until the next season. Dull green is the most satisfactory color. The underground section of the stake, which is apt to deteriorate first, should be treated with at least three coats of paint and a coat of tar or creosote.

For sweet peas, low climbers with tendrils,* gypsophila and carnations, branching twigs are better than stakes. The twigs cannot be used year after year, as can wooden and wire stakes, but they are cheap, easy to procure and inconspicuous, and preserve the natural beauty of the plant. — L. R.

**STALK.** Loosely, the stem of any organ, but stem is a term better restricted to the main axis or stalk of a plant. The term *stalk* has several specialized meanings when used accurately. Thus a leaf stalk is properly a petiole*; a flower stalk may be a peduncle,* pedicel,* or a scape*; the stalk of an anther is properly called a filament (see STAMEN); while the stalk of a fern frond is usually called a stipe.

**STALK BORER.** See Insect Pests at POTATO, CALLISTEPHUS (garden aster), DAHLIA, ROSE, and ZINNIA.

**STALK ROT.** See Diseases at CORN.

**STAMEN.** The male organ in a flower. The typical stamen consists of a shank-like stalk (the filament) and, at the summit, a small bulbous or oblongish organ (the anther), which secretes and discharges the male pollinating substance (the pollen). The latter is the familiar and usually yellow "dust" found in flowers. See FLOWER for the position and insertion of stamens. Some flowers bear infertile stamens. See STAMINODE.

**STAMINATE.** Bearing only stamens. See FEMALE.

**STAMINODE.** A functionless, sterile or infertile stamen. They often resemble a true stamen but produce no pollen. Some staminodes, however, are petal-like and showy, as in the canna and some peonies. The technical term is staminodium.

**STANDARD.** 1. A tree or shrub, which by grafting or training is restricted to a single, tree-like stem, usually shorter than normal, and in which all growth is concentrated in a terminal crown of foliage. Standards are popular in formal plantings, because their height and often umbrella-shaped form is fixed. Some standards have weeping branches, which have been grafted at the desired height, as in the weeping mulberry. Among other plants often grown as standards are forms of catalpa, rose, and several fruit trees.

A standard (1)

2. The upper, broad, and usually erect petal of a pea flower; called also a banner or vexillum. The term is also applied to the three erect petals of an iris flower to distinguish them from the three drooping ones known as "falls."

**STANDARD CATALPA** = *Catalpa bignonioides nana*.

**STANDARD WEIGHTS.** See WEIGHTS AND MEASURES.

**STANDING CYPRESS** = *Kochia scoparia*, also *Gilia rubra*.

**STANHOPEA** (stan-hope′ee-a). Tropical American orchids, comprising about 50 species, mostly tree-perching (epiphytes*), with thick branching stems and pseudobulbs,* which are sheathed with thin scales, each bearing one large leathery leaf. Flowers borne on leafless, drooping stalks which emerge from the under side of the plant. Flowers large, scented, mostly yellow, variously spotted with purple or red, to 7 in. across, in racemes.* Sepals and petals curved, similar to each other, excepting one, which forms the lip,* which is pouched or boat-shaped, with the middle part of the lobe fleshy and horn-shaped on either side. Fruit a 3-celled capsule. (Named for the Earl of Stanhope, of the Medico-Botanical Society of London.)

For cult. see ORCHID (greenhouse species).

**tigrina.** Flowers scented, large, to 7 in. across, in 2–4-flowered hanging racemes.* Sepals and petals yellow, marked purplish-blue, the lip white at tip. Mex. Aug.–Nov.

**wardi.** Leaves large, leathery. Flowers 6–10, in hanging racemes, to 16 in. long. Sepals and petals orange-yellow, spotted with purple. Inside of lip* dark purple and velvety. Guatemala to Venezuela. July–Sept.

**STANLEYA** (stan′lee-a). Perennial herbs, comprising about 10 species of the mustard family, natives of northwestern N.A. Leaves alternate,* bluish-green, the margins sometimes lobed. Flowers yellow, in long terminal racemes. Calyx of 4 sepals, narrow. Corolla of 4 petals, also narrow, alternating with the sepals. Stamens* 6, 4 long, 2 short. Fruit a long capsule.* (Named for Edward Stanley, Earl of Derby.)

Easily cult., the one below making a useful border plant. Propagated by seeds or division of the roots. Seeds should be sown ⅛ in. deep, in sandy soil, in a temperature of 50°–60° in the cool greenhouse, or cold frame in early spring. They should be gradually hardened off and planted in a sunny position. Division of the roots may be made in Sept., March or April.

**pinnata.** Growing to 5 ft. high. Leaves varying from ovalish to lance-shaped. Lower leaves usually cut into segments, upper leaves entire.* Flowers golden-yellow, in long, terminal racemes.* Western U.S.

*STANS* (stanz). Upright; erect.

**STANWELL PERPETUAL.** A rose variety. See ROSA SPINOSISSIMA.

**STAPEK.** A trademarked bird feeder, designed to hold suet where it may be used but not carried away by birds.

---

* Special articles on the subjects indicated by an asterisk (*) will be found at the words so marked.

STAPELIA (sta-pee'li-a). Carrion-flower. South African, cactus-like, desert plants, comprising over 100 species of the milkweed family. They are low-growing plants with thick, fleshy, green or colored stems which are 4-sided and grooved, sometimes with protuberances. There are no real leaves, which are represented by scales, spines or bristles. Flowers large with very unpleasant odor, curiously marked and barred with dull red, yellow or purple, growing from the angles of the stem. Calyx* of 5 sepals. Corolla of 5 petals, fleshy, spreading and variously colored, sometimes marbled or barred. The petals bear at the base 2 rows of outgrowths which are also colored, forming a crown or corona, the outer row petal-like, the inner scale-like. Fruit 2-celled. (Named for J. B. Van Stapel, Dutch physician.)

Stapelias are usually seen in botanic gardens, or specialists' collections of succulents, though a few species are grown in the greenhouse for their curious flowers. For cult. see SUCCULENTS. Perhaps two dozen other species are in cult. in America, mostly in desert gardens in Calif.

**gigantea.** Growing to 9 in. high. Stems dull green. Flowers to 11 in. across, salver-shaped, hairy, purple and light brown, marked with crimson lines. Summer.

**variegata.** Growing to 6 in. high. Stems green, often tinted purple. Flowers 1-5, growing at the base of the stem, to 3 in. across, under surface green, upper surface wrinkled and ridged, greenish-yellow, with dark purplish-brown spots.

**STAPHYLEA** (staf-i-lee'a). Bladder-nut. Shrubs or small trees comprising the only commonly cult. genus of the family **Staphyleaceae** (staf-i-lee-ā'see-ee) which includes 5 other genera and perhaps 25 species, all from the north temperate zone. The bladder-nuts, of which 11 species are known, but only the two below much cult., are small trees, or, as grown, more often shrubs with opposite,* compound* leaves, the leaflets arranged finger-fashion, with an odd one at the end. Flowers white, or greenish-white, not very showy, arranged in a terminal cluster (panicle*). Sepals,* petals, and stamens,* each 5. Fruit an inflated, membranous, usually 3-sided capsule,* the seeds bony (hence the name bladder-pod). The plants are more showy in fruit than in flower. (Staphylea is from the Greek for grape, in allusion to the grape-like branching of the flower cluster.)

One of the cult. species is from N.A., the other from the Caucasus. Both prefer partial shade and a reasonably moist, rich soil. There is little use of planting either on rocky or sandy, windswept slopes. Easily propagated by sowing fresh seed (or it may be stratified), or by cuttings.

**colchica.** Usually a shrub 8-12 ft. high. Leaflets 5 (or 3 on flowering twigs), oval-oblong, 2-3½ in. long, sharply toothed. Flower cluster 2-3 in. long, erect or a little pendulous. Flowers about ⅝ in. long. Fruit much inflated, 1¼-3½ in. long. Caucasus. May-June. Hardy from zone* 3 southward.

**trifolia.** A shrub or small tree, 8-14 ft. high. Leaflets 3, elliptic or ovalish, sharply, unequally, but somewhat irregularly finely toothed, 1½-3½ in. long. Flower cluster nodding, about 2 in. long, the flowers scarcely ½ in. long. Fruit 1½-3 in. long. Eastern N.A. May. Hardy from zone* 2 southward.

**STAR ANISE** = *Illicium verum*.

**STAR-APPLE.** Tropical, ornamental or fruit trees comprising the genus Chrysophyllum (kriss-o-fil'lum) of the family Sapotaceae, most of the 60 species from tropical America. They mostly have a milky juice and alternate,* leathery leaves, often golden-hairy on the under side, without marginal teeth, and with many transverse, lateral, parallel veins. Flowers small, inconspicuous, usually in nearly stalkless clusters. For details see SAPOTACEAE. Fruit a globe-shaped or oblongish berry, edible in some species. (Chrysophyllum is from the Greek for golden leaf, in allusion to the golden hairs on the under side of many of the leaves.)

The first species is grown chiefly for its fruit, although the under side of the foliage is very handsome. The satinleaf, as its name implies, has still more handsomely colored foliage, but is grown only for ornament. Neither species can be grown with safety north of zone* 8, which confines their cult. to the warmest parts of Fla. There they do well on a variety of sandy soils, which, however, should be manured if too poor in plant food. They are medium-sized trees and need not be spaced more than 25-30 ft. apart.

**C. cainito.** The common star-apple; called also cainito. A tree 25-30 ft. high, occasionally more. Leaves oval-oblong, 3-5 in. long, deep green above, golden and felty beneath. Fruit apple-shaped, 2-4 in. thick, smooth, greenish-purple, the flesh white and sweet when ripe. The cross-section of the fruit suggests a star (hence star-apple) in the arrangement of its seeds. Fruit ripening in late spring or early summer, and rarely seen in the North. Tropical America. Not safe north of zone* 9.

**C. oliviforme.** Satinleaf. A small, round-headed tree, rather compactly branched, the coppery under surface of the leaves very showy. Leaves ovalish or elliptic, 2-3½ in. long, deep green above. Fruit ovalish, scarcely ¾ in. long, deep purple, usually found at most seasons, due to the irregular flowering period. Fla. Bahamas and the W.I. Hardy as far north as protected parts of zone* 8. Grown only for ornament.

**STAR-BLOOM** = *Spigelia marilandica*.

**STAR CACTUS.** See ASTROPHYTUM.

**STARCH.** The first, and incomparably the most important, food manufactured in the green leaves of plants and never yet produced synthetically. It is made from a combination of sunshine, gases from the air, water and plant foods from the soil, worked upon by the green coloring matter of the leaves (chlorophyll*). For details of this process see PLANT FOODS. The starch in potatoes, rice, corn, etc., is not manufactured in the seeds or tubers, but in the leaves, and simply stored in other parts of the plant for future use.

**STARCH HYACINTH** = *Muscari botryoides*.

**STARFLOWER** = *Trientalis borealis*. For the spring starflower see BRODIAEA UNIFLORA.

**STAR-GRASS.** See ALETRIS FARINOSA and HYPOXIS.

**STAR HYACINTH** = *Scilla amoena*.

**STAR IPOMOEA** = *Quamoclit coccinea*.

**STAR JASMINE** = *Trachelospermum jasminoides*.

**STAR LILY** = *Leucocrinum montanum* and *Lilium concolor*.

**STARLINGS.** See Bird Nuisances at BIRDS.

**STAR-OF-BETHLEHEM** = *Ornithogalum umbellatum* and *O. nutans*.

**STAR-OF-JERUSALEM** = *Tragopogon pratensis*.

**STAR PHLOX** = *Phlox drummondi stellaris*.

**STAR PRIMROSE** = *Primula sinensis stellata*.

**STAR PULVERIZER.** See Section 1, TOOLS AND IMPLEMENTS.

**STARRY GRASSWORT** = *Cerastium arvense*.

**STARRY SOLOMON'S-SEAL** = *Smilacina stellata*.

**STAR VIOLET** = *Houstonia serpyllifolia*.

**STARWORT.** See STELLARIA and ASTER.

**STATE FLOWERS.** The different states of the Union have chosen floral emblems, sometimes by the legislature, sometimes by vote of the school children, or by suggestions from garden clubs. In many cases, as will be seen from the list below, the plant is not native in the state that chose it.

STATE FLOWERS

Alabama. Goldenrod
Arizona. Giant cactus
Arkansas. Apple blossom
California. California poppy
Colorado. Columbine
Connecticut. Mountain laurel
Delaware. Peach blossom
District of Columbia. American beauty rose
Florida. Orange blossom
Georgia. Cherokee rose
Idaho. Mock-orange
Illinois. Violet
Indiana. Zinnia
Iowa. Wild rose
Kansas. Sunflower
Kentucky. Goldenrod
Louisiana. Magnolia
Maine. White pine
Maryland. Black-eyed Susan
Massachusetts. Trailing arbutus
Michigan. Apple blossom
Minnesota. Showy lady's-slipper
Mississippi. Magnolia
Missouri. Hawthorn
Montana. Bitter-root
Nebraska. Goldenrod
Nevada. Sagebrush
New Hampshire. Lilac
New Jersey. Violet

* Special articles on the subjects indicated by an asterisk (*) will be found at the words so marked.

### STATE FLOWERS

| | |
|---|---|
| New Mexico. Spanish bayonet | South Dakota. Pasqueflower |
| New York. Wild rose | Tennessee. Maypop |
| North Carolina. Common white daisy | Texas. Lupine |
| | Utah. Globe tulip |
| North Dakota. Wild rose | Vermont. Red clover |
| Ohio. Carnation | Virginia. Flowering dogwood |
| Oklahoma. Mistletoe | |
| Oregon. Oregon grape | Washington. *Rhododendron californicum* |
| Pennsylvania. Mountain laurel | |
| | West Virginia. Great laurel |
| Rhode Island. Violet | Wisconsin. Violet |
| South Carolina. Carolina jasmine | Wyoming. Painted-cup |

All of these plants are in THE GARDEN DICTIONARY, mostly entered under the Latin name of the genera to which they belong. They are also entered under the common names given in the above list and should be sought in the body of the book if the Latin name is wanted for these state flowers. See also NATIONAL FLOWERS.

**STATICE** (stat'i-see). Thrift. Sea Pink. Summer-blooming, low, perennial herbs of the family Plumbaginaceae, comprising only a few species, although the names credited to *Statice* are many. Most of them belong to *Limonium* (which see). The true statices have small, evergreen leaves in basal rosettes, from which rises a rigid, stiff flowering stalk, at the end of which is a dense, globe-shaped head of chaffy flowers. Just below the head is a series of membranous colored bracts,* two of them united into a sort of sheath. The arrangement of this flower cluster is the chief difference between *Statice* and *Limonium*, where the cluster is open and branching. (*Statice* is the classical Greek name of the thrift.) The plants were long known as *Armeria* and are still so listed by some dealers.

The thrifts are good plants for the general border, the rock garden, or they are sometimes grown in pots (cool greenhouse) for their long-keeping flowers. They are of easy culture in most garden soils, but do better in light, sandy loams than in heavy clays. Easily propagated by division.

**armeria.** Common thrift. Not over 12 in. high. Leaves very narrow, 1-veined, scarcely ⅛ in. wide, in a dense basal rosette. Flowering stalk smooth, the head about ¾ in. in diameter, pink, purple or white (in hort. varieties). Eu., also rare in northern N.A. and in Chile. Sometimes offered as *Armeria maritima* or *A. vulgaris*. An old garden favorite, and known in several forms. The *var.* **laucheana** and its form known as Six Hills Hybrid are useful in the rock garden; they have light pink flowers. The *var.* **alba** has white flowers.

**caespitosa.** A rock garden plant, scarcely 2 in. high and densely tufted. Leaves very narrow and short. Flower heads nearly stalkless, small pink or pale lilac. Pyrenees.

**laucheana** = *Statice armeria laucheana.*

**plantaginea.** Resembling *S. armeria*, but the leaves about ¼ in. wide and 3–5-veined, and the stalk of the flower cluster may be 12–20 in. high. Flower heads about ¾ in. in diameter, pink, purple, crimson, or white. Eu.

**STATUARY.** See ORNAMENT AND FURNITURE.

**STAUNTONIA** (staun-tō-ni-a). A small, little-known genus of Asiatic, woody vines of the family Lardizabalaceae, with evergreen leaves. The only cult. species, S. **hexaphylla**, is a tall-growing vine, sometimes reaching 40 ft. in height, with alternate,* compound* leaves, the 3–7 leaflets arranged finger-fashion, more or less oval, and 3–4 in. long, pale green beneath. Male and female flowers separate, but on the same plant, white but tinged with violet, about ¾ in. wide, fragrant, borne in small clusters (racemes*) in the leaf-axils.* Stamens* 6, more or less connected. Petals none, the 6 sepals petal-like. Fruit fleshy and berry-like. Jap. and Korea. May–June. Hardy from zone* 6 southward, and best grown in partial shade and rich, moist soils. Propagated by greenwood cuttings under glass. (Named for Sir G. L. Staunton, English physician.)

**STECHADOS** = *Lavandula stoechas.*

**STECKLING.** A rare term for a slip or cutting; also a *steckling*, in sugar-beet regions, is a late-planted sugar beet, grown for seed production but not for its root.

**STEEPLEBUSH** = *Spiraea tomentosa.*

**STEIRONEMA** (sty-ro-nee'ma). Loosestrife. North American perennial herbs, comprising about 5 species, of the family Primulaceae. Leaves usually opposite,* sometimes in whorls,* lance-shaped. Flowers yellow, solitary or clustered, growing from the axils* of the leaves. Calyx of 5 sepals. Corolla of 5 petals, each petal curling inwards enclosing a stamen,* giving the flower a wheel-like appearance. Alternating with the petals are 5 sterile stamens (staminodes*). Fruit a dry capsule. (*Steironema* is from the Greek for sterile threads, in allusion to the staminodes.*) For other plants called loosestrife, see LYSIMACHIA and LYTHRUM.

They are not much in cultivation, but can be used in damp or shady places in the flower border or wild garden. Propagated by division of roots in Sept. or early spring.

**ciliatum.** Fringed loosestrife. Also known as *Lysimachia ciliata.* Strong-growing, to 4 ft. high, not much branched. Leaves opposite,* broadly lance-shaped, to 6 in. long. Flowers yellow, to 1 in. across. Moist places in U.S., naturalized in Eu. July.

**STELLARIA** (stell-lair'i-a). Starwort. Chickweed. Stitchwort. Annual or perennial herbs, comprising about 100 species, of the pink family, distributed throughout the world, chiefly in the temperate regions, and rather weedy. They are of spreading, tufted or scrambling habit, the stems weak and much-branched. Leaves opposite,* lance-shaped, sometimes hairy. Flowers small, generally white, in loose branching clusters. Calyx* of 5 sepals. Corolla of 5 petals, spreading, star-like. Stamens* 5–10. Fruit a dry capsule.* (*Stellaria* is from the Latin for star, in allusion to the shape of the flower.)

These plants are mostly garden weeds, the only cult. species, *S. holostea*, being the most showy. It may be used in the wild garden or for covering dry banks. Propagated by seeds.

**holostea.** Greater stitchwort. Easter-bell. Also known as *Alsine holostea.* Hardy perennial, with creeping rootstocks, and of scrambling habit, to 2 ft. high. Leaves lance-shaped, to 3 in. long, slightly hairy. Flowers white, showy, to ¾ in. across, numerous, in loose, branching terminal clusters. Calyx slightly hairy. Eurasia, naturalized in N.A.

**media.** Chickweed. See list at WEEDS.

**STELLARIS, -e** (stell-lar'is). Star-like.

**STELLATA, -us, -um** (stell-lay'ta). Star-like.

**STELLULATA, -us, -um** (stell-you-lay'ta). Somewhat, or a little, star-like.

**STEM.** The main axis of a plant, usually called the trunk in a tree, but mostly called the stem in shrubs or woody vines. In herbs the stem is sometimes known (loosely) as the stalk, but the latter term has, properly, a more restricted meaning. See STALK.

While most stems are aerial, *i.e.* above ground, there are many underground stems, which are commonly but incorrectly called roots. Actually they are rootstocks (which see), and often valuable propagative material for the gardener because they bear buds (which roots never do), from which new plants may arise. See also BULB.

The stems of woody plants differ from those of herbs in bearing buds which will survive the winter above ground. But the stems of all but a handful of herbs die down to the ground each winter. This fundamental difference in habit dictates our methods of propagating plants. See PROPAGATION.

While most stems are woody or herbaceous, there are a few families or genera of plants that bear most unusual stems. Some, as in the cacti, and in certain cactus-like spurges, function as do leaves, but are often much swollen and store large amounts of water. See CACTI, SUCCULENTS. Others are essentially leafless, or quite so, and such plants have green, wire-like, or flat leaf-like stems. See ACACIA, MUEHLENBECKIA, RUSCUS, and ASPARAGUS.

**STEM CLIMBER.** See VINES.

**STEM CUTTINGS.** See CUTTINGS.

**STEM-END-ROT.** See Diseases at ORANGE.

**STEM GRAFTING.** See GRAFTING.

**STEMMARIA** (stem-mair'i-a). An old generic name for certain ferns now included in *Platycerium* (which see).

**STEM NEMATODE.** See Diseases at PHLOX.

---

* Special articles on the subjects indicated by an asterisk (*) will be found at the words so marked.

**STEM ROT.** See Diseases at CARNATION and CLEMATIS.

**STENANTHIUM** (sten-an'thi-um). Perennial herbs with bulbous rootstocks, comprising about 5 species of the family Liliaceae, natives of the U.S. and Mex. Leaves mostly growing at the base of the stem. Flowers greenish-white or purple, often nodding, in loose or pyramidal clusters. Calyx* of 3 colored sepals, united at the base, forming a short top-shaped tube. Corolla of 3 petals alternating with the sepals attached to the short tube. Stamens* 6. Fruit a 3-celled capsule.* (*Stenanthium* is from the Greek for narrow flower, in allusion to the sepals and petals.)

These plants are of little garden importance, but occasionally grown in the wild garden, where they need a distinctly acid soil.

    **robustum.** Growing to 5 ft. high. Leaves to 1 ft. long, and ¾ in. wide, the upper ones reduced to bracts.* Flowers greenish-white, to ¾ in. across, numerous in pyramidal clusters to 2 ft. long. Southeastern U.S.

**STENOLOBIUM** (sten-o-lō'bi-um). A small genus of tropical American shrubs and trees of the family Bignoniaceae, **S. stans**, the yellow elder, is a very popular ornamental throughout zones* 8 and 9, and hardy even in protected parts of zone* 7. It is a large shrub or tree, scarcely over 20 ft. high, with opposite,* compound* leaves, the leaflets borne feather-fashion. Leaflets 5–13, lance-oval, 3–4 in. long, pointed at the tip, the margins toothed. Flowers showy, yellow, the corolla more or less funnel-shaped, about 2 in. long, the inside of the tube hairy toward the base. Fruit a narrow capsule,* 6–8 in. long. Of easy cult. and a deservedly popular ornamental, as its cluster of late-blooming flowers is borne in profusion. It is quick-growing, more often shrubby in the U.S. but a tree in the tropics. Other names for it are *Tecoma stans* and *Bignonia stans*. (*Stenolobium* is from the Greek for narrow lobes, in allusion to the narrow fruit.)

**STENOPHYLLA, -us, -um** (sten-o-fill'a). Narrow-leaved.

**STENOPTERA, -us, -um** (sten-op'ter-ra). Narrow-winged.

**STENOTAPHRUM** (sten-o-taff'rum). Tropical, or subtropical, perennial, creeping grasses of no hort. importance except that one of the three known species, **S. secundatum**, is the St. Augustine grass, widely used for lawns in the South where better lawn grasses will not thrive. See LAWN. It is a creeping grass, rooting at the joints, the leafy stems 3–12 in. high. Leaves grass-like, but short and flattish, blunt, rarely over 3 in. long. Flower spike stiff, terminal, 2–5 in. long, the spikelets borne in sunken pits on one side of the stalk of the spikelet. S. Car. to Tex. and throughout tropical America. (*Stenotaphrum* is from the Greek for narrow trench, in allusion to the pits in which the spikelets are borne.)

**STEPHANANDRA** (steff-a-nan'dra). Asiatic shrubs of the rose family, two of the four known species grown for ornament, although their spirea-like flowers are rather unimpressive. Leaves alternate,* more or less lobed and toothed. Flowers small, white, in terminal clusters (panicles* or corymbs*). Calyx* cup-shaped, its lobes 5. Petals 5, about the length of the calyx lobes. Stamens* 10–20. Fruit an oblique, scarcely splitting, dry pod (follicle*), with 1–2 shining seeds. (*Stephanandra* is from the Greek for crown and man, in allusion to the crown of rather persistent stamens.*)

Stephanandras are of easy culture in ordinary garden soils, but are not much grown because the closely related genus *Spiraea* provides far finer hort. material. They are easily propagated by seeds, cuttings or by division.

    **flexuosa** = *Stephanandra incisa*.

    **incisa.** An arching shrub 5–8 ft. high, the stems often drooping. Leaves ovalish, long-pointed, 2–2½ in. long, lobed almost to the middle, the lobes toothed. Flowers greenish-white, the stamens* 10. Jap. and Korea. June. Hardy from zone* 4 southward, possibly in zone* 3 with protection. Foliage reddish-purple in the fall. Sometimes offered as *S. flexuosa*.

    **tanakae.** Not over 6 ft. high. Leaves 2–4 in. long, shallowly 3-lobed or deeply toothed, the teeth also toothed. Flowers white, the stamens* 15–20. Jap. June–July. Hardy from zone* 4 southward, probably in zone* 3 with protection. Foliage yellow, orange, or scarlet in the fall.

**STEPHANOTIS** (steff-a-no'tis). Twining woody vines, comprising about 15 species of the family Asclepiadaceae, natives of Madagascar and the Malay Archipelago. Leaves opposite, thick and leathery. Flowers showy, large, white, in umbel*-like clusters growing from the axils* of the leaves. Calyx* of 5 sepals. Corolla of 5 lobes, opening salver-wise, the tube to 2 in. long, swollen at the base and sometimes at the throat. There is a small crown at the opening of the corolla tube. (*Stephanotis* is from the Greek for crown and ear, in allusion to the crown.)

Only *S. floribunda* is in general cultivation, and it makes one of the best greenhouse climbers or specimen plants. It should be grown in a winter temperature of 55°–65° and summer of 70°–90°. Propagated by cuttings made from half-ripened shoots. Shoots should be inserted in a mixture of ½ sand and ½ peat in individual pots in March, and placed in a confined, moist position, shaded from sun, until rooted. When pots are filled with roots they should be re-potted into potting mixture* 5, shaded from sun, given plenty of water and be syringed daily, as they are subject to mealybugs. They should be cut back occasionally to obtain several leads. These plants require shade and air through summer, but in the fall should be given less water until Feb. and a temperature of 55°–65°. They should be cut back and re-potted every year.

    **floribunda.** Madagascar jasmine. Wax flower. Stems twining. Leaves ovalish, thick and leathery, to 4 in. long. Flowers waxy-white, fragrant, in umbel-like clusters in the leaf-axils.* Madagascar. See VINES. It is grown outdoors in Fla.

**STEPPING STONES.** See PATHS AND PAVING.

**STEPS.** Steps are devices for making easier the passage on foot from one level to another. Therefore, no matter what the height of the ascent or the size of the building above, they must always be adapted to the human scale, by which is meant that they must be convenient for climbing both by children and grown-ups. Since their height and depth or width of tread can vary only within narrow limits, a dignified or imposing effect can only be obtained by increasing their length.

Outdoor steps should generally be less steep than indoor steps. Space within a building is usually so valuable that it cannot be spared to make steps of the easiest ascent. Steps of wood stairs in the average house are likely to be about 8 in. high and 10 in. deep, with a projecting nose increasing the width of tread to about 11 in. But a garden step of these dimensions will be neither comfortable to climb nor pleasant to look at, and since the quality of restfulness is indispensable to the well-designed garden, the proportions of the steps, which are usually conspicuous objects, are of much importance. For a 12-in.-wide step the height of the riser should not exceed 6 in., and this is a good general proportion for small garden steps and adjusts itself well to a bank of about 1 vertical: 2 horizontal.

A simple, built-up set of curved steps

Outdoor steps are frequently made of wider treads than 12 in. and when they are, the risers are usually lower. Thus a height or riser of 5 in. with a tread width of 14 in. or 15 in. makes a step pleasant both to look at and to climb, and many steps are found of still lower risers and wider treads.

The aesthetic value of garden steps is great. They express human uses and their strong horizontal and vertical lines are a good foil to the plant forms around them. A flight of a few steps may, of itself, often be just the constructed thing needed to accent and vitalize the plan of a simple garden, formal or informal.

---

*Special articles on the subjects indicated by an asterisk (*) will be found at the words so marked.

To anyone asking, When, where and how should garden steps be used? the answer might be made, Wherever they are necessary. That is to say, whenever and wherever it is felt to be better to pass from one level to another by a sudden transition rather than by a continuous slope. This, of course, is predicated on a good plan or layout in which all the lines have been laid down simply and constructively and the different levels foreseen. In such cases, steps will fall into their natural places on the plan: they will be put, in fact, where they will do most good. Not infrequently it is desirable to interrupt an easy grade by two or three steps, or even by a single step, making the grades still more easy; but such steps should be placed only where it is felt that, for some reason, a line of separation is appropriate. Such steps may be made either in narrow lawns or paved walks. Steps should be of the width of the walk which they terminate, sidewalls (if any) being outside of the walk lines. See also illust., page 386.

Solid stone steps with iron railings

Steps are usually straight (rectilinear) in all dimensions, but curved steps, either convex or concave, are common. In fact steps may be made to fit almost any desired lines. There are many effective flights of convex garden steps, especially in England, each step being of longer diameter than the one above it. Such steps should give on a wider open space below than the walk above them, so as to provide for the radiation or distribution of the traffic instead of confining it within the width of the walk.

As to materials and construction of steps. There are masonry steps of stone, brick or concrete which are likely to be part of a terrace wall or other structure. It is not possible within the limits of this article to go into details of construction of such steps, but it might be said that it should correspond with that of the wall or other structure of which they are part, their foundations or supports being laid below frost line.

Stone steps with parapet

But the most generally useful garden steps are those made of local materials, of stones that will split naturally into flat slabs, such as slate or bluestone, or, in fact, of any stones with one flat side. If flagstones with at least one straight edge are obtainable, these can be laid on other flagstones or bricks to make steps of the required height, while underneath should be a layer of broken stone or cinders 12 in. or more thick to make a good bed. The bottom of this bed should be horizontal or, better still, with a slight pitch forward to avoid sliding: this is in order to drain water away from under the steps. Stones for the treads should be large and heavy enough not to be easily displaced. Stones of each step should overlap those of the step below, say, an inch or more.

In many districts where there are no laminated or easily splittable stones there are waterworn stones with one flat side which can be made into practicable and attractive steps especially appropriate in natural or naturalistic compositions. But the building of these requires a good deal of ingenuity and patience, and it is not often that one can find a workman able to build such steps satisfactorily. It would be better for the garden owner to make them himself, with only the aid of the hired man. He is likely to get a thrill out of his work far exceeding that of some more expensive amusements. The general construction of such steps is similar in principle to that of flagstone steps described above. Useful tools to have around are a small and a larger crowbar and a pick and shovel.

A formal flight of garden steps with a balustrade

GRASS STEPS. An attractive alternative for any of those suggested above is a flight of grass steps. They cannot be used, of course, in places where there is much traffic, for the grass will not stand such concentrated wear and tear. But as infrequently used steps they are very charming, especially in secluded, partially shaded gardens. Make the steps broad and with shallow risers. Cut the earth very evenly and see that there is adequate topsoil. They must be turfed with the finest quality of turf, carefully laid and watered for the first few weeks. For details see TURF. — H. A. C.

**STERCULIA** (ster-kew′li-a). A large genus of tropical trees of the family Sterculiaceae, only S. foetida of hort. interest, and this little known outside of extreme southern Fla., perhaps because it is hardy nowhere else. It is a smooth-barked tree, 40–60 ft. high, the branches inclined to be in tiers (whorled*). Leaves alternate,* compound,* the leaflets arranged finger-fashion. Leaflets 5–9, oblongish or narrower, pointed, 5–9 in. long. Flowers blooming with the unfolding of the leaves, purplish-red, decidedly bad-smelling, and borne in clusters (panicles*) in the leaf-axils.* Flowers unisexual* or polygamous,* the 5 sepals petal-like, the petals lacking. Fruit a collection of 5 woody carpels, 3–4 in. long, green outside but bright red within, the seeds large, hard and black. Somewhat grown for ornament in Fla. and propagated by seeds or cuttings of green wood. For other trees, sometimes offered as *Sterculia*, see BRACHYCHITON and FIRMIANA SIMPLEX. (*Sterculia* is from the Latin for manure, in allusion to the unpleasant odor of some species.)

**STERCULIACEAE** (ster-kew-li-ā′see-ee). The chocolate family (50 genera and 750 species) is almost exclusively tropical and of more interest in commerce than as the source of garden plants. Mostly trees and shrubs, the outstanding economic genera are *Theobroma* (chocolate) and *Cola* (the kola nut), neither of which is much cult. outside of tropical plantations.

Ornamental tender plants are found in *Dombeya*, *Brachychiton*, *Firmiana* and *Sterculia*, some of which become trees if planted outdoors in frost-free areas. *Fremontia* and *Thomasia* (one a ground cover) are grown in Calif., rarely in greenhouses, while *Mahernia* is herbaceous and furnishes an attractive greenhouse herb for hanging baskets.

Leaves alternate,* simple,* or if compound,* the leaflets arranged finger-fashion. Flowers nearly always clustered, relatively showy and with petals in some genera (*Dombeya*,

* Special articles on the subjects indicated by an asterisk (*) will be found at the words so marked.

*Theobroma*, *Mahernia*, etc.), but without petals and relatively inconspicuous in *Firmiana* and *Cola*. Fruit dry, often a capsule,* nearly always splitting.

Technical flower characters: Flowers perfect* or unisexual.* Calyx tubular or bell-shaped, deeply 5-parted or cleft. Petals 5 or none. Stamens* 5 or more, and in two series, some sterile, the fertile ones united into a tube. Ovary superior,* 2-celled.

***STERILIS, -e*** (ster'ri-lis). Having no flowers or infertile ones.

**STERILITY.** The inability to produce normal living offspring. Varietal crosses are generally fertile; species hybrids are often sterile, and not infrequently fertile or partially so, especially if the hybrid is back-crossed to one of the parents. Crosses between genera are usually sterile. (*See* CROSSING, also SELF-STERILITY.) — O. E. W.

**STERILITY OF FRUIT TREES.** Unproductive fruit trees are often a problem to the home grower, but rarely so to the professional orchardist, because he avoids as many of the causes of it as possible. The failure to set fruit, or to set satisfactory amounts of it, may be due to three main causes:

(1) The flowers of certain fruit trees are sterile to their own pollen. In such cases it is essential to inter-plant other closely related varieties or forms, thus ensuring a supply of pollen that will effectively fertilize the ovules. There is no need to repeat the details of what fruits require this sort of planting, nor the varieties needed for inter-planting, because all such cases are noted in the special cultural articles on the different fruits. *See* the one you are having difficulty with.

(2) Improper culture and pruning will also cause trees to fail. Most orchard fruits do not require applications of fertilizer or manure, except in limited amounts and at special times. Too rich a soil will provoke more wood and foliage than fruit. *See* the directions regarding soils and fertilizers at the cultural articles on all the main fruit crops. It is easy to make the soils for fruit trees too rich.

Another common cause of fruit failure is incorrect pruning. This is covered in detail at the main fruit articles, and for the general principles of pruning fruit trees *see* PRUNING.

(3) In many early-flowering fruit trees there is the constant hazard of an untimely frost while they are in full flower. This, while it kills the blossoms in some tender sorts, practically stops insect visitors to all flowers and thus prevents pollination* even in those blossoms that survive the cold. There is, of course, no remedy for this unless you live in a region where orchard heating is possible (*see* FROST). For the small home grower, in the East, this is impossible. Then close proximity to a large body of water or the choosing of the most favorable site on the property is the only insurance one can provide against untimely frosts. *See* EXPOSURE. *See also* the general article on FRUIT CULTURE.

**STERNBERGIA** (stern-ber'ji-a). Winter daffodil. A genus of Eurasian bulbous herbs of the family Amaryllidaceae, one of them, **S. lutea**, the winter daffodil or lily-of-the-field, an attractive fall-blooming plant for the border or rock garden. Leaves basal, 8–12 in. long, about ¾ in. wide, without teeth, usually persisting over the winter. Flowers yellow, with a very short tube and erect, veined, oblongish segments, not over 1½ in. long. The flowers are solitary, rarely 2, at the end of a stalk 4–7 in. high. Stamens* 6. Southern Eu. and Asia Minor. For Culture *see* below. (Named for Count Caspar Sternberg, a botanist.)

WINTER DAFFODIL CULTURE

There are not many yellow-flowered bulbous plants blooming in the autumn, so the winter daffodil, aside from its other attractions, has a special color value. The dark green, strap-shaped leaves make their appearance in late August, and the glowing, orange-yellow, crocus-like blooms follow by the middle of September. The flowers, like the leaves, are of strong texture and will endure weather that would spoil the appearance of crocuses and colchicums.

Several flowers are produced by each bulb, carried on a stout stem to a height of from 4 to 7 in. The bulbs should be put in the ground as early in August as they may be procured and set about four inches deep. A gritty, nourishing soil suits them best and a sheltered position against a south-facing wall or in a warm nook in the rock garden where they will receive a good baking.

Seed is not always formed in this climate, but the bulbs increase readily by bulblets.* Frequent lifting and replanting is not recommended, but if they are not flowering well the bulbs may be lifted and replanted in fresh soil after the foliage has quite died away. The foliage usually persists over the winter, withering away in early spring. They are hardy as far north as zone* 4 and may be wintered in well-drained soil in sheltered places in zone* 3. Where they flower together, lavender-flowered *Crocus speciosus* makes a good companion for groups of *Sternbergia*. — L. B. W.

**STEVIA** (stee'vi-a). A very large genus of New World herbs of the family Compositae, none of which appear to be garden plants, although the name *Stevia* has also been applied to some rather commonly cult. plants. All the latter belong to the genus *Piqueria*, which *see* for garden plants offered as *Stevia*.

**STEWARTIA** (stew-art'i-a). Also spelled *Stuartia*. Showy, white-flowered shrubs or trees of the family Theaceae, comprising 6 species found in the southeastern U.S. or eastern Asia, two of them cult. for ornament, both shrubs. Leaves alternate,* short-stalked, toothed. Flowers solitary, mostly in the leaf-axils,* more or less cup-shaped, usually with one or two bracts* below the calyx* which is made up of 5 (rarely 6) sepals.* Petals 5 (rarely 6), roundish, finely round-toothed or wavy, blunt, silky on the outside. Stamens* numerous. Fruit a woody, 5-celled capsule.* (Named for John Stuart, Earl of Bute, a patron of botany.) Sometimes known as *Malachodendron*.

Both the shrubs below need partial shade and a moist, rich loam partly mixed with moderately acid peat. They may be propagated by seeds or by layers, or by cuttings of half-ripened wood taken in Aug. or Sept. and kept under glass.

**malachodendron.** Silky camellia. A shrub 8–12 ft. high, the twigs hairy. Leaves elliptic-oblong, 2½–4½ in. long, pointed at the tip, finely toothed and hairy on the margin. Flowers nearly 4 in. wide, white, but the anthers* bluish-purple. Fruit about ⅝ in. wide. Va. to Fla. and La. June–Aug. Hardy from zone* 5 southward.

**pentagyna.** Mountain camellia. A shrub 10–15 ft. high, the twigs smooth. Leaves ovalish or oblong, 2½–5½ in. long, remotely toothed. Flowers nearly 3 in. wide, white, but the anthers* orange. Fruit about ¾ in. long. Mostly in the mountains, N. Car. and Tenn. to Fla. July–Aug. Hardy from zone* 4 southward. The *var.* **grandiflora** has still larger and more handsome flowers. Autumn foliage orange-scarlet.

**STICK.** *See* BUD STICK.

**STICK-TIGHT** = *Bidens*.

**STICKY LEAVES.** Some leaves are normally sticky because they are covered with glandular* hairs. For generally smooth leaves that become sticky in warm weather *see* HONEY DEW.

**STIGMA.** The termination of the style* and ovary,* and the organ that receives the pollen at pollination. Stigmas may be forked or minutely globe-shaped, but they are usually sticky enough for pollen to adhere to them. *See* FLOWER.

**STIGMAPHYLLON** (stig-ma-fill'on). Tropical American, slender-stemmed, woody vines, comprising about 55 species of the family Malpighiaceae. Leaves generally opposite,* sometimes hairy, the margins toothed or not. Flowers yellow, in umbel*-like clusters growing from the axils* of the leaves. Calyx* of 5 sepals. Corolla of 5 glistening petals, unequal in size. Stamens* 10, 6 of them fertile, 4 sterile. Fruit 1–3-celled and winged. (*Stigmaphyllon* is from the Greek for stigma and leaf, in allusion to the leaf-like stigmas.)

Generally cult. in the warm greenhouse, but can be grown outdoors in the Far South. Propagated by cuttings of half-ripened wood in Feb. or March. Cuttings should be inserted in a mixture of ½ sand and ½ peat in a temperature of 65°–75°. When rooted pot into potting mixture* 5. In the summer months they require plenty of water and a temperature of 70°–85°, in winter months they require less water and a temperature of 55°–65°.

* Special articles on the subjects indicated by an asterisk (*) will be found at the words so marked.

**ciliatum.** Butterfly-vine. Stems slender and twining. Leaves smooth, bright green, heart-shaped, with hairy margins. Flowers large, bright yellow, in 3-6-flowered clusters. W.I. and S.A.

**STINGING NETTLE** = *Urtica dioica.* See NETTLE.

**STINK BUG.** See True Bugs at INSECT PESTS. See also Insect Pests at SNAPDRAGON and RICE.

**STINKING CEDAR** = *Torreya taxifolia.*

**STINKING CLOVER** = *Cleome serrulata.*

**STINKWEED** = *Ailanthus altissima.*

**STIPA** (sty'pa). Feather-grass. Perennial grasses comprising about 100 species, and distributed throughout the world, except in the colder regions. Leaves narrow, grass-like, the margins rolled. Flowers borne in loose branching clusters, each spikelet bearing a long feathery awn,* from 1½ in. to 1 ft. long. (*Stipa* is from the Greek for stipe, in allusion to the awns.)

Cult. for their feathery appearance, as they may be cut and dried for ornament. Propagated by seeds or division of roots, they may be grown in ordinary garden soil. The long awns of some species are dangerous to sheep and cattle.

**elegantissima.** Grows to 3 ft. high. Spikelets in loose branching clusters, to 8 in. long. Awns* feathery, to 1¼ in. long. Flower stalks hairy. Aust.

**pennata.** Growing in tufts to 3 ft. high. Spikelets in dense clusters. Awns* to 1 ft. long, the lower part smooth and twisted, the upper part feathery. Good ornamental species. Eu. and As.

**STIPE.** The stalk of a fern frond; more rarely, the stalk of an ovary. Such a stalked ovary, and the subsequent fruit, are said to be stipitate.

**STIPULATA, -us, -um** (stip-you-lay'ta). Having stipules,* often prominent ones.

**STIPULE.** One of the small, leaf-like or membranous organs found at the base of many leafstalks, usually in pairs. They may be conspicuous, as in the pea, inconspicuous as in many shrubs, or ephemeral when they drop off as soon as the leaf expands. In some plants the stipules are replaced by thorns as in *Pithecolobium dulce.*

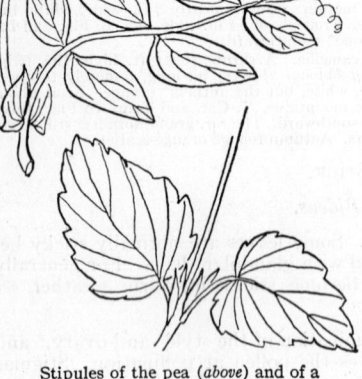

Stipules of the pea (*above*) and of a viburnum (*below*)

**STITCHWORT.** See STELLARIA.

**STIZOLOBIUM** (sty-zo-lō'bi-um). Velvet bean. Annual, chiefly Old World, tropical vines of the pea family, those below introduced into Fla. for ornament, but mostly as forage plants for regions too hot for good forage grasses. They are very strong-growing vines with alternate,* compound* leaves composed of 3 leaflets. Flowers showy, pea-like, white or deep purple, mostly in few-flowered clusters (racemes*). Fruit a heavy, ridged, hairy pod (legume*), with large, nearly round or oblongish seeds. (*Stizolobium* is from the Greek for stinging pods, in allusion to the stinging hairs found on the pods of some species.)

The velvet beans are coarse vines which will sprawl and completely cover the ground. If grown for ornament, and they grow very quickly, they must be given the support of a trellis or arbor. Sow the seeds only in warm, sandy soils, and in regions with much heat, a long growing season and no frost.

**deeringianum.** Florida velvet bean. A native of Indo-Malaya, but introduced into Fla. Vines very vigorous, sometimes 50 ft. long. Leaflets angled-ovalish, 2-6 in. long. Flowers purple, very showy, the cluster drooping, composed of 5-30 blooms, each about 1½ in. long. Pods black-hairy,

the hairs irritating to the skin. Seeds variously marbled or speckled, generally black, brown, and whitish.

**hasjoo.** Yokohama bean. Not over 20 ft. long, the ovalish leaflets 4-5 in. long. Flowers dark purple, about 1½ in. long, the clusters (racemes*) 4-6 in. long. Pods 3-4½ in. long, white-hairy, the seeds ashy. Jap.(?).

**niveum.** Lyon bean. Leaflets wavy-surfaced. Flowers white, the clusters showy, long-stalked, 1-2 ft. long. Pods 4-5 in. long, curved both ends, white-hairy, the seeds flattish. Southern As. and in the Philippines.

**pruritum.** Cowage; also called cowitch. A tropical vine little known in the U.S., but sometimes grown in southern Fla. Flowers brownish-purple. Pods reddish or blackish, nearly straight, bristly, 3-4 in. long, the seeds spotted, oblongish, used as cattle feed. The bristles on the pod are extremely irritating. Tropics.

**STOCK.** In a grafting or budding operation that part of a plant which is to receive the bud or cion (which see). Professionals usually refer to the operation of getting the stock ready for its cion or bud as "dressing" the stock. For the details of this *see* GRAFTING, BUDDING.

**STOCK** (*Mathiola incana*). The several varieties of stocks include Brampton, Intermediate, Queen and others, but the Ten-weeks fills every want and this variety is used generally either for the greenhouse or outdoors. It is not much subject to disease or destructive insects and makes a desirable plant for all to grow. Easily raised from seed, it makes a gorgeous show of color, many beautiful shades being now available in pastel colors.

Seed may be sown in Feb. or Mar. for outdoor use, and for greenhouse cultivation at any time, remembering that it takes 14 wks. to get them into flower. Seed should be sown in pans in any good soil not too finely sifted, free drainage being essential, and to ward against damping-off,* the seed should be sown thinly, covered lightly with soil, and watered sparingly, and this caution should be observed throughout the life of the plant, as stocks resent overwatering.

Prick-off into flats 3 in. apart when large enough to handle, and from these into pots for growing on, or into permanent benches or beds. It is important that the plants receive no check at any time, as upon this depends success or failure, and is chiefly the cause of an abnormal crop of single flowers. Beautiful spikes will be produced if all side shoots are carefully pinched out as they appear, and the large individual blooms may be used singly for design work. If a branching spike is preferred, the center should be pinched once, when the plants are 4 in. high, and the side shoots allowed to develop; these will make nice sprays for cut flowers.

Stocks require an even temperature of 50° and plenty of air at all times to keep the plants sturdy. Good plants can be grown in 5-in. and 6-in. pots and when they become filled with roots, applications of liquid manure once a week will prove beneficial. Plant in beds or benches 6 in. apart, 8 in. between the rows. There are many good strains of seed on the market, but it pays to save one's own seed. Select a single flower of good color, grow to a single spike, and allow it to develop its flowers fully. When a number of seed pods have formed, pinch out the end of the spike and allow the seeds to ripen naturally, save all the perfect seeds, and these will produce 90% double flowers. The seed may be kept several years in airtight containers, and still the germination will be 100%. — A. J. L.

INSECT PESTS. Some cabbage and general greenhouse insects attack stocks, both indoors and out. Leaf-eating caterpillars are checked by arsenicals, while mites, thrips, and aphids succumb to contact sprays.

DISEASES. Stocks are susceptible to a disease known as *wilt.* Caused by a soil-inhabiting fungus, the disease is characterized by yellowing, sudden wilting and death. Removal of infected plants and the use of clean or sterilized soil are measures for control.

**STOECHADIFOLIA, -us, -um** (stee-kad-i-fō'li-a). With leaves like the stechados (*Lavandula stoechas*); which was once assigned to the obsolete genus *Stoechas.*

**STOECHAS** (stee'kas). See STOECHADIFOLIA.

**STOKESIA** (sto-key'zi-a or stokes'i-a). American hardy perennial herbs of only 1 species, belonging to the family Compositae. Stems purplish, covered with white matted hairs. Leaves alternate.* Flower heads 1-4 in. across, solitary or several on a branching stalk. Flower heads surrounded by several rings of bracts,* the outermost bracts leaf-like with spine-like teeth, the inner bracts scale-like, sheathing the flowers. Flowers lavender-blue or purplish-

---

* Special articles on the subjects indicated by an asterisk (*) will be found at the words so marked.

blue. Ray florets* large, flattening into 5 lobes. Disk florets tubular, getting smaller toward the center. (Named for Jonathan Stokes, M.D., English botanist.)

Stokesia makes a good garden plant. Easily cult. in ordinary garden soil, which must be well drained, as it will not stand too much water at the roots during winter months. Propagated by seeds or division of roots. Seeds should be sown ⅛ in. deep in sandy soil in May in cold frame or outdoor seedbed. When large enough to handle they should be transplanted into nursery beds outdoors, transplanting to permanent positions the following spring. Division of roots should be made in early spring.

laevis. Stoke's aster. Stems purplish, covered with white-woolly hairs. Leaves lance-shaped to 10 in. long. Flowers lavender-blue, in heads 2-4 in. across. S.C. to La. The *var.* **alba** has white flowers; the *var.* **rosea** has pink flowers. The plant is sometimes sold as *S. cyanea*.

**STOKE'S ASTER** = *Stokesia laevis*.

**STOLON.** A horizontal stem, just above or beneath the soil, from the tip of which a new plant arises; also a bent shoot that takes root. Stolons are common in the blackberry and in many grasses. See RUNNER.

*STOLONIFERA, -us, -um* (stow-lo-niff'er-ra). Bearing stolons.*

**STOMA** (plural *stomata*). A pore-like opening in the surface of a leaf, through which it takes in gases and discharges other gases and water vapor.

**STOMACH POISONS.** See Stomach Poisons at INSECTICIDES.

**STONE.** For garden structures made of stone *see* BRIDGES, PATHS AND PAVING, WALLS AND WALL GARDENING, and STRUCTURES. For artificial stone *see* CONCRETE.

**STONE BRIDGE.** See BRIDGES.

**STONE CELLS.** The minute gritty cells found in the flesh of the pear; often called grit cells. In some varieties the number and size of the stone cells make the fruit too gritty for pleasant eating.

**STONE CRESS** = *Aethionema*.

**STONECROP.** See SEDUM.

**STONECROP FAMILY** = Crassulaceae.

**STONE FRUITS.** Any fruit having a stone, specifically the plums and cherries.

**STONE MINT** = *Cunila origanoides*.

**STONE OF TWO DEITIES.** See JAPANESE GARDEN.

**STONE OF WORSHIP.** See JAPANESE GARDEN.

**STONE PINE.** Several cult. trees are so called, notably *Pinus cembra* and *P. pinea*, both European, and *P. cembroides* and *P. cembroides edulis* of the western U.S. and adjacent Mex. The American stone pines are often called nut pines or piñons. See PINE.

**STONEROOT** = *Collinsonia canadensis*.

**STONE WALL.** See WALLS AND WALL GARDENING.

**STOOL.** The stump or base, or parent plant which gives rise to various propagative organs, such as shoots for layering, rootstocks for division, bulbs, buds, etc. A plant is sometimes said to *stool* freely when it produces a crop of such organs. Sometimes stooling is induced as in layering.

**STOOL LAYERING** = Mound layering. See LAYERING.

**STORAGE.** Storage facilities are divided into four classes — a vegetable room especially built for the purpose, a cellar, an outdoor pit or trench, and "cold storage" rooms. An abundance of vegetables may be stored by one of these methods for use in winter. It is easier and cheaper to store vegetables than to can them, and the quality is better.

Home storage includes the first three classifications. The conditions under which vegetables may be stored successfully are: crops of good quality, proper stage of maturity, right degree of temperature, and correct amount of moisture. The proper stage of maturity depends entirely upon the crop. Cabbage, onions, squash, pumpkins and potatoes should be fully matured when stored; beets, carrots, parsnips and turnips should be young and tender, as otherwise they become tough and woody. Beets, carrots, parsnips, turnips and celery require cool, moist conditions; potatoes and cabbage need more moisture, as in too dry an atmosphere they tend to excessive shrinkage; onions and dried beans keep best in a cool, dry atmosphere, while squash, pumpkins and sweet potatoes have better keeping qualities in a warm, dry place. The best keeping temperature for all vegetables except potatoes is just above freezing.

If space is available, the best way to keep vegetables for winter use is to build a special room with a dirt floor. If a corner of the cellar is used, the floor will probably be of concrete, in which case it should be wet down frequently. Size will depend upon the needs of the family, but a space six by eight feet usually will be ample. Two sides only need be partitioned, using the house walls as the other two, with a window to provide ventilation. Hinge the sash at the top so that it can be kept hooked open except in freezing weather. Screening is necessary to prevent the entry of flies and vermin, and burlap or sacking may be used over the window to darken the room. Cover each side of the studding with building paper and matched boards. This will leave an air space of approximately four inches between the walls, so that heat from the furnace will not affect the room temperature. The entrance door should fit tightly. Pieces of board should be laid loose on the floor along the wall, and slatted crates for potatoes set on these to allow circulation of air beneath. Tiering the crates will save space. Shelves should be built along the walls to hold canned products and fruits. Beneath the shelves may be built storage bins for vegetables. Many of the root crops keep best when placed on the dirt floor, covered with moist soil and dug as needed. Cabbage should be put on the shelves, so that air can freely circulate around it. Onions keep well in crates. Parsnips may be left in the garden all winter or stored, but not buried. Storage rooms may also be made under outbuildings or by excavating in banks. Any cellar without a furnace makes an excellent storage space.

Outdoor storage pits or trenches, although not so easy of access in freezing weather, may be used to bury root crops, potatoes and cabbage. The easiest way is to dig a shallow pit, 10 to 12 inches deep, and line it with leaves, straw or hay to a depth of eight inches. If the pit is located on a slight elevation, a ditch may be dug around it to facilitate drainage. Place the vegetables in the storage pit in a conical heap, and cover with a layer of leaves, straw or hay. Cover with soil to hold the material in place. Before freezing weather put on more soil, and extend a tuft of straw through the top of the pile for ventilation. Several small pits are better than one large one. Celery keeps better in a trench than any other way. It should be taken from the ground before freezing, the plants placed close together, and the trench covered with boards nailed together in the shape of a trough and inverted over it, and the whole covered with litter and soil.

Cold storage or refrigeration of vegetables is a lowering of the temperature to retard the deterioration of the crops. Some vegetables can be kept by this method for months, while others deteriorate in a week or less. Spoilage of vegetables in cold storage is due to diseases, wilting or chemical changes. Vegetables such as peas, asparagus and sweet corn, with a high sugar content, can be stored only a short time, due to chemical changes. Root crops can be stored for five or six months, but leafy vegetables for a much shorter period. Wilting, the chief danger with root and leafy crops, can be delayed by maintaining a low temperature with a high humidity. Mold and other storage diseases which affect tomatoes, muskmelons and similar crops are controlled by such treatment and the removal from storage of all diseased vegetables.

**STORAX.** See STYRAX.

**STORAX FAMILY** = Styracaceae.

---

* Special articles on the subjects indicated by an asterisk (*) will be found at the words so marked.

**STORK'S-BILL.** See PELARGONIUM and ERODIUM.

**STOVE.** An old hort. term for a warm, moist greenhouse. The plants grown in such a temperature were called stove plants. The modern equivalent for a stove house is the tropical house. See GREENHOUSE.

**STRAIN.** A not easily definable category of plants within a variety (which see). The word strain is most often used to indicate a group of plants, in a variety, with some character insufficient to make them worth describing as a distinct variety, but different enough to be entitled to some designation. There may thus be a tall, weak, strong, or sickly strain of a particular variety. *Strain*, as a hort. term, is not much used, and seldom with precision.

*STRAMINEOFRUCTA, -us, -um* (stra-min-ee-o-fruk'ta). With straw-colored fruit.

*STRAMONIUM* (stra-mō'ni-um). An obsolete generic name for plants now included in the genus *Datura*.

**STRAND PLANTS.** See SEASIDE GARDENS.

**STRANVAESIA** (stran-vee'zi-a). Asiatic, evergreen shrubs and trees of the rose family, comprising only 4 or 5 species, of which S. davidiana, of western China, is cult. for ornament. It is a broad-leaved evergreen shrub, 15-20 ft. high, with alternate,* oblongish leaves 3-4 in. long, pointed at the tip and wedge-shaped at the base, without marginal teeth. Flowers white, in a terminal, profuse cluster (corymb)*, nearly 4 in. wide, the calyx* turban-shaped and 5-toothed. Petals 5. Stamens* about 20. Fruit fleshy, nearly globe-shaped, about ⅓ in. wide, scarlet. June. Hardy from zone* 6 southward, possibly in protected places in zone* 5. Propagated by hardwood cuttings (see CUTTINGS). The *var.* **undulata** has wavy-margined leaves. (Named for William Fox-Strangways, English botanist.)

**STRAP-LEAVED TURNIP** = *Brassica rapa lorifolia*.

**STRATIFY, STRATIFICATION.** See SEEDS AND SEEDAGE.

**STRATIOTES** (stra-ti-ō'tees). European aquatic perennial herbs of only one species of the family Hydrocharitaceae. This is **S. aloides**, the water-soldier. Rootstocks short and thick. Leaves sword-shaped, fleshy and stiff, the margins sharply toothed. Flowering stalk 5-6 in. high, bearing at its summit a 2-leaved sheath, enclosing several white male flowers, or 1 white female flower. Fruit 6-celled, with many seeds. These plants rise to the surface before flowering and then after flowering sink to the bottom. They are not usually cult. except in botanic gardens. Easily propagated by the division of the rootstocks in early spring. (*Stratiotes* is from the Greek for soldier, in allusion to the sword-shaped leaves. It is also a specific name at *Pistia*.)

**STRATTON ARBORETUM.** See ARBORETUM.

**STRAWBERRY.** Perennial herbs comprising perhaps 20 species and constituting the genus **Fragaria** (fra-gair'i-a) of the rose family. They are essentially stemless plants except for the long runners,* and are chiefly found in the north temperate zone, but in the western part of the New World some extend southward to Patagonia and one of these, *F. chiloensis*, has entered largely into the making of the cult. strawberry. Leaves compound,* the leaflets 3. Flowers generally white (rarely reddish), in few-flowered clusters at the end of a slender stalk that arises from the ground. In some forms the flowers are unisexual.* Calyx* 5-toothed, the lobes spreading and forming the hull of the strawberry. Petals 5, mostly broad and rounded. Stamens* many. Fruit (in the ordinary sense) the much-enlarged, juicy, very fleshy and delicious receptacle,* in which or upon the surface of which are embedded the true fruits which are small achenes,* commonly but incorrectly called the seeds. (*Fragaria* is from the Latin for fragrance, in allusion to the pleasantly aromatic fruit.) "Fruit" as used below means the ripened receptacle* (see above). All flower in early spring.

For culture and varieties *see* below. The four species appear to be the ones most involved in the production of the cult. strawberry, which is the result of long years of breeding, mostly in France, upon plants of American origin. For the barren strawberry *see* WALDSTEINIA FRAGARIOIDES; for the mock or Indian strawberry *see* DUCHESNEA INDICA.

**F. chiloensis.** A low, bushy plant, its runners* usually forming after fruit is set. Leaves green and glossy above, pale bluish-white beneath, the leaflets broadly wedge-shaped, toothed. Flowers about ¾ in. wide, inclined to droop, standing below the foliage. Fruit firm, large, dark red, the hull* large. Alaska to Patagonia.

**F. moschata.** Hautbois strawberry. Resembling *F. vesca*, but taller, more hairy, the hull* of the fruit strongly bent backward. Fruit musky, dull red. Eu. More known abroad than here, but it has entered into some cult. varieties.

**F. vesca.** A sparsely hairy herb 9-12 in. high, the leaves thin and light green. Flower cluster forking, about the same height as the leaves, the leaflets of which are angularly wedge-shaped. Flowers about ½ in. wide, perfect,* standing above the foliage. Fruit small, hemispheric or slightly elongated, the hull* widely spreading. Eu. and possibly (in a form of it) in N.A. Very widely used in strawberry breeding, most of the late fruiting sorts (everbearing) having blood of *F. vesca* in them.

**F. virginiana.** The common wild strawberry of eastern N.A. A low herb, 4-8 in. high, making runners* from the start. Leaves thin, light green both sides, the leaflets wedge-shaped and toothed. Flower clusters long-stalked, usually erect, and standing below the foliage. Flowers about ¾ in. wide, perfect.* Fruit small, but very sweet, its small hull* spreading. Eastern N.A. It is rarely cult., but has entered into some modern hort. varieties of the strawberry.

### STRAWBERRY CULTURE

There is no region in North America in which agriculture is practiced where the strawberry may not find a place. It is everywhere a popular fruit because of the beauty and delectable quality of the berries; ease of culture, freedom from pests, short time to bring the plants to bearing age, large returns from small spaces of land, and the many uses which it serves.

The strawberry thrives on almost any agricultural land except dry sands and wet mucks. Perhaps a dark sandy loam is the best selection. A soil on which the potato grows well is usually suited to the strawberry. Surface drainage and under drainage are both essential. A goodly supply of organic matter makes tilth* an easy operation and gives the soil greater moisture-holding capacity. The strawberry thrives on both acid and alkaline soils and shows a slight preference to the acid ones — never use lime on strawberry lands.

A gentle slope is the best site for the strawberry patch and is always desirable; thus the grower may avoid spring frosts and do away with the danger of standing water, which would freeze and kill the plants in the winter. For an early crop a southern slope is best. To plant on land poorly prepared is to court failure. Rather deep fall-plowing is a prerequisite to spring planting. When the land is dry enough in the spring, use the disk and harrow until the soil is as fine and mellow as a bed for flower seed. Grass-land turned under harbors destructive white grubs that ruin a strawberry bed. A pure clover turned down in mid-autumn furnishes an excellent field for the strawberry.

PLANTING. Hill and matted row systems are used for beds. The hill system best suits one who wishes to grow handsome, delectable berries. It requires more plants to set in hills than in rows, and more labor in care. The loss of plants from pests and weather is more serious in a hilled than a matted row plantation. From these considerations, it becomes apparent that the matted row is best for large plantings.

Those who set in hills want from 12 to 18 in. between plants and rows 3 ft. apart. In matted rows the plants should stand from 18 to 30 in. apart in rows from 3 to 4 ft. apart, the distances depending upon whether the variety produces few or many runners.* Varieties making few runners should be set in hills; those making many runners in matted rows. Not more than two crops, usually but one, especially in commercial plantations, are taken from a planting.

There is less danger from winter injury and heaving of soil, from drought, and it is easier to get and to handle plants when they are set in the spring. If set in the fall they must be heavily mulched through the winter in the cold parts of the continent, and the bed must be carried through two winters to secure the doubtful advantage of two crops, the first one being a very light one. Runners, to be at their best for a new planting, should be taken from a bed that has not fruited. The fresher the young plants the better, and if they have come

---

* Special articles on the subjects indicated by an asterisk (*) will be found at the words so marked.

from a distance it is good to re-invigorate them by soaking in water for a few hours. In any case, plants ought to be heeled-in with earth firmly packed about the roots if they are not to be set in the permanent plantation almost immediately. All dead leaves and small offsets should be removed, leaving the young plant with a crown of one or two green leaves. Usually the roots may be shortened for greater convenience in planting.

In planting in the hill system, pride in having straight rows dictates marking both ways, but when the plants are to mat only the rows need be marked, leaving the planter to guess at distances between plants. In a large planting, a team of two men work to best advantage; one man opens the ground with a spade and the other sets the plant, after which one or the

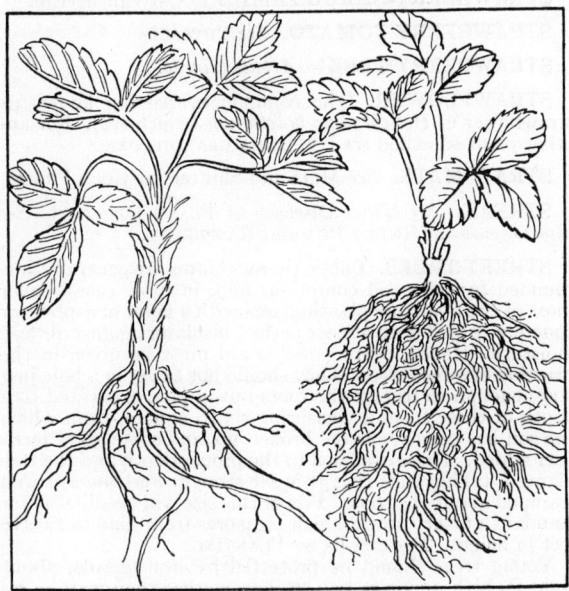

STRAWBERRY

At the left, an old plant not worth saving. At the right, a vigorous young plant upon which successful growers depend for new stock.

other firms the ground about the plant with his feet. In small areas a trowel is used to make the hole, possible only when the ground is loose and free from clods. The crown of the plant is set level with the surface of the ground. In dry weather, the plants must be "watered in."

The strawberry must have an abundance of plant food and without question this is best supplied by stable manure, at the rate of from 10 to 20 tons per acre, plowed under the fall before planting. Chemical fertilizers are not needed when manure has been used, and it is doubtful if they may be used with profit in any good soil which has been provided with organic matter by plowing under cover crops. Phosphoric acid and potash seldom show returns, lime never, but nitrate of soda applied the year the plants are set, at the rate of 200 lbs. per acre, much more than pays for its cost, especially in lands on the sandy side.

Cultivation should begin soon after the plants are set and should be frequent throughout the summer to keep the ground in good tilth* and to destroy all weeds. The hoe must supplement the cultivator to keep down weeds and cut out surplus runners. Too many runners weaken plants and reduce the size of both crop and fruit. Twelve to 18 inches is quite wide enough for a matted row. The cultivator should not be set deep.

Wherever the thermometer drops close to zero the strawberry bed must be mulched, although paradoxically enough in the coldest climate in which the strawberry grows on this continent a mulch is seldom used because snow may be depended upon to keep the plants from freezing. A mulch,*

however, is of value for other purposes than keeping out the winter's cold: it prevents freezing and thawing in winter and spring; it conserves moisture and keeps down weeds; it makes cultivation unnecessary until after the crop is picked; and berries from mulched plantings are much cleaner than those from fields unmulched. Straw of any of the cereals makes good mulch, of which wheat-and-oat-straw are best. Bean-vines and even corn-stalks can be used in a pinch. Usually it is best to leave the mulch on the plants in the spring until growth starts or before the leaves begin to bleach, when it is pulled from over the plants and left between rows.

As has been said it is best to renew the bed each year, but if two crops are to be taken, attention to renovation must be given after the first harvest. It suffices in most lands to plow between the rows reducing the mat to a width of 8 or 10 in. Plants in the row must then be thinned out to 10 in. apart. Lastly destroy all weeds and put on a top dressing of 200 lbs. of nitrate of soda per acre.

Strawberries, the country over, are marketed in quart baskets packed in 32-qt. crates. The cool of the day, if not too much dew, is the time to pick. The degree of ripeness depends on nearness to market — a little underripe for distant, fully ripe for local markets, dead ripe for home use. The calyx is left on the berry. Pick in carriers and grade and re-pack in a packing-shed.

Grown for home use, everbearing strawberries are well worth the extra care. Culture is similar to that given summer sorts, differing chiefly in that plants are set at less distances both ways since there are fewer runners. The blossoms are removed in the spring until summer kinds have been harvested, after which the plants are allowed to bear until frost comes. Retain the mulch to keep the berries clean.

The directions given so far have been for northern and eastern plantations. Cultural practices differ somewhat in the Gulf and Pacific states from those that have been given. In the Gulf states, the best strawberry land is often low and flat, and to secure good drainage, hills or matted rows are set on ridges 3 to 12 in. above the furrows which separate rows. Another outstanding difference is found in the time of planting. Because of serious troubles caused by eelworms and other pests parent plants in the Far South are imported from the North in late winter to produce runner-plants for the main plantation. These mother plants are grown through the summer, and in autumn, early or late, runners are taken from them for the fruit-bearing plantation.

The chief differences in strawberry culture in the Middle Western states and the Pacific states from eastern regions are those brought about by the necessity to irrigate, either by sprinkling or through furrows. Irrigation makes necessary changes in soil preparation, distance apart of plants, and tillage.

Before beginning a discussion of varieties, the reader must be reminded that strawberries have two types of flowers, perfect and imperfect. The perfect-flowered sorts have stamens* which produce pollen* and do not need cross-pollination. The imperfect-flowered varieties have no stamens,* produce no pollen* and must be cross-pollinated by a perfect variety which blooms at the same time. One row of a perfect-flowered variety will pollinate two or three rows of an imperfect variety.

Six strawberries only are grown largely in the commercial plantations of the whole country and these with about as many more supply the gardens. All have perfect flowers. Varieties of strawberries cannot well be referred to plant zones* since a winter mulch* or a protective snow cover overcomes the rigors of winter.

### VARIETIES

AROMA. Berry large, round-conic, firm, bright crimson, quality good, mid-season to late. Plants vigorous, healthy, make runners freely. Great Lakes to Missouri.

CHESAPEAKE. Berry large, round-conic to egg-shape, bright crimson, prominent seeds, very good, late. Foliage very healthy, few runners. Northeastern states to Maryland.

DUNLAP. Berry medium in size, conic, not very firm, dark crimson, deep red flesh, very good, early to mid-season.

---

* Special articles on the subjects indicated by an asterisk (*) will be found at the words so marked.

Plants healthy, make runners freely, very hardy to cold and drought. Plains states, east to Illinois and Wisconsin.

GANDY. Berry large, round-conic, firm, deep crimson with red flesh, subacid, quality good. Foliage healthy, makes runners freely. Season late. Maryland, Delaware, New Jersey, and north.

HOWARD 17. Berry medium to large, round-conic, firm, red flesh, subacid, very good, very early. Plants healthy, productive, make runners freely. New England southward to Virginia and westward to Michigan and Illinois.

JOE. Very large, round-conic, firm, dark crimson with red flesh, subacid, very good, mid-season to late. Plants healthy, make runners freely. Maryland, New Jersey, Delaware and Pennsylvania.

KLONDIKE. Berry medium in size, round-conic, very firm, deep crimson to center, acid, quality fair, mid-season. Plants healthy, make runners freely. Grown almost exclusively in the South Atlantic and Gulf states, in southern California and somewhat in other southern regions. Grown for northern markets.

MARSHALL. Berry large, round-conic to conic, soft, deep crimson to core, subacid, best in quality. Plants fairly healthy in the North, make runners freely. Adapted to heavy soils. Northeastern states to New Jersey and the Pacific Coast.

MISSIONARY. Berry below medium to large, conic, soft to firm, dark crimson with dark red flesh, acid, quality fair, early to mid-season. Plants resistant to disease, make runners freely, productive. Standard sort for Florida and grown northward to Virginia. Grown for northern markets.

OREGON. Berry medium to large, round-conic, fairly firm, dark crimson with light red flesh, mild subacid, very good, early to mid-season. Plants vigorous, productive, make runners freely. Pacific Northwest and parts of California.

### EVERBEARING STRAWBERRIES

MASTODON. Berry large to very large, round-conic, dark scarlet, firm, subacid, fair quality. Plants vigorous, make runners freely. Standard everbearing sort where sufficient rainfall permits culture of everbearing sorts.

PROGRESSIVE. Berry small to medium, dark crimson to the core, very good, better than Mastodon. Plant healthy, makes runners freely, hardy, and if planted in the spring yields some fruit the same year. Not adapted to southern strawberry regions. — U. P. H.

INSECT PESTS. Large white grubs, larvae of June bugs, are important pests which cut the roots. Strawberries should be planted on land that has been cultivated cleanly for a year previously, as grubs are not abundant in such ground, and the strawberry beds should be rotated.

Strawberry leaf rollers are small caterpillars that feed within folded leaves, which they web together; abundance is only occasional and seldom lasts long; arsenical spray will reduce their numbers considerably. A brown snout beetle, about 1/10 in. long, cuts off the blossom buds in spring, and may reduce the crop considerably; a spray of lead arsenate, 2 pounds to 50 gallons, before blossoming, will kill many of them. Winter burning around beds reduces their numbers. Several kinds of leaf beetles, and snout beetles, the larvae of which feed on roots, may be controlled with an arsenical. The snout beetles also succumb to poisoned bran bait. Slug-like, green sawfly larvae on leaves are easy to kill with arsenicals. A spray just before blossoming seems to check several pests; later sprays may be used as needed.

Root aphids sometimes injure strawberries; rotation of beds and the use of insect-free planting stock are advised.

DISEASES. Leafspot and leafblight are found almost everywhere the strawberry is grown. The older or the more depleted the bed the more likely that the leafspot will cause injury. Not only are the leaves affected, but lesions occur on the fruit stalks, causing the young berries to dry before ripening. The commercial practice of fruiting strawberry beds for only one year is the best practical method of control. On older plantings it may be desirable to apply bordeaux mixture, 3-3-50. Just after harvest the vines are mowed close to the ground, and the foliage removed and burned. Then when the new growth appears the spray applications are made at ten-day intervals.

Sometimes when powdery mildew, which produces a white talcum-like growth on the leaves and a curling of the foliage, is present, the spraying may have to be begun early in the season. It is not safe to apply sulphur to the plants. Strawberries when weakened by drought, too alkaline soil, or in any other way are very susceptible to black root-rot. The crop should always be planted on acid soil, and be supplied with plenty of moisture. During wet, hot seasons many berries may rot, due to an ashen-gray mold. The plants should have plenty of aeration, and the picked berries not permitted to become warm. Yellows has been reported on a few varieties. No definite control measures are known excepting that of changing varieties.

**STRAWBERRY BEGONIA** = Strawberry geraniums.

**STRAWBERRY-BLITE** = *Chenopodium capitatum.* See the list at WEEDS.

**STRAWBERRY-BUSH** = *Euonymus americanus* and *E. atropurpureus.*

**STRAWBERRY FAMILY** = Rosaceae.

**STRAWBERRY FERN** = *Hemionitis palmata.*

**STRAWBERRY GERANIUM** = *Saxifraga sarmentosa.*

**STRAWBERRY GUAVA** = *Psidium cattleianum.* See GUAVA.

**STRAWBERRY PEAR.** See *Hylocereus undatus.*

**STRAWBERRY-RASPBERRY** = *Rubus illecebrosus.*

**STRAWBERRY-SHRUB** = *Calycanthus.*

**STRAWBERRY-SHRUB FAMILY** = Calycanthaceae.

**STRAWBERRY TOMATO.** See PHYSALIS.

**STRAWBERRY TREE** = *Arbutus unedo.*

**STRAWFLOWER.** The common everlasting known as strawflower is *Helichrysum bracteatum* (which see). For another plant so called see UVULARIA GRANDIFLORA.

**STRAW MATS.** See Mats and Shutters at COLD FRAME.

**STREAK.** See Virus Diseases at PLANT DISEASES. See also Diseases at SWEET PEA and RASPBERRY.

**STREET TREES.** Public thoroughfares are generally surrounded by poor soil conditions and, in most cases, cover most of the available planting area with a layer of asphalt or concrete, which is an almost perfect insulator against air and moisture. Hence, every possible aid must be given in the planting of street trees. They should not be set in a hole just large enough to receive the roots but in pits, excavated to a depth of three ft. and measuring six ft. square, from which the soil has been removed, broken up, and some good fertilizer added. These are filled to the proper depth and the tree planted, taking care that it is set straight and the soil well tramped about the roots. Pits of this size will be suitable for standard nursery stock which measures from nine to twelve feet in height. For details see PLANTING.

Young trees should be protected by iron guards, about eight ft. high, made in two sections so that they may be removed. Leave them in place for about three years until the tree is established. In cases where young specimens lean, due to settling or mechanical injury, they should be supplied with guy wires, fastened about the trunk by means of sections of rubber hose passed over the wires to prevent cutting the bark. Where there is but a small space between the curb and sidewalk, or where the street and sidewalk completely surround the tree, iron gratings, three ft. square and made in two sections, so they may be removed, should be placed around the base of the tree. This permits all of the space about the tree to be available for use and, at the same time, allows for moisture, ventilation, and cultivation.

Safety is the first essential in the pruning of street trees and calls for the immediate removal of all dead and diseased trees or branches which might be a source of danger to the public. For much the same reason, the form and shape of street trees should be such that they will not hinder or endanger traffic. The trunk should be kept clean for a distance of at least twelve ft. from the ground. Branches should clear sidewalks by ten ft. and those over streets should be so pruned as to permit a clearance of at least fifteen ft.

Branches should never completely cover the street or adjacent properties. Avenues which are entirely shaded are damp and poorly aired. The same is true when street trees over-shade private property as well as often damaging roofs and chimneys by sweeping against them and clogging gutters or drains with leaves. When pruning street trees, the whole planting, rather than the individual specimen, should be considered. Only in this way is it possible to obtain symmetry. In many instances, the removal of lateral branches will stimulate top growth which should be trimmed back occasionally to prevent a lanky appearance.

Spraying requires both curative and preventive treat-

---

* Special articles on the subjects indicated by an asterisk (*) will be found at the words so marked.

ment. Those trees which have chronic diseases or infestations should be sprayed regularly. The appearance of a new pest calls for immediate action. Most of the common diseases and insects and their proper treatment will be found in the description of the various species.

### VARIETIES

The problem of selecting proper types of trees for avenue ornamentation should be carefully considered before such projects are undertaken. Gasoline fumes, smoke, and dust

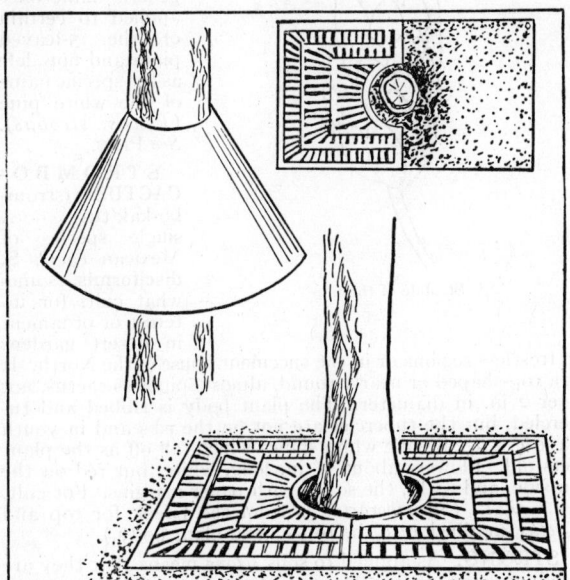

TREE GUARDS

At the left, a practical sheet-metal guard to keep animals from climbing tree trunks. At the right, a fine type of grating for street trees, removable, and allowing air and water to reach the soil.

have forced the discontinuance of much material which is well adapted in type of growth to street planting. In general public thoroughfares may be divided into three classes: wide streets, narrow streets, and parkways. In really congested districts where smoke and dust is rampant there is little choice, and the Tree-of-Heaven, *Ailanthus altissima*, or the London Plane, *Platanus acerifolia*, will probably have to be used. Sometimes, in Eu., the fluff or scurfiness from the leaves is irritating to the eyes and nose.

Wide avenues in residential districts are best planted with large trees such as: the American elm (*Ulmus americana*), the sugar maple (*Acer saccharum*), scarlet oak (*Quercus coccinea*), white oak (*Quercus alba*), Wych elm (*Ulmus glabra*), also *Tilia vulgaris*, and *Tilia euchlora*. In good soil, *Magnolia acuminata* may be used.

Narrow streets are not well supplied with suitable planting materials and, if those mentioned above are used, an excessive amount of pruning is necessary to prevent undue shade. Narrow growing trees are most desirable and, while plenty of such habit are in cultivation, comparatively few will withstand the hardships of roadside planting. Probably the easiest to obtain are the Norway maple (*Acer platanoides*), the pin oak (*Quercus palustris*), and the maidenhair-tree (*Ginkgo biloba*). The city of Rochester, New York, maintains its own nursery for the propagation of special street trees and is growing particularly erect or fastigiate* forms of the American elm, American linden, and Norway maple for this work.

The parkway allows the greatest possibilities in street planting. The sides may be planted with any of the materials already mentioned provided full sunlight may be per-

mitted to reach the center area. This may then be planted with some form of flowering tree. Magnolias are well suited for this purpose, as are the flowering crabapples.

The proper distance to space street trees varies greatly according to the material used. In general sixty to seventy-five ft. is proper for the larger species on wide streets with forty ft. as a minimum for narrow-growing forms on smaller thoroughfares.

In general flowering or heavy fruiting trees are not desirable for street work because they require good soil and plenty of nourishment for proper growth, conditions which are noticeably absent in most cases. Also their flowers and fruit clutter the street and are a nuisance. Trees which have vigorous root systems should not be employed, as they get into sewers and water mains, causing damage. The following, although sometimes used, cannot be recommended for this work: box-elder (*Acer negundo*), silver maple (*Acer saccharinum*), willows, poplars, birches, *Ulmus pumila*, *Catalpa*, *Gleditsia triacanthos*, *Platanus occidentalis*, and the horse-chestnut (*Aesculus hippocastanum*). Conifers are seldom a success in avenue ornamentation. See also TREES, TREE SURGERY. — A. D. S.

**STRELITZIA** (stre-lit′zi-a). Tender, South African perennials comprising about 5 species of the family Musaceae, with thick, underground, woody rootstocks, which in some species grow above the ground and become tree-like. Leaves large, banana-like, long-stalked. Flowering stalks terminal or growing from the axils* of the leaves, bearing 1–2 large, boat-shaped bracts* which are sometimes colored, enclosing the showy flowers. Calyx* of 3 colored sepals, not joined, keel-shaped. Corolla of 3 petals, 2 joined and tongue-shaped, generally blue, the odd petal white or yellow, and standing erect. (Named for the wife of King George III, Charlotte Sophia, of the Mecklenburg-Strelitz family.)

Not much in cultivation, but sometimes grown in the warm greenhouse for house or porch decoration. They can be grown outdoors where the temperature does not drop below 50°. Propagated by suckers or division of the rootstocks in spring. They can be grown in potting mixture* 4, in a winter temperature of 55°–65° and summer of 65°–90°. They prefer full sun all the year and plenty of water during summer months.

**nicolai.** Growing to 18 ft. high or more and with a woody stem. Leafstalks deeply grooved on the upper side. Leaves to 4 ft. long and 2 ft. wide. Bracts* purplish, boat-shaped, to 15 in. or more long, enclosing blue flowers.

**reginae.** Bird-of-paradise flower. Growing to 3 ft., with underground, woody rootstocks, but no trunk. Leaves basal, to 1½ ft. long, and 6 in. wide, stiff, with strong leafstalks. Bracts boat-shaped, purplish, to 8 in. long, enclosing the orange-yellow flowers, which have a blue tongue.

**STREPTOCARPUS** (strep-to-kar′pus). Cape primrose. Tender perennial herbs, comprising about 60 species of the family Gesneriaceae, natives of South Africa and Madagascar. They are low-growing plants, producing 1 or several spreading, basal leaves or sometimes with a short stem and opposite* leaves. Flowering stalks growing from the axils* of the leaves, bearing 1–several, pale purple, blue, or reddish flowers. Calyx* of 5 sepals. Corolla 5-lobed, tubular, opening obliquely into 2 lips,* upper of 2 petals, lower of 3, the throat sometimes hairy and veined with another color. Stamens* 2. Fruit a many-seeded capsule.* (*Streptocarpus* is from the Greek for compound and fruit, in allusion to the fruit.)

These are showy plants which can be grown for house decoration, and need a warm-temperate greenhouse. Easily propagated from seeds, which should be sown 1/16 in. deep in a mixture of equal parts of finely sifted sand, leaf mold and loam in pans, in a temperature of 55°–65° in Feb. or March. They should be kept in a moist, shady position. As soon as large enough to handle they should be pricked-off into pans 2 in. apart in a similar mixture, later potting into potting mixture* 4. They prefer cool, moist conditions at all times and a winter temperature of 40°–50° and summer of 55°–65°.

**hybridus.** = *Streptocarpus kewensis.*

**kewensis.** Leaves 2–3, dark green, ovalish, from 6–12 in. long, wrinkled, covered with soft hairs, the margins wavy. Flowering stalks several, each bearing 6–8 flowers in a cluster. Flowers bright purple, the throat striped dark brown. Corolla tube to 2 in. long. Of hybrid origin.

---

* Special articles on the subjects indicated by an asterisk (*) will be found at the words so marked.

**STREPTOPUS** (strep′to-pus). Twisted stalk. Hardy perennial herbs, comprising about 6 species of the lily family and natives of the temperate regions of the northern hemisphere. They have creeping rootstocks which are much-branched. Stems 2½–3 ft. high, hairy, and slightly branched. Leaves alternate, ovalish or lance-shaped, usually clasping the stem, parallel-veined. Flowers bell-shaped, nodding, pink or greenish-white, growing 1–2 on a short twisted stalk from the axils* of the leaves. Calyx* of 3 colored sepals. Corolla of 3 petals alternating with the sepals. Stamens* 6. Fruit a berry. (*Streptopus* is from the Greek for twisted stalk, in allusion to the twisted flower stalks.)

They are not of much garden importance, sometimes grown in the wild garden. Propagated by division of the rootstocks. They prefer damp, shady places, and rather acid soils.

**amplexifolius.** Growing to 3 ft. high. Leaves clasping the stem, ovalish, 3–6 in. long, bright green on under side. Flowers greenish-white, ½ in. long, 2 on a twisted stalk, growing from the axils* of the leaves. Berry red. N.A.

**roseus.** Growing to 2½ ft. high. Leaves partly clasping the stem, broadly lance-shaped, to 4 in. long. Flowers purplish-pink, ½ in. across, usually 1 flower growing from the axils of the leaves. Berry red. Eastern N.A.

**STREPTOSOLEN** (strep-to-so′len). Tender perennial shrubs of the family Solanaceae and natives of Colombia and Ecuador. The only species is S. jamesoni (also known as *Browallia jamesoni*) and is of sprawling habit, growing to 6 ft. Leaves alternate,* small, ovalish, wrinkled, slightly hairy, short-stalked. Flowers orange-red, short-stalked in terminal, umbel*-like clusters. Calyx tubular. Corolla tubular, opening salverwise, to ¾ in. across. Tube to 1¼ in. long and twisted. Stamens 4, in pairs, 2 long, and 2 short, growing on the calyx tube. Fruit a capsule.*

Mostly grown as greenhouse plants for house decoration, but excellent for the flower border where they can be lifted and taken care of in the greenhouse during the winter in a temperature of 50°–60°. They can of course be grown entirely outdoors in the extreme South and in Calif., where it makes a very beautiful plant when trained on a wall. Propagated by cuttings of the young shoots inserted in sand in early spring. When large enough to handle they should be potted into potting mixture* 1 and later into No. 3. They need staking and pinching and can be trained into any shape. (*Streptosolen* is from the Greek for twisted and tube, in allusion to the twisted corolla tube.)

*STRIATA, -us, -um* (stry-ā′ta). Striped.

*STRICTA, -us, -um* (strick′ta). Strict; *i.e.* rigid and upright, with few or no branches.

**STRIKE.** To root cuttings successfully; as in the phrase "to strike cuttings of carnations."

**STRING BEAN** = *Phaseolus vulgaris.* For culture see BEAN.

**STRINGLESS BEAN.** A very young string bean, or a relatively stringless variety of string beans, with little or no "string" along the seams of the pod. See BEAN.

**STRINGY-BARK.** See EUCALYPTUS.

**STRIPED MAPLE** = *Acer pennsylvanicum.* See MAPLE.

**STRIPED TULIPS.** See Garden Tulips at TULIPA.

**STROBILANTHES** (stro-bi-lan′theez). Perennial herbs or shrubs, comprising about 200 species of the family Acanthaceae, natives of Asia and tropical Africa. Leaves opposite.* Flowers blue, violet or white, solitary or in clusters, terminal or growing from the axils* of the leaves. Calyx of 5 sepals. Corolla irregular,* tubular, widely opening. Stamens* 2–4. Fruit a capsule.* (*Strobilanthes* is from the Greek for cone and flower, in allusion to the flower cluster, which is cone-like.)

Not of much garden importance, but sometimes grown in the warm greenhouse for their ornamental foliage. They are difficult to cultivate, as they require a constant warm temperature, moist conditions and syringing daily. Propagated by cuttings of young shoots in Feb. or March.

**dyerianus.** A hairy shrub. Leaves broadly lance-shaped, to 8 in. long, iridescent on the upper side and purplish on the under side, the margins toothed. Flowers purplish-blue, 1½ in. long, in terminal clusters. Burma.

**isophyllus.** A low-growing, bushy shrub. Leaves lance-shaped, to 4 in. long, the margins toothed. Flowers blue and white, to 1 in. long, growing in clusters from the axils* of the leaves. India.

**STROBILE.** Loosely, a small cone; specifically, the cone-like mass of scales and their fruits found in trees like the birch or in the fruits of the hop. See CONE.

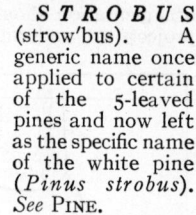

Strobile of the hop

*STROBUS* (strow′bus). A generic name once applied to certain of the 5-leaved pines and now left as the specific name of the white pine (*Pinus strobus*). See PINE.

**STROMBOCACTUS** (strom-bo-kak′tus). A single species of Mexican cacti, S. disciformis, somewhat cult. for interest or ornament in desert gardens in frostless regions or in the succulent house in the North. It is a top-shaped or nearly round, almost spineless cactus, not over 2 in. in diameter. The plant body is ribbed and tubercled, but the tubercles are not on the ribs and in youth have 1–4 needle-like white spines which fall off as the plant gets old. Flowers about ¾ in. long, white, but red on the outside, and scaly, the scales with paper margins. For cult. see CACTI. (*Strombocactus* is from the Greek for top and *Cactus*, in allusion to the top-shaped plant body.)

**STRONG.** As applied to soils *strong* means that they are productive or fertile. The term has greater validity among dirt gardeners and farmers than among the soil scientists; hence its wide and often cogent use.

**STROPHOLIRION CALIFORNICUM** = *Brodiaea volubilis.*

**STRUCTURES.** Since the early days of garden history, structures such as summer houses, garden pavilions, gazebos, pergolas and tool houses have been built, for the comfort of having such places has always been apparent. The need has been filled in many ways, from the classic temple of the Roman and eighteenth-century gardens to the humble, rustic tool house.

The gazebo is of Dutch origin and is a characteristic feature of old Dutch gardens. Built of brick or stone, gazebos were placed where the passing coach or boat could be easily seen. In the long summer evenings the men still bring their pipes to them and the women their sewing for a few hours of conversation and repose.

The pergola was originally designed to offer a shaded passageway from one building to another, or from one garden feature to another, and it is always at its best when serving this purpose. In modern parlance, however, any structure

Gazebo

---

* Special articles on the subjects indicated by an asterisk (*) will be found at the words so marked.

which has an open, vine-clad roof goes by that name. *See* ARBORS AND ARCHES.

The pergola has always been an important feature of Italian garden design and is capable of great elaboration. In Spain, too, the pergola is much used, but is usually of simple construction — rough beams supported by rustic posts, left natural in color or painted black or blue. Where wood is scarce, the posts may be of concrete, brick or stone, left exposed or whitewashed. These posts may well rest on a low wall.

Garden pavilion

Vines should not be allowed to grow too thickly over a pergola, but should clothe it scantily, to reveal its proportions. Two or three different kinds of vines may be grown on the same pergola if they are kept pruned or planted sufficiently far apart.

Garden structures serve a useful or an ornamental purpose and may preferably serve both. They should be considered as architectural features or ornaments, and should not be dotted about the grounds without reference to their surroundings and without regard to the general scheme. In fact, no feature of a garden can be considered as a thing apart, but all must be made to harmonize and fit naturally and inevitably into its proper place and be in keeping with its surroundings. The success of a garden structure depends more often on skill in placing than on form or material.

Such structures may dominate a view of the surrounding country or the color of an adjacent garden. They may terminate a garden path or allée or a cut through a wood. They may be arranged so that it is convenient to serve refreshments in them while enjoying the sight of a game of tennis and may also be useful to store the various "sporting goods" during bad weather. They may merely be quiet places in which to rest or read, away from the life of the house, or conversely they may be used as places in which to play noisy games so that the house itself may be more quiet. They may be filled with furniture and utensils for first lessons in housewifery, which will be the better learned under such pleasant conditions. They may shelter an object of value, as a spring or a statue.

Often, however, the primary reason for building a garden structure is that the designer feels the aesthetic need of an architectural object in a particular place — perhaps to close a vista or strengthen the corner of a garden wall and even the humble tool house may be successfully if skillfully, used in this way.

Not many tool houses are so good looking or so well placed as this one. *See* TOOL HOUSE.

In a landscape composition, the form of a structure should be considered not only in relation to its surroundings but also in relation to the other buildings in the same picture. In cases where it is near the main house or residence, or closely related by being a part of a formal scheme, it should have similar architectural treatment. It may repeat the architectural style or at least be made harmonious by the use of the same building material or the same color.

The question of the relative scale between the two is also important, as the house may tend to dwarf the garden structure and overpower it. French garden designers of the eighteenth century realized this in their lattice-work shelters, which, though frankly temporary pieces of stage scenery, were nevertheless sufficiently important as to be in scale with the adjacent château.

Summer house

Where a garden structure is placed in a remote part of the grounds and has no definite relationship to the main house, it should become a part of its wilder surroundings. Here shade or shelter is the primary consideration. The roof may be thatched, the supporting posts left rough or even with the bark on; the whole partly concealed by vines in order to obtain that rough and rustic look so charming in the right place. It may closely fit the ground and have an irregular shape. The gray-green of its painted woodwork may

---

* Special articles on the subjects indicated by an asterisk (*) will be found at the words so marked.

harmonize with the color of the surrounding foliage or its stonework may blend with the outcrop of stone appearing near it. It may be entirely or partly hidden by planting or reduced to comparative insignificance by one or more large, overhanging trees. As it grows old, it will always assume greater harmony with its surroundings.

The interior fittings of a garden structure will depend on circumstances, which should be well studied before the structure is built. As it is essential that the inside be clean in order to be attractive, only materials which are easily cleaned should be used. All these buildings should be convenient and efficient as well as beautiful. Fitness to local conditions and a simple form, obviously expressing a practical need, tend to make a building less expressive of man's fancy, more expressive of his necessity, and so less incongruous with its surroundings. — R. L. F., Jr.

**STRUMOSA, -us, -um** (strew-mō'sa). With cushion-like swellings.

**STRYCHNINE.** See STRYCHNOS NUX-VOMICA.

**STRYCHNOS** (strick'nos). A large genus of tropical shrubs and trees of the family Loganiaceae, some yielding valuable medicine, others arrow poisons more dangerous than any known, while *S. spinosa* yields an edible fruit. The two below are occasionally grown in extreme southern Fla. and are hardy nowhere else in the U.S. Leaves opposite.* Flowers small, yellowish-white, mostly in terminal, sometimes much-branched clusters (cymes*). For details of flower structure see LOGANIACEAE. Fruit fleshy and berry-like. (*Strychnos* is an old Greek name for a kind of nightshade, applied by Linnaeus to these plants, perhaps because so many of them are poisonous.)

**nux-vomica.** Strychnine. A medium-sized tree, not over 40 ft. high. Leaves ovalish, 2½-3½ in. long. Flower clusters (cymes*) nearly 2 in. wide. Fruit berry-like, about 1½ in. in diameter, its many seeds the source of strychnine. India.

**spinosa.** Natal Orange. A spiny shrub 7-10 ft. high, the spines about ¾ in. long. Leaves roundish, about 2 in. long, with 5 main veins. Flower clusters branched (a compound cyme*). Fruit yellow, berry-like, nearly 4 in. in diameter, its pulp sweet and edible. Central and South Africa.

**STUARTIA** = *Stewartia*.

**STUMPING.** See LAYERING.

**STUNT.** See Diseases at DAHLIA.

**STYLE.** The shank-like connection between the ovary and the stigma. See FLOWER.

**STYLOMA** = *Pritchardia*.

**STYLOPHORUM** (sty-loff'o-rum). Hardy perennial herbs comprising 3 species of the poppy family, one a native of North America, and 2 of China. They have thick rootstocks, yellow sap, and mostly basal leaves generally deeply cut almost to the midrib into several lobes. Flowers yellow or red, solitary or in clusters. Calyx* of 2 sepals. Corolla of 4 petals. Stamens* many. Fruit a capsule.* (*Stylophorum* is from the Greek for style, in allusion to the persistent style.)

Not generally cult., but sometimes grown in the wild garden. Propagated by seeds or division of the rootstocks in early spring, but it is often invasive and must be controlled rather than propagated. They prefer moist, rich, loose soil, and partial shade.

**diphyllum.** Celandine poppy. Growing to 1½ ft. high, with 2 leaves at top of flowering stalk. Leaves light green, deeply cut into lobes. Flowers deep yellow, to 2 in. across, in 2-5-flowered clusters. Capsules 1 in. long. Western Pa. to Wisc. and Tenn. April-May.

**STYLOSA, -us, -um** (sty-lō'sa). With a prominent style.*

**STYRACACEAE** (sty-ra-kay'see-ee). The storax family provides only three genera of hort. interest, *Halesia*, *Styrax* and *Pterostyrax*, all trees or shrubs and mostly hardy over much of the country. There are, in the whole family, perhaps 100 species in six genera which are widely distributed in the New World, Asia and southern Europe.

*Halesia* is an ornamental tree with profuse, bell-shaped flowers, and is much cult. Flowers white in all the cult. genera. Leaves alternate* and simple.* Fruit dry or fleshy.

Technical flower characters: Flowers perfect* and regular.* Calyx more or less united, its 4 or 5 segments cleft or lobed. Corolla generally bell-shaped, but of 4-8 petals, partly or wholly united at the base. Stamens* 4-8, or 8-16. Ovary superior* in *Styrax*, inferior in the two other cult. genera.

**STYRAX** (sty'racks). Storax. A large genus of ornamental shrubs and trees of the family Styracaceae, most of the 100 known species being found in tropical or warm regions, but the two below hardy in the temperate zone. Leaves alternate,* short-stalked, remotely and finely toothed (in ours). Flowers white, mostly in terminal clusters (racemes*), the calyx bell-shaped and slightly 5-toothed, usually persistent. Corolla united only at the base, the 5 lobes appearing as if 5 separate petals. Stamens* mostly 10. Fruit a rather dry drupe.* (*Styrax* is the old Greek name for one of the species.)

Both the plants below are handsome shrubs or small trees, thriving best in open sunlight and in a light, well-drained soil. Propagation is by seeds or by layers, but cuttings are difficult to strike. There are several native species in the southern states which may be transferred to grounds.

**japonica.** A shrub or small tree, 20-30 ft. high, often less as cult. Leaves broadly elliptic or oblongish, 2-3 in. long, pointed. Flowers about ½ in. long, fragrant, long-stalked, the few-flowered clusters drooping. Fruit egg-shaped, about ½ in. long. China and Jap. June-July. Hardy from zone* 3 southward. A very showy and desirable shrub, well suited to the lawn.

**obassia.** A shrub or small tree, 20-30 ft. high, usually less as cult. Leaves nearly round, or broadly oval, 3½-8 in. long, or even more on the main shoots, hairy on the under side. Flowers nearly 1 in. long, fragrant, in many-flowered clusters (racemes*) that may be 6-8 in. long, but are usually half hidden by the foliage. Fruit egg-shaped, nearly ¾ in. long. Jap. May-June. Hardy from zone* 3 southward.

**SUAVEOLENS** (swah-vee-ō'lenz). Pleasing.

**SUAVIS, -e** (swah'vis). Agreeable.

**SUBCARNOSA, -us, -um** (sub-kar-nō'sa). Somewhat fleshy.

**SUBCOERULEA, -us, -um** (sub-see-roo'lee-a). Almost dark blue.

**SUBCORDATA, -us, -um** (sub-kor-day'ta). Nearly heart-shaped.

**SUBDIVARICATA, -us, -um** (sub-dy-var-i-kay'ta). Somewhat divergent.

**SUBER** (soo'ber). An old name for the cork oak (*Quercus suber*). See OAK.

**SUBHIRTELLA, -us, -um** (sub-hir-tell'a). Slightly hairy.

**SUB-IRRIGATION.** See WATERING.

**SUBMERGED FLOWER ARRANGEMENT.** Clear glass and clear water are the chief essentials for a submerged flower arrangement, also called a submerged garden. Ordinary goldfish bowls, either oblong or round, are excellent receptacles. Color harmony, proportion, and balance must be kept in mind in selecting the plants. Orchids, camellias and similar flowers may be used, combined with ferns like the maidenhair, but smaller flowers give better results. Forget-me-nots, tiny rose buds, baby's-breath and small ferns are always good. The flower arrangement must be completed in the aquarium before any water is added. Light weights are attached to the flowers to prevent their rising to the top. Stem holders make good weights and may be concealed with moss or ferns. Pour the water in slowly and carefully, so that the flowers are not disturbed, until the top of the arrangement is at least one third below the surface.

Bubble bouquets are modified forms of submerged flower arrangements. Light weights are attached to the stems and they are arranged as desired so as to be anchored when water is put in. Then the holder upon which they are arranged is sunk in a tub of water, and a globe or bottle-shaped jar inverted over the flowers and stood in a shallow tray of water. The globe containing the submerged flower display is then removed from the tub of water, but its base must not be removed from the water-filled dish in which it stands. Small bubbles will soon form on the flower petals, leaves and stems. From these bubbles, this type of arrangement derives its name. Bubble bouquets do not last more than a day or two.

**SUBSESSILIS, -e** (sub-sess'i-lis). Nearly stalkless.

**SUB-SHRUB.** An under-shrub (which see).

---

* Special articles on the subjects indicated by an asterisk (*) will be found at the words so marked.

**SUBSOIL.** See SOILS.

**SUBSOIL PLOW.** See Section 1, TOOLS AND IMPLEMENTS.

**SUBSPECIES.** A somewhat technical designation for a race or form, especially a geographical race, of a species. It is more used by botanists than gardeners, for whom a subspecies is practically the same as a variety (which see).

**SUBTEND.** To stand close to, and just beneath; as many bracts* subtend the flowers or clusters just above them.

*SUBTOMENTOSA, -us, -um* (sub-to-men-tō′sa). Almost tomentose; *i.e.* covered with a soft, felt-like hairiness.

**SUB-TROPICAL GARDEN.** As the name implies, a sub-tropical region is one that borders on the tropics in climatic environment, but is not truly tropical because of the lower temperature means in winter and the occurrence of frosts of varying intensity at irregular intervals. In the U.S., the sub-tropical areas may be said to be confined to the warmer parts of Fla. and Calif., together with limited protected areas on the Gulf Coast that may be included for a few of the hardiest plants of tropical type.

In sub-tropical regions an opportunity is offered the gardener to create landscape effects that approach the tropical and to use to advantage a wide range of plants not adapted to cooler climates. Broad-leaved evergreen shrubs, palms, bamboos and flowering trees predominate and combine to lend a "tropical atmosphere." Instead of a bleak winter landscape of defoliated plants and an occasional conifer, the whole is distinctively full-foliaged and of a summery green the year round. A succession of flowering seasons provides a profusion of blossoms in every month, and the invitation into the garden extends its appeal at all seasons. Differences between the sub-tropical and tropical garden are mainly in magnitude of plant variety and may not be so great as between the typical northern garden and the sub-tropical.

Plants of the tropics are predominantly evergreen, and though complete defoliation for relatively short periods occurs with some, the period of leaf fall usually is coincident with the putting out of new foliage. Summer and winter seasons have little influence; moisture relations, rather than temperature, commonly determine the periods of growth and dormancy. Tropical gardens have no minimum temperature restrictions and consequently have access to the whole of the tropical world for variety; sub-tropical ones are confined to the hardier tropical species.

Plants adapted and now grown in sub-tropical gardens are legion. Presumably because of differences in rainfall, humidity and soils, they differ in variety between Fla. and Calif. A few of the commonly planted genera and species, exclusive of numerous herbaceous types, include:

| SHRUBS | TREES | VINES |
|---|---|---|
| Abelia grandiflora | Acacia | Abrus precatorius |
| Acacia | Albizzia | Allamanda cathartica |
| Acalypha | Araucaria | Antigonon leptopus |
| Azalea | Bamboos, in variety | Asparagus spp. |
| Breynia nivosa | Bauhinia | Beaumontia grandiflora |
| Buddleia | Cassia | Bougainvillaea |
| Callistemon | Casuarina | Clerodendron thomsonae |
| Camellia japonica | Cinnamomum | Cryptostegia |
| Carissa | Citrus | Ficus pumila |
| Cestrum | Dalbergia sissoo | Gelsemium sempervirens |
| Clerodendron | Delonix regia | Jasminum |
| Codiaeum | Eriobotrya japonica | Lonicera |
| Cotoneaster | Eucalyptus | Monstera deliciosa |
| Dombeya wallichi | Grevillea | Passiflora |
| Duranta repens | Ilex | Pereskia |
| Escallonia spp. | Jacaranda acutifolia | Petrea volubilis |
| Eugenia spp. | Mangifera indica | Porana paniculata |
| Hibiscus rosa-sinensis | Melaleuca leucadendron | Pyrostegia ignea |
| Ixora coccinea | Melia azedarach | Scindapsus aureus |
| Jasminum | Musa | Solandra guttata |
| Lagerstroemia | Palms, in variety | Solanum |
| Ligustrum (evergreen species) | Parkinsonia aculeata | Tecomaria capensis |
| Malvaviscus arboreus | Pithecolobium dulce | Thunbergia |
| Nandina domestica | Plumeria | Trachelospermum jasminoides |
| Nerium oleander | Quercus | |
| Pittosporum | Ravenala madagascariensis | |
| Plumbago capensis | Schinus | |
| Poinciana pulcherrima | Spathodea campanulata | |
| Poinsettia pulcherrima | Stenolobium stans | |
| Tabernaemontana | Tamarindus indica | |
| Viburnum spp. | Terminalia | |

All of these plants are entered at their proper alphabetical place in THE GARDEN DICTIONARY, and should be sought there for details of culture. See also PALM, BAMBOO. The design of a sub-tropical garden follows the main principles of good planning, as in any other garden. See LANDSCAPE ARCHITECTURE. See also PATIO GARDENS.

For the proper sequence of garden operations in the sub-tropical garden, which differ from those in cooler regions, see the heading **Sub-tropical**, under each month at GARDEN CALENDAR. — H. M.

*SUBULATA, -us, -um* (sub-you-lay′ta). Awl-shaped.

**SUBURBAN GARDEN.** See HOME GROUNDS.

**SUB-WATER.** To water by sub-irrigation. See WATERING.

**SUCCESSION CROPPING.** The planting of one crop immediately after the harvesting of another, on the same land, and in the same growing season. It is mostly practiced in the vegetable garden, and, with inter-cropping, provides a valuable method of getting the utmost return from the available space. For the details of succession cropping and inter-cropping see KITCHEN GARDEN.

**SUCCORY.** See CICHORIUM INTYBUS.

*SUCCULENTA, -us, -um* (suck-you-len′ta). With thick, fleshy leaves or stems.

**SUCCULENTS.** In nearly every country there is some region with deficient or periodic rainfall, where totally unrelated plants have been forced to adopt some mechanism to survive the dry season. The outstanding example, in the New World, is furnished by the cactus family, where leaves are usually lacking, and the plant body is green and functions as do leaves, in addition to storing large quantities of water. While the cacti are true succulents, they form such a distinct group that their culture and kinds are usually, and in this book, kept separate from all other succulents. See CACTI.

Three common types of succulents belonging to the genera *Stapelia* (right), *Aloe* (lower left), and HAWORTHIA (above)

Before discussing the different sorts of succulents it will be well to define the term, which is confusing to many and has a slightly misleading origin. Succulent is from the Latin *succus*, meaning juice. But if succulent, as a garden term, covered only those fleshy or juicy plants like cacti or the cactus-like spurges, it would be far more limited than usage has made it. For under the term succulent we include, rather loosely it must be admitted, two distinct classes of plants that have quite different ways of overcoming a deficiency of

---

* Special articles on the subjects indicated by an asterisk (*) will be found at the words so marked.

water. The only hort. reason for calling them all succulents is that their culture is approximately the same.

The two main groups of plants that are classed as succulents are those that store water and those that have become adapted to the lack of it, without special storage facilities. In the first group are the cacti and cactus-like spurges (as well as many others to be discussed presently). In these the very fleshy stems or leaves store considerable water upon which the plant draws during the dry season. Such plants are perhaps properly called succulents.

In the second group there are no special water-storage organs. But by reduction of leaf area, or actual leaflessness, or a varnished leaf surface, or ashy-gray foliage, or by other devices, the plants have so reduced their water requirements that they survive the long drought (lasting for years in some Peruvian deserts) just as well as those succulents that store water. This second group of succulents should perhaps not be called so, for they are what the botanist calls xerophytes. But the botanical term, among gardeners, is not likely to replace the word succulent for these drought-resistant plants, although it would make for greater accuracy if it did so. There are also some groups of succulents, like the agaves, that come under both categories. Generally speaking, however, it is possible to separate these two main groups of succulents into those that store water and those that get along without doing so; into other words, into the water-storing and drought-resistant succulents.

### WATER-STORING SUCCULENTS

Here belong the cacti (which see), all the cactus-like spurges (see EUPHORBIA), and many other plants with fleshy leaves or stems or both. Among the most common are those from the desert regions of South Africa and elsewhere, found in the genera *Gasteria, Haworthia, Aloe, Mesembryanthemum, Stapelia, Huernia, Huerniopsis, Echeveria, Crassula, Cotyledon, Sempervivum* (see HOUSELEEK), *Rochea, Sedum*, and *Pachyphytum* (see all these genera). There are also scattered succulents in various other genera and families, especially in the genus *Senecio*, and in the families Portulacaceae, Dioscoreaceae, Amaryllidaceae, and Liliaceae (see these entries).

Such plants are grown more for interest or oddity than for beauty, as many of them have grotesque plant forms. There are, however, very gorgeous flower colors in some of them, notably *Mesembryanthemum, Echeveria, Rochea, Kalanchoe, Sempervivum*, and *Pachyphytum*. In others the flowers are inconspicuous, and in *Stapelia, Huernia*, and *Huerniopsis* they are showy but disgusting, because of their foul, carrion-scented odor.

Not a few foliage plants are also found among these fleshy-leaved succulents. Especially in *Echeveria* and *Sedum* the carpet-bedding enthusiast will find many plants of low growth, colored leaves, and compact habit, well suited to this type of planting.

Overwhelmingly these water-storing succulents come from regions of intense summer heat, and equally intense dryness. Many of them will stand no frost and are consequently confined, so far as outdoor cult. is concerned, to the desert or semi-desert regions in southern Calif., Ariz., N. Mex., and western Tex. See DESERT GARDEN. See also CACTI. Their indoor culture will be discussed presently.

But some of these succulents will stand hard freezing so long as this is not interspersed with slush and moisture at their roots, which few or no succulents will stand. That is why only a handful of them can be grown in the northeastern states — mostly sedums, houseleeks, and a very few cacti.

### DROUGHT-RESISTANT SUCCULENTS

This group includes very different plants from the water-storing succulents, because they have, without special storage facilities, become habituated to long periods of dryness. Some, like the South American genera *Dyckia, Hechtia*, and *Puya*, all belonging to the pineapple family, have been known to grow for years without a single recorded rainfall. Naturally such plants may be said to exist rather than to grow, but grow they do, very slowly, and mostly when they do get a brief period of moisture.

Better known plants in these drought-resistant succulents will be found in the genera *Dasylirion, Yucca, Agave* (which also includes some fleshy-leaved species), *Fouquieria, Hesperaloe, Hesperoyucca, Samuela*, and *Furcraea*. Nearly all these have leathery or coarse foliage, some are very spiny, and generally their flowers are far less showy than in the water-storing succulents. But in some of these genera the flower cluster is very striking, notably in *Yucca*, and in *Agave* which includes the century plants.

These drought-resistant succulents, of which only some species of *Yucca* will stand wet, slushy winters, do not lend themselves to so many uses as the water-storing kinds. They are often tall, some have palm-like trunks, while others have immense basal rosettes of spiny-margined leaves. In other words, they need space and are more useful for accent* plants or for the rear of desert gardens than the generally lower, fleshy-leaved types, most of which are grown in pots.

### CULTURE

The culture of both types of succulents is properly based upon a study of the conditions under which they grow naturally. While temperature may, as in some upland Peruvian or Mexican deserts, fall far below freezing, the plants survive this easily if their roots are not rotted by slush or water. The whole secret in growing them is to see that this does not happen.

In desert gardens in the Southwest, sandy or gritty soils are easy to find, and in fact most of the local cacti will be found in such soils. The drainage is perfect and no stagnant water ever collects about the roots. These soil and moisture conditions are ideal, if, as nearly always happens, there is intense sunlight and great summer heat. All but a handful of succulents will thrive in such an environment.

When rains do come, the plants make a fair growth, but it is based upon the fact that while water is available, the plants are never bogged in it. They must, when the rain comes, or when you water them, get ample supplies of moisture, but all excess must drain away. And this can only be secured by a sandy or gritty soil.

In the greenhouse or in the home, very different conditions confront the succulent. There is far less sunshine, the plant grows much more slowly and there is grave danger from overwatering, especially in the winter in the comparative darkness of the living room. The first necessity is to see that your succulents, most of which will necessarily be pot plants of the fleshy-leaved type, get the proper soil conditions.

This is best approximated by potting mixture* 6, and the pot should have at least ¼ of its depth filled with broken flower pots, upon which the soil should be put. The lightness of the mixture and the ample drainage at the bottom will take care of any excess water.

There is one final caution for all soils used for succulents. They are peculiarly apt to harbor nematodes, and because the plants are inactive for so long a period, to accumulate trouble due to stagnation of water, this in spite of every care to secure proper drainage in the pots. To reduce these hazards many seasoned growers sterilize all soils for succulents. For the details of this see SOIL STERILIZATION.

The atmosphere in the greenhouse must be kept dry and airy; this is far more important than the temperature, although the latter should be around 55°–60° in the winter and 65°–75° in the summer. If possible, it is better to put the succulents outdoors in the summer, and if this is done, the pots should be plunged* in sand or ashes, in full sunshine.

Water requirements are much greater in the summer than in the dark days of winter. During the latter period the plants should be watered only enough to keep them from drying out — usually once a week is sufficient. If the plants are in the living room, they should be put as near the windows as possible for the best results, and watering will require more careful watching. More household succulents are lost from overwatering in the winter than from any other cause.

Poorly grown succulents have a pale and anemic appearance, which is especially likely to be the case when they are grown under glass or in dense shade. Expert growers have two methods for bringing out all the bright leaf colors. The first relates to plants grown in the sun and outdoors in the

---

* Special articles on the subjects indicated by an asterisk (*) will be found at the words so marked.

summer. Gradually stop watering them in the early fall and do not take the plants in until cold weather has really arrived. The second hint is for greenhouse cult. In preparing the plants for Christmas or Easter, diminish the heat until the houses are near the freezing point, at the same time withholding the water. A few days of this treatment will suffice. These suggestions do not apply to cacti.

### PROPAGATION

Many succulents, such as *Echeveria*, may be grown from single leaves, provided they are not watered, but are placed on top of dry sand. Nearly all other succulents may be grown from cuttings. These should be allowed to form a callus* or at least the wound should be dried over before planting. Then insert in dry sand and keep without water until growth or shriveling begins. Cuttings while rooting demand plenty of air and light. Some succulents can be propagated like geraniums.

Some of the more desirable aloes are hard to propagate. They may not perfect seed nor produce offshoots. Cutting the stem only causes it to rot and only the head can then be saved. In this case, a hot iron applied to the growing point will frequently cause development of shoots. Some agaves produce bulbils* instead of flowers. These are simply inserted in sand or, if roots have already formed, planted in potting mixture* 3.

Succulent species which have large seeds may be planted in potting mixture* 1 with an overlay of not too fine charcoal. Many of the succulents in the genera *Echeveria* and *Sempervivum* bear seed as fine as dust. These must be pressed firmly down on the surface of finely screened potting mixture* 1, and then sprinkled with a small amount of sifted charcoal dust, but not enough to form a covering layer. The pot is then immersed until evidence of moisture barely shows on the surface of the soil. Cover the pot with glass. Look twice a day for damping-off* which appears as a patch of fine, silky threads. Succulent seedlings are subject to this fungus, but spraying with Semesan will control it. It is good practice to keep a sprayer at hand, but it should have no rubber bulb to deteriorate.

Succulent plants frequently breed abnormal forms. Some of these, especially the crested or cockscombed forms, are highly prized by collectors. In these the stem tends to become fan-shaped, with a line of reduced leaves at the top. Globular growths form masses ranging from caterpillar-shape to those having the appearance of the human brain. As in the cacti, there is also a mania for producing bizarre plants by grafting, especially in forms of *Euphorbia lactea*.

Anyone interested in succulents or cacti is welcome to membership in the Cactus and Succulent Society in Calif. (which publishes a journal), or to membership in many local societies devoted to the same interest. For information as to your nearest society or club, write the Garden Editor, Houghton Mifflin Company, Boston, Mass.

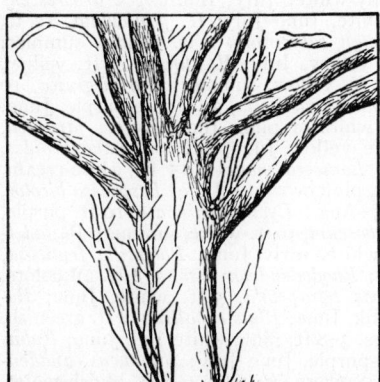

Suckers (*below*) and water sprouts (*above*) often steal much food from a tree.

**SUCKER.** A secondary shoot arising from the lower part of the trunk or from the ground, and usually growing at the expense of the plant producing it. Some plants sucker very freely and the growth of the suckers is so rampant as to suggest their other name of thieves.

Suckers that are produced higher up, on large branches or on the trunk, are usually called water sprouts. As in the basal suckers they should be removed, except where they have been induced, as in pollarding. *See also* SOBOLE.

**SUCKING-DISC (or DISK).** An adhesive enlargement at the tip of some tendrils.* It aids vines, like certain species of *Parthenocissus*, to cling to walls.

**SUCKING INSECTS.** *See* True Bugs at INSECT PESTS. For methods of control *see* Contact Insecticides at INSECTICIDES.

**SUDANENSIS, -e** (soo-dan-en'sis). From the Sudan.

**SUDAN GRASS** = *Holcus sudanensis*.

**SUECICA, -us, -um** (swee'si-ka). From Sweden.

**SUFFRUTICOSA, -us, -um** (suf-frew-ti-kō'sa). Suffruticose; *i.e.* a little shrubby. Mostly applied to herbs that are woody at the base.

**SUGAR-APPLE** = *Annona squamosa*.

**SUGAR BEET.** *See* BEET.

**SUGARBERRY** = *Celtis laevigata*. *See* HACKBERRY.

**SUGAR CANE.** The fact that *Saccharum officinarum* (which see) is a tropical crop explains why the culture of sugar cane in the U.S. has always been limited. Before the Civil War much cane was grown in the southern states, most of it of low sugar content, but competition from expert tropical growers did not then prevent the development of very considerable sugar estates in Ala., Fla., Ga., La., Miss., and southern Tex. Today practically all cane sugar produced in the U.S. is from extreme southern La. The total reduction of acreage in sugar cane is well illustrated by the last census figures — 291 thousand acres in 1930, but 476 thousand acres twenty years ago. The reason for this is higher sugar yields per acre in Cuba, Java, and the Philippines, and more expert extraction.

Sugar cane, as grown here, is mostly treated as an annual crop. Pieces of the woody stem are cut into lengths of 3-4 in. and planted about 18-20 in. apart, in a trench 4-5 in. deep. The rows should be 5-6 ft. apart, for the plant gets very tall and has ultimately a large head of corn-like leaves.

The soil does not seem to matter so much as the fact that it must be rich or have richness added to it. Fertilizers high in nitrogen and stable manure are the most useful. And the ground must be kept cultivated in the early months, as it will be difficult to get machinery between the rows later.

The leaves should be stripped from the cane before the latter is cut, and cutting must be done before there is a frost. It is chiefly this frost hazard and the lack of heat during the growing season which have held down the production of sugar cane in the U.S. It is now less than ½ of 1% of world production.

Growing certain varieties of sugar cane for syrup, however, is a worth-while enterprise, especially for those living in the states of Ga., Fla., Ala., Miss., and La., where such sugar cane cult. is still widely practiced (189 thousand acres). The varieties grown for this purpose are mostly Home Purple, a red-stemmed sort, and Ribbon Cane, which is striped. They are soft canes, popular for chewing, and useful for syrup extraction, but their sugar content does not make them profitable for sugar extraction.

These syrup type of canes usually sprout from ratoons* and consequently do not have to be planted fresh each year. But ratoon cane does not last indefinitely and cut pieces of the stem should be planted every second or third year, as in the cane varieties raised for sugar.

In some sections of the country there is confusion between these syrup sugar canes and the sugar sorghums. But there need not be, for sorghum does not produce a jointed stem, which, when cut, will produce a new plant. Also sorghum regularly flowers and fruits, while most sugar cane varieties do not, at least in the U.S. If they do, the seed should never be used, as it does not come true to variety.

INSECT PESTS. A whitish caterpillar bores in the stalks, killing young plants and injuring larger ones. Coarse grasses should be kept down and corn should not be planted near cane fields. Cane should be cut low, and old pieces of stalk cleaned up in the fall, but leaves and trash should be left on the ground, as they harbor a parasite. Planting stock

---

* Special articles on the subjects indicated by an asterisk (*) will be found at the words so marked.

can be freed from borers by keeping it under water for 72 hours prior to planting.

Mealybugs attack sugar cane all over the world. Clean-up methods, the use of clean planting stock, and ant control are advised. Snout beetles and other insects sometimes injuring cane are reduced in numbers by keeping down large-stemmed grasses. The little corn leaf aphid occurs on cane; it is not of itself seriously injurious, but it carries disease.

DISEASES. There is almost no end to the literature regarding sugar cane mosaic. There now are available high-yielding resistant strains for planting. Other troubles that cause losses are the Fiji disease, gummosis, rind disease, smut, sereh, red rot, sclerotium blight, root diseases, eye-spot, brown stripe, bacterial stripe, red stripe, and black rot. Some of the cane varieties are resistant to one or more of these, but in most cases only general recommendations in exclusion, eradication, and protection can be given.

**SUGAR CORN** = Sweet corn. *See* CORN.

**SUGAR FOR CUTTINGS.** *See* Aid of Chemicals at CUTTINGS.

**SUGAR GUM** = *Eucalyptus cladocalyx*.

**SUGAR-LOAF** = *Clematis douglasi*.

**SUGAR MAPLE** = *Acer saccharum*. *See* MAPLE.

**SUGAR PALM** = *Arenga saccharifera*.

**SUGAR PEA** = *Pisum sativum macrocarpon*. *See* PEA.

**SUGAR SORGHUM** = *Holcus sorghum saccharatus*.

**SUGI** = *Cryptomeria japonica*.

**SULCATE.** Grooved.

**SULFORON.** A trademarked fungicide, containing 95% sulphur, sold with directions for use as a dust against fungous diseases and mites.

**SULFOROTE.** A trademarked dust insecticide and fungicide, containing rotenone and sulphur, sold with directions for use against various insect pests, especially gladiolus thrips.

**SULLA CLOVER** = *Hedysarum coronarium*.

**SULPHATE OF AMMONIA.** *See* Nitrogen at FERTILIZERS.

**SULPHATE OF POTASH.** *See* Potash at FERTILIZERS.

**SULPHUR.** *See* Sulphur at FUNGICIDES, and at INSECTICIDES.

*SULPHUREA, -us, -um* (sul-fure′e-a). Yellow.

**SULPHUR-FLOWER** = *Eriogonum umbellatum*.

**SULPHUR-LIME.** *See* Sulphur at FUNGICIDES.

**SULPHUR SPRAY.** *See* Contact Spray at INSECTICIDES.

**SUMAC.** *See* RHUS.

**SUMAC FAMILY.** A family of woody plants, including shrubs, trees, and vines, and containing such unlike plants as the poison ivy, smoke-tree, pistache, and the mango. For the cult. genera *see* ANACARDIACEAE.

**SUMMER BEDDING.** The planting of tender ornamentals in flower beds during the summer, very widely done in public parks and in many private gardens. The only objection to it is the expense, as many plants used for summer bedding demand a greenhouse for winter care. Among such are palms, caladiums, crotons, dracaenas, and any other tropical shrubs or trees used in such a scheme. Many of the latter may be plunged* in the bed.

People without greenhouse equipment can, however, find a wide range of plants suitable for summer bedding. Most of the tender annuals (*see* ANNUALS) can be so used. So can the castor-oil plant, cannas, the elephant-ear, or other summer-blooming plants whose rootstocks or bulbs are stored over the winter.

**SUMMER CLOUD.** A trademarked powder sold with directions for use as a temporary shade for greenhouse glass.

**SUMMER CROOKNECK SQUASH** = *Cucurbita pepo melopepo*. For culture *see* SQUASH.

**SUMMER CYPRESS** = *Kochia scoparia*.

**SUMMER FIR** = *Artemisia sacrorum viride*.

**SUMMER GARDEN.** There is no difficulty in maintaining a full-flowered garden during June, July and August. The difficulty lies, rather, in avoiding monotony in the type of flowers used, the too frequent appearance of members of the daisy family (the Compositae) and the summer-flowering phloxes, with their wheel-like regularity of form. Also during this prodigal period, color is apt to get out of hand, with the result that the borders appear hot and restless.

Points to be aimed at in the summer garden are a pleasing arrangement of colors, employing to this end a good many flowers of cool tones, dim blues, lavenders, and numerous plants with gray foliage; the maintenance of a fresh, well-filled appearance by the use of such plants as have fine, lasting foliage. And neatness. The summer borders should appear trim, prosperous and well cared for. The plants should be firmly and inconspicuously staked and relieved of all spent blossoms and seed pods; the paths should be neatly raked and the grass cut short; borders and paths should be kept free of weeds and all climbers rigidly trained and fastened up.

During the summer season there are fewer flowering trees and shrubs than are available earlier in the season, but on the other hand there are a far greater number of annuals and perennials, as well as lilies, gladioli, dahlias, tritonias, and tuberoses. In selecting plants for the summer garden it is wise to employ a preponderance of those having a long season of bloom. There is no need to repeat here the long list of herbaceous plants in bloom during June, July and August, for all the important ones are mentioned at GARDEN CALENDAR, and their period of bloom specified. *See also* the special articles devoted to ANNUALS, BIENNIALS, and PERENNIALS.

SUMMER-FLOWERING SHRUBS

After the rush of spring bloom it is often difficult to maintain color in the shrub border, many of which are apt to be rather drab by midsummer. The list below, if followed carefully, will provide bloom in the shrub border from June until early Sept. All the plants mentioned will be found elsewhere in THE GARDEN DICTIONARY, and should be sought there for additional notes on culture and hardiness.

*Abelia chinensis*, 4–6 ft. pink, Aug.; *Amorpha canescens*, 3 ft. blue, June; *A. fruticosa*, 10 ft. blue, July; *Buddleia davidi*, 6 ft. purple, Aug.; *Callicarpa japonica*, 5 ft. pink, July; *Calluna vulgaris*, 15 ins. white, rose-carmine, Aug.; *Caragana arborescens*, 10 ft. yellow, June; *Ceanothus americanus*, 3 ft. white, July; *Cephalanthus occidentalis*, 5 ft. white, July; *Chionanthus virginica*, 15 ft. white, June; *Cladrastis lutea*, 50 ft. white, June; *Clethra alnifolia*, 6 ft. white, Aug.; *Cornus kousa*, 15 ft. white, June; *Deutzia* vars. 2–10 ft. white-pink, June; *Diervilla lonicera*, 4 ft. yellow, June; *Genista tinctoria plena*, 3–4 ft. yellow, July; *Hibiscus syriacus*, 18 ft. white, mauve, rose, purple, Aug.; *Holodiscus discolor*, 12 ft. creamy-white, July; *Hydrangea arborescens grandiflora*, 10 ft. white, June–July; *H. paniculata*, 12 ft. white, Aug.; *Hypericum calycinum*, 1 ft. yellow, summer; *H. densiflorum*, 6 ft. yellow, July; *H. aureum*, 4 ft. yellow, Aug.; *H. patulum*, 3 ft. yellow, summer; *Itea virginica*, 10 ft. white, July; *Kalmia angustifolia*, 3 ft. rose-purple, June; *K. latifolia*, to 8 ft. white or pink, June; *Kerria japonica*, 4–6 ft. double or single, yellow, June; *Laburnum anagyroides*, 30 ft. yellow, June; *Lonicera maacki*, 15 ft. white-cream, June; *L. tatarica*, 8 ft. pink or white, June; *Lespedeza bicolor*, 8 ft. purple-rose, July–Aug.; *Lycium chinense*, 10 ft. purple, July; *Oxydendrum arboreum*, 10 ft. white, summer; *Philadelphus* vars. 3–10 ft. white, early June; *Potentilla fruticosa*, 4 ft. yellow, summer; *Rhododendron* vars. 3–8 ft. all colors, June–July; *Rhodotypos tetrapetala*, 5 ft. white, June; *Robinia hispida*, 8 ft. pink, June; *Rhus copallina*, 8 ft. greenish, July; *Rosa*, many vars. 3–8 ft. pink, white, red, June; *Rubus odoratus*, 4–6 ft. rose-purple, June–July; *Sambucus canadensis*, 8 ft. white, July; *Sophora viciifolia*, 6–8 ft. bluish-violet, June; *Spiraea bumalda*, 2 ft. crimson, Aug.; *S.* Anthony Waterer, 3 ft. crimson, July; *S. salicifolia*, 6 ft. pink, July; *S. tomentosa*, 4–6 ft. rose-purple, July; *Stewartia pentagyna*, 12 ft. white, July; *Syringa josikaea*, 12 ft. violet, June; *S. reflexa*, 10–12 ft. soft pink, June; *S. sweginzowi superba*, 8–15

---

* Special articles on the subjects indicated by an asterisk (*) will be found at the words so marked.

ft. rose-pink, June; *S. villosa*, 10–12 ft. bright rose, June; *Tamarix gallica*, 8–10 ft. pinkish, June–July; *T. pentandra*, 15 ft. pink, Aug.; *Viburnum*, many species, white, early summer; *Vitex agnus-castus*, 8–10 ft. violet or white, summer; *V. negundo*, 10–15 ft. lavender, August. — L. B. W.

**SUMMER GRAFTING.** See GRAFTING.

**SUMMER GRAPE** = *Vitis aestivalis*.

**SUMMER HOUSE.** See STRUCTURES.

**SUMMER HYACINTH** = *Galtonia candicans*.

**SUMMER LILAC.** See BUDDLEIA DAVIDI.

**SUMMER SAVORY** = *Satureia hortensis*. See SAVORY.

**SUMMER SCALECIDE.** A trademarked miscible oil of light grade, suitable for summer spraying, and sold with directions for use as a contact spray.

**SUMMER SNOWFLAKE** = *Ornithogalum umbellatum*.

**SUMMER-SWEET** = *Clethra alnifolia*.

**SUMMER WORK.** See the summer months at GARDEN CALENDAR.

**SUNBERRY.** See SOLANUM NIGRUM.

**SUN BURN.** A burning or singeing of foliage in the greenhouse, due to concentration of the sun's rays; usually caused by imperfections in the glass. The obvious remedy is to provide temporary shade, or to get modern, clear glass. See GREENHOUSE.

**SUNDEW.** See DROSERA.

**SUNDEW FAMILY** = Droseraceae.

**SUNDIALS.** While the purely ornamental features of sundials come within the range of garden furniture and ornament, their ability to tell time needs a little study. Unless considerable care is used in setting them, their variation from true time may be appreciable.

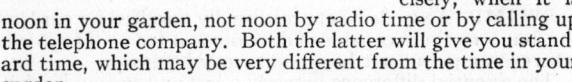
Armillary sundial

The first necessity is to have the plane of the sundial absolutely flat, and its base set on concrete or stone, so that there will be no settling. Determine its flatness with a spirit level. The next step is to determine, precisely, when it is noon in your garden, not noon by radio time or by calling up the telephone company. Both the latter will give you standard time, which may be very different from the time in your garden.

Much the simplest way to find when it is noon for you is to set the sundial temporarily on its bed and see when its gnomon (the shadow-casting part) throws no shadow on the dial except a mere slit straight north. At this moment (actually about 2 minutes) the shadow of the gnomon is exactly on a north-south axis, and it is noon.

The sundial can then be cemented in place. Do not think, however, that merely because it indicates noon in your garden that your sundial will be a perfect timepiece. For reasons of space it cannot be explained in detail here, but the sundial will only be exactly correct about 4 times a year, approximately Dec. 25, April 16, June 15, and Sept. 1, and even then it is only correct for sun time. An absolutely accurate sundial can be constructed only if especially made for your precise latitude and longitude. The usual commercial types are accurate only with the limitations outlined.

Sundial

It will not, of course, register daylight-saving time, and only in a very few places will it exactly register standard time, namely, if you happen to be on the time meridian for the particular time belt in which you live. These are the 75th meridian for Eastern Standard Time, the 90th for Central, the 105th for Mountain, and the 120th for Pacific Standard Time. If you live east or west of these degrees of longitude, your sundial will be earlier or later than the standard time for your region.

But if you live exactly on the line your sundial will register both sun and standard time with the limitations noted above which are due to the earth's inclination and the shape of its orbit. See also Section 7, TOOLS AND IMPLEMENTS.

**SUNDROPS.** See EVENING PRIMROSE.

**SUNFLOWER.** Rather coarse, hardy, annual or perennial herbs, comprising the genus **Helianthus** (he-li-an'thus) which contains about 60 species of the family Compositae, found mostly in N.A. They are very diverse in size and character, as they readily hybridize in their natural surroundings, and are therefore difficult to define. The perennial species have varied rootstocks, some thick, woody and compact, some thick, woody and spreading, others tuberous. Leaves alternate,* sometimes opposite* above, the margins usually coarsely toothed. Flowers in terminal heads, from 3–12 in. across, the ray florets* yellow, the disk florets yellow, brown or purple. (*Helianthus* is from the Greek for sun and a flower.)

For Culture see below.

**H. angustifolius.** Swamp sunflower. Perennial, growing to 7 ft. high, covered with stiff hairs. Leaves lance-shaped, to 7 in. long. Flower heads 2–3 in. across, solitary, or 2 or 3, yellow, the disk florets purple. Swamps, N.Y. to Fla. and west to Tex. Aug.–Oct.

**H. annuus.** Common sunflower. Annual, growing to 12 ft. high. Leaves ovalish, to 1 ft. long, hairy on both sides, the margins toothed. Flowers in heads to 1 ft. across, yellow, the disk florets* purplish-brown. Blooms July–Sept. Minn. to Wash. and Calif. The dwarf small-flowered forms are known as Cut-and-come-again.

**H. cucumerifolius** = *Helianthus debilis*.

**H. debilis.** Much-branched annual, growing to 4 ft. high, the stems covered with stiff hairs and sometimes marked purple and white. Leaves ovalish or triangular, to 4 in. long, the margins toothed. Flower heads solitary, to 3 in. across, yellow, the disk florets* purplish-brown. Fla. to Tex. July–Sept.

**H. decapetalus.** River sunflower. Perennial, growing to 5 ft. high. Leaves thin, broadly lance-shaped, to 8 in. long, hairy on the under side. Flower heads many, 2–3 in. across, yellow, the disk florets yellowish. Moist places, Quebec to Ga. and west to Mo. July–Sept.

**H. giganteus.** Giant sunflower. Tall sunflower. Wild sunflower. Strong-growing perennial, to 12 ft. high, with stiff, hairy stems. Leaves lance-shaped, to 6 in. long, covered with short, stiff hairs, the margins toothed. Flower heads several to 3 in. across, yellow, the disk florets yellowish. Moist places eastern N.A. Aug.–Oct.

**H. maximiliani.** Strong-growing, branching perennial, to 12 ft. high. Leaves lance-shaped, to 7 in. long, covered with rough hairs on both sides, the margins often toothed. Flower heads many, to 3 in. across, yellow, the disk florets yellowish. Dry plains, midwestern states. Aug.–Oct.

**H. mollis.** Strong-growing perennial, to 5 ft. high, covered with soft white hairs. Leaves broadly lance-shaped, to 5 in. long, the margins toothed. Flower heads solitary, or few, to 3 in. across, yellow, the disk florets yellowish. Dry places, Mass. to Ga. and Tex. Summer.

**H. orgyalis.** Strong-growing perennial, to 10 ft. high. Leaves lance-shaped, to 16 in. long, drooping, covered with stiff hairs, the margins sometimes slightly toothed. Flower heads many, to 2 in. across, yellow, the disk florets purplish-brown. Dry places, lower midwestern states. Sept.–Oct.

**H. scaberrimus.** Strong-growing perennial, to 8 ft. high, covered with stiff hairs. Leaves broadly lance-shaped, to 1 ft. long, the margins toothed. Flower heads solitary, or 2 or 3, to 3 in. across, yellow, the disk

* Special articles on the subjects indicated by an asterisk (*) will be found at the words so marked.

florets purplish-brown. Dry places, midwestern states and Ga. Aug.-Oct.

**H. tuberosus.** Jerusalem artichoke. Canada potato. Girasole. Strong-growing perennial, to 12 ft. high, with edible tuberous rootstocks. Leaves ovalish, to 8 in. long, covered with stiff hairs above and soft hairs beneath. Flower heads several, to 3½ in. across, yellow, the disk florets yellowish. Nova Scotia to Ga. and Ark. Widely cult. for its edible tubers and one of the few plants cult. by the North American Indians. It is neither an artichoke nor does it come from Jerusalem.

### Sunflower Culture

Sunflowers are grown both for ornament and use. Some species making very effective border plants or shrubbery plantings, while others are used commercially. The common sunflower, *H. annuus*, is the most useful, the dwarf small-flowered forms, commonly called Cut-and-come-again, are useful for the border and for cutting. The tall-growing forms are cult. for their seeds, especially in Russia. These seeds are eaten raw, used in poultry mixtures and as a parrot food. When dried and crushed, valuable oil is extracted, the finest of which is equal to olive oil, while the cruder forms are used for lighting, woolen dressing, soap and candlemaking. Oil cake made from this oil is used for fattening cattle.

These tall-growing forms are often grown in the cottage gardens of England, where wagers are made in the local inns as to which villager can grow the largest head, which, in this species, turn with the sun from east to west. There are several hort. forms with red or chestnut-colored ray florets,* and one with variegated leaves.

*Helianthus debilis* is very free-flowering and makes a good cut flower. *H. tuberosus*, Jerusalem artichoke, is widely grown for its potato-like tubers, and it may become a pest if not controlled.

Sunflowers are easily cult. They prefer moist, rich, deeply dug soil and are propagated by seeds or division of the rootstocks. For ordinary garden use, seeds should be sown where required to bloom, ½ in. deep, 1 ft. or more apart, according to the species, in early spring, or they may be sown in a cool greenhouse or cold frame in March and transplanted outdoors for early flowering. Strong supports should be provided for the tall-growing forms. Flower heads should be cut as soon as they are faded to ensure a longer flowering period. In commercial growing the annual form is cult. like corn, earthing up when 6 in. high to prevent stems from blowing down.

Perennial species, although they grow readily from seeds, are usually propagated by the division of the rootstocks in early spring.

In the Jerusalem artichoke, the tubers should be planted about 6 in. deep and 1 ft. apart in rows about 3 ft. wide. They should be taken up in the late fall and stored, like potatoes. Care should be taken in digging to take out every tuber or they become a pest in the garden. — H. R. M.

Insect Pests. Insect injury to sunflower is seldom serious. Leaf feeders, aphids, and a rather large leafhopper are only occasional pests. The plant harbors several borers. One, affecting many plants, is a moth larva; another is the larva of a red, black-spotted snout beetle, and is over ½ in. long. Borers may sometimes be cut out by carefully splitting the stem, but the chief measure against them is keeping down weeds and cleaning up old stems in the winter.

**SUNKEN GARDEN.** The lowest and usually central part of a garden built on different levels. Sunken gardens are most used in formal designs where the effect of looking *down* on a garden creates an entirely different appeal from that of one built on a single level.

**SUN MOSS** = *Portulaca grandiflora*.

**SUNOCO.** A trademarked miscible oil, sold with directions for use as a dormant contact spray.

**SUN-ROSE.** See Helianthemum.

**SUNSCALD.** Injury to woody plants caused by extremes of temperature, mostly affecting the bark. The sunscald of summer is caused by heat and may not be very serious as only small patches of bark are killed. It is sometimes serious in the orange (which see). Extremely low temperatures in the winter, however, may cause similar, but more serious injury, which is usually called winter sunscald. In both cases, disease organisms may attack the wounds caused by sunscald, which, if serious, should be thoroughly cleaned out.

The burning of plants in the greenhouse is sometimes called sunscald, but is usually mere mechanical burning, and is not followed by disease. See Sun Burn.

**SUPERACID.** A term for very acid soils with a pH of 4.0. For the details see Acid and Alkali Soils.

*SUPERBA, -us, -um* (soo-per'ba). Superb or showy.

**SUPERIOR.** As applied to flowers this term indicates that the ovary* is above the point of insertion of the calyx,* as in the buttercup, lily, and many other plants. Those having a superior ovary far outnumber the plants with an inferior ovary, which is inserted below the calyx.* See Inferior.

**SUPERPHOSPHATE.** For the garden uses of this invaluable material see Phosphoric Acid at Fertilizers; also Synthetic Manure at Manure.

**SUPPLEJACK** = *Berchemia scandens*.

**SUPPLY WOODLANDS.** See Forestry.

**SURINAM CHERRY** = *Eugenia uniflora*.

*SUSIANA, -us, -um* (soo-zi-ā'na). From Shushan, a Biblical, but now extinct city of Persia. See Crocus.

*SUSPENSA, -us, -um* (sus-pen'sa). Hung or suspended.

**SUTURE.** The line or seam that joins the valves of a fruit, or the similar line or seam down which the fruit splits, as in a pea pod. *Suture* is also applied to the furrow-like depression in some melon fruits which do not split.

**SUWARRO** = *Carnegiea gigantea*.

**SWAINSONA** (swain-sō'na). Darling pea. Poison bush. Australian herbs or under-shrubs of the pea family, comprising over 30 species, two grown for ornament in the cool greenhouse or outdoors in zones* 8 and 9. They have alternate,* compound* leaves, the leaflets arranged feather-fashion, with an odd one at the end. Flowers rather showy, pea-like, mostly in long-stalked clusters (racemes*) in the leaf-axils.* Fruit a much-inflated pod (legume*), usually leathery or membranous. (Named for Isaac Swainson, English horticulturist.)

The first species is an old favorite in northern greenhouses, where it should be grown in potting mixture* 4 and kept in the cool house. It is not so commonly grown outdoors in Fla. and Calif. as its handsome flowers warrant. Propagated by cuttings. In Aust. some species are serious cattle poisons.

**galegiflora.** A smooth shrub or under-shrub, not over 3 ft. high, its branches apt to sprawl or be partly climbing. Leaflets 11–21, oblongish, about ¾ in. long, blunt or notched at the tip. Flowers red, about ¾ in. long, the cluster usually longer than the leaves. Pod 1–2 in. long, stalked. It blooms nearly throughout the year, and is sometimes called winter sweet pea. There are varieties with white flowers (*var.* **albiflora**), with rose-pink flowers (*var.* **rosea**), and with rose-violet flowers (*var.* **violacea**).

**greyana.** An under-shrub or woody perennial, 2–3 ft. high, the young foliage white-felty, but losing it later. Leaflets 11–21, oblongish, ¾–1½ in. long, blunt or notched at the tip. Flowers about 1 in. wide, pink, in erect, stalked clusters (racemes*). Pod stalked, inflated, 1½–2 in. long.

**SWALLOW.** See Birds.

**SWAMP.** A wooded wet area usually unsuited for gardening, but sometimes capable of development for a wild garden, where swamp, but not bog, plants may be grown.

The essential difference between a bog and swamp is what determines the availability of the latter for plants that will not thrive in the acid soils of most bogs. The typical swamp usually has fairly good drainage through it, and its soil or water will rarely show more acidity than a pH of 6.0 or 6.5. Most bogs are much more acid than this. See Acid and Alkali Soils for the details of making these tests.

Having determined that the area is actually a swamp, that its tree canopy will provide shade, and its high and low water levels, one is ready to plan its development. If the place is too wet to walk through, it had better be left alone, because there are only two ways of making it available. The first is to lower the water level, which may be expensive or impossible. The other is to construct raised paths through it. The latter plan is probably the easiest in any case and can be done with cheap fill, such as cinders, house excavations, or old road metal.

---

* Special articles on the subjects indicated by an asterisk (*) will be found at the words so marked.

SWAMP | SWEET ORANGE

The lines of such paths should be as winding and informal as possible. Such a track as cows might make through a swamp would usually be an excellent guide for the future path.

Many wild flowers, ferns, shrubs, and even trees will be perfectly at home in a swamp of this sort. Of course all native material found growing in swamps in the vicinity may be used. Other plants suitable for such places will be found in the genera *Trillium, Arisaema, Lilium, Polemonium, Viola, Myosotis, Cimicifuga, Actaea,* and *Lobelia.* Others are marked with a dagger in the next entry, and still others will be found among the plants mentioned at WILD GARDEN. See also MUCKLAND GARDENING.

**SWAMP.** As an adjective swamp has been linked to the names of many cult. plants, some of which grow, not in swamps, but in marshes, bogs, or even in the salt marshes. In other words, those below, while commonly called swamp pink, swamp honeysuckle, etc., may merely be plants of wet places, often too acid to be candidates for a swamp garden. Those in THE GARDEN DICTIONARY and their proper equivalents are listed below. Those that may be classed as true swamp plants are marked with a dagger (†).

**Swamp andromeda** = *Xolisma ligustrina*; †**Swamp ash** = *Fraxinus pennsylvanica lanceolata* (see ASH); †**Swamp cabbage,** see SKUNK-CABBAGE; †**Swamp dewberry** = *Rubus hispidus*; **Swamp honeysuckle** = *Azalea viscosa*; **Swamp laurel** = *Magnolia virginiana*; **Swamp laurel** = *Kalmia polifolia*; †**Swamp lily** = *Crinum americanum*; **Swamp locust** = *Gleditsia aquatica* (see HONEY LOCUST); **Swamp loosestrife** = *Decodon verticillatus*; **Swamp mahogany** = *Eucalyptus robusta*; **Swamp mallow** = *Hibiscus moscheutos*; †**Swamp milkweed** = *Asclepias incarnata* (see MILKWEED); **Swamp pink** = *Calopogon pulchellus* and *Helonias bullata*; †**Swamp privet** = *Forestiera acuminata*; **Swamp reclamation** (see MUCKLAND GARDENING); †**Swamp rose** = *Rosa palustris*; †**Swamp spleenwort** = *Athyrium angustifolium*; †**Swamp sunflower** = *Helianthus angustifolius* (see SUNFLOWER); †**Swamp tickseed** = *Coreopsis rosea*; **Swamp white honeysuckle** = *Azalea viscosa*; **Swamp white oak** = *Quercus bicolor* (see OAK).

**SWAN RIVER DAISY** = *Brachycome iberidifolia.*

**SWAN RIVER EVERLASTING** = *Helipterum manglesi.*

**SWEDE** = *Brassica napobrassica.* For cult. see RUTABAGA.

**SWEDISH CLOVER** = *Trifolium hybridum.* See CLOVER.

**SWEDISH TURNIP** = *Brassica napobrassica.* For cult. see RUTABAGA.

**SWEET ALISON** = Sweet alyssum.

**SWEET ALYSSUM.** The ever-popular sweet alyssum is the only cult. species of a small group of Mediterranean herbs constituting the genus **Lobularia** (lob-you-lair'i-a) of the mustard family. The only cult. species is **L. maritima,** also known as snowdrift. It grows to 1 ft. high, and is much-branched and spreading. Leaves alternate,* small, lance-shaped to 1½ in. long. Flowers numerous, small, white or lilac in terminal racemes.* Calyx* of 4 sepals. Corolla of 4 petals. Stamens* 6, 4 long, 2 short. Fruit a 2-celled capsule. There are several hort. forms, some being more compact with larger flowers, some having double flowers, while others have variegated leaves. Grown as an annual and usually used for edging. Easily cult. Propagated by seeds, sown ⅛ in. deep in ordinary garden soil in a cool greenhouse or cold frame, in March or April. They should be pricked off into boxes and planted outdoors 6 in. apart, when danger of frost is over. They may be sown thinly where required to bloom, in April or May. Sometimes offered as *Koniga.* (*Lobularia* is from the Latin for a little lobe, perhaps in reference to the forked hairs of some species.) Also known as sweet Alison.

**SWEET BASIL** = *Ocimum basilicum.*

**SWEET BAY** = *Magnolia virginiana.* See also LAURUS.

**SWEET BIRCH** = *Betula lenta.* See BIRCH.

**SWEETBRIER** = *Rosa eglanteria.*

**SWEET BUCKEYE** = *Aesculus octandra.* See HORSE-CHESTNUT.

**SWEET-BUSH** = *Comptonia asplenifolia.*

**SWEET CASSAVA** = *Manihot dulcis.*

**SWEET CHERRY** = *Prunus avium.* For cult. see CHERRY.

**SWEET CICELY.** See MYRRHIS ODORATA.

**SWEET CLOVER.** See MELILOTUS.

**SWEET COLTSFOOT** = *Petasites fragrans.*

**SWEET CONEFLOWER** = *Rudbeckia subtomentosa.*

**SWEET CORN.** See CORN.

**SWEET CRABAPPLE** = *Malus coronaria.*

**SWEET FALSE CAMOMILE** = *Matricaria chamomilla.*

**SWEET FENNEL** = *Foeniculum vulgare dulce.* See FENNEL.

**SWEET-FERN.** See COMPTONIA.

**SWEET FLAG** = *Acorus calamus.*

**SWEET GALE** = *Myrica gale.*

**SWEET GUM.** Few trees turn such a gorgeous color as the native sweet gum, which is the only commonly cult. species of the genus **Liquidambar** (liquid-am'bar) of the family Hamamelidaceae. Only 3 other species are known, some of them Asiatic. Our native sweet gum, **L. styraciflua,** is a tree up to 120 ft. high, its twigs and young branches corky-winged. Leaves alternate,* star-like, stalked, much resembling a maple, the 3-7 lobes toothed. Flowers small, inconspicuous, mostly unisexual,* and in dense, globe-shaped clusters. Petals none. Fruit a globe-shaped collection of shining, brown capsules,* each tipped with a spine, the whole head, which may be 1¼ in. in diameter, thus prickly. An extremely handsome tree, its foliage brilliant scarlet in the fall. Conn. to Fla., Mo., Ill., and south to Mex. May. It prefers moist, rich soils and is hardy from zone* 3 southward. Propagated by seeds which, even if stratified, do not usually germinate for two years. (*Liquidambar* is from the Latin for liquid and Arabic for amber, in allusion to the fragrant resin of an Asiatic species.)

**SWEET HERBS.** Fragrant herbs used for condiments or for seasoning, sometimes sweet but often bitter or so considered by many. For the distinction between sweet and bitter herbs, their culture and uses *see* HERB GARDENING.

**SWEETLEAF** = *Symplocos tinctoria.*

**SWEET LEMON.** See LEMON.

**SWEET LIME.** See LIME (the citrus fruit).

**SWEET MARJORAM.** Old-fashioned, very fragrant, perennial herbs or under-shrubs comprising the genus **Majorana** (ma-jor-ray'na) of the mint family. The only commonly cult. species is the ordinary sweet marjoram, **M. hortensis,** sometimes called the annual marjoram because it is often grown as an annual. It has opposite,* stalked, elliptic leaves, about ½ in. long and without marginal teeth. Flowers small, purplish or whitish, crowded in dense, white-hairy whorls* which are grouped in spikes. Corolla 2-lipped,* not much protruding beyond the oblique calyx.* Eu. For uses and culture *see* HERB GARDENING. The plant is sometimes known as *Origanum majorana.* See ORIGANUM. (*Majorana* is perhaps derived from an Old French word *majoraine,* but of uncertain application to this plant.)

**SWEET McINTOSH.** An apple variety. See APPLE.

**SWEET MOCK-ORANGE** = *Philadelphus coronarius.* See MOCK-ORANGE.

**SWEET OLEANDER** = *Nerium indicum.* See OLEANDER.

**SWEET OLIVE.** See OSMANTHUS.

**SWEET ORANGE** = *Citrus sinensis.* For cult. *see* ORANGE.

---

* Special articles on the subjects indicated by an asterisk (*) will be found at the words so marked.

**SWEET PEA.** The sweet pea, *Lathyrus odoratus*, is perhaps the most highly developed of all annuals. Its culture affords pleasure to millions; the production of seeds is an important industry, while as a commercial cut flower it is one of the most popular of crops. The sweet pea was first introduced into England from Sicily in 1700, but not until some 150 years later was it seriously taken in hand by Henry Eckford who raised and introduced more than 200 varieties. To celebrate its 200th year in England, a great show was held in London in 1900, and large annual sweet pea shows have been held in London ever since. In 1904 Countess Spencer, a wavy-petaled sport of Eckford's Prima Donna, was introduced, and caused such a furore that within a few years the smooth-petaled varieties became obsolete. From the time Eckford began his work to the present time there are records of more than 3000 varieties, but not more than 300 are now in cultivation.

Early in the 20th century, too, the first early-flowering varieties appeared. These were later crossed with the waved Spencers. Their origin and development are entirely American. The early-flowering varieties are not important for outdoor culture; their principal value is that, under glass in a temperature of 50°, they can be flowered from September until the end of June. The late-flowering sorts, when grown under glass, cannot be made to flower before early Spring. Outdoors, the early-flowering kinds do not grow so vigorously, and they bloom but little earlier than the ordinary sorts.

Sweet peas are essentially cool weather plants, and they quickly fade away if the temperature persists for long above 75°. In the sea-cooled areas of New England and the Pacific Northwest, sweet peas can be grown successfully throughout the summer. In the central states from coast to coast, high-class sweet peas cannot be grown after mid-June, except at high elevations. In some of the southern states sweet peas can be had for a longer period than farther north, as the plants can make earlier growth and flower in May. In southern California sweet peas can be flowered still earlier, and it is in the neighborhood of Los Angeles that at least two-thirds of the world's sweet-pea seeds are produced. But while there are sections of the United States where it is almost impossible to get a worth-while crop of sweet-pea flowers because winter lingers late and summer comes with a rush, there are few places where it is too cool for this delightful annual.

It follows that in most parts of the United States the need for an early start is highly important. The plants must be well established before hot weather arrives, but if the heat is extreme and persistent, nothing will keep the plants growing vigorously, though it is possible to carry the plants through July and even later if a cheesecloth shading is erected over the plants. *See* CLOTH.

While in some seasons it is possible to make a sowing outdoors in the fall, this operation is hazardous. The seed should be sown 2 in. deep in rows in mid-November in the Atlantic states, so that the seeds will germinate but not appear above ground. When hard freezing starts, cover well with salt hay or other litter and remove when growth starts in early spring. Thin out if necessary, and provide support as soon as the plants are 3 or 4 in. tall. A safer plan is to sow the seeds in early October in a cold frame. Give all the ventilation possible until hard frost sets in, then heavily cover the frame with mats. Uncover when winter is departing and as soon as the ground is workable, carefully set the plants outdoors 4 to 6 in. apart.

The best plan for most sections is to sow in February indoors or in a greenhouse in flats of fairly sandy soil. The white-seeded kinds, which are liable to rot, should have pure sand as a covering; the seeds should not be covered more than one-half in. Water sparingly and place in a temperature of about 60°. As soon as they appear expose to full light and drop the temperature to about 50°. When 2 or 3 in. tall, pot into 2¼-in. pots, singly, and as soon as possible shift to a protected frame. Pinch out the tops when four or five sets of leaves have been made, and plant out, after thorough hardening, in well-prepared soil.

In some sections, even in the neighborhood of New York, if the season proves rather cool, it is possible to grow a respectable crop of sweet peas by sowing where they are to flower, in late March or early April. The soil, however, should be prepared in the fall so that it can settle. This is essential, as sweet peas like firm ground. Sow the seed 2 in. deep and cover with sandy soil.

Mention has been made of the tendency of white seeds to rot. Most white and cream varieties have white seeds, while lavender sorts usually have mottled seeds; these also are rather more weakly than the dark seeds which indicate varieties possessing a red tint. Very dark seeds are apt to be very hard and slow germinating. It is a good practice to soak all dark seeds in water before sowing, and plant after they have swelled. Any seeds that have not swelled after 24 hours should be "nicked" with a file, but not near the germ, or given a sulphuric-acid bath. From three to five minutes in pure acid is usually sufficient, and the seeds should then be well washed under the faucet before sowing.

To grow good sweet peas the entire plot, or at least rows 2 ft. wide, should be double dug, the whole depth of soil receiving a good dressing of well-rotted manure as well as a moderate application of some good fertilizer. Sweet peas are great feeders and must have nourishment and plenty of moisture.

There are two methods of culture or training, natural and exhibition. The former gives quantities of fair-sized flowers on medium stems. All the laterals are allowed to remain, except that it is sometimes advantageous to cut back the leading growths when they harden, and allow the younger growths to carry on. When once the vines become woody, short-stemmed flowers are certain. Exhibition or cordon growing means fewer but giant flowers, sometimes as many as five and six, on stems 18 inches or more in length. This system is not, however, worth while unless climatic or other conditions permit the plants to grow well into summer, as the finest flowers cannot be obtained until the plants attain a height of 4 ft. or more. The plants should be planted 9 in. or so apart and allowed to carry two or three main growths. All side shoots or laterals that appear in the leaf-axils* must be pinched out, leaving only the flower buds that likewise appear in the leaf-axils.* So treated, the plants, if conditions permit, grow 8 ft. or more, but can be kept down to a reasonable height by training. Exhibition plants need constant attention and much tying, especially if bamboo stakes are used for supports. To ensure continuous flowering no seed pods should be allowed to develop.

For general purposes, there is no better support for sweet peas than hazel or other twiggy branches flat trimmed, and pushed firmly into the ground on both sides of the plants. On no account should the young plants be allowed to stand without support after planting, as boisterous winds may damage them. Ordinary large-mesh chicken wire, fastened to strong posts, makes a good support, and for preference this should be on both sides of the rows, as the plants are better able to climb between a double support.

Among the finest summer-flowering varieties are: Ambition, lavender; Amethyst, blue; Damask, carmine; Charm, cerise; Mavis, salmon; Flamingo, cerise-scarlet; Grand National, cream; Floradale, cream-pink; Red Boy, crimson; Leviathan, maroon; International, mauve; Youth, white, edged pink; Sunkist, cream, edged pink; Pinkie, deep pink; Pacific, salmon-pink; Welcome, deep scarlet; Golden West, deep orange; Avalanche, white.

The culture of sweet peas under glass is comparatively simple. The plants are best grown in well-prepared beds, but in a small way they can be successfully flowered in 10-in. pots. For winter-flowering sow the seed early in August in 3-in. pots, thinning to two or three when well started. Shift into flower pots or plant out without disturbing the roots. For early spring-flowering sow in November and shift before the roots become pot-bound. Keep cool at all times; never run the night temperature above 50°, and 45° is sufficient. Ventilate freely and fumigate or spray regularly. Good early-flower sorts are: Columbia, pink and white; Ball Rose, deep rose; Harmony, lavender; Red Bird, crimson; White Harmony, white; Mrs. Hoover, blue; Eldorado, orange. — T. A. W.

---

* Special articles on the subjects indicated by an asterisk (*) will be found at the words so marked.

MODERN, LONG-STALKED, SWEET PEAS

INSECT PESTS. The principal outdoor pest is the aphid of garden peas (see PEA). In greenhouses, pests include aphids and leaf tiers (see CHRYSANTHEMUM), sowbugs and thousand-legs (see CINERARIA), and red spiders (see ROSE). Root pests cause loss of vigor; root aphids are checked by watering with nicotine solution and keeping down ants; eelworms (not insects) by steaming the soil before planting. Small white centipedes attack the roots of many greenhouse plants; they are checked by steaming the soil, and by the use of raised benches and clean soil.

DISEASES. Sweet peas are susceptible to mildew, root-knot, anthracnose, streak, root rot, mosaic, fasciation and bud drop. For *mildew* and *root-knot* see Mildew and Root-knot at PLANT DISEASES. *Anthracnose* affects stems, flowers, leaves and seed pods with white, dead areas as the chief symptom. For control, obtain seed from healthy pods, soak the seed for five minutes in 5% formaldehyde solution prior to planting, use clean soil and burn all refuse in the fall. *Streak*, a disease characterized by reddish-brown streaks along the stem, can be controlled as suggested for anthracnose. *Root rot* is caused by various soil-inhabiting fungi. Infected plants exhibit a yellow, sickly appearance with blackened and rotted roots. Soil sterilization and crop rotation are the only effective means of control.

When infected with *mosaic*, a virus disease, sweet peas are stunted, produce few flowers and exhibit distorted, mottled leaves. Infected plants should be removed immediately and nicotine or pyrethrum insecticides used to control the aphids which spread the disease. *Fasciation* is characterized by an abnormal production of short, fleshy stems. For control, improve environmental conditions and sterilize or replace the soil. *Bud drop* is a non-parasitic disease ascribed to various causes. In some cases it has been corrected by the use of artificial light and by applications of muriate of potash and acid phosphate.

**SWEET PEPPER** = *Capsicum frutescens grossum*.

**SWEET PEPPERBUSH** = *Clethra alnifolia*.

**SWEET PITAHAYA** = *Lemaireocereus thurberi*.

**SWEET POTATO** (*Ipomoea batatas*). Originally a tropical American morning-glory, the modern sweet potato is distinctly a warm-season crop or one for regions where there is continuous heat. It is grown commercially only in the South, but good crops may be secured in the East, as far north as southern New Jersey. Generally speaking, it should not be attempted above zone* 5 in the East, although occasional crops can be secured on western Long Island. In the Far West only southern and central Calif., Ariz., N. Mex. and southern and eastern Tex. are really suited to it. Good crops, however, are harvested in southern Ill.

The stems are very long, trailing vines which, as the crop matures, will completely cover the ground between the rows. Because of this, spacing and cultivation must be carefully arranged as in the subsequent directions.

SOILS AND FERTILIZERS. Sweet potatoes do best on very sandy, warm soils. They will not tolerate clay or muck soils, but good crops will often be raised on sandy loams. If the soil is too rich in nitrogen, most of the growth will be vine instead of the desired root. Some growers, because of this, use no fertilizer for sweet potatoes, especially if they follow other crops that were adequately fertilized the year before. An application of a commercial fertilizer with a ratio of 2-8-10 (see FERTILIZERS) at the rate of 1200 pounds per acre (4-5 pounds per 100-ft. row) should be used if none was used the year previous.

VARIETIES. If you are on or near the northern limits of sweet-potato culture by all means use Big-stem Jersey. It is a mealy, relatively dry-rooted sort that stands up better than the moist-fleshed kinds which can only be grown farther south. Other relatively hardy sorts for the northern part of the sweet-potato region are Yellow Jersey (yellow-skinned) and Red Jersey red-skinned).

For the moist-fleshed varieties, suited to farther south, the best selection should include: Yellow Belmont, Pumpkin, Porto Rico and Nancy Hall.

In Calif. Prolific and Priestly, besides those mentioned, are also used.

PLANTING. The home grower (and many commercial ones) rarely raise sweet-potato plants from "seed." Actually the plant does not flower nor set true seed as cultivated anywhere in the United States, except, possibly, near Key West. Plants are raised by specialists who utilize the habit of the sweet potato to throw off from its swollen root a shoot that develops from adventitious* buds. These slips or "draws," as they are called, are then separated from the old root and grown along until ready for planting outdoors. The whole process requires so much care and skillful handling that most growers are glad to use the plentiful supplies of such slips that the dealers offer at planting time.

The slips should not be set out before June 20 in southern N.J., but earlier farther southward. (March 1 in La., April 1 in Los Angeles.) The plant does not want merely absence of coolness, it needs more heat than almost any other garden crop. A soil temperature of 70°-85° is ideal. At a soil temperature of 60° the plant will often stop growth — at 50° it will die if that temperature is maintained.

For the northern varieties make the rows 30 in. apart and plant the slips 15 in. apart in the row. For the southern (mostly moist-fleshed) varieties the rows should be 4-5 ft. apart, and the slips set 20-24 in. apart. In both sorts a cupful of water should be poured over each planted slip.

CULTIVATION. This will be possible only in the early stages of growth because of the great spread of the vines. Do it often and thoroughly or weeds will be a serious problem when cultivation is no longer possible. Cultivation for the conservation of moisture is not very necessary, for the plant will stand dryness more than most vegetables. The period of cultivation may be increased by lifting the vines to prevent their rooting at the joints.

HARVESTING AND SUBSEQUENT CARE. It will take all the growing season for the roots to become big enough for harvesting. There is no surface indication (as in ordinary potatoes) when this time has arrived. When you think it has, dig up a plant and see. By so doing the home grower can harvest part of his crop and leave the rest for subsequent diggings.

If more than temporary needs are harvested, or if an early frost arrives, the sweet-potato grower must act quickly. The vines go black at the slightest touch of frost. If left in place, their juice will pass down into the root and ruin the crop. Cut frost-touched vines at once, leaving the potatoes in the ground for more leisurely digging.

When they are dug, or you have a surplus of roots from unfrosted vines, do not let the roots stand in the sun for more than an hour or two, and they must never be left on the surface of the ground overnight. They must be handled with extreme care, and all injured or cut roots used at once or thrown away. No crop rots quicker than sweet potatoes.

If the harvest is to be kept (as in nearly all commercial production), the roots must be cured at once. This is accomplished by placing them, uninjured, on frames or open-slat trays. Put the trays in a room (often specially constructed) in which the temperature can be kept between 80° and 86°. The heat (preferably applied at the bottom) will drive off much moisture. This must pass out of the room by proper ventilation, not condense on the walls and run down. Continue the process for 10 days or two weeks, after which the temperature is dropped to 55° and held there until the sweet potatoes are used.

Fresh sweet potatoes, without this curing, will last only a brief period without rotting, although their keeping period may, on a small scale, be lengthened by burying them in moist sand. *See also* BANKING.

In the South, the vine, or its root, is sometimes, but incorrectly, called a yam, which is a very different plant. (*See* DIOSCOREA).

INSECT PESTS. In the Gulf region white larvae of a slender snout beetle, the sweet potato weevil, bore in the roots. They are controlled by clean-up measures, and by the use of uninfested planting stock. Else-

*A draw of the sweet potato, and the most convenient way of starting a plantation.*

---

* Special articles on the subjects indicated by an asterisk (*) will be found at the words so marked.

where there are few pests of the sweet potato. Tortoise beetles with their trash-carrying larvae, as well as flea beetles, may be controlled with arsenicals if abundant.

DISEASES. The numerous diseases which attack sweet potatoes may be grouped into those that affect the young shoots in the seedbed, the field diseases, and the storage rots. In some cases, as black-rot, the same disease is found in the three divisions. Every disease requires slightly different control measures, but if the following yearly program is adhered to most of the maladies will be held in check satisfactorily. For seedling plants new soil should be placed in the hotbed after all diseased refuse has been destroyed and the bed disinfected. The seed should be selected from a healthy crop, the selection being made early enough in the fall to ensure recognition of the diseases present, seed treatment with corrosive sublimate (10 minutes in 1–1000 solution). Practice long rotations and be careful in harvesting to avoid bruising of the roots. Also provide the most careful sanitation about the storage house, including correct temperatures and moisture. See above.

**SWEET SCABIOUS** = *Scabiosa atropurpurea*.

**SWEET-SCENTED SHRUB** = *Calycanthus*.

**SWEET-SHRUB** = *Calycanthus*.

**SWEETSOP** = *Annona squamosa*.

**SWEET SORGHUM** = *Holcus sorghum saccharatus*.

**SWEET SULTAN** = *Centaurea moschata*. See also CNICUS BENEDICTUS.

**SWEET SYRINGA.** See MOCK-ORANGE.

**SWEET VERNAL GRASS** = *Anthoxanthum odoratum*.

**SWEET VIOLET** = *Viola odorata*.

**SWEET WHITE VIOLET** = *Viola blanda*.

**SWEET WILLIAM** = *Dianthus barbatus*. For the wild Sweet William see PHLOX DIVARICATA.

**SWEET WILLIAM CATCHFLY** = *Silene armeria*.

**SWEET WINES.** For the best grapes to be used in making sweet wines see *vinifera* varieties at GRAPE.

**SWEET WOODRUFF** = *Asperula odorata*.

**SWERTIA** = *Frasera*.

**SWIETENIA** (swy-tee′ni-a). Tropical American trees of the family Meliaceae, of no hort. interest except that one of the three known species, **S. mahagoni**, the mahogany, is occasionally planted for interest or shade in extreme southern Fla. It is the traditional mahogany (there are many African and Philippine Island substitutes) and is a large evergreen tree with hard wood, which becomes red-brown in age. Leaves alternate,* compound,* the 4–8 leaflets arranged feather-fashion, without an odd one at the end. Leaflets leathery, without teeth, 2–4 in. long. Flowers small, inconspicuous, whitish, in clusters (panicles*). Fruit a 5-valved woody capsule,* 3–4 in. long, its winged seeds nearly 2 in. long. (Named for Gerard van Swieten, Austrian botanist and physician.)

**SWISS CHARD.** See BEET.

**SWISS MOUNTAIN PINE** = *Pinus mugo*. See PINE.

**SWISS STONE PINE** = *Pinus cembra*. See PINE.

**SWITCH GRASS** = *Panicum virgatum*.

**SWORD BEAN** = *Canavalia gladiata*.

**SWORD FERN** = *Nephrolepis*.

**SWORD LILY.** See GLADIOLUS.

**SYAGRUS** (si-ag′rus). Chiefly Brazilian feather palms, comprising perhaps 40 species, and separated from *Cocos* only by technical characters. The outstanding one of hort. significance is **S. weddellianus** (long known as *Cocos weddelliana*), which is very widely grown by florists and is also planted outdoors in southern Fla. It is one of the most delicate, graceful, and feathery of all palms, never over 6–7 ft. high, but with a slender trunk. The drooping leaves usually touch the ground, the segments or leaflets long and narrow. In the usual young state (*i.e.* a florist's pot plant) the segments are scarcely ¼ in. wide and 4–6 in. long, gracefully drooping. Fruit oblongish or roundish, about ½ in. long, rarely or never produced in greenhouse specimens. Rio de Janeiro. For greenhouse cult. see PALM. In Fla. it is prized for outdoor planting, but is safe only in zone* 9, where it makes a very graceful lawn specimen. (*Syagrus* is from the Latin for wild pig, and a name for some sort of palm, but not this one.)

**SYCAMORE.** The traditional sycamore and the one mentioned in the Bible is *Ficus sycomorus*, a tree not usually cult. For the tree called sycamore in the U.S. see PLATANUS OCCIDENTALIS.

**SYCAMORE MAPLE** = *Acer pseudo-platanus*. See MAPLE.

**SYDNEY GOLDEN WATTLE** = *Acacia longifolia*.

*SYLVATICA, -us, -um* (sill-vat′i-ka). Wood-loving; *i.e.* a forest plant.

*SYLVESTER* (sill-ves′ter). Growing in forests.

*SYLVESTRIS, -e* (sill-ves′triss). Growing in forests.

**SYMMETRICAL.** See REGULAR FLOWER.

**SYMPHORICARPOS** (sim-for-i-kar′pos). Ornamental, hardy shrubs of the honeysuckle family, more showy in fruit than in flower. All but one Chinese species are American, and of the 15 known kinds, all of those below are in pretty frequent cult. here. Leaves opposite,* short-stalked, usually without teeth or lobes. Flowers small, not very showy, mostly in small clusters which are terminal or in the leaf-axils.* Corolla not over ⅓ in. long (in ours), bell-shaped or tubular, the limb* 4–5-lobed. Stamens* 4–5. Fruit a rather showy, 2-seeded berry, usually borne in pairs or small clusters. (*Symphoricarpos* is from the Greek for bearing together and fruit, in allusion to the clustered fruits.)

These are excellent shrubs for partly shady places or for the open; they are far more smoke-resistant than many other ornamental plants and thus excellent for city planting. They will also grow in a great variety of soils. Easily propagated by seeds, cuttings, or by division, or by detaching the numerous suckers.*

**albus.** Snowberry. Waxberry. Not over 3 ft. high, the branches slender and upright. Leaves ovalish or oblong, 1–2 in. long, blunt. Flowers pinkish. Fruit white. Throughout northern N.A. June–Aug. Hardy from zone* 2 southward. Well liked by bees. The var. **laevigatus** is nearly twice as tall, and has larger leaves. This is the form most common in cult., usually under the name **S. racemosus**.

**chenaulti.** A hybrid shrub derived from crossing *S. orbiculatus* with a Mexican species. It is 5–7 ft. high, the leaves hairy beneath. Flowers pinkish. Fruit red, but white-dotted. Hardy from zone* 3 southward and handsome in fruit.

**mollis.** Partly prostrate or decumbent* shrub, the twigs somewhat velvety. Leaves nearly round, ¾–2 in. wide, hairy both sides. Flowers pinkish or white. Fruit white. British Columbia to Calif. June–July. Hardy from zone* 3 southward.

**occidentalis.** Wolfberry; also called buckbrush. Not over 5 ft. high, the branches rather stiff and erect. Leaves ovalish, 2–3 in. long, gray-hairy beneath. Flowers pinkish. Fruit white. British Columbia and Colo. east to Mich. and Kan., probably far northward. June–July. Hardy everywhere.

**orbiculatus.** Indian currant. Coralberry. A shrub 5–7 ft. high, the branches erect. Leaves elliptic or ovalish, 1½–2½ in. long, pale and hairy beneath. Flowers white. Fruit reddish-purple, plentiful. N.J. to Ga. and westward to S. Dak. and Tex. July. Hardy from zone* 3 southward, and very attractive in the fall from the profusion of fruit and the long-persistent crimson foliage. There is also a variegated-leaved form. The plant is often sold as **S. vulgaris**.

**racemosus** = *Symphoricarpos albus laevigatus*.

**vulgaris** = *Symphoricarpos orbiculatus*.

**SYMPHYANDRA** (sim-fi-an′dra). Hardy biennial or perennial herbs, comprising about 8 species of the family Campanulacae, natives of eastern Eu. and western As. Leaves mostly basal, usually heart-shaped, hairy, and long-stalked. Stem leaves alternate,* few and smaller. Flowers white or yellowish, large, in terminal clusters (racemes*). Calyx of 5 sepals. Corolla bell-shaped. Stamens* 5, joined by their anthers,* forming a tube around the style, for this reason differing from *Campanula*. Fruit a 3-celled capsule.* (*Symphyandra* is from the Greek for anthers grown together.) For cultivation see CAMPANULA.

**hofmanni.** Hairy perennial, growing to 2 ft. high, with drooping branches. Leaves broadly lance-shaped, to 7 in. long, heart-shaped at base. Margins with small and large teeth. Flowers white, bell-shaped, 1½ in. long and wide, in terminal leafy clusters. Corolla hairy on the inside. Bosnia. July.

---

*Special articles on the subjects indicated by an asterisk (*) will be found at the words so marked.

**pendula.** Dwarf, hairy perennial, growing to 1 ft. high. Leaves heart-shaped, the lower long-stalked, the margins coarsely toothed. Flowers yellowish, bell-shaped, to 1¼ in. long, in terminal racemes.* Caucasus.

**SYMPHYTUM** (sim-fy'tum). Comfrey. Hardy perennial herbs, comprising about 25 species, belonging to the forget-me-not family (Boraginaceae), and natives of Eu., northern Af. and western As. Coarse-growing with thick rootstocks, sometimes tuberous. Stem and leaves covered with bristly hairs. Basal leaves large, the stem leaves alternate* or opposite.* Flowers yellowish, blue, white, rose or purple, in terminal, 1-sided, branching clusters. Calyx of 5 sepals, hairy on the outside. Corolla tubular. Stamens* 5. Fruit 2-celled, splitting into 4 when ripe. (*Symphytum* is from the Greek, to grow together, in allusion to the assumed healing properties.)

The comfrey is not of much garden importance, but sometimes grown in the border. Easily cult. Propagated by seeds or division of the rootstocks.

**asperrimum** = *Symphytum asperum*.
**asperum.** Prickly comfrey. Growing to 5 ft. high. Leaves ovalish, covered on both sides with stiff, bristly hairs, the stalks winged. Flowers rose, turning blue, about ½ in. long, in terminal, 1-sided clusters. Sometimes used as forage. Russia to Persia.
**officinale.** Growing to 3 ft. high and much-branched. Leaves broadly lance-shaped, covered with stiff, bristly hairs. Flowers yellowish, rose or white, in terminal, 1-sided clusters. Eu. and As., naturalized in N.A. The *var*. **variegatum** has leaves with creamy-white margins.

**SYMPLOCACEAE** (sim-plo-kay'see-ee). A family of shrubs or trees comprising only one genus, *Symplocos*, which see for a description of the only cult. species in the Symplocaceae.

**SYMPLOCARPUS.** See SKUNK-CABBAGE.

**SYMPLOCOS** (sim-plō'kos). A large genus (nearly 300 species) of trees and shrubs found in most tropical and warm regions (except Af.), at least one in the southeastern U.S. They constitute the family Symplocaceae, and two of them are somewhat cult. for ornament, although they are of secondary garden importance. Leaves alternate,* evergreen in some species. Flowers usually small and inconspicuous, but pleasantly fragrant, mostly in stalked or nearly stalkless clusters. Calyx* 5-lobed. Corolla 5–10-lobed, or (in ours) with as many nearly distinct petals. Stamens* 15 or more, often in bunches and fastened to the corolla. Fruit (in ours) an orange or blue drupe,* its stone 1–5-seeded. (*Symplocos* is from the Greek for connected, in allusion to the often united stamens.*)

The two below are rather unusual in cult. and are difficult to propagate, as the seeds are slow to germinate. Also propagated by cuttings of green wood under glass.

**paniculata.** A shrub or small tree, 20–35 ft. high. Leaves short-stalked, oblongish, 2–3 in. long, the margins finely toothed. Flowers fragrant, white, the clusters 2–3 in. long. Corolla about ⅓ in. long. Fruit about ½ in. long, bright blue. Jap., China, southward to the Himalayas. May-June. Hardy from zone* 3 southward.
**tinctoria.** Sweetleaf; also called horse sugar in the South. A shrub or small tree 15–25 ft. high, the foliage half-evergreen or evergreen in the deep South. Leaves elliptic to oblongish, thickish, 4–6 in. long, obscurely toothed or with no teeth. Flowers yellowish, fragrant, in dense, nearly stalkless clusters. Corolla about ⅜ in. wide. Fruit about ⅓ in. long, orange or brown. Del. to Fla. and La. May. Hardy from zone* 5 southward.

**SYNADENIUM** (sin-a-dee'ni-um). Fleshy-stemmed, African shrubs of the family Euphorbiaceae, the only one of hort. interest being **S. granti,** the African milk-bush. It is an erect shrub, 8–12 ft. high, the branches thick, fleshy, and with a milky juice (probably poisonous). Leaves alternate,* thick and fleshy, broadest toward the tip, 4–5 in. long. Flower clusters red. For details *see* EUPHORBIACEAE. The milk-bush is cult. as an interesting succulent in tropical regions, but it is scarcely hardy outside of zone* 9, where it is little grown. If grown in the greenhouse *see* the cultural notes at SUCCULENTS. (*Synadenium* is from the Greek for united, in allusion to a technical character in the involucral glands.)

**SYNCARP.** A collective fruit (*see* FRUIT). The term is more botanical than horticultural, although syncarps occur in plants like the mulberry, pineapple, and *Annona*. Perhaps the best-known one is the special sort of syncarp found in the fig (which see). All syncarps are the products of the ovaries of several flowers.

**SYNCARPIA** (sin-kar'pi-a). A small genus of Australian, evergreen, aromatic trees of the family Myrtaceae, one of them, **S. glomulifera,** the turpentine tree, occasionally grown as a shade tree in zones* 8 and 9. It is (in the wild) a huge tree, up to 200 ft. high. Leaves opposite,* broadly oval, 2–3 in. long and very thick, the under surface felty-hairy. Flowers in globe-like heads, white, not very showy. Calyx*-lobes mostly 4. Petals 4. Stamens* many. Fruit a capsule,* usually enclosed by the persistent calyx.* (*Syncarpia* is from the Greek for joined and fruit, in allusion to the head-like mass of capsules.*)

**SYNDESMON** = *Anemonella*.

**SYNGONANTHUS** (sin-go-nan'thus). Chiefly Brazilian or African herbs of no garden interest except that two of them have recently been widely imported in the dried state as delicate, very small, and beautiful everlastings. The two species are *S. niveus* and *S. elegans*, both natives of southern Brazil.

They have small, button-like heads of chaffy flowers and are conspicuous in florists' windows from their wide use as trimming for miniature trees and other stylistic decorations. The small clusters of *Syngonanthus* are wired onto the miniature tree and provide its "bloom." Some of these trees have been so skillfully covered with these Brazilian everlastings as to suggest a dried, dwarfed tree with its own bloom. Only recently has it been discovered that the "bloom" is made up of heads of *Syngonanthus*.

**SYNONYMS.** Latin plant names that are obsolete or incorrect. See PLANT NAMES.

**SYNTHETIC MANURE.** See MANURE.

**SYNTHYRIS** (sin-thy'riss). Hardy perennial herbs, comprising about 15 species, belonging to the snapdragon family (Scrophulariaceae), natives of N.A. and Eu. They are low-growing plants, with thick rootstocks and basal leaves. Leaves smooth or hairy, variously shaped, sometimes deeply cut, long-stalked, the margins toothed. Flowers white, blue or reddish in spikes or racemes.* Calyx of 4 sepals. Corolla shortly tubular, 4-lobed or sometimes undivided. Stamens* 2. Fruit a 2-celled capsule.* (*Synthyris* is from the Greek for together, and a little door or valve, in allusion to the fruit.)

They are not of much garden importance, but are sometimes used in the border. Propagated by seeds or division of the rootstocks.

**reniformis.** Growing to 9 in. high. Leaves basal, long-stalked, roundish or kidney-shaped, to 2 in. across, bright, shiny green, the margins deeply toothed. Flowers bluish-purple, ¼ in. long, numerous, in racemes* to 5 in. long. Calif. to Wash.
**rotundifolia.** Low-growing, to 5 in. high. Leaves basal, stalked, ovalish, heart-shaped at the base, to 2 in. long, slightly hairy, the margins with 2 rows of teeth. Flowers white, small, in few-flowered racemes.* Ore.

*SYPHILITICA, -us, -um* (siff-i-lit'i-ka). Reputedly useful as a remedy for syphilis.

*SYRIACA, -us, -um* (si-ri-ā'ka). From Syria.

**SYRINGA.** One of the most confusing names in hort. literature. The genus *Syringa* comprises the lilacs, but the common name syringa is widely used for the shrubs better known as mock-orange. See LILAC, MOCK-ORANGE.

*SYRINGANTHA, -us, -um* (sir-ing-gan'tha). With lilac-like flowers.

**SYRINGE.** See Section 6, TOOLS AND IMPLEMENTS.

---
* Special articles on the subjects indicated by an asterisk (*) will be found at the words so marked.

# T

**TABACUM** (ta-back'um). Latinized form of the original Indian word for tobacco.

**TABEBUIA** (ta-be-bew'i-a). Less than a dozen species of tropical American trees of the family Bignoniaceae, only one of them, **T. pallida** (sometimes known as *T. pentaphylla*), likely to be in cult. in the U.S. In the wild it may reach 60 ft. in height, as cult. in Fla. scarcely half this. Leaves long-stalked, compound,* the 3-5 leaflets arranged finger-fashion. Leaflets without teeth, more or less elliptic, 4-6 in. long. Flowers usually pink, sometimes white, and pink-veined, in large, showy, terminal clusters (panicles*), mostly blooming after the leaves fall in late winter or early spring. Corolla funnel-shaped, 2½-3 in. long, its limb* 5-lobed. Stamens* 4. Fruit a long pod (capsule*) with winged seeds. The tree is suited only to protected parts of zones* 8 and to zone* 9, and in the young state needs staking, without which it seems to be unable to keep upright, although perfectly erect in age. Propagated by seeds or by cuttings. (*Tabebuia* is derived from the Brazilian vernacular for some species.) Sometimes known as white cedar.

**TABERNAEMONTANA** (ta-ber-nee-mon-tan'a). A large genus of tropical shrubs and trees of the family Apocynaceae, two of them planted for ornament in zones* 8 and 9, possibly safe in protected parts of zone* 7. They have opposite* leaves, without marginal teeth, and terminal clusters (cymes*) of rather handsome, white or yellow flowers. Calyx* 5-parted. Corolla salver-shaped, its tube cylindrical, the lobes somewhat twisted to the left. Stamens* 5. Fruit a collection of 2 pods (follicles*) or fleshy. (Named for J. T. Tabernaemontanus, German botanist and physician, who is also commemorated by species named for him in *Scirpus* and *Amsonia*.)

The first species is a very popular plant for sub-tropical gardens. It should be planted in rich, sandy loam, not too dry, and preferably in the open. It is not easy to transplant, and potted specimens, derived from cuttings, are best grown along until a foot or two high and then planted with as little disturbance of the roots as possible. Young plants, freshly set out in Sept.-Oct., must be protected from frost (if in zones* 8 or 7), by banking with sand or soil for the first winter. Later they will usually stand without this protection. Propagated by cuttings.

**coronaria.** Crape jasmine; also called East Indian rose bay, Adam's-apple, and Nero's-crown. A beautifully fragrant shrub 5-8 ft. high. Leaves shining green, oblongish, 3-5 in. long. Flowers white, 1½-2 in. wide, the lobes crisped. Origin unknown, but cult. throughout the tropical and sub-tropical world, especially in the double-flowered form.

**grandiflora.** A shrub, 4-6 ft. high. Leaves oblongish, 3-5 in. long, pointed at the tip. Flowers yellow, not fragrant, about 1½ in. wide. Central and northern South America. Not much known in cult., but occasionally grown in southern Fla.

**TABLE GARDEN.** See TERRARIUM.

**TABULARIS, -e** (tab-you-lar'is). Flattened like a table.

**TAFT, L. R.** See America at GARDEN BOOKS.

**TAGETES.** See MARIGOLD.

**TAHITI LIME.** See Acid Lime at LIME (the citrus fruit).

**TAHITI ORANGE** = *Citrus taitensis*.

**TAIL-GRAPE** = *Artabotrys*.

**TAINUI** = *Pomaderris apetala*.

**TAITENSIS, -e** (ty-ten'sis). From Tahiti, one of the Society Islands in the south Pacific.

**TALINUM** (ta-ly'num). Rather fleshy-leaved, perennial herbs of the family Portulacaceae, comprising about 20 species, and of secondary hort. interest except for **T. calycinum**, the rock pink, a native from Kan. and Neb. to Mex., and occasionally grown in the rock garden. It is an erect plant, 6-12 in. high, from a thick rootstock. Leaves cylindrical, mostly clustered at the base, about 2 in. long, the leaf base broadened. Flowers pink, about 1 in. wide, in a loose, terminal, few-flowered cluster (cyme*). Petals, sepals, and stamens* usually 5 each. Fruit a 3-valved, nearly globe-shaped capsule.* The plant prefers a gritty or sandy soil, blooms in June, and repays a light, strawy mulch in winter. (*Talinum* is thought to be derived from a Senegal name for another species.)

**TALL BEARDED IRIS.** See IRIS.

**TALL FESCUE** = *Festuca elatior*.

**TALL MEADOW OAT** = *Arrhenatherum elatius*.

**TALL MEADOW RUE** = *Thalictrum polygamum*.

**TALL OAT GRASS** = *Arrhenatherum elatius*.

**TALL SUNFLOWER** = *Helianthus giganteus*. See SUNFLOWER.

**TALLOW SHRUB** = *Myrica cerifera*.

**TALLOW-TREE.** See SAPIUM.

**TAMARACK** = *Larix laricina*. See LARCH.

**TAMARICACEAE** (tam-a-ri-kay'see-ee). The tamarisk family comprises only 4 genera and about 100 species of curious, salt-resistant shrubs and trees, two of which, *Tamarix* and *Myricaria*, are of some hort. interest, especially to seashore gardeners. They are apparently leafless, cedar-like, arching shrubs which actually have innumerable scale-like, tiny leaves pressed flat against the twigs, which, especially the smaller ones, fall with the leaves.

Flowers very small, prevailingly pinkish, stalkless, in small spikes, these grouped in a terminal, branching cluster, and in the mass, quite attractive. Fruit a small pod (capsule*). Some species of *Tamarix*, especially *T. gallica*, are widely grown for ornament. Some species make excellent sand binders.

Technical flower characters: Flowers extremely small, regular* and perfect. Sepals 4 or 5. Stamens* 4 or more. Ovary superior,* 1-celled.

**TAMARIND** = *Tamarindus indica*. For the Manila tamarind see PITHECOLOBIUM DULCE.

**TAMARIND FAMILY.** See LEGUMINOSAE.

**TAMARINDUS** (tam-a-rin'dus). A single species of very widely cult. trees, **T. indica**, the tamarind, belonging to the pea family. Its edible fruit, long thought to come from India, resulted in its being named as from that country, although it is probably native in tropical Africa. Cult. in the U.S. only in zone* 9, as it will not stand the occasional frosts of zone* 8, and has never been a success in Calif. It is an immense, round-headed tree, casting an extremely dense shade. Leaves alternate,* compound,* the leaflets arranged feather-fashion, without an odd one at the end, small, numerous, about ⅝ in. long, more or less oblong. Flowers yellow, irregular,* but not pea-like, in terminal clusters (racemes*). Calyx tubular, 4-lobed, colored. Petals 5, the 3 upper overlapping, the 2 lower much reduced and hidden within the tube-like collection of stamens.* Fruit a pod which does not split, 3-8 in. long, somewhat constricted between its large seeds which are embedded in a brownish pulp. It is the latter for which the tree is grown, for it is of pleasing acid flavor, although its sugar content may be over 20%. Grown throughout the tropical world, and in Fla., more often for shade with us than for the pods. It thrives on the sandy soils of southern Fla., and is best propagated by the shield

---

* Special articles on the subjects indicated by an asterisk (*) will be found at the words so marked.

budding of desirable varieties on the stock of the common sorts. (*Tamarindus* is from the Arabic for Indian date, the plant or its fruit once having been so called.)

**TAMARISCIFOLIA**, *-us*, *-um* (tam-a-riss-i-fō'li-a). With leaves like a tamarisk.

**TAMARISK.** See TAMARIX.

**TAMARISK FAMILY** = Tamaricaceae.

**TAMARIX** (tam'a-ricks). The tamarisks comprise an interesting group of shrubs and trees of the family Tamaricaceae, all the 75 species from Eurasia or Asia Minor, and many of them salt-tolerant plants of semi-desert places, and growing naturally in pure sand. They have very slender branches, and the twigs, which are completely covered by the small, scale-like leaves, are shed with the leaves in the fall. The leaves are very small, hug the twigs, and are scarcely more than 1/16 in. long. Flowers very small, mostly crowded in dense racemes* which are grouped in terminal clusters (panicles*). Fruit a minute capsule.* (*Tamarix* is the old Latin name of these plants.)

The tamarisks are very feathery, slender plants providing a foliage character unlike most plants in cult. They appear superficially leafless because the scale-like leaves are so closely pressed against the twigs, suggesting *Casuarina* or heaths or some forms of juniper in this respect. But the foliage effect is finer with the tamarisks than in either *Casuarina* or the junipers. Because most species are salt- and sand-tolerant, they make excellent plants for the seaside garden, their slender branches swaying easily in the wind, and the plants not having, along the coast, the wind-wrenched appearance of stiffer-wooded plants. Cuttings root very easily in moist sand. Some of the species, in Calif., are useful bee plants.

**africana.** A shrub 6–10 ft. high. Flower clusters about 3 in. long, borne along the sides of last season's twigs. Mediterranean region. May. Hardy from zone* 6 southward, but little known in cult.

**articulata.** Athel tree. Salt tree. A tree or large shrub, 20–30 ft. high, the twigs jointed, usually covered with the persistent, scale-like leaves and the plant thus appearing evergreen. Flowers minute, pink, in terminal clusters (panicles*). Western As. and northern Af., especially in alkali and desert regions. Hardy from zone* 7 southward and useful in seaside gardens and as a windbreak.

**gallica.** Salt cedar; also called French tamarisk. A shrub or small tree 15–25 ft. high, the foliage bluish. Flowers white or pinkish. Mediterranean region. July–Aug. Hardy from zone* 3 southward, and the best known species in cult., suitable for a variety of soils.

**hispida.** Not over 4–5 ft. high, the twigs somewhat hairy. Flowers pink, the dense racemes* in a terminal cluster (panicle*). East of the Caspian Sea. Aug.–Sept. Hardy from zone* 5 southward.

**odessana.** A shrub 4–6 ft. high, the slender branches upright. Flowers pink, the slender racemes* about 1½ in. long. Caspian region. July–Sept. Hardy from zone* 3 southward.

**pentandra.** A shrub, 10–15 ft. high, the foliage purplish. Flowers pink or rose-pink, mostly in dense racemes,* which are grouped in a large terminal cluster (panicle*). Eurasia. Aug.–Sept. Hardy from zone* 3 southward.

**TANACETIFOLIA**, *-us*, *-um* (tan-a-see-ti-fō'li-a). With tansy-like leaves.

**TANACETUM** (tan-a-see'tum). Tansy. Very strongly-scented, rather weedy herbs of the family Compositae, all the 30 known species from the north temperate zone, and only T. vulgare, the common tansy, of any garden interest. It is a rank-growing herb, 2–3 ft. high, with alternate, much-dissected leaves. Flower heads small, button-like (hence its other name of bitter-buttons), yellow, exclusively of disk* flowers, the heads in a flat-topped cluster (cyme*). The var. **crispum** has more finely divided and crisped leaves. Eu. Common as a roadside weed over much of eastern U.S. For cult. and uses see HERB GARDENING. (*Tanacetum* is from the Greek for immortality, but of uncertain application here.)

**TANBARK OAK** = *Lithocarpus densiflora.*

**TAN BAY** = *Gordonia lasianthus.*

**TANGELO.** A citrus fruit derived from crossing the tangerine known as Dancy, with a grapefruit variety known as Bowen, in 1897. The tangelo is like neither of its parents, being a pear-shaped, thin-skinned, rather acid, juicy citrus fruit with an orange-colored pulp. Of no interest except to the breeders of citrus fruits. See CITRUS.

**TANGERINE** = *Citrus nobilis deliciosa.*

**TANGLEBERRY** = *Gaylussacia frondosa.* See HUCKLEBERRY.

**TANGUTICA**, *-us*, *-um* (tan-gew'ti-ka). From or near Tangut, Tibet.

**TANIA** = *Xanthosoma sagittaefolium.*

**TANKAGE.** See Nitrogen at FERTILIZERS.

**TANKS.** For contents of tanks *see* WEIGHTS AND MEASURES, 5.

**TAN OAK** = *Lithocarpus densiflora.*

**TANSY.** See TANACETUM.

**TANSY RAGWORT** = *Senecio jacobaea.*

**TANYOSHO** = *Pinus densiflora umbraculifera.* See PINE.

**TAPE-GRASS** = *Vallisneria spiralis.* See EEL-GRASS.

**TAPIOCA-PLANT** = *Manihot esculenta.*

**TAPROOT.** The main, central root of a plant, which usually goes straight down and is larger and stouter than the lateral roots. Plants with a deep taproot are harder to transplant than others, for they often lack the many small feeding roots found on the lateral root systems of most plants. While taproot is more often a characteristic of herbs, some trees, especially in the young stages, develop large taproots, as in the hickories. Such trees are notoriously difficult to move.

The dandelion is difficult to eradicate because of its taproot. Some trees also bear taproots and they are usually hard to transplant. See HICKORY.

**TARATA** = *Pittosporum eugenioides.*

**TARA VINE** = *Actinidia arguta.*

**TARAXACUM.** See DANDELION.

**TARDIFLORA**, *-us*, *-um* (tar-di-flow'ra). Late-flowering.

**TARE** = *Vicia sativa.*

**TARNISHED PLANT BUG.** See Insect Pests at DAHLIA, SNAPDRAGON, and ZINNIA.

**TARO** = *Colocasia esculenta.*

**TARRAGON** (*Artemisia dracunculus*). A little known, very pleasantly flavored, perennial herb, far more popular in Eu. than here. The French, particularly, grow it commercially as a source of an aromatic, pungent flavoring extract, which is widely used in flavoring pickles and in the making of tarragon vinegar. It is also the flavoring extract which gives the piquant and delightful tang to Dubonnet.

Tarragon is a perennial herb found wild from the Caspian Sea to Siberia, and is closely related to wormwood (*Artemisia absinthium*). As tarragon rarely, if ever, produces seeds, the plant must be propagated by division of its roots, preferably in early spring. The plant will grow in any ordinary garden soil, but the flavor for which it is famous is best produced when the plant is grown on rather poor, stony or sandy soil. As it is not a particularly decorative member of the genus *Artemisia*, its cult. really should be restricted to an attempt to produce its essential oil. This is rarely, if ever, done in America, most of our importations of tarragon coming from southern France.

---

* Special articles on the subjects indicated by an asterisk (*) will be found at the words so marked.

By keeping it on fairly poor soils, and restricting its cult. to regions where summer rainfall is not too great, there is no reason why a supply of tarragon leaves cannot be harvested in late Aug. and Sept. While they will not be so aromatic as the French product, the home gardener will have a supply of tarragon leaves, which may be used fresh or dried, as desired. For the details of drying see HERB GARDENING.

After harvesting, and if the region is a cold one, and with little snow cover, the plants should be cut down to the ground and given a light mulch of straw or leaves. Do not use manure, and do not apply any commercial fertilizer. Both would greatly increase the growth of tarragon, but decrease its flavor.

The plants should be grown about 1 ft. apart each way, and if division of the roots cannot be practiced, the plant may be propagated by cuttings, which can be made when desired. They root readily in moist sand.

**TARTARIAN ASTER** = *Aster tataricus*.

**TARTARIAN BUCKWHEAT** = *Fagopyrum tataricum*. See BUCKWHEAT.

**TARTARIAN DOGWOOD** = *Cornus alba*.

**TARTARIAN HONEYSUCKLE** = *Lonicera tatarica*.

**TARWEED.** See MADIA. See also GRINDELIA.

**TASAJILLO** = *Opuntia leptocaulis*.

**TASMANIAN STRINGY-BARK** = *Eucalyptus obliqua*.

**TASSEL-FLOWER** = *Amaranthus caudatus* and *Emilia sagittata*.

**TASSEL-HYACINTH** = *Muscari comosum*.

**TASSEL-TREE** = *Garrya elliptica*.

*TATARICA*, **-us, -um** (ta-tar'i-ka). From Central Asia, once called Tartary.

*TAURICA*, **-us, -um** (tau'ri-ka). From the ancient country of Tauris, now the Crimea (Krim).

**TAWHIWHI** = *Pittosporum tenuifolium*.

**TAXACEAE** (tacks-ā'see-ee). The yew family, next to the Pinaceae (which see), furnishes the most valuable evergreens for the hardy garden, and a few trees or shrubs for the greenhouse or for outdoor, frost-free regions. Of the 11 known genera at least five are in cult., but of the 100 widely distributed species of trees and shrubs, only a dozen or so are of any garden interest.

*Taxus*, the yew, with only a few species but many hort. varieties, is by far the most important genus. Its rich, lustrous, evergreen foliage is matched by few other plants. Other relatively hardy genera are *Torreya* and *Cephalotaxus*, but see these genera for exact notes on their hardiness. *Podocarpus* and *Dacrydium* can only be grown in relatively frost-free regions or in the cool greenhouse. The leaves are flat and relatively broad in some genera (*Podocarpus*), but needle-like or awl-shaped in *Taxus*, which unlike most of the genera is not resinous.

The only obvious difference between this family and the Pinaceae is that the former produces cones, while the fruit of the yew family is fleshy, part of the flesh being due to an aril.*

*TAXIFOLIA*, **-us, -um** (tacks-i-fō'li-a). With yew-like leaves.

**TAXODIUM** (tacks-ō'di-um). Three magnificent evergreen or deciduous trees of the pine family, one Mexican, the other two from the southeastern U.S., often, and in fact, usually called cypress in the U.S., but not the traditional cypress. They have light brown, scaly bark and bear two sorts of branchlets, the upper ones persistent, the lower ones on the shoot deciduous.* Leaves alternate,* flat, line-like, spreading. Male and female flowers separate, but on the same tree, the male flowers consisting of only 6–8 stamens, mostly in drooping clusters (panicles*). Female flowers ultimately producing a scaly, short-stalked cone, its seeds 3-angled and 3-winged. (*Taxodium* is from the Greek meaning *Taxus*-like.)

The first species is the bald cypress, and a valuable timber tree, as well as being most decorative. While its natural habitat is in the cypress swamps, it will grow on ordinary soils if they are in reasonably moist places. The second species is not hardy in the North, and is rarely grown even in southern Calif. or Fla.

**distichum.** Bald cypress; southern cypress. A deciduous* tree up to 150 ft. high, its trunk decidedly tapering, often buttressed at the base (in the wild), and in its native swamps producing the "cypress knees" which are woody projections of the roots, 4–6 ft. high and about a foot thick, which are thrust above the water. Leaves light green, about ¾ in. long, very numerous, the foliage graceful and feathery, orange in the autumn just before leaf-fall. Cones about 1 in. long. Del. to Fla. west to Ark. and La. Hardy from zone* 4, sometimes zone* 3, southward, but always a small tree northward. A closely related tree, *T. ascendens*, with less spreading leaves and rather upright branches, is sometimes cult.

**mucronatum.** Montezuma cypress; known in Mex. as ahuehuete. A magnificent evergreen tree, as famous in Aztec history as the oak in England. One of them, in the garden of Montezuma, and another in the churchyard at El Tule, were large trees at the time of the conquest and are still standing. The tree is lower than our bald cypress, but its crown far wider, one of the oldest being about 120 ft. high, its crown somewhat wider, and with a trunk diameter of over 50 ft. Leaves about ½ in. long, some of them often deciduous. Cones 1½–1¾ in. long. Central Mex. to Guatemala. Hardy only in zones* 8 and 9, and little grown outside of Mex., but occasionally planted in Fla. and southern Calif. It may be the oldest living thing in America, considered even older than the bigtree (*Sequoia gigantea*) by some authorities.

**TAXUS** (tacks'us). Yew. Beautiful, slow-growing evergreen shrubs and trees of the family Taxaceae, comprising perhaps 8 closely related species, but considered by some as merely forms of a single species which is found over much of the north temperate zone. They have, in age, scaly, reddish-brown bark, and spirally arranged, 2-ranked, typically dark green, narrow leaves, the foliage not resinous or aromatic as in so many conifers. Leaves with 2 yellowish or grayish-green bands on the under side. Male and female flowers on different plants, without sepals or petals, only the female producing the scarlet or brownish, berry-like fruit (a modified cone). The juice of the foliage, and the fruit, are dangerously poisonous. See POISONOUS PLANTS. (*Taxus* is the classical Latin name of the yew.)

For culture see EVERGREENS. The yews have been cult. since the days of the Greeks, especially *T. baccata*, the English yew. In its tree form this species is a very slow-growing plant, and is consequently rarely grown here. Its shrubby, cult. varieties, and the Japanese yew (*T. cuspidata*), are much better for evergreen plantings, their fine dark foliage and comparative freedom from disease making these shrubby yews among the most widely popular of all evergreens. Some of them, as noted below, are fine hedge plants and will stand the necessary shearing. Of course, like any other evergreen hedge plant, yews are expensive. For the details of setting out hedge plants see HEDGES.

**baccata.** English yew. A tree (in Eu.) up to 60 ft. high and with a broad, round head. Leaves 1–1¼ in. long, gradually tapering to a slender point. Fruit berry-like, olive-brown, just under ½ in. long. Eurasia and northern Af. Hardy from zone* 4 southward, but not happy in regions of dry, hot summers. This typical tree form rarely grown in the U.S., the following hort. varieties being much more useful hort. subjects:

*var.* **adpressa.** Low shrub or small tree, its leaves scarcely ½ in. long, and not spreading. |Comes in several color forms (*i.e.* foliage golden), and in erect or columnar forms, suited for hedge plants.

*var.* **argentea** = *var. variegata*.

*var.* **aurea.** Leaves yellow. Not much grown, and less desirable than some other varieties.

*var.* **fastigiata.** Irish yew. A very handsome columnar form with upright branches, the leaves spirally arranged, and of a fine dark green color. A good accent* plant. There are also variegated and golden-foliaged forms.

*var.* **repandens.** A beautiful, low, nearly prostrate form, with wide-spreading branches and bluish-green foliage.

*var.* **variegata** (also called *var. argentea*). A shrubby form with whitish-variegated foliage.

*var.* **washingtoni.** A wide-spreading, shrubby form with golden-yellow foliage.

Besides those listed above, there are perhaps 30 other hort. forms or varieties of this widely planted evergreen. Most of them are minor variations in habit or the color of the foliage.

**brevifolia.** The plants usually offered as this are *Taxus cuspidata nana*, the true *T. brevifolia* of western N.A. being rare in cult.

**canadensis.** Ground hemlock. A native American, straggling or half-prostrate, evergreen shrub, rarely over 3 ft. high. Leaves about 1 in. long, dark green, tapering suddenly to a minute, prickle-like point. Berry-like fruit scarlet. Eastern N.A. Hardy from zone* 2 southward. Less desir-

---

* Special articles on the subjects indicated by an asterisk (*) will be found at the words so marked.

able than the other two species, but useful as a ground cover under the shade of forest trees, especially evergreens. Not suited to open, windswept places.

**cuspidata.** Japanese yew. The most important horticulturally of all the yews, and the best for hedges. It is far more hardy than the English yew and faster-growing. A tree up to 40 ft. high, much more often a bushy shrub as cult. Leaves about 1 in. long, suddenly tapering to a short, dark green point. Berry-like fruit scarlet. Eastern As. Hardy from zone* 3, and possibly zone* 2, southward. Sometimes sold as *T. sieboldi*. The var. **capitata**, widely advertised, is apparently a seedling form of *T. cuspidata*. The var. **nana** (often offered as *T. brevifolia*) is a fine, shrubby form. The *var.* **densa** is a compact form scarcely over 3 ft. tall.

**sieboldi** = *Taxus cuspidata*.

**T-BUDDING.** See BUDDING.

**TEA.** For the true tea plant *see* Thea. But tea has been applied to many other cult. plants, or is a part of their name. Those in this book and their proper equivalents are:

**Appalachian tea** = *Viburnum cassinoides;* **Crystal tea** = *Ledum palustre;* **Labrador tea** = *Ledum groenlandicum;* **Mexican tea** = *Chenopodium ambrosioides;* **New Jersey tea** = *Ceanothus americanus;* **Oswego tea** = *Monarda didyma.* See also the next few entries.

**TEABERRY** = *Gaultheria procumbens* and *Mitchella repens.*

**TEA FAMILY** = Theaceae.

**TEA-OF-HEAVEN** = *Hydrangea serrata.*

**TEA OLIVE.** See OSMANTHUS.

**TEA ROSE** = *Rosa odorata.* For the garden forms of the tea rose *see* Group 1 at ROSE.

**TEASEL.** See DIPSACUS.

**TEASEL FAMILY** = Dipsacaceae.

**TEA-TREE.** See MELALEUCA and LEPTOSPERMUM.

*TECHNICA, -us, -um* (teck'ni-ka). Specialized or technical.

**TECOMA.** A tropical genus of shrubs or trees of no garden interest, except that the name *Tecoma* was long applied to the common trumpet-creeper (which see), now included in the genus *Campsis*. *Tecoma* has also been applied to several other garden plants now included in other genera. For:

| Tecoma australis | see | Pandorea pandorana. |
| " capensis | " | Tecomaria capensis. |
| " grandiflora | " | Trumpet-creeper (*Campsis chinensis*). |
| " jasminoides | " | Pandorea jasminoides. |
| " radicans | " | Trumpet-creeper (*Campsis radicans*). |
| " ricasoliana | " | Pandorea ricasoliana. |
| " stans | " | Stenolobium stans. |

**TECOMARIA** (teck-o-mair'i-a). A small genus of woody vines or scrambling shrubs of the family Bignoniaceae grown for ornament. Several are tropical American, but the only cult. one, **T. capensis**, the Cape honeysuckle, is from South Africa. It can be grown as a vine, or pruned as a scrambling shrub. It is an evergreen plant with opposite,* compound* leaves, the 7–9 leaflets toothed, ovalish, ¾–2 in. long. Flowers orange-red or scarlet, in showy, terminal, stalked clusters (racemes*), blooming over most of the year. Corolla slightly irregular, about 2 in. long, funnel-shaped, the upper lip* slightly notched. Stamens* 4, protruding. Fruit a narrow capsule,* about 1½ in. long. It grows profusely in the sandy soils of Fla. and should be propagated by seeds or cuttings. Not certainly hardy north of zones* 8 and 9, but possibly in protected places in zone* 7. A very handsome plant. (*Tecomaria*, derived from *Tecoma*, means resembling that genus.)

*TECTORA, -us, -um* (teck-tor'ra). Pertaining to a house roof.

**TEFF.** An important cereal in Abyssinia. See ERAGROSTIS ABYSSINICA.

**TELANTHERA** (tell-an'ther-ra). Low-growing foliage plants, belonging to the family Amaranthaceae, of little interest except to addicts of carpet bedding, who use them widely under the name *Alternanthera*. They are perennial plants, mostly Brazilian, and not well understood botanically. Of the 50 or more known species only the two below appear to be in common cult. They have opposite, narrow, small leaves, often colored, and minute, chaffy flowers in dense clusters in the leaf-axils,* but the flowers are rarely produced due to the shearing which must be done to keep them low enough for carpet bedding. (*Telanthera* is from the Greek for ten stamens, in allusion to the 5 fertile and 5 sterile stamens.)

These summer-bedding plants are not hardy and cannot be grown without a greenhouse for winter care. Their use as carpet-bedding plants is based upon their ability to stand shearing, which is done to keep them 4–6 in. high or even less. They need a warm, sunny place and not too rich a soil. Propagated by cuttings taken in Aug. and carried through the winter in the greenhouse, rarely in a hotbed. Or the plants may be divided when they are lifted in the fall. Whichever method is followed, the young plants should be potted up in March (in potting mixture* 3) and grown along in the temperate greenhouse until the season for outdoor bedding has arrived. They should then be planted close together and shearing started as soon as they become established.

**amoena.** A dwarf foliage plant, rarely over 4 in. high. Leaves more or less elliptic, green, but with orange or red blotches, or both. Brazil. There are several hort. forms with variously colored foliage.

**bettzickiana.** A somewhat higher plant than *T. amoena*, and the most popular for carpet bedding. Leaves narrowly spatula-shaped, mostly cream-yellow or red, but in the numerous hort. forms golden, striped, copper, olive-green, etc., and also available in a very dwarf form naturally, only 2–3 in. high. Probably Brazil.

**versicolor.** A medium-sized herb, 6–8 in. high. Leaves broadly spatula-shaped or roundish, blood-red or coppery. Probably Brazil.

**TELEGRAPH PLANT** = *Desmodium gyrans.*

*TELEPHIUM* (tell-ee'fi-um). An old name, of uncertain application, perhaps derived from Telephus of Greek mythology. It is now used for the specific name of *Sedum telephium* (which see).

**TELLIMA** (tel-ly'ma). Perhaps 10 species of hairy, perennial herbs of the family Saxifragaceae, from western N.A., one of them, **T. grandiflora**, the fringe-cups or false alum-root, cult. for ornament. It is a slender herb, 1–2 ft. high, resembling *Mitella*. Leaves chiefly basal, stalked, roundish or heart-shaped, and toothed, about 4 in. wide. Flowers nodding, greenish at first, ultimately pink or reddish, the calyx* inflated, more or less bell-shaped. Corolla of fringed petals. Calif. to Alaska. Suited only to the wild garden and needing shade and woods soil. (*Tellima* is an anagram of *Mitella*.) For the plant sometimes sold as *T. affinis* see LITHOPHRAGMA AFFINIS.

**TEMPERATE HOUSE.** A cool greenhouse. See GREENHOUSE.

**TEMPERATURE.** The total amount of heat and cold determines the wild flora of a region more than any other feature of the climate. This is also true for cult. plants. There are times when minor frosts can be held in check over limited areas (*see* FROST), but generally speaking heat and cold cannot be controlled, and upon the amount of each most gardening and farming must be based.

The wide-scale and long-continuing operation of a factor like low temperatures, for instance, dictates the hardiness of most cult. plants. And upon their response to this the country has been divided into 9 zones* of hardiness. For the details of this and a map *see* ZONE. See also HARDINESS.

The occurrence of killing frosts in spring and autumn, while not such a drastic factor as either extreme heat or cold, does control many hort. operations. And the figures for spring and autumn killing frosts have been tabulated for all the states. See the name of your state for the details of these frost dates.

* Special articles on the subjects indicated by an asterisk (*) will be found at the words so marked.

It would have been still more desirable to include here the figures for effective temperatures, perhaps the most important of all hort. criteria of temperature. But such figures are lacking, although they could be gleaned from weather bureau records if one had the time to do so. As understood by the experts, effective temperatures are those that are effective for plant growth. Between the freezing point and the amount when the plant begins to respond to increased heat, there is an accumulation of heat units of no use to most plants; — in other words, ineffective temperatures.

But at about 40°, plant activity does begin to stir, and barley, one of the hardiest of all cereals, will just germinate. The figure of about 40° has thus come to be the base upon which statistics of effective temperatures have been built. And 40° means that, during the day, the hourly maxima and hourly minima, divided by two, give the absolute mean temperature of 40°. And the effective temperatures are the accumulated degrees of heat above this base. Such a figure, for the growing season, at New York, totals 5,232°, for New Haven, Conn., 4,540°. And for Block Island, R.I., 4,444°. In other words, that many degrees of temperature, effective for plant growth, accumulated above the base of 40°. Similar figures from deserts and mountains would be extremely valuable, both to gardeners and foresters.

Another temperature factor of garden importance is the incidence of absolute maximal and absolute minimal temperatures. Even brief periods of intense cold or heat are of greater significance than comfortable average temperatures within which most plants grow perfectly well, assuming that rainfall or irrigations are adequate.

In the U.S. the absolute minimum and maximum temperatures are listed below for a few significant places:

|  | Absolute Minimum Temperatures | Absolute Maximum Temperatures |
|---|---|---|
| Boston | −17° | 95° |
| New York | −14° | 99° |
| Detroit | −20° | 105° |
| Chicago | −30° | 105° |
| Northern Montana | −60° | 105° |
| Northern Idaho | −50° | 100° |
| Seattle | 10° | 90° |
| San Francisco | 20° | 98° |
| Los Angeles | 25° | 105° |
| Northern Tex. | 0 | 110° |
| Southern Tex. | 10° | 110° |
| New Orleans | 10° | 100° |
| Key West | 41° | 95° |

Higher and lower temperatures than these have been recorded, as 65° below zero at Bismarck, N. Dak. and 115° at Yuma, Ariz. These figures, taken from the Atlas of American Agriculture, Part II. Climate, Section B. Temperature, Sunshine and Wind, published by the U.S. Weather Bureau, in 1928, may change somewhat in the future, but most of them are based on 60 years of temperature records.

**TEMPLETONIA** (tem-pel-tō'ni-a). Winter-blooming Australian shrubs of the pea family, only T. retusa, the coralbush, likely to be cult. and hardy only in zones* 8 and 9. It is sometimes grown outdoors for ornament in Calif. and Fla., rarely in the temperate greenhouse. It is a tall shrub with alternate,* simple leaves, which few plants of the pea family have. Leaves ovalish or wedge-shaped, about 1 in. long, notched or with a minute point at the tip. Flowers pea-like, red, solitary in the leaf-axils* or in clusters of 2–3, about 1 in. long. Pod (legume*) flattish, 1½–2 in. long. Propagated by cuttings. (Named for J. Templeton, Irish botanist.)

**TEMPLE TREE.** See PLUMERIA.

*TEMULENTA, -us, -um* (tem-you-len'ta). Unsteady or drunken.

*TENAX* (tee'nacks). Strong or tenacious.

**TENDER.** See HARDINESS. See also SUB-TROPICAL GARDEN.

**TENDER ANNUAL.** See ANNUALS.
**TENDER BORDER PLANTS.** See BORDER.
**TENDRIL.** A slender prolongation of the stem or leaf, of the greatest use to climbing plants, because tendrils cling to a support. Many vines have thread-like, herbaceous tendrils, most of which are highly sensitive to irritation. Much nonsense has been written about tendrils "seeking" a support. They consciously "seek" nothing, but their movements are none the less remarkable, as Darwin found after years of study. Some coil clockwise, others counter-clockwise. In

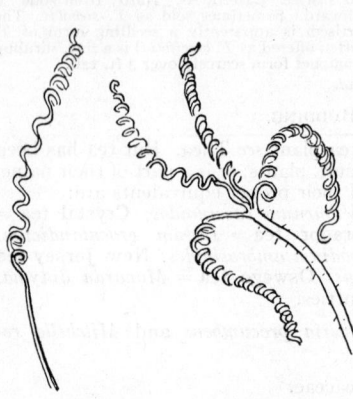

A simple and a branched tendril

some tropical vines tendrils are horribly prickly, while in others, as in *Antigonon*, the tendril is merely a slender tip of the inflorescence. Familiar examples of tendrils may be seen in the grape, pea, and in many relatives of the trumpet-creeper.

**TENNESSEE.** The state lies wholly in zones* 4, 5 and 6. It is ribbon-like in shape, extending over 400 miles from its eastern extreme to the western, and is less than 120 miles wide at its widest point. Areas of varying elevation extend in general from the north to the south and have important influences on the climate, soil type, and products of each section of the state.

East Tennessee is mountainous and variable in soil type. A given soil formation tends to extend parallel to the mountain ranges. While the soils of this area are fairly fertile, erosion is a serious problem on all cultivated upland.

Middle Tennessee is divided from the eastern section by a large area of higher elevation known as the Cumberland Plateau, where the soils are usually derived from sandstone and shale. These soils are low in fertility and require large applications of mineral fertilizers to produce satisfactory crops.

The central-basin area is comparable to the blue-grass sections of Kentucky. The soils were derived from limestone and are high in natural fertility.

Another plateau or "Highland rim" extends entirely around the central basin and extends over into west Tennessee. The soils of the "Rim" fall into two main groups, those derived from limestone and those derived from siliceous rock. The former are of good natural fertility, but the latter are usually very poor, and are often referred to as the "Barrens."

Large soil areas of west Tennessee are naturally of high fertility but have suffered much by erosion and one-crop farming. Silt loams are the prevailing types. Some of the alluvial lands are very productive, but drainage is often required.

FRUITS AND VEGETABLES. Differences in elevation give a wide range in climate in this state. Figs are grown in sheltered places in Knoxville, while spruce trees thrive and are a common forest tree at an elevation of 5000 feet in the Smoky Mountains near by. These variations in elevation furnish a certain amount of frost protection on the higher sites and largely account for the success of many apple and peach orchards in east Tennessee. The commercial peach section extends from Clinton and Harriman in the north to Sale Creek near Chattanooga on the south. Peach production varies greatly from year to year, but averages second in value among the fruits shipped out of the state.

---

* Special articles on the subjects indicated by an asterisk (*) will be found at the words so marked.

The great vegetable district of this state is in Gibson and five or six near-by counties of west Tennessee. Tomatoes, both for shipping north and for canning, lead among the truck crops. Milan, Humboldt, Gibson, Fruitland, and Trenton are the larger shipping points.

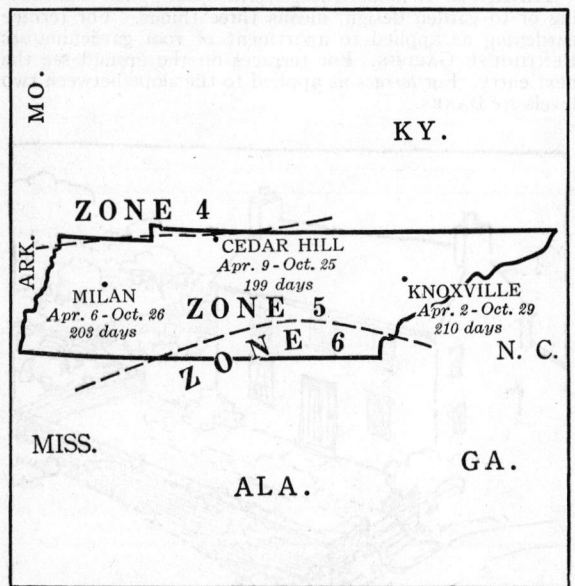

TENNESSEE

The zones of hardiness crossing Tennessee are those shown on the colored map at ZONE, which should be consulted for details. The dates are the average latest killing frost in spring and the first one in the fall. The figures below the dates show the average length of the growing season. Rainfall is adequate.

Sweet potatoes thrive in all parts of the state and are prominent in the diet of the people. Production varies from year to year, but usually ranks second to tomatoes in value. Weakley County in the northwestern part ships out the largest tonnage. The adjoining counties of Henry, Gibson, and Carroll rank next in sweet-potato production in the order named.

Early cabbage to ship to northern markets varies greatly in production from year to year, but usually ranks third among the vegetable crops. Gibson County is the center of cabbage production, with the towns of Humboldt, Gibson, and Medina the more important shipping points.

Irish or white potatoes are a small crop in this state compared with sweet potatoes, although from three to four hundred carloads of the spring crop are usually shipped out. Much of the spring crop and all the fall crop are used locally. In addition, large quantities of potatoes are shipped in to supply the local markets during the winter season. Columbia and Decherd in middle Tennessee are the more important shipping points.

The snap bean is usually one of the more important of the minor vegetable crops. In addition to production for home consumption, from 50 to over 125 carloads are shipped out annually. The center for exporting is in Weakley, Gibson, and Haywood counties of west Tennessee.

Strawberries lead among the fruit crops of Tennessee. From one thousand to over two thousand carloads are shipped out annually in addition to local consumption. About half of this tonnage is shipped from west Tennessee. Humboldt, Ripley, and Jackson are the larger shipping towns. The east Tennessee district centers around Rhea County, with Dayton, Evensville, and Spring City as the larger shipping points. The middle Tennessee district lies largely in Sumner County, with Portland, Mitchellville, and Westmoreland as shipping points.

Other fruits as apples, plums, pears, cherries, and raspberries are produced in small quantities and mostly for local consumption. Considerable quantities of these fruits are shipped or trucked into the state from other districts.

ORNAMENTALS. Tennessee is noted for its many kinds of flowers and ornamental trees and shrubs. Plant life furnishes one of the main attractions in the Smoky Mountains National Park, which lies partly within the state on its eastern border. Rhododendron, laurel, and the flame azalea attract tourists from long distances. Dogwood and redbud are the most attractive of the widely distributed, native flowering shrubs. Roses, both hybrid tea and climbing, are the most popular of the cultivated flowers. Many annuals, as cosmos and zinnias, will re-seed themselves from year to year. Jasmine, forsythia, and the various spireas are popular spring-blooming, cultivated shrubs. Crape myrtle, abelia, and hibiscus bloom in profusion during the late summer. Various hollies, cedars, euonymus, cherry laurels, junipers, and arborvitae are popular among evergreen shrubs.

CLIMATE. Elevation, both actual and above sea level, markedly influences the climate of many parts of Tennessee. Spring frosts occasionally destroy the first strawberry blossoms where air drainage is not good. Raspberries and rhubarb are more easily grown on the higher elevations where temperatures are lower and the rainfall more evenly distributed throughout the year.

KILLING FROSTS IN TENNESSEE

| Town | Average date of last killing frost in the spring | Latest known killing frost | Average date of earliest killing frost in the fall | Earliest known killing frost |
|---|---|---|---|---|
| Knoxville, in east Tennessee | April 2 | April 26 | Oct. 29 | Oct. 1 |
| Cedar Hill, in middle Tennessee | April 9 | April 26 | Oct. 25 | Oct. 9 |
| Milan, in west Tennessee | April 6 | April 26 | Oct. 26 | Oct. 9 |

The frost records of Knoxville as reported in the table were taken in the valley and are not comparable to those which could be taken on high elevations. The Cedar Hill records were taken near the Sumner County strawberry district and are fairly representative of that section. The Milan station is located in the west Tennessee trucking district.

Rainfall tends to vary with elevation and is especially heavy on the Cumberland Plateau. It averages less as a rule in May and in September and October than in other months, but is otherwise fairly evenly distributed. The Chattanooga station reports 32.68 inches of rainfall as their record low which occurred in 1904, while in 1929 it was 72.37 inches. This is a variation between years of nearly 40 inches while the average annual rainfall was 50.99 inches. The plateau section near Crossville averaged over 5 inches more of rainfall per year, and it was more evenly distributed both from season to season and within a given year.

The address of the Tennessee Agricultural Experiment Station, which has kindly supplied this information about the state, is Knoxville. The Station is always ready to answer gardening questions.

Garden club activities in the state include clubs of the Garden Club of America, the home office of which is 598 Madison Avenue, New York, N.Y. There are also nearly 50 clubs affiliated with the Tennessee Garden Club. For the one nearest your locality write the Garden Editor, Houghton Mifflin Company, Boston, Mass.

**TENNIS.** A lawn game, the standard court for which is 36 × 78 ft.

**TENT CATERPILLAR.** See Moths at INSECT PESTS. See also Insect Pests at APPLE.

*TENUIFOLIA, -us, -um* (ten-you-i-fō′li-a). Having slender or narrow leaves.

---

* Special articles on the subjects indicated by an asterisk (*) will be found at the words so marked.

**TEN-WEEKS STOCK** = *Mathiola incana annua*. For cult. see STOCK.

**TEOSINTE** = *Euchlaena mexicana*.

**TEPARY BEAN** = *Phaseolus acutifolius latifolius*.

**TEPHROSIA** (teff-rose'i-a). Ashy-leaved, perennial herbs, or, in the tropics, shrubs, of the pea family, comprising over 170 species, mostly from the warmer parts of the world and of little hort. interest. They have alternate,* compound* leaves, the leaflets arranged feather-fashion and with an odd one at the end. Flowers pea-like, white or yellowish-purple (in ours), mostly in racemes.* Pod (legume*) narrow and flattish. (*Tephrosia* is from the Greek for ashy or hoary, in allusion to the foliage.) The plants are often known as *Cracca*.

The first species is a tropical shrub sometimes planted for a windbreak in extreme southern Fla., and hardy nowhere else. The goat's-rue is a pretty little native plant suited only to dry, open, somewhat sandy places in the wild garden.

**candida.** A shrub, 8–10 ft. high, the foliage silky-hairy. Leaflets about 2 in. long. Flowers white, about 1 in. long. Pods 3–4 in. long. India.
**virginiana.** Goat's-rue; also called catgut and wild sweet pea. A showy-flowered, perennial herb, 1–2 ft. high. Leaflets 17–29, narrow, about 1 in. long, silky-hairy. Flowers yellowish-purple, about 1 in. long. Pods 1½–2 in. long. In open places, Me. to Fla. and N. Mex. June–July.

**TEQUILA MESCAL** = *Agave tequilana*.

*TEQUILANA*, *-us, -um* (te-key-lay'-na). From Tequila, Mexico.

*TEREBINTHIFOLIA*, *-us, -um* (te-re-bin-thi-fō'li-a). With leaves like the terebinth, a European tree scarcely known in cult. here.

**TERETE.** Round in cross-section, often not quite perfectly so, as in many leaves.

*TERETICORNIS*, *-e* (te-ree-ti-kor'nis). With round or terete horns.

**TERMINAL.** As used in hort. *terminal* has no special meaning other than the common one; *i.e.* at the end, not lateral. Many flower clusters are so designated to distinguish them from those borne in the leaf-axils,* which are hence never terminal.

**TERMINALIA** (ter-mi-nall'i-a). Chiefly Asiatic, tropical, and very handsome shade trees of the family Combretaceae, comprising over 100 species, some of which yield valuable products (gums, resins, myrobalans, tanning extracts, etc.), but only one in common cult. for ornament. This is the Indian almond, sometimes called tropical almond, and known to science as **T. catappa**, one of the most widely planted street trees in the tropics, and much used for that purpose in Fla. But as it is hardy only in zone* 9, it has not been grown in Calif. It is a tree up to 80 ft. high, with smooth, brownish-gray bark. Leaves alternate,* ovalish, 6–12 in. long, without teeth, but slightly eared toward the base, leathery, and glossy-green. Flowers small and inconspicuous, often unisexual* (for details see COMBRETACEAE). Fruit a dryish drupe,* greenish or reddish, angled, about 2 in. long, its seeds almond-like and edible. Malaya. Grows well in a variety of soils, and casts a denser shade than most tropical street trees. While the leaves turn a handsome copper-red before falling, the tree is never quite bare. (*Terminalia* is from the Latin for terminal, in allusion to the leaves often being borne toward the end of the shoot.)

**TERMINALIACEAE** = Combretaceae.

*TERMINALIS*, *-e* (ter-mi-nall'is). Terminal.*

**TERNARY** = ternate.*

*TERNATA*, *-us, -um* (ter-nay'ta). Ternate.*

**TERNATE.** Borne in threes, as are the leaflets in many compound leaves, notably in clover.

*TERNATEA*, *-us, -um* (ter-nay'te-a). From the island of Ternate in the Dutch East Indies.

*TERNIFOLIA*, *-us, -um* (ter-ni-fō'li-a). Three-leaved; or sometimes with ternate* leaflets.

**TERRACE.** In modern usage terrace, as applied to gardening or to garden design, means three things. For terrace gardening as applied to apartment or roof gardening see PENTHOUSE GARDEN. For terraces on the ground see the next entry. For *terrace* as applied to the slope between two levels see BANKS.

A house terrace (on a sloping plot) serves as a semi-architectural setting for the house. At the right, a sunken terrace, serving as an outdoor living room.

**TERRACES.** The house terrace forms an architectural base for the house, its clearly defined boundaries providing the necessary transition between the strictly architectural mass and lines of the house and the natural forms of the surrounding landscape. A terrace provides a space for use as an outdoor living room as well as serving to co-ordinate divergent lines of access to the house. It is therefore preferable to segregate it from surrounding outdoor areas by a low wall, balustrade or hedge, making it a single element of design.

Its size and proportions depend upon the mass of the house and the limits imposed by adjacent topography or other existing features, and should be related to the view which it commands. A broad terrace is restful and lends dignity to a large house. A small house calls for a terrace proportionately small and intimate in scale. Similarly, an extensive view suggests a large terrace, but it should not be so broad as to cut off part of the view from the house. Where there is no view, other factors control the design.

The question of use is of primary importance. If the owners entertain extensively, the terrace should be given ample proportions and should have convenient arrangements for service facilities. Its usefulness will be increased if it can be attractively illuminated at night. A large terrace of this type should be given a dignified, simple treatment. It is desirable to have a restful expanse of turf, unbroken save by one or two well-placed shade trees, and enclosed by an appropriate wall or balustrade or dwarf hedge. Where considerable use is to be made of certain parts of the terrace these areas should be paved with suitable material. A small house usually demands a more intimate terrace treatment.

---

* Special articles on the subjects indicated by an asterisk (*) will be found at the words so marked.

THE TERRACE, VIZCAYA (FLORIDA)
(From a water-color by John Singer Sargent)

(Courtesy of Worcester Art Museum)

If it commands an attractive view it is advisable to keep the terrace simple in order to avoid confusion of interests. Otherwise the terrace itself may be made the center of interest. In a small area it is more practical to use brick or flagstone paving than to attempt to maintain turf. Where they will not interfere with general use, soil pockets for plant material may be provided for in the paving. The terrace may be treated as a garden, with beds for shrubs or flowers surrounding the paved area. If space is limited, espaliered shrubs and potted plants would be more practical and equally effective. Further interest may be added by the introduction of such features as a fountain or pool, also certain unusual wall or paving treatments as well as treillage.* Trees for terrace planting should bear proportional relationship to the size of the terrace. For instance, a dogwood might be suitable for a small terrace and an elm tree in scale with a more ample area.

Being higher than the adjacent ground, the terrace usually requires some form of retaining wall. In an informal scheme a turf bank or dry stone wall may be adequate if suitably planted. More pretentious schemes require stone- or brick-masonry in harmony with the architecture of the house. Steps* and stairways usually add a definite interest to the terrace design. Where appropriate, sculptural features and jardinieres as well as certain architectural embellishments such as a niche or pavilion may supplement the simpler fundamentals of the design. All decorative features, however, should be in keeping with the life and character of the place as a whole. The terrace should be maintained as a functional unit, contributing toward the co-ordination of the more restricted life within the house and the greater freedom of out-of-doors. — A. F.

**TERRAPIN SCALE.** *See* Insect Pests at PEACH.

**TERRARIUM.** A terrarium is a transparent container, tightly fitted with an adjustable glass cover, in which plants are grown in earth instead of water. It is known also as a fernery, Wardian case, bottle garden, crystal garden, and glass garden. Terrariums may be bought in any number of sizes and shapes, or made at home by fitting pieces of glass, cut to the proper size, to a planting pan. The edges may be bound together with silk adhesive binding. Glass aquariums, fish globes, cracker and candy jars — in fact, any glass receptacle with a tight-fitting top can be used. The tight cover is to prevent the loss of interior humidity, as the terrarium actually answers the purpose of a miniature greenhouse.

The Wardian case is the oldest type of terrarium.

The uses of the terrarium are many: for home decoration, plant propagation, nature study, scientific observation, centerpiece, and table garden. Experiment with different sizes, shapes and planting materials will produce many odd and beautiful results. The size of the case will limit definitely the choice of the materials, but of more importance are the requirements of the plants. Woodland plantings of lichens, moss, trailing arbutus, violets, anemones, partridge-berries, trilliums, bloodroot, and wood ferns are desired by many as winter house decorations. But steam-heated living rooms, with temperatures of 70° to 75°, are much too warm for these cold-loving plants. These natural woodland plantings can be had, of course, if the temperature can be kept low enough, or the plants replaced easily from time to time.

If moss is used, place it face down in the container, so that a fresh green carpet will be visible from the outside. Then arrange your woodland plants and fill in around their roots with rich loam and more moss. Natural scenes may be copied from the woods, using stones for large boulders, a lichen-covered stick for a log, and a seedling evergreen for a tree. Colorful effects are obtained by the addition of bits of tree-growing fungi, twigs with incrusted growing plants, and low-growing flowering plants to force into bloom. Artificial furnishings should be used with discretion.

A bottle garden is a modern and probably ephemeral variant of the terrarium requiring much deftness in planting.

Sand and large pebbles may be used instead of moss as the drainage layer, with a little charcoal for sweetening. Above this spread an inch or more of topsoil.

Tropical plants with their wealth of color and love of heat and moisture are ideally suited to terrarium culture. Among the best of these are crotons, hoffmanias, all of the warm-house ferns, begonias, African violets, oxalis, peperomias, selaginellas, and creeping philodendrons. Tree-moss, liverworts and creeping nettles like *Helxine* make excellent carpets.

Terrariums require very little care. Watering must be done in moderation, perhaps once in ten days, unless the rooms are excessively hot. No water must be left standing around the roots, or the soil will become sour and soggy. If mold appears, increase the ventilation and it will disappear. If the lid fits very tightly, and the terrarium is given plenty of water, it may safely be left for a number of weeks without attention, as the moisture will condense on the cool glass and drip back into the garden.

**TERRESTRIAL.** Growing in the soil, not in the air as do epiphytes.*

**TESKIT.** A trademarked device for determining the acidity or alkalinity of soils, sold with directions for use.

***TESSELLATA**, -us, -um* (tes-sell-lay′ta). With a dice-like pattern.

***TESTACEA**, -us, -um* (tes-tay′see-a). Brick-colored; also light brown.

**TESTING SOILS.** There are three ways of testing soils, so far as their garden uses are concerned. The first is to determine the acidity or alkalinity of them. For the details of this *see* ACID AND ALKALI SOILS.

The second is to get some idea of their fertility. While growing crops upon them is the best method of determining this, those in a hurry will find a shorter (but not so satisfactory) method described at FERTILITY.

The mechanical constituents of your garden soil require attention, but its analysis is a job for a soil scientist. You can, however, determine its gross features by reading the article at SOILS. And its moisture-holding capacity, which is one of the most important things about all garden soils, is discussed at some length at HUMUS.

***TESTUDO*** (tes-too′do). A tortoise. *See* DEAMIA.

***TETRAGONA**, -us, -um* (tet-trag′o-na). Four-angled.

**TETRAGONIA.** *See* NEW ZEALAND SPINACH.

***TETRAGONOLOBA**, -us, -um* (tet-tra-go-nol′o-ba). With a 4-angled pod.

---

* Special articles on the subjects indicated by an asterisk (*) will be found at the words so marked.

**TETRALIX** (tet-tray'licks). Pre-Linnaean* name for *Erica tetralix*.

**TETRAPANAX** (tet-tra-pay'nacks). A single, Formosan species of shrubs or small trees of the family Araliaceae, generally known as the rice-paper tree, and to science as **T. papyriferum** (but long called *Aralia papyrifera* and *Fatsia papyrifera*). It is a shrub or small tree, without spines, the young foliage more or less felty-hairy. Leaves alternate, large, heart-shaped or ovalish, deeply 5–7-lobed, the margins toothed, the blade nearly 12 in. wide. Flowers greenish, in numerous small globe-shaped heads (umbels*), these arranged in a large woolly cluster (panicle*). Sepals, petals, and stamens* 4 each (5 in the closely related *Fatsia*). Fruit a small, globe-shaped berry. An extremely handsome plant for the shrubbery, but its large leaves, which are very striking, and spreading habit need considerable space. Propagated by seeds or cuttings. The plant is not certainly hardy north of zone* 6, and should have a wind-sheltered, preferably half-shady place. It is widely grown in Formosa as a source of rice-paper. (*Tetrapanax* is from the Greek for four and *Panax*, in allusion to the parts of the flowers being in fours.)

**TETRAPTERA, -us, -um** (tet-trap'ter-a). Four-winged.

**TETTERWORT** = *Sanguinaria canadensis*. See BLOODROOT.

**TEUCRIUM** (too'kri-um). Germander. Perennial herbs or under-shrubs of the mint family, comprising over 150 species, the few below grown for ornament or fragrance, but of secondary hort. interest. They have alternate* leaves, which become smaller and bract*-like near the flower clusters. Flowers in small whorls,* which are arranged in terminal clusters (mostly racemes* or spikes*). Corolla 2-lipped,* the lower lip much larger than the upper. Stamens* 4, conspicuously protruding. Fruit a collection of 4 small nutlets. (Named for King Teucer, first king of Troy; a species name at *Veronica*.)

The cult. germanders are partly herbaceous and hardy over most of the country, but two of them, *T. chamaedrys* and *T. marum*, are under-shrubs and not generally hardy north of zone* 6, although with protection they are grown north of this. None of the species are much grown. Propagated by division or by seeds, and of simple cult. in most garden soils, although *T. marum* appears to be lime-tolerant.

**canadense.** Wood sage. A native, perennial herb, 12–30 in. high. Leaves lance-shaped or ovalish, 3–5 in. long, toothed, hairy on the under side. Flowers purple or paler, about ¾ in. long, the spike 5–7 in. long. Eastern N.A. Summer.

**chamaedrys.** A prostrate or procumbent under-shrub. Leaves ovalish, about ¾ in. long, toothed and hairy. Flowers red-purple or rose, usually spotted with red and white, about ¾ in. long, the spikes loose. Eu. A good bedding plant blooming in late summer, but *see* above for hardiness.

**marum.** A small, white-felty shrub, not very showy but with pleasantly scented foliage. See FRAGRANCE. Leaves ovalish, scarcely ⅓ in. long, without teeth. Flowers purplish, mostly less than ½ in. long, the clusters (spikes*) about 1½ in. long. Mediterranean region. Summer. Grown mostly for its fragrant foliage. For hardiness *see* above.

**orientale.** A perennial herb not over 1 ft. high. Leaves 1½–2 in. long, cut feather-fashion into narrow segments. Flowers about ½ in. long, violet or blue. Western As.

**TEXANA, -us, -um** (teck-say'na). From Texas.

**TEXAN PRIDE** = *Phlox drummondi*.

**TEXAS.** The state lies wholly in zones* 4, 5, 6 and 7. It ranks high in the commercial production of winter and early spring vegetables. Leading summer vegetables are watermelon and sweet potatoes. Most fruits, including apples, berries, peaches, figs, and citrus, are grown commercially in some part of the state. It is unique in combining such diverse geographic conditions within its boundary. In the eastern part the timber belt is not greatly different from the southeastern states. The Gulf Coastal plain is quite distinct from this. The Lower Rio Grande Valley is subtropical. The Edwards plateau in the central western portion is sub-humid. The plains in the Panhandle occasionally experience zero weather. The extreme western portion is semi-arid and almost mountainous in character. With the exception of the apple area in the Davis Mountains, the irrigated region east of El Paso, and the pecan production along the streams of West Texas, the important commercial horticultural development lies east of a line drawn between Wichita Falls and San Antonio, and thence westward to Del Rio.

TEXAS

The zones of hardiness crossing Texas are those shown on the colored map at ZONE, which should be consulted for details. The dates are the average latest killing frost in spring and the first one in the fall. The figures below the dates show the average length of the growing season. Rainfall figures (in inches) are for total annual rainfall in the regions so indicated.

SOILS. The surface soils of the timber country are sandy loams and may be underlain either with a crumbly clay subsoil or a dense clay subsoil. The soils of the coastal plain may be either light or heavy; they are quite fertile and are inclined to be wet. The productive soils of the Rio Grande plain are similar to the coastal plain in character. Irrigation is necessary for fruit and vegetable production in this region. The soils of the large central area, including the Edwards plateau and the Panhandle, are calcareous in nature. An extensive black land strip occurs in the eastern portion. The fruit and vegetable developments are, in general, on the lighter soil types and those of alluvial origin.

CHIEF GARDENING CENTERS. The Ft. Worth–Dallas area, the Houston–Galveston area and the San Antonio area are among the important horticultural centers. This is due to the market for local produce and to a very evident interest in ornamental gardening. The farmers' markets are an important feature of the distributing system. The extensive parks contribute much to a better appreciation of landscape art. Tyler, in Smith County, should be mentioned as the center of an extensive rose industry.

FRUIT AREAS. Citrus growing in the Lower Rio Grande Valley has developed with amazing rapidity within the last few years. Emphasis is upon grapefruit because of its high quality. Grapes are grown commercially around Corpus Christi. Plantings here and elsewhere appear to be on the increase. Plums for the early market are grown south of San Antonio. Peaches are grown at scattered points over a vast area, covering approximately the northeastern quarter of the state. The Galveston–Houston region grows the most strawberries. There is also some production in the northeastern corner of the state and in the Winter Garden below Uvalde. Figures from the fifteenth census place Smith County first in the entire country in blackberry and dewberry production. Pecans are grown chiefly on bottom land

---

* Special articles on the subjects indicated by an asterisk (*) will be found at the words so marked.

in the central and eastern portions. Much of the yield comes from native trees. Figs are particularly well adapted to the Gulf Coast east of the Colorado River. Production depends almost entirely upon market conditions. Date growing appears to be a possibility in the country east of Eagle Pass, but this has yet to be demonstrated.

VEGETABLE AREAS. According to the fifteenth census Texas ranks first in area devoted to beets, onions and spinach, second in okra, parsley, radish, sweet potatoes, and watermelons, third in broccoli, carrots and rutabagas, and fourth in area devoted to cabbage, cantaloupe, and eggplant. In addition to citrus the Lower Rio Grande Valley grows large quantities of winter and spring vegetables. These include beets, carrots, cabbage, onions, potatoes, tomatoes, and green corn. Others, such as snap beans and spinach, are grown in somewhat smaller amounts. These are all under irrigation. In the Corpus Christi area most of these are grown under dry land conditions. The Winter Garden region, to the east of Eagle Pass, specializes in spinach and onions under irrigation. While individual plantings of early tomatoes are not large in east Texas, this crop is grown commercially over a wider area than any vegetable except Irish and sweet potatoes, and watermelons. Carlot shipments from the Lower Rio Grande Valley begin about May 1 and the harvest season moves northward as the season advances. The region around Palestine is the most important in east Texas. The largest sweet-potato acreage is found in the northeast corner of the state. Onion production is concentrated in the Laredo and Corpus Christi districts, in the Winter Garden and in Collin County north of Dallas, where onion seed is produced successfully. Seed production is a recent development. While watermelons are grown pretty much all over the state, the heaviest production is to the south of San Antonio. Brooks County, just north of the Lower Valley, is also a heavy producer.

ORNAMENTALS. Texas has a great deal of native material of ornamental value. The annuals and perennials are very numerous both as to number of species and especially as to number of individuals, since they literally cover the countryside with bloom in the spring. Perhaps the most noted of these is the Texas bluebonnet (*Lupinus texensis*). Other flowers which paint the landscape are the brilliant, red, Indian blanket, *Rudbeckia*, *Oenothera*, and *Verbena* to mention but a few. The Bluebell (*Eustoma*) is conspicuous for the size of its flowers. The cacti provide more variety of both form and color than any other single group. The agaves, yuccas and related types are characteristic of the southwest. Dry-land ferns are found in the hills of southwest Texas.

In the eastern timber belt the trees and shrubs are for the most part the same as those found farther east. They include the red cedar, the pines, which form the basis for a lumber industry, the broad-leaved evergreens, such as the magnolia, live oak and American holly, and many deciduous trees, such as sweet gum and tulip-tree. Yaupon (*Ilex vomitoria*) is perhaps the best native evergreen shrub. When established it is drought-resistant and hardy. Agarita (*Mahonia trifoliolata*) provides exceptionally interesting foliage. Selected individuals of both of these shrubs have very attractive berries. Deciduous shrubs with attractive fruits are the Coralberry (*Symphoricarpos orbiculatus*) and the French mulberry (*Callicarpa americana*).

Farther west in the range country the shrubs occupy a dominant position, not only in the landscape but in the lives of the people. "When the Bloom is on the Sage" is much more than a song. The leading spirits of the "Brush" are the acacias, huisache and many others, such as *Mimosa*, mesquite, and petama. Many of these brilliant-flowered shrubs are still called by their Mexican names.

CLIMATE. There is an immense range in climatic conditions within the state, which intimately affects the gardening activities of the various regions. The Lower Rio Grande Valley is sub-tropical; the Panhandle, which frequently has sub-zero weather in the winter, is very different. Similarly, the annual rainfall is much greater in the eastern than in the western part of the state. Important factors in garden-

ing here, as elsewhere, are the soil, the available water and variations in the temperature. More can be done to ameliorate the first two than is possible in the case of the latter. The extent of cold damage in the winter is largely dependent upon the extent of the preceding warm period. Plants that are easily seduced by a week or two of balmy weather must be placed on the north side of a building or some place where the winter growth will be discouraged. While the mild winters permit large acreages of the hardier vegetables and citrus in the southern areas, the peach growers in the northern part are dependent upon the winter cold to break the dormancy of their trees for a full crop. In the fertile irrigated valleys the disadvantage of light rainfall is partially offset by the small amount of disease present as a result of the low humidity.

The isotherms roughly parallel the coast except in the western part of the state. The following table gives some idea of the situation with respect to the growing season.

TEXAS FROST DATA

| Town | Average date of last killing frost in spring | Latest known killing frost | Average date of earliest killing frost in fall | Earliest known killing frost |
|---|---|---|---|---|
| Brownsville | Feb. 15 | Mar. 8, 1920 | Dec. 10 | Nov. 14, 1901 |
| Eagle Pass | Feb. 27 | Apr. 5, 1920 | Nov. 26 | Oct. 20, 1903 |
| Beaumont | Feb. 28 | Apr. 3, 1915 | Nov. 23 | Oct. 29, 1917 |
| Tyler | Mar. 16 | Apr. 25, 1910 | Nov. 18 | Oct. 20, 1917 |
| Lubbock | Apr. 9 | May 7, 1917 | Nov. 2 | Oct. 19, 1916 |

The greatest rainfall occurs in the eastern portion, decreasing farther west. This ranges from something over 50 inches in the southeast corner to 10 inches at El Paso. The eastern half of the state receives between 30 and 50 inches of rainfall annually. Just west of this is a sub-humid region receiving between 15 and 30 inches. It includes the Panhandle and extends a little east of south to the coast. The country west of a line extending from the southeast corner of New Mexico to Laredo is, in general, semi-arid with arid portions. Most horticultural crops, including apples, pears and a variety of vegetables, are grown under irrigation in this region. See IRRIGATION.

The address of the Agricultural Experiment Station, which has kindly supplied this information about the state, is College Station, and its staff is always ready to answer gardening questions.

Garden Club activities include clubs affiliated with the Garden Club of America, the home office of which is 598 Madison Avenue, New York, N.Y. There are also nearly 70 clubs affiliated with the Texas Federation of Garden Clubs. For the one in your vicinity write Garden Editor, Houghton Mifflin Company, Boston, Mass. See also HORTICULTURAL SOCIETIES.

**TEXAS BLUEBONNET** = *Lupinus texensis*.

**TEXAS BUCKTHORN OR JUJUBE** = *Zizyphus obtusifolia*.

**TEXAS MILLET** = *Panicum texanum*.

**TEXAS PLUME** = *Gilia rubra*.

**TEXAS SAGE** = *Salvia coccinea*.

**TEXAS UMBRELLA TREE** = *Melia azedarach umbraculiformis*.

*TEXENSIS, -e* (tecks-en′sis). From Texas.

*TEXTILIS, -e* (tecks′till-is). Woven; or useful for weaving textiles.

**THALIA** (thay′li-a). Canna-like, swamp or aquatic perennial herbs of the family Marantaceae, comprising about a dozen species from the warmer parts of America, one of them, **T. dealbata**, the water canna, often grown for ornament. It grows wild from S. Car. to Fla., but north of this it had better be grown in a greenhouse pool, or at least not allowed

---

* Special articles on the subjects indicated by an asterisk (*) will be found at the words so marked.

to freeze. It is a white-powdery, stemless herb, the slender leafstalks nearly 2 ft. long, the blade ovalish, 16-24 in. long, more or less heart-shaped at the base, and without teeth. Flowers dull violet, borne in spikes at the end of a hollow stalk 4-5 ft. high. Corolla very irregular,* and some of the sterile stamens* petal-like. It does best in wet soil or in shallow water. (Named for Johann Thalius, German naturalist.)

**THALICTRIFOLIA, -us, -um** (tha-lick-tri-fō′li-a). With leaves like the meadow rue.

**THALICTROIDES** (tha-lick-troy′deez, but *see* OÏDES). Like a meadow rue.

**THALICTRUM** (tha-lick′trum). Meadow rue. A large genus of graceful, perennial herbs of the buttercup family, most of the 100 species found in the temperate zone, and a few of them cult. for ornament. They have basal or alternate* leaves which are twice- or thrice-compound,* the ultimate leaflets of many species suggesting those of the maidenhair ferns. Flowers small, but handsome because of the usually large, terminal, often branching clusters (panicles* or racemes*). Petals none. Sepals sometimes colored and petal-like. Stamens* numerous and often providing most of the color. In many species the flowers are unisexual* or even dioecious (the male and female on different plants). Fruit a collection of small, ribbed or grooved achenes.* (*Thalictrum* is Latin for meadow rue.)

The European and Asiatic species below are far better garden plants than the native American sorts, most of which grow in moist meadows and are best suited to low, sunny places in the wild garden. All are of easy cult. and may be divided in the spring. While over 20 species are in cult. in the U.S., those below are among the best. Most of them, except *T. dipterocarpum*, bloom in early summer.

**aquilegifolium.** A branching herb 2-3 ft. high. Ultimate leaflets nearly round or oblongish, broadly few-toothed toward the tip. Male and female flowers on separate plants, the male flowers the more showy from the numerous pinkish-purple stamens,* which are longer than the white sepals. Eurasia. A handsome plant for the herbaceous border; known in several color forms, as white, dark purple and orange.

**dioicum.** Early meadow rue; also called silverweed. A native meadow plant, 1-2 ft. high. Ultimate leaflets roundish, bluntly 5-9-lobed. Male and female flowers on separate plants, the greenish-yellow stamens longer than the similarly colored sepals. Eastern U.S. Plant in low, open places in the wild garden.

**dipterocarpum.** A showy, Chinese plant, 1-2 ft. high, the roundish, notched, ultimate leaflets bluish-green on the under side. Flowers nodding, the cluster much-branched, the pale rose or lilac-lavender sepals nearly as long as the stamens. Western China. Late summer. *See* GRAY AND LAVENDER GARDEN.

**glaucum.** A bluish-green perennial, 3-4 ft. high. Ultimate leaflets ovalish, 3-lobed, and the lobes toothed. Flower clusters (panicles*) dense, the flowers yellow, the stamens longer than the sepals. Southern Eu.

**minus.** A low border plant 8-18 in. high, the ultimate leaflets very small, roundish and 3-lobed. Flowers greenish-yellow, drooping, in small, loose clusters. Eurasia and northern Af.

**polygamum.** Tall meadow rue. A branching, native meadow plant 6-8 ft. high. Ultimate leaflets roundish or oblongish, 3-lobed. Flowers small, but very numerous, in a large, branched, terminal cluster, the stamens and white sepals of about equal length. Eastern N.A. Suited to low, open places in the wild garden.

**THALLUS.** The plant body of the algae, mosses, lichens, and a few fungi, which, unlike that of flowering plants, has no true stem, leaves, or root. For the structure known as prothallus *see* Spores and Reproduction at FERNS AND FERN GARDENING.

**THAPSUS** (thap′sus). An old name for the mullein (*Verbascum thapsus*).

**THATCH PALM** = *Coccothrinax argentea*.

**THAWS AND THAWING.** Alternate thawing and freezing in late winter and early spring is usually more damaging than low temperatures. While no one can control this condition, there are things one can do in the garden to ward off its worst effects.

These are twofold. Perhaps the most serious is the opportunity it provides for susceptible woody plants to start into inopportune growth, which is often disastrous if followed by a hard freeze. It is also a particularly trying time for all broad-leaved evergreens and conifers, because a sudden warm spell puts a sudden demand for water upon the roots which they may not, and often cannot, meet. This impetuous water requirement, induced by a few warm, unseasonable days, kills or "burns," as the gardeners say, more plants than wintry blasts. To overcome the worst effects of thawing and freezing, it is necessary to understand just what hardiness is and what plant protection may do. Neither subject will be discussed here for both are fully covered at the articles HARDINESS and PROTECTING PLANTS.

The other effect of thawing and freezing is upon the soil, which in most reasonably moist soils results in heaving. Nothing can be more disastrous to shallow-rooted, perennial herbs, or to the lawn. For the first *see* HEAVING. For the heaving of lawns and what to do for it *see* Rolling at LAWN.

**THEA** (tee′a). Asiatic, mostly evergreen shrubs and trees of the family Theaceae, comprising about 14 species, only one of hort. significance, **T. sinensis**, the tea plant, grown more for interest than ornament, as no tea is produced commercially in the U.S. It is a shrub or small tree, never over 30 ft. high, and as cult. usually a small shrub. It has alternate,* leathery, more or less elliptic leaves (the source of tea), 2-5 in. long, and shallowly toothed. Flowers white, about 1½ in. wide, fragrant, nodding, solitary or in 2-4-flowered clusters. Sepals 5-7. Petals 5, partly united at the base. Stamens numerous, in 2 series. Fruit a woody capsule.* India and China. The tea plant is somewhat grown in the U.S., and needs the same cultural care as the closely related genus *Camellia* (which see). There are a few enthusiasts, notably in S. Car., who started the commercial growing of tea, but it has never been much more than an interesting experiment in the U.S. For the plant often advertised as *Thea japonica see* CAMELLIA JAPONICA. (*Thea* is the Latinized version of the Chinese name for tea.)

**THEACEAE** (tee-ā′see-ee). The tea family, besides the shrub yielding tea (*see* THEA), contains a few other genera of shrubs and trees of considerable garden interest. The family comprises only 16 genera and about 175 species, mostly from warm or tropical regions.

Of these *Camellia* is easily the most important. Requiring greenhouse culture also is *Eurya* (evergreen), although both genera can be grown outdoors in regions where the oleander will stand the winter. Two cult. genera with interesting American species are *Stewartia* and *Gordonia*, both with relatively showy flowers.

Leaves simple,* alternate,* usually leathery and often evergreen. Flowers solitary or a few together, often (*Stewartia, Gordonia* and especially *Camellia*) strikingly handsome. Fruit usually a dry, splitting pod (capsule*), but sometimes fleshy or dry and not splitting.

Technical flower characters: Flowers hermaphrodite.* Sepals 5-7, separate or united at the base, often with 2 bracts* below. Petals mostly 5, separate or united at the base (doubled in some hort. varieties of *Camellia*). Stamens* many (seldom 5), usually more or less joined at the base and joined often to the base of the petals. Ovary superior,* 2-10-celled.

**THE BRIDE.** *See* ANEMONE CORONARIA.

**THEIFERA, -us, -um** (tee-iff′er-ra). Tea-bearing; often merely tea-like or with the fragrance of tea.

**THELESPERMA** (thell-e-sper′ma). Coreopsis-like, and in ours, annual herbs of the family Compositae, comprising about 7 species, of which **T. burridgeanum**, from Tex., is a hardy flower garden annual. It has been called, at times, *Coreopsis atrosanguinea, Thelesperma hybridum,* and *Cosmidium burridgeanum.* It is a hardy annual (*see* ANNUALS) which should be sown where wanted, and a branching herb 12-18 in. high. Leaves alternate* and opposite,* much-divided into thread-like segments. Flower heads about 1½ in. wide, long-stalked, the ray* flowers reddish-brown or orange, the margins yellow. It differs only in technical characters from *Coreopsis*, and needs an open, sunny place. Aug.-Sept. (*Thelesperma* is from the Greek for wart and seed, in allusion to the warty achenes* of some species.)

**THELOCACTUS** (thell-o-kak′tus). Medium-sized, more or less globe-shaped cacti from Tex. and adjacent Mex., comprising about a dozen species, of which **T. bicolor,**

---

* Special articles on the subjects indicated by an asterisk (*) will be found at the words so marked.

closely related to *Echinocactus*, is cult. for ornament or interest in desert gardens in the Southwest, and in the succulent greenhouse northward. The plant body is globe-shaped or conical, about 3½ in. in diameter, usually with 8 low ribs. Spines very numerous, colored, 9–18 divaricating ones in a cluster, in the center of which are 4 stouter and erectish spines. Flowers pinkish-purple, nearly 2 in. long. For culture see CACTI. (*Thelocactus* is from the Greek for nipple and *Cactus*, in allusion to the nipple-like tubercles on the ribs.)

**THELYPTERIS** = *Dryopteris*.

*THELYPTEROIDES* (thell-lip-ter-roy'deez, but see OÏDES). Like a fern of the genus *Thelypteris*, here included within *Dryopteris*.

**THEOBROMA** (thee-o-brō'ma). A small, but commercially very important genus of tropical American shrubs and trees of the family Sterculiaceae. The chief species is **T. cacao**, the chocolate tree, and in the tropics widely cult. as the source of chocolate and cocoa. It is an evergreen tree, 20–25 ft. high, with alternate,* leathery, oblongish leaves, 8–12 in. long and without marginal teeth. Flowers small, yellowish, borne mostly on the bark of the larger branches and the trunk (for structure see STERCULIACEAE). Fruit a large, woody, ribbed, reddish-brown capsule,* filled with a whitish, rather evil-smelling paste in which are embedded the seeds (the cacao beans of commerce). These are about the size of a Lima bean and the source of both chocolate and cocoa. The plant can only be grown in zone* 9, and nowhere in the U.S. is there heat and moisture enough to make chocolate plantations profitable. (*Theobroma* is Greek for food of the gods, which the Aztecs and Mayans called it.) The name for the tree and its seeds in most tropical countries is cacao.

**THEOPHRASTUS.** See GARDEN BOOKS.

**THERMOMETER.** The only caution regarding thermometers, which are necessary for the mushroom bed, cold frames, hotbeds, and greenhouses, is to remember that in all these places there is much moisture at times. This means condensation on the thermometers, which, in consequence, had better be of glass and wood, or all glass, but not of metal, or of only rustless metal.

**THERMOPSIS** (ther-mop'sis). A genus of North American and Asiatic, rather showy-flowered, perennial herbs of the pea family, at least three of them grown in the herbaceous border for ornament. Leaves alternate,* compound,* with 3 leaflets. Flowers yellow (in ours), pea-like, in chiefly terminal, erect clusters (racemes*). Fruit an oblongish, straight or curved pod (legume*), flattened or inflated. (*Thermopsis* is from the Greek for lupine-like, in allusion to their resemblance to lupines.) Most of them have large, leaf-like, sometimes clasping stipules.*

Of simple culture in most garden soils, but doing better in light, well-drained soils than in heavy ones. They have deep roots and are more drought-resistant than most garden plants. Propagated by spring division of the rootstocks, or by seeds. But the seed should be sown when fresh, and is rather slow to germinate.

**caroliniana.** Aaron's-rod. A stout, smooth-stemmed, mostly unbranched herb 3–5 ft. high. Leaflets oblongish, silky-hairy beneath. Flower cluster 8–12 in. long, rather stiffly erect. Pod hoary, about 2 in. long. N. Car. to Ga. June–July.

**fabacea.** A somewhat silky-hairy herb, 12–18 in. high. Leaflets oblongish, 1–3 in. long. Flower cluster a long, spike-like raceme,* but mostly in the leaf-axils and not terminal. Pods hairy, not spreading, the seeds compressed. Siberia. May–June.

**mollis.** Bush pea. An erect, branched, hairy herb, 2–3 ft. high. Leaflets oblongish, 1–2 in. long. Flower cluster (raceme*) terminal, 6–9 in. long. Pod 2–4 in. long, somewhat curved at the tip. Va. to Ga. June–July.

**THESPESIA** (thess-pee'zi-a). Tropical Old World trees (rarely shrubs or herbs) of the mallow family, comprising about 10 species. The only one of hort. interest is **T. populnea**, the bendy tree, also called Portia tree and seaside mahoe, much planted in seaside gardens in Fla., the Gulf Coast, and in Calif., and not hardy elsewhere in the U.S. It is a dense-canopied tree, 30–50 ft. high, with alternate,* long-stalked, ovalish or heart-shaped leaves, which are 2½–4½ in. long and poplar-like. Flowers bell-shaped, showy, yellow, 2–3 in. wide, mostly in the leaf-axils.* Calyx* 5-parted. Petals 5. Fruit a woody, 5-valved capsule* which often does not split. Tropics of As., Af., and Pacific Islands, widely planted and naturalized in Fla., where it blooms in late spring or early summer, although in the tropics it may bloom continuously. Does well in sandy soils. Propagated by seed. (*Thespesia* is from the Greek for divine, and of uncertain application here.)

**THEVETIA** (thev-vee'shi-a). A genus of tropical American shrubs or small trees of the family Apocynaceae, one of the ten species commonly cult. in zones* 8 and 9 under the name of yellow oleander and known to science as **T. nereifolia**. It is an evergreen shrub or small tree with oleander-like foliage, and showy, yellow, fragrant flowers. Leaves alternate,* leathery, about 4 in. long and ¼ in. wide, the margins rolled. Flowers in a terminal, stalked cluster (cyme*), the corolla funnel-shaped, 2–3 in. long, the limb slightly twisted and longer than the tube. Fruit fleshy, black, about 1 in. wide, triangular (a drupe*), the flesh rather thin. A very popular ornamental for sub-tropical gardens, needing, in the young state, to be protected from occasional frosts by heaping up earth or sand around the base of the plant. It grows well in the sandy soils of the South and may be propagated by cuttings. (Named for André Thevet, French monk who explored Brazil.)

*THIBETICA, -us, -um* (ti-bet'i-ka). From Tibet.

**THIEF.** A somewhat fanciful, but not inappropriate name for a sucker.*

**THIMBLEBERRY** = *Rubus occidentalis*.

**THIMBLE-FLOWER** = *Rudbeckia hirta*.

**THIMBLE POT.** See FLOWER POTS.

**THINNING.** A common hort. operation having two objects. One involves the sacrificing of the plants or flowers removed for the benefit of the ones left behind. It is an operation widely practiced both in flower and fruit production where excellence rather than quantity is desired. For the details of this in fruit cult. see Thinning at PRUNING. In flowers, it is usually done by pinching out buds, and all commercial growers practice it. See DISBUDDING.

Thinning in another sense is equally important. It involves the pulling out of certain seedlings in a row for the sake of those left. Wherever this is necessary, it has been mentioned in the cultural articles throughout THE DICTIONARY. Where the thinned seedlings are to be saved and replanted, as in many young vegetable plants and flowers, the operation is usually known as pricking-out. See the Management of Seedlings at SEEDS AND SEEDAGE.

**THIN SOIL.** A poor soil, deficient in humus or plant food or both. See SOILS.

**THISTLE.** Usually prickly leaved herbs of the genera *Cirsium* or *Carduus*. See both genera. But many other plants have been called thistle or the word is part of their names. For those in THE GARDEN DICTIONARY see CNICUS, ECHINOPS, ONOPORDON, SALSOLA (see Russian thistle in the list at WEEDS), SCOLYMUS, and SILYBUM.

**THISTLE FAMILY.** See COMPOSITAE.

**THOMASIA** (toe-mass'i-a). A genus of 25 species of Australian, rather low, evergreen shrubs of the family Sterculiaceae, the two below occasionally grown for ornament in southern Calif., but otherwise little known in the U.S. They have alternate* leaves and white or purple flowers in terminal clusters (racemes*). Calyx of 5 sepals, more or less petal-like, and partly united. Petals none. Stamens* 5, or sometimes with 5 extra, sterile, ones. Fruit a capsule.* (Named for the brothers Thomas, who collected Swiss plants.)

The first species is somewhat grown as a ground cover in southern Calif. Propagated by cuttings of side shoots

---

* Special articles on the subjects indicated by an asterisk (*) will be found at the words so marked.

rooted under a bell-jar in sand. The species, as yet, are little known in America. Neither is over 3 ft. high.

**purpurea.** Leaves oblong or narrower, about ¾ in. long, hairy on the under side, less so above. Flowers purplish, the clusters longer than the leaves.

**rugosa.** Leaves heart-shaped or ovalish, lobed, 2–3 in. long and wrinkled, densely hairy or felty beneath, only slightly hairy above. Flowers white.

**THOMAS, J. J.** See America at GARDEN BOOKS.

**THORN.** As a common name thorn is properly applied to the hawthorns, for which *see* CRATAEGUS. But it has also been applied to many other plants or is part of their name. Those in THE GARDEN DICTIONARY and their proper equivalents are:

Blackthorn = *Prunus spinosa;* Box-thorn = *Lycium;* Buckthorn = *Rhamnus;* Christ's-thorn = *Paliurus spina-christi;* Jerusalem thorn = *Paliurus spina-christi* and *Parkinsonia aculeata;* Kangaroo thorn = *Acacia armata.*

**THORN.** A woody spine and nearly always a modified branch, as proved by the nearly universal origin in a bud (*see* SPINE). Technically, a rose does not have thorns but prickles, while true thorns are found on such plants as the hawthorn and honey locust (*Gleditsia*).

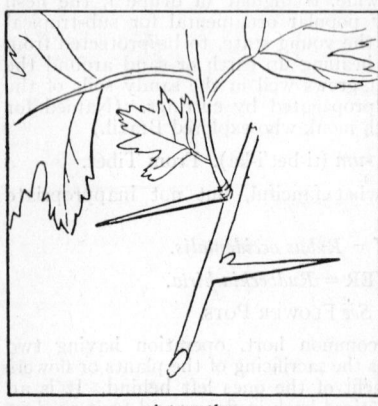

A true thorn

**THORNAPPLE** = *Datura stramonium.* See also CRATAEGUS.

**THORNY LOCUST** = *Robinia neo-mexicana.* See LOCUST.

**THOROUGHWORT.** See EUPATORIUM.

**THOUSAND-FLOWERED ASTER.** See BOLTONIA.

**THOUSAND-HEADED CABBAGE** = Brussels sprouts.

**THOUSAND-LEGS.** See Insect Pests at CINERARIA and SWEET PEA.

**THRASHER.** See BIRDS.

**THREE-QUARTER POT.** See FLOWER POTS.

**THREE-THORNED ACACIA** = *Gleditsia triacanthos.* See HONEY LOCUST.

**THREE-TOOTHED CINQUEFOIL** = *Potentilla tridentata.*

**THRIFT.** See STATICE. For the prickly thrift *see* ACANTHOLIMON.

**THRINAX** (thry'nacks). A small genus of unarmed fan palms of southern Fla., the W.I. and Central America, a few of which are occasionally dug from the wild in extreme southern Fla., but one of them, **T. microcarpa,** the silvertop palmetto (also called prickly thatch and brittle thatch), quite widely planted for ornament. It is 20–30 ft. high, the fan-like leaves nearly 2 ft. wide, and densely silvery on the under side, but pale green above, divided into many deeply cleft, pointed and stiffish segments. Flower cluster from among the leaves, not long, the perfect* flowers borne on short, thick stalks. Fruit white-fleshed, scarcely ⅓ in. in diameter. The palm grows well on sandy soils, but is not certainly hardy north of zone* 9. For the palm sometimes called *Thrinax argentea see* COCCOTHRINAX ARGENTEA. (*Thrinax* is Greek for a fan, in allusion to the fan-like leaves.)

**THRIPS.** See Thrips at INSECT PESTS. Notes on their control will be found at the Insect Pests at AVOCADO, BLUEBERRY, ORANGE, PEAR, CARNATION, CYCLAMEN, and GLADIOLUS.

**THROAT.** The opening to the tubular part of a corolla, usually at the point where the limb* and tube meet.

**THROATWORT** = *Trachelium caeruleum.*

**THRUM-EYED.** See PIN-EYED.

**THRUSH.** See BIRDS.

**THRYALLIS** (thry-all'is). Horticulturally desirable shrubs of the family Malpighiaceae, some 15 species being scattered from Tex. and Calif. to Brazil. Only one of them, **T. glauca** (sometimes mistakenly called *T. brasiliensis*), is occasionally cult. for ornament from zone* 7 southward. It is a shrub 3–5 ft. high, with bluish-green foliage, the leaves opposite,* without marginal teeth, more or less oblong, 1–2 in. long. Flowers yellow, about ¾ in. wide, borne in slender-stalked clusters (for details *see* MALPIGHIACEAE). Fruit a 3-valved capsule.* A handsome but little cult. shrub, sometimes grown under glass. Use potting mixture* 4 and keep in the warm-temperate greenhouse. (*Thryallis* is an old Greek name for some plant, but adopted by Linnaeus for this genus.)

**THUJA** (thew'ya). Arborvitae. Extremely valuable, evergreen, hort. and timber trees of the pine family, found in N.A. and eastern As., comprising only 6 species but with innumerable hort. varieties, most of which are low or at

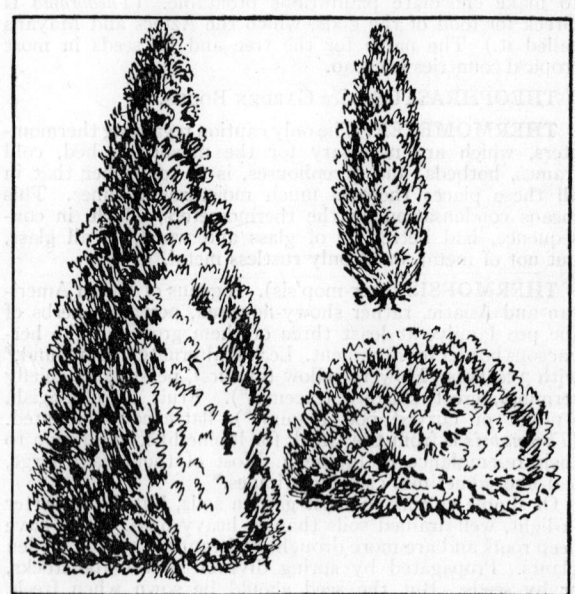

Various outlines of the American arborvitae: Tree form (*left*), and the globular and columnar dwarf hort. forms at the right.

least not tree-like. The wild trees are magnificent forest evergreens and widely cut for timber, especially in the Pacific Northwest. They usually form a pyramidal head. Twigs densely covered with the tiny, scale-like leaves, and standing in flat, fan-like sprays or fronds, the leaves completely covering the twigs. Flowers none, in the usual garden sense, being represented by 6–12 stamens* in the male flower, the female flowers ultimately forming an egg-shaped or oblongish cone with its scales green and keeled, and not resembling the familiar pine cone. (*Thuja* is the old Greek name for them, and is sometimes spelled *Thuya*.)

The hort. forms of *T. occidentalis* and *T. orientalis* are among the most widely planted evergreens in the country.

---

* Special articles on the subjects indicated by an asterisk (*) will be found at the words so marked.

As will be seen below, they come in a large variety of shapes and colors. The low or dwarf or bushy kinds are very widely used for foundation planting, for evergreen groups at gateways, and for specimens on the lawn.

Wherever arborvitae grows naturally there is coolness and moisture, and the cult. species will always do best in such regions. But there are millions of them cult. in city courtyards, for accent* plants, in window boxes (dwarf forms) and wherever a handsome evergreen is needed for winter decoration.

While many thousands of *Thuja* are annually set out in cities, the plants do not like wind, dust, or smoke, and few of them survive such an environment for more than a season or two. Away from these conditions, and in places without too much summer heat and too little rain, the arborvitae is one of the finest cult. evergreens. They do especially well along the coast from L.I. to Canada, and in the Pacific Northwest, but indifferently in the central U.S. where their cult. is at least hazardous. For their culture and propagation *see* EVERGREENS. Of the six known species three are grown quite generally in the U.S.

**dolobrata** = *Thujopsis dolobrata*.

**occidentalis.** The American arborvitae; called also white cedar and northern white cedar. A medium-sized evergreen tree, rarely over 60 ft. high, the trunk buttressed at the base, the bark reddish-brown and furrowed. Leaves dark green or golden-green, the frond-like, fan-shaped, leaf-clothed twigs very handsome. Cones oblong, about ½ in. long, green at first, ultimately brownish, angled. Eastern N.A. Hardy from zone* 2 southward, but not in the warm, dry parts of the coastal plain. The common tree form, described above, is rather rare in cult., but has been the origin of innumerable hort. varieties, all of them much lower, shrubby or even dwarf. There are also many forms with variously colored foliage. Of the many varieties in cult. (perhaps over 100) the leading and most horticulturally useful are:

*var.* **alba.** Queen Victoria arborvitae. Tips of the young foliage white.

*var.* **boothi.** A low, compact form with larger leaves than some of the others.

*var.* **columbia.** Foliage variegated with silver; a shrubby form.

*var.* **compacta.** A form with dense, low habit.

*var.* **douglasi aurea.** Foliage bronzy-yellow.

*var.* **douglasi pyramidalis.** A low form with pyramidal habit and handsome, fern-like twigs.

*var.* **ellwangeriana.** A low shrub with juvenile* and adult leaves.

*var.* **ellwangeriana aurea.** Similar to the one above, but the foliage yellow.

*var.* **fastigiata.** A columnar shrub, the branches short and upright. A good accent* plant.

*var.* **globosa.** A very common form in cult., with a nearly perfect dome-shaped habit; useful for accent* plants.

*var.* **hoveyi.** A dwarf form with a globe-shaped head of bright green foliage.

*var.* **lutea.** George Peabody arborvitae. A moderate-sized, shrubby form, of pyramidal habit and bright yellow foliage.

*var.* **umbraculifera.** A dwarf form with an umbrella-shaped outline.

*var.* **variegata.** A shrubby form with white-variegated foliage.

*var.* **vervaeneana.** A small, dense-foliaged form with bronzy leaves.

**orientalis.** Oriental arborvitae. A rather low, bushy tree, often branching near the base, the bark reddish-brown and scaly. Leaves all alike, the frond-like foliage bright green. Cones egg-shaped, about 1 in. long, rather fleshy and bluish in youth. China and Korea. Hardy from zone* 4 southward, and sometimes sold as *Biota*. Its leading hort. varieties are:

*var.* **aurea-compacta.** A low, compact form with yellow foliage, especially in spring, gradually becoming green.

*var.* **aurea-nana.** A dwarf form with yellow, spring foliage, ultimately becoming green.

*var.* **compacta.** A dwarf and compact form.

*var.* **elegantissima.** A compact form, the foliage in early spring bright yellow.

*var.* **semperaurescens.** A shrubby form, the leaves more or less permanently golden.

**plicata.** Western red cedar; also called red cedar and giant arborvitae. A magnificent forest evergreen, and an extremely valuable timber tree, reaching up to 200 ft. high — never in cult. anything like this. Leaves bright green, but white-marked below. Cones oblong, about ¾ in. long. An extremely ornamental tree, native from Alaska to northern Calif. and Mont., mostly in regions of copious rainfall and fog. Hardy in the East only in zones* 3, 4, and 5, and precariously so if winter winds are bitter and summer droughts too protracted. Its leading hort. varieties are:

*var.* **atrovirens.** Foliage dark green.

*var.* **aurea.** Leaves yellowish.

*var.* **fastigiata.** A columnar form with erect branches.

*var.* **pendula.** A form with drooping branches.

**THUJOPSIS** (thew-yop'sis). A single species of Japanese evergreen trees of the pine family, **T. dolobrata**, the false or Hiba arborvitae, often grown for ornament. It resembles, and is closely related to, the true arborvitae (*Thuja*), differing in having woody, instead of somewhat herbaceous cone scales. It is a tree up to 50 ft. high, the foliage in flat, frond-like sprays, the leaves glossy above, but with a broad white band beneath. Cones egg-shaped, scarcely ½ in. long, the scales flat and woody. For culture *see* EVERGREENS. Hardy from zone* 4 southward, but only in regions of adequate summer moisture. It does not do well, or fails, in regions of summer heat and dryness. There are dwarf and variegated-leaved forms. Sometimes known as *Thuja dolobrata*. (*Thujopsis* is from the Greek, meaning like *Thuja*.)

**THUMB POT.** See FLOWER POTS.

**THUNBERGIA** (thune-ber'ji-a). Mostly Asiatic or African, tender, woody or herbaceous vines or shrubs of the family Acanthaceae, comprising over 75 species, those below grown for ornament. Leaves opposite,* often arrow-shaped at the base. Flowers showy, solitary in the leaf-axils,* variously colored, and below them 2 or more leafy bracts.* Corolla funnel-shaped or bell-shaped, sometimes curved, the limb regular* or nearly so, not 2-lipped.* Fruit a beaked capsule.* (Named for Carl Peter Thunberg, noted Swedish botanical author, a traveler in Jap. and South Af., and a student of Linnaeus.*)

These are popular vines in Calif. and the South, and are sometimes grown in the warm greenhouse northward. Use potting mixture* 3, or plant directly in the soil if possible. They are fairly rampant vines and will cover trellises or porches in a short time. Some of the species are more hardy than others, as noted below. Propagated by cuttings or by layering.

**alata.** Black-eyed Susan. An herbaceous vine, actually a perennial, but it will bloom from seed in one year if the growing season is long. Leaves ovalish or triangular, toothed, 2-3 in. long, the stalk winged. Flowers long-stalked, solitary, about 1½ in. long, white but purple-throated. Tropical Africa. Midsummer and later. See VINES.

**erecta.** A shrubby, vine-like plant, not usually over 6 ft. high. Leaves ovalish, 2-3 in. long, the marginal teeth few or none. Flowers nearly 2½ in. long, bluish-purple, the tube white. Tropical Africa. Not hardy north of zone* 8.

**fragrans.** Mountain creeper. An evergreen, woody vine, somewhat resembling *T. grandiflora*, but more delicate in growth. Flowers pure white, about 1½ in. long, the tube slender, the limb flaring. India. Not certainly hardy north of zone* 9, possibly in zone* 8 with protection.

**gibsoni.** A perennial, herbaceous vine, the ovalish leaves 2-3 in. long, and with winged stalks. Flowers about 1¾ in. long, orange, solitary and long-stalked, the stalks hairy. Tropical Africa. In Calif. it may be grown as a biennial or annual if the growing season is long.

**grandiflora.** Sky-flower. The best known of the genus and a handsome, evergreen, woody vine. Leaves ovalish, 6-8 in. long, rough, 3-veined, the margins angularly toothed. Flowers blue (rarely white) nearly 3 in. long, in drooping clusters (racemes*), very showy. Corolla distinctly, but not deeply, 2-lipped.* India. Aug.-Dec. A rapidly growing, handsome, evergreen creeper, much planted in Fla. and Calif. Hardy from protected parts of zone* 7 southward.

**THURLOW'S WEEPING WILLOW** = *Salix elegantissima*. See WILLOW.

**THUYA** = *Thuja*.

**THYME.** Pleasantly aromatic woody perennials, or under-shrubs of the mint family, comprising the genus **Thymus** (ty'mus) which contains over 50 species, most of them from the Mediterranean region. Two are widely grown for ornament or for their fragrant herbage, used as seasoning. They are erect or nearly prostrate plants with small, opposite* leaves without marginal teeth, diminishing in the flower cluster to tiny, leaf-like bracts.* Flowers lilac or purplish (in ours), small, mostly clustered in few-flowered whorls,* these distant, or the clusters in the leaf-axils.* Calyx tubular, but 2-lipped.* Corolla usually half hidden by the calyx, slightly 2-lipped. Fruit a collection of 4 smooth nutlets. (*Thymus* is an old Greek name for some fragrant plant, perhaps savory or these.)

For the culture of the first species *see* ROCK GARDEN. For the culture and use as seasoning of the second *see* HERB GARDENING.

**T. azoricus** = *Thymus serpyllum*.

**T. serpyllum.** Mother-of-thyme. Creeping thyme. A much-branched, rather woody, prostrate or tufted herb, the stems wiry and rooting at the joints. Leaves short-stalked, more or less elliptic, scarcely ½ in. long. Flowers small, purplish, scarcely protruding beyond the calyx. Eurasia and northern Africa. Summer. For cult. *see* ROCK GARDEN. Of the many hort. varieties of this old-time favorite the best are:

---

* Special articles on the subjects indicated by an asterisk (*) will be found at the words so marked.

THYMELAEACEAE 804 TILIACEAE

*var.* **albus.** Flower white.
*var.* **aureus.** Foliage variegated with yellow.
*var.* **citriodorus** = *Thymus serpyllum vulgaris.*
*var.* **coccineus.** Taller than the type, the flowers crimson.
*var.* **lanuginosus.** Woolly thyme. Whole plant gray-hairy.
*var.* **splendens.** Flowers red.
*var.* **vulgaris.** Lemon thyme. With smaller, lemon-scented leaves. Sometimes known as *T. serpyllum citriodorus.*
**vulgaris.** Common thyme. An erect, woody herb 6–8 in. high, the stems white-hairy. Leaves nearly stalkless, ovalish or narrower, scarcely ½ in. long, the margins rolled. Flowers scarcely ¼ in. long, lilac or purplish. Southern Eu. June. For culture and use see HERB GARDENING.

**THYMELAEACEAE** (ty-me-lee-ā'see-ee). The mezereon family, sometimes called Daphnaceae, is much larger than its hort. importance indicates. Of its 40 genera and over 450 species of shrubs and trees only a handful are of garden interest. Most of them have tough, acrid bark, especially *Dirca* (the leatherwood) of eastern N.A., which is sometimes cult.

The other cult. genera are *Edgeworthia*, *Pimelea* and *Daphne*, of which the last is much the most important because it furnishes several attractive (sometimes evergreen) low shrubs for the rock garden, border or greenhouse. The other two genera are mostly tender northward.

Leaves mostly alternate,* but opposite in a few. Flowers small, but often attractively clustered in heads, panicles* or spikes,* mostly without petals. Fruit various, fleshy in *Daphne* and *Dirca*; nut-like or dry in some others.

Technical flower characters: Flower regular* and hermaphrodite.* Calyx-tube or receptacle* often petal-like, the sepals 4–5 (sometimes 6), also petal-like. Petals none or reduced to mere scales. Stamens* mostly 4–5. Ovary superior,* 1-celled or rarely 2-celled.

**THYMIFOLIA, -us, -um** (ty-mi-fō'li-a). With leaves like thyme.

**THYMUS.** See THYME.

**THYOIDES** (thee-oy'deez, but see OïDES). Like the arborvitae (*Thuja*).

**THYRSE.** A rather dense flower cluster, usually considered as a compound panicle.* It is technically an inflorescence which is branched, the main branch never ending in a flower, but the other branches always ending in one. Common examples are the lilac and horse-chestnut.

**THYRSIFLORA, -us, -um** (thir-si-flow'ra). Bearing flowers in a thyrse.*

**THYRSOIDES** (thir-soy'deez, but see OïDES). Like a thyrse.*

**TIARELLA** (ty-a-rell'a). A small group of chiefly woodland, perennial herbs of the family Saxifragaceae, found in N.A. and eastern As., and suited to the wild garden. The only commonly cult. species is **T. cordifolia**, the false mitrewort or foam flower, sometimes called the coolwort. It is a beautiful native wild flower with chiefly basal, broadly heart-shaped leaves, 3–4 in. wide, the margins lobed and toothed. Flowers small, white, in a dense, finger-shaped cluster (raceme*) at the end of a slender stem about 8 in. high. Petals 5, with a claw.* Stamens* 10. Fruit a small, membranous, 2-valved capsule.* Eastern N.A., mostly in rich woods, and needing similar conditions in the wild garden, but not difficult to grow. The *var.* **major** is larger and has salmon-pink or red flowers. (*Tiarella* is a Greek diminutive for turban, in allusion to the shape of the pistil.)

*A thyrse (diagrammatic)*

**TIBETICA, -us, -um** (ti-bet'i-ka). From Tibet.

**TIBOUCHINA** (ti-boo-ky'na). Spiderflower. Chiefly Brazilian, bristly or hairy shrubs of the family Melastomaceae, comprising over 200 species, only one of which, **T. semidecandra**, is of much hort. interest, and grown outdoors in sub-tropical gardens, or in the North in the warm-temperate greenhouse. It is a handsome, hairy shrub, 4–6 ft. high, with opposite,* densely hairy, ovalish-oblong leaves, 2–4 in. long, pale beneath, and with 3–7 main veins. Flowers showy, 3–5 in. wide, solitary or in few-flowered, terminal clusters, beneath them 2 nearly round bracts.* Petals 5, violet or reddish-purple. Stamens* 10, of unequal length, some of them sticky-hairy. Fruit a 5-valved capsule,* surrounded by the calyx* tube. Not hardy outdoors north of zone* 8, perhaps in the warmest parts of zone* 7. In the greenhouse use potting mixture* 4. (*Tibouchina* is a Latinized version of the name for some species in the Guianas.)

**TICK CLOVER.** See DESMODIUM.

**TICKSEED** = *Coreopsis* and *Bidens.*

**TICK TREFOIL.** See DESMODIUM.

**TIDY-TIPS** = *Layia elegans.*

**TI-ES** = *Lucuma nervosa.*

**TIGERFLOWER.** See TIGRIDIA.

**TIGER LILY** = *Lilium tigrinum.*

**TIGERTAIL SPRUCE** = *Picea polita.* See SPRUCE.

**TIGRIDIA** (ty-grid'i-a). Tigerflower. Showy, tender, bulbous herbs of the iris family, the dozen or so species scattered from Mex. to Chile. One of them, **T. pavonia**, is grown for ornament, although its large, handsome flowers are rather fugitive. The bulb (actually a corm*) is about 1½ in. in diameter, very starchy, and a favorite food of certain Mexican Indians. Leaves basal, stiffish, more or less sword-shaped, 12–18 in. long. Flowers 3–5 in. wide, red, but with conspicuous spots, generally cup-shaped, and growing from between leaf-like spathes* which are 3–5 in. long. Petals and sepals scarcely distinguishable as such, but the inner segments shorter than the outer, the narrow claw* purple or yellow. Fruit a capsule.* The plant is cult. in several varieties, one of them, the *var.* **conchiflora**, having bright yellow flowers. Others with lavender or white flowers are also known. The plants should be grown like *Gladiolus* (which see), as their bulbs will not stand severe frosts. (*Tigridia* is the Latin for tiger, in allusion to the markings on the flowers.)

**TIGRINA, -us, -um** (ty-gry'na). Colored or marked like a tiger.

**TILE DRAINING.** See DRAINING.

**TILE WALL.** See WALLS AND WALL GARDENING.

**TILIA.** See LINDEN.

**TILIACEAE** (tilly-ā'see-ee). The cult. genera of the linden or jute family well represent its diversity as to habit and distribution. Of its 35 genera and 370 species, some are herbs, some hardy trees (the lindens), while most are purely tropical plants.

Only four genera are of hort. interest. By far the most important is *Tilia* (see LINDEN), also called basswood and lime, which yields some of our finest shade trees. *Corchorus*, an herb, which yields jute, is grown in warm regions. *Sparmannia* contains one African, greenhouse, white-flowered shrub, while *Entelea* is from New Zealand and is planted outdoors in Calif., as is *Sparmannia*.

The bark is usually fibrous and often mucilaginous. Leaves simple* and alternate.* Flowers regular, very fragrant and bee-visited in the lindens, always in clusters. Fruit various; in the linden, the stalk of the fruit and flower cluster arises from the middle of a leaf-like appendage.

Technical flower characters: Sepals 5 (rarely 4 or 3), usually soon falling. Petals 5, or less (in the cult. genera). Stamens* many, free, or united in bunches of 5–10, often a few infertile. Ovary superior,* 2–10-celled.

---

* Special articles on the subjects indicated by an asterisk (*) will be found at the words so marked.

**TILLAGE.** See CULTIVATION.

**TILLANDSIA** (till-and′zi-a). A very large genus of chiefly tree-perching (epiphytic*) plants of the family Bromeliaceae, nearly all from tropical America, but a few entering the U.S., and one of them, the Spanish or long moss, a familiar sight throughout the southeastern U.S. They are of very various habit, sometimes stemless and with a basal rosette of narrow leaves, sometimes, as in the Spanish moss, with long-trailing, thread-like stems and very narrow, thread-like leaves. In some species the basal rosette, by the flaring of the leaf bases and their overlapping edges, makes a cup-like cavity which holds water. The leaves of many species are colored or grayish and usually scurfy. Flowers showy in some species, but very small and inconspicuous in the Spanish moss. See BROMELIACEAE. Fruit a capsule.* (Named for Elias Tillands, Swedish physician and botanist.)

The tillandsias and the related genus *Guzmania* are nearly all epiphytes,* and consequently light-demanding plants. They must be grown in the warm-temperate or tropical greenhouse in the North, and potted up, if at all, in a mixture of peat fiber or orchid peat. Many of them will grow perfectly if the plant is wired by its roots to a board upon which some orchid peat is fastened. Such boards may be hung from the greenhouse roof or nailed, as high as possible, to a greenhouse wall. They need frequent watering in the spring and summer, but should be allowed to become partially dormant, by reducing their water, during the dark winter months. The Spanish moss needs no attention other than to throw strands of it over the branch of a tree. It absorbs most of its food directly from the atmosphere.

In the collections of fanciers there are many other species than those below, but the three here listed are the only ones commonly grown.

**fasciculata.** A stiffish plant with a basal rosette of gray-green, narrow leaves 12–18 in. long. Flowers blue, the spike 4–6 in. long, borne mostly in branched clusters which are bracted, the bracts* greenish, but red-tinged. Central America and the W.I.

**lindeneana.** A showy plant with a basal rosette of leaves, which are about 12 in. long and ¾ in. wide. Flowers in large spikes, bluish-purple. Bracts* on the flowering stalks carmine-red. Ecuador and Peru.

**usneoides.** Spanish or long moss (not a true moss). An extraordinary, lichen-like plant which drapes trees, especially live oaks and cypresses from southern Va. southward. Stems and leaves long and thread-like, gray, the dense festoons often hanging over 20 ft. from the branches over which they are hung. Flowers extremely small, yellow. Va. to Fla. and Tex., also in tropical America. It adds, to garden pictures in the South, an extraordinarily weird and misty note, suggesting in the distance a dense fog.

**TILTH.** That condition of the soil in which it is fit to produce good crops; most often used in the phrase that such a soil is in good *tilth*. There is, however, no precise definition of tilth. As ordinarily understood by gardeners, it means a soil that, having been plowed (or dug) and harrowed (or raked), is sufficiently workable or friable* so that seeds or plants may be planted with ease, and a reasonable expectation that they will grow. But the etymology of the word implies that it should be restricted to the cultivation of the soil after the crop is planted. In this sense tilth is the same as cultivation (which see).

**TILTON.** An apricot variety. See APRICOT.

**TIME OF FLOWERING.** For the factors that control the time of flowering see PHENOLOGY. For the progress of bloom from month to month see GARDEN CALENDAR.

**TIME TO?** For the proper sequence of garden operations, both in the North and in the sub-tropical garden, see GARDEN CALENDAR.

**TIMOTHY** = *Phleum pratense*.

**TINCTORIA, -us, -um** (tink-tor′i-a). Used by dyers, or for dyeing; hence, usually, handsomely colored.

**TINKER'S-WEED** = *Triosteum perfoliatum*.

**TINUS** (ty′nus). Pre-Linnaean* name for the laurustinus (*Viburnum tinus*).

**TIP-BURN.** See Environmental Influences at PLANT DISEASES. See also Diseases at POTATO.

**TIP CUTTINGS.** See Softwood Cuttings at CUTTINGS.

**TIRED SOIL.** A term scarcely sanctioned by the soil scientists, but of considerable cogency among practical gardeners to indicate a soil exhausted of nourishment for a particular crop. It usually implies that a crop has been grown for too long a period in one spot, and the obvious remedy is to move it. See ROTATION OF CROPS.

**TISSWOOD** = *Halesia monticola*.

**TITHONIA** (ti-thō′ni-a). Tall, sunflower-like shrubs or woody, perennial herbs of the family Compositae, found in Mex., Central America, and the W.I. Only one species, *T. rotundifolia* (sometimes known as *T. speciosa*), is of any garden interest, and its cult. is confined to zones* 8 and 9. It is a shrub or woody herb, 4–6 ft. high, with alternate,* broadly ovalish leaves 7–10 in. long, 3-lobed or coarsely round-toothed. Flower heads nearly 3 in. wide, the ray and disk flowers orange-yellow and resembling a sunflower. It is little known in cult. here, but grown in Mex. (Named for Tithonus, a mythological character.)

*TITHYMALOIDES* (ti-thi-ma-loy′deez, but *see* OÏDES). Like a spurge of the genus *Tithymalus* which is of no hort. interest, and is often included in *Euphorbia*. See PEDILANTHUS.

**TI TREE** = *Cordyline australis*.

**TOAD.** A frog-like, perfectly harmless, mostly land-inhabiting animal, common in many gardens and a most welcome visitor. They do not cause warts, but do feed on many injurious insects, slugs, and worms.

**TOADFLAX.** See LINARIA.

**TOAD LILY** = *Fritillaria meleagris*, *Tricyrtis hirta*, and *Nymphaea odorata*.

**TOAD'S-MOUTH.** See SNAPDRAGON.

**TOBACCO** (*Nicotiana tabacum;* for the plant called Indian tobacco see LOBELIA INFLATA). The commercial production of tobacco lies quite outside the scope of this book, for much of the most valuable varieties cannot be grown in the U.S. But in spite of being a tender, tropical annual, several varieties are grown on a large scale in Va. and southward, and others in Pa., Conn., and even in Canada. All such cult. is based upon the raising of plants under glass, in anticipation of maturing them in the warm growing season outdoors.

VARIETIES. The leading kinds for cigar wrappers are Sumatra and Connecticut Havana. Most of the fillers for cigars are Cuban varieties, but Cuban is also grown in Fla., Texas, and a few other states.

For cigarettes the best variety is White Burley, largely grown in Ky., Tenn., southern Ohio and somewhat in Va. and N. Car. Pipe tobacco varieties are North Carolina Bright Yellow, and Maryland Smoking.

CULTURE. Seeds should be sown in a seedbed in Feb. or March and the seeds are so fine that they must be mixed with corn meal or fine sand to secure an even distribution of them. The soil must be finely pulverized and kept moist. It should also be rich in plant food, because the smallness of the seeds leaves little room for nourishment from that source. The hotbed in which the seeds are started should range from 70°–90°, but never below 70° during the night. The growing of tobacco for cigar wrappers is best done under a cloth shade (see CLOTH). This not only serves as a protection against insect pests, but by cutting off direct sunlight tends to make the leaves thinner.

No crop requires more care and feeding than tobacco if really desirable leaves are to be produced. The soil must be rich, preferably a sandy loam, deeply plowed, and brought to the utmost condition of tilth,* before the plants are set out. These should be 12 in. apart in the row and the rows 3 ft. 3 in. apart.

In the early stages frequent cultivation is absolutely essential — at least once a week. Later it will become impossible, due to the growth of the plants. If, however, early cultivation has been thorough, weeds in the later weeks will

---

* Special articles on the subjects indicated by an asterisk (*) will be found at the words so marked.

easily be kept down by the crowding of the tobacco plants.

As the plants are about to come into flower the tops should be pinched off and no flowers allowed to bloom except those which are to produce seed. The latter are best kept separate and allowed to flower as a unit.

HARVESTING AND CURING. Leaves are usually ready for harvesting when light yellowish patches begin to appear on them. Usually this discoloration occurs on the lowest leaves first, and harvesting of these should begin first, waiting for a few days until the upper leaves also begin to discolor.

The leaves are hung, stem up, in a specially constructed curing barn, the sides of which can be opened in sections to permit free circulation of air during the day, but closed at night. For some varieties and in moist weather it is also necessary to use heat. Conditions vary so widely that no general statement is safe to give for curing, which is a very expert business requiring years of experience. The whole crop can be ruined in a few hours of improper curing.

INSECT PESTS. Small black flea beetles, the same as those on potato, attack tobacco in seedbed and field in the spring. They can be controlled by a light dusting of strong arsenical; 1 part of Paris green to 4 parts of lime is suggested. Smooth green caterpillars feed in the terminals, boring through leaves. Corn-ear-worm larvae sometimes work in the same way. A mixture of 1 part of lead arsenate to 75 parts of corn meal, sifted into the terminals every few days during the summer, has been used. The large green worms that attack tomato also feed on tobacco, and may be controlled by hand-picking or with arsenical dust. Cutworms attacking transplants are usually controlled with poisoned bran bait sown in the evening.

DISEASES. The diseases of tobacco are very numerous, so that they can be named only in groups; the root rots, as black and brown root rots; mildews; leafspots, particularly wild fire and angular leafspot; stem diseases, as bacterial wilt and black shank; degeneration diseases, mosaic and ring spot; and storage shed injuries. Control measures include healthy seed, seed treatment (mercuric chloride, 1–1000 for 15 minutes), seedbed soil sterilization, dusting seedlings with copper-lime, and the selection of good tobacco soil in the field. This includes good drainage, proper fertilizer, long rotations, and well-decayed humus.

**TOBACCO FAMILY** = Solanaceae.

**TOBACCO TEA.** An infusion of tobacco stems and leaves. See Contact Sprays at INSECTICIDES.

***TOBIRA*** (toe-by'ra). Japanese vernacular name for *Pittosporum tobira*.

**TOBIRA FAMILY** = Pittosporaceae.

**TOCOCA** (toe-kō'ka). Very beautiful, but culturally difficult shrubs of the family Melastomaceae, all the 50 species from the steaming, hot forests of northern S.A. The only cult. species, and this little known, is **T. platyphylla**, a low shrub with rather fleshy, hairy stems. Leaves opposite,* broadly ovalish, nearly 1 ft. long, very finely toothed and hairy on the margin, and with 7 main veins. Flowers red, in terminal clusters (panicles*), with 5–6 oblongish petals and 10–12 stamens.* Fruit a fleshy berry. The plant needs a tropical greenhouse, plenty of moisture, and the glass should be shaded, as the plant does not like direct sunlight. Use ½ potting mixture* 3 and ½ orchid peat or other fibrous material, and see that there is plenty of drainage in the bottom of the pot (see POTTING). Propagated by cuttings consisting of a single bud, the leaf rolled around the cutting and inserted in a thumb pot filled with a mixture of sand and chopped orchid peat. Plunge the pots in a propagating bench with bottom-heat* of about 80°. (*Tococa* is the Latin version of a native name for a related species.)

**TODDY PALM** = *Caryota urens*.

**TOLMIEA** (toll'me-a). A single species of perennial herbs of the family Saxifragaceae, **T. menziesi**, a somewhat sticky-hairy herb, native from Alaska to Calif. and closely related to *Tiarella*. It differs from the latter in having only 2 or 3 stamens.* Leaves chiefly basal, heart-shaped, more or less lobed or bluntly round-toothed. Stem leaves (when present) 2–4, alternate.* Flowers greenish, the petals very narrow, the terminal cluster (raceme*) 8–15 in. long. Fruit a capsule.* It needs shade and woods soil and is suited only to the wild garden or rock garden. Easily propagated from the runners which are produced freely in summer. (Named for a Doctor Tolmie, a surgeon of the Hudson's Bay Company.)

***TOLPIS*** (toll'pis). A genus of small annual and perennial herbs of the family Compositae, chiefly from the Mediterranean region, one of them, **T. barbata,** occasionally grown as a hardy annual (see ANNUALS) in the flower garden. It is a slender herb 8–12 in. high, with a milky juice, and basal, lance-shaped, remotely toothed leaves. Flowers yellow, in small heads, not over ½ in. wide, and composed only of ray* flowers, not particularly showy. Beneath the head is a series of thread-like bracts,* some of which are also on the upper part of the flowering stalk. The plant is of secondary garden interest, flowers from midsummer to frost, and is sometimes listed as *Crepis barbata*. (*Tolpis* is of unknown origin.)

**TOMATILLO** = *Physalis ixocarpa*.

**TOMATO.** The garden tomato, and its relatives, all belong to the genus **Lycopersicum** (ly-ko-per'si-kum). This is a group of 10 or 12 species of South American herbs, mostly with strong-smelling foliage, belonging to the potato family (see SOLANACEAE). Only the two below are of any garden interest.

*Lycopersicum* (sometimes written *Lycopersicon*) has compound* leaves (the leaflets sometimes curly), or merely deeply divided leaves and the foliage is often sticky (glandular). It is closely related to the genus *Solanum* (which see), but wholly lacks the prickles often found in that genus. Flowers yellow, the corolla shallowly bell-shaped or wheel-shaped. Fruit a pulpy berry. (*Lycopersicum* is Greek for wolf peach, perhaps in allusion to its once being thought poisonous.) The only two hort. species are:

**L. esculentum.** The type from which the common tomato has been derived. It is a spreading, hairy, strong-smelling herb, 3–6 ft. high. Leaves compound, often with smaller leaflets interspersed with larger ones. Flowers 3–7, usually nodding. Fruit red or yellow, 2–3 in. in diameter, the sides more or less grooved. This plant (known also as *Solanum esculentum*) is scarcely grown in cult., but from it the following varieties have been derived:

*var.* **cerasiforme**, the cherry tomato. The fruit about ¾ in. in diameter, red or yellow, nearly round. Oblong-fruited forms are often called plum tomato.

*var.* **commune**, the common garden tomato. Its leaflets are scarcely curled. Fruit (very large in some cult. forms), nearly round, but flattened at the ends, the sides not much (or not at all) grooved or furrowed.

*var.* **grandifolium**, the large-leaved or potato-leaved tomato. This plant has usually 5 rather large leaflets, without teeth or lobes, and few or no smaller scattered leaflets.

*var.* **pyriforme**, the pear tomato, has pear-shaped fruit usually about 1½ in. long.

**L. pimpinellifolium.** Currant tomato. A weak, almost smooth herb, with little odor, many flowers (10–25), and small red fruit suggesting currants. A curiosity from Peru and little grown. Of these species and varieties much the most important is the tomato.

### TOMATO CULTURE (*Lycopersicum esculentum commune*)

The tomato is perhaps more tender than any other garden plant in such general cult. It is blackened by the least touch of frost, and will grow well only where there is plenty of heat.

The foliage of it is also extraordinarily sensitive to illuminating gas. Concentrations of gas too small to be detected chemically (1–1,000,000 parts of air), will injure or kill tomato leaves, and potted plants are used as gas indicators by some florists who suspect, but could not otherwise prove, that gas is seeping into their greenhouses. See GAS INJURY.

The outdoor culture of the tomato (once, and sometimes still called love-apple) is based upon treating it as a tender annual, plants of which are raised under glass in anticipation of being later put outdoors. Many commercial growers and some home gardeners (in their anxiety to get the earliest possible yields) put the plants outdoors before they really should, and rely upon various devices to protect them from the cold (see below).

VARIETIES. Tomato varieties are divided into two groups, early and general season. The former (the only ones possible for zones* 1, 2, and the upper part of zone* 3) are grown for the quickness of development; the latter for the supply that should last until frost.

Early varieties: Bonny Best. John Baer. Chalk Jewel. Pritchard.

General season varieties: Globe. Stone. Marglobe. Greater Baltimore.

Many other varieties are offered. Some, like Ponderosa, yield immense fruit. But this and several others are open to

---

* Special articles on the subjects indicated by an asterisk (*) will be found at the words so marked.

the objection that the fruit is apt to split or show cracks as it matures.

RAISING TOMATO PLANTS. While many home gardeners will prefer to buy potted plants offered by dealers at the time they should be planted out, there is little need to do this, for tomatoes are among the easiest of vegetables to raise from seed. In your calculations for the early varieties, allow 7–8 weeks from the time of sowing seed to the proper date in your locality for setting the plants in the garden (see below).

Plant the seeds in flats or boxes in a greenhouse where the temperature does not fall much below 70°. If you have no greenhouse, the boxes may be set in the kitchen window, but if there is a gas stove, put the boxes in the bathroom window (assuming the latter is at ordinary room temperature). The usually dry air of a living room is decidedly less favorable.

The seed should be sown in fine, not too rich soil, about ¼ inch deep, either in tiny drills or broadcast as you prefer. Keep the soil moist but not wet. When the seedlings are about 2½ in. high, prick them out and replant on 2 × 2 in. intervals and allow them to grow until they are 4 or 5 in. high. For details see SEEDS AND SEEDAGE.

The seedlings are then replanted in individual containers — discarded paper drinking cups, old berry boxes, tomato cans (with a hole in the bottom), or into 3-in. flower pots. At this time also must begin the process of gradually checking their growth so that they will be fit to meet the outdoor temperature. The best method is to transfer the pots from the house or greenhouse to the cold frame or hotbed, keeping the temperature at first around 60°, later around 55°. This will check, but not stop their growth and so harden-off the plants.

Tomato plants which have not followed this routine become spindling and weak — wholly unsuited for planting in the garden. If you purchase plants from dealers, see that they are stocky, have been hardened-off, and are generally no more than 8–12 in. high. If your own plants show signs of becoming higher than this, pinch them back to keep them stocky.

General season plants (which are set out three weeks after the early ones) are grown in the same way, but may usually be started in a hotbed or cold frame. These are also, by some, merely thinned to secure stockiness. They are less likely to meet cool nights than the early sorts and there is less need for the routine of hardening them off.

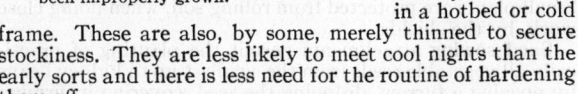

A stocky tomato plant fit for outdoor cult. (left) and a leggy* one which has been improperly grown.

OUTDOOR PLANTING. Left to itself a tomato plant is weak and sprawling. Commercial growers let them sprawl and there is no doubt the yield is heavier when so grown. If you decide to adopt this method, the plants must be set 4 ft. apart each way.

The alternative is to tie each plant to a 4-ft. (above ground) stake and pinch off many superfluous leaves. Many home growers prefer this to save space. If you adopt it, set the plants 2½ ft. apart each way. Still another method is to use two stakes fastened to a barrel hoop over which the plant sprawls or is tied.

The date of planting outdoors is of the greatest importance for the early varieties. The plants need heat, both as to air temperature and soil temperature. You, on the other hand, want to set out the plants at the earliest safe date, or even a bit earlier.

In your locality a fair criterion is when the average daily temperature (maximum and minimum divided by two) is at least 60°. Many commercial growers plant earlier than this, well knowing that unprotected plants will be seriously checked by cool night temperatures. To overcome this they cover the plants every night (and on cool days) with one of a number of paper, cardboard or cellophane plant protectors. Some (in the haste to get early tomatoes) even use these protectors to keep out frost. But the latter is a hazardous business, the likelihood of a killing frost proving you are starting too early. See PROTECTING PLANTS.

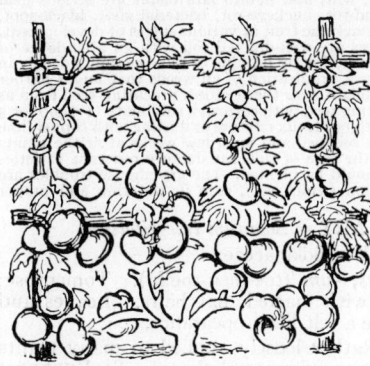

Tomato plants grown on a simple support. They produce more fruit if allowed to sprawl.

For most home gardeners the best method is to wait until protectors are no longer necessary.

CULTIVATION AND SOILS. Tomatoes need constant cultivation to keep down weeds and conserve soil moisture, upon which they draw heavily. This is especially true in the early stages of the plants allowed to sprawl. Later these cannot be cultivated without injury to the tender, rather brittle stems.

The home grower should keep on pinching off the extra amount of foliage which staked plants are sure to develop. Pinch off enough leaves so that the sun can easily reach the developing fruit. Staked plants, well grown, ought to produce 6–8 tomatoes per plant (more in some of the general season varieties); unstaked plants from 9–12. These figures make calculation of the number of plants you need reasonably easy. But cold, rainy weather in midsummer would greatly decrease the yield, so it is safer to plant more than seems advisable from statistical evidence. Fruits harvested green just before frost will ripen if left on a sunny window sill.

Any good garden soil will grow tomatoes. Experience has shown that too much (especially nitrogenous) fertilizer or manure close to the plants makes them more likely to produce leafage than fruit. If you are prepared to pinch off the excess leaves, they may be fertilized as for any other rich-feeding crop.

TOMATOES IN WINTER. The all-year market supply is based upon utilizing the comparatively warm winters of the Far South or sections of Calif. But northern gardeners with a greenhouse or conservatory may have home-grown tomatoes from November to March. These plants are started from seed 10 weeks before the plants are set in the greenhouse bench, and handled as outdoor seedlings are to ensure stockiness, but of course are not hardened-off. Plant them at 3½ ft. intervals. Keep the night temperature around 60°, the day temperature 65°–70°.

Greenhouse plants are usually grown (by pinching) to a single erect stem tied at intervals to a wire stretched to the roof. When they are in flower they must be pollinated, as this will not be taken care of by insects as in outdoor plants. To pollinate, choose a warm, sunny day and have the air in the house reasonably dry. Gently shake the plants when the pollen is in condition to fall. Usually this jarring will distribute enough. But if you are not certain, use a camel's-hair brush (see CROSSING).

For the preferred position and sequence of your outdoor tomato plants see KITCHEN GARDEN.

INSECT PESTS. Cutworms often destroy tomato plants and other garden plants. These smooth caterpillars curl up in the soil during the day and cut off plants at night. Bran bait sown thickly in the garden and around its borders in the evening kills many. Arsenicals will check flea beetles. The large green tomato worm may be hand-picked or poisoned with lead arsenate. An arsenical spray as fruits begin setting will reduce numbers of the corn ear worm, which may bore in fruits.

DISEASES. Among the long list of diseases which affect tomatoes are

---

* Special articles on the subjects indicated by an asterisk (*) will be found at the words so marked.

nematode root-galls, timber-rot and leaf-mold as probably the most serious troubles in the greenhouse or occasionally outdoors where the temperature and moisture permit; leafblight, Grand Rapids disease, western yellow blight, mosaic, wilt, and potato late blight are serious field maladies; and blossom end-rot, buckeye-rot, bacterial spot, black-spot, and innumerable others attack the fruit at various stages of development.

General control measures are well-drained soil with an abundance of humus, long rotations, destruction by burning or plowing under deeply in the fall of all diseased refuse, eradication of all weeds that might harbor mosaic or western yellow blight near the seedbed, procuring seed from as far north as possible, treating seed with corrosive sublimate (1–3000 for 5 minutes), and spraying with bordeaux mixture or dusting with copper lime at weekly intervals in the seedbed and for a few weeks after the plants are set into the field. In the case of wilt, satisfactory resistant varieties have been selected and should be planted. The greenhouse troubles are reduced by soil sterilization (which see), care in watering and proper ventilation.

**TOMATO EGGPLANT** = *Solanum integrifolium*.

**TOMATO FAMILY** = Solanaceae.

*TOMENTOSA, -us, -um* (toe-men-toe'sa). Tomentose; *i.e.* densely covered with matted, flat hairs. Leaves and stems so clothed have a felt-like appearance.

**TOM THUMB.** Rather loosely applied to many plants which are low, dwarf, or produce small flowers. See BERBERIS WILSONAE.

**TON.** See WEIGHTS AND MEASURES, 4.

**TONGUE-FERN** = *Cyclophorus lingua*.

**TONGUE GRAFT.** A whip graft. See GRAFTING.

**TOOG** = *Bischofia javanica*.

**TOOL HOUSE.** In any garden beyond the smallest, some sort of a tool house is much the best solution of the problem of what to do with the tools and implements listed in the next article.

A tool house may be as attractive as the one shown in the picture at STRUCTURES, but more often it must be a simple affair of wood, preferably hidden from the garden proper by planting, or if space does not permit a thick screen of shrubs and trees, the tool house should be covered with vines. See VINES.

The interior of the house should have floor space for roller, lawn mower, wheel-barrow, or other large equipment, and it should have several shelves for storing boxes or baskets, and if it has running water and a sink, it will often save the kitchen from much rough washing of vegetables, trimming of flowers, and other jobs better done in the garden.

If possible, the floor should be of cement and there should be pegs or nails on the walls for hanging up everything possible. Because vermin are hard to control in such places, all seeds, bulbs, or tubers should be kept in tin boxes while waiting for planting day. But remember that the house will have no heat and tender bulbs should not be left out over the winter in regions of severe cold.

One of the best tool houses known has not only plenty of pegs or nails for hanging things up, but overhead crossbeams so arranged that stakes, poles, and other bulky material can be put up there for the winter. In some busy planting seasons the floor of the tool house may be the most convenient place to do many jobs, and the aim should consequently be to keep it as clear as possible.

**TOOLS AND IMPLEMENTS.** Have you the right tools for your gardening problems? Garden makers throughout the country will have fewer backaches if they select them with care. Only a few are actually needed in the home garden. Many good gardeners, with years of experience, get along with only a hoe, a rake, and a spade. But in this era of time- and labor-saving devices, many tools have been invented, all of which serve a useful purpose under some conditions. Most tools are made by professionals for professionals. Each one is as large and heavy as the man who uses it each and every day can manage. But amateurs — office men and women who garden as a hobby, evenings and Sundays — are less skilled in the use of their tools. They require smaller, lighter variations of many of the standard articles. Not toys, but good, light-weight, sensible gardening tools and implements. In the selection of these there will always be differences of opinion. Every gardener must buy the kind which seems to meet his individual needs.

From the tools named in the following discussion the garden maker will have considerable latitude in choosing the equipment necessary to carry on all ordinary gardening operations. In trying new tools, too, one may find something which will make a greater appeal than those especially recommended for the purpose. In addition, the widespread garden movement has resulted in the invention of many articles, commonly called "garden gadgets," which are as distinctly worth-while for the actual dirt gardener as for the amateur. Therefore, to the list of practical tools has been added a number of appliances, which will serve as useful gifts to the garden-minded, as well as fulfilling their utilitarian purpose.

### 1. VEGETABLE GARDEN

The best vegetables grow in gardens that are properly plowed and cultivated. If the garden is large there is definite economy of time, labor and money in having it plowed and harrowed either by tractor or horse power. A **garden tractor**, with its adaptability to almost any job or condition, due to the large number of attachments that can be used with it, will reduce costs considerably for any person raising truck crops for a living. It replaces a horse for almost any job, does as much work as fifteen or more men with hoes, or four or five men with wheel-hoes.

All **plows** used in tillage operations may be included under three classes: subsoil, trench, and ordinary plows. **Subsoil plows** are used to break and fine subsoil without bringing it to the surface. **Trench plows** are designed for deep plowing. Ordinary plows, such as the landside and swivel, with a coulter attachment to cut litter-like cornstalks, if necessary, are used for general garden plowing.

There is no single **harrow** suited to all classes of work. The **disk harrow** is used immediately after plowing to do the rough pulverizing of the soil. This should be followed by the **spike-tooth harrow,** to give the finish necessary for most kinds of seeds. This harrow is of use also in cultivating. The **spring-tooth harrow** tears up the ground by means of curved spring teeth, which are set at various angles according to the kind of work required. These are not much used for ordinary gardens, except in rough ground where there are rocks or roots.

Unless gardening is to be done on a large scale, the most important tool for the home gardener is a combined **wheel-hoe cultivator**. The single wheel-hoe is the best for use in small garden plots. Commercial growers generally use a type with two wheels, which makes it possible to straddle the rows, cultivating both sides at once, until the plants are more than a foot and a half high. The handles of both the double and single wheel-hoes are adjustable for height to suit the operator, and bent handles can be substituted for the "saw-grip." Plow attachments are used to plow up very small gardens; also for opening furrows, covering seeds, smothering weeds, and for plowing away from and hilling up corn, potatoes, and other growing crops. Cultivator teeth turn over weeds and are good for both deep and shallow cultivation. Hoes are very useful attachments. They are obtainable in various sizes and are used for weeding, mulching, etc. Small plants are protected from rolling soil, when doing close work, by the shields.

**Seed sowing** attachments permit the planting of practically all vegetable seeds from the smallest up to kidney beans by opening a furrow, dropping the seed, covering it, firming the soil above it, and marking out the next row, all in one operation. Seed can be sown either in hills or in continuous rows. In a small garden where only one row or so of each vegetable is planted, this will have little value. Many other attachments are obtainable for the wheel-hoes.

Farmers and commercial vegetable growers with insufficient acreage to warrant the use of large tractors or horse-drawn outfits will find it economical to use a **drill seeder** with a **fertilizer spreader**. There are two types, one for muck and the other for ordinary soils. They plant in continuous rows only, so that thinning-out is necessary, but the seeds are planted evenly and accurately and with a uniform depth of covering. The attachment for fertilizing sows fertilizer on both sides of the row, either mixing it in the soil or leaving it on the surface as preferred. Formaldehyde dust can be applied directly to the seed when planted; or the same attachment can be used for drilling fertilizer in a furrow, or side

---

\* Special articles on the subjects indicated by an asterisk (\*) will be found at the words so marked.

dressing one side each of two rows. For the grower who plants several acres of a single vegetable crop there is a Four, Six and Eight Seeder which will plant on beds or on the flat with equal facility, and is adaptable to use with tractor or horse power.

A separate **hand cultivator,** the **Norcross,** with three or five prongs, can be had in light weight, with a four-foot hardwood handle. Another good cultivator, the **Star Pulverizer,** is weeder, cultivator, and mulcher in one. It works on the order of a carpet sweeper. As it is pushed back and forth between vegetables and flowers, or around trees and shrubs, the star disks crumble the soil while the scuffle blade, which cuts on both the backward and forward stroke, cuts off the weeds. It is especially valuable for preparing seedbeds and breaking up freshly spaded ground. A handy little cultivator especially suitable for backyard gardening is the **Jiffy-hoe.** It is equipped either with three teeth for deep cultivation or a scuffle blade for shallow work. The wheel steadies the tool and keeps the depth of cultivation even.

The common **hoe** must not be overlooked, although there are several new forms which are very desirable. In many places it is almost indispensable. Select carefully, as it must have proper balance and the right "feel" in the hand. The New England type is heavy but in common use; some people prefer the narrow-bladed or round-top **onion hoe.** Practically all gardeners consider the **scuffle hoe,** also called the **English scuffle hoe, D-hoe** and **Dutch hoe,** a necessity. It has a straight flat blade attached to a long handle and can be pushed back and forth just beneath the surface to break up the crust and destroy weeds. Handle this hoe carefully, as there is danger of cutting off outside plants when using it close to the rows. The **Warren hoe,** triangular in shape with a sharp point at the bottom, takes the place of a trowel with those who prefer to work around small plants, or make holes for setting them out, without stooping. The small beet weeding hoe, with one or two points as preferred, is one of the most useful for light work. Other good ones are the combination rake-and-hoe, **half-moon,** and the potato hoe or manure drag. The "pull" hoe is drawn toward the user, who steps back instead of forward in working new ground.

The **pickax** is extremely useful in loosening heavy or sunbaked soil, removing sod, and for general work where neither trowel nor spading fork will serve. A **mattock,** which is a pickax-like tool having blades instead of points, will be found very useful to cut out large roots, old clumps of plants, and will even act as an edger, if need be.

Strong, well-made, but not too heavy **spades** and forks are needed by all gardeners. The D-handled spades are made with either long or short handles and are light enough to be managed easily by ladies. For transplanting, digging, and general work there is the heavier nursery spade, which is reinforced in the handle for its entire length with steel straps. A hand weeding fork, which can also be used for cultivating, is a strong serviceable tool with a four-foot handle. The best **manure fork** is probably that with a D-handle; it comes with extra heavy tines. A regular **spading fork,** with flat-pointed steel tines, and an English digging fork with four pointed, solid steel, square tines are both desirable tools. The trench shovel, such as was made during the war, can be used either as a trowel or spade, and is heavy enough so that when it is used like a mattock it answers the same purpose. In buying **shovels** for use in the garden be sure to get the round-nosed type, as the square-nosed ones are good only for cleaning up litter, shoveling away ashes, etc.

**Rakes,** like hoes, must be properly balanced and "feel" just right in the hand. An iron one is necessary for smoothing over seedbeds and breaking up rough ground. An excellent sort now on the market has slender wire teeth about eight inches long, set three-quarters of an inch apart, and is one of the best for the final raking of seedbeds. Most women prefer the **bamboo rake,** as it is light and easy to handle. The improved form has metal grips which make it much stronger. Besides being flexible, the new type is so constructed that every tooth rests evenly on the ground, rather than moving in opposite directions over uneven spots, causing the binding to break, as in the old models. The newest rake is made with rubber teeth which are flexible but still strong enough to do their work well. The only use for these is for the lawn, as they will not tear up the grass, and to remove dead leaves and mulch from among young vegetable plants without injury. One is known as the "Gumfinger" rake.

It goes without saying that good **trowels** are very important tools, and although the so-called rust-proof ones now on the market cost a little more, it is economy in the end. They must be strong and well made, and even though made of metal throughout may bend or snap off at the shank. Wooden-handled ones can be bought, as well as those made all in one piece. Those used for bulb planting should have a flat, broad blade forged together with the shank from one piece of high-grade steel. The best trowel for transplanting is the "hoe" trowel. It also comes with an extra-narrow blade.

For bulb-setting, in large quantities, the "hole-in-one" planting tool removes the soil and makes a perfect planting hole, in one operation. Another good bulb planter can be used from a standing position and has an adjustable feature which controls various planting depths. **Dibbles** (or **dibbers**) are extremely useful in setting seedlings into their permanent beds. The handles are of wood, with the points of either iron or brass, and come in two sizes. Care must be taken in using this tool not to make the holes too deep so that the plant is "hung." In other words, if the hole in which the seedling is planted is too deep, an air pocket is left which allows air to get at the roots of the young plants.

Nothing gives any garden such a forlorn look as crooked, slovenly planted rows. At a small cost a **garden line,** marked off into one-foot sections for easy measuring, can be bought, or an iron garden line reel can be used with common garden twine. A hemp line can be had if preferred. Straight lines in planting save time and work also in cultivating with hoes or hand cultivators. Garden stakes and fasteners, made of redwood so they are impervious to rot, play a large part in the well-kept garden (see STAKES AND STAKING). A heavy mallet will be found beneficial in driving the stakes firmly into the ground. Plant labels, weatherproofed, and protected in a celluloid case, are now on the market. More than fifty different kinds of labels can be bought, so that each gardener can satisfy his own whims regarding them. See LABELS.

Many new weeders have been invented of late — not exactly one for each weed, but enough to satisfy the most ardent weeding fan. Some of these are of rust-proof, malleable galvanized iron, with wooden handles. The following are all good weeders and will serve a number of purposes: three-tined weeder with two- or four-foot handle; claw weeder with short handle; beet weeder — also used for radishes, carrots and similar vegetables that are drilled in rows; so-called "Magic" weeder with fingers made of tempered wire, flattened out at the points. The "fingers" may be drawn closely together or used widespread. The Wonder weeder is made of two different-sized loops of band steel an inch wide, which are reversible, carried on a four-foot pole. This is light, loosens the ground and lifts the weeds out when small. The Cape Cod weeder is a good tool for getting out crab-grass. Insert the tip of the blade under the grass crown, press the shaft back on its elbow, and lift up the grass mat intact. This method does not destroy the good grass roots. It can be used also for cultivating between plants and for loosening roots that need to be pulled out. Some people make use of the **asparagus knife** for cutting out weeds that grow close to small plants; others use a sharp-pointed steel ice pick, for getting out weeds with long taproots from between walk flags, etc. Cultivator teeth may also be used for weeding. There is a good dandelion and plantain extractor which can be used anywhere.

There are many small accessories which add materially to successful vegetable gardening. The asparagus buncher comes in two sizes, and the tape for tying in various colors. The knife for cutting has a total length of fourteen inches. The miniature hothouse-like protectors which are placed over the plants to protect them against cold are useful, but of different degrees of efficiency (see PROTECTING PLANTS). Paper mulch (see MULCH AND MULCHING) is an excellent way of conserving moisture and discouraging weed growth, and can be

---

\* Special articles on the subjects indicated by an asterisk (\*) will be found at the words so marked.

bought in two or more types of durable paper impregnated with asphalt. Mole and gopher traps (see ANIMAL INJURY) are made in a number of designs. Pumps and sprayers for insect control are a necessity. See SPRAYING AND DUSTING.

Without an adequate supply of water gardens perish, and artificial watering, in one way or another, must be given to many gardens. The overhead system is the quickest and easiest, and it may be either permanent, or set up on tripods and each section of pipe joined with a hand union (see IRRIGATION). **Sprinkling cans** or **watering cans** are best for caring for seedlings in frames or small seedbeds. Both the English and French types of can are equipped with long spouts and supplied with two roses, one having fine perforations for the seedlings and seeds and the other with coarse openings for general work. A special style, made of copper with a brass handle, and an extra-long spout of seamless copper tubing, has been designed for watering window gardens. The garden **hose** will put on more water in a few minutes than can be carried in a can in hours, and large operations should be cared for by this method. Good rubber hose comes in a number of brands with innumerable nozzles which will give any kind of spray from a solid stream to a fine mist. A Siamese connection permits the use of two lines of hose from a single outlet. Clamps, couplings which snap together and part instantly, and hose menders to take care of leaks and breaks are all easily obtainable. A hose holder is a great convenience, as it is hard to hold a hose long enough to water the garden thoroughly. Different sorts are for sale; one gadget has a spike that goes into the ground, a galvanized wire device to hold the nozzle, and a handle above so that it can be turned without shutting off the water.

Every well-ordered garden should have its quota of wheelbarrows and baskets. The **baskets** are used for many purposes — to cover up plants before a freeze, for holding and transporting leaves to the compost pile, making up potting soil, and holding waste matter for the brush pile previous to burning.

**Barrows** or **wheelbarrows** are an absolute necessity. The wooden and all metal ones are useful for transporting rocks, dirt and debris. The garden barrow has high, removable sides, and leaf or litter racks may be added and increase its load capacity threefold. Dump-carts, whether hand, horse, or motor, are used the same as the barrows, but the latter two are valuable only on large places. The hand dump-cart is merely a two-wheeled cart with two handles and a crossbar, which enables the operator either to draw or push it. It empties forward, instead of backward. The horse and motor carts are used for heavy loads, the motor dump-cart carrying from three-quarters to a ton load easily.

All of these tools and implements can be used to advantage in other forms of gardening. Additional ones for the vegetable garden may be found also in the sections below.

## 2. FLOWER GARDEN

As with the vegetable garden, preparation of the soil is of prime importance, and many of the tools and implements discussed above will be required to care for it properly in the flower garden. Plowing and harrowing will not be necessary unless the garden is very large or flowers are to be grown for commercial purposes.

Many tools for the flower garden are designed especially for women. A four-piece set which is durable and useful, at the same time made of light-weight materials, consists of a fork, spade, hoe and rake. There is also a combination trowel and weeder with an efficient sawtooth edge, a dibble made of aluminum, two sizes of aluminum trowels, a small hand seedsower for even sowing, a transplanting trowel with notches for matching the depth, and heavy garden gloves with metal fingers attached for cultivating around small plants.

A fertilizing distributor which is equally good for vegetable or flower plot is a hand machine that will take care of any commercial fertilizer and distribute it evenly in any desired quantity. In backyard gardens, or the like, the fertilizer may of course be spaded in. A small fertilizer distributor, to care for golf greens, lawns, parks and cemeteries has a rotor attachment which spreads the fertilizer in an even band thirty-six inches wide. Rakes, weeders, grass hooks and shears are all covered in this article at Section 1, the vegetable garden, or Section 3, the lawn. Gathering shears are useful when flowers with either long or short stems are being picked. With them it is possible to reach into a rose bush, and cut a flower without being scratched. The stem is cleanly cut and the upper part of the stem containing the flower has two thin metal bands clamped about it which holds but does not crush. Another oddity has handles thinly wrapped in straw; this scissor comes in three sizes. **Gloves** made for use rather than looks are to be had in different styles and colors; they are thorn-proof.

Adjustable plant supports are obtainable for practically all flowers. Some are painted green and are practically invisible when in place; others are of wire and galvanized metal. (See STAKES AND STAKING.) Flower pots can be acquired for every need and purpose (see FLOWER POTS). **Kneeling pads,** waterproofed, save much wear on clothing, as well as preventing dampness from the ground to penetrate. Wire guards for protecting choice bulbs and plants come in different sizes and mesh.

Nonkinkable hose (see the discussion at vegetable garden and lawn in this article), with a number of nozzles suited to seedbeds, fragile flowers, etc., is more feasible for a flower garden than the underground sprinkler system. A pipe line may be run along the edge of the border, through the fern bed, and among the rock garden, with the nozzles set two or three inches above the ground. A line of pipe mounted on wheels may be fitted with fine rose sprays, some of which are designed especially for rose bushes, which will spray the under as well as the upper foliage. A special nozzle to hold a cartridge of fertilizer is made to use with a garden hose.

A decorative refuse can should be placed at some convenient spot in the garden, to care for the debris which collects during the day.

## 3. LAWNS

Any new lawn has to have a firm seedbed. This is often made by rolling the soil before sowing the seed. An easy running **roller,** with rounded edges to prevent tearing the sod on established lawns, is the water ballast type. This can be adjusted to varying weights with water. A good substitute for the roller consists of planks fastened together in the form of a drag, or, as they are known in some parts of the country, a boat. These **plank drags** often take the place of the harrow, discussed in the making of the vegetable garden above.

If an old lawn is to be renovated it will need food, and the iron rake mentioned in the vegetable garden above will clean the surface of refuse, loosen the surface soil, and eliminate many of the spreading type of weeds. Wooden rakes, either the self-cleaning sort which do not clog up with debris, or a heavier one with three steel reinforcing bows, may be used to gather up leaves and light litter. **Lawncombs** with flat steel teeth, and a grass rake with curved teeth, will clean the lawn of the smallest particles. Bamboo and rubber rakes are excellent (see vegetable garden above). A small fertilizer distributor will apply plant food to the lawn evenly and quickly.

There are many types of **lawn mowers,** including the horse-drawn and gasoline power motors for large estates. For small backyard or terraced gardens one of the best mowers obtainable is made of tough aluminum alloy castings. This make is approximately fourteen pounds lighter in weight than the average lawn mower. The width of the cut varies from twelve to twenty-one inches, depending upon the type selected. **Lawn trimmers,** working on the same basis as the lawn mowers, may be had in different designs. One is constructed with a slanting side plate which makes it possible to cut grass in places heretofore accessible only to hand shears. Another, with an eight-inch cut, trims along walks, walls and flower beds which are out of the reach of the ordinary mower. Still another make is a combination trimmer and edger for turf. A lawn cleaner will remove not only cut grass, but litter, leaves and trash. It works on the same principle as the vacuum cleaner operates on carpet. Lawn cultivators are

---

* Special articles on the subjects indicated by an asterisk (*) will be found at the words so marked.

expensive, but for large plots which need re-seeding, fertilizing or top-dressing they are invaluable. The disks aerate the soil, break up hard-baked surfaces, and destroy moss and fungous growths.

For lawn edging the most convenient tool is the revolving disk edger. It has a long handle and can be used by the operator in a standing position. Either the English or American **edging knives** are good. These are fitted with strong, straight, wooden handles. A D-shaped handle can also be obtained. **Grass hooks** or **sickles** of either English or American manufacture are a necessity for clearing out weedy spots, trimming around places where the grass is too long to be cut with grass shears, etc. Scythes must be used for heavy mowing or large stands of long grass. **Grass shears,** of domestic, English or German make, must be selected with handles which fit the contour of the hand; the best ones are of malleable iron, japanned, or Sheffield steel. **Lawn shears** can be bought with two wheels and a blade which lies flat against the ground, for cutting grass under trees and fences. A **turfing spade** or **sod lifter** must be kept very sharp in order to do good work. The blade, when correctly sharpened, cuts rapidly and to an even thickness. Another good tool for use as a grass and weeding implement is two-edged and cuts equally well on either the forward or backward swing. This swings easily on a three-foot steel handle, much the same as a golf club.

The best system for thoroughly watering a lawn is the underground system which can be operated with a turn of a valve. Unfortunately these are not possible for all gardens, but a good substitute for the underground sprinkling system can be bought at small cost. These portable sets are obtainable in sets of three tees, square spray heads, and one hose cap. When used between lengths of nonkinkable hose of about fifteen feet, the one set will care for about 675 square feet of lawn. For small lawns there are the whirligig, and for large ones the oscillating, types of sprinkler. This latter is mounted on rollers so it can be moved from place to place without shutting off the water. A heavy spray but not a solid stream is desirable for a lawn, as too coarse a stream digs the soil from between the grass plants. A waterfan will distribute water from seventeen nozzles at once, over a rectangular area forty by forty-five feet. Another good sprinkler is of the revolving or stationary spray type, while a large circle sprinkler for golf courses and large lawns will cover an area of 125 feet in diameter, and delivers up to forty gallons of water per minute. There are all sorts of fine rose or large spray nozzles which can be attached to different types of sprinklers.

### 4. Shrubs and Hedges

While fixed rules for the pruning and shaping of shrubs and hedges are mentioned at Pruning and Hedges, there are many appliances on the market to make these tasks easy, and grouped here for convenience.

**Pruning shears** for pruning, and trimming (even for bulb or tuber separation), come in a number of designs. Some of these are made of lightweight materials for use by women, and others with curved, pointed, double cutting blades for rugged work. The blades of one type of **hedge shears** are fitted with a spring tension that keeps them in position on heavy work. **Secateurs,** a very sharp type of pruning shears, are ideal for shearing evergreens. Electric hedge trimmers will do the work much faster than hand shears. Attachments come with these machines to adapt them to flat, round, or pivot tops, as well as side cuttings. In the pruning of old wood on shrubs a sharp saw does a cleaner job than shears. These **pruning saws** come in various sizes, with straight or curved blades; some have extra long, needle-point, special-shaped teeth. These saws are of use also in the orchard. See Orchard, below.

Espalier shrubs, as well as young fruit trees, can be fastened up without injury by means of **wall nails.** A soft metal extension clasps the plant to the wall. These are also used as climbing vine supports.

### 5. Orchard

The pruning and trimming tools, with the exception of those mentioned specifically for hedge work, are also of use in the orchard. In addition, the following are of value in the fruit orchard and in the care of shade trees: a ten-foot pole pruner, which the operator can handle from the ground; extra large tree-pruning shears for heavy wood; horticultural **knives** for budding, propagating and also for pruning. In a great many cases a chisel will be found a helpful tool — this can be bought in the same matching design as the **grafting knife.** Grafting wax (*see* Grafting Wax) and pruning compound, an antiseptic dressing for use on pruning wounds and cavities in trees, can be bought in large or small quantities, as preferred.

Although the poison bait method is used by many orchardists as the main control of protecting their young trees from mice, wire guards are commonly used also. An asbestos torch is the best for burning caterpillars' nests.

Baskets are essential for picking and storing fruit and vegetables. A half-bushel size is the best for pears and apples; market baskets, also useful for gathering flowers, are best for grapes and peaches, which will bruise easily if carelessly piled on top of each other.

### 6. Greenhouse, Hotbeds and Cold Frames

Frames, mats, glass and shutters for cold frames and hotbeds are thoroughly discussed under Cold Frames. To keep frames, hotbeds and greenhouses in order, however, many small tools are required. Among these is the **putty bulb,** with a tube for applying liquid putty to glazing glass, or a **mastica** machine for applying mastica which, unlike putty, does not crack. Glass cutters and glazing points are also required. Special thermometers for greenhouse, hotbed, and mushroom growing cost little and are essential for keeping proper temperatures (*see* Thermometers).

Flower pots and tubs (*see* Flower Pots) come in all sizes, according to the type of plant for which they are adapted. They should be kept clean, the tubs painted when necessary, and may be kept either in the tool house or greenhouse proper. Watering cans, such as were discussed in the vegetable garden above, may be used also for the greenhouse. A special type sprinkler, shaped like a bulb syringe, with an angle neck, is made especially for greenhouse plants. Other types of **syringes** can be bought, in varying sizes. Raffia fiber and tape are useful in tying up plants. Spraying apparatus is discussed at Spraying and Dusting.

Garden flats for seed sowing and forcing are so designed that the front is removable. They come in different sizes and take either two- or three-inch pots, or, more often, are filled with soil for starting seedlings. The standard flat is a shallow box, 3 in. deep, 18 in. long, and 12 in. wide. It will easily grow from 800–1000 seedlings if the seeds are sown 10–12 seeds to the inch and the rows are 2 in. apart. Of course such densely crowded seedlings must be thinned almost immediately. *See* Management of Seedlings at Seeds and Seedage

### 7. Garden Gadgets

Garden gadgets is the term applied to numerous little accessories of gardening which are not actual necessities but which do much toward making the life of a gardener more easy and pleasant. They make nice holiday gifts, being both practical and ornamental. Some are for house decoration only and others are for the garden proper. More than one hundred of these gadgets were on display recently at the show given by the Horticultural Society of New York.

The name **Sunclock** has been given to a new type of sundial which is weatherproof and color-fast. It has a gnomon at the base, which is adjustable for various altitudes. It is utterly unlike other sundials but inexpensive and practical.

A number of small watering pots have been designed for the indoor gardener. Brass and copper have been used in a French design, so that they are ornamental as well as useful. Another design is in the form of an old ship's bell, finished in heavy pewter.

All women who weed or plant gardens will be pleased with the combination tool-bag and pad. It is waterproofed material in red and white and has a pocket to hold scissors, trowel, seeds, and other small garden tools. Gloves and hat may be bought to match.

---

\* Special articles on the subjects indicated by an asterisk (\*) will be found at the words so marked.

Although flower holders are thoroughly covered in this book (see FLOWER ARRANGING), the ones mentioned here are novelties only, and must be considered as such. An excellent one is made of heavy wire in three different sizes and resembles a mass of hairpins closed side up. The flowers can be stuck in at any angle. Another is a group of enameled tubes of different types, to be set in odd parts of flower dishes, as wanted. Lead holders are made to represent different flowers, such as chrysanthemums. Others of lead are heavy enough to hold branches of forsythia, rhododendron, laurel and sprays of berried shrubs.

Fertilized transplanting pots are for the amateur dirt gardener. The seeds are planted in the little pots and when ready for transplanting the entire container is set in the ground. The container itself disintegrates and acts as fertilizer for the young seedling. A set of forty glass vials were arranged for the storage of seeds. Three glass tubes for planting seeds go with the set; the seed is placed in the tube and dropped as wished. Green and silver paper covers for milk bottles, used at flower shows as containers for cut flowers, are unique. Another gadget admirable for use at flower shows is brownskin paper. This is waterproof and amply protects the table, can be used many times, and fits well with any background.

To combat the dry atmosphere of steam-heated houses and apartments, an humidifier is shown in which all that is necessary to operate it is to plug into an electric switch. Moist air is then thrown into the room at all times.

Lamps, in various designs, have attachments for plants. Houses made of straw for all types of birds are extremely attractive. A miniature feeding station has a special arrangement for holding a large piece of suet; other suet holders are especially designed to hang from trees.

A wire shrub protector has three prongs which push into the ground and thus keep dogs and other animals from coming into contact with the young plants. A woven wire screen which fastens at the top is to protect flowers in beetle-infested regions. It is set over the entire plant and the base rests upon the ground, in the same fashion as plants are covered by baskets to protect them from frost. A kit for soil testing, with notebook, is for testing various kinds of soil by chemical analysis.

Artistic wrought-iron wall brackets and stands are now made with floral decorations, and an attachment to hold either flowers or a hanging vine goes with them. An electrically heated case, with straight sides of glass and a flat top, is for the purpose of starting choice seeds in early spring. It is good-looking and can be placed in the living room if necessary.

### 8. PROPER CARE OF TOOLS

During the frenzy of spring gardening there is little time to give your tools the care and attention they deserve. But when the gardening season is over all tools and implements should be put away in a clean condition. A well-kept tool makes any job easier and gives a better result. Dirty, rusty spades and hoes do not slide into the soil or make clean cuts. It is also important to keep these and similar tools with a cutting edge sharp throughout the season; a file can be carried in the pocket for use when necessary. Any tool which comes into contact with the soil should be cleaned after each job, as soil will adhere to a dull and rusty tool, with the result that the gardener will find himself lifting twice as heavy a load as he should. An oily rag may be run over blades and handles and the metal parts rubbed dry and clean with a rag. Oil lawn mowers thoroughly and have the blades sharpened and the machine overhauled. This will save a lot of time and bother next spring. Trimmers and grass knives should be sharpened and a few drops of oil applied to clippers, scissors and pruning shears.

If you are lucky enough to have a tool house (for exterior design see STRUCTURES) all the small tools can be conveniently hung in racks. Shelves can be used if preferred. The larger tools can be stood up on end or hung on the wall. If bands in some bright color are painted on the handles, and initialed in a contrasting shade, there will be less chance of their being lost or not returned by a borrower. See TOOL HOUSE.

A great deal of damage is done to the garden hose by allowing water to stand in it, especially during the hot summer months. Especially is this true if the hose is left in the sun; when the water gets hot the rubber rots and hardens on the outside as well, which shortens its usefulness considerably. If the hose is mounted on a reel, on wheels, and wound every time after using, most of the water will be eliminated. Before storing for the winter drain the hose thoroughly and coil it in a three- or four-foot circle. After tying it together in three or four places hang it up in a cool place, but not where it will have to stand freezing weather.

When the wheelbarrow is put up for the winter give it a good coat of paint or clean and oil it, if it does not need redoing. Cold frame and hotbed sash should be gone over at some slack time. — C. H. M.

**TOON, TOONA.** See CEDRELA TOONA.

**TOOTHACHE TREE.** See ZANTHOXYLUM.

**TOOTHWORT** = *Plumbago scandens*. See also DENTARIA.

**TOP-DRESS.** As the name implies, top-dressing is the application of a dressing of manure, fertilizer, humus or the proceeds of the compost* pile to crops without plowing. In the garden the material that is used for top-dressing would, or should, be raked in. And in top-dressing a lawn the fertilizer or manure or humus would usually be better distributed if the lawn is thoroughly raked with a steel rake. See LAWN.

The great advantage of top-dressing is that the material used for it can be scattered or sown, depending on its consistency, without any disturbance of the crop in place, and to its very decided advantage. Care should be used in top-dressing a border or vegetable garden not to get raw fertilizer or manure on the plants. Spread or scatter it carefully between the rows.

To the amateur top-dressing may seem very like mulching.* But the latter is often, especially in the growing season, for the purpose of conserving moisture or to keep down weeds, neither of which is accomplished by top-dressing. While it is true that a winter mulch of manure may feed the plant, this is not the primary function of a mulch, while top-dressing is purely this or the improvement of the physical condition of the soil.

Materials for top-dressing and the amount used will vary with the crop. On lawns some form of non-acid, weed-free humus (which see) is often of the greatest benefit. It should be scattered about 1 in. thick and raked in. If a commercial fertilizer is indicated, this should be sown like grass seed (no thicker), preferably before a rain.

For the flowers and vegetable garden a good material for top-dressing would be:

2 Parts of thoroughly rotted material from the compost* pile.

1 Part well-rotted stable manure.

1 Part of leaf mold or commercial humus.

The three ingredients should be thoroughly mixed, all lumps broken up, and spread when reasonably dry to ensure an even distribution. Generally such a mixture should not be applied more than ¾ in. thick, and worked into the soil with a rake or cultivator.

Top-dressing is especially valuable on sandy soil, or for crops which are rich feeders, or where speed, as in lettuce growing, is particularly desirable. It is also very beneficial for pot plants where constant watering is apt to leach out much food.

For special sorts of top-dressing, such as those needed for the azaleas and rhododendrons (which are really permanent mulches), for the rock garden, and where commercial fertilizers are used, see AZALEA, ROCK GARDEN, FERTILIZERS. See also MULCH AND MULCHING.

**TOPEPO.** A little-known, tomato-like vegetable, assumed to be a hybrid between the red pepper and the tomato. It is of no garden significance.

---

* Special articles on the subjects indicated by an asterisk (*) will be found at the words so marked.

**TOPER'S-PLANT** = *Sanguisorba minor*.

**TOP-GRAFTING.** See GRAFTING.

**TOPIARY.** Topiary work is the clipping and training of shrubs into ornamental or grotesque figures — which they really are depends upon whether you think topiary work artistic or not. Ever since the days of the Romans, who were expert topiarists, there has always been a prejudice against it, one English writer describing topiary as a "monument of perverted taste." It is undeniably effective only when held within rigid limits and it often has not been. To see an English countryside peppered up with vegetative foxes, birds, children, and all sorts of grotesque geometrical figures is not artistic, but it does show a high degree of hort. skill. Topiary is far more common there than here, and only in a few of the oldest and finest estates is topiary work in America likely to be seen.

The basic material, in the North, is usually privet, but far finer effects may be secured from yew or arborvitae, if you live in the region where they are thoroughly hardy. See THUJA and TAXUS. See also HEDGES for the initial care of privet.

**TOP ONION** = *Allium cepa viviparum*.

**TOPSOIL.** See SOILS.

**TOP-WORK.** To make over the top of a shrub or tree by substituting better varieties for the existing one. It is usually done by grafting or budding the desirable varieties upon the existing stock. For the details see Top-grafting at GRAFTING. See also BUDDING.

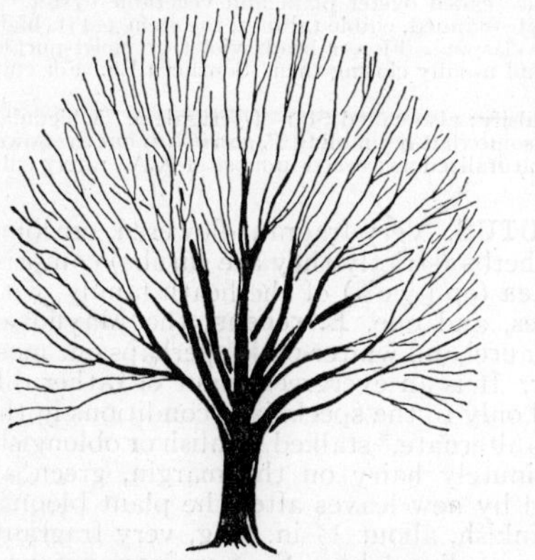

**TORCH LILY.** See KNIPHOFIA and DORYANTHES EXCELSA.

**TORCH TREE FAMILY.** The Fouquieriaceae. See FOUQUIERIA.

**TORENIA** (tor-ren'i-a). African and Asiatic perennial or annual herbs of the family Scrophulariaceae, comprising over 30 species, of which T. fournieri, from Cochin-China, is a flower-garden plant grown as a tender annual (see ANNUALS). It is a much-branched herb, 10–12 in. high, with a 4-angled stem, and opposite,* ovalish, toothed, stalked leaves, 1½–2 in. long. Flowers blue, or blue-violet and yellow, in stout, stalked clusters in the leaf-axils,* or terminal. Corolla 2-lipped,* the upper lip* faintly 2-lobed, the lower lip 3-lobed, the central lobe blotched yellow at the base. Fruit an oblong capsule.* A useful and attractive annual, good for the border, for the rock garden, for edging, and for hanging baskets. The *var.* **compacta**, the blue wing flower, is a lower form particularly suited for edging (which see). A related species, T. flava, with yellow and purple flowers, a native of eastern As., is sometimes seen in rare collections. It should be grown also as a tender annual. (Named for Olaf Toren, Swedish clergyman and botanist.)

**TORII.** See JAPANESE GARDEN.

**TORINGO CRABAPPLE** = *Malus sieboldi*.

**TORINGOIDES** (tor-ring-goy'deez, but see OÏDES). Resembling the toringo crabapple.

**TORREYA** (tor'ree-a). Six species of Asiatic or eastern North American evergreen trees of the family Taxaceae, three of them grown for ornament. They are handsome trees with fissured bark and the branches in whorled* tiers. Leaves 2-ranked, narrow, stiff, and almost prickle-tipped, with two white or brownish bands beneath. Flowers in the garden sense none, being represented by a collection of 6–8 groups of 4 stamens* each in the male flowers, and stalkless ovules in the female flowers followed by drupe*-like, slightly fleshy fruit. The male and female flowers usually on separate plants. (Named for John Torrey, American botanist.) Also known as *Tumion*.

These plants are closely related to the yews (*Taxus*), being chiefly distinguished by the drupe-like fruit. For cult. see EVERGREENS.

**californica.** California nutmeg. A tree up to 60 or even 75 ft. high, the bark gray-brown, the branches drooping. Leaves line-like, 2–2½ in. long, shining green. Fruit egg-shaped or oblongish, about 1¼ in. long, light green, but streaked with purple. Calif. March–May. Hardy from zone* 6 southward, occasionally dropping its leaves near the northern edge of its cultural range.

**nucifera.** A Japanese tree up to 75 ft. high, less as cult. Leaves lance-shaped, ¾–1¼ in. long, dark, shining green above. Fruit stalkless, oblongish, about 1¼ in. long, green, but faintly streaked with purple. May. Hardy from zone* 3 southward.

**taxifolia.** Stinking cedar. An evergreen tree not over 45 ft. high, usually half that. Leaves narrow, line-like, almost spine-tipped, about 1¼ in. long, dark shining green above, of decidedly unpleasant odor when bruised. Fruit inverted egg-shaped, about 1¼ in. long, purple. Fla. Hardy from zone* 7 southward, possibly in protected parts of zone* 6.

*TORTUOSA, -us, -um* (tor-tew-ō'sa). Tortuose.*

**TORTUOSE** = Flexuous; *i.e.* more or less twisting or zigzag.

**TORUS.** See RECEPTACLE.

*TOTAI* (toe'ty, also toe-tah'ee). A South American vernacular name for the palm *Acrocomia totai*.

**TOUCH-ME-NOT.** See IMPATIENS.

*TOVARENSIS, -e* (toe-var-ren'sis). From Tovar, Colombia.

**TOWNSENDIA** (town-zen'di-a). Western North American perennial (or biennial) herbs of the family Compositae, of secondary garden interest, but the two below occasionally taken from the wild for the informal border or rock garden. They have alternate,* narrow leaves without marginal teeth, and solitary, but usually numerous aster-like heads composed of both ray* and disk* flowers. (Named for David Townsend, Pennsylvania botanist.)

The two below are chiefly Rocky Mountain plants suited to the rock garden, where the first species flowers earlier than almost any other plant of the daisy family. They need a gritty soil, and in the East may not be hardy, for while they can stand any amount of cold, summer heat and moisture do not agree with them.

**exscapa.** Easter daisy. A practically stemless perennial, the stalkless flower heads nestled in a rosette of very narrow leaves. Flower head with white or purplish rays. Rocky Mountain regions. Feb.–April (in Colo.).

**grandiflora.** A spreading perennial (sometimes biennial) 9–15 in. high, usually branched. Leaves narrow, line-like. Flower heads about 1 in. wide, blue or violet. Western Neb., Colo., and N. Mex., but not so high in the mountains as the last. Summer.

*TOXICODENDRON* (tock-si-ko-den'dron). An old, and now obsolete generic name for the poison ivy and its relatives. See RHUS.

*TOXYLON* = *Maclura*.

**TOYON.** A single species of beautiful evergreen shrubs from California and Lower California, constituting the genus **Heteromeles** (het-er-om'e-leez) of the rose family. It is an important bee plant, called also (in Calif.) the Christmasberry, redberry, and California holly, and known to science as **H. arbutifolia.** It is a shrub up to 15 ft. high, occasionally tree-like, with alternate,* thick, leathery, oblongish, sharply toothed and abruptly pointed leaves, 2–4 in. long. Flowers white, scarcely ¼ in. wide, in dense clusters (panicles*) 2–3 in. high. Petals 5. Stamens* 10. Fruit bright red (rarely yellow), oblongish, about ¼ in. long, persistent and decorative. Summer. Not hardy north of zone* 7, but widely planted in Calif. for ornament, and much used for Christmas decorations. Propagated by seeds or by layers or cuttings. (*Heteromeles* is from the Greek for different apple, in allusion to the fruit being unlike related genera with apple-like fruit.)

A top-worked tree, the heavy lines showing the original stock, the light lines the new growth resulting from the budding or grafting. Such wholesale top-working takes a few years to complete.

---

* Special articles on the subjects indicated by an asterisk (*) will be found at the words so marked.

**TRACHELIUM** (tra-kee'li-um). Little-grown perennial herbs of the family Campanulaceae, comprising about half a dozen species from the Mediterranean region, one of which, **T. caeruleum**, the throatwort, is somewhat cult. for ornament. It is a biennial or short-lived perennial, 12–30 in. high, with alternate,* ovalish, unequally toothed leaves, 2–3 in. long. Flowers blue (rarely white), in a dense terminal cluster (cyme*). Corolla tubular, about ⅓ in. long, its limb 5-lobed, the lobes narrow. Fruit an angled capsule.* Southern Eu. Summer. Not hardy in the North, where it may be treated as a greenhouse annual, or cuttings may be made of old plants. (*Trachelium* is from the Greek for neck, in allusion to its supposed value for throat trouble.) The genus is closely related to *Campanula*, one of which is called *Campanula trachelium*, but the true bellflowers are finer garden plants than the cult. species of *Trachelium*.

**TRACHELOSPERMUM** (tra-kell-o-sper'mum). Indo-Malayan or Chinese, mostly showy-flowered, woody vines of the family Apocynaceae, one of them, **T. jasminoides**, the star or Confederate jasmine, widely grown for ornament from zone* 6 southward, and also a favorite greenhouse plant in the North. It is a high-climbing vine, without tendrils* or aerial roots, which climbs by twining and is rather slow-growing. Leaves evergreen, opposite,* ovalish, short-stalked, narrowed both ends, 2–3 in. long, without marginal teeth. Flowers white, star-like, about ¾ in. wide, most beautifully fragrant, grouped in rather sparse, long-stalked clusters (cymes*). Corolla short-tubed, its 5 oblong lobes twisted to the left. Fruit consisting of 2 long, slender pods (follicles*), which are round in cross-section. The plant, a long-time favorite throughout the South, will grow in a variety of soils, but is slow in getting established. In the greenhouse it should be planted in a tub (using potting mixture* 4), where, by clipping, it can be made into a handsome, bushy plant 3–4 ft. high. It needs a warm-temperate house and moisture during spring and summer, but a cooler house and less water in the winter. Southern China. Blooming outdoors in April–May. (*Trachelospermum* is from the Greek for neck and seed, in allusion to the seed having a neck.)

**TRACHYCARPUS** (tra-kee-kar'pus). Rather low-growing Asiatic, fan palms, among the hardiest known, and generally not thriving in the tropics, nor does the only cult. species do well in zone* 9 in Fla. In zone* 8, and over the warmest parts of zone* 7, the one below is perfectly hardy and has been known to stand temperatures of 20°, thus hardy up to the coasts of the Carolinas, and nearly throughout the Pacific Coast. Of the half-dozen or so known species, only **T. fortunei**, the hemp or windmill palm, is commonly cult., but this is widely planted outdoors, and tubbed specimens are much used for patios, porches, and for indoor decoration northward. As cult. it is a low, slow-growing palm, the trunk rarely over 10 ft. high (40 ft. in the wild), and densely clothed with the remains of the old leaf sheaths. Leaves nearly round, fan-like, stiffish, 2–4 ft. wide, divided nearly to the middle into many narrow, pointed segments, the leafstalk roughish. Flower cluster among the crown of leaves, short, the flowers unisexual* or polygamous* (*see* PALMACEAE). Fruit drupe*-like, pea-sized, bluish. Burma, Indo-China, perhaps in Jap. (*Trachycarpus* is from the Greek for rough and rigid, in allusion to the lobed fruit of some species.) The plant is often known as *T. excelsa*, and is just as often offered as *Chamaerops* (which see).

**TRACHYMENE** (tra-kee-mee'ne). Chiefly Australian, annual or perennial herbs of the carrot family, comprising over 25 species, one of which, **T. coerulea**, the blue lace-flower has become, in the last 25 years, a very popular flower garden and greenhouse annual. It is grown for its beautiful flowers which strongly suggest a pale blue or lavender edition of the common wild carrot or Queen Anne's-lace (*see* CARROT). It is an erect, but weak-stemmed plant, 18–30 in. high, with twice- or thrice-compound leaves, the ultimate segments narrow, and cut into 3 narrow lobes. Flowers minute, but numerous and borne in a flat umbel,* 2–3 in. wide. Fruit flat (*see* UMBELLIFERAE). The blue lace-flower can be grown as a tender annual, or the seed can be sown directly where wanted (*see* ANNUALS). It is not particular as to soil, but flowers better if the plants are a bit crowded. Commonly grown also in the cool greenhouse, where flowers may be had almost throughout the year by planting a succession of seed. It is commonly grown by florists. (*Trachymene* is from the Greek for rough membrane, in allusion to the fruit of some species.) It is often offered as *Didiscus*.

**TRACHYPLEURA, -us, -um** (tra-kee-ploor'ra). With rough ribs or veins.

**TRACTOR.** *See* Section 1, at TOOLS AND IMPLEMENTS.

**TRADESCANTIA.** *See* SPIDERWORT.

**TRAGOPOGON** (tra-go-pō'gon). Goatsbeard. Rather coarse, taprooted, biennial or perennial, Old World herbs of the family Compositae, comprising nearly 40 species, of which only two are of garden interest, one a root vegetable, the other a weedy plant, sometimes cult. for ornament. They are milky-juiced herbs, with narrow, grass-like, sometimes keeled leaves, the base often clasping. Flower heads solitary, large, yellow or purple, all the flowers strap-shaped, with no disk florets.* Fruit a longish, stick-like achene.* (*Tragopogon* is Greek for a goat's beard.)

The first species is cult. only for its edible taproot* (*see* SALSIFY). The second, often a mere weed, is a hardy biennial seldom cult. for ornament and scarcely worth growing.

porrifolius. Salsify; also called oyster plant and vegetable oyster. A biennial with a deep, white-skinned, edible taproot, the stem 3–4 ft. high. Leaves keeled, the base clasping. Flower heads violet or violet-purple, blooming before noon, and usually closing then. Southern Eu. For cult. *see* SALSIFY.

pratensis. Meadow salsify; also called Star-of-Jerusalem. A biennial, weedy herb, 2–3 ft. high, somewhat resembling *T. porrifolius* but the flower head yellow. Eu., but naturalized as a weed in most of N.A., rarely cult. for ornament.

**TRAILING ARBUTUS.** Very fragrant-flowered, creeping or prostrate woody herbs (strictly they are shrubs) comprising the genus **Epigaea** (ep-i-jee'a) of the heath family, with one Japanese species, and one, **E. repens**, the Mayflower (also called ground laurel and winter pink), perhaps our most fragrant wild flower. It is an evergreen plant of rather difficult culture, suited only to the specialized conditions in the wild garden. Leaves alternate,* stalked, ovalish or oblongish, ¾–2½ in. long, minutely hairy on the margin, green all winter, but replaced by new leaves after the plant blooms. Flowers white or pinkish, about ½ in. long, very fragrant, the corolla with 5 spreading lobes. Stamens* 10, not protruding. Sometimes male and female flowers are separate and on different plants. Fruit a small capsule,* which becomes berry-like after it splits. Seeds extremely minute, often lacking. Eastern N.A. but westward to Mich. and Saskatchewan, mostly in dry woods. April–May. Hardy everywhere, but not easy to grow. For cult. *see* Wild Garden. (*Epigaea* is from the Greek for upon the earth, in allusion to its prostrate habit.)

**TRAILING AZALEA** = *Loiseleuria procumbens*.

**TRAILING BEGONIA** = *Cissus discolor*.

**TRAILING FIRE** = *Gilia rubra*.

**TRAILING FUCHSIA** = *Fuchsia procumbens*.

**TRAILING PLANTS.** *See* VINES.

**TRAINING GARDENERS.** *See* GARDEN SCHOOLS.

**TRAINING PLANTS.** The term *training*, as applied to plants, is indicative of the fact that the cultivator can control the habit of his plants more or less as he sees fit, but in the main, training is confined to subjects of long-lived character. It can, however, be practiced on some herbs by pinching.

PINCHING. Some annual flowering plants are to some extent so trained. Many, notably *Schizanthus*, mignonette, *Calendula*, etc., are apt to run to flower without branching if the point of the leading growth is not nipped out after they reach 16 in. or so in height. Pinching out the tip induces branching, and by repeated pinching of the succeeding growths

---

* Special articles on the subjects indicated by an asterisk (*) will be found at the words so marked.

it is possible to develop huge specimens of *Schizanthus* or *Nemesia*.

Pinching naturally delays flowering, but when such plants are grown in pots, under glass, it enables the grower to time the flowering when wanted. The greenhouse carnation, if not pinched after the rooted cutting is 6 in. tall, will run up to flower during early summer and few or no blooms would be secured during winter. By successive pinches up to July or Aug., many shoots that will flower from October on are secured. Marguerites, fuchsias, geraniums (*Pelargonium*) and similar soft and semi-hardwooded plants grown in pots, especially when desired as large specimens more than one year old, are repeatedly pinched during the growing season, and in some cases the shoots are tied to wire framework to develop formal designs.

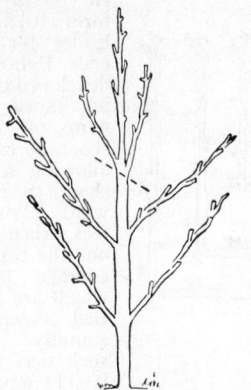
A whip or one-year maiden. See text for details.

Some varieties of Chrysanthemums are similarly trained by repeated pinching and tying in various shapes such as domes, pyramids, boats, airplanes and so forth. The so-called Japanese cascade type of Chrysanthemum, easily raised from seed, can in one season be grown to form, when in bloom, a veritable cascade, with branches hanging downward several feet and bearing many hundreds of small, single flowers. Large-flowered varieties, particularly one known as Felton, have been trained in circular form with a spread of 16 ft. and bearing up to 600 or more flowers. Infinite skill and patience and ample greenhouse space are necessary to obtain such specimens. The vogue for these phenomena of culture was more general 40 or 50 years ago than it is today.

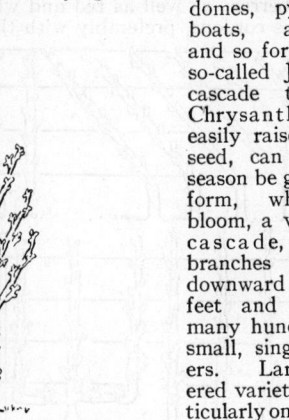
The same plant the second year

The general principles of training by pinching are simple. At the base of every leaf on the stem is one or more dormant growth buds or eyes. Some of these will naturally develop into side branches or laterals, but the removal of the top of a main stem encourages these dormant buds to grow sooner than they otherwise would. If the tips of these side growths are again pinched, still more shoots will develop. In most cases the first pinch is done when a young plant has six or eight leaf joints, but when a tree-shaped or standard fuchsia, geranium, lantana, or marguerite is desired, the leading shoot is encouraged to go upward until it reaches 3 ft. or more in height, all side shoots being removed as soon as they appear. When a clear stem of the desired height is attained, the point is nipped out, and all succeeding shoots that appear are similarly pinched when they have four to eight leaves until a tree-like head is secured. Careful staking at all times is necessary.

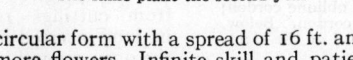
Horizontal cordon

Various climbing plants are trained into globes or other designs by pinching and tying. The English Ivy is quite commonly trained over a wire framework when grown in pots or tubs, such specimens being used for outdoor decoration during the summer months. Another system of training entails the use of shears as well as tying the growths on to the framework, this being termed topiary work. It is confined mostly to hardy evergreens and is a long and tedious process.

## Fruit Trees

The training of fruit trees is an art worthy of far greater attention in gardens than it receives. Practiced in France and other European countries for well over a century the cultivation of trained fruit trees is scarcely known to the average American home gardener and but few commercial nurserymen offer such trees. The most common patterns or designs adopted for apples and pears are **cordons**, oblique, upright and horizontal; **espalier, fan or gridiron; pyramid** and **bush.** Fan or espalier shapes are used for plums, cherries, and peaches, but these subjects so trained usually do best if grown upon walls. Many large European gardens are surrounded by high brick walls, these invariably being devoted to trained fruits, the shelter afforded serving to ward off frosts when the trees are blooming. Brick or stone dwelling houses, too, are frequently to be seen supporting trained fruit trees, the entire side of a house perhaps being covered by one pear tree.

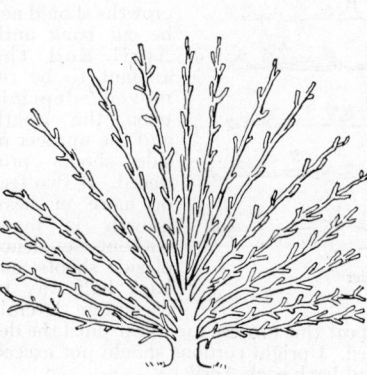
Fan-trained fruit tree

The training of fruit trees is essentially French, hence the term cordon, meaning cord or rope, and espalier, taken from epaulet or shoulder strap, the branches of an espalier tree being more or less at right angles or shoulder-like. Fan and gridiron are English terms used for trees that are modified forms of the espalier.

To obtain success with trained fruits, especially if small, early-fruiting trees are desired, it is essential that they be budded or grafted on dwarfing rootstocks, viz. paradise for apples, quince for pears, mahaleb for Plums, and mazzard for cherries. Peaches are scarcely worth considering since they are too short-lived in most parts of the United States.

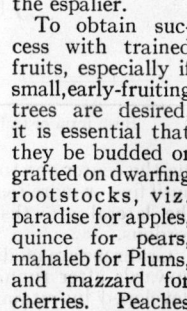
Pyramid

---

* Special articles on the subjects indicated by an asterisk (*) will be found at the words so marked.

Trained, fruiting-size trees, three or more years old, may be secured from some nurseryman, but if the gardener would raise his own he must either secure the necessary material and bud his own or buy one-year-old trees known as maidens or whips, and train them himself. One-year trees usually have straight stems without branches. If to be grown as cordons, they may be planted where they are to stand, in rows 18 in. apart and 5 ft. between the rows. Cut them back to 18 in. or so, and when the new growths start, decide whether to be one- or two-stemmed and carry up the strongest, tying to a cane or stake to keep them straight.

Any shoots that appear below the leaders should be cut back to the last eye or leaf at the end of June. All side shoots or laterals that appear on the leaders should also be cut back to one leaf when they reach 12 in. The top of the leading growth or growths should not be cut back until April and the amount to be removed depends upon the length and the number of side shoots produced. If two feet or more of head growth is made without evidence of side shoots, cut back half way to encourage laterals or fruiting spurs. Repeat this process each year until the desired length is attained. Upright cordons should not exceed 10 ft. After that, head back each April.

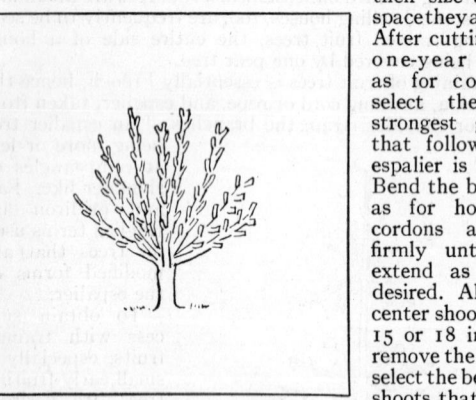
Espalier

Horizontal cordons consist of two stems which should be tied down in their second year. Horizontal cordons are used for edging paths, and since the bending down encourages side growths it may not be necessary to cut back the leaders until they reach their full length which may be 10 ft. or more.

Espalier, gridiron and fan trees require more attention and their training may be spread over some years, depending on their size and the space they are to fill. After cutting back one-year whips as for cordons, select the three strongest growths that follow if an espalier is desired. Bend the best pair as for horizontal cordons and tie firmly until they extend as far as desired. Allow the center shoot to run 15 or 18 in., then remove the top and select the best three shoots that follow, training two horizontally and allowing the center one to go upward. Repeat in successive years until five or more tiers are attained. During this training all the lateral growths must be cut back as suggested for cordons.

Bush form of training fruit trees

Gridirons are modified espaliers, the branches being turned upwards after running horizontally several feet. Fans are developed by retaining all the shoots of even strength the first year, cutting back the center one hard the following year to encourage as many shoots from near one point as possible.

Bush trees are secured by selecting six or seven of the best growths that follow the cutting-back of a maiden tree, training them outwards in basin-shaped form with no center leader for preference. Pyramids are developed by bending down six or more of the first shoots horizontally, allowing a center shoot to run upward about two feet, then taking out the top to encourage branches which are likewise tied down horizontally. Several such tiers may be built up, each somewhat shorter than the preceding one, until a complete pyramid is obtained. The laterals that develop must be suppressed as for cordons.

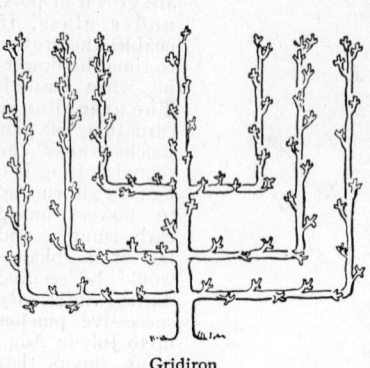
Gridiron

It will be understood that such trained trees must be supported, especially in their early stages. Cordons and espaliers may be kept tied to stakes or supported upon tightly drawn wire treillage or trellis. If grown on walls, choose an east or northerly position so that the trees are not subjected to the fierce summer sun.

Gooseberries, as well as red and white currants, may be trained as cordons, preferably with three or four stems. If borers destroy a stem it is easy to carry up a new one, as these fruits constantly produce new shoots from the base; these should be removed as they appear unless needed for renewals. These berry fruits may also be grown as short-legged standards or tree-fashion. Gooseberries and currants, unlike other fruits, are propagated from cuttings 12 in. long inserted in the open ground in October.

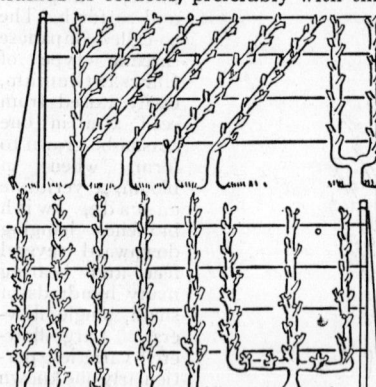
Above, at the left, the oblique cordon; at the right, a twin cordon. Below, the upright cordon; and at the right, a triple cordon.

If standards are desired, allow one stem to run upward, removing all side growths. The following year reserve all the branches that develop near the top, removing all that push forth below. A good head can be developed in two or three years. — T. A. W. See also QUENOUILLE TRAINING, and the Kniffin system of training grapes at GRAPE.

**TRANSPIRATION.** The normal escape of water vapor through the pores of the leaf. It directly affects growth and wilting, and the plant regulates the rate of transpiration according to its water requirements and the weather. It differs in this regulatory control from the purely mechanical process of evaporation with which many confuse it. Water evaporates from the soil or a pond, but is *transpired* by leaves, the latter being a highly complicated physiological process.

**TRANSPLANTING.** Moving plants from one place to another requires the same care as, and does not really differ from, the operation of planting (which see). See also Moving Trees at TREES.

**TRANSVAAL DAISY** = *Gerbera jamesoni*.

---
* Special articles on the subjects indicated by an asterisk (*) will be found at the words so marked.

**TRAPA** (trap′a). A genus of only 3 species of aquatic herbs of the family Onagraceae, all from the warmer parts of the Old World, one of them, **T. natans,** the water chestnut, grown for ornament in pools or aquaria, but also yielding an edible fruit for which it is cult., mostly in China. It is a beautiful floating aquatic with opposite,* much-dissected, submerged leaves, and clustered, floating ones, which are borne in rosette-like clusters, and have roundish, toothed blades, often beautifully variegated or mottled, and spongy, buoyant leafstalks. Flowers very small and inconspicuous, followed by the 4-pronged, fleshy, but ultimately nut-like fruit which is nearly 2 in. long, and delicious when young. Eurasia, but somewhat naturalized in the eastern U.S. and perfectly hardy. Its seeds fall to the bottom in autumn and sprout in the spring. (*Trapa* is from the Greek for a 4-pronged instrument of war, in allusion to the 4-pronged fruit.) The plant is also called water caltrop and Jesuit's-nut.

**TRAPS.** See Animal Injury.

**TRAUTVETTERIA** (traut-vet-teer′i-a). Rather inconspicuous, perennial herbs of the buttercup family, comprising one Asiatic species and another from the southeastern U.S., **T. carolinensis,** the false bugbane, sometimes grown in the shady, moist parts of the wild garden. It is a stout, branching plant, 2–3 ft. high, with basal, long-stalked leaves, 6–8 in. wide, deeply 7–11-lobed, the lobes pointed and sharply toothed. Flowers scarcely ¼ in. wide, without petals, but 3–5 concave, whitish sepals which soon fall. Stamens* numerous. Fruit a head-like collection of small achenes.* The plant is closely related to *Thalictrum*, although of very different habit. (Named for E. R. von Trautvetter, Russian botanist.)

**TRAVELER'S-JOY** = *Clematis vitalba.*

**TRAVELER'S-TREE.** See Ravenala.

**TREACLEBERRY** = *Smilacina racemosa.*

**TREBIZOND DATE** = *Elaeagnus angustifolia.*

**TREE.** It is impossible to draw a technical definition of a tree. As ordinarily understood it is a woody plant, of some considerable size, with a single stem or trunk. But some palms have several trunks. And many shrubs have only a single stem, and others are taller than many plants that are unmistakable trees. See Shrub.

Trees as part of the landscape are of far more importance than the attempt to draw sharp distinctions between them and shrubs. For their supreme importance in design and the making of permanent pictures of beauty *see* Trees.

**TREE ASTER.** See Olearia.

**TREE AZALEA** = *Azalea arborescens.*

**TREEBINE.** See Cissus.

**TREE CELANDINE** = *Macleaya cordata.*

**TREE COLLECTIONS.** See Arboretum.

**TREE COTTON.** In America, *Gossypium barbadense;* in the Old World, *G. arboreum.*

**TREE CRICKET.** See Insect Pests at Blackberry.

**TREE CYPRESS** = *Gilia rubra.*

**TREE DAHLIA** = *Dahlia imperialis* and *D. maxoni.*

**TREE FERN.** See Cyathea and Alsophila. For other tree-like ferns *see also* Cibotium and Dicksonia.

**TREE GUARDS.** See Street Trees.

**TREE HEATH** = *Erica arborea.*

**TREE HEIGHT.** See Garden Tables III.

**TREE MALLOW.** See Lavatera.

**TREE MYRTLE** = *Ceanothus arboreus.*

**TREE-OF-HEAVEN** = *Ailanthus altissima.*

**TREE-OF-SADNESS** = *Nyctanthes arbor-tristis.*

**TREE PEONY** = *Paeonia suffruticosa.* See Peony.

**TREE-PERCHING.** See Epiphytes.

**TREE POPPY** = *Dendromecon rigidum.*

**TREES.** No garden of permanent value is possible without trees. They furnish the most lasting material not only for shade and ornament, but as definite elements in any garden design. Their form and outline, their branching, the winter effects of those with distinctive bark character or colored fruits and, above all, the evergreens* contribute to the garden picture what nothing else can. And this quite apart from their more utilitarian uses as screens, windbreaks, or for street planting. The latter features are dealt with elsewhere (*see* Screen Planting, Street Trees and Windbreaks); — here we are concerned only with the ornamental value of trees in the Garden. This is very different from the culture of trees for forest purposes, or as a supply for firewood, an art or science generally known as silviculture, and in this book treated briefly (for it is not a garden project) at Forestry.

Like many other divisions of horticulture, the growing of trees for ornament has a special name, dear to the pedantic, but not so well liked by the public — arboriculture. From this root *arbor*, a tree, came the now widely observed Arbor Day, first established in Nebraska in 1872. Special effort is made to plant trees on this day, usually as a community enterprise for school children, and a very useful activity for any garden club.

### Trees in the Landscape

While trees are an indispensable feature of any garden, many people think that because they are big and permanent they must be costly. Fortunately there are ample facts and figures to disprove such an illusion. Over a period of years, and taking into account their initial cost and the expense of planting them, they cost far less than a lawn, flower border, vegetable garden or almost any other garden feature. The reason is that over a long period of years the upkeep expense for trees (including proper spraying, pruning, and feeding, where necessary) is very slight, while most other forms of gardening require constant attention. The lack of it will soon ruin most gardens, but many long-neglected places still have splendid trees upon them which only need a minimum of attention when such an abandoned estate or farm property is again transformed into a garden. In other words trees will stand years of neglect, but a garden becomes a wilderness in two seasons without care.

This economic feature of trees *vs.* other forms of gardening should not be ignored by those to whom steady maintenance expense must be considered. A good grouping of trees, a lawn, and the house, and one has the cheapest, and by no means the least desirable of landscape effects. And, as we shall see presently, such a scheme need not be without color, winter and summer, even if, from motives of economy, shrubs, borders, and beds are omitted. And trees will give a stately dignity to such a place that no riot of midsummer color can approach.

### Kinds to Plant

Throughout The Garden Dictionary, there are described at their proper alphabetical entries all the trees admitted into the book — several hundred species. Their inclusion was based upon their availability (through the ordinary trade channels, *i.e.* nursery catalogues), their beauty, or their special adaptability on account of soils, climate, showy flowers, fruits, and especially upon their value for shade and as permanent features of all good gardens.

It is obviously impossible to treat them all here, and it would be useless repetition of notes on their hardiness, period of flowering, propagation, etc., and other details which should be sought at the different tree entries. But from them it is desirable to mention here those of outstanding use, and these can be grouped into five general classes: (1) Hardy Trees grown mostly for shade; (2) Trees grown mostly for flowers; (3) Trees grown mostly for showy fruits, often winter-persistent, or for colored bark; (4) Trees for sub-tropical regions like Fla., the Gulf Coast and southern Calif.; and (5) Trees for the prairies.

(1) Shade Trees. These are the main features of any

---

* Special articles on the subjects indicated by an asterisk (*) will be found at the words so marked.

tree planting, and generally speaking they are the sorts which drop their leaves each fall (deciduous*). The kinds and culture of the evergreen, or coniferous trees, which are rarely planted for shade, are treated at EVERGREENS. They are chiefly used as specimen plants, for decorative groups, accent* plants, but not for shade, except a few pines and the hemlock.

Among the generally hardy shade trees those of most permanent value, all the subjects of special articles which should be sought for details, are: OAK, BEECH, LINDEN, ELM and MAPLE, each of them containing a few or many different kinds. These are, generally speaking, trees of relatively slow growth, but of lasting value in any garden. Other long-lived trees, some of them of great beauty, will be found at *Liquidambar* (sweet gum), *Nyssa* (sour gum), *Platanus* (plane tree or sycamore), Tulip-tree (*Liriodendron*, also with beautiful flowers), Horse-chestnut (*Aesculus*, also grown for flowers), Hornbean (*Carpinus*), and *Sassafras*, which also has delightfully fragrant flowers. Less can be said for the Honey Locust, and of secondary importance among the permanent species are trees which will be found at *Broussonetia*, Hackberry, *Koelreuteria, Maackia, Maclura*, Mulberry, *Ostrya, Phellodendron, Planera*, and *Zanthoxylum*.

No one should plant any of the above with an expectation of quick results, although some of the oaks and the tulip-tree are not so slow-growing as others in this group which are selected for permanent value. *See also* GINKGO.

There are places where quicker growing trees are demanded and some gardeners are so impatient that they will plant nothing else. A few are listed here, but they should be used with the distinct understanding that they are not long-lived, and that whatever effect you get from them should be reinforced by planting among them some of those listed above.

Relatively quick-growing trees will be found at BIRCH, POPLAR, WILLOW, ASH and *Ailanthus*, the latter especially good for city conditions (for others *see* SMOKE). Others will be found among the next group.

(2) FLOWERING TREES. While all trees must, of course, have flowers of some sort, there are a few that are far more showy or even spectacular than the common run of shade trees. They are planted primarily for their flowers, and generally speaking they are not as long-lived as the more permanent type of shade trees. All those listed below should be sought in the body of THE DICTIONARY for additional notes upon culture, hardiness, and time of flowering, as these details cannot be repeated here. The most desirable flowering trees will be found at:

Ash (only *Fraxinus ornus*)
Catalpa (catalpa)
Cladrastis (yellow-wood)
Cornus (flowering dogwood)
Crataegus (hawthorn)
Halesia (snowdrop tree)
Horse-chestnut (*Aesculus*)
Laburnum (golden chain)
Locust (*Robinia*)
Magnolia (magnolia)
Malus (flowering crabapples)
Mountain-ash (*Sorbus*)
Oxydendrum (sourwood)
Paulownia (paulownia)
Prunus (Japanese flowering cherries and others)
Redbud (*Cercis*)
Sophora (Japanese pagoda tree)
Styrax (storax)
Tulip-tree (*Liriodendron*)

To these, of course, should be added the incomparably fine blossom of the fruit trees in the rose family, notably apple, pear, peach, plum, cherry, apricot and almond, the last two only in climatically favorable places. *See* each of these fruits for varieties and culture.

(3) TREES WITH SHOWY FRUITS (or with colored bark). Late autumn and winter effects, especially if those below are massed with evergreens, can be secured by using trees in this group. They are all described in detail elsewhere in THE DICTIONARY, and additional notes on culture and hardiness should be sought at the names listed below:

Beech (handsome pearl-gray bark)
Birch (white-barked species)
Cotinus (plumy fruits)
Crataegus (showy fruits)
Honey Locust (large flat pods)
Maple (some with colored bark)
Mountain-ash (colored fruits)
Oak (several with long-persistent, autumnal-colored leaves)
Platanus (peeling bark and persistent fruits)
Willow (several with yellow twigs)

Those seeking such effects should also consult the list of shrubs and trees with striking autumnal foliage at AUTUMN FOLIAGE. There are, too, many other trees with handsome fruits, such as *Ailanthus* (female trees only), but often these are less conspicuous than those listed above because the leaves are still on while they are in fruit.

(4) SUB-TROPICAL TREES. In frostless or relatively frostless regions many other trees than those so far mentioned can be grown. As pretty complete lists of such are found elsewhere, they will not be repeated here. *See* SUB-TROPICAL GARDEN, CALIFORNIA, NEW MEXICO, LOUISIANA, and TEXAS. In this region, also, can be grown some of the tall bamboos and many palms. *See* BAMBOO, PALM.

(5) TREES FOR THE PRAIRIES. From the western edge of the naturally forested area of the U.S. to the eastern escarpment of the Rocky Mountains is a vast tract that is unsuited to many of the trees so far mentioned. There is, in the first place, too little rainfall, too much wind, and often extremely cold winter temperatures. The combination of these and the annual prairie fires of the old days made or kept this huge grassland bare of trees, except in the river valleys.

It is no better suited to most trees today. Evergreens, especially, find such conditions particularly trying, and many other fine forest trees of eastern N.A. and eastern Asia do not thrive in this region. Those that do, therefore, are of outstanding importance in the prairie and plain states. The trees which have best stood these conditions are the following:

Ailanthus (tree-of-heaven)
Ash (only *Fraxinus pennsylvanica lanceolata*)
Catalpa (catalpa)
Elm (only *Ulmus parvifolia* and *U. pumila*)
Hackberry (*Celtis occidentalis*)
Honey Locust (*Gleditsia*)
Maclura (Osage orange)
Maple (only *Acer negundo*, less surely *A. saccharinum* and *A. platanoides*)
Mulberry (only *Morus alba* and its varieties)
Platanus (the London plane, and less surely *P. occidentalis*)
Poplar (several species, *see* POPLAR)
Willow (only *Salix nigra*, and some native species)

Even these trees will need far more care than if grown in more favorable places, especially when young and if in an unprotected (*i.e.* windswept) place. For such sites it is better, before serious tree planting, to consider the possibility of making a windbreak (which see).

PLANTING AND CARE

The planting of ornamental trees which are meant to be permanent features of the garden should be done with care. It is, after all, done but once, and it is far better to see that both the plant itself and the soil in which it is to go get the needed attention. The details of planting trees and shrubs have all been carefully described elsewhere, and need not be repeated here. *See* PLANTING. The only further caution is to see, until the tree is thoroughly established, that it does not suffer for water, at least during the first year or two. After that it should need no water beyond rainfall, assuming you have picked the right sort of a tree for your locality. *See* the Lists above.

Subsequent care is divided into two main categories: (1) Fighting Pests and (2) Pruning and Injury.

(1) Insect Pests and Plant Diseases are so various and the number of trees so many that no general directions are possible. Throughout THE DICTIONARY, the contributing editors in charge of diseases and insect pests have inserted notes on their control at the end of each article on important crops — trees among the rest. If you have disease or insect trouble turn first to the name of your tree in THE DICTIONARY,

---

* Special articles on the subjects indicated by an asterisk (*) will be found at the words so marked.

where you will find what to do. It is also advisable to read the general articles on INSECT PESTS, PLANT DISEASES, and SPRAYING AND DUSTING. For the few animal pests that injure trees see ANIMAL INJURY.

(2) Pruning and Injury. Shade trees do not usually need pruning beyond the initial cutting-back at planting time, as do many fruit trees and shrubs. The exception to this statement, sometimes seen in old trees, is where two branches rub against each other. One of these, whichever is the easiest to remove, should be cut off as near the trunk or branch to which it is attached as possible. For details of this, and for other injuries or wounds, see the next article, TREE SURGERY. At that entry, also, will be found what to do when a change of grade may endanger existing trees.

## MOVING TREES

Moving very large trees is obviously outside the skill and equipment of the average home gardener, as it is generally, also, outside the scope of even pretentious estates. For any tree with a trunk diameter of 5 in. or more, moving it is then a job for a professional who provides his own equipment, and if he is competent and reliable will guarantee the result. Naturally such experience and service is expensive, and even the very rich will not move many big trees unless there is adequate reason.

Trees of less than 5 in. in diameter can be moved by the careful and intelligent amateur, with a few men and great care. Generally a tree of this size has been growing for a considerable time in one place and its root system is widely ramified. Merely to dig up such a tree and re-plant in another site is inviting disaster, because its feeding roots are at the ends of its main roots and most of them will be lost no matter how carefully dug.

If such a tree is to be moved, you should make up your mind at least a year before the move is to be made. Then dig a trench about 3 ft. deep and 18 in. wide completely around the tree, and at about 5 ft. from the trunk. Remove from this circular trench all the soil and cut with an axe or heavy pruning shears all roots that pass through and beyond the trench. This should be done in March or April and the trench filled with a mixture of ⅔ good garden loam and ⅓ well-rotted cow or horse manure, thoroughly mixed. If the following growing season is dry, see that the trench of fresh soil is thoroughly watered.

The effect of this operation is to force the tree to produce a lot of new young feeding roots either in the trench or even nearer the trunk. In other words you have been root pruning your tree, exactly as any competent nurseryman does smaller ones every two years or so, well knowing that such a procedure will greatly help the tree when final moving time arrives.

For you that will be the following March or April. Start digging (with a digging fork, not a spade), and carefully uncover all the roots possible, keeping the uncovered ones tied up in wet bagging if the operation lasts more than a few hours. If in digging you come to downward-pointing large roots that cannot be easily removed, do not hesitate to cut them off, leaving a nice, smooth-cut end, which will often, and in fact usually, put out a lot of fresh young feeding roots in the new site.

Great care must be used in this digging operation; both to prevent destruction of as few roots as possible, and, when the tree is finally tipped down and put on a truck, to see that the bark is not rubbed or injured. There must be an ample supply of bagging, old quilts or plenty of straw to prevent this.

Before actual planting, which is the same as for small trees, only on a larger scale, tip the tree down and thoroughly head it back;— which means that about ¼ or ⅓ of all final twigs and small branches should be removed by pruning. This sounds drastic, but to neglect it will greatly promote failure. You put upon the tree without the heading-back the same burden of water requirements as in its old site, and ask it to ignore the shock of removal. And make no mistake — the move is a shock, which it is your business to lessen as much as possible. For planting operation see PLANTING.

When the hole is filled up and the tree started on its new venture, give it a thorough soaking and see that it is carefully guyed by wires. While young trees need only 3 guy wires, it is better to use 4 or even 5 on a large tree. Even with heading-back it will have a large crown of foliage, and no sudden gust from summer showers, nor a steady gale must be allowed to move the trunk in the least. Keep the guy wires tight and see that they don't girdle the trunk or branches, as noted at PLANTING. For the first winter or two it will also pay to give your tree a heavy mulch* of well-rotted manure.

The operation above described is quite possible for most trees that drop their leaves, and do not need to have their roots in soil while being moved. But some deciduous trees, and all evergreens and broad-leaved evergreens cannot be moved in this way. They can only be safely moved by the ball and burlap method described at PLANTING. Among deciduous* trees which should be moved only with the ball and burlap method are magnolias, tulip-tree, sour gum, and the white oak. And all evergreens must be so cared for. The weight of soil to be moved, the risks involved, and the much greater cost of the operation make moving trees of this sort an undertaking to be considered very carefully. It is primarily a job for professionals. See Ball and Burlap at PLANTING.

## MOUNT VERNON

Before leaving the general subject of trees, it may be worth recording how much our greatest country gentleman was interested in them. His diary is full of notes on those he planted, many of which are still growing at Mount Vernon. Among the trees which General Washington planted, or were already on the property during his lifetime, and are alive today, are:

| | | |
|---|---|---|
| Ash | Hemlock | Mulberry |
| Beech | American Holly | Pear |
| Box | Honey Locust | Pecan |
| Buckeye | Horse-chestnut | Redbud |
| Kentucky Coffee-tree | Linden | Red and Sugar Maple |
| American Elm | Magnolia | Tulip-tree |
| | Mountain-ash | |

All but three are native American trees which he planted, or were on the place, between 1783 and 1785, just after the ending of the war and before he became the first president. There are now over 50 specimens at Mt. Vernon which were either planted by Washington or mentioned in his diary. In addition he tried 25 other species, some tender exotics, all of which have since died, one being the mahogany! For other collections of trees in this country see ARBORETUM.

For statistics on trees, their height, rate of growth, number of seeds per pound, etc., see GARDEN TABLES II and III. See also DRIP, SMOKE, and SHADE.

**TREE SURGERY.** Under this general term the garden public has come to group many things in the after-care of trees, whether it involves "surgery" or not. Originally the tree surgeons were developed because the butchery of street trees by public service employees called for trained men and better methods. As the service has now grown, it is of far wider usefulness, and many reliable firms offer complete protection to existing trees, involving necessary pruning, spraying, feeding where necessary, and most of all the repair of old injuries and those caused by sudden and very destructive ice storms. Many public utility companies now employ tree surgeons for clearing wires or poles of interfering branches.

As in the case of big tree moving, the tree surgeons, by training and equipment, can do many things which are either impossible for the home gardener to do himself, or are so dangerous that it is far better to let the trained man do them. In all large trees there are times when cat-like agility at considerable heights is necessary, the risks considerable, and the chances of skimped work pretty certain if the operator is not thoroughly at home in the air.

But all owners should understand what is being done, the need for it, and the principles upon which competent

---

* Special articles on the subjects indicated by an asterisk (*) will be found at the words so marked.

and reliable firms do the work. As in any other lucrative business there are many fakirs and downright crooks who, merely because they call themselves "tree surgeons," filch the public. A comprehensive program for the after-care tree demands attention to the following details: (1) Pruning, (2) Repair of injury, (3) Spraying, (4) Feeding when necessary, and (5) Saving trees from changes of grade.

(1) PRUNING. Shade trees do not need pruning as do many fruit trees and shrubs. Beyond the initial cutting-back or heading-in at planting time, they may be left to follow their natural development, and will in a few years assume the normal shape of canopy peculiar to each. There are many reasons for not interfering with this process.

Of course the remedy is to leave no stumps, as the illustrations show.

Nearly always, in removing a large branch, it is unwise to make the cut as close to the trunk as possible at first. For, as the saw is finishing its work, the weight of the branch will almost certainly tear loose the remnant of uncut wood, and along with it a section of the bark of the trunk, leaving a large gaping wound. The remedy here is to make the first cut at least a foot from the trunk, having previously under-cut it as shown in the illustrations. And then, when the weight of the pruned branch is no longer a danger, make a second and final cut as close as possible. *See* the illustrations.

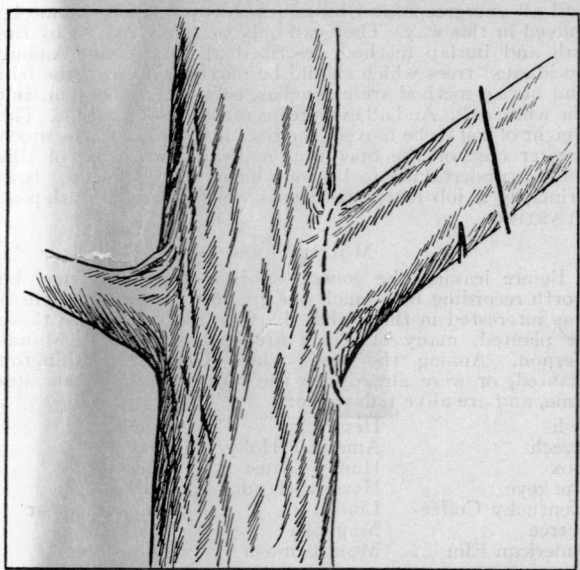

Pruning an old branch. Start by a small under-cut. Then saw off the branch, leaving a stub which must be finally cut as shown by the dotted line, as close to the trunk as possible.

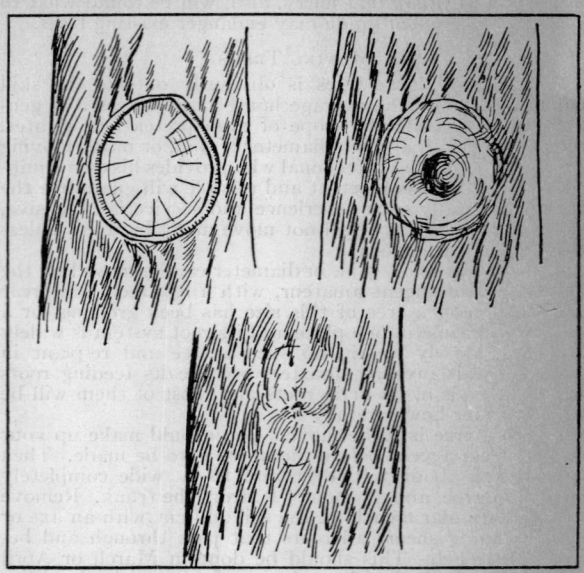

The three stages in the healing process when limbs are properly removed, as shown in the illustration before this one: Upper left, the cambium starting to cover the wound; upper right, nearly covering it; the final stage is the bark-like covering of the wound. This process cannot be completed if a stub is left.

But in any garden there are times when trees should be pruned because of overhanging branches, interference with buildings, clearance for driveways, diseased branches, and other causes. Most of such pruning can be done by the owner unless the branches to be pruned are very heavy and high up, in which case a professional is by far the best solution.

In removing branches the thing to keep in mind is that trees do everything in their power to repair damage and heal over cut ends. The thing to do is to aid the tree in this process of self-preservation and not hinder it, and an understanding of wound response is all that is necessary.

Trees have an outer, mostly dead bark, and an inner, usually green layer known as cambium (*see* BARK). This cambium layer, usually very thin and just beneath the outer bark, is active and growing every day. As soon as there is an injury (a pruned branch is an injury to the tree) the cambium layer will start at once to grow around all edges of the wound and will, if not prevented, cover the whole wound in a few years with a protective coating that will completely seal the wound, and will later turn into outer bark.

But what if the cambium layer cannot complete its job because there is a stump left of the pruned branch? The cambium cannot grow up and around a stub of this sort, and is forced to stop where it strikes the base of the stub. There is then left a fast-dying (or perhaps dead) stub of an old branch, through which organisms of decay and insect pests can easily get past the protective guard which the cambium layer has been prevented from completing.

(2) REPAIR OF INJURY. Many injuries are simply of the sort caused by gales in summer or ice storms in winter. This usually means many torn branches which must be cleaned up and their stumps pruned in accordance with the details mentioned just above.

Other injuries, however, call for different methods. One of the commonest, especially in old trees, are cavities often of years' standing, filled with punk instead of good wood, and a definite menace to the tree. When these are very large, and near the base of the trunk, they may have so weakened the tree that it is no longer safe to leave. If the tree is in this condition it is wiser to call in professional advice as to whether it can be saved, or whether it is safer to take it down forthwith.

But long before trees reach this stage of decay the watchful gardener should have prevented it. Most of it is caused by fungi which have invaded the sapwood or heartwood through what looked like minor injuries or through the holes left by borers (*see* WOOD ROT). The moment such a cavity is noted it should be cleaned out completely, even cutting out some of the uncontaminated wood. In other words we should try to make the cavity as sterile of the organisms of decay as the dentist does with a decayed tooth. If the tree cavity is large it will have to be filled, and that is much better done by a professional who comes with the proper tools for thoroughly cleaning and disinfecting the wound, and skillful advice as to whether a composition or cement filling is wisest.

The principal upon which such work must be done is that all decayed material must be removed. It is sometimes

---

* Special articles on the subjects indicated by an asterisk (*) will be found at the words so marked.

soil (5–8 in.) from a 1-ft. strip and throw it in the bottom of the first trench, which should have been loosened, and enriched with a layer of manure. Then take the lower level of soil from the second trench and use it to make the top layer of the first. Keep on doing this until you reach the last trench, which will be filled with the soil you wheeled there for the purpose.

Bastard trenching, a modification of the above, is done by making the initial and all subsequent trenches 2 ft. wide. The soil in each operation is separated into three instead of two layers and manure is put between layers as it is put back. In this case there are three trenches open all the time, and as in ordinary trenching no surface soil is left at the surface. Trench number 1 gets part of its soil from trench 2 and part from trench 3, and so on to the end. Neither method is likely to find favor with those who can have the garden plowed yearly. But in small gardens it can be profitably employed. In fact, with care to bring up only about 1 in. of subsoil at each annual trenching, you will ultimately have a far deeper, finer soil than even a subsoil plowing can give. The only real objection to trenching is the labor.

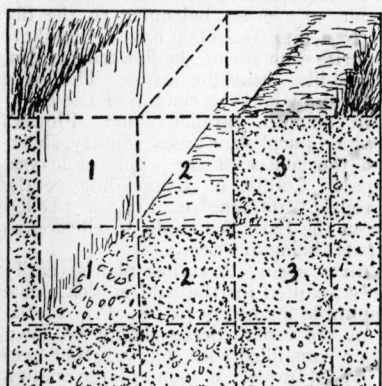
Bastard trenching. There are three trenches open at a time. See text.

**TRENCH PLOW.** See Section 1, TOOLS AND IMPLEMENTS.

*TRIACANTHOPHORA, -us, -um* (try-a-kan-thoff'o-ra). Bearing three spines.

*TRIACANTHOS* (try-a-kan'thoss). With three spines.

*TRIANDRA, -us, -um* (try-an'dra). With three stamens.

*TRIANGULARIS, -e* (try-ang-you-lar'is). Three-angled.

*TRIBULOIDES* (trib-you-loy'deez, but *see* OÏDES). Resembling the genus *Tribulus*, which contains the sandbur. See Sandbur in the list at WEEDS.

*TRICHOCALYX* (try-ko-kay'licks). With a hairy calyx.*

*TRICHOCARPA, -us, -um* (try-ko-kar'pa). Hairy-fruited.

**TRICHOLAENA** (try-ko-lee'na). Chiefly tropical, Old World grasses, comprising about 15 species, of which **T. rosea**, the Natal or ruby grass, is the only one of hort. significance. It is grown in the South, but not widely, both as forage and for ornament. Grown as an annual, although a perennial plant, it is a handsome grass, 3–4 ft. high, the grass-like leaves 5–8 in. long and about ¼ in. wide. Flowering spikelets softly hairy, arranged in a shining, branched, pink or reddish-brown, terminal cluster (panicle*) nearly 12 in. long and very attractive. South Africa. (*Tricholaena* is from the Greek for hair mantle, in allusion to the softly hairy spikelets.)

*TRICHOMANES* (try-ko-man'eez). A specific name derived from the genus *Trichomanes*, which is scarcely of garden interest. See ASPLENIUM.

**TRICHOME.** A hair or hair-like bristle.

*TRICHOPHYLLA, -us, -um* (try-ko-fill'a). Hairy-leaved; or with hair-like leaves.

*TRICHOSANTHA, -us, -um* (try-ko-san'tha). With hairy flowers.

**TRICHOSANTHES** (try-ko-san'theez). Indo-Malayan, herbaceous vines of the cucumber family, comprising over 40 species, one of them, **T. anguina**, the serpent or snake gourd, and sometimes known as the club gourd. It is a tall-growing annual vine (needing support or it will sprawl) with angled, hairy stems and branched tendrils.* Leaves alternate,* broadly angled or lobed, or sometimes unlobed, 5–9 in. long, the margins with weak-prickled, remote teeth. Flowers unisexual,* sometimes on different plants, long-stalked, 2–3 in. wide, white, the corolla more or less cup-shaped, the limb fringed. Fruit 1–5 ft. long, greenish-white, cucumber-like (and used as food in India), very various as to shape, always slender and tapering, but sometimes curved, coiled, or club-shaped and grown for these curious fruits in the U.S. It is one of the oddest of the ornamental gourds (which see). (*Trichosanthes* is from the Greek for hair and flower, in allusion to the fringed corolla lobes.) Sometimes offered as *T. colubrina*.

**TRICHOSPORUM** (try-kos'po-rum). Blushwort. Also known as *Aeschynanthus*. Tropical shrubby plants generally of trailing or scrambling habit, comprising about 55 species of the family Gesneriaceae, natives of tropical As., and found growing on trees and pieces of dead wood. Leaves opposite,* smooth or covered with hairs, fleshy or leathery, ovalish, the margins sometimes toothed. Flowers showy, scarlet, greenish-yellow or yellow, in dense clusters, borne in the axils* of the leaves. Calyx of 5 sepals. Corolla tubular, opening into 2 lips* which are usually oblique. Stamens* 4. Fruit a long, 2-celled capsule.* (*Trichosporum* is from the Greek for hair and seed, in allusion to the hairy-tailed seeds.)

These plants are not much in cult., but sometimes grown in the warm greenhouse in a winter temperature of 60°–70°. Propagated from cuttings of firm shoots about 3 in. long, inserted in equal parts of osmunda* peat and sphagnum* moss interspersed with plenty of charcoal, in a propagating frame in a close temperature of 75°–85° until rooted, which generally takes about 4 weeks. They are best grown in shallow pans suspended from the greenhouse roof in the same mixture. Care must be taken to shade from strong sun. They are free of insect pests.

**lobbianum.** Trailing plant. Leaves opposite,* ovalish, the margins slightly toothed. Flowers velvety, scarlet, with yellow throat. Calyx* covered with soft, purplish hairs. Java.

**pulchrum.** A trailing plant. Leaves opposite,* broadly ovalish, the margins slightly toothed. Flowers scarlet, with yellow throat. Corolla 3 times as long as the green calyx.* Java.

**TRICHOSTEMA.** See BLUECURLS.

*TRICHOTOMA, -us, -um* (try-kot'o-ma). Thrice-forked.

**TRICKER, WILLIAM.** See America at GARDEN BOOKS.

*TRICOLOR* (try'color). Three-colored.

*TRICOSTATA, -us, -um* (try-kos-tay'ta). Three-ribbed.

*TRICUSPIDATA, -us, -um* (try-kus-pi-day'ta). With three sharp, stiff points.

**TRICYRTIS** (try-sir'tis). Half-hardy perennial herbs, comprising about 9 species, of the lily family, natives of Japan and Formosa. They have short, thick rootstocks, usually spreading. Leaves alternate,* simple, ovalish, not stalked, clasping the stem. Flowers solitary, or in small clusters, stalked, terminal or growing in the axils* of the leaves, large, bell-shaped, whitish or purplish and spotted, star-like when fully open. Calyx* of 3 colored sepals. Corolla of 3 petals, alternating with the sepals. Stamens* 6. Fruit a 3-celled capsule.* (*Tricyrtis* is from the Greek for 3 cavities, in allusion to the 3 nectar-bearing sacs at the base of the sepals.)

*Tricyrtis* make useful garden plants, and are sometimes grown in pots in the cool greenhouse. Propagated by division of the rootstocks. They may be grown like lilies except that they should be gradually dried off in the fall and be kept dry through the winter. When grown outdoors in the North they should be lifted before hard frost and stored.

**hirta.** Toad lily. Hairy perennial growing to 3 ft. high. Leaves alternate,* ovalish, to 6 in. long. Flowers 1 in. long, whitish, spotted with purple and black on the inside, growing in small clusters in the axils* of the leaves. Jap. See AUTUMN GARDEN.

**macropoda.** Growing to 3 ft. Leaves alternate,* broadly lance-shaped, slightly hairy on the under side. Flowers in terminal clusters, pale purple, with small purple spots on the inside, bell-shaped, ¾ in. long. Jap. and China.

---

* Special articles on the subjects indicated by an asterisk (*) will be found at the words so marked.

**TRIDENTATA, -us, -um** (try-den-tay'ta). Three-toothed.

**TRIENTALIS** (try-en-tay'lis). Hardy perennial herbs, comprising 2 species of the family Primulaceae, one Eurasian, the other in N.A. They have creeping rootstocks with slender stems to 9 in. high. Leaves 5-9 in a whorl* at the top of the stem. Flowers white or pink, generally 2, with thread-like stalks growing from the center of the leaves. Calyx* of 5-9 sepals. Corolla of 5-9 petals, wheel-shaped. Stamens* 5-9. Fruit a capsule.* (*Trientalis* is from the Greek for 1/3 of a ft., in allusion to the height.)

These plants are not generally cult., but are interesting for the wild garden or moist, shady places in the rock garden. Propagated from seeds or division of the rootstocks. Seeds should be sown in April, 1/8 in. deep, in light, sandy soil in cool greenhouse or cold frame. They may be transplanted to permanent positions when large enough to handle. They must be shaded from midday sun at all times. Division of rootstocks may be made in Nov. or early spring.

**americana** = *Trientalis borealis*.
**borealis.** Starflower. Chickweed wintergreen. Grows 6-9 in. high. Leaves 5-9 in a whorl at top of stem, lance-shaped, pointed each end, to 4 in. long, bright green, thin and shiny. Flowers 2, white, star-shaped, 1/2 in. across, growing on thin, thread-like stalks 2 in. long. Labrador to Va. and Ill. June.

**TRIFASCIATA, -us, -um** (try-fas-i-ā'ta). In three bunches or clusters.

**TRIFIDA, -us, -um** (triff'i-da). Thrice-cut or parted.

**TRIFLORA, -us, -um** (try-flow'ra). Three-flowered.

**TRIFOLIA, -us, -um** (try-fō'li-a). Three-leaved; less correctly, with three leaflets.

**TRIFOLIATA, -us, -um** (try-fō-li-ā'ta). Three-leaved; often with three leaflets.

**TRIFOLIATE ORANGE** = *Poncirus trifoliata*.

**TRIFOLIOLATA, -us, -um** (try-fo-li-o-lay'ta). With three leaflets.

**TRIFOLIUM.** See CLOVER.

**TRIGENERIC HYBRID.** A hybrid derived from crossing plants in three different genera. While such hybrids are rare there are some among the orchids. See BRASSOCATTLAELIA and SOPHROCATLAELIA.

**TRIGONELLA** (try-go-nell'a). Annual or perennial herbs comprising about 55 species of the pea family, natives of Eu., As., Aust. and tropical Af. Leaves compound,* the leaflets 3, usually with the midrib ending in teeth. Flowers pea-like, yellow, blue or white, solitary or in umbel*-like clusters or in short, many-flowered racemes.* Fruit a pod (legume*) with long point or beak. (*Trigonella* is from the Latin for a little triangle, believed in allusion to the flowers.)

These plants are not much in cultivation, but the annual species are sometimes grown in the sunny border. Propagated from seeds. Seeds should be sown 1/4 in. deep in April, in patches where required to bloom. They should be thinned to about 3 in. apart.

**caerulea.** Blue melilot. Annual, growing to 2 ft. high. Leaflets 3, lance-shaped. Flowers blue and white in long-stalked clusters. Pods short, with a long beak. Eu. Also offered as *Melilotus caerulea*.
**foenum-graecum.** Fenugreek. Annual to 2 ft. high, the stems not branched. Leaflets 3, ovalish. Flowers whitish, the calyx covered with soft hairs. Pods sickle-shaped, twice as long as the beak. South Eu. and As.

**TRIGYNA, -us, -um** (try-gy'na). With three pistils.

**TRILISA** (tri-liss'a). American perennial herbs, comprising 2 species of the family Compositae, closely allied to *Liatris*. Roots thin and fibrous. Stems erect, sometimes covered with sticky hairs. Leaves alternate,* simple, the margins sometimes toothed. Flowers rose, purple or white, the heads of disk flowers only and borne in loose-branching clusters. Flower heads surrounded by 2-3 rows of bracts.* (*Trilisa* is an anagram of *Liatris*.)

These plants are of easy cultivation, and suitable for the flower border. Propagated by seeds or division of the roots. Seeds should be sown 1/8 in. deep, in spring in cold frame or outside seedbed, in ordinary garden soil. They may be transplanted as soon as large enough to handle. Division of the roots should be made in early spring.

**odoratissima.** Carolina vanilla. Vanilla-leaf. Strong-growing, smooth perennial to 3 ft. high. Leaves lance-shaped or spoon-shaped, to 10 in. long, vanilla-scented when crushed, the margins sometimes toothed. Flowers rose-purple, in heads, in loose-branching clusters. N.C. to Fla. and La.

**TRILLIUM** (trill'i-um). Wakerobin. Hardy perennial herbs, comprising about 30 species, belonging to the lily family, and natives of N.A. and As. They have thick, short rootstocks from which arise each spring the flowering stalks, bearing at the base scale-like sheathing leaves. The three true leaves are arranged in a whorl* at the top of the stalk. Leaves simple, ovalish, smooth, parallel-veined. Flowers pink, white, greenish-white, purplish or green, solitary, short-stalked, growing from the center of the whorl of leaves. Calyx* of 3 green sepals. Corolla of 3 spreading petals, alternating with the sepals. Stamens* 6. Fruit a 3-celled berry. (*Trillium* is from the Latin for triple, in allusion to the leaves and flower parts being in threes.)

The trilliums are early spring flowering plants, easily cult. and are admirably adapted for the wild garden, some of the species being suitable for boggy places. Propagated by seeds or division of the roots. Seeds should be sown in well-drained boxes or pans filled with sandy, rather acid peat, placed in shade in cold frame. As soon as large enough to handle they should be planted out in shady places in similar soil. Division of the roots may be made in Nov. or early spring.

**cernuum.** Nodding trillium. Ground lily. Jew's-harp. Grows 1-1½ ft. high. Leaves 3, in a whorl at the top of the stem, not stalked, ovalish, to 5 in. long. Flowers white or pinkish, on short recurved stalks, often hidden by the leaves. Petals wavy, to 3/4 in. long. Newfoundland to Ga. and Mo.
**erectum.** Purple trillium. Birthroot. Bethroot. Strong-growing, 12-15 in. high. Leaves 3, in a whorl at the top of the stem, ovalish to 7 in. long, abruptly pointed. Flowers on stalks 4 in. long, white to pink or brownish-purple, unpleasantly scented. Petals to 1½ in. long. Green flies are greatly attracted by this species. Nova Scotia to N.C. and west to Tex.
**erythrocarpum** = *Trillium undulatum*.
**grandiflorum.** Great white trillium. Trinity lily. Strong-growing, to 1½ ft. Leaves in a whorl at the top of the stem, ovalish, to 6 in. long. Flowers erect, on stalks 3 in. long, waxy-white, fading to pink. Petals 1½-2 in. long, curving backwards. Quebec to N.C. and Mo. and one of the finest for the wild garden.
**nivale.** Snow trillium. Not over 8 in. high, the ovalish, blunt leaves 1½-2 in. long. Flowers scarcely over 1 in. long, white, the stalk erect or drooping, and about 1 in. long. A woodland plant from Pa. and Ky. to Minn. and Iowa. March-May.
**ovatum.** Coast trillium. Growing to 1½ ft. high. Leaves 3, in a whorl* at the top of the stem, ovalish to 6 in. long. Flowers erect, on stalks 3 in. long, white fading to rose. Petals narrower than in *T. grandiflora*, to 2 in. long. British Columbia to Calif.
**sessile.** Red trillium. Nosebleed. Bloody butchers. Grows to 1 ft. high. Leaves 3 in a whorl* at the top of the stem, ovalish, often blotched with lighter and darker green. Flowers erect, not stalked, purple or green. Petals narrow, to 2 in. long. Pa. to Fla. and Miss. Color forms of this species are found in Calif. and Ore.
**stylosum.** Slender-growing plant to 1½ ft. high. Leaves 3, growing in a whorl* at the top of the stem, ovalish. Flowers pink, on drooping stalks, to 2 in. long. Petals to 2 in. long. N.C. to Ga. and Ala.
**undulatum.** Painted trillium. Smiling wakerobin. Grows to 1½ ft. high. Leaves 3, growing in a whorl* at the top of the stem, ovalish, tapering to a sharp point. Flowers white, on stalks to 2 in. long. Petals 1½ in. long, marked with a crimson V. This is one of the most beautiful of the species. Nova Scotia to Ga. and Mo. Sometimes offered as *T. erythrocarpum*.

**TRILOBA, -us, -um** (try-low'ba, *also* trill'o-ba). Three-lobed.

**TRILOBATA, -us, -um** (try-low-bay'ta). Three-lobed.

**TRIMESTRIS, -e** (try-mes'tris). Pertaining to three months.

**TRINERVIA, -us, -um** (try-ner'vi-a). Three-veined.

**TRINITY LILY** = *Trillium grandiflorum*.

**TRINOMIAL.** See VARIETY.

**TRI-OGEN.** A trademarked insecticide and fungicide, sold with directions for use against black spot and rose insects.

---
*Special articles on the subjects indicated by an asterisk (*) will be found at the words so marked.

**TRIONUM** (try-ō'num). A specific name for a species of *Hibiscus*, of uncertain origin, but perhaps from its three-lobed leaves.

**TRIOSTEUM** (try-os'te-um). Horse gentian. Feverwort. A small genus of horticulturally unimportant perennial herbs of the family Caprifoliaceae, mostly from N.A. but a few from eastern Asia. They are rather rank-growing herbs with opposite,* stalkless, usually fiddle-shaped leaves, in the axils* of which are the not very attractive, nearly stalkless flowers. Calyx tubular, its 5 lobes narrow and persistent. Corolla tubular or bell-shaped, its limb somewhat oblique. Stamens* 5. Fruit a rather leathery capsule.* (*Triosteum* is a contraction of a Greek word for three bony seeds, in allusion to the usually 3 seeds.)

The horse gentians are not worth growing in the perennial border, but are sometimes cult. in more informal parts of the wild garden. The only cult. species are easily grown in a variety of soils, and are found wild along the edges of woods or in thickets. They are rather coarse, almost weedy plants. Easily propagated by division.

**aurantiacum.** Orange horse gentian. Erect herb 3-4 ft. high. Leaves generally oblongish, 7-10 in. long, narrowed to a broad, stalkless base. Flowers about ¾ in. long, dull red. Fruit orange-red. Eastern N.A. May-June.

**perfoliatum.** Horse gentian; also called horse ginseng, wild ipecac, and tinker's-weed. Erect, 3-4 ft. high. Leaves joined at the base, the stem passing through them, somewhat smaller than in the species above. Flowers about ⅝ in. long, dull purplish-brown. Fruit orange-yellow. Eastern U.S. June-July.

*TRIPARTITA, -us, -um* (try-par'ti-ta). Three-parted.

**TRIPHASIA** (try-fay'zi-a). A single, fragrant species of tropical, Asiatic, spiny shrubs of the family Rutaceae, **T. trifolia**, not distantly related to *Citrus*. It is variously called limeberry, bergamot lime, orangeberry, and limoncito, and is widely cult. throughout the tropical and sub-tropical world for ornament. Leaves compound,* the leaflets 3, round-toothed, about 1½ in. long. Spines short, stiff, forked. Flowers resembling an orange blossom, about 1 in. wide, very fragrant. Fruit red, about ½ in. in diameter, fragrant, its pulp spicy, but little used as a fruit. The plant is slightly more hardy than the orange and is sometimes used as a hedge plant in zones* 8 and 9, possibly safe over much of zone* 7. (*Triphasia* is from the Greek for triple, in allusion to the 3 leaflets, 3 sepals, and 3 petals.)

*TRIPHYLLA, -us, -um* (try-fill'a). With three leaves; less correctly, with three leaflets.

**TRIPLET LILY.** See BRODIAEA.

**TRIPTERYGIUM** (trip-ter-rij'i-um). Hardy, eastern Asiatic, deciduous shrubs, comprising about 3 species of the family Celastraceae. They are of straggling habit with flexible, reddish stems, growing to 6 ft. or more. Leaves shiny, bright green, alternate,* stalked. Flowers fragrant, small, white or greenish-white, in terminal branching clusters, to 10 in. long. Calyx* of 5 sepals. Corolla of 5 petals. Stamens* 5. Fruit 3-sided and winged, 1-seeded. (*Tripterygium* is from the Greek for three and wing, in allusion to the fruit.)

These shrubs are not much in cultivation. Propagated from seeds in ordinary garden soil.

**regeli.** Handsome shrub, growing to 6 ft., with warty, scrambling, reddish-brown branches. Leaves stalked, bright green, ovalish, 3-6 in. long, the margins toothed. Flowers greenish-white, ⅓ in. across, in terminal branching clusters to 8 in. long. Fruit ½ in. long, broadly winged. Manchuria, Korea and Jap. July-Aug. Hardy from zone* 3 southward.

*TRISTACHYA, -us, -um* (try-stack'i-a). Three-spiked.

**TRISTANIA** (tris-tay'ni-a). Chiefly Australasian trees and shrubs of the family Myrtaceae, only **T. conferta**, the Brisbane box, likely to be much cult., although there are 25 other species known. It is, as cult. in Calif., a medium-sized tree somewhat resembling a eucalyptus, with alternate,* ovalish or narrower leaves, 3-6 in. long, which are often grouped at the ends of the twigs. Flowers about ¾ in. wide, white, mostly in small clusters (cymes*) in the leaf-axils.* Calyx turban-shaped. Petals 5, widespreading. Stamens numerous, usually grouped in clusters. Fruit a capsule* more or less enclosed by the persistent calyx. Aust. The tree is somewhat cult. in Calif., but scarcely known elsewhere, although it is very attractive in flower. Not certainly hardy north of zone* 8 or the warmest parts of zone* 7. Propagated by seeds or by cuttings of half-ripened wood. (Named for Jules M. C. Tristan, French botanist.)

*TRISTIS, -e* (triss'tis). Sad, bitter, or dull.

**TRITELEIA** = *Brodiaea*.

**TRITERNATE.** Thrice-compound* and with each main division having three leaflets or ultimate segments.

**TRITHRINAX** (try-thry'nacks). A small genus of very spiny, medium-sized fan palms from southern S.A., three of them occasionally planted in southern Calif., but not definitely known to be cult. elsewhere in the U.S. Those below have a short or almost no trunk, and the old, persistent leaf bases which clothe the trunk are covered with sharp spines. Leaves fan-like, cut nearly halfway down into many segments, the leafstalk not spiny. Flowers perfect,* solitary, and stalkless on the short, branched flower cluster which is borne among the leaves. Stamens* 6. Fruit globe-shaped, about 1 in. in diameter. (*Trithrinax* is a compound of *tri*, three, and *Thrinax*, perhaps in allusion to thrinax-like leaves that are, in some species, split into three main divisions.)

These are rare palms in the U.S. and little is known regarding their cult. See PALM.

**acanthocoma.** Trunk solitary, covered with downward-pointing, stiff spines, 3-6 in. long. Leaves green both sides, paler beneath, about 3 ft. wide, cut into about 40 narrow segments, each cleft a little at the tip. Southern Brazil.

**brasiliensis.** Trunk solitary, not over 12 ft. high, spiny as in *T. acanthocoma*. Leaves about 3 ft. wide, green above, bluish-green beneath, cut into about 30 narrow segments, each more deeply cleft at the tip than in *T. acanthocoma*. Southern Brazil and Paraguay.

**campestris.** Trunk solitary in age and in the wild, as cult. nearly wanting, the plant making a crown-like mass of foliage from a very spiny base. Spines 6 in. long or more. Leaves 2-3 ft. wide, gray or bluish-green, cut into about 20 stiffish segments that are cleft at the tip and spiny-pointed. Argentina.

**TRITICUM** (trit'i-kum). Wheat. Annual or biennial grasses of no garden interest, but **T. sativum** (sometimes called *T. aestivum*) the source of flour and hence the most important cereal grass in the world. Cult. since antiquity, wheat is now unknown as a wild plant and even its original home is in doubt, but it appears to have been somewhere in western Asia. Modern wheat is a cultigen* and an annual grass about 4 ft. high, its flat, grass-like leaves 12-16 in. long, and about ½ in. wide. Flower spikes terminal, about 4 in. long, awned in some varieties, but without an awn* in others. Fruit a caryopsis* (the wheat grain) about ¼ in. long, grooved. Included in the above are the common winter and spring wheats. There are many other varieties for special purposes, macaroni among them, but these belong to agriculture and not to gardening. (*Triticum* is the classical Latin name of wheat.)

**TRITOMA.** See KNIPHOFIA.

**TRITONIA** (try-tō'ni-a). Blazing star. Handsome, South African, bulbous plants of the iris family, known to many gardeners as montbretias, and cult. like the closely related gladiolus. Of the 50 known species only the three below are in common cult. and they are showy, summer-blooming plants with short stems, narrow, sword-shaped leaves, and growing from fibrous or sheathed corms.* Flowering spike 2-3 ft. high, its spathe*-like bracts often 3-toothed. From between these bracts the tubular or bell-shaped corolla emerges, its lobes nearly regular. Fruit a membranous capsule.* (*Tritonia* is explained by its author to refer to a weather-cock, in allusion to the variable direction of the stamens* of some species.)

The culture of montbretias is the same as for gladiolus (which see). They should be planted 3-4 in. deep, and about 5 in. apart each way. Among the many named hort. forms, all derived from the second species, are James Coey, Lord Nelson, and Princess, handsome red varieties. See RED GARDEN.

---

* Special articles on the subjects indicated by an asterisk (*) will be found at the words so marked.

**crocata.** A few-leaved, slender, mostly unbranched plant. Flowers nearly 2 in. wide, yellowish-brown or orange-red, in few-flowered, 1-sided clusters (racemes*). There are also light red, scarlet, and purple forms.

**crocosmaeflora.** The common montbretia of the garden and derived from crossing the next species with *Crocosmia aurea* (which see). It is a much-branched plant, 3-4 ft. high, its sword-shaped leaves several to many. Flowers about 2 in. wide, orange-crimson in the typical form, in a long, loose, more or less 2-ranked (distichous*) cluster, the tube of the corolla curved. There are many color forms of this most popular flower garden plant. The original cross which produced this favorite was not made until about 1880.

**pottsi.** A few- or several-leaved, branching herb, 2-4 ft. high. Flowers about 1 in. long, funnel-shaped, the tube twice as long as the slightly unequal limb. Corolla yellow but tinged with red. Transvaal and Natal. One of the parents of the common montbretia (*T. crocosmaeflora*).

**TRI-TOX-CIDE.** A trademarked combination fungicide and insecticide, containing Rotenone, and sold with directions for use against gladiolus pests and the Mexican bean beetle.

***TRIVIALIS, -e*** (triv-i-ā'lis). Ordinary; common or trivial.

**TROCHODENDRACEAE** (tro-ko-den-dray'see-ee). A family of fairly unimportant trees or shrubs, both genera of which, *Cercidiphyllum* and *Euptelea*, are Asiatic, and somewhat cult. for ornament.

Leaves alternate* in *Euptelea*, opposite* or nearly so in *Cercidiphyllum*. Flowers small, appearing before the leaves in both genera, perfect* in *Euptelea*, but with male and female flowers on separate plants in the other genus. Fruit winged in *Euptelea*, a dry pod in *Cercidiphyllum*, which has very handsome autumnal foliage.

Technical flower characters: Petals and sepals none in *Euptelea* or in *Cercidiphyllum*. Stamens* many and usually providing the only color to the flower (sometimes red). Ovary of separate carpels (*see* PISTIL), sometimes partly immersed in the fleshy receptacle.*

***TROJANA, -us, -um*** (tro-jay'na). Relating to Troy.

**TROLLIUS** (trŏl'i-us). Globeflower. Hardy perennial herbs, comprising about 12 species of the family Ranunculaceae, found in damp places throughout the temperate regions of the Northern Hemisphere. Rootstocks thick and spreading. Leaves dark green or bronzy-green, deeply cut into lobes, each lobe coarsely toothed. Flowers showy, whitish, orange, yellow or purple, usually solitary at the ends of the branches. Calyx* of 5-15 large, colored, petal-like sepals. Corolla of 5-15 inconspicuous petals. Stamens* many. Fruit a collection of 1-celled, 1-seeded follicles.* (*Trollius* is from the old German word *trol*, round, in allusion to the ball-like flowers.)

*Trollius* is easily cult. and thrives best in moist, half-shady places. Suitable for the sunken garden and edges of water gardens, though they may be used in the flower border if given similar conditions. Propagated by seeds or division of rootstocks. Seeds should be sown ⅛ in. deep in a moist, shady seedbed, outdoors, in Sept. or April. They may be transplanted as soon as large enough to handle. Division of rootstocks may be made in Oct. or early spring.

**asiaticus.** Asiatic globeflower. Strong-growing plant, to 2 ft. or more high. Leaves bronze-green, finely lobed, and cut. Flowers solitary, with 10 orange-colored spreading sepals and 10 orange, short, narrow petals. Siberia.

**europaeus.** European globeflower. Strong-growing, to 2 ft. high, much-branched. Basal leaves on short stalks. Leaves dark green, 5-lobed, cut and coarsely toothed. Flowers 1-2, at the ends of the branches, globular, 2 in. across. Sepals 10-15, lemon-yellow, incurved. Petals lemon-yellow, shorter than the sepals, spoon-shaped. Eu.

**laxus.** American globeflower. Weak-growing plant to 2 ft. high. Leaves stalked, cut into 5-7 lobes, which are again cut and toothed. Flowers generally solitary, 1-2 in. across. Sepals 5-7, yellowish-green, spreading. Petals 5-15, short and narrow. Wet places, eastern U.S. May.

**ledebouri.** Golden queen. Strong-growing plant, to 2 ft. high. Leaves deeply lobed, each lobe being again cut and toothed. Flowers yellow, with 5 spreading sepals, and 10-12 short petals. Siberia.

**pumilus.** Low-growing, to 1 ft. high. Leaves small, 1-2 in. across, cut into 5 lobes, each lobe again cut into 3 segments. Flowers solitary, 1 in. across, yellow. Sepals 5-6, spreading and notched. Petals 10-12, short. High Himalayas.

**TROPAEOLACEAE** (tro-pee-o-lay'see-ee). A restricted family of chiefly climbing herbs found in the upper elevations of the Andes and Mex., comprising only one genus, *Tropaeolum*. *See* NASTURTIUM.

**TROPAEOLUM.** *See* NASTURTIUM.

**TROPICAL ALMOND** = *Terminalia catappa*.

**TROPICAL GARDEN.** There are, strictly speaking, no true tropical gardens in the U.S., the only place where such a garden might be even possible being near Key West, Fla. For the gardens loosely called tropical, *see* SUB-TROPICAL GARDEN.

**TROPICAL LILAC** = *Duranta repens*.

***TROUTBECKIANA, -us, -um*** (trout-beck-i-ā'na). From "Troutbeck," an estate at Amenia, N.Y. *See* CLEMATIS.

**TROUT FLOWER.** *See* ERYTHRONIUM.

**TROWEL.** *See* Section 1, TOOLS AND IMPLEMENTS.

**TRUCK GARDENING.** *See* VEGETABLE GARDENING.

**TRUE ALOE** = *Aloe vera*.

**TRUFFLE.** An underground fungus, perhaps the greatest delicacy of the mushroom world, and neither cult. nor wild in the U.S. or in England. Truffle culture is confined to certain districts in France where dogs and pigs are trained to help harvest them. They grow mostly in association with the roots of young oak trees, thousands of acres of which are planted in France for the purpose. The truffle "spawn" is sown in deep trenches. It often fails and much of the truffle industry is merely harvesting wild plants.

**TRUMPET-CREEPER.** Very handsome, rampant-growing, woody vines comprising the genus **Campsis** (kamp'sis) of the family Bignoniaceae, both the species cult. for ornament, especially the native one. They are tall-growing vines, without tendrils,* but climbing by aerial rootlets. Leaves opposite,* compound,* the leaflets arranged feather-fashion with an odd one at the end. Flowers showy, orange or scarlet, in terminal clusters (cymes* or panicles*), the calyx tubular or somewhat bell-shaped, the corolla funnel-shaped, its spreading limb oblique, the flowers thus slightly irregular. Stamens* 4, curved. Fruit a long, stalked capsule, its many seeds flattened and with 2 wings. (*Campsis* is from the Greek for curved, in allusion to the curved stamens.*)

Handsome vines, especially the second, which climbs higher than the Asiatic species, but does not flower until an older plant than *C. chinensis*. They grow easily in a variety of soils, but do best in open places with fertile soil, especially the American species which thrives very well over chicken houses and other outbuildings. Both may be propagated very readily by seed, layers, or by cuttings.

**C. chinensis.** Chinese trumpet-creeper. Not so high-climbing as the next species and with fewer aerial rootlets. Leaflets 7-9, more or less ovalish, 1½-2½ in. long. Flowers nearly 3 in. wide, scarlet, the tube about half the length of the flower. China. Aug.-Sept. Hardy from zone* 5 southward. Long known as *Tecoma grandiflora* and *Bignonia grandiflora*. A hybrid between this and the next species, known as *C. hybrida*, is a little more hardy than *C. chinensis* and nearly as showy.

**C. hybrida.** *See* CAMPSIS CHINENSIS.

**C. radicans.** Trumpet-creeper; also known as trumpet-vine. A stout, woody vine, often climbing to 30 ft. high, the aerial rootlets numerous. Leaflets 9-11, elliptic or ovalish, 1½-2½ in. long, hairy on the midrib beneath. Flowers orange-scarlet, about 2 in. wide, the tube thrice as long as the expanded part of the corolla. Pa. to Mo., Fla., and Tex. July-Sept. Hardy from zone* 3 southward, and an excellent vine for smoke-ridden cities as well as for the country. It clings firmly to tree trunks or rough walls, and is nearly as showy as the Chinese species. It is sometimes called trumpet-honeysuckle, a name better applied to *Lonicera sempervirens*. Long known as *Tecoma radicans*, and *Bignonia radicans*.

**TRUMPET-CREEPER FAMILY.** A large and diverse group of plants, comprising such unlike garden subjects as the trumpet-creeper, catalpa, and the calabash. For the many genera and their garden uses *see* BIGNONIACEAE.

**TRUMPET-FLOWER** = *Bignonia capreolata*.

**TRUMPET-HONEYSUCKLE** = *Lonicera sempervirens*. But *see* Campsis radicans at TRUMPET-CREEPER.

**TRUMPET-LEAF** = *Sarracenia flava*. *See* PITCHER-PLANT.

**TRUMPET-LILY** = *Lilium longiflorum*.

**TRUMPET NARCISSUS** = *Narcissus pseudo-narcissus*.

**TRUMPETS** = *Sarracenia flava*. *See* PITCHER-PLANT.

**TRUMPET-VINE** = *Campsis radicans*. *See* TRUMPET-CREEPER.

---

* Special articles on the subjects indicated by an asterisk (*) will be found at the words so marked.

**TRUNCATA**, *-us, -um* (trun-kay′ta). Truncate; *i.e.* cut squarely off.

**TRUSS.** A common garden term, without technical significance, for a more or less compact flower cluster at the end of a stalk, as in the lilac.

**TSUGA.** *See* HEMLOCK.

**TSUS-SIMENSIS**, *-e* (sus-sy-men′sis). From the Japanese island of Tsus-sima.

**TSUTAI-OCHI.** A glide-falling waterfall. *See* JAPANESE GARDEN.

**TSUTSUTSI.** A small group of garden azaleas, mostly derived from *Azalea indica* and *A. yedoensis*, and popular, especially in Jap., for their showy bloom.

**TUBE.** The usually narrow, cylindric or funnel-shaped part of a united calyx or corolla.

**TUBER.** A swollen, mostly underground stem which bears buds as in the potato. Tubers are often confused with a tuberous (*i.e.* swollen) root, such as those of the dahlia, but the latter are true roots just as is the sweet potato, while true tubers are always modified stems. While most tubers are underground, some are borne in the air. *See* DIOSCOREA.

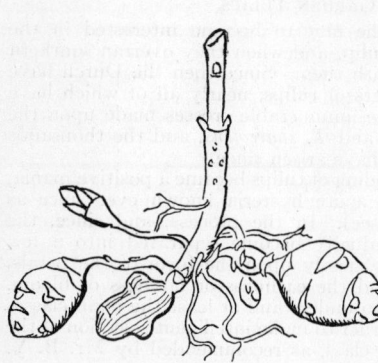
Tuber of the Jerusalem artichoke, showing the eyes (buds).

**TUBERCLE.** A small tuber. The word is also applied to the pealike nodules on the roots of most legumes, and to the rounded, knob-like outgrowths on the ridge or face of many cacti.

**TUBER CROPS.** *See* ROOT CROPS.

**TUBERCULOSA**, *-us, -um* (too-ber-kew-lō′sa). Tuberculate; *i.e.* bearing tubercles (which see).

**TUBER FERN** = *Nephrolepis cordifolia*.

**TUBEROSA**, *-us, -um* (too-ber-rō′sa). Bearing tubers; or merely tuberous.*

**TUBEROSE.** The common garden tuberose is the only cult. species of the genus **Polianthes** (po-li-anth′eez) of the family Amaryllidaceae. They are tender, tuberous, perennial herbs, comprising about 12 species, all natives of Mex. The only cult. species, *P. tuberosa*, the common tuberose, however, has not been found wild. It grows to 3½ ft. high and has basal leaves 1-1½ ft. long and ½ in. wide, bright green, reddish at base. Stem leaves clasping the stem, smaller. Flowers waxy-white, fragrant in short terminal racemes.* Calyx* of 3 white sepals. Corolla of 3 white petals. Stamens* 6. Fruit a 3-celled capsule.* (*Polianthes* is probably from the Greek for white, shining flowers, in allusion to the waxy-white corolla.)

The tuberose is easily cult. and propagated by offsets* of the tubers. Offsets should be planted as soon as danger of frost is over or may be started in the cool greenhouse. They should be planted about 2 in. deep and 4 in. apart in rich garden soil. These will not flower the first year so the tubers must be taken up and stored in a dry, frost-free place during winter, and planted 3 in. deep and 6 in. apart the following year, when they will bloom in Oct. Tubers must show signs of life to be worth planting. The double-flowered forms are the ones usually cult.

**TUBEROUS.** Having a swollen root, usually known as a tuberous root, as in the dahlia; but also applied to true tubers (which see).

**TUBER ROT.** *See* Diseases at POTATO.

**TUB GARDENING.** An easy method of growing flowers and certain fruits and vegetables for home consumption is by planting them in barrels. Many persons with limited space may thus have pleasures which would otherwise be denied them. Trailing plants such as petunias, nasturtiums, oxalis, and Kenilworth ivy should be used in connection with small annuals, to secure decorative effects. Plants may be bought from florists or raised from seeds sown in flats. Dewberries, strawberries and tomatoes, when grown in barrels, ripen two weeks or more before those raised in the garden. They are easily cared for and have less tendency to become diseased. Runners should be cut back drastically. Small fruiting varieties of tomatoes give the best crops. Save the main stem and two branches of each tomato plant, cutting the others off just beyond the first cluster of blossoms. This treatment allows all the fruits to develop to perfection without rotting.

Strawberries are ideal fruit for this form of gardening. The berries are easily protected from birds, kept clean and they ripen evenly. The holes for the plants should not be over 4 in. in diameter and 12 in. apart from center to center, staggered, which gives a diagonal spacing of 13½ in. A full-sized barrel will thus accommodate 15 plants on the sides and 3 on the top. Through center of barrel run three boards about 4 in. in width, fastened together in the shape of a triangle. Bore holes down the length of these to aerate the soil, which without ventilation might become sour; close these apertures loosely with hay or excelsior. Water given by means of a sprinkling can must be distributed evenly over the surface soil. Five or six small holes bored in the bottom of the barrel will allow drainage of any superfluous water. Set in a sheltered location on brick 3 in. from the ground. Keep the plants well watered and use new ones each year, as second year plants give smaller fruits, although they may be carried over one season. Late varieties are usually more robust than the earlier sorts.

If you have no other space, tub gardening is an alternative. Strawberries or flowers may be so grown.

**TUBIFLORA**, *-us, -um* (too-bi-flow′ra). Having tubular flowers.

**TUBS.** For all greenhouse or conservatory plants too big for a 12-in. flower pot a wooden tub is essential. They may be of any size, round or square, and should have handles for lifting. Very large tubs should have hooks or rings near the top through which an iron pipe may be inserted. The pipe will allow several men to work at once in lifting heavy tubs.

All tubs are best made of cypress and painted outside but not in. Unless, as in small ones they have short legs, they should be set on bricks or blocks of wood, not flat on the ground or greenhouse floor. Large, square tubs should be made so that one panel or board near the bottom can be unscrewed to allow examination of the roots and soil. All tubs must be provided with several holes in the bottom to permit of perfect drainage. *See* POTTING.

---

* Special articles on the subjects indicated by an asterisk (*) will be found at the words so marked.

**TUBULOSA, -us, -um** (too-bew-lō′sa). Having tubes.

**TUFA.** A porous, pitted limestone used in making rock gardens, but it should be used with caution. *See* Kind of Rock at Rock Garden.

**TUFTED.** Growing in more or less dense tufts or clusters. No single-stemmed plant can ever be tufted, but many plants with several stems, such as some grasses, saxifrages, sedums, etc., are always tufted. When the congestion of stems becomes such as to make the plant into a tight, ball-like cushion, such densely tufted specimens are called cushion plants. They are common in dry or alpine situations, the cushion-like habit helping to reduce transpiration.*

**TUFTED PANSY.** *See* Viola cornuta.

**TUFT TREE** = *Cordyline australis*.

**TULE POTATO.** *See* Sagittaria latifolia.

**TULIP.** For the common tulip *see* Tulipa. For the globe tulip *see* Calochortus.

**TULIPA** (too′li-pa). Tulip. Bulbous herbs of the lily family, comprising over 60 species, and several thousand horticultural forms, the latter including all the common garden tulips. The wild forms all come from the Old World, from an area stretching from the Mediterranean region to Jap. Bulb generally pointed, the stem single (rarely branched in some species), the leaves mostly basal, but a few on the stem in some tall sorts, generally thick, bluish-green, without teeth. Flowers usually solitary, chiefly erect, bell-shaped or saucer-shaped, the petals and sepals indistinguishable as such, totaling 6 (except in double-flowered forms). Stamens* 6. Fruit a many-seeded capsule.* (*Tulipa* is a Latinized version of an Arabic word for a turban, in allusion to the shape of the flower.)

Tulips are divided into two main divisions — the "species" tulips, derived from wild species and generally breeding true, and the common garden tulips which are the result of centuries of breeding, mostly upon the two species *Tulipa suaveolens* and *T. gesneriana*. Most garden tulips do not breed true and are propagated by their bulbs.

In the discussion of the tulips of hort. significance it will simplify matters to first dispose of the "species" sorts, and then take up the common garden tulips. As the proper method of planting has already been described at Bulbs, it will not be repeated here. All are planted in the late fall — Oct.–Nov.

Nearly 40 different species of *Tulipa* have, at times, been grown in the U.S., but of these the selection below will be found the most generally useful. They are nothing like so much grown as the common garden sorts to be discussed at the end of the "species" tulips.

**clusiana.** Not over 15 in. high, the bulb hairy and small. Leaves narrow. Flowers fragrant, small, the base purple, the pointed tips white or yellowish. Southern Eu. and Persia.

**dasystemon.** Not over 5 in. high, the flowers small, usually several, yellow, but the petals edged with white, and greenish on the back. Turkestan. For culture *see* Rock Garden.

**eichleri.** A low plant, 6–12 in. high, the leaves broad, but long-tapering. Flowers bluish-black at the base, scarlet above, the petals blunt but with a minute point. Southwestern Asia. For culture *see* Rock Garden.

**fosteriana.** A stout plant with broad leaves. Flower large, bright crimson, but darker at the base. Turkestan. *See* Rock Garden.

**gesneriana.** The origin of most of the common garden tulips (*see* below). From 12–24 in. high, the leaves broad and ample. Flowers now very variable as to shape, color, and markings (*see* below), Armenia and Persia.

**greigi.** A low tulip, 6–9 in. high, with rather broad, wavy-margined, dark leaves. Flowers orange-red, the base darker and yellow-margined, the petals minutely pointed. Turkestan.

**ingens.** Not over 10 in. high, the hairy leaves broad. Flowers vermilion-red, but darker at the base, the petals blunt but with a minute point. Bokhara.

**kaufmanniana.** A showy tulip, 5–10 in. high, the leaves broad but abruptly tapering. Flowers spreading, white or pale yellow, with a yellow center that is red-marked. Turkestan. For culture *see* Rock Garden.

**linifolia.** A low tulip, 5–10 in. high, with narrow, grass-like leaves. Flowers crimson, the base bluish, the petals pointed. Bokhara.

**montana.** Not over 8 in. high, the leaves bluish-green and long-tapering. Flowers about 2 in. wide, dark crimson, but paler outside, the outer petals pointed. Persia and Afghanistan. For culture *see* Rock Garden.

**patens** = *Tulipa persica*.

**persica.** Not over 8 in. high, the leaves curved and narrow. Flowers in clusters of 1–3, fragrant, whitish or pale yellow, with a yellow base, the petals narrow and bluntish. Siberia. Sometimes listed as *T. patens*. For culture *see* Rock Garden.

**praestans.** A medium-sized tulip, usually 12–18 in. high, the leaves broad and short-tapering. Flowers light red, the petals blunt but with a minute point. Bokhara.

**sprengeri.** Medium-sized, mostly 8–15 in. high, the pointed leaves long and narrow. Flowers orange-red, the base darker and the petals almost prickle-tipped. Armenia.

**suaveolens.** The origin of the Duc van Thol tulips (*see* below). Mostly 4–8 in. high and very early flowering. Leaves broad. Flowers fragrant, bright yellow, the petals pointed. Southern Eu.

These "species" tulips, sometimes referred to as botanical tulips, are not usually grown in quantity as are the garden tulips, but mostly planted in groups in the border, or rock garden. They are fine plants for special color gardens, especially for borders or gardens in which red predominates. Their season of bloom stretches from early April to late May so their color is often the most reliable material to use for such effects at this early season. *See* Red Garden. Many of them are also much at home in the rock garden, where their early bloom is most welcome. *See* Rock Garden.

### Garden Tulips

The Turks were the first to become interested in the development of the tulip, and when they overran southern Eu. the tulip went with them. Since then the Dutch have been the great breeders of tulips, nearly all of which have been derived from the innumerable crosses made upon the species *T. gesneriana* and *T. suaveolens*, and the thousands of named forms that have arisen since.

In Holland the breeding of tulips became a positive mania, finally leading to an acute hysteria known ever since as tulipomania (which see). In the process, and since, the garden tulip has gradually become separated into a few special classes, based mostly upon the form of the petals, the color of them, and the earliness or lateness of bloom. It is rather essential to understand at least the main classes of modern tulips, in order to make intelligent selection of the varieties, under each class, as recommended by Mr. B. Y. Morrison in the section below.

**Main Classes.** From the garden standpoint the principal classes of tulips are divided into 4 groups.

1. Early Tulips.
2. Breeder Tulips.
3. Cottage Tulips.
4. Darwin Tulips.

Each of these main classes has several subdivisions, and in some cases hundreds of varieties. The characteristics and principal subdivisions under each class are briefly outlined below.

1. **Early Tulips.** The first of the garden tulips to bloom, usually before the end of April. They are chiefly of dwarf habit. They may be single or double-flowered, and of a variety of colors. An especially early strain, rarely over 6 in. high, is known as the Duc van Thol.

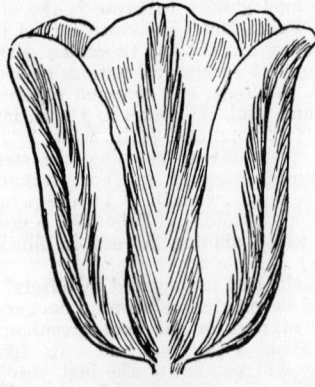

Early tulip

Among desirable varieties with single flowers are Brilliant Star (vermilion), Diadem (pink), Moonbeam (yellow), Thomas Moore (apricot), and White Hawk (white). Double-flowered varieties include Electra (carmine), Mr. Van Tubergen (yellow), Murillo (pink), Orange Nassau (orange-red), and Vuubaak (scarlet).

---

* Special articles on the subjects indicated by an asterisk (*) will be found at the words so marked.

**2. Breeder Tulips.** Tall-stemmed, May-flowering tulips, with rounded or square-tipped petals, resembling the Darwins but the flower not rectangular at the base. The flowers are self-colored, except as regards the base.

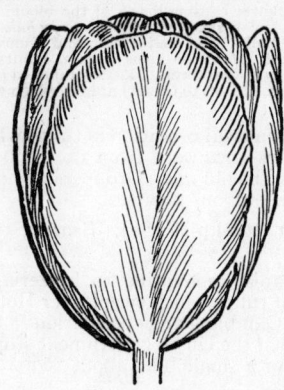
Breeder tulip

The Breeder tulips are divided into at least two main groups, the Dutch Breeders and the English Breeders. The Dutch varieties have oval or cup-shaped flowers, mostly in shades of brown, purple, bronze, or red, but the base of the flower is white or yellow, often stained blue, green or bluish-black. The English Breeders have nearly ball-like flowers, the base of which is yellow or white but not stained with any other color.

**3. Cottage Tulips.** Tall-stemmed, May-flowering tulips, with self-colored, mostly pointed petals but sometimes with rounded petals. As now understood cottage tulips comprise a somewhat heterogeneous class including many garden tulips not conveniently classed elsewhere.

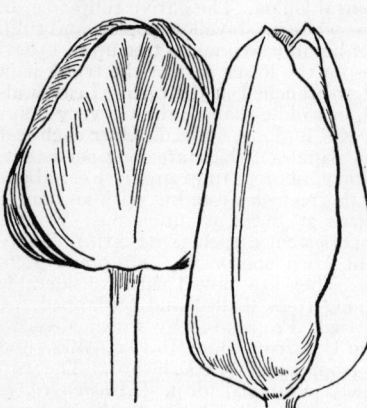
Two types of Cottage tulips

Among well-known varieties of Cottage Tulips, most of them of English origin but commonly sold here, are: Albino (white), Ellen Willmot (yellow), Fulgens (scarlet), Glare of the Garden (scarlet), Marjorie Bowen (salmon, later orange-pink), Union Jack (light violet, streaked purple and white), General French (cerise), Moonlight (yellow), Sirene (pink), and many recently introduced novelties from Holland.

**4. Darwin Tulips.** The tallest of the self-colored, May-flowering tulips and very popular. The lower part of the flower is usually somewhat rectangular, the petals rounded or square-tipped.

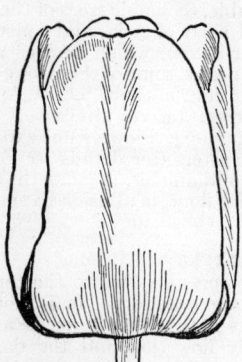
Darwin tulip

The Darwins are often divided into Giant Darwins and ordinary Darwins. The first have generally larger flowers and are taller plants. The distinction between the two groups does not always hold, however, as some varieties could be classed as of either group. Among the most popular varieties of Darwin tulips are: Clara Butt (salmon-pink), Matchless (pink), Faust (purple-maroon), William Pitt (dark crimson), Afterglow (apricot-orange), Aphrodite (silvery-rose), Dream (lilac), La Tulipe Noire (nearly black), and White Giant and White Queen, both white. There are also many fine novelties imported from Holland every year, which, for the first few years, are relatively expensive.

Nearly all the varieties in these classes are what is known as self-colored, *i.e.* without splashes of other color in the petals which in some classes to be discussed presently are variously edged, feathered, streaked or blotched with other colors. Such are called "broken" tulips, but the causes of the breaking-up of the colors is wholly unknown. Once "broken" a variety never again becomes self-colored.

SECONDARY CLASSES. Among the classes of secondary importance, but widely planted in certain varieties are:

1. **Lily-flowered Tulips.** Tall-stemmed, May-flowering tulips with pointed petals.
2. **Triumph Tulips.** Early-flowering tulips, following just after the group known as Early tulips (*see* above), but much taller. Most Triumph tulip varieties are nearly as tall as the Darwins.
3. **Mendel Tulips.** Rather early-flowering tulips derived from crossing the Duc Van Thol (*see* Early Tulips above) with the Darwins.
4. **Special Groups or Terms.** In addition to those listed above there are still several classes of garden tulips and some terms used to characterize others. The names are common throughout tulip literature, although some of the plants are not now as popular as they once were. The chief of these terms or groups are the following:

Bizarres. Tulips with broken colors. They have a generally yellow ground-color, with splashes of scarlet and brown. Bizarre tulips may occur in any of several of the classes above, notably among cottage tulips.

Bybloems. Tulips with broken colors, the ground-color of which is generally white, but with splashes of rose or purple.

Parrot Tulips. An old race of garden tulips with streaked or feathered petals, which are fringed or notched on the edges.

Rembrandt Tulips. Darwin tulips in which the color is broken.

Retroflexa. A cottage or lily-flowered tulip in which the outer petals are recurved.

Striped Tulips. A somewhat loose characterization of tulip classes in which the flowers are not self-colored. It thus includes any in which the petals are variously marked, streaked, or feathered with other colors like the Bizarres and Bybloems.

While the average home gardener will ignore most of the classes under the heading SECONDARY CLASSES as outlined above, they contain many charming varieties well known and still better liked by tulip-lovers. It is quite true, however, that for the beginner the four main groups of Early, Breeder, Cottage and Darwin will provide a complete succession of tulip flowers throughout the season of their bloom. For the individual varieties to plant and their colors see the final section of this article.

### TULIP VARIETIES

Garden tulips are the products of many years of breeding and selection and in most cases of somewhat uncertain origin. Their classification is a purely horticultural one and not a botanical one, and recognizes chiefly time of bloom, shape of flower and habit of plant. Among them is almost every conceivable color and combination of color, save the true blues, while even these are found in some of the inner markings.

The first to bloom are the **Early Tulips,** either single or double, that open their flowers on sunny days almost as soon as the leaves push up through the ground. Artis, scarlet; Cottage Maid, rose flushed on white; De Wet,

---

* Special articles on the subjects indicated by an asterisk (*) will be found at the words so marked.

orange; Fred Moore, terra-cotta; Mon Tresor, yellow; White Hawk, white, will serve as singles, and Yellow Rose should represent the doubles if no other is chosen.

Immediately after these come the **Triumph Tulips** with stems almost as tall as the later Darwins. Of these, Lord Carnarvon, clear pink, and Boston, rose, tinged lilac and salmon, will serve as examples. Almost simultaneously appear the **Mendel Tulips,** the result of crossing the early **Duc van Thols** and Darwins. Here the choice might include Dodoaeus, mahogany with gold margin; Hildegarde, deep red; Krelage's Triumph, dark geranium-red; Mozart, bright pink; Mrs. E. H. Krelage, rose-pink.

By this time, usually May in the North, the full mass of tall-stemmed tulips will dominate the scene, Darwins, Breeders, Cottage and Lily-flowered, according to one's preference in color and form, for the first two groups have broad petals with square or rounded tips and the latter two have pointed and sometimes reflexed petals.

As a group the **Darwin** varieties run through color ranges that do not exactly include yellow, although there are now some yellow varieties. They range from white through pale pinks to rose and crimson, through pinks to pinkish-scarlets, through pale rather gray-lavender to dark purple and maroon-purples that approach black. The Breeder tulips parallel them in their darker hues with an undertone of yellow and orange that produces warm bronzes, browns and chocolates, as well as yellow and orange flushed thinly with darker colors that give metallic overtones.

A choice of varieties among Darwin tulips is almost impossible, but the following will do for a first choice until the gardener can choose his or her own favorites by sight: White Queen, white; Gretchen, pale silvery-pink; Baronne de la Tonnaye, bright pink paler on margin; City of Haarlem, deep blood-red; King Harold, crimson-maroon; Prof. Rauwenhoff, cardinal-red; Rev. H. Ewbank, heliotrope; William Copeland, mauve to lilac; The Bishop, purple; Valentine, rich violet; La Tulipe Noire, blackish-purple.

Among the **Breeder** tulips — Bacchus, plum color; Bronze Queen, brownish-bronze; Cardinal Manning, rose-violet flushed orange at margin; Dom Pedro, coffee-brown; Indian Chief, coppery brown-red; Louis XIV, rich purple flushed golden-bronze; and Panorama, terra-cotta.

Among the **Cottage** tulips with their clearer colors and more delicate form, choice is even harder, for, in addition to the usual colors, they give a fine sequence of pure yellows: Avis Kennicott, deep yellow; Carrara, white; *Gesneriana spathulata*, vivid scarlet; John Ruskin, orange flushed salmon and mauve; La Rêve, flesh-tinged buff; Moonlight, pale yellow; The Fawn, dove color; and Walter T. Ware, deep orange-yellow.

The **Lily-flowered** tulips all go back doubtless to the old but still lovely light yellow Retroflexa and Picotee with its white ground edged with a line of rose that suffuses the petals as the flower ages; but there are newer forms, Artemis, deep rose; Marcellina, even deeper rose; Palemon, orange-scarlet; and Siren, cerise-pink, that merit attention.

Of the **Striped Tulips** little need be said save that either one likes them or he does not. The **Rembrandts** are "broken" Darwins much like their sources but flaked with white, and some of us still prefer the older **Bizarres** and **Byblooms** with their clearer ground and finer flames and featherings. For a bit of old-fashioned border, well away from the other tulips, or for a plot that can be used for cutting, they are charming, if one likes variegated blooms at all.

The other garden curiosity in the tulip tribe is the **Parrot Tulip** which not only has flakes and feathers of broken color but fringed and notched petal edges, making flowers of almost barbaric splendor too huge to hold erect. Admiral van Constantinople in orange-scarlet; Cramoisi Brilliant, dark vermilion-scarlet; Lutea Major, yellow; and Fantasy, rose-pink, will offer a reasonable beginning. — B. Y. M.

INSECT PESTS. The insect pests of tulip will be found at BULBS.
DISEASES. Botrytis blight, blossom blight, gray bulb rot and mosaic are the common diseases. *Botrytis blight* is characterized by small, whitish-gray spots on the leaves, buds and flowers. Yellow-brown circular lesions also occur on the bulbs. Soil sterilization (which see), the use of healthy bulbs, removal of early infections, crop rotation, early digging and sanitation are measures for control. When *blossom blight* is present, the flower stalk shrivels below the flower causing death of the bloom. For control, avoid planting tulips in low or shady situations. *Gray bulb rot* is characterized by a decay of the bulbs. Soil sterilization and removal of infected plants will afford control. *Mosaic*, a virus disease, results in a distinct, broken, feathered coloring of the flowers. Destroy infected plants and use nicotine or pyrethrum insecticides to control aphids which transmit the virus.

**TULIP DROPPER.** An unusual condition in tulips whereby a vegetative shoot grows downward from the bulb and produces a new bulb below the old one. Droppers are occasionally found also in other bulbous plants.

*TULIPIFERA, -us, -um* (too-lip-iff'er-a). Bearing tulip-like flowers.

**TULIPOMANIA.** A mania, amounting to hysteria, for the raising and breeding of tulips which swept over Holland in the early 17th century. Gambling and speculation in tulip bulbs reached such a pass that the Dutch government stopped it after $10,000 was paid for a single bulb about 1630.

**TULIP ORCHID** = *Cattleya citrina*.

**TULIP POPLAR** = *Liriodendron tulipifera*. See TULIP-TREE.

**TULIP POPPY** = *Papaver glaucum*. See POPPY.

**TULIP-TREE.** A magnificent, North American forest tree of the genus **Liriodendron** (lir-i-o-den'dron), belonging to the magnolia family. There are only 2 species; one in the New World, the other in central China. The native tulip-tree, **L. tulipifera**, also known as whitewood, yellow poplar, and tulip poplar, is a columnar or broadly pyramidal tree up to 150 ft. high, without branches on the lower part of the trunk if in the forest, but often low-branched in the open. Leaves alternate,* broadly oval, or saddle-shaped, the tip very blunt and deeply notched, 3–5½ in. long, stalked. Over each leaf bud are 2 conspicuous stipules* which are long-persistent. Flowers terminal, solitary, showy, tulip or lily-like, about 2½ in. wide, the 6 petals greenish-white but with an orange band at the base. Sepals 3. Stamens* numerous. Fruit a cone-like mass of long-persistent carpels (*see* PISTIL). Tulip-trees make magnificent lawn specimens, and prefer rich, reasonably moist sites. They are moved with considerable difficulty and only young trees (balled and burlapped, *see* PLANTING) should be tried. Propagated by stratified seeds, or by grafting. Eastern U.S. from Mass. to Fla., Miss., and Wisc. June. Hardy from zone* 3 southward. The *var.* **pyramidalis** is a narrowly pyramidal form. (*Liriodendron* is from the Greek for lily and tree, in allusion to the shape of the flowers.) For a tree called tulip-tree in Aust. see LAGUNARIA PATERSONI.

**TUMION** = *Torreya*.

*TUNA* (too'na). Tropical American name for several edible prickly pears. *See* OPUNTIA.

**TUNG-OIL TREE.** Valuable, economic trees of the spurge family, chiefly from tropical parts of Asia, and constituting the genus **Aleurites** (al-your-i'teez), which besides the one below contains only 5 other species, some of them long cult. in China and Jap. The only one cult. in the U.S. is **A. fordi**, the tung-oil or China wood-oil tree. Leaves alternate,* ovalish and sometimes 3-lobed, 3–5 in. long. Flowers unisexual,* not showy, mostly in terminal clusters (for details *see* EUPHORBIACEAE). Fruit 2–3 in. in diameter, a smooth drupe.* (*Aleurites* is from the Greek for flour, in allusion to the mealy appearance of some species.)

## CULTURE

In 1934 there were 40,000 acres devoted to the tung-tree, although its requirements are exacting. It is not satisfactory in the warmer parts of Fla., as it needs a period of winter chilling. Its early flowering and the danger of these flowers being killed by early frosts is great. Its most favorable sites are found in a belt scarcely 75 miles wide, along the Gulf Coast, the northern part of Fla. and extreme southern and southwestern Ga. This new hort. industry is

* Special articles on the subjects indicated by an asterisk (*) will be found at the words so marked.

based upon importations made by explorers of the U.S. Department of Agriculture.

Tung-oil (China wood-oil) is the oil expressed from the seed of the tung-oil (*Aleurites fordi*) and another Asiatic tree not cult. here. This oil has been used for centuries in China, the native habitat of the trees, and is imported into the U.S. in amounts exceeding 100 million pounds annually. It has numerous uses but is utilized chiefly in the manufacture of varnishes and in insulating and waterproofing compounds. A recent development has been the successful incorporation of the oil as a vehicle in high-grade paints.

In America, only the tung-oil tree (*A. fordi*) is grown commercially. The tree grows rapidly, attaining a mature size in about 10 years, and begins fruiting at an early age. Its span of life is not yet known; the first tree planted has reached its 28th year. Maturing in late Sept. and Oct., the apple-like fruits fall to the ground and harvesting consists merely in picking them up. They are allowed to dry and are then ready for oil expression, but may be kept for several months without deterioration. Oil extraction is wholly a mechanical process, the hulls being removed by a decorticator and oil expressed from the ground seed by an expeller. Air-dried seeds contain approximately ⅓ their weight in oil.

Although planted on a wide range of soils, including sands, clays and loams, the preference tends toward loamy types, mostly somewhat acid. Thorough drainage is essential and fertilizers are required. Fertilizer kind and quantity will depend on the soils on which planted; usually nitrogen is applied at first, followed with complete mixtures on bearing trees. Leguminous summer cover crops, chiefly the crotalarias, are extensively planted. Pruning requirements are limited to shaping the development of the young tree and later removal of dead wood. Thorough and regular cultivation of young trees is practiced, amounts decreasing with attainment of maturity in the planting.

Propagation is by seeds and budding. Seeds are planted in Feb. and require about 60 days for germination. Seedlings attain a height of 3 to 5 ft. in one season and are of sufficient size and preferred age for transplanting that winter. Planting distances are from 12½ × 30 ft. to 30 × 30 ft. Varieties are mainly based on whether fruits are borne singly or in clusters; the latter yields larger crops and is preferred. Pests and diseases are of little consequence and no spraying has been required. Three scale insects, 2 diseases and root-knot have been reported. The last seriously affects young seedlings, but not older trees, on nematode-infested soils, and is overcome by planting seeds on newly cleared lands. — H. M.

**TUNICA** (too'ni-ka). Hardy annual or perennial herbs, comprising about 20 species of the family Caryophyllaceae, natives of Eurasia, grown for ornament. They are low-growing plants of tufted and spreading habit. Leaves alternate, small, lance-shaped, about ½ in. long. Flowers pale pink, lilac or white in terminal-branching clusters. Calyx of 5 sepals. Corolla of 5 petals. Stamens* 10. Fruit a capsule.* (*Tunica* is from the Latin for a tunic, in allusion to the close-fitting calyx.*)

The saxifrage pink is easily cult. in any ordinary garden soil. Propagated by seeds or division of roots. Seeds should be sown 1/16 in. deep in early spring in cold frame or outdoor seedbed in ordinary garden soil. As soon as large enough to handle they may be planted out in permanent positions. Division of roots may be made in early spring.

saxifraga. Saxifrage pink. Hardy perennial, growing to 10 in. high, of tufted* and spreading habit. Stems thin and wiry. Leaves small, lance-shaped, to ½ in. long. Flowers pink or lilac, in terminal-branching clusters. Petals deeply notched. Eu. There are several hort. color forms. July to frost.

**TUNICATED BULB.** See BULB.

**TUNKA** = *Benincasa hispida*.

**TUPELO, TUPELO GUM** = *Nyssa sylvatica*.

**TUPIDANTHUS** (too-pi-dan'thus). A genus of woody plants containing only one anomalous species from India, belonging to the family Araliaceae. It is a small tree of shining appearance which becomes a climber with age. (*Tupidanthus* is from the Greek for mallet and flower, in allusion to the shape of the flower buds.)

The only species is not of much garden importance, but sometimes grown in the warm greenhouse for its foliage.

calyptratus. Leaves compound,* the leaflets 7–9 and arranged finger-fashion, broadly lance-shaped, drooping, stalked, the stalks 2 in. long. Flowers green in compound umbels.* Calyx of 3 sepals. Corolla of 3 petals joined in a hood. Stamens many. Fruit a berry.

**TURBAN BUTTERCUP** = *Ranunculus asiaticus*. See BUTTERCUP.

***TURBANIFORMIS, -e*** (tur-ban-i-for'mis). Turban-shaped.

**TURBAN SQUASH** = *Cucurbita maxima turbaniformis*. For culture see SQUASH.

***TURBINATA, -us, -um*** (tur-bi-nay'ta). Top-shaped.

**TURF.** Good turf is the final reward for having made a good lawn, kept it fresh and green and reasonably free from weeds. See LAWN.

Such a reward is the finest possible source of sods for repairing lawns, laying along the edges of roads or paths, for steep banks, or for making the attractive grass steps.

Sods should be cut about 12 in. wide and 15 in. long and either used at once, or stacked face to face, in the shade. In no case should they be kept stacked for more than two days, or the grass will become yellowish or whitish, and if left too long killed outright.

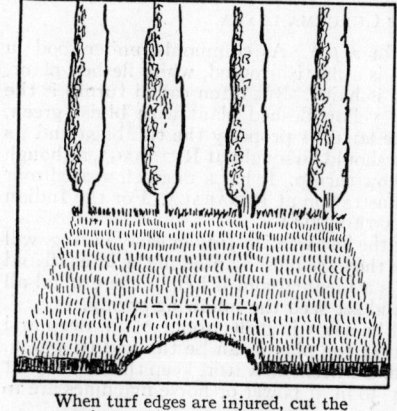

When turf edges are injured, cut the piece as shown by dotted line.

In laying turf there are only two important things to remember. (1) Prepare the soil where it is going, just as carefully as if seeding down a lawn, but enough below finished grade to take care of the thickness of the sods (2–3 in.). (2) In laying the sods see that their edges touch as closely as possible and if there are broken corners fill in with good topsoil, after which the sod should be thoroughly tamped down with a rammer. Merely patting it with the back of a spade is not enough. It must be firmly packed down on the fresh soil and then well watered.

If the turfing is on a very steep bank or on the rim of a grass step, the sods had better be pegged down (wooden meat skewers will do), until its roots have gotten firm hold. Fresh sod on steep banks may otherwise be washed away in a downpour.

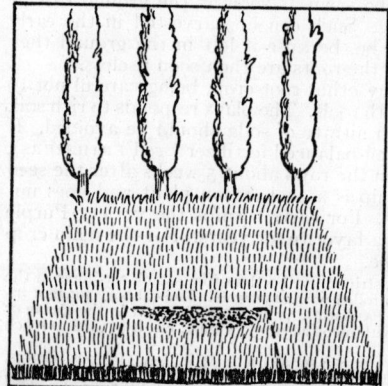

Reverse the broken sod, making a clean edge, and do the re-seeding or re-sodding away from the edge.

If large areas are to be sodded, which, of course, is the quickest way to get a lawn, the freshly laid sod, instead of being rammed, may be thoroughly sprinkled and then rolled with a heavy roller. All holes should be filled with soil or with the mixture of soil and grass seed mentioned in the section on

---

* Special articles on the subjects indicated by an asterisk (*) will be found at the words so marked.

repairing lawns at LAWN. Old or broken sods are, of course, the finest sort of material for the compost* pile.

*TURGIDA, -us, -um* (tur′gi-da). Turgid, *i.e.* inflated or full; used mostly of plant cells which are swollen because distended with water.

**TURION.** A shoot developing from the underground bud of a rootstock. Turions are often scaly, but as applied to blackberries and raspberries turions may not be scaly. They are merely young canes which flower and fruit the second year and then die down.

**TURKESTAN MILLET** = *Setaria italica rubrofructa*.

**TURKEY-BEARD.** See XEROPHYLLUM.

**TURKEY-CORN** = *Dicentra canadensis*.

**TURKEY OAK** = *Quercus cerris*. See OAK.

**TURKISH HAZEL** = *Corylus colurna*. See HAZEL.

**TURK'S-CAP.** See MALVAVISCUS.

**TURK'S-CAP or TURK'S-HEAD CACTUS** = *Melocactus communis*.

**TURK'S-CAP LILY.** See LILIUM CHALCEDONICUM, L. MARTAGON, and L. SUPERBUM.

**TURMERIC.** See CURCUMA LONGA.

**TURNIP** (*Brassica rapa*). As commonly understood in America, the turnip is a flattish-rooted, white-fleshed plant, the foliage of which is hairy. But often called turnip is the much larger-rooted, yellow-fleshed plant with bluish-green, smooth foliage. The latter is properly the rutabaga and its culture and varieties should be sought at RUTABAGA, although it is often called yellow turnip. It has a more elongated root with a neck.* See illustration at RUTABAGA. For the Indian turnip see ARISAEMA TRIPHYLLUM.

Seeds sown about the last week in July or early in Aug. will provide a crop when they are most wanted in the late fall and winter. The plant is a biennial and if left in the ground all winter will bloom and set seed the following spring.

The seeds should be sown in drills about ¾ in. deep and thickly enough so that the plants can be thinned to 5–6 in. apart. For hoeing or a wheel cultivator, keep the rows about 15 in. apart, but 24–30 in. if power or horse machines are to be used.

The plant does best in a loose friable* loam, and the product is much better if quickly grown. While it is primarily a late fall and winter vegetable, very early varieties have been developed which may be sown as soon as the ground can be worked in the spring. Such can be harvested in the early summer, and should be, because if left in the ground they will go to flower and the roots are then soon useless.

Cultivate as for any other root crop, being careful not to injure young roots with tools. The plant responds to rich soil, but top-dressing with nitrate of soda should be avoided. If necessary, use any well-balanced fertilizer (*see* FERTILIZERS), working it in between the rows about 5 weeks after the seed is planted. The turnip is a cool season plant and does not like hot, dry regions. For early turnips the variety Purple Top Milan has been a favorite for years. For the main crop use Purple Top Globe.

INSECT PESTS. Small, striped flea beetles often attack seedlings in the spring; they may be controlled with arsenicals. The cabbage maggot injures spring turnips (*see* CABBAGE). Aphids attack either in the spring or the fall; they are killed with nicotine spray or dust, but it is hard to reach them under the leaves.

The vegetable weevil, a brown snout beetle ⅓ in. long, injures turnips, carrots, and many other plants in the Gulf states. Summer cultivation, crop clean-up, and crop rotation are of value. A mash consisting of 1 pound of sodium fluoride, 15 pounds of bran, and 8 pounds of chopped turnips, mixed with water, scattered in the evening, will kill many.

DISEASES. (*See also* CABBAGE DISEASES.) There are four rather common leafblights which may kill much of the foliage when weather conditions are favorable. Two of these blight fungi also cause cankers on the roots. They apparently are carried with the seed. There are still other rots which affect the roots in storage. The suggested control measures are treating the seed with hot water (122° F. for 15 minutes), then dusting with an organic mercury compound, well-drained soil, three or more year rotations of crops, destruction by plowing under deeply diseased refuse, and proper sanitation* and temperature control in storage.

**TURNIP CABBAGE.** A name applied both to the kohlrabi and the rutabaga. See both vegetables.

**TURNIP PARSNIP.** See PARSNIP.

**TURNIP-ROOTED CABBAGE.** See KOHLRABI.

**TURNIP-ROOTED CELERY** = Celeriac. See CELERY.

**TURNIP-ROOTED CHERVIL** = *Chaerophyllum bulbosum*.

**TURNIP-ROOTED PARSLEY.** See PARSLEY.

**TURPENTINE TREE** = *Syncarpia glomulifera*.

**TURTLEHEAD** = *Chelone glabra*.

**TUSSIE-MUSSIE.** An Old English word for a nosegay. See FLOWER ARRANGING.

**TUSSILAGO** (tuss-i-lay′go). Perennial herbs of only 1 species of the family Compositae, and a native of Eurasia. The only species, *T. farfara*, is the coltsfoot; also called clayweed and coughwort. Rootstocks thick, and spreading entirely underground. Flowering stem appearing before the leaves, 1–1½ ft. high, covered with scaly bracts.* Flowers bright yellow in solitary flat heads, ½–¾ in. across, each head surrounded by a single row of bracts.* Leaves basal, long-stalked, heart-shaped at first becoming angular, upper side cobwebby, under side covered with long white, woolly, matted hairs. Blooms in March. The plant is of no garden importance. Once introduced it is difficult to eradicate. Sometimes used for covering dry banks. Propagated by division of the roots. (*Tussilago* is from the Latin, for cough and go, in allusion to the medicinal use of the leaves.)

**TUSSOCK MOTH.** See Insect Pests at ELM and MAPLE.

**TUTSAN.** See St. John's-wort at SAINT.

**TWAYBLADE.** See LIPARIS.

**TWENTY-OUNCE.** An apple variety. See APPLE.

**TWICE-COMPOUND.** Leaves that are compound* and have the major divisions again compound, as in many ferns and plants of the carrot family.

**TWIG BUDDING.** An erroneous term for a form of grafting (which see).

**TWINBERRY** = *Mitchella repens* and *Lonicera involucrata*.

**TWINFLOWER.** See LINNAEA.

**TWINING PLANTS.** See VINES.

**TWIN-LEAF** = *Jeffersonia diphylla*.

**TWIN SISTERS** = *Linnaea americana*.

**TWISTED EGLANTINE** = *Lonicera periclymenum*.

**TWISTED HEATH** = *Erica cinerea*.

**TWISTED STALK.** See STREPTOPUS.

**TWO-LIPPED.** See LIP.

**TWO-RANKED.** See DISTICHOUS.

**TYPHA, TYPHACEAE.** See CAT-TAIL.

*TYPHINA, -us, -um* (ty-fy′na). Relating to fever; *i.e.* typhus.

---

* Special articles on the subjects indicated by an asterisk (*) will be found at the words so marked.

# U

**UCRANICA, -us, -um** (you-kray′ni-ka). From the Ukraine.

**UGNI** (ug′ni). An obsolete generic name for the Chilean guava (*Myrtus ugni*).

**ULE** = *Castilla elastica*.

**ULEX.** See FURZE.

**ULIGINOSA, -us, -um** (you-li-ji-nō′sa). Of wet or marshy places.

**ULMACEAE** (ul-may′see-ee). The elm family has only 15 genera and about 140 species, nearly all trees, some of the cult. sorts being among our most valuable shade trees. Four genera are in cult. *Ulmus* (see ELM) is by far the most important. *Celtis* (see HACKBERRY) is quite secondary, while *Planera* (the water elm) and *Zelkova* (Asiatic trees and shrubs) are chiefly of botanical interest.

Trees with a watery juice, differing in this respect from the closely related, milky-juiced Moraceae. Leaves alternate,* prevailingly lopsided (inequilateral) at the base. Flowers inconspicuous, without petals, the male and female ones sometimes separate, but on the same tree, often appearing before the leaves unfold. Fruit winged in the elm — nut-like or fleshy in other genera.

Technical flower characters: Calyx of 4–5, rarely more or fewer, sepals, which are usually more or less united. Petals none. Stamens* 4–5, rarely twice as many. Ovary superior,* 1-celled.

**ULMARIA.** See FILIPENDULA.

**ULMOIDES** (ul-moy′deez, but see OÏDES). Like an elm (*Ulmus*).

**ULMUS.** See ELM.

**UMBEL.** A flower cluster in which all the individual flower stalks arise at one point, the cluster being flat-topped or ball-like, depending on the length of the individual stalks. Umbels are found throughout the carrot family (hence called Umbelliferae), also among the onions and in some of its relatives and in a few milkweeds. In some plants the smaller umbels are themselves grouped in a large umbel which is then said to be a compound umbel.

Umbel

**UMBELLATA, -us, -um** (um-bel-lay′ta). Umbellate; *i.e.* bearing umbels.*

**UMBELLIFERAE** (um-bel-lif′fer-ee). The carrot, celery or parsnip family is far more important for its herbs, condiments or vegetables than for ornamental garden plants. It is by some called Ammiaceae, or Apiaceae.

The family is a huge one (250 genera and probably 2000 species), easily recognized from its prevailingly compound leaves and the arrangement of its flowers in an umbel.* Sometimes the umbel is twice- or thrice-compound, and in a few genera the whole cluster is very large. Each individual flower (often wrongly called a "ray") of the umbel is very small. In *Eryngium* the flowers are in heads. The characters separating the genera reside in the peculiar, usually aromatic fruit (often called "seed") of this family, and are wholly technical.

From the gardening standpoint the cult. genera may be easily divided upon their use, as follows:
1. Furnishing vegetables:
    *Apium* (see CELERY), *Arracacia*, *Chaerophyllum*, *Daucus* (see CARROT), *Pastinaca* (see PARSNIP).
2. Furnishing seasonings, condiments, garnishes and herbs:
    *Anethum* (see DIL), *Anthriscus*, *Angelica*, *Carum* (see CARAWAY), *Coriandrum* (see CORIANDER), *Cuminum*, *Ferula*, *Foeniculum* (see FENNEL), *Levisticum*, *Petroselinum* (see PARSLEY), *Pimpinella* (see ANISE). In this connection see also HERB GARDENING.
3. Garden flowers for the less important parts of the open border or wild garden, none very showy:
    *Aegopodium*, *Astrantia*, *Cicuta*, *Conium* (juice deadly poisonous), *Erigenia*, *Eryngium* (most showy of this group), *Harbouria* (chiefly for the rock garden), *Heracleum* and *Sium*.

There are only two other cult. genera: *Myrrhis*, which is the sweet cicely of Eu., and the Australian *Trachymene*, which is the beautiful little blue lace-flower of the florists' shops.

The stems of many of these plants are hollow, and the leaf-stalk is often sheath-like or expanded as in the edible celery. The whole umbel* (see above) often has a series of bracts* beneath each subdivision of the whole cluster. This is a very characteristic feature of some genera, and is found in nearly every genus.

Technical flower characters: Flowers regular,* sometimes the outer ones in the umbel sterile and ray-like. Sepals very small or none. Petals 5. Stamens* 5, alternate with the petals and inserted on a ring-like disk. Ovary inferior,* 2-celled. Styles 2. Fruit consisting of 2, ribbed or winged, 1-seeded carpels which separate at the base, but are attached at the top, often provided internally with (aromatic) oil tubes.

**UMBELLULARIA** (um-bel-you-lair′i-a). A single species of aromatic, evergreen trees, known as the Calif. laurel, spice tree, bay tree, or balm-of-heaven, and to science as **U. californica**, of the family Lauraceae. It is a handsome, medium-sized tree, rarely over 25 ft. high, with alternate,* short-stalked, ovalish or oblongish leaves, 3–5 in. long and without marginal teeth. Flowers perfect, yellowish-green, in dense clusters (umbels*) which are ¾ in. thick. Calyx and corolla indistinguishable as such, soon falling. Stamens* many. Fruit a fleshy, egg-shaped, yellowish-green drupe* about 1 in. long. Calif. to Ore. Jan.–May. Hardy along the Pacific Coast and in the East from zone* 6 southward. It prefers reasonably moist soils and is propagated by seeds. (*Umbellularia* is Latin for a little umbel, in allusion to the flower clusters.)

**UMBILICUS** = *Cotyledon*.

**UMBONATE.** With a rounded or bluntish, boss-like projection, arising from an otherwise smooth surface. Umbos are not often found in plants, but a common example is the fruit of the lemon. The cone-scales of some trees in the pine family are also umbonate.

**UMBRA** = *Phytolacca dioica*.

**UMBRACULIFERA, -us, -um** (um-brack-you-liff′er-a). Umbrella-bearing, hence, umbrella-like.

**UMBRACULIFORMIS, -e** (um-brack-you-ly-for′mis). Umbrella-shaped.

**UMBRELLA CATALPA** = *Catalpa bignonioides nana*.

**UMBRELLA LEAF** = *Diphylleia cymosa*.

**UMBRELLA PALM** = *Hedyscepe canterburyana*.

**UMBRELLA PINE.** A single species of Japanese evergreen trees of the pine family constituting the genus **Sciadop-**

---
* Special articles on the subjects indicated by an asterisk (*) will be found at the words so marked.

itys (sy-a-dop'i-tis), widely planted for ornament. The only species, **S. verticillata**, is, in Jap., a tree up to 120 ft. high, but much less as cult. here. It is a beautiful evergreen with nearly smooth bark and horizontal branches. Leaves of two sorts, some short and scale-like, the others very handsome, dark glossy-green, and growing in umbrella-like whorls of 15-35 leaves. These are narrow, line-like, nearly 6 in. long, rather soft-textured, furrowed, and with 2 light bands beneath. Flowers none in the garden sense, consisting only of bunches of stamens,* and the female flowers only of naked ovules* between scales. Fruit a woody cone, 3-5 in. long. The umbrella pine is a very handsome, but slow-growing tree, hardy from zone* 3 southward, and does best in places not too dry and windy. For culture *see* EVERGREENS. (*Sciadopitys* is from the Greek for umbrella and pine, in allusion to the leaf arrangement.)

**UMBRELLA PLANT** = *Cyperus alternifolius*.

**UMBRELLA TREE** = *Magnolia tripetala*. For the Texas umbrella tree see MELIA AZEDARACH UMBRACULIFORMIS.

*UMBROSA, -us, -um* (um-brō'sa). Shade-enduring.

**UMKOKOLO** = *Dovyalis caffra*.

*UNCINATA, -us, -um* (un-si-nay'ta). Having a hooked tip.

*UNDATA, -us, -um* (un-day'ta). Wavy.

**UNDER-SHRUB.** A low shrub, or sometimes a stout herb that is woody at the base; sometimes called sub-shrub.

*UNDULATA, -us, -um* (un-dew-lay'ta). Undulate; *i.e.* wavy or wavy-margined.

*UNEDO* (you-nee'do). Classical name of the strawberry tree (*Arbutus unedo*).

*UNGUICULARIS, -e* (un-gwi-kew-lay'is). With a narrowed base or shank (*i.e.* clawed*).

*UNGUIS-CATI* (un-gwis-kat'i). A cat's claw.

**UNICORN-PLANT.** See PROBOSCIDEA.

*UNIFLORA, -us, -um* (you-ni-flow'ra). One-flowered.

*UNILATERALIS, -e* (you-ni-lat-er-ral'is). One-sided.

**UNIOLA** (you-ny'o-la). American perennial grasses, comprising 5 species, the one below a good ornamental grass. It is a strong-growing plant 4-5 ft. high. Leaves grass-like, about 9 in. long and 1 in. wide, clasping the stem. Flower spikes in flat, terminal, loose-branching clusters. (*Uniola* is an ancient Latin name for an unknown plant and of little significance here.)

*U. latifolia* is sometimes cult. for the showy ornamental spikes which can be cut and dried in Aug. for house decoration. Easily cult. Propagated by seeds or division of roots. Seeds should be sown ⅛ in. deep in open border where required to bloom. They prefer sandy soil. Division of roots may be made in Oct. or early spring.

**latifolia.** Flower spikes on slender, drooping stalks, the clusters graceful, about 8 in. long, the stalks very slender. One of the best native ornamental grasses. Pa. to Fla. and Tex.

**UNIOLOIDES** (you-ni-o-loy'deez, but see OÏDES). Like a grass of the genus *Uniola*.

**UNION.** The proper uniting of a stock and cion* in a grafting operation. See GRAFTING.

**UNISEXUAL.** As to flowers, of one sex only; that is, bearing only stamens in one flower and pistils in another. *See also* MONOECIOUS, DIOECIOUS, and PERFECT.

**UNPRODUCTIVE FRUIT TREES.** See STERILITY OF FRUIT TREES.

**UNSHIU.** Japanese name of the satsuma orange.

**UP-BUDDING.** See Shield Budding at BUDDING.

**UPLAND COTTON** = *Gossypium hirsutum*.

**UPLAND CRESS.** See BARBAREA and LEPIDIUM SATIVUM.

**URBINIA** (ur-bin'i-a). Mexican fleshy herbs, comprising about 3 species of the family Crassulaceae. They are low-growing, tender plants with short thick stems, crowded with fleshy leaves forming rosettes. Flowering stalk to 1 ft. high, thick, sometimes reddish, covered with small leaves. Flowers generally in a forked cluster (raceme*). Calyx of 5 sepals. Corolla of 5 lobes, urn-shaped, pink or red below, yellow above. Stamens* 10. Fruit 1-celled, many-seeded. (Named for Dr. Manuel Urbinia.)

Easily cult. and usually grown as pot plants in the cool greenhouse for house decoration. Sometimes grown outdoors in the South, but may be grown outdoors in the North if taken inside during winter. Propagated by seeds or division of the rootstock. Seeds should be sown 1/16 in. deep in pans of fine sandy soil. They should be pricked-off as soon as large enough to handle into pans or boxes, about 2 in. apart in potting mixture* 6. They may be placed in separate pots in the same mixture as soon as large enough. Division of the rootstocks may be made any time during spring and summer.

**agavoides.** Low-growing plant with short, thick stem. Leaves in a rosette overlapping each other, ovalish, to 2 in. long, the midrib ending in a spine. Flowering stalk crowded with small leaves. Flowers in coiled clusters. Corolla reddish, tipped yellow. Mex. Also known as *Echeveria agavoides*.

**URD** = *Phaseolus mungo*.

**UREA.** See Nitrogen at FERTILIZERS.

*URENS* (your'enz). Stinging or burning.

**URGINEA** (ur-gin'e-a). Half-hardy bulbous perennials, comprising about 75 species, belonging to the lily family, and natives of the Mediterranean region, India and S. Af. Bulbs large and scaly. Leaves basal, long and narrow. Leafless flowering stalk appearing before the leaves. Flowers whitish, yellowish or pink, small, growing in the axils* of bracts* in terminal racemes.* Calyx of 3 colored sepals. Corolla of 3 petals, alternating with the sepals. Stamens* 6. Fruit a 3-sided capsule,* many-seeded. (*Urginea* was named from an Arabian tribe in Algeria known as Ben Urgin.)

These bulbs are not usually cult. The bulbs of *U. maritima* are gathered in their wild state for their drug properties, and also contain a large amount of sugar, for which reason they are sometimes used for making whiskey in Sicily.

**maritima.** Sea onion. Sea squill. Bulbs 4-6 in. thick. Leaves to 1½ ft. long and 4 in. wide, lance-shaped, fleshy, shiny green. Flowers numerous, whitish, ½ in. long in a raceme to 1½ ft. long. Flowering stalk leafless, to 3 ft. long. Canary Islands to Syria and S. Af.

**URNS.** See ORNAMENT AND FURNITURE.

**URSINIA** (ur-sin'i-a). Annual or perennial herbs or sub-shrubs, comprising about 60 species of the family Compositae, and natives of S. Af. Leaves alternate,* usually deeply cut into narrow lobes, the margins toothed. Flowers in solitary heads, daisy-like. Ray* florets orange or yellow, sometimes purplish-brown at base, the disk florets dark bluish-purple or brown. (Named for John Ursinus of Regensburg, 17th century botanical author.) Sometimes spelled *Ursinea*.

Ursinias make showy garden plants, but only the tender annual species are cult. *See* ANNUALS. They may be grown in the greenhouse as pot plants for early spring flowering, in which case seeds should be sown in Jan.

**anethoides.** Sometimes written *anthemoides*. Also known as *Sphenogyne anthemoides*. Annual, growing to 1 ft. high, of bushy habit. Leaves deeply cut into narrow lobes. Flowering stalk thin and wiry. Flowers in numerous, solitary heads. Ray florets orange, purple at base; the disk florets* purple.

**pulchra.** Also known as *Sphenogyne speciosa*. Bushy annual growing to 2 ft. high. Leaves deeply cut into lobes, each lobe again cut. Flowering stalks bearing small lobed leaves. Flowers in solitary heads about 2 in. across. Ray florets* yellow or orange, marked purple at the base. Disk florets purple.

**URTICA.** See NETTLE.

**URTICACEAE** (ur-ti-kay'see-ee). The nettle family is of secondary hort. significance, although it has over 40 genera and perhaps 500 species, largely tropical. The only cult. genera, little grown, are *Boehmeria* (a tree-like, woody herb yielding ramie), *Helxine* (a moss-like, prostrate herb of greenhouse or terrarium* culture), *Pilea*, and the nettle (*Urtica*), largely weedy and with stinging foliage. Many of the non-hort. tropical trees have violently stinging hairs on the leaves and twigs.

---

* Special articles on the subjects indicated by an asterisk (*) will be found at the words so marked.

Leaves opposite* or alternate.* Flowers always greenish and inconspicuous, in all the cult. genera, unisexual,* in various sorts of clusters. Fruit dry, 1-seeded (an achene*), sometimes surrounded by the fleshy calyx.

Technical flower characters: Male flowers with the calyx 4–5-parted. Female flowers with a tubular, or 3–5-parted calyx. Petals none. Stamens* 4–5. Ovary superior,* 1-celled.

**URTICAEFOLIA, -us, -um** (ur-ti-kee-fō′li-a). Having nettle-like leaves.

**USAMBARA VIOLET** = *Saintpaulia ionantha*.

**USITATISSIMA, -us, -um** (you-si-ta-tiss′i-ma). Most useful.

**USNEOIDES** (uz-nee-oy′deez, but *see* OÏDES). Resembling a lichen of the genus *Usnea*. See TILLANDSIA.

**UTAH** The state lies wholly in zones* 3 and 4.

Many soil types occur in the state of Utah. Since most of the garden areas lie immediately west of the Wasatch Mountains the garden soils are predominately sandy loams to clay loams. They are almost entirely shore-line or river deposits. Immediately adjacent to the mountains the soils contain considerable sharp rock and much organic matter; consequently, they are gravelly and very black in color. The larger deltas that have been built by the Bear, Weber, and Provo River systems consist of relatively fine-textured sands, underlain and interspersed with more or less heavy clays. Much of the best agricultural soil occur where these sandy areas merge with the clay areas. Beyond these margins in one direction the soils become quite sandy in some places, while in the opposite direction they may be too heavy for garden purposes.

Most of the soils in the Great Basin tend to be alkaline. There are no decidedly acid soils in the state, with the possible exception of a few small mountain areas. In a few places near the mountains where the soils are derived from igneous materials the soil reaction is approximately neutral.

All of the sandy loam and clay loam soils that are not alkaline are extremely fertile and with sufficient irrigation produce abundantly.

FRUITS. The fruit industry of the state produces an annual income of approximately two and a half to three million dollars. It consists largely of peaches, cherries, apricots, and apples. Market garden and home orchards also contain pears and plums, and a few pears are produced for export. Utah's so-called "Dixie," located in the southwest corner of the state, also produces figs, pomegranates, some nuts, and many *vinifera* grapes. The principal stone* fruit areas are located on the gravelly loam soils of the Old Lake Bonneville terraces and on the gravelly deltas at the foot of the Wasatch Mountains in Salt Lake and Utah valleys. Peaches and cherries are also grown extensively in the Virgin River Valley in Washington County. The most important fruit-growing counties are Boxelder, Weber, Davis, Salt Lake, Utah and Washington counties. Less important areas are located in Emery, Juab, Cache and Grand counties. Apples and pears are also grown in these same general areas. However, they occupy the heavier soils and as a rule are situated farther from the mountains than are the stone fruits. Peaches, apples, cherries, and some apricots and pears are shipped out of the state as fresh fruit; in addition, large quantities of cherries and apricots and some apples are canned.

Small fruits are grown in the same territory as the stone fruits. They are grown mostly for local markets, although considerable quantities of strawberries are cold-packed and exported. Strawberries are by far the most important of the small fruits, with raspberries second.

VEGETABLES. Vegetable production occupies an important position in the agriculture of the state. The 1929 farm value was in excess of seven million dollars and the cash income value nearly six millions of dollars. While some home gardens and small market gardens are located in all counties of the state, Davis, Utah, Weber, Boxelder, and Sevier counties are the most important vegetable-growing counties. These counties are listed in the order of their relative importance.

Other less important vegetable-growing counties are Salt Lake, Cache, and Morgan counties.

Potato growing is the most important vegetable enterprise. The sandy loam soils and the lighter clay loam soils of Boxelder, Weber, Davis, and Salt Lake counties are admirably adapted to potato growing and large yields are produced. Morgan, Sevier, Beaver, and Iron counties also produce potatoes on a commercial scale.

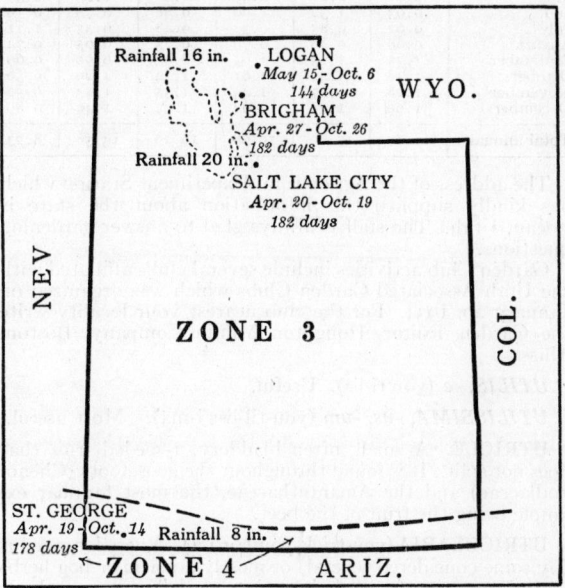

UTAH

The zones of hardiness crossing Utah are those shown on the colored map at ZONE, which should be consulted for details. The dates are the average latest killing frost in spring and the first one in the fall. The figures below the dates show the average length of the growing season. Rainfall figures (in inches) are for total annual rainfall in the regions so indicated.

Next to potato growing, canning crop production is important. Since canning crops are grown almost entirely on a contract basis, this industry affords the most certain source of cash income. The cool mountain valleys in Cache, Weber, Wasatch and Sanpete counties produce sweet, tender peas of the highest quality. Tomato growing is an important industry on the sandy soils in Weber and Davis counties. Ogden is the center of the canning industry. Both peas and tomatoes are grown to some extent in Boxelder, Salt Lake, and Utah counties, and some peas are grown in Davis County. Beans and cabbage are also grown for canning.

Cabbage, cauliflower, and Spanish onions are produced for exporting from the state. In fact, the soil and climate of various parts of Utah are admirably adapted to growing many high-quality fruits and vegetables. The chief limitations are limited supplies of irrigation water and high transportation costs to consuming markets.

FROST AND RAINFALL DATA

| Place | Average date of last killing frost | Latest known killing frost | Average date of earliest killing frost in fall | Earliest known killing frost |
|---|---|---|---|---|
| Logan | May 15 | June 17 | October 6 | September 13 |
| Brigham | April 27 | About May 15 | October 26 | About October 1 |
| Farmington | May 10 | June 16 | September 30 | September 8 |
| Salt Lake City | April 20 | June 18 | October 19 | September 22 |
| Provo | May 24 | June 17 | September 21 | August 31 |
| St. George | April 19 | May 20 | October 14 | September 13 |

* Special articles on the subjects indicated by an asterisk (*) will be found at the words so marked.

| Month | Average precipitation by months in inches ||||||
| --- | --- | --- | --- | --- | --- | --- |
| | Logan | Brigham | Farmington | Salt Lake City | Provo | St. George |
| January | 1.75 | 2.17 | 2.01 | 1.32 | 1.55 | 1.04 |
| February | 1.37 | 1.37 | 2.25 | 1.48 | 1.69 | 0.98 |
| March | 1.98 | 2.33 | 2.62 | 2.06 | 1.71 | 1.76 |
| April | 1.66 | 1.50 | 2.15 | 2.08 | 1.44 | 0.44 |
| May | 2.27 | 2.28 | 2.49 | 2.01 | 1.63 | 0.37 |
| June | 0.93 | 1.32 | 1.06 | 0.88 | 0.78 | 0.10 |
| July | 0.62 | 0.85 | 0.56 | 0.48 | 0.35 | 1.11 |
| August | 0.68 | 0.46 | 0.70 | 0.75 | 0.65 | 0.74 |
| September | 1.25 | 1.15 | 1.05 | 0.94 | 0.90 | 0.69 |
| October | 1.38 | 1.42 | 1.61 | 1.44 | 1.29 | 0.59 |
| November | 1.28 | 1.67 | 1.44 | 1.35 | 1.13 | 0.52 |
| December | 1.00 | 1.28 | 2.04 | 1.37 | 1.46 | 0.89 |
| Total annual | 16.17 | 17.80 | 19.98 | 16.20 | 14.58 | 8.23 |

The address of the Agricultural Experiment Station which has kindly supplied this information about the state is Logan, Utah. The staff is always glad to answer gardening questions.

Garden Club activities include several clubs affiliated with the Utah Associated Garden Clubs which was organized on January 20, 1934. For the club nearest your locality write the Garden Editor, Houghton Mifflin Company, Boston, Mass.

**UTILIS, -e** (you'ti-lis). Useful.

**UTILISSIMA, -us, -um** (you-til-liss'i-ma). Most useful.

**UTRICLE.** A small, often bladdery, 1-seeded fruit that does not split. It is found throughout the goosefoots (Chenopodiaceae) and the Amaranthaceae, the most familiar example being the fruit of the beet.

**UTRICULARIA** (you-trick-you-lair'i-a). A very large genus (by some considered several) of mostly aquatic or bog herbs more interesting for their insectivorous habit than as hort. subjects. Of over 200 species, belonging to the family Lentibulariaceae, many tropical species are epiphytes,* and some live in the water found in the pitcher-like rosette formed by certain plants of the pineapple family. Some of the tropical species are almost orchid-like, in their showy flowers, but are very rare in cult. All the temperate zone species grow in pools, in bogs, or on wet shores. Of these only U. vulgaris, the common bladderwort, is of any general hort. interest and it is grown as an aquarium plant. It has finely dissected floating or submerged leaves, about ¾ in. long, and provided with numerous, small, insect-catching bladders. See INSECTIVOROUS PLANTS. Flowers yellow, about ½ in. long, very irregular,* borne in a few-flowered cluster (raceme*) which stands above the water 5–7 in. (For flower structure see LENTIBULARIACEAE.) The bladderwort is a good aquarium plant, a native of the north temperate zone, and some authorities consider the American plant different from the Eurasian form. It is perfectly hardy, and is propagated naturally by seeds and winter buds. (*Utricularia* is Latin for a little bladder, in allusion to the small, insect-catching bladders.)

**UTRICULATA, -us, -um** (you-trick-you-lay'ta). Having a small, bladdery, 1-seeded fruit.

**UVARIA** (you-vair'i-a). Resembling a bunch of grapes.

**UVA-URSI** (you-va-ur'si). Latin for grape and bear; *i.e.* the "bear's grape," now called bearberry. See ARCTOSTAPHYLOS.

**UVIFERA, -us, -um** (you-viff'er-a). Grape-bearing; or bearing fruits in a grape-like cluster.

**UVULARIA** (you-vew-lair'i-a). Bellwort. North American hardy perennial herbs, comprising about 4 species, belonging to the lily family (Liliaceae). They have thick, creeping rootstocks, the alternate leaves not stalked, sometimes clasping the stem, lance-shaped, light green, parallel-veined. Flowers yellow, bell-shaped, or tubular, drooping, solitary, at the ends of the branches. Calyx of 3 colored sepals. Corolla of 3 petals alternating with the sepals. Stamens* 6. Fruit a 3-celled capsule.* (*Uvularia* is from the Latin for palate, in allusion to the hanging flowers.)

These spring-flowering plants are not usually cult., but if grown in light, peaty soil and shade make useful plants for the border or wild garden. They are useful for planting against a north wall. Propagated by division in Oct.

**grandiflora.** Strawflower. Cornflower. Wood daffodil. Strong-growing, hardy perennial to 1½ ft. high. Stem forked. Leaves not stalked, clasping the stem, lance-shaped, to 5 in. long, dark green, covered with fine white hairs on the under side. Flowers pale yellow, bell-shaped to 1½ in. long, drooping at the ends of the branches. Quebec to Ga. and Kans. April–May.

**perfoliata.** Mealy bellwort. Mohawkweed. Slender perennial to 1½ ft. high. Stem forked. Leaves not stalked, clasping the stem, broadly lance-shaped, to 5 in. long, dark green. Flowers pale yellow, bell-shaped, 1 in. long, drooping at the ends of the branches. Quebec to Fla. and Miss.

**sessilifolia.** Wild oats. Also known as *Oakesia sessilifolia*. Perennial to 1 ft. high. Leaves lance-shaped, to 3 in. long, deep green, covered with fine hairs on the under side. Flowers greenish-yellow, tube-shaped, to 1¼ in. long, drooping at the ends of the branches. Eastern N.A.

# V

**VACCARIA** (vak-kair'i-a). An obsolete generic name for certain plants now included in *Saponaria* (which see).

**VACCINIACEAE.** See ERICACEAE.

**VACCINIUM** (vak-sin'i-um). A very large genus of erect or prostrate shrubs of the family Ericaceae (by some considered as of the separate family Vacciniaceae), one grown for ornament, but of chief hort. interest because it contains both the blueberry and cranberry. Of over 130 species, which range from the Arctic Circle to the summits of tropical mountains, only those below are of garden interest, and all are of special growth requirements, as noted below. Leaves alternate,* short-stalked, often minutely hairy on the margins. Flowers generally small, not showy, urn-shaped in the blueberries, but deeply 4-parted and with recurved corolla-lobes in the cranberry. Stamens* 8 or 10. Fruit a true, many-seeded berry, crowned with the often persistent lobes of the calyx.* (*Vaccinium* is the Latin name for the whortleberry or the blueberry.)

The blueberries need special cultural requirements which are described in detail at BLUEBERRY. The cranberry, needing special conditions such as are found in natural cranberry bogs, can only be grown where these conditions occur naturally or can be controlled. See CRANBERRY. The only remaining species of hort. interest is *V. vitis-idaea*, an evergreen, prostrate plant, the culture of which is described at WILD GARDEN. No plant of the genus *Vaccinium* can be grown under ordinary garden conditions, as they need acid soils ranging from pH 4.0–5.0 (see ACID AND ALKALI SOILS). Some confuse the true blueberries with the huckleberries. For the distinctions see BLUEBERRY.

Several other wild species of *Vaccinium*, all of the blueberry type, may occasionally be transferred to the garden, but they are scarcely hort. subjects.

**corymbosum.** High-bush blueberry. A spreading, bushy shrub, 8–12 ft. high, the young twigs yellowish-green and warty. Leaves ovalish or elliptic, 2–3 in. long. Flowers about ⅓ in. long, urn-shaped, white or pinkish. Fruit bluish-black, with a bloom. Eastern U.S., mostly in swamps or bogs. May. Hardy from zone* 2 southward. There are several, closely related wild species which are sometimes gathered for *V. corymbosum*. For culture see BLUEBERRY.

**macrocarpon.** Cranberry. Similar to *V. oxycoccus*, but with blunt leaves, longer stems, and the fruit nearly ¾ in. in diameter. Northern N.A. June–July. Hardy from zones* 2 to 5, and the commercial source of cranberry. For culture and varieties see CRANBERRY. Sometimes known as *Oxycoccus macrocarpus*.

**oxycoccus.** A wild, small-fruited cranberry, and a prostrate, creeping vine with very slender stems. Leaves pointed, evergreen, about ⅓ in. long, bluish-green beneath. Flowers pinkish, about ¼ in. long, deeply 4-

* Special articles on the subjects indicated by an asterisk (*) will be found at the words so marked.

parted, and borne in small terminal clusters. Fruit bright red, about ⅓ in. in diameter. Arctic and colder regions of the north temperate zone. May–June. Hardy from zone* 4 northward. Not a commercial cranberry, but the fruits harvested from the wild and used for preserves or jellies. Sometimes known as *Oxycoccus oxycoccus.*

**virgatum.** Blueberry. A shrub somewhat resembling *V. corymbosum,* but with the corolla more cylindric, and with black fruit having only a slight bloom. Southern Va. to Fla. and La. April–May. Hardy from zone* 6 southward. Of chief interest as the source of some of the improved strains of blueberry cult. in Fla. See BLUEBERRY.

**vitis-idaea.** Cowberry; also called red whortleberry and lignon-berry. A prostrate, evergreen plant, the rootstocks creeping, but the stems erect, 4–9 in. high. Leaves ovalish, shining green, about 1 in. long. Flowers bell-shaped or urn-shaped, about ¼ in. long, pink, and grouped in nodding clusters (racemes*). Cooler parts of Eurasia. An American representative, the *var.* **minus**, the mountain cranberry, is a beautiful dwarf, evergreen, mat-forming plant, found wild from mountain summits in New England to Alaska. For culture *see* WILD GARDEN.

**VAGANS** (vay'ganz). Wandering or vagrant.

**VAGNERA** = *Smilacina.*

**VALDIVIENSIS, -e** (val-di-vi-en'sis). From Valdivia, an old name for Chile.

**VALERIAN.** For the true valerian *see* VALERIANA. For other plants to which the name valerian is sometimes applied *see* CENTRANTHUS, FEDIA, and POLEMONIUM.

**VALERIANA** (va-leer-i-ā'na). Tender and hardy perennial herbs, under-shrubs or shrubs, comprising about 260 species of the family Valerianaceae, found distributed mostly in the temperate and colder regions of the northern hemisphere and the tropical and warm regions of the southern hemisphere. Rootstocks thick, spreading, and strong-scented. Stem leaves opposite,* lance-shaped, sometimes cut into lobes, the margins sometimes toothed. Flowers small, white or rose, in compact roundish clusters at the ends of the branches. Calyx not conspicuous at first, but later it develops 5–15 hairy appendages. Corolla narrowly tubular, to ½ in. long, opening into 5 distinct lobes. Stamens* 3. Fruit 3-celled, each cell 1-seeded. (*Valeriana* is from the Latin to be strong, in allusion to medicinal uses.)

Valerianas make good border plants and are easily cult. and only the herbaceous species are grown. Propagated by seeds or division of the rootstocks. Seeds should be sown 1/16 in. deep, in light sandy soil, in sunny positions in cold frame or outdoor seedbed. They may be transplanted as soon as large enough to handle. Division of the rootstocks may be made in Oct. or early spring.

**officinalis.** Common valerian. Garden heliotrope. Cherry pie. Strong-growing perennial herb, 2–5 ft. high. Rootstocks thick and spreading. Leaves broadly lance-shaped, the upper leaves cut into 7–10 pairs of lance-shaped, sometimes toothed segments. Flowers pink, white or lavender, fragrant, in compact roundish clusters at the ends of the branches. The roots of this species are used medicinally. Eu. and northern As., naturalized in N.A.

**phu.** Cretan spikenard. Stout-growing perennial, to 3 ft. high. Basal leaves long-stalked, sometimes toothed at the base. Stem leaves divided into 3–4 pairs of lance-shaped segments. Flowers white or flesh-pink, in compact, roundish clusters at the ends of the branches. Caucasus.

**rubra** = *Centranthus ruber.*

**VALERIANACEAE** (va-leer-i-a-nay'see-ee). The valerian family comprises 9 genera and possibly 300 species of chiefly herbs, most abundant in the north temperate zone. Four genera are in cult. for ornament, or as in *Valerianella,* the corn salad, for food.

The other cult. genera are ornamentals, but not very important ones. *Centranthus* contains the familiar red valerian, *Fedia* is the African valerian, while *Valeriana* includes the garden heliotrope (not *Heliotropium*).

Leaves opposite.* Flowers small, usually unisexual,* sometimes irregular, and attractively clustered (cymes* or heads*). Fruit small, dry, not splitting, achene*-like, often crowned with the remains of the calyx.

Technical flower characters: Calyx tubular, 5-parted or lobed. Corolla more or less tubular, 5-lobed, sometimes irregular* and spurred,* or swollen at the base. Stamens 1–3, rarely 4, borne on the corolla. Ovary inferior,* 1–3-celled, two of the cells empty, the third with a single ovule.

**VALERIANELLA** (va-leer-i-a-nell'a). Annual herbs comprising about 58 species of the family Valerianaceae, found distributed throughout the temperate regions of the northern hemisphere, mostly in the Mediterranean region. Basal leaves spoon-shaped or roundish, in a rosette. Stem leaves toothed, sometimes deeply cut. Flowers small, white, pale blue or pink, in dense roundish clusters at the ends of the branches. Calyx not conspicuous, but later producing 1–4 appendages. Corolla of 5 spreading lobes. Stamens* usually 3. Fruit 3-celled, each cell 1-seeded. (*Valerianella* is a diminutive of *Valeriana.*)

Valerianellas are usually cult. for their leaves, which are used for salads. Propagated by seeds, which should be sown ½ in. deep, in drills 8 in. apart in ordinary garden soil, from April to Sept. They should be thinned out to 3 in. apart. *See* SALAD PLANTS.

**eriocarpa.** Italian corn salad. Leaves to 5 in. long, spoon-shaped, slightly hairy, the margins toothed at the base. Flowers pale blue, in dense round clusters at the ends of the branches. Southern Eu. Best species for warm localities.

**locusta.** The typical form of the species is rarely grown, although it is sometimes a weed in the eastern states. The *var.* olitoria, the corn salad or field salad, is the common garden sort. It grows to 1 ft. high. Leaves spoon-shaped, in a dense rosette, the veins prominent. Flowers light blue, in roundish terminal clusters. Eu. and the Orient. A round-leaved variety is grown extensively for the Paris market.

**VALIDA, -us, -um** (val'i-da). Strong.

**VALLARIS** (val-lar'is). Milky-juiced, woody vines, comprising about 6 species of the family Apocynaceae, natives of tropical As. and Malaya. Stems woody and twining. Leaves opposite,* ovalish or lance-shaped. Flowers whitish, in clusters growing from the axils* of the leaves. Calyx of 5 sepals. Corolla tubular at first, opening salver-wise, 5-lobed. Stamens* 5. Fruit 1-celled, many-seeded. (*Vallaris* is believed to be from the Latin to enclose, perhaps from their use as fences in Java.)

Sometimes grown in the extreme South as an ornamental climber.

**heynei.** Tall, strong-growing, climbing vine. Leaves ovalish, to 4 in. long, the veins prominent, sometimes covered with hairs. Flowers white, ⅔ in. across, scented, in 3–10-flowered clusters. Flower stalks covered with soft hairs. Fruits large, to 6 in. long. India.

**VALLEY WHITE OAK** = *Quercus lobata. See* OAK.

**VALLISNERIA.** *See* EEL-GRASS.

**VALLOTA** (val-low'ta). South African bulbous herbs of only one species of the family Amaryllidaceae, **V. speciosa,** the Scarborough lily. It has large bulbs and basal leaves to 2 ft. long and 1 in. wide, appearing at the same time as the flowering stalk, dying down in the autumn. Flowering stalks leafless, stout, hollow, flattish, to 3 ft. Flowers scarlet, funnel-shaped, to 3 in. across, in terminal umbels.* Calyx of 3 colored sepals. Corolla of 3 petals alternating with the sepals. Stamens* 6. Fruit a 3-celled capsule.* (Named for Pierre Vallot, French botanist.)

For culture *see* AMARYLLIS.

**VALVE.** The units or separable parts of a splitting pod. Familiar examples are the two valves of a pea pod or the three valves of an iris pod.

**VANCOUVERIA** (van-koo-veer'i-a). Low-growing, evergreen under-shrubs or woody herbs, comprising 3 species belonging to the barberry family, and natives of the woods of northwestern America. Rootstocks thick and creeping. Leaves alternate,* compound,* the leaflets 3, ovalish, bright glossy-green. Flowers small, white or yellow, in drooping terminal clusters. Calyx of 6 small, colored sepals, bending outward. Corolla of 6 small, narrow petals. Stamens* 6. Fruit 1-celled. (Named for Captain George Vancouver, commander of the Discovery, who landed at Vancouver in 1791.)

The cult. species makes an excellent ground cover and can also be used in the border. It will not stand strong sun, although easily cult. Propagated by division of the rootstocks. It requires a deep rich soil.

**hexandra.** Grows to 18 in. high. Leaves compound.* Leaflets 3, ovalish, to 1½ in. long, glossy. Flowers white to ½ in. long. Woods British Columbia to northern Calif.

**VANDA** (van'da). Large-flowered, tree-perching orchids, comprising about 25 species found in India, the Malay Islands, China and New Guinea. They have aerial* roots growing from the stems, and are varied in habit, some being dwarf and erect, covered with numerous leaves arranged in two rows on the stem, while others are taller and of straggling

---

* Special articles on the subjects indicated by an asterisk (*) will be found at the words so marked.

habit, branching and climbing round other plants. Leaves long and narrow, flat or fleshy and grooved, the tip sometimes slightly cut. Flowers showy in various colors, in racemes* growing from the axils* of the leaves. Calyx of 3 colored, spreading sepals. Corolla of 3 petals alternating with the sepals, 2 similar to the sepals and 1 forming a 3-lobed lip,* the middle lobe spreading, the side lobes small and erect. Fruit a 3-celled capsule. (*Vanda* is a native Indian name for some species.)

These handsome orchids are general favorites. Propagated by cuttings. Cuttings should be made of pieces of the tops of the stem cut below 3 or 4 of the aerial roots. They are best grown in teakwood baskets. Compost must be composed of live sphagnum* moss, interspersed with large pieces of charcoal. They should be suspended from the roof of a greenhouse in a winter night temperature of 60°–70° and summer of 70°–85°. They should be shaded from midday sun from Feb.–Nov. They require a humid atmosphere at all times, but ventilation should be given whenever weather conditions permit. These plants are subject to scale, which can be kept in check by frequent syringing or spongings with soapy sprays.

**caerulea.** Erect plant, growing to 2 ft. high. Leaves opposite,* to 10 in. long and 1 in. wide. Flowers light blue, to 4 in. across, in 7–15-flowered racemes* on a flowering stalk to 1½ ft., drooping at the tip. Himalayas.

**tricolor.** Strong-growing, erect plant to 3 ft. high. Leaves many, growing in 2 rows, to 18 in. long and 1½ in. wide. Flowers 2 in. across, in 8–10-flowered racemes* on flowering stalk to 1 ft. long. Petals and sepals wavy, yellow, marked with brown spots. Lip* light purple, veined purple with white side lobes. Java. The *var.* **suavis** has white sepals and petals marked purple, with the lip* marked purple at the base.

**VANILLA** (va-nill'a). Nearly thirty species of tropical, climbing orchids, of no hort. interest save for the Mexican **V. fragrans**, widely cult. in the tropics for its fruit which is the source of vanilla. It is a tall-climbing, fleshy-stemmed vine with oblong, thick, fleshy leaves, 6–8 in. long and about 2 in. wide. Flowers greenish-yellow, about 3 in. wide, grouped in a raceme.* Sepals and petals narrow, the lip* trumpet-shaped, shorter than the petals, its lobes somewhat scalloped. Fruit a slender, bean-like pod. The vanilla was well known to the Aztecs who cultivated the plant for its fragrant, aromatic pods. Its commercial production (much reduced since the production of synthetic vanilline) is now chiefly centered in the East Indies. A vanilla vine will, when mature, bear 40–50 vanilla beans a year for many years. The plant is occasionally grown in greenhouses, but rarely sets pods, as it needs artificial pollination. *See* Greenhouse Orchids at ORCHID for cult. notes. (*Vanilla* is the Spanish word for a little sheath or pod.) The plant was long known as *V. planifolia*, and is now found through much of tropical America. For the plant known as Carolina vanilla *see* TRILISA ODORATISSIMA.

**VANILLA GRASS** = *Hierochloë odorata*.

**VANILLA-LEAF** = *Trilisa odoratissima*.

**VAN RENSSELAER, MRS. SCHUYLER.** *See* America at GARDEN BOOKS.

**VAN THOL** = Duc van Thol. *See* Early Tulips at TULIPA.

**VAN TOL.** A valuable, grafted variety of the English holly which is reasonably sure to set fruit. *See Ilex aquifolium* at HOLLY.

**VAR.** The abbreviation for variety (which see).

**VARIA**, *-us*, *-um* (vair'i-a). Variable.

**VARIATION.** Differences between plants, or variations, are brought about, genetically speaking, in three different ways. (1) Differences due to changes in environment,* heredity* remaining unchanged — environment being such phenomena as soil, temperature, moisture and a host of other things external to the plant itself. Commonly these produce changes in size, shape, color, and many other characters. A certain primrose species has white flowers at one temperature and red ones at another and one may see both these flower colors on the same plant at the same time in such an experiment. Many flowers are pink in one soil type and blue in another, as occurs in certain varieties of hydrangea. Some characters are less sensitive to change than others, but it is difficult to generalize on this subject. Height in sorghum and corn is sensitive to both soil and moisture, while height in peas is much less so.

(2) Differences due to changes in heredity, the environment remaining unchanged, are, as regards the plant as a whole, of two sorts — (*a*) mutations* and allied phenomena — in which something hereditarily new has been produced (double flowers from single-flowered plants), and (*b*) new combinations of old character-determiners, producing at times new associations of old characters, such as dwarf yellow four-o'clocks from crosses between tall yellow and dwarf white varieties; or at other times new characters, as exemplified by dwarf light yellow four-o'clocks from this same type of cross.

(3) Heredity* and environment* may both change, from a formerly recognized state, at the same time or during the same season, so that one might secure a dwarf (environmental), white (hereditary) oat from a tall black variety. — O. E. W.

**VARICOSA**, *-us*, *-um* (vair-i-kō'sa). Irregularly swollen.

**VARIEGATA**, *-us*, *-um* (vair-i-e-gay'ta). Variegated.*

**VARIEGATED.** Having marks, stripes, or blotches of some color other than the basic ground-color, which is usually green. Variegated leaves are rare among wild plants but pretty common in hort. forms, especially in privet, holly, *Vinca*, many evergreens, and in a host of ornamental foliage plants.

While, generally speaking, the ground-color of variegated leaves is green, there are many very showy foliage plants, especially among the begonias and caladiums, where it is red, orange, yellow, or almost any other color. Some authorities would restrict the term variegation to those instances where the ground-color is green, but there does not seem sufficient evidence for this. Variegation, as used throughout this book, means exactly what it says in the first sentence of this definition.

**VARIETY.** Scarcely any term in botany or hort. is so variable in its meaning as *variety*. Strictly, from the botanical standpoint, the word denotes a group or class of plants, within a species, which have constant characters that separate them slightly from the typical form and from other possible varieties found within that species. An illustration:

*Rosa chinensis* is the China rose, and a good species. But contained within that species are four groups or classes of rose, all differing from the typical *R. chinensis*, but not enough to make them entitled to species names. To these four groups are attached what are called *varietal* names. In other, and strictly correct, words, they are each a *variety* of the China rose. Throughout this book a true variety is indicated by *var.*, which is merely the abbreviation for the word variety. The varieties of the China rose thus appear as

    *var.* **manetti.** The manetti rose.
    *var.* **minima.** The fairy rose.
    *var.* **semperflorens.** The Chinese monthly rose.
    *var.* **viridiflora.** The green rose. *See Rosa chinensis* at ROSA.

Not all cult. species have as many varieties as the China rose, but some have many more, as in corn, sorghum, heather, and several others. The thing to keep in mind throughout this book is that wherever the abbreviation *var.* appears it always means variety used in this technical sense, which is almost synonymous with a subspecies.

Most unfortunately, however, the word has several other meanings, neither precise nor adhered to by gardeners. In this looser and very general use of *variety* the word applies to any race, strain, or named horticultural form which is obviously different from the species to which it belongs. In such a sense it is commonly used to describe a red-flowered form of a white species, or a sour-juiced race of a sweet-juiced species, or to say that Duc van Thol is a *variety* of early tulip. Most hort. named forms, like American Beauty rose, are varieties in this sense.

These technical and popular uses of the word *variety* for

---

\* Special articles on the subjects indicated by an asterisk (\*) will be found at the words so marked.

any chance variation on the one hand, and for a strict botanical *var.* on the other, have resulted in widespread confusion, a confusion from which there is no escape, because of lack of adherence to any scheme for hort. nomenclature below the rank of a species. In this book the abbreviation *var.* means a variety in the technical sense, but the word *variety*, written in full, is still an indefinite category such as outlined above. *See* CLONE, PLANT NAMES.

While the usual method of indicating a variety is as shown above (*i.e. Rosa chinensis* var. *manetti*, etc.), there are many times when convenience or lack of space (as in lists) makes it necessary to omit the abbreviation *var.* In such cases, the name appears as *Rosa chinensis manetti* — a three-combination name known as a trinomial.

**VARIETY HYBRID.** *See* CROSS-BREED.

**VARIIFOLIA, -us, -um** (var-i-i-fō'li-a). With various or variable leaves.

**VARNISH-TREE** = *Koelreuteria paniculata*.

**V.-C. FAIRWAY.** *See* FAIRWAY FOOD.

**VECTOR.** The insect carrier of a virus disease. *See* Virus Disease at PLANT DISEASES.

**VEGECULTURE.** Vegetable gardening.

**VEGETA, -us, -um** (vej'e-ta). Vigorous; a luxuriant grower.

**VEGETABLE.** Scarcely needing a definition but often demanding one in the courts, where there is confusion as between the word fruit* and vegetable. No popular definition that is precise can be given of either word. Watermelon is considered a fruit in some sections but a vegetable in others. So are rhubarb and several other plants.

For a list of what everyone understands to be the leading vegetables *see* KITCHEN GARDEN.

**VEGETABLE BRAIN.** *See* BLIGHIA SAPIDA.

**VEGETABLE GARDENING.** As the name implies, this is merely the raising of vegetables. The pedantic call it olericulture or vegeculture, while those who do it for profit know it as truck gardening or market gardening. From these purely commercial activities the home gardener may learn much. Their methods, wherever applicable, will be found at the article KITCHEN GARDEN. Vegetables first enter the house through the kitchen. That is why the garden from which they come is properly called a kitchen garden. Thus, for the main details of raising vegetables *see* KITCHEN GARDEN. For the culture of individual crops, *see* CABBAGE, ONION, PEA, POTATO, etc.

**VEGETABLE GOLD** = *Crocus sativus*.

**VEGETABLE MARROW.** *See* CURCURBITA PEPO. *See also* BLIGHIA SAPIDA.

**VEGETABLE ORANGE** = Mango melon. *See* MELON.

**VEGETABLE OYSTER** = *Tragopogon poriifolius*. For culture *see* SALSIFY.

**VEGETABLE PEACH OR PEAR** = *Sechium edule*.

**VEGETABLE SHOWS.** *See* EXHIBITIONS AND SHOWS.

**VEGETABLE SILK.** *See* BEAUMONTIA GRANDIFLORA.

**VEGETABLE SPONGE.** *See* LUFFA.

**VEGETABLE TALLOW** = *Sapium sebiferum*.

**VEGETABLE WEEVIL.** *See* Insect Pests at TURNIP.

**VEINS.** *See* VENATION.

**VELAMEN.** The white or greenish outer covering of the aerial roots of some tree-perching orchids, and a few other epiphytes.* It has the unusual faculty of condensing and absorbing atmospheric moisture. Almost no plants can do this, but it is an extremely useful capacity for an epiphyte* in a tropical forest.

**VELUTINA, -us, -um** (vel-loo'ti-na). Velvety.

**VELVET BEAN.** *See* STIZOLOBIUM.

**VELVET BENT** = *Agrostis canina*.

**VELVET GRASS** = *Notholcus lanatus*.

**VELVET PLANT** = *Verbascum thapsus* and *Gynura aurantiaca*.

**VENATION.** The arrangement of the veins, usually in leaves, but many petals and not a few fruits have veins. The way veins are arranged in leaves is of prime importance in the classification of plants. In monocotyledons the veins are usually parallel, while most dicotyledonous plants have netted-veined leaves. *See* MONOCOTYLEDON, DICOTYLEDON.

**VENIDIUM** (ve-nid'i-um). South African annual or perennial herbs, comprising about 18 species of the family Compositae. Leaves alternate,* deeply cut, stalked, grayish-green, of cobwebby appearance when young. Flowers in solitary heads 4–5 in. across, daisy-like. Ray florets* yellow or orange, sometimes with purple band at the base. Disk florets purplish-black. (Origin of name unknown.)

Venidiums make showy plants for the border and are sometimes grown as pot plants in the greenhouse. They make excellent cut flowers, opening in the morning and closing at night in the same manner as when growing on the plant. Usually treated as tender annuals. Propagated by seeds. Seeds should be sown in April, ⅛ in. deep, in light sandy soil in greenhouse or cold frame, or later they may be sown outdoors where needed, in full sun. Care should be taken not to overwater at any time as plants are subject to stem rot.

**decurrens.** Perennial, of branching habit, growing to 2 ft. high. Leaves stalked, generally lyre-shaped, grayish, covered with soft hairs. Flowers in solitary heads, to 2½ in. across. Ray florets golden-yellow. Disk florets* purplish-black.

**fastuosum.** Annual, growing 2–3 ft. high. Leaves lyre-shaped, grayish, cobwebby when young. Flowers in solitary heads, 4–5 in. across. Ray florets bright orange with purplish band at the base. Disk florets purplish-black.

**VENTILATION.** For the ventilation of cold frames and hotbeds *see* COLD FRAME. For greenhouse and conservatory ventilation *see* GREENHOUSE.

**VENTRAL.** The front, inside, or upper side of an organ. *See* DORSAL.

**VENTRICOSA, -us, -um** (ven-tri-kō'sa). Ventricose; *i.e.* unequally swollen, as are some flowers or fruits.

**VENUS'S-FLYTRAP** = *Dionaea muscipula*.

**VENUS'S-HAIR** = *Adiantum capillus-veneris*.

**VENUS'S-LOOKING-GLASS** = *Specularia speculum-veneris*.

**VENUSTA, -us, -um** (ve-nus'ta). Charming.

**VERA, -us, -um** (ver'ra). True.

**VERATRUM** (ver-rah'trum). False hellebore. Hardy perennial herbs comprising about 18 species, belonging to the lily family, found throughout the northern hemisphere. Rootstocks thick and highly poisonous. Leaves alternate,* clasping the stem, large, parallel-veined. Flowers greenish-white or purplish, in terminal branching clusters. Calyx of 3 colored sepals. Corolla of 3 petals alternating with the sepals. Stamens* 6. Fruit a 3-celled capsule. (*Veratrum* is an old name for hellebore.)

These plants are not generally cult., but sometimes grown in the shady border or wild garden. Easily cult. Propagated by seeds or division of the rootstocks. They prefer damp and shady places.

**album.** European white hellebore. Hardy perennial, growing to 4 ft. high. Rootstock thick and fleshy. Leaves to 1 ft. long, and 5–6 in. wide, stiff, clasping the stem. Flowers in terminal clusters to 2 ft. long, greenish outside, white inside. Petals wavy and toothed. Eu. and northern As.

**viride.** White hellebore. American white hellebore. Indian poke. Strong-growing plant to 8 ft. high. Leaves clasping the stem, to 1 ft. long and 6 in. wide, narrowing toward the tip. Flowers greenish-yellow, hairy, to 1 in. across in terminal branching clusters, to 2 ft. long. Eastern N.A., and very common in swampy woods.

**VERBASCUM** (ver-bas'kum). Mullein. Hardy biennial or perennial herbs comprising about 270 species of the family Scrophulariaceae, found mostly in the Mediterranean region

---

* Special articles on the subjects indicated by an asterisk (*) will be found at the words so marked.

but naturalized throughout the northern hemisphere. Basal leaves large. Stem leaves alternate* and smaller, generally grayish-green and velvety, being often covered with soft hairs. Flowers yellow, tawny-red, or purple, sometimes white, numerous in showy spikes or racemes.* Calyx of 5 sepals. Corolla of 5 spreading lobes. Stamens* 5, the filaments being covered with showy hairs. Fruit a 2-celled capsule.* (*Verbascum* is an old Latin name used by Pliny for these plants.)

Verbascums are suitable for the large border, edges of shrubberies or the wild garden. Usually treated as biennials. Easily propagated by seeds. Seeds should be sown ⅛ in. deep in light sandy soil in April or May in cold frame or outdoor seedbed. They may be transplanted as soon as large enough to handle. These plants do not like wet, cold soil.

**blattaria.** Moth mullein. Strong-growing biennial to 6 ft. high. Leaves smooth, dark green, ovalish, to 2½ in. long, the margins toothed or cut. Flowers in a long, loose raceme,* yellow, marked purple at the base with lilac hairs on the stamen filaments. Eu. and northern As.; naturalized in N.A.

**chaixi.** Biennial, growing to 3 ft. high, and covered with white-woolly hairs. Leaves ovalish, to 6 in. long, coarsely toothed. Flowers yellow, with purple hairs on the stamen filaments, borne in a raceme with small, side, flower-bearing branches. Southern Eu.

**olympicum.** Biennial, growing 3–6 ft. high and covered with white-woolly hairs. Leaves ovalish, to 1 ft. long. Flowering stalk thick. Flowers bright yellow, with white-woolly hairs on the stamen filaments, arranged in bunched clusters in the axils* of leafy bracts in a raceme. Greece.

**phoeniceum.** Purple mullein. Biennial, growing to 5 ft. high. Leaves basal, in a rosette, ovalish, wrinkled, dark green on the upper side, covered with short hairs on the under side, the margins with rounded teeth. Flowers reddish-purple, with purplish-woolly hairs on the stamen filaments, borne in a slender, sometimes branched raceme. S.E. Eu. and As.

**thapsus.** Common mullein. Velvet plant. Candlewick. Flannel-leaf. Strong-growing biennial, to 6 ft. high and covered with felty, yellowish hairs. Basal leaves large, to 1 ft. long. Stem leaves smaller, clasping the stem. Flowers yellow, to 1 in. across, in bunched clusters arranged in a spike. Eurasia. Usually considered a weed, and widely so naturalized in N.A.

**VERBENA** (ver-bee'na). Vervain. Tender or hardy annual or perennial herbs, comprising about 80 species of the family Verbenaceae, natives of America with the exception of 1 species found in Eurasia. Leaves generally opposite,* usually lobed or toothed. Flowers in various shades of white, lilac, rose and purple, small, sometimes stalked, in terminal spikes* or terminal, roundish clusters. Calyx tubular, 5-toothed. Corolla tubular, opening salver-wise, its lobes 5, the tube long and narrow. Stamens* 4, in pairs. Fruit 4-celled which when ripe separates into 4 parts, each part containing 1 seed. (*Verbena* is the ancient Latin name of the European vervain.) For the lemon verbena see LIPPIA CITRIODORA, for the sand verbena see ABRONIA.

Verbenas are useful garden plants for the border and are sometimes grown in the greenhouse as pot plants for house decoration. Usually only the perennial species are grown but they are best treated as tender annuals (*see* ANNUALS). Propagated by seeds or cuttings. Seeds should be sown in March, ⅛ in. deep, in light sandy soil, in cool greenhouse or cold frame and pricked-off into boxes or small pots as soon as large enough to handle. They may be transplanted to permanent positions as soon as danger of frost is over. Cuttings are usually made only when it is desired to retain a particular color. To do this plants should be cut down in early Sept. when young shoots will form. Cuttings may then be made from these shoots which should be rooted under glass and kept in cool greenhouse through the winter.

**canadensis.** A perennial with creeping rootstocks, the branches growing to 18 in. high, and covered with stiff hairs. Leaves ovalish, to 4 in. long, often cut into 3 lobes. Flowers reddish, purple, lilac or white, to ⅔ in. across, stalked, in terminal heads. Va. and south and west to Colo.

**erinoides** = *Verbena laciniata* and *Verbena pulchella*.

**hastata.** Blue vervain. Hardy erect perennial, with square stems, growing 4–5 ft. high. Leaves lance-shaped, to 6 in. long, the margins toothed. Flowers blue, small, in slender spikes. Eastern N.A. *See* BLUE GARDEN.

**hortensis.** Garden verbena. Tender trailing perennial, growing to 1 ft. high. Leaves broadly lance-shaped, 2–4 in. long, the margins bluntly toothed. Flowers pink, red, yellow or white in terminal compact clusters. Of hybrid origin. Among the hort. forms of this old garden favorite are Miss Willmott (*see* PINK GARDEN), and Etna and Spectrum Red (*see* RED GARDEN).

**laciniata.** Tender perennial, of spreading habit, the stems hairy and rooting, the branches erect. Leaves ovalish, deeply cut into 3 lobes, each lobe cut into narrow segments. Flowers lilac, in short, dense, head-like clusters. Argentina and Chile.

**pulchella.** Perennial, of spreading habit, the stem somewhat woody at the base, hairy and rooting. Branches erect, to 20 in. high. Leaves ovalish, cut into narrow lobes. Flowers blue or lilac, in terminal dense clusters. Southern S.A.

**VERBENACEAE** (ver-be-nay'see-ee). The vervain or verbena family includes many old garden favorites among its 67 genera and over 750 species. It is largely tropical or sub-tropical, although some cult. genera such as *Verbena* and *Callicarpa* are mostly hardy. Some of the most attractive shrubby genera are not quite hardy over extreme winters, especially *Lippia*, *Vitex* and *Caryopteris*.

*Citharexylum*, *Clerodendron* (one or two hardy), *Duranta*, *Holmskioldia*, *Lantana*, *Petrea* (a woody vine), and *Oxera* (also a vine) are generally tropical. They require greenhouse culture or outdoor sites in southern Fla. and southern Calif. (zones* 8 and 9).

*Vitex*, *Caryopteris*, and *Callicarpa* are easily, and deservedly, the most popular hort. genera. All are profuse bloomers.

Leaves prevailingly opposite,* simple* or compound.* Flowers usually irregular* and often 2-lipped,* very ornamental in most of the cult. genera. Fruit nearly always fleshy, none edible.

Technical flower characters: Calyx* united, mostly 4–5-toothed. Corolla tubular or funnel-shaped, its 4–5 lobes irregular* or two-lipped in most genera (nearly regular in *Verbena*). Stamens* generally 4, two shorter than the others. Ovary superior.*

**VERBESINA** (ver-be-sy'na). American annual or perennial herbs and shrubs, the shrubby species tropical, comprising about 50 species of the family Compositae. Leaves opposite* or alternate,* often running down the stem (decurrent*). Flower heads solitary, or in clusters. Ray florets* usually absent. Disk florets yellow, orange or white. (*Verbesina* is believed to be a meaningless alteration of *Verbena*.)

These plants are not of any garden importance, although they are sometimes used in the wild garden. Propagated by seeds or cuttings.

**encelioides.** Golden crown-beard. Annual, growing to 3 ft. high. Leaves alternate, ovalish, to 4 in. long, pale green on the under side, the margins toothed. Flowers in solitary heads 2 in. across. Ray florets* golden-yellow. Fla.–Mex.

**VERDEX.** A trademarked green surfacing material for garden walks, driveways, and tennis courts.

*VERIS* (ver'is). True.

**VERMONT.** The state lies in zones* two and three.

SOILS. The soils of Vermont are much diversified. On cultivable land they are best suited to the culture of grass and, therefore, well adapted for the most part to garden plants. The major soils are of different kinds of loam such as clay, silty clay, stony loam, shale loam, fine sandy loam, and there are places where gravelly loam prevails. The soils of the Mohawk group occur on low, smooth ridges throughout the Champlain Valley and are derived from glacial, limy shales and are limy at shallow depths. The Merrimac soils prevail on the terraced areas along the larger streams. They are free from stone, level, and their excellent texture makes a good medium for crops. Most of the potatoes in the state are grown on these soils. Agawam soil is found on the terraces in the Connecticut River section, and possesses the best structure of any soil in this region. The Bristol soils, derived from quartz, etc., are sandy and less productive and occur on the plains of Chittenden County where market gardening is successful.

FRUITS AND VEGETABLES. The main fruit and vegetable areas are in the Champlain Valley on the western border and in the lower Connecticut Valley on the eastern border. Orchards abound in the first and market gardens in the second district. Potato culture, with reference to table stock and certified potato stock, is the largest vegetable enterprise in the state.

The climate of Vermont is well adapted to apple culture. The leading varieties are, in order of importance: McIntosh, Northern Spy, North Western Greening, Delicious, Wealthy. The culture of this fruit has assumed commercial proportions. The largest orchard covers 1000 acres, and there are many of over 200 acres in extent. Apple culture is general over the state but there is more of it on the west side.

---

* Special articles on the subjects indicated by an asterisk (*) will be found at the words so marked.

About 5000 acres of land are set to orchards, and there are over 300,000 trees in the commercial orchards, and nearly as many more in home orchards and smaller plantings. Small fruit culture is practiced to a limited extent in the western and north central sections of the state in areas sufficient to meet local demands, except for very early markets. The leading varieties of raspberries are Latham, Cuthbert, Viking, Chief and Dike. Strawberry culture is most practiced in the Connecticut Valley section on the higher areas along the Connecticut River. The leading varieties are Howard 17, Dunlap, Burrill, Fairfax, Dorset and Green Mountain. Small fruits, as raspberries and strawberries, are grown with success on small areas throughout the state.

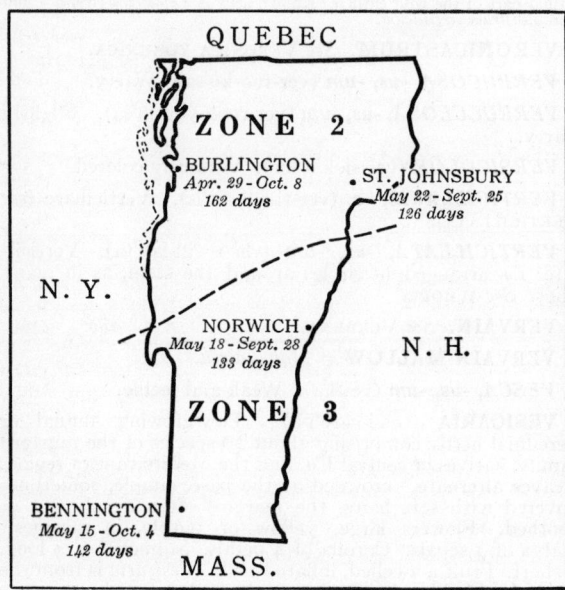

VERMONT

The zones of hardiness crossing Vermont are those shown on the colored map at ZONE, which should be consulted for details. The dates are the average latest killing frost in spring and the first one in the fall. The figures below the dates show the average length of the growing season.

All of the cool season crops can be grown with success, but such warm temperature crops as eggplant, pepper, etc., are not generally successful, with the exception of tomatoes, unless advanced under glass and short season varieties are selected.

The Irish potato is the major vegetable crop. Irish Cobbler and Green Mountain are the chief varieties both for table stock and for certified seed sale.

The market-garden enterprises, aside from the potato, are for the most part located near St. Johnsbury in Caledonia County, near Burlington in Chittenden County, near Brattleboro, Vernon and Westminster in Windham County, near St. Albans in Franklin County, near Middlebury and Vergennes in Addison County, and in the environs of Bennington in Bennington County.

CLIMATE. The general climatic factors in Vermont are wind, sunshine, length of growing period and rainfall. The winds over most of the state are moderate and destructive gales of large extent are not on record. The average hourly velocity of wind in Burlington over a 25-year period is 10:8 miles per hour. The highest velocity on record for a five-minute period was 57 miles. The prevailing wind was from the South.

Vermont receives about 45% of possible sunshine. The highest monthly average in Burlington is 59% in July, and the lowest is 22% in December.

The humidity is not excessive. It is lowest from April to June, inclusive. Fogs are not frequent, the average number of foggy days in Burlington being eight per year. An all-day fog is rare. There are more foggy days in the valleys than in the upland sections. Thunderstorms are frequent but not destructive. The average annual number at Burlington is thirty.

FROST DATA

| | Average date of last killing frost in spring | Latest known killing frost | Average date of earliest killing frost in fall | Earliest known killing frost |
|---|---|---|---|---|
| Burlington | April 29 | May 21 | October 8 | Sept. 15 |
| Bennington | May 15 | May 26 | October 4 | Sept. 14 |
| St. Johnsbury | May 22 | June 20 | September 25 | Sept. 6 |
| Norwich (Hanover, N.H.) | May 18 | June 20 | September 28 | Sept. 7 |

The average growing season of frost-free weather is as follows: At Burlington in Chittenden County, 162 days; at St. Johnsbury in Caledonia County, 126 days; at Bennington in Bennington County, 142 days; at Norwich in Windsor County, 133 days. The latest spring frost is May 31 in northern towns and April 20 in other towns; the earliest frost in the fall is September 6 and October 18. The total rainfall at Burlington is 32.28; St. Johnsbury, 34.68; Bennington, 37.71; Norwich (Hanover, N.H.), 33.78. The rainfall in the growing season (May to October) is 17.09 in Burlington; 15.40 in St. Johnsbury; 18.91 in Bennington; 16.64 in Norwich (Hanover, N.H.). There is more rainfall in the Connecticut Valley sections, especially in the southern part, than in the Champlain Valley.

The address of the Agricultural Experiment Station which has kindly supplied this information about the state is Burlington. The station is always glad to answer gardening questions.

Garden Club activities include clubs of the Garden Club of America, the home office of which is 598 Madison Avenue, New York.

**VERNA, -us, -um** (ver'na). Spring.

**VERNALIS, -e** (ver-nal'is). Having to do with spring; *i.e.* spring-blooming.

**VERNATION.** The arrangement of leaves in a bud. Botanists have many special terms for the different methods of folding, curling, twisting, or coiling of young leaves in an unopened bud, but they are scarcely garden terms.

**VERNONIA** (ver-no'ni-a). Ironweed. Perennial herbs, shrubs or trees, comprising about 560 species of the family Compositae, distributed throughout the world, the shrubs and trees tropical. Leaves alternate,* simple, lance-shaped, sometimes hairy, the margins toothed. Flowers in heads, in terminal clusters, composed of disk florets* only, purple, pink or white. Flower heads surrounded by numerous overlapping bracts,* their tips sometimes bristle-like. (Named for Wm. Vernon, English botanist.)

A few herbaceous species are cult. for use in the back of the border or wild garden for their autumn flowers. Easily cult. Propagated by division of the rootstocks in early spring. They prefer damp, deep, rich soil.

**altissima.** Strong-growing perennial, 5–9 ft. high. Leaves deep green, lance-shaped, to 1 ft. long, the margins finely toothed. Flowers purple, in heads ½ in. across. Heads in loose, terminal clusters. Mass. to Fla. and La. See AUTUMN GARDEN.

**crinita.** Strong-growing perennial to 12 ft. high. Leaves narrowly lance-shaped, to 1 ft. long, sometimes covered with hairs, the margins finely toothed. Flowers purple, in heads 1 in. across. Bracts* surrounding the heads green, sometimes tipped red. Mo. to Tex. See GRAY AND LAVENDER GARDEN.

**noveboracensis.** Perennial, growing 3–7 ft. high. Leaves lance-shaped, to 10 in. long, dark green, the margins finely toothed. Flowers deep purple, in heads ⅓ in. across, the heads in terminal clusters. Bracts* surrounding the heads bristle-tipped. Mass. to N.C. and Miss.

**VERONICA** (ver-ron'i-ka). Speedwell. A very large genus of rather unlike plants of the family Scrophulariaceae, some of them hardy herbs for the border or rock garden, but many of them shrubs or small trees, chiefly from New Zea-

---

* Special articles on the subjects indicated by an asterisk (*) will be found at the words so marked.

land, and cult. here outdoors only in zones* 7, 8, and 9, especially in Calif., where they are very popular. Some authorities (with a good deal of reason) consider these New Zealand plants as a separate genus, to which the name *Hebe* is applied. But they have for so long been retained as of the genus *Veronica*, and are so generally still known by that name that they are here included within it. Stem leaves opposite,* (rarely alternate* or whorled*), the upper nearly always alternate.* Flowers mostly in terminal clusters (spikes or racemes*), but these sometimes in the axils* of the leaves. Calyx* united, mostly 4-parted. Corolla almost or completely regular,* mostly with a short tube and a spreading, 4–5-lobed limb. Stamens* 2. Fruit a 2-grooved capsule.* (Named for Saint Veronica.)

Culturally, the two sections of *Veronica* must be treated very differently. The herbs are attractive garden plants for the border or rock garden, nearly all perennials and of easy culture under most ordinary garden conditions. Some are attractively flowering, prostrate plants good for ground cover or for edging. All the herbs should be increased by division, which should be done after flowering, and the plants re-set in good rich soil.

The shrubby species from New Zealand grow well in a variety of soils in Calif., where some of them can be clipped into informal hedges. They may be propagated by cuttings of mature wood in fall, most of which will bloom the following season. Some, like *V. traversi*, are occasionally grown in northern greenhouses, where they need a temperate house and potting mixture* 4. All these New Zealand species in the list below (species of *Hebe* to those who maintain that genus) are marked with a dagger (†).

† **amplexicaulis.** A partly prostrate or decumbent shrub, 1–3 ft. high. Leaves very numerous, overlapping, about 1 in. long, without teeth, bluish-green. Flowers white, about ¼ in. long, in spikes about 1 in. long. N. Zeal.

† **andersoni.** A hybrid veronica, and a much-branched shrub 5–8 ft. high. Leaves 4–5 in. long. Flowers very small, but showy from the handsome clusters (racemes*) which are 4–6 in. long. Corolla white, but violet-tipped. The *var.* **variegata** has the leaves blotched creamy-white.

**austriaca.** A perennial herb, 1–2 ft. high, the leaves cut feather-fashion into oblong or narrower segments. Flowers blue, in showy, terminal clusters (racemes*). Eurasia. *See* BLUE GARDEN.

† **buxifolia.** A shrub, 3–5 ft. high, with very numerous, overlapping, small, stiff leaves, scarcely ⅓ in. long. Flowers about ⅓ in. long, the clusters (spikes*) about 1 in. long. N. Zeal.

† **cupressoides.** A stiffish shrub, its twigs covered by scale-like leaves which in maturity are scarcely 1/10 in. long, but large (¼ in.) on young twigs. Flowers pale purple, about ⅙ in. long, in head-like clusters. N.Z.

**decussata** = *Veronica elliptica.*

† **elliptica.** A much-branched shrub, 15–20 ft. high. Leaves about 1¼ in. long, and half as wide. Flowers nearly ⅔ in. wide, white, but often veined with purple or blue, the clusters nearly 2 in. long. N. Zeal.

**fruticulosa.** A woody, perennial herb, 4–6 in. high. Leaves oblongish, nearly ½ in. long. Flowers small, blue or rarely pale pink, in short clusters (racemes*). In the mountains of Eu. and in Greenland. Best suited to the rock garden (which see).

**gentianoides.** A perennial herb, 1–2 ft. high, the leaves oblongish or narrower, 2–3 in. long. Flowers blue, veined with darker blue, in rather showy, loose, terminal clusters (racemes*). Southeastern Eu. For culture *see* ROCK GARDEN.

† **hulkeana.** A shrub, 2–3 ft. high, the ovalish, toothed leaves 1½–2 in. long. Flowers about ¼ in. long, white, in a showy, terminal cluster (panicle*) nearly 1 ft. long. N. Zeal.

**incana.** A white-hairy herb, mostly 8 in. high or less, occasionally up to 18 in. high. Leaves oblongish, toothed, 2–3 in. long. Flowers blue, the clusters (racemes*) nearly 6 in. long. Northern As. A good edging plant. For culture *see* ROCK GARDEN.

**longifolia** = *Veronica maritima.*

**maritima.** A perennial herb, 1–2 ft. high. Leaves oblongish or tapering, toothed, 3–4 in. long. Flowers lilac-blue in dense, terminal clusters (racemes*). Eurasia, naturalized in N.A. and often known as *V. longifolia.* The *var.* **subsessilis** has deeper blue flowers and nearly stalkless leaves. *See* BLUE GARDEN.

**officinalis.** A prostrate, perennial, weedy herb with oblongish leaves and pale blue flowers. Eurasia and N.A. *See* Speedwell in the list at WEEDS.

**pectinata.** A prostrate, white-hairy perennial with ovalish or oblong, coarsely toothed leaves. Flowers deep blue, white-eyed, in profuse clusters (racemes*). Asia Minor. For culture *see* ROCK GARDEN.

**repens.** A moss-like, prostrate perennial, the leaves about ½ in. long and shining. Flowers small, rose-pink or bluish, the clusters few-flowered. Corsica. There is also a white-flowered form. *See* ROCK GARDEN.

**rupestris.** *See* VERONICA TEUCRIUM DUBIA.

**spicata.** Cat's-tail speedwell. A perennial, 15–24 in. high. Leaves lance-shaped, toothed, 1½–2 in. long. Flowers blue, the clusters (racemes*) dense. Eurasia. *See* BLUE GARDEN. The *var.* **rosea** has pink flowers. *See* PINK GARDEN.

**spuria.** Bastard speedwell. A perennial, 12–20 in. high, covered with dense hairs. Leaves line-like, scarcely 1 in. long. Flowers blue, the clusters branched (panicled racemes). Eurasia. *See* BLUE GARDEN.

**subsessilis** = *Veronica maritima subsessilis.*

**teucrium.** Germander speedwell, and the best known of all the herbaceous species. It is 12–18 in. high, the leaves oblongish or narrower, coarsely toothed. Flowers generally blue, but sometimes white or pinkish. Eurasia. It is a fine border plant, especially the form known as Royal Blue. The *var.* **prostrata** is a nearly prostrate form useful for ground cover. The *var.* **dubia,** a low form popular for the rock garden, is of uncertain identity and is sometimes called *V. rupestris.*

† **traversi.** A thrifty but small, much-branched shrub. Leaves about 1 in. long, scarcely ⅓ in. wide. Flowers white, about ¼ in. long, the cluster (raceme*) 2–3 in. long. N. Zeal.

**virginica.** Culver's-root; also called blackroot. A native American, perennial herb, 4–6 ft. high. Leaves lance-shaped, 4–6 in. long, mostly in whorls. Flowers scarcely ⅕ in. long, in a loose, terminal cluster, 6–9 in. long. Eastern U.S. but west to Tex. Summer. Suited to the more informal part of the wild garden. Known also as *Leptandra virginica* and *Veronicastrum virginicum.*

**VERONICASTRUM.** *See* VERONICA VIRGINICA.

***VERRUCOSA, -us, -um*** (ver-roo-kō'sa). Warty.

***VERRUCULOSA, -us, -um*** (ver-rook-you-lō'sa). Slightly warty.

***VERSICOLOR*** (ver-sick'o-lor). Variously colored.

***VERTICILLARIS, -e*** (ver-ti-sill-air'is). Verticillate (*see* VERTICILLATA).

***VERTICILLATA, -us, -um*** (ver-ti-sill-lay'ta). Verticillate; *i.e.* arranged in circles around the stem, as in many lilies. *See* WHORL.

**VERVAIN.** *See* VERBENA.

**VERVAIN MALLOW** = *Malva alcea.*

***VESCA, -us, -um*** (ves'ka). Weak and feeble.

**VESICARIA** (ves-i-care'i-a). Low-growing annual or perennial herbs, comprising about 20 species of the mustard family, natives of central Eu. and the Mediterranean region. Leaves alternate,* crowded at the base, simple, sometimes covered with soft hairs, the margins often deeply cut or toothed. Flowers large, yellow or purple, in racemes.* Calyx of 4 sepals. Corolla of 4 petals. Stamens* 6, 4 long, 2 short. Fruit a 2-celled, inflated pod. (*Vesicaria* is from the Latin for bladder, in allusion to the pods.)

Not much in cult., the species below being the one generally grown. It should be treated as a hardy annual. Propagated by seeds sown in early spring where required to bloom.

**utriculata.** Bladder-pod. Perennial, but grown as an annual; of branching habit, slightly woody at the base, and growing to 18 in. high. Lower leaves ovalish, crowded on the stem. Upper leaves lance-shaped. Flowers yellow, in racemes.* Mediterranean region. Grown mostly for its pods.

**VESPERTINE.** Flowering toward dusk.

***VESTITA, -us, -um*** (ves-ty'ta). Clothed or covered, often with hairs, scales, etc.

**VETCH.** *See* VICIA. For other plants occasionally called vetch *see* ANTHYLLIS, ASTRAGALUS, and CORONILLA.

**VETCHLING.** *See* LATHYRUS.

**VETIVER** = *Vetiveria zizanioides.*

**VETIVERIA** (vet-i-veer'i-a). Tropical, perennial grasses of only 1 species, and a native of the E. Indies, but naturalized in the southern states and scarcely known elsewhere. (*Vetiveria* is the native Tamil name for this grass.)

Vetiver is important in the East, the roots being used for centuries for perfumery and medicinal purposes. Propagated by division of the rootstocks.

**zizanioides.** Vetiver. Khus-khus. Strong-growing perennial, to 8 ft. high, with thick, aromatic rootstocks. Leaves to 3 ft. long and ⅓ in. wide, clasping the stem, the margins saw-like. Flowers in pairs in short spikes arranged in a raceme a foot long. Also known as *Anatherum.*

**VETKOUSIE.** *See* MESEMBRYANTHEMUM POMERIDIANUM.

***VEXILLARIA, -us, -um*** (veck-sill-ar'i-a). Relating to the standard (a petal). *See* STANDARD, 2.

**VEXILLUM.** *See* STANDARD, 2.

**VIABILITY OF SEED.** *See* GARDEN TABLES II for the

* Special articles on the subjects indicated by an asterisk (*) will be found at the words so marked.

usual length of time for seeds to keep the power of germinating.

**VI-APPLE** = *Spondias cytherea*.

**VIBURNUM** (vy-bur'num). A large and valuable genus of shrubs and small trees of the honeysuckle family, many of the 120 known species cult. for ornament. They are chiefly deciduous shrubs of the north temperate zone, with opposite leaves and small, generally white flowers in showy, terminal clusters (panicles* or cymes*). Calyx with 5 very small teeth. Corolla bell-shaped or wheel-shaped, or even tubular. Stamens* 5. Fruit a 1-seeded, fleshy drupe,* often colored handsomely, persistent, and a favorite food of birds. (*Viburnum* is the classical Latin name of *V. lantana*, the wayfaring tree.)

The viburnums are generally of the easiest culture and consequently widely popular. Their attractive flower clusters, especially in some sorts known as snowball, and their often showy fruits make them very attractive shrubs. As the list of species indicates, they are found in a variety of heights, and their flowering period stretches over a considerable period. All of them have fine autumnal color in their foliage except *V. odoratissimum*, *V. tinus*, *V. rhytidophyllum*, and *V. suspensum*, which are evergreen. Propagated by stratified seeds, cuttings, or by layering. All are white-flowered unless otherwise mentioned. Some of them are known as haw. Some of the species resemble *Cornus* (which see for the differences).

**acerifolium.** Dockmackie. Not over 5-6 ft. high. Leaves maple-like, 3-lobed, and coarsely toothed. Flower clusters long-stalked, about 3 in. wide. Fruit black-purple. May-June. Eastern N.A. Hardy from zone* 3 southward.

**alnifolium.** Hobblebush; also called American wayfaring tree and witch-hobble. A spreading shrub 6-10 ft. high. Leaves nearly round, nearly 7 in. wide, irregularly toothed. Flower cluster flat-topped, nearly 5 in. wide, the marginal flowers nearly 1 in. wide and sterile. Fruit purplish-black. Eastern N.A. May-June. Hardy from zone* 2 southward.

**americanum** = *Viburnum trilobum*.

**carlesi.** A shrub 3-5 ft. high. Leaves ovalish, 2-3½ in. long, hairy both sides. Flowers fragrant, white, the clusters (cymes*) dense. Fruit bluish-black. Korea. April-May. Hardy from zone* 3 southward. It is a useful shrub for forcing, especially because of its handsome, fragrant flowers. See FORCING.

**cassinoides.** Withered. Appalachian tea. A shrub 8-12 ft. high. Leaves ovalish, 3-4 in. long, finely toothed. Flowers in short-stalked clusters (cymes*). Fruit bluish-black. Eastern N.A. June-July. Hardy from zone* 2 southward.

**dentatum.** Arrow-wood. A shrub 10-15 ft. high. Leaves ovalish or round, 2-3 in. long, coarsely toothed. Flowers in long-stalked clusters (cymes*), which are about 3 in. wide. Fruit bluish-black. Eastern N.A. May-June. Hardy from zone* 2 southward. This and *V. cassinoides* are both good, if informal, hedge plants.

**dilatatum.** A shrub 6-10 ft. high. Leaves nearly round, about 4½ in. wide, hairy both sides and coarsely toothed. Flower clusters about 5 in. wide. Fruit scarlet. Jap. May-June. Hardy from zone* 3 southward, and an attractive shrub in the fall as the fruit is long-persistent.

**lantana.** Wayfaring-tree. A tree-like shrub 10-15 ft. high. Leaves ovalish, 3-5 in. long, hairy both sides, coarsely toothed. Flower clusters nearly 4 in. wide. Fruit red, but later turning black. Eurasia, but naturalized in the eastern U.S. June-July. Hardy from zone* 3 southward.

**lentago.** Nannyberry. Sheepberry. A shrub, but more often tree-like, 20-30 ft. high. Leaves ovalish, 3-4 in. long, finely toothed. Flower clusters nearly 5 in. wide, stalkless. Fruit bluish-black, with a slight bloom. N.A. May-June. Hardy from zone* 2 southward.

**molle.** Poison haw. A shrub 8-12 ft. high. Leaves nearly round, 3-5 in. long, coarsely toothed and heart-shaped at the base. Flower clusters long-stalked, about 3 in. wide. Fruit bluish-black. Central U.S. June. Hardy from zone* 3 southward.

**odoratissimum.** A handsome evergreen shrub 7-10 ft. high. Leaves ovalish, 4-6 in. long, practically without teeth, shining green above. Flowers fragrant, the clusters (panicles*) about 4 in. high. Fruit red, later black. India to Jap. May-June. Hardy from zone* 6 southward.

**opulus.** Cranberry tree. A shrub 8-12 ft. high, useful in cities as it stands smoke very well. Leaves maple-like, 3-5-lobed, about 3½ in. wide, hairy on the under side. Flower clusters nearly 4 in. wide, stalked, the outer flowers nearly ¾ in. wide and sterile. Fruit red. Eurasia and northern Af. May-June. Hardy from zone* 2 southward. The *var.* **nanum** is a dwarf form with smaller leaves and is a good accent plant (*see* ACCENT PLANT). The *var.* **sterile**, the common snowball or Guelder rose, is by far the most common in cult. Its ball-like flower clusters are wholly made up of sterile flowers. The plant is sometimes offered as *V. opulus roseum*. It is useful for forcing (which see).

**prunifolium.** Black haw; also known as stag bush. A shrub or small tree 10-15 ft. high. Leaves broadly ovalish, 2-3 in. long, finely toothed. Flower clusters nearly 4 in. wide, stalkless. Fruit bluish-black, with a slight bloom. Conn. to Fla. and Tex. April-May. Hardy from zone* 3 southward.

**pubescens.** A spreading shrub 6-10 ft. high. Leaves ovalish or broader, 3-4 in. long, coarsely toothed, hairy on the under side. Fruit bluish-black. Mass. to Va. June-July. Hardy from zone* 3 southward.

**rhytidophyllum.** An evergreen shrub 7-10 ft. high. Leaves ovalish or oblong, 5-7 in. long, nearly without marginal teeth, wrinkled above, grayish or yellowish beneath, with felty hairs. Flowers yellowish-white, the clusters nearly 8 in. wide. Fruit red, later black. China. June. Hardy from zone* 4 southward.

**sieboldi.** A shrub 8-10 ft. high. Leaves generally ovalish or broader towards the tip, 4-6 in. long, coarsely toothed, hairy beneath, of unpleasant odor when crushed. Flower cluster (panicle*) about 4 in. high. Fruit pink, later bluish-black. Jap. May-June. Hardy from zone* 3 southward.

**suspensum.** An evergreen shrub 4-6 ft. high. Leaves ovalish, 3-4 in. long, toothed towards the tip. Flower cluster dense (a panicle*), pinkish, about 1½ in. wide. Fruit red. Liu-Kiu Islands, near Hongkong, China. Hardy from zone* 6 southward.

**tinus.** Laurestinus. A handsome evergreen shrub 7-10 ft. high. Leaves oblongish or broader, 2-3 in. long, without marginal teeth, dark green. Flower clusters about 3 in. wide, often faintly pinkish. Fruit black. Mediterranean region. July-Aug. Hardy from protected parts of zone* 6 southward. Long in cult. and a beautiful evergreen shrub, also known in several hort. forms, one with variegated leaves.

**tomentosum.** A shrub 7-10 ft. high. Leaves ovalish, 3-4 in. long, hairy on the under side and toothed. Flower cluster long-stalked, more or less flat-topped, nearly 4 in. wide, the marginal flowers sterile and about 1 in. wide. Fruit red, ultimately bluish-black. China and Jap. May-June. Hardy from zone* 3 southward. The *var.* **sterile**, the Japanese snowball, has a large ball-shaped flower cluster wholly of sterile flowers. It is often offered as *V. tomentosum plicatum*, and is a useful shrub for forcing.

**trilobum.** Cranberry bush; also called high cranberry. A shrub 8-12 ft. high. Leaves broadly oval, 3-lobed and toothed, 3-5 in. long. Flower cluster short-stalked, nearly 4 in. wide, the marginal flowers sterile, and larger than the others. Fruit scarlet. Northern N.A. May-June. Fruit ripening in late July and persistent over most of the winter. Hardy from zone* 4 northward. Closely related to *V. opulus* and perhaps not really separable, but the leaves of *V. trilobum* are smooth on the under side. The plant is sometimes known as *V. americanum*.

**VICIA** (viss'i-a). Vetch. Annual or perennial herbs, comprising about 150 species, belonging to the pea family, found distributed throughout the northern hemisphere and S.A. They are mostly hardy, climbing plants, a few erect. Leaves alternate,* compound,* stalked, with 2 small leaf-like appendages (stipules*) at the base. Leaflets usually in 1-12 pairs, ovalish or lance-shaped, in the climbing species the end leaflet modified into a tendril* by means of which the plant climbs. Flowers blue, violet, yellowish or white, pea-like, usually small, in short racemes* growing from the axils* of the leaves. Stamens* 10, 9 joined by their filaments* and 1 free. Fruit a flat pod (legume*), sometimes white-woolly within. (*Vicia* is the classical Latin name of the vetch.)

For cultivation *see* below.

**cracca.** Cow vetch. Climbing perennial, to 5 ft. high. Leaflets lance-shaped, in 9-12 pairs. Flowers violet-purple, sometimes white, ½ in. long, in many-flowered, 1-sided racemes.* Fruit to 1 in. long. A most showy species. Eurasia and N.A.

**ervilia.** Ervil. Bitter vetch. Erect, slightly hairy annual, growing to 2 ft. high. Leaflets lance-shaped, in 8-12 pairs, tendril* absent. Flowers rose-color, in 2-4-flowered racemes.* Fruit yellowish, to 1 in. long. Eu.

**faba.** Broad bean. Horse bean. Strong-growing, erect, hardy annual growing to 5 ft. high, or more. Stipules* at the base of the leafstalk marked with a black spot. Leaflets ovalish, in 2-6 pairs, not always opposite, tendril* absent. Flowers in short racemes, white with purplish-black spot on the 2 side petals. Fruit a pod, sometimes 6-12 in. long, with a white-woolly lining in which the seeds are embedded. Seeds edible (*see* cult. below). Cult. from the earliest times. Northern Af. and southwestern As.

**sativa.** Common vetch. Spring vetch. Tare. Half-hardy, slightly hairy annual or biennial, growing 2-3 ft. high, of climbing habit. Leaflets lance-shaped, in 3-7 pairs. Flowers purplish, usually in a 2-flowered raceme.* Fruits to 3 in. long. Grown for forage, also as green manure (*see* cult. below). Eu.; naturalized in N.A.

**villosa.** Winter vetch. Hardy, hairy annual or biennial of climbing habit. Leaflets narrowly lance-shaped, in 5-10 pairs. Flowers violet-blue, numerous, in long, 1-sided racemes.* Fruit an in. long. Eurasia.

### VETCH CULTURE

The common and winter vetches and their varieties are used as cover crops in orchards, but more often for their value as a green manure and for forage. Plowing in green vetch crops is very beneficial to the soil, the green part forming humus, which helps to hold moisture in the soil, while their nitrogen-fixing root tubercles add nitrogen to the soil (*see* LEGUMINOSAE). Seed should be sown broadcast, then harrowed and raked. The crop may be plowed under in about 3 months. It is sometimes cut and used as green fodder.

The cow vetch (*V. cracca*) can be used as an ornamental climber. Propagated by seeds sown in early spring.— H. R. M.

INSECT PESTS. Few insects are recorded from vetch. Cutworms are likely to be harbored by its winter growth. Corn ear worms feed on leaves early in the summer; they may be combated with a dust of calcium arsenate, or by use of poisoned bran bait. The pea aphid has been

---

* Special articles on the subjects indicated by an asterisk (*) will be found at the words so marked.

abundant at times on winter crops of vetch in Calif. The vetch bruchid has recently gained a foothold in the eastern part of this country; it attacks the seeds, working like the bean weevil (*see* BEAN).

**VICIAEFOLIA, -us, -um** (vis-i-ee-fo'li-a). With vetch-like foliage. The name is sometimes spelled *viciifolia*.

**VICTORIA** (vick-tor'i-a). A remarkable genus of South American aquatic plants of the family Nymphaeaceae, two of the three known species cult. for ornament, and the largest water lilies in the world. They have thick rootstocks and long-stalked, huge, floating leaves, the margins turned up at the edges, the leaf thus appearing like a large, shallow, cir-

*Victoria*, the largest water lily in the world. In the foreground, some ordinary water lilies to show the size of *Victoria*.

cular, floating pan, beautifully colored and veined; hence the name water platter, which is often applied to them. The stalk of the leaves and flowers and the under side of the leaves covered with stout, usually reddish prickles. Flowers floating, 7-18 in. wide, fragrant, white as they open towards evening, becoming pink or red the second day, after which they wither. Petals 50 or more, the stamens* thrice as numerous. Fruit berry-like. (Named for Queen Victoria.)

Of the two species below *V. cruziana* is the chief one in cult. and is to be attempted only if you can give it the conditions described at WATER GARDEN, otherwise, it cannot be forced into bloom in the North. *Victoria regia*, a more spectacular plant, is found in the hot, steaming lagoons of the Amazon and neighboring regions and is rare in cult. outside the tropics.

**cruziana.** Santa Cruz water lily, or water platter. Floating leaves 2-5 ft. wide, the upturned margins 6-8 in. high, the under side of the blade densely hairy, the radiating veins very large and conspicuous. Flowers deep pink or red the second day, the sepals with prickles only at the base. Paraguay.

**regia.** Royal water lily, or water platter. Floating leaves 3-6 ft. across, the upturned margin 2-4 in. high, the under side of the blade only slightly hairy. Flowers turning dull crimson the second day, the sepals prickly throughout. Amazon River and in British Guiana. More difficult to cult. than *V. cruziana* as it needs greater heat.

**VICTORIAN BOX** = *Pittosporum undulatum*.

**VIGNA** (vig'na). Rather showy, chiefly tropical vines of the pea family, but cult. mostly as cover crops or for green manuring or forage in the South, where they are sown as annuals, like beans, to which they are closely related. They are herbaceous vines with compound* leaves, having 3 leaflets. Flowers mostly in pairs at the ends of long stalks, pea-like, the pods (legumes*) long and cylindric. (Named for Dominicus Vigna, Italian scientist.) The species, if planted for the first time, need a culture of the proper sort of bacteria. *See* LEGUME INOCULATION.

**catjang.** Catjang. Strong-growing, long-stemmed vine, much resembling *V. sesquipedalis*, but its erect pods 3-5 in. long. Asia (?); not so much cult. as the other two.

**sesquipedalis.** Asparagus bean. Yard-long bean. A trailing, long-stemmed vine, the leaflets angularly ovalish, 3-5 in. long. Flowers yellow or violet, nearly 1 in. long, usually 2, but sometimes 3, at the end of a long stalk. Pod (legume*) 1-3 ft. long, hanging or often flat on the ground, fleshy and flabby when young. Asia (?), but widely cult. throughout the tropics and in the southern U.S.

**sinensis.** Cowpea. Resembling *V. sesquipedalis*, but the hanging pods 8-12 in. long, not flabby when young. Asia (?). Grown in warm regions for green manure and for forage.

**VILLA.** *See* HOME GROUNDS.

**VILLOSA, -us, -um** (vil-lō'sa). Villous; *i.e.* softly hairy.

**VILLOSULA, -us, -um** (vil-lō'su-la). Somewhat softly hairy.

**VIMINALIS, -e** (vim-i-nay'lis). Osier-like; *i.e.* willow-like.

**VIMINEA, -us, -um** (vim-i-nee'a). Twiggy; like a wicker-work of osiers.

**VIMLITE.** A trademarked substitute for glass. *See* Sash at COLD FRAME.

**VINCA** (vin'ka). Evergreen, erect or trailing perennial herbs or under-shrubs, comprising about 12 species of the family Apocynaceae, natives of the Mediterranean region, tropical America, India and Madagascar. Leaves opposite,* simple, ovalish, shining green, leathery. Flowers blue, pink or white, salver-shaped, solitary, stalked, growing in the axils* of the leaves. Calyx small, with 5 lobes. Corolla tubular, its 5 lobes slightly twisted to the left. Stamens* 5, growing on the corolla. Fruit 1-celled, 6-8-seeded. (*Vinca* is the name used by Pliny for the periwinkle.)

The species commonly cult. are *Vinca major* and *Vinca minor*. The latter is a trailing evergreen plant, quite hardy, and makes excellent ground cover under trees, and is good covering for shady banks. *Vinca major* is widely used for window boxes and commonly sold by florists. Both are easily cult. and propagated chiefly by cuttings or division.

Cuttings of young shoots may also be made during the summer months. They should be inserted in a mixture of ½ sand and ½ soil in a cold frame, kept well watered and shaded from sun. The sash should be kept closed except for an hour each day until rooted, when they may be planted out in ordinary garden soil in a shady position. Tips should be pinched to make plants bushy.

*Vinca rosea* is used for bedding purposes and for pot plants, and is usually treated as a tender annual. Propagated by seeds sown ⅛ in. deep in pans in Feb. or March under glass in a temperature of 60°-70°. As soon as large enough to handle, they should be potted into 3-in. pots, using potting mixture* 3, and be kept under glass until danger of frost is over. If kept through the winter, cuttings may be taken in early spring.

**major.** A trailing evergreen, the stems thin and wiry. Leaves opposite, simple, ovalish, heart-shaped at base, shiny dark green. Flowers blue, 1-2 in. across. Eu. The most widely grown form is *var.* **variegata**, much used in window boxes. Not hardy in the North.

**minor.** Periwinkle. Creeping myrtle. Running myrtle. Trailing, hardy evergreen, the stems thin and wiry. Leaves opposite, broadly lance-shaped, to 2 in. long, shiny dark green. Flowers light blue, ¾ in. across. Eu., naturalized in the U.S. There are several hort. color forms. A good ground cover for shady places.

**rosea.** Madagascar periwinkle. Tender, erect, ever-blooming perennial, growing to 2 ft., mostly grown as a tender annual. Leaves opposite, lance-shaped, prominently veined. Flowers showy, pink or white with reddish eye, 1½ in. across. Madagascar.

**VINCETOXICUM ACUMINATUM** = *Cynanchum acuminatifolium*.

**VINE.** The vine of antiquity and history is always the grape. *See* GRAPE for culture and VITIS for the wild species of grape. *Vine* as a general hort. term includes all woody or herbaceous plants that creep, climb, or trail, as distinguished from those that stand without support. For their garden uses *see* VINES.

**VINE BOWER** = *Clematis viticella*.

---

* Special articles on the subjects indicated by an asterisk (*) will be found at the words so marked.

VINE CACTUS = *Fouquieria splendens.*

VINEGARWEED = *Trichostema lanceolatum.* See BLUE CURLS.

VINE MAPLE = *Acer circinatum.* See MAPLE.

VINE PEACH = mango melon. See MELON.

VINES. Under this term the gardener includes all plants, whether woody or herbaceous, that require some support for their proper development. While some climb by tendrils,* others are self-twiners, while still others need to be tied or nailed to the structure they are to cover.

By whatever method grown, all the vines of garden interest may be grouped into six classes:

1. WALL-TOP TUMBLERS. This includes familiar favorites suitable for planting on retaining walls, to drape and veil an old ruin, or sprawl gracefully over unsightly objects and tumble about outcroppings of stone and rocky elevations.

2. CREEPERS AND TRAILERS. These resemble carpets, but the growth takes root at frequent intervals and establishes separate colonies of plants quite independent of the parent group. They resemble ground covers, often sprawling about as undergrowth in woods and natural plantings. *See also* GROUND COVER.

3. TWINING PLANTS AND STEM CLIMBERS. Here come plants that support themselves by the spiral action of leaf or stem and climb upon anything near them.

4. WOODY VINES. The grape and many others with tendrils* or sucking disks, upon which they depend for support.

5. ANNUAL VINES. Includes many tender perennials treated as annuals. They are valuable as quick summer fillers and of great decorative value.

6. SOUTHERN AND GREENHOUSE VINES. Many good plants are put to walls and fences in a mixed and careless manner, hence losing their true character and crowding each other out of recognition. Some of these vines have nearly tropical luxuriance and are most valuable in hiding unsightly objects, covering ruins, or traveling to great heights on dead trees. These lusty growers should be kept away from buildings which would otherwise require constant cleaning.

From the six groups of vines below the gardener can pick nearly everything he needs in the way of herbaceous or woody vines. Remember that every one has additional information at its generic name in the DICTIONARY. Turn to these entries for special notes on hardiness or culture, too extensive to duplicate here.

### 1. WALL-TOP TUMBLERS

These generally need no special fastening and will cling without tying. The plants listed here are very effective in the situations already mentioned, namely, straight bare walls and ruins, which then take on variety and color never before possible.

The Dutchman's-pipe has handsome leaves for covering a porch or arbor.

**Rosa wichuraiana.** Memorial Rose. This is either a creeper or may be used to grow over walls.

**Forsythia suspensa.** The most graceful of the early golden bells if left unpruned. It is scarcely a vine, but becomes vine-like on steep banks.

**Clematis vitalba** and *C. paniculata* are two profuse, white-flowered favorites. *See also* CLEMATIS.

**Clematis montana.** Well known for its pure white garlands festooning over old ruins, trees and fences. The *var.* **rubens** is considered one of the most successful to grow. *See also* CLEMATIS.

**Lycium chinense** and the English ivy will succeed if the wall is shady.

**Parthenocissus vitacea** is most suitable as a tumbler because it does not cling to supports, and has the most brilliant autumn coloring.

**Celastrus scandens.** The bittersweet has a poor reputation in a confined area, but for wilderness beauty on poor soil it has no equal. In the autumn it exposes its orange and scarlet fruits.

**Ampelopsis japonica** yields a decorative berry that changes from white to purple and blue.

**Vitis kaempferi** is the most ornamental and healthy of the ornamental grapevines.

**Rosa setigera.** The Prairie rose, if planted in good soil and in an open position, will provide two show seasons, first, in late June with its great wealth of clear pink single flowers. In autumn and winter it is covered with orange-scarlet fruit which provides winter food for birds.

### 2. CREEPERS AND TRAILERS

This group are mostly prostrate vines or trailers. Perhaps the best known and most easily grown are:

**Lysimachia nummularia.** Yellow flowers in summer; prostrate.

**Lonicera japonica aureo-reticulata.** This is the smallest of all the Japanese honeysuckles; sprawling.

**Vinca minor.** Periwinkle. Prefers shade. Flowers usually blue; common also as a ground cover.

**Hedera helix.** English ivy. Prefers shade. Protect from direct sun after sharp frost; will also cover walls.

**Cotoneaster.** The genus provides many prostrate vines for covering rocks or banks and all bear attractive fruits. *See* COTONEASTER.

Creeping vines such as English ivy and periwinkle do well under the shade of trees, but the ivy will also climb if it has a chance.

**Coronilla varia.** Crown vetch. Pink, pea-like flowers and feathery foliage; prostrate or sprawling.

**Lantana sellowiana.** Beautiful, nearly prostrate or trailing shrub with mauve flowers all summer. Useful only from zone* 6 southward.

**Saponaria ocymoides.** Lavender-flowered or pink-flowered prostrate herb. Prefers moisture, but good drainage.

### 3. TWINING PLANTS AND STEM CLIMBERS

**Actinidia arguta.** Tara vine. Woody; foliage glossy, with red stalks. Flowers brownish-white.

**Actinidia chinensis.** Yangtao. Even finer than *A. arguta*, but more tender. Leaf-veins covered with reddish hairs.

**Akebia quinata.** Flowers purplish-brown, fragrant.

**Aristolochia durior.** Dutchman's-pipe. Large-leaved, handsome woody vine with yellow-brown flowers.

**Celastrus articulatus.** Resembles the native bittersweet.

**Centrosema virginianum.** Butterfly-pea. Flowers purple and white in midsummer; a perennial.

**Decumaria barbara.** Hydrangea-like, white-flowered vine, safe only from zone* 5 southward.

---

* Special articles on the subjects indicated by an asterisk (*) will be found at the words so marked.

**Eccremocarpus scaber.** Showy Chilean vine with orange-red flowers. Not hardy northward except as an annual. See ECCREMOCARPUS.

A climbing rose grown against a wall

**Humulus lupulus.** Hop. Covers almost anything with its profuse foliage in a single season. Flowers inconspicuous. See HOP for other species.

**Lathyrus grandiflorus.** Everlasting pea. Pink and white flowers resembling the sweet pea, but our plant is a perennial.

**Menispermum canadense.** Canada moonseed. Woody vine with white and yellow flowers.

**Passiflora incarnata.** Beautiful vine with white and purple flowers in midsummer. Not hardy northward.

**Periploca graeca.** Silk vine. Flowers greenish-brown. Hardy from zone* 5 southward.

**Polygonum auberti.** Silver-lace vine. Profuse summer-blooming, white-flowered vine.

**Lonicera.** Among the climbing honeysuckles the best evergreen ones are *L. japonica*, *L. henryi*, and *L. sempervirens*. The best deciduous climbing honeysuckle is *L. periclymenum*. Of the native or hybrid species *L. heckrotti* will bloom from June to frost and *L. flava* has yellow flowers. For other species see LONICERA.

Among the most showy of all vines, usually needing a trellis or wall for proper support, are the various forms of the climbing roses. See the colored plate (herewith) for some of the best varieties. Others, and the culture of them, are treated at Group 6 (Hardy climbing roses) at ROSE.

4. WOODY VINES LIKE THE GRAPE AND OTHERS WITH TENDRILS* OR SUCKING-DISKS*

For this group provide wire for safe attachment, especially as they get older and their large woody stems become heavy.

**Vitis.** The most ornamental species of grape, easily grown, is *V. kaempferi*. See VITIS.

**Euonymus radicans vegetus.** An evergreen, red-berried creeper, with fine leathery foliage. Suitable for walls.

**Wistaria sinensis** is the commonest of the cult. wisterias. It is a fine woody vine with an almost tropical cast of foliage. Some plants do not always flower. To help them bloom, the vine should be pruned at least three times during spring and summer. After August 1st the new growth can be left for the next spring's pruning. For other fine species see WISTARIA.

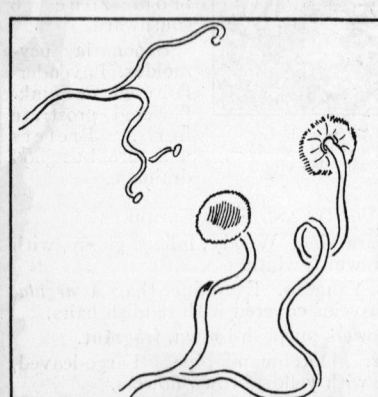
The sucking disks (*enlarged*) at the ends of Boston ivy tendrils which help it to cling to walls.

**Hydrangea petiolaris.** Climbing hydrangea. A woody vine from Japan which sticks to wood or brick with considerable firmness.

**Parthenocissus quinquefolia,** the Virginia creeper, and *P. tricuspidata*, the Boston ivy, will both cling to buildings easily and provide brilliant autumnal color. *P. tricuspidata lowi*, a small-leaved form of the Boston ivy, has young foliage which is purplish.

**Pyracantha coccinea lalandi.** A white-flowered, orange-fruited shrub that does well trained on a wall.

**Schizophragma hydrangeoides.** A Japanese woody vine somewhat resembling *Hydrangea petiolaris* and more difficult to grow. Scarcely hardy north of zone* 4.

**Tripterygium regeli.** An Asiatic sprawling shrub or woody vine with small, white flowers, brilliant green foliage and winged fruit.

Another group of woody vines, especially suited for limited wall spaces and hardy only in Calif. and other warm regions, comprise the following:

**Azara microphylla.** A Chilean shrub easily trained on a wall, with greenish flowers and orange fruit.

**Jasminum humile.** Italian jasmine. Its weak branches are almost vine-like and can be trained on a wall. Flowers yellow.

**Ficus pumila.** Climbing fig. A slender vine with numerous small leaves. Will completely cover small brick or cement walls, and cling safely in the early stages. Older and larger leaves will not cling, and the plant must be tied to a support.

Many wall-climbing vines, even if they have the sucking-disks of the Boston ivy, are best secured by staples driven into the mortar between bricks or stones, when the vines are old and the stems heavy. They may be fastened to the staple by wires run through old pieces of hose, and care must be taken to see that the stems are not pinched in the process.

5. ANNUAL VINES AND PERENNIALS TREATED AS ANNUALS

These find a place in nearly every garden because they are of quick growth, often produce showy bloom, or, as in the gourds,* handsome or even grotesque fruit. Those scarcely needing itemized mention are the morning-glory and the related convolvulus, also the ornamental gourds, which are curious colored-fruited relatives of the pumpkin, squash, melon or cucumber. (See GOURDS.)

Other vines in this group, some of tropical origin but hardy as summer annuals, are:

**Quamoclit lobata** and *Q. coccinea*. Crimson-flowered herbaceous vines from tropical America. Very showy and quick-growing.

**Tropaeolum.** Any of the tall-growing hort. varieties of nasturtium*; also *T. peregrinum*, the Canary creeper.

**Humulus japonicus.** Japanese relative of the common hop. Useful only for foliage. See HOP.

**Thunbergia alata.** Showy, white-purple flowers in midsummer. See THUNBERGIA for other species.

A quick-growing, tropical, annual vine is *Cobaea scandens*.

**Echinocystis lobata.** Wild balsam apple. A native climber with lobed leaves and profuse white flowers.

**Cobaea scandens.** Very handsome Mexican vine, usually treated as an annual, with large violet or greenish-purple flowers.

**Dolichos lablab.** Hyacinth bean. Showy purple or white flowers, pea-like pods, and large leaflets.

**Ecballium elaterium.** Squirting cucumber. Yellow-flow-

---

* Special articles on the subjects indicated by an asterisk (*) will be found at the words so marked.

CLIMBING ROSES

Paul's Scarlet Climber
Madame Grégoire Staechelin
Golden Dawn

La Rêve
New Dawn
Excelsa

ered vine with peculiar fruit which ejects its seeds explosively.

**Cardiospermum halicacabum.** Balloon-vine. Flowers small, white, but numerous. Fruit inflated like a miniature balloon.

### 6. Southern and Greenhouse Vines

These are mostly woody plants of the tropics, not to be grown outdoors north of zone* 7 and preferably in zones* 8 and 9, except where noted. All can be grown in the greenhouse.

**Abrus precatorius.** Rosary-pea. Flowers reddish-purple. Seeds black and red, very striking. Not hardy north of zone* 8.

**Allamanda cathartica hendersoni.** Handsome woody vine with showy yellow flowers.

**Antigonon leptopus.** Coral vine. Tall-growing vine with a profusion of bright pink flowers.

**Aristolochia elegans.** Calico-flower. Tropical relative of the Dutchman's-pipe with flowers 3 in. across.

**Bignonia capreolata.** Cross-vine. Related to the common trumpet-creeper. Hardy to zone* 4.

**Bougainvillaea** (see that genus). These are among the finest and most showy of all tropical vines, often growing 50–60 ft. in height.

**Clerodendron thomsonae.** Bag-flower. A west African woody vine with very showy white and red flowers.

**Clianthus dampieri.** Glory-pea. Low-growing vine or weak shrub with scarlet, purple-blotched flowers.

**Doxantha unguis-cati.** Cat's-claw. Tropical American woody vine with bright yellow flowers and spiny, claw-like tendrils.

**Gloriosa superba.** Tuberous-rooted, tropical, herbaceous vine with red and yellow flowers.

**Hoya carnosa.** Wax-plant. Thick-leaved, low-growing vine with white and pink flowers.

**Jasminum grandiflorum.** Spanish jasmine. Fragrant white flowers. A shrub to 20 ft. with weak, vine-like branches.

**Lapageria rosea.** Chilean bellflower. Showy rose-colored flowers nearly 4 in. long. There is a white-flowered hort. variety.

**Stephanotis floribunda.** Madagascar jasmine. A woody vine with white, fragrant, waxy flowers.

**Tecomaria capensis.** Cape honeysuckle. Very showy relative of the native trumpet-creeper, with red, orange or scarlet flowers.

**Thunbergia grandiflora.** Sky-flower. A woody vine from India with blue flowers.

**Trachelospermum jasminoides.** Star jasmine. A fragrant, white-flowered vine common throughout the South and hardy to zone* 6.

No account of garden vines would be complete without mention of *Clematis.* But there are so many species and varieties of these handsome plants that there is no space to repeat an account of them here. See CLEMATIS. — W. J. I.

**VINE WEEVIL.** See Insect Pests at CAMELLIA and CYCLAMEN.

*VINIFERA, -us, -um* (vy-niff′er-a). Wine- or grape-bearing. The *vinifera* grapes are *Vitis vinifera,* the leading sorts used for making wine. See GRAPE.

**VIOLA** (vy-ō′la). Violet. Hardy perennial, and a few annual herbs, comprising about 300 species of the family Violaceae, found distributed throughout the temperate regions of the world, and including the violet and the pansy. They are low-growing plants, generally of tufted* habit, some species producing runners. Leaves basal or growing on the stems. Basal leaves simple, heart-shaped or ovalish, sometimes cut into finger-like lobes, slightly wrinkled, stalked, the stalks grooved, the margins coarsely toothed. Stem leaves alternate,* simple, ovalish, usually stalked, the margins with rounded teeth. Two stipules* (leafy appendages) at base of the stem leaves are usually cut into 3 lobes. Flowers stalked, solitary, sometimes nodding, violet, blue, reddish-purple, lilac, yellow or white. Calyx of 5 sepals. Corolla of 5 petals, 4 arranged in pairs, each pair differing, the lower petal spurred.* Stamens 5, with an orange, shield-shaped appendage at the top of each anther. Fruit a 3-celled, many-seeded capsule. Some species have two kinds of flowers, non-fertile, the showy spring flowers, and fertile, the summer flowers, which are completely closed, never open and are self-fertilizing (cleistogamous*). (*Viola* is the classical Latin name of the violet.)

For Culture see below. All bloom early in the spring, except some of the hort. varieties, which bloom later.

**blanda.** Sweet white violet. Low-growing, tufted perennial. Leaves basal, ovalish, slightly hairy on the upper side, stalked. Flowers white, solitary. Petals narrow and reflexed. Quebec to Ga. and La.

**canadensis.** Canada violet. Tufted perennial, growing 1 ft. or more. Leaves broadly heart-shaped, stalked, the margins toothed. Flowers white with yellow eye, tinged purple on the outside. Canada and northern U.S.

**cornuta.** Horned violet. Bedding pansy. Tufted pansy. Tufted perennial with branching stems. Leaves alternate, ovalish, slightly wrinkled, stalked, the margins with rounded teeth. Stipules* (leafy appendages) at the base of the leaves, triangular, cut into 3 or more segments. Flowers violet, solitary, stalked. Spain and the Pyrenees. There are many color forms in cult. See ROCK GARDEN.

**culcullata.** Blue violet. Strong-growing, tufted* perennial to 6 in. high. Leaves basal, broadly heart-shaped, stalked, the margins coarsely toothed. Flowers violet, with white or greenish eye, solitary. Eastern N.A.

**gracilis.** Hairy perennial of straggling habit, growing to 1 ft. high. Leaves simple, alternate, ovalish, slightly toothed. Stipules* (leafy appendages) at the base of the leaves, deeply cut into segments. Flowers violet, long-spurred. (See GRAY AND LAVENDER GARDEN.) Macedonia and Asia Minor.

**odorata.** Sweet violet. Florist's violet. Garden violet. Tufted perennial, producing long runners which root at the joints. Leaves basal, broadly heart-shaped and stalked, the margins with rounded teeth. Flowers deep violet or white, sweet-scented, the spur short. Eu., Af., and As. The hort. *var.* alba is a white form. The *var.* pallida plena, the Neapolitan violet, is pale lavender and with double flowers. A hort. variety, Marie Louise, a double-flowered, reddish-purple, very fragrant plant, can be substituted here for the Parma violet, a form of the Neapolitan violet, which is apparently not in cult. in the U.S.

**pedata.** Bird's-foot violet. Perennial of tufted* habit, with short, thick crown. Leaves basal, cut into lobes shaped like a bird's foot, the lobes cut and toothed near the tip. Flowers usually with 2 upper petals dark violet and 3 lower soft lilac. Eastern and mid-western states, especially in dry, open places. April–May. There is also a variety with narrower leaf lobes and more showy flowers than the type. See WILD GARDEN.

**pubescens.** Yellow violet. A softly hairy, branching herb, 8–12 in. high, most of the leaves near the top, kidney-shaped and with finely toothed margins. Flowers generally solitary or few, yellow. In rich woods, eastern N.A. April–May. Other yellow violets are occasionally dug from the wild.

**tricolor hortensis.** Pansy. Hearts-ease. Johnny jump-up. Short-lived perennial of straggling habit, growing to 1 ft. or more. Stems branching and usually square. Basal leaves heart-shaped, the stem leaves alternate, ovalish or lance-shaped, the margins toothed. Stipules* (leafy appendages) at the base of the leaves, large, cut into small segments near the base. Flowers 3-colored, blue, white and yellow, solitary, stalked, growing in the axils of the leaves. They differ from the other violas in that the corolla is flattish and roundish and the petals overlap. For cult. see PANSY.

### Viola Culture

Violas are among the most popular and useful spring- and summer-flowering plants.

The hort. varieties that are similar to the pansy in appearance and commonly called tufted pansies or horned violets are used extensively for bedding purposes, in fact fulfill the uses of the pansy, as they withstand the summer heat better and have a longer flowering period. Among the best are:

| | |
|---|---|
| Arkwright Ruby. | Wallflower red with dark central markings. |
| Yellow Queen. | Large, deep yellow. |
| Avalanche. | White. |
| Blue Butterfly. | Blue. |

The smaller flowering violas, with violet type flowers, are the kind mostly used for the rock garden or edges of the border. Good varieties are:

| | | | |
|---|---|---|---|
| Jersey Gem. | Blue. | Lutea splendens. | Yellow. |
| Apricot Gem. | | White Perfection. | |
| Mauve Queen. | | | |

---

* Special articles on the subjects indicated by an asterisk (*) will be found at the words so marked.

Violas are easily cult., but for best results should have partially shaded positions in rich, moist soil. Propagated by seeds, division of rootstocks, and cuttings. Seeds should be sown in boxes, ⅛ in. deep, in cold frame or cool greenhouse in Sept. or early spring. If sown in the fall they must be transplanted to cold frame and kept there during winter, if sown in spring they may be transplanted to permanent positions as soon as large enough to handle. Division of rootstocks may be made in Sept. or early spring. Cuttings of young shoots 2–3 in. long may be made in Sept. They should be inserted in sandy soil in a cold frame, shaded from sun. Sash should be kept closed except for an hour each day until rooted. They must be left in the cold frame during the winter, admitting air whenever possible.

The native violets are usually distinguished from violas by having basal leaves, although some, like *V. canadensis* and *V. pubescens*, have stem leaves. They are used extensively for naturalizing in the wild garden. The best species are:

| | |
|---|---|
| *V. pedata.* | Violet-mauve. |
| *V. cucullata.* | Violet. |
| *V. canadensis.* | White with purple. |
| *V. blanda.* | White. |

There are also many other wild species which may be transferred to the garden.

These are propagated by seeds and runners. Seeds should be sown ⅛ in. deep, in boxes, and be placed outdoors or in open cold frame in the fall. Exposure to the weather is necessary, as freezing assists germination of the seed. Runners, which some of them produce freely, may be separated from the parent plant as soon as rooted.

Varieties of *Viola odorata*, the sweet or florist's violet, are grown for flowering during the cool months, and sold by the florists under various names. They should be planted in early spring in deep, rich soil outdoors, in semi-shady position, and be kept well watered.

They should be removed to cold frame or cool greenhouse in Sept. If grown in cold frame they must be protected from frost. Winter greenhouse temperature should be 35°–50°. If given heat, the atmosphere must be kept moist or plants will be attacked with red spider. Fertilizer should be given occasionally. — H. R. M.

INSECT PESTS. The violet sawfly is injurious outdoors (*see* PANSY). Several kinds of aphids occurring in the greenhouse can be controlled by derris spray or calcium cyanide fumigation. Violets are attacked by red spiders and are often a source of infestation of other plants both in greenhouses and outside. Lime-sulphur spray, washed off after a few hours, or derris spray, is effective.

DISEASES. Leafspot and root rot are the common diseases. For *leafspot*, remove infected leaves, spray with weak bordeaux mixture and burn all refuse in the fall. *Root rot*, caused by various fungi, results in sickly, stunted plants with black, rotted roots. The use of healthy plants with soil sterilization (which see) or crop rotation is advised for control.

**VIOLACEA, -us, -um** (vy-o-lay'see-a). Violet-colored.

**VIOLACEAE** (vy-o-lay'see-ee). The violet family comprises some 15 genera of herbs, or in the tropics, shrubs and even trees, of which the only cult. genus is *Viola*, which includes the violets and the pansy. See VIOLA.

**VIOLET.** See VIOLA. For other plants to which the name violet is sometimes applied see ERYTHRONIUM, HESPERIS, and SAINTPAULIA.

**VIOLET SAGE** = *Salvia nemorosa*.

**VIOLET WOOD SORREL** = *Oxalis violacea*.

**VIORNA.** See CLEMATIS.

**VIPER'S-BUGLOSS.** See ECHIUM.

*VIRGATA, -us, -um* (vir-gay'ta). Wand-like; also twiggy.

*VIRGINALIS, -e* (vir-ji-nal'is). Virginal; *i.e.* white.

**VIRGINIA.** The state lies wholly in zones* 4, 5, and 6.

SOILS. The natural regions of the state embrace the coastal plain, the piedmont plateau and the limestone valleys, and each of these regions has its own particular types of soil. The limestone valleys lie between the Blue Ridge Mountains on the southeast and the Allegheny Mountains on the northwest.

Only the well-drained soils of the coastal plain now have horticultural possibilities for truck farming and for floriculture, and they include the following series of soils: Norfolk, Moyock, Onslow, Craven, Kalmia, Rustin, and Sassafras. These soils are all derived from a parent material of unconsolidated sands and clays of marine deposit and they vary in topography from smooth to rolling.

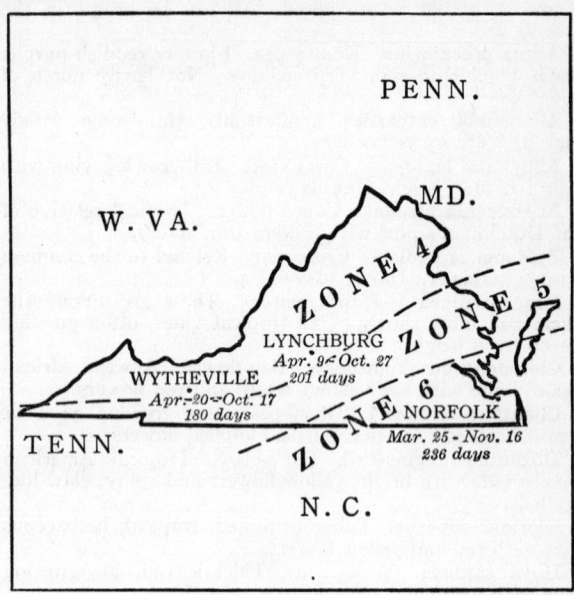

VIRGINIA

The zones of hardiness crossing Virginia are those shown on the colored map at ZONE, which should be consulted for details. The dates are the average latest killing frost in spring and the first one in the fall. The figures below the dates show the average length of the growing season.

In the piedmont plateau region the soils of greatest horticultural possibilities are derived from granite and basic rocks. Among the soils of granitic origin, the most extensive are Cecil fine sandy loam and Appling fine sandy loam; and the principal difference between these two types is that the subsoil of Appling is lighter in color than that of Cecil. Davidson loam or clay loam is derived from diorites or other basic rock and is known locally as red land and is one of the most productive soils in this region.

The principal types of soil in the limestone valleys are Frederick silt loam and Hagerstown loam, and both types are suitable for the growing of fruits, vegetables and flowers.

GARDENING. The region around Norfolk is one of the important trucking regions of the United States. Water, railroad and motor truck transportation place this region in an advantageous position with respect to the great centers of population in our country including the cities of Washington, Baltimore, Philadelphia, New York, and Boston; and truck crops are also shipped to many inland cities. Early potatoes (particularly in Accomac and Northampton counties on the eastern shore), sweet potatoes, cabbage, kale, spinach and strawberries are grown here on a large scale.

There is an important cabbage-growing industry centered around Rural Retreat in southwestern Virginia. In the vicinity of every city and town in the state, there are market gardens to supply the local demand for vegetables in season.

Home gardens are found without exception everywhere in the rural parts of the state, and many of the householders in towns and cities have vegetable gardens. Some of these home gardens have a large assortment of vegetables, in

---

* Special articles on the subjects indicated by an asterisk (*) will be found at the words so marked.

some cases thirty to forty kinds in order to provide the table with fresh vegetables throughout the year. The gardener may choose varieties to suit his taste from a long list of vegetables, including asparagus, bush beans, lima beans, beets, cabbage, carrots, cauliflower, celery, corn, cucumber, eggplant, kale, lettuce, muskmelon, mustard, okra, onions, parsnips, peas, peppers, potatoes, pumpkins, radish, rhubarb, salsify, spinach, squash, sweet potato, Swiss chard, tomatoes, turnips, and watermelon. The home garden is not only an economy in the affairs of the farmer but it is also a great benefit to the comfort and health of the farm family. The county agricultural agents, home demonstration agents, and agricultural high schools are stimulating rural folk to place greater emphasis on the home garden.

FRUIT GROWING. The growing of apples and peaches on a commercial scale is an important industry in the piedmont plateau region along the foothills of the Blue Ridge Mountains and even in the coves of the mountains. The Albemarle Pippin and Winesap apples made this region famous for fruit growing in the early history of commercial fruit growing in the United States. Among the centers of fruit growing here should be mentioned Rappahannock, Albemarle, Nelson, Amherst, Bedford, Franklin and Patrick counties. Commercial fruit growing has developed extensively in several sections of the limestone valleys (which lie between the Blue Ridge and Allegheny Mountains), notably in Frederick, Clarke, Shenandoah, Rockingham, Augusta, Botetourt, Roanoke, Smyth and Washington counties. The York is the leading variety of apple in the limestone valleys, although Stayman, Winesap, Grimes, Delicious, Ben Davis, and many other varieties find a place in the orchards.

Small orchards that furnish fruit for the use of the family are found on about 90% of the farms in the state, and fruit of some kind could readily be grown on every farm in Virginia, for fruit of one sort or another may be grown on practically all of the soil types of the state. Among the fruits grown successfully in home orchards are apple, apricot, cherry, fig (southeastern part of state), peach, pear, plum, quince, grape, persimmon, chestnut (now disappearing), hazelnut, pecan, walnut, blackberry, dewberry, blueberry, cranberry, currant, gooseberry, raspberry, strawberry, and a few others. There is a considerable range of varieties in most of these species from which the farmer may choose the kinds that will serve his needs. The health-giving qualities of fruits make the home orchard a necessary adjunct to the homestead. Nurseries are found at strategic points in the state from which the farmer may secure trees and plants adapted to local conditions.

ORNAMENTALS. Growing conditions in the state change appreciably with changes in altitude. The coastal plain region has a sufficiently mild and equable climate for the cultivation of live oak, cedar-of-Lebanon, sweet bay magnolia; for shrubs or small trees like Portuguese laurel, yaupon, *Eurya, Osmanthus, Viburnum tinus, Gardenia*, and the tender azaleas; for vines like *Wistaria*, and Carolina jasmine; for flowers like *Iris*, sea lavender, thrift, rosemary, *Hibiscus*, and Cape fuchsia, also the Tea Roses.

Most of these plants, were they moved into the less mild climate of the piedmont plateau, would not tolerate the change in exposure without a good deal of protection in winter. Whereas shingle oak, *Cryptomeria* and *Mimosa*; boxwoods, evergreen barberries, evergreen loniceras, American hollies (except yaupon), cherry laurel, and crape myrtle; lavenders, lupines, *Salvia patens*, and pentstemons would probably prove adaptable. The piedmont plateau is well adapted to the growing of willow oaks, swamp maple, *Nyssa*, elm, and hackberries; hollies, bayberries, blueberries, groundsel-bush and gorse; Cherokee, McCartney and Lady Bank's roses; magnolias, azaleas, laurels, jasmines and gardenias; heathers, lilies, and bulbs in general.

In the limestone valleys which are bounded on the southeast by the Blue Ridge Mountains and on the northwest by the Allegheny Mountains, the natural growth includes such ornamental species as balsams, white pine, hemlocks, arborvitae, sugar maple, mountain maple, mountain-ash, mountain laurels, rhododendrons, andromedas, hardy azaleas, *Calycanthus*, viburnums, hawthorns, crabapple, hypericums, and hardy roses; bleeding-heart, turk's-cap lily, marsh-marigold, celandine, *Mertensia, Gillenia, Tradescantia, Trillium*, and mountain phlox. Most of these are plants so attached to their native region that it is difficult to transplant them to a new environment, but *see*, in this connection, WILD GARDEN. Hardy garden shrubs and perennials are adapted here and many half-hardy sorts will thrive in sheltered spots in soil properly prepared, especially if slight protection is given in winter and early spring.

There is a remarkable variety of ornamental plants temptingly within reach of lovers of flowers in the state. The interest of our people in this most fascinating avocation is growing year by year. As one looks upon the homes beautified by appropriate flowers, trees and shrubs, he sees a symbol of the taste, refinement and culture of the people who live in those homes.

CLIMATE. The state has a long growing season with adequate rainfall well distributed through the year. The following weather records cover 50 years at Norfolk and Lynchburg and 27 years at Wytheville.

SIGNIFICANT FROST DATES

| Name of city | Average date of last killing frost in spring | Latest known killing frost | Average date of earliest killing frost in fall | Earliest known killing frost |
|---|---|---|---|---|
| Norfolk | Mar. 25 | Apr. 26 | Nov. 16 | Oct. 11 |
| Lynchburg | Apr. 9 | May 7 | Oct. 27 | Oct. 2 |
| Wytheville | Apr. 20 | May 27 | Oct. 17 | Sept. 19 |

RAINFALL IN THREE REGIONS OF THE STATE

| Name of city | Average annual rainfall (inches) | Apr. | May | June | July | Aug. | Sept. |
|---|---|---|---|---|---|---|---|
| Norfolk | 46.43 | 3.43 | 3.89 | 4.24 | 5.83 | 5.46 | 3.66 |
| Lynchburg | 41.75 | 3.11 | 3.71 | 3.97 | 4.14 | 4.07 | 3.54 |
| Wytheville | 46.71 | 3.66 | 3.91 | 4.11 | 4.44 | 4.54 | 3.29 |

Since the topography of the state ranges in elevation from sea level to about 4000 feet above sea level, there is a corresponding variation in climate which in turn makes possible the growing of many sorts of vegetables, fruits, and ornamental plants.

The address of the Agricultural Experiment Station, which has kindly supplied this information about the state, is Blacksburg, Virginia. The station is always ready to answer gardening questions.

As one of the oldest settled parts of the country, Va. has long been famous for magnificent estates landscaped upon the English plan, many of which are still among the finest gardens in America. The interest in gardening is so great that garden club activities are very extensive. There are several clubs affiliated with the Garden Club of America, the home office of which is 598 Madison Avenue, New York. There are also over 60 clubs affiliated with the Virginia Federation of Garden Clubs, The Garden Club of Virginia or with the Southwestern Virginia Garden Clubs. For the club nearest your locality write the Garden Editor, Houghton Mifflin Company, Boston, Mass.

**VIRGINIA COWSLIP** = *Mertensia virginica*.

**VIRGINIA CREEPER** = *Parthenocissus quinquefolia*. See also POISON IVY, for which it is often mistaken.

*VIRGINIANA, -us, -um* (vir-gin-i-ā'na). From Virginia.

**VIRGINIA SNAKEROOT** = *Aristolochia serpentaria*.

**VIRGINIA STOCK** = *Malcomia maritima*.

---

* Special articles on the subjects indicated by an asterisk (*) will be found at the words so marked.

**VIRGINIA WILLOW** = *Itea virginica*.

**VIRGINICA, -us, -um** (vir-gin'i-ka). From Virginia.

**VIRGIN'S-BOWER.** See CLEMATIS.

**VIRIDIFLORA, -us, -um** (vi-ri-di-flow'ra). Green-flowered.

**VIRIDIFOLIA, -us, -um** (vi-ri-di-fō'li-a). Green-leaved.

**VIRIDIS, -e** (vi'ri-dis). Green.

**VIRIDISSIMA, -us, -um** (vi-ri-diss'i-ma). Very or most green.

**VIRUS DISEASES.** See Virus Diseases at PLANT DISEASES.

**VISCARIA.** An obsolete genus name for plants now included in *Lychnis*.

**VISCOSA, -us, -um** (vis-kō'sa). Sticky.

**VISTA.** A vista is a focalized view. This term is used to discriminate between a broad panoramic view and one which is limited in its scope by a frame. A view between hills which fold together framing a view toward a distant horizon, or an opening through the forest giving glimpses of the landscape beyond are typical natural vistas.

No other element of landscape composition commands as much attention as the vista. Wherever there is a restrained glimpse of something beyond the immediate range of vision the eye quickly focuses on the distant point of interest. The same point of interest might go unnoticed in a panoramic view where there is no vista to pick it out.

Not all vistas terminate with distant views, although this is the origin of the idea. Where property is limited and there is no control over surroundings similar effects may be created by shortening the vista with an artificial terminus. A fountain playing in the sunlight beyond a shaded avenue of trees, a sculptural figure silhouetted against the sky at the end of an allée,* a small garden, pavilion or any other feature of architectural interest seen between borders of tall planting, or the view of a specimen tree framed by surrounding trees in the foreground, are all variations of the vista idea.

An open vista

Aside from its own beauty the vista is a valuable means of arranging other elements in the landscape scheme; it is the backbone or axis on which the skeleton of design is formed. Since it is the most potent means of centering interest the vista is often used as the approach to a garden, as a connecting link between buildings, or as an entrance drive. Wherever a vista appears there is an irresistible impulse to go in that direction. By this means interest may unconsciously lead from one point to another creating a logical circulation through a city, an estate, a monumental garden, or a modest home grounds.

In cases where it is not possible, because of interfering obstructions, to plan open vistas it may be possible to create an aerial vista. By topping out certain trees in a woodland the vision may be directed over some intervening object to a distant view. The use of aerial vistas often extends the apparent size of a property far beyond its own limits. This scheme also eliminates the "middle ground" which is always the least interesting element of any view. The foreground is usually interesting because of its detail, and the distance because of its simple mass effect. When the foreground is seen silhouetted directly against distance, without the interference of middle ground, a view is always more interesting.

A closed vista

In planning a vista the effect must be visualized in perspective since the picture is always to be viewed that way. The level of the horizon in relation to the observer, the height of the framework in relation to the height of the terminal feature, as well as the length and breadth of the plan, all must be considered in the design. Beautiful vistas often occur accidentally in nature, but when they are deliberately planned satisfactory results are sometimes just as fine as natural vistas. — R. E. G.

**VITACEA, -us, -um** (vy-tay'see-a). Resembling the grape (*Vitis*).

**VITACEAE** (vy-tay'see-ee). The grape family, nearly always vines in the garden plants, contains about 12 genera and over 500 species, many of which are shrubs or trees in the tropics, but prevailingly woody vines in those from the temperate zone.

From the garden standpoint the grape (*Vitis*) is by far the most important. But *Cissus*, *Parthenocissus* and *Ampelopsis* yield many widely cult. vines grown for ornament, especially the Virginia creeper and Boston ivy. See VINES. *Leea* is a greenhouse shrub grown for its ornamental foliage.

In all but *Leea*, they are tendril*-bearing vines. Leaves usually alternate,* sometimes a tendril* opposite the leaf, simple or compound. Flowers small, numerous, mostly inconspicuous, sometimes unisexual,* nearly always clustered. Fruit a berry.

Technical flower characters. Calyx* entire or with very small teeth. Petals separate, or united and withering as an apparently tubular flower. Stamens* 4 or 5, opposite the petals. Ovary superior,* mostly 2-celled.

**VITALBA, -us, -um** (vy-tal'ba). A white or white-flowered vine.

**VITAMINS.** Many of the most important of these necessities of our diet are found in fruits and vegetables. Vitamins A, B, C, and D are common in nearly all fresh fruits and vegetables.

**VITELLINA, -us, -um** (vy-tell-eye'na). Dull yellowish-red.

**VITEX** (vy'tex). Ornamental trees or shrubs comprising about 60 species of the family Verbenaceae, found distributed chiefly in the tropical and warmer regions of the world. Leaves opposite,* compound,* long-stalked, the leaflets 3–7, arranged finger-fashion, sometimes stalked, often grayish-green, and slightly hairy. Flowers small, white, blue, yellowish or red in dense, showy, terminal clusters (spikes*). Calyx of 5 sepals. Corolla tubular, 4 of its lobes equal, 1 larger, forming a lip.* Stamens* 4, 2 long, 2 short. Fruit plum-like, 4-seeded. (*Vitex* is an ancient Latin name.)

The shrubby species make good plants for the shrubbery or back of the herbaceous border, and *V. negundo* is especially grown for bees. In the North the stems are often winter-killed, but the roots send up new shoots which flower the same year. Propagated by seeds but chiefly by cuttings. Cuttings of young shoots should be inserted in

---

* Special articles on the subjects indicated by an asterisk (*) will be found at the words so marked.

½ sand and ½ soil, shaded from sun and kept in a humid atmosphere until rooted. They should be kept in a cool greenhouse or cold frame during winter months.

**agnus-castus.** Chaste tree. Hemp tree. Monk's pepper-tree. Deciduous shrub growing to 10 ft. high. Leaves long-stalked, the leaflets 5-7, lance-shaped, the middle leaflets to 4 in. long, covered with short gray hairs on the under side, pleasantly scented when bruised. Flowers pale lilac-blue, in dense, showy, terminal spikes. Southern Eu. July-Aug. The *var.* alba is a white form, while the *var.* macrophylla has larger leaves and deeper colored flowers and is the best of the cult. *vitex.*

**negundo.** Deciduous shrub growing to 15 ft. high, the branches 4-sided. Leaves, long-stalked. Leaflets 3-5, broadly lance-shaped, covered with small gray hairs on the under side, the margins sometimes toothed. Flowers deep lavender-blue, ¼ in. long, stalked, in dense, showy, terminal spikes.* China and India. Aug.-Sept. In the *var.* incisa (also known as *laciniata*) the leaflets are much cut, and the flowers less showy. It is hardier than the species, being reasonably safe up to zone* 4.

**VITICELLA** (vy-ti-sell'a). A diminutive of *Vitis*, the grape; hence a slender vine. See CLEMATIS.

**VITICETUM.** A plantation of vines.

**VITICULTURE.** The growing of the grape (which see).

**VITIFOLIA, -us, -um** (vy-ti-fō'li-a). Having leaves like the grape (*Vitis*).

**VITIS** (vy'tis). Grape. Woody vines, climbing by tendrils,* belonging to the family Vitaceae, and comprising about 60 species from the north temperate zone. While a few of them are somewhat decorative, the species are of outstanding importance as the source of all the grapes used as fruit or for wine-making. They have usually shreddy bark, a brown pith separated by cross partitions, except in *V. rotundifolia.* Tendrils* forked except in *V. rotundifolia.* Leaves alternate,* often lobed finger-fashion, always toothed. Flowers small, greenish, unisexual* or polygamous,* the male and female sometimes on different plants, in small clusters mostly opposite the leaves. For details of flower structure see VITACEAE. Fruit the familiar grape (a true berry), 2-4-seeded, the seeds pear-shaped and grooved. (*Vitis* is the Latin name of the grape.)

For the culture and best hort. varieties see GRAPE. The vine dimensions given below are for the wild plants, which as ordinarily grown under cult. conditions are very much shorter, due to the different systems of pruning and training described at GRAPE. Many of the cult. varieties are hardier than the wild species from which they have been derived.

**aestivalis.** Summer grape. Pigeon grape. A high-climbing vine, the leaves broadly oval, deeply 3-5-lobed, 4½-8 in. wide, dull above, rusty beneath. Flower cluster (panicle*) 4½-6 in. long. Fruit black with somewhat of a bloom, usually juicy and sweet, sometimes dryish and sourish. Eastern U.S. June. Hardy from zone* 3 southward.

**coignetiae** = *Vitis kaempferi glabrescens.*

**cordifolia.** Frost grape; also called chicken, winter, and raccoon grape. A very stout, high-climbing vine, the stem sometimes a foot or even more in diameter in old plants. Leaves broadly ovalish, heart-shaped at the base, otherwise undivided or shallowly 3-lobed, green both sides, toothed. Flower cluster (panicle*) 5-7 in. long. Fruit black, thick-skinned, slightly bloomy, sweet after a frost. Pa. to Fla. and Tex. July. Hardy from zone* 3 southward.

**kaempferi.** A strong-growing vine grown for ornament, as its purplish-black, bloomy fruit is inedible. Leaves roundish or ovalish, 4½-9 in. wide, deeply heart-shaped at the base, unequally and shallowly toothed, generally grayish or rusty beneath. Flower cluster (panicle*) short. Jap. June-July. Hardy from zone* 3 southward, and a handsome vine grown mostly for its foliage which turns a bright crimson in the fall. The *var.* glabrescens, the crimson glory vine, is an especially fine form often sold as *V. coignetiae.*

**labrusca.** Fox grape. A strong-growing vine with a leaf, tendril* or flower cluster at nearly every joint. Leaves nearly round or broadly ovalish, 3-6½ in. wide, sometimes slightly 3-lobed, green above but whitish or pale-rusty beneath. Flower cluster 2-4½ in. long. Fruit purplish-black (rarely amber), thick-skinned, the pulp sweet but musky. Eastern U.S. June. Hardy from zone* 3 southward. Little grown as a wild plant, but the origin of many fine varieties of American grapes.

**rotundifolia.** Muscadine or bullace grape; also called scuppernong, and the origin of many grape varieties generally called *rotundifolia* grapes. A strong-growing vine, the stems sometimes 90 ft. long, the tendrils* not forked. Leaves nearly round or broadly oval, 2½-5 in. wide, coarsely and triangularly toothed, green above, yellowish-green beneath. Flower cluster (panicle*) short and dense. Fruit dull purple, thick-skinned, the pulp decidedly musky. Del. to Fla. and westward to Tex., Kan., and Mo. July. Hardy from zone* 4 or 5 southward.

**vinifera.** The source of all the finer wine grapes, commonly called *vinifera* grapes. A strong-growing vine, the stems 45-60 ft. long. Leaves nearly round, 3½-6 in. wide, heart-shaped at the base, 3-5-lobed, the lobes toothed and often overlapping. Flower cluster (panicle*) long and much-branched. Fruit slightly football-shaped, black and with a bloom, or red or green in many varieties. Originally wild in the Caucasus (?), but cult. for centuries throughout much of Eu. and As., and the leading grape in Calif. While cult. sporadically elsewhere in the U.S., the wine grape is practically confined to Calif. so far as commercial wine production is concerned. See GRAPE for varieties and hardiness.

**vulpina.** Riverbank grape; also called frost grape. A high-climbing vine. Leaves broadly ovalish, or narrower, 3½-8 in. long, mostly 3-lobed and with a cleft at the base, coarsely toothed. Flower cluster 3½-7 in. long, fragrant. Fruit nearly black, densely covered with a bloom. Eastern N.A., west to Tex. and Colo. June. Hardy from zone* 1 southward.

**VITIS-IDAEA** (vy-tis-eye-dee'a). A specific name meaning, literally, the grape of Mt. Ida (Greece), and applied to the mountain cranberry (*Vaccinium vitis-idaea*).

**VITTADINIA** (vit-a-din'i-a). Perennial herbs or undershrubs, comprising about 12 species of the family Compositae, and natives of Aust., N.Z., S.A. and the Hawaiian Islands. They are low-growing plants with thick rootstocks. Leaves alternate,* lance-shaped or spoon-shaped, sometimes deeply cut or toothed. Flowers in small heads, solitary, or in loose-branching clusters. Heads surrounded by several rows of overlapping bracts.* Ray florets* white or blue. Disk florets yellow. (Named for Dr. C. Vittadini, Austrian botanist.)

The plant below is not much in cultivation, is closely related to *Erigeron*, and often sold under the name of *Erigeron karvinskianus.* Propagated by seeds or division of the rootstocks.

**australis.** Slightly hairy plant, growing to 1 ft. high, woody at the base. Leaves lance-shaped or spoon-shaped, sometimes cut into 3 lobes. Flowers in solitary heads, the rays white, the disk florets yellow. Aust. and N.Z.

**triloba** = *Vittadinia australis.*

**VITTATA, -us, -um** (vit-tay'ta). Striped.

**VIVIPARA, -us, -um** (vy-vip'a-ra). Viviparous; i.e. freely producing organs of reproduction while still growing on the parent plant. Notable examples are the bulbils* of some onions and the sprouting leaf margins of *Bryophyllum* (which see).

**VOLK.** A trademarked, emulsified oil of light grade, suitable for summer spraying, sold with directions for use as a contact spray.

**VOLUBILIS, -e** (vol-loo'bill-is). Twining.

**VOMITORIA, -us, -um** (vom-i-tor'i-a). Emetic.

**VRIESIA** (vree'zi-a). Tropical American, tree-perching foliage plants, comprising about 80 species of the pineapple family, with stiff, erect, fleshy, green, often marbled leaves growing in a rosette, which sometimes holds water. Flowers yellow, green, pink or white in terminal, flattish spikes,* each flower growing in the axil* of a showy, colored bract.* Calyx of 3 colored sepals. Corolla of 3 petals, alternating with the sepals. Stamens* 6. Fruit a 3-celled capsule.* (Named for Dr. W. de Vriese, Dutch botanist.)

*Vriesia* and the genus *Aechmea* are grown in the greenhouse in a warm, moist atmosphere, in pots or in wire or wooden baskets. Propagated by offshoots. They can be grown in potting mixture* 4, in a winter temperature of 50°-70°. They require plenty of water during summer months while making their growth, and should be shaded from March-Oct.

**saundersi.** Leaves many, in a rosette, stiff, fleshy, narrow, recurving, grayish, marked white on the upper side and reddish-brown on the under side. Flowering stalk to 1½ ft. high. Flowers yellow, cylindrical. Brazil.

**splendens.** Strong-growing, to 3 ft. high. Leaves to 1 ft. long, and 3 in. wide, stiff, fleshy, growing in a rosette, banded-brown. Bracts* enclosing the flowers bright red. Flowers yellowish-white. Guiana.

**VULCANICA, -us, -um** (vul-kay'ni-ka). Pertaining to a volcano.

**VULGARIS, -e** (vul-gar'is). Common.

**VULGATA, -us, -um** (vul-gay'ta). Common.

**VULNERARIA, -us, -um** (vul-ner-rair'i-a). Pertaining to wounds; often an assumed cure for them.

**VULPINA, -us, -um** (vul-py'na). Relating to a fox.

**VYN-TACK.** A trademarked fastener used to attach vines to a wall.

---

* Special articles on the subjects indicated by an asterisk (*) will be found at the words so marked.

# W

**WAFER ASH** = *Ptelea trifoliata*.

**WAHLENBERGIA** (wall-en-ber′ji-a). Annual or perennial herbs, comprising about 100 species of the family Campanulaceae, widely distributed throughout the world, mostly in the warmer regions. Leaves alternate,* or sometimes opposite,* lance-shaped or ovalish, sometimes heart-shaped at the base. Flowers bell-shaped or tubular, blue, nodding, usually solitary, stalked, terminal or growing in the axils* of the leaves. Corolla funnel-shaped. Stamens* 5. Fruit a capsule.* (Named for George Wahlenberg, Swedish botanist.)

The species generally cult. is used in the rock garden, but may also be grown in the border. Propagated by seeds or division of the roots. Seeds should be sown in a cold frame, ⅛ in. deep, in sandy soil, in early spring. They may be transplanted to permanent positions as soon as large enough to handle.

**dalmatica** = *Edraianthus tenuifolius*.

**gracilis**. Annual, growing to 1 ft. high. Leaves alternate,* narrowly lance-shaped, to ½ in. long, the margins toothed. Flowers solitary, blue, long-stalked. N.Z., Aust., and South Af.

**WAHOO** = *Euonymus atropurpureus*.

**WAKEROBIN.** See TRILLIUM. See also ARUM MACULATUM.

**WALDSTEINIA** (wald-sty′ni-a). A small genus of horticulturally unimportant, strawberry-like herbs of the rose family, and closely related to the strawberry, but with dry, hairy fruits. The only cult. species, **W. fragarioides**, the barren or dry strawberry, is sometimes grown in the wild garden. It looks very like a small strawberry plant, has 3 leaflets and a small cluster (corymb*) of white flowers that are about ⅓ in. wide. It is of easy culture in partially shaded places. Eastern N.A. May–June. (Named for Francis Adam, Count of Waldstein-Wartenburg, a German botanist.)

**WALKING FERN; WALKING LEAF.** See CAMPTOSORUS.

**WALKS.** See PATHS AND PAVING.

**WALL.** For the various uses that can be made of garden walls see WALLS AND WALL GARDENING.

**WALL CRESS** = *Arabis albida*.

**WALL FERN** = *Polypodium vulgare*.

**WALLFLOWER** = *Cheiranthus cheiri*. See also ERYSIMUM.

**WALL NAILS FOR VINES.** See Section 4, TOOLS AND IMPLEMENTS. See also VYN-TACK.

**WALL PEPPER** = *Sedum acre*.

**WALLS AND WALL GARDENING.** As a distinctive structural element in landscape design, a wall may separate or unify space relationships. When its primary purpose is to set up a protective barrier, a wall should induce a sense of security against intrusion; and when it is desirable to segregate an area by an enclosure, a wall materially contributes toward visual unity. The type and style of a wall as well as its height and extent are influenced somewhat by local traditions and environment but more specifically by the requirements of a given problem.

The architectural snap and definition that a wall contributes to a landscape effect should be softened by judicious planting so that the wall will harmonize with the general atmosphere and adjacent surroundings. Plant material for walls might be divided into two general groups: plants to grow within the wall structure, such as rock plants, and secondly, plants to be trained over the surface of the wall, such as espalier trees or climbing or trailing vines.

EARTH WALL. A simple wall of earth suitably planted might be appropriate within the confines of a property when used to define the limits of an area such as a rock garden

A double wall with a topsoil core upon which a hedge or other plants may be grown.

or a children's outdoor playroom. This type of wall requires the use of a rich, loamy soil thoroughly tamped and compacted. Turf sods or moss or thick, matted roots of suitable perennials can readily be wired to the slopes of either or both sides. To insure an adequate water supply, a one-inch galvanized iron pipe perforated every few inches might be run along the crest of the wall, and connected to the nearest supply with a control valve. Where a hedge surmounts the earth wall, such irrigation may prove to be a necessity, especially where the side walls as well as the crest are thickly planted.

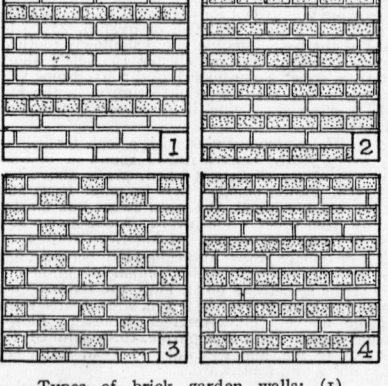

Types of brick garden walls: (1) Common bond; (2) English bond; (3) Dutch bond; (4) Cross-bond.

RIP-RAP WALL. Where large rocks and boulders are available for rip-rap, this type of wall affords an economical way of retaining a steep slope. A liberal batter should be provided and all stones tilted back against the bank to allow rain water to seep into the soil.

Rocks should be so placed that they bind on one another, and all voids filled with good topsoil and thoroughly tamped. Native bayberry or dwarf huckleberry or roses, for instance,

---

* Special articles on the subjects indicated by an asterisk (*) will be found at the words so marked.

might be suitable to plant between the rocks along a driveway embankment. Dwarf evergreen creepers such as periwinkle or euonymus would be more suitable where a rich, compact effect is desired.

HA-HA WALL. Suitable for use against pasture land where a definite barrier is required, yet where an uninterrupted view is desired, is a Ha-ha wall. It usually takes the form of a dry retaining wall constructed on the near side of a ditch or dry moat so that it is only visible from the outside area. Where one wishes to see only a quiet stretch of lawn from the inside looking out, but would like to see a jolly bit of color from the outside looking in, this sunken wall would be the suitable type to use.

DRY STONE WALL. A free-standing stone wall laid up dry, with no cement in the joints, requires a more highly skilled mason than a wall whose joints are filled with cement. Where long, flat stones are available, a dry wall may be laid up very effectively. If an old dry stone wall is to be converted into a wall garden, it would be necessary to remove sufficient stone to fill interior voids with topsoil. Plants are liable to dry out from lack of moisture where capillary action cannot take place due to the soil pockets having no direct soil contact with the ground.

Types of stone garden walls: (1) Random rubble. (2) Random coursed rubble. (3) Broken coursed rubble. (4) Irregular coursed rubble.

DRY DOUBLE WALL. This type is admirably suited to wall gardening, as it provides two stone faces laid up dry with exposed earth pockets as required and with a central core of topsoil to act as a reservoir of cool, moist earth where deep, penetrating roots may feed. A hedge might readily be planted along the top of this type of wall, affording added height and protection. For a low thick tangle, a hedge of *Rosa setigera* would be effective. For a restrained formal hedge, Mugho pines, dwarf evergreen azaleas, or barberry would be suitable. A thorn, beech, or hornbeam hedge would be very formidable on a long run of wall where the element of protection is a factor. Various types of junipers should thrive in such a location, and if provided sufficient moisture, pines and hemlocks should prove very effective. Where both faces of the double dry wall are to be planted, the central core of soil should be adequate to sustain vigorous growth on both sides as well as top. Suitable types for planting in large drifts on both faces might be *Dianthus plumarius*, *Nepeta mussini*, *Iberis sempervirens*, or *Euonymus radicans*.

MASONRY WALL. A masonry wall makes a most suitable background for espalier fruits or flowering trees and shrubs. An easterly exposure is generally considered ideal. Even a southern exposure, however, is feasible for this purpose if the lines of supporting wires are run sufficiently far out from the wall surface to prevent the plant from being burned by the reflected heat from the sun. Regular, trained trees and shrubs espaliered against a wall are most suitable for formal effects such as might be required for an entrance court treatment or a garden wall or the plain exposed wall surfaces of a house. Shrubs such as forsythia, cotoneaster, buddleia, and *Euonymus alatus* lend themselves admirably to espalier treatment. (See TRAINING PLANTS.) Vines, of course, are ideal for softening hard construction lines of a masonry wall. Hybrids of the *wichuraiana* rose have good foliage and make excellent cover and can be trained on diagonal wires to give an architectural effect.

STONE VENEER ON CONCRETE WALL. Where laminated stone is laid up in layers facing down a concrete retaining wall, soil pockets may be provided in any location or series of locations desired. A most effective planting display may be created by organizing the material in subtly related rhythmical patterns in form and texture and color.

BRICK WALL. The wall texture of a definitely repeated small unit, such as a brick, creates a background scale of uniform pattern which forms an interesting contrast with the lively lines of branches and more dynamic patterns of living foliage masses. An effective treatment for a brick wall is to divide the wall into a series of panels, possibly varying in width. Alternate panels might be planted with an evergreen vine like English ivy and the wall space or panel between might be embellished with such espaliered material as *Viburnum sieboldi*, or perhaps *Cornus florida* or *Pyracantha coccinea lalandi*. Where protected, buddleia and jasmine are ideal shrubs for training against a wall. See VINES.

Informal wall garden

CONCRETE WALL. By itself, a concrete wall may be said to lack distinction. It needs planting to give it character. Co-ordinating patterns of evergreens when established on a concrete wall tend to enliven an otherwise dull surface and also tend to integrate the whole lifeless expanse. A flat colortone of soft lavender-pink or a warm beige applied to the concrete enriches the effect. Shrubs such as weigelas, Regel's privet and forsythias may readily be trained against a concrete wall, and alternate with such vines as wisteria or *Celastrus articulatus* to bring new life and light to play on such a static background.

Espaliered fruits on a brick wall

---

* Special articles on the subjects indicated by an asterisk (*) will be found at the words so marked.

TERRACED WALLS OF TILE OR BLOCK. A wall garden may be constructed of a series of terraced groups of terra-cotta tiles or concrete blocks. They may be laid up in varying patterns, such as pyramidal or winged formations, and filled with topsoil and planted with rock plants, ferns, or dwarf evergreens. A stunning effect might be produced by building a terraced wall of glass brick with adequate provision for rock-plant pockets and adequate arrangements for lighting the glass at night from below so as to give the effect of a softly glowing wall.

CITY WALLS: The following plants have been successfully grown in backyard gardens trained on walls or fences: *Cotoneaster simondsi, Ilex crenata, Forsythia suspensa, Forsythia intermedia, Ligustrum obtusifolium regelianum*. The following vines also do well on city walls: *Polygonum auberti, Campsis radicans, Wistaria sinensis*, and in shady, protected places, the English ivy will often thrive.

HERBS FOR SUNNY WALL GARDENS: *Ajuga, Alyssum, Aster*, Mauve Cushion, *Campanula, Cerastium, Dianthus, Gypsophila, Helianthemum, Iberis, Phlox subulata, Ceratostigma plumbaginoides, Sedum, Silene, Thymus, Tunica saxifraga, Veronica.*

PLANTS FOR SHADY WALL GARDENS: *Ajuga, Campanula carpatica, Hypericum, Euonymus radicans minimus, Potentilla tridentata, Saxifraga, Sedum, Veronica repens, Viola.* — A. F.

**WALNUT.** Valuable nut trees constituting the genus **Juglans** (jug'lanz) of the family Juglandaceae, and comprising only about 15 species found mostly in N.A. and Eurasia, and including, besides the walnuts, the butternut. They are usually tall trees closely related to the hickory, but not having the shaggy bark of some hickories. Leaves alternate,* compound,* the leaflets arranged featherfashion, with an odd one at the end. Male and female flowers separate, on the same tree, the male flowers in hanging catkins, the female in few-flowered, erect clusters (racemes*). Petals none. Fruit a large, fleshy, non-splitting drupe,* within which is the seed (the walnut or butternut), commonly but incorrectly called a nut. In some species, especially the butternut, the outer husk of the fruit is aromatic, and the bruised foliage of all species is also aromatic. (*Juglans* is the old Latin name of the English walnut, and means, literally, the acorn of Jupiter.)

For Culture *see* below. Nut as used below means nut in the ordinary sense, although it is actually the seed. All species flower with or before the expansion of the leaves.

**J. californica.** A shrub or small tree, the leaflets 11–15, oblongish, pointed, 1½–3 in. long, smooth. Fruit round, about ¾ in. in diameter, the nut deeply grooved. Southern Calif. Hardy from zone* 6 southward, and of little interest except as breeding stock for English walnut varieties. This and a related Californian tree, *J. hindsi* (which is a street tree in Calif.), have been much used by walnut breeders. *J. hindsi* has 15–19 leaflets, and a faintly grooved nut.

**J. cinerea.** Butternut; sometimes called white walnut. A round-headed tree, sometimes 90 ft. high, usually less, the bark deeply fissured. Leaflets 11–19, oblongish, 2½–5 in. long, the blade and stalk sticky-hairy. Fruit egg-shaped or football-shaped, about 3½ in. long, the nut ridged and with smaller ridges or furrows between the main ridges, the meat oily, rich, and spicy. Eastern N.A. Hardy from zone* 2 southward.

**J. hindsi.** See JUGLANS CALIFORNICA.

**J. nigra.** Black walnut. A tall tree, sometimes 150 ft. high, its brown bark deeply fissured, and its timber highly prized. Leaflets 15–23, ovalish or narrower, rounded at the base, 2½–5 in. long, irregularly toothed, minutely hairy but not sticky. Fruit nearly round or slightly pear-shaped, about 2 in. thick, hairy, the nut strongly and irregularly sculptured. Mass. to Fla. west to Tex. and Minn. Hardy from zone* 3 southward. An ornamental tree, but valued chiefly for its fine, rich, oily nuts.

**J. regia.** English walnut; also, and more correctly, called Persian walnut, as it is native there and not in England. A tree up to 100 ft. high, the bark silvery-gray. Leaflets 5–9, rarely 11, elliptic or oblongish, without marginal teeth except on young leaves. Fruit nearly round, green, smooth, about 2 in. in diameter, the nut much sculptured. Southeastern Eu. and Asia Minor to the Himalayas and China. Hardy, in some of its forms, from zone* 4 southward. Long cult. and the origin, after centuries of breeding, of the modern varieties of the English walnut. *See* below.

**J. sieboldiana.** A Japanese walnut of chief interest for breeding with the English walnut, as it is hardier than that species. Leaflets 9–17, ovalish or oblong, minutely toothed. Fruit nearly round, or egg-shaped, but pointed, about 2½ in. long, the nut 8-ridged, and sculptured between the ridges. Hardy from zone* 3 southward.

## WALNUT CULTURE

Of the important genus *Juglans*, to which the walnuts belong, two representatives are of principal importance in the United States; the English or Persian walnut (*Juglans regia*), which is grown in California and Oregon, and the native black walnut (*Juglans nigra*), grown in the central and eastern U.S. Although, because of climatic conditions and the blight disease, commercial culture of the former is restricted to the Pacific Coast, there are hardy varieties which succeed reasonably well in the Middle Atlantic states and Great Lake region.

ENGLISH WALNUT. On the basis of climatic requirements and tolerances the English walnuts grown in this country are of two kinds; the so-called Santa Barbara group, a hardy sub-tropical type of Chilean origin, and the French group, a hardy warm-temperate type. The former requires a longer growing season and is less resistant to both heat and cold. Its commercial culture is restricted, therefore, to those parts of the coastal plain area of southern California and adjoining valleys where the equable summer climate favors high quality and the winters are cool enough to break the rest period. The latter has a much higher requirement for winter cold and hence its commercial culture is restricted to central and northern California and parts of Oregon. This type is sufficiently hardy to withstand the winters of all save the coldest parts of eastern United States, but bears poorly because of killing of the small fruit-wood. Both kinds require more winter cold than the pecan, for which reason they do not succeed in the Gulf Coast states. The principal climatic hazards to which the southern California industry is occasionally subject are frosts, summer heat, and winters too mild to break the rest. In northern California and Oregon the major hazards are early fall frost and rain during the harvesting period. Orchard heating is practiced to some extent in southern California (for details *see* FROST).

The English walnut is one of the most exacting of all orchard trees with reference to soil requirements. While the tree itself succeeds reasonably well on a wide variety of soils, and notably so on relatively light soils, good crops of well-filled, high quality nuts are produced only on deep, fertile soils of medium-heavy texture. Because of the deep extension of the roots, soils of less than 10 to 12 feet in depth should not be planted to this nut. It is also intolerant of wet soils, for which reason excellent under-drainage must exist and heavy soils should be avoided. The English walnut is markedly sensitive to alkali, even in low concentration, which requires the avoidance of such soils and the use of irrigation water of the best possible quality. Because of its exacting soil requirement no greater mistake can be made than to plant the walnut on any soil but the best.

All varieties appear to be both self-fertile and cross-fertile, and provision for cross-pollination is ordinarily not made, though there is some evidence of benefits therefrom. Satisfactory overlapping of the bloom periods of the male and female flowers usually occurs, but not always. The benefits of pollinators are most evident in the central and northern California sections.

Nursery trees are propagated mainly by whip-grafting year-old seedlings, though patch-budding in summer or fall is favored in the northern sections. The rootstock most employed in the past is the northern California black walnut (*Juglans hindsi*), but the trend is now toward the use of the English walnut seedling, which appears to be immune to the crown-rot disease. Top-grafting orchard trees is of considerable importance either for changing varieties or converting seedling trees to standard sorts. The English walnut top-grafts with greater difficulty than the black walnuts. For the former, modified cleft-grafting is the most successful method; for the latter, cutting back and patch-budding the new shoots is equally satisfactory. Successful conversion depends largely on the care with which the follow-up work is done.

The walnut requires wide spacing for satisfactory yield and quality. On good soils the permanent trees should not be closer than 60 to 70 feet apart. Intercropping the young walnut orchard and the use of filler trees, which are removed when crowding becomes imminent, are common and recommended practices. Many of the older orchards were

---

* Special articles on the subjects indicated by an asterisk (*) will be found at the words so marked.

planted too close, with the result that the trees have become crowded, and yield and quality have declined. Removal of part of the trees is invariably followed by improvement in production and quality.

Of soil-management practices irrigation is undoubtedly the most important. An adequate soil moisture supply must be maintained at all times. Failure to wet the soil deeply in winter causes dieback, a form of drought injury. On good soils the response to nitrogen fertilizers is not sufficient to pay for the costs; no response to other elements has been noted. Cultivation is necessary only to turn under cover crops or weeds and to facilitate irrigation and harvesting. Pruning is of minor importance and is confined to the removal of suckers* and declined lower limbs, and to light thinning of the tops.

Early harvesting and rapid curing enhance the quality of the nuts and are recommended. The nuts are shaken from the trees by hooked poles operated from the ground or portable towers. They are hand-hulled as gathered, in so far as necessary and practicable; those to which the hulls stick are machine-hulled.

The principal varieties in southern California are Placentia, Eureka, Chase and Ehrhardt. In northern California the major varieties are Concord, Payne, Franquette and Blackmer. Mayette and Franquette are the hardiest to winter cold and hence best adapted to Oregon and eastern United States.

AMERICAN BLACK WALNUT. This nut is a hardy temperate-zone forest tree grown mainly for lumber, though the harvesting of the nuts is an industry of some importance. In recent years small plantings have been made primarily for the nuts, which are of distinctive flavor and are sold mainly in shelled form. Several comparatively thin-shelled varieties have been selected and propagated, of which the most important are Thomas, Ohio, Stabler and Ten Eyck; the two latter have the thinnest shells and are the most promising. — R. W. H.

INSECT PESTS. The dark, hairy, ugly walnut caterpillars up to 1½ in. long feed in conspicuous groups late in the summer. The groups may be destroyed mechanically or poisoned with arsenicals. They also attack hickory and pecan. A weevil or snout beetle attacks the young nuts; fallen nuts should be destroyed.

English walnuts on the Pacific Coast are attacked by a strain of codling moth; it is controlled in the same way as on apple, but a basic lead arsenate is used in preference to the ordinary form. A yellowish plant louse is a serious pest there, and is controlled with nicotine dust. A fruit maggot burrows in the husk of English walnut in the West; adults may be killed with an arsenical spray early in August.

DISEASES. Bacterial blight causes black, irregular spots on the leaves and fruits of walnuts, blights the young shoots and causes failure to set fruit. Control has been obtained by two applications of bordeaux spray 3-3-50, one before and one just after the blooming of the panicle flowers. Walnut and butternut are often damaged by a twig blight and dieback of fungous origin. Control involves increasing vigor of the tree and cutting out infected parts as they appear. Several leafspots afflict walnut. Two or three applications of bordeaux 4-4-50 at two-week intervals after the leaves are half grown will help to protect the foliage. A canker causes large, open wounds, particularly on the cultivated variety, Thomas. Removal of the affected parts is the most effective control known. Infection through wounds induces cankers and wood rots, and all openings in the bark should be treated so as to protect them from such invasion.

**WALPOLE TEA** = *Ceanothus americanus*.

**WANDERING JEW** = *Tradescantia fluminensis*. See SPIDERWORT. See also ZEBRINA.

**WAND-FLOWER.** See SPARAXIS.

**WAPATOO** = *Sagittaria latifolia*.

**WARDIAN CASE.** See TERRARIUM.

**WARS OF THE ROSES.** See ROSA DAMASCENA VERSICOLOR.

**WASHINGTON.** For the trees planted by George Washington *see* Mount Vernon at TREES.

**WASHINGTON.** The state lies wholly in zones* 3, 4, 5, and 6, which, instead of running east and west as in most parts of America, run approximately north and south, due to the proximity of high mountains and the warm sea water.

SOILS. In western Washington the most productive soils are the dark silt or sandy loam soils, high in organic matter, found in the alluvial river valleys and the reclaimed tidal flats. In the upland areas the soils, sandy and a light-yellowish in color, are not quite so productive as the first soil type. East of the Cascade Mountains the soils are predominately of volcanic origin, modified by ice, water, and wind. In the larger and lower valleys of central Washington the soil is a productive sandy loam. In the southeast section the soil is a deep fertile brown silt loam, in many respects resembling a loess* soil. Certain northern areas of the state have been glaciated and such soils vary from a stony, gravelly type to a sandy loam structure.

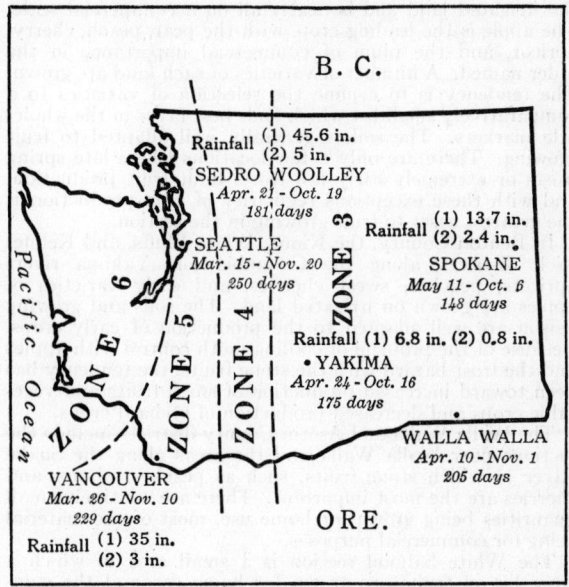

WASHINGTON

The zones of hardiness crossing Washington are those shown on the colored map at ZONE, which should be consulted for details. The dates are the average latest killing frost in spring and the first one in the fall. The figures below the dates show the average length of the growing season. Rainfall figures (in inches) show (1) the total annual rainfall and (2) the amount falling in the growing season at the places indicated.

FRUIT AREAS. The Spokane Valley is the principal fruit district of zone* 3 in the state of Washington. Apples are the leading tree fruit crop with cherries closely following. Midseason and early varieties of apples are primarily grown. Of the small fruits, raspberries and strawberries are grown both commercially and for home use. The Kettle Falls district in the upper Columbia River and the central part of Stevens County around Colville produce some small fruits.

Zone* 4 includes the principal fruit-growing areas with Okanogan on the north and White Salmon on the south. The principal fruits of the Okanogan Valley are apples and pears grown under irrigation near Okanogan, Omak, and Oroville, and in other smaller districts.

The Methow Valley is a small, irrigated apple-growing district in the valley of the Methow River, extending from Pateros to Methow.

The Wenatchee section, extending from Wenatchee to Leavenworth up the Wenatchee River, to Orondo on the east side of the Columbia River and to Rock Island in the southeastern direction from Wenatchee, is a large district confined to the narrow irrigated lands near the rivers. Apples are the leading crop with pears, cherries, apricots, and peaches following in approximately the order named. There are relatively few fruits, chiefly apricots, grown on the non-irrigated lands. Regularity of crop production is one of the principal features of this district.

Moses Lake in Grant County is the center of the apple production of that county. A few orchards are near Soap Lake. In this section the land is level, irrigated mostly by

---

* Special articles on the subjects indicated by an asterisk (*) will be found at the words so marked.

pumping projects from the lake. There is little fruit grown outside of the commercial orchards.

The Ellensburg and Kittitas community has a commercial orchard area in which fruit of good quality is grown. On the irrigated farms fruit is grown for home use and there is considerable irrigated land devoted to general farming. The apples grown are nearly all of the mid-season and early-ripening varieties.

The Yakima fruit district extends from Tieton and Naches, at the upper limits, to Grandview, the lower limit of the section. Fruit growing is confined almost entirely to the irrigated land and is nearly all on a commercial scale. The apple is the leading crop, with the pear, peach, cherry, apricot, and the plum of commercial importance in the order named. A number of varieties of each kind are grown. The tendency is to confine the selection of varieties to a comparatively small list which finds best favor in the wholesale markets. The soil is generally well adapted to fruit growing. There are only a few locations where late spring frosts or extremely early fall frosts limit fruit production, and with these exceptions regularity of crop production is the greatest asset to fruit growing in the section.

In Benton County, the Kiona, White Bluffs, and Kennewick districts, along the Columbia and Yakima rivers apricots, peaches, sweet cherries, and early varieties of apples are grown on irrigated land. The soils and growing season are well adapted to the production of early crops. Because of the problem of codling moth control with apples and the frost hazard with the stone fruits, the tendency has been toward increased production of small fruits and vegetable crops and decreased production of orchard crops.

The Walla Walla and Asotin County districts include the sections near Walla Walla and the areas along the Snake River in which stone fruits, such as peaches, plums, and cherries are the most important. There are relatively small quantities being grown for home use, most of the material being for commercial purposes.

The White Salmon section is a small area in which a large list of fruits are grown for home use, and the commercial production of fruits is confined almost entirely to apples. Only a part of the commercial orchards are irrigated and usually none of the home orchards.

In zone* 6 are found three districts. In Clark County prunes and small fruits, such as raspberries and strawberries, filberts and walnuts are grown. Rainfall is depended upon for the water supply, but the semi-coastal climate has given protection against injury from late spring frosts and early autumn frosts. Rains at blossom time have been the most destructive element of climate.

In the Puyallup summer district, which extends from Tacoma to near Seattle, raspberries and blackberries form the principal fruit crops. Some pears and sour cherries are also grown. Commercial plantings are successful and also nearly every farm home has a goodly supply of tree and bush fruits for family use.

VEGETABLE AREAS. In zone* 3 the principal vegetable-gardening center is in the Spokane Valley, near the city of Spokane. The vegetables best suited are tomatoes, cabbage, muskmelons, squash, sweet corn, late potatoes, carrots, cucumbers, string beans, and celery. The soils of the Spokane Valley are generally somewhat shallow, with the surface soil tending to be a gravelly loam in character, while the subsoil is somewhat gravelly to very gravelly.

In zone* 4 the principal vegetable-gardening centers are the Yakima Valley, especially around Wapato, Toppenish, Sunnyside, and Kennewick. About Wapato, spinach, carrots, potatoes, string beans, tomatoes, eggplants, peppers, watermelons, muskmelons, cucumbers, and sweet corn are grown. In the Toppenish region, spinach, onions, potatoes, tomatoes, cucumbers, muskmelons, watermelons, and sweet corn are produced. Around Sunnyside, the principal vegetables are asparagus, spinach, onions, potatoes, tomatoes, pumpkins, squash, and sweet corn, while at Kennewick asparagus, head lettuce, potatoes, and muskmelons are important vegetables. The soils of Wapato, Toppenish, and Sunnyside are deep to very deep, with the surface soil tending to be a fine, silty loam and the subsoil a silt. In the Kennewick area the soils are medium in depth with the subsoil tending to be a sandy gravel. Occasionally a hardpan is found near the surface in some of the areas.

Vegetables are also grown in the Walla Walla Valley, around the city of Walla Walla, the principal crops being asparagus, rhubarb, spinach, head lettuce, onions, potatoes, beans, peas, tomatoes, eggplants, peppers, cucumbers, and sweet corn. The soils of the vegetable-producing areas of the Walla Walla Valley are generally deep to very deep and of a silty loam to a silt nature.

Other principal vegetable-growing areas are in the White River Valley, from Puyallup to Seattle, and about the cities of Monroe and Bellingham. In the White River Valley, rhubarb, spinach, celery, head lettuce, cabbage, cauliflower, root crops, green beans, peas, eggplants, peppers, and cucumbers are grown. In the Monroe section any of the market garden crops can be grown except those requiring a high degree of heat, such as do tomatoes, melons, and sweet corn, but the principal crops are head lettuce, cabbage, and potatoes. In the vicinity of Bellingham, the vegetables grown are rhubarb, head lettuce, celery, cabbage, cauliflower, carrots, beets, parsnips, beans, peas, eggplants, peppers, and cucumbers.

ORNAMENTAL PLANTS. No extensive study has been made in the state of Washington concerning the preference of ornamental plants for certain soil types. One reason for this is that the soil in most sections where ornamentals are grown is relatively good, reasonably fertile, and sufficiently deep to maintain the plant materials grown. Water and climate, rather than soil, are the two limiting factors in the selection and choice of ornamental plant materials, especially for the eastern section of the state. Thus, the state may be divided into two rather distinct areas from the standpoint of growing ornamental plants. West of the Cascades the winters are relatively mild, with an abundant rainfall. The soils in most of this area give a distinct acid reaction. East of the Cascades the winters are comparatively cold, the summers warm and dry. The soil gives a neutral or in some cases a distinctly alkaline reaction.

Some of the trees which do particularly well on the coast are: Alaska cedar, arborvitae, Douglas fir, hemlock, incense cedar, juniper, Oregon maple, pine, spruce, vine maple, and white fir.

The shrubs are: azaleas, boxwood, barberry, dogwood, English holly, hydrangea, laurel, madroña, Oregon grape, rose, and rhododendron.

The trees commonly grown east of the Cascades are: ash, birch, black locust, linden, maple, mountain ash, pine, poplar, Siberian or Chinese elm, spruce, and sycamore.

The shrubs are: barberry, bush honeysuckle, hawthorn, lilac, mock-orange, cream bush, Russian olive, serviceberry, pea tree, snowberry, spirea, and sumac.

CLIMATE. The climate varies widely with the proximity to the Pacific Ocean, the topography, the altitude, and latitude. West of the Cascades, because of the proximity to large bodies of water, the climate is mild and humid, and the rainfall varies from 35 to over 100 inches annually. East of the Cascades the winters are more severe and the day summer temperatures hotter and relative humidity lower than in western Washington. At the extreme lower end of the Yakima Valley the rainfall may average only about 6.5 inches, but in the higher elevations elsewhere east of the Cascades the rainfall may exceed 25 inches per annum.

KILLING FROSTS

| Towns | Average date of last killing frost in spring | Latest known spring killing frost | Average date of the earliest killing frost in fall | Earliest known fall killing frost |
| --- | --- | --- | --- | --- |
| Spokane | May 11 | May 25 | October 6 | September 5 |
| Yakima | April 24 | May 10 | October 16 | September 5 |
| Walla Walla | April 10 | May 10 | November 1 | September 20 |
| Seattle | March 15 | April 20 | November 20 | November 1 |
| Sedro Woolley | April 21 | May 15 | October 19 | September 15 |
| Vancouver | March 26 | April 25 | November 10 | October 10 |

* Special articles on the subjects indicated by an asterisk (*) will be found at the words so marked.

RAINFALL

| Places | Total yearly rainfall | Approximate amount falling in June, July, August |
|---|---|---|
| Spokane | 13.7 in. | 2.4 in. |
| Yakima | 6.8 in. | 0.8 in. |
| Walla Walla | 15.6 in. | 2.2 in. |
| Seattle | 29.6 in. | 3.5 in. |
| Sedro Woolley | 45.6 in. | 5.0 in. |
| Vancouver | 35.0 in. | 3.0 in. |

FOG. During the growing season fog occurs quite generally in zones* 5 and 6 throughout the spring and early summer months. By 9:00 to 10:00 o'clock in the morning, however, the fog generally rises. The humidity is unusually high during the summer months.

SNOW COVER. In zone* 4, snow covers the ground during parts of December and January, affording considerable protection to the perennial crops. If it were not for the snowfall, the area would have a deficient water supply.

Zone* 3 depends on irrigation as a source of water supply. The streams from which much of the irrigation water is taken have their origin in the Cascade Mountains. Whether or not there is a water shortage depends on the annual snowfall. Some water for irrigation comes from reservoirs in the mountains which are filled by the melting snows. Little if any snow falls in the area to the west of the Cascades.

CASCADE MOUNTAINS. The chief climatic control is the Cascade range of mountains. The rains from the Pacific fall mostly on the western slopes of the mountains, and that carried over is diverted high into the air and does not begin to fall until it reaches the extreme eastern section of Washington, known as the Palouse region. As a consequence, a great part of eastern Washington is arid.

The address of the Agricultural Experiment Station, which has kindly supplied this information about the state, is the State College of Washington, Pullman, Washington. The station is always ready to answer gardening questions.

Garden Club activities include clubs of the Garden Club of America at Tacoma and Seattle. The home office is at 598 Madison Avenue, New York. There are also many clubs affiliated with the Washington State Federation of Garden Clubs. For the one nearest your locality write the Garden Editor, Houghton Mifflin Company, Boston, Mass.

**WASHINGTON ASPARAGUS.** See ASPARAGUS.

**WASHINGTONIA** (wash-ing-tō'ni-a). Fan palms with massive trunks, comprising only 2 (or perhaps 3) species native in Calif., northern Mex., and in southwestern Ariz. and widely planted there; also planted less commonly along the Gulf Coast and in Fla. Trunks unarmed, shaggy in the second species, but densely clothed with a "petticoat" of hanging withered leaves in the first. Leaves fan-like, but cut into numerous narrow segments. Flowers perfect,* nearly stalkless on the flowering branches which are long, slender, and usually longer than the foliage. Stamens* 6. Fruit 1-seeded, thin-fleshed, scarcely ⅓ in. long (a drupe*). The individual flower clusters suggest a corn-tassel. (Named for General George Washington.) Long known as *Neowashingtonia* and closely related to *Brahea* (which see).

The California fan palms are widely planted and make extremely handsome avenue trees throughout central and southern Calif. While, for palms, they are relatively hardy, they are not safe above zone* 7. See PALM.

**filifera.** A stout palm, 60–80 ft. high, the upper part of the trunk clothed with the long-persistent, withered or dead, hanging leaves. Living leaves long-stalked, erect, the stalks prickly, the blade 3–5 ft. wide, grayish-green, cut to nearly the middle into many, narrow, drooping, thready segments. Moist places near the Colorado Desert, Calif. Less planted than the next species, and less satisfactory near the Calif. coast, but superior in dry soils in Fla.

**robusta.** California fan palm. Taller than the last, the trunk more slender, usually clothed above with a dense, shaggy, fibrous network, through which protrude the old, spiny leafstalks, but the trunk naked toward the base. Leaf blades cut only about ⅓ of the way to the middle, the stiffish or drooping segments not thready as in *W. filifera*.

**WASHINGTONIANA, -us, -um** (wash-ing-tō-ni-a'na). From the state of Washington.

**WASHINGTON LILY** = *Lilium washingtonianum*.
**WASHINGTON PLANT** = *Cabomba caroliniana*.
**WASHINGTON THORN** = *Crataegus phaenopyrum*
**WASHOUT.** See EROSION.

**WATER.** Without water no plant can live and grow, and without water as a landscape feature few gardens are as attractive as they might be. For this purely aesthetic feature of water see the next entry which includes notes on the landscape value of pools, streams, fountains, etc. For the cultivation of aquatic or water plants *see* WATER GARDEN. For supplying water to gardens deficient in it *see* IRRIGATION. For the purely physical water-needs of plants all gardeners should consult the articles on WATERING, SOIL MOISTURE, CULTIVATION, and PLANT FOODS. For the amount of water in some common fruits and vegetables *see* WATER CONTENT.

**WATER.** Although water has no tangible form of its own, it will assume the shape of any form into which it flows, and may be made to take on a great variety of predictable shapes and characters by the direction of forces upon it. Responsive to such outside influences, water may vary endlessly in type and character as well as in emotional appeal. Whatever form it may take, however, water retains certain constant attributes such as moisture and the ability to reflect light. Throughout all its various manifestations, water retains its identity and unity of spirit, making it an ideal element in landscape design.

Electrical illumination for night lighting effects is an intriguing problem. Blue light seems to have the greatest appeal and yellow follows for colored lighting effects. A crystal white light is most satisfactory for general use, however, and is more symbolic of the attributes of water — refreshing purity and cleanliness. See LIGHTING.

LAKE OR POND. With its extended surface area, a lake or pond can reflect greater play of light and shade and color tone and provide wider scope for dramatic mood, than smaller water features.

Introducing water-loving plants in organized groups along the shoreline and backing these up with naturalized masses of shrubby growth whose flowering season synchronizes with the water plants, creates a lovely splash of color in the water, and this effect is greatly strengthened if the shrub growth is supplemented with flowering trees. One should bear in mind an essential principle of landscape design, that a very simple and restrained initial grouping that is rich in color will make the most beautiful reflections in the water. See WATER GARDEN.

POOLS AND BASINS. Where the purpose of a pool is to reflect, one should use great restraint in adding supplementary details such as balustrades, hedge-like edgings or water lilies and other aquatic plants. Should a pool be built under a canopy of trees, care should be taken to let the light play through onto the water so that there would be reflected light coming up out of darkness. Adjacent planting material might well be evergreen so as to avoid staining and littering the pool by deciduous tree leaves. However, a spreading dogwood tree arching over a pool or basin is most effective.

STREAM AND BROOK. The essential quality of a stream is continuity of flow, and it is very helpful to keep this constantly in mind when constructing an artificial brook or stream. An exaggerated expression of water action should be suggested in the bed and banks of the stream to imply a greater flow in times of freshet. The careful placement of a selected group of waterside plants should produce interesting reflections.

CASCADE. There is a sweetly melancholy aspect about a cascade which is soothing and relaxing. In constructing such a watercourse the source of the water must either be very frankly displayed or very cleverly concealed. Falling in thinly veiled sheets from basin to basin, the water playfully

---

* Special articles on the subjects indicated by an asterisk (*) will be found at the words so marked.

may create a dramatic effect with a small supply. To avoid any tendency toward mechanical setness, one should endeavor to have a slightly different light aspect for each individual waterfall by subtle variations in orientation and height. All lip stones should be undercut to insure a direct fall and prevent the water from dribbling down the underside of the rock.

An artificial but skillfully contrived cascade, making a fine site for water plants in a naturalistic setting.

WATER RAMP. There are interesting possibilities in the treatment of a runnel which follows the course of a ramp. A series of small pools, overflowing to join the runnel again, together with specially constructed sides to create a gurgling sound along the runnel's course, suggest a refreshing tonal symphony.

WATERFALL. Where a fairly large stream is provided, a very satisfying effect is produced by letting it fall directly into the pool below. Where the stream has only a small flow, it is well to make the most of what is given and so distribute the rocks that they catch the falling water and dash and splash it from one face to another, thereby employing the element of light to amplify the interest and playfulness of the waterfall.

WALL FOUNTAIN. A wall fountain usually takes the form of a basin architecturally related to a building or wall and the basin is fed by a spouting sculptural feature of various types and descriptions. Such a fountain would be appropriate on a terrace or in an intimate garden. One of the most attractive uses of fountains is indoors. The water provides a good atmosphere in which to grow plants and the pool into which the water tumbles may be used for aquatics (see WATER GARDEN). See also HOUSE PLANTS.

FREESTANDING FOUNTAIN. Where a freestanding fountain jet is concerned, it is the architectural or sculptural effect of the water mass itself that is to be considered primarily. The pool or basin which holds the jet may express to a minor degree the mood the designer wishes to create. The character the fountain is to assume may vary endlessly. Upspringing into the light, and joyously welling up from within, a fountain is usually inspiring and emotionally stimulating. Through sight and sound simultaneously playing together, a reaction of emotional tenseness is stirred within the beholder — if he is sensitive. There seems to be a universal quality about a fountain that recalls all fountains everywhere, and serves to give its eternal message as a symbol of the water of life. — A. F.

**WATER ARUM** = *Calla palustris.*

**WATER BEECH** = *Carpinus caroliniana.* See HORNBEAM.

**WATER BLISTER.** A usually discolored spot on the leaves of greenhouse plants caused by the concentration of sunlight through a drop of water, or by imperfections in the glass, often called a burn.

**WATER CALTROP, WATER CHESTNUT** = *Trapa natans.*

**WATER CANNA.** See THALIA.

**WATER CHINQUAPIN** = *Nelumbium luteum.*

**WATER CONTENT.** The water content of fresh fruits and vegetables is a fair index of the water needs of the plants that produce them. While grains like rice or wheat may be only 12–14% water, fruits and vegetables contain far more than this.

Percentage of water in some common vegetables.

| Artichoke | 81 | Onion | 86 |
|---|---|---|---|
| Asparagus | 93 | Parsnip | 79 |
| Bean | 15 | Pea | 14 |
| Beet | 85 | Potato | 75 |
| Cabbage | 90 | Pumpkin | 90 |
| Carrot | 85 | Rhubarb | 91 |
| Cauliflower | 90 | Rutabaga | 87 |
| Celery | 84 | Spinach | 92 |
| Cucumber | 95 | Turnip | 92 |
| Lettuce | 94 | | |

Percentage of water in some common fruits.

| Apple | 83 | Pear | 83 |
|---|---|---|---|
| Cherry | 82 | Plum | 83 |
| Gooseberry | 90 | Strawberry | 90 |
| Grape | 83 | | |

**WATERCRESS** (*Roripa nasturtium-aquaticum*). This extremely hardy, European perennial can be grown wherever there is standing or quietly flowing water, but it prefers cool to warm water and so does better in the northern part of the country, where it is widely naturalized. It may be gathered from the wild and will easily root from broken-off stems inserted in wet sand, or it often, in quiet pools, begins to grow without attachment to the soil. Often it will completely choke such pools, and this should be kept in mind when introducing it.

If pools are not available, watercress may be planted in wet sand or sandy soil, and the flats put in the cold frame and kept constantly wet.

**WATER DAFFODIL.** See STERNBERGIA.

**WATER DOCK** = *Orontium aquaticum.*

**WATER ELM** = *Ulmus americana.* See ELM. See also PLANERA AQUATICA.

**WATER FERN.** See CERATOPTERIS.

**WATER GARDEN.** Under the term water gardening is included the cultivation and grouping of aquatic or waterside plants for the best effect. The value of water gardening lies in its extreme ease of care and culture, and its wide adaptability to all kinds of gardens. Aquatic gardens vary from small tub gardens and artificial or natural brooks to the large formal or informal pools, but in each and every case, they all share the same joyful lack of weeding, cultivation and spraying. Their only demands are for as much sun as possible, and for proper construction in the first place. With these two factors taken care of, by selecting the plants which are suitable to your own climate and garden, your water garden will be a constant delight all summer long, being of especial value in those localities where the summers are hot and dry, and any water feature of maximum importance.

CONSTRUCTION

The best mixture for concrete brooks or pools is one part Portland cement, two parts sharp sand, and three parts ½ inch gravel. The sand should be well graded, the particles varying in size from the finest up to that which screens through a ½-inch mesh. For every cubic yard needed, this 1–2–3 mixture will require 7 sacks of cement, 14 cubic feet of sand and 21 cubic feet of gravel. If the sand and gravel are absolutely dry, it will require about 5½ gallons of water to each sack of cement; if moist, 4½ gallons; if wet, 3¾ gallons. Use only pure water.

In order to form a winter-proof pool, it should be built on compact ground, with a six-inch layer of cinders or gravel beneath the concrete. The floor and walls must be poured at the same time to avoid any construction joints, and the concrete should be about six inches thick, with a layer of reinforcement in the middle. The reinforcement should be bent to the shape of the pool and raised as the concrete is poured until it is approximately in the center of the six-inch layer.

---

\* Special articles on the subjects indicated by an asterisk (\*) will be found at the words so marked.

Allow for ledges or pockets to hold the shallow-growing plants, and be sure that there is plenty of area where the required two feet of depth needed for the growing of water lilies will be available. If you use forms to hold your mixture, oil the sides which come in contact with the concrete. Used motor oil will do for this, and will insure an easy removal of the forms after they have remained in contact with the cement for the required forty-eight hours or more. Smooth down the surface with a brick when the forms are removed, or finish off with a thin coat of cement applied with a trowel or paint brush.

Protect the new concrete from wind and sun, which would otherwise evaporate the water still contained in it and prevent its hardening properly. Moist earth or straw will accomplish this, if it is kept wet for a week or ten days. Walls may have wet canvas or burlap hung over them. If the weather is cold, it is not necessary to maintain the moisture in the protecting layer; merely keep the work covered for a week or ten days. It takes about four weeks for a pool to cure completely — with a minimum of two weeks at least. If possible, wait a month before filling the pool for the first time. *It is very important* to remember that the first water put into a pool will absorb the alkali from the new concrete, and it is absolutely essential to fill the pool at least two weeks to permit the complete absorption of this free alkali into the water. Then drain and refill with fresh water before planting or stocking with fish.

### Brooks

For the small home owner who does not care for the little tub-garden, or wishes something more striking for his small available space, the answer is found in an artificial brook. For satisfactory aquatic culture, a brook, like a pool, should be about two feet deep, at least in spots. Both width and depth may vary along its course, simulating nature wherever possible. An inlet and outlet drain are advisable, and in all construction details the artificial brook follows the same rules as the conventional pool.

It is in planting that the most noticeable difference arises. There is no such thing as a formal brook; it must be as natural as space and material permit. For this reason, your choice of material will be decided by your particular geographical location. Water lilies will need a two-foot depth to accommodate the boxes in which they grow and still maintain the required 8 to 12 inches above their bulb crown. The aquatics which do not call for so much water covering may be grown in the shallower portions of the brook, while the submerged oxygenating plants (*see* AQUARIUM) will assist your snails and other scavengers in keeping the water clean and pure for the plants and fish.

The surface of the brook may be still further enhanced by the floating plants like *Salvinia* and *Azolla*, and along the edges and in the bends of the brook, the marsh-loving cat-tails, lotus (*Nelumbium*), *Acorus*, *Thalia* (water canna) etc., may be used to bring accent and height. Be sure to confine the roots of these, however, to limited areas, or they will take over your whole brook in a season or two.

### Winter Care

A well-reinforced pool will not crack over the winter even if left uncovered, but it is safer either to drain the pool or to cover it with boards, topped by leaves, straw or other mulching material. This is also adequate protection for pools in which hardy lilies, water plants and fish are left, provided the water level is kept up. If the pool is to be drained, and the plants left in, place a covering of manure, straw or leaves directly on the soil bottom. The most satisfactory method is to have the lilies in tubs, which can be taken out and covered in a trench or brought into the cool basement and kept covered with moist wrappings of burlap to prevent the destructive dry rot attacking the dormant roots. Tropical lilies can be carried over in heated aquaria, or in greenhouse pools, according to instructions given later under *propagation*, though it is easier to treat them as annuals, replacing them each year. Tub gardens should be drained and covered with leaves and boards, holding the leaves in place. Leave them in the ground if possible; if not, heap up leaves around them

### Planting Design

Your arrangement of plants will depend on whether you have decided upon a formal or informal pool. A formal pool is regular in outline, and requires great care in planting to retain the proportion of the pool itself in relation to the rest of the garden. If it is squared or oblong, the corners will be available for tall plantings of water canna, lotus, cat-tails or any of the water plants which grow several feet above the surface of the water. If it is round or oval, any height must be gained from the center. The outline of a formal pool should be a thing of beauty in itself, and never obscured by poor planting. If a fountain is built either at one end or in the center, a very valuable plant will be found in the parrot's-feather (*Myriophyllum proserpinacoides*).

An informal pool must be just as carefully planted as the formal, but with a different end in view. Proportion must be observed, of course, but with the idea of attaining as naturalistic an effect as possible, drawing the pool into its surroundings rather than bringing it into prominence. Conspicuous edgings of up-ended rock should be avoided. Either lay the rock flat, covering it with rock plants, moss, fern or any other suitable planting; or avoid its use altogether, and bring the turf right down to the brink of the pool. It is usually found advisable to locate a naturalistic pool against a background of shrubbery, rock garden, or some other terminating feature of the garden, unless the garden is of estate proportions, and the pool then becomes a pond. A formal pool may be isolated as a central feature, but a naturalistic pool is seldom successfully handled unless it is closely tied in with the general plan of the marginal planting. Its outline is frequently irregular, and gives plenty of opportunity for the use of the tall water plants in the nooks and pockets of the "shore-line" as well as in the background. However, in a small pool, it is necessary to use extreme care with the larger, coarser plant material, to keep the planting in scale. The desired effect is one of harmony with the surroundings, and any too-obvious rock work, or misplaced cat-tail clump will appear definitely grotesque.

### Plant Materials

A. Aquatics, other than lilies.
  I. Hardy aquatics: — 2–4 ft. tall.
    Nelumbium (lotus)
    Thalia dealbata (water canna)
    Pontederia cordata (pickerelweed)
    Typha latifolia (cat-tail)
    Typha angustifolia (cat-tail)
    Sagittaria sagittifolia *fl. pl.*
    Acorus calamus variegata (sweet flag)
  II. Tender aquatics
    a. *Free-floating*
      Salvinia auriculata
      Azolla caroliniana (azolla)
    b. *Plants that float, but do best if planted in shallow water where they may take root.*
      Eichhornia (water hyacinth)
      Pistia stratiotes (water lettuce)
      Ceratopteris pteridoides (water fern)
    c. *Plants that must take root in shallow water.*
      Hydrocleis nymphoides (water poppy)
      Myriophyllum proserpinacoides (parrot's-feather)
      Colocasia esculenta (taro)
      Cyperus papyrus (papyrus)
      Cyperus alternifolius (umbrella plant)
B. Water Lilies (*Nymphaea*); for the species *see* NYMPHAEA; those below are all hort. hybrids.
  I. Hardy water lilies
    a. *Red*
      N. James Brydon
      N. Attraction
    b. *Yellow*
      N. Sunrise
      N. marliacea chromatella

---

\* Special articles on the subjects indicated by an asterisk (\*) will be found at the words so marked.

    c. *Pink*
        N. formosa
        N. Eugenia de Land
    d. *Rose-orange*
        N. Sioux
        N. Paul Hariot
    e. *White*
        N. Gladstone
        N. Gonnere
II. Tropical water lilies
    a. Day-bloomers
        Viviparous (see VIVIPAROUS below)
        1. *Dark blue*
            N. August Koch
            N. Missouri Botanical Garden 151
        2. *Light blue*
            N. Mrs. Woodrow Wilson gigantea
        3. *Purple*
            N. Panama Pacific
        4. *White*
            Missouri Botanical Garden 197
        5. *Yellow*
            Missouri Botanical Garden 162
        6. *Light pink*
            Missouri Botanical Garden 104
        Non-viviparous (see VIVIPAROUS below)
        1. *Dark blue*
            N. Henry Shaw
            N. Blue Beauty (Pennsylvania)
        2. *Lavender-blue*
            N. Mrs. Edward Whitaker
        3. *White*
            N. Mrs. G. H. Pring
        4. *Yellow*
            N. St. Louis
        5. *Pink*
            N. General Pershing
    b. Night-bloomers
        1. *White*
            N. Missouri
        2. *Red*
            N. Frank Trelease
            N. H. C. Haarstick
        3. *Pink*
            N. Omarana
            N. Emily Grant Hutchings
            N. Mrs. Geo. C. Hitchcock
III. Pigmies (for tubs and small pools)
    A wide range of colors is available in the following types
        N. tetragona....white
        N. tetragona helvola....yellow

## WATER LILIES

Water lilies will make up the main feature in a water garden, since they bloom all summer long, and are quite capable of providing a lovely spectacle with no help from any other plants. There are the hardy types of lilies, which may be left in the ground all winter long; and there are the tropical lilies, which provide the large, fragrant blooms so much admired in any pool large enough to accommodate their size. A pool 6 to 8 feet will hold three comfortably. The tropical lilies are divided into day and night bloomers. When the temperature is above 70° the night bloomers will be open from 7 P.M. to about 9 A.M., the day bloomers opening at 8 A.M. and closing at 6 P.M. A cooler temperature and cloudy weather will often keep the day bloomers asleep, and waken the night bloomers to full activity all day long... so there is no possibility of missing a glorious all-summer display if both types of the tropical lilies are planted.

VIVIPAROUS LILIES. Another division of the tropical lilies is found in the day-blooming class, which is now divided into viviparous and non-viviparous types. Due to the extreme ease of propagation of the viviparous types, they are becoming increasingly popular, particularly since they are now available in a full range of colors. These viviparous day-blooming tropical lilies produce in the center of each mature leaf a tiny new plant, complete from roots to leaves. Details are given in the section on propagation of the treatment of this new plant. Non-viviparous tropical lilies are best treated as annuals, being replaced every spring.

PLANTING. The time for planting will be governed by your geographical location. The water must be at least 70°, as a minimum, since the tropical lilies especially are susceptible to chilling in cooler water, and will become dormant. Frequently dealers are blamed for sending poor plants, when in reality the lilies have merely gone back to sleep in water which was too cold.

In planting, the tuber* should be set with the crown just below the surface of the soil. As the lily grows, the water level should be raised until it is a foot above the roots. The plants will bloom about July 1st, and continue until killed back by frost. The hardy lilies grow from continuously dividing rhizomes, like iris, and require transplanting every four years. When grown in boxes, fresh soil should be added at the time of removal. Plant the rhizomes* in early spring about 2-3 inches deep.

SOIL. Where the pool is given a natural bottom, the soil should be very well fertilized before the lilies are planted. Both tropical and hardy water lilies are rank feeders, and require plenty of rich food. When a concrete pool has been built, spread about two inches of manure over the bottom, followed by eight inches of sod-soil. The lilies will do well in this, but if the pool is small the gardener is not so likely to be satisfied. It is absolutely essential in a small pool to keep it well stocked with fish to prevent the mosquito menace, and fish will so stir up a pond whose bottom is covered with soil that the water will be constantly muddy. To avoid this, plant your lilies in boxes two to three feet square and a foot deep, or in half-barrels, placing manure in the bottom and filling up with sod soil. The concrete bottom can then be left clear, and the surface of the water covered with floating plants. In the corners and along the edges of the pool it is possible to construct ledges or pockets for the larger plants like lotus and cat-tails, whose root-space must be restricted to keep them from usurping the entire area. By carrying up the wall of the pocket almost to the surface, the roots of the plants may be protected from the nibbling fish.

PROPAGATION. The hardy lilies which grow from a creeping rhizome or underground stem may be propagated merely by dividing the clump in early spring and planting the growing tips, exactly as the familiar garden iris is handled. The tricks of propagation are called into play only with the tropical lilies. Here the old tubers are of little use, and it is actually a waste of time to dig them up. For new lilies, then, it is necessary either to buy new plants or to make use of one of the three available methods for propagating the tropical lilies. These are (1) seeds, (2) leaf propagation, (3) tubers, the second being confined to the viviparous hybrids from *N. micrantha* parentage.

(1) *Seeds*. In view of the mongrel ancestry of our cultivated lilies their seeds will be valueless if you expect them to produce plants like their father or mother. You may obtain a lily worth growing, but you will almost never get one which really resembles one of its immediate parents, even in controlled pollination. However, if you have the space for experimenting and are interested in producing new varieties, you may check up on the vagaries of the ancestors by keeping a record of crosses you make and seeing what comes out in the children. Pick out two lilies which you wish to cross, and remove the stamens from the one you decide to use as a seed-bearer. This will prevent self-pollination. The time to place the pollen from the stamens of the one flower on the pistil of the seed-bearing lily from which the stamens have been removed can be judged by the condition of the pistil, and will be somewhere between 10 A.M. and 12 noon on the first day.

After dusting the pollen from the one flower onto the pistil of the other, cover the pollinated flower with thin muslin and attach it to a stake, with enough string to permit the flower lowering itself under the water. This is the natural position for it to assume while the seed is developing. After about three weeks the seed-pod will again rise to the surface, and

---

* Special articles on the subjects indicated by an asterisk (*) will be found at the words so marked.

unless the pod has been wrapped with muslin as indicated above, the seeds will have been broadcast over the surface of the water by the natural opening of the seed-pod.

In order to disintegrate the fleshy covering of the seeds, place them in a battery jar of water for three or four days to ripen them. When they are fully ripened, the virile seeds will sink to the bottom, and should be removed from the water at once to prevent premature germination. Dry them for two or three days, and when they separate readily, sow them in sandy soil in shallow pans or in glass battery jars half filled with water. Barely cover the seeds with fine sand, and gently firm the soil to prevent the seeds rising when water is placed in the pan or jar. Place the container in tanks heated to about 75° to 80° F., and as soon as the seedlings develop their floating leaves, transplant them to small pots for development, maintaining the same temperature all winter.

(2) *Leaf propagation.* As has been stated, this is limited to the viviparous varieties, but in view of the extreme ease of multiplying lilies in this fashion, it is suggested that the amateur confine his list to these forms for re-stocking his pool with tropical lilies, until he becomes sufficiently familiar with his plants to use their tubers. The tiny plants formed in the center of each mature leaf may be cut out when the old leaf begins to turn yellow. Remove a small portion of the stem with the little plant, to act as a brace in the pot. The pots may be left in the pool all summer and brought inside into heated tanks at about the end of September.

(3) *Tuber propagation.* This is the only method of producing true type lilies from the non-viviparous tropical forms. The original tubers which are planted out of doors are of no use in carrying the lilies over the winter; but at their base during the summer are formed small nut-like tubers which will bring forth new plants in great numbers if properly handled. At the end of August or early September, remove these tubers from the base of the old one, and place each one of them in sand for two or three weeks to rest. Be sure to keep them in a tin container with a firmly attached top during this resting period, since both rats and mice relish them.

After the resting period, place each tuber in the bottom of a pot filled with sandy soil. The depth of planting will induce the tuber to grow a long radicle* when placed in a tank of water heated to a temperature of about 80°. The young leaves will appear in about two weeks, and when the plants have formed two floating leaves the time is ripe for removing them from their tubers. Dig into the soil with thumb and finger; locate the radicle or stem by feeling the top of the tuber; and pinch off the stem just above the tuber, removing the young plant with roots and all, and potting it up immediately to prevent drying out. Leave the tuber in its pot, and it will continue to send off these young plants.

VICTORIA CRUZIANA (The water platter)

This lily, while belonging to the night-blooming tropical group, is so distinctive in habit as to require a separate treatment. It has enormous circular leaves with up-turned edges, strengthened underneath by a net-work of veins which makes it capable of supporting a great weight. The writer, who weighs 160 pounds, has stood upon a leaf on which a cotton pad and wooden frame or composition board was placed to equalize his weight and prevent the leaf from being torn. The exterior of the flowers, stems, leaves and seed-pods are covered with dagger-like spines, which necessitates the use of great care in handling; but as a curiosity it is unequaled in water-gardening, and is worth the trouble it causes.

The flowers bloom at night, being white when opening, and turning gradually to a darker pink. The older blooms have a fragrance similar to the pineapple, and are very large, often measuring a foot or more in diameter. The plant attains a great size when grown in rich soil and given plenty of room, but it will remain small if limited in space and food; so it is possible to grow it even in a small pool. However, to accommodate its full beauty, the pool should be at least 20 feet in diameter, and the soil thoroughly enriched with fertilizer. These plants will frequently produce from eight to ten of their enormous leaves at one time, all growing from the center, and as the stems develop it is necessary to peg them down to prevent the giant leaves from tearing and turning over during wind storms. The flowers are proportionally large and handsome, and it is well worth while to turn over a large pool to one of these tropical beauties.

Since they are a pure species, they will come true from seed, but the growing season is only about four months, except in the southern states, which is not sufficient time to ripen the pods in the pool. When the first light freeze comes, cut off the seed-pods and bring them into a tub of water in the greenhouse. In about six weeks the seeds will free themselves from the pod and show a light yellow color, and may then be separated from the pulp and spines by screening... being even more careful of the spines than usual, since they are most dangerous in this free state.

Pack the seeds in a covered tin box between layers of moist sand, keeping them at a temperature of about 60°. When the seeds are fully ripened, they will be about the size of an ordinary garden pea, and dark brown or black in color. This process may take as long as two years, but it is essential for them to be fully ripe to germinate. Seeds have germinated in the pool at the Missouri Botanical Garden in St. Louis three years after the plant had been grown in the pond, even though it was drained each winter.

When the seeds are ripe, plant them about March 1st at twice their depth in a medium of half sand and half soil, screened through a ½-inch mesh. Use a shallow pan as a container, submerging it in a tank of water about three inches above the top of the pan, and keeping at a temperature of 80°. In three or four weeks, a needle-like shoot will appear, followed by a submerged, lance-shaped leaf and an ovate floating leaf. When two floating leaves appear, separate the seedlings and plant in 3-inch pots in a mixture of ¾ sod-soil and ¼ sand. When the roots have filled the pot, transplant to a shallow, 8-inch pot, which should be large enough to contain the plant until it may be placed outside.

The period of outdoor planting depends upon your geographical location. The water must be about 75°–80°, which in St. Louis is usually between June 1st and June 15th. When a natural pond is available, an area of 100 square feet should be covered with 2 inches of cow manure or one ounce per cubic foot of an inorganic fertilizer consisting of 15 parts of nitrogen, 30 of phosphoric acid and 15 of potash. Spade in to a depth of one foot, and mound it up slightly at the center of the area to indicate the place of planting. Fertilizing may be done also while the plant is still potted up indoors, and the leaves when brought outside should be about one foot in diameter if the plant is to be forced to a maximum size. With plenty of room for the roots, and the free use of manure, the plant may be brought to giant proportions in eight weeks. — G. H. P.

**WATER HAWTHORN** = *Aponogeton distachyus*.

**WATER HEMLOCK.** See CICUTA.

**WATER HOLLY** = *Mahonia nervosa*.

**WATER HOREHOUND.** See LYCOPUS.

**WATER HYACINTH.** Very showy, chiefly South American, floating aquatic plants constituting the genus **Eichhornia** (ike-hor′ni-a) of the family Pontederiaceae, often grown for ornament in warm pools, or outdoors in the Far South, but unable to stand frost. In Fla. and in several tropical countries the water hyacinth has become a major pest, completely choking otherwise navigable streams. This should be kept in mind in planting it.

They have floating leaves, the stalk of *E. crassipes* much inflated and spongy with air-chambers, the blade more or less erect. Flowers in a terminal cluster on a fleshy stalk, rising well above the water. Corolla irregular,* of 6 segments, more or less funnel-shaped. Stamens* 6, some of them protruding. Fruit a 3-celled capsule.* (Named for J. A. F. Eichhorn, Prussian minister.) The plants are often known as *Piaropus*.

These extremely attractive aquatics are easily grown in shallow pools or even in tubs of water. They may be propagated by division, but in all warm regions the difficulty is to prevent them from propagating too fast.

---

* Special articles on the subjects indicated by an asterisk (*) will be found at the words so marked.

**E. azurea.** Leaves variable, generally broadly oval or roundish, the stalk not inflated. Flower stalk gradually inflated into a hood-like organ, the lavender-blue, purple-centered flowers scattered or in pairs along the hairy stalk. Brazil.

**E. crassipes.** The common water hyacinth, upon which Fla. has spent thousands of dollars for eradication. Leafstalk much inflated and spongy, the blade ovalish or roundish, 2-5 in. wide. Flower spikes profuse, the flowers violet, the upper lobes blue-patched and yellow-spotted. Throughout tropical America, and naturalized in Fla. An extremely handsome aquatic with fine feathery roots which show attractively in an aquarium.

**WATERING.** Water is not only a plant nutrient in itself, but also the conveyer of other food constituents taken up in solution through the medium of the root hairs. Its proper application calls for good judgment on the part of the grower, especially in the cultivation of plants under glass, where it becomes a matter of daily importance. Skill in watering comes from practice and close observation of the conditions which govern the amount of water each plant requires. Neither the amount nor the frequency of its application can be definitely stated, weather conditions alone being too variable.

Large-leaved and actively growing softwooded plants require more than those of slower and harder growth, while any plant should be watered less frequently when in a state of rest. Plants get dry much faster under the influence of strong light and dry air, due to the more rapid loss of water by transpiration through the leaves. Subdued light and a moisture-laden atmosphere tend to reduce the amount of water needed at the roots, and are important factors in the growth of many plants. Leaf wilting follows when the soil becomes so dry that the roots are unable to supply enough water to keep the cells distended.

Some plants will recover from an occasional flagging with no apparent injury, but hardwooded plants in pots may not readily recover if allowed to get so dry. Complete immersion of the pot for a few minutes is the best way to assist recovery, but it is well to avoid the need for such treatment. Strong sunlight following a cloudy period sometimes causes the leaves of fast-growing plants to wilt when there is no lack of water at the roots. In such a case the proper balance is restored by spraying the leaves or otherwise creating atmospheric moisture to check the rate of transpiration, and so avoid overwatering.

Plants set out in beds or benches will not require such frequent watering as those in pots, but in any case it should be well done when needed. Mere surface waterings will not supply the needs. On the other hand, except for aquatics, plants object to soil that is continually saturated. Proper drainage is therefore necessary to allow the free passage of water which the soil does not readily absorb. Benches may be watered by sub-irrigation, in which case the water is distributed through lines of tile laid on water-tight bottoms. While effective, it increases construction costs. Plants should be thoroughly soaked before being re-potted. It is generally best to water immediately after, then wait for the soil to get somewhat dry before repeating. Overwatering before the roots get working freely in the new soil is likely to cause trouble.

Excessive moisture about the plants at night during winter is likely to cause trouble, so watering is best done early in the day. In late spring and summer, water may be needed more than once on bright days, but with free ventilation late watering will do no harm. In the watering of seedpans special care is needed. Some prefer to water well before sowing the seeds, and have found boiling water used at this time efficacious in preventing troubles which may bother seedlings, especially those of slow germination. Overhead watering of seeds through the fine rose of a carefully handled watering can is generally safe. With very fine seeds it may be safer to water from below by partial immersion of the soil container as required.

A question often asked by those wishing to keep plants in the home is, How often should I water my plants? Conditions are so variable that the only safe reply is, "When needed." One thing is certain, never give water in driblets, but enough to ensure a thorough soaking all the way through. The frequency of watering will depend on the kind of plant, its condition of growth, the temperature of the room, and the moisture content of the air. It is chiefly the hot and dry air of the average room that is so detrimental to the well-being of many plants in the home. Anything that can be done to modify this condition, such as standing the pots on a tray of moist sand or gravel, will be of material help to the plants. On the other hand, except for such moisture-loving plants as the calla lily, it is not good for plants to be kept standing in water in a jardiniere.* Succulent plants are so constructed that they lose moisture very slowly by transpiration, and many of these are excellent plants for the home if placed in good light. While needing to be watered less often than leafy plants, good drainage is essential.

Where pot plants are used to furnish inside window boxes, filling the spaces between the pots with sphagnum moss helps to check dryness. Such boxes may be made with a false bottom, from which surplus water can be drawn off through a stopcock. Window boxes and hanging baskets with devices for watering by sub-irrigation work out very well in places where drip would be a nuisance. Wire hanging baskets lined with moss need to be immersed occasionally to ensure sufficient moisture. Large plants in tubs will need careful attention, especially in exposed positions. A removable outer shell of larger size, to allow of an insulation of damp moss, would be of help in keeping the roots cool and moist.

It has long been known by plantsmen that soft rain-water has a more kindly effect on plants than hard water, and also that they prefer it at about the same temperature in which they are growing.—H. E. D.

**WATERING POT OR CAN.** See Section I, TOOLS AND IMPLEMENTS.

**WATERLEAF.** See HYDROPHYLLUM.

**WATER LEMON** = *Passiflora laurifolia*.

**WATER LETTUCE** = *Pistia stratiotes*.

**WATER LILY.** See NYMPHAEA. See also WATER GARDEN.

**WATER LOCUST** = *Gleditsia aquatica*. See HONEY LOCUST.

**WATERMELON.** The common watermelon is the only cult. species of the genus Citrullus (sit-trull'us) of the cucumber family. A variety of it is the citron, sometimes called the preserving melon. *Citrullus* contains only 4 or 5 species, all from tropical Africa, but one of them also found in Asia. The watermelon is **C. vulgaris**, a long-running, annual, very tender, prostrate vine with branched tendrils* (the tendrils are unbranched in the closely related muskmelon; see CUCUMIS). Leaves alternate,* broad, but divided into segments. Flowers light yellow, about 1½ in. wide, solitary in the leaf-axils,* the male and female separate, but on the same plant. Corolla shallowly funnel-shaped, deeply 5-parted. Stamens* 5, but apparently 3 because two pairs are united. Fruit berry-like, but with a hard rind (a pepo), green in the familiar watermelon in which the flesh is red or pink and very watery. In the *var.* **citroides,** the citron or preserving melon, the fruit is much smaller and the flesh is hard, white, and useful only when cooked. Tropical and South Africa. (*Citrullus* is a diminutive of *Citrus*, probably in some unknown allusion to the fruit.) For the Chinese watermelon see BENINCASA.

### WATERMELON CULTURE

The watermelon requires a long, hot growing season; it does not succeed as far north as the cantaloupe, but does well under high humidity and is grown extensively in the southern sections of the U.S. When grown in northern sections, early-maturing varieties must be selected or the plants started under protection and set in the field after frost. A fertile sandy loam is a preferable soil type; it must be well drained and free from alkali.

The culture of the watermelon is similar to that of the cantaloupe or muskmelon except that it requires more room. See MELON.

For highest quality the watermelon should be picked when fully ripe but not over-ripe. It is difficult to determine the proper stage, as the fruit shows very few external changes in

---

* Special articles on the subjects indicated by an asterisk (*) will be found at the words so marked.

size or color as it ripens. When green, the fruit gives forth a metallic ring when thumped; this sound becomes more muffled or deader with increasing ripeness. It is advisable to test this and other criteria of ripeness by cutting occasional melons in the field to secure the knack of picking at the proper stage.

The most important varieties are Tom Watson (shipping), Stone Mountain or Dixie Bell, Rattlesnake, Irish Grey, Kleckly Sweet, Cole's Early, Halbret Honey, and Klondyke and Striped Klondyke (Calif. only).

Pumpkins or squash can have no possible effect on flavor or quality of adjacent melons.

Because of the size and length of the vines watermelons cannot be grown where space is limited. The vines should be at least 6 ft. apart each way. — G. W. S.

INSECT PESTS. The most important pests are cucumber beetles and melon aphids. Pickle worms have little effect on watermelon (see CUCUMBER and MELON).

DISEASES. The diseases of the cantaloupe and watermelon are very similar. One of the worst is foot-rot for which there is no control. By far the most common disease is bacterial wilt, which is carried by various beetles. In young plants destroy the beetles. Older plants may be sprayed with bordeaux mixture. Do not put old vines on the compost pile as the disease may winter-over.

Downy mildew also affects melon vines and the best control is spraying with bordeaux mixture. There are many other diseases of the melon, most of them similar to the disease of cucumber (which see for control, especially the treatment of seed before planting).

**WATER-MILFOIL.** See MYRIOPHYLLUM.

**WATER OAK** = *Quercus nigra*. See OAK.

**WATER PLANTAIN** = *Alisma plantago-aquatica*.

**WATER PLANTS.** See WATER GARDEN, BOG GARDEN.

**WATER PLATTER.** See VICTORIA.

**WATER POPPY** = *Hydrocleis nymphoides*.

**WATER RICE** = *Zizania aquatica*.

**WATER SHIELD.** See CABOMBA and BRASENIA SCHREBERI.

**WATER SNOWFLAKE** = *Nymphoides indicum*.

**WATER-SOLDIER.** See STRATIOTES.

**WATER SPROUT.** See SUCKER.

**WATER SUPPLY.** See IRRIGATION.

**WATER-WEED** = *Elodea canadensis*.

**WATER WILLOW** = *Decodon verticillatus*.

**WATSONIA** (wat-sō'ni-a). Bugle-lily. South African, gladiolus-like herbs of the iris family, comprising perhaps 30 species, of which three are sometimes cult. for ornament, but better known in Calif. than in the East. They have basal, sword-shaped leaves, sometimes a few on the stem, and rather showy flowers in a terminal cluster (raceme*), the corolla differing from the closely related *Gladiolus* in being nearly regular,* the tube curved. Fruit a 3-celled capsule.* (Named for Sir William Watson, English botanist.)

The culture of watsonias, which are summer-blooming, is the same as for gladiolus (which see).

**angusta.** Nearly 4 ft. high. Flowers scarlet, the tube not expanding upward, the segments tapering, about 1 in. long.

**iridifolia.** Nearly 4 ft. high. Flowers nearly 3 in. long, pink, the tube longer than the segments. The var. **o'brieni** has white flowers.

**rosea.** From 3-6 ft. high. Flowers rose-red, the tube flaring towards the top and as long as the segments.

**WATTLE.** See ACACIA.

**WAUKEGAN JUNIPER** = *Juniperus horizontalis douglasi*.

**WAX.** The chief use of wax is in grafting. For the preparation of the sort so used see GRAFTING WAX. The other use of wax is to cover young whips,* buds, cions, etc., with a thin film in packing them for transportation. The wax prevents them drying out and can easily be removed by melting, without injury to the buds.

**WAX BEAN** = *Phaseolus vulgaris*. For culture see BEAN.

**WAXBERRY** = *Symphoricarpos albus*.

**WAX DOLLS** = *Fumaria officinalis*. See FUMITORY.

**WAX FLOWER** = *Stephanotis floribunda*.

**WAX GOURD** = *Benincasa hispida*.

**WAX MYRTLE** = *Myrica cerifera*.

**WAX PALM** = *Ceroxylon andicolum*.

**WAX PINK** = *Portulaca grandiflora*.

**WAX-PLANT** = *Hoya carnosa*.

**WAX PRIVET** = *Ligustrum japonicum*. See PRIVET.

**WAXWINGS.** See BIRDS.

**WAXWORK** = *Celastrus scandens*.

**WAYFARING-TREE** = *Viburnum lantana*.

**WAYTHORN** = *Rhamnus cathartica*.

**WEATHER.** See CLIMATE.

**WEAVER'S BROOM** = *Spartium junceum*.

**WEBWORMS.** See Insect Pests at APPLE, MULBERRY, and PERSIMMON.

**WEEDS AND WEEDING.** Weeds are plants out of place. The effects of weeds are many. They flourish more readily than most cultivated plants. They have a direct influence on

In hoeing out weeds, remember that they quickly die if left on the surface of the soil.

the devaluation of property — and often the reputation of the owner. The expense of clearing weeds will often adversely impress a prospective buyer. Some weeds are hosts* for fungi, rusts, and insects which may spread to garden plants. Others, like poison ivy and black nightshade, are poisonous either externally or internally.

### THE KINDS

Weeds, for the practical gardener, may be put under two main headings, annual* and perennial.* Neither should be tolerated in any garden, and in commercial nurseries or market gardens few are found, for they are a costly extravagance. Because of their different life spans annual and perennial weeds must be treated differently, but for both cultivation* is always right in their early stages, for it leaves the roots exposed. The list of weeds at the end gives special directions for both classes, where cultivation is not sufficient.

---

* Special articles on the subjects indicated by an asterisk (*) will be found at the words so marked.

## Annual Weeds

Because of their short life span, many gardeners think annual weeds may be neglected because they will soon die out or can be easily exterminated. A dense crop of several generations, however, means a costly clearing not only locally, but wherever the seed has had time to scatter. Annual weeds are the most persistent in cultivated gardens, but are fortunately very easily controlled if cultivation is regular and well done. Even winter annuals,* while more difficult to control, can be destroyed by early spring cultivation.

## Perennial Weeds

These invade and persist in lawns and permanent crops like strawberry, asparagus and perennial flower borders. When full grown they have to be individually hand-weeded or dug out. In the case of lawn infestation, strong weed killers (see below) are necessary.

The most effective means of control in a regularly cropped garden is annual trenching or deep digging of all spare ground. While many weeds have powerful and long-lived rootstocks, the great majority will not survive deep burial. The turned-up soil will reveal any deep-rooted ones which should be picked out whole. Regular cultivation after this will take care of any seed blown from neglected lots, whether annual or perennial, but the cultivation must be prompt to prevent deep-rooted perennials from getting a start.

A continual cutting of the green leaves will effectively remove the most vital source of nourishment to some weed roots and thus starve them out.

Should a plot harbor weeds like thistles and dandelions, the cleanest method to reclaim the soil would be deep plowing or trenching.*

Weeds in paths, drives, crazy paving and rock gardens present other problems. In the hands of a careful distributor, the commercial weed killers are easy and effective (see Weed Killers below). Weeding annuals from crazy paving and rock gardens may be simple, but perennials follow the half-buried stones so thoroughly that it is often most effective to take up and relay the stones in a crazy path. Around large rocks a constant warfare must be kept up to break the heart of any persistent weed roots, such as sheep's-sorrel, knotweed or quack grass.

For surface weeds, where weed killers are impossible, a Dutch or "D" hoe is the most effective and quickest tool to use. By working backwards the soil is not trodden down and the weeds in the surface mulch, with their necks broken, do not revive after a shower.

## Lawn Weeds

Weedy lawns present a problem by themselves. Perennials are the main source of trouble, but if annuals like chickweed or crab grass once invade the lawn, they outrun all perennials in exasperating persistency. The latter pest has become most notorious. A condition of high acidity, however, discourages its growth, and this may be secured by the liberal use of peat moss and sheep manure. This not only benefits a poor soil but will also check chickweed, which will often disappear with the use of sheep manure alone. If the lawn is of Kentucky bluegrass, however, the acidity cannot be increased too much. See Lawn.

If the lawn grasses are strong, but invaded by deep-rooting dandelions, plantains or prickly lettuce, the best method would be to apply sulphate of iron through a spring gun to the heart of every weed or to dust it on the tender, flat weed leaves. Grass itself is most resistant to this weed killer, owing to the fineness of its blades. Any damaged grass leaves are quickly removed by mowing.

Lawn sand, which includes sulphate of iron, is a favorite spring dressing. Spread broadcast, it invigorates the grass and burns up all flat weed leaves it touches.

For persistent, shallow-rooted lawn weeds there is a long-handled weeder that grips like long pincers, with two inches of steel thrust on either side of the weed. See Section 1, Tools and Implements.

One of the main sources of weeds is cheap grass seed and the penalty of one year's bad seeding may be seven years' weeding. Just as clean seed should be used for lawns, equal care should be taken in the use of lawn dressings. (See Lawn.) Heat and fermentation are the main destroyers of weed seed, but do not trust too much to farmyard manures. Many new weeds have traveled long distances by way of the manure heap.

## Weed Killers

Chemical weed killers are most effective in places where cultivation is impossible, as on roadways, tennis courts and garden paths. They may be used as liquids (plainly labeled "poison") through a rose-spouted watering pot or as a powder dusted on the damp weed foliage. Take care not to pour these poisons within six inches of grass edges or borders with live surface roots. The untreated six inches must be hand-weeded or hoed off. Dwarf shrub borders may be protected from splashes by light boards placed alongside. Apply weed killer after a rain or after wetting the weeds down first. Do not walk from the treated places to borders or the vegetable garden. The leading weed killers are:

1. Sulphate of Iron (sometimes called copperas). Fifty gallons will spray an acre of grass or road surface, applied when the soil is moist but in fair weather, so that the solution is not in danger of being washed from the foliage. Mix 75 pounds of sulphate of iron to 50 gallons of water and allow it to dissolve. The speediest killing is done when the leaves are bruised, so they should be rolled or brush-harrowed before treatment. A power sprayer is more effective and economical on a large area, but it can be applied with a watering pot over small ones. Caution: Do not use sulphate of iron on a lawn planted with creeping bent. See Lawn.

2. Chlorate of Soda. This is a familiar weed killer for deep-rooted and obnoxious weeds in places where there is no other herbage. It is sometimes confused with caustic soda. Chlorate of Soda is very useful for drives and paths, especially bluestone walks. One pound of Chlorate of Soda to four gallons of water is a good mixture for deep-rooted weeds and its effects will last all summer. For shallow-rooted weeds use it at half the strength. It dissolves very rapidly, and should be stirred with a wooden stick or metal rod. It must be kept away from garden plants.

3. Carbolic Acid (commercial) is extensively used for deep-rooted weeds. It should be controlled from a needle syringe or an oil can. It is quick-acting but expensive and dangerously poisonous. It can be used with any kind of metal can or pump, but must be constantly stirred.

Four common garden weeds, numbered as in the list on pages 865 and 866. No. 10 — chickweed; No. 11 — Crab grass; No. 13 — Curled dock; No. 35 — Purslane.

* Special articles on the subjects indicated by an asterisk (*) will be found at the words so marked.

4. COMMON SALT is the most convenient and safest killer for a small garden and where dangerous poisons are a worry. It is applied in hot weather when nourishment is more easily absorbed by the weeds, and for this reason it cannot be used carelessly on a lawn. One pound of salt to a gallon of water made into a hot brine will eradicate bad weeds very quickly.

5. BLUESTONE OR COPPER SULPHATE is used for clearing fungus and toadstools from lawns. Mix twelve pounds of Bluestone with fifty gallons of water, use through a mist spray on a fine day.

There are commercial weed killers that are ready to use if these mixtures cannot be easily made and stored. All of them have directions, and in addition many seedsmen carry all sorts of pumps and dusters for applying them. — W. J. I.

### THE FIFTY WORST GARDEN WEEDS

Of the hundreds of naturalized weeds in America, mostly of European or Asiatic origin, the following appear to be either the most common or most troublesome. It should not be forgotten, however, that they seldom trouble good gardeners who know that constant cultivation will kill all weed seedlings and so prevent permanent infestation.

Those marked with a dagger (†) are annual.* All the rest are perennial,* except a few noted as biennial.*

To aid in identifying them they may be grouped thus:
Grasses: Numbers 11, 36, 39
Low or prostrate weeds: Numbers 2, 10, 12, 16, 20, 21, 23, 26, 34, 35, 40, 41, 45, 46, 47
Obviously creeping or climbing plants: Numbers 3, 15, 16, 17, 32
Erect weeds prickly on the stems, leaves or flower-cluster: Numbers 6, 7, 18, 33, 38, 44
Erect weeds of varying heights but never prickly.
White flowered: Numbers 4, 24, 43, 50
Yellow flowered: Numbers 1, 5, 8, 14, 24, 27, 49
Blue or purple: Numbers 9, 41
Red, pink or orange: Numbers 9, 29, 41, 50
Greenish, or inconspicuous: Numbers 13, 22, 25, 28, 30, 31, 37, 42, 48

†1. **Beggar-ticks** (*Bidens frondosa*). Called also boot-jack and Spanish needles. Yellow-flowered stout herb with compound* leaves and barbed fruit that sticks to clothing. Tillage is the remedy.

2. **Bird's-foot trefoil** (*Lotus corniculatus*). Low clover-like herb with yellow flower heads. Spray iron sulphate for lawn infestation; cultivate it out of the garden. *See* LOTUS CORNICULATUS.

†3. **Black bindweed** (*Polygonum convolvulus*). A rampant twining vine with heart-shaped or halberd-shaped leaves on long stalks. Often called wild buckwheat. Easily killed by cultivation. *See also* 21, 22.

†4. **Black nightshade** (*Solanum nigrum*). Wilted foliage very poisonous. Erect herb with oval leaves, small white flowers in drooping clusters and black fruit. Very common but easily controlled by cultivation. *See also* 18.

5. **Bulbous buttercup** (*Ranunculus bulbosus*). Deep-rooted buttercup with the familiar yellow flowers. Often a serious pest in lawns from which it must be dug. Cultivation will control it in the garden. There are many other species. *See also* 12.

6. **Burdock** (*Arctium lappa*). A coarse biennial,* resembling a thistle but with only the flower-head and fruits prickly. Leaves large, green above and whitish beneath, the stalks deeply furrowed. Flower-heads loosely clustered, purplish or whitish. Its bur-like fruit sticks to clothing by minute hooked prickles. Cut it off below ground. Called, also, gobo and great burdock.

7. **Canada thistle** (*Cirsium arvense*). A deep-rooted, smooth-stemmed but prickly leaved herb with showy purple flowers in a tight head. Perhaps the most pernicious European weed ever introduced into America. Proof against most chemicals, and cultivation does not reach deep enough to kill the root. It must be dug out.

8. **Cat's-ear** (*Hypochaeris radicata*). Called also gosmore and California dandelion. Erect herb with dandelion-like, but smaller, flower heads and leaves like a cat's ear. Cultivate or apply caustic soda.

9. **Chicory** (*Cichorium intybus*). Deep-rooted plant with alternate cut leaves and handsome blue, pink or purplish flowers in solitary stalkless heads. Must be dug, when old, but cultivation will kill young plants. *See* CICHORIUM INTYBUS.

†10. **Chickweed** (*Stellaria media*). A general garden pest. Low, with oval leaves on hairy stalks and tiny white flowers with 4 or 5 petals. Cultivation for the garden or spraying sulphate of iron on the lawn. It must sometimes (*i.e.* in times when the soil is too moist to cult.) be pulled out by hand from seedbeds or borders. *See also* Lawn Weeds above.

†11. **Crab grass** (*Digitaria sanguinalis*). A bad lawn pest, often called finger-grass. It spreads and roots at the joints, and sends up a long stalk with finger-like, spreading spikes. Hand weed it or spray sulphate of iron. *See also* Lawn Weeds above.

12. **Creeping buttercup** (*Ranunculus repens*). Low prostrate herb with small yellow flowers. Mostly a lawn weed and there treated with sulphate of iron or dilute solution of caustic soda. Called also creeping crowfoot and sitfast. *See also* 5.

13. **Curled dock** (*Rumex crispus*). Deep-rooted, pernicious weed with wavy-margined narrow leaves and a dense terminal cluster of greenish, small flowers. Must be dug out. There are many other species. *See also* 42.

14. **Dandelion** (*Taraxacum officinale*). Golden-headed tramp with a deep root. Apply caustic soda, in drops, in the lawn or dig out. Cultivate it out of the garden.

15. **Field bindweed** (*Convolvulus arvensis*). A creeping vine with arrow-shaped leaves and flowers resembling a small, whitish-pink morning-glory. It has deep white rootstocks which must be dug or killed with caustic soda. A persistent and pernicious pest. *See also* 17.

16. **Ground ivy** (*Nepeta hederacea*). Creeping plant with roundish, scalloped leaves and small, light blue flowers clustered in the axils.* Easily killed by cultivation. Spray sulphate of iron on lawns. Called also Gill-over-the-ground and field balm. *See* NEPETA HEDERACEA.

17. **Hedge bindweed** (*Convolvulus sepium*). Resembling the field bindweed but with leaves and flowers nearly twice the size and with the leaves roundish. It is sometimes called Rutland Beauty. Treatment same as field bindweed (No. 15).

18. **Horse nettle** (*Solanum carolinense*). Deep-rooted, pernicious, prickly pest. Erect or straggling stems, irregularly lobed or cut leaves, potato-like, blue or white flowers followed by yellow berries. Cultivate or kill with caustic soda. *See also* 4.

19. **Horsetail** (*Equisetum arvense*). Leafless herb having whorls* of thread-like branches and a terminal yellowish cone. Very persistent and must be frequently cultivated.

†20. **Knawel** (*Scleranthus annuus*). Low, spreading weed with tiny thread-like leaves and very small green flowers. Cultivate or spray sulphate of iron on lawns.

21. **Knotweed** (*Polygonum aviculare*). Prostrate, very wiry herb with bluish-gray very small leaves and still smaller greenish, pink-margined flowers. Cultivate it out of the garden and pull it out of the lawn, filling the space with white clover. *See also* 3, 22.

†22. **Lady's-thumb** (*Polygonum persicaria*). Erect herb with a conspicuous dark spot on the leaves and a spike of small, inconspicuous, pinkish-white flowers. Kill it by cultivation. *See also* 3, 21.

23. **Mallow** (*Malva rotundifolia*). Really a biennial.* Low, nearly prostrate herb with alternate, roundish, long-stalked leaves and white solitary flowers in the axils.* Cultivate from the garden and spray lawn with sulphate of iron, or use the dilute solution of caustic soda. Called also cheeses.

†24. **Mayweed** (*Anthemis cotula*). Called also dog fennel. A rank-smelling, upright weed with dissected leaves and white-flowered heads with a yellow center. Decorative, but should be exterminated by cultivation.

25. **Mexican tea** (*Chenopodium ambrosioides*). The strongest-smelling of all our weeds. Stout herb (sometimes an annual) with cut or merely toothed, nearly stalkless leaves

---

* Special articles on the subjects indicated by an asterisk (*) will be found at the words so marked.

and a terminal leafy cluster of minute, very numerous, greenish flowers. Cultivation kills it. Common in the garden or dooryards, rare in the lawn. See also 30, 48.

26. **Mouse-ear chickweed** (*Cerastium vulgatum*). Low, creeping weed with opposite* leaves and small white flowers on erect stalks. Most common in lawns where it must be dug, or spray with sulphate of iron.

27. **Mouse-ear hawkweed** (*Hieracium pilosella*). Somewhat resembling the orange hawkweed, but with yellow flowers. Treat as for orange hawkweed, No. 29.

†28. **Orach** (*Atriplex patula*). A dry-soil weed, pale green and often somewhat scurfy or mealy on its slender-stalked, narrowly arrow-shaped leaves. It has inconspicuous flowers in slender, discontinuous spikes. Easily killed by cultivation.

29. **Orange hawkweed** (*Hieracium aurantiacum*). A persistent, very prolific weed in fields and lawns, less common in gardens. It has basal hairy leaves and long-stalked heads of very showy orange flowers. Shallow-rooted and easily controlled by cultivation. Spray lawns with sulphate of iron. Called also devil's-paintbrush. See also 27.

†30. **Pigweed** (*Chenopodium album*). One of the commonest weeds in America, with mealy, toothed leaves and greenish-white flower spikes in the axils.* Often called lamb's-quarters. Pull up, or, in young state, cultivate. See also 25, 48.

31. **Plantain** (*Plantago major* and *P. lanceolata*). One of these has broad leaves; the other, narrow ones, but in both species they are basal and ribbed. Flowers small and inconspicuous, in erect, close clusters. Dig out of the garden and apply caustic soda on lawns.

32. **Poison ivy** (*Rhus toxicodendron*). A deep-rooted woody vine, or often shrubby, with glossy, compound* leaves, tiny greenish flowers and white fruit. Poisonous by contact. Dig out (with gloves on) or burn, in dormant season, with Chlorate of Soda. See also Poison Ivy.

33. **Prickly lettuce** (*Lactuca scariola*). Nearly five feet high when full grown. Leaves bluish-green, prickly margined and with scattered prickles on the midrib.* Flowers pale yellow in a huge, branched, rather sparse inflorescence.* Dig out, or cut off below ground. It will continue to grow if cut above ground.

†34. **Prostrate pigweed** (*Amaranthus blitoides*). Spreading over the ground, often in dense mats, and very quickly. Nearly stalkless green leaves and tiny greenish flowers in the axils.* Cultivation is the only remedy. There are several other species, often erect and coarse.

†35. **Purslane** (*Portulaca oleracea*). Commonly called "pussley." Fleshy-leaved pest, perhaps the most notorious weed in the world. Flowers very small, yellow. Never let it set seed, as they have long keeping qualities. Cultivation is a sure cure.

36. **Quack grass** (*Agropyron repens*). A grass most easily distinguished by its ivory-white, sharp-pointed rootstocks. Perhaps the most troublesome weed known. Only digging out will control it. Broken rootstocks simply make new plants. Some think it can be smothered by straw mulch.

†37. **Ragweed** (*Ambrosia elatior*). A coarse, roughish herb from 3 to 12 ft. high. Leaves large, 3- to 5-lobed. Flowers very numerous in tall, often branching, spike-like clusters, the individual heads turban-shaped and apparently upside down. Its profuse pollen is one of the leading causes of hay fever. Kill by cultivation. There is another species, also annual.

†38. **Russian thistle** (*Salsola pestifer*). A red-stemmed herb that becomes prickly, profusely branched into a dome-shaped plant. Most serious in the Middle and Far West. Cultivate it out of gardens and mow all roadsides and fence-rows to prevent its copious seeding.

†39. **Sandbur** (*Cenchrus tribuloides*). A spreading grass easily recognized by its prickly burs. Common in sandy soils, shallow-rooted and easily controlled by cultivation.

†40. **Scarlet pimpernel** (*Anagallis arvensis*). A low, often nearly prostrate herb with tiny bell-shaped, red or white flowers. Called also poor man's weatherglass. Cultivate it out.

41. **Self-heal** (*Prunella vulgaris*). Low or sprawling herb with opposite, stalked leaves and head-like, mostly terminal clusters of violet or pinkish flowers. Easily exterminated by cultivation. Called also heal-all.

42. **Sheep's-sorrel** (*Rumex acetosella*). A bitter-tasting herb with halberd-shaped leaves and slender spikes of small flowers. Cultivating it out of the garden is difficult or almost impossible. Spray sulphate of iron on lawn. See also 13.

†43. **Shepherd's-purse** (*Capsella bursa-pastoris*). Erect herb with root leaves clustered, small white flowers in spreading clusters and small, purse-shaped pods that taper towards the base. Easily controlled by cultivation, but a prolific seeder.

†44. **Sow thistle** (*Sonchus oleraceus*). A coarse, leafy herb with smooth stems, yellow, dandelion-like flowers in sparse clusters and cut leaves with a large terminal lobe and finely prickly teeth. Sulphate of iron in fields and cultivate in the garden. There are other, sometimes perennial, species.

45. **Speedwell** (*Veronica officinalis*). Rare in the garden, but common on lawns where spraying with sulphate of iron is best. It is a semi-prostrate plant with ascending clusters of small blue flowers.

†46. **Spotted spurge** (*Euphorbia maculata*). Hugs the ground in flat mats. Leaves small, with a conspicuous red dot. Cultivation is the remedy. There are many other species, some erect.

†47. **Spurry** (*Spergula arvensis*). A small, nearly prostrate, very common, white-flowered herb with thread-like whorled* leaves. Easily killed by cultivation.

†48. **Strawberry-blite** (*Chenopodium capitatum*). A coarse weed with fleshy red fruit. Cultivation. See also 25, 30.

†49. **Wild mustard** (various species of *Brassica*). Serious weed in grain fields and in ill-kept gardens. Various forms are known, all resembling mustard and with yellow flowers. Spray with sulphate of iron, or cultivate.

50. **Yarrow** (*Achillea millefolium*). Erect herb with finely dissected, strong-smelling, leaves and flat-topped clusters of small white flowers. Dig old plants out or cultivate. Spray lawns with sulphate of iron. There is a pink-flowered form.

**WEEPING AMERICAN ELM** = *Ulmus americana pendula*. See ELM.

**WEEPING BEECH** = *Fagus sylvatica pendula*. See BEECH.

**WEEPING GOLDEN BELL** = *Forsythia suspensa*.

**WEEPING MULBERRY.** See *Morus alba* at MULBERRY.

**WEEPING TREES.** Besides the four just above, and the weeping willow which follows, there are several other shrubs and trees with drooping branches, although they are not all so named. Among the best of them are weeping forms of the white birch, ash, *Sophora japonica pendula*, and *Sorbus aucuparia pendula* (see MOUNTAIN-ASH). Among trees that flower showily the finest weeping tree is probably *Prunus subhirtella pendula* whose weeping branches are loaded with showy bloom in spring. Many of the weeping trees are grafted or budded as standards (see STANDARD, 1), which ensures their being kept at the desired height, while the weeping branches often reach the ground. If you need a weeping tree on the lawn, it is well to specify whether you want a natural weeping tree like the weeping beech or weeping willow, or whether one grown as a standard is needed.

An old weeping mulberry. Few of them reach this degree of perfection.

---

* Special articles on the subjects indicated by an asterisk (*) will be found at the words so marked.

**WEEPING WILLOW.** The common weeping willow is *Salix babylonica*, but *S. blanda* and *S. elegantissima* both have pendulous branches and are sometimes called weeping willows. See WILLOW.

**WEIGELA** (wy-gee'la). Very handsome, mostly May-June flowering shrubs of the honeysuckle family, closely related to *Diervilla* and by some not considered distinct, but differing in the larger, much more showy flowers. Leaves opposite.* Flowers more or less funnel-shaped, about 1½ in. long, borne very profusely on short shoots of the season, mostly in clusters of 1-3. Corolla slightly irregular.* Stamens* 5. Fruit a rather woody, 2-valved capsule,* splitting from the top downward. All of the 10 species are Asiatic and the identity of the cult. sorts is in considerable confusion, as there are many hybrids and named forms. (Named for C. E. Weigel, Swedish physician.)

These very showy bushes are of the easiest cult. in any ordinary garden soil, which fact, with their attractive bloom, accounts for their wide popularity. They root easily from cuttings taken in summer and put in moist sand in the cold frame or in boxes under the trees. Their profuse bloom is borne on shoots of the season which start from last year's twigs. They should only be pruned, therefore, if this is necessary at all, after flowering is over. The Latin names below are still in much doubt, and they have no common names. All are hardy from zone* 3 southward.

**amabilis.** The plants offered as this are usually *Weigela florida*.
**floribunda.** A shrub 7-10 ft. high. Leaves elliptic or oblongish, 3-4½ in. long, toothed, hairy both sides. Flowers dark crimson, nearly stalkless, the stamens* as long as the corolla, but the style* protruding. Jap.
**florida.** The most widely planted sort, and a shrub 8-10 ft. high, the branches spreading. Leaves generally elliptic, tapering at the tip, 3-4 in. long, hairy only on the veins beneath. Flowers rose-pink in the typical form, but in the many hort. varieties white, pink, or darker. Northern China and Korea. More than a dozen different names have been applied to this old favorite, among them *amabilis, candida* (white), *rosea, versicolor,* etc.
**hortensis.** Resembling *W. floribunda*, but the carmine flowers are distinctly stalked and rather narrowly bell-shaped. Jap.
**hybrida.** A group name for many named forms of *Weigela*, some of which may belong to *W. florida*. One of the best is Eva Rathke, a fine, red-flowered shrub; others include plants known as Abel Carrière, Dr. Baillon, Madame Lemoine, etc. Some have variegated leaves.
**japonica.** A shrub 8-10 ft. high, the leaves oblongish, 3-4 in. long, hairy on the under side, especially on the veins. Flowers generally in clusters of 3, narrowly bell-shaped, white at first, ultimately carmine. Jap.
**praecox.** Plants so named appear to be early-flowering forms of *W. florida*.
**rosea** = *Weigela florida*.

**WEIGHTS AND MEASURES.** Here are included the purely arithmetical dimensions of land, or of the contents of containers, useful for ready reference in the garden. Elsewhere are grouped an entirely different set of garden statistics having to do with yields, seeds, plants per acre, longevity of seeds, height and age of trees, and many other figures of use in making calculations for planting. See GARDEN TABLES.

In the tables below are grouped, according to sections, the following:

1. Acre.
2. Linear, square and cubic measures.
3. Volume of containers (Liquid and Dry Measures).
4. Standard Weights.
5. Contents of Cisterns.

### 1. ACRE

An acre contains 43,560 square ft. or 4840 square yards. It is almost exactly 209 × 209 ft. Hence, some of the ordinary-shaped gardens are:

100 × 200 ft. = ½ acre
100 × 100 = ¼ acre
50 × 100 = ⅛ acre  } approximately.
25 × 100 = 1/16 acre
33 × 66 = 1/20 acre exactly.

For the number of plants needed for an acre, at intervals of from 1 × 1 in. to 100 × 100 ft., see GARDEN TABLES, 1. There are 640 acres in a square mile.

### 2. LINEAR, SQUARE, AND CUBIC MEASURES

Linear.
12 in. = 1 ft.         320 rods = 1 mile
3 ft. = 1 yard       1760 yards = 1 mile
16½ ft. = 1 rod       5280 ft. = 1 mile

Square.
144 square in. = 1 square ft.
9 " ft. = 1 " yard
30¼ square yards = 1 " rod
160 " rods = 1 acre

Cubic.
1 cubic ft. = 1728 cubic in.
1 cubic yard = 27 " ft.
A cubic yard contains 43,656 cubic in.
A cubic foot of water weighs about 62½ pounds, and is almost 7½ gallons.

### 3. VOLUMES OF CONTAINERS
(Liquid and Dry Measures)

Liquid Measure:
4 gills = 1 pint, which is just over 1 pound of water
2 pints = 1 quart
4 quarts = 1 gallon, which is 8.34 pounds of water, and contains 231 cubic in.

Dry Measure:
2 pints = 1 quart
8 quarts = 1 peck
4 pecks = 1 bushel, which, in the U.S., should contain 2150 cubic in. For the weight of a bushel see next table.

### 4. STANDARD WEIGHTS
(avoirdupois)

16 drams = 1 ounce
16 ounces = 1 pound
100 pounds = hundredweight
2000 " = 1 ton
2240 " = 1 long ton

These are some figures of weights that gardeners often find useful.

Bushel of Apples = 48-50 pounds
Barley = 48 "
Beets = 56-60 "
Buckwheat = 42-50 "
Corn = 56-60 "
Onions = 52-57 "
Potatoes = 60 " (except in Va., where it is 56)
Turnips = 55-60 "
Wheat = 60 "
Gallon of Water = 8.34 pounds
Pint of Water = Just over 1 pound
Cubic foot of water = 62.42 pounds.

### 5. CONTENTS OF CISTERNS

Gallons in Round Tanks

| Diameter ft. | Depth 3 ft. | 4 ft. | 5 ft. | 6 ft. | 7 ft. | 8 ft. | 9 ft. | 10 ft. |
|---|---|---|---|---|---|---|---|---|
| 4 | 282 | 376 | 470 | 564 | 658 | 752 | 846 | 940 |
| 5 | 440 | 587 | 734 | 881 | 1028 | 1175 | 1321 | 1468 |
| 6 | 634 | 846 | 1057 | 1269 | 1480 | 1692 | 1903 | 2115 |
| 7 | 863 | 1151 | 1439 | 1727 | 2015 | 2303 | 2590 | 2878 |
| 8 | 1128 | 1504 | 1880 | 2256 | 2632 | 3008 | 3384 | 3760 |
| 9 | 1427 | 1903 | 2379 | 2855 | 3331 | 3807 | 4282 | 4758 |
| 10 | 1762 | 2350 | 2937 | 3525 | 4112 | 4700 | 5287 | 5875 |
| 11 | 2132 | 2843 | 3554 | 4265 | 4976 | 5687 | 6397 | 7108 |
| 12 | 2538 | 3384 | 4230 | 5076 | 5922 | 6768 | 7614 | 8460 |

Gallons in Rectangular Tanks

| Size of Tank in Feet | 1 Ft. Deep | 3 Ft. Deep | 4 Ft. Deep | 5 Ft. Deep |
|---|---|---|---|---|
| 4 by 4 | 119 | 359 | 478 | 598 |
| 5 by 5 | 187 | 561 | 748 | 935 |
| 6 by 4 | 179 | 538 | 718 | 897 |
| 6 by 6 | 269 | 807 | 1077 | 1346 |

* Special articles on the subjects indicated by an asterisk (*) will be found at the words so marked.

Gallons in Rectangular Tanks

| Size of Tank in Feet | 1 Ft. Deep | 3 Ft. Deep | 4 Ft. Deep | 5 Ft. Deep |
|---|---|---|---|---|
| 7 by 5 | 261 | 785 | 1047 | 1309 |
| 7 by 6 | 314 | 942 | 1256 | 1570 |
| 7 by 7 | 366 | 1099 | 1466 | 1832 |
| 8 by 4 | 239 | 718 | 957 | 1196 |
| 8 by 6 | 359 | 1077 | 1436 | 1795 |
| 8 by 8 | 478 | 1436 | 1915 | 2393 |
| 9 by 6 | 403 | 1211 | 1615 | 2019 |
| 9 by 8 | 538 | 1615 | 2154 | 2692 |
| 9 by 9 | 605 | 1817 | 2423 | 3029 |
| 10 by 5 | 374 | 1122 | 1496 | 1870 |
| 10 by 6 | 448 | 1346 | 1795 | 2244 |
| 10 by 8 | 598 | 1795 | 2393 | 2992 |
| 10 by 10 | 748 | 2244 | 2992 | 3740 |
| 11 by 6 | 493 | 1481 | 1974 | 2468 |
| 11 by 9 | 740 | 2221 | 2962 | 3702 |
| 11 by 11 | 905 | 2715 | 3620 | 4525 |
| 12 by 6 | 538 | 1615 | 2154 | 2692 |
| 12 by 8 | 718 | 2154 | 2872 | 3590 |
| 12 by 10 | 897 | 2692 | 3590 | 4488 |
| 12 by 12 | 1077 | 3231 | 4308 | 5385 |

**WELSH ONION** = *Allium fistulosum.*

**WELSH POPPY** = *Meconopsis cambrica.*

**WESTERN HEMLOCK** = *Tsuga heterophylla.* See HEMLOCK.

**WESTERN JUNIPER** = *Juniperus occidentalis.*

**WESTERN RED CEDAR** = *Juniperus scopulorum* and *Thuja plicata.*

**WESTERN YELLOW PINE** = *Pinus ponderosa.* See PINE.

**WEST INDIAN CEDAR** = *Cedrela odorata.*

**WEST INDIAN GHERKIN** = *Cucumis anguria.*

**WEST INDIAN KALE** = *Xanthosoma atrovirens.*

**WEST INDIAN LIME.** See Acid Lime at LIME (the citrus fruit).

**WEST INDIAN LOCUST** = *Hymenaea courbaril.*

**WEST VIRGINIA.** The state lies wholly in zones* 3 and 4.

SOILS. The U.S. Bureau of Soils has divided the United States into thirteen soil provinces or regions, three of which are found in West Virginia; viz. Limestone Valleys and Upland Province, Appalachian Mountains and Plateau Province, and the River Flood Plains Province. The Limestone Valleys and Upland Province soils are derived for the most part from limestone, are generally productive and are easily worked. They are found in the eastern panhandle, in the southern part of the state and in restricted areas in the northern panhandle. From the standpoint of a permanent agriculture these soils are the most important in the state. The commercial fruit industry is, for the most part, located on these soils. The Appalachian Mountains and Plateau Province soils are derived from sandstones and shales. They are not very productive, generally heavy in texture, so that they are difficult to cultivate and shallow in depth, particularly where eroded on the hillsides. Soils belonging to this series constitute the hilly, mountainous and high plateau areas of the state and are, therefore, the most important from the standpoint of total area. They are, however, of relatively little importance horticulturally, except in potato production. The soils belonging to the River Flood Plains Province series are alluvial in nature, and generally light in texture. Their productivity varies, depending on the series from which they have been derived. Although limited in area, from the standpoint of vegetable production they are the most important soils of the state.

CHIEF GARDENING CENTERS. For more than a hundred years West Virginia has been known as an apple-producing state, and the industry has grown until at the present time it ranks eighth in total production. The commercial apple industry has largely developed within the past thirty-five years. Peaches and sour cherries are also grown to a considerable extent. Between 1899 and 1919 railroad shipments of apples from the major apple-growing sections of the state increased more than five times. In recent years production has remained about stationary — the drought of 1930 being one of the main contributing causes. The commercial tree fruit sections of the state are located (1) in the Eastern Panhandle, which is part of the great Potomac-Shenandoah fruit region, (2) in the Northern Panhandle of the state, and (3) on the hills overlooking the Ohio River Valley.

WEST VIRGINIA

The zones of hardiness crossing West Virginia are those shown on the colored map at ZONE, which should be consulted for details. The dates are the latest known killing frost in spring and the average earliest one in the fall. The figures below the dates show the length of the growing season based on this data. Rainfall figures (in inches) are for total annual rainfall in the regions so indicated.

Raspberries and strawberries are also grown to a considerable extent. With these fruits greatest acreages are near large centers of consumption, indicating that they are grown chiefly for local markets.

The vegetable industry is located chiefly in the valleys of the Ohio and Kanawha rivers. Products are shipped north to Pittsburgh, Ohio cities, south to the West Virginia coal fields, and to some extent marketed in near-by West Virginia towns. Cabbage, tomatoes, melons, and sweet corn are the most important crops.

Geographically the state is intermediate between the large vegetable areas of the South and North and, enjoying a corresponding climate, is able easily to market her crop without much competition from these areas. West Virginia is also well situated with reference to the large eastern centers of population, being within easy trucking distance of our more important cities. Should the industry expand, the increased production could be easily marketed.

Potato growing is increasing rapidly in importance, since soil and climatic conditions are admirably adapted to the crop and the problem of marketing has not been a serious one. Chief centers of production are in the Ohio River Valley, where early varieties are grown, and the higher altitude counties such as Preston, Randolph, Pocahontas, etc.

Generally speaking, West Virginia is well adapted to the culture of the various ornamental plants normally growing in this latitude, but with altitudes varying from near sea level

---

* Special articles on the subjects indicated by an asterisk (*) will be found at the words so marked.

to near 4800 ft., marked differences in temperature and rainfall have a profound effect on the adaptability of the different kinds of plants. Native plants widely used in landscape work are: flowering dogwood (*Cornus florida*), flame azalea (*Azalea calendulacea*), great laurel (*Rhododendron maximum*), mountain rose bay (*Rhododendron catawbiense*), redbud (*Cercis canadensis*), and bittersweet (*Celastrus scandens*).

CLIMATE. Due to physical conditions — latitude and particularly altitude — the climate of West Virginia is markedly varied, although genial and healthful. Winters are mild at the low altitudes with occasional periods of prolonged hot weather during the summer. As the altitude increases the winters increase in severity, approaching those of northern New York at altitudes of 3500 ft. and above. Summers are correspondingly cool and delightful.

The rainfall is ample and well distributed, with periods of severe drought uncommon except at the low altitudes along the Ohio River, and in the Eastern Panhandle near the foothills of the Alleghenies.

Total annual rainfall corresponds roughly to altitude. Thus, at Martinsburg (435 ft. elevation) the average annual rainfall is 37.59 inches, at Morgantown (1300 ft. elevation) 43.73 inches, while at Davis (3093 ft. elevation) it is 53.62 inches.

FROST DATA

| City | Elevation | Latest known killing frost in spring | Average date of earliest killing frost in fall | Earliest known killing frost in fall |
|---|---|---|---|---|
| Terra Alta | 2559 | June 8 | Sept. 26 | Sept. 7 |
| Elkins | 1947 | May 26 | Oct. 12 | Sept. 20 |
| Martinsburg | 435 | May 16 | Oct. 16 | Sept. 23 |
| Point Pleasant | 595 | May 23 | Oct. 16 | Sept. 23 |
| Charleston | 600 | May 12 | Oct. 23 | Sept. 26 |

The address of the Agricultural Experiment Station, which has kindly supplied this information, is Morgantown, W. Va. The station is always ready to answer gardening questions.

Garden Club activities include clubs of the Garden Club of America, the home office of which is 598 Madison Avenue, New York. There are also over 40 clubs affiliated with the Federated Garden Club of West Virginia.

**WET FEET.** That condition in potted plants caused by excessive watering and insufficient drainage. It is most evident in house plants which begin to turn yellow and drop their leaves. See POTTING.

**WEYMOUTH PINE** = *Pinus strobus*. See PINE.

**WHALE-OIL SOAP.** An obsolescent insecticide replaced by fish-oil soap. See Contact Sprays at INSECTICIDES.

**WHEAT.** See TRITICUM.

**WHEELBARROW.** See Section 1, TOOLS AND IMPLEMENTS.

**WHEEL-HOE CULTIVATOR.** See Section 1, TOOLS AND IMPLEMENTS.

**WHIN.** See FURZE.

**WHIP.** A young, unbranched shoot of a woody plant, especially the first year's growth from a graft or bud. *See also* MAIDEN.

**WHIP GRAFTING.** See GRAFTING.

**WHIP-TAIL.** A cauliflower disease discussed at the diseases at CABBAGE.

**WHISPERING BELLS** = *Emmenanthe penduliflora*.

**WHITE.** As an adjective, white is applied to many things in the garden. Those that occur in THE GARDEN DICTIONARY and their proper equivalents are:

White alder (see CLETHRA); White alder family (see ERICACEAE); White ash = *Fraxinus americana* (see ASH); White azalea = *Azalea viscosa*; White baneberry = *Actaea alba*; White bay = *Magnolia virginiana*; Whitebeam = *Sorbus aria* (see MOUNTAIN-ASH); White bedstraw = *Galium mollugo*; White beech = *Fagus grandifolia* (see BEECH); White birch. In America, *Betula papyrifera*; in Europe, *Betula pendula* (see BIRCH); White campion = *Lychnis alba*; White cedar = *Thuja occidentalis*; White cedar (see TABEBUIA PALLIDA); White cedar = *Libocedrus decurrens* (see INCENSE CEDAR); White Cedar. In the West, *Chamaecyparis lawsoniana*; in the East, *C. thyoides*. It is also used for *Cupressus macnabiana*; White clover = *Trifolium repens* (see CLOVER); White cohosh = *Actaea alba*; White corallita (see PORANA PANICULATA; White daisy = *Layia glandulosa*; White daisy = *Chrysanthemum leucanthemum*; White Dutch clover = *Trifolium repens* (see CLOVER); White Dutch runner = *Phaseolus coccineus albus*; White eardrops = *Dicentra cucullaria*; White elm = *Ulmus americana* (see ELM); White fir = *Abies concolor* (see FIR); Whiteflies (see True Bugs at INSECT PESTS; also the Insect Pests at GRAPEFRUIT, ORANGE, BEGONIA, COLEUS, and AZALEA); White-flowered gourd = *Lagenaria leucantha*; White fringed orchis = *Habenaria blephariglottis*; White garden (see first main entry below); White globe lily = *Calochortus albus*; White goldenrod = *Solidago bicolor* (see GOLDENROD); White gourd = *Benincasa hispida*; White grubs (see Beetles at INSECT PESTS); White hellebore = *Veratrum viride*; White holly = *Ilex opaca* (see HOLLY); White kerria = *Rhodotypos tetrapetala*; White jasmine = *Jasminum officinale*; White linden = *Tilia tomentosa* (see LINDEN); White lotus = *Nymphaea lotus*; White mariposa lily = *Calochortus venustus*; White melilot = *Melilotus alba*; White mulberry = *Morus alba* (see MULBERRY); White mustard = *Brassica alba*; White oak = *Quercus alba* (see OAK); White osier = *Leucothoë racemosa*; White pickle virus (see Diseases at CUCUMBER); White pine. In the East, *Pinus strobus*; in the West, *P. flexilis* (see PINE); White popinac = *Leucaena glauca*; White poplar = *Populus alba*; White rose mallow = *Hibiscus oculiroseus*; White rot (see Diseases at GRAPE); White sage = *Audibertia polystachya*; White sapote = *Casimiroa edulis*; White snakeroot = *Eupatorium urticaefolium*; White spruce = *Picea glauca* (see SPRUCE); White swamp azalea = *Azalea viscosa*; White tassel-flower = *Petalostemon candidum*; White trumpet-lily = *Lilium longiflorum*; White trumpet narcissus = *Narcissus moschatus*; White upland aster = *Aster ptarmicoides*; White walnut = *Juglans cinerea* (see WALNUT); White water lily = *Nymphaea odorata*; White willow = *Salix alba* (see WILLOW); White wine grapes (see *vinifera* varieties at GRAPE); Whitewood = *Liriodendron tulipifera* (see TULIP-TREE); White wood aster = *Aster divaricatus*.

**WHITE GARDEN.** A garden, or a section of it, planted wholly with white flowers, has far more distinction and variety than might be supposed. Few flowers are pure white throughout, nearly all being flushed or veined or otherwise marked with green, rose, mauve or yellow. The effect of a white garden is tranquil and cool and is especially lovely at night. In planting such a garden or border, dark evergreens make the most effective background, and much gray foliage may be used. In the following lists only white-flowered forms of the plants named are intended, so the variety name *alba* has been omitted to save space.

SHRUBS OR SMALL TREES TO BE USED AS ACCENTS OR BACKGROUND

SPRING-FLOWERING: *Amelanchier canadensis*, 10 ft.; *Aronia arbutifolia*, 10 ft.; *Chamaedaphne calyculata*, 3 ft., evergreen; *Cornus florida*, 10–20 ft., *C. kousa*, 10–15 ft.; *Crataegus oxyacantha*, hawthorn, 10–20 ft., *Cytisus albus* (see BROOM), 4–8 ft., *C. kewensis*, low-growing; *Deutzia gracilis*, 1½ ft., *D. lemoinei*; *Exochorda racemosa*, 10 ft.; *Halesia tetraptera*, 20 ft.; *Leucothoë catesbaei* (evergreen), 4 ft.; *Lonicera bella albida*, 10 ft., *L. fragrantissima*, 8 ft.; *Magnolia soulangeana alba superba*, 20 ft., *M. stellata*, 8–10 ft.; *Philadelphus* (mock-orange) many vars. tall and dwarf, single and double; *Pieris floribunda* and *P. japonica* (evergreen), 3–6 ft.; *Prunus glandulosa* (white, flowering almond), 4–5 ft., *P. maritima* (beach plum), 2–5 ft., *P. tomentosa*, 5 ft.; Japanese cherries, 20–30 ft., *Malus sargenti*, 8 ft., *M. toringoides*, 25 ft.; *Rhodo-*

* Special articles on the subjects indicated by an asterisk (*) will be found at the words so marked.

dendron carolinianum, 4–6 ft.; many hybrid varieties; *Rhodotypos tetrapetala*, 5–6 ft.; *Rubus deliciosus*, 3–6 ft.; *Spiraea arguta*, 6 ft., *S. prunifolia*, 5 ft., *S. thunbergi*, 3–5 ft., *S. vanhouttei*, 8 ft.; *Viburnum carlesi*, 3–5 ft., *V. lantana*, 15 ft.

SUMMER- AND AUTUMN-FLOWERING: *Abelia chinensis*, 4 ft.; *Calluna vulgaris*, 15 ins.; *Ceanothus americanus*, 2–5 ft.; *Chionanthus virginica*, 15 ft.; *Clethra alnifolia*, 4–8 ft.; *Cornus nuttalli*, 8–10 ft.; *Deutzia scabra*, 8 ft.; *Hibiscus syriacus* Jeanne d'Arc (double), and Snowstorm (single), 12 ft.; *Hydrangea arborescens grandiflora*, 5 ft., *H. radiata*, 6 ft.; *Itea virginica*, 4 ft.; *Kalmia latifolia* (evergreen), 4–8 ft.; *Lonicera ruprechtiana*, 12 ft.; *L. tatarica*, 10 ft.; *Azalea viscosa*, 4–6 ft.; *Rosa multiflora*, 10 ft., *R. rugosa* and varieties, 5 ft., *R. spinosissima*, 4–5 ft.; *Sambucus canadensis* (elder), 10 ft.; *Syringa* (lilac), many varieties; *Viburnum trilobum*, 12 ft.; *V. cassinoides*, 12 ft., *V. tomentosum*, 8 ft.; *Weigela florida*, 7 ft.

TALL PLANTS FOR USE AT BACK OF BORDER

SUMMER-FLOWERING: *Althaea rosea* (hollyhock), double and single; *Aruncus sylvester*; *Macleaya cordata*; *Campanula lactiflora*; *C. pyramidalis*; *Cimicifuga simplex*, *C. racemosa*; *Delphinium*; *Filipendula camtschatica*; *Thalictrum aquilegifolium*, *T. dipterocarpum*.

FALL-FLOWERING: Asters; *Boltonia asteroides*; *Chrysanthemum uliginosum*; Phlox, several varieties; *Veronica virginica*.

PLANTS OF MEDIUM HEIGHT

SPRING-FLOWERING: *Aquilegia vulgaris*; *Astilbe japonica*; *Dianthus barbatus* (Sweet William); *Hesperis matronalis*; *Linum perenne*; *Polemonium caeruleum*.

SUMMER-FLOWERING: *Achillea ptarmica* Boule de Neige, and Perry's White; *Campanula alliariaefolia*, *C. latifolia*, *C. medium* (Canterbury bells), *C. persicifolia*; *Centranthus ruber*; *Centaurea montana*; *Chrysanthemum maximum* varieties; *Chelone glabra*; *Clematis recta*; *Dictamnus albus*; *Filipendula hexapetala* (dropwort), *F. ulmaria* (queen-of-the-meadow), *F. purpurea*; *Galega officinalis*; *Geranium pratense*, *G. sanguineum*; *Gypsophila paniculata*, double and single; *Iris* (bearded), many varieties; *Iris* (Japanese); *Iris sibirica* and varieties; *Lobelia syphilitica*; *Lupinus polyphyllus*; *Monarda fistulosa*; *Papaver orientale* Perry's White; *Paeonia*, double and single, many varieties; *Pentstemon digitalis*; *Physostegia virginiana*; *Platycodon grandiflorum*; *Sidalcea candida*; *Stenanthium robustum*; *Veronica maritima*, *V. spicata*; *Yucca filamentosa*.

FALL-FLOWERING: *Anemone japonica*; Aster; *Chrysanthemum coreanum*; *Eupatorium urticaefolium*; *Hosta plantaginea*.

LOW-GROWING PLANTS FOR FOREGROUND

SPRING-FLOWERING: *Aquilegia flabellata nana*; *Arenaria montana*; *Arabis albida*; *Asperula odorata*; *Cerastium tomentosum*; *Convallaria majalis* (lily-of-the-valley); *Dianthus deltoides*; *Epimedium macranthum*; *Erinus alpinus*; *Gypsophila cerastioides*; *Iberis sempervirens*; *Iris*, dwarf varieties; *Myosotis*; *Phlox subulata*; *Sanguinaria canadensis*; *Silene alpestris*; *Statice armeria* (thrift); *Tiarella cordifolia*; *Veronica teucrium dubia*; *Viola cornuta*.

SUMMER-FLOWERING: *Anemone sylvestris*; *Campanula carpatica*; *Delphinium grandiflorum*; *Erigeron coulteri*; *Galium boreale*; *Helianthemum*; *Heuchera* Perry's White; *Lychnis viscaria*; *Nierembergia rivularis*; *Primula japonica*; *Scabiosa caucasica*; *Sedum album*; *Stokesia laevis*; *Thymus serpyllum*; *Tunica saxifraga*.

AUTUMN-FLOWERING: *Aster ericoides*; *A. ptarmicoides*; *Chrysanthemum arcticum*; *Helleborus niger*.

ANNUALS FOR SUMMER FLOWERING

Ageratum; *Lobularia maritima*; Antirrhinum, tall and dwarf; *Argemone mexicana*; Asters, tall and dwarf; *Bellis*; Candytuft; Sweet Sultan; Cornflower, double; *Clarkia*; Cosmos, early and late; Chinese Pinks; *Godetia*; *Gypsophila elegans*; Heliotrope; *Lavatera trimestris splendens*; Larkspur; Lobelia; Mignonette; *Nicotiana affinis*; *Omphalodes linifolia*; Pansies; *Petunia*, double and single; *Phlox drummondi*; Poppies; Sweet Peas; Stocks; Verbenas; Zinnias.

SPRING AND SUMMER-FLOWERING BULBS

*Allium neapolitanum*; *Camassia leichtlini*; *Chionodoxa luciliae*; *Colchicum autumnale*, *C. speciosum* (autumn); *Crocus biflorus*, and hybrid crocuses (spring-flowering), *C. speciosus* (autumn-flowering); *Eremurus elwesi*, 10–12 ft.; *Erythronium californicum*; *Fritillaria meleagris*; *Galanthus* (snowdrop) species; Hyacinths, double and single; *Leucojum aestivum*, *L. vernum* (see SNOWFLAKE); *Lilium auratum* (summer), *L. browni* (early summer), *L. candidum*, *L. martagon*, *L. speciosum* (late summer); *L. regale* (July); Narcissus, many varieties; *Ornithogalum umbellatum*; Tulips, many varieties; *Scilla hispanica*, *S. nutans*, *S. sibirica*.

SUMMER-FLOWERING BULBS AND ROOTS
TO BE PLANTED IN SPRING

Dahlias, tall and dwarf; Gladioli; *Galtonia candicans*; tuberoses, double and single; *Zephyranthes*.

CLIMBERS

*Actinidia arguta*; *Clematis*, Duchess of Edinburgh, *C. montana*, *C. paniculata*, *C. veitchiana*; *Calonyction aculeatum* (moonflower); *Lonicera halliana*; *Lathyrus latifolius*; *Polygonum auberti*; Roses, many varieties; *Wistaria sinensis*. — L. B. W.

**WHITLAVIA** = *Phacelia whitlavia*.

**WHITLOW GRASS.** See DRABA.

**WHITSUN GILLYFLOWER.** See HESPERIS MATRONALIS.

**WHORL; WHORLED.** Having three or more leaves, flowers, twigs, etc., all inserted at one point and in a circle. This arrangement, known as a whorl, is verticillate. See VERTICILLATA.

**WHORLED MILKWEED** = *Asclepias verticillata*. See MILKWEED.

**WHORL-FLOWER** = *Morina longifolia*.

**WHORTLEBERRY.** See VACCINIUM.

**WICKSON, E. J.** See America at GARDEN BOOKS.

**WICOPY** = *Dirca palustris* and *Xolisma mariana*.

**WIDOW'S-CROSS** = *Sedum pulchellum*.

**WIDOW'S-TEAR.** See SPIDERWORT.

**WIEGELA.** Incorrect spelling of *Weigela*.

**WIER'S CUT-LEAVED MAPLE** = *Acer saccharinum wieri*. See MAPLE.

**WIGANDIA** (wi-gan'di-a). Tropical American foliage plants of the family Hydrophyllaceae, comprising only six species, of which **W. caracasana** is planted for ornament outdoors in southern Calif. and similar climates. It is a bold plant, 7–10 ft. high or more, sometimes nearly tree-like. Leaves (for which it is grown) heart-shaped, nearly 18 in. long, covered with glistening and stinging hairs, coarsely and doubly toothed, long-stalked. Flowers small, tubular, blue or violet, but the tube white, scarcely over ½ in. long, and borne in terminal 1-sided clusters (cymes*). A very handsome foliage plant, especially the **var. macrophylla**, which has still larger leaves, and is fine for the sub-tropical garden. It can be raised from seed sown in winter in the greenhouse, or increased from root cuttings in spring. (Named for Johannes Wigand, a Prussian bishop who wrote on plants.)

**WILCOXIA** (will-kocks'i-a). Slender-stemmed cacti of Mex. and adjacent Tex., comprising 4 species, of which only **W. poselgeri**, the sacasil, is likely to be in cult. It is a branched cactus from a tuberous, dahlia-like root, the stems scarcely ½ in. thick and 1–2 ft. long, faintly 8–10-ribbed, the very numerous flattened spines nearly hiding the stems. Each spine cluster consists of a single central, erect spike, and 9–12 widely divaricating lateral spines. Flowers about 2 in. long, purple or pink. For cult. see CACTI. (Named for Timothy E. Wilcox, American army officer.)

**WILD.** As an adjective, wild still clings to the name of many garden plants or things to do with the garden. Those occurring here and their proper equivalents are:

---

* Special articles on the subjects indicated by an asterisk (*) will be found at the words so marked.

Wild balsam apple = *Echinocystis lobata;* Wild bean = *Apios tuberosa;* Wild bergamot = *Monarda fistulosa;* Wild black cherry = *Prunus serotina;* Wild bleeding-heart = *Dicentra eximia;* Wild buckwheat = black bindweed (*see* list at WEEDS); Wild buckwheat = *Eriogonum fasciculatum;* Wild calla = *Calla palustris;* Wild camomile (*see* MATRICARIA); Wild carrot (*see* CARROT); Wild celery = *Vallisneria spiralis* (*see* EEL-GRASS); Wild clove = *Pimenta acris;* Wild coffee (*see* PSYCHOTRIA); Wild corn = *Clintonia umbellata;* Wild cucumber = *Echinocystis lobata;* Wild date = *Phoenix sylvestris;* Wild flag = *Iris versicolor;* Wild garden (*see* first main entry below); Wild geranium = *Geranium maculatum;* Wild ginger = *Asarum;* Wild ginger family = Aristolochiaceae; Wild hoarhound = *Eupatorium aromaticum;* Wild hollyhock = *Sidalcea malvaeflora;* Wild hyacinth = *Brodiaea lactea;* Wild hydrangea = *Hydrangea arborescens;* Wild indigo (*see* BAPTISIA); Wilding (*see* second main entry below); Wild ipecac = *Apocynum androsaemifolium;* also *Triosteum perfoliatum;* Wild lantana (*see* ABRONIA); Wild lilac (*see* CEANOTHUS); Wild lily-of-the-valley = *Maianthemum canadense;* Wildling (*see* Wilding, at second main entry below); Wild lupine = *Lupinus perennis;* Wild madder = *Galium mollugo;* Wild marjoram = *Origanum vulgare;* Wild monkshood = *Aconitum uncinatum* (*see* MONKSHOOD); Wild mulberry = *Morinda royoc;* Wild mustard (*see* list at WEEDS); Wild oat = *Avena fatua;* Wild oats = *Uvularia sessilifolia;* Wild oleander = *Decodon verticillatus;* Wild oleaster = *Shepherdia argentea;* Wild orange = *Laurocerasus caroliniana;* Wild passion-flower = *Passiflora incarnata;* Wild pennyroyal = *Mentha arvensis* (*see* MINT); Wild pink = *Arethusa bulbosa;* Wild plantain = *Heliconia bihai;* Wild plum = *Prunus americana;* Wild pumpkin = *Cucurbita foetidissima;* Wild red cherry = *Prunus pennsylvanica;* Wild rice (*see* ZIZANIA); Wild rosemary = *Ledum palustre;* Wild rye (*see* ELYMUS); Wild sage = *Artemisia frigida;* Wild sarsaparilla = *Aralia nudicaulis;* Wild senna = *Cassia marylandica;* Wild spikenard = *Smilacina racemosa;* Wild sunflower = *Helianthus giganteus* (*see* SUNFLOWER); Wild sweet pea = *Tephrosia virginiana;* Wild sweet potato = *Ipomoea pandurata;* Wild Sweet William = *Phlox divaricata* and *P. maculata;* Wild wormwood = *Artemisia canadensis;* Wild yam = *Dioscorea villosa.*

**WILD GARDEN.** Broadly speaking, the term wild gardening signifies the use of native American plants as the dominant note in ornamental planting. In actual practice it is generally construed as applying to the creation of more or less naturalistic effects in which no plant of foreign origin is used, reliance being placed solely on species indigenous to N.A., although not necessarily to that part of the country where the garden in question is located. It is in this second and more specific sense that the term is here used. *See also* INFORMAL GARDEN.

Properly conceived and executed plantings of native material, besides being pleasing to the eye, are relatively novel and offer wide scope for the originality of the gardener. They are particularly appropriate to the American scene and American life, especially in country regions, and the less populous suburbs, where it frequently happens that they can be developed with little or no alteration of already existing land characteristics and contours.

Another advantage of this type of planting is its value from the conservation standpoint. Through extension of real estate development and the general opening up of land, the habitats of many species are being altered and the less resistant types of local flora eliminated. Despite efforts to control their depredations, plant vandals continue to destroy stands of the choicer flowers, with the result that over many large areas such formerly abundant species as the trailing arbutus, pink lady's-slipper and the eastern columbine have been completely exterminated. Intelligent wild flower gardening suggests the possibilities of establishing private sanctuaries where such threatened plants can be perpetuated and may conceivably lead to their large-scale re-establishment in suitable regions.

Native plants of definite merit can be successfully chosen for practically any type of site—wet or dry, sunny or shaded, sloping or level. Among the conifers a wide selection is available, ranging from the low, trailing types of junipers to such forest trees as the Douglas fir, white pine and the American and Carolina hemlocks. Worth-while deciduous trees are too numerous for even a partial listing in this discussion; a study of any unspoiled natural woodland will disclose many of them. The same can be said of the flowering woody material, although one cannot refrain from specific mention of such outstanding examples as our native rhododendrons, viburnums, flowering dogwood, *Magnolia virginiana,* various hawthorns, redbud and the incomparable mountain laurel. In vines the choice is more limited, but even so there are many possibilities among the grape, clematis, *Parthenocissus, Passiflora, Gelsemium,* and trumpet-creeper, which are indigenous to various regions.

### WILD FLOWERS

As a rule, the really desirable native plants demand at least approximately the conditions of soil, moisture and light to which they are accustomed in their natural habitats. It becomes necessary, therefore, to determine definitely what these conditions are in the site of the proposed planting and then either select plants which fit them or change the conditions to conform to the needs of desired plants which are not already met. Failure to provide the right surroundings will lead to disappointment and the loss of plants which would better have been left growing in their wild state.

SOILS. Particular attention should be paid to the acidity or alkalinity of the soil, and its physical condition. Many desirable native plants have marked preference for a heavy, a sandy or a leaf-moldy soil and refuse to thrive unless these predilections are satisfied. Similarly, the degree of moisture, especially subsoil moisture, is a prominent factor in numerous cases. Methods of providing for these various needs are obvious and need not be discussed here. *See* ACID AND ALKALI SOILS.

When it comes to the actual securing of plants for a wild-flower garden, three general courses are open. The first and most obvious plan is to collect them directly from the wild, a perfectly permissible and satisfactory method, with easily transplanted species, of which a plentiful supply exists. Digging may be done in either spring or fall — the former for late summer- and autumn-bloomers, the latter for those which flower in spring and early summer.

Secondly, nursery-grown plants may be secured from reliable concerns which specialize in native material. As a rule

A corner in a real wild garden

* Special articles on the subjects indicated by an asterisk (*) will be found at the words so marked.

these are superior in root development and top growth to those collected from field or woodland. This fact is of special importance in connection with trees and shrubs which, in a natural state, are often poorly rooted and leggy* as a result of the crowded conditions in which they have developed.

The third plan is to propagate the plants yourself from seed, top-growth cuttings, root division or whatever special method may fit the species in question. Comparatively little has been written on the propagation of native plants, so the field is a rich one for original investigation. Certain species are so constituted that they rarely succeed when transplanted from the wild, so that some form of propagation is essential if one is to get them established in the native planting. As a truly constructive conservation move, of course, experimentation along these lines may be invaluable.

In general, a sowing mixture of one-third good garden loam, one-third woods leaf mold and one-third rather coarse, clean sand should be used. Seeds of plants of the heath family may be sown in a mixture of one part sand and two parts Michigan peat, the trade name of which is Soil Sponge. All sowing soils should be finely screened, very thoroughly mixed and firmed down evenly in the flats when somewhat damp. Well-drained wooden flats are the best containers; pots, pans and other earthenware containers dry out too rapidly and are likely to crack and spill their contents under the influence of the hard winter freezing to which many seeds must be subjected. Some of the tree and shrub seeds, especially, lie dormant for two full years, so substantial containers are obviously necessary.

Use fresh seed — as fresh as possible. Nature has a reason for making seed fall as soon as it is fully ripe. Most seeds should be covered about twice their own depth. In the case of very small ones, broadcast rather than sow in drills, and barely cover them with a dusting of the sowing soil mixture, shaken on through a small-mesh kitchen sifter.

Watering must be carefully done, to avoid washing out some of the seeds and covering others too deeply. It is hard to find a watering can with a rose fine enough to forestall risks like this. A safe job can be done with a compressed-air sprayer of the flit-gun type for one or two flats, or the large plunger pump brand, with rubber hose and trigger nozzle, for more extensive operations. Either of these, used with reasonable care and allowing time for the mist-like spray to sink into the soil, will obviate the need for all the paraphernalia of watering from below. *See* WATERING.

When the flats have been sown and watered and installed in the frame, a screen made of laths or laths and cheesecloth is laid over the sash to shade it, the sash itself being left on to protect the seeds from beating rains. The seed of most worth-while native plants takes its time about germinating — two, three or four weeks, six months, a year or two. During this time the soil in which it lies must not be allowed to become bone-dry; sometimes weekly or semi-weekly watering will be required.

There is nothing mysterious or particularly tricky about handling most of the seedlings, once they are up — the procedure is similar to that for regular garden flowers. In other words, they are pricked-off* to other flats or to small individual pots when they have made their second pair of true leaves, kept protected from heavy rains, and in all respects given more than a fair chance to live long and prosper. The soil into which they are shifted must of course match that selected by their parents in the wild — sandy, acid, alkaline, clayey, well furnished with leaf mold, moist or dry, as the case may be. Here again arises the importance of knowing the requirements of the species and following them with reasonable fidelity. The one liberty which can be taken with safety — with actual benefit — is to give the young plants an occasional dose of weak liquid manure. Most of them like it and will repay the attention with more rapid growth.

In the case of other methods of propagation, such as cuttings, the various forms of division, etc., the accepted nursery procedures should be followed as a basis.

As has been intimated, the cultural conditions required by different choice native plants vary widely and are best learned by observation and the study of books. Certain ones may be set down here, however, because of their highly specialized character and the fact that specific data on them are scattered, inadequate or unrecorded elsewhere.

### Wild Garden Plants

Bearberry (*Arctostaphylos uva-ursi*). Evergreen trailer, scarlet berries. Sandy, acid or nearly neutral soil, very well drained. Sun or part shade. Very hard to transplant from the wild, unless frozen clumps are used, but not difficult with pot-grown plants. Propagation by late fall, or winter cuttings under glass, or by seeds (very slow) exposed in winter.

Columbine (*Aquilegia canadensis*). Rather poor, dry soil (moisture and feeding promotes too rank growth), strongly acid to neutral. Full sun to ¾ shade. Propagation by seed.

*Chimaphila umbellata* and *C. maculata*. Very choice, low, half-woody evergreens, fragrant white to pinkish flowers. Shade, good drainage, highly acid, leaf-moldy soil. Practically impossible to transplant; must be pot-grown. Propagation by summer cuttings; difficult.

Bunchberry (*Cornus canadensis*). Dwarf, nearly herbaceous dogwood, only a few inches high. Rich woods soil, highly acid. Shade, good drainage, cool location. May be transplanted in large sods, but pot-grown plants are better.

Pink lady's-slipper (*Cypripedium acaule*). Well-drained, woods soil, intensely acid. Full shade. Often difficult to transplant from the wild, but possible if large amount of soil from the site is taken with it; best seasons after flowering or in early October. In planting, do not cover crown more than ½ in. Satisfactory propagation method unknown at time of writing. If possible keep well-mulched with pine needles. They provide acidity and prevent soil splashing on the leaves, which this plant resents.

Larger yellow lady's-slipper (*Cypripedium parviflorum pubescens*). Woods soil, neutral to moderately acid, well drained. Half to full shade. Not difficult to transplant.

Fringed gentian (*Gentiana crinita*). Heavy, somewhat sandy muck soil, preferably neutral. Full sun to half shade, abundant subsoil moisture. Character of root system makes transplanting extremely difficult. Propagation by strictly fresh seed broadcast in autumn on prepared soil in suitable location, lightly covered with clean sand and protected for the winter with single thickness of burlap laid on. Remove burlap about mid-April. As species is biennial, sow seed every year. Has been grown successfully in pots.

*Hepatica americana*. Acid woods soil, full shade, good drainage. Not difficult to transplant, but takes time to become fully re-established. Propagation by division or seed.

Trailing arbutus (*Epigaea repens*). Very acid, sandy, leaf-moldy soil, excellent drainage. Full shade (will live in part sun, but foliage is injured and small and plants are stubby). Extremely difficult to transplant. Pot-grown plants move readily and should always be used. Propagation by cuttings or strictly fresh seed.

Mountain laurel (*Kalmia latifolia*). Acid soil containing plenty of humus, good drainage. Shade or sun. Shelter from heavy winds desirable. Nursery-grown plants preferable. Propagation by fall or early spring-sown seed.

Twinflower (*Linnaea borealis* and *L. americana*). Very choice evergreen creeper with fragrant blossoms in pairs. Rich, acid, woods soil. Full shade. Propagation by cuttings.

Sand myrtle (*Leiophyllum buxifolium*). Fine evergreen flowering shrublet. Acid, rather sandy soil, half sun. Propagation by cuttings; difficult.

Partridge berry (*Mitchella repens*). Acid woods soil. Can be acclimated to either sun or shade. Transplanted easily.

*Phyllodoce glanduliflora*. One of the choice northwestern alpine heaths. Withstands eastern conditions if given some winter protection from sun and wind. Acid, gritty soil containing good supply of peat moss.

Gaywings (*Polygala paucifolia*). Very acid, leaf-moldy soil, shade, moist or dry. Transplants readily in large sods. Propagation by root division.

Bloodroot (*Sanguinaria canadensis*). Well-drained soil, neutral to acid. Shade to ¾ sun. Transplants readily. Propagation by seed (slow) or root division.

---

* Special articles on the subjects indicated by an asterisk (*) will be found at the words so marked.

Mountain cranberry (*Vaccinium vitis-idaea minus*). Excellent, low, evergreen ground cover, only a few inches high. Acid, gritty soil, sun to half shade. Propagation by seed or cuttings.

*Viola pedata*. There is a narrow-leaved and particularly showy form of the always lovely bird's-foot violet. Acid, sandy, well-drained soil, in full sun. Propagation by division.

For the exact definition of the terms acid, very acid, neutral, etc., as applied to soils for the wild garden *see* ACID AND ALKALI SOILS. — R. S. L.

**WILDING AND WILDLING.** These mean almost exactly the same thing. Both are applied to wild or uncultivated plants of natural origin. But *wildling* is also used for a cultivated plant that has run wild, otherwise known as an escape (which see).

**WILLOW.** For the true willows *see* the next entry. Several other plants, however, have *willow* as part of their name. For those in this book *see* CHILOPSIS, DECODON, EPILOBIUM, ITEA, JUSSIAEA, LYTHRUM and the next few entries.

**WILLOW.** A huge group of quick-growing, often brittle-wooded shrubs and trees, comprising the genus **Salix** (say'-licks) of the family Salicaceae. More than 300 species are known, chiefly from the cooler parts of the north temperate zone, but a few in the southern hemisphere, none in Aust. Besides the great number of very similar species there are innumerable natural and induced hybrids, so that exact naming of willows is difficult even for the experts. For this reason only a few of the best known ones are here included, although others are known to be in cult. in America, where there are over 100 wild species of willow. They are closely related to the poplars, which, however, have mostly drooping catkins, while in willows the catkins are erect. *See* POPULUS.

Leaves alternate,* usually narrow, mostly lance-shaped and tapering both ends. Male and female flowers on separate plants, both in catkins* which bloom before or when the leaves expand. Petals and sepals none, the flowers thus naked, but each flower borne in the axil* of a bract,* the collection of which forms the catkin* (the female is the familiar pussy willow). Fruit a 2-valved capsule.* (*Salix* is the classical Latin name for a willow.)

While most willows grow best in moist places, most of them will do well in any ordinary garden soil and they are probably the easiest of all plants to propagate. Cuttings will root almost anywhere, but best, of course, in moist sand. There are a few dry land species and among the cult. sorts the best of these is *Salix tristis*. While the best known of the weeping willows is *S. babylonica*, other weeping sorts are *S. blanda* and *S. elegantissima*. Some, like the osier willow, are cult. for basket making, and a few species are useful for the drug salicin, one of the ingredients of aspirin.

**S. alba.** White willow. A tree 30–60 ft. high. Leaves 3–4 in. long, finely toothed, the under side silky-hairy. Eurasia and northern Af., often an escape* in N.A. Hardy everywhere. There are several varieties differing mostly in the shape of the leaves and the amount of hairiness of them.

**S. babylonica.** Weeping willow. A tree up to 40 ft. high, the branches long and pendulous, yellowish-brown when young. Leaves 5–6 in. long, finely toothed, grayish-green beneath. China. Hardy from zone* 3 southward. Often confused with *S. elegantissima*.

**S. blanda.** Wisconsin weeping willow. A hybrid between the ordinary weeping willow (*S. babylonica*) and a Eurasian species. It is a round-headed tree with long, pendulous branches, the young twigs dull green or brown. Leaves 3½–6 in. long, finely toothed, bluish-green beneath. Hardy from zone* 3 southward.

**S. caprea.** Goat willow; also called sallow. Not over 25 ft. high, usually much less and a shrub. Leaves oblongish, or broader, 3–4 in. long, faintly toothed. Catkins bright yellow, conspicuous. Eurasia and northern Persia. Hardy from zone* 3 southward. There is a variegated-leaved form, and another with pendulous branches.

**S. discolor.** Common pussy willow. A shrub or small tree 10–18 ft. high. Leaves elliptic or oblongish, 3–4 in. long, finely wavy-toothed or without teeth, bluish-green beneath. The female catkins are the familiar pussy willow which can be easily forced by bringing them into a warm room after Jan. 15. Eastern N.A. Hardy everywhere.

**S. elegantissima.** Thurlow's weeping willow. A medium-sized tree with long, pendulous branches, the twigs brown. Leaves narrow, 4–6 in. long, sharply toothed, bluish-green beneath. Jap.(?) Hardy from zone* 3 southward.

**S. nigra.** Black willow. A tree up to 35 ft. high, the bark very dark purple, almost black, the branches erect, the twigs yellowish. Leaves narrow, 3–5 in. long, finely toothed, pale beneath. Nearly throughout N.A. Hardy from zone* 2 southward. An extremely effective combination with the nearly black bark of this tree are the white flowers of some of the Japanese flowering cherries or of white crabapples.

**S. pentandra.** Laurel or bay willow. A tree 40–60 ft. high, the leaves elliptic, shining green, 3–5 in. long and finely toothed. Catkins showy, golden-yellow. Southeastern Eu., sometimes an escape in the eastern U.S. Hardy from zone* 2 southward.

**S. tristis.** A shrub scarcely 2 ft. high, the leaves 1½–2 in. long, without marginal teeth, densely white-felty beneath. In dry, sandy places, eastern U.S. Hardy from zone* 2 southward. *See* SAND GARDEN.

**S. viminalis.** Common osier or osier willow. The young twigs densely hairy. Leaves very narrow, 7–10 in. long, practically without teeth. Eurasia, but naturalized in the eastern U.S. Much cult. for basket making, especially the *var. gmelini*, a Siberian form.

**S. vitellina.** Golden osier. Considered by many to be only a variety of *S. alba*, but its bright yellow twigs make it sufficiently distinct for garden purposes. Its winter and early spring color, due to these showy twigs, is very handsome. Eurasia. Hardy everywhere, and much grown for ornament.

**WILLOW CACTUS.** *See* RHIPSALIS.

**WILLOW-HERB.** *See* EPILOBIUM.

**WILLOW-LEAVED JASMINE** = *Cestrum parqui*.

**WILLOW MYRTLE** = *Agonis*.

**WILLOW OAK** = *Quercus phellos*. *See* OAK.

**WILLOW-WORT** = *Lysimachia vulgaris*.

**WILT.** A plant disease mostly resulting from some disturbance in the water-carrying tubes in the structure of the plant, the main symptom of which is that leaves begin to wilt and finally wither. For its control *see* the Plant Diseases at CALLISTEPHUS, CHRYSANTHEMUM, DAHLIA, CABBAGE, EGGPLANT, PEA, BANANA, etc.

**WILTING.** The flagging of leaves or flowers due to improper moisture conditions, too great heat, or too much wind. Wilting is actually a lack of turgidity in the cells of the plant, which instead of being distended with water become partly dried out, causing leaves or petals to become flaccid.

Reviving wilted plants is often easy if wilting has not gone too far. In the case of potted plants it is usually sufficient to set them in a moist atmosphere for a few hours. If you have no greenhouse, the proper atmosphere can be arranged by standing the pot in a glass-covered carton at the bottom of which is a pail of water. Put a brick in the pan and stand the pot on the brick, as the soil in the pot, while needing moisture, must not get soggy.

Vegetable or flower seedlings set out in the open ground are harder to revive, because one cannot control the atmosphere. See that the flagged plants have plenty of water, and if the plantation is not too extensive cover it for a day or two with lath shades. *See* SHADES AND SHADING. Or they may be covered with cheesecloth or newspaper. The object in all cases is to try and prevent too rapid transpiration* which is the real cause of all wilting. Merely drowning the soil will not answer, because plants, except aquatics, cannot absorb "free water." They can only use the capillary water around each soil particle, and excess water, because it fills up space which should be filled with air, is worse than useless. Instead of reviving wilted plants this excess water is itself the cause of wilting.

Wilted flowers can often be revived by submerging their stems, and making a fresh cut, under water, never allowing the freshly cut stem to come out of the water until the flowers have revived. Some flowers, especially dahlias, poppies, and heliotrope may be revived by making a fresh cut and dipping the end of the flower stalk for a few seconds in hot water (150°–170°). *See also* CUT FLOWERS.

**WIND.** Even more than too much heat, wind is an unfavorable factor in any garden, and most garden operations should never be attempted in a high wind. Some of the things that should never be done in a high wind are:

| | |
|---|---|
| Seeding a Lawn | Spreading Lime or Fertilizer |
| Cutting Flowers | Planting Trees or Shrubs |
| Planting Seedlings | Moving Evergreens or Broad-leaved Evergreens |

Some of these things can be done in a wind, if you don't mind a thorough dusting from lime or fertilizer, or are

---

* Special articles on the subjects indicated by an asterisk (*) will be found at the words so marked.

resigned to losing much of your grass seed. But planting operations of any sort are far better postponed to a quiet or cloudy day. Wind greatly increases the rate of transpiration, and the shock of transplanting.

Another feature of wind to observe closely, particularly in the prairie states and along the seacoast, is to watch the prevailing direction of the summer and winter winds. If either is violent some protection against them must be provided before a good garden is possible. *See* WINDBREAKS. Also, in towns or cities it is equally desirable to watch the prevailing wind direction, in order to avoid if possible the steady fumes of factory smoke. *See* SMOKE.

Still another feature of wind is the necessity to exclude as much as possible from the wild garden. Plants of the cool, moist forest floor do not tolerate winds, and the wild garden should be screened by planting, even more than most garden sites. *See* WILD GARDEN.

**WINDBREAK.** In regions of high winds, such as prairies or along the seashore, it is necessary to plant wind-resistant trees to form a screen behind which the better kinds of gardening are possible. Such shelter trees, or in more extensive plantings what are called protection woods, must be spaced so thickly that even in their early years they form some protection against wind. By crowding they also protect each other.

For a small garden one of the best windbreaks is a high, thick hedge, preferably of the California privet. For the details of planting and care *see* HEDGES.

Where higher protection is needed a dense growth of the following trees is by far the best, but they are better adapted to regions from zone* 5 northward than south of this. All are extremely wind-resistant and grow fairly rapidly:

| | |
|---|---|
| Russian Mulberry | Box-elder (a maple) |
| Osage Orange | Silver Maple |
| London Plane | Cottonwood |
| Pea tree | Certinensis Poplar |

In regions of more heat, from zones* 6 and 7 southward, very effective shelter belts can be made with *Tamarix articulata*, or *Cupressus arizonica*, and in Calif. the Monterey cypress is often so used. Also in Calif. various eucalyptus trees will make a good screen against wind. Some fruit crops, especially lemons, demand such protection from wind. In Fla. good wind-resistant trees will be found in the genus *Casuarina*, and a useful shrub for that purpose is *Tephrosia candida*.

Some Californian gardeners, for low (5–6 ft.) windbreaks, use the showy *Lavatera assurgentiflora*, but the plant is not hardy in cold regions.

In regions of very heavy snowfall a windbreak will act as a snow trap, just as the snow guards do along the highway or railroad. If protection from snow is desired the windbreak must be located at right angles to the prevailing direction of the winter winds. Otherwise windbreaks are more often used as a protection for late spring or hot summer winds which, because of normal growth of leaves, are often more destructive than winter winds.

**WIND BURN.** A withered, apparently blasted condition of foliage, due to violent winds. It is often seen along the seashore or on prairies, and leaves so affected do not usually recover. Wind-burned privet, looking as though fired in Aug., will, however, leaf out the following season with little or no permanent damage to the hedge. The term is also applied, not very accurately, to the bronzed condition of some evergreens in winter, from which they usually recover.

**WINDFLOWER** = *Anemone*.

**WINDMILL PALM** = *Trachycarpus fortunei*.

**WINDOW GARDENING.** The garden at our windows allows much leeway both as to variety in the type of garden and the construction of window boxes. Plants grown in the house for interior decoration (*see* HOUSE PLANTS), the raising of seedlings, etc. (*see* HOUSE PLANTS and TERRARIUM), or the placing of geraniums on the window sill or fire escape are sometimes included in window gardening, but in this article the window box or vest-pocket garden is considered only in its relation to the exterior beautification of the house.

WINDOW BOXES. Moisture and drainage must be considered in the construction of all window boxes. If a simple wooden one, it should be of some moisture-resistant material, such as white pine, cypress or cedar, and at least one and one quarter inches thick. Outside spar varnish, three coats, applied to the inside will help in making the box water-resistant. Brass or copper screws are essential because they are rust proof. Metal brackets are more practical than wooden ones, but on brick or stone buildings they must be fastened with expansion bolts.

A simple window box of annuals

Wooden boxes may be made to fit any size of window sill, as far as length is concerned, but they should be at least eight or ten inches wide and deep. Bore a half-dozen three-quarter-inch holes in the bottom, through which the water can escape. Place broken crocks, cinders or gravel over the holes, to ensure good drainage.

There are many variations of the simple window box, such as those made of metal, terra cotta, concrete, stucco, stone or tile. A pleasant fiction exists regarding the so-called "self-watering" qualities of the metal boxes now on the market. These are actually sub-irrigating boxes in which the water, poured through a tube into the bottom of the box, is drawn up through the gravel and soil in the same manner that moisture is drawn to the surface of the ground by capillary attraction. This is a decided advantage over the other type of box, as it eliminates daily watering of the plants, prevents hardening of the surface soil from top watering, and promotes root growth. In the city, stone or tile boxes are often used with excellent effect.

PLANTING. The city dweller can buy many varieties of potted plants from the florist, and in some cases it is wiser to plunge* these pots in the soil, rather than to take the risk of transplanting. Where the climate is mild, or in the advent of an early spring, bulbs can precede the more tender plants, and thus give a month's earlier bloom. In choosing your combinations do so with an eye to the general effect when viewed also from the inside.

In selecting your plants, divide them into three general groups: those taller growing ones which will form a suitable background; those which grow upright to reach a few inches above the top of the box; and those which trail down over the edges. The plants chosen will depend also in large part upon the exposure, especially in the city where the amount of sunlight is often limited to an hour or two a day. For shaded positions the following plants are suitable: pansies, snapdragons, Swan River daisies, fuchsias, begonias, astilbe and forget-me-nots. Foliage plants for shaded boxes are English ivy, *Asparagus sprengeri*, crotons, wandering Jew, coleus, ferns, and caladiums. *Euonymus radicans* and *Lonicera japonica halliana* are good climbers for shaded locations.

In midsummer the sun beats with relentless fury on all exposed positions, but petunias, portulaca, ageratum, candytuft, heliotrope, lantana, annual phlox, marigolds, nemophila, verbena, sedum, and California poppies, all stand heat and sun well. Balcony petunias (*see* PETUNIA), trailing nasturtiums and begonias may be used for drooping or trailing effects, as well as English and German ivy.

Winter boxes, especially in the city, may be planted with

---

* Special articles on the subjects indicated by an asterisk (*) will be found at the words so marked.

dwarf evergreens. Yew, box, *Juniperus communis hibernica*, Mugo pine, and the dwarf heathers are all good; sink young specimens of the larger kinds in pots into the earth so that they are easily removable in spring.

Certain plants seem to belong to formal effects, while other flowers, old-fashioned and intimate, belong to small houses and suburban cottages. A purely formal arrangement, such as might grace the splendor of an Italian terra cotta or Spanish tile window box, is closely clipped dwarf box alternating with pale yellow and white tuberous-rooted begonias, which are double, single, crested and fringed, with a fine leaf type of English ivy for the trailer. Dwarf evergreens or aucubas could be used instead of box, in combination with the rich mahogany shades of dwarf marigolds and purple fuchsias. Other rather formal combinations are small pink and blue hydrangeas with the pale green-scented lemon verbena and *Cissus capensis*; Rex begonias, *Vinca major variegata* for the trailer, and *Pteris* or dwarf forms of the Boston fern for the inner edge; and carefully chosen plants of coleus, which if used for foliage alone, with the unattractive flowers kept picked off, gives a fine color effect. Should there be a ground planting of shrubs or evergreens directly beneath the window box, omit long trailing effects, as a bit of intervening wall space and an upright planting avoids a crowded appearance.

A formal window box for a city house or apartment, with evergreens, ivy, etc.

A less elaborate box, but slightly more informal, may be had by using carefully chosen potted plants. Geraniums do double duty for either formal or informal usage, but for greatest effectiveness mix the single and double varieties, and give them plenty of sun. The semi-double S. A. Nutt has rich dark crimson flowers of a large size and combines beautifully with the double pure white La Favorite. Another good white is Mme. Recamier. The old-fashioned Dryden has blossoms of a brilliant cherry-red, with white eyes, and is an exceptionally free bloomer. Another semi-double is Beauté Poitevine with large salmon-pink blossoms, which combines well with white, and perhaps two or three dracaenas, for accent and height. The single geraniums may be had in all shades, but they drop their petals easily, although very free-blooming. Zinnias, marigolds, dwarf salvia, lobelia, petunias and practically all medium-sized potted plants may be used.

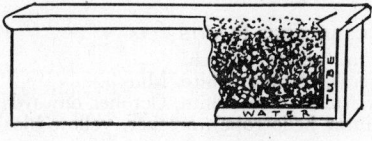

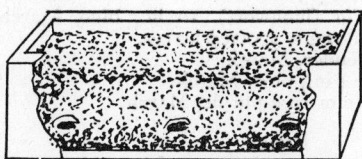

Below, an old-fashioned window box ready for planting (note the holes in the bottom and drainage crocks below the soil). Above, a sub-irrigated window box (for details see text).

*Vinca*, English ivy, wandering Jew with variegated leaves, or any other suitable climber or trailer might be used as the pendant vine. If a trellis is used in connection with a window box plant some of the many varieties of morning-glories (Heavenly Blue is one of the finest blues, while Rose Marie is a lovely soft pink), *Cobaea scandens*, cypress vine, climbing nasturtiums (these must be sprayed), or sweet peas.

Those who live in the country or suburbs have doubtless planned and planted in the fall previous, so that early in spring the window boxes will be gay with pastel shades of hyacinths in lavender, blue, rose and yellow. These will probably be followed by tulips in shades of rosy-pink and buttercup-yellow, or salmon-pink tulips and forget-me-nots. An easy way to fill the window boxes with spring-blooming things is to dig them from the garden when the buds appear. Disturb the roots as little as possible, and plant them close enough together to get a good colorful effect. Fluffy blue ageratum and pink candytuft combined with the Allegheny vine, which makes a mass of feathery foliage the first year, is charming against a white New England cottage. Brown and gold schemes are lovely near the sea. A stained cottage might have boxes filled with bronze and yellow marigolds combined with orange nemesia, or brown and yellow pansies and a mass of tiny marigolds (*Tagets*).

The cheapest way to fill the window box is to plant seeds of annuals directly into the soil in the box. Calendulas, African marigolds, nicotiana, zinnias, stock, sweet alyssum, ageratum, portulaca — in fact almost all of the annuals that grow easily in the garden.

Porch and flower boxes are planted the same and require the same care as window boxes. It is best to place the porch boxes upon cleats, rather than to set them flat down on the porch rail, as in this way air circulates beneath the box and keeps the bottom of it from rotting. It allows also free escape of surplus water. For porch decoration potted plants, such as palms, may be used, and fern balls and hanging baskets (*see* HANGING BASKETS) add variety. In this connection the golden *Scindapsus aureus* may be used wherever a pendant plant is wanted.

Planting requirements are very simple, providing ample allowance is made for good drainage conditions. An inch layer of coarse ashes or pebbles over the broken crocks or cinders which cover the drainage holes will further facilitate good drainage. Then fill the box with soil. Potting mixture* 3 will care for most of the plants grown in window boxes. Fill the box nearly to the rim, water, and set aside for a day or two, so that the soil will settle considerably before planting. The plants must be set closer together than is usual when placing them in the garden, but not so close that they appear crowded.

Evaporation is rapid in hot weather and the boxes must be thoroughly watered every morning and every evening after sundown. Pour the water on slowly and allow it to soak well into the soil, rather than to stand on the surface. A little liquid manure or some good commercial fertilizer applied once a week will help in producing large and free-blooming plants. As with indoor plants, insects and pests must be controlled with sprays, syringing, and other methods of control. For the details *see* PLANT DISEASES and INSECT PESTS. — C. H. M.

**WIND-POLLINATED.** Having the pollen carried by wind instead of insects, which is the usual procedure. Plants, such as the pines, grasses, birches, and many others, are wind-pollinated, and are hence often said to be anemophilous.

**WIND POPPY** = *Meconopsis heterophylla*.

**WINEBERRY** = *Rubus phoenicolasius*. *See also* ARISTOTELIA.

**WINE GRAPE.** All the best wines are derived from varieties of *Vitis vinifera*, generally called *vinifera* grapes. But many other varieties or species of grapes are also used to make wine and brandy. *See* GRAPE.

**WINE PALM.** Several palms with a sweet juice are used to make wine, especially in India and the East Indies. Among cult. palms so used and usually called wine palm are *Caryota urens* and *Jubaea spectabilis* (*see* both genera).

---

* Special articles on the subjects indicated by an asterisk (*) will be found at the words so marked.

**WINE PLANT.** The common garden rhubarb (which see).

**WINESAP.** An apple variety. *See* APPLE.

**WING.** A membranous or leaf-like appendage found on many fruits as in the stone cress, ash, maple, *Ptelea trifoliata*, etc. Wings are often found on leafstalks, as in most citrus fruits. There are also corky-winged twigs, as in the sweet gum and in *Euonymus alatus*.

**WINGED EVERLASTING** = *Ammobium alatum*.

**WINGED PEA** = *Lotus tetragonolobus*.

**WINGED PETIOLE.** A winged leafstalk. *See* PETIOLE.

**WINGED SPINDLE-TREE** = *Euonymus alatus*.

**WINTER.** As part of the name of many plants, and not a few garden activities, *winter* is very common. Those that occur here and their proper equivalents are:

Winter aconite = *Eranthis hyemalis*; Winter annual (see first main entry below); Winterberry = *Ilex glabra* and *I. verticillata* (see HOLLY); Winter-bloom (see HAMAMELIS); Winter bouquet (see DRIED FLOWERS); Winter bud (see BUDS); Winter cauliflower = *Brassica oleracea botrytis* (for culture see CAULIFLOWER); Winter cherry = *Physalis alkekengi*; Winter cress (see BARBAREA); Winter crookneck squash = *Cucurbita moschata* (for culture see SQUASH); Winter daffodil = *Sternbergia lutea*; Winter fern (see POISON HEMLOCK); Winter garden (see second main entry below); Winter grafting (see GRAFTING); Winter grape = *Vitis cordifolia*; Wintergreen (see WINTERGREEN below); Winter hazel (see CORYLOPSIS); Winter heath = *Erica carnea*; Winter heliotrope = *Petasites fragrans*; Wintering (see PROTECTING PLANTS); Winter jasmine = *Jasminum nudiflorum*; Winter-kill (see WINTER-KILL below); Winter melon (see MELON); Winter pink = *Epigaea repens* (see TRAILING ARBUTUS); Winter protection (see PROTECTING PLANTS); Winter purslane = *Montia perfoliata*; Winter radish = *Raphanus sativus longipinnatus* (see RADISH); Winter rose = *Helleborus niger*; Winter savory = *Satureia montana* (see SAVORY); Winter squash = *Cucurbita maxima* (for cult. see SQUASH); Winter sunscald (see SUNSCALD); Winter-sweet = *Origanum vulgare*; Winter sweet pea (see SWAINSONA GALEGIFLORA); Winter vetch = *Vicia villosa*; Winter work (see GARDEN CALENDAR).

**WINTER ANNUAL.** An annual plant, sown late in the summer or early fall, which lies dormant over the winter and completes its growth the following season. Such annuals may be protected with a light mulch of straw or leaves, in severe climates, and really approach biennials in their method of handling. Unfortunately many weeds are winter annuals, and in the late fall and early spring are hard to control because the ground is usually too wet for cult.

**WINTER GARDEN.** It is not usual in northern latitudes to plan for flowers in the open air in winter, yet it is possible to contrive a winter garden even in cold climates that will give shelter from cold winds and refreshment to the eye, and even produce a few flowers during the so-called flowerless months. Evergreens, both broad and narrow-leaved, will play an important part in its furnishing, as will shrubs that have colored bark, and such as carry their berries late.

The choice of a situation must be carefully made. It is imperative that it be open to the south and cut off by some means from the prevailing winter winds. A south-facing wall provides a comfortable back, or the angle of house walls may be utilized for two sides, and if there is a chimney in the wall greater warmth will be furnished. The remaining sides may be made of some close-knit evergreens, such as hemlock or spruce, planted close together and kept clipped so that they will grow the thicker.

If no wall is available an inclosure of evergreens may be made in any part of the grounds and left open to the south so the full force of the sun may enter. It is wise not to make this inclosure too large but to keep it small enough to seem a snug refuge, not only for the plants, but for individuals who enjoy sitting out of doors in the winter sunshine.

If only a very small winter garden is desired one may easily be built into the rock garden, for it is a simple matter to arrange sheltered hollows and heat-retaining surfaces among the rocks.

In connection with the winter garden it must be remembered that while it is warmer in winter than the rest of the garden it is also warmer and probably drier in summer. Plants growing there must be watered during dry periods and the soil kept stirred to form a mulch. Bulbs and herbaceous plants may be scattered about at the base.

Flowering dates given in the following lists are for the neighborhood of New York. Plants marked † are tender in that locality, but may be grown southward.

### FLOWERING SHRUBS AND TREES

*Mahonia japonica*, 6 ft., and a broad-leaved evergreen. Yellow flowers. March.
*Mahonia bealei*, much like the foregoing, but flowers smell of lily-of-the-valley.
†*Meratia praecox*, yellow, blossoms in winter.
*Cornus mas*, tree, 15–20 ft., yellow blossoms in February and March.
*Corylopsis spicata*, yellow cowslip-scented flowers in Feb.–March.
*Chaenomeles japonica* (flowering quince), scarlet flowers in March–April.
†*Daphne mezereum*, 3–4 ft., white or pink flowers, fragrant, March–April.
*Daphne odora*, evergreen, white fragrant flowers in March–April.
*Epigaea repens*, creeper, pink, March–April.
*Erica carnea*, 6–8 in., white or rose flowers throughout winter (with protection).
*Hamamelis japonica*, *H. mollis* and *H. vernalis* (witch-hazels), slender shrubs or small trees, with yellow flowers.
*Jasminum nudiflorum* (winter jasmine), slender and sprawling; yellow flowers in Feb. and March.
*Lonicera fragrantissima* and *L. standishi*, creamy flowers in March–April.
*Magnolia stellata*, March.
*Pieris floribunda* and *P. japonica*, evergreens, creamy flowers in March.
*Salix discolor* (pussy willow), catkins in Feb.–March.

### HERBACEOUS PLANTS

*Adonis amurensis*, 18 in., yellow, March.
*Arabis albida* (wall cress), trailing, white, March.
*Helleborus niger* (Christmas rose), white, October onwards.
*Petasites fragrans* (winter heliotrope), creeper, yellow blossom, March.
*Primula denticulata*, purple or white, March; *P. vulgaris* (common primrose).
*Pulmonaria angustifolia* (lungwort), 10 in., blue, March; *P. saccharata*, pink flowers, spotted leaves.
*Pulsatilla vernalis*, lavender, March.
*Synthyris rotundifolia*, 4 in., blue, March.
*Bergenia ligulata*, white or rose-purple, March.

### BULBS

*Anemone blanda*, blue, pink or white, late March.
*Bulbocodium vernum*, pinkish, Feb., March.
*Chionodoxa luciliae*, *C. sardensis*, blue, 3 in., March.
*Crocus longiflorus*; *C. pulchellus*, flowering in late autumn; *C. biflorus*; *C. imperati*; *C. susianus*; *C. tomassinianus*; *C. verna*, flowering Feb., March, April.
*Eranthis hyemalis* (winter aconite), yellow, 3 in., Feb., March.
*Galanthus* (snowdrop); *G. byzantinus*; *G. elwesi*; *G. nivalis*, double and single, Dec., Jan., Feb., March.
*Hyacinthus azureus*, pale blue, 3–4 in., March.
*Leucojum vernum*, white, March, 8 in.
*Narcissus cyclamineus*, 3 in., March; *N. minor*, 4 in., March.
*Scilla sibirica*, blue, 3–4 in., March. Shade.
*Sisyrinchium grandiflorum*, 10 ins., rose, March.
*Tulipa kaufmanniana*, 8 in., rose and cream, March.— L. B. W.

---

* Special articles on the subjects indicated by an asterisk (*) will be found at the words so marked.

WINTERGREEN = *Gaultheria procumbens* and *Chimaphila umbellata*. For flowering wintergreen see POLYGALA PAUCIFOLIA.

WINTERGREEN BARBERRY = *Berberis julianae*.

WINTER-KILL. The killing of twigs unfit to survive the winter, usually because the wood was not sufficiently ripened to withstand severe weather. Unless very badly winter-killed, most old wood of shrubs and trees will put out new shoots the following year, when the winter-killed twigs should be pruned. The real cause of winter-killing is lack of hardiness (which see). For ways of guarding against winter-killing see PROTECTING PLANTS.

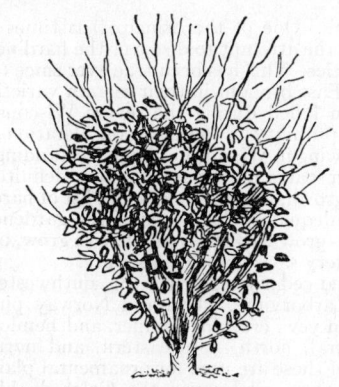

A typically winter-killed shrub as it appears in May before the dead wood has been removed.

WIRE GRASS = *Poa compressa* and *Eleusine indica*.

WIRE-STEM. See DAMPING-OFF.

WIRE-VINE = *Muehlenbeckia complexa*.

WISCONSIN. The state lies principally in zones* 1 and 2, a small portion in the southeastern corner falling in zone* 3.

CLIMATE. Climatic zone lines in Wisconsin are greatly affected by the water influences of Lakes Michigan and Superior, and the Mississippi and Wisconsin Rivers. Plant hardiness in Wisconsin is not entirely a matter of minimum temperatures, but is influenced by the atmospheric moisture and soil conditions prevailing in a given section, the latter being particularly important in the growing of tree fruits.

Variations in the length of the growing season make a considerable difference in the crops successfully grown in various sections. The average maximum growing season of 170 days is found in the southeastern corner of the state in Kenosha, Racine, and Milwaukee counties; and the shortest, under 100 days, in the extreme north central part. The shorter season of this section and the lower mean summer temperature make it very difficult and in some cases impossible to grow successfully the long-season crops which require relatively high temperatures.

Dates of killing frosts do not follow latitude lines. Frost lines are irregularly sharply crescent-shaped with the base of the crescent lying in the center of the state east and west. Lines showing the same late frost dates will have the two horns of the crescent, 50 to 100 miles north of the base, and the difference in early fall frosts is even greater. For example, Marinette, Portage, and New Richmond have nearly the same date for the last killing frost in spring and first killing frost in fall. The following table gives some significant data as to the range of frost occurrence and its variability as to latitude due to water and altitude influence.

| Town | Average date of last killing frost in spring | Latest killing frost | Average date of first killing frost in fall | Earliest killing frost |
|---|---|---|---|---|
| Marinette | May 8 | May 25 | Oct. 7 | Sept. 25 |
| Portage | May 3 | June 8 | Oct. 5 | Sept. 10 |
| New Richmond | May 10 | May 28 | Oct. 3 | Sept. 10 |
| Milwaukee | Apr. 26 | May 29 | Oct. 18 | Sept. 25 |
| Prentice | June 2 | June 29 | Sept. 9 | Aug. 15 |
| Grantsburg | May 22 | June 11 | Sept. 19 | Aug. 26 |

RAINFALL. The distribution of rainfall is quite uniform over the entire state. The mean for the state is 31 inches, the average varying for different sections from 28 to 34 inches. (These figures do not include the recent drought years.) The heaviest rainfall is in the elevated sections of the southwestern part of the state, and the smallest in the north central highlands. Wisconsin is fortunate in the amount of rainfall occurring during the growing season. Nearly 70 % of the precipitation is from April to September inclusive, which covers the growing season for most plants. Under ordinary conditions, the summer rainfall is adequate to produce satisfactory growing conditions making irrigation or watering unnecessary except for occasional brief intervals on lawns and gardens. Since the advent of the newer types of irrigation, there is an increasing tendency to utilize artificial watering.

SOILS. A wide variety of soils is found in the state. They range from the very heavy clays to light sands. There are also considerable areas of peat and muck. The lighter sandy soils are largely confined to four sections. The largest is the central section lying mostly in an area bounded by Portage and Wisconsin Dells on the south; Stevens Point and Wisconsin Rapids on the north; Waupaca and Berlin on the east; and Black River Falls and Sparta on the west. A much smaller section is found in the northeastern part of the state beginning near Shawano and extending northeasterly to the Wisconsin-Michigan state line. The third section is in the northwest corner of the state beginning in the vicinity of Grantsburg in Burnett County and extending northeasterly into Douglas and Bayfield counties. The fourth area is one in which the sandy lands are interspersed with areas of heavier soil. It lies in parts of Lincoln, Langlade, Oneida, Forest, and Vilas counties.

There is a large area of fine sandy loam soil northwest of Black River Falls extending across Jackson, Eau Claire, Chippewa, and Dunn counties and into southern Barron County. The soils in the remaining portion of the state are largely silt loams, with clay along Lake Superior and Lake Michigan from near Milwaukee north to Algoma, and extending west at Manitowoc to include the area around Lake Winnebago and the Fox River Valley to Green Bay.

PRINCIPAL GARDENING CENTERS. Amateur gardening is most highly developed in the eastern part of the state. This is due largely to the more favorable climatic conditions, greater density of population, and an earlier development of the summer resort possibilities which resulted in the development of country estates and summer homes, which served as stimuli and examples for the decorative gardening of many less pretentious year-round homes. Lake Geneva, Delavan, Milwaukee, the summer home section lying between Milwaukee and Watertown, Madison, around Lake Winnebago, Green Bay, Sheboygan, and Manitowoc are the principal centers of decorative gardening. It should not be inferred that gardening is largely confined to the eastern area, as in most of the cities of western Wisconsin excellent examples of good landscape art are to be found.

Amateur vegetable gardening is general throughout the state. While all sections are not equally adapted to growing vegetables, excellent results may be had in most sections if the proper selection of crops and proper cultural practices are observed.

FRUITS. The successful growing of fruits is more restricted. Climatic conditions and soils make the growing of most of the tree fruits and some of the small fruits hazardous in considerable areas. Tree fruit growing, with the possible exception of the native plum, is usually not very successful in those sections having light soils and low winter temperatures. Native plums, or hybrids of native plums, and the hardier varieties of apples are the only tree fruits which are adapted to the greater part of the state. Peaches are not adapted to any section even as a home orchard fruit. Hardy varieties of pears are grown to a limited extent as far north as La Crosse in the Mississippi Valley, in the two or three southern tiers of counties, and along Lake Michigan as far north as Manitowoc. They come more nearly being adapted in Racine and

* Special articles on the subjects indicated by an asterisk (*) will be found at the words so marked.

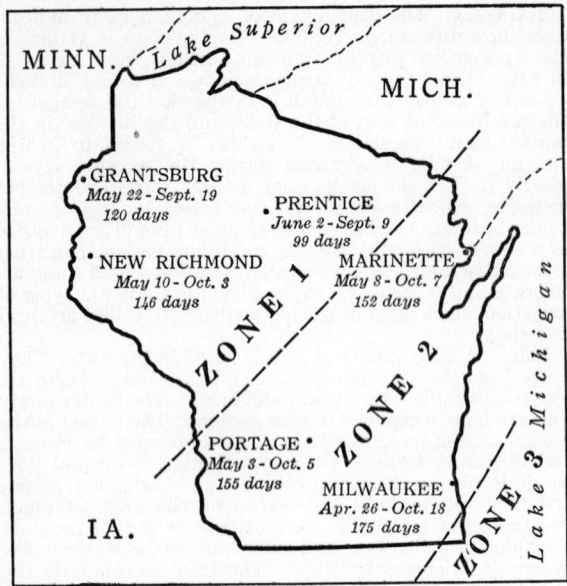

WISCONSIN

The zones of hardiness crossing Wisconsin are those shown on the colored map at ZONE, which should be consulted for details. The dates are the average latest killing frost in spring and the first one in the fall. The figures below the dates show the average length of the growing season.

Kenosha counties, but even there are not well enough adapted to be successful commercially.

The Wisconsin sour cherry is probably the best known of Wisconsin tree fruits. However, the area of successful commercial culture is quite limited. Even for home use its culture is largely limited to the section given for pear culture. There are two notable exceptions, however, the Green Bay Peninsula, and the Bayfield Peninsula. Sturgeon Bay is the center of commercial sour cherry growing in the state. The commercial area is found largely north of the body of water called Sturgeon Bay, but the cherry can be grown commercially along Lake Michigan from Washington Island to the southern state line. The cherry section in the Bayfield Peninsula is much smaller. It is confined to a rather narrow strip of land along the shore of Lake Superior from Washburn to Port Wing.

The strawberry may be said to be universally grown in Wisconsin. It is the most important fruit of the amateur garden. Currants and gooseberries can be grown quite generally, but are less satisfactory in the areas with light soils. The culture of raspberries and blackberries is more limited. Only the very hardiest varieties of blackberries can be successfully grown and these with reasonable certainty of success only in the southern two-thirds of the state. Black raspberries may be grown in about the same areas as blackberries. The red raspberry has a wider range and when the hardiest varieties are used, can be grown in most sections.

Grapes are almost entirely an amateur fruit in Wisconsin. The possibility of growing grapes is largely determined by the varieties selected. Varieties of the hardiness of Concord, Worden, and Moore's Early can be grown in the east half of the state south of Green Bay except in the sandy area; and in the three southern tiers of counties and the counties along the Mississippi to Saint Croix County. Covering is practiced quite extensively in the less favored sections to reduce the liability of winter injury. Hardier varieties, as Janesville and Wyoming, have a slightly wider range. Beta, which is the hardiest variety, gives evidence of succeeding reasonably well even under the most trying conditions, although its adaptability to all sections has not been definitely determined.

VEGETABLES. Wisconsin grows successfully all of the vegetables usually considered adapted to the northern states. Certain limitations do occur, however, in the northern part of the state because of lower mean summer temperature and a relatively short growing season. The cucurbits, tomatoes, peppers, and eggplant, are most affected, and to grow most of them successfully requires selecting the earlier varieties and starting them under glass. On the other hand, these same sections are better adapted to growing such crops as rutabagas, head lettuce, and cauliflower than the more southern sections.

ORNAMENTAL PLANTS. One of the principal pastimes of Wisconsin gardeners is the attempt to discover the hardiness of new kinds and varieties. This has been true ever since the early settlers from the East brought in their eastern varieties and had most of them killed during the severe Wisconsin winters. Climatic adaptability is the first consideration in selecting plants for growing in Wisconsin. Notwithstanding a winter climate in most parts of the state which definitely limits the plants to be grown, there is a sufficient list of hardy plants to meet quite adequately the needs of the gardener. He is not always able to grow what he would like to grow, but he usually can find a very satisfactory substitute.

Of the evergreens, red cedar is native in the southwestern and western sections; arborvitae, white and Norway pine, white spruce, American yew, creeping juniper, and hemlock are found in the central, north, northeastern, and northwestern sections. All of these are used for ornamental planting. In addition to native evergreens, the Colorado blue spruce, Douglas fir, white fir, Norway spruce, and mugo pine are quite generally adapted and used in ornamental plantings.

There is a wealth of native shrubs which are found well distributed over the state and which are constantly becoming more important in shrub plantings. The principal ones are red, gray, and blue dogwood; smooth and staghorn sumach; various viburnums; hazel, winterberry; ninebark, New Jersey tea, and the European elder in the south and red-berried elder in the north. Numerous introduced plants are used to supplement the natives. Those of widest adaptation to Wisconsin conditions are *Spiraea vanhouttei*, mock-orange, lilacs, honeysuckles, Japanese barberry, and the hardier species of roses. All of these are fairly hardy in most sections and are well adapted to the southern area and in the vicinity of large bodies of water except in the extreme north. Many of the tenderer shrubs do well in the southern, and in the eastern sections south of Green Bay, and in the western sections as far north as Hudson.

HERBACEOUS PLANTS. The peony, iris, coreopsis, Michaelmas daisy, delphinium, gaillardia, liatris, violet, columbine, several lilies, both native and introduced, are generally adapted throughout the state and serve as the foundation of herbaceous perennial plantings. The list of annuals which are available is limited only by their adaptability to soil conditions, prevalency of parasites; and in those of long season, to starting them under glass to adapt them to the shorter growing season which prevails in some sections. See ANNUALS.

The address of the Agricultural Experiment Station which has supplied the above information is Madison. The Station is always glad to answer questions requiring more detailed information than that given above.

Garden Club activities are extensive, especially in the regions of ornamental gardening. They include clubs of the Garden Club of America, the home office of which is 598 Madison Avenue, New York. There are also over 50 clubs affiliated with the Wisconsin Federation of Garden Clubs. For the nearest one to your locality write the Garden Editor, Houghton Mifflin Company, Boston, Mass. *See also* HORTICULTURAL SOCIETIES.

**WISCONSIN WEEPING WILLOW** = *Salix blanda*. See WILLOW.

**WISETONENSIS, -e** (wise-to-nen'sis). A name applied by its originator to *Schizanthus wisetonensis* and derived from Wiseton, a village in Nottinghamshire, England.

**WISTARIA** (wis-tair'i-a). Wisteria (which is the preferred spelling of the common name). Beautiful woody vines of the pea family, two of the species native in the U.S., the other 5

---

* Special articles on the subjects indicated by an asterisk (*) will be found at the words so marked.

Asiatic. They are widely planted for their profuse, spring bloom and often reach to the house-top when old. Leaves alternate,* compound,* the leaflets arranged feather-fashion, with an odd one at the end, the leaflets also alternate.* Flowers pea-like, in showy, drooping clusters (racemes*). Fruit a stalked, flattened pod (legume*) usually constricted between the seeds. (Named for Caspar Wistar, Pennsylvania professor of anatomy.) The plants are sometimes known as *Millettia* and *Kraunhia*, and the generic name is occasionally spelled *Wisteria*.

For Culture *see* below.

**floribunda.** Japanese wisteria. A tall-climbing vine, but not usually so high as the Chinese wisteria. Leaflets 13-19, ovalish or oblong, 1¾-3½ in. long. Flowers violet-blue or violet, about ¾ in. long, the cluster nearly 18 in. long. Pod velvety, 4½-7 in. long. Jap. May. Hardy from zone* 3 southward. There are several hort. varieties, one with white flowers, another with variegated leaves, but the most striking is *var.* **macrobotrys,** where the hanging flower cluster may be 3 ft. long. This variety is often offered as *W. multijuga*, and is very popular.

**frutescens.** A native American wisteria found wild from Va. to Fla. and Tex. It climbs 20-30 ft. high, and has 9-15 elliptic or ovalish leaflets ¾-2 in. long. Flowers about ½ in. long, lilac-purple, the hairy cluster scarcely over 4 in. long. Pod smooth, 2-4 in. long. June-July. Hardy from zone* 4 southward. Not much cult. The plant often listed as the *var. magnifica* is *W. macrostachya*.

**macrostachya.** A native American wisteria found wild from Tenn. to Ill., Mo., and Tex. Leaflets 9, ovalish, 1-2½ in. long. Flowers lilac-purple, but with a yellow spot, the individual flower stalks sticky-hairy, the clusters nearly 1 ft. long. Pod smooth, 3-6 in. long. June-July. Hardy from zone* 4 southward. Usually offered as *W. frutescens magnifica*.

**multijuga** = *Wistaria floribunda macrobotrys*.

**sinensis.** Chinese wisteria, and, with *W. floribunda*, the usual one in cult. It is a high-climbing vine reaching, in old specimens, the tops of trees or houses. Leaflets 7-13 (mostly 11), ovalish or oblong, 2½-4 in. long. Flowers bluish-violet, fragrant, about 1 in. long, the cluster about 12 in. long. Pods 5-7 in. long, densely velvety. China. May. Generally hardy from zone* 3 southward, but not so hardy as *W. floribunda*. The *var.* **alba** has pure white flowers.

### Wisteria Culture

These, probably the most desirable of all hardy woody vines, are difficult to transplant and quite apt to be without flowers for the first few years unless precautions are taken. In starting, it is always better to buy a small potted vine from a reliable nurseryman and so avoid the risk of field-dug specimens. While wisteria vines will grow in most ordinary garden soils, it is far better to make a special mixture for such a permanent vine which, if you want it to flower freely, must be richly fed. Dig out enough soil (about a barrelful) and replace with rich garden loam to which about ⅓ its bulk of old, well-rotted manure has been added. Thoroughly mix up the soil, pack it in well and plant the potted wisteria (with of course the pot removed). See that it gets water enough the first season and that you do not injure the roots while planting, nor afterwards by cultivation or otherwise.

The young vine will have to be tied up at first until it begins to twine around its support, for the wisterias have no tendrils.* Later it will look after its own climbing.

Many beautiful old wisteria vines are growing up the trunks of trees. If you pick such a site for your vine, do not start it under a young, vigorous, densely canopied tree, but choose an old, slowly dying one. Wisterias do not like shade, at least the best of the Asiatic species do not. If the vine is to grow against the house see that it is securely fastened for the first few years, or better yet, start it on a trellis.

While many nurserymen offer plants that have already bloomed once or twice, it is not unusual for a wisteria to grow vigorously for a few years and produce no flowers or only a few. While few gardeners take the trouble, more and better bloom will be produced by a careful system of pruning. In the summer prune out the long, straggling growths except those needed for climbing purposes. This is more likely to induce fine bloom than anything else. The straggling shoots should be cut back from ½-⅓ their length, which will induce the production of short spurs upon which next season's flower clusters will be borne. It is also necessary to give the vine an annual mulch of rich manure each fall and to dig it in carefully in the spring.

While normal wisterias are always vines, very beautiful effects can be had by the shrubby, weeping forms. These are the result of long training. The height is held at a definite point by pinching out young shoots, and after a trunk-like stem is produced (it takes years) the leaders are then allowed to droop to the ground.

In choosing wisterias it is well to remember that the finest of them are the two Asiatic species, *W. sinensis* and *W. floribunda*, and that both of them bloom before or with the unfolding of the leaves. The native American *W. frutescens* and *W. macrostachya* bloom later and after the leaves are grown. They are consequently never as showy as the Asiatic kinds, but they do prolong wisteria bloom.

**WISTERIA.** The preferred spelling of the common name for vines of the genus *Wistaria* (which see).

**WITCH-ALDER.** See FOTHERGILLA.

**WITCHES'-BROOM.** An abnormal, bush-like growth caused by a parasitic fungus, found on cedars, blueberries, and several other woody plants. They are not usually serious and the best remedy is to cut them out.

**WITCH-HAZEL.** See HAMAMELIS.

**WITCH-HOBBLE** = *Viburnum alnifolium*.

**WITCH'S-TEETH** = *Hosackia gracilis*.

**WITHE.** A slender, whip-like twig, especially a willow twig.

**WITHERING.** See WILTING.

**WITHEROD** = *Viburnum cassinoides*.

**WITHERTIP.** See Diseases at ORANGE.

**WITHY.** Any willow, especially the osier willow.

**WITHYWIND** = *Clematis vitalba* and *Solanum dulcamara*.

**WITLOOF.** A form of chicory grown as a salad plant. For description *see* CICHORIUM. For culture *see* CELLAR GARDENING. Another name for witloof is French endive.

**WOAD.** See ISATIS.

**WOADWAXEN** = *Genista tinctoria*.

**WOLFBERRY** = *Symphoricarpos occidentalis* and *Elaeagnus argentea*.

**WOLFSBANE** = Monkshood.

**WOMAN'S-TONGUE TREE** = *Albizzia lebbek*.

**WOMEN GARDENERS.** The gardening movement in America is very largely in the hands of women. For the chief manifestation of it *see* GARDEN CLUBS. For the training of professional women gardeners and landscape architects *see* GARDEN SCHOOLS.

**WONDERBERRY.** See SOLANUM NIGRUM.

**WONGA-WONGA** = *Pandorea pandorana*.

**WOOD ANEMONE** = *Anemone nemorosa* and *A. quinquefolia*.

**WOOD ASHES.** See ASH AND ASHES.

**WOOD BETONY.** See PEDICULARIS.

**WOODBINE.** A very old name for any number of vines. Those in this book are *Parthenocissus quinquefolia* (the Virginia creeper), *Clematis virginiana* (the common wild clematis), and *Lonicera periclymenum* (an Old World honeysuckle).

**WOOD CUDWEED** = *Gnaphalium sylvaticum*.

**WOOD DAFFODIL** = *Uvularia grandiflora*.

**WOOD HYACINTH** = *Scilla nonscripta*.

**WOODLANDS.** See FORESTRY.

**WOODLAND STAR** = *Lithophragma affinis*.

**WOOD LILY** = *Lilium philadelphicum*.

**WOOD MEADOW GRASS** = *Poa nemoralis*.

**WOOD-OIL TREE.** See TUNG-OIL TREE.

**WOOD ROT.** The wood of all trees, living or dead, is subject to decay or disintegration by micro-organisms, among

---

* Special articles on the subjects indicated by an asterisk (*) will be found at the words so marked.

which fungi are the most numerous and of greatest importance. Wood-destroying fungi use the wood as food and the materials which serve to make wood strong and hard are wholly or partly removed in the process, decay being the result. In the case of living trees, decay fungi enter through wounds or other openings in the bark. The reproductive bodies or spores of the wood-rotting fungi are nearly everywhere in the air. The number is naturally greater near heavily forested regions where there is an abundance of decaying wood, but the spores* may be carried for long distances by air currents. The fact that many wood-destroying fungi are the same the world over indicates that the spores* travel widely.

Although all of the wood of the tree is subject to decay, certain fungi show a preference for certain parts of the tree. Reference may then be made to sapwood rots, heartwood rots, root rot, butt rots and the like. It follows that certain organisms thus become associated with definite types of decay and thus are recognizable. It may happen, however, that a fungus having become established in one region of the trunk, may subsequently invade other adjacent regions so that the above distinctions apparently disappear.

If the wound penetrates a short distance, so that only a few rings of the outer (sapwood) are exposed, the opportunity is given for a sapwood rot to start. Such rots are characterized by rapid development and superficial, though often serious effect on the tree. The outer wood layers are invaded, next to the vulnerable cambium, and death of the overlying bark soon follows. Sapwood rots frequently follow fire scarring or winter injury. Rots of the sapwood are sometimes admitted through wounds which may be described as bruises or contusions where the tree has been struck a blow by a falling object, a motor vehicle or other agent.

The bulk of the wood of mature trees is heartwood and decay of this portion of the tree is of great importance in the deterioration of older individuals, since to a large extent these trees depend upon the heartwood for mechanical support. Heartwood-rotting fungi gain entrance mainly through larger wounds, which extend deeply into the tree. Broken branches or tops where the heartwood is exposed are common avenues of entry. The invasion of the decay is slow but continuous and profound changes occur in the physical and chemical properties of the wood. It becomes softer and lighter in weight and rapidly loses its strength. Color changes and certain types of fracture and fragmentation furnish the distinguishing characteristics of the various rots and some may with a little experience be recognized on sight. *See* illustration at PLANT DISEASES.

Structural timber, fence posts, bedding frames, wooden sills and like materials are subject to decay if constantly exposed to weather and in contact with other decaying wood or moist ground. The decay of wood apart from the tree is essentially the same process but is caused by different fungi.

Some time before the final stage in the disintegration of the wood is reached, most decay-producing fungi form fruiting bodies on the outside of the tree or piece of rotting wood. The spores* which serve to perpetuate the fungus are borne on these mature fungi and liberated into the air in enormous numbers in such a way that they are easily carried away by wind and air currents. In this manner, some spores find places favorable for initiating decay anew.

As most of the decay of wood starts at some injured part of the tree, the remedy and prevention is always to see that such injuries are repaired. The details of this will be found at TREE SURGERY. — D. S. W.

**WOODRUFF** = *Asperula*.

**WOOD SAGE** = *Teucrium canadense*.

**WOODSIA** (wood'zi-a). Tufted,* mostly rock-inhabiting ferns of the family Polypodiaceae, comprising over 25 species, and natives of the cooler and cold regions, mostly from the northern hemisphere. They have stout rootstocks and numerous fronds which (in ours) are once- or twice-compound and often with a shaggy stalk. Spore cases scattered on the under side of the leaf segments, usually at the forking of the veins. (Named for Joseph Woods, English botanist and architect.)

The cult. woodsias are plants for the hardy fern garden, and prefer rocky, shady places. For culture *see* FERNS AND FERN GARDENING.

ilvensis. Rootstocks growing in masses, the plant densely tufted.* Stalk of the frond rusty and chaffy. Leaves compound,* generally lance-shaped, 5–10 in. long, the stalkless segments coarsely toothed, the teeth themselves toothed, rusty on the under side. Northern N.A., south to Ky. and Iowa. Also in Greenland and Eurasia, chiefly on exposed rocks.

obtusa. Rootstock slender and creeping, the stalk of the frond smooth. Fronds twice-compound,* 1–3 ft. long, more or less triangular-lance-shaped, pointed at the tip, its main segments cut into sharply toothed ultimate segments which are themselves toothed, the foliage hence fine and feathery. Eastern N.A., mostly in rocky woods.

**WOOD SORREL.** *See* OXALIS.

**WOODWARDIA** (wood-war'di-a). Chain fern. Rather coarse marsh ferns of the family Polypodiaceae with creeping rootstocks,* and often bearing both infertile foliage fronds and other spore*-bearing fertile fronds. The fronds are once- or twice-compound* or divided, the spore cases borne in chain-like lines along the midrib of the fertile fronds. (Named for Thomas J. Woodward, English botanist.)

The cult. chain ferns are not of much hort. importance and present no difficulties in growing. *Woodwardia areolata* grows best in rather acid wet places, but the others are not particular so long as the place is moist. They require less shade than most ferns and in the wild often grow in full sun.

areolata. Rootstock creeping and chaffy. Foliage fronds triangular-ovalish, the segments narrow, minutely toothed on the margins. Fertile or spore-bearing fronds similar but larger than the foliage fronds, the segments narrower, the under side with a double row of chain-like spore cases. Eastern U.S.

virginica. Rootstock creeping, chaffy only at the end. Fronds of one sort, 2–3 ft. high, the stalks polished. Fronds twice-compound,* the main segments narrow, deeply toothed, but the teeth not again toothed. Spore cases in chain-like lines on the lower side of the ultimate segments, mostly along the midrib. Eastern N.A., also in Bermuda. Sometimes known as *Anchistea virginica*.

**WOODWAXEN** = *Genista tinctoria*.

**WOODY PLANTS.** Shrubs, trees, and woody vines are distinguished from all herbaceous plants by the fact that they produce wood, and have buds which survive above ground during the winter. Fleshy-stemmed herbs do neither (except in rare cases), and their buds are underground during the winter. For Woody Vines *see* VINES.

**WOOLLY.** Covered with soft, loose, somewhat matted hairs, hence resembling wool. The technical term is lanate. *See also* TOMENTOSA.

**WOOLLY MANZANITA** = *Arctostaphylos tomentosa*.

**WOOLLY SUNFLOWER.** *See* ERIOPHYLLUM.

**WOOLLY THYME** = *Thymus serpyllum lanuginosus*. *See* THYME.

**WORM.** For true worms *see* EARTHWORM. For the caterpillars often incorrectly called worms *see* INSECT PESTS.

**WORM-GRASS** = *Spigelia marilandica* and *Sedum album*.

**WORMWOOD.** Any species of *Artemisia*, especially *A. absinthium*.

**WORMWOOD SAGE** = *Artemisia frigida*.

**WOUNDS.** *See* TREE SURGERY.

**WOUNDWORT** = *Anthyllis vulneraria*. *See also* STACHYS.

**WREATH GOLDENROD** = *Solidago caesia*. *See* GOLDENROD.

**WULFENIA** (wool-fen'ia). Eurasian, little known, perennial herbs of the family Scrophulariaceae, comprising about 8 species, of which only **W. carinthiaca** from the Carinthian Mountains is occasionally cult. in the rock garden. It needs a gritty soil, moist in the growing season but not too wet in the winter as the plant rots easily. It is about 9 in. high with basal, oblongish, toothed leaves, 6–8 in. long. Flowers tubular, blue, about ⅓ in. long, in a dense terminal cluster (ra-

* Special articles on the subjects indicated by an asterisk (*) will be found at the words so marked.

ceme*-like), the stalk of which may be 2 ft. high. Corolla cylindrical, 4-lobed, the stamens* 2. Fruit a 4-valved capsule. (Named for F. X. von Wulfen, Austrian mineralogist.)

**WYCH ELM** = *Ulmus glabra.* See ELM.

**WYETHIA** (wy-ee'thi-a). Mule-ears. Sunflower-like perennial herbs of the family Compositae, all the 8 known species from western N.A., two of them of secondary hort. interest, but occasionally planted in the wild garden. They have basal or alternate* stem leaves which are narrow and without marginal teeth. Flower heads yellow, solitary, or a few in a cluster, the ray flowers in a single row. (Named for N. J. Wyeth, American botanical explorer.)

They are plants of similar culture to the sunflower (which see).

**amplexicaulis.** A smooth herb 1–2 ft. high. Leaves glossy-green, oblongish, 8–12 in. long, the upper nearly stalkless or clasping the stem. Flower heads nearly 3 in. wide, bright yellow. British Columbia to Colo.

**angustifolia.** Not over 2 ft. high, the stem hairy. Leaves oblongish or narrower, 8–12 in. long, the upper nearly stalkless but not clasping, sometimes stalked. Flower heads about 4 in. wide. Calif.

**WYOMING.** The state lies wholly in zones* 2 and 3.

SOILS. Wyoming soils covering an area of 62.5 million acres are derived from a great variety of crystalline, shale, sandstone and limestone rocks which have been weathered by an arid or semi-arid climate and vegetation.

Owing to the limited rainfall and vegetation, 49 million acres of this area are best adapted to grazing and livestock production. About 2 million acres are irrigated near the mountain ranges and streams. Although about three times this area could be irrigated, most of the available water is already pre-empted. About 8 million acres could be dry-farmed more or less intensively in the eastern and northeastern counties. Nine million acres are in mountain forests.

Most of the irrigated soils are mature brown loams and fine sandy loams developed upon level high terraces bordering the streams or upon level bench lands coated with loamy and gravelly soil transported from the mountains near by. A very small part of the heavy soils from shales are farmed or irrigated, in part because of the trouble caused by soluble alkali salts in the shales and in the soils developed upon them.

WYOMING

The zones of hardiness crossing Wyoming are those shown on the colored map at ZONE, which should be consulted for details. The dates are the average latest killing frost in spring and the first one in the fall. The figures below the dates show the average length of the growing season. Rainfall figures (in inches) show (1) the total annual rainfall and (2) the amount falling in the growing season at the places indicated.

Most soils are gray-colored on the surface with a relatively sandy texture from one to four inches deep overlying heavier brown subsoils. All bench and terrace lands contain much gravel, especially in the subsoil, and a lime horizon which makes them suitable for alfalfa, sugar beets, grain and root crops. New land needs to be tamed and organic matter incorporated in it by growing alfalfa until the land reaches its full productivity.

FLOWERS AND SHRUBS. All of the common varieties of flowers including the columbine, snapdragon, *Phlox, Lychnis, Campanula, Coreopsis,* bleeding-heart, *Delphinium,* both annual and perennial, dahlias, gladioli, peony, *Anchusa, Papaver,* and asters are adapted to localities in the state where the elevation is 6000 feet or less. The list for higher elevations includes many varieties such as pansy, *Portulaca, Cosmos, Rudbeckia, Alyssum,* and *Centaurea.*

Ornamental trees for all sections of the state include *Picea pungens,* and *Juniperus communis depressa.*

Many native shrubs are suitable in all parts of the state. These include *Cornus, Ribes, Sambucus, Shepherdia, Elaeagnus, Betula, Amelanchier, Potentilla, Symphoricarpos, Acer,* and many of the low-growing willows.

*Caragana, Syringa,* and *Cotoneaster* are dependable introduced shrubs, especially *Caragana,* which is useful for windbreaks.

The above-named varieties of plants are suitable for the irrigated sections of the state. They ordinarily will not grow well on dry land. The farmers in some dry land sections of the state, however, are growing gardens and flowers with a supply of water from the windmill or from favorably located springs. Where there is an ample supply of water available from such sources, in addition to that used for stock water, satisfactory flowers and shrubs may be grown. Cultivation is the principal precaution against failure in order that every bit of moisture may be conserved and held for the use of the growing plants.

In towns having a municipal water supply it is possible to grow all the plants listed in the foregoing paragraphs and others in addition, unless the towns are located in the highest elevations of the state, where the seasons are short and the nights cool.

CLIMATE. The variation in climate of different places in the state is associated for the most part with differences in altitude.

The length of time between killing frosts is shown for several places in the following table.

| Name of town | Average date of last killing frost in spring | Latest known killing frost | Average date of earliest killing frost in fall | Earliest known killing frost |
|---|---|---|---|---|
| Torrington | May 20 | June 10 | September 24 | September 8 |
| Worland | May 14 | June 7 | September 26 | September 11 |
| Lovell | May 20 | June 21 | September 16 | August 10 |
| Sheridan | May 18 | June 6 | September 20 | August 25 |
| Eden | June 18 | July 9 | September 8 | August 15 |
| Riverton | May 17 | June 1 | September 20 | August 7 |
| Powell | May 18 | June 13 | September 20 | August 25 |

RAINFALL

| Name of town | No. years recorded | Yearly total (inches) | Growing season total (5 mo.) (inches) |
|---|---|---|---|
| Torrington | 10 | 16.26 | 10.29 |
| Worland | 22 | 7.89 | 4.73 |
| Lovell | 21 | 7.84 | 4.65 |
| Sheridan | 38 | 15.21 | 8.02 |
| Eden | 23 | 6.41 | 3.74 |
| Riverton | 19 | 10.19 | 6.32 |
| Powell | 24 | 5.87 | 4.03 |

The address of the Agricultural Experiment Station, which has kindly supplied this information, is Laramie, Wyoming. The station is always ready to answer gardening questions.

---

* Special articles on the subjects indicated by an asterisk (*) will be found at the words so marked.

# X

**XANTHINA, -us, -um** (zan-thy′na). Yellow.

**XANTHISMA** (zan-this′ma). Little-known Texas herbs of the family Compositae, one of the two known species, **X. texanum**, occasionally grown for ornament. It is an annual (or biennial), 2–4 ft. high, with wand-like stems and narrow, alternate* leaves 1½–2½ in. long. Flower heads long-stalked, mostly solitary, about 2½ in. wide, the 18–20 rays yellow. The plant is not much grown, but as it grows naturally on dry, open prairies, it is well suited to open places with poorish soil. Seeds should be sown where wanted as the plant will bloom the first year, although often biennial in habit. (*Xanthisma* is from the Greek for yellow dyed, in allusion to the color of the flowers.)

**XANTHOCERAS** (zan-tho-seer′ras). A single species of rather handsome Chinese shrubs of the family Sapindaceae, **X. sorbifolia** grown for ornament. It is a shrub 10–15 ft. high with compound* leaves composed of 9–17 narrow, toothed leaflets which are 1–2 in. long and pale beneath. Flowers polygamous,* whitish, about ¾ in. wide, the base of each of the 5 petals with a yellow or reddish blotch. The flower cluster (raceme*) is rather showy, 6–10 in. long, upright, its individual flower stalks slender. Stamens* 8. Fruit a 3-valved capsule. It is an attractive shrub, holding its bright green foliage late in the fall. Not particular as to soils and propagated by root cuttings over bottom-heat, or by stratified seeds. April–May. Hardy from zone* 3 southward. (*Xanthoceras* is from the Greek for yellow horn, in allusion to the horn-like projections on the receptacle or disk.)

**XANTHORRHIZA, -us, -um** (zan-tho-ry′za). Yellow-rooted. For the plant sometimes known as *Xanthorhiza* see ZANTHORHIZA.

**XANTHOSOMA** (zan-tho-sō′ma). Tropical American, thick, fleshy-leaved herbs of the arum family, related to the elephant-ear, grown chiefly in the tropics for their starchy, edible rootstocks, but also grown for ornament in warm regions, and in the greenhouse. They have large, arrowhead-shaped leaves, sometimes cut or divided, and thick, channeled leafstalks. Flowers minute, unisexual,* crowded on a spadix* which is usually shorter than the spathe.* (For details see ARACEAE.) A somewhat diversified hort. group of plants as some are only grown for food, and in tropical America replace the taro for that purpose, while *X. lindeni* is an old favorite as a greenhouse foliage plant. (*Xanthosoma* is from the Greek for yellow body, in reference to the yellow stigma.)

*Xanthosoma atrovirens* and *X. sagittaefolium* are food plants in tropical America and can only be grown outdoors in extreme southern Fla. They need a rich, moist soil and should have frequent top-dressings of well-rotted manure. The two other species are foliage plants for the tropical greenhouse where they need the same conditions as *Caladium* (which see). While not such a showy foliage plant, *Xanthosoma lindeni* is a better house plant than the caladiums.

**atrovirens.** Malanga; also called West Indian kale. Leaves 2–3 ft. long and nearly 2 ft. wide, green above, bluish-green below, the grooved stalks nearly 2 ft. long. S.A.; widely planted in the W.I. for food.

**lindeni.** A handsome foliage plant producing a mass of white-veined leaves which are about 12 in. long, 4–6 in. wide, the stalks nearly 12 in. long. Spathe* nearly 6 in. long, white. Colombia. A good plant for the tropical greenhouse, or it can be used for summer bedding.

**sagittaefolium.** Tania. Yautia. A tropical American food plant, replacing the taro in the W.I. It has a distinct stem, 2–3 ft. high, but often appears stemless, the leafstalks arising from the ground. Leaves 2–3 ft. wide and long, green both sides, the stalks nearly 3 ft. long. Spathe* 7–9 in. long, greenish-white.

**violaceum.** A purplish-veined foliage plant, the leaves 18–24 in. long and nearly as wide, the purple stalks even longer. Spathes* about 12 in. long, yellowish-white. Tropical America.

**XANTHOXYLUM** = *Zanthoxylum*.

**XERANTHEMUM** (zer-ran′the-mum). Everlasting. A small group of Mediterranean annual herbs of the daisy family, **X. annuum** the common everlasting or immortelle, and perhaps the best-known of all everlastings. It is a white-felty annual 2–3 ft. high, with oblongish leaves 1–2 in. long, without marginal teeth. Flower heads long-stalked, solitary, about 1½ in. wide, composed wholly of white, purple, or violet disk flowers. Surrounding the head is a collection of small, papery or chaffy bracts* colored like the heads. There are several varieties, some with double flower heads. Should be grown as a hardy annual, or if wanted especially early, it may be started as a tender annual. See ANNUALS. For the best method of preserving the flowers for winter use see DRIED FLOWERS. (*Xeranthemum* is from the Greek for dry flower.)

**XEROPHYLLUM** (zer-o-fill′um). Turkey-beard. An unimportant group of North American herbs of the lily family, two of the 3 known species occasionally grown in the wild garden. They have woody rootstocks and wiry, basal, grass-like leaves. Flowers small, white, in a long-stalked, dense cluster (raceme*) which rises from the leaf rosette. Petals soon withering. Stamens* 6. Fruit a 3-valved capsule.* (*Xerophyllum* is from the Greek for dry leaf, in allusion to the wiry leaves.)

The eastern turkey-beard (*X. asphodeloides*) prefers moist, acid sand such as that found along the edges of pine-barren bogs. The western *X. tenax* is certainly hardy only in its own region. The two species are much alike.

**asphodeloides.** Leaves tough, wiry, rough-margined, about 15 in. long and 1/10 in. wide. Flowering stalk 4–5 ft. high, the terminal cluster (raceme*) dense, about 6 in. long. Pine-barrens. N.J. to Fla. June.

**tenax.** Elk-grass; also known as fire-lily. Leaves nearly 24 in. long, about ⅙ in. wide. Flowering stalk 4–5 ft. high, the terminal cluster (raceme*) nearly 20 in. long, the stamens* violet and longer than the petals. British Columbia to Calif. June–July.

**XEROPHYTE.** A plant adapted to a deficiency of water or to only periodic occurrence of it. While most xerophytes are desert plants, not all of them store large quantities of water as do the cacti. Many xerophytes have ashy or white foliage, or drop their leaves, or have varnished or tightly rolled leaves — all devices to reduce the plant's water needs. See SUCCULENTS.

**XIPHIUM** (zy′fi-um). A group name for a section of *Iris*.

**XOLISMA** (zo-liz′ma). A genus of handsome shrubs of the heath family, comprising about 30 species found in N.A. and eastern As., 3 of them cult. for ornament. They are closely related to *Pieris*, but the latter are evergreens, while only the fetter-bush is evergreen among the xolismas. They have alternate,* short-stalked leaves and small flowers in dense clusters (racemes*) which may be in the leaf-axils* or terminal. Corolla white or pinkish, mostly urn-shaped or bell-shaped. Stamens* 10. Fruit a small capsule* opening by terminal pores. (*Xolisma* is of unknown origin.) Sometimes known as *Lyonia*.

The xolismas need a distinctly acid soil, preferably sandy and with a pH of about 5.0 (see ACID AND ALKALI SOILS). They should have a permanent mulch of dried leaves and do not like disturbance of their roots. They are chiefly shrubs for the more informal border, the closely related genera *Pieris* and *Leucothoë* furnishing horticulturally more desirable shrubs. Propagated by cuttings.

**ligustrina.** Swamp andromeda; also called maleberry, he-huckleberry, and privet andromeda. A spreading shrub 7–10 ft. high. Leaves elliptic or oblongish, 2–3 in. long, nearly without marginal teeth. Flower cluster terminal, leafless, composed of racemes* grouped in a panicle, white. Eastern N.A. May–June. Hardy from zone* 2 southward. Prefers moist sand. Sometimes offered as *Andromeda ligustrina*.

**lucida.** Fetter-bush. An evergreen shrub 4–6 ft. high. Leaves broadly elliptic, 2–3 in. long, shining. Flowers in a terminal, leafy cluster (ra-

---

* Special articles on the subjects indicated by an asterisk (*) will be found at the words so marked.

ceme*), white or pinkish. Va. to Fla. and La. April-May. Hardy from zone* 6 southward. Sometimes sold as *Pieris lucida* and *Xolisma nitida*.

**mariana.** Stagger-bush. Wicopy. A shrub 4-6 ft. high. Leaves ovalish or elliptic, 1-2½ in. long, without teeth. Flowers white, nodding, in clusters (racemes*) from the leaf axils,* the clusters a little leafy. R.I. to Fla. to Ark. May-June. Hardy from zone* 3 southward. Sometimes sold as *Pieris mariana*.

**XYLOPHYLLA** (zy-lo-fill′a). A small genus of secondary hort. importance comprising about 10 species of tropical American shrubs of the spurge family, two of them occasionally grown as oddities in the greenhouse. They are spreading plants, the branches flattened into leaf-like organs. True leaves none, or borne only in youth, and soon falling. Flowers not conspicuous, without petals, borne in clusters along the margins of the leaf-like branches. (For flower structure see EUPHORBIACEAE.) Fruit a capsule.* (*Xylophylla* is from the Greek for woody leaf, in allusion to the leaf-like branches.)

Best grown in the warm-temperate greenhouse in potting mixture* 4. Propagated by cuttings of the leaf-like branches. Not certainly grown outdoors in the U.S.

**angustifolia.** A branching shrub 7-10 ft. high. Leaf-like branches about 3½ in. long and ½ in. wide, the small reddish flowers borne on the margins. Jamaica.

**speciosa.** Seaside laurel. A shrub, or even tree-like, 15-20 ft. high. Leaf-like branches 2-3 in. long, nearly 1 in. wide, the whitish flowers borne on the margins. Jamaica.

**XYLOSTEUM** (zy-los′te-um). Pre-Linnaean* name for some bush honeysuckles. See LONICERA.

# Y

**YAM.** The true yam is *Dioscorea* (which see). In the southeastern U.S. yam is often, but incorrectly, applied to the sweet potato.

**YAM BEAN.** Tropical herbaceous vines of the pea family, comprising the genus **Pachyrhizus** (pack-i-ry′zus), two of the 3 known species grown for the edible tubers and pods in warm countries but little known in the U.S. They have long, twining stems, often thickened and woody at the base, and compound* leaves with 3, often lobed, leaflets. Flowers pea-like, white or violet, borne in clusters (racemes*) which have swollen joints. Fruit a large, beaked, reddish-hairy pod (legume*), somewhat constricted between the flat seeds. (*Pachyrhizus* is from the Greek for thick root, in allusion to the tubers.)

The vines need support or they will sprawl over the ground. Grown from seeds.

**erosus.** Common yam bean. Tubers large, the stems 15-20 ft. long. Leaflets 3-6 in. long, the lateral ones somewhat oblique, the central one with angular lobes. Flowers violet or reddish-pink. Pod 4-6 in. long, the seeds 6-8. Tropical Regions.

**tuberosus.** Similar to the above, but the flowers white, the central leaflet scarcely lobed and the pods twice as large. S.A. (?).

**YAM FAMILY** = Dioscoreaceae.

**YAMPEE** = *Dioscorea trifida*.

**YANGTAO** = *Actinidia chinensis*.

**YANKEE CORN** = *Zea mays indurata*. See CORN.

**YARD.** See BACKYARD GARDEN. For the dimension see WEIGHTS AND MEASURES, 2.

**YARD-LONG BEAN** = *Vigna sesquipedalis*.

**YARROW** = *Achillea millefolium*.

**YATE-TREE** = *Eucalyptus cornuta*.

**YAUPON** = *Ilex vomitoria;* and sometimes, but less correctly, *I. cassine*. See HOLLY.

**YAUTIA** = *Xanthosoma sagittaefolium*.

**YAW-WEED** = *Morinda royoc*.

**YEDDO HAWTHORN** = *Raphiolepis umbellata*.

**YEDDO SPRUCE** = *Picea jezoensis*. See SPRUCE.

**YEDOENSIS, -e** (yed-o-en′sis). From Yeddo, Japan.

**YELLOW.** As an adjective, *yellow* is part of the name of many plants and things to do with a garden. Those that occur in here and their proper equivalents are:

Yellow adder′s-tongue = *Erythronium americanum;* Yellow aster = golden aster (see CHRYSOPSIS). See also note at ASTER); Yellow bedstraw = *Galium verum;* Yellow bell = *Allamanda neriifolia;* Yellow bells = *Emmenanthe penduliflora;* Yellow birch = *Betula lutea* (see BIRCH); Yellow buckthorn = *Rhamnus caroliniana;* Yellow calla lily = *Zantedeschia elliottiana* (see CALLA LILY); Yellow camomile = *Anthemis tinctoria;* Yellow cedar = *Juniperus occidentalis;* Yellow cypress = *Chamaecyparis nootkatensis;* Yellow daisy (see RUDBECKIA); Yellow dwarf (see Diseases at POTATO); Yellow elder = *Stenolobium stans;* Yellow-eyed grass = *Hypoxis hirsuta;* Yellow flat (see Diseases at LILIUM); Yellow flax = *Reinwardtia indica;* Yellow-flowering pea (see CROTALARIA); Yellow foxglove = *Digitalis ambigua* (see FOXGLOVE); Yellow fringed orchis = *Habenaria ciliaris;* Yellow fritillary = *Fritillaria pudica;* Yellow garden (see first main entry below); Yellow gentian = *Gentiana lutea;* Yellow gourds (see CUCURBITA PEPO OVIFERA); Yellow granadilla = *Passiflora laurifolia;* Yellow honeysuckle = *Lonicera flava;* Yellow jasmine = *Gelsemium sempervirens;* Yellow lady′s-slipper = *Cypripedium parviflorum;* Yellow leaf (see Diseases at CHERRY); Yellow locust = *Robinia pseudo-acacia* (see LOCUST); Yellow melilot = *Melilotus officinalis;* Yellow mombin = *Spondias mombin;* Yellow mosaic (see Diseases at RASPBERRY); Yellow Newtown (see APPLE); Yellow oak = *Quercus velutina* (see OAK); Yellow oleander = *Thevetia nereifolia;* Yellow oxide (see Mercury at FUNGICIDES); Yellow perilla = *Menispermum canadense;* Yellow pine = *Pinus ponderosa* (see PINE); Yellow pitcher-plant = *Sarracenia flava* (see PITCHER-PLANT); Yellow plum = *Prunus americana;* Yellow pond lily = *Nymphozanthus advenus;* Yellow poplar = *Liriodendron tulipifera* (see TULIP-TREE); Yellow puccoon = *Lithospermum angustifolium;* Yellow puccoon = *Hydrastis canadensis* (see GOLDENSEAL); Yellowroot = *Hydrastis canadensis* (see GOLDENSEAL. See also ZANTHORHIZA APIIFOLIA and COPTIS TRIFOLIA); Yellow rot (see Diseases at HYACINTH); Yellows (see Virus Diseases at PLANT DISEASES); Yellow sage = *Lantana camara;* Yellow skunk-cabbage = *Lysichitum camtschatensis;* Yellow star = *Helenium autumnale;* Yellow stonecrop = *Sedum reflexum;* Yellow trumpet narcissus (see NARCISSUS MINOR); Yellow tuft = *Alyssum argenteum;* Yellow violet = *Viola pubescens;* Yellow water lily = *Nymphaea mexicana;* Yellow-weed = *Solidago canadensis* (see GOLDENROD); Yellow-wood (see CLADRASTIS).

**YELLOW GARDEN.** Generally speaking, flowers of the yellow scale, ranging from pale yellow to orange, appear best in full sunshine. An evergreen hedge makes a good background for them as does a white stucco wall. Fences, trellis-work, arbors and furniture may be painted pure white, light or dark green or gray-blue. Other accessories should be in harmony. Introduced as foils, a few white, sky-blue or deep purple flowers bring about an excellent effect.

SHRUBS OR SMALL TREES TO BE USED AS ACCENTS OR BACKGROUND

SPRING-FLOWERING: *Benzoin aestivale*, 6-10 ft.; *Berberis*, many species, 3-10 ft.; *Cornus mas*, 10-15 ft.; *Corylopsis pauciflora*, 4-6 ft., *C. spicata*, 4-6 ft.; *Enkianthus campanulatus*, 6-10 ft.; *Forsythia*, all species, 6-10 ft.; *Hamamelis mollis*, 10-15 ft., *H. vernalis*, 6-10 ft.; *Kerria japonica;* Ma-

---

* Special articles on the subjects indicated by an asterisk (*) will be found at the words so marked.

*honia aquifolium*, 3–6 ft., *M. repens*, 1–2 ft.; *Azalea calendulacea*, 4–10 ft. and many hybrid azaleas; *Ribes odoratum*.
  SUMMER-FLOWERING: *Caragana arborescens*, 10–15 ft.; *Cytisus nigricans*, 3–6 ft., *C. scoparius*, 4–8 ft.; *Genista pilosa*, 2–3 ft., *G. tinctoria*, 2–3 ft.; *Hypericum prolificum*, 4–8 ft.; *Laburnum anagyroides*, 6–10 ft.; *Potentilla fruticosa*, 2–3 ft.; *Rosa hugonis*, 5–6 ft.; *R. xanthina* (yellow).
  AUTUMN-FLOWERING: *Hamamelis virginiana*, 10–15 ft.

### TALL PLANTS FOR USE IN BACKGROUND

  SPRING-FLOWERING: *Doronicum plantagineum*; *Fritillaria imperialis* (bulb).
  SUMMER-FLOWERING: *Achillea filipendulina*; *Althaea ficifolia* (Antwerp hollyhock); *Asphodeline lutea*; *Baptisia tinctoria*; *Buphthalmum salicifolium*; *Dahlia*, many varieties; *Helianthus annuus* (annual sunflower), *H. mollis*; *Hemerocallis* varieties (see DAYLILY); *Inula helenium*; *Lilium hansoni*, *L. henryi*, *L. superbum*; *Lysimachia vulgaris*; *Oenothera biennis*; *Rudbeckia laciniata*; *Tagetes erecta* (African marigold); *Thalictrum glaucum*; *Verbascum chaixi*, *V. olympicum*; *Zinnia*, many varieties (annual).
  AUTUMN-FLOWERING: *Cosmos* (annual); *Dahlia*; *Helenium autumnale*; *Helianthus decapetalus*, single and double, *H. maximiliani*, *H. scaberrimus*; *Rudbeckia subtomentosa*.

### PLANTS OF MEDIUM HEIGHT, 1½–4 FT.

  SPRING-FLOWERING: *Euphorbia epithymoides*; *Doronicum caucasicum*; *Helenium hoopesi*; *Trollius asiaticus*, *T. europaeus*.
  SUMMER-FLOWERING: *Aconitum anthora*, *A. lycoctonum*; *Allium moly* (bulb); *Anthemis tinctoria*; *Aquilegia chrysantha*; *Argemone mexicana* (annual); *Asclepias tuberosa*; *Antirrhinum* (annual) lemon to orange; *Calendula officinalis* (annual) lemon to orange; *Centaurea moschata* (annual); *Chrysanthemum* (annual) varieties; *Coreopsis grandiflora*, *C. tinctoria* (annual), *C. verticillata*; *Digitalis ambigua*; *Dimorphotheca aurantiaca* (annual); *Erysimum perofskianum* (annual); *Gaillardia* varieties; *Gladiolus* varieties; *Glaucium flavum* (biennial); *Helenium autumnale pumilum*; *Heliopsis helianthoides*; *Hemerocallis*, species and varieties; *Lilium canadense*, *L. croceum*, *L. elegans*; *Linaria dalmatica*; *Lysimachia punctata*; *Oenothera fruticosa*; *Rudbeckia hirta*, *R. speciosa*.
  AUTUMN-FLOWERING: *Chrysanthemum* (hardy) yellow to orange.

### LOW GROWING PLANTS, 6 IN. TO 1½ FT.

  SPRING-FLOWERING: *Adonis amurensis*, *A. vernalis*; *Alyssum saxatile*; *Brodiaea ixioides* (bulb); *Crocus aureus*, *C. susianus* (Dutch yellow); *Doronicum clusi*; *Epimedium pinnatum colchicum*; *Eranthis hyemalis* (tuber); *Erythronium grandiflorum* (bulb); *Euphorbia myrsinites*; *Geum montanum*; *Helianthemum nummularium*; *Hyacinthus orientalis* varieties (bulb); *Lysimachia nummularia*; *Lotus corniculatus*; *Narcissus* (daffodils), many varieties; *Primula auricula*, *P. elatior*, *P. vulgaris*; *Tulipa persica*, and garden tulips.
  SUMMER-FLOWERING: *Achillea tomentosa*; *Alyssum argenteum*; *Arnica montana*; *Antirrhinum*, low varieties (annual); *Belamcanda chinensis*; *Coreopsis drummondi* (golden wave, annual); *Corydalis cheilanthifolia*, *C. lutea*; *Dianthus knappi*; *Erigeron aurantiacus*; *Erysimum pulchellum*; *Eschscholtzia californica* (annual); *Hemerocallis middendorfi*, *H. minor*; *Inula ensifolia*; *Linum flavum*; nasturtiums (annual); *Nemesia* varieties; *Papaver nudicaule*; *Phlox drummondi* (annual); *Potentilla pyrenaica*; *Sanvitalia procumbens*; *Tagetes*.
  AUTUMN-FLOWERING: *Crocus*, several species (bulb); *Sternbergia lutea* (bulb).

### CLIMBERS

  *Clematis orientalis* (autumn), *C. tangutica* (summer); *Jasminum nudiflorum* (spring); *Lonicera flava* (summer), *L. japonica halliana* (summer); nasturtiums (climbing annual, summer and autumn); rose, climbing numerous varieties (summer); sweet pea (summer). — L. B. W.

**YERBA BUENA** = *Micromeria chamissonis*.

**YEW.** See TAXUS. For the plum-yew see CEPHALOTAXUS.

**YEW FAMILY** = Taxaceae.

**YIELDS.** See GARDEN TABLES I.

**YLANG-YLANG** = *Cananga odorata*. See also ARTABOTRYS.

**YODOGAVA, -us, -um** (yo-do-ga′va). From Yodogawa, Japan.

**YOKOHAMA BEAN** = *Stizolobium hasjoo*.

**YONG, W.** See America at GARDEN BOOKS.

**YORK AND LANCASTER ROSE** = *Rosa damascena versicolor*.

**YOSEMITENSIS, -e** (yo-sem-i-ten′sis). From Yosemite National Park, California.

**YOUTH-AND-OLD-AGE** = *Zinnia elegans*.

**YUCCA** (yuck′a). Semi-desert plants of the lily family, chiefly Mexican, but a few in the southern states and in the W.I. cult. for their striking flower clusters. Most of them are stemless with a basal rosette of sword-shaped, tough, leathery leaves, but *Y. brevifolia* and *Y. glauca* have distinct trunks. Flowers white (rarely purple-tinged), waxy, cup-shaped, nodding, usually fragrant at night, some blooming only at night, and borne in showy, erect, terminal clusters (panicles*). Petals (or sepals) 6. Stamens* 6. Fruit usually a capsule.* (*Yucca* is the Latinized version of a Spanish vernacular for some other desert plant.)

The yuccas are bold striking plants which are very common in the southwestern U.S., culminating in the extraordinary Joshua-tree (*Y. brevifolia*) which ranges from Calif. to Utah. It has a grotesquely branching trunk and often is 30–40 ft. high. The other cult. species with an obvious trunk are *Y. glauca* and *Y. aloifolia*. *Y. aloifolia* and *Y. brevifolia* are not hardy in regions of wet slushy winters. They need the same culture as desert cacti.

The other species have no evident trunk and are hardy over much of the U.S. south of zone* 3, and sometimes in zone* 3 if they are protected from too much winter moisture. All of them do best in light, sandy or gritty soils, and may be propagated by seeds or offsets* which are frequently produced. Several Mexican (non-hort.) species yield fibers.

  **aloifolia.** Spanish bayonet. Spanish dagger. Producing a simple or branched trunk, 10–25 ft. high. Leaves stiff, about 2½ ft. long, 2 in. wide and prolonged into a very sharp point. Flowers nearly 4 in. wide, white, or purple-tinged, the cluster often 2 ft. long and very showy; it is particularly good for its late flowering. Southern U.S. to Mex. and the W.I.
  **brevifolia.** Joshua-tree; also called tree yucca. An extraordinary, grotesquely branching desert plant, often 30–40 ft. high, the leaves in dense terminal rosettes. Leaves 6–9 in. long, toothed. Flowers greenish-white, about 2 in. long, the cluster not over 18 in. long. Calif. to Utah.
  **filamentosa.** Adam's-needle. Bear grass. Spanish bayonet. The commonest yucca in cult. in the East, and native from N. Car. to Fla. and Miss. It is practically stemless, but the stalk of the flower cluster may be 8–12 ft. high. Leaves 2–2½ ft. long, about 1 in. wide, thready on the margin. Flowers white or cream-white, about 2 in. long. There is also a form with variegated leaves. For hardiness see above.
  **glauca.** Bear grass. Trunk short and usually prostrate. Leaves nearly 3 ft. long, scarcely ½ in. wide, white-margined and also finely thready on the margin. Flowers greenish-white, about 2 in. long. New Mex., northward to Iowa and S. Dak., and one of the hardiest of the yuccas.
  **gloriosa.** Spanish dagger. Stemless, or with a very short trunk in the South. Leaves nearly 2½ ft. long, about 2 in. wide, prolonged into a stiff, sharp point, but not thready on the margin. Flowers nearly 4 in. wide, greenish-white or reddish. N. Car. to Fla.
  **whipplei** = *Hesperoyucca whipplei*.

**YULAN** = *Magnolia denudata*.

**YUNNANENSIS, -e** (you-nan-en′sis). From Yunnan, China.

**YUQUILLA** = *Manihot carthaginensis*.

---

* Special articles on the subjects indicated by an asterisk (*) will be found at the words so marked.

# Z

**ZALUZIANSKYA** (zal-oo-zi-an'ski-a). Beautifully fragrant, chiefly night-blooming, South African plants of the family Scrophulariaceae, two of the 20 known species grown in the flower garden as tender annuals. They have opposite* leaves, or the upper ones alternate,* and reduced upward to mere bracts.* Flowers in terminal spikes, the calyx 2-lipped.* Corolla tubular, the tube much longer than the regular, 5-lobed limb.* Fruit an oblong capsule.* (Named for Adam Zaluziansky von Zaluzian, Polish physician.)

Both the cult. species should be grown as tender annuals. See ANNUALS.

**capensis.** Not over 18 in. high, the leaves narrow, about 1½ in. long. Flowers about 1½ in. long, the corolla white inside, but purplish-black and hairy outside. Summer.

**villosa.** Not over 12 in. high, the stems hairy. Leaves ovalish or broader toward the tip, about 1 in. long. Flowers white or pale lilac inside, but purple outside and the corolla only slightly hairy, if at all. Summer.

**ZAMAN.** See SAMANEA SAMAN.

**ZAMIA** (zay'mi-a). Stiff-leaved, fern-like or palm-like plants comprising over 40 species of the family Cycadaceae, all from tropical or sub-tropical America. They have generally underground, woody trunks (obviously above ground in some old specimens), and a terminal crown of evergreen compound* leaves. Flowers none in the usual garden sense, the male and female organs borne in dense, woody cones or close clusters (for details see CYCADACEAE). (*Zamia* is a Latin word for a barren pine cone and was adopted by Linnaeus for these plants because of the cone-like inflorescence.)

The zamias are of secondary hort. importance and the two below can only be grown outdoors in zone* 9. Some of the Florida species were used by the Indians to make soap, and the plants are sometimes now grown for ornament or interest. They do well in the light, sandy soils of southern Fla. If grown in the greenhouse, they require the same conditions as *Cycas* (which see).

**floridana.** Coontie. Trunk mostly underground. Leaves with 14-20, mostly opposite leaflets, which are slightly arched, rolled on the margin and blunt at the tip. Female cones 5-6 in. long. Southern Fla.

**integrifolia.** Trunk more obvious, generally above ground and sometimes 12 in. high. Leaflets 14-32, oblongish or narrower, blunt at the tip, mostly without teeth, but sometimes toothed toward the tip. W.I.

**ZANTEDESCHIA.** See CALLA LILY.

**ZANTHORHIZA** (zan-tho-ry'za), sometimes spelled *Xanthorhiza*. A single species of low shrubs of the buttercup family, Z. apiifolia, the yellowroot or shrub yellowroot, a native of the eastern U.S. It is scarcely 2 ft. high and has yellow, bitter roots. Leaves compound,* long-stalked, the usually 5 leaflets ovalish, deeply cut, sometimes 3-lobed, 2-4 in. long. Flowers perfect or unisexual,* brownish-purple, about ⅓ in. long, in drooping clusters (racemes*). Sepals 5, petal-like. Petals none, but the 5 nectaries 3-lobed and petal-like. Stamens* 5-10. Fruit a collection of 10, 1-seeded, small pods (follicles*). A useful shrub for low, moist, shady banks, but not thriving in open, wind-swept places. N.Y. to Ky. and Fla. April–May. Hardy from zone* 3 southward. Easily propagated by division. (*Zanthorhiza* is from the Greek for yellow root.)

**ZANTHOXYLUM** (zan-thocks'i-lum), also spelled *Zanthoxylon* and *Xanthoxylum*. Aromatic, prickly shrubs or trees of the family Rutaceae, comprising over 150 species from both hemispheres, but chiefly tropical, although the cult. species are natives of the U.S. They have alternate,* compound* leaves, the leaflets arranged feather-fashion and opposite each other, with an odd one at the end. Flowers small, greenish, the male and female on different plants, or polygamous* (for details see RUTACEAE). Fruit a collection of 2-valved, ripened carpels (see PISTIL), each with 1 shining, black seed. (*Zanthoxylum* is from the Greek for yellow wood, in allusion to the yellow wood of some species.)

These shrubs present no difficulties and thrive in any ordinary garden soil, although they are hardy only as indicated below. Propagated by seeds, or by root cuttings.

**americanum.** Prickly ash; also called angelica tree and toothache tree. A shrub or small tree, 10-20 ft. high, the prickles about ½ in. long. Leaflets 5-11, ovalish, about 2 in. long, hairy beneath. Flowers small, blooming before the leaves unfold, in small clusters in the leaf-axils.* Eastern N.A. April–May. Hardy from zone* 3 southward.

**clava-herculis.** Hercules'-club; also called prickly ash and toothache tree. A tree 30-50 ft. high, the trunk and branches prickly. Leaflets 7-19, toothed, the stalk and main axis usually prickly. Flowers in rather large, terminal clusters (panicles*). Southern Va. to Fla. and Tex. April. Hardy from zone* 5 southward, sometimes north of this. It is often shrubby in the young state.

**ZANZIBARIENSIS, -e** (zan-zi-bar-i-en'sis). From Zanzibar, Africa.

**ZAPOTA** (za-po'ta). The common name in Latin America for the marmalade plum (*Achras zapota*).

**ZAUSCHNERIA** (zaush-near'i-a). A small genus of Californian perennial herbs of the family Onagraceae, Z. californica, the Calif. fuchsia or hummingbird's-trumpet, cult. for its late-blooming, brilliant scarlet flowers. It is a decumbent or partly erect, branched herb, 8-15 in. high, the foliage densely hairy. Leaves generally alternate,* oblongish or narrower, ½-1½ in. long. Calyx tubular, scarlet, flaring above. Petals scarlet, not much exceeding the calyx* lobes. Stamens* 8, protruding. Fruit a 4-valved, many-seeded capsule.* A showy garden plant with fuchsia-like flowers, but not certainly hardy in the eastern states. It may be propagated by division or by seeds. In Calif. it is remarkably drought-resistant. (Named for H. Zauschner, once a botanist at Prague.)

**ZEA.** See CORN.

**ZEBRA-GRASS** = *Miscanthus sinensis zebrinus*.

**ZEBRA-PLANT** = *Calathea zebrina*.

**ZEBRINA** (zee-bry'na). A genus of only 2 species of the family Commelinaceae, one of them, Z. pendula, the wandering Jew, a Mexican, watery-juiced herb widely cult. in greenhouses and often spreading under the benches. It is closely related to *Tradescantia fluminensis* (also called wandering Jew), a Brazilian plant, from which it differs chiefly in having the petals united into a tube (see SPIDERWORT). *Zebrina pendula* is a decumbent or prostrate plant, rooting very easily at the joints and grown mostly for its foliage and handsome reddish-purple flowers from between 2 boat-shaped, unequal bracts.* The var. quadricolor, with its leaves striped green, white, and red, is a particularly showy form. The plant will stand no frost, but is a handsome subject for hanging baskets or window boxes. (*Zebrina* is from the Latin for zebra, in allusion to the striped foliage.)

**ZELKOVA** (zel-ko'va). Elm-like, Asiatic shrubs and trees of the family Ulmaceae, comprising about 5 species, the two below of secondary garden interest but occasionally cult. for ornament. They have alternate,* toothed leaves which are slightly unequal at the base. Flowers small, polygamous,* without petals, not showy, solitary, or the male flowers in small clusters in the leaf-axils,* all blooming early in the spring with the opening of the leaves. Fruit a 2-edged, oblique drupe,* winged on the upper half. (*Zelkova* is a Latinized version of a common name in the Caucasus for the first species.)

**carpinifolia.** A tree up to 80 ft. high in the wild, as cult. usually with a short trunk which splits into several main branches, making a round-headed tree. Leaves elliptic or oblongish, pointed, 1-2 in. long, toothed and hairy on the veins beneath. Fruit about ⅓ in. wide. Caucasus. Hardy from zone* 4 southward. Sometimes offered as Z. ulmoides.

**serrata.** A similar tree, but the leaves more sharply toothed, tapering at the tip, broader and about twice as long, and without hairs on the veins beneath. Jap. Hardy from zone* 3 southward.

---

* Special articles on the subjects indicated by an asterisk (*) will be found at the words so marked.

**ZENOBIA** (zen-ō′bi-a). A single species of little-known shrubs of the heath family, *Z. pulverulenta* of the southeastern U.S. occasionally grown for ornament, and sometimes forced in the greenhouse for its white, bell-shaped flowers. See FORCING. It is a partly evergreen shrub, 4–6 ft. high, the alternate* ovalish leaves very bluish-green, 2–3 in. long. Flowers about ½ in. wide, in a terminal cluster made up of racemes.* Fruit a small capsule.* N. Car. to Fla. May–June. Hardy from zone* 4 southward. It is closely related to *Pieris* and needs the same conditions for growth. See PIERIS. (Named for Queen Zenobia of Palmyra.)

**ZEPHYRANTHES** (zeff-i-ran′theez). Zephyr-flower. Zephyr lily. A large genus of New World, bulbous herbs of the family Amaryllidaceae, a few grown for ornament and of uncertain hardiness over most of the country north of zone* 5. They have narrow, basal leaves, more or less grass-like, usually appearing with the flowers and persistent in some species over the winter, or in others appearing after the flowers. Flower solitary, its stalk hollow, and appearing from a tubular spathe* which is notched at the tip. Corolla erect, more or less funnel-shaped, the segments nearly of equal length, the flower thus faintly irregular. Stamens* 6. Fruit a nearly round, 3-celled capsule.* (*Zephyranthes* is from the Greek for the west-wind flower, in allusion to the plants being wholly American.) They are sometimes known under the genus name *Atamosco*.

The first species is the hardiest and will ordinarily survive the winters up to zone* 4 if given a site not too wet and slushy in the winter months. The others are best planted in the spring, allowed to flower, and dug up and stored over the winter. Storage should not allow the bulbs to dry out, and they should be kept in dry or moistish sand. South of zone* 5 they can stay in the ground all year; they will sometimes survive this treatment northward, but not usually. All the half-hardy species can be grown in the cool greenhouse.

**atamasco.** Atamasco lily. Leaves about 12 in. long, very narrow. Flowering stalk nearly 1 ft. long, the flowers white or tinged with purple, nearly 3 in. long. Pa. to Fla. and Ala. April–May.

**candida.** Leaves thick, stiffish, about 1 ft. long. Flowers summer-blooming, about 2 in. long, white or rarely rose-tinged. Argentine.

**carinata.** Common zephyr lily. Leaves flat, narrow, about 12 in. long. Flowers blooming in late spring and summer, about 3 in. long, red or pink. Tropical America.

**rosea.** Resembling *Z. carinata* and sometimes mistaken for it, but with broader, blunter leaves, and smaller flowers which do not bloom until autumn. Cuba, and the least hardy of the zephyr lilies.

**ZEPHYR-FLOWER; ZEPHYR LILY.** See ZEPHYRANTHES.

**ZEYLANICA, -us, -um** (zee-lan′i-ka). From Ceylon.

**ZIGZAG CLOVER** = *Trifolium medium*. See CLOVER.

**ZINC-LIME.** A recently devised spraying mixture used for leafspot and other bacterial diseases of the peach during the summer when other remedies are not safe. It is made by mixing 8 pounds of zinc sulphate crystals and 8 pounds of hydrated lime (see LIME) to 100 gallons of water. See Diseases at PEACH.

**ZINGIBER.** See GINGER.

**ZINGIBERACEAE** (zin-ji-ber-ray′see-ee). The ginger family comprises aromatic tropical herbs grown for their flavoring products and for ornament. All require greenhouse culture, or some can be grown outdoors in completely frost-free parts of the country (zone* 9). There are over 40 genera and 400 species, mostly from the Old World tropics. The family was once included in the Scitamineae.

Of the six cult. genera two are the most important, *Zingiber* (see GINGER) and *Elettaria* (see CARDAMON). The others, grown mostly for ornament, are *Alpinia, Amomum, Curcuma,* and *Hedychium,* the latter including the popular ginger-lily, also called butterfly-lily.

Nearly all are stout herbs with large aromatic rootstalks (ginger). Leaves mostly with sheathing bases or leafstalks, always without marginal teeth, often very large. Flowers irregular, usually in bracted* clusters, often from between sheath-like bracts (a spathe*). Fruit a dry pod (capsule*).

Technical flower characters: Flowers hermaphrodite,* irregular.* Calyx tubular or spathe*-like of 3 segments. Corolla tubular, but unequal, 3-lobed. Stamen 1, but there are often sterile ones and sometimes these are petal-like or form a lip.* Ovary inferior,* mostly 1-celled.

**ZINNIA** (zin′i-a). Annual or perennial herbs or undershrubs comprising about 15 species of the family Compositae, chiefly found in Mex., but also from Tex. and Colo. and Chile. They have rather stiff, erect stems covered with short bristly hairs and somewhat woody at the base. Leaves opposite,* ovalish or lance-shaped, usually stem-clasping. Flowers in solitary, flattish or cone-shaped, showy heads, each flower growing in the axil of a scale-like bract,* the tip of which is often colored. Ray florets of every shade except blue, the under side often greenish, arranged in 1-many rows. Disk florets* yellow or purplish-brown. (Named for Johann Gottfried Zinn, Professor of Medicine at Göttingen.) For cult. and varieties, see below.

**angustifolia.** Stiff-growing, erect annual, up to 18 in. high, covered with short stiff hairs. Leaves broadly lance-shaped, not stalked. Flowers in terminal heads to 1½ in. across. Ray florets orange. Disk florets yellow, red or orange. Mex.

**elegans.** Youth-and-old-age. Stiff-growing, erect annual to 3 ft. high, covered with short stiff hairs. Leaves ovalish, clasping the stem, prominently veined. Flowers in solitary heads to 4½ in. across. Ray florets purple or reddish-lilac. Disk florets yellow or orange. There are hort. varieties of every shade except blue. Disk florets often absent in hort. forms. Mex.

**haageana** = *Zinnia angustifolia*.
**mexicana** = *Zinnia angustifolia*.

### ZINNIA CULTURE

Zinnias are among the most popular summer- and autumn-flowering plants. The various shades and heights now obtainable make effective showy plantings for the sunny or semi-shady borders. As they last well in the hot weather they are much grown for cutting. The giant forms of *Zinnia elegans* growing to 3 ft. high, are especially adapted for the back of the border, while the free-flowering, smaller-flowered Liliputian varieties, with their cone-shaped heads, growing to 18 in. high, are useful for the front of the border and for table decoration when cut. Zinnias are easily cult. and will grow in almost any soil. Best results are obtained when grown in deep rich soil which has been well dug and manured. They should be given water freely in hot, dry weather; a mulch of strawy manure or hay placed round the plants will help retain the moisture and keep soil from packing during heavy rains.

Seeds should be sown in cool greenhouse or cold frame in boxes of light sandy soil, ⅛ in. deep, in early April. When plants are large enough to handle they should be transplanted in the same kind of soil to 3 in. apart in boxes and placed near the glass if grown in greenhouse to keep them from becoming leggy,* but if started in the cold frame they may be transplanted into the frame, keeping the sash closed at night until danger of frost is over when they may be transplanted.

Those started in the greenhouse must be hardened off by admitting air whenever possible and placing boxes outside for a few days before planting. The giant forms should be planted 1½–2 ft. apart, the Liliputian varieties may be planted 1 ft. apart. Seeds may also be sown outdoors from the end of April to the middle of May, or earlier in the southern states. They may be sown where required to bloom, 3–4 seeds should be planted about 1 ft. apart. When 3 in. high they should be thinned out, leaving the plants about a foot apart each way. — H. R. M.

INSECT PESTS. Not many pests occur, but occasionally stem borers (see CALLISTEPHUS), tarnished plant bugs (see DAHLIA), and leaf feeders (checked by arsenicals) are found.

DISEASES. For mildew, see Powdery Mildew at PLANT DISEASES.

**ZINNIAEFLORA, -us, -um** (zin-i-ee-flow′ra). With zinnia-like flowers.

**ZIT-KWA** = *Benincasa hispida*.

**ZIZANIA** (zy-zay′ni-a). Tall, and in ours, annual marsh grasses comprising two American and one Asiatic species, of which **Z. aquatica,** the wild rice of eastern N.A., is much cult. for its nutritious grain, and for ornament, as it is a handsome grass 7–10 ft. high. It is often called water, Indian, or Canada rice, and besides its use for food is widely grown by sportsmen for wild fowl food. Leaves grass-like, 12–18 in. long and about 2 in. wide. Flower cluster terminal (a panicle*),

* Special articles on the subjects indicated by an asterisk (*) will be found at the words so marked.

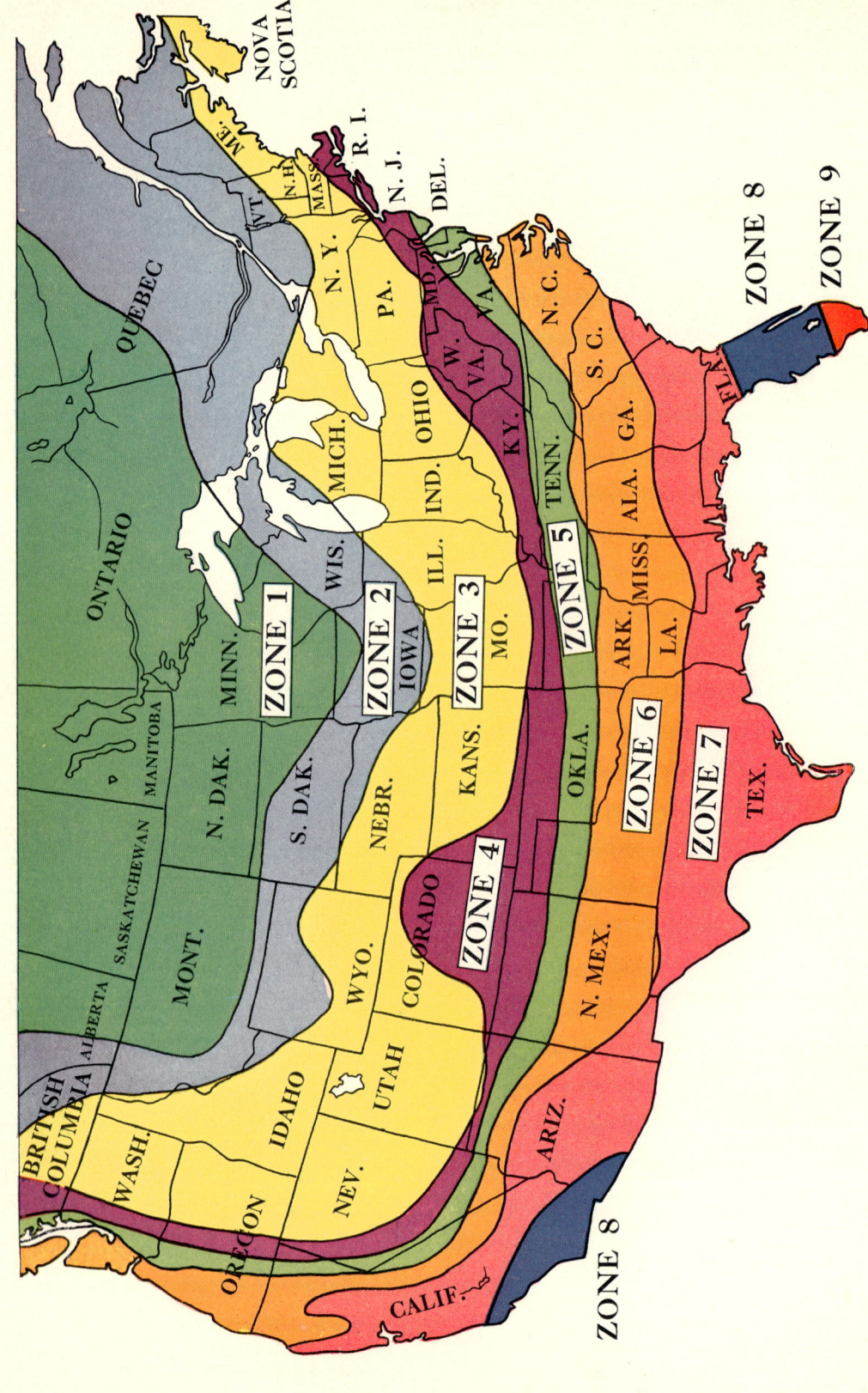

ZONES OF HARDINESS IN THE UNITED STATES AND SOUTHERN CANADA
(For details see text)

nearly 2 ft. long, the upper spikelets furnished with awns* nearly 3 in. long. Grain rice-like, but narrower. The plant grows best in water from 5 in. to 3 ft. deep, but can be made to grow also along the edges of pools, marshes, or bogs. The seed should be soaked for a day, in coarse cotton bags, submerged in the water it is to be planted in. Sow the seeds in May on the muddy bottom (not on sandy bottoms), or plant them in mud which can later be flooded, as the plant does better in standing (not running) water than anywhere else. There is a *var.* **angustifolia** with narrower leaves, which is sometimes offered as *Z. palustris*. (*Zizania* is a Greek name for some wild grain, but not certainly for this one.)

**ZIZANIOIDES** (zy-zay-ni-oy'deez, but *see* OÏDES). Like the wild rice (*Zizania*).

**ZIZYPHUS** (ziz'i-fuss). A genus of over 40 species of somewhat spiny shrubs and trees of the family Rhamnaceae, one of the three below a promising but little-known fruit in the U.S. — the jujube. The species are natives of the warmer regions of both the Old and New Worlds and are not generally satisfactory in the cooler parts of the country. Leaves alternate,* short-stalked, 3–5-veined from the base. Flowers small, yellowish or greenish-yellow, perfect,* in small clusters (cymes*) in the leaf-axils.* For details *see* RHAMNACEAE. Fruit oblong, or nearly round, fleshy (a drupe*). (*Zizyphus* is the old Greek name for the first species.) *See* LOTUS.

The common or Chinese jujube (*Z. jujuba*) is the only one of commercial importance, and this is slight as the fruits of the jujube are little known in the U.S. Another species, *Z. mauritiana*, is suited to the warmer parts of Fla. The common jujube is most satisfactory in regions of great summer heat, notably southern Tex., N. Mex., Ariz., and especially Calif. Trees should be planted 20 × 20 ft. apart, and they have a wide soil tolerance, if there is sufficient summer heat, being more alkali-tolerant than most fruit trees. So far the jujube, which is of comparatively recent introduction in the U.S., has not been much troubled with pests. While isolated trees have been grown here for many years, the introduction of the improved Chinese varieties noted below has greatly increased the demand for jujubes. Its use here has been held back by lack of knowledge as to its qualities. It is not the best of all fruits to be eaten fresh, but a very fine confection is made by scoring the skin of the fruit with a sharp knife (or razor blade) just before it is dropped into boiling syrup, where it should stay 20–30 minutes. Cool the fruit and syrup and then repeat the boiling. The fruit is then removed from the syrup and dried about to the consistency of a prune.

**jujuba.** Common or Chinese jujube. A shrub or small tree, not over 30 ft. high, one spine of each group of 2, curved. Leaves oblongish, 1–2 in. long, bluntly toothed. Fruits oblong or nearly round or sometimes egg-shaped, about 1 in. long, acid, when ripe brownish. Eurasia. Among the best varieties for Calif. and similar climates, all originating in China where the fruit is highly prized, are: Mu Shing Hong, Lang, Sui Meu, and Li, all of them imported by the U.S. Department of Agriculture.

**mauritiana.** Indian or cottony jujube. Usually an evergreen shrub or small tree with broadly oval leaves, 1¾–2½ in. long, the under side rusty-hairy. Fruit nearly round, red when ripe, acid, about 1 in. in diameter. India. Suited only to zone* 9, and does well on a variety of soils in southern Fla., but not much known, and with no outstanding hort. forms.

**obtusifolia.** Texas jujube or buckthorn; also called lote bush. A stiff, spiny, much-branched shrub. Leaves generally ovalish, ¾–1¼ in. long, smooth, a little toothed or without teeth. Fruit about ⅓ in. long, black, edible, but of inferior quality. Tex. and Ariz. to northern Mex.

**ZONATA, -us, -um** (zo-nay'ta). Banded or zoned.

**ZONE.** As outlined in the article HARDINESS, the ability of woody plants to grow in any particular place is a combination of many factors. But of these the average minimum temperature of the coldest month is probably the most critical. As a criterion for the hardiness of woody plants in this country it was adopted by Mr. Alfred Rehder of the Arnold Arboretum, and, with modifications to be explained presently, has been used throughout THE GARDEN DICTIONARY.

The advantage of such a method is that it creates, upon the reasonably accurate basis of the Weather Bureau figures rather fixed zones of hardiness, within which certain plants will grow and north of which they usually perish. Rehder divided the regions north of a line from northern S. Car. to northern Tex. into 8 zones.

Because THE GARDEN DICTIONARY includes all of the U.S. it was necessary to re-zone the country in accordance with the accompanying map — there being 9 zones in all. These zones are all based upon Weather Bureau figures kept for a period of many years, and show the average minimum temperatures of the coldest month.

The nine zones and their average minimum temperatures are:

|  |  |
| --- | --- |
| Zone 1. | zero or below |
| Zone 2. | zero to 10° above. |
| Zone 3. | 10°–20° |
| Zone 4. | 20°–25° |
| Zone 5. | 25°–30° |
| Zone 6. | 30°–40° |
| Zone 7. | 40°–50° |
| Zone 8. | 50°–60° |
| Zone 9. | 60° or above. |

**Zone 1.** This includes the region of the northern spruce and fir forests in the East, some prairie in the north central area, and in addition to intense cold has a short growing season.

**Zone 2.** In the East this includes the southern edge of the spruce and fir forests as well as much of the red and white pine country. In the central section it cuts across large sections of prairie.

**Zone 3.** In the East the heart of the beech — birch — maple forests of the North are found in this zone, which, in the central section covers a large area of prairie.

**Zone 4.** While the natural vegetation is not greatly different from zone 3, the line between zones 3 and 4 seems to be a critical one for many cult. woody plants, especially plants like box and English holly.

**Zone 5.** It is in this zone that many southern plants reach about the northern limits of their hardiness.

**Zone 6.** This is the upper limit for the commercial culture of cotton and for many garden plants.

**Zone 7.** The great cotton belt, and the largest area in the country with such a warm winter temperature. Many plants from zone 8 are safe in zone 7 if local conditions are favorable. *See* LOUISIANA.

**Zone 8.** A limited region, where citrus fruits are relatively safe, confined to central Fla. and extreme southern Calif. and adjacent Ariz. Horticulturally an extremely important zone. *See* special account of the conditions as outlined at CALIF., ARIZ. and FLA.

**Zone 9.** The only absolutely frost-free, relatively tropical section of the U.S. is found in this zone and comprises only the region around Key West, Fla. The rest of zone 9 may have a rare frost, but it contains all the really tropical plants cult. outdoors in the country, with the possible exception of some particularly favored places in zone 8 in Calif. (which see).

If North America were flat and the oceans that bathe the eastern and western coasts did not exist, the zones of hardiness would extend across the country in relatively even bands. The map shows how far they deviate from such regularity, where the zones cross the two main mountain ranges and approach the eastern and western oceans. This is particularly true in the western third of the area, and in this region it is safer to consult the detailed account of local gardening possibilities which will be found at the name of your state or province. All who intend to use the map as a guide for planting should read the article on HARDINESS, as other things besides temperature have a strong bearing upon hardiness.

HOW TO USE THE MAP

The zoning system here adopted is designed only for one purpose — to show the relative hardiness of woody plants as cult. outdoors in America. The map does not show the onset of spring, the time of flowering, nor the proper planting times for gardens. All the latter information will be found at GARDEN CALENDAR and the very different map that accompanies that article.

* Special articles on the subjects indicated by an asterisk (*) will be found at the words so marked.

Throughout this book there are thousands of references reading "Hardy from zone* 3 southward" — etc. Such statements mean that the plant is hardy in zone 3 and south of it. The validity of the statement is based upon records kept at the Arnold Arboretum at Boston, the Central Experimental Farm at Ottawa, as well as many scattered records from Agricultural Experiment Stations, botanic gardens and some private gardeners.

While no scheme of this sort is infallible, wherever there was a doubt as to the hardiness of a particular plant for a particular zone, it has been assigned to the next warmest zone for safety. Venturesome gardeners will always try growing plants in regions unfit for them. While THE DICTIONARY wishes these pioneers the best of luck, it cannot be in a position of recommending such apparently doomed experiments. Additional records of hardiness will always be welcome and should be addressed to the Garden Editor, Houghton Mifflin Company, Boston, Mass.

There is one final caution about the zones. Many northern plants appear to need a more or less prolonged chilling in winter. When, as happens in the extreme South, they cannot get it, they either grow very poorly or die. Whenever, in THE DICTIONARY, it says, that a plant is "Hardy from zone* 4 southward," it should be understood that such a plant may not be suitable for extreme southern localities, not because of cold but because of too much winter heat. *See*, in this connection especially, the articles on LOUISIANA and CALIFORNIA.

No country-wide scheme of plotting temperature records can hope to be accurate for a particular locality, so that judgment will have to be used in applying the map. This is especially true if you happen to live on the edge of a zone, or if some local feature of altitude, topography or proximity to water is likely to alter your conditions. At each state there is a special map which shows where the particular zone lines cross the state, as affected by local conditions. If in doubt it will be well to consult these more detailed maps, after which you may plant or not as courage dictates.

**ZOYSIA** (zoy'si-a). Asiatic or Australasian, creeping grasses comprising only 4 species, two of them of minor importance as lawn grasses for the extreme South. They are perennial grasses with creeping rootstocks and fine, wiry, grass-like leaves. Flowering spikelets flattened, without awns,* crowded in a dense spike-like cluster (panicle*). (Named for Karl von Zoys, Austrian botanist.)

Both species are suited to open, sandy regions and should be planted by bits of rootstocks as in creeping bent (for details *see* LAWN). Neither is much used, except in the extreme South. They are sometimes offered as *Osterdamia*.

**japonica.** Korean lawn grass; also called Japanese lawn grass. A creeping grass, its rootstocks sending up numerous tough, wiry shoots. Leaves 1–3 in. long, sharp-pointed. Spikelets purplish, about 1 in. long. Jap. and China. Useful in the southeastern states.

**tenuifolia.** Mascarene grass. A creeping grass, the shoots and leaves much finer than in *Z. japonica*, and making a flat, beautiful turf in Calif., but little known elsewhere. It is said to smother out all other plants, including other grasses, but does not seed in Calif. Mascarene Islands.

**ZUMI** (zoo'mi). Japanese common name for *Malus zumi*.

**ZYGADENUS** (zig-a-den'us). A genus of perennial herbs of the lily family, two of the 25 species Asiatic, all the rest from the New World. They are of secondary garden interest, although the three below are occasionally planted in the wild garden. They have a collection of basal, long, narrow, grass-like leaves and a tall flowering stalk crowned with a simple or branched cluster (raceme* or panicle*) of white or yellowish-green flowers which soon wither but persist. Corolla of petal-like sepals. Stamens* 6. Fruit a 3-celled capsule.* (*Zygadenus* is from the Greek for yoke and gland, in allusion to the pair of glands found at the base of the sepals.) Sometimes known as *Amianthium*. The foliage and rootstock of most species contain a poisonous juice, and some non-hort. species are deadly. The second species is from Calif. and not certainly hardy in the eastern states. The other two are suited to moist, somewhat acid sites in the wild garden or in the bog.

**elegans.** Alkali-grass. Leaves tough and wiry, nearly 12 in. long, very bluish-green. Flower stalk 2–3 ft. high, the cluster about 12 in. long and branched. Flowers greenish, about ½ in. wide. Eastern N.A., southwestward to N. Mex. Summer.

**fremonti.** Leaves about 12 in. long, nearly ⅓ in. wide, only slightly bluish-green. Flowers similar to those of *Z. elegans*, but the cluster often not branched. Calif.

**leimanthoides.** With a slender, leafy stem about 4 ft. high, the leaves mostly basal, about 12 in. long and ⅓ in. wide. Flowers greenish-white, about ⅓ in. wide, the cluster branched, nearly 12 in. long. N.Y. to Ga. Summer.

**ZYGOCACTUS** (zy-go-kak'tus). A single Brazilian species of tree-perching, spineless cacti, **Z. truncatus**, widely grown and popular under the name of crab cactus or Christmas cactus. It is a much-branched, hanging plant, the broad, leaflike stems or joints sharply cut off at the tip, 1½–2 in. long, about ¾ in. wide, the margins with 1–3 coarse, blunt teeth, the two upper ones a little incurved. Flowers very showy, 2½–3½ in. wide, red and very irregular.* Fruit about ¾ in. in diameter, red and pear-shaped. Often sold as *Epiphyllum truncatum*, and the genus *Zygocactus* is often confused with *Epiphyllum*, but the latter has regular flowers. Unlike most cacti the crab cactus can be easily grown in potting mixture* 3, and is a favorite house plant. It needs more water than other cacti and is a fine plant for the window sill or for hanging baskets. (*Zygocactus* is from the Greek for yoke and *Cactus*, in allusion to the irregular* flowers.) Sometimes offered as *Phyllocactus*, and blooming about Christmas time.

**ZYGOPETALUM** (zy-go-pet'a-lum). Tropical American tree-perching (epiphytic*) orchids, comprising about a dozen species, of which **Z. mackai** of Brazil is often cult. in greenhouses for its showy bloom. It has egg-shaped pseudobulbs,* 2–3 in. long, from which arise 2–3 narrow, sheathing leaves about 12 in. long. Flower stalk about 18 in. long, the 5–8 flowers separate, each about 3 in. wide. Sepals and petals somewhat similar, yellowish-green and white, spotted with purple-brown. Lip* notched, more or less fan-shaped, white, but streaked and spotted with bluish-purple. An extremely handsome orchid of comparatively easy culture. See Epiphytic Orchids at ORCHID. The *var*. **crinitum** has greenish flowers spotted with brown and a hairy, wavy lip.* (*Zygopetalum* is from the Greek for yoke and petal, in allusion to the irregular* flower.)

**ZYGOPHYLLACEAE** (zy-go-fill-lay'see-ee). A chiefly tropical family of herbs, shrubs, and trees, all of little or no hort. interest except *Larrea*, which see for the only cult. plants in the family Zygophyllaceae.

**ZYKLON DISCOIDS.** A trademarked insecticide containing liquid hydrocyanic acid absorbed in an inert carrier; sold with directions for fumigation.

---

## SOME STATISTICS

| | |
|---|---:|
| Total number of **boldface** entry words | 11,292 |
| Plant Families | 190 |
| Genera | 1,751 |
| Species, varieties and named horticultural forms | 7,785 |
| Common or vernacular plant names | 4,403 |
| Species names defined and pronounced | 1,912 |
| Cross-references and miscellaneous short definitions | 6,966 |
| Cultural and special articles | 473 |

---

* Special articles on the subjects indicated by an asterisk (*) will be found at the words so marked.

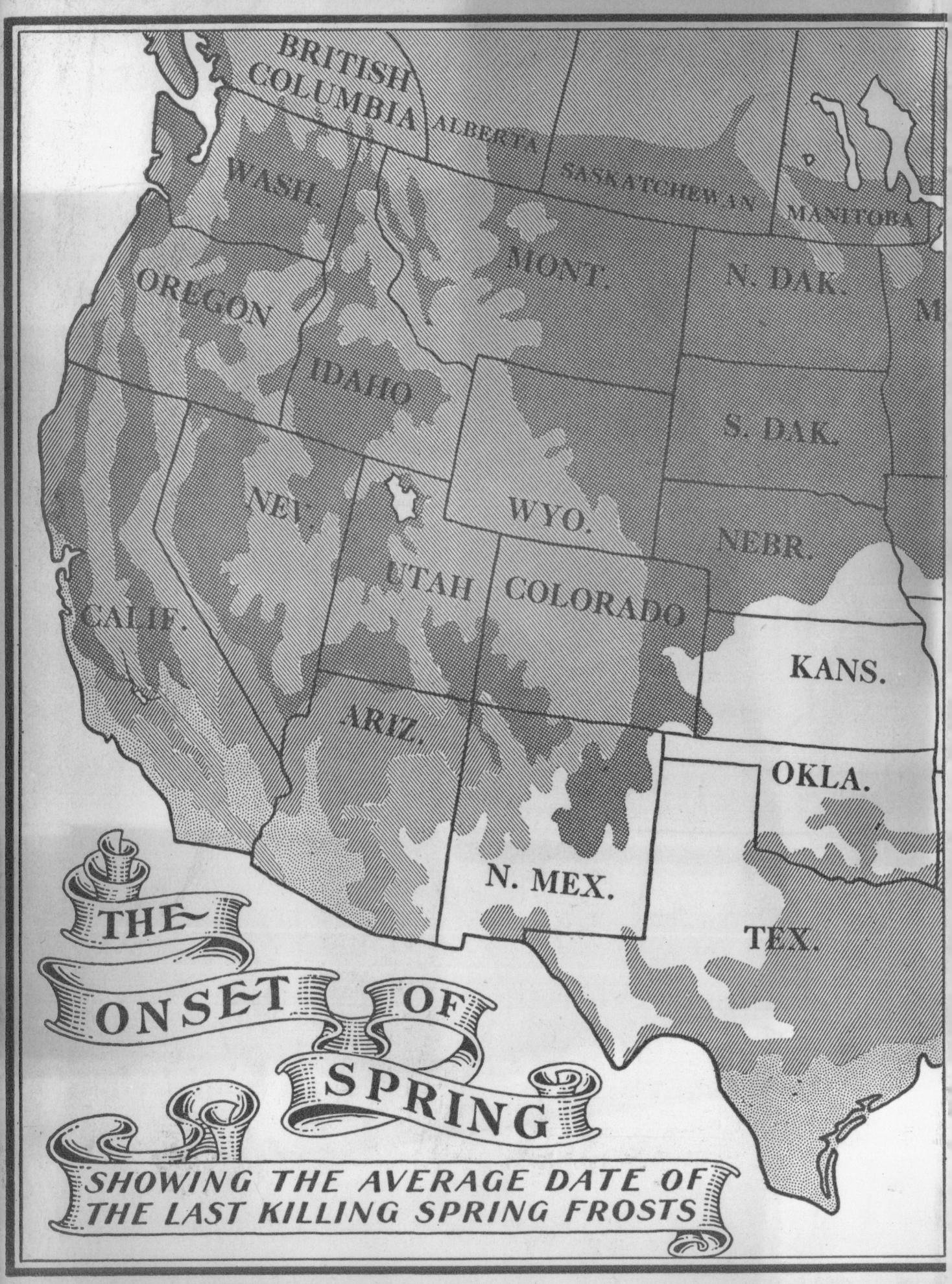